VideoHound's® GOLDEN MOVIE RETRIEVER®

VideoHound's® GOLDEN MOVIE RETRIEVER®

Jim Craddock, Editor

Detroit • New York • San Francisco • New Haven, Conn • Waterville, Maine • London

VideoHounds Golden Movie Retriever® 2011

Project Editor: James Craddock

Editorial: Tom Burns, Michael J. Tyrkus

Editorial Support Services: Wayne Fong

Manufacturing: Rita Wimberley

Composition and Prepress: Gary Leach

Gale
27500 Drake Rd.
Farmington Hills, MI, 48331-3535

ISBN-13: ISBN 978-1-4144-4286-0
ISBN-10: ISBN 1-4144-4286-6

ISSN 1095-371X

Printed in the United States of America
1 2 3 4 5 6 7 14 13 12 11 10

Credits:
or Who Does What

Project Editor
Jim Craddock

Editorial Coordinator
Dawn DesJardins

Editorial
Tom Burns
Michael J. Tyrkus

Editorial Support Services
Wayne Fong

Product Design
Pam Galbreath

Manufacturing
Rita Wimberley

Animal Control Officer:
Joyce Nakamura

Review Crew
Tom Burns
James A. Cook
Martin Craddock
Dawn Desjardins
Lisa DeShantz-Cook
Scott Estes
Beth A. Fhaner
Jeff Hermann
Lynne Konstantin
Keith Lindsay
Peter Tigger Lunney
Stuart Mammel
Robyn Parton
Joel Potrykus
Chris Scanlon
Amanda Scheid
Chris Tomassini
Mike Tyrkus
Hilary White

Special Assignment Research:
Keith Lindsay

Typesetter Extraordinaire:
Gary Leach

Makin' Copy:
PJ Butland

Licensing/Special Markets:
Jerry Moore

Contents

Introduction

"Reality leaves a lot to the imagination"

-John Lennon

Judging by the past year's big movies (and the most recent Oscars), reality *brought* a lot to Hollywood's imagination. Reality, or at least Hollywood's idea of reality, played a big part in some of the most successful and critically lauded films of the year.

Between stories based on actual events, such as the inspirational sports drama *The Blind Side* to the harrowing but quietly hopeful *Precious: Based on the Novel 'Push' by Sapphire*, and biopic/day-in-the-blog-life story *Julie & Julia*, and true-to-life stories such as the Iraq War dramas *The Messenger* and *The Hurt Locker*, the tender country music tale *Crazy Heart*, and coming-of-age story *An Education*, the movies are concentrating on "keeping it real." *Up in the Air* focused not only on real-life relationships, but the very harsh, persistent reality of corporate downsizing. Of course, documentaries are always focused on true events, and one of the most entertaining was *Anvil! The Story of Anvil* about a faded, never-was-but-shoulda-been heavy metal band.

Of course, man cannot live by reality alone, especially if he works in Hollywood. The fantastical, and creative, side of the movies was once again well-represented this year. Nowhere more clearly than in James Cameron's long-awaited CGI game-changer *Avatar*, which featured a completely computer-generated new world and species, dazzling to the senses and thrilling to the techno-geek. The plot was a little more Earth-bound, but nobody seemed to mind too much. *District 9* took a real life situation and turned it on it's ear with its tale of apartheid of an alien species in South Africa. Not to be outdone, Quentin Tarantino changed the ending of not only a 1970's era exploitation war movie, but changed the ending of World War II with the spectacular *Inglourious Basterds.* Reality never stood a chance...

Pixar once again warmed hearts and tickled funny bones with the imaginative *Up*, while another animated feast *Cloudy with a Chance of Meatballs,* brought laughter and cravings to movie audiences everywhere in a year that was particularly blessed with strong animated films that included *Coraline* and *Monsters vs. Aliens* as well. *Up* even snagged an Oscar nomination in the expanded (to ten nominees) Best Picture category.

That wasn't the only reason this award season was historic. Kathryn Bigelow made history as the first woman to take home the Best Director Oscar for the aforementioned *The Hurt Locker,* which also garnered awards for Best Picture, Original Screenplay, Editing, Sound, and Sound Effects Editing. *Avatar* (helmed by Bigelow's ex, James Cameron) took home most of the technical awards while long-time favorites Jeff Bridges (Best Actor for *Crazy Heart*) and Sandra Bullock (Best Actress for *The Blind Side*) finally took home statuettes. The painful, but ultimately hopeful story of *Precious* produced the best work of Mo'Nique's career, and she was rewarded for her role as the abusive mother with a Best Supporting Actress Oscar. *Precious* also won the award for Best Adapted Screenplay. Christoph Waltz's by turns chilling and sublime role as an SS officer in *Inglourious Basterds* won him the Best Supporting Actor Oscar. You can see a full list of winners and nominees in the Awards Index of this very book.

One person whose life and career seemed to blur the line between reality and the fantastic was Michael Jackson. His death in July of 2009 shocked the world, and like much of his life, was surrounded by controversy. In addition to Jackson, the entertainment world lost some luster and talent with the passing of legends such as David Carradine, John Hughes, Patrick Swayze, Farrah Fawcett, Dom DeLuise, and Ricardo Montalban. Particularly surprising was the death of one-time starlet Brittany Murphy.

In less dire news, *VideoHound* continues to add more and more movies to the book (and our web site www.movieretriever.com). We're fairly bursting at the seams with new movies. They're coming from everywhere! Direct-to-video, Asian cult flicks, classic black-and-white films made to order, everything on-demand...it seems that that there are more ways to acquire and watch movies than ever. This presents something of a problem for us, since there are physical limits to binding capabilities. We're sure we'll figure it out, but we're also not above soliciting suggestions from outside the doghouse. So, if you have an idea of how we could save space, features or content we could (or should) remove (as loathe as we are to do that), let us know. In the meantime, we'll be here, providing you with all the fun and informative reviews and indexes you've come to expect from us through the years.

As always, let us know how we're doing, what you think (about movies and the book, please!), and how great we are.

Here's how to contact us: VideoHound's Golden Movie Retriever 27500 Drake Rd. Farmington Hills, MI 48331-3535 or email at jim.craddock@cengage.com or at the website (once again, that's www.movieretriever.com) Thanks for your continued support and assistance. P.S. For those of you who have asked, Robert De Niro is indeed listed in the Cast Index. He is under De(space)N, not DeN.

Using VideoHound

Alphabetization

Titles are arranged on a word-by-word basis, including articles and prepositions. Leading articles (A, An, The) are ignored in English-language titles. The equivalent foreign articles are not ignored, however: *The Abyss* appears under "A" while *Les Miserables* appears under "L." **Other points to keep in mind:**

- Acronyms appear alphabetically as if regular words. For example, *C.H.U.D.* is alphabetized as "Chud"; *M*A*S*H* as "Mash."
- Common abbreviations in titles file as if they were spelled out, so *St. Elmo's Fire* will be found under "Saint Elmo's Fire" and *Mr. Holland's Opus* will be alphabetized as "Mister Holland's Opus."
- Proper names in titles are alphabetized beginning with the individual's first name; for instance, *Monty Python's The Meaning of Life* is under "M"; *Eddie Murphy: Raw* is under "E."
- Titles with numbers (*2001: A Space Odyssey*) are alphabetized as if the number were spelled out under the appropriate letter, in this case "Two Thousand One." When numeric titles gather in close proximity to each other (*2000 Year Old Man, 2001, 2010: The Year We Make Contact*), the titles will be arranged in a low (*2000*) to high (*2010*) numeric sequence.

Indexes

Alternate Title Index. A number of videos, particularly older, foreign, or B-type releases, may have variant titles. Alternate titles are listed alphabetically and refer the reader to the title under which the entry is listed. The alternate titles are also noted within the review.

Category Index. Subject categories ranging from the orthodox to slightly eccentric permit you to video sleuth from broad type to significant themes to signature scenes. The mix, arranged alphabetically by category, includes hundreds of traditional film genres and sub-genres as well as a feast of *VideoHound* exclusives. Integrated into the index are cross references, while preceding the index is a list of definitions. Release year will help differentiate between titles of the same name. **A tipped triangle (▸) indicates a movie rated three bones or above.**

Kibbles and Series Index. Not your everyday categories, Kibbles span the literary side of movie-making (Adapted from a Play, Books to Film: Ernest Hemingway) and point out key producers and special effects masters. Yearly box-office winners (that are now on video) since 1939 are listed, along with classic movies, four-bone delights, trash films, modern Shakespeare, Disney fare, significant on-screen and director/actor pairings. The Series portion of this index provides listings of major movie series, ranging from James Bond to National Lampoon to Indiana Jones. Recurring cinematic collaborations and partnerships of note are also listed, including Hope & Crosby, Abbott & Costello, De Niro & Scorsese, and Rafelson & Nicholson. A complete list of the categories precedes the index. Release year will help differentiate between titles of the same name. **As in the Category Index, tipped triangles (▸) indicate quality views.**

Awards Index. The Awards Index lists almost 7,000 films honored by national and international award bodies, representing some 90 categories of competition. This information is also contained in the review following the credits. Nominations are also included in this index. A star (★) denotes the winner. **Only features available on video and reviewed in the main section are listed in this index; movies not yet released on video are not covered.** As award-winning and nominated films find their way to video, they will be added to the review section and covered in this index. Awards listed include the American Academy Awards; British Academy of Film and Television Arts; Golden Globes; Directors Guild of America; Independent Spirit; Writers' Guild of America; National Film Registry; and the Golden Raspberries.

Cast/Director Indexes. The Cast Index provides full videographies for all actors and actresses listed in *VideoHound* with more than two movies on their resume. The Director Index lists the works of any director who has made it to video and to *VideoHound*. Although listed in a first name, last name sequence, the names are alphabetized by last name. Film titles, complete with initial year of release, are arranged in chronological order, starting with their most recent. A (V) designation after a film title indicates that the actor lent only vocal talents to that movie, as in animation features. An (N) depicts narration duties. Birth and death dates (year only) have been added to the citations. While they are not yet complete, they will continue to be updated, with more added to every edition. **Cross-references for actors and actresses who have appeared under more than one name have been added for this edition.**

Writer Index. Screenwriters and script doctors are listed with their vital works. Names are arranged alphabetically by last name. Works are arranged chronologically.

Cinematographer Index. Directors of Photography are listed alphabetically by last name, along with their work, which is arranged chronologically.

Composer Index. Videographies of movie music composers, arrangers, lyricists, and so on are listed. Arranged alphabetically by last name.

The **Video Sources Guide:** Lists a number of mail order and independent video dealers where videos and DVDs can be obtained.

Web Site Guide. Lists Internet web sites for studios; general entertainment information; film festivals; and filmmaker resources; as well as sites for gossip, upcoming releases, video ordering outlets, and trivia.

Sample Review

Each *VideoHound* review contains up to 19 items, ranging from title, to the review, to cast listings, to awards received. The information in these reviews is designed to help you choose a video you'll like, increase your enjoyment of a movie as you watch (especially by answering that nagging question of "What else have I seen that guy in?"), and increase your knowledge of movie trivia.

1 Tainted 2 🦴🦴 **3** *Angry Young Vampires* **4 1998 5 (R) 6** Ever wonder what would happen if the guys from "Clerks" fell in with a bunch of vampires? Well, lucky you. Now you can find out. Video clerks Ryan and J.T. hitch a ride to the midnight movie with their new co-worker Alex, who just happens to be a vampire whose ex is shacking up with the new vamp in town, who wants to taint the city's blood supply with undead blood. Script has many laughs, lots of attitude, and plenty of pop-culture knowledge, but gets a bit windy at times. Sometimes the actors seem to be trying a little too hard, but it doesn't detract from the story. Filmed in Detroit with lots of excellent local product placement. **7** ♫Bottoms Up; Rats!; One More for the Road.

8&9 64m/C 10 VHS, DVD. 11 ***GB*** **12** Brian Evans, Sean Farley, Dusan "Dean" Cechvala, Greg James, Jason Brouwer, Tina Kapousis; **13** ***D:*** Brian Evans; **14** ***W:*** Sean Farley; **15** ***C:*** Brian Evans; **16** ***M:*** Jessie McClear. **17** ***Nar:*** Bela Lugosi. **18** Academy Awards '98: Best Adapted Screenplay; Independent Spirit Awards '99: Best First Feature; Writers Guild of America '98: Best Original Screenplay. **19 VIDEO**

1. Title
2. One- to four-bone rating (or *Woof!*)
3. Alternate Title (we made this up)
4. Year released
5. MPAA rating
6. Description/review
7. Songs (made these up, too)
8. Length (in minutes)
9. Black & White (B) or Color (C)
10. Format (VHS, DVD, CD-I, Widescreen, closed captioned, or 8mm)
11. Country of origin (made up)
12. Cast (*V:* indicates voiceovers; also includes cameos)
13. Director
14. Writer(s)
15. Cinematographer(s)
16. Composer(s)/Lyricist(s)
17. Narrator (made up)
18. Awards (yet again, made up)
19. Made-for-Television/Cable/Video identification

The movie used in this sample is a real movie, it was filmed in Detroit, released by Troma, and is available from Thomas Video.

Alternate Titles Index

The Alternate Titles Index provides variant and foreign titles for movies with more than one name. Titles are listed in alphabetical order, followed by a cross-reference to the appropriate entry in the main video review section. If you don't find a movie you're looking for in the main section, this is the best place to look next.

Ahava Ilemeth *See* Secret of Yolanda (1982)

Ai-Fak *See* The Judgement (2004)

Ai Mei *See* Ghosted (2009)

Ai No Corrida *See* In the Realm of the Senses (1976)

Aideista Parhain *See* Mother of Mine (2005)

Aime Ton Pere *See* A Loving Father (2002)

Aimez-Vous Brahms *See* Goodbye Again (1961)

Ain't No Way Back *See* No Way Back (1990)

Aiqing Wansui *See* Vive l'Amour (1994)

Airport '79 *See* The Concorde: Airport '79 (1979)

Akage *See* Red Lion (1969)

Akahige *See* Red Beard (1965)

Akarui mirai *See* Bright Future (2003)

Akasen Chitai *See* Street of Shame (1956)

Akira Kurosawa's The Quiet Duel *See* A Quiet Duel (1949)

Akumu Tantei *See* Nightmare Detective (2006)

Al Di La Della Legge *See* Beyond the Law (1968)

Al-Jenna-An *See* Paradise Now (2005)

Al-Massir *See* Destiny (1997)

Al-Ris-Alah *See* The Message (1977)

Al 33 di Via Orologio fa Sempre Freddo *See* Shock (1979)

Alas de Mariposa *See* Butterfly Wings (1991)

Alem Da Paixao *See* Happily Ever After (1986)

Alfie Darling *See* Oh, Alfie (1975)

Ali Baba et les Quarante Voleurs *See* Ali Baba and the 40 Thieves (1954)

Alias Bulldog Drummond *See* Bulldog Jack (1935)

The Alibi *See* Lies & Alibis (2006)

Alice and Martin *See* Alice et Martin (1998)

Alicja *See* Alice (1986)

Alien 2 *See* Aliens (1986)

Alien P.I. *See* Alien Private Eye (1987)

Alien Terror *See* The Sinister Invasion (1968)

Alien Thunder *See* Dan Candy's Law (1973)

Alien vs. Alien *See* Showdown at Area 51 (2007)

Alien Within *See* Evil Spawn (1987)

The Alien Within *See* Unknown Origin (1995)

Alien Women *See* Zeta One (1969)

Alien Zone *See* House of the Dead (1978)

The Alien's Return *See* The Return (1980)

Alistair MacLean's Death Train *See* Detonator (1993)

Alistair MacLean's Night Watch *See* Detonator 2: Night Watch (1995)

Alive by Night *See* Evil Spawn (1987)

All for Love *See* St. Ives (1998)

All for One *See* Return to Paradise (1998)

All Forgotten *See* Lover's Prayer (1999)

All Good Citizens *See* All My Good Countrymen (1968)

All in Place *See* All Screwed Up (1974)

All Monsters Attack *See* Destroy All Monsters (1968)

All Night Long *See* Toute Une Nuit (1982)

All Our Fault *See* Nothing Personal (1995)

All That Money Can Buy *See* The Devil & Daniel Webster (1941)

All the Mornings of the World *See* Tous les Matins du Monde (1992)

All the Rage *See* It's the Rage (1999)

All the Way *See* The Night We Called It a Day (2003)

All This and Glamour Too *See* Vogues of 1938 (1937)

All Weekend Lovers *See* The Killing Game (1967)

Alla vi barn i Bullerby *See* The Children of Noisy Village (1986)

Aller-Simple Pour Manhattan *See* Petty Crimes (2002)

Alles Auf Zucker! *See* Go for Zucker (2005)

The Alley of Miracles *See* Midaq Alley (1995)

Alley of Nightmares *See* She-Freak (1967)

Alligators *See* The Great Alligator (1981)

Almok a hazrol *See* 25 Fireman's Street (1973)

Almost Human *See* Shock Waves (1977)

Alone *See* Horton Foote's Alone (1997)

Alone *See* Solas (1999)

Alone Together *See* Crisscross (1992)

Alphaville, a Strange Case of Lemmy Caution *See* Alphaville (1965)

Alphaville, Une Etrange Aventure de Lemmy Caution *See* Alphaville (1965)

Alter Ego *See* Murder by the Book (1987)

The Alternate *See* Agent of Death (1999)

The Alzheimer Affair *See* The Memory of a Killer (2003)

Am zhan 2 *See* Running Out of Time 2 (2006)

Am zin 2 *See* Running Out of Time 2 (2006)

Amantes *See* Lovers: A True Story (1990)

Amanti d'Oltretomba *See* Nightmare Castle (1965)

Amarelo Manga *See* Mango Yellow (2002)

Amateur Hour *See* I Was a Teenage TV Terrorist (1987)

The Amateurs *See* The Moguls (2005)

Amator *See* Camera Buff (1979)

The Amazing Panda Rescue *See* The Amazing Panda Adventure (1995)

The Amazing Quest of Ernest Bliss *See* Amazing Adventure (1937)

Amazon: Savage Adventure *See* Cut and Run (1985)

Amazon Women *See* Gold of the Amazon Women (1979)

Amazonia: The Catherine Miles Story *See* White Slave (1986)

Ambush in Waco *See* In the Line of Duty: Ambush in Waco (1993)

Amelia and the King of Plants *See* Bed of Roses (1995)

Amelie from Montmartre *See* Amelie (2001)

American Beauty Hostages *See* She Devils in Chains (1976)

An American Daughter *See* Trial by Media (2000)

American Dragons *See* Double Edge (1997)

American Fork *See* Humble Pie (2007)

American Nightmares *See* Combat Shock (1984)

American Pie 3 *See* American Wedding (2003)

American Pie 5: The Naked Mile *See* American Pie Presents: The Naked Mile (2006)

American Raspberry *See* Prime Time (1977)

American Rickshaw *See* American Tiger (1989)

American Warrior *See* American Ninja (1985)

The American Way *See* Riders of the Storm (1988)

Amerikaner Shadkhn *See* American Matchmaker (1940)

L'Ami de Mon Ami *See* Boyfriends & Girlfriends (1988)

Amigo/Amado *See* Beloved/Friend (1999)

Amityville 3-D *See* Amityville 3: The Demon (1983)

The Amityville Horror: The Evil Escapes, Part 4 *See* Amityville 4: The Evil Escapes (1989)

Amok *See* Schizo (1977)

Amor Estranho Amor *See* Love Strange Love (1982)

Amor Perjudica Seriamente la Salud *See* Love Can Seriously Damage Your Health (1996)

Amore in Citta *See* Love in the City (1953)

Amores Possiveis *See* Possible Loves (2000)

The Amorous General *See* Waltz of the Toreadors (1962)

The Amorous Sex *See* Sweet Beat (1959)

L'Amour a Mort *See* Love Unto Death (1984)

L'Amour Chez les Poids Lourds *See* Truck Stop (1978)

Amour de Poche *See* Girl in His Pocket (1957)

L'Amour l'Apres-midi *See* Chloe in the Afternoon (1972)

Amy Fisher: My Story *See* Lethal Lolita—Amy Fisher: My Story (1992)

Amy Foster *See* Swept from the Sea (1997)

Amy's Orgasm *See* Amy's O (2002)

Anacardium *See* Deranged (2001)

Anatomie *See* Anatomy (2000)

Anatomie de L'Enfer *See* Anatomy of Hell (2004)

And Comes the Dawn...But Colored Red *See* Web of the Spider (1970)

And Life Goes On ... *See* Life and Nothing More ...(1992)

And Once Upon a Love *See* Fantasies (1973)

And Then There Were None *See* Ten Little Indians (1975)

...And They Lived Happily Ever After *See* Happily Ever After (2004)

And Woman...Was Created *See* And God Created Woman (1957)

And Your Mother Too *See* Y Tu Mama Tambien (2001)

An Andalusian Dog *See* Un Chien Andalou (1928)

Anders Als du und Ich *See* The Third Sex (1957)

Anderson's Angels *See* Chesty Anderson USN (1976)

Andoromedia *See* Andromedia (2000)

Andrews' Raiders *See* The Great Locomotive Chase (1956)

Andy Colby's Incredibly Awesome Adventure *See* Andy and the Airwave Rangers (1989)

Andy Warhol's Flesh *See* Flesh (1968)

Andy Warhol's Heat *See* Heat (1972)

Andy Warhol's Young Dracula *See* Andy Warhol's Dracula (1974)

Angel *See* Danny Boy (1982)

Angel in Red *See* Uncaged (1991)

Angel of Vengeance *See* Ms. 45 (1981)

Angel of Vengeance *See* WarCat (1988)

An Angel Passed Over Brooklyn *See* The Man Who Wagged His Tail (1957)

Angel Sharks *See* Marie Baie des Anges (1997)

Angel Street *See* Gaslight (1940)

Angelique et le Roy *See* Angelique and the King (1966)

Angelique et le Sultan *See* Angelique and the Sultan (1968)

Angelique, Marquise des Anges *See* Angelique (1964)

Angelique, Marquise of Angels *See* Angelique (1964)

Angelos *See* Angel (1982)

Angels for Kicks *See* Wild Riders (1971)

Angels in the Attic *See* The Robin Hood Gang (1998)

Anglagard *See* House of Angels (1992)

Angst Essen Selle auf *See* Ali: Fear Eats the Soul (1974)

Angst vor der Angst *See* Fear of Fear (1975)

Animal House *See* National Lampoon's Animal House (1978)

Animale Chiamato Uomo *See* Animal Called Man (1972)

Anita—Tanze des Lasters *See* Anita, Dances of Vice (1987)

Anna: From Six Till Eighteen *See* Anna (1993)

Anna: Ot Shesti do Vosemnadtsati *See* Anna (1993)

Anne and Muriel *See* Two English Girls (1972)

Anne Frank *See* Anne Frank: The Whole Story (2001)

Anne of Green Gables: The Sequel *See* Anne of Avonlea (1987)

Annie's Coming Out *See* A Test of Love (1984)

Anno Domini *See* A.D. (1985)

Anno Zero - Guerra Nello Spazio *See* War in Space (1977)

Anoche Sone Contigo *See* Dreaming About You (1992)

Anonyma: Eine Frau in Berlin *See* A Woman in Berlin (2008)

Ansikte mot Ansikte *See* Face to Face (1976)

The Anti-Extortion Woman *See* Minbo—Or the Gentle Art of Japanese Extortion (1992)

The Antichrist *See* The Tempter (1974)

L'Anticristo *See* The Tempter (1974)

Antikorper *See* Antibodies (2005)

Antinea, l'Amante Della Citta Sepolta *See* Journey Beneath the Desert (1961)

Anton der Zauberer *See* Anton, the Magician (1978)

The Anxious Years *See* Dark Journey (1937)

Any Special Way *See* Business is Business (1971)

Anyone for Venice? *See* The Honey Pot (1967)

Anything for Love *See* 11 Harrowhouse (1974)

Apa *See* Father (1967)

Apache Vengeance *See* The Desperados (1970)

The Apartment on the 13 Floor *See* Cannibal Man (1971)

Apocalipsis Canibal *See* Hell of the Living Dead (1983)

The Apprentices *See* Les Apprentis (1995)

Apres l'Amour *See* Love After Love (1994)

Apres-Ski *See* Snowballin' (1971)

April One *See* Stand Off (1993)

Apu Sansat *See* The World of Apu (1959)

Apur Sansar *See* The World of Apu (1959)

The Aqua Sex *See* The Mermaids of Tiburon (1962)

Aranyer Din Ratri *See* Days and Nights in the Forest (1970)

Arctic Heat *See* Born American (1986)

Are You Dying Young Man? *See* Beast in the Cellar (1970)

L'Argent de Poche *See* Small Change (1976)

Arizona Ripper *See* Terror at London Bridge (1985)

Arlen Faber *See* The Answer Man (2009)

L'Arma *See* The Sniper (1978)

Beasts *See* Twilight People (1972)

The Beating of the Butterfly's Wings *See* Happenstance (2000)

Beatlemania *See* Beatlemania! The Movie (1981)

Beatsville *See* The Rebel Set (1959)

Beaumarchais L'Insolent *See* Beaumarchais the Scoundrel (1996)

Beautiful But Dangerous *See* She Couldn't Say No (1952)

Beautiful But Deadly *See* The Don Is Dead (1973)

The Beautiful Ordinary *See* Remember the Daze (2007)

A Beautiful Place to Kill *See* Paranoia (1969)

The Beautiful Troublemaker *See* La Belle Noiseuse (1990)

Because He's My Friend *See* Love Under Pressure (1978)

Beethoven's Great Love *See* Beethoven (1936)

Before It Had a Name *See* The Black Widow (2005)

Beggars' Opera *See* The Threepenny Opera (1931)

The Beginners *See* The First Time (1969)

The Beginners Three *See* The First Time (1969)

Behind Enemy Lines *See* The P.O.W. Escape (1986)

Behind Locked Doors *See* Human Gorilla (1948)

Behind the Blue *See* L'Enfant d'Eau (1995)

Behind the Forbidden City *See* East Palace, West Palace (1996)

Behind the Iron Mask *See* The Fifth Musketeer (1979)

Believe Me *See* Hollow Reed (1995)

The Bell *See* Rough Justice (1970)

Bella Martha *See* Mostly Martha (2001)

Belleville Rendez-Vous *See* The Triplets of Belleville (2002)

Bells *See* Murder by Phone (1982)

The Beloved *See* Restless (1972)

Below Utopia *See* Body Count (1997)

Belphegar: Le Fantome du Louvre *See* Belphegar: Phantom of the Louvre (2001)

Berlinguer Ti Voglio Bene *See* Berlinguer I Love You (1977)

Berry Gordy's The Last Dragon *See* The Last Dragon (1985)

The Best Way to Walk *See* The Best Way (1976)

Beta House *See* American Pie Presents: Beta House (2007)

Bethune, The Making of a Hero *See* Dr. Bethune (1990)

Betrayal *See* Lady Jayne Killer (2003)

Betrayal *See* Trahir (1993)

Betty Fisher and Other Stories *See* Alias Betty (2001)

Betty Fisher et Autres Histoires *See* Alias Betty (2001)

Between the Walls *See* The Class (2008)

Between Us *See* Entre-Nous (1983)

Betzilo Shel Helem Krav *See* Shell Shock (1963)

Beverly Hills Nightmare *See* Housewife (1972)

Beware of Children *See* No Kidding (1960)

Bewitching Scatterbrain *See* Ravishing Idiot (1964)

Beyond Bedlam *See* Nightscare (1993)

Beyond Control *See* The Amy Fisher Story (1993)

Beyond Justice *See* Guardian Angel (1994)

Beyond Loch Ness *See* Loch Ness Terror (2007)

Beyond Obsession *See* Beyond the Door (1975)

Beyond the City Limits *See* Rip It Off (2002)

Beyond the Door 2 *See* Shock (1979)

Beyond the Fog *See* Tower of Evil (1972)

Beyond the Gates *See* Shooting Dogs (2005)

Beyond the Living *See* Hospital of Terror (1978)

Beyond the Living Dead *See* The Hanging Woman (1972)

Beyond the Rising Moon *See* Star Quest (1989)

Bez Konca *See* No End (1984)

Bez Znieczulenia *See* Without Anesthesia (1978)

Biandan, Guniang *See* So Close to Paradise (1998)

The Big Bang Theory *See* Bang (1995)

The Big Bankroll *See* The King of the Roaring '20s: The Story of Arnold Rothstein (1961)

The Big Boss *See* Fists of Fury (1973)

The Big Boss *See* Rulers of the City (1976)

The Big Carnival *See* Ace in the Hole (1951)

The Big Dance *See* DC 9/11: Time of Crisis (2004)

The Big Day *See* Jour de Fete (1948)

Big Deal at Dodge City *See* A Big Hand for the Little Lady (1966)

Big Duel in the North *See* Godzilla vs. the Sea Monster (1966)

Big Enough and Old Enough *See* Savages from Hell (1968)

The Big Escape *See* Eagles Attack at Dawn (1970)

The Big Grab *See* Any Number Can Win (1963)

The Big Heart *See* Miracle on 34th Street (1947)

The Big Lobby *See* Rosebud Beach Hotel (1985)

Big Monster on Campus *See* Boltneck (1998)

Big Monster War *See* Spook Warfare (1968)

The Big One: The Great Los Angeles Earthquake *See* The Great Los Angeles Earthquake (1991)

The Big Payoff *See* Win, Place, or Steal (1972)

The Big Risk *See* Classe Tous Risque (1960)

The Big Search *See* East of Kilimanjaro (1957)

Big Time Operators *See* The Smallest Show on Earth (1957)

Big Town Scandal *See* Underworld Scandal (1947)

The Biggest Fight on Earth *See* Ghidrah the Three Headed Monster (1965)

Biggles: Adventures in Time *See* Biggles (1985)

Bijita Q *See* Visitor Q (2001)

Bijo to Ekitainigen *See* H-Man (1959)

Bikini Genie *See* Wildest Dreams (1990)

Bikur Ha-Tizmoret *See* The Band's Visit (2007)

Bill *See* Meet Bill (2007)

Billy the Kid in Texas *See* Battling Outlaw (1940)

Billy the Kid's Fighting Pals *See* Trigger Men (1941)

Billy the Kid's Law and Order *See* Law and Order (1942)

Billy the Kid's Range War *See* Texas Trouble (1941)

Bio-Force I *See* Mutant Species (1995)

The Bird with the Glass Feathers *See* The Bird with the Crystal Plumage (1970)

Birds of a Feather *See* The Birdcage (1995)

Birds of a Feather *See* La Cage aux Folles (1978)

Birds of Prey *See* Beaks: The Movie (1987)

Birth of Octopuses *See* Water Lilies (2007)

Birthmark *See* The Omen (1976)

Birumano Tategoto *See* The Burmese Harp (1956)

Bis ans Ende der Welt *See* Until the End of the World (1991)

The Bitch *See* La Chienne (1931)

The Bitter End *See* Love Walked In (1997)

Bitter Harvest *See* How Harry Became a Tree (2001)

Bittere Ernte *See* Angry Harvest (1985)

Black Angels *See* Black Bikers from Hell (1970)

Black Arrow Strikes *See* Black Arrow (1948)

The Black Book *See* Reign of Terror (1949)

The Black Bounty Hunter *See* Boss (1974)

The Black Bounty Killer *See* Boss (1974)

The Black Buccaneer *See* The Black Pirate (1926)

Black Cat's Revenge *See* Blind Woman's Curse (1970)

Black Christmas *See* Black Sabbath (1964)

Black Dragon *See* Miracles (1989)

Black Eliminator *See* Kill Factor (1978)

Black Emmanuelle *See* Emmanuelle, the Queen (1979)

Black Emmanuelle, White Emmanuelle *See* Naked Paradise (1978)

Black Evil *See* Ganja and Hess (1973)

Black Fist *See* Fist (1976)

Black Fist *See* Homeboy (1975)

Black Flowers for the Bride *See* Something for Everyone (1970)

Black Forest: Rage in Space *See* Hyper Space (1989)

Black Frankenstein *See* Blackenstein (1973)

Black Gauntlet *See* Black Starlet (1974)

Black Jack *See* Captain Blackjack (1951)

Black Jesus *See* Super Brother (1968)

Black Kingpin *See* Hit Men (1973)

Black Love, White Love *See* Sweet Love, Bitter (1967)

Black Out *See* Midnight Heat (1995)

Black Out: The Moment of Terror *See* Ganja and Hess (1973)

Black Rage *See* Sunshine Run (1979)

Black Rider *See* Joshua (1976)

Black River *See* Dean Koontz's Black River (2001)

Black Rose of Harlem *See* Machine Gun Blues (1995)

Black Scorpion 2: Aftershock *See* Black Scorpion 2: Ground Zero (1996)

The Black Streetfighter *See* Fist (1976)

The Black Torrent *See* Estate of Insanity (1964)

Black Valor *See* Savage! (1973)

Black Vampire *See* Ganja and Hess (1973)

Black Velvet *See* Naked Paradise (1978)

The Black Velvet Gown *See* Catherine Cookson's The Black Velvet Gown (1992)

Black Vengeance *See* Poor Pretty Eddie (1973)

Black Werewolf *See* The Beast Must Die (1975)

Blackboard Massacre *See* Massacre at Central High (1976)

Blackout *See* Contraband (1940)

Blackout in Rome *See* Era Notte a Roma (1960)

Blade of Steel *See* The Far Pavilions (1984)

Blair Witch 2 *See* Book of Shadows: Blair Witch 2 (2000)

Blake Edwards' Son of the Pink Panther *See* Son of the Pink Panther (1993)

Blast-Off *See* Those Fantastic Flying Fools (1967)

Blazing Arrows *See* Fighting Caravans (1931)

Blazing Magnums *See* Strange Shadows in an Empty Room (1976)

Bless 'Em All *See* The Act (1982)

Blikende Lygter *See* Flickering Lights (2001)

Blind Alley *See* Perfect Strangers (1984)

The Blind Dead *See* Tombs of the Blind Dead (1972)

Blind Fairies *See* His Secret Life (2001)

Blind Man's Bluff *See* Cauldron of Blood (1967)

The Blind Swordsman: Zatoichi *See* Zatoichi (2003)

Blind Terror *See* See No Evil (1971)

Blink of an Eye *See* Blink of an Eye (1992)

Bl,.m *See* Bloom (2003)

Blonde Bombshell *See* Bombshell (1933)

Blonde for Danger *See* Sois Belle et Tais-Toi (1958)

The Blonde From Peking *See* The Peking Blond (1968)

A Blonde in Love *See* Loves of a Blonde (1965)

Blondie Has Servant Trouble *See* Blondie Has Trouble (1940)

Blood and Bullets *See* Rulers of the City (1976)

Blood and Sand *See* Sand and Blood (1987)

The Blood Baron *See* Torture Chamber of Baron Blood (1972)

Blood Bath *See* Track of the Vampire (1966)

Blood Beast from Outer Space *See* Night Caller from Outer Space (1966)

Blood Brides *See* Hatchet for the Honeymoon (1970)

The Blood Brother *See* Texas Pioneers (1932)

Blood Castle *See* The Blood Spattered Bride (1972)

Blood Ceremony *See* The Legend of Blood Castle (1972)

Blood Couple *See* Ganja and Hess (1973)

Blood Creature *See* Terror Is a Man (1959)

The Blood Crowd *See* The McMasters (1970)

The Blood Cult of Shangri-La *See* The Thirsty Dead (1974)

Blood Demon *See* The Torture Chamber of Dr. Sadism (1969)

Blood Doctor *See* Mad Doctor of Blood Island (1968)

The Blood Drinkers *See* The Vampire People (1966)

Blood Evil *See* Demons of the Mind (1972)

Blood Feast *See* Night of a Thousand Cats (1972)

Blood Fiend *See* Theatre of Death (1967)

Blood for Dracula *See* Andy Warhol's Dracula (1974)

Blood Freaks *See* Blood Freak (1972)

Blood Hunger *See* Vampyres (1974)

Blood Hunt *See* The Thirsty Dead (1974)

Blood Is My Heritage *See* Blood of Dracula (1957)

Blood Mad *See* The Glove (1978)

Blood Money *See* The Killer's Edge (1990)

Blood Money *See* Requiem for a Heavyweight (1962)

Blood Money *See* Under Oath (1997)

Blood Moon *See* The Werewolf vs. the Vampire Woman (1970)

Blood Oath *See* Prisoners of the Sun (1991)

Blood of Frankenstein *See* Dracula vs. Frankenstein (1971)

Blood of Fu Manchu *See* Kiss and Kill (1968)

Blood of the Demon *See* Blood of Dracula (1957)

Blood of the Man Devil *See* House of the Black Death (1965)

Blood of the Undead *See* Schizo (1977)

Blood on His Lips *See* Hideous Sun Demon (1959)

Blood Orange *See* Three Stops to Murder (1953)

Blood Orgy *See* The Gore-Gore Girls (1972)

A Blood Pledge: Broken Promise *See* Blood Pledge (2009)

Blood Rust *See* Space Master X-7 (1958)

The Blood Seekers *See* Cain's Cutthroats (1971)

Blood Snow *See* Lady Snowblood (1973)

Blood Song *See* Haunted Symphony (1994)

Blood Splash *See* Nightmare (1982)

The Blood Suckers *See* Alien Massacre (1967)

The Blood Suckers *See* Dr. Terror's House of Horrors (1965)

Blood Thirst *See* Salem's Lot (1979)

Blood Waters of Dr. Z *See* Attack of the Swamp Creature (1975)

Blood Will Have Blood *See* Demons of the Mind (1972)

Bloodline *See* Hush (1998)

Bloodline *See* Sidney Sheldon's Bloodline (1979)

Bloodrage *See* Never Pick Up a Stranger (1979)

Bloodsilver *See* Beyond the Law (1968)

Bloodsucking Nazi Zombies *See* Oasis of the Zombies (1982)

The Bloody Bushido Blade *See* The Bushido Blade (1980)

Bloody Fiance *See* The Blood Spattered Bride (1972)

Bloody Pom Poms *See* Cheerleader Camp (1988)

The Bloody Scream of Dracula *See* Dracula, Prince of Darkness (1966)

Bloody Weekend *See* Loaded (1994)

Bloomfield *See* The Hero (1971)

The Blow-Out *See* La Grande Bouffe (1973)

Blue *See* Trois Couleurs: Bleu (1993)

Blue and the Gold *See* An Annapolis Story (1955)

Blue Beach *See* Beach Hotel (1992)

Blue Eyes *See* Retribution Road (2007)

Blue Eyes of the Broken Doll *See* House of Psychotic Women (1973)

Blue Heat *See* The Last of the Finest (1990)

Blue Jean Cop *See* Shakedown (1988)

Blue Manhattan *See* Hi, Mom! (1970)

Blue Sierra *See* Courage of Lassie (1946)

Blue Vision *See* In Dreams (1998)

Blues for Lovers *See* Ballad in Blue (1966)

Blues La-Chofesh Ha-Godol *See* Late Summer Blues (1987)

Bluff Storia di Truffe e di Imbroglioni *See* The Switch (1976)

Blut an den Lippen *See* Daughters of Darkness (1971)

Bo biu *See* Have Sword, Will Travel (1969)

The Boat *See* Das Boot (1981)

The Boat That Rocked *See* Pirate Radio (2009)

Bob the Gambler *See* Bob le Flambeur (1955)

Boca a Boca *See* Mouth to Mouth (1995)

Bodas de Sangre *See* Blood Wedding (1981)

Bodres Bear Traces of Carnal Violence *See* Torso (1973)

Body Parts *See* Harold Robbins' Body Parts (1999)

The Body Stealers *See* Invasion of the Body Stealers (1969)

The Bodyguard *See* Have Sword, Will Travel (1969)

The Bodyguards *See* La Scorta (1994)

Bog Bodies *See* Legend of the Bog (2008)

Bogus Bandits *See* The Devil's Brother (1933)

Bohemian Life *See* La Vie de Boheme (1993)

Boksuneun naui geot *See* Sympathy for Mr. Vengeance (2002)

A Bold Affair *See* Interlocked (1998)

The Bold Cavalier *See* The Bold Caballero (1936)

Bolero: An Adventure in Ecstasy *See* Bolero (1984)

Bolt *See* Rebel Run (1994)

Bom Yeorum Gaeul Gyeoul Geurigo...Bom *See* Spring, Summer, Fall, Winter... and Spring (2003)

Bombsight Stolen *See* Cottage to Let (1941)

Bone *See* Housewife (1972)

Boogiepop wa Wawaranai *See* Boogiepop and Others (2000)

Book of Beasts *See* Merlin and the Book of Beasts (2009)

Book of Blood *See* Clive Barker's Book of Blood (2008)

Bookworm *See* The Edge (1997)

Bor Lei Jun *See* Gorgeous (1999)

Bordello of Blood *See* Tales from the Crypt Presents Bordello of Blood (1996)

Border Heat *See* Deadly Stranger (1988)

Born Natturunnar *See* Children of Nature (1991)

Born to Be Sold *See* Baby Broker (1981)

Born to Kill *See* Cockfighter (1974)

Born to the West *See* Helltown (1938)

Bosambo *See* Sanders of the River (1935)

Bosque de Sombras *See* The Backwoods (2006)

Boss Nigger *See* Boss (1974)

Boudu Sauve des Eaux *See* Boudu Saved from Drowning (1932)

Bound by Honor *See* Blood In ...Blood Out: Bound by Honor (1993)

The Bounty *See* The Bounty Hunter (2010)

Bourbon St. Shadows *See* The Invisible Avenger (1958)

Bowfinger's Big Thing *See* Bowfinger (1999)

The Boxer *See* Blade Boxer (1997)

The Boxer *See* Counter Punch (1971)

The Boy in the Golden Kimono *See* Karate Warrior (1988)

The Boy Who Had Everything *See* Winner Takes All (1984)

The Boyfriend School *See* Don't Tell Her It's Me (1990)

Boyichi and the Supermonster *See* Gamera vs. Gaos (1967)

The Boynton Beach Bereavement Club *See* The Boynton Beach Club (2005)

The Boys are Back in Town *See* The Boys Are Back (2009)

The Boys from Brooklyn *See* Bela Lugosi Meets a Brooklyn Gorilla (1952)

The Boys From County Clare *See* The Boys and Girl From County Clare (2003)

Brain Damage *See* Brain of Blood (1971)

The Brain Machine *See* Mind Warp (1972)

The Brain of Frankenstein *See* Abbott and Costello Meet Frankenstein (1948)

Braindead *See* Dead Alive (1993)

The Brainsnatchers *See* The Man Who Lived Again (1936)

Brainwash *See* Circle of Power (1983)

Bram Stoker's Burial of the Rats *See* Burial of the Rats (1995)

Bram Stoker's Count Dracula *See* Count Dracula (1971)

Bram Stoker's Dracula *See* Dracula (1973)

Brand New Day *See* Love Happens (2009)

Branded *See* Bad Boy (1939)

Brandy Ashore *See* Green Grow the Rushes (1951)

Brat *See* Brother (1997)

The Brave and the Beautiful *See* The Magnificent Matador (1955)

The Brave Young Men of Weinberg *See* Up the Academy (1980)

Breach of Faith: A Family of Cops 2 *See* Family of Cops 2: Breach of Faith (1997)

Break In *See* Loophole (1983)

Breakdance *See* Breakin' (1984)

Breakdance 2: Electric Boogaloo *See* Breakin' 2: Electric Boogaloo (1984)

The Breakup *See* La Rupture (1970)

Brendan and the Secret of Kells *See* The Secret of Kells (2009)

Brenn, Hexe, Brenn *See* Mark of the Devil (1969)

Brennendes Geheimnis *See* Burning Secret (1989)

Briar Patch *See* Plain Dirty (2004)

Bride of Fengriffen *See* And Now the Screaming Starts (1973)

Bride of the Atom *See* Bride of the Monster (1955)

The Bride of the Lake *See* Lily of Killarney (1934)

Brides of Blood *See* Brides of the Beast (1968)

Bridge Across Time *See* Terror at London Bridge (1985)

Brodre *See* Brothers (2004)

Broken April *See* Behind the Sun (2001)

Broken Hearts and Noses *See* Crimewave (1985)

Broken Lizard's Club Dread *See* Club Dread (2004)

Broken Lizard's Super Troopers *See* Super Troopers (2001)

Bronenosets Potemkin *See* The Battleship Potemkin (1925)

Bronx Warriors *See* 1990: The Bronx Warriors (1983)

Brooklyn Love Story *See* Who Shot Pat? (1992)

Brothel 8 *See* Sandakan No. 8 (1974)

Brotherhood of the Yakuza *See* The Yakuza (1975)

Brothers Five *See* Sword Masters: Brothers Five (1970)

Bruce Brown's The Endless Summer 2 *See* The Endless Summer 2 (1994)

Bruce Brown's The Endless Summer Revisited *See* The Endless Summer 2 (1994)

Bruce Lee's Game of Death *See* Game of Death (1979)

Bruno *See* The Dress Code (1999)

The Brute *See* El Bruto (1952)

Brutti, Sporchi, e Cattivi *See* Down & Dirty (1976)

Bu san *See* Goodbye, Dragon Inn (2003)

Buck Rogers *See* Destination Saturn (1939)

Buckaroo Banzai *See* The Adventures of Buckaroo Banzai Across the Eighth Dimension (1984)

Bud Abbott and Lou Costello In Hollywood *See* Abbott and Costello in Hollywood (1945)

Budbringeren *See* Junk Mail (1997)

Budding Love *See* L'Amour en Herbe (1977)

The Buddy Factor *See* Swimming with Sharks (1994)

Buenos Aires, 1977 *See* Chronicle of an Escape (2006)

The Bug *See* Bug (1975)

Bui bun si mun *See* The Master (1980)

Build a Fort Set It on Fire *See* Basquiat (1996)

Build My Gallows High *See* Out of the Past (1947)

A Bullet from God *See* God's Gun (1975)

Bullfighter *See* Torero (1956)

Bump in the Night *See* The Final Terror (1983)

Bundy: An American Icon *See* Bundy: A Legacy of Evil (2008)

Bunhongsin *See* The Red Shoes (2005)

Bunman *See* The Untold Story (1993)

The Bunny Caper *See* Games Girls Play (1975)

Buon Funerale, Amigos! *See* Gunslinger (1970)

The Burden of Proof *See* Scott Turow's The Burden of Proof (1992)

Bure Baruta *See* Cabaret Balkan (1998)

Buried on Sunday *See* Northern Extremes (1993)

Burn, Hollywood, Burn *See* An Alan Smithee Film: Burn, Hollywood, Burn (1997)

Burn Out *See* Journey into Fear (1974)

Burn, Witch, Burn *See* Mark of the Devil (1969)

Burning Cross *See* The Klansman (1974)

Burning Hearts *See* Kolberg (1945)

The Burning Man *See* Dangerous Summer (1982)

The Burning Question *See* Reefer Madness (1938)

The Bus Is Coming *See* Ghetto Revenge (1971)

Bush Christmas *See* Prince and the Great Race (1983)

Bushwhacked *See* French Twist (1995)

Bustin' Bonaparte: The Story of an African Farm *See* The Story of an African Farm (2004)

The Butcher *See* Le Boucher (1969)

The Butcher *See* Psycho from Texas (1975)

Butcher Baker (Nightmare Maker) *See* Night Warning (1982)

The Butchers *See* Murderer's Keep (1970)

The Butterfly Affair *See* Queen of Diamonds (1970)

Butterfly on a Wheel *See* Shattered (2007)

The Butterfly Revolution *See* Summer Camp Nightmare (1986)

Butterfly's Tongue *See* Butterfly (1998)

Buzzy and the Phantom Pinto *See* The Phantom Pinto (1941)

Bvongiorno, Elefante *See* Pardon My Trunk (1952)

By Hook or By Crook *See* I Dood It (1943)

By Rocket to the Moon *See* Woman in the Moon (1929)

Ca Va Barder *See* There Goes Barder (1954)

Caballos Salvajes *See* Wild Horses (1995)

Cabiria *See* Nights of Cabiria (1957)

Caccia Ai Violenti *See* One Step to Hell (1967)

Caccia alla Volpe *See* After the Fox (1966)

Caceria *See* Manhunt (2001)

Cache *See* Hidden (2005)

Cactus Jack *See* The Villain (1979)

A Cada Lado *See* On Each Side (2007)

Cafe of the Seven Sinners *See* Seven Sinners (1940)

The Cage *See* My Sister, My Love (1978)

Caged Females *See* Caged Heat (1974)

Caged Heart *See* L'Addition (1985)

Cain's Way *See* Cain's Cutthroats (1971)

Calhoun *See* Nightstick (1987)

California Axe Massacre *See* Axe (1974)

The California Dolls *See* ...All the Marbles (1981)

California Holiday *See* Spinout (1966)

California Hot Wax *See* The Bikini Car Wash Company (1990)

California in 1878 *See* Fighting Thru (1930)

California Man *See* Encino Man (1992)

The Californian *See* The Gentleman from California (1937)

Call Harry Crown *See* 99 & 44/100 Dead (1974)

Call It Love *See* She's So Lovely (1997)

Call It Murder *See* Midnight (1934)

The Call of the Savage *See* Savage Fury (1935)

The Call of the Wild: Dog of the Yukon *See* Jack London's The Call of the Wild (1997)

Call the Cops *See* Find the Lady (1976)

The Calling *See* Murder by Phone (1982)

Calling Northside 777 *See* Call Northside 777 (1948)

Cama Adentro *See* Live-In Maid (2004)

Campanadas a Medianoche *See* Chimes at Midnight (1967)

Camper John *See* Gentle Savage (1973)

Campsite Massacre *See* The Final Terror (1983)

A Candle for the Devil *See* It Happened at Nightmare Inn (1970)

Canicule *See* Dog Day (1983)

Cannabis *See* French Intrigue (1970)

Cannibal Orgy, or the Maddest Story Ever Told *See* Spider Baby (1964)

The Cannibal's Daughter *See* Lucia, Lucia (2003)

Cannibals in the City *See* Cannibal Apocalypse (1980)

Cannibals in the Streets *See* Cannibal Apocalypse (1980)

Can't Be Heaven *See* Forever Together (2000)

Caos Calmo *See* Quiet Chaos (2008)

Capers *See* The Brooklyn Heist (2008)

Capitaine Morgan *See* Morgan the Pirate (1960)

Capitalismo Salvaje *See* Savage Capitalism (1993)

Captain Conan *See* Capitaine Conan (1996)

Captain Hurricane *See* Captain Calamity (1936)

Captain Mephisto and the Transformation Machine *See* Manhunt of Mystery Island (1945)

Captain Midnight *See* On the Air Live with Captain Midnight (1979)

Captain Yankee *See* Jungle Raiders (1985)

Captive *See* Sex and the Other Man (1995)

Captive Planet *See* Metallica (1985)

Captive Women 3: Sweet Sugar *See* Sweet Sugar (1972)

Captured *See* Agent Red (2000)

The Car *See* El Carro (2004)

Caravan *See* Himalaya (1999)

Caravans West *See* Wagon Wheels (1934)

The Card *See* The Promoter (1952)

Cardigan's Last Case *See* State's Attorney (1931)

Care of the Spitfire Grill *See* The Spitfire Grill (1995)

A Caribbean Mystery *See* Agatha Christie's A Caribbean Mystery (1983)

Caricies *See* Caresses (1997)

Carlo Collodi's Pinocchio *See* The Adventures of Pinocchio (1996)

Carmen of the Streets *See* As Tears Go By (1988)

Carnage *See* Twitch of the Death Nerve (1971)

Carne per Frankenstein *See* Andy Warhol's Frankenstein (1974)

Carne Tremula *See* Live Flesh (1997)

Carnival of Fools *See* Death Wish Club (1983)

Carnival of Thieves *See* Caper of the Golden Bulls (1967)

Carosello Napoletano *See* Neapolitan Carousel (1954)

Carquake *See* Cannonball (1976)

Carrie 2 *See* The Rage: Carrie 2 (1999)

Carry On, Don't Lose Your Head *See* Don't Lose Your Head (1966)

Carry On Follow That Camel *See* Follow That Camel (1967)

Carry On 'Round the Bend *See* Carry On at Your Convenience (1971)

Carry On Venus *See* Carry On Jack (1963)

The Cars That Eat People *See* The Cars That Ate Paris (1974)

Cartagine in Fiamme *See* Carthage in Flames (1960)

Cartas del Parque *See* Letters from the Park (1988)

Carter's Army *See* Black Brigade (1969)

Cartes sur Table *See* Attack of the Robots (1966)

Carthage en Flammes *See* Carthage in Flames (1960)

Casa de Areia *See* House of Sand (2005)

Casa Privata per le SS *See* SS Girls (1977)

Casanova Falling *See* Giving It Up (1999)

Case of Evil *See* Sherlock: Case of Evil (2002)

The Case of Jonathan Drew *See* The Lodger (1926)

The Case of the Hillside Stranglers *See* The Hillside Strangler (1989)

Case of the Missing Switchboard Operator *See* The Love Affair, or The Case of the Missing Switchboard Operator (1967)

Cash *See* If I Were Rich (1933)

Cash Crop *See* Harvest (1998)

Cassanova and Co. *See* Sex on the Run (1978)

Castle in the Sky *See* Yidl Mitn Fidl (1936)

Castle of Doom *See* Vampyr (1931)

Castle of Dracula *See* Blood of Dracula's Castle (1969)

Castle of Terror *See* Castle of Blood (1964)

Castle of Terror *See* The Virgin of Nuremberg (1965)

The Castle of the Spider's Web *See* Throne of Blood (1957)

Castle of the Walking Dead *See* The Torture Chamber of Dr. Sadism (1969)

The Cat *See* Le Chat (1975)

The Cat Ate the Parakeet *See* Pot, Parents, and Police (1971)

The Cat in the Hat *See* Dr. Seuss' The Cat in the Hat (2003)

Cat Murkil and the Silks *See* Cruisin' High (1975)

C.A.T. Squad *See* Stalking Danger (1986)

C.A.T. Squad: Python Wolf *See* Python Wolf (1988)

The Cat With the Jade Eyes *See* Watch Me When I Kill (1977)

Catacombs *See* Curse 4: The Ultimate Sacrifice (1990)

Catastrophe 1999 *See* Last Days of Planet Earth (1974)

Catch Me If You Can *See* Deadly Game (1998)

Catchfire *See* Backtrack (1989)

Caterina va in citta *See* Caterina in the Big City (2003)

Catholic Boys *See* Heaven Help Us (1985)

Cathy Tippel *See* Katie Tippel (1975)

Cats *See* Night of a Thousand Cats (1972)

Cattle Call *See* National Lampoon Presents Cattle Call (2006)

Cauchemares *See* Cathy's Curse (1977)

Caught in the Act *See* Cosi (1995)

Cauldron of Death *See* Mean Machine (1973)

A Cause d'un Garcon *See* You'll Get Over It (2002)

Cause Toujours, Mon Lapin *See* Keep Talking Baby (1961)

Cavalleria Commandos *See* Cavalry Command (1963)

The Cave Dwellers *See* One Million B.C. (1940)

Cave Man *See* One Million B.C. (1940)

Cavegirl *See* Cave Girl (1985)

Cell Block Girls *See* Thunder County (1974)

Cell Block Girls *See* Women's Prison Escape (1974)

Celos *See* Jealousy (1999)

Cemetery Girls *See* The Vampire Hookers (1978)

Cemetery Girls *See* The Velvet Vampire (1971)

Cento Dollari D'Odio *See* Uncle Tom's Cabin (1969)

Central Do Brasil *See* Central Station (1998)

Ceremonia Sangrienta *See* The Legend of Blood Castle (1972)

Cerny Petr *See* Black Peter (1963)

A Certain Mr. Scratch *See* The Devil & Daniel Webster (1941)

Ces Dames Preferent le Mambo *See* Dishonorable Discharge (1957)

C'est Arrive pres de Chez Vous *See* Man Bites Dog (1991)

Cet Obscur Objet du Desir *See* That Obscure Object of Desire (1977)

Ceux Qui M'Aiment Predront le Train *See* Those Who Love Me Can Take the Train (1998)

Cha no aji *See* The Taste of Tea (2004)

Chacun Cherche Son Chat *See* When the Cat's Away (1996)

Chacun sa Nuit *See* One to Another (2006)

Chained Heat 3 *See* Chained Heat 3: Hell Mountain (1998)

Chained Heat 3: The Horror of Hell Mountain *See* Chained Heat 3: Hell Mountain (1998)

Chaingang Girls *See* Sweet Sugar (1972)

Chakushin ari *See* One Missed Call (2003)

Chakushin ari 2 *See* One Missed Call 2 (2005)

Chakushin ari Final *See* One Missed Call 3: Final (2006)

Chaliapin: Adventures of Don Quixote *See* Don Quixote (1935)

The Challenge *See* It Takes a Thief (1959)

The Challenge of Rin Tin Tin *See* Courage of Rin Tin Tin (1957)

Chamber of Fear *See* The Fear Chamber (1968)

Chamber of Tortures *See* Torture Chamber of Baron Blood (1972)

The Chambermaid *See* The Chambermaid on the Titanic (1997)

Champ d'Honneur *See* Field of Honor (1987)

Change Moi Ma Vie *See* Change My Life (2001)

Changes *See* Danielle Steel's Changes (1991)

Chaos *See* Kaos (1985)

Charades *See* First Degree (1998)

Charles: Mort ou Vif *See* Charles: Dead or Alive (1969)

Charlie's Ghost Story *See* Charlie's Ghost: The Secret of Coronado (1994)

Charterhouse at Parma *See* La Chartreuse de Parme (1948)

Chastnaya Zhizn *See* Private Life (1982)

The Chautauqua *See* The Trouble with Girls (and How to Get into It) (1969)

Che? *See* Diary of Forbidden Dreams (1973)

Cheaters *See* Tricheurs (1984)

Cheeseburger Film Sandwich *See* Amazon Women on the Moon (1987)

Chek law dak gung *See* Naked Weapon (2003)

Chelovek s Kinoapparatom *See* The Man with the Movie Camera (1929)

Chernobyl: The Final Warning *See* Final Warning (1990)

Cherry Blossoms: Hanami *See* Cherry Blossoms (2008)

Cherry Pink *See* Just Looking (1999)

Cheun Gwong Tsa Sit *See* Happy Together (1996)

Cheung Fo *See* The Mission (1999)

Chevy Van *See* The Van (1977)

Chi Bi *See* Red Cliff (2008)

Chi l'Ha Vista Morire *See* Who Saw Her Die? (1972)

Chi Sei *See* Beyond the Door (1975)

The Chief Wants No Survivors *See* No Survivors, Please (1963)

Chik yeung tin si *See* So Close (2002)

Chikamatsu Monogatari *See* The Crucified Lovers (1954)

Chiklo Gouyeung *See* Naked Killer (1992)

Chikyu Boelgun *See* The Mysterians (1958)

Child of Satan *See* To the Devil, a Daughter (1976)

Child of the Night *See* What the Peeper Saw (1972)

Childhood of Maxim Gorky *See* My Childhood (1938)

Childish Things *See* Confessions of Tom Harris (1972)

The Children of Bullerby Village *See* The Children of Noisy Village (1986)

Children of the Dust *See* A Good Day to Die (1995)

Child's Play *See* Love Me if You Dare (2003)

Chilled in Miami *See* New in Town (2009)

Chin gei bin *See* Vampire Effect (2003)

China 9, Liberty 37 *See* Gunfire (1978)

China Ranch *See* Shell Shock (1963)

Chinchero *See* The Last Movie (1971)

Chine, Ma Douleur *See* China, My Sorrow (1989)

The Chinese *See* La Chinoise (1967)

Chinese Super Ninjas *See* Five Element Ninjas (1982)

Chinese Superman *See* Super Inframan (1976)

Cho kowai hanashi A: yami no karasu *See* Cursed (2004)

Chocolate for Breakfast *See* Four and a Half Women (2005)

Chong xiao lou *See* House of Traps (1981)

Chongqing Senlin *See* Chungking Express (1995)

Choyonghan kajok *See* The Quiet Family (1998)

Chrissa Stands Strong *See* American Girl: Chrissa Stands Strong (2009)

A Christmas Memory *See* ABC Stage 67: Truman Capote's A Christmas Memory (1966)

Christmas Miracle in Caulfield, U.S.A. *See* The Christmas Coal Mine Miracle (1977)

Christmas Mountains *See* Story of a Cowboy Angel (1981)

Christmas Rush *See* Breakaway (2002)

The Christmas Tree *See* When Wolves Cry (1969)

Christmas Vacation *See* National Lampoon's Christmas Vacation (1989)

Christmas Vacation 2: Cousin Eddie *See* National Lampoon's Christmas Vacation 2: Cousin Eddie's Big Island Adventure (2003)

Christmas Vacation 2: Cousin Eddie's Island Adventure *See* National Lampoon's Christmas Vacation 2: Cousin Eddie's Big Island Adventure (2003)

A Christmas Wish *See* The Great Rupert (1950)

Chrome Hearts *See* C.C. & Company (1970)

Chronicle of a Lonely Child *See* Chronicle of a Boy Alone (1964)

Chronos *See* Cronos (1994)

Chuck Norris vs. the Karate Cop *See* Slaughter in San Francisco (1981)

Chuecatown *See* Boystown (2007)

Chuen jik sat sau *See* Full Time Killer (2001)

Chui Ma Lau *See* Drunken Monkey (2002)

Chum thaang rot fai phii *See* Diecovery (2003)

Chunchik satsau *See* Full Time Killer (2001)

Chunfeng Chenzuide Yewan *See* Spring Fever (2009)

Chung siu lau *See* House of Traps (1981)

Chungon Satluk Linggei *See* Organized Crime & Triad Bureau (1993)

Chupacabra: Dark Seas *See* Chupacabra Terror (2005)

Ci Qing *See* Spider Lilies (2006)

Ciao! Manhattan *See* Edie in Ciao! Manhattan (1972)

Cica Tomina Koliba *See* Uncle Tom's Cabin (1969)

Cidade de Deus *See* City of God (2002)

Cidade des Homens *See* City of Men (2007)

Cien *See* Shadow (1956)

The Cinder Path *See* Catherine Cookson's The Cinder Path (1994)

Cing shao nian nuo jha *See* Rebels of the Neon God (1992)

Cinq fois deux *See* 5x2 (2004)

Cipolla Colt *See* Spaghetti Western (1975)

The Circle *See* The Fraternity (2001)

The Circle *See* The Vicious Circle (1957)

The Circle *See* Woman in Brown (1948)

Circuit Breaker *See* Inhumanoid (1996)

Circuitry Man 2 *See* Plughead Rewired: Circuitry Man 2 (1994)

The Cisco Kid in Old New Mexico *See* In Old New Mexico (1945)

Citadel of Crime *See* Wheel of Fortune (1941)

The Citizen Rebels *See* Street Law (1974)

Citizen's Band *See* FM (1978)

City in Fear *See* A Place Called Today (1972)

The City Jungle *See* The Young Philadelphians (1959)

The City of the Dead *See* Horror Hotel (1960)

City of the Living Dead *See* Gates of Hell (1980)

City with No Mercy *See* Flash Point (2007)

Ciudad de M *See* City of M (2001)

Civility *See* Malicious Intent (1999)

The Clairvoyant *See* The Evil Mind (1934)

The Clairvoyant *See* Killing Hour (1984)

The Clansman *See* The Birth of a Nation (1915)

Class of '86 *See* National Lampoon's Class of '86 (1986)

Class Reunion *See* National Lampoon's Class Reunion (1982)

Claude *See* The Two of Us (1968)

Claude et Greta *See* Her and She and Him (1969)

Claudine's Return *See* Kiss of Fire (1998)

Claustrophobia *See* Serial Slayer (2003)

Clean Slate *See* Coup de Torchon (1981)

The Cleaner *See* The Professional (1994)

Cleo de 5 a 7 *See* Cleo from 5 to 7 (1961)

Clickety Clack *See* Dodes 'ka-den (1970)

Clinton & Nadine *See* Blood Money: The Story of Clinton and Nadine (1988)

Clive Barker Presents: Hellraiser *See* Hellraiser (2009)

Clive Barker's Lord of Illusions *See* Lord of Illusions (1995)

The Cloak *See* The Overcoat (1959)

The Closed Door *See* Bandh Darwaza (1990)

The Closer You Get *See* American Women (2000)

The Closest of Kin *See* All the Lovin' Kinfolk (1970)

Club Dead *See* Terror at Red Wolf Inn (1972)

Clubland *See* Introducing the Dwights (2007)

Coast of Terror *See* Summer City (1977)

Coastwatcher *See* The Last Warrior (1989)

Cobra Nero *See* The Black Cobra (1987)

Cobweb Castle *See* Throne of Blood (1957)

Cockles and Muscles *See* Cote d'Azur (2005)

Coco avant Chanel *See* Coco Before Chanel (2009)

Cocozza's Way *See* Strictly Sinatra (2001)

Code Inconnu: Recit Incomplet De Divers Voyages *See* Code Unknown (2000)

Code Name: Operation Crossbow *See* Operation Crossbow (1965)

Code Name: Trixie *See* The Crazies (1973)

Code Name: Wolverine *See* Wolverine (1996)

Code 645 *See* G-Men Never Forget (1948)

Code Unknown: Incomplete Tales of Several Journeys *See* Code Unknown (2000)

Codename: The Soldier *See* The Soldier (1982)

Coeurs *See* Private Fears in Public Places (2006)

Coffin of Terror *See* Castle of Blood (1964)

Cold Night Into Dawn *See* Bomb Squad (1997)

Colin Nutley's House of Angels *See* House of Angels (1992)

Collision Course *See* The Bamboo Saucer (1968)

Colonel Blimp *See* The Life and Death of Colonel Blimp (1943)

Colorado Ranger *See* Guns of Justice (1950)

Colossus and the Amazons *See* Colossus and the Amazon Queen (1964)

Colour Blind *See* Catherine Cookson's Colour Blind (1998)

Combien Tu M'Aimes? *See* How Much Do You Love Me? (2005)

Come Back Peter *See* The Seducer (1969)

Come Back to Me *See* Doll Face (1946)

Come Dance with Me *See* Voulez-Vous Danser avec Moi? (1959)

Come 'n' Get It *See* Lunch Wagon (1981)

Come On Ranger *See* Come on Rangers (1938)

A Comedia de Deus *See* God's Comedy (1995)

Comedie de L'Innocence *See* Comedy of Innocence (2000)

Comizi d'Amore *See* Love Meetings (1964)

Comme des Voleurs *See* Stealth (2006)

Comme Tout le Monde *See* Mr. Average (2006)

Comme un Frere *See* Like a Brother (2005)

Comme un Poisson Hors de'Eau *See* Like a Fish Out of Water (1999)

Comme une image *See* Look at Me (2004)

Comment J'ai Tue Mon Pere *See* How I Killed My Father (2003)

Comment le Desir Vient aux Filles *See* I Am Frigid... Why? (1972)

Communion *See* Alice Sweet Alice (1976)

Como Agua para Chocolate *See* Like Water for Chocolate (1993)

Como Era Gostoso O Meu Frances *See* How Tasty Was My Little Frenchman (1971)

Como ser Mujer y No Morir en El *See* How to Be a Woman and Not Die in the Attempt (1991)

Compagna di Viaggio *See* Traveling Companion (1996)

The Company of Strangers *See* Strangers in Good Company (1991)

Complicity *See* Retribution (1998)

Computer Killers *See* Horror Hospital (1973)

Comrades *See* The Organizer (1964)

Comradeship *See* Kameradschaft (1931)

The Con Artists *See* The Switch (1976)

Con Man *See* Freelance (1971)

The Con Man *See* The Con Artists (1980)

Concerto *See* I've Always Loved You (1946)

A Condemned Man Has Escaped *See* A Man Escaped (1957)

Condenados a Vivir *See* Bronson's Revenge (1972)

Confesion a Laura *See* Confessing to Laura (1990)

Confession *See* Repentance (1987)

The Confession *See* Quick, Let's Get Married (1971)

Confessions of A Peeping John *See* Hi, Mom! (1970)

Confessions of a Prostitute *See* The Immoral One (1980)

Confessions of a Sex Maniac *See* The Slasher (1972)

Confidences trop intimes *See* Intimate Strangers (2004)

Confidential Report *See* Mr. Arkadin (1955)

Conflagration *See* Enjo (1958)

The Conflict *See* Catholics (1973)

Conqueror of the Desert *See* The Conqueror (1956)

Conquest *See* El Barbaro (1984)

The Conquests of Peter the Great *See* Peter the First: Part 2 (1938)

The Conspiracy *See* Le Complot (1973)

Contamination *See* Alien Contamination (1981)

Conte d'Automne *See* Autumn Tale (1998)

Conte d'Ete *See* A Summer's Tale (1996)

Conte D'Hiver *See* A Tale of Winter (1992)

Continuavamo A Chiamarlo Trinita *See* Trinity Is Still My Name (1975)

Contra el Viento *See* Against the Wind (1990)

Contracorriente *See* Undertow (2010)

Contract in Blood *See* Le Choc (1982)

Control *See* Kontroll (2003)

Control Factor *See* The Big Game (1972)

Convention City *See* Sons of the Desert (1933)

Conviene far Bene L'Amore *See* The Sex Machine (1975)

The Cook in Love *See* A Chef in Love (1996)

Coolangatta Gold *See* The Gold & Glory (1988)

Coonskin *See* Streetfight (1975)

A Cop for the Killing *See* In the Line of Duty: A Cop for the Killing (1990)

Cop Killers *See* Corrupt (1984)

Cop Tips Waitress 2 Million *See* It Could Happen to You (1994)

Copenhagen's Psychic Loves *See* The Psychic (1968)

Copland *See* Cop Land (1997)

Cord *See* Hide and Seek (2000)

The Corporation *See* Subliminal Seduction (1996)

A Corps Perdu *See* Straight for the Heart (1988)

The Corpse *See* Crucible of Horror (1969)

Corpse Bride *See* Tim Burton's Corpse Bride (2005)

A Corpse Hangs in the Web *See* Horrors of Spider Island (1959)

Corta Notte delle Bambole di Vetro *See* Short Night of Glass Dolls (1971)

Cosi Dolce...Cosi Perversa *See* Kiss Me, Kill Me (1973)

The Cosmic Man Appears in Tokyo *See* Warning from Space (1956)

Cosmo 2000: Planet Without a Name *See* Cosmos: War of the Planets (1980)

Cost of Dying *See* Taste of Death (1968)

Cottonmouth *See* Lethal Force (2000)

Count Dracula and His Vampire Bride *See* The Satanic Rites of Dracula (1973)

Count Dracula's Great Love *See* Dracula's Great Love (1972)

Country Blue *See* On the Run (1973)

Country Music *See* Las Vegas Hillbillys (1966)

Country Music Daughter *See* Nashville Girl (1976)

Country Nurse *See* Emmanuelle in the Country (1978)

Country of My Skull *See* In My Country (2004)

Coup de Foudre *See* Entre-Nous (1983)

Coup de Tete *See* Hothead (1978)

A Couple of Dicks *See* Cop Out (2010)

Courage *See* Raw Courage (1984)

The Courage of Kavik, the Wolf Dog *See* Kavik the Wolf Dog (1980)

The Courier *See* Outta Time (2001)

Cours Toujours *See* Dad On the Run (2000)

The Court *See* Bamako (2006)

Court Martial *See* Carrington, V.C. (1954)

Courtesan *See* Dangerous Beauty (1998)

The Courtneys of Curzon Street *See* The Courtney Affair (1947)

Covek Nije Tica *See* Man Is Not a Bird (1965)

Covert One: The Hades Factor *See* The Hades Factor (2006)

Cowboy Dad *See* A Father's Choice (2000)

Cows *See* Vacas (1991)

Coyote Moon *See* Desert Heat (1999)

Crack *See* Strike Force (1975)

Crackerjack 2: Hostage Train *See* Crackerjack 2 (1997)

Cradle of Crime *See* Dead End (1937)

Crank 2: High Voltage *See* Crank: High Voltage (2009)

Crash Landing: The Rescue of Flight 232 *See* A Thousand Heroes (1992)

Crash of Silence *See* Mandy (1953)

Crawlers *See* They Crawl (2001)

The Crawling Monster *See* Creeping Terror (1964)

Crazy Doll Trick *See* Murders in the Doll House (1979)

Crazy for You *See* Vision Quest (1985)

Crazy Horse *See* Friends, Lovers & Lunatics (1989)

Crazy House *See* Night of the Laughing Dead (1975)

Crazy Jack and the Boy *See* Silence (1973)

Crazy Joe *See* Dead Center (1994)

Crazy Knights *See* Ghost Crazy (1944)

Crazy Streets *See* Forever, Lulu (1987)

Crazy World *See* Mondo Cane 2 (1964)

Created to Kill *See* Embryo (1976)

Creature from Galaxy 27 *See* Night of the Blood Beast (1958)

The Creature Wasn't Nice *See* Spaceship (1981)

Creatures *See* From Beyond the Grave (1973)

Creatures of the Devil *See* Dead Men Walk (1943)

Creatures of the Prehistoric Planet *See* Horror of the Blood Monsters (1970)

Creatures of the Red Planet *See* Horror of the Blood Monsters (1970)

The Creature's Revenge *See* Brain of Blood (1971)

The Creeper *See* Dark Side of Midnight (1986)

The Creeper *See* Rituals (1979)

Creepers *See* They Live (1988)

The Creepers *See* Assault (1970)

The Creepers *See* Island of Terror (1966)

The Creeping Unknown *See* The Quatermass Experiment (1956)

Creeps *See* Bloody Birthday (1980)

Creeps *See* Night of the Creeps (1986)

Cria Cuervos *See* Cria (1976)

The Cricket *See* La Cicada (1983)

Crime and Punishment *See* Dostoevsky's Crime and Punishment (1999)

Crime Boss *See* New Mafia Boss (1972)

The Crime Doctor's Vacation *See* The Millerson Case (1947)

Crime et Chatiment *See* Crime and Punishment (1935)

Crimen Ferpecto *See* El Crimen Perfecto (2004)

Crimes in the Wax Museum *See* Nightmare in Wax (1969)

Crimes, Inc. *See* Gangs, Inc. (1941)

The Crimes of Dr. Mabuse *See* Testament of Dr. Mabuse (1962)

The Criminal *See* The Concrete Jungle (1982)

The Crimson Altar *See* The Crimson Cult (1968)

Crimson Executioner *See* The Bloody Pit of Horror (1965)

The Crimson Ghost *See* Cyclotrode "X" (1946)

Cristo si e fermato a Eboli *See* Christ Stopped at Eboli (1979)

Crocodile *See* Blood Surf (2000)

Cronaca di un Amore *See* Story of a Love Affair (1950)

Cronica de un Nino Solo *See* Chronicle of a Boy Alone (1964)

Cronica de una Fuga *See* Chronicle of an Escape (2006)

Cronicamente Inviavel *See* Chronically Unfeasible (2000)

Crooked River *See* Last Bullet (1950)

Crooks in Clover *See* Penthouse (1933)

Crossed Swords *See* The Prince and the Pauper (1978)

Crossed Tracks *See* Roman de Gare (2007)

Crossfire *See* The Bandits (1967)

Crossing the Line *See* The Big Man: Crossing the Line (1991)

The Crown Caper *See* The Thomas Crown Affair (1968)

Cruel Swamp *See* Swamp Women (1955)

Crusade in Jeans *See* Crusade: A March through Time (2006)

Crustaces et Coquillages *See* Cote d'Azur (2005)

The Cry *See* Il Grido (1957)

Crying Out Loud *See* Cotton Queen (1937)

Crypt of Dark Secrets *See* Mardi Gras Massacre (1978)

Crypt of the Blind Dead *See* Tombs of the Blind Dead (1972)

C.S. Lewis Through the Shadowlands *See* Shadowlands (1985)

Csillagosok, Katonak *See* The Red and the White (1968)

C't'a Ton Tour, Laura Cadieux *See* It's My Turn, Laura Cadieux (1998)

Cuatro Dolares de Venganza *See* Four Dollars of Revenge (1966)

Cuba Crossing *See* The Mercenaries (1980)

Cuban Rebel Girls *See* Assault of the Rebel Girls (1959)

Cult of the Dead *See* The Snake People (1968)

Cumbres Borrascosas *See* Wuthering Heights (1953)

Cupid in the Rough *See* Aggie Appleby, Maker of Men (1933)

The Cure *See* Cure (1997)

Curley and His Gang in the Haunted Mansion *See* Who Killed Doc Robbin? (1948)

The Curse *See* Xala (1975)

Curse of Dark Shadows *See* Night of Dark Shadows (1971)

The Curse of Demon Mountain *See* Shadow of Chikara (1977)

The Curse of Dr. Phibes *See* The Abominable Dr. Phibes (1971)

The Curse of Dracula *See* Return of Dracula (1958)

The Curse of Green Eyes *See* Cave of the Living Dead (1965)

Curse of Melissa *See* The Touch of Satan (1970)

Curse of the Blood-Ghouls *See* The Slaughter of the Vampires (1962)

Curse of the Crimson Altar *See* The Crimson Cult (1968)

The Curse of the Dragon *See* Bruce Lee: Curse of the Dragon (1993)

Curse of the Living Dead *See* Kill, Baby, Kill (1966)

Curse of the Mushroom People *See* Attack of the Mushroom People (1963)

Curse of the Mushroom People *See* Matango (1963)

Curses of the Ghouls *See* The Slaughter of the Vampires (1962)

The Cusp *See* Falling Fire (1997)

Cut-Throats Nine *See* Bronson's Revenge (1972)

Cutter and Bone *See* Cutter's Way (1981)

The Cutting Edge 2: Going for the Gold *See* The Cutting Edge: Going for the Gold (2005)

Cybele *See* Sundays & Cybele (1962)

Cyber-Chic *See* Robo-Chic (1989)

Cyberjack *See* Virtual Assassin (1995)

Cyborg 2: Glass Shadow *See* Cyborg 2 (1993)

Cyborg Cop 2 *See* Cyborg Soldier (1994)

D-Day-Eonneunal kabjagi cheotbeonjjae iyagi *See* My Bloody Roommates (2006)

D-Day on Mars *See* The Purple Monster Strikes (1945)

D-Tox *See* Eye See You (2001)

D-War *See* Dragon Wars (2007)

Da Bancarella a Bancarotta *See* Peddlin' in Society (1947)

Da Wan *See* Big Shot's Funeral (2001)

Da Zdravstvuyet Meksika *See* Que Viva Mexico (1932)

Da zhi lao *See* Running on Karma (2003)

Da zui xia *See* Come Drink with Me (1965)

Daai chek liu *See* Running on Karma (2003)

Daai Si Gin *See* Breaking News (2004)

Daddy *See* Danielle Steel's Daddy (1991)

Daddy Nostalgie *See* Daddy Nostalgia (1990)

Daddy's Deadly Darling *See* Pigs (1973)

Daddy's Girl *See* Cravings (2006)

Dad's Week Off *See* National Lampoon's Dad's Week Off (1997)

Daehakno-yeseo maechoon-hadaka tomaksalhae danghan yeogosang ajik Daehakno-ye Issda *See* Killing Machine (2002)

Dagboek Van Een Oude Dwaas *See* Diary of a Mad Old Man (1988)

Dagora *See* Dagora, the Space Monster (1965)

Dai Koesu Yongkari *See* Yongkari Monster of the Deep (1967)

Dai Nipponjin *See* Big Man Japan (2007)

Daibosatsu Toge *See* Sword of Doom (1967)

Daikaiju Baran *See* Varan the Unbelievable (1961)

Daikaiju Gamera *See* Gamera, the Invincible (1966)

Daikaiju Masura *See* Mothra (1962)

Daikyoju Gappa *See* Gappa the Trifibian Monster (1967)

Daimajin 2: Wrath of Daimajin *See* Wrath of Daimajin (1966)

Daimajin gyakushu *See* Return of Daimajin (1966)

Daimajin ikaru *See* Wrath of Daimajin (1966)

Dairy Queens *See* Drop Dead Gorgeous (1999)

Dakhtaran-e Khorshid *See* Daughters of the Sun (2000)

Dalle Ardenne All'Inferno *See* Dirty Heroes (1971)

The Dalton Gang *See* Outlaw Gang (1949)

Dance Academy *See* Body Beat (1988)

Dance of the Dwarfs *See* Jungle Heat (1984)

Dance of the Vampires *See* The Fearless Vampire Killers (1967)

Dancer *See* Billy Elliot (2000)

Dancing about Architecture *See* Playing by Heart (1998)

Dandelion *See* Tampopo (1986)

Danger Rides the Range *See* Three Texas Steers (1939)

Dangerous Charter *See* Creeping Terror (1964)

Dangerous Female *See* The Maltese Falcon (1931)

A Dangerous Friend *See* The Todd Killings (1971)

Dangerous Isolation *See* Trapped (2006)

Dangerous Kiss *See* True Crime (1995)

Dangerous Love Affairs *See* Dangerous Liaisons (1960)

Daniel Defoe's Robinson Crusoe *See* Robinson Crusoe (1996)

Danielle Steel's Jewels *See* Jewels (1992)

Danielle Steel's Safe Harbour *See* Safe Harbour (2007)

Danielle Steel's Vanished *See* Vanished (1995)

Danny the Dog *See* Unleashed (2005)

Danny Travis *See* The Last Word (1980)

Dans la Ville Blanche *See* In the White City (1983)

Dans les Griffes du Maniaque *See* The Diabolical Dr. Z (1965)

Dans Paris *See* Inside Paris (2006)

Danza Macabra *See* Castle of Blood (1964)

Dao huo xian *See* Flash Point (2007)

Daoma Zei *See* The Horse Thief (1987)

Dare mo shiranai *See* Nobody Knows (2004)

The Daring Caballero *See* Guns of Fury (1949)

Dario Argento's Phantom of the Opera *See* The Phantom of the Opera (1998)

Dark Angel *See* I Come in Peace (1990)

The Dark Avenger *See* The Warriors (1955)

Dark Empire *See* Dark City (1997)

Dark Encounters *See* The Black Gate (1995)

Dark Eyes *See* Demon Rage (1982)

Dark Eyes of London *See* Dead Eyes of London (1961)

Dark Eyes of London *See* The Human Monster (1939)

Dark Prince: Intimate Tales of Marquis de Sade *See* Marquis de Sade (1996)

Dark Prince: The True Story of Dracula *See* Dracula: The Dark Prince (2001)

Dark Red *See* Fatal Passion (1994)

Dark Sands *See* Jericho (1938)

Dark Summer *See* Innocents (2000)

Dark Waters *See* Dead Waters (1994)

Dark World *See* Dark City (1997)

The Darkening *See* The Black Gate (1995)

Darkness Falling *See* Dark Side (2002)

Darkness in Tallinn *See* City Unplugged (1995)

D'Artagnan *See* The Three Musketeers (1916)

D'Artagnan and the Three Musketeers *See* The 4 Musketeers (2005)

D'Artagnan Contro I Tre Moschettieri *See* Revenge of the Musketeers (1963)

D'Artagnan et les Trois Mousquietaires *See* The 4 Musketeers (2005)

D'Artagnan's Daughter *See* Revenge of the Musketeers (1994)

Das Amulett des Todes *See* Cold Blood (1975)

Das Bildness des Dorian Gray *See* Dorian Gray (1970)

Das Blaue Licht *See* The Blue Light (1932)

Das Boot Ist Voll *See* The Boat Is Full (1981)

Das Cabinet des Dr. Caligari *See* The Cabinet of Dr. Caligari (1919)

Das Indische Grabmal *See* The Indian Tomb (1959)

Das Kabinett des Doktor Caligari *See* The Cabinet of Dr. Caligari (1919)

Das Kaninchen Bin Ich *See* The Rabbit Is Me (1965)

Das Leben der Anderen *See* The Lives of Others (2006)

Das Phantom von Soho *See* The Phantom of Soho (1964)

Deutschland im Herbst *See* Germany in Autumn (1978)

Deux ou Trois Choses Que Je Sais d'Elle *See* Two or Three Things I Know about Her (1966)

Deux Secondes *See* 2 Seconds (1998)

The Devil and Dr. Frankenstein *See* Andy Warhol's Frankenstein (1974)

The Devil and the Dead *See* Lisa and the Devil (1975)

The Devil and the Nun *See* Mother Joan of the Angels (1960)

The Devil in the House of Exorcism *See* Lisa and the Devil (1975)

Devil Master *See* The Demon Lover (1977)

Devil Rider *See* Master's Revenge (1971)

The Devil Walks at Midnight *See* The Devil's Nightmare (1971)

The Devil within Her *See* Beyond the Door (1975)

The Devil Within Her *See* I Don't Want to Be Born (1975)

The Devil Woman *See* Onibaba (1964)

The Devil's Bride *See* The Devil Rides Out (1968)

The Devil's Commandment *See* I, Vampiri (1956)

Devil's Doll *See* The Devil's Hand (1961)

The Devil's Envoys *See* Les Visiteurs du Soir (1942)

Devil's Express *See* Gang Wars (1975)

The Devil's Men *See* Land of the Minotaur (1977)

Devil's Odds *See* The Wild Pair (1987)

The Devils of Loudun *See* The Devils (1971)

The Devil's Own *See* The Witches (1966)

The Devil's Plot *See* Counterblast (1948)

The Devil's Undead *See* Nothing But the Night (1972)

The Devil's Weed *See* She Shoulda Said No (1949)

Devil's Witch *See* Kiss Me, Kill Me (1973)

Di san lei da dou *See* Heaven & Hell (1978)

Di yu *See* Heaven & Hell (1978)

Dia de los Muertos *See* All Souls Day (2005)

Diabolica Malicia *See* What the Peeper Saw (1972)

The Diabolical Dr. Mabuse *See* The Thousand Eyes of Dr. Mabuse (1960)

Diabolik *See* Danger: Diabolik (1968)

Diaboliquement Votre *See* Diabolically Yours (1967)

Dial 999 *See* The Way Out (1956)

Dial Rat for Terror *See* Housewife (1972)

Diamond Alley *See* Little Ladies of the Night (1977)

Diamond Dog Caper *See* Dog Gone (2008)

Diamond Earrings *See* The Earrings of Madame De... (1954)

Diamond Skulls *See* Dark Obsession (1990)

Diamond Thieves *See* The Squeeze (1980)

Diamonds and Crime *See* Hi Diddle Diddle (1943)

Dian Zhi Gong Fu Gan Chian Chan *See* Half a Loaf of Kung Fu (1978)

Diario Segreto Di Un Carcere Femminele *See* Women in Cell Block 7 (1977)

Diarios de motocicleta *See* The Motorcycle Diaries (2004)

Diary of a Hooker *See* Business is Business (1971)

Diary of Oharu *See* Life of Oharu (1952)

Dias Contados *See* Running Out of Time (1994)

Dick Tracy Meets Karloff *See* Dick Tracy Meets Gruesome (1947)

Dick Tracy's Amazing Adventure *See* Dick Tracy Meets Gruesome (1947)

Die Abenteuer des Werner Holt *See* The Adventures of Werner Holt (1965)

Die Angst Tormannes beim Elfmeter *See* The Goalie's Anxiety at the Penalty Kick (1971)

Die, Beautiful Marianne *See* Die Screaming, Marianne (1973)

Die Bitteren Traenen der Petra von Kant *See* The Bitter Tears of Petra von Kant (1972)

Die Blechtrommel *See* The Tin Drum (1979)

Die Bleierne Zeit *See* Marianne and Juliane (1982)

Die Brucke *See* The Bridge (1959)

Die Buechse der Pandora *See* Pandora's Box (1928)

Die Dreigroschenoper *See* The Three Penny Opera (1962)

Die Dreigroschenoper *See* The Threepenny Opera (1931)

Die Ehe Der Maria Braun *See* The Marriage of Maria Braun (1979)

Die Erotische Geschichten *See* Tales of Erotica (1993)

Die Falscher *See* The Counterfeiters (2007)

Die Fetten Jahre sind vorbei *See* The Edukators (2004)

Die Finanzen des Grossherzogs *See* The Finances of the Grand Duke (1924)

Die Flambierte Frau *See* A Woman in Flames (1984)

Die Folterkammer des Dr. Fu Manchu *See* The Castle of Fu Manchu (1968)

Die Frau und der Fremde *See* The Woman and the Stranger (1984)

Die Freudlosse Gasse *See* Joyless Street (1925)

Die Geschichte vom Weinenden Kamel *See* The Story of the Weeping Camel (2003)

Die Geschwister Oppermann *See* The Oppermann Family (1982)

Die Hard 3 *See* Die Hard: With a Vengeance (1995)

Die Holle von Macao *See* The Corrupt Ones (1967)

Die Holle von Manitoba *See* A Place Called Glory (1966)

Die Legende von Paul und Paula *See* The Legend of Paul and Paula (1973)

Die Letzte Brucke *See* The Last Bridge (1954)

Die Lustigen Weiber von Windsor *See* The Merry Wives of Windsor (1950)

Die Marquise Von O *See* The Marquise of O (1976)

Die Morder Sind Unter Uns *See* The Murderers Are Among Us (1946)

Die Nibelungen *See* Kriemhilde's Revenge (1924)

Die Now, Pay Later *See* Fort Yuma Gold (1966)

Die Regenschirme von Cherbourg *See* Umbrellas of Cherbourg (1964)

Die Reise nach Kafiristan *See* The Journey to Kafiristan (2001)

Die Saege des Todes *See* Bloody Moon (1983)

Die Schachnovelle *See* Brainwashed (1960)

Die Schlangengrube und das Pendel *See* The Torture Chamber of Dr. Sadism (1969)

Die Sehns Ucht Der Veronika Voss *See* Veronika Voss (1982)

Die Siebtelbauern *See* The Inheritors (1998)

Die Stille Nach Dem Schuss *See* The Legend of Rita (1999)

Die Tausend Augen des Dr. Mabuse *See* The Thousand Eyes of Dr. Mabuse (1960)

Die Toten Augen von London *See* Dead Eyes of London (1961)

Die Unsichtbaren Krallen des Dr. Mabuse *See* The Invisible Dr. Mabuse (1962)

Die Verfehlung *See* The Mistake (1991)

Die Verlorene Ehre Der Katharina Blum *See* The Lost Honor of Katharina Blum (1975)

Die Verruckten Reichen *See* Twist (1976)

Die Vierde Man *See* The 4th Man (1979)

Die Weisse Rose *See* The White Rose (1983)

Die Xue Jie Tou *See* A Bullet in the Head (1990)

Die Xue Shuang Xiong *See* The Killer (1990)

Die Zartlichkeit der Wolfe *See* Tenderness of the Wolves (1973)

Die Zwolfte Stunde *See* Nosferatu (1922)

The Digital Prophet *See* Cyberstalker (1996)

Dillinger 70 *See* Carbon Copy (1969)

Dillinger e Morto *See* Dillinger Is Dead (1969)

Dillo con Parole Mie *See* Ginger and Cinnamon (2003)

Dimensions in Death *See* Castle of Blood (1964)

Dio Mio, Come Sono Caduta in Basso *See* Till Marriage Do Us Part (1974)

Dio, Sei Proprio un Padrenterno! *See* Escape from Death Row (1973)

Direktoren for Det Hele *See* The Boss of It All (2006)

Dirt Nap *See* Two Tickets to Paradise (2006)

Dirty Hands *See* Innocents with Dirty Hands (1976)

A Dirty Knight's Work *See* Choice of Weapons (1976)

Dirty Mary *See* A Very Curious Girl (1969)

Dirty, Mean and Nasty *See* Down & Dirty (1976)

The Dirty Mob *See* Mean Machine (1973)

Dirty Work *See* Bad City (2006)

The Disappearance of Nora *See* High Stakes (1993)

Disaster at Valdez *See* Dead Ahead: The Exxon Valdez Disaster (1992)

Disciple of Dracula *See* Dracula, Prince of Darkness (1966)

Disco Godfather *See* Avenging Disco Godfather (1976)

Disco Madness *See* Toga Party (1977)

The Discreet *See* La Discrete (1990)

Disney's A Christmas Carol *See* A Christmas Carol (2009)

Disney's Blank Check *See* Blank Check (1993)

Dispara *See* Outrage (1993)

Disparen a Matar *See* Shoot to Kill (1990)

Distant Cousins *See* Desperate Motives (1992)

A Distant Scream *See* The Dying Truth (1986)

Dites-Lui Que Je L'Aime *See* This Sweet Sickness (1977)

Divertimento *See* La Belle Noiseuse (1990)

Divine Emmanuelle *See* Love Camp (1981)

Divine Obsession *See* Dangerous Obsession (1988)

Divorzio All'Italiana *See* Divorce—Italian Style (1962)

Django 2: Il Grande Ritorno *See* Django Strikes Again (1987)

Django Spara per Primo *See* Django Shoots First (1974)

Djavulens Oga *See* The Devil's Eye (1960)

Djoflaeyjan *See* Devil's Island (1996)

Dnevnoi Dozor: Mel Sudbi *See* Day Watch (2006)

Do Not Disturb *See* Silent Witness (1999)

Do You Want to Dance with Me? *See* Voulez-Vous Danser avec Moi? (1959)

Doches Froides *See* Cold Showers (2005)

The Dock Brief *See* Trial & Error (1962)

Docteur Chance *See* Doctor Chance (1997)

Docteur M. *See* Club Extinction (1989)

Docteur Popaul *See* High Heels (1972)

Doctor Beware *See* Teresa Venerdi (1941)

Dr. Black and Mr. White *See* Dr. Black, Mr. Hyde (1976)

Doctor Blood Bath *See* Horror Hospital (1973)

Dr. Cadman's Secret *See* The Black Sleep (1956)

The Doctor from Seven Dials *See* Corridors of Blood (1958)

Doctor Gore *See* The Body Shop (1972)

Dr. Jekyll vs. the Werewolf *See* Dr. Jekyll and the Wolfman (1971)

Dr. Jekyll y el Hombre Lobo *See* Dr. Jekyll and the Wolfman (1971)

Dr. Jekyll's Dungeon of Darkness *See* Dr. Tarr's Torture Dungeon (1975)

Dr. Mabuse, Parts 1 & 2 *See* Dr. Mabuse, The Gambler (1922)

Dr. Maniac *See* The Man Who Lived Again (1936)

Doctor Maniac *See* House of the Living Dead (1973)

Dr. Orloff's Invisible Monster *See* Orloff and the Invisible Man (1970)

Dr. Phibes *See* The Abominable Dr. Phibes (1971)

Dr. Sleep *See* Close Your Eyes (2002)

Dr. Terror's Gallery of Horrors *See* Alien Massacre (1967)

Dr. Terror's Gallery of Horrors *See* Gallery of Horrors (1967)

Doctors Wear Scarlet *See* The Bloodsuckers (1970)

The Does *See* Les Biches (1968)

A Dog, a Mouse, and a Sputnik *See* Sputnik (1961)

Dog Soldiers *See* Who'll Stop the Rain? (1978)

Dogboys *See* Tracked (1998)

A Dog's Life *See* Mondo Cane (1963)

Dogwater *See* Since You've Been Gone (1997)

Doin' It *See* The First Time (1969)

Doin' It *See* First Time (1982)

Doing Life *See* Truth or Die (1986)

Doing Time *See* Porridge (1991)

Doktor Mabuse der Spieler *See* Dr. Mabuse, The Gambler (1922)

Dolphins *See* Octane (2007)

Dolwyn *See* The Last Days of Dolwyn (1949)

Dom Durakov *See* House of Fools (2002)

Dom Za Vesanje *See* Time of the Gypsies (1990)

Domestic Import *See* Nanny Insanity (2006)

Domicile Conjugal *See* Bed and Board (1970)

Dominick Dunne Presents Murder in Greenwich *See* Murder in Greenwich (2002)

The Domino Killings *See* The Domino Principle (1977)

Don Juan *See* Private Life of Don Juan (1934)

Don Juan 73 *See* Don Juan (Or If Don Juan Were a Woman) (1973)

Don Juan, Mi Querido Fantasma *See* Don Juan, My Love (1990)

Don Kikhot *See* Don Quixote (1957)

Dona Flor e Seus Dois Maridos *See* Dona Flor and Her Two Husbands (1978)

Dona Herlinda y Su Hijo *See* Dona Herlinda & Her Son (1986)

Donato and Daughter *See* Dead to Rights (1993)

Dong *See* The Hole (1998)

Dong Fang San Xia *See* The Heroic Trio (1993)

Dong Mau Anh Hung *See* The Rebel (2008)

Donggong, Xigong *See* East Palace, West Palace (1996)

Donne facili *See* Les Bonnes Femmes (1960)

The Don's Analyst *See* National Lampoon's The Don's Analyst (1997)

Don't Go Near the Park *See* Nightstalker (1981)

Don't Look Now, We've Been Shot At *See* La Grande Vadrouille (1966)

Don't Tempt Me! *See* No News from God (2001)

Don't Touch the Axe *See* The Duchess of Langeais (2007)

Donzoko *See* The Lower Depths (1957)

Doomed *See* Ikiru (1952)

The Doomsday Machine *See* Escape from Planet Earth (1967)

The Door with Seven Locks *See* Chamber of Horrors (1940)

Dope Addict *See* Reefer Madness (1938)

Doped Youth *See* Reefer Madness (1938)

Dopo mezzanotte *See* After Midnight (2004)

Doppelganger *See* Journey to the Far Side of the Sun (1969)

Doppleganger *See* Doppelganger: The Evil Within (1990)

Dos Tipos Duros *See* Two Tough Guys (2003)

Dos Veces Judas *See* Twice a Judas (1969)

Dou fo sin *See* Flash Point (2007)

The Double *See* Kagemusha (1980)

Double Cross *See* Motorcycle Squad (1941)

Double Down *See* Stacy's Knights (1983)

Double Hit *See* The Arab Conspiracy (1976)

Double Possession *See* Ganja and Hess (1973)

Double Trouble *See* No Deposit, No Return (1976)

Double Your Pleasure *See* The Reluctant Agent (1989)

Doubting Thomas *See* Spy School (2008)

Douce Violence *See* Sweet Ecstasy (1962)

Doulos—The Finger Man *See* Le Doulos (1961)

Down *See* The Shaft (2001)

Down Among the Z Men *See* Goon Movie (1952)

Down Went McGinty *See* The Great McGinty (1940)

Dracula *See* Bram Stoker's Dracula (1992)

Dracula *See* The Horror of Dracula (1958)

Dracula and the Seven Golden Vampires *See* The Legend of the 7 Golden Vampires (1973)

Dracula Cerca Sangue di Vergine e...Mori de Sete *See* Andy Warhol's Dracula (1974)

Dracula Contra Frankenstein *See* Dracula vs. Frankenstein (1971)

Dracula in the Castle of Blood *See* Web of the Spider (1970)

Dracula Is Dead and Well and Living in London *See* The Satanic Rites of Dracula (1973)

Dracula Pere et Fils *See* Dracula and Son (1976)

Dracula Saga *See* The Saga of the Draculas (1972)

Dracula 71 *See* Count Dracula (1971)

Dracula: The Bloodline Continues... *See* The Saga of the Draculas (1972)

Dracula: The Love Story *See* To Die For (1989)

Dracula, the Terror of the Living Dead *See* The Hanging Woman (1972)

Dracula Today *See* Dracula A.D. 1972 (1972)

Dracula vs. Frankenstein *See* The Screaming Dead (1972)

Dracula Vuole Vivere: Cerca Sangue de Vergina *See* Andy Warhol's Dracula (1974)

Dracula's Castle *See* Blood of Dracula's Castle (1969)

Dracula's Dog *See* Zoltan... Hound of Dracula (1978)

Dracula's Virgin Lovers *See* Dracula's Great Love (1972)

The Dragon and the Cobra *See* Fist of Fear, Touch of Death (1980)

Dragon Chow *See* Drachenfutter (1987)

Dragon Forever *See* Dragons Forever (1988)

Dragon Lady *See* G.I. Executioner (1971)

Dragon Wars: D-War *See* Dragon Wars (2007)

Dragonfly *See* One Summer Love (1976)

Dragon's Food *See* Drachenfutter (1987)

Drawing Blood *See* Sergio Lapel's Drawing Blood (1999)

Draws *See* American Tickler (1976)

The Dreaded Persuasion *See* The Narcotics Story (1958)

Dream Slayer *See* Blood Song (1982)

The Dreamcatcher *See* The Dream Catcher (1999)

Dreaming of Julia *See* Cuban Blood (2003)

Dreams *See* Akira Kurosawa's Dreams (1990)

Dreamworld *See* Covergirl (1983)

Drei Sterne *See* Mostly Martha (2001)

Dripping Deep Red *See* Deep Red: Hatchet Murders (1975)

Drivers to Hell *See* Wild Ones on Wheels (1962)

Droid Gunner *See* Cyberzone (1995)

Drole de Drama *See* Bizarre Bizarre (1939)

Drole de Felix *See* The Adventures of Felix (1999)

Drops of Blood *See* Mill of the Stone Women (1960)

The Drug *See* Kids in the Hall: Brain Candy (1996)

The Drum *See* Drums (1938)

Drunken Master 2 *See* The Legend of Drunken Master (1994)

Du bi quan wang da po xue di zi *See* Master of the Flying Guillotine (1975)

Du Rififi Chez les Hommes *See* Rififi (1954)

Du Saram-yida *See* Voices (2008)

Duck, You Sucker *See* A Fistful of Dynamite (1972)

The Duckweed Story *See* Drifting Weeds (1959)

Due Er Ikke Alene *See* You Are Not Alone (1978)

Due Notti Con Cleopatra *See* Two Nights with Cleopatra (1954)

Due Occhi Diabolici *See* Two Evil Eyes (1990)

Due Volte Guida *See* Twice a Judas (1969)

Duel of the Gargantuas *See* War of the Gargantuas (1970)

Duel of the Masters *See* Gods of Wu Tang (1983)

Duel of the Space Monsters *See* Frankenstein Meets the Space Monster (1965)

Duello Nel Texas *See* Gunfight at Red Sands (1963)

Duk bei kuen wong daai poh huet dik ji *See* Master of the Flying Guillotine (1975)

Dumb Dicks *See* Detective School Dropouts (1985)

Dumbo Drop *See* Operation Dumbo Drop (1995)

Dun Hun Ling *See* Bells of Death (1968)

D'Une Femme a L'Autre *See* A Business Affair (1993)

Dung che sai duk *See* Ashes of Time (1994)

Dungeons and Dragons *See* Mazes and Monsters (1982)

Duoluo Tianshi *See* Fallen Angels (1995)

Dura Deka *See* The Rug Cop (2006)

Dusting Cliff Seven *See* The Last Assassins (1996)

Dutchess of Doom *See* Blacksnake! (1973)

Duvar *See* The Wall (1983)

The Dwelling Place *See* Catherine Cookson's The Dwelling Place (1994)

Dynamite Women *See* The Great Texas Dynamite Chase (1976)

Dyrygent *See* The Conductor (1980)

E Dio Disse a Caino *See* And God Said to Cain (1969)

E Tu Vivrai Nel Terrore—L'aldila *See* The Beyond (1982)

E venne il giorno dei limoni neri *See* Black Lemons (1970)

Each Man For Himself *See* The Ruthless Four (1970)

Each One For Himself *See* The Ruthless Four (1970)

The Eagle with Two Heads *See* The Eagle Has Two Heads (1948)

Earth *See* Tierra (1995)

Earth Defense Forces *See* The Mysterians (1958)

The Earth Will Tremble *See* La Terra Trema (1948)

East Great Falls High *See* American Pie (1999)

East of Shanghai *See* Rich and Strange (1932)

East of the Bowery *See* Follow the Leader (1944)

East of the Rising Sun *See* Malaya (1949)

Easy Go *See* Free and Easy (1930)

Eat Your Heart Out *See* Skinned Alive (2008)

Eaten Alive *See* Emerald Jungle (1980)

Eaten Alive by Cannibals *See* Emerald Jungle (1980)

Eaters of the Dead *See* The 13th Warrior (1999)

Eating Pattern *See* Tales from a Parallel Universe: Eating Pattern (1997)

Ebirah, Terror of the Deep *See* Godzilla vs. the Sea Monster (1966)

Eboli *See* Christ Stopped at Eboli (1979)

Ebony, Ivory, and Jade *See* She Devils in Chains (1976)

Echte Kerle *See* Regular Guys (1996)

Ecks vs. Sever *See* Ballistic: Ecks vs. Sever (2002)

Ecstasy *See* Extasis (1996)

Edgar Allan Poe's Conqueror Worm *See* The Conqueror Worm (1968)

Edgar Allen Poe's House of Usher *See* The House of Usher (1988)

Edgar Allen Poe's The Oblong Box *See* The Oblong Box (1969)

The Edge of Hell *See* Rock 'n' Roll Nightmare (1985)

Edipo Re *See* Oedipus Rex (1967)

Edison *See* Edison Force (2005)

Edogawa Rampo ryoki-kan: Yaneura no sanpo sa *See* The Watcher in the Attic (1976)

Edogawa Rampo taizen: Kyofu kikei ningen *See* Horrors of Malformed Men (1969)

Edwards & Hunt: The First American Road Trip *See* Almost Heroes (1997)

Efter Bryllupet *See* After the Wedding (2006)

Efter Repetitionen *See* After the Rehearsal (1984)

Eight Arms to Hold You *See* Help! (1965)

8 Crazy Nights *See* Adam Sandler's 8 Crazy Nights (2002)

8 femmes *See* 8 Women (2002)

800 Balas *See* 800 Bullets (2002)

18 Shades of Dust *See* Hitman's Journal (1999)

Ein Lied von Liebe und Tod *See* Gloomy Sunday (2002)

Ein Mann wie Eva *See* A Man Like Eva (1983)

Ein Toter Hing im Netz *See* Horrors of Spider Island (1959)

Eine Liebe in Deutschland *See* A Love in Germany (1984)

Eine Reise ins Licht *See* Despair (1978)

Einer Frisst den Anderen *See* Dog Eat Dog (1964)

Einer Trage des Anderen Last... *See* Bear Ye One Another's Burden... (1988)

Ekstase *See* Ecstasy (1933)

El Abrazo Partido *See* Lost Embrace (2004)

El Abuelo *See* The Grandfather (1998)

El Angel exterminador *See* The Exterminating Angel (1962)

El Ataque de los Muertos Sin Ojos *See* Return of the Evil Dead (1975)

El Ataud Del Coffin *See* The Vampire's Coffin (1958)

El Ataud Del Vampiro *See* The Vampire's Coffin (1958)

El Baron del Terror *See* The Brainiac (1961)

El Beso Que Me Diste *See* The Kiss You Gave Me (2000)

El Buque Maldito *See* Horror of the Zombies (1974)

El Callejon de los Milagros *See* Midaq Alley (1995)

El Camino *See* The Road (2000)

El Cazador de la Muerte *See* Deathstalker (1983)

El Che Guevara *See* Diary of a Rebel (1968)

El Cobra *See* The Cobra (1968)

El Coleccionista de Cadaveres *See* Cauldron of Blood (1967)

El Crimen del Padre Amaro *See* The Crime of Father Amaro (2002)

El Crimen Ferpecto *See* El Crimen Perfecto (2004)

El Dedo En El Gatillo *See* Finger on the Trigger (1965)

El Dia Que Murio el Silencio *See* The Day Silence Died (1998)

El Diablo se Lleva a los Muertos *See* Lisa and the Devil (1975)

El Espanto Surge de la Tumba *See* Horror Rises from the Tomb (1972)

El Espinazo del Diablo *See* The Devil's Backbone (2001)

El Espiritu de la Colmena *See* Spirit of the Beehive (1973)

El Grito de la Muerte *See* The Living Coffin (1958)

El Hijo de la Novia *See* The Son of the Bride (2001)

El la Nave Va *See* And the Ship Sails On (1983)

El Laberinto del Fauno *See* Pan's Labyrinth (2006)

El Lado Oscuro del Corazon *See* The Dark Side of the Heart (1992)

El Lago de los Muertos Vivientes *See* Zombie Lake (1980)

El Lazarillo de Tormes *See* Lazarillo (1959)

El Maquinista *See* The Machinist (2004)

El Mariachi 2 *See* Desperado (1995)

The Fall of the House of Usher *See* La Chute de la Maison Usher (1928)

Fallen *See* Falling (2006)

Fallen Knight *See* The Minion (1998)

Falltime *See* Fall Time (1994)

False Face *See* Scalpel (1976)

False Faces *See* Let 'Em Have It (1935)

Falstaff *See* Chimes at Midnight (1967)

Familia Rodante *See* Rolling Family (2004)

The Familiar Stranger *See* My Husband's Double Life (2001)

Family Resemblances *See* Un Air de Famille (1996)

Family Wedding *See* Our Family Wedding (2010)

Fanatic *See* Die! Die! My Darling! (1965)

Fanfan the Tulip *See* Fanfan la Tulipe (1951)

Fang Shi Yu *See* Kick of Death: The Prodigal Boxer (1973)

Fangelse *See* Devil's Wanton (1949)

Fanny by Gaslight *See* Man of Evil (1948)

Fanny Och Alexander *See* Fanny and Alexander (1983)

Fan's Video *See* Otaku No Video (1991)

The Fantastic Disappearing Man *See* Return of Dracula (1958)

The Far Country *See* Nevil Shute's The Far Country (1985)

Farewell Bender *See* Wasted (2006)

Farewell, Friend *See* Honor Among Thieves (1968)

Farewell, My Love *See* Murder, My Sweet (1944)

Farinelli Il Castrato *See* Farinelli (1994)

Farinelli the Castrato *See* Farinelli (1994)

The Farm *See* The Curse (1987)

Farm Girl *See* The Farmer's Other Daughter (1965)

Farm of the Year *See* Miles from Home (1988)

The Farmhouse *See* Eye of the Storm (1998)

Fashion House of Death *See* Blood and Black Lace (1964)

Fashions *See* Fashions of 1934 (1934)

Fast Fortune *See* 11 Harrowhouse (1974)

Fast on the Draw *See* Sudden Death (1950)

Fast Track *See* The Ex (2007)

Fatal Affair *See* Stalker (1998)

Fatal Assassin *See* African Rage (1978)

Fatal Woman *See* Femme Fatale (1990)

Fate Ignoranti *See* His Secret Life (2001)

The Father *See* Baba (1973)

Father & Son: Dangerous Relations *See* Dangerous Relations (1993)

Father Brown *See* The Detective (1954)

Father Damien: The Leper Priest *See* Damien: The Leper Priest (1980)

Father Goose *See* Fly Away Home (1996)

Father Jackleg *See* Sting of the West (1972)

The Father Kino Story *See* Mission to Glory (1980)

Father Master *See* Padre Padrone (1977)

Father, Son and the Mistress *See* For Richer, for Poorer (1992)

Faubourg 36 *See* Paris 36 (2008)

Faust-Eine deutsche Volkssage *See* Faust (1926)

Faustrecht der Freiheit *See* Fox and His Friends (1975)

Fauteuils d'Orchestre *See* Avenue Montaigne (2006)

The FBI Murders *See* In the Line of Duty: The FBI Murders (1988)

Fear *See* Night Creature (1979)

The Fear *See* Gates of Hell (1980)

Fear 2 *See* The Fear: Halloween Night (1999)

fear dot com *See* Feardotcom (2002)

Fear Eats the Soul *See* Ali: Fear Eats the Soul (1974)

Fear in the City of the Living Dead *See* Gates of Hell (1980)

Fear in the Night *See* Dynasty of Fear (1972)

Fear: Resurrection *See* The Fear: Halloween Night (1999)

Fearless *See* Jet Li's Fearless (2006)

Fearless Little Soldier *See* Fanfan la Tulipe (1951)

The Feast of All Saints *See* Anne Rice's The Feast of All Saints (2001)

Feast of Flesh *See* Blood Feast (1963)

Feast of Satan *See* Feast for the Devil (1971)

Federico Fellini: Sono un gran bugiardo *See* Fellini: I'm a Born Liar (2003)

Federico Fellini's 8 1/2 *See* 8 1/2 (1963)

Federico Fellini's Intervista *See* Intervista (1987)

Feel the Heat *See* Catch the Heat (1987)

Fei cheung goh hiu *See* Gods of Wu Tang (1983)

A Fei jing juen *See* Days of Being Wild (1991)

Fei xiang guo he *See* Gods of Wu Tang (1983)

Fei yan jin dao *See* Vengeance is a Golden Blade (1969)

Fei yin gam do *See* Vengeance is a Golden Blade (1969)

Fei Ying *See* Silver Hawk (2004)

A Fei zheng zhuan *See* Days of Being Wild (1991)

Fellini: Je suis un grand menteur *See* Fellini: I'm a Born Liar (2003)

Fellini: Sono un gran bugiardo *See* Fellini: I'm a Born Liar (2003)

Felons *See* First Degree (1998)

Female *See* The Violent Years (1956)

The Female Butcher *See* The Legend of Blood Castle (1972)

Female Fiend *See* Theatre of Death (1967)

Female Prisoner: Cage *See* Female Prisoner: Caged (1983)

Femmine Infernali *See* Escape from Hell (1979)

Feng Yue *See* Temptress Moon (1996)

Fengriffen *See* And Now the Screaming Starts (1973)

Ferpect Crime *See* El Crimen Perfecto (2004)

Festen *See* The Celebration (1998)

Feux rouges *See* Red Lights (2004)

A Few Days in the Life of I.I. Oblomov *See* Oblomov (1981)

Fibra Optica *See* Optic Fiber (1997)

The Fiend with the Atomic Brain *See* Blood of Ghastly Horror (1972)

The Fiend with the Electronic Brain *See* Blood of Ghastly Horror (1972)

Fiendish Ghouls *See* The Flesh and the Fiends (1960)

Fierce *See* Fighting Mad (1977)

The Fifteen Streets *See* Catherine Cookson's The Fifteen Streets (1990)

The Fifth Chair *See* It's in the Bag (1945)

The Fifth Season *See* Profile for Murder (1996)

The 51st State *See* Formula 51 (2001)

50 Violins *See* Music of the Heart (1999)

50 Ways to Leave Your Lover *See* How to Lose Your Lover (2004)

Figaros Hochzeit *See* The Marriage of Figaro (1949)

The Fighting Men *See* Men of Steel (1977)

The Fighting Phantom *See* The Mysterious Rider (1933)

The Fighting Pimpernel *See* The Elusive Pimpernel (1950)

The Fighting Seventh *See* Little Big Horn (1951)

Fighting Thru *See* Fightin' Ranch (1930)

Figli de Annibale *See* Children of Hannibal (1998)

A Film about Love *See* Love Film (1970)

Film d'Amore et d'Anarchia *See* Love and Anarchy (1973)

Filofax *See* Taking Care of Business (1990)

Fin Aout Debut Septembre *See* Late August, Early September (1998)

Final Call *See* One Missed Call 3: Final (2006)

The Final Crash *See* Steelyard Blues (1973)

Final Cut *See* Death Games (1980)

Final Destination 4 *See* The Final Destination (2009)

Final Destination: Death Trip 3D *See* The Final Destination (2009)

Finally, Sunday *See* Confidentially Yours (1983)

Finding Kelly *See* Mystery Kids (1999)

Fine and Dandy *See* The West Point Story (1950)

Fine Mrtve Djevojke *See* Fine Dead Girls (2002)

Fine Things *See* Danielle Steel's Fine Things (1990)

Fire Festival *See* Himatsuri (1985)

Fire in Eden *See* Tusks (1989)

Fire on the Mountain *See* Volcano: Fire on the Mountain (1997)

The Firebird *See* Phoenix (1978)

The First and the Last *See* 21 Days (1937)

The First Great Train Robbery *See* The Great Train Robbery (1979)

The First Hello *See* High Country (1981)

The First of the Few *See* Spitfire (1942)

The First Rebel *See* Allegheny Uprising (1939)

First Strike *See* Jackie Chan's First Strike (1996)

The First Time *See* The Fighter (1952)

First Woman into Space *See* Space Monster (1964)

Fischia il sesso *See* Loose in New York (1974)

Fish Out of Water *See* The Witness (1999)

A Fist Full of Chopsticks *See* They Call Me Bruce? (1982)

Fist of Fear *See* Fist of Fear, Touch of Death (1980)

Fist of Fury *See* Chinese Connection (1973)

Fist Right of Freedom *See* Fox and His Friends (1975)

A Fistful of Feathers *See* Fowl Play (1975)

Fistful of the Dragon *See* Chinese Connection 2 (1977)

Fists of Fury 2 *See* Chinese Connection 2 (1977)

Five Angles on Murder *See* The Woman in Question (1950)

The Five at the Funeral *See* House of Terror (1972)

Five Bloody Days to Tombstone *See* Gun Riders (1969)

Five Bloody Graves *See* Gun Riders (1969)

The Five Day Lover *See* Time Out for Love (1961)

Five Days *See* Paid to Kill (1954)

5 Fingers of Death *See* King Boxer (1972)

Five Minutes to Live *See* Door to Door Maniac (1961)

Five Savage Men *See* The Desperados (1970)

Five Times Two *See* 5x2 (2004)

Five Women *See* Gonin 2 (1996)

Five Women Around Utamaro *See* Utamaro and His Five Women (1946)

Fixing the Shadow *See* Beyond the Law (1992)

Flagrant Desir *See* Trade Secrets (1986)

The Flame of Torment *See* Enjo (1958)

Flanagan *See* Walls of Glass (1985)

Flash Gordon: Rocketship *See* Rocketship (1936)

Flash Gordon's Trip to Mars *See* Flash Gordon: Mars Attacks the World (1939)

Flashpoint *See* Flash Point (2007)

Flatbed Annie *See* Flatbed Annie and Sweetiepie: Lady Truckers (1979)

The Flesh Creatures *See* Horror of the Blood Monsters (1970)

Flesh Creatures of the Red Planet *See* Horror of the Blood Monsters (1970)

Flesh for Frankenstein *See* Andy Warhol's Frankenstein (1974)

Fleur Bleue *See* The Apprentice (1971)

The Flight *See* The Taking of Flight 847: The Uli Derickson Story (1988)

Flight of the Dove *See* The Spy Within (1994)

The Flight of the White Stallions *See* The Miracle of the White Stallions (1963)

Flip Out *See* Get Crazy (1983)

Flipper and the Pirates *See* Flipper's New Adventure (1964)

Floating Weeds *See* Drifting Weeds (1959)

Flood *See* Hard Rain (1997)

Flower of the Arabian Nights *See* Arabian Nights (1974)

Flowers and Snakes *See* Flower & Snake '74 (1974)

Flu Bird Horror *See* Flu Birds (2008)

Flugel und Fesseln *See* The Future of Emily (1985)

Flying Aces *See* The Flying Deuces (1939)

The Flying Dutchman *See* Frozen in Fear (2000)

Flying Wild *See* Fly Away Home (1996)

Focus *See* Shot (2001)

Fog *See* A Study in Terror (1966)

Folies Bourgeoises *See* Twist (1976)

The Folks at Red Wolf Inn *See* Terror at Red Wolf Inn (1972)

Follow That Bird *See* Sesame Street Presents: Follow That Bird (1985)

Follow the Hunter *See* Fangs of the Wild (1954)

Follow Your Dreams *See* Independence Day (1983)

Fontane Effi Briest *See* Effi Briest (1974)

Footprints *See* Primal Impulse (1974)

For a Few Bullets More *See* Any Gun Can Play (1967)

For a Few Extra Dollars *See* Fort Yuma Gold (1966)

For Better or For Worse *See* Honeymoon Academy (1990)

For Love or Money *See* If I Were Rich (1933)

For Men Only *See* Tall Lie (1953)

For the Cause *See* Final Encounter (2000)

For We Too Do Not Forgive *See* Death Is Called Engelchen (1963)

Forbidden Alliance *See* The Barretts of Wimpole Street (1934)

Forbidden Floor: 4 Horror Tales *See* Hidden Floor (2006)

Forbidden Love *See* Freaks (1932)

Forbidden Paradise *See* Hurricane (1979)

Forbidden Passions *See* The Sensuous Teenager (1970)

Forbidden Son *See* Bulldance (1988)

The Forbin Project *See* Colossus: The Forbin Project (1970)

Forbrydelsens Element *See* The Element of Crime (1984)

Ford Fairlane *See* The Adventures of Ford Fairlane (1990)

A Foreign Affair *See* 2 Brothers & a Bride (2003)

Foreign Skin *See* Unveiled (2005)

The Forest Primeval *See* The Final Terror (1983)

Forgotten Prisoners: The Amnesty Files *See* Forgotten Prisoners (1990)

The Forsyte Saga *See* That Forsyte Woman (1950)

Fortune in Diamonds *See* The Adventurers (1951)

The Fortunes and Misfortunes of Moll Flanders *See* Moll Flanders (1996)

47 Samurai *See* 47 Ronin, Part 1 (1942)

Forward March *See* Doughboys (1930)

The Fotographer of Panic *See* Peeping Tom (1960)

Four Dark Hours *See* The Green Cockatoo (1937)

Four Dollars for Vengeance *See* Four Dollars of Revenge (1966)

The Four Just Men *See* The Secret Four (1940)

4 Luni, 3 Saptamani si 2 Zile *See* 4 Months, 3 Weeks and 2 Days (2007)

A Fourth for Marriage *See* What's Up Front (1963)

4...3...2...1...Morte *See* Mission Stardust (1968)

Foxforce *See* She Devils in Chains (1976)

F.P. 1 Antwortet Nicht *See* F.P. 1 Doesn't Answer (1933)

Fra Diavolo *See* The Devil's Brother (1933)

Frameup *See* Jon Jost's Frameup (1993)

Francesco, giullare di Dio *See* The Flowers of St. Francis (1950)

Francis *See* Francis the Talking Mule (1949)

Francis Ford Coppola Presents: The Legend of Suriyothai *See* The Legend of Suriyothai (2002)

Francis, God's Jester *See* The Flowers of St. Francis (1950)

Frank Herbert's Dune *See* Dune (2000)

Frank Miller's Sin City *See* Sin City (2005)

Frankenstein *See* Andy Warhol's Frankenstein (1974)

Frankenstein *See* Mary Shelley's Frankenstein (1994)

Frankenstein '88 *See* The Vindicator (1985)

The Frankenstein Experiment *See* Andy Warhol's Frankenstein (1974)

Frankenstein Made Woman *See* Frankenstein Created Woman (1966)

Frankenstein Meets the Giant Devil Fish *See* Frankenstein Conquers the World (1964)

Frankenstein Meets the Spacemen *See* Frankenstein Meets the Space Monster (1965)

Frankenstein Monsters: Sanda vs. Gairath *See* War of the Gargantuas (1970)

Frankenstein vs. Baragon *See* Frankenstein Conquers the World (1964)

Frankenstein vs. the Giant Devil Fish *See* Frankenstein Conquers the World (1964)

Frankenstein vs. the Subterranean Monster *See* Frankenstein Conquers the World (1964)

Frasier the Lovable Lion *See* Frasier the Sensuous Lion (1973)

Fraternally Yours *See* Sons of the Desert (1933)

The Freak from Suckweasel Mountain *See* Geek Maggot Bingo (1983)

Freak Talks About Sex *See* Blowin' Smoke (1999)

Freddie as F.R.O.7 *See* Freddie the Frog (1992)

Free to Live *See* Holiday (1938)

Freedom for Us *See* A Nous la Liberte (1931)

The Freedom Seekers *See* The Bloodsuckers (1970)

Freefall *See* Firefall (1994)

The Freeze Bomb *See* Kill Factor (1978)

Fremde Haut *See* Unveiled (2005)

Frenzy *See* Torment (1944)

Fresa y Chocolate *See* Strawberry and Chocolate (1993)

Fresh Bait *See* L'Appat (1994)

Freylekhe Kabtsonim *See* The Jolly Paupers (1938)

A Friday Night Date *See* Road Rage (2001)

The Fright *See* Visiting Hours (1982)

Frightened City *See* The Killer That Stalked New York (1947)

The Frightened Lady *See* The Case of the Frightened Lady (1939)

Frightmare 2 *See* Frightmare (1974)

Frissons *See* They Came from Within (1975)

Friz Freleng's Looney Looney Looney Bugs Bunny Movie *See* Looney Looney Looney Bugs Bunny Movie (1981)

The Frog Prince *See* The French Lesson (1986)

Frogmen Operation Stormbringer *See* U.S. SEALs: Dead or Alive (2002)

Froken Julie *See* Miss Julie (1950)

From a Whisper to a Scream *See* The Offspring (1987)

From Broadway to Cheyenne *See* Broadway to Cheyenne (1932)

From Hell to Victory *See* Eagles Attack at Dawn (1970)

From the Mixed-Up Files of Mrs. Basil E. Frankweiler *See* The Hideaways (1973)

Frozen Terror *See* Macabre (1980)

Fruhlingssinfonie *See* Spring Symphony (1986)

The Fruit Machine *See* Wonderland (1988)

F.T.W. *See* The Last Ride (1994)

Fu Gui Lie Che *See* The Millionaire's Express (1986)

Fuera de Carta *See* Chef's Special (2008)

Fugitive Lovers *See* Runaways (1975)

Fukkatsu no Hi *See* Virus (1982)

Fukusho Suruwa Ware Ni Ari *See* Vengeance Is Mine (1979)

The Fulfillment of Mary Gray *See* Fulfillment (1989)

Full Moon of the Virgins *See* Devil's Wedding Night (1973)

Fulltime Killer *See* Full Time Killer (2001)

The Fun House *See* Last House on Dead End Street (1977)

Fun Loving *See* Quackser Fortune Has a Cousin in the Bronx (1970)

Funeral Rites *See* The Funeral (1984)

Funf Patronenhulsen *See* Five Cartridges (1960)

Fungus of Terror *See* Attack of the Mushroom People (1963)

Funny Little Dirty War *See* Funny, Dirty Little War (1983)

Fuoco Fatuo *See* The Fire Within (1964)

Fuori dal Mondo *See* Not of This World (1999)

Furankenshutain No Kaiju: Sanda tai Gailah *See* War of the Gargantuas (1970)

Furankenshutain tai chitai kaiju Baragon *See* Frankenstein Conquers the World (1964)

Furankensuten to Baragon *See* Frankenstein Conquers the World (1964)

Furin Kazan *See* Samurai Banners (1969)

The Further Adventures of Ma and Pa Kettle *See* Ma and Pa Kettle (1949)

A Further Gesture *See* The Break (1997)

Fury Is a Woman *See* Siberian Lady Macbeth (1961)

Fury of Samson *See* The Fury of Hercules (1961)

Fury of the Succubus *See* Demon Rage (1982)

Fury of the Vikings *See* The Invaders (1963)

Furyo anego den: Inoshika Ocho *See* Sex and Fury (1973)

Future Cop *See* Trancers (1984)

Future Ninja *See* Cyber Ninja (1994)

Gadjo Dilo *See* The Crazy Stranger (1998)

A Gai Waak *See* Project A (1983)

Gake no Ue no Ponyo *See* Ponyo (2008)

The Gallery Murders *See* The Bird with the Crystal Plumage (1970)

Gallery of Horror *See* Alien Massacre (1967)

Gambara vs. Barugon *See* Gamera vs. Barugon (1966)

Gamblers in Okinawa *See* Sympathy for the Underdog (1971)

Gamblin' Man *See* Cockfighter (1974)

The Gambling Man *See* Catherine Cookson's The Gambling Man (1998)

Game *See* Gamer (2009)

The Game of Death *See* Robert Louis Stevenson's The Game of Death (1999)

Gamera *See* Gamera, the Invincible (1966)

Gamera: Chiisaki yusha-tachi *See* Gamera the Brave (2006)

Gamera: Little Braves *See* Gamera the Brave (2006)

Gamera Tai Barugon *See* Gamera vs. Barugon (1966)

Gamera Tai Gaos *See* Gamera vs. Gaos (1967)

Gamera Tai Guiron *See* Gamera vs. Guiron (1969)

Gamera Tai Shinkai Kaiju Jigara *See* Gamera vs. Zigra (1971)

Gamera Tai Uchukaiju Bairasu *See* Destroy All Planets (1968)

Gamera Tai Viras *See* Destroy All Planets (1968)

Gamera vs. Gyaos *See* Gamera vs. Gaos (1967)

Gamera Vs. Outer Space Monster Viras *See* Destroy All Planets (1968)

Gamera vs. the Deep Sea Monster Zigra *See* Gamera vs. Zigra (1971)

Gamera Vs. Viras *See* Destroy All Planets (1968)

Gamma Sango Uchu Daisakusen *See* The Green Slime (1968)

Gamma 693 *See* The Chilling (1989)

Gamma 693 *See* Night of the Zombies (1981)

Gammera *See* Gamera, the Invincible (1966)

Gang War *See* Odd Man Out (1947)

Gangland *See* Mean Machine (1973)

Gangland Boss *See* A Better Tomorrow, Part 1 (1986)

Gangster *See* Hoodlum (1996)

The Gangster's Moll *See* Minbo—Or the Gentle Art of Japanese Extortion (1992)

The Gardener *See* Seeds of Evil (1976)

The Gargon Terror *See* Teenagers from Outer Space (1959)

Garou Garou le Passe Muraille *See* Mr. Peek-A-Boo (1950)

Gas-s-s-s... or, It May Become Necessary to Destroy the World in Order to Save It *See* Gas-s-s-s! (1970)

A Gathering of Old Men *See* Murder on the Bayou (1991)

Gatto Rossi In Un Labirinto Do Vetro *See* Eyeball (1978)

Gawi *See* Nightmare (2000)

Gawi: The Nightmare *See* Nightmare (2000)

The Gay Divorce *See* The Gay Divorcee (1934)

The Gay Mrs. Trexel *See* Susan and God (1940)

The Gaze of Ulysses *See* Ulysses' Gaze (1995)

Gazon Maudit *See* French Twist (1995)

Gebroken Spiegels *See* Broken Mirrors (1985)

Gegen die Wand *See* Head On (2004)

Geheimecode Wildganse *See* Codename: Wildgeese (1984)

Gei Ba Ba de Xin *See* Jet Li's The Enforcer (1995)

Gekko no sasayaki *See* Moonlight Whispers (1999)

The Gemini Twins *See* Twins of Evil (1971)

Genealogies d'un Crime *See* Genealogies of a Crime (1997)

Genie of Darkness *See* Curse of Nostradamus (1960)

A Gentle Creature *See* A Gentle Woman (1969)

The Gentleman Tramp *See* La Collectionneuse (1967)

Gentlemen Don't Eat Poets *See* Grave Indiscretions (1996)

Gently Before She Dies *See* Your Vice is a Closed Room and Only I Have the Key (1972)

Geomeun jip *See* Black House (2007)

Geomi Sup *See* Spider Forest (2004)

George A. Romero's Diary of the Dead *See* Diary of the Dead (2007)

George A. Romero's Survival of the Dead *See* Survival of the Dead (2009)

The George McKenna Story *See* Hard Lessons (1986)

Georgia's Friends *See* Four Friends (1981)

The German Sisters *See* Marianne and Juliane (1982)

Gestapo *See* Night Train to Munich (1940)

Get Down and Boogie *See* Darktown Strutters (1974)

Get Rita *See* Lady of the Evening (1975)

Get Well Soon *See* Visiting Hours (1982)

Getting Even *See* Fight for Your Life (1977)

Getting Even *See* Utilities (1983)

Getting Married in Buffalo Jump *See* Buffalo Jump (1990)

Gharbar *See* The Householder (1963)

Ghare Baire *See* The Home and the World (1984)

Ghidora, the Three-Headed Monster *See* Ghidrah the Three Headed Monster (1965)

Ghidorah Sandai Kaiju Chikyu Saidai No Kessan *See* Ghidrah the Three Headed Monster (1965)

Ghidrah *See* Ghidrah the Three Headed Monster (1965)

The Ghost Creeps *See* Boys of the City (1940)

The Ghost of Fletcher Ridge *See* Ain't No Way Back (1989)

The Ghost of John Holling *See* Mystery Liner (1934)

Ghost Riders of the West *See* The Phantom Rider (1946)

The Ghost Steps Out *See* The Time of Their Lives (1946)

Ghost Story *See* Madhouse Mansion (1974)

Ghost Story of the Snake Woman *See* Snake Woman's Curse (1968)

Ghost Taxi *See* Terror Taxi (2004)

Ghosthouse 2 *See* Witchery (1988)

The Ghostly Rental *See* The Haunting of Hell House (1999)

Ghosts from the Past *See* Ghosts of Mississippi (1996)

Ghosts of Mars *See* John Carpenter's Ghosts of Mars (2001)

Ghosts on Parade *See* Spook Warfare (1968)

The Ghoul in School *See* Werewolf in a Girl's Dormitory (1961)

The Giant Leeches *See* Attack of the Giant Leeches (1959)

The Giant Majin *See* Daimajin (1966)

The Gift *See* Echelon Conspiracy (2009)

Giga Shadow *See* Tales from a Parallel Universe: Giga Shadow (1997)

Gigantis, the Fire Monster *See* Godzilla Raids Again (1955)

Gilbert Grape *See* What's Eating Gilbert Grape (1993)

Gill Woman *See* Voyage to the Planet of Prehistoric Women (1968)

Gill Women of Venus *See* Voyage to the Planet of Prehistoric Women (1968)

Gin Gwai 2 *See* The Eye 2 (2004)

Gin Gwai 3 *See* The Eye 3 (2005)

Gin Gwai 10 *See* The Eye 3 (2005)

Ging Chaat Goo Si *See* Police Story (1985)

Ginger Snaps 2: The Sequel *See* Ginger Snaps: Unleashed (2004)

Ginger Snaps 3 *See* Ginger Snaps Back: The Beginning (2004)

Gingerbread House *See* Who Slew Auntie Roo? (1971)

Gion Bayashi *See* A Geisha (1953)

Gion Festival Music *See* A Geisha (1953)

Gion No Shimai *See* Sisters of the Gion (1936)

Giormi *See* Days (2002)

Giorni e Nuvole *See* Days and Clouds (2007)

The Girl *See* Catherine Cookson's The Girl (1996)

The Girl Gets Moe *See* Love to Kill (1997)

Girl in Pawn *See* Little Miss Marker (1934)

The Girl in the Case *See* The Girl in the News (1941)

Girl in the Leather Suit *See* Hell's Belles (1969)

Girl in the Moon *See* Woman in the Moon (1929)

Girl in the Park *See* Sanctuary of Fear (1979)

Girl in the Street *See* London Melody (1937)

The Girl of the Nile *See* Emerald of Artama (1967)

The Girl Was Young *See* Young and Innocent (1937)

The Girl with the Thunderbolt Kick *See* Golden Swallow (1968)

The Girl You Want *See* Boys (1995)

Girlfriends *See* Les Biches (1968)

The Girls *See* Les Bonnes Femmes (1960)

Girls for Rent *See* I Spit on Your Corpse (1974)

The Girls He Left Behind *See* The Gang's All Here (1943)

Girls Hotel *See* Black Heat (1976)

Girls in Uniform *See* Maedchen in Uniform (1931)

Girls Will Be Girls *See* Fish Without a Bicycle (2003)

Giro City *See* And Nothing But the Truth (1982)

Giu la Testa *See* A Fistful of Dynamite (1972)

Giu la Testa...Hombre *See* Fistful of Death (1971)

Giulietta Degli Spiriti *See* Juliet of the Spirits (1965)

Giulio Cesare, il conquistatore delle Gallie *See* Caesar the Conqueror (1963)

Give Me Back My Skin *See* Rendez-Moi Ma Peau (1981)

Gladiatorerna *See* The Gladiators (1970)

Glass Bottle *See* Gorgeous (1999)

The Glass Cage *See* Glass Tomb (1955)

The Glass Virgin *See* Catherine Cookson's The Glass Virgin (1995)

Glen or Glenda: The Confessions of Ed Wood *See* Glen or Glenda? (1953)

Gli Amori di Ercole *See* The Loves of Hercules (1960)

Gli Indifferenti *See* Time of Indifference (1964)

Gli Invasori *See* The Invaders (1963)

Gli Orrori del Castello di Norimberga *See* Torture Chamber of Baron Blood (1972)

Global Heresy *See* Rock My World (2002)

Glorious Sacrifice *See* The Glory Trail (1936)

Glory at Sea *See* The Gift Horse (1952)

Glory Glory *See* Hooded Angels (2000)

The Glove: Lethal Terminator *See* The Glove (1978)

Glump *See* Please Don't Eat My Mother (1972)

G'mar Giviya *See* Cup Final (1992)

Gnaw: Food of the Gods 2 *See* Food of the Gods: Part 2 (1988)

A Gnome Named Gnorm *See* The Adventures of a Gnome Named Gnorm (1993)

Go and See *See* Come and See (1985)

The Goat *See* La Chevre (1981)

The Goddess *See* Devi (1960)

God's Gift *See* Wend Kuuni (1982)

Godson *See* Le Samourai (1967)

Godz of Wu Tang *See* Gods of Wu Tang (1983)

Godzilla Fights the Giant Moth *See* Godzilla vs. Mothra (1964)

Godzilla Versus the Bionic Monster *See* Godzilla vs. the Cosmic Monster (1974)

Godzilla vs. Gigan *See* Godzilla on Monster Island (1972)

Godzilla vs. Hedora *See* Godzilla vs. the Smog Monster (1972)

Godzilla vs. Mechagodzilla *See* Godzilla vs. the Cosmic Monster (1974)

Godzilla vs. the Giant Moth *See* Godzilla vs. Mothra (1964)

Godzilla vs. the Thing *See* Godzilla vs. Mothra (1964)

Godzilla's Counter Attack *See* Godzilla Raids Again (1955)

Gohatto *See* Taboo (1999)

Going Ape *See* Where's Poppa? (1970)

Going Back *See* Under Heavy Fire (2001)

Going West in America *See* Switchback (1997)

Gojira *See* Godzilla, King of the Monsters (1956)

Gojira no Musuko *See* Son of Godzilla (1966)

Gojira tai Biorante *See* Godzilla vs. Biollante (1989)

Gojira Tai Hedora *See* Godzilla vs. the Smog Monster (1972)

Gojira tai Megaro *See* Godzilla vs. Megalon (1976)

Gojira Tai Meka-Gojira *See* Godzilla vs. the Cosmic Monster (1974)

Goke, Body Snatcher from Hell *See* Body Snatcher from Hell (1969)

Goke the Vampire *See* Body Snatcher from Hell (1969)

Gokiburi *See* Twilight of the Cockroaches (1990)

Gokudo kyofu dai-gekijo *See* Gozu (2003)

Gokudo sengokushi: Fudo *See* Fudoh: The New Generation (1996)

Gold Coast *See* Elmore Leonard's Gold Coast (1997)

The Golden Age *See* L'Age D'Or (1930)

Golden Hands of Kurigal *See* Federal Agents vs. Underworld, Inc. (1949)

The Golden Heist *See* Inside Out (1975)

The Golden Hour *See* Pot o' Gold (1941)

Golden Ivory *See* White Huntress (1957)

Golden Marie *See* Casque d'Or (1952)

The Golden Trail *See* Riders of the Whistling Skull (1937)

Golden Virgin *See* The Story of Esther Costello (1957)

Golden Years *See* Stephen King's Golden Years (1991)

Golemata voda *See* The Great Water (2004)

Goliat Contra Los Gigantes *See* Goliath Against the Giants (1963)

Goliath and the Giants *See* Goliath Against the Giants (1963)

Goliath and the Golden City *See* Samson and the 7 Miracles of the World (1962)

Goliath Contro I Giganti *See* Goliath Against the Giants (1963)

Goliath, King of the Slaves *See* The Beast of Babylon Against the Son of Hercules (1963)

Goliathon *See* The Mighty Peking Man (1977)

Golpes a Mi Puerta *See* Knocks at My Door (1993)

Gomar the Human Gorilla *See* Night of the Bloody Apes (1968)

Gomi Sup *See* Spider Forest (2004)

Gone are the Days! *See* Purlie Victorious (1963)

Gong fu *See* Kung Fu Hustle (2004)

Gongdong gyeongbi guyeok JSA *See* JSA: Joint Security Area (2000)

Gonggongui jeog *See* Public Enemy (2002)

Gonggongui Jeog 2 *See* Another Public Enemy (2005)

Gongpo Taxi *See* Terror Taxi (2004)

The Good Girls *See* Les Bonnes Femmes (1960)

Good Idea *See* It Seemed Like a Good Idea at the Time (1975)

Good Luck, Miss Wyckoff *See* The Shaming (1979)

A Good Marriage *See* Le Beau Mariage (1982)

Good Morning Babilonia *See* Good Morning, Babylon (1987)

Good Ole Boy: A Delta Boyhood *See* The River Pirates (1988)

The Good Shepherd *See* The Confessor (2004)

The Good Time Girls *See* Les Bonnes Femmes (1960)

Good to Go *See* Short Fuse (1988)

Goodbye Bafana *See* The Color of Freedom (2007)

Goodbye Bruce Lee: His Last Game of Death *See* Game of Death (1979)

Goodbye, Children *See* Au Revoir les Enfants (1987)

Goodbye Gemini *See* Twinsanity (1970)

Goodbye to the Hill *See* Paddy (1970)

The Goods: The Don Ready Story *See* The Goods: Live Hard, Sell Hard (2009)

Gordon il Pirata Nero *See* The Black Pirate (1926)

Gorilla *See* Nabonga (1944)

Gosta Berling's Saga *See* The Atonement of Gosta Berling (1924)

Gotter der Pest *See* Gods of the Plague (1969)

Gouttes d'Eau sur Pierres Brulantes *See* Water Drops on Burning Rocks (1999)

Goyangileul butaghae *See* Take Care of My Cat (2001)

Grace Under Pressure *See* Something to Talk About (1995)

The Grail *See* Lancelot of the Lake (1974)

Gran Amore del Conde Dracula *See* Dracula's Great Love (1972)

The Grand Highway *See* Le Grand Chemin (1987)

The Grand Maneuvers *See* Les Grandes Manoeuvres (1955)

Grandmother *See* Yaaba (1989)

Grandmother's House *See* Grandma's House (1988)

The Grass is Singing *See* Killing Heat (1984)

The Grasshopper *See* The Passing of Evil (1970)

Grave Desires *See* Brides of the Beast (1968)

Grave Robbers from Outer Space *See* Plan 9 from Outer Space (1956)

The Graveside Story *See* The Comedy of Terrors (1964)

Graveyard Tramps *See* Invasion of the Bee Girls (1973)

The Great Adventure *See* The Adventurers (1951)

The Great Balloon Adventure *See* Olly Olly Oxen Free (1978)

The Great Day *See* A Special Day (1977)

The Great Decision *See* Men of America (1932)

Great Drunken Hero *See* Come Drink with Me (1965)

Great Freedom No. 7 *See* Die Grosse Freiheit Nr. 7 (1945)

The Great Georgia Bank Hoax *See* Great Bank Hoax (1978)

The Great Goblin War *See* The Great Yokai War (2005)

The Great Hope *See* Submarine Attack (1954)

Great Japanese *See* Big Man Japan (2007)

The Great Lester Boggs *See* Hootch Country Boys (1975)

The Great Manhunt *See* The Doolins of Oklahoma (1949)

Great Moments in Aviation *See* Shades of Fear (1993)

The Great Monster War *See* Godzilla vs. Monster Zero (1968)

Great Monster Yongkari *See* Yongkari Monster of the Deep (1967)

The Great Ride *See* Greedy Terror (1978)

The Great Schnozzle *See* Palooka (1934)

The Great Spy Mission *See* Operation Crossbow (1965)

The Great Wall is a Great Wall *See* A Great Wall (1986)

The Greatest Battle *See* Battleforce (1978)

The Greatest Battle on Earth *See* Ghidrah the Three Headed Monster (1965)

The Greatest Love *See* Europa '51 (1952)

Greed *See* Axe (2006)

The Greeks Had a Word for Them *See* Three Broadway Girls (1932)

The Green Carnation *See* The Trials of Oscar Wilde (1960)

Green Flash *See* Beach Kings (2008)

Green Monkey *See* Blue Monkey (1987)

The Green Ray *See* Summer (1986)

The Greenhouse *See* The Green House (1996)

Greta *See* According to Greta (2008)

Greta the Mad Butcher *See* Ilsa, the Wicked Warden (1978)

Grey Knight *See* The Ghost Brigade (1993)

Grey Matter *See* Mind Warp (1972)

Greystoke 2: Tarzan and Jane *See* Tarzan and the Lost City (1998)

Gridlock *See* Great American Traffic Jam (1980)

Grijpstra and de Gier *See* Fatal Error (1983)

Grim Weekend *See* S.I.C.K. Serial Insane Clown Killer (2003)

Grimm Brothers' Snow White *See* Snow White: A Tale of Terror (1997)

The Grinch *See* Dr. Seuss' How the Grinch Stole Christmas (2000)

Grindhouse: Death Proof *See* Death Proof (2007)

Grindhouse: Planet Terror *See* Planet Terror (2007)

Grine Felder *See* Green Fields (1937)

Gringo *See* Gunfight at Red Sands (1963)

The Grip of the Strangler *See* The Haunted Strangler (1958)

The Grip of the Vampire *See* Curse of the Undead (1959)

Gritos en la Noche *See* The Awful Dr. Orloff (1962)

The Groove Room *See* A Man with a Maid (1973)

The Grotesque *See* Grave Indiscretions (1996)

The Grudge *See* Ju-On: The Grudge (2003)

The Gruesome Shock of the Devil *See* Devil Hunter (2008)

Gruner Felder *See* Green Fields (1937)

Gruppo di Famiglia in un Interno *See* Conversation Piece (1975)

Guardian of the Wilderness *See* Mountain Man (1977)

Guardians of the Deep *See* Shark Hunter (1979)

Guerreros *See* Warriors (2002)

Gui yu *See* Re-Cycle (2006)

Guilty Assignment *See* Big Town (1947)

Guizi Laile *See* Devils on the Doorstep (2000)

Gun Man from Bodie *See* Gunman from Bodie (1941)

Gun Moll *See* Get Rita (1975)

Gun Moll *See* Jigsaw (1949)

Gun Moll *See* Lady of the Evening (1975)

Guney's The Wall *See* The Wall (1983)

Gunki hataweku motoni *See* Under the Flag of the Rising Sun (1972)

Gunpoint *See* At Gunpoint (1955)

Guns in the Afternoon *See* Ride the High Country (1962)

Guns, Sin and Bathtub Gin *See* Lady in Red (1979)

Gwai wik *See* Re-Cycle (2006)

Gwendoline *See* The Perils of Gwendoline (1984)

Gwoemul *See* The Host (2006)

Gycklarnas Afton *See* Sawdust & Tinsel (1953)

The Gypsy *See* Le Gitan (1975)

H2 : Halloween 2 *See* Halloween II (2009)

Ha Buah *See* The Bubble (2006)

Ha-Gilgul *See* The Unmistaken Child (2008)

Ha-Sodot *See* The Secrets (2007)

Haakon Haakonsen *See* Shipwrecked (1990)

Hab Og Karlighed *See* Twist & Shout (1984)

Habitaciones para Turistas *See* Rooms for Tourists (2004)

Hable con Ella *See* Talk to Her (2002)

Habricha el Hashemesh *See* Escape to the Sun (1972)

Hachi: A Dog's Tale *See* Hachiko: A Dog's Tale (2009)

Hachigatsu no Kyoshikyoku *See* Rhapsody in August (1991)

Hacia la Oscuridad *See* Towards Darkness (2007)

Hacks *See* Sink or Swim (1997)

Hadaka No Shima *See* The Island (1961)

Hadduta Misriya *See* An Egyptian Story (1982)

Haebyeoneuro gada *See* Bloody Beach (2000)

Hail to the Chief *See* Hail (1973)

Hairshirt *See* Too Smooth (1998)

The Hairy Bird *See* All I Wanna Do (1998)

Haishang Hua *See* Flowers of Shanghai (1998)

Hak Hap *See* Black Mask (1996)

Hak Hap 2 *See* Black Mask 2: City of Masks (2002)

Ha'Kohavim Shel Shlomi *See* Bonjour Monsieur Shlomi (2003)

Half a Sinner *See* Half a Soldier (1940)

The Half Life of Timofey Berezin *See* PU-239 (2006)

Half Slave, Half Free 2 *See* Charlotte Forten's Mission: Experiment in Freedom (1985)

Hallam Foe *See* Mister Foe (2007)

Hallelujah, I'm a Tramp *See* Hallelujah, I'm a Bum (1933)

Halloween 7 *See* Halloween: H20 (1998)

Halloween: H20 (Twenty Years Later) *See* Halloween: H20 (1998)

Halloween Night *See* Hack O'Lantern (1987)

Halloween: The Origin of Michael Myers *See* Halloween 6: The Curse of Michael Myers (1995)

Halloweentown 3 *See* Halloweentown High (2004)

Halloweentown 4 *See* Return to Halloweentown (2006)

Hallucination Generation *See* Hallucination (1967)

Ham Ham *See* Jamon, Jamon (1993)

Hamam: Il Bagno Turco *See* Steam: A Turkish Bath (1996)

Ha'Matarah Tiran *See* Sinai Commandos (1968)

The Hammond Mystery *See* The Undying Monster (1942)

Han Cheng Gong Lue *See* Seoul Raiders (2005)

Hana-Bi *See* Fireworks (1997)

Hana to Arisu *See* Hana & Alice (2004)

Hana to hebi *See* Flower & Snake (2004)

Hana to hebi *See* Flower & Snake '74 (1974)

Hana to hebi 2: Pari/Shizuko *See* Flower & Snake 2 (2005)

Hand of Death *See* King Boxer (1972)

Hand of Night *See* Beast of Morocco (1966)

Handgun *See* Deep in the Heart (1983)

Handle With Care *See* Citizens Band (1977)

Hands of a Killer *See* Planets Against Us (1961)

Hands of a Strangler *See* The Hands of Orlac (1960)

Hands of Blood *See* Stepsisters (1974)

The Hands of Orlac *See* Mad Love (1935)

Hands of the Strangler *See* The Hands of Orlac (1960)

Handsome Antonio *See* Il Bell'Antonio (1960)

Handsome Serge *See* Le Beau Serge (1958)

The Hangover *See* The Female Jungle (1956)

Hans Christian Andersen's Thumbelina *See* Thumbelina (1994)

Hanzo the Razor: Sword of Justice *See* The Razor: Sword of Justice (1972)

Hao xia *See* Last Hurrah for Chivalry (1978)

Happiness *See* Le Bonheur (1965)

Happiness *See* Le Bonheur Est Dans le Pre (1995)

Happiness Is In the Fields *See* Le Bonheur Est Dans le Pre (1995)

Happy as the Grass Was Green *See* Hazel's People (1973)

Happy Go Lucky *See* Hallelujah, I'm a Bum (1933)

Happy Mother's Day, Love, George *See* Run, Stranger, Run (1973)

The Happy New Year Caper *See* Happy New Year (1973)

Happy Times *See* The Inspector General (1949)

Hard Driver *See* The Last American Hero (1973)

Hard Knocks *See* Mid Knight Rider (1979)

Hard Stick *See* A Real American Hero (1978)

Hard 10 *See* She's Out of My League (2010)

Hard Times for Vampires *See* Uncle Was a Vampire (1959)

Hard to Die *See* Crime Story (1993)

Hard Vice *See* Vegas Vice (1994)

Hard Way Out *See* Bloodfist 8: Hard Way Out (1996)

Hardball *See* Bounty Hunters 2: Hardball (1997)

The Hardcore Life *See* Hardcore (1979)

Harem Holiday *See* Harum Scarum (1965)

Harem Suare *See* Harem (1999)

Harlem Hot Shot *See* The Black King (1932)

Harlequin *See* Dark Forces (1983)

Harold Robbins' The Betsy *See* The Betsy (1978)

Harp of Burma *See* The Burmese Harp (1956)

Harrison Bergeron *See* Kurt Vonnegut's Harrison Bergeron (1995)

Harry, A Friend Who Wishes You Well *See* With a Friend Like Harry (2000)

Harry Black *See* Harry Black and the Tiger (1958)

Harry, He's Here to Help *See* With a Friend Like Harry (2000)

Harry Potter and the Philosopher's Stone *See* Harry Potter and the Sorcerer's Stone (2001)

Harry Tracy—Desperado *See* Harry Tracy (1983)

Harry, un Ami Qui Vous Veut du Bien *See* With a Friend Like Harry (2000)

Harry's Game *See* Belfast Assassin (1984)

Harry's Machine *See* Hollywood Harry (1986)

Harvest *See* Cash Crop (2001)

Hasta Clerto Punto *See* Up to a Certain Point (1983)

The Hatchet Murders *See* Deep Red: Hatchet Murders (1975)

Hatouna Mehuheret *See* Late Marriage (2001)

Hatred *See* Hate (1995)

The Haunted *See* Curse of the Demon (1957)

The Haunted and the Hunted *See* Dementia 13 (1963)

Haunted by the Past *See* Secret Passions (1987)

The Haunted Planet *See* Planet of the Vampires (1965)

The Haunting of Hamilton High *See* Hello Mary Lou: Prom Night 2 (1987)

The Haunting of Hill House *See* The Haunting (1999)

The Haunting of Julia *See* Full Circle (1977)

Hauru no ugoku shiro *See* Howl's Moving Castle (2004)

Haus Der Tausend Freuden *See* The House of 1000 Dolls (1967)

Ha'Ushpizin *See* Ushpizin (2004)

Haut Bas Fragile *See* Up/Down/Fragile (1995)

Haute tension *See* High Tension (2003)

Have a Nice Funeral *See* Gunslinger (1970)

Hawk of Bagdad *See* Ali Baba and the Seven Saracens (1964)

The Hawk of Castile *See* Hawk and Castile (1967)

Haxan *See* Haxan: Witchcraft through the Ages (1922)

Hayanbang *See* Unborn but Forgotten (2002)

He Lived to Kill *See* Night of Terror (1933)

He Loved an Actress *See* Mad About Money (1937)

He Ni Zaiyiqi *See* Together (2002)

He or She *See* Glen or Glenda? (1953)

He, She or It *See* The Doll (1962)

Head On *See* Fatal Attraction (1980)

Head Over Heels *See* Chilly Scenes of Winter (1979)

The Head that Wouldn't Die *See* The Brain that Wouldn't Die (1963)

A Heart in Winter *See* Un Coeur en Hiver (1993)

The Heart Is Elsewhere *See* Incantato (2003)

The Heart of New York *See* Hallelujah, I'm a Bum (1933)

Heartbeat *See* Danielle Steel's Heartbeat (1993)

Heartbeat *See* Le Schpountz (1938)

Heartbreak Motel *See* Poor Pretty Eddie (1973)

Hearts and Minds *See* Master Touch (1974)

Heartstone *See* Demonstone (1989)

Heaven and Hell Gate *See* Heaven & Hell (1978)

Heaven on a Shoestring *See* The Night of Nights (1939)

Heaven Only Knows *See* For Heaven's Sake (1979)

Heavenly Pursuits *See* The Gospel According to Vic (1987)

Heaven's Pond *See* Devil's Pond (2003)

Hector Servadac's Ark *See* On the Comet (1968)

Hei Ma *See* A Mongolian Tale (1994)

Hei xia 2 *See* Black Mask 2: City of Masks (2002)

Heimat-Eine deutsche Chronik *See* Heimat 1 (1984)

The Heir to Genghis Khan *See* Storm over Asia (1928)

Heisei tanuki gassen pompoko *See* Pom Poko (1994)

Heisser Sommer *See* Hot Summer (1968)

The Heist *See* Carbon Copy (1969)

The Heist *See* Dollars (1971)

The Heist *See* The Squeeze (1980)

Held Hostage *See* Fight for Your Life (1977)

Heldorado *See* Helldorado (1946)

Hell Bent for Glory *See* Lafayette Escadrille (1958)

Hell Creatures *See* Invasion of the Saucer Men (1957)

Hell Fire *See* They (1977)

Hell in Normandy *See* Special Forces (1968)

Hell in the City *See* And the Wild, Wild Women (1959)

Hell to Macao *See* The Corrupt Ones (1967)

Hellborn *See* Asylum of the Damned (2003)

Hellborn *See* The Sinister Urge (1960)

Hellcab *See* Chicago Cab (1998)

Hellcamp *See* Opposing Force (1987)

Hellfire *See* Haunted Symphony (1994)

Hellfire *See* Primal Scream (1987)

Hellfire on Ice, Part 2: Escape from Hell *See* Escape from Hell (1979)

Hello Elephant *See* Pardon My Trunk (1952)

Hellraiser 2 *See* Hellbound: Hellraiser 2 (1988)

Hellraiser 7: Deader *See* Hellraiser: Deader (2005)

Hell's Beacon *See* Predator Island (2005)

Hemoglobin *See* Bleeders (1997)

Henry 2: Portrait of a Serial Killer *See* Henry: Portrait of a Serial Killer 2: Mask of Sanity (1996)

Henry James' The Ghostly Rental *See* The Haunting of Hell House (1999)

Her Bridal Night *See* The Bride Is Much Too Beautiful (1958)

Her Mad Night *See* Held for Murder (1932)

Her Majesty Mrs. Brown *See* Mrs. Brown (1997)

Her Secret Life *See* Code Name: Dancer (1987)

Her Third *See* The Third (1972)

Her Wicked Ways *See* Lethal Charm (1990)

Hercules Against the Sons of the Sun *See* Hercules vs. the Sons of the Sun (1964)

Hercules and the Conquest of Atlantis *See* Hercules and the Captive Women (1963)

Hercules and the Haunted Women *See* Hercules and the Captive Women (1963)

Hercules and the Hydra *See* The Loves of Hercules (1960)

Hercules and the Ten Avengers *See* The Triumph of Hercules (1966)

Hercules Goes Bananas *See* Hercules in New York (1970)

Hercules: The Movie *See* Hercules in New York (1970)

Hercules vs. the Giant Warriors *See* The Triumph of Hercules (1966)

Hercules vs. the Hydra *See* The Loves of Hercules (1960)

Hercules vs. the Moloch *See* Conquest of Mycene (1963)

Here Come the Tigers *See* Manny's Orphans (1978)

Here Is a Man *See* The Devil & Daniel Webster (1941)

Here Lies Love *See* The Second Woman (1951)

Here We Go Again *See* Pride of the Bowery (1941)

Hero of Babylon *See* The Beast of Babylon Against the Son of Hercules (1963)

The Hero of Pine Ridge *See* Yodelin' Kid from Pine Ridge (1937)

The Heroes *See* The Invincible Six (1968)

Heroes Die Hard *See* Mr. Kingstreet's War (1971)

Herr Tartuff *See* Tartuffe (1925)

Herz aus Glas *See* Heart of Glass (1974)

Herzbube *See* King, Queen, Knave (1972)

Hets *See* Torment (1944)

L'Heure d'Ete *See* Summer Hours (2008)

Hex *See* The Shrieking (1973)

Hexen bis aufs Blut Gequaelt *See* Mark of the Devil (1969)

H.G. Wells' New Invisible Man *See* The New Invisible Man (1958)

Hi No Tori *See* Phoenix (1978)

Hidden Face *See* Jail Bait (1954)

Hidden Power *See* Sabotage (1936)

Hidden Rage *See* Perfect Victims (1987)

The Hidden Room of 1,000 Horrors *See* The Tell-Tale Heart (1960)

Hidden Vision *See* Night Eyes (1990)

Hidden War 2 *See* Running Out of Time 2 (2006)

Hide and Shriek *See* American Gothic (1988)

Hideous Mutant Freekz *See* Freaked (1993)

Hifazaat *See* In Custody (1994)

High Risk *See* Meltdown (1995)

High Rolling *See* High Rolling in a Hot Corvette (1977)

Highbinders *See* The Medallion (2003)

A Higher Form of Learning *See* Kill Switch (2008)

Higher Love *See* Uncorked (1998)

The Highest Bidder *See* Woman Hunt (1972)

Highlander 2: Renegade Version *See* Highlander 2: The Quickening (1991)

Highlander 3: The Magician *See* Highlander: The Final Dimension (1994)

Highlander 3: The Sorcerer *See* Highlander: The Final Dimension (1994)

Highway to Hell *See* Running Hot (1983)

Hillbillys in a Haunted House *See* Hillbillies in a Haunted House (1967)

Him *See* Only You (1994)

Himalaya - L'Enfance d'un Chef *See* Himalaya (1999)

Himalaya - The Youth of a Chief *See* Himalaya (1999)

The Hindu *See* Sabaka (1955)

His Other Woman *See* Desk Set (1957)

Histoire de Marie et Julien *See* The Story of Marie and Julien (2003)

Histoires Extraordinaires *See* Spirits of the Dead (1968)

History is Made at Night *See* Spy Games (1999)

Hit & Run *See* Hot Blooded (1998)

Hit Man *See* La Scoumoune (1972)

Hitlerjunge Salomon *See* Europa, Europa (1991)

Hitler's Gold *See* Inside Out (1975)

Hitman *See* American Commandos (1984)

HMS Defiant *See* Damn the Defiant (1962)

The Hoary Legends of the Caucasus *See* Ashik Kerib (1988)

Hobgoblins & the Great War *See* The Great Yokai War (2005)

Hol Volt, Hol Nem Volt *See* A Hungarian Fairy Tale (1987)

The Hole *See* Le Trou (1959)

Holiday *See* Jour de Fete (1948)

Hollow Point *See* The Wild Pair (1987)

Hollow Triumph *See* The Scar (1948)

Hollyweird *See* Flicks (1985)

Hollywood Cowboy *See* Hearts of the West (1975)

Hollywood Hoodlum *See* Hollywood Mystery (1934)

Hollywood, I Love You *See* Hollywood, Je T'Aime (2009)

Hollywood Knight *See* Mid Knight Rider (1979)

The Hollywood Strangler *See* Don't Answer the Phone (1980)

Hollywood Stunt Man *See* Movie Stuntmen (1953)

Hollywood Thrillmakers *See* Movie Stuntmen (1953)

Hollywood Vixens *See* Beyond the Valley of the Dolls (1970)

Holocaust 2000 *See* The Chosen (1977)

The Holy Child *See* Holy Girl (2004)

Holy Terror *See* Alice Sweet Alice (1976)

Holy Week *See* Angel of Death (2002)

Holy Year *See* L'Annee Sainte (1976)

Homa ke Nero *See* Earth & Water (1999)

Hombre Mirando Al Sudeste *See* Man Facing Southeast (1986)

Home Fires Burning *See* The Turning (1992)

Home Front *See* Morgan Stewart's Coming Home (1987)

Home in Oklahoma *See* Big Show (1937)

Home Is Where the Heart Is *See* Where the Heart Is (2000)

Home is Where the Heart Is *See* Square Dance (1987)

Home of Phobia *See* Freshman Orientation (2004)

Homeboy *See* Fist (1976)

Homecoming Night *See* Night of the Creeps (1986)

L'Homme de Sa Vie *See* The Man of My Life (2006)

L'Homme du Minnesota *See* Minnesota Clay (1965)

Homo Erectus *See* National Lampoon's The Stoned Aged (2007)

The Honest Courtesan *See* Dangerous Beauty (1998)

Honeymoon in Bali *See* My Love For Yours (1939)

Honeymoon of Fear *See* Dynasty of Fear (1972)

Hong Kong Express *See* Chungking Express (1995)

Hong quan da shi *See* Opium and Kung-Fu Master (1984)

Hong Yan *See* Dam Street (2005)

Hong Ying Tao *See* Red Cherry (1995)

Hongfen *See* Blush (1995)

Honogurai mizu no soko kara *See* Dark Water (2002)

Honor Betrayed *See* Fear (1988)

Honor They Father *See* A Loving Father (2002)

The Honorary Consul *See* Beyond the Limit (1983)

Honour Among Thieves *See* Grisbi (1953)

Hoodlum Girls *See* Youth Aflame (1944)

Hoods *See* Hoodlum (1996)

Hoodwinked 2: Hood vs. Evil *See* Hoodwinked Too! Hood vs. Evil (2010)

The Hooker Cult Murders *See* The Pyx (1973)

Hopalong Cassidy Enters *See* Hopalong Cassidy (1935)

The Hopeless Ones *See* The Round Up (1966)

A Hora Da Estrela *See* The Hour of the Star (1985)

Horem Padem *See* Up and Down (2004)

Hori, ma panenko *See* The Firemen's Ball (1968)

L'Horloger de Saint-Paul *See* The Clockmaker (1973)

The Horrible House on the Hill *See* Devil Times Five (1974)

The Horrible Mill Women *See* Mill of the Stone Women (1960)

Horror Castle *See* The Virgin of Nuremberg (1965)

Horror Convention *See* Nightmare in Blood (1975)

Horror Creatures of the Prehistoric Planet *See* Horror of the Blood Monsters (1970)

Horror Game Movie *See* Nightmare (2000)

Horror High *See* Twisted Brain (1974)

Horror Hotel Massacre *See* Eaten Alive (1976)

Horror in the Midnight Sun *See* Invasion of the Animal People (1962)

Horror Maniacs *See* The Greed of William Hart (1948)

Horror of a Deformed Man *See* Horrors of Malformed Men (1969)

Horror of the Stone Women *See* Mill of the Stone Women (1960)

Horror on Snape Island *See* Tower of Evil (1972)

Horror Planet *See* Inseminoid (1980)

Hors de Prix *See* Priceless (2006)

Horse, My Horse *See* The Horse (1982)

A Horse Named Comanche *See* Tonka (1958)

Horse Thieves *See* In the Arms of My Enemy (2007)

Horsie *See* Queen for a Day (1951)

Horton Hears a Who! *See* Dr. Seuss' Horton Hears a Who! (2008)

Hostage *See* Savage Attraction (1983)

Hostage: Dallas *See* Getting Even (1986)

Hostage: The Christine Maresch Story *See* Savage Attraction (1983)

Hostage Train *See* Crackerjack 2 (1997)

Hostages in the Gulf *See* Eagles Attack at Dawn (1970)

Hostile Country *See* Outlaw Fury (1950)

Hostile Force *See* The Heist (1996)

Hostsonaten *See* Autumn Sonata (1978)

Hot and Cold *See* Weekend at Bernie's (1989)

Hot Blooded *See* Red Blooded 2 (1996)

Hot Car Girl *See* Hot Rod Girl (1956)

Hot Lead *See* Run of the Arrow (1956)

The Hot One *See* Corvette Summer (1978)

Hot Seat *See* The Chair (1987)

Hot Sex in Bangkok *See* Inn of Temptation (1973)

Hot Spot *See* I Wake Up Screaming (1941)

The Hot Spur *See* Love Desperados (1968)

Hot Sweat *See* Katie Tippel (1975)

Hotaru no Haka *See* Grave of the Fireflies (1988)

Hotel des Ameriques *See* Hotel America (1981)

Hotel Paraiso *See* Zus & Zo (2001)

Hotel Sorrento *See* Sorrento Beach (1995)

The Houghland Murder Case *See* Murder by Television (1935)

The Hounds of Zaroff *See* The Most Dangerous Game (1932)

Hour of Glory *See* The Small Back Room (1949)

The Hour of the Pig *See* The Advocate (1993)

House 3 *See* The Horror Show (1989)

The House Across the Lake *See* Heat Wave (1954)

House by the Lake *See* Death Weekend (1976)

House in Nightmare Park *See* Night of the Laughing Dead (1975)

The House in the Square *See* I'll Never Forget You (1951)

House of Crazies *See* Asylum (1972)

House of Doom *See* The Black Cat (1934)

House of Evil *See* Dance of Death (1968)

House of Evil *See* The House on Sorority Row (1983)

The House of Exorcism *See* Lisa and the Devil (1975)

House of Fear *See* Fearmaker (1971)

House of Fright *See* Black Sunday (1960)

House of Fright *See* The Two Faces of Dr. Jekyll (1960)

House of Insane Women *See* Exorcism's Daughter (1974)

House of Mortal Sin *See* The Confessional (1975)

House of Mystery *See* Night Monster (1942)

House of Pleasure *See* Le Plaisir (1952)

House of Terror *See* Face of the Screaming Werewolf (1959)

House of Terror *See* The Hanging Woman (1972)

House of the Damned *See* Spectre (1996)

House of the Dark Stairway *See* A Blade in the Dark (1983)

The House of the Screaming Virgins *See* Bloodsucking Freaks (1975)

House of Usher *See* The Fall of the House of Usher (1960)

The House on Sorority Row *See* Sorority Row (2009)
The House on Turk Street *See* No Good Deed (2002)
House Transformations *See* The Heirloom (2005)
The House Where Death Lives *See* Delusion (1980)
The House Where Hell Froze Over *See* Keep My Grave Open (1980)
House Without Windows *See* Seven Alone (1975)
Housebound *See* Kitchen Privileges (2000)
How Is It Going? *See* Comment Ca Va? (1976)
How Long Can You Fall? *See* Till Marriage Do Us Part (1974)
How the Grinch Stole Christmas *See* Dr. Seuss' How the Grinch Stole Christmas (2000)
How to Be a Player *See* Def Jam's How to Be a Player (1997)
How to Be a Woman and Not Die Trying *See* How to Be a Woman and Not Die in the Attempt (1991)
How to Get the Man's Foot Outta Your Asss! *See* Baadasssss! (2003)
How to Irritate People *See* John Cleese on How to Irritate People (1968)
How to Save a Life *See* To Save a Life (2010)
How to Steal a Diamond in Four Easy Lessons *See* The Hot Rock (1970)
How to Steal a Million Dollars and Live Happily Ever After *See* How to Steal a Million (1966)
Howard Beach: Making the Case for Murder *See* Skin (1989)
Howard Stern's Private Parts *See* Private Parts (1996)
Howling 2: Stirba—Werewolf Bitch *See* Howling 2: Your Sister Is a Werewolf (1985)
Howling 7 *See* The Howling: New Moon Rising (1995)
H.P. Lovecraft's Beyond the Wall of Sleep *See* Beyond the Wall of Sleep (2006)
H.P. Lovecraft's The Unnamable Returns *See* The Unnamable 2: The Statement of Randolph Carter (1992)
Hrafninn Flygur *See* Revenge of the Barbarians (1985)
Hsi Yen *See* The Wedding Banquet (1993)
Hua Pi Zhi Yinyang Fawang *See* Painted Skin (1993)
Huang Jia Zhan Shi *See* Royal Warriors (1986)
Huang Tudi *See* Yellow Earth (1989)
Huggers *See* Crazy Moon (1987)
Hula garu *See* Hula Girls (2006)
The Human Beast *See* La Bete Humaine (1938)
Human Cargo *See* Escape: Human Cargo (1998)
Human Meat Pies *See* The Untold Story (1993)
The Human Question *See* Heartbeat Detector (2007)
Human Skin Lanterns *See* Human Lanterns (1982)
The Human Tornado *See* Dolemite 2: Human Tornado (1976)
Hunchback *See* The Hunchback of Notre Dame (1982)
The Hundred Monsters *See* 100 Monsters (1968)
Hung Kuen Dai See *See* Opium and Kung-Fu Master (1984)
Hungry Pets *See* Please Don't Eat My Mother (1972)
Hungry Wives *See* Season of the Witch (1973)
Hunt to Kill *See* The White Buffalo (1977)
The Hunted *See* Touch Me Not (1974)
Hunter of the Apocalypse *See* The Last Hunter (1980)
Hunters Are For Killing *See* Hard Frame (1970)
Huo Shao Dao *See* The Prisoner (1990)
Huo Yuan Jia *See* Jet Li's Fearless (2006)
Huozhe *See* To Live (1994)
Hurricane *See* Hurricane Streets (1996)
Hustler Squad *See* The Doll Squad (1973)
Hydra *See* Attack of the Swamp Creature (1975)
Hyeol-ui nu *See* Blood Rain (2005)
Hypercube *See* Cube 2: Hypercube (2002)
Hypnotic *See* Close Your Eyes (2002)
I Accuse *See* J'Accuse (1937)
I Accuse! *See* J'accuse! (1919)
I Am a Fugitive From the Chain Gang *See* I Am a Fugitive from a Chain Gang (1932)
I Am the Rabbit *See* The Rabbit Is Me (1965)
I Bambini Ci Guardano *See* The Children Are Watching Us (1944)
I Became a Criminal *See* They Made Me a Criminal (1939)
I Became a Criminal *See* They Made Me a Fugitive (1947)
I Breathe *See* Respiro (2002)
I Call First *See* Who's That Knocking at My Door? (1968)
I Can Make You Love Me *See* Stalking Laura (1993)
I Changed My Sex *See* Glen or Glenda? (1953)
I Cinque Della Vendetta *See* Five Giants from Texas (1966)
I Coltelli Del Vendicatore *See* Knives of the Avenger (1965)
I Compagni *See* The Organizer (1964)
I Corpi Presentano Tracce Di Violenza Carnale *See* Torso (1973)
I Crossed the Line *See* The Black Klansman (1966)
I Due Gladiatori *See* Two Gladiators (1964)
I Fak *See* The Judgement (2004)
I Fidanzati *See* Fiances (1963)
I Fought the Law *See* Dead Heat (2001)
I Giorni Dell'Inferno *See* Days of Hell (1984)
I Guardiani del Cielo *See* Tower of the Firstborn (1998)
I Hate Your Guts *See* Shame (1961)
I Have a New Master *See* Passion for Life (1948)
I Have a Stranger's Face *See* Face of Another (1966)
I Have Lived *See* After Midnight (1933)
I Have No Mouth But I Must Scream *See* And Now the Screaming Starts (1973)
I Led Two Lives *See* Glen or Glenda? (1953)
I Live for Your Death *See* A Long Ride From Hell (1968)
I Love a Man in Uniform *See* A Man in Uniform (1993)
I Love to Kill *See* Impulse (1974)
I Married a Shadow *See* I Married a Dead Man (1982)
I Married Too Young *See* Married Too Young (1962)
I Masnadieri *See* The Mercenaries (1962)
I Nuovi Barbari *See* Warriors of the Wasteland (1983)
I Padroni della Citta *See* Rulers of the City (1976)
I Pianeti Contro di Noi *See* Planets Against Us (1961)
I Racconti di Canterbury *See* The Canterbury Tales (1971)
I Remember *See* Amarcord (1974)
I Saw a Dream Like This *See* Akira Kurosawa's Dreams (1990)
I Skiachtra *See* The Enchantress (1985)
I Soliti Ignoti *See* Big Deal on Madonna Street (1958)
I Tre Volti della Paura *See* Black Sabbath (1964)
I Want Her Dead *See* W (1974)
I Was a Teenage Boy *See* Something Special (1986)
I Was a Teenage Teenager *See* Clueless (1995)
I Worship His Shadow *See* Tales from a Parallel Universe: I Worship His Shadow (1997)
I You She He *See* Je Tu Il Elle (1974)
I Zitelloni *See* The Inveterate Bachelor (1958)
The Iceberg *See* L'Iceberg (2005)
Ich und Er *See* Me and Him (1989)
Ich War Neunzehn *See* I Was Nineteen (1968)
Ich Will Doch Nur, Dass Ihr Mich Liebt *See* I Only Want You to Love Me (1976)
Ici et Ailleurs *See* Here and Elsewhere (1976)
Identificazione di una Donna *See* Identification of a Woman (1982)
Identikit *See* Driver's Seat (1973)
Idi i Smotri *See* Come and See (1985)
The Idiot *See* L'Idiot (1946)
Idioterne *See* The Idiots (1999)
Ido Zero Daisakusen *See* Latitude Zero (1969)
Iedereen Beroemd! *See* Everybody's Famous! (2000)
Ieri, Oggi E Domani *See* Yesterday, Today and Tomorrow (1964)
If He Hollers, Let Him Go *See* Dead Right (1968)
If I Didn't Care *See* Blue Blood (2007)
If Only *See* Twice upon a Yesterday (1998)
If You Can't Say It, Just See It *See* Whore (1991)
If You Feel Like Singing *See* Summer Stock (1950)
Ignorant Fairies *See* His Secret Life (2001)
Ika resuraa *See* The Calamari Wrestler (2004)
Ike: The War Years *See* Ike (1979)
Iki-jigoku *See* Living Hell: A Japanese Chainsaw Massacre (2000)
Iklimler *See* Climates (2006)
Il Boia Scarlatto *See* The Bloody Pit of Horror (1965)
Il Buco *See* Le Trou (1959)
Il Buco *See* Night Watch (1972)
Il Cacciatore di Squali *See* Shark Hunter (1979)
Il Castello de Morti Vivi *See* Castle of the Living Dead (1964)
Il Cielo Cade *See* The Sky Is Falling (2000)
Il Cittadino si Ribella *See* Street Law (1974)
Il Cobra *See* The Cobra (1968)
Il Conformista *See* The Conformist (1971)
Il Conte Dracula *See* Count Dracula (1971)
Il Cristo Proibito *See* The Forbidden Christ (1950)
Il Crudeli *See* Hellbenders (1967)
Il Cuore Altroe *See* Incantato (2003)
Il Decameron *See* The Decameron (1970)
Il Deserto dei Tartari *See* The Desert of the Tartars (1976)
Il Deserto Rosso *See* The Red Desert (1964)
Il Diario di una Cameriera *See* Diary of a Chambermaid (1964)
Il Diavolo e i Morti *See* Lisa and the Devil (1975)
Il Diavolo in Corpo *See* Devil in the Flesh (1987)
Il Dio Chiamato a Dorian *See* Dorian Gray (1970)
Il Disprezzo *See* Contempt (1964)
Il Etait une Fois un Pays *See* Underground (1995)
Il Fantasma dell'Opera *See* The Phantom of the Opera (1998)
Il Figlio del Capitano Blood *See* Son of Captain Blood (1962)
Il Fiore delle Mille e Una Notte *See* Arabian Nights (1974)
Il Fiume del Grande Caimano *See* The Great Alligator (1981)
Il Gatto Dagli Occhi di Giada *See* Watch Me When I Kill (1977)
Il Gatto Nero *See* The Black Cat (1981)
Il Gattopardo *See* The Leopard (1963)
Il Generale Della-Rovere *See* Generale Della Rovere (1960)
Il Giardino Del Finzi-Contini *See* The Garden of the Finzi-Continis (1971)
Il Gigante Di Metropolis *See* The Giant of Metropolis (1961)
Il Giorno e L'Ora *See* The Day and the Hour (1963)
Il Gladiatore che Sfido l'Impero *See* Challenge of the Gladiator (1965)
Il Gladiatore Di Roma *See* Gladiator of Rome (1963)
Il Gladiatore Invincible *See* The Invincible Gladiator (1962)
Il Gladiatore Invincible *See* The Invincible Gladiator (1963)
Il Ladro Di Bagdad *See* Thief of Baghdad (1961)
Il Ladro di Bambini *See* The Stolen Children (1992)
Il Lago di Satana *See* The She-Beast (1965)
Il Mercante di Pietre *See* The Stone Merchant (2006)
Il Messia *See* The Messiah (1975)
Il Mio Nome e Nessuno *See* My Name Is Nobody (1974)
Il Mio West *See* Gunslinger's Revenge (1998)
Il Mondo Di Yor *See* Yor, the Hunter from the Future (1983)
Il Monstro *See* The Monster (1996)
Il Montagna di Dio Cannibale *See* Mountain of the Cannibal God (1979)
Il Mostro e in Tavola...Barone Frankenstein *See* Andy Warhol's Frankenstein (1974)
Il Mulino delle Donne di Pietra *See* Mill of the Stone Women (1960)
Il Natale Che Quasi Non Fu *See* The Christmas That Almost Wasn't (1966)
Il Pianeta Degli Uomini Spenti *See* Battle of the Worlds (1961)
Il Portiere de Notte *See* The Night Porter (1974)
Il Postino *See* The Postman (1994)
Il Processo *See* The Trial (1963)
Il Quartetto Basileus *See* Basileus Quartet (1982)
Il Ragno *See* The Killer Must Kill Again (1975)
Il Re Dei Criminali *See* Superargo (1967)
Il Regina di Matrimoni *See* The Wedding Director (2006)
Il Rosso Segmo della Follia *See* Hatchet for the Honeymoon (1970)
Il Segreto del Vestito Rosso *See* Assassination in Rome (1965)
Il Sicario *See* The Hit Man (1960)
Il Sigillo de Pechino *See* The Corrupt Ones (1967)
Il Sole Anche di Notte *See* Night Sun (1990)

L'Aigle a Deux Tetes *See* The Eagle Has Two Heads (1948)

Laitakaupungin Valot *See* Lights in the Dusk (2006)

The Lake of the Living Dead *See* Zombie Lake (1980)

Lakposhtha ham parvaz mikonand *See* Turtles Can Fly (2004)

L'Albero Degli Zoccoli *See* The Tree of Wooden Clogs (1978)

L'Amant *See* The Lover (1992)

L'Amant de Lady Chatterley *See* Lady Chatterley's Lover (1955)

The Lament of the Path *See* Pather Panchali (1954)

L'Amour en Fuite *See* Love on the Run (1978)

The Lamp *See* The Outing (1987)

Lan Feng Zheng *See* The Blue Kite (1993)

Lancelot and Guinevere *See* Sword of Lancelot (1963)

Lancelot du Lac *See* Lancelot of the Lake (1974)

Land of the Dead *See* George A. Romero's Land of the Dead (2005)

Landru *See* Bluebeard (1963)

The Lane Frost Story *See* 8 Seconds (1994)

L'Anee Derniere a Marienbad *See* Last Year at Marienbad (1961)

L'Anglaise et le Duc *See* The Lady and the Duke (2001)

The Langoliers *See* Stephen King's The Langoliers (1995)

L'Annulaire *See* The Ring Finger (2005)

Larceny Lane *See* Blonde Crazy (1931)

Large as Life *See* Larger Than Life (1996)

Larsen, Wolf of the Seven Seas *See* The Legend of the Sea Wolf (1958)

Las Cartas de Alou *See* Letters from Alou (1990)

Las Luchadoras Contra la Momia *See* Wrestling Women vs. the Aztec Mummy (1959)

Las Vegas Strip War *See* The Vegas Strip Wars (1984)

Lashou Shentan *See* Hard-Boiled (1992)

Lasky Jedne Plavovlasky *See* Loves of a Blonde (1965)

L'Associe *See* The Associate (1979)

The Last Adventurers *See* Down to the Sea in Ships (1922)

The Last Battle *See* Le Dernier Combat (1984)

Last Chance For a Born Loser *See* Stateline Motel (1975)

The Last Dance *See* The Hole (1998)

The Last Days of John Dillinger *See* Dillinger (1991)

The Last Days of Man on Earth *See* The Final Programme (1973)

The Last Days of Sodom and Gomorrah *See* Sodom and Gomorrah (1962)

The Last Elephant *See* Ivory Hunters (1990)

The Last Frontier *See* Savage Wilderness (1955)

The Last Great Treasure *See* Mother Lode (1982)

The Last Horror Film *See* Fanatic (1982)

Last House on the Left, Part 2 *See* Twitch of the Death Nerve (1971)

Last Man Standing *See* Circle Man (1987)

Last Message From Saigon *See* Operation C.I.A. (1965)

Last of the Cowboys *See* Great Smokey Roadblock (1976)

The Last Outpost *See* Cavalry Charge (1951)

The Last Page *See* Man Bait (1952)

Last Resurrection *See* Haunted Symphony (1994)

Last Rites *See* Dracula's Last Rites (1979)

The Last Shot *See* Carbon Copy (1969)

The Last Train of the Night *See* Night Train Murders (1975)

The Last Victim *See* Forced Entry (1975)

The Last Warrior *See* The Final Executioner (1983)

The Last Will of Dr. Mabuse *See* Crimes of Dr. Mabuse (1932)

The Last Will of Dr. Mabuse *See* Testament of Dr. Mabuse (1962)

The Last Witness *See* Caracara (2000)

Lat den Ratte Komma In *See* Let the Right One In (2008)

The Late Edwina Black *See* The Obsessed (1951)

Later *See* One Day You'll Understand (2008)

Latin Love *See* Greek Street (1930)

Latin Quarter *See* Frenzy (1946)

Latitude Zero: Big Military Operation *See* Latitude Zero (1969)

Latitude Zero Military Tactics *See* Latitude Zero (1969)

Laughterhouse *See* Singleton's Pluck (1984)

Laure *See* Forever Emmanuelle (1975)

The Law *See* Tilai (1990)

The Law *See* Where the Hot Wind Blows (1959)

Law Breakers *See* Les Assassins de L'Ordre (1971)

Lawless: Beyond Justice *See* Beyond Justice (2001)

Lawless: Dead Evidence *See* Dead Evidence (2000)

Lawnmower Man 2: Jobe's War *See* Lawnmower Man 2: Beyond Cyberspace (1995)

The Lay of the Land *See* The Student Affair (1997)

Lazarus and the Hurricane *See* The Hurricane (1999)

Lazy Bones *See* Hallelujah, I'm a Bum (1933)

LD 50 Lethal Dose *See* Lethal Dose (2003)

Le Battement d'Ailes du Papillon *See* Happenstance (2000)

Le Blonde de Pekin *See* The Peking Blond (1968)

Le Bossu *See* On Guard! (2003)

Le Caporal Epingle *See* The Elusive Corporal (1962)

Le Carrosse D'Or *See* The Golden Coach (1952)

Le Cerveau *See* The Brain (1969)

Le Chaland qui Passe *See* L'Atalante (1934)

Le Charme Discret de la Bourgeoisie *See* The Discreet Charm of the Bourgeoisie (1972)

Le Chat et la Souris *See* Cat and Mouse (1978)

Le Chateau de Ma Mere *See* My Mother's Castle (1991)

Le Cheval D'Orgeuil *See* The Horse of Pride (1980)

Le Ciel et le Boue *See* The Sky Above, the Mud Below (1961)

Le Coeur au Poing *See* Street Heart (1998)

Le Comte de Monte Cristo *See* The Count of Monte Cristo (1999)

Le Confessionnal *See* The Confessional (1995)

Le Corniauds *See* The Sucker (1965)

Le Cri du Hibou *See* The Cry of the Owl (1987)

Le Crime de Monsieur Lange *See* The Crime of Monsieur Lange (1936)

Le Danger Vient de l'Escape *See* The Day the Sky Exploded (1957)

Le Declin De L'Empire Americain *See* The Decline of the American Empire (1986)

Le Dejeuner sur l'Herbe *See* Picnic on the Grass (1959)

Le Dernier Metro *See* The Last Metro (1980)

Le Dernier Tango a Paris *See* Last Tango in Paris (1973)

Le Desert des Tartares *See* The Desert of the Tartars (1976)

Le Diable au Corps *See* Devil in the Flesh (1946)

Le Diable, Probablement *See* The Devil, Probably (1977)

Le Diner de Cons *See* The Dinner Game (1998)

Le Distrait *See* The Daydreamer (1975)

Le Docteur Petiot *See* Dr. Petiot (1990)

Le Fabuleux Destin d'Amelie Poulain *See* Amelie (2001)

Le Fantome de la Liberte *See* Phantom of Liberty (1974)

Le Fantome D'henri Langlois *See* Henri Langlois: The Phantom of the Cinematheque (2004)

Le Feu Follet *See* The Fire Within (1964)

Le Fille sure le Pont *See* The Girl on the Bridge (1998)

Le Fils de L'Epicier *See* Grocer's Son (2007)

Le Fils du Requin *See* The Son of the Shark (1993)

Le Fils Prefere *See* The Favorite Son (1994)

Le Fruit Defendu *See* Forbidden Fruit (1952)

Le Gai Savoir *See* The Joy of Knowledge (1965)

Le Geant de la Vallee Das Rois *See* Son of Samson (1962)

Le Genou de Claire *See* Claire's Knee (1971)

Le Gentleman d'Epsom *See* Duke of the Derby (1962)

Le Gout des Autres *See* The Taste of Others (2000)

Le Graal *See* Lancelot of the Lake (1974)

Le Grand Bleu *See* The Big Blue (1988)

Le Grand Blond avec une Chassure Noire *See* The Tall Blond Man with One Black Shoe (1972)

Le Grand Meaulnes *See* The Wanderer (1967)

Le Grande Role *See* The Grand Role (2004)

Le Huitieme Jour *See* The Eighth Day (1995)

Le Hussard sur le Toit *See* The Horseman on the Roof (1995)

Le Infedeli *See* The Unfaithfuls (1960)

Le Jardin des Plantes *See* The Green House (1996)

Le Joueur d'Echecs *See* The Chess Player (1927)

Le Jour et L'Heure *See* The Day and the Hour (1963)

Le Journal du Seducteur *See* Diary of a Seducer (1995)

Le Journal d'un Cure de Campagne *See* Diary of a Country Priest (1950)

Le Journal d'un Suicide *See* Diary of a Suicide (1973)

Le Journal d'une Femme de Chambre *See* Diary of a Chambermaid (1964)

Le Juge et L'assassin *See* The Judge and the Assassin (1975)

Le Locataire *See* The Tenant (1976)

Le Maitre de Musique *See* The Music Teacher (1988)

Le Mandat *See* Mandabi (1968)

Le Mari de la coiffeuse *See* The Hairdresser's Husband (1992)

Le Mepris *See* Contempt (1964)

Le Meraviglie Di Aladino *See* The Wonders of Aladdin (1961)

Le Moine et la Sorciere *See* Sorceress (1988)

Le Monstre *See* The Monster (1996)

Le Mur *See* The Wall (1983)

Le Mura di Malapaga *See* The Walls of Malapaga (1949)

Le Neveu de Beethoven *See* Beethoven's Nephew (1988)

Le Notti Bianche *See* White Nights (1957)

Le Notti de Cabiria *See* Nights of Cabiria (1957)

Le Nouveau Monde *See* New World (1995)

Le Pacte des Loups *See* Brotherhood of the Wolf (2001)

Le Papillon *See* The Butterfly (2002)

Le Parfum d'Yvonne *See* The Perfume of Yvonne (1994)

Le Pays Bleu *See* Blue Country (1977)

Le Peau Douce *See* The Soft Skin (1964)

Le Petit Monde de Don Camillo *See* Little World of Don Camillo (1951)

Le Peuple Migrateur *See* Winged Migration (2001)

Le Placard *See* The Closet (2000)

Le Plus Vieux Metier du Monde *See* Oldest Profession (1967)

Le Proces *See* The Trial (1963)

Le Quatrieme Sexe *See* The Fourth Sex (1961)

Le Rayon Vert *See* Summer (1986)

Le Regle du Jeu *See* The Rules of the Game (1939)

Le Retour de Martin Guerre *See* The Return of Martin Guerre (1983)

Le Retour du Grand Blond *See* Return of the Tall Blond Man with One Black Shoe (1974)

Le Roi de Coeur *See* The King of Hearts (1966)

Le Rouble a Deux Faces *See* The Hot Line (1969)

Le Rouge aux Levres *See* Daughters of Darkness (1971)

Le Rouge et le Noir *See* The Red and the Black (1957)

Le Salaire de la Peur *See* Wages of Fear (1955)

Le Sang d'un Poete *See* The Blood of a Poet (1930)

Le Sant de l'Ange *See* Cobra (1971)

Le Sauvage *See* Lovers Like Us (1975)

Le Sauvage *See* The Savage (1975)

Le Scaphandre et le Papillon *See* The Diving Bell and the Butterfly (2007)

Le Silence de Lorna *See* Lorna's Silence (2008)

Le Sirene du Mississippi *See* Mississippi Mermaid (1969)

Le Soleil des Voyous *See* Action Man (1967)

Le Temps des Loups *See* Carbon Copy (1969)

Le Temps du Loup *See* Time of the Wolf (2003)

Le Temps Retrouve *See* Time Regained (1999)

Le Testament D'Orphee *See* The Testament of Orpheus (1959)

Le Testament du Docteur Cordelier *See* The Testament of Dr. Cordelier (1959)

Le Teur Invisible *See* Curse of the Undead (1959)

Le Tournoi dans la Cite *See* Tournament (1929)

Le Train *See* The Train (1965)

Le Trio Infernal *See* The Infernal Trio (1974)

Le Trou *See* Night Watch (1972)

Le Trou Normand *See* Crazy for Love (1952)

Le Vieil Homme Et L'Enfant *See* The Two of Us (1968)

Le Vieux Fusil *See* Old Gun (1976)
Le Violon Rouge *See* The Red Violin (1998)
Le Voleur *See* The Thief of Paris (1967)
Le Voleur De Bagdad *See* Thief of Baghdad (1961)
Le Voyage du Ballon Rouge *See* Flight of the Red Balloon (2008)
Leader of the Pack *See* Unholy Rollers (1972)
Leather and Nylon *See* Action Man (1967)
The Leather Girls *See* Faster, Pussycat! Kill! Kill! (1965)
The Leatherboys *See* The Leather Boys (1963)
Lebenszeichen *See* Signs of Life (1968)
L'eclisse *See* The Eclipse (1966)
L'Ecole Buissonniere *See* Passion for Life (1948)
Legacy of Blood *See* Blood Legacy (1973)
The Legacy of Maggie Walsh *See* The Legacy (1979)
The Legend *See* James Dean (1976)
Legend in Leotards *See* Return of Captain Invincible (1983)
Legend of Cougar Canyon *See* The Secret of Navajo Cave (1976)
Legend of Dinosaurs and Ominous Birds *See* Legend of the Dinosaurs and Monster Birds (1977)
The Legend of Gosta Berling *See* The Atonement of Gosta Berling (1924)
The Legend of Machine Gun Kelly *See* Melvin Purvis: G-Man (1974)
Legend of the Bayou *See* Eaten Alive (1976)
Legend of the Dinosaurs *See* Legend of the Dinosaurs and Monster Birds (1977)
Legend of the Mummy *See* Bram Stoker's The Mummy (1997)
The Legend of the Pianist on the Ocean *See* The Legend of 1900 (1998)
The Legend of the Zaat Monster *See* Attack of the Swamp Creature (1975)
Legend of Witch Hollow *See* The Witchmaker (1969)
The Legend of Zu *See* Zu Warriors (2001)
Legenda Del Rudio Malese *See* Jungle Raiders (1985)
Legenda Suramskoi Kreposti *See* The Legend of Suram Fortress (1985)
The Legendary Curse of Lemora *See* Lemora, Lady Dracula (1973)
Legion of the Damned *See* Battle of the Commandos (1971)
Lejonsommar *See* Vibration (1968)
Lemmy Pour les Dames *See* Ladies' Man (1962)
Lemon Popsicle V *See* Baby Love (1983)
Lemora: A Child's Tale of the Supernatural *See* Lemora, Lady Dracula (1973)
Len Deighton's Bullet to Beijing *See* Bullet to Beijing (1995)
Lenexa, 1 Mile *See* Full Count (2006)
L'Enfant Sauvage *See* The Wild Child (1970)
Leo Tolstoy's Anna Karenina *See* Leo Tolstoy's Anna Karenina (1996)
Leon *See* The Professional (1994)
Leona Helmsley: The Queen of Mean *See* The Queen of Mean (1990)
Leonera *See* Lion's Den (2008)
Lepa Sela, Lepo Gore *See* Pretty Village, Pretty Flame (1996)
Lepassager de la Pluie *See* Rider on the Rain (1970)
L'Eredita Ferramonti *See* The Inheritance (1976)
Les Adventures de Rabbi Jacob *See* The Mad Adventures of Rabbi Jacob (1973)
Les Amants Criminels *See* Criminal Lovers (1999)
Les Amants du Pont-Neuf *See* The Lovers on the Bridge (1991)
Les Amities Particulieres *See* This Special Friendship (1967)
Les Amours d'Astree et de Celadon *See* The Romance of Astrea and Celadon (2007)
Les Avaleuses *See* Female Vampire (1973)
Les Aventuriers *See* The Last Adventure (1967)
Les Bananes Mecaniques *See* Erotic Escape (1972)
Les Bas Fonds *See* The Lower Depths (1936)
Les Belles de Nuit *See* Beauties of the Night (1952)
Les Bijoutiers du Clair de Lune *See* The Night Heaven Fell (1957)
Les Boys *See* The Boys (1997)
Les Bronzes *See* French Fried Vacation (1979)
Les Cent et Une Nuits *See* One Hundred and One Nights (1995)
Les Cent et Une Nuits de Simon Cinema *See* One Hundred and One Nights (1995)
Les Chansons d'Amour *See* Love Songs (2007)
Les Choristes *See* The Chorus (2004)
Les Choses De La Vie *See* The Things of Life (1970)
Les Collegiennes *See* The Twilight Girls (1957)
Les Corrompus *See* The Corrupt Ones (1967)
Les Cousins *See* The Cousins (1959)
Les Dames du Bois de Bologne *See* The Ladies of the Bois de Bologne (1944)
Les Demoiselles de Rochefort *See* The Young Girls of Rochefort (1968)
Les Demons *See* The Demons (1974)
Les Destinees Sentimentales *See* Les Destinees (2000)
Les Deux Anglaises et le Continent *See* Two English Girls (1972)
Les Deux Rivales *See* Time of Indifference (1964)
Les Diabolique *See* Diabolique (1955)
Les Dimanches de Ville d'Arvay *See* Sundays & Cybele (1962)
Les Egares *See* Strayed (2003)
Les Enfants du Paradis *See* Children of Paradise (1944)
Les Enfants du Siecle *See* Children of the Century (1999)
Les Enfants Gates *See* Spoiled Children (1977)
Les Felins *See* Joy House (1964)
Les Feluettes *See* Lilies (1996)
Les Femmes *See* The Women (1968)
Les Filles Ne Savent Pas Nager *See* Girls Can't Swim (1999)
Les Fils de Gascogne *See* Son of Gascogne (1995)
Les Fils du Vent *See* The Great Challenge (2004)
Les Gaspards *See* The Holes (1972)
Les Grandes Gueules *See* Jailbird's Vacation (1965)
Les Grandes Personnes *See* Time Out for Love (1961)
Les Griffes du Vampire *See* Curse of the Undead (1959)
Les Innocents aux Mains Sales *See* Innocents with Dirty Hands (1976)
Les Invasions Barbares *See* The Barbarian Invasions (2003)
Les Jeux Interdits *See* Forbidden Games (1952)
Les Liaisons Dangereuses *See* Dangerous Liaisons (1960)
Les Liaisons dangereuses *See* Dangerous Liaisons (2003)
Les Liens de Sang *See* Blood Relatives (1977)
Les Louves *See* Letters to an Unknown Lover (1984)
Les Mille Et Une Nuits *See* The Wonders of Aladdin (1961)
Les Mille et Une Recettes du Cuisinier Amoureux *See* A Chef in Love (1996)
Les Mongols *See* The Mongols (1960)
Les Noces de Papier *See* A Paper Wedding (1989)
Les Noces Rouges *See* Wedding in Blood (1974)
Les Nuits de la Pleine *See* Full Moon in Paris (1984)
Les Orgueilleux *See* The Proud Ones (1953)
Les Parapluies de Cherbourg *See* Umbrellas of Cherbourg (1964)
Les Parents Terribles *See* The Storm Within (1948)
Les Passagers *See* Intruder (1976)
Les Possedes *See* The Possessed (1988)
Les Poupees Russes *See* Russian Dolls (2005)
Les Predateurs de la Nuit *See* Faceless (1988)
Les Quartre Cents Coups *See* The 400 Blows (1959)
Les Rendez-vous de Paris *See* Rendezvous in Paris (1995)
Les Repos du Guerrier *See* Love on a Pillow (1962)
Les Revenants *See* They Came Back (2004)
Les Ripoux *See* My New Partner (1984)
Les Rivieres Pourpres *See* The Crimson Rivers (2001)
Les Rivieres Pourpres II: Les Anges de L'apocalypse *See* Crimson Rivers 2: Angels of the Apocalypse (2005)
Les Roseaux Sauvages *See* Wild Reeds (1994)
Les Routes du Sud *See* Roads to the South (1978)
Les Silences du Palais *See* The Silences of the Palace (1994)
Les Somnambules *See* Mon Oncle d'Amerique (1980)
Les Sorcieres de Salem *See* The Crucible (1957)
Les Temoins *See* The Witnesses (2007)
Les Temps Qui Changent *See* Changing Times (2004)
Les Temps Qui Reste *See* Time to Leave (2005)
Les Triplettes de Belleville *See* The Triplets of Belleville (2002)
Les Trois Visages de la Peur *See* Black Sabbath (1964)
Les Vacances de Monsieur Hulot *See* Mr. Hulot's Holiday (1953)
Les Valseuses *See* Going Places (1974)
Les Visiteurs *See* The Visitors (1995)
Les Yeux Noirs *See* Dark Eyes (1987)
Les Yeux sans Visage *See* The Horror Chamber of Dr. Faustus (1959)
Lesbian Twins *See* The Virgin Witch (1970)
Lesbian Vampire Killers *See* Vampire Killers (2009)
L'Ete Meurtrier *See* One Deadly Summer (1983)
L'Ete Prochain *See* Next Summer (1984)
L'Eternel Retour *See* Eternal Return (1943)
Lethal *See* The KGB: The Secret War (1986)
Let's Kill Bobby Z *See* Bobby Z (2007)
Let's Make Friends *See* I Love You, Man (2009)
Letter to Daddy *See* Jet Li's The Enforcer (1995)
A Letter to Mama *See* A Brivele der Mamen (1938)
A Letter to Mother *See* A Brivele der Mamen (1938)
Letyat Zhuravit *See* The Cranes Are Flying (1957)
L'Evangile Selon Saint-Matthieu *See* The Gospel According to St. Matthew (1964)
Levres de Sang *See* Lips of Blood (1975)
L'Histoire d'Adele H. *See* The Story of Adele H. (1975)
L'Homme de Rio *See* That Man from Rio (1964)
L'Homme du Train *See* The Man on the Train (2002)
L'Homme Qui Aimait les Femmes *See* The Man Who Loved Women (1977)
L'Homme Qui J'aime *See* The Man I Love (1997)
L'Humanite *See* Humanity (1999)
L'Hypothese du Tableau Vole *See* The Hypothesis of the Stolen Painting (1978)
Liar *See* Deceiver (1997)
Libido *See* The Sensuous Teenager (1970)
Licensed to Kill *See* Second Best Secret Agent in the Whole Wide World (1965)
The Lie Detector *See* Le Polygraphe (1996)
Lie to Me *See* Fling (2008)
Liebe Ist Kalter Als Der Tod *See* Love Is Colder Than Death (1969)
The Life and Adventures of Nicholas Nickleby *See* Nicholas Nickleby (1946)
The Life and Death of Bobby Z *See* Bobby Z (2007)
The Life and Death of King Richard III *See* Richard III (1912)
The Life and Loves of Beethoven *See* Beethoven (1936)
The Life and Music of Giuseppe Verdi *See* Verdi (1953)
Life at Stake *See* The Key Man (1957)
Life Combat *See* Life Gamble (2004)
Life/Drawing *See* Apartment 12 (2006)
Life During Wartime *See* The Alarmist (1998)
Life in the Food Chain *See* Age Isn't Everything (1991)
Life Is a Fairy Tale *See* Life Is a Bed of Roses (1983)
Life Is Rosy *See* La Vie Est Belle (1987)
Life of Brian *See* Monty Python's Life of Brian (1979)
The Life of Jack London *See* Jack London (1944)
Lifebreath *See* Last Breath (1996)
Lifesavers *See* Mixed Nuts (1994)
The Light Fantastic *See* Love Is Better Than Ever (1952)
Lighthouse *See* Dead of Night (1999)
Lightning Fists of Shaolin *See* Opium and Kung-Fu Master (1984)
Lights of Variety *See* Variety Lights (1951)
Like a Crow on a June Bug *See* Sixteen (1972)
Like Father, Like Son *See* The Executioner (1978)
Like Minds *See* Murderous Intent (2006)
Lila *See* Mantis in Lace (1968)
Lila Dit Ca *See* Lila Says (2004)
Lilacs in the Spring *See* Let's Make Up (1955)
The Limb Salesman *See* Re-Generation (2004)
The Limit *See* Gone Dark (2003)
Limonadovy Joe aneb Konska Opera *See* Lemonade Joe (1964)
L'Inafferrabile Invincible *See* Mr. Superinvisible (1973)
Lincoln *See* Gore Vidal's Lincoln (1988)
Linkeroever *See* Left Bank (2008)
The Lion *See* La Leon (2007)

A Lion Is in the Streets *See* A Lion in the Streets (1953)

The Lion's Den *See* La Boca del Lobo (1989)

The Liquid Sword *See* Legend of the Liquid Sword (1993)

Lisa e il Diavolo *See* Lisa and the Devil (1975)

Lisa, Lisa *See* Axe (1974)

Lisbon *See* Lisboa (1999)

L'Isola Degli Uomini Pesce *See* Screamers (1980)

Little Fellas *See* Petits Freres (2000)

Little Jerusalem *See* La Petite Jerusalem (2005)

Little Lili *See* La Petite Lili (2003)

The Little Martyr *See* The Children Are Watching Us (1944)

The Little Mermaid *See* La Petite Sirene (1980)

Little Miss Millions *See* Home for Christmas (1993)

Little Mother *See* Mamele (1938)

Little Pal *See* Healer (1936)

Little Panda *See* The Amazing Panda Adventure (1995)

The Little Sister *See* The Tender Age (1984)

Live a Little, Steal a Lot *See* Murph the Surf (1975)

Live Bait *See* L'Appat (1994)

Live to Love *See* The Devil's Hand (1961)

Live Virgin *See* American Virgin (1998)

The Liver Eaters *See* Spider Baby (1964)

Livers Ain't Cheap *See* The Real Thing (1997)

Living *See* Ikiru (1952)

The Living Dead at Manchester Morgue *See* Let Sleeping Corpses Lie (1974)

Living Hell *See* Organizm (2008)

Living Nightmare *See* Echoes (1983)

Ljubarni Slucaj *See* The Love Affair, or The Case of the Missing Switchboard Operator (1967)

Lo Chiamavano King *See* His Name Was King (1971)

Lo Chiamavano Trinita *See* They Call Me Trinity (1972)

Lo Que Vendra *See* Times to Come (1981)

Lo Sbarco di Anzio *See* Anzio (1968)

Lo Scatenato *See* Catch as Catch Can (1968)

Lo Sceicco Bianco *See* The White Sheik (1952)

Lo Spettro *See* The Ghost (1963)

Lo Spettro de Dr. Hitchcock *See* The Ghost (1963)

Lo Squartatore de New York *See* New York Ripper (1982)

Lo Strangolatore di Vienna *See* The Mad Butcher (1972)

Lo Strano Vizio della Signora Ward *See* Blade of the Ripper (1970)

Lo Strano Vizio Della Signora Wardh *See* The Next Victim (1971)

Lo Zio Indegno *See* The Sleazy Uncle (1989)

Loaded Weapon 1 *See* National Lampoon's Loaded Weapon 1 (1993)

Lock Your Doors *See* The Ape Man (1943)

The Lodger: A Case of London Fog *See* The Lodger (1926)

L'Oeuvre au Noir *See* The Abyss (1989)

Lola + Bilikid *See* Lola and Billy the Kid (1998)

Lola Rennt *See* Run Lola Run (1998)

Lolita 2000 *See* Lolida 2000 (1997)

The Lone Troubador *See* Two-Gun Troubador (1937)

Lone Wolf and Cub: Baby Cart to Hades *See* Shogun Assassin 2: Lightning Swords of Death (1973)

The Lonely Hearts Killers *See* Honeymoon Killers (1970)

The Lonely Maiden *See* The Maiden Heist (2008)

Lonely Man *See* Gun Riders (1969)

The Lonely Wife *See* Charulata (1964)

The Lonely Woman *See* Voyage in Italy (1953)

The Loner *See* Ruckus (1981)

Lonesome Dove: Streets of Laredo *See* Larry McMurtry's Streets of Laredo (1995)

The Long Arm *See* The Third Key (1957)

The Long, Dark Night *See* The Pack (1977)

Long John Silver Returns to Treasure Island *See* Long John Silver (1954)

The Long Night of '43 *See* That Long Night in '43 (1960)

The Long Ride *See* Brady's Escape (1984)

The Long Shot *See* African Rage (1978)

Long Time, Nothing New *See* No Looking Back (1998)

Long Way Home *See* Raising Victor Vargas (2003)

Long Weekend *See* Nature's Grave (2008)

Longshot *See* Long Shot Kids (1981)

Longxiong Hudi *See* Operation Condor 2: The Armour of the Gods (1986)

Look Beautiful and Shut Up *See* Sois Belle et Tais-Toi (1958)

Look Down and Die *See* Steel (1980)

The Look of Ulysses *See* Ulysses' Gaze (1995)

Lookin' Italian *See* Showdown (1994)

Loonies on Broadway *See* Zombies on Broadway (1944)

Loose Joints *See* Flicks (1985)

Looters *See* Trespass (1992)

L'Opera De Quat'Sous *See* The Threepenny Opera (1931)

Lorca *See* The Disappearance of Garcia Lorca (1996)

Lorca and the Outlaws *See* Starship (1987)

Lord Mountbatten: The Last Viceroy *See* Mountbatten: The Last Viceroy (1986)

Lords of Treason *See* Secret Honor (1985)

L'Oro Di Napoli *See* The Gold of Naples (1954)

L'Orribile Segreto del Dr. Hichcock *See* The Horrible Dr. Hichcock (1962)

Los Abrazos Rotos *See* Broken Embraces (2009)

Los Amantes del Circulo Polar *See* Lovers of the Arctic Circle (1998)

Los Ambiciosos *See* Fever Mounts at El Pao (1959)

Los Cronocrimenes *See* Timecrimes (2007)

Los Demonios *See* The Demons (1974)

Los Despiadados *See* Hellbenders (1967)

Los Doctores las Prefieren Desnudas *See* Naked Is Better (1973)

Los Lunes al Sol *See* Mondays in the Sun (2002)

Los Ojos Azules de la Muneca Rota *See* House of Psychotic Women (1973)

Los Santos Inocentes *See* The Holy Innocents (1984)

Loser Take All *See* Strike It Rich (1990)

The Lost Glory of Troy *See* The Avenger (1962)

The Lost Illusion *See* The Fallen Idol (1949)

Lost in Time *See* Waxwork 2: Lost in Time (1991)

Lost Island of Kioga *See* Hawk of the Wilderness (1938)

Lost Planet Airmen *See* King of the Rocketmen (1949)

Lost Women *See* Mesa of Lost Women (1952)

Lost Women of Zarpa *See* Mesa of Lost Women (1952)

The Lost World *See* Sir Arthur Conan Doyle's The Lost World (1998)

The Loudest Whisper *See* The Children's Hour (1961)

Louis L'Amour's Conagher *See* Conagher (1991)

Louis L'Amour's "The Shadow Riders" *See* The Shadow Riders (1982)

Louis 19, le Roi des Ondes *See* King of the Airwaves (1994)

Love and Death in Saigon *See* A Better Tomorrow, Part 3 (1989)

Love and Hate: The Story of Colin and Joanne Thatcher *See* Love and Hate: A Marriage Made in Hell (1990)

Love and the Midnight Auto Supply *See* Midnight Auto Supply (1978)

The Love Cage *See* Joy House (1964)

Love Eternal *See* Eternal Return (1943)

The Love Factor *See* Zeta One (1969)

Love in Las Vegas *See* Viva Las Vegas (1963)

Love is Blind *See* Love at First Sight (1976)

Love Lessons *See* All Things Fair (1995)

Love Letter *See* When I Close My Eyes (1995)

Love Madness *See* Reefer Madness (1938)

The Love Maniac *See* Blood of Ghastly Horror (1972)

The Love of a Man *See* Amor de Hombre (1997)

Love Scenes *See* Ecstasy (1984)

A Love Story *See* Song of Love (1947)

Love, the Magician *See* El Amor Brujo (1986)

Love Trap *See* Curse of the Black Widow (1977)

Love You to Death *See* Deadly Illusion (1987)

The Lovelorn Minstrel *See* Ashik Kerib (1988)

Lover of the Great Bear *See* Smugglers (1975)

Lover, Wife *See* Wifemistress (1979)

Lovers from Beyond the Tomb *See* Nightmare Castle (1965)

Lovers Must Learn *See* Rome Adventure (1962)

The Lovers of Montparnasse *See* Modigliani (1958)

Love's a Bitch *See* Amores Perros (2000)

Loves of a Scoundrel *See* Death of a Scoundrel (1956)

The Loves of Count Yorga, Vampire *See* Count Yorga, Vampire (1970)

The Loves of Irina *See* Female Vampire (1973)

The Loves of Isadora *See* Isadora (1968)

Loving Moments *See* Bleak Moments (1971)

Low Rent *See* Apartment 12 (2006)

The Loyal 47 Ronin *See* 47 Ronin, Part 1 (1942)

Luca il Contrabbandiere *See* Contraband (1980)

Luce Dei Miei Occhi *See* Light of My Eyes (2001)

L'Ucello dalle Plume di Cristallo *See* The Bird with the Crystal Plumage (1970)

Luci del Varieta *See* Variety Lights (1951)

Lucia y el Sexo *See* Sex and Lucia (2001)

The Lucifer Project *See* Barracuda (1978)

Lucky Boots *See* Gun Play (1936)

Lucky Break *See* Paperback Romance (1996)

Lucky 13 *See* Running Hot (1983)

Lucky to Be a Woman *See* What a Woman! (1956)

The Lullaby *See* The Sin of Madelon Claudet (1931)

L'Ultimo Bacio *See* The Last Kiss (2001)

L'Ultimo Uomo Della Terra *See* The Last Man on Earth (1964)

Lulu *See* Pandora's Box (1928)

Lunch on the Grass *See* Picnic on the Grass (1959)

Lunch Wagon Girls *See* Lunch Wagon (1981)

L'Une Chante, l'Autre Pas *See* One Sings, the Other Doesn't (1977)

L'Uomo Dalle Due Ombre *See* Cold Sweat (1971)

L'Uomo di Rio *See* That Man from Rio (1964)

Lure of the Jungle *See* Boy of Two Worlds (1959)

Lust for Evil *See* Purple Noon (1960)

Lust och Fagring Stor *See* All Things Fair (1995)

Lust of the Vampires *See* I, Vampiri (1956)

Lycanthropus *See* Werewolf in a Girl's Dormitory (1961)

Lysets Hjerte *See* Heart of Light (1997)

M. Hire *See* Monsieur Hire (1989)

M:I 2 *See* Mission: Impossible 2 (2000)

M1187511 *See* In This World (2003)

Ma and Pa Kettle Go to Paris *See* Ma and Pa Kettle on Vacation (1953)

Ma Femme est une Actrice *See* My Wife is an Actress (2001)

Ma Nuit Chez Maud *See* My Night at Maud's (1969)

Ma Vie Sexuelle...Comment Je Me Suis Dispute *See* My Sex Life... Or How I Got into an Argument (1996)

Ma Vraie Vie a Rouen *See* My Life on Ice (2002)

Maboroshi no Hikari *See* Maborosi (1995)

Macabra *See* Demonoid, Messenger of Death (1981)

Macabre Serenade *See* Dance of Death (1968)

Maccheroni *See* Macaroni (1985)

Maciste Alla Corte Del Gran Khan *See* Samson and the 7 Miracles of the World (1962)

Maciste at the Court of the Great Khan *See* Samson and the 7 Miracles of the World (1962)

Maciste Contro i Mostri *See* Fire Monsters Against the Son of Hercules (1962)

Maciste Contro lo Sceicco *See* Samson Against the Sheik (1962)

Maciste, Il Gladiatore piu Forte del Monte *See* Colossus of the Arena (1962)

Maciste la Regina di Samar *See* Hercules against the Moon Men (1964)

Maciste, L'Eroe Piu Grande Del Mondo *See* Goliath and the Sins of Babylon (1964)

Maciste Nella Terra dei Ciclopi *See* Atlas in the Land of the Cyclops (1961)

The Mad Butcher of Vienna *See* The Mad Butcher (1972)

Mad Dog *See* Mad Dog Morgan (1976)

Mad Dog Time *See* Trigger Happy (1996)

Mad Dogs and Englishmen *See* Shameless (1994)

The Mad Hatter *See* Breakfast in Hollywood (1946)

Mad Jake *See* Blood Salvage (1990)

Mad Magazine's Up the Academy *See* Up the Academy (1980)

Mad Max 2 *See* The Road Warrior (1982)

Mad Trapper of the Yukon *See* Challenge To Be Free (1976)

Mad Wednesday *See* The Sin of Harold Diddlebock (1947)

Madame *See* Madame Sans-Gene (1962)

Madame De... *See* The Earrings of Madame De... (1954)

Madame Frankenstein *See* Lady Frankenstein (1972)

Madeleine Tel. 13 62 11 *See* Naked in the Night (1958)

Mademoiselle France *See* Reunion in France (1942)

Mademoiselle Striptease *See* Plucking the Daisy (1956)

Madmen of Mandoras *See* They Saved Hitler's Brain (1964)

Madness of Love *See* Mad Love (2001)

Madonna Truth or Dare *See* Truth or Dare (1991)

Mafia Docks *See* Desperate Crimes (1993)

Mafia Junction *See* Super Bitch (1973)

Mafia Lady *See* Smokey & the Hotwire Gang (1979)

The Mafu Cage *See* My Sister, My Love (1978)

The Magic Hour *See* Twilight (1998)

The Magic Roundabout *See* Doogal (2005)

The Magnificent One *See* Le Magnifique (1976)

The Magnificent Seven *See* Seven Samurai (1954)

The Magnificent Showman *See* Circus World (1964)

Mahanagar *See* The Big City (1963)

Majin *See* Daimajin (1966)

Majin Strikes Again *See* Return of Daimajin (1966)

Major Movie Star *See* Private Valentine: Blonde & Dangerous (2008)

Making It *See* Going Places (1974)

Mako: The Jaws of Death *See* Jaws of Death (1976)

Malastrana *See* Short Night of Glass Dolls (1971)

Malenka, the Vampire *See* Fangs of the Living Dead (1968)

Malenkaya Vera *See* Little Vera (1988)

Malibu Hot Summer *See* Sizzle Beach U.S.A. (1974)

Malice in Wonderland *See* The Rumor Mill (1986)

Malizia *See* Malicious (1974)

Malli *See* The Terrorist (1998)

Mamba Snakes *See* Fair Game (1989)

Mamoru Oshii's - Talking Head *See* Talking Head (1992)

Man Against the Mob: The Chinatown Murders *See* The Chinatown Murders: Man against the Mob (1989)

Man and His Mate *See* One Million B.C. (1940)

A Man Betrayed *See* Wheel of Fortune (1941)

Man Cheng Jin Dai Huang Jin Jia *See* Curse of the Golden Flower (2006)

Man-Eater *See* Shark! (1968)

A Man Escaped, or the Wind Bloweth Where It Listeth *See* A Man Escaped (1957)

The Man from C.O.T.T.O.N. *See* Purlie Victorious (1963)

The Man From C.O.T.T.O.N., Purlie Victorious *See* Gone Are the Days (1963)

Man from Music Mountain *See* Texas Legionnaires (1943)

The Man From Nevada *See* The Nevadan (1950)

The Man Hunter *See* Devil Hunter (2008)

Man in a Cocked Hat *See* Carlton Browne of the F.O. (1959)

A Man in Mommy's Bed *See* With Six You Get Eggroll (1968)

The Man in Possession *See* Personal Property (1937)

Man in the Middle *See* 48 Hours to Live (1960)

Man Looking Southeast *See* Man Facing Southeast (1986)

Man of Bronze *See* Jim Thorpe: All American (1951)

Man of Mystery *See* End of the Road (1944)

Man of the Frontier *See* Red River Valley (1936)

Man of the Hour *See* Colonel Effingham's Raid (1945)

Man on the Move *See* Jigsaw (1971)

Man Som Hatar Kvinnor *See* The Girl With the Dragon Tattoo (2009)

The Man Who Changed His Mind *See* The Man Who Lived Again (1936)

The Man Who Cried *See* Catherine Cookson's The Man Who Cried (1993)

The Man Who Watched Trains Go By *See* Paris Express (1953)

The Man With Rain in His Shoe *See* Twice upon a Yesterday (1998)

The Man With The Deadly Lens *See* Wrong Is Right (1982)

The Man with the Green Carnation *See* The Trials of Oscar Wilde (1960)

The Man with the Synthetic Brain *See* Blood of Ghastly Horror (1972)

The Man with the X-Ray Eyes *See* X: The Man with X-Ray Eyes (1963)

The Man with the Yellow Eyes *See* Planets Against Us (1961)

The Man with Thirty Sons *See* The Magnificent Yankee (1950)

Manchester Prep *See* Cruel Intentions 2 (1999)

Mandingo Manhunter *See* Devil Hunter (2008)

Manen Pa Taket *See* The Man on the Roof (1976)

Mangiati Vivi dai Cannibali *See* Emerald Jungle (1980)

Manhattan Project: The Deadly Game *See* The Manhattan Project (1986)

Manhunt *See* Hit Men (1973)

Manhunt in the Dakotas *See* Midnight Murders (1991)

Manhunt: The Search for the Night Stalker *See* The Hunt for the Night Stalker (1991)

Mania *See* The Flesh and the Fiends (1960)

The Maniacs Are Loose *See* The Thrill Killers (1965)

Manifesto *See* A Night of Love (1987)

Manly Love *See* Amor de Hombre (1997)

Mannen fran Mallorca *See* Man from Mallorca (1984)

Mannequins for Rio *See* Party Girls for Sale (1954)

Manner wie wir *See* Guys and Balls (2004)

Manon 70 *See* Manon (1968)

Manon des Sources *See* Manon of the Spring (1987)

Mansion of Madness *See* Dr. Tarr's Torture Dungeon (1975)

Mansquito *See* Mosquitoman (2005)

The Manster—Half Man, Half Monster *See* The Manster (1959)

Manuela's Loves *See* Le Jupon Rouge (1987)

Mar Adentro *See* The Sea Inside (2004)

Marc Bolan and T-Rrex: Born to Boogie *See* Born to Boogie (1972)

Marc Mato, Agent S.077 *See* Espionage in Tangiers (1965)

Marcelino *See* The Miracle of Marcelino (1955)

Marcelino, Pan y Vino *See* The Miracle of Marcelino (1955)

Marching Along *See* Stars and Stripes Forever (1952)

Marco Polo Junior Versus the Red Dragon *See* Marco Polo, Jr. (1972)

The Marconi Bros. *See* The Wedding Bros. (2008)

Margaret Bourke-White *See* Double Exposure: The Story of Margaret Bourke-White (1989)

Maria di Mi Corazon *See* Mary, My Dearest (1983)

Maria Larssons Eviga Ogonblick *See* Everlasting Moments (2008)

Maria, llena eres de gracia *See* Maria Full of Grace (2004)

Maria Marten *See* Murder in the Old Red Barn (1936)

Maria-nap *See* Maria's Day (1984)

Marie Bay of Angels *See* Marie Baie des Anges (1997)

Marie Walewska *See* Conquest (1937)

Marijuana the Devil's Weed *See* She Shoulda Said No (1949)

Marijuana: The Devil's Weed *See* Marihuana (1936)

Marijuana, Weed with Roots in Hell *See* Marihuana (1936)

Marilyn *See* Roadhouse Girl (1953)

Marine Issue *See* Instant Justice (1986)

Mario Puzo's The Last Don *See* The Last Don (1997)

Mario Puzo's The Last Don 2 *See* The Last Don 2 (1998)

Marius et Jeannette: Un Conte de L'Estaque *See* Marius and Jeannette (1997)

Mark of Terror *See* Drums of Jeopardy (1931)

Mark of the Avenger *See* The Mysterious Rider (1938)

Mark of the Beast *See* Curse of the Undead (1959)

Mark of the Claw *See* Dick Tracy's Dilemma (1947)

Mark of the Vampire *See* The Vampire (1957)

Mark of the West *See* Curse of the Undead (1959)

Mark Twain *See* The Adventures of Mark Twain (1985)

Married in Haste *See* Consolation Marriage (1931)

A Married Woman *See* Une Femme Mariee (1964)

Marrionnier: Doll Horror Movie *See* Marrionnier (2005)

Mars Invades Puerto Rico *See* Frankenstein Meets the Space Monster (1965)

The Marseille Contract *See* The Destructors (1974)

Marshal of Heldorado *See* Blazing Guns (1950)

The Marsupials: Howling 3 *See* Howling 3: The Marsupials (1987)

Marte, Dio Della Guerra *See* Venus Against the Son of Hercules (1962)

Martha, Meet Frank, Daniel and Laurence *See* The Very Thought of You (1998)

Martin Lawrence You So Crazy *See* You So Crazy (1994)

Marusa No Onna *See* A Taxing Woman (1987)

Marusa No Onna II *See* A Taxing Woman's Return (1988)

The Marvelous Visit *See* La Merveilleuse Visite (1974)

The Marx Brothers at the Circus *See* At the Circus (1939)

Marx Brothers Go West *See* Go West (1940)

Mary Bryant *See* The Incredible Journey of Mary Bryant (2005)

Mary Jane's Last Dance *See* New Best Friend (2002)

Mascskajatek *See* Cat's Play (1974)

Masculin Feminin *See* Masculine Feminine (1966)

Mask of Dust *See* Race for Life (1955)

Mask of Fury *See* First Yank into Tokyo (1945)

Mask of Satan *See* Black Sunday (1960)

Massacre at Fort Holman *See* A Reason to Live, a Reason to Die (1973)

Massacre Hill *See* Eureka Stockade (1949)

Massacre Mafia Style *See* The Executioner (1978)

Massa'ot James Be'eretz Hakodesh *See* James' Journey to Jerusalem (2003)

The Master Killer *See* The 36th Chamber of Shaolin (1978)

The Master Mystery *See* The Houdini Serial (1920)

Master of Evil *See* The Demon Lover (1977)

Master of Lassie *See* The Hills of Home (1948)

Master of the Crimson Armor *See* The Promise (2005)

Mat i Syn *See* Mother and Son (1997)

Matango *See* Attack of the Mushroom People (1963)

Matango the Fungus of Terror *See* Matango (1963)

Matar al Abuelito *See* Killing Grandpa (1991)

Mater Dolorosa *See* The Torture of Silence (1917)

The Mating of the Sabine Women *See* The Rape of the Sabines (1961)

Matir Moina *See* The Clay Bird (2002)

Matka Joanna Od Aniolow *See* Mother Joan of the Angels (1960)

Matt Riker *See* Mutant Hunt (1987)

A Matter of Life and Death *See* Stairway to Heaven (1946)

Mauri *See* Big Mo (1973)

Maurice Richard *See* The Rocket (2005)

Mausoleum *See* One Dark Night (1982)

Mauvais Genres *See* Transfixed (2001)

Mauvaises Frequentations *See* Bad Company (1999)

Mavri Emmanouella *See* Emmanuelle, the Queen (1979)

Max, My Love *See* Max, Mon Amour (1986)

Maxie *See* Murderer's Keep (1970)

Mayerling to Sarajevo *See* De Mayerling a Sarajevo (1940)

The Mayfair Bank Caper *See* The Big Scam (1979)

Mazel Tov Ou le Mariage *See* Marry Me, Marry Me (1969)

McKlusky *See* White Lightning (1973)

The McMasters...Tougher Than the West Itself *See* The McMasters (1970)

M.D.C. Maschera di Cera *See* Wax Mask (1997)

Me Faire ca a Moi *See* It Means That to Me (1960)

Meachorei Hasoragim *See* Beyond the Walls (1984)

Meat Is Meat *See* The Mad Butcher (1972)

Mecaniques Celestes *See* Celestial Clockwork (1994)

Mechanical Bananas *See* Erotic Escape (1972)

The Medicine Hat Stallion *See* Peter Lundy and the Medicine Hat Stallion (1977)

The Medieval Dead *See* Army of Darkness (1992)

Medusa vs. the Son of Hercules *See* Medusa Against the Son of Hercules (1962)

Meet Miss Marple *See* Murder She Said (1962)

Meet Ruth Stoops *See* Citizen Ruth (1996)

Meet the Applegates *See* The Applegates (1989)

Meet the Browns *See* Tyler Perry's Meet the Browns (2008)

Meet the Ghosts *See* Abbott and Costello Meet Frankenstein (1948)

Meet Whiplash Willie *See* The Fortune Cookie (1966)

The Meetings of Anna *See* Les Rendez-vous D'Anna (1978)

Mega Snake *See* Megasnake (2007)

Megall Az Ido *See* Time Stands Still (1982)

A Meia-Noite Levarei Sua Alma *See* At Midnight, I'll Take Your Soul (1963)

Mein Fuhrer: Die Wirklich Wahrste Wahrheit Ueber Adolf Hitler *See* My Fuhrer (2007)

Mekagojira No Gyakushu *See* Terror of Mechagodzilla (1978)

Melanie Rose *See* High Stakes (1989)

Melodie en Sous-Sol *See* Any Number Can Win (1963)

Melody of Youth *See* They Shall Have Music (1939)

Meltdown *See* American Meltdown (2004)

Mem om oss barn i Bullerby *See* More about the Children of Noisy Village (1987)

Memorias del Subdesarrollo *See* Memories of Underdevelopment (1968)

The Men *See* Killing in the Sun (1973)

Men Don't Quit *See* Grilled (2006)

Men in Tights *See* Robin Hood: Men in Tights (1993)

Men of Steel *See* Steel (1980)

Men with Guns *See* Hombres Armados (1997)

Meng zhong ren *See* Dream Lovers (1986)

The Mercenaries *See* Dark of the Sun (1968)

Merchant of Death *See* Mission of Death (1997)

Mermaid Chronicles Part 1: She Creature *See* She Creature (2001)

Merry Christmas *See* Felicidades (2000)

Merry Christmas *See* Joyeux Noel (2005)

A Merry Little Christmas *See* The Town That Banned Christmas (2006)

Merveilleuse Angelique *See* Angelique: The Road to Versailles (1965)

Mery per Sempre *See* Forever Mary (1989)

Messer Im Kopf *See* Knife in the Head (1978)

Metalmeccanico e Parrucchiera in un Turbine di Sesso e di Politica *See* The Worker and the Hairdresser (1996)

Metempsycose *See* Tomb of Torture (1965)

Meteor Monster *See* Teenage Monster (1957)

Meteoro Kai Skia *See* Meteor & Shadow (1985)

Metisse *See* Cafe au Lait (1994)

Meurtre en 45 Tours *See* Murder at 45 R.P.M. (1965)

Mi Casa, Su Casa *See* Loco Love (2003)

Mi Familia *See* My Family (1994)

A mi madre le gustan las mujeres *See* My Mother Likes Women (2002)

Mia Eoniotita Ke Mia Mera *See* Eternity and a Day (1997)

MIB *See* Men in Black (1997)

Mibu gishi den *See* When the Last Sword is Drawn (2002)

Michael Almereyda's The Mummy *See* The External (1999)

Michael Angel *See* The Apostate (1998)

Michael Shayne *See* Too Many Winners (1947)

Mickey Spillane's Margin for Murder *See* Margin for Murder (1981)

Micmac a Tire-Larigot *See* Micmacs (2009)

Microscopia *See* Fantastic Voyage (1966)

Midare Karakuri *See* Murders in the Doll House (1979)

Midnight at Madame Tussaud's *See* Midnight at the Wax Museum (1936)

Midnight Heat *See* Sunset Heat (1992)

Midnight Man *See* Jack Higgins' Midnight Man (1996)

Midnight Movie Massacre *See* Attack from Mars (1988)

A Midsummer Night's Dream *See* William Shakespeare's A Midsummer Night's Dream (1999)

Miel et Cendres *See* Honey & Ashes (1996)

Mies Vailla Menneisyytta *See* The Man Without a Past (2002)

Mifune's Last Song *See* Mifune (1999)

Mifunes Sidste Sang *See* Mifune (1999)

The Mighty Ducks 2 *See* D2: The Mighty Ducks (1994)

The Mighty Thunder *See* Tundra (1936)

The Mighty Ursus *See* Ursus in the Valley of the Lions (1962)

The Mighty Warrior *See* The Trojan Horse (1962)

Mikan No Taikyoku *See* The Go-Masters (1982)

Mike Leigh's Naked *See* Naked (1993)

Mikres Aphrodites *See* Young Aphrodites (1963)

Milagro en Roma *See* Miracle in Rome (1988)

Milczaca Gwiazda *See* First Spaceship on Venus (1960)

Mile a Minute Love *See* Roaring Speedboats (1937)

Milou en Mai *See* May Fools (1990)

Milou in May *See* May Fools (1990)

Mimi Metallurgico Ferito Nell'Onore *See* Seduction of Mimi (1972)

Minaccia d'Amore *See* Dial Help (1988)

Minbo No Onna *See* Minbo—Or the Gentle Art of Japanese Extortion (1992)

Mind Games *See* The Agency (1981)

Mind Rage *See* Mind Lies (2000)

Mind Ripper *See* Wes Craven Presents Mind Ripper (1995)

Mindwarp: An Infinity of Terror *See* Galaxy of Terror (1981)

Minna von Barnhelm oder das Soldatengluck *See* Minna von Barnhelm or The Soldier's Fortune (1962)

Mio Fratello e Figlio Unico *See* My Brother Is an Only Child (2007)

Mio in the Land of Faraway *See* The Land of Faraway (1987)

A Miracle Can Happen *See* On Our Merry Way (1948)

The Miracle of Fatima *See* Miracle of Our Lady of Fatima (1952)

Miracle of Life *See* Our Daily Bread (1934)

Miracolo a Milano *See* Miracle in Milan (1951)

Mirage *See* Maborosi (1995)

Mirai Ninja *See* Cyber Ninja (1994)

The Mischief-Makers *See* Les Mistons (1957)

Miss Castaway and the Island Girls *See* Miss Cast Away (2004)

Miss Europe *See* Prix de Beaute (1930)

Miss Muerte *See* The Diabolical Dr. Z (1965)

Miss Shumway *See* Rough Magic (1995)

The Mission of the Yogi *See* The Indian Tomb (1921)

The Mrs. Bradley Mysteries: Speedy Death *See* Speedy Death (1999)

Mrs. Parker and the Round Table *See* Mrs. Parker and the Vicious Circle (1994)

Mr. Ashton was Indiscreet *See* The Senator Was Indiscreet (1947)

Mr. Bug Goes to Town *See* Hoppity Goes to Town (1941)

Mr. Celebrity *See* Turf Boy (1942)

Mr. Forbush and the Penguins *See* Cry of the Penguins (1971)

Mr. Fox of Venice *See* The Honey Pot (1967)

Mr. Invisible *See* Mr. Superinvisible (1973)

Mr. Murder *See* Dean Koontz's Mr. Murder (1998)

Mr. Quilp *See* The Old Curiosity Shop (1975)

Mister Scarface *See* Rulers of the City (1976)

Mr. Sebastian *See* Sebastian (1968)

Mr. 247 *See* A Modern Affair (1994)

Mister V *See* Pimpernel Smith (1942)

Mr. Wrong *See* Dark of the Night (1985)

Misterios del Ultratumba *See* Black Pit of Dr. M (1947)

Mit Eva Fing Die Sunde An *See* The Bellboy and the Playgirls (1962)

Mitt Liv Som Hund *See* My Life As a Dog (1985)

Miyazaki's Spirited Away *See* Spirited Away (2001)

Mme. Olga's Massage Parlor *See* Olga's Girls (1964)

Mo *See* Natural City (2003)

Moartea Domnului Lazarescu *See* The Death of Mr. Lazarescu (2005)

The Model Killer *See* The Hollywood Strangler Meets the Skid Row Slasher (1979)

Model Massacre *See* Color Me Blood Red (1964)

Modelo Antiguo *See* Vintage Model (1992)

A Modern Bluebeard *See* Boom in the Moon (1946)

A Modern Hero *See* Knute Rockne: All American (1940)

Modesty Blaise: The Beginning *See* My Name is Modesty: A Modesty Blaise Adventure (2004)

Modigliani of Montparnasse *See* Modigliani (1958)

Mogan Do *See* Infernal Affairs (2002)

Mogliamante *See* Wifemistress (1979)

The Mogul *See* Ratings Game (1984)

Mohammad: Messenger of God *See* The Message (1977)

Moise: L'Affaire Roch Theriault *See* Savage Messiah (2002)

Mojave *See* Death Valley (2004)

Molding Clay *See* River's End (2005)

Molly Louvain *See* The Strange Love of Molly Louvain (1932)

Mon Idole *See* Whatever You Say (2002)

Mon Meilleur Ami *See* My Best Friend (2006)

Mon Pere, Ma Mere, Mes Freres et Mes Soeurs *See* My Father, My Mother, My Brothers and My Sisters (1999)

Mon seung *See* Diary (2006)

Mon tresor *See* Or (My Treasure) (2004)

Monday Morning *See* Class of Fear (1991)

Mondo Insanity *See* Mondo Cane 2 (1964)

Mondo Pazzo *See* Mondo Cane 2 (1964)

Money *See* L'Argent (1983)

The Money Order *See* Mandabi (1968)

Monique and Julie *See* Sweet Young Thing (1979)

A Monkey in Winter *See* Un Singe en Hiver (1962)

Monkey Shines: An Experiment in Fear *See* Monkey Shines (1988)

Monsieur Hulot's Holiday *See* Mr. Hulot's Holiday (1953)

Monsieur Ibrahim and the Flowers of the Koran *See* Monsieur Ibrahim (2003)

Monsieur Ibrahim et les Fleurs du Coran *See* Monsieur Ibrahim (2003)

Monsoon *See* Isle of Forgotten Sins (1943)

Monster *See* Humanoids from the Deep (1980)

The Monster Baran *See* Varan the Unbelievable (1961)

The Monster Demolisher *See* Curse of Nostradamus (1960)

Monster from a Prehistoric Planet *See* Gappa the Trifibian Monster (1967)

Monster from Mars *See* Robot Monster (1953)

Monster from the Surf *See* The Beach Girls and the Monster (1965)

Monster in the Night *See* Monster on the Campus (1959)

Monster in the Surf *See* The Beach Girls and the Monster (1965)

Monster Island's Decisive Battle: Godzilla's Son *See* Son of Godzilla (1966)

Monster Maker *See* Monster from the Ocean Floor (1954)

The Monster Meets the Gorilla *See* Bela Lugosi Meets a Brooklyn Gorilla (1952)

Monster of Monsters *See* Ghidrah the Three Headed Monster (1965)

Monster of Terror *See* Die, Monster, Die! (1965)

Monster of the Island *See* Island Monster (1953)

The Monster Show *See* Freaks (1932)

The Monster Walked *See* The Monster Walks (1932)

The Monster with Green Eyes *See* Planets Against Us (1961)

Monster Yongkari *See* Yongkari Monster of the Deep (1967)

Monster Zero *See* Godzilla vs. Monster Zero (1968)

The Monsters Are Loose *See* The Thrill Killers (1965)

Monsters from the Moon *See* Robot Monster (1953)

Monsters from the Unknown Planet *See* Terror of Mechagodzilla (1978)

Monsters of the Night *See* Navy vs. the Night Monsters (1966)

Monstrosity *See* The Atomic Brain (1964)

Montana Justice *See* Man from Montana (1941)

Monte Carlo or Bust *See* Those Daring Young Men in Their Jaunty Jalopies (1969)

Montenegro—Or Pigs and Pearls *See* Montenegro (1981)

Montparnasse 19 *See* Modigliani (1958)

More About the Children of Bullerby Village *See* More about the Children of Noisy Village (1987)

More Tales of the City *See* Armistead Maupin's More Tales of the City (1997)

Morgan! *See* Morgan: A Suitable Case for Treatment (1966)

Morgan il Pirata *See* Morgan the Pirate (1960)

Morgen Grauen *See* Time Troopers (1989)

Morir (O No) *See* To Die (Or Not) (1999)

Moriras en Chafarinas *See* Zafarinas (1994)

The Mormon Peril *See* Trapped by the Mormons (1922)

Morning Terror *See* Time Troopers (1989)

Mortal Sins *See* Dangerous Obsession (1988)

Morte a Venezia *See* Death in Venice (1971)

Mosaic *See* Frankenstein '80 (1979)

The Moscow Chronicle *See* Final Assignment (1980)

Moscow Distrusts Tears *See* Moscow Does Not Believe in Tears (1980)

Moscow Nights *See* I Stand Condemned (1936)

Moskwa Sljesam Nje Jerit *See* Moscow Does Not Believe in Tears (1980)

Most Dangerous Man in the World *See* The Chairman (1969)

The Most Desired Man *See* Maybe… Maybe Not (1994)

Mosura *See* Mothra (1962)

Mosura *See* Rebirth of Mothra (1996)

Mosura 2 *See* Rebirth of Mothra 2 (1997)

Mosura tai Gojira *See* Godzilla vs. Mothra (1964)

Motel *See* Pink Motel (1982)

Motel Vacancy *See* Talking Walls (1985)

Motevalede Mahe Mehr *See* Born Under Libra (2001)

The Moth *See* Catherine Cookson's The Moth (1996)

Mother *See* Madeo (2009)

Mother Goose A Go-Go *See* The Unkissed Bride (1966)

Mother Riley Meets the Vampire *See* My Son, the Vampire (1952)

A Mother's Fight for Justice *See* Crash Course (2000)

Mothra *See* Rebirth of Mothra (1996)

Mothra 2 *See* Rebirth of Mothra 2 (1997)

Mothra vs. Godzilla *See* Godzilla vs. Mothra (1964)

Motor Rods and Rockers *See* Motor Psycho (1965)

Mou gaan dou II *See* Infernal Affairs 2 (2003)

Mou gaan dou III: Jung mik mou gaan *See* Infernal Affairs 3 (2003)

The Moustache *See* La Moustache (2005)

Movie Struck *See* Pick a Star (1937)

The Moving Target *See* Harper (1966)

Mowgli and Baloo: Jungle Book 2 *See* Rudyard Kipling's the Second Jungle Book: Mowgli and Baloo (1997)

Mr. Scarface *See* Big Boss (1977)

Ms. Don Juan *See* Don Juan (Or If Don Juan Were a Woman) (1973)

Mua Len Trau *See* Buffalo Boy (2004)

Much Ado about Murder *See* Theatre of Blood (1973)

Mud *See* The Stick-Up (1977)

Muhomatsu no Issho *See* Rikisha-Man (1958)

Mui du du Xanh *See* The Scent of Green Papaya (1993)

Mujeres al Borde de un Ataque de Nervios *See* Women on the Verge of a Nervous Breakdown (1988)

The Mummy *See* Bram Stoker's The Mummy (1997)

Mumsy, Nanny, Sonny, and Girly *See* Girly (1970)

Mundo Depravados *See* World of the Depraved (1967)

Munkbrogreven *See* The Count of the Old Town (1934)

Mur *See* Wall (2004)

Murder by Mail *See* Schizoid (1980)

Murder by Proxy *See* Blackout (1954)

Murder: By Reason of Insanity *See* My Sweet Victim (1985)

The Murder Gang *See* Black Heat (1976)

Murder in the Ring *See* Counter Punch (1971)

The Murder in Thorton Square *See* Gaslight (1944)

Murder, Inc. *See* The Enforcer (1951)

Murder is Easy *See* Agatha Christie's Murder is Easy (1982)

Murder Near Perfect *See* Dagger Eyes (1983)

Murder on Diamond Row *See* The Squeaker (1937)

Murder One *See* Death Sentence (1974)

The Murder Room *See* P.D. James: The Murder Room (2004)

Murder Rooms: The Dark Origins of Sherlock Holmes *See* Dr. Bell and Mr. Doyle: The Dark Beginnings of Sherlock Holmes (2000)

Murder Will Out *See* The Voice of Merrill (1952)

Murder with Mirrors *See* Agatha Christie's Murder with Mirrors (1985)

Murder with Music *See* Mistaken Identity (1941)

The Murderer Dmitri Karamazov *See* The Brothers Karamazov (1958)

Muriel, Or the Time of Return *See* Muriel (1963)

Muriel, Ou le Temps d'Un Retour *See* Muriel (1963)

The Murri Affair *See* La Grande Bourgeoise (1974)

Musa *See* The Warrior (2001)

Musa: The Warrior *See* The Warrior (2001)

Music in Darkness *See* Night Is My Future (1947)

The Music Room *See* Jalsaghar (1958)

Musime si Pomahat *See* Divided We Fall (2000)

Mussolini: The Decline and Fall of Il Duce *See* Mussolini & I (1985)

Mutant *See* Forbidden World (1982)

The Mutation *See* The Freakmaker (1973)

Mutations *See* The Freakmaker (1973)

Mute Love *See* Secret of Yolanda (1982)

The Mutilator *See* The Dark (1979)

The Mutineers *See* Pirate Ship (1949)

Mutter Kusters Fahrt Zum Himmel *See* Mother Kusters Goes to Heaven (1976)

Mutter und Sohn *See* Mother and Son (1997)

Mutters Courage *See* My Mother's Courage (1995)

MVP 3 *See* MXP: Most Xtreme Primate (2003)

My Bollywood Bride *See* My Faraway Bride (2006)

My Brother, the Outlaw *See* My Outlaw Brother (1951)

My Brother's Keeper *See* Brother's Keeper (2002)

My Brother's Wife *See* La Mujer de Mi Hermano (2006)

My Crazy Life *See* Mi Vida Loca (1994)

My Darling Shiksa *See* Over the Brooklyn Bridge (1983)

My Father Is a Hero *See* Jet Li's The Enforcer (1995)

My Father, My Master *See* Padre Padrone (1977)

My Favorite Season *See* Ma Saison Preferee (1993)

My Favourite Year *See* My Favorite Year (1982)

My Forgotten Man *See* Flynn (1996)

My Fuhrer: The Truly Truest Truth About Adolf Hitler *See* My Fuhrer (2007)

My Girlfriend's Boyfriend *See* Boyfriends & Girlfriends (1988)

My Hero *See* A Southern Yankee (1948)

My Idol *See* Whatever You Say (2002)

My Life in Pink *See* Ma Vie en Rose (1997)

My Love Letters *See* Love Letters (1983)

My Man *See* Mon Homme (1996)

My Name is John *See* The Legend of Hillbilly John (1973)

My Name Is Zora *See* Zora Is My Name! (1990)

My Neighbor's Daughter *See* Angel Blue (1997)

My Night with Maud *See* My Night at Maud's (1969)

My Palikari *See* Silent Rebellion (1982)

My Posse Don't Do Homework *See* Dangerous Minds (1995)

My Son Alone *See* American Empire (1942)

My Teenage Daughter *See* Teenage Bad Girl (1959)

My Uncle *See* Mon Oncle (1958)

My Uncle, Mr. Hulot *See* Mon Oncle (1958)

My World Dies Screaming *See* Terror in the Haunted House (1958)

Mystere *See* Dagger Eyes (1983)

Mystere Alexina *See* The Mystery of Alexina (1986)

Mysterious Invader *See* The Astounding She-Monster (1958)

The Mysterious Rider *See* Badmen of Nevada (1933)

The Mysterious Satellite *See* Warning from Space (1956)

The Mystery of Kaspar Hauser *See* Every Man for Himself & God Against All (1975)

The Mystery of Spoon River *See* The Ghost of Spoon River (2000)

Mystery of the Black Jungle *See* The Black Devils of Kali (1955)

The Mystery of the Marie Celeste *See* The Mystery of the Mary Celeste (1935)

Mystique *See* Circle of Power (1983)

Na Cidade Vazia *See* Hollow City (2004)

Na Komete *See* On the Comet (1968)

Na Samyn Dnie *See* Deep End (1970)

Nabbeun namja *See* Bad Guy (2001)

Nachts wenn Dracula Erwacht *See* Count Dracula (1971)

Nagooa *See* Drifting (1982)

Naissance des Pieuvres *See* Water Lilies (2007)

Naisu no mori: The First Contact *See* Funky Forest: The First Contact (2006)

The Naked Goddess *See* The Devil's Hand (1961)

Naked Island *See* The Island (1961)

Naked Massacre *See* Born for Hell (1976)

The Naked Night *See* Sawdust & Tinsel (1953)

Naked Space *See* The Creature Wasn't Nice (1981)

Naked Space *See* Spaceship (1981)

Naked under Leather *See* The Girl on a Motorcycle (1968)

Naked Warriors *See* The Arena (1973)

The Naked Weekend *See* Circle of Power (1983)

Naked Youth *See* The Cruel Story of Youth (1960)

Nama-natsu *See* Raw Summer (2006)

Nam's Angels *See* The Losers (1970)

Namu, My Best Friend *See* Namu, the Killer Whale (1966)

Nanguo Zaijian, Nanguo *See* Goodbye South, Goodbye (1996)

Nankai No Daikaiju *See* Yog, Monster from Space (1971)

Nankai No Kai Ketto *See* Godzilla vs. the Sea Monster (1966)

Nanny McPhee and the Big Bang *See* Nanny McPhee 2 (2010)

NaPolA *See* Before the Fall (2004)

Nara Livet *See* Brink of Life (1957)

Narayama-Bushi-Ko *See* The Ballad of Narayama (1983)

Nathaniel Hawthorne's "Twice Told Tales" *See* Twice-Told Tales (1963)

National Lampoon's Cousin Eddie's Christmas Vacation Lost *See* National Lampoon's Christmas Vacation 2: Cousin Eddie's Big Island Adventure (2003)

Nattens Engel *See* Angel of the Night (1998)

Nattvardsgaesterna *See* The Winter Light (1962)

Nature's Mistakes *See* Freaks (1932)

Naughty Girl *See* Mam'zelle Pigalle (1958)

Navy Cross *See* G.I. Jane (1997)

Navy Diver *See* Men of Honor (2000)

The Navy Steps Out *See* A Girl, a Guy and a Gob (1941)

Ne le Dis a Personne *See* Tell No One (2006)

Ne Touchez pas la Hache *See* The Duchess of Langeais (2007)

Neat and Tidy *See* Adventures Beyond Belief (1987)

Nebeonjjae cheung-Eoneunal kabjagi doobeonjjae *See* Hidden Floor (2006)

Neco Z Alenky *See* Alice (1988)

Necromancy *See* The Witching (1972)

Necronomicon *See* H.P. Lovecraft's Necronomicon: Book of the Dead (1993)

Ned Blessing: The Story of My Life and Times *See* Lone Justice 2 (1993)

Ned Kelly, Outlaw *See* Ned Kelly (1970)

Neil Simon's Biloxi Blues *See* Biloxi Blues (1988)

Neil Simon's Brighton Beach Memoirs *See* Brighton Beach Memoirs (1986)

Neil Simon's Broadway Bound *See* Broadway Bound (1992)

Neil Simon's Lost in Yonkers *See* Lost in Yonkers (1993)

Neil Simon's The Slugger's Wife *See* The Slugger's Wife (1985)

Nella Cita L'Inferno *See* And the Wild, Wild Women (1959)

Nella Stretta M Orsa Del Ragno *See* Web of the Spider (1970)

Nelly and Mr. Arnaud *See* Nelly et Monsieur Arnaud (1995)

Nemesis 3: Prey Harder *See* Nemesis 3: Time Lapse (1996)

The Neptune Disaster *See* Neptune Factor (1973)

Nes en 68 *See* Born in 68 (2008)

Neskolko Dnel iz Zhizni I.I. Oblomov *See* Oblomov (1981)

Netforce *See* Tom Clancy's Netforce (1998)

Nettoyage a Sec *See* Dry Cleaning (1997)

Neurosis *See* Revenge in the House of Usher (1982)

Nevada Heat *See* Fake Out (1982)

Never Cry Devil *See* Night Visitor (1989)

The Never Dead *See* Phantasm (1979)

Never Ever *See* Circle of Passion (1997)

Never Give an Inch *See* Sometimes a Great Notion (1971)

NeverWhere *See* Neil Gaiman's NeverWhere (1996)

The New Adventures of Don Juan *See* Adventures of Don Juan (1949)

New Adventures of Tarzan *See* Tarzan and the Green Goddess (1938)

The New Barbarians *See* Warriors of the Wasteland (1983)

New Girl in Town *See* Nashville Girl (1976)

New Moon *See* The Twilight Saga: New Moon (2009)

New Tales of the Taira Clan *See* Shin Heike Monogatari (1955)

New Wave *See* Nouvelle Vague (1990)

New Wine *See* Melody Master (1941)

The Newcomers *See* The Wild Country (1971)

Next! *See* Blade of the Ripper (1970)

The Next Man *See* The Arab Conspiracy (1976)

The Next Victim *See* Blade of the Ripper (1970)

Ng fu tiu lung *See* Sword Masters: Brothers Five (1970)

Ngo Hai Sui *See* Jackie Chan's Who Am I (1998)

Nicholas Nickleby *See* The Life and Adventures of Nicholas Nickleby (1981)

Nickel and Dime *See* Larger Than Life (1996)

The Niece of the Vampire *See* Fangs of the Living Dead (1968)

Olga's Massage Parlor *See* Olga's Girls (1964)

Olga's Parlor *See* Olga's Girls (1964)

Oltre la Porta *See* Beyond Obsession (1982)

Omar Mukhtar *See* Lion of the Desert (1981)

Omen 3: The Final Conflict *See* The Final Conflict (1981)

On Connait la Chanson *See* Same Old Song (1997)

On Dangerous Ground *See* Jack Higgins' On Dangerous Ground (1995)

On Eagle's Wings *See* Black Horizon (2001)

On the Great White Trail *See* Renfrew on the Great White Trail (1938)

On the Other Side *See* The Edge of Heaven (2007)

On the Road Again *See* Honeysuckle Rose (1980)

On the Run *See* Nowhere to Hide (1983)

On to Mars *See* Abbott and Costello Go to Mars (1953)

Once Upon a Texas Train *See* Texas Guns (1990)

Once Upon a Time There Was a Country *See* Underground (1995)

Ondskan *See* Evil (2003)

A One and a Two... *See* Yi Yi (2000)

One Armed Boxer II *See* Master of the Flying Guillotine (1975)

One Armed Boxer vs. the Flying Guillotine *See* Master of the Flying Guillotine (1975)

One Born Every Minute *See* Flim-Flam Man (1967)

One Cup of Coffee *See* Pastime (1991)

One For All *See* The President's Mystery (1936)

One for Sorrow, Two for Joy *See* Signs of Life (1989)

One for the Money, Two for the Show *See* On the Run (1973)

One Horse Town *See* Small Town Girl (1953)

One Hundred Percent Pure *See* The Girl from Missouri (1934)

One in a Million *See* Dangerous Appointment (1934)

One-Man Mutiny *See* The Court Martial of Billy Mitchell (1955)

One Man Out *See* Erik (1990)

One Missed Call Final *See* One Missed Call 3: Final (2006)

One Plus One *See* Sympathy for the Devil (1970)

One Point O *See* Paranoia 1.0 (2004)

One Silver Dollar *See* Blood for a Silver Dollar (1966)

One Way Out *See* Crazed Cop (1988)

Ong Bak: The Beginning *See* Ong Bak 2 (2008)

Onkel Toms Hutte *See* Uncle Tom's Cabin (1969)

Only Blackness *See* The Bloodstained Shadow (1978)

Only for Love *See* Please Not Now! (1961)

Only the French Can! *See* French Can-Can (1955)

Onmyoji: The Yin Yang Master *See* Onmyoji (2001)

Onna Ga Kaidan O Agaru Toki *See* When a Woman Ascends the Stairs (1960)

Oopsie Poopsie *See* Get Rita (1975)

Oopsie Poopsie *See* Lady of the Evening (1975)

Oorlogswinter *See* Winter in Wartime (2010)

OpenCam *See* Open Cam (2005)

Operacione Paura *See* Kill, Baby, Kill (1966)

Operation Cicero *See* Five Fingers (1952)

Operation Espionage *See* Billion Dollar Brain (1967)

Operation Kid Brother *See* Secret Agent 00 (1967)

Operation M *See* Hell's Bloody Devils (1970)

Operation Monsterland *See* Destroy All Monsters (1968)

Operation Overthrow *See* Power Play (1978)

Operation Serpent *See* Fer-De-Lance (1974)

Operation Snafu *See* On the Fiddle (1961)

Operation Undercover *See* Report to the Commissioner (1974)

Operation Warhead *See* On the Fiddle (1961)

Operazione Goldman *See* Lightning Bolt (1967)

Opium Connection *See* The Poppy Is Also a Flower (1966)

Oprah Winfrey Presents: Mitch Albom's For One More Day *See* For One More Day (2007)

L'ora di religione *See* My Mother's Smile (2002)

The Oracle *See* The Horse's Mouth (1958)

Orazi e Curiazi *See* Duel of Champions (1961)

Orca—Killer Whale *See* Orca (1977)

Orchestra Seats *See* Avenue Montaigne (2006)

Order of Death *See* Corrupt (1984)

Ore Ni Sawaru to Abunaize *See* Black Tight Killers (1966)

Orfeu Negro *See* Black Orpheus (1958)

Orgasmo *See* Paranoia (1969)

Orgy of the Dead *See* The Hanging Woman (1972)

The Original Fabulous Adventures of Baron Munchausen *See* Fabulous Adventures of Baron Munchausen (1961)

Orkobefogadas *See* Adoption (1975)

Orlacs Hande *See* The Hands of Orlac (1925)

Orloff Against the Invisible Man *See* Dr. Orloff and the Invisible Man (1972)

Orloff Against the Invisible Man *See* Orloff and the Invisible Man (1970)

Orphee *See* Orpheus (1949)

Orson Welles' Don Quixote *See* Don Quixote (1992)

Orson Welles's Othello *See* Othello (1952)

Oru Kaiju Daishingeki *See* Godzilla's Revenge (1969)

Oscar *See* Forbidden Passion: The Oscar Wilde Movie (1985)

Osenny Marafon *See* Autumn Marathon (1979)

Ososhiki *See* The Funeral (1984)

OSS 117: Le Caire Nid d'Espions *See* OSS 117: Cairo, Nest of Spies (2006)

OSS 177 - Double Agent *See* Murder for Sale (1968)

Ost und West *See* East and West (1924)

Ostre Sledovane Vlaky *See* Closely Watched Trains (1966)

Otac na Sluzbenom Putu *See* When Father Was Away on Business (1985)

Otets I Syn *See* Father and Son (2003)

Other People's Business *See* Way Back Home (1932)

The Other Side of Paradise *See* Foxtrot (1976)

Otto E Mezzo *See* 8 1/2 (1963)

Our Daily Bread *See* City Girl (1930)

Our Girl Friday *See* The Adventures of Sadie (1955)

Our Music *See* Our Music (2004)

Our Story *See* Notre Histoire (1984)

L'Ours *See* The Bear (1989)

Ourselves Alone *See* River of Unrest (1936)

Out of Omaha *See* California Dreaming (2007)

Out of Rosenheim *See* Bagdad Cafe (1988)

Out of Sight, Out of Mind *See* Out of Sight, Out of Her Mind (1989)

Out of Synch *See* Lip Service (2000)

Out of the Darkness *See* Night Creature (1979)

Out of the Darkness *See* Teenage Caveman (1958)

Out of the Frying Pan *See* Young and Willing (1942)

Out of the Night *See* Strange Illusion (1945)

Out of the Shadow *See* Murder on the Campus (1952)

Out of Time *See* Iris (1989)

Out on Probation *See* Daddy-O (1959)

Outback Vampires *See* The Wicked (1989)

The Outcast *See* Man in the Saddle (1951)

The Outcry *See* Il Grido (1957)

Outer Reach *See* Spaced Out (1980)

Outlaw Gun *See* A Minute to Pray, a Second to Die (1967)

The Outlawed Planet *See* Planet of the Vampires (1965)

Outlaws of the Marsh *See* The Water Margin (1972)

Outomlionnye Solntsem *See* Burnt by the Sun (1994)

Outside In *See* Red, White & Busted (1975)

The Outsider *See* Fatal Error (1983)

The Outsider *See* The Guinea Pig (1948)

Outsider in Amsterdam *See* Fatal Error (1983)

The Outsiders *See* Band of Outsiders (1964)

Over Her Dead Body *See* Enid Is Sleeping (1990)

The Pace That Kills *See* Cocaine Fiends (1936)

Paid to Dance *See* Hard to Hold (1937)

Painted Angels *See* The Wicked, Wicked West (1997)

The Painting *See* Soldiers of Change (2006)

Paksa wayu *See* Garuda (2004)

The Palace Thief *See* The Emperor's Club (2002)

The Pale Horse *See* Agatha Christie's The Pale Horse (1996)

Palomino *See* Danielle Steel's Palomino (1991)

Pamela Principle 2 *See* Seduce Me: Pamela Principle 2 (1994)

Pan Jin Lian Zhi Qian Shi Jin Sheng *See* The Reincarnation of Golden Lotus (1989)

Pan si dong *See* The Cave of the Silken Web (1967)

Pane, Amore e Fantasia *See* Bread, Love and Dreams (1953)

Pane e Cioccolata *See* Bread and Chocolate (1973)

Pane e Tulipani *See* Bread and Tulips (2001)

Panga *See* Curse 3: Blood Sacrifice (1990)

Panic *See* Panique (1947)

Panic at Lakewood Manor *See* Ants (1977)

Panic in the Trans-Siberian Train *See* Horror Express (1972)

Panic on the Trans-Siberian Express *See* Horror Express (1972)

Panico en el Transiberiano *See* Horror Express (1972)

Panny z Wilka *See* Maids of Wilko (1979)

Panther Squadron *See* Men of the Fighting Lady (1954)

Paoda Shuang Deng *See* Red Firecracker, Green Firecracker (1993)

Paper Bullets *See* Gangs, Inc. (1941)

Par-dela les Nuages *See* Beyond the Clouds (1995)

Paralyzed *See* Short Night of Glass Dolls (1971)

The Parasite Murders *See* They Came from Within (1975)

Pardon Me, Your Teeth Are in My Neck *See* The Fearless Vampire Killers (1967)

Parfait Amour *See* Perfect Love (1996)

The Pariah *See* La Scoumoune (1972)

Paris Brule-t-il? *See* Is Paris Burning? (1966)

Paris Does Strange Things *See* Elena and Her Men (1956)

Paris, I Love You *See* Paris, je t'aime (2006)

Paris is Ours *See* Paris Belongs to Us (1960)

Paris Nous Appartient *See* Paris Belongs to Us (1960)

Paris Qui Dort *See* The Crazy Ray (1922)

Paris vu Par *See* Six in Paris (1968)

Park Plaza *See* Norman Conquest (1953)

Paroles et Musique *See* Love Songs (1984)

Paroxismus *See* Venus in Furs (1970)

Parts: The Clonus Horror *See* The Clonus Horror (1979)

The Party *See* Can't Hardly Wait (1998)

The Party at Kitty and Stud's *See* The Italian Stallion (1973)

Party Girls *See* Party Incorporated (1989)

Pas de Probleme! *See* No Problem (1975)

Pasazerka *See* Passenger (1961)

Pasqualino Settebellezze *See* Seven Beauties (1976)

Pasqualino: Seven Beauties *See* Seven Beauties (1976)

The Pass *See* Highway Hitcher (1998)

Passages from "Finnegans Wake" *See* Finnegan's Wake (1965)

Passages from James Joyce's "Finnegans Wake" *See* Finnegan's Wake (1965)

The Passerby *See* La Passante (1983)

The Passion Flower Hotel *See* Boarding School (1983)

Passion Play *See* Love Letters (1983)

Passione d'Amore *See* Passion of Love (1982)

Passions *See* The Passing of Evil (1970)

Passkey to Danger *See* The Undercover Woman (1946)

Passport to Shame *See* Room 43 (1958)

The Patsy *See* L'Addition (1985)

Patterns of Power *See* Patterns (1956)

Patton: A Salute to a Rebel *See* Patton (1970)

Patton—Lust for Glory *See* Patton (1970)

Paul Bowles: Halbmond *See* Halfmoon (1995)

Pauline a la Plage *See* Pauline at the Beach (1983)

Paura in citta *See* Street War (1976)

Paura Nella Citta Dei Morti Viventi *See* Gates of Hell (1980)

Pavilion 6 *See* Ward Six (1978)

Paws *See* Boy of Two Worlds (1959)

Pay the Devil *See* Man in the Shadow (1957)

Pazzi borghesi *See* Twist (1976)

P.D. James: A Mind to Murder *See* A Mind to Murder (1996)

P.D. James: Devices & Desires *See* Devices and Desires (1991)

The Peace Game *See* The Gladiators (1970)

Peace Virus *See* Terminal Error (2002)

Peacemaker *See* The Ambassador (1984)

Peau d'Ane *See* Donkey Skin (1970)
Peccato Che Sia una Canaglia *See* Too Bad She's Bad (1954)
The Peking Medallion *See* The Corrupt Ones (1967)
Pellet *See* El Bola (2000)
Pelvis *See* Toga Party (1977)
Penn of Pennsylvania *See* The Courageous Mr. Penn (1941)
Pensionat Oskar *See* Like It Never Was Before (1995)
People Toys *See* Devil Times Five (1974)
People's Enemy *See* Prison Train (1938)
Pepi, Luci, Bom y Otras Chicas del Monton *See* Pepi, Luci, Bom and Other Girls on the Heap (1980)
Per Pochi Dollari Ancora *See* Fort Yuma Gold (1966)
Per Saldo Mord *See* Swiss Conspiracy (1977)
Perceval Le Gallois *See* Perceval (1978)
Perche Quelle Strane Gocce di Sangre sul Corpo di Jennifer? *See* The Case of the Bloody Iris (1972)
Percy's Progress *See* It's Not the Size That Counts (1974)
Perdita Durango *See* Dance with the Devil (1997)
The Perfect Man *See* Heartstrings (1993)
The Perfect Model *See* Sweet Perfection (1990)
Perfect Strangers *See* Almost Strangers (2001)
The Perfect You *See* Crazy Little Thing (2002)
The Perfumed Garden *See* Tales of the Kama Sutra: The Perfumed Garden (1998)
Peril en la Demeure *See* Peril (1985)
Perils from Planet Mongo *See* Flash Gordon: Rocketship (1940)
The Perils of Gwendoline in the Land of the Yik-Yak *See* The Perils of Gwendoline (1984)
Perils of Nyoka *See* Nyoka and the Tigermen (1942)
Perros Callejeros *See* Street Warriors (1977)
Perros Callejeros II *See* Street Warriors, Part 2 (1979)
Persecution *See* The Graveyard (1974)
Perseo l'Invincibile *See* Medusa Against the Son of Hercules (1962)
Perseus the Invincible *See* Medusa Against the Son of Hercules (1962)
Personally Yours *See* Wilderness Love (2002)
Persons Unknown *See* Big Deal on Madonna Street (1958)
Peter and Pavla *See* Black Peter (1963)
Peter Benchley's The Beast *See* The Beast (1996)
Peter Rabbit and Tales of Beatrix Potter *See* Tales of Beatrix Potter (1971)
Petersen *See* Jock Petersen (1974)
Petroleum Girls *See* Legend of Frenchie King (1971)
Phantom *See* O Fantasma (2000)
Phantom Fiend *See* The Return of Dr. Mabuse (1961)
The Phantom of Terror *See* The Bird with the Crystal Plumage (1970)
Phantom of the Air *See* The Phantom Broadcast (1933)
The Phantom Ship *See* The Mystery of the Mary Celeste (1935)
Phar Lap: Heart of a Nation *See* Phar Lap (1984)
Phenomena *See* Creepers (1985)
Philo Vance Returns *See* Infamous Crimes (1947)
Phoebe *See* Zelly & Me (1988)
Phoenix *See* War of the Wizards (1983)
Phorpa *See* The Cup (1999)
The Piano Player *See* The Target (2002)
Picking up the Pieces *See* Bloodsucking Pharoahs of Pittsburgh (1990)
Pickup on 101 *See* Where the Eagle Flies (1972)
Pictures of Baby Jane Doe *See* Jane Doe (1996)
Pido nunmuldo eobshi *See* No Blood No Tears (2002)
Piggy Banks *See* Born Killers (2005)
Pigsty *See* Porcile (1969)
Pilgrimage to Rome *See* L'Annee Sainte (1976)
The Pill *See* Test Tube Babies (1948)
The Pilot *See* Danger in the Skies (1979)
Pin Down Girl *See* Pin Down Girls (1951)
The Pinata: Survival Island *See* Survival Island (2002)
Pinball Pick-Up *See* Pick-Up Summer (1979)
Pinball Summer *See* Pick-Up Summer (1979)
Ping Guo *See* Lost in Beijing (2007)
Pinocchio *See* The Adventures of Pinocchio (1996)
Pinochet in Suburbia *See* Pinochet's Last Stand (2006)
Pioneers *See* Pioneer Woman (1973)
Pippi Langstrump Pa de Sju Haven *See* Pippi in the South Seas (1970)
Piranha 2: Flying Killers *See* Piranha 2: The Spawning (1982)
Pirate's Fiancee *See* A Very Curious Girl (1969)
Pirate's Harbor *See* Haunted Harbor (1944)
Pistol Blues *See* Machine Gun Blues (1995)
Pisutoru opera *See* Pistol Opera (2002)
Pitch Black 2: Chronicles of Riddick *See* The Chronicles of Riddick (2004)
Pixote: A Lei do Mais Fraco *See* Pixote (1981)
The Pizza Connection *See* The Sicilian Connection (1985)
The Plains of Heaven *See* Panic Station (1982)
Plane Dead *See* Flight of the Living Dead: Outbreak on a Plane (2007)
Planet of Blood *See* Planet of the Vampires (1965)
Planet of Horrors *See* Galaxy of Terror (1981)
Planet of Incredible Creatures *See* Fantastic Planet (1973)
The Planet of Junior Brown *See* Junior's Groove (1997)
Planet of Love *See* Galaxies Are Colliding (1992)
Planet of Terror *See* Planet of the Vampires (1965)
Planet of the Damned *See* Planet of the Vampires (1965)
Planet of the Lifeless Men *See* Battle of the Worlds (1961)
Plankton *See* Creatures from the Abyss (1994)
The Plants Are Watching *See* The Kirlian Witness (1978)
Plata Quemada *See* Burnt Money (2000)
Play of the Month: MacBeth *See* Macbeth (1970)
Playa Azul *See* Beach Hotel (1992)
Players *See* The Club (1981)
Playgirl Gang *See* Switchblade Sisters (1975)
The Playgirls and the Bellboy *See* The Bellboy and the Playgirls (1962)
Playing for Keeps *See* Lily in Love (1985)
Playtime *See* Love Play (1960)
Please! Mr. Balzac *See* Plucking the Daisy (1956)
The Pleasure of Your Company *See* Wedding Daze (2006)
Pledge of Allegiance *See* Players (2003)
Plein Soleil *See* Purple Noon (1960)
Plein Sud *See* Heat of Desire (1984)
Pluck of the Irish *See* Great Guy (1936)
Plus Tard *See* One Day You'll Understand (2008)
Po Dezju *See* Before the Rain (1994)
Po jun *See* Flash Point (2007)
Pocomania *See* The Devil's Daughter (1939)
Podranki *See* The Orphans (1977)
Poe's Tales of Terror *See* Tales of Terror (1962)
The Poet *See* Hearts of War (2007)
Poisoned by Love: The Kern County Murders *See* Murder So Sweet (1993)
Pokayaniye *See* Repentance (1987)
Poketto Monsutaa: Maboroshi No Pokemon X: Lugia Bakudan *See* Pokemon the Movie 2000: The Power of One (2000)
Pokolenie *See* A Generation (1954)
Police Assassins *See* Royal Warriors (1986)
Police Connection *See* The Mad Bomber (1972)
Police Force *See* Police Story (1985)
Police Story 3, Part 2 *See* Supercop 2 (1993)
Police Story 3: Supercop *See* Supercop (1992)
Police Story 4 *See* Jackie Chan's First Strike (1996)
Police Woman *See* Young Tiger (1974)
Politist, Adj. *See* Police, Adjective (2009)
Polk County Pot Plane *See* In Hot Pursuit (1977)
Polly Tix in Washington *See* Kid 'n' Hollywood and Polly Tix in Washington (1933)
Pon *See* Phone (2002)
Pony Express *See* Peter Lundy and the Medicine Hat Stallion (1977)
Ponyo on the Cliff by the Sea *See* Ponyo (2008)
Pookie *See* The Sterile Cuckoo (1969)
Poopsie *See* Get Rita (1975)
Poor Albert and Little Annie *See* I Dismember Mama (1974)
Poor Boy's Game *See* Poor Man's Game (2006)
The Poor Outlaws *See* The Round Up (1966)
The Pope Must Die *See* The Pope Must Diet (1991)
Popiol i Diament *See* Ashes and Diamonds (1958)
Poppies Are Also Flowers *See* The Poppy Is Also a Flower (1966)
Popsy Pop *See* Queen of Diamonds (1970)
Por Que Lo Llaman Amor Cuando Quieren Decir Sexo? *See* Why Do They Call It Love When They Mean Sex? (1992)
Porcherie *See* Porcile (1969)
Porno jidaigeki: Bohachi bushido *See* Bohachi Bushido: Code of the Forgotten Eight (1973)
A Pornographic Liaison *See* An Affair of Love (1999)
Porte Aperte *See* Open Doors (1989)
Portrait of a Hitman *See* The Last Contract (1977)
Portrait of a Sinner *See* The Rough and the Smooth (1959)
Portrait of a Woman, Nude *See* Nudo di Donna (1983)
Portrait of Alison *See* Postmark for Danger (1956)
Portrait of Maria *See* Maria Candelaria (1946)
Portraits of Innocence *See* Portraits of a Killer (1995)
The Possessed *See* P (2004)
Post Coitum *See* After Sex (1997)
Post Coitum, Animal Triste *See* After Sex (1997)
The Post Grad Survival Guide *See* Post Grad (2009)
Postal Worker *See* Going Postal (1998)
Potemkin *See* The Battleship Potemkin (1925)
Potop *See* The Deluge (1973)
Poulet au Vinaigre *See* Cop Au Vin (1985)
The Powder Keg *See* Cabaret Balkan (1998)
Practice Makes Perfect *See* Le Cavaleur (1978)
Prague Duet *See* Lies and Whispers (1998)
Prairie Outlaws *See* Wild West (1946)
Pratldwandi *See* The Adversary (1971)
Pre *See* Without Limits (1997)
Precious *See* Citizen Ruth (1996)
Pred dozhdot *See* Before the Rain (1994)
Prega il Morto e Ammazza il Vivo *See* Shoot the Living, Pray for the Dead (1970)
The Prehistoric Sound *See* Sound of Horror (1964)
Prehistoric World *See* Teenage Caveman (1958)
Prenom: Carmen *See* First Name: Carmen (1983)
Preparez Vous Mouchoirs *See* Get Out Your Handkerchiefs (1978)
Preppies *See* Making the Grade (1984)
The President's Women *See* Foreplay (1975)
Presque Rien *See* Come Undone (2000)
Preston Tylk *See* Bad Seed (2000)
Pret-a-Porter *See* Ready to Wear (1994)
Prete-Moi ta Main *See* I Do (2006)
Pretty When You Cry *See* Seduced: Pretty When You Cry (2001)
Prey *See* Alien Prey (1978)
Pride of Kentucky *See* The Story of Seabiscuit (1949)
Prima della Rivoluzione *See* Before the Revolution (1965)
Prince of Jutland *See* Royal Deceit (1994)
Priority Red One *See* Delta Force Commando 2 (1990)
Prison *See* Devil's Wanton (1949)
Prison Heat *See* Female Prisoner: Caged (1983)
The Prisoner *See* Cold Room (1984)
Prisoner of the Caucasus *See* Prisoner of the Mountains (1996)
Prisoner of Zenda Inc. *See* Double Play (1996)
Private House of the SS *See* SS Girls (1977)
The Private Life of Paul Joseph Goebbels *See* Enemy of Women (1944)
The Private Lives of Elizabeth and Essex *See* Elizabeth, the Queen (1968)
Private Snuffy Smith *See* Snuffy Smith, Yard Bird (1942)
The Private Wore Skirts *See* Never Wave at a WAC (1952)
Pro Urodov i Lyudej *See* Of Freaks and Men (1998)
The Prodigal Boxer *See* Kick of Death: The Prodigal Boxer (1973)
The Prodigious Hickey *See* The Lawrenceville Stories (1988)
Profession: Reporter *See* The Passenger (1975)
The Professional *See* Le Professionnel (1981)
The Profile of Terror *See* The Sadist (1963)
Profumo di Donna *See* The Scent of a Woman (1975)

Profundo Carmesi *See* Deep Crimson (1996)

Profundo Rosso *See* Deep Red: Hatchet Murders (1975)

Project Greenlight's Stolen Summer *See* Stolen Summer (2002)

Project Greenlight's The Battle of Shaker Heights *See* The Battle of Shaker Heights (2003)

Project Shadowchaser 2 *See* Night Siege Project: Shadowchaser 2 (1994)

Prom Night 2 *See* Hello Mary Lou: Prom Night 2 (1987)

Promenons Nous dans les Bois *See* Deep in the Woods (2000)

The Promise *See* La Promesse (1996)

Promise Her Anything *See* Promises! Promises! (1963)

A Promise Kept *See* The Gunman (2003)

The Promise of Red Lips *See* Daughters of Darkness (1971)

The Promised Land *See* Legal Deceit (1995)

The Promised Life *See* La Vie Promise (2002)

Prophecies of Nostradamus *See* Last Days of Planet Earth (1974)

A Proposito Luciano *See* Lucky Luciano (1974)

Prorva *See* Moscow Parade (1992)

Protection *See* Moolaade (2004)

The Protectors, Book One *See* Angel of H.E.A.T. (1982)

Proud, Damned, and Dead *See* The Proud and the Damned (1972)

Prova d'Orchestra *See* Orchestra Rehearsal (1978)

Przesluchanie *See* The Interrogation (1982)

Psycho a Go Go! *See* Blood of Ghastly Horror (1972)

Psycho-Circus *See* Circus of Fear (1967)

Psycho Killers *See* The Flesh and the Fiends (1960)

Psycho Puppet *See* Delirium (1977)

Psycho Sex Fiend *See* The House that Vanished (1973)

Psycho Sisters *See* The Sibling (1972)

Psychotic *See* Driver's Seat (1973)

Ptang, Yang, Kipperbang *See* Kipperbang (1982)

Public Be Damned *See* The World Gone Mad (1933)

The Public Be Hanged *See* The World Gone Mad (1933)

Pulse: Afterlife and Invasion *See* Pulse 2: Afterlife (2008)

Pun see dung *See* The Cave of the Silken Web (1967)

Puo Una Morta Rivivere Per Amore? *See* Venus in Furs (1970)

The Pupil *See* L'Eleve (1995)

Purei *See* Pray (2005)

The Purim Player *See* Der Purimshpiler (1937)

Purple Death from Outer Space *See* Flash Gordon Conquers the Universe (1940)

The Purple Riders *See* Purple Vigilantes (1938)

The Purple Shadow Strikes *See* The Purple Monster Strikes (1945)

Pursuit *See* Apache Blood (1975)

Pussycat *See* Faster, Pussycat! Kill! Kill! (1965)

Putyovka V Zhizn *See* The Road to Life (1931)

Q *See* Q (The Winged Serpent) (1982)

Q Planes *See* Clouds over Europe (1939)

Qian Li Zou Dan Ji *See* Riding Alone for Thousands of Miles (2005)

Qiji *See* Miracles (1989)

Qin Song *See* The Emperor's Shadow (1996)

Qiu Ju Da Guansi *See* The Story of Qiu Ju (1991)

Qiuyue *See* Autumn Moon (1992)

Qu mo dao zhang *See* Exorcist Master (1993)

Quai des Orfevres *See* Jenny Lamour (1947)

Qualcosa di Biondo *See* Aurora (1984)

Quality of Life *See* Against the Wall (2004)

Quando De Donne Avevando La Coda *See* When Women Had Tails (1970)

Quante Volte...Quella Notte *See* Four Times That Night (1969)

Quanto Costa Morire *See* Taste of Death (1968)

Quattro Moschi di Velluto Grigio *See* Four Flies on Grey Velvet (1972)

Que He Hecho Yo Para Merecer Estol? *See* What Have I Done to Deserve This? (1985)

Que La Bete Meure *See* This Man Must Die (1970)

Queen of Blood *See* Planet of Blood (1966)

Queen of Broadway *See* Kid Dynamite (1943)

Queen of the Cannibals *See* Doctor Butcher M.D. (1980)

Queen of the Gorillas *See* The Bride & the Beast (1958)

The Queen's Husband *See* The Royal Bed (1931)

Quei Temerari Sulle Loro Pazze, Scatenate, Scalcinate Carriole *See* Those Daring Young Men in Their Jaunty Jalopies (1969)

Quel Maldetto Treno Blindato *See* The Inglorious Bastards (1978)

Quel Maledetto Treno Blindato *See* Deadly Mission (1978)

Quella Villa Accanto Al Cimitero *See* The House by the Cemetery (1983)

Quelqu' Un Derriere la Porte *See* Someone Behind the Door (1971)

Quelques Jours en Septembre *See* A Few Days in September (2006)

Quemimada! *See* Burn! (1970)

Quentin Tarantino's Death Proof *See* Death Proof (2007)

The Quest *See* The Captive: The Longest Drive 2 (1976)

The Quest *See* The Longest Drive (1976)

Qui a tu Bambi? *See* Who Killed Bambi? (2003)

Quien Sabe? *See* A Bullet for the General (1968)

A Quiet Little Neighborhood, A Perfect Little Murder *See* A Perfect Little Murder (1990)

A Quiet Place to Kill *See* Paranoia (1969)

Quoi De Neuf, Pussycat? *See* What's New Pussycat? (1965)

The Raccoon War *See* Pom Poko (1994)

Race for the Yankee Zephyr *See* Treasure of the Yankee Zephyr (1983)

Race Gang *See* The Green Cockatoo (1937)

Racket Girls *See* Pin Down Girls (1951)

The Radical *See* Katherine (1975)

Radio Ranch *See* The Phantom Empire (1935)

Radon *See* Rodan (1956)

Radon the Flying Monster *See* Rodan (1956)

Rafferty and the Highway Hustlers *See* Rafferty & the Gold Dust Twins (1975)

The Rag Nymph *See* Catherine Cookson's The Rag Nymph (1996)

Rage *See* Rabid (1977)

Rage of the Buccaneers *See* The Black Pirate (1926)

Ragewar *See* Dungeonmaster (1983)

Ragged Angels *See* They Shall Have Music (1939)

The Raging Moon *See* Long Ago Tomorrow (1971)

Raging Waters *See* The Green Promise (1949)

Ragno Gelido *See* Dial Help (1988)

Rags to Riches *See* Callie and Son (1981)

Rain *See* Baran (2001)

Rainbow Boys *See* The Rainbow Gang (1973)

Rainbow on the River *See* It Happened in New Orleans (1936)

The Rainmaker *See* John Grisham's The Rainmaker (1997)

Raise Ravens *See* Cria (1976)

Ramblin' Man *See* The Concrete Cowboys (1979)

Rancho del Miedo *See* Fearmaker (1971)

Rane *See* The Wounds (1998)

Rang-e Khoda *See* The Color of Paradise (1999)

The Ranger, The Cook and a Hole in the Sky *See* Hole in the Sky (1995)

Ransom *See* Maniac (1977)

Rape Me *See* Baise Moi (2000)

Rape of Innocence *See* Dupont Lajoie (1974)

The Rape of Richard Beck *See* Broken Badge (1985)

Rape Squad *See* Act of Vengeance (1974)

Rasputin: The Mad Monk *See* Rasputin and the Empress (1933)

Rat Pfink and Boo Boo *See* Rat Pfink a Boo-Boo (1966)

The Rats *See* Deadly Eyes (1982)

Rats: Night of Terror *See* Rats (1983)

The Rats of Tobruk *See* The Fighting Rats of Tobruk (1944)

The Raven *See* Le Corbeau (1943)

Raye Makhfi *See* Secret Ballot (2001)

Re-Animator 2 *See* Bride of Re-Animator (1989)

RE: Lucky Luciano *See* Lucky Luciano (1974)

The Reader *See* La Lectrice (1988)

Real Men *See* Regular Guys (1996)

The Rebel *See* The Bushwackers (1952)

Rebel of the Road *See* Hot Rod (1979)

Rebel with a Cause *See* The Loneliness of the Long Distance Runner (1962)

Rebellion *See* Samurai Rebellion (1967)

Rece do Gory *See* Hands Up (1981)

Recoil *See* Silent Venom (2008)

Record of a Living Being *See* I Live in Fear (1955)

Red *See* Trois Couleurs: Rouge (1994)

Red Blooded American Girl 2 *See* Hot Blooded (1998)

The Red Circle *See* Le Cercle Rouge (1970)

Red Dragon *See* Code Name Alpha (1967)

Red Dragon *See* Manhunter (1986)

The Red Hangman *See* The Bloody Pit of Horror (1965)

The Red Head *See* Poil de Carotte (1931)

The Red Headed Corpse *See* Sweet Spirits (1971)

Red Hot Tires *See* Racing Luck (1935)

Red Hot Wheels *See* To Please a Lady (1950)

Red-Light District *See* Street of Shame (1956)

The Red Lips *See* Daughters of Darkness (1971)

Red Nightmare *See* The Commies Are Coming, the Commies Are Coming (1957)

Red on Red *See* Scarred (1984)

The Red Phone: Manhunt *See* Anti-Terrorist Cell: Manhunt (2001)

The Red Sign of Madness *See* Hatchet for the Honeymoon (1970)

The Red Tide *See* Blood Tide (1982)

The Redeemer *See* Class Reunion Massacre (1977)

Redheads *See* Desperate Prey (1994)

Redneck County *See* Hootch Country Boys (1975)

Redneck County *See* Poor Pretty Eddie (1973)

Reed, Mexico Insurgente *See* Reed: Insurgent Mexico (1973)

Reflections on a Crime *See* Reflections in the Dark (1994)

The Refugee *See* Three Faces West (1940)

Regain *See* Harvest (1937)

Regeneration *See* Behind the Lines (1997)

Regina Roma *See* Regina (1983)

Rehearsal for a Crime *See* The Criminal Life of Archibaldo de la Cruz (1955)

Reine Geschmacksache *See* Fashion Victims (2007)

Rejuvenatrix *See* The Rejuvenator (1988)

Rekopis Znaleziony W Saragossie *See* The Saragossa Manuscript (1965)

Religious Racketeers *See* Mystic Circle Murder (1939)

Remando al Viento *See* Rowing with the Wind (1988)

The Remarkable Mr. Kipps *See* Kipps (1941)

Remembrance of Love *See* Holocaust Survivors... Remembrance of Love (1983)

Remo: Unarmed and Dangerous *See* Remo Williams: The Adventure Begins (1985)

Remorques *See* Stormy Waters (1941)

Remove Lum & Abner *See* So This Is Washington (1943)

Ren pi deng long *See* Human Lanterns (1982)

Renacer *See* Reborn (1981)

Renegade Girls *See* Caged Heat (1974)

Renfrew of the Royal Mounted on the Great White Trail *See* Renfrew on the Great White Trail (1938)

Reprieved *See* Sing Sing Nights (1935)

Requiem fur Dominic *See* Requiem for Dominic (1991)

The Rescue *See* Let's Get Harry (1987)

Rescue Force *See* Terminal Force (1988)

Respectable Families *See* Un Air de Famille (1996)

Respiro: Grazia's Island *See* Respiro (2002)

The Rest of the Warrior *See* Love on a Pillow (1962)

Rest Stop 2 *See* Rest Stop: Don't Look Back (2008)

Rest Stop: Dead Ahead *See* Rest Stop (2006)

The Resurrection Syndicate *See* Nothing But the Night (1972)

Retaliator *See* Programmed to Kill (1986)

Retik, the Moon Menace *See* Radar Men from the Moon (1952)

Return from the Past *See* Alien Massacre (1967)

The Return of Captain America *See* Captain America (1944)

The Return of Giant Majin *See* Wrath of Daimajin (1966)

Return of Majin *See* Return of Daimajin (1966)

The Return of Maxwell Smart *See* The Nude Bomb (1980)

The Return of Mr. H. *See* They Saved Hitler's Brain (1964)

The Return of She *See* The Vengeance of She (1968)

Return of the Blind Dead *See* Return of the Evil Dead (1975)

The Return of the Duchess Dracula *See* Devil's Wedding Night (1973)

The Return of the Giant Majin *See* Return of Daimajin (1966)

The Return of the Giant Monsters *See* Gamera vs. Gaos (1967)

Return of the Living Dead *See* Messiah of Evil (1974)

Return of the Seven *See* Return of the Magnificent Seven (1966)

Return of the Texas Chainsaw Massacre *See* The Texas Chainsaw Massacre 4: The Next Generation (1995)

Return of the Wolfman *See* The Craving (1980)

Return of the Zombies *See* The Hanging Woman (1972)

Return to Sender *See* Convicted (2004)

Reunion *See* Reunion in France (1942)

Revelations of a Sex Maniac to the Head ot the Criminal Investigation Division *See* The Slasher (1972)

Revenant *See* Modern Vampires (1998)

Revenge *See* Blood Feud (1979)

Revenge *See* Fallen Angel (1999)

The Revenge *See* Zemsta (2002)

Revenge of a Kabuki Actor *See* An Actor's Revenge (1963)

The Revenge of Al Capone *See* Capone (1989)

Revenge of Dracula *See* Dracula, Prince of Darkness (1966)

The Revenge of Dracula *See* Dracula vs. Frankenstein (1971)

The Revenge of Milady *See* The Four Musketeers (1975)

The Revenge of the Blood Beast *See* The She-Beast (1965)

Revenge of the Dead *See* Night of the Ghouls (1959)

Revenge of the Dead *See* Zeder (1983)

Revenge of the Innocents *See* South Bronx Heroes (1985)

Revenge of the Living Dead *See* Children Shouldn't Play with Dead Things (1972)

Revenge of the Ninja Warrior *See* The Dagger of Kamui (1985)

Revenge of the Savage Bees *See* Terror Out of the Sky (1978)

Revenge of the Screaming Dead *See* Messiah of Evil (1974)

Revenge of the Vampire *See* Black Sunday (1960)

Revenge of the Zombie *See* Kiss Daddy Goodbye (1981)

Revenge Squad *See* Hit & Run (1982)

Revenge! The Killing Fist *See* The Street Fighter's Last Revenge (1974)

The Revengers' Comedies *See* Sweet Revenge (1998)

Rex: Le cyber chien *See* Cybermutt (2002)

Rhen zhe wu di *See* Five Element Ninjas (1982)

Rhodes of Africa *See* Rhodes (1936)

Rhosyn A Rhith *See* Coming Up Roses (1987)

Rhythm on the Ranch *See* Rootin' Tootin' Rhythm (1938)

Ricco *See* Mean Machine (1973)

Rice, Beans and Ketchup *See* Manhattan Merenque! (1995)

Rich, Young, and Deadly *See* Platinum High School (1960)

Riches and Romance *See* Amazing Adventure (1937)

The Richest Man in the World: The Story of Aristotle Onassis *See* Onassis (1988)

Richie *See* The Death of Richie (1976)

Rickshaw Man *See* Rikisha-Man (1958)

Ride a Dark Horse *See* Man & Boy (1971)

Riders *See* Guerilla Brigade (1939)

Rien ne va plus *See* The Swindle (1997)

Riffraff *See* Riff Raff (1935)

Riget *See* The Kingdom (1995)

Riget II *See* The Kingdom 2 (1997)

The Right Man *See* Her First Romance (1940)

Rih Essed *See* Man of Ashes (1986)

Rika the Mixed Blood Girl *See* Rica (1972)

Ring of Fire *See* Cowboy Up (2000)

Ringu 0: Basudei *See* Ringu 0 (2001)

Rinjin 13-go *See* The Neighbor No. Thirteen (2005)

Rinne *See* Reincarnation (2005)

Rio Vengeance *See* Motor Psycho (1965)

Riot *See* Riot in the Streets (1996)

Rip-Off *See* The Squeeze (1980)

Ripped Off *See* Counter Punch (1971)

The Ripper *See* New York Ripper (1982)

Riri Shushu no subete *See* All About Lily Chou-Chou (2001)

Risate de Gioia *See* Passionate Thief (1960)

Risate di Gioia *See* Joyful Laughter (1960)

The Rise of Catherine the Great *See* Catherine the Great (1934)

The Rise of Helga *See* Susan Lenox: Her Fall and Rise (1931)

Rising to Fame *See* Susan Lenox: Her Fall and Rise (1931)

Riso Amaro *See* Bitter Rice (1949)

Ritana *See* Returner (2002)

Riten *See* The Rite (1969)

Rites of Summer *See* White Water Summer (1987)

Ritoru Champion *See* My Champion (1981)

The Ritual *See* The Rite (1969)

Ritual Dos Sadicos *See* Awakenings of the Beast (1968)

Ritual of the Maniacs *See* Awakenings of the Beast (1968)

Rivelazioni di un Maniaco Sessuale al Capo Della Squadra Mobile *See* The Slasher (1972)

The Road *See* La Strada (1954)

The Road to Frisco *See* They Drive by Night (1940)

Roaring Timber *See* Come and Get It (1936)

Rob-B-Hood *See* Robin-B-Hood (2006)

Rob Roy *See* Rob Roy—The Highland Rogue (1953)

Robert A. Heinlein's The Puppet Masters *See* The Puppet Masters (1994)

Robert B. Parker's Jesse Stone: Death in Paradise *See* Jesse Stone: Death in Paradise (2006)

Robert B. Parker's Jesse Stone: Night Passage *See* Jesse Stone: Night Passage (2006)

Robert B. Parker's Jesse Stone: Stone Cold *See* Jesse Stone: Stone Cold (2005)

Robert B. Parker's Thin Air *See* Thin Air (2000)

Robert Louis Stevenson's St. Ives *See* St. Ives (1998)

Robert Louis Stevenson's The Suicide Club *See* Robert Louis Stevenson's The Game of Death (1999)

Robert Ludlum's Covert One: The Hades Factor *See* The Hades Factor (2006)

Robert Ludlum's the Apocalypse Watch *See* The Apocalypse Watch (1997)

Robert Rodriguez's Planet Terror *See* Planet Terror (2007)

Robinson Crusoeland *See* Utopia (1951)

Robo Ninja *See* Cyber Ninja (1994)

RoboDoc *See* National Lampoon Presents RoboDoc (2008)

Rocco E I Suoi Fratelli *See* Rocco and His Brothers (1960)

Rocco et Ses Freres *See* Rocco and His Brothers (1960)

Rock and Roll Wrestling Women vs. the Aztec Mummy *See* Wrestling Women vs. the Aztec Mummy (1959)

Rocket and Roll *See* Abbott and Costello Go to Mars (1953)

Rocket Man *See* RocketMan (1997)

Rocket to the Moon *See* Cat Women of the Moon (1953)

Rocky Mountain Mystery *See* The Fighting Westerner (1935)

Rodents *See* Ratas, Ratones, Rateros (1999)

Rodgers & Hammerstein's Cinderella *See* Cinderella (1997)

Roger Corman Presents: Alien Avengers *See* Alien Avengers (1996)

Roger Corman Presents: Black Scorpion *See* Black Scorpion (1995)

Roger Corman Presents Burial of the Rats *See* Burial of the Rats (1995)

Roger Corman Presents: House of the Damned *See* Spectre (1996)

Roger Corman Presents: Humanoids from the Deep *See* Humanoids from the Deep (1996)

Roger Corman Presents: Inhumanoid *See* Inhumanoid (1996)

Roger Corman Presents Last Exit to Earth *See* Last Exit to Earth (1996)

Roger Corman Presents Subliminal Seduction *See* The Corporation (1996)

Roger Corman Presents: Subliminal Seduction *See* Subliminal Seduction (1996)

Roger Corman Presents: Suspect Device *See* Suspect Device (1995)

Roger Corman Presents: The Alien Within *See* Unknown Origin (1995)

Roger Corman Presents: Vampirella *See* Vampirella (1996)

Roger Corman's Frankenstein Unbound *See* Frankenstein Unbound (1990)

Rois et reine *See* Kings and Queen (2004)

Rokugatsu no hebi *See* A Snake of June (2002)

Rolf *See* Last Mercenary (1984)

Roma *See* Fellini's Roma (1972)

Roma, Citta Aperta *See* Open City (1945)

Romance and Riches *See* Amazing Adventure (1937)

Romance da Empregada *See* The Story of Fausta (1988)

Romauld et Juliet *See* Mama, There's a Man in Your Bed (1989)

Rome, Open City *See* Open City (1945)

Romeo and Juliet *See* William Shakespeare's Romeo and Juliet (1996)

Romeo in Pyjamas *See* Parlor, Bedroom and Bath (1931)

Romeo, Julia a Tma *See* Sweet Light in a Dark Room (1960)

Romeo, Juliet and Darkness *See* Sweet Light in a Dark Room (1960)

Rommel—Desert Fox *See* The Desert Fox (1951)

Rona Jaffe's Mazes and Monsters *See* Mazes and Monsters (1982)

Ronin-Gai *See* Ronin Gai (1990)

The Rook *See* Something for Everyone (1970)

Rookies *See* Buck Privates (1941)

Rookies Come Home *See* Buck Privates Come Home (1947)

Roommates: 4 Horror Tales *See* My Bloody Roommates (2006)

Rosamunde Pilcher's Coming Home *See* Coming Home (1998)

The Rose and the Sword *See* Flesh and Blood (1985)

The Rose of Baghdad *See* The Singing Princess (1949)

Rose Red *See* Stephen King's Rose Red (2002)

Roseanna's Grave *See* For Roseanna (1996)

Rosemary's Killer *See* The Prowler (1981)

The Rotten Apple *See* Five Minutes to Love (1963)

Rouge Baiser *See* Red Kiss (1985)

Rouge Face *See* Dam Street (2005)

Rough Company *See* The Violent Men (1955)

Rough Treatment *See* Without Anesthesia (1978)

The Round Tower *See* Catherine Cookson's The Round Tower (1998)

Roveh Huliot *See* The Wooden Gun (1979)

Roxanne: The Prize Pulitzer *See* The Prize Pulitzer (1989)

The Royal Game *See* Brainwashed (1960)

Ruang rak noi nid mahasan *See* Last Life in the Universe (2003)

Ruang talok 69 *See* 6ixtynin9 (1999)

Ruby Cairo *See* Deception (1992)

Rudyard Kipling's Jungle Book *See* The Jungle Book (1942)

Rue Cases Negres *See* Sugar Cane Alley (1983)

Ruggero Deodato's Cannibal Holocaust *See* Cannibal Holocaust (1980)

Ruguo Ai *See* Perhaps Love (2005)

Rukajarven Tie *See* Ambush (1999)

Rules of Obsession *See* A Passion to Kill (1994)

Rumble in Hong Kong *See* Young Tiger (1974)

Rumpo Kid *See* Carry On Cowboy (1966)

Run for the Money *See* Hard Cash (2001)

Run, Simon, Run *See* Savage Run (1970)

The Runaways *See* South Bronx Heroes (1985)

Russ Meyer's SuperVixens *See* Supervixens (1975)

Russicum *See* Third Solution (1989)

Rustler's Roundup *See* Rustler's Hideout (1944)

The Rutles *See* All You Need Is Cash (1978)

Ryeong *See* The Ghost (2004)

S21: La Machine De Mort Khmere Rouge *See* S21: The Khmer Rouge Killing Machine (2003)

S21: The Khmer Rouge Death Machine *See* S21: The Khmer Rouge Killing Machine (2003)

Saam Gaang *See* 3 Extremes 2 (2002)

Sababa *See* Private Manoeuvres (1983)

The Saboteur *See* Morituri (1965)

Saboteur: Code Name Morituri *See* Morituri (1965)

The Sabre and the Arrow *See* Last of the Comanches (1952)

The Sabre Tooth Tiger *See* Deep Red: Hatchet Murders (1975)

Sabrina Fair *See* Sabrina (1954)

Sacco e Vanzetti *See* Sacco & Vanzetti (1971)

Sadie & Son *See* Detective Sadie & Son (1984)

Sadko *See* The Magic Voyage of Sinbad (1952)

The Saga of Dracula *See* The Saga of the Draculas (1972)

The Saga of Gosta Berling *See* The Atonement of Gosta Berling (1924)

The Saga of the Road *See* Pather Panchali (1954)

Saga of the West *See* When a Man's a Man (1935)

Saikaku Ichidai Onna *See* Life of Oharu (1952)

St. George and the Dragon *See* The Magic Sword (1962)

St. George and the Seven Curses *See* The Magic Sword (1962)

St. Martin's Lane *See* Sidewalks of London (1938)

Sakebi *See* Retribution (2006)

Sakima and the Masked Marvel *See* The Masked Marvel (1943)

The Salamander *See* La Salamandre (1971)

Salem's Ghost *See* Witchcraft 8: Salem's Ghost (1995)

Salerno Beachhead *See* A Walk in the Sun (1946)

Salinui chueok *See* Memories of Murder (2003)

Sally Lockhart Mysteries: Ruby in the Smoke *See* Ruby in the Smoke (2006)

Salmer fra Kjokkenet *See* Kitchen Stories (2003)

The Salute of the Jugger *See* The Blood of Heroes (1989)

Salvation! Have You Said Your Prayers Today? *See* Salvation! (1987)

Sam Cooper's Gold *See* The Ruthless Four (1970)

Sam Marlowe, Private Eye *See* The Man with Bogart's Face (1980)

Samaria *See* Samaritan Girl (2004)

Samehada otoko to momojiri onna *See* Shark Skin Man and Peach Hip Girl (1998)

Sam's Song *See* The Swap (1971)

The Samurai *See* Le Samourai (1967)

San Fernando *See* San Fernando Valley (1944)

San Ging Chaat Goo Si *See* New Police Story (2004)

San Michele Aveva un Gallo *See* St. Michael Had a Rooster (1972)

Sanda tai Gailah *See* War of the Gargantuas (1970)

Sandakan House 8 *See* Sandakan No. 8 (1974)

Sandkings *See* The Outer Limits: Sandkings (1995)

Sandokan alla Riscossa *See* The Conqueror & the Empress (1964)

The Sandpit Generals *See* Defiant (1970)

Sandra *See* Sandra of a Thousand Delights (1965)

Sang sei dau *See* Life Gamble (2004)

Sanma No Aji *See* An Autumn Afternoon (1962)

Sans Toit Ni Loi *See* Vagabond (1985)

Sansho Dayu *See* Sansho the Bailiff (1954)

Santa Claus Defeats the Aliens *See* Santa Claus Conquers the Martians (1964)

Santo en el Museo de Cera *See* Samson in the Wax Museum (1963)

Santo in the Wax Museum *See* Samson in the Wax Museum (1963)

Sarajevo *See* De Mayerling a Sarajevo (1940)

Sardonicus *See* Mr. Sardonicus (1961)

Sars Wars *See* Sars Wars: Bangkok Zombie Crisis (2004)

Sasayaki *See* Moonlight Whispers (1999)

Sasom I En Spegel *See* Through a Glass Darkly (1961)

The Sasquatch Dumpling Gang *See* The Sasquatch Gang (2006)

Satan *See* Mark of the Devil (1969)

Satan *See* Sheitan (2006)

Satanic Mechanic *See* Perfect Killer (1977)

Satan's Bloody Freaks *See* Dracula vs. Frankenstein (1971)

Satan's Claw *See* The Blood on Satan's Claw (1971)

Satan's Daughters *See* Vampyres (1974)

Satan's Dog *See* Play Dead (1981)

Satan's Mistress *See* Demon Rage (1982)

Satan's Satellites *See* Zombies of the Stratosphere (1952)

Satan's Skin *See* The Blood on Satan's Claw (1971)

Satan's Supper *See* Cataclysm (1981)

Satansbraten *See* Satan's Brew (1976)

Satellite of Blood *See* First Man into Space (1959)

Satin Vengeance *See* Naked Vengeance (1985)

Satree lek 2 *See* The Iron Ladies 2 (2003)

Satree Lex *See* The Iron Ladies (2000)

Satsujim-ken *See* The Street Fighter (1974)

Satsujin-ken 2 *See* Return of the Street Fighter (1974)

Saturday Island *See* Island of Desire (1952)

Saturn *See* Speed of Life (1999)

Saturno Contro *See* Saturn in Opposition (2007)

Satyricon *See* Fellini Satyricon (1969)

Saul e David *See* Saul and David (1964)

Sauve qui peut *See* Every Man for Himself (1979)

Sauve qui peut la vie *See* Every Man for Himself (1979)

The Savage *See* In Hell (2003)

The Savage *See* Lovers Like Us (1975)

Savage Abduction *See* Cycle Psycho (1972)

Savage Apocalypse *See* Cannibal Apocalypse (1980)

Savage Beasts *See* The Wild Beasts (1985)

Savage Nights *See* Les Nuits Fauves (1992)

The Savage Planet *See* Fantastic Planet (1973)

The Savage State *See* L'Etat Sauvage (1978)

Sayat Nova *See* The Color of Pomegranates (1969)

The Scalper *See* Just the Ticket (1998)

Scaramouche *See* Loves & Times of Scaramouche (1976)

Scared Stiff *See* Treasure of Fear (1945)

The Scaremaker *See* Girls Night Out (1983)

Scarface: The Shame of a Nation *See* Scarface (1931)

Scarlet Buccaneer *See* Swashbuckler (1976)

The Scarlet Buccaneer *See* Swashbuckler (1984)

Scary Movie *See* Scream (1996)

The Scavengers *See* Rebel Vixens (1969)

The Scent of Yvonne *See* The Perfume of Yvonne (1994)

Schatten der Engel *See* Shadow of Angels (1976)

Scherben *See* Shattered (1921)

Schlafes Bruder *See* Brother of Sleep (1995)

Schloss Vogelod *See* The Haunted Castle (1921)

The School That Ate My Brain *See* Zombie High (1987)

Schrei - denn ich werde dich toten! *See* School's Out (1999)

Schwestern Oder die Balance des Glucks *See* Sisters, Or the Balance of Happiness (1979)

The Scotland Yard Mystery *See* The Living Dead (1933)

Scoundrel in White *See* High Heels (1972)

The Scoundrel's Wife *See* The Home Front (2002)

Scream *See* The Night God Screamed (1971)

Scream Again *See* Scream 2 (1997)

Scream and Die *See* The House that Vanished (1973)

Scream Bloody Murder *See* House of Terror (1972)

Scream Bloody Murder *See* My Brother Has Bad Dreams (1972)

Scream Free! *See* Free Grass (1969)

Screamer *See* Scream and Scream Again (1970)

Screwface *See* Marked for Death (1990)

Scrooge *See* A Christmas Carol (1951)

Scum of the Earth *See* Poor White Trash 2 (1975)

Se, Jie *See* Lust, Caution (2007)

Sea Change *See* Jesse Stone: Sea Change (2007)

The Sea Witches *See* The Sea is Watching (2002)

Sea Wyf and Biscuit *See* Sea Wife (1957)

Search for the Mother Lode *See* Mother Lode (1982)

Searchers of the Voodoo Mountain *See* Warriors of the Apocalypse (1985)

Season of Dreams *See* Stacking (1987)

Seated At His Right *See* Black Jesus (1968)

The Second Arrival *See* The Arrival 2 (1998)

Second Breath *See* Le Deuxieme Souffle (1966)

Second Chances *See* Probation (1932)

The Second Coming *See* Messiah of Evil (1974)

The Second Jungle Book: Mowgli and Baloo *See* Rudyard Kipling's the Second Jungle Book: Mowgli and Baloo (1997)

The Second Lieutenant *See* The Last Lieutenant (1994)

Secondloitnanten *See* The Last Lieutenant (1994)

Seconds to Live *See* Viva Knievel (1977)

The Secret *See* Catherine Cookson's The Secret (2000)

The Secret Cinema *See* Paul Bartel's The Secret Cinema (1969)

Secret File: Hollywood *See* Secret File of Hollywood (1962)

Secret Honor: A Political Myth *See* Secret Honor (1985)

Secret Honor: The Last Testament of Richard M. Nixon *See* Secret Honor (1985)

The Secret of Dr. Mabuse *See* The Thousand Eyes of Dr. Mabuse (1960)

The Secret of Dorian Gray *See* Dorian Gray (1970)

The Secret Pact *See* The Pact (1999)

Secret Paper WB1 *See* Geheimakte WB1 (1942)

Secret Service in Darkest Africa *See* Manhunt in the African Jungles (1943)

The Secret Stranger *See* Rough Riding Ranger (1935)

Secret Weapon *See* Sherlock Holmes and the Secret Weapon (1942)

Secretos del Corazon *See* Secrets of the Heart (1997)

Secrets of the Red Bedroom *See* Secret Weapons (1985)

Seddok, l'Erede di Satana *See* Atom Age Vampire (1961)

Sedotta e Abbandonata *See* Seduced and Abandoned (1964)

The Seducer's Diary *See* Diary of a Seducer (1995)

The Seductress *See* The Teacher (1974)

Seduta Alla Sua Destra *See* Black Jesus (1968)

Seed of Terror *See* Grave of the Vampire (1972)

Seeds of Wrath *See* Man in the Shadow (1957)

The Seekers *See* Land of Fury (1955)

Segunda Piel *See* Second Skin (1999)

Sei Donne per l'Assassino *See* Blood and Black Lace (1964)

Seishun Zanoku Monogatari *See* The Cruel Story of Youth (1960)

Semana Santa *See* Angel of Death (2002)

Sen to Chihiro—No Kamikakushi *See* Spirited Away (2001)

Sengoku Gunto-Den *See* Saga of the Vagabond (1959)

Senior Trip *See* National Lampoon's Senior Trip (1995)

Senki *See* Shadows (2007)

Sensations *See* Sensations of 1945 (1944)

Sensuous Vampires *See* The Vampire Hookers (1978)

Sentimental Destinies *See* Les Destinees (2000)

The Sentinel *See* La Sentinelle (1992)

Seom *See* The Isle (2001)

Separate Beds *See* The Wheeler Dealers (1963)

Separate Rooms *See* Notre Histoire (1984)

Separation *See* Don't Hang Up (1990)

Seppuku *See* Harakiri (1962)

Sept Fois Femme *See* Woman Times Seven (1967)

Sergeant Steiner *See* Breakthrough (1978)

Serial Killing 4 Dummys *See* Serial Killing 101 (2004)

The Serpent *See* Night Flight from Moscow (1973)

Seryozha *See* A Summer to Remember (1961)

Sette Uomini d'Oro Nello Spazio *See* Metallica (1985)

Sette Volte Donna *See* Woman Times Seven (1967)

Seul contre tous *See* I Stand Alone (1998)

Seunlau Ngaklau *See* Time and Tide (2000)

Se7en *See* Seven (1995)

Seven Bad Men *See* Rage at Dawn (1955)

Seven Blows of the Dragon *See* The Water Margin (1972)

The Seven Brothers Meet Dracula *See* The Legend of the 7 Golden Vampires (1973)

Seven Different Ways *See* Quick, Let's Get Married (1971)

Seven Doors of Death *See* The Beyond (1982)

Seven Graves for Rogan *See* Time to Die (1983)

Seven Sisters *See* The House on Sorority Row (1983)

7-10 Split *See* Strike (2007)

Seven Waves Away *See* Abandon Ship (1957)

75 Degrees in July *See* 75 Degrees (2000)

Sex Crime of the Century *See* Last House on the Left (1972)

The Sex of the Stars *See* Le Sexe des Etoiles (1993)

Sex Play *See* Games Girls Play (1975)

The Sex Racketeers *See* Man of Violence (1971)

Sexo canibal *See* Devil Hunter (2008)

Sexton Blake and the Hooded Terror *See* The Hooded Terror (1938)

SF: Episode One *See* Samurai Fiction (1999)

Sha chu di yu mun *See* Heaven & Hell (1978)

Shadow *See* Unsane (1982)

The Shadow *See* Webmaster (1998)

The Shadow Army *See* Army of Shadows (1969)

Shadow of the Werewolf *See* The Werewolf vs. the Vampire Woman (1970)

Shadow Play *See* Portraits Chinois (1996)

The Shadow Versus the Thousand Eyes of Dr. Mabuse *See* The Thousand Eyes of Dr. Mabuse (1960)

The Shadow Warrior *See* Kagemusha (1980)

Shadow Zone: My Teacher Ate My Homework *See* My Teacher Ate My Homework (1998)

Shadowbuilder *See* Bram Stoker's Shadowbuilder (1998)

Shadows in an Empty Room *See* Strange Shadows in an Empty Room (1976)

Shadows of Our Ancestors *See* Shadows of Forgotten Ancestors (1964)

Shadows of Our Forgotten Ancestors *See* Shadows of Forgotten Ancestors (1964)

Shadows of the Peacock *See* Echoes of Paradise (1986)

Shaft Returns *See* Shaft (2000)

Shakespeare's Sister *See* The Proposition (1997)

Shalimar *See* Deadly Thief (1978)

Shall We Dansu? *See* Shall We Dance? (1996)

Shame of the Sabine Women *See* The Rape of the Sabines (1961)

Shanghai Express *See* The Millionaire's Express (1986)

Shao Lin shan shi liu fang *See* The 36th Chamber of Shaolin (1978)

Shao Lin yu Wu Dang *See* Shaolin & Wu Tang (1981)

Shao Lin yu Wu Dang *See* Sword Masters: Two Champions of Shaolin (1980)

Shao Nian Huang Fei Hong Zhi Tie Ma Liu *See* Iron Monkey (1993)

Shaolin Avenger *See* King Boxer (1972)

Shaolin Hellgate *See* Heaven & Hell (1978)

Shaolin Master Killer *See* The 36th Chamber of Shaolin (1978)

The Shaolin Swallow *See* Golden Swallow (1968)

Shaolin Temple, Part II *See* Shaolin & Wu Tang (1981)

Shaolin Wu Tang *See* Shaolin & Wu Tang (1981)

Shark: Red on the Ocean *See* Devilfish (1984)

Shark Reef *See* She Gods of Shark Reef (1956)

Shatter *See* Call Him Mr. Shatter (1974)

Shatterhand *See* Apache's Last Battle (1964)

She Demons of the Swamp *See* Attack of the Giant Leeches (1959)

She Devil *See* Drums O'Voodoo (1934)

She Devils of the S.S. *See* The Cut Throats (1969)

She Drives Me Crazy *See* Friends, Lovers & Lunatics (1989)

She Gets What She Wants *See* Slap Her, She's French (2002)

She Got What She Asked For *See* Yesterday, Today and Tomorrow (1964)

She Knew No Other Way *See* Last Resort (1986)

She Monster of the Night *See* Frankenstein's Daughter (1958)

She Should Have Stayed in Bed *See* I Am Frigid... Why? (1972)

She Was a Hippy Vampire *See* The Wild World of Batwoman (1966)

She-Wolf *See* The Legend of the Wolf Woman (1977)

Sheba *See* The Graveyard (1974)

Sheer Bliss *See* Winter Break (2002)

Shelf Life *See* Subhuman (2004)

She'll Be Sweet *See* Magee and the Lady (1978)

Shenanigans *See* Great Bank Hoax (1978)

Sheng si dou *See* Life Gamble (2004)

Sherlock Holmes *See* The Adventures of Sherlock Holmes (1939)

Sherlock Holmes and the Prince of Crime *See* Hands of a Murderer (1990)

Sherlock Holmes and the Scarlet Claw *See* Scarlet Claw (1944)

Sherlock Holmes and the Spider Woman *See* Spider Woman (1944)

Sherlock Holmes and the Woman in Green *See* The Woman in Green (1949)

Sherlock Holmes Grosster Fall *See* A Study in Terror (1966)

Sherlock Holmes in The Hound of London *See* The Hound of London (1993)

Sherlock Holmes: The Silver Blaze *See* Murder at the Baskervilles (1937)

Sherlock Holmes Und Das Halsband des Todes *See* Sherlock Holmes and the Deadly Necklace (1962)

She's De Lovely *See* De-Lovely (2004)

She's De Lovely *See* She's So Lovely (1997)

Shi gan *See* Time (2006)

Shi qi sui de tian kong *See* Formula 17 (2004)

Shichinin No Samurai *See* Seven Samurai (1954)

Shifshuf Naim *See* Hot Bubblegum (1981)

Shijie *See* The World (2004)

Shimian Maifu *See* House of Flying Daggers (2004)

Shimmering Light *See* Mutual Respect (1977)

Shimotsuma monogatari *See* Kamikaze Girls (2004)

Shin Jingi No Hakaba *See* Graveyard of Honor (2002)

Shin Kanashiki Hittoman *See* Another Lonely Hitman (1995)

Shinel *See* The Overcoat (1959)

Shinju Ten No Amijima *See* Double Suicide (1969)

Shinobi: Heart Under Blade *See* Shinobi (2005)

Ship of Fools *See* The Imposters (1998)

The Ship was Loaded *See* Carry On Admiral (1957)

Ships of the Night *See* Ships in the Night (1928)

Shiqisuide Danche *See* Beijing Bicycle (2001)

Shiryo No Wana 2: Hideki *See* Evil Dead Trap 2: Hideki (1991)

Shiver *See* Night Train to Terror (1984)

Shivers *See* They Came from Within (1975)

Shiza *See* Schizo (2004)

Shizuka Naru Ketto *See* A Quiet Duel (1949)

Shnat Effes *See* Year Zero (2004)

Shock *See* Le Choc (1982)

Shock (Transfer Suspense Hypnos) *See* Shock (1979)

Shocked *See* Mesmerized (1984)

Shockwave *See* The Arrival (1996)

Shogun Assassin 2: Lightning Swords of Death *See* Shogun Assassin 2: Lightning Swords of Death (1973)

Shogun Island *See* Raw Force (1981)

The Shogun's Samurai *See* Shogun's Samurai—The Yagyu Clan Conspiracy (1978)

Shoot the Pianist *See* Shoot the Piano Player (1962)

The Shooter *See* Hidden Assassin (1994)

Shootout *See* Shoot Out (1971)

The Shop on High Street *See* The Shop on Main Street (1965)

Shu Dan Long Wei *See* Meltdown (1995)

Shu Shan *See* Zu: Warriors from the Magic Mountain (1983)

Shu shan zheng zhuan *See* Zu Warriors (2001)

Shuang Long Hui *See* Twin Dragons (1992)

Shuang Tong *See* Double Vision (2002)

Shuban *See* Scandal (1950)

Shui Hu Zhuan *See* The Water Margin (1972)

Shunpuden *See* Story of a Prostitute (1965)

Shura Yukihime *See* The Princess Blade (2002)

Shurayukihime *See* Lady Snowblood (1973)

Shussho Iwai *See* The Wolves (1982)

Shut Up and Dance *See* Dance with Me (1998)

Shutter: They Are Around Us *See* Shutter (2005)

The Shuttered Room *See* Blood Island (1968)

Shvil Hahalav *See* The Milky Way (1997)

Si Don Juan Etait une Femme *See* Don Juan (Or If Don Juan Were a Woman) (1973)

Si J'Etais Toi *See* The Secret (2007)

Si Te Dicen Que Cai *See* If They Tell You I Fell (1989)

Sibirska Ledi Magbet *See* Siberian Lady Macbeth (1961)

Sid & Nancy: Love Kills *See* Sid & Nancy (1986)

Sidney Sheldon's Windmills of the Gods *See* Windmills of the Gods (1988)

Siegfried's Death *See* Siegfried (1924)

Siegfrieds Tod *See* Siegfried (1924)

Signal One *See* Bullet Down Under (1994)

Signe Charlotte *See* Sincerely Charlotte (1986)

Significant Other *See* When a Man Loves a Woman (1994)

The Silence After the Shot *See* The Legend of Rita (1999)

The Silence of the Sea *See* La Silence de la Mer (1947)

Silencio de Neto *See* The Silence of Neto (1994)

Silencio Roto *See* Broken Silence (2001)

The Silent Flute *See* Circle of Iron (1978)

Silent Night, Evil Night *See* Black Christmas (1975)

Silken Skin *See* The Soft Skin (1964)

Silver Blaze *See* Murder at the Baskervilles (1937)

The Silver Brumby *See* The Silver Stallion: King of the Wild Brumbies (1993)

Silver Devil *See* Wild Horse (1931)

Simbad Contro I Sette Saraceni *See* Ali Baba and the Seven Saracens (1964)

Simon del Desierto *See* Simon of the Desert (1966)

Simson Magus *See* Simon the Magician (1999)

Simone Barbes ou la Vertu *See* Simone Barbes (1980)

Simoom: A Passion in the Desert *See* Passion in the Desert (1997)

Simple Lies *See* Rx (2006)

The Sin *See* The Shaming (1979)

Sin Eater *See* The Order (2003)

Sin Noticias de Dios *See* No News from God (2001)

Sinai Commandos: The Story of the Six Day War *See* Sinai Commandos (1968)

Sinbad Against the Seven Saracens *See* Ali Baba and the Seven Saracens (1964)

The Singing Musketeer *See* The Three Musketeers (1939)

Sinister House *See* Who Killed Doc Robbin? (1948)

The Sinners *See* La Piscine (1969)

Sins of Love *See* Test Tube Babies (1948)

Siren's Kiss *See* Body Strokes (1995)

Sista Dansen *See* The Last Dance (1993)

The Sister of Satan *See* The She-Beast (1965)

Sisters *See* Some Girls (1988)

Sitting Bull's History Lesson *See* Buffalo Bill & the Indians (1976)

Siu hap Cho Lau Heung *See* Legend of the Liquid Sword (1993)

Siu lam juk kau *See* Shaolin Soccer (2001)

Siulam Chukkau *See* Shaolin Soccer (2001)

Siunin Wong Fei-hung Tsi Titmalau *See* Iron Monkey (1993)

Six Inches Tall *See* Attack of the Puppet People (1958)

Six Women for the Murderer *See* Blood and Black Lace (1964)

The Sixth of June *See* D-Day, the Sixth of June (1956)

Skate! *See* Blades of Courage (1988)

Ski Lift to Death *See* Snowblind (1978)

Skip Tracer *See* Deadly Business (1977)

Skipper *See* The Todd Killings (1971)

Sky is Falling *See* Bloodbath (1976)

Skyggen *See* Webmaster (1998)

Skyggen af Emma *See* Emma's Shadow (1988)

Skylark *See* Sarah, Plain and Tall: Skylark (1993)

The Slammer *See* Short Eyes (1979)

The Slasher *See* Cosh Boy (1952)

Slasher in the House *See* Home Sweet Home (1980)

Slaughter *See* Kinatay (2009)

The Slaughterers *See* Cannibal Apocalypse (1980)

Slave Coast *See* Cobra Verde (1988)

Slave Girls *See* Prehistoric Women (1967)

Slave of the Cannibal God *See* Mountain of the Cannibal God (1979)

Slaves *See* Blacksnake! (1973)

Slaves of the Invisible Monster *See* The Invisible Monster (1950)

Slay It Again, Sam *See* Codename: Foxfire (1985)

Sleep No More *See* Invasion of the Body Snatchers (1956)

Slip Slide Adventures *See* Water Babies (1979)

Slit-Mouthed Woman *See* Carved (2007)

Slow Motion *See* Every Man for Himself (1979)

A Small Miracle *See* Simon Birch (1998)

Small Town Massacre *See* Strange Behavior (1981)

Smart Alec *See* Movie Maker (1986)

Smashing the Crime Syndicate *See* Hell's Bloody Devils (1970)

Smokey and the Bandit Ride Again *See* Smokey and the Bandit 2 (1980)

Smorgasbord *See* Cracking Up (1983)

Smultron-Stallet *See* Wild Strawberries (1957)

Snake Eyes *See* Dangerous Game (1993)

Snake Fist Fighter *See* Master with Cracked Fingers (1971)

The Snake King *See* Snakeman (2005)

Snapshot *See* The Night After Halloween (1979)

Snitch *See* Monument Ave. (1998)

Snow Days *See* Let It Snow (1999)

Snow White and the Three Clowns *See* Snow White and the Three Stooges (1961)

Snow White in the Black Forest *See* Snow White: A Tale of Terror (1997)

Snuff *See* Thesis (1996)

Snuffy Smith *See* Snuffy Smith, Yard Bird (1942)

So Evil, My Sister *See* The Sibling (1972)

So Naked, So Dead *See* The Slasher (1972)

So Sad About Gloria *See* Visions of Evil (1975)

So Sweet, So Dead *See* The Slasher (1972)

So Sweet, So Perverse *See* Kiss Me, Kill Me (1973)

So This Is Romance? *See* Romance and Rejection (1996)

Social Suicide *See* Pre-Madonnas: Rebels Without a Clue (1995)

Sodome et Gomorrhe *See* Sodom and Gomorrah (1962)

Solamente Nero *See* The Bloodstained Shadow (1978)

Soldaat van Oranje *See* Soldier of Orange (1978)

Soldier Duroc *See* Soldat Duroc... Ca Va Etre Ta Fete! (1975)

Soldier in Skirts *See* Triple Echo (1977)

The Soldier Who Declared Peace *See* Tribes (1970)

The Soldiers *See* Les Carabiniers (1963)

Sole Nella Pelle *See* Summer Affair (1971)

Solo de Otono *See* Autumn Sun (1998)

Solomon Northrup's Odyssey *See* Half Slave, Half Free (1985)

Solyaris *See* Solaris (1972)

Sombra, the Spider Woman *See* The Black Widow (1947)

Some Like It Cool *See* Sex on the Run (1978)

Some Like It Hot *See* Rhythm Romance (1939)

Some Like It Sexy *See* The Seducer (1969)

Someone Behind You *See* Voices (2008)

Someone is Killing the Great Chefs of Europe *See* Who Is Killing the Great Chefs of Europe? (1978)

Someone's Killing the World's Greatest Models *See* She's Dressed to Kill (1979)

Something Fishy *See* Pas Tres Catholique (1993)

Something Is Out There *See* Day of the Animals (1977)

Something Like the Truth *See* The Offence (1973)

Something to Hide *See* Shattered (1972)

Something Waits in the Dark *See* Screamers (1980)

Something's Gotta Give *See* Move Over, Darling (1963)

Somewhere in France *See* The Foreman Went to France (1942)

Somewhere in Paris *See* The Spy Ring (1938)

Sommarlek *See* Summer Interlude (1950)

Sommarnattens Leende *See* Smiles of a Summer Night (1955)

Sommer '04 *See* Summer of '04 (2006)

Son of Blob *See* Beware! The Blob (1972)

Son of Darkness: To Die For 2 *See* To Die For 2: Son of Darkness (1991)

Sondagsengler *See* The Other Side of Sunday (1996)

The Song of the Road *See* Pather Panchali (1954)

Song of the Sierra *See* Springtime in the Sierras (1947)

The Songs of My Homeland *See* Marooned in Iraq (2002)

Sono Otoko, Kyobo ni Tsuki *See* Violent Cop (1989)

Sons and Warriors *See* Some Mother's Son (1996)

Sons of the Legion *See* Sons of the Desert (1933)

Sons of the Musketeers *See* At Sword's Point (1951)

Sons of the Wind *See* The Great Challenge (2004)

Sophie Scholl: Die Letzten Tage *See* Sophie Scholl: The Final Days (2005)

Sophie's Place *See* Crooks & Coronets (1969)

Soreum *See* Sorum (2001)

Sorstalansag *See* Fateless (2005)

So's Your Aunt Emma *See* Meet the Mob (1942)

Sotto gli Occhi dell'Assassino *See* Unsane (1982)

Soul *See* Earth (1930)

Soul Man 2 *See* Far Out Man (1989)

Soulmates *See* Evil Lives (1992)

Sound From a Million Years Ago *See* Sound of Horror (1964)

Sound of Fury *See* Try and Get Me (1950)

Soup to Nuts *See* Waitress (1981)

Sous le Sable *See* Under the Sand (2000)

Sous le Soleil de Satan *See* Under Satan's Sun (1987)

Sous les Bombes *See* Under the Bombs (2007)

Sous les Toits de Paris *See* Under the Roofs of Paris (1929)

South of Panama *See* Panama Menace (1941)

South Pacific *See* Rodgers & Hammerstein's South Pacific (2001)

South Sea Woman *See* Pearl of the South Pacific (1955)

South Seas *See* South Seas Massacre (1974)

Southside *See* Cock & Bull Story (2003)

Southwest to Sonora *See* The Appaloosa (1966)

Soy Cuba *See* I Am Cuba (1964)

Space 2074 *See* Star Quest (1989)

Space: 2100 *See* Destination Moonbase Alpha (1975)

The Space Amoeba *See* Yog, Monster from Space (1971)

Space Avenger *See* Alien Space Avenger (1991)

Space Invasion from Lapland *See* Invasion of the Animal People (1962)

Space Invasion of Lapland *See* Invasion of the Animal People (1962)

Space Men *See* Assignment Outer Space (1961)

Space Men Appear in Tokyo *See* Warning from Space (1956)

Space Mission of the Lost Planet *See* Horror of the Blood Monsters (1970)

Space Monster Dagora *See* Dagora, the Space Monster (1965)

Space Mutants *See* Planet of the Vampires (1965)

Space Odyssey *See* Metallica (1985)

Space Soldiers *See* Flash Gordon: Rocketship (1940)

Space Station *See* Black Horizon (2001)

Space Travellers *See* Marooned (1969)

The Space Vampires *See* The Astro-Zombies (1967)

Spacemen Saturday Night *See* Invasion of the Saucer Men (1957)

Spaceship *See* The Creature Wasn't Nice (1981)

Spaceship to the Unknown *See* Flash Gordon: Rocketship (1940)

The Spanish Apartment *See* L'Auberge Espagnole (2002)

Spanish Rose *See* Point of Impact (1993)

Spara Forte, Piu Forte...Non Capisco *See* Shoot Loud, Louder, I Don't Understand! (1966)

Sparkling Cyanide *See* Agatha Christie's Sparkling Cyanide (1983)

Spawn *See* Todd McFarlane's Spawn (1997)

Spawn of the Slithis *See* Slithis (1978)

The Spawning *See* Piranha 2: The Spawning (1982)

Special Unit AT 13 *See* Anti-Terrorist Cell: Manhunt (2001)

The Specter of Freedom *See* Phantom of Liberty (1974)

The Spectre *See* The Ghost (1963)

Speed Brent Wins *See* Breed of the Border (1933)

The Spell of Amy Nugent *See* Spellbound (1941)

Spell of the Hypnotist *See* Fright (1956)

Spettri *See* Specters (1987)

The Spider *See* Earth vs. the Spider (1958)

The Spider *See* The Killer Must Kill Again (1975)

Spider Baby, or the Maddest Story Ever Told *See* Spider Baby (1964)

Spider-Man *See* The Amazing Spider-Man (1977)

Spies-A-Go-Go *See* Nasty Rabbit (1964)

Spies, Lies, and Alibis *See* Code Name: Chaos (1990)

Spinal Tap *See* This Is Spinal Tap (1984)

Spione *See* Spies (1928)

Spiral *See* Uzumaki (2000)

Spirit of Tattoo *See* Irezumi (1983)

Spirit of the Dead *See* The Asphyx (1972)

Spirit of the People *See* Abe Lincoln in Illinois (1940)

The Spiritualist *See* The Amazing Mr. X (1948)

Spivs *See* I Vitelloni (1953)

The Split *See* The Manster (1959)

Spook Warfare *See* The Great Yokai War (2005)

The Spooky Movie Show *See* The Mask (1961)

Spoorloos *See* The Vanishing (1988)

Spot *See* Dog Pound Shuffle (1975)

Spotlight on Scandal *See* Spotlight Scandals (1943)

Spotlight Revue *See* Spotlight Scandals (1943)

Spotswood *See* The Efficiency Expert (1992)

Spring Break USA *See* Lauderdale (1989)

Spring Fever USA *See* Lauderdale (1989)

Spur der Steine *See* Trace of Stones (1966)

The Spy in White *See* Secret of Stamboul (1936)

Spyder *See* Blackbelt 2: Fatal Force (1993)

Spymaker *See* Spymaker: The Secret Life of Ian Fleming (1990)

Spymaster *See* Goldeneye: The Secret Life of Ian Fleming (1989)

Squadron of Doom *See* Ace Drummond (1936)

Stacey and Her Gangbusters *See* Stacey (1973)

Stadt ohne Mitleid *See* Town without Pity (1961)

Stakeout 2 *See* Another Stakeout (1993)

The Stand *See* Stephen King's The Stand (1994)

Stand and Deliver *See* Bowery Blitzkrieg (1941)

Stand Easy *See* Goon Movie (1952)

Standard Time *See* Anything But Love (2002)

Stanno Tutti Bene *See* Everybody's Fine (1990)

Star *See* Danielle Steel's Star (1993)

Star Child *See* Space Raiders (1983)

The Star Man *See* The Star Maker (1995)

Star Odyssey *See* Metallica (1985)

Star Runner *See* The Kumite (2003)

Star Trek: The Future Begins *See* Star Trek (2009)

Star Trek: The IMAX Experience *See* Star Trek (2009)

Star Wars: Episode 4—A New Hope *See* Star Wars (1977)

Star Wars: Episode 5—The Empire Strikes Back *See* The Empire Strikes Back (1980)

Star Wars: Episode 6—Return of the Jedi *See* Return of the Jedi (1983)

Stardust *See* Mad About Money (1937)

Starflight: the Plane that Couldn't Land *See* Starflight One (1983)

Starknight *See* Star Knight (1985)

Starlight Slaughter *See* Eaten Alive (1976)

A State of Shock *See* Power Play (1978)

The Statutory Affair *See* Lola (1969)

Stauffenberg *See* Operation Valkyrie (2004)

Stay *See* Sleeping Dogs Lie (2006)

Staying Alive *See* Fight for Your Life (1977)

The Steam Experiment *See* The Chaos Experiment (2009)

Steel Edge of Revenge *See* Goyokin (1969)

Steiner—Das Eiserne Kreuz *See* Cross of Iron (1976)

Stella Star *See* Star Crash (1978)

Stepfather *See* Beau Pere (1981)

Stephen King's Cat's Eye *See* Cat's Eye (1985)

Stephen King's Graveyard Shift *See* Graveyard Shift (1990)

Stephen King's Silver Bullet *See* Silver Bullet (1985)

Stephen King's Sleepwalkers *See* Sleepwalkers (1992)

Stesti *See* Something Like Happiness (2005)

Steven Spielberg Presents: Taken *See* Taken (2002)

Still Smokin' *See* Cheech and Chong: Still Smokin' (1983)

Stinky *See* Fistful of Death (1971)

Sto Dnej Do Pri Kaza *See* 100 Days Before the Command (1990)

Stolen Hearts *See* Two If by Sea (1995)

Stone Cold *See* Jesse Stone: Stone Cold (2005)

The Stone House *See* Red Sands (2009)

Storia de Ragazzi e di Ragazze *See* The Story of Boys & Girls (1991)

Storm *See* Storm Tracker (1999)

Storm of the Century *See* Stephen King's The Storm of the Century (1999)

Storm Riders *See* Wind and Cloud: The Storm Riders (2004)

Stormbreaker *See* Alex Rider: Operation Stormbreaker (2006)

Stormy Crossing *See* Black Tide (1958)

Story of a Marriage *See* On Valentine's Day (1986)

The Story of Gosta Berling *See* The Atonement of Gosta Berling (1924)

The Story of Robin Hood *See* The Story of Robin Hood & His Merrie Men (1952)

A Story of the Cruelties of Youth *See* The Cruel Story of Youth (1960)

The Story Without A Name *See* Without Warning (1952)

Strafsache 4 Ks 2/63: Auschwitz Vor Dem Frankfurter Schwurgericht *See* Verdict on Auschwitz: The Frankfurt Auschwitz Trial 1963—1965 (1993)

Straight Jacket *See* Dark Sanity (1982)

Straight on Till Morning *See* Dressed for Death (1974)

Straight to Hell *See* Cut and Run (1985)

Straightheads *See* Closure (2007)

Strakarnir Okkar *See* Eleven Men Out (2005)

Stranded *See* Black Horizon (2001)

A Strange Adventure *See* Wayne Murder Case (1932)

The Strange Adventure of David Gray *See* Vampyr (1931)

Strange Affection *See* The Scamp (1957)

The Strange Case of Dr. Jekyll and Mr. Hyde *See* Dr. Jekyll and Mr. Hyde (1968)

Teen Monster *See* Boltneck (1998)

Teenage Hooker Becomes a Killing Machine *See* Killing Machine (2002)

Teenage Norcha *See* Rebels of the Neon God (1992)

The Teenage Psycho Meets Bloody Mary *See* Incredibly Strange Creatures Who Stopped Living and Became Mixed-Up Zombies (1963)

Tejing Xinrenlei *See* Gen-X Cops (1999)

The Telegian *See* The Secret of the Telegian (1961)

Tell It To the Marines *See* Here Come the Marines (1952)

Tell Your Children *See* Reefer Madness (1938)

Tema *See* The Theme (1979)

Tempi Duri per i Vampiri *See* Uncle Was a Vampire (1959)

Tempo di Charleston - Chicago 1929 *See* They Paid with Bullets: Chicago 1929 (1969)

Tempo di Uccidere *See* Time to Kill (1989)

Temporada de patos *See* Duck Season (2004)

Tempting Fate *See* The Proposition (1997)

Tender Love *See* L'Amour en Herbe (1977)

The Tenderfoot *See* Bushwhacked (1995)

Tenderfoots *See* Bushwhacked (1995)

Tendre Poulet *See* Dear Detective (1977)

Tenebrae *See* Unsane (1982)

Tenebre *See* Unsane (1982)

Tengoku To Jigoku *See* High & Low (1962)

Tennessee Valley *See* The Only Thrill (1997)

Tennessee Williams: The Roman Spring of Mrs. Stone *See* The Roman Spring of Mrs. Stone (2003)

Tentacoli *See* Tentacles (1977)

Tenue de Soiree *See* Menage (1986)

Terminal *See* Robin Cook's Terminal (1996)

Terminal Station Indiscretion *See* Indiscretion of an American Wife (1954)

Terminus Station *See* Indiscretion of an American Wife (1954)

Terra *See* Battle for Terra (2009)

Terra em Transe *See* Earth Entranced (1966)

Terra Estrangeira *See* Foreign Land (1995)

Terreur dans l'Espace *See* Planet of the Vampires (1965)

Terror at the Opera *See* Opera (1988)

Terror Castle *See* The Virgin of Nuremberg (1965)

Terror Circus *See* Barn of the Naked Dead (1973)

Terror Eyes *See* Night School (1981)

Terror from the Sun *See* Hideous Sun Demon (1959)

Terror Hospital *See* Hospital of Terror (1978)

Terror House *See* The Night Has Eyes (1942)

Terror House *See* Terror at Red Wolf Inn (1972)

Terror in Space *See* Planet of the Vampires (1965)

Terror in the Midnight Sun *See* Invasion of the Animal People (1962)

Terror in Toyland *See* Christmas Evil (1980)

Terror of Dracula *See* Nosferatu (1922)

Terror of Sheba *See* The Graveyard (1974)

Terror of the Hatchet Men *See* The Terror of the Tongs (1961)

The Terror Strikes *See* The War of the Colossal Beast (1958)

Terror under the House *See* Revenge (1971)

Terrore *See* Castle of Blood (1964)

Terrore nello Spazio *See* Planet of the Vampires (1965)

Terry Pratchett's The Color of Magic *See* The Color of Magic (2008)

Tesis *See* Thesis (1996)

Testament in Evil *See* The Testament of Dr. Cordelier (1959)

The Testament of Dr. Mabuse *See* Crimes of Dr. Mabuse (1932)

Tetsujin niju-hachigo *See* Tetsujin 28 (2004)

Texas Blood Money *See* From Dusk Till Dawn 2: Texas Blood Money (1998)

Texas Chainsaw Massacre 3: Leatherface *See* Leatherface: The Texas Chainsaw Massacre 3 (1989)

Texas Desperadoes *See* Drift Fence (1936)

Texas Hill Killings *See* Stepsisters (1974)

Texas in Flames *See* She Came to the Valley (1977)

Texas Layover *See* Blazing Stewardesses (1975)

Texas Road Agent *See* Road Agent (1926)

Texas Serenade *See* Old Corral (1936)

Teyve der Milkhiker *See* Tevye (1939)

Thank God He Met Lizzie *See* The Wedding Party (1997)

Thanks to Gravity *See* Love and Debate (2006)

Thanksgiving Family Reunion *See* National Lampoon's Holiday Reunion (2003)

Thar Figlio di Attila *See* Tharus Son of Attila (1962)

That Man Mr. Jones *See* The Fuller Brush Man (1948)

That They May Live *See* J'Accuse (1937)

That's the Way of the World *See* Shining Star (1975)

These Dangerous Years *See* Dangerous Youth (1958)

These Foolish Things *See* Daddy Nostalgia (1990)

They *See* They Watch (1993)

They *See* Wes Craven Presents: They (2002)

They Call Me Hallelujah *See* Guns for Dollars (1973)

They Call Me Macho Woman *See* Savage Instinct (1989)

They Came From Upstairs *See* Aliens in the Attic (2009)

They Don't Wear Pajamas at Rosie's *See* The First Time (1969)

They Loved Life *See* Kanal (1956)

They Made Me a Criminal *See* They Made Me a Fugitive (1947)

They Made Me a Fugitive *See* They Made Me a Criminal (1939)

They Passed This Way *See* Four Faces West (1948)

They Who Step on the Tiger's Tail *See* The Men Who Tread on the Tiger's Tail (1945)

They're Coming to Get You *See* Dracula vs. Frankenstein (1971)

Thick as Thieves *See* The Code (2009)

Thieves *See* Les Voleurs (1996)

Thieves Holiday *See* A Scandal in Paris (1946)

Thin Air *See* Invasion of the Body Stealers (1969)

Thin Ice *See* Jesse Stone: Thin Ice (2009)

The Thing from Another World *See* The Thing (1951)

Thinner *See* Stephen King's Thinner (1996)

The Third Mother *See* Mother of Tears (2008)

Third Party Risk *See* Big Deadly Game (1954)

Thirst *See* Three Strange Loves (1949)

The Thirst of Baron Blood *See* Torture Chamber of Baron Blood (1972)

Thirteen at Dinner *See* Agatha Christie's Thirteen at Dinner (1985)

The Thirteen Chairs *See* 12 Plus 1 (1970)

Thirteen Steps to Death *See* Why Must I Die? (1960)

37.2 Degrees in the Morning *See* Betty Blue (1986)

37.2 le Matin *See* Betty Blue (1986)

36 Hours *See* Terror Street (1954)

36th Chamber *See* The 36th Chamber of Shaolin (1978)

This and That *See* Zus & Zo (2001)

This Is It *See* Michael Jackson's This Is It (2009)

This Side of the Truth *See* The Invention of Lying (2009)

This Strange Passion *See* El (1952)

This Time Forever *See* The Victory (1981)

Thomas Crown and Company *See* The Thomas Crown Affair (1968)

Thomas Est Amoureux *See* Thomas in Love (2001)

Thomas Kinkade's Home for Christmas *See* The Christmas Cottage (2008)

Thomas Kinkade's The Christmas Cottage *See* The Christmas Cottage (2008)

Thomas Mann's Doktor Faustus *See* Doktor Faustus (1982)

Thoroughbred *See* Run for the Roses (1978)

Those Dear Departed *See* Ghosts Can Do It (1987)

Those Were the Happy Times *See* Star! (1968)

Thou Shall Not Kill *See* Avenging Conscience (1914)

Thou Shalt Honour Thy Wife *See* Master of the House (1925)

A Thousand and One Nights *See* Arabian Nights (1974)

Thralls *See* Blood Angels (2005)

3x Jugatsu *See* Boiling Point (1990)

Three Bad Men in the Hidden Fortress *See* The Hidden Fortress (1958)

Three Colors: Blue *See* Trois Couleurs: Bleu (1993)

Three Colors: Red *See* Trois Couleurs: Rouge (1994)

Three Colors: White *See* Trois Couleurs: Blanc (1994)

Three Crazy Legionnaires *See* Three Legionnaires (1937)

Three Evil Masters *See* The Master (1980)

The Three Faces of Fear *See* Black Sabbath (1964)

The Three Faces of Terror *See* Black Sabbath (1964)

Three For the Money *See* Win, Place, or Steal (1972)

Three Golden Serpents *See* Island of Lost Girls (1968)

Three Moves to Freedom *See* Brainwashed (1960)

Three Ninjas: Showdown at Mega Mountain *See* 3 Ninjas: High Noon at Mega Mountain (1997)

Three of a Kind *See* Cooking Up Trouble (1944)

Three Rascals in the Hidden Fortress *See* The Hidden Fortress (1958)

Three Steps to the Gallows *See* White Fire (1953)

The Three Stooges Go Around the World in a Daze *See* Around the World in a Daze (1963)

Three Way Split *See* 3-Way (2004)

The Threepenny Opera *See* Mack the Knife (1989)

Thriller: An Echo of Teresa *See* Anatomy of Terror (1974)

Thriller: Kill Two Birds *See* Cry Terror (1976)

Through the Looking Glass *See* The Velvet Vampire (1971)

Through the Magic Pyramid *See* Tut & Tuttle (1981)

Throwing Stars *See* Who's Your Monkey (2007)

Thunder *See* Thunder Warrior (1985)

Thunder County *See* Women's Prison Escape (1974)

Thunder Mountain *See* Shadow of Chikara (1977)

Thunder on the Trail *See* Thundering Trail (1951)

Thunder Point *See* Jack Higgins' Thunder Point (1997)

Thursday the 12th *See* Pandemonium (1982)

Thy Neighbor's Wife *See* Poison (2001)

Ti Kniver I Hjertet *See* Cross My Heart and Hope to Die (1994)

Tian di ying xiong *See* Warriors of Heaven and Earth (2003)

Tian long ba bu *See* Sword Masters: The Battle Wizard (1977)

Tian Tang Kou *See* Blood Brothers (2007)

Tian xia *See* Wind and Cloud: The Storm Riders (2004)

Tian xia di yi quan *See* King Boxer (1972)

Tian Yu *See* Xiu Xiu: The Sent Down Girl (1997)

Tianguo Niezi *See* The Day the Sun Turned Cold (1994)

Ticket to Ride *See* Post Grad (2009)

Tidal Wave *See* Portrait of Jennie (1948)

The Tide of Life *See* Catherine Cookson's The Tide of Life (1996)

The Ties That Bind *See* The Unsaid (2001)

The Tiger *See* Tiger Warsaw (1987)

Tiger in the Sky *See* The McConnell Story (1955)

Tiger of Bengal *See* Journey to the Lost City (1958)

The Tiger of Eschanapur *See* The Indian Tomb (1921)

The Tiger Woman *See* Perils of the Darkest Jungle (1944)

Tigers Don't Cry *See* African Rage (1978)

Tight Little Island *See* Whiskey Galore (1948)

The Tigress *See* Ilsa, the Tigress of Siberia (1979)

'Til Christmas *See* Breathing Room (1996)

Til Dawn Do Us Part *See* Dressed for Death (1974)

Till Death Us Do Part *See* The Blood Spattered Bride (1972)

Till Gladje *See* To Joy (1950)

Tilly Trotter *See* Catherine Cookson's Tilly Trotter (1999)

Tim Burton's The Nightmare Before Christmas *See* The Nightmare Before Christmas (1993)

Timber Tramps *See* The Big Push (1975)

Time Bomb *See* Spy Train (1943)

Time Flyers *See* The Blue Yonder (1986)

A Time For Caring *See* Generation (1969)

The Time of Return *See* Muriel (1963)

Time of the Beast *See* Mutator (1990)

Time of the Wolves *See* Carbon Copy (1969)

Time Raiders *See* Warriors of the Apocalypse (1985)

Time Trap *See* The Time Travelers (1964)

Time Warp Terror *See* Bloody New Year (1987)

Timecode *See* Time Code (2000)

The Timeshifters *See* Thrill Seekers (1999)

Timeslip *See* The Atomic Man (1956)

Timewarp *See* Day Time Ended (1980)

Tin lung bat bou *See* Sword Masters: The Battle Wizard (1977)

Tini Zabutykh Predkiv *See* Shadows of Forgotten Ancestors (1964)

Tintorera *See* Tintorera… Tiger Shark (1978)

Tintorera...Bloody Waters *See* Tintorera… Tiger Shark (1978)

Tirez sur le Pianiste *See* Shoot the Piano Player (1962)

Titan Find *See* Creature (1985)

Tito and I *See* Tito and Me (1992)

Tito i Ja *See* Tito and Me (1992)

To Be a Man *See* Cry of Battle (1963)

To Catch a Spy *See* Catch Me a Spy (1971)

To Die For *See* Heaven's a Drag (1994)

To Elvis, With Love *See* Touched by Love (1980)

To Have and to Hold *See* When a Man Loves a Woman (1994)

To Koritsi Me Ta Mavra *See* Girl in Black (1956)

To Live *See* Ikiru (1952)

To Love a Vampire *See* Lust for a Vampire (1971)

To Our Loves *See* A Nos Amours (1984)

To Return *See* Volver (2006)

To Telefteo Psemma *See* A Matter of Dignity (1957)

To Viemma Tou Odyssea *See* Ulysses' Gaze (1995)

Toca Para Mi *See* Play for Me (2001)

Today We Live *See* The Day and the Hour (1963)

Todo Sobre Mi Madre *See* All About My Mother (1999)

Toemarok *See* The Soul Guardians (1998)

A Toi de Faire, Mignonne *See* Your Turn Darling (1963)

Toi et Moi *See* You and Me (2006)

Tokaido obake dochu *See* Along with Ghosts (1969)

Tokyo Bad Girls *See* Delinquent Girl Boss: Blossoming Night Dreams (1970)

Tokyo Monogatari *See* Tokyo Story (1953)

Tokyo Nagaremono *See* Tokyo Drifter (1966)

Tokyo Raiders 2 *See* Seoul Raiders (2005)

Tokyo zankoku keisatsu *See* Tokyo Gore Police (2008)

Tomb of the Cat *See* Tomb of Ligeia (1964)

Tomb of the Living Dead *See* Mad Doctor of Blood Island (1968)

Tomb Raider *See* Lara Croft: Tomb Raider (2001)

The Tommyknockers *See* Stephen King's The Tommyknockers (1993)

Ton Kero Ton Hellinon *See* When the Greeks (1981)

Tong Nien Wang Shi *See* A Time to Live and a Time to Die (1985)

Tonight's the Night *See* The Game of Love (1987)

Too Many Chefs *See* Who Is Killing the Great Chefs of Europe? (1978)

Too Much *See* Wish You Were Here (1987)

Top of the Food Chain *See* Invasion! (1999)

Topio Stin Omichli *See* Landscape in the Mist (1988)

Tora No O Wo Fumu Otokotachi *See* The Men Who Tread on the Tiger's Tail (1945)

Torment *See* L'Enfer (1993)

Torpedo Zone *See* Submarine Attack (1954)

Torture Chamber *See* The Fear Chamber (1968)

Torture Zone *See* The Fear Chamber (1968)

Toto the Hero *See* Toto le Heros (1991)

Tou Ming Zhuang *See* Warlords (2008)

The Touch of Flesh *See* You've Ruined Me, Eddie (1958)

The Touch of Melissa *See* The Touch of Satan (1970)

Touchez Pas Au Grisbi *See* Grisbi (1953)

Touchez pas au Grisbi *See* Grisbi (1953)

Tough Guy *See* Counter Punch (1971)

Tout Contre Leo *See* Close to Leo (2002)

A Toute Vitesse *See* Full Speed (1996)

Tower of Terror *See* Assault (1970)

Tower of Terror *See* Hard to Die (1990)

A Town Called Bastard *See* A Town Called Hell (1972)

Town Creek *See* Blood Creek (2009)

The Town That Cried Terror *See* Maniac (1977)

T.R. Sloane *See* Death Ray 2000 (1981)

Trackers *See* Space Rage (1986)

The Tragedy of Othello: The Moor of Venice *See* Othello (1952)

Trail of the Royal Mounted *See* Mystery Trooper (1932)

Train de Vie *See* Train of Life (1998)

Train of Terror *See* Terror Train (1980)

Train 2419 *See* The Return of Casey Jones (1934)

Traitement de Choc *See* Shock Treatment (1981)

Trance *See* The External (1999)

Trancers *See* Future Cop (1976)

Transport Z Raje *See* Transport from Paradise (1965)

The Transvestite *See* Glen or Glenda? (1953)

Tras el Cristal *See* In a Glass Cage (1986)

Trauma *See* Dario Argento's Trauma (1993)

Trauma *See* The House on Straw Hill (1976)

Traveling Birds *See* Winged Migration (2001)

Travels with Anita *See* Lovers and Liars (1981)

Tre Fratelli *See* Three Brothers (1980)

Tré Passi nel Delirio *See* Spirits of the Dead (1968)

Treasure of the Living Dead *See* Oasis of the Zombies (1982)

Tredowata *See* Leper (1976)

The Tree of Hands *See* Innocent Victim (1990)

Tree of Liberty *See* The Howards of Virginia (1940)

Tres Dias *See* Before the Fall (2008)

Trial by Combat *See* Choice of Weapons (1976)

Trial by Fire *See* Smoke Jumpers (2008)

Trick of the Eye *See* Primal Secrets (1994)

Trilogia: To Livadi pou dakryzei *See* Weeping Meadow (2004)

Trilogy: The Weeping Meadow *See* Weeping Meadow (2004)

A Trip with Anita *See* Lovers and Liars (1981)

Triple Trouble *See* Kentucky Kernels (1934)

Tristan and Isolde *See* Lovespell (1979)

Triumph des Willens *See* Triumph of the Will (1934)

Trmavomodry Svet *See* Dark Blue World (2001)

Troglodyte *See* Sea Beast (2008)

Trois Histoires Extraordinaires d'Edgar Poe *See* Spirits of the Dead (1968)

Trois Hommes et un Couffin *See* Three Men and a Cradle (1985)

Trois Vies et Une Seule Mort *See* Three Lives and Only One Death (1996)

The Trojan Brothers *See* Murder in the Footlights (1946)

The Trojan War *See* The Trojan Horse (1962)

The Trollenberg Terror *See* The Crawling Eye (1958)

Trolosa *See* Faithless (2000)

Tromba *See* Tromba, the Tiger Man (1952)

Trop Belle pour Toi *See* Too Beautiful for You (1988)

Trop Jolie pour Etre Honette *See* Too Pretty to Be Honest (1972)

Tropicana *See* The Heat's On (1943)

Trottie True *See* The Gay Lady (1949)

Trouble at 16 *See* Platinum High School (1960)

Trouble Chaser *See* Li'l Abner (1940)

The Trout *See* La Truite (1983)

The True Story of My Life in Rouen *See* My Life on Ice (2002)

Truman Capote's A Christmas Memory *See* ABC Stage 67: Truman Capote's A Christmas Memory (1966)

Truman Capote's One Christmas *See* One Christmas (1995)

Truman Capote's The Glass House *See* The Glass House (1972)

The Truth About Tully *See* Tully (2000)

Try and Find It *See* Hi Diddle Diddle (1943)

Try Seventeen *See* All I Want (2002)

Trzeci *See* The Third (2004)

Tsarskaya Nevesta *See* The Tsar's Bride (1966)

Tsubaki Sanjuro *See* Sanjuro (1962)

Tsvet Granata *See* The Color of Pomegranates (1969)

Tudor Rose *See* Nine Days a Queen (1936)

Tueur de Ch Icago *See* Scarface Mob (1962)

Tulitkkutehtaan Tytto *See* The Match Factory Girl (1990)

The Tunnel *See* Transatlantic Tunnel (1935)

Tunnels *See* Criminal Act (1988)

Turkey Shoot *See* Escape 2000 (1981)

Turn Your Pony Around *See* Mortal Danger (1994)

Turnaround *See* The Big Turnaround (1988)

Turtle Beach *See* The Killing Beach (1992)

Tuzolto utca 25 *See* 25 Fireman's Street (1973)

Twee Vrouwen *See* Twice a Woman (1979)

Twelve Miles Out *See* The Second Woman (1951)

Twenty-One Days Together *See* 21 Days (1937)

Twenty Twelve *See* 2012 (2009)

2012 : Supernova *See* Supernova (2009)

24 Hours *See* Trapped (2002)

Twice Bitten *See* The Vampire Hookers (1978)

Twilight: New Moon *See* The Twilight Saga: New Moon (2009)

Twilight of the Dead *See* Gates of Hell (1980)

Twinkle, Twinkle, Killer Kane *See* The Ninth Configuration (1979)

Twinky *See* Lola (1969)

The Twins Effect *See* Vampire Effect (2003)

Twins of Dracula *See* Twins of Evil (1971)

Twist of Fate *See* Psychopath (1997)

Twisted *See* Medusa (1974)

The Twisted Road *See* They Live by Night (1949)

Two Champions of Death *See* Sword Masters: Two Champions of Shaolin (1980)

Two Champions of Shaolin *See* Sword Masters: Two Champions of Shaolin (1980)

2 Cries in the Night *See* Funeral Home (1982)

Two Guys Talkin' About Girls *See* At First Sight (1995)

The Two-Headed Monster *See* The Manster (1959)

Two If By Sea *See* Stolen Hearts (1995)

Two Minds for Murder *See* Someone Behind the Door (1971)

2 S.I.C.K. (Serial Insane Clown Killer) *See* Mr. Jingles (2006)

2002: The Rape of Eden *See* Bounty Hunter 2002 (1994)

Two Weeks in September *See* A Coeur Joie (1967)

2BPerfectlyHonest *See* 2B Perfectly Honest (2004)

Tyler Perry's Daddy's Little Girls *See* Daddy's Little Girls (2007)

Tyler Perry's I Can Do Bad All By Myself *See* I Can Do Bad All By Myself (2009)

Tyler Perry's Madea Goes to Jail *See* Madea Goes to Jail (2009)

Tyler Perry's The Family That Preys *See* The Family That Preys (2008)

Tystnaden *See* The Silence (1963)

Tyubeu *See* Tube (2003)

U-Boat *See* In Enemy Hands (2004)

U-Boat 29 *See* Spy in Black (1939)

U-238 and the Witch Doctor *See* Jungle Drums of Africa (1953)

Uccellacci e Uccellini *See* The Hawks & the Sparrows (1967)

Uccidero Un Uomo *See* This Man Must Die (1970)

Uchu Daikaiiju Dogora *See* Dagora, the Space Monster (1965)

Uchudai Dogorá *See* Dagora, the Space Monster (1965)

Uchujin Tokyo Ni Arawaru *See* Warning from Space (1956)

Ugetsu Monogatari *See* Ugetsu (1953)

Ugly, Dirty and Bad *See* Down & Dirty (1976)

Ukigusa *See* Drifting Weeds (1959)

Ulisse *See* Ulysses (1955)

The Ultimate Chase *See* The Ultimate Thrill (1974)

Ultimate Desires *See* Beyond the Silhouette (1990)

The Ultimate Solution of Grace Quigley *See* Grace Quigley (1984)

Ultimi Giorni di Pompeii *See* The Last Days of Pompeii (1960)

L'Ultimo Tango a Parigi *See* Last Tango in Paris (1973)

L'Ultimo Treno della Notte *See* Night Train Murders (1975)

Ultra Force *See* Royal Warriors (1986)

Umarete Wa Mita Keredo *See* I Was Born But… (1932)

The Umbrella Woman *See* The Good Wife (1986)

Umi wa miteita *See* The Sea is Watching (2002)

Un Amour De Swann *See* Swann in Love (1984)

Un Amour En Allemagne *See* A Love in Germany (1984)

Un Angelo e Sceso a Brooklyn *See* The Man Who Wagged His Tail (1957)

Un Angelo per Satan *See* An Angel for Satan (1966)

Un Ano Perdido *See* A Lost Year (1993)

Un Ano Sin Amor *See* A Year Without Love (2005)

Un Arma de Dos Filos *See* Shark! (1968)

Un Autre Homme, Une Autre Chance *See* Another Man, Another Chance (1977)

Un Baiser S'il Vous Plait? *See* Shall We Kiss? (2007)

Un Chapeau de Paille d'Italie *See* Italian Straw Hat (1927)

Un Complicato Intrigo Di Donne, Vicoli E Delitti *See* Camorra: The Naples Connection (1985)

Un Condamne a Mort s'est Echappe, Ou le Vent Souffle ou il Vent *See* A Man Escaped (1957)

Un Conte de Noel *See* A Christmas Tale (2008)

Un, Deux, Trois, Quatre! *See* Black Tights (1960)

Un dia sin mexicanos *See* A Day Without a Mexican (2004)

Un Dimanche a la Campagne *See* A Sunday in the Country (1984)

Un Divan a New York *See* A Couch in New York (1995)

Un Dollar Troue *See* Blood for a Silver Dollar (1966)

Un Elephant a Trompe Enormement *See* Pardon Mon Affaire (1976)

Un Grand Amour de Beethoven *See* Beethoven (1936)

Un Heros Tres Discret *See* A Self-Made Hero (1995)

Un Hombre vino a matar *See* Rattler Kid (1968)

Un Homme Amoureux *See* A Man in Love (1987)

Un Homme Est Mort *See* The Outside Man (1973)

Un Homme et Un Femme *See* A Man and a Woman (1966)

Un Homme Et Une Femme: Vingt Ans Deja *See* A Man and a Woman: 20 Years Later (1986)

Un Indien dans la Ville *See* Little Indian, Big City (1995)

Un long dimanche de fiancailles *See* A Very Long Engagement (2004)

Un Minuto Per Pregare, Un Istante Per Morire *See* A Minute to Pray, a Second to Die (1967)

Un monde presque paisible *See* Almost Peaceful (2002)

Un Paraiso Bajo las Estrellas *See* A Paradise Under the Stars (1999)

Un Partie de Plaisir *See* A Piece of Pleasure (1974)

Un Prophete *See* A Prophet (2009)

Un Senor Muy Viejo Con Unas Alas Enormes *See* A Very Old Man with Enormous Wings (1988)

Un Tipo con Una Faccia Strana ti Cerca per Ucciderti *See* Mean Machine (1973)

Un Trem Para as Estrelas *See* Subway to the Stars (1987)

Un Uomo da Rispettare *See* Master Touch (1974)

Un Week-end sur Deux *See* Every Other Weekend (1991)

Un Zoo, La Nuit *See* Night Zoo (1987)

Una Bruja Sin Escoba *See* A Witch Without a Broom (1968)

Una Giornata Speciale *See* A Special Day (1977)

Una Hacha para la Luna de Miel *See* Hatchet for the Honeymoon (1970)

Una Lucertola con la Pelle di Donna *See* A Lizard in a Woman's Skin (1971)

Una Pura Formalita *See* A Pure Formality (1994)

Una Ragione Per Vivere e Una Per Morire *See* A Reason to Live, a Reason to Die (1973)

Una Sombra Ya Pronto Seras *See* A Shadow You Soon Will Be (1994)

Unagi *See* The Eel (1996)

Unakrsna Vatra *See* Operation Cross Eagles (1969)

Uncle Harry *See* The Strange Affair of Uncle Harry (1945)

Uncle Silas *See* Inheritance (1947)

Unconventional Linda *See* Holiday (1938)

Undead Pool *See* Attack Girls' Swim Team vs. the Undead (2007)

Under California Skies *See* Under California Stars (1948)

Under Heaven *See* In the Shadows (1998)

Under Siege *See* Hostages (1980)

Under Solen *See* Under the Sun (1998)

Under the Banner of Samurai *See* Samurai Banners (1969)

Under the Clock *See* The Clock (1945)

Under the Olive Trees *See* Through the Olive Trees (1994)

Under the Sun of Satan *See* Under Satan's Sun (1987)

Underground *See* The Lower Depths (1936)

An Underwater Odyssey *See* Neptune Factor (1973)

Underworld *See* Transmutations (1985)

Underworld After Dark *See* Big Town After Dark (1947)

Une Affaire de Femmes *See* The Story of Women (1988)

Une Femme a sa Fentre *See* A Woman at Her Window (1977)

Une Femme de Menage *See* The Housekeeper (2002)

Une Femme Douce *See* A Gentle Woman (1969)

Une Femme Est une Femme *See* A Woman Is a Woman (1960)

Une Femme Fidele *See* Game of Seduction (1976)

Une Femme ou Deux *See* One Woman or Two (1985)

Une Hirondelle a Fait le Printemps *See* The Girl from Paris (2002)

Une Histoire Simple *See* A Simple Story (1979)

Une Liaison d'Amour *See* An Affair of Love (1999)

Une Liaison Pornographique *See* An Affair of Love (1999)

Une Noire de... *See* Black Girl (1966)

Une Partie de Campagne *See* A Day in the Country (1946)

Une Pure Formalite *See* A Pure Formality (1994)

The Unfaithful Wife *See* La Femme Infidele (1969)

The Ungodly *See* The Perfect Witness (2007)

U.S. SEALs 3: Frogmen *See* U.S. SEALs: Dead or Alive (2002)

U.S. Vice *See* Black Heat (1976)

The Unknown *See* Clawed: The Legend of Sasquatch (2005)

Unknown Satellite Over Tokyo *See* Warning from Space (1956)

The Unnamable Returns *See* The Unnamable 2: The Statement of Randolph Carter (1992)

Unseen Evil 2 *See* Alien 3000 (2004)

Untel Pere et Fils *See* Heart of a Nation (1943)

Unter dem Pflaster Ist der Strand *See* Under the Pavement Lies the Strand (1975)

Unterm Birnbaum *See* Under the Pear Tree (1973)

The Untold *See* Sasquatch (2002)

The Untold Story: Human Meat Roast Pork Buns *See* The Untold Story (1993)

The Unvanquished *See* Aparajito (1958)

Uomini Uomini Uomini *See* Men Men Men (1995)

Uomo Dalla Pelle Dura *See* Counter Punch (1971)

L'Uomo delle Stelle *See* The Star Maker (1995)

Up Frankenstein *See* Andy Warhol's Frankenstein (1974)

Up in Smoke *See* Cheech and Chong's Up in Smoke (1979)

Up in the Cellar *See* Three in the Cellar (1970)

Up 'n Coming *See* Cassie (1983)

Up the Chastity Belt *See* Naughty Knights (1971)

Up to a Point *See* Up to a Certain Point (1983)

The Upstate Murders *See* Savage Weekend (1980)

Urban Justice *See* Under Oath (1997)

Urga *See* Close to Eden (1990)

Ursus *See* Ursus in the Valley of the Lions (1962)

The Usual Unidentified Thieves *See* Big Deal on Madonna Street (1958)

Utamaro O Meguru Gonin No Onna *See* Utamaro and His Five Women (1946)

Utvandrarna *See* The Emigrants (1972)

Uvidet Parizh i Umeret *See* To See Paris and Die (1993)

Vacation *See* National Lampoon's Vacation (1983)

Vagabond Violinist *See* Broken Melody (1934)

Vaghe Stelle Dell'Orsa *See* Sandra of a Thousand Delights (1965)

Valborgmassoafton *See* Walpurgis Night (1941)

The Valdez Horses *See* Chino (1975)

Valdez the Half Breed *See* Chino (1975)

Vale Abraao *See* Abraham's Valley (1993)

Valentine's Day *See* Protector (1997)

Valley of Abraham *See* Abraham's Valley (1993)

Valley of Fear *See* Sherlock Holmes and the Deadly Necklace (1962)

Valley of the Swords *See* The Castilian (1963)

Vals in Bashir *See* Waltz with Bashir (2008)

The Vampire *See* Vampyr (1931)

The Vampire and the Robot *See* My Son, the Vampire (1952)

The Vampire-Beast Craves Blood *See* Blood Beast Terror (1967)

Vampire Castle *See* Captain Kronos: Vampire Hunter (1974)

Vampire Conspiracy *See* Vampire Centerfolds (1998)

Vampire Hunters *See* Tsui Hark's Vampire Hunters (2002)

Vampire Men of the Lost Planet *See* Horror of the Blood Monsters (1970)

Vampire Orgy *See* Vampyres (1974)

Vampire Over London *See* My Son, the Vampire (1952)

Vampire Playgirls *See* Dracula's Great Love (1972)

Vampires *See* John Carpenter's Vampires (1997)

The Vampire's Assistant *See* Cirque du Freak: The Vampire's Assistant (2009)

Vampires: Los Muertos *See* John Carpenter Presents Vampires: Los Muertos (2002)

The Vampire's Niece *See* Fangs of the Living Dead (1968)

Vampire's Night Orgy *See* Orgy of the Vampires (1973)

Vampires of Prague *See* Mark of the Vampire (1935)

Vampire's Thirst *See* The Body Beneath (1970)

Vampyr, Der Traum des David Gray *See* Vampyr (1931)

Vampyr, Ou l'Etrange Aventure de David Gray *See* Vampyr (1931)

Vampyres, Daughters of Dracula *See* Vampyres (1974)

Van Wilder *See* National Lampoon's Van Wilder (2002)

Van Wilder 2: The Rise of Taj *See* National Lampoon's Van Wilder 2: The Rise of Taj (2006)

Vanishing Body *See* The Black Cat (1934)

Vargtimmen *See* Hour of the Wolf (1968)

Variete *See* Variety (1925)

The Varrow Mission *See* Teen Alien (1978)

Vasectomy *See* Vasectomy: A Delicate Matter (1986)

Vaudeville *See* Variety (1925)

V.C. Andrews' Rain *See* Rain (2006)

Vegas, Baby *See* Bachelor Party Vegas (2005)

The Veil *See* Haunts (1977)

Veillees d'armes *See* The Troubles We've Seen (1994)

Velka voda *See* The Great Water (2004)

Velocity *See* The Wild Ride (1960)

The Velocity of Gary* (*Not His Real Name) *See* The Velocity of Gary (1998)

Velvet House *See* Crucible of Horror (1969)

Vendetta: Secrets of a Mafia Bride *See* A Family Matter (1991)

A Vendre *See* For Sale (1998)

Vendredi Soir *See* Friday Night (2002)

Venere Imperiale *See* Imperial Venus (1963)

Vengeance *See* The Brain (1962)

Vengeance of a Soldier *See* Soldier's Revenge (1984)

Vengeance One by One *See* Old Gun (1976)

Vengeance: The Demon *See* Pumpkinhead (1988)

Vengeance: The Story of Tony Cimo *See* Vengeance (1989)

The Vengeful Dead *See* Kiss Daddy Goodbye (1981)

Venice *See* Dangerous Beauty (1998)

Venkovsky Ucitel *See* The Country Teacher (2008)

Venus in Peltz *See* Venus in Furs (1970)

The Venusian *See* The Stranger from Venus (1954)

Vercingetorix *See* Druids (2001)

Verdi *See* Life of Verdi (1982)

The Veritas Project: Hangman's Curse *See* Hangman's Curse (2003)

Vers le Sud *See* Heading South (2005)

A Very Big Weekend *See* A Man, a Woman, and a Bank (1979)

A Very Cool Christmas *See* Too Cool for Christmas (2004)

A Very Discreet Hero *See* A Self-Made Hero (1995)

Vesnicko Ma Strediskova *See* My Sweet Little Village (1986)

Vessel of Wrath *See* Beachcomber (1938)

The Veteran *See* Deathdream (1972)

Viagem ao Principio do Mundo *See* Voyage to the Beginning of the World (1996)

Viaggio in Italia *See* Voyage to Italy (1953)

Viaje Fantastico en Globo *See* Fantastic Balloon Voyage (1976)

The Vicious Circle *See* Woman in Brown (1948)

Victims of the Beyond *See* Sucker Money (1934)

Viehjud Levi *See* Jew-Boy Levi (1999)

The Vienna Strangler *See* The Mad Butcher (1972)

Vig *See* Money Kings (1998)

Viking Massacre *See* Knives of the Avenger (1965)

Viktor Vogel: Commercial Artist *See* Advertising Rules! (2001)

Vincent, Francois, Paul et les Autres *See* Vincent, Francois, Paul and the Others (1976)

Vindicator *See* Wheels of Fire (1984)

Violated *See* Party Girls for Sale (1954)

Violence et Passion *See* Conversation Piece (1975)

Violent City *See* The Family (1970)

Violent Journey *See* The Fool Killer (1965)

Violent Midnight *See* Psychomania (1963)

Violent Rage *See* Fearmaker (1971)

Violent Streets *See* Thief (1981)

Violette Noziere *See* Violette (1978)

Viperes *See* Posers (2002)

Virgin Hunters *See* Test Tube Teens from the Year 2000 (1993)

The Virgin Vampires *See* Twins of Evil (1971)

The Virgin Wife *See* You've Got to Have Heart (1977)

The Virtuous Tramps *See* The Devil's Brother (1933)

Virus *See* Cannibal Apocalypse (1980)

Virus Undead *See* Beast Within (2008)

Viskingar Och Rop *See* Cries and Whispers (1972)

Vita Privata *See* A Very Private Affair (1962)

Vital Parts *See* Harold Robbins' Body Parts (1999)

Vitelloni *See* I Vitelloni (1953)

Viva Las Nowhere *See* Dead Simple (2001)

Vivement Dimanche! *See* Confidentially Yours (1983)

The Vivero Letter *See* Forgotten City (1998)

Vivi O, Prefeibilmente, Morti *See* Sundance and the Kid (1969)

Viviamo Oggi *See* The Day and the Hour (1963)

Vivid *See* Luscious (1997)

Vivo per la Tua Morte *See* A Long Ride From Hell (1968)

Vivre Sa Vie *See* My Life to Live (1962)

The Vixen *See* The Women (1968)

Vixens *See* Supervixens (1975)

Vlci Jama *See* Wolf Trap (1957)

Voces inocentes *See* Innocent Voices (2004)

Voci dal Profondo *See* Voices from Beyond (1990)

Vogues *See* Vogues of 1938 (1937)

Voices *See* Voices from a Locked Room (1995)

Voleurs de Chevaux *See* In the Arms of My Enemy (2007)

Voodoo Blood Bath *See* I Eat Your Skin (1964)

Voor een Verloren Soldaat *See* For a Lost Soldier (1993)

Vor *See* The Thief (1997)

Voros Fold *See* Red Earth (1982)

Vortex *See* Day Time Ended (1980)

Voskhozhdeniye *See* The Ascent (1976)

Voyage beyond the Sun *See* Space Monster (1964)

Voyage to a Prehistoric Planet *See* Voyage to the Prehistoric Planet (1965)

Voyage to Italy *See* Voyage in Italy (1953)

Vrazda Po Cesky *See* Murder Czech Style (1966)

Vredens Dag *See* Day of Wrath (1943)

Vsichni Moji Blizci *See* All My Loved Ones (2000)

Vudu Sangriento *See* Voodoo Black Exorcist (1973)

Vulcan, Son of Jupiter *See* Vulcan God of Fire (1962)

Vzlomschik *See* Burglar (1987)

W Pustyni I W Puszczy *See* In Desert and Wilderness (2001)

Wages of Fear *See* Sorcerer (1977)

Waiting Women *See* Secrets of Women (1952)

Wajda: Czlowiek Z Zelaza *See* Man of Iron (1981)

The Waking Hour *See* The Velvet Vampire (1971)

Wakusei daikaiju Negadon *See* Negadon: The Monster from Mars (2005)

Waldo Warren: Private Dick Without a Brain *See* Maximum Thrust (1988)

Walkers on the Tiger's Tail *See* The Men Who Tread on the Tiger's Tail (1945)

Wandafuru Raifu *See* After Life (1998)

Wang jiao ka men *See* As Tears Go By (1988)

The Wannabes *See* Criminal Ways (2003)

Wannseekonferenz *See* The Wannsee Conference (1984)

Want a Ride, Little Girl? *See* Impulse (1974)

Wanted *See* Crime Spree (2003)

Wanted Women *See* Jessi's Girls (1975)

The Wanton Contessa *See* Senso (1954)

War Between the Planets *See* Planet on the Prowl (1965)

War Games *See* Suppose They Gave a War and Nobody Came? (1970)

The War Is Over *See* La Guerre Est Finie (1966)

The War of the Monsters *See* Gamera vs. Barugon (1966)

War of the Monsters *See* Godzilla vs. Monster Zero (1968)

War of the Planets *See* Cosmos: War of the Planets (1980)

War of the Robots *See* Reactor (1978)

War Shock *See* Battle Shock (1956)

Ward 13 *See* Hospital Massacre (1981)

Warlock *See* Skullduggery (1979)

The Warm-Blooded Spy *See* Ravishing Idiot (1964)

Warnung Vor Einer Helligen Nutte *See* Beware of a Holy Whore (1970)

Warrior *See* Mexican Blow (2002)

The Warrior of Waverly Street *See* Star Kid (1997)

The Warrior Princess *See* The Warrior (2001)

Warrior's Rest *See* Le Repos du Guerrier (1962)

Waru Yatsu Hodo Yoku Nemuru *See* The Bad Sleep Well (1960)

Warum Lauft Herr R Amok? *See* Why Does Herr R. Run Amok? (1969)

Was Tun, Wenn's Brennt? *See* What to Do in Case of Fire (2002)

Washington, B.C. *See* Hail (1973)

Watch That Man *See* The Man Who Knew Too Little (1997)

Watchtower *See* Cruel and Unusual (2001)

Water Child *See* L'Enfant d'Eau (1995)

Water Cyborgs *See* Terror Beneath the Sea (1966)

The Watts Monster *See* Dr. Black, Mr. Hyde (1976)

The Way *See* Yol (1982)

The Way Ahead *See* Immortal Battalion (1944)

The Way of Life *See* They Call It Sin (1932)

The Way We Are *See* Quiet Days in Hollywood (1997)

Ways of Love *See* The Miracle (1948)

WAZ *See* The Killing Gene (2007)

We Met on the Vineyard *See* The Big Day (1999)

We Will All Meet in Paradise *See* Pardon Mon Affaire, Too! (1977)

Weapon *See* Cyborg Soldier (2008)

Wedding Bells *See* Royal Wedding (1951)

Wedding Breakfast *See* The Catered Affair (1956)

A Wedding for Bella *See* The Bread, My Sweet (2001)

Wednesday's Child *See* Family Life (1971)

Wee Geordie *See* Geordie (1955)

Week of the Killer *See* Cannibal Man (1971)

Weekend Babysitter *See* Weekend with the Babysitter (1970)

Welcome Home Brother Charles *See* Soul Vengeance (1975)

Welcome to Jericho *See* Last Man Standing (1996)

Welcome to Oblivion *See* Ultra Warrior (1992)

Welcome to Planet Earth *See* Alien Avengers (1996)

The Well-Made Marriage *See* Le Beau Mariage (1982)

Wendy Cracked a Walnut *See* ...Almost (1990)

We're in the Army Now *See* Pack Up Your Troubles (1932)

The Werewolf and the Yeti *See* Night of the Howling Beast (1975)

Werewolf Warrior *See* Kibakichi (2004)

Werewolf Woman *See* The Legend of the Wolf Woman (1977)

Wes Craven Presents Carnival of Souls *See* Carnival of Souls (1998)

Wes Craven Presents: Don't Look Down *See* Don't Look Down (1998)

Wes Craven Presents Dracula 2: Ascension *See* Dracula 2: Ascension (2003)

Wes Craven Presents: Dracula 2000 *See* Dracula 2000 (2000)

Wes Craven Presents Wishmaster *See* Wishmaster (1997)

West Beyrouth *See* West Beirut (1998)

West of the Badlands *See* The Border Legion (1940)

West of the Brazos *See* Rangeland Empire (1950)

The Westing Game *See* Get a Clue! (1998)

Whare Are Those Strange Drops of Blood on the Body of Jennifer? *See* The Case of the Bloody Iris (1972)

What *See* The Whip and the Body (1963)

What? *See* Diary of Forbidden Dreams (1973)

What a Chassis! *See* Belle Americaine (1961)

What a Drag *See* Pedale Douce (1996)

What a Man *See* Never Give a Sucker an Even Break (1941)

What Changed Charley Farthing *See* Bananas Boat (1978)

What Ever Happened to Baby Jane *See* What Ever Happened To... (1993)

What Happened to Tully *See* Tully (2000)

What Lola Wants *See* Damn Yankees (1958)

What the Swedish Butler Saw *See* A Man with a Maid (1973)

What We Did That Night *See* Murder at Devil's Glen (1999)

The Wheel *See* La Roue (1923)

The Wheelchair *See* El Cochecito (1960)

Wheels of Terror *See* The Misfit Brigade (1987)

When Knighthood Was in Flower *See* The Sword & the Rose (1953)

When Michael Calls *See* Shattered Silence (1971)

When the Girls Meet the Boys *See* Girl Crazy (1943)

When the Raven Flies *See* Revenge of the Barbarians (1985)

When Youth Conspires *See* Old Swimmin' Hole (1940)

Where is the Friend's Home? *See* Where Is My Friend's House? (1987)

Where the Hell's the Gold? *See* Dynamite and Gold (1988)

Where the River Bends *See* Bend of the River (1952)

While Plucking the Daisy *See* Plucking the Daisy (1956)

While the Children Sleep *See* The Sitter (2007)

The Whipping Boy *See* Prince Brat and the Whipping Boy (1995)

Whispering Corridors 3 *See* The Wishing Stairs (2003)

Whispering Corridors 5: Suicide Pact *See* Blood Pledge (2009)

White *See* Trois Couleurs: Blanc (1994)

White Paws *See* Pattes Blanches (1949)

The White River Kid *See* White River (1999)

White Room *See* Unborn but Forgotten (2002)

White Trash on Moonshine Mountain *See* Moonshine Mountain (1964)

A White White Boy *See* The Mirror (1975)

Whiteboys *See* White Boyz (1999)

Who? *See* Roboman (1975)

Who Am I *See* Jackie Chan's Who Am I (1998)

Who Dares Wins *See* The Final Option (1982)

Who Fears the Devil *See* The Legend of Hillbilly John (1973)

Who Is Killing the Stuntman *See* Stunts (1977)

Who Killed Atlanta's Children? *See* Echo of Murder (2000)

Who Knows? *See* Va Savoir (2001)

Who Murdered Joy Morgan? *See* Killjoy (1981)

Who Shot Patakango? *See* Who Shot Pat? (1992)

Whoever Slew Auntie Roo? *See* Who Slew Auntie Roo? (1971)

The Who's Tommy *See* Tommy (1975)

Why Did I Get Married? *See* Tyler Perry's Why Did I Get Married? (2007)

Why Did I Get Married Too *See* Tyler Perry's Why Did I Get Married Too? (2010)

Why Not? *See* Eijanaika (1981)

The Wicked Caresses of Satan *See* Devil's Kiss (1975)

Wicked Wife *See* Grand National Night (1953)

Wide-Eyed and Legless *See* The Wedding Gift (1993)

The Widow and the Gigolo *See* Roman Spring of Mrs. Stone (1961)

Wilbur Falls *See* Dead Silence (1998)

Wild Beds *See* Tigers in Lipstick (1980)

Wild Drifters *See* Cockfighter (1974)

Wild Flower *See* Fiorile (1993)

Wild Flower *See* Flor Silvestre (1958)

Wild Flowers *See* Wildflowers (1999)

Wild for Kicks *See* Beat Girl (1960)

Wild Geese *See* Mistress (1953)

Wild Horse Mesa *See* When the West Was Young (1932)

Wild Horses of Fire *See* Shadows of Forgotten Ancestors (1964)

The Wild McCullochs *See* The McCullochs (1975)

Wild Oats *See* The Errors of Youth (1978)

The Wild Pack *See* Defiant (1970)

The Wild Side *See* Suburbia (1983)

Wild Weed *See* She Shoulda Said No (1949)

Wild West Comedy Show *See* Vince Vaughn's Wild West Comedy Show (2006)

Wild Youth *See* Naked Youth (1959)

Wildcat *See* Great Scout & Cathouse Thursday (1976)

Wildchild 2 *See* Silk 'n' Sabotage (1994)

Wilderness Family, Part 2 *See* Further Adventures of the Wilderness Family, Part 2 (1977)

A Wilderness Station *See* Edge of Madness (2002)

William Shakespeare's The Merchant of Venice *See* The Merchant of Venice (2004)

Youth Takes a Hand *See* Behind Prison Walls (1943)

Yukinojo Henge *See* An Actor's Revenge (1963)

Yume *See* Akira Kurosawa's Dreams (1990)

Yun pei dung lung *See* Human Lanterns (1982)

Yup-Yup Man *See* Dark Justice (2000)

Zaat *See* Attack of the Swamp Creature (1975)

Zabudnite na Mozarta *See* Forget Mozart (1985)

Zambo, King of the Jungle *See* Jungle Inferno (1972)

Zamri Oumi Voskresni *See* Freeze-Die-Come to Life (1990)

Zanan Bedoone Mardan *See* Women Without Men (2009)

Zankoku Hoten *See* Cruel Restaurant (2008)

Zato Ichi To Yojimbo *See* Zatoichi vs. Yojimbo (1970)

Zatoichi and the Fugitives *See* Zatoichi: The Blind Swordsman and the Fugitives (1968)

Zatoichi Meets Yojimbo *See* Zatoichi vs. Yojimbo (1970)

Zatoichi's Vengeance *See* Zatoichi: The Blind Swordsman's Vengeance (1966)

Zayn Vaybs Lubovnik *See* His Wife's Lover (1931)

Zazie in the Subway *See* Zazie dans le Metro (1961)

Zazie in the Underground *See* Zazie dans le Metro (1961)

Zeburaman *See* Zebraman (2004)

Zeder: Voices from Beyond *See* Zeder (1983)

Zee & Co. *See* X, Y & Zee (1972)

Zeiram *See* Zeram (1991)

Zeiram 2 *See* Zeram 2 (1994)

Zeiramu *See* Zeram (1991)

Zeiramu *See* Zeram 2 (1994)

Zeisters *See* Fat Guy Goes Nutzoid (1986)

Zemlya *See* Earth (1930)

Zendegi Va Digar Hich ...*See* Life and Nothing More ...(1992)

Zerkalo *See* The Mirror (1975)

Zero de Conduit *See* Zero for Conduct (1933)

Zero Kelvin *See* Zero Degrees Kelvin (1995)

Zhaibian *See* The Heirloom (2005)

Zhifu *See* Uniform (2003)

Zhing hua jing hua *See* China Heat (1990)

Zhong Nan Hai Bao Biao *See* The Body-guard from Beijing (1994)

Zhou Yu de Huoche *See* Zhou Yu's Train (2002)

Zi Hudie *See* Purple Butterfly (2003)

Ziemia Obiecana *See* Land of Promise (1974)

Zigs *See* Double Down (2001)

Zire Darakhtan Zeyton *See* Through the Olive Trees (1994)

Zits *See* Spy Trap (1988)

Zoku akutokui: Joi-hen *See* Madame O (1967)

Zoku shinobi no mono *See* Shinobi no Mono 2: Vengeance (1963)

Zombi *See* Dawn of the Dead (1978)

Zombi 2 *See* Zombie (1980)

Zombie *See* Dawn of the Dead (1978)

Zombie *See* I Eat Your Skin (1964)

Zombie 5 *See* Revenge in the House of Usher (1982)

Zombie Creeping Flesh *See* Hell of the Living Dead (1983)

Zombie Flesh-Eaters *See* Zombie (1980)

Zombie Holocaust *See* Doctor Butcher M.D. (1980)

Zombie ja Kummitusjuna *See* Zombie and the Ghost Train (1991)

Zombies *See* Dawn of the Dead (1978)

Zombies *See* I Eat Your Skin (1964)

Zong guo chhao ren *See* Super Inframan (1976)

Zong Heng Si Hai *See* Once a Thief (1990)

Zoot Suit Jesus *See* Greaser's Palace (1972)

Zormba *See* Zorba the Greek (1964)

Zorro *See* The Mask of Zorro (1998)

Z.P.G. *See* Zero Population Growth (1972)

Zubeko bancho: yume wa yoru hiraku *See* Delinquent Girl Boss: Blossoming Night Dreams (1970)

Zuckerbaby *See* Sugarbaby (1985)

Zuihaode Shiguang *See* Three Times (2005)

Zuo You *See* In Love We Trust (2007)

Zura Deka *See* The Rug Cop (2006)

Zwartboek *See* Black Book (2006)

Zycie Rodzinne *See* Family Life (1971)

A Coeur Joie ✗✗ *Two Weeks in September* **1967** Beautiful 30-something Cecile is married to a much older Englishman. She's content with her peaceful life until she meets a young man who rekindles her passions. Will Cecile run off with her new lover or stay with the man who makes her secure? French with subtitles. **96m/C VHS, DVD.** *GB FR* Brigitte Bardot, Laurent Terzieff, Jean Rochefort, James Robertson Justice, Michael Sarne, Murray Head; ***D:*** Serge Bourguignon; ***W:*** Serge Bourguignon, Pascal Jardin.

A. I.: Artificial Intelligence ✗✗ **2001 (PG-13)** Definitely an acquired taste—the uneasy melding of a long-cherished idea by late director Stanley Kubrick and the homage directed by Spielberg. Global warming has submerged the world's coastal cities but advanced humanoid robots, or "mechas," keep things going. Professor Hobby (Hurt) has made a child mecha, David (Osment), designed to be loving and extremely loyal—in this case to his human mother Monica (O'Connor) who eventually abandons him to the cruel wide world. Having heard the Pinocchio story, David (and his mecha bear Teddy) go in search of the Blue Fairy who can make David a "real" boy. Along the way, David meets mecha Gigolo Joe (Law), who profers good advice about the perfidity of human beings. It's long, it's dark, it's confusing, it's sometimes boring, and sometimes touching. Law's role is small but, as usual, Osment carries the picture. Based on the 1969 short story "Supertoys Last All Summer Long" by Brian Aldiss. **145m/C VHS, DVD.** *US* Haley Joel Osment, Jude Law, Frances O'Connor, Sam Robards, Brendan Gleeson, William Hurt, Jake Thomas, Clara Bellar, Enrico Colantoni, Adrian Grenier, Emmanuelle Chriqui; ***D:*** Steven Spielberg; ***W:*** Steven Spielberg; ***C:*** Janusz Kaminski; ***M:*** John Williams; ***V:*** Robin Williams, Chris Rock, Meryl Streep, Jack Angel; ***Nar:*** Ben Kingsley.

A la Mode ✗✗ ½ *In Fashion* **1994 (R)** It's Paris in the '60s as shy 17-year-old orphan Fausto (Higelin) is apprenticed to fatherly Jewish tailor Mietek (Yanne). But Fausto is transfixed by lovely mechanic Tonie (Darel) and decides what he really wants (besides the girl) is to design women's fashions. Very frothy coming-of-age tale, anchored by Yanne's veteran charm. Based on the novel "Fausto" by Richard Morgieve. French with subtitles. **89m/C VHS, DVD.** *FR* Ken Higelin, Jean Yanne, Florence Darel, Francois Hautesserre; ***D:*** Remy Duchemin; ***W:*** Remy Duchemin, Richard Morgieve; ***M:*** Denis Barbier.

A Lot Like Love ✗ **2005 (PG-13)** More like "A Lot Like a Million Other Disposable Romantic Comedies." On a plane from New York to L.A., shy Oliver (Kutcher) meets aggressive Emily (Peet), who goads Oliver into joining the Mile High Club and unceremoniously dumps him once they land, claiming that he's just not her type. Apparently the universe and the writers (who've obviously seen "When Harry Met Sally" a few times) disagree, because over the next seven years, Oliver and Emily's paths keep crossing, making them both wonder if they've found their true love. Kutcher and Peet do their best to fake on-screen chemistry, but instead come off as the poor man's Tom Hanks and Meg Ryan. **95m/C DVD.** *US* Ashton Kutcher, Amanda Peet, Kathryn Hahn, Kal Penn, Taryn Manning, James Read, Molly Cheek, Gabriel Mann, Ty(rone) Giordano, Aimee Garcia, Ali Larter, Amy Aquino, Jeremy Sisto, Holmes Osborne, Lee Garlington, Linda Hunt, Melissa van der Schyff; ***D:*** Nigel Cole; ***W:*** Colin Patrick Lynch; ***C:*** John de Borman; ***M:*** Alex Wurman.

A Nos Amours ✗✗✗ *To Our Loves* **1984 (R)** Craving the attention she is denied at home, a young French girl searches for love and affection from numerous boyfriends in hopes of eradicating her unhappy home. Occasional lapses in quality and slow pacing hamper an otherwise excellent effort. The characterization of the girl Suzanne is especially memorable. In French with English subtitles. **99m/C VHS, DVD.** *FR* Sandrine Bonnaire, Dominique Besnehard, Maurice Pialat, Evelyne Ker; ***D:*** Maurice Pialat; ***W:*** Arlette Langmann, Maurice Pialat; ***C:*** Jacques Loiseleux; ***M:*** Henry Purcell.

A Nous la Liberte ✗✗✗✗ *Freedom for Us* **1931** Two tramps encounter industrialization and automation, making one into a wealthy leader, the other into a nature-loving iconoclast. A poignant, fantastical masterpiece by Clair, made before he migrated to Hollywood. Though the view of automation may be dated, it influenced such films as Chaplin's "Modern Times." In French with English subtitles. **87m/B VHS, DVD.** *FR* Henri Marchand, Raymond Cordy, Rolla France, Paul Olivier, Jacques Shelly, Andre Michaud; ***D:*** Rene Clair; ***W:*** Rene Clair; ***C:*** Georges Perinal; ***M:*** Georges Auric.

A Propos de Nice ✗✗✗ *Nizza* **1929** First film by French director Vigo, the silent film parodies French travelogues in a manner that indicates the director's later brilliance. **25m/B VHS.** *FR* ***D:*** Jean Vigo; ***W:*** Jean Vigo; ***C:*** Boris Kaufman.

The A-Team 2010 The 1983-87 TV series takes its chances on the big screen, and its four members are now Iraq War vets. They still escape from a military prison after a false conviction to become do-gooder mercenaries though. Stephen J. Cannell, who created and produced the TV show, is a producer of the film version. **m/C DVD.** *US* Liam Neeson, Bradley Cooper, Sharlto Copley, Quinton 'Rampage' Jackson, Jessica Biel, Patrick Wilson, Brian Bloom, Gerald McRaney; ***Cameos:*** Dirk Benedict, Dwight Schultz; ***D:*** Joe Carnahan; ***W:*** Skip Woods, Michael Brandt, Derek Haas; ***C:*** Mauro Fiore; ***M:*** Alan Silvestri.

Aaron Loves Angela ✗✗ **1975 (R)** Puerto Rican girl falls in love with a black teen amidst the harsh realities of the Harlem ghetto. "Romeo and Juliet" meets "West Side Story" in a cliched comedy drama. **99m/C VHS.** Kevin Hooks, Irene Cara, Moses Gunn, Robert Hooks; ***Cameos:*** Jose Feliciano; ***D:*** Gordon Parks Jr.; ***C:*** Richard Kratina; ***M:*** Jose Feliciano.

Abandon ✗✗ ½ **2002 (PG-13)** "Traffic" screenwriter Stephen Gaghan makes his directorial debut in this psychological thriller that centers on bookworm college student Katie (Holmes) and her mysteriously missing boyfriend Embry (Hunnam). When police detective Wade (Bratt) arrives to question Katie two years after the disappearance of the eccentric Embry, she begins to see glimpses of him all over campus. The "twist" ending is fairly predictable, but the cast, particularly Union, Mann and Deschanel as Katie's classmates, get the most out of the script. Based on the book "Adam's Fall" by Sean Desmond. **99m/C VHS, DVD.** *US* Katie Holmes, Benjamin Bratt, Charlie Hunnam, Zooey Deschanel, Gabrielle Union, Gabriel Mann, Mark Feuerstein, Melanie Lynskey, Will McCormack, Philip Bosco, Tony Goldwyn, Fred Ward; ***D:*** Stephen Gaghan; ***W:*** Stephen Gaghan; ***C:*** Matthew Libatique; ***M:*** Clint Mansell.

Abandon Ship ✗✗ ½ *Seven Waves Away* **1957** A luxury liner hits a derelict mine and sinks within minutes, leaving 27 survivors clinging to one tiny lifeboat. Ship's officer Alex Holmes (Power) knows that the amount of food and water they have is limited, the waters are shark-infested, and the injured stand little chance, so he must decide who will survive. **97m/B VHS.** *GB* Tyrone Power, Mai Zetterling, Lloyd Nolan, Stephen Boyd, Moira Lister, James Hayter, Marie Lohr, Gordon Jackson, Laurence Naismith, John Stratton, Victor Maddern, Eddie Byrne, Noel Willman, Ralph Michael, David Langton, Ferdinand "Ferdy" Mayne, Austin Trevor, Finlay Currie, Jill Melford; ***D:*** Richard Sale; ***W:*** Richard Sale; ***C:*** Wilkie Cooper; ***M:*** Arthur Bliss.

Abandoned ✗ ½ *Abandoned Woman* **1947** A young woman goes missing in Los Angeles, and her sister starts searching. Turns out the missing girl had a baby—but the baby is nowhere to be found. The police are disinterested until a local crime reporter gets involved and winds up finding a shady detective and black market baby ring. **78m/B DVD.** Dennis O'Keefe, Gale Storm, Marjorie Rambeau, Raymond Burr, Will Kuluva, Jeff Chandler, Meg Randall, Jeannette Nolan; ***D:*** Joseph M. Newman; ***W:*** Irwin Gielgud, William Bowers.

The Abandoned ✗✗ **2006 (R)** Euro-horror. Marie and her twin brother Nicolai were abandoned as babies and only meet again when they must deal with their parents' abandoned farmhouse, located in a creepy Russian forest. The haunted house is the site of the 40-year-old murder of their mother, and the siblings soon find themselves trapped by ghostly images that want to recreate the past and make sure that this time they die. **99m/C DVD.** *BL SP* Anastasia Hille, Karel Roden, Valentin Ganev, Carlos Reig-Plaza; ***D:*** Nacho Cerda; ***W:*** Richard Stanley, Nacho Cerda, Karim Hussani; ***C:*** Xavi Gimenez; ***M:*** Alfons Conde.

Abbott and Costello Go to Mars 1/2 *On to Mars; Rocket and Roll* **1953** Poor parody of sci-fi films finds the frantic duo aboard a rocket ship and accidentally heading off into outer space. They don't land on Mars, but Venus, which is populated by lots of pretty women and no men. Even this duo looks good to the ladies. Cheapie production and uninspired buffoonery. **77m/B VHS, DVD.** Bud Abbott, Lou Costello, Mari Blanchard, Robert Paige, Martha Hyer, Horace McMahon, Jack Kruschen, Anita Ekberg, Jean Willes, Joe (Joseph) Kirk, Jackie Loughery, James Flavin; ***D:*** Charles Lamont; ***W:*** John Grant, D.D. Beauchamp; ***C:*** Clifford Stine; ***M:*** Joseph Gershenson.

Abbott and Costello in Hollywood *Bud Abbott and Lou Costello In Hollywood* **1945** Bud and Lou appear as a barber and porter of a high-class tonsorial parlor in Hollywood. A rather sarcastic look at backstage Hollywood, Abbott & Costello style. Ball makes a guest appearance. **111m/B VHS, DVD.** Bud Abbott, Lou Costello, Frances Rafferty, Warner Anderson, Jean Porter, Robert Stanton, Mike Mazurki; ***D:*** S. Sylvan Simon; ***M:*** George Bassman.

Abbott and Costello in the Foreign Legion 1/2 **1950** Fight promoters Jonesy and Max trail their runaway fighter to Algiers where they're tricked into joining the French Foreign Legion. They have to cope with a sadistic sergeant, a sexy spy, and still find their man. Most amusement comes from Lou's wild desert mirages. **80m/B VHS, DVD.** Bud Abbott, Lou Costello, Walter Slezak, Patricia Medina, Douglass Dumbrille, Leon Belasco, Marc Lawrence, Tor Johnson; ***D:*** Charles Lamont; ***W:*** John Grant, Martin Ragaway, Leonard Stern; ***C:*** George Robinson.

Abbott and Costello Meet Captain Kidd **1952** With pirates led by Captain Kidd on their trail, Abbott and Costello follow a treasure map. Bland A&C swashbuckler spoof with a disinterested Laughton impersonating the Kidd. One of the duo's few color films. **70m/C VHS.** Bud Abbott, Lou Costello, Charles Laughton, Hillary Brooke, Fran Warren, Bill (William) Shirley, Leif Erickson; ***D:*** Charles-Lamont.

Abbott and Costello Meet Dr. Jekyll and Mr. Hyde **1952** Slim (Abbott) and Tubby (Costello) are a couple of cops sent to London, who become involved with crazy Dr. Jekyll (Karloff), who has transformed himself into Mr. Hyde via an experimental serum, and is terrorizing London. Naturally, he goes after the boys. A lame attempt at recapturing the success of "Abbott and Costello Meet Frankenstein" but Karloff is top-notch as always. **77m/B VHS, DVD.** Bud Abbott, Lou Costello, Boris Karloff, Craig Stevens, Helen Westcott, Reginald Denny, John Dierkes, Marjorie Bennett, Lucille Lamarr, Patti McKay; ***D:*** Charles Lamont; ***W:*** John Grant, Leo Loeb, Howard Dimsdale; ***C:*** George Robinson.

Abbott and Costello Meet Frankenstein *Abbott and Costello Meet the Ghosts; Meet the Ghosts; The Brain of Frankenstein* **1948** Big-budget A&C classic is one of their best efforts and was rewarded handsomely at the boxoffice. Unsuspecting baggage clerks Chick (Abbott) and Wilbur (Costello) deliver a crate containing the last but not quite dead remains of Dracula (Lugosi) and Dr. Frankenstein's monster (Strange) to a wax museum. When Drac revives, he decides to replace the monster's brain with Wilbur's so he'll be easier to control. Chaney Jr. makes a special wolfish appearance to warn the boys that trouble looms. Last film to use the Universal creature pioneered by Karloff in 1931. **83m/B VHS, DVD.** Bud Abbott, Lou Costello, Lon Chaney Jr., Bela Lugosi, Glenn Strange, Lenore Aubert, Jane Randolph, Frank Ferguson, Charles Bradstreet, Howard Negley, Clarence Straight; ***D:*** Charles T. Barton; ***W:*** John Grant, Robert Lees, Frederic Rinaldo; ***C:*** Charles Van Enger; ***M:*** Frank Skinner; ***V:*** Vincent Price. Natl. Film Reg. '01.

Abbott and Costello Meet the Invisible Man **1951** Abbott and Costello play newly graduated detectives who take on the murder case of a boxer (Franz) accused of killing his manager. Using a serum that makes people invisible, the boxer helps Costello in a prizefight that will frame the real killers, who killed the manager because the boxer refused to throw a fight. Great special effects and hilarious gags make this one of the best from the crazy duo. **82m/B VHS, DVD.** Bud Abbott, Lou Costello, Nancy Guild, Adele Jergens, Sheldon Leonard, William Frawley, Gavin Muir, Arthur Franz, Syd Saylor, Bobby Barber; ***D:*** Charles Lamont; ***W:*** Frederic Rinaldo, John Grant, Robert Lees; ***C:*** George Robinson; ***M:*** Hans J. Salter.

Abbott and Costello Meet the Keystone Kops 1/2 **1954** It's 1912 and the boys are bilked into buying a fake movie studio by a clever con man. When they find out they've been tricked, the duo head to Hollywood to track him down and find out the crook is trying to cheat Sennett's film company. Sennett himself trained A&C and the new Keystone Kops in their recreations of his silent screen routines. Good final chase sequence but the earlier work is tired. **79m/B VHS, DVD.** Bud Abbott, Lou Costello, Fred Clark, Lynn Bari, Mack Sennett, Maxie "Slapsie" Rosenbloom, Frank Wilcox, Harold Goodwin; ***D:*** Charles Lamont; ***W:*** John Grant; ***C:*** Reggie Lanning; ***M:*** Joseph Gershenson.

Abbott and Costello Meet the Killer, Boris Karloff *Abbott and Costello Meet the Killer* **1949** Unremarkable Abbott and Costello murder mystery. Karloff plays a psychic who tries to frame Lou for murder. Pleasant enough but not one of their best. **84m/B VHS, DVD.** Bud Abbott, Lou Costello, Boris Karloff, Lenore Aubert, Gar Moore, Donna (Dona Martel) Martell, Alan Mowbray, James Flavin, Roland Winters, Nicholas Joy, Mikel Conrad, Morgan Farley, Victoria Horne; ***D:*** Charles T. Barton; ***W:*** John Grant, Hugh Wedlock Jr., Howard Snyder; ***C:*** Charles Van Enger; ***M:*** Milton Schwarzwald.

Abbott and Costello Meet the Mummy 1/2 **1955** Okay comedy from the duo has them stranded in Egypt with a valuable medallion which will lead to secret treasure and the mummy who guards the tomb. The last of the films the twosome made for Universal. **90m/B VHS, DVD.** Bud Abbott, Lou Costello, Marie Windsor, Michael Ansara, Dan Seymour, Kurt Katch, Richard Deacon, Mel Welles, Edwin Parker, Richard Karlan, George Khoury; ***D:*** Charles Lamont; ***W:*** John Grant; ***C:*** George Robinson; ***M:*** Joseph Gershenson, Hans J. Salter.

ABC Stage 67: Truman Capote's A Christmas Memory 1/2 *Truman Capote's A Christmas Memory; A Christmas Memory* **1966** Capote narrates his remembered childhood experience of baking dozens of fruitcakes for friends at Christmas with his elderly distant cousin, Miss Sook Faulk (Page). She is quiet, lovely, and true in this sensitive portrait of why we give and what we have to be thankful for. Adapted from a short story by Capote and Eleanor Perry. **51m/B VHS.** Geraldine Page, Donnie Melvin; ***D:*** Frank Perry; ***W:*** Truman Capote; ***Nar:*** Truman Capote. **TV**

ABCD 1/2 **1999** Touching story of an Asian Indian-American family living in New York. Siblings Raj and Nina have grown up in America, and have struggled with the competing pressures of their peers and their parent's old-world expectations. Their widowed mother wants them to settle down with suitable Indian spouse. Patel shows humor, and largely avoids stereotypes (although the mother ventures dangerously close), and the kids manage to be fully-realized characters. **102m/C VHS, DVD.** *US* Madhur Jaffrey, Faran Tahir, Sheetal Sheth, Aasif Mandvi, Adriane Forlana Erdos, Rex Young; ***D:*** Krutin Patel; ***W:*** Krutin Patel, James McManus; ***C:*** Milton Kam; ***M:*** Deirdre Broderick.

The Abdication 1/2 **1974** Unconvincing historical bio of Sweden's Queen Christina (Ullmann) who relinquishes her 17th-century throne after converting to Catholicism. She heads to Rome but rather than finding herself dedicated to God, Christina becomes more interested in Cardinal Azzolino (Finch). Wolff adapted from her play. Garbo did it much better in 1933's "Queen Christina." **102m/C DVD.** *GB* Peter Finch, Cyril Cusack, Graham Crowden, Michael Dunn, Liv Ullman, Kathleen Byron; ***D:*** Anthony Harvey; ***W:*** Ruth Wolff; ***C:*** Geoffrey Unsworth; ***M:*** Nino Rota.

Abducted 1/2 **1986 (PG)** A woman jogger is abducted by a crazed mountain man in the Canadian Rockies. Weird and unbelievably tedious film is nevertheless highlighted by some spectacular wilderness footage of the Vancouver area, a travelogue bonus for those in the mood. **87m/C VHS.** *CA* Dan Haggerty, Roberta Weiss, Lawrence King Phillips; ***D:*** Boon Collins.

Abducted 2: The Reunion 1/2 **1994 (R)** Three girlfriends decide to go camping for their reunion trip. Oops—psycho mountain man alert! **91m/C VHS.** Dan Haggerty, Jan-Michael Vincent, Donna Jason, Raquel Bianca, Debbie Rochon, Lawrence King; ***D:*** Boon Collins; ***W:*** Boon Collins; ***C:*** Danny Nowak.

Abduction 1/2 **1975 (R)** Exploitative account of the Patty Hearst kidnapping, loosely adapted from the Harrison James novel written before the kidnapping. A young woman from a wealthy capitalist family is kidnapped by black radicals and held for an unusual ransom. Oh, and she tangles with lesbians, too. **100m/C VHS.** Judith-Marie Bergan, David Pendleton, Gregory Rozakis, Leif Erickson, Dorothy Malone, Lawrence Tierney; ***D:*** Joseph Zito.

The Abduction 1/2 **1996** Fact-based melodrama about Kate Olavsky (Principal) and her abusive marriage to cop Paul (Hays). Afraid to press charges, she finally manages to leave him and get on with her life. But Paul refuses to let Kate go, constantly hounding her, until he takes Kate hostage at gunpoint. **91m/C VHS, DVD.** Victoria Principal, Robert Hays, Christopher Lawford, William Greenblatt; ***D:*** Larry Peerce; ***W:*** Marshall Goldberg; ***C:*** Tony Imi; ***M:*** Fred Mollin. **CABLE**

The Abduction of Allison Tate 1/2 **1992 (R)** Rich developer takes land belonging to a group of Native Americans. Three young tribe members retaliate by kidnapping the developer's daughter. But when their plans go awry and one of the trio is killed, Allison finds herself sympathizing more with them than with her father's ambitions. **95m/C VHS.** Leslie Hope, Bernie (Bernard) White; ***D:*** Paul Leder.

The Abduction of Kari Swenson 1/2 **1987** An account of the true-life (it really happened) kidnapping of Olympic biathalon hopeful Swensen by a pair of mischievous Montana mountain men with matrimony in mind. The movie details the abduction of Swenson by the scruffy father and son duo and the massive manhunt. As the put-upon Kari, Pollan exceeds script expectations in this exercise in stress avoidance. **100m/C VHS.** Joe Don Baker, M. Emmet Walsh, Ronny Cox, Michael Bowen, Geoffrey Blake, Dorothy Fielding, Tracy Pollan; ***D:*** Stephen Gyllenhaal. **TV**

Abduction of St. Anne **1975** An almost interesting mystical thriller about a detective and a bishop trying to track down a gangster's daughter, who may have nifty supernatural healing powers the Church would be very interested in having documented. **78m/C VHS.** Robert Wagner, E.G. Marshall, William Windom, Lloyd Nolan; ***D:*** Harry Falk; ***M:*** George Duning. **TV**

The Abductors **1972 (R)** Caffaro's super-agent takes on international white slavery, a worthy target for any exploitation effort. While the novelty is a tough and intelligent on-screen heroine, sufficient sleaze and violence bring it all down to the proper level of swampland video. Sequel to the never-to-be-forgotten "Ginger." **90m/C VHS, DVD.** Cheri Caffaro, William Grannel, Richard Smedley, Patrick Wright, Laurie Rose, Jeramie Rain; ***D:*** Don Schain; ***W:*** Don Schain; ***C:*** R. Kent Evans; ***M:*** Robert G. Orpin.

Abdulla the Great *Abdullah's Harem* **1956** A dissolute Middle Eastern monarch falls for a model, who spurns him for an army officer. While distracted by these royal shenanigans, the king is blissfully unaware of his subjects' disaffection—until they revolt. Dares to lampoon Egypt's dead King Farouk, going against conventional Hollywood wisdom ("Farouk in film is boxoffice poison"). **89m/C VHS.** *GB* Gregory Ratoff, Kay Kendall, Sydney Chaplin, Alexander D'Arcy; ***D:*** Gregory Ratoff; ***C:*** Lee Garmes; ***M:*** Georges Auric.

Abe Lincoln in Illinois *Spirit of the People* **1940** Massey considered this not only his finest film but a part he was "born to play." Correct on both counts, this Hollywood biography follows Lincoln from his log cabin days to his departure for the White House. The Lincoln-Douglass debate scene and Massey's post-presidential election farewell to the citizens of Illinois are nothing short of brilliant. Written by Sherwood from his Pulitzer-Prize winning play. Contrasted with the well-known "Young Mr. Lincoln" (Henry Fonda), its relative anonymity is perplexing. **110m/B VHS.** Raymond Massey, Gene Lockhart, Ruth Gordon, Mary Howard, Dorothy Tree, Harvey Stephens, Minor Watson, Alan Baxter, Howard da Silva, Maurice Murphy, Clem Bevans, Herbert Rudley; ***D:*** John Cromwell; ***W:*** Robert Sherwood; ***C:*** James Wong Howe; ***M:*** Roy Webb.

The Abe Lincoln of Ninth Avenue 1/2 *Streets of New York* **1939** All-American tale of a poor young man making good in New York. His role model is Abraham Lincoln. Cooper is exceptional, supported by effective performances by the rest of the cast. **68m/B VHS, DVD.** Jackie Cooper, Martin Spelling, Marjorie Reynolds, Dick Purcell, George Cleveland, George Irving; ***D:*** William Nigh.

Aberdeen **2000** Ambitious London attorney Kaisa (Headey) gets a call from her terminally ill mother Helen (Rampling), who lives in Aberdeen, Scotland. Helen wants Kaisa to travel to Oslo and retrieve Tomas (Skargard), her alcoholic and estranged father, so Helen and he can have a deathbed reconciliation. Assertive Kaisa tracks the drunk down and makes him come with her on a nightmare trip back. Lead performances are utterly unsentimental. **103m/C VHS, DVD.** *NO GB* Stellan Skarsgard, Lena Headey, Ian Hart, Charlotte Rampling; ***D:*** Hans Petter Moland; ***W:*** Hans Petter Moland, Kristin Amundsen; ***C:*** Philip Ogaard; ***M:*** Zbigniew Preisner.

Aberration **1997 (R)** Amy (Gidley) has traveled to her parents remote cabin and notices a lizard infestation. So she heads to the store for some exterminating equipment and meets biologist Marshall (Bossell), who studies eco-abnormalities. Seems the lizards are vicious mutants who eat Amy's cat and are working their way up the food chain. Doesn't offer many scares. **93m/C VHS.** *AU GB* Pamela Gidley, Simon Bossell, Valery (Valeri Nikolayev) Nikolaev; ***D:*** Tim Boxell; ***W:*** Darrin Oura, Scott Lew; ***C:*** Allen Guilford. **VIDEO**

Abigail's Party **1977** Steadman plays the hostess for a very ill-fated dinner party, especially when she realizes her husband has just died on her new carpet. **105m/C VHS, DVD.** *GB* Alison Steadman; ***D:*** Mike Leigh. **TV**

Abilene Town **1946** In a post-Civil War Kansas town far from the freeway, Scott is the tough marshal trying to calm the conflict between cattlemen and homesteaders. He also finds time to participate in a romantic triangle with dance hall vixen Dvorak and heart-of-gold Fleming. Snappy pace keeps it interesting. Based on a novel by Ernest Haycox. **90m/B VHS, DVD.** Randolph Scott, Ann Dvorak, Edgar Buchanan, Rhonda Fleming, Lloyd Bridges; ***D:*** Edwin L. Marin; ***W:*** Harold Shumate; ***C:*** Archie Stout.

Ablaze 1/2 **2000 (R)** Greedy developer Wendell Mays (Arnold) arranges for his industrial refinery to be torched and the ensuing fire and explosion taxes both the fire fighters and the hospital that has to deal with the casualties. Wynorski directs under the pseudonym Jay Andrews. **97m/C VHS, DVD.** John Bradley, Tom Arnold, Michael Dudikoff, Ice-T, Amanda Pays, Cathy Lee Crosby, Pat Harrington, Edward Albert, Mary Jo Catlett, Richard Biggs; ***D:*** Jim Wynorski; ***W:*** Steve Latshaw; ***C:*** Andrea V. Rossotto; ***M:*** Neal Acree. **VIDEO**

The Abominable Dr. Phibes 🦴🦴🦴 *Dr. Phibes; The Curse of Dr. Phibes* **1971 (PG)** After being disfigured in a freak car accident that killed his wife, an evil genius decides that the members of a surgical team let his wife die and shall each perish by a different biblical plague. High camp with the veteran cast in top form. **90m/C VHS, DVD.** *GB* Vincent Price, Joseph Cotten, Hugh Griffith, Terry-Thomas, Virginia North, Susan Travers, Alex Scott, Caroline Munro, Peter Jeffrey, Peter Gilmore, Edward Burnham, Sean Bury, David Hutcheson, Maurice Kaufmann, Charles Farrell; ***D:*** Robert Fuest; ***W:*** William Goldstein, James Whiton; ***C:*** Norman Warwick; ***M:*** Basil Kirchin, Jack Nathan.

The Abominable Snowman 🦴🦴 *The Abominable Snowman of the Himalayas* **1957** Corny Hammer horror about adventurer Tom Friend (Tucker), Dr. John Rollason (Cushing), and guide Ed Shelley (Brown) searching for the legandary Yeti. The harsh conditions cause the explorers to lose their grip and, after Shelley shoots a Yeti, Rollason begins to suspect that the creatures practice mind control. **91m/B VHS, DVD.** *GB* Peter Cushing, Forrest Tucker, Robert Brown, Richard Wattis, Maureen Connell; ***D:*** Val Guest; ***W:*** Nigel Kneale; ***C:*** Arthur Grant; ***M:*** Humphrey Searle.

The Abomination 🦴 **1988 (R)** After a 5,000-year-old creature possesses him during a nightmare, a boy goes on an eye-gouging frenzy. Only the audience gets hurt. **100m/C VHS.** Van Connery, Victoria Chaney, Gaye Bottoms, Suzy Meyer, Jude Johnson, Blue Thompson, Scott Davis; ***D:*** Max Raven.

About a Boy 🦴🦴🦴 **2002 (PG-13)** After "Bridget Jones's Diary," Grant continues to take on the role of charming cad. This time, he's Will, a 38-year-old bachelor who doesn't work thanks to a legacy from his father and has never made a lasting emotional commitment to anyone. Will's latest dating scheme is to pretend to be a single parent and join support groups so he can hit on the single mums. This is how he meets Marcus (Hoult), the 12-year-old misfit son of the seriously depressed Fiona (Collette). Will likes Marcus despite himself and becomes his confidante. And he finds a romance with single mum Rachel (Weitz) but that's almost besides the point. Adapted from the novel by Nick Hornby. **100m/C VHS, DVD.** *US GB* Hugh Grant, Rachel Weisz, Toni Collette, Nicholas Hoult, Isabel Brook, Victoria Smurfit; ***D:*** Chris Weitz, Paul Weitz; ***W:*** Chris Weitz, Paul Weitz, Peter Hedges; ***C:*** Remi Adefarasin; ***M:*** Badly Drawn Boy.

About Adam 🦴🦴 **2000 (R)** Adam (Townsend) is a duplicitous Dublin charmer who worms his way into the Owens family. Waitress Lucy (Hudson) falls in love with Adam and takes him to meet her family and before anyone realizes what's happening, Adam seduces both her sisters, telling each woman exactly what she needs to hear. And no one holds a grudge! **98m/C VHS, DVD.** *IR GB* Stuart Townsend, Kate Hudson, Frances O'Connor, Charlotte Bradley, Rosaleen Linehan, Brendan F. Dempsey, Alan Maher, Tommy Tiernan, Cathleen Bradley; ***D:*** Gerard Stembridge; ***W:*** Gerard Stembridge; ***C:*** Bruno de Keyzer; ***M:*** Adrian Johnston.

About Last Night... 🦴🦴🦴 **1986 (R)** Semi-realistic comedy-drama which explores the ups and downs of one couple's (Lowe, Moore) relationship. Mostly quality performances, especially Perkins and Belushi as friends of the young lovers. Based on David Mamet's play "Sexual Perversity in Chicago," but considerably softened so that more people would buy tickets at the boxoffice, the film acts as a historical view of contemporary mating rituals before the onset of the AIDS crisis. **113m/C VHS, DVD.** Rob Lowe, Demi Moore, Elizabeth Perkins, James Belushi, George DiCenzo, Robin Thomas, Michael Alldredge; ***D:*** Edward Zwick; ***W:*** Tim Kazurinsky, Denise DeClue; ***C:*** Andrew Dintenfass; ***M:*** Miles Goodman.

About Schmidt 🦴🦴🦴 ½ **2002 (R)** Jack's back and playing against type as Warren Schmidt, a man left with virtually no identity once he retires from his ho-hum insurance job. Left only with time to reflect on a meaningless life, he questions everything he once took for granted, including Helen (Squibb), his wife of 42 years. The day after his retirement, the couple shares breakfast before Helen suddenly dies. With nothing left to lose, Schmidt hits the road in a Winnebago to visit his daughter and try to find some meaning in his poorly thought-out life. In Denver, he meets and immediately hates his daughter's cheesy salesman fiance Randall (Mulroney), while Randall's flowsy mother Roberta (Bates) tries to seduce the lonely introvert in a hot tub. Combines humor, pathos, and hope with a first rate performance by Nicholson, who quashes any of his characteristic animation. Davis, Mulroney, and especially Bates are also excellent. **124m/C VHS, DVD.** *US* Jack Nicholson, Hope Davis, Dermot Mulroney, Kathy Bates, Len Cariou, Howard Hesseman, June Squibb; ***D:*** Alexander Payne; ***W:*** Alexander Payne, Jim Taylor; ***C:*** James Glennon; ***M:*** Rolfe Kent. Golden Globes '03: Actor—Drama (Nicholson), Screenplay; L.A. Film Critics '02: Actor (Nicholson), Film, Screenplay; Natl. Bd. of Review '02: Support. Actress (Bates).

Above and Beyond 🦴🦴🦴 **1953** Good performance by Taylor as Col. Paul Tibbets, the man who piloted the Enola Gay, which dropped the atomic bomb on Hiroshima. Focuses on the secrecy of the mission and the strain this puts on Tibbets marriage. Exciting action sequences of the mission itself. **122m/B VHS.** Robert Taylor, Eleanor Parker, James Whitmore, Larry Keating, Larry Gates, Robert Burton, Jim Backus, Marilyn Erskine, Steve (Stephen) Dunne, John Pickard, Hayden Rorke, Lawrence (Larry) Dobkin, Jack Raine, Jeff Richards, Barbara Ruick, Harlan Warde, John Close, Frank Gerstle, Dabbs Greer, Ewing Mitchell, Gregory Walcott, John Baer, Jonathon Cott, Dick Simmons, John McKee, G. Pat Collins, John Hedloe, Mack Williams, Dorothy Kennedy; ***D:*** Melvin Frank, Norman Panama; ***W:*** Melvin Frank, Norman Panama, Beirne Lay Jr.; ***C:*** Ray June; ***M:*** Hugo Friedhofer.

Above Suspicion 🦴🦴🦴 **1943** MacMurray and Crawford are American honeymooners (poor Fred!) asked to assist an international intelligence organization. They engage the Nazis in a tense battle of wits. Well-made and engaging. **91m/B VHS.** Joan Crawford, Fred MacMurray, Conrad Veidt, Basil Rathbone, Reginald Owen, Richard Ainley, Cecil Cunningham; ***D:*** Richard Thorpe; ***W:*** Patricia Coleman; ***C:*** Robert Planck; ***M:*** Bronislau Kaper.

Above Suspicion 🦴🦴 **1995 (R)** Dempsey Cain (Reeve) seems to be the perfect cop, as well as a loving husband and father and a mentor to his younger brother. But when Cain is paralyzed by a drug dealer's bullet, he begins to notice just how close his wife (Cattrall) and brother (Kerr) are. There's adultery, there's murder, and there's the cop who just may be a cold-blooded killer. Unnervingly, Reeve plays a paraplegic in the last movie he made before his own paralyzing riding accident. **92m/C VHS, DVD.** Christopher Reeve, Kim Cattrall, Joe Mantegna, Edward Kerr; ***D:*** Steven Schachter. **CABLE**

Above Suspicion 🦴🦴 **2000 (R)** James Stockton (Bakula) seems like the perfect family man but his wife Lisa (Sciorra) starts becoming suspicious of his past—fearing that he's a killer on the lam. **99m/C VHS, DVD.** Scott Bakula, Annabella Sciorra, George Dzundza, Ed Asner, Jack Blessing; ***D:*** Steven La Rocque.

Above the Law 🦴🦴 **1988 (R)** In his debut, Seagal does his wooden best to portray a tough Chicago police detective planning an enormous drug bust of one of the biggest felons in the state. Unfortunately, the FBI has ordered him to back off and find another bust. The reasons are almost as complex as Seagal's character, and like most details of the flick, stupid. However, people don't watch these movies for the acting or the plot, but for the fight scenes, which are well-choreographed and violent. Watch it with someone you love. **99m/C VHS, DVD.** Steven Seagal, Pam Grier, Henry Silva, Sharon Stone, Ron Dean, Daniel Faraldo, Chelcie Ross, Thalmus Rasulala, Michael Rooker; ***D:*** Andrew Davis; ***W:*** Andrew Davis, Steven Pressfield; ***C:*** Robert Steadman; ***M:*** David Michael Frank.

Above the Rim 🦴🦴 ½ **1994 (R)** Vulgar, violent hoopster drama about a fiercely competitive inner-city playground game. Kyle-Lee Watson (Martin), a self-involved high school star raised by a saintly single mom (Pinkins), is torn between the lure of the streets and his college recruiting chances. His odds aren't made any easier by homeboy hustler Birdie (Shakur), who wants to improve his chances of making money on the local games by making sure Watson plays for his team. Energetic b-ball sequences, strong performances lose impact amid formulaic melodrama and the usual obscenities. Debut for director Pollack. **97m/C VHS, DVD.** Duane Martin, Tupac Shakur, Leon, Marlon Wayans, Tonya Pinkins, Bernie Mac; ***D:*** Jeff Pollack; ***W:*** Jeff Pollack, Barry Michael Cooper; ***M:*** Marcus Miller.

Above Us the Waves 🦴🦴🦴 **1956** During WWII, the British navy immobilizes a huge German battleship off the coast of Norway. Effectively dramatizes the British naval preparations for what seemed a suicidal mission: using midget submarines to plant underwater explosives on the hull of the German vessel and detonating them before the Germans could detect the danger. **92m/C VHS.** *GB* John Mills, John Gregson, Donald Sinden, James Robertson Justice, Michael Medwin, James Kenney, O.E. Hasse, Theodore Bikel, Thomas Heathcote, Lee Patterson, Lyndon Brook, Anthony Newley; ***D:*** Ralph Thomas.

Abraham 🦴🦴 ½ **1994** Biblical epic chronicling the Old Testament story of humble shepherd Abraham (Harris), who's commanded by God to lead his family into the promised land of Canaan. Among his family's many trials will be God's command that Abraham sacrifice his son Isaac as a test of faith and obedience. Filmed on location in Morocco with a commanding performance by Harris that somewhat redeems the film's dullness. **175m/C VHS, DVD.** Richard Harris, Barbara Hershey, Maximilian Schell, Vittorio Gassman, Carolina Rosi, Gottfried John, Kevin McNally; ***D:*** Joseph Sargent; ***W:*** Robert McKee; ***C:*** Raffaele Mertes; ***M:*** Ennio Morricone, Marco Frisina. **CABLE**

Abraham Lincoln 🦴🦴 ½ **1930** Griffith's first talking movie takes Abraham Lincoln from his birth through his assassination. This restored version includes the original slavery sequences which were believed to be lost, but obviously were not. Musical score included. **97m/B VHS, DVD.** Walter Huston, Una Merkel, Kay Hammond, E. Alyn (Fred) Warren, Hobart Bosworth, Henry B. Walthall, Russell Simpson, Ian Keith, Frank Campeau; ***D:*** D.W. Griffith; ***C:*** Karl Struss.

Abraham's Valley 🦴🦴 *Vale Abraao; Valley of Abraham* **1993** Beautiful Ema (Silveira) is forced into a wealthy marriage to a friend of her father's and they move to the vineyards of Abraham's Valley where the bride knows no one. Unhappy, Ema refuses to submit to her husband and decides to take a lover of her own. Based on the novel by Augustina Bessa-Luis. Portuguese with subtitles. **180m/C VHS, DVD.** *PT* Leonor Silveira, Luis Miguel Cintra, Diogo Doria, Ruy de Carvalho, Luis Lima Barreto; ***D:*** Manoel de Oliveira; ***W:*** Manoel de Oliveira; ***C:*** Mario Barroso.

Abraxas: Guardian of the Universe 🦴 ½ *Abraxas* **1990 (R)** Good space cop versus bad space cop with an ecological twist. Good-guy Abraxas (Ventura) has the task of stopping planets from destroying their environments and fighting senseless wars. His ex-partner Secundas (Ole-Thorsen) has his own mission, seeking an anti-life power which could destroy the universe. They decide to fight it out, using Earth as the battleground. Also available in an edited PG-13 version. **90m/C VHS, DVD.** Jesse Ventura, Sven-Ole Thorsen, Damian Lee, Marjorie Bransfield, Ken Quinn, Marilyn Lightstone, Moses Znaimer, Layne Coleman, Sonja Belliveau, James Belushi; ***D:*** Damian Lee; ***W:*** Damian Lee; ***C:*** Curtis Petersen.

Abroad with Two Yanks 🦴🦴 **1944** Two Marine buddies on furlough exhibit slapstick tendencies while competing for the same girl. Along the way a big chase ensues with the two soldiers in drag. Typical wartime shenanigans likely to incite only weak chuckling or inspired snoozing. **81m/B VHS.** William Bendix, Dennis O'Keefe, Helen Walker, John Loder, George Cleveland, Janet Lambert, James Flavin, Arthur Hunnicutt; ***D:*** Allan Dwan.

Absence of Malice 🦴🦴 ½ **1981 (PG)** High-minded story about the harm that the news media can inflict. Field is the earnest reporter who, after being fed some facts by an unscrupulous federal investigator, writes a story implicating Newman in a murder he didn't commit. Field hides behind journalistic confidentiality privilege to put off the outraged Newman, who loses a friend to suicide during the debacle. Interesting performances by Field and Newman. **116m/C VHS, DVD.** Paul Newman, Sally Field, Bob Balaban, Melinda Dillon, Luther Adler, Barry Primus, Josef Sommer, John Harkins, Don Hood, Wilford Brimley; ***D:*** Sydney Pollack; ***W:*** Kurt Luedtke; ***C:*** Owen Roizman; ***M:*** Dave Grusin.

Absence of the Good 🦴🦴 **1999 (R)** Homicide detective Caleb Barnes (Baldwin) is mourning the accidental death of his only child while investigating a series of murders in Salt Lake City. He's under pressure to solve the case, even as his home life is disintegrating, and Caleb's investigation leads to a family's malignant history. **99m/C VHS, DVD.** Stephen Baldwin, Tyne Daly, Allen (Goorwitz) Garfield, Robert Knepper; ***D:*** John Flynn; ***W:*** James Reid.

The Absent-Minded Professor 🦴🦴🦴 ½ **1961** Classic dumb Disney fantasy of the era. A professor accidentally invents an anti-gravity substance called flubber, causing inanimate objects and people to become airborne. Great sequence of the losing school basketball team taking advantage of flubber during a game. MacMurray is convincing as the absent-minded genius in this newly colored version. Followed by "Son of Flubber." **97m/C VHS, DVD.** Fred MacMurray, Nancy Olson, Keenan Wynn, Tommy Kirk, Leon Ames, Ed Wynn, Edward Andrews, Wally Brown, Wendell Holmes; ***D:*** Robert Stevenson; ***W:*** Bill Walsh; ***C:*** Edward Colman; ***M:*** George Bruns.

Absent Without Leave 🦴🦴 ½ **1995** Ed (McLachlan) marries his pregnant girlfriend Daisy (Hobbs) in 1942 before joining the army. When Daisy miscarries, Ed pledges to take her home even though it means leaving the army wihout permission. As the newleyweds travel across the New Zealand countryside, they struggle with the new demands of their relationship. **104m/C VHS.** *NZ* Craig McLachlan, Katrina Hobbs; ***D:*** John Laing.

Absolute Beginners 🦴🦴 **1986 (PG)** Fervently stylish camp musical exploring the lives of British teenagers in the 1950s never quite gets untracked, although MTV video moments fill out a spare plotline. Based on a novel by Colin MacInnes. ♫ Absolute Beginners; That's Motivation; Volare; Killer Blow; Have You Ever Been Blue?; Quiet Life; Having It All; Selling Out; Va Va Voom. **107m/C VHS, DVD.** *GB* David Bowie, Ray Davies, Mandy Rice-Davies, James Fox, Eddie O'Connell, Patsy Kensit, Anita Morris, Sade Adu, Sandie Shaw; ***D:*** Julien Temple; ***W:*** Richard Burridge, Don MacPherson; ***C:*** Oliver Stapleton.

Absolute Power 🦴🦴 ½ **1997 (R)** Eastwood is "In the Line of Fire," (against the very agents he previously glorified) as an expert thief being pursued by rogue Secret Service men in this fast-paced thriller. While looting a Washington official's place, Luther (Eastwood) inadvertently witnesses a murder committed by none other than U.S. President Richmond (Hackman) and his goons. Immediately, a cover-up is organized by his unbalanced chief-of-staff (Davis) and Luther becomes the prime suspect. Harris gives his usual solid performance as the homicide detective. Eastwood's simple directorial style keeps up the suspense and propels the film steadily forward, alongside a generally solid plot that gets a bit improbable near the end. Based on the novel by David Baldacci. **120m/C VHS, DVD.** Clint Eastwood, Gene Hackman, Ed Harris, Laura Linney, Judy Davis, Scott Glenn, Dennis Haysbert, E.G. Marshall, Melora Hardin; ***D:*** Clint Eastwood; ***W:*** William Goldman; ***C:*** Jack N. Green; ***M:*** Lennie Niehaus.

Absolutely Fabulous: The Last Shout 🦴🦴 ½ **1996** The first TV movie from the British comedy series finds Edina (Saunders) selling her fashion PR business after a near-death experience and doing some soul-searching—AbFab style, which involves shopping, travel, and champagne. Naturally, Patsy (Lumley) goes along for the ride. The duo's favorite designer Christian LaCroix even has a cameo. **90m/C VHS.** *GB* Jennifer Saunders, Joanna Lumley; ***Cameos:*** Marianne Faithfull. **TV**

Absolution 1981 **(R)** Two English boys trapped in a Catholic boarding school conspire to drive a tyrannical priest over the edge of sanity. As a result, bad things (including murder) occur. Burton is interesting in sadistic character study. Not released in the U.S. until 1988 following Burton's death, maybe due to something written in the will. **105m/C VHS, DVD.** *GB* Richard Burton, Dominic Guard, Dai Bradley, Andrew Keir, Billy Connolly, Willoughby Gray, Preston Lockwood, James Ottaway, Brook Williams, Jon Plowman, Robin Soans, Trevor Martin; ***D:*** Anthony Page; ***W:*** Anthony Shaffer; ***C:*** John Coquillon; ***M:*** Stanley Myers.

Abuse 1982 Fourteen-year-old Tommy (Sbarge) is the victim of child abuse. After a beating causes convulsions, his parents rush him to a New York hospital where the intern on duty phones his student filmmaker friend Larry (Ryder), who's doing a documentary on child abuse as his master thesis. When Tommy learns that Larry is also gay, he agrees to discuss his problems but their continuing contact leads the duo to fall in love and Larry to worry about exploiting Tommy's affections. Interspersed with their story are interviews and photos of child abuse victims and their abusers. Not necessarily for the squeamish. **93m/B VHS.** Richard Ryder, Raphael Sbarge; ***D:*** Arthur J. Bressan Jr.; ***W:*** Arthur J. Bressan Jr.; ***C:*** Douglas Dickinson; ***M:*** Shawn Phillips.

The Abyss *L'Oeuvre au Noir* **1989 (PG-13)** Underwater sci-fi adventure about a team of oil-drilling divers pressed into service by the navy to locate and disarm an inoperative nuclear submarine. A high-tech thriller with fab footage underwater and pulsating score. **140m/C VHS, DVD.** Ed Harris, Mary Elizabeth Mastrantonio, Todd Graff, Michael Biehn, John Bedford Lloyd, J.C. Quinn, Leo Burmester, Kidd Brewer Jr., Kimberly Scott, Adam Nelson, George Robert Kirk, Chris Elliott, Jimmie Ray Weeks; ***D:*** James Cameron; ***W:*** James Cameron; ***C:*** Mikael Salomon; ***M:*** Alan Silvestri. Oscars '89: Visual FX.

Acapulco Gold ½ **1978 (PG)** Mockumentary follows Gortner as he's framed for drug smuggling and becomes entangled in a Hawaiian drug deal. Not worth the time it'll take to track down a copy. **105m/C DVD.** Marjoe Gortner, Robert Lansing, Ed Nelson, John Harkins, Lawrence Casey, Phil Hoover; ***D:*** Burt Brinckerhoff; ***W:*** Don Enright; ***C:*** Robert Steadman; ***M:*** Craig Safan.

Accatone! **1961** Accatone (Citti), a failure as a pimp, tries his luck as a thief. Hailed as a return to Italian neo-realism, this is a gritty, despairing, and dark look at the lives of the street people of Rome. Pasolini's first outing, adapted by the director from his novel, "A Violent Life." Pasolini served as mentor to Bernardo Bertolucci, listed in the credits as an assistant director. **116m/B VHS, DVD.** *IT* Franco Citti, Franca Pasut, Roberto Scaringelli, Silvana Corsini, Paolo Guidi, Adriana Asti; ***D:*** Pier Paolo Pasolini; ***W:*** Pier Paolo Pasolini; ***C:*** Tonino Delli Colli.

Acceptable Risk **2001** Pharmaceutical scientist Edward Wells (Lowe) discovers a strange fungus in a walled-in part of his basement. He takes it into the lab, finds unusual healing properties in the substance, and immediately begins to test it on himself. At first, he feels superhuman, but monstrous side effects quickly surface. There is some suspense in this TV movie, but the inconsistent story and poor performances are hard to get past. **92m/C DVD.** Chad Lowe, Kelly Rutherford, Sean Patrick Flanery, Patty McCormack, Danielle von Zerneck; ***D:*** William A. Graham; ***W:*** Michael J. Murray; ***C:*** Eyal Grodin. **TV**

Acceptable Risks ½ **1986 (R)** Toxic disaster strikes when a plant manager is ordered to cut costs and sacrifice safety at the Citichem plant. Predictable plot stars Dennehy as the plant manager who risks all and fights politicians to reinstate the safety standards. Meanwhile, Tyson is the city manager who tries to warn the town of a possible chemical accident that could have devastating effects on the community. TV drama that shamelessly preys on audience fears. **97m/C VHS.** Brian Dennehy, Cicely Tyson, Kenneth McMillan, Christine Ebersole, Beah Richards, Richard Gilliland; ***D:*** Rick Wallace. **TV**

Accepted ½ **2006 (PG-13)** Flunky campus farce about what to do after getting one too many thin envelopes from college admissions offices: create your own university. Bartleby (Long) and his buds pretend to matriculate at the fictitious South Harmon Institute of Technology. So-so jokes about beer and babes and that oh-so-hilarious acronym abound, until the tale attempts to take an unexpectedly touching turn. Ultimately lands on the failing side of the campus-movie bell curve (with "Animal House" and "Back to School" at the top of the class). **92m/C DVD.** *US* Justin Long, Blake Lively, Mark Derwin, Anthony Heald, Adam Herschman, Jonah Hill, Columbus Short, Maria Thayer, Lewis Black, Ann Cusack, Travis Van Winkle, Hannah Marks, Diora Baird; ***D:*** Steve Pink; ***W:*** Mark Perez, Adam Cooper, Bill Collage; ***C:*** Matthew F. Leonetti; ***M:*** David Schommer.

Access Code **1984** Government agents attempt to uncover a private organization that has gained control of nuclear weapons for the purpose of world domination. A ragged patchwork of disconnected scenes meant to test the virtue of patience. **90m/C VHS.** Martin Landau, Michael Ansara, MacDonald Carey; ***D:*** Mark Sobel.

Accident ½ **1967** A tangled web of guilt, remorse, humor and thwarted sexuality is unravelled against the background of the English countryside in this complex story of an Oxford love triangle. An inside view of English repression at the university level adapted for the screen by Pinter from the novel by Nicholas Mosley. Long-winded but occasionally engrossing character study with interesting performances. **100m/C VHS, DVD.** *GB* Dirk Bogarde, Michael York, Stanley Baker, Jacqueline Sassard, Delphine Seyrig, Alexander Knox, Vivien Merchant, Freddie Jones, Harold Pinter; ***D:*** Joseph Losey; ***W:*** Harold Pinter; ***C:*** Gerry Fisher; ***M:*** John Dankworth. Cannes '67: Grand Jury Prize.

Accident ½ **1983** Skate for your life. A hockey game turns into a nightmare when the roof over the arena collapses under the weight of too much ice and snow. One of the few hockey disaster films. **104m/C VHS.** Terence Kelly, Fiona Reid, Frank Perry; ***D:*** Donald Britain.

The Accidental Husband ½ **2008 (PG-13)** In this feeble romcom, New York firefighter Patrick Sullivan (Morgan) is incensed when his fiancee dumps him, thanks to the advice of frigid radio therapist Emma Lloyd (Thurman). In an unlikely chain of events, Patrick forges a marriage license between himself and the doc that throws a wrench into Emma's plans with her own stuffy fiance Richard (Firth). Morgan is hunky but Thurman is boring. **91m/C DVD.** Uma Thurman, Jeffrey Dean Morgan, Colin Firth, Justina Machado, Sam Shepard, Lindsay Sloane, Ajay Naidu, Keir Dullea; ***D:*** Griffin Dunne; ***W:*** Mimi Hare, Clare Naylor, Bonnie Sikowitz; ***C:*** William Rexer; ***M:*** Andrea Guerra. **VIDEO**

Accidental Meeting ½ **1993 (R)** A female version of "Strangers on a Train." Two women meet because of an auto accident and wind up talking about their lives. The main topic is man trouble and both "jokingly" plot to murder each other's man. Only, one woman does the deed and the other soon finds herself on the murderess' hit list. **91m/C VHS.** Linda Gray, Linda Purl, Leigh McCloskey, David Hayward, Ernie Lively, Kent McCord; ***D:*** Michael Zinberg; ***W:*** Pete Best, Christopher Horner.

The Accidental Spy ½ **2001 (R)** Salesman Bei (Chan) longs for some excitement in his life but gets more than anticipated when he foils the plans of two bank robbers. The resulting publicity leads Bei to discover that he's the long-lost son of a wealthy Korean businessman who also turns out to be a spy and Bei decides to join the family profession. **87m/C VHS, DVD.** *HK* Jackie Chan, Eric Tsang, Vivian Hsu, Alfred Cheung, Min-jeong Kim, Hsing-kuo Wu; ***D:*** Teddy Chen; ***W:*** Ivy Ho; ***C:*** Wing-Hung Wong; ***M:*** Peter Kam.

The Accidental Tourist ½ **1988 (PG)** A bittersweet and subtle story, adapted faithfully from Anne Tyler's novel, of an introverted, grieving man who learns to love again after meeting an unconventional woman. After his son's death and subsequent separation from wife Turner, Macon Leary (Hurt) avoids emotional confrontation, burying himself in routines with the aid of his obsessive-compulsive siblings. Kooky dog-trainer Muriel Pritchett (an exuberant Davis) wins his attention, but not without struggle. Hurt effectively uses small gestures to describe Macon's emotional journey, while Davis grabs hearts with her open performance. Outstanding supporting cast. **121m/C VHS, DVD.** William Hurt, Geena Davis, Kathleen Turner, Ed Begley Jr., David Ogden Stiers, Bill Pullman, Amy Wright; ***D:*** Lawrence Kasdan; ***W:*** Lawrence Kasdan; ***C:*** John Bailey; ***M:*** John Williams. Oscars '88: Support. Actress (Davis); N.Y. Film Critics '88: Film.

Accidents ½ **1989 (R)** A scientist discovers that his invention has been stolen and is going to be used to cause worldwide havoc. He becomes concerned and spends the remainder of the movie trying to relieve himself of anxiety. **90m/C VHS.** Edward Albert, Leigh Taylor-Young, Jon Cypher; ***D:*** Gideon Amir.

The Accompanist ½ *L'Accompagnatrice* **1993 (PG)** Centers around a Parisian diva Irene's (Safonova) relationship with her talented pianist Sophie (Romane Bohringer), amidst the clamor of WWII Europe. Sophie impresses Irene with her musical abilities, and takes on additional work as her housekeeper. Meanwhile, Charles (Richard Bohringer), Irene's husband, schmoozes with the Nazis to line his own pockets while she helps the war effort by having an affair with a member of the resistance (Labarthe). Unfortunately, Sophie starts to resent living in Irene's shadow. Adapted from the novel by Nina Berberouva. The Bohringers are father and daughter. French with subtitles. **111m/C VHS.** *FR* Elena Safonova, Romane Bohringer, Richard Bohringer, Samuel Labarthe, Nelly Borgeaud, Julien Rassam; ***D:*** Claude Miller; ***W:*** Claude Miller, Luc Beraud, Claude Rich; ***C:*** Yves Angelo; ***M:*** Alain Jomy.

Accomplice ½ **1946** Plodding whodunit with Arlen as a shy, bookish private eye hired by his old flame to locate her missing husband. His investigations uncover several murders and long after the viewers have put 2 + 2 together, the P.I. smells a rat. The missing husband was a ruse to divert him from the real scam-a bank heist. Painfully low-level excitement. **66m/B VHS.** Richard Arlen, Veda Ann Borg, Tom Dugan, Francis Ford; ***D:*** Walter Colmes.

According to Greta *Greta* **2008 (PG-13)** Duff acquits herself quite well as a suicidal teen who's fobbed off on her grandparents for the summer by her preoccupied mother. Greta gets a job as a waitress and starts an interracial romance with the unfortunately-named Julie (Ross), the cook. But her grandparents really freak when they find out the boy has a criminal past. **91m/C DVD.** Hilary Duff, Evan Ross, Ellen Burstyn, Michael Murphy, Melissa Leo; ***D:*** Nancy Bardawil; ***W:*** Michael Gilvary; ***C:*** Dietrich Lohmann; ***M:*** Joseph E. Nordstrom.

Accused ½ **1936** Married dancers Fairbanks and Del Rio are working in a Parisian revue when the show's sultry leading lady (Desmond) makes a pass at Fairbanks. Though he's turned her down, through a series of misunderstandings Del Rio believes the worst and the two women get into a vicious argument. When the star is found dead guess who gets the blame? Del Rio is lovely, Desmond is spiteful, and Fairbanks serves as a fine object of two women's affections. **83m/B VHS.** *GB* Douglas Fairbanks Jr., Dolores Del Rio, Florence Desmond, Basil Sydney, Athole Stewart, Esme Percy, Googie Withers, Cecil Humphreys; ***D:*** Thornton Freeland.

The Accused ½ *Strange Deception* **1948** Young is cast against character in this story of a college professor who is assaulted by one of her students and kills him in self-defense. A courtroom drama ensues, where Young is defended by the dead man's guardian. Film noir with nice ensemble performance. **101m/B VHS.** Loretta Young, Robert Cummings, Wendell Corey, Sam Jaffe, Douglas Dick, Sara Allgood, Ann Doran; ***D:*** William Dieterle; ***C:*** Milton Krasner.

The Accused **1988 (R)** Provocative treatment of a true story involving a young woman gang raped in a bar while onlookers cheer. McGillis is the assistant district attorney who takes on the case and must contend with the victim's questionable past and a powerful lawyer hired by a wealthy defendant's parents. As the victim with a past, Foster gives an Oscar-winning performance that won raves for its strength and complexity. **110m/C VHS, DVD.** Jodie Foster, Kelly McGillis, Bernie Coulson, Leo Rossi, Ann Hearn, Carmen Argenziano, Steve Antin, Tom O'Brien, Peter Van Norden, Woody Brown; ***D:*** Jonathan Kaplan; ***W:*** Tom Topor; ***C:*** Ralf Bode; ***M:*** Brad Fiedel. Oscars '88: Actress (Foster); Golden Globes '89: Actress—Drama (Foster); Natl. Bd. of Review '88: Actress (Foster).

Ace Drummond *Squadron of Doom* **1936** The complete 13-chapter serial about a murder organization that tries to stop several countries from forming a worldwide clipper ship air service and government troubleshooter Ace Drummond who's out to stop them. **260m/B VHS, DVD.** John "Dusty" King, Jean Rogers, Noah Beery Jr.; ***D:*** Ford Beebe.

Ace High ½ **1968** Spaghetti western about a ruthless outlaw named Cat Stevens trying to save himself from the noose. Patterned after the famous Sergio Leone-Clint Eastwood westerns, with less of a budget and more camp tendencies. **120m/C VHS, DVD.** *IT* Eli Wallach, Terence Hill, Bud Spencer, Brock Peters, Kevin McCarthy; ***D:*** Giuseppe Colizzi.

Ace in the Hole *The Big Carnival* **1951** Moralist Wilder brilliantly captures a cynical media circus. Alcoholic SOB reporter Chuck Tatum (Douglas) is bored crazy working a podunk paper in New Mexico when he gets a big scoop. Unhappy Lorraine (Sterling) tells Tatum her husband Leo (Benedict) was searching for Indian artifacts and is now trapped in a cave-in. Tatum teams up with corrupt local sheriff Gus Kretzer (Teal) to delay rescue operations to milk the story for maximum exposure while poor Leo suffers and the public come to gawk. Based on the Floyd Collins mining disaster of the 1920s. **111m/B DVD.** Kirk Douglas, Richard Benedict, Ray Teal, Jan Sterling, Robert Arthur, Porter Hall, Frank Cady, Gene Evans, Lewis Martin, Harry Harvey, Richard Gaines; ***D:*** Billy Wilder; ***W:*** Billy Wilder, Lesser Samuels, Walter Newman; ***C:*** Charles B(ryant) Lang Jr.; ***M:*** Hugo Friedhofer.

Ace of Aces **1933** An American sculptor is reviled, particularly by his girlfriend, when he does not join fellows in enlisting in what becomes WWI. Out to prove he's not lacking testosterone, he becomes a pilot in France, but is embittered by his experiences. Dated but well-acted war melodrama. **77m/B VHS.** Richard Dix, Elizabeth Allan, Theodore Newton, Ralph Bellamy, William Cagney, Frank Conroy; ***D:*** J. Walter Ruben; ***C:*** Henry Cronjager; ***M:*** Max Steiner.

Ace of Hearts **1985** A seedy story about a rich guy in the South Pacific who pays heavily to have himself killed. **90m/C VHS.** Mickey Rooney, Chris Robinson, Pilar Velasquez.

Ace of Hearts ½ **2008 (PG)** Officer Daniel Harding (Cain) is a member of the K-9 unit with his German Shepherd police partner, Ace. When Ace is unjustly accused of mauling a suspect, an over-zealous DA wants the dog euthanized. But Dan and his family are determined to clear Ace's name and save his furry life. **99m/C DVD.** Dean Cain, Mike Dopud, Anne Marie Deluise, Matthew Harrison, Britt Mckillip, David Patrick Green; ***D:*** David McKay; ***W:*** Frederick Ayeroff; ***C:*** Gordon Verheul; ***M:*** Michael Richard Plowman. **VIDEO**

Ace Ventura Jr.: Pet Detective **2008 (PG)** Eccentric 12-year-old Ace Jr. (Flitter) is following in his dad's footsteps when his mom (Cusack) is falsely accused of stealing a zoo's baby panda. He teams up with girl-next-door Laura (Lockhart) and gizmo-crazy pal A-Plus (Rogers) to clear the family name. Alrighty then! **93m/C DVD.** Josh Flitter, Emma Lockhart, Austin Rogers, Ann Cusack, Ralph Waite, Brian Patrick Clarke, Art LaFleur, Reed Alexander, Cullen Douglas; ***D:*** David Mickey Evans; ***W:*** David Mickey Evans, Jeffrey Sank, Jason Heimberg, Justin Heimberg; ***C:*** Mark Irwin; ***M:*** Laura Karpman. **VIDEO**

Ace Ventura: Pet Detective **1993 (PG-13)** Shamelessly silly comedy casts human cartoon Carrey, he of the rubber limbs and spasmodic facial muscles, as Ace, the guy who'll find missing pets, big or small. When the Miami Dolphins' mascot Snowflake is kidnapped, he abandons his search for an albino pigeon to save the lost dolphin just in time for the Super Bowl. This is brain candy, running full throttle with juvenile humor, some charm, and the hyper-energetic Carrey, not to mention Young as the police chief with a secret. Critically trashed boxoffice smash catapulted Carrey into nearly instant stardom after seven seasons as the geeky white guy on "In Living Color." **87m/C VHS, DVD.** Jim Carrey, Courteney Cox, Sean Young, Tone Loc, Noble Willingham, Troy Evans, Udo Kier; ***Cameos:*** Dan Marino; ***D:*** Tom Shadyac; ***W:*** Tom Shadyac, Jack Bernstein, Jim Carrey; ***C:*** Julio Macat; ***M:*** Ira Newborn. Blockbuster '95: Male Newcomer, V. (Carrey), Comedy Actor, V. (Carrey).

Ace Ventura: When Nature Calls 🦴🦴 *Ace Ventura Goes to Africa* **1995 (PG-13)** Ace is back on the case as the pet dick (Carrey) ventures to Africa to restore peace among rival tribes by finding an albino bat that's M.I.A. Plot is secondary, however, to multi-million dollar man Carrey's outrageous brand of physical comedy combined with his unique ability to deliver junior high level lines with pseudo-suave savoir-faire. Contains only a handful of outstanding gags, the best with Ace and a mechanical rhino. Mainly for Carrey aficionados (of which there are many) and original "Ace" fans—the lowbrow humor runs a bit thin by the end. **94m/C VHS, DVD.** Jim Carrey, Ian McNeice, Simon Callow, Maynard Eziashi, Bob Gunton, Sophie Okonedo, Tommy Davidson; ***D:*** Steve Oedekerk; ***W:*** Steve Oedekerk; ***C:*** Donald E. Thorin; ***M:*** Robert Folk. MTV Movie Awards '96: Male Perf. (Carrey), Comedic Perf. (Carrey); Blockbuster '96: Comedy Actor, T. (Carrey).

Aces and Eights 🦴🦴 ½ **1936** Gambler McCoy catches a fellow cardsharp cheating and the marshal runs the varmint out of town. When the cheater is murdered, the lawman suspects McCoy, who sets out to prove his innocence. Title refers to the "death hand" held by Wild Bill Hickok, killed while playing poker. Film opens with a shot of Hickok and a speech about gambler's luck. **62m/B VHS, DVD.** Tim McCoy, Jimmy Aubrey, Luana Walters, Wheeler Oakman, Earle Hodgins, Frank Glennon, Rex Lease, Joseph Girard, John Merton; ***D:*** Sam Newfield.

Aces: Iron Eagle 3 🦴🦴 **1992 (R)** Colonel "Chappy" Sinclair returns once again in this air adventure. He's been keeping busy flying in air shows when he stumbles across the nefarious activities of a Peruvian drug baron working out of a remote village. Sinclair recruits a team of maverick air circus pilots and they "borrow" a fleet of WWII vintage aircraft to raid the village, coming up against a fellow Air Force officer who turns out to be another villain. Lots of action and a stalwart cast. **98m/C VHS, DVD.** Louis Gossett Jr., Rachel McLish, Paul Freeman, Horst Buchholz, Christopher Cazenove, Sonny Chiba, Fred Dalton Thompson, Mitchell Ryan, Robert Estes, J.E. Freeman; ***D:*** John Glen.

Aces 'n Eights 🦴🦴 **2008** Luke Rivers (Van Dien) has retired as a gunslinger and is now working on an Arizona ranch owned by crusty Thurmond Prescott (Borgnine). The local land owners band together to fight ruthless railroad mogul Howard (Atherton), who uses intimidation and murder to seize their land. Looks like Rivers is going to have to strap on his six-guns and go up against some of his old saddle-mates in order to defend his new life. Title refers to poker's so-called "dead man's hand," held by Wild Bill Hickok when he was killed. **87m/C DVD.** Casper Van Dien, Bruce Boxleitner, Ernest Borgnine, William Atherton, Jeff Kober, Jack Noseworthy, Jake Thomas, Rodney Scott, Deirdre Quinn; ***D:*** Craig R. Baxley; ***W:*** Ronald M. Cohen, Dennis Shryack; ***C:*** Yaron Levy. **TV**

Aces Wild 🦴 ½ **1937** Another poker title. Outlaws menace an honest newspaper until the lawmen show up and send them on their way. **62m/B VHS.** Harry Carey Sr., Gertrude Messinger, Edward Cassidy, Roger Williams; ***D:*** Harry Fraser.

The Acid Eaters 🦴 **1967** Straight-laced desk jockeys spend their weekends exploring the realm of the senses. Includes nudity. **62m/C VHS, DVD.** Buck Kartalian, Pat (Barringer) Barrington; ***D:*** B. Ron Elliott; ***W:*** B. Ron Elliott, Carl Monson; ***M:*** William Allen Castleman.

The Acid House 🦴🦴 ½ **1998** Trilogy of tales written by Irving Welsh, author of "Trainspotting," similarly centers on down-on-their-luck Scottish hooligans ravaged by drugs and drink. Its tone, however, makes its predecessor look like a light-hearted romp in the countryside. In "The Granton Star Cause," freeloading loser Boab (McCole) gets turned into a fly by God during a trip to the pub. He proceeds to exact some disgusting revenge on those he feels have wronged him. "A Soft Touch" depicts the twisted relationship between brow-beaten Johnny (McKidd) and kinky wife Catriona (Gomez), who is sleeping with psycho neighbor Larry (McCormack). In the last chapter, "The Acid House," tripped-out rave party boy Coco (Bremner) exchanges personalities with the newborn baby of suburban couple Rory (Clunes) and Jenny (Redgrave). First-time director McGuigan does a good job of translating the material to the screen, but sometimes goes over the top in showing these skanky Scots. Also, be warned that the Scottish accents are so thick that the movie ran with subtitles during its limited U.S. theatre run. If you liked "Trainspotting," however, you'll probably like this similar entry in the "if it's Scottish, it's crap!" genre. **118m/C VHS, DVD.** Stephen McCole, Maurice Roeves, Garry Sweeney, Kevin McKidd, Ewen Bremner, Martin Clunes, Jemma Redgrave, Arlene Cockburn, Jenny McCrindle, Michelle Gomez, Tam Dean Burn, Gary McCormack, Jane Stabler; ***D:*** Paul McGuigan; ***W:*** Irvine Welsh; ***C:*** Alasdair Walker.

Acla's Descent into Floristella 🦴🦴 *Acla* **1987** Twelve-year-old Acla (Cusimano) is sold by his father to work underground in the sulfur mines for eight years. Repeatedly beaten by his owner, Acla runs away, but there are dire consequences for him and his family. Set in 1930s Sicily. Italian with subtitles. **86m/C VHS.** *IT* Francesco Cusimano, Tony Sperandeo; ***D:*** Aurelio Grimaldi; ***W:*** Aurelio Grimaldi; ***C:*** Maurizio Calvesi; ***M:*** Dario Lucantoni.

Acorn People 🦴🦴 **1982** An unemployed teacher takes a summer job at a camp for handicapped children and learns sensitivity. Weeper adapted by Tewkesbury from the book by Ron Jones. **97m/C VHS.** Ted Bessell, Cloris Leachman, LeVar Burton, Dolph Sweet, Cheryl Anderson; ***D:*** Joan Tewkesbury. **TV**

Acqua e Sapone 🦴 ½ **1983 (PG)** A young innocent model goes to Rome under the watchful eyes of an appointed priest-chaperon, but finds love, fun and other sinful things. Sudsy/romantic comedy. **100m/C VHS.** *IT* Carlo Verdone, Natasha Hovey, Florinda Bolkan, Elena Bolkan; ***D:*** Carlo Verdone.

Across 110th Street 🦴🦴 **1972 (R)** Gritty, violent cop thriller in the blaxploitation genre. Both the Mafia and the cops hunt down three black hoods who, in a display of extremely bad judgment, knocked over a mob-controlled bank while disguised as police. Lots of bullets create buckets of blood. Filmed on location in Harlem. **102m/C VHS, DVD.** Anthony Quinn, Yaphet Kotto, Anthony (Tony) Franciosa, Paul Benjamin, Ed Bernard, Antonio Fargas, Tim O'Connor, Lewis Gilbert, Richard Ward; ***D:*** Barry Shear; ***W:*** Luther Davis; ***C:*** Jack Priestley.

Across the Bridge 🦴🦴 ½ **1957** A man on the run from Scotland Yard for stealing a fortune flees to Mexico, in the process killing a man and assuming his identity. An ironic twist and his love for a dog seal his final destiny. Steiger's psychological study as the fugitive is compelling. Based on a novel by Graham Greene. **103m/B VHS, DVD.** *GB* Rod Steiger, David Knight, Marla Landi, Noel Willman, Bernard Lee; ***D:*** Ken Annakin; ***M:*** James Bernard.

Across the Great Divide 🦴🦴 ½ **1976 (G)** Two orphans must cross the rugged snow-covered Rocky Mountains in 1876 in order to claim their inheritance—a 400-acre plot of land in Salem, Oregon. Pleasant coming-of-age tale with majestic scenery. **102m/C VHS, DVD.** Robert F. Logan, George "Buck" Flower, Heather Rattray, Mark Hall; ***D:*** Stewart Raffill; ***W:*** Stewart Raffill; ***M:*** Angelo Badalamenti.

Across the Line 🦴🦴 ½ **2000 (R)** Miranda (Erez) crosses the border from Mexico into the U.S. and immediately witnesses the murder of a tourist and her husband by corrupt Border Patrol officers. A sheriff (Johnson) tries to protect his witness even as he falls in love with her. **97m/C VHS, DVD.** Brad Johnson, Sigal Erez, Brian Bloom, Marshall Teague, Adrienne Barbeau; ***D:*** Martin Spottl; ***W:*** Sigal Erez. **VIDEO**

Across the Moon 🦴🦴 **1994 (R)** A road trip to the desert takes Carmen and Kathy away from their incarcerated boyfriends but into troubles with cowboys and prospectors. **88m/C VHS, DVD.** Jack Kehler, Elizabeth Pena, Christina Applegate, Tony Fields, Peter Berg, James Remar, Michael McKean, Burgess Meredith, Jack Nance; ***D:*** Lisa Gottlieb; ***W:*** Stephen Schneck; ***C:*** Andrzej Sekula; ***M:*** Christopher Tyng, Exene Cervenka.

Across the Pacific 🦴🦴🦴 ½ **1942** Classic Bogie/Huston vehicle made on the heels of "The Maltese Falcon." Bogie is an American Army officer booted out of the service on false charges of treason. When no other military will accept him, he sails to China (via the Panama Canal) to offer his services to Chiang Kai-Shek. On board, he meets a variety of seedy characters who plan to blow up the canal. Huston again capitalizes on the counterpoint between the rotundly acerbic Greenstreet, who plays a spy, and stiff-lipped Bogart, who's wooing Astor. Great Bogie moments and fine direction make this an adventure classic. When he departed for the service just prior to filming the final scenes, Huston turned over direction to Vincent Sherman. Also available colorized. **97m/B VHS, DVD.** Humphrey Bogart, Mary Astor, Sydney Greenstreet, Charles Halton, Victor Sen Yung, Roland Got, Keye Luke, Richard Loo, Frank Wilcox, Paul Stanton, Lester Matthews, Tom Stevenson, Roland (Walter Goss) Drew, Monte Blue, Rudy Robles, Lee Tung Foo, Chester Gan, Kam Tong, Spencer Chan, Philip Ahn, Frank Faylen, Frank Mayo; ***D:*** John Huston; ***W:*** Richard Macaulay; ***C:*** Arthur Edeson; ***M:*** Adolph Deutsch.

Across the Plains 🦴 ½ **1939** Predictable oater about two brothers who are raised separately after their parents are murdered by outlaws. One is brought up by Indians, the other by the outlaws responsible for wiping out the folks, who tell the boy that Indians did in his ma and pa. Eventually the brothers meet and fight. Odds favor the good one winning, aided by Indian pals. **59m/B VHS.** Addison "Jack" Randall, Frank Yaconelli, Joyce Bryant, Hal Price, Dennis Moore, Glenn Strange, Bud Osborne; ***D:*** Spencer Gordon Bennet.

Across the Tracks 🦴🦴 **1989 (PG-13)** Two brothers, Billy (Schroder), a juvie-home rebel, and Joe (Pitt), a straight-A jock, are at odds when the black sheep is pressured into selling drugs. In an attempt to save his brother from a life of crime, saintly Joe convinces Billy to join him on the school track team, and the brothers are forced to face off in a big meet. Fairly realistic good guy/bad guy who's really a good guy teen drama. **101m/C VHS, DVD.** Rick Schroder, Brad Pitt, Carrie Snodgress; ***D:*** Sandy Tung; ***W:*** Sandy Tung; ***C:*** Michael Delahoussaye; ***M:*** Joel Goldsmith.

Across the Universe 🦴🦴 **2007 (PG-13)** Director Julie Taymor has certainly crafted a mystical tour, from middle America to bohemian Greenwich Village to Vietnam. Whether this portrayal of the Vietnam era, using gorgeous visuals, a stylized 60s aesthetic, a nice chunk of the Beatles songbook, and surprisingly little spoken dialogue, is also magical is debatable. Lucy Even (Wood) moves from a small town to New York City, where she and her brother Max (Anderson) meet and befriend a number of predictable characters including Jude (Sturgess), a Brit from—where else?—Liverpool. The music has been tasked with propelling the plot along via a vision of this revolutionary time from hippie idealism through the duty of military service to the anti-war counter culture, which is where the message of the film finally lands. See it for the stunning visuals and the fresh interpretation of Beatles classics. **133m/C DVD, Blu-ray Disc.** *US* Evan Rachel Wood, Joe Anderson, Jim Sturgess, Dana Fuchs, Martin Luther McCoy, T.V. Carpio; ***Cameos:*** Bono; ***D:*** Julie Taymor; ***W:*** Dick Clement, Ian La Frenais; ***C:*** Bruno Delbonnel; ***M:*** Elliot Goldenthal.

Across the Wide Missouri 🦴🦴 ½ **1951** Pioneer epic stars Gable as a rugged fur trapper who marries an Indian woman (Marques) so he can trap beaver pelts on her people's rich land. On the journey to the Indian territory however, the trapper truly falls in love with his bride. Superior historical drama is marred slightly by the use of narration (provided by Howard Keel). Look for lively performances from Menjou as a French tippler and Naish as the quirky Indian Chief. Beautiful scenery filmed in the spectacular Rocky Mountains. **78m/C VHS.** Clark Gable, Ricardo Montalban, John Hodiak, Adolphe Menjou, Maria Elena Marques, J. Carrol Naish, Jack Holt, Alan Napier; ***D:*** William A. Wellman; ***C:*** William Mellor; ***Nar:*** Howard Keel.

Across to Singapore 🦴🦴 **1928** Convoluted family/romantic drama based on the Ben Ames Williams novel "All the Brothers Were Valiant." Childhood friends Joel Shore (Novarro) and Priscilla Crowninshield (Crawford) have grown up in seafaring New England. When Joel's older brother Mark (Torrence) returns home from a long voyage, he's immediately smitten by Priscilla and both fathers agree to their marriage (without consulting Priscilla). Joel refuses to hear Priscilla's pleas that she loves only him and agrees to join his brothers on a voyage to Singapore where multiple tragedies strike. **85m/B DVD.** Ramon Novarro, Joan Crawford, Ernest Torrence, Jim Mason, Frank Currier, Louis Wolheim, Duke Martin, Edward Connelly, Anna May Wong; ***D:*** William Nigh; ***W:*** Joe Farnham; ***C:*** John Seitz.

The Act 🦴🦴 *Bless 'Em All* **1982 (R)** A muddled satire about political double dealing and union corruption further muddled by a twangy musical score manufactured by folksy Sebastian. **90m/C VHS.** Jill St. John, Eddie Albert, Pat Hingle, Robert Ginty, Sarah Langenfeld, Nicolas Surovy; ***D:*** Sig Shore; ***M:*** John Sebastian.

Act of Aggression 🦴🦴 *L'Agression* **1973 (R)** When a Parisian man finds his wife and daughter murdered at a summer resort, he takes the law into his own hands, with predictable results. **100m/C VHS.** *FR* Jean-Louis Trintignant, Catherine Deneuve, Claude Brasseur, Milena Vukotic, Jacques Rispal, Philippe Brigaud, Michele Grellier, Robert Charlebois, Franco Fabrizi; ***D:*** Gerard Pires; ***C:*** Silvano Ippoliti.

Act of Passion: The Lost Honor of Kathryn Beck 🦴🦴 ½ **1983** A woman meets a man at a party and has the proverbial one-night stand. Her privacy is shattered when she discovers that he's a terrorist under surveillance by the police and press. Strong performances by Thomas and Kristofferson help turn this into an interesting American TV remake of the German "Lost Honor of Katharina Blum," based loosely on a novel by Heinrich Boll. **100m/C VHS.** Marlo Thomas, Kris Kristofferson, George Dzundza, Jon (John) DeVries; ***D:*** Simon Langton. **TV**

Act of Piracy 🦴 ½ **1989 (R)** A bankrupt contractor reunites with his estranged wife to track down the brutal terrorists who have kidnapped their son. **105m/C VHS.** Gary Busey, Belinda Bauer, Ray Sharkey, Nancy Mulford, Dennis Casey Park, Arnold Vosloo, Ken Gampu; ***D:*** John Cardos; ***W:*** Hal Reed; ***C:*** Vincent Cox; ***M:*** Morton Stevens.

Act of Vengeance 🦴🦴 *Rape Squad* **1974 (R)** A group of women band together to hunt down and exact revenge on the man who raped them. Exploitative action-filled thriller. **90m/C VHS.** Jo Ann Harris, Peter Brown, Jennifer Lee, Lisa Moore, Connie Strickland, Pat Estrin; ***D:*** Bob Kelljan.

Act of Vengeance 🦴🦴 ½ **1986** Drama about Jock Yablonski, a United Mine Workers official who challenged the president, Tony Boyle. Based on fact, showing the events that led up to the murder of Yablonski and his family. Intriguing story lacking cinematic drive. **97m/C VHS.** Charles Bronson, Ellen Burstyn, Wilford Brimley, Hoyt Axton, Robert Schenkkan, Ellen Barkin, Keanu Reeves; ***D:*** John MacKenzie; ***W:*** Scott Spencer. **CABLE**

Act of Violence 🦴🦴 ½ **1948** Postwar melodrama. Small-town businessman and war hero Frank Enley (Heflin) has a pretty wife (Leigh), a young son, and a good life that gets him recognition. But this brings Frank to the attention of embittered, crippled vet Joe Parkson (Ryan), who's got a beef. Seems both were POWs in a German camp and Enley informed on the men's escape plans, which got everyone but Parkson killed. As Parkson pursues Enley through the seedier sides of L.A., Astor enters the picture as a down-heels dame at a dive bar who offers Enley some assistance that results in a lot more trouble. **82m/B DVD.** Van Heflin, Robert Ryan, Janet Leigh, Mary Astor, Phyllis Thaxter, Berry Kroeger, Taylor Holmes; ***D:*** Fred Zinnemann; ***W:*** Robert L. Richards; ***C:*** Robert L. Surtees; ***M:*** Bronislau Kaper.

Act of War 🦴🦴 **1996** Disgraced diplomat/spy Jack Gracey (Scalia) has to stop renegade communists who've taken over a remote nuclear missile site from pressing the button on a missle aimed directly at the White House. Lots of action should hold viewers' interest. **100m/C VHS, DVD.** *CA CZ* Jack Scalia, Ingrid Torrance, Douglas Arthurs; ***D:*** Robert Lee; ***W:*** Michael Bafaro; ***C:*** David Pelletier; ***M:*** Peter Allen. **VIDEO**

Acting on Impulse 🦴🦴 **1993 (R)** Impulsive, troublemaking movie star (Fiorentino) becomes a murder suspect when her producer is killed. This doesn't slow her down. She checks into a hotel with a major party attitude and manages to seduce a conservative businessman (Howell) and his junior exec (Allen) into helping her forget her troubles. And then the businessman's fiancee turns up dead. Any connection? **94m/C VHS.** Linda Fiorentino, C. Thomas Howell, Nancy Allen, Adam Ant, Judith Hoag, Patrick Bauchau, Isaac Hayes, Paul Bartel, Donny Most, Miles O'Keeffe, Dick Sargent, Charles Lane, Mary Woronov, Zelda Rubinstein, Nicholas Sadler, Peter Lupus, Kim McGuire, Cassandra Peterson, Brinke Stevens, Michel Talbot, Robert Alan Golub, Cliff Dorfman, Craig Shoemaker, Scott Thompson Stevens; ***D:*** Sam Irvin; ***W:*** Mark Pittman, Alan Moskowitz; ***C:*** Dean Lent; ***M:*** Daniel Licht. **CABLE**

Action for Slander 🦴🦴 ½ **1938** A British army officer sporting the typical stiff upper lip is accused of cheating during a card game, and the slander mars his reputation until the case is taken to court. Dryly earnest and honest in its depiction of class differences in pre-war England. Based on a novel by Mary Borden. **84m/B VHS.** *GB* Clive Brook, Ann Todd, Margaretta Scott, Ronald Squire, Francis L. Sullivan, Felix Aylmer, Googie Withers; ***D:*** Tim Whelan.

Action in Arabia 🦴🦴 **1944** A newsman uncovers a Nazi plot to turn the Arabs against the Allies while investigating a colleague's murder in Damascus. The desert teems with spies, double agents, and sheiks as suave Sanders goes about his investigative business. Quintessential wartime B-movie. **75m/B VHS.** George Sanders, Virginia Bruce, Lenore Aubert, Gene Lockhart, Robert Armstrong, H.B. Warner, Alan Napier, Michael Ansara; ***D:*** Leonide Moguy.

Action in the North Atlantic 🦴🦴 **1943** Massey and Bogart are the captain and first mate of a Merchant Marine vessel running the lone supply route to the Soviet Union. Eventually they wind up locking horns with a Nazi U-boat. Plenty of action and strenuous flag waving in this propagandorama. Gordon fans won't want to miss her as Massey's wife. Also available colorized. **126m/B VHS, DVD.** Humphrey Bogart, Raymond Massey, Alan Hale, Julie Bishop, Ruth Gordon, Sam Levene, Dane Clark, Peter Whitney, Minor Watson, J.M. Kerrigan, Dick Hogan, Kane Richmond, Chick Chandler, Donald "Don" Douglas, Creighton Hale, Iris Adrian, Elliott Sullivan, Glenn Strange; ***D:*** Lloyd Bacon; ***W:*** A(lbert) I(saac) Bezzerides, W.R. Burnett, John Howard Lawson; ***C:*** Ted D. McCord; ***M:*** Adolph Deutsch.

Action Jackson 🦴🦴 **1988 (R)** Power-hungry auto tycoon Nelson tries to frame rebellious black police sergeant Weathers for murder. Being a graduate of Harvard and a tough guy, the cop doesn't go for it. Nelson eats up the screen as the heavy with no redeeming qualities, while Weathers is tongue-in-cheek as the resourceful good guy who keeps running afoul of the law in spite of his best efforts. Lots of action, violence, and a few sexy women help cover the plot's lack of common sense. **96m/C VHS, DVD.** Carl Weathers, Vanity, Craig T. Nelson, Sharon Stone, Thomas F. Wilson, Mary Ellen Trainor; ***D:*** Craig R. Baxley; ***W:*** Robert Reneau; ***C:*** Matthew F. Leonetti; ***M:*** Herbie Hancock, Michael Kamen.

Action Man 🦴🦴 *Le Soleil des Voyous; Leather and Nylon* **1967** Ferrand (Gabin) has reformed his criminal ways to run a restaurant but he's bored and ready to get involved in one last caper with crooked pal Beckley (Stack). The bank job goes fine but drug dealers kidnap Ferrand's wife and want the loot in exchange for her life. French with subtitles. **95m/C DVD.** *FR IT* Jean Gabin, Robert Stack, Suzanne Flon, Georges Aminel, Walter Giller, Jean Topart, Margaret Lee; ***D:*** Jean Delannoy; ***W:*** Jean Delannoy, Alphonse Boudard; ***C:*** Walter Wottitz; ***M:*** Francis Lai.

Action U.S.A. 🦴 ½ **1989** A young woman witnesses the murder of her boyfriend by gangsters, who then pursue her to make sure she will never tell what she saw. Throughout Texas she rambles with the mob sniffing at her heels, grateful for the opportunity to participate in numerous stunts and car crashes. **90m/C VHS.** Barri Murphy, Gregory Scott Cummins, William Knight, William (Bill) Smith, Cameron Mitchell; ***D:*** John Stewart; ***W:*** David Reskin; ***C:*** Thomas Callaway.

Active Stealth 🦴🦴 **1999 (R)** The Army's most secret weapon, an undetectable fighter jet, is hijacked by terrorists during a training mission. Now, it's up to Jefferson Pike (Baldwin) to lead a team into the Central American jungles to retrieve the military's property. **99m/C VHS, DVD.** Daniel Baldwin, Fred Williamson, Hannes Jaenicke, Chick Vennera, Lisa Vidal; ***D:*** Fred Olen Ray. **VIDEO**

Actor: The Paul Muni Story 🦴🦴 **1978** Musical biography of Paul Muni, from his beginnings as a traveling actor in Hungary to his New York theatre and movie career. **105m/C VHS.** Herschel Bernardi, Georgia Brown, Harold Gould.

Actors and Sin 🦴🦴 ½ **1952** Two-part film casting a critical eye toward actors and Hollywood. "Actor's Blood" is the melodramatic story of Shakespearean actor Robinson and his unhappy actress daughter. She commits suicide and he sets out to prove it was murder. Heavy going. Lighter and more entertaining is "Woman of Sin," which relates a Hollywood satire involving a theatrical agent and his newest client, a precocious nine-year-old. **82m/B VHS.** Edward G. Robinson, Marsha Hunt, Eddie Albert, Alan Reed, Dan O'Herlihy, Tracey Roberts, Rudolph Anders, Paul Guilfoyle, Alice Key, Douglas Evans, Rick Roman, Jenny Hecht, Jody Gilbert, John Crawford; ***D:*** Lee Garmes, Ben Hecht; ***W:*** Ben Hecht; ***C:*** Lee Garmes; ***M:*** George Antheil.

An Actor's Revenge 🦴🦴 *Yukinojo Henge; Revenge of a Kabuki Actor* **1963** In the early 19th century, a female impersonator in a Kabuki troupe takes revenge on the three men who killed his parents. Fascinating study of opposites—male/female, stage/life, love/hate. In Japanese with English subtitles. **110m/C VHS.** *JP* Kazuo Hasegawa, Fujiko Yamamoto, Ayako Wakao, Ganjiro Nakamura; ***D:*** Kon Ichikawa; ***W:*** Teinosuke Kinugasa, Daisuke Ito, Natto Wada; ***C:*** Setsuo Kobayashi; ***M:*** Yashushi Akutagawa.

The Actress 🦴🦴 ½ **1953** Solid performances from Tracy and Wright as the concerned parents although Simmons seems out of her depth (although it befits the character). Working-class Clinton Jones is dismayed that his daughter Ruth is stagestruck and tries to persuade her to a more conventional life. When she is rejected for theater roles in Boston, dad finally realizes how much being an actress means to his little girl and he gives Ruth his only valuable possession to sell so she can move to New York. Film debut of Perkins as the suitor. Based on Gordon's autobiographical play "Years Ago." **90m/B DVD.** Spencer Tracy, Jean Simmons, Teresa Wright, Anthony Perkins, Ian Wolfe, Mary Wickes; ***D:*** George Cukor; ***W:*** Ruth Gordon; ***C:*** Harold Rosson.

Acts of Betrayal 🦴🦴 **1998** Alonso is about to divulge wise guy secrets and for her protection, she's paired with FBI agent McColm to make certain the bad guys don't silence her first. **112m/C VHS.** Maria Conchita Alonso, Matt McColm, Muse Watson, David Groh, Gregory Alan Williams, Susan Lee Hoffman, Joe Estevez; ***D:*** Joakim (Jack) Ersgard; ***W:*** Patrick Highsmith; ***C:*** Jerry Sidell; ***M:*** Roger Neill. **VIDEO**

Acts of Worship 🦴🦴 ½ **2001 (R)** Kicked out by her boyfriend, junkie Alix finds a safe haven with Digna, a former addict. But her attempt to straighten Alix out leads Digna back to her old, bad habits. **94m/C VHS, DVD.** Ana Reeder, Michael Hyatt, Nestor Rodriguez, Christopher Kadish; ***D:*** Rosemary Rodriguez; ***W:*** Rosemary Rodriguez; ***C:*** Luke Geissbuhler; ***M:*** Jim Coleman. **VIDEO**

A.D. 🦴🦴 ½ *Anno Domini* **1985** Set shortly after Jesus' death, this rather low-budget miniseries chronicles the life and adventures of Christ's disciples (especially Peter and Paul) and the growing conflicts between Jewish zealots, early Christians, and the power of the Roman empire. Based on the Acts of the Apostles. **540m/C VHS, DVD.** Denis Quilley, Philip Sayer, Anthony Andrews, Colleen Dewhurst, Ava Gardner, Richard Kiley, James Mason, David Hedison, John Houseman, John McEnery, Ian McShane, Jennifer O'Neill, Fernando Rey, Richard Roundtree, Ben Vereen, Susan Sarandon, Diane Venora, Anthony Zerbe, Jack Warden, Amanda Pays, Millie Perkins, Michael Wilding Jr.; ***D:*** Stuart Cooper; ***W:*** Anthony Burgess; ***C:*** Ennio Guarnieri; ***M:*** Lalo Schifrin. **TV**

Adam 🦴🦴🦴 ½ **1983** Docu-drama based on a tragic, true story. John and Reve Williams (Travanti and Williams) desperately search for their six-year-old son abducted during an outing. During their long search and struggle, they lobby Congress for use of the FBI's crime computer. Eventually their efforts led to the creation of the Missing Children's Bureau. Sensitive, compelling performances by Travanti and Williams as the agonized, courageous parents. **100m/C VHS.** Daniel J. Travanti, JoBeth Williams, Martha Scott, Richard Masur, Paul Regina, Mason Adams; ***D:*** Michael Tuchner. **TV**

Adam 🦴🦴 ½ **2009 (PG-13)** New York-set romantic drama with a twist. Having just moved into her apartment building, teacher Beth (Byrne) becomes intrigued by good-looking neighbor Adam (Dancy) although he's ill at ease socially. After gaining his trust, Adam explains to Rose that he has Asperger's syndrome (a form of autism) and doesn't understand empathy or what people are thinking. Still recovering from a painful break-up, Rose is uncertain if she wants to get involved or how much Adam can participate in a romantic relationship, especially when her parents' reservations and problems begin interfering. Dancy never overdoes his role and Byrne is sympathetic without being cloying. **97m/C DVD.** *US* Hugh Dancy, Rose Byrne, Frankie Faison, Amy Irving, Peter Gallagher, Mark Linn-Baker; ***D:*** Max Mayer; ***W:*** Max Mayer; ***C:*** Seamus Tierney; ***M:*** Christopher Lennertz.

Adam & Steve 🦴🦴 **2005** Contrived but generally amusing gay romance begins in 1987 when shy goth boy Adam (writer/director Chester) meets glittery party boy Steve (Gets) and their trick turns into disaster. They meet cute 17 years later, don't recognize each other, and start a romance fraught with individual neuroses that stem from that fateful night. Each man also comes complete with the prerequisite straight best friend: for Adam, it's former-fatty turned skinny comic Rhonda (Posey) and for Steve it's caustic roommate Michael (Kattan). A couple of musical fantasy sequences provide some unexpected distraction. **99m/C DVD.** *US* Craig Chester, Malcolm Gets, Parker Posey, Chris Kattan, Sally Kirkland, Noah Segan; ***D:*** Craig Chester; ***W:*** Craig Chester; ***C:*** Carl F. Bartels; ***M:*** Roddy Bottum.

Adam at 6 a.m. 🦴🦴 **1970 (PG)** Douglas is a young college professor who decides to spend a summer laboring in Missouri, where life, he thinks, is simpler. Of course, he learns that life in the boonies has its own set of problems, but unfortunately it takes him the entire movie before he catches the drift. **100m/C VHS, DVD.** Michael Douglas, Lee Purcell, Joe Don Baker, Charles Aidman, Marge Redmond, Louise Latham, Grayson Hall, Dana Elcar, Meg Foster, Richard Derr, Anne Gwynne; ***D:*** Robert Scheerer.

Adam Had Four Sons 🦴🦴 ½ **1941** Satisfying character study involving the typical turn-of-the-century family nearly consumed by love, jealousy, and hatred. In the early part of the century, a goodly governess (Bergman in her second U.S. film) watches sympathetically over four sons of an American businessman after their mother dies. Economic necessity separates Bergman from the family for several years. Upon her return, she tangles with scheming bride-to-be Hayward, a bad girl intent on dividing and conquering the family before walking down the aisle with one of the sons. Based on a novel by Charles Bonner. **81m/B VHS, DVD.** Ingrid Bergman, Warner Baxter, Susan Hayward, Fay Wray, Richard Denning, June Lockhart, Robert Shaw, Johnny Downs; ***D:*** Gregory Ratoff.

Adam Resurrected 🦴 ½ **2008 (R)** An unsettling story, with a brilliant lead performance by Goldblum, but Schrader's tone veers uncertainly. Adam Stein (Goldblum) was a successful Jewish cabaret performer in Berlin until the Nazis came to power. Sent to a concentration camp, Adam survives because the camp's Commandant (Defoe) is an admirer. But he also treats Adam (literally) like a dog so it's no wonder that Adam eventually winds up in an Israeli mental hospital for Holocaust survivors. He's still using humor as a coping mechanism but circumstances and survivors' guilt undermine an already shaky foundation. Based on the novel by Yoram Kaniuk. **106m/C DVD.** *GE IS* Jeff Goldblum, Willem Dafoe, Derek Jacobi, Ayelet Zurer, Moritz Bleibtreu, Hanna Laslo, Tudor Rapiteanu; ***D:*** Paul Schrader; ***W:*** Noah Stollman; ***C:*** Sebastian Edscmid; ***M:*** Gabriel Yared.

Adam Sandler's 8 Crazy Nights 🦴🦴 *8 Crazy Nights* **2002 (PG-13)** Parents should be warned that Adam Sandler's foray into animated holiday fare is more for the big kids than the tiny tots. When eyes are aglow, it's usually the bloodshot peepers of party animal Davey Stone (voiced by Sandler), who harbors a grudge against the holiday season. After he goes on a spree of booze-soaked vandalism, the judge is about to throw the book at Davey until Whitey, the ref of a youth basketball league, intercedes for him. Davey proceeds to torment Whitey and his sister Eleanor (both also voiced by Sandler) until the last act less-than-believably transforms him into a good guy. At turns offensive and interesting, this foul-mouthed cartoon does manage to set a record for animated product placement. **71m/C VHS, DVD.** *US* ***D:*** Seth Kearsley; ***W:*** Adam Sandler, Allen Covert, Brooks Arthur, Brad Isaacs; ***M:*** Marc Ellis, Ray Ellis, Teddy Castellucci; ***V:*** Adam Sandler, Kevin Nealon, Rob Schneider, Norm Crosby, Jackie Titone, Austin Stout, Jon Lovitz.

Adam's Apples 🦴🦴 *Adams Aebler* **2005 (R)** Danish black comedy about a Neo-Nazi forced to finish a prison sentence doing community service at a church. Adam (Thomsen) is EVIL and meets his opposite in the positive-to-a-fault priest Ivan (Mikkelsen). Adam promises Ivan that he'll make a pie from the apples that grow in the churchyard, but as crows and disease peck away at the apples, Adam decides to break Ivan down, mentally and physically. Alternately bleak and ludicrous, the movie is mostly style over substance and rarely digs deeper than the basic absurdity of its premise. **93m/C DVD.** *CZ* Ulrich Thomsen, Mads Mikkelsen, Paprika Steen, Nikolaj Lie Kaas, Nicolas Bro, Ali Kazim, Ole Thestrup; ***D:*** Anders Thomas Jensen; ***W:*** Anders Thomas Jensen; ***C:*** Sebastian Blenkov; ***M:*** Jeppe Kaas.

Adam's Rib 🦴🦴🦴🦴 **1950** Classic war between the sexes cast Tracy and Hepburn as married attorneys on opposite sides of the courtroom in the trial of blonde bombshell Holliday, charged with attempted murder of the lover of her philandering husband. The battle in the courtroom soon takes its toll at home as the couple is increasingly unable to leave their work at the office. Sharp, snappy dialogue by Gordon and Kanin with superb direction by Cukor. Perhaps the best of the nine movies pairing Tracy and Hepburn. Also available colorized. **101m/B VHS, DVD.** Spencer Tracy, Katharine Hepburn, Judy Holliday, Tom Ewell, David Wayne, Jean Hagen, Hope Emerson, Polly Moran, Marvin Kaplan, Paula Raymond, Tommy Noonan; ***D:*** George Cukor; ***W:*** Garson Kanin, Ruth Gordon; ***C:***

George J. Folsey; *M:* Miklos Rozsa. Natl. Film Reg. '92.

Adaptation 🦴🦴🦴 1/2 **2002 (R)** Quirky but highly entertaining comedy about blocked L.A. screenwriter Charlie Kaufman (Cage), hired to adapt author Susan Orlean's (Streep) book "The Orchid Thief." The book recounts the story of John Laroche (Cooper), one of a breed of orchid-obsessed con men who schemes to steal the desirable plants from the Florida Everglades. At a loss as to how to treat the story, the neurotic Charlie becomes obsessed with Orlean, gazing at her picture while his lesser twin brother Donald (also Cage), breezily announces the sales of his own million dollar screenplay, which he wrote after one seminar. Meanwhile, Orlean travels to Florida to interview the gap-toothed Laroche and begins her own minor obsession. Plot twists keep you on your toes right down to the surprise ending. Cage is at his best as the twin writers, while Streep shows off her comic chops and Cooper turns in a career-making performance. Deftly directed by Jonze. **114m/C VHS, DVD.** *US* Nicolas Cage, Meryl Streep, Chris Cooper, Tilda Swinton, Cara Seymour, Brian Cox, Judy Greer, Maggie Gyllenhaal, Ron Livingston, Stephen Tobolowsky, Jay Tavare, Litefoot, Gary Farmer, Peter Jason, Curtis Hanson; *D:* Spike Jonze; *W:* Charlie Kaufman; *C:* Lance Acord; *M:* Carter Burwell. Oscars '02: Support. Actor (Cooper); British Acad. '02: Adapt. Screenplay; Golden Globes '03: Support. Actor (Cooper), Support. Actress (Streep); L.A. Film Critics '02: Support. Actor (Cooper); Natl. Bd. of Review '02: Screenplay, Support. Actor (Cooper); N.Y. Film Critics '02: Screenplay.

The Addams Family 🦴🦴 1/2 **1991 (PG-13)** Everybody's favorite family of ghouls hits the big screen, but something is lost in the translation. An imposter claiming to be long-lost Uncle Fester (Lloyd), who says he was in the Bermuda Triangle for 25 years, shows up at the Addams' home to complete a dastardly deed—raid the family's immense fortune. Although Fester's plan is foiled, a series of plot twists highlight the ghoulish family's eccentricities. Darkly humorous but eventually disappointing: Julia, Huston, and Ricci (as Gomez, Morticia, and Wednesday, respectively) are great in their roles and the sets look good, but the plot is thin. Much closer to the original comic strip by Charles Addams than the popular TV show ever was. **102m/C VHS, DVD.** Anjelica Huston, Raul Julia, Christopher Lloyd, Dan Hedaya, Elizabeth Wilson, Judith Malina, Carel Struycken, Dana Ivey, Paul Benedict, Christina Ricci, Jimmy Workman, Christopher Hart, John Franklin; ***Cameos:*** Marc Shaiman; *D:* Barry Sonnenfeld; *W:* Caroline Thompson, Larry Thompson; *C:* Owen Roizman; *M:* Marc Shaiman. Golden Raspberries '91: Worst Song ("Addams Groove").

Addams Family Values 🦴🦴 1/2 **1993 (PG-13)** The creepy Addams' are back, but this time they leave the dark confines of the mansion to meet the "real" world. New baby Pubert causes homicidal jealousy in sibs Wednesday and Pugsley, causing Mom and Dad to hire a gold-digging, serial-killing nanny (Cusack) with designs on Uncle Fester to watch over the tot. A step above its predecessor, chock full of black humor, subplots, and one-liners. Cusack fits right in with an outrageously over the top performance and Ricci nearly steals the show again as the deadpan Wednesday. **93m/C VHS, DVD.** Anjelica Huston, Raul Julia, Christopher Lloyd, Joan Cusack, Carol Kane, Christina Ricci, Jimmy Workman, Kaitlyn Hooper, Kristen Hooper, Carel Struycken, David Krumholtz, Christopher Hart, Dana Ivey, Peter MacNichol, Christine Baranski, Mercedes McNab; *D:* Barry Sonnenfeld; *W:* Paul Rudnick; *M:* Marc Shaiman. Golden Raspberries '93: Worst Song ("WHOOMP! There It Is").

Addicted 🦴🦴 *Jungdok* **2002** Ho-jin (Eol Lee) and Dae-jin (Byung-hun Lee) are brothers so close that even after Dae-jin marries Eun-su (Mi-yeon Lee), his brother continues to live with them. At least until they both have tragic car accidents on the same day and end up in comas. After a year only Dae-jin awakens, but he goes home to keep the same routine his brother always had. Even weirder he has his brother's skills as a cook, and knows things only Ho-jin would know. **112m/C DVD.** *KN* Byung-hun Lee, Mi-yeon Lee, Eol Lee, Seon-Yeong Park, Byung-hun Lee, Mi-yeon Lee, Eol Lee, Young-hoon Park; *D:* Young-hoon Park, Young-hoon Park; *W:* Won-mi Byun, Won-mi Byun; *C:* Byeong-il Kim, Byeong-il Kim; *M:* Jae-hyeong Jeong, Jae-hyeong Jeong.

Addicted to Love 🦴🦴 1/2 **1996 (R)** Warning: Do not rent this movie with your significant other if you're thinking about breaking up with them. After they're both dumped, mild-mannered Sam (Broderick) and wild woman Maggie (Ryan) discover they have a lot in common. First of all, their exes Linda (Preston) and Anton (Karyo) are dating each other. Secondly, they're both stalkers! Yep! A romantic comedy about stalking. Sam wants nothing more than to reclaim Linda as his own. Maggie wants nothing less than Anton's head on a plate. Interesting comedy wavers between dark and light moments, aided by the rather murky sets and lighting. Directorial debut for Dunne, who makes his father eat a bug in one scene. **100m/C VHS, DVD.** Meg Ryan, Matthew Broderick, Kelly Preston, Tcheky Karyo, Maureen Stapleton, Remak Ramsay, Nesbitt Blaisdell, Dominick Dunne; *D:* Griffin Dunne; *W:* Robert Gordon; *C:* Andrew Dunn; *M:* Rachel Portman.

Addicted to Murder 🦴🦴 **1995** Joel Winter (McCleery) was abused as a child and now takes his anger out on women by killing them. Then he meets vampire Angie (Graham), who decides to transform him since he's already a predator. But Joel develops a conscience and tries to reform, which ticks Angie off and she frames him for a murder he didn't commit. Which ticks Joel off so he becomes a vampire (and a vampire hunter) to get even. **90m/C VHS, DVD.** Michael (Mick) McCleery, Sasha Graham, Laura McLaughlin; *D:* Kevin J. Lindenmuth; *W:* Kevin J. Lindenmuth; *C:* Kevin J. Lindenmuth. **VIDEO**

Addicted to Murder 2: Tainted Blood 🦴 1/2 **1997** It's a case of diminishing returns as is usual with sequels in this plotwise mishmash. New York City is the happy hunting grounds for a rogue vamp who's turning others whom Angie (Graham) doesn't considered worthy of getting "The Gift." So she intends to put a stop to it. And just around for more laughs is Joel (McCleery)—the serial killer turned vampire turned vampire hunter. **80m/C VHS, DVD.** Sasha Graham, Michael (Mick) McCleery, Sarah K. Lippmann, Robbi Firestone, Ted Grayson, Joe Moretti, Joel D. Wynkoop, Tom NonDorf; ***Cameos:*** Ted V. Mikels; *D:* Kevin J. Lindenmuth; *W:* Kevin J. Lindenmuth. **VIDEO**

Addicted to Murder 3: Bloodlust 🦴 1/2 **1999** Serial killer Joel Winter (McCleery) continues his quest to eliminate vampires in revenge for his own transformation. One master vamp thinks he has a secure haven but he's very wrong. **85m/C VHS, DVD.** Michael (Mick) McCleery, Sarah K. Lippmann, Nick Kostopoulos, Cloud Michaels, Grant Cramer, Frank Lopez, Joe Zaso, Jon Sanborne, Reid Ostrowski; *D:* Kevin J. Lindenmuth, Tom Vollmann; *W:* Kevin J. Lindenmuth, Tom Vollmann. **VIDEO**

The Addiction 🦴🦴 1/2 **1995 (R)** Ph.D. candidate Kathleen Conklin (Taylor, in a haunting performance) gets bitten by more than the philosophy bug while attending university in Manhattan. When attacked by a female vampire (Sciorra), Kathleen quickly becomes driven by a ferocious blood need, beginning with an attack that parallels drug addiction when she stabs a derelict with a hypodermic needle and injects his blood into her own veins. Bitingly pretentious, themes experiment with the philosophy of Kirkegaard, Nietzsche, and Sartre, and exploitative glimpses of the Holocaust and the My Lai massacre attempt to connect Kathleen's struggle to resist evil to historical atrocities. **82m/B VHS.** Lili Taylor, Christopher Walken, Annabella Sciorra, Edie Falco, Paul Calderon, Fredro Starr, Kathryn Erbe, Michael Imperioli; *D:* Abel Ferrara; *W:* Nicholas St. John; *C:* Ken Kelsch; *M:* Joe Delia.

Address Unknown 🦴🦴 1/2 **1996 (PG)** A ten-year-old letter and a priceless stamp provide a teenager with clues to dad's mysterious death. **92m/C VHS.** Kyle Howard, Johna Stewart, Patrick Renna, Corbin Allred, Michael Flynn; *D:* Shawn Levy.

Adelheid 🦴🦴 **1969** Viktor, a Czech soldier, returns home after WWII and is told to inventory the contents of a mansion that was owned by a wealthy German family. Adelheid, the daughter of the previous owner, is now a servant there and though Viktor falls in love, the lingering bitterness of the war ruins the romance. Czech with subtitles. **99m/C DVD.** *CZ* Petr Cepek, Emma Cerna; *D:* Frantisek Vlacil; *W:* Frantisek Vlacil, Vladimir Korner; *C:* Frantisek Uldrich; *M:* Zdenek Liska.

Adios Amigo 🦴🦴 **1975 (PG)** Offbeat western comedy has ad-libbing Pryor hustling as a perennially inept con man. Script and direction (both provided by Williamson) are not up to Pryor's level, although excessive violence and vulgarity are avoided in a boring attempt to provide good clean family fare. **87m/C VHS, DVD.** Fred Williamson, Richard Pryor, Thalmus Rasulala, James Brown, Robert Phillips, Mike Henry; *D:* Fred Williamson; *W:* Fred Williamson.

Adios, Hombre 🦴 **1968** An innocent man who was imprisoned for murder escapes from prison and seeks revenge. You'll be saying adios as well. **90m/C VHS.** *IT* Craig Hill, Giulia Rubini; *D:* Mario Caiano.

Adios, Sabata 🦴 1/2 **1971 (PG-13)** Brynner took over the role for one sequel. In 1873, Sabata comes to the aid of a band of Mexican revolutionaries who want to steal a wagonload of gold from sadistic Austrian interloper, Colonel Von Skimmel. **102m/C DVD.** *IT* Yul Brynner, Ignazio Spalla, Gerard Herter, Dean Reed, Sal Borgese, Franco Fantasia; *D:* Gianfranco Parolini; *W:* Gianfranco Parolini, Renato Izzo; *C:* Sandro Moncori; *M:* Bruno Nicolai.

The Adjuster 🦴🦴 1/2 **1991 (R)** Critics either loved or hated this strange film. Insurance adjuster Noah Render's clients look to him for all sorts of comfort, so much so that his own identity becomes a blurred reflection of their tragedies. Wife Hera is a film censor who secretly tapes the pornographic videos she watches at work. Their carefully organized lives are invaded by Bubba and Mimi, a wealthy couple who pass themselves off as filmmakers who want to use the Render house as a movie set. They are instead looking to involve the Renders in their latest and most elaborate erotic fantasy. Lots of symbolism, but little substance. **102m/C VHS, DVD.** *CA* Elias Koteas, Arsinee Khanjian, Maury Chaykin, Gabrielle Rose, David Hemblen, Jennifer Dale, Don McKellar, Raoul Trujillo; *D:* Atom Egoyan; *W:* Atom Egoyan; *C:* Paul Sarossy; *M:* Mychael Danna. Toronto-City '91: Canadian Feature Film.

The Adjustment Bureau **2010** Expect the weird since the movie is based on a story by Philip K. Dick. Rising congressman David Norris (Damon) discovers strange forces are keeping him apart from potential lover, ballet dancer Elise (Blunt). **m/C DVD.** *US* Matt Damon, Emily Blunt, Anthony Mackie, Terence Stamp, Daniel Dae Kim, John Slattery, David Alan Basche, Anthony Michael Ruivivar, Michael Kelly, Shohreh Aghdashloo; *D:* George Nolfi; *W:* George Nolfi; *C:* John Toll.

The Admirable Crichton 🦴🦴 1/2 **1957** Social satire about an aristocratic family and their butler who are marooned on a tropical island. Crichton (More), the butler, has a good deal more practical experience and sense than his employers so he's soon in charge of their survival. Filmed in Bermuda and based on the play by James M. Barrie. **93m/C VHS.** *GB* Kenneth More, Cecil Parker, Sally Ann Howes, Diane Cilento, Martita Hunt, Jack Watling, Peter Graves, Gerald Harper; *D:* Lewis Gilbert; *W:* Vernon Harris; *C:* Wilkie Cooper; *M:* Douglas Gamley.

The Admiral Was a Lady 🦴🦴 **1950** Four ex-GIs try to get by in life without going to work. Hendrix walks into their lives as a winning ex-Wave gifted with a knack for repartee who is disgusted by their collective lack of ambition. Nevertheless, she is pursued by the zany quartet with predictable results. **87m/B VHS, DVD.** Edmond O'Brien, Wanda Hendrix, Rudy Vallee, Steve Brodie; *D:* Albert Rogell.

Adomas Nori Buti Zmogumi 🦴🦴 *Adam Wants to Be a Man* **1959** Soviet Lithuanian feature in its original form, with dialogue in Lithuanian. A young worker scrapes together money for a ticket to Buenos Aires, but the money is stolen by the manager of the travel office. **90m/B VHS.** *RU LI* Donatas Banionis, Juozas Miltinis; *D:* V. Zhalakyavichus; *W:* V. Zhalakyavichus; *C:* Algimantas Mockus.

Adoption 🦴🦴🦴 *Orkobefogadas* **1975** The third of Meszaros's trilogy, involving a middle-aged Hungarian woman who longs for a child and instead forms a deep friendship with a 19-year-old orphan. In Hungarian with English subtitles. **89m/B VHS, DVD.** *HU* Kati Berek, Laszlo Szabo, Gyongyver Vigh, Dr. Arpad Perlaky; *D:* Marta Meszaros; *W:* Marta Meszaros, Gyula Hernadi; *C:* Lajos Koltai; *M:* Gyorgy Kovacs. Berlin Intl. Film Fest. '75: Golden Berlin Bear.

The Adorable Cheat 🦴🦴 **1928** A low-budget, late-silent melodrama about a young woman who tries to get involved in the family business, despite her father's refusal of her help. Once in the business, she finds love. **76m/B VHS.** Lila Lee, Cornelius Keefe, Burr McIntosh; *D:* Burton King.

Adorable Julia 🦴🦴 **1962** When an actress takes on a lover many years younger than herself, the laughs begin to fly in this sex comedy based on W. Somerset Maugham's novel. **97m/C VHS.** *FR* Lilli Palmer, Charles Boyer; *D:* Alfred Weidenmann.

Adoration 🦴🦴 **2008 (R)** High-school French teacher Sabine (Khanjian) gives her class a translation exercise based on a news story about a terrorist and his pregnant girlfriend. Student Simon (Bostick) has a lot of unresolved feelings about his parents' death in a car crash, especially since his bigoted grandfather (Welsh) has led Simon to believe that his Lebanese father deliberately caused the accident. Simon uses the article to imagine himself as the terrorist's now-grown son but presents his work as fact not fiction when he uses a webcam to take the story to internet chat rooms, which has the deception spiraling out of control. English and French with subtitles. **101m/C DVD.** *CA FR* Arsinee Khanjian, Scott Speedman, Rachel Blanchard, Noam Jenkins, Kenneth Welsh; *D:* Atom Egoyan; *W:* Atom Egoyan; *C:* Paul Sarossy; *M:* Mychael Danna.

Adrenalin: Fear the Rush 🦴 **1996 (R)** Dull future thriller in the deadly virus category. In 2007, a plague in Eastern Europe causes those that survive to turn into cannabalistic killers. The U.S. has started quarantine camps, one of which is in Boston, and two cops (Henstridge and Lambert) must track down an infected killer who's escaped. Not worth your time. **77m/C VHS, DVD.** Christopher Lambert, Natasha Henstridge, Norbert Weisser, Craig Davis, Elizabeth Barondes, Xavier DeClie; *D:* Albert Pyun; *W:* Albert Pyun; *C:* George Mooradian; *M:* Tony Riparetti.

Adrenaline Drive 🦴🦴 *Adorenarin Doraibu* **1999** Sad sack Suzuki (Ando), who's working for a car rental company, accidentally plows a car into the Jaguar of yakuza big guy Kuroiwa (Matushige). Before punishment can be exacted, there's an explosion that lands them in the hospital. Three shy nurse Shizuko (Ishida) latches on both to Suzuki and to a yakuza suitcase full of money and drags both on a road trip to freedom. Silly, good-natured comedy. Japanese with subtitles. **111m/C VHS, DVD.** *JP* Hikari Ishida, Mansanobu Ando, Yutaka Matushige, Kazue Tsunogae; *D:* Shinobu Yaguchi; *W:* Shinobu Yaguchi; *C:* Takashi Hamada; *M:* Seiichi Yamamoto.

Adrift 🦴🦴 1/2 **1993** Yet another couple-in-terror-from-psychos-on-the-high-seas flick. Katie and Guy Nast (Jackson and Welsh) are on an anniversary sailing adventure intended to shore up their shaky marriage. They discover a boat adrift with two survivors (Greenwood and Rowan) who have a suspicious story but they help them nonetheless. Big mistake. **92m/C VHS.** Kate Jackson, Kenneth Welsh, Bruce Greenwood, Kelly Rowan; *D:* Christian Duguay. **TV**

Adrift in Manhattan 🦴🦴 **2007 (R)** Chance encounters change the lives of three lonely New Yorkers. Simon (Rasuk) is a young man with a passion for photography. Snapping street pics, he finds his muse in depressed optometrist Rose (Graham), who's estranged from her husband (Baldwin) after their young child's death. Rose's patient Tommaso (Chianese), a painter, is going blind and she encourages him to find comfort with someone, deciding to take her own advice after Simon gets the courage to introduce himself. **91m/C DVD.** Heather Graham, William Baldwin, Victor Rasuk, Dominic Chianese, Elizabeth Pena, Marta Colon, Erika Michels; ***D:*** Alfredo de Villa; ***W:*** Alfredo de Villa, Nat Moss; ***C:*** John Foster; ***M:*** Michael A. Levine.

The Adultress **1977 (R)** When a husband and wife cannot satisfy their desire to have a family, they hire a young man to help them in this dumb melodrama. **85m/C VHS.** Tyne Daly, Eric (Hans Gudegast) Braeden, Gregory Morton; ***D:*** Norbert Meisel. **TV**

Adventure **1945** Gable's first post-war film has him as a roughneck sailor romancing a shy and reserved librarian (Garson). Dull and disappointing—both stars deserve better. However, there is a touching scene of Gable with newborn child that might be of interest to some. Based on the novel by Clyde Brion Davis. **130m/B VHS.** Clark Gable, Greer Garson, Joan Blondell, Thomas Mitchell, Tom Tully, John Qualen, Richard Haydn, Lina Romay; ***D:*** Victor Fleming; ***W:*** Vincent Lawrence, Frederick Hazlitt Brennan; ***C:*** Joseph Ruttenberg.

Adventure in Sahara 1/2 **1938** Typical desert soldier saga. Savatt (Gordon) is the cruel commander of a detachment of Foreign Legionnaires. Most of his brutalized men eventually mutiny and send him and a few loyalists off into the desert. They survive, and Savatt vows revenge, but when they arrive back at their outpost it is under siege. **60m/B DVD.** Paul Kelly, C. Henry Gordon, Adrian Booth, Robert (Fisk) Fiske, Marc Lawrence, Dick Curtis, Robert (Fisk) Fiske; ***D:*** David Ross Lederman; ***W:*** Maxwell Shane; ***C:*** Franz Planer.

Adventure Island 1/2 **1947** En route to Australia, a small ship stops at a remote island for supplies. The crew is greeted by a crazed, tyrannical leader who makes their lives difficult. Dull low-budget remake of 1937's "Ebb Tide." **66m/C VHS.** Rory Calhoun, Rhonda Fleming, Paul Kelly, John Abbott, Alan Napier; ***D:*** Sam Newfield.

Adventure of the Action Hunters **1987 (PG)** A dying sailor leaves a tourist couple a message leading to a treasure, and they vie for it along with gangsters, mercenaries and other unsavory types. **81m/C VHS.** Ronald Hunter, Sean Murphy, Joe Cimino; ***D:*** Lee Bonner.

Adventureland **2009 (R)** With his post-college dreams of a European trip squashed by his dad's financial problems, James (Eisenberg) instead must move back home to Pennsylvania in the summer of 1987 and with his limited degree can only find work at the "Adventureland," the ragged local amusement park. Still a virgin, James encounters Em (Stewart), a sexually-experienced though troubled young woman who can't stand her stepmother and is having an affair with the park's married handyman (Reynolds). The pair genuinely connect, in large part to the actors, particularly Stewart. Yes, it's a coming-of-age comedy and has the usual sophomoric jokes, vulgarity, and drug use but they are just background to a charming love story. Based in part on writer-director Mottola's own life, also features a great '80s soundtrack and a fun pairing of SNLers Wiig and Hader as the park's married owners. **107m/C DVD.** *US* Jesse Eisenberg, Kristen Stewart, Martin Starr, Bill Hader, Bill Hader, Kristen Wiig, Ryan Reynolds; ***D:*** Greg Mottola; ***W:*** Greg Mottola; ***C:*** Terry Stacey.

The Adventurer 1/2 **1917** An escaped convict saves two wealthy women from death. They mistake him for a gallant sportsman and bring him home. Early Chaplin silent with music track. **20m/B VHS, DVD.** Charlie Chaplin, Charles Halton; ***D:*** Charlie Chaplin.

The Adventurers *Fortune in Diamonds; The Great Adventure* **1951** At the turn of the century, two Boers and an English officer set out to recover stolen jewels hidden in the jungles of South Africa. On the way, greed and anger take their toll a la "The Treasure of Sierra Madre," only on a less convincing scale. **82m/B VHS.** *GB* Dennis Price, Jack Hawkins, Siobhan McKenna, Peter Hammond, Bernard Lee; ***D:*** David MacDonald.

The Adventurers **WOOF!** **1970 (R)** Sleazy Harold Robbins novel retains its trashy aura on film. Unfortunately, this turkey is also long and boring. Set in South America, it tells the tale of a rich playboy who uses and destroys everyone who crosses his path. His vileness results from having seen his mother murdered by outlaws, but his obsession is to avenge his father's murder. Blood, gore, revolutions, and exploitive sex follow him everywhere. Watch and be amazed at the big-name stars who signed on for this one. **171m/C VHS, DVD.** Candice Bergen, Olivia de Havilland, Bekim Fehmiu, Charles Aznavour, Alan Badel, Ernest Borgnine, Leigh Taylor-Young, Fernando Rey, Thommy Berggren, John Ireland, Sydney Tafler, Rossano Brazzi, Anna Moffo, Christian Roberts, Yorgo Voyagis, Angela Scoular, Yolande Donlan, Ferdinand "Ferdy" Mayne, Jaclyn Smith, Peter Graves, Roberta Haynes; ***D:*** Lewis Gilbert.

Adventures Beyond Belief *Neat and Tidy* **1987** An irreverent motorcyclist is chased across Europe for a murder he didn't commit. Firmly within the boundaries of belief. **95m/C VHS.** Elke Sommer, Jill Whitlow, Graham Stark, Stella Stevens, Larry Storch, Thick Wilson, Skyler Cole, Edie Adams, John Astin; ***D:*** Marcus Thompson.

Adventures in Babysitting 1/2 **1987 (PG-13)** Pleasant comedy has its moments when a babysitter and her charges leave peaceful suburbia for downtown Chicago to rescue a friend in trouble. After a flat tire strands them on the freeway, trouble takes on a new meaning. Shue is charming as the hapless sitter, unexpectedly dateless, who finds herself doing a lot more than just watching the kids. Ludicrous at times, but still fun to watch. **102m/C VHS, DVD.** Elisabeth Shue, Keith Coogan, Maia Brewton, Anthony Rapp, Calvin Levels, Vincent D'Onofrio, Penelope Ann Miller, George Newbern, John Ford Noonan, Lolita (David) Davidovich, Albert Collins; ***D:*** Chris Columbus; ***W:*** David Simkins; ***C:*** Ric Waite; ***M:*** Michael Kamen.

Adventures in Dinosaur City **1992 (PG)** Expect to see lots of movies riding on the coattails of the dino mania sweeping the land. Some will be good, others will not. "Adventures" falls into the latter category. Modern-day pre-teen siblings are transported back in time to the stone age. There they meet their favorite TV characters (they're dinosaurs) and help them solve prehistoric crimes. Family film may amuse kids, but adults should stick to "Jurassic Park." **88m/C VHS.** Omri Katz, Shawn Hoffman, Tiffanie Poston, Pete Koch, Megan Hughes, Tony Doyle, Mimi Maynard; ***D:*** Brett Thompson; ***W:*** Willie Baronet, Lisa Morton; ***M:*** Fredric Teetsel.

Adventures in Spying **1992 (PG-13)** Brian McNichols is just trying to enjoy his summer vacation when he discovers that a notorious drug lord is living in his neighborhood. After realizing there is a $50, 000 reward for his capture, he enlists the help of his friend (Schoelen) to get the man's picture for the police. Action-packed film is geared towards the junior high set, but relies too heavily on coincidence and other plot connivances to compete with espionage flicks directed at an older market. **92m/C VHS.** Jill Schoelen, Bernie Coulson, Seymour Cassel, G. Gordon Liddy, Michael Emil; ***D:*** Hil Covington; ***W:*** Hil Covington; ***M:*** James Stemple.

The Adventures of a Gnome Named Gnorm 1/2 *A Gnome Named Gnorm* **1993 (PG)** Silly cop caper finds LAPD detective Casey (Hall) stuck with a very strange new partner—a bark-wearing gnome named Gnorm. The two team up to go after a diamond smuggling ring. The special-effects creature may hold the kiddies interest. **86m/C VHS.** Anthony Michael Hall, Jerry Orbach, Claudia Christian; ***D:*** Stan Winston.

Adventures of a Private Eye **1977** A self-mocking British detective farce about an inept private eye who takes his time tracking down a beautiful girl's blackmailer, bedding down with all the women he meets along the way. **96m/C VHS.** *GB* Christopher Neil, Suzy Kendall, Irene Handl; ***D:*** Stanley Long; ***W:*** Michael Armstrong, Stanley Long; ***C:*** Peter Sinclair.

Adventures of a Taxi Driver **WOOF!** **1976** Cabbie finds sex, crime, sex, adventure and sex on the road in this off-duty comedy. **89m/C VHS.** *GB* Barry Evans, Judy Geeson, Adrienne Posta, Diana Dors, Liz Fraser; ***D:*** Stanley Long.

The Adventures of Baron Munchausen 1/2 **1989 (PG)** From the director of "Time Bandits," "Brazil," and "The Fisher King" comes an ambitious, imaginative, chaotic, and under-appreciated marvel based on the tall (and often confused) tales of the Baron. Munchausen encounters the King of the Moon, Venus, and other odd and fascinating characters during what might be described as a circular narrative in which flashbacks dovetail into the present and place and time are never quite what they seem. Wonderful special effects and visually stunning sets occasionally dwarf the actors and prove what Gilliam can do with a big budget. **126m/C VHS, DVD.** *GB GE* John Neville, Eric Idle, Sarah Polley, Valentina Cortese, Oliver Reed, Uma Thurman, Sting, Jonathan Pryce, Bill Paterson, Peter Jeffrey, Alison Steadman, Charles McKeown, Winston Dennis, Jack Purvis, Don Henderson, Andrew MacLachlan; ***Cameos:*** Robin Williams; ***D:*** Terry Gilliam; ***W:*** Terry Gilliam, Charles McKeown; ***C:*** Giuseppe Rotunno; ***M:*** Michael Kamen.

The Adventures of Buckaroo Banzai Across the Eighth Dimension *Buckaroo Banzai* **1984 (PG)** A man of many talents, Buckaroo Banzai (Weller) travels through the eighth dimension in a jet-propelled Ford Fiesta to battle Planet 10 aliens led by the evil Lithgow. Buckaroo incorporates his vast knowledge of medicine, science, music, racing, and foreign relations to his advantage. Offbeat and often humorous cult sci-fi trip. **100m/C VHS, DVD.** Peter Weller, Ellen Barkin, Jeff Goldblum, Christopher Lloyd, John Lithgow, Lewis Smith, Rosalind Cash, Robert Ito, Pepe Serna, Vincent Schiavelli, Dan Hedaya, Yakov Smirnoff, Jamie Lee Curtis, Ronald Lacey, Matt Clark, Clancy Brown, Carl Lumbly, Boyd 'Red' Morgan, Damon Hines, Billy Vera, Bill Henderson, Jonathan Banks, John Ashton, James Saito; ***D:*** W.D. Richter; ***W:*** Earl MacRauch; ***C:*** Fred W. Koenekamp; ***M:*** Michael Boddicker.

The Adventures of Bullwhip Griffin 1/2 **1966** A rowdy, family-oriented comedy-adventure set during the California Gold Rush. Light Disney farce catches Russell at the tail end of his teenage star days. Pleshette and McDowall embark upon an ocean trip from Boston to San Francisco to find her brother, Russell, who's out west digging for gold. Assorted comedic adventures take place. **110m/C VHS, DVD.** Roddy McDowall, Suzanne Pleshette, Karl Malden, Harry Guardino, Bryan Russell; ***D:*** James Neilson; ***C:*** Edward Colman; ***M:*** George Bruns.

Adventures of Captain Fabian 1/2 **1951** When the captain of the "China Sea" learns that a beautiful woman has been falsely imprisoned, he comes to her rescue. Not one of Flynn's better swashbucklers, with typically low-quality Republic production. **100m/B VHS.** Errol Flynn, Vincent Price, Agnes Moorehead, Micheline Presle; ***D:*** William Marshall.

The Adventures of Captain Marvel 1/2 **1941** A 12-episode cliff-hanging serial based on the comic book character. Details the adventures of klutzy Billy Batson, who transforms into superhero Captain Marvel by speaking the magic word, "Shazam!" **240m/B VHS, DVD.** Tom Tyler, Frank "Junior" Coghlan, Louise Currie; ***D:*** William Witney.

Adventures of Don Juan 1/2 *The New Adventures of Don Juan* **1949** Flynn's last spectacular epic features elegant costuming and loads of action. Don Juan saves Queen Margaret from her evil first minister. He then swashbuckles his way across Spain and England in an effort to win her heart. Grand, large-scale fun and adventure with Flynn at his self-mocking best. **111m/C VHS, DVD.** Errol Flynn, Viveca Lindfors, Robert Douglas, Romney Brent, Alan Hale, Raymond Burr, Aubrey Mather, Ann Rutherford; ***D:*** Vincent Sherman; ***M:*** Max Steiner. Oscars '49: Costume Des. (C).

Adventures of Eliza Fraser 1/2 **1976** A young shipwrecked couple move from bawdy pleasures to cannibalism after being captured by aborigines. **114m/C VHS.** Susannah York, Trevor Howard, Leon Lissek, Abigail, Noel Ferrier, Carole Skinner; ***D:*** Tim Burstall.

The Adventures of Felix *Drole de Felix* **1999** Felix (Bouajila) is a gay, HIV-positive Frenchman of Arab descent who decides to go on a road trip to Marseilles after finding some old letters from the father he never knew. Felix has a number of adventures while hitchhiking and makes an impromptu family of those he meets along the way, which leads him to wonder if he really needs to meet his biological dad after all. French with subtitles. **95m/C VHS, DVD.** *FR* Sami Bouajila, Patachou, Ariane Ascaride, Pierre-Loup Rajot, Charly Sergue, Clement Reverend, Maurice Benichou; ***D:*** Olivier Ducastel, Jacques Martineau; ***W:*** Olivier Ducastel, Jacques Martineau; ***C:*** Mathieu Poirot-Delpech.

The Adventures of Ford Fairlane **WOOF!** *Ford Fairlane* **1990 (R)** The Diceman plays an unusual detective specializing in rock 'n' roll cases. When a heavy metal singer dies on stage, he takes the case in his own inimitable fashion, pursuing buxom gals, sleazy record executives, and even his ex-wife. Not surprisingly, many of his stand-up bits are worked into the movie. Clay, the ever-so-controversial comic in his first (and likely last) starring role haplessly sneers his way through this rock 'n' roll dud of a comedy thriller. A quick effort to cash in on Clay's fading star. Forget about it. **101m/C VHS, DVD.** Andrew (Dice Clay) Silverstein, Wayne Newton, Priscilla Presley, Morris Day, Lauren Holly, Maddie Corman, Gilbert Gottfried, David Patrick Kelly, Brandon Call, Robert Englund, Ed O'Neill, Sheila E, Kari Wuhrer, Tone Loc; ***D:*** Renny Harlin; ***W:*** David Arnott, Daniel Waters, James Cappe. Golden Raspberries '90: Worst Picture, Worst Actor (Silverstein), Worst Screenplay.

The Adventures of Frank and Jesse James **1948** The bad brothers of the Wild West are trying to make good for rip-offs committed in their names, so they're hoping to hit pay-dirt with a silver mine. A 13-episode serial on two cassettes. **180m/B VHS.** Steve Darrell, Clayton Moore, Noel Neill, Stanley Andrews; ***D:*** Yakima Canutt.

The Adventures of Frontier Fremont **1975** A rough and tumble story of a man who leaves the city, grows a beard, and makes the wilderness his home (and the animals his friends). Mountain life, that's the life for me. Almost indistinguishable from Haggerty's "Grizzly Adams," with the usual redeeming panoramic shots of majestic mountains. **95m/C VHS.** Dan Haggerty, Denver Pyle; ***D:*** Richard Friedenberg.

The Adventures of Gallant Bess **1948** The time-honored story of a rodeo man torn between his girl and his talented horse (the Bess of the title). **73m/C VHS, DVD.** Cameron Mitchell, Audrey Long, Fuzzy Knight, James Millican; ***D:*** Lew Landers.

The Adventures of Huck Finn **1993 (PG)** Decent Disney attempt at adapting an American favorite by Mark Twain. Mischievous Huck and runaway slave Jim travel down the muddy Mississippi, working on life and friendship and getting into all sorts of adventures in the pre-Civil War era. Fast-paced and amusing with good performances by Wood (in the title role) and Broadway trained Vance (as Jim). Racial epithets and minstrel show dialect have been eliminated in this version. Some material, including Jim's close call with a lynch mob and Huck's drunken, brutal father may be too strong for immature children. **108m/C VHS, DVD.** Elijah Wood, Courtney B. Vance, Robbie Coltrane, Jason Robards Jr., Ron Perlman, Dana Ivey, Anne Heche, James Gammon, Paxton Whitehead, Tom Aldredge, Curtis Armstrong, Mary Louise Wilson, Frances Conroy; ***D:*** Stephen Sommers; ***W:*** Stephen Sommers; ***C:*** Janusz Kaminski; ***M:*** Bill Conti.

The Adventures of Huckleberry Finn **1939** Mark Twain's classic story about a boy who runs away and travels down the Mississippi on a raft, accompanied by a runaway slave, is done over in MGM-style. Rooney is understated as Huck (quite a feat), while the production occasionally floats aimlessly down the Mississippi. An entertaining follow-up to "The Adventures of Tom Sawyer." **89m/B VHS.** Mickey Rooney, Lynne Carver, Rex Ingram, William Frawley, Walter Connolly; ***D:*** Richard Thorpe.

The Adventures of Huckleberry Finn 1/2 **1960** A lively adaptation of the Twain saga in which Huck and runaway slave Jim raft down the Mississipi in search of freedom and adventure. Miscasting of Hodges as Huck hampers the proceedings, but Randall shines as the treacherous King. Strong supporting cast includes Keaton as a lion-tamer and boxing champ Moore as Jim. **107m/C VHS, DVD.** Tony Randall, Eddie Hodges, Archie Moore, Patty McCormack, Neville Brand, Mickey Shaughnessy, Judy Canova, Andy Devine, Sherry Jackson, Buster Keaton, Finlay Currie, Josephine Hutchinson, Parley Baer, John Carradine, Royal Dano, Sterling Holloway, Harry Dean Stanton; ***D:*** Michael Curtiz.

The Adventures of Huckleberry Finn **1978** The classic adventure by Mark Twain of an orphan boy and a runaway slave done again as a TV movie and starring "F-Troop" regulars Tucker and Storch. Lacks the production values of earlier versions. **100m/C VHS.** Forrest Tucker, Larry Storch, Kurt Ida, Mike Mazurki, Brock Peters; ***D:*** Jack B. Hively. **TV**

The Adventures of Huckleberry Finn 1/2 **1985** An adaptation of the Mark Twain story about the adventures encountered by Huckleberry Finn and a runaway slave as they travel down the Mississippi River. Top-notch cast makes this an entertaining version. Originally made in a much longer version for PBS's "American Playhouse." **121m/C VHS, DVD.** Sada Thompson, Lillian Gish, Richard Kiley, Jim Dale, Barnard Hughes, Patrick Day, Frederic Forrest, Geraldine Page, Butterfly McQueen, Samm-Art Williams; ***D:*** Peter H. Hunt. **TV**

The Adventures of Ichabod and Mr. Toad 1/2 **1949** Disney's wonderfully animated versions of Kenneth Grahame's "The Wind in the Willows" and "The Legend of Sleepy Hollow" by Washington Irving. Rathbone narrates the story of Mr. Toad, who suffers from arrogance and eventually must defend himself in court after being charged with driving a stolen vehicle (Disney did take liberties with the story). Crosby provides all the voices for "Ichabod," which features one of the all-time great animated sequences—Ichabod riding in a frenzy through the forest while being pursued by the headless horseman. A treat for all ages. **68m/C VHS, DVD.** ***D:*** James Nelson Algar, Clyde Geronimi; ***W:*** Winston Hibler, Erdman Penner, Joe Rinaldi, Ted Sears, Homer Brightman, Harry Reeves; ***M:*** Oliver Wallace; ***V:*** Eric Blore, Pat O'Malley, Jack Kinney, Bing Crosby; ***Nar:*** Basil Rathbone.

The Adventures of Marco Polo 1/2 **1938** Lavish Hollywood production based on the exploits of 13th-century Venetian explorer Marco Polo (Cooper). He becomes the first white man to record his visit to the Eastern court of Kublai Khan, where he falls for a beautiful princess also desired by the evil Rathbone. Lots of action, though its hard to picture the laconic Cooper in the title role. **100m/B VHS, DVD.** Gary Cooper, Sigrid Gurie, Basil Rathbone, Ernest Truex, George Barbier, Binnie Barnes, Alan Hale, H.B. Warner; ***D:*** Archie Mayo; ***W:*** Robert Sherwood; ***M:*** Hugo Friedhofer.

The Adventures of Mark Twain **1944** March stars as Mark Twain, the nom de plume of Samuel Clemens, the beloved humorist and writer. His travels and adventures along the Mississippi and on to the California gold rush would later result in the books and stories which would make him so well-known. March attains a quiet nobility as he goes from young man to old sage, along with Smith, who plays Olivia, Twain's beloved wife. **130m/B VHS.** Fredric March, Alexis Smith, Donald Crisp, Alan Hale, Sir C. Aubrey Smith, John Carradine, William Henry, Robert Barrat, Walter Hampden, Percy Kilbride; ***D:*** Irving Rapper; ***W:*** Alan LeMay, Harry Chandlee; ***M:*** Max Steiner.

The Adventures of Mark Twain *Mark Twain* **1985 (G)** A clay-animated fantasy based on, and radically departing from, the life and work of Mark Twain. Story begins with Twain flying into outer space in a blimp with stowaways Huck Finn, Tom Sawyer and Becky Thatcher and takes off from there. Above average entertainment for kids and their folks. **86m/C VHS, DVD.** ***D:*** Will Vinton; ***W:*** Susan Shadburne; ***V:*** James Whitmore, Chris Ritchie, Gary Krug, Michele Mariana.

The Adventures of Milo & Otis *Koneko Monogatari; The Adventures of Chatran* **1989 (G)** Delightful Japanese children's film about a farm-dwelling dog and cat and their odyssey after the cat is accidentally swept away on a river. Notable since no humans appear in the film. A record-breaking success in its homeland. Well received by U.S. children. Narrated by Dudley Moore. **76m/C VHS, DVD.** *JP* ***D:*** Masanori Hata; ***W:*** Mark Saltzman; ***C:*** Hideo Fujii, Shinji Tomita; ***M:*** Michael Boddicker; ***Nar:*** Dudley Moore.

The Adventures of Nellie Bly **1981** "Classics Illustrated" story of Nellie Bly, a strong-willed female reporter doing her best to expose wrongdoings in the late 19th century. A decent performance by Purl is overshadowed by the general lack of direction. **100m/C VHS.** Linda Purl, Gene Barry, John Randolph, Raymond Buktenica, J.D. Cannon, Elayne Heilveil, Cliff Osmond; ***D:*** Henning Schellerup. **TV**

The Adventures of Picasso **1980** A Swedish satire on the life of Picasso, dubbed in English. Don't look for art or facts here, or, for that matter, many laughs. **88m/C VHS.** *SW* Gosta Ekman Jr., Lena Nyman, Hans Alfredson, Margareta Krook, Bernard Cribbins, Wilfrid Brambell; ***D:*** Tage Danielsson.

The Adventures of Pinocchio 1/2 *Pinocchio; Carlo Collodi's Pinocchio* **1996 (G)** Live-action version of Carlo Collodi's story about woodcarver Gepetto (Landau) who carves himself a puppet son (Thomas) who longs to be a real boy. Story differs from the Disney cartoon version in that it's a little darker and the cat, the fox, and the cricket have larger roles. Jim Henson's Creature Shop provided the animatronic magic to bring Pinocchio to life. His head alone was jammed with wiring and 18 tiny motors to give the "boy" a full range of facial expressions. It took as many as five puppeteers at a time to animate the character. So lifelike was the puppet that some of the crew actually spoke to it as they did the human actors. **88m/C VHS, DVD.** Martin Landau, Jonathan Taylor Thomas, Rob Schneider, Bebe Neuwirth, Udo Kier; ***D:*** Steven Barron; ***W:*** Steven Barron, Tom Benedek, Sherry Mills; ***C:*** Juan Ruiz-Anchia; ***M:*** Rachel Portman.

The Adventures of Pluto Nash **WOOF! 2002 (PG-13)** Pluto Nash (Murphy) owns a nightclub on the moon in the year 2087, and some gangsters want it. Murphy should save us all a lot of time, trouble, and wasted effort and hand it over. On the shelf for two years (and some good reasons), this steaming pile of "action-comedy" has nothing going for it. The performances are "collecting-a-paycheck" quality, the script and direction are a mess, and it's howlingly unfunny. If you avoid seeing one movie this year, make it this one. **97m/C VHS, DVD.** *US* Eddie Murphy, Rosario Dawson, Randy Quaid, Joe Pantoliano, Jay Mohr, John Cleese, Pam Grier, Peter Boyle, Luis Guzman, James Rebhorn, Burt Young, Miguel A. Nunez Jr., Illeana Douglas, Victor Varnado; ***D:*** Ron Underwood; ***W:*** Neil Cuthbert; ***C:*** Oliver Wood; ***M:*** John Powell.

Adventures of Power 1/2 **2008 (PG-13)** Underdog satire (that's not very adventurous) about an aging misfit with a fixation on air-drumming. After getting fired, Power (Gold) finally makes his way from New Mexico to New Jersey where he finds some soulmates in Newark and faces off in a New York competition to be the best darn air drummer anywhere. Comedy is inconsistent and triple-duty Gold is more irksome than weirdo appealing. **96m/C DVD.** *US* Ari Gold, Michael McKean, Jane Lynch, Soshannah Stern, Adrian Grenier, Steven Williams, Jimmy Jean-Louis, Chi Ling Chiu, Richard Fancy; ***D:*** Ari Gold; ***W:*** Ari Gold; ***C:*** Lisa Weigand; ***M:*** Ethan Gold.

The Adventures of Priscilla, Queen of the Desert **1994 (R)** Quirky down-under musical-comedy follows two drag queens and a transsexual across the Australian Outback on their way to a gig in a small resort town. They make the drive in a pink bus nicknamed Priscilla. Along the way they encounter, and perform for, the usual unusual assortment of local characters. Scenes depicting homophobic natives play out as expected. Finest moments occur on the bus or onstage (all hail ABBA). Strong performances, especially by usually macho Stamp as the widowed Bernadette, rise above the cliches in what is basically a bitchy, cross-dressing road movie, celebrating drag as art and the nonconformity of its heroes. Costumes (by Lizzy Gardner and Tim Chappel) are a lark, the photography's surreal, and the soundtrack fittingly campy. **102m/C VHS, DVD.** *AU* Terence Stamp, Hugo Weaving, Guy Pearce, Bill Hunter, Sarah Chadwick, Mark Holmes, Julia Cortez, Rebel Russell, June Marie Bennett, Alan Dargin, Al Clark, Margaret Pomeranz; ***D:*** Stephan Elliott; ***W:*** Stephan Elliott; ***C:*** Brian J. Breheny; ***M:*** Guy Gross. Oscars '94: Costume Des.; Australian Film Inst. '94: Costume Des.

Adventures of Red Ryder **1940** The thrills of the rugged West are presented in this 12-episode serial. Based on the then-famous comic strip character. **240m/B VHS, DVD.** Tommy Cook, Harry Worth, Wally Wales, William Farnum, Carleton Young, Donald (Don "Red") Barry, Noah Beery Sr.; ***D:*** John English, William Witney; ***W:*** Frank (Franklyn) Adreon, Norman S. Hall, Barney A. Sarecky; ***C:*** William Nobles; ***M:*** Cy Feuer.

The Adventures of Robin Hood **1938** Rollicking technicolor tale of the legendary outlaw, regarded as the swashbuckler standard-bearer. The justice-minded Saxon knight battles the Normans, outwits evil Prince John, and gallantly romances Maid Marian. Grand Castle sets and lush forest photography display ample evidence of the huge (for 1938) budget of $2 million plus. Just entering his prime, Flynn enthusiastically performed most of his own stunts, including intricate swordplay and advanced tree and wall climbing. His Robin brims with charm and bravura. THe rest of the cast likewise attacks with zest: de Havilland, a cold, but ultimately sympathetic Marian; Rains's dastardly Prince John; and Rathbone's convincing Sir Guy to Robin's band of very merry men. Based on the many Robin Hood legends, as well as Sir Walter Scott's "Ivanhoe" and the opera "Robin Hood" by De Koven-Smith. **102m/C VHS, DVD, HD DVD.** Errol Flynn, Olivia de Havilland, Claude Rains, Basil Rathbone, Alan Hale, Una O'Connor, Patric Knowles, Eugene Pallette, Herbert Mundin, Melville Cooper, Ian Hunter, Montagu Love; ***D:*** Michael Curtiz; ***W:*** Seton I. Miller, Norman Reilly Raine; ***C:*** Gaetano Antonio "Tony" Gaudio, Sol Polito; ***M:*** Erich Wolfgang Korngold. Oscars '38: Film Editing, Orig. Score, Natl. Film Reg. '95.

The Adventures of Rocky & Bullwinkle 1/2 **2000 (PG)** Flying squirrel and his moose pal, who have been living on residuals since their TV show was cancelled, discover that their old enemies, spies Boris Badenov (Alexander), Natasha Fatale (Russo) and their Fearless Leader (De Niro), have escaped from their two-dimensional existence. Now the trio are headed for Hollywood and a plot to—what else—take over the world. Someone seriously miscalculated in aiming this one at the Pokemon set (the show is 35 years old, and the majority of the jokes were always aimed at adults anyway), but it still provides a few good laughs, and is much more effective back home on the small screen. **88m/C VHS, DVD.** Robert De Niro, Jason Alexander, Rene Russo, Janeane Garofalo, Randy Quaid, Piper Perabo, Carl Reiner, Jonathan Winters, John Goodman, Kenan Thompson, Kel Mitchell, James Rebhorn, David Alan Grier, Norman Lloyd, Jon Polito, Whoopi Goldberg, Billy Crystal, Don Novello, Harrison Young, Dian Bachar, Paget Brewster; ***D:*** Des McAnuff; ***W:*** Kenneth Lonergan; ***C:*** Thomas Ackerman; ***M:*** Mark Mothersbaugh; ***V:*** June Foray, Keith Scott.

The Adventures of Rusty 1/2 **1945** Forties family film series begins with this classic boy-meets-dog story. Danny's dog dies in an accident and his widowed father has just remarried so the kid's feeling pretty bad. Then he meets neglected German Shepherd Rusty, a former police dog with an undeservedly bad rep. Naturally, boy and dog bond and even capture a couple of escaped convicts (and Danny learns to love his stepmom too). **67m/B VHS.** Ted Donaldson, Margaret Lindsay, Conrad Nagel, Gloria Holden; ***D:*** Paul Burnford; ***W:*** Aubrey Wisberg.

The Adventures of Sadie 1/2 *Our Girl Friday* **1955** Collins is stranded on a desert island with three men, two of whom continuously chase her around. Naturally, she falls for the guy who ignores her. Obvious sex comedy which plays on Collins' scantily clad physical assets. Based on the novel "The Cautious Amorist" by Norman Lindsay. **87m/C VHS.** *GB* Joan Collins, George Cole, Kenneth More, Robertson Hare, Hermione Gingold, Walter Fitzgerald; ***D:*** Noel Langley; ***W:*** Noel Langley.

The Adventures of Sebastian Cole 1/2 **1999 (R)** Sebastian (Grenier) is a misfit highschooler in upstate New York in 1983. Not only does he have to deal with the usual trials of adolescence but there's his unusual family problems. His mother, Joan (Colin), returns to her native England upon learning that Sebastian's stepdad, Hank (Gregg), has decided to become a woman. Sebastian eventually winds up living with Hank, who is now known as Henrietta, and who's still the most stable adult in the teen's fractured world. **99m/C VHS, DVD.** Adrian Grenier, Clark Gregg, Aleksa Palladino, Margaret Colin, John Shea, Joan Copeland, Marni Lustig, Tom Lacy; ***D:*** Tod Williams; ***W:*** Tod Williams; ***C:*** John Foster; ***M:*** Lynne Geller.

The Adventures of Sharkboy and Lavagirl in 3-D 1/2 **2005 (PG)** Multi-hyphenate Rodriguez uses a story from son Racer as the basis for this kid-friendly adventure. Ten year-old misfit Max (Boyd) dreams up a couple of young superheroes and finds them coming to life. Sharkboy (Lautner) and Lavagirl (Dooley) need Max's help to save their home world, Planet Drool, from the evil Mr. Electric (Lopez). The cartoonish gee-wizardry will no doubt appeal to its target audience, but might struggle to hold the attention of older kids. **94m/C DVD, UMD.** *US* Kristin Davis, David Arquette, George Lopez, Taylor Lautner, Taylor Dooley, Cayden Boyd, Jacob Davich, Sasha Pieterse, Rico Torres, Rebel Rodriquez, Racer Rodriguez, Rocket Rodriguez; ***D:*** Robert Rodriguez; ***W:*** Robert Rodriguez; ***C:*** Robert Rodriguez; ***M:*** John Debney, Graeme Revell.

The Adventures of Sherlock Holmes 1/2 *Sherlock Holmes* **1939** The immortal Sherlock Holmes and his assistant Dr. Watson conflict with Scotland Yard as they both race to stop arch-criminal Professor Moriarty. The Yard is put to shame as Holmes, a mere amateur sleuth, uses his brilliant deductive reasoning to save the damsel in distress and to stop Moriarty from stealing the Crown Jewels. Second in the series. **83m/B VHS, DVD.** Basil Rathbone, Nigel Bruce, Ida Lupino, George Zucco, E.E. Clive, Mary Gordon; ***D:*** Alfred Werker; ***W:*** Edwin Blum; ***C:*** Leon Shamroy.

The Adventures of Sherlock Holmes' Smarter Brother **1978 (PG)** The unknown brother of the famous Sherlock Holmes takes on some of his brother's more disposable excess cases and makes some hilarious moves. Moments of engaging farce borrowed from the Mel Brooks school of parody (and parts of the Brooks ensemble as well). **91m/C VHS, DVD.** Gene Wilder, Madeline Kahn, Marty Feldman, Dom DeLuise, Leo McKern, Roy Kinnear, John Le Mesurier, Douglas Wilmer, Thorley Walters; ***D:*** Gene Wilder; ***W:*** Gene Wilder.

Adventures of Smilin' Jack **1943** WWII flying ace Smilin' Jack Martin comes to life in this action-packed serial. Character from the Zack Mosley comic strip about air force fighting over China. **90m/B VHS, DVD.** Tom Brown, Sidney Toler; ***D:*** Ray Taylor.

The Adventures of Tartu 1/2 *Tartu* **1943** A British secret agent, sent to blow up a Nazi poison gas factory in Czechoslovakia, poses as a Romanian. One of Donat's lesser films, in the style of "The 39 Steps." **103m/C VHS, DVD.** *GB* Robert Donat, Valerie Hobson, Glynis Johns; ***D:*** Harold Bucquet.

The Adventures of Tarzan **1921** The screen's first Tarzan in an exciting jungle thriller. Silent. **153m/B VHS.** Elmo Lincoln, Louise Lorraine, Lilian Worth, Frank Whitson, Frank Merrill; ***D:*** Robert F. "Bob" Hill; ***W:*** Robert F. "Bob" Hill.

The Adventures of the Wilderness Family 1976 **(G)** The story of a modern-day pioneer family who becomes bored with the troubles of city life and heads for life in the wilderness. There, they find trouble in paradise. Family-oriented adventure offering pleasant scenery. Followed by "The Wilderness Family, Part 2." **100m/C VHS, DVD.** Robert F. Logan, Susan Damante-Shaw; ***D:*** Stewart Raffill; ***W:*** Stewart Raffill.

The Adventures of Tom Sawyer 1938 The vintage Hollywood adaptation of the Mark Twain classic, with art direction by William Cameron Menzies. Not a major effort from the Selznick studio, but quite detailed and the best Tom so far. **91m/C VHS.** Tommy Kelly, Walter Brennan, Victor Jory, May Robson, Victor Kilian, Jackie Moran, Donald Meek, Ann Gillis, Marcia Mae Jones, David Holt, Margaret Hamilton; ***D:*** Norman Taurog; ***C:*** James Wong Howe; ***M:*** Max Steiner.

The Adventures of Tom Sawyer 1/2 1973 Tom Sawyer is a mischievous Missouri boy who gets into all kinds of trouble in this white-washed, made for TV adaptation of the Mark Twain classic. **76m/C VHS.** Jane Wyatt, Buddy Ebsen, Vic Morrow, John McGiver, Josh Albee, Jeff Tyler; ***D:*** James Neilson. **TV**

The Adventures of Werner Holt *Die Abenteuer des Werner Holt* **1965** Two teenagers, Werner Holt and Gilbert Wolzow, are taken out of school and conscripted into Hitler's army. Gilbert is a fanatical soldier, while the horrors of the front call Werner's loyalties into question. But when Gilbert is executed by the SS, Werner turns his gun on his own side. Based on the novel by Dieter Noll. German with subtitles. **163m/B VHS.** *GE* Klaus-Peter Thiele, Manfred Karge, Arno Wyzniewski, Gunter Junghans, Peter Reusse, Wolfgang Langhoff; ***D:*** Joachim Kunert.

The Adventurous Knights WOOF! **1935** An athlete learns he is the heir to a Transylvanian throne. **60m/B VHS.** David Sharpe, Mary Kornman, Mickey Daniels, Gertrude Messinger; ***D:*** Edward Roberts.

The Adversary 1/2 *Pratidwandi* **1971** A young man must quit college because of his father's death. He struggles to find employment in Calcutta but his hardships are magnified by the impersonal society. In Bengali with English subtitles. **110m/C VHS.** *IN* Dhritiman Chatterjee, Jayshree Roy, Debraj Roy, Krishna Bose; ***D:*** Satyajit Ray; ***W:*** Satyajit Ray; ***C:*** Soumendu Roy, Purnendu Bose; ***M:*** Satyajit Ray.

Advertising Rules! *Viktor Vogel: Commercial Artist* **2001 (R)** Graphic artist Viktor Vogel actually lands a job after sneaking into an ad agency board meeting. And his luck continues when he meets sexy artist Rosa and helps her with an idea for her debut art exhibition. Then Viktor inadvertantly pitches the same idea for the ad campaign and has to find a way to satisfy both work and Rosa. German with subtitles. **109m/C VHS, DVD.** *GE* Gudrun Landgrebe, Alexander Scheer, Goetz George, Chulpan Khamatova, Maria Schrader, Vadim Glowna; ***D:*** Lars Kraume; ***W:*** Lars Kraume, Tom Schlessinger; ***C:*** Andreas Daub; ***M:*** Robert Jan Meyer.

Advise and Consent 1962 An interesting political melodrama with a fascinating cast, based upon Allen Drury's novel. The President chooses a candidate for the Secretary of State position which divides the Senate and causes the suicide of a senator. Controversial in its time, though somewhat turgid today. Laughton's last film. **139m/B VHS, DVD.** Don Murray, Charles Laughton, Henry Fonda, Walter Pidgeon, Lew Ayres, Burgess Meredith, Gene Tierney, Franchot Tone, Paul Ford, George Grizzard, Betty White, Peter Lawford, Edward Andrews; ***D:*** Otto Preminger; ***W:*** Wendell Mayes; ***C:*** Sam Leavitt. Natl. Bd. of Review '62: Support. Actor (Meredith).

The Advocate *The Hour of the Pig* **1993 (R)** Bizarre black comedy about 15th-century Paris lawyer Richard Courtois (Firth) who decides to ply his trade in the country, only to find things stranger than he can imagine. His first case turns out to be defending a pig that's accused of murdering a child. And the pig is owned by beautiful gypsy Samira (Annabi), so the idealistic lawyer can fall in love (or lust). There's religion and superstition, there's power struggles, there's ignorance versus knowledge—things sound very modern indeed. **102m/C VHS, DVD.** *GB* Colin Firth, Amina Annabi, Nicol Williamson, Ian Holm, Lysette Anthony, Donald Pleasence, Michael Gough, Harriet Walter, Jim Carter, Dave Atkins; ***D:*** Leslie Megahey; ***W:*** Leslie Megahey.

Aelita: Queen of Mars *Aelita: The Revolt of the Robots* **1924** Though the title has blockbuster potential, "Aelita" is a little-known silent Soviet sci-fi flick destined to remain little known. After building a rocket to fly to Mars, a Russian engineer finds it's no Martian holiday on the fourth planet from the sun, with the Martians in the midst of a revolution. Silent, with a piano score. **113m/B VHS, DVD.** *RU* Yulia Solntseva, Nikolai Batalov, Nikolai Tseretelli, Nikolai Tseretelli, Vera Orlova, Pavel Poi, Konstantin Eggert, Yuri Zavadski, Valentina Kuindzi, N. Tretyakova; ***D:*** Yakov Protazanov; ***W:*** Fedor Ozep, Aleksey Fajko; ***C:*** Yuri Zhelyabuzhsky, Emil Schoenemann.

Aeon Flux 1/2 **2005 (PG-13)** It's hard to fault a movie that's ostensibly about Charlize Theron in spandex shooting people, so why bother trying? Based on the MTV cartoon, Kusama's sci fi/actioner is a goofy guilty pleasure that succeeds largely due to Theron's on-screen charisma. Set 400 years in the future, after a plague has wiped out most of humanity, survivors live in a walled city called Bregna, ruled by the fascist government of Trevor Goodchild (Csokas). A resistance movement sends their top assassin, Aeon Flux (Theron), to dispatch Goodchild, but Aeon soon realizes that there might be some disturbing truths behind her brave new world. Sure, things get cheesy, but Kusama has a lot of fun with her wonky futuristic designs. **95m/C DVD, Blu-ray Disc, HD DVD.** *US* Charlize Theron, Marton Csokas, Jonny Lee Miller, Sophie Okonedo, Frances McDormand, Pete Postlethwaite, Amelia Warner, Nikolai Kinski, Caroline Chikezie; ***D:*** Karyn Kusama; ***W:*** Phil Hay, Matt Manfredi; ***C:*** Stuart Dryburgh; ***M:*** Graeme Revell.

The Affair 1973 Songwriter/polio victim Wood falls in love for the first time with attorney Wagner. Delicate situation handled well by a fine cast. **74m/C VHS, DVD.** Natalie Wood, Robert Wagner, Bruce Davison, Kent Smith, Frances Reid, Pat Harrington; ***D:*** Gilbert Cates. **TV**

The Affair 1/2 **1995 (R)** It's 1944 in a small English town, where a troop of black American soldiers are billeted prior to the D-Day invasion. Travis (Vance) falls for the married Maggie (Fox)—whose husband, Edward (Hinds), is supposed to be away at sea—and they begin an affair. Unfortunately, Edward arrives home unexpectedly and accuses Travis of raping his wife. If Maggie denies the accusation, she'll lose her home and family but if she confirms it, Travis, according to Army law, will be condemned to death. **105m/C VHS, DVD.** *GB* Courtney B. Vance, Kerry Fox, Ciaran Hinds, Beatie Edney, Leland Gantt, Bill Nunn, Ned Beatty; ***D:*** Paul Seed; ***W:*** Pablo F. Fenjves, Bryan Goluboff; ***C:*** Ivan Strasburg; ***M:*** Christopher Gunning. **CABLE**

An Affair in Mind 1989 A professional writer falls in love with a beautiful woman who tries to convince him to assist her in murdering her husband. **88m/C VHS.** *GB* Amanda Donohoe, Stephen (Dillon) Dillane, Matthew Marsh, Jean-Laurent Cochot; ***D:*** Michael Baker. **TV**

Affair in Trinidad 1952 Fun in the tropics as nightclub singer Hayworth enlists the help of brother-in-law Ford to find her husband's murderer. The trail leads to international thieves and espionage in a romantic thriller that reunites the stars of "Gilda." Hayworth sings (with Jo Ann Greer's voice) "I've Been Kissed Before." **98m/B VHS.** Rita Hayworth, Glenn Ford, Alexander Scourby, Torin Thatcher, Valerie Bettis, Steven Geray; ***D:*** Vincent Sherman.

An Affair of Love 1/2 *Une Liaison Pornographique; A Pornographic Liaison; Une Liaison d'Amour* **1999 (R)** French love story sounds like "Last Tango in Paris" but really owes more to "sex, lies and videotape." Elle (Baye) places an ad in a sex magazine and arranges to meet a respondent, Lui (Lopez), for afternoon sexual encounters in a hotel. Virtually all of the physical action takes place behind a closed door. The point is emotional and so, in after-the-fact monologues, they both discuss (separately) what's happened. French with subtitles. **80m/C VHS, DVD.** *FR BE LU* Nathalie Baye, Sergi Lopez, Paul Pavel; ***D:*** Frederic Fonteyne; ***W:*** Philippe Blasband; ***C:*** Virginie Saint-Martin; ***M:*** Andre Dziezuk, Marc Mergen, Jeannot Sanavia.

The Affair of the Necklace 1/2 **2001 (R)** Louis XVI-era history is given a tabloid treatment in this costume drama concerning the vengeful efforts of orphaned Jeanne de la Motte-Valois to restore nobility to her family name. She conspires with a court rogue to hatch a sophisticated scam involving the cardinal of France, Marie Antoinette, German Illuminati, and the fabulous necklace of the title, paving the way for the French Revolution. Excessive narration and flashbacks bog the plot; film offers little other than eye candy in the form of intricate set pieces and fancy dress. Intriguing story potential is mishandled, and Swank is terribly miscast but looks nice in a corset. The remaining actors are underused, except Walken in a scene-chewing role as a Svengali-like mesmerist. **120m/C VHS, DVD.** *US* Hilary Swank, Jonathan Pryce, Simon Baker, Adrien Brody, Brian Cox, Joely Richardson, Christopher Walken, Paul Brooke, Peter Eyre, Simon Kunz, Hayden Panettiere; ***D:*** Charles Shyer; ***W:*** John Sweet; ***C:*** Ashley Rowe; ***M:*** David Newman.

An Affair to Remember 1/2 **1957** McCarey remakes his own "Love Affair, " with less success. Nightclub singer Kerr and wealthy bachelor Grant discover love on an ocean liner and agree to meet six months later on top of the Empire State Building to see if their feelings are the same. Not as good as the original, but a winner of a fairy tale just the same. Notable for causing many viewers to sob uncontrollably. "Affair" was gathering dust on store shelves until "Sleepless in Seattle" used it as a plot device and rentals skyrocketed. In 1994 real life couple Warren Beatty and Annette Bening attempted a third "Love Affair" remake. **115m/C VHS, DVD.** Cary Grant, Deborah Kerr, Richard Denning, Cathleen Nesbitt, Neva Patterson, Robert Q. Lewis, Fortunio Bonanova, Matt Moore, Nora Marlowe, Sarah Selby; ***D:*** Leo McCarey; ***W:*** Leo McCarey, Delmer Daves, Donald Ogden Stewart; ***C:*** Milton Krasner; ***M:*** Hugo Friedhofer.

Affairs of Anatol 1921 Philandering playboy Anatol Spencer (Reid) finds no luck with women. He's robbed by one (Ayres), two-timed by another (Hawley), and even madam Satan Synne (Daniels) isn't what she seems. Then Anatol decides to return to his wife, Vivian (Swanson), only to discover that she's being amusing herself with another. Based on a play by Arthur Schnitzler. **117m/B VHS, DVD.** Wallace Reid, Gloria Swanson, Bebe Daniels, Wanda (Petit) Hawley, Agnes Ayres, Monte Blue, Theodore Roberts, Elliott Dexter; ***D:*** Cecil B. DeMille; ***W:*** Beulah Marie Dix; ***C:*** Karl Struss, Alvin Wyckoff.

The Affairs of Annabel 1/2 **1938** The first of the popular series of Annabel pictures Lucy made in the late 1930s. Appealing adolescent is zoomed to movie stardom by her press agent's stunts. A behind-the-scenes satire on Hollywood, stars, and agents. **68m/B VHS.** Lucille Ball, Jack Oakie, Ruth Donnelly, Fritz Feld, Bradley Page; ***D:*** Ben Stoloff.

The Affairs of Dobie Gillis 1/2 **1953** Light musical-comedy about a group of college kids and their carefree antics. Complete with big-band tunes, dance numbers, and plenty of collegiate shenanigans, this '50s classic inspired a hit TV series, "The Many Loves of Dobie Gillis." ♫ I'm Through with Love; All I Do Is Dream of You; You Can't Do Wrong Doing Right; Those Endearing Young Charms. **72m/B VHS.** Debbie Reynolds, Bobby Van, Barbara Ruick, Bob Fosse, Lurene Tuttle, Hans Conried, Charles Lane; ***D:*** Don Weis; ***W:*** Max Shulman; ***C:*** William Mellor.

Affinity 2008 In 1870s Victorian England, a woman of Margaret Prior's (Madeley) upper social class and age should be married. Instead, she lives with her mother and is suffering a deep depression after the recent death of her father and the marriage of her best friend (and secret lover) Helen (Young) to her brother. Encouraged to do good works, Margaret mentors the female inmates of Milbank prison and becomes curious about Selina Dawes (Tapper), a so-called spirit medium incarcerated for murder after a seance gone wrong. At first skeptical of Selina's alleged gifts, Margaret becomes fascinated by the allure of the unknown. Based on the novel by Sarah Waters. **94m/C DVD.** *GB* Anna Madeley, Zoe Tapper, Domini Blythe, Anne Reid, Amanda Plummer, Anna Massey, Ferelith Young, Vincent Leclerc; ***D:*** Tim Fywell; ***W:*** Andrew Davies; ***C:*** Bernard Couture; ***M:*** Frederic Weber. **TV**

Affliction 1/2 **1997 (R)** Nolte, Schrader, and Coburn turn in the finest work of their careers in this bleak tale of one man's battle with the demons of his past and the failures of the present. Nolte is small-town, small-time sheriff Wade Whitehouse, who wants to do the right things, but never does. Damaged beyond repair by his abusive alcoholic father (Coburn), he alienates or scares away anyone who might care for him, including his daughter (Tierney) and his girlfriend (Spacek). When a local businessman dies under mysterious circumstances, Wade sees a chance at redemption, but the investigation turns out to be the catalyst for his final degradation. Schrader has studied the beaten-down male psyche before, but never with this much discipline or implicit knowledge. He adapted the screenplay from Russell Banks' 1989 novel. **113m/C VHS, DVD.** Nick Nolte, James Coburn, Sissy Spacek, Willem Dafoe, Mary Beth Hurt, Jim True-Frost, Marian Seldes, Brigid Tierney, Sean McCann, Wayne Robson, Holmes Osborne; ***D:*** Paul Schrader; ***W:*** Paul Schrader; ***C:*** Paul Sarossy; ***M:*** Michael Brook. Oscars '98: Support. Actor (Coburn); N.Y. Film Critics '98: Actor (Nolte); Natl. Soc. Film Critics '98: Actor (Nolte).

Afghan Knights 1/2 **2007 (R)** An ex-Navy SEAL recruits some former comrades to go back to Afghanistan as mercenaries in order to sneak a warlord out of the country. They meet some opposition and are forced to hide out in a cave where they find some weapons that contain the spirit of Genghis Khan and his Mongol warriors. Said ghostly hordes are looking for some new recruits. Surprisingly, not as ridiculous as it sounds. **90m/C DVD.** Francesco Quinn, Steve Bacic, Gary Stretch, Michael Madsen, Chris Kramer; ***D:*** Allan Harmon; ***W:*** Christine Stringer; ***C:*** Randal Platt; ***M:*** Jon Lee, Stu Goldberg. **VIDEO**

Afraid of the Dark 1992 **(R)** Convoluted psycho-thriller from a child's point of view. Young Lucas is fearful for his blind mother. It seems a vicious slasher has been attacking blind women and Lucas' father, a policeman, has yet to apprehend the criminal. But...Lucas it seems has a problem with reality. With his fantasies and realities mixed, all the people in his life also play entirely different roles. Characters are so detached and unreal that a viewer is prevented from a clear understanding of anything that may, or may not, be going on. Directorial debut of Peploe. **91m/C VHS, DVD.** *FR GB* Ben Keyworth, James Fox, Fanny Ardant, Paul McGann, Clare Holman, Robert Stephens; ***D:*** Mark Peploe; ***W:*** Mark Peploe; ***C:*** Bruno de Keyzer.

Africa Screams 1/2 **1949** Abbott and Costello go on an African safari in possession of a secret map. Unheralded independent A&C film is actually quite good in the stupid vein, with lots of jungle slapstick, generally good production values, and a supporting cast of familiar comedy faces. **79m/B VHS, DVD.** Lou Costello, Bud Abbott, Shemp Howard, Hillary Brooke, Joe Besser, Clyde Beatty, Max Baer Sr.; ***D:*** Charles T. Barton; ***W:*** Earl Baldwin; ***M:*** Walter Schumann.

Africa Texas Style 1967 An East African rancher hires an American cowboy and his Navajo sidekick to help run his wild game ranch. Decent family adventure which served as the pilot for the short-lived TV series "Cowboy in Africa." Features lots of wildlife footage and a cameo appearance by Hayley Mills. **109m/C VHS.** Hugh O'Brian, John Mills, Nigel Green, Tom Nardini, Adrienne Corri; ***Cameos:*** Hayley Mills; ***D:*** Andrew Marton; ***M:*** Malcolm Arnold. **TV**

An African Dream 1/2 **1990 (PG)** A period tale about a black man and a white woman fighting against repression in South

Africa. **94m/C VHS.** Kitty Aldridge, John Kani, Dominic Jephcott, John Carson, Richard Haines, Joy Stewart Spence; ***D:*** John Smallcombe.

African Journey 1989 A moving, cross-cultural drama of friendship. A young black American goes to Africa for the summer to be with his divorced father who is working in the diamond mines. There he meets a young black African like himself; they overcome cultural clashes and learn respect for one another. Beautiful scenery, filmed in Africa. Part of the "Wonderworks" series. **174m/C VHS.** Jason Blicker, Pedzisai Sithole.

The African Queen 🦴🦴🦴🦴 **1951** After Bible-thumping spinster Hepburn's missionary brother is killed in WWI Africa, hard-drinking, dissolute steamer captain Bogart offers her safe passage. Not satisfied with sanctuary, she persuades him to destroy a German gunboat blocking the British advance. The two spend most of their time battling aquatic obstacles and each other, rather than the Germans. Time alone on a African river turns mistrust and aversion to love, a transition effectively counterpointed by the continuing suspense of their daring mission. Classic war of the sexes script adapted from C.S. Forester's novel makes wonderful use of natural dialogue and humor. Shot on location in Africa. **105m/C VHS, DVD.** *GB* Humphrey Bogart, Katharine Hepburn, Robert Morley, Theodore Bikel, Peter Bull, Walter Gotell, Peter Swanwick, Richard Marner; ***D:*** John Huston; ***W:*** John Huston, James Agee; ***C:*** Jack Cardiff. Oscars '51: Actor (Bogart); AFI '98: Top 100, Natl. Film Reg. '94.

African Rage 🦴🦴 *Tigers Don't Cry; The Long Shot; Target of an Assassin; Fatal Assassin* **1978** Little known release about an aging male nurse (yes, Quinn) who discovers he's dying of an incurable disease. With nothing left to lose, he plans the kidnapping of an African leader, hoping that the ransom will support his family. Meanwhile, another man is plotting the same leader's death. Decent performances help move along the improbable plot. **90m/C VHS, DVD.** *SA* Anthony Quinn, John Phillip Law, Simon Sabela, Ken Gampu, Marius Weyers, Sandra Prinsloo; ***D:*** Peter Collinson.

After Dark, My Sweet 🦴🦴🦴 **1990 (R)** A troubled young man in search of a little truth ends up entangled in a kidnapping scheme. Muddled direction is overcome by above average performances and gritty realism. Based on the novel by Jim Thompson. **114m/C VHS, DVD.** Jason Patric, Rachel Ward, Bruce Dern, George Dickerson, James Cotton, Corey Carrier, Rocky Giordani; ***D:*** James Foley; ***W:*** Robert Redlin, James Foley; ***C:*** Mark Plummer; ***M:*** Maurice Jarre.

After Darkness 🦴 **1985** Slow-moving psycho-suspenser about a man obsessed with trying to remedy his twin brother's schizophrenia. **104m/C VHS.** *SI GB* John Hurt, Julian Sands, Victoria Abril, Pamela Salem; ***D:*** Dominique Othenin-Girard.

After Hours 🦴🦴🦴 1/2 **1985 (R)** An absurd, edgy black comedy that's filled with novel twists and turns and often more disturbing than funny. An isolated uptown New York yuppie (Dunne) takes a late night stroll downtown and meets a sexy woman in an all-night coffee shop. From there he wanders through a series of threatening and surreal misadventures, leading to his pursuit by a vigilante mob stirred by ice cream dealer O'Hara. Something like "Blue Velvet" with more Catholicism and farce. Or similar to "Something Wild" without the high school reunion. Great cameos from the large supporting cast, including Cheech and Chong as burglars. A dark view of a small hell-hole in the Big Apple. **97m/C VHS, DVD.** Griffin Dunne, Rosanna Arquette, John Heard, Teri Garr, Catherine O'Hara, Verna Bloom, Linda Fiorentino, Dick Miller, Bronson Pinchot, Will Patton, Rockets Redglare, Rocco Sisto, Larry Block, Victor Argo; ***Cameos:*** Richard "Cheech" Marin, Thomas Chong, Martin Scorsese; ***D:*** Martin Scorsese; ***W:*** Joe Minion; ***C:*** Michael Ballhaus; ***M:*** Howard Shore. Cannes '86: Director (Scorsese); Ind. Spirit '86: Director (Scorsese), Film.

After Innocence 🦴🦴🦴 **2005** Sanders exposes the cracks in the criminal justice system by examining the cases of seven men—four white and three black—who were convicted on murder and rape charges. Eventually, after spending many years in prison, each was exonerated because of DNA evidence. Also examined are the roadblocks thrown up by authorities who don't want to admit to mistakes, the question of compensation after wrongful imprisonment, and life after release. Documentary was made in collaboration with the nonprofit legal clinic, the Innocence Project, now expanded into the Innocence Network. Since its founding in 1992 more than 160 people have been exonerated through DNA testing. **95m/C DVD.** *US* ***D:*** Jessica Sanders; ***W:*** Jessica Sanders, Marc H. Simon; ***C:*** Buddy Squires, Shana Hagan; ***M:*** Charles Bernstein.

After Julius 🦴🦴 **1978** Twenty years after Julius Grace's death, his memory still hovers over his wife's and daughters' lives. British soap opera moves with glacier-like speed. Adapted from the book by Elizabeth Jane Howard. **150m/C VHS.** *GB* Faith Brook, John Carson, Cyd Hayman; ***D:*** John Glenister.

After Life 🦴🦴 *Wandafuru Raifu* **1998** A drab office building turns out to be a metaphysical doorway and those who pass through are the recently deceased. Each person is assigned a caseworker and told that they have three days to decide on one particular memory to take with them into the after life. If they cannot chose, they will be forced to remain in the limbo of the processing center until they can do so. Japanese with subtitles. **118m/C VHS, DVD.** *JP* Taketoshi Naito, Susumu Terajima, Arata, Erika Oda, Takashi Naito, Hisako Hara; ***D:*** Hirokazu Kore-eda; ***W:*** Hirokazu Kore-eda; ***C:*** Yutaka Yamazaki, Masayoshi Sukita; ***M:*** Yasuhiro Kasamatsu.

After Midnight 🦴 *I Have Lived* **1933** An aspiring playwright tries to get his work produced, only to meet with dead ends. Eventually, he hooks up with a talented young actress with whom he finds romance and success. **69m/B VHS.** Alan Dinehart, Anita Page, Allen Vincent, Gertrude Astor; ***D:*** Richard Thorpe.

After Midnight 🦴🦴 **1989 (R)** Suspended in a central story about an unorthodox professor who preys upon the deepest fears of his students, a trio of terror tales come to life. From the writers of "The Fly II" and "Nightmare on Elm Street 4." Some chills, few thrills. **90m/C VHS, DVD.** Marg Helgenberger, Marc McClure, Alan Rosenberg, Pamela Segall, Nadine Van Der Velde, Ramy Zada, Jillian McWhirter, Billy Ray Sharkey, Judie Aronson, Tracy Wells, Ed Monaghan, Monique Salcido, Penelope Sudrow; ***D:*** Jim Wheat, Ken Wheat; ***W:*** Jim Wheat, Ken Wheat; ***M:*** Marc Donahue.

After Midnight 🦴🦴 *Dopo mezzanotte* **2004** Quiet Martino lives a simple life as the night watchman for the National Museum of Cinema at the Mole Antonelliana in Turin, Italy, with the film aficionado spending his spare time dabbling on a pieced-together project of the city's history on film. But the entrance of eye-catching Amanda—on the lam from the police for scalding her boss with hot cooking fat—changes all that, especially once she's cleared of the charges and free to return to her car-thief boyfriend. The romantic triangle, in the end, doesn't offer much sizzle. In Italian, with English subtitles. **99m/C** Giorgio Pasotti, Silvio Orlando, Francesca Inaudi, Fabio Troiano, Francesca Picozza; ***D:*** Davide Ferrario; ***W:*** Davide Ferrario; ***M:*** Banda Ionica, Daniele Sepe, Fabio Barovero.

After Pilkington 🦴🦴 **1988** Thriller about an uptight Oxford professor who runs into his bewitching childhood sweetheart after many years. She persuades him to help search for a missing archaeologist. **100m/C VHS.** *GB* Bob Peck, Miranda Richardson, Barry Foster; ***D:*** Christopher Morahan. **TV**

After Sex 🦴🦴 *Post Coitum, Animal Triste; Post Coitum* **1997** Passion and madness—French style. Confident, middleaged Diane (Rouan) has a successful career and a complacent marriage. Then she meets twentysomething hunk Emilio (Terral) and all bets are off. The twosome have a delirious affair but Diane's passion teeters towards obsession, with reckless disregard for her family. Then the affair ends and Diane falls apart. French with subtitles. **97m/C VHS.** *FR* Brigitte Rouan, Boris Terral, Patrick Chesnais, Nils (Niels) Tavernier, Jean-Louis Richard, Francoise Arnoul; ***D:*** Brigitte Rouan; ***W:*** Santiago Amigorena, Guy Zilberstein, Brigitte Rouan, Jean-Louis Richard; ***C:*** Pierre Dupouey; ***M:*** Michel Musseau, Umberto Tozzi.

After the Deluge 🦴🦴🦴 **2003** Dogged with their own problems, three brothers must deal with their distant father's decline from Alzheimer's while he is painted by flashbacks of his WWII tour of duty. **103m/C VHS, DVD.** David Wenham, Hugo Weaving, Samuel Johnson, Aden Young, Catherine McClements, Ray Barrett, Rachel Griffiths, Essie Davis, Kate Beahan, Vince Colosimo, Marta Dusseldorp, Bob Franklin, Marco Chiappi, Simon Burke; ***D:*** Brendan Maher; ***W:*** Deb Cox, Andrew Knight; ***C:*** Geoff Burton; ***M:*** Cezary Skubiszewski. **TV**

After the Fall of New York WOOF! **1985 (R)** Dim-witted post-apocalyptic tale set in New York after the fall of the "Big Bomb." A man, driven to search for the last normal woman, has reason to believe she is frozen alive and kept in the heart of the city. His mission: locate her, thaw her, engage in extremely limited foreplay with her, and repopulate the planet. A poorly dubbed dating allegory. **95m/C VHS, DVD.** *IT FR* Michael Sopkiw, Valentine Monnier, Anna Kanakis, Roman Geer, Edmund Purdom, George Eastman; ***D:*** Sergio Martino.

After the Fox 🦴🦴 *Caccia alla Volpe* **1966** Sellers is a con artist posing as a film director to carry out a bizarre plan to steal gold from Rome. Features occasional backhand slaps at Hollywood, with Mature turning in a memorable performance as the has-been actor starring in Sellers' movie. Though the screenplay was co-written by Neil Simon, the laughs are marginal. **103m/C VHS, DVD.** *GB IT* Peter Sellers, Victor Mature, Martin Balsam, Britt Ekland; ***D:*** Vittorio De Sica; ***W:*** Neil Simon, Cesare Zavattini; ***C:*** Leonida Barboni; ***M:*** Burt Bacharach.

After the Promise 🦴🦴 **1987** During the Depression, a poor carpenter tries to regain custody of his four sons following the death of his wife. Maudlin melodrama based on a true story. **100m/C VHS.** Mark Harmon, Diana Scarwid, Rosemary Dunsmore, Donnelly Rhodes, Mark Hildreth, Trey Ames, Richard Billingsley; ***D:*** David Greene; ***M:*** Ralph Burns. **TV**

After the Rain 🦴🦴 **1999 (R)** Hard-hitting apartheid story that unfortunately descends into melodrama. In 1970s South Africa, Steph (Bettany) is a conflicted soldier in love with dancer Emma (Lombard). After his brigade is posted, lonely Emma befriends a black co-worker, Joseph (Bakare). Upon learning that he is living on the streets, Emma invites Joseph to stay with her. Of course that just happens to be when Steph, who's deserted, returns and assumes the worst. Writer/director Kettle adapted the film from his play "Soweto's Burning." **110m/C DVD.** *SA* Paul Bettany, Louise Lombard, Ariyon Bakare; ***D:*** Ross Kettle; ***W:*** Ross Kettle; ***C:*** Koos Roets; ***M:*** Hummie Mann.

After the Rehearsal 🦴🦴🦴 *Efter Repetitionen* **1984 (R)** Two actresses, one young, the other at the end of her career, challenge their director with love and abuse. Each questions his right to use them on stage and off. A thoughtful discussion of the meaning and reason for art originally made for Swedish TV. Swedish with English subtitles. **72m/C VHS.** *SW* Erland Josephson, Ingrid Thulin, Lena Olin; ***D:*** Ingmar Bergman; ***W:*** Ingmar Bergman; ***C:*** Sven Nykvist. **TV**

After the Revolution 🦴🦴 **1990** A struggling novelist decides to write his next book from the viewpoint of his cat. In Hungarian with English subtitles. **82m/C VHS.** *HU* Io Tillett Wright; ***D:*** Andras Szirtes.

After the Shock 🦴🦴 **1990 (PG)** Documentary-like dramatization of the San Francisco-Oakland earthquake of October 1989 and, of course, its aftermath. Incorporates actual footage of the disaster. **92m/C VHS.** Yaphet Kotto, Rue McClanahan, Jack Scalia, Scott Valentine; ***D:*** Gary Sherman; ***W:*** Gary Sherman. **CABLE**

After the Storm 🦴🦴 1/2 **2001 (R)** Beachcomber Arno (Bratt) discovers a sunken yacht but can't salvage the loot, even with the help of girlfriend Coquina (Avital). So he hooks up with Jean-Pierre (Assante) and his wife Janine (Girard), but greed gets the best of everyone. Based on a story by Ernest Hemingway; filmed in Belize. **103m/C VHS, DVD.** Benjamin Bratt, Armand Assante, Mili Avital, Simone-Elise Girard, Stephen Lang; ***D:*** Guy Ferland; ***W:*** A.E. Hotchner; ***C:*** Gregory Middleton; ***M:*** Bill Wandel. **CABLE**

After the Sunset 🦴🦴 **2004 (PG-13)** Lightweight crime caper is as memorable as a soap bubble, although the scenery (Hayek in a variety of skimpy attire and the sun-drenched island setting) is appealing. Max (Brosnan) is a suave thief who, with partner Lola (Hayek), has pulled off a successful diamond heist that ruins the career of FBI agent Stan (Harrelson). The thieves then retire to the Bahamas where Max is soon bored, bored, bored, and ready for some action when an ocean liner docks in port with a priceless jewel exhibit onboard. Stan, of course, shows up, determined to finally outwit Max. Hayek plays another firecracker while Brosnan slums charmingly; Cheadle is wasted in a throwaway role as a gangster. **93m/C VHS, DVD.** *US* Pierce Brosnan, Salma Hayek, Woody Harrelson, Don Cheadle, Naomie Harris, Christopher Penn, Mykelti Williamson, Obba Babatunde, Russell Hornsby, Rex Linn, Kate Walsh, Troy Garity; ***D:*** Brett Ratner; ***W:*** Craig Rosenberg, Paul Zbyszewski; ***C:*** Dante Spinotti; ***M:*** Lalo Schifrin.

After the Thin Man 🦴🦴🦴 **1936** Second in a series of six "Thin Man" films, this one finds Nick, Nora and Asta, the lovable terrier, seeking out a murderer from Nora's own blue-blooded relatives. Fast-paced mystery with a witty script and the popular Powell/Loy charm. Sequel to "The Thin Man," followed by "Another Thin Man." **113m/B VHS, DVD.** William Powell, Myrna Loy, James Stewart, Elissa Landi, Joseph Calleia, Jessie Ralph, Alan Marshal; ***D:*** Woodbridge S. Van Dyke.

After the Wedding 🦴🦴🦴 *Efter Bryllupet* **2006 (R)** Jacob (Mikkelsen), director of a struggling Indian orphanage, is given the opportunity to solve all his problems via a rich benefactor back in Denmark. Once he returns home, however, he finds things much more complicated than he expected, and he must choose between the world he knows in India and the obligations towards an ex-girlfriend and illegitimate daughter in Denmark. Oscar-nominated, poignant film teeters on the fine line between melodrama and soap opera. **120m/C DVD.** *CZ* Mads Mikkelsen, Rolf Lassgard, Sidse Babett Knudsen, Stine Fischer Christensen, Christian Tafdrup; ***D:*** Suzanne (Susanne) Bier; ***W:*** Anders Thomas Jensen; ***C:*** Morten Soborg; ***M:*** Johan Soderqvist.

After Tomorrow 🦴🦴 **1932** In this Depression-era film, Peter (Farrell) and Sidney (Nixon) struggle to work and save their money to get married but are frequently separated by hardship. Fearing she's losing her beau, Sidney suggests they go away together (there's a sex talk) while Peter nobly insists they wait until marriage. **70m/B DVD.** Charles Farrell, Marion (Marian) Nixon, Minna Gombell, Josephine Hull, William Collier Sr., William Pawley; ***D:*** Frank Borzage; ***W:*** Sonya Levien; ***C:*** James Wong Howe.

Afterburn 🦴🦴🦴 **1992 (R)** When Ted, her Air Force pilot husband, is killed in a crash of his F-16 fighter, Janet Harduvel learns the official explanation is pilot error. Convinced that something was wrong with his plane, Janet sets out to investigate, and eventually sue, military contractor General Dynamics. Dern turns in a great performance as the tough widow determined to clear her husband's name. Based on a true story. **103m/C VHS, DVD.** Laura Dern, Robert Loggia, Vincent Spano, Michael Rooker, Andy Romano; ***D:*** Robert Markowitz; ***W:*** Elizabeth Chandler. **CABLE**

Afterglow 🦴🦴 **1997 (R)** Romantic quadrangle skates by on the performances of its two veterans. Lucky Mann (Nolte) is experiencing marital boredom with his longtime wife Phyllis (the ever-beautiful Christie), a former B-movie actress. Meanwhile twenty-something Marianne Byron (Boyle), who is desperate to have a baby, is sexually frustrated by her workaholic hubby, Jeffrey (Miller). Repairman Lucky happens to come along to work on the Bryon's apartment and Marianne decides to throw herself at him.

Then Jeffrey meets the sophisticated Phyllis and soon both couples have uncoupled and re-formed. **113m/C VHS, DVD.** Nick Nolte, Julie Christie, Lara Flynn Boyle, Jonny Lee Miller, Jay Underwood, Domini Blythe; ***D:*** Alan Rudolph; ***W:*** Alan Rudolph; ***C:*** Toyomichi Kurita; ***M:*** Mark Isham. Ind. Spirit '98: Actress (Christie); N.Y. Film Critics '97: Actress (Christie); Natl. Soc. Film Critics '97: Actress (Christie).

Aftermath ½ **1985** Three astronauts return to Earth and are shocked to discover that the planet has been ravaged by a nuclear war. Quickly they make new plans. **96m/C VHS.** Steve Barkett, Larry Latham, Lynne Margulies, Sid Haig, Forrest J Ackerman; ***D:*** Ted V. Mikels.

Afterschool **2008** Feature film debut for writer/director Campos who was 24 at the time of filming. Socially awkward, self-absorbed teen Robert (Miller) is boarding at a New England prep school where he's generally ignored and his roommate deals drugs. Repressed, Robert finds his sexual outlet in violent Internet porn. During an afterschool student film project, Robert accidentally films the drug overdose deaths of twin sisters who die in his arms. The school tries to cover up the scandal and Robert is asked to supply a tasteful memorial film, which turns out to be truthful and wildly inappropriate—much like the movie. **121m/C DVD.** *US* Ezra Miller, Jeremy White, Emory Cohen, Christopher McCann, Michael Stuhlbarg, Addison Timlin, Lee Wilkof; ***D:*** Antonio Campos; ***W:*** Antonio Campos; ***C:*** Jody Lee Lipes; ***M:*** Rakotondrabe Gael.

Aftershock ½ **1988 (R)** A beautiful alien and a mysterious stranger battle the Earth's repressive, evil government. **90m/C VHS, DVD.** Jay Roberts Jr., Elizabeth Kaitan, Chris Mitchum, Richard Lynch, John Saxon, Russ Tamblyn, Michael Berryman, Chris De Rose, Chuck Jeffreys; ***D:*** Frank Harris; ***W:*** Michael Standing; ***M:*** Kevin Klinger, Bob Mamet.

Aftershock: Earthquake in New York ½ **1999** Typical TV disaster movie based on the novel by Chuck Scarborough. You're introduced to a bunch of nice people (there's quite a good cast), disaster strikes, death and destruction are everywhere and all it brings out (rather than hysteria, looting, violence and assorted evilness) is good deeds and rescues. Nifty special effects though. **139m/C VHS, DVD.** Tom Skerritt, Sharon Lawrence, Charles S. Dutton, Lisa Nicole Carson, Cicely Tyson, Jennifer Garner, Rachel Ticotin, Frederick Weller, Erika Eleniak, Mitchell Ryan; ***D:*** Mikael Salomon; ***W:*** David Stevens, Paul Eric Meyers, Loren Boothby; ***C:*** Jon Joffin; ***M:*** Irwin Fisch. **TV**

Afterwards ½ **2008** Sentimental and slow-paced (and a little creepy). Successful New York lawyer Nathan Del Amico (Duris) encounters mysterious hospice physician, Dr. Kay (Malkovich), who claims to have supernatural abilities to see a white aura around people who will soon die. Thinking he's next, Nathan decide to make peace with his past, including his ex-wife Claire (Lilly), while trying to thwart what he thinks is supposed to be his destiny. **107m/C DVD.** *FR GE* Romain Duris, John Malkovich, Evangeline Lilly, Pascale Bussieres, Reece Thompson, Sara Waisglass; ***D:*** Gilles Bourdos; ***W:*** Gilles Bourdos, Michel Spinosa; ***C:*** Mark Lee Ping-Bin; ***M:*** Alexandre Desplat.

Against a Crooked Sky **1975 (G)** A young boy sets out with an elderly trapper to find his sister, who was captured by the Indians. Similiar story to "The Searchers," but no masterpiece. **89m/C VHS, DVD.** Richard Boone, Stewart Petersen, Jewel Blanch, Geoffrey Land, Henry Wilcoxon; ***D:*** Earl Bellamy.

Against All Flags **1952** An enjoyable Flynn swashbuckler about a British soldier slashing his way through the Spanish fleet at the turn of the 18th century. Though the story has been told before, tight direction and good performances win out. O'Hara is a tarty eyeful as a hot-tempered pirate moll. **81m/C VHS, DVD.** Errol Flynn, Maureen O'Hara, Anthony Quinn, Mildred Natwick; ***D:*** George Sherman.

Against All Odds ½ **1984 (R)** An interesting love triangle evolves when recently cut quarterback Terry Brogan (Bridges) is asked by his nightclub owning/bookie buddy, Jack (Woods), to travel to Mexico and bring back Jack's sultry girlfriend, Jessie (Ward). Then Terry discovers that Jessie is the daughter of Mrs. Wyler, the football team owner. Contains complicated plot, numerous double crosses, sensual love scenes, and a chase scene along Sunset Boulevard. As the good friend sans conscience, Woods stars. A remake of 1947's "Out of the Past." **122m/C VHS, DVD.** Jeff Bridges, Rachel Ward, James Woods, Alex Karras, Jane Greer, Richard Widmark, Dorian Harewood, Swoosie Kurtz, Bill McKinney, Saul Rubinek; ***D:*** Taylor Hackford; ***W:*** Eric Hughes; ***C:*** Donald E. Thorin; ***M:*** Larry Carlton, Michel Colombier.

Against the Dark **2008 (R)** Seagal vs. the vampires. In a post-apocalyptic world the few human survivors are being sucked dry by vampires. Trapped in a hospital, Commander Tao and his group of ex-military vigilantes are about to make their last stand. **94m/C DVD.** Skye Bennett, Emma Catherwood, Keith David, Jenna Harrison, Linden Ashby, Steven Seagal, Tanoai Reed; ***D:*** Richard Crudo; ***W:*** Matthew Klickstein; ***C:*** William Trautvetter; ***M:*** Philip White. **VIDEO**

Against the Law ½ **1998** Criminal Rex (Grieco) prides himself on his abilities with a gun—leaving a trail of dead cops in his wake. His wants notoriety and, after spotting detective John Shepard (Mancuso) on a news show, decides that TV is the perfect medium to get his 15 minutes of infamy. **85m/C VHS.** Richard Grieco, Nick Mancuso, Nancy Allen, Steven Ford; ***D:*** Jim Wynorski; ***W:*** Steve Mitchell, Bob Sheridan; ***C:*** Andrea V. Rossotto; ***M:*** Kevin Kiner. **VIDEO**

Against the Ropes **2004 (PG-13)** "Erin Brockovich" meets "Rocky" in this biopic loosely based on the life of Detroit boxing manager Jackie Kallen (although for some reason, they set it in Cleveland). Jackie (Ryan) is a tough, harried secretary for the Cleveland Coliseum who's smarter than her skimpy outfits would indicate. She sees her chance to go somewhere in the boxing world when she buys crackhead/boxer Luther's (Epps) contract from mobbed-up manager Sam (Shalhoub) for a dollar. Ryan plays Jackie as a walking cliche spouting lousy dialogue. Shalhoub injects the movie with a bit of fun doing his best Snidley Whiplash. Dutton does better playing Luther's trainer, Felix, than he does directing fight scenes that don't show the action with much clarity. There's no clear winner here, but the audience is definitely the loser. Paramount shelved the movie for a year and a half. **111m/C VHS, DVD.** *US* Meg Ryan, Omar Epps, Tony Shalhoub, Timothy Daly, Charles S. Dutton, Kerry Washington, Joe Cortese; ***D:*** Charles S. Dutton; ***W:*** Cheryl Edwards; ***C:*** Jack N. Green; ***M:*** Michael Kamen.

Against the Wall **1994** Compelling and tense dramatization of the 1971 Attica, New York prison uprising in which 10 guards were held hostage and state troopers and the National Guard killed 29 prisoners before regaining control. Partially fictionalized version of the story told from the viewpoints of a young prison guard (MacLachlan) and a politicized prisoner (Jackson). Filmed at a prison in Clarksville, Tennessee. **115m/C VHS, DVD.** Kyle MacLachlan, Samuel L. Jackson, Clarence Williams III, Frederic Forrest, Harry Dean Stanton, Tom Bower, Philip Bosco, Anne Heche, David Ackroyd; ***D:*** John Frankenheimer; ***W:*** Ron Hutchinson; ***M:*** Gary Chang. **CABLE**

Against the Wall *Quality of Life* **2004 (R)** Mikey (Garrison) and Curtis (Burnam) make their claim to fame as graffiti artists in San Francisco's hard-luck Mission District. But when their illegal activity gets them arrested, Mikey starts thinking about the future and going legit while Curtis violates his probation and his self-destructive behavior shatters their friendship. Debut for Morgan. **84m/C DVD.** MacKenzie Firgens, Luis Saguar, Lane Garrison, Brian Burnam; ***D:*** Benjamin Morgan; ***W:*** Benjamin Morgan; ***C:*** Kev Robertson.

Against the Wind ½ **1948** A motley crew is trained for a mission into Nazi Germany to blow up records and rescue a prisoner. The first half of the film focuses on the group's training, but despite its intensity they win only a pyrrhic victory. A well-done production with solid performances from the cast. **96m/B VHS.** Robert Beatty, Jack Warner, Simone Signoret, Gordon Jackson, Paul Dupuis, Peter Illing; ***D:*** Charles Crichton.

Against the Wind *Contra el Viento* **1990** Juan (Banderas) takes refuge in a remote area of Andalusia in an effort to get away from a mutally obsessive love. But his exile is in vain when his lover appears—his sister (Suarez). Spanish with subtitles. **117m/C VHS, DVD.** *SP* Antonio Banderas, Emma Suarez; ***D:*** Paco Perinan.

Agata and the Storm *Agata et la Tempesta* **2004** Determinedly cheerful, middle-aged Genoa bookstore owner Agata is surprised when she is suddenly wooed by young customer Nico, who turns out to be married. But her pleasure at the unexpected romance literally causes electrical sparks. Meanwhile, Agata's brother Gustavo learns he was adopted, so he leaves his troubled marriage to meet his newly-discovered brother Romeo, a traveling salesman whose dream is to start a trout farm. Italian with subtitles. **118m/C DVD.** *IT* Licia Maglietta, Emilio Solfrizzi, Guiseppe Battiston, Claudio Santamaria, Marina Massironi, Giselda Volodi; ***D:*** Silvio Soldini; ***W:*** Silvio Soldini, Doriana Leondeff, Francesco Piccolo; ***C:*** Arnaldo Catinari; ***M:*** Giovanni Venosta.

Agatha ½ **1979 (PG)** A speculative period drama about Agatha Christie's still unexplained disappearance in 1926, and a fictional American reporter's efforts to find her. Beautiful but lackluster mystery. Unfortunately, Hoffman and Redgrave generate few sparks. **98m/C VHS.** Pam(ela) Austin, Dustin Hoffman, Vanessa Redgrave, Timothy Dalton, Helen Morse, Tony Britton, Timothy West, Celia Gregory; ***D:*** Michael Apted.

Agatha Christie: A Life in Pictures ½ **2004** In 1926, famed mystery writer Agatha Christie (Williams) went missing for 11 days. She was found at a hotel and couldn't remember what had happened to her, although hypnosis revealed that Christie knew her husband Archie (Coulthard) was an unfaithful wastrel. But Christie also left clues in her writings and, in 1962, the aged Agatha (Massey) speaks of her disappearance to a journalist. **90m/C DVD.** *GB* Olivia Williams, Anna Massey, Raymond Coulthard, Stephen Boxer, Anthony O'Donnell; ***D:*** Richard Curson Smith; ***W:*** Richard Curson Smith; ***C:*** Jeff Baynes; ***M:*** Andrew Phillips. **TV**

Agatha Christie's A Caribbean Mystery ½ *A Caribbean Mystery* **1983** Miss Marple's vacation turns into another sluething adventure when she must solve the murder of a retired British Army officer. Faithful adaptation updates the action form the 1950s to the '80s in fine fashion. **96m/C VHS, DVD.** Helen Hayes, Barnard Hughes, Jameson Parker, Season Hubley, Swoosie Kurtz, Cassie Yates, Zakes Mokae, Stephen Macht, Maurice Evans, Lynne Moody, George Innes, Brock Peters; ***D:*** Robert Lewis; ***W:*** Sue Grafton, Steve Humphrey; ***C:*** Ted Voightlander; ***M:*** Lee Holdridge. **TV**

Agatha Christie's Murder is Easy *Murder is Easy* **1982** Luke Williams (Bixby), an American computer expert, is on a train to London when he meets an old woman (Hayes) who confides that she is going to Scotland Yard to report some mysterious deaths in her village. When she is killd by a hit-and-run driver after leaving the train, he decides to investigate. When he reaches the village, he is aided by a local girl who also suspects foul play. So-so mystery suffers from attempts to update the mystery with computer technology. Adapted from the Agatha Christie novel "Easy to Kill." **95m/C VHS, DVD.** Bill Bixby, Lesley-Anne Down, Olivia de Havilland, Helen Hayes, Patrick Allen, Freddie Jones, Shane Briant, Leigh Lawson, Jonathan Pryce, Carol MacReady; ***D:*** Claude Whatham; ***W:*** Carmen Culver; ***C:*** Brian Tufano; ***M:*** Gerald Fried. **TV**

Agatha Christie's Murder with Mirrors *Murder with Mirrors* **1985** Lightweight TV mystery has Miss Marple (Hayes) once again sleuthing about to help an old friend (Davis) who thinks she's going to be killed for her estate. Hayes is once again delightful, but things begin to fade about half way through. Look for Tim Roth spicing things up in an early role. **96m/C VHS, DVD.** Helen Hayes, Bette Davis, Leo McKern, John Mills, John Laughlin, Dorothy Tutin, Anton Rodgers, John Woodvine, James Coombes, Tim Roth; ***D:*** Dick Lowry; ***W:*** George Eckstein; ***C:*** Brian West; ***M:*** Richard Rodney Bennett. **TV**

Agatha Christie's Sparkling Cyanide *Sparkling Cyanide* **1983** Somebody spiked the champagne—with cyanide! This really brings down a socialite couple's anniversary party as they have to set aside the hor's douvres to solve the whodunit. Cheesy but enjoyable, the twist ending adds to the fun. **96m/C VHS.** Anthony Andrews, Deborah Raffin, Pamela Bellwood, Nancy Marchand, Josef Sommer, David Huffman, Christine Belford, June Chadwick, Harry (Henry) Morgan, Michael Woods; ***D:*** Robert Lewis; ***W:*** Robert M. Young, Sue Grafton, Steve Humphrey; ***C:*** Ted Voightlander. **TV**

Agatha Christie's The Pale Horse ½ *The Pale Horse* **1996** When writer Mark Easterbrook is accused of murdering a priest, the only clue to clearing himself is a mysterious list of names. Now he has to figure out the connection between the names if he expects to clear himself. **100m/C VHS, DVD.** *GB* Michael Byrne, Ruth Madoc, Leslie Phillips, Jean Marsh; ***D:*** Charles Beeson. **TV**

Agatha Christie's Thirteen at Dinner *Thirteen at Dinner* **1985** Hercule Poirot must solve the case when an actress's ex-husband dies shortly after granting her a divorce. Lack of character development hurt this otherwise solid outing. Fine cast is highlighted by Ustinov and Dunaway. **91m/C VHS, DVD.** Peter Ustinov, Faye Dunaway, David Suchet, Jonathan Cecil, Bill Nighy, Lee Horsley, Diane Keen, Allan Cuthbertson, John Barron, Amanda Pays, Lesley Dunlop; ***Cameos:*** David Frost; ***D:*** Lou Antonio; ***W:*** Rod Browning; ***C:*** Curtis Clark; ***M:*** John Addison. **TV**

Age Isn't Everything *Life in the Food Chain* **1991 (R)** An appalling clumsy comedy about a recent college graduate who abruptly becomes an old man while retaining his youthful exterior. He looks the same, but walks slowly and talks with a thick Yiddish accent, get it? The cast just marks time until an inexplicable ending. **91m/C VHS.** Jonathan Silverman, Robert Prosky, Rita Moreno, Paul Sorvino, Rita Karin, Robert Cicchini, Brian Williams, Dee Hoty, Dr. Joyce Brothers, Bella Abzug; ***D:*** Douglas Katz; ***W:*** Douglas Katz; ***C:*** Michael Spiller.

Age of Consent **1969** Disillusioned painter Bradley Morahan (Mason) leaves his successful career in New York to return to his Australian homeland. He rents a house on a sparsely populated Great Barrier Reef island and promptly notices the fleshy beauty of teenager Cora (Mirren), who agrees to pose nude for him, which reinvigorates Morahan in more than one way. Morahan's paradise is invaded by a mooching old friend (MacGowran) who steals from him, and Cora's alcoholic granny (Carr-Glynn) makes trouble. **103m/C DVD.** *AU* James Mason, Helen Mirren, Jack MacGowran, Andonia Katsaros, Neva Carr-Glynn, Michael Bodde; ***D:*** Michael Powell; ***W:*** Peter Yeldham; ***C:*** Hannes Staudinger; ***M:*** Peter Sculthorpe.

The Age of Innocence **1993 (PG)** Magnificently lavish adaptation of Edith Wharton's novel of passion thwarted by convention is visually stunning, but don't expect action since these people kill with a word or gesture. In 1870s New York, proper lawyer Newland Archer (Day-Lewis) is engaged to the equally proper May Welland (Ryder). He discovers unexpected romance when May's cousin, the rather scandalous Ellen Olenska (Pfeiffer), returns to the city from Europe but his hesitancy costs them dearly. Woodward's narration of Wharton's observations helps sort out what goes on behind the facades. Although slow, see this one for the beautiful period authenticity, thanks to Scorsese, who obviously labored over the small details. He shows up as a photographer; his parents appear in a scene on a train. **138m/C VHS, DVD.** Martin Scorsese, Daniel Day-Lewis, Michelle Pfeiffer, Winona Ryder, Richard E. Grant, Alec McCowen, Miriam Margolyes, Mary Beth Hurt, Geraldine Chaplin, Stuart Wilson,

Michael Gough, Alexis Smith, Jonathan Pryce, Robert Sean Leonard; **D:** Martin Scorsese; **W:** Martin Scorsese, Jay Cocks; **C:** Michael Ballhaus; **M:** Elmer Bernstein; **Nar:** Joanne Woodward. Oscars '93: Costume Des.; British Acad. '93: Support. Actress (Margolyes); Golden Globes '94: Support. Actress (Ryder); Natl. Bd. of Review '93: Director (Scorsese), Support. Actress (Ryder).

Age Old Friends 1/2 **1989** Crusty octogenarian Cronyn must choose. His daughter (played by real-life offspring Tandy) wants him to move out of a retirement home and into her house. But he's struggling to keep neighbor and increasingly senile friend Gardenia from slipping into "zombieland." An emotional treat with two fine actors deploying dignity and wit in the battle against old age. Originally adapted for HBO from the Broadway play, "A Month of Sundays" by Bob Larbey. **89m/C VHS, DVD.** Vincent Gardenia, Hume Cronyn, Tandy Cronyn, Esther Rolle, Michelle Scarabelli; **D:** Allen Kroeker.

The Agency *Mind Games* **1981 (R)** An advertising agency attempts to manipulate public behavior and opinion through the use of subliminal advertising. A good premise is bogged down by a dull script and plodding performances by all concerned. Based on a Paul Gottlieb novel. **94m/C VHS, DVD.** *CA* Robert Mitchum, Lee Majors, Valerie Perrine, Saul Rubinek, Alexandra Stewart; **D:** George Kaczender; **M:** Lewis Furey.

Agent Cody Banks 1/2 **2003 (PG)** Muniz is Cody Banks, a seemingly normal 15-year-old kid who lives a secret life as a CIA spy. After training for a few years at a "junior spy" summer camp, he's given his first mission: talk to a girl! He must befriend and protect classmate Natalie (Duff), the daughter of a scientist (Donovan) who's created a nanotechnology that could help villains McShane and Vosloo CONTROL THE WORLD!!! Much junior 007 action ensues, mixed with some quirky comedy and innocent teen romance. "Spy Kids" had more charm, but the target audience probably won't mind the difference. Harmon keeps things interesting for the older set with her vavoom-ish wardrobe and surprising knack for comedy. If the characters aren't exactly fleshed out, at least the actors playing them seem to be enjoying themselves. **95m/C VHS, DVD.** *US* Frankie Muniz, Hilary Duff, Angie Harmon, Keith David, Cynthia Stevenson, Arnold Vosloo, Martin Donovan, Daniel Roebuck, Ian McShane, Darrell Hammond; **D:** Harald Zwart; **W:** Scott M. Alexander, Ashley Edward Miller, Zack Stentz, Larry Karaszewski; **C:** Denis Crossan; **M:** John Powell.

Agent Cody Banks 2: Destination London **2004 (PG)** Banks is back to take on more evildoers who want to RULE THE WORLD!!! AGAIN!!! Now it's British industrialist Lord Kenworth (Faulkner) and Diaz (Allen), Banks's CIA camp commander turned traitor, who have a device that allows them to control what people do and say. Off to London for the big showdown. Cody goes undercover in a youth symphony where he meets his handler (the funny Anderson, who's not given much to work with) and Hilary Duff fill-in Spearritt as Emily, the prerequisite pretty girl (albeit a drab one here). While the first effort thrived on the normal-teenager-becomes-secret-agent concept the second surprisingly ignores the first part and focuses on the at-times hard-to-follow action scenes. Muniz puts in another fine performance and the kids will probably still find it a fun ride, but a trilogy is probably not needed. **99m/C VHS, DVD.** *US* Frankie Muniz, Anthony Anderson, Cynthia Stevenson, Daniel Roebuck, Hannah Spearritt, Anna Chancellor, Keith Allen, James Faulkner, David Kelly, Santiago Segura, Connor Widdows, Keith David; **D:** Kevin Allen; **W:** Don Rhymer, Harald Zwart; **C:** Denis Crossan; **M:** Mark Thomas.

Agent of Death *The Alternate* **1999 (R)** Philandering President Beck is not Mr. Popularity and there's an election coming up. So his PR head arranges for a fake kidnapping to garner sympathy. But the plans goes wrong and he winds up in the hands of a psycho Secret Service agent (Genesse). And the one man (Roberts) who might be able to rescue the Prez doesn't want the job. **105m/C VHS, DVD.** Ice-T, Eric Roberts, Michael Madsen, Bryan Genesse, John Beck; **D:** Sam Firstenberg; **W:** Bryan Genesse. **VIDEO**

Agent on Ice **1986 (R)** Hockey team is stalked by lawyers. No, wait. An ex-CIA agent is stalked for cover-up purposes by the agency and the mob. One slippery fellow. **96m/C VHS.** Tom Ormeny, Clifford David, Louis Pastore, Matt Craven; **D:** Clark Worswick.

Agent Red 1/2 *Captured* **2000 (R)** Oh so typical story done in a less-than-enthralling manner. Naval Specials Ops Commander Matt Hendricks (Lundgren) is aboard a U.S. sub, escorting a deadly chemical weapon to a safe storage facility. Then the sub is boarded by Russian terrorists who want to unleash the virus on New York City. Naturally, Hendricks must prevent that. **95m/C VHS, DVD.** Dolph Lundgren, Randolph Mantooth, Meilani Paul, Alexander Kuznitsov, Natalie Radford, Steve Eastin, Tony Becker; **D:** Damian Lee; **W:** Damian Lee; **C:** Ken Blakey; **M:** David Wurst, Eric Wurst. **VIDEO**

Aggie Appleby, Maker of Men 1/2 *Cupid in the Rough* **1933** A wimpy society boy transforms himself into a tough guy, all for the love of a dame. Based on a play by Joseph O. Kesselring. Very slight comedy. **73m/B VHS.** Charles Farrell, Wynne Gibson, William Gargan, Zasu Pitts, Betty Furness; **D:** Mark Sandrich; **M:** Max Steiner.

Agnes and His Brothers *Agnes und Seine Bruder* **2004** Transsexual Agnes has little in common with her two brothers, Hans-Jorg and Werner, except for their loathing of their weirdo recluse father, Gunther. Agnes has man trouble (she's always a victim) and Hans-Jorg and Werner are sexually desperate, albeit for different reasons. These are strange, unlikable people and you will be very glad they're not part of your family. German with subtitles. **115m/C DVD.** *GE* Moritz Bleibtreu, Herbert Knaup, Vadim Glowna, Katja Riemann, Martin Weiss, Tom Schilling; **D:** Oskar Roehler; **W:** Oskar Roehler; **C:** Carl F. Koschnick; **M:** Martin Todsharow.

Agnes Browne 1/2 **1999 (R)** Sentimental, old-fashioned saga concerning recent widow Agnes Browne (Huston), who's trying to cope with her seven children under difficult circumstances in Dublin in 1967. Agnes, who works a market stall, has one personal dream—she wants to see Tom Jones in an upcoming concert. Guess what happens. Director Huston does try to keep the bathos under control. Based on the novel "The Mammy" of Brendan O'Carroll. **91m/C VHS, DVD.** Anjelica Huston, Ray Winstone, Arno Chevrier, Marion O'Dwyer, Ciaran Owens, Tom Jones; **D:** Anjelica Huston; **W:** John Goldsmith, Brendan O'Carroll; **C:** Anthony B. Richmond; **M:** Paddy Moloney.

Agnes of God **1985 (PG-13)** Stage to screen translation of John Pielmeier's play loses something in the translation. Coarse chain-smoking psychiatrist Fonda is sent to a convent to investigate whether young nun Tilly is fit to stand trial. Seems that the nun may have given birth to and then strangled her baby, although she denies ever having sexual relations and knows nothing about an infant. Naive Tilly is frightened by probing Fonda, while worldly mother-superior Bancroft is distrusting. Melodramatic stew of Catholicism, religious fervor, and science features generally good performances, although Fonda often seems to be acting (maybe it's the cigarettes). **98m/C VHS, DVD.** Jane Fonda, Anne Bancroft, Meg Tilly, Anne Pitoniak, Winston Rekert, Gratien Gelinas; **D:** Norman Jewison; **W:** John Pielmeier; **C:** Sven Nykvist; **M:** Georges Delerue. Golden Globes '86: Support. Actress (Tilly).

The Agony and the Ecstasy 1/2 **1965** Big-budget (for 1965 anyway at $12 million) adaptation of the Irving Stone book recounts the conflict between Michelangelo and Pope Julius II after His Holiness directs the artist to paint the Sistine Chapel. Follow the tortured artist through his unpredictable creative process and the hours (it seems literal due to movie length) of painting flat on his back. Heston exudes quiet strength in his sincere interpretation of the genius artist, while Harrison has a fling as the Pope. Slow script is not up to the generally good performances. Disappointing at the boxoffice, but worth a look on the small screen for the sets alone. **136m/C VHS, DVD.** Charlton Heston, Rex Harrison, Harry Andrews, Diane Cilento, Alberto Lupo, Adolfo Celi; **D:** Carol Reed; **W:** Philip Dunne; **C:** Leon Shamroy; **M:** Jerry Goldsmith, Alex North. Natl. Bd. of Review '65: Support. Actor (Andrews).

Agony of Love **1966** An unhappy homemaker rents a nearby apartment to live out her wildest fantasies and bring some excitment into her otherwise dull life. **?m/C VHS, DVD.** Pat (Barringer) Barrington, William Rotsler; **D:** William Rotsler; **W:** William Rotsler.

Aguirre, the Wrath of God 1/2 *Aguirre, der Zorn Gottes* **1972** Herzog at his best, combining brilliant poetic images and an intense narrative dealing with power, irony, and death. Spanish conquistadors in 1590 search for the mythical city of gold in Peru. Instead, they descend into the hell of the jungle. Kinski is fabulous as Aguirre, succumbing to insanity while leading a continually diminishing crew in this compelling, extraordinary drama shot in the jungles of South America. Both English- and German-language versions available. **94m/C VHS, DVD.** *GE* Klaus Kinski, Ruy Guerra, Del Negro, Helena Rojo, Cecilia Rivera, Peter Berling, Danny Ades; **D:** Werner Herzog; **W:** Werner Herzog; **C:** Thomas Mauch; **M:** Popul Vuh. Natl. Soc. Film Critics '77: Cinematog.

Ah, Wilderness! 1/2 **1935** Delightful tale of a teen boy coming of age in small town America. Watch for the hilarious high school graduation scene. Based on the play by Eugene O'Neill. Remade in 1948 as "Summer Holiday," a musical with Mickey Rooney in the lead. **101m/B VHS.** Wallace Beery, Lionel Barrymore, Aline MacMahon, Eric Linden, Cecilia Parker, Spring Byington, Mickey Rooney, Charley Grapewin, Frank Albertson; **D:** Clarence Brown; **C:** Clyde De Vinna.

Aileen: Life and Death of a Serial Killer **2003** Documentary studies the life and crimes of serial killer Aileen Wuornos. In-depth work recounts her horrible childhood and the psychoses that led to her murderous spree. Chilling. **89m/C VHS, DVD.** *US* **D:** Joan Churchill, Nick Broomfield; **C:** Joan Churchill; **M:** Robert (Rob) Lane.

Aimee & Jaguar **1998** In 1943 Berlin, Jewish Felice (Schrader) is hiding her identity and working for a Nazi newspaper where she can gather information to leak to the resistance. She leads a hedonistic night life with a group of lesbian friends and, one night, encounters Lilly (Koehler), the unfaithful wife of an SS soldier who's away at the Russian front. The odd couple begin a risky affair (the title refers to the nicknames the women gave each other) until the inevitable discovery. Based on a true story from the 1994 book by Erica Fischer. German with subtitles. **125m/C VHS, DVD.** *GE* Maria Schrader, Juliane Kohler, Johanna Wokalek, Heike Makatsch, Elisabeth Degen, Detlev Buck; **D:** Max Farberbock; **W:** Rona Munro, Max Farberbock; **C:** Tony Imi; **M:** Jan A.P. Kaczmarek.

Ain't No Way Back *The Ghost of Fletcher Ridge* **1989** Two hunters stumble upon a feudin' bunch of moonshiners and must leave their city ways behind if they plan to survive. **90m/C VHS, DVD.** Campbell Scott, Virginia Lantry, Bernie (Bernard) White, John Durbin, Len Lesser, Joe Mays; **D:** Michael Borden.

Air America **1990 (R)** It's the Vietnam War and the CIA is operating a secret drug smuggling operation in Southeast Asia to finance the effort. Flyboys Gibson and Downey drop opium and glib lines all over Laos. Big-budget Gibson vehicle with sufficient action but lacking much of a story, which was adapted from a book by Christopher Robbins. **113m/C VHS, DVD.** Mel Gibson, Robert Downey Jr., Marshall Bell, Nancy Travis, David Marshall Grant, Tim Thomerson, Lane Smith; **D:** Roger Spottiswoode; **W:** Richard Rush; **C:** Roger Deakins; **M:** Charles Gross.

Air Bud 1/2 **1997 (PG)** Buddy's a basketball-playing golden retriever (no relation) who befriends lonely misfit Josh (Zegers) and teaches him the nuances of the layup, fade-away J, and pick-and-roll. It's good to see dog athletes getting to stretch beyond the usual frisbee and stick-fetching roles. Teaming animals (especially canines) with kids usually adds up to success. This one's no exception, especially for the grade school crowd. **92m/C VHS, DVD.** Kevin Zegers, Michael Jeter, Bill Cobbs, Wendy Makkena, Eric Christmas, Brendan Fletcher, Jay Brazeau, Stephen E. Miller, Nicola Cavendish; **D:** Charles Martin Smith; **W:** Paul Tamasy, Aaron Mendelsohn; **C:** Mike Southon; **M:** Brahm Wenger.

Air Bud 2: Golden Receiver **1998 (G)** Buddy, the canine Michael Jordan of last year's "Air Bud," is back for more organized team sports with small children. His owner, Josh (Zegers) is still mourning the death of his father and isn't ready to deal with his mother's budding romance with the new veterinarian in town (Harrison). Meanwhile, Josh joins the school's football team and finds himself thrust into the spotlight as the team's quarterback when the starter is injured (big surprise!), only to be bailed out by his multi-sport pooch. Actually, Buddy is played by four different Golden Retrievers, as the original died shortly after completing the original. This rehash tries to take itself seriously, with lessons about overcoming tragedy and adjusting to change, but isn't much more than sappy melodrama and cute dog tricks. **90m/C VHS, DVD.** Kevin Zegers, Cynthia Stevenson, Gregory Harrison, Nora Dunn, Robert Costanzo, Tim Conway, Dick Martin, Perry Anzilotti, Suzanne Ristic, Jay Brazeau; **D:** Richard Martin; **W:** Paul Tamasy, Aaron Mendelsohn; **C:** Mike Southon; **M:** Brahm Wenger.

Air Bud 3: World Pup 1/2 **2000 (G)** Buddy went from basketball to football and now to soccer in this third installment. This time he teams up with the U.S. Women's Soccer Team and also becomes a dad. And wouldn't you know—just before the championship game, dad Buddy must rescue one of his pups from a gang of dog-nappers. **83m/C VHS, DVD.** Kevin Zegers, Dale Midkiff, Caitlin Wachs, Martin Ferrero, Duncan Regehr, Brittany Paige Bouck, Briana Scurry, Brandi Chastain, Tisha Venturini; **D:** Bill Bannerman. **VIDEO**

Air Bud 4: Seventh Inning Fetch 1/2 **2002 (G)** Since Josh is off at college, it's his little sis Andrea who needs Buddy's help on her baseball team. But Buddy's got other problems—Rocky the Raccoon has kidnapped Buddy's puppies! **93m/C VHS, DVD.** Richard Karn, Cynthia Stevenson, Kevin Zegers, Caitlin Wachs; **D:** Robert Vince. **VIDEO**

Air Bud 5: Buddy Spikes Back **2003 (G)** After her best friend moves to California, Andrea (Wachs) takes up volleyball so she can win a chance to visit. Naturally, all-around sports dog Buddy can do a little spiking of his own. **87m/C VHS, DVD.** *CA* Caitlin Wachs, Katija Pevec, Jake D. Smith, Tyler Boissonnault, Edie McClurg, Patrick Cranshaw, Cynthia Stevenson, Rob Tinkler; **D:** Mike Southon; **C:** Adam Sliwinski. **VIDEO**

Air Bud 6: Air Buddies **2006 (PG)** When doggie parents Buddy and Molly are abducted, their five talking puppies—B-Dawg, RoseBud, Bud-dha, Mudbud, and Budderball—must come to the rescue. Yeah, it's cute—you expected more? **80m/C DVD.** Slade Pearce, Trevor Wright; **D:** Robert Vince; **W:** Robert Vince, Anna McRoberts; **C:** Mike Southon; **M:** Brahm Wenger; **V:** Abigail Breslin, Spencer Breslin, Josh Flitter, Spencer Fox, Michael Clarke Duncan, Don Knotts, Mike Southon. **VIDEO**

Air Force 1/2 **1943** One of the finest of the WWII movies, Hawks' exciting classic has worn well through the years, in spite of the Japanese propaganda. It follows the hazardous exploits of a Boeing B-17 bomber crew who fight over Pearl Harbor, Manila, and the Coral Sea. Extremely realistic dogfight sequences and powerful, introspective real guy interfacing by the ensemble cast are masterfully combined by Hawks. **124m/B VHS, DVD.** John Garfield, John Ridgely, Gig Young, Arthur Kennedy, Charles Drake, Harry Carey Sr., George Tobias, Ray Montgomery, James Brown, Stanley Ridges, Willard Robertson, Moroni Olsen, Edward Brophy, Richard Lane, Faye Emerson, Addison Richards, James Flavin, Ann Doran, Dorothy Peterson, William Forrest, Ward Wood; **D:** Howard Hawks; **W:** Dudley Nichols, William Faulkner; **C:** James Wong Howe, Elmer Dyer, Charles A. Marshall; **M:** Franz Waxman. Oscars '43: Film Editing.

Air Force One *AFO* **1997 (R)** Ford stars as U.S. President James Marshall, who is not only tough on crime but tough, period. His policy is to not negotiate with terrorists. Then Air Force One, with him, the First Lady and their daughter aboard is hijacked by Russian nationalists, led by ice cold Ivan (Oldman). Close is first woman Veep, Kathryn Bennett, stuck in D.C. coping with the situation. Ford is in fine form as the President who's forced to kick some Commie butt to save the day. Director Petersen ("In The Line of Fire") is becoming a master of building tension in confined places and puts his strong cast to good use. Nail-biting suspense and breath-taking action sequences cap off tour-de-force adventure. **124m/C VHS, DVD, UMD.** Harrison Ford, Gary Oldman, Glenn Close, Dean Stockwell, William H. Macy, Wendy Crewson, Xander Berkeley, Paul Guilfoyle, Liesl Matthews, Bill Smitrovich, Elya Baskin, David Vadim, Tom Everett, Philip Baker Hall, Spencer Garrett, Donna Bullock; ***Cameos:*** Jurgen Prochnow; ***D:*** Wolfgang Petersen; ***W:*** Andrew Marlowe; ***C:*** Michael Ballhaus; ***M:*** Jerry Goldsmith.

Air Guitar Nation **2006 (R)** Suit up, grab your guitars...wait, you don't need them. First time director (and reality TV vet) Lipsitz follows rivals David "C. Diddy" Jung and Dan "Bjorn Turoque" Crane as they air guitar-battle their way from American competitions to the World Championships in Finland. Lipsitz doesn't push many boundaries with her direction or narrative, but still manages to create a film that's often hilarious without making its subjects the butt of the joke. **81m/C DVD.** *US* ***D:*** Alexandra Lipsitz; ***C:*** Anthony Sacco; ***M:*** Dan Crane.

Air Hawk **1984** Australian made for TV release details the adventures of an outback pilot involved with stolen diamonds. **90m/C VHS.** *AU* Eric Oldfield, Louise Howitt, Ellie MacLure, David Robson, David Baker; ***D:*** David Baker. **TV**

The Air I Breathe **2007 (R)** Four interlocking stories are delivered in the form of an allegorical gangster movie that ends up an overwrought mess. Characters Happiness (Whitaker), Pleasure (Fraser), Sorrow (Gellar), and Love (Bacon), named for the key emotions of a Chinese proverb, muddle through individual challenges while the menacing gangster Fingers (Garcia) casts a shadow over all their lives. Standout cast fails to overcome the challenges presented by such a poorly executed, pretentious movie. **97m/C DVD, Blu-ray Disc.** *US* Forest Whitaker, Brendan Fraser, Sarah Michelle Gellar, Kevin Bacon, Andy Garcia, Emile Hirsch, Julie Delpy; ***D:*** Jieho Lee; ***W:*** Jieho Lee, Bob DeRosa; ***C:*** Walt Lloyd; ***M:*** Marcelo Zarvos.

Air Rage **2001 (R)** General Prescott (Cord) screwed over five Marines, setting them up and sending them to prison in order to advance his career. Now they're out and have just hijacked a 747 with the general on board—they not only want revenge but $100 million as well. Captain Marshall (Ice-T) and his team are sent on a rescue mission but things go wrong and Marshall is left to tackle the bad guys on his own. Familiar but fast-paced. **99m/C VHS, DVD.** Ice-T, Cyril O'Reilly, Steve Hytner, Gil Gerard, Alex Cord, Kim Oja; ***D:*** Fred Olen Ray; ***W:*** Sean O'Bannon; ***C:*** Mac Ahlberg. **VIDEO**

Air Raid Wardens **1/2 1943** Laurel & Hardy play a couple of small-town failures who become the local air raid wardens during WWII. They even manage to make a mess of this but redeem themselves when they overhear a spy plot and save the town's munitions factory from a German spy ring. A so-so effort from the comic duo. **67m/B VHS, DVD.** Stan Laurel, Oliver Hardy, Edgar Kennedy, Jacqueline White, Stephen McNally, Russell Hicks, Howard Freeman, Donald Meek, Henry O'Neill; ***D:*** Edward Sedgwick.

The Air Up There **1994 (PG)** Assistant basketball coach Jimmy Dolan (Bacon) heads to the African village of Winabi to recruit talented (and tall) Saleh (Maina) to play b-ball in the U.S. But Saleh is next in line to be the tribe's king and doesn't want to leave. Stupid American in foreign country learning from the natives story is lighthearted, but relies heavily on formula—and borders on the stereotypical, though climatic game is a lot of fun. **108m/C VHS, DVD.** Kevin Bacon, Charles Gitona Maina, Sean McCann, Dennis Patrick; ***D:*** Paul Michael Glaser; ***W:*** Max Apple; ***C:*** Elliot Davis; ***M:*** David Newman.

Airborne **1/2 1993 (PG)** Cool California rollerblade dude gets transplanted to Cincinnati for a school year, and has to prove himself when those good ol' midwestern boys come after him. Nothing short of a skate vehicle appealing largely, if not solely, to the high school contingent. **91m/C VHS.** Jack Black, Chris Conrad, Alanna Ubach, Jacob Vargas, Shane McDermott, Seth Green, Brittney Powell, Edie McClurg; ***D:*** Rob Bowman; ***W:*** Bill Apablasa; ***M:*** Stewart Copeland.

Airborne **1998 (R)** Members of a covert Special Forces team are targeted for assassination after recovering a biochemical weapon from terrorists. But their leader (Guttenberg) decides to use the virus as bait to find out who wants them dead. Guttenberg tries but can't convince as a tough guy but there's lots of action to make up for this casting quirk. **94m/C VHS, DVD.** Steve Guttenberg, Sean Bean, Colm Feore; ***D:*** Julian Grant. **VIDEO**

Airboss **1/2 1997 (R)** A special forces team of FBI agents and the military must track down a hijacked shipment of plutonium before it falls into terrorist hands. When a team member is killed, fighter pilot Frank White (Zagarino) is called in. Lots of machinery, guns, and explosions make up for the lack of believable story. **90m/C VHS, DVD.** Frank Zagarino, John Christian, Kayle Watson, Caroline Strong, Jerry Kokich; ***D:*** J. Christian Ingvordsen. **VIDEO**

Airheads **1/2 1994 (PG-13)** "Wayne's World" meets "Dog Day Afternoon." Silly farce has three metal heads (Buscemi, Fraser, Sandler) holding a radio station hostage in order to get their demo tape played. Events snowball and they receive instant fame. Cast and crew rich with subversive comedic talents, including Sandler and Farley from "Saturday Night Live." Soundtrack authenticity supplied by White Zombie and The Galatic Cowboys. **81m/C VHS, DVD.** Brendan Fraser, Steve Buscemi, Adam Sandler, Chris Farley, Michael McKean, Judd Nelson, Joe Mantegna, Michael Richards, Ernie Hudson, Amy Locane, Nina Siemaszko, John Melendez, Harold Ramis, Marshall Bell, David Arquette, Reg E. Cathey, Allen Covert, Sam Whipple, China Kantner; ***D:*** Michael Lehmann; ***W:*** Rich Wilkes; ***C:*** John Schwartzman; ***M:*** Carter Burwell.

Airplane! **1/2 1980 (PG)** Classic lampoon of disaster flicks is stupid but funny and launched a bevy of wanna-be spoofs. Former pilot Ted Striker (Hays), who's lost both his stewardess girlfriend Elaine (Hagerty) and his nerve, takes over the controls of a jet when the crew is hit with food poisoning. The passengers become increasingly crazed and ground support more surreal as our hero struggles to land the plane. Clever, fast-paced, and very funny parody mangles every Hollywood cliche within reach. The gags are so furiously paced that when one bombs it's hardly noticeable. Launched Nielsen's second career as a comic actor. And it ain't over till it's over: don't miss the amusing final credits. Followed by "Airplane 2: The Sequel." **88m/C VHS, DVD.** Jerry Zucker, Jim Abrahams, David Zucker, Robert Hays, Julie Hagerty, Lloyd Bridges, Peter Graves, Robert Stack, Kareem Abdul-Jabbar, Leslie Nielsen, Stephen Stucker, Ethel Merman, Barbara Billingsley, Lorna Patterson, Joyce Bulifant, James Hong, Maureen McGovern, Jimmie Walker, Rossie (Ross) Harris; ***D:*** Jerry Zucker, Jim Abrahams, David Zucker; ***W:*** Jerry Zucker, Jim Abrahams, David Zucker; ***C:*** Joseph Biroc; ***M:*** Elmer Bernstein. Writers Guild '80: Adapt. Screenplay.

Airplane 2: The Sequel **1982 (PG)** Not a Zucker, Abrahams and Zucker effort, and sorely missing their slapstick and script finesse. The first passenger space shuttle has taken off for the moon and there's a mad bomber on board. Given the number of stars mugging, it's more of a loveboat in space than a fitting sequel to "Airplane." Nonetheless, some funny laughs and gags. **84m/C VHS, DVD.** Robert Hays, Julie Hagerty, Lloyd Bridges, Raymond Burr, Peter Graves, William Shatner, Sonny Bono, Chuck Connors, Chad Everett, Stephen Stucker, Rip Torn, Kent McCord, Sandahl Bergman, Jack Jones, John Dehner, Richard Jaeckel; ***Cameos:*** Ken Finkleman; ***D:*** Ken Finkleman; ***W:*** Ken Finkleman; ***C:*** Joseph Biroc; ***M:*** Elmer Bernstein.

Airport **1970 (G)** Old-fashioned disaster thriller built around an all-star cast, fairly moronic script, and an unavoidable accident during the flight of a passenger airliner. A boxoffice hit that paved the way for many lesser disaster flicks (including its many sequels) detailing the reactions of the passengers and crew as they cope with impending doom. Considered to be the best of the "Airport" series; adapted from the Arthur Hailey novel. **137m/C VHS, DVD.** Dean Martin, Burt Lancaster, Jean Seberg, Jacqueline Bisset, George Kennedy, Helen Hayes, Van Heflin, Maureen Stapleton, Barry Nelson, Lloyd Nolan, Dana Wynter, Barbara Hale, Gary Collins, Jessie Royce Landis; ***D:*** George Seaton; ***W:*** George Seaton; ***C:*** Ernest Laszlo; ***M:*** Alfred Newman. Oscars '70: Support. Actress (Hayes); Golden Globes '71: Support. Actress (Stapleton).

Airport '75 **1975 (PG)** After a mid-air collision, a jumbo 747 is left pilotless. Airline attendant Black must fly da plane. She does her cross-eyed best in this absurd sequel to "Airport" built around a lesser "all-star cast." Safe on the ground, Heston tries to talk the airline hostess/pilot into landing, while the impatient Kennedy continues to grouse as leader of the foam-ready ground crew. A slick, insincere attempt to find box office magic again (which unfortunately worked, leading to two more sequels). **107m/C VHS, DVD.** Charlton Heston, Karen Black, George Kennedy, Gloria Swanson, Helen Reddy, Sid Caesar, Efrem Zimbalist Jr., Susan Clark, Dana Andrews, Linda Blair, Nancy Olson, Roy Thinnes, Myrna Loy, Ed Nelson, Larry Storch; ***D:*** Jack Smight; ***W:*** Don Ingalls; ***C:*** Philip Lathrop; ***M:*** John Cacavas.

Airport '77 **1977 (PG)** Billionaire Stewart fills his converted passenger jet with priceless art and sets off to Palm Beach for a museum opening, joined by an uninvited gang of hijackers. Twist to this in-flight disaster is that the bad time in the air occurs underwater, a novel (and some might say, desperate) twist to the old panic in the plane we're all gonna die formula. With a cast of familiar faces, some of them stars and some of them just familiar faces, this is yet another sequel to "Airport" and another boxoffice success, leading to the last of the tired series in 1979. **114m/C VHS, DVD.** Jack Lemmon, James Stewart, Lee Grant, Brenda Vaccaro, Joseph Cotten, Olivia de Havilland, Darren McGavin, Christopher Lee, George Kennedy, Kathleen Quinlan, Monte Markham; ***D:*** Jack Smight.

Ajami **1/2 2009** A non-professional cast, many from Jaffa's multi-ethnic Ajami neighborhood, are featured in Copti and Shani's intense story of culture clash in Israel. A revenge killing has many repercussions that involve Palestinians and Israelis, Christians, Muslims, and Jews—all of whom are hostile to the differing communities. Moving, powerful portrait of a society where violence permeates even the most insignificant aspects of daily life. Arabic and Hebrew with subtitles. **120m/C DVD.** *IS* Shahir Kabaha, Fouad Habash, Ibrahim Frege, Youseff Sahwani, Ramin Karim, Eran Naim, Scandar Copti; ***D:*** Scandar Copti, Yaron Shani; ***W:*** Scandar Copti, Yaron Shani; ***C:*** Boaz Yehonatan Yaacov; ***M:*** Rabiah Buchari.

AKA **2002 (R)** Unhappy with his family life, young man Dean leeches off of rich socialite Lady Gryffoyn until her son, Alex, smells a rat and Dean scampers away to Paris. Unable to forgo his taste for the good life, he opts to pass himself off as Alex—causing him to face his sexuality. British writer-director Roy uses offbeat three-screen device to tell his own real-life tale. **107m/C VHS, DVD.** *GB* Diana Quick, Blake Ritson, Bill Nighy, Geoff Bell, Matthew Leitch, George Asprey, Lindsey Coulson; ***D:*** Duncan Roy; ***W:*** Duncan Roy. **VIDEO**

Akeelah and the Bee **1/2 2006 (PG)** Inspirational story focuses on 11-year-old Akeelah (Palmer), a vocabulary whiz (thanks to her late father's Scrabble prowess) who doesn't want to be humiliated as a brainiac at her tough South Central L.A. school. But after a couple of spelling bee wins, and the coaching of no-nonsense UCLA English professor Larabee (Fishburne), Akeelah is encouraged to dream big and head for the National Spelling Bee. Bassett plays her overworked widow mom, who has too many other worries to help her daughter (at least at first). Palmer's character is both sweet and determined although the film may seem overly familiar. **107m/C DVD.** *US* Laurence Fishburne, Angela Bassett, Keke Palmer, Curtis Armstrong, Tzi Ma, Lee Thompson Young, Sahara Garey, J.R. Villarreal, Sean Michael Afable; ***D:*** Doug Atchison; ***W:*** Doug Atchison; ***C:*** M. David Mullen; ***M:*** Aaron Zigman.

Akira **1989** Secret government experiments on children with ESP go awry, resulting in an cataclysmic explosion on Tokyo. The city in turn builds itself up into a Megalopolis and the experiments continue. Animated; in Japanese with English subtitles or dubbed. **124m/C VHS, DVD, UMD.** *JP* ***D:*** Katsuhiro Otomo, Sheldon Renan; ***W:*** Katsuhiro Otomo, Izo Hashimoto; ***C:*** Katsuji Misawa; ***M:*** Shoji Yamashiro; ***V:*** Mitsuo Iwata, Nozomu Sasaki, Mami Koyama.

Akira Kurosawa's Dreams **1/2** *Dreams; Yume; I Saw a Dream Like This; Konna Yume Wo Mita* **1990 (PG)** An anthological lesson regarding the simultaneous loss of humanity and nature that threatens us all from the renowned Japanese director. Although the startling and memorable imagery is still present, Kurosawa's lessons are strangely trite and consequently lack the power that is normally associated with his work. Watch for Scorsese as Van Gogh. With English subtitles. **120m/C VHS, DVD.** *JP* Akira Terao, Mitsuko Baisho, Meiko Harada, Chishu Ryu, Hisashi Igawa, Mitsunori Isaki, Toshihiko Nakano, Yoshitaka Zushi, Toshie Negishi, Martin Scorsese; ***D:*** Akira Kurosawa; ***W:*** Akira Kurosawa; ***C:*** Kazutami Hara, Takao Saito, Masaharu Ueda; ***M:*** Shinichiro Ikebe.

Al Capone **1959** Film noir character study of one of the most colorful gangsters of the Roaring '20s. Sort of an underworld "How to Succeed in Business." Steiger chews scenes and bullets as they fly by, providing the performance of his career. Plenty of gangland violence and mayhem and splendid cinematography keep the fast-paced period piece sailing. **104m/C VHS, DVD.** Rod Steiger, Fay Spain, Murvyn Vye, Nehemiah Persoff, Martin Balsam, Al Ruscio, Joe De Santis; ***D:*** Richard Wilson.

Al Franken: God Spoke **2007** Documentary following comedian Al Franken's career after his two-decade stint on "Saturday Night Live" to his decision to enter politics. **84m/C DVD.**

Alabama's Ghost **1/2 1972 (PG)** Musician steals a dead master magician's secrets, incurring the wrath of the paranormal underworld. Far from the best of the "blaxploitation" films of the '70s. **96m/C VHS.** Christopher Brooks, E. Kerrigan Prescott; ***D:*** Fredric Hobbs.

Aladdin *Superfantagenio* **1986 (PG)** A comedic Italian modernization of the Aladdin fable. **97m/C VHS, DVD.** *IT* Bud Spencer, Luca Venantini, Janet Agren, Julian Voloshin, Umberto Raho; ***D:*** Bruno Corbucci.

Aladdin **1/2 1992 (G)** Boy meets princess, loses her, finds her, wins her from evil vizier and nasty parrot, while being aided by big blue genie. Superb animation triumphs over average songs and storyline by capitalizing on Williams' talent for ad-lib with lightning speed genie changes, lots of celebrity spoofs, and even a few pokes at Disney itself. Adults will enjoy the 1,001 impersonations while kids will get a kick out of the big blue genie and the songs, three of which are the late Ashman's legacy. Kane and Salonga are responsible for the singing voices of Aladdin and Jasmine; Gottfried is a riot as the obnoxious parrot sidekick. Be forewarned: small children may be frightened by some of the scarier sequences. ♫A Whole New World; Prince Ali; Friend Like Me; One Jump Ahead; Arabian Nights. **90m/C VHS, DVD.** ***D:*** Ron Clements, John Musker; ***W:*** Ron Clements, John Musker, Ted Elliott, Terry Rossio; ***M:*** Alan Menken, Howard Ashman, Tim Rice; ***V:*** Robin Williams, Scott Weinger, Linda Larkin, Jonathan Freeman, Frank Welker, Gilbert Gottfried, Douglas Seale, Brad Caleb Kane, Lea Salonga. Oscars '92: Song ("A Whole New World"), Orig. Score; Golden Globes '93: Song ("A Whole New World"), Score; MTV Movie Awards '93: Comedic Perf. (Williams).

Aladdin and His Wonderful Lamp 1/2 **1984** The story of Aladdin, a young man who finds a magical oil lamp when he is trapped in a tiny cave. From the "Faerie Tale Theatre" series and director of "Beetlejuice" and "Batman" Tim Burton. **60m/C VHS, DVD.** Valerie Bertinelli, Robert Carradine, Leonard Nimoy, James Earl Jones; ***D:*** Tim Burton.

Aladdin and the King of Thieves **1996** Second-direct-to-video saga (following "The Return of Jafar") once again features Williams as the voice of the genie (after settling a dispute with Disney). On the eve of Aladdin's marriage to Jasmine, theives try to steal a magic talisman, sending Aladdin on a mission to find the thieves—and his father. Disney had such terrific success with "Return" that it was inevitable they would try again. **82m/C VHS, DVD.** ***D:*** Ted Stones; ***W:*** Mark McCorkle, Robert Schooley; ***M:*** Mark Watters; ***V:*** Robin Williams, Scott Weinger, Jerry Orbach, John Rhys-Davies, Gilbert Gottfried, Linda Larkin, CCH Pounder, Frank Welker.

The Alamo **1960** Old-fashioned patriotic battle epic recounts the real events of the 1836 fight for independence in Texas. The usual band of diverse and contentious personalities, including Wayne as a coonskin-capped Davy Crockett, defend a small fort against a very big Mexican raiding party outside of San Antonio. Before meeting mythic death, they fight with each other, learn the meaning of life, and ultimately come to respect each other. Just to make it more entertaining, Avalon sings. Big-budget production features an impeccable musical score by Tiomkin and an impressive 7,000 extras for the Mexican army alone. Wayne reportedly received directorial assistance from John Ford, particularly during the big massacre finale. **161m/C VHS, DVD.** John Wayne, Richard Widmark, Laurence Harvey, Frankie Avalon, Richard Boone, Carlos Arruza, Chill Wills, Veda Ann Borg, Linda Cristal, Patrick Wayne, Joan O'Brien, Joseph Calleia, Ken Curtis, Jester Hairston, Denver Pyle, John Dierkes, Guinn "Big Boy" Williams, Olive Carey, William Henry, Hank Worden, Ruben Padilla, Jack Pennick; ***D:*** John Wayne; ***W:*** James Edward Grant; ***C:*** William Clothier; ***M:*** Dimitri Tiomkin, Paul Francis Webster. Oscars '60: Sound; Golden Globes '61: Score.

The Alamo 1/2 **2004 (PG-13)** Dry as a tumbleweed epic is the latest and not so greatest in a dozen odd big-screen tries of dubious success at depicting the historic Texas battle. Thornton stars as Davy Crockett along with Wilson, Patric, and Quaid as William Travis, Jim Bowie, and Sam Houston who, along with 189 others, form the "Texican" holdouts who, after nearly two weeks of anxious waiting, battle the Mexican army of nearly 2,500 and their General, Santa Anna (Echevarria). Mostly tedious waiting, while the actual battle is surprisingly sterile. Thornton (if not his character) emerges unscathed with an excellent performance, especially in the winning rooftop fiddle serenade scene. Supporting work is more uneven. Big-budgeter looks great and is exacting in historical accuracy but ultimately lacks dramatic punch and a cohesive plot. **137m/C DVD.** Dennis Quaid, Billy Bob Thornton, Jason Patric, Patrick Wilson, Emilio Echeverria, Jordi Molla, Leon Rippy, Marc Blucas, Tom Davidson, Robert Prentiss, Ken Page, Joe Stevens, Steven Prince, Tom Everett, Brandon Smith, Rance Howard, Stephen Bruton, Emily Deschanel, Laura Clifton, Edward "Blue" Deckert; ***D:*** John Lee Hancock; ***W:*** John Lee Hancock, Leslie Bohem, Stephen Gaghan; ***C:*** Dean Semler, John O'Connor; ***M:*** Carter Burwell.

Alamo Bay 1/2 **1985** A slow-moving but sincere tale of contemporary racism. An angry Vietnam veteran and his red-neck buddies feel threatened by Vietnamese refugees who want to go into the fishing business. Set in Texas, filled with Texas-sized characters, and based on a true Texas story, as interpreted by the French Malle. **99m/C VHS.** Ed Harris, Ho Nguyen, Amy Madigan, Donald Moffat, Cynthia Carle, Truyen V. Tran, Rudy Young; ***D:*** Louis Malle; ***W:*** Alice Arlen; ***M:*** Ry Cooder.

The Alamo: Thirteen Days to Glory **1987** The legendary Davy Crockett (Keith), Colonel William Travis (Baldwin), and Jim Bowie (Arness) overcome personal differences to unite against the Mexican Army, vowing to hold down the fort or die. It takes a true Texan to fully appreciate the merits of this rather pedestrian retelling of a familiar story, but the battle scenes are pretty heady (although they lose some of their froth on the small screen). If nothing else, the ever-versatile Julia is worth seeing as Santa Anna in this made-for-TV rendering of J. Lon Tinkle's "Thirteen Days to Glory." You may not want to remember the Alamo this way. **180m/C VHS.** James Arness, Lorne Greene, Alec Baldwin, Brian Keith, Raul Julia, Laura Elena Harring; ***D:*** Peter Werner; ***M:*** Peter Bernstein.

Alamut Ambush **1986** A federal agent is stalked by assassins, and decides to hunt them in return. Sequel to "Cold War Killer." **94m/C VHS, DVD.** *GB* Terence Stamp, Michael Culver; ***D:*** Ken Grieve.

Alan & Naomi 1/2 **1992 (PG)** In 1944, 14-year-old Alan Silverman is more concerned with his Brooklyn stickball team than the war raging across Europe. This changes when his upstairs neighbor offers refuge to a French-Jewish mother and her young daughter and he is asked to befriend the girl. Naomi witnessed the brutal death of her father by the Nazis and retreated into a world of her own. Together the two build a sweet, if unlikely, friendship. Fine performances save this average coming of age tale. Based on the novel by Myron Levoy. **95m/C VHS.** Lukas Haas, Vanessa Zaoui, Michael Gross, Amy Aquino, Kevin Connolly, Zohra Lampert; ***D:*** Sterling Van Wagenen; ***W:*** Jordan Horowitz; ***M:*** Dick Hyman.

An Alan Smithee Film: Burn, Hollywood, Burn 1/2 *Burn, Hollywood, Burn* **1997 (R)** Follows a British director (Idle), whose given name is Alan Smithee, as he kidnaps the reels of his own picture when he realizes he hates the movie but can't remove his name from it since the Directors Guild of America's official pseudonym for disputed films is "Alan Smithee." O'Neal stars as the boorish producer who drives Smithee to the desperate act. This extended in-joke ran into its own problem when director Arthur Hiller, in what seemed like a publicity stunt, repudiated the version producer/writer Eszterhas recut and had his own name removed from the film, thus making "An Alan Smithee Film" one of the more than 30 Alan Smithee films in as many years. The tedious mockumentary style is relentless in narrating the story to the audience, who is never allowed to just watch what happens. Only interest is the parade of star cameos, including Stallone, Goldberg, and Chan (as themselves), along with writer Eszterhas in a scene with the director who declined credit for the film, Hiller. **86m/C VHS, DVD.** Eric Idle, Ryan O'Neal, Coolio, Richard Jeni, Sandra Bernhard, Cherie Lunghi, Harvey Weinstein, M.C. Lyte, Stephen Tobolowsky, Chuck D, Leslie Stefanson, Gavin Polone, Marcello Thedford, Nicole Nagel, Dina Spybey; ***Cameos:*** Joe Eszterhas, Sylvester Stallone, Whoopi Goldberg, Jackie Chan, Larry King, Billy Bob Thornton, Dominick Dunne, Robert Evans, Shane Black; ***D:*** Arthur Hiller; ***W:*** Joe Eszterhas; ***C:*** Reynaldo Villalobos; ***M:*** Gary G-Wiz. Golden Raspberries '98: Worst Picture, Worst Support. Actor (Eszterhas), Worst Screenplay, Worst Song ("I Wanna Be Mike Ovitz!"), Worst New Star (Eszterhas).

The Alarmist *Life During Wartime* **1998** Tommy Hudler (Arquette) is the eager beaver new employee at the L.A. home-security company owned by slick supersalesman Heinrich Grigoris (Tucci). But Tommy's soon shocked to learn that Heinrich makes certain clients continue to need his services by breaking into their homes. Tommy makes his first sale to fortysomething widow Gale (Capshaw), who enjoys seducing the boyish innocent, and the two embark on a torrid affair. Then Gale and her teenaged son are murdered after a home break-in and Tommy suspects Heinrich went a little too far. Arquette's amusingly geeky but Tucci steals the film as his sleazy boss. **93m/C VHS, DVD.** Stanley Tucci, David Arquette, Kate Capshaw, Ryan Reynolds, Mary McCormack, Tricia Vessey; ***D:*** Evan Dunsky; ***W:*** Evan Dunsky; ***C:*** Alex Nepomniaschy; ***M:*** Christophe Beck.

Alaska 1/2 **1996 (PG)** Fourteen-year-old Vincent Barnes (Kartheiser) and his 12-year-old sister Jessie (Birch) try to rescue their bush pilot father Jake (Benedict) whose plane has crashed in the wilderness. They also rescue an orphaned polar bear cub from an evil poacher (Heston) that manages to help them out along the way. See this flick if only to enjoy the lush backdrop of Alaska and British Columbia and, of course, the absolutely adorable polar cub. Director Fraser C. Heston directs dad Charlton, appropriate payback for landing him the role as the infant Moses in "The Ten Commandments." **109m/C VHS, DVD.** Thora Birch, Vincent Kartheiser, Dirk Benedict, Charlton Heston; ***D:*** Fraser Heston; ***W:*** Andy Burg, Carol Fuchs; ***C:*** Tony Westman.

Alberto Express 1/2 **1992** Black comedy explores the debts children owe their parents—literally. Alberto's family has a peculiar tradition. It seems that now he's married and about to become a father, he's expected to pay back every cent spent on his own upbringing. Cash poor (and panicky) Alberto hops a train from Paris to Rome and frantically tries to raise the necessary cash by preying, in a series of increasingly bizarre ways, on his fellow passengers before he faces his father once again. In French and Italian with English subtitles. **90m/C VHS.** *FR* Sergio Castellitto, Nino Manfredi, Marie Trintignant, Jeanne Moreau, Michel Aumont, Dominique Pinon, Marco Messeri, Eugenia Marruzzo; ***D:*** Arthur Joffe; ***W:*** Arthur Joffe.

Albino WOOF! **1976 (R)** Albino chief leads African terrorists to murder white settlers, one of whom is an ex-policeman's fiancee. So the ex-cop pursues the bad guys, who are fairly easy to identify (just look for the big group hanging with the albino). Danning, Lee, and Howard only briefly show faces and collect checks. **85m/C VHS.** Christopher Lee, Trevor Howard, Sybil Danning, Horst Frank, James Faulkner; ***D:*** Jurgen Goslar.

Albino Alligator **1996 (R)** Three small-time crooks bungle a robbery and inadvertently run down a federal officer in Academy Award-winning actor Spacey's directorial debut. The trio, consisting of leader Dova (Dillon), brains Milo (Sinise) and brawn Law (Fichtner) hole up in a seedy bar and grab the occupants as hostages. The police soon surround the dive, and the crooks begin arguing among themselves and with brash barmaid Janet (Dunaway) about their chances and means for escape. All, however, is not as it seems. The claustrophobic setting seems more suitable for the stage than the screen, and the plot twists don't bend very far from predictable. Screenwriter Forte is the son of '60s teen idol Fabian. **94m/C VHS, DVD.** Matt Dillon, Gary Sinise, Faye Dunaway, William Fichtner, Joe Mantegna, Viggo Mortensen, John Spencer, Skeet Ulrich, M. Emmet Walsh; ***D:*** Kevin Spacey; ***W:*** Christian Forte; ***C:*** Mark Plummer; ***M:*** Michael Brook.

The Alchemist WOOF! **1981 (R)** See humans transformed into murderous zombies! A bewitched man seeks revenge upon the evil magician who placed a curse on him, causing him to live like an animal. Painfully routine, with a few chills along the way. Amonte is an alias for Charles Band. Filmed in 1981 and released four years later. **86m/C VHS.** Robert Ginty, Lucinda Dooling, John Sanderford, Viola Kate Stimpson, Bob Glaudini; ***D:*** Charles Band; ***W:*** Alan J. Adler; ***M:*** Richard Band.

The Alchemists 1/2 **1999 (PG-13)** The world's leading pharmaceutical company is covering up the fact that their fertility drug has some serious side effects. Employees Show and Gemmell try to expose the corporate conspiracy. Based on the novel by Peter James. **150m/C VHS, DVD.** Grant Show, Ruth Gemmell, Edward Hardwicke; ***D:*** Peter Smith; ***C:*** Peter Middleton; ***M:*** Rick Wentworth.

Alchemy 1/2 **2005 (PG-13)** Slight romantic comedy that gets a little extra oomph from its appealing leads. Professor Mal Downey (Cavanaugh) uses his new computer software to woo struggling actress Samantha Rose (Chalke) based on the responses the program generates. **85m/C DVD.** Sarah Chalke, Nadia Dajani, Illeana Douglas, Celeste Holm, Tom Cavanaugh, James Barbour, Anna Belknap, Erik Palladino; ***D:*** Evan Oppenheimer; ***W:*** Evan Oppenheimer; ***C:*** Luke Geissbuhler; ***M:*** Peter Lurye.

Aldrich Ames: Traitor Within 1/2 **1998 (PG)** Hutton stars as Aldrich Ames, a longtime, second-rate CIA employee with an expensive Colombian-born second wife, Rosario (Pena), and a lot of debts. So Ames turns weasel and begins to sell secrets to the Russians in the mid-'80s, which resulted in the deaths of at least 10 agents. Plowright is the CIA analyst in charge of plugging the leak. Both Ames' were arrested and sent to prison in 1994; Rosario was released in 1999 and returned to Bogota. **97m/C VHS.** Timothy Hutton, Joan Plowright, Elizabeth Pena, Eugene Lipinski, C. David Johnson; ***D:*** John MacKenzie; ***W:*** Michael Burton; ***C:*** Walter McGill. **CABLE**

Alex 1/2 **1992** Inspirational story about 15-year-old New Zealand swimmer Alex Archer (Jackson), who is working towards a spot at the 1960 Rome Olympics. But her goal is threatened by an accident and a new rival and Alex struggles to overcome her obstacles with the help of her boyfriend Andy (Picker). Based on the novel by Tessa Duder. **92m/C VHS.** *AU* Lauren Jackson, Chris Haywood, Josh Picker, Catherine Godbold, Elizabeth Hawthorne; ***D:*** Megan Simpson.

Alex & Emma 1/2 **2003 (PG-13)** The original unwieldy title was "Loosely Based on a True Love Story" because it's loosely based on writer Fyodor Dostoyevsky's story "The Gambler," which was based on a true incident in his life. Or at least that's what the original hype for the movie maintained. Writer Alex (Wilson) has big gambling debts so he takes an advance from his publisher (Reiner) in exchange for churning out a book in 30 days. He hires stenographer Emma (Hudson) to take dictation of his very bad novel, which is set in 1924 and comes to life as Alex spins a story that Emma heartily criticizes. Lame romantic comedy wastes its leads, who have been much more charming in other films (and who have no chemistry together). Lovely blond Hudson is forced into a drab brunette persona that's as unappealing as her wardrobe. **96m/C VHS, DVD.** *US* Luke Wilson, Kate Hudson, Sophie Marceau, David Paymer, Francois Giroday, Rob Reiner, Cloris Leachman, Rip Taylor; ***D:*** Rob Reiner; ***W:*** Jeremy Leven; ***C:*** Gavin Finney; ***M:*** Marc Shaiman.

Alex in Wonderland 1/2 **1970 (R)** A semi-autobiographical and satirical look at Hollywood from the standpoint of a young director who's trying to follow up his recent hit (in real life, "Bob & Carol & Ted & Alice") with a picture of some integrity that will keep the mass audience away. The confused plot provides obvious parallels to Fellini (who appears in a cameo) and some sharp, often bitter insights into the Hollywood of the early '60s. Strong performances by Sutherland and Burstyn compensate somewhat for the patience-trying self-indulgent arty whining of the script. **109m/C VHS.** Donald Sutherland, Ellen Burstyn, Paul Mazursky; ***Cameos:*** Jeanne Moreau, Federico Fellini; ***D:*** Paul Mazursky; ***W:*** Larry Tucker, Paul Mazursky.

Alex Rider: Operation Stormbreaker *Stormbreaker* **2006 (PG)** Horowitz adapted the story from the first book in his own young adult series about 14-year-old Alex Rider (newcomer Pettyfer), who's basically a junior James Bond. Alex is orphaned and living with his spy uncle Ian (McGregor), who's quickly killed off, thus leaving Alex himself to be recruited by MI-6 boss Blunt (Nighy). Good thing the teen's already had all that special ops training. The villain is the ever-creepy Rourke, here playing some evil tycoon with a grudge, and Silverstone is Alex's helpful housekeeper, Jack. There's gadgets and action galore for the undemanding youngster while the adults can stick with Ian Fleming. **93m/C DVD.** *GE* Ewan McGregor, Mickey Rourke, Bill Nighy, Sophie Okonedo, Alex Pettyfer, Alicia Silverstone, Missi Pyle, Sarah Bolger, Damian Lewis, Andy Serkis, Robbie Coltrane, Stephe Fry; ***D:*** Geoffrey Sax; ***W:*** Anthony Horowitz; ***C:*** Chris Seager; ***M:*** Alan Parker.

Alexander **2004 (R)** Looooong and somewhat farcical bio of Macedonian conqueror Alexander the Great. In Stone's depiction, Alexander (Farrell) is the pawn in a marital war between his swaggering, drunken father Philip (Kilmer) and his snake-worshipping mother Olympias (a sultry Jolie), who implies that her boy is really the progeny of the god Zeus. Tutored by Aristotle (Plummer), Alexander believes it's his destiny to subjugate as much of the known world as is possible. Lots of big battles ensue as Alexander forcibly unites the squabbling Greek city-states before challenging the might of the Persian empire. He does take some time out to marry hot-blooded Eastern princess, Roxanne (Dawson), while the ruler's relationship with constant companion Hephaistion (Leto) is reduced to meaningful glances. Farrell cannot overcome the fact that he isn't forceful enough to portray an epic figure. **175m/C VHS, DVD.** *US* Colin Farrell, Angelina Jolie, Val Kilmer, Christopher Plummer, Jared Leto, Rosario Dawson, Anthony Hopkins, Brian Blessed, Jonathan Rhys Meyers, Tim Pigott-Smith, Gary Stretch, John Kavanagh, Ian Beattie, Feodor Atkine, Connor Paolo, Nick Dunning, Marie Meyer, Elliot Cowan, Joseph Morgan, Denis Conway, Neil Jackson, Rory McCann, Raz Degan, Annelise Hesme; ***D:*** Oliver Stone; ***W:*** Oliver Stone, Laeta Kalogridis, Christopher Kyle; ***C:*** Rodrigo Prieto; ***M:*** Vangelis.

Alexander Nevsky 1/2 **1938** A story of the invasion of Russia in 1241 by the Teutonic Knights of Germany and the defense of the region by good old Prince Nevsky. Eisenstein's first completed project in nearly ten years, it was widely regarded as an artistic disappointment upon release and as pro-war propaganda for the looming conflict with the Nazis. Fabulous Prokofiev score illuminates the classic battle scenes, which used thousands of Russian army regulars. Russian with subtitles. **110m/B VHS, DVD.** *RU* Nikolai Cherkassov, Nikolai P. Okhlopkov, Andrei Abrikosov, Alexandra Danilova, Dmitri Orlov, Vera Ivasheva, Sergei Blinnikov, Lev Fenin, Vladimir Yershov, Nikolai Arsky, Naum Rogozhin, Varvara O. Massalitinova, Vasili Novikov, Ivan Lagutin; ***D:*** Sergei Eisenstein; ***W:*** Sergei Eisenstein, Pyotr Pavlenko; ***C:*** Eduard Tisse; ***M:*** Sergei Prokofiev.

Alexander the Great 1/2 **1955** A lavish epic about the legendary Greek conqueror of the fourth century B.C., which provides Burton a rare chance at an adventure role. Here we find Alexander is the product of a dysfunctional royal family who hopes to create an idealized world modeled after Greek culture to make up for the love he lacks from daddy. This he does by conquering everything before dying at the age of 33. The great cast helps to overcome the sluggish pacing of the spectacle, while numerous battle scenes featuring loads of spears and arrows are staged effectively. **135m/C VHS, DVD.** Richard Burton, Fredric March, Claire Bloom, Harry Andrews, Peter Cushing, Danielle Darrieux, Helmut Dantine; ***D:*** Robert Rossen; ***C:*** Robert Krasker.

Alexander: The Other Side of Dawn **1977** Tired sequel to the television movie "Dawn: Portrait of a Teenage Runaway." A young man turns to prostitution to support himself on the street of Los Angeles. **100m/C VHS.** Leigh McCloskey, Eve Plumb, Earl Holliman, Juliet Mills, Jean Hagen, Lonny (Lonnie) Chapman; ***D:*** John Erman. **TV**

Alexander's Ragtime Band *Irving Berlin's Alexander's Ragtime Band* **1938** Energetic musical that spans 1915 to 1938 and has Power and Ameche battling for Faye's affections. Power is a society nabob who takes up ragtime. He puts together a band, naming the group after a piece of music (hence the title), and finds a singer (Faye). Ameche is a struggling composer who brings a Broadway producer to listen to their performance. Faye gets an offer to star in a show and becomes an overnight success. Over the years the trio win and lose success, marry and divorce, and finally end up happy. Corny but charming. ♫ Alexander's Ragtime Band; All Alone; Blue Skies; Easter Parade; Everybody's Doin' It; Everybody Step; For Your Country and My Country; Heat Wave; I Can Always Find a Little Sunshine at the YMCA. **105m/B VHS, DVD.** Tyrone Power, Alice Faye, Don Ameche, Ethel Merman, Jack Haley, Jean Hersholt, Helen Westley, John Carradine, Paul Hurst, Joe King, Ruth Terry; ***D:*** Henry King; ***W:*** Kathryn Scola, Lamar Trotti; ***M:*** Irving Berlin. Oscars '38: Score.

Alexandria Again and Forever *Iskanderija, Kaman oue Kaman* **1990** Yehia (Chahine) remembers his win as best director at the Berlin Film Festival a decade before for his political film "Alexandria...Why?" and thinks about that film's leading man with whom he fell in love. But when he meets and falls for Nadia, Yehia decides he will launch her career as the star of his new film. The final part of Chahine's Alexandria trilogy, following "Alexandria...Why?" and "An Egyptian Story." Arabic with subtitles. **105m/C VHS, DVD.** *EG* Youssef Chahine, Zaki Abdel Wahab, Menha Batraoui, Teheya Cariocca, Amr Abdel Guelil, Yousra; ***D:*** Youssef Chahine; ***W:*** Youssef Chahine; ***C:*** Ingy Assolh; ***M:*** Mohammed Nouh.

Alexandria... Why? **1978** Schoolboy (director Chahine uses his adolescent recollections) tries to ignore the war in Alexandria in 1942 by escaping into the movies and his dreams of becoming a star. He also witnesses two love affairs—one between a Muslim man and a Jewish woman and the second betweeen an Arab nationalist and an English soldier. Part 1 of Chahine's Alexandria trilogy, followed by "An Egyptian Story" and "Alexandria Again and Forever." Arabic with subtitles. **133m/C VHS, DVD.** *EG* Gerry Sundquist, Naglaa Fathi, Farid Shawki, Mohsen Mohiedine; ***D:*** Youssef Chahine; ***W:*** Youssef Chahine; ***C:*** Mohsen Nasr; ***M:*** Foad El Zaheri.

Alfie **1966 (PG)** What's it all about, Alfie? Caine, in his first starring role, plays the British playboy out of control in mod London. Alfie is a despicable, unscrupulous and vile sort of guy who uses woman after woman to fulfill his basic needs and then casts them aside until...tragedy strikes. Though this box office hit was seen as a sophisticated take on current sexual mores upon release, it now seems a dated but engaging comedy, notable chiefly for its performances. From the play by Bill Naughton. The title song "Alfie," sung by Dionne Warwick, was a top ten hit. **114m/C VHS, DVD.** *GB* Michael Caine, Shelley Winters, Millicent Martin, Vivien Merchant, Julia Foster, Jane Asher, Shirley Anne Field, Eleanor Bron, Denholm Elliott, Alfie Bass, Graham Stark, Murray Melvin, Sydney Tafler; ***D:*** Lewis Gilbert; ***W:*** Bill Naughton; ***C:*** Otto Heller; ***M:*** Burt Bacharach, Sonny Rollins. Cannes '67: Grand Jury Prize; Golden Globes '67: Foreign Film; Natl. Bd. of Review '66: Support. Actress (Merchant); Natl. Soc. Film Critics '66: Actor (Caine).

Alfie 1/2 **2004 (R)** Law plays a kinder, gentler lothario in this contemporary update of the 1966 film (which helped make Michael Caine a star), although Alfie still engages in a somewhat self-conscious running commentary directed to the camera. The charming, handsome Alfie is now a limo driver in New York who indulges himself with as many beautiful birds as will put up with him. These include the lonely, married Dorie (Krakowski); single mom Julie (Tomei), who kicks him out after realizing Alfie is a horn-dog; sexy, self-destructive party girl Nikki (Miller); and foxy Lonette (Long), the ex-girlfriend of his best friend Marlon (Epps). But even Alfie must pay for his dalliances when he suffers a bout of impotence and then meets his sexual match in worldly mature beauty Liz (Sarandon). While Alfie remains a narcissist (though ever-so-appealing as played by Law) at least the women characters are no longer complaisant or compliant. **106m/C VHS, DVD.** *US* Jude Law, Marisa Tomei, Omar Epps, Nia Long, Jane Krakowski, Sienna Miller, Susan Sarandon, Renee Taylor, Dick Latessa, Jefferson Mays, Gedde Watanabe; ***D:*** Charles Shyer; ***W:*** Charles Shyer, Elaine Pope; ***C:*** Ashley Rowe; ***M:*** Mick Jagger, David A. Stewart, John Powell. Golden Globes '05: Song ("Old Habits Die Hard").

Alfredo, Alfredo **1972 (R)** Hoffman plays a mild-mannered bank clerk who regrets marrying a sexy woman. Lightweight domestic comedy. In Italian with English subtitles (Hoffman's voice was dubbed). **97m/C VHS.** *IT* Dustin Hoffman, Stefania Sandrelli, Carla Gravina, Clara Colosimo, Daniela Patella, Dulio Del Prete; ***D:*** Pietro Germi; ***W:*** Pietro Germi, Leonardo Benvenuti; ***C:*** Aiace Parolini; ***M:*** Carlo Rustichelli.

Algiers **1938** Nearly a scene-for-scene Americanized remake of the 1937 French "Pepe Le Moko" about a beautiful rich girl (Lamarr) who meets and falls in love with a notorious thief (Boyer, then a leading sex symbol). Pursued by French police and hiding in the underworld-controlled Casbah, Boyer meets up with Lamarr in a tragically fated romance done in the best tradition of Hollywood. Boyer provides a measured performance as Le Moko, while Lamarr is appropriately sultry in her American film debut (which made her a star). Later remade as the semi-musical "Casbah." **96m/B DVD.** Charles Boyer, Hedy Lamarr, Sigrid Gurie, Gene Lockhart, Joseph Calleia, Alan Hale; ***D:*** John Cromwell; ***C:*** James Wong Howe.

Ali 1/2 **2001 (R)** Mann, a notorious obsessive, couldn't have picked a more ambitious topic. The herculean task proves too much, yielding a film that lacks focus or insight into its subject. Ali is depicted during a contentious decade (1964-1974), in which he converted to Islam, befriended civil rights icons, refused the draft, was stripped of his title, married three times, and blurred lines between sport, ethics and society. Perhaps it's no coincidence that screenwriter Roth, who previously penned "Forrest Gump," was chosen to chronicle Ali amid such historic happenings. Mann's visual skills are apparent, and Smith gives an inspired performance in and out of the ring. Other noteworthies include Foxx as cornerman "Bundini" Brown, and Voight as verbose sportscaster Cosell. Despite the charisma of its subject (and its lead), film feels distant and subdued. Lands a few clean blows, but certainly not a knockout. **158m/C VHS, DVD.** *US* Will Smith, Jamie Foxx, Jon Voight, Mario Van Peebles, Ron Silver, Jeffrey Wright, Mykelti Williamson, Jada Pinkett Smith, Michael Michele, Joe Morton, Paul Rodriguez, Nona Gaye, Bruce McGill, Barry (Shabaka) Henley, Giancarlo Esposito, Laurence Mason, LeVar Burton, Albert Hall, David Cubitt, Ted Levine, David Elliott, Michael Bentt, James N. Toney, Charles Shufford, Malick Bowens, Shari Watson, Victoria Dillard, Kim Robillard, Gailard Sartain, Rufus Dorsey, Robert Sale, Damien "Bolo" Wills, Michael Dorn; ***D:*** Michael Mann; ***W:*** Michael Mann, Stephen J. Rivele, Christopher Wilkinson, Eric Roth; ***C:*** Emmanuel Lubezki; ***M:*** Lisa Gerrard, Pieter Bourke.

Ali Baba and the Forty Thieves 1/2 **1943** Ali Baba and his gang of thieves do battle against Hulagu Khan, leader of the Mongols, to save Baghdad and its citizens from ruin and death. **87m/C VHS.** Jon Hall, Turhan Bey, Maria Montez, Andy Devine, Kurt Katch, Frank Puglia, Fortunio Bonanova, Moroni Olsen, Scotty Beckett; ***D:*** Arthur Lubin; ***W:*** Edmund Hartmann; ***C:*** William Howard Greene.

Ali Baba and the 40 Thieves *Ali Baba et les Quarante Voleurs* **1954** French adaptation of the popular novel "A Thousand and One Nights." Servant boy Ali Baba discovers the magic cave holding the stolen treasure of Abdul and his 40 thieves. Shot on location in Morocco. Also available dubbed. **92m/C VHS.** *FR* Samia Gamal, Dieter Borsche, Henri Vilbert; ***D:*** Jacques Becker; ***W:*** Jacques Becker.

Ali Baba and the Seven Saracens *Sinbad Against the Seven Saracens; Simbad Contro I Sette Saraceni; Hawk of Bagdad* **1964** The hero is either Sinbad or Ali Baba but it's never really clear (maybe it's the atrocious dubbing)—not that it matters anyway. The leaders of eight tribes must battle to the death until a winner is left to be the new ruler to the Golden Throne of the Majii. And whoever our hero is, he's a prime candidate. Dubbed. **92m/C DVD.** *IT* Gordon Mitchell, Bella Cortez, Bruno Piergentili, Carla Calo, Tony Di Mitri; ***D:*** Emmimo Salvi.

Ali: Fear Eats the Soul *Fear Eats the Soul; Angst Essen Selle auf* **1974** A widow cleaning woman in her 60s has a love affair with a Moroccan man 30 years her junior. To no one's surprise, both encounter racism and moral hypocrisy in West Germany. Serious melodrama from Fassbinder, who wrote it and appears as the squirmy son-in-law. In German with English subtitles. **68m/C VHS, DVD.** *GE* Brigitte Mira, El Hedi Ben Salem, Irm Hermann; ***D:*** Rainer Werner Fassbinder; ***W:*** Rainer Werner Fassbinder; ***C:*** Jurgen Jurges.

Alias Betty *Betty Fisher and Other Stories; Betty Fisher et Autres Histoires* **2001** Writer Betty (Kiberlain) has recently returned to Paris after separating from her lover. She is uneasily waiting for the arrival of her mother Margot (Garcia), a disturbed woman who abused Betty as a child. Betty's own young son Joseph (Setbon) suddenly dies in an accidental fall and she suffers a breakdown. Jose (Chatrian) is the abused young son of single mother Carole (Seigner). When Margot notices Jose alone in the streets, she takes him back to Betty as a replacement child and Betty debates whether to go along or go to the cops. Based on the book "The Tree of Hands" by Ruth Rendell. French with subtitles. **101m/C VHS, DVD.** *FR CA* Sandrine Kiberlain, Nicole Garcia, Mathilde Seigner, Alexis Chatrian, Edouard Baer, Arthur Setbon, Luck Mervil, Stephane Freiss; ***D:*** Claude Miller; ***W:*** Claude Miller; ***C:*** Christophe Pollock.

Alias Billy the Kid **1946** Western adventure with Carson posing as a famous outlaw to find out who's behind the scam involving the Denton City cattle trade. **54m/B VHS.** Sunset Carson, Peggy Stewart, Tom London, Roy Barcroft; ***D:*** Thomas Carr; ***C:*** Bud Thackery.

Alias Jesse James **1959 (PG)** Insurance agent Milford Farnsworth (Hope) is an eastern tenderfoot who holds a policy on Jesse James (Corey). So he heads west to make certain the outlaw doesn't get killed. Only Jesse sets Milford up as himself, hoping to collect on his own policy. Fleming's the local beauty. A number of western stars have cameos, coming to Hope's rescue. **92m/C VHS.** Bob Hope, Rhonda Fleming, Wendell Corey, Jim Davis, Gloria Talbott, Will Wright, Mary (Marsden) Young, Joseph (Joe) Vitale; ***Cameos:*** Hugh O'Brian, Ward Bond, James Arness, Roy Rogers, Fess Parker, Gail Davis, James Garner, Gene Autry, Jay Silverheels, Bing Crosby, Gary Cooper; ***D:*** Norman Z. McLeod; ***W:*** William Bowers, D.D. Beauchamp; ***C:*** Lionel Lindon.

Alias John Law **1935** The Good Guy fights for oil rights against the bad guys. Confused program western with an especially convoluted plot. **54m/B VHS, DVD.** Bob Steele; ***D:*** Robert North Bradbury.

Alias John Preston 1/2 **1956** Yet another one of those pseudo-psychological to sleep perchance to dream movies. Lee plays a man haunted by dreams in which he's a murderer, and soon starts to question whether his dreams might not imitate life. It's been done before, it's been done since, and it's been done better. **66m/B VHS, DVD.** *GB* Betta St. John, Alexander Knox, Christopher Lee, Sandra Dorne, Patrick Holt, Betty Ann Davies, John Longden, Bill Fraser, John Stuart; ***D:*** David MacDonald.

Alias, La Gringa **1991** Follows the adventures of La Gringa, a likeable criminal capable of escaping from any Peruvian jail. After being aided in his latest escape by a political prisoner, La Gringa decides to return in disguise to pay back the favor. But the prison is rocked by rioting and La Gringa finds himself in a situation out of his control. Spanish with subtitles. **100m/C VHS.** *PV* Orlando Sacha, German Gonzalez, Elsa Olivero, Juan Manuel Ochoa; ***D:*** Alberto Durant; ***W:*** Alberto Durant; ***C:*** Mario Garcia Joya; ***M:*** Pochi Marambio.

Alibi **1929** Low-budget crime drama from independent producer/director West. Gangster Chick Williams (Morris) reclaims his mob role after being released from prison. But when a cop is killed during a robbery, Williams is suspected of the crime and the detective squad will employ any method to bring him to justice. Noted for its experimental use of sound, its dazzling Art Deco sets, and its eccentric composition. **84m/B VHS.** Chester Morris, Mae Busch, Regis Toomey, Harry Stubbs; ***D:*** Roland West; ***W:*** Roland West, C. Gardner Sullivan; ***C:*** Ray June; ***M:*** Hugo Riesenfeld.

Alibi for Murder 1/2 **1936** Radio newsman Perry Travis (Gargan) turns amateur sleuth when his scientist interviewee is murdered and Travis becomes the prime suspect. **61m/B DVD.** William Gargan, Marguerite Churchill, Gene Morgan, John Gallaudet, Romaine Callender; ***D:*** David Ross Lederman; ***W:*** Tom Van Dycke; ***C:*** George Meehan Jr.

Alibi Ike 1/2 **1935** Baseball comedy about rookie Cubs pitcher Frank Farrell (rubbery-faced comedian Brown), who is known as "Alibi Ike" because he's always making excuses, driving his manager Cap (Frawley) and his teammates crazy. He can't even be straight with his gal, Dolly (de Havilland).

Next, Frank gets into trouble with gamblers who want him to throw games but he comes through in the end. Adapted from a story by Ring Lardner. **73m/B VHS.** Joe E. Brown, Olivia de Havilland, William Frawley, Ruth Donnelly, Roscoe Karns, Joseph King, Paul Harvey, Selmer Jackson; ***D:*** Ray Enright; ***W:*** William Wister Haines; ***C:*** Arthur L. Todd.

Alice *Alicja* **1986** A twist on the "Alice in Wonderland" tale. Alice witnesses an attempted murder, faints, and awakens in a weird, yet strangely familiar environment. Adapted from the stage production. **80m/C VHS, DVD.** Sophie Barjac, Susannah York, Jean-Pierre Cassel, Paul Nicholas; ***D:*** Jacek Bromski, Jerzy Gruza.

Alice 1/2 *Neco Z Alenky* **1988** An acclaimed surreal version of Lewis Carroll's already surreal "Alice in Wonderland," with the emphasis on Carroll's obsessiveness. Utilizing animated puppets and a live actor for Alice, Czech director Svankmajer injects grotesque images and black comedy into Wonderland. Not for the kids. **84m/C VHS, DVD.** *CZ SI GB GE* Kristina Kohoutova; ***D:*** Jan Svankmajer; ***W:*** Jan Svankmajer; ***C:*** Svatopluk Maly.

Alice **1990 (PG-13)** Farrow is "Alice," a woman plagued with doubts about her lifestyle, her religion, and her happiness. Her perfect children, husband, and apartment don't prevent her backaches, and she turns to an Oriental "herbalist" for aid. She finds his methods unusual and the results of the treatments surprising. Lightweight fairytale of Yuppiedom gone awry. Fine performances, but superficial and pointed story that may leave the viewer looking for more. (Perhaps that's Allen's point.) Farewell performance from charactor actor Luke, unbilled cameo from Judith Ivey, and first time out for Dylan O'Sullivan Farrow, adopted daughter of Allen and Farrow, as Kate. **106m/C VHS, DVD.** Mia Farrow, William Hurt, Joe Mantegna, Keye Luke, Alec Baldwin, Cybill Shepherd, Blythe Danner, Gwen Verdon, Bernadette Peters, Judy Davis, Patrick O'Neal, Julie Kavner, Caroline Aaron, Holland Taylor, Robin Bartlett, David Spielberg, Bob Balaban, Dylan O'Sullivan Farrow, Elle Macpherson; ***D:*** Woody Allen; ***W:*** Woody Allen; ***C:*** Carlo Di Palma. Natl. Bd. of Review '90: Actress (Farrow).

The Alice 1/2 **2004** A disparate group of characters come from all corners of Australia to the outback town of Alice Springs in order to witness a total eclipse of the sun in hopes that it will changes their lives. Apparently intended as an Australian TV pilot although it never went any farther. **98m/C DVD.** *AU* Erik Thomson, Jessica Napier, Brett Stiller, Simon Burke, Caitlin McDougall, Luke Carroll, Kyas Sherriff; ***D:*** Kate Dennis; ***W:*** Justin Mongo; ***C:*** Louis Irving. **TV**

Alice **2009** Syfy pic derived from "Alice in Wonderland" goes psychedelic with uneven results. This time Alice (Scorsone) is not only an adult but a martial arts instructor who tumbles through a mirror with the help of a ring given to her by beau Jack (Winchester). Wonderland is under the totalitarian control of the Queen of Hearts (Bates) and Alice teams up with such rebels as the Hatter (Potts) and the White Knight (Frewer) to battle the regime, which tends to turn unwelcome guests into zombies. **180m/C DVD.** Caterina Scorsone, Kathy Bates, Philip Winchester, Andrew Lee Potts, Matt Frewer, Colm Meaney, Tim Curry, Allan Gray, Eugene Lipinski, Harry Dean Stanton; ***D:*** Nick Willing; ***W:*** Nick Willing; ***C:*** Jon Joffin; ***M:*** Ben Mink. **CABLE**

Alice Adams 1/2 **1935** Based on the classic Booth Tarkington novel about a poor girl from a small Midwestern town who falls in love with a man from the upper level of society. She tries desperately to fit in and nearly alienates her family and friends. The sets may be dated, but the insight on human behavior is timeless. **99m/B VHS, DVD.** Katharine Hepburn, Fred MacMurray, Evelyn Venable, Fred Stone, Frank Albertson, Ann Shoemaker, Charley Grapewin, Grady Sutton, Hedda Hopper, Hattie McDaniel; ***D:*** George Stevens; ***M:*** Max Steiner.

Alice Doesn't Live Here Anymore 1/2 **1974 (PG)** Scorsese marries road opera with pseudo-feminist semi-realistic melodrama and produces uneven but interesting results. When Alice's husband dies suddenly, leaving her with their 11-year-old son, she leaves for California, but finds herself stranded in Phoenix, down to her last few bucks. There she lands a job as a waitress in a diner where she meets kindly rancher Kristofferson. Notable for its female point of view, it was also the basis for the once-popular TV show "Alice." Burstyn and Ladd lend key performances, while Kristofferson is typically wooden. **105m/C VHS, DVD.** Ellen Burstyn, Kris Kristofferson, Diane Ladd, Jodie Foster, Harvey Keitel, Vic Tayback, Billy Green Bush, Laura Dern; ***D:*** Martin Scorsese; ***W:*** Robert Getchell; ***C:*** Kent Wakeford; ***M:*** Richard LaSalle. Oscars '74: Actress (Burstyn); British Acad. '75: Actress (Burstyn), Film, Screenplay, Support. Actress (Ladd).

Alice et Martin 1/2 *Alice and Martin* **1998 (R)** Director Andre Techine examines the complexity of relationships through the lives of nervous violinist Alice (Binoche) and psychologically fragile model Martin (Loret). The story opens in Martin's childhood, when he is sent by his free-spirited mother to live with his cold and distant father Victor (Maguelon). Martin flees his father's house after an unrevealed trauma, showing up at the door of his half-brother Benjamin (Amalric), who is Alice's roommate. Despite initial reluctance from Alice, the pair become lovers. During a trip to Spain Alice tells Martin that she's pregnant, and he goes off the deep end, haunted by memories of his father and the fateful event that will continue to affect their lives. Slow-moving but beautifully filmed. **123m/C VHS.** *FR SP* Juliette Binoche, Alexis Loret, Carmen Maura, Pierre Maguelon, Mathieu Amalric; ***D:*** Andre Techine; ***W:*** Andre Techine, Gilles Taurand, Olivier Assayas; ***C:*** Caroline Champetier; ***M:*** Philippe Sarde.

Alice in the Cities 1/2 **1974** American and German culture are compared and contrasted in this early Wenders road work about a German journalist in the USA on assignment who suddenly finds himself custodian to a worldly nine-year-old girl abandoned by her mother. Together they return to Germany and search for the girl's grandmother. Along the way they learn about each other, with many distinctive and graceful Wenders moments. **110m/B VHS.** Ruediger Vogler, Yella Rottlaender, Elisabeth (Lisa) Kreuzer, Edda Kochi; ***D:*** Wim Wenders; ***W:*** Wim Wenders.

Alice in Wonderland 1/2 **1950** Another version of the Lewis Carroll classic which combines the usage of Lou Bunin's puppets and live action to tell the story. Released independently to cash in on the success of the Disney version. Takes a more adult approach to the story and is worth viewing on its own merits. **83m/C VHS.** *FR* Carol Marsh, Stephen Murray, Pamela Brown, Felix Aylmer, Ernest Milton; ***D:*** Dallas Bower.

Alice in Wonderland **1951 (G)** Classic Disney dream version of Lewis Carroll's famous children's story about a girl who falls down a rabbit hole into a magical world populated by strange creatures. Beautifully animated with some startling images, but served with a strange dispassion warmed by a fine batch of songs. Wynn's Mad Hatter and Holloway's Cheshire Cat are among the treats in store. ♫ Alice in Wonderland; I'm Late; A Very Merry Un-Birthday. **75m/C VHS, DVD.** ***D:*** Hamilton Luske, Wilfred Jackson, Clyde Geronimi; ***V:*** Kathryn Beaumont, Ed Wynn, Sterling Holloway, Jerry Colonna.

Alice in Wonderland 1/2 **1985** All-star updated adaptation of the Lewis Carroll classic. This time instead of Alice falling down a rabbit hole she falls through her television set. But her adventures still include the White Rabbit, Mad Hatter, March Hare, Cheshire Cat, and the King and Queen of Hearts. Followed by "Alice Through the Looking Glass." **90m/C VHS, DVD.** Natalie Gregory, Anthony Newley, Ringo Starr, Telly Savalas, Robert Morley, Sammy Davis Jr., Steve Allen, Steve Lawrence, Eydie Gorme, Red Buttons, Ann Jillian, Scott Baio, Sid Caesar, Ernest Borgnine, Beau Bridges, Lloyd Bridges, Tom McLoughlin, Harvey Korman, Patrick Duffy, Donald O'Connor, Arte Johnson, Carol Channing, Sherman Hemsley, Roddy McDowall, Donna Mills, Imogene Coca, Karl Malden, Noriyuki "Pat" Morita, Sally Struthers, Martha Raye, Merv Griffin, Jack Warden, Louis Nye, Shelley Winters, John Stamos, Jonathan Winters, George Savalas; ***D:*** Harry Harris; ***W:*** Paul Zindel; ***C:*** Fred W. Koenekamp; ***M:*** Morton Stevens. **TV**

Alice in Wonderland 1/2 **1999** Visually elaborate but somewhat tedious version of the popular Lewis Carroll tale filled with scenery chewing by the real actors and the welcome presence of animatronic wonders from the Jim Henson Creature Shop. This time Alice is the poised Majorino, who seems more annoyed by the denizens of Wonderland than amazed at her adventures. **129m/C VHS, DVD.** Tina Majorino, Martin Short, Miranda Richardson, Whoopi Goldberg, Ben Kingsley, Gene Wilder, Christopher Lloyd, Pete Postlethwaite, Peter Ustinov, George Wendt, Robbie Coltrane; ***D:*** Nick Willing; ***W:*** Peter Barnes; ***C:*** Giles Nuttgens; ***M:*** Richard Hartley. **TV**

Alice in Wonderland 1/2 **2010 (PG)** Burton's visually stunning flick combines Lewis Carroll's novels of Wonderland with his poem "The Jabberwocky" to tell the tale of an older Alice (Wasikowska). Now 19 years old and resisting an arranged marriage to an upper-class twit, Alice flees her engagement party and once again falls down the rabbit hole. She's reunited with her old friends the Mad Hatter (Depp) and the White Queen (Hathaway), as well as her old enemy the Red Queen (Bonham-Carter). The climactic battle scene seems forced and cribbed from other recent fantasy epics, but the characters retain their demented quirkiness. The movie was not actually shot in 3-D, which makes its release in this format (with sub-par results) seem curiouser and curiouser. **108m/C DVD.** Mia Wasikowska, Johnny Depp, Anne Hathaway, Helena Bonham Carter, Crispin Glover, Michael Sheen, Alan Rickman, Christopher Lee, Stephen Fry, Matt Lucas, Marton Csokas, Lindsay Duncan; ***D:*** Tim Burton; ***W:*** Linda Woolverton; ***C:*** Darius Wolski; ***M:*** Danny Elfman.

Alice Sweet Alice 1/2 *Holy Terror; Communion* **1976 (R)** Mediocre, gory who-killed-her, best remembered as the debut of Shields (in a small role). **112m/C VHS, DVD.** Linda Miller, Paula Sheppard, Mildred Clinton, Niles McMaster, Jane Lowry, Rudolph Willrich, Brooke Shields, Alphonso de Noble, Gary Allen, Tom Signorelli, Lillian Roth; ***D:*** Alfred Sole; ***W:*** Alfred Sole, Rosemary Ritvo; ***C:*** John Friberg, Chuck Hall; ***M:*** Stephen Lawrence.

Alice Through the Looking Glass 1/2 **1966** Based on Lewis Carroll's classic adventure. Follows the further adventures of young Alice. After a chess piece comes to life, it convinces Alice that excitement and adventure lie through the looking glass. **72m/C VHS.** Judi Rolin, Ricardo Montalban, Nanette Fabray, Robert Coote, Agnes Moorehead, Jack Palance, Jimmy Durante, Tom Smothers, Roy Castle, Richard Denning; ***D:*** Alan Handley.

Alice to Nowhere **1986** Concerns a running argument in the Outback over a fortune in gems unknowingly carried by a young woman. Based on a novel by Evan Green. **210m/C VHS.** *AU* Rosie Jones, Steve Jacobs, John Waters, Ruth Cracknell; ***D:*** John Power. **TV**

Alice Upside Down 1/2 **2007** Preteen Alice McKinley (Stoner) and her older brother Lester (Grabeel) struggle when their widowed dad Ben (Perry) decides to make a fresh start in St. Louis. Alice has a tough time adjusting to her new school and gets into trouble with her stern homeroom teacher Mrs. Plotkin (Marshall). But Alice learns two important lessons as adolescence hits: don't be judgmental and don't jump to conclusions. Adapted from Phyllis Reynolds Naylor's "Alice" novels. **90m/C DVD.** Alyson Stoner, Luke Perry, Lucas Grabeel, Penny Marshall, Ann Dowd, Dylan McLaughlin, Parker McKenna Posey; ***D:*** Stanley Tung; ***W:*** Stanley Tung, Meghan Heritage; ***C:*** Mark Mervis.

Alice's Restaurant 1/2 **1969 (PG)** Based on the popular and funny 20-minute Arlo Guthrie song "Alice's Restaurant Massacre" about a Flower Child during the Last Big War who gets hassled for littering, man. Step back in time and study the issues of the hippie era, including avoiding the draft, dropping out of college, and dealing with the local pigs. Sort of a modern movie in the cinematic ambling genre, in that nothing really happens. **111m/C VHS, DVD.** Arlo Guthrie, James Broderick, Pat Quinn, Geoff Outlaw, Pete Seeger, Lee Hays, Michael McClanathan, Tina Chen, Kathleen Dabney, William Obanhein, Graham Jarvis, M. Emmet Walsh; ***D:*** Arthur Penn; ***W:*** Arthur Penn, Venabel Herndon; ***C:*** Michael Nebbia; ***M:*** Garry Sherman, Arlo Guthrie.

Alien 1/2 **1979 (R)** Terse direction, stunning sets and special effects, and a well-seasoned cast save this from being another "Slimy monster from Outerspace" story. Instead it's a grisly rollercoaster of suspense and fear (and a huge boxoffice hit). Intergalactic freighter's crew is invaded by an unstoppable carnivorous alien intent on picking off the crew one by one. While the cast mostly bitches and banters while awaiting the horror of their imminent departure, Weaver is exceptional as Ripley, a self-reliant survivor who goes toe to toe with the Big Ugly. Futuristic, in the belly of the beast visual design creates a vivid sense of claustrophobic doom enhanced further by the ominous score. Oscar-winning special effects include the classic baby alien busting out of the crew guy's chest routine, a rib-splitting ten on the gore meter. Successfully followed by "Aliens" and "Alien 3." **116m/C VHS, DVD, UMD.** *GB* Tom Skerritt, Sigourney Weaver, Veronica Cartwright, Yaphet Kotto, Harry Dean Stanton, Ian Holm, John Hurt, Bolaji Badejo; ***D:*** Ridley Scott; ***W:*** Dan O'Bannon; ***C:*** Derek Vanlint; ***M:*** Jerry Goldsmith; ***V:*** Helen Horton. Oscars '79: Visual FX, Natl. Film Reg. '02.

Alien 3 **1992 (R)** Picks up where "Aliens" left off as Ripley crash lands on Fiorina 161, a planet that serves as a penal colony for 25 celibate but horny men who smell bad. Ripley is forced to shave her head because of the planet's lice problem, and she sets out to survive on the cold, unfriendly planet until a rescue ship can come for her. Fending off sexual advances from the men, Ripley soon discovers she wasn't the only survivor of the crash—the alien survived too and has somehow implanted her with an alien of her own. Dark and disturbing, filled with religious allegories, and a universe removed from the two earlier Aliens. Intended as the final installment of the series. **135m/C VHS, DVD.** Sigourney Weaver, Charles S. Dutton, Charles Dance, Paul McGann, Brian Glover, Ralph Brown, Danny (Daniel) Webb, Christopher John Fields, Holt McCallany, Lance Henriksen; ***D:*** David Fincher; ***C:*** Alex Thomson; ***M:*** Elliot Goldenthal.

The Alien Agenda: Endangered Species 1/2 **1997** Tabloid TV reporter Megan Cross has a too-close encounter with extraterrestrials that frightens her enough to have her join a secret organization that keeps tabs on alien activity. Along with mercenary Cope Ransom and operative Fritz, Megan is sent to infiltrate the mutant wasteland that used to be Florida and see what the aliens are plotting. **102m/C VHS.** Debbie Rochon, Joel D. Wynkoop, Joe Zaso, Candice Meade; ***D:*** Kevin J. Lindenmuth, Ron Ford, Gabriel Campisi, Tim Ritter; ***W:*** Kevin J. Lindenmuth, Ron Ford, Gabriel Campisi, Tim Ritter. **VIDEO**

The Alien Agenda: Out of the Darkness WOOF! **1996** Cheesy sci-fi with a narrator who ruminates about mysterious aliens who enjoy tormenting humans and can travel through time (and send humans back and forth). You won't care. **80m/C VHS.** Sasha Graham, Michael (Mick) McCleery, Scooter McCrae, T.J. Miller, Marcus Zanders; ***D:*** Michael (Mick) McCleery, Kevin J. Lindenmuth; ***W:*** Michael (Mick) McCleery, Kevin J. Lindenmuth. **VIDEO**

The Alien Agenda: Under the Skin 1/2 **1997** Scientist Alfred Malone is kidnapped by the mystery guys in black and taken to their hideaway in Puerto Rico, where vicious aliens roam around outside just looking for a tasty earthling snack. Then there's Victor who's a smalltime hood who's not only got the cops after him but the new head of Chicago's crime syndicate, who's not exactly what he seems. **75m/C VHS.** Nick Kostopoulos, Arthur Lundquist, Leslie Body, Steven Jon White, Conrad Brooks; ***D:*** Kevin J. Lindenmuth, Mike Legge; ***W:*** Kevin J. Lindenmuth, Mike Legge. **VIDEO**

Alien Agent 1/2 **2007 (R)** Agent Rykker (Dacascos) is sent to stop a renegade military unit that is building a portal between its dying homeworld and Earth. Seem Saylon (Zane), Isis (Cooke), and their band have decided they will exterminate the humans and move in. Good fights (director Johnson got his start as a stunt coordinator) but not much true sci-fi despite the plot. **95m/C DVD.** Mark Dacascos, Billy Zane, Kim Coates, Amelia Cooke, Emma Lahana; ***D:*** Jesse Johnson; ***W:*** Vlady Pildysh; ***C:*** C. Kim Miles; ***M:*** Michael Richard Plowman. **VIDEO**

Alien Avengers 1/2 *Roger Corman Presents: Alien Avengers; Welcome to Planet Earth* **1996 (R)** Naive, poor Joseph Collins (Brown) inherits a rundown roominghouse and before he knows it, he has his first tenants—Charlie (Wendt), Rhonda (Reed), and their teenaged daughter Daphne (Sakelaris). What Joseph doesn't know is the friendly trio are aliens (on vacation), who are fond of killing lowlifes and bringing home human parts for snacks. Goofy and gory cable movie. **120m/C VHS, DVD.** George Wendt, Shanna Reed, Christopher Brown, Anastasia Sakelaris; ***D:*** Lev L. Spiro; ***W:*** Michael James McDonald; ***C:*** Christopher Baffa; ***M:*** Tyler Bates.

Alien Cargo **1999 (PG)** The crew of a Mars transport ship has just awakened from eight months in hypersleep to discover something they're off-course and in big trouble. Standard issue plot makes for boring entertainment. **89m/C VHS.** Jason London, Missy (Melissa) Crider, Simon Westaway, Elizabeth (Liz) Alexander; ***D:*** Mark Haber. **TV**

Alien Chaser **1996 (R)** Alien android Zagarino, who crashed in the African desert 5000 years ago, returns to life thanks to the unwitting aid of archeologists Jensen and MacDonald. They literally hold the key to stopping his destruction of mankind. **95m/C VHS, DVD.** Frank Zagarino, Todd Jensen, Jennifer MacDonald, Brian O'Shaughnessy; ***D:*** Mark Roper; ***W:*** B.J. Nelson; ***C:*** Rod Stewart; ***M:*** Robert O. Ragland.

Alien Contamination WOOF! *Contamination* **1981 (R)** Tale of two astronauts who return to Earth from an expedition on Mars carrying some deadly bacterial eggs. Controlled by a Martian intent on conquering the world, the eggs squirt a gloppy juice that makes people explode on contact (a special effect). A cheap and sloppy attempt to cash in on the success of "Alien." Dubbed. **90m/C VHS, DVD.** *IT* Ian McCulloch, Louise Monroe, Martin Mase, Siegfried Rauch, Lisa Hahn, Louise Marleau, Al Cliver, Carlo De Mejo, Gisela Hahn; ***D:*** Lewis (Luigi Cozzi) Coates; ***W:*** Lewis (Luigi Cozzi) Coates; ***M:*** The Goblins.

Alien Dead *It Fell from the Sky* **1979 (R)** The teenage victims of a bizarre meteor crash reincarnate as flesh-eating ghouls anxious for a new supply of human food in this extremely low-budget sleep inducer. **75m/C VHS, DVD.** Buster Crabbe, Linda Lewis, Ray Roberts, Mike Bonavia, Dennis Underwood; ***D:*** Fred Olen Ray; ***W:*** Fred Olen Ray, Martin Allen Nicholas; ***C:*** Fred Olen Ray.

The Alien Factor 1/2 **1978 (PG)** Another low-budget crazed critter from outerspace dispatch, this one featuring multiple aliens, one of whom is good, who have the misfortune of crash landing near Baltimore. The grotesque extraterrestrials jolt a small town out of its sleepy state by wreaking havoc (except for the good one, of course). Decent special effects. **82m/C VHS, DVD.** Don Leifert, Tom Griffith, Mary Mertens, Richard Dyszel, Richard Geiwitz, Eleanor Herman, Anne Frith, Christopher Gummer, George Stover, John Walker, Donald M. Dohler; ***D:*** Donald M. Dohler; ***W:*** Donald M. Dohler; ***M:*** Ken Walker.

Alien from L.A. WOOF! **1987 (PG)** Awesomely inept comedy about a California girl who unwittingly stumbles onto the famed continent of Atlantis and can't find a yogurt stand. Weakly plotted and acted and filmed. Like, really. **88m/C VHS, DVD.** Kathy Ireland, Thom Mathews, Don Michael Paul, Linda Kerridge, William R. Moses, Richard Haines, Janie du Plessis, Russel Savadier, Simon Poland, Locher de Kock, Deep Roy; ***D:*** Albert Pyun; ***W:*** Albert Pyun, Debra Ricci, Regina Davis; ***C:*** Tom Fraser; ***M:*** James Saad.

Alien Fury: Countdown to Invasion **2000 (PG-13)** Bill Templer (Midkiff) is upset when budget cuts threaten to close his government defense office, which sends probes into space looking for aliens. So he fakes some satellite photos of an alien armada poised to attack Earth from the dark side of the moon. Only, ha ha, the threat turns out to be real. This movie is so lame, you'll hope the aliens do attack and wipe these fools out. **88m/C VHS.** Dale Midkiff, Stephen Tobolowsky, Dondre T. Whitfield, Joanie Laurer, Grace Phillips, Scott Lowell, Paul Schulze, Troy Evans; ***D:*** Rob Hedden; ***W:*** Rob Hedden; ***C:*** John Newby; ***M:*** John Beal, Dennis McCarthy. **TV**

Alien Intruder **1993 (R)** What happens when an evil demon appears before the soldiers of the future in the guise of a beautiful woman? Futuristic trash B-movie emerges from the depths. **90m/C VHS, DVD.** Billy Dee Williams, Tracy Scoggins, Maxwell Caulfield; ***D:*** Ricardo Jacques Gale.

Alien Massacre WOOF! *Dr. Terror's Gallery of Horrors; Return from the Past; The Blood Suckers; Gallery of Horror* **1967** One of the worst films of all time—five short horror stories about zombies and vampires. Goes by many names—stinks in all of them. **90m/C VHS, DVD.** Lon Chaney Jr., John Carradine, Rochelle Hudson, Roger Gentry, Mitch Evans, Joey Benson, Vic McGee; ***D:*** David L. Hewitt; ***W:*** Gary Heacock, David Prentiss; ***C:*** Austin McKinney.

Alien Nation 1/2 **1988 (R)** A few hundred thousand alien workers land accidentally on Earth and slowly become part of its society, although widely discriminated against. One of the "newcomers" teams with a surly and bigoted human cop to solve a racially motivated murder. An inconsistent and occasionally transparent script looks at race conflicts and includes some humorous parallels with contemporary American life. Basis for the TV series. Producer Hurd was also the force behind "The Terminator" and "Aliens." **89m/C VHS, DVD.** James Caan, Mandy Patinkin, Terence Stamp, Kevyn Major Howard, Peter Jason, Jeff Kober, Leslie Bevis; ***D:*** Graham Baker; ***W:*** Rockne S. O'Bannon; ***C:*** Adam Greenberg; ***M:*** Curt Sobel.

Alien Nation: Body and Soul 1/2 **1995** The second TV movie sequel to the series finds detectives Francisco (Pierpoint) and Sykes (Graham) on a murder investigation that leads to a Newcomer scientist whose secret research deals with interspecies breeding. Meanwhile, Sykes' romance with Cathy (Treas) is heating up and he's becoming painfully aware of the sexual differences between humans and Newcomers. **?m/C VHS.** Gary (Rand) Graham, Eric Pierpoint, Terri Treas, Michelle Scarabelli, Sean Six, Lauren Woodland, Kristin Davis, Tiny Ron; ***D:*** Kenneth Johnson; ***C:*** Shelly Johnson; ***M:*** David Kurtz.

Alien Nation: Dark Horizon 1/2 **1994 (PG)** The alien Newcomers have successfully adapted to life on Earth but face continuing dangers when a human-supremacy group develops a virus to wipe them out and an alien infiltrator is plotting to return them to slavery on Tencton. Naturally, it's up to detectives Sykes and Francisco to save the day. Based on the TV series. **90m/C VHS.** Gary (Rand) Graham, Eric Pierpoint, Scott Patterson, Terri Treas, Michelle Scarabelli, Lee Bryant, Sean Six, Lauren Woodland, Ron Fassler, Jeff Marcus; ***D:*** Kenneth Johnson; ***W:*** Diane Frolov, Andrew Schneider; ***M:*** David Kurtz.

Alien Nation: Millennium 1/2 **1996** In this third TV sequel Matt (Graham) and George's (Pierpoint) latest police investigation hits very close to the Francisco home. Rebellious teenager Buck (Six) gets involved with a suspicious cult, lead by Newcomer Jennifer (Keane), that offers spiritual enlightenment at a very heavy price. **?m/C VHS.** Eric Pierpoint, Gary (Rand) Graham, Sean Six, Kerrie Keane, Michelle Scarabelli, Terri Treas, Lauren Woodland, Jeff Marcus, Jenny Gago, David Faustino; ***D:*** Kenneth Johnson; ***W:*** Kenneth Johnson; ***C:*** Shelly Johnson; ***M:*** David Kurtz.

Alien Nation: The Enemy Within 1/2 **1996** George (Pierpont) must deal with his own bigotry when he and Matt (Graham) investigate the death of an Eenos Newcomer. The underground-dwelling Eenos are shunned as an ignorant and savage subclass by other Newcomers but the detectives gradually discover some sinister goings-on involving a fierce Eenos/Newcomer mutant. Meanwhile, George's wife Susan (Scarabelli) is feeling neglected and Cathy (Treas) and Matt find living together causes a strain on their relationship. The fourth TV movie from the series. **?m/C VHS.** Eric Pierpoint, Gary (Rand) Graham, Michelle Scarabelli, Terri Treas, Sean Six, Lauren Woodland, Joe Lando, Kerrie Keane, Tiny Ron, Ron Fassler; ***D:*** Kenneth Johnson.

Alien Predators WOOF! **1980 (R)** Three friends encounter a malevolent alien in this dull reworking of the plot of "The Andromeda Strain" with laughable special effects tossed in for those outwitted by the script. **92m/C VHS.** Dennis Christopher, Martin Hewitt, Lynn-Holly Johnson, Luis Prendes; ***D:*** Deran Sarafian.

Alien Prey 1/2 *Prey* **1978 (R)** Two lesbians are making love when they are unexpectedly devoured by a hungry and indiscreet alien. No safe sex there. Graphic sex, violence, and cannibalism abound. Interesting twist to the old eat 'em and leave 'em genre. **85m/C VHS, DVD.** *GB* Glory Annen, Sandy Chinney, Barry Stokes, Sally Faulkner; ***D:*** Norman J. Warren; ***W:*** Max Cuff; ***C:*** Derek V. Browne; ***M:*** Ivor Slaney.

Alien Private Eye *Alien P.I* **1987** An extraterrestrial detective searches Los Angeles for a missing magic disk while investigating an intergalactic crime ring. **90m/C VHS.** Nikki Fastinetti; ***D:*** Nik Rubenfeld.

Alien Raiders **2008 (R)** A family-owned supermarket in a small Arizona town is getting ready to close when it is taken over by armed men. They aren't robbers but scientists who have tracked an alien infestation to that store. Now the scientists have to discover who among the employees and customers were infected. Fast-paced and reasonably clever with a few twists. **85m/C DVD.** Matthew St. Patrick, Rockmond Dunbar, Jeff(rey) Licon, Bonita Friedericy, Carlos Bernard, Courtney Ford, Derek Basco, Bryan Krasner; ***D:*** Ben Rock; ***W:*** David Simkins, Julia Fair; ***C:*** Walt Lloyd; ***M:*** Kays Alatrakchi. **VIDEO**

Alien: Resurrection **1997 (R)** Despite her fiery end in the last film, Ripley is brought back, through cloning, by a team of scientist anxious to get their hands on the alien embryo that invaded her. A more buffed and equally strange Ripley (Weaver) results as some of her DNA gets mixed with her alien friend. Injecting new life into the franchise, director Jeunet creates a freaky and macabre journey as the aliens get loose on board the mysterious space craft Auriga and create messy havoc for new alien appetizers including Call (Ryder), who has a personal agenda of her own with Ripley. Ryder may be somewhat out of place, but the humor and energy from the supporting cast, along with the film's dank look raises this one from the bowels of formulaic action/horror. Includes some decent scares with a tense underwater sequence. **108m/C VHS, DVD.** Sigourney Weaver, Winona Ryder, Ron Perlman, Dominique Pinon, Michael Wincott, Kim Flowers, Leland Orser, Brad Dourif, Dan Hedaya, J.E. Freeman, Raymond Cruz; ***D:*** Jean-Pierre Jeunet; ***W:*** Joss Whedon; ***C:*** Darius Khondji; ***M:*** John (Gianni) Frizzell.

Alien Seed **1989** Aliens kidnap a woman and impregnate her. Estrada is the government scientist hot on her trail. (How far could a woman carrying alien offspring wander?) **88m/C VHS, DVD.** Erik Estrada, Heidi Paine, Steven Blade; ***D:*** Bob James.

Alien Siege 1/2 **2005 (R)** Aliens descend upon Earth seeking human blood, which is the only cure for a virus killing their race. They destroy some cities to show they mean business. Since they need 8 million bodies, a lottery system is devised and the unlucky get to become alien vaccine. Scientist Steven Chase (Johnson) decides no fair when his only child, Heather (Ross), is chosen. Naturally, there's a resistance group that feels earthlings should be fighting the alien fiends and Steve joins. A Sci-Fi Channel original. **90m/C DVD.** Brad Johnson, Carl Weathers, Nathan Anderson, Erin Ross, Lilas Lane; ***D:*** Robert Stadd; ***W:*** Robert Stadd; ***C:*** Lorenzo Senatore; ***M:*** Matthias Weber, Chris Walden. **CABLE**

Alien Space Avenger 1/2 *Space Avenger* **1991** A spaceship piloted by four alien convicts crash lands in New York City. Stalked by an intergalatic bounty hunter whose job is to kill them, the aliens attack and hide inside human bodies to avoid discovery. It's a race against time as the preservation of the human race depends on the avenger's ability to seek and destroy the alien invaders. Bland ripoff of "Aliens" is reminiscent of old-time "B" sci-fi flicks, with more gore and violence. Shot with the old 3-strip Technicolor method. **88m/C VHS.** Robert Prichard, Mike McClerie, Charity Staley, Gina Mastrogiacomo, Kick Fairbanks Fogg, Angela Nicholas, Marty Roberts, James Gillis; ***D:*** Richard W. Haines; ***W:*** Richard W. Haines, Linwood Sawyer; ***M:*** Richard Fiocca.

Alien Terminator **1995 (R)** Scientists experimenting with DNA find themselves creating an organism capable of instant regeneration that also likes to nosh on living flesh. To make matters worse, the scientists are trapped in their lab complex, which happens to be located five miles below Los Alamos. **95m/C VHS, DVD.** Maria Ford, Kevin Alber, Rodger Halston, Cassandra Leigh, Emile Levisetti; ***D:*** Dave Payne.

Alien 3000 WOOF! *Unseen Evil 2* **2004 (R)** This woofer is dull as well as stupid. A commando unit is sent into the forest to search for an invisible alien creature that is supposed to be guarding an unknown treasure in a cave no one can find. Ummm, maybe that's because it's really hard to tell what's going on and not worth the effort anyway. **81m/C DVD.** Lorenzo Lamas, Priscilla Barnes, Corbin Timbrook, Scott Schwartz; ***D:*** Jeff Leroy; ***W:*** Garrett Clancy; ***C:*** Rachel Wyn Dunn; ***M:*** Collin Simon. **VIDEO**

Alien Trespass 1/2 *It Came From Beyond Space* **2009 (PG)** In 1957, a spaceship crash-lands in the Mohave desert, witnessed only by a waitress and an astronomer. The occupants are a vicious omnivorous alien, Ghota, and its captor, Urp. In order to save mankind, Urp (McCormack) must take over the astronomer's body and capture the beast, with the waitress's help. Earnest tribute to 1950s drive-in movie monster flicks. **90m/C DVD.** *US* Eric McCormack, Robert Patrick, Dan Lauria, Jenni Baird, Jody Thompson, Aaron Brooks, Sarah Smyth, Andrew Dunbar; ***D:*** R.W. Goodwin; ***W:*** Steve(n) Fisher; ***C:*** David Moxness; ***M:*** Louis Febre.

Alien vs. Predator *AvP* **2004 (PG-13)** How to classify "AvP?" Is it an "Alien" or "Predator" movie? It doesn't really matter since it's the worst offering that either franchise has produced to date. Predictable, effects-laden prequel to the four-part "Alien" saga and a sequel to the two "Predator" films has a bunch of humans finding an arctic training base for adolescent Predators that uses Aliens as their prey. Of course, the silly humans get caught between them and bad things happen. Monster fest fails to enhance either franchise. **110m/C VHS, DVD, Blu-ray Disc, UMD.** *US* Sanaa Lathan, Raoul Bova, Lance Henriksen, Ewen Bremner, Colin Salmon, Tommy Flanagan, Joseph Rye, Agathe de la Boulaye, Carsten Norgaard, Sam Troughton, Ian Whyte; ***D:*** Paul W.S. Anderson; ***W:*** Paul W.S. Anderson, Dan O'Bannon; ***C:*** David C(lark) Johnson; ***M:*** Harald Kloser.

Alien Visitor *Epsilon* **1995 (PG-13)** Beautiful alien woman lands on Earth in the Australian outback where she meets a guy and is disappointed in her destination since Earth is considered so backwards. But he manages to show her some things that make Earth life worth living. **92m/C VHS, DVD.** *AU* Syd Brisbane, Alethea McGrath, Chloe Ferguson, Phoebe Ferguson, Ulli Birve; ***D:*** Rolf de Heer; ***W:*** Rolf de Heer; ***C:*** Tony Clark; ***M:*** Graham Tardif.

Alien Warrior WOOF! **1985 (R)** An extraterrestrial fights a street pimp to save a crime-ridden Earth neighborhood. Low-brain rip-off of Superman. **92m/C VHS.** Brett (Baxter) Clark, Pamela Saunders; ***D:*** Ed(ward) Hunt.

Alienator **1989 (R)** In the improbable future, an unstoppable android killer is sent after an intergalactic villain. An intentional "Terminator" rip-off. **93m/C VHS, DVD.** Jan-Michael Vincent, John Phillip Law, Ross Hagen, Dyana Ortelli, Dawn Wildsmith, P.J. Soles, Teagan Clive, Robert Clarke, Leo Gordon, Robert

Quarry, Fox Harris, Hoke Howell, Jay Richardson; *D:* Fred Olen Ray.

Aliens 🦴🦴🦴 1/2 *Alien 2* **1986 (R)** The bitch is back, some 50 years later. Popular sequel to "Alien" amounts to non-stop, ravaging combat in space. Contact with a colony on another planet has mysteriously stopped. Fresh from deep space sleep, Ripley and a slew of pulsar-equipped Marines return to confront the mother alien at her nest, which is also inhabited by a whole bunch of the nasty critters spewing for a fight. Something's gotta give, and the Oscar-winning special effects are especially inventive (and messy) in the alien demise department. Dimension (acting biz talk) is given to our hero Ripley, as she discovers maternal instincts lurking within her space suit while looking after a young girl, the lone survivor of the colony. Tension-filled gore blaster. Followed by "Aliens 3." **138m/C VHS, DVD.** Sigourney Weaver, Michael Biehn, Lance Henriksen, Bill Paxton, Paul Reiser, Carrie Henn, Jenette Goldstein, William Hope, Al Matthews, Mark Rolston, Ricco Ross, Colette Hiller; *D:* James Cameron; *W:* James Cameron, Walter Hill; *C:* Adrian Biddle; *M:* James Horner. Oscars '86: Sound FX Editing, Visual FX.

Aliens Are Coming 🦴 1/2 **1980** A spaceship crash lands on Earth, and its devious denizens begin invading human bodies. TV movie that's a dull echo of "Invasion of the Body Snatchers." **100m/C VHS.** Tom Mason, Melinda Fee, Max Gail, Eric (Hans Gudegast) Braeden, Matthew Laborteaux; *D:* Harvey Hart; *M:* William Goldstein.

Aliens from Spaceship Earth 🦴 1/2 **1977** Are strange, celestial forces invading our universe? If they are, is man prepared to defend his planet against threatening aliens of unknown strength? Lame docudrama featuring the Hurdy Gurdy man himself, Donovan. **107m/C VHS, DVD.** Donovan, Lynda Day George; *D:* Don Como.

Aliens in the Attic 🦴 1/2 *They Came From Upstairs* **2009 (PG)** Youngsters will probably be at least mildly entertained by this live-action/(mediocre) CGI concoction. The extended Pearson family is staying at their vacation home in Michigan although the teens are less than thrilled about being there. Then brainiac Tom (Jenkins) discovers four pint-sized aliens have taken over the attic. The nasty aliens have a device (resembling a videogame joystick) that can control the minds and actions of the adults so it's up to the kids to improvise and save the planet. Silly and generally harmless, although Roberts as a martial arts-kicking granny is somewhat unnerving. **86m/C DVD.** *US* Carter Jenkins, Ashley Tisdale, Austin Butler, Ashley Boettcher, Doris Roberts, Robert Hoffman III, Kevin Nealon, Andy Richter, Tim Meadows, Henri Young, Regan Young, Malese Jow, Maggie VandenBerghe, Megan Parker; *D:* John Schultz; *W:* Mark Burton, Adam F. Goldberg; *C:* Don Burgess; *M:* John Debney; *V:* Thomas Haden Church, Josh Peck, Ashley Peldon, Kari Wahlgren, J.K. Simmons.

Aliens vs. Predator: Requiem 🦴 1/2 **2007 (R)** In this sequel to the 2004 flick, the extraterrestrial beasties are cool and the humans are interchangeable incubators and fodder. A mutant alien-predator crash-lands near a small Colorado town and begins using convenient humans for procreation vessels and a super-Predator shows up to dispatch the new critters. The locals are collateral damage. Everything moves along at a snappy pace and there's some action pieces that are watchable, which means if you're a fan you probably won't be disappointed. **86m/C DVD.** *US* Reiko Aylesworth, John Ortiz, Johnny Lewis, Ariel Gade, Steven Pasquale, Sam Trammell, Robert Joy; *D:* Colin Strause, Greg Strause; *W:* Shane Salerno; *C:* Daniel Pearl; *M:* Brian Tyler.

Alison's Birthday 🦴🦴 **1979** A teenage girl learns that some of her family and friends are Satan worshipers at a terrifying birthday party. Meanwhile, the ghost of her dad hovers about, asking for more lines. **99m/C VHS.** *AU* Joanne Samuel, Lou Brown, Bunny Brooke; *D:* Ian Coughlan.

Alive 🦴🦴 1/2 **1993 (R)** Recounts the true-life survival story of a group of Uruguayan rugby players in 1972. After their plane crashes in the remote, snowy Andes (in a spectacular sequence) they're forced to turn to cannibalism during a 10-week struggle to stay alive. Marshall doesn't focus on the gruesome idea, choosing instead to focus on all aspects of their desperate quest for survival. The special effects are stunning, but other parts of the film are never fully realized, including the final scene. Based on the non-fiction book by Piers Paul Read. **127m/C VHS, DVD.** Ethan Hawke, Vincent Spano, Josh Hamilton, Bruce Ramsay, John Haymes Newton, David Kriegel, Kevin Breznahan, Sam Behrens, Illeana Douglas, Jack Noseworthy, Christian Meoli, Jake Carpenter; *D:* Frank Marshall; *W:* John Patrick Shanley; *C:* Peter James; *M:* James Newton Howard; *Nar:* John Malkovich.

Alive and Kicking 🦴🦴 1/2 *Indian Summer* **1996 (R)** Tonio (Flemyng) is a handsome, vain ballet dancer with AIDS, who hides his emotions beneath a witty facade and his work. At a club he meets the older, equally driven Jack (Sher), an AIDS counselor, who pursues him. Though they become lovers, Tonio's obsession with his latest (and last) dance role causes a rift between them. Subplot between Tonio and lesbian dancer Millie (Parish) is self-conscious and Tonio's theatrics can become annoying but both Flemyng and Sher do their best in somewhat one-note roles. **100m/C VHS, DVD.** *GB* Jason Flemyng, Anthony Sher, Dorothy Tutin, Anthony (Corlan) Higgins, Diane Parish, Bill Nighy; *D:* Nancy Meckler; *W:* Martin Sherman; *C:* Chris Seager; *M:* Peter Salem.

All About Eve 🦴🦴🦴🦴 **1950** One of the wittiest (and most cynical) flicks of all time follows aspiring young actress Eve Harrington (Baxter) as she ingratiates herself with a prominent group of theatre people so she can become a Broadway star without the usual years of work. The not-so-innocent babe becomes secretary to aging star Margo Channing (Davis) and ruthlessly uses everyone in her climb to the top, much to Davis' initial disbelief and eventual displeasure. Satirical, darkly funny view of the theatre world features exceptional work by Davis, Sanders, and Ritter. Based on "The Wisdom of Eve" by Mary Orr. Later staged as the musical "Applause." **138m/B VHS, DVD.** Bette Davis, Anne Baxter, George Sanders, Celeste Holm, Gary Merrill, Thelma Ritter, Marilyn Monroe, Hugh Marlowe, Gregory Ratoff, Eddie Fisher; *D:* Joseph L. Mankiewicz; *W:* Joseph L. Mankiewicz; *C:* Milton Krasner; *M:* Alfred Newman. Oscars '50: Costume Des. (B&W), Director (Mankiewicz), Picture, Screenplay, Sound, Support. Actor (Sanders); AFI '98: Top 100; British Acad. '50: Film; Cannes '51: Actress (Davis), Grand Jury Prize; Directors Guild '50: Director (Mankiewicz); Golden Globes '51: Screenplay, Natl. Film Reg. '90;; N.Y. Film Critics '50: Actress (Davis), Director (Mankiewicz), Film.

All About Lily Chou-Chou 🦴🦴🦴 *Riri Shushu no subete* **2001** Yuichi's (Hayato Ichihara) mother has remarried, and he doesn't exactly like it. At school he is bullied horrifically, and he has to resort to crime to pay off the demands of his assailants, one of whom pimps out the other school boys to older men. His only respite is the website he runs about his favorite singer Lily Chou-Chou. Pic boasts some of the most beautiful cinematography to come out of Japan, but its subject matter is brutal and unforgiving, and the nonlinear story will cause some confusion. **146m/C DVD.** *JP* Hayato Ichihara, Yu Aoi, Shugo Oshinari, Ayumi Ito, Takao Osawa, Miwako Ichikawa, Izumi Inamori, Kazusa Matsuda, Ryo Katsuji; *D:* Shunji Iwai; *W:* Shunji Iwai; *C:* Noboru Shinoda; *M:* Takeshi Kobayashi.

All About My Mother 🦴🦴🦴 *Todo Sobre Mi Madre* **1999 (R)** Manuela (Roth) is a single mom, emotionally dependent on her 17-year-old son, Esteban (Azorin). After seeing him killed in a car accident, the grief-stricken mom seeks to find Esteban's father—now a transvestite named Lola (Canto)—and meets an old friend, tranvestite prostitute Agrado (San Juan), who offers comfort. Adding to the female roundelay are Huma Rojo (Paredes), Esteban's favorite actress, and Sister Rosa (Cruz), a pregnant nun who runs a shelter. As Manuela encounters each of them, they help give her a renewed sense of hope and the strength to carry on. Spanish with subtitles. **102m/C VHS, DVD.** *SP* Cecilia (Celia) Roth, Penelope Cruz, Marisa Paredes, Eloy Azorin, Toni Canto, Antonia San Juan, Candela Pena; *D:* Pedro Almodovar; *W:* Pedro Almodovar; *C:* Alfonso Beato; *M:* Alberto Iglesias. Oscars '99: Foreign Film; British Acad. '99: Director (Almodovar), Foreign Film; Cannes '99: Director (Almodovar); Cesar '00: Foreign Film; Golden Globes '00: Foreign Film; L.A. Film Critics '99: Foreign Film; N.Y. Film Critics '99: Foreign Film; Broadcast Film Critics '99: Foreign Film.

All About Steve 🦴 **2009 (PG-13)** Mary Magdalene Horowitz is a boring, clingy, delusional, cruciverbalist (crossword-puzzle designer) who after one blind date with cable news cameraman Steve (Cooper) misinterprets an innocent comment that leads her to relentlessly follow him across the country, egged on by a self-serving reporter, Hartman Hughes (Church). Amid the trek she befriends a variety of socially inept characters like herself that bring nothing but more uncomfortable irritation. Feature debut from director Traill falls seriously short of anything remotely funny, even with his notable cast, while writer Barker vies for the "most annoying character ever created" award. Even Bullock's charm and Cooper's hunky-ness can't spare this from being, in a five-letter word—"awful." **98m/C DVD.** *US* Sandra Bullock, Bradley Cooper, Thomas Haden Church, Ken Jeong, DJ Qualls, Katy Mixon; *D:* Phil Traill; *W:* Kim Barker; *C:* Tim Suhrstedt; *M:* Christophe Beck. Golden Raspberries '09: Worst Actress (Bullock).

All About the Benjamins 🦴🦴 **2002 (R)** Cube and Epps re-team (2000's "Next Friday") as bounty hunter Bucum (Ice Cube) and two-bit con Reggie (Epps) who meet mobsters and mayhem in Miami in this hip-hop buddy flick. Bucum, who dreams of opening his own private-eye agency, is sent to track down Reggie, who seeks a lost lottery tickets which gets the mismatched duo mixed up in a diamond heist. As usual, Cube, straight man to Epps's clown, have the usual chemistry and deliver some amusing moments in this light caper comedy, but the director's penchant for gory violence interrupts the otherwise slapstick mood. The two leads would shine if not for being stuck in this nod to "Miami Vice" and Elmore Leonard without the character development and plot. Cube co-wrote with Levy. **98m/C VHS, DVD.** *US* Ice Cube, Mike Epps, Tommy Flanagan, Eva Mendes, Carmen Chaplin, Roger Guenveur Smith, Anthony Michael Hall, Valarie Rae Miller, Bow Wow; *D:* Kevin Bray; *W:* Ice Cube, Ronald Lang; *C:* Glen MacPherson; *M:* John Murphy.

All About You 🦴 1/2 **2001 (PG)** Tired tale takes Nicole from lost love Robbie in L.A. to blossoming romance with Brian in San Fran. Naturally the new guy is the old guy's alienated brother. **100m/C VHS, DVD.** Terron Brooks, Debbie Allen, LisaRaye, Renee Goldsberry, Lou Myers, Vanessa Bell Calloway, Bobby Hosea, Chris Spencer, Tico Wells, Adam Lazarre-White, Emily Liu; *D:* Christine Swanson; *W:* Christine Swanson; *C:* Wolf Baschung, David Scardina; *M:* John Bickerton. **VIDEO**

All-American Murder 🦴🦴 **1991 (R)** A rebellious young man is enrolled in a typical, all-American college for one last shot at mainstream life. Things start out okay, as he meets an attractive young coed. Hours later, he finds himself accused of her grisly murder. The youth is then given 24 hours to prove his innocence by a canny homicide detective. Average performances highlight this film, which isn't able to rise above the mediocre. **94m/C VHS, DVD.** Christopher Walken, Charlie Schlatter, Josie Bissett, Joanna Cassidy, Richard Kind, Woody Watson, J.C. Quinn, Amy Davis; *D:* Anson Williams; *W:* Barry Sandler.

All Creatures Great and Small 🦴🦴🦴 **1974** Taken from James Herriot's bestselling novels, this is a delightful, quiet drama of a veterinarian's apprentice in rural England. Fine performance by Hopkins. Followed by "All Things Bright and Beautiful" and a popular British TV series. **92m/C VHS, DVD.** *GB* Simon Ward, Anthony Hopkins, Lisa Harrow, Brian Stirner, Freddie Jones, T.P. McKenna; *D:* Claude Whatham; *W:* Hugh Whitemore; *C:* Peter Suschitzky; *M:* Wilfred Josephs.

All Dogs Go to Heaven 🦴🦴 **1989 (G)** Somewhat heavy-handed animated musical (Reynolds sings) about a gangster dog who is killed by his partner in business. On the way to Heaven, he discovers how to get back to Earth to seek his revenge. When he returns to Earth, he is taken in by a little girl and learns about something he missed in life the first time around: Love. Expertly animated, but the plot may not keep the grown-ups engrossed, and the kids may notice its lack of charm. **85m/C VHS, DVD.** *D:* Don Bluth; *W:* Don Bluth, David N. Weiss; *M:* Ralph Burns; *V:* Burt Reynolds, Judith Barsi, Dom DeLuise, Vic Tayback, Charles Nelson Reilly, Melba Moore, Candy Devine, Loni Anderson.

All Dogs Go to Heaven 2 🦴🦴 1/2 **1995 (G)** Animated musical finds lovable scamp Charlie (Sheen) the dog discovering that the afterlife is not all it's cracked up to be and pining for dysfunction aplenty back on earth. He gets his chance when Gabriel's Horn is stolen and Charlie is assigned to retrieve it. Charlie teams up again with old buddy Itchy (Deluise) as the two come down from Dog Heaven to stop the villainous Carface (Borgnine) and demonic cat Red (Hearn). Along the way, Charlie falls in love with sexy Irish Setter Sasha (Easton), and finds a chance for redemption by helping a little boy in trouble. Animation not outstanding, but should keep the attention of small children. **82m/C VHS, DVD.** *D:* Paul Sabella, Larry Leker; *W:* Arne Olsen, Kelly Ward, Mark Young; *M:* Mark Watters, Barry Mann, Cynthia Weil; *V:* Charlie Sheen, Sheena Easton, Ernest Borgnine, Dom DeLuise, George Hearn, Bebe Neuwirth, Hamilton Camp, Wallace Shawn, Bobby DiCicco, Adam Wylie.

All Fall Down 🦴🦴 1/2 **1962** A young man (de Wilde) idolizes his callous older brother (Beatty) until a tragedy forces him to grow up. Saint plays the older woman taken in by the brothers' family, who is seduced and abandoned. When she finds herself pregnant and alone, she commits suicide causing the younger brother, who loved her from afar, to vow to kill his older sibling. A well-acted melodrama. Also available colorized. **111m/B VHS, DVD.** Eva Marie Saint, Brandon de Wilde, Warren Beatty, Karl Malden, Angela Lansbury, Constance Ford, Barbara Baxley; *D:* John Frankenheimer; *W:* William Inge; *C:* Lionel Lindon; *M:* Alex North.

All God's Children 🦴🦴 1/2 **1980** Drama about the controversial forced busing issue and two families who must face it. Top-notch cast is occasionally mislead by meandering script attempting to stay true to a sensitive issue. **100m/C VHS.** Richard Widmark, Ned Beatty, Ossie Davis, Ruby Dee, Mariclare Costello, George Spell, Trish Van Devere, Ken Swofford; *D:* Jerry Thorpe; *M:* Billy Goldenberg. **TV**

All Good Things **2009** The son (Gosling) of a New York real estate dynasty falls for a wrong-side-of-the-tracks girl (Dunst). When she disappears, a down-and-out PI (Morgan) investigates and people turn up dead. Set in the 1980s. **m/C DVD.** *US* Ryan Gosling, Kirsten Dunst, Frank Langella, Jeffrey Dean Morgan, Lily Rabe, Kristen Wiig, Diane Venora, Trini Alvarado, Philip Baker Hall, John Doman; *D:* Andrew Jarecki; *W:* Andrew Jarecki, Marcus Hinchey, Marc Smerling; *C:* Michael Seresin.

All Hat 🦴 1/2 **2007 (R)** And no particular brains or heart. Hot-head Ray Doakes (Kirby) just got out of prison. He returns to his Ontario hometown to find that lowdown land developer Sonny Stanton (Jenkins), who helped put Ray away, is still up to no good. When an expensive thoroughbred from Stanton's racing stables goes missing, the scumball uses it as an excuse to squeeze the local farmers into selling their property for his golf resort. Only Ray comes up with a plan to stop him. **91m/C DVD.** *CA* Rachael Leigh Cook, Luke Kirby, Noam Jenkins, Keith Carradine, Ernie Hudson, David Alpay, Graham Greene, Gary Farmer, Lisa Ray, Stephen McHattie, Michelle Nolden; *D:* Leonard Farlinger; *W:* Brad Smith; *C:* Paul Sarossy; *M:* Bill Frisell. **VIDEO**

All I Desire 🦴🦴 1/2 **1953** Estranged wife and mother (Stanwyck) returns to her hometown after fleeing years ago to pursue a stage career. She desires a new beginning with her family, but finds things have changed in her absence. The story examines the will of a strong woman and small town values. Director Sirk disagreed with the happy ending demanded by producers, but the drama is still noteworthy. **80m/B VHS.** Barbara Stanwyck, Richard Carlson, Lyle Bettger, Maureen O'Sullivan; *D:* Douglas Sirk; *W:* James Gunn,

Robert Blees, Carl Guthrie, Gina Kaus; ***M:*** Joseph Gershenson.

All I Wanna Do 1/2 *The Hairy Bird; Strike!* **1998 (PG-13)** The students of an exclusive, and financially troubled, East Coast girls' school, circa 1963, are vigorously opposed to the merger of their school with a boys' academy. So they decide to stage a protest strike. Rather typical coming of age tale with a notable cast of up-and-comers. Film was briefly released in 1998 at 110 minutes under the title "Strike" and then re-edited and re-released under its current title in 2000. **94m/C VHS, DVD.** Kirsten Dunst, Gaby Hoffman, Heather Matarazzo, Rachael Leigh Cook, Monica Keena, Merritt Wever, Lynn Redgrave, Vincent Kartheiser, Tom Guiry, Matthew Lawrence, Robert Bockstael; ***D:*** Sarah Kernochan; ***W:*** Sarah Kernochan; ***C:*** Anthony C. "Tony" Jannelli; ***M:*** Graeme Revell.

All I Want *Try Seventeen* **2002 (R)** Jones Dillon (Wood) is a 17-year-old wide-eyed Kansas university freshman who soon decides that dorm life is not for him. So he moves into the boarding house of Ma Mabley (Harry) and is soon pining after a couple of his neighbors—sweet would-be actress Lisa (Moore) and experienced photographer Jane (Potente). Coming of ager hasn't anything new to say but the three leads do well with their limited material. **96m/C VHS, DVD.** Elijah Wood, Franka Potente, Mandy Moore, Deborah Harry, Aaron Pearl, Elizabeth Perkins; ***D:*** Jeffrey Porter; ***W:*** Charles Kephart; ***C:*** Blake T. Evans; ***M:*** Andrew Gross.

All I Want for Christmas **1991 (G)** Low-budget, sappy holiday tale of a young girl (Birch) who wants to reunite her divorced parents. Determined to fulfill her Christmas wish, Hallie seeks out the Santa Claus at Macy's department store to tell him the one thing she truly wants for Christmas. Birch is charming as are Bacall as her grandmother and Nielsen as Santa but the story is too squishy and bland to be believable. **92m/C VHS, DVD.** Thora Birch, Leslie Nielsen, Lauren Bacall, Jamey Sheridan, Harley Jane Kozak, Ethan (Randall) Embry, Kevin Nealon, Andrea Martin; ***D:*** Ron Lieberman; ***W:*** Richard Kramer, Thom Eberhardt, Neal Israel, Gail Parent; ***C:*** Robbie Greenberg; ***M:*** Bruce Broughton.

All I Want for Christmas 1/2 **2007** Wanting to help out his overworked, widowed mom Sarah (O'Grady), young Jesse (Pinchak) enters a national contest sponsored by a toy company with an essay about wanting a new husband to take care of his mom. When Jesse wins, it thrusts them into a national spotlight and Sarah just may wind up with the wrong guy. A Hallmark Channel original. **89m/C DVD.** Gail O'Grady, Robert Mailhouse, Greg Germann, Amanda Foreman, Jimmy Pinchak, Bess Meyer, Robert Pine; ***D:*** Harvey Frost; ***W:*** Marc Rey; ***C:*** Dane Peterson; ***M:*** Stephen Graziano. **CABLE**

All In **2006 (R)** Alice "Ace" Anderson (Swain) has been raised by her poker-playing father (Madsen) in the world of backstreet gambling. With mounting debts from med school, Ace decides to recruit some fellow students to take on the best players and win at the World Series of Poker. Lame effort with some confusing and unnecessary subplots. **?m/C DVD.** Dominique Swain, Michael Madsen, James Russo, Louis Gossett Jr., Kristen Miller, Colleen Porch, Scott Whyte, Michelle Lombardo, Chris Backus, Johann Urb, Hayley DuMond; ***D:*** Nick Vallelonga; ***W:*** Loren Comitor; ***C:*** Jeff Baustert; ***M:*** Harry Manfredini.

All in a Night's Work 1/2 **1961** The founder of a one-man publishing empire is found dead with a smile on his face. His nephew inherits the business and finds himself caught in a series of big and small business misunderstandings. He's also falling in love with the woman he suspects was responsible for his uncle's grin. Nicely paced sex and business comedy with warm performances. **94m/C VHS, DVD.** Dean Martin, Shirley MacLaine, Cliff Robertson, Charlie Ruggles; ***D:*** Joseph Anthony; ***W:*** Sidney Sheldon; ***M:*** Andre Previn.

All Mine to Give 1/2 *The Day They Gave the Babies Away* **1956** Sad saga of a Scottish family of eight who braved frontier hardships, epidemics, and death in the Wisconsin wilderness more than a century ago. Midway through, mom and dad die, leaving the oldest child struggling to keep the family together. A strange, though often effective, combination of pioneer adventures and tear-jerking moments that avoids becoming hopelessly soapy due to fine performances. Unless you're pretty weathered, you'll need some hankies. Based on the reminiscences of Dale and Katherine Eunson as detailed in a "Cosmopolitan" magazine article. **102m/C VHS.** Glynis Johns, Cameron Mitchell, Rex Thompson, Patty McCormack, Ernest Truex, Hope Emerson, Alan Hale Jr., Royal Dano, Reta Shaw, Rita Johnson, Ellen Corby, Jon(athan) Provost; ***D:*** Allen Reisner; ***M:*** Max Steiner.

All My Good Countrymen 1/2 *All Good Citizens* **1968** A lyrical, funny film about the eccentric denizens of a small Moravian village soon after the socialization of Czechoslovakia in 1948. Completed during the Soviet invasion of 1968 and immediately banned. In Czech with English subtitles. **115m/C VHS.** *CZ* Vladimir Mensik, Radoslav Brozobohaty, Pavel Pavlovsky; ***D:*** Vojtech Jasny. Cannes '69: Director (Jasny).

All My Loved Ones *Vsichni Moji Blizci* **2000** Moving fictionalized account by director Minac of his mother's recollections of being one of nearly 700 Czech Jewish children saved in the Kindertransport trains. Briton Nicholas Winton (Graves) is on holiday in Prague in 1938; recognizing the worsening situation for the Jews in Czechoslovakia, he discovers that both Sweden and Britain are willing to take in child refugees if he can transport them out of the country. One of these potential transportees is 10-year-old David (Holicek), a member of a weathy family who fail to recognize the seriousness of their situation. Czech with subtitles. **91m/C VHS, DVD.** *CZ* Rupert Graves, Libuse Safrankova, Josef Abrham, Jiri Bartoska, Brano Holicek, Jiri Menzel; ***D:*** Matej Minac; ***W:*** Jiri Hubac; ***C:*** Dodo Simoncic; ***M:*** Janusz Stoklosa.

All My Sons **1948** Joe Keller (Robinson) is a small-town manufacturer enjoying the profits he made from his WWII contracts. But his family is pulled apart by guilt and shame when son Chris (Lancaster) discovers his father sold defective parts to the military that resulted in loss of life and then covered up the crime. Excellent performances; adapted from the play by Arthur Miller. Remade in 1986 with James Whitmore and Aidan Quinn. **94m/B VHS.** Edward G. Robinson, Burt Lancaster, Mady Christians, Louisa Horton, Howard Duff, Frank Conroy, Arlene Francis, Harry (Henry) Morgan; ***D:*** Irving Reis; ***W:*** Chester Erskine; ***C:*** Russell Metty; ***M:*** Leith Horton.

All My Sons **1986** A wealthy family is distraught when their eldest son is listed as missing-in-action during WWII. They must cope with guilt, as well as grief, because the father's business reaped profits from the war. Adapted from the acclaimed Arthur Miller play. **122m/C VHS.** James Whitmore, Aidan Quinn, Joan Allen, Michael Learned; ***D:*** John Power. **TV**

All New Adventures of Laurel and Hardy: For Love or Mummy 1/2 **1998 (PG)** Stan Laurel (Pinchot) and Oliver Hardy (Sartain) are the equally bumbling nephews of the original comedic duo. The would-be movers are hired to transport an Egyptian mummy to an American museum, where archeologist Leslie (Danford) is the unwitting object of an ancient curse that fortells her marrying the reanimated corpse. **84m/C VHS, DVD.** Bronson Pinchot, Gailard Sartain, F. Murray Abraham, Susan Danford; ***D:*** John R. Cherry III, Larry Harmon.

All Night **1918** A rare comedy starring newcomer Valentino. Struggling William and Maude Harcourt invite young friends Richard and Elizabeth to a dinner party, with the Harcourts pretending to be servants since their own hired help have walked out. But the joke is on them when millionaire Bradford suddenly decides to take the Harcourts up on a previous invitation. So they have Richard and Elizabeth host instead and Bradford is so charmed by the faux-Harcourts that it causes more trouble, including a quite suggestive bedroom scene. **57m/B DVD.** Rudolph Valentino, Carmel Myers, Charles Dorian, Mary Warren, William J. Dyer, Wadsworth Harris; ***D:*** Paul Powell; ***W:*** Edgar Franklin, Fred Myton.

All Night Long **1981 (R)** Offbeat middle-age crisis comedy about a burned-out and recently demoted drugstore executive in L.A. who leaves his wife, takes up with his fourth cousin by marriage, and begins a humorous rebellion, becoming an extremely freelance inventor while joining the drifters, weirdos and thieves of the night. An obscure, sometimes uneven little gem with Hackman in top form and an appealing supporting performance by Streisand. Highlighted by delightful malapropisms and sataric inversion of the usual cliches. **100m/C VHS, DVD.** Gene Hackman, Barbra Streisand, Diane Ladd, Dennis Quaid, Kevin Dobson, William Daniels; ***D:*** Jean-Claude Tramont; ***W:*** W.D. Richter; ***M:*** Ira Newborn.

All of Me 1/2 **1984 (PG)** A wealthy woman (Tomlin) dies and her guru accidentally transfers her soul to the right side of her lawyer's body, a modern version of existential hell. Lawyer Martin indulges in some funny slapstick as he discovers that his late client is waging an internal war for control of his body. Flat and cliched at times, but redeemed by the inspired clowning of Martin and witty Martin/Tomlin repartee. Based on the novel "Me Too" by Ed Davis. **93m/C VHS, DVD.** Steve Martin, Lily Tomlin, Victoria Tennant, Madolyn Smith, Richard Libertini, Dana Elcar, Selma Diamond, Jason Bernard, Eric Christmas, Peggy (Margaret) Feury; ***D:*** Carl Reiner; ***W:*** Phil Alden Robinson; ***C:*** Richard H. Kline; ***M:*** Patrick Williams. N.Y. Film Critics '84: Actor (Martin); Natl. Soc. Film Critics '84: Actor (Martin).

All or Nothing **2002 (R)** A depressing tale about depressed and desperate people set in a grotty housing project in South London. Hangdog minicab driver Phil (Spall) can't even earn a decent wage to support his family, cashier common-law wife Penny (Manville), and their layabout son Rory (Corden) and misfit daughter Rachel (Garland). Their neighbors aren't any better off—stuck with abusive boyfriends, unplanned pregnancy, alcoholism, and the general dreariness of their daily lives. Leigh is known for his slice-of-life dramas but this just stays one-dimensional. **128m/C VHS, DVD.** *GB FR* Timothy Spall, Lesley Manville, Alison Garland, James Corden, Paul Jesson, Ruth Sheen, Marion Bailey, Sally Hawkins, Ben Crompton, Helen Coker, Daniel Mays; ***D:*** Mike Leigh; ***W:*** Mike Leigh; ***C:*** Dick Pope; ***M:*** Andrew Dickson.

All or Nothing at All **1993** Leo Hopkins (Laurie) is a charming con man with a successful career and a wife and kids. He's also a gambling addict who can't help living life on the edge, until he finds himself about to fall off. **150m/C DVD.** *GB* Hugh Laurie, Bob Monkhouse, Pippa Guard, Caroline Quentin, Jessica Turner, Steve Steen, Phyllida Law; ***D:*** Andrew Grieve; ***W:*** Guy Andrews. **TV**

All Over Me **1996 (R)** Teen angst/coming of age set in New York's Hell's Kitchen. Ungainly wanna-be guitarist, 15-year-old Claudia-AKA-Claude (Folland), is best friends with flirty blonde Ellen (Subkoff). But their relationship changes when Ellen begins dating the macho older Mark (Hauser) and is soon into sex and drugs, while Claude's sexual quandries lead her to a lesbian bar and an interest in singer Lucy (Hailey). Good performances but a moody and somewhat awkward first feature from Sichel, whose sister wrote the screenplay. **90m/C VHS, DVD.** Alison Folland, Tara Subkoff, Cole Hauser, Wilson Cruz, Leisha Hailey, Pat Briggs, Ann Dowd; ***D:*** Alex Sichel; ***W:*** Sylvia Sichel; ***C:*** Joe DeSalvo; ***M:*** Miki Navazio.

All Over the Guy 1/2 **2001 (R)** Writer/director Roos served as executive producer on this film, which re-unites some of the personnel from his hit "The Opposite of Sex." Unfortunately, the quality of that film isn't reproduced here. Eli (writer Bucatinsky adapted from his play) and Tom (Ruccolo) are two gay men who are set up on a blind date by Brett (Goldberg) and Jackie (Alexander). They don't really get along, but they find themselves very attracted to one another. The film then explores the ups and downs of their courtship, as each tries to deal with the baggage from the past which keeps them from succeeding in the present. The problem is it's incredibly unoriginal. There doesn't seem to be any real chemistry between the couple, so whether or not they stay together may become a moot point to some viewers. Some of the performances are good (Goldberg has some good lines), but Ruccolo looks very uncomfortable at times. **95m/C VHS, DVD.** Dan Bucatinsky, Richard Ruccolo, Adam Goldberg, Sasha Alexander, Doris Roberts, Andrea Martin, Tony Abatemarco, Joanna Kerns, Nicolas Surovy, Christina Ricci, Lisa Kudrow; ***D:*** Julie Davis; ***W:*** Dan Bucatinsky; ***C:*** Goran Paviceric; ***M:*** Peter Stuart, Andrew Williams.

All Over Town 1/2 **1937** Two vaudevillians with a trained seal find themselves involved in a murder when they are kidnapped by a gang of thugs. A lesser Olsen and Johnson comedy with scattered funny moments. **52m/B VHS, DVD.** Ole Olsen, Chic Johnson, Mary Howard, Franklin Pangborn, James Finlayson; ***D:*** James W. Horne; ***W:*** Jack Townley, Jerome Chodorov.

All Quiet on the Western Front **1930** Extraordinary and realistic anti-war epic based on the novel by Erich Maria Remarque. Seven patriotic German youths go together from school to the battlefields of WWI. They experience the horrors of war first-hand, stuck in the trenches and facing gradual extermination. Centers on experiences of one of the young men, Paul Baumer, who changes from enthusiastic war endorser to battle-weary veteran in an emotionally exact performance by Ayres. Boasts a gigantic budget (for the time) of $1.25 million, and features more than 2000 extras swarming about battlefields set up on ranchland in California. Relentless anti-war message is emotionally draining and startling with both graphic shots and haunting visual poetry. Extremely controversial in the U.S. and Germany upon release, the original version was 140 minutes long (some versions are available with restored footage) and featured ZaSu Pitts as Ayres mother (later reshot with Mercer replacing her). Remarque, who had fought and been wounded on the Western Front, was eventually forced to leave Germany for the U.S. due to the film's ongoing controversy. **103m/B VHS, DVD.** Lew Ayres, Louis Wolheim, John Wray, Slim Summerville, Russell Gleason, Raymond Griffith, Ben Alexander, Beryl Mercer, Arnold Lucy, William "Billy" Bakewell, Scott Kolk, Owen Davis Jr., Walter Rodgers, Richard Alexander, Harold Goodwin, G. Pat Collins, Edmund Breese; ***D:*** Lewis Milestone; ***W:*** Maxwell Anderson, George Abbott, Del Andrews; ***C:*** Arthur Edeson, Karl Freund; ***M:*** David Broekman. Oscars '30: Director (Milestone), Picture; AFI '98: Top 100, Natl. Film Reg. '90.

All Quiet on the Western Front 1/2 **1979** A big-budget TV remake of the 1930 masterpiece starring John Boy. Sensitive German youth Thomas plunges excitedly into WWI and discovers its terror and degradation. Nowhere near the original's quality. **150m/C VHS, DVD.** Richard Thomas, Ernest Borgnine, Donald Pleasence, Patricia Neal; ***D:*** Delbert Mann; ***W:*** Paul Monash; ***C:*** John Coquillon; ***M:*** Allyn Ferguson. **TV**

All Roads Lead Home 1/2 **2008 (PG)** Twelve-year-old Belle (Cardone) begins acting out after her mother's death in a car accident. She thinks her father Cody (London), who must euthanize unwanted pets as part of his animal control job, is in some way responsible. Cody decides to send Belle to her maternal grandfather Hock's (Coyote) farm but Hock is having trouble dealing with his own grief and it has turned him indifferent to the plight of the animals on the property. Of course as Belle helps care for the various critters, she and her family begin to reach out to one another. Boyle's last film role. **112m/C DVD.** Vivien Cardone, Peter Coyote, Jason London, Evan Dexter Parke, Peter Boyle, Patton Oswalt, Vanessa Branch, Shannon Knopke; ***D:*** Dennis Fallon; ***W:*** Douglas Delaney; ***C:*** Fred Paddock; ***M:*** Korey Ireland.

All Saint's Day **1998** Tired of his going-nowhere life, Marco (Blatt) recruits four of his screw-up friends to help him rob the Brooklyn fish market where he works. Of course, since they're all losers this doesn't work out as planned. **82m/C VHS, DVD.** Mickey Blatt, Thomas J. La Sorsa, James Patrick McArdle, Mark Love, Christopher Lynn, Anthony Mangano, Ray Garvey, Howard Simon; ***D:*** Thomas J. La Sorsa; *W:* Thomas J. La Sorsa, Christopher Lynn; *C:* Daniel Marracino.

All Screwed Up 🦴🦴🦴 *All in Place; Nothing in Order* **1974** A group of young immigrants come to Milan and try to adjust to city life; they soon find that everything is in its place, but nothing is in order. Wertmuller in a lighter vein than usual. **104m/C VHS.** *IT* Luigi Diberti, Lina Polito; *D:* Lina Wertmuller; *W:* Lina Wertmuller.

All Souls Day 🦴 1/2 *Dia de los Muertos* **2005** Vargas Diaz's 1892 brutal rampage in a small Mexican town on the symbolic "Day of the Dead" causes his murderous soul to haunt the locals for years, leading them to perform certain acts to keep the zombies at bay. First up to be terrorized is a 1950's family with a sick boy and a hot teenaged girl who takes the standard "something-bad-is-about-to-happen" steamy bath. Then, in the present, Joss (Wester) and Alicia (Ramirez) seem doomed when they unknowingly interrupt the long-standing rite and must flee the same creepy hotel. Sci-Fi Channel original should have let the walking dead lie. **90m/C DVD.** Travis Wester, Nichole Hiltz, Laz Alonso, Laura Elena Harring, Marisa Ramirez, David Keith, Jeffrey Combs, Ellie Cornell, Julia Vera, Daniel Burgio, Mircea Monroe, Danny Trejo, Noah Luke; *D:* Jeremy Kasten; *W:* Mark Altman; *C:* Christopher Duddy; *M:* Joseph Gutowski. **CABLE**

All That Heaven Allows 🦴🦴🦴 **1955** Attractive, wealthy middleaged widow Cary Scott (Wyman) falls for her 15-years-younger gardener, Ron Kirby (Hudson), and becomes the target of small-minded gossips and her disapproving family. Ron's no gigolo or fortune-hunter but societal pressure still gets to Cary and she breaks things off. But loneliness makes her realize what she's missing and she decides to make things up with Ron and forget her critics. Hopeful Sirk romance that still takes some jabs at conformity. **89m/B VHS, DVD.** Jane Wyman, Rock Hudson, Conrad Nagel, Agnes Moorehead, Virginia Grey, Gloria Talbott, William Reynolds; *D:* Douglas Sirk; *W:* Peggy Fenwick; *C:* Russell Metty; *M:* Frank Skinner, Joseph Gershenson. Natl. Film Reg. '95.

All That Jazz 🦴🦴🦴 1/2 **1979 (R)** Fosse's autobiographical portrait with Scheider fully occupying his best role as the obsessed, pill-popping, chain-smoking choreographer/director dancing simultaneously with love and death. But even while dying, he creates some great dancing. Vivid and imaginative with exact editing, and an eerie footnote to Fosse's similar death almost ten years later. Egocentric and self-indulgent for sure, but that's entertainment. ♫On Broadway; Everything Old is New Again; After You've Gone; There'll Be Some Changes Made; Some of These Days; Bye Bye Love. **120m/C VHS, DVD.** Roy Scheider, Jessica Lange, Ann Reinking, Leland Palmer, Cliff Gorman, Ben Vereen, Erzebet Foldi, John Lithgow, Max Wright, Deborah Geffner, Michael (Lawrence) Tolan, Keith Gordon, David Margulies, Nicole Fosse, Anthony Holland; *D:* Bob Fosse; *W:* Bob Fosse, Robert Alan Aurthur; *C:* Giuseppe Rotunno; *M:* Ralph Burns. Oscars '79: Art Dir./Set Dec., Costume Des., Film Editing, Orig. Song Score and/or Adapt.; Cannes '80: Film, Natl. Film Reg. '01.

All the Brothers Were Valiant 🦴🦴 1/2 **1953** Brothers Taylor and Granger are New England whaling captains but Granger decides to treasure hunt instead. He finds a priceless cache of black pearls on an island but angers the locals who regard the gems as sacred. When Taylor rescues him, Granger promptly turns his brother's crew into mutineers in order to return to the island and retrieve his prize. Lots of brawling and there's an incidental love story with Blyth desired by both men (she's married Taylor and just happens to be aboard). Last role for Stone. Based on the novel by Ben Ames Williams. **101m/C VHS.** Robert Taylor, Stewart Granger, Ann Blyth, Betta St. John, Keenan Wynn, James Whitmore, Kurt Kasznar, Lewis Stone, Robert Burton, Peter Whitney, John Lupton, Billie Dove; *D:* Richard Thorpe; *W:* Harry Brown; *C:* George J. Folsey; *M:* Miklos Rozsa.

All the Good Ones Are Married 🦴 1/2 **2007** Alex (Hannah) is going through an amicable divorce from Ben (McGowan) until his mistress (Douglas) shows up at her door. Having been dumped herself, she thinks the two women scorned should team up, but Alex is naturally wary. Lifetime drama. **89m/C DVD.** Daryl Hannah, Deborah Odell, Matthew Knight, Nick Baillie, James McGowan, Joanna Douglas, Matthew Broderick, Brittany Snow, Maura Tierney, Peter Facinelli; *D:* Terry Ingram; *C:* Marcus Elliott. **CABLE**

All the Kind Strangers 🦴🦴 *Evil in the Swamp* **1974** Traveling photographer Keach picks up a young hitchhiker and takes him to the boy's home. He discovers six other children there who want him as a father, his alternative being death. He and "Mother" Eggar plot their escape from the dangerous orphans. Thriller short on suspense. **72m/C VHS, DVD.** Stacy Keach, Robby Benson, John Savage, Samantha Eggar; *D:* Burt Kennedy. **TV**

All the King's Men 🦴🦴🦴🦴 **1949** Grim and graphic classic set in the Depression follows the rise of a Louisiana farm-boy from angry and honest political hopeful to powerful but corrupt governor. Loosely based on the life (and death) of Huey Long and told by a newsman who's followed his career (Ireland). Willy Stark (Crawford, in his breakthrough role) is the politician who, while appearing to improve the state, rules dictatorially, betraying friends and constituents and proving once again that power corrupts. In her first major role, McCambridge delivers a powerful performance as the cunning political aide. Potent morality play based on the Robert Penn Warren book. **109m/B VHS, DVD.** Broderick Crawford, Mercedes McCambridge, John Ireland, Joanne Dru, John Derek, Anne Seymour, Shepperd Strudwick; *D:* Robert Rossen; *W:* Robert Rossen; *C:* Burnett Guffey; *M:* Louis Gruenberg. Oscars '49: Actor (Crawford), Picture, Support. Actress (McCambridge); Golden Globes '50: Actor—Drama (Crawford), Director (Rossen), Film—Drama, Support. Actress (McCambridge), Natl. Film Reg. '01;; N.Y. Film Critics '49: Actor (Crawford), Film.

All the King's Men 🦴🦴 1/2 **1999** In 1915, Frank Beck (Jason), the manager of the royal estate of Sandringham, trains a company of servants to be volunteer soldiers. Unfortunately, the raw recruits are posted to the disaster of Gallipoli and a battle against the Turks. The true fate of the company was unknown for many years and their disappearance became the stuff of myth (recent discoveries proved much grimmer) but the storyline is muddled and it's not easy to distinguish one youthful character from another (although the veterans do a notable job). Based on the novel by Nigel McCrery. **110m/C VHS, DVD.** *GB* David Jason, Maggie Smith, Stuart Bunce, William Ash, James Murray, Sonya Walger, Eamon Boland, David Troughton, Emma Cunniffe, Adam Kotz, Patrick Malahide, Ed Waters, Tom Burke, Ben Crompton, Jo Stone-Fewings, James Hillier, Ian McDiarmid, Phyllis Logan; *D:* Julian Jarrold; *W:* Alma Cullen; *C:* David Odd; *M:* Adrian Johnston. **TV**

All the King's Men 🦴 1/2 **2006 (PG-13)** Based on Robert Penn Warren's 1946 novel, this bungled remake of the 1949 film focuses on the rise and fall of a Huey P. Long-like politician, with Penn all bug-eyed sputterings as southern demagogue Willie Stark. Besides the out-of-place Penn, there's a bunch of miscast Brits, including narrator Law as boozy journalist Jack Burden, Winslet as Stark's unrequited love Anne, and Hopkins as a judge that Willie wants dirt on. Louisiana native Clarkson and former child actor Haley are about the only two actors who probably won't make you squirm. **128m/C DVD, Blu-ray Disc.** *US* Sean Penn, Jude Law, Kate Winslet, James Gandolfini, Mark Ruffalo, Patricia Clarkson, Kathy Baker, Jackie Earle Haley, Anthony Hopkins, Kevin Dunn, Frederic Forrest, Talia Balsam, Glenn Morshower; *D:* Steven Zaillian; *W:* Steven Zaillian; *C:* Pawel Edelman; *M:* James Horner.

All the Little Animals 🦴🦴 1/2 **1998 (R)** Twenty-four-year old Bobby (Bale) is brain damaged from a childhood accident. After his mother's death, he's left in the less-than-tender care of his malevolent stepfather, De Winter (Benzali), who's only interested in Bobby's inheritance. So Bobby runs away and is taken in by hermit, Mr. Summers (Hurt), who is devoted to burying the remains of animals killed in road accidents. But Bobby's idyll cannot last when his stepfather finds him—and Mr. Summers is also not quite what he seems. Based on the novel by Walker Hamilton. **104m/C VHS, DVD.** *GB* John Hurt, Christian Bale, Daniel Benzali, James Faulkner, Amy Robbins; *D:* Jeremy Thomas; *W:* Eski Thomas; *C:* Mike Molloy; *M:* Richard Hartley.

All the Lovin' Kinfolk 🦴 *Kin Folk; Kinfolk; The Closest of Kin* **1970 (R)** Two recent Hillbilly High graduates decide to take on the big city, but find themselves in dire situations. For those with time to kill. **80m/C VHS.** Mady Maguire, Jay Scott, Anne Ryan, John Denis, Donna Young, Marland Proctor, Uschi Digart; *D:* John Hayes; *W:* John Hayes.

...All the Marbles 🦴🦴 *The California Dolls* **1981 (R)** A manager of two beautiful lady wrestlers has dreams of going to the top. Aldrich's last film, and an atypical one, with awkward pacing and a thin veil of sex exploitation. Falk provides needed grace and humor as the seedy manager, with Young contributing his usual competent bit as a hustling promoter dabbling in criminal activity. One of the few tag-team women wrestling pictures, it builds to a rousing finale match in the "Rocky" tradition, although the shift in tone and mounting cliches effectively body slam the intent. **113m/C VHS.** Peter Falk, Burt Young, Richard Jaeckel, Vicki Frederick, Claudette Nevins, Lenny Montana; *D:* Robert Aldrich; *C:* Joseph Biroc.

All the President's Men 🦴🦴🦴 1/2 **1976 (PG)** True story of the Watergate break-in that led to the political scandal of the decade, based on the best-selling book by Washington Post reporters Bob Woodward and Carl Bernstein. Intriguing, terse thriller is a nail-biter even though the ending is no secret. Expertly paced by Pakula with standout performances by Hoffman and Redford as the reporters who slowly uncover and connect the seemingly isolated facts that ultimately lead to criminal indictments of the Nixon Administration. Deep Throat Holbrook and Robards as executive editor Ben Bradlee lend authenticity to the endeavor, a realistic portrayal of the stop and go of journalistic investigations. **135m/C VHS, DVD.** Dominic Chianese, David Arkin, Polly Holliday, James Karen, Robert Redford, Dustin Hoffman, Jason Robards Jr., Martin Balsam, Jane Alexander, Hal Holbrook, F. Murray Abraham, Stephen Collins, Lindsay Crouse, Meredith Baxter, Ned Beatty, Penny Fuller; *D:* Alan J. Pakula; *W:* William Goldman; *C:* Gordon Willis; *M:* David Shire. Oscars '76: Adapt. Screenplay, Art Dir./Set Dec., Sound, Support. Actor (Robards); Natl. Bd. of Review '76: Director (Pakula), Support. Actor (Robards); N.Y. Film Critics '76: Director (Pakula), Film, Support. Actor (Robards); Natl. Soc. Film Critics '76: Film, Support. Actor (Robards); Writers Guild '76: Adapt. Screenplay.

All the Pretty Horses 🦴🦴 **2000 (PG-13)** John Grady Cole (Damon) is a dispossessed Texas cowboy in the late 1940s who, along with his buddy Lacey Rawlins (Thomas) and teen misfit Blevins (Black), crosses the border for, he hopes, a better life in Mexico. What he finds is an ill-fated romance with the beautiful daughter (Cruz) of a possessive rancher (Blades). It's pretty, all right. But thanks to Thornton's uneven pacing and inability to settle on a visual style, the story, and splendor, of the book is lost somewhere along the way. Of the young (and also pretty) cast, Damon and especially Black fare the best. Based on the first book of Cormac McCarthy's Border Trilogy. **117m/C VHS, DVD.** Matt Damon, Penelope Cruz, Ruben Blades, Lucas Black, Henry Thomas, Robert Patrick, Julio Oscar Mechoso, Miriam Colon, Bruce Dern, Sam Shepard; *D:* Billy Bob Thornton; *W:* Ted Tally; *C:* Barry Markowitz; *M:* Marty Stuart. Natl. Bd. of Review '00: Screenplay.

All the Queen's Men 🦴🦴 **2002** After his mission to steal a German Enigma encoding machine is torpedoed by an arrogant British officer, American OSS agent O'Rourke (LeBlanc) is assigned to multinational commando team to try again. Only this time they'll be infiltrating a Nazi factory—as female workers. Cross-dressing comic Izzard, as team member Tony, is invaluable here, as he's the only one who looks comfortable in a dress or supplies any comic flair. Jumbled plot and bumbled comedic opportunities combine to thwart a good premise and excellent cast. **99m/C VHS, DVD.** Matt LeBlanc, Eddie Izzard, James Cosmo, Udo Kier, Edward Fox, Nicolette Krebitz, David Birkin, Oliver Korittke, Karl Markovics; *D:* Stefan Ruzowitzky; *W:* David Schneider; *C:* Wedigo von Schultzendorff; *M:* Joern-ewe Fahrenkrog-Petersen.

All the Real Girls 🦴🦴🦴 1/2 **2003 (R)** Sophomore effort of writer-director Green is a sincere and poignant look at youthful love. Paul (Schneider), a twentysomething Romeo who's broken more than a few hearts in town, finds the real thing in Noel (played wonderfully by Deschanel), the 18-year-old sister of his best friend, fresh out of boarding school. Fully captures the real and often awkward moments of young love and the pain and confusion that can come with it. Schneider also helped conceive and write the story. **108m/C VHS, DVD.** *US* Paul Schneider, Zooey Deschanel, Patricia Clarkson, Maurice Compte, Benjamin Mouton, Shea Whigham, Danny McBride; *D:* David Gordon Green; *W:* Paul Schneider, David Gordon Green; *C:* Tim Orr; *M:* David Wingo, Michael Linnen.

All the Right Moves 🦴🦴 1/2 **1983 (R)** Cruise is the high school football hero hoping for a scholarship so he can vacate pronto the dying Pennsylvania mill town where he grew up. At least he thinks that's what he wants to do. Further mixing up his own mixed feelings are his pushy, ambitious coach (Nelson, doing what he does best), his understanding dad (Cioffi) and supportive girlfriend (Thompson, in a notable early role). Strong performances push the relatively cliched melodrama into field goal range. Cinematographer Chapman's directorial debut. **90m/C VHS, DVD.** Tom Cruise, Lea Thompson, Craig T. Nelson, Christopher Penn, Charles Cioffi, Paul Carafotes, Dick Miller; *D:* Michael Chapman; *W:* Michael Kane; *C:* Jan De Bont; *M:* David (Richard) Campbell.

All the Rivers Run **1984** First made-for-cable miniseries. A young Australian girl spends her inheritance on a river boat and becomes the first female river captain in Australian history. Directed by George Miller of "Man from Snowy River" fame. **400m/C VHS.** *AU* Sigrid Thornton, John Waters, Diane Craig, Charles "Bud" Tingwell, Gus Mercurio; *D:* George Miller, Pino Amenta; *C:* David Connell. **CABLE**

All the Vermeers in New York 🦴🦴🦴 1/2 **1991** A stressed-out Wall Street broker flees to the soothing recesses of the Metropolitan Museum's Vermeer Room. There he meets a beautiful, manipulative French actress dreaming of success in Manhattan. Amidst the opulent art world of New York, the two pursue their relationship to an ultimately tragic end. Jost offers an inside look at the collision of commerce and art and the corrupt underside of New York in this elegant contemporary film. **87m/C VHS, DVD.** Emmanuelle Chaulet, Stephen Lack, Grace Phillips, Katherine Bean, Laurel Lee Kiefer, Gracie Mansion, Gordon Joseph Weiss, Roger Ruffin; *D:* Jon Jost; *W:* Jon Jost.

All the Way, Boys 🦴 1/2 **1973 (PG)** Two inept adventurers crash-land a plane in the Andes in the hope of discovering slapstick, but find none. "Trinity" cast up to no good. **105m/C VHS.** *IT* Terence Hill, Bud Spencer, Cyril Cusack, Michel Antoine; *D:* Giuseppe Colizzi.

All the Wrong Places 🦴 1/2 **2000** Twenty-somethings Marisa (Hillis) and Paul (Klavens), the children of successful parents, are struggling to find their own identities and careers. Marisa is trying to make it as a filmmaker, while spending much of her time on her therapist's couch, while Paul is working on his first novel. They've got a lot in common but most of it is little above slacker whining. **95m/C DVD.** *US* Ali Hillis, Alyce LaTourelle, Brian Patrick Sullivan, Jeremy Klavens, Judy Del Guidice; *D:* Martin Edwards; *W:* Martin Edwards; *C:* Bing Rao; *M:* Jody Elff.

All the Young Men 🦴🦴🦴 **1960** Fairly powerful men-uniting-in-battle story with an interesting cast, highlighted by Poitier in an early role. A tiny marine squadron overrun by the Chinese in the Korean War attempts to resist the numerous attackers. In their spare time, the men confront racial prejudice when a black man (guess who) takes command.

86m/B VHS. Alan Ladd, Sidney Poitier, James Darren, Glenn Corbett, Mort Sahl, Ana St. Clair, Paul (E.) Richards, Richard (Dick) Davalos, Lee Kinsolving, Joseph (Joe) Gallison, Paul Baxley, Charles Quinlivan, Michael Davis; ***D:*** Hall Bartlett; ***W:*** Hall Bartlett; ***C:*** Daniel F. Fapp; ***M:*** George Duning.

All Things Fair 1/2 *Lust och Fagring Stor; Love Lessons; Laererinden* **1995** Coming of age story set in neutral Sweden in 1943. Fifteen-year-old Stig (Widerberg, the director's son) has just arrived in Malmo to begin classes at his all-male school—a situation filled with sexual curiosity and repression. Stig is attracted to his beautiful teacher Viola (Lagercrantz), whose marriage to alcoholic traveling salesman Frank (von Bromssen) is less than ideal, and the duo begin an affair. Frank not only seems not to care but befriends his wife's youthful lover, although the situation is ripe for tragedy. Excellent performances, sensual air, though somewhat lacking in logical narrative. Swedish with subtitles. **128m/C VHS, DVD.** *DK SW* Johan Widerberg, Marika Lagercrantz, Tomas von Bromssen, Bjorn Kjellman, Charles A. Palmer; ***D:*** Bo Widerberg; ***W:*** Bo Widerberg; ***C:*** Morten Bruus.

All This and Heaven Too **1940** When a governess arrives at a Parisian aristocrat's home in the 1840s, she causes jealous tension between the husband and his wife. The wife is soon found murdered. Based on Rachel Field's best-seller. **141m/B VHS.** Charles Boyer, Bette Davis, Barbara O'Neil, Virginia Weidler, Jeffrey Lynn, Helen Westley, Henry Daniell, Harry Davenport, June Lockhart, Montagu Love, Anne Howard; ***D:*** Anatole Litvak; ***M:*** Max Steiner.

All Through the Night **1942** A very funny spy spoof as well as a thrilling crime story with Bogart playing a gambler who takes on a Nazi spy ring. Features memorable double-talk and a great auction scene that inspired the one with Cary Grant in "North by Northwest." Suspense builds throughout the film as Lorre appears in a sinister role as Pepi and Veidt gives a fine performance as the spymaster. **107m/B VHS, DVD.** Humphrey Bogart, Conrad Veidt, Karen Verne, Jane Darwell, Frank McHugh, Peter Lorre, Judith Anderson, William Demarest, Jackie Gleason, Phil Silvers, Barton MacLane, Martin Kosleck, Wallace Ford; ***D:*** Vincent Sherman; ***C:*** Sid Hickox; ***M:*** Adolph Deutsch.

All Tied Up 1/2 **1992 (R)** Ladies man Brian (Galligan) thinks he's found true love with Linda (Hatcher) but that doesn't mean he's stopped seeing other women. And when Linda finds out, she breaks it off. So Brian goes over to her house to work things out and gets tied up—literally—by Linda and her girlfriends. Talk about teaching a guy a lesson. **90m/C VHS, DVD.** Zach Galligan, Teri Hatcher, Tracy Griffith, Lara Harris; ***D:*** John Mark Robinson; ***W:*** Robert Madero, I. Markie Lane; ***M:*** Bernardo Bonezzi.

All You Need Is Cash *The Rutles* **1978** "The Rutles" star in this parody of The Beatles' legend, from the early days of the "Pre-Fab Four" in Liverpool to their worldwide success. A marvelous pseudo-documentary, originally shown on NBC-TV and with various SNL alumni, which captures the development of the Beatles and '60s rock with devastating effect. Served as the inspiration for "This Is Spinal Tap." **70m/C VHS, DVD.** *GB* Eric Idle, Neil Innes, Ricky Fataar, Dan Aykroyd, Gilda Radner, John Belushi, George Harrison, Paul Simon, Mick Jagger, John Halsey, Michael Palin, Bianca Jagger, Bill Murray, Gwen Taylor, Ron Wood, Jeannette Charles, Al Franken, Lorne Michaels, Tom Davis; ***D:*** Gary Weis, Eric Idle; ***W:*** Eric Idle; ***C:*** Gary Weis; ***M:*** Neil Innes. **TV**

Allan Quatermain and the Lost City of Gold 1/2 **1986 (PG)** While trying to find his brother, Quatermain discovers a lost African civilization, in this weak adaptation of an H. Rider Haggard adventure. An ostensible sequel to the equally shallow "King Solomon's Mines." **100m/C VHS, DVD.** Richard Chamberlain, Sharon Stone, James Earl Jones; ***D:*** Gary Nelson; ***W:*** Gene Quintano, Lee Reynolds; ***C:*** Frederick Elmes.

Allegheny Uprising 1/2 *The First Rebel* **1939** Set in 1759, the story of a frontiersman who clashes with a British military commander in order to stop the sale of firearms to Indians. The stars of "Stagecoach" are back on board in this lesser effort. Also available colorized. **81m/B VHS.** John Wayne, Claire Trevor, George Sanders, Brian Donlevy, Chill Wills, Moroni Olsen; ***D:*** William A. Seiter.

Allegro 1/2 **2005** Emotionally frigid pianist Zetterstrom (Thomson) is unable to tell his girlfriend Andrea (Christensen) that he loves her, which causes some bizarre time rupture. He loses his memories, which are sealed-off in a special section of Copenhagen called the Zone. When Zetterstrom returns to Copenhagen after ten years, he's instructed to go to Zone and see if he can recapture his past. Since the romantic leads have zero chemistry, this doesn't seem too important but the visual effects are kinda cool. Danish with subtitles. **88m/C DVD.** *CZ* Ulrich Thomsen, Henning Moritzen, Helena Christensen, Svetoslav Korolev; ***D:*** Christoffer Boe; ***W:*** Christoffer Boe, Mikawel Wulff; ***C:*** Manuel Alberto Claro; ***M:*** Thomas Knak.

Allegro Non Troppo **1976 (PG)** An energetic and bold collection of animated skits set to classical music in this Italian version of Disney's "Fantasia." Watch for the evolution of life set to Ravel's Bolero, or better yet, watch the whole darn movie. Features Nichetti (often referred to as the Italian Woody Allen, particularly by people in Italy) in the non-animated segments, who went on to write, direct, and star (he may have sold concessions in the lobby as well) in "The Icicle Thief." **75m/C VHS, DVD.** *IT* Maurizio Nichetti, Nestor Garay, Maria Giovannini; ***D:*** Bruno Bozzetto; ***W:*** Bruno Bozzetto, Guido Manuli, Maurizio Nichetti; ***C:*** Mario Masini.

Alley Cat **1984 (R)** Woman uses martial arts to fight back against a street gang that attacked her. **82m/C VHS, DVD.** Karin Mani, Robert Torti, Brit Helfer, Michael Wayne, Jon Greene; ***D:*** Edward Victor.

The Alley Cats **1965** Leslie, a part of Berlin's swinging '60s set, is being ignored by fiance Logan in favor of his affair with her friend Agnes. So Leslie decides to retaliate by having an affair with a painter, Christian, but since Leslie just can't stand to be alone, when Christian is called away on business, she succumbs to the charms of socialite Irena. **83m/B VHS, DVD.** Anna Arthur, Sabrina Koch, Karin (Karen) Field, Chaz Hickman, Harold Baerow, Uta Levka; ***D:*** Radley Metzger; ***W:*** Radley Metzger.

Alley Cats Strike 1/2 **2000** Four teen misfits have an interest in bowling that makes them outcasts among their hipper classmates. But then their skills could win them a major trophy and school glory. **88m/C VHS.** Robert Ri'chard, Kyle Schmid, Kaley Cuoco, Mimi Paley, Daphne Maxwell; ***D:*** Rod Daniel. **CABLE**

Allie & Me **1997** Gullible beautician Allie (Baron) wants to make some changes in her life but doesn't quite expect what happens when she teams up with wronged wife Michelle (Benson). They decide to take out their frustrations by committing a burglary but find the Beverly Hills abode occupied by stud Rodney (Wilder), whom they take as a hostage, and then Allie decides to fall in love with him. Lots of recognizable faces but the comedy doesn't quite come together. **86m/C VHS, DVD.** Joanne Baron, Lyndie Benson, James Wilder, Steven Prince, Ed Lauter, Lainie Kazan, Dyan Cannon, Harry Hamlin, Julianne Phillips; ***D:*** Michael Rymer; ***W:*** Michael Rymer; ***C:*** Rex Nicholson.

Alligator **1980 (R)** Dumped down a toilet 12 long years ago, lonely alligator Ramon resides in the city sewers, quietly eating and sleeping. In addition to feasting on the occasional stray human, Ramon devours the animal remains of a chemical plant's experiment involving growth hormones and eventually begins to swell at an enormous rate. Nothing seems to satisfy Ramon's ever-widening appetite: not all the people or all the buildings in the whole town, but he keeps trying, much to the regret of the guilt-ridden cop and lovely scientist who get to know each other while trying to nab the gator. Mediocre special effects are only a distraction in this witty eco-monster take. **94m/C VHS, DVD.** Robert Forster, Robin Riker, Jack Carter, Henry Silva, Dean Jagger, Michael V. Gazzo, Perry Lang, Bart Braverman, Angel Tompkins, Sue Lyon, Sydney Lassick, James Ingersoll, John Lisbon Wood, Robert Doyle, Patti Jerome; ***D:*** Lewis Teague; ***W:*** John Sayles, Frank Ray Perilli; ***C:*** Joseph Mangine; ***M:*** Craig Hundley.

Alligator 2: The Mutation **1990 (PG-13)** Not a sequel to 1980's surprisingly good "Alligator," but a bland rehash with a decent cast. Once again a toxic alligator grows to enormous size and menaces a community. A Donald-Trump-like villain and pro wrestlers (!) bring this up to date, but it's all on the level of a TV disaster movie; even the PG-13 rating is a bit too harsh. **92m/C VHS.** Steve Railsback, Dee Wallace, Joseph Bologna, Woody Brown, Bill Daily, Brock Peters, Richard Lynch, Holly Gagnier; ***D:*** Jon Hess; ***W:*** Curt Allen; ***C:*** Joseph Mangine.

Alligator Alley **1972** When two young divers witness a major drug deal, they become entangled in a web of danger they never expected. **92m/C VHS, DVD.** Steve Alaimo, John Davis Chandler, Willie Pastrano, Jeremy Slate, Cece Stone; ***D:*** William Grefe.

Alligator Eyes 1/2 **1990 (R)** Stranger wearing trouble like a cheap perfume enters the midst of a vacationing trio of New Yorkers. Their vulnerabilities are exposed by a young hitchhiker sporting a slinky polka dot ensemble and way cool sunglasses who insinuates herself into their vacation plans (not to mention their private lives), before the three realize she's blind and full of manipulative and vindictive tricks, thanks to the usual brutal childhood. Psycho-sexo-logical thriller has some fine performances and a promising beginning, before fizzling into celluloid cotton candy. **101m/C VHS.** Annabelle Larsen, Roger Kabler, Mary McLain, Allen McCullough, John MacKay; ***D:*** John Feldman; ***W:*** John Feldman; ***M:*** Sheila Silver.

The Allnighter **1987 (PG-13)** A college coed searches through the hypersexed beach-party milieu of her senior year for Mr. Right. Bangle Hoffs is directed by her mom, to no avail. **95m/C VHS, DVD.** Susanna Hoffs, John Terlesky, Joan Cusack, Michael Ontkean; ***D:*** Tamar Simon Hoffs; ***W:*** Tamar Simon Hoffs; ***C:*** Joseph D. Urbanczyk; ***M:*** Charles Bernstein.

Allonsanfan 1/2 **1973** Early Taviani, in which a disillusioned Jacobin aristocrat in 1816, after Napoleon has fallen, struggles with his revolutionary ideals and his accustomed lifestyle. Exciting score. In Italian with English subtitles. **115m/C VHS.** *IT* Marcello Mastroianni, Laura Betti, Renato de Carmine, Lea Massari, Mimsy Farmer, Claudio Cassinelli, Bruno Cirino, Michael Berger; ***D:*** Paolo Taviani, Vittorio Taviani; ***W:*** Paolo Taviani, Vittorio Taviani; ***C:*** Giuseppe Ruzzolini; ***M:*** Ennio Morricone.

All's Fair **1989** Silly and predictable comedy about executives who take on their spouses at weekend war games. An unfortunate waste of a good cast. **89m/C VHS.** George Segal, Sally Kellerman, Robert Carradine, Jennifer Edwards, Jane Kaczmarek, John Kapelos, Lou Ferrigno; ***D:*** Rocky Lane; ***C:*** Peter Lyons Collister.

Almanac of Fall **1985** Set in a claustrophobic apartment, where the occupants reveal all their deepest hostilies, fears, and obsessions. In Hungarian with English subtitles. **119m/C VHS, DVD.** *HU* Hedi Temessy, Erika Bodnar, Miklos B. Szekely, Pal Hetenyi, Janos Derzsi; ***D:*** Bela Tarr; ***W:*** Bela Tarr.

...Almost *Wendy Cracked a Walnut* **1990 (PG)** Arquette plays a curiously giddy bookworm with a vivid imagination. When her husband disappears on their anniversary, the man of her dreams shows up to sweep her off her feet. Is he real or is he simply another daydream? Almost a good time. **87m/C VHS, DVD.** *AU* Rosanna Arquette, Bruce Spence; ***D:*** Michael Pattinson.

Almost an Angel 1/2 **1990 (PG)** Another in a recent spate of angels and ghosts assigned back to earth by the head office. A life-long criminal (Hogan) commits a heroic act and finds himself a probationary angel returned to earth to gain permanent angel status. He befriends a wheelchair-bound man, falls in love with the guy's sister, and helps her out at a center for potential juvenile delinquents. Melodramatic and hokey in places, relying too much on Hogan's crocodilian charisma. **98m/C VHS, DVD.** Paul Hogan, Linda Kozlowski, Elias Koteas, Doreen Lang, Charlton Heston, David Alan Grier, Larry Miller, Douglas Seale, Parley Baer, Hank Worden; ***D:*** John Cornell; ***W:*** Paul Hogan; ***C:*** Russell Boyd; ***M:*** Maurice Jarre.

Almost Angels **1962** Two boys romp in Austria as members of the Vienna Boys Choir. Lesser sentimental Disney effort that stars the actual members of the Choir; not much of a draw for today's Nintendo-jaded young viewers. **85m/C VHS.** Vincent Winter, Peter Weck, Hans Holt; ***D:*** Steve Previn.

Almost Blue 1/2 **1993 (R)** A gigantic, slow-moving, movie cliche. Madsen is a sulky, hard-living sax player going off the deep end because of his wife's death. Walden is the good woman who comes along to save him from himself. Tenor saxman Ernie Watts doubles for Madsen. Do yourself a favor—skip the movie and listen to some good jazz instead. **98m/C VHS.** Michael Madsen, Lynette Walden, Garrett Morris, Gale Mayron, Yaphet Kotto; ***D:*** Keoni Waxman.

Almost Dead 1/2 **1994** Psychiatrist Katherine Roshak's (Doherty) mother committed suicide four years ago and suddenly her corpse is appearing to Katherine. When she visits Mom's grave, Katherine finds an empty coffin. So she teams up with a skeptical cop (Mandylor) to figure out what's going on. Lots of loose ends. Based on the novel "Resurrection" by William Valtos. **92m/C VHS.** Shannen Doherty, Costas Mandylor, John Diehl, William R. Moses; ***D:*** Ruben Preuss; ***W:*** Miguel Tejada-Flores; ***C:*** Zoran Hochstatter.

Almost Famous **2000 (R)** Fifteen-year-old budding rock critic William Miller's (Fugit) dream comes true after he bluffs his way into a Rolling Stone writing assignment covering a rising '70s rock band on tour. This ode to the music and youth culture of that decade may lack grit, but its sympathetic treatment of young Miller's coming-of-age amid groupies, drugs, rock and roll, and a worried, undupable mother (McDormand) achieves director Crowe's ends. The film's adoration of the music's energy and emotion appear to be the headliner here, but it never outperforms its devotion to character and relationship. Delicate performances by first-timer Fugit, and by Hudson as the more-than-a-groupie groupie, plus a memorable portrayal of the wise and slightly surly critic Lester Bangs by Hoffman. Based on Crowe's own experiences. **202m/C VHS, DVD.** Patrick Fugit, Philip Seymour Hoffman, Frances McDormand, Jason Lee, Billy Crudup, Kate Hudson, John Fedevich, Mark Kozelek, Fairuza Balk, Bijou Phillips, Anna Paquin, Noah Taylor, Jimmy Fallon, Zooey Deschanel, Liz Stauber, Eion Bailey, Mark Pellington, Terry Chen, Peter Frampton, Zack (Zach) Ward; ***Cameos:*** Jann Wenner; ***D:*** Cameron Crowe; ***W:*** Cameron Crowe; ***C:*** John Toll; ***M:*** Nancy Wilson. Oscars '00: Orig. Screenplay; Golden Globes '01: Film—Mus./Comedy, Support. Actress (Hudson); L.A. Film Critics '00: Actor (Douglas), Support. Actress (McDormand); Broadcast Film Critics '00: Orig. Screenplay, Support. Actress (McDormand).

Almost Heaven **2006** Alcoholic Canadian director Mark Brady (Logue) is hired for a low-rated fishing program in Scotland that's hosted by his bitter ex-wife Taya (Collins). The village is filled with the usual quirky characters and Mark finds romance with independent fishing guide Nicki (Mitchell) but is she enough to help keep him sober? **102m/C DVD.** *CA* Donal Logue, Tom Conti, Kirsty Mitchell, Joely Collins, Erin Karpluk; ***D:*** Shel Piercy; ***W:*** Shel Piercy, Richard Beattie; ***C:*** Oliver Cheesman; ***M:*** Richard G. Mitchell.

Almost Heroes 1/2 *Edwards & Hunt: The First American Road Trip* **1997 (PG-13)** Farley's last screen appearance teams him with Perry as explorers Edwards and Hunt, who are racing Lewis and Clark to the Pacific Ocean in 1804. Edwards (Perry) is a glory-seeking fop who's totally out of his league, Hunt (Farley) is a slovenly, clumsy tracker with a soft spot for toilet (or would that be outhouse?) humor. Along with a team of misfits and losers, the duo wreaks havok on the American frontier. Perry and Farley show some flashes of comic chemistry, but their left to fend for themselves by a script that's lost in the wilderness, sadly relying too much on Farley's patented self-destructive schtick. **87m/C VHS, DVD.** Chris Farley, Matthew Perry, Eugene Levy, Bokeem Woodbine, Lisa Barbuscia, Kevin Dunn, Hamilton Camp, Lewis Arquette; ***D:*** Christopher Guest; ***W:*** Tom Wolfe, Mark Nutter, Boyd Hale; ***C:*** Adam Kimmel, Kenneth Macmillan; ***M:*** C.J. Vanston; ***V:*** Harry Shearer.

Almost Human WOOF! *The Kidnap of Mary Lou* **1979 (R)** An Italian Mafia gorefest about a second-class don who kidnaps a businessman's daughter, and then has trouble trying to collect a ransom. For aficionados of Italian Mafia gorefests only (check your weapons at the door). **90m/C VHS, DVD.** *IT* Henry Silva, Tomas Milian, Laura Belli; ***D:*** Umberto Lenzi; ***M:*** Ennio Morricone.

Almost Partners 1987 Grandpa's ashes are in trouble. His urn and remains have been stolen. Fortunately, his teenage granddaughter and a detective are on the case. From the PBS "Wonderworks" series. **58m/C VHS.** Paul Sorvino, Royana Black, Mary Wickes; ***D:*** Alan Kingsberg. **TV**

Almost Peaceful *Un monde presque paisible* **2002** In 1946, a Jewish tailor is restarting his business and attempting to regain a life of normalcy. Deville quietly follows the Jewish employees—some who have survived the camps, some who have escaped the horrors but have fought their own war—as they stitch, sew, and try to restore themselves. Intertwined stories flow marvelously, providing poignant observation of the Holocaust aftermath. **90m/C DVD.** *FR* Simon Abkarian, Zabou Breitman, Denis Podalydes, Vincent Elbaz, Lubna Azabal, Stanislas Merhar, Clotilde Courau, Julie Gaynet, Malik Zidi; ***D:*** Michel DeVille; ***C:*** Andre Diot.

An Almost Perfect Affair 1979 (PG) Taxing romantic comedy about an ambitious independent American filmmaker who, after finishing a movie about an executed murderer, travels to the Cannes festival and proceeds to fall in love or lust with the wife of an Italian producer. Numerous inside jokes and capable performances nearly overcome script lethargy. **92m/C VHS, DVD.** Keith Carradine, Monica Vitti, Raf Vallone, Christian de Sica, Dick Anthony Williams; ***D:*** Michael Ritchie; ***W:*** Walter Bernstein; ***M:*** Georges Delerue.

Almost Pregnant 1/2 1991 (R) Linda Anderson (Roberts) desperately wants a baby, but her husband, Charlie (Conaway) is unable to get her pregnant. Dead set against artificial insemination, Linda decides to take a lover. Charlie doesn't want to lose her, so he goes along with her idea. Linda falls in love with the new guy; discovers he's had a vasectomy and takes yet another lover while continuing to see the other two guys. Hilarious complications abound in her outrageous quest for a baby. An unrated version containing explicit scenes is also available. **90m/C VHS.** Tanya Roberts, Jeff Conaway, Joan Severance, Dom DeLuise; ***D:*** Michael DeLuise; ***W:*** Fred Stroppel.

Almost Strangers *Perfect Strangers* **2001** Compelling thriller about family ties. Ernest Symon (Howell) arranges a complicated three-day family reunion at a London hotel, which is reluctantly attended by black sheep Raymond (Gambon) and his curious son Daniel (Macfadyen). Both see family photos of events neither of them can remember and then Daniel meets his up-to-no-good cousins Rebecca (Skinner) and Charles (Stephens). Are those family skeletons we hear rattling? **237m/C DVD.** *GB* Michael Gambon, Matthew MacFadyen, Claire Skinner, Toby Stephens, Lindsay Duncan, Peter Howell, Anton Lesser; ***D:*** Stephen Poliakoff; ***W:*** Stephen Poliakoff; ***C:*** Cinders Forshaw; ***M:*** Adrian Johnston. **TV**

Almost You 1985 (R) Normal marital conflicts and uncertainties grow exponentially when a wealthy New York City 30-something couple hires a lovely young nurse to help care for the wife after a car accident. An unsentimental marital comedy with a good cast that still misses. **91m/C VHS, DVD.** Brooke Adams, Griffin Dunne, Karen Young, Marty Watt, Christine Estabrook, Josh Mostel, Laura Dean, Dana Delany, Miguel Pinero, Joe Silver, Suzzy Roche, Spalding Gray; ***D:*** Adam Brooks; ***M:*** Jonathan Elias.

Aloha, Bobby and Rose 1/2 1974 (PG) A mechanic and his girlfriend in L.A. become accidentally involved in an attempted robbery and murder and go on the run for Mexico, of course. Semi-satisfying drama in the surf, with fine location photography. **90m/C VHS, DVD.** Paul LeMat, Dianne Hull, Robert Carradine, Tim McIntire, Noble Willingham, Leigh French; ***D:*** Floyd Mutrux; ***W:*** Floyd Mutrux; ***C:*** William A. Fraker.

Aloha Summer 1988 (PG) Six surfing teenagers of various ethnic backgrounds learn of love and life in 1959 Hawaii while riding the big wave of impending adulthood, with a splash of Kung Fu thrown in for good measure. Sensitive and bland. **97m/C VHS.** Chris Makepeace, Lorie Griffin, Don Michael Paul, Sho Kosugi, Yuji Okumoto, Tia Carrere; ***D:*** Tommy Lee Wallace; ***W:*** Bob Benedetto.

Alone Against Rome 1/2 1962 A muscle-bound warrior takes on the forces of Rome to avenge himself against a scornful woman. **100m/B VHS.** *IT* Lang Jeffries, Rossana Podesta, Phillippe LeRoy; ***D:*** Herbert Wise.

Alone in the Dark 1982 (R) Slash and dash horror attempt featuring four escaped patients from a mental hospital who decide that they must kill their doctor because they don't like him. Conveniently, a city-wide blackout provides the opportunity, as the good doctor defends home and family against the aging stars intent on chewing up as much scenery as possible. **92m/C VHS, DVD.** Jack Palance, Donald Pleasence, Martin Landau, Dwight Schultz; ***D:*** Jack Sholder; ***W:*** Jack Sholder.

Alone in the Dark WOOF! 2005 (R) If there's any justice, Tim Burton's grandson will one day film a lovingly campy biopic about director Uwe Boll. Heir apparent to Ed Wood, Boll follows up 2003's "House of the Dead" with yet another incoherent video game adaptation. Paranormal detective Edward Carnby (Slater) represses memories of an orphanage trauma as he travels the globe collecting mystical chotchkies and fighting poorly-lit bad guys. When his fellow orphans start disappearing, Carnby and his scientist girlfriend (Reid) team up to battle bargain-basement CGI terror dogs. The monsters are somehow tied to an extinct Indian tribe, but you'll be too busy groaning at Reid's phonetically sounded-out science talk or the ridiculously inane opening crawl to care. **96m/C DVD.** *US US CA GE* Christian Slater, Tara Reid, Stephen Dorff, Matthew (Matt) Walker, Will Sanderson, Darren Shahlavi, Karin Konoval, Ed Anders, Frank C. Turner, Mark Acheson, Craig Bruhnanski, Kwesi Ameyaw, Catherine Lough Haggquist; ***D:*** Uwe Boll; ***W:*** Elan Mastai, Michael Roesch, Peter Scheerer; ***C:*** Mathias Neumann; ***M:*** Bernd Wendlandt.

Alone in the Neon Jungle 1987 A glamorous big-city police captain is assigned to clean up the most corrupt precinct in town. Pleshette is untypically cast but still manages to make her role believable in a serviceable TV cop drama with more dialogue than action. **90m/C VHS, DVD.** Suzanne Pleshette, Danny Aiello, Georg Stanford Brown, Frank Converse, Joe Morton; ***D:*** Georg Stanford Brown.

Alone in the T-Shirt Zone 1986 A maniacal T-shirt designer lands in a mental institution. **81m/C VHS.** Michael Barrack, Taylor Gilbert, Bill Barron; ***D:*** Mikel B. Anderson; ***W:*** Mikel B. Anderson.

Alone in the Woods 1995 (PG) Ten-year-old Justin mistakenly gets into the wrong van while on his way to his family's annual mountain vacation. Turns out the duo in the van are would-be kidnappers after Chelsea Stuart, the daughter of a toy magnate and now Justin must escape and rescue Chelsea. **81m/C VHS, DVD.** Brady Bluhm, Chick Vennera, Matthias Hues, Laraine Newman, Daniel McVicar, Krystee Clark; ***D:*** John Putch; ***W:*** J. Riley Lagesen; ***C:*** Frank Johnson; ***M:*** David Lawrence. **VIDEO**

Alone with a Stranger 1999 (R) Long lost Evil Twin (Moses) learns that he has a rich brother. Evil Twin and girlfriend (Peeples) plan to kidnap Good Twin, sell his company, and scoot with the loot. But what about Good Twin's wife (Niven) and family? **90m/C DVD.** William R. Moses, Barbara Niven, Priscilla Barnes, Nia Peeples, Mindy Cohn; ***D:*** Peter Paul Liapis; ***W:*** Peter Paul Liapis, Richard Dana Smith; ***C:*** M. David Mullen; ***M:*** Alan Howarth.

Alone With Her 1/2 2007 Clumsy thriller with camera as voyeur. Doug (Hanks) is obsessed with Amy (Talancon) and sets up surveillance on her with hidden cameras after breaking into her apartment. He orchestrates nasty little surprises and then turns up as Amy's concerned friend but the tension never particularly increases, even when Doug goes to what should have been more creepy extremes. **78m/C DVD.** *US* Ana Claudia Talancon, Colin Hanks, Jordana Spiro, Jonathan Trent; ***D:*** Eric Nicholas; ***W:*** Eric Nicholas; ***C:*** Nathan Wilson; ***M:*** David E. Russo.

Along Came a Spider 2001 (R) Sequel to 1997's "Kiss the Girls" is actually a prequel storywise but Freeman does reprise his character of Detective Alex Cross. This time he must save a U.S. Senator's daughter who's been kidnapped by a serial killer. Freeman is easily the best thing in this convoluted, plot-deficient, murky mess. He makes every "yeah, right" moment (and there are many) palatable. Based on the novel by James Patterson. **103m/C VHS, DVD.** *US* Morgan Freeman, Monica Potter, Michael Wincott, Penelope Ann Miller, Michael Moriarty, Dylan Baker, Billy Burke, Jay O. Sanders, Kim Hawthorne, Mika Boorem, Anton Yelchin; ***D:*** Lee Tamahori; ***W:*** Marc Moss; ***C:*** Matthew F. Leonetti; ***M:*** Jerry Goldsmith.

Along Came Jones 1945 Cowboy Cooper, who can't handle a gun and is saddled with grumpy sidekick Demarest, is the victim of mistaken identity as both the good guys and the bad guys pursue him thinking he is a vicious killer. Young is the woman who rides to his defense. Offbeat and charming western parody based on a novel by Alan le May. **93m/B VHS, DVD.** Gary Cooper, Loretta Young, Dan Duryea, William Demarest; ***D:*** Stuart Heisler; ***W:*** Nunnally Johnson; ***C:*** Milton Krasner; ***M:*** Arthur Lange.

Along Came Polly 2004 (PG-13) There's something about Polly. Neurotic risk analyst (Stiller) meets wild child Polly (Aniston) and learns to let loose. Has the requisite number of sight gags involving bodily fluids and embarrassing situations (Stiller is a master at squeezing the humor out of both), but breaks no new ground and quickly become formulaic. Generic romantic comedy with a few laughs is otherwise forgettable. **91m/C VHS, DVD.** *US* Ben Stiller, Jennifer Aniston, Philip Seymour Hoffman, Debra Messing, Alec Baldwin, Hank Azaria, Bryan Brown, Michele Lee, Jsu Garcia, Bob (Robert) Dishy, Missi Pyle, Judah Friedlander, Kym E. Whitley, Kevin Hart; ***D:*** John Hamburg; ***W:*** John Hamburg; ***C:*** Seamus McGarvey; ***M:*** Theodore Shapiro.

Along for the Ride 1/2 2000 (R) Seriously disturbed Lulu (Griffith) checks herself out of the mental hospital and informs old boyfriend Ben (Swayze) that when she was a teen, she gave birth to their son and put him up for adoption. Somehow she manages to persuade him on a cross-country journey to Wisconsin to meet the now-teenaged kid. Naturally, this idea doesn't sit that well with Ben's wife Claire (Miller) who decides to put a stop to the nonsense. Goopy sentiment. **99m/C VHS, DVD.** Melanie Griffith, Patrick Swayze, Penelope Ann Miller, Joseph Gordon-Levitt, Richard Schiff, Annie Corley, Lee Garlington, Michael J. Pollard, Steven Bauer; ***D:*** John Kaye; ***W:*** John Kaye; ***C:*** Dion Beebe; ***M:*** Serge Colbert.

Along the Great Divide 1951 A U.S. marshal and his deputy battle pursuing vigilantes and the untamed frontier to bring a falsely accused murderer to trial (and of course, find the real bad guy). Douglas' first western has the usual horse opera cliches supported by excellent cinematography. **88m/B VHS.** Kirk Douglas, John Agar, Walter Brennan, Virginia Mayo; ***D:*** Raoul Walsh.

Along the Navaho Trail 1945 A cattle syndicate is threatening the local ranchers and Roy, aided by a band of gypsies, helps thwart the bad guys. **66m/B VHS.** Roy Rogers, Dale Evans, George "Gabby" Hayes, Douglas Fowley; ***D:*** Frank McDonald; ***W:*** Gerald Geraghty; ***C:*** William Bradford.

Along the Sundown Trail 1/2 1942 Standard western escapades as cowboy G-men round up the villains. **59m/B VHS.** William Boyd, Art Davis, Lee Powell, Julie Duncan, Kermit Maynard, Charles "Blackie" King; ***D:*** Sam Newfield.

Along with Ghosts *Tokaido obake dochu; Yokai Monsters 3: Along with Ghosts; Journey With Ghost Along Yokaido Road* **1969** A young girl discovers proof of corruption in her town, and her grandfather is murdered because of it. She flees in search of her father. Because her grandfather was murdered on holy ground, the Yokai agree to protect her and take revenge on her behalf. This is the third film in the Yokai trilogy. The monsters are finally a little less cutesy looking for this sequel, which is fitting considering the mythological reputation of the Yokai. **90m/C DVD.** *JP* Kojiro Hongo, Bokuzen Hidari, Pepe Hozumi, Masami Burukido, Mutsuhiro, Yoshito Yamaji; ***D:*** Yoshiyuki Kuroda, Kimiyoshi Yasuda; ***W:*** Tetsuro Yoshida; ***C:*** Hiroshi Imai; ***M:*** Michiaki Watanabe.

Alpha Beta 1/2 1973 A stage production set to film studying the break-up of a marriage, where all the husband and wife have in common is the children. Finney and Roberts efficiently carry the load. **70m/C VHS.** Albert Finney, Rachel Roberts; ***D:*** Anthony Page.

Alpha Dog 2006 (R) True crime saga resulting from sheer stupidity. Wannabe white gangsta drug dealer Johnny Truelove (Hirsch) feels dissed when customer Jake (Foster) refuses to pay his tab. So Johnny and his equally wasted posse take advantage of a run-in with Jake's naive 15-year-old half brother Zack (Yelchin) and decide to hold him as collateral. Cohort Frankie (a convincing Timberlake) becomes Zack's de-facto babysitter and introduces him to their indulgent SoCal life—that is until someone finally realizes that kidnapping is a serious crime. A "River's Edge" for 21st-century teens. **117m/C DVD, HD DVD.** *US* Emile Hirsch, Justin Timberlake, Ben Foster, Anton Yelchin, Shawn Hatosy, Bruce Willis, Sharon Stone, David Thornton, Fernando Vargas, Amanda Seyfried, Dominique Swain, Olivia Wilde, Lukas Haas, Vincent Kartheiser, Harry Dean Stanton, Alex Kingston, Heather Wahlquist; ***D:*** Nick Cassavetes; ***W:*** Nick Cassavetes; ***C:*** Robert Fraisse; ***M:*** Aaron Zigman.

The Alpha Incident 1/2 1976 (PG) Time-worn doomsday drama about an alien organism with the potential to destroy all living things. Government works hard to cover up. **86m/C VHS, DVD.** Ralph Meeker, Stafford Morgan, John Goff, Carol Irene Newell, John Alderman; ***D:*** Bill Rebane.

Alpha Male 1/2 2006 The time switch between the present and 10 years in the past can be confusing but this is an otherwise decent family drama. Wealthy Jim (Huston) has made a good life for wife Alice (Ehle) and their two children, despite his temper and domineering attitude. After Jim dies from cancer, officious son Jack (Wells) takes it badly when Alice decides to remarry, especially since widower Clive (Baladi) is his father's polar opposite. The situation comes to a boil when Alice throws Jack a lavish 21st birthday party. **100m/C DVD.** *GB* Danny Huston, Jennifer Ehle, Amelia Warner, Christopher Egan, Mark Wells, Patrick Baladi, Trudie Styler; ***D:*** Dan Wilde; ***W:*** Dan Wilde; ***C:*** Shane Daly; ***M:*** Stephen Warbeck.

Alphabet City 1984 (R) A drug kingpin who runs New York's Lower East Side has decided to turn over a new leaf, but first he must survive his last night as a criminal while figuring out a way to pay off his large debts. Very stylish and moody, but light on content and plot. **85m/C VHS, DVD.** Vincent Spano, Michael Winslow, Kate Vernon, Jami Gertz, Zohra Lampert, Raymond Serra, Ken Marino, Daniel Jordano, Miguel Pinero; ***D:*** Amos Poe; ***W:*** Amos Poe.

The Alphabet Killer 2008 (R) Loosely-based on the true story of a 1970s serial killer in Rochester, New York. Police detective Megan Paige (Dushku) becomes obsessed with a child killer case and has a breakdown after suffering hallucinations. Diagnosed as schizophrenic, Megan eventually returns to the force just as the killer, who chooses victims whose first and last names begin with the same letter, gets active again. Can she hold it together long enough to catch the killer this time? **100m/C DVD.** Eliza Dushku, Cary Elwes, Timothy Hutton, Tom Malloy, Michael Ironside, Martin Donovan, Melissa Leo, Bill Moseley, Carl Lumbly, Tom Noonan; ***D:*** Rob Schmidt; ***W:*** Tom Malloy; ***C:*** Joe DeSalvo; ***M:*** Eric Perlmutter.

The Alphabet Murders 🦴🦴 *ABC Murders* **1965** Picture this: Randall playing Agatha Christie's famous Belgian sleuth, Hercule Poirot, and Rutherford—in a cameo—as Miss Marple. As if that wouldn't be enough to make Dame Agatha roll over in her grave, there's plenty of cloying wisecracking and slapsticking throughout. An adaptation of "The ABC Murders" in which Poirot stalks a literate killer who snuffs out his victims in alphabetical order. Hardly a must-see, unless you're hellbent on viewing the entire Randall opus. **90m/B VHS.** Tony Randall, Anita Ekberg, Robert Morley, Maurice Denham, Guy Rolfe, Sheila Allen, Margaret Rutherford, Julian Glover; ***D:*** Frank Tashlin.

Alphaville 🦴🦴🦴 *Alphaville, a Strange Case of Lemmy Caution; Alphaville, Une Etrange Aventure de Lemmy Caution* **1965** Engaging and inimitable Godard attempt at science fiction mystery. P.I. Lemmy Caution searches for a scientist in a city (Paris as you've never seen it before) run by robots and overseen by a dictator. The futuristic techno-conformist society must be upended so that Caution may save the scientist as well as nonconformists everywhere. In French with subtitles. **100m/B VHS, DVD.** *FR* Eddie Constantine, Anna Karina, Akim Tamiroff, Howard Vernon, Laszlo Szabo, Michel Delahaye, Jean-Pierre Leaud; ***D:*** Jean-Luc Godard; ***W:*** Jean-Luc Godard; ***C:*** Raoul Coutard; ***M:*** Paul Misraki. Berlin Intl. Film Fest. '65: Golden Berlin Bear.

Alpine Fire 🦴🦴 1/2 **1989 (R)** Coming of age story about an adolescent girl and her deaf-mute brother living an isolated life in the Swiss Alps. When life on the mountain overwhelms them, they turn to each other for love. Sharply observed with a naturalistic style, elevating the proceedings above mere voyeurism. **119m/C VHS.** *SI* Thomas Knock, Johanna Lier, Dorothea Moritz, Rolf Illig; ***D:*** Fredi M. Murer.

Already Dead 🦴 1/2 **2007 (R)** Thomas Archer (Eldard) has a great job and a beautiful wife and son. Then the Archer home is robbed, his wife is brutalized, and his son is killed. The police can't find the criminals so Archer turns to a shadow group that promises to deliver those responsible and then give Archer the opportunity to deal with them as he sees fit. **93m/C DVD.** Ron Eldard, Til Schweiger, Christopher Plummer, Patrick Kilpatrick, Marisa Coughlan; ***D:*** Joe Otting; ***W:*** Joe Chappelle; ***C:*** Eric Trageser; ***M:*** Nathan Furst. **VIDEO**

Alsino and the Condor 🦴🦴🦴 **1982 (R)** An acclaimed Nicaraguan drama about a young boy, caught in war-torn Nicaragua between the Somoza government and the Sandinista rebels, who dreams of flying above the human strife. In Spanish with English subtitles. **89m/C VHS.** *NI* Dean Stockwell, Alan Esquivel; ***D:*** Miguel Littin; ***W:*** Miguel Littin.

Altered States 🦴🦴🦴 **1980 (R)** Obsessed with the task of discovering the inner man, Hurt's ambitious researcher ignores his family while consuming hallucinogenic drugs and floating in an immersion tank. He gets too deep inside, slipping way back through the evolutionary order and becoming a menace in the process. Confusing script based upon Chayefsky's (alias Sidney Aaron) confusing novel is supported by great special effects and the usual self-indulgent and provocative Russell direction. Chayefsky eventually washed his hands of the project after artistic differences with the producers. Others who departed from the film include initial director William Penn and special effects genius John Dykstra (relieved ably by Bran Ferren). Hurt's a solemn hoot in his first starring role. **103m/C VHS, DVD.** William Hurt, Blair Brown, Bob Balaban, Charles Haid, Dori Brenner, Drew Barrymore, Miguel Godreau, Thaao Penghlis, Peter Brandon, Charles White Eagle, Meghan Jeffers, Jack Murdock, John Larroquette; ***D:*** Ken Russell; ***W:*** Paddy Chayefsky, Sidney Aaron; ***C:*** Jordan Cronenweth; ***M:*** John Corigliano.

Alternative 🦴🦴 **1976** A female magazine editor finds herself unmarried and quite pregnant. She is caught in a tug-of-war between the baby's father and her current lover. Dated liberated woman and career snoozer. **90m/C VHS.** *AU* Wendy Hughes, Peter Adams, Alwyn Kurts, Carla Hoogeveen, Tony Bonner; ***D:*** Paul Eddy; ***W:*** Tony Morphett; ***C:*** Russell Boyd; ***M:*** Bob Young.

Alvarez Kelly 🦴🦴 1/2 **1966** Offbeat western with Holden as the Mexican-Irish Kelly who has just sold a herd of cattle to the North during the Civil War. Confederate officer Widmark kidnaps Holden in an effort to have the cattle redirected to the South. Aided by the traditional women in the midst of men intent on double-crossing each other, a fierce hatred develops between the two, erupting into violence. Sleepy performance by Holden is countered by an intensive Widmark. Based on a true Civil War incident, the script occasionally wanders far afield with the cattle, who cleverly heighten the excitement by stampeding. **109m/C VHS, DVD.** William Holden, Richard Widmark, Janice Rule, Patrick O'Neal, Harry Carey Jr., Victoria Shaw, Roger C. Carmel, Indus Arthur; ***D:*** Edward Dmytryk; ***W:*** Elliott Arnold, Franklin Coen; ***C:*** Joe MacDonald; ***M:*** Johnny Green.

Alvin and the Chipmunks 🦴🦴 1/2 **2007 (PG)** Alvin, Simon, and Theodore (now digitally rendered) bring their chipmunk schtick into the twenty-first century, and mostly pull it off. Dave Seville (Lee) finds the trio in a muffin basket, quickly discovering their ability not only to speak, but to sing. Soon enough, a hustling promoter (Cross) takes their act on the road, where, sadly, the chipmunks fall victim to burn-out and must lip-sync the rest of their shows. (It ain't the '50s.) Lots of fun for nostalgic baby-boomers and kiddies alike; featuring techno and hip-hop remixes of the Chipmunks' classics. **92m/C DVD.** *US* Jason Lee, David Cross, Cameron Richardson, Jane Lynch; ***D:*** Tim Hill; ***W:*** Jon Vitti, Will McRobb, Chris Viscardi; ***C:*** Peter Lyons Collister; ***M:*** Christopher Lennertz; ***V:*** Justin Long, Matthew Grey Gubler, Jesse McCartney.

Alvin and the Chipmunks: The Squeakuel 🦴 1/2 **2009 (PG)** The unruly rodent trio of Alvin, Simon, and Theodore are back! This time around, Dave Seville (Lee) is laid up in a French hospital (thanks to Alvin) and the boys are inevitably left in the care of Dave's lazy video-game playing cousin Toby (Levi). Former promoter Ian (Cross) is angry that the Chipmunks aren't his to manage anymore but soon comes across the female Chipettes—Eleanor, Jeanette, and Brittany—who he pits against the boys. Mayhem ensues with plenty of pop music mixes to entertain the kiddies though its weak and predictable plot makes it a far squeak from the original. **88m/C DVD.** *US* Jason Lee, Zachary Levi, David Cross, Bridgit Mendler, Wendie Malick; ***D:*** Betty Thomas; ***W:*** Jonathan Aibel, Glenn Berger, Will McRobb, Chris Viscardi, Jon Vitti; ***C:*** Anthony B. Richmond; ***M:*** Brian Bulman; ***V:*** Justin Long, Matthew Grey Gubler, Jesse McCartney, Anna Faris, Christina Applegate, Amy Poehler.

Alvin Purple 🦴 1/2 **1973 (R)** Pedestrian comedy about a Mr. Purple, an ordinary Aussie who sells waterbeds and is for some reason constantly being pursued by throngs of sexually insatiable women. Fortunately, he too enjoys sex, even though complications abound. Sexual situations, double entendres, and a script that aims for cleverness (but rarely attains it) somehow made the lust romp a hit in its native Australia, while worldwide it helped establish a market for Down Under cinema. Shot in Melbourne, and followed by "Alvin Rides Again." **97m/C VHS.** *AU* Graeme Blundell, George Whaley, Ellie MacLure, Penne Hackforth-Jones; ***D:*** Tim Burstall; ***W:*** Alan Finney, Alan Hopgood, Tim Burstall.

Alvin Rides Again 🦴🦴 **1974** The sexually insatiable Alvin Purple is asked to impersonate an American gangster who was accidentally killed. Another Aussie sex farce from the original writers, who conspire to create a decent sequel to "Alvin Purple," with much of the same cast and crew. **89m/C VHS.** *AU* Graeme Blundell, Alan Finney, Briony Behets, Frank Thring Jr., Jeff Ashby, Chantal Contouri; ***D:*** David Bilcock, Robin Copping; ***W:*** Tim Burstall, Alan Hopgood, Alan Finney; ***C:*** Robin Copping.

Always 🦴🦴🦴 **1985 (R)** Jaglom fictionally documents his own divorce and reconciliation with Patrice Townsend: set in the director's home and starring his friends and family, the film provides comic insight into the dynamics of married/about-to-be-married/and used-to-be-married relationships. Set at a Fourth of July barbecue, this bittersweet romantic comedy is a veritable feast for Jaglom fans, but not everyone will find the director's free-form narrative to their taste. **105m/C VHS, DVD.** Henry Jaglom, Patrice Townsend, Bob Rafelson, Melissa Leo, Andre Gregory, Michael Emil, Joanna Frank, Alan Rachins, Jonathan Kaufer; ***D:*** Henry Jaglom; ***W:*** Henry Jaglom; ***C:*** Hanania Baer.

Always 🦴🦴 1/2 **1989 (PG)** A hotshot pilot (Dreyfuss) meets a fiery end and finds that his spirit is destined to become a guardian angel to the greenhorn fire-fighting flyboy (Johnson) who steals his girl's heart. Warm remake of "A Guy Named Joe," one of Spielberg's favorite movies. Sparks between Dreyfuss and Hunter eventually ignite, but Goodman delivers the most heat. Hepburn makes an appearance as the angel who guides Dreyfuss. An old-fashioned tree-burner romance that includes actual footage of the 1988 Yellowstone fire. **123m/C VHS, DVD.** Holly Hunter, Richard Dreyfuss, John Goodman, Audrey Hepburn, Brad Johnson, Marg Helgenberger, Keith David, Roberts Blossom, Dale Dye; ***D:*** Steven Spielberg; ***W:*** Jerry Belson; ***C:*** Mikael Salomon; ***M:*** John Williams.

Always Outnumbered Always Outgunned 🦴🦴🦴 **1998 (R)** Character study follows ex-con Socrates Fortlow (Fishburne in a dynamic performance). A convicted murderer, he's now trying to lead a non-violent life on the violent streets of L.A.'s Watts, maintain his dignity, and find a job. But none of this is easy. Adapted from the book by Mosley, who wrote the teleplay. **110m/C VHS, DVD.** Laurence Fishburne, Bill Cobbs, Natalie Cole, Daniel Williams, Laurie Metcalf, Bill Nunn, Cicely Tyson, Isaiah Washington IV; ***D:*** Michael Apted; ***W:*** Walter Mosley; ***C:*** John Bailey; ***M:*** Michael Franti. **CABLE**

Always Will 🦴🦴 1/2 **2006 (PG)** High-school senior Will discovers his elementary school's time capsule and it allows him to revisit his past and change decisions he now regrets. But his changes impact his present in unexpected ways and Will wonders if selfishness is the true problem and if he needs to accept his past and move on. **95m/C DVD.** Andrew Baglini, John Schmidt, Mark Schroeder, Noelle Meixell, Bart Mallard, Jody Seymour; ***D:*** Michael Sammaciccia; ***W:*** Michael Sammaciccia; ***C:*** Michael Sammaciccia; ***M:*** Michael Aharon. **VIDEO**

Amadeus 🦴🦴🦴 1/2 **1984 (PG)** Entertaining adaptation by Shaffer of his play about the intense rivalry between 18th century composers Antonio Salieri and Wolfgang Amadeus Mozart. Abraham's Salieri is a man who desires greatness but is tortured by envy and sorrow. His worst attacks of angst occur when he comes into contact with Hulce's Mozart, an immature, boorish genius who, despite his gifts, remains unaffected and delighted by the beauty he creates while irking the hell out of everyone around him. Terrific period piece filmed on location in Prague; excellent musical score, beautiful sets, nifty billowy costumes, and realistic American accents for the 18th century Europeans. ♫ Concert No. 27 for Pianoforte and Orchestra in B Flat Major; Ave Verum Corpus; A Quintet For Strings in E Flat; A Concerto for Clarinet and Orchestra in A Major; Number 39 in E-Flat Major; Number 40 in G Minor; Number 41 in C Major. **158m/C VHS, DVD, Blu-ray Disc.** F. Murray Abraham, Tom Hulce, Elizabeth Berridge, Simon Callow, Roy Dotrice, Christine Ebersole, Jeffrey Jones, Kenny Baker, Cynthia Nixon, Vincent Schiavelli; ***D:*** Milos Forman; ***W:*** Peter Shaffer; ***C:*** Miroslav Ondricek; ***M:*** John Strauss. Oscars '84: Actor (Abraham), Adapt. Screenplay, Art Dir./Set Dec., Costume Des., Director (Forman), Makeup, Picture, Sound; AFI '98: Top 100; Cesar '85: Foreign Film; Directors Guild '84: Director (Forman); Golden Globes '85: Actor—Drama (Abraham), Director (Forman), Film—Drama, Screenplay; L.A. Film Critics '84: Director (Forman), Film, Screenplay.

Amanda and the Alien 🦴 1/2 **1995 (R)** Dumb saga finds flaky Californian Amanda (Eggert) taking care of a sex-starved, shape-changing extraterrestrial (Meneses) while a couple of feds hunt him down. Based on a story by Robert Silverberg. **94m/C VHS.** Alex Meneses, Nicole Eggert, Michael Dorn, Stacy Keach, Michael C. Bendetti, Richard Speight Jr., David Millbern; ***D:*** Jon Kroll; ***W:*** Jon Kroll. **CABLE**

Amarcord 🦴🦴🦴 1/2 *I Remember* **1974 (R)** Semi-autobiographical Fellini fantasy which takes place in the village of Rimini, his birthplace. Focusing on the young Zanin's impressions of his town's colorful slices of life, Fellini takes aim at fascism, family life, and religion in 1930s Italy. Visually ripe, delivering a generous, occasionally uneven mix of satire, burlesque, drama, and tragicomedic lyricism. Considered by people in the know as one of Fellini's best films and the topic of meaningful discussions among art film students everywhere. **124m/C VHS, DVD.** *IT* Magali Noel, Bruno Zanin, Pupella Maggio, Armando Brancia; ***D:*** Federico Fellini; ***W:*** Federico Fellini, Tonino Guerra; ***C:*** Giuseppe Rotunno; ***M:*** Nino Rota. Oscars '74: Foreign Film; N.Y. Film Critics '74: Director (Fellini), Film.

Amarilly of Clothesline Alley 🦴🦴 1/2 **1918** Amarilly (Pickford) gets a job as a New York dance hall cigarette girl and is around to help wealthy slumming playboy Gordon Phillips (Kerry) after he gets into a fight. Phillips becomes convinced he loves Amarilly, despite her social inferiority, but Amarilly comes to realize she should stick with those that know her best, including neighborhood beau, Terry (Scott). **77m/B VHS, DVD.** Mary Pickford, William Scott, Norman Kerry, Ida Waterman, Kate Price, Margaret Landis; ***D:*** Marshall Neilan; ***W:*** Frances Marion; ***C:*** Walter Stradling.

The Amateur 🦴 1/2 **1982 (R)** Computer technologist for the CIA dives into a plot of international intrigue behind the Iron Curtain when he investigates the death of his girlfriend, murdered by terrorists. Confused and ultimately disappointing spy drama cursed with a wooden script written by Littell, based on his novel. **112m/C VHS, DVD.** John Savage, Christopher Plummer, Marthe Keller, Arthur Hill, Ed Lauter; ***D:*** Charles Jarrott; ***W:*** Robert Littell.

Amateur 🦴🦴🦴 **1994 (R)** Former nun Huppert, trying to make a living writing pornography, hooks up with an amnesiac (Donovan) who turns out to have a criminal past and a porno actress wife (Lowensohn) who wants him dead. Blackmail plot has oddball characters racing through dark and evocative settings while unfolding a tale loaded with offbeat oppositions and an irresistibly bizarre romantic triangle. Lively and playful without becoming pretentious, Hartley's self-described "action thriller... with one flat tire" evokes his typical deadpan subtle style. **105m/C VHS, DVD.** Isabelle Huppert, Martin Donovan, Elina Lowensohn, Damian Young, Chuck Montgomery, David Simonds, Pamela Stewart, Terry Alexander; ***D:*** Hal Hartley; ***W:*** Hal Hartley; ***C:*** Michael Spiller; ***M:*** Hal Hartley, Jeff Taylor.

Amateur Night 🦴 **1985** Sloppy musical comedy about the backstage bickering occuring during the amateur night at a famous nightclub. **91m/C VHS.** Geoffrey Deuel, Dennis Cole, Allen Kirk; ***D:*** Eddie Beverly Jr.; ***W:*** Tom Dempsey.

Amazing Adventure 🦴🦴 *Romance and Riches; The Amazing Quest of Ernest Bliss; Riches and Romance* **1937** A millionaire wins a bet when he rises from a chauffeur's position to the executive board room without using his wealth. Though not particularly amazing, lightweight English comedy has Grant working hard to charm over and above the demands of the dated formula, a performance he undertook during a vacation from Hollywood. Adapted from a novel by E. Phillips Oppenheim. **63m/C VHS, DVD.** Cary Grant, Mary Brian, Henry Kendall, Leon M. Lion, Ralph Richardson; ***D:*** Alfred Zeisler.

The Amazing Colossal Man 🦴🦴 **1957** A standard '50s sci-fi film about atomic radiation. Colonel Manning is exposed to massive doses of plutonium when an experiment backfires (literally). The former good-guy grows to 70 feet and starts taking out his anger on a helpless Las Vegas. Can anything stop his murderous rampages? Followed by "War of the Colossal Beast." **79m/B VHS.** Glenn Langan, Cathy Downs, William (Bill) Hudson, James Seay, Russ Bender, Lyn Osborn, Frank Jenks, Hank Patterson; ***D:*** Bert I. Gordon; ***W:*** Bert I. Gordon, Mark Hanna; ***C:*** Joseph Biroc; ***M:*** Albert Glasser.

The Amazing Dobermans 1976 **(G)** Family-oriented pooch performance piece featuring Astaire in one of his lesser roles. Ex-con man Astaire and his five trained Dobermans assist an undercover agent in foiling a small-time criminal's gambling and extortion racket. The last in a series that includes "The Daring Dobermans" and "The Doberman Gang." **96m/C VHS.** Fred Astaire, Barbara Eden, James Franciscus, Jack Carter, Billy Barty, Parley Baer; ***D:*** Byron Ross Chudnow; ***M:*** Alan Silvestri.

Amazing Dr. Clitterhouse

1938 Satirical gangster saga has criminologist Dr. Clitterhouse (Robinson) so fascinated by crime that he commits a few jewel robberies just to test out that bad guy rush. He contacts a fence, luscious Jo Keller (Trevor), who gets Clitterhouse an in with gangster Rocks Valentine (Bogart). Clitterhouse sucessfully masterminds some heists for Valentine—who becomes jealous of Clitterhouse's brain power and things just get more wacky from there (including a farcical trial). This is definitely Robinson's show. **87m/B VHS.** Edward G. Robinson, Claire Trevor, Humphrey Bogart, Gale Page, Donald Crisp, Maxie "Slapsie" Rosenbloom, Thurston Hall, Allen Jenkins, John Litel, Henry O'Neill, Ward Bond, Curt Bois; ***D:*** Anatole Litvak; ***W:*** John Huston, John Wexley; ***C:*** Gaetano Antonio "Tony" Gaudio; ***M:*** Max Steiner.

Amazing Grace 1974 Some righteous mothers led by Moms Mabley go up against corrupt city politics in this extremely dated comedy that was cast with a sense of the absurd. **99m/C VHS, DVD.** Moms (Jackie) Mabley, Slappy (Melvin) White, Moses Gunn, Rosalind Cash, Dolph Sweet, Butterfly McQueen, Stepin Fetchit; ***D:*** Stan Lathan; ***W:*** Matt Robinson; ***C:*** Edward R. Brown, Sol Negrin.

Amazing Grace 1992 Eighteen-year-old Jonathan leaves home to share his friend Mickey's apartment. He meets Thomas, who has just returned to Israel after years in New York, and they begin a tentative relationship. But Thomas is hiding the fact that he may be HIV-positive and tries to keep a distance from the eager Jonathan. Hebrew with subtitles. **95m/C VHS.** *IS* Rivka Michaely, Sharon Alexander, Gal Hoyberger, Hina Rozovska; ***D:*** Amos Guttman.

Amazing Grace **2006 (PG)** Sincere and forceful bio of evangelical Christian William Wilberforce (Gruffudd), a member of the House of Commons, who spent his years in the British Parliament introducing antislavery legislation. Tells the crusader's story with flashbacks, introducing both foes and friends, including former slave trader John Newton (Finney), who wrote the title hymn (rousingly sung by Gruffudd), as part of his atonement. Senegalese singer N'Dour makes his film debut as freed slave and author Oloudah Equiano. **111m/C DVD.** *GB* Ioan Gruffudd, Romola Garai, Albert Finney, Michael Gambon, Rufus Sewell, Ciaran Hinds, Toby Jones, Nicholas Farrell, Sylvestria Le Touzel, Stephan Campbell Moore, Benedict Cumberbatch, Youssou N'Dour; ***D:*** Michael Apted; ***W:*** Steven Knight; ***C:*** Remi Adefarasin; ***M:*** David Arnold.

Amazing Grace & Chuck 1987 **(PG)** Perhaps the only anti-war/sports fantasy ever made. After a visit to a Minuteman missile site in Montana, 12-year-old Little Leaguer Chuck learns of the dangers of nuclear arms. He begins a protest by refusing to play until the nations come to a peace agreement. In a sudden surge of social conscience, athletes worldwide put down their equipment and join in droves, starting with pro-basketball star Amazing Grace Smith (Denver Nugget English). Capra-like fantasy has good intentions but ultimately lacks two key elements: coherency and plausibility. **115m/C VHS.** Jamie Lee Curtis, Gregory Peck, William L. Petersen, Joshua Zuehlke, Alex English; ***D:*** Mike Newell; ***C:*** Robert Elswit; ***M:*** Elmer Bernstein.

The Amazing Howard Hughes 1/2 **1977** Reveals the full story of the legendary millionaire's life and career, from daring test pilot to inventor to Hollywood film producer to isolated wealthy paranoiac with a germ phobia. Lingers on the rich guy with big problems theme. Big-budget TV drama with a nice performance by Jones. **119m/C VHS, DVD.** Tommy Lee Jones, Ed Flanders, James Hampton, Tovah Feldshuh, Lee Purcell; ***D:*** William A. Graham. **TV**

The Amazing Mrs. Holiday 1/2 **1943** Pleasant Durbin outing finds the star playing the daughter of missionaries working in China. Ruth accompanies a group of Chinese orphans aboard a ship bound for San Francisco, aided by steward Timothy (Fitzgerald). She wants the children to stay together, so Timothy passes Ruth off as the wife of a shipping magnate, who's been lost at sea. Ruth admits her deception to the man's grandson Tom (O'Brien) and convinces him that it's okay that she and the children stay in the family mansion. **98m/B VHS.** Deanna Durbin, Edmond O'Brien, Barry Fitzgerald, Arthur Treacher, Harry Davenport, Grant Mitchell, Frieda Inescort, Elisabeth Risdon; ***D:*** Bruce Manning; ***W:*** Frank Ryan, John Jacoby; ***C:*** Elwood "Woody" Bredell; ***M:*** Frank Skinner, Hans J. Salter.

Amazing Mr. Blunden 1/2 **1972 (G)** Solid kidvid about two youngsters aided by a ghost who travel back in time to save the lives of two murdered children. Adapted by Jeffries from Antonia Barber's novel, "The Ghosts." **100m/C VHS.** Laurence Naismith, Lynne Frederick, Garry Miller, Marc Granger, Rosalyn London, Diana Dors; ***D:*** Lionel Jeffries; ***M:*** Elmer Bernstein.

The Amazing Mr. X 1/2 *The Spiritualist* **1948** When a woman's husband dies, she tries to contact him via a spiritualist. Things are not as they seem however, and the medium may just be part of an intricate scheme to defraud the woman. **79m/B VHS, DVD.** Turhan Bey, Lynn Bari, Cathy O'Donnell, Richard Carlson, Donald Curtis, Virginia Gregg; ***D:*** Bernard Vorhaus; ***W:*** Ian McLellan Hunter, Muriel Roy Boulton; ***C:*** John Alton.

The Amazing Panda Adventure 1/2 *Little Panda; The Amazing Panda Rescue* **1995 (PG)** Ryan (Slater) is off to China during his spring break to visit dad Michael (Lang), who's working on a project to rescue the dwindling panda population. But there's poacher trouble and Ryan and young translator Ling (Ding) decide to rescue the preserve's panda cub, which has been animal-napped (where's Ace Ventura when you need him). Family fare, with a mixture of totally adorable real and animatronic pandas; filmed in the Sichuan province of China, home to the Wolong Nature Reserve which is famous for its successful breeding of the endangered giant pandas. Slater, in his first starring role, is the younger brother of Christian. **84m/C VHS, DVD.** Ryan Slater, Stephen Lang, Yi Ding, Wang Fei; ***D:*** Christopher Cain; ***W:*** Laurice Elehwany, Jeff Rothberg; ***C:*** Jack N. Green; ***M:*** William Ross.

The Amazing Spider-Man *Spider-Man* **1977** The Marvel Comics superhero's unique powers are put to the test when he comes to the rescue of the government by preventing an evil scientist from blackmailing the government for big bucks. The wall-walking webslinger has his origins probed (a grad student bit by a radioactive spider develops superhuman powers) in his live-action debut, which led to a short-lived TV series. **94m/C VHS.** Nicholas Hammond, David White, Lisa Eilbacher, Michael Pataki; ***D:*** E.W. Swackhamer. **TV**

Amazing Stories **1985** From the Steven Spielberg produced TV series. "The Mission" sees a WWII turret gunner trapped in an unusual predicament. In "The Wedding Ring," a man gives his wife a strange ring and bizarre situations ensue. **70m/C VHS.** Kevin Costner, Casey Siemaszko, Kiefer Sutherland, Danny DeVito, Rhea Perlman; ***D:*** Danny DeVito, Steven Spielberg. **TV**

The Amazing Transparent Man **WOOF! 1960** A mad scientist makes a crook invisible in order to steal the radioactive materials he needs. The crook decides to rob banks instead. Shot at the Texas State Fair for that elusive futuristic look. For Ulmer fans only. **58m/B VHS, DVD.** Douglas Kennedy, Marguerite Chapman, James J. Griffith, Ivan Triesault, Boyd 'Red' Morgan, Carmel Daniel, Jonathan Ledford, Norman Smith, Patrick Cranshaw, Kevin Kelly; ***D:*** Edgar G. Ulmer; ***W:*** Jack Lewis; ***C:*** Meredith Nicholson; ***M:*** Darrell Calker.

The Amazing Transplant **WOOF!** **1970** A sleaze-bag psycho has a "love enhancing" transplant, much to the pleasure of his sexual partners. Much to their and our dismay, however, he then kills them and bores us. **90m/C VHS, DVD.** Juan Fernandez, Linda Southern, Larry Hunter, Kim Pope; ***D:*** Doris Wishman; ***W:*** Doris Wishman; ***C:*** C. Davis Smith.

Amazon **1990 (R)** An adventure movie filmed in the Brazilian rainforest with an environmental message. A businessman being chased by the police in the Amazon jungle is rescued by a bush pilot who dreams of mining the Amazon's riches. A Brazilian woman enters the picture and persuades the businessman to help save the rainforest. Portions of the proceeds from the sale of this film go to the Rainforest Action Network. **88m/C VHS.** Kari Vaananen, Robert Davi, Rae Dawn Chong; ***D:*** Mika Kaurismaki.

Amazon Jail **1985** Scantily clad women go over the wall and promptly get caught by devil worshiping men in the jungle. They should have known better. Redeemed only by lingerie selection. **94m/C VHS, DVD.** Elisabeth Hartmann, Mauricio Do Valle, Sondra Graffi; ***D:*** Oswald De Oliveira.

Amazon Warrior **1997** Tara is a mercenary in a future world ruled by violence. The last survivor of her Amazon tribe, she sells her fighting skills to the highest bidder while searching for the leader of the rebel Marauder army, which massacred her people. Tara's well-equipped when that final showdown comes. **85m/C VHS.** J.J. Rodgers, Christine Lydon, Jimmy Jerman, Al Spencer, Raymond Storti; ***D:*** Dennis Devine; ***W:*** Steve Jarvis; ***M:*** David De Palo.

Amazon Women on the Moon *Cheeseburger Film Sandwich* **1987 (R)** A plotless, irreverent media spoof, depicting the programming of a slipshod TV station as it crams weird commercials and shorts around a comical '50s science fiction film. Inconsistent, occasionally funny anthology hangs together very loosely. Produced by Landis, with the usual amount of in-joke cameos and allusions to his other works of art. **85m/C VHS, DVD.** Rosanna Arquette, Steve Guttenberg, Steve Allen, B.B. King, Michelle Pfeiffer, Arsenio Hall, Andrew (Dice Clay) Silverstein, Howard Hesseman, Lou Jacobi, Carrie Fisher, Griffin Dunne, Sybil Danning, Henny Youngman, Monique Gabrielle, Paul Bartel, Kelly Preston, Ralph Bellamy, Russ Meyer, Steve Forrest, Joey Travolta, Ed Begley Jr., Forrest J Ackerman, Archie Hahn, Phil Hartman, Peter Horton, Charlie Callas, T.K. Carter, Dick Miller, Roxie Roker; ***D:*** John Landis, Joe Dante, Carl Gottlieb, Robert Weiss, Peter Horton; ***W:*** Michael Barrie, Jim Mulholland; ***C:*** Daniel Pearl; ***M:*** Ira Newborn.

The Amazons 1/2 **1984** Goofy drama about a beautiful doctor who discovers an underground organization of Amazon-descended women bent on taking over the world or at least making life hard for men while investigating a Congressman's mysterious death. **100m/C VHS.** Tamara Dobson, Jack Scalia, Stella Stevens, Madeleine Stowe, Jennifer Warren; ***D:*** Paul Michael Glaser; ***M:*** Basil Poledouris. **TV**

Amazons **1986 (R)** Tall, strong women who occasionally wander around nude search for a magical talisman that will overthrow an evil magician. **76m/C VHS, DVD.** Mindi Miller, Penelope Reed, Joseph Whipp, Willie Nelson, Danitza Kingsley; ***D:*** Alex Sessa.

Amazons and Gladiators **2001 (R)** The title just says it all, doesn't it? Beautiful slave girl joins up with an Amazon queen and her band of warriors to fight an evil Roman governor. **89m/C VHS, DVD.** *US GE* Jennifer Rubin, Patrick Bergin, Nichole Hiltz, Wendi Winburn, Melanie Gutteridge, Richard Norton; ***D:*** Zachary Weintraub; ***W:*** Zachary Weintraub; ***C:*** Thomas Hencz; ***M:*** Timothy S. (Tim) Jones. **VIDEO**

The Ambassador 1/2 *Peacemaker* **1984** An American ambassador (Mitchum) is sent to the Middle East to try to solve the area's deep political problems. He quickly becomes the target of terrorist attacks, and is blamed for the nation's unrest. To make matters worse, his wife is having an affair with a PLO leader. The President ignores him, forcing the ambassador to fend for himself. Talk about your bad days. Hudson's last feature. Based on Elmore Leonard's "52 Pickup," and remade a year later under its own title. **97m/C VHS, DVD.** Robert Mitchum, Ellen Burstyn, Rock Hudson, Fabio Testi, Donald Pleasence; ***D:*** J. Lee Thompson.

Ambassador Bill **1931** An Oklahoma rancher is appointed ambassador to a country in revolt. Rogers, of course, saves the day with his rustic witticisms. Based on the story "Ambassador from the United States" by Vincent Sheean. **68m/B VHS.** Will Rogers, Marguerite Churchill, Greta Nissen, Ray Milland, Tad Alexander, Gustav von Seyffertitz; ***D:*** Sam Taylor.

The Ambassador's Daughter

1956 The Parisian adventures of an American ambassador's daughter De Havilland and soldier Forsythe, who, unaware of her position, falls in love with her. Faltering comedy is supported by an expert cast (although nearly 40, De Havilland is charming as the young woman) with especially good performances from Menjou and Loy. **102m/C VHS.** Olivia de Havilland, John Forsythe, Myrna Loy, Adolphe Menjou, Edward Arnold, Francis Lederer, Tommy Noonan, Minor Watson; ***D:*** Norman Krasna; ***W:*** Norman Krasna.

Amber Waves 1/2 **1982** Credible drama about a generation-gap conflict between a Midwestern farmer (Weaver) and an irresponsible male model (Russell) who has coasted through life on con and charm. **98m/C VHS.** Dennis Weaver, Kurt Russell, Rossie (Ross) Harris, Mare Winningham, Wilford Brimley; ***D:*** Joseph Sargent. **TV**

Ambition 1/2 **1991 (R)** Scriptwriter/star Phillips gets a bone for chutzpah by taking an unsavory lead role; his character torments a paroled psycho so that the killer will kill again and inspire a true-crime bestseller. The plot looks good on paper, but onscreen it's padded and unconvincing. **99m/C VHS.** Lou Diamond Phillips, Clancy Brown, Cecilia Peck, Richard Bradford, Willard Pugh, Grace Zabriskie, Katherine Armstrong, John David (J.D.) Cullum, Haing S. Ngor; ***D:*** Scott Goldstein; ***W:*** Lou Diamond Phillips; ***M:*** Leonard Rosenman.

The Ambulance 1/2 **1990 (R)** A New York cartoonist witnesses a mysterious ambulance at work and decides to investigate. His probings uncover a plot to sell the bodies of dying diabetics. A surprisingly good no-money feature from low-budget king Cohen. Includes an appearance by Marvel Comics' Stan Lee as himself. **95m/C VHS.** Eric Roberts, James Earl Jones, Megan Gallagher, Richard Bright, Janine Turner, Eric (Hans Gudegast) Braeden, Red Buttons, Laurene Landon, Jill Gatsby, Nicholas Chinlund, James Dixon, Stan Lee; ***D:*** Larry Cohen; ***W:*** Larry Cohen; ***C:*** Jacques Haitkin; ***M:*** Jay Chattaway.

Ambush *Rukajarven Tie* **1999** Young lieutenant Eero is serving in the Finnish Army in 1941 pursuing Russian troops along the border. During his mission, Eero is able to briefly spend some time with his lovely fiancee Irina but must soon leave to go on a recon. He receives word that Irina has been killed by Russian soldiers and seeks revenge on any Russians he finds—turning from innocent soldier to dehumanized killer. Co-writer Tuuri adapted from his novel. Finnish with subtitles. **117m/C VHS, DVD.** *FI* Peter Franzen, Irina Bjorklund, Kari Vaananen, Kari Heiskanen, Taisto Reimalvoto; ***D:*** Olli Saarela; ***W:*** Olli Saarela, Antti Tuuri; ***C:*** Kjell Lagerros; ***M:*** Tuomas Kantelinen.

Ambush at Tomahawk Gap

1953 Three released prisoners go in search of hidden loot and tempers rise when the goods don't turn up. Then the Apaches show up. **73m/C VHS.** John Hodiak, John Derek, David Brian, Maria Elena Marques, Ray Teal; ***D:*** Fred F. Sears.

The Ambush Murders 1/2 **1982** True story of a stalwart white attorney defending a black activist accused of killing two cops. Not the compelling TV drama it could be, but still enjoyable. From Ben Bradlee Jr.'s novel. **100m/C VHS.** James Brolin, Dorian Harewood, Alfre Woodard, Louis Giambalvo, John McLiam, Teddy Wilson, Antonio Fargas, Amy Madigan; ***D:*** Steven Hilliard Stern. **TV**

Ambush Trail **1946** Stranger-in-town Steele metes out justice to help local ranchers while sidekick Saylor leaves 'em laughing. **60m/B VHS.** Bob Steele, Syd Saylor, I. Stanford Jolley, Lorraine Miller, Charles "Blackie" King, Kermit Maynard; ***D:*** Harry Fraser.

The Ambushers WOOF! 1967 Martin's third Matt Helm farce finds him handling a puzzling case involving the first United States spacecraft. When the craft is hijacked with Rule on board, it's Matt to the rescue, regaining control before unfriendly forces can take it back to Earth. Tired formula seems to have worn Martin out while the remainder of the cast goes to camp. Followed by "The Wrecking Crew." **102m/C VHS, DVD.** Dean Martin, Janice Rule, James Gregory, Albert Salmi, Senta Berger, Kurt Kasznar, Beverly Adams; ***D:*** Henry Levin; ***W:*** Herbert Baker; ***C:*** Burnett Guffey, Edward Colman; ***M:*** Hugo Montenegro.

Amelia 1/2 **2009 (PG)** Good-looking, if old-fashioned, biography of famed celebrity aviatrix Amelia Earhart based on Susan Butler's "East to the Dawn" and Elgin Long's "Amelia Earhart: The Mystery Solved." Director Nair highlights the wonder (and danger) of flying in the 1920s and 30s through Swank's sparkling lead performance and how the adventuresome Amelia dealt with worldwide fame as well as her unconventional marriage to New York publisher George Putnam (Gere). **111m/C DVD.** *US* Hilary Swank, Richard Gere, Ewan McGregor, Christopher Eccleston, Mia Wasikowska, Joe Anderson, Cherry Jones, William Cuddy; ***D:*** Mira Nair; ***W:*** Ronald Bass, Anna Hamilton Phelan; ***C:*** Stuart Dryburgh; ***M:*** Gabriel Yared.

Amelia Earhart: The Final Flight 1/2 **1994** Investigates the mysterious disappearance of pioneering aviatrix Amelia Earhart's 1937 flight to become the first pilot to circumnavigate the globe. Earhart (Keaton) and her navigator Fred Noonan (Hauer) disappeared over the Pacific Ocean and their fate has never been determined. Dern plays Earhart's husband, publisher George B. Putnam, who served as Amelia's manager and publicist. Based on the biography by Doris L. Rich. **95m/C VHS.** Diane Keaton, Rutger Hauer, Bruce Dern, Paul Guilfoyle, Denis Arndt, David Carpenter, Diana Bellamy; ***D:*** Yves Simoneau; ***W:*** Anna Sandor; ***M:*** George S. Clinton. **TV**

Amelie 1/2 *Amelie from Montmartre; The Fabulous Destiny of Amelie Poulain; Le Fabuleux Destin d'Amelie Poulain* **2001 (R)** Paris waitress Amelie (Tautou) has led a solitary, but not wholly unpleasant, existence. When she finds a box of childhood treasures behind a wall in her apartment, she sets out to return them to their original owner. Accomplishing this, she begins to secretly intervene in the lives of neighbors and coworkers, helping some find romance, others retribution for past wrongs. When her "missions" bring her into contact with a quirky local (Kassovitz), she begins a roundabout courtship involving a treasure hunt instead of approaching him directly. Director Jeunet leaves intact his stunning, and very stylized visual talents, but marshals them in service of a fresh, lighthearted comedy, in contrast to his previous, downcast work. Tautout has no problem carrying the movie and has the look of a budding major star. **120m/C VHS, DVD.** *FR GE* Audrey Tautou, Mathieu Kassovitz, Rufus, Yolande Moreau, Dominique Pinon, Maurice Benichou, Artus de Penguern, Urbain Cancellier, Isabelle Nanty, Claire Maurier, Claude Perron, Clothilde Mollet, Serge Merlin, Jamel Debbouze, Flora Guiet; ***D:*** Jean-Pierre Jeunet; ***W:*** Jean-Pierre Jeunet, Guillaume Laurant; ***C:*** Bruno Delbonnel; ***M:*** Yann Tiersen; ***Nar:*** Andre Dussollier. British Acad. '01: Orig. Screenplay; Cesar '01: Art Dir./Set Dec., Director (Jeunet), Film, Score; Broadcast Film Critics '01: Foreign Film.

Amen **2002 (R)** Costa-Gavras dramatizes a Holocaust story with a somewhat heavy hand. SS. Lt. Kurt Gerstein (Tukur) is a chemist who uses prussic acid Zyklon B for fumigating camp barracks. Sent to a Polish concentration camp, he witnesses the deaths of Jewish prisoners by the gas. Appalled, Gerstein rishes reprisals by informing various church leaders, although no one is willing to speak out until he reaches the young Italian priest, Father Riccardo Fontana (Kassovitz), who has family ties to Pope Pius XII (Iures). As head of the the Hygiene Institute, the SS expects Gerstein to continue to eliminate vermin of all kinds while Father Fontana heads to the Vatican in the hopes of getting the Pope to expose the genocide. An adaptation of Rolf Hochhuth's 1963 play, "The Deputy." **130m/C DVD.** *FR* Ulrich Tukur, Mathieu Kassovitz, Marcel Iures, Ulrich Muhe, Michel Duchaussoy, Ion Caramitru; ***D:*** Constantin Costa-Gavras; ***W:*** Constantin Costa-Gavras, Jean-Claude Grumberg; ***C:*** Patrick Blossier; ***M:*** Armand Amar.

America 1/2 **1924** Young patriot Nathan Holden (Hamilton) is torn between his political beliefs and his love for the daughter of a Virignia Tory (Dempster). Meanwhile, evil redcoat Captain Butler (Barrymore) and his band of murderous Mohawks ruthlessly attack the colonists. **141m/B VHS, DVD.** Neil Hamilton, Carol Dempster, Lionel Barrymore, Erville Alderson, Charles Bennett, Arthur Donaldson, Charles Emmet Mack, Frank McGlynn, Henry O'Neill, Ed Roseman, Harry Semels, Louis Wolheim, Hugh Baird, Lee Beggs, Downing Clarke, Sydney Deane, Arthur Dewey, Michael Donavan, Paul Doucet, John Dunton, Riley Hatch, Emil Hoch, Edwin Holland, W.W. Jones, William S. Rising, Frank Walsh; ***D:*** D.W. Griffith; ***W:*** Robert W. Chambers; ***C:*** Marcel Le Picard, Hendrik Sartov, Billy (G.W.) Bitzer.

America 1/2 **1986 (R)** New York cable station receives worldwide fame when their signal bounces off of the moon. Uninspired piece of fluff from otherwise talented director Downey. **83m/C VHS.** Zack Norman, Tammy Grimes, Michael J. Pollard, Monroe Arnold, Richard Belzer, Liz Torres, Howard Thomashefsky, Laura Ashton, Robert Downey Jr.; ***D:*** Robert Downey.

America 1/2 **2009** Outstanding performance by newcomer Philip Johnson in the title role highlights this message movie that's based on the novel by E.R. Frank. Therapist Dr. Marie Brennan (O'Donnell) tries to help sullen 17-year-old America (Johnson), who's caught up in the overburdened foster care system. Flashbacks detail some of the abuse he's suffered while in the present America struggles to adjust to a group home. **90m/C DVD.** Rosie O'Donnell, Phil Johnson, Raquel Castro, Timothy Edward Rhoze, Jade Yorker, Ruby Dee; ***D:*** Yves Simoneau; ***W:*** Joyce Eliason; ***C:*** John Aronson; ***M:*** Normand Corbeil. **TV**

America at the Movies 1/2 **1976** Scenes from more than 80 of the finest American motion pictures fly by in an effort to tell the story of the cinema and provide a portrait of America as it has been seen on screen for half a century. Clips from "The Birth of a Nation," "Citizen Kane," "Dr. Strangelove," "East of Eden," "The French Connection," and "From Here to Eternity" are among the many included. Some black-and-white scenes; produced by the American Film Institute. **116m/C VHS.** John Wayne, Orson Welles, Peter Sellers, James Dean, Gene Hackman, Burt Lancaster, Julie Harris, Deborah Kerr, Al Pacino, Robert De Niro; ***M:*** Nelson Riddle; ***Nar:*** Charlton Heston.

America First 1/2 **1970** A group of seven travelers try to build an "Eden" with the inhabitants of an Appalachian hollow. **90m/C VHS.** Michael Kennedy, Walter Keller, Pat Estrin, Lois McGuire; ***D:*** Joseph L. Anderson.

America 3000 **1986 (PG-13)** Hundreds of years in the holocaust-torn future, men rebel against a brutal, overpowering race of women, with predictable results. **94m/C VHS.** Chuck Wagner, Laurene Landon; ***D:*** David Engelbach.

The American **2001** Heavy-handed adaptation of Henry James's 1877 novel. Christopher Newman (Modine) makes a fortune in California and heads to Paris in the 1870s where he hopes to acquire both culture and a wife. He meets mysterious widow Claire de Cintre (Sullivan) but his proposal is rejected by her snobby aristocratic family, which is headed by Claire's imperious mother, Madame de Bellegarde (Rigg). Then Newman learns a family secret that could win him Claire's hand. **90m/C VHS, DVD.** Matthew Modine, Aisling O'Sullivan, Diana Rigg, Brenda Fricker, Andrew Scott, Eva Birthistle; ***D:*** Paul Unwin; ***W:*** Michael Hastings. **TV**

American Adobo 1/2 **2002 (R)** An adobo is the Philippines' national dish, a savory concoction that must marinate to bring its flavors together. As it does five Filipino-American long-time friends around a dinner table in Queens. They are all doing well professionally but their personal lives could definitely use work. **99m/C VHS, DVD.** Dina Bonnevie, Randy Becker, Cherry Pie Picache, Sol Ocoa, Christopher De Leon, Susan Valdez-LeGoff, Ricky Davao, Wayne Maugans, Paolo Montalban, Gloria Romero; ***D:*** Laurice Guillen; ***W:*** Vincent R. Nebrida; ***C:*** Lee Meily.

An American Affair 1/2 **1999** Washington, D.C., District Attorney Sam Brady (Bernsen) marries Genevieve (D'Abo) even though he's having an affair with her best friend, Barbara (Heitmeyer). But after Genevieve is murdered, her ghost begins to haunt him. And to make things more complicated, a senator seems to have it in for Sam. The two plotlines take too long to intersect, so the story never makes much sense. **90m/C VHS, DVD.** *CA* Corbin Bernsen, Maryam D'Abo, Jayne Heitmeyer, Robert Vaughn; ***D:*** Sebastian Shah. **VIDEO**

An American Affair 1/2 **2009 (R)** In 1963, 13-year-old Adam (Bright), suffering from raging teen hormones, takes to peeping on his beautiful new Washington, DC neighbor Catherine (Mol), even working odd jobs in order to be near her. She's got lots of problems, including over-indulging in drugs and alcohol. Catherine, a divorced socialite artist, is also having an affair with the President and is a pawn for the CIA. Mol gives off that Marilyn Monroe vibe but the story is probably drawn from a tryst JFK had with a Washington socialite who was later murdered. **93m/C DVD.** Gretchen Mol, Cameron Bright, Perrey Reeves, Noah Wyle, James Rebhorn, Mark Pellegrino, Kris Arnold; ***D:*** William Sten Olsson; ***W:*** Alex Metcalf; ***C:*** David Insley; ***M:*** Dustin O'Halloran.

The American Angels: Baptism of Blood **1989 (R)** Three beautiful young women, each with a personal dream, strive to make it in the world of professional wrestling. Hackneyed plot devices, but those simply watching for the wrestling scenes won't be disappointed. **99m/C VHS.** Jan MacKenzie, Tray Loren, Mimi Lesseos, Trudy Adams, Patricia Cavoti, Susan Sexton, Jean Kirkland, Jeff Lundy, Lee Marshall; ***D:*** Beverly Sebastian, Ferd Sebastian.

American Anthem **1986 (PG-13)** A young gymnast must choose between family responsibilities or the parallel bars. Olympic gymnast Gaylord makes his movie debut but doesn't get the gold. Good fare for young tumblers, but that's about it. Followed by two of the films' music videos and tape-ads featuring Max Headroom. **100m/C VHS.** Mitch Gaylord, Janet Jones, Michelle Phillips, Michael Pataki; ***D:*** Albert Magnoli; ***W:*** Evan P. Archerd, Jeff Benjamin; ***M:*** Alan Silvestri.

American Aristocracy 1/2 **1917** A silent comic romp in which Fairbanks, an old moneyed dandy, wreaks havoc on an island resort whose clientele is composed of the nouveau well-to-do. **52m/B VHS.** Douglas Fairbanks Sr., Jewel Carmen, Albert Parker; ***D:*** Lloyd Ingraham.

American Autobahn 1/2 **1984** A low-budget independent actioner about a journalist who discovers an underworld weapons ring that hits the highway in pursuit of him. **90m/C VHS.** Jan Jalenak, Michael von der Goltz, Jim Jarmusch; ***D:*** Andre Degas.

American Beauty 1/2 **1999 (R)** Lester Burnham (Spacey) is dead. This isn't any shock—Lester tells you this himself in his opening narration. It's the time leading up to his death Lester wants to remember. Lester is a middle-aged drone with a brittle, status-conscious wife, Carolyn (Bening), and a sullen teenaged daughter, Jane (Birch). Lester's world is rocked when he meets Jane's Lolita-like friend, Angela (Suvari), and his fantasies find him quitting his job, pumping iron, and smoking dope with Ricky (Bentley), the voyeuristic kid next door who has a thing for videotaping Jane. It's a suburban nightmare writ large with an excellent cast and some unexpected twists. **118m/C VHS, DVD.** Kevin Spacey, Annette Bening, Mena Suvari, Thora Birch, Wes Bentley, Peter Gallagher, Chris Cooper, Allison Janney, Scott Bakula, Sam Robards; ***D:*** Sam Mendes; ***W:*** Alan Ball; ***C:*** Conrad L. Hall; ***M:*** Thomas Newman. Oscars '99: Actor (Spacey), Cinematog., Director (Mendes), Film, Orig. Screenplay; British Acad. '99: Actor (Spacey), Actress (Bening), Cinematog., Film, Film Editing, Score; Directors Guild '99: Director (Mendes); Golden Globes '00: Director (Mendes), Film—Drama, Screenplay; L.A. Film Critics '99: Director (Mendes); Natl. Bd. of Review '99: Film; Screen Actors Guild '99: Actor (Spacey), Actress (Bening), Cast; Writers Guild '99: Orig. Screenplay; Broadcast Film Critics '99: Director (Mendes), Film, Orig. Screenplay.

American Blue Note *Fakebook* **1989 (PG-13)** Loosely plotted, bittersweet account of a struggling jazz quartet in the early 1960s, as its leader (MacNicol) must decide if their fruitless tours of sleazy bars and weddings are still worth it. The debut of director Toporoff. **96m/C VHS.** Peter MacNichol, Carl Capotorto, Tim Guinee, Bill Christopher-Myers, Jonathan Walker, Charlotte d'Amboise, Louis Guss, Zohra Lampert, Trini Alvarado, Sam Behrens; ***D:*** Ralph Toporoff; ***W:*** Gilbert Girion, Larry Schanker.

American Born 1/2 **1989** Murder Inc. returns to the dismay of one idealist who embarks on a battle he doesn't intend to lose. The mob had better look out. **90m/C VHS.** Joey Travolta, Andrew Zeller; ***D:*** Raymond Martino; ***W:*** Raymond Martino.

American Boyfriends **1989 (PG-13)** An ostensible sequel to "My American Cousin," in which two Canadian girls go to California and discover innocent romance and friendship. **90m/C VHS.** *CA* Margaret Langrick, John Wildman, Jason Blicker, Lisa Repo Martell; ***D:*** Sandy Wilson; ***W:*** Sandy Wilson; ***C:*** Brenton Spencer.

American Buffalo 1/2 **1995 (R)** Somewhat lackluster but decent screen adaptation of a classic American drama. Franz's junk shop owner Donny plans to steal back a rare Buffalo-head nickel that he feels he was swindled out of, with the help of his protege Bobby (Nelson). Hoffman's ferret-like Teach, one of Donny's card-playing buddies and an arrogant opportunist, tries to weasel in on the plan that never comes to fruition. Set in Corrente's hometown of Pawtucket, the director's reverence for the material is obvious and he plays it too safe. Top-notch performances raise the level. Mamet adapts his play for the screen. **88m/C VHS, DVD.** Dustin Hoffman, Dennis Franz, Sean Nelson; ***D:*** Michael Corrente; ***W:*** David Mamet; ***C:*** Richard Crudo; ***M:*** Thomas Newman.

An American Carol WOOF! 2008 (PG-13) An anti-American filmmaker named Michael Malone (Farley)—a shameless parody of real-life documentarian Michael Moore, down to the ubiquitous baseball cap—is out to abolish the 4th of July holiday when he is visited by three ghostly historic figures who try to get him to appreciate his country ala "A Christmas Carol." An overtly biased skewering of supposedly "liberal" politics and ideologies is ultimately a smear campaign masquerading as entertainment—and it's not even funny. Kevin Farley is the brother of the late Chris Farley. **84m/C DVD, Blu-ray Disc.** *US* Kevin Farley, Kelsey Grammer, Jon Voight, Robert Davi, Chriss Anglin, Leslie Nielsen, Gail O'Grady, Trace Adkins; ***D:*** David Zucker; ***W:*** David Zucker, Lewis Freidman, Myrna Sokoloff; ***C:*** Brian Baugh; ***M:*** James L. Venable.

American Chinatown 1/2 **1996** Orphaned tough guy is taken in by a powerful Chinatown mob family but gets into trouble when he falls for the head man's sister. He has a chance to redeem himself when he learns about a plot to overthrow the triad clan but will he take it? **90m/C VHS, DVD.** Henry Lee, Robert Z'Dar, Liat Goodson; ***D:*** Richard W. Park.

An American Christmas Carol **1979** Charles Dickens' classic story is retold with limited charm in a

TV effort. This time a greedy American financier (Winkler) learns about the true meaning of Christmas. **98m/C VHS, DVD.** Henry Winkler, David Wayne, Dorian Harewood; ***D:*** Eric Till; ***M:*** Hagood Hardy. **TV**

American Commandos *Hitman* **1984 (R)** An ex-Green Beret slaughters the junkies who killed his son and raped his wife, and then joins his old buddies for a secret, Rambo-esque mission in Vietnam providing a tired rehash of Vietnam movie cliches. **96m/C VHS, DVD.** Chris Mitchum, John Phillip Law, Franco Guerrero; ***D:*** Bobby Suarez.

American Cop 1/2 **1994 (PG-13)** Elmo LaGrange is an ordinary cop taking a vacation, when his layover in the Moscow airport becomes a lesson in mistaken identities. He teams up with the pre-requisite beautiful woman to outwit and outrun the Russian mafia. **91m/C VHS.** Wayne Crawford, Ashley Laurence, Daniel Quinn, William Katt, Olga Vodin, Vladimir Shpoudeiko, Nickolai Nedovodin; ***D:*** Wayne Crawford; ***W:*** Carlos Brooks; ***C:*** Nicholas Josef von Sternberg.

American Cousins 1/2 **2002** New Jersey gangsters Gino and Settimo Bazaglia get into trouble with the Ukrainian mob while in Europe and are instructed to lay low in Glasgow with their distant cousin Roberto. Roberto is a mild-mannered, stamp-collecting fish & chips shop proprietor, who is clueless about his American cousins' true business. But they decide to repay his hospitality by helping Roberto out with some local thugs who are trying to muscle in on his business. Light-hearted culture clash comedy. **89m/C DVD.** *GB* Danny Nucci, Dan Hedaya, Shirley Henderson, Vincent Pastore, Gerald Lepkowski, Russell Hunter, Stevan Remkus; ***D:*** Donald Coutts; ***W:*** Sergio Casci; ***C:*** Jerry Kelly; ***M:*** Don Shaw.

An American Crime **2007 (R)** A cringing, sordid true crime story set in 1965 in Indianapolis. Sylvia (Page) and her younger sister Jennie (McFarland) are left by their carny parents in the paid care of single mother Gertrude (Keener), who already has seven kids. Gert needs the money but she's soon over the edge (although booze and drugs help). Soon, the crazy sadist accuses Sylvia of all sorts of crimes and locks her in the basement. Then the real abuse starts until things end tragically with a trial. **92m/C DVD.** Catherine Keener, Ellen Page, James Franco, Bradley Whitford, Ari Gaynor, Nick Searcy, Michael O'Keefe, Romy Rosemont, Hayley McFarland; ***D:*** Tommy O'Haver; ***W:*** Tommy O'Haver, Irene Turner; ***C:*** Byron Shah; ***M:*** Alan Ari Lazar. **CABLE**

American Crude **2007 (R)** That would be crude as in unfunny sex comedy and not as in oil production. Johnny (Livingston) is married to Jane (Watros) and they are both throwing separate engagement parties for their friends Bill (Schneider) and Olivia (Detmer) on the same night. There's also a bunch of other characters, including an amateur porn maker, a 'ho, and a runaway teen, and of course their stories will converge but you won't care in the slightest. **98m/C DVD.** Ron Livingston, Cynthia Watros, Rob Schneider, Amanda Detmer, Jennifer Esposito, Michael Clarke Duncan, Missi Pyle, Raymond J. Barry, Sarah Foret, Nancy Marlow; ***D:*** Craig Sheffer; ***W:*** Craig Sheffer; ***C:*** James Mathers; ***M:*** Dennis Hamlin.

American Cyborg: Steel Warrior 1/2 **1994 (R)** Basic evil-machine-bent-on-mankind's-destruction movie—with a hero bent on rescuing the world. **95m/C VHS.** Joe Lara, John P. Ryan; ***D:*** Boaz Davidson; ***W:*** Bill Crounse.

American Dream **1981** A mid-western family leaves the suburbs and moves into a Chicago inner-city neighborhood. Good TV-movie pilot for the short-lived series that was Emmy nominated for direction and writing. **90m/C VHS.** Stephen Macht, Karen Carlson, John Karlen, Andrea Smith, John Malkovich, John McIntire; ***D:*** Mel Damski; ***M:*** Artie Butler. **TV**

American Dreamer **1984 (PG)** A housewife wins a trip to Paris as a prize from a mystery writing contest. Silly from a blow on the head, she begins living the fictional life of her favorite literary adventure. Sporadic comedy with a good cast wandering about courtesy of a clumsy screenplay. **105m/C VHS, DVD.** JoBeth Williams, Tom Conti, Giancarlo Giannini, Coral Browne, James Staley; ***D:*** Rick Rosenthal; ***M:*** Lewis Furey.

American Dreamz **2006 (PG-13)** Weitz's obvious satire has self-loathing, smarmy Brit Martin Tweed (Grant) hosting the universally popular reality show of the title. This latest version will be highlighted by the appearance of dim-witted, affable American President Staton (Quaid) as a guest judge. He has the time because the country is actually being run by his power-hungry chief of staff (Dafoe). Vying for celebrity status are small-town blonde Sally Kendoo (Moore), who hides her unholy ambitions behind a girl-next-door smile, and Omer (Golzari), a showtune-loving Iraqi who has been chosen as a suicide bomber. Grant and Moore fare best as conniving players who recognize and respect the dark streak in each other. **107m/C DVD.** *US* Hugh Grant, Dennis Quaid, Mandy Moore, Willem Dafoe, Chris Klein, Jennifer Coolidge, Marcia Gay Harden, John Cho, Sam Golzari, Seth Meyers, Judy Greer, Shohreh Aghdashloo, Bernie (Bernard) White, Tony Yalda, Marley Shelton, Lawrence Pressman, Noureen DeWulf; ***D:*** Paul Weitz; ***W:*** Paul Weitz; ***C:*** Robert Elswit; ***M:*** Stephen Trask.

American Eagle 1/2 **1990 (R)** A veteran goes crazy and seeks sadistic, bloody revenge on his war buddies. Now his war buddies are the only ones who can stop him. **92m/C VHS, DVD.** Asher Brauner, Robert F. Lyons, Vernon Wells, Kai Baker; ***D:*** Robert J. Smawley.

American East **2007 (R)** Arab-American Moustafa is having a very bad day. He has problems with his children and sister and the customers at his rundown L.A. diner insist on arguing about politics. Then when he goes to pick up his cousin at the airport, Moustafa is detained and questioned by an FBI agent. His one dream is to open a classy Middle Eastern restaurant with his Jewish pal Sam (Shalhoub), but no one believes he can do that either. **110m/C DVD.** Sayed Badreya, Tony Shalhoub, Anthony Azizi, Kais Nashef, Amanda Detmer, Erik Avari, Ray Wise, Tay Blessey, Sarah Shahi; ***D:*** Hesham Issawi; ***W:*** Sayed Badreya, Hesham Issawi; ***C:*** Michael G. Wojciechowski; ***M:*** Tony Humecke.

American Empire 1/2 *My Son Alone* **1942** Two Civil War heroes struggle to build a cattle empire in Texas and are hampered by rustlers, one of whom was their partner. A fine, veteran cast and a tight script keep things moving, including the cattle. **82m/B VHS, DVD.** Preston Foster, Richard Dix, Frances Gifford, Leo Carrillo; ***D:*** William McGann.

American Fabulous 1/2 **1992** The posthumously released autobiography of an eccentric homosexual who lived life in the fast lane. Jeffrey Strouth performs his monologue from the back seat of a 1957 Cadillac, where the images of small-town America are seen to contrast sharply with his flamboyant style. His grotesque and candid recollections include his alcoholic Elvis-impersonator father, a stint as a teenage prostitute, drag queen friends, and drug addiction in New York. Strouth puts a comic twist on even the most brutal of his memories. He died of AIDS at the age of 33 in 1992. **105m/C VHS.** Jeffrey Strouth; ***D:*** Reno Dakota; ***W:*** Jeffrey Strouth.

American Flyers 1/2 **1985 (PG-13)** Two competitive brothers train for a grueling three-day bicycle race in Colorado while tangling with personal drama, including the spectre that one of them may have inherited dad's tendency for cerebral aneurisms and is sure to drop dead during a bike race soon. Written by bike movie specialist Tesich ("Breaking Away") with a lot of the usual cliches (the last bike ride, battling bros, eventual understanding), which are gracefully overridden by fine bike-racing photography. Interesting performances, especially Chong as a patient girlfriend and Amos as the trainer. **113m/C VHS, DVD.** Kevin Costner, David Marshall Grant, Rae Dawn Chong, Alexandra Paul, John Amos, Janice Rule, Robert Kevin Townsend, Jennifer Grey, Luca Bercovici; ***D:*** John Badham; ***W:*** Steve Tesich; ***M:*** Lee Ritenour, Greg Mathieson.

The American Friend 1/2 *Der Amerikanische Freund* **1977** Tribute to the American gangster film helped introduce Wenders to American moviegoers. Young Hamburg picture framer thinks he has a terminal disease and is set up by American expatriate Hopper to become a hired assassin in West Germany. The lure is a promise of quick money that the supposedly dying man can then leave his wife and child. After the first assasination, the two bond. Hopper is the typical Wenders protagonist, a strange man in a strange land looking for a connection. Great, creepy thriller adapted from Patricia Highsmith's novel "Ripley's Game." Fuller and Ray (better known as directors) appear briefly as gangsters. **127m/C VHS, DVD.** *FR GE* Bruno Ganz, Dennis Hopper, Elisabeth (Lisa) Kreuzer, Gerard Blain, Jean Eustache, Samuel Fuller, Nicholas Ray, Daniel Schmid, Lou Castel, Rudolf Schuendler, Sandy Whitelaw; ***Cameos:*** Wim Wenders; ***D:*** Wim Wenders; ***W:*** Wim Wenders; ***C:*** Robby Muller; ***M:*** Jurgen Knieper.

American Friends **1991 (PG)** Genteel story masquerades as high comedy. Palin is a fussy middle-aged Oxford classics tutor. On a holiday he meets American Hartley (Booth) and her adopted daughter, Elinor (Alvarado). Both women are immensely attracted to the don (for reasons that are unclear) and follow him back to Oxford, where he's engaged in a battle of succession with his rival Molina. Dismal screenplay lacks logic and urgency, making it difficult to care about the story or the characters. Script is said to have been inspired by an incident in the life of Palin's great-grandfather. If this sounds like your cup of tea, save your time and watch a Merchant Ivory film instead. **95m/C VHS.** *GB* Michael Palin, Connie Booth, Trini Alvarado, Alfred Molina; ***D:*** Tristam Powell; ***W:*** Michael Palin, Tristam Powell; ***M:*** Georges Delerue.

American Fusion 1/2 **2005 (PG-13)** Charming romance in a culture clash comedy. Middle-aged, divorced Yvonne (Chang) is the frustrated daughter in a crazy Chinese-American family. She falls in love with Hispanic dentist Jose (Morales) but her family disapproves and his family isn't too happy with the cultural diversity either. **107m/C DVD.** Sylvia Chang, Esai Morales, Collin Chou, James Hong, Lan Yeung, Noriyuki "Pat" Morita, Randall Park; ***D:*** Frank Lin; ***W:*** Randall Park, Frank Lin; ***C:*** Jason Inouye; ***M:*** Dave Iwataki.

American Gangster **2007 (R)** Director Ridley Scott's shot at the gangster genre hits the mark, transcending the tough-guy norm in its purposeful juxtaposition of the two main characters: Frank Lucas (Washington), the near-perfect, respectable, yet cold-blooded criminal genius who is pursued by the unkempt, womanizing, but razor-straight cop, Ritchie Roberts (Crowe). Washington and Crowe are mesmerizing in this powerful story of the brutality and excess of the '70s era Harlem drug trade that would be over-the-top if it weren't true, and that revolutionized both the drug trade and the law enforcement of the period. **157m/C DVD.** *US* Denzel Washington, Russell Crowe, Chiwetel Ejiofor, Cuba Gooding Jr., Josh Brolin, Ted Levine, Armand Assante, Clarence Williams III, Lymari Nadal, John Ortiz, RZA, Ruby Dee, Idris Elba, Carla Gugino, Common, Joe Morton, Jon Polito, Kevin Corrigan, Ruben Santiago-Hudson, Roger Bart, KaDee Strickland; ***D:*** Ridley Scott; ***W:*** Steven Zaillian; ***C:*** Harris Savides; ***M:*** Marc Streitenfeld. Screen Actors Guild '07: Support. Actress (Dee).

American Gigolo **1979 (R)** A Los Angeles loner who sexually services the rich women of Beverly Hills becomes involved with the wife of a California state senator and is then framed for a murder he did not commit. A highly stylized but empty view of seamy low lives marred by a contrived plot, with decent romp in the hay readiness displayed by Gere. **117m/C VHS, DVD.** Richard Gere, Lauren Hutton, Hector Elizondo, Nina Van Pallandt, Bill Duke, K. Callan; ***Cameos:*** Paul Schrader; ***D:*** Paul Schrader; ***W:*** Paul Schrader; ***C:*** John Bailey; ***M:*** Giorgio Moroder.

American Girl: Chrissa Stands Strong 1/2 *Chrissa Stands Strong* **2009** When fourth-grader Chrissa's family moves in to help out her recently-widowed grandma, she's most afraid that she won't make friends at her new school. Chrissa's fears seem well-founded when Tara, queen of the mean girl clique, starts tormenting Chrissa and turns out to be her main rival on the swim team. Finally, Chrissa has to decide what's the best way to stand up to Tara's bullying. **90m/C DVD.** Michael Learned, Annabeth Gish, Timothy Bottoms, Jennifer Tilly, Don Franklin, Sammi Hanratty, Adair Tishler, Austin Thomas; ***D:*** Martha Coolidge; ***W:*** Christine Coyle Johnson, Julie Prendiville Roux; ***C:*** Johnny E. Jensen; ***M:*** Jennie Muskett. **VIDEO**

American Gothic WOOF! *Hide and Shriek* **1988 (R)** Three couples headed for a vacation are instead stranded on an island and captured by a demented family headed by Steiger and De Carlo, a scary enough proposition in itself. Even worse, Ma and Pa have three middle-aged moronic offspring who still dress as children and are intent on killing the thwarted vacationers (who are none too bright themselves) one by bloody one. A stultifying career low for all involved. **89m/C VHS, DVD.** *CA GB* Rod Steiger, Yvonne De Carlo, Michael J. Pollard, Sarah Torgov, Fiona Hutchinson, William Hootkins, Terry Kelly, Mark Ericksen, Caroline Barclay, Mark Lindsay Chapman; ***D:*** John Hough; ***W:*** Michael Vines, Bert Wetanson; ***C:*** Harvey Harrison; ***M:*** Alan Parker.

American Graffiti 1/2 **1973 (PG)** Atmospheric, episodic look at growing up in the innocence of America before the Kennedy assassination and the Vietnam War. It all takes place on one hectic but typical night in the life of a group of recent California high school grads unsure of what the next big step in life is. So they spend their time cruising, listening to Wolfman Jack, and meeting at the drive-in. Slice of '60s life boasts a prudent script, great set design, authentic soundtrack, and consistently fine performances by the young cast. Catapulted Dreyfuss, Ford, and Somers to stardom, branded Lucas a hot directorial commodity with enough leverage to launch "Star Wars," and steered Howard and Williams towards continued age-of-innocence nirvana on "Happy Days." **112m/C VHS, DVD.** Richard Dreyfuss, Ron Howard, Cindy Williams, MacKenzie Phillips, Paul LeMat, Charles Martin Smith, Suzanne Somers, Candy Clark, Harrison Ford, Bo Hopkins, Joe Spano, Kathleen Quinlan, Wolfman Jack; ***D:*** George Lucas; ***W:*** George Lucas, Gloria Katz, Willard Huyck; ***C:*** Jan D'Alquen, Ron Everslage. AFI '98: Top 100; Golden Globes '74: Film—Mus./Comedy, Natl. Film Reg. '95;; N.Y. Film Critics '73: Screenplay; Natl. Soc. Film Critics '73: Screenplay.

American Gun **2002 (R)** Coburn, in his last performance, is Martin Tillman, an anguished father whose daughter has recently been killed during a violent crime. He decides to trace the history of the gun that was used, and along the way deals with an incident from his service in the Korean War that still haunts him. Coburn's performance is magnificent, even if the material itself is a little uneven. **89m/C VHS, DVD.** James Coburn, Barbara Bain, Virginia Madsen, Alexandra Holden; ***D:*** Alan Jacobs; ***W:*** Alan Jacobs; ***C:*** Phil Parmet; ***M:*** Anthony Marinelli.

American Gun 1/2 **2005 (R)** Three generally uninvolving stories about guns from debuting director Avelino. In Oregon, Janet (Harden) and her teen son David (Marquete) are guilt-wracked community outcasts three years after her older son participated in a high school shooting rampage. At a gang-ridden Chicago school, Principal Carter (Whitaker) expels student Jay (Escarpeta) for having a handgun, and the pic follows the teen to his convenience store job where he tries to use the (fake) weapon as intimidation against would-be thieves. In Virginia, co-ed Mary Ann (Cardellini) sets aside her dislike of firearms and learns to shoot after a friend is date-raped. **94m/C DVD.** *US* Donald Sutherland, Forest Whitaker, Marcia Gay Harden, Linda Cardellini, Tony Goldwyn, Christopher Marquette, Nikki Reed, Garcelle Beauvais, Amanda Seyfried, Melissa Leo, Arlen Escarpeta; ***D:*** Aric Avelino; ***W:*** Aric Avelino, Steven Bagatourian; ***C:*** Nancy Schreiber; ***M:*** Peter Golub.

An American Haunting 1/2 **2005 (PG-13)** Fictionalized account of Tennessee's "Bell Witch," adapted from Brent Monahan's novel. In 1818, a neighbor curses the prosperous Bell family for their greed and soon they are haunted by a poltergeist that eventually takes possession of pretty teen daughter Betsy (Hurd-Ward). Parents John (Sutherland) and Lucy (Spacek) try to fight the evil spirit. Lots of hokum, not many frights. **82m/C DVD.** *US* Donald Sutherland, Sissy Spacek, Rachel Hurd-Wood, James D'Arcy, Matthew Marsh, Thom Fell, Gaye Brown; ***D:*** Courtney Solomon; ***W:*** Courtney Solomon; ***C:*** Adrian Biddle; ***M:*** Caine Davidson.

American Heart 1/2 **1992 (R)** Jack (Bridges) is a suspicious ex-con, newly released from prison, with few prospects and little hope. He also has a teenage son, Nick (Furlong), he barely remembers but who desperately wants to have his father back in his life. Jack is reluctantly persuaded to let Nick stay with him in his cheap hotel where Nick befriends fellow resident, Molly (Kaprisky), a teenage hooker, and other cast-off street kids. Superb performances by both male leads—Furlong, both yearning and frustrated as he pursues his dream of having a family, and Bridges as the tough parolee, unwilling to open his heart. Hardboiled, poignant, and powerful. **114m/C VHS, DVD.** Jeff Bridges, Edward Furlong, Lucinda Jenney, Tracey Kapisky, Don Harvey, Margaret Welsh; ***D:*** Martin Bell; ***W:*** Peter Silverman; ***C:*** James R. Bagdonas; ***M:*** James Newton Howard. Ind. Spirit '94: Actor (Bridges).

American History X 1/2 **1998 (R)** Former skinhead Derek (Norton) is released from prison after a three-year stint for killing two black teens. He returns home having renounced his neo-Nazi ideology and lifestyle, only to find his younger brother Danny (Furlong) involved in a skinhead gang. Controversial not only due to its touchy subject matter and startling violence, but also because director Kaye waged a public war with New Line to remove his name from the film, believing his vision had been compromised by the studio. Ultimately, the fuss is much ado about not much, as the film falls short of expectations. The story is predictable and rather simplistic, the script uneven and sometimes preachy, and most of the characters are wafer-thin. Only Norton's mesmerizing, forceful performance and a commendable job by Furlong as the impressionable younger brother lend credibility. **118m/C VHS, DVD.** Edward Norton, Edward Furlong, Fairuza Balk, Beverly D'Angelo, Avery Brooks, Stacy Keach, Jennifer Lien, Elliott Gould, William Russ, Joe Cortese, Ethan Suplee, Guy Torry, Giuseppe Andrews, Jordan Marder, Anne Lambton, Paul LeMat; ***D:*** Tony Kaye; ***W:*** David McKenna; ***C:*** Tony Kaye; ***M:*** Anne Dudley.

An American in Paris **1951** Lavish, imaginative musical features a sweeping score, and knockout choreography by Kelly. Ex-G.I. Kelly stays on in Paris after the war to study painting, supported in his efforts by rich American Foch, who hopes to acquire a little extra attention. But Kelly loves the lovely Caron, unfortunately engaged to an older gent. Highlight is an astonishing 17-minute ballet which holds the record for longest movie dance number—and one of the most expensive, pegged at over half a million for a month of filming. For his efforts, the dance king won a special Oscar citation. While it sure looks like Paris, most of it was filmed in MGM studios. ♫ S'Wonderful; I Got Rhythm; Embraceable You; Love Is Here To Stay; Tra-La-La; I'll Build a Stairway to Paradise; Nice Work If You Can Get It; By Strauss; Concerto in F (3rd Movement). **113m/C VHS, DVD.** Gene Kelly, Leslie Caron, Oscar Levant, Nina Foch, Georges Guetary; ***D:*** Vincente Minnelli; ***W:*** Alan Jay Lerner; ***C:*** John Alton; ***M:*** Ira Gershwin. Oscars '51: Art Dir./Set Dec., Color, Color Cinematog., Costume Des. (C), Picture, Story & Screenplay, Scoring/Musical; AFI '98: Top 100; Golden Globes '52: Film—Mus./Comedy, Natl. Film Reg. '93.

American Justice *Jackals* **1986 (R)** Two cops, one of whom looks suspiciously like a Simon of "Simon and Simon," fight political corruption and white slavery near the Mexican border. The chief white slaver bears a full resemblance to the other Simon. Sufficient action but less than original. **96m/C VHS, DVD.** Jameson Parker, Gerald McRaney, Wilford Brimley, Jack Lucarelli; ***D:*** Gary Grillo.

American Kickboxer 1 1/2 **1991 (R)** Barrett stars as B.J. Quinn, a down on his luck kickboxing champion who spends much of his time onscreen aimlessly wandering (apparently searching for the meaning of his life). Lackluster script and performances will make this one trying—even for kickboxing fans. Barrett is Chuck Norris' former workout partner, but there isn't enough action often enough for him to show off his formidable skills. **93m/C VHS.** John Barrett, Keith Vitali, Brad Morris, Terry Norton, Ted Leplat; ***D:*** Frans Nel; ***W:*** Emil Kolbe; ***M:*** Frank Becker.

American Kickboxer 2: To the Death 1/2 **1993 (R)** Lillian must find a way to get her cop ex-husband and her kickboxer ex-lover to work together to save her kidnapped daughter's life. **91m/C VHS, DVD.** Dale "Apollo" Cook, Evan Lurie, Kathy Shower, Ted Markland; ***D:*** Jeno Hodi.

American Madness 1/2 **1932** Benevolent banker Dickson (Huston) has been making loans without sufficient collateral. The bank's board of directors give him a warning and then a robbery causes a run on the bank. The directors are ready to oust Dickson when the small businessmen he's helped rally to his defense. Tedious romantic subplot has Dickson's unhappy wife (Johnson) accusing him of neglect and dallying with unscrupulous bank clerk Cluett (Gordon). **75m/B VHS, DVD.** Walter Huston, Pat O'Brien, Kay Johnson, Gavin Gordon, Constance Cummings, Robert Ellis, Walter Walker, Arthur Hoyt; ***D:*** Frank Capra; ***W:*** Robert Riskin; ***C:*** Joseph Walker.

The American Mall 1/2 **2008** An MTV-produced teen musical that finds songwriter Ally (Dobrev) working at her mother's failing mall music store. She falls for janitor/musician Joey (Mayes) and they would make beautiful music together if not for rich witch Madison (Reeser), whose daddy owns the property. A would-be fashion designer, Madison wants Joey to be her model and she wants to kick out Ally's mom so she can have the space to expand her own store. Satisfyingly chipper—if predictable—with cute leads and bright songs. **100m/C DVD.** Nina Dobrev, Autumn Reeser, Al Sapienza, Rob Mayes, Yassmin Alers, Wade Allain-Marcus, Neil Haskell, Brooke Lyons; ***D:*** Shawn Ku; ***W:*** Margaret Grieco Oberman; ***C:*** Matthew Williams. **CABLE**

American Matchmaker 1/2 *Amerikaner Shadkhn* **1940** Nat Silver decides to go into the matchmaking business, after his own marriages fail miserably, hoping to experience happiness vicariously. However, he soon begins to realize that one of his clients is a better match for him than the man he chose for her. In Yiddish with English subtitles. **87m/B VHS, DVD.** Leo Fuchs, Judith Abarbanel, Rosetta Bialis, Yudel Dubinsky, Abe Lax; ***D:*** Edgar G. Ulmer; ***W:*** S. (Shirley Ulmer) Castle; ***C:*** Edgar G. Ulmer.

American Me **1992 (R)** Violent and brutal depiction of more than 30 years of gang wars and drugs in East Los Angeles. Santana founded a street gang as a teenager, but has spent the last 18 years in prison, where he's the boss of the so-called Mexican Mafia, which oversees the drugs, scams, murders, and violence that are an everyday fact of prison life. Released from Folsom, Santana goes back to his old neighborhood and attempts to distance himself from his old life but finds his gang ties are stronger than any other alliance. Unsparing and desolate directorial debut from Olmos. **119m/C VHS, DVD, HD DVD.** Edward James Olmos, William Forsythe, Pepe Serna, Danny De La Paz, Evelina Fernandez, Daniel Villarreal, Cary-Hiroyuki Tagawa, Sal Lopez, Tony Giorgio; ***D:*** Edward James Olmos; ***W:*** Floyd Mutrux, Desmond Nakano; ***C:*** Reynaldo Villalobos; ***M:*** Dennis Lambert.

American Meltdown *Meltdown* **2004** In this tense thriller six terrorists take over the San Juan nuclear power plant and the government tries to figure out how to respond to the threat without it leading to a meltdown. However, the terrorists aren't exactly who they seem. **90m/C DVD.** Bruce Greenwood, Leslie Hope, Arnold Vosloo, James Remar, Susan Merson, Will Lyman; ***D:*** Jeremiah S. Chechik; ***W:*** Larry Barber, Paul Barber; ***C:*** Douglas Koch; ***M:*** Tomandandy. **CABLE**

American Movie 1/2 **1999 (R)** Would-be filmmaker Mark Borchardt's American Dream is to make his own independent film in his home of Menomonee Falls, Wisconsin. He doesn't have the money (or a particularly workable idea) but he does have lots of self-confidence and enthusiasm, as well as his mom, his 82-year-old Uncle Bill, and a cast of eccentrics. Smith's unlimited access shows Borchardt's almost limitless failures and obstacles, making the whole affair seem like a "Spinal Tap"-esque spoof, even though the people are sometimes painfully, sometimes hilariously real. **104m/C VHS, DVD.** Mike Schank, Mark Borchardt; ***D:*** Chris Smith; ***C:*** Chris Smith; ***M:*** Mike Schank.

American Nightmare 1/2 **1981** Young man searches for his missing sister against a background of pornography, drug peddling, and prostitution in the slums of a city. The usual titillating squalid urban drama. **85m/C VHS.** Lawrence S. Day, Lora Staley, Lenore Zann, Michael Ironside, Alexandra Paul; ***D:*** Don McBrearty.

American Nightmare 1/2 **2000 (R)** To commemorate the killings of four college students on Halloween the year before, pirate radio show "American Nightmare" is broadcasting all night. The program's host, Caligari (Ryan), has listeners calling in with their worst fears and seven friends take turns calling. Too bad, the killer is also listening and decides to make their nightmares come true. **91m/C VHS, DVD.** Debbie Rochon, Brandy Little, Johnny Sneed, Christopher Ryan, Brinke Stevens; ***D:*** Jon Keeyes; ***W:*** Jon Keeyes; ***C:*** Brad Walker; ***M:*** Peter Gannan, David Rosenblad.

American Ninja *American Warrior* **1985 (R)** American Dudikoff is G.I. Joe, a martial-arts expert stationed in the Philippines who alienates most everyone around him (he's a rebel). Deadly black-belt war begins with Joe confronting the army which is selling stolen weapons to the South American black market. Aided by one faithful pal, Joe uses his head-kicking martial arts skills to stop hundreds of ninja combatants working for the corrupt arms dealer. In his spare time he romances the base chief's daughter. Efficient rib-crunching chop-socky action wrapped in no-brainer plot and performed by nonactors. Cannon epic mercilessly followed by at least three sequels. **96m/C VHS, DVD.** Michael Dudikoff, Guich Koock, Judie Aronson, Steve James; ***D:*** Sam Firstenberg; ***W:*** Gideon Amir; ***C:*** Hanania Baer; ***M:*** Michael Linn.

American Ninja 2: The Confrontation **1987 (R)** Soldiers Dudikoff and James are back again using their martial arts skills (in lieu of any acting) to take on a Caribbean drug-lord. Apparently he has been kidnapping Marines and taking them to his island, where he genetically alters them to become fanatical ninja assassins eager to do his dirty work. The script hardly gets in the way of the rib-crunching action, but is an improvement upon Ninja Number One. **90m/C VHS.** Michael Dudikoff, Steve James, Larry Poindexter, Gary Conway; ***D:*** Sam Firstenberg; ***W:*** Gary Conway, James Booth.

American Ninja 3: Blood Hunt **WOOF! 1989 (R)** Second sequel in the American Ninja series. Bradley replaces Dudikoff as the martial arts good guy fighting the martial arts bad guys on a Caribbean island. He's pursued by ex-evangelist Marjoe, who wants to inject him with a nasty virus before unloading the germs to bad buys worldwide. Less ninjitsu; more uninspired martial arts. **90m/C VHS, DVD.** David Bradley, Steve James, Marjoe Gortner, Michele Chan, Calvin Jung; ***D:*** Cedric Sundstrom; ***W:*** Paul DeMielche, Gary Conway; ***M:*** George S. Clinton.

American Ninja 4: The Annihilation **WOOF! 1991 (R)** Dudikoff returns after noticeable absence in last sequel. He should have stayed away from #4—it's a rehash of tired ideas that never gets off the ground. Forget this and see "American Ninja 2: The Confrontation," the best of this series. **99m/C VHS, DVD.** Michael Dudikoff, David Bradley, James Booth, Dwayne Alexandre, Robin Stille, Ken Gampu; ***D:*** Cedric Sundstrom; ***W:*** David Geeves; ***M:*** Nicolas Tenbroek.

American Outlaws **2001 (PG-13)** Look kids, it's N'Sync as the James Gang! Remember "Young Guns" (1988)? By the end of this, you'll be begging for Emilio Estevez's constant mugging and Kiefer Sutherland's ridiculous brooding. Jesse (Farrell) and Frank James (Macht), along with cousins Cole (Caan), Bob (McCormack) and Jim Younger (Smith) return from the Civil War to find Ma (Bates) and the family farm threatened by the railroad. So they commence to robbin' banks to help out the poor folk who been done wrong. Along the way Jesse courts purty young filly Zee (Larter). People have been writing the obituary of the Western for a few years now, but "Outlaws" may be the bullet in the genre's back. **95m/C VHS, DVD.** *US* Colin Farrell, Gabriel Macht, Scott Caan, Gregory Edward Smith, Will McCormack, Timothy Dalton, Kathy Bates, Nathaniel Arcand, Ali Larter, Ronny Cox, Harris Yulin, Terry O'Quinn, Ty O'Neal, Joe Stevens; ***D:*** Les Mayfield; ***W:*** John Rogers, Roderick Taylor; ***C:*** Russell Boyd; ***M:*** Trevor Rabin.

American Pie *East Great Falls High* **1999 (R)** And you thought you loved dessert! Four high school seniors led by pastry molesting Jim (Biggs) vow to lose their virginity before the Prom. Unfortunately for them, the girls that they're chasing aren't your usual teenage sex comedy tarts. These smart little cookies make sure that the boys' quest is chock full of humiliation. The sensitivity to the female point-of-view is balanced by a heapin' helpin' of crude and disgusting humor for the guys. An absolute must-see for baked goods and the men who love them. **95m/C VHS, DVD, UMD.** Jason Biggs, Thomas Ian Nicholas, Chris Owen, Chris Klein, Natasha Lyonne, Tara Reid, Mena Suvari, Alyson Hannigan, Shannon Elizabeth, Eugene Levy, Seann William Scott, Jennifer Coolidge, Eddie Kaye Thomas, Lawrence Pressman, Eric Lively, Molly Cheek, Clyde Kusatsu, John Cho, Eli Marienthal, Casey Affleck, Tara Subkoff, Christina Milian; ***D:*** Chris Weitz, Paul Weitz; ***W:*** Adam Herz; ***C:*** Richard Crudo; ***M:*** David Lawrence.

American Pie 2 1/2 **2001 (R)** No pie is abused in this movie, although everyone (including exec producers Chris and Paul Weitz) is back for a second helping. The story picks up a year later while everyone is on summer vacation from college and sharing a beach house. Jim (Biggs) is nervously anticipating a visit from Nadia, while getting sex tips from band camp geek Michelle (Hannigan). Entertaining sequel shares the original's appealing and effective combination of gross-out situations and sweet silliness, and while it's not quite as good, it doesn't miss by much. **105m/C VHS, DVD, UMD.** *US* Jason Biggs, Shannon Elizabeth, Alyson Hannigan, Chris Klein, Natasha Lyonne, Thomas Ian Nicholas, Tara Reid, Chris Owen, Seann William Scott, Mena Suvari, Eddie Kaye Thomas, Eugene Levy, Jennifer Coolidge, Christopher Penn, Eli Marienthal, Casey Affleck, Denise Faye, Molly Cheek; ***D:*** James B. Rogers; ***W:*** Adam Herz; ***C:*** Mark Irwin; ***M:*** David Lawrence.

American Pie Presents Band Camp *Band Camp* **2005** Stiffler's equally obnoxious and horny younger brother Matt (Hilgenbrink) is sent to summer band camp as punishment for a prank gone wrong. He decides to liven up his stay by shooting "girls gone wild"-type videos of the band chicks, only to have a change of heart when he hooks up with old friend Elyse (Kebbel). Levy's the only original cast member to sheepishly show up in this drivel. **94m/C DVD.** Tad Hilgenbrink, Arielle Kebbel, Crystle Lightning, Eugene Levy, Jason Earles; ***D:*** Steve Rash; ***W:*** Brad Riddell; ***C:*** Victor Kemper; ***M:*** Robert Folk. **VIDEO**

American Pie Presents: Beta House *Beta House* **2007 (R)** And the franchise just gets lamer and grosser. Dwight Stifler is the head of the infamous Beta frat, just pledged by his cousin Erik and his buds. But their house superiority is challenged by newcomer Geek House and power-hungry nerd Edgar. **89m/C DVD.** Jake Siegel, John White, Steven Talley, Meghan Heffern, Nic Nac, Tyrone Savage, Sarah Power, Eugene Levy, Christopher McDonald; ***D:*** Andrew Waller; ***W:*** Erik Lindsay; ***M:*** Jeff Cardoni. **VIDEO**

American Pie Presents: The Naked Mile *American Pie 5: The Naked Mile* **2006 (R)** Raunchy and surprisingly funny sex comedy. Erik Stifler (White) is a high school virgin since sweet girlfriend Tracy (Schram) won't put out. Erik and his buddies are visiting his cousin Dwight (Talley) at college for the weekend in order to run in the annual naked mile. Feeling guilty, Tracy gives him a free pass to do whatever he wants—and then worries that what Erik wants is sex with some other girl. Humiliation and a wide variety of bodily fluids follow. Also available unrated. **97m/C DVD.** John White, Steven Talley, Ross Thomas, Christopher McDonald, Jessy Schram, Jake Siegel, Eugene Levy, Candace Kroslak; ***D:*** Joe Nussbaum; ***W:*** Erik Lindsay; ***C:*** Eric Haase; ***M:*** Jeff Cardoni. **VIDEO**

American Pluck **1925** Before he can inherit anything, a playboy millionaire's son must go out into the world and prove he can make his own way. He meets a beautiful princess, who is pursued by a villainous count. Walsh, as the dashing hero, was the younger brother of director Raoul. Silent with original organ music. **91m/B VHS.** George Walsh, Wanda (Petit) Hawley, Frank Leigh, Sidney De Grey; ***D:*** Richard Stanton.

American Pop **1981 (R)** Animated story of four generations of men told in music. Immigrant Zalmie starts off in vaudeville and winds up involved in the mob, his pianist son Benny gets killed in WWII, Benny's son Tony winds up in the early psychedelic rock scene in Haight-Asbury, and Tony's son Little Pete becomes a rock idol. ♫A Hard Rain's A-Gonna Fall; Don't Think Twice It's All Right; People Are Strange; Purple Haze; Hell is for Children; Free Bird; I'm Waiting for the Man; Night Moves; You Send Me. **95m/C VHS, DVD.** ***D:*** Ralph Bakshi; ***W:*** Ronni Kern; ***M:*** Lee Holdridge; ***V:*** Ron Thompson, Marya Small, Lisa Jane Persky, Roz Kelly, Richard Singer, Jeffrey Lippa.

The American President **1995 (PG-13)** Widower president Andrew Shepherd (Douglas) decides it's time to get back into the dating game. But just what woman wants to find her romance in the public eye? Well, it turns out to be feisty environmental lobbyist Sydney Wade (the ever-charming Bening). But the Prez also has to put up with nasty opponent Bob Rumson (Dreyfuss), who's using their courtship as political fodder, approval ratings, and a nosy press. Glossy fairytale material expertly handled by both cast and director. **114m/C VHS, DVD.** Michael Douglas, Annette Bening, Martin Sheen, Michael J. Fox, David Paymer, Samantha Mathis, John Mahoney, Anna Deavere Smith, Nina Siemaszko, Wendie Malick, Shawna Waldron, Richard Dreyfuss, Gabe Jarret, Anne Haney, Gail Strickland, Joshua Malina, Ron Canada, Jennifer Crystal Foley, Taylor Nichols; ***D:*** Rob Reiner; ***W:*** Aaron Sorkin; ***C:*** John Seale; ***M:*** Marc Shaiman.

American Psycho **1999 (R)** Trimmed-down and (slightly) cleaned-up version of Bret Easton Ellis's widely hated 1991 novel has Bale as '80s hotshot Wall Street exec and apparent serial-killer Patrick Bateman. Bateman is the poster child for Reaganera excess and preference for style over substance, a theme with which the film, while shooting for satire, beats you over the head. Like the decade it portrays, "Psycho" is far from subtle, and the characters barely register as two-dimensional, let alone three. They got the look right, but then, that's the point, isn't it? The production drew protests in Toronto, where some scenes were shot, and Leo DiCaprio was rumored to be in line to play the lead for a time. **103m/C VHS, DVD, Blu-ray Disc, UMD.** Christian Bale, Willem Dafoe, Jared Leto, Reese Witherspoon, Samantha Mathis, Chloe Sevigny, Justin Theroux, Josh(ua) Lucas, Guinevere Turner, Matt Ross, William Sage, Cara Seymour; ***D:*** Mary Harron; ***W:*** Mary Harron, Guinevere Turner; ***C:*** Andrzej Sekula; ***M:*** John Cale.

American Psycho 2: All American Girl **2002 (R)** Rachelle Newman (Kunis) is the only victim who managed to escape from serial killer Patrick Bateman. But her ordeal left her obsessed with such killers and when she learns that college prof Robert Strickland (Shatner) was an FBI profiler specializing in the subject, Rachelle is determined to become his teaching assistant. Even if it means killing the competition. **88m/C VHS, DVD.** Mila Kunis, William Shatner, Geraint Wyn Davies, Lindy Booth, Robin Dunne; ***D:*** Morgan J. Freeman; ***W:*** Karen Craig, Alex Sanger; ***C:*** Vanja Cernjul; ***M:*** Norman Orenstein. **VIDEO**

An American Rhapsody **2001 (PG-13)** A mother/daughter conflict steeped in history and based on the experiences of writer/director Gardos. Margit (Kinski) and her family flee Hungary during the communist takeover of the 1950s but she is forced to leave her infant daughter behind. While the family settles in L.A., Suzanne is being raised in the country by adoptive parents and knows nothing of her origins. She gets a rude awakening at the age of 6 when her grandmother Helen (Banfalvy) makes arrangements to reunite Suzy with her unknown "real" family. The child grows into a sullen teenager (Johansson) who longs to return to Budapest. Her father finally agrees to a solo trip and Suzanne learns just what her family suffered and where she truly belongs. **106m/C VHS, DVD.** *US HU* Nastassja Kinski, Scarlett Johansson, Tony Goldwyn, Kelly Endresz-Banlaki, Agnes Banfalvy, Zsuzsi Czinkoczi, Balazs Galko, Zoltan Seress, Mae Whitman, Lisa Jane Persky, Emmy Rossum; ***D:*** Eva Gardos; ***W:*** Eva Gardos; ***C:*** Elemer Ragalyi; ***M:*** Cliff Eidelman.

American Roulette **1988 (R)** Garcia is the exiled president of a Latin American country living in London in this thin political thriller. A plot riddled with weaknesses and poor direction make this potentially interesting film dull and lifeless. **102m/C VHS.** *GB AU* Andy Garcia, Kitty Aldridge, Robert Stephens, Al Matthews, Susannah York; ***D:*** Maurice Hatton; ***M:*** Michael Gibbs.

American Samurai **1/2 1992 (R)** Drew is the adopted son of a Japanese samurai, who gives him the family's sacred sword. This gesture angers his stepbrother who gets involved with Japanese gangsters and illegal live-blade fighting, and who also vows revenge on this American upstart. Lots of sword play to go with the chop-socky action. **89m/C VHS, DVD.** David Bradley, Mark Dacascos, John Fujioka, Valarie Trapp; ***D:*** Sam Firstenberg; ***W:*** John Corcoran.

The American Scream **1/2 1988** An innocent family vacationing in the mountains stumbles on to a satanic cult. And that can really ruin a vacation. **85m/C VHS.** Jennifer Darling, Pons Marr, Blackie Dammett, Kimberly Kramer, Jean Sapienza, Kevin Kaye, Matt Borlenghi, James Cooper; ***D:*** Mitchell Linden.

American Shaolin: King of the Kickboxers 2 **1/2 1992 (PG-13)** When Drew gets his butt kicked in a karate tournament he decides to head to China and learn some fight-winning moves from a group of warrior monks. **103m/C VHS.** Reese Madigan, Trent Bushy, Daniel Dae Kim, Billy Chang, Cliff Lenderman, Zhang Shi Yen, Kim Chan, Alice Zhang Hung; ***D:*** Lucas Lowe.

The American Soldier **1/2** *Der Amerikanische Soldat* **1970** Fassbinder's homage to the American gangster film tells the story of Ricky, a charismatic hit man. Ricky always wears a gun in a shoulder holster, sports a fedora and a white double-breasted suit, and drinks Scotch straight from the bottle. He also carries out his assigned murders with complete efficiency and no emotion. In German with English subtitles. **80m/C VHS, DVD.** *GE* Rainer Werner Fassbinder, Karl Scheydt, Elga Sorbas, Jan George, Ingrid Caven, Ulli Lommel, Kurt Raab; ***D:*** Rainer Werner Fassbinder; ***W:*** Rainer Werner Fassbinder; ***C:*** Dietrich Lohmann; ***M:*** Peer Raben.

American Soldiers WOOF! 2005 (R) Incompetent mess mangles a serious subject and is only worth a groan for its ineptitude. In April 2004, an army platoon is ambushed by insurgents in Iraq and the surviving soldiers must make their way back to base through enemy territory. Filmed in Hamilton, Ontario, which cannot in any way pass for Iraq. **103m/C DVD.** *CA* Curtis Morgan, Zan Calabretta, Jordan Brown, Eddie Della Siepe; ***D:*** Sidney J. Furie; ***W:*** Greg Mellott. **VIDEO**

American Son **1/2 2008 (R)** Well-done drama focuses on the personal rather than the military aspects of the Iraq War. Marine Pvt. Mike Holland (Cannon) gets a four-day Thanksgiving leave before shipping out to Iraq. While taking the bus from Camp Pendleton to Bakersfield, Mike is instantly smitten by fellow passenger Cristina (Diaz), a Mexican-American college student. Mike keeps postponing the moment he has to tell his troubled family he's leaving while dealing with his volatile friend, drug dealer Jake (O'Leary), who's upset that Mike has changed. Meanwhile, Mike tries to persuade Cristina to be his girlfriend despite his upcoming departure. **86m/C DVD.** Nick Cannon, Melonie Diaz, Matt O'Leary, Jay Hernandez, Chi McBride, Tom Sizemore, April Grace; ***D:*** Neil Abramson; ***W:*** Eric Schmid; ***C:*** Kris Kachikis; ***M:*** Tim Bolland, Sam Retzer. **VIDEO**

American Splendor **1/2 2003 (R)** Giamatti is brilliant as Harvey Pekar, a life-long file clerk in Cleveland who authored the R. Crumb-illustrated autobiographical graphic novels of the film's title. The unlikely courtship of misfits Pekar and his third wife Joyce Brabner (Davis) is comically portrayed as the two kindred souls mysteriously come together. Their unlikely romance mirrors the unlikelihood that a comic filled with the pessimism, cynicism, and wry comic observations of Pekar's admitted hum-drum life would somehow translate just as well onto the big screen. But it does. Documentarian directors Berman and Pulcini weave fiction with fact as the real Pekar narrates and cameos. They also make use of illustrated comic segments and footage from Pekar's frequent appearances on David Letterman's show. **101m/C VHS, DVD.** *US* Paul Giamatti, Hope Davis, Harvey Pekar, Joyce Brabner, Earl Billings, James Urbaniak, Judah Friedlander, Donal Logue, Molly Shannon, James McCaffrey, Shari Springer Berman, Robert Pulcini; ***D:*** Shari Springer Berman, Robert Pulcini; ***W:*** Shari Springer Berman, Robert Pulcini; ***C:*** Terry Stacey; ***M:*** Mark Suozzo. L.A. Film Critics '03: Film, Screenplay; N.Y. Film Critics '03: Actress (Davis); Natl. Soc. Film Critics '03: Film, Screenplay; Writers Guild '03: Adapt. Screenplay.

An American Story **1/2 1992 (PG)** Earnest but predictable story based on an actual incident. Six WWII vets return to their small Texas town as heroes. But when they find a corrupt mayor and a brutal sheriff running things they decide to campaign to unseat the local politicos, in spite of some dire warnings. Meade (Johnson), their commanding officer in Europe, is the designated leader in the plan but his ambitious wife and father-in-law want him to align himself with the status quo instead. Hallmark Hall of Fame production is enjoyable and better than most made for TV movies, but fails to reach the heights of many other HHF offerings. **97m/C VHS.** Brad Johnson, Kathleen Quinlan, Tom Sizemore, Josef Sommer, Patricia Clarkson, Lisa Blount, G.W. Bailey, John M. Jackson; ***D:*** John Gray; ***W:*** John Gray; ***C:*** Johnny E. Jensen. **TV**

American Strays **1/2 1996 (R)** Episodic black comedy about various oddballs (most of them violent) who cross paths (usually in Kane's roadside diner) in an isolated desert town. There's a masochist who wants help committing suicide, an unemployed family man on the verge of a breakdown, a serial killer, and more—mostly strange. **97m/C VHS, DVD.** Jack Kehler, Carol Kane, Jennifer Tilly, Eric Roberts, John Savage, Luke Perry, Joe (Johnny) Viterelli, James Russo, Vonte Sweet, Sam Jones, Brion James, Toni Kalem, Melora Walters; ***D:*** Michael Covert; ***W:*** Michael Covert; ***C:*** Sead Muhtarevic; ***M:*** John Graham.

American Streetfighter **1996** Martial arts expert Jake Tanner gets involved with an illegal streetfighting ring to rescue his brother, Randy, who's the target of a drug courier. But what happens when his next opponent is his sibling? **80m/C VHS, DVD.** Gary Daniels, Ian Jacklin, Tracy Dali; ***D:*** Steve Austin.

American Streetfighter 2: The Full Impact **1/2 1997** Ex-cop becomes a bounty hunter tracking a serial killer who likes to kill his victims with his bare hands. **90m/C VHS, DVD.** Gary Daniels, Graciela Casillas; ***D:*** Marc Messenger. **VIDEO**

An American Summer **1990** A Chicago kid spends a summer with his aunt in beach-rich Los Angeles in this coming-of-age tale filled with '90s teen idols. **100m/C VHS, DVD.** Brian Austin Green, Joanna Kerns, Michael Landes, Tony Crane, Brian Krause, Wayne Pere, Amber Susa; ***D:*** James Slocum; ***W:*** James Slocum; ***C:*** Bruce Dorfman; ***M:*** Roger Neill.

An American Tail **1/2 1986 (G)** While emigrating to New York in the 1880s, a young Russian mouse (Fievel) is separated from his family. He matures as he learns to live on the Big Apple's dirty boulevards. The bad guys are of course cats. Excellent animation and a high-minded (though sentimental and stereotypical) plot keep it interesting for adults. Produced by Spielberg and the first big hit for the Bluth factory, a collection of expatriate Disney artists. Knowing better than to let a money-making mouse tale languish, Bluth followed with "An American Tale: Fievel Goes West." **81m/C VHS, DVD.** ***D:*** Don Bluth; ***M:*** James Horner; ***V:*** Dom DeLuise, Madeline Kahn, Phillip Glasser, Christopher Plummer, Nehemiah Persoff, Will Ryan, John Finnegan, Cathianne Blore.

An American Tail: Fievel Goes West **1991 (G)** Fievel and the Mousekewitz family continue their pursuit of the American dream by heading West, where the intrepid mouse seeks to become a famous lawman while his sister looks to make it big as a dance hall singer. The score is performed by the London Symphony Orchestra. Unfortunately released at the same time as "Beauty and the Beast," "Fievel Goes West" suffers from comparison. Worthwhile viewing for the whole family, but it won't ever reach the heights of "B&B." The laser edition is letterboxed and features chapter stops. **75m/C VHS, DVD.** ***D:*** Phil Nibbelink, Simon Wells; ***W:*** Flint Dille; ***M:*** James Horner; ***V:*** John Cleese, Dom DeLuise, Phillip Glasser, Amy Irving, Jon Lovitz, Catherine Cavadini, Nehemiah Persoff, Erica Yohn, James Stewart.

American Teen **1/2 2008 (PG-13)** Slick documentary following four teens through their senior year of high school in Warsaw, Indiana. Director Burstein shot 1000 hours of footage over 10 months, piecing together her version of "The Breakfast Club" for MTV. The popular girl, the basketball star, the band geek, and the art chick all suspiciously play exactly to stereotype, making it seem more like reality TV than a documentary. Nothing too thought provoking or unusual (zits, prom jitters, the big game, Internet drama) but it still touches a nerve and may bring back a few memories, good or bad. **95m/C DVD.** *US* ***D:*** Nanette Burstein; ***C:*** Laela Kilbourn, Wolfgang Held, Robert Hanna; ***M:*** Michael Penn.

American Tickler **1/2** *Draws* **1976 (R)** A thigh-slappin' (or is it head-whacking?) series of satirical pastiches in the grand style of "Kentucky Fried Movie," only more sophomoric. A tasteless collection of yearning to be funny sketches about American institutions. **77m/C VHS.** W.P. Dremak, Joan Sumner, Marlow Ferguson, Jeff Allin, Joe Piscopo; ***D:*** Chuck Vincent.

American Tiger *American Rickshaw* **1989 (R)** The collegiate hero of "American Tiger" is, like so many college students, framed for murder, and he applies himself to clearing his sullied name. Somewhere during this process, he finds himself in the middle of a battle between good and evil on a football field. About what you'd expect from a supernatural kung-fu teen-action drama. **93m/C VHS.** Mitch Gaylord, Donald Pleasence, Daniel Greene, Victoria Prouty; ***D:*** Sergio Martino.

An American Tragedy **1931** Straightforward retelling of the Theodore Dreiser novel (although Dreiser sued Paramount because he didn't approve of the script). Ambitious factory boss Clyde Griffiths (Holmes) takes advantage of his distant connection to some wealthy relatives to hang around the fringes of high society. He romances moneyed beauty Sondra (Dee) but his plans are thrown into disarray when working-class Roberta (Sidney) tells Clyde she's pregnant. After a boating trip, Clyde becomes a criminal suspect leading to a long trial sequence. Remade as 1951's "A Place in the Sun." **96m/B DVD.** Phillips Holmes, Sylvia Sidney, Frances Dee, Irving Pichel, Lucille LaVerne, Frederick Burton, Charles Middleton, Emmett Corrigan; ***D:*** Irving Pichel, Josef von Sternberg; ***W:*** Samuel Hoffenstein; ***C:*** Lee Garmes.

American Tragedy **1/2 2000 (PG-13)** Remember the O.J. Simpson trial? Well, if you don't, this cable drama is here to remind you as it explores the egos and infighting of Simpson's four defense lawyers: Johnny Cochran (Rhames), Bob Shapiro (Silver), F. Lee Bailey (Plummer), and Barry Scheck (Kirby). Based on the book by Schiller, who also directed. **170m/C VHS, DVD.** Ving Rhames, Ron Silver, Christopher Plummer, Bruno Kirby, Nicholas Pryor, Robert LuPone, Ruben Santiago-Hudson, Richard Cox, Clyde Kusatsu, Jeff Kober; ***D:*** Lawrence Schiller;

W: Norman Mailer; *C:* Bruce Surtees; *M:* Bill Conti. **CABLE**

American Vampire 🦴🦴 1/2 **1997 (R)** Teenager Frankie (Lussauer) has been left alone while his parents are on vacation. One night on the beach, he and his friend Bogie (Hitt) meet Moondoggie (Venokur), who promises to help them party the summer away. He soon reappears with two babes (Electra and Xavier) who appear to be undead. Frankie must turn to The Big Kahuna (West) to stop the vampires. Yes, the plot strictly follows the formula, but the effects are not bad for a low-budget production; the photography is better than it needs to be; and the humor is intentional. **99m/C VHS, DVD.** Trevor Lissauer, Danny Hitt, Johnny Venokur, Carmen Electra, Debora Xavier, Adam West, Sydney Lassick; *D:* Luis Esteban; *W:* Rollin Jarrett; *C:* Jurgen Baum, Goran Paviceric. **VIDEO**

American Venus 🦴 1/2 **2007** Celia Lane (De Mornay) is the ultimate in crazy, controlling mothers. When her ice skating daughter Jenna (McGregor) chokes during a national-level competition, Jenna decides she's had enough and quits for good—much to coach/mom Celia's fury. So Jenna sneaks out of Spokane to live the college life in Vancouver, British Columbia—until Celia tracks her down. Celia's also the ultimate in ugly Americans in a foreign country and the viewer is never quite sure if Sweeney is aiming for satire or not. **80m/C DVD.** *CA* Rebecca De Mornay, Jane McGregor, Matt Craven, Nicholas Lea, Agam Darshi, Anna Amoroso; *D:* Bruce Sweeney; *W:* Bruce Sweeney; *C:* David Pelletier; *M:* James Jandrisch. **VIDEO**

American Violet 🦴🦴 1/2 **2009 (PG-13)** Docudrama of Dee Roberts (Beharie), a 24 year-old African-American single mother of four young girls living in a small Texas town barely able to make ends meet. While police drag Dee from work in handcuffs on trumped-up charges, dumping her in the women's county prison, the powerful local district attorney (O'Keefe) leads an extensive drug bust, sweeping her housing project and ultimately charging Dee as a drug dealer. With few choices, Dee and her ACLU attorney decide to sue the DA for unjust practices. Predictable outcome but does well in its portrayal of the plight of poor minorities caught up, legitimately or not, in a racially tainted justice system. Newcomer Beharie shines alongside veterans Woodard, Dutton, and Blake Nelson. Based on a true story that's set during the 2000 presidential campaign. **103m/C DVD.** *US* Michael O'Keefe, Tim Blake Nelson, Will Patton, Alfre Woodard, Nicole Beharie, Xzibit, Scott A. Martin; *D:* Tim Disney; *W:* Bill Haney; *C:* Steve Yedlin.

American Virgin 🦴 *Live Virgin* **1998 (R)** Ronny Bartoloti (Loggia) is a successful Hollywood adult film director who has upset his virginal 18-year-old daughter, Katrina (Suvari), with his double-standard attitudes. So she decides to get even by sharing her first sexual experience with millions—by going live on camera on closed-circuit—with the help of Ronny's rival Joey Quinn (Hoskins). But can daddy get his determined little darling to change her mind? Exploitative would-be satire falls flat. **87m/C VHS, DVD.** Mena Suvari, Robert Loggia, Bob Hoskins, Gabriel Mann, Sally Kellerman, Bobbie Phillips, Lamont Johnson, Rick Peters, O-lan Jones, Alexandra Wentworth; *D:* Jean Pierre Marois; *W:* Jean Pierre Marois, Ira Israel; *C:* Eagle Egilsson.

American Virgin 🦴 **2009 (R)** Yeah, it's a stupid, low-budget, direct-to-DVD college sex comedy (and the female leads keep their clothes on) but said female leads try hard and even Schneider isn't completely offensive. Chaste college freshman Priscilla (Dewan) is horrified that her roommate Natalie (Davis) is the biggest slut on campus. Then Priscilla gets drunk (thanks to Natalie) at a frat party and displays her ta-tas for a "Girls Gone Crazy" video. Humiliated, she scrambles to get the footage back from sleazy producer Ed (Schneider), who's now down in New Orleans filming more unseemly behavior at Mardi Gras. **88m/C DVD.** Jenna Dewan, Brianne Davis, Rob Schneider, Ebon Moss-Bachrach, Chase Ryan Jeffery, Ben Marten, Ashley Schneider, Bo Burnham; *D:* Clare Kilner; *W:* Lucas Jarach, Jason Price, Jeff Seeman; *C:* Oliver Curtis; *M:* John Hunter. **VIDEO**

American Wedding 🦴🦴 1/2 *American Pie 3* **2003 (R)** In the finale of the epic trilogy Annakin and Amidala, no, wait. Frodo and Gollum...no, Neo and Trinity...that's not it either. Jim and Michelle are getting married, with the dubious help of most of the gang. Kevin and Finch are still around, but it's Stifler who has the biggest impact, throwing the bachelor party, battling Finch for the affections of Michelle's sister Cadence (Jones), and almost putting the kibosh on the whole wedding. Like the other two, it's pretty gross in parts, uproarious in others, but still has its sweet, charming moments. Levy and Willard make the most of their scenes as the father of the groom and bride, respectively. **96m/C VHS, DVD, UMD.** *US* Jason Biggs, Alyson Hannigan, Seann William Scott, Eddie Kaye Thomas, January Jones, Eugene Levy, Thomas Ian Nicholas, Fred Willard, Molly Cheek, Eric Allen Kramer, Deborah Rush, Jennifer Coolidge, Angela Paton, Lawrence Pressman, Amanda Swisten, Nikki Schieler Ziering; *D:* Jesse Dylan; *W:* Adam Herz; *C:* Lloyd Ahern II; *M:* Christophe Beck.

An American Werewolf in London 🦴🦴🦴 **1981 (R)** Strange, darkly humorous version of the classic man-into-wolf horror tale became a cult hit, but never clicked with most American critics. Two American college students, David (Naughton) and Jack (Dunne), are backpacking through England when thy're viciously attacked by a werewolf one foggy night. Jack is killed, but keeps appearing (in progressively decomposed form) before the seriously wounded David, warning him of impending werewolfdom when the moon is full; Jack advises suicide. Seat-jumping horror and gore, highlighted by intensive metamorphosis sequences orchestrated by Rick Baker, are offset by wry humor, though the shifts in tone don't always work. Great moon songs permeate the soundtrack, including CCR's "Bad Moon Rising" and Van Morrison's "Moondance." Followed by "An American Werewolf in Paris" (1997). **97m/C VHS, DVD, HD DVD.** *GB* David Naughton, Griffin Dunne, Jenny Agutter, Frank Oz, Brian Glover, Lila Kaye, David Schofield, John Woodvine, Don McKillop, Paul Kember, Colin Fernandes, Rik Mayall, Paddy Ryan; *D:* John Landis; *W:* John Landis; *C:* Robert Paynter; *M:* Elmer Bernstein. Oscars '81: Makeup.

An American Werewolf in Paris 🦴🦴 **1997 (R)** More of a remake than a sequel, horror-comedy fails to live up to the wit and quirkiness of the original. Andy (Scott) is on a daredevil tour of Europe along with buddies Brad (Vieluf) and Chris (Buckman). As he attempts to bungee jump off of the Eiffel Tower, he spots a French femme attempting to plungee jump nearby. He saves her and immediately falls in love with her. The girl, Serafine (Delpy) warns him to stay away, but he keeps sniffing around. They tail her to a creepy house she shares with a guy named Claude (Cosso), where Andy secures a date and his friends are invited to a dinner party. Claude, however, is top dog in a pack of racist werewolves, and Andy's pals end up as the main course. Bitten himself, Andy learns that he's now a werewolf. Brad and the other victims pop up now and again to remind Andy that they're doomed to walk the earth until the werewolves that killed them are destroyed. Special effects have advanced a long way since the original and it shows, although the computer generated wolves are difficult to tell apart. **100m/C VHS, DVD.** Anthony Waller, Julie Delpy, Tom Everett Scott, Julie Bowen, Pierre Cosso, Thierry Lhermitte, Vince Vieluf, Phil Buckman, Tom Novembre, Isabelle Constantini; *D:* Anthony Waller; *W:* Anthony Waller, Tim Burns, Tom Stern; *C:* Egon Werdin; *M:* Wilbert Hirsch.

American Women 🦴🦴 *The Closer You Get* **2000 (PG-13)** Poor schlub County Donegal lads, weary of their lack of female companionship, send an ad to the Miami Herald, looking for young, nubile American women to come over and "see what happens." Hoping to see the American lasses in time for the social event of the season, the St. Martha's Day dance, they're disappointed when the day arrives but the girls don't. To make matters worse, the local ladies have brought in some Spanish fishermen to play music at the dance. Old fashioned ethnic comedy tries to cash in on the successes of "The Full Monty" and "Waking Ned Devine," but contains a wee bit too many Irish cliches, and the charm is squeezed out by the patronizing view of what is supposed to be modern-day Ireland. **90m/C VHS, DVD.** *IR GB* Ian Hart, Sean McGinley, Niamh Cusack, Ruth McCabe, Ewan Stewart, Maureen O'Brien, Pat Laffan, Britta Smith, Pat Shortt, Cathleen Bradley, Sean McDonagh, Risteard Cooper; *D:* Aileen Ritchie; *W:* William Ivory; *C:* Robert Alazraki; *M:* Rachel Portman.

American Yakuza 🦴🦴 **1994 (R)** FBI agent Nick Davis (Mortensen) is sent to L.A. to infiltrate the American arm of the Yakuza, Japan's dangerous criminal underworld. He rises through the ranks and is adopted into the powerful Tendo family. Now Davis finds himself caught between the FBI, the Yakuza, and the vengeful American mafia. **95m/C VHS, DVD.** Viggo Mortensen, Michael Nouri, Ryo Ishibashi, Franklin Ajaye; *D:* Frank Cappello; *W:* Max Strom, John Allen Nelson; *C:* Richard Clabaugh; *M:* David Williams.

Americana 🦴🦴 1/2 **1981 (PG)** A troubled Vietnam vet tries to restore himself by rebuilding a merry-go-round in a small mid-western town, while dealing with opposition from the local residents. Offbeat, often effective post-Nam editorial that was produced and directed in 1973 by Carradine and then shelved. Hershey and Carradine were a couple back then. **90m/C VHS, DVD.** David Carradine, Barbara Hershey, Michael Greene, John Drew (Blythe) Barrymore Jr.; *D:* David Carradine; *W:* Richard Carr.

The Americanization of Emily 🦴🦴🦴 **1964** A happy-go-lucky American naval officer (Garner) with no appetite for war discovers to his horror that he may be slated to become the first casualty of the Normandy invasion as part of a military PR effort in this black comedy-romance. Meanwhile, he spreads the charisma in an effort to woo and uplift Emily (Andrews), a depressed English woman who has suffered the loss of her husband, father, and brother during the war. A cynical, often funny look at military maneuvers and cultural drift that was adapted by Paddy Chayefsky from William Bradford Huie's novel. Also available colorized. **117m/B VHS, DVD.** James Garner, Julie Andrews, Melvyn Douglas, James Coburn, Joyce Grenfell, Keenan Wynn, Edward Binns, Liz Fraser, William Windom; *D:* Arthur Hiller; *W:* Paddy Chayefsky.

The Americano 🦴🦴 1/2 **1917** Ever-suave Fairbanks frees a South American politician locked in a dungeon, returns him to political success, and captures the heart of his beautiful daughter. Based on Eugene P. Lyle Jr.'s "Blaze Derringer." **58m/B VHS.** Douglas Fairbanks Sr., Alma Rubens, Spottiswoode Aitken, Lillian Langdon, Carl Stockdale, Tom Wilson; *D:* John Emerson.

Americano 🦴🦴 **1955** A cowboy travelling to Brazil with a shipment of Brahma bulls discovers the rancher he's delivering them to has been murdered. An odd amalgam of western cliches and a South American setting. **85m/C VHS.** Glenn Ford, Frank Lovejoy, Abbe Lane, Cesar Romero; *D:* William Castle.

Americano 🦴🦴 **2005 (R)** Recent college grad Chris (Jackson) and his friends Ryan (Sharp) and Michelle (Ruthanna Hopper) have been backpacking through Europe and wind up at the end of their trip in Pamplona, Spain, for the annual running of the bulls. Chris meets beautiful Adela (Varela), who takes pity on him and lets Chris stay at her house after his backpack is stolen. His feelings quickly turn romantic. Dennis Hopper plays an ex-pat bar owner proffering advice when Chris wonders if he's really ready to return home. **95m/C DVD.** Joshua Jackson, Leonor Varela, Dennis Hopper, Timm Sharp, Ruthanna Hopper; *D:* Kevin Noland; *W:* Kevin Noland; *C:* Robert Christopher Webb; *M:* Peter Golub.

America's Deadliest Home Video 🦴🦴 **1991** Camp spoof about America's obsession with videotaping everything in sight. Video enthusiast Doug is taken hostage by the Clint Dryer gang who want him to tape their crime spree. Every aspect is only seen through the lens of the video camera. **90m/C VHS.** Danny Bonaduce, Mick Wynhoff, Mollena Williams, Melora Walters; *D:* Jack Perez; *W:* Jack Perez.

America's Dream 🦴🦴🦴 **1995 (PG-13)** Trilogy of short stories covering black life from 1938 to 1958. In "Long Black Song," based on a short story by Richard Wright, Alabama farmer Silas (Glover) lives with lonely wife Sarah (Lifford), who succumbs to the charms of white travelling salesman, David (Donovan). "The Boy Who Painted Christ Black" is young Aaron (Golden), who gives the drawing to his teacher, Miss Williams (Calloway). But the portrait causes a great deal of controversy in Aaron's 1948 Georgia school, especially for ambitious principal George Du Vaul (Snipes). Based on a story by John Henrich Clarke. The last story is Maya Angelou's "The Reunion," about Chicago jazz pianist Philomena (Toussaint), who encounters her childhood nemesis, Beth Ann (Thompson), the daughter of the white family who employed her parents as servants. **87m/C VHS, DVD.** Danny Glover, Tina Lifford, Tate Donovan, Dan Kamin, Wesley Snipes, Jasmine Guy, Vanessa Bell Calloway, Norman D. Golden II, Timothy Carhart, Yolanda King, Rae'ven (Alyia Larrymore) Kelly, Lorraine Toussaint, Susanna Thompson, Carl Lumbly, Phyllis Cicero; *D:* Bill Duke, Kevin Rodney Sullivan, Paris Barclay; *W:* Ron Stacker Thompson, Ashley Tyler; *C:* Karl Herrmann; *M:* Patrice Rushen.

America's Heart and Soul 🦴🦴 **2004 (PG)** Series of vignettes seeks to capture the diversity and indomitable spirit of America, as a saccharine and ineffective answer to "Fahrenheit 9/11." Viewers literally fly over the U.S. and swoop down to meet a cowboy in Colorado, a rug weaver in Appalachia, a dairy farmer in Vermont, a trombone prodigy in Louisiana, a Methodist pastor in San Francisco, an Olympic boxer in Chicago and so on. Although the scenery is gorgeous and the people compelling, you're never with them for very long or reach any sort of depth. **84m/C DVD.** *D:* Louis Schwartzberg; *C:* Louis Schwartzberg; *M:* Joel McNeely.

America's Sweethearts 🦴🦴 **2001 (PG-13)** This just in: Hollywood is shallow and fake, Julia Roberts is pretty, and entertainment reporters are freeloading numbskulls. These are the themes covered in this disappointing romantic comedy in which America's favorite on- and off-screen couple Eddie (Cusack) and Gwen (Zeta-Jones) pretend to reconcile during a disaster-filled press junket cooked up by desparate publicist Lee (Crystal). Complicating matters are the developing relationship between Gwen's sister and assistant Kiki (Roberts) and Eddie. Roth hasn't directed a film in over 10 years, and it shows here. But beneath the rust, there are some funny moments, mostly including Walken as the crazy director who has taken his own film hostage. **103m/C VHS, DVD.** *US* Julia Roberts, Catherine Zeta-Jones, John Cusack, Billy Crystal, Hank Azaria, Christopher Walken, Seth Green, Stanley Tucci; *Cameos:* Larry King; *D:* Joe Roth; *W:* Billy Crystal, Peter Tolan; *C:* Phedon Papamichael; *M:* James Newton Howard.

Americathon **WOOF!** **1979 (PG)** It is the year 1998 and the United States is almost bankrupt, so President Chet Roosevelt decides to stage a telethon to keep the country from going broke. Interesting satiric premise with a diverse cast, but a poor script and slack pacing spoil all the fun. The soundtrack features music by The Beach Boys and Elvis Costello while the narration is by George Carlin. **85m/C VHS.** Terence McGovern, Allan Arbus, David Opatoshu, John Lone, Cybill Shepherd, Dorothy Stratten, Peter Riegert, John Ritter, Nancy Morgan, Harvey Korman, Fred Willard, Meat Loaf Aday, Elvis Costello, Chief Dan George, Howard Hesseman, Jay Leno; *Cameos:* Tommy Lasorda, Peter Marshall; *D:* Neal Israel; *W:* Monica Johnson, Neal Israel; *M:* Earl Brown Jr.; *Nar:* George Carlin.

Amin: The Rise and Fall **WOOF!** **1982** Excessively violent and ultimately pointless dramatization of Idi Amin's eight-year reign of terror in Uganda, which resulted in the deaths of a half million people and the near ruin of a nation. **101m/C VHS.** Joseph Olita, Geoffrey Keen; *D:* Sharad Patel.

Amistad 🦴🦴🦴 **1997 (R)** Spielberg again creates an epic from another historic example of man's inhumanity, although not quite as effectively this time around. In 1839, African captives aboard the slaveship Amistad, led by a Mende tribesman named Cinque (Hounsou), free themselves and take over the ship in a bloody mutiny. Property attorney Robert Baldwin (McConaughey) must prove in lengthy court battles that the Africans were rightfully freed individuals in the eyes of the law. John Quincy Adams (Hopkins) presents the Africans' defense to the Supreme Court. Sequences depicting the horrors of slavery are bogged down with heavy handed musical orchestrations that elicit emotion, but at the price of storytelling. McConaughey seems a bit too Californian to be colonial and Morgan Freeman is reduced to periodic cameos as an abolitionist. Fortunately, thanks to an eye for rich detail and superb acting by dynamic newcomer Hounsou, the film nearly escapes the clutches of melodrama to emerge educational and moving. Film's release was marred by a French author accusing Spielberg and his Dreamworks studio of plagiarism. **152m/C VHS, DVD.** Djimon Hounsou, Anthony Hopkins, Matthew McConaughey, Morgan Freeman, Nigel Hawthorne, David Paymer, Pete Postlethwaite, Stellan Skarsgard, Anna Paquin, Austin Pendleton, Tomas Milian, Paul Guilfoyle; ***D:*** Steven Spielberg; ***W:*** David Franzoni; ***C:*** Janusz Kaminski; ***M:*** John Williams. Broadcast Film Critics '97: Support. Actor (Hopkins).

The Amityville Horror 🦴🦴 **1979 (R)** Sometimes a house is not a home. Ineffective chiller that became a boxoffice biggie, based on a supposedly real-life occurrence in Amityville, Long Island. The Lutz family moves into the house of their dreams only to find it full of nightmares. Once the scene of a grisly mass murder, the house takes on a devilish attitude, plunging the family into supernatural terror. Pipes and walls ooze icky stuff, flies manifest in the strangest places, and doors mysteriously slam while exorcist Steiger staggers from room to room in scene-chewing prayer. Based on the Jay Anson book and followed by a number of sequels. **117m/C VHS, DVD.** James Brolin, Margot Kidder, Rod Steiger, Don Stroud, Murray Hamilton, Helen Shaver, Amy Wright, Val Avery, Natasha Ryan, John Larch, K.C. Martel, Meeno Peluce; ***D:*** Stuart Rosenberg; ***W:*** Sandor Stern; ***C:*** Fred W. Koenekamp; ***M:*** Lalo Schifrin.

Amityville 2: The Possession **WOOF! 1982 (R)** More of a prequel than a sequel to "The Amityville Horror" (1979). Relates the story of the house's early years as a haven for demonic forces intent on driving a father to beat the kids, a mother to prayer, and a brother to lust after his sister (before he murders them all). Young etc. portray an obnoxious family that you're actually glad to see wasted by the possessed son. A stupid, clumsy attempt to cash in on the success of the first film, which was also stupid and clumsy but could at least claim novelty in the bad housing development genre. Followed by "Amityville 3: The Demon" in 1983. **110m/C VHS.** James Olson, Burt Young, Andrew Prine, Moses Gunn, Rutanya Alda, Jack Magner, Diane Franklin; ***D:*** Damiano Damiani; ***W:*** Tommy Lee Wallace; ***C:*** Franco Di Giacomo; ***M:*** Howard Blake, Lalo Schifrin.

Amityville 3: The Demon 🦴 1/2 *Amityville 3-D* **1983 (R)** America's worst real-estate value dupes another funky buyer. The infamous Amityville house is once again restless with terror and gore, though supported with even less plot than the usual smidgin. Cynical reporter Roberts moves in while trying to get to the bottom of the story by way of the basement. Courtesy of 3-D technology, monsters sprang at theatre patrons but the video version is strictly two-dimensional, forcing the viewer to press his or her face directly onto the TV screen in order to derive similar effect. **98m/C VHS, DVD.** Tony Roberts, Tess Harper, Robert Joy, Candy Clark, John Beal, Leora Dana, John Harkins, Lori Loughlin, Meg Ryan, Rikke Borge, Jack Cardiff; ***D:*** Richard Fleischer; ***W:*** William Wales, David Ambrose; ***C:*** Fred Schuler; ***M:*** Howard Blake.

Amityville 4: The Evil Escapes 🦴 1/2 *The Amityville Horror: The Evil Escapes, Part 4* **1989 (R)** It's an unusual case of house-to-house transference as the horror from Amityville continues, now lodged in a Californian residence. The usual good-house-gone-bad story has the place creating a lot of unusual creaks and rattles before deciding to use its inherited powers to attack and possess a little girl. Special effects from Richard Stutsman ("The Lost Boys" and "Jaws"). **95m/C VHS, DVD.** Patty Duke, Jane Wyatt, Norman Lloyd, Frederic Lehne, Brandy Gold; ***D:*** Sandor Stern; ***W:*** Sandor Stern; ***M:*** Rick Conrad. **TV**

Amityville: A New Generation 🦴 1/2 **1993 (R)** And the bad sequels just go on and on and on. Terry is a young photographer who's given an old mirror by a crazy homeless man (tell me why he took it). He shares a loft with three friends and all begin experiencing vivid and terrifying dreams of murder. Seems the mirror is tied to Amityville and its evil legacy and Terry is the designated inheritor. **92m/C VHS, DVD.** Ross Partridge, Julia Nickson-Soul, David Naughton, Richard Roundtree, Terry O'Quinn; ***D:*** John Murlowski; ***W:*** Christopher DeFaria, Antonio Toro.

The Amityville Curse **WOOF! 1990 (R)** The possessed house is yet again purchased by a pathetically uninformed family. The usual ghostly shenanigans occur with low-budget regularity in this fifth film in the series. Never released theatrically, for good reason. **91m/C VHS.** *CA* Kim Coates, Dawna Wightman, Helen Hughes, David Stein, Cassandra Gava, Jan Rubes; ***D:*** Tom Berry; ***W:*** Michael Krueger, Norvell Rose.

Amityville Dollhouse 🦴 1/2 **1996 (R)** Family moves into their Victorian dream home in Amityville, which comes complete with a replica dollhouse that charms the daughter. But the Amityville curse inhabits the plaything and soon the poltergeists make their nasty appearance. **97m/C VHS, DVD.** Robin Thomas, Starr Andreeff, Allen (Culter) Cutler, Rachel Duncan, Jarrett Lennon, Clayton Murray, Frank Ross, Lenora Kardorf, Lisa Robin Kelly; ***D:*** Steve White; ***W:*** Joshua Michael Stern; ***C:*** Thomas Callaway.

The Amityville Horror 🦴🦴 1/2 **2005 (R)** Revamp of the Amityville tale swaps the understated chills of the original 1979 film with faster editing, more gore, and lots of goth imagery. George and Kathy Lutz (Reynolds and George) learn the meaning of "buyer beware" when they move their family into a lakeside colonial home, a real bargain thanks to the house's history of bone-chilling mass murders. After a series of strange incidents and ghostly visitations, Kathy begins catching on, just in time to watch her husband start channeling Jack Nicholson in "The Shining." The scares are familiar, but Douglas does an admirable job of creating a pervasively creepy, claustrophobic atmosphere throughout. **89m/C DVD, Blu-ray Disc, UMD.** *US* Ryan Reynolds, Melissa George, Jesse James, Jimmy Bennett, Rachel Nichols, Philip Baker Hall, Rich Komenich, Scott Kosar, Brendan Donaldson, Annabel Armour, Chloe Grace Moretz, Isabel Conner, Jose Taitano, David Gee, Danny McCarthy, Nancy Lollar; ***D:*** Andrew Douglas; ***C:*** Peter Lyons Collister; ***M:*** Steve Jablonsky.

Amityville 1992: It's About Time 🦴🦴 **1992 (R)** Time is of the essence in the sixth installment of the Amityville flicks. A vintage clock (from Amityville, of course), causes creepy goings-on in a family's house. Actually a halfway decent horror film with high-grade special effects, and much, much better than previous Amityville sequels, which isn't saying much. **95m/C VHS, DVD.** Stephen Macht, Shawn Weatherly, Megan Ward, Damon Martin, Nita Talbot, Dick Miller; ***D:*** Tony Randel; ***W:*** Christopher DeFaria, Antonio Toro.

Amnesia 🦴🦴 **1996 (R)** Minister Paul Keller (Walker) is having an affair with his son's teacher, Veronica Dow (Tomanovich). Paul decides to fake his death, leaving wife Martha (Sheedy) with the insurance money, and allowing him to start a new life with Veronica. Only he has an accident that causes amnesia and runs into more trouble than he can imagine. Has more humor than you might imagine, thanks to its wacky characters, but as usual Kirkland is way over the top as a love-starved motel owner. **92m/C VHS, DVD.** Nicholas Walker, Ally Sheedy, Sally Kirkland, John Savage, Dara Tomanovich, Vincent Berry; ***D:*** Kurt Voss.

Among Brothers 🦴🦴 **2005** A "what if" based on a true crime from 1994. South Carolina frat boy Ethan doesn't take it well when co-ed Jennifer just wants to be friends, and she winds up dead in her apartment. Ethan whines to frat brothers Miles and Billy that it was an accident, so they torch the place to cover things up. Only the cops figure out Jennifer was murdered, so the boys try to shift the blame elsewhere. The real crime remains unsolved. **85m/C DVD.** Matt Mercer, Lauren Schneider, Corey Cicci, Daniel J. Watts, Lindsay Ayliffe; ***D:*** John Schwert; ***W:*** John Schwert; ***C:*** Brad Hoover.

Among Giants 🦴🦴 **1998 (R)** Postlethwaite is Ray, the foreman of a crew of painters assigned to slap a new coat on the electrical towers that line the Yorkshire countryside. When a female Australian rock climber (Griffiths) wanders into town, joins the crew, and starts sleeping with Ray, she causes static between him and his best friend (Thornton). Understated to the point of being comatose, nothing much happens with the romance or the dangerous occupation angle. Postlethwaite does a fine job as the unlikely romantic lead, though. **93m/C VHS.** *GB* Pete Postlethwaite, Rachel Griffiths, James Thornton, Lennie James, Andy Serkis, Rob Jarvis; ***D:*** Sam Miller; ***W:*** Simon Beaufoy; ***C:*** Witold Stok; ***M:*** Tim Atack.

Among the Cinders 🦴🦴 **1983** Sometimes interesting coming of age drama about a 16-year-old New Zealand boy who runs away to his grandfather's farm to forget about his friend's accidental death. At the farm, he meets an older woman and compromises his virtue. **103m/C VHS.** *GE NZ* Paul O'Shea, Derek Hardwick, Rebecca Gibney, Yvonne Lawley, Amanda Jones; ***D:*** Rolf Haedrich.

Amongst Friends 🦴🦴 **1993 (R)** Three boyhood buddies, Trevor (McGaw), Billy (Lindsey), and Andy (Parlavecchio), from a nice Long Island neighborhood turn to crime out of boredom. Trevor gets busted and goes to prison for two years. Upon getting out, he finds his old cronies still share the taste for crime and general aimlessness but also still want that one big score. Trevor finally agrees to join Andy and Billy in a drug deal but the jealous Billy, who wants Trevor's old girlfriend Laura (Sorvino), plans a double-cross that will affect them all. Filled with cutting attacks on the society that spawns aimless youth. Debut of then 26-year-old writer/director Weiss. **88m/C VHS, DVD.** Louis Lombardi, Patrick McGaw, Steve Parlavecchio, Joseph Lindsey, Mira Sorvino, David Stepkin, Michael Artura; ***D:*** Rob Weiss; ***W:*** Rob Weiss; ***C:*** Michael Bonvillain; ***M:*** Mick Jones.

Amongst Women 🦴🦴 **1998** Embittered ex-IRA soldier Michael Moran (Doyle) is desperate to keep his family together, but the widower's brutality only succeeds in driving his children to strong measures to make their own lives. Set in 1950s rural Ireland; based on the novel by John McGahern. **219m/C DVD.** *IR* Tony Doyle, Susan Lynch, Ger Ryan, Geraldine O'Rawe, Anne-Marie Duff, Brian F. O'Byrne; ***D:*** Tom Cairns; ***W:*** Adrian Hodges; ***C:*** Sue Gibson; ***M:*** Niall Byrne. **TV**

Amor Bandido 🦴🦴 1/2 **1979** When cab drivers in Rio are turning up dead, a young prostitute is torn between her detective father and her prime suspect boyfriend. Drama based on a true story. In Portuguese with English subtitles. **95m/C VHS.** *BR* Paulo Gracindo, Cristina Ache, Paulo Guarniero; ***D:*** Bruno Barreto.

Amor de Hombre 🦴🦴 *The Love of a Man; Manly Love* **1997** Ramon is a gay man with a lot of bedroom action. His best friend is Esperanza, who goes home alone since she always falls for gay guys. Trouble starts when Ramon meets Esperanza's fellow teacher Roberto and their relationship turns into more than a one-night stand. Suddenly, Esperanza is really the odd woman out. Spanish with subtitles. **88m/C VHS, DVD.** *SP* Loles Leon, Andrea Occhipinti, Pedro Mari Sanchez, Armando Del Rio; ***D:*** Juan Luis Iborra, Yolanda Garcia Serrano; ***W:*** Juan Luis Iborra, Yolanda Garcia Serrano; ***C:*** Paco Femenia.

Amore 🦴🦴🦴 **1948** Rossellini's tribute to actress Magnani consists of the short films "The Human Voice" and "The Miracle." In "The Human Voice," Magnani is shown alone, speaking to her lover on the telephone. Based on Jean Cocteau's one-act drama. In "The Miracle," she is a simple peasant girl who believes her illegitimate child is acutally the new Messiah. In Italian with English subtitles. **78m/B VHS.** *IT* Anna Magnani; ***D:*** Roberto Rossellini.

Amore! 🦴🦴 1/2 **1993 (PG-13)** Wealthy investment banker Saul Schwartz (Scalia) hates his job, his wife, and his life. The only way he loses himself is by watching movies starring Italian matinee idol Rudolfo Carbonera (Hamilton). So Saul gets divorced and decides to change his life—by going to Hollywood and becoming an actor like his debonair idol. With the help of some newfound friends he transforms himself into suave leading man material (under the name of Salvatore Guiliano III) but promptly winds up falling for a writer (Ireland), who couldn't care less. **93m/C VHS.** Jack Scalia, Kathy Ireland, Elliott Gould, George Hamilton, Brenda Epperson, James Doohan, Katherine Helmond, Betsy Russell, Norm Crosby, Frank Gorshin; ***D:*** Lorenzo Doumani; ***W:*** Lorenzo Doumani.

Amores Perros 🦴🦴🦴 *Love's a Bitch* **2000 (R)** A Mexico City car accident and the fortunes of a dog bring together three stories of love, loss, and redemption in director/producer Gonzalez Inarritu's impressive feature debut. Octavio's love for his brother's wife leads him to enter his dog, Cofi, in a dogfight for elopement money. When Cofi is wounded, it leads to a car chase, and the central accident. A woman, Valeria, is injured and permanently scarred in the accident. This affects her beau, who has just left his family to be with her. A homeless man, a former revolutionary turned hitman, witnesses the crash and rescues the dog, who becomes a part of his search for his estranged daughter. The plot structure invites comparisons to Tarantino, but these characters inhabit a more consequences-and-morality-oriented world than Q's characters ever did. Film came under fire from animal rights activists for the dogfight scenes, although it was made clear from the start that no animals were actually harmed. **153m/C VHS, DVD.** *MX* Vanessa Bauche, Emilio Echeverria, Gael Garcia Bernal, Goya Toledo, Alvaro Guerrero, Jorge Salinas, Marco Perez, Rodrigo Murray, Humberto Busto, Gerardo Campbell, Rosa Maria Bianchi, Dunia Saldivar, Adriana Barraza; ***D:*** Alejandro Gonzalez Inarritu; ***W:*** Guillermo Arriaga; ***C:*** Rodrigo Prieto; ***M:*** Gustavo Santaolalla. British Acad. '01: Foreign Film; Natl. Bd. of Review '01: Foreign Film.

The Amorous Adventures of Moll Flanders 🦴🦴 **1965** An amusing romp set in 18th century England focusing on a poor orphan girl who seeks wealth. Moll plots to get ahead through an advantageous series of romances and marriages. Her plan is ruined when she falls in love and he turns out to be a wanted highwayman, landing her in prison. Not surprisingly, love (and money) conquers all. Based on the novel by Daniel Defoe. Novak tries in this female derivative of "Tom Jones," but this period piece isn't her style. **126m/C VHS.** Kim Novak, Richard Johnson, Angela Lansbury, Vittorio De Sica, Leo McKern, George Sanders, Lilli Palmer; ***D:*** Terence Young; ***C:*** Ted Moore; ***M:*** John Addison.

Amos 🦴🦴 1/2 **1985** Douglas is Amos, an aging baseball coach confined most reluctantly to a nursing home. He's disturbed by recent suspicious events there, his concern causing him to take on Montgomery, the staunch head nurse. Well-acted drama produced by Douglas's son Peter, offering an echo of "One Flew Over the Cuckoo's Nest," which Dad starred in on Broadway and son Michael helped produced as a movie classic. **100m/C VHS.** Kirk Douglas, Elizabeth Montgomery, Dorothy McGuire, Noriyuki "Pat" Morita, James Sloyan, Ray Walston; ***D:*** Michael Tuchner; ***M:*** Georges Delerue.

Amos and Andrew 🦴 1/2 **1993 (PG-13)** Embarrassing attempt at comedy stops short of endorsing the stereotypes it tries to parody. Prizewinning African-American author Andrew Sterling (Jackson) is seen moving into a house on an island previously reserved for the uptight white, and the neighbors call the cops, assuming he's a thief. Chief of police (Coleman) eagerly gets into the act, then exploits drifter Amos (Cage) in a cover-up attempt when he realizes his mistake. Talented cast can't overcome lame jokes and transparent plot that serves as an opportunity to bring black and white together for a "see how much we have in common" bonding session. **96m/C VHS, DVD.** Nicolas Cage, Samuel L. Jackson, Michael Lerner, Margaret Colin, Giancarlo Esposito, Dabney Coleman, Bob Balaban, Aimee Graham, Brad Dourif, Chelcie Ross, Jodi Long; ***D:*** E. Max Frye; ***W:*** E. Max Frye; ***M:*** Richard Gibbs.

The Amphibian Man 🦴🦴 **1961** What does a scientist do once he's created a young man with gills? Plunge him in the real world of aqua pura to experience life and love, albeit underwater. Trouble is, the protagonist, who's come to be known as the Sea Devil, takes a dive for a young pretty he's snatched from the jaws of death. A '60s Soviet sci-fi romance originally seen on American TV. **93m/C VHS, DVD.** *RU* K. Korieniev, M. Virzinskaya, Mikhail Kozakov, Vladlen Davydov; *D:* Y. Kasancki; *W:* Aleksei Kapler.

Amreeka 𝒮𝒮𝒮 **2009 (PG-13)** Palestinian divorced mom Muna (Faour), who lives on the West Bank, decides she and her 16-year-old son Fadi (Muallem) will have a better life joining her married sister Raghda (Abbass) in suburban Chicago. However, the U.S. has just invaded Iraq so all Arabs are under suspicion and Muna and her family face a number of indignities. Despite her professional background, the only job Muna can find is working at White Castle (a fact she keeps from her family) while Fadi tries to make his way through the hazards of high school. The cast is excellent with Faour expressing a particularly warm, bright, and strong presence. English and Arabic with subtitles. **96m/C DVD.** *US CA* Nisreen Faour, Melkar Muallem, Hiam Abbass, Yussef Abu-Warda, Alia Shawkat, Joseph Ziegler; *D:* Cherien Dabis; *W:* Cherien Dabis; *C:* Tobias Datum; *M:* Kareem Roustom.

The Amsterdam Connection 𝒮 **1978** Film company acts as a cover for prostitution and drug smuggling, with the girls acting as international couriers. **90m/C VHS, DVD.** *HK* Chen Shing, Kid Sherrif, Yeung Sze, Jason Pai Piu, Fang Mui San; *D:* Fang Mui San, Lo Ke.

The Amsterdam Kill 𝒮𝒮 **1978 (R)** A washed-up ex-agent of the U.S. Drug Enforcement Agency is hired by a desperate U.S. Drug Enforcement Agency to hunt down the kingpin of a narcotics syndicate in Hong Kong. Tedious pace with occasional spells of violence fails to awaken somnambulent Mitchum. Shot on location in Hong Kong. **93m/C VHS.** *HK* Robert Mitchum, Richard Egan, Keye Luke, Leslie Nielsen, Bradford Dillman; *D:* Robert Clouse; *W:* Robert Clouse.

Amsterdamned 𝒮𝒮 **1988 (R)** A crime thriller taking place on the canals of Amsterdam featuring a serial skindiver killer who surfaces periodically to slash and splash. A steely detective fishes for clues. Dubbed. **114m/C VHS.** *NL* Monique Van De Ven, Huub Stapel, Hidde Maas, Serge-Henri Valcke, Wim Zomer, Tatum Dagelet; *D:* Dick Maas; *W:* Dick Maas; *C:* Marc Felperlaan.

Amuck! 𝒮𝒮 **1/2 1971** Vintage early '70s Euro-sleaze makes a belated debut on home video. Greta (Bouchet) is hired to be a secretary to world-famous author Richard Stuart (Granger). But Stuart's wife Eleanora (Neri) has designs on the young woman, and Greta has secrets of her own. Nostalgic treat for fans of the era. **98m/C DVD.** *IT* Farley Granger, Barbara Bouchet, Rosalba Neri, Umberto Raho, Patrizia Viotti, Dino Mele, Petar Martinovic, Nino Segurini; *D:* Silvio Amandio; *W:* Silvio Amandio; *C:* Aldo Giordani; *M:* Teo Usuelli.

Amusement 𝒮 **2008 (R)** There's nothing amusing about it. Longtime friends Tabitha, Shelby, and Lisa are held hostage in a maze of cells and traps as someone wants revenge for a long-past incident from their school days. **85m/C DVD.** Katheryn Winnick, Laura Breckenridge, Jessica Lucas, Tad Hilgenbrink, Reid Scott; *D:* John Simpson; *W:* Jake Wade Hall; *C:* Mark Garret; *M:* Marco Beltrami. **VIDEO**

Amy 𝒮𝒮 **1/2 1981 (G)** Set in the early 1900s, the story follows the experiences of a woman after she leaves her well-to-do husband to teach at a school for the deaf and blind. Eventually she organizes a football game between the handicapped kids and the other children in the neighborhood. Good Disney family fare. **100m/C VHS.** Jenny Agutter, Barry Newman, Kathleen Nolan, Margaret O'Brien, Nanette Fabray, Chris Robinson, Louis Fant; *D:* Vincent McEveety; *M:* Robert F. Brunner.

Amy 𝒮𝒮 **1/2 1998** Quirky to say the least. Nine-year-old Amy (De Roma) has been an elective deaf-mute since witnessing the death of her rock star father Will (Barker), who was electrocuted during a concert. The only way Amy does communiate is through music—something discovered by luckless musician Robert (Mendelsohn). Meanwhile, Amy's bitter mom Tanya (Griffiths) is trying to avoid the welfare authorities who want to take charge of Amy's schooling and treatment. Uneasy mix of genres but the performance by child actress De Roma is remarkable. **103m/C VHS.** *AU* Rachel Griffiths, Alana De Roma, Ben Mendelsohn, Nick Barker, Kerry Armstrong; *D:* Nadia Tass; *W:* David Parker; *C:* David Parker; *M:* Phil Judd.

The Amy Fisher Story 𝒮𝒮 *Beyond Control* **1993** Amy Fisher wishes she looked this good. Perhaps if she did, she could be acting in TV movies like Barrymore instead of providing fodder for them. The ABC account draws from a variety of sources to dramatize the relationship between Amy and her married, ahem, friend, and Amy's subsequent attack on his wife. Although it tries not to take sides, it does include some pretty hot sex scenes which could be why this docudrama garnered the highest ratings of the three network productions released on TV. See also: "Casualties of Love: The 'Long Island Lolita' Story" and "Lethal Lolita—Amy Fisher: My Story." **93m/C VHS, DVD.** Drew Barrymore, Anthony John (Tony) Denison, Harley Jane Kozak, Tom Mason, Laurie Paton, Ken Pogue, Linda Darlow, Garry Davey, Dwight McFee, Gabe Khouth, Philip Granger, Stephen Cooper; *D:* Andy Tennant; *W:* Janet Brownell; *C:* Glen MacPherson; *M:* Michael Hoenig. **TV**

Amy's O 𝒮𝒮 *Amy's Orgasm* **2002** Amy (Davis) is a twentysomething L.A. single who has penned a self-help book about why women don't need men to feel complete. She's successful but doesn't believe her own work and is lonely and looking. She meets radio shock jock Matthew Starr (Chinlund), who turns out to be a pretty decent guy, although he's got some personal quirks Amy comes to resent. And Matthew finds some things about Amy he could live without. Of course, they're meant to be together if they could just get past their own egos. **87m/C VHS, DVD.** Julie Davis, Nicholas Chinlund, Caroline Aaron, Mitchell Whitfield, Mary Ellen Trainor, Charles Cioffi, Tina Lifford, Jennifer Bransford; *D:* Julie Davis; *W:* Julie Davis; *C:* Mark Mervis, Goran Paviceric.

Anaconda 𝒮𝒮 **1/2 1996 (PG-13)** Snakes—lots and lots of snakes. Teeny baby snakes, little snakes, medium-sized snakes, large snakes, and one gigantic 40-foot long snake that likes to swallow people and then vomit them up again (the better to have room to swallow somebody else). Oh yeah, the minimal plot concerns a documentary film crew traveling the Amazon River looking for a legendary Indian tribe. They not only have to contend with the snakes but with crazy, snake-obsessed guide Paul Sarone (Voight). The actors react appropriately to becoming snake food. **90m/C VHS, DVD.** Jon Voight, Jennifer Lopez, Ice Cube, Eric Stoltz, Owen Wilson, Kari Wuhrer, Jonathan Hyde, Vincent Castellanos, Danny Trejo; *D:* Luis Llosa; *W:* Jim Cash, Jack Epps Jr., Hans Bauer; *C:* Bill Butler; *M:* Randy Edelman.

Anaconda 3: The Offspring 𝒮 **2008 (R)** It was filmed in Romania, has bad CGI, and a nonsensical plot—yep, it's another Sci-Fi Channel treasure. Scientist Amanda (Allen) has been working with Murdoch (Rhys-Davies), who has done some genetic tinkering that resulted in a mutated 60-foot long anaconda with a machete growing out of its tail (good for the gore factor but really silly looking). Of course the beastie gets loose and must be eradicated, which is where Hammett (Hasselhoff) and his mercenaries come in. **91m/C DVD.** John Rhys-Davies, David Hasselhoff, Anthony Green, Crystal Allen, Patrick Regis; *D:* Don E. Fauntleroy; *W:* Nicholas Davidoff, David C. Olson; *C:* Don E. Fauntleroy; *M:* Peter Meisner. **CABLE**

Anacondas: The Hunt for the Blood Orchid 𝒮𝒮 **2004 (PG-13)** An enjoyably trashy quasi-sequel to the 1997 flick finds even more (and bigger) snakes to swallow the generally no-name cast. A pharmaceutical company sponsors a scientific expedition along a Borneo river to hunt for the rare title flower, which may extend life and youth. There's the usual mix of characters: fearless riverboat captain (Messner), arrogant scientist (Marsden), computer geek (Bryd), babe (Strickland), etc., and the standard situations: ramshackle boat, dense jungle, hungry snakes, and a really clever monkey for a little variety. The director and cast handle their parts efficiently and they know enough not to take it too seriously. Neither should you. **93m/C VHS, DVD, UMD.** *US* Johnny Messner, KaDee Strickland, Matthew Marsden, Eugene Byrd, Denis Arndt, Morris Chestnut, Salli Richardson, Nicholas Gonzalez; *D:* Dwight Little; *W:* Michael Miner, John Claflin, Daniel Zelman, Edward Neumeier; *C:* Stephen Windon; *M:* Nerida Tyson-Chew.

Anacondas: Trail of Blood 𝒮 **2009 (R)** Yep, SciFi Channel does it again with cheap CGI that can't even get the snakes right (there's a couple of decent deaths which is why this isn't a woofer). In this fourth entry, scientist Amanda (Allen) has turned into a good girl and is trying to foil a corporate plot to get the super-snake's priceless venom. **88m/C DVD.** John Rhys-Davies, Linden Ashby, Crystal Allen, Calin Stanciu, Danny Midwinter, Ana Ularu; *D:* Don E. Fauntleroy; *W:* David C. Olson; *C:* Don E. Fauntleroy; *M:* Peter Meisner. **CABLE**

Analyze That 𝒮 **1/2 2002 (R)** Woefully inferior sequel finds shrink Dr. Sobel (Crystal, becoming more irritating with every film), who's trying to deal with his father's death, also helping out mobster Vitti (De Niro), whose life is being threatened by mob factions with boundary issues. After Vitti fakes a breakdown to escape jailhouse hitmen, Sobel is forced by the FBI to house and rehabilitate him, incurring the wrath of his loving but running-out-of patience wife Laura (the sadly underused Kudrow). There are a few laughs to be had, mostly compliments of De Niro, but not enough to keep the inevitable "Analyze the Other Thing" off the Least Wanted list. **95m/C VHS, DVD.** *US* Billy Crystal, Robert De Niro, Lisa Kudrow, Joe (Johnny) Viterelli, Reg Rogers, Cathy Moriarty, John Finn, Kyle Sabihy, Callie (Calliope) Thorne, Pat Cooper, Frank Gio, Donnamarie Recco; *D:* Harold Ramis; *W:* Harold Ramis, Peter Steinfeld, Peter Tolan; *C:* Ellen Kuras; *M:* David Holmes.

Analyze This 𝒮𝒮𝒮 **1998 (R)** Robert De Niro stars as anxiety-stricken mob boss Paul Vitti. He begins to see suburban shrink Ben (Crystal), and is so pleased with the results that he strong-arms the doc into seeing him whenever he wants. Unfortunately for Ben and fiance Laura (Kudrow), that usually happens to be when they're trying to get married. Palminteri is a rival gangster with whom Vitti "seeks closure." De Niro expertly winks at the mob genre (which he helped create) without losing the air of menace that surrounds the good fella character. His performance carries the movie despite the somewhat hokey ending. It's De Niro's underworld, Billy's just living in it. **110m/C VHS, DVD.** Robert De Niro, Billy Crystal, Lisa Kudrow, Chazz Palminteri, Joe (Johnny) Viterelli, Bill Macy, Leo Rossi, Rebecca Schull, Molly Shannon, Max Casella, Pat Cooper, Richard C. Castellano, Jimmie Ray Weeks, Elizabeth Bracco, Tony Darrow, Kyle Sabihy, Donnamarie Recco; *D:* Harold Ramis; *W:* Harold Ramis, Peter Tolan, Kenneth Lonergan; *C:* Stuart Dryburgh; *M:* Howard Shore.

Anamorph 𝒮 **1/2 2007 (R)** Psycho-thriller gets too arty for its own good. Stan Aubray (Dafoe) is an OCD NYC police detective assigned to the case of a serial killer who arranges his victims using an artistic technique called anamorphosis (manipulating perspective). The killings may be related to a closed case where Aubray killed the prime suspect. Are the new murders being done by a copycat or did Aubray kill the wrong person? **107m/C DVD.** Willem Dafoe, Scott Speedman, Clea DuVall, James Rebhorn, Peter Stormare, Amy Carlson; *D:* H.S. Miller; *W:* H.S. Miller, Tom Phelan; *C:* Fred Murphy; *M:* Reinhold Heil, Johnny Klimek.

Anastasia 𝒮𝒮𝒮 **1/2 1956** Bergman won her second Oscar, and deservedly so, for her classic portrayal of the amnesia victim chosen by Russian expatriate Brynner to impersonate Anastasia, the last surviving member of the Romanoff dynasty. As such, she becomes part of a scam to collect millions of rubles deposited in a foreign bank by her supposed father, the now-dead Czar. But is she just impersonating the princess? Brynner as the scheming White General and Hayes as the Grand Duchess who needs to be convinced turn in fine performances as well. Based on Marcelle Maurette's play. **105m/C VHS, DVD.** Ingrid Bergman, Yul Brynner, Helen Hayes, Akim Tamiroff, Martita Hunt, Felix Aylmer, Ivan Desny, Sacha (Sascha) Pitoeff; *D:* Anatole Litvak; *W:* Arthur Laurents; *C:* Jack Hildyard. Oscars '56: Actress (Bergman); Golden Globes '57: Actress—Drama (Bergman); N.Y. Film Critics '56: Actress (Bergman).

Anastasia 𝒮𝒮 **1/2 1997 (G)** Let's face it, this is a pretty weird story to turn into a cartoon fairy tale. Fox's first entry into the Disney-dominated full-length animated musical fray is the story of Princess Anastasia and the fall of the Romanov empire. She has been missing ever since the evil Rasputin put a curse on the Romanov family and started the Russian Revolution (Lenin must have flunked the screen test. Not "toon" enough). Ten years later, con artist Dimitri and ex-aristocrat Vladimir try to convince orphaned 18-year-old Anya that she's the ex-royal so they can claim a reward from the princess' grandmother. Little do they know that she actually is the lost princess, but they must battle Rasputin and his albino bat henchman to put things right. Among the big names lending their voices are Meg Ryan, John Cusack (Cossack?), and Christopher Lloyd. Now let me tell you how the Katzenjammer Kids started WWII... **90m/C VHS, DVD.** *D:* Don Bluth, Gary Goldman; *W:* Bruce Graham, Susan Guathier, Bob Tzudiker, Noni White; *M:* David Newman; *V:* Meg Ryan, John Cusack, Kelsey Grammer, Angela Lansbury, Christopher Lloyd, Hank Azaria, Bernadette Peters, Kirsten Dunst.

Anastasia: The Mystery of Anna 𝒮𝒮 **1/2 1986** Irving stars as Anna Anderson, a woman who claimed to be the Grand Duchess Anastasia, the sole surviving daughter of Russian Czar Nicholas II. A powerful epic reliving her experience of royalty, flight from execution, and struggle to retain her heritage. The story of Anastasia remains as one of the greatest dramatic mysteries of the 20th century. Adapted from the book "Anastasia: The Riddle of Anna Anderson" by Peter Kurth. **190m/C VHS, DVD.** Amy Irving, Olivia de Havilland, Jan Niklas, Nicolas Surovy, Susan Lucci, Elke Sommer, Edward Fox, Claire Bloom, Omar Sharif, Rex Harrison; *D:* Marvin J. Chomsky; *W:* James Goldman. **CABLE**

Anatomy 𝒮𝒮𝒮 *Anatomie* **2000 (R)** Medical student Paula Henning (Potente) is accepted into a prestigious Heidelberg anatomy class. She's carrying on the family tradition of her grandfather, who's dying in the hospital he built, and her father, with whom she disagrees on almost everything. But when she gets to the new university, she finds that very creepy stuff is going on. Medical horror/thriller is right up there with "Coma." It's inventive, grotesque, and the special effects work very well. Franka Potente shows that the impression she made in "Run, Lola, Run" was no fluke. **100m/C VHS, DVD.** *GE* Franka Potente, Benno Furmann, Anna Loos, Holger Spechhahn, Sebastian Blomberg; *D:* Stefan Ruzowitzky; *W:* Stefan Ruzowitzky; *C:* Peter von Haller; *M:* Marius Ruhland.

Anatomy of a Murder 𝒮𝒮𝒮𝒮 **1959** Considered by many to be the best courtroom drama ever made. Small-town lawyer in northern Michigan faces an explosive case as he defends an army officer who has killed a man he suspects was his philandering wife's rapist. Realistic, cynical portrayal of the court system isn't especially concerned with guilt or innocence, focusing instead on the interplay between the various courtroom characters. Classic performance by Stewart as the down home but brilliant defense lawyer who matches wits with Scott, the sophisticated prosecutor; terse and clever direction by Preminger. Though tame by today's standards, the language used in the courtroom was controversial. Filmed in upper Michigan; based on the bestseller by judge Robert Traver. **161m/B VHS, DVD.** James Stewart, George C. Scott, Arthur O'Connell, Ben Gazzara, Lee Remick, Orson Bean, Eve Arden, Duke Ellington, Kathryn Grant, Murray Hamilton, Joseph Welch; *D:* Otto Preminger; *W:* Wendell Mayes; *C:* Sam Leavitt; *M:* Duke Ellington. N.Y. Film Critics '59: Actor (Stewart), Screenplay.

Anatomy of a Psycho 𝒮 **1961** A man plans to avenge his gas chambered brother by committing mass murder. Very cheaply and poorly produced. **75m/B VHS, DVD.**

Ronnie Burns, Pamela Lincoln, Darrell Howe, Russ Bender; *D:* Boris L. Petroff.

Anatomy of a Seduction 1979 TV formula melodrama of a middle-aged divorcee's affair with her son's best friend. Age knows no boundaries when it comes to television lust. **100m/C VHS.** Susan Flannery, Jameson Parker, Rita Moreno, Ed Nelson, Michael LeClair; *D:* Steven Hilliard Stern; *M:* Hagood Hardy. **TV**

Anatomy of Hell WOOF! *Anatomie de L'Enfer* **2004** French pretentiousness at its most full-blown. An unnamed straight woman (Casar)—bored, stupid, mentally unbalanced or all three—slits her wrists in a gay disco and is attended to by a nameless gay man (Italian porn stud Siffredi) whom she then propositions. She'll pay him to accompany her to her creepy isolated house and look at her naked. This will help her confront her problems with intimacy or sexuality or something. Unless you're as masochistic as the characters, you won't care. Oh, and Casar has a body double for the more, ummm, close-up views but that's all Siffredi all the time. Adapted from Breillat's novel "Pornocratie"; French with subtitles. **87m/C DVD.** *FR* Amira Casar, Rocco Siffredi, Catherine Breillat; *D:* Catherine Breillat; *W:* Catherine Breillat; *C:* Yorgos Arvanitis, Guillaume Schiffman, Miguel Malherios, Pedro da Santos; *M:* D'juiz.

Anatomy of Terror *Thriller: An Echo of Teresa* **1974** Drama about an army vet going bonkers (what? really?) and revealing espionage secrets in his home life. **73m/C VHS.** Paul Burke, Polly Bergen, Dinsdale Landen, Basil Henson, Roger Hume, William Job; *D:* Brian Clemens, Peter Jefferies; *M:* Laurie Johnson. **TV**

Anchorman: The Legend of Ron Burgundy 1/2 **2004 (PG-13)** Back in the '80s, Chevy Chase specialized in clueless all-American goofs who thought they were smarter than they were. The crown has now been passed to Ferrell. Here, he plays Ron Burgundy, the top-rated anchorman in '70s-era San Diego. Ron is the booze swilling, cigarette smoking, female ogling, narcissistic leader of an all-male news team whose world is rocked by the arrival of a new female reporter—beautiful, talented, and ambitious Veronica Corningstone (Applegate). Ron falls for the babe even as he tries to retain his chauvinistic place at the top of the news chain. It's amusing shtick and a fair send-up of a time when men were pigs and women decided to bring home the bacon themselves. Besides Applegate, Ferrell is well supported by Koechner, Carell, and Rudd as his equally macho-wannabe news boys. **91m/C DVD, HD DVD.** Will Ferrell, Christina Applegate, David Koechner, Steve Carell, Paul Rudd, Fred Willard, Vince Vaughn, Chad Everett, Tara Subkoff, Stephen (Steve) Root, Danny Trejo, Jack Black, Ben Stiller, Missi Pyle, Chris Parnell, Tim Robbins, Luke Wilson, Laura Kightlinger, Kevin Corrigan, Fred Armisen; *D:* Adam McKay; *W:* Will Ferrell, Adam McKay; *C:* Thomas Ackerman; *M:* Alex Wurman.

Anchors Aweigh **1945** Snappy big-budget (for then) musical about two horny sailors, one a girl-happy dancer and the other a shy singer. While on leave in Hollywood they return a lost urchin to his sister. The four of them try to infiltrate a movie studio to win an audition for the girl from maestro Iturbi. Kelly's famous dance with Jerry the cartoon Mouse (of "Tom and Jerry" fame) is the second instance of combining live action and animation. The young and handsome Sinatra's easy crooning and Grayson's near operatic soprano are blessed with music and lyrics by Styne and Cahn. Lots of fun, with conductor-pianist Iturbi contributing and Hollywood-style Little Mexico also in the brew. ♫ We Hate to Leave; I Fall in Love Too Easily; The Charm of You; The Worry Song; Jalousie; All of a Sudden My Heart Sings; I Begged Her; What Makes the Sun Set?; Waltz Serenade. **139m/C VHS, DVD.** Frank Sinatra, Gene Kelly, Kathryn Grayson, Jose Iturbi, Dean Stockwell, Carlos Ramirez, Pamela Britton, Sharon McManus, Leon Ames; *D:* George Sidney; *M:* Jule Styne, Sammy Cahn. Oscars '45: Scoring/Musical.

Ancient Evil: Scream of the Mummy 1/2 **2000 (R)** Six archeology students discover accidentally revive an Aztec mummy and unleash a deadly curse that could destroy mankind. **86m/C VHS, DVD.** Ariauna Albright, Jeff Peterson, Russell Richardson, Christopher Cullen; *D:* David DeCoteau. **VIDEO**

Ancient Relic 1/2 *The Jesus Video* **2002 (R)** Confusing German miniseries focuses on a startling archeological discovery. Steffen Vogt is helping out at a dig site in Israel when he finds a 2,000-year-old skeleton holding instructions for a video camera. He leaps to the conclusion that the skeleton belongs to a time traveler who got actual footage of Jesus. His crackpot idea is given credence by expert Kaun, who's convinced the camera is hidden somewhere in Jerusalem's Wailing Wall. Then Steffen is abducted by your basic secret Vatican society who doesn't want the status quo upset. German with subtitles. **182m/C DVD.** *GE* Naike Rivelli, Hans Diehl, Matthias Koeberlin, Heinrich Giskes; *D:* Sebastian Niemann; *W:* Martin Ritzenhoff; *C:* Gerhard Schirlo; *M:* Egon Riedel. **TV**

And a Nightingale Sang 1/2 **1991** WWII England is the scene of this sweet romance, a sad and humorous tale of a woman who gives everything for the war effort. Stunning recreation of the final days of the Blitzkreig. Originally produced for Masterpiece Theatre. **90m/C VHS.** *GB* Joan Plowright, Tom Watt, Phyllis Logan, John Woodvine, Pippa Hinchley, Stephen Tompkinson; *D:* Robert Knights.

And Baby Makes Six 1/2 **1979** An unexpected pregnancy creates new challenges for a couple with grown children. Dewhurst is excellent as usual. Followed by "Baby Comes Home." **100m/C VHS.** Colleen Dewhurst, Warren Oates, Maggie Cooper, Mildred Dunnock, Timothy Hutton, Allyn Ann McLerie; *D:* Waris Hussein; *W:* Shelley List. **TV**

And God Created Woman 1/2 *And Woman...Was Created; Et Dieu Crea la Femme* **1957 (PG)** Launching pad for Bardot's career as a sex siren, as she flits across the screen in a succession of scanty outfits and hangs out at the St. Tropez beach in what is euphemistically known as a swimsuit while turning up the heat for the males always in attendance. The plot concerns an 18-year-old nymphomaniac who is given a home by a local family with three handsome young sons. A cutting-edge sex film in its time that was boffo at the boxoffice. In French with English subtitles. **93m/C VHS, DVD.** *FR* Brigitte Bardot, Curt Jurgens, Jean-Louis Trintignant, Christian Marquand; *D:* Roger Vadim; *W:* Roger Vadim, Raoul Levy; *C:* Armand Thirard; *M:* Paul Misraki.

And God Created Woman 1/2 **1988 (R)** Loose, dull remake by Vadim of his own 1957 softcore favorite about a free-spirited woman dodging men and the law while yearning for rock and roll stardom. DeMornay is a prisoner who hopes to marry one of the local hunks (Spano) so she can be paroled. They marry, she strips, he frets, while political hopeful Langella smacks his lips in anticipation. Available in an unrated 100-minute version. **98m/C VHS, DVD.** Rebecca De Mornay, Vincent Spano, Frank Langella, Donovan Leitch, Judith Chapman, Thelma Houston; *D:* Roger Vadim; *M:* Tom Chase, Steve Rucker.

And God Said to Cain *E Dio Disse a Caino* **1969** Another Biblically titled western from the prolific Kinski, about a put-upon gunman who must fight for his life. **95m/C VHS.** *IT* Klaus Kinski, Antonio Cantafora, Peter Carsten, Marcella Michelangeli, Alan Collins, Giuliano Raffaelli; *D:* Anthony M. Dawson; *W:* Anthony M. Dawson, Giovanni Addessi; *C:* Riccardo (Pallton) Pallottini, Luciano Trasatti; *M:* Carlo Savina.

...And God Spoke **1994 (R)** Low budget spoof takes on both religion and moviemaking with two schlockmeisters filming a biblical epic. Since the duo have no budget and are basic hacks with pretensions, they have to settle...so Sales plays Moses, "The Incredible Hulk" Ferrigno gets cast as Cain, while Plumb ("Jan" on "The Brady Bunch") does Mrs. Noah. Has some lulls but also covers very recognizable territory. Directorial debut of Borman. **82m/C VHS, DVD.** Michael Riley, Stephen Rappaport, Soupy Sales, Lou Ferrigno, Eve Plumb, Andy Dick, R(ichard) C(arlos) Bates, Fred Kaz, Daniel Tisman; *D:* Arthur Borman; *W:* Gregory S. Malins, Michael Curtis; *C:* Lee Daniel.

And Hope to Die 1/2 **1972** Moody, muddled crime drama with a good cast about a fleeing Frenchman who joins a gang of hardened criminals in Canada. They go ahead with their plans to kidnap a retarded girl even though she is already dead. Standard caper film is enhanced by arty camera work and some unusual directorial touches. **95m/C VHS.** *FR* Robert Ryan, Jean-Louis Trintignant, Aldo Ray, Tisa Farrow, Lea Massari; *D:* Rene Clement.

And I Alone Survived **1978** True story of a woman who survives a leisure-plane crash in the Sierra Nevadas and her struggle to get to the village below. Brown does her best to elevate the proceedings above the usual I-hope-I-don't-die cliches. **90m/C VHS.** Blair Brown, David Ackroyd, Vera Miles, G.D. Spradlin; *D:* William A. Graham; *C:* Jordan Cronenweth. **TV**

And Justice for All 1/2 **1979 (R)** Earnest attorney Pacino questions the law and battles for justice in and out of the courtroom. He's hired to defend a detested judge from a rape charge, while dealing with a lost-soul caseload of eccentric and tragedy-prone clients. Overly melodramatic, an odd mix of satire, cynicism, and seemingly sincere drama that hits with a club when a stick will do. Jewison aims for black surrealism, permitting both Pacino and Warden (as a judge losing his sanity) to veer into histriohics, to the detriment of what is essentially a gripping behind-the-scenes story. Excellent cast creates sparks, including Lahti in her film debut. And Baltimore never looked lovelier. **120m/C VHS, DVD.** Dominic Chianese, Al Pacino, Jack Warden, Christine Lahti, Thomas G. Waites, Craig T. Nelson, John Forsythe, Lee Strasberg, Jeffrey Tambor; *D:* Norman Jewison; *W:* Barry Levinson, Valerie Curtin; *C:* Victor Kemper; *M:* Dave Grusin.

And Nothing But the Truth 1/2 *Giro City* **1982** A multinational corporation is out to ruin the investigative TV report team trying to do a story on the company. **90m/C VHS.** *GB* Glenda Jackson, Jon Finch, Kenneth Colley, James Donnelly; *D:* Karl Francis.

And Now for Something Completely Different **1972 (PG)** A compilation of skits from BBC-TV's "Monty Python's Flying Circus" featuring Monty Python's own weird, hilarious brand of humor. Sketches include "The Upper Class Twit of the Year Race," "Hell's Grannies," and "The Townswomen's Guild Reconstruction of Pearl Harbour." A great intro to Python for the uninitiated, or a chance for the converted to see their favorite sketches again. **89m/C VHS, DVD.** *GB* John Cleese, Michael Palin, Eric Idle, Graham Chapman, Terry Gilliam, Terry Jones, Carol Cleveland, Connie Booth; *D:* Ian McNaughton, Terry Gilliam; *W:* John Cleese, Michael Palin, Eric Idle, Graham Chapman, Terry Gilliam, Terry Jones; *C:* David Muir; *M:* Douglas Gamley.

And Now Ladies and Gentlemen **2002 (PG-13)** Englishman Valentin (Irons) is a jewel thief who likes disguises and is suffering from mysterious blackouts. In Paris, jazz singer Jane Lester (Kaas) is also suffering from blackouts. They both wind up in Morocco, staying at the same hotel and seeing the same doctor (both turn out to have brain tumors). They flirt, there's a robbery at the hotel, a cop investigates...and the film continues to meander on and on. It all looks lovely but doesn't amount to much. English and French with subtitles. **126m/C VHS, DVD.** *FR GB* Jeremy Irons, Patricia Kaas, Alessandra Martines, Thierry Lhermitte, Ticky Holgado, Yvan Attal, Claudia Cardinale, Amidou, Jean-Marie Bigard; *D:* Claude Lelouch; *W:* Claude Lelouch, Pierre Uytterhoeven, Pierre Leroux; *C:* Pierre William Glenn; *M:* Michel Legrand.

And Now Miguel **1966** Plodding tale of a young boy who wants to take over as head shepherd of his family's flock. Filmed in New Mexico, but the over-long outdoor shots make it drag a bit in spite of Cardi's competent performance. **95m/C VHS.** Pat Cardi, Michael Ansara, Guy Stockwell, Clu Gulager, Joe De Santis, Pilar Del Rey, Buck Taylor; *D:* James B. Clark.

And Now My Love 1/2 **1974 (PG)** A French couple endeavor to maintain their romance despite interfering socio-economic factors—she's a millionaire and he's an ex-con filmmaker. Keller plays three roles spanning three generations, as Lelouch invests autobiographical details to invent a highly stylized, openly sentimental view of French folks in love with love. Along the way he comments on social mores and changing attitudes through the years. Dubbed in English. **121m/C VHS, DVD.** *FR* Marthe Keller, Andre Dussollier, Carla Gravina; *D:* Claude Lelouch; *W:* Claude Lelouch. L.A. Film Critics '75: Foreign Film.

And Now the Screaming Starts 1/2 *Bride of Fengriffen; Fengriffen; I Have No Mouth But I Must Scream* **1973 (R)** The young bride-to-be of the lord of a British manor house is greeted by bloody faces at the window, a severed hand, and five corpses. Then Cushing shows up to investigate. Good-looking, sleek production with genuine chills. **91m/C VHS, DVD.** *GB* Peter Cushing, Herbert Lom, Patrick Magee, Ian Ogilvy, Stephanie Beacham, Rosalie Crutchley, Guy Rolfe, Janet Key, Gillian Lind; *D:* Roy Ward Baker; *W:* Roger Marshall; *C:* Denys Coop; *M:* Douglas Gamley.

And Soon the Darkness **1970 (PG)** One of two vacationing young nurses disappears in France where a teenager was once murdered and the search is on. Predictable, ineffective suspenser. **94m/C VHS, DVD.** *GB* Pamela Franklin, Michele Dotrice, Sandor Eles, John Nettleton, Claire Kelly, Hanna-Marie Pravda; *D:* Robert Fuest; *W:* Terry Nation, Brian Clemens; *C:* Ian Wilson; *M:* Laurie Johnson.

And Starring Pancho Villa as Himself **2003** It's 1914, and Mexican revolutionary Pancho Villa finds himself in dire need of funding for his campaign against the military-run government. He strikes a deal with American filmmakers D.W. Griffith (Feore) and Harry Aiken (Broadbent) that provides them with full access to his war. Based upon actual events, their efforts resulted in the first feature length film. Splendid portrayal by the charismatic and superbly-cast Banderas in the title role of the complex and compelling Villa. **115m/C VHS, DVD.** Antonio Banderas, Eion Bailey, Alan Arkin, Jim Broadbent, Matt(hew) Day, Colm Feore, Michael McKean, Alexa Davalos, Anthony Head, Kyle Chandler, Saul Rubinek, Damian Alcazar, Pedro Armendariz Jr.; *D:* Bruce Beresford; *W:* Larry Gelbart; *C:* Andre Fleuren, Peter James; *M:* Joseph Vitarelli. **CABLE**

And the Band Played On **1993 (PG-13)** Randy Shilts's monumental, and controversial, 1987 book on the AIDS epidemic comes to TV in an equally controversial cable movie. Details the intricate medical research undertaken by doctors in France and the U.S. who fought to isolate and identify the mystery virus despite governmental neglect, red tape, clashing egos, and lack of funding. Various aspects of gay life are shown objectively, without sensationalizing. Celebrity cameos are somewhat distracting though most acquit themselves well. The script went through numerous rewrites; director Spottiswoode reportedly objected to HBO interference at the editing stage. **140m/C VHS, DVD.** Matthew Modine, Alan Alda, Ian McKellen, Lily Tomlin, Glenne Headly, Richard Masur, Saul Rubinek, Charles Martin Smith, Patrick Bauchau, Nathalie Baye, Christian Clemenson; ***Cameos:*** Richard Gere, David Clennon, Phil Collins, Alex Courtney, David Dukes, David Marshall Grant, Ronald Guttman, Anjelica Huston, Ken Jenkins, Richard Jenkins, Tcheky Karyo, Swoosie Kurtz, Jack Laufer, Steve Martin, Dakin Matthews, Peter McRobbie, Lawrence Monoson, B.D. Wong, Donal Logue, Jeffrey Nordling, Stephen Spinella; *D:* Roger Spottiswoode; *W:* Arnold Schulman; *C:* Paul Elliott; *M:* Carter Burwell. **CABLE**

... And the Earth Did Not Swallow Him 1/2 *...Y No Se Lo Trago La Tierra* **1994** Family trials of migrant farm workers from the perspective of 12-year-old Marcos, who travels with his parents on their annual (it's 1952) move from Texas throughout the midwest during harvest season. Balances their struggles with the strong family bonds that allow them to endure. Based on the semi-autobiographical novel by Tomas Rivera. **99m/C VHS.** Jose Alcala, Rose Portillo, Marco Rodriguez; *D:* Severo Perez; *W:* Severo Perez; *C:* Virgil Harper; *M:* Marcos Loya.

And the Ship Sails On *E la Nave Va* **1983 (PG)** On the eve of WWI, a group of devoted opera lovers take a luxury cruise to pay their respects to a recently deceased opera diva. Also on board is a group of fleeing Serbo-Croation freedom fighters. A charming and absurd autumnal homage-to-life by Fellini shot entirely in the studio. **130m/C VHS, DVD.** *IT* Freddie Jones, Barbara Jefford, Janet Suzman, Peter Cellier, Philip Locke, Victor Poletti, Norma West; ***D:*** Federico Fellini; ***W:*** Federico Fellini, Tonino Guerra; ***C:*** Giuseppe Rotunno; ***M:*** Gianfranco Plenizio.

And the Wild, Wild Women *Hell in the City; Nella Cita L'Inferno* **1959** Italian women-behind-bars potboiler. Young Lina (Masina) is falsely convicted of robbery and sent to the slammer in Rome, where seasoned cellmate Egle (Magnani) decides to look after her. Lina is finally exonerated but, to Egle's regret, that doesn't mean Lina's life gets any better. Dubbed. **85m/B DVD.** *IT FR* Anna Magnani, Giulietta Masina, Renato Salvatori, Alberto Sordi, Myriam Bru, Cristina Gaioni; ***D:*** Renato Castellani; ***W:*** Renato Castellani; ***C:*** Leonida Barboni; ***M:*** Roman Vlad.

And Then Came Lola **2009** Lesbian rom com inspired by the 1998 German film "Run, Lola, Run." This Lola is a talented but unreliable San Francisco photographer who is asked by her girlfriend to deliver some important photos to a meeting. Lola has three chances but gets waylaid by a no-nonsense meter maid, crazy dog owners, and beautiful babes, which could ruin both her personal and professional lives if she screws up. **70m/C DVD.** Ashleigh Sumner, Jill Bennett, Cathy DeBuono, Jessica Graham, Candy Tolentino, Linda Ignazi, Angelyna Martinez, Jenoa Harlow; ***D:*** Ellen Seidler, Megan Siler; ***W:*** Ellen Seidler, Megan Siler; ***C:*** Jennifer Derbin.

And Then Came Love **2007** When Julie (Williams) decides to search for the anonymous sperm donor father of her six-year old son, her idyllic world is suddenly turned upside-down. This color-blind romantic comedy provides unadulterated insight into complex relationships without being overly sappy or contrary. **98m/C DVD.** Vanessa L(ynne) Williams, Kevin Daniels, Ben Vereen, Michael Boatman, Eartha Kitt, Tommy Nelson, Stephen Spinella; ***D:*** Richard Schenkman; ***W:*** Caytha Jentis; ***C:*** Timothy Naylor; ***M:*** Rebecca Lloyd.

And Then There Were None 1/2 **1945** An all-star cast makes up the ten colorful guests invited to a secluded estate in England by a mysterious host. What the invitations do not say, however, is the reason they have been specifically chosen to visit—to be murdered, one by one. Cat and mouse classic based on Agatha Christie's book with an entertaining mix of suspense and black comedy. Remade in 1966 and again in 1975 as "Ten Little Indians," but lacking the force and gloss of the original. **97m/B VHS, DVD.** Louis Hayward, Barry Fitzgerald, Walter Huston, Roland Young, Sir C. Aubrey Smith, Judith Anderson, Mischa Auer, June Duprez; ***D:*** Rene Clair; ***W:*** Rene Clair, Dudley Nichols; ***C:*** Lucien N. Andriot; ***M:*** Mario Castelnuovo-Tedesco.

And Then You Die **1988 (R)** An intense crime drama about a Canadian drug lord who amasses a fortune from the cocaine and marijuana trade. His empire is threatened as the Mafia, Hell's Angels, and the police try to bring him down. **115m/C VHS.** *CA* Kenneth Welsh, R.H. Thomson, Wayne Robson, Tom Harvey, George Bloomfield, Graeme Campbell; ***D:*** Francis Mankiewicz.

And You Thought Your Parents Were Weird! 1/2 **1991 (PG)** A pair of introverted, whiz kid brothers invent a lovable robot to provide fatherly guidance as well as companionship for their widowed mother. Surprisingly charming, sentimental film is only slightly hampered by low-budget special effects. **92m/C VHS.** Marcia Strassman, Joshua John Miller, Edan Gross, John Quade, Sam Behrens, Susan Gibney, Gustav Vintas, Eric Walker; ***D:*** Tony Cookson; ***W:*** Tony Cookson; ***C:*** Paul Elliott; ***M:*** Randy Miller; ***V:*** Alan Thicke, Richard Libertini.

The Anderson Tapes **1971 (PG)** Newly released from prison, an ex-con assembles his professional pals and plans the million-dollar robbery of an entire luxury apartment house on NYC's upper east side. Of course, he's unaware that a hoard of law men from federal, state, and local agencies are recording their activities for a wide variety of reasons, though none of the surveillance is coordinated and it has nothing to do with the planned robbery. Based on the novel by Lawrence Sanders, the intricate caper is effectively shaped by Lumet, who skillfully integrates broad satire with suspense. Shot on location in New York City. Walken is The Kid, his first major role. **100m/C VHS.** Sean Connery, Dyan Cannon, Martin Balsam, Christopher Walken, Alan King, Ralph Meeker, Garrett Morris, Margaret Hamilton, Val Avery, Dick Anthony Williams, Richard B. Shull, Conrad Bain, Paul Benjamin; ***D:*** Sidney Lumet; ***W:*** Frank Pierson; ***M:*** Quincy Jones.

Andersonville **1995** Andersonville was an infamous Confederate prison camp in Georgia that by August, 1864 contained more than 32,000 Union POWs—and was planned to hold 8,000 men. One in four soldiers died in the camp. The story is told through the eyes of Massachusetts Corporal Josiah Day (Emick), who is captured in 1864 and struggles to survive the hellish conditions. The commander of the Andersonville was a deranged German-Swiss captain named Wirz (Triska)—who became the only Civil War soldier to be hanged for war crimes (depicted in "The Andersonville Trial"). The TV miniseries was filmed some 150 miles from the original site. **168m/C VHS, DVD.** Thomas F. Wilson, Jarrod Emick, Frederic Forrest, Ted Marcoux, Jan Triska, Cliff DeYoung, Tom Aldredge, Frederick Coffin, Justin Henry, Kris Kamm, William H. Macy, Gabriel Olds, William Sanderson, Bud Davis, Carmen Argenziano, Peter Murnik; ***D:*** John Frankenheimer; ***W:*** David W. Rintels; ***C:*** Ric Waite; ***M:*** Gary Chang. **TV**

The Andersonville Trial 1/2 **1970** Details the atrocities experienced by captured Union soldiers who were held in the Confederacy's notorious Andersonville prison during the American Civil War. Provides an interesting account of the war-crimes trial of the Georgia camp's officials, under whom more than 14,000 prisoners died. Moving, remarkable TV drama based on the book by Pulitzer prize-winner MacKinlay Kantor. **150m/C VHS, DVD.** Martin Sheen, William Shatner, Buddy Ebsen, Jack Cassidy, Richard Basehart, Cameron Mitchell; ***D:*** George C. Scott. **TV**

Andre 1/2 **1994 (PG)** More human-animal interaction from the director of "The Man from Snowy River," telling the true story of an orphaned seal that was adopted by the local Maine harbormaster (Carradine) and his family. As they raise their houseguest, the question arises whether Andre should be returned to the wild. It'll remind you of "Free Willy" with an appealing smaller sea mammal and the equally appealing Majorino, as the youngster who befriends Andre. For those who are sticklers for accuracy, Andre is actually portrayed by a sea lion and not a seal. **94m/C VHS, DVD.** Keith Carradine, Tina Majorino, Chelsea Field, Keith Szarabajka, Shane Meier, Joshua Jackson; ***D:*** George Miller; ***W:*** Dana Baratta; ***C:*** Thomas Burstyn; ***M:*** Bruce Rowland.

Andrei Rublev **1966** A 15th-century Russian icon painter must decide whether to record history or participate in it as Tartar invaders make life miserable. During the black and white portion, he becomes involved in a peasant uprising, killing a man in the process. After a bout of pessimism and a vow of silence, he goes forth to create artistic beauty as the screen correspondingly blazes with color. A brilliant historical drama censored by Soviet authorities until 1971. In Russian with English subtitles. **185m/C VHS, DVD.** *RU* Anatoli (Otto) Solonitzin, Ivan Lapikov, Nikolai Grinko, Nikolai Sergeyev; ***D:*** Andrei Tarkovsky; ***W:*** Andrei Tarkovsky, Andrei Konchalovsky; ***C:*** Vadim Yusov; ***M:*** Vyacheslav Ovchinnikov.

Androcles and the Lion 1/2 **1952** Stage-bound Hollywood version of the George Bernard Shaw story about a tailor in Imperial Rome who saves Christians from a hungry lion he had previously befriended. Sharp dialogue and a plot that's relatively (within the bounds of Hollywood) faithful help a great play become a semi-satisfying cinematic morsel. Harpo Marx was originally cast as Androcles, but was fired by producer Howard Hughes five weeks into the shooting. **105m/B VHS.** Jean Simmons, Alan Young, Victor Mature, Robert Newton, Maurice Evans, Elsa Lanchester; ***D:*** Chester Erskine; ***C:*** Harry Stradling Sr.

Android 1/2 **1982 (PG)** When an android who has been assisting a quirky scientist in space learns that he is about to be permanently retired, he starts to take matters into his own synthetic hands. Combines science fiction, suspense and cloned romance. A must for Kinski fans. **80m/C VHS, DVD.** Klaus Kinski, Don Opper, Brie Howard, Norbert Weisser, Crofton Hardester, Kendra Kirchner; ***D:*** Aaron Lipstadt; ***W:*** James Reigle, Don Opper; ***C:*** Tim Suhrstedt; ***M:*** Don Preston.

The Android Affair 1/2 **1995 (PG-13)** Karen Garrett (Kozak) is studying at the Institute for Surgical Research where doctors practice experimental techniques on lifelike androids. Her next patient is William (Dunne), a handsome and charming android with a heart defect, who doesn't want to "die" during Karen's risky surgical procedure. What's worse is Karen finds this 'droid all too humanly appealing and decides to help him escape the Institute. From a story by Isaac Asimov and screenwriter Kletter. **90m/C VHS.** Harley Jane Kozak, Griffin Dunne, Ossie Davis, Saul Rubinek, Peter Outerbridge, Natalie Radford; ***D:*** Richard Kletter; ***W:*** Richard Kletter; ***C:*** Berhard Salzmann; ***M:*** Simon Boswell.

The Andromeda Strain 1/2 **1971 (G)** A satellite falls back to earth carrying a deadly bacteria that must be identified in time to save the population from extermination. The tension inherent in the bestselling Michael Crichton novel is talked down by a boring cast. Also available in letterbox format. **131m/C VHS, DVD.** Arthur Hill, David Wayne, James Olson, Kate Reid, Paula Kelly, Ramon Bieri, George Mitchell; ***D:*** Robert Wise; ***W:*** Nelson Gidding; ***C:*** Richard H. Kline; ***M:*** Gil Melle.

The Andromeda Strain **2008** Creepy, updated, but over-extended adaptation of Michael Crichton's 1969 novel that was previously filmed for the big screen in 1971. An alien pathogen—code-named Andromeda—hitches a ride aboard a satellite that crashes near a small desert town in Utah. It either quickly kills the inhabitants or turns them into homicidal zombies. Dr. Jeremy Stone (Bratt) and his team are responsible for finding a cure but their efforts are hindered by government conspiracies as well as environmental activism and potential bioterrorism. Then a military snafu leads to an outbreak within the scientists' underground lab. **177m/C DVD.** Benjamin Bratt, Christa Miller, Rick Schroder, Andre Braugher, Eric McCormack, Viola Davis, Justin Louis, Daniel Dae Kim; ***D:*** Mikael Salomon; ***W:*** Robert Schenkkan; ***C:*** Jim Joffin; ***M:*** Joel J. Richard. **CABLE**

Andromedia 1/2 *Andoromedia* **2000** Horribly sappy teen romance drama from director Takashi Miike featuring two Japanese pop bands as actors. A father resurrects his dead teen daughter as a computer program only to be murdered by a mega-corporation hell-bent on world domination. How they intend to achieve said domination with the archived memories of a dead teenager is anyone's guess. **109m/C DVD.** *JP* Hiroko Shimabukoro, Eriko Imai, Takako Uehara, Hitoe Arakaki, Kenji Harada, Ryo Karato, Christopher Doyle, Tomorowo Taguchi, Issa Hentona, Shinobu Miyara, Yukinari Tamaki, Ken Okumoto; ***D:*** Takashi Miike; ***W:*** Itaru Era, Masa Nakamura, Kozy Watanabe; ***C:*** Christopher Doyle, Hideo Yamamoto.

Andy and the Airwave Rangers *Andy Colby's Incredibly Awesome Adventure* **1989** Andy is whisked into the TV!! He finds adventure and excitement—car chases, intergalactic battles, and cartoons. **75m/C VHS, DVD.** Dianne Kay, Vince Edwards, Bo Svenson, Richard Thomas, Erik Estrada, Randy Josselyn, Jessica Puscas, Chuck Kovacic; ***D:*** Deborah Brock.

Andy Hardy Gets Spring Fever **1939** Andy falls for a beautiful acting teacher, and then goes into a funk when he finds she's engaged. Judge Hardy and the gang help heal the big wound in his heart. A lesser entry (and the seventh) from the popular series. **88m/B VHS.** Mickey Rooney, Lewis Stone, Ann Rutherford, Fay Holden, Cecilia Parker, Sara Haden, Helen Gilbert; ***D:*** Woodbridge S. Van Dyke.

Andy Hardy Meets Debutante 1/2 **1940** Seems like there should be an article in that title. Garland's second entry in series, wherein Andy meets and falls foolishly for glamorous debutante Lewis with Betsy's help while family is on visit to New York. Judy/Betsy sings "I'm Nobody's Baby" and "Singing in Rain." **86m/B VHS.** Mickey Rooney, Judy Garland, Lewis Stone, Ann Rutherford, Fay Holden, Sara Haden, Cecilia Parker, Diana Lewis, Tom Neal; ***D:*** George B. Seitz.

Andy Hardy's Double Life 1/2 **1942** In this entertaining installment from the Andy Hardy series, Andy proposes marriage to two girls at the same time and gets in quite a pickle when they both accept. Williams makes an early screen splash. **91m/B VHS.** Mickey Rooney, Lewis Stone, Ann Rutherford, Fay Holden, Sara Haden, Cecilia Parker, Esther Williams, William Lundigan, Susan Peters, Robert (Bobby) Blake; ***D:*** George B. Seitz; ***C:*** George J. Folsey.

Andy Hardy's Private Secretary **1941** After Andy fails his high school finals he gets help from a sympathetic faculty member. As the secretary, Grayson makes a good first impression in one of her early screen appearances. The Hardy series was often used as a training ground for new MGM talent. **101m/B VHS.** Mickey Rooney, Kathryn Grayson, Lewis Stone, Fay Holden, Ian Hunter, Gene Reynolds, Ann Rutherford; ***D:*** George B. Seitz.

Andy Warhol's Bad **1977 (R)** In the John Waters' school of "crime is beauty," a Queens housewife struggles to make appointments for both her home electrolysis clinic and her all-female murder-for-hire operation, which specializes in children and pets (who are thrown out of windows and knived, respectively). Her life is further complicated by a boarder (King) who's awaiting the go-ahead for his own assignment, an autistic child unwanted by his mother. One of Warhol's more professional-appearing films, and very funny if your tastes run to the tasteless. **100m/C VHS, DVD.** Perry King, Carroll Baker, Susan Tyrrell, Stefania Casini, Cyrinda Foxe, Lawrence Tierney, Tito Goya; ***D:*** Jed Johnson; ***C:*** Alan Metzger; ***M:*** Michael Bloomfield.

Andy Warhol's Dracula *Blood for Dracula; Young Dracula; Dracula Cerca Sangue di Vergine e...Mori de Sete; Dracula Vuole Vivere: Cerca Sangue de Vergina; Andy Warhol's Young Dracula* **1974 (R)** Sex and camp humor, as well as a large dose of blood, highlight Warhol's treatment of the tale. As Dracula can only subsist on the blood of pure, untouched maidens ("were-gins"), gardener Dallesandro rises to the occasion in order to make as many women as he can ineligible for Drac's purposes. Very reminiscent of Warhol's "Frankenstein," but with a bit more spoofery. Look for Roman Polanski in a cameo peek as a pub patron. Available in R and unrated versions. **106m/C VHS, DVD.** *IT FR* Udo Kier, Arno Juerging, Maxine McKendry, Joe Dallesandro, Vittorio De Sica, Milena Vukotic, Dominique Darel, Stefania Casini, Silvia Dionisio; ***Cameos:*** Roman Polanski; ***D:*** Paul Morrissey, Anthony M. Dawson; ***W:*** Paul Morrissey; ***C:*** Luigi Kuveiller; ***M:*** Claudio Gizzi.

Andy Warhol's Frankenstein 1/2 *Flesh for Frankenstein; The Frankenstein Experiment; Up Frankenstein; The Devil and Dr. Frankenstein; Carne per Frankenstein; Frankenstein; Il Mostro e in Tavola...Barone Frankenstein* **1974 (X)** A most outrageous parody of Frankenstein, featuring plenty of gore, sex, and bad taste in general. Baron von Frankenstein (Kier) derives sexual satisfaction from his corpses (he delivers a particularly thought-provoking philosphy on life as he lustfully fondles a gall bladder); his wife seeks her pleasure from the monster himself (Dallesandro). Originally made in 3-D, this is one of Warhol's campiest outings. Also available on video in an R-rated version. **95m/C VHS, DVD.** *GE FR IT* Udo Kier, Monique Van Vooren, Joe Dallesandro, Dalia di Lazzaro, Arno Juerging, Srdjan Zelenovic, Nicoletta Elmi, Marco Liofredi, Cristina Gajoni, Carla Mancini, Liu Bozizio; ***D:*** Paul Morrissey; ***W:*** Paul Morrissey; ***C:*** Luigi Kuveiller; ***M:*** Claudio Gizzi.

Angel 1/2 **1937** Melodrama finds Maria Barker (Dietrich) the bored wife of British diplomat Sir Frederick (Marshall). So she heads off to Paris to visit a friend and meets the dashing Anthony Halton (Douglas), with whom she has a fling. Too bad Halton's next stop is jolly old England where he runs into an old military chum (Sir Fred, of course). High gloss but no heart. **91m/B VHS.** Marlene Dietrich, Herbert Marshall, Melvyn Douglas, Edward Everett Horton, Laura Hope Crews; ***D:*** Ernst Lubitsch; ***W:*** Guy Bolton, Samson Raphaelson, Russell Medcroft; ***C:*** Charles B(ryant) Lang Jr.; ***M:*** Frederick "Friedrich" Hollander.

Angel *Angelos* **1982** Angel (Maniatis) falls for a sailor (Xanthos) who promises a better life away from his abusive father and the poverty that surrounds him. Instead, Angel winds up on the Athens' streets as a transvestite prostitute, a situation that eventually lead the distraught young man to a shocking act of violence. Explicit but not prurient and based on a true story. Greek with subtitles. **126m/C VHS, DVD.** *GR* Michael Maniatis, Dionyssis Xanthos, Maria Alkeou, Katerina Helmi; ***D:*** George Katakouzinos; ***W:*** George Katakouzinos; ***C:*** Tassos Alexakis; ***M:*** Stamatis Spanoudakis.

Angel 1/2 **1984 (R)** Low-budget leerer about a 15-year-old honor student who attends an expensive Los Angeles private school during the day and by night becomes Angel, a streetwise prostitute making a living amid the slime and sleaze of Hollywood Boulevard. But wait, all is not perfect. A psycho is following her, looking for an opportunity. **94m/C VHS, DVD.** Donna Wilkes, Cliff Gorman, Susan Tyrrell, Dick Shawn, Rory Calhoun, John Diehl, Elaine Giftos, Ross Hagen; ***D:*** Robert Vincent O'Neil; ***W:*** Joseph M. Cala.

Angel 3: The Final Chapter WOOF! 1988 (R) Former hooker Angel hits the streets to save her newly discovered sister from a life of prostitution. Trashy sequel with a better cast to tepid "Avenging Angel," which was the inept 1985 follow-up to 1984's tasteless "Angel." **100m/C VHS, DVD.** Maud Adams, Mitzi Kapture, Richard Roundtree, Mark Blankfield, Kin Shriner, Tawny (Ellis) Fere, Toni Basil; ***D:*** Tom De Simone; ***M:*** Eric Allaman.

Angel-A **2005 (R)** Andre (Debbouze), a small-time crook, owes thugs all over Paris and he's at the end of the line. Contemplating a leap from a bridge to end his woes, a gorgeous blonde in a miniskirt beats him to it and leaps first. Of course he saves her. Of course she's his angel (a la "It's a Wonderful Life") and it's really her mission to save him. The spectacular Angela (Rasmussen) and Andre then traipse around town fixing Andre's mistakes, as well as Andre himself. Shot in black and white, with stunning images of Paris; the film's plot and actors, alas, do not fare as well. **91m/B DVD.** *FR* Jamel Debbouze, Rie Rasmussen, Gilbert Melki, Serge Riaboukine; ***D:*** Luc Besson; ***W:*** Luc Besson; ***C:*** Thierry Arbogast.

Angel and the Badman **1947** When notorious gunslinger Wayne is wounded during a shoot-out, a pacifist family takes him in and nurses him back to health. While he's recuperating, the daughter in the family (Russell) falls for him. She begs him not to return to his previous life. But Wayne, though smitten, thinks that a Duke's gotta do what a Duke's gotta do. And that means finding the dirty outlaw (Cabot) who killed his pa. Predictable but nicely done, with a good cast and script. Wayne provides one of his better performances (and also produced). **100m/B VHS, DVD.** John Wayne, Gail Russell, Irene Rich, Harry Carey Sr., Bruce Cabot; ***D:*** James Edward Grant; ***W:*** James Edward Grant; ***C:*** Archie Stout; ***M:*** Richard Hageman.

Angel and the Badman 1/2 **2009 (PG-13)** Wounded gunslinger Quirt Evans (Phillips) takes refuge with a family of Quakers and immediately starts romancing eldest daughter Temperance (Unger). But if he really expects to win her heart, he has to lay down his gun and not take revenge against bad guy Loredo (Perry). Dull remake of the 1947 western, which starred John Wayne, features Wayne's grandson Brendan in a small role. **92m/C DVD.** Lou Diamond Phillips, Deborah Kara Unger, Luke Perry, Brendan Wayne; ***D:*** Terry Ingram; ***W:*** Jack Nasser; ***C:*** Anthony C. Metchie; ***M:*** Stu Goldberg. **CABLE**

An Angel at My Table **1989 (R)** New Zealand TV miniseries chronicling the life of Janet Frame, New Zealand's premiere writer/poet. At once whimsical and tragic, the film tells of how a mischievious, free-spirited young girl was wrongly placed in a mental institution for eight years, yet was ultimately able to cultivate her incredible storytelling gifts, achieving success, fame and happiness. Adapted from three of Frame's novels: "To the Is-land," "An Angel at My Table," and "The Envoy From Mirror City." Highly acclaimed the world over, winner of over 20 major international awards. **157m/C VHS, DVD.** *NZ* Kerry Fox, Alexia Keogh, Karen Fergusson, Iris Churn, K.J. Wilson, Martyn Sanderson; ***D:*** Jane Campion; ***W:*** Laura Jones; ***C:*** Stuart Dryburgh. Ind. Spirit '92: Foreign Film. **TV**

Angel Baby 1/2 **1961** A mute girl struggles to re-define her faith when she is cured by preacher, but then sees him fail with others. Fine performances all around, notably Reynolds in his screen debut. Adapted from "Jenny Angel" by Elsie Oaks Barber. **97m/B VHS.** George Hamilton, Salome Jens, Mercedes McCambridge, Joan Blondell, Henry Jones, Burt Reynolds; ***D:*** Paul Wendkos, Hubert Cornfield; ***C:*** Haskell Wexler.

Angel Baby **1995 (R)** Psychiatric out patients Kate (McKenzie) and Harry (Lynch) fall in love and move in together despite some misgivings from family and the medical bureaucracy. When Kate becomes pregnant, they decide to stop taking their medication so the baby has a better chance of being born healthy. Kate's doctors believe she's not capable of dealing with a child, although she is equally determined to have her baby, while Harry struggles to make a life for all of them. Strong performances and an assured debut by writer/director Rymer. Film won all seven of the Australian Film Institute Awards for which it was nominated. **101m/C VHS.** *AU* John Lynch, Jacqueline McKenzie, Colin Friels, Deborra-Lee Furness, Robyn Nevin; ***D:*** Michael Rymer; ***W:*** Michael Rymer; ***C:*** Ellery Ryan; ***M:*** John Clifford Ryan. Australian Film Inst. '95: Actor (Lynch), Actress (McKenzie), Cinematog., Director (Rymer), Film, Film Editing, Orig. Screenplay.

Angel Blue 1/2 *My Neighbor's Daughter* **1997** All-around married nice guy Dennis Cromwell (Bottoms) lives with his wife, Jill (Eichhorn) and newborn child in his California hometown. He befriends newcomer Enrique (Rodriguez) and soon Enrique's daughter Angela (Behrens) is babysitting for the infant Cornwell. David should really know better when his friendship with the teen turns sexual and their secret gets out. **91m/C VHS, DVD.** Karen Black, Sandor Tecsy, Sam Bottoms, Yeniffer Behrens, Lisa Eichhorn, Marco Rodriguez; ***D:*** Steven Kovacs; ***W:*** Steven Kovacs; ***C:*** Mickey Freeman; ***M:*** Joel Lindheimer. **CABLE**

Angel City 1/2 **1980** A Florida labor camp is the setting for this made-for-TV drama. A family of rural West Virginia migrant workers find themselves trapped inside the camp and exploited by the boss-man. Adapted from Patricia Smith's book. **90m/C VHS.** Ralph Waite, Paul Winfield, Jennifer Warren, Jennifer Jason Leigh, Mitchell Ryan; ***D:*** Philip Leacock; ***W:*** James Lee Barrett.

Angel Dust **1996** Nightmare noir about a serial killer who haunts Tokyo's subways. Setsuko (Minami) is a criminal psychologist investigating the murders of several young women, all committed during rush hour at various commuter stops. Each victim has been killed with a poisonous injection. Setsuko learns the first victim was psychologically deprogrammed after leaving a religious cult and contacts her ex-lover, Rei (Wakamatsu), who runs a clinic specializing in such deprogramming. But Rei also becomes the chief suspect when he begins to play sadistic mind games with Setsuko. Is she paranoid or truly in danger? Japanese with subtitles. **116m/C VHS.** *JP* Kaho Minami, Takeshi Wakamatsu; ***D:*** Sogo Ishii; ***W:*** Sogo Ishii, Yorozu Ikuta; ***C:*** Norimichi Kasamatsu; ***M:*** Hiroyuki Nagashima.

Angel Eyes 1/2 **2001 (R)** Although the film's marketing campaign implied some supernatural elements, there's nothing unworldly about this romantic drama. And despite some capable performances by the leads, the film is utterly predictable as well. Tough Chicago police officer Sharon Pogue (Lopez) is still dealing with the effects of an abusive childhood when she meets another lost soul, Catch (Caviezel), who's grappling with the death of his wife and child. He saves her life, they fall for each other, but things are hardly that simple. They both have emotional issues and a past connection that's all too easy to determine. **104m/C VHS, DVD.** Jennifer Lopez, James (Jim) Caviezel, Sonia Braga, Terrence Howard, Jeremy Sisto, Monet Mazur, Victor Argo, Shirley Knight, Jeremy Ratchford, Peter MacNeill, Stephen Kay; ***D:*** Luis Mandoki; ***W:*** Gerald Di Pego; ***C:*** Piotr Sobocinski; ***M:*** Marco Beltrami.

Angel Face **1952** An angel's face with a devil's heart is psycho rich girl Diane (Simmons), who wants to get rid of her hated stepmommy (O'Neil) so she can have daddy (Marshall) all to herself. Diane is infatuated with new chauffeur Frank (Mitchum) and he becomes an unwitting accomplice in her deadly scheme. Both are brought up on murder charges but Frank doesn't realize how far this crazy chick will go to keep what—and who—she wants. Wild noir melodrama from Preminger that gave good girl Simmons a chance to unleash her inner bad femme. Mitchum is his usual cool self. **92m/B DVD.** Jean Simmons, Robert Mitchum, Herbert Marshall, Mona Freeman, Leon Ames, Barbara O'Neil, Kenneth Tobey; ***D:*** Otto Preminger; ***W:*** Frank Nugent, Oscar Millard; ***C:*** Harry Stradling Sr.; ***M:*** Dimitri Tiomkin.

An Angel for Satan 1/2 *Un Angelo per Satan* **1966** Steele plays a dual role in her last major, Italian horror film. She gives a strong performance as a woman possessed by the spirit of a statue. In Italian with no subtitles. **90m/B VHS, DVD.** *IT* Barbara Steele, Anthony Steffen, Aldo Berti, Mario Brega, Ursula Davis, Claudio Gora; ***D:*** Camillo Mastrocinque; ***W:*** Camillo Mastrocinque; ***M:*** Francesco De Masi.

Angel Heart 1/2 **1987 (R)** Exotic, controversial look at murder, voodoo cults, and sex in 1955 New Orleans. Bonet defiantly sheds her image as a young innocent (no more Cosby Show for you, young lady). Rourke is slimy as marginal NYC private eye Angel, hired by the devilish De Niro to track a missing big band singer who violated a "contract." His investigation leads him to the bizarre world of the occult in New Orleans, where the blood drips to a different beat. Visually stimulating, with a provocative sex scene between Bonet and Rourke, captured in both R-rated and unrated versions. Adapted by Parker from "Falling Angel" by William Hjortsberg. **112m/C VHS, DVD.** Mickey Rourke, Robert De Niro, Lisa Bonet, Charlotte Rampling, Michael Higgins, Charles Gordone, Kathleen Wilhoite, Stocker Fountelieu, Brownie McGhee, Elizabeth Whitcraft, Eliott Keener, Dann Florek; ***D:*** Alan Parker; ***W:*** Alan Parker; ***C:*** Michael Seresin; ***M:*** Trevor Jones.

Angel in a Taxi **1959** A six-year-old boy in an orphanage decides to choose his own mother, a beautiful ballerina he sees in a magazine, when an ugly couple try to adopt him. Italian film dubbed in English. **89m/B VHS.** *IT* Wera Cecova, Ettore Manni, Vittorio De Sica, Marietto, Gabriele Ferzetti; ***D:*** Antonio Leonviola.

The Angel Levine 1/2 **1970 (PG)** Morris (Mostel) is an old Jewish man who has lost his faith in God after a series of personal and professional losses. Alexander Levine (Belafonte) is a black angel who can earn his wings if he can convince Morris that his life does have meaning. As sentimental as it sounds but the leads are pros. Based on a story by Bernard Malamud. **104m/C VHS, DVD.** Zero Mostel, Harry Belafonte, Ida Kaminska, Milo O'Shea, Gloria Foster, Eli Wallach, Anne Jackson; ***D:*** Jan Kadar; ***W:*** Bill Gunn, Ronald Ribman; ***C:*** Richard Kratina; ***M:*** William Eaton.

Angel of Death WOOF! 1986 (R) A small mercenary band of Nazi hunters attempt to track down Josef Mengele in South America. Stupid entry in the minor "let's find the darn Nazi before he really causes trouble" genre. Director Franco is also known as A. Frank Drew White. **92m/C VHS.** Chris Mitchum, Fernando Rey, Susan Andrews; ***D:*** Jess (Jesus) Franco.

Angel of Death *Semana Santa; Holy Week* **2002** Detective Maria Delgado (Sorvino) comes to Seville during Holly Week to investigate a series of ritual killings. With cops Quemada (Martinez) and Torillo (Atkine) assisting, Maria discovers a mysterious religious order, The Brotherhood of Christ, and an old woman (Valli) keeping a secret since the Spanish Civil War. Lackluster, miscast thriller adapted from the novel by David Hewson. **94m/C DVD.** *GE SP GB FR IT DK* Mira Sorvino, Olivier Martinez, Feodor Atkine, Alida Valli, Luis Tosar; ***D:*** Pepe Danquart; ***W:*** Roy Mitchell; ***C:*** Ciro Cappellari; ***M:*** Andrea Guerra.

Angel of Death 1/2 **2009 (R)** Originally a 10-episode web series starring Bell as remorseless assassin Eve. After suffering severe head trauma, the hitwoman begins to hallucinate and is haunted by her victims. So Eve decides to seek revenge on her mob employers, who ordered the hits. **90m/C DVD.** Zoe Bell, Lucy Lawless, Doug Jones, Vail Bloom, Theodore (Ted) Raimi, Brian Poth, Justin Huen, Jake Abel; ***D:*** Paul Etheredge-Ouzts; ***W:*** Ed Brubaker; ***C:*** Carl Herse.

Angel of Destruction 1/2 **1994 (R)** Undercover cop is assigned to protect controversial rock star from psycho fan. Cop gets killed and cop's sister decides to go after the killer. **80m/C VHS, DVD.** Maria Ford, Charlie Spradling; ***D:*** Charles Philip Moore.

Angel of Fury 1/2 **1993 (R)** Rothrock plays the head of security of a computer corporation who must battle terrorists after the company's top-secret computer. And there's no one she can trust. Lots of martial arts action with the competent Rothrock. **91m/C VHS.** Cynthia Rothrock, Christopher Barnes, Peter O'Brien; ***D:*** Ackyl Anwary.

Angel of H.E.A.T. WOOF! *The Protectors, Book One* **1982 (R)** Porn-star Chambers is Angel, a female super-agent on a mission to save the world from total destruction. Sex and spies abound with trashy nonchalance. **90m/C VHS, DVD.** Marilyn Chambers, Mary Woronov, Steve Johnson; ***D:*** Helen Sanford, Myrl A. Schreibman.

Angel of the Night *Nattens Engel* **1998 (R)** Rebecca inherits her grandmother's creepy mansion and invites her best friend and her boyfriend for a visit. While exploring, Rebecca discovers that great-grandpa Rico was a vampire and she inadvertently releases him from his tomb. Dubbed from Danish. **98m/C VHS, DVD.** *DK* Ulrich Thomsen, Maria Karlsen, Erik Holmey; ***D:*** Shakey Gonzaless; ***W:*** Shakey Gonzaless; ***C:*** Jacob Kusk; ***M:*** Soren Hyldgaard.

Angel on My Shoulder **1946** A murdered convict makes a deal with the Devil (Rains) and returns to earth for revenge as a respected judge who's been thinning Hell's waiting list. Occupying the good judge, the murderous Muni has significant problems adjusting. Amusing fantasy with Muni in a rare and successful comic role. Co-written by Segall, who scripted "Here Comes Mr. Jordan," in which Rains played an angel. Remade in 1980. **101m/B VHS, DVD.** Paul Muni, Claude Rains, Anne Baxter, Onslow Stevens; ***D:*** Archie Mayo; ***W:*** Harry Segall; ***C:*** James Van Trees; ***M:*** Dimitri Tiomkin.

Angel on My Shoulder **1980** A small-time hood wrongfully executed for murder comes back as district attorney. He owes the devil, but he's finding it tough to be evil enough to repay his debt. O.K. TV remake of the better 1946 film starring Paul Muni. **96m/C VHS.** Peter Strauss, Richard Kiley, Barbara Hershey, Janis Paige; ***D:*** John Berry; ***M:*** Artie Butler. **TV**

Angel Rodriguez 1/2 **2005** Unsentimental story about the problems facing the trouble-prone title character. Angel (Everett) is a smart Brooklyn high schooler whose temper often gets the best of him. After getting into a fight with his dad's girlfriend, he's thrown out of the house and taken in for the night by his pregnant guidance counselor Nicole (Griffiths). But good intentions have a way of going wrong. **87m/C DVD.** Rachel Griffiths, Denis O'Hare, David Zayas, Jonan Everett, Wallace Little, Jon Norman Schneider,

Denise Burse; *D:* Jim McKay; *W:* Jim McKay, Hannah Weyer; *C:* Chad Davidson. **CABLE**

Angel Square **1992** A Canadian production from the director of the acclaimed "Bye Bye Blues." When the father of a neighborhood boy is brutally attacked, the community bands together to search for the culprit. **106m/C VHS.** *CA* Ned Beatty; *D:* Anne Wheeler; *W:* James DeFelice.

Angel Town **1989 (R)** A foreign exchange student, who happens to be a champion kick-boxer, is forced into combat with LA street gangs. **90m/C VHS, DVD.** Olivier Gruner, Theresa Saldana, Frank Aragon, Tony Valentino, Peter Kwong, Mike Moroff; *D:* Eric Karson.

Angel Unchained 1/2 **1970** Typical biker exploitation flick has bikers and hippies joining together to fend off small-town redneck hostility. **92m/C VHS, DVD.** Don Stroud, Tyne Daly, Luke Askew, Larry Bishop, Aldo Ray, Bill McKinney; *D:* Lee Madden; *W:* Jeffrey Alladin Fiskin.

Angel with the Trumpet **1950** Depressing character study of a woman who marries to please her family, rather than herself. When the Gestapo finds out about her Jewish ancestry, she must make the most important decision of her life. **98m/B VHS.** *GB* Eileen Herlie, Basil Sydney, Norman Wooland, Maria Schell, Olga Edwards, Oskar Werner, Anthony Bushell, Wilfrid Hyde-White; *D:* Anthony Bushell.

Angela **1977** Twisted love story about a young man (Railsback) who jumps the bones of an older woman, unaware that she is the mother he's been separated from for 23 long years. Seems that way back when, the boy was kidnapped by crime boss Huston from mom Loren, an ex-prostitute, who then turned in the boy's dad, who was something of a criminal. Mom thought son was dead, dad vowed revenge from prison, and son went about his unwitting business. It all comes together insipidly, at the expense of the cast and viewer. **91m/C VHS.** *CA* Sophia Loren, Steve Railsback, John Huston, John Vernon; *D:* Boris Sagal; *M:* Henry Mancini.

Angela **1994** Exceedingly mystical film focuses on religiously obsessed 10-year-old Angela (Rhyne), who tells her six-year-old sister Ellie (Blythe) that unless they are very good the Devil will come to take them away. Meanwhile, she tries to cope with volatile family relationships, including their unstable mother. Good performances in a sometimes sluggish and abstract drama. **105m/C VHS, DVD.** Miranda Stuart Rhyne, Charlotte Blythe, Anna Thomson, John Ventimiglia, Vincent Gallo; *D:* Rebecca Miller; *W:* Rebecca Miller; *C:* Ellen Kuras; *M:* Michael Rohatyn. Sundance '95: Cinematog., Filmmakers Trophy.

Angela **2002 (R)** Angela (Finochiarro) is married to the older Saro (Pupella), who runs the mob in Palermo. Angela helps out by using her shoe store as a front for his drug deals, but she's frustrated by being shut out of all the business decisions. Then hunky hood Masino (di Stefano) is hired and the two are soon hitting the sheets. A bad idea, not only because of what Saro will do but because it gives the cops, who have the mobsters under surveillance, the leverage they need to take Saro down. Italian with subtitles. **100m/C DVD.** *IT* Andrea Di Stefano, Donatella Finochiarro, Mario Pupella, Toni Gambino; *D:* Roberta Torre; *W:* Roberta Torre, Massimo D'Anolfi; *C:* Daniele Cipri; *M:* Andrea Guerra.

Angela's Ashes 1/2 **1999 (R)** Frank McCourt's devastating memoir covers growing up poverty-stricken in Limerick during the 1930s, with an alcoholic father (Carlyle) and a mother (Watson) struggling to hold the family together while dealing with her own deep depression. The book had the saving graces of lyricism and wit. Unfortunately, the film misses all that and is merely bleak despite the talented cast (including the three actors who play Frank through the years). **145m/C VHS, DVD.** Emily Watson, Robert Carlyle, Joe Breen, Ciaran Owens, Michael Legge, Ronnie Masterson, Pauline McLynn; *D:* Alan Parker; *W:* Robert Carlyle, Laura Jones; *C:* Michael Seresin; *M:* John Williams; *Nar:* Andrew Bennett.

Angele **1934** A lovely, naive country girl is lured to the city by a cunning pimp who knows that she wants to escape her oppressive father. With her illegitimate baby, she's discovered in a whorehouse and taken in disgrace back home to dad, who promptly locks her in the barn. One special guy, however, appreciates her purity and plots to rescue her. What he lacks in material resources he makes up for in character. An overlong but moving story of lost innocence and intolerance. In French with English subtitles. Based on the novel "Un de Baumugnes" by Jean Giono. **130m/B VHS.** *FR* Orane Demazis, Fernandel, Henri Poupon, Edouard Delmont; *D:* Marcel Pagnol.

Angelique 1/2 *Angelique, Marquise des Anges; Angelique, Marquise of Angels* **1964** The first of a five-picture series of mildly racy, bodice-ripping costumed pulp. Beautiful Angelique (Mercier) is forced to leave her lover Nicolas (Gemma) to marry wealthy (but disfigured) Count Joffrey de Peyrac (Hossein). A marriage of convenience turns into true love but Joffrey has powerful enemies, including a jealous Louis XIV (Toja), who accuses Joffrey of sorcery. Loosely based on the novels by Anne and Serge Colon; French with subtitles. **117m/C DVD.** *FR* Michele Mercier, Robert Hossein, Jean Rochefort, Claude Giraud, Giuliano Gemma, Charles Regnier, Jacques Toja; *D:* Bernard Borderie; *W:* Claude Brule, Francis Cosne; *C:* Henri Persin; *M:* Michel Magne.

Angelique and the King 1/2 *Angelique et le Roy* **1966** The third in the series following "Angelique: The Road to Versailles." The Persian ambassador (Frey) falls in love with Angelique and holds her captive, hoping that she'll return his affections. When she finally returns to the court of King Louis (Toja) it's to rumors that she's his new mistress. Followed by "Untamable Angelique." French with subtitles. **104m/C DVD.** *FR* Michele Mercier, Robert Hossein, Sami Frey, Jean Rochefort, Estella Blain, Jacques Toja; *D:* Bernard Borderie; *W:* Bernard Borderie, Francis Cosne, Alain Decaux; *C:* Henri Persin; *M:* Michel Magne.

Angelique and the Sultan 1/2 *Angelique et le Sultan* **1968** The fifth and last in the series, following "Untamable Angelique." Angelique continues to be threatened by d'Escrainville, who holds her aboard his ship. A battle ensues between the kidnapper and Joffrey but Angelique has already been sold to the Sultan of Morocco, so Joffrey must go rescue his wife. French with subtitles. **97m/C DVD.** *FR* Michele Mercier, Robert Hossein, Roger Pigaut, Ettore Manni, Helmuth Schneider, Jean-Claude Pascal, Jacques Santi, Aly Ben-Ayed; *D:* Bernard Borderie; *W:* Bernard Borderie, Francis Cosne; *C:* Henri Persin; *M:* Michel Magne.

Angelique: The Road to Versailles 1/2 *Merveilleuse Angelique* **1965** The second in the series, following "Angelique." Believing her husband Joffrey is dead, Angelique hides out in Paris with her old love Nicolas but discovers he's changed from a sweet youth to a ruthless criminal. Still, Nicolas offers her protection and when Angelique is reunited with her children, she decides to try respectability by becoming a shop owner under an assumed name. Followed by "Angelique and the King." French with subtitles. **105m/C DVD.** *FR* Michele Mercier, Robert Hossein, Giuliano Gemma, Claude Giraud, Jean Rochefort, Charles Regnier, Claire Maurier, Jacques Toja, Jean-Louis Trintignant; *D:* Bernard Borderie; *W:* Claude Brule, Francis Cosne; *C:* Henri Persin; *M:* Michael Magne.

Angelo My Love **1983 (R)** Compassionate docudrama about New York's modern gypsy community. Follows the adventures of 12-year-old Angelo Evans, the streetwise son of a fortune teller, who, with a fresh view, explores the ups and downs of his family's life. Duvall financed the effort and cast non-professional actors in this charming tale of reality and fairy-tale. **91m/C VHS.** Angelo Evans, Michael Evans, Steve "Patalay" Tsiginoff, Cathy Kitchen, Millie Tsiginoff; *D:* Robert Duvall; *M:* Michael Kamen.

Angels & Demons **2009** In this prequel to Dan Brown's "The Da Vinci Code," Harvard symbologist Robert Langdon (Hanks) is in Rome trying to prevent the secret society, the Illuminati, from destroying the Vatican. **m/C DVD.** *US* Tom Hanks, Ayelet Zurer, Ewan McGregor, Stellan Skarsgard, Armin Mueller-Stahl; *D:* Ron Howard; *W:* Akiva Goldsman, David Koepp; *C:* Salvatore Totino; *M:* Hans Zimmer.

Angels and Insects **1995 (R)** Very strange Victorian-era romantic drama is definitely an acquired taste. The mysteries of nature are nothing compared to the mysteries of human life as naturalist William Adamson (Rylance) comes to discover when he takes up a position at the home of amateur insect collector, Sir Harald Alabaster (Kemp). He falls in love and quickly marries blondly beautiful Eugenia (Kensit), whose outward propriety hides a sensual nature and some decadent family secrets. Based on A.S. Byatt's novella "Morpho Eugenia." Take particular note of the costumes by Paul Brown, which mimic the exoticness of insects. **116m/C VHS, DVD.** *GB* Mark Rylance, Patsy Kensit, Kristin Scott Thomas, Jeremy Kemp, Douglas Henshall, Chris Larkin, Annette Badland, Anna Massey, Saskia Wickham; *D:* Philip Haas; *W:* Belinda Haas, Philip Haas; *C:* Bernard Zitzermann; *M:* Alexander Balanescu.

Angel's Brigade **1979 (PG)** Seven models get together to stop a big drug operation. Drive-in vigilante movie fare fit for a rainy night. **97m/C VHS.** Jack Palance, Peter Lawford, Jim Backus, Arthur Godfrey; *D:* Greydon Clark; *W:* Greydon Clark; *C:* Dean Cundey.

Angel's Dance 1/2 **1999 (R)** Tony (Chandler) works for mobster Uncle Vinnie (Polito) and wants to be a hit man. So, Vinnie sends him to L.A. for training with Stevie Rossellini (Belushi) who, despite appearances, is an expert. Part of Tony's education is to choose and kill a victim at random and he selects Angel (Lee). This is Tony's big mistake, since this Angel is turns out to be the avenging kind. Gets a little too goofy but does provide some action. **102m/C VHS, DVD.** James Belushi, Sheryl Lee, Kyle Chandler, Jon Polito, Ned Bellamy, Mac Davis, Frank John Hughes, Mark Carlton; *D:* David Corley; *W:* David Corley; *C:* Michael G. Wojciechowski; *M:* Tim Truman.

Angels Die Hard **1970 (R)** Novel biker story with the cyclists as the good guys intent on helping a town during a mining disaster. Grizzly Adams makes an early film appearance. **86m/C VHS.** Tom Baker, R.G. Armstrong, Dan Haggerty, William (Bill) Smith; *D:* Richard Compton; *W:* Richard Compton; *M:* Bill Cone.

Angels Don't Sleep Here **2000** Forensic pathologist Michael Daniels returns to his hometown when his twin brother disappears. He gets involved with district attorney Kate, who was his brother's childhood girlfriend, and whose father is the town's mayor. Michael thinks his brother is stalking him and when the mayor is killed, he believes his brother is the culprit. But local detective Russell Stark thinks Michael is the real criminal. **97m/C VHS, DVD.** Dana Ashbrook, Robert Patrick, Roy Scheider, Susan Allison, Gary Farmer, Kelly Rutherford, Christina Pickles; *D:* Paul Cade. **VIDEO**

Angels Fall 1/2 **2007** Reece Gilmore (Locklear) was the sole survivor of a mass killing at the Boston restaurant where she worked. Desperate for a fresh start, Reece hits the road until her car breaks down in a Wyoming town and she takes a diner job to get some cash. Settling in, Reece becomes interested in writer Brody (Schaech), who is the only one to help her when Reece claims she witnessed a murder, although the cops don't find any evidence of a crime. A Lifetime original movie based on the novel by Nora Roberts. **95m/C DVD.** Heather Locklear, Johnathon Schaech, Gary Hudson, Derek Hamilton, Linda Darlow; *D:* Ralph Hamecker; *W:* Janet Brownell; *C:* Joel Ransom; *M:* Chris P. Bacon, Stuart M. Thomas. **CABLE**

Angels from Hell **1968** Early application in the nutso 'Nam returnee genre. Disillusioned Vietnam veteran forms a massive biker gang for the sole purpose of wreaking havoc upon the Man, the Establishment and anyone else responsible for sending him off to war. The big gang invades a town, with predictably bloody results. Sort of a follow-up to "Hell's Angels on Wheels." **86m/C VHS.** Tom Stern, Arlene Martel, Ted Markland, Stephen Oliver, Paul Bertoya, James Murphy, Jack Starrett, Pepper Martin, Luana Talltree; *D:* Bruce Kessler.

Angels Hard As They Come **1971 (R)** Opposing Hell's Angels leaders clash in a hippie-populated ghost town. A semi-satiric spoof of the biker genre's cliches features an early Glenn appearance and Busey's film debut. **86m/C VHS, DVD.** Gary Busey, Scott Glenn, James Iglehart, Gary Littlejohn, Charles Dierkop, Larry Tucker, Gilda Texter, Janet Wood, Brendan Kelly; *D:* Joe Viola; *W:* Jonathan Demme, Joe Viola; *M:* Richard Hieronymous.

Angels in America **2003** Kushner exquisitely adapts his two-part award-winning play into this six-part miniseries that vividly intertwines the lives and sufferings of several New Yorkers as they grapple with such issues as AIDS, drug addiction, homosexuality, and abandonment during the mid-80s. Masterfully directed by Nichols, it presents a spiritual perspective featuring Thompson as an angel of mercy to a man dying of AIDS while Streep appears as an apparition to another. **360m/C DVD.** Meryl Streep, Emma Thompson, Justin Kirk, Ben Shenkman, Mary-Louise Parker, Jeffrey Wright, Patrick Wilson, James Cromwell, Michael Gambon, Simon Callow, Brian Markinson; *D:* Mike Nichols; *W:* Al Pacino, Tony Kushner; *C:* Stephen Goldblatt; *M:* Thomas Newman. **CABLE**

Angels in the Endzone 1/2 **1998** TV follow-up to Disney's 1994 "Angels in the Outfield" finds the heavenly troops trying to aid a failing high school football squad, especially the leading players (Gallagher and Lawrence) who are also trying to also handle the death of their father. **85m/C VHS, DVD.** Matthew Lawrence, David Gallagher, Paul Dooley, Christopher Lloyd; *D:* Gary Nadeau. **TV**

Angels in the Infield 1/2 **2000** Third in the Disney series finds former baseball player Bob "The Bungler" Bugler (Grier) trying to earn his Guardian Angels wings by looking out for pitcher Eddie Everett (Warburton) who's lost his self-confidence. But with daughter Laurel (Irvin) praying for some heavenly intervention, things are certainly looking up. **93m/C VHS, DVD.** David Alan Grier, Patrick Warburton, Kurt Fuller, Rebecca Jenkins, Colin Fox, Peter Keleghan, Duane Davis, Brittney Irvin; *D:* Robert King. **TV**

Angels in the Outfield **1951** Enjoyable comedy fantasy about the lowly Pittsburgh Pirates who get a little celestial help in their race for the pennant. Naturally, it takes the prayers of young Bridget (Corcoran) to get the angel Gabriel to assist. Oh yeah, only the kid can actually see the angels (no special effects in this movie). Great performances all around, especially Douglas as gruff losing manager Guffy McGovern, with Janet Leigh as the reporter he makes a play for. Based on a story by Richard Conlin. **102m/C VHS, DVD.** Paul Douglas, Janet Leigh, Keenan Wynn, Donna Corcoran, Lewis Stone, Spring Byington, Bruce Bennett, Marvin Kaplan, Ellen Corby, Jeff Richards; *D:* Clarence Brown; *W:* Dorothy Kingsley, George Wells; *C:* Paul Vogel.

Angels in the Outfield 1/2 **1994 (PG)** Remake of the 1951 fantasy about a lowly baseball team who, along with some heavenly animated help find themselves on a winning streak. The new lineup includes Glover as manager of the hapless California Angels, Danza as a washed-up pitcher, and Lloyd as captain of the celestial spirits. Gordon-Levitt plays the foster child who believes he'll get his family back together if the Angels win the pennant. Familar ground still yields good, heartfelt family fare. Oakland A's third baseman Carney Lansford served as technical advisor, molding actors into fair semblance of baseball team. **105m/C VHS, DVD.** Danny Glover, Tony Danza, Christopher Lloyd, Brenda Fricker, Ben Johnson, Joseph Gordon-Levitt, Jay O. Sanders, Dermot Mulroney; *D:* William Dear; *W:* Holly Goldberg Sloan; *C:* Matthew F. Leonetti; *M:* Randy Edelman.

Angels of the City **1989** What's a girl got to do to join a sorority? A house prank turns vicious when two coeds take a walk on the wild side and accidentally observe a murder, making them the next targets. Credible exploitation effort, if that's not an oxymoron. **90m/C VHS.** Lawrence-Hilton Jacobs, Cynthia Cheston, Kelly Galindo, Sandy Gershman; ***D:*** Lawrence-Hilton Jacobs; ***W:*** Lawrence-Hilton Jacobs, Raymond Martino, Joseph Merhi.

Angels One Five **1954** A worm's-eye view of British air power in WWII. What little "excitement" there is, is generated by flashing lights, plotting maps, and status boards. Hawkins and Denison are the only bright spots. **97m/B VHS.** *GB* Jack Hawkins, Michael Denison, Dulcie Gray, John Gregson, Cyril Raymond, Veronica Hurst, Geoffrey Keen, Vida Hope, Andrew Osborn; ***D:*** George More O'Ferrall; ***W:*** Derek Twist; ***C:*** Christopher Challis, Stanley Grant; ***M:*** John Wooldridge.

Angels Over Broadway **1940** Slick, fast-paced black comedy about con man Fairbanks, who plans to hustle suicidal thief Qualen during a poker game, but has a change of heart. With the help of call-girl Hayworth and drunken playwright Mitchell, he helps Qualen turn his life around. Ahead of its time with an offbeat morality, but a delight in the '90s. **80m/B VHS, DVD.** Douglas Fairbanks Jr., Rita Hayworth, Thomas Mitchell, John Qualen, George Watts; ***D:*** Ben Hecht, Lee Garmes; ***W:*** Ben Hecht; ***C:*** Lee Garmes.

Angels' Wild Women WOOF! **1972** From the man who brought you "Dracula vs. Frankenstein" comes an amalgamation of hippies, motorcycle dudes, evil desert gurus and precious little plot. **85m/C VHS, DVD.** Kent Taylor, Regina Carrol, Ross Hagen, Maggie Bemby, Vicki Volante; ***D:*** Al Adamson.

Angels with Dirty Faces **1938** Rousing classic with memorable Cagney twitches and the famous long walk from the cell to the chair. Two young hoods grow up on NYC's lower East Side with diverse results—one enters the priesthood and the other opts for crime and prison. Upon release from the pen, famed gangster Cagney sets up shop in the old neighborhood, where Father O'Brien tries to keep a group of young toughs (the Dead End Kids) from following in his footsteps. Bogart's his unscrupulous lawyer and Bancroft a crime boss intent on double-crossing Cagney. Reportedly they were blasting real bullets during the big shootout, no doubt helping Cagney's intensity. Adapted from a story by Rowland Brown. **97m/B VHS, DVD.** James Cagney, Pat O'Brien, Humphrey Bogart, Ann Sheridan, George Bancroft, Billy Halop, Leo Gorcey, Huntz Hall, Bobby Jordan, Bernard Punsley, Gabriel Dell, Adrian Morris; ***D:*** Michael Curtiz; ***W:*** John Wexley, Warren Duff, Rowland Brown; ***C:*** Sol Polito; ***M:*** Max Steiner. N.Y. Film Critics '38: Actor (Cagney).

Anger Management **2003 (PG-13)** Disappointing comedy has mild-mannered, confrontation-averse Dave (Sandler) forced to attend anger management therapy after a misunderstanding on an airplane. Crazed anger therapist Dr. Buddy Rydell (Nicholson) is of the opinion that Dave isn't angry enough on the outside, so he proceeds, in increasingly ridiculous ways, to make him...angry, disrupting Dave's life and his relationship with girlfriend Linda (Tomei). While attempting to play off the two leads' screen and public personas, it succeds only rarely, due mainly to a weak script that takes the easy way out whenever it's offered, and by-the-numbers direction. Nicholson's obvious glee at not having to be restrained makes some scenes work on a pure comic level, while Sandler seems right at home, back in his element, after the smart comedy of "Punch-Drunk Love." **101m/C VHS, DVD, Blu-ray Disc, UMD.** *US* Adam Sandler, Jack Nicholson, Marisa Tomei, Luis Guzman, Allen Covert, Lynne Thigpen, Kurt Fuller, Jonathan Loughran, Krista Allen, January Jones, Woody Harrelson, John Turturro, Heather Graham, John C. Reilly, Kevin Nealon, Harry Dean Stanton; ***Cameos:*** Bobby Knight, John McEnroe; ***D:*** Peter Segal; ***W:*** David Dorfman; ***C:*** Donald McAlpine; ***M:*** Teddy Castellucci.

Angi Vera **1978** Naive 18-year-old Angi (Papp) is living in 1948 Hungary during the early days of socialism. Sent to a re-education school, she falls in love with her married Party leader but gradually loses her personal integrity to a corrupt system. Hungarian with subtitles. **96m/C VHS.** *HU* Veronika Papp, Erszi Pasztor, Eva Szabo, Tamas Dunai, Laszlo Horvath; ***D:*** Pal Gabor; ***W:*** Pal Gabor; ***C:*** Lajos Koltai; ***M:*** Gyorgy Selmeczi.

Angie **1994 (R)** Brassy Angie finds herself pregnant and unmarried. Tired of the advice and criticism she receives from her close knit neighborhood she strikes out of Brooklyn to find a new life for herself. Average "woman's movie" wrought with messages of pregnancy, childbirth, friendship, love, and family has far too much going on and relies too heavily on formula soap. Davis, in what could have been a juicy (read "Oscar") role is strong, but her performance is drowned by all the melodrama. Madonna was originally cast as Angie, but was bounced when the filming of "Snake Eyes" conflicted. Adapted from the book "Angie, I Says" by Avra Wing. **108m/C VHS, DVD.** Geena Davis, Aida Turturro, Stephen Rea, Philip Bosco, James Gandolfini, Jenny O'Hara; ***D:*** Martha Coolidge; ***W:*** Todd Graff.

AngKor: Cambodia Express **1981** An American journalist travels back to Vietnam to search for his long lost love. **96m/C VHS, DVD.** Robert Walker Jr., Christopher George; ***D:*** Lek Kitiparaporn.

Angry Harvest *Bittere Ernte* **1985** During the WWII German occupation of Poland, a gentile farmer shelters a young Jewish woman on the run, and a serious, ultimately interdependent relationship forms. Acclaimed; Holland's first film since her native Poland's martial law imposition made her an exile to Sweden. In German with English subtitles. Contains nudity and violence. **102m/C VHS, DVD.** *GE* Armin Mueller-Stahl, Elisabeth Trissenaar, Wojciech Pszoniak, Margit Carstensen, Kurt Raab, Kathe Jaenicke, Hans Beerhenke, Isa Haller; ***D:*** Agnieszka Holland; ***W:*** Agnieszka Holland. Montreal World Film Fest. '85: Actor (Mueller-Stahl).

Angry Joe Bass **1976** Contemporary Native American Joe Bass faces government officials who continually usurp his fishing rights. Something like "Billy Jack" without the intelligence. **82m/C VHS.** Henry Bal, Molly Mershon; ***D:*** Thomas G. Reeves.

The Angry Red Planet *Invasion of Mars; Journey to Planet Four* **1959** An unintentionally amusing sci-fi adventure about astronauts on Mars fighting off aliens and giant, ship-swallowing amoebas. Filmed using bizarre "Cinemagic" process, which turns almost everything pink. Wild effects have earned the film cult status. **83m/C VHS, DVD.** Gerald Mohr, Les Tremayne, Jack Kruschen, Nora Hayden, Paul Hahn, J. Edward McKinley, Tom Daly, Don Lamond; ***D:*** Ib Melchior; ***W:*** Ib Melchior, Sidney W. Pink; ***C:*** Stanley Cortez; ***M:*** Paul Dunlap.

Anguish 1/2 **1988 (R)** Well-done horror thriller about a lunatic who, inspired to duplicate the actions of an eyeball-obsessed killer in a popular film, murders a movie audience as they watch the movie. Violence and gore abound. **89m/C VHS, DVD.** *SP* Zelda Rubinstein, Michael Lerner, Talia Paul, Clara Pastor; ***D:*** Bigas Luna; ***W:*** Bigas Luna; ***C:*** Josep Civit; ***M:*** J(ose) M(anuel) Pagan.

Angus **1995 (PG-13)** Dull teen comedy about self-esteem revolves around the overweight Angus (Talbert), a friendly kid tormented by the usual school bullies. His best bud is twerp Troy (Owen), who tries to help Angus out with his crush on cute blonde Melissa (Ariana). There's even a schmaltzy prom scene. The profanity, though mild, and the boys sexual interests make this questionable for the pre-teen audience that could actually enjoy it. **87m/C VHS.** Charlie Talbert, Kathy Bates, George C. Scott, Chris Owen, Ariana Richards, Lawrence Pressman, Rita Moreno, James Van Der Beek, Anna Thomson; ***D:*** Patrick Read Johnson; ***W:*** Jill Gordon; ***C:*** Alexander Grusynski; ***M:*** David E. Russo.

Angus, Thongs and Perfect Snogging 1/2 **2008 (PG-13)** Angus is a feral cat and 'snogging' is kissing in Brit-speak in this cheerful adaptation of the first two books in Louise Rennison's teen girl series. Plain 14-year-old Georgia (Groome) is obsessed with both her looks and inexperience with boys, which she writes about in her diary. Things look up in the boy department when two handsome brothers move into the neighborhood and she and Robbie (Johnson) bond over their fondness for cats. Too bad that he's already been claimed by her school rival Lindsay (Nixon). **100m/C DVD.** *GB* Aaron Johnson, Kimberly Nixon, Eleanor Tomlinson, Sean Bourke, Liam Hess, Alan J. Dachman, Karen Taylor, Manjeevan Grewal, Georgia Henshaw, Eva Drew; ***D:*** Gurinder Chadha; ***W:*** Gurinder Chadha, Paul Mayeda Berges, Will McRobb, Chris Viscardi; ***C:*** Richard Pope; ***M:*** Joby Talbot.

Anima **1998** Sam and Iris have long left their pasts in Nazi Germany behind them for a secluded life in a New England farmhouse. At least until young journalist Bill discovers them while researching an article on taxidermy and mummification and sees their bizarre private world. **88m/C VHS, DVD.** Bray Poor, George Bartenieff, Jacqueline Bertrand; ***D:*** Craig Richardson; ***W:*** Craig Richardson; ***C:*** Randy Drummond; ***M:*** Joel Diamond, Adam Hurst.

The Animal 1/2 **2001 (PG-13)** Meek clerk Schneider is injured in a serious car accident and is rescued by a mad scientist who surgically replaces his damaged organs with animal parts. These animalistic traits tend to surface at the worst possible time for Schneider, just as he's realizing his dream of becoming a supercop. Haskell (from TV's first "Survivor") is pleasant in her big screen debut as the animal-rights advocate girlfriend, but Schneider is the one who makes this surprisingly enjoyable comedy work with his affable loser persona and willingness to go with the joke. **83m/C VHS, DVD.** *US* Rob Schneider, Guy Torry, John C. McGinley, Colleen Haskell, Michael Caton, Louis Lombardi, Ed Asner, Michael (Mike) Papajohn; ***D:*** Luke Greenfield; ***W:*** Rob Schneider, Tom Brady; ***C:*** Peter Lyons Collister; ***M:*** Teddy Castellucci.

Animal 1/2 **2005 (R)** James "Animal" Allen is a violent gangsta sent to prison, leaving behind young son Darius (Howard), who grows up following in pop's footsteps. When Animal emerges from prison reformed, he attempts to get Darius out of the life. Thoughtful and intelligent, with excellent performances by leads Howard and Rhames. **93m/C DVD.** Ving Rhames, Terrence Howard, Jim Brown, Chazz Palminteri, Paula Jai Parker, Faizon Love, Wes Studi, Beverly Todd; ***D:*** David J. Burke; ***W:*** David C(lark) Johnson. **VIDEO**

Animal 2 **2007** Lifer James "Animal" Allen's (Rhames) prison transfer finds him doing time with younger son James Jr. (Collins), who was framed for murder by Animal's old foe Kasada (Dunn), who wants Animal to get back into the prison fight game. On the outside, elder son Darius (Shannon) is trying to find the evidence to clear his bro. **93m/C DVD.** Ving Rhames, Vicellous Shannon, Conrad Dunn, K.C. Collins; ***D:*** Ryan Combs; ***W:*** Jacob L. Adams; ***M:*** Craig McConnell. **VIDEO**

Animal Behavior **1989 (PG)** An animal researcher and a music professor fall in love on a college campus. Bowen's (she actually released it under the alias Riley H. Anne) comedy was filmed in 1985 and edited/shelved for over four years, with good reason. **79m/C VHS.** Karen Allen, Armand Assante, Holly Hunter, Josh Mostel, Richard Libertini; ***D:*** Jenny (H. Anne Riley) Bowen; ***W:*** Susan Rice; ***C:*** Richard Bowen; ***M:*** Cliff Eidelman.

Animal Called Man *Animale Chiamato Uomo* **1972** Two crooked buddies join a big western gang in pillaging a small town and get in too deep. **83m/C VHS.** *IT* Vassilli Karis, Craig Hill, Gillian Bray; ***D:*** Robert (Roberto) Mauri; ***W:*** Robert (Roberto) Mauri; ***C:*** Luis Ciccarese; ***M:*** Carlo Savina.

Animal Crackers 1/2 **1930 (G)** The second and possibly the funniest of the 13 Marx Brothers films, "Animal Crackers" is a screen classic. Groucho is a guest at the house of wealthy matron Margaret Dumont and he, along with Zeppo, Chico, and Harpo, destroy the tranquility of the estate. Complete with the Harry Ruby music score—including Groucho's "Hooray for Captain Spaulding" with more quotable lines than any other Marx Brothers film: "One morning I shot an elephant in my pajamas. How he got into my pajamas, I'll never know." Based on a play by George S. Kaufman. **98m/B VHS, DVD.** Groucho Marx, Chico Marx, Harpo Marx, Zeppo Marx, Lillian Roth, Margaret Dumont, Louis Sorin, Hal Thompson, Robert Greig, Margaret Irving, Edward Metcalf, Kathryn Reece; ***D:*** Victor Heerman; ***W:*** Morrie Ryskind; ***C:*** George J. Folsey; ***M:*** Bert Kalmar, Harry Ruby.

Animal Factory 1/2 **2000 (R)** When first-time felon Ron Decker (Furlong) is sentenced to two years in a decaying prison, he is introduced to a world where violence is a way of life. After witnessing a riot, Ron is taken under the wing of Earl Copen (Dafoe), the main-man on the cellblock, but the younger man soon discovers that life in prison is not about rehabilitation, it's about survival. Bunker wrote the screenplay based on his novel of the same name. **94m/C VHS, DVD.** Edward (Eddie) Bunker, Willem Dafoe, Edward Furlong, Danny Trejo, John Heard, Mickey Rourke, Tom Arnold, Mark Boone Jr., Steve Buscemi, Seymour Cassel; ***D:*** Steve Buscemi; ***W:*** Edward (Eddie) Bunker, John Steppling; ***C:*** Phil Parmet; ***M:*** John Lurie.

Animal Farm **1955** An animated version of George Orwell's classic political satire about a barnyard full of animals who parallel the growth of totalitarian dictatorships. Not entirely successful, but probably best translation of Orwell to film. **73m/C VHS, DVD.** ***D:*** John Halas, Joy Batchelor; ***V:*** Maurice Denham, Gordon Heath.

Animal Farm 1/2 **1999** Orwell's political satire is given the "Babe" treatment in this live-action version. Drunken farmer Mr. Jones (Postlethwaite) has his power overthrown by his barnyard animals, who in turn are ruled by the farm's pig population. Only porker Napoleon (Stewart) turns out to be as big a tyrant as his human counterpart. Far beyond the scope of children, this retelling is clunky and its propaganda value has certainly come and gone. (Orwell was originally satirizing Stalinist Russia.) **91m/C VHS, DVD.** Pete Postlethwaite; ***D:*** John Stephenson; ***W:*** Martyn Burke, Alan Janes; ***C:*** Mike Brewster; ***M:*** Richard Harvey; ***V:*** Patrick Stewart, Kelsey Grammer, Ian Holm, Julia Ormond, Julia Louis-Dreyfus, Paul Scofield, Peter Ustinov. **CABLE**

Animal Instincts **1992 (R)** A woman takes a prescription drug that makes her a nymphomaniac, and her police officer husband discovers that he's turned on by videotaping her in bed with other men and women. One of the many in her constant stream of lovers is a politician whose campaign is based on shutting down all the town's sex clubs. Another in the string of sexual thrillers riding on the coattails of "Basic Instinct." **94m/C VHS, DVD.** Maxwell Caulfield, Jan-Michael Vincent, Mitch Gaylord, Shannon Whirry, Delia Sheppard, John Saxon, David Carradine; ***D:*** Alexander Gregory (Gregory Dark) Hippolyte; ***W:*** Jon Robert Samsel, Georges des Esseintes; ***C:*** Paul Desatoff; ***M:*** Joseph Smith.

Animal Instincts 2 **1994 (R)** Joanna leaves her overbearing husband and moves into a supposedly quiet community. Neighbor Steve is a security expert—and a voyeur. He's hidden a camera in Joanna's bedroom but she knows he's watching. **92m/C VHS, DVD.** Shannon Whirry, Woody Brown, Elizabeth Sandifer, Al Sapienza; ***D:*** Alexander Gregory (Gregory Dark) Hippolyte.

Animal Instincts 3: The Seductress **1995 (R)** Joanna (Schumacher) finds a new kind of sexual excitement when she gets involved with rock music promoter Alex (Matthew), whose kicks include feining blindness. The unrated version contains 12 more minutes of footage. **96m/C VHS, DVD.** Wendy Schumacher, James Matthew, Marcus Graham, John Bates, Anthony Lesa; ***D:*** Alexander Gregory (Gregory Dark) Hippolyte; ***W:*** Selwyn Harris; ***C:*** Ernest Paul Roebuck.

The Animal Kingdom *The Woman in His House* **1932** A romantic triangle develops when Howard, married to Loy, has an affair with Harding. The problem is Harding acts more like a wife and Loy a mistress. Intelligently written and directed, with a marvelous performance from veteran character actor Gargan. **95m/B VHS, DVD.** Ann Harding, Leslie Howard, Myrna Loy, Neil Hamilton, William Gargan, Henry Stephenson, Ilka Chase; ***D:*** Edward H. Griffith; ***W:*** Horace Jackson; ***C:*** George J. Folsey.

Animal Room **1995** When high school student Arnold Mosk (Harris) is caught using drugs, he's place in the school's controversial isolation program that's nicknamed "The Animal Room." There are no rules and Arnold's life is threatened by delinquent thug, Doug (Lillard). But if Arnold expects to survive, he's going to have to learn how to fight. **98m/C VHS, DVD.** Neil Patrick Harris, Matthew Lillard, Gabriel Olds, Catherine Hicks, Brian Vincent; ***D:*** Craig Singer.

Anita, Dances of Vice 🦴🦴 *Anita—Tanze des Lasters* **1987** German avant-garde film celebrates Anita Berber, the "most scandalous woman in 1920s Berlin." Berber was openly bisexual, used drugs, and danced nude in public. In von Praunheim's film, she rises from the dead and creates yet more scandal. **85m/C VHS.** *GE* Lotti Huber, Ina Blum, Mikhael Honesseau; ***D:*** Rosa von Praunheim.

The Ann Jillian Story 🦴 ½ **1988** Jillian stars as herself in this melodrama recounting her battle with breast cancer. Several musical numbers are included. **96m/C VHS.** Ann Jillian, Tony LoBianco, Viveca Lindfors, Leighton Bewley; ***D:*** Corey Allen. **TV**

Ann Vickers 🦴🦴 ½ **1933** A dashing young army captain wins over the heart of a dedicated social worker. Okay adaptation of a Sinclair Lewis novel, with Dunne suffering more than usual. **76m/B VHS.** Irene Dunne, Walter Huston, Bruce Cabot, Conrad Nagel, Edna May Oliver; ***D:*** John Cromwell; ***M:*** Max Steiner.

Anna 🦴🦴 **1951** Novitiate nun Anna (Mangano) is forced to confront her sordid past (as a nightclub entertainer), and her love for two very different men, when her seriously injured former fiancee is brought to the hospital where she is a nurse. Anna must finally deal with her feelings and decide which path her life will take. Dubbed in English. **111m/B VHS.** *IT* Silvana Mangano, Raf Vallone, Vittorio Gassman; ***D:*** Alberto Lattuada; ***C:*** Otello Martelli; ***M:*** Nino Rota.

Anna 🦴🦴🦴 **1987 (PG-13)** Age, envy, and the theatrical world receive their due in an uneven but engrossing drama about aging Czech film star Anna, making a sad living in New York doing commercials and trying for off-Broadway roles. She takes in Krystyna, a young Czech peasant girl who eventually rockets to model stardom. Modern, strongly acted "All About Eve" with a story partially based on a real Polish actress. Kirkland drew quite a bit of flak for shamelessly self-promoting for the Oscar. She still lost. **101m/C VHS, DVD.** Sally Kirkland, Paulina Porizkova, Robert Fields, Stefan Schnabel, Larry Pine, Ruth Maleczech; ***D:*** Yurek Bogayevicz; ***W:*** Yurek Bogayevicz, Agnieszka Holland; ***C:*** Bobby Bukowski; ***M:*** Greg Hawkes. Golden Globes '88: Actress—Drama (Kirkland); Ind. Spirit '88: Actress (Kirkland); L.A. Film Critics '87: Actress (Kirkland).

Anna 🦴🦴🦴 ½ *Anna: From Six Till Eighteen; Anna: Ot Shesti do Vosemnadtsati* **1993** Director Nikhalkov follows Russian history from the early 1980s through the early 1990s by following the development of his daughter during these years. He does this by annually asking her a series of questions about her views, likes, loves, hates, and outlook. Effectively paints a portrait of a country and a person experiencing life and the accompanying growing pains and triumphs. **99m/C VHS.** *RU FR* Nikita Mikhalkov, Nadia Mikhalkov, Anna Mikhalkov; ***D:*** Nikita Mikhalkov; ***W:*** Nikita Mikhalkov; ***C:*** Pavel Lebeshev, Vadim Yusov; ***M:*** Eduard Artemyev.

Anna and the King 🦴🦴 ½ **1999 (PG-13)** Based on the story of English widow and schoolteacher Anna Leonowens (Foster) who, in 1862, is hired by the King Mongkut of Siam (Yun-Fat) to introduce his 58 children to the ideas of the West. The film looks stunning (it was filmed in Malaysia) and Yun-Fat is regal and charismatic but Foster is too stiff upper-lipped and remote and there's respect rather than any hint of romance. Previously filmed as 1946's "Anna and the King of Siam" and the 1956 musical "The King and I." **147m/C VHS, DVD.** Jodie Foster, Chow Yun-Fat, Bai Ling, Tom Felton, Syed Alwi; ***D:*** Andy Tennant; ***W:*** Steve Meerson, Peter Krikes; ***C:*** Caleb Deschanel; ***M:*** George Fenton.

Anna and the King of Siam 🦴🦴🦴 ½ **1946** Splendid adaptation, from the book by Margaret Landon, about the true life adventures of 33-year-old English widow Anna Leonowens. In 1862 Anna and her son travelled to the exotic kingdom of Siam to educate the harem and children of the king. Dunne is splendid as the strong-willed governess as is Harrison (in his first American film) as the authoritarian eastern ruler. Remade as the musical "The King and I." **128m/B VHS, DVD.** Irene Dunne, Rex Harrison, Linda Darnell, Lee J. Cobb, Gale Sondergaard, Mikhail Rasumny, Dennis Hoey, Richard Lyon, John Abbott; ***D:*** John Cromwell; ***W:*** Sally Benson, Talbot Jennings; ***C:*** Arthur C. Miller; ***M:*** Bernard Herrmann. Oscars '46: Art Dir./Set Dec., B&W, B&W Cinematog.

Anna Christie 🦴🦴🦴 ½ **1923** Silent production of Eugene O'Neill's play that even he liked. A young girl is sent away by her father, a seaman, and finds her way to Chicago, where she becomes a prostitute. Later she visits her father's barge and falls for a sailor. She shares her past life story, hoping they will understand. This film was acclaimed when it was released, and still remains a touching work of art. Remade in 1930. **75m/B VHS.** Blanche Sweet, George F. Marion Sr., William Russell, Eugenie Besserer, Chester Conklin, George Siegmann, Victor Potel, Fred Kohler Sr.; ***D:*** John Griffith Wray.

Anna Christie 🦴🦴 ½ **1930** Garbo is the ex-prostitute who finds love with sailor Bickford. Bickford is unaware of his lover's tarnished past and she does her best to keep it that way. Garbo's first sound effort was advertised with the slogan "Garbo Talks." Adapted from the classic Eugene O'Neill play, the film is a slow but rewarding romantic drama. **90m/B VHS, DVD.** Greta Garbo, Marie Dressler, Charles Bickford, George F. Marion Sr.; ***D:*** Clarence Brown; ***C:*** William H. Daniels.

Anna Karenina 🦴🦴🦴 ½ **1935** Cinematic Tolstoy with Garbo as sad, moody, married Anna willing to give up everything to be near Vronsky (March), the cavalry officer she's obsessed with. And since it's Russian, expect tragedy. A classic Garbo vehicle with March and Rathbone (as the cuckhold husband) providing excellent support. Interestingly, a remake of the Garbo and John Gilbert silent, "Love." **85m/B VHS, DVD.** Greta Garbo, Fredric March, Freddie Bartholomew, Maureen O'Sullivan, May Robson, Basil Rathbone, Reginald Owen, Reginald Denny; ***D:*** Clarence Brown; ***W:*** S.N. Behrman, Clemence Dane, Salka Viertel; ***C:*** William H. Daniels; ***M:*** Herbert Stothart. N.Y. Film Critics '35: Actress (Garbo).

Anna Karenina 🦴🦴 ½ **1948** Stiff version of Tolstoy's passionate story of illicit love between a married woman and a military officer. In spite of exquisite costumes, and Leigh and Richardson as leads, still tedious. **123m/C VHS, DVD.** *GB* Vivien Leigh, Ralph Richardson, Kieron Moore, Sally Ann Howes, Niall MacGinnis, Martita Hunt, Michael Gough; ***D:*** Julien Duvivier; ***W:*** Julien Duvivier; ***C:*** Henri Alekan; ***M:*** Constant Lambert.

Anna Karenina 🦴🦴 ½ **1985 (PG)** TV version of Tolstoy's novel of betrayal, intrigue, and forbidden love. Anna, defying all social practices of the time, falls into the arms of a dashing count. Features an excellent performance from Paul "A Man for All Seasons" Scofield. **96m/C VHS.** Jacqueline Bisset, Christopher Reeve, Paul Scofield, Ian Ogilvy, Anna Massey, Judi Bowker; ***D:*** Simon Langton. **TV**

Anna Karenina 🦴🦴 ½ **2000** Well-done British adaptation of the familiar Tolstoy drama although, frankly, Anna (McCrory) is a pill. Less tragic than headstrong, this willful Russian beauty runs from her passionless marriage to Karenin (Dillane) straight into the arms of dashing seducer Vronsky (McKidd). Of course, once they turn each other's lives to misery, what else is left but a tragic end. This version also includes the secondary love affair of Kitty (Baeza) and Levin (Henshall). **240m/C VHS, DVD.** Helen McCrory, Kevin McKidd, Stephen (Dillon) Dillane, Douglas Henshall, Paloma Baeza, Amanda Root, Mark Strong; ***D:*** David Blair; ***W:*** Allan Cubitt; ***C:*** Ryszard Lenczewski; ***M:*** John Keane. **TV**

Anna to the Infinite Power 🦴🦴 ½ **1984** Sci fi based on the book of the same name follows a young girl with telepathic powers. When the girl discovers that she has sisters as the result of a strange scientific experiment, she sets out to find them, drawing on her own inner strength. **101m/C VHS.** Dina Merrill, Martha Byrne, Mark Patton; ***D:*** Robert Wiemer.

Annapolis 🦴 **1928** Life's in the pink for two guys at the U.S. naval academy until jealousy rears its loathsome head when they fall for the same gal. Just when it's beginning to look like love and honor is an either-or proposition, the lovelorn rivals find that although love transcends all, a guy's gotta do what a guy's gotta do, even if it means sticking up for his romantic nemesis. Lots of sub-par male bonding. **63m/B VHS.** Johnny Mack Brown, Hugh Allan, Hobart Bosworth, William "Billy" Bakewell, Charlotte Walker, Jeanette Loff; ***D:*** Christy Cabanne.

Annapolis 🦴 ½ **2006 (PG-13)** Predictable military/boxing flick finds hot-headed, working-class Jake Huard (Franco) set on entering the U.S. Naval Academy at Annapolis. He's finally accepted and finds himself subjected to the berating of disciplinarian Lt. Cole (Gibson), who is certain Jake doesn't have what it takes. However, Jake is a really good boxer and starts training for the Academy's Brigades competition, hoping for a shot at the reigning champ—Cole. The fetching Brewster serves as Jake's superior officer, questionable trainer, and romantic object. **108m/C DVD, Blu-ray Disc.** *US* James Franco, Tyrese Gibson, Jordana Brewster, Donnie Wahlberg, Vicellous Shannon, Roger Fan, Chi McBride, Brian Goodman, Charles Napier, Zachery Ty Bryan; ***D:*** Justin Lin; ***W:*** Dave Collard; ***C:*** Phil Abraham; ***M:*** Brian Tyler.

An Annapolis Story 🦴 ½ *Blue and the Gold* **1955** Cliche-ridden WWII drama about two naval cadets romancing the same lucky girl. Low-rent time for director Siegel which wastes a decent cast. **81m/C VHS.** John Derek, Kevin McCarthy, Diana Lynn, Pat Conway, L.Q. Jones, Alvy Moore, Betty Lou Gerson, Robert Osterloh, George Eldredge, Dabbs Greer, Sam Peckinpah, William Schallert; ***D:*** Donald Siegel; ***W:*** Daniel Mainwaring, Daniel Ullman; ***C:*** Sam Leavitt; ***M:*** Marlin Skiles.

Anne Frank: The Whole Story 🦴🦴🦴 *Anne Frank* **2001** Solid made-for-TV entry into the pantheon of Anne Frank pathos, legend, or tragedy—take your pick. Romanian-born director Robert Dornhelm does his best work to date by taking a more intimate look at the day-to-day life of the young Anne Frank (played with great precision by Hannah Taylor-Gordon) during the years she and her family spent in hiding from the German invaders. Anne, as a human being, is fleshed out and painted with more detail than in other bio-pics covering the same ground (story is based on Melissa Muller's biography, and not on the famous diary). This has the effect of making her ultimate fate at Auschwitz all the more painful. **189m/C DVD.** Ben Kingsley, Brenda Blethyn, Hannah Taylor Gordon, Joachim Krol, Lili Taylor, Tatjana Blacher; ***D:*** Richard Dornhelm; ***W:*** Kirk Ellis; ***C:*** Elemer Ragalyi; ***M:*** Graeme Revell. **TV**

Anne of Avonlea 🦴🦴🦴 ½ *Anne of Green Gables: The Sequel* **1987** Equally excellent miniseries sequel to "Anne of Green Gables" in which the romantic heroine grows up and discovers romance. The same cast returns and Sullivan continues his tradition of lavish filming on Prince Edward Island and beautiful costumes. Based on the characters from L.M. Montgomery's classic novels "Anne of Avonlea," "Anne of the Island," and "Anne of Windy Poplars." CBC, PBS, and Disney worked together on this WonderWorks production. **224m/C VHS, DVD.** *CA* Megan Follows, Colleen Dewhurst, Wendy Hiller, Frank Converse, Patricia Hamilton, Schuyler Grant, Jonathan Crombie, Rosemary Dunsmore; ***D:*** Kevin Sullivan; ***W:*** Kevin Sullivan; ***M:*** Hagood Hardy. **TV**

Anne of Green Gables 🦴🦴🦴 **1934** A lonely Canadian couple adopts an orphan who keeps them on their toes with her animated imagination, and wins a permanent place in their hearts. Warm (but loose) adaptation of Lucy Maud Montgomery's popular novel is entertaining although 1985 remake is far superior. Followed by "Anne of Windy Poplars." **79m/B VHS.** Anne Shirley, Tom Brown, O.P. Heggie, Helen Westley, Sara Haden, Charley Grapewin; ***D:*** George Nicholls Jr.; ***M:*** Max Steiner.

Anne of Green Gables 🦴🦴🦴 ½ **1985** Splendid production of the famous Lucy Maud Montgomery classic about a young orphan girl growing to young adulthood with the help of a crusty brother and sister duo. The characters come to life under Sullivan's direction, and the movie is enhanced by the beautiful Prince Edward Island scenery and wonderful costumes. One of the few instances where an adaptation lives up to (if not exceeds) the quality of the original novel. A WonderWorks presentation that was made with the cooperation of the Disney channel, CBC, and PBS. Followed by "Anne of Avonlea." On two tapes. **197m/C VHS, DVD.** *CA* Megan Follows, Colleen Dewhurst, Richard Farnsworth, Patricia Hamilton, Schuyler Grant, Jonathan Crombie, Marilyn Lightstone, Charmion King, Rosemary Radcliffe, Jackie Burroughs, Robert E. Collins, Joachim Hansen, Cedric Smith, Paul Bown, Miranda de Pencier, Jennifer Inch, Wendy Lyon, Christiane Kruger, Trish Nettleton, Morgan Chapman; ***D:*** Kevin Sullivan; ***W:*** Kevin Sullivan, Joe Wiesenfeld; ***C:*** Rene Ohashi; ***M:*** Hagood Hardy. **TV**

Anne of Green Gables: The Continuing Story 🦴🦴 ½ **1999** Anne (Follows) learns that fiance Gilbert (Blythe) has accepted a job in a New York hospital. She takes a job in a publishing house where she meets fast-living journalist Jack Garrison (Daddo). Gilbert and Anne return to Avonlea to marry just before WWI and Gilbert joins the army as a doctor and is sent to France. When he's declared MIA, Anne heads overseas with the Red Cross to search for him and runs into Jack again, who leads Anne into numerous intrigues. This far-fetched story is not based on one of Lucy Maud Montgomery's books but Anne at least retains her spunkiness and determination. **185m/C VHS, DVD.** *CA* Megan Follows, Jonathan Crombie, Cameron Daddo, Schuyler Grant, Patricia Hamilton, Rosemary Radcliffe, Miranda de Pencier, Barry Morse, Martha Henry, Janet-Laine Green, Nigel Bennett, Shannon Lawson; ***D:*** Stefan Scaini; ***W:*** Kevin Sullivan, Laurie Pearson; ***C:*** Robert Saad; ***M:*** Peter Breiner. **TV**

Anne of the Thousand Days 🦴🦴🦴 ½ **1969 (PG)** Lavish retelling of the life and loves of Henry the VIII. In 1526, Henry tosses aside his current wife for the young and devastatingly beautiful Anne Boleyn (Bujold). But after the birth of Princess Elizabeth, Henry tires of Anne and wishes to marry another. So he decides to rid himself of her presence—permanently. Burton's performance of the amoral king garnered him an Oscar nomination. Based on the 1948 play by Maxwell Anderson. Watch for Elizabeth Taylor as a masked courtesan at the costume ball. **145m/C VHS.** Richard Burton, Genevieve Bujold, Irene Papas, Anthony Quayle, John Colicos, Michael Hordern, Michael Johnson; ***D:*** Charles Jarrott; ***W:*** Bridget Boland, John Hale; ***M:*** Georges Delerue. Oscars '69: Costume Des.; Directors Guild '70: Director (Jarrott); Golden Globes '70: Actress—Drama (Bujold), Director (Jarrott), Film—Drama, Screenplay.

Anne Rice's The Feast of All Saints 🦴🦴 ½ *The Feast of All Saints* **2001** It's not about vampires. Rice's novel is set in pre-Civil War New Orleans among free people of color. They enjoy certain privileges of middleclass society while still dealing with class, race, and sex. Cecil St. Marie (Rueben) is the mistress of white plantation owner Philippe Ferronnaire (Gallagher). He makes certain promises to his children by Cecil—Marcel (Ri'chard) and Marie (Lyn)—which he fails to keep, thus causing family dissension. As the children grow into adults they face romantic and societal dilemmas of their own. Excellent cast does well by the sometimes melodramatic story. Title refers to the day for remembering the dead. **212m/C VHS, DVD.** Robert Ri'chard, Peter Gallagher, Gloria Reuben, Nicole Lyn, Jennifer Beals, Ossie Davis, Ruby Dee, Pam Grier, Jasmine Guy, Victoria Rowell, James Earl Jones, Eartha Kitt, Ben Vereen, Forest Whitaker, Bianca Lawson, Daniel Sunjata; ***D:*** Peter Medak; ***W:*** John Wilder; ***C:*** Edward Pei; ***M:*** Patrick Seymour. **CABLE**

Annie 🦴🦴 **1982 (PG)** Stagy big-budget adaption of the Broadway musical, which was an adaptation of the comic strip. A major financial disaster upon release, still it's an entertaining enterprise curiously directed by Huston and engagingly acted by Finney and

Quinn. ♫ Tomorrow; It's the Hard Knock Life; Maybe; I Think I'm Gonna Like It Here; Little Girls; We Got Annie; Let's Go to the Movies; You're Never Fully Dressed Without a Smile; Easy Street. **128m/C VHS, DVD.** Aileen Quinn, Carol Burnett, Albert Finney, Bernadette Peters, Ann Reinking, Tim Curry; ***D:*** John Huston; ***W:*** Thomas Meehan; ***C:*** Richard Moore; ***M:*** Ralph Burns. Golden Raspberries '82: Worst Support. Actress (Quinn).

Annie **1999** Lively and amusing adaptation of the smash Broadway musical that will make you forget that dud 1982 movie version. Scrappy urchin Annie (newcomer Morton) is incarcerated in a Depression-era orphange run by despotic Miss Hannigan (Bates) when she's offered the chance to spend the holidays with chilly moneybags Oliver Warbucks (Garber). Naturally, Annie thaws his frosty demeanor. Able support is provided by Warbucks' faithful assistant Grace (McDonald) and Miss Hannigan's wastrel brother Rooster (Cumming) and his floozy Lily (Chenoweth). **120m/C VHS, DVD.** Alicia Morton, Victor Garber, Kathy Bates, Alan Cumming, Audra McDonald, Kristin Chenoweth; ***Cameos:*** Andrea McArdle; ***D:*** Rob Marshall; ***W:*** Irene Mecchi; ***C:*** Ralf Bode; ***M:*** Charles Strouse, Martin Charnin. **TV**

Annie: A Royal Adventure 1/2 **1995** TV sequel to "Annie" finds the red-haired heroine (Johnson) traveling to England with her Daddy Warbucks (Hearn), who's about to be knighted in London. But the evil Lady Edwina Hogbottom (played to a high-camp hilt by Collins) has a plan to blow up Buckingham Palace and take over as queen. Naturally, it's up to Annie to defeat her and have a happy ending. **92m/C VHS, DVD.** Ashley Johnson, George Hearn, Joan Collins, Emily Ann Lloyd, Camilla Belle, Ian McDiarmid; ***D:*** Ian Toynton; ***W:*** Trish Soodik; ***C:*** Alan Hume; ***M:*** David Michael Frank.

Annie Get Your Gun **1950** A lavish production of Irving Berlin's Broadway hit musical. Sharpshooting Annie Oakley (Hutton) is the queen of Buffalo Bill's Wild West show though her talents leave her loveless. Seems fellow marksman Frank Butler's (Keel) ego can't handle the fact that Annie keeps beating him. Lots of singing, with an enthusiastic lead performance by Hutton. ♫ There's No Business Like Show Business; My Defenses Are Down; I'm an Indian Too; Doin' What Comes Natur'lly; Colonel Buffalo Bill; The Girl That I Marry; You Can't Get a Man with a Gun; They Say It's Wonderful; I Got the Sun in the Morning. **107m/C VHS, DVD.** Betty Hutton, Howard Keel, Keenan Wynn, Louis Calhern, J. Carrol Naish, Edward Arnold, Clinton Sundberg; ***D:*** George Sidney; ***W:*** Sidney Sheldon; ***C:*** Charles Rosher; ***M:*** Irving Berlin. Oscars '50: Scoring/Musical.

Annie Hall **1977 (PG)** Acclaimed coming-of-cinematic-age film for Allen is based in part on his own life. His love affair with Hall/Keaton is chronicled as an episodic, wistful comedy commenting on family, love, loneliness, communicating, maturity, driving, city life, careers, and various other topics. Abounds with classic scenes, including future star Goldblum and his mantra at a cocktail party; Allen and the lobster pot; and Allen, Keaton, a bathroom, a tennis racket, and a spider. The film operates on many levels, as does Keaton's wardrobe, which started a major fashion trend. Don't blink or you'll miss several future stars in bit parts. Expertly shot by Gordon Willis. **94m/C VHS, DVD.** Woody Allen, Diane Keaton, Tony Roberts, Carol Kane, Paul Simon, Colleen Dewhurst, Janet Margolin, Shelley Duvall, Christopher Walken, Marshall McLuhan, Dick Cavett, John Glover, Jeff Goldblum, Beverly D'Angelo; ***D:*** Woody Allen; ***W:*** Woody Allen, Marshall Brickman; ***C:*** Gordon Willis. Oscars '77: Actress (Keaton), Director (Allen), Orig. Screenplay, Picture; AFI '98: Top 100; British Acad. '77: Actress (Keaton), Director (Allen), Film, Screenplay; Directors Guild '77: Director (Allen); Golden Globes '78: Actress—Mus./Comedy (Keaton); L.A. Film Critics '77: Screenplay; Natl. Bd. of Review '77: Support. Actress (Keaton), Natl. Film Reg. '92;; N.Y. Film Critics '77: Actress (Keaton), Director (Allen), Film, Screenplay; Natl. Soc. Film Critics '77: Actress (Keaton), Film, Screenplay; Writers Guild '77: Orig. Screenplay.

Annie O 1/2 **1995 (PG)** 15-year-old Annie Rojas (Yares) runs into problems when she joins the boys' basketball team (since her school doesn't have a girls team). Her teammates are jealous and so are her brother and boyfriend. **93m/C VHS.** Coco Yares, Chad Willet, Robert Stewart; ***D:*** Michael McClary.

Annie Oakley **1935** Energetic biographical drama based on the life and legend of sharpshooter Annie Oakley and her on-off relationship with Wild Bill Hickok. Stanwyck makes a great Oakley. Later musicalized as "Annie Get Your Gun." **90m/B VHS.** Barbara Stanwyck, Preston Foster, Melvyn Douglas, Pert Kelton, Andy Clyde, Moroni Olsen, Chief Thundercloud; ***D:*** George Stevens.

The Annihilators WOOF! 1985 (R) A group of Vietnam vets band together in an extremely violent manner to protect their small town from a gang of thugs. **87m/C VHS.** Gerrit Graham, Lawrence-Hilton Jacobs, Paul Koslo, Christopher Stone, Andy Wood, Sid Conrad, Dennis Redfield; ***D:*** Charles E. Sellier.

The Anniversary **1968** One-eyed monster mom Mrs. Taggart (Bette at her baddest) gives new meaning to the word "possessive." Thoroughly cowing her three grown sons, she manages to get them to come home each year on the wedding anniversary to the husband she despised. Only this time, the trio tell her they're going to live their own lives. Hah—not if mom has anything to do with it. Based on the play by Bill MacIlwraith. **93m/C VHS, DVD.** *GB* Bette Davis, Jack Hedley, James Cossins, Christian Roberts, Sheila Hancock, Elaine Taylor; ***D:*** Roy Ward Baker; ***W:*** Jimmy Sangster; ***C:*** Henry Waxman; ***M:*** Philip Martell.

The Anniversary Party **2001 (R)** Leigh and Cumming co-write, co-direct, and star as the central couple in this impressive ensemble comedy-drama about a group of Hollywood friends celebrating said couple's sixth anniversary. Amid much career and personal angst, drug use, and sometimes nasty air-clearing, most of the characters are fleshed out nicely and the dialogue remains sharp throughout. The air is thick with genuine personal dread and interpersonal tension. Among the uniformly excellent performances, two especially stand out: Leigh as the aging actress on the cusp of career oblivion, and Cates as a former actress who's given up her career to focus on being a wife (to just-beyond-leading-man-status hubby Kline) and mother. Filmed in digital video in 19 days under the Dogme 95 guidelines. **117m/C VHS, DVD.** *US* Jennifer Jason Leigh, Alan Cumming, Gwyneth Paltrow, Kevin Kline, Phoebe Cates, John C. Reilly, Jane Adams, John Benjamin Hickey, Parker Posey, Denis O'Hare, Jennifer Beals, Mina (Badiyi) Badie, Michael Panes; ***D:*** Jennifer Jason Leigh, Alan Cumming; ***W:*** Jennifer Jason Leigh, Alan Cumming; ***C:*** John Bailey; ***M:*** Michael Penn.

Anonymous Rex **2004** So dinosaurs didn't actually die off, they adapted and live side-by-side with humans. They wear holographic suits as disguises. Dino-detectives Vince Rubio and Ernie Watson are out to stop a mutant sect that wants to wipe out mankind. Based on the comic mysteries by Eric Garcia. **89m/C DVD.** Sam Trammell, Daniel Baldwin, Faye Dunaway, Isaac Hayes, Tamara Gorski, Stephanie Lemelin; ***D:*** Julian Jarrold; ***W:*** Joe Menosky; ***C:*** Albert J. Dunk, Kit Whitmore; ***M:*** David Bergeaud. **CABLE**

Another Chance **1988 (R)** Girl-crazy bachelor is returned from heaven for a second chance and has to choose between a "bad" girl and a "good" girl. What a choice! **99m/C VHS.** Bruce Greenwood, Frank Annese, Jeff East, Anne Ramsey, Barbara (Lee) Edwards; ***D:*** Jerry Vint.

Another Cinderella Story 1/2 **2008 (PG)** Same basic plot as 2004's "A Cinderella Story" with different characters. Our Cinderella is Mary (Gomez), whose mean stepsisters are trying to stop her from putting on her dancing shoes and going to a costume ball. But Mary makes it and dances with Joey (Seeley), the most popular guy around, who recognizes that this is his dream girl even behind a mask. When Mary has to make a quick exit to meet her curfew, Joey's only clue is the phone she left behind. **90m/C DVD, Blu-ray Disc.** Jane Lynch, Katharine Isabelle, Emily Perkins, Marcus T. Paulk, Selena Gomez, Andrew Seeley, Jessica Parker Kennedy; ***D:*** Damon Santostefano; ***W:*** Masahiro Asakawa, Jessica Scott; ***C:*** Jon Joffin; ***M:*** John Paesano. **VIDEO**

Another Country 1/2 **1984** Mitchell's adaptation of his play based on the life of Guy Burgess, who became a spy for the Soviet Union. Guy Bennett (Everett) is an English boarding school upperclassman whose affected mannerisms and barely disguised homosexuality cause dissension among his schoolmates, while his one friend, Tommy Judd (Firth), is a fervant Marxist. Rather fancifully depicted and loving recreation of 1930s English life. Although the film is inferior to the award-winning play, director Kanievska manages to transform a piece into a solid film, and Everett's performance as Bennett/Burgess is outstanding. **90m/C VHS, DVD.** *GB* Rupert Everett, Colin Firth, Michael Jenn, Robert Addie, Anna Massey, Betsy Brantley, Rupert Wainwright, Cary Elwes, Arthur Howard, Tristan Oliver, Frederick Alexander, Adrian Ross-Magenty, Geoffrey Bateman, Philip Dupuy, Jeffrey Wickham, Gideon Boulting, Ivor Howard, Charles Spencer; ***D:*** Marek Kanievska; ***W:*** Julian Mitchell; ***C:*** Peter Biziou; ***M:*** Michael Storey.

Another Day in Paradise **1998 (R)** Tulsa teen junkies Bobbie (Kartheiser) and Rosie (Wagner) team up with older junkie couple Mel (Woods) and Sidney (Griffith) and go from bad to worse. Mel's also a dealer and thief and is glad to add two would-be partners in crime to his and Sidney's traveling road to hell. Woods is all sly confidence while Griffith shows some seductive tough-chick grit and the younger twosome manage to hold their own nicely. Not a pic for the faint of heart or queasy of stomach. Based on the book by Eddie Little. **101m/C VHS, DVD.** James Woods, Melanie Griffith, Vincent Kartheiser, Natasha Gregson Wagner, Paul Hipp, Brent Briscoe, Lou Diamond Phillips; ***D:*** Larry Clark; ***W:*** Christopher Landon, Stephen Chin; ***C:*** Eric Alan Edwards.

Another 48 Hrs. 1/2 **1990 (R)** Continuing chemistry between Nolte and Murphy is one of the few worthwhile items in this stodgy rehash. Any innovation by Murphy seems lost, the story is redundant of any other cop thriller, and violence and car chases abound. Pointlessly energetic and occasionally fun for only the true devotee. **98m/C VHS, DVD.** Eddie Murphy, Nick Nolte, Brion James, Kevin Tighe, Bernie Casey, David Anthony Marshall, Ed O'Ross; ***D:*** Walter Hill; ***W:*** Jeb Stuart; ***C:*** Matthew F. Leonetti; ***M:*** James Horner.

Another Life 1/2 **2001** Based on the 1920s Thompson-Bywaters criminal case. Fanciful Edith (Little) makes a grave mistake by marrying staid Percy Thompson (Moran), whom she soon feels is dull, resentful, and cold. When Edith re-connects with exciting family friend Frederick Bywaters (Gruffudd), she strays, eventually confessing to Freddy that she wishes Percy were dead. He soon is and the adulterers stand trial for his murder. **101m/C DVD.** *GB* Natasha Little, Nick Moran, Ioan Gruffudd, Imelda Staunton, Rachael Stirling, Tom Wilkinson, Liz McKechnie; ***D:*** Philip Goodhew; ***W:*** Philip Goodhew; ***C:*** Simon Archer; ***M:*** James McConnel.

Another Lonely Hitman *Shin Kanashiki Hittoman* **1995** Character study rather than a typical gangster flick. Old-school yakuza and former junkie Tachibana (Ishibashi) finds his ways badly out-of-date after he's released from a 10-year prison stretch. He tries to do the right thing by helping young druggie/hooker Yuki (Sawada) clean up (and the withdrawal scenes aren't pretty) and teach the younger hoods some manners. Based on the book by Yamanouchi, who did the screenplay; Japanese with subtitles. **105m/C DVD.** *JP* Ryo Ishibashi, Asami Sawada, Kazuhiko Kanayama, Tatsuo Yamada; ***D:*** Rokuro Mochizuki; ***W:*** Yukio Yamanouchi; ***C:*** Naoki Imaizumi; ***M:*** Kazutoki Umezu.

Another Man, Another Chance *Un Autre Homme, Une Autre Chance* **1977 (PG)** Remake of Lelouch's "A Man and a Woman," set in the turn-of-the-century American West, pales by comparison to the original. Slow-moving tale casts widow Bujold and widower Caan as lovers. **132m/C VHS.** *FR* James Caan, Genevieve Bujold, Francis Huster, Jennifer Warren, Susan Tyrrell; ***D:*** Claude Lelouch; ***W:*** Claude Lelouch.

Another Man's Poison 1/2 **1952** Melodramatic crime drama with a showy, if stereotypical role, for Davis. She's mystery writer Janet Frobisher and lives on a secluded Yorkshire farm. Too bad her escaped con husband suddenly shows up (and gets killed by Janet). Her troubles aren't over. Hubby's partner, George Bates (Merrill), comes a-lookin' and agrees to dispose of the body if Janet will let him hide out. She tries to kill Bates as well but her scheming comes to an unexpected conclusion. Adapted from the play "Deadlock" by Leslie Sands. **90m/B VHS, DVD.** *GB* Bette Davis, Gary Merrill, Emlyn Williams, Anthony Steel, Barbara Murray, Reginald Beckwith, Edna Morris; ***D:*** Irving Rapper; ***W:*** Val Guest; ***C:*** Robert Krasker; ***M:*** Paul Sawtell.

Another 9 1/2 Weeks WOOF! 1996 (R) Uninteresting sequel finds suicidal John (Rourke) overwhelmed by his kinky memories of Elizabeth, so he flies to Paris determined to find her. Instead, he meets fashion designer Lea (Everhart), who claims to be Elizabeth's friend and who puts the sexual tease on the S/M devotee. Monotony sets in early and there's no real heat generated between the duo. **104m/C VHS, DVD.** Mickey Rourke, Angie Everhart, Steven Berkoff, Agathe de la Fontaine, Dougray Scott; ***D:*** Anne Goursaud; ***W:*** Mick Davis; ***C:*** Robert Alazraki; ***M:*** Stephen Parsons, Francis Haines.

Another Pair of Aces: Three of a Kind **1991** Nelson and Kristofferson team up to clear the name of Torn, a Texas Ranger accused of murder. Video contains some scenes deemed too racy for TV. Sequel to "A Pair of Aces." **93m/C VHS, DVD.** Willie Nelson, Kris Kristofferson, Joan Severance, Rip Torn, Dan Kamin, Ken Farmer, Richard Jones; ***D:*** Bill Bixby. **TV**

Another Public Enemy *Gonggongui Jeog 2* **2005 (R)** Prosecutor Kang investigates corrupt businessman Han, who is laundering his ill-gotten real estate gains in the U.S. Only his superiors suspect Kang's motives since the two were bitter high school rivals. Really, really, really long, which dilutes any action and suspense. Korean with subtitles. **148m/C DVD.** *KN* Kyung-gu Sol, Jun-ho Jeong, Shin-il Kang; ***D:*** Woo-suk Kang; ***W:*** Woo-suk Kang; ***M:*** Jawe-kwon Han.

Another Stakeout 1/2 *Stakeout 2* **1993 (PG-13)** Sequel six years after the original finds Dreyfuss and Estevez partnered again for another stakeout, this time to keep an eye on Moriarty, a reluctant witness against the Mob. The two spying detectives find themselves in an upscale neighborhood where blending in is a hard thing to do. O'Donnell is a breath of fresh air as a wisecracking assistant district attorney. Stowe briefly reprises her role as Dreyfuss' girlfriend. Writer Kouf reportedly had difficulty penning the script, surprising since there isn't much new here. **109m/C VHS, DVD.** Richard Dreyfuss, Emilio Estevez, Rosie O'Donnell, Cathy Moriarty, Madeleine Stowe, John Rubinstein, Marcia Strassman, Dennis Farina, Miguel Ferrer; ***D:*** John Badham; ***W:*** Jim Kouf; ***C:*** Roy Wagner.

Another Thin Man 1/2 **1939** Powell and Loy team up for the third in the delightful "Thin Man" series. Slightly weaker series entry takes its time, but has both Powell and Loy providing stylish performances. Nick Jr. is also introduced as the newest member of the sleuthing team. Sequel to "After the Thin Man"; followed by "Shadow of the Thin Man." **105m/B VHS, DVD.** William Powell, Myrna Loy, Virginia Grey, Otto Kruger, Sir C. Aubrey Smith, Ruth Hussey; ***D:*** Woodbridge S. Van Dyke.

Another Time, Another Place **1958** Sappy melodrama about an American journalist who suffers an emotional meltdown when her married British lover is killed during WWII. So she heads for Cornwall to console the widow and family. **98m/B VHS, DVD.** *GB* Lana Turner, Barry Sullivan, Glynis Johns, Sean Connery, Terence Longdon; ***D:*** Lewis Allen; ***C:*** Jack Hildyard.

Another Time, Another Place **1983 (R)** Bored young Scottish housewife married to an older fella falls in love with an Italian prisoner-of-war who works on her farm during WWII. Occasionally quirky, always finely crafted view of wartime Britain and the little-known life of POWs in England. **101m/C VHS.** *GB* Phyllis Logan, Giovanni Mauriello, Gian Luca Favilla, Paul Young, Tom Watson; ***D:*** Michael Radford; ***W:*** Michael Radford; ***C:*** Roger Deakins.

Another Way ½ *Olelkezo Tekintetek* **1982** The director of 1971's much-lauded "Love" sets this politically charged love story in Hungary in 1958. Opening with a view of a female corpse, the story flashes backward to look at the woman's journalistic career and her relationship with a women colleague. Candid love scenes between women in Hungary of 1958, considered a cinematic novelty in many places outside Hungary. In Hungarian with English subtitles. **100m/C VHS, DVD.** *HU* Jadwiga Jankowska Cieslak, Grazyna Szapolowska, Josef Kroner, Hernadi Judit, Andorai Peter; ***D:*** Karoly Makk. Cannes '82: Actress (Cieslak).

Another Woman **1988 (PG)** The study of an intellectual woman whose life is changed when she begins to eavesdrop. What she hears provokes her to examine every relationship in her life, finding things quite different than she had believed. Heavy going, with Rowlands effective as a woman coping with an entirely new vision of herself. Farrow plays the catalyst. Although Allen's comedies are more popular than his dramas, this one deserves a look. **81m/C VHS, DVD.** Gena Rowlands, Gene Hackman, Mia Farrow, Ian Holm, Betty Buckley, Martha Plimpton, Blythe Danner, Harris Yulin, Sandy Dennis, David Ogden Stiers, John Houseman, Philip Bosco, Frances Conroy, Kenneth Welsh, Michael Kirby; ***D:*** Woody Allen; ***W:*** Woody Allen; ***C:*** Sven Nykvist.

Another Woman ½ **1994** Lisa Temple (Bateman) was attacked and left for dead in an alley. She wakes up in the hospital with amnesia but her bitter husband Paul (Outerbridge) still wants a divorce. Lisa learns things about herself she doesn't like and vows to change but as her memories start to return she realizes just what put her in that alley in the first place. From the Harlequin Romance Series; adapted from the Margot Dalton novel. **91m/C DVD.** *CA* Justine Bateman, Peter Outerbridge, Amy Stewart, Kenneth Welsh, James Purcell, Jackie Richardson, Michael Copeman, Elizabeth Lennie; ***D:*** Alan Smythe; ***W:*** Jim Henshaw, Lee Langley, Lyle Slack; ***C:*** Michael Storey; ***M:*** David Blamires. **TV**

Another Woman's Husband ½ **2000** Traumatized as a child by the drowning death of her brother, Laurel (Rinna) finally decides to get over her fear of water by taking swimming lessons. Susan (O'Grady) is her swimming instructor and they become best friends. Until the women realize they also share the same man (Midkiff), who happens to be Susan's husband. Based on the novel "Swimming Lessons" by Anna Villegas and Lynne Hugo. **91m/C VHS, DVD.** Lisa Rinna, Gail O'Grady, Dale Midkiff, Sally Kirkland, Charlotte Rae; ***D:*** Noel Nosseck; ***W:*** Susan Arnout Smith; ***C:*** Alan Caso; ***M:*** Mark Snow. **CABLE**

Another You **1991 (R)** Con man Wilder takes pathological liar Pryor under his care and decides to use his talents to his fullest advantage. Posing as successful businessmen, the duo initiate a scam so complicated that they may end up being double-crossed or worse yet, dead! Can the pair see their plan through without losing their lives? Sad to see how far these two gifted comedians have fallen. Their collaboration is tired and the movie generally dreadful. **98m/C VHS, DVD.** Richard Pryor, Gene Wilder, Mercedes Ruehl, Vanessa L(ynne) Williams, Stephen Lang, Kevin Pollak; ***D:*** Maurice Phillips.

The Answer Man *Arlen Faber* **2009 (R)** Arlen Faber (Daniels) has suffered for 20 years as the author of a spiritual self-help guide that became a mass-media sensation. Unable to handle the fame, Arlen is a misanthropic recluse with back trouble that drives him into the arms of single mom/chiropractor Elizabeth (Graham) who thinks maybe Arlen could also be the new dad figure in her young son's life. Also having father issues is bookstore owner Kris (Pucci), just out of alcohol rehab, who turns to the reluctant Arlen for guidance. Pic skates on the emotional surface of some big issues but does have some nice turns by the leads. **96m/C DVD.** *US* Jeff Daniels, Lauren Graham, Lou Taylor Pucci, Olivia Thirlby, Kat Dennings, Nora Dunn, Tony Hale; ***D:*** John Hindman; ***W:*** John Hindman; ***C:*** Oliver Bokelberg; ***M:*** Teddy Castellucci.

The Ant Bully ½ **2006 (PG)** Warner Bros. entry in the CGI-created insect category comes eight years after Pixar and DreamWorks set the standard with "A Bug's Life" and "Antz," respectively, and delivers nothing new. New kid on the block and neighborhood punching-bag Lucas, vents his frustration by picking on something smaller than him—an ant colony in his yard—only to be magically shrunken and transported into the ant's world to face his victims. Predictable life lessons about acceptance and teamwork, along with uninspired voice work from the star-studded cast drag down this visually impressive but all too familiar story. Based on the book by John Nickle. **88m/C DVD, Blu-ray Disc.** *US* ***D:*** John A. Davis; ***W:*** John A. Davis; ***M:*** John Debney; ***V:*** Zach Tyler, Jake T. Austin, Nicolas Cage, Bruce Campbell, Meryl Streep, Julia Roberts, Paul Giamatti, Myles Jeffrey, Regina King, Cheri Oteri, Lily Tomlin, Rob Paulsen, Allison Mack, Ricardo Montalban, Larry Miller, Austin Majors, Mark DeCarlo, Frank Welker, Nicole Sullivan, Vernee Watson-Johnson.

Antarctica **1984** Due to unfortunate circumstances, a group of scientists must leave their pack of huskies behind on a frozen glacier in the Antarctic. The film focuses on the dogs' subsequent struggle for survival. Dubbed. **112m/C VHS.** *JP* Ken Takakura, Masako Natsume, Keiko Oginome; ***D:*** Koreyoshi Kurahara; ***M:*** Vangelis.

Anthony Adverse ½ **1936** March is a young man in the 19th century who searches for manhood across America and Mexico. He grows slowly as he battles foes, struggles against adversity and returns home to find his lover in this romantic swashbuckler. A star-studded cast, lush costuming, and an energetic musical score. Highly acclaimed in its time, but now seems dated. Based on the novel by Hervey Allen. **141m/B VHS.** Fredric March, Olivia de Havilland, Anita Louise, Gale Sondergaard, Claude Rains, Edmund Gwenn, Louis Hayward, Anne Howard; ***D:*** Mervyn LeRoy; ***C:*** Gaetano Antonio "Tony" Gaudio; ***M:*** Erich Wolfgang Korngold. Oscars '36: Cinematog., Film Editing, Support. Actress (Sondergaard), Score.

Anti-Terrorist Cell: Manhunt *The Red Phone: Manhunt; Special Unit AT 13* **2001** The ATC is an international covert organization that hunts terrorists who escape government, military, and police agencies although this case involves a group of greedy mercenaries. Made as a TV pilot for the European market, it failed to sell—probably because it's cheap and boring. **92m/C DVD.** *GE* Joe Penny, Michael Wincott, Arnold Vosloo, Michael Ironside, Ben Cross, Colin Salmon; ***D:*** Jerry Jameson; ***W:*** Terry Thompson, Steven Whitney; ***C:*** Fernando Arguelles; ***M:*** Martin Locker.

Antibodies *Antikorper* **2005** Captured serial killer Gabriel Engel (Hennicke) admits to the murders of 13 boys and is suspected in the death of a young girl in a rural community. Naive local cop Michael Martens (Mohring) travels to the city to question the now wheelchair-bound Engel and close his case. But Engel tries to convince him that someone else killed the girl and Michael learns more about the killer and himself that he could have imagined. German with subtitles. **128m/C DVD.** *GE* Andre Hennicke, Wotan Wilke Mohring, Heinz Hoenig, Ulrike Krumbiegel, Jurgen Schornagel; ***D:*** Christian Alvart; ***W:*** Christian Alvart; ***C:*** Hagen Bogdanski; ***M:*** Michi Britsch.

Antibody **2002 (R)** Terrorist Moran (Vergov) has a nuclear bomb and the detonator chip is inside his body. He's shot and if he dies, the chip will go off. So it's up to security expert Richard Gaynes (Henriksen) and a team of scientists to send an experimental tracking craft inside Moran's bloodstream to find and extract the chip in time. **90m/C VHS, DVD.** Lance Henriksen, Robin Givens, William Zabka, Julian Vergov; ***D:*** Christian McIntire; ***W:*** Michael Baldwin; ***C:*** Adolfo Bartoli; ***M:*** Scott Clausen. **VIDEO**

Antichrist **2009** Challenging in all the wrong ways, Von Tier's self-conscious, symbolic, misogynistic, psychosexual arthouse horror is divided into four chapters and begins with the accidental death of a toddler. The nameless traumatized mother (Gainsbourg) and her domineering husband (Dafoe), a professional therapist, go to their isolated home in the country in an effort to deal with their grief. Soon, her sanity is in question and Von Tier eventually tips over the edge in a graphically-depicted mutilation scene. In black and white and color. **105m/C DVD.** *DK GE FR SW IT PL* Charlotte Gainsbourg, Willem Dafoe; ***D:*** Lars von Trier; ***W:*** Lars von Trier; ***C:*** Anthony Dod Mantle.

Antitrust ½ **2000 (PG-13)** Supernerd code writer Milo (Phillippe) leaves the garage for a Pacific Northwest software giant only to discover the company's mega-monied leader, Winston (Robbins), may not be on the up and up—in fact, the things he's doing to maintain industry supremacy could be downright evil. Robbins's bespectacled techie villain is spot-on Bill Gates, but the film borrows heavily from its paranoid predecessors and offers little of its own to the field. A mediocre thriller among other mediocre thrillers. **120m/C VHS, DVD.** Ryan Phillippe, Tim Robbins, Rachael Leigh Cook, Claire Forlani, Douglas McFerran, Richard Roundtree, Yee Jee Tso, Tygh Runyan; ***D:*** Peter Howitt; ***W:*** Howard Franklin; ***C:*** John Bailey; ***M:*** Don Davis.

Antoine et Antoinette ½ **1947** Antoine (Pigaut) is a shop foreman and his wife, Antoinette (Maffei), a clerk, who lead a somewhat tempestuous life in Paris. Then the situation worsens when Antoine loses the couple's winning lottery ticket. The first of Becker's romantic trilogy, followed by "Rendez-vous de Juillet" and "Edward and Caroline." French with subtitles; originally released at 95 minutes. **78m/B VHS.** *FR* Roger Pigaut, Claire Maffei, Noel Roquevert; ***D:*** Jacques Becker; ***W:*** Jacques Becker, Maurice Griffe, Francoise Giroud; ***C:*** Pierre Montazel; ***M:*** Jean Jacques Grunenwald.

Anton, the Magician *Anton der Zauberer* **1978** Anton likes to live by his wits. A car mechanic, he marries the boss' daughter, Liesel, and uses his skills to make a pile of illegal dough that he hides at the home of the widowed Sabine, with whom he's also involved. When Anton's schemes catch up with him, he ends up in prison, and Sabine takes off to Switzerland with the cash. But this isn't the end of their story. German with subtitles. **101m/C VHS.** *GE* Ulrich Thein, Barbara Dittus, Anna Dymna, Erwin Geschonneck, Erik S. Klein; ***D:*** Guenther Reisch; ***W:*** Guenther Reisch, Karl-Georg Egel; ***C:*** Gunter Haubold; ***M:*** Wolfram Heicking.

Antonia and Jane **1991 (R)** Enjoyable film tells the story of a longstanding, heavily tested friendship between two women. From the very beginning, they are a study in contrasts—Jane as rather plain, frumpy, and insecure; Antonia as glamorous, elegant, and successful. Both believe that each other's lives are more interesting and exciting than their own. Kidron, who directed this smart witty comedy for British TV, offers an honest look into the often complex world of adult friendships. **75m/C VHS.** *GB* Imelda Staunton, Saskia Reeves, Patricia Leventon, Alfred Hoffman, Maria Charles, John Bennett, Richard Hope, Alfred Marks, Lila Kaye, Bill Nighy, Brenda Bruce; ***D:*** Beeban Kidron; ***W:*** Marcy Kahan; ***C:*** Rex Maidment; ***M:*** Rachel Portman. **TV**

Antonia's Line ½ **1995 (R)** 90-year-old Antonia (Van Ammelrooy) has decided that she is going to die today and so begins a 50-year-long flashback of her nonconformist life in a Dutch village. Her lesbian daughter Danielle (Dottermans) wants a child without bothering about a husband and Antonia obliging arranges a brief interlude that produces child prodigy Therese (Van Overloop), who eventually has her own daughter, Sarah (Ravesteijn). Lots of female bonding (the male characters are mostly on the periphery of the action) and a certain magic realism abound. Dutch with subtitles. **102m/C VHS, DVD.** *NL* Willeke Van Ammelrooy, Els Dottermans, Veerle Van Overloop, Thyrza Ravesteijn, Jan Decleir, Mil Seghers, Jan Steen, Marina De Graaf; ***D:*** Marleen Gorris; ***W:*** Marleen Gorris; ***C:*** Willy Stassen; ***M:*** Ilona Sekacz. Oscars '95: Foreign Film.

Antonio **1973** A Texas millionaire on the run from his wife and her divorce lawyer alights in a small Chilean village and turns it upside down. **89m/C VHS.** Larry Hagman, Trini Lopez, Noemi Guerrero, Pedro Becker; ***D:*** Claudio Guzman.

Antonio Das Mortes ½ *O Dragao da Maldade contra o Santo Guerreiro* **1968** Antonio is a savage mercenary hired to kill rebels against the Brazilian government. Belatedly he realizes he sympathizes with the targets and turns his guns the other way for an incredible shootout finale. A visually lavish poltical polemic, espousing revolutionary guerrilla action within the format of a South American western. In Portuguese with English subtitles. **100m/C VHS.** *BR* Mauricio Do Valle, Odete Lara, Jofre Soares, Othon Bastos; ***D:*** Glauce Rocha; ***W:*** Glauce Rocha; ***C:*** Alfonso Beato.

Antony and Cleopatra **1973 (PG)** Heston wrote, directed, and starred in this long, dry adaptation of the Shakespeare play that centers on the torrid romance between Mark Antony and Cleopatra. **150m/C VHS, DVD.** Charlton Heston, Hildegard(e) Neil, Fernando Rey, Eric Porter, John Castle, Freddie Jones, Warren Clarke, Julian Glover; ***D:*** Charlton Heston.

Ants ½ *Panic at Lakewood Manor; It Happened at Lakewood Manor* **1977** A mad bug parable for our planet-obsessed society. Insecticide-infected ants turn militant and check into a local hotel to vent their chemically induced foul mood on the unsuspecting clientele. The guest register includes a gaggle of celebrities who probably wish they'd signed on the Love Boat instead. Made for TV (an ant farm would probably be just too horrible on the big screen). **100m/C VHS, DVD.** Suzanne Somers, Robert Foxworth, Myrna Loy, Lynda Day George, Gerald Gordon, Bernie Casey, Barry Van Dyke, Karen Lamm, Anita Gillette, Moosie Drier, Steve Franken, Brian Dennehy, Bruce French, Stacy Keach Sr., Rene Enriquez, James Storm; ***D:*** Robert Scheerer; ***W:*** Guerdon (Gordon) Trueblood; ***C:*** Bernie Abramson; ***M:*** Ken Richmond. **TV**

Antwone Fisher **2002 (PG-13)** Washington's directorial debut is a drama based on the true story of Antwone Fisher, who also wrote the screenplay. Washington also stars as Jerome Davenport, the naval psychiatrist who helps the angry young Fisher (Luke) get past the demons of his foster childhood. The two knock heads and are both forced to change their own ideas, slowly coming to understand and trust one another. Davenport learns that Fisher was born in prison, his father murdered and his mother a convict. Davenport urges Fisher to confront his past, and some of the best scenes are with Fisher's aunt (Johnson), uncle (Billings) and mother (Davis), which resonate. Subplot with Davenport and wife Berta (Richardson) shows they have their own issues to work out, as well. A tearjerker in the best sense, the simply told tale is a triumph for Luke, who is impressive in his debut role. **113m/C VHS, DVD, Blu-ray Disc.** *US* Derek Luke, Denzel Washington, Joy Bryant, Salli Richardson, Earl Billings, Kevin Connolly, Viola Davis, Rainoldo Gooding, Novella Nelson, Vernee Watson-Johnson, Kente Scott, Yolonda Ross, Stephen Snedden, Malcolm David Kelly; ***D:*** Denzel Washington; ***W:*** Antwone Fisher; ***C:*** Philippe Rousselot; ***M:*** Mychael Danna. Ind. Spirit '03: Actor (Luke).

Antz **1998 (PG)** Malcontent worker ant, Z (Allen), moans to his therapist about his insignificance and the depressing anonymity of "being born in the middle of five million." But after meeting the colony's princess, Bala (Stone), who is facing her own bleak future thanks to an arranged marriage with the colony's power-hungry General Mandible (Hackman), Z and Princess Bala embark on a dangerous mission to the surface in search of the mythical "Insectopia." Only the second film ever created entirely through computer animation ("Toy Story" being the first), pic is visually amazing. The fact that the ant characters do not resemble their performers' appearances makes the relationship between Z and the princess plausible, and actually adds depth to the characters' personalities. An interesting, rather elaborate storyline, along with excellent voice performances (even Stallone!) make this one fun for all ages. **83m/C VHS, DVD.** ***D:*** Eric Darnell, Tim Johnson; ***W:*** Chris Weitz, Paul Weitz, Todd Alcott; ***M:*** Harry Gregson-Williams, John Powell; ***V:*** Woody Allen, Sharon Stone, Sylvester

Stallone, Anne Bancroft, Danny Glover, Christopher Walken, Jane Curtin, Jennifer Lopez, John Mahoney, Dan Aykroyd, Paul Mazursky, Gene Hackman.

Anvil! The Story of Anvil **2009** Rockumentary about the aging, working-class Canadian metal band that seemed on the brink of stardom in the mid-1980s and instead faded into obscurity. Lead vocalist Steve 'Lips' Kudlow and drummer Robb Reiner have been playing together since the age of 14 and their early LPs influenced more successful speed-metal bands. But with only modest hits and a mismanaged European tour, they were dropped by their label. Still playing clubs (with two additional rotating members), they have day jobs to support their families while working on a comeback album. You have to admire their persistence and optimism if nothing else. **90m/C DVD.** *US* Steve "Lips" Kudlow, Robb Reiner; ***D:*** Sacha Gervasi; ***C:*** Christopher Soos. Ind. Spirit '10: Feature Doc.

Any Given Sunday **1999 (R)** Stone sets aside his conspiracy theories on war and politics and effectively shines a spotlight on a different kind of battlefield to come up with the most commerical and entertaining film of his career. Pacino heads an all-star cast as the battered, yet wise and resilient coach of a struggling Miami football team who locks horns with not only young quarterback Foxx, but ruthless, ballbuster team owner Diaz. Epic-like runtime (which sprints along thanks to Stone's potent mix of raw camera work and hip-hop soundtrack) allows much of the cast plenty of room, with comedian Foxx holding his own with the big boys in a star-making performance as the hotdog player with a bad case of ego. With an intelligent script and a perfect cast, Stone creates the most realistic look at pro football since 1979's "North Dallas Forty." **170m/B VHS, DVD, Blu-ray Disc.** Al Pacino, Dennis Quaid, Cameron Diaz, Jamie Foxx, Charlton Heston, James Woods, Matthew Modine, Ann-Margret, Lauren Holly, Lela Rochon, LL Cool J, Aaron Eckhart, Jim Brown, Bill Bellamy, Elizabeth Berkley, John C. McGinley; ***D:*** Oliver Stone; ***W:*** Oliver Stone, John Logan; ***C:*** Salvatore Totino; ***M:*** Robbie Robertson.

Any Gun Can Play *For a Few Bullets More* **1967** Typical spaghetti western. Three men (banker, thief, and bounty hunter) compete for a treasure of gold while wandering about the Spanish countryside. **103m/C VHS, DVD.** *IT SP* Edd Byrnes, Gilbert Roland, George Hilton, Kareen O'Hara, Pedro Sanchez, Gerard Herter; ***D:*** Enzo G. Castellari.

Any Man's Death **1990 (R)** Savage is a globe-trotting reporter on the trail of a worldwide conspiracy who accidentally uncovers a Nazi war criminal in Africa. Well-meaning but confused tale. **105m/C VHS, DVD.** John Savage, William Hickey, Mia Sara, Ernest Borgnine, Michael Lerner; ***D:*** Tom Clegg.

Any Number Can Play 1/2 **1949** Fast-moving drama about an ailing gambler who faces a series of crises. Gable gives a commanding performance as the noble dice-roller. Based on the novel by Edward Harris Heath. **102m/B VHS.** Clark Gable, Alexis Smith, Wendell Corey, Audrey Totter, Frank Morgan, Mary Astor, Lewis Stone, Barry Sullivan; ***D:*** Mervyn LeRoy; ***W:*** Richard Brooks.

Any Number Can Win *Melodie en Sous-Sol; The Big Grab* **1963** Two ex-convicts, aging Charles (Gabin) and his former cellmate Francis (Delon), risk their lives and freedom for one last major heist: a gambling casino on the French Riviera. French with English subtitles. **118m/B VHS, DVD.** *FR* Claude Cerval, Jean Gabin, Alain Delon, Viviane Romance, Maurice Biraud, Carla Marlier, Jose-Luis De Villalonga, Jean Carmet; ***D:*** Henri Verneuil; ***W:*** Henri Verneuil, Michel Audiard, Albert Simonin; ***C:*** Louis Page; ***M:*** Michel Magne.

Any Place But Home 1/2 **1997 (PG-13)** Roberta (Keller) and Lucas (Lando) Dempsey find themselves in big trouble when Roberta's sister Carrie Miller (Conway) and her low-life hubby Carl (Midkiff) try to involve them in a plan to kidnap 12-year-old John Danforth (Norris), figuring John's rich dad August (Thicke) will be happy to pay the ransom. Roberta manages to get the kid and the money away from the Millers but she and Lucas discover John is an abused child and terrified of his father. The threesome go on the run with the Millers, August's hired help, and the FBI on their trail. **90m/C VHS.** Joe Lando, Mary Page Keller, Alan Thicke, Dale Midkiff, Cristie Conway, Richard Roundtree; ***D:*** Rob Hedden; ***W:*** Bart Baker. **CABLE**

Any Wednesday 1/2 *Bachelor Girl Apartment* **1966** Okay sex farce about powerful industrialist Robards' use of his mistress's apartment as a tax write-off. When a young company executive learns of the "company" apartment, he meets Robards' nonchalant wife for a tryst of their own. Based on Muriel Resnik's Broadway play; similar to the 1960 "The Apartment." **110m/C VHS.** Jane Fonda, Jason Robards Jr., Dean Jones, Rosemary Murphy; ***D:*** Robert Ellis Miller; ***W:*** Julius J. Epstein; ***M:*** George Duning.

Any Which Way You Can **1980 (PG)** Bad brawler Philo Beddoe and his buddy Clyde, the orangutan, are back again in the sequel to "Every Which Way But Loose." This time Philo is tempted to take part in a big bout for a large cash prize. Clyde steals scenes, brightening up the no-brainer story. **116m/C VHS, DVD.** Clint Eastwood, Sondra Locke, Ruth Gordon, Harry Guardino, William (Bill) Smith, Geoffrey Lewis, Barry Corbin; ***D:*** Buddy Van Horn; ***W:*** Stanford Sherman; ***C:*** David Worth.

Anything But Love 1/2 *Standard Time* **2002 (PG-13)** Predictable Hollywood love story. Writer/actor Isabel Rose plays Billie Golden, a not-so-young wanna-be torch singer wrestling with the choice of whether to marry her old high school crush (Bancroft) for security, or stay with her anguished true love (McCarthy), who better understands her. Meager budget is best spent on the elaborate dream sequences. Eartha Kitt appears as herself, providing crucial advice and a shining example of a true star. **99m/C VHS, DVD.** *US* Isabel Rose, Andrew McCarthy, Cameron Bancroft, Alix Korey, Victor Argo, Ilana Levine, Sean Arbuckle, Eartha Kitt; ***D:*** Robert Cary; ***W:*** Isabel Rose, Robert Cary; ***C:*** Horacio Marquinez; ***M:*** Andrew Hollander, Steven Lutvak.

Anything Else 1/2 **2003 (R)** With his last few outings, Allen has shown that he's a shadow of his former creative self, so he's logically picked Biggs to play a shadow of his former self. Biggs doesn't seem comfortable in his role as a neurotic psychoanalyst-dependent joke-writer trying to break up with the quirky, torturing girlfriend (Ricci) he's smitten with. The Woodman shows up as his alter-ego's paranoid, mean-spirited mentor and confidant. Flick is so short on new ideas that the young couple can only agree on their love of Bogie and old jazz records. Ricci spends most of the film walking around her apartment in her underwear, which isn't bad if you can keep the image of Allen leering just off-camera out of your head. If you insist on a Woody Allen movie, make it almost anything else but this mess. **108m/C VHS, DVD.** *US* Jason Biggs, Christina Ricci, Woody Allen, Stockard Channing, Danny DeVito, Jimmy Fallon, Erica Leerhsen, David Conrad, KaDee Strickland, Adrian Grenier; ***D:*** Woody Allen; ***W:*** Woody Allen; ***C:*** Darius Khondji.

Anything for a Thrill **1937** Two kids save a cameraman's career, make friends with a millionairess, and foil some crooks. **59m/B VHS.** Frankie Darro, Kane Richmond; ***D:*** Leslie Goodwins.

Anything for Love 1/2 *Just One of the Girls* **1993** Teen musician is the object of a school bully's rage so he decides to dress up as a girl to escape the guy's fists. **90m/C VHS, DVD.** *CA* Corey Haim, Nicole Eggert, Cameron Bancroft, Kevin McNulty, Wendy Van Riesen, Lochlyn Munro, Rachel Hayward, Molly Parker; ***D:*** Michael Keusch; ***M:*** Amin Bhatia.

Anywhere But Here 1/2 **1999 (PG-13)** Just who's the Mom here? It certainly doesn't seem to be flaky Adele (Sarandon), who suddenly uproots teen daughter Ann (Portman) from provincial Wisconsin to relocate in sunny L.A., where Adele wants Ann to become an actress. Ann's definitely the practical one of the duo and she tries to rein in Adele's loopier flights of fantasy. Of course, Ann does have some plans (and dreams) of her own. The leads are both pros and there are enough tear-jerking moments to satisfy in this somewhat stereotypical drama. Based on the 1986 novel by Mona Simpson. **114m/C VHS, DVD.** Susan Sarandon, Natalie Portman, Shawn Hatosy, Hart Bochner, Bonnie Bedelia, Eileen Ryan, Ray Baker, John Diehl, Caroline Aaron, Paul Guilfoyle, Mary Ellen Trainor, Ashley Johnson; ***D:*** Wayne Wang; ***W:*** Alvin Sargent; ***C:*** Roger Deakins; ***M:*** Danny Elfman.

Anzacs: The War Down Under **1985** Well-made Australian TV miniseries about the Australian and New Zealand Army Corps during WWI. Follows the men from the time they enlist to the campaigns in Gallipoli and France. **165m/C VHS.** *AU* Paul Hogan, Andrew Clarke, Jon Blake, Megan Williams; ***D:*** George Miller. **TV**

Anzio *The Battle for Anzio; Lo Sbarco di Anzio* **1968** The historic Allied invasion of Italy during WWII as seen through the eyes of American war correspondent Mitchum. Fine cast waits endlessly to leave the beach, though big battle scenes are effectively rendered. Based on the book by Wynford Vaughan Thomas. **117m/C VHS, DVD.** Giancarlo Giannini, Robert Mitchum, Peter Falk, Arthur Kennedy, Robert Ryan, Earl Holliman, Mark Damon, Reni Santoni, Patrick Magee; ***D:*** Edward Dmytryk; ***W:*** H.A.L. Craig, Frank De Felitta; ***C:*** Giuseppe Rotunno; ***M:*** Riz Ortolani.

Apache 1/2 **1954** Lancaster is the only Indian in Geronimo's outfit who refuses to surrender in this chronicle of a bitter battle between the Indians and the U.S. cavalry in the struggle for the West. First western for Aldrich is a thoughtful piece for its time that had the original tragic ending reshot (against Aldrich's wishes) to make it more happy. Adapted from "Bronco Apache" by Paul I. Wellman. **91m/C VHS, DVD.** Burt Lancaster, John McIntire, Jean Peters, Charles Bronson, John Dehner, Paul Guilfoyle; ***D:*** Robert Aldrich; ***C:*** Ernest Laszlo.

Apache Blood 1/2 *Pursuit* **1975 (R)** An Indian Brave, the lone survivor of an Indian massacre by the U.S. Army, squares off with a cavalry scout in the forbidding desert. **92m/C VHS.** Ray Danton, DeWitt Lee, Troy Neighbors, Diane Taylor, Eva Kovacs, Jason Clark; ***D:*** Thomas Quillen.

Apache Chief **1950** Two Apache tribe leaders, one good, the other evil clash. Ultimately, and perhaps predictably, they face each other in hand-to-hand combat and peace prevails. **60m/B VHS.** Alan Curtis, Tom Neal, Russell Hayden, Carol Thurston, Fuzzy Knight; ***D:*** Frank McDonald.

Apache Kid's Escape **1930** The Apache Kid leads the cavalry on a wild chase across the plains in this saga of the old west. **60m/B VHS.** Jack Perrin, Fred Church, Josephine Hill, Virginia Ashcroft, Bud Osborne, Henry Roquemore, Buzz Barton; ***D:*** Robert J. Horner.

Apache Rose **1947** Gambling boat owner plots to gain control of oil found on Vegas Ranch. Roy and Dale oppose the idea. First of the series in color; the original, unedited version of the film. **75m/B VHS, DVD.** Roy Rogers, Dale Evans, Olin Howlin, George Meeker; ***D:*** William Witney.

Apache Uprising 1/2 **1966** A standard western with Calhoun as the lawman up against gunfighters and stagecoach robbers as well as the usual Indians. **60m/C VHS.** Rory Calhoun, Corinne Calvet, DeForest Kelley, John Russell, Lon Chaney Jr., Gene Evans, Richard Arlen, Robert H. Harris, Arthur Hunnicutt, Jean Parker, Johnny Mack Brown; ***D:*** R.G. Springsteen.

Apache Woman 1/2 **1955** Bridges stars as a government agent sent to investigate some crimes committed by a group of Apache Indians. As he tries to calm the townspeople, Bridges discovers that the group is made up of white people led by an educated half-breed. He instigates the help of the half-breed's sister (and also Bridges' love interest) to stop the gang. Some good action, but lots of dull spots. **82m/C VHS.** Lloyd Bridges, Joan Taylor, Lance Fuller, Morgan Jones, Paul Birch, Jonathan Haze, Paul Dubov, Lou Place; ***D:*** Roger Corman.

Apache's Last Battle *Old Shatterhand; Shatterhand* **1964** A boundary scout discovers the ward of an Apache chief has been framed for murder by a cavalry officer who wants to start an Indian war in this exciting Euro western. **122m/C VHS.** *GE YU FR IT* Lex Barker, Pierre Brice, Daliah Lavi, Guy Madison, Ralf Wolter, Gustavo Rojo, Rick (Rik) Battaglia, Bill Ramsey; ***D:*** Hugo Fregonese; ***W:*** Ladislas Fodor, Robert A. Stemmle; ***C:*** Siegfried Hold; ***M:*** Riz Ortolani.

Aparajito 1/2 *The Unvanquished* **1958** The second of the Apu trilogy, about a boy growing up in India, after "Pather Panchali," and before "The World of Apu." Apu is brought to Benares and his education seriously begins. The work of a master; in Bengali with English subtitles. **108m/B VHS, DVD.** *IN* Pinaki Sen Gupta, Karuna Bannerjee, Kanu Bannerjee, Ramani Sen Gupta; ***D:*** Satyajit Ray; ***W:*** Satyajit Ray; ***C:*** Subrata Mitra; ***M:*** Ravi Shankar. Venice Film Fest. '57: Film.

Apart from Hugh **1994** Collin and Hugh have been living together for a year and to celebrate the occasion, Hugh decides to plan an anniversary party. Unfortunately, Collin hasn't told Hugh he's having second thoughts about their relationship. Directorial debut of FitzGerald. **87m/B VHS, DVD.** Steve Arnold, David Merwin, Jennifer Reed; ***D:*** Jon FitzGerald; ***W:*** Jon FitzGerald; ***C:*** Randy Allred; ***M:*** James Clarke.

The Apartment 1/2 **1960** Lowly insurance clerk C.C. Baxter (Lemmon) tries to climb the corporate ladder by "loaning" his apartment out to executives having affairs. Problems arise, however, when he unwittingly falls for sweet elevator operator Fran Kubelik (MacLaine), the most recent girlfriend of his unfeeling boss J.D. Sheldrake (MacMurray). Highly acclaimed social satire. **125m/B VHS, DVD.** Jack Lemmon, Shirley MacLaine, Fred MacMurray, Ray Walston, Jack Kruschen, Joan Shawlee, Edie Adams, Hope Holiday, David Lewis; ***D:*** Billy Wilder; ***W:*** I.A.L. Diamond, Billy Wilder; ***C:*** Joseph LaShelle; ***M:*** Adolph Deutsch. Oscars '60: Art Dir./Set Dec., B&W, Director (Wilder), Film Editing, Picture, Story & Screenplay; AFI '98: Top 100; British Acad. '60: Actor (Lemmon), Actress (MacLaine), Film; Directors Guild '60: Director (Wilder); Golden Globes '61: Actor—Mus./Comedy (Lemmon), Actress—Mus./Comedy (MacLaine), Film—Mus./Comedy, Natl. Film Reg. '94;; N.Y. Film Critics '60: Director (Wilder), Film, Screenplay.

Apartment Complex 1/2 **1998 (R)** An assortment of Hollywood weirdos occupy Dr. Caligari's Wonder View Apartments where psych grad student Stan Warden (Lowe) has just taken a job as the building manager. There's a hot-to-trot psychic, a paranoid ex-government agent, and a recluse, among others and then Stan discovers the body of the previous super. Strange things begin happening (including the appearance of a giant snake), even as hapless Stan becomes the prime suspect and potential victim. Creepy and comic. **99m/C VHS.** Chad Lowe, Fay Masterson, Obba Babatunde, Patrick Warburton, Ron Canada, Amanda Plummer, Miguel (Michael) Sandoval, Jon Polito, R. Lee Ermey, Charles Martin Smith; ***D:*** Tobe Hooper; ***W:*** Karl Schaefer; ***C:*** Jacques Haitkin; ***M:*** Mark Adler. **CABLE**

Apartment 1303 **2007** Sayaka throws an apartment-warming party, during which she freaks out and throws herself from the balcony after sucking down some dog food for no apparent reason, leaving her friends to wonder what the heck they just witnessed as the little kid from the hall says, "There goes another one". Sayaka's curious sister learns suicides happen pretty regularly among the tenants in that building, and of course there are ghosts involved. **94m/C DVD.** *JP* Eriko Hatsune, Yuka Itaya, Naoko Otani; ***D:*** Byeong-ki Ahn; ***W:*** Byeong-ki Ahn, Brian O'Hara; ***C:*** Seok-hyeon Lee; ***M:*** Tae-beon Lee.

Apartment 12 1/2 *Low Rent; Life/Drawing* **2006 (R)** Artisan Alex (Ruffalo) is stunned when a gallery curator trashes his work and pulls his show, causing his shallow bombshell of a girlfriend to lose interest. Dejected and homeless, he takes a pizza shop job and moves into more affordable digs where he meets several interesting characters, including goofy and loveable Lori (Ulrich). They start dating but Alex's cold feet mess things up, though the neighbors can't avoid one another. Solid work by leads Ruffalo and Ulrich keep this average romantic tale from getting evicted. **90m/C DVD.** Mark Ruffalo, Alan Gelfant, Manuel Cabral, Beth Ulrich, Mary Coleston; ***D:*** Dan Bootzin; ***W:*** Dan Bootzin, Elizabeth Rivera Bootzin. **VIDEO**

Apartment Zero 1/2 **1988 (R)** A decidedly weird, deranged psychological drama about the parasite/host-type relationship between two roommates in downtown Buenos Aires: one, an obsessive British movie nut, the other, a sexually mesmerizing stud who turns out to be a cold-blooded psycho. **124m/C VHS, DVD.** *GB* Hart Bochner, Colin Firth, Fabrizio Bentivoglio, Liz Smith, Dora Bryan, James Telfer, Mirella D'Angelo, Juan Vitale, Francesca D'Aloja, Miguel Ligero, Elvia Andreoli, Marikeva Monti; ***D:*** Martin Donovan; ***W:*** Martin Donovan, David Koepp; ***C:*** Miguel Rodriguez; ***M:*** Elia Cmiral.

The Ape **1940** When his daughter dies of a crippling disease, Karloff becomes fixated with the mission to cure paralysis. Obviously distraught, he begins donning the hide of an escaped circus ape whose spinal fluid is the key to the serum. Hide-bedecked, he slays unknowing townspeople to tap them of their spinal fluid and cure his latest patient. **62m/B VHS, DVD.** Boris Karloff, Maris Wrixon, Henry Hall, Gertrude Hoffman; ***D:*** William Nigh.

A*P*E* WOOF! *Attack of the Giant Horny Gorilla* **1976 (PG)** A*P*E* is 36 feet tall and ten tons of animal fury who destroys anything that comes between him and the actress he loves. Cheap rip-off of Kong. **87m/C VHS, DVD.** *KN* Rod Arrants, Joanna Kerns, Alex Nicol, Francis Lee; ***D:*** Paul Leder; ***W:*** Paul Leder, Reuben Leder.

The Ape **2005** In search of solitude as he struggles to write his first great novel, Harry (Franco, also debuting as writer and director) leaves his wife and child for a studio apartment in NYC, where he is shocked to find that an ape already lives there—one that talks and wears a gaudy Hawaiian t-shirt. He somehow serves as Harry's inspiration despite stooping to lowbrow jokes and gags such as throwing poop. **93m/C DVD.** James Franco, Brian Lally, Allison Bibicoff, Stacey Miller, Vince Jolivette; ***D:*** James Franco; ***W:*** James Franco, Merriwether Williams. **VIDEO**

The Ape Man *Lock Your Doors* **1943** With the aid of a secret potion, a scientist turns himself into a murderous ape. The only way to regain his human side is to ingest human spinal fluid. Undoubtedly inspired by Boris Karloff's 1940 film, "The Ape." **64m/B VHS, DVD.** Henry Hall, Minerva Urecal, Wheeler Oakman, J. Farrell MacDonald, Wallace Ford, Bela Lugosi, Louise Currie; ***D:*** William Beaudine; ***W:*** Barney A. Sarecky; ***C:*** Mack Stengler.

A.P.E.X. **1994 (R)** Nicholas Sinclair (Keats), a researcher from 2073, time travels back to 1973 to retrieve a faulty robot probe called A.P.E.X. (Advanced Prototype Extermination Unit). Unwittingly he has been infected with a mysterious virus and when he returns it's to a version of his own time where humans are dying from the virus and robots are sent to eradicate the few survivors. It also seems Sinclair is now a guerilla in an anti-robot army. Yes, it sounds like "The Terminator" but the action moves and though the budget is limited the special effects are still impressive. **103m/C VHS.** Richard Keats, Mitchell Cox, Lisa Ann Russell, Marcus Aurelius, Adam Lawson; ***D:*** Phillip J. Roth; ***W:*** Phillip J. Roth, Ronald Schmidt; ***M:*** Jim Goodwin.

The Apocalypse **1996 (R)** Space pilot J.T. Wayne (Bernhard) teams up with salvage operator Suarez (McCoy) and his crew to retrieve a cargo ship lost in space for 25 years. But crewman Vendler (Zagarino) hijacks the cargo for himself, with only Wayne and Lennon (Dye) as survivors. But it turn's out the ship is one big booby-trap rigged to crash into earth. Now Wayne and Lennon must not only save themselves but the planet as well. Low-budget, with a confusing plot. **96m/C VHS, DVD.** Sandra Bernhard, Laura San Giacomo, Cameron Dye, Frank Zagarino, Matt McCoy; ***D:*** Hubert de la Bouillerie; ***C:*** Greg Gardiner.

Apocalypse Now **1979 (R)** Coppola's $40 million epic vision of the Vietnam War was inspired by Joseph Conrad's novella "Heart of Darkness," and continues to be the subject of debate. Disillusioned Army captain Sheen travels upriver into Cambodia to assassinate overweight renegade colonel Brando. His trip is punctuated by surrealistic battles and a terrifying descent into a land where human rationality seems to have slipped away. Considered by some to be the definitive picture of war in its overall depiction of chaos and primal bloodletting; by others, over-wrought and unrealistic. May not translate as well to the small screen, yet worth seeing if for nothing more than Duvall's ten minutes of scenery chewing as a battle-obsessed major ("I love the smell of napalm in the morning!"), a study in manic machismo. Stunning photography by Vittorio Storaro, awe-inspiring battle scenes, and effective soundtrack montage. Both Sheen and Coppola suffered emotional breakdowns during the prolonged filming, and that's a very young Fishburne in his major film debut. Available in a remastered version in letterbox on VHS with a remixed soundtrack that features Dolby Surround stereo. In 1991 a documentary detailing the making of the film, "Hearts of Darkness: A Filmmaker's Apocalypse," was released. **153m/C VHS, DVD.** Francis Ford Coppola, Marlon Brando, Martin Sheen, Robert Duvall, Frederic Forrest, Sam Bottoms, Scott Glenn, Albert Hall, Laurence Fishburne, Harrison Ford, G.D. Spradlin, Dennis Hopper, Cynthia Wood, Colleen Camp, Linda Carpenter, Tom Mason, James Keane, Damien Leake, Jack Thibeau, R. Lee Ermey, Vittorio Storaro; ***D:*** Francis Ford Coppola; ***W:*** Francis Ford Coppola, John Milius, Michael Herr; ***C:*** Vittorio Storaro; ***M:*** Carmine Coppola. Oscars '79: Cinematog., Sound; AFI '98: Top 100; British Acad. '79: Director (Coppola), Support. Actor (Duvall); Cannes '79: Film; Golden Globes '80: Director (Coppola), Support. Actor (Duvall), Score, Natl. Film Reg. '00;; Natl. Soc. Film Critics '79: Support. Actor (Forrest).

The Apocalypse Watch *Robert Ludlum's the Apocalypse Watch* **1997** CIA analyst Drew (Bergin) takes over his field agent brother's assignment when the latter is killed. Drew hooks up with his bro's girlfriend/partner (Madsen) and their spying leads to a neo-Nazi organization. Based on the novel by Ludlum. **176m/C VHS, DVD.** Patrick Bergin, Virginia Madsen, John Shea, Benedick Blythe, Christopher Neame, Malcolm Tierney; ***D:*** Kevin Connor; ***W:*** John Goldsmith, Christopher Canaan; ***C:*** Dennis C. Lewiston; ***M:*** Ken Thorne. **TV**

Apocalypto **2006 (R)** Set during ancient times against a lavish, peaceful backdrop in the Yucatan Peninsula. Producer/director/co-writer Gibson unleashes a savage nightmare that somehow surpasses the bloodbaths of his other works, "Passion of the Christ" and "Braveheart." Jaguar Paw (Youngblood, part of the all-native cast) and his forest tribe are viciously rounded up by Mayan attackers as their rulers desperately attempt to save their decaying civilization by sacrificing Paw's people to the gods. As the graphic slaughter begins, Paw slips away and triggers an intense 45-minute jungle chase as he tries to outrun his captors and return to his pregnant wife and young son who he'd hidden in a village well. Gibson's talent at creating no-holds-barred action is on full display. In the Mayan language of the Yucatec, with English subtitles. **137m/C DVD, Blu-ray Disc.** *US* Rudy Youngblood, Dalia Hernandez, Jonathan Brewer, Morris Birdyellowhead, Carlos Emilio Baez, Raoul Trujillo, Rodolfo Palacios; ***D:*** Mel Gibson; ***W:*** Mel Gibson, Farhad Safinia; ***C:*** Dean Semler; ***M:*** James Horner.

Apollo 13 1/2 **1995 (PG)** Realistic big-budget reenactment of the 1970 Apollo lunar mission that ran into a "problem" 205,000 miles from home reunites Hanks and Sinese from "F. Gump" and Howard and Hanks from "Splash." And an enjoyable reunion it is. Explosion in one of two oxygen tanks helping power the spacecraft leaves the three astronauts (led by Hanks) tumbling through space. With the electrical system kaput and oxygen running low, the men seek refuge in the Lunar Excursion Module. Since it's based on the real event and the outcome is known, director Howard concentrates on the personalities and the details of the seven-day adventure at Mission Control and in space, in the process delivering the dramatic payload. Weightless shots are the real deal as crew filmed for ten days and made 600 parabolic loops in a KC-135 jet, NASA's "Vomit Comet," the long plunge creating 25 seconds of weightlessness. Special effects (by James Cameron's Digital Domain) and set design do the rest; no NASA footage is used, though original TV footage is used to dramatic effect. Script, with an uncredited rewrite by John Sayles, is based on the 1994 book, "Lost Moon," written by 13's Jim Lovell (who has a cameo as the Navy captain welcoming the astronauts aboard the recovery ship), while Apollo 15 commander David Scott served as a consultant. **140m/C VHS, DVD, HD DVD.** Tom Hanks, Kevin Bacon, Bill Paxton, Gary Sinise, Ed Harris, Kathleen Quinlan, Brett Cullen, Emily Ann Lloyd, Miko Hughes, Max Elliott Slade, Jean Speegle Howard, Tracy Reiner, Michelle Little, David Andrews, Mary Kate Schellhardt, Gabe Jarret, Chris Ellis, Joe Spano, Xander Berkeley, Marc McClure, Clint Howard, Loren Dean, Todd Louiso; ***D:*** Ron Howard; ***W:*** William Broyles Jr., Al Reinert; ***C:*** Dean Cundey; ***M:*** James Horner. Oscars '95: Film Editing, Sound; Directors Guild '95: Director (Howard); Screen Actors Guild '95: Support. Actor (Harris), Cast; Blockbuster '96: Drama Actor, T. (Hanks).

Apology **1986** A psychotic killer stalks Warren, an experimental artist, in Manhattan while a detective stalks the killer. Written by Medoff, author of "Children of a Lesser God." **98m/C VHS.** Lesley Ann Warren, Peter Weller, John Glover, George Loros, Jimmie Ray Weeks, Christopher Noth, Harvey Fierstein; ***D:*** Robert Bierman; ***W:*** Mark Medoff; ***M:*** Maurice Jarre. **CABLE**

The Apostate *Michael Angel* **1998 (R)** A young Jesuit priest, whose gay prostitute brother has been murdered by a serial killer, heads home to Puerto Rico and offers his assistance to his police inspector uncle in catching the killer, who seems driven by religious torment. But the priest himself is torn by spiritual doubts about his calling and is plunged into a world of temptation and vengeance. **94m/C VHS, DVD.** Richard Grieco, Dennis Hopper, Kristin Minter, Frank Medrano, Michael Cole, Efrain Figueroa, Bridget Ann White; ***D:*** Bill Gove; ***W:*** Bill Gove; ***C:*** Reinhart Pesche; ***M:*** Thomas Morse. **VIDEO**

The Apostle **1997 (PG-13)** No-holds-barred look at one man's search for religious redemption. Eulis Dewey (Duvall) is a devout, middle-aged, Pentecostal preacher in Texas, with a true gift for inspiring his congregation. Unfortunately, he's not so inspiring to his wife Jessie (Fawcett), who's cheating on him with younger minister, Horace (Allen). When Eulis discovers the infidelity, he strikes Horace with a bat, sending the man into a coma. Eulis escapes and winds up in the predominantly black town of Bayou Boutte, Louisiana, having shed his old identity for that of E.F., "The Apostle" of God. He zealously starts up a new church, seeking salvation, but his past comes back to haunt him. **134m/C VHS, DVD.** Robert Duvall, Miranda Richardson, Farrah Fawcett, John Beasley, Todd Allen, June Carter Cash, Billy Bob Thornton, Rick Dial, Walton Goggins, Billy Joe Shaver; ***D:*** Robert Duvall; ***W:*** Robert Duvall; ***C:*** Barry Markowitz; ***M:*** David Mansfield. Ind. Spirit '98: Actor (Duvall), Director (Duvall), Film; L.A. Film Critics '97: Actor (Duvall); Natl. Soc. Film Critics '97: Actor (Duvall).

The Appaloosa 1/2 *Southwest to Sonora* **1966** A lamenting loner who decides to begin anew by breeding Appaloosas is ripped off by a desperate woman who steals his horse in order to get away from her abusive amour. Brando falls in love with the girl and the two amazingly survive a wealth of obstacles in their battle against Mexican bandits. **99m/C VHS, DVD.** Marlon Brando, Anjanette Comer, John Saxon; ***D:*** Sidney J. Furie; ***W:*** James Bridges; ***C:*** Russell Metty.

Appaloosa **2008 (R)** Director, co-writer, co-producer, and star Harris brings the 2005 Robert B. Parker novel to the big screen with grit and grandeur. In 1880s New Mexico, two friends, Virgil Cole (Harris) and Everett Hitch (Mortensen), are hired to uphold the law in a small town overtaken by a tyrannical rancher (Irons). Their duty, as well as their friendship, is put to the test as a fetching young widow (Zellweger) strolls into town, stirring the hearts of both men. Beautifully shot and perfectly acted, with a smart and funny screenplay that keeps it above the genre cliches. **114m/C DVD, Blu-ray Disc.** *US* Ed Harris, Viggo Mortensen, Renee Zellweger, Jeremy Irons, Rex Linn, Tom Bower, Timothy Spall, James Gammon, Lance Henriksen, Ariadna Gil; ***D:*** Ed Harris; ***W:*** Ed Harris, Robert Knott; ***C:*** Dean Semler; ***M:*** Jeff Beal.

Appetite **1998 (R)** Try to stick with this slow-moving suspenser because it's got a wicked ending. A group of strangers, staying at the same hotel, play a game of cards where the loser must sleep in the reputedly haunted Room 207. **99m/C VHS, DVD.** Ute Lemper, Trevor Eve, Christien Anholt, Edward Hardwicke; ***D:*** George Milton; ***W:*** Dominik Scherrer; ***C:*** Peter Thwaites.

Applause **1929** Morgan plays a down-and-out burlesque star trying to protect her fresh from the convent daughter. Definitely dated, but a marvelous performance by Morgan. Film buffs will appreciate this early talkie. **78m/B VHS, DVD.** Helen Morgan, Joan Peers, Fuller Mellish Jr., Henry Wadsworth, Dorothy (Dorothy G. Cummings) Cumming; ***D:*** Rouben Mamoulian; ***C:*** George J. Folsey. Natl. Film Reg. '06.

The Apple 1/2 **1980 (PG)** Futuristic musical filmed in Berlin that features a young, innocent, folk-singing couple who nearly become victims of the evil, glitzy record producer who tries to recruit the couple into a life of sex and drugs. **90m/C VHS, DVD.** Catherine Mary Stewart, Alan Love, Grace Kennedy, Joss Ackland; ***D:*** Menahem Golan; ***W:*** Menahem Golan.

The Apple Dumpling Gang **1975 (G)** Three frisky kids strike it rich and trigger the wildest bank robbery in the gold-mad West. Unmistakably Disney, a familial subplot and a wacky duo are provided. Mediocre yet superior to its sequel, "The Apple Dumpling Gang Rides Again." **100m/C VHS, DVD.** Bill Bixby, Susan Clark, Don Knotts, Tim Conway, David Wayne, Slim Pickens, Harry (Henry) Morgan; ***D:*** Norman Tokar; ***M:*** Buddy (Norman Dale) Baker.

The Apple Dumpling Gang Rides Again **1979 (G)** Two lovable hombres terrorize the West in their bungling attempt to go straight. Fans of Conway or Knotts may appreciate this sequel to Disney's "The Apple Dumpling Gang." **88m/C VHS, DVD.** Tim Conway, Don Knotts, Tim Matheson, Kenneth Mars, Harry (Henry) Morgan, Jack Elam; ***D:*** Vincent McEveety; ***M:*** Buddy (Norman Dale) Baker.

The Applegates 1/2 *Meet the Applegates* **1989 (R)** Ecologically correct Amazonian beetles are more than a little miffed about the slash-and-burn tactics in their home and decide to establish a kinder, gentler habitat. Bug Begley and his brood transform themselves into average Americans, but then don't want to leave their decadent life: even insects aren't immune to the lure of sex, drugs, and cable shopping networks. Imaginative, often quite funny one-joke flick should've been shorter. Fits quite well as a double feature with Lehmann's earlier "Heathers." **90m/C VHS.** Ed Begley Jr., Stockard Channing, Dabney Coleman, Camille (Cami) Cooper, Bobby Jacoby, Glenn Shadix, Susan Barnes, Adam Biesk, Savannah Smith Boucher; ***D:*** Michael Lehmann; ***W:*** Michael Lehmann, Redbeard Simmons; ***C:*** Mitchell Dubin; ***M:*** David Newman.

The Appointment WOOF! **1982** A supernatural force enters the bodies and minds of people and suddenly everyone begins going crazy. **90m/C VHS.** Edward Woodward, Jane Merrow; ***D:*** Lindsey C. Vickers; ***C:*** Carlo Di Palma.

Appointment in Honduras **1953** An adventurer goes on a dangerous trek through the Central American jungles to deliver funds to the Honduran President. **79m/C VHS, DVD.** Glenn Ford, Ann Sheridan, Zachary Scott; ***D:*** Jacques Tourneur.

Appointment with Crime 1/2 **1945** After serving a prison sentence, an ex-con sets out to avenge himself against the colleagues who double crossed him. Well done, highlighted by superior characterizations. Based on the story by Michael Leighton. **91m/B VHS.** *GB* William Hartnell, Raymond Lovell, Robert Beatty, Herbert Lom, Joyce Howard, Alan Wheatley, Cyril Smith; ***D:*** John Harlow; ***W:*** John Harlow.

Appointment with Death 1/2 **1988 (PG)** Disappointing Agatha Christie mystery with Hercule Poirot solving the murder of a shrewish widow in 1937 Palestine. **103m/C VHS.** Peter Ustinov, Lauren Bacall, Carrie Fisher, John Gielgud, Piper Laurie, Hayley Mills, Jenny Seagrove, David Soul; ***D:*** Michael Winner; ***W:*** Anthony Shaffer, Peter Buckman, Michael Winner; ***M:*** Pino Donaggio.

Appointment with Fear **1985 (R)** A tough detective investigates a murder and all of the clues lead him mysteriously to a comatose asylum inmate. **95m/C VHS.** Michael Wyle, Michelle Little, Kerry Remsen, Douglas Rowe, Garrick Dowhen, Deborah Voorhees; ***D:*** Alan Smithee, Razmi Thomas; ***W:*** Gideon Davis, Bruce Mead.

The Apprentice 1/2 *Fleur Bleue* **1971** A directionless young French-Canadian man, growing up in Montreal, is involved with both his fanatical French separatist girlfriend and a free-spirited English-Canadian model. It's a love triangle that doesn't end well. An early role for Sarandon and a time capsule of the '70s separatist movement in Quebec. English and French with subtitles. **81m/C DVD.** *CA* Susan Sarandon, Carole Laure, Gerard Parkes, Steve Fiset, Celine Bernier, Jean-Pierre Cartier; ***D:*** Larry Kent; ***W:*** Edward Steward; ***C:*** Jean-Claude Labrecque.

Apprentice to Murder **1988 (PG-13)** A small Pennsylvania Dutch town is shaken by a series of murders, thought to be associated with a bizarre local mystic and healer. Based on a true story, sort of. **97m/C VHS.** Donald Sutherland, Mia Sara, Chad Lowe, Eddie Jones; ***D:*** Ralph L. (R.L.) Thomas; ***W:*** Allan Scott, Wesley Moore.

The Apprenticeship of Duddy Kravitz 1/2 **1974 (PG)** Young Jewish man in Montreal circa 1948 is driven by an insatiable need to be the "somebody" everyone has always told him he will be. A series of get-rich-quick schemes backfire in different ways, and he becomes most successful at driving people away. Young Dreyfuss is at his best. Made in Canada with thoughtful detail, and great cameo performances. Script by Richler, from his novel. **121m/C VHS, DVD.** *CA* Richard Dreyfuss, Randy Quaid, Denholm Elliott, Jack Warden, Micheline Lanctot, Joe Silver; ***D:*** Ted Kotcheff; ***W:*** Mordecai Richler, Lionel Chetwynd. Berlin Intl. Film Fest. '74: Golden Berlin Bear; Writers Guild '74: Adapt. Screenplay.

Apres Lui *After Him* **2007** Divorcee Camille (Deneuve) is devastated when her 20-year-old son Mathieu (Jolivet) is killed in a car accident. She turns to her son's grief-stricken best friend Franck (Dumerchez), who was the driver of the car, and starts helping the less-privileged young man out with college, also giving him a job in her bookstore. Franck's bewildered by her concern, which becomes obsessive, especially when Camille follows him on vacation. French with subtitles. **89m/C DVD.** *FR* Catherine Deneuve, Guy Marchand, Elodie Bouchez, Adrien Jolivet, Thomas Dumerchez; ***D:*** Gael Morel; ***W:*** Gael Morel, Christophe Honore; ***C:*** Jean-Max Bernard; ***M:*** Louis Sclavis.

Apres-Vous *After You* **2003 (R)** Sometimes you should just mind your own business. Parisian maitre d' Antoine (Auteuil) saves depressive loser Louis (Garcia) from hanging himself in a park and then feels responsible for making the man happy. He gets Louis a wine steward job, though he has no abilities whatsoever, and seeks to reconcile the sad sack with ex-lover Blanche (Kiberlain), except that Antoine falls for her himself. Auteuil is so good he can make any character believable (even this overzealous nice guy), but this familiar farce doesn't do much to stretch his talents. French with subtitles. **110m/C DVD.** *FR* Daniel Auteuil, Jose Garcia, Sandrine Kiberlain, Marilyne Canto, Michele Moretti, Garance Clavel, Fabio Zenoni, Ange Ruze; ***D:*** Pierre Salvadori; ***W:*** Pierre Salvadori, Benoit Graffin, David Colombo Leotard; ***C:*** Gilles Henry; ***M:*** Camille Bazbaz.

April Fool 1/2 **1926** A man makes a fortune in the umbrella business and then discovers his daughter has fallen in love with the son of a nouveaux riche neighbor, resulting in all sorts of complications. **63m/B VHS.** Alexander Carr, Mary Alden, Raymond Keane, Snitz Edwards; ***D:*** Nat Ross; ***W:*** Zion Myers.

April Fools **1969 (PG)** A bored stockbroker falls in love with a beautiful woman who turns out to be married to his boss. **95m/C VHS.** Jack Lemmon, Catherine Deneuve, Sally Kellerman, Peter Lawford, Harvey Korman, Melinda Dillon, Kenneth Mars; ***D:*** Stuart Rosenberg; ***M:*** Marvin Hamlisch.

April Fool's Day 1/2 **1986 (R)** Rich girl Muffy (Foreman) invites eight college friends to spend the April Fool's weekend with her at her family's isolated island mansion. Everyone is subjected to an endless series of practical jokes when things apparently turn deadly and several of the kids begin disappearing. Twist ending. Lame spoof of "Friday the 13th" and other teenagers-in-peril slasher films. **90m/C VHS, DVD.** Deborah Foreman, Jay Baker, Pat Barlow, Lloyd Berry, Deborah Goodrich, Ken Olandt, Griffin O'Neal, Tom Heaton, Mike Nomad, Leah K. Pinsent, Clayton Rohner, Amy Steel, Thomas F. Wilson; ***D:*** Fred Walton; ***W:*** Danilo Bach; ***C:*** Charles Minsky; ***M:*** Charles Bernstein.

April Fool's Day WOOF! **2008 (R)** You'll be the fool if you're conned into watching this dreck done by the duo appropriately calling themselves the Butcher Brothers. Rich bitch Desiree (Cole) plays a prank on rival Milan (Aldridge) at a party, only things go way too far and Milan dies. A year later, the partygoers receive invitations to Milan's gravesite and are then warned that they too will die unless someone accepts responsibility for Milan's death. Shares nothing but the title with the 1986 slasher flick. **91m/C DVD.** Sabrina Aldridge, Josh Henderson, Scout Taylor-Compton, Joe Egender, Samuel Child, Jennifer Siebe, Joseph McKelheer; ***D:*** Phil Flores, Mitchell Altieri; ***W:*** Phil Flores, Mitchell Altieri; ***C:*** Michael Maley; ***M:*** James Stemple. **VIDEO**

April in Paris **1952** Dynamite Jackson (Day), a chorus girl accidentally sent by the State Department to perform in Paris, meets S. Winthrop Putnam (Bolger), a timid fellow trapped in an unpleasant marriage. They eventually sing and dance their way to warm feelings as they begin a lifelong romance and live happily ever after. **100m/C VHS.** Doris Day, Ray Bolger, Claude Dauphin, Eve Miller, George Givot, Paul Harvey; ***D:*** David Butler; ***W:*** Jack Rose, Melville Shavelson.

April's Shower 1/2 **2003 (R)** April's about to get married, but what few know is that April's been a lesbian most of her life. Her ex-lover, and now bridesmaid, has even kept it a secret. Up until now. A slew of one-dimensional stereotypes parade across the screen, almost like they're at a John Waters audition, to ruin the emotional core. Tries too hard to be comedic and outrageous and oh, so culturally hip, assuming it can elude criticism by playing the indie card. Nope. Even the gay and lesbian crowds will find little amusement. **98m/C DVD.** *US* Maria Cina, Zack (Zach) Ward, Lara Harris, Molly Cheek, Trish Doolan, Frank Grillo, Randall Batinkoff, Arly Jover; ***D:*** Trish Doolan; ***W:*** Trish Doolan; ***C:*** Kristian Bernier, Rory King; ***M:*** Jeff Cardoni.

Apt Pupil **1997 (R)** In 1984, high school senior Todd Bowden (Renfro) becomes fascinated by the Holocaust during a school project and is able to discern from an old photo that neighbor Kurt Dussander (McKellen) was a Nazi concentration camp commander and is a war criminal. Todd agrees to keep quiet if the old man will tell exactly what he did during the war. But Dussander hasn't stayed quiet all these years to have his secrets revealed by a nosy teen, so Todd gets an up close and personal lesson about the nature of evil. Very creepy adaptation of the Stephen King novella with a standout performance by McKellen. **111m/C VHS, DVD.** Ian McKellen, Brad Renfro, Jan Triska, Bruce Davison, Joe Morton, Elias Koteas, David Schwimmer, Michael Byrne, Heather McComb, Ann Dowd, Joshua Jackson, Michael Artura; ***D:*** Bryan Singer; ***W:*** Brandon Boyce; ***C:*** Newton Thomas (Tom) Sigel; ***M:*** John Ottman.

Aqua Teen Hunger Force Colon Movie Film for Theaters 1/2 **2007 (R)** As intentionally nonsensical as its title. This component of the Cartoon Network's "Adult Swim" feature has New Jersey roomies (and fast-food items) Frylock, Master Shake, and Meatwad going full-length and big screen, battling the Insane-O-Flex home exercise machine that's actually an alien (the outer space kind). Familiar characters like Carl, Dr. Weird, Err, and others make their appearances. Only for those who already know "Aqua Teen" or just can't stand to be out of the pop culture loop. **86m/C DVD.** *US* ***D:*** Matt Maiellaro, Dave Willis; ***W:*** Matt Maiellaro, Dave Willis; ***V:*** Bruce Campbell, Matt Maiellaro, Dave Willis, Dana Snyder, Carey Means, Mike Schatz, Andy Merrill, C. Martin Croker.

Aquamarine 1/2 **2006 (PG)** Sweet tweener flick about best friends and a girl with a tail. Mermaid Aquamarine (Paxton) washes into a Florida beach club pool after a storm. She's discovered by 13-year-olds Claire (Roberts) and Hailey (Levesque) and the trio make a pact: Aqua needs to prove to her stern father that true love exists within three days or she will be forced to marry, and the girls want her to grant their wish to stop Hailey from moving away. Fortunately, Aqua is a blonde babe (her tail can conveniently vanish during daylight) who falls for cute lifeguard, Raymond (McDorman)—a romance the younger girls eagerly encourage. Generally comic calamities ensue. Based on the book by Alice Hoffman. **109m/C DVD.** *US* Sara Paxton, Emma Roberts, Arielle Kebbel, Claudia Karvan, Joanna "JoJo" Levesque, Jake McDorman, Bruce Spence, Roy Billing, Tammin Sursok, Julia Blake, Shaun Micallef; ***D:*** Elizabeth Allen; ***W:*** Jessica Bendinger, John Quaintance; ***C:*** Brian J. Breheny; ***M:*** David Hirschfelder.

The Arab Conspiracy *The Next Man; Double Hit* **1976 (R)** Sharpe plays a hit-woman conspiring with assassins from all over the world to kill Arab leaders. One problem—she falls in love with Saudi Arabian ambassador Connery as he tries to gain peace with Palestine. **108m/C VHS, DVD.** Sean Connery, Cornelia Sharpe, Albert Paulsen, Adolfo Celi, Charles Cioffi; ***D:*** Richard Sarafian; ***W:*** Alan R. Trustman; ***C:*** Michael Chapman; ***M:*** Michael Kamen.

Arabesque 1/2 **1966** A college professor is drawn into international espionage by a beautiful woman and a plot to assassinate an Arab prince. Stylish and fast moving. From the novel "The Cipher" by Gordon Cotler. **105m/C VHS.** Gregory Peck, Sophia Loren, George Coulouris, Alan Badel, Kieron Moore; ***D:*** Stanley Donen; ***M:*** Henry Mancini.

Arabian Nights **1942** Two brothers fight for the throne of Turkey and the affection of the sultry dancing girl Scheherazade. Enchanting costumes and lavish sets augment the fantasy atmosphere. **87m/C VHS, DVD.** Jon Hall, Maria Montez, Sabu, Leif Erickson, Edgar Barrier, Richard Lane, Turhan Bey; ***D:*** John Rawlins; ***W:*** Michael Hogan; ***C:*** Milton Krasner.

Arabian Nights *Il Fiore delle Mille e Una Notte; Flower of the Arabian Nights; A Thousand and One Nights* **1974** The third of Pasolini's epic, explicit adaptations of classic portmanteau, featuring ten of the old Scheherazade favorites adorned by beautiful photography, explicit sex scenes and homoeroticism. In Italian with English subtitles; available dubbed. **130m/C VHS, DVD.** *IT* Ninetto Davoli, Franco Merli, Ines Pellegrini, Luigina Rocchi, Franco Citti; ***D:*** Pier Paolo Pasolini; ***W:*** Pier Paolo Pasolini; ***C:*** Giuseppe Ruzzolini; ***M:*** Ennio Morricone.

Arabian Nights 1/2 **2000** Lavish spectacle and good casting overcomes the somewhat sluggish storytelling that combines a number of familiar tales. Sultan Schahriar's (Scott) grip on reality is slim ever since his greedy brother (Frain) and his first (and now late) wife plotted to assassinate him. Although he agrees to marry lovely Scheherezade (Avital), he also plans to kill her the morning after. But the lady is bright and desperate, she sooths her savage sultan with a number of stories involving genies, flying carpets, 40 thieves, and magic in order to stay alive until his sanity returns. Filmed on location in Turkey and Morocco. **175m/C VHS, DVD.** Mili Avital, Dougray Scott, James Frain, John Leguizamo, Rufus Sewell, Jason Scott Lee, Alan Bates, Tcheky Karyo; ***D:*** Steven Barron; ***W:*** Peter Barnes; ***C:*** Remi Adefarasin; ***M:*** Richard Harvey. **TV**

Arachnid 1/2 **2001 (R)** Plane carrying a rescue crew on a mission to find a downed pilot crashes on a tropical island that contains a gigantic, carnivorous alien spider. Nothing that hasn't been seen before. **95m/C VHS, DVD.** Chris Potter, Neus Asensi, Jose Sancho, Alex Reid; ***D:*** Jack Sholder; ***W:*** Mark Sevi; ***C:*** Carlos Gonzalez; ***M:*** Francesc Gener.

Arachnophobia 1/2 **1990 (PG-13)** Big-budget big-bug horror story has a few funny moments as lots and lots of spiders wreak havoc in a white picket fence community somewhere off the beaten track. Lethal South American spider makes a trek to sunny California, meets up with local spiders, and rapidly multiplies. Utterly arachnophobic (read: totally scared of spiders) town doctor Daniels pairs with gung-ho exterminator Goodman to try and track down the culprits. The script's a bit yawn-inspiring but the cast and effects will keep you from dozing off. Directorial debut for Marshall, a longtime friend and producer for Spielberg. **109m/C VHS, DVD.** Jeff Daniels, John Goodman, Harley Jane Kozak, Julian Sands, Roy Brocksmith, Stuart Pankin, Brian McNamara, Mark L. Taylor, Henry Jones, Peter Jason, James Handy; ***D:*** Frank Marshall; ***W:*** Wesley Strick, Don Jakoby; ***C:*** Mikael Salomon; ***M:*** Trevor Jones.

Ararat **2002 (R)** The slaughter of more than one million Armenians by the Turks in 1915 is the difficult subject matter of Canadian/Armenian director Egoyan's historically-themed drama. Excellent ensemble cast portrays characters in modern-day Toronto who deal with pasts that have been affected by the event in different ways. A director (Aznavour) revisits his roots by making a movie about the Armenian genocide. An expert (Egoyan's wife Khanjian) on Armenian painter Gorky deals with her son (Alpay), whose father was killed after attempting to assassinate a Turkish diplomat, and stepdaughter (Croze), who's father committed suicide. Frequent Egoyan collaborator Greenwood turns up as an actor portraying a real-life U.S. doctor in Turkey during that era who published a book about the events. Stylistically intricate, which may leave some confused, but the heartfelt message is not lost in the crowd. **116m/C VHS, DVD.** *CA* Charles Aznavour, Eric Bogosian, Brent Carver, David Alpay, Marie Josee Croze, Arsinee Khanjian, Bruce Greenwood, Elias Koteas, Christopher Plummer, Simon Abkarian; ***D:*** Atom Egoyan; ***W:*** Atom Egoyan; ***C:*** Paul Sarossy; ***M:*** Mychael Danna. Genie '02: Actress (Khanjian), Costume Des., Film, Support. Actor (Koteas), Score.

Arc **2006** Former L.A. cop Paris Pritchert (Facinelli) is now a junkie and drug dealer. In a last ditch effort at redemption, he tries to find a missing child, which leads to deceit, betrayal, and his own past. First-time director Gunnerson drags out the story and gets overly self-important for what should be a tight crime drama. **113m/C DVD.** Peter Facinelli, Jonah Blechman, Ann Cusack, Logan Grove, Mel Harris, Ken Howard, Simone Moore; ***D:*** Robert Ethan Gunnerson; ***W:*** Robert Ethan Gunnerson; ***C:*** David J. Frederick; ***M:*** Monte Montgomery.

Arcade 1/2 **1993 (R)** All the kids in town are desperate to play the new virtual reality game Arcade, only the game is just a little too real. Seems it can transport you into another world with its stunning graphics and sound effects but you really put your life on the line. Only Alex (Ward) worries when kids start to disappear and she decides to battle the game for their lives. **85m/C VHS.** Megan Ward, Peter Billingsley, John de Lancie, Sharon Farrell, Seth Green, Humberto Ortiz, Jonathan Fuller, Norbert Weisser; ***D:*** Albert Pyun; ***W:*** David S. Goyer; ***M:*** Alan Howarth.

Arch of Triumph **1948** In Paris, an Austrian refugee doctor falls in love just before the Nazis enter the city. Big-budget boxoffice loser featuring fine cast but sluggish pace. Based on the Erich Maria Remarque novel. **120m/B VHS.** Ingrid Bergman, Charles Boyer, Charles Laughton, Louis Calhern, Ruth Warrick; ***D:*** Lewis Milestone; ***W:*** Lewis Milestone, Harry Brown; ***C:*** Russell Metty.

Arch of Triumph 1/2 **1985** A refugee doctor falls in love with a mystery woman as the Nazis enter Paris. TV remake of the 1948 film. **95m/C VHS, DVD.** Anthony Hopkins, Lesley-Anne Down, Donald Pleasence, Frank Finlay; ***D:*** Waris Hussein; ***W:*** Charles Israel; ***M:*** Georges Delerue. **TV**

Archangel 𝒥𝒥 1/2 **2005 (R)** Based on the novel by Robert Harris, this thriller follows British historian Kelso (Craig), an expert on the Stalin-era USSR, to a Moscow conference. He's approached by an elderly man (Chernvak) claiming to know the whereabouts of Stalin's lost diary and he's plausible enough to have Kelso haring off to the port city of Archangel, accompanied by the man's daughter Zinaida (Rednikova) and reporter O'Brian (Macht). Only their search leads them to a dangerous underground movement to restore Stalinism to modern Russia. Originally broadcast as a BBC miniseries. **120m/C DVD.** Daniel Craig, Yekaterina Rednikova, Gabriel Macht, Valery Chernvak; ***D:*** Jon Jones; ***W:*** Dick Clement, Ian La Frenais; ***C:*** Chris Seager; ***M:*** Robert (Rob) Lane. **TV**

Archer: The Fugitive from the Empire 𝒥 **1981** A young warrior battles the forces of evil. Lots of strange names to learn even if you already know who's going to win the final battle. **97m/C VHS.** Lane Caudell, Belinda Bauer, George Kennedy, Victor Campos, Kabir Bedi, George Innes, Marc Alaimo, Allan Rich, John Hancock, Priscilla Pointer, Sharon Barr; ***D:*** Nicholas J. Corea. **TV**

Archer's Adventure 𝒥 1/2 **1985** An Australian family film based on a true story. A horsetrainer's young apprentice delivers a prize racehorse to Melbourne, through 600 miles of tough frontier, devious bush rangers, and disaster. **120m/C VHS, DVD.** *AU* Brett Climo, Nicole Kidman; ***D:*** Denny Lawrence.

Archie: Return to Riverdale 𝒥𝒥 1/2 **1990 (PG)** Archie, Reggie, Betty, Veronica, and Jughead return to Riverdale for their 15-year class reunion. Made for TV; based on the comic book. **85m/C VHS.** Christopher Rich, Lauren Holly, Karen Kopins, Sam Whipple, Gary Kroeger, Matt McCoy, David Doyle, Fran Ryan; ***D:*** Dick Lowry; ***C:*** Frank Byers; ***M:*** Mark Snow. **TV**

The Architect 𝒥𝒥 **2006 (R)** Rickety construction undermines the cast. Affluent white architect Leo Waters (LaPaglia) lives with his dysfunctional family on Chicago's North Shore. Black activist Tonya Neely (Davis) is an occupant of a South Side housing tower that Leo designed, which in now gang-controlled and falling apart. Tonya, who has her own family issues, wants the towers torn down for new housing and thinks Leo's signature on her petition will help her efforts, but he's reluctant to participate. Based on a play by David Grieg. **82m/C DVD.** Anthony LaPaglia, Viola Davis, Isabella Rossellini, Hayden Panettiere, Sebastian Stan, Paul James, Serena Reeder, Walton Goggins; ***D:*** Matt Tauber; ***W:*** Matt Tauber; ***C:*** John Bailey; ***M:*** Marcelo Zarvos.

Arctic Blue 𝒥 1/2 **1993 (R)** Alaskan biologist Walsh gets stuck being the local lawman when he's the only one willing to escort Hauer, a homicidal trapper, to a Fairbanks jail. But nothing's that easy—their plane crashes atop a glacier and the duo must battle each other and the elements to survive, while Hauer's brutal partners hunt Walsh. **95m/C VHS, DVD.** Dylan Walsh, Rutger Hauer, Richard Bradford; ***D:*** Peter Masterson; ***W:*** Ross LaManna; ***C:*** Thomas Burstyn; ***M:*** Peter Melnick.

Arctic Tale 𝒥𝒥 1/2 **2007 (G)** We love pretending animals are just like us, don't we? Just add some disco music ("We Are Family") and a narrator (Queen Latifah) we all recognize and watch those wacky things animals do in the wild (like fart). Flick follows a polar bear and a walrus over six years, starting with their birth. The message is clear beyond our compulsion to humanize them, however; climate change, possibly caused by us, is dramatically affecting their habitat. Lush (if not chilly) backdrops and the directors' passion make this a fine family film. **96m/C DVD, HD DVD.** *US* ***D:*** Adam Ravetch, Sarah Robertson; ***W:*** Linda Woverton, Moses Richards, Kristin Gore; ***C:*** Adam Ravetch; ***M:*** Joby Talbot; ***Nar:*** Queen Latifah.

Are Parents People? 𝒥𝒥 **1925** Lighthearted silent comedy about a young girl's successful attempts to reunite her feuding parents. It all begins as she runs away and spends the night in the office of a doctor she has grown to like. After a frantic night of searching, her parents are reunited through their love for her. **60m/B VHS.** Betty Bronson, Adolphe Menjou, Florence Vidor, Andre Beranger, Lawrence Gray, Mary Beth Milford, Emily Fitzroy, William Courtwright; ***D:*** Malcolm St. Clair; ***W:*** Frances Agnew, Alice Duer Miller; ***C:*** Bert Glennon.

Are We Done Yet? 𝒥 1/2 **2007 (PG)** Apparently this sequel to "Are We There Yet?" is based on the 1948 Cary Grant comedy "Mr. Blandings Builds His Dream House" but don't count on it. Nick's (Ice Cube) married to divorcee-with-kids Suzanne (Long) and she announces she's preggers. Nick decides the family needs larger digs and leaves city life for a deceptively beautiful country house sold to them by slick/crazy contractor/building inspector/real estate salesman Chuck (scene-stealer McGinley). Of course their new abode is actually a homeowner's worst nightmare. If you liked the first Ice Cube family flick, this is more of the same. **92m/C DVD, Blu-ray Disc.** *US* Ice Cube, Nia Long, John C. McGinley, Aleisha Allen, Philip Daniel Bolden; ***D:*** Steve Carr; ***W:*** Hank Nelken; ***C:*** Jack N. Green; ***M:*** Teddy Castellucci.

Are We There Yet? 𝒥 **2005 (PG)** Ice Cube is Nick Persons, an easygoing, charming ladies' man with a self-professed hatred of kids, when in walks his dream woman in the form of Suzanne (Long), an event planner. Suzanne, unfortunately for Nick, is a divorcee with two children, 11-year-old Lindsey (Allen) and 8-year-old Kevin (Bolden). Nick reconsiders his anti-kid rule, and decides to court Suzanne anyway. However, the two kids, who stubbornly believe that their parents will get back together, have decided to thwart any of their mother's would-be boyfriends. As luck would have it, their mother is needed in Vancouver to plan a New Year's Eve party and needs Nick to bring the kids to her. While Ice Cube is certainly enjoyable to watch, the kids are so obnoxious that the obvious question is, "is this movie done yet?" **91m/C DVD, UMD.** *US* Ice Cube, Nia Long, Jay Mohr, M.C. Gainey, Aleisha Allen, Philip Daniel Bolden, Tracy Morgan, Nichelle Nichols; ***D:*** Brian Levant; ***W:*** Steven Banks, Claudio Grazioso, J. David Stem, David N. Weiss; ***C:*** Thomas Ackerman; ***M:*** David Newman.

Are You in the House Alone? 𝒥𝒥 **1978** Adaptation of Richard Peck's award-winning novel. Story of a high school coed who becomes the target of a terror campaign. **100m/C VHS.** Blythe Danner, Kathleen Beller, Tony Bill, Scott Colomby; ***D:*** Walter Grauman; ***M:*** Charles Bernstein. **TV**

Are You Lonesome Tonight 𝒥𝒥 1/2 **1992 (PG-13)** Suspense thriller casts Seymour as a wealthy socialite who discovers her husband is having an affair with a phone-sex girl. His sudden and mysterious disappearance forces her to hire a private detective (Stevenson) to track him down, with only the taped conversations as clues. Average cable TV fare. **91m/C VHS.** Jane Seymour, Parker Stevenson, Beth Broderick, Joel Brooks, Robert Pine; ***D:*** E.W. Swackhamer; ***W:*** Wesley Moore. **CABLE**

Are You Scared? **WOOF!** **2006** Scared only by this movie—a dire rip-off/combination of "Saw" and TV's "Fear Factor." Six young people wake up in an abandoned factory and learn they are contestants on the reality TV show of the title. They all have to face their worst fear—or die trying. **79m/C DVD.** Aletha Kutscher, Erin Consolvi, Carlee Avers, Soren Bowie, Kariem Marbury, Brad Ashten, Caia Coley, Brent Fidler; ***D:*** Andy Hurst; ***W:*** Andy Hurst; ***C:*** Jeffrey Smith. **VIDEO**

The Arena 𝒥𝒥 *Naked Warriors* **1973 (R)** Ancient Romans capture beautiful women from around the world and force them to compete in gladiatorial games. New World exploitation gem featuring mostly Italian cast, including Bay, who starred in the previous year's "Lady Frankenstein." **75m/C VHS, DVD.** Margaret Markov, Pam Grier, Lucretia Love, Paul Muller, Daniel Vargas, Marie Louise, Mary Count, Rosalba Neri, Vic Karis, Sid Lawrence, Peter Cester, Anna Melita; ***D:*** Steve Carver; ***W:*** John W. Corrington, Joyce H. Corrington; ***C:*** Joe D'Amato; ***M:*** Francesco De Masi.

Arena 𝒥𝒥 **1989 (PG-13)** Remember old boxing melodramas about good-natured palookas, slimy opponents, gangsters and dames? This puts those cliches in a garish sci-fi setting, with handsome Steve Armstrong battling ETs and the astro-mob to be the first human pugilistic champ in decades. A really cute idea (from the screenwriters of "The Rocketeer"), but it conks out at the halfway point. Worth a look for buffs. **97m/C VHS.** *IT* Paul Satterfield, Claudia Christian, Hamilton Camp, Marc Alaimo, Armin Shimerman, Shari Shattuck, Jack Carter; ***D:*** Peter Manoogian; ***W:*** Danny Bilson, Paul DeMeo; ***M:*** Richard Band.

Argentine Nights 𝒥 1/2 **1940** The Ritz Brothers arrive broke in Argentina with their all-girl band and try to save a local hotel from a con man. Debut of The Andrews Sisters. **75m/B VHS.** Al Ritz, The Andrews Sisters, George Reeves, Peggy Moran, Anne Nagel, Constance Moore, Harry Ritz, Jimmy Ritz; ***D:*** Albert Rogell; ***W:*** Ray Golden, Arthur T. Horman, Sid Kuller; ***C:*** Elwood "Woody" Bredell.

Aria 𝒥𝒥 **1988 (R)** Ten directors were given carte blanche to interpret ten arias from well-known operas. Henry and D'Angelo star in Julian Temple's rendition of Verdi's "Rigoletto." In Fonda's film debut, she and her lover travel to Las Vegas and eventually kill themselves in the bathtub, just like "Romeo & Juliet." Jarman's piece (a highlight) shows an aged operatic star at her last performance remembering an early love affair. "I Pagliacci" is the one aria in which the director took his interpretation in a straightforward manner. **90m/C VHS, DVD.** *GB* Theresa Russell, Anita Morris, Bridget Fonda, Beverly D'Angelo, Buck Henry, John Hurt; ***D:*** Ken Russell, Charles Sturridge, Robert Altman, Bill Bryden, Jean-Luc Godard, Bruce Beresford, Nicolas Roeg, Franc Roddam, Derek Jarman, Julien Temple; ***W:*** Ken Russell, Charles Sturridge, Robert Altman, Bill Bryden, Jean-Luc Godard, Bruce Beresford, Nicolas Roeg, Franc Roddam, Derek Jarman, Julien Temple; ***C:*** Caroline Champetier, Oliver Stapleton, Gale Tattersall.

Ariel 𝒥𝒥𝒥 **1989** Refreshing, offbeat Finnish comedy by highly praised newcomer Kaurismaki. Hoping to find work in Southern Finland, an out-of-work miner from Northern Finland (Pajala) jets off in his white Cadillac convertible given to him in a cafe by a friend, who promptly shoots himself. There's no linear progression toward a happy ending, although antiheroic subject does find employment and romances a meter maid. Mostly, though, he's one of those it's hell being me guys who wouldn't have any luck if it weren't for bad luck. Strange slice-of-life sporting film noir tendencies, although essentially antistylistic. **74m/C VHS.** *FI* Susanna Haavisto, Turo Pajala, Matti Pellonpaa; ***D:*** Aki Kaurismaki; ***W:*** Aki Kaurismaki; ***C:*** Timo Salminen. Natl. Soc. Film Critics '90: Foreign Film.

The Aristocats 𝒥𝒥𝒥 **1970** Typically entertaining Disney animated story about pampered pussy Duchess (Gabor) and her three kittens, who are left a fortune in their mistress' will. The fortune goes to the butler if the cats don't survive, so he dumps them in the country hoping they won't find their way home. The cats are aided by tough alley denizen O'Malley (Harris)—it's kind of the feline version of "Lady and the Tramp." Maurice Chevalier sings the title tune. **78m/C VHS, DVD.** ***D:*** Wolfgang Reitherman; ***M:*** George Bruns; ***V:*** Eva Gabor, Phil Harris, Sterling Holloway, Roddy Maude-Roxby, Bill Thompson, Hermione Baddeley, Carol(e) Shelley, Pat Buttram, Nancy Kulp, Paul Winchell.

The Aristocrats 𝒥𝒥 1/2 **1999** True story of the scandalous 18th-century aristocratic Lennox family, including the four beautiful sisters whose elopements, liaisons, and intrigues provided ample English gossip. Based on the novel by Stella Tillyard. Three cassettes. **255m/C VHS, DVD.** *GB* Jodhi May, Geraldine Somerville, Serena Gordon, Anne-Marie Duff, Alun Armstrong, Julian Fellowes, Ben Daniels, Diane Fletcher, Clive Swift, Sian Phillips, Richard Dempsey; ***D:*** David Caffrey; ***W:*** Harriet O'Carroll. **TV**

The Aristocrats 𝒥𝒥𝒥 **2005** "A family walks into a talent agency..." and so begins the raunchiest joke in cinematic history. It might seem odd to dedicate an entire documentary to one joke, but co-directors Provenza and Jillette excel at demonstrating how different comedians bring their own unique interpretations to the same material. The all-star interviewees (George Carlin, Chris Rock, and Robin Williams, among many others) speak elegantly about the joys of working "blue," although the true tour-de-force performances come from Bob Saget, Gilbert Gottfried, and Sarah Silverman, who all give blisteringly filthy renditions of the titular joke that you'll be talking about for weeks to come. **87m/C DVD.** *US* ***D:*** Paul Provenza; ***M:*** Gary Stockdale.

Arizona 𝒥𝒥 1/2 **1940** Arthur is a hellion in wild 1860 Tucson who falls for the wandering Holden. He's headed for California and she can't keep him in town so Arthur throws herself into business by establishing a freight line. Only warring Apaches try to burn her out and Holden rides in to save the day (with the cavalry and a stampeding cattle herd). Holden's first western is lively but long. **121m/B VHS, DVD.** Jean Arthur, William Holden, Warren William, Porter Hall, Paul Harvey, George Chandler, Regis Toomey, Edgar Buchanan; ***D:*** Wesley Ruggles; ***W:*** Claude Binyon; ***M:*** Victor Young.

Arizona 𝒥 1/2 **1986** A group of illegal aliens struggle for survival after they cross the border into the harsh desert. **94m/C VHS.** *MX* Anna De Sade, Gilberto Trujillo, Roberto "Flaco" Guzman, Juan Valentin; ***D:*** Fernando Duran Rojas; ***W:*** Hector Kiev; ***C:*** Manuel Tejada; ***M:*** Gustavo Cesar Carrion.

Arizona Bound 𝒥 **1941** Mesa City is infested with a villain and our "Rough Rider" trio must rid the town of him. **57m/B VHS, DVD.** Buck Jones, Tim McCoy, Raymond Hatton, Dennis Moore, Luana Walters; ***D:*** Spencer Gordon Bennet.

Arizona Bushwackers 𝒥 1/2 **1967** Routine western that has Confederate spy Keel taking job as sheriff in small Arizona town. Once there, he has to straighten out a few bad guys who have been selling weapons to the Apaches. Notable for presence of old western-movie veterans Ireland, Donlevy, Brady, and MacLane. Based on a story by Steve Fisher. **87m/C VHS.** Howard Keel, Yvonne De Carlo, John Ireland, Marilyn Maxwell, Scott Brady, Brian Donlevy, Barton MacLane; ***D:*** Lesley Selander.

Arizona Cowboy 𝒥 **1949** An ex-G.I., now the rodeo's big attraction, gets involved in a robbery. **57m/B VHS.** Rex Allen, Gordon Jones, Roy Barcroft; ***D:*** R.G. Springsteen.

Arizona Cyclone 𝒥 1/2 **1941** Tom Baxter runs the freight lines for George Randolph and his daughter Claire against competitor Quirt Crenshaw. Town banker Adam Draper, in cahoots with Crenshaw, wants to discredit the Randolphs because he knows a lucrative hauling contract is about to be awarded. So he hires a gang of outlaws to steal a gold shipment and Baxter must save the day. **59m/B DVD.** Johnny Mack Brown, Fuzzy Knight, Nell O'Day, Herbert Rawlinson, Dick Curtis, Robert Strange, Glenn Strange, Kathryn Adams; ***D:*** Joseph H. Lewis; ***W:*** Sherman Lowe; ***C:*** Charles Van Enger.

Arizona Days 𝒥 1/2 **1937** Cowboys join a minstrel group and rescue the show when a group of toughs try to break it up. **56m/B VHS, DVD.** Tex Ritter, Eleanor Stewart, Syd Saylor, Snub Pollard; ***D:*** John English.

Arizona Dream 𝒥𝒥 **1994 (R)** Alex (Depp) is a New York drifter who gets stuck working for his uncle's (Lewis) car dealership in a small Arizona town. He meets an eccentric older woman (Dunaway) with a homemade plane and some dreams of her own. Tends toward the surreal and confusing. **119m/C VHS.** Johnny Depp, Faye Dunaway, Jerry Lewis, Lili Taylor, Paulina Porizkova, Tricia Leigh Fisher, Vincent Gallo; ***D:*** Emir Kusturica; ***W:*** Emir Kusturica, David Atkins; ***C:*** Vilko Filac.

Arizona Gangbusters 𝒥 **1940** Below-average oater has real-life cowboy McCoy fighting city hall in order to fight other baddies. Newfield directed under the pseudonym "Peter Stewart." **57m/B VHS.** Tim McCoy, Pauline Hadden, Forrest Taylor, Julian Rivero; ***D:*** Sam Newfield; ***C:*** Jack Greenhalgh.

Arizona Gunfighter 𝒥 **1937** A young cowhand seeks revenge against the man who murdered his father in this western. **60m/B VHS, DVD.** Bob Steele, Ted Adams, Ernie Adams; ***D:*** Sam Newfield.

Arizona Heat 𝒥𝒥 **1987 (R)** A violent cop is teamed up with a tough, but tender female cop in this all-too-familiar tale of two cops chasing a cop killer. **91m/C VHS.** Michael Parks, Denise Crosby, Hugh Farrington; ***D:*** John G. Thomas.

Arizona Kid 1939 Another sagebrush saga featuring Roy in singin' and fightin' action. **54m/B VHS, DVD.** Roy Rogers, George "Gabby" Hayes; ***D:*** Joseph Kane.

Arizona Mahoney 1936 Weird mixture of circus adventure and serious western doesn't work too well. Confused film with farfetched reasons for having the paths of circus performers and cowboys cross. Based on a Zane Grey novel. **58m/B VHS, DVD.** Joe Cook, Robert Cummings, June Martel, Marjorie Gateson, John Miljan; ***D:*** James Hogan; ***W:*** Robert Yost, Stuart Anthony.

Arizona Raiders 1965 Arizona rangers hunt down killers who have been terrorizing the territory. **88m/C VHS.** Audie Murphy, Buster Crabbe, Gloria Talbott; ***D:*** William Witney.

Arizona Roundup 1/2 1942 Good vs. bad amid tumbleweed, bleached-white chaps, bloodless shoot-outs and happy endings. **54m/B VHS.** Tom Keene, Sugar Dawn, Jack Ingram; ***D:*** Robert Emmett Tansey.

Arizona Sky 2008 Kyle and Jake were teenaged best friends who could never follow through with their feelings for each other because of hometown prejudice. A stressed-out Jake returns to their desert community after 20 years and discovers Kyle hasn't been happy with his choices either. So the men decide to see if those old emotions are worth pursuing. **91m/C DVD.** Patricia Place, Eric Dean, Jayme McCabe, Bernadette Murray; ***D:*** Jeff London; ***W:*** Jeff London; ***C:*** Matthew Skala. **VIDEO**

Arizona Stagecoach 1942 The Range Busters set out to bust a notorious, guiltless, devil-may-care outlaw gang. **58m/B VHS, DVD.** Ray Corrigan, Max Terhune, Kermit Maynard, Charles "Blackie" King, John "Dusty" King; ***D:*** S. Roy Luby.

Arizona Summer 1/2 2003 (PG) Brent (Barnett) makes friends and gets some life lessons at a summer camp run by Travers (Majors). Simple family entertainment. **90m/C DVD.** *US* Lee Majors, Greg Evigan, Morgan Fairchild, Bug Hall, Gemini Barnett, David Henrie, Lorenzo Henrie, Scott Clifton; ***D:*** Joey Travolta; ***W:*** Bill Blair.

Arizona Terror 1/2 1931 Our hero is on a quest for vengeance, seeking the posse that killed his partner. **64m/B VHS.** Ken Maynard, Lena Basquette, Hooper Atchley, Michael Visaroff, Tom London, Jack Natteford; ***D:*** Phil Rosen; ***W:*** Jack Natteford; ***C:*** Arthur Reed.

Arizona Whirlwind 1944 Our intrepid heroes must battle torrents of gunfire in order to prevent a stage hold-up in this western saga. **59m/B VHS.** Ken Maynard, Hoot Gibson, Bob Steele; ***D:*** Robert Emmett Tansey.

Ark of the Sun God 1982 Another adventurer battles the Nazis and nutsies for a 2000-year-old ark buried in the Sahara. **95m/C VHS.** David Warbeck, John Steiner, Susie Sudlow, Alan Collins, Riccardo Palacio; ***D:*** Anthony M. Dawson.

Arlington Road 1/2 1999 (R) The tranquility of surburban life is shattered for college professor Faraday (Bridges) when he suspects the picket fence and overly friendliness of new neighbor Lang (Robbins) is a cover for his right-wing terrorism. As Faraday slowly uncovers Lang's true identity, it becomes harder for him to convince friends to believe the conspiracy. Impressive nail-biter with an interesting twist has a solid performance from Bridges as the paranoid professor, and an eerie one from the otherwise affable Robbins. Director Pellington, with the aide of Badalamenti's haunting score maintains the film's objective of showing how evil can come from the most unlikely place. **119m/C VHS, DVD, Blu-ray Disc.** Jeff Bridges, Tim Robbins, Joan Cusack, Hope Davis, Mason Gamble, Stanley Anderson, Robert Gossett, Spencer (Treat) Clark; ***D:*** Mark Pellington; ***W:*** Ehren Kruger; ***C:*** Bobby Bukowski; ***M:*** Angelo Badalamenti, Tomandandy.

Armageddon 1/2 1998 (PG-13) A Texas-sized asteroid is hurtling towards earth, NASA gets nervous, and it's up to oil driller Harry Stamper (Willis) and his misfit crew to turn astronaut, blast off into space, land on that rock, and blow the sucker to kingdom come. Ya get a little romance as hotshot A.J. Frost (Affleck) smooches with babe Grace (Tyler), who's Harry's nubile daughter. Lots of action (naturally), some humor, and some sappy, heart-tugging moments for perfect put-your-brain-on-hold entertainment. The second "space rock hits earth" movie, following the somber "Deep Impact." **150m/C VHS, DVD, Blu-ray Disc.** Bruce Willis, Ben Affleck, Billy Bob Thornton, Steve Buscemi, Liv Tyler, Will Patton, Peter Stormare, Keith David, Owen Wilson, William Fichtner, Jessica Steen, Grayson McCouch, Jason Isaacs, Michael Clarke Duncan, Erik Per Sullivan; ***D:*** Michael Bay; ***W:*** Jonathan Hensleigh, J.J. (Jeffrey) Abrams; ***C:*** John Schwartzman; ***M:*** Trevor Rabin. MTV Movie Awards '99: Song ("I Don't Want to Miss a Thing"), Action Seq.; Golden Raspberries '98: Worst Actor (Willis).

Armageddon: The Final Challenge 1/2 1994 After a nuclear holocaust, evil forces rule the Earth in the guise of "The Future Bank." They send out Fear-Permutator Clones to keep order and kill undesirables but naturally there's a rebel ready to do battle. **85m/C VHS.** Todd Jensen, Graham Clarke, Tony Caprari, Joanna Rowlands; ***D:*** Michael Garcia; ***W:*** George Garcia, Michael Garcia; ***M:*** Johan Lass.

Armed and Dangerous 1986 (PG-13) Candy and Levy are incompetent security guards assigned to a do-nothing job. Things get spiced up when a mobster tries to run a crime ring under their nose. Candy catches on and winds up in a full-fledged chase. Not as funny as it sounds, though occasionally has moments of genuine comedy. **88m/C VHS, DVD.** John Candy, Eugene Levy, Kenneth McMillan, Brion James, Robert Loggia, Meg Ryan, Don Stroud, Jonathan Banks, Steve Railsback, Bruce Kirby, Tony Burton, Larry Hankin, Judy Landers, David Wohl; ***D:*** Mark L. Lester; ***W:*** Harold Ramis, Peter Torokvei, James Keach, Brian Grazer.

Armed for Action 1992 Routine action thriller casts Estevez as Sgt. Phil Towers who gets more than he bargained for when his prisoner, Mafia hitman David Montel, escapes while en route from New York to Los Angeles. When he finally catches up with them, Towers leads a small army of locals on a brutal assault. **88m/C VHS.** Joe Estevez, Rocky Patterson, Barri Murphy, David Harrod, J. Scott Guy; ***D:*** Shane Spaulding.

Armed Response 1986 (R) Carradine leads a group of mercenaries in a battle against Chinatown mobsters. They race to locate a priceless jade statue before it can fall into the wrong hands. **86m/C VHS, DVD.** David Carradine, Lee Van Cleef, Mako, Lois Hamilton, Ross Hagen, Brent Huff; ***D:*** Fred Olen Ray; ***C:*** Paul Elliott.

Armistead Maupin's More Tales of the City 1/2 *More Tales of the City* **1997** More risque and odd adventures for the inhabitants of Barbary Lane. Sequel picks up some six weeks after the first adventures. In 1977 San Francisco, Mary Ann (Linney) and Mouse (Hopkins) hunt for romance on a Mexican cruise. Mary Ann falls for handsome amnesiac Burke (Ferguson) and tries to help him regain his memory, while Mouse reunites with ex-lover, Dr. Jon (Campbell). Meanwhile, Mona (Siemszko) searches for her roots, which leads to revelations from Mrs. Madrigal (Dukakis). Brian (Hubley) becomes a voyeur and DeDe (Garrick) awaits the birth of twins—whose father is not her supercilious husband Beauchamp (Gibson). **330m/C VHS, DVD.** Laura Linney, Olympia Dukakis, Colin Ferguson, Billy Campbell, Paul Hopkins, Whip Hubley, Thomas Gibson, Barbara Garrick, Nina Siemaszko, Jackie Burroughs, Swoosie Kurtz, Francoise Robertson, Dan E. Butler; ***Cameos:*** Parker Posey, Ed Asner, Paul Bartel, Brian Bedford, Sheila McCarthy, Scott Thompson; ***D:*** Pierre Gang; ***W:*** Nicholas Wright; ***C:*** Serge Ladouceur; ***M:*** Richard Gregoire.

Armistead Maupin's Tales of the City 1/2 *Tales of the City* **1993** Carefree '70s San Francisco is the setting for the interconnected stories of the inhabitants of 28 Barbary Lane. There's mysterious landlady Mrs. Madrigal (Dukakis); free-spirit Mona Ramsey (Webb); her gay roomie, Michael "Mouse" Tolliver (D'Amico); hetero lawyer-turned-waiter Brian (Gross); nerdy, secretive Norman (DeSantis); and the naively sweet Mary Ann Singleton (Linney). Definite time-warp factor in this pre-AIDS depiction of sex and drugs, but also the timeless search for love and happiness. Maupin first wrote the stories as an ongoing serial for the "San Francisco Chronicle" and they were later turned into six novels. Made for British TV. **360m/C VHS, DVD.** *GB* Olympia Dukakis, Donald Moffat, Chloe Webb, Laura Linney, Marcus D'Amico, Billy Campbell, Thomas Gibson, Paul Gross, Barbara Garrick, Nina Foch, Edie Adams, Meagen Fay, Lou Liberatore, Country Joe McDonald, Mary Kay Place, Parker Posey, Kevin Sessums, McLean Stevenson, Stanley DeSantis, Cynda Williams, Karen Black, Michael Jeter, Paul Bartel, Lance Loud, Ian McKellen, Bob Mackie, Marissa Ribisi, Mother Love, Don Novello, Rod Steiger, Janeane Garofalo, Armistead Maupin; ***D:*** Alastair Reid; ***W:*** Richard Kramer; ***M:*** John Keane. **TV**

Armored 1/2 2009 (PG-13) Unpretentious but generic heist movie. A six-man crew at an L.A. armored transport security firm are in on a robbery against their company with a $42 million dollar payoff. If only planner Cochrane (Dillon) can persuade Iraqi war vet Hackett (Short) to go along by reassuring him that nobody will get hurt. Of course, that turns out to be wrong and a conflicted Hackett then tries to do the right thing. **88m/C DVD.** *US* Columbus Short, Jean Reno, Laurence Fishburne, Skeet Ulrich, Amaury Nolasco, Fred Ward, Matt Dillon, Milo Ventimiglia, Andre Jamal Kinney; ***D:*** Nimrod Antal; ***W:*** James V. Simpson; ***C:*** Andrzej Sekula; ***M:*** John Murphy.

Armored Car Robbery 1950 Talman and his buddies plot to rob an armored car but are foiled by McGraw and his crime-fighters. Surprisingly good B-crime drama. **68m/B VHS.** Charles McGraw, Adele Jergens, William Talman, Steve Brodie, Douglas Fowley, Don McGuire, James Flavin, Gene Evans; ***D:*** Richard Fleischer; ***W:*** Gerald Drayson Adams, Earl Felton; ***C:*** Guy Roe; ***M:*** Paul Sawtell.

Armored Command 1/2 1961 A beautiful German spy infiltrates an American outpost during the Battle of the Bulge. Tepid WWII fare made too long after the fact. **105m/B VHS.** Burt Reynolds, Tina Louise, Howard Keel, Earl Holliman, Warner Anderson, Carleton Young; ***D:*** Byron Haskin.

Army Brats 1/2 1984 In this Dutch film a military family goes bloodily and comically to war with itself. Even in a welfare state, parents can't control their wee ones. **105m/C VHS.** *NL* Akkemay, Frank Schaafsma, Peter Faber; ***D:*** Ruud Van Hemert.

Army of Darkness *Evil Dead 3; The Medieval Dead* **1992 (R)** Campbell returns for a third "Evil Dead" round as the square-jawed, none too bright hero, Ash in this comic book extravaganza. He finds himself hurled back to the 14th-century through the powers of an evil book. There he romances a babe, fights an army of skeletons, and generally causes all those Dark Age knights a lot of grief, as he tries to get back to his own time. Raimi's technical exuberance is apparent and, as usual, the horror is graphic but still tongue-in-cheek. **77m/C VHS, DVD, HD DVD.** Bruce Campbell, Embeth Davidtz, Marcus Gilbert, Ian Abercrombie, Richard Grove, Michael Earl Reid, Tim Quill, Bridget Fonda, Patricia Tallman, Theodore (Ted) Raimi, Ivan Raimi, Donald Campbell, William Lustig, Josh Becker; ***D:*** Sam Raimi; ***W:*** Sam Raimi, Ivan Raimi; ***C:*** Bill Pope; ***M:*** Joseph LoDuca, Danny Elfman.

Army of One 1/2 1994 (R) Santee (Lundgren) and his pal are hauling stolen cars across the desert when a cop pulls them over. Soon there's two dead bodies and Santee's in big trouble. An unrated version is also available. **102m/C VHS, DVD.** Dolph Lundgren, George Segal, Kristian Alfonso, Geoffrey Lewis, Michelle Phillips; ***D:*** Vic Armstrong; ***W:*** Steven Pressfield, Joel Goldsmith.

Army of Shadows 1/2 *L'Armee des Ombres; Army in the Shadows; The Shadow Army* **1969** Melville's stunning adaptation of the 1943 Joseph Kessel novel focuses on members of the French Resistance in 1942. They lead shadow lives under false identities, struggling to survive while living in fear of betrayal. The head of this cell is Luc Jardie (Meurisse) but the most necessary of its members is field commander Philippe Gerbier (Ventura,) who metes out punishment for such betrayals. It's grim and dangerous and morally ambivalent and no one has time to be heroic (though they are) because there's too much at stake. You can't look away even if you want to. Melville himself was a member of the Resistance. French with subtitles. **140m/C DVD.** *FR IT* Lino Ventura, Simone Signoret, Paul Meurisse, Jean-Pierre Cassel, Claude Mann, Paul Crauchet, Christian Barbier, Alain Libolt, Jean-Marie Robain; ***D:*** Jean-Pierre Melville; ***W:*** Jean-Pierre Melville; ***C:*** Pierre Lhomme; ***M:*** Eric Demarsen.

Arnold 1/2 1973 (PG) Outrageous black comedy involving a woman who marries a cadaver to gain his large inheritance. Lots of bizarre and creative deaths in this horror spoof. Unusual wedding scene is a must-see. **96m/C VHS.** Stella Stevens, Roddy McDowall, Elsa Lanchester, Victor Buono, Bernard Fox, Farley Granger, Shani Wallis, Jamie Farr, Patric Knowles, John McGiver, Norman Stuart; ***D:*** Georg Fenady; ***W:*** Jameson Brewer, John Fenton Murray; ***C:*** William B. Jurgensen; ***M:*** George Duning.

Around the Bend 2004 (R) Dying patriarch Henry Lair (Caine) is being cared for by his grandson Jason (Lucas), who is also looking after his own young son, Zach (Bobo). Jason's black sheep father, Turner (Walken), abandoned him to Henry's care when he was a child. But Turner suddenly shows up, just in time to fulfill Henry's last request—he wants to be buried in a bizarre ritual that will mean a generational road trip from L.A. to Albuquerque. So does some male bonding occur? Boy, howdy, you betcha, but with Walken around the trip is never completely mundane. Feature debut of director/writer Roberts. **83m/C DVD.** *US* Christopher Walken, Josh(ua) Lucas, Michael Caine, Glenne Headly, Jonah Bobo; ***D:*** Jordan Roberts; ***W:*** Jordan Roberts; ***C:*** Michael Grady; ***M:*** David Baerwald.

Around the Fire 1998 (R) At boarding school, Simon (Sawa) tries to escape his emotional troubles by getting in with the school druggies, including Andrew (Mabius). He also begins a foray into the neo-hippie world of the Grateful Dead, where he falls for the free-spirited Jennifer (Reid). Simon does wind up in rehab, looking back on his life. **107m/C VHS, DVD.** Devon Sawa, Eric Mabius, Bill Smitrovich, Tara Reid, Charlaine Woodard, Michael McKeever; ***D:*** John Jacobsen; ***W:*** John Comerford, Tommy Rosen; ***M:*** B.C. Smith. **VIDEO**

Around the World 1/2 1943 Kyser leads a USO-like tour to entertain troops. Interesting only in a historical sense. ♫ Doodle-Ee-Doo; He's Got a Secret Weapon; Candlelight and Wine; Great News in the Making; They Chopped Down the Old Apple Tree; A Moke from Shamokin. **80m/B VHS.** Kay Kyser, Ish Kabibble, Mischa Auer, Joan Davis, Marcy McGuire; ***D:*** Allan Dwan.

Around the World in 80 Days 1956 (G) Niven is the unflappable Victorian Englishman who wagers that he can circumnavigate the earth in four-score days. With his faithful manservant Cantinflas they set off on a spectacular journey. A perpetual favorite providing ample entertainment. Star-gazers will particularly enjoy the more than 40 cameo appearances by many of Hollywood's biggest names. Adapted from the novel by Jules Verne. **178m/C VHS, DVD.** David Niven, Shirley MacLaine, Cantinflas, Robert Newton, Charles Boyer, Joe E. Brown, Martine Carol, John Carradine, Charles Coburn, Ronald Colman; ***Cameos:*** Melville Cooper, Noel Coward, Andy Devine, Reginald Denny, Fernandel, Marlene Dietrich, Hermione Gingold, Cedric Hardwicke, Trevor Howard, Glynis Johns, Buster Keaton, Evelyn Keyes, Peter Lorre, John Gielgud, Victor McLaglen, John Mills, Robert Morley, Jack Oakie, George Raft, Cesar Romero, Gilbert Roland, Red Skelton, Frank Sinatra, Beatrice Lillie, Ava Gardner; ***D:*** Michael Anderson Sr.; ***W:*** James Poe, John Farrow, S.J. Perelman; ***C:*** Lionel Lindon; ***M:*** Victor Young. Oscars '56: Adapt. Screenplay, Color Cinematog., Film Editing, Picture, Orig. Dramatic Score; Golden Globes '57: Actor—

Mus./Comedy (Cantinflas), Film—Drama; N.Y. Film Critics '56: Film, Screenplay.

Around the World in 80 Days 🦴🦴 1/2 **1989** TV adaptation of the Jules Verne adventure novel that finds Victorian gentleman Phineas Fogg (Brosnan) wagering that he can circle the globe in 80 days. He's pursued by private detective Fix (Ustinov), who suspects him of a daring bank robbery, and faces many trials and much excitement along the way. On two cassettes. **270m/C VHS, DVD.** Pierce Brosnan, Peter Ustinov, Eric Idle, Arielle Dombasle, Henry Gibson, John Hillerman, Jack Klugman, Christopher Lee, Patrick Macnee, Roddy McDowall, Darren McGavin, John Mills, Robert Morley, Lee Remick, Pernell Roberts, James B. Sikking, Jill St. John, Robert Wagner, Julia Nickson-Soul; ***D:*** Buzz Kulik.

Around the World in 80 Days 🦴🦴 **2004 (PG)** Phileas Fogg (Coogan) bets the London science community that he can circumnavigate the earth in 80 days, aided by assistant Passpartout (Chan). Surprising no one, a few people don't want him to make it. This time around Passpartout steals the show as a martial arts expert trying to return a stolen sacred heirloom to his village in China. In fact, Fogg's unworldly inventor seems at times like the sidekick. While departing wildly from the source material, it's lightweight fun better suited to the lowered expectations of a rental. As in the previous version, entertaining cameos add to the humor. Schwarzenegger is especially silly as an over-the-top lusty Turkish prince. **125m/C DVD.** *GB IR GE* Steve Coogan, Jackie Chan, Cecile de France, Jim Broadbent, Kathy Bates, Arnold Schwarzenegger, John Cleese, Ian McNeice, Luke Wilson, Owen Wilson, Ewen Bremner, Rob Schneider, Mark Addy, Sammo Hung, Roger Hammond, David Ryall, Macy Gray, Daniel Wu, Will Forte, Robert Fyfe, Karen Joy Morris, Richard Branson; ***D:*** Frank Coraci; ***W:*** David Benullo, David Titcher, David Goldstein; ***C:*** Phil Meheux; ***M:*** Trevor Jones.

Around the World in 80 Ways 🦴🦴 1/2 **1986 (R)** Sometimes clever, sometimes crude Australian comedy about an aging man rescued from a nursing home and taken on a phony trip around the world by his sons. Odd, but genuinely funny at times. **90m/C VHS.** *AU* Philip Quast, Alan Penney, Diana Davidson, Kelly Dingwall, Gosia Dobrowolska; ***D:*** Stephen MacLean; ***W:*** Stephen MacLean, Paul Leadon; ***M:*** Chris Neal.

Around the World in a Daze 🦴🦴 1/2 *The Three Stooges Go Around the World in a Daze* **1963** The Stooges are servants for Phileas Fogg's great-grandson, who has decided to repeat his ancestor's famous feat. Mayhem ensues when the three help out in their usual efficient, competent way. **93m/B VHS, DVD.** Moe Howard, Larry Fine, Joe DeRita, Jay Sheffield; ***D:*** Norman Maurer.

Around the World Under the Sea 🦴🦴 **1965** Bunch of men and one woman scientist plunge under the ocean in an experiment to predict earthquakes. They plant earthquake detectors along the ocean floor and discover the causes of tidal waves. They have men-women battles. They see big sea critters. **111m/C VHS.** David McCallum, Shirley Eaton, Gary Merrill, Keenan Wynn, Brian Kelly, Lloyd Bridges; ***D:*** Andrew Marton.

Aroused 🦴 **1966** Hollister is an apparently dedicated policeman who commits a number of blunders in the pursuit of a serial killer, including leaving his wife with the sociopath while he cavorts with the prostitute assigned to his protection. Director Holden's psychothriller was gorily ahead of its time. Includes heart-stopping castration sequence. **78m/B VHS, DVD.** Janine Lenon, Steve Hollister, Fleurette Carter, Joanna Mills, Tony Palladino, Ted Gelanza; ***D:*** Anton Holden.

The Arousers 🦴🦴 1/2 *Sweet Kill; A Kiss from Eddie* **1970 (R)** Cult item starring hunk Hunter as a handsome California psycho. Tab travels the coast searching for a woman he is able to make love to; those who fail to arouse him come to tragic, climactic ends. Definitely underground and moderately interesting. **85m/C VHS.** Tab Hunter, Nadyne Turney, Roberta Collins, Isabel Jewell, John Aprea, Angel Fox, Sandy Kenyon, Cherie Latimer; ***D:*** Curtis Hanson; ***W:*** Curtis Hanson; ***C:*** Daniel Lacambre; ***M:*** Charles Bernstein.

The Arrangement 🦴 1/2 **1969 (R)** Veteran advertising executive Douglas attempts suicide and then sets out to search for the meaning of life. Along the way he attempts to patch up his "arrangements" with his wife, his mistress and his father. Forced, slow, and self-conscious, though well acted. Adapted by Kazan from the director's own novel. **126m/C VHS, DVD.** Kirk Douglas, Faye Dunaway, Deborah Kerr, Richard Boone, Hume Cronyn; ***D:*** Elia Kazan; ***W:*** Elia Kazan; ***C:*** Robert L. Surtees; ***M:*** David Amram.

The Arrangement 🦴🦴🦴 **1999 (R)** Jake (Keskhemnu) lives in Los Angeles. Luhann (James) is in New York. They're engaged until he admits to a one-night stand and invites her to experiment herself before the wedding. When she accepts, he is not pleased. Low-budget independent production is a bit obvious and slow moving in some respects, much more sophisticated in others. The details of everyday life are well observed and ring true. Editing is zippy and the characters are treated seriously. **90m/C DVD.** Billie James, Keskhemnu; ***D:*** H.H. Cooper; ***W:*** H.H. Cooper; ***C:*** Douglas W. Shannon; ***M:*** Michael Bearden.

Arrest Bulldog Drummond 🦴🦴 **1938** Captain Drummond is accused of killing the inventor of a futuristic detonator machine and must track down the real killers. Part of the "Bulldog Drummond" series. **57m/B VHS, DVD.** John Howard, Heather Angel, George Zucco, H.B. Warner, E.E. Clive, Reginald Denny, John Sutton; ***D:*** James Hogan.

The Arrival 🦴 **1990 (R)** An never-seen alien parasite turns an old man into a vampiric young stud after female blood. Plot and characterizations never do arrive. Horror director Stuart Gordon cameos as a hairy biker. **107m/C VHS.** John Saxon, Joseph Culp, Robert Sampson, Michael J. Pollard; ***Cameos:*** David Schmoeller; ***D:*** David Schmoeller; ***W:*** David Schmoeller; ***M:*** Richard Band.

The Arrival 🦴🦴 1/2 *Shockwave* **1996 (PG-13)** Radio astronomer Zane (Sheen) picks up a message from deep space and discovers a planned alien invasion. When he brings evidence of such to his boss Gordian (Silver) he finds himself on the run from both government operatives and morphing aliens. Starts off slow, but an intelligent script and premise makes this a grade above cheesy. The aliens, with their kooky flaps of skin and back bending knees, are fun to watch. Directorial debut for Twohy. **109m/C VHS, DVD.** Charlie Sheen, Ron Silver, Lindsay Crouse, Teri Polo; ***D:*** David N. Twohy; ***W:*** David N. Twohy; ***C:*** Hiro Narita; ***M:*** Arthur Kempel.

The Arrival 2 🦴🦴 *The Second Arrival* **1998 (R)** Computer programmer Muldoon receives information describing an extraterrestrial conspiracy against earth. Dull story, dull cast. **101m/C VHS, DVD.** Patrick Muldoon, Michael Sarrazin, Jane Sibbett; ***D:*** Kevin S. Tenney; ***W:*** Mark David Perry; ***C:*** Bruno Philip; ***M:*** Ned Bouhalassa. **VIDEO**

Arrivederci, Baby! 🦴 **1966** An unfunny sex comedy with Curtis as a modern Bluebeard who weds rich women and kills them for their money. His last mate plans to turn the tables and kill him first. **100m/C VHS.** Tony Curtis, Rosanna Schiaffino, Lionel Jeffries, Zsa Zsa Gabor, Nancy Kwan, Fenella Fielding, Anna Quayle, Warren Mitchell, Mischa Auer; ***D:*** Ken Hughes; ***W:*** Ken Hughes.

Arrowhead 🦴🦴 1/2 **1953** A long-running argument between a tough Cavalry scout and an Apache chief pits the cowboys against the Indians in this western fantasy. The personal battles that become all-out wars turn back to fist-fights before the matter is finally settled. **105m/C VHS, DVD.** Charlton Heston, Jack Palance, Katy Jurado, Brian Keith, Milburn Stone; ***D:*** Charles Marquis Warren; ***C:*** Ray Rennahan.

Arrowsmith 🦴🦴 1/2 **1932** A small-town medical researcher battles his conscience as he juggles his selfish and unselfish motivations for the work he does. He travels to the West Indies to confront the issues of his life and come to terms with himself once and for all. A talented cast takes their time. Based on the classic Sinclair Lewis novel. Two edited versions available (99 and 89 minutes), both of which delete much of Loy. **95m/B VHS, DVD.** Ronald Colman, Helen Hayes, Myrna Loy; ***D:*** John Ford.

Arsenal 🦴🦴🦴 **1929** Classic Russian propagandist drama about strikes affecting the Russian home front during WWI, marking Dovzhenko's first great achievement in the realm of Eisenstein and Pudovkin. Silent. **75m/B VHS, DVD.** *RU* Semyon Svashenko, Luciano Albertini; ***D:*** Alexander Dovzhenko; ***W:*** Alexander Dovzhenko; ***C:*** Daniil Demutsky.

The Arsenal Stadium Mystery 🦴🦴 1/2 **1939** Inspector Banks of Scotland Yard tracks down the killer of a football star in this clever but unassuming murder mystery. **85m/B VHS.** *GB* Leslie Banks, Greta Gynt, Ian MacLean, Liane Linden, Anthony Bushell, Esmond Knight; ***D:*** Thorold Dickinson.

Arsenic and Old Lace 🦴🦴🦴 1/2 **1944** Set-bound but energetic adaptation of the classic Joseph Kesselring play. Easy-going drama critic Mortimer Brewster (Grant) is caught in a sticky situation when he learns of his aunts' favorite pastime. Apparently the kind, sweet, lonely spinsters lure gentlemen to the house and serve them elderberry wine with a touch of arsenic, then they bury the bodies in the cellar—a cellar which also serves as the Panama Canal for Mortimer's cousin (who thinks he's Theodore Roosevelt). Massey, as Brewster cousin Jonathan, and Lorre, as his plastic surgeon, excel in their sinister roles. One of the best madcap comedies of all time—a must-see. Shot in 1941 and released a wee bit later. **118m/B VHS, DVD.** Cary Grant, Josephine Hull, Jean Adair, Raymond Massey, Jack Carson, Priscilla Lane, John Alexander, Edward Everett Horton, Peter Lorre, James Gleason, John Ridgely; ***D:*** Frank Capra; ***W:*** Julius J. Epstein, Philip G. Epstein; ***C:*** Sol Polito; ***M:*** Max Steiner.

Art for Teachers of Children 🦴🦴 **1995** Autobiographical account of 14-year-old Jennifer (McDonnell) who becomes a model for married photographer John (Hannah), who's also her boarding school dorm advisor. He's well-known for his nude portraits of young women as well as his affairs with his models and Jennifer's both confused and excited by her emerging sexuality as she and John become lovers. Remarkably detached considering the provocative subject matter. **82m/B VHS.** Caitlin Grace McDonnell, Duncan Hannah, Coles Burroughs, Bryan Keane; ***D:*** Jennifer Montgomery; ***W:*** Jennifer Montgomery; ***C:*** Jennifer Montgomery.

Art Heist 🦴🦴 1/2 **2005 (R)** The theft of a precious painting from a Barcelona art gallery causes art expert Sandra (Pompeo) to leave New York to work with Daniel (Folk), an old love interest, to investigate the crime. This doesn't sit well with her tough-guy ex-husband Bruce (Baldwin), an NYPD cop, who tracks Sandra down, only to find her in over her head with the menacing Russian mafia. **98m/C VHS, DVD.** *SP* Ellen Pompeo, William Baldwin, Abel Folk, Simon Andreu, Ed Lauter; ***W:*** Diane Fine, Evan Spiliotopolos; ***C:*** Jacques Haitkin. **VIDEO**

Art House 🦴 1/2 **1998 (R)** Ray (O'Donahue) and his irritating pal Weston (irritating Hardwick) aspire to be filmmakers, but the road to success is blocked by rocky relationships, money problems, and lack of talent. The comic elements are fitfully funny but the image is so rough that only the most dedicated fans of low-budget ($200,000 according to the director) independent productions will be willing to stick with it. Those hoping to see a lot of Internet babe Weber will be disappointed. **89m/C DVD.** Dan O'Donahue, Chris Hardwick, Luigi Amodeo, Rebecca McFarland, Adam Carolla, Cheryl Pollak, Amy Weber; ***D:*** Leigh Slawner; ***W:*** Dan O'Donahue, Leigh Slawner; ***C:*** Billy Beaird; ***M:*** Christopher Lennertz.

The Art of Crime 🦴🦴 1/2 **1975** A gypsy/detective is drawn into a homicide case when one of his fellow antique dealers is charged with murder. Maintains an atmospheric edge over others of the crime art genre. A pilot for a prospective TV series based on the novel "Gypsy in Amber." **72m/C VHS.** Ron Leibman, Jose Ferrer, David Hedison, Jill Clayburgh; ***D:*** Richard Irving; ***W:*** Bill Davidson, Martin Smith. **TV**

The Art of Dying 🦴🦴🦴 **1990** A loony videophile decides to start staging productions of his all-time favorite scenes. Trouble is, his idea of a fabulous film moment calls for lots of blood and bile as he lures teenage runaways to his casting couch. Director Hauser stars as the cop who's none too impressed with the cinematic remakes, while cult favorite Pollard is his partner. If you like a little atmosphere and psychological depth in your slashers, you'll find this to be the stuff that populates film noir nightmares. **90m/C VHS, DVD.** Wings Hauser, Michael J. Pollard, Sarah Douglas, Kathleen Kinmont, Sydney Lassick, Mitch Hara, Gary Werntz; ***D:*** Wings Hauser.

The Art of Murder 🦴🦴 **1999 (R)** Married Elizabeth (Pacula) has a wealthy hubby (Moriarty) and a younger lover (Kesnter) to keep her motor running. But then sleazy Willie (Onorati) threatens to show her husband dirty pictures of the affair and blackmail is just the beginning. **97m/C VHS, DVD.** Joanna Pacula, Michael Moriarty, Boyd Kestner, Peter Onorati; ***D:*** Ruben Preuss; ***W:*** Shawn Smith, Anthony Stark; ***C:*** John Tarver. **VIDEO**

The Art of Travel 🦴🦴 **2008 (R)** When Conner Layne (Masterson) finds his fiancee cheating, he dumps her at the altar and takes off for a solo Central American honeymoon. First he gets robbed, but then he's befriended by adventure junkies Darlene (Burns) and Christopher (Messner), who are planning to cross Darien Gap, 100 miles of roadless jungle separating Panama and Columbia. They invite Conner along and he's soon hooked on the travel and decides not to stop. **101m/C DVD.** Christopher K. Masterson, Brooke Burns, Johnny Messner, James Duval, Angelika Baran, Jake Muxworthy, Maria Conchita Alonso, Salim Ortiz; ***D:*** Thomas Whelan; ***W:*** Thomas Whelan, Brian LaBelle; ***C:*** Lawson Deming; ***M:*** Steve Bartek.

The Art of War 🦴 1/2 **2000 (R)** Disappointingly formulaic thriller has Snipes starring as top-secret U.N. operative Neil Shaw, who is framed for the assassination of a Chinese ambassador (Hong). Also involved is his boss, Eleanor Hooks (Archer), Chinese power broker David Chan (Tagawa), and interpreter Julia (Matiko), whom Shaw kidnaps to help him prove his innocence. Plot is both convoluted and obvious (you can pretty much guess what's coming) and you learn so little about the players that you won't be very interested in what happens to them. **117m/C VHS, DVD.** Wesley Snipes, Marie Matiko, Cary-Hiroyuki Tagawa, Anne Archer, Maury Chaykin, Michael Biehn, Donald Sutherland, Liliana Komorowska, James Hong; ***D:*** Christian Duguay; ***W:*** Wayne Beach, Simon Davis Barry; ***C:*** Pierre Gill; ***M:*** Normand Corbeil.

Art of War 2: The Betrayal 🦴 **2008 (R)** Dull plot isn't even redeemed by any good action and everyone looks bored. Neil Shaw (Snipes) is called out of retirement by his friend Garret (Munro), a senatorial candidate. Seems senators with oversight on defense spending are either being blackmailed or killed and Garret doesn't want to wind up a statistic. **103m/C DVD.** Wesley Snipes, Lochlyn Munro, Athena Karkanis, Winston Rekert, Clifford W. Stewart, Ryan McDonald; ***D:*** Josef Rusnak; ***W:*** Jason Bourque, Keith Shaw; ***C:*** Neil Cerrin; ***M:*** Peter Allen. **VIDEO**

The Art of War 3: Retribution 🦴 1/2 *Intervention* **2008 (R)** Agent Shaw is on a mission to prevent North Korean terrorists from obtaining a nuclear bomb. Framed for murder and hunted on the streets, Shaw has to stop the terrorists before they can detonate the bomb at a U.N. peace conference. **88m/C DVD.** Anthony Criss, Sung Hi Lee, Warren DeRosa; ***D:*** Gerry Lively; ***W:*** Joe Halpin; ***C:*** Suki Medencevic; ***M:*** James Bairian, Louis Castle. **VIDEO**

Art School Confidential 🦴🦴 **2006 (R)** Underdeveloped and frequently flat satire about the art world. Idealistic Jerome (Minghella) wants to be the next Picasso when he enters art school. He soon learns it's not about art, it's about hype and commerce. Generic character types include pretentious professor Sandiford (Malkovich), no-talent filmmaker Vince (Suplee), shallow-but-beautiful artists' model Audrey (Myles), drunken failed artist Jimmy (Broadbent), and Jerome's own cynical guide Bardo (Moore). Jerome becomes disillusioned and desperate, and not just because a serial killer is working the neighborhood. Clowes adapted from his comic strip. Buscemi is uncredited as trendy restaurant owner Broadway Bob. **102m/C DVD.** *US* Max Minghella, Sophia Myles, John Malkovich, Jim Broadbent, Matt Keeslar, Ethan Suplee, Anjelica Huston, Joel David Moore, Nick Swardson, Steve Buscemi; ***D:*** Terry Zwigoff; ***W:*** Daniel Clowes; ***C:*** Jamie Anderson; ***M:*** David Kitay.

Artemisia **1997 (R)** Artemisia (Cervi) is the teenaged daughter of well-known artist Orazio Gentileschi (Serrault), who encourages her artistic pursuits. He bullies the local art academy to admit Artemisia, a no-no in 17th-century Rome, and she even tries the forbidden territory of the male nude. Soon her artistic passion is matched by a sexual passion for fellow artist Agostino Tassi (Manojlovic), but this time her father isn't so understanding and Artemisia becomes the center of a rape trial. The real Artemisia is considered to be the first known female artist. French with subtitles. **95m/C VHS, DVD.** *FR* Valentina Cervi, Michel Serrault, Miki (Predrag) Manojlovic, Luca Zingaretti, Brigitte Catillon, Frederic Pierrot, Maurice Garrel, Yann Tregouet, Jacques Nolot; ***D:*** Agnes Merlet; ***W:*** Agnes Merlet; ***C:*** Benoit Delhomme; ***M:*** Krishna Levy.

Arthur **1981 (PG)** Spoiled, alcoholic billionaire Moore stands to lose everything he owns when he falls in love with a waitress. He must choose between wealth and a planned marriage, or poverty and love. Surprisingly funny, with an Oscar for Gielgud as Moore's valet, and great performance from Minnelli. Arguably the best role Moore's ever had, and he makes the most of it, taking the one-joke premise to a Oscar nomination. ♫ Arthur's Theme; Blue Moon; If You Knew Susie; Santa Claus Is Coming to Town. **97m/C VHS, DVD.** Dudley Moore, Liza Minnelli, John Gielgud, Geraldine Fitzgerald, Stephen Elliott, Jill Eikenberry, Lou Jacobi, Ted Ross, Barney Martin; ***D:*** Steve Gordon; ***W:*** Steve Gordon; ***C:*** Fred Schuler; ***M:*** Burt Bacharach, Peter Allen, Peter Allen. Oscars '81: Song ("Arthur's Theme"), Support. Actor (Gielgud); Golden Globes '82: Actor—Mus./Comedy (Moore), Film—Mus./Comedy, Song ("Arthur's Theme"), Support. Actor (Gielgud); L.A. Film Critics '81: Support. Actor (Gielgud); N.Y. Film Critics '81: Support. Actor (Gielgud); Writers Guild '81: Orig. Screenplay.

Arthur 2: On the Rocks **½ 1988 (PG)** When Arthur finally marries his sweetheart, it may not be "happily ever after" because the father of the girl he didn't marry is out for revenge. When Arthur discovers that he is suddenly penniless, a bit of laughter is the cure for the blues and also serves well when the liquor runs out. A disappointing sequel with few laughs. **113m/C VHS, DVD.** Dudley Moore, Liza Minnelli, John Gielgud, Geraldine Fitzgerald, Stephen Elliott, Ted Ross, Barney Martin, Jack Gilford; ***D:*** Bud Yorkin; ***W:*** Andy Breckman; ***C:*** Stephen Burum; ***M:*** Burt Bacharach. Golden Raspberries '87: Worst Actress (Minnelli).

Arthur and the Invisibles *Arthur et les Minimoys* **2006 (PG)** Maybe it makes sense to the French. Besson tackles kiddie fantasy in this mishmash combo of CGI and live-action. Arthur (Highmore) lives with his grandma (Farrow), who is about to lose their debt-ridden home. Arthur needs to follow clues left by grandpa to some rubies hidden in the land of the Minimoys, who look like fairies and happen to live in the backyard. A little hocus-pocus, and Arthur becomes mini, gets some help from the inhabitants, and goes after the gems, which are held by evil Maltazard (Bowie). Film's voices are frequently out of sync (it was dubbed from French) and since it's remarkably talky, this is a notable distraction (at least to adult eyes). **102m/C DVD.** *FR* Freddie Highmore, Mia Farrow, Adam LeFevre, Douglas Rand, Penny Balfour; ***D:*** Luc Besson; ***W:*** Luc Besson, Celine Garcia; ***C:*** Thierry Arbogast; ***M:*** Eric Serra; ***V:*** David Bowie, Madonna, Jimmy Fallon, Robert De Niro, Anthony Anderson, Chazz Palminteri, Snoop Dogg, Jason Bateman, Harvey Keitel, Emilio Estevez.

Arthur's Hallowed Ground **1984** A cricket field caretaker battles the board of directors over the fate of his favorite plot of sod. **75m/C VHS.** Jimmy Jewel, Jean Boht, Michael Elphick; ***D:*** Frederick A. (Freddie) Young.

Arthur's Quest **½ 1999 (PG)** In this switcheroo on Mark Twain's "A Connecticut Yankee in King Arthur's Court" a five-year-old Arthur is transported by Merlin from his medieval home to the modern age because the wizard fears for the boy's safety. Merlin doesn't reappear for 10 years, so Arthur has become a typical American teen. Now, how do you convince a 15-year-old that he's really a medieval monarch who must return to save Camelot? **91m/C VHS, DVD.** Kevin Elston, Zach Galligan, Arye Gross, Clint Howard, Brion James, Katie Johnston, Neil Mandt; ***D:*** Neil Mandt. **VIDEO**

Article 99 **1992 (R)** Doctors in a Kansas City Veteran's Administration hospital try to heal patients while putting up with bureaucratic red tape and a stingy administrator. When rogue physician Sturgess (Liotta) is dismissed, the patients hold a siege. Sort of son of "M.A.S.H." (Big Daddy Sutherland did Hawkeye) that gets its title from a fictional rule that says veterans can be treated only for conditions related to military service. Erstwhile cast labors to combine comedic and dramatic intentions of script. **100m/C VHS, DVD.** Ray Liotta, Kiefer Sutherland, Forest Whitaker, Lea Thompson, John C. McGinley, John Mahoney, Keith David, Kathy Baker, Eli Wallach, Noble Willingham, Julie Bovasso, Troy Evans, Lynne Thigpen, Jeffrey Tambor, Rutanya Alda; ***D:*** Howard Deutch; ***W:*** Ron Cutler; ***C:*** Rick Bota; ***M:*** Danny Elfman.

Artifacts *Artefacts* **2008 (R)** A young blonde has just broken up with her boyfriend to devote herself to her work. Then all her friends get murdered by their own look-alikes, and the boyfriend suddenly doesn't look so bad. Oh, and they both have the same weird chest implant that all their dead friends have. Is it the aliens? Is it the government? Will the boyfriend get wise and ditch her when he realizes he's being used as a meat shield? **75m/C DVD.** Mary Stockley, Cecile Boland, Max Digby, Jason Morell, Felix Scott, Martin Swabey, Veronique Van de Ven; ***D:*** Giles Daoust, Emmanuel Jespers; ***W:*** Giles Daoust, Emmanuel Jespers; ***C:*** Bernard Vervoort; ***M:*** Ernst Meinrath. **VIDEO**

Artists and Models **½ 1955** Martin is a struggling comic book artist and Lewis his idiot roommate. The pair become mixed up in both romance and intrigue when Lewis begins talking in his sleep about spys and such. One of the duo's more pleasant cinematic outings. ♫ Inamorata; Lucky Song; You Look So Familiar; Why You Pretend. **109m/C VHS.** Dean Martin, Jerry Lewis, Shirley MacLaine, Dorothy Malone, Eddie Mayehoff, Eva Gabor, Anita Ekberg, George Winslow, Jack Elam, Herbert Rudley, Nick Castle; ***D:*** Frank Tashlin; ***W:*** Frank Tashlin, Hal Kanter, Herbert Baker; ***C:*** Daniel F. Fapp.

As Good as Dead **½ 1995 (PG-13)** A young woman allows her sick friend to assume her identity but when her friend is murdered, she realizes the killer was really after her. **88m/C VHS.** Crystal Bernard, Traci Lords, Judge Reinhold; ***D:*** Larry Cohen; ***W:*** Larry Cohen.

As Good As It Gets *Old Friends* **1997 (PG-13)** Entertaining and enjoyable outing from Brooks racked up an impressive list of Oscar noms (including Best Picture). Obsessive-compulsive romance novelist Melvin Udall (Nicholson) is also the meanest guy in New York, liked by nobody and hating all. The only exception is single-mother/waitress Carol (Hunt), who puts up with his annoying habits at the local restaurant where he dines. Forced to look after gay neighbor Kinnear's fussy-but-cute dog, Udall falls into an improbable quest for love, friendship, and a life as "normal as it gets" in this sort of extended-sitcom universe. Snappy dialogue by Brooks and co-writer Andrus, and an easy-going non-stereotypical performance by Kinnear are highlights, almost overshadowing both Hunt's Jodie Foster-like portrayal, and Nicholson's typical but delightful role (both of which won Oscars). **130m/C VHS, DVD.** Jack Nicholson, Helen Hunt, Greg Kinnear, Cuba Gooding Jr., Skeet Ulrich, Shirley Knight, Yeardley Smith, Lupe Ontiveros, Bibi Osterwald, Brian Doyle-Murray, Randall Batinkoff, Shane Black, Missi Pyle, Tara Subkoff, Danielle Brisebois, Harold Ramis, Jimmy Workman; ***Cameos:*** Lawrence Kasdan, Todd Solondz, Tom McGowan; ***D:*** James L. Brooks; ***W:*** Mark Andrus, James L. Brooks; ***C:*** John Bailey; ***M:*** Hans Zimmer. Oscars '97: Actor (Nicholson), Actress (Hunt); Golden Globes '98: Actor—Mus./Comedy (Nicholson), Actress—Mus./Comedy (Hunt), Film—Mus./Comedy; Natl. Bd. of Review '97: Actor (Nicholson), Support. Actor (Kinnear); Screen Actors Guild '97: Actor (Nicholson), Actress (Hunt); Writers Guild '97: Orig. Screenplay; Broadcast Film Critics '97: Actor (Nicholson).

As If It Were Raining **1963** Constantine gets involved in an embezzlement scheme in Spain in this espionage thriller. **85m/C VHS.** *FR* Eddie Constantine, Henri Cogan, Elisa Montes, Jose Nieto, Silvia Solar; ***D:*** Jose Monter.

As Is **½ 1985** Two gay New Yorkers deal with a troubled romance and AIDS. Adapted from the William M. Hoffman play. **86m/C VHS.** Jonathan Hadary, Robert Carradine; ***D:*** Michael Lindsay-Hogg. **CABLE**

As Summers Die **1986** Louisiana attorney Glenn fights in the late 1950s to protect the rights of a black family, against the wishes of a powerful local clan. Glenn finds support in surprising places, though. From Winston Groom's acclaimed novel. **100m/C VHS.** Scott Glenn, Jamie Lee Curtis, Penny Fuller, Bette Davis, John Randolph, Beah Richards, Ron O'Neal, John McIntire; ***D:*** Jean-Claude Tramont. **CABLE**

As Tears Go By *Wong gok ka moon; Carmen of the Streets; Wang jiao ka men* **1988** A young gangster is visited by his pretty young cousin from the country because she needs medical treatment for her lung problems. He begins to fall for her but this is complicated by his unstable friend who has a habit of angering mob bosses. Soon he finds himself roped into a scheme to assassinate a witness before he can testify, in order to apologize for his friends' mistakes. **102m/C DVD.** *HK* Andy Lau, Maggie Cheung, Jacky Cheung; ***D:*** Kar-Wai Wong; ***W:*** Kar-Wai Wong; ***C:*** Wai Keung (Andrew) Lau; ***M:*** Teddy Robin Kwan, Ting Yat Chung.

As You Desire Me **1932** Garbo plays an amnesia victim who returns to a husband she doesn't even remember after an abusive relationship with a novelist. An interesting, if not down-right bizarre movie, due to the pairing of the great Garbo and the intriguing von Stroheim. An adaption of Luigi Pirandello's play. **71m/B VHS.** Greta Garbo, Melvyn Douglas, Erich von Stroheim, Owen Moore, Hedda Hopper; ***D:*** George Fitzmaurice.

As You Like It **½ 1936** A Duke's banished daughter poses as a man to win the attentions of one of her father's attendants in this highly stylized Shakespearean comedy adapted by J.M. Barrie and Robert Cullen. Early Shakespearean Olivier. **96m/B VHS, DVD.** *GB* Elisabeth Bergner, Laurence Olivier, Henry Ainley, Felix Aylmer; ***D:*** Paul Czinner; ***W:*** J.M. Barrie, Robert Cullen; ***C:*** Jack Cardiff, Harold Rosson; ***M:*** William Walton.

As You Like It **½ 2006 (PG)** Branagh sets this version of Shakespeare's romantic fantasy in 18th-century Japan with a group of Europeans who live in a trade colony. Because of a family conflict, Rosalind (Howard) and her entourage are forced to flee into the enchanted forest of Arden. Disguising herself (fetchingly unconvincingly) as a boy, Rosalind then proceeds to confuse the heck out of would-be love interest Orlando (Oyelowo). Kline is along as the melancholy Jacques with the "all the world's a stage" speech. **135m/C DVD.** Bryce Dallas Howard, David Oyelowo, Kevin Kline, Alfred Molina, Adrian Lester, Brian Blessed, Janet McTeer, Romola Garia, Jade Jefferies; ***D:*** Kenneth Branagh; ***W:*** Kenneth Branagh; ***C:*** Roger Lanser; ***M:*** Patrick Doyle. **CABLE**

As You Were **1951** A girl with a photographic memory enlists in the Army, becoming both a nuisance and comedic victim to her sergeant. **57m/B VHS.** Joseph (Joe) Sawyer, William Tracy, Sondra Rogers, Joan Vohs, Russell Hicks, John Ridgely; ***D:*** Bernard Girard; ***W:*** Edward E. Seabrook.

As Young As You Feel **1951** A 65-year-old man is forced to retire from his job. He poses as the head of the conglomerate and convinces them to repeal their retirement policy. He then gains national publicity when he makes a speech about the dignity of man. Watch for Monroe as the boss's secretary. Fine comic performances enhance the script; based on a story by Chayefsky. **77m/C VHS, DVD.** Monty Woolley, Thelma Ritter, David Wayne, Jean Peters, Constance Bennett, Marilyn Monroe, Allyn Joslyn, Albert Dekker, Clinton Sundberg, Minor Watson; ***D:*** Harmon Jones; ***W:*** Paddy Chayefsky.

The Ascent *Voskhozhdeniye* **1976** During WWII, two Soviet partisans leave their comrades in order to obtain supplies from a nearby farm. Only the Germans have gotten there first, forcing the Soviets deeper into occupied territory, which leads to their eventual capture and interrogation. Russian with subtitles. **105m/B VHS.** *RU* Boris Plotnikov, Vladimir Gostyukhin; ***D:*** Larisa Shepitko; ***W:*** Larisa Shepitko, Yuri Klepikov; ***C:*** Pavel Lebeshev, Vladimir Chukhnov; ***M:*** Alfred Schnittke.

The Ascent **½ 1994 (PG)** Based on the true story of Franco (Spano), a WWII Italian POW who's held in a camp in Africa. The prisoners enjoy making fun of the camp commander (Cross), who consistently fails at his attempts to climb the 15,500 peak of Mt. Kenya. Meanwhile, Franco decides to escape and climb the mountain himself—with the commander right behind. Beware if you suffer from vertigo. **96m/C VHS.** Vincent Spano, Ben Cross, Tony LoBianco, Rachel Ward; ***D:*** Donald Shebib; ***C:*** David Connell.

Ash Wednesday **1973 (R)** Taylor endures the pain of cosmetic surgery in an effort to rescue her floundering union with Fonda. Another undistinguished performance by Liz. Fonda is especially slimy as the philandering husband, but only appears in the latter stages of the film. **99m/C VHS.** Elizabeth Taylor, Henry Fonda, Helmut Berger, Keith Baxter, Margaret Blye, Maurice Teynac, Monique Van Vooren; ***D:*** Larry Peerce; ***M:*** Maurice Jarre.

Ash Wednesday **2002 (R)** On Ash Wednesday, 1983, ex-Hell's Kitchen tough Francis Sullivan (Burns) is working in his bar when his younger brother Sean (Wood) suddenly turns up. Three years ago to the day, Sean killed some thugs after his bro and went into exile, allowing everyone to think he was dead, including his wife Grace (Dawson). In the intervening time, Grace and Francis have become more than just in-laws. Oh, and gangster Moran (Platt) still wants revenge on Sean for killing his goons. The penance references are all too obvious and Wood's an odd casting choice since he looks too young and innocent for his role. **98m/C VHS, DVD.** Edward Burns, Elijah Wood, Rosario Dawson, Oliver Platt, Pat McNamara, James Handy, Michael Mulheren, Malachy McCourt; ***D:*** Edward Burns; ***W:*** Edward Burns; ***C:*** Russell Fine; ***M:*** David Shire.

Ashanti, Land of No Mercy *Ashanti* **1979** Caine of the week movie with Michael portraying a doctor acting as a missionary in South Africa who finds himself alone in a battle to rescue his wife from a band of slave traders. The chase spans many Middle Eastern countries and begins to look bleak for our man. Talented cast and promising plot are undone by slow pace. Based on the novel "Ebano" by Alberto Vasquez-Figueroa. **117m/C VHS, DVD.** Michael Caine, Omar Sharif, Peter Ustinov, Rex Harrison, William Holden, Beverly Johnson; ***D:*** Richard Fleischer.

Ashes and Diamonds **½** *Popiol i Diament* **1958** In the closing days of WWII, young Polish resistance fighter Maciek (Cybulski) is sent to a small town to assassinate a Communist Party official. Waiting around in a hotel, Maciek romances the beautiful barmaid, Krystyna (Krzysewska), and questions the meaning of struggle. A seminal Eastern European masterpiece that defined a generation of pre-solidarity Poles. The last installment of the trilogy that includes "A Generation" and "Kanal" and based on a novel by Jerzy Andrzewski. Polish with subtitles. **105m/B VHS, DVD.** *PL* Zbigniew Cybulski, Eva Krzyzewska, Adam Pawlikowski, Bogumil Kobiela, Waclaw Zastrzezynski; ***D:*** Andrzej Wajda; ***W:*** Andrzej Wajda, Jerzy Andrzejewski; ***C:*** Jerzy Wojcik; ***M:*** Jan Krenz, Filip Nowak.

Ashes and Embers 1982 A black Vietnam vet in Los Angeles has trouble fitting into society, eventually running afoul of the police. Ethiopian-born director Gerima endows vital subject matter with a properly alienated mood. **120m/C VHS.** John Anderson, Evelyn Blackwell; ***D:*** Haile Gerima.

Ashes of Time *Dung che sai duk* **1994** Mystical, brooding, and sumptiously lensed martial arts epic was filmed in mainland China, with respect paid to Sergio Leone. A swordsman, played by Tony Leung, is going blind and wants to see his wife one last time before the lights go out completely. Another, played by the other Tony Leung, possesses a magic wine that allows him to forget his haunted past. The two swordsmen are hired to kill and protect, respectively, the same person. The plot simmers and occasionally explodes into chaotic action peppered with sparkling geysers and such. **95m/C DVD.** *CH* Tony Leung Chiu-Wai, Tony Leung Ka-Fai, Brigitte Lin, Jacky Cheung, Leslie Cheung, Maggie Cheung, Carina Lau; ***D:*** Wong Kar-Wai; ***W:*** Wong Kar-Wai; ***C:*** Christopher Doyle; ***M:*** Frankie Chan.

Ashes of Time Redux **2008 (R)** Hong Kong director Wong was never satisfied with his 1994 wuxia epic, feeling he didn't do his vision justice (though it originally took two years to film). Over the years the movie was subjected to various bootleg versions and the original negative was disintegrating, so Wong spent five years reassembling, restoring, color-correcting, and rescoring before releasing his updated cut. Not that the dense narrative is any easier to follow (though the subtitles are good). Set over five seasons, Ouyang (Cheung), disappointed that his true love married his brother, moves to the desert and becomes a middleman for those who want to hire a swordsman to settle a wrong. Chinese with subtitles. **93m/C DVD.** *HK* Leslie Cheung, Maggie Cheung, Brigitte Lin, Carina Lau, Tony Leung Ka-Fai, Jacky Cheung, Tony Leung Chiu-Wai; ***D:*** Wong Kar-Wai; ***W:*** Wong Kar-Wai; ***C:*** Christopher Doyle; ***M:*** Wu Tong.

Ashik Kerib *The Lovelorn Minstrel; The Hoary Legends of the Caucasus* **1988** Ashik Kerib is a wandering minstrel who is rejected by a rich merchant as his daughter's suitor. He then journeys for 1,000 days trying to earn enough money to marry his beloved. Along the way he's imprisoned by an evil sultan and rides a flying horse, among other adventures. Wonderful use of exotic makeup and costumes highlight this Arabian Nights tale. Adapted from a story by Mikhail Lermontov. Paradjanov's last film. In Russian with English subtitles. **75m/C VHS, DVD.** *RU* Yiur Mgoyan, Veronkia Metonidze, Levan Natroshvili, Sofiko Chiaureli; ***D:*** Dodo Abashidze, Sergei Paradjanov; ***W:*** Giya Badridze; ***M:*** Djavashir Kuliev.

Asian Stories 1/2 *Asian Stories: Book 3* **2006** Not particularly interesting story about a man who thinks he wants to die. Chinese-American Jim (Lee) has been dumped by his fiancee two weeks before their Valentine's Day wedding. Depressed and in debt, Jim asks his hitman best friend Alex (Kishita) to kill him and they decide to head off to a mountain cabin for some quiet contemplation under the condition that the deed must be done before the dreaded lovers' holiday. Think Jim will change his mind? **98m/C DVD.** James Kyson Lee, Kirt Kishita, Kathy Uyen; ***D:*** Ron Oda, Kris Chin; ***W:*** Ron Oda; ***C:*** Jonathan Hall; ***M:*** Thomas' Apartment.

Ask Any Girl 1/2 **1959** Lighthearted fluff about a small-town girl who moves to Manhattan. MacLaine plays the bright Meg who gets a job at an ad agency and decides to set her sights on marrying her boss (Young). She asks his older brother's (Niven) help in her quest and the inevitable happens. **101m/C VHS.** Shirley MacLaine, David Niven, Gig Young, Rod Taylor, Jim Backus, Claire Kelly, Elisabeth Fraser; ***D:*** Charles Walters. British Acad. '59: Actress (MacLaine).

Ask the Dust **2006 (R)** Chasing an aspiring novelist's dream in 1930s Los Angeles, Arturo Bandini (Farrell)—the son of Italian immigrants but desperate to leave his heritage behind—collides into a turbulent love/hate affair with Camilla (Hayek), a Latina waitress with her own agenda to quickly ascend the social ladder. When Arturo comes into money to write his book, their relationship oddly cools off, while later he struggles with what success has cost him. Taken from John Fantes' 1939 novel of the same name and highlighted by brilliant desert scenery shot in South Africa. **117m/C DVD.** *US* Colin Farrell, Salma Hayek, Donald Sutherland, Eileen Atkins, Idina Menzel, Justin Kirk, Jeremy Crutchley, Richard Schickel; ***D:*** Robert Towne; ***W:*** Robert Towne; ***C:*** Caleb Deschanel; ***M:*** Ramin Djawadi, Hector Pereira.

Aspen Extreme **1993 (PG-13)** Former Aspen ski instructor writes and directs a movie on (what else?) ski instructors in (where?) Aspen! Long on ski shots and short on plot, this movie never leaves the bunny hill. Two Detroiters leave Motown for Snowtown to pursue a life on the slopes. T.J (Gross) soon has his hands full with two beautiful women (Polo and Hughes) who encourage his dream of becoming a writer. His friend Dexter (Berg), however, acquires a few bad habits, and the whole movie just goes downhill from there. **128m/C VHS, DVD.** Paul Gross, Peter Berg, Finola Hughes, Teri Polo, Martin Kemp, Nicolette Scorsese, William Russ, Will MacMillan; ***D:*** Patrick Hasburgh; ***W:*** Patrick Hasburgh; ***C:*** Steven Fierberg; ***M:*** Michael Convertino.

The Asphalt Jungle **1950** An aging criminal emerges from his forced retirement (prison) and assembles a gang for one final heist. A very realistic story line and a superb cast make this one of the best crime films ever made. Highly acclaimed. **112m/B VHS, DVD.** Sterling Hayden, Louis Calhern, Jean Hagen, James Whitmore, Sam Jaffe, John McIntire, Marc Lawrence, Barry Kelley, Anthony Caruso, Teresa Celli, Marilyn Monroe; ***D:*** John Huston; ***W:*** W.R. Burnett, Ben Maddow; ***M:*** Miklos Rozsa. Natl. Bd. of Review '50: Director (Huston), Natl. Film Reg. '08;; Venice Film Fest. '50: Actor (Hayden).

The Asphyx *Spirit of the Dead* **1972 (PG)** Nineteenth century doctor Stephens is studying death when he discovers The Asphyx, an aura that surrounds a person just before they die. Stephens delves deeper into his research and finds the keys to immortality. However, his irresponsibility in unleashing the obscure supernatural power on the world brings a swarm of unforeseen and irreversible troubles. High-class sci fi. **98m/C VHS, DVD.** *GB* Robert Stephens, Robert Powell, Jane Lapotaire, Alex Scott, Ralph Arliss, Fiona Walker, John Lawrence, Paul Bacon, Terry Scully; ***D:*** Peter Newbrook; ***W:*** Brian Comfort; ***C:*** Frederick A. (Freddie) Young; ***M:*** Bill McGuffie.

Assassin **1986 (PG-13)** Made for TV drama about a mad scientist who creates a bionic killer for a bizarre plot to take over the world. He programs the cyborg to assassinate the President and other key people to help carry out his plan. A retired CIA operative emerges to stop the scientist by trying to destroy the robot. **94m/C VHS, DVD.** Robert Conrad, Karen Austin, Richard Young, Jonathan Banks, Robert Webber; ***D:*** Sandor Stern; ***W:*** Sandor Stern; ***C:*** Chuck (Charles G.) Arnold; ***M:*** Anthony Guefen. **TV**

Assassin **1989 (R)** Fairly lame thriller about a CIA agent protecting a Senator who falls under suspicion when his charge is shot by an assassin. In investigating the killing the agent discovers the usual governmental conspiracy. **92m/C VHS.** Steve Railsback, Nicholas Guest, Xander Berkeley, Elpidia Carrillo; ***D:*** Jon Hess.

Assassin of Youth 1/2 **1935** Girl is introduced to marijuana and soon becomes involved in "the thrills of wild parties," and the horrors of the "killer weed." Camp diversion. **70m/B VHS, DVD.** Luana Walters, Arthur Gardner, Earl Dwire, Fern Emmett, Dorothy Short; ***D:*** Elmer Clifton.

Assassination **1987 (R)** A serious threat has been made to First Lady Ireland and no one is taking it lightly. Secret Service agent Bronson has been called as Ireland's personal bodyguard and suddenly they are both the target of terrorist attacks. Strangely though, the attacks seem to be directed from inside the White House. Bronson as you've seen him many times before. **93m/C VHS, DVD.** Charles Bronson, Jill Ireland, Stephen Elliott, Michael Ansara; ***D:*** Peter Hunt; ***W:*** Richard Sale; ***C:*** Hanania Baer.

The Assassination Bureau **1969** Set in Victorian-era London, this amusing farce concerns a society of international assassins led by the charming Reed. Rigg is an intrepid reporter who pays Reed to have his own organization try to kill him. Reed in turn will try to get them first. A cross-European chase ends in a battle aboard a Zeppelin. Tongue-in-cheek whimsey with a fine cast. Based on a short story by Jack London. **106m/C VHS, DVD.** *GB* Oliver Reed, Diana Rigg, Telly Savalas, Curt Jurgens, Philippe Noiret, Warren Mitchell, Beryl Reid, Clive Revill, Kenneth Griffith, Vernon Dobtcheff, Annabella Incontrera; ***D:*** Basil Dearden; ***C:*** Geoffrey Unsworth.

The Assassination File **1996 (R)** FBI agent Lauren Jacobs (Fenn) quits the Bureau after the first African-American President (Winfield) is killed on her watch. But two years later, when she encounters former co-workers, there's talk of a conspiracy and things turn even more dangerous. **106m/C VHS.** Sherilyn Fenn, Dan E. Butler, Tom Verica, Victor Love, Kevin Corrigan, Paul Winfield, Diedrich Bader; ***D:*** John Harrison; ***W:*** Bruce Miller; ***C:*** Rob Draper.

The Assassination Game **1992 (R)** Rookie CIA agent teams up with a veteran KGB agent to prevent the assassination of a world leader. **90m/C VHS.** Robert Rusler, Theodore Bikel, Doug Wert, Denise Bixler; ***D:*** Jonathan Winfrey.

Assassination in Rome *Il Segreto del Vestito Rosso* **1965** American Shelley North (Charisse) and her husband are vacationing in Rome when he suddenly disappears. When she goes to the American embassy for help, Shelley is reunited with ex-lover, reporter Dick Sherman (O'Brian), who decides to help her out. A dead body in the Trevi fountain isn't the missing Mr. North but Dick thinks there's a connection and he and Shelley take their investigation to Venice. Available as a Drive-In Double Feature with "Espionage in Tangiers." **104m/C DVD.** *IT SP* Cyd Charisse, Hugh O'Brian, Mario Feliciani, Juliette Mayniel, Alberto Closas; ***D:*** Silvio Amadio; ***W:*** Giovanni Simonelli, Silvio Amadio; ***C:*** Mario Pacheco; ***M:*** Armando Trovajoli.

The Assassination of Jesse James by the Coward Robert Ford **2007 (R)** Calling this film a western is like calling a transcontinental railroad journey a trip to the coast. Tightly wound epic, brooding and dark yet visually spectacular, unfolds at a deliberate pace as a case study of James (Pitt) and his clinging young sycophant admirer, Robert Ford (Affleck), who would become the man who finally takes James' life. Ford's hero worship turns into jealousy and then disdain in the shadow of James' tabloid celebrity. A true film lover's film, director Dominik brings a style and texture that transcends the genre. See it if you worship the craft or Pitt, or both. **152m/C DVD.** *US* Brad Pitt, Casey Affleck, Sam Shepard, Mary-Louise Parker, Sam Rockwell, Paul Schneider, Jeremy Renner, Garret Dillahunt, Zooey Deschanel, Michael Parks, Ted Levine, Alison Elliott, James Carville, Tom Aldredge; ***D:*** Andrew Dominik; ***W:*** Andrew Dominik; ***C:*** Roger Deakins; ***M:*** Nick Cave, Warren Ellis; ***Nar:*** Hugh Ross.

The Assassination of Richard Nixon 1/2 **2005 (R)** Sam Bicke (Penn), a hopeless loser who shoots himself in the foot at every turn, ends up blaming Nixon for his downfall and decides to hijack a jet and fly it into the White House. Based on the true story of a failed plot, film focuses on showing Bicke's gradual but certain descent, played by Penn with gutwrenching nakedness. Incredibly dismal but revealing look at the making of a potential terrorist. **95m/C DVD.** *US* Sean Penn, Don Cheadle, Naomi Watts, Jack Thompson, Michael Wincott, Mykelti Williamson, Nick Searcy, Brad William Henke, Lily Knight, Tracy Middendorf, April Grace, Eileen Ryan, Jared Dorrance; ***D:*** Niels Mueller; ***W:*** Niels Mueller, Kevin Kennedy; ***C:*** Emmanuel Lubezki; ***M:*** Steven Stern.

Assassination of Trotsky **1972** Middling attempt to dramatize the last days of the Russian Revolutionary leader in Mexico before he's done in with an ice pick. **113m/C VHS, DVD.** *FR GB IT* Richard Burton, Alain Delon, Romy Schneider, Valentina Cortese, Jean Desailly; ***D:*** Joseph Losey; ***C:*** Pasqualino De Santis.

The Assassination Run **1984** A retired British spy is involved against his will in an intricate plot of terrorism, counter-terrorism and espionage. **111m/C VHS.** *GB* Malcolm Stoddard, Mary Tamm; ***D:*** Ken Hannam.

Assassination Tango **2003 (R)** Aging Brooklyn hit man John J. (Duvall), who dotes on girlfriend Maggie (Baker), and her daughter Jenny (Miller), and likes to hang out at the local dance hall, is sent to Argentina to kill a general. When the hit is delayed, he meets and is enchanted by Tango instructor Manuela, as well as the dance she teaches to him. Deep character study, beautifully shown in Duvall's performance, redeems film's slow, at times maddening pace. Duvall's direction, while not perfect, makes the proceedings interesting to watch, but requires patience. **114m/C VHS, DVD.** *US* Robert Duvall, Ruben Blades, Kathy Baker, Luciana Pedraza, Julio Oscar Mechoso, James Keane, Frank Gio, Katherine Micheaux Miller; ***D:*** Robert Duvall; ***W:*** Robert Duvall; ***C:*** Felix Monti; ***M:*** Luis Bacalov.

Assassins 1/2 **1995 (R)** Stallone gets to play elder statesman in the very deadly rivalry between two contract killers. Robert Rath (Stallone) is the man—number one with a bullet—whose reputation has caught up with him. Hot-headed Miguel Bain (the ever-smoldering Banderas) wants to off Rath and assume the position of top hitman. Caught in the middle of this macho posturing is surveillance expert—and potential murderee—Electra (Moore). It's Stallone to the rescue but his character pays more attention to Pearl, Electra's pampered Persian cat than to the lovely lady herself. But then romance isn't what this film is about—and director Donner does know his action. **132m/C VHS, DVD.** Sylvester Stallone, Antonio Banderas, Julianne Moore, Anatoly Davydov; ***D:*** Richard Donner; ***W:*** Brian Helgeland, Andy Wachowski, Larry Wachowski; ***C:*** Vilmos Zsigmond; ***M:*** Mark Mancina.

Assault 1/2 *In the Devil's Garden; Tower of Terror; The Creepers* **1970** Violent sex murders in a girl's school have the police baffled. The school's pretty art teacher offers to act as bait in order to catch the murderer. **89m/C VHS.** *GB* Suzy Kendall, Frank Finlay, Freddie Jones, James Laurenson, Lesley-Anne Down, Tony Beckley; ***D:*** Sidney Hayers.

The Assault 1/2 *De Aanslag* **1986 (PG)** Powerful and disturbing drama about a Dutch boy who witnesses the arbitrary murder of his family by Nazis. The memory tortures him and leaves him empty as he matures. Years later he meets other victims and also the perpetrators of the incident, each of them changed forever by it. Thought-provoking consideration of WWII and the horrors of living in Nazi Germany from many points of view. Based on a novel by Harry Mulisch. Dutch language dubbed into English. **149m/C VHS.** *NL* Derek de Lint, Marc Van Uchelen, Monique Van De Ven; ***D:*** Fons Rademakers. Oscars '86: Foreign Film; Golden Globes '87: Foreign Film.

Assault and Matrimony 1/2 **1987** Real-life married people Tucker and Eikenberry play a married couple fighting tooth and nail. Lots of slapstick and general nonsense. Based on James Anderson's novel. **100m/C VHS.** John Hillerman, Michelle Phillips, Joe Cortese, Michael Tucker, Jill Eikenberry; ***D:*** James Frawley; ***C:*** Dick Bush. **TV**

Assault at West Point: The Court-Martial of Johnson Whittaker 1/2 **1994 (PG-13)** In 1880, Johnson C. Whittaker, a black West Point cadet, is found beaten, mutilated, and tied to his bed. Instead of seeking his attackers, the Academy sets up a court martial to expel Whittaker, claiming he faked his own attack. Clashes also ignite between Whittaker's defense counsel—white abolitionist lawyer Chamberlain, whose own racism is thinly disguised, and black lawyer Greener, who originally encouraged Whittaker to enroll at the Point. Interesting case but a shallow production. Based on a true story and adapted from the book by John Marszalek. **98m/C VHS.** Seth Gilliam, Samuel L. Jackson, Sam Waterston, John Glover, Al Freeman Jr.; ***D:***

Harry Moses; *W:* Harry Moses; *M:* Terence Blanchard. **TV**

Assault of the Killer Bimbos 1/2 **1988 (R)** A show girl gets framed for the murder of her boss and takes off for the border with a couple of girlfriends. On the way they get pursued by the expected dumb cops and meet up with horny, clean-cut hunks. In Mexico they encounter the villain and extract comic vengeance. Watchable mainly due to the likable female leads and pleasant, lightly camp execution, although it might prove too tame for most of its target audience. **85m/C VHS, DVD.** Patti Astor, Christina Whitaker, Elizabeth Kaitan, Griffin O'Neal, Nick Cassavetes, Clayton Landey, Eddie Deezen, Arell Blanton, David Marsh, Tammara Souza, Jamie Bozian, Mike Muscat, Jeffrey Orman, John Quern, Jay O. Sanders; *D:* Anita Rosenberg; *W:* Ted Nicolaou; *C:* Thomas Callaway; *M:* Fred Lapides, Marc Ellis.

Assault of the Party Nerds **1989 (R)** Nerds throw a wild party to try and attract new members to their fraternity, while a jock frat plots against them. Sound familiar? Little more than a ripoff of "Revenge of the Nerds" made especially for video. **82m/C VHS, DVD.** Michelle (McClellan) Bauer, Linnea Quigley, Troy Donahue, Richard Gabai, C. Paul Demsey, Marc Silverberg, Robert Mann, Richard Rifkin, Deborah Roush; *D:* Richard Gabai. **VIDEO**

Assault of the Party Nerds 2: Heavy Petting Detective **1995** Detective tries to save a beauty from her scheming husband. **87m/C VHS, DVD.** Linnea Quigley, Richard Gabai, Michelle (McClellan) Bauer, Arte Johnson, Burt Ward; *D:* Richard Gabai; *W:* Richard Gabai.

Assault of the Rebel Girls 1/2 *Cuban Rebel Girls; Attack of the Rebel Girls* **1959** A reporter gets involved with smuggling in Castro's Cuba. Flynn's last film, saving the worst for last. **66m/B VHS.** Errol Flynn, Beverly Aadland, John MacKay, Jackie Jackler, Marie Edmund; *D:* Barry Mahon; *W:* Errol Flynn.

Assault on a Queen **1966** Stupid Sinatra vehicle about a group of con men who plot together to rob the Queen Mary on one of her trips. Their attack vessel is a renovated WWII German U-boat. The producers tried to capitalize on the popularity of "Ocean's Eleven," but they didn't even come close. Based on a novel by Jack Finney. **106m/C VHS.** Frank Sinatra, Virna Lisi, Anthony (Tony) Franciosa, Richard Conte, Reginald Denny; *D:* Jack Donohue; *W:* Rod Serling; *C:* William H. Daniels.

Assault on Agathon **1975 (PG)** Amid the scenic Greek isles, an "executed" WWII guerilla leader returns to lead a revolution, and bloodshed and bombings ensue. **95m/C VHS.** *GB IT* Nina Van Pallandt, Marianne Faithfull, John Woodvine, Nico Minardos; *D:* Laszlo Benedek.

Assault on Precinct 13 **1976** Urban horror invades LA. Lt. Bishop (Stoker) is assigned to oversee the final shutdown of Precinct 13. Nearly abandoned, except for a couple of secretaries and a few officers, the phones and electricity have already been shut off. First problem: a busload of criminals and officers are forced to make a stop to look after a sick prisoner. Second problem: a father, who just witnessed his daughter's murder by a brutal street gang, stumbles in. Then said street gang surrounds the precinct to get the witness. Paranoia abounds as the police are attacked from all sides and can see no way out. Carpenter's musical score adds to the excitement of this low-budget police exploitation story. Semi-acclaimed cult feature and very gripping. **91m/C VHS, DVD, Blu-ray Disc.** Austin Stoker, Darwin Joston, Martin West, Tony Burton, Nancy Loomis, Kim Richards, Henry (Kleinbach) Brandon, Laurie Zimmer, Charles Cyphers, Peter Bruni; *D:* John Carpenter; *W:* John Carpenter; *C:* Douglas Knapp; *M:* John Carpenter.

Assault on Precinct 13 1/2 **2005 (R)** Richet's remake of the Carpenter cult classic has the cons and cops, led by burned-out Sgt. Roenick (Hawke) and criminal kingpin Bishop (Fishburne) holed up in a soon-to-be-closed Precinct 13 on a snowy New Year's Eve against a squad of corrupt cops intent on eliminating Bishop, their not-quite-silent-enough partner. Generally solid, if standard, updating loses much credibility by plopping a forest in the middle of a heavily industrial part of Detroit, where this one is set. Hawke and Fishburne are appropriately conflicted and heroic as it's called for, but it's the supporting cast that gives this rendition its zest. Stick around for the helpful plot-summarizing rap song that plays over the closing credits. **109m/C VHS, DVD, UMD, HD DVD.** *US* Ethan Hawke, Laurence Fishburne, Brian Dennehy, Drea De Matteo, Maria Bello, Gabriel Byrne, Ja Rule, Matt Craven, John Leguizamo, Fulvio Cecere, Currie Graham, Dorian Harewood, Kim Coates, Hugh Dillon, Titus Welliver, Aisha Hinds; *D:* Jean-Francois Richet; *W:* James DeMonaco; *C:* Robert Gantz; *M:* Graeme Revell.

Assault with a Deadly Weapon **1982** When the police budget is cutback, crime runs rampant in an unnamed American city. **86m/C VHS.** Sandra Foley, Richard Holliday, Lamont Jackson; *D:* Arthur Kennedy.

The Assignment **1978** The assassination of a high-ranking officer in an uneasy Latin American nation spurs violence and political instability. A Swedish diplomat is assigned the tremendous task of restoring peace and stability between the political factions. **92m/C VHS.** *SW* Christopher Plummer, Thomas Hellberg, Carolyn Seymour, Fernando Rey; *D:* Mats Arehn.

The Assignment 1/2 **1997 (R)** Workmanlike thriller is a case of deadly impersonation. Infamous terrorist Carlos the Jackal (Quinn) is shown plying his trade in Europe under the nose of CIA counterterrorism expert Jack Shaw (Sutherland). Later, in Israel, Mossad agent Amos (Kinglsey) captures a man whom he thinks is Carlos, only it's his double—U.S. Navy officer Annibal Ramirez (Quinn again). So Shaw and Amos decide to turn the seaman into the terrorist, in an elaborate plot to have Carlos' Russian handlers think the terrorist has betrayed them. There's a very long setup for a somewhat lame payoff. **115m/C VHS, DVD.** *CA* Aidan Quinn, Donald Sutherland, Ben Kingsley, Liliana Komorowska, Claudia Ferri, Celine Bonnier, Vlasta Vrana, Von Flores, Al Waxman; *D:* Christian Duguay; *W:* Don Gordon, Sabi H. Shabtai; *C:* David Franco; *M:* Normand Corbeil.

Assignment Outer Space *Space Men* **1961** A giant spaceship with bytes for brains is on a collision course with Earth. A team of astronauts is sent to save the world from certain peril. Seems they take the task lightly, though, and their mission (and hence the plot) revolves more around saving sexy sultress Farinon from certain celibacy. If you're into stultifying Italian space operas with a gratuitous sex sub-plot then look up this assignment, but don't say we didn't warn you. Director Margheriti is also known as Anthony Dawson, not to be confused with the actor of the same name. **79m/B VHS, DVD.** *IT* Rik van Nutter, Gabriella Farinon, Archie Savage, Dave Montresor, Alan Dijon; *D:* Anthony M. Dawson; *Nar:* Jack Wallace.

The Assisi Underground **1984** True but boringly told story of how the Catholic Church helped to save several hundred Italian Jews from being executed by the Nazis during the 1943 German occupation of Italy. Edited from 178 minutes, a good-will gesture from the producers. **115m/C VHS.** James Mason, Ben Cross, Maximilian Schell, Irene Papas, Angelo Infanti; *D:* Alexander Ramati; *M:* Pino Donaggio.

The Assistant **1997** The Jewish Bober family have escaped the anti-Semitism of their homeland and emigrated to the U.S. where they are struggling to run a small grocery store during the depression. Drifter Frank (Bellows) hooks up with thief Ward (Woolvet) and they rob the store, with Ward attacking Morris Bober (Mueller-Stahl). A guilty Frank later returns and offers to help out. Morris doesn't know Frank was part of the robbery and agrees and Frank soons falls for the Bober's daughter, Helen (Greenhouse). Then Morris discovers the truth. Based on a novel by Bernard Malamud. **105m/C VHS.** *CA* Gil Bellows, Armin Mueller-Stahl, Joan Plowright, Kate Greenhouse, Jaimz Woolvett; *D:* Daniel Petrie; *W:* Daniel Petrie; *C:* Philip Earnshaw.

The Associate *L'Associe* **1979 (R)** French farce about penniless financial consultant Julien Pardot (Serrault) who invents a fictitious partner, Mr. Davis, in order to get his business rolling. When his clients, his wife, and even his mistress are all more intrigued by the partner than Julien, he becomes so jealous he decides to "murder" his creation. Based on the novel "My Partner, Mr. Davis" by Jenaro Prieto. French with subtitles; remade in 1996 with Whoopi Goldberg. **93m/C VHS.** *FR* Michel Serrault, Claudine Auger, Catherine Alric, Matthieu Carriere; *D:* Rene Gainville; *W:* Jean-Claude Carriere.

The Associate **1996 (PG-13)** Whoopi drags a 20-minute premise over almost two hours when she invents an elderly, white, male business partner to give her fledgling financial consulting business some prestige. After having all her moneymaking ideas appropriated by male colleagues, Laurel Ayres (Goldberg) starts her own business, only to find that no one wants to hire her. She creates the genius and the money comes rolling in. Everyone clamors to meet the mystery man, so she goes undercover as the elusive Robert S. Cutty. The sight of Goldberg in old white guy garb and makeup is jarring, and the payoff doesn't merit the overlong build up. Based on the French film "L'Associate" and the Jenaro Prieto novel "El Socio." **113m/C VHS, DVD.** Whoopi Goldberg, Timothy Daly, Bebe Neuwirth, Dianne Wiest, Eli Wallach; *D:* Donald Petrie; *W:* Nick Thiel; *C:* Alex Nepomniaschy; *M:* Christopher Tyng.

Asteroid **1997** Re-edited version of the NBC TV miniseries emphasizes the special effects and action, which should help this routine disaster flick. Astronomer Lily McKee (Sciorra) discovers that several giant asteroids are on a collision course with Kansas City. She contacts FEMA and gets hotshot director Jack Wallach (Biehn) anxious to help out (and not just with the rock problem). Naturally, the citizens freak and one asteroid hits but there's an even bigger one on the way. **120m/C VHS, DVD.** Michael Biehn, Annabella Sciorra, Don Franklin, Anne-Marie Johnson, Anthony Zerbe, Carlos Gomez, Jensen (Jennifer) Daggett, Michael Weatherly, Frank McRae, Denis Arndt; *D:* Bradford May; *W:* Robbyn Burger, Scott Sturgeon; *C:* David Hennings, Thomas Del Ruth; *M:* Shirley Walker. **TV**

Astoria **2000 (R)** The Astoria section of Queens is heavily Greek-American with all its ethnic traditions. Alex (Stear) is 28 and wants to escape his stagnant life by joining an archeological expedition to find the lost tomb of Alexander the Great. His father Demo (Setrakian) expects Alex to help with the family business. Alex isn't happy until Greek art restorer Elena (Turco) pays a visit and suddenly things look a lot brighter. **103m/C DVD.** Rick Stear, Ed Setrakian, Paige Turco, Joseph (Joe) D'Onofrio; *D:* Nick Efteriades; *W:* Nick Efteriades; *C:* Elia Lyssey; *M:* Nikos Papazoglou.

The Astounding She-Monster WOOF! *Mysterious Invader* **1958** How can you not love a movie with a title like this? A bad script and snail-paced plot are a good start. A geologist wanting only to be left alone with his rocks survives a brush with the kidnappers of a wealthy heiress only to happen upon an alien spacecraft that's crashed nearby. At the helm is a very tall, high-heeled fem-alien in an obligatory skintight space outfit. Excellent, our rock jock thinks, but it seems she kills with the slightest touch. For connoisseurs of truly bad movies. **60m/B VHS, DVD.** Robert Clarke, Kenne Duncan, Marilyn Harvey, Jeanne Tatum, Shirley Kilpatrick, Ewing Miles Brown; *D:* Ronnie Ashcroft; *W:* Frank Hall; *C:* William C. Thompson; *M:* Guenther Kauer.

Astro Boy 1/2 **2009 (PG)** Energetic—if somewhat violent—adaptation of the Japanese manga books and the 1963 anime TV series. Set in Metro City, an orbiting world above a polluted Earth, robot Astro Boy (Highmore) is created by grieving scientist Dr. Tenma (Cage) as a replacement for his deceased son. When he can't fulfill his "father's" expectations, the rejected Astro Boy finds a home amidst Earth's scavengers but must return to Metro City when he learns everyone is in danger from polluting red energy (Astro Boy is powered by clean blue energy) and save the day. **94m/C DVD.** *US HK* *D:* David Bowers; *W:* Timothy Harris; *C:* Pepe Valencia; *M:* John Ottman; *V:* Freddie Highmore, Nicolas Cage, Donald Sutherland, Kristen Bell, Bill Nighy, Nathan Lane, Eugene Levy, Matt Lucas, Samuel L. Jackson; *Nar:* Charlize Theron.

The Astro-Zombies WOOF! *The Space Vampires* **1967** A contender as one of the worst movies of all time. Carradine plays a mad scientist creating zombies who eat people's guts. Cult favorite Satana stars. Co-written and co-produced by Rogers of "M*A*S*H" fame. **83m/C VHS, DVD.** Tura Satana, Wendell Corey, John Carradine, Tom Pace, Joan Patrick, Rafael Campos, William Bagdad, Joseph Hoover, Victor Izay, Vincent Barbi, Rod Wilmoth; *D:* Ted V. Mikels; *W:* Ted V. Mikels, Wayne Rogers; *C:* Robert Maxwell; *M:* Nico Karaski.

The Astronaut Farmer 1/2 **2007 (PG)** NASA engineer Charlie Farmer (Thornton) left the space program for his family's failing Texas ranch but never gave up his dream of being an astronaut. He's got his very own shiny silver space suit and is building an actual rocket in his barn. His family and friends see Charlie as a larger-than-life eccentric but when he tries to buy rocket fuel the feds think Charlie's some kind of homegrown terrorist. Film treats Charlie and his dreams matter-of-factly as does Thornton, with Madsen luminous as his devoted wife and Simmons blustering as his fed nemesis. **104m/C DVD.** *US* Billy Bob Thornton, Virginia Madsen, Bruce Dern, J.K. Simmons, Tim Blake Nelson, Max Thieriot, Jon(athan) Gries, Mark Polish, Jasper Polish, Logan Polish; *Cameos:* Bruce Willis; *D:* Michael Polish; *W:* Mark Polish, Michael Polish; *C:* M. David Mullen; *M:* Stuart Matthewman.

The Astronaut's Wife 1/2 **1999 (R)** Astronaut Spencer Armacost (Depp) just isn't the same guy after he returns from a nearly fatal space shuttle mission. He and his wife, Jillian (Theron), suddenly move to New York and she definitely notices some behavorial changes (he likes to listen to the test pattern on the TV screen). Oh, and then the little woman discovers she's pregnant and things get very "Rosemary's Baby." Theron's role is also very much like her beleaguered wife in "The Devil's Advocate," since everyone seems to think Jillian's nuts. Disappointingly formulaic; Depp's more believable in quirky roles in quirky movies. **109m/C VHS, DVD.** Johnny Depp, Charlize Theron, Joe Morton, Tom Noonan, Blair Brown, Nick Cassavetes, Clea DuVall, Donna Murphy, Samantha Eggar; *D:* Rand Ravich; *W:* Rand Ravich; *C:* Allen Daviau; *M:* George S. Clinton.

Asunder 1/2 **1999** Slick thriller with a familiar storyline. Michael (Beach) and wife Lauren (Morgan) are at the fairground with best friends Chance (Underwood) and his pregnant wife Roberta (Hicks). Roberta is tragically killed in a fall while riding the Ferris wheel. Michael and Lauren invite Chance to stay with them and the viewer learns that Lauren and Chance once had an extramarital affair. Then Chance decides to wreck her marriage and get Lauren back. **102m/C VHS, DVD.** Blair Underwood, Debbi (Deborah) Morgan, Michael Beach, Marva Hicks; *D:* Tim Reid; *W:* Eric Lee Bowers; *C:* Johnny (John W.) Simmons; *M:* Lionel Cole.

Asylum 1/2 *House of Crazies* **1972 (PG)** Four strange and chilling stories weave together in this film. A murderer's victim seeks retribution. A tailor seems to be collecting his bills. A man who makes voodoo dolls...only to become one later on. A woman plagued by a double. A doctor visiting the asylum tells each tale. Horrifying and grotesque, not as humorless as American horror films. **100m/C VHS, DVD.** *GB* Peter Cushing, Herbert Lom, Britt Ekland, Barbara Parkins, Patrick Magee, Barry Morse, Robert Powell, Richard Todd, Charlotte Rampling, Ann(e) Firbank, Sylvia Syms, James Villiers, Geoffrey Bayldon, Megs Jenkins; *D:* Roy Ward Baker; *W:* Robert Bloch; *C:* Denys Coop.

Asylum 1/2 **1997 (R)** Unstable investigator Nick Tordone (Patrick) looks into his shrink's supposed suicide by become a patient at the doctor's mental hospital. By what he finds is serial killer Sullivan Rane (McDowell) and a doctor (Gibson) doing dangerous mind control experiments. Tension holds up well until the unfortunate finale. **92m/C VHS.** Jason Schombing, Kevin Anthony Cole,

Peter Brown, Robert Patrick, Malcolm McDowell, Henry Gibson, Sarah Douglas; ***D:*** James Seale; ***W:*** James Seale; ***C:*** David Rakoczy; ***M:*** Alan Williams.

Asylum **2005 (R)** Sex in the loony bin. In 1959, frustrated Stella Raphael (Richardson) accompanies her hubby Max (Bonneville) to the titular Victorian heap where he is the new superintendent. Stella meets hottie patient Edgar (Csokas), who helps out around the grounds, and the two are soon helping themselves to each other. Despite the fact that Edgar's locked up because he beat his wife to death in a jealous rage. Add to the mix Edgar's manipulative doctor, Peter Cleave (McKellen), and you've got a melodrama at high boil, just waiting to bubble over. As over-the-top as it sounds; adapted from the novel by Patrick McGrath. **90m/C DVD.** *IR GB* Natasha Richardson, Ian McKellen, Marton Csokas, Hugh Bonneville, Judy Parfitt, Sean Harris, Gus Lewis, Wanda Ventham, Joss Ackland; ***D:*** David Mackenzie; ***W:*** Patrick Marber, Chrys Balis; ***C:*** Giles Nuttgens; ***M:*** Mark Mancina.

Asylum of Satan **1972** A beautiful concert pianist is savagely tortured by a madman in the Asylum of Satan. Filmed on location in Louisville, Kentucky. **87m/C VHS, DVD.** Charles Kissinger, Carla Borelli, Nick Jolly, Sherry Steiner; ***D:*** William Girdler; ***W:*** William Girdler.

Asylum of the Damned *Hellborn* **2003 (R)** Naive psychologist believes he can tackle the worst offenders at the criminally insane asylum but isn't ready to deal with the hideous truth behind the high volume of vanishing inmates. **85m/C VHS, DVD.** Bruce Payne, Tracy Scoggins, Tommy (Tiny) Lister, Gregory Wagrowski, Bill McKinney, Randall England, Kyle T. Heffner, Michael Earl Reid, David Thomas, Matt Stasi, Julia Lee, Joe Sabatino, Deborah Flora, Stefan Marchand; ***D:*** Philip Jones; ***W:*** Matthew McCombs; ***C:*** Mark Melville; ***M:*** Valentine Leone, Steve Bauman. **VIDEO**

At Any Cost 1/2 **2000 (R)** Ah, the music business. Austin, Texas band Beyond Gravity has a shot at a major recording career in L.A. when they're signed by an indie label. Leader Lance (Mills) vows to wife/bandmember Chelsea (Flannigan) that they won't blow their big chance but problems arise quickly. Seems Lance's brother Mike (Franco) can't control his drug problem and ambitious pal Ben (Quinn) wants to strike out on his own when the band starts to go south. Typical price-of-fame cable drama. **92m/C VHS.** Eddie Mills, James Franco, Glenn Quinn, Maureen Flannigan, Cyia Batten; ***D:*** Charles Winkler; ***W:*** Bruce Taylor, Roderick Taylor; ***C:*** Robert Steadman. **CABLE**

At Close Range **1986 (R)** Based on the true story of Bruce Johnston Sr. and Jr. in Brandywine River Valley, Pennsylvania. Father, Walken, tempts his teenaged son, Penn, into pursuing criminal activities with talk of excitement and high living. Penn soon learns that his father is extremely dangerous and a bit unstable, but he's still fascinated by his wealth and power. Sometimes overbearing and depressing, but good acting and fancy camera work. A young cast of stars includes Masterson as the girl Penn tries to impress. Features Madonna's "Live to Tell." **115m/C VHS, DVD.** Sean Penn, Christopher Walken, Christopher Penn, Mary Stuart Masterson, Crispin Glover, Kiefer Sutherland, Candy Clark, Tracey Walter, Millie Perkins, Alan Autry, David Strathairn, Eileen Ryan; ***D:*** James Foley; ***W:*** Nicholas Kazan; ***C:*** Juan Ruiz-Anchia; ***M:*** Patrick Leonard.

At First Sight 1/2 *Two Guys Talkin' About Girls* **1995 (R)** Yakky pedestrian comedy about schleppy Lenny (Silverman) and his best friend, macho Joey (Cortese), trying to help each other out with their romantic crises. Lenny meets cute when he picks up Rhonda (Smith) at the planetarium while Joey beds a string of girls, all of whom are named Cindy, in an effort to get over the first Cindy who broke his heart. It's been done before—and better. **90m/C VHS.** Jonathan Silverman, Dan Cortese, Allison Smith, Monte Markham, Kathleen Freeman; ***D:*** Steven Pearl; ***W:*** Ken Copel; ***C:*** Glenn Kershaw; ***M:*** Richard Gibbs.

At First Sight 1/2 **1998 (PG-13)** Slow-paced romantic drama stars Kilmer as a blind masseuse who falls for high-strung architect Sorvino. She persuades him to have an operation that restores his sight, and he's forced to adapt to a world he has never seen. Excellent supporting performances by McGillis as Kilmer's sister and Lane as the doctor that eases his transition. Kilmer does an outstanding job in making his character neither pitiful nor over-sentimental, which is rare in movies that center on disabilities. Based loosely on a case study by Dr. Oliver Sacks, whose work was also the basis for "Awakenings." **128m/C VHS, DVD.** Val Kilmer, Mira Sorvino, Kelly McGillis, Steven Weber, Bruce Davison, Nathan Lane, Ken Howard; ***D:*** Irwin Winkler; ***W:*** Steve Levitt; ***C:*** John Seale; ***M:*** Mark Isham.

At Gunpoint *Gunpoint* **1955** A store owner becomes the town hero when, by accident, he shoots and kills a bank robber. **81m/C VHS.** Fred MacMurray, Dorothy Malone, John Qualen, Walter Brennan; ***D:*** Alfred Werker; ***C:*** Ellsworth Fredericks.

At Gunpoint 1/2 **1990** A no-account bank robber spends his six year stint in the slammer plotting his revenge. Having gone thoroughly stircrazy, the vengeful criminal stalks the lawman who put him away, like so many vengeful criminals before him. Run of the mill addition to big list of bad-guy-hunting-for-revenge flicks. **90m/C VHS.** Frank Kanig, Tain Bodkin, Scott Claflin; ***D:*** Steven Harris; ***W:*** Steven Harris.

At Home with the Webbers **1994 (R)** Gerald, Emma, Johnny, and Miranda Webber win a contest to star in a cable TV series about their lives. What they don't expect is that the series will become a hit or that all the family idosyncrasies will be exaggerated by stardom (the manipulative TV producer doesn't help). Over-the-top comedy requires tolerance but does have some amusing performances. **109m/C VHS.** Jeffrey Tambor, Rita Taggart, Jennifer Tilly, David Arquette, Robby Benson, Brian Bloom, Caroline Goodall; ***D:*** Brad (Sean) Marlowe; ***W:*** Brad (Sean) Marlowe.

At Midnight, I'll Take Your Soul *A Meia-Noite Levarei Sua Alma* **1963** Brazilian import about sadistic gravedigger Coffin Joe (alter ego of director Jose Mojica Marins), who wanders the streets of his hometown in order to meet a desirable woman. His mission is to sire a son to continue his legacy and wiggle his lips at screaming women. A study in psycho-sexual horror, this makes "Apocalypse Now" look like a beach party. Coffin Joe, or "Ze do Caixao," is a kind of South American Freddy or Jason; Mojica Marin's movies—which are graphically sadistic—were banned by the Brazilian government. In Portugese with English subtitles. Followed by "Tonight I'll Be Incarnated in Your Corpse." **92m/B VHS, DVD.** *BR* Jose Mojica Marins, Magda Mei, Nivaldo de Lima; ***D:*** Jose Mojica Marins; ***W:*** Jose Mojica Marins; ***C:*** Giorgio Attili.

At Play in the Fields of the Lord **1991 (R)** A thoughtful epic that never quite lives up to its own self-importance—or length. Two yankee missionary couples try to evangelize a fearsome tribe of Brazilian rain-forest dwellers. One of the Christian families suffers a crisis of faith that's well-acted but not as powerful as a co-plot regarding a modern American Indian (Berenger) who joins the jungle natives with calamitous results. Based on the novel by Peter Matthiessen. **186m/C VHS.** Tom Berenger, Aidan Quinn, Kathy Bates, John Lithgow, Daryl Hannah, Tom Waits, Stenio Garcia, Nelson Xavier, Jose Dumont, Niilo Kivirinta; ***D:*** Hector Babenco; ***W:*** Hector Babenco, Jean-Claude Carriere; ***M:*** Zbigniew Preisner.

At Sword's Point *Sons of the Musketeers* **1951** Adventure tale based on characters from Alexandre Dumas's "The Three Musketeers," although the story is original. The French Queen (Cooper) is disturbed by sinister Duke Lavalle (Douglas) who wishes to marry Princess Henriette (Gates) and gain power to the throne. But the children of the four original musketeers come to her rescue, including swordswoman Claire (O'Hara). **81m/C VHS.** Cornel Wilde, Maureen O'Hara, Robert Douglas, Dan O'Herlihy, Alan Hale Jr., Blanche Yurka, Gladys Cooper, June Clayworth, Nancy Gates; ***D:*** Lewis Allen; ***W:*** Walter Ferris, Joseph Hoffman; ***C:*** Ray Rennahan; ***M:*** Roy Webb.

At the Circus 1/2 *The Marx Brothers at the Circus* **1939** Marx Brothers invade the circus to save it from bankruptcy and cause their usual comic insanity, though they've done it better before. Beginning of the end for the Marxes, a step down in quality from their classic work, though frequently darn funny. ♫ Lydia the Tattooed Lady; Step Up and Take a Bow; Two Blind Loves; Blue Moon. **87m/B VHS, DVD.** Groucho Marx, Chico Marx, Harpo Marx, Margaret Dumont, Kenny L. Baker, Florence Rice, Eve Arden, Nat Pendleton, Fritz Feld, James Burke, Barnett Parker; ***D:*** Edward Buzzell; ***W:*** Irving Brecher; ***C:*** Leonard Smith; ***M:*** Harold Arlen.

At the Earth's Core **1976 (PG)** A Victorian scientist invents a giant burrowing machine, which he and his crew use to dig deeply into the Earth. To their surprise, they discover a lost world of subhuman creatures and prehistoric monsters. Based on Edgar Rice Burrough's novels. **90m/C VHS, DVD.** *GB* Doug McClure, Peter Cushing, Caroline Munro, Cy Grant, Godfrey James, Keith Barron; ***D:*** Kevin Connor; ***W:*** Milton Subotsky; ***C:*** Alan Hume; ***M:*** Michael Vickers.

At the Midnight Hour 1/2 **1995** Elizabeth Guinness (Kensit) is hired as the new nanny to care for the troubled young son of widowed scientist Richard Keaton (MacCorkindale). She finds herself falling in love but then uncovers a secret about the death of Keaton's wife. From the Harlequin Romance series; adapted from the novel by Alicia Scott. **95m/C DVD.** *CA* Patsy Kensit, Simon MacCorkindale, Keegan Macintosh, Lindsay Merrithew, Cynthia Dale, Kay Hawtrey; ***D:*** Charles Jarrott; ***W:*** Joe Wiesenfeld; ***C:*** Robert Fresco; ***M:*** Charles T. Cozens. **TV**

At War with the Army **1950** Serviceable comedy from Martin and Lewis in their first starring appearance, as the recruits get mixed up in all kinds of wild situations at their army base. Based on the play by James Allardice. **93m/B VHS, DVD.** Dean Martin, Jerry Lewis, Polly Bergen, Mike Kellin; ***D:*** Hal Walker; ***W:*** Fred Finklehoffe; ***C:*** Stuart Thompson; ***M:*** Jerry Livingston.

Atalia **1985** Relates the love between Atalia, a war widow, and the younger man she loves. The problem stems from the fact that she lives in a Kibbutz, and the lifestyle contradicts sharply from that of her beliefs in love, forcing her to eventually make a momentous decision. **90m/C VHS.** Michal Bat-Adam, Yftach Katzur, Dan Toren; ***D:*** Akiva Tevet.

Athena 1/2 **1954** Two sisters (Powell and Reynolds) from an eccentric, health-faddist family fall in love with their opposites. Purdom is the stuffy Boston lawyer who goes off with Powell and Reynolds entices a TV crooner (Damone). Routine romance with routine songs. Reeves, who would become a star as a movie muscleman, appears in a brief role. ♫ Love Can Change the Stars; The Girl Next Door; Imagine; Venezia; Chacun le Sait; I Never Felt Better; Vocalize. **96m/C VHS.** Jane Powell, Debbie Reynolds, Edmund Purdom, Vic Damone, Louis Calhern, Evelyn Varden, Linda Christian, Virginia Gibson, Nancy Kilgas, Dolores Starr, Jane Fischer, Cecile Rogers, Steve Reeves; ***D:*** Richard Thorpe; ***W:*** William Ludwig, Leonard Spigelgass; ***M:*** Hugh Martin, Ralph Blane.

ATL **2006 (PG-13)** A pack of roller-skating Atlanta outsiders battle the streets and get their groove on to a bumpin' soundtrack (certain to be the perfect corporate tie-in). High-octane dazzle should satisfy most looking for a safe urban-teen flick not loaded with the normally obligatory f-bomb. But the poor-boy-meets-rich-girl romance is too fluffy, and an evil drug-dealer conflict still doesn't add the bite it needs. Music-video director Chris Robinson makes his wildly disobedient big-screen debut with bling and hoopla, but a lack of grit and coherence is all too apparent. **105m/C DVD, Blu-ray Disc, UMD, HD DVD.** Lonette McKee, Mykelti Williamson, Keith David, Jason Weaver, Tip "T.I." Harris, Lauren London, Evan Ross, Antwan Andre Patton, Jackie Long, Albert Daniels, Malika Khadijah, Tyree Simmons; ***D:*** Chris Robinson; ***W:*** Tina Gordon Chism, Antwone Fisher; ***M:*** Aaron Zigman.

Atlantic City 1/2 *Atlantic City U.S.A* **1981 (R)** A small-time, aging Mafia hood falls in love with a young clam bar waitress, and they share the spoils of a big score against the backdrop of Atlantic City. Wonderful character study that becomes something more, a piercing declaration about a city's transformation and the effect on the people who live there. Lancaster, in a sterling performance, personifies the city, both of them fading with time. **104m/C VHS, DVD.** *FR CA* Burt Lancaster, Susan Sarandon, Kate Reid, Michel Piccoli, Hollis McLaren, Robert Joy, Al Waxman; ***D:*** Louis Malle; ***W:*** John Guare; ***C:*** Richard Ciupka; ***M:*** Michel Legrand. British Acad. '81: Actor (Lancaster), Director (Malle); Genie '81: Support. Actress (Reid); L.A. Film Critics '81: Actor (Lancaster), Film, Screenplay, Natl. Film Reg. '03;; N.Y. Film Critics '81: Actor (Lancaster), Screenplay; Natl. Soc. Film Critics '81: Actor (Lancaster), Director (Malle), Film, Screenplay.

Atlantis, the Lost Continent **1961** If anything could sink the fabled lost continent of Atlantis it's this cheap fantasy flick. A greek sailor saves a princess and takes her back to her Atlantis home where he's promptly enslaved by the island's evil ruler. But this hero won't put up with any nonsense so he leads his fellow slaves in a revolt and gains his freedom before sinking both evil ruler and island (using atomic power no less!). **90m/C VHS.** *US* Anthony Hall, Joyce Taylor, John Dall, William (Bill) Smith, Edward Platt, Frank De Kova; ***D:*** George Pal; ***W:*** Daniel Mainwaring; ***C:*** Harold E. Wellman; ***M:*** Russell Garcia; ***Nar:*** Paul Frees.

Atlantis: The Lost Empire 1/2 **2001 (PG)** Fast-paced and action-packed animated Disney adventure about inexperienced explorer Milo Thatch (Fox) who uses his grandfather's secret journals to discover the whereabouts of the submerged city of Atlantis. Submarine Captain Rourke (Garner) leads the expedition, but the eccentric and multi-ethnic crew are not entirely who or what they seem to be. Once found, the city holds a love interest (Summer) for Milo, and treasures to tempt the less benevolent members of the crew. The animation is old-fashioned and the plotting is reminiscent of adventure movies such as "Raiders of the Lost Ark" and "20,000 Leagues Under the Sea," but these should be considered merits instead of liabilities, especially if you're under 13 years old. **95m/C VHS, DVD.** ***D:*** Gary Trousdale, Kirk Wise; ***W:*** Tab Murphy; ***M:*** James Newton Howard; ***V:*** Michael J. Fox, James Garner, Claudia Christian, Cree Summer, John Mahoney, Leonard Nimoy, David Ogden Stiers, Jim Varney, Phil Morris, Don Novello, Florence Stanley, Corey Burton, Jacqueline Obradors.

Atlas **1960** The mighty Atlas takes on massive armies, one of which includes director Corman, in a bid to win the hand of a princess. About as cheap as they come, although it is one of the few Sword & Sandal epics that isn't dubbed. **84m/C VHS, DVD.** Michael Forest, Frank Wolff, Barboura Morris, Walter Maslow, Christos Exarchos, Miranda Kounelaki, Theodore Dimitriou, Charles B. Griffith, Roger Corman, Dick Miller; ***D:*** Roger Corman; ***W:*** Charles B. Griffith; ***C:*** Basil Maros; ***M:*** Ronald Stein.

Atlas in the Land of the Cyclops **WOOF!** *Atlas Against the Cyclops; Maciste Nella Terra dei Ciclopi* **1961** Atlas takes on a hideous one-eyed monster to save a baby from an evil queen. Not a divorce custody drama. **100m/C VHS.** *IT* Mitchell Gordon, Chelo Alonso, Vira (Vera) Silenti; ***D:*** Antonio Leonviola.

Atom Age Vampire **WOOF!** *Seddok, l'Erede di Satana* **1961** Mad scientist doing research on Japanese nuclear bomb victims falls in love with a woman disfigured in an auto crash. To remove her scars, he treats her with a formula derived from the glands of freshly killed women. English dubbed. Not among the best of its kind (a low-rent district if ever there was one), but entertaining in a mischievous, boy-is-this-a-stupid-film sort of way. **71m/B VHS, DVD.** *IT* Alberto Lupo, Susanne Loret, Sergio Fantoni, Franca Parisi Strahl, Ivo Garrani, Andrea Scotti, Rina Franchetti; ***D:*** Anton Giulio Majano; ***W:*** Anton Giulio Majano, Alberto Bevilacqua, Gino De Santis; ***C:*** Aldo Giordani.

Atom Man vs. Superman **1950** Superman saves Metropolis from the machinations of his deadly foe, Atom Man, in this long-unseen second theatrical serial. Contains all

15 episodes on two tapes. **251m/B VHS.** Kirk Alyn, Lyle Talbot, Noel Neill, Tommy "Butch" Bond, Pierre Watkin; ***D:*** Spencer Gordon Bennet.

The Atomic Brain WOOF! *Monstrosity* **1964** An old woman hires a doctor to transplant her brain into the body of a beautiful young girl. Of the three girls who are abducted, two become homicidal zombies and the third starts to act catty when she is given a feline brain. A must-see for bad-brain movie fans. **72m/B VHS, DVD.** Frank Gerstle, Erika Peters, Judy Bamber, Marjorie Eaton, Frank Fowler, Margie Fisco; ***D:*** Joseph Mascelli; ***W:*** Jack Pollexfen, Vivian Russell, Dean Dillman Jr., Sue Bradford.

The Atomic Cafe 🦴🦴🦴 **1982** A chillingly humorous compilation of newsreels and government films of the 1940s and '50s that show America's preoccupation with the A-Bomb. Some sequences are in black and white. Includes the infamous training film "Duck and Cover," which tells us what to do in the event of an actual bombing. **92m/C VHS, DVD.** ***D:*** Kevin Rafferty, Jayne Loader, Pierce Rafferty; ***M:*** Miklos Rozsa.

The Atomic City 🦴🦴 ½ **1952** Barry plays a nuclear physicist at Los Alamos whose son is kidnapped by terrorists who want his bomb-making formulas. The bad guys hide out in the nearby mountains which at least makes for some pleasant scenery in this average thriller. **84m/B VHS.** Gene Barry, Lee Aaker, Michael D. Moore, Lydia Clarke, Nancy Gates, Milburn Stone; ***D:*** Jerry Hopper.

Atomic Dog 🦴 ½ **1998 (PG-13)** The Yates family (Hugh-Kelly and Pickett) move to a new town near a nuclear power plant. Soon, the family dog is having puppies—only the sire turns out to be a radioactive hound who wants his offspring and he's a very determined doggie indeed. **86m/C VHS.** Daniel Hugh-Kelly, Isabella Hofmann, Cindy Pickett, Katie Stuart, Micah Gardener; ***D:*** Brian Trenchard-Smith; ***W:*** Miguel Tejada-Flores; ***C:*** David Lewis; ***M:*** Peter Bernstein. **CABLE**

The Atomic Kid 🦴 ½ **1954** A man survives an atomic blast because of a peanut butter sandwich he was eating. As a result, he himself becomes radioactive and discovers that he has acquired some strange new powers which get him into what pass for hilarious predicaments. **86m/B VHS.** Mickey Rooney, Robert Strauss, Elaine Davis, Bill Goodwin, Whit Bissell; ***D:*** Leslie Martinson; ***W:*** Blake Edwards; ***M:*** Van Alexander.

The Atomic Man 🦴 ½ *Timeslip* **1956** Owing to radioactive experimentation, a scientist exists for a short time in the future. Once there, both good and evil forces want to use him for their own purposes. **78m/B VHS.** *GB* Gene Nelson, Faith Domergue, Joseph Tomelty, Peter Arne; ***D:*** Ken Hughes.

Atomic Submarine 🦴🦴 **1959** Futuristic sci fi plots government agents against alien invaders. The battle, however, takes place in the ocean beneath the Arctic and is headed by an atomic-powered submarine clashing with a special alien underwater saucer. We all live on the atomic submarine: fun for devotees. **80m/C VHS, DVD.** Arthur Franz, Dick Foran, Bob Steele, Brett Halsey, Joi Lansing, Tom Conway, Paul Dubov; ***D:*** Spencer Gordon Bennet; ***W:*** Orville H. Hampton; ***C:*** Gilbert Warrenton; ***M:*** Alexander Laszlo.

Atomic Train 🦴 ½ **1999 (PG-13)** Silly two-part TV mini about a runaway train that's packed with toxic waste and a nuclear bomb, which is headed straight for Denver. Lowe (who makes a surprisingly good action hero) is National Transportation Safety Board investigator John Seger, who must derail the disaster. Meanwhile, the relentless media coverage has brought on widespread panic (those fiends!). **168m/C VHS, DVD.** Rob Lowe, Kristin Davis, Esai Morales, John Finn, Mena Suvari, Sean Smith, Edward Herrmann, Erik King, Blu Mankuma; ***D:*** Dick Lowry, David S. Jackson; ***C:*** Steven Fierberg; ***M:*** Lee Holdridge. **TV**

Atonement 🦴🦴🦴 **2007 (R)** In 1935 England, 13-year-old Briony (Ronan) sees her sister Cecilia (Knightley) and their cook's son Robbie (McAvoy) together (literally) and, out of jealousy, accuses Robbie of a crime he didn't commit. The once beloved Robbie is sent to jail and the family, who had been paying for him to attend college, rejects him. Only Cecilia believes he is innocent, and cannot forgive her sister. Five years later, the now grown Briony (Garai) and Cecilia are nurses in London and Robbie has been released from prison to fight in the war. Desperate for forgiveness for ruining Robbie's life, Briony tries to find a way to fix her mistake, but it may be too late. Knightley and McAvoy shine as the long-lost lovers, and Ronan's Briony is stellar. Beautifully shot period film is faithful to McEwan's novel, and to the tone and style of 1930s and '40s-era melodramas. **122m/C DVD.** *US GB* James McAvoy, Keira Knightley, Saoirse Ronan, Romola Garai, Vanessa Redgrave, Brenda Blethyn, Juno Temple, Patrick Kennedy, Benedict Cumberbatch, Harriet Walter, Gina McKee; ***D:*** Joe Wright; ***W:*** Christopher Hampton; ***C:*** Seamus McGarvey; ***M:*** Dario Marianelli. Oscars '07: Orig. Score; British Acad. '07: Film; Golden Globes '08: Film—Drama, Orig. Score.

The Atonement of Gosta Berling 🦴🦴🦴 *Gosta Berling's Saga; The Legend of Gosta Berling; The Story of Gosta Berling; The Saga of Gosta Berling* **1924** A priest, forced to leave the priesthood because of his drinking, falls in love with a young married woman. Garbo shines in the first role which brought her critical acclaim; Hanson's performance also makes this a memorable drama. Adapted from the novel by Selma Lagerlof. **91m/B VHS, DVD.** *SW* Lars Hanson, Greta Garbo, Ellen Cederstrom, Mona Martenson, Jenny Hasselquist, Gerda Lundequist; ***D:*** Mauritz Stiller.

Ator the Fighting Eagle WOOF! 1983 (PG) Styled after "Conan The Barbarian" this mythical action fantasy stars O'Keeffe as Ator, son of Thorn. Ator must put an end to the tragic Dynasty of the Spiders, thereby fulfilling the legend of his family at the expense of the viewer. Goofy low-budget sword and sandal stuff. D'Amato used the pseudonym David Hills. Followed by "The Blade Master." **98m/C VHS, DVD.** *IT* Miles O'Keeffe, Sabrina Siani, Ritza Brown, Edmund Purdom, Laura Gemser; ***D:*** Joe D'Amato.

Attack! 🦴🦴🦴 **1956** Cowardly Captain Cooney (Albert) is order to move one of his platoons into a forward position in 1944 Belgium. They are slowly surrounded by the enemy as platoon leader, Lt. Costa (Palance), calls headquarters for reinforcements. But Cooney won't commit his reserves even as the platoon is decimated. Expert portrayals of men under pressure. **107m/B VHS, DVD.** Eddie Albert, Jack Palance, Lee Marvin, Robert Strauss, Richard Jaeckel, Buddy Ebsen, William (Bill) Smithers, Strother Martin; ***D:*** Robert Aldrich; ***W:*** James Poe; ***C:*** Joseph Biroc; ***M:*** Frank DeVol.

Attack Force WOOF! 2006 (R) Even judging by the low standards set by Seagal movies, this dreck isn't worth the effort to figure out what might be going on. After Special Agent Marshall Lawson's strike team is wiped out by a super-strong, drugged-out prostie, he's determined to figure out how it happened. This leads to a military/political conspiracy to infect the water supply with a drug that turns its users ultra-violent. Even the dialogue over-dubbing is ludicrous, with someone else obviously substituting for Seagal in various scenes. **95m/C DVD.** Steven Seagal, David Kennedy, Danny (Daniel) Webb, Andrew Bicknell, Lisa Lovbrand, Matthew Chambers; ***D:*** Michael Keusch; ***W:*** Steven Seagal, Joe Halpin; ***C:*** Sonja Rom; ***M:*** Barry Taylor. **VIDEO**

Attack Force Z 🦴🦴 **1984** An elite corps of Australian military is Force Z. Volunteers are chosen for a dangerous mission: find the plane that crashed somewhere in the South Pacific and rescue the defecting Japanese government official on board, all before the end of WWII and the feature. Talented cast is effectively directed in low-key adventure featuring young Gibson. **84m/C VHS, DVD.** *AU* Sam Neill, Chris Haywood, Mel Gibson, John Phillip Law, John Waters; ***D:*** Tim Burstall.

Attack from Mars 🦴🦴 ½ *Midnight Movie Massacre* **1988** Retro splatterama has really gross vampire alien land outside a Burbank movie theatre in 1956, and the really weird movie patrons try to terminate it. **86m/C VHS, DVD.** Robert Clarke, Ann (Robin) Robinson; ***D:*** Mark Stock; ***W:*** Mark Stock, David Houston.

Attack Girls' Swim Team vs. the Undead WOOF! *Joshikyoei hanrangun; Attack Girls' Swim Team vs the Unliving Dead; Nihonbi 2; Undead Pool* **2007** Second in a series of zombie-themed horror comedies (the others are to date unavailable in the United States). A villain convinces a local school of a virus outbreak, and they allow him to vaccinate the students—which actually turns them into flesh-eating zombies. Chlorine renders one immune to the vaccine, and thankfully the school's new lesbian leads the girls swim team on an all-out assault against them. **80m/C DVD.** *JP* Sasa Handa, Yuria Hidaka; ***D:*** Koji Kawano; ***W:*** Satoshi Owada; ***C:*** Mitsuaki Fujimoto; ***M:*** Hideto Takematsu.

Attack of the Beast Creatures WOOF! 1985 The survivors of a wrecked ocean liner are stranded on a desert island overrun by savage creatures. This makes them anxious. **82m/C VHS.** Robert Nolfi, Robert Langyel, Julia Rust, Lisa Pak; ***D:*** Michael Stanley.

Attack of the 50 Foot Woman 🦴🦴 ½ **1958** A beautiful, abused housewife has a frightening encounter with a giant alien, causing her to grow to an enormous height. Then she goes looking for hubby. Perhaps the all-time classic '50s sci fi, a truly fun movie highlighted by the sexy, 50-foot Hayes in a giant bikini. Has intriguing psychological depth and social commentary done in a suitably cheezy manner. **72m/B VHS.** Allison Hayes, William (Bill) Hudson, Roy Gordon, Yvette Vickers, George Douglas, Ken Terrell, Michael Ross, Frank Chase, Eileen Stevens, Otto Waldis; ***D:*** Nathan "Jerry" Juran; ***W:*** Mark Hanna; ***C:*** Jacques "Jack" Marquette; ***M:*** Ronald Stein.

Attack of the 50 Ft. Woman 🦴🦴 ½ **1993** Campy remake of the 1958 sci-fi cult classic features the statuesque Hannah in the title role. Nancy's a put-upon hausfrau with zero self-esteem thanks to her domineering father (Windom) and loutish hubby (Baldwin). They should have been sweet to her because after an encounter with a flying saucer Nancy starts to grow...and grow...and grow. And then she decides to get some revenge. **90m/C VHS, DVD.** Daryl Hannah, Daniel Baldwin, William Windom, Frances Fisher, Cristi Conaway, Paul Benedict, Lewis Arquette, Xander Berkeley, Hamilton Camp, Richard Edson, Victoria Haas, O'Neal Compton; ***D:*** Christopher Guest; ***W:*** Joseph Dougherty; ***M:*** Nicholas Pike. **TV**

Attack of the Giant Leeches 🦴 *The Giant Leeches; She Demons of the Swamp; Demons of the Swamp* **1959** Cheapo Corman fare about giant leeches in a murky swamp who suddenly decide to make human flesh their new food supply. Perturbed inn keeper plays along by forcing his wife and lover into the murk. Leeches frolic. Sometimes tedious, sometimes chilling, always low budget and slimy. Although the special effects aren't top notch, this might be a fine choice for a late night scare/laugh. **62m/B VHS, DVD.** Ken Clark, Yvette Vickers, Gene Roth, Bruno VeSota, Michael Emmet, Tyler McVey, Jan Shepard, George Cisar, Dan(iel) White; ***D:*** Bernard L. Kowalski; ***W:*** Leo Gordon; ***C:*** John M. Nickolaus Jr.; ***M:*** Alexander Laszlo.

Attack of the Killer Tomatoes WOOF! 1977 (PG) Candidate for worst film ever made, deliberate category. Horror spoof that defined "low budget" stars several thousand ordinary tomatoes that suddenly turn savage and begin attacking people. No sci-fi cliche remains untouched in this dumb parody. A few musical numbers are performed in lieu of an actual plot. Followed by "Return of the Killer Tomatoes." Originally released at 87 minutes. **87m/C VHS, DVD.** Georges Wilson, Jack Riley, Rock Peace, Eric Christmas, David Miller, Sharon Taylor, Jerry Anderson, Nigel Barber, John DeBello; ***D:*** John DeBello; ***W:*** Costa Dillon, John DeBello; ***C:*** John K. Culley.

Attack of the Mayan Mummy WOOF! 1963 A greedy doctor gets his patient to channel her former self so that she can show him where to find an ancient tomb that is filled with treasure. Good idea. **77m/B VHS.** *MX* Richard Webb, Nina Knight, Norman Burton, Steve Conte; ***D:*** Jerry Warren.

Attack of the Mushroom People 🦴🦴 *Matango; Fungus of Terror; Curse of the Mushroom People* **1963** Secluded island is the site where people eating mysterious mushrooms have been turning into oversized, killer 'shrooms' themselves. Trouble is, the only witness to this madness has gone insane. Will anyone believe him before it's too late? **70m/B VHS, DVD.** *JP* Akira Kubo, Kenji Sahara, Yoshio Tsuchiya, Hiroshi Koizumi, Kumi Mizuno, Miki Yashiro, Eisei Amamoto, Hiroshi Tachikawa; ***D:*** Inoshiro Honda; ***W:*** Takeshi Kimura; ***C:*** Hajime Koizumi.

Attack of the Puppet People 🦴🦴 *Six Inches Tall* **1958** This alternative classic from the prolific Bert I. Gordon, a rival to Ed Wood Jr. in the schlock hall of fame, will not make anyone forget "The Incredible Shrinking Man." The insane dollmaker Dr. Franz (Hoyt) shrinks six people (including our heroes Agar and Kenny) to the size of Ken and Barbie. Can they escape the mad scientist? The dog? The rat? The effects are nostalgically charming. **79m/B DVD.** John Agar, John Hoyt, June Kenney, Sally Reynolds, Susan Gordon; ***D:*** Bert I. Gordon; ***W:*** George Worthing Yates; ***C:*** Ernest Laszlo; ***M:*** Albert Glasser.

Attack of the Robots 🦴 ½ *Cartes sur Table* **1966** Silly spy spoof about powerful government officials who are being killed off by a mad scientist's robots. Interpol agent Lemmy Caution comes to the rescue. **88m/B VHS.** *FR SP* Eddie Constantine, Fernando Rey; ***D:*** Jess (Jesus) Franco; ***W:*** Jean-Claude Carriere.

Attack of the Sabretooth 🦴 ½ **2005 (R)** Think cheap "Jurassic Park." Niles (Bell) invests his moolah in a combo tropical paradise resort and wildlife refuge that contains cloned sabretooth tigers. Naturally they escape and maul and munch any human in reach. **88m/C DVD.** *AU* Robert Carradine, Nicholas Bell, Billy Aaron Brown, Brian Wimmer, Stacy Haiduk, Natalie Avital, Amanda Stephens; ***D:*** George Miller; ***W:*** Tom Woosley; ***C:*** Mark Melville; ***M:*** Timothy S. (Tim) Jones. **CABLE**

Attack of the 60-Foot Centerfold 🦴 ½ **1995 (R)** Angel Grace wants to be Centerfold of the Year so badly that she gets a doctor to enhance her endowments even more through a mystery formula. Only there's a little complication. Cheesy, with pretty women and no discernable acting (and a spoof of that '58 gem "Attack of the 50 Ft. Woman"). **83m/C VHS, DVD.** J.J. North, Tammy Parks, John Lazar, Russ Tamblyn, Tommy Kirk, Stanley Livingston, Michelle (McClellan) Bauer, George Stover, Forrest J Ackerman, Ted Monte, Jim Wynorski, Raelyn Saalman, Tim Abell, Jay Richardson, Nikki Fritz; ***D:*** Fred Olen Ray; ***W:*** Steve Armogida; ***C:*** Gary Graver, Howard Wexler; ***M:*** Jeff Walton.

Attack of the Swamp Creature WOOF! *Blood Waters of Dr. Z; Zaat; The Legend of the Zaat Monster; Hydra* **1975** A deranged scientist transforms himself into a swamp critter and terrorizes a small town. **96m/C VHS.** Marshall Grauer, Nancy Lien, Paul Galloway, Wade Popwell, Frank Crowell, David Robertson, Doug Thomas; ***D:*** Don Barton, Arnold Stevens; ***W:*** Lee Larew, Ron Kivett.

Attack Squadron 🦴 ½ *Kamakazi* **1963** Story of Japan's suicidal WWII pilots. **105m/C VHS.** *JP* Toshiro Mifune, Yuzo Kayama, Takashi Shimura, Yosuke Natsuki, Makoto Sato; ***D:*** Shue Matsubayashi; ***W:*** Shinobu Hashimoto; ***C:*** Takao Saito; ***M:*** Ikuma Dan.

Attack the Gas Station 🦴🦴 ½ *Juyuso seubgyuksageun* **1999 (R)** Four young slackers who have been successful at robbing gas stations take one over and pose as the attendants while keeping the real workers in back as hostages. They then indulge in other brilliant behavior by beating up the local gangsters, robbing the guys who deliver their takeout food, and cheesing off anyone they encounter. Eventually this ends in a comic slugfest between them, the cops, the mob, and several local Chinese restaurants. The police and organized crime are survivable but they're pretty brave taking on Chinese delivery boys. **109m/C DVD.** *KN* Ji-tae Yu, Jun Jeong, Yu-won Lee, Sung-jae Lee, Oh-seong Yu, Seong-jin Kang, Yeong-gyu Park; ***D:*** Sang-jin Kim; ***W:*** Jeong-woo Park; ***C:*** Jeong-won Choi; ***M:*** Mu-hyeon Son.

Attention Shoppers 1999 **(R)** Latin sitcom heartthrob Carbonell angers his wife and threatens his hunk status during a K-Mart publicity appearance in Houston that's taken over by his rival, soap star Perry. **87m/C VHS, DVD.** Nestor Carbonell, Luke Perry, Martin Mull, Kathy Najimy, Michael Lerner, Cara Buono, Lin Shaye, Casey Affleck; ***D:*** Philip Charles MacKenzie; ***W:*** Nestor Carbonell. **VIDEO**

The Attic 1/2 **1980 (R)** Psychodrama about an overbearing invalid father and his insecure and unmarried daughter. The girl learns to escape her unhappy life by hiding in the attic. Not horrifying, but a clear analytical look into the game of control. **92m/C VHS, DVD.** Carrie Snodgress, Ray Milland, Rosemary Murphy, Ruth Cox, Frances Bay, Marjorie Eaton; ***D:*** George Edwards.

The Attic **2006 (R)** Not very scary horror flick that also suffers in the script and acting departments. Emma Callan (Moss) and her family move into what seems to be a perfect Victorian home. Only Emma begins to have visions of her twin, who's supposedly dead, evil, and hiding in the attic. **85m/C DVD.** Elisabeth (Elissabeth, Elizabeth, Liz) Moss, Jason Lewis, John Savage, Catherine Mary Stewart, Tom Malloy; ***D:*** Mary Lambert; ***W:*** Tom Malloy; ***C:*** James Callanan; ***M:*** Mario Grigorov. **VIDEO**

The Attic: The Hiding of Anne Frank 1/2 **1988** Steenburgen is wonderful in the true story of Miep Gies, the Dutch woman who hid Otto Frank, her employer, and his family from the Nazis. Unusual because it is told from Gies's perspective, rather than from the more familiar Anne Frank story. Based on Gies's book, "Anne Frank Remembered." **95m/C VHS.** Mary Steenburgen, Paul Scofield, Huub Stapel, Eleanor Bron, Miriam Karlin, Lisa Jacobs, Ronald Pickup; ***D:*** John Erman; ***W:*** William Hanley; ***M:*** Richard Rodney Bennett. **TV**

Attica **1980** Tense depiction of the infamous Attica prison takeover in 1971 and the subsequent bloodbath as state troops were called in. Although edited due to the searing commentary by Nelson Rockefeller, it remains powerful and thought-provoking. Adapted from the Tom Wicker bestseller "A Time to Die." **97m/C VHS.** George Grizzard, Charles Durning, Anthony Zerbe, Roger E. Mosley; ***D:*** Marvin J. Chomsky. **TV**

Attila 1/2 **1954** Silly historical costumer. Attila (Quinn) and his brother Bleda (Manni) battle for control over the Huns. Attila wants to conquer Rome next but Bleda wants to make the Romans their allies. The weakling Roman emperor (Laydu) is willing to make peace and his ambitious sister Honoria (Loren) offers to wed Attila, but their powerful mother (Regis) refuses and tells Roman general Aetius (Vidal) to prepare the legions for battle. Italian with subtitles. **87m/C DVD.** *IT* Anthony Quinn, Sophia Loren, Henri Vidal, Ettore Manni, Irene Papas, Christian Marquand, Claude Laydu, Colette Regis; ***D:*** Christian Marquand, Pietro Francisci; ***W:*** Primo Zeglio, Ennio De Concini; ***C:*** Aldo Tonti; ***M:*** Enzo Masetti.

Attila 1/2 **2001** Epic miniseries takes on the life of Attila the Hun. Early years of Attila are swiftly dealt with as his family is slaughtered and the boy is raised by his uncle—with his cousin as his rival for leadership. The adult Attila (Butler) is tough, charismatic, and bloodthirsty enough to unite the Hun tribes and challenge the domination of the Roman empire, which leads to the politically savvy Roman general Flavius Aetius (Boothe) being dispatched to get Attila on Rome's side. Lots of big battles as this part of history is treacherous indeed. **177m/C VHS, DVD.** Gerard Butler, Powers Boothe, Alice Krige, Simmone Jade MacKinnon, Tim Curry, Reg Rogers, Steven Berkoff, Tommy Flanagan, Pauline Lynch, Liam Cunningham, Jolyon Baker, Sian Phillips, Jonathan Hyde; ***D:*** Dick Lowry; ***W:*** Robert Cochran; ***C:*** Steven Fierberg; ***M:*** Nick Glennie-Smith. **CABLE**

Au Pair 1/2 **1999** MBA grad Jenny Morgan learns the job she's been hired for by widowed, wealthy business exec Oliver Caldwell is that of nanny to his two bratty kids, Kate and Alex. When the kids bond with Jenny, they decide she'd make a much-better stepmom than their dad's witchy fiancee, Vivian (Sibbert), and play matchmaker when they all travel to Paris. Originally shown on the Fox Family Channel. **90m/C DVD.** Heidi Lenhart Seban, Gregory Harrison, Katie Volding, Jake Dinwiddie, John Rhys-Davies, Jane Sibbett, Michael Woolson, Richard Riehle; ***D:*** Mark Griffiths; ***W:*** Jeffrey C. Sherman, Cheryl Seban; ***C:*** Blake T. Evans; ***M:*** Inon Zur. **CABLE**

Au Pair 2: The Fairy Tale Continues 1/2 **2001** Nanny Jenny and her boss Oliver are keeping their romance a secret for fear of upsetting imperious Nell, his late wife's mother, who's willing to believe the worst about Jenny. But the bigger obstacle is the would-be merger of Oliver's firm with that of Karl Sennhauser, whose greedy grown children plan to use Jenny to ruin Oliver so they can take over instead. However, Oliver's smarter, younger kids have different ideas. Originally shown on the Fox Family Channel. **93m/C DVD.** Gregory Harrison, Heidi Lenhart Seban, June Lockhart, Katie Volding, Jake Dinwiddie, Rachel York, Robin Dunne, Rory Johnston, Celine Massuger, Cliff Bemis; ***D:*** Mark Griffiths; ***W:*** Jeffrey C. Sherman, Cheryl Seban; ***C:*** Thomas Callaway; ***M:*** Inon Zur. **CABLE**

Au Pair 3: Adventure in Paradise **2009** Oliver and Jenny are married with a baby and they and his children Kate and Alex go on vacation to Puerto Rico. But it's not all fun in the sun as Jake refuses to be groomed to take over the family business and both Jake and Kate would rather go off on their own than hang out with the 'rents. An eight-year gap between sequels wasn't exactly kind to the cable family comedy and the brother/sister duo were more appealing characters when they were younger. Originally shown on ABC Family. **99m/C DVD.** Heidi Lenhart Seban, Gregory Harrison, Jake Dinwiddie, Katie Volding; ***D:*** Mark Griffiths; ***W:*** Jeffrey C. Sherman. **CABLE**

Au Pair Girls 1/2 **1972** Four sexy young ladies leave their various homelands to embark on careers as au pair girls, making friends and love along the way. **86m/C VHS, DVD.** *GB* Gabrielle Drake, Astrid Frank, Nancie Wait, Me Me Lai, Richard O'Sullivan, Johnny Briggs, Ferdinand "Ferdy" Mayne; ***D:*** Val Guest; ***W:*** Val Guest, David Adnopoz; ***C:*** John Wilcox; ***M:*** Roger Webb.

Au Revoir les Enfants *Goodbye, Children* **1987 (PG)** During the Nazi occupation of France in the 1940s, the headmaster of a Catholic boarding school hides three Jewish boys among the other students by altering their names and identities. Two of the students, Julien (Manesse) and Jean (Fejto), form a friendship that ends tragically when Jean and the other boys are discovered and taken away by the Gestapo. Compelling and emotionally wrenching coming of age tale based on an incident from director Malle's childhood is considered to be his best film to date and quite possibly the best he will ever make. In French with English subtitles. Other 1987 movies with similar themes are "Hope and Glory" and "Empire of the Sun." **104m/C VHS, DVD.** *FR GE* Gaspard Manesse, Raphael Fejto, Francine Racette, Stanislas Carre de Malberg, Philippe Morier-Genoud, Francois Berleand, Peter Fitz, Francois Negret, Irene Jacob, Pascal Rivet, Benoit Henriet, Richard Leboeuf, Xavier Legrand, Arnaud Henriet, Jean-Sebastien Chauvin, Luc Etienne; ***D:*** Louis Malle; ***W:*** Louis Malle; ***C:*** Renato Berta. British Acad. '88: Director (Malle); Cesar '88: Art Dir./Set Dec., Cinematog., Director (Malle), Film, Sound, Writing; L.A. Film Critics '87: Foreign Film; Venice Film Fest. '87: Film.

Audition 1/2 *Odishon* **1999** Director Miike successfully illustrates a middle-aged widower's worst nightmares about remarrying a younger woman. The benign first half of the film, in which businessman Aoyama (Ishibashi) is persuaded by a producer friend to stage a fake movie audition in order to find a new bride, belies the gruesome turn of events revealed later. Seven years single, Aoyama wants a traditional, submissive young girl, which he finds in one of the actresses, Asami (Shiina). Aoyama's smitten, but buddy Yoshikawa (Kunimura) is decidedly less so, sensing something a tad askew in the graceful beauty. Something definitely is amiss, as numerous flashbacks showing the girl's sadistic bent attest. Soon enough, Aoyama is on the business end of Asami's macabre doings. Based on a story by Ryu Murakami. In Japanese with subtitles. **115m/C VHS, DVD.** *JP* Ryo Ishibashi, Eihi Shiina, Tetsu Sawaki, Jun Kunimura, Miyuki Matsuda; ***D:*** Takashi Miike; ***W:*** Daisuke Tengan; ***C:*** Hideo Yamamoto; ***M:*** Koji Endo.

The Audrey Hepburn Story **2000 (PG)** When you play a movie icon, expect the critical brickbats to fly. Sweet Hewitt does her best in the title role (Hepburn's her longtime idol) but it's all surface gloss. Bio covers 1935 to 1960 as Hepburn deals with family crises (dad's a two-timing Nazi sympathizer who abandons his family), war years in Nazi-occupied Holland, Hepburn's beginnings as a dancer in England and her first small roles. Then it's onto New York and the world of theatre and films. Along the way there's a little romance, a marriage to actor Mel Ferrer (McCormack), and various re-creations of some Hepburn movie roles. **133m/C VHS, DVD.** Jennifer Love Hewitt, Eric McCormack, Frances Fisher, Peter Giles, Keir Dullea, Gabriel Macht, Marcel Jeannin, Swede Svensson, Michael J. Burg, Ryan Hollyman; ***D:*** Steve Robman; ***W:*** Marsha Norman; ***C:*** Pierre Letarte; ***M:*** Lawrence Shragge. **TV**

Audrey Rose **1977 (PG)** Parents of a young girl are terrified when their darling daughter is having dreadful dreams. Mysterious friend Hopkins cements their fears when he declares that his dead daughter has been reincarnated in their child. The nightmares continue suggesting that none other than Lucifer could be at work. Good cast is hampered by slow-moving take-off on "The Exorcist" with a weak staged ending. Adapted by DeFelitta from his novel. **113m/C VHS, DVD.** Marsha Mason, Anthony Hopkins, John Beck, John Hillerman, Susan Swift, Norman Lloyd; ***D:*** Robert Wise; ***W:*** Frank De Felitta; ***C:*** Victor Kemper.

Audrey's Rain **2003** Audrey (Smart) is already caring for her younger, mentally challenged sister Marguerite (Wilhoite) when she must take in her orphaned niece and nephew after another sister commits suicide. No wonder Audrey is grateful for the attentions of old boyfriend Terry Lloyd (Smart's husband Gilliland). But can they overcome their troubles to take a second chance on love? Packs too much story into a too-short run time but Smart is always a pleasure to watch. **88m/C DVD.** *US* Jean Smart, Richard Gilliland, Kathleen Wilhoite, Angus T. Jones, Carol Kane; ***D:*** Sam Pillsbury; ***W:*** Jennifer Schwalbach Smith, Kate Smith; ***C:*** James W. Wrenn; ***M:*** Stephen (Steve) Edwards. **CABLE**

August 1/2 **1995 (PG)** Yet another version of Chekov's "Uncle Vanya," this time transported to 1890s Wales. Hopkins (who makes his directorial debut and composed the score) stars as Ieuan Davies, a bitter drinker who manages the estate of brother-in-law Alexander Blathwaite (Phillips). Blathwaite arrives for his annual summer stay with unhappy, young second wife Helen (Burton), who's the object of desire for both Ieuan and the local doctor, Michael Lloyd (Grainger). It's a perfectedly adequate rendition but offers little that's new except a change of scenery. **93m/C VHS.** *GB* Anthony Hopkins, Kate Burton, Leslie Phillips, Gawn Grainger, Rhian Morgan, Hugh Lloyd, Rhoda Lewis, Menna Tussler; ***D:*** Anthony Hopkins; ***W:*** Julian Mitchell; ***C:*** Robin Vidgeon; ***M:*** Anthony Hopkins.

August 1/2 **2008 (R)** In 2001, Tom Sterling (Hartnett) is riding the dot-com bubble as CEO of Landshark, a New York internet startup company whose services are actually created by his married brother Josh (Scott). The cracks begin to show, precipitating a cash-flow crisis Tom prefers to ignore. There's no particular urgency or surprise to the story and Tom is a hollow, unlikeable character blankly played by Hartnett. **88m/C DVD.** Josh Hartnett, Adam Scott, Robin Tunney, Emmanuelle Chriqui, Andre Royo, Naomie Harris, Rip Torn, Caroline Lagerfelt, David Bowie; ***D:*** Austin Chick; ***W:*** Howard A. Rodman; ***C:*** Andrij Parekh; ***M:*** Nathan Larson.

August Rush **2007 (PG)** Lyla (Russell) is a classical cellist who falls for club-band musician Louis (Rhys Myers) and soon finds herself pregnant with his child. Her overbearing stage father tells her the baby has died and ships him off to an orphanage. Fast-forward 11 years and little orphan Evan (adorable Highmore) hears music in everything. He thinks if he learns how to play an instrument, his parents—who he knows are musicians—will find him. Through sheer force, a few side players, a healthy dose of appropriately sappy music, and a whole lotta far-fetched coincidences, the family is reunited. Utterly and unapologetically predictable, but it won't matter a bit if your idea of a good film is one in which you need an entire box of tissues. **113m/C DVD.** *US* Freddie Highmore, Keri Russell, Jonathan Rhys Meyers, Terrence Howard, Robin Williams, William Sadler, Leon G. Thomas III, Jamia Simone Nash; ***D:*** Kristen Sheridan; ***W:*** Nick Castle, James V. Hart; ***C:*** John Mathieson; ***M:*** Mark Mancina, Hans Zimmer.

Augustin **1995** Very short comedy about aspiring actor Augustin (Sibertin-Blanc), who may just get his break when he hears about a part for a room-service waiter and prepares himself rigorously by actually getting a job in a Paris hotel. Pathetically earnest and dignified, at the actual audition he bewilders actor Lhermitte, when instead of just reading the scene, Augustin proceeds to act it out in detail. Very slight but charming thanks to a deadpan performance by Sibertin-Blanc (who's also director Fontaine's brother). French with subtitles. **61m/C VHS.** *FR* Jean-Chretien Sibertin-Blanc, Thierry Lhermitte, Stephanie Zhang, Nora Habib, Guy Casabonne; ***D:*** Anne Fontaine; ***W:*** Anne Fontaine; ***C:*** Jean-Marie Dreujou.

Augustine of Hippo *Agostino di Ippona* **1972** One of Rossellini's later historical epics, depicting the last years of St. Augustine and how they exemplify the growing conflicts between Church and State, Christian ethic and societal necessity. In Italian with subtitles. **120m/C VHS.** *IT* ***D:*** Roberto Rossellini.

Auntie WOOF! *Keep It Up, Jack* **1973 (R)** Entertainer must dress and act like his madam aunt who has died, in order to fool her former employees in a house of prostitution. **85m/C VHS.** *GB* Mark Jones, Sue Longhurst, Frank Thornton, Linda Regan; ***D:*** Derek Ford; ***W:*** Derek Ford, Alan Selwyn; ***C:*** Geoff Glover; ***M:*** Terry Warr.

Auntie Lee's Meat Pies 1/2 **1992 (R)** Auntie Lee's meat pie business is booming thanks to her five beautiful nieces. They help keep their aunt supplied with the secret ingredient—gorgeous young men! Four Playboy Playmates are featured in this cannibalistic horror comedy. **100m/C VHS.** Karen Black, Noriyuki "Pat" Morita, Pat Paulsen, Huntz Hall, Michael Berryman, David Parry, Stephen Quadros, Ava Fabian, Teri Weigel; ***D:*** Joseph F. Robertson; ***W:*** Joseph F. Robertson; ***C:*** Arledge Armenaki.

Auntie Mame **1958** A young boy is brought up by his only surviving relative—flamboyant and eccentric Auntie Mame. Mame is positive that "life is a banquet and most poor suckers are starving to death." Based on the Patrick Dennis novel about his life with "Auntie Mame." Part of the "A Night at the Movies" series, this tape simulates a 1958 movie evening, with a Road Runner cartoon, "Hook, Line and Stinker," a newsreel and coming attractions for "No Time for Sergeants" and "Chase a Crooked Shadow." **161m/C VHS, DVD.** Rosalind Russell, Patric Knowles, Roger Smith, Peggy Cass, Forrest Tucker, Coral Browne; ***D:*** Morton DaCosta; ***W:*** Betty Comden, Adolph Green; ***C:*** Harry Stradling Sr. Golden Globes '59: Actress—Mus./Comedy (Russell).

The Aura **2005** To escape his bleak life in Buenos Aires, Esteban (Darin)—a quiet, reserved taxidermist—has fantasies of carrying out the perfect crime using his photographic memory even though he's plagued by epileptic seizures that at first give him great clarity (the "aura") but then cause blackouts. Despite this, Esteban seizes a chance to make his crime dream come true when he figures out that Dietrich (Rodal), who he mistakenly kills while on a hunting trip, was plotting a real heist. He's able to convince Dietrich's wife and gang members that he's also in on the gig but much like his seizures the events that follow get out of control. Tense thriller was only the second movie directed by Bielinsky, who died of a heart attack after its completion. In Spanish with subtitles. **138m/C DVD.** *AR FR SP* Ricardo Darin, Dolores Fonzi, Alejandro Awada, Pablo Cedron, Jorge d'Elia, Nahuel Perez, Walter Reyno, Manuel Rodal, Rafael Castejon; ***D:*** Fabian Bielinsky; ***W:*** Fabian Bielinsky; ***C:*** Checco Varese; ***M:*** Lucio Godoy.

Aurora 🦴🦴 ½ *Aurora by Night; Qualcosa di Biondo* **1984** Single mom Aurora (Loren) will do anything for her blind son Ciro (played by Loren's son Edoardo Ponti). When she discovers that there's a possible operation that could restore his sight, Aurora decides to call up all Ciro's possible fathers and get them to finance the surgery. This plan also reunites Aurora with the one man she truly loved. Made for Italian TV. **91m/C VHS.** *IT* Sophia Loren, Daniel J. Travanti, Ricky Tognazzi, Philippe Noiret, Anna Strasberg, Franco Fabrizi; ***D:*** Maurizio Ponzi; ***M:*** Georges Delerue. **TV**

Aurora Borealis 🦴🦴 ½ **2006 (R)** Sutherland happily chews scenery as aged Ronald, whose increasingly ill health is proving too much for his wife Ruth (Fletcher) to handle. Fortunately, their slacker grandson Duncan (Jackson) gets a handyman's job at their apartment building to help out. Ruth also hires free-spirited home healthcare worker Kate (Lewis), whom Duncan immediately fancies. But Kate doesn't like to stay in one place for too long so Duncan may have to make a tough decision about where his future lies. Title refers to Ronald's belief that he can see the northern lights from his window. **110m/C DVD.** *US* Joshua Jackson, Donald Sutherland, Juliette Lewis, Louise Fletcher; ***D:*** James C.E. Burke; ***W:*** Brent Boyd; ***C:*** Alar Kivilo; ***M:*** Mychael Danna.

The Aurora Encounter 🦴🦴 **1985 (PG)** Aliens surreptitiously infiltrate a small town in 1897, and spread benevolence everywhere. Family fare. **90m/C VHS, DVD.** Jack Elam, Peter Brown, Carol Bagdasarian, Dottie West, George "Spanky" McFarland; ***D:*** Jim McCullough Sr.; ***W:*** Jim McCullough Jr.

Aussie and Ted's Great Adventure 🦴🦴 ½ **2009 (G)** Michael Brooks returns from Australia with a dog that immediately bonds with his young daughter Laney. However, Michael later buys Laney a very special teddy bear from a friend in Chinatown. Aussie gets jealous and manages to 'lose' Ted on the streets of their San Francisco hometown. Then doggie guilt sets in and Aussie hunts to find Ted, only to have the Brooks' move out to their aunt's farm in the meantime. **89m/C DVD.** Dean Cain, Alyssa Shafer, Leo Howard, Kristin Eggers, Beverly D'Angelo, Emily Kuroda, Vanessa Bell Calloway, Timothy Starks; ***D:*** Shuki Levy; ***W:*** Shuki Levy, Tori Avey; ***C:*** James Mathers; ***M:*** Shuki Levy, Gil Feldman; ***V:*** James Ryan, Nick Shafer. **VIDEO**

Austin Powers: International Man of Mystery 🦴🦴🦴 **1997 (PG-13)** Hilarious spoof of '60s spy and babe movies. Groovy '60s spy Austin Powers (Myers) discovers that his arch-enemy, Dr. Evil (Myers again) has frozen himself in order to elude capture, so the swingin' dentally challenged Brit decides to do the same. They awaken 30 years later in the same state: woefully out of touch. Dr. Evil is attempting to blackmail the British government and deal with his Gen-X son, Scott Evil (Green), who wants more quality time and less world conquest. Austin, on the other hand, is trying to "shag" every "groovy bird" he sees. He is teamed with Vanessa (Hurley), the daughter of his former partner, and they try to stop the evil machinations of...well..Evil. A festival of crushed velvet, political incorrectness, and female robots with lethal breasts. Myers revels in playing the fool, and he may step over the line every once in a while, but he gets plenty of mileage out of the one-joke premise. **88m/C VHS, DVD, UMD.** Mike Myers, Elizabeth Hurley, Michael York, Seth Green, Mimi Rogers, Robert Wagner, Fabiana Udenio, Paul Dillon, Charles Napier, Will Ferrell, Mindy Sterling; ***Cameos:*** Tom Arnold, Carrie Fisher; ***D:*** Jay Roach; ***W:*** Mike Myers; ***C:*** Peter Deming; ***M:*** George S. Clinton. MTV Movie Awards '98: Villain (Myers), Dance Seq. (Mike Myers/Londoners).

Austin Powers 2: The Spy Who Shagged Me 🦴🦴🦴 **1999 (PG-13)** Old snaggle-tooth (Myers) returns and time travels back to 1969 in order to foil his look-alike nemesis, Dr. Evil, who steals Powers' mojo. Myers wisely highlights the not-so-good Dr., along with some hilarious new characters, instead of the periodically wearisome Powers. Again plot takes a back seat to the great dialogue, characters (including Rob Lowe doing a dead-on Robert Wagner and a third Myers incarnation, Fat Bastard), and kitchy eye candy. It all still works because of Myers' winking good nature. **95m/C VHS, DVD.** Mike Myers, Heather Graham, Elizabeth Hurley, Seth Green, Robert Wagner, Rob Lowe, Verne Troyer, Kristen Johnston, Mindy Sterling, Gia Carides, Clint Howard, Michael York, Will Ferrell, Muse Watson, Charles Napier, Tim Robbins, Fred Willard, Jack Kehler; ***Cameos:*** Burt Bacharach, Elvis Costello, Rebecca Romijn, Woody Harrelson, Willie Nelson, Jerry Springer; ***D:*** Jay Roach; ***W:*** Michael McCullers, Mike Myers; ***C:*** Ueli Steiger; ***M:*** George S. Clinton. MTV Movie Awards '00: On-Screen Duo (Mike Myers/Verne Troyer), Villain (Myers).

Austin Powers In Goldmember 🦴🦴 ½ **2002 (PG-13)** Shag-happy superspy Austin Powers is back for the third installment of the spy-spoof franchise. Austin travels back to the 70's to find his secret agent dad Nigel (Caine), hook up with new love interest and fellow spy Foxxy Cleopatra (Knowles), and rescue the world. Myers again takes on numerous roles, this time adding new villain Goldmember, a disco-clad Dutchman with a gilded prosthetic and a penchant for world domination. Dr. Evil is in good form but soft newcomer Goldmember comes up short, and Myers is running out of funny ideas. Bond studio MGM raised a stink about the title (too close to "Goldfinger") but finally saw the light and allowed the parody to continue. **94m/C VHS, DVD.** *US* Mike Myers, Michael Caine, Seth Green, Beyonce Knowles, Verne Troyer, Michael York, Robert Wagner, Mindy Sterling, Fred Savage, Tommy (Tiny) Lister, Clint Howard, Nathan Lane; ***Cameos:*** Steven Spielberg, Gwyneth Paltrow, Tom Cruise, Kevin Spacey, Danny DeVito, John Travolta, Quincy Jones, Burt Bacharach, Britney Spears, Ozzy Osbourne, Donna D'Errico, Susanna Hoffs; ***D:*** Jay Roach; ***W:*** Mike Myers, Michael McCullers; ***C:*** Peter Deming; ***M:*** George S. Clinton.

Australia 🦴🦴 ½ **2008 (PG-13)** Luhrmann's near-three-hour epic, set in northern Australia shortly before WWII, finds English aristocrat Lady Sarah Ashley inheriting a sprawling cattle station, eyed by local barons looking to take over. So Lady Sarah joins forces with a stockman known only as The Drover to drive 2,000 head of cattle to market, only to then face the bombing of Darwin by the Japanese. Long and melodramatic all-things-Down-Under story is beautiful to watch, with astonishing photography, sweeping vistas, and easy-on-the-eyes leads in Kidman and Jackman, but is ultimately overwhelmed by its own grandiose ambitions (note the similarities between posters for "Australia" and "Gone With the Wind"). **165m/C DVD.** *AU US GB* Nicole Kidman, Hugh Jackman, David Wenham, Bryan Brown, Jack Thompson, Ben Mendelsohn, David Gulpilil, David Ngoombujarra, Yuen Wah, Barry Otto, Bruce Spence, Brandon Walters, Lillian Crombie; ***D:*** Baz Luhrmann; ***W:*** Baz Luhrmann, Stuart Beattie, Ronald Harwood, Richard Flanagan; ***C:*** Mandy Walker; ***M:*** David Hirschfelder.

Author! Author! 🦴🦴 ½ **1982 (PG)** Sweet, likable comedy about playwright Pacino who is about to taste success with his first big hit. Suddenly his wife walks out, leaving him to care for her four children and his own son. His views shift as he begins to worry about, among other things, who will watch the obnoxious kids on opening night. **100m/C VHS, DVD.** Al Pacino, Tuesday Weld, Dyan Cannon, Alan King, Andre Gregory; ***D:*** Arthur Hiller; ***W:*** Israel Horovitz; ***M:*** Dave Grusin.

Auto Focus 🦴🦴🦴 **2002 (R)** Paul Schrader examines the sordid life and death of "Hogan's Heroes" star Bob Crane (Kinnear). Kinnear's portrayal of Crane from the seemingly normal father and husband to the sexaholic who was found bludgeoned to death amongst his amateur pornography is startling. The trouble starts when he meets creepy pal (and possible murderer) Carpenter (Dafoe), who gets him drumming gigs in strip clubs. This easy access to women, along with his affable manner and Carpenter's array of video equipment lead to a torrent of carnal acts that the two obsessively commit to tape. Crane loses two wives (Wilson, Bello) and his wholesome image while remaining oblivious to the descent that his sex addiction is causing in his personal and professional life. The cast does a great job with difficult material, especially Kinnear and Ron Leibman as Crane's weary agent. **104m/C VHS, DVD.** *US* Greg Kinnear, Willem Dafoe, Rita Wilson, Maria Bello, Ron Leibman, Kurt Fuller, Ed Begley Jr., Michael E. Rodgers, Michael McKean, Bruce Solomon, Christopher Neiman, Lyle Kanouse; ***D:*** Paul Schrader; ***W:*** Michael Gerbosi; ***C:*** Fred Murphy; ***M:*** Angelo Badalamenti.

Autobiography of a Princess 🦴🦴 **1975** A brief character study shot by Merchant-Ivory in six days. An East Indian princess, living in self-enforced exile in London, invites her father's former tutor to tea. They watch old movie footage of royal India together and dream of a happier past. **59m/C VHS.** James Mason, Madhur Jaffrey; ***D:*** James Ivory; ***W:*** Ruth Prawer Jhabvala.

The Autobiography of Miss Jane Pittman 🦴🦴🦴 ½ **1974** The history of blacks in the South is seen through the eyes of a 110-year-old former slave. From the Civil War through the Civil Rights movement, Miss Pittman relates every piece of black history, allowing the viewer to experience the injustices. Tyson is spectacular in moving, highly acclaimed drama. Received nine Emmy awards; adapted by Tracy Keenan Wynn from the novel by Ernest J. Gaines. **110m/C VHS, DVD.** Cicely Tyson, Odetta, Joseph Tremice, Richard Dysart, Michael Murphy, Katherine Helmond; ***D:*** John Korty; ***W:*** Tracy Keenan Wynn; ***C:*** James A. Crabe; ***M:*** Fred Karlin. **TV**

Automatic 🦴 ½ **1994 (R)** Renegade RobGen Industries android Gruner saves Ashbrook from the loathsome sexual advances of the boss but kills the scum in the process. So the duo are targeted for death by company head Glover with killers, led by Kober, sent to do the mopping up. **90m/C VHS.** Olivier Gruner, Daphne Ashbrook, John Glover, Jeff Kober, Dennis Lipscomb; ***D:*** John Murlowski; ***W:*** Susan Lambert, Patrick Highsmith.

Automaton Transfusion WOOF! **2006 (R)** Dumb title, worse movie. It's cheap, gory zombie horror that has the advantage of at least having a short run-time. Teens in some backwater Florida burg find their town is being overrun by bloodthirsty zombies that are result of a misbegotten military experiment. **75m/C DVD.** Garrett Jones, Juliet Reeves, Kendra Farner, Joel Hebner, Rowan Bousaid, William Howard Bowman; ***D:*** Steven C. Miller; ***W:*** Steven C. Miller; ***C:*** Jeff Dolan; ***M:*** Jamey Scott. **VIDEO**

Autopsy 🦴 ½ *Tarot* **1974 (R)** Forensic pathologist Farmer is working at a morgue compiling statistics concerning suicides and murders staged to look like suicides. Farmer begins to go nuts when it seems a stalker is killing people around her using the fake suicide method. Then there's the fact that the pathological pathologist is also sexually repressed and everything and everyone starts to scream sex to her and things get really kinky (and gory). **100m/C VHS, DVD.** *IT FR SP* Mimsy Farmer, Barry Primus, Angela Goodwin, Ray Lovelock; ***D:*** Armando Crispino; ***W:*** Armando Crispino, Lucio Battistrada; ***C:*** Carlo Carlini; ***M:*** Ennio Morricone.

Autopsy 🦴 *Tarot* **1974** A young gold-digger and a millionaire marry, and then cheat on each other, provoking blackmail and murder. **90m/C VHS, DVD.** *FR SP* Sue Lyon, Fernando Rey, Gloria Grahame, Christian Hay; ***D:*** Jose Maria Forque; ***W:*** Rafael Azcona; ***C:*** Alejandro Ulloa; ***M:*** Michel Colombier.

Autopsy: A Love Story 🦴🦴 ½ **2002** Life is a cold, lonely place for morgue-worker Charlie, whose pushy boss has him knee-deep in the bootlegged organs business. Meanwhile, his cross, crippled girlfriend torments him. The arrival of a hot new amour at the office livens things up—even though she's dead—but the pitiful lad is thrown when her (living) twin sister shows up. **90m/C VHS, DVD.** Joe Estevez, Paul DeGruccio, Dina Osmussen, Ginny Harman, Wendy Crawford, Robert McClure, Jill Seitz, Greg Hanson, Mike Watkis, Keith Arbo, Ashley Smith, John Scott Mills; ***D:*** Guy Crawford; ***W:*** Guy Crawford, Tamarie Hargrove. **VIDEO**

Autopsy of a Ghost 🦴 ½ *Autopsia de un Fantasma* **1967** Comedy/horror film stars Rathbone as a ghost and Mitchell as a mad scientist. Notable as Rathbone's last screen appearance. In Spanish with no subtitles. **110m/C VHS.** *SP* Basil Rathbone, John Carradine, Cameron Mitchell, Amadee Chabot; ***D:*** Ismael Rodriguez; ***W:*** Armando Crispino, Lucio Battistrada.

An Autumn Afternoon 🦴🦴🦴 ½ *Sanma No Aji* **1962** Ozu's final film is a beautiful expression of his talent. In postwar Tokyo, an aging widower loses his only daughter to marriage and begins a life of loneliness. A heart-wrenching tale of relationships and loss. In Japanese with English subtitles. **112m/C VHS.** *JP* Chishu Ryu, Shima Iwashita, Shin-Ichiro Mikami, Mariko Okada, Keiji Sada; ***D:*** Yasujiro Ozu; ***W:*** Yasujiro Ozu; ***C:*** Yuuharu Atsuta; ***M:*** Kojun Saito.

Autumn Born 🦴 ½ **1979 (R)** Young heiress is abducted by her guardian and imprisoned while she's taught to obey his will. Ill-fated ex-Playmate Dorothy Stratton's first film. **76m/C VHS.** Dorothy Stratten, Ihor Procak, Dory Jackson, Gisselle Fredette, Nate MacIntosh, Joanna McClelland Glass, Roberta Weiss, Roman Buchok, Sharon Elder; ***D:*** Lloyd A. Simandl; ***W:*** Sharon Christensen, Shannon Lee, Ihor Procak; ***C:*** Lloyd A. Simandl.

Autumn Hearts: A New Beginning 🦴🦴 *Emotional Arithmetic* **2007** A notable cast in a story that's sentimental and somewhat familiar. In 1945, Jewish dissident Jakob protected youngsters Melanie and Christopher when they were all interred at a detention camp outside Paris. After 35 years, the trio is unexpectedly reunited at Melanie's (Sarandon) rural home in Quebec, where she lives unhappily with husband David (Plummer). Christopher (Byrne) has never gotten over his first love for Melanie and the strong emotional bonds of the past prove to be equally potent in the present. **100m/C DVD.** *CA* Susan Sarandon, Christopher Plummer, Gabriel Byrne, Max von Sydow, Roy Dupuis, Kris Holden-Ried, Dakota Goya, Regan Jewitt, Alexandre Nachi; ***D:*** Paolo Barzman; ***W:*** Jefferson Lewis; ***C:*** Luc Montpellier; ***M:*** Normand Corbeil.

Autumn in New York 🦴 ½ **2000 (PG-13)** Start with one clunky love story with no chemistry, then mix in cheesy melodrama and a dash of creepy Freudian undertones and what do you get? This recipe for disaster about a doomed May-December romance. Middle-aged Will Keane (Gere) leads a playboy's life as the owner of one of New York's most fashionable restaurants. He falls for much younger sensitive gal Charlotte (Ryder) after finding out that he dated her mother. Unfortunately, Charlotte is afflicted with a life-threatening disease whose symptoms include saying "Wow!" a lot and fainting at overly dramatic moments. Will's life is changed, and he rushes around trying to find some medical miracle or plot device which might be able to save her. Rent "Love Story" instead. Because love means never having to say you're sorry you wasted two hours of your life on this movie. **104m/C VHS, DVD.** Richard Gere, Winona Ryder, Anthony LaPaglia, Elaine Stritch, Vera Farmiga, Sherry Stringfield, Jill(ian) Hennessey; ***D:*** Joan Chen; ***W:*** Allison Burnett; ***C:*** Changwei Gu; ***M:*** Gabriel Yared.

Autumn Leaves 🦴🦴 ½ **1956** Crawford plays a middle-aged typist grasping at her last chance for love. She marries a younger man who's been romancing her, then finds him more and more unstable and violent. Weak story material that could turn melodramatic and tawdry, but doesn't because of Crawford's strength. **108m/B VHS.** Cliff Robertson, Joan Crawford, Vera Miles, Lorne Greene; ***D:*** Robert Aldrich; ***W:*** Robert Blees, Lewis Meltzer, Hugo Butler, Jean Rouveral; ***C:*** Charles B(ryant) Lang Jr. Berlin Intl. Film Fest. '56: Director (Aldrich).

Autumn Marathon 🦴🦴 ½ *Osenny Marafon* **1979** To say that this is one of the better Russian movies of the past three decades is sort of faint praise, given the state of

Soviet cinema. Written by playwright Volodin, it's just another paint-by-number version of the philandering man who's really an OK Joe who loves his kids comedy. In Russian with English subtitles. **100m/C VHS, DVD.** *RU* Oleg Basilashvili, Natalia Gundareva, Marina Neyolova; ***D:*** Georgi Daniela; ***W:*** Alexander Volodin.

Autumn Moon *Qiuyue* **1992** Young Japanese tourist (Nagase) travels to Hong Kong to enjoy some sexual fun but instead he befriends a 15-year-old girl (Wai), who's afraid of her family's impending emigration to Canada. Not much happens but the Hong Kong setting is eye-catching. English and Cantonese with subtitles. **108m/C VHS.** *HK* Masatoshi Nagase, Li Pui Wai; ***D:*** Clara Law; ***C:*** Tony Leung Siu Hung.

Autumn Sonata *Hostsonaten* **1978** Nordic family strife as famed concert pianist Bergman is reunited with a daughter she has not seen in years. Bergman's other daughter suffers from a degenerative nerve disease and had been institutionalized until her sister brought her home. Now the three women settle old scores, and balance the needs of their family. Excellent performance by Bergman in her last feature film. **97m/C VHS, DVD.** *SW* Ingrid Bergman, Liv Ullmann, Halvar Bjork, Lena Nyman, Gunnar Bjornstrand, Erland Josephson; ***D:*** Ingmar Bergman; ***W:*** Ingmar Bergman; ***C:*** Sven Nykvist. Golden Globes '79: Foreign Film; Natl. Bd. of Review '78: Actress (Bergman), Director (Bergman); N.Y. Film Critics '78: Actress (Bergman); Natl. Soc. Film Critics '78: Actress (Bergman).

Autumn Sun *Solo de Otono* **1998** This is a love story for appreciative adults. Clara (Aleandro) is a middleaged Buenos Aires accountant whose personal ad for a Jewish gentleman caller is answered by older widower (and non-Jew) Raul Ferraro (Luppi). Still, they're attracted to each other, and since Clara needs a man to pose as her admirer for a visit from her long-absent brother, Raul agrees to the ruse and undergoes a crash course in Jewish customs. This isn't actually played for laughs but as a reflection on expanding one's horizons and taking chances. Spanish with subtitles. **103m/C VHS, DVD.** *AR* Norma Aleandro, Federico Luppi, Jorge Luz, Cecilia Rossetto; ***D:*** Eduardo Mignogna; ***W:*** Eduardo Mignogna, Santiago Carlos Oves; ***C:*** Marcelo Camorino; ***M:*** Edgardo Rudnitzky.

Autumn Tale ½ *Conte d'Automne* **1998 (PG)** Middleaged, widowed winegrower Magali (Romand) is lonely now that her children are grown, so her best friend Isabelle (Riviere) secretly places a personal ad and decides to meet the respondents herself in order to find someone suitable for her friend. Isabelle decides saleman Gerald (Libolt) is a likely prospect and schemes to introduce them. Meanwhile, Rosine (Portal), the live-wire girlfriend of Magali's son Leo (Darmon), thinks that her older philosophy professor (and ex-lover), Etienne (Sandre), might be a match. Magali is simply mortified by the entire situation. The fourth film in Rohmer's "Tales of the Four Seasons." French with subtitles. **110m/C VHS.** *FR* Beatrice Romand, Marie Riviere, Alexia Portal, Alain Libolt, Didier Sandre, Stephane Darmon; ***D:*** Eric Rohmer; ***W:*** Eric Rohmer; ***C:*** Diane Baratier; ***M:*** Claude Marti. Natl. Soc. Film Critics '99: Foreign Film.

Avalanche ½ **1978 (PG)** Disasterama as vacationers at a new winter ski resort find themselves at the mercy of a monster avalanche leaving a so-called path of terror and destruction in its wake. Talented cast is buried by weak material, producing a snow-bound adventure yawn. **91m/C VHS, DVD.** Rock Hudson, Mia Farrow, Robert Forster, Rick Moses; ***D:*** Corey Allen; ***W:*** Corey Allen; ***C:*** Pierre William Glenn; ***M:*** William Kraft.

Avalanche ½ **1999 (PG-13)** Prototypical cheesy disaster flic. Alaskan chopper pilot Neil (Griffith) helps out Lia (Feeney), the widow of an old pal, who works for the EPA. She believes the establishment of an oil company's overland pipeline through the mountains will trigger an avalanche that could destroy the city of Juneau. Naturally, no one believes her until there's an avalanche. (Considering the movie's title, you could have guessed this.) **105m/C VHS, DVD.** Thomas Ian Griffith, Caroleen Feeney, R. Lee Ermey, C. Thomas Howell, John Ashton, Hilary Shepard; ***D:*** Steve Kroschel; ***W:*** Steve Kroschel; ***C:*** Steve Kroschel, Richard Pepin; ***M:*** K. Alexander (Alex) Wilkinson.

Avalanche Express **1979 (PG)** Marvin is a CIA agent who uses a defector (Shaw) to lure a scientist (Schell), specializing in biological warfare, aboard a European train. Marvin wants to eliminate Schell but all plans go awry when the snow begins to fall. Ineffective thriller. Director Robson's and actor Shaw's last film—much of Shaw's dialogue was dubbed due to his death before the film's soundtrack was completed. Based on a novel by Colin Forbes. **89m/C VHS.** Lee Marvin, Robert Shaw, Maximilian Schell, Linda Evans, Mike Connors, Joe Namath, Horst Buchholz, David A(lexander) Hess; ***D:*** Mark Robson; ***W:*** Abraham Polonsky; ***C:*** Jack Cardiff.

Avalon **1990 (PG)** Powerful but quiet portrait of the break-up of the family unit as seen from the perspective of a Russian family settled in Baltimore at the close of WWII. Initally, the family is unified in their goals, ideologies, and social lives. Gradually, all of this disintegrates; members move to the suburbs and TV replaces conversation at holiday gatherings. Levinson based his film on experiences within his own family of Russian Jewish immigrants. **126m/C VHS, DVD.** Armin Mueller-Stahl, Aidan Quinn, Elizabeth Perkins, Joan Plowright, Lou Jacobi, Leo Fuchs, Eve Gordon, Kevin Pollak, Israel Rubinek, Elijah Wood, Grant Gelt, Bernard Hiller; ***D:*** Barry Levinson; ***W:*** Barry Levinson; ***C:*** Allen Daviau; ***M:*** Randy Newman. Writers Guild '90: Orig. Screenplay.

Avanti! ½ **1972 (R)** Stuffy businessman Wendell Armbruster (Lemmon) heads to Italy to claim his father's body when the old man dies while on vacation. Then he discovers dad has been visiting his mistress lo these many years. While trying to get through mountains of red tape, Wendell finds himself romancing the woman's daughter (Mills). Too long but still amusing. **144m/C VHS, DVD.** Jack Lemmon, Juliet Mills, Clive Revill, Edward Andrews, Gianfranco Barra, Franco Angrisano; ***D:*** Billy Wilder; ***W:*** I.A.L. Diamond, Billy Wilder.

Ava's Magical Adventure ½ **1994 (PG)** Ten-year-old Eddie decides to take Ava on a little adventure. Too bad she's a 2-ton elephant he's stolen from the circus. Based on the Mark Twain story "The Stolen White Elephant." **97m/C VHS.** Timothy Bottoms, Georg Stanford Brown, Patrick Dempsey, Priscilla Barnes, David Lander, Kaye Ballard, Remi Ryan; ***D:*** Patrick Dempsey, Rocky Parker; ***W:*** Susan D. Nimm; ***M:*** Mark Holden.

Avatar **2009 (PG-13)** Cameron's first directorial effort since "Titanic" is an elaborate 3-D sci-fi adventure with dazzling technique and a behind-the-scenes story more interesting than what appears onscreen. When Cameron created (in collaboration) advanced motion-capture at an alleged cost of more than $200 million and four years of actual production. The plot itself is fairly standard, set in 2154 when Earth (as usual) has suffered some disaster. Paraplegic ex-Marine Jake Sully (Worthington) is taken to the human outpost on Pandora where a shady corporation is trying to mine a rare mineral. Only the indigenous Na'vi (gigantic blue beings with tails) are in the way. Because the atmosphere is toxic, humans are mind-linked to a remote-controlled biological body called an avatar. Jake's avatar allows him to walk again and he's supposed to infiltrate the Na'vi. Too bad Jake becomes completely intrigued with their civilization and warrior Neytiri (Saldana) and is torn between duty and the exotic alien world. **163m/C DVD.** *US* Sam Worthington, Zoe Saldana, Michelle Rodriguez, Sigourney Weaver, Giovanni Ribisi, Laz Alonso, Wes Studi, Stephen Lang, CCH Pounder, Joel David Moore; ***D:*** James Cameron; ***W:*** James Cameron; ***C:*** Mauro Fiore, Mauro Fiore; ***M:*** James Horner. Oscars '09: Art Dir./Set Dec., Cinematog., Visual FX; British Acad. '09: Visual FX; Golden Globes '10: Director, Film—Drama.

The Avenger ½ **1960** The story of a criminal who cuts off the heads of people and mails them off makes for a shocker. Graphic violence will appeal to those who like a good mail-order gorefest and are not employed by the post office. **102m/B VHS, DVD.** *GE* Ingrid van Bergen, Heinz Drache, Ina Duscha, Mario Litto, Klaus Kinski; ***D:*** Karl Anton.

The Avenger *The Lost Glory of Troy* **1962** This time muscleman Reeves plays Aeneas and leads the Trojans in battle against the Greeks. It's supposedly an adaptation of "The Aeneid" by Virgil. **108m/C VHS, DVD.** *FR IT* Steve Reeves, Giacomo "Jack" Rossi-Stuart, Carla Marlier, Gianni "John" Garko, Liana Orfei; ***D:*** Giorgio Rivalta.

The Avengers **1998 (PG-13)** Based on the culty '60s Brit TV series, this unfortunate big screen adaptation fails by choosing style over campy charm. Set in a surreal 1999 London, scientist (and leather-girl) Mrs. Emma Peel (Thurman) teams up with dapper secret agent John Steed (Fiennes) to defeat maximum baddie, Sir August de Wynter (Connery). Seems de Wynter has a machine that can manipulate the world's weather—and he's not intending to do good deeds. It's dull, the leads have no chemistry together (although they have their separate charms), and the creators have chosen to include some lesser aspects of the series, such as the boring character of Mother (Broadbent). Unforgiveably, Laurie Johnson's memorable TV theme is not used for the film's opening—replaced instead by generic music by McNeely. (Johnson's theme is heard later.) Original Steed, Patrick MacNee, does have an amusing cameo. **90m/C VHS, DVD.** Ralph Fiennes, Uma Thurman, Sean Connery, Jim Broadbent, Fiona Shaw, Eileen Atkins, John Wood, Eddie Izzard, Carmen Ejogo, Keeley Hawes; ***Cameos:*** Patrick Macnee; ***D:*** Jeremiah S. Chechik; ***W:*** Don MacPherson; ***C:*** Roger Pratt; ***M:*** Joel McNeely. Golden Raspberries '98: Worst Remake/Sequel.

The Avenging **1992 (PG)** Horse comes home from college to run the family ranch but has problems with his two resentful brothers. **100m/C VHS.** Michael Horse, Efrem Zimbalist Jr., Sherry Hursey, Joseph Runningfox, Taylor Lacher; ***D:*** Lyman Dayton; ***W:*** Lyman Dayton.

Avenging Angel **WOOF!** **1985 (R)** Law student Molly "Angel" Stewart is back on the streets to retaliate against the men who killed the policeman who saved her from a life of prostitution. Worthless sequel to 1984's "Angel," exploiting the original's exploitative intent. Followed listlessly by "Angel III: The Final Chapter." **94m/C VHS, DVD.** Betsy Russell, Rory Calhoun, Susan Tyrrell, Ossie Davis, Barry Pearl, Ross Hagen, Karin Mani, Robert Tessier; ***D:*** Robert Vincent O'Neil; ***W:*** Joseph M. Cala; ***C:*** Peter Lyons Collister; ***M:*** Paul Antonelli.

The Avenging Angel ½ **1995** Unusual take on religion and western justice. Brigham Young (Heston) and his Mormon sect have established themselves in Utah—with the aid of some sharpshooting vigilantes, including Miles Utley (Berenger). When an assassination attempt is made on Young's life, Utley finds he's stumbled into an ever-widening church conspiracy that threatens to consume him. Based on the novel by Gary Stewart. **100m/C VHS.** Tom Berenger, Charlton Heston, James Coburn, Kevin Tighe, Jeffrey Jones, Tom Bower, Joanna Miles; ***D:*** Craig R. Baxley; ***W:*** Dennis Nemec; ***C:*** Mark Irwin; ***M:*** Gary Chang.

Avenging Angel ½ **2007** Cliches abound in this oater about a nameless preacher (Sorbo) who suffered a personal tragedy at the hands of greedy land baron Col. Cusack (Hauser) and his evil minions. The preacher turns bounty hunter before rethinking his path thanks to outcast single mother Maggie (Watros). But when Cusack turns to violence again to get rid of some pesky settlers, the preacher straps on his trusty six-shooter. **81m/C DVD.** Kevin Sorbo, Cynthia Watros, Wings Hauser, Nicholas Chinlund, Richard Lee Jackson, Jim Haynie; ***D:*** David S. Cass Sr.; ***W:*** William Sims Myers; ***C:*** Maximo Munzi; ***M:*** Joe Kraemer. **CABLE**

Avenging Angelo **2002 (R)** The Hound thinks this flick is supposed to be a mobster comedy with some romance and, well, it's such a mess who knows what was intended, except it's not gonna revive Stallone's career. He's bodyguard Frankie Delano. He works for mob boss Angelo Allighieri (Quinn), who gets whacked. Frankie then decides Angelo's daughter Jennifer (Stowe) is in danger, so he goes to protect her. Only Jennifer was adopted and doesn't know she's a mobster's daughter and thinks Frankie is nuts—until she nearly gets whacked. Then she believes him and wants revenge. **96m/C VHS, DVD.** Sylvester Stallone, Madeleine Stowe, Harry Van Gorkum, Raoul Bova, Anthony Quinn; ***D:*** Martyn Burke; ***W:*** Will Aldis, Steve Mackall; ***C:*** Ousama Rawi; ***M:*** Bill Conti.

Avenging Conscience *Thou Shall Not Kill* **1914** An early eerie horror film, based on tales of Edgar Allan Poe. D.W. Griffith's first large-scale feature. Silent. **78m/B VHS.** Henry B. Walthall, Blanche Sweet; ***D:*** D.W. Griffith.

Avenging Disco Godfather ½ *Avenging Godfather; Disco Godfather* **1976 (R)** Moore parodies the "Godfather" and martial arts movies. **99m/C VHS, DVD.** Rudy Ray Moore, Carol Speed, Jimmy Lynch, Jeny Jones, Lady Reeds, James H. Hawthorne, Frank Finn, Julius J. Carry III; ***D:*** J. Robert Wagoner; ***W:*** J. Robert Wagoner, Cliff Roquemore; ***C:*** Arledge Armenaki; ***M:*** Ernie Fields Jr.

Avenging Force **1986 (R)** Okay actioner about retired CIA agent Dudikoff returning to the force to help colleague James run for political office. A group of right-wing terrorists called "Pentangle" threatens James, so Dudikoff adds his name to their wanted list. Conflict leads to a forest manhunt where the avenging force does its avenging. **104m/C VHS.** Michael Dudikoff, Steve James, John P. Ryan; ***D:*** Sam Firstenberg; ***W:*** Mercer Ellington, James Booth; ***M:*** George S. Clinton.

The Avenging Hand ½ **1936** Leaden suspense story about a hotel filled with thieves all searching for stolen loot. **56m/B VHS.** Noah Beery Jr., Kathleen Kelly, Louis Borell, James Harcourt, Charles Oliver, Reginald Long; ***D:*** Victor Hanbury.

Avenue Montaigne ½ *Fauteuils d'Orchestre; Orchestra Seats* **2006 (PG-13)** Sweet provincial gamine Jessica (De France) comes to Paris and gets a job at a cafe along the titular street. The cafe is particularly busy because three major events will be happening nearby: classical pianist Jean-Francois (Dupontel) is giving a concert; popular TV actress Catherine (Lemercier) is starring onstage; and aging businessman Jacques (Brasseur) is going to auction off his extensive art collection. Each are having personal difficulties, which come to a boil over a three-day period, with Jessica providing her common-sense reactions. French with subtitles. **100m/C DVD.** *FR* Cecile de France, Valerie Lemercier, Albert Dupontel, Claude Brasseur, Dani, Laura Morante, Sydney Pollack, Annelise Hesme, Suzanne Flon; ***D:*** Daniele Thompson; ***W:*** Daniele Thompson; ***C:*** Jean-Marc Fabre; ***M:*** Nicola Piovani.

The Average Woman **1924** Gritty journalist consults plain Jane for "Modern Woman" story and finds a major rewrite in order when he falls with a thud for Miss Jane. **52m/B VHS.** Pauline Garon, David Powell, Burr McIntosh, Harrison Ford, De Sacia Mooers; ***D:*** Christy Cabanne.

The Aviator **1985 (PG)** Pilot Reeve, haunted by the memory of a fatal crash, tries to find a new line of work. Large sums of money persuade him to transport spoiled Arquette to Washington. When the biplane crashes in the mountain wilderness, the two fall in love between scavenging for food and fighting wild animals. From the director of "Man From Snowy River." **98m/C VHS, DVD.** Christopher Reeve, Rosanna Arquette, Jack Warden, Tyne Daly, Marcia Strassman, Sam Wanamaker, Scott Wilson; ***D:*** George Miller; ***W:*** Marc Norman; ***C:*** David Connell; ***M:*** Dominic Frontiere.

The Aviator ½ **2004 (PG-13)** Scorsese's sweeping, rich biopic of eccentric movie producer/aviation pioneer Howard Hughes soars on many levels. The film follows Hughes from maverick producer taking Hollywood by storm in the '20s through his successes in aviation and the founding of TWA, and finally battling Pan Am and Congress in the '40s. Di Caprio, in full-on movie idol mode, captures the drive and intensity of Hughes, letting the audience see glimpses of the coming breakdown, but mostly keeping it bubbling below the surface (until a slightly over-the-top sequence about 90 minutes in).

Blanchett also shines in a dazzling portrayal of Katharine Hepburn. Scorsese's eye for detail and love of Old Hollywood serve the proceedings well, providing fascinating peeks into the workings of the old studio system, the testing and building of experimental aircraft, and the wheeling and dealing of high-stakes politics. **166m/C VHS, DVD, Blu-ray Disc, HD DVD.** *US* Leonardo DiCaprio, Cate Blanchett, Kate Beckinsale, John C. Reilly, Alec Baldwin, Alan Alda, Ian Holm, Danny Huston, Jude Law, Adam Scott, Matt Ross, Kelli Garner, Frances Conroy, Brent Spiner, Stanley DeSantis, Edward Herrmann, Willem Dafoe, J.C. MacKenzie, Kenneth Welsh, Amy Sloan, Kevin O'Rourke, Lisa Bronwyn Moore, Gwen Stefani, Vincent Laresca, Josie Maran; ***D:*** Martin Scorsese; ***W:*** John Logan; ***C:*** Robert Richardson; ***M:*** Howard Shore. Oscars '04: Art Dir./Set Dec., Cinematog., Costume Des., Film Editing, Support. Actress (Blanchett); British Acad. '04: Film, Makeup, Support. Actress (Blanchett); Golden Globes '05: Actor—Drama (DiCaprio), Film—Drama, Orig. Score; Screen Actors Guild '04: Support. Actress (Blanchett).

The Aviator's Wife 🦴🦴🦴 *La Femme de L'Aviateur* **1980** The first in Rohmer's Comedies and Proverbs series is a comedy of errors involving a post-office worker (Marlaud) who believes that his older girlfriend (Riviere) is seeing another man, a pilot (Carriere). He enlists the aid of a young girl (Meury) to help him spy on his romantic obsession. French with subtitles. **104m/C VHS, DVD.** *FR* Philippe Marlaud, Marie Riviere, Anne-Laure Meury, Matthieu Carriere; ***D:*** Eric Rohmer; ***W:*** Eric Rohmer; ***C:*** Bernard Lutic; ***M:*** Jean-Louis Valero.

Awake 🦴 1/2 **2007 (R)** Wealthy Clayton Beresford (Christensen), stricken with a heart defect, must undergo a transplant to save his life. Unfortunately, something goes wrong, and he experiences "anesthesia awareness," which means that he appears asleep but is actually awake and fully aware of everything going on during his operation. Rather than build suspense and tension from such an intense premise, the story's twists and surprises (including an absurd-even-by-horror-movie-standards plot for poor Clay to die on the operating table) pile on ad nauseum, and Christensen is expected to carry much of the movie while flat on his back. **78m/C DVD.** *US* Hayden Christensen, Jessica Alba, Terrence Howard, Lena Olin, Arliss Howard, Christopher McDonald, Fisher Stevens, Sam Robards, Georgina Chapman; ***D:*** Joby Harold; ***W:*** Joby Harold; ***C:*** Russell Carpenter; ***M:*** Graeme Revell.

The Awakening 🦴 1/2 **1980 (R)** An archeologist discovers the tomb of a murderous queen, but upon opening the coffin, the mummy's spirit is transferred to his baby daughter, born at that instant. They call that bad luck. **101m/C VHS.** *GB* Charlton Heston, Susannah York, Stephanie Zimbalist, Patrick Drury, Ian McDiarmid, Bruce Myers, Nadim Sawalha, Jill Townsend; ***D:*** Mike Newell; ***W:*** Allan Scott, Chris Bryant, Clive Exton; ***C:*** Jack Cardiff; ***M:*** Claude Bolling.

The Awakening 🦴 1/2 **1995** Smalltown Sara (Geary) has had to turn the family home into a boardinghouse in order to meet expenses. Bounty hunter Flynn (Beecroft) moves in while pursuing an antiques smuggler and he and Sara join forces to find romance as well as adventure. From the Harlequin Romance Series; adapted from the Patricia Coughlin novel. **95m/C DVD.** *CA* Cynthia Geary, David Beecroft, Sheila McCarthy, Maurice Godin; ***D:*** George Bloomfield; ***W:*** Maria Nation; ***C:*** Manfred Guthe; ***M:*** Amin Bhatia. **TV**

Awakening of Candra WOOF! **1981** Based on a real 1975 incident, a young couple honeymooning in the mountains is assaulted by a lunatic fisherman. The psycho kills the husband and rapes the girl, then he brainwashes poor Candra into thinking it was all an accident. Intense subject matter should be horrifying, but falls short of the mark in this flop. **96m/C VHS.** Blanche Baker, Cliff DeYoung, Richard Jaeckel, Jeffrey Tambor, Paul Regina, Elizabeth Cheshire; ***D:*** Paul Wendkos; ***C:*** Richard C. Glouner; ***M:*** Billy Goldenberg. **TV**

Awakenings 🦴🦴🦴 1/2 **1990 (PG-13)** Marshall's first dramatic effort is based on the true story of Dr. Oliver Sacks, from his book of the same title. It details his experimentation with the drug L-dopa which inspired the "awakening" of a number of catatonic patients, some of whom had been "sleeping" for as long as 30 years. Occasionally oversentimental, but still providing a poignant look at both the patients—who find themselves confronted with lost opportunities and faded youth—and at Sacks, who must watch their exquisite suffering as they slip away. De Niro's performance as the youngest of the group is heart-rending, while Williams offers a subdued, moving performance as the doctor. **120m/C VHS, DVD.** Robin Williams, Robert De Niro, John Heard, Julie Kavner, Penelope Ann Miller, Max von Sydow, Anne Meara, Dexter Gordon, Alice Drummond, Richard Libertini, Judith Malina, Barton Heyman, Bradley Whitford, Peter Stormare, Laura Esterman, Vincent Pastore, Vin Diesel; ***D:*** Penny Marshall; ***W:*** Steven Zaillian; ***M:*** Randy Newman. Natl. Bd. of Review '90: Actor (De Niro), Actor (Williams); Natl. Soc. Film Critics '90: Actor (De Niro).

Awakenings of the Beast 🦴 *Ritual Dos Sadicos; Ritual of the Maniacs* **1968** Documents the protracted sufferings of an LSD drug user who is beset with hallucinatory visions and is prone to fits of frenzied violence. Director Jose Mojica Marins (AKA Coffin Joe) steps out of his Ze do Ciaxia character in this disjointed mix of drugs and sex intercut with Mojica Marins himself on trial for his offensive movies, followed by a case study on drugs and sexual behavior. By the end of the movie, there is a point—that drugs aren't the cause of evil behavior—but it's very painful getting there. In Portugese with English subtitles. **93m/B VHS, DVD.** *BR* Jose Mojica Marins, Sergio Hinst, Andrea Bryan, Mario Lima; ***D:*** Jose Mojica Marins; ***W:*** Jose Mojica Marins, Rubens Francisco Lucchetti; ***C:*** Giorgio Attili.

Away All Boats 🦴🦴 1/2 **1956** The true story of one Captain Hawks, who led a crew of misfits to victory in WWII Pacific aboard transport USS Belinda. Battle scenes are well done; look for early (and brief) appearance by young Clint Eastwood. **114m/B VHS, DVD.** Jeff Chandler, George Nader, Richard Boone, Julie Adams, Keith Andes, Lex Barker, Clint Eastwood; ***D:*** Joseph Pevney; ***W:*** Ted Sherdeman; ***C:*** William H. Daniels; ***M:*** Frank Skinner.

Away From Her 🦴🦴🦴 **2006** Polley makes her directorial debut with this adaptation of the Alice Munro story "The Bear Who Came Over the Mountain." Grant (Pinsent) and Fiona (Christie) have been married more than 40 years when she is diagnosed with Alzheimer's. As her mental acuity deteriorates, Fiona insists on entering a nursing home, where she befriends another married patient (Murphy), while Grant struggles to cope with the changes. Gracefully aging '60s British icon Christie is well-matched by Canadian actor Pinsent in a tender story about love and loss that shouldn't be seen by cynics. **110m/C DVD.** *CA* Julie Christie, Gordon Pinsent, Olympia Dukakis, Michael Murphy, Wendy Crewson, Alberta Watson, Kristen Thomson; ***D:*** Sarah Polley; ***W:*** Sarah Polley; ***C:*** Luc Pontpellier; ***M:*** Jonathan Goldsmith. Golden Globes '08: Actress—Drama (Christie); Screen Actors Guild '07: Actress (Christie).

Away We Go 🦴🦴 **2009 (R)** Thirty-somethings Burt (Krasinski) and Verona (Rudolph) are a longtime unmarried couple who are expecting their first child. Uncommitted to their life in Colorado, they decide to travel around the U.S., visiting various cities to see if any appeal as the perfect place to start their family. Along the way, they have misadventures and find fresh connections with an assortment of relatives and old friends who just might help them discover "home" for the first time. The leads are appealing but the writers seem determined to showcase various domestic hells and condescending caricatures with their secondary characters. **97m/C DVD.** *US* John Krasinski, Jeff Daniels, Maggie Gyllenhaal, Melanie Lynskey, Maya Rudolph, Allison Janney, Catherine O'Hara, Jim Gaffigan, Carmen Ejogo, Josh Hamilton, Chris Messina, Paul Schneider; ***D:*** Sam Mendes; ***W:*** Dave Eggers, Vendela Vida; ***C:*** Ellen Kuras; ***M:*** Alex Murdoch.

Awesome! I F*in' Shot That!** 🦴🦴🦴 **2006 (R)** Combination of professional and fans' footage of The Beastie Boys' October 9, 2004 show at Madison Square Garden. The band encouraged fans to film the concert and send them the results. Works as both a document of the show and as an experiment in cooperation and collaboration between the artists and their fans. **90m/C DVD.** ***D:*** Adam "MCA" Yauch; ***C:*** Alexis Boling; ***M:*** Adam "MCA" Yauch, Adam Horovitz, Mike D.

The Awful Dr. Orloff 🦴 *Gritos en la Noche; The Demon Doctor* **1962** Set in a bygone era, Dr. Orloff (Vernon) is a retired prison physician who needs unblemished skin to remedy the horrible disfigurement of his daughter Melissa (Lorys), injured by fire. He abducts promising young women candidates with the help of his blind zombie henchman Morpho (Valle), who simply cannot be trusted with a scalpel. After several surgical mishaps, they kidnap the perfect specimen, a woman who bears an uncanny resemblance to Melissa. Unfortunately, she is engaged to suspicious police Inspector Tanner (San Martin). French version with English subtitles that includes more explicit gore is also available. **86m/B VHS, DVD.** *SP FR* Howard Vernon, Diana Lorys, Frank Wolff, Riccardo Valle, Conrado San Martin, Perla Cristal, Maria Silva, Mara Laso; ***D:*** Jess (Jesus) Franco; ***W:*** Jess (Jesus) Franco; ***C:*** Godofredo Pacheco; ***M:*** Jose Pagan, Antonio Ramirez Angel.

The Awful Truth 🦴🦴🦴🦴 **1937** Lucy (Dunne) and Jerry (Grant) Warriner are a young couple who discard their marriage made in heaven and go their separate ways in search of happiness. Meticulously sabotaging each others' new relationships, they discover they really were made for each other. Grant is at his most charming with dead-on comic timing while Dunne is brilliant as his needling ex. The scene where Dunne poses as Grant's prodigal fan-dancing sister who pays a surprise cocktail-hour visit to the family of his stuffy, upper-class girlfriend (Lamont) is among the most memorable screwball vignettes of all time. And don't miss the custody battle they have over the family dog (Asta of "The Thin Man" fame). Based on Arthur Richman's 1922 play. Preceded by 1925 and 1929 versions; remade in 1953 as "Let's Do It Again." **92m/B VHS, DVD.** Irene Dunne, Cary Grant, Ralph Bellamy, Alexander D'Arcy, Cecil Cunningham, Molly Lamont, Esther Dale, Joyce Compton, Robert "Tex" Allen, Robert Warwick, Mary Forbes; ***D:*** Leo McCarey; ***W:*** Vina Delmar. Oscars '37: Director (McCarey), Natl. Film Reg. '96.

An Awfully Big Adventure 🦴🦴 **1994 (R)** Coming-of-age saga set in postwar Liverpool around a provincial reperatory company. Stage-struck 16-year-old Stella (Cates) gets work as a company apprentice, immediately getting a crush on arch, callous theatre manager Meredith Potter (a deliciously nasty Grant), who enjoys degrading everyone around him. The company's chance for success rests on a production of "Peter Pan," with visiting actor P.L. O'Hara (dashing Rickman), who immediately seduces Stella and has more than a few secrets of his own. Theatrically exaggerated; based on the novel by Beryl Bainbridge. **113m/C VHS, DVD.** *GB* Georgina Cates, Hugh Grant, Alan Rickman, Peter Firth, Alun Armstrong, Prunella Scales, Rita Tushingham, Alan Cox, Edward Petherbridge, Nicola Pagett, Carol Drinkwater, Clive Merrison, Gerard McSorley; ***D:*** Mike Newell; ***W:*** Charles Wood; ***C:*** Dick Pope; ***M:*** Richard Hartley.

Axe 🦴 1/2 *Lisa, Lisa; California Axe Massacre* **1974 (R)** After a group of thugs kill a man (on an embarrassingly shoddy set), they flee to the country, where they take over a farmhouse. The only residents of this farmhouse are a young girl, Lisa (Lee), and her invalid grandfather. The criminals force Lisa to cook a chicken dinner (NO!) and then generally terrorize the girl and her grandfather. Eventually, Lisa (who is actively hallucinating throughout this episode) gets the titular axe and seeks her revenge. The film is slow and boring, and the sub-amateur acting doesn't help. The only positive aspect is the suspense that mounts over the course of the movie. Having seen films like this before, and given the fact that nothing else is happening, the audience knows that Lisa is going to strike back at some time. **68m/C DVD.** Leslie Lee, Jack Canon, Frederick Friedel, Frank Jones; ***D:*** Frederick Friedel; ***W:*** Frederick Friedel; ***C:*** Austin McKinney.

Axe WOOF! *Greed* **2006** Underwear acting. Babes Raven and Ashley (who spend a lot of time in their scanties) hit a desert bar after a rock-climbing expedition. After being harassed by a biker gang, they steal one of the bikes and wind up at a lonely motel with a satchel of cash. Oh, and there's an escaped con, Ivan the Axeman, on the loose as well. London has limited screen time as the bar owner in this incredibly stupid mishmash of genres. **92m/C DVD.** Tim Sitarz, Jason London, Joe Goodrich, Andrea Bogart, Darlena Tejeiro; ***D:*** Ron Wolotzky; ***W:*** Eyal Sher, Dred Ross; ***C:*** Moshe Levin, Scott Carrithers; ***M:*** Erik Godal, Mark Fontana. **VIDEO**

Ay, Carmela! 🦴🦴🦴 **1990** During the Spanish Civil War, two vaudevillians with strong anti-Franco views are captured by Franco forces and sentenced to execution. They are reprieved when a theatre-loving Lieutenant offers to spare their lives if they will entertain the troops. Clever and entertaining farce, with poignant undertones. **105m/C VHS.** *SP IT* Carmen Maura, Andres Pajares, Gabino Diego, Maurizio De Razza, Miguel Rellan, Edward Zentara, Jose Sancho, Antonio Fuentes; ***D:*** Carlos Saura; ***W:*** Rafael Azcona; ***C:*** Jose Luis Alcaine.

Azumi 🦴🦴🦴 **2003 (R)** In 19th century Japan, Azumi, a young orphan girl is raised, along with other orphans, to become an assassin. Azumi (Ueto) soon becomes the best of them. When they come of age, they are cruelly tested, and the survivors are given a mission to eliminate warlords who are tearing the country apart. The action is top-notch, as expected, and the script manages to show both the beauty and brutality of the end of the Samurai era in Japan. Not all Western audience will appreciate the humor, fatalism, or meandering storytelling, but patience and attention is definitely rewarded. **128m/C DVD.** Shun Oguri, Yoshio Harada, Masato Ibu, Joe Odagiri, Naoto Takenaka, Aya Ueto, Hiroki Narimiya, Kenji Kohashi, Takatoshi Kaneko, Yuma Ishigaki, Yasuomi Sano, Shinji Suzuki, Eita Nagayama, Shogo Yamaguchi, Kazuki Kitamura, Kenichi Endo, Kazuya Shimizu, Ryo, Michael P. Greco, Shoichiro Masumoto, Minoru Matsumoto, Aya Okamoto, Tak Sakaguchi, Hideo Sakaki; ***D:*** Ryuhei Kitamura; ***W:*** Yu Koyama, Rikiya Mizushima, Isao Kiriyama; ***C:*** Takumi Furuya; ***M:*** Taro Iwashiro.

Azumi 2 🦴🦴 1/2 *Azumi 2: Death or Love; Azumi 2: Love or Duty...An Assassin Must Choose* **2005** Beginning directly where the first film leaves off, Azumi (Ueto) and Nagara (Ishigaki) continue their pursuit of their assigned target Masayuki Sanada (Nagasawa). He hires the Koga Ninja clan, a band of specialized assassins to take them out before they can reach him. The first film is required viewing for this one as there are no flashbacks or explanations given. Fans of "Kill Bill" should look for Chiaki Kuriyama (she played Go Go) as one of the ninja super assassins. **108m/C DVD.** *JP* Aya Ueto, Yuma Ishigaki, Chiaki Kuriyama, Shun Oguri, Kenichi Endo, Kai Shishido, Tak Sakaguchi, Shoichiro Masumoto, Eugene Nomura, Aki Maeda, Toshie Negishi, Toshiya Nagasawa, Kenji Takechi, Shigeru Koyama, Mikijiro Hira, Kazuki Kitamura, Reiko Takashima; ***D:*** Shusuke (Shu) Kaneko; ***W:*** Yu Koyama, Yoshiaki Kawajiri, Mataichiro Yamamoto; ***C:*** Yoshitaka Sakamoto.

B. Monkey 🦴🦴 **1997 (R)** B—AKA Beatrice—(Argento) hopes she can escape her world of drugs and crime (she's a thief) with the romantic aid of schoolteacher Alan (Harris). But her past catches up with her when ex-partners Paul (Everett) and Bruno (Rhys Meyers) convince her to do one last job (she misses the rush). Based on the novel by Andrew Davies, this one is mainly cool Brit style over substance. **91m/C VHS, DVD.** *GB* Asia Argento, Jared Harris, Rupert Everett, Jonathan Rhys Meyers, Tim Woodward, Ian Hart; ***D:*** Michael Radford; ***W:*** Michael Thomas, Chloe King; ***C:*** Ashley Rowe; ***M:*** Jennie Muskett.

Baadasssss! 🦴🦴🦴 1/2 *How to Get the Man's Foot Outta Your Ass!* **2003 (R)** Mario Van Peebles' fictionalized biopic of his father Melvin's efforts to get his influential indie film "Sweet Sweetback's Baadasssss Song" (the forerunner of the blaxploitation genre) made. Melvin (Mario, who also directed, co-wrote, and produced) is plagued with money and health problems, union troubles and lack of studio interest. Well-made and highly entertaining film was adapted from Melvin's "making of" book. Mario honors his father's work without over-romanticizing the often-imperfect man behind it. **108m/C DVD.** *US* Mario Van

Peebles, Nia Long, David Alan Grier, Ossie Davis, Terry Crews, Rainn Wilson, Joy Bryant, Saul Rubinek, T.K. Carter, Paul Rodriguez, Vincent Schiavelli, Khleo Thomas, Len Lesser, Sally Struthers, Adam West, Glenn Plummer, Khalil Kain, Pamela Gordon, Joseph Culp, Karimah Westbrook, Ralph Martin, Robert Peters, Wesley Jonathan, John Singleton; ***D:*** Mario Van Peebles; ***W:*** Mario Van Peebles, Dennis Haggerty; ***C:*** Robert Primes; ***M:*** Tyler Bates.

The Baader Meinhof Complex **2008 (R)** Overstuffed drama crams ten years worth of history on the notorious 1960-70s West German terrorist group, the Red Army Faction (RAF), reducing it to re-enactments (albeit with some ferocious acting) with not much explanation for those not already familiar with the history. Left-wing journalist Ulricke Meinhof (Gedeck) uses the German government's heavy-handed reaction to student demonstrations to leave behind her life as a prosaic middle-class wife and mother. Instead, she becomes involved in the political activities of Andreas Baader (Bleibtrue) and Gudrun Ensslin (Wokalek) that were transformed from idealism to nihilism and violence, including bombings, hijackings, kidnappings, jailbreaks, and assassinations. Adapted from the book by Stefan Aust. English, German, French, and Arabic with subtitles. **150m/C DVD.** *GE* Martina Gedeck, Moritz Bleibtreu, Johanna Wokalek, Bruno Ganz, Nadja Uhl, Jan Josef Liefers, Stipe Erceg, Niels Bruno Schmidt, Vinzenz Kiefer, Simon Licht; ***D:*** Uli Edel; ***W:*** Uli Edel, Bernd Eichinger; ***C:*** Rainer Klausmann; ***M:*** Peter Hindertuer, Florian Tesslof.

Ba'al: The Storm God WOOF! 2008 (PG-13) An archaeologist gathers four ancient amulets, designed to reawaken the storm god Ba'al, hoping their mystical properties will cure his terminal cancer. Cheapo Sci-Fi Channel movie with a lousy script and equally bad acting. **90m/C DVD.** Jeremy London, Lexa Doig, Michael Kopsa; ***D:*** Paul Ziller; ***W:*** Paul Ziller, Andrew Black; ***C:*** Mahlon Todd Williams; ***M:*** Pinar Toprak. **CABLE**

Baaria 2009 Focuses on the Sicilian Torrenuova clan, a family of shepherds who survive through Fascism, WWII, and the political chaos of postwar Italy as seen through the eyes of socially conscious and ambitious Peppino. Italian with subtitles. **150m/C DVD.** *IT* Angela Molina, Enrico Lo Verso, Lina Sastri, Francesco Scianna, Margareth Made, Lollo Franco, Giovanni Gambino, Davide Viviani; ***D:*** Giuseppe Tornatore; ***W:*** Giuseppe Tornatore; ***C:*** Enrico Lucidi; ***M:*** Ennio Morricone.

Baba *The Father* **1973** A poor boatman agrees to be the fall guy in a murder in exchange for the actual murderer supporting his family. But after 24 years in prison, the boatman finds all his sacrificing has been in vain. His daughter has become a prostitute and his son is working as one of the murderer's henchman. In Turkish with English subtitles. **95m/C VHS.** *TU* ***D:*** Yilmaz Guney.

Babar: The Movie **1/2 1988 (G)** The lovable Babar, king of the elephants, must devise a plan to outwit an angry hoard of attacking rhinos. Based on the characters of Jean and Laurent de Brunhoff. **75m/C VHS, DVD.** *CA FR* ***D:*** Alan Bunce; ***W:*** Alan Bunce, John deKlein; ***V:*** Gavin Magrath, Gordon Pinsent, Sarah Polley, Chris Wiggins, Elizabeth Hanna.

Babe! **1/2 1975** A fine TV movie about the life of one of America's most famous woman athletes, Babe Didrickson. Adapted by Joanna Lee from Didrickson's autobiography "The Life I've Led." The movie was nominated for Outstanding Special of 1975-76 and Clark won an Emmy for her work. **120m/C VHS.** Susan Clark, Alex Karras, Slim Pickens, Jeannette Nolan, Ellen Geer, Ford Rainey; ***D:*** Buzz Kulik; ***M:*** Jerry Goldsmith. **TV**

The Babe **1/2 1992 (PG)** Follows the life of legendary baseball player Babe Ruth, portrayed as a sloppy drunkard whose appetites for food, drink, and sex were as large as he was. Alvarado and McGillis do well as the Babe's first and second wives, but this is Goodman's show from start to finish. He's excellent as Ruth, and looks the part, but his fine performance can't make up for a lackluster script filled with holes. **115m/C VHS, DVD.** Michael (Mike) Papajohn, John Goodman, Kelly McGillis, Trini Alvarado, Bruce Boxleitner, Peter Donat, J.C. Quinn, Richard Tyson, James Cromwell, Joe Ragno, Bernard Kates, Michael McGrady, Stephen Caffrey; ***D:*** Arthur Hiller; ***W:*** John Fusco; ***C:*** Haskell Wexler; ***M:*** Elmer Bernstein.

Babe **1/2** *Babe, the Gallant Pig* **1995 (G)** Totally charming fable has intelligent piglet Babe being raised by matriarch sheepdog Fly, and learning the art of sheep herding along with his new canine brothers. Farmer Hoggett (Cromwell), Babe's owner by virtue of a winning raffle ticket, sees that he's more than just a ham, and enters them in the world sheepdog herding championship. Whimsy that never crosses the line into treacle. Four different special effects houses were used to make the barnyard animals talk and walk. Filmed on location in Australia; based on Dick King-Smith's book "The Sheep-Pig." **91m/C VHS, DVD.** *AU* James Cromwell, Magda Szubanski; ***D:*** Chris Noonan; ***W:*** Chris Noonan, George Miller; ***C:*** Andrew Lesnie; ***M:*** Nigel Westlake; ***V:*** Christine Cavanaugh, Miriam Margolyes, Danny Mann, Hugo Weaving; ***Nar:*** Roscoe Lee Browne. Oscars '95: Visual FX; Golden Globes '96: Film—Mus./Comedy; Natl. Soc. Film Critics '95: Film.

Babe: Pig in the City **1/2 1998 (PG)** Miller takes over the director's chair for this trip. And he brings along more money, more effects, more animals, and more unsettling images, including Mickey Rooney in a creepy clown suit, than anyone who saw the original would expect. Babe returns home to a hero's welcome, but the joy doesn't last long. Farmer Hoggett (Cromwell) is injured, and with foreclosure imminent, Babe and Mrs. Hoggett (Szubanski) head out to turn Babe's fame into a little cash. Along the way, they miss their connecting flight in "the city" and are forced to stay at a hotel that caters to animals. There, they meet the aforementioned Rooney and his three chimp partners, along with various dogs and cats. Technically well-done, and sporting an imaginative story, but may be a little dark for the younger kiddies. **96m/C VHS, DVD.** James Cromwell, Magda Szubanski, Mickey Rooney, Mary Stein, Julie Godfrey; ***D:*** George Miller; ***W:*** Judy Morris, Mark Lamprell; ***C:*** Andrew Lesnie; ***M:*** Nigel Westlake; ***V:*** Elizabeth (E.G. Dailey) Daily, Danny Mann, Glenne Headly, Steven Wright, James Cosmo, Stanley Ralph Ross, Russi Taylor, Adam Goldberg, Nathan Kress, Myles Jeffrey; ***Nar:*** Roscoe Lee Browne.

Babe Ruth Story **1948** An overly sentimental biography about the famed baseball slugger. Bendix is miscast as the Bambino, but the actual film clips of the Babe are of interest. A movie to be watched during those infrequent bouts of sloppy baseball mysticism. **107m/B VHS.** William Bendix, Claire Trevor, Charles Bickford, William Frawley, Sam Levene, Gertrude Niesen; ***D:*** Roy Del Ruth.

Babel **1/2 2006 (R)** A father in a Moroccan village allows his two young sons to shoot his hunting rifle and an international incident is sparked. The boys innocently aim at a tourist bus, never believing the bullets could actually hit someone. They do, of course, and this one foolish act leads to complications that will encompass a Mexican nanny and her Anglo charges back in California and an angry deaf-mute teenaged girl in Tokyo. Somehow director Gonzalez Inarritu manages to tie the stories together (with a certain amount of unbelievability). Pitt and Blanchett join an impressive international cast who live up to this gritty, realistic dramatic puzzle. **142m/C DVD, Blu-ray Disc, HD DVD.** *US* Brad Pitt, Cate Blanchett, Gael Garcia Bernal, Adriana Barraza, Elle Fanning, Koji Yakusho, Nathan Gamble, Rinko Kikuchi, Said Tarchani, Boubker Ait El Caid, Mustapha Rachidi, Abdelkader Bara; ***D:*** Alejandro Gonzalez Inarritu; ***W:*** Guillermo Arriaga; ***C:*** Rodrigo Prieto; ***M:*** Gustavo Santaolalla. Oscars '06: Orig. Score; British Acad. '06: Orig. Score; Golden Globes '07: Film—Drama.

Babes in Arms **1/2 1939** The children of several vaudeville performers team up to put on a show to raise money for their financially impoverished parents. Loosely adapted from the Rodgers and Hart Broadway musical of the same name; features some of their songs as well as new additions. ♫Babes in Arms; I Cried for You; Good Morning; You Are My Lucky Star; Broadway Rhythm; Where or When; Daddy Was a Minstrel Man; I'm Just Wild About Harry; God's Country. **91m/B VHS.** Judy Garland, Mickey Rooney, Charles Winninger, Guy Kibbee, June Preisser; ***D:*** Busby Berkeley; ***M:*** George Bassman, Richard Rodgers, Lorenz Hart.

Babes in Toyland **1961** A lavish Disney production of Victor Herbert's timeless operetta, with Toyland being menaced by the evil Barnaby and his Bogeymen. Yes, Annette had a life after Mickey Mouse and before the peanut butter commercials. Somewhat charming, although the roles of the lovers seem a stretch for both Funicello and Kirk. But the flick does sport an amusing turn by Wynn. **105m/C VHS, DVD.** Annette Funicello, Ray Bolger, Tommy Sands, Ed Wynn, Tommy Kirk; ***D:*** Jack Donohue; ***C:*** Edward Colman; ***M:*** George Bruns.

Babes in Toyland **1/2 1986** Young girl must save Toyland from the clutches of the evil Barnaby and his monster minions. Bland TV remake of the classic doesn't approach the original. **96m/C VHS.** Drew Barrymore, Noriyuki "Pat" Morita, Richard Mulligan, Eileen Brennan, Keanu Reeves, Jill Schoelen, Googy Gress; ***D:*** Clive Donner; ***W:*** Paul Zindel; ***M:*** Leslie Bricusse.

Babes on Broadway **1/2 1941** Mickey and Judy put on a show to raise money for a settlement house. Nearly the best of the Garland-Rooney series, with imaginative numbers staged by Berkeley. ♫Babes on Broadway; Anything Can Happen in New York; How About You?; Hoe Down; Chin Up! Cheerio! Carry On!; Mama Yo Quiero; F.D.R. Jones; Waiting for the Robert E. Lee. **118m/B VHS.** Mickey Rooney, Judy Garland, Fay Bainter, Richard Quine, Virginia Weidler, Ray Macdonald, Busby Berkeley; ***D:*** Busby Berkeley; ***M:*** George Bassman.

Babette's Feast **1/2** *Babettes Gaestebud* **1987** A simple, moving pageant-of-life fable. Philippa (Kjer) and Martina (Federspiel) took over their late father's ministry in a small Danish coastal town. Widowed Frenchwoman Babette (Audran) has spent 14 years in their service and, after winning a lottery prize, decides she will prepare a lavish banquiet in honor of their father's 100th birthday. The religiously conservative villagers don't know what to make of such bounty—or the pleasure it brings to their senses. Adapted from a tale by Isak Dinesen. French and Danish with subtitles. **102m/C VHS, DVD.** *DK FR* Stephane Audran, Bibi Andersson, Bodil Kjer, Birgitte Federspiel, Jean-Philippe LaFont, Ebbe Rode, Jarl Kulle; ***D:*** Gabriel Axel; ***W:*** Gabriel Axel; ***C:*** Henning Kristiansen; ***M:*** Per Norgard; ***Nar:*** Ghita Norby. Oscars '87: Foreign Film; British Acad. '88: Foreign Film.

The Baby **1972 (PG)** Bizarre story of a social worker who resorts to swinging an ax to cut the apron strings of "baby," a retarded man-child, from his over-protective and insane (bad combination) mother and sisters. Low-budget production looks and feels like a low-budget production, but any movie featuring a grown man wandering about in diapers can't be all bad. **85m/C VHS, DVD.** Anjanette Comer, Ruth Roman, Marianna Hill, Suzanne Zenor, David Manzy, Michael Pataki, Erin O'Reilly, Virginia Vincent; ***D:*** Ted Post; ***W:*** Abe Polsky; ***C:*** Michael D. Margulies; ***M:*** Gerald Fried.

Baby **2000** John (Carradine) and Lily (Fawcett) Malone are unsuccessful in coping with their grief over the death of their infant son and in helping their 12-year-old daughter, Larkin (Pill), to deal with her own pain. Then a baby girl is abandoned on the Malone doorstep and Lily immediately wants to keep the child—much to the others' dismay. Formulaic weepie based on the novel by Patricia MacLachlan. **93m/C VHS.** Farrah Fawcett, Keith Carradine, Jean Stapleton, Alison Pill, Vincent Berry, Ann Dowd; ***D:*** Robert Allan Ackerman; ***W:*** Kerry Kennedy, Patricia MacLachlan, David Manson; ***C:*** Ron Garcia; ***M:*** Jeff Danna; ***Nar:*** Glenn Close. **CABLE**

The Baby and the Battleship **1/2 1956** The old baby out of (on the?) water plot. While on liberty in Italy, a sailor, after a series of complications, becomes custodian of a baby and attempts to hide the tyke aboard his battleship (hence the title). More complications ensue. Some funny moments. Great cast. **96m/C VHS.** *GB* John Mills, Richard Attenborough, Andre Morell, Bryan Forbes, Lisa Gastoni, Michael Hordern, Lionel Jeffries, Gordon Jackson, John Le Mesurier; ***D:*** Jay Lewis.

Baby Boom **1/2 1987 (PG)** J.C. Wiatt (Keaton) is a hard-charging exec who becomes the reluctant mother to an orphaned baby girl (a gift from a long-lost relative). She adjusts with great difficulty to motherhood and life outside the rat race and New York City when J.C. decides she must make some radical changes to her routine. A fairly harmless collection of cliches bolstered by Keaton's usual nervous performance as a power-suited yuppie ad queen saddled with a noncareer-enhancing baby, who moves from manic career woman to jelly-packing Vermont store-owner/mom. Shepherd serves as her new, down-home, doctor beau. To best appreciate flick, see it with a bevy of five- and six-year-olds (a good age for applauding the havoc that a baby creates). **103m/C VHS, DVD.** Diane Keaton, Sam Shepard, Harold Ramis, Sam Wanamaker, James Spader, Pat Hingle, Mary Gross, Victoria Jackson, Paxton Whitehead, Annie Golden, Dori Brenner, Robin Bartlett, Christopher Noth, Britt Leach; ***D:*** Charles Shyer; ***W:*** Charles Shyer, Nancy Meyers; ***C:*** William A. Fraker; ***M:*** Bill Conti.

Baby Boy **1/2 2001 (R)** Singleton's candid look at a culture that fosters and tolerates lack of emotional maturity in young African-American males. Jody (Gibson) is a 20-year-old manchild who still lives with his mother (Johnson), has two children with two different women, no job, and cheats on his current girl, Yvette. Jody's life changes when his mother's boyfriend moves in. Melvin (Rhames), an ex-con who's been down the road Jody is heading, shows no tolerance for his attitude. Real trouble starts when Rodney (Snoop Dogg), a street thug and Yvette's ex, is released from prison and refuses to leave her house. Singleton toys with two endings, but finishes the story with the message that the means to fix the problems he's described are within reach. **129m/C VHS, DVD, UMD.** *US* Tyrese Gibson, Omar Gooding, Taraji P. Henson, Adrienne-Joi (AJ) Johnson, Snoop Dogg, Tamara La Seon Bass, Ving Rhames, Angell Conwell; ***D:*** John Singleton; ***W:*** John Singleton; ***C:*** Charles Mills; ***M:*** David Arnold.

Baby Broker **1/2** *Born to Be Sold* **1981** Dated TV melodrama finds social worker Kate Carlin (Carter) learning that a 14-year-old client has agreed to a private adoption. When the teen tries to change her mind, a greedy lawyer who's arranging the black market baby sales hands the tyke over to paying-but-unfit parents anyway. Naturally Kate's in jeopardy when she starts investigating. **94m/C DVD.** Lynda Carter, Harold Gould, Dean Stockwell, Sharon Farrell, Philip Sterling, Lloyd Haynes, Ed Nelson, Donna Wilkes; ***D:*** Burt Brinckerhoff; ***W:*** Karen Harris; ***C:*** William Cronjager; ***M:*** Johnny Harris. **TV**

The Baby Dance **1998** Well-off, middleaged Hollywood marrieds Rachel (Channing) and Richard (Reigert) Luckman have unsuccessfully tried to have a baby for years. Finally they place an adoption ad and receive a response from poor Louisiana trailer park inhabitants Wanda (Dern) and Art (Lineback) LeFauvre, who have an unwanted fifth child on the way. A meeting between the couples soon points out monetary, religious, and cultural differences that may derail their bargain. The two leading ladies carry the picture, which is based on director Anderson's Off-Broadway play. **95m/C VHS, DVD.** Stockard Channing, Laura Dern, Peter Riegert, Richard Lineback; ***D:*** Jane Anderson; ***W:*** Jane Anderson; ***C:*** Jan Kiesser; ***M:*** Terry Allen. **CABLE**

Baby Doll **1956** Suggestive sex at its best, revolving around the love of cotton in Mississippi. Nubile Baker is married to slow-witted Malden, who runs a cotton gin. His torching of Wallach's cotton gin begins a cycle of sexual innuendo and tension, brought to exhilarating life on screen, without a single filmed kiss. Performers and sets ooze during the steamy exhibition, which was considered highly erotic when released. Excellent performances from entire cast, with expert pacing by director Kazan. Screenplay is based on Tennessee Williams' "27 Wagons Full of Cotton." **115m/B VHS, DVD.** Eli Wallach, Carroll Baker, Karl Malden, Mildred Dunnock, Rip Torn; ***D:*** Elia Kazan; ***W:*** Tennessee Williams; ***C:*** Boris Kaufman. Golden Globes '57: Director (Kazan).

The Baby Doll Murders 1992 **(R)** Someone in L.A. is killing beautiful young women and then leaving a broken baby doll at the scene of the crime. The gruesome murderer manages to elude everyone, until Detective Benz discovers a link between the victims and a pattern begins to form. He also discovers that his partner's wife is going to be the next victim unless he can stop this ruthless serial killer from striking again. **90m/C VHS.** Jeff Kober, Melanie Smith, John Saxon, Tom (Thomas E.) Hodges, Bobby DiCicco; ***D:*** Paul Leder; ***W:*** Paul Leder.

Baby Face **1933** A small town girl moves to the city when her father dies. There she gets a job at a bank and sleeps her way to the top of the business world, discarding used men left and right. The Hays Office was extremely upset with the then risque material and forced Warner to trim the first cut. **70m/B VHS, DVD.** Barbara Stanwyck, George Brent, Donald Cook, John Wayne, Henry Kolker, Margaret Lindsay, Douglass Dumbrille, James Murray; ***D:*** Alfred E. Green; ***W:*** Gene Markey, Kathryn Scola; ***C:*** James Van Trees; ***M:*** Leo F. Forbstein. Natl. Film Reg. '05.

Baby Face Morgan **1942** Poor comedy about gangsters who attempt to take advantage of the FBI's preoccupation with saboteurs and spies by muscling in on an insurance firm. **60m/B VHS, DVD.** Mary Carlisle, Richard Cromwell, Robert Armstrong, Chick Chandler, Charles (Judel, Judells) Judels, Warren Hymer, Vince Barnett, Ralf Harolde; ***D:*** Arthur Dreifuss.

Baby Face Nelson ½ **1997 (R)** Lame Depression-era gangster flick with George "Baby Face" Nelson (Howell) and his moll Helen Womack (Zane) fighting rival Al Capone (Abraham) in Chicago. Kove comes off well as gangster John Dillinger. **80m/C VHS.** C. Thomas Howell, Lisa Zane, F. Murray Abraham, Doug Wert, Martin Kove; ***D:*** Scott Levy; ***W:*** Joseph Farrugia, Craig J. Nevius; ***C:*** Christopher Baffa; ***M:*** Christopher Lennertz.

Baby Geniuses ½ **1998 (PG)** Steals the most irritating parts of "Look Who's Talking," "Home Alone" and that creepy dancing baby and pastes them onto a lame good kids vs. evil adults plot. Turner and Lloyd are evil scientists attempting to crack the secret language of babies, which they believe holds the secrets of the universe (such as how to enjoy drooling and making in your pants). Standing in their way are nursery school operators Cattrall and MacNichol and an array of babies that spout inane dialogue thanks to an abuse of computer morphing. The effect is more disturbing than cute, and an excellent supporting cast is wasted. More interesting things can be found inside a diaper. **94m/C VHS, DVD.** Kathleen Turner, Christopher Lloyd, Kim Cattrall, Peter MacNichol, Dom DeLuise, Ruby Dee, Kyle Howard, Leo Fitzgerald, Myles Fitzgerald, Gerry Fitzgerald; ***D:*** Bob (Benjamin) Clark; ***W:*** Bob (Benjamin) Clark, Steven Paul, Francisca Matos, Robert Grasmere, Greg Michael; ***C:*** Stephen M. Katz; ***M:*** Paul Zaza.

Baby Girl Scott ½ **1987** Hurt and Lithgow play the parents of an extremely premature infant who is being kept alive by technology. They make a heartrending decision and then must battle doctors and the system to let their daughter die with dignity. **97m/C VHS.** John Lithgow, Mary Beth Hurt, Linda Kelsey; ***D:*** John Korty. **TV**

Baby It's You **1982 (R)** In New Jersey in the '60s, the relationship between a smart, attractive Jewish girl who yearns to be an actress and a street-smart Catholic Italian boy puzzles their family and friends. It all works due to Arquette's strong acting and Sayles' script, which explores adolescent dreams, the transition to adulthood, class differences, and the late 1960s with insight and humor. Interesting period soundtrack (Woolly Bully and, for some reason, Bruce Springsteen) helps propel the film, a commercial job which helped finance Sayles' more independent ventures. **105m/C VHS.** Rosanna Arquette, Vincent Spano, Jack Davidson, Joanna Merlin, Nick Ferrari, Leora Dana, Robert Downey Jr., Tracy Pollan, Matthew Modine; ***D:*** John Sayles; ***W:*** John Sayles; ***C:*** Michael Ballhaus.

Baby Love WOOF! 1969 (R) A softcore fluff-fest about a trollop seducing a doctor's family. The doctor may or may not be her father. Hayden tantalizes the doctor, the doctor's son, and the doctor's wife, as well as the neighbors, leaving only those in adjoining communities untouched. Based on the novel by Tina Chad Christian. **98m/C VHS.** *GB* Ann Lynn, Keith Barron, Linda Hayden, Derek Lamden, Diana Dors, Patience Collier; ***D:*** Alastair Reid.

Baby Love WOOF! *Lemon Popsicle V* **1983** Nerds get revenge against the freshmen who run the local frat house. **80m/C VHS.** *IS* Dolly Dollar, Bea Fiedler, Jesse Katzur, Yftach Katzur, Dvora Kedar, Renate Langer, Zachi Noy, Jonathan Sagalle; ***D:*** Dan Wolman; ***C:*** Ilan Rosenberg.

The Baby Maker **1970 (R)** A couple who cannot have children because the wife is sterile decides to hire a woman to have a child for them. However, the relationship between the husband and the surrogate progresses beyond what either of them wanted. Hershey stars as the free-love surrogate mama (just before she underwent the supreme 60s transformation into Barbara Seagull) and Bridges makes his directorial debut. Flick is interesting as a combo critique/exploitation of those wild and groovy 1960s. **109m/C VHS.** Barbara Hershey, Collin Wilcox-Paxton, Sam Groom, Scott Glenn, Jeannie Berlin; ***D:*** James Bridges; ***W:*** James Bridges.

Baby Mama ½ **2008 (PG-13)** Predictable mom com starring Fey and Poehler, who got comfortable doing skits together on SNL. Single, 37-year-old workaholic Kate Holbrook (Fey) determines she now has the time and resources to have a baby, but dang if her biological clock hasn't stopped ticking. So Kate goes the surrogacy route and chooses an unlikely candidate—South Philly good-time gal Angie (Poehler), who's unwilling to follow Kate's precise pregnancy plans when the duo wind up as roommates. Naturally, over the course of nine months and lots of preggo jokes, they bond. The leads sell the weak material and are backed up by such pros as Weaver, Kinnear, and Martin. **99m/C DVD, Blu-ray Disc.** *US* Tina Fey, Amy Poehler, Greg Kinnear, Dax Shepard, Romany Malco, Holland Taylor, Sigourney Weaver, Maura Tierney, Steve Martin, Siobhan Fallon Hogan; ***D:*** Michael McCullers; ***W:*** Michael McCullers; ***C:*** Daryn Okada; ***M:*** Jeff Richmond.

Baby Monitor: Sound of Fear ½ **1997 (R)** Matt (Beghe) makes the mistake of falling in love with nanny Ann (Bissett), which makes his wife Carol (Tyson) go psychotic. She overhears everyhing thanks to that darn baby monitor and decides to have Ann killed in a botched kidnapping attempt. But Ann discovers the evil goings-on (because of the baby monitor, natch) and works to save the good guys. **91m/C VHS.** Josie Bissett, Jason Beghe, Barbara Tyson, Jeffrey Noah, Vincent Gale, Gerard Plunkett; ***D:*** John L. Roman; ***W:*** Edgar van Cossart. **CABLE**

Baby of the Bride ½ **1991** Follow-up to "Children of the Bride," has McClanahan settling into wedded bliss with younger husband Shackleford when she discovers she's pregnant. Not only is she unsure about wanting to be a mom again at her age but then grown—and single—daughter McNichol announces she is also pregnant. The sheer silliness of this TV fare makes it fun to watch. **93m/C VHS, DVD.** Rue McClanahan, Ted Shackleford, Kristy McNichol, John Wesley Shipp, Anne Bobby, Conor O'Farrell; ***D:*** Bill Bixby; ***W:*** Bart Baker. **TV**

Baby on Board **1992 (PG)** Kane plays the wife of a Mafia bookkeeper who is accidentally killed in a gangland murder. Out for revenge, she tracks her husband's killer to JFK airport with her four-year-old daughter in tow. Just as she pulls the loaded gun from her purse and takes aim, a pickpocket snatches her purse, accidentally firing the gun. Now she's on the run and she jumps into the first cab she can find, driven by Reinhold. New York City is turned upside down as mother, daughter, and cabbie try to elude the mob in this funny but predictable comedy. **90m/C VHS.** Carol Kane, Judge Reinhold, Geza Kovacs, Errol Slue, Alex Stapley, Holly Stapley; ***D:*** Francis Schaeffer.

Baby on Board **2008 (R)** Witless pregnancy comedy. Chicago ad exec Angela (Graham), half of a power couple along with dopey husband Curtis (O'Donnell), is confounded by her unexpected pregnancy, which she feels will derail her career. Angela goes all hormonal and you won't really care what happens over the next nine months. **94m/C DVD.** Heather Graham, Jerry O'Connell, Lara Flynn Boyle, John Corbett, Kate Finneran, Anthony Starke; ***D:*** Brian Herzinger; ***W:*** Russell Sealise; ***C:*** Denis Maloney; ***M:*** Teddy Castellucci. **VIDEO**

Baby... Secret of the Lost Legend **1985 (PG)** A sportswriter and his paleontologist wife risk their lives to reunite a hatching brontosaurus with its mother in the African jungle. Although this Disney film is not lewd in any sense, beware of several scenes displaying frontal nudity and some violence. **95m/C VHS.** William Katt, Sean Young, Patrick McGoohan, Julian Fellowes; ***D:*** Bill W.L. Norton.

The Baby-Sitters' Club ½ **1995 (PG)** Centering on the summer vacation of seven enterprising Connecticut 13-year-olds and their teen trials with parents, boys, and babysitting, this film is sure to hit home with a crowd that is rarely featured, pre-teen girls. Director Mayron claims, "It's the 'Mystic Pizza' of their age." Young girls and girls young at heart should enjoy this touching look at the fragile years of our youth, leaving baby dolls behind and heading towards dating. Based on the best-selling book series by Ann Martin. Fisk, who plays club leader Kristy, is the daughter of actress Sissy Spacek and director Jack Fisk. **92m/C VHS, DVD.** Schuyler Fisk, Bre Blair, Rachael Leigh Cook, Larisa Oleynik, Tricia Joe, Stacey Linn Ramsower, Zelda Harris, Brooke Adams, Peter Horton, Bruce Davison, Ellen Burstyn, Austin O'Brien, Aaron Michael Metchik; ***D:*** Melanie Mayron; ***W:*** Dalene Young; ***C:*** Willy Kurant; ***M:*** David Michael Frank.

Baby, Take a Bow **1934 (PG)** Temple's first starring role. As a cheerful Pollyanna-type she helps her father, falsely accused of theft, by finding the true thief. **76m/B VHS, DVD.** Shirley Temple, James Dunn, Claire Trevor, Alan Dinehart; ***D:*** Harry Lachman.

Baby, the Rain Must Fall **1964** A rockabilly singer, paroled from prison after serving time for a knifing, returns home to his wife and daughter, but his outbursts of violence make the reunion difficult. Unsentimental with realistic performances, but script is weak (although written by Foote, based on his play, "The Traveling Lady"). Theme song was a Top 40 hit. **100m/B VHS.** Steve McQueen, Lee Remick, Don Murray; ***D:*** Robert Mulligan; ***W:*** Horton Foote; ***C:*** Ernest Laszlo; ***M:*** Elmer Bernstein.

Babycakes ½ **1989** A marshmellow romance between an overweight mortuary attendant who decides to follow her heart when she falls for a hunky ice skater. Can she make him appreciate her inner beauty instead of just her not-the-normal-beauty-standard outward appearance? (Happy ending guaranteed.) TV remake of the darker German film "Sugarbaby." **94m/C VHS, DVD.** Ricki Lake, Craig Sheffer, Paul Benedict, Betty Buckley, John Karlen, Nada Despotovich; ***D:*** Paul Schneider. **TV**

Babyfever ½ **1994 (R)** Women gather at a baby shower and tell stories about motherhood and related topics. May be viewed as a babblefest with video accompaniment or as an overdue cinematic exploration of a fairly important aspect of life (where would we be without mom?). That said, pace of the comedy drama is less than feverish, although director Jaglom captures the essence of the stories without disturbing their flow. Foyt, Jaglom's wife and co-screenwriter, makes her acting debut. **110m/C VHS, DVD.** Matt Salinger, Eric Roberts, Frances Fisher, Victoria Foyt, Zack Norman, Dinah Lenney, Elaine Kagan; ***D:*** Henry Jaglom; ***W:*** Victoria Foyt, Henry Jaglom; ***C:*** Hanania Baer.

Babylon A.D. **2008 (PG-13)** See if this sounds familiar: War-torn, post-apocalyptic, bleak future finds mercenary loner who is forced into a seemingly impossible transglobal mission where he is accosted by bad guys every step of the way. Thought so. In this version, Diesel plays Toorop, the brooding ex-pat who must transport Aurora (Thierry), a young woman with a potentially lethal secret, from Russia to New York by whatever means necessary, including a snowmobile! Someone forgot to tell French co-writer/director Kassovitz that Diesel cannot carry a movie, even with a decent French cast and a few visually interesting sets. Kassovitz disowned it in the end, calling it "stupid." Who are we to disagree? **90m/C DVD, Blu-ray Disc.** *FR* Vin Diesel, Melanie Thierry, Gerard Depardieu, Charlotte Rampling, Mark Strong, Lambert Wilson, Michelle Yeoh, Jerome Le Banner; ***D:*** Mathieu Kassovitz; ***W:*** Mathieu Kassovitz, Eric Besnard; ***C:*** Thierry Arbogast; ***M:*** Atli Orvarsson.

Baby's Day Out ½ **1994 (PG)** Poor man's "Home Alone" refits tired Hughes formula using little tiny baby for original spin. Adorable Baby Bink crawls his way onto the city streets, much to his frantic mother's dismay, and unwittingly outsmarts his would-be kidnappers. As in "HA I and II," the bad guys fall victim to all sorts of cataclysmic Looney Tunes violence. Small kids will get a kick out of this one. Particular problem for the moviemakers was that the nine-month old Worton twins were past the year mark by the end of the shoot, a world of difference in infantdom. Blue screens and out-of-sequence shooting were used to overcome the developmental gap. **99m/C VHS, DVD.** Adam Worton, Jacob Worton, Joe Mantegna, Lara Flynn Boyle, Joe Pantoliano, Fred Dalton Thompson, John Neville, Brian Haley, Matthew Glave; ***D:*** Patrick Read Johnson; ***W:*** John Hughes; ***C:*** Thomas Ackerman; ***M:*** Bruce Broughton.

The Babysitter **1980** A family hires the mysterious but ingratiating Johanna (Zimbalist) as live-in help without checking on her references (who'd all checked out). The babysitter is the answer to all their problems—Mom's an alcoholic, Dad's a workaholic, and their daughter's just plain maladjusted—but once Johanna's gained their trust (or, in Dad's case, lust), she sets out to manipulate and exploit the family for her own psychotic purposes. Houseman plays the nosy neighbor who's on to her evil plan. Fair made-for-TV treatment of a common suspense plot. **96m/C VHS.** William Shatner, Patty Duke, Stephanie Zimbalist, Quinn Cummings, John Houseman, David Wallace; ***D:*** Peter Medak.

The Babysitter ½ **1995 (R)** All-American teen Jennifer (Silverstone) becomes the unexpected object of desire for family man Harry (Walsh), whose wife Dolly (Garlington) is fantasizing about having an affair with a neighbor (Segal). But then Jennifer's boyfriend (London) gets caught up in a malicious prank that turns bad for everyone involved. Based on a short story by Robert Coover. **90m/C VHS, DVD.** Alicia Silverstone, Jeremy London, J.T. Walsh, Lee Garlington, Nicky Katt, Lois Chiles, George Segal; ***D:*** Guy Ferland; ***W:*** Guy Ferland; ***M:*** Loek Dikker.

The Babysitters ½ **2007 (R)** Married men in midlife crises turn to teen girls for sex. Babysitter Shirley (Waterston) is having an affair with married dad Mike (Leguizamo), who tips her very generously. Mike tells pal Jerry (Comeau) while Shirley tells friend Melissa (Birkell), who's willing to oblige Jerry with special services. Soon Shirley is recruiting a couple of other gals into her little sex ring and things start to get dicey before director Ross completely loses control of his sexcapade. **90m/C DVD.** John Leguizamo, Andy Comeau, Denis O'Hare, Cynthia Nixon, Ethan Phillips, Katherine Waterston, Lauren Birkell, Louisa Krause, Halley Wegryn, Jason Dubin; ***D:*** David Ross; ***W:*** David Ross; ***C:*** Michael McDonough; ***M:*** Chad Fischer.

The Bacchantes **1963** Poorly dubbed account of a ballerina, her life and loves. Based on the play by Euripides. **100m/B VHS.** *IT* Taina Elg, Pierre Brice, Alessandra Panaro, Alberto Lupo, Akim Tamiroff; ***D:*** Giorgio Ferroni.

The Bachelor **1993** Beautiful, seductive period drama about a shy and solitary physician who is forced into a new life when a family tragedy changes everything he once took for granted. Richardson and Carradine give brilliant performances in this provocative story of one man's sexual awakening. Based on a novel by Arthur Schnitzler. **105m/C VHS.** Keith Carradine, Miranda Richardson, Mari Torocsik, Max von Sydow, Kristin Scott Thomas, Sarah-Jane Fenton, Franco Dio-gene; ***D:*** Roberto Faenza; ***W:*** Roberto Faenza, Ennio de Concini, Hugh Fleetwood; ***M:*** Ennio Morricone.

The Bachelor **1999 (PG-13)** Exec producer/star Chris O'Donnell's remake of Buster Keaton's 1925 silent comedy "Seven Chances" falls short of bringing the story to a modern audience. Well, an audience that's aware of the discovery of talkies, feminism and plot holes anyway. O'Donnell plays Jimmy, who stands to inherit a fortune from his grandfather (Ustinov) if he marries before the age of 30. Unfortunately, he receives this news immediately after his odious proposal to girlfriend Anne (Zellweger) is rejected...and of course his 30th birthday happens to be 27 hours away. Madcap antics allegedly ensue as Jimmy trolls for a wife from the pool of his ex-girlfriends and flees the husband-hunting horde who respond to a front-page ad placed by his pal Marco (Lange). **101m/C VHS, DVD.** Chris O'Donnell, Renee Zellweger, Hal Holbrook, James Cromwell, Artie Lange, Ed Asner, Marley Shelton, Stacy Edwards, Rebecca Cross, Jennifer Esposito, Peter Ustinov, Mariah Carey, Brooke Shields; ***D:*** Gary Sinyor; ***W:*** Steve Cohen; ***C:*** Simon Archer; ***M:*** David A. Hughes, John Murphy.

The Bachelor and the Bobby-Soxer *Bachelor Knight* **1947** Playboy Grant is brought before Judge Loy for disturbing the peace and sentenced to court her teenage sister Temple. Cruel and unusual punishment? Maybe, but the wise Judge hopes that the dates will help Temple over her crush on handsome Grant. Instead, Loy and Grant fall for each other. **95m/B VHS, DVD.** Cary Grant, Myrna Loy, Shirley Temple, Rudy Vallee, Harry Davenport, Ray Collins, Veda Ann Borg; ***D:*** Irving Reis; ***W:*** Sidney Sheldon. Oscars '47: Orig. Screenplay.

Bachelor Apartment **½ 1931** Once at the leading edge of the bachelor on the loose genre, this one's hopelessly dated. The scandalous womanizing of a wealthy '30s Lothario just doesn't have the same impact on the "men just don't understand" generation. Nevertheless, as vintage if-the-walls-could-talk fluff, it's good for a giggle. **77m/B VHS.** Lowell Sherman, Irene Dunne, Norman Kerry, Claudia Dell, Noel Francis, Charles Coleman, Mae Murray, Claudia Dell, Ivan Lebedeff, Purnell Pratt, Kitty Kelly; ***D:*** Lowell Sherman; ***W:*** John Howard Lawson, J. Walter Ruben; ***C:*** Leo Tover; ***M:*** Max Steiner.

Bachelor Bait **½ 1934** A marriage license clerk who's tired of just handing out licenses opens a matrimonial service for men. **75m/B VHS.** Stuart Erwin, Rochelle Hudson, Pert Kelton, Richard "Skeets" Gallagher, Berton Churchill, Grady Sutton, Clarence Wilson; ***D:*** George Stevens; ***W:*** Glenn Tryon; ***C:*** Dave Abel; ***M:*** Max Steiner.

Bachelor in Paradise **½ 1969** Silly tale starring Hope as a writer of books to the lovelorn who decides to do firsthand research on the sexual goings-on of a suburban California community. All the married ladies find him charming (much to their husbands' disgust) and the lone single woman, Turner, isn't single by the end of the movie. **109m/C VHS.** Bob Hope, Lana Turner, Janis Paige, Jim Hutton, Paula Prentiss, Don Porter, Virginia Grey, Agnes Moorehead, John McGiver; ***D:*** Jack Arnold; ***W:*** Hal Kanter, Valentine Davies; ***M:*** Henry Mancini.

Bachelor Mother **1939** A single salesgirl causes a scandal when she finds an abandoned baby and is convinced by her boss to adopt the child. Smart, witty comedy with nice performance by Rogers. **82m/B VHS.** Ginger Rogers, David Niven, Charles Coburn; ***D:*** Garson Kanin.

Bachelor of Hearts **½ 1958** Sophomoric British comedy set at Cambridge University, with a German exchange student whose difficulty with English brings him to date several women in one evening. Notable for horror fans as the debut of femme fright fave Barbara Steele. **94m/C VHS.** *GB* Hardy Kruger, Sylvia Syms, Ronald Lewis; ***D:*** Wolf Rilla; ***W:*** Frederic Raphael, Leslie Bricusse.

Bachelor Party **1984 (R)** Rick (Hank) is silly, cute, and poor. Debbie (Kitaen) is intelligent, beautiful, and rich. It must be a marriage made in heaven, because no one in their right mind would put these two together. All is basically well, except that her parents hate him and his friends dislike her. Things are calm until right before the big event, when the bride-to-be objects to Rick's traditional pre-nuptial partying and with good reason. Light and semi-entertaining with scattered laughs. **105m/C VHS, DVD.** Tom Hanks, Tawny Kitaen, Adrian Zmed, George Grizzard, Robert Prescott, William Tepper, Wendie Jo Sperber, Barry Diamond, Michael Dudikoff, Deborah Harmon, John Bloom, Toni Alessandra, Monique Gabrielle, Angela Aames, Rosanne Katon, Bradford Bancroft; ***D:*** Neal Israel; ***W:*** Pat Proft; ***C:*** Hal Trussel; ***M:*** Robert Folk.

Bachelor Party 2: The Last Temptation **2008** Has, of course, nothing to do with the 1984 Tom Hanks comedy. Ron (Cooke) gets engaged to wealthy Melinda (Foster). Her scheming brother Todd (Christie) is convinced that the affable Ron will be anointed heir to the family business so he takes Ron and his buds to South Beach hoping some compromising situations will lead to the wedding being called off. An excuse for a lot of topless women to be on parade and men-behaving-badly stupidity. **103m/C DVD.** Sara Foster, Danny A. Jacobs, Harland Williams, Emmanuelle Vaugier, Audrey Landers, Josh Cooke, Warren Christie, Greg Pitts, Major Mike Russell; ***D:*** James Ryan; ***W:*** Jay Longino; ***C:*** Roy Wagner; ***M:*** James Dooley. **VIDEO**

Bachelor Party in the Bungalow of the Damned **½ 2008** A wild bachelor party at a house in the Hamptons (complete with a creepy caretaker) goes awry amid the jiggle and debauchery when the gates of hell open up mid-bash, leaving some to wonder, can I get my shower present back? **90m/C DVD.** Trina Analee, Monique Dupree, Gregg Aaron Greenburg, Kaitlyn Gutkes, Zoe Hunter, Sean Parker, Joseph Parker, Gelu Dan Rusu, Joe Testa; ***D:*** Brian Thomson; ***W:*** Brian Thomson; ***C:*** Demian Barba; ***M:*** Brian Thomson. **VIDEO**

Bachelor Party Vegas **WOOF!** *Vegas, Baby* **2005 (R)** Things go wrong for five friends when they head to Vegas and discover their bachelor party planner is a casino thief, which leads to all sorts of misunderstandings. Unbelievably crass and unfunny comedy that should have stayed in Vegas, preferably so the master print could have been shredded by one of Siegfried & Roy's white tigers. **90m/C DVD.** *US* Kal Penn, Jonathan Bennett, Donald Adeosun Faison, Charlie Talbert, Vincent Pastore, Jaime Pressly, Aaron Himelstein, Diora Baird, Lin Shaye, Graham Beckel, Daniel Stern, Steve Hytner, Kathy Griffin; ***D:*** Eric Bernt; ***W:*** Eric Bernt; ***C:*** Robert Primes.

BachelorMan **2003 (R)** Easygoing Ted Davis (DeLuise) considers himself an authority on bachelorhood. But when hot brunette Heather (Pyle) becomes his next-door neighbor, all Ted's tricks to woo her fail. Even worse, Ted realizes he's actually fallen in love. Based on the sketch comedy act of Rodney Lee Conover, who plays Ted's outspoken buddy Gordie. **90m/C DVD.** David DeLuise, Missi Pyle, Karen Bailey, Rodney Lee Conover; ***D:*** John Putch; ***W:*** Jeffrey Hause, David Hines; ***C:*** Keith J. Duggan; ***M:*** Steve Bauman, J. Lynn Duckett. **VIDEO**

Back Door to Heaven **½ 1939** Traces the path of a young boy who is born into a poor family and the reasons for his turning to a life of crime. A grim and powerful drama with many convincing performances. **85m/B VHS, DVD.** Wallace Ford, Aline MacMahon, Stuart Erwin, Patricia Ellis, Kent Smith, Van Heflin, Jimmy Lydon; ***D:*** William K. Howard.

Back from Eternity **1956** Eleven survivors of a plane crash are stranded in a headhunter region of South America's jungle. Remake of "Five Came Back" (1939), which was also directed by Farrow. **97m/B VHS.** Robert Ryan, Rod Steiger, Anita Ekberg, Phyllis Kirk, Keith Andes, Gene Barry, Jon(athan) Provost, Beulah Bondi, Barbara Eden; ***D:*** John Farrow; ***C:*** William Mellor.

Back Home **½ 1990** A family reunion movie with pure Disney sentiment. A 12-year-old English girl, who has been living in America during WWII, is reunited with her family in postwar England. **103m/C VHS, DVD.** Hayley Carr, Hayley Mills, Jean Anderson, Rupert Frazer, Brenda Bruce, Adam Stevenson, George Clark; ***D:*** Piers Haggard. **CABLE**

Back in Action **½ 1994 (R)** Veteran LA detective Rossi (Piper) is out to bust the ruthless drug gang who gunned down his partner. But he's got company—martial-arts expert Billy (Blanks) whose young sister has fallen prey to the same gang. So the two action junkies reluctantly team up to cause some major damage. **93m/C VHS, DVD.** Roddy Piper, Billy Blanks, Bobbie Phillips, Matt Birman, Nigel Bennett, Damon D'Oliveira, Kai Soremekun; ***D:*** Paul Ziller, Steve DiMarco; ***W:*** Karl Schiffman.

Back in Business **1996 (R)** Joe Elkhart's (Bosworth) life is down the drain. After failing to expose a fellow police officer as corrupt, he's kicked off the force, abandoned by his friends, and divorced by his wife. Now working as a mechanic, Joe gets pulled back into the action when his ex-partner, Tony (Torry), goes undercover to bring down a major drug dealer and Joe discovers the corrupt cops that framed him are also behind the current heroin deal. **93m/C VHS.** Brian Bosworth, Joe Torry, Dara Tomanovich, Alan Scarfe, Brion James, Ron Glass; ***D:*** Philippe Mora; ***W:*** Ed Decatur, Ash Staley; ***C:*** Walter Bal.

Back in Business **2006** Lame Brit crime caper. Con man Will Spencer (Kemp) and his various allies plot to steal a technologically advanced space exploration device developed by Britain and sought after by a number of foreign investors. But is ex-detective Jarvis (Waterman) planning to double-cross the crew or make the scam his own? **82m/C DVD.** *GB* Martin Kemp, Dennis Waterman, Chris Barrie, Brian Blessed, Stefan Booth, Joanna Taylor; ***D:*** Chris Munro; ***W:*** Chris Munro; ***C:*** Martin Kenzie; ***M:*** Mark Thomas.

Back in the Day **½ 2005 (R)** Reggie Cooper (Ja Rule) is living with his successful, divorced father (Esposito) in an effort to stay away from the 'hood that nearly cost him his life. But when Reggie reconnects with gangster mentor J-Bone (Rhames) it can only mean trouble because J-Bone has some scores to settle. Reggie gets involved in the murder of a local preacher (Morton), but tries to keep his part a secret after he falls for the man's daughter (Ali). Now he must choose between old loyalties and new love. Decent effort with a familiar cast doing professional work. **103m/C DVD.** *US* Ja Rule, Ving Rhames, Tatyana Ali, Giancarlo Esposito, Pam Grier, Joe Morton, Tia Carrere, Frank Langella, Debbi (Deborah) Morgan, Al Sapienza, Lahmard Tate; ***D:*** James Hunter; ***W:*** James Hunter, Michael Raffanello; ***C:*** Donald M. Morgan; ***M:*** Robert Folk. **VIDEO**

Back in the Saddle **½ 1941** Autry is a ranch foreman who discovers a nearby copper mine is poisoning his cattle. Gene manages to do a lot of singing in between the fist fights. **71m/B VHS.** Gene Autry, Smiley Burnette, Mary Lee, Edward Norris; ***D:*** Lew Landers; ***W:*** Richard Murphy, Jesse Lasky Jr.; ***C:*** Ernest Miller.

Back in the USSR **½ 1992 (R)** Danger follows two lovers caught up in the Moscow underworld. When young American touring Russia unwittingly gets involved with a beautiful art thief. Lots of fast-paced action in an otherwise muddled film. The first American film shot entirely on location in Moscow. **87m/C VHS.** Frank Whaley, Natalia (Natalya) Negoda, Roman Polanski, Claudia Robinson, Dey Young, Andrew Divoff, Brian Blessed, Ravil Isyanov; ***D:*** Deran Sarafian; ***C:*** Yuri Neyman.

Back of Beyond **1995 (R)** Spectacular setting in the Australian outback can't make up for unfocused plot and characters with little impact. Tom (Mercutio) ran a remote desert gas station with his sister, Susan (Elmalogulou), before she was killed on his motorbike. When Connor's (Friels) car breaks down by the derelict station, he, girlfriend Charlie (Smart), and sidekick Nick (Polson) must wait while Tom tries to fix it. Only Connor is a diamond thief and patience isn't one of his virutes, especially when he notices the unhappy Charlie making friends with Tom. Mystical/supernatural elements involving ghosts and Aboriginal sites only add to the confusion. **85m/C VHS.** *AU* Paul Mercurio, Colin Friels, Dee Smart, John Polson, Rebekah Elmaloglou, Bob Maza, Terry Serio; ***D:*** Michael Robertson; ***W:*** Paul Leadon, A.M. Brooksbank, Richard I. Sawyer; ***C:*** Stephen Dobson; ***M:*** Mark Moffatt, Wayne Goodwin.

Back Roads **1981 (R)** Southern hooker meets a down-on-his-luck boxer and both head out for a better life in California, finding love along the way. Ritt road trip lacks any comedic rhythm and survives on Field and Jones working to entertain. **94m/C VHS, DVD.** Sally Field, Tommy Lee Jones, David Keith; ***D:*** Martin Ritt; ***W:*** Gary De Vore; ***C:*** John A. Alonzo; ***M:*** Henry Mancini.

Back Street **½ 1941** Pretty Rae Stevens (Sullavan) falls in love with Walter Saxel (Boyer) but, thanks to a misunderstanding, they part company. They meet again five years later and, although Walter is married and has children, begin an affair. Over the years, Rae is to learn that the life of a mistress is a lonely one. Based on the novel by Fannie Hurst; also filmed in 1932 and 1961. **89m/B VHS.** Margaret Sullavan, Charles Boyer, Richard Carlson, Frank McHugh, Tim Holt, Frank Jenks, Esther Dale, Samuel S. Hinds; ***D:*** Robert Stevenson; ***W:*** Bruce Manning, Felix Jackson; ***C:*** William H. Daniels; ***M:*** Frank Skinner.

Back Street **1961** The forbidden affair between a married man and a beautiful fashion designer carries on through many anxious years to a tragic end. The lavish third film version of the Fannie Hurst novel. **107m/C VHS.** Susan Hayward, John Gavin, Vera Miles; ***D:*** David Miller; ***C:*** William H. Daniels.

Back to Back **1990 (R)** A beautiful young vigilante embarks on a rampage to clear her family's name and make her town's redneck crooks pay for their crimes. Never released in theatres. **95m/C VHS.** Bill Paxton, Todd Field, Apollonia, Luke Askew, Ben Johnson, David Michael-Standing, Susan Anspach, Sal Landi; ***D:*** John Kincade; ***C:*** James L. Carter.

Back to Back **½ 1996 (R)** Ex-cop Malone (Rooker) must team up with hitman Koji (Ishibashi), who's holding Malone's daughter hostage, to double-cross a corrupt cop and stay alive while being hunted by the Mafia. **95m/C VHS, DVD.** Michael Rooker, Ryo Ishibashi, John Laughlin, Danielle Harris, Bob-(cat) Goldthwait, Vincent Schiavelli; ***D:*** Roger Nygard; ***W:*** Lloyd Keith; ***C:*** Mark W. Gray; ***M:*** Walter Werzowa.

Back to Bataan **½ 1945** Colonel forms guerrilla army to raid Japanese in the Philippines and to help Americans landing on Leyte. Also available in a colorized version. **95m/B VHS, DVD.** John Wayne, Anthony Quinn, Beulah Bondi, Fely Franquelli, Richard Loo, Philip Ahn, Lawrence Tierney; ***D:*** Edward Dmytryk.

Back to Hannibal: The Return of Tom Sawyer and Huckleberry Finn **½ 1990** Mark Twain's characters Tom Sawyer and Huckleberry Finn are reunited as adults to solve a murder mystery. Tom is a lawyer, Finn a newspaper man, and it's Becky Thatcher's husband who's been murdered. Did a freed slave really commit the crime? **92m/C VHS.** Raphael Sbarge, Mitchell Anderson, Megan Follows, William Windom, Ned Beatty, Paul Winfield; ***D:*** Paul Krasny; ***M:*** Lee Holdridge. **TV**

Back to School **½ 1986 (PG-13)** Dangerfield plays an obnoxious millionaire who enrolls in college to help his wimpy son, Gordon, achieve campus stardom. His motto seems to be "if you can't buy it, it can't be had." At first, his antics embarrass his shy son, but soon everyone is clamoring to be seen with the pair as Gordon develops his own self confidence. **96m/C VHS, DVD.** Rodney Dangerfield, Keith Gordon, Robert Downey Jr., Sally Kellerman, Burt Young, Paxton Whitehead, Adrienne Barbeau, M. Emmet Walsh, Severn Darden, Ned Beatty, Sam Kinison, Kurt Vonnegut Jr., Robert Picardo, Terry Farrell, Edie McClurg, Jason Hervey, William Zabka; ***D:*** Alan Metter; ***W:*** Will Aldis, Steven Kampmann, Harold Ramis, Peter Torokvei; ***C:*** Thomas Ackerman; ***M:*** Danny Elfman.

Back to the Beach **½ 1987 (PG)** Frankie and Annette return to the beach as self-parodying, middle-aged parents with rebellious kids, and the usual run of sunbleached, lover's tiff comedy ensues. Plenty of songs and guest appearances from television past. Tries to bring back that surf, sun, and sand feel of the original "Beach Party" movies, but fails. ♫ Absolute Perfection; California Sun; Catch a Ride; Jamaica Sky; Papa-Oom-Mow-Mow; Sign of Love; Sun, Sun, Sun, Sun, Sun; Surfin' Bird; Wooly Bully. **92m/C VHS, DVD.** Frankie Avalon, Annette Funicello, Connie Stevens, Lori Loughlin, Tommy Hinkley, Demian Slade, John Calvin, Joe Holland, David Bowe, Paul (Pee-wee Herman) Reubens, Don Adams, Bob Denver, Alan Hale Jr., Tony Dow, Jerry Mathers, Dick Dale, Stevie Ray Vaughan, Edd Byrnes, Barbara Billingsley; ***D:*** Lyndall Hobbs; ***W:*** James Komack, Bill W.L. Norton; ***C:*** Bruce Surtees; ***M:*** Steve Dorff.

Back to the Future 🦴🦴🦴 **1985 (PG)** When neighborhood mad scientist Doc Brown (Lloyd) constructs a time machine from a DeLorean, his youthful companion Marty (Fox) accidentally transports himself to 1955. There, Marty must do everything he can to bring his high-school age parents together (so he can be born), elude the local bully, and get back...to the future. Solid fast-paced entertainment is even better due to Lloyd's inspired performance as the loony Doc while Fox is perfect as the boy completely out of his element. Soundtrack features Huey Lewis and the News. Followed by two sequels. **116m/C VHS, DVD.** Michael J. Fox, Christopher Lloyd, Lea Thompson, Crispin Glover, Wendie Jo Sperber, Marc McClure, Thomas F. Wilson, James Tolkan, Casey Siemaszko, Billy Zane, George DiCenzo, Courtney Gains, Claudia Wells, Jason Hervey, Harry Waters Jr., Maia Brewton, J.J. (Jeffrey Jay) Cohen; ***Cameos:*** Huey Lewis; ***D:*** Robert Zemeckis; ***W:*** Robert Zemeckis, Bob Gale; ***C:*** Dean Cundey; ***M:*** Alan Silvestri. Natl. Film Reg. '07.

Back to the Future, Part 2 🦴🦴 1/2 **1989 (PG)** Taking up exactly where Part 1 left off, Doc Brown and Marty time-hop into the future (2015 to be exact) to save Marty's kids, then find themselves returning to 1955 to retrieve a sports almanac that causes havoc for the McFly family. Clever editing allows for Marty Part 2 to see Marty Part 1 at the school dance. Most of the cast returns, although Glover appears only in cuts from the original and Shue steps in as girlfriend Jennifer. Not up to the original, but still satisfying. Cliffhanger ending sets up Part 3, which was shot simultaneously with this. **107m/C VHS, DVD.** Michael J. Fox, Christopher Lloyd, Lea Thompson, Thomas F. Wilson, Harry Waters Jr., Charles Fleischer, Joe Flaherty, Elisabeth Shue, James Tolkan, Casey Siemaszko, Jeffrey Weissman, Flea, Billy Zane, J.J. (Jeffrey Jay) Cohen, Darlene Vogel, Jason Scott Lee, Crispin Glover, Ricky Dean Logan; ***D:*** Robert Zemeckis; ***W:*** Robert Zemeckis, Bob Gale; ***C:*** Dean Cundey; ***M:*** Alan Silvestri.

Back to the Future, Part 3 🦴🦴🦴 **1990 (PG)** Picks up where Part 2 climaxed a la cliffhanger. Stuck in 1955, time-traveling hero Marty frantically searches for Doc Part 1 so he can return to 1985. Instead, he finds himself in the Wild West circa 1885, trying to save Doc's life. Plot is related to earlier BTTFs, so first time viewers might be confused. For those who've seen previous incarnations, the clever interconnections are really nifty. Nearly matches the original for excitement and offers some snazzy special effects. The complete trilogy is available as a boxed set. **118m/C VHS, DVD.** Michael J. Fox, Christopher Lloyd, Mary Steenburgen, Thomas F. Wilson, Lea Thompson, Elisabeth Shue, Matt Clark, Richard Dysart, Pat Buttram, Harry Carey Jr., Dub Taylor, James Tolkan, Marc McClure, Wendie Jo Sperber, J.J. (Jeffrey Jay) Cohen, Ricky Dean Logan, Jeffrey Weissman; ***D:*** Robert Zemeckis; ***W:*** Robert Zemeckis, Bob Gale; ***C:*** Dean Cundey; ***M:*** Alan Silvestri.

Back to the Secret Garden 🦴🦴 1/2 **2001** Well-meaning but dull sequel based on characters from the novel by Frances Hodgson Burnett. It's now the 1940s and sullen Mary has grown into the elegant Lady Mary (Lunghi), the wife of the ambassador to the U.S. Mistlethwaite has turned into a sunny English orphanage that is run by Martha (Plowright). Lady Mary arranges for Brooklyn-born orphan Lizzie (Buelle) to join their little band, and the young girl just happens to be a gardening whiz. Which is a good thing, since Mary's special garden been badly neglected once again. **100m/C VHS, DVD.** Camilla Belle, Cherie Lunghi, Joan Plowright, David Warner, Leigh Lawson, Florence Hoath; ***D:*** Michael Tuchner; ***W:*** Joe Wiesenfeld; ***C:*** Ian Wilson. **CABLE**

Back to the Wall 🦴🦴 **1956** Moreau is an adulturous wife whose web of deceit results in a suspenseful tale of murder and blackmail. **94m/B VHS.** *FR* Jeanne Moreau, Gerard Oury, Claire Maurier; ***D:*** Edouard Molinaro.

The Back-Up Plan 2010 Zoe is tired of waiting for the right man to father her child so she goes the sperm donor route. Of course just when she gets pregnant, Zoe meets Stan who may be a keeper since he's willing to stick around and help her with the pregnancy. But then the realization of upcoming parenthood sinks in, causing both of them to question the suddenness of their relationship. **m/C DVD.** Jennifer Lopez, Eric Christian Olsen, Danneel Harris, Melissa McCarthy; ***D:*** Alan Poul; ***W:*** Kate Angelo.

Backbeat 🦴🦴🦴 **1994 (R)** Backed by the beat of early Beatle tunes as rendered by some of today's top alternative musicians, the debut for director Softley explores the Fab Four's beginnings in Hamburg's underground music scene. Storyline is driven by the complications of a romantic triangle between John Lennon, Astrid Kirchherr (the photographer who came up with the band's signature look) and Stu Sutcliffe, Lennon's best friend and the original bass player for the Beatles. Hart's dead-on as Lennon, playing him a second time (check out "The Hours and Times"). Energetic and enjoyable, particularly when the Was-produced music takes center stage. **100m/C VHS, DVD.** *GB* Stephen Dorff, Sheryl Lee, Ian Hart, Gary Bakewell, Chris O'Neill, Scot Williams, Kai Wiesinger, Jennifer Ehle; ***D:*** Iain Softley; ***W:*** Michael Thomas, Stephen Ward, Iain Softley; ***C:*** Ian Wilson; ***M:*** Don Was.

Backdraft 🦴🦴 1/2 **1991 (R)** High action story of Chicago firemen has some of the most stupendous incendiary special effects ever filmed. But then there's that plot, B-movie hokum about a mystery arsonist torching strategic parts of the community with the finesse of an expert and a brother-against-brother conflict. Straight-forward performances from most of the cast in spite of the weak storyline. Writer Widen wrote from experience—he used to be a fireman; real-life Chicago firefighters were reportedly very happy with the realistic and intense fire scenes. Forget the plot and just watch the fires. Also available in a letterboxed version. **135m/C VHS, DVD, HD DVD.** Kurt Russell, William Baldwin, Robert De Niro, Donald Sutherland, Jennifer Jason Leigh, Scott Glenn, Rebecca De Mornay, Jason Gedrick, J.T. Walsh, Tony Mockus Sr., Clint Howard, David Crosby; ***D:*** Ron Howard; ***W:*** Gregory Widen; ***C:*** Mikael Salomon; ***M:*** Hans Zimmer.

Backfield in Motion 🦴🦴 1/2 **1991** Silly but harmless comedy about a widowed mom who tries to get closer to her high-schooler son by organizing a mother-son football game. But it's the boys' football coach who really wants to get close—to mom. TV movie debut of both Arnolds (past and present). **95m/C VHS, DVD.** Roseanne, Tom Arnold, Colleen Camp, Conchata Ferrell, Johnny Galecki, Kevin Scannell; ***D:*** Richard Michaels. **TV**

Backfire 🦴🦴 **1922** If you're gonna rob a bank, you shouldn't let anyone hear you plan it, and if you're not gonna rob a bank, you shouldn't let anyone hear you plan one. This vintage "Lightning" Carson crime western has Carson and friend suspected of bank robbery because someone heard them planning one. The sheriff follows their every footstep as they search for the real perpetrators. **56m/B VHS.** Jack Hoxie, George Sowards, Lew Meehan, Florence Gilbert; ***D:*** Alan James.

Backfire 🦴🦴 **1988 (R)** A mysterious stranger enters the lives of a disturbed 'Nam vet and his discontented wife, setting a pattern of murder and double-cross in motion. **90m/C VHS, DVD.** Karen Allen, Keith Carradine, Jeff Fahey, Bernie Casey, Dinah Manoff, Dean Paul (Dino Martin Jr.) Martin; ***D:*** Gilbert Cates; ***W:*** Larry Brand; ***M:*** David Shire.

Backfire! 🦴 1/2 **1994 (PG-13)** Silly spoof finds Jeremy (Mosby) wanting to join New York City's all-female fire brigade who are trying to stop an arsonist from blowing up the city's toilets. Mitchum is the fire marshal and Ireland the mayor's charming assistant. **88m/C VHS.** Josh Mosby, Kathy Ireland, Robert Mitchum, Shelley Winters; ***D:*** A. Dean Bell.

Backflash 🦴🦴 **2001 (R)** Ray (Patrick) runs a videostore and needs a little excitement in his life. He picks up pretty hitchhiker Harley (Esposito), who's just out of jail, and gets more than he's bargained for since Harley needs Ray to pretend to be her husband so she can get into a safety deposit box. But just who's conning who? **90m/C VHS, DVD.** Robert Patrick, Jennifer Esposito, Melissa Joan Hart; ***D:*** Philip Jones; ***W:*** Philip Jones, Jennifer Farrell, Lillian Jackson; ***C:*** Maximo Munzi; ***M:*** Valentine Leone, Carl Wurtz.

Background to Danger 🦴🦴🦴 **1943** A suspenseful WWII actioner about American agent Raft who travels to Turkey to receive secret documents from the soon-to-be-murdered Massen. Greenstreet is the Nazi master spy who also wants the documents as do Russian spies, Lorre and Marshall. Somewhat confusing plot but fast-paced. Based on the thriller "Uncommon Danger" by Eric Ambler. This film was Warner Bros.' follow-up to "Casablanca" with Raft in the Bogie role he had turned down in that cinema classic. **80m/B VHS.** George Raft, Sydney Greenstreet, Peter Lorre, Brenda Marshall, Osa Massen, Turhan Bey, Kurt Katch; ***D:*** Raoul Walsh; ***W:*** W.R. Burnett.

Backlash 🦴🦴 1/2 **1986 (R)** An aborigine barmaid is raped. When her assailant turns up dead, she's charged with murder and winds up in the custody of two police officers on a trip across the outback. Holes in the plot undermine this interesting, although graphic, drama with racial overtones. **88m/C VHS.** *AU* David Argue, Gia Carides, Lydia Miller, Brian Syron, Anne Smith; ***D:*** Bill Bennett; ***W:*** Bill Bennett; ***M:*** Michael Atkinson, Michael Spicer.

Backlash 🦴🦴 *Justice* **1999 (R)** Federal prosecutor Gina Gallagher (Needham) has gotten on the wrong side of the Colombian drug cartel. After her partner is killed, Gina works with veteran homicide detective Moe Ryan (Durning) and uncovers a government conspiracy—so maybe trusting a convict (Belushi) to protect her isn't such a bad idea. **103m/C VHS, DVD, UMD.** Tracey Needham, Charles Durning, James Belushi, JoBeth Williams, Patrick Ersgard, Tony Plana, Henry Silva, Warren Berlinger; ***D:*** Joakim (Jack) Ersgard; ***W:*** Patrick Ersgard. **VIDEO**

Backlash: Oblivion 2 🦴🦴 1/2 *Oblivion 2* **1995 (PG-13)** Galactic supervillainess Lash stakes her claim to a rare derconium mine on the remote space outpost of Oblivion. Will cave monsters thwart her evil plan before space cowboys come to the town's rescue? **82m/C VHS, DVD.** Andrew Divoff, Meg Foster, Isaac Hayes, Julie Newmar, Carel Struycken, George Takei, Musetta Vander, Jimmie F. Skaggs, Irwin Keyes, Maxwell Caulfield; ***D:*** Sam Irvin; ***W:*** Peter David; ***M:*** Pino Donaggio.

Backstab 🦴🦴 1/2 **1990 (R)** A spellbinding tale of work, lust, and murder. Architect Brolin finds himself unable to get over the death of his wife, until a seductive and mysterious woman helps him over his grief. They spend the night together, engulfed in passion, but in the morning he wakes to find himself sleeping with the corpse of his boss. Only the first twist in this intriguing thriller. **91m/C VHS.** James Brolin, Meg Foster, Isabelle Truchon; ***D:*** Jim Kaufman.

Backstairs 🦴🦴 **1921** An obscure German silent film about urban degradation and familial strife. **44m/B VHS.** *GE* Henny Porten, Fritz Kortner, William Dieterle; ***D:*** Leopold Jessner.

Backstairs at the White House 🦴🦴🦴 1/2 **1979** Drawn from Lillian Rogers Parks' 1961 novel "My Thirty Years Backstairs at the White House" and originally aired on NBC, recounts the head maid's real life as she works for eight presidents—from Taft through Eisenhower—and narrates a wide array of historical events during her 52 years of service. **540m/C DVD.** Olivia Cole, Leslie Uggams, Louis Gossett Jr., Robert Hooks, Leslie Nielsen, Cloris Leachman, Hari Rhodes, Paul Winfield, Julie Harris, Victor Buono, David Downing, Helen Carroll, Robert Vaughn, Kim Hunter, James A. Watson Jr., Claire Bloom, Celeste Holm, George Kennedy, Ed Flanders, Lee Grant, Larry Gates, Eileen Heckart, John Anderson, Harry (Henry) Morgan, Estelle Parsons, Jan Sterling, Barbara Barrie, Andrew Duggan, Heather Angel, Matthew "Stymie" Beard, Bibi Besch, Gerry Black, Marilyn Chris, Tom Clancy, Ann Doran, BeBe Drake, Kevin Hooks, Nancy Morgan, Harrison Page, Woodrow Parfrey, Bill Quinn, Ford Rainey, John Randolph, Noble Willingham, Dana Wynter, Ian Abercrombie, Louise Latham; ***D:*** Michael O'Herlihy; ***W:*** Paul Dubov; ***C:*** Robert L. Morrison; ***M:*** Morton Stevens. **TV**

Backstreet Dreams 🦴🦴 **1990 (R)** The young parents of an autistic child find themselves torn apart due to their feelings of guilt. The father has an affair with a specialist hired to help the boy, causing further strife. Interesting story possibilities never get far. **104m/C VHS.** Brooke Shields, Jason O'Malley, Sherilyn Fenn, Tony Fields, Burt Young, Anthony (Tony) Franciosa, Nick Cassavetes, Ray "Boom Boom" Mancini; ***D:*** Rupert Hitzig; ***M:*** Bill Conti.

Backstreet Justice 🦴🦴 1/2 **1993 (R)** Pittsburgh PI Keri Finnegan (Kozlowski) is investigating a series of murders in her neighborhood when she uncovers ties to police corruption dating back 30 years. This doesn't make her popular since it involves her dead cop father and a number of old friends (and enemies). Kozlowski is appropriately feisty and the plot twists will hold your attention. **91m/C VHS.** Linda Kozlowski, Hector Elizondo, John Shea, Paul Sorvino, Viveca Lindfors, Tammy Grimes; ***D:*** Chris T. McIntyre; ***W:*** Chris T. McIntyre.

Backtrack 🦴🦴🦴 *Catchfire* **1989 (R)** Foster co-stars in this thriller about an artist who accidentally witnesses a mob hit. The mob puts a hitman (Hopper) on her trail, and after studying her background and listening to audio tapes she recorded, he finds himself falling in love. Originally intended for a theatrical release, it hit the European screens in a different cut as "Catchfire"; Hopper restored his original version and it was released on cable TV in the U.S. **102m/C VHS, DVD.** Dennis Hopper, Jodie Foster, Dean Stockwell, Vincent Price, John Turturro, Fred Ward, G. Anthony "Tony" Sirico, Julie Adams, Frank Gio, Sy Richardson, Helena Kallianiotes, Bob Dylan; ***Cameos:*** Charlie Sheen, Joe Pesci; ***D:*** Dennis Hopper; ***W:*** Ann Louise Bardach; ***M:*** Michel Colombier.

Backwoods 🦴 **1987 (R)** Two campers wish they had never encountered a mountain man when he begins to stalk them with murder in mind. **90m/C VHS, DVD.** Jack O'Hara, Dick Kreusser, Brad Armacot; ***D:*** Dean Crow.

The Backwoods 🦴 1/2 *Bosque de Sombras* **2006 (R)** Weak, schlocky psychothriller. In 1978, Norman (Considine) and his unhappy wife Lucy (Ledoyen) visit Spain's Basque Country to stay at the isolated house that's being renovated by their friends Paul (Oldman) and Isabel (Sanchez-Gijon). When the guys go out hunting, they find a hut where a disfigured, feral young girl (Esteve) is chained. After freeing her, they bring her back to the house but for some reason this makes the locals very upset. English and Spanish with subtitles. **97m/C DVD.** *GB FR SP* Gary Oldman, Paddy Considine, Virginie Ledoyen, Aitana Sanchez-Gijon, Lluis Homar, Yaiza Esteve, Andres Gertrudix, Jon Arino; ***D:*** Koldo Serra; ***W:*** Koldo Serra, Jon Sagala; ***C:*** Unax Mendia; ***M:*** Fernando Verazquez.

Backwoods 🦴 **2008 (R)** Despite the rating and subject matter, this is a remarkably tame horror show about computer programmers on a corporate wilderness retreat in Northern California. They are preyed on by religious fanatics/survivalists who are interested in the women for breeding purposes. The men are expendable. **84m/C DVD.** Haylie Duff, Ryan Merriman, Danny Nucci, Mark Rolston, Troy Winbush, Deborah Van Valkenburgh; ***D:*** Marty Weiss; ***W:*** Anthony Jaswinski; ***C:*** James W. Wrenn; ***M:*** Paul D'Amour. **VIDEO**

The Bad and the Beautiful 🦴🦴🦴 1/2 **1952** The rise and fall of a Hollywood producer. Douglas stars as the ruthless, arrogant Jonathan Shields, who alienates actress Georgia (Turner), writer James Lee Bartlow (Powell), and director Fred Amiel (Sullivan) as he pursues his career. Much speculation at the time as to who the real-life models for the insider story actually were. Winner of five Oscars, a splendid drama. **118m/B VHS, DVD.** Kirk Douglas, Lana Turner, Dick Powell, Gloria Grahame, Barry Sullivan, Walter Pidgeon, Gilbert Roland, Leo G. Carroll; *D:* Vincente Minnelli; *W:* Charles Schnee; *C:* Robert L. Surtees; *M:* David Raksin. Oscars '52: Art Dir./Set Dec., B&W, B&W Cinematog., Costume Des. (B&W), Screenplay, Support. Actress (Grahame), Natl. Film Reg. '02.

Bad Attitude **1993 (R)** Leon is a narcotics officer on a mission to restore his badge after his careless pistol work gets him booted off the force. The quick-tempered cop relentlessly pursues druglord Finque with the help of an open-minded preacher (De Veaux) and his sexy, streetwise assistant (Lim). **87m/C VHS, DVD.** Leon, Gina Lim, Nathaniel DeVeaux, Susan Finque; *D:* Bill Cummings.

Bad Behavior 1/2 **1992 (R)** Unscripted character-driven drama. Gerry and Ellie McAllister are an Irish couple living in North London. He's tired of working for the local planning commission, she's bored being just a mum at home, and both are still a little uneasy living in England. When they decide to remodel the family bath, the unexpected problems lead to an emotional shakeup. Don't expect a lot of drama, the film works only if you accept the decency of the characters and the small moments of recognizable daily life. Director Blair wrote a basic script outline and had the actors improvise their dialogue, in character, over a long rehearsal period to develop their roles. **103m/C VHS, DVD.** *GB* Stephen Rea, Sinead Cusack, Philip Jackson, Clare Higgins, Phil Daniels, Saira Todd; *D:* Les Blair; *M:* John Altman.

Bad Blood **1981** The true story of Stan Graham, who went on a killing spree in the New Zealand bush when his farm was foreclosed and his life ruined. **104m/C VHS, DVD.** *NZ* Jack Thompson, Carol Burns, Dennis (Denis) Lill; *D:* Mike Newell; *W:* Andrew Brown; *C:* Gary Hansen; *M:* Richard Hartley.

Bad Blood 1/2 **1994 (R)** Travis Blackstone (Lamas) will use any methods to protect his brother Franklin, who's targeted for death by a ruthless drug lord. Lots of action and violence. **90m/C VHS.** Lorenzo Lamas, Hank Cheyne, Frankie Thorn, Kimberley Kates, Joe Son; *D:* Tibor Takacs; *W:* Neil Ruttenberg; *C:* Berhard Salzmann.

Bad Boy 1/2 *Branded* **1939** A country boy goes to the big city, and succumbs to urban evils and temptations, but is eventually saved by motherly love. **60m/B VHS.** Johnny Downs, Helen MacKellar, Rosalind Keith, Holmes Herbert; *D:* Kurt Neumann.

Bad Boy Bubby **1993** Bizarre black comedy about the extremely maladjusted Bubby (Hope), who becomes a pop culture phenomena. The 35-year-old childlike Bubby has been kept a virtual prisoner by his monstrous mom, who has told him the world outside is filled with poisonous gas. Wondering how his cat survived, Bubby wraps it in plastic wrap and is puzzled when it dies. Still, this gives Bubby an idea—he wraps mom in plastic and escapes outside, where he's soon adopted by a struggling rock band that writes a cult song hit about his experiences. It's even stranger than it sounds. **114m/C VHS, DVD.** *IT AU* Nicholas Hope, Claire Benito, Carmel Johnson, Ralph Cotterill, Norman Kaye, Paul Philpot, Graham Duckett, Bridget Walters; *D:* Rolf de Heer; *W:* Rolf de Heer; *M:* Graham Tardif. Australian Film Inst. '94: Actor (Hope), Director (de Heer), Film Editing, Orig. Screenplay.

Bad Boys **1983 (R)** When a gang member's little brother is killed in a rumble, the teen responsible (Penn, who else?) goes to a reformatory, where he quickly (though somewhat reluctantly) takes charge. Meanwhile, on the outside, his rival attacks Penn's girlfriend (Sheedy, in her feature film debut) in retaliation, is incarcerated, and ends up vying with Penn for control of the cell block. Backed into a corner by their mutual hatred and escalating peer pressure, the two are pushed over the brink into a final and shattering confrontation. Not as violent as it could be, to its credit; attempts to communicate a message. **104m/C VHS, DVD.** Sean Penn, Esai Morales, Reni Santoni, Jim Moody, Eric Gurry, Ally Sheedy, Clancy Brown; *D:* Rick Rosenthal; *W:* Richard Dilello; *C:* Donald E. Thorin; *M:* Bill Conti.

Bad Boys 1/2 **1995 (R)** And you thought the old buddy-cop formula was played out. Well, Hollywood sticks with what works, and pairing the two TV personalities definitely works at the minimalist level required. Mike (Smith) and Marcus (Lawrence) are Miami cops who must track down $100 million worth of heroin stolen from their evidence room before internal affairs shuts down the precinct. The case leads them to a vicious thief and a beautiful female witness to his murderous handiwork. Plot lacks depth, but high energy and dazzling action sequences keep things moving. Loud adventure is made louder still by cranking soundtrack. Satisfying addition to the odd-couple cops genre with potential to spawn a "Lethal Weapon"-type franchise. Feature film debut for director Bay. **118m/C VHS, DVD.** Martin Lawrence, Will Smith, Tcheky Karyo, Tea Leoni, Theresa Randle, Marg Helgenberger, Joe Pantoliano, John Salley, Nestor Serrano, Michael Imperioli, Julio Oscar Mechoso; *D:* Michael Bay; *W:* Michael Barrie, Jim Mulholland; *C:* Howard Atherton; *M:* Mark Mancina. Blockbuster '96: Male Newcomer, T. (Smith).

Bad Boys 2 **2003 (R)** Bombastic sequel finds Miami narcs Mike Lowrey (Smith) and Marcus Burnett (Lawrence) going after a violent network of Ecstasy dealers. The duo also has personal problems when Mike falls for Marcus' sister, Syd (Union), an undercover cop. Meanwhile, Marcus ponders whether he wants to remain partners with Mike, and whether, in classic Det. Murtaugh style, he's getting too old for this...stuff. Typical action-flick paper-thin plot doesn't stop Smith and Lawrence from clicking as a comedy-action team. Since this flick is basically the original, amped up to a ridiculous degree, your enjoyment will hinge on your opinion of that one, and your tolerance for the Bruckheimer-Bay "make-go-boom!" style. **146m/C VHS, DVD, UMD.** *US* Will Smith, Martin Lawrence, Gabrielle Union, Joe Pantoliano, Theresa Randle, Jordi Molla, Peter Stormare, Michael Shannon, Jon Seda, Yul Vazquez, Henry Rollins, Jason Manuel Olazabel, Otto Sanchez; *D:* Michael Bay; *W:* Ron Shelton, Jerry Stahl; *C:* Amir M. Mokri.

Bad Bunch **1976** A white liberal living in Watts tries to befriend a ruthless black street gang, but is unsuccessful. **82m/C VHS.** Greydon Clark, Tom Johnigam, Pamela Corbett, Jacqulin Cole, Aldo Ray, Jock Mahoney; *D:* Greydon Clark.

B.A.D. Cats **1980** Two members of a police burglary auto detail team chase after a group of car thieves who are planning a million-dollar gold heist. **74m/C VHS.** Asher Brauner, Michelle Pfeiffer, Vic Morrow, Jimmie Walker, Steve Hanks, LaWanda Page; *D:* Bernard L. Kowalski.

Bad Channels **1992 (R)** Radio goes awry when female listeners of station KDUL are shrunk and put into speciman jars by a way-out disc jockey and a visiting alien, who plans to take the women back to his planet. Mildly amusing comedy features ex-MTV VJ Quinn and score by Blue Oyster Cult. Also available with Spanish subtitles. **88m/C VHS.** Paul Hipp, Martha Quinn, Aaron Lustig, Ian Patrick Williams, Charlie Spradling, Tim Thomerson, Sonny Carl Davis, Robert Factor, Michael Huddleston; *D:* Ted Nicolaou; *W:* Jackson Barr; *C:* Adolfo Bartoli.

Bad Charleston Charlie WOOF! 1973 (PG) Dud of a gangster comedy with terrible acting. A comedy? **91m/C VHS.** Ross Hagen, Kelly Thordsen, John Carradine, Hoke Howell, Carmen Zapata; *D:* Ivan Nagy; *W:* Ross Hagen, Ivan Nagy, Stan Kamber; *C:* Albert Aley; *M:* Luchi De Jesus.

Bad City *Dirty Work* **2006 (R)** Yes, gnomish Pendleton is playing a depraved Chicago crime lord named Julian Healy and he's scarily effective. Derek Manning (Reddick) is a tough detective with a gambling problem who is in debt to Healy, which makes investigating the murder of hooker Bridgette (McDonough) difficult. Then there's too-slick politico Frank Sullivan (McGlone) whose troublesome wife (Anglin) is also killed. **97m/C DVD.** Lance Reddick, Mike McGlone, Austin Pendleton, Nutsa Kukhianidze, Tim Decker, Meghan Maureen McDonough, Karin Anglin; *D:* Bruce Terris; *W:* Bruce Terris, Rick Rose; *C:* David Blood; *M:* Mark Messing.

Bad Company 1/2 **1972 (PG)** Thoughtful study of two very different Civil War draft dodgers roaming the Western frontier and eventually turning to a fruitless life of crime. Both the cast and script are wonderful in an entertaining film that hasn't been given the attention it's due. **94m/C VHS, DVD.** Jeff Bridges, Barry Brown, Jim Davis, John Savage; *D:* Robert Benton; *W:* Robert Benton, David Newman; *C:* Gordon Willis.

Bad Company **1994 (R)** Cynical thriller pits the bad against the worst. Vic Grimes (Langella) and Margaret Wells (Barkin) run a company of former secret agents who specialize in corporate dirty work. Nelson Crowe (Fishburne) is an ex-CIA agent who's their latest recruit. But maybe he's not so ex and maybe Margaret doesn't like sharing power and maybe the cold-blooded duo will get together to make some changes. Everything is stylish, including the leads, but there's a definite chill in the air. **118m/C VHS, DVD.** Ellen Barkin, Laurence Fishburne, Frank Langella, Michael Beach, Gia Carides, David Ogden Stiers, Spalding Gray, James Hong, Daniel Hugh-Kelly; *D:* Damian Harris; *W:* Ross Thomas; *C:* Jack N. Green; *M:* Carter Burwell.

Bad Company 1/2 *Mauvaises Frequentations* **1999** Delphine (Forget) is a typically dissatisfied middle-class teen susceptible to her more-worldly peers, which include the attitudinal, punked-out Olivia (Doillon). Olivia takes Delphine clubbing and she meets requisite smoldering bad boy, Laurent (Stevenin). Delphine's hormones are soon out of control and she agrees to some very questionable suggestions to prove her "love." Frank and unsettling. French with subtitles. **98m/C VHS, DVD.** *FR* Maud Forget, Lou Doillon, Robinson Stevenin, Maxime Mansion, Delphine Rich, Rene Berleand, Micheline Presle, Cyril Cagnat; *D:* Jean-Pierre Ameris; *W:* Alain Layrac; *C:* Yves Vanderemeeren; *M:* Lene Marlin, Giya Kanchell.

Bad Company **2002 (PG-13)** Hustler Rock discovers his twin brother was a CIA operative who has just been murdered. He gets recruited by agency honcho Hopkins to take over his bro's assignment, which involves terrorists, bombs, and New York City. Considering these elements, it's no wonder this one got delayed. Rock deserves a better movie, but he almost salvages this one, anyway...almost. He's up against a standard-issue plot that merely serves to get to the next action set piece which, this being a Bruckheimer production, are done well, but done too often. Schumacher manages to (mostly) subdue his worst instincts (see "Batman & Robin" to watch him surrender to them completely), but it doesn't really help. **111m/C VHS, DVD.** *US* Chris Rock, Anthony Hopkins, Matthew Marsh, Garcelle Beauvais, Kerry Washington, Gabriel Macht, Peter Stormare, John Slattery, Adoni Maropis, Brooke Smith; *D:* Joel Schumacher; *W:* Michael Browning, Jason Richman; *C:* Darius Wolski; *M:* Trevor Rabin.

Bad Day at Black Rock 1/2 **1954** Story of a one-armed man uncovering a secret in a Western town. Wonderful performances from all concerned, especially Borgnine. Fine photography, shot using the new Cinemascope technique. Based on the novel by Howard Breslin. **81m/C VHS, DVD.** Spencer Tracy, Robert Ryan, Anne Francis, Dean Jagger, Walter Brennan, John Ericson, Ernest Borgnine, Lee Marvin; *D:* John Sturges; *C:* William Mellor; *M:* Andre Previn. Cannes '55: Actor (Tracy).

Bad Dreams 1/2 **1988 (R)** The only surviving member of a suicidal religious cult from the '60s awakens in 1988 from a coma. She is pursued by the living-dead cult leader, who seeks to ensure that she lives up (so to speak) to the cult's pact. Blood begins flowing as her fellow therapy group members begin dying, but the only bad dreams you'd get from this flick would be over the money lost on the video rental. **84m/C VHS, DVD.** Bruce Abbott, Jennifer Rubin, Richard Lynch, Harris Yulin, Dean Cameron, Elizabeth (E.G. Dailey) Daily, Susan Ruttan, Charles Fleischer, Sy Richardson; *D:* Andrew Fleming; *W:* Andrew Fleming, Steven E. de Souza; *C:* Alexander Grusynski; *M:* Jay Ferguson.

Bad Education *La Mala Educacion* **2004** Complicated film noir begins in 1980 Madrid where young movie director Enrique (Martinez) is seeking inspiration. It comes to him, literally, when old school friend Ignacio (Garcia Bernal) turns up and hands Enrique a story he's written about the sexual abuse he suffered at the hands of the principal of their Catholic boys' school. But something is wrong—and it's not just the fact that the wannabe actor returns demanding to play the part of transsexual prostitute Zahara (Garcia Bernal again—making quite a pretty woman) in the film, which plays out in Enrique's mind so you're watching two films at once. And if that's not confusing enough, the film has flashbacks to the boys' schooldays and a subsequent meeting in 1977. Somehow Almodovar makes it work. Spanish with subtitles. **104m/C DVD.** Fele Martinez, Gael Garcia Bernal, Lluis Homar, Javier Camara, Petra Martinez, Nacho Perez, Raul Garcia Forneiro, Juan Fernandez, Daniel Gimenez Cacho, Lluis Homar, Alberto Ferreiro, Francisco Boira; *D:* Pedro Almodovar; *W:* Pedro Almodovar; *C:* Jose Luis Alcaine; *M:* Alberto Iglesias.

Bad Georgia Road 1/2 **1977 (R)** A New Yorker inherits a moonshine operation from her uncle, and fights off the syndicate for its profits. **85m/C VHS.** Gary Lockwood, Carol Lynley, Royal Dano, John Wheeler, John Kerry; *D:* John Broderick.

Bad Girl **1931** Apparently sassy model Dorothy (Eilers) is a bad girl because she has sex with Eddie (Dunn) before marriage and gets herself into trouble. Eddie does the right thing and they get married, although he doesn't really want to be a father and isn't happy to give up his dreams to support his unexpected family. So they have to struggle to make things work amidst hard times. **90m/B DVD.** James Dunn, Sally Eilers, Minna Gombell, William Pawley, Frank Darien; *D:* Frank Borzage; *W:* Edwin Burke; *C:* Chester Lyons.

Bad Girls 1/2 **1994 (R)** Latest in the current western craze turns the tables as women take their turns being the gunslingers. Four hooker chums hastily flee town after one kills a nasty customer—only to find the bank where their cash was stashed was robbed by baddies Loggia and Russo. Wearing stylish duds and with each hair perfectly in place the beauties manage to recover their loot. Unexciting script leaves a lot to be desired, but a strong performance from Stowe makes this nearly worthwhile. Lots of off-set drama with original director Tamra Davis fired, and the actresses reportedly having a less-than-bonding experience. **99m/C VHS, DVD.** Andie MacDowell, Madeleine Stowe, Mary Stuart Masterson, Drew Barrymore, James Russo, Dermot Mulroney, Robert Loggia, James LeGros, Nicholas Chinlund, Will MacMillan, Jim Beaver; *D:* Jonathan Kaplan; *W:* Ken Friedman, Yolande Finch; *M:* Jerry Goldsmith.

Bad Girls Do Cry WOOF! 1954 Unbelievably bad exploitation film. Idiotic plot with long scenes of girls stripping down to their undies. Although an American film, the voice track was dubbed in later. **59m/B VHS, DVD.** Bill Page, Misty Ayers, Heather English, Ben Frommer; *D:* Sid Melton.

Bad Girls Dormitory **1984 (R)** At the New York Female Juvenile Reformatory, suicide seems a painless and welcome escape. Utilizes standard genre identifiers, including rape, drugs, soapy showers, bad docs, and desperate young women trapped in a web of frustration and desire. Cheap and mindless titillation. **95m/C VHS, DVD.** Carey Zuris, Teresa Farley; *D:* Tim Kincaid.

Bad Girls from Mars WOOF! 1990 (R) "B" movie sleaze-o-rama in which everyone is murdered, either before, after, or during sex, just like in real life. When the director of the film within this film hires an actress who is, shall we say, popular, to be the heroine of his latest sci-fier, the fun, slim as it is, begins. **86m/C VHS, DVD.** Edy Williams, Brinke Stevens, Jay Richardson, Oliver Darrow, Dana Bentley, Jeffrey Culver, Jasae; *D:* Fred Olen Ray; *W:* Sherman Scott, Mark Thomas McGee; *C:* Gary Graver; *M:* Chuck Cirino.

Bad Girls Go to Hell WOOF! 1965 From the sultana of sleaze, Wishman, comes this winning entry into Joe Bob Briggs' "Sleaziest Movies in the History of the World" series. A ditsy-but-sexy housewife accidentally commits murder and what follows is a plethora of perversion involving hirsute men and gender-bending women who are hell-bent on showing her how hot it is where bad girls go. **98m/B VHS, DVD.** Gigi Darlene, George La Rocque, Sam Stewart, Sandee Norman, Alan Yorke, Bernard L. Sankett, Darlene Bennett, Marlene Starr, Harold Key; ***D:*** Doris Wishman; ***W:*** Doris Wishman, Dawn Whitman; ***C:*** C. Davis Smith.

Bad Guy 1/2 *Nabbeun namja* **2001** Han-ki (Jae-hyeon Jo) is a brutal thug and a pimp who one day sees Sun-hwa (Won Seo) on a park bench and becomes obsessed with her. Forcibly kissing her, he is beaten by bystanders. Han-ki then sets her up in a sting, and blackmails her into becoming a prostitute when she is caught breaking the law. After which he watches her through a peephole. **100m/C DVD.** *KN* Jae-hyeon Jo, Won Seo, Yun-tae Kim, Duek-mun Choi, Yoo-jin Shin, Jung-young Kim; ***D:*** Kim Ki Duk; ***W:*** Kim Ki Duk; ***C:*** Cheol-hyeon Hwang; ***M:*** Ho-jun Park.

Bad Guys **1979** A goulash western about the outlaw days of Hungary in the 1860s. A gang of bandits terrorizes the Transdanubian countryside. In Hungarian with English subtitles. For those seeking the Eastern European Wild West experience. **93m/C VHS.** *HU* Janos Derzsi, Djoko Rosic, Mari Kiss, Gyorgy Dorner, Laszlo Szabo, Miklos Benedek; ***D:*** Gyorgy Szomjas.

Bad Guys **1986 (PG)** An inane comedy about two ridiculous policemen who decide to take the wrestling world by storm after being kicked off the police force. Featuring scenes with many of the world's most popular wrestlers. **86m/C VHS.** Adam Baldwin, Mike Jolly, Michelle Nicastro, Ruth Buzzi, James Booth, Gene LeBell, Norman Burton; ***D:*** Joel Silberg; ***C:*** Hanania Baer; ***M:*** William Goldstein.

Bad Influence 1/2 **1990 (R)** A lackluster effort in the evil-doppelganger school of psychological mystery, where a befuddled young executive (Spader) is led into the seamier side of life by a mysterious stranger (Lowe). **99m/C VHS, DVD.** Rob Lowe, James Spader, Lisa Zane, Christian Clemenson, Kathleen Wilhoite; ***D:*** Curtis Hanson; ***C:*** Robert Elswit; ***M:*** Trevor Jones.

Bad Jim 1/2 **1989 (PG)** A cowpoke buys Billy the Kid's horse and, upon riding it, becomes an incorrigible outlaw himself. First feature film for Hollywood legend Clark Gable's son. **110m/C VHS.** James Brolin, Richard Roundtree, John Clark Gable, Harry Carey Jr., Ty Hardin, Pepe Serna, Rory Calhoun; ***D:*** Clyde Ware.

Bad Lands 1/2 **1939** A small cowboy posse finds themselves trapped by a band of Apache Indians in the Arizona desert. A remake of "The Lost Patrol." **70m/B VHS.** Robert Barrat, Guinn "Big Boy" Williams, Douglas Walton, Andy Clyde, Addison Richards, Robert Coote, Paul Hurst, Noah Beery Jr.; ***D:*** Lew Landers.

Bad Lieutenant **1992 (NC-17)** Social chaos and degeneration characterize story as well as nameless loner lieutenant Keitel, who is as corrupt as they come. Assigned to a case involving a raped nun, he's confronted by his own lagging Catholic beliefs and the need for saving grace. From cult filmmaker Ferrara ("Ms. 45") and filled with violence, drugs, and grotesque sexual situations. Tense, over-the-top, urban drama is not intended for seekers of the subtle. Rent it with "Reservoir Dogs" and prepare yourself for a long tense evening of top-rated Keitel and screen-splitting violence. "R" rated version is also available at 91 minutes. **98m/C VHS, DVD.** Harvey Keitel, Brian McElroy, Frankie Acciario, Peggy Gormley, Stella Keitel, Victor Argo, Paul Calderon, Leonard Thomas, Frankie Thorn; ***D:*** Abel Ferrara; ***W:*** Zoe Lund, Abel Ferrara; ***C:*** Ken Kelsch; ***M:*** Joe Delia. Ind. Spirit '93: Actor (Keitel).

Bad Lieutenant: Port of Call New Orleans **2009 (R)** Loopy director Herzog does his 'reimaging' of Abel Ferrara's 1992 guilt-ridden cult flick "Bad Lieutenant" that starred an over-the-top Harvey Keitel. This time it's Cage as New Orleans homicide detective Terence McDonaugh, who's a gambling and drug addict who hallucinates evil iguanas. He also has a beautiful drug-addicted hooker girlfriend (Mendes) and a gangland slaying (that's drug related) to investigate. It's all just secondary to watching Cage act bizarrely, which (for a change) is actually in keeping with his erratic character. **121m/C DVD.** *US* Nicolas Cage, Val Kilmer, Eva Mendes, Fairuza Balk, Jennifer Coolidge, Brad Dourif, Michael Shannon, Shawn Hatosy, Denzel Whitaker, Shea Whigham, Xzibit, Tom Bower, Irma P. Hall, Vondie Curtis-Hall, Brandi Coleman, Katie Chonacas, Lance E. Nichols; ***D:*** Werner Herzog; ***W:*** William M. Finkelstein; ***C:*** Peter Zeitlinger; ***M:*** Mark Isham.

Bad Love 1/2 **1995 (R)** Unlucky Eloise (Gidley) stays true to nature when she falls for loser Lenny (Sizemore), who decides the big score lies with robbing the fading movie star (O'Neill) Eloise works for. Naturally, things go badly. Slick production for anyone who likes fringe romances. **93m/C VHS, DVD.** Tom Sizemore, Pamela Gidley, Debi Mazar, Jennifer O'Neill, Margaux Hemingway, Richard Edson, Seymour Cassel, Joe Dallesandro; ***D:*** Jill Goldman; ***C:*** Gary Tieche; ***M:*** Rick Cox.

Bad Man of Deadwood **1941** A man-with-a-past joins a circus as a sharpshooter, and is threatened with disclosure. **54m/B VHS, DVD.** Roy Rogers, George "Gabby" Hayes, Carol Adams, Henry (Kleinbach) Brandon, Herbert Rawlinson, Sally Payne, Wally Wales, Jay Novello, Horace Murphy, Monte Blue; ***D:*** Joseph Kane; ***W:*** James R. Webb; ***C:*** William Nobles; ***M:*** Cy Feuer.

Bad Manners **1984 (R)** When an orphan is adopted by a wealthy but entirely selfish couple, a group of his orphan friends try to free him from his new home and lifestyle. **85m/C VHS.** Martin Mull, Karen Black, Anne DeSalvo, Murphy Dunne, Pamela Segall, Edy Williams, Susan Ruttan, Richard Deacon; ***D:*** Bobby Houston; ***C:*** Jan De Bont.

Bad Manners **1998 (R)** Pompous musicologist Matt (Rubinek) returns to Boston with his razor-tongued girlfriend Kim (Feeney) to give a lecture and check in on his old girlfriend, brittle unhappy Nancy (Bedelia), and her prissy academic husband Wes (Strathairn). It's a weekend in hell for houseguests and hosts as they play not-so-adult games of truth-or-dare. Based on Gilman's play "Ghost in the Machine." **88m/C VHS, DVD.** David Strathairn, Bonnie Bedelia, Saul Rubinek, Caroleen Feeney, Julie Harris; ***D:*** Jonathan Kaufer; ***W:*** David Gilman; ***C:*** Denis Maloney; ***M:*** Ira Newborn.

Bad Man's River **1972** A Mexican revolutionary leader hires a gang of outlaws to blow up an arsenal used by the Mexican Army. **92m/C VHS, DVD.** *IT SP* Lee Van Cleef, James Mason, Gina Lollobrigida; ***D:*** Eugenio (Gene) Martin; ***W:*** Philip Yordan; ***C:*** Alejandro Ulloa; ***M:*** Waldo de los Rios.

Bad Medicine **WOOF!** **1985 (PG-13)** A youth who doesn't want to be a doctor is accepted by a highly questionable Latin American school of medicine. Remember that it was for medical students like these that the U.S. liberated Grenada. **97m/C VHS.** Steve Guttenberg, Alan Arkin, Julie Hagerty, Bill Macy, Curtis Armstrong, Julie Kavner, Joe Grifasi, Robert Romanus, Taylor Negron, Gilbert Gottfried; ***D:*** Harvey Miller; ***W:*** Harvey Miller.

Bad Men of the Border 1/2 **1945** Routine oater has Kirby posing as a bandit in order to infiltrate an outlaw band passing counterfeit money. He rounds up the bad guys and finds time to romance Armida too. **56m/B VHS.** Kirby Grant, Fuzzy Knight, Armida, John Eldridge, Francis McDonald; ***D:*** Wallace Fox; ***W:*** Adele Buffington.

Bad Moon 1/2 **1996 (R)** Let's put it this way, the werewolf in this movie is not the only thing that bites. Shortest (mercifully) studio release in recent history is a horror (in more ways than one) film with Pare leading the pack as Ted, a photojournalist who comes back from the Amazon a different, more nocturnally hirsute man. Fleeing from the site of his nightly gore, Ted takes refuge with his loving sister Janet (Hemingway) and her son Brett (Gamble). The real hero (and best actor) is a German shepherd named Thor (Primo) who discovers that Ted's a werewolf. Dog steals the show paws down (naturally). Decent special FX. Adapted from Wayne Smith's novel "Thor." **79m/C VHS, DVD.** Mariel Hemingway, Michael Pare, Mason Gamble, Ken Pogue; ***D:*** Eric Red; ***W:*** Eric Red; ***C:*** Jan Kiesser; ***M:*** Daniel Licht.

The Bad News Bears **1976 (PG)** Family comedy about a misfit Little League team that gets whipped into shape by a cranky, sloppy, beer-drinking coach who recruits a female pitcher. O'Neal and Matthau are top-notch. Spawned two sequels and a TV series. **102m/C VHS, DVD.** Walter Matthau, Tatum O'Neal, Vic Morrow, Joyce Van Patten, Jackie Earle Haley, Chris Barnes, Erin Blunt, Gary Cavagnaro, Alfred Lutter, David Stambaugh, Brandon Cruz, Jaime Escobedo, Scott Firestone, George Gonzales, Brett Marx, David Pollock, Quinn Smith; ***D:*** Michael Ritchie; ***W:*** Bill Lancaster; ***C:*** John A. Alonzo; ***M:*** Jerry Fielding. Writers Guild '76: Orig. Screenplay.

The Bad News Bears **2005 (PG-13)** Here's some bad news: Indie darling Linklater hit a home run with his kid-friendly "School of Rock," but he couldn't squeeze any life of out this watered-down remake of the 1976 Walter Matthau classic. It's disturbing that the updated "Bears" is a million times less subversive, vulgar, and (let's face it) funny than the original, a film that was released almost thirty years ago. Isn't society supposed to be declining? Shouldn't Linklater's movie be raunchier than a film released during the Carter administration? Casting Thornton in the lead was an inspired choice, but the toothless script just forces him to do the PG version of his "Bad Santa" routine. Do yourself a favor and rent the original. **111m/C DVD, UMD.** *US* Billy Bob Thornton, Greg Kinnear, Marcia Gay Harden, Tyler Patrick Jones, Sammi Kraft, Timmy Deters, Ridge Canipe, Brandon Craggs, Jeff Davies, Carter Jenkins, Jeffrey Tedmori, Troy Gentile, Carlos Estrada, Emmanuel Estrada, Kenneth "K.C." Harris, Aman Johal; ***D:*** Richard Linklater; ***W:*** Glenn Ficarra, John Requa, Bill Lancaster; ***C:*** Rogier Stoffers; ***M:*** Ed Shearmur, Randall Poster.

The Bad News Bears Go to Japan **1978 (PG)** The second sequel, in which the famed Little League team goes to the Little League World Series in Tokyo. Comic adventure features Curtis as a talent agent out to exploit the team's fame. **92m/C VHS, DVD.** Tony Curtis, Jackie Earle Haley, Tomisaburo Wakayama, George Wyner, Erin Blunt, George Gonzales, Brett Marx, David Pollock, David Stambaugh, Regis Philbin; ***D:*** John Berry; ***W:*** Bill Lancaster; ***C:*** Gene Polito; ***M:*** Paul Chihara.

The Bad News Bears in Breaking Training 1/2 **1977 (PG)** With a chance to take on the Houston Toros for a shot at the little league baseball Japanese champs, the Bears devise a way to get to Texas to play at the famed Astrodome. Disappointing sequel to "The Bad News Bears"; followed by "The Bad News Bears Go to Japan" (1978). **99m/C VHS, DVD.** William Devane, Clifton James, Jackie Earle Haley, Jimmy Baio, Chris Barnes, Erin Blunt, George Gonzales, Jaime Escobedo, Alfred Lutter, Brett Marx, David Pollock, Quinn Smith, David Stambaugh, Dolph Sweet; ***D:*** Michael Pressman; ***W:*** Paul Brickman; ***C:*** Fred W. Koenekamp; ***M:*** Craig Safan.

The Bad Pack 1/2 **1998 (R)** Soldier of fortune puts together a team when he's hired to defend a town beseiged by a sadistic militia. **93m/C VHS, DVD.** Robert Davi, Ralph (Ralf) Moeller, Roddy Piper, Brent Huff, Larry B. Scott, Patrick Dollaghan, Marshall Teague; ***D:*** Brent Huff. **VIDEO**

Bad Reputation **2005 (R)** Chillingly disturbing portrayal of victim's revenge. Michelle, though poor, attends an affluent school on scholarship. She chooses to keep buried in a book rather than mix with the shallow class populous. One night at a party, she is drugged and gang-raped. A metamorphosis follows, as the shy, smart, attractive girl becomes an avenging assassin, swiftly wiping out all who humiliated her. Excellent character development, smart script, and bright directing make for a very satisfying retaliation tale. **90m/C DVD.** Angelique Hennessy, Jerad Anderson, Danielle Noble, Mark Kunzman, Kristina Conzen; ***D:*** Jim Hemphill; ***W:*** Jim Hemphill; ***C:*** Forrest Allison; ***M:*** John LeBec, Eric Choronzy. **VIDEO**

Bad Ronald **1974** No, not a political biography of Ronald Reagan... Fascinating thriller about a disturbed teenager who kills a friend after being harassed repeatedly. The plot thickens after the boy's mother dies, and he is forced to hide out in a secret room when an unsuspecting family with three daughters moves into his house. The story is accurately recreated from the novel by John Holbrook Vance. **78m/C VHS.** Scott Jacoby, Pippa Scott, John Larch, Dabney Coleman, Kim Hunter, John Fiedler; ***D:*** Buzz Kulik. **TV**

Bad Santa 1/2 **2003 (R)** This is not your grandparents' Christmas movie. Or your kids' for that matter. Thornton is Willie Stokes, an alcoholic, vulgarian, self-loathing department store Santa who uses the gig to rob the store safe on Christmas Eve. His partner is sidekick/elf Marcus, the brains of the duo, who berates Willie for letting his liquor-soaked ways interfere with the job. When they set up shop in Phoenix, things get complicated when a doughy outcast kid leeches onto Willie. Sentimentality is crushed beneath the boot of bitter misanthropy as the movie swerves from tasteless to merely outrageous and back. Luckily, the commitment of the cast to their unsavory roles makes most of the comedy works. Zwigoff and the script let in a little light at the end, but not so much that it betrays what came before. Ritter is excellent in his final role, as the meek store manager. **91m/C VHS, DVD.** *US* Billy Bob Thornton, Tony Cox, Lauren Graham, Brett Kelly, John Ritter, Bernie Mac, Lauren Tom, Cloris Leachman; ***D:*** Terry Zwigoff; ***W:*** Glenn Ficarra, John Requa; ***C:*** Jamie Anderson; ***M:*** David Kitay.

The Bad Seed 1/2 **1956** A mother makes the tortuous discovery that her cherubic eight-year-old daughter harbors an innate desire to kill. Based on Maxwell Anderson's powerful Broadway stage play. **129m/B VHS, DVD.** Patty McCormack, Nancy Kelly, Eileen Heckart, Henry Jones, Evelyn Varden, Paul Fix, Jesse White, Gage Clark, Joan Croyden, Frank Cady, William Hopper; ***D:*** Mervyn LeRoy; ***W:*** John Lee Mahin; ***C:*** Harold Rosson; ***M:*** Alex North. Golden Globes '57: Support. Actress (Heckart).

The Bad Seed **1985** TV remake of the movie with the same name. Story about a sadistic little child who kills for her own evil purposes. Acting is not up to par with previous version. **100m/C VHS.** Blair Brown, Lynn Redgrave, David Carradine, Richard Kiley, David Ogden Stiers, Carrie Wells, Chad Allen, Christa Denton, Anne Haney, Eve Smith; ***D:*** Paul Wendkos; ***M:*** Paul Chihara. **TV**

Bad Seed *Preston Tylk* **2000 (R)** Mild-mannered Preston (Wilson) storms out of the house when he discovers wife Emily (Avital) is having an affair. He returns home to find her murdered—maybe by her boyfriend Jonathan (Reedus) whom Preston then tries to track down. There's another murder, both men go on the lam, and Preston turns to a hard-luck PI, Dick (Farina), for help. Too bad the film doesn't hang together better since it had the makings of a fine little thriller. **92m/C VHS, DVD.** Luke Wilson, Norman Reedus, Dennis Farina, Mili Avital, Vincent Kartheiser; ***D:*** Jon Bokenkamp; ***W:*** Jon Bokenkamp; ***C:*** Joey Forsyte; ***M:*** Kurt Kuenne.

The Bad Sleep Well 1/2 *The Worse You Are, the Better You Sleep; Waru Yatsu Hodo Yoku Nemuru* **1960** Japanese variation of the 1940 Warner Bros. crime dramas. A tale about corruption in the corporate world as seen through the eyes of a rising executive. **135m/B VHS, DVD.** *JP* Toshiro Mifune, Masayuki Kato, Masayuki Mori, Takashi Shimura, Akira Nishimura; ***D:*** Akira Kurosawa; ***W:*** Akira Kurosawa, Shinobu Hashimoto, Ryuzo Kikushima, Hideo Oguni; ***C:*** Yuzuru Aizawa; ***M:*** Masaru Sato.

Bad Taste **1988** A definite pleaser for the person who enjoys watching starving aliens devour the average, everyday human being. Alien fast-food manufacturers come to earth in hopes of harvesting all of mankind. The earth's fate lies in the hands of the government who must stop these rampaging creatures before the whole human race is gobbled up. Terrific make-up jobs on the aliens add the final touch to this gory, yet humorous cult horror flick. **90m/C VHS, DVD.** *NZ* Peter Jackson, Pete O'Herne, Mike Minett, Terry Potter, Craig Smith, Doug Wren, Dean Lawrie, Peter Vere-Jones, Ken Hammon,

Michael Gooch; *D:* Peter Jackson; *W:* Tony Hiles, Peter Jackson, Ken Hammon; *C:* Peter Jackson; *M:* Michelle Scullion.

The Badge **2002 (R)** Small-town sheriff Darl (Thornton) must set aside his personal distaste to investigate the murder of a local transsexual, who was once married to stripper Scarlett (Arquette). But the deeper Darl digs, the more the powers that be want the incident covered up. Mediocre mystery despite the name cast. **103m/C VHS, DVD.** Billy Bob Thornton, Patricia Arquette, Sela Ward, William Devane, Jena Malone, Tom Bower, Ray McKinnon, Julie Hagerty, Hill Harper; *D:* Robby Henson; *W:* Robby Henson; *C:* Irek Hartowicz; *M:* David Bergeaud.

Badge of the Assassin **1985** True story of a New York assistant DA who directed a campaign to catch a pair of cop-killers from the '70s. **96m/C VHS.** James Woods, Yaphet Kotto, Alex Rocco, David Harris, Pam Grier, Steven Keats, Richard Bradford, Rae Dawn Chong; *D:* Mel Damski. **TV**

Badge 373 1/2 **1973 (R)** In the vein of "The French Connection," a New York cop is suspended and decides to battle crime his own way. **116m/C VHS.** Robert Duvall, Verna Bloom, Eddie Egan; *D:* Howard W. Koch.

Badland 1/2 **2007 (R)** Overly-solemn and way too long. Marine reservist Jerry wound up with a dishonorable discharge and PTSD after a stint in Iraq. Now he's got a nothing job in a nowhere Wyoming town when his boss falsely accuses him of theft. When shrewish wife Nora nags once too often—well, Jerry takes young daughter Celia and hits the road. **165m/C DVD.** Jamie Draven, Vinessa Shaw, Joe Morton, Chandra West, Grace Fulton, Patrick Richards; *D:* Francesco Lucente; *W:* Francesco Lucente; *C:* Carlo Varini; *M:* Ludek Drizhal.

The Badlanders **1958** A western remake of the 1950 crime drama "The Asphalt Jungle." In 1898, Peter 'The Dutchman' Van Hoek (Ladd) and John McBain (Borgnine) are released from Yuma state prison. Both wind up in Prescott, Arizona where the Dutchman is unwelcome since the mining engineer was framed and sent to the pen by gold mine owner Cyril Lounsberry (Smith). McBain wants to go straight but is drawn into the Dutchman's revenge scheme. **83m/C DVD.** Alan Ladd, Ernest Borgnine, Kent Smith, Claire Kelly, Katy Jurado, Nehemiah Persoff; *D:* Delmer Daves; *W:* Richard Collins; *C:* John Seitz.

Badlands 1/2 **1974 (PG)** Based loosely on the Charlie Starkweather murders of the 1950s, this impressive debut by director Malick recounts a slow-thinking, unhinged misfit's killing spree across the midwestern plains, accompanied by a starry-eyed 15-year-old schoolgirl. Sheen and Spacek are a disturbingly numb, apathetic, and icy duo. **94m/C VHS, DVD.** Martin Sheen, Sissy Spacek, Warren Oates, Ramon Bieri, Alan Vint, Gary Littlejohn, Charles Fitzpatrick, Howard Ragsdale, John Womack Jr., Dona Baldwin; ***Cameos:*** Terrence Malick; *D:* Terrence Malick; *W:* Terrence Malick; *C:* Tak Fujimoto, Stevan Larner, Brian Probyn; *M:* Carl Orff. Natl. Film Reg. '93.

Badman's Territory **1946** A straight-shooting marshal has to deal with such notorious outlaws as the James and Dalton boys in a territory outside of government control. **79m/B VHS.** Randolph Scott, Ann Richards, George "Gabby" Hayes, Steve Brodie; *D:* Tim Whelan.

Badmen of Nevada 1/2 *The Mysterious Rider* **1933** Badmen roam Nevada in the early days before law and order. **57m/B VHS.** Kent Taylor, Lona Andre, Warren Hymer, Irving Pichel, Gail Patrick, Clarence Wilson, Niles Welch, Berton Churchill; *D:* Fred Allen; *W:* Robert N. Lee, Harvey Gates, Robert Niles; *C:* Archie Stout.

Baffled 1/2 **1972** Nimoy is a race car driver who has visions of people in danger. He must convince an ESP expert (Hampshire) of the credibility of his vision, and then try to save the lives of the people seen with his sixth sense. **90m/C VHS.** Leonard Nimoy, Susan Hampshire, Vera Miles, Rachel Roberts, Jewel Blanch, Christopher Benjamin; *D:* Philip Leacock. **TV**

Bagdad **1949** Arabian nights story with the lovely O'Hara starring as Princess Marjan, the daughter of a sheik. She returns from England to find her father murdered and Hassan (Christian), the leader of a suspicious group known as The Black Riders, the main suspect. But then there's Turkish Pasha Al Nadim (Price) lurking sinisterly, as well. **83m/C VHS.** Maureen O'Hara, Paul (Christian) Hubschmid, Vincent Price, John Sutton, Jeff Corey, Frank Puglia, David Wolfe, Fritz Leiber; *D:* Charles Lamont; *C:* Russell Metty.

Bagdad Cafe *Out of Rosenheim* **1988 (PG)** A large German woman, played by Sagebrecht, finds herself stranded in the Mojave desert after her husband dumps her on the side of the highway. She encounters a rundown cafe where she becomes involved with the off-beat residents. A hilarious story in which the strange people and the absurdity of their situations are treated kindly and not made to seem ridiculous. Spawned a short-lived TV series with Whoopi Goldberg. **91m/C VHS, DVD.** *GE* Marianne Saegebrecht, CCH Pounder, Jack Palance, Christine Kaufmann, Monica Calhoun, Darron Flagg; *D:* Percy Adlon; *W:* Percy Adlon, Eleonore Adlon; *C:* Bernd Heinl; *M:* Bob Telson. Cesar '89: Foreign Film.

Baghead **2008 (R)** Four wannabe actor/writers take a weekend retreat to a woodsy cabin so they can come up with a screenplay they can star in. The two sorta couples are having relationship issues and then some peeper, wearing a bag on his head, starts peering in the windows. But no one's sure if it's just a prank or something more sinister. A mumblecore indie mash-up of genres best appreciated by those who enjoy watching the self-absorbed yammer. **84m/C DVD.** Ross Partridge, Greta Gerwig, Elise Muller, Steve Zissis; *D:* Mark Duplass, Jay Duplass; *W:* Mark Duplass, Jay Duplass; *C:* Jay Duplass; *M:* J. Scott Howard.

Bahama Passage 1/2 **1942** Trite story of one lady's efforts to win the affection of a macho Bahamas stud. **83m/C VHS.** Madeleine Carroll, Sterling Hayden, Flora Robson, Leo G. Carroll, Dorothy Dandridge, Mary Anderson, Cecil Kellaway, Fred Kohler Jr.; *D:* Edward H. Griffith; *W:* Virginia Van Upp; *C:* Leo Tover.

Bail Jumper **1989** A story of love and commitment against incredible odds; some of which happen to be a swarm of locusts, a tornado, and falling meteorites. Joe and Elaine are small-time hoods escaping their dreary lives in Murky Springs Missouri by heading for that great bastion of idyllism and idealism—New York City. But even as the world starts to crumble around them, get the message that love prevails. **96m/C VHS.** Eszter Balint, B.J. Spalding, Tony Askin, Joie Lee; *D:* Christian Faber.

Bail Out **1990 (R)** Three bounty hunters, armed to the teeth, run a car-trashing police gauntlet so they may capture a valuable crook. **88m/C VHS, DVD.** David Hasselhoff, Linda Blair, John Vernon, Tom Rosales, Charlie Brill; *D:* Max Kleven.

Bail Out at 43,000 **1957** Movie about the lifestyles and love affairs of your average, everyday parachutist. **80m/B VHS.** John Payne, Karen Steele, Paul Kelly; *D:* Francis D. Lyon; *W:* Paul Monash.

Bailey's Billion$ 1/2 **2005 (G)** Bailey (voiced by Lovitz) is a golden retriever who has been left a fortune by his late owner. Naturally, the woman's greedy nephew Caspar (Curry) and his scheming wife Dolores (Tilly) plot to get the money by kidnapping the dog. However, Bailey's guardian Theodore (Cain), a geeky animal behaviorist who can speak dog, and animal-rights activist Marge (Holden) team up to do right by him. **93m/C DVD.** *CA* Dean Cain, Laurie Holden, Tim Curry, Jennifer Tilly, Angela Vallee, Max Baker, Sheila McCarthy, Kenneth Welsh; *D:* David Devine; *W:* Heather Conkie, Mary Walsh; *C:* Gavin Finney; *M:* Lou Pomanti; *V:* Jon Lovitz.

Baise Moi **WOOF!** *Rape Me* **2000** French porn dressed up for the arthouse crowd had critics spinning like tops to justify not calling the film what it is—exploitative trash, even if it is done by women. After Manu (Anderson) gets gang raped, she kills her boyfriend, steals his money, and hooks up with prostitute Nadine (Bach) to go on a sex and murder spree. Very, very graphic sex and violence and the literal translation of the French title is not "rape" but another four-letter word beginning with "f." Based on the novel by co-writer/director Despentes; French with subtitles. **77m/C VHS, DVD.** *FR* Raffaela Anderson, Karen Bach; *D:* Virginie Despentes, Coralie Trinh Thi; *W:* Virginie Despentes, Coralie Trinh Thi; *C:* Benoit Chamaillard; *M:* Varou Jan.

Bait **2000 (R)** Bait is what you use to catch bigger fish, and hopefully star Foxx can use his performance in this otherwise by-the-book action-comedy to snag bigger and better roles. Petty thief Alvin (Foxx) winds up in the clink after a botched seafood robbery. His cellmate Jaster (Pastorelli) is the double-crossing partner of prancing archvillain Bristol (Hutchinson), who has stolen $40 million in gold. Unfortunately for Alvin, Jaster winds up in the Big House in the sky before he can tell anyone where the hidden loot is stashed. Head Fed Clenteen (Morse), thinking that Alvin knows where the gold is hidden, has him unwittingly equipped with surveillance devices and springs him from the pokey. Alvin, now followed by Bristol and the feds, tries to find the stashed loot by piecing together the cryptic clues that Jaster has left him. Lots of action on a minimal (for these types of movies) budget. **119m/C VHS, DVD.** Jamie Foxx, Doug Hutchison, David Morse, Jamie Kennedy, Robert Pastorelli, Kimberly Elise, David Paymer, Tia Texada, Mike Epps, Nestor Serrano, Megan Dodds, Jeffrey Donovan, Kirk Acevedo; *D:* Antoine Fuqua; *W:* Tom Gilroy, Jeff Nathanson, Adam Scheinman, Andrew Scheinman; *C:* Tobias Schliessler; *M:* Mark Mancina.

Bait 1/2 **2002** Jack Blake does a good deed on a cold, rainy night, taking in Pam and her daughter Stephanie when their car breaks down. Their gratitude is short-lived as Jack, still anguished over his daughter's unsolved murder years before, realizes that Stephanie looks like her and holds them captive so he can use her to catch the killer. **98m/C VHS, DVD.** John Hurt, Sheila Hancock, Rachael Stirling, Angeline Ball, Jonathan Firth, Nicholas Farrell, Matthew Scurfield; *D:* Nicholas Renton; *W:* Daniel Boyle; *C:* Oliver Curtis; *M:* John Keane. **TV**

Bait Shop 1/2 **2008 (PG)** Good ole boy bait shop owner Bill (Engvall) is going to lose his business to the bank unless he can come up 15,000 smackers. His one chance is to win the annual Bass Tournament, which he's lost every previous year to smug rival Hot Rod Johnson (Cyrus). **85m/C DVD.** Bill Engvall, Billy Ray Cyrus, Vincent Martella, Harve Presnell, Billy Joe Shaver; *D:* C.B. Harding; *W:* Bear Aderhold, Tom Sullivan; *C:* Jamie Barber; *M:* Steven R. Phillips. **VIDEO**

Baja **1995 (R)** Bebe (Ringwald) hides out in Baja with her beau Alex (Logue) after a drug deal goes bad. They hold up in a sleazy motel while Bebe waits for dad, John (Bernsen), to bail her out. But instead, John persuades estranged hubby Michael (Nickles) to track down the runaways and Michael finds out that hitman Tom (Henriksen) is hunting for Alex. Must be the desert heat causing all the ensuing commotion. **92m/C VHS, DVD.** Molly Ringwald, Lance Henriksen, Michael A. (M.A.) Nickles, Donal Logue, Corbin Bernsen; *D:* Kurt Voss; *W:* Kurt Voss; *C:* Denis Maloney; *M:* Reg Powell.

Baja Oklahoma **1987** A country barmaid has dreams of being a country singer. Songs by Willie Nelson, Emmylou Harris, and Billy Vera. **97m/C VHS.** Lesley Ann Warren, Peter Coyote, Swoosie Kurtz, Willie Nelson, Julia Roberts; *D:* Bobby Roth; *W:* Bobby Roth; *C:* Michael Ballhaus. **CABLE**

Baker's Hawk **1976** A young boy befriends a red-tailed hawk and learns the meaning of family and caring. **98m/C VHS, DVD.** Clint Walker, Diane Baker, Burl Ives, Lee Montgomery, Alan Young, Danny Bonaduce; *D:* Lyman Dayton; *W:* Dan Greer, Hal Harrison Jr.; *C:* Bernie Abramson; *M:* Lex de Azevedo.

The Baker's Wife 1/2 *La Femme du Boulanger* **1933** There's a new baker in town, and he brings with him to the small French village an array of tantalizing breads, as well as a discontented wife. When she runs off with a shepherd, her loyal and naive husband refuses to acknowledge her infidelity; however, in his loneliness, the baker can't bake, so the townspeople scheme to bring his wife back. Panned as overly cute Marcel Pagnol peasant glorification, and hailed as a visual poem full of wit; you decide. In French with subtitles. Also available for French students without subtitles; a French script booklet is also available. **101m/B VHS.** *FR* Raimu, Ginette LeClerc, Charles Moulton, Charpin, Robert Vattier; *D:* Marcel Pagnol; *W:* Marcel Pagnol; *C:* Georges Benoit; *M:* Vincent Scotto. N.Y. Film Critics '40: Foreign Film.

Balalaika **1939** Rather dull operetta about the Russian revolution with Eddy playing a Russian prince. Eddy masquerades as a member of the proletariat in order to romance Massey, who was expected to become the next Garbo. Didn't happen, though. Eddy's rendition of "Stille Nacht" ("Silent Night") is highlight of film. Based on the operetta by Eric Maschwitz, George Ponford, and Bernard Gruen. **102m/B VHS.** Nelson Eddy, Ilona Massey, Charlie Ruggles, Frank Morgan, Lionel Atwill, Sir C. Aubrey Smith, Joyce Compton; *D:* Reinhold Schunzel; *W:* Leon Gordon, Charles Bennett, Jacques Deval; *C:* Karl Freund.

Balance of Power 1/2 **1996 (R)** Martial arts master Matsumoto (Mako) prepares fighter Niko (Blanks) for a death match against a former student who's gone bad. **92m/C VHS.** Billy Blanks, Mako, James Lew; *D:* Rick Bennet; *W:* Phil Good, Rick Bennet; *C:* Gilles Corbeil.

Balboa **WOOF!** **1982** Set on sun-baked Balboa Island, this is a melodramatic tale of high-class power, jealousy, and intrigue. Never-aired pilot for a TV miniseries, in the night-time soap tradition (even features Steve Kanaly from TV's "Dallas"). Special appearance by Cassandra Peterson, also known as horror hostess Elvira; and if that interests you, look for Sonny Bono, as well. **92m/C VHS.** Tony Curtis, Carol Lynley, Chuck Connors, Sonny Bono, Steve Kanaly, Jennifer Chase, Lupita Ferrer, Martine Beswick, Henry Jones, Cassandra Peterson; *D:* James Polakof. **TV**

The Balcony **1963** A film version of the great Jean Genet play about a surreal brothel, located in an unnamed, revolution-torn city, where its powerful patrons act out their fantasies. Scathing and rude. **87m/B VHS, DVD.** Peter Falk, Shelley Winters, Lee Grant, Kent Smith, Peter Brocco, Ruby Dee, Jeff Corey, Leonard Nimoy, Joyce Jameson; *D:* Joseph Strick; *W:* Ben Maddow; *C:* George J. Folsey.

Ball & Chain 1/2 **2004 (PG-13)** Although raised in America, Ameet (Malhotra) and Saima (Ray) can't escape the customs of India when their respective parents arrange their marriage. They want to break their engagement, so Ameet decides that if he behaves outrageously enough, his prospective in-laws will be so dismayed that they will call things off. Only the more time Ameet and Saima spend together, the more they realize that the arrangement could actually work. **90m/C DVD.** Lisa Ray, Kal Penn, Purva Bedi, Suni Malhotra, Ismail Bashey; *D:* Shriaz Jafri; *W:* Thomas Mortimer; *C:* Peter Simonite; *M:* Deane Ogden.

Ball of Fire **1941** A gang moll hides out with a group of mundane professors, trying to avoid her loathsome boyfriend. The professors are busy compiling an encyclopedia and Stanwyck helps them with their section on slang in the English language. Cooper has his hands full when he falls for this damsel in distress and must fight the gangsters to keep her. Stanwyck takes a personal liking to naive Cooper and resolves to teach him more than just slang. **111m/B VHS, DVD.** Gary Cooper, Barbara Stanwyck, Dana Andrews, Gene Krupa, Oscar Homolka, Dan Duryea, S.Z. Sakall, Henry Travers; *D:* Howard Hawks; *W:* Billy Wilder, Charles Brackett; *C:* Gregg Toland; *M:* Alfred Newman.

Ball of Wax 1/2 **2003** Superstar baseball player Bret Packard (Mench) is a domination freak who plots the downfall of his teammates basically because he's a wealthy, arrogant sociopath and he can. Then manager Ingels (Morris) brings in motivational speaker Bob Tower (Tobias) to get the team back on track and Packard flips to find he's losing control of the situation. **90m/C DVD.** Larry Tobias, Mark Mench, Justin Smith, Traci Dinwiddie, Cullen Moss, Daniel Morris, Kevin Scanlon, Stephanie Wallace; *D:* Daniel Kraus; *W:* Daniel Kraus; *C:* Michael Caporale; *M:* Eric Bachman.

Ballad in Blue ✂✂ *Blues for Lovers* **1966** Real life story of Ray Charles and a blind child. Tearjerker also includes some of Charles' hit songs. ♫ I Got a Woman; What'd I Say?. **89m/B VHS.** *GB* Ray Charles, Tom Bell, Mary Peach, Dawn Addams, Piers Bishop, Betty McDowall; *D:* Paul Henreid.

Ballad of a Gunfighter ✂ **1964** A feud between two outlaws reaches the boiling point when they both fall in love with the same woman. **84m/C VHS.** Marty Robbins, Bob (Robert) Barron, Joyce Redd, Nestor Paiva, Laurette Luez, Michael Davis; *D:* Bill Ward; *W:* Bill Ward; *C:* Brydon Baker; *M:* Jaime Mendoza-Nava.

Ballad of a Soldier ✂✂✂ 1/2 *Ballada o Soldate* **1960** As a reward for demolishing two German tanks, a 19-year-old Russian soldier receives a six-day pass so he can see his mother; however, he meets another woman. Well directed and photographed, while avoiding propaganda. Russian with subtitles. **88m/B VHS, DVD.** *RU* Vladimir Ivashov, Shanna Prokhorenko, Antonina Maximova, Nikolai Kryuchkov; *D:* Grigori Chukhraj; *W:* Grigori Chukhraj, Valentin Yezhov; *C:* Sergei Mukhin; *M:* Mikhail Ziv. British Acad. '61: Film.

The Ballad of Andy Crocker ✂✂ 1/2 **1969** Early TV movie take on vets returning home from Vietnam. Andy (Majors) comes home to find his girlfriend has married someone else, his small business is in ruins, and his friends and family haven't a clue as to what has happened or what to expected from the disillusioned ex-soldier. **80m/C VHS, DVD.** Lee Majors, Joey Heatherton, Jimmy Dean, Marvin Gaye, Agnes Moorehead, Pat Hingle, Jill Haworth, Peter Haskell, Bobby Hatfield; *D:* George McCowan; *W:* Stuart Margolin; *C:* Henry Cronjager Jr.; *M:* Billy May. **TV**

Ballad of Cable Hogue ✂✂✂ **1970 (R)** A prospector, who had been left to die in the desert by his double-crossing partners, finds a waterhole. A surprise awaits his former friends when they visit the remote well. Not the usual violent Peckinpah horse drama, but a tongue-in-cheek comedy romance mixed with tragedy. Obviously offbeat and worth a peek. **122m/C VHS, DVD.** Jason Robards Jr., Stella Stevens, David Warner, L.Q. Jones, Strother Martin, Slim Pickens; *D:* Sam Peckinpah; *C:* Lucien Ballard; *M:* Jerry Goldsmith.

Ballad of Gregorio Cortez ✂✂✂ **1983 (PG)** Tragic story based on one of the most famous manhunts in Texas history. A Mexican cowhand kills a Texas sheriff in self-defense and tries to elude the law, all because of a misunderstanding of the Spanish language. Olmos turns in a fine performance as Cortez. **105m/C VHS.** Edward James Olmos, James Gammon, Tom Bower, Alan Vint, Barry Corbin, Rosanna Desoto, Bruce McGill, Brion James, Pepe Serna, William Sanderson; *D:* Robert M. Young; *W:* Robert M. Young; *C:* Reynaldo Villalobos; *M:* W. Michael Lewis.

The Ballad of Jack and Rose ✂✂✂ **2005 (R)** Absorbing story about an idealistic father and daughter living on their own like the last two hippies on earth in an abandoned commune. Rose (Belle) loves her father, Jack (Day-Lewis). A lot. Actually, she's probably in love with him. This is a touchy subject (not literally, don't worry) for Jack. Jack knows his daughter is too attached, is going to lose him one day, and may not make it on her own. After venturing into the real world for six months Jack begins dating a woman, mother to two boys, and asks her and the boys to move into the commune. Rose reacts with jealousy, trying to anger her father by seducing the sons. Writer/director Rebecca Miller, daughter of playwright Arthur Miller, sidesteps any cliches but piles on a few too many tricks at the end. **138m/C DVD.** *US* Daniel Day-Lewis, Catherine Keener, Camilla Belle, Beau Bridges, Jason Lee, Jena Malone, Paul Franklin Dano, Susanna Thompson, Ryan McDonald; *D:* Rebecca Miller; *W:* Rebecca Miller; *C:* Ellen Kuras; *M:* Michael Rohatyn. L.A. Film Critics '05: Actress (Keener).

The Ballad of Little Jo ✂✂ 1/2 **1993 (R)** Inspired by a true story set during the 1866 gold rush. Easterner Josephine Monaghan is cast out of her wealthy family after she has a baby out of wedlock. Heading west, she passes herself off as a man—Little Jo—in an attempt to forestall harrassment. Solemn and overly earnest attempt by Greenwald to demystify the old west and bring a feminist viewpoint to a familiar saga. **110m/C VHS, DVD.** Suzy Amis, Bo Hopkins, Ian McKellen, Carrie Snodgress, David Chung, Rene Auberjonois, Heather Graham, Anthony Heald, Sam Robards, Ruth Maleczech; *D:* Maggie Greenwald; *W:* Maggie Greenwald; *C:* Declan Quinn; *M:* David Mansfield.

The Ballad of Narayama ✂✂✂✂ *Narayama-Bushi-Ko* **1983** Director Imamura's subtle and vastly moving story takes place a vague century ago. In compliance with village law designed to control population among the poverty-stricken peasants, a healthy 70-year-old woman must submit to solitary starvation atop a nearby mountain. We follow her as she sets into motion the final influence she will have in the lives of her children and grandchildren, a situation described with detachment and without imposing a tragic perspective. In Japanese with English subtitles. **129m/C VHS.** *JP* Ken Ogata, Sumiko Sakamoto, Takejo Aki, Tonpei Hidari, Shoichi Ozawa; *D:* Shohei Imamura; *W:* Shohei Imamura; *C:* Maseo Tochizawa; *M:* Shinichiro Ikebe. Cannes '83: Film.

The Ballad of the Sad Cafe ✂✂ 1/2 **1991 (PG-13)** Unusual love story set in a small Southern town during the Depression. The everday lives of its townspeople are suddenly transformed when a distant relation of the town's outcast (Redgrave) unexpectedly shows up. A moving story that tries to portray both sides of love and its power to enhance and destroy simultaneously. Emotion never seems to come to life in a movie that's nice to watch, but is ultimately disappointing. Adapted from the play by Edward Albee, which was based on the critically acclaimed novella by Carson McCullers. A British/U.S. co-production. **100m/C VHS, DVD.** *GB* Vanessa Redgrave, Keith Carradine, Cork Hubbert, Rod Steiger, Austin Pendleton, Beth Dixon, Lanny Flaherty, Mert Hatfield, Earl Hindman, Anne Pitoniak; *D:* Simon Callow; *W:* Michael Hirst; *C:* Walter Lassally; *M:* Richard Robbins.

Ballast ✂✂ **2008** Hammer's debut follows the misfortunes of a poor Mississippi Delta family and the little bit of hope that sustains them. Lawrence (Smith, Sr.) shot himself after his twin brother Darius OD'd. He's slowly recovering at home where he's confronted by Darius' reckless 12-year-old son James (Ross), who believes he and his ex-druggie mother Marlee (Riggs) are owed money from the small business the brothers ran. They need the cash since Marlee has just lost her job but there's a lot of bitterness on both sides to overcome. **96m/C DVD.** *US* Tarra Riggs, JimMyron Ross, Michael J. Smith Sr., Johnny McPhail; *D:* Lance Hammer; *W:* Lance Hammer; *C:* Lol Crawley.

Ballbuster ✂ 1/2 **1989** Cops take on gangs in an all-out high-stakes battle to win back the streets. **100m/C VHS.** Ivan Rogers, Bonnie Paine, W. Randolph Galvin, Bill Shirk, Brenda Banet; *D:* Eddie Beverly Jr.; *W:* Eddie Beverly Jr.

Ballet Russes ✂✂✂ **2005** Documentary covering the history of the various ballet companies who have used the Ballet Russes name, from its founding by impresario Serge Daghilev in 1909 to the last performance in 1962, including its legendary choreographers, dancers, and designers. Although there's footage of various performances, the most appealing aspects are the interviews of dancers, who were in their 80s and 90s when reunited in 2000, recalling their lives on stage. **118m/C DVD.** *US* *D:* Dan Geller, Dayna Goldfine; *W:* Dan Geller, Dayna Goldfine, Gary Weimberg; *C:* Dan Geller; *M:* Todd Boekelheide, David Conte.

Ballet Shoes ✂✂ 1/2 **2007** Orphans Pauline (Watson), Petrova (Paige), and Posy (Boynton) are adopted by eccentric paleontologist Great Uncle Matthew (Griffiths), who leaves their raising to his niece Sylvia (Fox) while he's off exploring. Each girl has an ambition: Pauline wants to act, Posy wants to be a ballet dancer, and Petrova wants to be an aviatrix. Times are tough in 1930s London and Sylvia is forced to take boarders. Luckily dance teacher Theo (Cohu) is able to help out with the girls' desire to raise some money. Sweet adaptation of the novel by Noel Streatfeild. **84m/C DVD.** *GB* Emma Watson, Yasmin Paige, Emilia Fox, Richard Griffiths, Victoria Wood, Lucy Cohu, Marc Warren, Eileen Atkins, Gemma Jones, Harriet Walter, Lucy Boynton; *D:* Sandra Goldbacher; *W:* Heidi Thomas; *C:* Peter Greenhalgh; *M:* Kevin Sargent. **TV**

Ballistic ✂ 1/2 **1994 (R)** L.A. cop Jesse Gavin (Holden) gets in trouble when the government witness she's supposed to be protecting gets murdered. So she teams up with her ex-con father and her boyfriend to track the mobster responsible for the hit. **86m/C VHS.** Marjean Holden, Richard Roundtree, Sam Jones, Joel Beeson, Charles Napier; *D:* Kim Bass.

Ballistic: Ecks vs. Sever ✂ 1/2 *Ecks vs. Sever* **2002 (R)** Awkwardly titled actioner stars Banderes as Ecks, a disillusioned former FBI manhunter mourning his dead wife. Liu is code-name Sever, a former government-trained assassin. Ecks has been rehired to track Sever for kidnapping the son of her former boss Gant (Henry), chief of the Defense Intelligence Agency. Both agents are also on the lookout for a supposedly dangerous and supremely ridiculous techno virus. Once the operatives find they have a lot in common, including a common enemy, they join forces to gun down and blow up everything in sight. Superb, if overdone stunts take top billing, while dim lighting matches equally dim plot. Neophyte director Kaos (short for Kaosayananda) cops all the moves of "The Matrix." Based on the far more entertaining video game. **95m/C VHS, DVD.** *US* Antonio Banderas, Lucy Liu, Gregg Henry, Ray Park, Talisa Soto, Miguel (Michael) Sandoval, Terry Chen, Sandrine Holt, Roger R. Cross, Steve Bacic, Aidan Drummond; *D:* Kaos; *W:* Alan B. McElroy; *C:* Julio Macat; *M:* Don Davis.

Balloon Farm ✂✂ 1/2 **1997** Harvey Potter (Torn), using some magic, raises a crop of balloons on cornstalks. His drought-stricken fellow farmers see the miraculous crop as symbols of hope but grumpy farmer Wheezle (Blossom) is suspicious. And his suspcions begin to infect the rest of the community, except for spunky young Willow (Wilson). Based on Jerdine Nolen's children's book "Harvey Potter's Balloon Farm." **89m/C VHS, DVD.** Rip Torn, Mara Wilson, Roberts Blossom, Laurie Metcalf, Neal McDonough, Frederic Lehne, Adam Wylie; *D:* William Dear; *W:* Steven M. Karczynski. **TV**

Balls of Fury ✂✂ 1/2 **2007 (PG-13)** Former child prodigy ping-pong star Randy Daytona (Fogler) finds himself fat and washed up at the ripe old age of 32. He's approached by the feds (Lopez as FBI agent) to take on a dangerous mission—infiltrate an underground ping-pong tournament run by shifty Chinese crime boss Feng (Walken), who also happens to be responsible for Randy's fathers' (Patrick) death. But Randy finds his mission has a dual purpose: avenge his father's murder, and attempt a high-stakes comeback. Of course every would-be hero needs a little help, and Randy's crackpot team includes blind restaurateur and ping-pong sage Master Wong (Hong) and his totally hot niece Maggie (Maggie Q). Some funny moments intertwine with a backdrop of Def Leppard in this ode to '80s nostalgia and martial arts, but it never fully takes off. **90m/C DVD, HD DVD.** *US* Dan Fogler, Christopher Walken, George Lopez, James Hong, Terry Crews, Robert Patrick, Diedrich Bader, Aisha Tyler, Thomas Lennon, Maggie Q; *D:* Robert Ben Garant; *W:* Thomas Lennon, Robert Ben Garant; *C:* Thomas Ackerman; *M:* Randy Edelman.

Balls Out: Gary the Tennis Coach ✂ 1/2 **2009 (R)** Raunchy, dumb sports comedy about a loser with dreams of greatness. High school janitor Gary Houseman (Scott) decides to coach the long-neglected, losing tennis team. Soon, despite his crude behavior, his unorthodox methods actually get the team to the state championships. **93m/C DVD.** Seann William Scott, Randy Quaid, Leonor Varela, Deke Anderson, Justin Chon, Brent Anderson; *D:* Danny Leiner; *W:* Andy Stock, Rick Stempson; *C:* Rogier Stoffers; *M:* John Swihart. **VIDEO**

Baltic Deputy ✂✂✂ 1/2 **1937** An early forerunner of Soviet historic realism, where an aging intellectual deals with post-revolution Soviet life. In Russian with subtitles. **95m/B VHS.** *RU* Boris Livanov, Marta Domasheva, Oleg Zhakov, Nikolai Cherkassov; *D:* Iosif Kheifits, Alexander Zarkhi, Yosif Heifitz; *W:* Iosif Kheifits, Alexander Zarkhi; *C:* Edgar Shtyrtskober; *M:* Nikolai Timofeyev.

The Baltimore Bullet ✂✂ **1980 (PG)** Two men make their living traveling through the country as pool hustlers, bilking would-be pool sharks. Features ten of the greatest pool players in the world. **103m/C VHS.** James Coburn, Omar Sharif, Bruce Boxleitner, Ronee Blakley, Jack O'Halloran; *D:* Robert Ellis Miller; *W:* Robert Vincent O'Neil, John F. Brascia.

Balto ✂✂ 1/2 **1995 (G)** Animated adventure, based on a true story, of a half-husky, half-wolf sled dog, Balto, who faces overwhelming odds to bring life-saving medicine to Nome, Alsaka. It's 1925, there's a diptheria epidemic, and Balto is the lead team dog on the final leg of the race to get the serum to Nome in time. Balto and the rest of the team dogs became instant heroes and even journeyed to Hollywood to star in their own silent film "Balto's Race to Nome." **78m/C VHS, DVD.** *D:* Simon Wells; *W:* Cliff Ruby, Elana Lesser, David Steven Cohen, Roger S.H. Schulman; *M:* James Horner; *V:* Kevin Bacon, Bob Hoskins, Bridget Fonda, Jim (Jonah) Cummings, Phil Collins, Juliette Brewer, Danny Mann, Miriam Margolyes.

Balzac: A Life of Passion ✂✂✂ **1999** Bio of French writer Honore de Balzac (1799-1850)—a larger-then-life figure played by the larger-than-life Depardieu. He has mom problems (she never loved him) and turns to women who encourage him as his writing consumes him. There are balls and duels and all sorts of high and low society life during the Napoleonic era to enjoy. French with subtitles. **210m/C VHS, DVD.** *FR* Gerard Depardieu, Jeanne Moreau, Fanny Ardant, Virna Lisi, Katja Riemann, Claude Rich; *D:* Josee Dayan; *W:* Didier Decoin; *C:* Willy Stassen; *M:* Bruno Coulais. **TV**

Balzac and the Little Chinese Seamstress ✂✂ *Balzac et la petite tailleuse Chinois; Xiao cai feng* **2002** Sijie dreamily adapts his own autobiographical novel depicting life in a remote Chinese mountain village in 1971. City boys Luo (Chen) and Ma (Liu) are sent to be re-educated under Mao's Cultural Revolution. The young men perform manual labor under the watchful eyes of the village chief (Wang) and both become attracted to the nameless young woman (Zhou) of the title, reading to her from a secreted cache of Western books (including Balzac, Flaubert, and Dumas) and teaching her to read and write. There is eventual separation and loss and an abrupt epilogue that shows the men 20 years later wondering whatever happened to the girl they once knew. Mandarin and French with subtitles. **111m/C DVD.** *CH FR* Liu Ye, Hongwei Wang, Ziiou Xun, Chen Kun, Wang Shuangbao, Chung Zhijun; *D:* Dai Sijie; *W:* Dai Sijie, Nadine Perront; *C:* Jean-Marie Dreujou; *M:* Wang Pujian.

Bam Bam & Celeste ✂✂✂ **2005** Margaret Cho's screenplay features herself as Celeste, a social outcast on a quest to win a makeover on "Trading Faces," a popular show filmed in New York. On the road trip from Illinois to the Big Apple with her gay hairdresser, boyfriend/buddy Bam Bam (Daniels), the pair encounter offbeat characters and situations and a showdown with their high school rivals, while discovering beauty is more than skin deep. Cheeky, loose, cry-while-you're-laughing entertainment. **85m/C DVD.** Margaret Cho, Bruce Daniels, Alan Cumming, Elaine Hendrix, Jane Lynch, John Cho, Wilson Cruz, Kathy Najimy, Butch Klein; *D:* Lorene Machado; *W:* Margaret Cho; *C:* Matthew Clark; *M:* Pat Irwin.

Bamako ✂✂ *The Court* **2006** Didactic drama that pits African debt against the International Monetary Fund (IMF) and the World Bank. A makeshift courtroom is set up in the courtyard of Mele (Maiga) and Chaka's (Traore) home in a poor section of Bamako.

Because of international monetary policies, African nations are in serious debt and cannot meet their obligations to their own people while paying exorbitant interest rates. Lawyers listen to witness testimony while life goes on around them. It's important, but most Westerners will probably go "huh?" French and Bambara with subtitles. **115m/C DVD.** *FR* Aissa Maiga, Maimouna Helene Diarra, Tiecoura Traore, Habib Dembele; *D:* Abderrahmane Sissako; *W:* Abderrahmane Sissako; *C:* Jacques Besse.

Bambi 1942 (G) A true Disney classic, detailing the often harsh education of a newborn deer and his friends in the forest. Proves that Disney animation was—and still is—the best to be found. Thumper still steals the show and the music is delightful, including "Let's Sing a Gay Little Spring Song," "Love is a Song," "Little April Shower," "The Thumper Song," and "Twitterpated." Stands as one of the greatest children's films of all time; a genuine perennial from generation to generation. Based very loosely on the book by Felix Salten. **69m/C VHS, DVD.** *D:* David Hand; *W:* Larry Morey; *M:* Frank Churchill, Edward Plumb; *V:* Bobby Stewart, Peter Behn, Stan Alexander, Cammie King, Donnie Dunagan, Hardie Albright, John Sutherland, Tim Davis, Sam Edwards, Sterling Holloway, Ann Gillis, Perce Pearce.

Bambi II ½ 2006 (G) The sequel might not be up to the standards of the original but it will keep the tykes occupied. Bambi's dad, the Great Prince, takes over the raising of his fawn when mom gets killed but he's having a tough time. Still, Bambi tries his best to learn despite clumsiness and teasing with some help from his pals Thumper and Flower. **72m/C DVD.** *D:* Brian Pimental; *W:* Alicia Kirk; *M:* Bruce Broughton; *V:* Patrick Stewart, Alexander Gould, Brendon Baerg, Nicky Jones. **VIDEO**

The Bamboo Blonde ½ 1946 Wartime romance in which nightclub singer Louise (Langford) meets cute with B-29 pilot Patrick (Wade). She gives him her photograph and when he heads to Saipan, his bomber crew decides to paint Louise's picture on the nose of their plane for good luck. When the crew starts sinking Japanese ships and shooting down Zeros, the "Bamboo Blonde" becomes famous and Eddie (Edwards), the huckster club owner who employs Louise, gets rich by exploiting that fact. Told in flashbacks. **67m/B DVD.** Frances Langford, Ralph Edwards, Russell Wade, Iris Adrian, Jane Greer, Richard Martin, Paul Harvey; *D:* Anthony Mann.

The Bamboo Saucer ½ *Collision Course* 1968 Russian and American scientists race to find a U.F.O. in Red China. **103m/C VHS.** Dan Duryea, John Ericson, Lois Nettleton, Nan Leslie; *D:* Frank Telford.

Bamboozled ½ 2000 (R) Spike Lee aims for controversy once again as he criticizes Hollywood's portrayal of African-Americans as well as pointing the finger at the black community's complicity in the process. Fed-up black writer Pierre Delacroix (Wayans) comes up with a series idea for a fledgling TV network as a form of protest—a modern day minstrel show complete with performers in burnt cork blackface. Fully expecting the show to fail, he hires struggling street performers Manray (Glover) and Womack (Davidson), changing their names to Mantan and Sleep 'N Eat (a reference to '30s and '40s black actors Mantan Moreland and Stepin Fetchit). The show becomes a surprise hit but also riles a militant black group, resulting in chaos in the lives of Delacroix and his assistant Sloan (Pinkett). The feel of the movie sways toward melodrama halfway through, but the wry observations of the artistic treatment of AfricanAmericans ring eerily true. Don't say it couldn't happen these days. **135m/C VHS, DVD.** Damon Wayans, Jada Pinkett Smith, Savion Glover, Tommy Davidson, Michael Rapaport, Thomas Jefferson Byrd, Paul Mooney, Susan Batson, Mos Def, Sarah Jones, Gillian Iliana Waters; *D:* Spike Lee; *W:* Spike Lee; *C:* Ellen Kuras; *M:* Terence Blanchard.

Bananas 1971 (PG-13) Intermittently hilarious pre-"Annie Hall" Allen fare is full of the director's signature angst-ridden philosophical comedy. A frustrated product tester from New York runs off to South America, where he volunteers his support to the revolutionary force of a shaky Latin-American dictatorship and winds up the leader. Don't miss an early appearance by Stallone. Witty score contributes much. **82m/C VHS, DVD.** Woody Allen, Louise Lasser, Carlos Montalban, Howard Cosell, Charlotte Rae, Conrad Bain, Allen (Goorwitz) Garfield, Sylvester Stallone; *D:* Woody Allen; *W:* Mickey Rose, Woody Allen; *C:* Andrew M. Costikyan; *M:* Marvin Hamlisch.

Bananas Boat WOOF! *What Changed Charley Farthing* 1978 A captain takes a man and his daughter away from the collapsing government of their banana republic. The cast and director take a few risks but fail in this would-be comedy. **91m/C VHS.** *GB* Doug McClure, Hayley Mills, Lionel Jeffries, Dilys Hamlett, Warren Mitchell; *D:* Sidney Hayers.

Band of Angels ½ 1957 Orphaned Amantha (De Carlo) learns she has African-American blood and since it's the pre-Civil War era she promptly winds up on the auction block. She becomes both the property and the mistress of mysterious New Orleans landowner Hamish Bond (Gable). Then the Civil War comes along bringing threats and revelations. De Carlo looks properly sultry but this is a weak attempt at costume drama. Based on the novel by Robert Penn Warren. **127m/C VHS, DVD.** Clark Gable, Yvonne De Carlo, Sidney Poitier, Efrem Zimbalist Jr., Rex Reason, Patric Knowles, Torin Thatcher, Andrea King, Ray Teal; *D:* Raoul Walsh; *W:* John Twist, Ivan Goff; *M:* Max Steiner.

Band of Brothers ½ 2001 Steven Spielberg and Tom Hanks executive produced this excellent adaptation of Stephen Ambrose's epic tale of the 101 Airborne's Easy Company as they made their way from D-Day through Operation Market-Garden, The Battle of the Bulge, and finally, the capture of Hitler's "Eagle's Nest" compound. Although uniformly showing the influence of "Saving Private Ryan," each episode focuses on a separate sub-theme or character while not losing sight of the big-picture depth. Some characters are given short shrift, and sometimes it's hard to tell which characters lived or died during a battle, but that's a minor quibble with such a large and, in most cases, unknown, cast. Although they're young and mostly anonymous, they do give excellent, and in some cases, breakout performances (with the exception of one of the few "name" actors, David Schwimmer). The battle scenes are bracing, harrowing, and well-constructed, and the quiet moments serve to underscore the bond that develops between the men as they become battle tested. **600m/C VHS, DVD.** Eion Bailey, Jamie Bamber, Michael Cudlitz, Dale Dye, Scott Grimes, Frank John Hughes, Ron Livingston, James Madio, Neal McDonough, Rene L. Moreno, David Schwimmer, Donnie Wahlberg, Colin Hanks, Marc Warren, Damian Lewis, Kirk Acevedo, Rick Gomez, Richard Speight Jr., Jimmy Fallon, Ian Virgo, Thomas (Tom) Hardy; *D:* David Frankel, Tom Hanks, Richard Loncraine, Phil Alden Robinson, Mikael Salomon, David Nutter, David Leland, Tony To; *W:* Tom Hanks, E. Max Frye, Erik Jendresen, Bruce McKenna, Graham Yost, Stephen E. Ambrose, Erik Bork, John Orloff; *C:* Remi Adefarasin; *M:* Michael Kamen. **CABLE**

Band of Gold 1995 Unflinching British miniseries follows the lives of Yorkshire prostitutes Rosie (James), Carol (Tyson), and Gina (Gemmell). They try to survive the streets of Bradford while a serial killer is targeting the local hookers. On six cassettes. **312m/C VHS.** *GB* Geraldine James, Cathy Tyson, Ruth Gemmell, Barbara Dickson, David Schofield, Richard Moore, Rachel Davies, Samantha Morton; *D:* Richard Standeven, Richard Laxton; *W:* Kay Mellor; *C:* Peter Jessop; *M:* Hal Lindes.

Band of Outsiders ½ *Bande a Part; The Outsiders* 1964 A woman hires a pair of petty criminals to rip off her aunt; Godard vehicle for expousing self-reflexive comments on modern film culture. In French with English subtitles. **97m/B VHS, DVD.** *FR* Sami Frey, Anna Karina, Claude Brasseur, Louisa Colpeyn; *D:* Jean-Luc Godard; *W:* Jean-Luc Godard; *C:* Raoul Coutard; *M:* Michel Legrand.

Band of the Hand 1986 (R) A "Miami Vice" type melodrama about five convicts who are trained to become an unstoppable police unit. The first feature film by Glaser, last seen as Starsky in "Starsky & Hutch." **109m/C VHS, DVD.** Stephen Lang, Michael Carmine, Lauren Holly, Leon Robinson; *D:* Paul Michael Glaser; *W:* Jack Baran, Leo Garen.

The Band Wagon 1953 A Hollywood song-and-dance man finds trouble when he is persuaded to star in a Broadway musical. Charisse has been called Astaire's most perfect partner, perhaps by those who haven't seen Rogers. ♫ That's Entertainment; Dancing in the Dark; By Myself; A Shine On Your Shoes; Something to Remember You By; High and Low; I Love Louisa; New Sun in the Sky; I Guess I'll Have to Change My Plan. **112m/C VHS, DVD.** Fred Astaire, Cyd Charisse, Oscar Levant, Nanette Fabray, Jack Buchanan, Bobby Watson; *D:* Vincente Minnelli; *W:* Betty Comden; *M:* Arthur Schwartz, Howard Dietz. Natl. Film Reg. '95.

Bandh Darwaza ½ *The Closed Door* 1990 A woman who desperately wishes to have a child visits the Black Mountain and conceives with the help of a monster who resembles a western vampire (Bandh Darwaza is often referred to as the Indian Dracula). She is told that if the child is female it must be given to the mountain, and the consequences will be horrible if she refuses. Of course it's a girl, and of course she refuses. Pic veers into musical dance numbers at random moments; it was one of the last films to come out of the late 1980s/early 1990s horror boom in India. **145m/C DVD.** *IN* Viyajendra Ghatge, Anirudh Agarwal, Beena Banerjee, Raza Murad, Aruna Irani, Kunika; *D:* Shyam Ramsay, Tulsi Ramsay; *W:* Shyam Ramsay, Dev Kishan; *C:* Gangu Ramsay; *M:* Anand Chitragupth, Milind Chitragupth.

Bandit King of Texas ½ 1949 A varmint is swindling unsuspecting settlers in a land scheme and then robbing and murdering them when they go to visit their supposed property. Rocky and friends come to the rescue. **60m/B VHS, DVD.** Allan "Rocky" Lane, Eddy (Eddie, Ed) Waller, Helene Stanley, Robert Bice, Harry Lauter, Jim Nolan, John Hamilton, Lane Bradford; *D:* Fred Brannon; *W:* Olive Cooper.

Bandit Queen ½ 1951 Spanish girl forms a band to stop seizure of Spanish possessions by lawless Californians. **71m/B VHS.** Barbara Britton, Willard Parker, Philip Reed, Jack Perrin; *D:* William Berke.

Bandit Queen 1994 Phoolan Devi (Biswas) is a female Robin Hood in modern-day India. A lower-caste woman, Devi is sold into marriage at 11, brutalized by her husband (and many others throughout the film), and eventually winds up with an equally brutal group of hill bandits. Only this time around, Devi takes action by aiding the group in robbing, kidnapping (and murdering) the rich and higher castes. Devi surrendered to authorities in 1983 and spent 11 years in jail. Based on screenwriter Sen's biography "India's Bandit Queen: The True Story of Phoolan Devi" and Devi's diaries. In Hindi with subtitles. **119m/C VHS, DVD.** *GB IN* Seema Biswas, Nirmal Pandey, Manoj Bajpai, Raghuvir Yadav, Rajesh Vivek, Govind Namdeo; *D:* Shekhar Kapur; *W:* Mala Sen; *C:* Ashok Mehta; *M:* Nusrat Fateh Ali Khan, Roger White.

The Bandits ½ *Crossfire* 1967 (PG) Three cowboys team up with a band of Mexican outlaws to find a traitor in the midst of the Mexican revolution. **83m/C VHS.** *MX* Robert Conrad, Jan-Michael Vincent, Roy Jenson, Manuel Lopez Ochoa; *D:* Alfredo Zacharias, Robert Conrad.

Bandits ½ 1986 Simon Verini (Yanne), a sophisticated fence, is given the loot from a $10 million Cartier heist to exchange for cash by Mozart (Bruel) the leader of the thieves. But two of Mozart's gang want to keep the jewels instead and kidnap Verini's wife as ransom. She's killed, even after he returns the goods, and Verini is then framed for the theft and spends 10 years in prison. He's sent his daughter Marie-Sophie to a Swiss boarding school and upon his release works to both establish a relationship with her and to find those responsible for his wife's death. Director Lelouch's wife portrays the adult Marie-Sophie. In French with English subtitles. **98m/C VHS.** *FR* Jean Yanne, Marie-Sophie L(elouch), Patrick Bruel, Charles Gerard, Corinne Marchand, Christine Barbelivien; *D:* Claude Lelouch; *W:* Pierre Uytterhoeven, Claude Lelouch.

Bandits 1999 (R) Talk about your band on the run! Four young women form a prison rock-and-roll band called the Bandits. Their first gig on the outside is the policeman's ball, where they escape. They become folk heroes as they elude the police and a clandestine recording they sent to a music exec zooms up the charts. German with subtitles. **109m/C VHS, DVD.** *GE* Katja Riemann, Jutta Hoffmann, Jasmin Tabatabai, Nicolette Krebitz, Hannes Jaenicke, Werner Schreyer; *D:* Katja von Garnier; *W:* Katja von Garnier, Uwe Wilhelm; *C:* Torsten Breuer.

Bandits ½ 2001 (PG-13) Willis and Thornton are Joe and Terry, quirky bank robbers known as the "sleepover bandits" for their unusual but non-violent heists. With Willis as the smirky brawn and Thornton as the neurotic brain, the two play the Butch-and-Sundance act until fate puts bored housewife Kate (Blanchett) in their path. She talks her way into their little gang, but can't decide which of the two she should fall for most. The plot then slams on the brakes, although Levinson adds enough padding to cushion the blow. Blanchett is excellent as the sultry, vulnerable Kate, but Thornton steals the show (and chomps on considerable scenery) as the omniphobic hypochondriac Terry (his fear of antique furniture is actually one of Thornton's well-documented quirks as well). **123m/C VHS, DVD.** *US* Bruce Willis, Billy Bob Thornton, Cate Blanchett, Troy Garity, Bobby Slayton, Brian F. O'Byrne, Azura Skye, Stacey Travis, William Converse-Roberts, Richard Riehle, Micole Mercurio, January Jones; *D:* Barry Levinson; *W:* Harley Peyton; *C:* Dante Spinotti; *M:* Christopher Young. Natl. Bd. of Review '01: Actor (Thornton).

Bandits of Orgosolo ½ *Banditi a Orgosolo* 1961 An acclaimed, patient drama about a Sardinian shepherd who shelters a band of thieves from the police. When one of the cops is killed the shepherd panics and flees into the hills for survival. Dubbed in English. **98m/B VHS.** *IT* Michele Cossu, Peppeddu Cuccu; *D:* Vittorio de Seta; *W:* Vittorio de Seta, Vera Gherarducci; *C:* Vittorio de Seta, Luciano Tovoli; *M:* Valentino Bucchi.

Bandolero! ½ 1968 (PG) In Texas, Stewart and Martin are two fugitive brothers who run into trouble with their Mexican counterparts. **106m/C VHS, DVD.** James Stewart, Raquel Welch, Dean Martin, George Kennedy, Will Geer, Harry Carey Jr., Andrew Prine; *D:* Andrew V. McLaglen; *C:* William Clothier; *M:* Jerry Goldsmith.

The Band's Visit *Bikur Ha-Tizmoret* 2007 (PG-13) Eight members of an Egyptian police orchestra are accidentally stranded in the Israeli desert, far away from their intended destination. They end up in an Israeli town where they are anything but welcome. Through the culture clash, connections are made, and an unlikely attraction develops between band members and the beautiful restaurant owner who gives them a place to stay. Director Kolirin draws comedy out of the isolated, sad characters and their awkward situation without exploiting them. **89m/C DVD.** *FR IS US* Sasson Gabai, Ronit Elkabetz, Saleh Bakri, Shlomi Avraham, Khalifa Natour, Rubi Muscovich; *D:* Eran Kolirin; *W:* Eran Kolirin; *C:* Shai Goldman; *M:* Habib Shehadeh Hanna.

Bandslam ½ 2009 (PG) Awkward but pleasant teen musical. Geek introvert Will (Connell) is the new kid at Van Buren HS after he and mom Karen (Kudrow) move to suburban New Jersey. He bonds over shared musical tastes with sullen Sam (Hudgens) and cheerleader-turned-singer Charlotte (Michalka) who decides Will's love of vintage rock makes him the perfect manager for her garage band. After a few changes and a lot of practice, Will figures they have a shot at the tri-state battle-of-the-bands competition. Music isn't terribly memorable but everyone is just so darn cute. **111m/C DVD.** *US* Alyson Michalka, Scott Porter, Vanessa Anne Hudgens, Lisa Kudrow, Ryan Donowho, Gaelen Connell, Charlie Saxton; ***Cameos:*** David Bowie; *D:* Todd Graff; *W:* Todd Graff, Josh A. Cagan; *C:* Eric Steelberg; *M:* Junkie XL.

Bandwagon 1995 Four unlikely twentysomething guys decide to form a band in Raleigh, NC. Tony Ridge (Holmes) is the lead singer-songwriter who's so shy he practices in a closet; chatty drummer Charlie Flagg (Hennessey) has the rehearsal space; Wynn Knapp (Corrigan) is the band's perpetually stoned guitarist; and bass player Eric Ellwood's (Parlavecchio) hot temper has him in big trouble with a local loan shark. They finally come up with a name (Circus Monkey), get a gig (a raucous frat party), and are on their way when they acquire Zen-like road manager Linus Tate (MacMillan) and a battered van. Of course, life on the road proves to be a challenge. **99m/C VHS.** Kevin Corrigan, Steve Parlavecchio, Lee Holmes, Matthew Hennessey, Doug MacMillan, Lisa Keller; ***D:*** John Schultz; ***W:*** John Schultz; ***C:*** Shawn Maurer; ***M:*** Greg Kendall.

Bang 🦴🦴 *The Big Bang Theory* **1995** This $20,000 indie concerns a nameless, powerless Asian-American would-be actress (Narita) in L.A. She gets kicked out of her apartment, accosted by a homeless crazy (Greene), and sexually propositioned by a sleazy producer (Graff). Finally, she's accused of causing a public disturbance by a cop (Newland), who'll let her off in exchange for sexual favors. Instead, she grabs his gun, forces him to strip, ties him to a tree, puts on the cop's uniform, and steals his motorcycle. In uniform, she's suddenly viewed with authority and decides to take some time to see what that's like. **98m/C VHS, DVD.** Darling Narita, Peter Greene, Michael Newland, David Allen Graff, Eric Schrody, Michael Arturo, James Sharpe, Luis Guizar, Art Cruz, Stanley Herman; ***D:*** Ash; ***W:*** Ash; ***C:*** Dave Gasperik.

Bang Bang Kid 🦴🦴 *Bang Bang* **1967 (G)** A western spoof about a klutzy gunfighter defending a town from outlaws. **78m/C VHS.** Tom Bosley, Guy Madison, Sandra Milo; ***D:*** Stanley Prager.

Bang Rajan 🦴🦴🦴 1/2 **2000** Kind of a Thai version of the Alamo. The small village of Bang Rajan, circa 1765, finds itself geographically in the path of a very angry Burmese army on their way to the warring city of Ayudhay. With no outside help, the community must band together in hopes of protecting their land. One of the country's most legendary battles, told with Hollywood-like epic production helped the film become Thailand's biggest box office hit ever. One-upping "Braveheart," the film arguably contains the most violent images of warfare to date. Fan Oliver Stone helped secure U.S. release. **119m/C DVD.** *TH* Winai Kraibutr, Bin Bunluerit, Chumphorn Thepphithak, Jaran Ngamdee, Suntharee Maila-or; ***D:*** Thanit Jitnukul; ***W:*** Thanit Jitnukul, Kongkiat Khomsiri, Bunthin Thuaykaew, Patikarn Phejmunee, Suttipong Muttanavee; ***C:*** Wichian Ruangwijchayakul; ***M:*** Chartachai Phongpraphaphan.

Bang the Drum Slowly 🦴🦴 **1956** The original TV adaptation of a Mark Harris novel about baseball. A ball player stricken by a terminal illness strikes an unlikely friendship with a teammate. Interesting role for an actor (Newman) who claims to have been driven to acting by running away from the sporting goods business. **60m/B VHS.** Paul Newman, George Peppard, Albert Salmi; ***D:*** Daniel Petrie. **TV**

Bang the Drum Slowly 🦴🦴🦴 **1973 (PG)** The touching story of a major league catcher who discovers that he is dying of Hodgkins disease and wants to play just one more season. De Niro is the weakening baseball player and Moriarty is the friend who helps him see it through. Based on a novel by Mark Harris. **97m/C VHS, DVD.** Robert De Niro, Michael Moriarty, Vincent Gardenia, Phil Foster, Ann Wedgeworth, Heather MacRae, Selma Diamond, Danny Aiello; ***D:*** John Hancock. N.Y. Film Critics '73: Support. Actor (De Niro).

The Banger Sisters 🦴🦴 **2002 (R)** Fast forward "Almost Famous" thirty years and you'll find Kate Hudson has turned into her real-life mother, Hawn, who plays Suzette, a middle-aged former '60s/'70s "band-aid" turned, well, not turned at all, still living the wild, free-spirit life. Her partner in rock n' roll groupie-dom, Vinnie (Sarandon), however, has grown up and uptight; now she's suburban mom Lavinia living in the 'burbs. When Suzette loses her job, she drifts back into Vinnie's life and helps her get back to her sleazy, but more honest, roots. Sanitized-for-your-protection version of groupie life rings false throughout. Characters are essentially modeled on groupie legends the Plaster Casters. Material isn't worthy of these A-listers and nostalgia appeal runs thin. Amurri is Sarandon's real-life daughter. **97m/C VHS, DVD.** *US* Goldie Hawn, Susan Sarandon, Geoffrey Rush, Erika Christensen, Robin Thomas, Eva Amurri, Matthew Carey; ***D:*** Bob Dolman; ***W:*** Bob Dolman; ***C:*** Karl Walter Lindenlaub; ***M:*** Trevor Rabin.

Bangkok Dangerous 🦴🦴 **2000 (R)** A moderately interesting action film that inspired a horrible Hollywood remake that was somehow done by the same team of directors (you'd think they'd get it better the second time around). A deaf mute assassin who doesn't know sign language (good thing he can read) becomes a one-man army after deciding to leave the business for his girlfriend. **105m/C DVD.** *TH* Pawalit Mongkolpisit, Premsinee Ratanasopha, Patharawarin Timkul, Pisek Intrakanchit; ***D:*** Oxide Pang Chun, Danny Pang; ***W:*** Oxide Pang Chun, Danny Pang; ***C:*** Decha Srimantra; ***M:*** Orange Music.

Bangkok Dangerous 🦴 1/2 **2008 (R)** The Pang Brothers come to Hollywood for the remake of their 1999 Hong Kong cult classic. Hitman Joe (Cage), not deaf like the original hitman, is sent to Thailand to complete four last jobs before he can retire. Struggling with culture shock, he hires street rat Kong (Yamnarm) as an interpreter/assistant. Each kill brings him closer to ending his career, but the progressive difficulties bring him closer to ending his life. Shelved for almost two years after production, with execs hoping Cage's career would pick up enough to guarantee box-office success. Instead, Cage's tendency towards wildly inconsistent performances continues, and he's utterly awful and joyless, not to mention silly-looking in his leather jacket and lousy haircut. Awkward title likely comes from studio heads assuming a semicolon would turn off American audiences. **100m/C DVD, Blu-ray Disc.** *US* Nicolas Cage, Charlie Yeung, Shahkrit Yamnarm, Panward Hemmanee, James With, Dom Hetrakul, Philip Waley, Shaun Delaney; ***D:*** Danny Pang, Oxide Pang; ***W:*** Jason Richman; ***C:*** Decha Srimantra; ***M:*** Brian Tyler.

Banjo Hackett 🦴🦴 1/2 *Banjo Hackett: Roamin' Free* **1976** Banjo (Meredith) and his orphaned nephew (Eisenmann) travel the West in search of a rare Arabian horse that was stolen from the boy's mother before she died. Also in pursuit are a millionaire and a devious bounty hunter who will stop at nothing to capture the missing steed. Although the storyline is as rambling as the West, it's heartfelt all the same. **100m/C DVD.** Don Meredith, Ike Eisenmann, Carol Connors, Gloria De Haven, Jeff Corey, L.Q. Jones, Jan Murray, Dan O'Herlihy, Jennifer Warren, David Young, Richard Young, Anne Francis, Slim Pickens; ***D:*** Andrew V. McLaglen; ***W:*** Ken Trevey; ***C:*** Al Francis; ***M:*** Morton Stevens.

The Bank 🦴🦴 1/2 **2001** Geeky mathematician/computer whiz Jim Doyle (Wenham) is offered a job by unscrupulous Centrabank CEO Simon O'Reilly (LaPaglia) to set up a computer program that will predict stock market fluctuations and increase the bank's profits. Victims of Centrabank's drive for profits are Wayne (Rodgers) and Diane (McElhinney) Davis, who are suing the bank as a cause of a family tragedy. The two stories come to overlap when O'Reilly pressures Doyle into questionable practices to resolve the various situations. **103m/C VHS, DVD.** *AU* David Wenham, Anthony LaPaglia, Steve Rodgers, Mandy McElhinney, Mitchell Butel, Sibylla Budd; ***D:*** Robert Connolly; ***W:*** Robert Connolly; ***C:*** Tristan Milani; ***M:*** Alan John.

The Bank Dick 🦴🦴🦴🦴 *The Bank Detective* **1940** Fields wrote the screenplay (using an alias) and stars in this zany comedy about a man who accidentally trips a bank robber and winds up as a guard. Fields' last major role is a classic, a worthy end to his great career. **73m/B VHS, DVD.** W.C. Fields, Cora Witherspoon, Una Merkel, Evelyn Del Rio, Jack Norton, Jessie Ralph, Franklin Pangborn, Shemp Howard, Grady Sutton, Russell Hicks, Richard Purcell, Reed Hadley; ***D:*** Edward F. (Eddie) Cline; ***W:*** W.C. Fields; ***C:*** Milton Krasner. Natl. Film Reg. '92.

The Bank Job 🦴🦴🦴 **2008 (R)** Terry (Statham) thinks his ex-lover Martine (Burrows) has recruited him to assemble a crew including his number two guy, porn king Kevin (Campbell Moore), for a straightforward cash heist. They end up involved in one of the greatest bank robberies in British history: the 1971 tunneled break in at the Baker Street branch of Lloyd's. The real-life investigation produced no arrests and recovered no loot, thus allowing writers Clement and La Frenais to construct an elaborate albeit fictionalized account that ties the crime to a conspiracy to retrieve sexually-compromising photos of a British royal from the safe deposit box of a black power operative (De Jersey). A near-perfect period heist-caper film that extracts terrific effect from the fashion and technology of the 70's. Particularly humorous are the giant walkie-talkies alleged to have played a role in the crime. **111m/C DVD.** *GB US* Jason Statham, Saffron Burrows, Daniel Mays, David Suchet, Richard Lintern, James Faulkner; ***D:*** Roger Donaldson; ***W:*** Dick Clement, Ian La Frenais; ***C:*** Michael Coulter; ***M:*** J. Peter Robinson.

Bank Robber 🦴🦴 **1993 (R)** Billy (Dempsey) is a thief who will retire after one final bank heist, if only he hadn't forgotten to break that surveillance camera. Holed up in a New York hotel he's subjected to extortion schemes and finds himself a new outlaw celebrity to newshounds. Bonet is a sweet hooker who falls in love with him. Satire on crooks and fame is too mild-mannered for its own good but not without charm. Directorial debut of Mead. Unedited NC-17 version also available. **94m/C VHS.** Patrick Dempsey, Lisa Bonet, Olivia D'Abo, James Garde, Forest Whitaker, Judge Reinhold, Michael Jeter, Joe Alaskey, John Chappoulis; ***D:*** Nick Mead; ***W:*** Nick Mead; ***M:*** Stewart Copeland.

Bank Shot 🦴🦴🦴 **1974** Hilarious comedy about a criminal who plans to rob a bank by stealing the entire building. Based on the novel by Donald Westlake, and the sequel to "The Hot Rock." **83m/C VHS, DVD.** George C. Scott, Joanna Cassidy, Sorrell Booke, G(eorge) Wood, Clifton James, Bob Balaban, Bibi Osterwald; ***D:*** Gower Champion; ***W:*** Wendell Mayes; ***C:*** Harry Stradling Jr.

The Banker 🦴🦴 **1989 (R)** A cop, played by Forster, suspects a wealthy, highly influential banker of brutal serial killings. **90m/C VHS.** Robert Forster, Jeff Conaway, Leif Garrett, Duncan Regehr, Shanna Reed, Deborah Richter, Richard Roundtree, Teri Weigel, E.J. Peaker, Michael Fairman, Juan Garcia; ***D:*** William Webb; ***C:*** John Huneck; ***M:*** Reg Powell, Sam Winans.

Banshee 🦴 1/2 **2006 (R)** Kind of a woman-in-peril/action/psycho-thriller. Pro car thief Sage (Manning), nicknamed Banshee, is always in competition with boyfriend Tony (Kelly) for the hottest cars to boost. She steals a 1966 Dodge Charger, knowing it will bring top dollar, but not knowing the ride belongs to serial killer/DJ Larch (Campbell). Larch has this little kink about recording the screams of his victims and then mixing them in with his techno sounds. Larch not only wants his car back but he wants to teach Sage a very unpleasant lesson. **9m/C DVD.** Taryn Manning, Christian Campbell, Morgan Kelly, Tony Calabretta, Mike Lombardi; ***D:*** Keri Skogland; ***W:*** Kirsten Elms; ***C:*** David Franco; ***M:*** Ned Bouhalassa. **CABLE**

Banzai Runner 🦴🦴 **1986** A cop whose brother was killed in an exclusive desert-highway race decides to avenge by joining the race himself. **88m/C VHS, DVD.** Dean Stockwell, John Shepherd, Charles Dierkop; ***D:*** John G. Thomas; ***W:*** Phil Harnage; ***C:*** Howard Wexler; ***M:*** Joel Goldsmith. **VIDEO**

B.A.P.'s 🦴 1/2 **1997 (PG-13)** Ghetto to riches story about Georgia waitresses Nisi (Berry) and Mickey (Desselle) who dream about opening their own business—a combo restaurant and hair salon. An L.A. audition offering $10,000 gets them to the sunny coast and eventually into the Beverly Hills mansion of Mr. Blakemore (Landau), where Nisi's persuaded to pose as the granddaughter of his lost love by Blakemore's money-grubbing nephew, Isaac (Fried). Everybody bonds and butler Manley (Richardson) instructs the women in taste and etiquette. Good cast is wasted and the comedy's lame when not offensive. **91m/C VHS, DVD.** Halle Berry, Natalie Desselle, Martin Landau, Ian Richardson, Troy Beyer, Luigi Amodeo, Jonathan Fried, A.J. (Anthony) Johnson; ***D:*** Robert Kevin Townsend; ***W:*** Troy Beyer; ***C:*** Bill Dill; ***M:*** Stanley Clarke.

Bar-B-Q **WOOF!** **2000** A pro-ball player turned actor needs a break and heads home to have a Bar-B-Q with his girl and old homies. When word gets out the entire neighborhood shows up for the party. A lot of music and a lot of crude jokes and infantile humor make this poorly made, horribly acted film practically unwatchable. The 102-minute running time includes nearly 15 minutes of credits and what the cast and crew apparently considered humorous outtakes. **102m/C DVD.** Layzie Bone, John West, Chanda Watts, Lea Griggs; ***D:*** Amanda Moss, John West; ***W:*** John West.

Bar Girls 🦴🦴 **1995 (R)** Mating rituals, set in L.A. wateringhole "The Girl Bar," finds usually tough cookie Loretta (Wolfe) spotting new face Rachael (D'Agostino) and deciding she likes what she sees. There's various mind games as they chart a rocky course to true love—with jealousy, possessiveness, and past romance all playing their parts. Hoffman adapted from her play and the staginess remains; film debut for director Giovanni. **95m/C VHS, DVD.** Nancy Allison Wolfe, Liza D'Agostino, Justine Slater, Paula Sorge, Camila Griggs, Pam Raines; ***D:*** Marita Giovanni; ***W:*** Lauran Hoffman; ***C:*** Michael Ferris; ***M:*** Lenny Meyers.

Bar Hopping 🦴 **2000** Disjointed series of vignettes about the singles scene in L.A. centered around a bar with Arnold as the bartender, narrating the action (or lack thereof). Lame. **88m/C VHS, DVD.** Tom Arnold, Nicole Sullivan, Scott Baio, John Henson, Sally Kellerman, Kevin Nealon, Kelly Preston, Roy Thinnes, Linda Favila, Anson Downes; ***D:*** Steve Cohen; ***W:*** Linda Favila, Anson Downes; ***C:*** Joe Montgomery; ***M:*** Nick Loren. **CABLE**

Barabbas 🦴🦴 1/2 **1962** Barabbas, a thief and murderer, is freed by Pontius Pilate in place of Jesus. He is haunted by this event for the rest of his life. Excellent acting, little melodrama, lavish production make for fine viewing. Based on the novel by Lagerkvist. **144m/C VHS, DVD.** Anthony Quinn, Silvana Mangano, Arthur Kennedy, Jack Palance, Ernest Borgnine, Katy Jurado, Vittorio Gassman; ***D:*** Richard Fleischer; ***W:*** Diego Fabbri, Christopher Fry, Ivo Perilli, Nigel Balchin; ***C:*** Aldo Tonti; ***M:*** Mario Nascimbene.

Baraka 🦴🦴🦴 **1993** Time-lapse photography transforms a fascinating array of scenic panoramas into a thought-provoking experience. No dialogue, but the captivating visuals, shot in 24 countries, are a feast for the eyes. Points of interest include Iguacu Falls in Argentina, Ayers Rock in Australia, the temples of Angkor Wat in Cambodia, and the Grand Canyon. Also tours Auschwitz and the streets of Calcutta, in an effort to warn the viewer of the planet's fragility. Filmed in 70mm. **96m/C VHS, DVD.** ***D:*** Ron Fricke; ***W:*** Ron Fricke, Mark Magidson, Bob Green; ***C:*** Ron Fricke; ***M:*** Michael Stearns.

Baran 🦴🦴 1/2 *Rain* **2001 (PG)** Latif (Abedini) works as a tea boy and cook on a construction site in Iran where many of the other laborers are illegal Afghan emigres. When one of his co-workers is injured, the man's young son, Baran (Bahrami), comes to take his place, although he's too frail to do the job. So Baran takes Latif's place and he must move to a more strenuous job, which he doesn't mind when he discovers that Baran is actually a girl; so Latif begins an awkward courtship while trying to keep her secret. Farsi with subtitles. **94m/C VHS, DVD.** *IA* Hossein Abedini, Zahra Bahrami, Mohammad Reza Naji, Hossein Rahimi; ***D:*** Majid Majidi; ***W:*** Majid Majidi; ***C:*** Mohammad Davudi; ***M:*** Ahmad Pejman.

Barb Wire 🦴 1/2 **1996 (R)** "Don't call me babe!" That'll be difficult when the figure in question is Anderson Lee's big-screen take on Dark Horse comic book heroine Barb Wire. Barb runs the sleazy Hammerhead Bar & Grille in Steel Harbor, the only neutral city in an America torn by a second civil war, and reluctantly agrees to aid hunky resistance leader Axel (Morrison) on a dangerous peace mission. Pambo gives Stallone a fight for the action title—fetching in high heels and black leather—with lots of fire power and a take-no-prisoners attitude. Plot's secondary to pulchritude but, unfortunately, the movie's just not a lotta fun. **98m/C VHS, DVD.** Pamela Anderson, Temuera Morrison, Jack Noseworthy, Victoria Rowell, Xander Berkeley, Udo Kier, Steve Railsback, Clint Howard, Tony Bill; *D:* David Hogan; *W:* Chuck Pfarrer, Ilene Chaiken; *C:* Rick Bota; *M:* Michel Colombier. Golden Raspberries '96: Worst New Star (Anderson).

Barbarella 1/2 *Barbarella, Queen of the Galaxy* **1968 (PG)** Based on the popular French sci-fi comic strip drawn by Jean-Claude Forest, this cult classic details the bizarre adventures of a space nymphette (Fonda) encountering fantastic creatures and super beings. You'll see sides of Fonda you never saw before (not even in the workout videos). Notorious in its day; rather silly, dated camp now. Don't miss the elbow-sex scene. Terry Southern contributed to the script. **98m/C VHS, DVD.** *FR IT* Jane Fonda, John Phillip Law, David Hemmings, Marcel Marceau, Anita Pallenberg, Milo O'Shea, Ugo Tognazzi, Veronique Vendell, Giancarlo Cobelli, Serge Marquand; *D:* Roger Vadim; *W:* Roger Vadim, Terry Southern, Vittorio Bonicelli, Claude Brule, Tudor Gates, Clement Biddle Wood, Brian Degas, Jean-Claude Forest; *C:* Claude Renoir; *M:* Charles Fox.

The Barbarian **1933** Diana (Loy) travels to Cairo with her Uncle Cecil (Smith) and sharp-tongued companion Powers (Hale) to meet stuffy fiance Gerald (Denny). Arab guide Jamil (Navarro) is immediately attracted to the beauty, eventually kidnapping her and taking Diana on a desert trek to further his romantic plans after revealing to her that he's actually a prince. Pre-Code MGM production has a risque bathing scene by Loy and a questionable seduction scene common to the milieu. Based on Edgar Selwyn's racy play "The Arab." **84m/B DVD.** Myrna Loy, Reginald Denny, Louise Closser Hale, Sir C. Aubrey Smith, Edward Arnold, Ramon Novarro; *D:* Sam Wood; *W:* Anita Loos, Elmer Harris; *C:* Harold Rosson; *M:* Herbert Stothart.

Barbarian and the Geisha **1958** The first US diplomat in Japan undergoes culture shock as well as a passionate love affair with a geisha, circa 1856. **104m/C VHS.** John Wayne, Eiko Ando, Sam Jaffe, So Yamamura; *D:* John Huston; *M:* Hugo Friedhofer.

The Barbarian Invasions *Les Invasions Barbares* **2003 (R)** Writer/director Arcand reunites characters from his 1986 film "The Decline of the American Empire" to capture the last days of lecherous, lustful divorced academic Remy (Girard), hospitalized with terminal cancer in his fifties. Through some pleading by his ex-wife (Berryman), estranged son Sebastian (Rousseau) reconnects with his father and deftly orchestrates his twilight days. He upgrades his medical care, persuades ex lovers and colleagues to come and see him off, and sneaks him heroin to ease the physical pain. Takes a few jabs at the Canadian health care system while showing how life and death can be celebrated. Sparkling performances by all, with clever writing that avoids being overly sentimental or maudlin, well deserving of its win in Cannes. **110m/C VHS, DVD.** *CA FR* Remy Girard, Stephane Rousseau, Marie Josee Croze, Marina Hands, Dorothee Berryman, Johanne-Marie Tremblay, Dominique Michel, Louise Portal, Yves Jacques, Pierre Curzi; *D:* Denys Arcand; *W:* Denys Arcand; *C:* Guy Dufaux; *M:* Pierre Aviat. Oscars '03: Foreign Film; British Acad. '03: Orig. Screenplay; Cannes '03: Actress (Croze), Screenplay; Natl. Bd. of Review '03: Foreign Film.

Barbarian Queen **1985 (R)** Female warriors led by beauteous babe seek revenge for the capture of their men in this sword-and-sorcery epic. Low-budget rip-off "Conan the Barbarian" is laughable. Also available in an unrated version. Followed by "Barbarian Queen 2: The Empress Strikes Back." **71m/C VHS, DVD.** *IT* Lana Clarkson, Frank Zagarino, Katt Shea, Dawn Dunlap, Susana Traverso; *D:* Hector Olivera; *W:* Howard R. Cohen; *C:* Rudy Donovan; *M:* Christopher Young.

Barbarian Queen 2: The Empress Strikes Back **1989 (R)** Apparently one movie wasn't enough to tell the beautiful Princess Athalia's story. This time she fights her evil brother Ankaris. He throws her in prison, she escapes, joins a band of female rebels, and leads them into battle. No better than the first attempt. **87m/C VHS, DVD.** *IT* Lana Clarkson, Greg Wrangler, Rebecca Wood, Elizabeth Jaegen, Roger Cundy; *D:* Joe Finley; *W:* Howard R. Cohen; *C:* Francisco Bojorquez; *M:* Christopher Young.

The Barbarians *The Barbarians and Co* **1987 (R)** Two bodybuilder siblings in animal skins battle wizards and warlords in this dumb-but-fun U.S./Italian co-production. **88m/C VHS.** *IT* David Paul, Peter Paul, Richard Lynch, Eva LaRue, Virginia Bryant, Sheeba Alahani, Michael Berryman; *D:* Ruggero Deodato; *M:* Pino Donaggio.

Barbarians at the Gate 1/2 **1993 (R)** In the "greed is good" financial climate of the '80s, this movie chronicles the $25 billion battle in 1988 for RJR Nabisco, which at the time was working on developing a "smokeless cigarette." Garner is CEO F. Ross Johnson, who is confident that their "smokeless cigarette" will boost the stock's value—until he gets the test-marketing results. Unwilling to risk the product's failure, Johnson decides to buy the company and is challenged by master dealer Kravis (Pryce). Fascinating social commentary on the nastiest mega-deal in history. Based on the book by Bryan Burrough and John Helyar. **107m/C VHS, DVD.** James Garner, Jonathan Pryce, Peter Riegert, Joanna Cassidy, Fred Dalton Thompson, Leilani Sarelle Ferrer, Matt Clark, Jeffrey DeMunn; *D:* Glenn Jordan; *W:* Larry Gelbart; *C:* Thomas Del Ruth, Nicholas D. Knowland; *M:* Richard Gibbs. **CABLE**

Barbarosa **1982 (PG)** Offbeat western about an aging, legendary outlaw constantly on the lam who reluctantly befriends a naive farmboy and teaches him survival skills. Nelson and Busey are a great team, solidly directed. Lovely Rio Grande scenery. **90m/C VHS.** Willie Nelson, Gilbert Roland, Gary Busey, Isela Vega; *D:* Fred Schepisi; *C:* Ian Baker; *M:* Bruce Smeaton.

Barbary Coast **1935** A ruthless club owner tries to win the love of a young girl by building her into a star attraction during San Francisco's gold rush days. **90m/B VHS, DVD.** Edward G. Robinson, Walter Brennan, Brian Donlevy, Joel McCrea, Donald Meek, David Niven, Miriam Hopkins; *D:* Howard Hawks.

The Barbary Coast **1974** A turn-of-the-century detective sleuths the streets of San Francisco in this average TV movie. **100m/C VHS.** William Shatner, Dennis Cole, Lynda Day George, John Vernon, Charles Aidman, Michael Ansara, Neville Brand, Bill Bixby; *D:* Bill Bixby. **TV**

The Barber Shop **1933** Fields portrays the bumbling, carefree barber Cornelius O'Hare, purveyor of village gossip and problem solver. Havoc begins when a gangster enters the shop and demands that Cornelius change his appearance. **21m/B VHS, DVD.** W.C. Fields, Elise Cavanna, Harry Watson, Dagmar Oakland, Frank Yaconelli; *D:* Arthur Ripley.

Barbershop **2002 (PG-13)** Ensemble comedy looks at the unique culture found in barbershops in the black male community. Cube plays Calvin, discontented owner of a barbershop he inherited from his father. In debt, Calvin sells the shop to a loan shark, which sends all the shop's regulars reeling, as their haven will be turned into a strip club. During the shop's final day, when the film takes place, Calvin must come to grips with his mistake and recognize the value of his father's legacy. Though two lesser subplots detract from the engrossing barbershop talk, a host of interesting characters mesh with an original and entertaining story. **102m/C VHS, DVD, UMD.** *US* Ice Cube, Anthony Anderson, Cedric the Entertainer, Eve, Sean Patrick Thomas, Troy Garity, Michael Ealy, Leonard Earl Howze, Keith David, Lahmard Tate, Tom Wright, Jazzmin Lewis; *D:* Tim Story; *W:* Mark Brown, Don D. Scott, Marshall Todd; *C:* Tom Priestley; *M:* Terence Blanchard.

Barbershop 2: Back in Business **2004 (PG-13)** Calvin and the rest of the crew are back. This time around, the shop faces a community crisis in the form of franchise cutters Nappy Cutz moving in across the street, threatening to put Calvin's shop out business. Lacks the fresh charm of the first one, but the strong cast and crisp writing save the day. **106m/C VHS, DVD.** *US* Ice Cube, Cedric the Entertainer, Sean Patrick Thomas, Eve, Troy Garity, Michael Ealy, Leonard Earl Howze, Harry J. Lennix, Robert Wisdom, Jazsmin Lewis, Carl Wright, Kenan Thompson, Queen Latifah, Garcelle Beauvais; *D:* Kevin Rodney Sullivan; *W:* Don D. Scott; *C:* Tom Priestley; *M:* Richard Gibbs.

Barcelona **1994 (PG-13)** Old-fashioned talkfest about two neurotic Americans experiencing sibling rivalry in Spain. Serious Ted (Nichols) is an American sales rep, posted to Barcelona, who can't quite get into the city's pleasure-loving rhythm. This is not a problem for Ted's cousin Fred (Eigeman), an obnoxious naval officer, with whom Ted has had a rivalry dating back to their boyhood. Set in the 1980s, the two must also deal with anti-Americanism, which leads both to violence and romantic developments. Tart dialogue, thoughtful performances, and exotic locales prove enticing in low-budget sleeper that effectively mixes drama and dry comedy. Watch for Eigeman in Tom Cruise's uniform from "A Few Good Men." **102m/C VHS, DVD.** Taylor Nichols, Christopher Eigeman, Tushka Bergen, Mira Sorvino, Pep Munne, Francis Creighton, Thomas Gibson, Jack Gilpin, Nuria Badia, Hellena Schmied; *D:* Whit Stillman; *W:* Whit Stillman; *C:* John Thomas; *M:* Tom Judson, Mark Suozzo. Ind. Spirit '95: Cinematog.

The Barcelona Kill 1/2 **1977** When a journalist and her boyfriend get in too deep with the Barcelona mob, their troubles begin. **86m/C VHS.** Linda Hayden, John Astin, Simon Andreu, Maximo Valverde; *D:* Jose Antonio De La Loma.

Bardelys the Magnificent **1926** Boastful, womanizing swashbuckler the Marquis de Bardelys (Gilbert) sets out to woo Roxalanne (Boardman) who has already rejected the advances of sinister Chatellerault (D'Arcy). Bardelys assumes the disguise of a rebel leader, gets into trouble, and winds up on the gallows thanks to his rival. A gap in the surviving print is bridged with stills and footage from the original trailer. Based on the novel by Rafael Sabatini. **90m/B DVD.** John Gilbert, Eleanor Boardman, Roy D'Arcy, Arthur Lubin, Lionel Belmore, Emily Fitzroy; *D:* King Vidor; *W:* Dorothy Farnum; *C:* William H. Daniels.

Bare Essentials **1991 (PG)** Made for TV yuppie Club Med nightmare in which a high-strung couple from New York find themselves marooned on a desert isle with only two other inhabitants. With no cellular telephoning ability and an absence of large-ticket consumer goods to purchase, the two turn their reluctant sights on each other, focusing on the bare essentials, as it were. Great soul-searching scenes for the inarticulate. **94m/C VHS.** Gregory Harrison, Lisa Hartman Black, Mark Linn-Baker, Charlotte Lewis; *D:* Martha Coolidge. **TV**

Bare Knees **1928** A woman causes a scandal in her family when she arrives at her sister's birthday party with bare knees, cigarettes, and other flapper items. The quintessential flapper movie. **61m/B VHS.** Virginia Lee Corbin, Donald Keith, Jane Winton, Johnnie Walker, Forrest Stanley, Maude Fulton; *D:* Erle C. Kenton.

Bare Knuckles **1977 (R)** The adventures of a low-rent bounty hunter. **90m/C VHS.** Robert Viharo, Sherry Jackson, Michael Heit, Gloria Hendry, John Daniels; *D:* Don Edmonds; *C:* Dean Cundey.

The Barefoot Contessa **1954** The story, told in flashback, of a Spanish dancer's rise to Hollywood stardom, as witnessed by a cynical director. Shallow Hollywood self-examination. **128m/C VHS, DVD.** Ava Gardner, Humphrey Bogart, Edmond O'Brien, Valentina Cortese, Rossano Brazzi, Warren Stevens, Marius Goring; *D:* Joseph L. Mankiewicz; *W:* Joseph L. Mankiewicz; *C:* Jack Cardiff. Oscars '54: Support. Actor (O'Brien); Golden Globes '55: Support. Actor (O'Brien).

The Barefoot Executive **1971** A mailroom boy who works for a national TV network finds a chimpanzee that can pick hit shows in this Disney family comedy. **92m/C VHS, DVD.** Kurt Russell, John Ritter, Harry (Henry) Morgan, Wally Cox, Heather North, Joe Flynn; *D:* Robert Butler; *M:* Robert F. Brunner.

Barefoot in Athens **1966** TV presentation from "George Schaefer's Showcase Theatre" chronicles the last years of the philosopher Socrates who, barefoot and unkempt, is an embarrassment to his wife, and a dangerous critic to the corrupt Athenian leaders, nevertheless believes that democracy and truth are all-important in his city. **76m/C VHS.** Peter Ustinov, Geraldine Page, Anthony Quayle; *D:* George Schaefer. **TV**

Barefoot in the Park **1967** Neil Simon's Broadway hit translates well to screen. A newly wedded bride (Fonda) tries to get her husband (Redford, reprising his Broadway role) to loosen up and be as free-spirited as she is. **106m/C VHS, DVD.** Robert Redford, Jane Fonda, Charles Boyer, Mildred Natwick, Herb Edelman, Mabel Albertson; *D:* Gene Saks; *W:* Neil Simon; *C:* Joseph LaShelle; *M:* Neal Hefti.

Barfly **1987 (R)** Bukowski's semi-autobiographical screenplay is the story of a talented writer who chooses to spend his time as a lonely barfly, hiding his literary abilities behind glasses of liquor. Dunaway's character is right on target as the fellow alcoholic. **100m/C VHS, DVD.** Mickey Rourke, Faye Dunaway, Alice Krige, Frank Stallone, J.C. Quinn, Jack Nance, Charles Bukowski, Pruitt Taylor Vince, Fritz Feld, Sandy Martin, Damon Hines; *D:* Barbet Schroeder; *W:* Charles Bukowski; *C:* Robby Muller; *M:* Jack Baran.

The Bargain 1/2 **1915** Hart's first feature, in which he portrays a bandit desperately trying to go straight. Original titles with musical score. **50m/B VHS.** William S. Hart, J. Frank Burke, J. Barney Sherry, Clara Williams, Joseph J. Dowling, Roy Laidlaw, Herschel Mayall, Charles Swickard, Charles French; *D:* Reginald Barker; *W:* William H. Clifford, Thomas Ince; *C:* Joseph August.

Baritone **1985** Concerned Polish drama about a prominent opera singer who promises to deliver a grand concert upon returning to his small town, only to lose his voice just before the show is to start. Proof positive that the opera ain't over 'til the fat lady sings. **100m/C VHS.** *PL* Zbigniew Zapasiewicz; *D:* Janusz Zaorski.

Barjo **1993** In a bland and isolated French suburb lives willful housewife Fanfan (Bouchet) with her older businessman husband Charles (Bohringer) and her eccentric twin brother Barjo (Girardot). Barjo is obsessed with lists and extraterrestrials and his sister's affair with their next-door neighbor, which he likes to spy on. Her husband naturally begins to go crazy. Deadpan satire based on the novel "Confessions of a Crap Artist" by Philip K. Dick. The post-WWII American setting of the novel makes a decidedly uneasy transistion to contemporary French life. In French with English subtitles. **85m/C VHS.** *FR* Anne Brochet, Hippolyte Girardot, Richard Bohringer, Consuelo de Haviland, Renaud Danner, Nathalie Boutefeu; *D:* Jerome Boivin; *W:* Jerome Boivin, Jacques Audiard; *M:* Hugues LeBars.

Bark! 1/2 **2002 (R)** L.A. dog walker Lucy (Morgan) begins to overly-identify with her clients when she stops speaking and begins barking and displaying other canine behavior. Her baffled husband Peter (Tergesen) consults Lucy's equally odd parents as well as a vet (Kudrow) and a shrink (D'Onofrio) and decides to have his wife committed. But when Lucy becomes catatonic in the hospital, Peter decides to take her home and learn to adapt. He's a lot more understanding than the viewer will be. **100m/C VHS, DVD.** *US* Lee Tergesen, Lisa Kudrow, Vincent D'Onofrio, Heather Morgan, Hank Azaria, Mary Jo Deschanel, Scott Wilson, Aimee Graham, Wade Andrew Williams; *D:* Kasia Adamik; *W:* Heather Morgan; *C:* Irek Hartowicz; *M:* Eric Colvin.

The Barkleys of Broadway **1949** The famous dancing team's last film together; they play a quarreling husband/wife showbiz team. ♫ They Can't Take That Away From Me; The Sabre Dance; Swing Trot; Manhattan Downbeat; A Weekend in the Country; My One and Only Highland Fling; You'd Be Hard to Replace; Bouncin' the Blues; Shoes With Wings On. **109m/C VHS, DVD.** Fred Astaire, Ginger Rogers, Gale Robbins, Oscar Levant, Jacques Francois, Billie Burke; ***D:*** Charles Walters; ***W:*** Adolph Green, Betty Comden; ***C:*** Harry Stradling Sr.; ***M:*** Ira Gershwin, Harry Warren.

Barn of the Naked Dead WOOF! *Nightmare Circus; Terror Circus* **1973** Prine plays a sicko who tortures women while his radioactive monster dad terrorizes the Nevada desert. Rudolph's first film, directed under the pseudonym Gerald Comier. **86m/C VHS, DVD.** Andrew Prine, Manuella Thiess, Sherry Alberoni, Gylian Roland, Al Cormier, Jennifer Ashley; ***D:*** Alan Rudolph; ***W:*** Alan Rudolph, Roman Valenti.

Barnaby and Me 🦴🦴 **1977** Australian star Barnaby the Koala Bear joins an international con-man in this romantic adventure. The mob is chasing the con-man when he meets and falls for a lovely young woman and her daughter. **90m/C VHS.** *AU* Sid Caesar, Juliet Mills, Sally Boyden; ***D:*** Norman Panama.

Barney's Great Adventure 🦴🦴 **1998 (G)** First the bad news: that big purple dweebosaur made a movie and your three-year-old is going to make you buy the video. Now the good news: since it's on video you can cue it up for the young-uns and run screaming from the room. You see, they don't care what you think about Barney, who looks a little like a big lug in a purple felt suit, actually. In this extravaganza of not so special effects, Barney and two little girls chase a magical egg around town and encounter a parade, a circus and other allegedly wonderful things, all while trying to convince the older Kyle that Barney is "cool." In a surprise move, the egg hatches to reveal....that new stuffed animal you're going to have to buy! **75m/C VHS, DVD.** George Hearn, Shirley Douglas, Kyla Pratt, Trevor Morgan, Diana Rice, Renee Madeleine Le Guerrier; ***D:*** Steve Gomer; ***W:*** Stephen White; ***C:*** Sandi Sissel; ***V:*** Bob West, Julie Johnson.

Barnum 🦴🦴 **1/2 1986** P.T. Barnum's life is focused upon in this biography about the man who helped to form "The Greatest Show On Earth." **100m/C VHS, DVD.** Burt Lancaster, Hanna Schygulla, Jenny Lind, John Roney; ***D:*** Lee Philips.

Barnyard 🦴🦴 **2006 (PG)** Young Otis the cow (James) is unconcerned about keeping the secret that animals can not only talk, but like to dance, sing, party, and play pranks. But when the farmer's away, Otis is given the unexpected responsibility of looking after things. Cute, but probably more enjoyable for younger kids. Some jokes click for older kids and adults, but not quite enough. **89m/C DVD.** *US* ***D:*** Steve Oedekerk; ***W:*** Steve Oedekerk; ***M:*** John Debney; ***V:*** Kevin James, Courteney Cox, Sam Elliott, Danny Glover, Andie MacDowell, Wanda Sykes, David Koechner, Steve Oedekerk, Rob Paulsen, Dom Irrera, Maria Bamford, Laraine Newman, Maurice LaMarche, Jeff Garcia.

Barocco 🦴🦴 **1976** Crook kills his lookalike and takes his place and his girlfriend. Together the duo try blackmail to get the money they need to start a new life. Self-conscious would-be film noir. French with subtitles. **102m/C VHS, DVD.** *FR* Gerard Depardieu, Isabelle Adjani, Marie-France Pisier, Jean-Claude Brialy; ***D:*** Andre Techine; ***W:*** Andre Techine, Marilyn Goldin; ***C:*** Bruno Nuytten; ***M:*** Philippe Sarde.

The Baron 🦴 **1/2 1988** Vengeance is the name of the game when an underworld boss gets stiffed on a deal. Fast-paced no-brainer street drama. **88m/C VHS, DVD.** Calvin Lockhart, Charles McGregor, Joan Blondell, Richard Lynch, Marlene Clark; ***D:*** Philip Fently.

The Baron and the Kid 🦴 **1984** A pool shark finds out that his opponent at a charity exhibition game is his long-lost son. Based on Johnny Cash's song. Made for TV. **100m/C VHS, DVD.** Johnny Cash, Darren McGavin, June Carter Cash, Richard Roundtree; ***D:*** Gary Nelson; ***M:*** Brad Fiedel. **TV**

Baron Munchausen 🦴🦴🦴 **1943** The German film studio UFA celebrated its 25th anniversary with this lavish version of the Baron Munchausen legend, starring a cast of top-name German performers at the height of the Third Reich. Filmed in Agfacolor; available in English subtitled or dubbed versions. **120m/C VHS, DVD.** *GE* Hans Albers, Kaethe Kaack, Hermann Speelmanns, Leo Slezak; ***D:*** Josef von Baky.

Baron of Arizona 🦴🦴🦴 **1951** Land office clerk almost succeeds in convincing the U.S. that he owned the state of Arizona. **99m/B VHS, DVD.** Vincent Price, Ellen Drew, Beulah Bondi, Reed Hadley, Vladimir Sokoloff; ***D:*** Samuel Fuller; ***W:*** Samuel Fuller; ***C:*** James Wong Howe.

Barracuda WOOF! *The Lucifer Project* **1978 (R)** Lots of innocent swimmers are being eaten by crazed killer barracudas. **90m/C VHS.** Wayne Crawford, Jason Evers, Roberta Leighton; ***D:*** Harry Kerwin.

The Barretts of Wimpole Street 🦴🦴🦴 *Forbidden Alliance* **1934** The moving, almost disturbing, account of poetess Elizabeth Barrett, an invalid confined to her bed, with only her poetry and her dog to keep her company. She is wooed by poet Robert Browning, in whose arms she finds true happiness and a miraculous recovery. Multi-faceted drama expertly played by all. **110m/B VHS.** Fredric March, Norma Shearer, Charles Laughton, Maureen O'Sullivan, Katherine Alexander, Una O'Connor, Ian Wolfe; ***D:*** Sidney Franklin; ***C:*** William H. Daniels.

Barricade 🦴🦴 **1949** Massey practically twirls a mustache of evil in this odd western that's an alleged adaptation of Jack London's "The Sea Wolf." Gold mine owner Boss Kruger uses fugitives on the lam to dig for his ore, including new arrivals Bob (Clark) and Judith (Roman). They befriend lawyer Milburn (Douglas) who wants revenge on Kruger for murdering his brother, the mine's original owner. **75m/C DVD.** Raymond Massey, Dane Clark, Ruth Roman, Robert Douglas, Morgan Farley; ***D:*** Peter Godfrey; ***W:*** William Sackheim; ***C:*** Carl Guthrie.

Barrio Wars 🦴 **1/2 2002 (R)** Hip hop Latino Romeo and Juliet staged on the mean streets of L.A. Plato and Angelina are the star-crossed lovers from rival gangs sparking violence and turmoil all over the city. Nice try, but the standard no-budget acting style and a rather jarring soft-core sex scene defeats any intended purpose. But really, what's the point? Leonardo DiCaprio and Claire Danes have already done modern-day Shakespeare much better. **90m/C VHS, DVD.** Sevier Crespo, Luchana Gatica, Anthony Martins, Beny Mena, Chino XL; ***D:*** Paul Wynne; ***W:*** Paul Wynne. **VIDEO**

Barry Lyndon 🦴🦴🦴 **1/2 1975 (PG)** Ravishing adaptation of the classic Thackeray novel about the adventures of an Irish gambler moving from innocence to self-destructive arrogance in the aristocracy of 18th Century England. Visually opulent. Kubrick received excellent performances from all his actors, and a stunning display of history, but the end result still overwhelms. O'Neal has seldom been better. **185m/C VHS, DVD.** Ryan O'Neal, Marisa Berenson, Patrick Magee, Hardy Kruger, Guy Hamilton; ***D:*** Stanley Kubrick; ***W:*** Stanley Kubrick; ***C:*** John Alcott. Oscars '75: Art Dir./Set Dec., Cinematog., Costume Des., Orig. Song Score and/or Adapt.; British Acad. '75: Director (Kubrick); L.A. Film Critics '75: Cinematog.; Natl. Bd. of Review '75: Director (Kubrick); Natl. Soc. Film Critics '75: Cinematog.

Barry McKenzie Holds His Own 🦴🦴 **1974** In this sequel to "The Adventures of Barry McKenzie," we find that after a young man's aunt is mistaken for the Queen of England, two emissaries of Count Plasma of Transylvania kidnap her to use as a Plasma tourist attraction. Based on the 'Private Eye' comic strip, this crude Australian film is as disappointing as the first of the Barry McKenzie stories. **93m/C VHS.** *AU* Barry Humphries, Barry Crocker, Donald Pleasence; ***D:*** Bruce Beresford; ***W:*** Barry Humphries, Bruce Beresford.

Bart Got a Room 🦴 **1/2 2008 (PG-13)** All-too familiar plot overdoes the fact that Hollywood, Florida high school nerd Danny (Kaplan) lives in a geriatric haven. Danny spends a fortune renting a room for the prom (after he learns ever dweebier Bart has apparently scored) with the expectation of losing his virginity. But first he has to get a date and he keeps overlooking his best friend Camille (Shawkat). Maybe he can't think of her 'that way.' Funniest thing in the movie is Macy's (Danny's divorced, dating dad) Jewish 'fro. **80m/C DVD.** Alia Shawkat, William H. Macy, Cheryl Hines, Ashley Benson, Jennifer Tilly, Steve Kaplan, Brandon Hardesty, Chad Jamian Williams; ***D:*** Brian Hecker; ***W:*** Brian Hecker; ***C:*** Hallvard Braein; ***M:*** Jamie Lawrence.

Bartleby 🦴🦴 **1/2 1970** A new version of the classic Herman Melville short story. McEnery is Bartleby the clerk, who refuses to leave his job even after he's fired; Scofield is his frustrated boss. **79m/C VHS, DVD.** Paul Scofield, John McEnery, Colin Jeavons, Thorley Walters; ***D:*** Anthony Friedman; ***W:*** Rodney Carr-Smith.

Bartleby 🦴🦴 **2001 (PG-13)** Contempo version of Herman Melville's 1856 novella "Bartleby the Scrivener." Eccentric Bartleby (Glover) is the model of efficiency when first hired to do clerical work in a nondescript records office. But gradually Bartleby begins to refuse tasks, then to do anything at all—even firing him has no effect to the consternation of his boss (Paymer) and the bewilderment of his co-workers. **83m/C VHS, DVD.** *US* Crispin Glover, David Paymer, Glenne Headly, Joe Piscopo, Maury Chaykin, Seymour Cassel, Carrie Snodgress, Dick Martin; ***D:*** Jonathan Parker; ***W:*** Jonathan Parker, Catherine Di Napoli; ***C:*** Wah Ho Chan; ***M:*** Jonathan Parker, Seth Asarnow.

Barton Fink 🦴🦴🦴 **1991 (R)** This eerie comic nightmare comes laden with awards (including the Palme D'Or from Cannes) but only really works if you care about the time and place. Fink is a trendy New York playwright staying in a seedy Hollywood hotel in the 1940s, straining to write a simple B-movie script. Macabre events, both real and imagined, compound his writer's block. Superb set design from Dennis Gassner complements an unforgettable cast of grotesques. **116m/C VHS, DVD.** John Turturro, John Goodman, Judy Davis, Michael Lerner, John Mahoney, Tony Shalhoub, Jon Polito, Steve Buscemi, David Warrilow, Richard Portnow, Christopher Murney; ***D:*** Joel Coen; ***W:*** Joel Coen, Ethan Coen; ***C:*** Roger Deakins; ***M:*** Carter Burwell. Cannes '91: Actor (Turturro), Director (Coen), Film; L.A. Film Critics '91: Cinematog., Support. Actor (Lerner); N.Y. Film Critics '91: Cinematog., Support. Actress (Davis); Natl. Soc. Film Critics '91: Cinematog.

The Base 🦴🦴 **1/2 1999 (R)** Army Intelligency officer Major John Murphy (Dacascos) is sent undercover to Fort Tilman to investigate the murder of an army operations officer. Murphy is assigned to a border patrol unit and discovers his fellow soldiers are muscling in on the Mexican/American drug trade. When he discovers who's behind the operation, Murphy's cover is blown and he's in for the fight of his life. **101m/C VHS, DVD.** Mark Dacascos, Tim Abell, Paula Trickey, Noah Blake, Frederick Coffin; ***D:*** Mark L. Lester; ***W:*** Jeff Albert, William Martell; ***C:*** Jacques Haitkin; ***M:*** Paul Zaza. **VIDEO**

Based on an Untrue Story 🦴🦴 **1/2 1993** Campy spoof of popular "true story" TV docudramas in which powerful Satin Chau (Fairchild), a perfume mogul, loses her sense of smell. Satin leaves her mentor Varda (Cannon) to discovery herself but finds that only her two separated-at-birth sisters, Velour (Lake) and Corduroy (Jackson), hold the secrets to the past. It's hard to spoof a genre that's become a cliche but this TV movie does its best. **90m/C VHS.** Morgan Fairchild, Dyan Cannon, Victoria Jackson, Ricki Lake, Harvey Korman, Robert Goulet, Dan Hedaya; ***D:*** Jim Drake.

BASEketball 🦴🦴 **1/2 1998 (R)** Dude! Three slacker buddies ("South Park"'s Parker and Stone plus Bachar) invent a new game in their driveway—a combo of basketball with baseball rules—and see it turn into big business. Parkere gets to romance Jenna Reed (Bleeth), a social worker who helps "health-challenged" kids. Stone and Parker's penchant for gross-out humor and having their characters say whatever's on their minds (no matter how offensive) mixes well with Zucker's talent for sight gags and physical humor to create an enjoyably guilty pleasure. Based on a game that Zucker invented with friends. **103m/C VHS, DVD.** Trey Parker, Matt Stone, Yasmine Bleeth, Jenny McCarthy, Ernest Borgnine, Dian Bachar, Robert Vaughn, Bob Costas, Al Michaels, Reggie Jackson, Robert Stack, Steve Garvey, Kareem Abdul-Jabbar; ***D:*** David Zucker; ***W:*** David Zucker, Robert Locash, Jeffrey Wright, Lewis Friedman; ***C:*** Steve Mason; ***M:*** Ira Newborn.

The Bashful Bachelor 🦴🦴 **1942** Yokel joker Abner trades his delivery car for a race horse, hoping to win a big race. **78m/B VHS, DVD.** Chester Lauck, Norris Goff, Zasu Pitts, Grady Sutton, Louise Currie, Irving Bacon, Earle Hodgins, Benny Rubin; ***D:*** Malcolm St. Clair.

Basic 🦴🦴 **2003 (R)** Travolta, swallowing scenery and his fellow actors in one gulp, is DEA agent and ex-Army Ranger Tom Hardy, brought in to investigate how a training mission ended in all but two soldiers being killed. Over the objections of the base's top cop, Capt. Julia Osborne (Nielsen, sporting an inconsistent Southern accent), he interrogates both survivors and gets two completely differing accounts, "Rashomon" style. In flashback, it's learned that the platoon's commander, Sgt. West, was universally hated, and the men were killed by each other, and some kind of drug smuggling ring may have been involved. Convoluted and confusing are two words you could use for this script, but both are woefully inadequate to describe how it messes with your head, and not in that good, "Wow, that was clever" way. It seems that the actors are as confused as the audience, and decide to cover that with epidemic over-acting. **95m/C VHS, DVD.** *US* John Travolta, Samuel L. Jackson, Connie Nielsen, Giovanni Ribisi, Brian Van Holt, Taye Diggs, Christian de la Fuente, Dash Mihok, Timothy Daly, Roselyn Sanchez, Harry Connick Jr.; ***D:*** John McTiernan; ***W:*** James Vanderbilt; ***C:*** Steve Mason; ***M:*** Klaus Badelt.

Basic Instinct 🦴🦴 **1/2 1992 (R)** Controversial thriller had tongues wagging months before its theatrical release. Burnt-out detective Douglas falls for beautiful, manipulative murder suspect Stone, perfectly cast as a bisexual ice queen who may or may not have done the deed. Noted for highly erotic sex scenes and an expensive (3 million bucks) script; ultimately the predictable plot is disappointing. Gay activists tried to interrupt filming because they objected to the depiction of Stone's character but only succeeded in generating more free publicity. The American release was edited to avoid an "NC-17" rating, but an uncut, unrated video version is also available. **123m/C VHS, DVD, Blu-ray Disc.** Michael Douglas, Sharon Stone, George Dzundza, Jeanne Tripplehorn, Denis Arndt, Leilani Sarelle Ferrer, Bruce A. Young, Chelcie Ross, Dorothy Malone, Wayne Knight, Stephen Tobolowsky; ***D:*** Paul Verhoeven; ***W:*** Joe Eszterhas; ***C:*** Jan De Bont; ***M:*** Jerry Goldsmith. MTV Movie Awards '93: Female Perf. (Stone), Most Desirable Female (Stone).

Basic Instinct 2 🦴 **2006 (R)** It took 14 years for a sequel and this glossy, laughably overwrought mess is what we get? Stone tries too hard reprising her role as cold-blooded vamp Catherine Tramell, who's now living in London. After a fatal car crash, suspicious Scotland Yard detective Washburn (Thewlis) asks criminologist Michael Glass (Morrissey) to evaluate Catherine for possible criminal charges. His diagnosis is "risk addiction." Gee, doc, no kidding. Soon Michael is drawn into Catherine's possibly deadly web. Maybe this effort will become a midnight movie, just waiting to be mocked. **114m/C DVD, Blu-ray Disc.** *US* Sharon Stone, David Morrissey, David Thewlis, Charlotte Rampling, Hugh Dancy, Flora Montgomery, Iain Robertson, Indira Varma, Anne Caillon, Stan Collymore, Heathcote Williams; ***D:*** Michael Caton-Jones; ***W:*** Leora Barish, Henry Bean; ***C:*** Gyula Pados; ***M:*** John Murphy. Golden Raspberries '06: Worst Picture, Worst Actress (Stone), Worst Screenplay, Worst Sequel/Prequel.

Basic Training WOOF! 1986 (R) Three sexy ladies wiggle into the Pentagon in their efforts to clean up the government. **85m/C VHS, DVD.** Ann Dusenberry, Rhonda Shear, Angela Aames, Walter Gotell; ***D:*** Andrew Sugarman.

Basil 🦴🦴 **1/2 1998 (R)** Turn of the century English aristocrat Basil (Leto) strives for the approval of his overbearing father (Jacobi) while also trying to please the selfish woman he loves (Forlani). Based on the novel by Wilkie Collins. **113m/C VHS.** Jared Leto, Claire Forlani, Christian Slater, Derek Jacobi; *D:* Radha Bharadwaj.

Basileus Quartet ✓✓✓ *Il Quartetto Basileus* **1982** The replacement for a violinist in a well-established quartet creates emotional havoc. Beautiful music, excellent and evocative photography. **118m/C VHS.** *FR IT* Pierre Malet, Hector Alterio, Omero Antonutti, Michel Vitold, Alain Cuny, Gabriele Ferzetti, Elisabeth (Lisa) Kreuzer; *D:* Fabio Carpi; *W:* Fabio Carpi; *C:* Dante Spinotti.

The Basket ✓✓ 1/2 **1999 (PG)** There's a lot going on in a small Washington community, circa 1918. Martin Conlon (Coyote) is the new teacher (he's from Boston) at the one-room schoolhouse who introduces opera and basketball into the curriculum. Then German orphans Helmut (Burke) and Brigitta (Willenborg) come to live with the local doctor and are persecuted for their nationality because of WWI. Mr. Emery (MacDonald) is especially hostile since his son was wounded in the war but Mrs. Emery (Allen) is willing to give the newcomers a chance. Helmut turns out to be a hoops natural and the team has a chance to compete in a national championship—if they can set their differences aside. **104m/C VHS, DVD.** Karen Allen, Peter Coyote, Robert Karl Burke, Amber Willenborg, Jock MacDonald, Eric Dane, Casey Cowan, Brian Skala, Tony Lincoln, Patrick Treadway, Ellen Travolta; *D:* Rich Cowan; *W:* Rich Cowan, Frank Swoboda, Tessa Swoboda; *C:* Dan Heigh; *M:* Don Caron.

Basket Case ✓✓✓ **1982** A gory horror film about a pair of Siamese twins—one normal, the other gruesomely deformed. The pair is surgically separated at birth, and the evil disfigured twin is tossed in the garbage. Fraternal ties being what they are, the normal brother retrieves his twin—essentially a head atop shoulders—and totes him around in a basket (he ain't heavy). Together they begin twisted and deadly revenge, with the brother-in-a-basket in charge. Very entertaining, if you like this sort of thing. Followed by two sequels, if you just can't get enough. **89m/C VHS, DVD.** Kevin Van Hentenryck, Terri Susan Smith, Beverly Bonner, Robert Vogel, Diana Browne, Lloyd Pace, Bill Freeman, Joe Clarke, Ruth Neuman, Richard Pierce, Dorothy Strongin; *D:* Frank Henenlotter; *W:* Frank Henenlotter; *C:* Bruce Torbet; *M:* Gus Russo.

Basket Case 2 ✓✓ 1/2 **1990 (R)** Surgically separated teenage mutant brothers Duane and Belial are back! This time they've found happiness in a "special" family—until they're plagued by the paparazzi. Higher production values make this sequel slicker than its low-budget predecessor, but it somehow lacks the same charm. **90m/C VHS, DVD.** Kevin Van Hentenryck, Annie Ross, Kathryn Meisle, Heather Rattray, Jason Evers, Ted (Theodore) Sorel, Matt Mitler, Ron Fazio, Leonard Jackson, Beverly Bonner; *D:* Frank Henenlotter; *W:* Frank Henenlotter; *C:* Robert M. "Bob" Baldwin Jr.; *M:* Joe Renzetti.

Basket Case 3: The Progeny ✓✓ 1/2 **1992 (R)** In this sequel to the cult horror hits "Basket Case" and "Basket Case 2," Belial is back and this time he's about to discover the perils of parenthood as the mutant Mrs. Belial delivers a litter of bouncing mini-monsters. Everything is fine until the police kidnap the little creatures and chaos breaks out as Belial goes on a shocking rampage in his newly created mechanical body. Weird special effects make this a cult favorite for fans of the truly outrageous. **90m/C VHS, DVD.** Annie Ross, Kevin Van Hentenryck, Gil Roper, Tina Louise Hilbert, Dan Biggers, Jim O'Doherty, Jackson Faw, Jim Grimshaw; *D:* Frank Henenlotter; *W:* Frank Henenlotter, Robert Martin; *C:* Bob Paone; *M:* Joe Renzetti.

The Basketball Diaries ✓✓ **1995 (R)** Disappointing adaptation of undeground writer/musician Jim Carroll's 1978 cult memoirs, with DiCaprio starring as the teen athlete whose life spirals into drug addiction and hustling on the New York streets. Carroll and friends Mickey (Wahlberg), Neutron (McGaw), and Pedro (Madio), form the heart of St. Vitus' hot hoopster team. But the defiant quartet really get their kicks from drugs, dares, and petty crime—leading to an ever-downward turn. The book takes place in the '60s but the film can't make up its mind what the decade is, although DiCaprio (and Wahlberg) are particularly effective in a self-conscious first effort from Kalvert. **102m/C VHS, DVD.** Leonardo DiCaprio, Mark Wahlberg, Patrick McGaw, James Madio, Bruno Kirby, Ernie Hudson, Lorraine Bracco, Juliette Lewis, Josh Mostel, Michael Rapaport, Michael Imperioli, James Dennis (Jim) Carroll; *D:* Scott Kalvert; *W:* Bryan Goluboff; *C:* David Phillips; *M:* Graeme Revell.

Basquiat ✓✓✓ *Build a Fort Set It on Fire* **1996 (R)** First-time writer/director and re-knowned '80s pop artist Schnabel paints a celluloid portrait of African-American artist Jean Michel Basquiat, who went from grafitti artist to overnight sensation in the mid-1980s before dying of a drug overdose at 27. Schnabel's first-hand knowledge provides details of the painters, the dealers, and the patrons of the whirlwind New York art scene of the time, using an all-star cast (no mean feat on a $3 million budget). Making the move from stage to screen, Wright is an aptly deep and elusive Basquiat and Bowie stands out in a marvelously concevied portrayal of Basquiat's pseudo-mentor, the equally sensational Warhol. Features authentic works of the artists portrayed and some very convincing Basquiat reproductions done by Schnabel. **108m/C VHS, DVD.** Jeffrey Wright, David Bowie, Dennis Hopper, Gary Oldman, Christopher Walken, Michael Wincott, Benicio Del Toro, Parker Posey, Elina Lowensohn, Courtney Love, Claire Forlani, Willem Dafoe, Paul Bartel, Tatum O'Neal, Chuck Pfeiffer; *D:* Julian Schnabel; *W:* Julian Schnabel; *C:* Ron Fortunato; *M:* John Cale. Ind. Spirit '97: Support. Actor (Del Toro).

The Bastard ✓✓ 1/2 *The Kent Chronicles* **1978** Dashing (but alas, illegitimate) nobleman roams Europe on futile, "Roots"-like search; then settles for America during the Revolutionary War in this long-winded TV adaptation of John Jakes's equally cumbersome bestseller (part of his popular Bicentennial series). Stevens stars, along with many supporting performers merely keeping active. Followed by "The Rebels" and "The Seekers." **189m/C VHS.** Andrew Stevens, Tom Bosley, Kim Cattrall, Buddy Ebsen, Lorne Greene, Olivia Hussey, Cameron Mitchell, Harry (Henry) Morgan, Patricia Neal, Eleanor Parker, Donald Pleasence, William Shatner, Barry Sullivan, Noah Beery Jr., William Daniels, Keenan Wynn, Peter Bonerz, James Gregory, Mark Neely, Ike Eisenmann, Charles Haid, Russell Johnson, James Whitmore Jr., Alan Napier, Stephen Furst, Philip Baker Hall; *D:* Lee H. Katzin; *W:* Guerdon (Gordon) Trueblood; *C:* Michael Hugo; *M:* John Addison; *Nar:* Raymond Burr. **TV**

Bastard out of Carolina ✓✓ **1996 (R)** Huston's steeped-in-controversy directorial debut tells the story of young mom Anney (Leigh), who lives a hardscrabble life in Greenville, South Carolina, with an illegitimate daughter nicknamed Bone (Malone). Working as a waitress, Anney's eager to find love and succumbs to the charms of laborer Glen (Eldard), despite his nasty temper. Eleven-year-old Bone and Glen are immediately at odds and he begins to beat her, with Anney unwilling to face the truth, until a final horrific event. Based on the 1992 semiautiobiographical novel by Dorothy Allison, the film was originally made for Ted Turner's TNT network but was rejected as unsuitable because of its graphic depiction of child abuse. **97m/C VHS, DVD.** Sonny Shroyer, Jennifer Jason Leigh, Jena Malone, Ron Eldard, Glenne Headly, Lyle Lovett, Dermot Mulroney, Christina Ricci, Michael Rooker, Diana Scarwid, Susan Traylor, Grace Zabriskie; *D:* Anjelica Huston; *W:* Anne Meredith; *C:* Anthony B. Richmond; *M:* Van Dyke Parks. **TV**

The Bat ✓✓✓ **1926** A bat-obsessed killer stalks the halls of a spooky mansion in this early film version of the Mary Roberts Rinehart novel. **81m/B VHS, DVD.** Andre de Beranger, Charles Herzinger, Emily Fitzroy, Louise Fazenda, Arthur Houseman, Robert McKim, Jack Pickford, Jewel Carmen; *D:* Roland West; *W:* Roland West.

The Bat ✓✓ **1959** A great plot centering around a murderer called the Bat, who kills hapless victims by ripping out their throats when he isn't busy searching for $1 million worth of securities stashed in the old house he is living in. Adapted from the novel by Mary Roberts Rinehart. **80m/B VHS, DVD.** Vincent Price, Agnes Moorehead, Gavin Gordon, John Sutton, Lenita Lane, Darla Hood; *D:* Crane Wilbur; *W:* Crane Wilbur; *C:* Joseph Biroc; *M:* Louis Forbes.

The Bat People ✓ *It Lives By Night* **1974 (R)** Less-than-gripping horror flick in which Dr. John Bech is bitten by a bat while on his honeymoon. He then becomes a sadistic bat creature, compelled to kill anyone who stumbles across his path. The gory special effects make for a great movie if you've ever been bitten by that sort of thing. **95m/C VHS.** Stewart Moss, Marianne McAndrew, Michael Pataki, Paul Carr; *D:* Jerry Jameson; *C:* Matthew F. Leonetti; *M:* Artie Kane.

Bat 21 ✓✓ **1988 (R)** Hackman, an American officer, is stranded in the wilds of Vietnam alone after his plane is shot down. He must rely on himself and Glover, with whom he has radio contact, to get him out. Glover and Hackman give solid performances in this otherwise average film. **112m/C VHS, DVD.** Gene Hackman, Danny Glover, Jerry Reed, David Marshall Grant, Clayton Rohner, Erich Anderson, Joe Dorsey; *D:* Peter Markle; *W:* Marc Norman, William C. Anderson; *C:* Mark Irwin; *M:* Christopher Young.

The Bat Whispers ✓✓ 1/2 **1930** A masked madman is stalking the halls of a creepy mansion; eerie tale that culminates in an appeal to the audience to keep the plot under wraps. Unusually crafted film for its early era. Comic mystery based on the novel and play by Mary Roberts Rinehart and Avery Hopwood. **82m/B VHS, DVD.** Chester Morris, Chance Ward, Richard Tucker, Wilson Benge, DeWitt Jennings, Una Merkel, Spencer Charters; *D:* Roland West; *W:* Roland West; *C:* Ray June, Robert Planck.

Bataan ✓✓ 1/2 **1943** A rugged war-time combat drama following the true story of a small platoon in the Philippines endeavoring to blow up a pivotal Japanese bridge. Also available in a colorized version. **115m/B VHS, DVD.** Robert Taylor, George Murphy, Thomas Mitchell, Desi Arnaz Sr., Lee Bowman, Lloyd Nolan, Robert Walker, Barry Nelson, Phillip Terry, Tom Dugan, Roque Espiritu, Kenneth Spencer, Alex Havier, Donald Curtis, Lynne Carver, Bud Geary, Dorothy Morris; *D:* Tay Garnett; *W:* Robert D. (Robert Hardy) Andrews; *C:* Sidney Wagner; *M:* Bronislau Kaper, Eric Zeisl.

Bathing Beauty ✓✓ 1/2 **1944** This musical stars Skelton as a pop music composer with the hots for college swim teacher Williams. Rathbone is a music executive who sees the romance as a threat to Skelton's career and to his own profit margin. Full of aquatic ballet, Skelton's shtick, and wonderful original melodies. The first film in which Williams received star billing. ♫I Cried for You; Bim, Bam, Boom; Tico-Tico; I'll Take the High Note; Loch Lomond; By the Waters of Minnetonka; Magic is the Moonlight; Trumpet Blues; Hora Staccato. **101m/C VHS, DVD.** Red Skelton, Esther Williams, Basil Rathbone, Bill Goodwin, Jean Porter, Carlos Ramirez, Donald Meek, Ethel Smith, Helen Forrest; *D:* George Sidney; *C:* Harry Stradling Sr.; *M:* Xavier Cugat.

Batman ✓✓ 1/2 **1966** Holy television camp, Batman! Will the caped crusader win the Bat-tle against the combined forces of the Joker, the Riddler, the Penguin, and Catwoman? Will Batman and Robin save the United World Security Council from dehydration? Will the Bat genius ever figure out that Russian journalist Miss Kitka and Catwoman are one and the same? Biff! Thwack! Socko! Not to be confused with the Michael Keaton version of the Dark Knight, this is the potbellied Adam West Batman, teeming with Bat satire and made especially for the big screen. **104m/C VHS, DVD.** Burt Ward, Adam West, Burgess Meredith, Cesar Romero, Frank Gorshin, Lee Meriwether, Alan Napier, Neil Hamilton, Stafford Repp, Madge Blake, Reginald Denny, Milton Frome; *D:* Leslie Martinson; *W:* Lorenzo Semple Jr.; *C:* Howard Schwartz; *M:* Nelson Riddle.

Batman ✓✓✓ 1/2 **1989 (PG-13)** The blockbuster fantasy epic that renewed Hollywood's faith in media blitzing. The Caped Crusader (Keaton) is back in Gotham City, where even the criminals are afraid to walk the streets alone. There's a new breed of criminal in Gotham, led by the infamous Joker (Nicholson). Their random attacks via acid-based make-up are just the beginning. Keaton is surprisingly good as the dual personality hero though Nicholson steals the show with his campy performance. Basinger is blonde and feisty as photog Vicki Vale, who falls for mysterious millionaire Bruce Wayne (and the bat). Marvelously designed and shot. Followed by three sequels. **126m/C VHS, DVD, UMD.** Michael Keaton, Jack Nicholson, Kim Basinger, Robert Wuhl, Tracey Walter, Billy Dee Williams, Pat Hingle, Michael Gough, Jack Palance, Jerry Hall; *D:* Tim Burton; *W:* Sam Hamm, Warren Skaaren; *C:* Roger Pratt; *M:* Danny Elfman, Prince. Oscars '89: Art Dir./Set Dec.

Batman and Robin ✓ 1/2 **1997 (PG-13)** Includes lots of flash but, as usual, not much substance in this fourth adventure, which features a less angst-ridden caped crusader in the charming persona of Clooney. O'Donnell, who apparently knows a good gig when he's got one, returns as Robin. They must battle evil industrialist, Mr. Freeze (an impressively costumed Schwarzenegger), and his partner-with-the-deady-kiss (but what a way to go!), Poison Ivy (Thurman), who have plans to freeze Gotham City. Our heroes have some additional help in the person of Batgirl (Silverstone), who's now butler Alfred's (Gough) niece (she was Commissioner Gordon's daughter in the comics). Story's simplified but the secondary characters still get lost in the crowd. Director Schumacher's already agreed to helm a fifth film, but don't hold your breath since he succeeded in doing the impossible: killing the franchise. **125m/C VHS, DVD.** George Clooney, Chris O'Donnell, Arnold Schwarzenegger, Uma Thurman, Alicia Silverstone, Michael Gough, Pat Hingle, John Glover, Elle Macpherson, Vivica A. Fox, Vendela Thommessen, Jeep Swenson; *D:* Joel Schumacher; *W:* Joel Schumacher, Akiva Goldsman; *C:* Stephen Goldblatt; *M:* Elliot Goldenthal. Golden Raspberries '97: Worst Support. Actress (Silverstone).

Batman Begins ✓✓✓ **2005 (PG-13)** They got rid of the Bat-nipples? Joel Schumacher will be so disappointed. Fortunately for everyone else, Nolan rejects the other Bat-sequels' lame campiness and returns Batman to his gritty roots, showing us how a young Bruce Wayne (Bale) first became the Caped Crusader. After training abroad with the mysterious Ducard (Neeson) and Ra's Al Ghul (Watanabe), Wayne begins his one-man war on crime with the help of his butler Alfred (Caine), good cop Jim Gordon (Oldman), and tech-savvy Lucius Fox (Freeman). The cast is beyond stellar, and Nolan does an amazing job of making Batman's world seem almost plausible. There's a bit too much angsty pondering about the nature of fear, but you'll forget all that once you see the Lamborghini-inspired Batmobile. **141m/C DVD, Blu-ray Disc, UMD, HD DVD.** *US* Christian Bale, Michael Caine, Ken(saku) Watanabe, Cillian Murphy, Tom Wilkinson, Morgan Freeman, Katie Holmes, Gary Oldman, Liam Neeson, Rutger Hauer, Mark Boone Jr., Linus Roache, Gus Lewis; *D:* Christopher Nolan; *W:* Christopher Nolan, David S. Goyer; *C:* Wally Pfister; *M:* Hans Zimmer, James Newton Howard.

Batman Forever ✓✓✓ **1995 (PG-13)** Holy franchise, Batman! Third-time actioner considerably lightens up Tim Burton's dark vision for a more family-oriented Caped Crusader (now played by Kilmer, who fills out lip requirement nicely). The Boy Wonder also makes a first-time appearance in the bulked-up form of O'Donnell, a street-smart Robin with revenge on his mind. Naturally, the villains still steal the show in the personas of maniacal Carrey (the Riddler) and the sartorially splendid Jones as Harvey "Two-Face" Dent. Rounding out this charismatic cast is Kidman's slinky psychologist Chase Meridian, who's eager to find the man inside the bat (and who can blame her). Lots of splashy toys for the boys and awe-inspiring sets to show you where the money went. A Gotham City gas that did $53 million at it's opening weekend boxoffice—breaking the "Jurassic Park" record, testimony to the power of aggressive marketing. **121m/C VHS, DVD.** Val Kilmer, Tommy Lee Jones, Jim Carrey, Chris O'Donnell, Nicole Kidman, Drew Barrymore, Debi Mazar, Michael Gough, Pat Hingle, Jon Favreau, George Wallace, Don "The Dragon" Wilson, Ed Begley Jr., Rene Auberjonois, Joe Grifasi, Jessica Tuck, Kimberly Scott; *D:* Joel Schumacher; *W:* Janet Scott Batchler, Akiva Goldsman, Lee Batchler; *C:* Stephen Goldblatt; *M:* Elliot Goldenthal. Blockbuster '96: Action Actress, T. (Kidman).

Batman: Mask of the Phantasm 1/2 *Batman: The Animated Movie* **1993 (PG)** Based on the Fox TV series with the animated Batman fending off old enemy the Joker, new enemy the Phantasm, and dreaming of his lost first love. Cartoon film noir set in the 1940s but filled with '90s sarcasm. Complicated storyline with a stylish dark look may be lost on the kiddies but adults will stay awake. **77m/C VHS, DVD.** *D:* Eric Radomski, Bruce W. Timm; *W:* Michael Reaves, Alan Burnett, Paul Dini, Martin Pako; *M:* Shirley Walker; *V:* Kevin Conroy, Dana Delany, Mark Hamill, Stacy Keach, Hart Bochner, Abe Vigoda, Efrem Zimbalist Jr., Dick Miller.

Batman Returns 1/2 **1992 (PG-13)** More of the same from director Burton, with Batman more of a supporting role overshadowed by provocative villains. DeVito is the cruely misshapen Penguin who seeks to rule over Gotham City; Pfeiffer is the exotic and dangerous Catwoman—who has more than a passing purr-sonal interest in Batman; Walken is the maniacal tycoon Max Shreck. Pfeiffer fares best in her wickedly sexy role and second-skin costume (complete with bullwhip). Plot is secondary to special effects and nightmarish settings. Despite a big budget, this grandiose sequel is of the love it or leave it variety. **126m/C VHS, DVD.** Michael Keaton, Danny DeVito, Michelle Pfeiffer, Christopher Walken, Michael Gough, Michael Murphy, Cristi Conaway, Pat Hingle, Vincent Schiavelli, Jan Hooks, Paul (Pee-wee Herman) Reubens, Andrew Bryniarski; *D:* Tim Burton; *W:* Daniel Waters; *C:* Stefan Czapsky; *M:* Danny Elfman.

Baton Rouge **1988** Gigolo Antonio (Banderas) gets together with psychiatrist Anao (Abril) in a scheme to seduce one of her patients, the wealthy Isabel (Maura), who suffers from terrible nightmares. They plan to kill her wealthy ex-husband and accuse her of the crime in order to get her fortune. But there's an elaborate double-cross and things go back for all concerned. The spanish trio, all veterans of director Pedro Almodovar's films, certainly know how to steam up the screen. Spanish with subtitles. **90m/C VHS.** *SP* Antonio Banderas, Victoria Abril, Carmen Maura; *D:* Rafael Moleon; *W:* Rafael Moleon, Agustin Diaz Yanes; *C:* Angel Luis Fernandez.

Bats 1/2 **1999 (PG-13)** B-grade comedy/thriller proves that people with a warped vision can create something that'll suck the life right out of you. Unfortunately, they use dialogue and plot, and not the winged critters in the title. A mad scientist (Gunton) working for the military genetically engineers some extra-nasty super-intelligent bats. Mad scientists being notoriously bad at cage maintenance, they escape. They then rile up a bunch of normally docile bats, turning them into vicious killers through some type of rodent peer pressure. After several attacks on his small Texas town, Sheriff Kimsey (Phillips) summons the nearest beautiful female bat expert (Meyer) and comic relief sidekick (Leon) so the bats have someone to chase around until the finale. They decide to freeze the bats in their cave, at the risk of trudging through a lot of guano to reach the end. You'll know how they feel. **91m/C VHS, DVD.** Lou Diamond Phillips, Dina Meyer, Bob Gunton, Leon, Carlos Jacott, Oscar Rowland, David Shawn McConnell, Marcia Dangerfield; *D:* Louis Morneau; *W:* John Logan; *C:* George Mooradian; *M:* Graeme Revell.

Bats: Human Harvest **WOOF!** **2007 (R)** Basically an in-name-only sequel to 1999's "Bats" (well, except for the genetically mutated flying rodents). A special ops squad is sent to Chechnya to retrieve a renegade doctor (Arana). Seems the doc has turned bats into flesh-eating monsters that are now infesting the local woods. Just terrible in every possible way, including its bad CGI. **84m/C DVD.** Tomas Arana, Michael Jace, David Chokachi, Melissa De Sousa; *D:* Jamie Dixon; *W:* Chris Denk; *C:* Ivo Peitchev; *M:* James Bairian, Louis Castle. **CABLE**

***batteries not included** 1/2 **1987 (PG)** As a real estate developer fights to demolish a New York tenement, the five remaining residents are aided by tiny metal visitors from outer space in their struggle to save their home. Each resident gains a renewed sense of life in this sentimental, wholesome family film produced by Spielberg. Cronyn and Tandy keep the schmaltz from getting out of hand. Neat little space critters. **107m/C VHS, DVD.** Hume Cronyn, Jessica Tandy, Frank McRae, Michael Carmine, Elizabeth Pena, Dennis Boutsikaris, James LeGros; *D:* Matthew Robbins; *W:* Matthew Robbins, Brad Bird, Brent Maddock, S.S. Wilson; *C:* John McPherson; *M:* James Horner.

Battle Beneath the Earth **1968** The commies try to undermine democracy once again when American scientists discover a Chinese plot to invade the U.S. via a series of underground tunnels. Perhaps a tad jingoistic. **112m/C VHS.** *GB* Kerwin Mathews, Peter Arne, Viviane Ventura, Robert Ayres; *D:* Montgomery Tully.

Battle Beyond the Stars 1/2 **1980 (PG)** The planet Akir must be defended against alien rapscallions in this intergalactic Corman creation. Sayles authored the screenplay and co-authored the story on which it was based. **105m/C VHS, DVD.** Richard Thomas, Robert Vaughn, George Peppard, Sybil Danning, Sam Jaffe, John Saxon, Darlanne Fluegel, Jeff Corey, Morgan Woodward, Marta Kristen, Ron Ross, Eric Morris; *D:* Jimmy T. Murakami; *W:* John Sayles; *C:* Daniel Lacambre; *M:* James Horner.

Battle Beyond the Sun **1963** Former Russian movie "Nebo Zowet" is Americanized. Everyone is trying to send a mission to Mars. Roger Corman was the producer, director Coppola used the pseudonym Thomas Colchart. **75m/C VHS, DVD.** Edd Perry, Arla Powell, Bruce Hunter, Andy Stewart; *D:* Francis Ford Coppola; *W:* Nicholas Colbert, Edwin Palmer; *M:* Les Baxter.

Battle Circus 1/2 **1953** Sappy drama casts Bogart as a surgeon at a M*A*S*H unit during the Korean War. Allyson is a combat nurse who finds love amongst the harsh reality of a war zone. Bogart was badly miscast and his performance proves it. Weak script and uninspired performances don't help this depressing story. **90m/B VHS.** Humphrey Bogart, June Allyson, Keenan Wynn, Robert Keith, William Campbell, Perry Sheehan, Patricia Tiernan, Adele Longmire, Jonathon Cott, Ann Morrison, Helen Winston, Sarah Selby, Danny Chang, Philip Ahn, Steve Forrest, Jeff Richards, Dick Simmons; *D:* Richard Brooks; *W:* Richard Brooks; *C:* John Alton; *M:* Lennie Hayton.

Battle Cry **1955** A group of U.S. Marines train, romance, and enter battle in WWII. But it takes 'em a while to do it. Walsh's film focuses on the psychology of training men to fight, and to wait for the chance. Uris's script (from his own novel) also spends an inordinate amount of time on the love lives of the soldiers. **169m/C VHS, DVD.** Van Heflin, Aldo Ray, Mona Freeman, Tab Hunter, Dorothy Malone, Anne Francis, James Whitmore, Raymond Massey, William Campbell, John Lupton, L.Q. Jones, Perry Lopez, Fess Parker, Jonas Applegarth, Tommy Cook, Felix Noriego, Nancy Olson, Susan Morrow, Carleton Young, Rhys Williams, Gregory Walcott, Frank Ferguson, Sarah Selby, Willis Bouchey; *D:* Raoul Walsh; *W:* Leon Uris; *C:* Sid Hickox; *M:* Max Steiner.

Battle for Terra *Terra* **2009 (PG)** A sci-fi story with a moral and some great 3-D animation. Having ruined Earth, human survivors are seeking another planet to colonize. This leads them to peaceful Terra, where the Terrans have set aside weapons and war long ago. Rebellious teen Mala (Wood) saves the life of human pilot Jim (Wilson) and, in return, asks for his help in rescuing her father who is a prisoner. The Terrans themselves are in danger since General Hammer (Cox) wants to get rid of the pesky natives and make the planet Earthlings-only. Don't worry, it's still fun as well. **85m/C DVD.** *US* *D:* Aristomenis Tsirbas; *W:* Evan Spiliotopolos; *M:* Abel Korzeniowski; *V:* Evan Rachel Wood, Luke Wilson, Brian Cox, James Garner, Chris Evans, Dennis Quaid, David Cross.

Battle for the Planet of the Apes **1973 (G)** A tribe of human atomic bomb mutations are out to make life miserable for the peaceful ape tribe. The story is told primarily in flashback with the opening and closing sequences taking place in the year A.D. 2670. Final chapter in the five-movie simian saga. **96m/C VHS, DVD.** Roddy McDowall, Lew Ayres, John Huston, Paul Williams, Claude Akins, Severn Darden, Natalie Trundy, Austin Stoker, Noah Keen, Michael Stearns, John Landis; *D:* J. Lee Thompson; *W:* John W. Corrington, Joyce H. Corrington; *C:* Richard H. Kline; *M:* Leonard Rosenman.

Battle Heater *Electric Kotatsu Horror; Battle Heater: Kotatsu* **1989** Two junk collectors who spend their days rummaging through landfills find a kotatsu heater (a Japanese table) with a sacred seal on it. Once they remove the seal it becomes a man-eating monster and begins devouring the tenants of the apartment building they live in. Fortunately a punk rock band lives there, and they specialize in whoopin' animated house appliances. **93m/C DVD.** *JP* Pappara Kawai, Yasuko Tomita; *D:* Joji Iida.

Battle Hell *Yangtse Incident* **1956** The true story of how a British ship was attacked by the Chinese Peoples Liberation Army on the Yangtze River in 1949. **112m/B VHS.** *GB* Richard Todd, Akim Tamiroff, Keye Luke; *D:* Michael Anderson Sr.; *W:* Eric Ambler.

Battle Hymn 1/2 **1957** After accidentally bombing an orphanage as a WWII fighter pilot, Dean Hess (Hudson) becomes a minister. He returns to the Air Force in 1950 to train Korean pilots in Seoul and winds up building a home for the local orphans. True story on which the real Hess served as technical advisor. **109m/C VHS, DVD.** Rock Hudson, Dan Duryea, Martha Hyer, Anna Kashfi, Don DeFore, Jock Mahoney, Carl Benton Reid, Alan Hale Jr., Richard Loo, Philip Ahn; *D:* Douglas Sirk; *W:* Charles Grayson, Vincent B. Evans; *C:* Russell Metty; *M:* Frank Skinner.

Battle in Heaven *Batalla En El Cielo* **2005** Set in Mexico, Marcos (Hernandez) is a general's chauffeur whose life collapses around him when the baby he and his wife kidnapped for ransom unexpectedly dies. He seeks out Ana (Mushkadiz)—the general's daughter and a prostitute in her spare time—to ease his pain. She in turn entrusts Marcos, her driver since she was a young child, with her secret life. For some, this is cutting edge art house material that lays bare the lives of Mexico's haves and have-nots; others may view the nonprofessional actors and blandly graphic sex scenes as a big yawn. **94m/C DVD.** Marcos Hernandez, Anapola Mushkadiz, Berta Ruiz, David Bornstien, Rosalinda Ramirez, El Abuelo; *D:* Carlos Reygadas; *W:* Carlos Reygadas; *C:* Diego Martinez Vignatti; *M:* John Tavener, Marcha Cordobesa.

Battle in Seattle **2007 (R)** Dramatic (and heavily biased) reenactment of five days in 1999 when the World Trade Organization convened in Seattle and was met with tens of thousands of activists upset with the corporate entity's globalization policies and damage to the environment. Soon, however, the protests turned violent, with the police donning riot gear and the National Guard swooping in to clean up the mess. All the players get their turn: good-guy cop Dale (Harrelson) and his pregnant wife Ella (Theron), protest leader Jay (Henderson) and his angry girlfriend Lou (Rodriguez), over-zealous newswoman Jean (Nielsen), and finally, non-fictionalized Mayor Tobin (Liotta) to ineffectively calm both groups' fears. Despite writer-director Townsend's attempt for grit and realism, silly monologues and overt melodrama reek of pure Hollywood. **100m/C DVD.** *US* Andre Benjamin, Jennifer Carpenter, Michelle Rodriguez, Martin Henderson, Ray Liotta, Woody Harrelson, Charlize Theron, Connie Nielsen, Channing Tatum, Isaach de Bankole, Joshua Jackson, Rade Sherbedgia; *D:* Stuart Townsend; *W:* Stuart Townsend; *C:* Barry Ackroyd; *M:* One Point Six.

The Battle of Algiers 1/2 *La Bataille d'Alger; La Battaglia di Algeri* **1966** Famous, powerful, award-winning film depicting the uprisings against French Colonial rule in 1954 Algiers. A seminal documentary-style film which makes most political films seem ineffectual by comparison in its use of non-professional actors, gritty photography, realistic violence, and a boldly propagandistic sense of social outrage. **123m/B VHS, DVD.** *AL IT* Yacef Saadi, Jean Martin, Brahim Haggiag, Tommaso Neri, Samia Kerbash, Fawzia el Kader, Michele Kerbash, Mohamed Ben Kassen; *D:* Gillo Pontecorvo; *W:* Gillo Pontecorvo, Franco Solinas; *C:* Marcello Gatti; *M:* Gillo Pontecorvo, Ennio Morricone. Venice Film Fest. '66: Film.

The Battle of Austerlitz *Austerlitz* **1960 (PG)** Ambitious but numbing costume drama about the events leading up to the epic battle between Napoleon and the overwhelming forces of the Czar and the Austrian Emperor at Austerlitz. Napoleon won. Film has been drastically cut from original 166 minute release. Watch director Gance's silent version, "Napoleon," for a truly epic experience. **123m/C VHS.** *FR IT YU* Claudia Cardinale, Martine Carol, Rossano Brazzi, Vittorio De Sica, Jean Marais, Ettore Manni, Jack Palance, Orson Welles; *D:* Abel Gance.

The Battle of Blood Island **1960** Two G.I.s, one Christian and one Jewish, face death at the hands of the Japanese during WWII. Still, they bicker incessantly before finally pulling together to save themselves. **64m/B VHS, DVD.** Richard Devon, Ron Kennedy; *D:* Joel Rapp.

Battle of Britain 1/2 **1969 (G)** A powerful retelling of the most dramatic aerial combat battle of WWII, showing how the understaffed Royal Air Force held off the might of the German Luftwaffe. **132m/C VHS, DVD, Blu-ray Disc.** Harry Andrews, Michael Caine, Laurence Olivier, Trevor Howard, Kenneth More, Christopher Plummer, Robert Shaw, Susannah York, Ralph Richardson, Curt Jurgens, Michael Redgrave, Nigel Patrick, Edward Fox, Ian McShane, Patrick Wymark; *D:* Guy Hamilton; *W:* James Kennaway, Wilfred Greatorex; *C:* Frederick A. (Freddie) Young; *M:* Malcolm Arnold, Ronald Goodwin, William Walton.

The Battle of El Alamein **1968** Action filled movie about the alliance of Italy and Germany in a war against the British, set in a North African desert in the year 1942. Ferroni used the pseudonym Calvin Jackson Padget. **105m/C VHS, DVD.** *IT FR* Frederick Stafford, Ettore Manni, Robert Hossein, Michael Rennie, George Hilton, Ira Furstenberg; *D:* Giorgio Ferroni.

Battle of Elderbush Gulch 1/2 **1913** An ancient pioneering western short famous for innocently employing the now-established cliches of bad guy, good guy, and helpless frontier heroine. One of Gish's first films. **22m/B VHS, DVD.** Mae Marsh, Alfred Paget, Robert "Bobbie" Harron, Lionel Barrymore, Leslie Loveridge, Lillian Gish; *D:* D.W. Griffith; *C:* Billy (G.W.) Bitzer.

Battle of Neretva **1969** During WWII, Yugoslav partisans are facing German and Italian troops and local Chetniks as they battle for freedom. Big budget war film lost continuity with U.S. cut. **106m/C VHS.** *YU* Yul Brynner, Curt Jurgens, Orson Welles, Hardy Kruger, Franco Nero, Sergei Bondarchuk; *D:* Veljko Bulajic.

The Battle of Shaker Heights 1/2 *Project Greenlight's The Battle of Shaker Heights* **2003 (PG-13)** Disappointing sophomore effort from the HBO series "Project Greenlight," backed once again by producers Ben Affleck and Matt Damon. Kelly Ernswiler (LaBeouf) is bright, middle-class Midwestern teen whose hobby is military re-enactment. He becomes best friends with Bart (Henson) after "saving his life" in a mock battle. He soon develops a crush on Bart's older sister Tabby, an engaged Yale grad student, much to the dismay of his supermarket co-worker Sarah (Appleby). This only adds to Kelly's mounting problems, which include myriad family problems with ex-addict dad (Sadler) and "art" entrepreneur mom (Quinlan). LaBeouf is appealing, rising above the disjointed, uninspired mess. If there is another "Project," they should look for a director who will provide satisfying drama on the big screen as well as on the show. **85m/C VHS, DVD.** *US* Shia LaBeouf, Elden (Ratliff) Henson, Amy Smart, Billy Kay, Shiri Appleby, Kathleen Quinlan, William Sadler, Ray Wise, Anson Mount, Philipp Karner; *D:* Kyle Rankin, Efram Potelle; *W:* Erica Beeney; *C:* Thomas Ackerman; *M:* Richard (Rick) Marvin.

Battle of the Bulge **1965** A re-creation of the famous offensive by Nazi Panzer troops on the Belgian front during

1944-45, an assault that could have changed the course of WWII. **141m/C VHS, DVD, Blu-ray Disc, HD DVD.** Henry Fonda, Robert Shaw, Robert Ryan, Dana Andrews, Telly Savalas, Ty Hardin, Pier Angeli, George Montgomery, Charles Bronson, Barbara Werle, Hans-Christian Blech, James MacArthur, Karl Otto Alberty; ***D:*** Ken Annakin; ***W:*** Philip Yordan, John Melson; ***C:*** Jack Hildyard; ***M:*** Benjamin Frankel.

Battle of the Commandos *Legion of the Damned* **1971** A tough Army colonel leads a group of convicts on a dangerous mission to destroy a German-built cannon before it's used against the Allied Forces. **94m/C VHS.** *IT* Jack Palance, Curt Jurgens, Thomas Hunter, Robert Hunter; ***D:*** Umberto Lenzi.

Battle of the Eagles 1/2 **1979** Follows the true adventures of the "Partisan Squadron," the courageous airmen known as the "Knights of the Sky" during WWII in Yugoslavia. **102m/C VHS, DVD.** Bekim Fehmiu, George Taylor, Gloria Samara; ***D:*** Tom Raymonth.

The Battle of the Japan Sea **1970 (G)** A Japanese epic, dubbed in English, centering around the historic WWII battle between Japan and Russia. **120m/C VHS.** *JP* Tatsuya Nakadai, Yuzo Kayama, Chishu Ryu, Susumu Fujita, Mitsuko Kusabe, Toshiro Mifune; ***D:*** Seiji Maruyama; ***W:*** Toshio Yasumi; ***C:*** Masaru Sato; ***M:*** Hiroshi Murai.

Battle of the Rails *La Bataille du Rail* **1946** Docudrama based on actual events of French Resistance fighters who worked on the railways and, at great peril, stymied the Nazis efforts throughout World War II and aided the Allies during the D-Day invasion. Powerful debut feature film for French director Clement, who included real railroad workers in recreating events. In French with subtitles. **85m/B DVD.** Marcel Barnault, Jean Clarieux, Jean Daurand, Jacques Desagneaux, Francois Joux; ***D:*** Rene Clement; ***W:*** Rene Clement. **VIDEO**

Battle of the Sexes **1928** Real estate tycoon Judson (Hersholt) abandons his wife (Bennett) and home for money-hungry flapper Marie (Haver). Based on the novel "The Single Standard" by Daniel Carson Goodman. Griffith's remake of his own 1913 film. **88m/B VHS, DVD.** Jean Hersholt, Phyllis Haver, Belle Bennett, Don Alvarado, William "Billy" Bakewell, Sally O'Neil; ***D:*** D.W. Griffith; ***W:*** Gerrit J. Lloyd; ***C:*** Billy (G.W.) Bitzer, Karl Struss.

The Battle of the Sexes **1960** Sophisticated British comedy has mild-mannered Sellers trying to prevent a business takeover by the brash American Cummings. A good supporting cast and the impeccable Sellers make this one unique. Adapted from the James Thurber short story "The Catbird Seat." **88m/B VHS.** *GB* Peter Sellers, Robert Morley, Constance Cummings, Jameson Clark, Ernest Thesiger, Donald Pleasence, Moultrie Kelsall, Alex Mackenzie, Roddy McMillan, Michael Goodliffe, Norman MacOwen, William Mervyn; ***D:*** Charles Crichton; ***W:*** Monja Danischewsky; ***C:*** Freddie Francis; ***M:*** Stanley Black; ***Nar:*** Sam Wanamaker.

Battle of the Worlds *Il Pianeta Degli Uomini Spenti; Planet of the Lifeless Men* **1961** Typical low-budget science fiction. A scientist tries to stop an alien planet from destroying the Earth. Even an aging Rains can't help this one. Poorly dubbed in English. **84m/C VHS, DVD.** *IT* Claude Rains, Maya Brent, Bill Carter, Marina Orsini, Jacqueline Derval; ***D:*** Anthony M. Dawson.

Battle of Valiant **1963** Thundering hordes of invading barbarians trample the splendor of ancient Rome beneath their grimy sandals. **90m/C VHS.** Gordon Mitchell, Ursula Davis, Massimo Serato; ***D:*** John Gentil.

Battle Queen 2020 **1999 (R)** In a frozen post-apocalyptic future (eternal winter after asteroid crash), Gayle (Strain) leads the downtrodden masses in a revolution against the Elites who live above ground. She's a courtesan by day, freedom fighter by night...or is the other way around? This one is at least as good as "Battlefield Earth." It's certainly shorter and was made by people who were under no illusions about what they were doing. **80m/C DVD.** *CA* Julie Strain, Jeff Wincott; ***D:*** Daniel D'or; ***W:*** Michael B. Druxman, William Hulkower, William D. Bostjancic, Caron Nightengale; ***C:*** Billy Brao; ***M:*** Robert Duncan. **VIDEO**

Battle Shock *A Woman's Devotion; War Shock* **1956** Ex-GI painter is accused of murdering a cantina waitress while on his honeymoon in Mexico. Soon other women are turning up dead and he realizes he is having blackouts. Solid work all around. **88m/C VHS.** Ralph Meeker, Janice Rule, Paul Henreid, Rosenda Monteros, Jose Torvay, Yerye Beirut; ***D:*** Paul Henreid; ***W:*** Robert J. Hill; ***C:*** Jorge Stahl Jr.; ***M:*** Les Baxter.

Battlefield Baseball 1/2 *Jigoku koshien; Battlefield Stadium* **2003** Seido High School has a chance to make it to the championships, but their next opponent, Gedo High, fields a baseball team of flesh-eating zombie mutants. Technically a spoof of cliched sports films, it goes off into the Twilight Zone pretty quickly and never comes back. Ultra campy with cyborgs, zombies, random naked men, senseless death, and superhumanly powered high school baseball players. **87m/C DVD.** *JP* Tak Sakaguchi, Hideo Sakaki, Atsushi Ito; ***D:*** Yudai Yamaguchi; ***W:*** Yudai Yamaguchi, Isao Kiriyama, Gataro Man, Ryuichi Takatsu; ***M:*** Daisuke Yano.

Battlefield Earth **WOOF! 2000 (PG-13)** In the year 3000, the Earth has been decimated by 10-foot tall aliens known as Psychlos who are stripping the planet of its natural resources. Only a few humans survive, including Pepper who becomes the leader of a rebellion. Travolta plays the leader of the bad aliens and is extremely evil-lookng but in a strangely campy way. Based on a 1982 novel by Scientology founder L. Ron Hubbard. Film generated controversy for that reason and supposedly "subliminal" church messages but you'll simply be stunned into submission by how badly it blows. **117m/C VHS, DVD.** John Travolta, Barry Pepper, Forest Whitaker, Kelly Preston, Kim Coates, Richard Tyson, Sabine Karsenti, Michael Byrne, Sean Hewitt, Michel Perron, Shaun Austin-Olsen, Marie Josee Croze; ***D:*** Roger Christian; ***W:*** J. David Shapiro, Cory Mandell; ***C:*** Giles Nuttgens; ***M:*** Elia Cmiral. Golden Raspberries '00: Worst Picture, Worst Actor (Travolta), Worst Support. Actor (Pepper), Worst Support. Actress (Preston), Worst Director (Christian), Worst Screenplay.

Battleforce *The Battle of the Mareth Line; The Greatest Battle* **1978** Exciting battle scenes lose their power in the confusion of this mixed-up WWII film about Rommel's last days. Dubbed sequences, news-reel vignettes and surprise performances by big name stars are incomprehensibly glued together. **97m/C VHS, DVD.** *GE YU* Henry Fonda, Stacy Keach, Helmut Berger, Samantha Eggar, Giuliano Gemma, John Huston; ***D:*** Umberto Lenzi; ***Nar:*** Orson Welles.

Battleground **1949** A tightly conceived post-WWII character drama, following a platoon of American soldiers through the Battle of the Bulge. Available in a Colorized version. **118m/B VHS, DVD.** Van Johnson, John Hodiak, James Whitmore, George Murphy, Ricardo Montalban, Marshall Thompson, Jerome Courtland, Don Taylor, Bruce Cowling, Leon Ames, Douglas Fowley, Richard Jaeckel, Scotty Beckett, Herbert Anderson, Thomas E. Breen, Denise Darcel, James Arness, Brett King; ***D:*** William A. Wellman; ***W:*** Robert Pirosh; ***C:*** Paul Vogel; ***M:*** Lennie Hayton. Oscars '49: B&W Cinematog., Story & Screenplay; Golden Globes '50: Screenplay, Support. Actor (Whitmore).

The Battleship Potemkin *Potemkin; Bronenosets Potemkin* **1925** Eisenstein's best work documents mutiny aboard the Russian battleship Potemkin in 1905 which led to a civilian uprising against the Czar in Odessa, and the resulting crackdown by troops loyal to the Czar. Beautiful cinematography, especially the use of montage sequences, changed filmmaking. In particular, a horrifying sequence depicting the slaughter of civilians on an Odessa beach by soldiers coming down the stairs leading to it is exceptional; many movies pay homage to this scene including "The Untouchables" and "Love and Death." Viewers should overlook obvious Marxist overtones and see this film for what it is: a masterpiece. **71m/B VHS, DVD.** *RU* Alexander Antonov, Vladimir Barsky, Grigori Alexandrov, Mikhail Gomorov, Sergei Eisenstein, I. Brobov, Beatrice Vitoldi, N. Poltavseva, Alexandr Levshin, Repnikova, Korobei, Levchenko; ***D:*** Grigori Alexandrov, Sergei Eisenstein; ***W:*** Nina Agadzhanova Shutko, Sergei Eisenstein; ***C:*** Eduard Tisse.

Battlestar Galactica 1/2 **1978 (PG)** Plot episode of the sci-fi TV series which was later released in the theatres. The crew of the spaceship Galactica must battle their robot enemies in an attempt to reach Earth. Contains special effects designed by John "Star Wars" Dykstra. Individual episodes are also available. **125m/C VHS, DVD.** Lorne Greene, Dirk Benedict, Maren Jensen, Jane Seymour, Patrick Macnee, Terry Carter, John Colicos, Richard A. Colla, Laurette Spang, Richard Hatch; ***D:*** Richard A. Colla; ***W:*** Glen Larson, Richard A. Colla; ***C:*** Ben Colman; ***M:*** Stu Phillips. **TV**

Battlestar Galactica: The Plan **2009** The human-Cylon war, as seen through the eyes of the machines, opens with their destruction of Caprica. It then wanders off to show backstory on too many of the series's pivotal events in order to try and tie up some loose ends. A fans-only watch. **112m/C DVD.** Edward James Olmos, Tricia Helfer, Dean Stockwell, Grace Park, Michael Hogan, Michael Trucco, Callum Keith Rennie, Kate Vernon; ***D:*** Edward James Olmos; ***W:*** Jane Espenson; ***C:*** Stephen McNutt; ***M:*** Bear McCreary. **VIDEO**

Battling Bunyon 1/2 **1924** A wily youngster becomes a comedy boxer for profit, and eventually gets fed up and battles the champ. Silent. **71m/B VHS.** Chester Conklin, Wesley Barry, Mollie Malone, Jackie Fields, Paul Hurst, Frank Campeau, Johnny Relasco, Landers Stevens, Harry Mann, Pat Kemp; ***D:*** Paul Hurst.

Battling Butler 1/2 **1926** Rich young Keaton tries to impress a young lady by impersonating a boxer. All goes well until he has to fight the real thing. Mostly charming if uneven; one of Keaton's more unusual efforts, thought to be somewhat autobiographical. Silent. **70m/B VHS, DVD.** Buster Keaton, Sally O'Neil, Snitz Edwards, Francis McDonald, Mary O'Brien, Tom Wilson, Walter James; ***D:*** Buster Keaton; ***W:*** Al Boasberg, Lex Neal, Charles Henry Smith, Paul Girard Smith; ***C:*** Bert Haines, Devereaux Jennings.

Battling for Baby **1992** It's the war of the Grandmas. New mother Katherine decides to return to work and both her mother and mother-in-law want to look after the little tyke. Silly made-for-TV fluff. **93m/C VHS, DVD.** Courteney Cox, Suzanne Pleshette, Debbie Reynolds, John Terlesky, Doug McClure, Leigh Lawson, Mary Jo Catlett; ***D:*** Art Wolff; ***W:*** Walter Lockwood, Nancy Silvers.

Battling Marshal 1/2 **1948** Carson battles bad guys out to steal a family's gold-rich land. He foils a fake smallpox scare, thugs, and cheapo production values. **52m/B VHS, DVD.** Sunset Carson, Lee Roberts, Pat Gleason; ***D:*** Oliver Drake.

Battling Orioles 1/2 **1924** The once scrappy baseball team is now a bunch of grumpy old men, that is until Glenn whips them into shape. Silent. **58m/B VHS.** Glenn Tryon, Blanche Mehaffey, Noah Young; ***D:*** Ted Wilde, Fred Guiol.

Battling Outlaw 1/2 *Billy the Kid in Texas* **1940** Billy is made sheriff of a lawless Texas town after standing up to the local gang. Then he and his friend Fuzzy set out to retrieve money stolen by the gang. **64m/B VHS.** Bob Steele, Al "Fuzzy" St. John, John Merton, Terry Walker, Carleton Young, Charles "Blackie" King, Charles "Slim" Whitaker, Frank LaRue; ***D:*** Sam Newfield; ***W:*** Joseph O'Donnell; ***C:*** Jack Greenhalgh.

Battling with Buffalo Bill **1931** Twelve episodes of the vintage serial concerning the exploits of the legendary Indian fighter. **180m/B VHS.** Tom Tyler, Rex Bell, Franklyn Farnum, Lucille Browne, Francis Ford, William Desmond, Jim Thorpe, Yakima Canutt, Chief Thunderbird, Bud Osborne; ***D:*** Ray Taylor; ***W:*** Ella O'Neill, George Plympton.

The Bawdy Adventures of Tom Jones 1/2 **1976 (R)** An exploitive extension of the Fielding novel about the philandering English lad, with plenty of soft-core skin and lewdness. **89m/C VHS.** *GB* Joan Collins, Trevor Howard, Terry-Thomas, Arthur Lowe, Murray Melvin; ***D:*** Cliff Owen.

Baxter 1/2 **1989** A bull terrier lives his life with three different sets of masters. He examines all of humankind's worst faults and the viewer quickly realizes that Baxter's life depends on his refusal to obey like a good dog should. Based on the novel by Ken Greenhall. Funny, sometimes erotic, quirky comedy. In French with English subtitles. **82m/C VHS.** *FR* Lisa (Lise) Delamare, Jean Mercure, Jacques Spiesser, Catherine Ferran, Jean-Paul Roussillon, Sabrina Leurquin; ***D:*** Jerome Boivin; ***W:*** Jerome Boivin, Jacques Audiard; ***C:*** Yves Angelo; ***M:*** Marc Hillman, Patrick Roffe.

The Baxter **2005 (PG-13)** Elliot Sherman (Showalter) is so CPA mega-nerd even his sweet grandmother knows he's "the Baxter," the also-ran, the nice, safe, dull guy who never gets the girl. In the opening scene he's dumped at the altar by his beautiful fiancee Caroline (Banks) when her high school flame Bradley (Theroux) reappears. You might want to feel something for Elliot, but he's so unlikable that sympathy will be hard to find. Soon it becomes apparent that Elliot's office temp Cecil (Williams), who has been right there under his nose, is the perfect woman for him. **91m/C DVD.** *US* Michael Showalter, Elizabeth Banks, Michelle Williams, Justin Theroux, Zak Orth, Michael Ian Black, Catherine Lloyd Burns, Peter Dinklage, Paul Rudd; ***D:*** Michael Showalter; ***W:*** Michael Showalter; ***M:*** Theodore Shapiro, Craig (Shudder to Think) Wedren.

The Bay Boy 1/2 **1985 (R)** Set in the 1930s in Nova Scotia, this period piece captures the coming-of-age of a rural teenage boy. Young Sutherland's adolescent angst becomes a more difficult struggle when he witnesses a murder, and is tormented by the secret. **107m/C VHS.** *CA* Liv Ullmann, Kiefer Sutherland, Peter Donat, Matthieu Carriere, Joe MacPherson, Isabelle Mejias, Alan Scarfe, Chris Wiggins, Leah K. Pinsent; ***D:*** Daniel Petrie; ***M:*** Claude Bolling. Genie '85: Film, Support. Actor (Scarfe).

Bayou Romance **1986** Painter inherits a Louisiana plantation, moves in, and falls in love with a young gypsy. **90m/C** Annie Potts, Michael Ansara, Barbara Horan, Paul Rossilli; ***D:*** Alan Myerson.

Baywatch the Movie: Forbidden Paradise 1/2 **1995 (PG)** The "Baywatch" babes and their fellow lifesaving hunks-in-trunks head off to Hawaii to study the latest search and rescue techniques from the state's premier lifeguard team. **90m/C VHS.** David Hasselhoff, Pamela Anderson, Alexandra Paul, Yasmine Bleeth, David Charvet, Gregory Alan-Williams, Jeremy Jackson; ***D:*** Douglas Schwartz.

Be Cool **2005 (PG-13)** Paging Dr. Tarantino STAT! This turgid sequel to "Get Shorty" proves that Travolta is in need of another new-career-ectomy. Jettisoning anything even mildly cool about the witty original, director Gray instead focuses on bombast and pointless cameos in the continuing adventures of Hollywood shylock Chili Palmer (Travolta). This time, Chili tries to break into the music business with the help of a widowed record producer (Thurman) and a young ingenue (Milian). Standing in their way are Russian mobsters, gangsta rap kingpins, and Vince Vaughn doing the tired white-guy-who-thinks-he's-black routine. Even The Rock as a flamboyantly gay bodyguard can't inject any life into such a flat, unfunny mess. **112m/C VHS, DVD, UMD.** *US* John Travolta, Uma Thurman, Vince Vaughn, Cedric the Entertainer, Andre Benjamin, Robert Pastorelli, Christina Milian, Paul Adelstein, Debi Mazar, Gregory Alan Williams, Harvey Keitel, Dwayne "The Rock" Johnson, Danny DeVito, James Woods; ***D:*** F. Gary Gray; ***W:*** Peter Steinfeld; ***C:*** Jeffrey L. Kimball; ***M:*** John Powell.

Be Kind Rewind 1/2 **2008 (PG-13)** Simple guy Jerry (Black) lives in a trailer, works at a junkyard, and likes to hang out at Mr. Fletcher's (Glover) titular video rental store,where his buddy Mike (Def) works.

After a mishap at a local power plant magnetizes Jerry, accidentally erases all of the videotapes (the store is VHS only), so Jerry and Mike enlist the talents of the very cute Alma (Diaz) from the nearby dry cleaner to help them re-enact and re-record all of the movies for rental as usual. The oddball store regulars get wise to their shenanigans and everyone wants to play a part, which makes Jerry, Mike and the video store unlikely celebrities. Black is Black and the whole thing is often silly and obvious, but entertaining nonetheless. **100m/C DVD, Blu-ray Disc.** *US* Jack Black, Mos Def, Danny Glover, Mia Farrow, Melonie Diaz, Arjay Smith, Sigourney Weaver, Chandler Parker, Irv Gooch; ***D:*** Michel Gondry; ***W:*** Michel Gondry; ***C:*** Ellen Kuras; ***M:*** Jean-Michel Bernard.

Be Yourself 1/2 **1930** Thin plot contrived for Ziegfeld Follies star Brice, who stars as nightclub entertainer Fanny Field. Fanny falls for a down-and-out-boxer (Armstrong) trying to make a comeback. Brice, who was married to impresario Billy Rose at the time, sings several songs co-written by Rose, including "Cookin' Breakfast for the One I Love." **65m/B VHS.** Fanny Brice, Robert Armstrong, Harry Green, Gertrude Astor, G. Pat Collins, Marjorie "Babe" Kane; ***D:*** Thornton Freeland; ***W:*** Thornton Freeland; ***C:*** Karl Struss, Robert Planck.

The Beach **2000 (R)** DiCaprio's follow-up to the blockbuster "Titantic" is an uneven adaptation of the novel by Alex Garland concerning a group of hedonists trying to find paradise and destroying their ideal in the process. Cynical young journalist Richard (DiCaprio) meets the manic Daffy (Carlyle) in a Bangkok dive and is given a map to a supposedly unspoiled island off the Thai coast. Impulsively, Richard asks French acquaintances Francoise (Ledoyen) and Etienne (Canet) to accompany him and they discover an odd settlement of Euro-trash, headed by Sal (Swinton), amidst a marijuana plantation guarded by gun-wielding thugs. Paradise turns out to be less than paradisical. **120m/C VHS, DVD.** Leonardo DiCaprio, Tilda Swinton, Virginie Ledoyen, Guillaume Canet, Robert Carlyle, Paterson Joseph, Peter Youngblood Hills, Jerry Swindall; ***D:*** Danny Boyle; ***W:*** John Hodge; ***C:*** Darius Khondji; ***M:*** Angelo Badalamenti.

Beach Babes 2: Cave Girl Island **1995** The babes crash land on a prehistoric planet populated by horny cavemen. **78m/C VHS, DVD.** Sara Bellomo, Stephanie Hudson, Rodrigo Botero; ***D:*** David DeCoteau. **VIDEO**

Beach Babes from Beyond **1993 (R)** "HOT. TAN. ALIEN." Three words that would send shivers through the body of any red-blooded American boy. And as if alien silicone isn't enough to draw a crowd, this piece of fluff also features the relatives of big name stars hoping to cash in on the family name. Typical Hollywood cheese and sleaze should be fun for those who still can't get this kind of quality entertainment on cable. **78m/C VHS.** Joe Estevez, Don Swayze, Joey Travolta, Burt Ward, Jacqueline Stallone, Linnea Quigley, Sara Bellomo, Tamara Landry, Nicole Posey; ***D:*** David DeCoteau.

Beach Blanket Bingo **1965** Fifth entry in the "Beach Party" series (after "Pajama Party") is by far the best and has achieved near-cult status. Both Funicello and Avalon are back, but this time a very young Evans catches Avalon's eye. Throw in a mermaid, some moon-doggies, skydiving, sizzling beach parties, and plenty of nostalgic golly-gee-whiz fun and you have the classic '60s beach movie. Totally implausible, but that's half the fun when the sun-worshipping teens become involved in a kidnapping and occasionally break into song. Followed by "How to Stuff a Wild Bikini." ♫ Beach Blanket Bingo; The Cycle Set; Fly Boy; The Good Times; I Am My Ideal; I Think You Think; It Only Hurts When I Cry; New Love; You'll Never Change Him. **96m/C VHS, DVD.** Frankie Avalon, Annette Funicello, Linda Evans, Don Rickles, Buster Keaton, Paul Lynde, Harvey Lembeck, Deborah Walley, John Ashley, Jody McCrea, Marta Kristen, Timothy Carey, Earl Wilson, Bobbi Shaw, Brian Wilson; ***D:*** William Asher; ***W:*** William Asher, Sher Townsend, Leo Townsend; ***C:*** Floyd Crosby; ***M:*** Les Baxter.

Beach Girls **1982 (R)** Three voluptuous coeds intend to re-educate a bookish young man and the owner of a beach house. **91m/C VHS, DVD.** Debra Blee, Val Kline, Jeana Tomasina, Adam Roarke, Paul Richards; ***D:*** Patrice Townsend; ***C:*** Michael D. Murphy.

The Beach Girls and the Monster *Monster in the Surf; Monster from the Surf* **1965** Here's one on the cutting edge of genre bending: while it meticulously maintains the philosophical depth and production values of '60s beach bimbo fare, it manages to graft successfully with the heinous critter from the sea genre to produce a hybrid horror with acres o' flesh. **70m/B VHS, DVD.** Jon Hall, Sue Casey, Walker Edmiston, Arnold Lessing, Elaine DuPont, Dale Davis; ***D:*** Jon Hall; ***W:*** Joan Gardner; ***C:*** Dale Davis; ***M:*** Frank Sinatra Jr.

Beach Hotel *Playa Azul; Blue Beach* **1992** Accused of fraud, a politican escapes to a remote and semi-abandoned hotel that he owns. He summons his family to decide what to do next, hoping his friends will also assist him. But his friends refuse their aid, and even his family eventually abandons him to his fate. Spanish with subtitles. **96m/C VHS, DVD.** *SP* Sergio Bustamante, Pilar Pellicer, Mercedes Olea; ***D:*** Alfredo Joskowicz; ***W:*** Alfredo Joskowicz; ***C:*** Rodolfo Sanchez; ***M:*** Amparo Rubin.

Beach House **1982** In this boring comedy, adolescents frolic on the beach, get inebriated, and listen to rock 'n' roll. **76m/C VHS.** Kathy McNeil, Richard Duggan, Ileana Seidel, John Cosola, Spence Waugh, Paul W.S. Anderson, John A. Gallagher; ***D:*** John A. Gallagher; ***W:*** Marino Amaruso, John A. Gallagher.

Beach Kings 1/2 *Green Flash* **2008 (PG-13)** Thirty-year-old Cameron Day (Charvet) is a former college basketball star who couldn't stand the pressure of trying to make a pro career. A chance meeting with Mia (DeVitto) has Cam returning to sports as a pro beach volleyball player but as the pressures build again so do his own insecurities. **95m/C DVD.** David Charvet, Torrey DeVitto, Brody Hutzler, Kristin Cavallari, Court Young, Jaleel White, Bret Roberts; ***D:*** Paul Nihipali; ***W:*** Paul Nihipali; ***C:*** David Waldman; ***M:*** Craig Eastman. **VIDEO**

Beach Party **1963** Started the "Beach Party" series with the classic Funicello/Avalon combo. Scientist Cummings studying the mating habits of teenagers intrudes on a group of surfers, beach bums, and bikers, to his lasting regret. Typical beach party bingo, with sand, swimsuits, singing, dancing, and bare minimum in way of a plot. Followed by "Muscle Beach Party." ♫ Beach Party; Don't Stop Now; Promise Me Anything; Secret Surfin' Spot; Surfin' and a-Swingin'; Treat Him Nicely. **101m/C VHS, DVD.** Frankie Avalon, Annette Funicello, Harvey Lembeck, Robert Cummings, Dorothy Malone, Morey Amsterdam, Jody McCrea, John Ashley, Candy Johnson, Dolores Wells, Yvette Vickers, Eva Six, Brian Wilson, Vincent Price, Peter Falk, Dick Dale; ***D:*** William Asher; ***W:*** Lou Rusoff; ***C:*** Kay Norton; ***M:*** Les Baxter.

Beachcomber *Vessel of Wrath* **1938** Comedy set in the Dutch East Indies about a shiftless beachcomber (Laughton) who falls in love with a missionary's prim sister (Lanchester), as she attempts to reform him. The real-life couple of Laughton and Lanchester are their usual pleasure to watch. Remade in 1954. Story by W. Somerset Maugham. **88m/B VHS.** *GB* Charles Laughton, Elsa Lanchester, Robert Newton, Tyrone Guthrie; ***D:*** Erich Pommer.

Beaches 1/2 **1988 (PG-13)** Based on the novel by Iris Rainer Dart about two girls whose friendship survived the test of time. The friendship is renewed once more when one of the now middle-aged women learns that she is dying slowly of a fatal disease. **123m/C VHS, DVD.** Bette Midler, Barbara Hershey, John Heard, Spalding Gray, Lainie Kazan, James Read, Mayim Bialik; ***D:*** Garry Marshall; ***W:*** Mary Agnes Donoghue; ***C:*** Dante Spinotti; ***M:*** Georges Delerue.

Beaks: The Movie **WOOF!** *Birds of Prey* **1987 (R)** Two TV reporters try to figure out why birds of prey are suddenly attacking humans. Owes nothing to Hitchcock's "The Birds." **86m/C VHS, DVD.** Christopher Atkins, Michelle Johnson; ***D:*** Rene Cardona Jr.

Bean **1997 (PG-13)** Big screen adaptation of rubber-faced Atkinson's Mr. Bean character finds disaster-magnet hero working as a guard in London's National Gallery. When a famous painting is purchased by a museum in L.A., the Gallery's curators jump at the chance to send Bean along with the painting as an "expert," although he is nearly mute and definitely not qualified. David (MacNicol), the American curator, invites him to stay at his house, much to the dismay of his wife and children. Bean, of course, wrecks the painting, ruins David's marriage and career, and generally makes an ass out of himself. He then resourcefully (and sometimes accidentally) puts things right. Atkinson proves himself a master of the almost lost art of slapstick comedy. **92m/C VHS, DVD.** *GB* Rowan Atkinson, Peter MacNichol, Pamela Reed, Harris Yulin, Burt Reynolds, Larry Drake, Johnny Galecki, Richard Gant, Tom McGowan, Dakin Matthews, Peter Capaldi, Sandra Oh, Tricia Vessey, Peter Egan; ***D:*** Mel Smith; ***W:*** Richard Curtis, Robin Driscoll; ***C:*** Francis Kenny; ***M:*** Howard Goodall.

Beanstalk 1/2 **1994 (PG)** Modern-day version of the fairytale finds young Jack Taylor (Daniels) scheming to make it big to help his hardworking single mom. He meets up with a wacky scientist (Kidder), who gives Jack some recently discovered seeds that naturally grow into an enormous beanstalk. And what does Jack find when he climbs the beanstalk—why an entire family of silly giants. **80m/C VHS.** J.D. Daniels, Margot Kidder, Richard Moll, Amy Stock-Poynton, Patrick Renna, Richard Paul, David Naughton, Stuart Pankin, Cathy McAuley; ***D:*** Michael Davis; ***W:*** Michael Davis; ***M:*** Kevin Bassinson.

The Bear *L'Ours* **1989 (PG)** Breathtaking, effortlessly entertaining family film (from France) about an orphaned bear cub tagging after a grown Kodiak male and dealing with hunters. The narrative is essentially from the cub's point of view, with very little dialogue. A huge money-maker in Europe; shot on location in the Dolomites and the Candian Arctic. Based on the 1917 novel "The Grizzly King" by James Oliver Curwood. **92m/C VHS, DVD.** *FR* Jack Wallace, Tcheky Karyo, Andre Lacombe; ***D:*** Jean-Jacques Annaud; ***W:*** Gerard Brach, Michael Kane; ***C:*** Philippe Rousselot; ***M:*** Bill Conti.

Bear Island 1/2 **1980 (PG)** Group of secret agents cleverly disguising themselves as U.N. weather researchers converge upon Bear Island in search of a Nazi U-Boat. Looks like rain. **118m/C VHS.** Donald Sutherland, Richard Widmark, Barbara Parkins, Vanessa Redgrave, Christopher Lee, Lloyd Bridges; ***D:*** Don Sharp.

Bear Ye One Another's Burden... *Einer Trage des Anderen Last* **1988** In the early 50s, communist police officer Josef Heilinger (Pose) is sent to a private sanitorium for consumptives. He's forced to share a room with a young Protestant curate, Hubertus Koschenz (Mock). Their ill health is the only thing they have in common, and they deliberately seem to annoy each other, but soon their situation has them grudgingly developing a mutual respect and even friendship. German with subtitles. **118m/C VHS.** *GE* Jorg Pose, Manfred Mock, Susanne Luning, Dieter Knaup; ***D:*** Lothar Warneke; ***C:*** Peter Ziesche; ***M:*** Gunther Fischer.

The Bears & I **1974 (G)** A young Vietnam vet helps Indians regain their land rights while raising three bear cubs. Beautiful photography in this Disney production. **89m/C VHS, DVD.** Patrick Wayne, Chief Dan George, Andrew Duggan, Michael Ansara; ***D:*** Bernard McEveety; ***W:*** Jack Speirs, John Whedon; ***C:*** Ted D. Landon; ***M:*** Buddy (Norman Dale) Baker.

The Beast 1/2 *La Bete* **1975** Long considered taboo due to its erotic subject matter, this 1975 French film from director Borowczyk arrives in its uncensored form for the first time in 2000. Young heiress Lucy Broadhurst (Hummel) arrives at the de l'Esperance chateau, where she is to marry the young Mathurn de l'Esperance (Benedetti). After retiring to her room, Lucy finds herself dreaming of the 18th-century lady of the chateau, Romilda de l'Esperance (Lane), who according to legend, encountered a wild, sexual monster in the forest near the manor. Was this an isolated incident or does the Beast still roam the grounds? The once shocking sex scenes will be considered quite tame by today's audience, and some of them come across as quite silly. **94m/C DVD.** Sirpa Lane, Lisbeth Hummel, Elizabeth Kaza, Pierre Benedetti, Guy Trejan; ***D:*** Walerian Borowczyk; ***W:*** Walerian Borowczyk; ***C:*** Bernard Daillencourt, Marcel Grignon.

The Beast 1/2 *The Beast of War* **1988 (R)** Violent and cliche-driven war drama notable for its novel twist: wild Russian tank officer becomes lost in the Afghanistan wilderness while being tracked by Afghan rebels with revenge in mind. Filmed in the Israel desert and adapted by William Mastrosimone from his play. **93m/C VHS, DVD.** George Dzundza, Jason Patric, Steven Bauer, Stephen Baldwin, Don Harvey, Kabir Bedi, Erik Avari, Haim Gerafi; ***D:*** Kevin Reynolds; ***W:*** William Mastrosimone; ***C:*** Doug Milsome; ***M:*** Mark Isham.

The Beast *Peter Benchley's The Beast* **1996 (PG-13)** Benchley once again terrorizes a small coastal community with a giant sea creature that preys on sailors and divers. When a poacher's attempts to capture the creature result in further disaster, a fishing boat captain, a Coast Guard officer, and a marine biologist set sail to to kill the critter. **116m/C VHS.** William L. Petersen, Karen Sillas, Charles Martin Smith, Ronald Guttman, Missy (Melissa) Crider, Sterling Macer, Denis Arndt, Larry Drake; ***D:*** Jeff Bleckner; ***W:*** J.B. White; ***C:*** Geoff Burton; ***M:*** Don Davis. **TV**

The Beast from Haunted Cave **1960** Gold thieves hiding in a wilderness cabin encounter a spiderlike monster. Surprisingly good performances from Sinatra (Frank's nephew) and Carol. Produced by Gene Corman, Roger's brother. **64m/B VHS, DVD.** Michael Forest, Sheila Carol, Frank Wolff, Richard Sinatra, Wally Campo; ***D:*** Monte Hellman; ***W:*** Charles B. Griffith; ***C:*** Andrew M. Costikyan.

The Beast from 20,000 Fathoms 1/2 **1953** Atomic testing defrosts a giant dinosaur in the Arctic; the hungry monster proceeds onwards to its former breeding grounds, now New York City. Oft-imitated saurian-on-the-loose formula is still fun, brought to life by Ray Harryhausen special effects. Based loosely on the Ray Bradbury story "The Foghorn." **80m/B VHS, DVD.** Paul (Christian) Hubschmid, Paula Raymond, Cecil Kellaway, Kenneth Tobey, Donald Woods, Lee Van Cleef, Steve Brodie, Mary Hill, Jack Pennick, Ross Elliot; ***D:*** Eugene Lourie; ***W:*** Eugene Lourie, Fred Freiberger, Louis Morheim, Robert Smith; ***C:*** John L. "Jack" Russell; ***M:*** David Buttolph.

Beast in the Cellar 1/2 *Are You Dying Young Man?* **1970 (R)** Every family has something to hide, and in the case of two spinster sisters, it's their murderous inhuman brother, whom they keep chained in the cellar. Like all brothers, however, the "beast" rebels against his sisters' bossiness and escapes to terrorize their peaceful English countryside. The sisters' (Reid and Robson) performances aren't bad, but rest of effort is fairly disappointing. **85m/C VHS, DVD.** *GB* Beryl Reid, Flora Robson, T.P. McKenna; ***D:*** James Kelly.

The Beast Must Die *Black Werewolf* **1975 (PG)** A millionaire sportsman invites a group of men and women connected with bizarre deaths or the eating of human flesh to spend the cycle of a full moon at his isolated lodge. **93m/C VHS, DVD.** *GB* Peter Cushing, Calvin Lockhart, Charles Gray, Anton Diffring, Marlene Clark, Ciaran Madden, Tom Chadbon, Michael Gambon; ***D:*** Paul Annett; ***W:*** Michael Winder; ***C:*** Jack Hildyard; ***M:*** Douglas Gamley.

The Beast of Babylon Against the Son of Hercules *Goliath, King of the Slaves; Hero of Babylon; L'Eroe di Babilonia* **1963** Nippur (Gordon) probably doesn't have any filial bond to Hercules but it's a convenient hook for this dubbed Italian flick. Tyrant Balthazar (Lulli) rules Assyria, sacrificing virgins to the goddess Istar. Nippur, the rightful heir to the throne, leads a slave revolt to overthrow the bloodthirsty ruler. **98m/C DVD.** *IT* Gordon Scott, Genevieve Grad, Pierro Lulli, Andrea Scotti, Moira Orfei, Mario Petri; ***D:***

Siro Marcellini; *W:* Siro Marcellini, Gian Paolo Callegari, Albert Valentin; *C:* Pier Ludovico Pavoni; *M:* Carlo Franci.

Beast of Morocco *Hand of Night* **1966** Interesting vampire film about a Morrocan vampire princess who sets her sights on seducing a noted archaeologist. Of course his girlfriend ends up being abducted by the vampire's servant. **88m/C VHS.** *GB* William Sylvester, Alizia Gur, Terence de Marney, Diane Clare, Edward Underdown, William Dexter, Sylvia Marriott; *D:* Frederick Goode; *W:* Bruce Stewart; *C:* William Jordan; *M:* John Shakespeare.

The Beast of the City **1932** Crime melodrama that ends in a violent machine-gun rubout, making you wonder just who the good guys are. Chicago police captain Jim Fitzpatrick (Huston) is obsessed with cleaning up the city but crime boss Belmonte (Hersholt) gets off because he has city and police officials on his payroll. When Jim becomes a hero foiling a bank robbery, public opinion demands he be appointed the new police commissioner and his first order is to get Belmonte by any means necessary. Harlow plays gun moll Daisy. **85m/B DVD.** Walter Huston, Jean Harlow, Jean Hersholt, Wallace Ford, Dorothy Peterson, Tully Marshall, Emmett Corrigan; *D:* Charles Brabin; *W:* John Lee Mahin; *C:* Norbert Brodine.

Beast of the Yellow Night WOOF! **1970 (R)** A dying soldier sells his soul to Satan at the close of WWII. Years later, existing without aging, he periodically turns into a cannibal monster. Although the first half is tedious, the monster turns things around when he finally shows up. Decent gore effects. **87m/C VHS, DVD.** *PH* John Ashley, Mary Wilcox, Eddie Garcia, Vic Diaz; *D:* Eddie Romero.

The Beast of Yucca Flats WOOF! **1961** A really cheap, quasi-nuclear protest film. A Russian scientist is chased by communist agents into a nuclear testing area and is caught in an atomic blast. As a result, he turns into a club-weilding monster. Voice over narration is used in lieu of dialogue as that process proved too expensive. **53m/B VHS, DVD.** Tor Johnson, Douglas Mellor, Larry Aten, Barbara Francis, Conrad Brooks, Anthony Cardoza, Bing Stafford, John Morrison; *D:* Coleman Francis; *W:* Coleman Francis; *C:* John Cagle; *M:* Irwin Nafshun, Al Remington.

The Beast That Killed Women 1/2 **1965** Colonists at a sunny Florida nudist camp have their beach party interrupted by an escaped gorilla. Director Mahon, in his first color effort, stretches this panicky moment into an hour of fleshy fun and games. **60m/C VHS, DVD.** Darlene Bennett, Gigi Darlene, June Roberts; *D:* Barry Mahon; *W:* Barry Mahon; *C:* Barry Mahon.

The Beast with Five Fingers 1/2 **1946** After a pianist mysteriously dies and leaves his fortune to his private nurse, the occupants of his villa are terrorized by a creature that turns out to be the pianist's hand which was severed by his personal secretary (Lorre). Lorre is also terrorized by hallucinations of the hand, and no matter what he does to stop it (nail it to a desk, throw it in the fire, etc.), nothing can keep the hand from carrying out its mission. A creepy thriller with inventive shots of the severed hand. **88m/B VHS.** Robert Alda, Andrea King, Peter Lorre, Victor Francen, J. Carrol Naish, Charles Dingle; *D:* Robert Florey; *W:* Curt Siodmak; *M:* Max Steiner.

The Beast Within **1982 (R)** Young woman has the misfortune of being raped by an unseen creature in a Mississippi swamp. Seventeen years later, her son conceived from that hellish union begins to act quite strange, developing a penchant for shedding his skin before turning into an insect-like critter with a cannibalistic appetite. First film to use the air "bladder" type of prosthetic make-up popularized in later, and generally better, horror films. Contains some choice cuts in photo editing: the juxtaposition of hamburger and human "dead meat" is witty. Based on Edward Levy's 1981 novel. **98m/C VHS, DVD.** Ronny Cox, Bibi Besch, L.Q. Jones, Paul Clemens, Don Gordon, Katherine Moffat, John Dennis Johnston, R.G. Armstrong, Logan Ramsey, Ron Soble, Meshach Taylor; *D:* Philippe Mora; *W:* Tom Holland; *C:* Jack L. Richards; *M:* Les Baxter.

Beast Within *Virus Undead* **2008 (R)** Yet another zombie flick with a too-predictable plot (this time from Germany). Medical student Robert and his friends are whooping it up in his grandfather's country mansion when zombies (infected by diseased birds) come a-callin'. **93m/C DVD.** *GE* Philipp Danne, Anna Breuer, Marvin Gronen, Birthe Wolter, Alex Attimoneilli; *D:* Wolf Wolff; *W:* Wolf Janke; *C:* Heiko Rahnenfuhrer.

Beastly **2010 (PG-13)** Modern retelling of the "Beauty and the Beast" story that's based on the novel by Alex Finn. Wealthy and handsome Kyle Kingson (Pettyfer) also has a mean streak, but he humiliates the wrong classmate when Kendra (Olsen) uses a spell to transform Kyle into a repulsive character. Banished to Brooklyn seclusion, his curse can only be lifted if Kyle can find someone to love him as he is. So he makes a deal with desperate Linda Taylor (Hudgens) who moves in and becomes his companion. **m/C DVD.** *US* Vanessa Anne Hudgens, Alex Pettyfer, Mary-Kate Olsen, Peter Krause, Neil Patrick Harris, Lisa Gay Hamilton; *D:* Daniel Barnz; *W:* Daniel Barnz; *C:* Mandy Walker; *M:* Marcelo Zarvos.

Beastmaster **1982 (PG)** Adventure set in a wild and primitive world. The Beastmaster is involved in a life-and-death struggle with overwhelming forces of evil. Campy neanderthal flesh flick. **119m/C VHS, DVD.** Marc Singer, Tanya Roberts, Rip Torn, John Amos, Josh Milrad, Billy Jacoby, Ben Hammer; *D:* Don A. Coscarelli; *W:* Don A. Coscarelli, Paul Pepperman; *C:* John Alcott; *M:* Lee Holdridge.

Beastmaster 2: Through the Portal of Time 1/2 **1991 (PG-13)** This time the laughs are intentional as the Beastmaster follows an evil monarch through a dimensional gate to modern-day L.A., where the shopping is better for both trendy clothes and weapons. Fun for genre fans, with a behind-the-scenes featurette on the tape. **107m/C VHS.** Marc Singer, Kari Wuhrer, Sarah Douglas, Wings Hauser, James Avery, Robert Fieldsteel, Arthur Malet, Robert Z'Dar, Michael Berryman; *D:* Sylvio Tabet; *M:* Robert Folk.

Beastmaster 3: The Eye of Braxus 1/2 **1995 (PG)** Heroic hunk Dar the Beastmaster (Singer) returns to battle evil. Lord Agon (Warner) needs to obtain a jeweled eye that will bring the demon Braxus back to life—and he'll stop at nothing, including kidnapping Dar's brother King Tal (Van Dien), to reach his terrifying goal. But Dar isn't alone—he's got the bewitching sorceress Morgana (Down), tempting warrioress Shada (Hess), and loyal advisor Seth (Todd) to help him out. **92m/C VHS.** Marc Singer, David Warner, Lesley-Anne Down, Tony Todd, Casper Van Dien, Keith Coulouris, Sandra Hess, Patrick Kilpatrick; *D:* Gabrielle Beaumont; *W:* David Wise; *C:* Barbara Claman; *M:* Jan Hammer.

Beasts **1983** A young couple's plans for a romantic weekend in the Rockies are slightly changed when the pair are savagely attacked by wild beasts. **92m/C VHS.** Tom Babson, Kathy Christopher, Vern Potter; *D:* Don Hawks.

The Beat **1988** Unrealistic film about a bookish new kid who intercedes in the tension between two rival street gangs, changing their lives in his literary way. **101m/C VHS.** John Savage, Kara Glover, Paul Dillon, David Jacobson, William McNamara; *D:* Peter Mones; *W:* Peter Mones; *M:* Carter Burwell.

Beat **2000** Disappointing look at the events leading up to William S. Burroughs's shooting of his wife in Mexico in 1951. Tangled hetero- and homosexual relationships and unrequited longings between future literarati Burroughs (Sutherland), his wife (Love), Allen Ginsberg (Livingston), Lucien Carr (Reedus), and Jack Kerouac (Martinez) should've provided more spark, but the indifferent direction and poor script give the actors little to work with. **89m/C VHS, DVD.** Courtney Love, Kiefer Sutherland, Ron Livingston, Kyle Secor, Daniel Martinez, Sam Trammell; *D:* Gary Walkow; *W:* Gary Walkow; *C:* Ciro Cabello; *M:* Ernest Troost.

Beat Girl *Wild for Kicks* **1960** Pouty rebellious teen Jennifer (Hill) spends her days in art school and her nights at a London beat hangout. She's jealous when daddy (Farrar) marries sexy French Nichole (Adam) and plots to break them up. When Jennifer discovers Nichole's sordid past she winds up in a burlesque club, attracting the unsavory attentions of owner Kenny (Lee). Then Kenny winds up dead. Singer Adam Faith performs and Reed has a bit as a youthful tough. **85m/B VHS, DVD.** *GB* Gillian Hills, David Farrar, Noelle Adam, Christopher Lee, Shirley Anne Field, Oliver Reed, Nada Beall, Adam Faith, Nigel Green, Claire Gordon; *D:* Edmond T. Greville; *W:* Dail Ambler; *C:* Walter Lassally; *M:* John Barry.

The Beat My Heart Skipped *De batter mon coeur s'est arrete* **2005** In adapting James Toback's 1978 "Fingers," French director Audiard changed the place (from New York to Paris), the pace (more somber and less high-strung), and the names—but the heart of the story stayed the same. Here Thomas Seyr (Duris, in Harvey Keitel's "Johnny Fingers" role) does his dad's dirty collections work in crooked real estate schemes though it repulses him. But when his long-discarded dreams of becoming a concert pianist reemerge, the pull between his two lives proves more than he can bear. **107m/C DVD.** *FR* Romain Duris, Niels Arestrup, Linh Dan Pham, Emmanuelle Devos, Jonathan Zaccai, Gilles Cohen, Anton Yakovlev, Melanie Laurent; *D:* Jacques Audiard; *W:* Jacques Audiard, Tonino Benaquista; *C:* Stephane Fontaine. British Acad. '05: Foreign Film.

Beat Street 1/2 **1984 (PG)** Intended as a quick cash-in on the break dancing trend, this essentially plotless musical features kids trying to break into local show biz with their rapping and dancing skills. Features the music of Afrika Bambaata and the Soul Sonic Force, Grand Master Melle Mel and the Furious Five, and others. ♫Beat Street Breakdown; Baptize the Beat; Stranger in a Strange Land; Beat Street Strut; Us Girls; This Could Be the Night; Breakers Revenge; Tu Carino (Carmen's Theme); Frantic Situation. **106m/C VHS, DVD.** Rae Dawn Chong, Leon Grant, Saundra Santiago, Guy Davis, Jon Chardiet, Duane Jones, Kadeem Hardison; *D:* Stan Lathan; *W:* Andrew Davis.

Beat the Devil **1953** Each person on a slow boat to Africa has a scheme to beat the other passengers to the uranium-rich land that they all hope to claim. An unusual black comedy which didn't fare well when released, but over the years has come to be the epitome of spy-spoofs. **89m/C VHS, DVD.** Humphrey Bogart, Gina Lollobrigida, Peter Lorre, Robert Morley, Jennifer Jones, Edward Underdown, Ivor Barnard, Bernard Lee, Marco Tulli; *D:* John Huston; *W:* John Huston, Truman Capote; *C:* Oswald Morris; *M:* Franco Mannino.

Beatlemania! The Movie *Beatlemania* **1981** Boring look at the Fab Four. Not the real Beatles, but impersonators who do a very inadequate job. Based on the equally disappointing stage show. **86m/C VHS.** Mitch Weissman, Ralph Castelli, David Leon, Tom Teeley; *D:* Joseph Manduke.

The Beatniks **1960** Story about the dark secrets of the beat generation in which a man is promised fame and fortune by an agent, but his dreams are dashed when his friend commits murder. A big waste of time. **78m/B VHS, DVD.** Tony Travis, Peter Breck, Karen Kadler, Joyce Terry, Sam Edwards, Bob Wells; *D:* Paul Frees; *W:* Paul Frees; *C:* Murray Deatley; *M:* Stanley Wilson.

Beatrice 1/2 *La Passion Beatrice* **1988 (R)** In France during the Middle Ages, a barbaric soldier of the Hundred Years' War returns to his estate that his daughter has maintained, only to brutalize and abuse her. In French with English subtitles. **132m/C VHS.** *FR* Julie Delpy, Barnard Pierre Donnadieu, Nils (Niels) Tavernier; *D:* Bertrand Tavernier; *W:* Colo Tavernier O'Hagan; *C:* Bruno de Keyzer; *M:* Lili Boulanger. Cesar '88: Costume Des.

Beau Brummel 1/2 **1924** The famous silent adaptation of the Clyde Fitch play about an ambitious English dandy's rise and fall. **80m/B VHS.** John Barrymore, Mary Astor, Willard Louis, Irene Rich, Carmel Myers, Alec B. Francis, William Humphreys; *D:* Harry Beaumont.

Beau Brummel **1954** Lavish production casts Granger in the role of the rags-to-riches dandy and chief adviser to the Prince of Wales. Born into a life of poverty, George Bryan Brummel uses wit and intelligence to meet the vain Prince and ingratiate himself to the future king (George IV). He also manages to catch the eye of Taylor, who falls in love with him. Outstanding period piece cinematography, sets, and costumes. Shot on location in England's beautiful countryside, many of the interior shots are from a 15th-century mansion, Ockwell Manor, located near Windsor Castle. Remake of the 1924 silent film starring John Barrymore. Based on the play by Clyde Fitch. **113m/C VHS.** Stewart Granger, Elizabeth Taylor, Peter Ustinov, Robert Morley, James Donald, James Hayter, Rosemary Harris, Paul Rogers, Noel Willman, Peter Dyneley, Charles Carson; *D:* Curtis Bernhardt; *W:* Karl Tunberg; *C:* Oswald Morris.

Beau Brummell: This Charming Man 1/2 **2006** Brummell (Purefoy) is a Regency dandy who changes the powders, perfumes, and foppery of male dress to one of elegance and expensive simplicity. He does a makeover on the Prince of Wales (Bonneville) and uses his royal connection to further his extravagant lifestyle. Then Beau meets the much more fascinating Lord Byron (Rhys), falls out of royal favor, and winds up in greatly-reduced circumstances. Based on Ian Kelly's biography. **79m/C DVD.** *GB* James Purefoy, Hugh Bonneville, Matthew Rhys, Anthony Calf, Nicholas (Nick) Rowe, Philip Davis, Zoe Telford; *D:* Philippa Lowthorpe; *W:* Simon Bent; *C:* Graham Smith; *M:* Peter Salem. **TV**

Beau Geste 1/2 **1939** The classic Hollywood adventure film based on the Percival Christopher Wren novel. To protect aging Lady Patricia (Thatcher), who raised the orphaned brothers, Beau Geste (Cooper) takes the blame for a jewel theft and decides to enlist in the Foreign Legion. He's followed by his brothers John (Milland) and Digby (Preston), and all face desert wars and despicable officers, including the psychotic Sgt. Markoff (Donlevy). A rousing, much-copied epic. **114m/B VHS, DVD.** Gary Cooper, Ray Milland, Robert Preston, Brian Donlevy, Donald O'Connor, J. Carrol Naish, Susan Hayward, James Stephenson, Albert Dekker, Broderick Crawford, Charles T. Barton, Heather Thatcher, James Burke, G.P. (Tim) Huntley Jr., Harold Huber, Harvey Stephens, Stanley Andrews, Harry Woods, Arthur Aylesworth, Henry (Kleinbach) Brandon, Nestor Paiva, George Chandler, George Regas; *D:* William A. Wellman; *W:* Robert Carson; *C:* Theodor Sparkuhl, Louis Clyde Stouman, Archie Stout; *M:* Alfred Newman.

Beau Pere *Stepfather* **1981** Bittersweet satiric romp from Blier about the war zone of modern romance, wherein 14-year-old Besse pursues her 30-year-old irresponsible, widowed stepfather (Dewaere). Sharp-edged and daring. In French with subtitles. **125m/C VHS, DVD.** *FR* Patrick Dewaere, Nathalie Baye, Ariel Besse, Maurice Ronet, Genevieve Mnich, Maurice Risch, Macha Meril, Rose Thiery; *D:* Bertrand Blier; *W:* Bertrand Blier; *C:* Sacha Vierny; *M:* Philippe Sarde.

Beau Revel 1/2 **1921** Critically acclaimed romantic drama of the silent era. A passionate dancing girl played by Vidor, one of the '20s' more prolific romantic leads (and erstwhile wife of director King Vidor) is the object of romantic interest of a father and son, which leaves the threesome lovelorn, suicidal, and emotionally scarred. You might recognize Stone from his later role as Judge Hardy in the MGM "Hardy Family" series. **70m/B VHS.** Lewis Stone, Florence Vidor, Lloyd Hughes, Katherine Kirkham, William Conklin; *D:* John Griffith Wray.

Beau Travail 1/2 **1998** Very loose adaptation of Melville's "Billy Budd" is set in the French Foreign Legion at an outpost near Djibouti in Africa. Second-in-command Galoup (Lavant) tries to break popular new soldier Sentain (Colin) before he can become the Commandant's favorite. Visual style and attention to the male form take precedence over the story itself, which is mostly provided in Galoup's flashback narration. French with subtitles. **89m/C VHS, DVD.** *FR* Denis Lavant,

Michel Subor, Gregoire Colin; *D:* Claire Denis; *W:* Claire Denis, Jean-Pol Fargeau; *C:* Agnes Godard.

Beaufort 1/2 **2007** A fascinating, intense look at the strife in the Middle East through the eyes of soldiers who have lived their entire lives under the shadow of conflict. As the 18-year Israeli occupation of the medieval Lebanese castle Beaufort comes to an end, the soldiers pray to survive random Hezbollah bombing attacks while waiting out the days until withdrawal. As the bombings increase, commander Liberti (Cohen) and his troops must hold on to hope while trying to manage the tedium of holding a castle for largely symbolic purposes. Film avoids political commentary and instead explores the minds of soldiers on the ground, to excellent effect. **125m/C DVD.** *IS* Oshri Cohen, Ohad Knoller, Eli Eltonyo, Gal Friedman, Nevo Kimchi, Daniel Brook; *D:* Joseph Cedar; *W:* Joseph Cedar; *C:* Ofer Inov; *M:* Ishai Adar.

Beaumarchais the Scoundrel 1/2 *Beaumarchais L'Insolent* **1996** Adapted from an unpublished play by Sacha Guitry. Beautifully filmed romp of the social-climbing and political-spying gadfly Pierre Augustin Caron de Beaumarchais. Molinaro has simplified the fantastic life of the 18th-century dramatist, courtier, and watchmaker to Louis XV (and author of the comic masterpieces "The Barber of Seville" and "The Marriage of Figaro") but the result is still dizzying. French with subtitles. **100m/C VHS.** *FR* Fabrice Luchini, Jacques Weber, Michel Piccoli, Claire Nebout, Jean-Francois Balmer, Florence Thomassin, Michel Serrault, Dominique Besnehard, Jean-Claude Brialy, Murray Head, Jeff Nuttal, Jean Yanne, Manuel Blanc, Sandrine Kiberlain, Axelle Laffont; *D:* Edouard Molinaro; *W:* Edouard Molinaro, Jean-Claude Brisville; *C:* Michael Epp; *M:* Jean-Claude Petit.

The Beautician and the Beast **1997 (PG)** Evita meets Lucille Ball when TV's "Nanny" enters Eastern Europe whining to conquer fictional "Slovetzia" royalty. Camp comedy casts Drescher as Joy, a beautician who becomes a local hero after a fire in her beauty class and is subsequently hired by a visiting emissary to tutor the children of despotic dictator Pochenko (Dalton). Overridingly well-known caricatures, loosely based on the fairy tale "Beauty and the Beast," as well as a host of old-time, culture clash movies ("The King and I," "Sound of Music"), where the humble nanny attempts to bring joy (get it?) into the life of a man who carries the weight of the world on his shoulders. Lensed in Prague inside a Gothic, 17th-century castle. Pleasant enough, if not original, time-killer. **105m/C VHS, DVD.** Fran Drescher, Timothy Dalton, Ian McNeice, Patrick Malahide, Lisa Jakub, Michael Lerner, Phyllis Newman; *D:* Ken Kwapis; *W:* Todd Graff; *C:* Peter Lyons Collister; *M:* Cliff Eidelman.

Beauties of the Night *Night Beauties; Les Belles de Nuit* **1952** Dreamy fantasy finds a shy music teacher (Philipe) escaping from his boring life into romantic adventures with beautiful women. But his dreams slowly turn nightmarish and he's forced to deal with reality—and real love. French with subtitles. **89m/B VHS.** *FR* Gerard Philipe, Gina Lollobrigida, Martine Carol, Magali Vendeuil, Paolo Stoppa, Raymond Bussieres, Raymond Cordy; *D:* Rene Clair; *W:* Rene Clair; *C:* Armand Thirard; *M:* Georges Van Parys.

Beautiful **2000 (PG-13)** Field's directorial debut is a cloying beauty pageant satire that wants you to like it. REALLY wants you to like it. Unfortunately, the jokes and characters are U-G-L-Y and they ain't got no alibi. Minnie Driver is Mona, a bright girl from an abusive home who escapes her grim reality by trying to win beauty pageants. She's shown as a little ugly duckling who uses any means necessary to win her way up the escalating ladder of swimsuitability. Finally, she qualifies for the Holy Grail of beauty pageants, the Miss American Miss competition. Along the way, however, she has become a single mother, which automatically disqualifies her as a contestant. She comes up with a plan where her daughter Vanessa (Pepsi prodigy and demon-child Hallie Kate Eisenberg) is passed off as the child of her patient best friend Ruby (Adams). Mona then screeches complaints about the kid's behavior being a distraction to her goal (which is no way to treat your child, even if she is Satan's hand-puppet) while an ambitious reporter (Stefanson) tries to reveal her secret. Overly padded, and it doesn't even have a nice personality. **112m/C VHS, DVD.** Minnie Driver, Hallie Kate Eisenberg, Joey Lauren Adams, Kathleen Turner, Leslie Stefanson, Bridgette Wilson-Sampras, Kathleen Robertson, Michael McKean, Gary Collins, Brent Briscoe; *D:* Sally Field; *W:* Jon Bernstein; *C:* Robert Yeoman; *M:* John (Gianni) Frizzell.

Beautiful Beast *XX: Utukushiki Gakuen; XX Beautiful Beast* **1995** Mysterious Chinese warrior woman known as Black Orchid arrives in Japan and rubs out mob boss Ishizuka. Fleeing the scene, she hides out with bartender Yoichi Fujinami, who becomes torn between helping his old pal Yaguchi and the mystery girl that he's falling in love with. Foregoes a lot of empty soft-core sex in favor of providing more action. Director Toshiharu Ikeda is no John Woo, but at least Black Orchid's trunk full of high-powered weaponry provides a little fun. **87m/C DVD.** *JP* Kaori Shimamura, Takanori Kikuchi, Hakuryu, Minako Ogawa; *D:* Toshiharu Ikeda; *W:* Tamiya Takehashi, Hiroshi Takehashi; *C:* Seizo Sengen.

The Beautiful Blonde from Bashful Bend 1/2 **1949** Charming comedy-western gets better with age. Grable is the pistol packing mama mistaken for the new school teacher. Fun performances by all, especially Herbert. **77m/C VHS.** Betty Grable, Cesar Romero, Rudy Vallee, Olga San Juan, Hugh Herbert, Porter Hall, Sterling Holloway, El Brendel; *D:* Preston Sturges.

The Beautiful Country 1/2 **2004 (R)** In 1990, 20-year-old Binh (Nguyen) lives with poverty and discrimination in Vietnam because of his mixed ancestry: his father was an American solider. Binh's dying mother sends him on an illegal journey to the U.S. in hopes of tracking down his dad in Houston. There's an extended sequence involving a Malaysian refugee camp (with Ling as a friendly prostitute) and a trip on a freighter (captained by Roth) before the young man makes it to the States and finally meets his dad (Nolte). Earnest, gentle, and sometimes harrowing (and rather too long). **137m/C DVD.** *NO US* Nick Nolte, Tim Roth, Bai Ling, Temuera Morrison, Damien Nguyen, Nguyen Thi Huong Dung, Chau Thi Kim Xuan, Anh Thu, Khong Duc Thuan, Chapman To, Vu Tang, Nguyen Than Kien, Bui Ti Hong, John Hussey; *D:* Hans Petter Moland; *W:* Larry Gross, Sabina Murray; *C:* Stuart Dryburgh; *M:* Zbigniew Preisner.

Beautiful Creatures **2000 (R)** Fitful comedy/thriller follows the adventures of Petulia (Weisz) and Dorothy (Lynch), two Glasgow lasses with abusive boyfriends. Dorothy escapes a beating from her druggie boyfriend Tony (Glen), only to wind up aiding Petulia, who is being attacked in the street by drunken Brian (Mannion). Unfortunately, Brian dies and the women decides to make it look like he's been kidnapped and ask a ransom from his equally violent brother Ronnie (Roeves) so they can get out of town. Then a crooked detective (Norton) enters the scene and the women's plans turn a little complicated. **88m/C VHS, DVD.** *GB* Rachel Weisz, Susan Lynch, Alex Norton, Iain Glen, Maurice Roeves, Tom Mannion; *D:* Bill Eagles; *W:* Simon Donald; *C:* James Welland; *M:* Murray Gold.

Beautiful Dreamers 1/2 **1992 (PG-13)** Maurice Bucke is a young Canadian physician who runs the London Insane Asylum. After a chance meeting with poet Walt Whitman, both men discover their mutual outrage for current treatment of the mentally ill. Bucke persuades Whitman to visit his asylum in order to try Whitman's theory of human compassion on the asylum's inmates. However, Bucke runs into opposition from the local townspeople, scandalized by Whitman's radical reputation. Fairly humdrum with a larger-than-life performance by Torn as Whitman. Based on Whitman's visit to Canada in 1880. **108m/C VHS.** *CA* Rip Torn, Colm Feore, Wendel Meldrum, Sheila McCarthy, Colin Fox; *D:* John Kent Harrison; *W:* John Kent Harrison.

Beautiful Girls **1996 (R)** Slow but easy-going film highlights the differences between men, women, and relationships. A 10-year high school reunion brings together buddies Tommy (Dillon), Kev (Perlich), Paul (Rapaport), Mo (Emmerich), and Willie (Hutton). They ice-fish, drink, and talk about women (about whom they haven't a clue). All are smitten by Andera (Thurman), the gorgeous visiting cousin of another friend, and Willie becomes intrigued by Marty (Portman), his precociously tantalizing 13-year-old neighbor. The guys' whining gets annoying and the women are strictly secondary characters, but O'Donnell's tirade about fake femininity is just one of many amusing examples of smart dialogue. The Afghan Whigs are featured as the bar band. **110m/C VHS, DVD.** Matt Dillon, Timothy Hutton, Michael Rapaport, Max Perlich, Noah Emmerich, Lauren Holly, Uma Thurman, Natalie Portman, Mira Sorvino, Martha Plimpton, Rosie O'Donnell, Annabeth Gish, Pruitt Taylor Vince, Sam Robards, David Arquette, Anne Bobby, Richard Bright; *D:* Ted (Edward) Demme; *W:* Scott Rosenberg; *C:* Adam Kimmel; *M:* David A. Stewart.

Beautiful Hunter *XX Beautiful Hunter* **1994** Shion has been raised since birth to be the perfect assassin and executioner for the Magnificat crime family, a devoutly Catholic gang that do their criminal business in the vestments of priests and nuns. Blind Father Kano fully controls the life of his adopted daughter, until photographer Ito gets photos of her. The lethal yet naive heroine finds herself attracted to Ito, but Father Kano Sister Mitsuko and a squad of killers after them. Kuno looks—well, beautiful, in and out of a series of foxy outfits, but doesn't display any kind of martial arts to convince us of her master assassin status. **91m/C DVD.** *JP* Makiko Kuno, Koji Shimizu; *D:* Masaura Konuma.

Beautiful Joe **2000 (R)** Joe (Connolly) decides to hit the road for adventure and discovers it in Louisville, Kentucky when he meets Hush (Stone), an ex-stripper turned con artist. Then Joe gets in trouble when he tries to help Hush with her debt to crime boss George the Geek (Holm) and the twosome take off to Vegas with Geek's henchman (Bellows) on their trail. **98m/C VHS, DVD.** Billy Connolly, Sharon Stone, Gil Bellows, Ian Holm, Dann Florek, Barbara Tyson; *D:* Stephen Metcalfe; *W:* Stephen Metcalfe; *C:* Thomas Ackerman.

A Beautiful Mind 1/2 **2001 (PG-13)** Loose adaptation of Sylvia Nasar's 1998 bio of Nobel Prize winning mathematician John Forbes Nash Jr. An anti-social genius at Princeton University, Nash wrote his thesis on game theory at 21 and worked for the government in the 1950s before succumbing to paranoid schizophrenia, necessitating his confinement to a mental institution. (The treatment scenes are not for the faint-hearted.) His apparent recovery, after some 30 years, led to sharing a Nobel award in economics in 1994. Director Howard manages to keep the inherent sentimentality and sensationalism generally under control thanks to some powerful performances from Crowe (as Nash), Connelly (as wife Alicia), and Harris (as a sinister government official). The usual controversies swirled about the accuracy of the biopic and what was left out. Ignore the petty carping. **129m/C VHS, DVD.** *US* Russell Crowe, Jennifer Connelly, Ed Harris, Paul Bettany, Christopher Plummer, Judd Hirsch, Adam Goldberg, Josh(ua) Lucas, Anthony Rapp, Austin Pendleton, Vivien Cardone; *D:* Ron Howard; *W:* Akiva Goldsman; *C:* Roger Deakins; *M:* James Horner. Oscars '01: Adapt. Screenplay, Director (Howard), Film, Support. Actress (Connelly); British Acad. '01: Actor (Crowe), Support. Actress (Connelly); Directors Guild '01: Director (Howard); Golden Globes '02: Actor—Drama (Crowe), Film—Drama, Screenplay, Support. Actress (Connelly); Screen Actors Guild '01: Actor (Crowe); Writers Guild '01: Adapt. Screenplay; Broadcast Film Critics '01: Actor (Crowe), Director (Howard), Film, Support. Actress (Connelly).

Beautiful Ohio **2006** Coming-of-age age story about sibling rivalry, set in the 1970s. Clive Messerman (Call) is a teen math prodigy who's grown distant from his once-idolized older brother William (Davern). William is not only jealous of his parents' hopes for Clive but covets his troubled girlfriend Sandra (Trachtenberg), which leads to an unexpected revelation. Directorial debut of Lowe. **90m/C DVD.** Rita Wilson, William Hurt, Michelle Trachtenberg, Julianna Margulies, Thomas (Tom) McCarthy, David Call, Brett Davern, Hale Appleman; *D:* Chad Lowe; *W:* Ethan Canin; *C:* Stephen Kazmierski; *M:* Craig (Shudder to Think) Wedren.

Beautiful People **1999 (R)** The war in Bosnia (circa 1993) comes to London when former neighbors-turned-enemies, one a Serbian and the other a Croatian, accidentally meet on a bus and try to kill each other. This chaos leads to a variety of intersecting situations: Portia (Coleman), a doctor and daughter of a snobby Tory MP, falls for a refugee; another doctor (Farrell) counsels a pregnant refugee who wants to abort her baby, who is the product of a rape; a druggy skinhead (Nussbaum) winds up experiencing battle firsthand, and on and on and on. **107m/C VHS, DVD.** *GB* Charlotte Coleman, Nicholas Farrell, Danny Nussbaum, Edin Dzandzanovic, Charles Kay, Rosalind Ayres, Heather Tobias, Siobhan Redmond, Gilbert Martin, Linda Bassett, Steve Sweeney; *D:* Jasmin Dizdar; *W:* Jasmin Dizdar; *C:* Barry Ackroyd; *M:* Gary Bell.

The Beautiful, the Bloody and the Bare **1964** Sordid screamer in the Herschell Gordon Lewis tradition. Set in New York City in the '60s, a depraved artist kills the nude models who pose for him. **?m/C VHS, DVD.** Adela Rogers St. John, Marlene Denes, Debra Page, Jack Lowe; *D:* Sande N. Johnsen; *W:* Sande N. Johnsen; *C:* Jerry Denby; *M:* Steve Karmen.

Beautiful Thing **1995 (R)** Sweet, fairytalish, gay coming-of-age story set in a working-class southeast London housing estate. Shy teenager Jamie (Berry) lives with his barmaid mum, Sandra (Henry), and her lover, Tony (Daniels). Next-door is his best mate, the stoic Ste (Neal), who's regularly abused by his father and brother. But when things get too bad, he sleeps over with Jamie. And one night, nature hesitantly takes its course. Their tart-tongued, Mama Cass fanatic, friend Leah (Empson) starts rumors about the twosome that lead to some uneasy (but ultimately conciliatory) confrontations. Fine performances; Harvey adapted from his play. **89m/C VHS, DVD.** *GB* Glen Berry, Scott Neal, Linda Henry, Tameka Empson, Ben Daniels; *D:* Hettie Macdonald; *W:* Jonathan Harvey; *C:* Chris Seager.

Beauty and the Beast *La Belle et la Bete* **1946** The classic medieval fairy tale is brought to life on the big screen for the first time. Beauty takes the place of her father after he is sentenced to die by the horrible Beast and falls in love with him. Cocteau uses the story's themes and famous set-pieces to create a cohesive and captivating surreal hymn to romantic love that is still the definitive version of B&B. In French with subtitles. **90m/B VHS, DVD.** *FR* Jean Marais, Josette Day, Marcel Andre, Mila Parely, Nane Germon, Michel Auclair; *D:* Jean Cocteau; *W:* Jean Cocteau; *C:* Henri Alekan; *M:* Georges Auric.

Beauty and the Beast **1983** From "Faerie Tale Theatre" comes the story of a Beauty who befriends a Beast and learns a lesson about physical appearance and true love. **60m/C VHS, DVD.** Susan Sarandon, Anjelica Huston, Klaus Kinski, Stephen Elliott; *D:* Roger Vadim. **CABLE**

Beauty and the Beast **1991 (G)** Wonderful Disney musical combines superb animation, splendid characters, and lively songs about a beautiful girl, Belle, and the fearsome and disagreeable Beast. Supporting cast includes the castle servants (a delightful bunch of household objects). Notable as the first animated feature to be nominated for the Best Picture Oscar. Destined to become a classic. The deluxe video version features a work-in-progress rough film cut, a compact disc of the soundtrack, a lithograph depicting a scene from the film, and an illustrated book. ♫Beauty and the Beast; Belle; Something There; Be Our Guest. **84m/C VHS, DVD.** *D:* Kirk Wise, Gary Trousdale; *W:* Linda Woolverton; *M:* Alan Menken, Howard Ashman; *V:* Paige O'Hara, Robby Benson, Rex Everhart, Richard White, Jesse Corti, Angela Lansbury, Jerry Orbach, David Ogden Stiers, Bradley Michael Pierce, Jo Anne Worley, Kimmy Robertson. Oscars '91: Song ("Beauty and the Beast"), Orig. Score; Golden Globes '92: Film—Mus./Comedy, Natl. Film Reg. '02.

Beauty and the Devil *La Beaute du Diable* **1950** Ambitious retelling of the Faust legend finds old Faust (Simon) willing to sell his soul to the Devil, courtesy of his agent Mephistopheles (Philipe), in return for youth and beauty to pursue the beautiful woman he loves. Clair has his actors trade roles midway through as Faust makes his bargain. French with subtitles. **97m/B VHS.** *FR* Michel Simon, Gerard Philipe, Simone Valere, Raymond Cordy, Gaston Modot, Paolo Stoppa, Nicole Besnard; ***D:*** Rene Clair; ***W:*** Rene Clair, Armand Salacrou; ***C:*** Michel Kelber; ***M:*** Roman Vlad.

Beauty for the Asking **1939** It sounds like a workable Lucille Ball vehicle—a beautician develops a bestselling skin cream—and even the title sounds like something you'd like to love Lucy in. But somehow the numerous plot implausibilities managed to get by the story's five writers, and the idea of a jilted woman making millions while being financed by her ex's wife just doesn't fly (perhaps it was an idea ahead of its time). Die-hard Lucy fans may find this interesting. **68m/B VHS.** Lucille Ball, Patric Knowles, Donald Woods, Frieda Inescort, Frances Mercer; ***D:*** Glenn Tryon.

Beauty on the Beach **1961** A comedy about a mad psychologist, his bizarre experiments with women, and his eventual descent into insanity. In Italian with English subtitles. **90m/C VHS.** *IT* Ennio Girolami, Gloria Milland, Alberto Talegalli, Lorella De Luca, Valeria Fabrizi; ***D:*** Romolo Guerrieri; ***W:*** Tito Carpi, Fabio Dipas, Carlo Moscovini; ***C:*** Mario Fioretti; ***M:*** Carlo Savina.

Beauty School *Sylvia Kristel's Beauty School* **1993 (R)** The promise of an advertising contract pits the owners of rival beauty schools against each other. **95m/C VHS.** Sylvia Kristel, Kevin Bernhardt, Kimberly Taylor, Jane (Veronica Hart) Hamilton; ***D:*** Ernest G. Sauer; ***W:*** Merrill Friedman; ***M:*** Jonathan Hannah.

Beauty Shop **2005 (PG-13)** Spinning off from the "Barbershop" series, familiar tale of female empowerment succeeds, thanks to Queen Latifah's classy, charismatic lead performance. Beautician Gina moves to Atlanta, landing a job working for pretentious upscale salon owner Jorge (Bacon). Frustrated with Jorge's lack of respect, Gina opens her own beauty shop in a working-class black neighborhood, gathering a group of good-natured, eccentric stylists like outspoken Ms. Josephine (Woodard) and clueless white girl Lynn (Silverstone). All of the community pride themes from the "Barbershop" movies are touched on here, but "Beauty" distinguishes itself with genuine characters. Bacon and Suvari are exceptions, choosing instead to go ridiculously broad. **105m/C DVD, UMD.** *US* Queen Latifah, Alicia Silverstone, Andie MacDowell, Alfre Woodard, Mena Suvari, Della Reese, Golden Brooks, Paige Hurd, LisaRaye, Keisha Knight Pulliam, Bryce Wilson, Kevin Bacon, Djimon Hounsou, Adele Givens, Miss Laura Hayes, Little JJ, Sherri Shepherd, Kimora Lee Simmons, Sheryl Underwood; ***D:*** Bille Woodruff; ***W:*** Kate Lanier, Norman Vance, Jr.; ***C:*** Theo van de Sande; ***M:*** Christopher Young.

Beavis and Butt-Head Do America 1/2 **1996 (PG-13)** Moronic MTV metalheads go on the road in search of their stolen TV and are somehow mistaken for criminal masterminds. Okay, enough about plot. If you're thinking of renting this one, you don't care about that stuff anyway. Director/writer/voice of B&B Judge is smart enough not to change our "heroes" just because they're on a bigger screen. They're still stupid, obsessed with chicks, (Yeah! Chicks are cool!) and blissfully unaware of what's happening around them. The opening sequence, a parody of 70s cop shows, is hilarious (and cool). For those who like the show, and for people who just don't admit that they do, the boys' movie debut (he said "but") doesn't suck. **82m/C VHS, DVD.** ***D:*** Mike Judge; ***W:*** Joe Stillman, Mike Judge; ***M:*** John (Gianni) Frizzell; ***V:*** Mike Judge, Robert Stack, Cloris Leachman, Demi Moore, Eric Bogosian, Richard Linklater, Pamela Blair, Tim Guinee, David Letterman, David Spade, Bruce Willis, Toby Huss.

Bebe's Kids 1/2 **1992 (PG-13)** When ladies' man Robin falls for the lovely Jamika, he gets some unexpected surprises when he takes her out on a first date to an amusement park—and she brings along four kids. Animated comedy takes some funny pot-shots at both black and white culture and Disneyland. The children are amusing, especially baby PeeWee, a tot with chronically dirty diapers and Tone Loc's gravelly voice. Based on characters created by the late comedian Robin Harris. The video includes the seven-minute animated short "Itsy Bitsy Spider." **74m/C VHS, DVD.** ***D:*** Bruce Smith; ***W:*** Reginald (Reggie) Hudlin; ***M:*** John Barnes; ***V:*** Faizon Love, Vanessa Bell Calloway, Wayne Collins, Jonell Green, Marques Houston, Tone Loc, Nell Carter, Myra J.

Because I Said So **2007 (PG-13)** Keaton stars as Daphne, a well-intentioned but overprotective and meddling mom to three beautiful daughters. Maggie (Graham) and Mae (Perabo) are safely married and successful, but youngest chick Milly (Moore) has terrible taste in men, so Daphne places a personal ad and screens the replies. Daphne approves of architect Jason (Scott) but Milly is drawn to musician and single dad Johnny (Macht), whose own dad, Joe (Collins), strikes unexpected sparks with Daphne. Much over-the-top shtick follows but everything (and everyone) looks gorgeous. **102m/C DVD.** *US* Diane Keaton, Mandy Moore, Lauren Graham, Piper Perabo, Gabriel Macht, Tom Everett Scott, Stephen Collins, Ty Panitz, Colin Ferguson, Tony Hale, Matt Champagne; ***D:*** Michael Lehmann; ***W:*** Karen Leigh Hopkins, Jessie Nelson; ***C:*** Julio Macat; ***M:*** David Kitay.

Because of Him 1/2 **1945** Actress Kim Walker (Durbin) fakes a letter of introduction from famous thespian John Sheridan (Laughton) in order to impress Broadway producer Charles Gilbert (Ridges). It works and she's given the lead, much to the dismay of the playwright, Paul Taylor (Tone). Naturally, Kim turns out to be an opening night success and Paul comes around and realizes what a swell gal she is. Laughton is at his best as the hammy veteran performer. **88m/B VHS.** Deanna Durbin, Franchot Tone, Charles Laughton, Stanley Ridges, Helen Broderick, Donald Meek; ***D:*** Richard Wallace; ***W:*** Edmund Beloin; ***C:*** Hal Mohr; ***M:*** Miklos Rozsa.

Because of the Cats 1/2 **1974** Police inspector uncovers an evil cult within his seaside village while investigating a bizarre rape and burglary. **90m/C VHS.** Bryan Marshall, Alexandra Stewart, Alex Van Rooyen, Sylvia Kristel, Sebastian Graham Jones; ***D:*** Fons Rademakers.

Because of Winn-Dixie 1/2 **2005 (PG)** Based on the popular children's book by Kate DiCamillo of the same name about a lonely young girl who adopts a stray dog. India Opal Buloni (played by Robb) is a lonely 10 year-old who's just moved to Florida with her preacher father (Daniels). Without friends, and missing her mother, who left her when she was three, Opal encounters a stray dog at the local grocery store. She adopts the dog as her own, naming him Winn-Dixie after the store. Slowly, the dog helps Opal ease her loneliness and she discovers some rare friendships in unusual places. While not perfect, the movie has more hits than misses and is helped along with a strong supporting cast, including Dave Matthews as a singing pet store clerk. **105m/C DVD.** *US* Jeff Daniels, Cicely Tyson, Eva Marie Saint, Courtney Jines, Elle Fanning, AnnaSophia Robb, Dave Matthews, Nick Price, Luke Benward; ***D:*** Wayne Wang; ***W:*** Joan Singleton; ***C:*** Karl Walter Lindenlaub; ***M:*** Rachel Portman.

Because of You 1/2 **1952** Parolee Christine Carroll (Young) marries Steve Kimberly (Chandler) without revealing her sordid past. Then said past bites her in the butt when her criminal associates find and involve her in another crime. Lots of tears. **95m/B VHS.** Loretta Young, Jeff Chandler, Alex Nicol, Frances Dee, Alexander Scourby, Lynne Roberts, Mae Clarke; ***D:*** Joseph Pevney; ***W:*** Ketti Frings; ***C:*** Russell Metty; ***M:*** Frank Skinner.

Because of You *Kyoko* **1995 (R)** Jose (Osorio), a Cuban-American serviceman stationed in Japan, taught the young Kyoko how to do latin dancing. When she's 21, Kyoko (Takaoka) travels to New York to see Jose again. When she does find him, she discovers Jose has AIDS and no longer remembers much of his past, including Kyoko. Terminally ill, his one wish is to be reunited with his family in Miami. Kyoko decides to drive Jose home, hoping somehow he'll come to remember her. **85m/C VHS, DVD.** Saki Takaoka, Carlos Osorio, Scott Whitehurst, Mauricio Bustamante, Oscar Colon, Bradford West, Angel Stephens; ***D:*** Ryu Murakami; ***W:*** Ryu Murakami; ***C:*** Sarah Cawley.

Because Why? **1993** After travelling abroad for five years, Alex (Riley) returns to Montreal with a back pack, a skateboard, and an old girlfriend's address. The address only leads to a demolished building, so Alex finds himself a new home and—longing to belong somewhere—a potentially new family and friends. **104m/C VHS, DVD.** *CA* Michael Riley, Martine Rochon, Doru Bandol, Heather Mathieson; ***D:*** Arto Paragamian; ***W:*** Arto Paragamian; ***C:*** Andre Turpin; ***M:*** Nana Vasconcelos.

Because You're Mine **1952** Lanza plays an opera star who is drafted and falls in love with Morrow, his top sergeant's sister. Plenty of singing—maybe too much at times, but Lanza's fans will enjoy it nonetheless. ♫All the Things You Are; Because You're Mine; Be My Love; Granada; Lee-Ah-Loo; The Lord's Prayer; The Song Angels Sing; You Do Something to Me. **103m/C VHS, DVD.** Mario Lanza, James Whitmore, Doretta Morrow, Dean Miller, Rita (Paula) Corday, Jeff Donnell, Spring Byington; ***D:*** Alexander Hall.

Becket **1964** Adaptation of Jean Anouilh's play about the tumultuous friendship between Henry II of England and the Archbishop of Canterbury Thomas Becket. Becket views his position in the church of little relation to the sexual and emotional needs of a man, until he becomes archbishop. His growing concern for religion and his shrinking need of Henry as friend and confidant eventually cause the demise of the friendship and the resulting tragedy. Flawless acting from every cast member, and finely detailed artistic direction make up for the occasional slow moment. **148m/C VHS, DVD, Blu-ray Disc.** Richard Burton, Peter O'Toole, John Gielgud, Donald Wolfit; ***D:*** Peter Glenville; ***W:*** Edward Anhalt; ***C:*** Geoffrey Unsworth. Oscars '64: Adapt. Screenplay; Golden Globes '65: Actor—Drama (O'Toole), Film—Drama.

Becky Sharp 1/2 **1935** This premiere Technicolor film tells the story of Becky Sharp, a wicked woman who finally performs one good deed. **83m/C VHS, DVD.** Miriam Hopkins, Frances Dee, Cedric Hardwicke, Billie Burke, Nigel Bruce, Pat Nixon; ***D:*** Rouben Mamoulian; ***C:*** Ray Rennahan.

Becoming Colette **1992 (R)** Tedious flashbacking bio of French writer Colette, from her innocent days in the country to her (bad) marriage to writer/publisher Willy and on and on to her own growing career as a writer. She begins writing stories, using an alter-ego character, Claudine, which detail her sexual escapades. Lots of naked flesh but little passion. A postscript notes that Colette wrote "Gigi" and was the first woman to receive the French Legion of Honor. **97m/C VHS.** Mathilda May, Klaus Maria Brandauer, Virginia Madsen, Paul Rhys, Jean-Pierre Aumont, John van Dreelen, Lucienne Hamon; ***D:*** Danny Huston; ***W:*** Ruth Graham; ***M:*** John Scott.

Becoming Jane 1/2 **2007 (PG)** Jane Austen's writing has withstood the test of time, but films about the writer and her writings are still fledgling. This one's a love story—supposedly her own—and takes place before Jane (Hathaway) is, well, Jane Austen as we know her. Penniless mom and dad (Walters and Cromwell) don't take the whole writing thing seriously and expect 20-year-old Jane to choose a wealthy suitor from among those that come calling. Then Thomas Lefroy (McAvoy) shows up, dashing and pushy, and Jane—after initial annoyance—entertains the thought of shelving her writing, at least temporarily. Alas, relatives from both sides disapprove of the match. No matter, she becomes a fantastic writer whom we still read, speak of, and make films about nearly 200 years later. Pretty costumes, but with a been-there-done-that (think "Pride and Prejudice" remake) feel. Still worthwhile for Austen fans and non-fans alike. **120m/C DVD, Blu-ray Disc.** *US GB* Anne Hathaway, James McAvoy, Julie Walters, James Cromwell, Laurence Fox, Maggie Smith, Ian Richardson, Anna Maxwell Martin, Joe Anderson, Helen McCrory, Leo Bill; ***D:*** Julian Jarrold; ***W:*** Kevin Hood, Sarah Williams; ***C:*** Eigil Bryld; ***M:*** Adrian Johnston.

Bed and Board *Domicile Conjugal* **1970** The fourth film in the Antoine Doinel (Leaud) cycle finds him marrying Christine (Jade) and becoming a father. The responsibilities of adulthood upset him so much that Antoine leaves his new family and begins an affair. French with subtitles. **100m/C VHS, DVD.** *FR* Jean-Pierre Leaud, Claude Jade, Barbara Laage, Hiroko Berghauer, Daniel Boulanger, Pierre Maguelon, Jacques Jouanneau, Jacques Rispal, Jacques Robiolles, Pierre Fabre, Billy Kearns, Daniel Ceccaldi, Daniele Girard, Claire Duhamel, Sylvana Blasi, Claude Vega, Christian de Tiliere, Annick Asty, Marianne Piketi, Guy Pierauld, Marie Dedieu, Marie Irakane, Yvon Lec, Ernest Menzer, Christophe Vesque; ***D:*** Francois Truffaut; ***W:*** Francois Truffaut, Bernard Revon, Claude de Givray; ***C:*** Nestor Almendros; ***M:*** Antoine Duhamel.

Bed & Breakfast 1/2 **1992 (PG-13)** Three generations of women lead quiet lives while running a failing Nantucket bed and breakfast. When a mystery man washes up on their beach, he charms them all, but it seems that he has a past that could endanger everyone. Lightweight final role for Dewhurst, though she provides some sparks as the strong and loving matriarch. Gentle romantic comedy skims the surface, but is still enjoyable. **97m/C VHS.** Roger Moore, Talia Shire, Colleen Dewhurst, Nina Siemaszko, Ford Rainey, Stephen (Steve) Root, Jamie Walters, Victor Slezak; ***D:*** Robert Ellis Miller; ***W:*** Cindy Myers; ***M:*** David Shire.

Bed and Sofa 1/2 **1927** Adultery, abortion, and women's rights are brought about by a housing shortage which forces a man to move in with a married friend. Famous, ground-breaking Russian silent. **73m/B VHS, DVD.** *RU* Nikolai Batalov, Vladimar Fogel; ***D:*** Abram Room.

Bed of Roses 1/2 *Amelia and the King of Plants* **1995 (PG)** Wistful romance finds workaholic investment banker Lisa Walker (Masterson) receiving lavish floral tributes from an unknown admirer. When Lisa tracks her giver down, it turns out to be lovestruck widowed florist Lewis Farrell (Slater), who noticed Lisa crying through her apartment window and sent the flowers to cheer her up. Best friend Kim (Seagall) urges Lisa to go for Lewis but a problematic past has Lisa distrusting her emotions and their romantic path has a few bumps (easily overcome). Appealing leads, lots of cliches. Goldenberg's debut. **88m/C VHS, DVD.** Christian Slater, Mary Stuart Masterson, Pamela Segall, Josh Brolin, Ally Walker, Debra Monk; ***D:*** Michael Goldenberg; ***W:*** Michael Goldenberg; ***C:*** Adam Kimmel; ***M:*** Michael Convertino.

The Bed You Sleep In **1993** Ray (Blair) is a struggling lumber mill owner, living with his wife Jean (McLaughlin) in a small Oregon town. The couple are torn apart when they receive a letter from their daughter, who's away at college, accusing her father of sexual abuse. The secrets and lies of the family soon echo throughout their community. **117m/C VHS, DVD.** Tom Blair, Ellen McLaughlin, Kathryn Sannella; ***D:*** Jon Jost; ***W:*** Jon Jost; ***C:*** Jon Jost.

Bedazzled **1968 (PG)** Short-order cook Stanley Moon (Moore) is saved from suicide by the devil, here known as George Spiggot (Cook), who makes Stanley an offer: seven wishes in exchange for his soul. What Stanley wants is waitress Margaret (Bron) but each of Stanley's wishes is granted with surprising consequences. Cult comedy is a sometimes uneven, but thoroughly entertaining and funny retelling of the Faustian story. **107m/C VHS, DVD.** *GB* Dudley Moore, Peter Cook, Eleanor Bron, Michael Bates, Raquel Welch, Bernard Spear, Parnell McGarry, Howard Goorney, Daniele Noel, Barry Humphries, Lockwood West, Robert Russell, Michael Trubshawe, Robin Hawdon, Evelyn Moore, Charles Lloyd-Pack; ***D:*** Stanley Donen; ***W:*** Dudley Moore, Peter Cook; ***C:*** Austin Dempster; ***M:*** Dudley Moore.

Bedazzled 1/2 **2000 (PG-13)** Mortals have been falling for this scam for centuries: seven wishes in exchange for your eternal soul. Once again the Devil finds a taker. Fraser plays Elliot, a nice but hopeless geek who will do anything to improve his lowly stature in life and nab the girl of his dreams (O'Connor). The Devil's (Hurley) misinterpretations of his requests result in Elliot becoming, among other things, a drug lord, an NBA star, and a much too sensitive bore. Will Elliot find a way out of his hellish obligation? Is there a lesson to be learned from his experiences? You probably know the answers. Ramis occasionally misfires, but the hits outnumber the misses. An updated remake of the Dudley Moore/Peter Cook film. **105m/C VHS, DVD.** Brendan Fraser, Elizabeth Hurley, Frances O'Connor, Rudolf Martin, Orlando Jones, Gabriel Casseus, Miriam Shor, Brian Doyle-Murray; ***D:*** Harold Ramis; ***W:*** Harold Ramis, Larry Gelbart, Peter Tolan; ***C:*** Bill Pope.

Bedelia 1946 Lockwood well-plays a black widow. Bedelia is living happily in Monte Carlo with hubby Charlie (Hunter) until Ben Chaney (Barnes) shows up. Posing as an artist—but really a private eye—Ben has questions about Bedelia's past. Seems she poisoned three previous husbands for the insurance money and Charlie is a good bet to be her next victim. Based on the novel by Vera Caspary. **90m/B VHS.** Margaret Lockwood, Ian Hunter, Barry Barnes, Anne Crawford, Beatrice Varley, Jill Esmond, Julien Mitchell, Kynaston Reeves, Louise Hampton; ***W:*** Isadore Goldsmith, Herbert Victor; ***C:*** Frederick A. (Freddie) Young; ***M:*** Hans May.

Bedford Incident 1/2 1965 The U.S.S. Bedford discovers an unidentified submarine in North Atlantic waters. The Bedford's commander drives his crew to the point of exhaustion as they find themselves the center of a fateful controversy. **102m/B VHS, DVD.** Richard Widmark, Sidney Poitier, James MacArthur, Martin Balsam, Wally Cox, Donald Sutherland, Eric Portman; ***D:*** James B. Harris.

Bedknobs and Broomsticks 1/2 1971 (G) A novice witch and three cockney waifs ride a magic bedstead and stop the Nazis from invading England during WWII. Celebrated for its animated art. **117m/C VHS, DVD.** Angela Lansbury, Roddy McDowall, David Tomlinson, Bruce Forsyth, Sam Jaffe; ***D:*** Robert Stevenson; ***W:*** Don DaGradi, Bill Walsh; ***C:*** Frank Phillips; ***M:*** Richard M. Sherman, Robert B. Sherman. Oscars '71: Visual FX.

Bedlam 1945 Creeper set in the famed asylum in 18th-century London. A woman, wrongfully committed, tries to stop the evil doings of the chief (Karloff) of Bedlam, and endangers herself. Fine horror film co-written by producer Lewton. **79m/B VHS, DVD.** Jason Robards Sr., Ian Wolfe, Glenn Vernon, Boris Karloff, Anna Lee, Billy House, Richard Fraser, Elizabeth Russell, Skelton Knaggs, Robert Clarke, Ellen Corby, Leyland Hodgson, Joan Newton; ***D:*** Mark Robson; ***W:*** Mark Robson, Val Lewton; ***C:*** Nicholas Musuraca; ***M:*** Roy Webb.

Bedroom Eyes 1986 (R) A successful businessman becomes a voyeur by returning nightly to a beautiful woman's window, until she is killed and he is the prime suspect. Part comic, part disappointing thriller. **90m/C VHS, DVD.** Kenneth Gilman, Dayle Haddon, Christine Cattall; ***D:*** William Fruet.

Bedroom Eyes 2 1989 (R) After discovering his wife has had an affair, a stockbroker takes a lover. When she turns up dead, he and his wife become murder suspects. Provides some suspenseful moments. **85m/C VHS.** Wings Hauser, Kathy Shower, Linda Blair, Jane (Veronica Hart) Hamilton, Jennifer Delora; ***D:*** Chuck Vincent.

The Bedroom Window 1/2 1987 (R) Guttenberg is having an illicit affair with his boss' wife (Huppert), who witnesses an assault on another woman (McGovern) from the bedroom window. To keep the affair secret Guttenberg reports the crime, but since it is secondhand, the account is flawed and he becomes a suspect. Semi-tight thriller reminiscent of Hitchcock mysteries isn't always believable, but is otherwise interesting. **113m/C VHS, DVD.** Steve Guttenberg, Elizabeth McGovern, Isabelle Huppert, Wallace Shawn, Paul Shenar, Carl Lumbly, Frederick Coffin, Brad Greenquist; ***D:*** Curtis Hanson; ***W:*** Curtis Hanson; ***C:*** Gilbert Taylor; ***M:*** Patrick Gleeson, Michael Shrieve, Felix Mendelessohn.

Bedrooms and Hallways 1/2 1998 Single gay Leo (McKidd) is urged to join a new agey men's therapy group where, during one of their meetings, he expresses his interest in Brendan (Purefoy), who's breaking up with longtime lover, Sally (Ehle). After Leo and Brendan get together, Leo realizes that Sally is his old high school girlfriend and there's still a certain spark between them. And things just get more complicated. Zippy if glib humor, although the film tends to lose steam at the end. **96m/C VHS, DVD.** *GB* Kevin McKidd, James Purefoy, Jennifer Ehle, Tom Hollander, Hugo Weaving, Simon Callow, Harriet Walter, Christopher Fulford, Julie Graham; ***D:*** Rose Troche; ***W:*** Robert Farrar; ***C:*** Ashley Rowe; ***M:*** Alfredo Troche.

Bedtime for Bonzo 1/2 1951 A professor adopts a chimp to prove that environment, not heredity, determines a child's future. Fun, lighthearted comedy that stars a future president. Followed by "Bonzo Goes to College." **83m/B VHS, DVD.** Ronald Reagan, Diana Lynn, Walter Slezak, Jesse White, Bonzo the Chimp, Lucille Barkley, Herbert (Hayes) Heyes, Herb Vigran, Harry Tyler, Edward Clark; ***D:*** Fred de Cordova; ***W:*** Lou Breslow, Val Burton; ***C:*** Carl Guthrie; ***M:*** Frank Skinner.

Bedtime Stories 1/2 2008 (PG) Skeeter (Sandler) is a lowly maintenance guy at the hotel now standing on the site of the motel he and his sister (Cox) grew up in. Skeeter's lifelong dream of running it as his father (Pryce) once did seems unlikely as he toils under the loathsome hotel manager, Kendall (Pearce), a pompous dream-crusher who's double-timing his girlfriend Violet (Palmer)—the hotel owner's daughter who Skeeter has a colossal crush on. Skeeter's luck begins to change when he realizes, while caring for his sister's kids, that his wild bedtime stories of heroic daring can show up in real life. Thus he concocts tales giving him the upper hand with his boss and catching the eye of his girl. Uneven story but the outrageous special effects deliver a wholesome family comedy. **99m/C DVD.** *US* Adam Sandler, Keri Russell, Guy Pearce, Courteney Cox, Teresa Palmer, Russell Brand, Lucy Lawless, Richard Griffiths, Jonathan Pryce, Aisha Tyler, Laura Ann Kesling, Madisen Beaty; ***D:*** Adam Shankman; ***W:*** Tim Herlihy, Matt Lopez; ***C:*** Michael Barrett; ***M:*** Rupert Gregson-Williams.

Bedtime Story 1963 Two con artists attempt to fleece an apparently wealthy woman and each other on the French Riviera. Re-made in 1988 as "Dirty Rotten Scoundrels." One of Brando's thankfully few forays into comedy. **99m/C VHS, DVD.** Marlon Brando, David Niven, Shirley Jones, Dody Goodman, Marie Windsor; ***D:*** Ralph Levy.

Bee Movie 2007 (PG) A bee named Barry B. Benson (Seinfeld) finds himself on a mission when he learns that humans have been profiting off bees forever. Wanting more out of life than his job at a honey-production company can offer, Barry goes out in search of adventure and meets florist Vanessa (Zellweger), a former lawyer wannabe. A budding legal eagle himself, Barry ends up taking on the honey industry with Vanessa's help, and by recruiting all sorts of folks to further his cause (Sting and Larry King, among others). The environmental tones are sound, but the big names behind this film (Seinfeld also co-wrote and co-produced) are the only real buzz. There are bursts of cuteness and the kids will enjoy it, but the frenetic pace and endless string of one-liners tend to come off as just too much busyness. **90m/C DVD, Blu-ray Disc.** *US* ***D:*** Simon J. Smith, Steve Hickner; ***W:*** Jerry Seinfeld, Spike Feresten, Barry Marder, Andy Robin; ***M:*** Rupert Gregson-Williams; ***V:*** Jerry Seinfeld, Renee Zellweger, Matthew Broderick, John Goodman, Patrick Warburton, Chris Rock, Kathy Bates, Barry Levinson, Oprah Winfrey, Larry Miller, Megan Mullally, Rip Torn, Michael Richards, Larry King, Ray Liotta, Sting.

Bee Season 2005 (PG-13) Based on the bestselling novel by Myla Goldberg. Eleven-year-old Eliza (Cross), an average kid who lacks attention from her bright but aptly troubled parents, finds she's got a gift for spelling. Dad Saul (Gere), a religious studies professor and follower of Kabbalah mysticism, is at a loss as scientist wife Miriam (Binoche) teeters on the edge of instability. Meanwhile Eliza has fantastical visions of the words she is to spell as she wins local spelling bees and heads toward the national competition in Washington, D.C. Dad becomes obsessed with Eliza's gift, ignoring Miriam and their other child, Aaron (Minghella). Viewers who didn't read the book may be set adrift in this somewhat pretentious, but earnest film. **104m/C DVD.** *US* Richard Gere, Juliette Binoche, Flora Cross, Max Minghella, Kate (Catherine) Bosworth; ***D:*** Scott McGehee, David Siegel; ***W:*** Naomi Foner; ***C:*** Giles Nuttgens.

Beefcake 1999 Campy docudrama set in 1950s L.A. covers the muscle (or men's physique) magazine culture. Doting mama's boy Bob Mizer (MacIvor) found his talents as a still photographer and filmmaker, who also published Physique Pictorial, all of which featured chiseled studs. While Mizer insisted that his models were just clean-cut, all-American boys, he still fell afoul of pornography charges and operating a prostitution ring. The mock style turns harder-edged with Mizer's tribulations. To further confuse things, the film also includes present-day interviews with some of Mizer's one-time models and others familiar with the culture. **93m/C VHS, DVD.** Daniel MacIvor, Josh Peace, Carroll Godsman; ***D:*** Thom Fitzgerald; ***W:*** Thom Fitzgerald; ***C:*** Thomas M. Harting; ***M:*** John Roby.

Beer 1985 (R) A female advertising executive devises a dangerous sexist campaign for a cheap beer, and both the beer and its nickname become nationwide obsessions. Not especially amusing. **83m/C VHS.** Loretta Swit, Rip Torn, Dick Shawn, David Alan Grier, William Russ, Kenneth Mars, Peter Michael Goetz; ***D:*** Patrick Kelly; ***C:*** Bill Butler; ***M:*** Bill Conti.

Beer for My Horses 2008 (PG-13) Country singer Toby Keith writes and stars in this dim comedy adaptation of one of his songs. Rack and Lonnie are deputies in a usually quiet small southern town. Then Rack's girlfriend is kidnapped by a drug lord whose brother has been arrested, and the duo, joined by fellow lawman Skunk, go on a rescue mission. Stick to the music career, Toby. **86m/C DVD.** Ted Nugent, Tom Skerritt, Claire Forlani, Greg Serano, Toby Keith, Rodney Carrington, Carlos Sanz, Barry Corbin, Willie Nelson, Gina Gershon; ***D:*** Mikael Salomon; ***W:*** Toby Keith, Rodney Carrington; ***C:*** Paul Elliott; ***M:*** Toby Keith, Jeff Cardoni. **VIDEO**

Beer League *Artie Lange's Beer League* 2006 (R) Howard Stern sidekick Lange sticks to his booze, smokes, and broads persona as Artie DeVanzo, the head of a lousy New Jersey softball team at war with their perennial winning cross-town rivals. The deadbeat team of losers can't win a game, but that's okay, they've got beer and brawls. Except that the local law is fed up and demands the team either win or be forced to disband. Oh, the horror. If you actually know who Lange is, you know what to expect, and criticism is beside the point. Sit back and have another beer. **86m/C DVD.** *US* Artie Lange, Ralph Macchio, Anthony De Sando, Seymour Cassel, Cara Buona, Jimmy Palumbo, Joe Lo Truglio, Laurie Metcalf; ***D:*** Frank Sebastiano; ***W:*** Frank Sebastiano; ***C:*** David Phillips; ***M:*** B.C. Smith.

Beerfest 2006 (R) It's from those Broken Lizard boys, so don't go looking for sophistication. American brothers Todd and Jan Wolfhouse travel to Germany's Oktoberfest and stumble across a secret, long-standing beer competition. They also meet the arrogant German branch of the family who humiliate the brothers when they attempt to enter the contest and stand up for American males' ability to drink themselves stupid. "Strange Brew" meets "Fight Club" as this raucous comedy will probably become an instructional video to aspiring frat boys everywhere. **111m/C DVD.** *US* Jay Chandrasekhar, Kevin Heffernan, Steve Lemme, Paul Soter, Erik Stolhanske, Eric Christian Olsen, Cloris Leachman, Donald Sutherland, Mo'Nique, Jurgen Prochnow, M.C. Gainey, Will Forte, Blanchard Ryan, Ralph (Ralf) Moeller; ***D:*** Jay Chandrasekhar; ***W:*** Jay Chandrasekhar, Kevin Heffernan, Steve Lemme, Paul Soter, Erik Stolhanske; ***C:*** Frank DeMarco; ***M:*** Nathan Barr.

The Bees WOOF! 1978 (PG) Sting of a poor movie is painful. A strain of bees have ransacked South America and are threatening the rest of the world. The buzz is that no one is safe. Cheap rip-off of "The Swarm," which is saying something. **93m/C VHS.** John Saxon, John Carradine, Angel Tompkins, Claudio Brook, Alicia Encinas; ***D:*** Alfredo Zacharias.

Bees in Paradise 1944 Typical wartime comedy from Askey. Four airmen are forced to parachute out of their plane and they land on a tropical isle populated entirely by women. They think this is wonderful until they realize why there are no other men around. The women practice a marriage ceremony that requires the new hubby to commit suicide after the honeymoon. Arthur and his fellows try to convince the ladies that part of the ritual really isn't necessary. **72m/B DVD.** *GB* Arthur Askey, Peter Graves, Jean Kent, Max Bacon, Ronald Shiner, Antoinette Cellier, Joy Shelton, Beatrice Varley, Anne Shelton; ***D:*** Val Guest; ***W:*** Val Guest, Marriott Edgar; ***C:*** Phil Grindrod.

Beethoven *Beethoven's Great Love; The Life and Loves of Beethoven; Un Grand Amour de Beethoven* 1936 Startling biography of the musical genius, filled with opulent, impressionistic visuals. French with subtitles. **116m/B VHS, DVD.** *FR* Harry Baur, Jean-Louis Barrault, Marcel Dalio; ***D:*** Abel Gance; ***W:*** Abel Gance; ***C:*** Marc Fossard, Robert Lefebvre.

Beethoven 1/2 1992 (PG) Adorable St. Bernard puppy escapes from dognappers and wanders into the home of the Newtons, who, over dad's objections, adopt him. Beethoven grows into a huge, slobbering dog who sorely tries dad's patience. To make matters worse, two sets of villains also wreak havoc on the Newton's lives. Evil veterinarian Dr. Varnick plots to steal Beethoven for lab experiments, and yuppie couple Brad and Brie plot to take over the family business. Enjoyable cast, particularly Grodin as dad and Chris as Beethoven enable this movie to please more than the milk and cookies set. Followed by "Beethoven's 2nd." **89m/C VHS, DVD.** Charles Grodin, Bonnie Hunt, Dean Jones, Oliver Platt, Stanley Tucci, Nicholle Tom, Christopher Castile, Sarah Rose Karr, David Duchovny, Patricia Heaton, Laurel Cronin; ***D:*** Brian Levant; ***W:*** John Hughes, Amy Holden Jones; ***C:*** Victor Kemper; ***M:*** Randy Edelman.

Beethoven Lives Upstairs 1/2 1992 In 19th century Vienna 10 year-old Christoph's life is turned upside-down when the family's eccentric new tenant turns out to be composer Ludwig Van Beethoven. In time, Christoph comes to appreciate the beauty of the music and the tragedy of the composer's deafness. Features more than 25 excerpts of Beethoven's works. **52m/C VHS, DVD.** Neil Munro, Ilya Woloshyn, Fiona Reid, Paul Soles, Sheila McCarthy, Albert Schultz; ***D:*** David Devine; ***W:*** Heather Conkie.

Beethoven's 2nd 1/2 1993 (PG) Sequel has awwww factor going for it as new daddy Beethoven slobbers over four adorable and appealing St. Bernard pups and his new love Missy. Same basic evil subplot as the first, with wicked kidnappers replacing evil vet. During the upheaval, the Newtons take care of the little yapping troublemakers, providing the backdrop for endless puppy mischief and exasperation on Grodin's part. Silly subplots and too many human moments tend to drag, but the kids will find the laughs (albeit stupid ones). **87m/C VHS, DVD.** Charles Grodin, Bonnie Hunt, Nicholle Tom, Christopher Castile, Sarah Rose Karr, Debi Mazar, Christopher Penn, Ashley Hamilton; ***D:*** Rod Daniel; ***W:*** Len Blum; ***C:*** Bill Butler; ***M:*** Randy Edelman.

Beethoven's 3rd 1/2 2000 (PG) Dad Richard Newton (Reinhold) wants to take the family on vacation and, naturally, huge St. Bernard Beethoven is coming along. Suddenly, that rented luxury RV doesn't seem very big and dad's idea of fun is lame to the kids. Of course, it's not a typical vacation anyway, seems thieves Tommy (Ciccolini) and Bill (Marsh) need to retrieve a videotape that Richard has rented. Beethoven tries to protect his family while being blamed for every little mishap. A dog's life, indeed! **99m/C VHS, DVD.** Judge Reinhold, Julia Sweeney, Joe Pichler, Michaela Gallo, Jamie Marsh, Michael Ciccolini, Frank Gorshin, Danielle Wiener; ***D:*** David Mickey Evans; ***W:*** Jeff Schechter; ***C:*** John Aronson; ***M:*** Philip Giffin. **VIDEO**

Beethoven's 4th ☞ 1/2 **2001** Unruly Beethoven is sent to obedience school where he's accidentally switched with a well-behaved St. Bernard. Imagine the family's confusion. **94m/C VHS, DVD.** Judge Reinhold, Julia Sweeney, Joe Pichler, Michaela Gallo, Matt McCoy, Veanne Cox, Mark Lindsay Chapman, Art LaFleur, Kaleigh Krish, Natalie Marston; ***D:*** David Mickey Evans; ***W:*** John Loy; ***C:*** John Aronson. **VIDEO**

Beethoven's 5th ☞☞ **1/2 2003** Twelve-year-old Sara (Chase) and Beethoven spend the summer with eccentric Uncle Freddy (Thomas) in the old mining town of Quicksilver. Beethoven manages to dig up an old $10 bill that apparently comes from some loot buried by a couple of crooks in the 1920s and soon everyone in town is looking for the rest of the cash. **90m/C VHS, DVD.** Daveigh Chase, Dave Thomas, Faith Ford, John Larroquette, Kathy Griffin, Tom Poston, Katherine Helmond, Clint Howard; ***D:*** Mark Griffiths; ***W:*** Elana Lesser, Cliff Ruby; ***C:*** Christopher Baffa; ***M:*** Adam Berry. **VIDEO**

Beethoven's Big Break ☞☞ **1/2 2008 (PG)** Struggling animal trainer Eddie gets his big break as the wrangler for a movie star St. Bernard. But the dog's fame means some criminal-types have come up with a kidnapping and ransom scheme. **101m/C DVD.** Jonathan Silverman, Moises Arias, Rhea Perlman, Stephen Tobolowsky, Eddie Griffin, Osmar Nunez, Joey Fatone, Jennifer Finnigan; ***D:*** Mike Elliott; ***W:*** Derek Rydall; ***C:*** Stephen Campbell; ***M:*** Robert Folk. **VIDEO**

Beethoven's Nephew ☞ **1/2** *Le Neveu de Beethoven* **1988** A tepid pseudo-historical farce about Beethoven's strange obsession with his only nephew. Directed by erstwhile Warhol collaborator Morrissey. **103m/C VHS.** *FR* Wolfgang Reichmann, Ditmar Prinz, Jane Birkin, Nathalie Baye; ***D:*** Paul Morrissey; ***W:*** Paul Morrissey, Matthieu Carriere.

Beetlejuice ☞☞☞ **1/2 1988 (PG)** The after-life is confusing for a pair of ultra-nice novice ghosts Adam Maitland (Baldwin) and his wife Barbara (Davis), who are faced with chasing an obnoxious family of post-modern art lovers who move into their house. Then they hear of a poltergeist who promises to rid the house of all trespassers for a price. Things go from bad to impossible when the maniacal Keaton (as the demonic "Betelgeuse") works his magic. The calypso scene is priceless. A cheesy, funny, surreal farce of life after death with inventive set designs popping continual surprises. Ryder is striking as the misunderstood teen with a death complex, while O'Hara is hilarious as the yuppie art poseur. **92m/C VHS, DVD.** Michael Keaton, Geena Davis, Alec Baldwin, Sylvia Sidney, Catherine O'Hara, Winona Ryder, Jeffrey Jones, Dick Cavett, Glenn Shadix, Robert Goulet; ***D:*** Tim Burton; ***W:*** Michael McDowell, Warren Skaaren; ***C:*** Thomas Ackerman; ***M:*** Danny Elfman. Oscars '88: Makeup; Natl. Soc. Film Critics '88: Actor (Keaton).

Before and After ☞ **1/2 1995 (PG-13)** Disjointed drama depicts well-off suburban couple, Carolyn (Streep) and Ben (Neeson), who are thrown into chaos when their teenaged son Jacob (Furlong) is accused of murdering his girlfriend. Upon notification by the police that his son is the prime suspect and on the lam, Ben finds what seems to be bloody evidence in the family's car, which he destroys. The story loses steam from there. Based on the novel by Rosellen Brown, the focus is on the effect the death has on this picture book Massachusetts family. Neeson and Streep fall short of usually deliverable goods and director Schroeder takes the middle-of-the-road sentimental approach. **107m/C VHS, DVD.** Meryl Streep, Liam Neeson, Edward Furlong, Alfred Molina, John Heard, Julia Weldon, Daniel von Bargen, Ann Magnuson, Alison Folland, Kaiulani Lee; ***D:*** Barbet Schroeder; ***W:*** Ted Tally; ***C:*** Luciano Tovoli; ***M:*** Howard Shore.

Before I Forget ☞☞ *Avant que J'oubile* **2007** When his wealthy benefactor dies after 30 years of support and he doesn't get an expected inheritance, former gigolo Pierre (Nolot) struggles insouciantly to cope with age, poverty, and the increasing complications of his HIV status. He pursues sex with rent boys though he doesn't seem to take any pleasure in it, except for gossiping with his friend Georges (Pommier) about the cost, and takes an unsentimental look back on his life while writing his memoirs. French with subtitles. **108m/C DVD.** *FR* Jacques Nolot, Jean Pommier, Bastien d'Asnieres, Marc Rioufol, Jean-Pol Dubois; ***C:*** Josee Desaies.

Before I Hang ☞☞☞ **1940** When a doctor invents a youth serum from the blood of a murderer, he'll stop at nothing to keep his secret. Karloff himself stands the test of time, and is satisfying as the mad scientist, giving this horror flick its appeal. **60m/B VHS, DVD.** Boris Karloff, Evelyn Keyes, Bruce Bennett, Edward Van Sloan, Ben Taggart, Pedro de Cordoba, Wright Kramer, Bertram Marburgh, Don Beddoe, Robert (Fisk) Fiske; ***D:*** Nick Grinde; ***W:*** Robert D. (Robert Hardy) Andrews; ***C:*** Benjamin (Ben H.) Kline.

Before I Say Goodbye ☞ **1/2 2003** Political hopeful Nell's (Young) hubby faces accusations of crooked business deeds when he and his boat are blown to bits. But her desperate search for the truth might make her the next victim. A Mary Higgins Clark adaptation. **95m/C VHS, DVD.** Sean Young, Lloyd Bochner, Peter DeLuise, Ursula Karven; ***D:*** Michael Storey; ***W:*** John Benjamin Martin, Jon Cooksey, Ali Matheson; ***C:*** David Pelletier. **TV**

Before Morning ☞ **1/2 1933** Police officer poses as a blackmailer to find out which of the two women in the murder victim's life are guilty. **68m/B VHS.** Leo Carrillo, Lora Baxter, Taylor Holmes, Blaine Cordner, Louise Prussing, Russell Hicks, Louis Jean Heydt, Jules Epailly, Constance Bertrand, Terry Carroll; ***D:*** Arthur Hoerl; ***C:*** Walter Strenge.

Before Night Falls ☞☞☞ **2000 (R)** Director Schnabel takes a quantum leap in skill in his second film (after "Basquiat"). This time his tortured artist is the literally tortured late Cuban poet Reinaldo Arenas (Bardem), who falls victim to Castro's repression against both his writings and his sexuality (he's gay). Arenas gets thrown into prison, eventually gets released after confessing his "crimes," and makes his escape as part of the 1980 Mariel boatlift. Ironically, freedom offers little solace to Arenas either in Miami or his last home in New York. Spanish actor Bardem is outstanding as the poet who only seeks to be true to himself and pays a tragic price. Based on the writer's autobiography. **134m/C VHS, DVD.** Javier Bardem, Olivier Martinez, Andrea Di Stefano, Johnny Depp, Michael Wincott, Sean Penn, Hector Babenco, Najwa Nimri; ***D:*** Julian Schnabel; ***W:*** Julian Schnabel, Lazaro Gomez Carilles, Cunningham O'Keefe; ***C:*** Xavier Perez Grobet, Guillermo Rosas; ***M:*** Carter Burwell. Ind. Spirit '01: Actor (Bardem); Natl. Bd. of Review '00: Actor (Bardem); Natl. Soc. Film Critics '00: Actor (Bardem).

Before Sunrise ☞☞ **1/2 1994 (R)** Light, "getting-to-know-you," romance unfolds as two 20-somethings share an unlikely 14-hour date. Gen-Xer Jesse (Hawke) and French beauty (Delpy) meet on the Eurail and he convinces her to join him in exploring Vienna and their mutual attraction before he heads back to the States in the morning. The two exchange life experiences and philosophies in the typical Linklater conversational fashion, but the film strays from the comical accounts of earlier works "Slacker" and "Dazed and Confused." Cinematographer Daniel captures the Old World with finesse, especially in the inevitable "first kiss" atop the Ferris wheel made famous in Orson Welles' "The Third Man." **101m/C VHS, DVD.** Ethan Hawke, Julie Delpy; ***D:*** Richard Linklater; ***W:*** Richard Linklater, Kim Krizan; ***C:*** Lee Daniel. Berlin Intl. Film Fest. '94: Director (Linklater).

Before Sunset ☞☞☞ **1/2 2004 (R)** Sequel to Linklater's "Before Sunrise" reunites Jesse (Hawke) and Celine (Delpy), nine years after their Viennese fling, on the sidewalks of Paris. He's a writer promoting his book about their brief affair. She, a Parisian, shows up at his book signing. The two have only a few hours to catch up before Jesse has to fly back to America. In real time, they walk through Paris together, just talking. But what talking! They begin awkwardly polite and impersonal, but as the minutes slip away their questions and responses take on more urgency. Hawke and Delpy co-wrote the screenplay (with Hawke using his real-life divorce as inspiration) and there's real chemistry between them. Movie veers cleverly back and forth between them and ends ambiguously. Great date film (Sorry, guys). **80m/C VHS, DVD.** Ethan Hawke, Julie Delpy, Rodolphe Pauly; ***D:*** Richard Linklater; ***W:*** Ethan Hawke, Julie Delpy, Richard Linklater; ***C:*** Lee Daniel; ***M:*** Julie Delpy, Glover Gill.

Before the Devil Knows You're Dead ☞☞☞ **2007 (R)** At 83, director Lumet shows he still has crime chops in this grubby tragedy about a botched heist. Calculating, fleshy Andy (Hoffman) has a drug problem and a trophy wife, Gina (Tomei), while his sad-sack, skinny baby bro Hank (Hawke), who happens to be hitting the sheets with Gina, needs cash for his shrewish ex (Ryan). Andy plans a heist on their family's jewelry store but Hank manages to screw it up and things just get more complicated. Good performances by all concerned. **117m/C DVD.** *US* Philip Seymour Hoffman, Ethan Hawke, Marisa Tomei, Albert Finney, Rosemary Harris, Brian F. O'Byrne, Amy Ryan, Michael Shannon, Aleksa Palladino; ***D:*** Sidney Lumet; ***W:*** Kelly Masterson; ***C:*** Ron Fortunato; ***M:*** Carter Burwell.

Before the Fall ☞☞ *NaPolA* **2004** In 1942, teenager Friedrich Weimer (Riemelt) goes against his father's wishes to enter an exclusive Berlin school designed to educate future Nazi leaders. Friedrich distinguishes himself with his boxing prowess but eventually begins to question his indoctrination. German with subtitles. **110m/C DVD.** *GE* Tom Schilling, Max Riemelt, Michael Schenk, Jonas Jagermeyr, Leon A. Kersten, Thomas Dreschel; ***D:*** Dennis Gansel; ***W:*** Dennis Gansel, Maggie Peren; ***C:*** Torsten Brewer; ***M:*** Angelo Badalamenti, Normand Corbeil.

Before the Fall ☞ *Tres Dias* **2008** Predictable and dull wannabe apocalypse thriller. A giant meteorite is headed to apparently destroy the Earth, which has everyone freaking out except for lazy screw-up Alejandro (Clavijo). His mom is more worried that a prison escapee is on his way to kill her absent older son and insists that Alejandro must guard his kids who live out in the country. Spanish with subtitles. **96m/C DVD.** *SP* Victor Clavijo, Eduardo Fernandez, Mariana Cordero; ***D:*** F. Javier Gutierrez; ***W:*** F. Javier Gutierrez, Juan Velarde; ***C:*** Miguel Angel Mora; ***M:*** Antonio Meliveo.

Before the Rain ☞☞☞ *Po Dezju; Pred dozhdot* **1994** War-torn Macedonia is the backdrop for Manchevski's first film (and first made in the newly declared republic of Macedonia). Powerful circular narrative joins three stories about the freedom of love and the pervasiveness of violence. "Words" finds young Macedonian monk Kiril (Colin) distracted from his spiritual duties by young Albanian Muslim Zamira (Mitevska), who takes refuge in his monastery. In "Faces," pregnant picture editor Anne (Cartlidge) is torn between her estranged husband and her lover, Aleksander (Serbedzija), a London-based war photographer who left his native Macedonia years before. "Pictures" finds Aleksandar returning to his old village—now torn by ethnic strife. In Macedonian, Albanian, and English, with subtitles. **120m/C VHS, DVD.** *GB FR MA* Rade Serbedzija, Katrin Cartlidge, Gregoire Colin, Labina Mitevska, Phyllida Law; ***D:*** Milcho Manchevski; ***W:*** Milcho Manchevski; ***C:*** Manuel Teran; ***M:*** Anastasia. Ind. Spirit '96: Foreign Film; Venice Film Fest. '94: Golden Lion.

Before the Rains ☞☞ **2007 (PG-13)** Lavishly photographed period piece about Brits behaving badly in India. In 1937, spice baron Henry Moores (Roache) plans to build a road that will help expand his business but it needs to be completed before monsoon season. His right-man man T.K. (Bose) smooths the way but Moores is having an affair with married housemaid Sajani (Das), whose suspicious husband (Paul) beats her. When Sajani comes to Moores for help, he coldly turns her over to the loyal T.K. to deal with, causing more turmoil and eventual tragedy. **98m/C DVD.** Linus Roache, Rahul Bose, Nandita Das, Jennifer Ehle, Lal Paul, John Standing, Leopold Benedict; ***D:*** Santosh Sivan; ***W:*** Cathy Rabin; ***C:*** Santosh Sivan; ***M:*** Mark Kilian.

Before the Revolution ☞☞ *Prima della Rivoluzione* **1965** One of Bertolucci's first films. Love and politics are mixed when the young Fabrizio, who is dabbling in communism, is also flirting with his young aunt. Striking and powerful film that has yet to lose its effect despite the times. Italian with subtitles. **115m/C VHS.** *IT* Francesco Barilli, Adriana Asti, Alain Midgette, Morando Morandini, Domenico Alpi; ***D:*** Bernardo Bertolucci; ***W:*** Bernardo Bertolucci; ***C:*** Aldo Scavarda; ***M:*** Ennio Morricone, Gino Paoli.

Beggars in Ermine ☞☞ **1934** A handicapped, impoverished man organizes all the beggars in the world into a successful corporation. Unusual performance from Atwill. **70m/B VHS, DVD.** Lionel Atwill, Henry B. Walthall, Betty Furness, Jameson Thomas, James Bush, Astrid Allwyn, George "Gabby" Hayes; ***D:*** Phil Rosen.

Beggars of Life ☞☞ **1928** In a panic, Nancy (Brooks) kills her abusive stepfather. She disguises herself as a boy and, with fellow runaway Jim (Arlen) serving as her protector, decides to hop a train to Canada. They wind up spending the night in a hobo camp, looked after by Oklahoma Red (Beery) who aids in their escape at great cost to himself. **100m/B VHS.** Louise Brooks, Richard Arlen, Wallace Beery, Robert Perry, Roscoe Karns, Edgar "Blue" Washington; ***D:*** William A. Wellman; ***W:*** Benjamin Glazer, Jim Tully; ***C:*** Henry W. Gerrard; ***M:*** Karl Hajos.

Beggar's Opera ☞☞ **1954** Brooks' directorial debut was this adaptation of John Gay's 18th-century comic opera. Highwayman MacHeath (Olivier), a prisoner in Newgate who's condemned to hang, regales a beggar (Griffith) with his life story and the beggar decides to write an opera about him. Olivier did his own singing (badly) while most of the other performers were dubbed. **93m/C DVD.** *GB* Laurence Olivier, Hugh Griffith, Stanley Holloway, Dorothy Tutin, George Devine, Mary Clare, Athene Seyler, Daphne Anderson; ***D:*** Peter Brooks; ***W:*** Christopher Fry, Denis Cannan; ***C:*** Guy Green; ***M:*** Arthur Bliss.

Beginning of the End ☞ **1/2 1957** Produced the same year as "The Deadly Mantis," Gordon's effort adds to 1957's harvest of bugs on a rampage "B"-graders. Giant, radiation-spawned grasshoppers attack Chicago causing Graves to come to the rescue. Easily the best giant grasshopper movie ever made. **73m/B VHS, DVD.** Peggy Castle, Peter Graves, Morris Ankrum, Richard Benedict, James Seay, Thomas B(rowne). Henry, Larry J. Blake, John Close, Frank Wilcox; ***D:*** Bert I. Gordon; ***W:*** Lester Gorn, Fred Freiberger; ***C:*** Jack Marta; ***M:*** Albert Glasser.

The Beguiled ☞☞☞ **1970 (R)** During the Civil War a wounded Union soldier is taken in by the women at a girl's school in the South. He manages to seduce both a student and a teacher, and jealousy and revenge ensue. Decidedly weird psychological melodrama from action vets Siegel and Eastwood. **109m/C VHS, DVD.** Clint Eastwood, Geraldine Page, Elizabeth Hartman, Jo Ann Harris; ***D:*** Donald Siegel; ***W:*** Albert (John B. Sherry) Maltz, Irene (Grimes Grice) Kamp; ***C:*** Bruce Surtees; ***M:*** Lalo Schifrin.

Behave Yourself! ☞ **1/2 1952** A married couple adopts a dog who may be the key for a million-dollar hijacking setup by a gang of hoodlums. **81m/B VHS, DVD.** Shelley Winters, Farley Granger, William Demarest, Lon Chaney Jr., Hans Conried, Elisha Cook Jr., Francis L. Sullivan; ***D:*** George Beck.

Behind Enemy Lines ☞ **1/2 1985 (R)** Special Forces soldier goes on a special mission to eliminate a possible Nazi spy. **83m/C VHS, Blu-ray Disc, UMD.** Hal Holbrook, Ray Sharkey, David McCallum, Tom Isbell, Anne Twomey, Robert Patrick; ***D:*** Sheldon Larry. **TV**

Behind Enemy Lines ☞☞ **1996 (R)** Ex-Marine Mike Weston (Griffith) believes he was responsible for the death of his friend Jones (Mulkey) during assignment in Vietnam. When Weston discovers Jones is actually being hostage, he decides on a rescue mission. **89m/C VHS, DVD.** Thomas Ian Griffith, Chris Mulkey, Courtney Gains; ***D:*** Mark Griffiths; ***W:*** Andrew Osborne, Dennis Cooley; ***C:*** Blake T. Evans; ***M:*** Arthur Kempel.

Behind Enemy Lines ☞☞ **2001 (PG-13)** Balkan civil war is mere scenery, and soldiers only caricatures, in this cartoonish cat-and-mouse chase movie. Ace Navy navigator Lt. Burnett (Wilson), tired of flying peace missions, yearns for some real action. When a routine reconnaissance operation goes awry—his plane shot down over Serbian territory and his pilot ruthlessly executed—Burnett gets his wish. Crusty Admiral Reigart (Hackman) wants to rescue his flyboy, but a pesky international peace agreement gets in the way. First-time director Moore, best known for Sega promos, takes a video game approach to war. Utterly unconvincing suspense, but action sequences do their duty. Despite a clear connection to the ordeal of real-life Air Force captain Scott O'Grady, this is no true story. **106m/C VHS, DVD.** *US* Owen Wilson, Gene Hackman, Joaquim de Almeida, David Keith, Gabriel Macht, Charles Malik Whitfield, Olek Krupa, Vladimir Mashkov, Marko Ogonda; ***D:*** John Moore; ***W:*** David Veloz, Zak Penn; ***C:*** Brendan Galvin; ***M:*** Don Davis.

Behind Enemy Lines 2: Axis of Evil 🦴 1/2 **2006 (R)** Navy SEALs are on a covert op to North Korea to take out a nuclear missile site. The mission is aborted when they are already on the ground so the soldiers decide to get it done anyway despite the bad guys hunting for them. Dumb but generally fast-paced escapist fare. **96m/C DVD.** Nicholas Gonzalez, Keith David, Denis Arndt, Ben Cross, Bruce McGill, Peter Coyote, Glenn Morshower, Matt Bushell, Dennis James Lee; ***D:*** James Dodson; ***W:*** James Dodson; ***C:*** Lorenzo Senatore; ***M:*** Pinar Toprak. **VIDEO**

Behind Enemy Lines 3: Colombia 🦴 1/2 **2008 (R)** An in-name-only sequel that finds a team of Navy SEALS, on assignment in Colombia, falsely accused of assassinating the leaders of two opposing factions. With the U.S. government disavowing their mission, the commandoes are left to sort out the mess on their own. **94m/C DVD.** Joe Manganiello, Kenneth Anderson, Keith David, Channon Roe, Yancey Arias, Steven Bauer, Tim Matheson; ***D:*** Tim Matheson; ***W:*** Tobias Iaconis; ***C:*** Claudio Chea; ***M:*** Joseph Conlan. **VIDEO**

Behind Locked Doors 🦴🦴 1/2 **1948** A journalist fakes mental illness to have himself committed to an asylum, where he believes a crooked judge is in hiding. A superior "B" mystery/suspense feature, with some tense moments. **61m/B VHS, DVD.** Lucille Bremer, Richard Carlson, Tor Johnson, Douglas Fowley, Herbert (Hayes) Heyes, Ralf Harolde; ***D:*** Budd Boetticher; ***W:*** Eugene Ling, Malvin Wald; ***C:*** Guy Roe; ***M:*** Irving Friedman.

Behind Office Doors 🦴🦴 **1931** Astor stars as the secretarial "power behind the throne" in this look at who really wields power in an office. Her boss takes her for granted until things go wrong. **82m/B VHS, DVD.** Mary Astor, Robert Ames, Ricardo Cortez, Charles Sellon; ***D:*** Melville Brown; ***W:*** Carey Wilson.

Behind Prison Walls 🦴🦴 *Youth Takes a Hand* **1943** A steel tycoon and his son are sent to prison, and the son tries to convert his dad to socialism. A fun, light hearted film, the last for veteran Tully. **64m/B VHS.** Alan Baxter, Gertrude Michael, Tully Marshall, Edwin Maxwell, Jacqueline Dalya, Matt Willis; ***D:*** Steve Sekely.

Behind That Curtain 🦴 1/2 **1929** Charlie Chan (Park) makes a brief appearance as a Scotland Yard detective in this melodrama. Wealthy Eve Mannering (Moran) marries rotter Eric Durand (Strange) and they go off to India. Soon unhappy, Eve is eager to leave Eric behind when old friend John Beetham (Baxter) assures her of his love. They travel to San Francisco with a murderous Eric in pursuit. Boris Karloff makes an appearance in his first sound picture as a nameless servant. **91m/B DVD.** Warner Baxter, Lois Moran, Philip Strange, Charles King, Gilbert Emery, E.L. Park; ***D:*** Irving Cummings; ***W:*** Sonya Levien, Clarke Silvernail; ***C:*** Conrad Wells.

Behind the Front 🦴🦴 1/2 **1926** Two friends tumble in and out of trouble in this comic Army film. One of the most profitable films of the late '20s. **60m/B VHS.** Wallace Beery, Raymond Hatton, Richard Arlen, Mary Brian, Chester Conklin; ***D:*** Edward Sutherland.

Behind the Lines 🦴🦴 *Regeneration* **1997 (R)** Focuses on the friendship between WWI soldier/poets Siegfried Sassoon (Wilby) and Wilfred Owen (Bunce), who receive a brief reprieve from the war when they're treated for shell shock at Edinburgh's Craiglockhart Hospital in 1917. Another patient is working-class soldier Billy Prior (Miller), made mute from the horrors he's witnessed. But their compassionate doctor, William Rivers (Pryce), is himself becoming increasingly unstable over the ethical concerns his work engenders. If he cures his patients, they go back to the front to fight again. The first book in Pat Barker's war trilogy. **96m/C VHS, DVD.** *GB CA* Jonathan Pryce, James Wilby, Jonny Lee Miller, Stuart Bunce, Tanya Allen, John Neville, Dougray Scott, David Hayman, David Robb, Julian Fellowes, Kevin McKidd, Jeremy Child; ***D:*** Gilles Mackinnon; ***W:*** Allan Scott; ***C:*** Glen MacPherson; ***M:*** Mychael Danna.

Behind the Mask 🦴🦴 1/2 **1946** Lamont Cranston, better known as do-gooder "The Shadow," finds himself accused of murdering a blackmailing newspaper reporter. Based on the radio serial. **68m/C VHS.** Kane Richmond, Barbara Read, George Chandler, Dorothea Kent, Robert Shayne, June Clyde; ***D:*** Phil Karlson.

Behind the Mask 🦴🦴 1/2 **1999** Mentally challenged janitor James Jones (Fox) is employed at a center run by workaholic doctor Bob Shushan (Sutherland). When the doc suffers a heart attack, it's James who saves him. Shushan takes this as a wake-up call and decides to help James find the father who abandoned him while reconnecting with his own neglected adult son, Brian (Whitford). Based on a true story. **90m/C DVD.** Donald Sutherland, Matthew Fox, Bradley Whitford, Mary McDonnell, Sheila Larkin, Currie Graham, Lorena Gale, Ron Sauve; ***D:*** Tom McLoughlin; ***W:*** Gregory Goedell; ***C:*** Arthur Albert. **TV**

Behind the Red Door 🦴🦴 **2002 (R)** Natalie (Sedgwick) hasn't spoken to her arrogant older brother Roy (Sutherland) for 10 years. A New York photographer, Natalie is tricked by her friend and agent Julia (Channing) into accepting an assignment in Boston that turns out to be for her brother's company. Roy then bullies Natalie into staying for his birthday party—later revealing to her that he's dying of AIDS. He wants to reconcile but a shaken Natalie (who blames Roy for some childhood traumas) insists she must return home. Good cast, but Sutherland's character is so secretive and obnoxious it's hard to dredge up any sympathy for him. **105m/C VHS, DVD.** Kyra Sedgwick, Kiefer Sutherland, Stockard Channing, Jason Carter, Philip Craig; ***D:*** Matia Karrell; ***W:*** Matia Karrell, C.W. Cressler; ***C:*** Robert Elswit; ***M:*** David Fleury. **CABLE**

Behind the Rising Sun 🦴🦴 1/2 **1943** A Japanese publisher's political views clash with those of his American-educated son in 1930s Japan. Well done despite pre-war propaganda themes. **88m/B VHS.** Tom Neal, J. Carrol Naish, Robert Ryan, Mike Mazurki, Margo, Gloria Holden, Donald "Don" Douglas; ***D:*** Edward Dmytryk.

Behind the Sun 🦴🦴 *Abril Despedacado; Broken April* **2001 (PG-13)** A blood feud between two families nearly destroys them both in Salles' adaptation of Ismail Kadare's novel, which the director relocated to Brazil in 1910. The Ferreiras and the Breveses are both sugarcane planters determined to protect their honor if nothing else. Tonho Breves (Santoro) is expected to avenge the death of his older brother at the hands of the Ferreiras. Tonho's young brother (Lacerda) can't understand why the pointless violence continues and when Tonho falls in love with traveling circus performer Clara (Antonio), the boy becomes determined to see his brother safe and happy. Portuguese with subtitles. **91m/C VHS, DVD.** *BR FR SI* Jose Dumont, Rita Assemany, Rodrigo Santoro, Ravi Ramos Lacerda, Luiz Carlos Vasconcelos, Othon Bastos, Flavia Marco Antonio; ***D:*** Walter Salles; ***W:*** Walter Salles, Karim Ainouz, Sergio Machado; ***C:*** Walter Carvalho; ***M:*** Antonio Pinto. British Acad. '01: Foreign Film.

Behind the Wall 🦴 1/2 **2008 (R)** A small community in Maine has decided to renovate a local lighthouse that's reputed to be haunted because of a 20-year-old murder case, despite the objections of an elderly priest. The pace picks up in the latter half of this low-budget horrorfest. **94m/C DVD.** Souleymane Sy Savane, Diana Franco-Galindo, Jody Richardson, Lindy Booth, Lawrence Dane, James Thomas, Andy Jones; ***D:*** Paul Schneider; ***W:*** Anna Singer, Michael Bafaro; ***C:*** Larry Lynn. **VIDEO**

Behind Two Guns 🦴 1/2 **1924** A medicine show doctor and his trusty Indian sidekick help a frontier town's citizens discover who's constantly robbing the strongbox from the stagecoach. **62m/B DVD.** Otto Lederer, J.B. Warner, Guillermo Calles, Hazel Newman, Jim Welch; ***D:*** Robert North Bradbury; ***W:*** Robert North Bradbury; ***C:*** Bert Longenecker.

Behold a Pale Horse 🦴🦴 1/2 **1964** A Spanish police captain attempts to dupe Peck into believing that his mother is dying and he must visit her on her deathbed. Loyalist Spaniard Peck becomes privy to the plot against him, but goes to Spain anyway in this post Spanish Civil War film. **118m/B VHS, DVD.** Gregory Peck, Anthony Quinn, Omar Sharif, Mildred Dunnock; ***D:*** Fred Zinnemann; ***W:*** J(ames) P(inckney) Miller; ***M:*** Maurice Jarre.

Beijing Bicycle 🦴🦴 *Shiqisuide Danche* **2001 (PG-13)** Guei (Lin) leaves his provincial home and gets a job as a bike messenger in Beijing where most of his meager wages go to purchase his mountain bike. His bike is stolen and Guei loses his job. He finally discovers that petulant high schooler Jian (Bin), whose father wouldn't buy him a bike of his own, has purchased Geui's from a flea market and, because he can now join his friends riding after school, he refuses to let it go. Their confrontation turns violent as more and more people become involved. Chinese with subtitles. **113m/C VHS, DVD.** *TW FR* Cui Lin, Bin Li, Zhou Xun, Gao Yuanyuahn, Li Shuang, Zhao Yiwel, Pang Yan; ***D:*** Xiaoshuai Wang; ***W:*** Xiaoshuai Wang, Danian Tang, Peggy Chiao, Hsiang-Ming Hsu; ***C:*** Jie Liu; ***M:*** Wang Hsiao Feng.

The Being 🦴 **1983 (R)** People in Idaho are terrorized by a freak who became abnormal after radiation was disposed in the local dump. Another dull monster-created-by-nuclear-waste non-event. Of limited interest is Buzzi. However, you'd be more entertained (read: amused) by Troma's "The Toxic Avenger," which takes itself much (much!) less seriously. **82m/C VHS, DVD.** Ruth Buzzi, Martin Landau, Jose Ferrer; ***D:*** Jackie Kong.

Being at Home with Claude 🦴🦴 **1992** Yves (Dupuis) is a 22-year-old Montreal hustler being interrogated by a nameless inspector (Godin) for the murder of his lover, Claude (Pichette). Yves has admitted his guilt but the inspector wants to reconstruct the event and determine a motive. Lots of black-and-white flashbacks as Yves dwells on his work and his psychologically love-death relationship with Claude. Rather pretentious and long-winded. Based on the play by Rene-Daniel DuBois. In French with English subtitles. **86m/C VHS.** *CA* Roy Dupuis, Jacques Godin, Jean-Francois Pichette, Gaston Lepage; ***D:*** Johanne Boisvert; ***W:*** Jean Boudin. Genie '92: Score.

Being Human 🦴🦴 1/2 **1994 (PG-13)** Ambitious comedy drama promises more than it delivers, and shackles Williams in the process. Hector (Williams) is a regular guy continuously reincarnated throughout the milennia. He plays a caveman, a Roman slave, a Middle Ages nomad, a crew member on a 17th century new world voyage, and a modern New Yorker in separate vignettes that echo and/or extend the main themes of family, identity, and random fate. But he manages to emerge from each sketch as an unassuming everyman who never learns his lesson. One of Williams' periodic chancy ventures away from his comedic roots occasionally strikes gold, but often seems overly restrained. **122m/C VHS.** Robin Williams, John Turturro, Anna Galiena, Vincent D'Onofrio, Hector Elizondo, Lorraine Bracco, Lindsay Crouse, Kelly Hunter, William H. Macy, Grace Mahlaba, Theresa Russell, Charles Miller, Helen Miller, Robert Carlyle, Tony Curran, Bill Nighy, David Morrissey, Ewan McGregor, David Proval; ***D:*** Bill Forsyth; ***W:*** Bill Forsyth; ***C:*** Michael Coulter; ***M:*** Michael Gibbs.

Being John Malkovich 🦴🦴🦴 **1999 (R)** Very weird comedy is the debut feature for Jonze. High-strung street puppeteer Craig Schwartz (Cusack) is married to frumpy pet-store worker Lotte (an unrecognizable Diaz). Forced to take a job as an office clerk in a building on floor seven-and-a-half, Craig falls for office vixen, Maxine (Keener), but his big discovery is a sealed door that reveals a tunnel leading directly into actor John Malkovich's mind. Craig views the world through the actor's eyes for 15 minutes at a time and decides to profit on his findings. Things just get more surreal when both Lotte and Maxine get involved. **112m/C VHS, DVD, HD DVD.** John Cusack, Cameron Diaz, Catherine Keener, John Malkovich, Orson Bean, Mary Kay Place, Charlie Sheen; ***D:*** Spike Jonze; ***W:*** Charlie Kaufman; ***C:*** Lance Acord; ***M:*** Carter Burwell. British Acad. '99: Orig. Screenplay; Ind. Spirit '00: First Feature, First Screenplay; L.A. Film Critics '99: Screenplay; MTV Movie Awards '00: New Filmmaker (Jonze); N.Y. Film Critics '99: Support. Actor (Malkovich), Support. Actress (Keener); Natl. Soc. Film Critics '99: Film, Screenplay.

Being Julia 🦴🦴🦴 **2004 (R)** Bening triumphs in the title role as a larger-than-life stage actress suffering a midlife dip. But this delightful diva still has the deviousness to show a couple of whippersnappers what it means to be a star. Swanning about in 1938 London, Julia has a strong support system, led by her unfaithful but loving manager/husband Michael (Irons). However, she's bored and ready for a little fling with Tom (Evans), a fawning young fan with an agenda of his own, involving his ambitious actress girlfriend (Punch). When Julia discovers she's been used, she takes the opportunity not only to get revenge but as a step in revitalizing her life. Based on the novel "Theatre" by W. Somerset Maugham. **105m/C DVD.** *HU CA GB* Annette Bening, Jeremy Irons, Bruce Greenwood, Miriam Margolyes, Juliet Stevenson, Shaun Evans, Lucy Punch, Maury Chaykin, Sheila McCarthy, Michael Gambon, Leigh Lawson, Rosemary Harris, Rita Tushingham, Thomas Sturridge; ***D:*** Istvan Szabo; ***W:*** Ronald Harwood; ***C:*** Lajos Koltai; ***M:*** Mychael Danna. Golden Globes '05: Actress—Mus./Comedy (Bening).

Being There 🦴🦴🦴 1/2 **1979 (PG)** A feeble-minded gardener, whose entire knowledge of life comes from watching TV, is sent out into the real world when his employer dies. Equipped with his prize possession, his remote control unit, the gardener unwittingly enters the world of politics and is welcomed as a mysterious sage. Sellers is wonderful in this satiric treat adapted by Jerzy Kosinski from his novel. **130m/C VHS, DVD, Blu-ray Disc.** Peter Sellers, Shirley MacLaine, Melvyn Douglas, Jack Warden, Richard Dysart, Richard Basehart; ***D:*** Hal Ashby; ***W:*** Jerzy Kosinski; ***C:*** Caleb Deschanel; ***M:*** Johnny Mandel. Oscars '79: Support. Actor (Douglas); Golden Globes '80: Actor—Mus./Comedy (Sellers), Support. Actor (Douglas); L.A. Film Critics '79: Support. Actor (Douglas); Natl. Bd. of Review '79: Actor (Sellers); N.Y. Film Critics '79: Support. Actor (Douglas); Natl. Soc. Film Critics '79: Cinematog.; Writers Guild '79: Adapt. Screenplay.

Being Two Isn't Easy 🦴🦴 1/2 **1962** Director Ichikawa shows the world through the eyes of a two-year-old as a young couple struggle to raise their son. In Japanese with English subtitles. **88m/C VHS.** *JP* Fujiko Yamamoto, Eiji Funakoshi; ***D:*** Kon Ichikawa.

Bela Lugosi Meets a Brooklyn Gorilla **WOOF!** *The Boys from Brooklyn; The Monster Meets the Gorilla* **1952** Two men who look like Dean Martin and Jerry Lewis (but aren't) get lost in the jungle, where they meet mad scientist Lugosi. Worse than it sounds. Real Jerry sued for unflattering imitation. **74m/B VHS, DVD.** Bela Lugosi, Duke Mitchell, Sammy Petrillo, Charlita, Martin Garralaga, Al Kikume, Muriel Landers, Milton Newberger; ***D:*** William Beaudine; ***W:*** Tim Ryan; ***C:*** Charles Van Enger; ***M:*** Richard Hazard.

Belfast Assassin 🦴 *Harry's Game* **1984** A British anti-terrorist agent goes undercover in Ireland to find an IRA assassin who shot a British cabinet minister. **130m/C VHS.** Derek Thompson, Ray Lonnen, Gil Brailey, Benjamin Whitrow; ***D:*** Lawrence Gordon-Clark.

Believe 🦴🦴 1/2 **1999 (PG-13)** Teen prankster Ben Stiles (Mabe) loves to scare people. In fact, his behavior gets him kicked out of prep school and sent to live with his no-nonsense grandfather (Rubes). But the fright's on him when Ben and his friend

Katherine (Cuthbert) decide to turn the abandoned Wickwire House into a haunted mansion and a ghostly figure suddenly starts making appearances. **97m/C VHS, DVD.** Ricky Mabe, Elisha Cuthbert, Jan Rubes, Ben Gazzara, Andrea Martin, Jayne Heitmeyer; ***D:*** Robert Tinnell. **VIDEO**

Believe in Me 🦴🦴 **2006 (PG)** Formulaic, standard "inspiring story" sports film plays like a distaff "Hoosiers" but occasionally conjures up an interesting twist. Clay Driscoll (Donovan) moves to small-town America to discover that his new job coaching a high school boy's team has been taken from him and he's been given the girl's team instead. At first offended, he takes the young women from zeros (giggling losers) to heroes (state finals) through hard work, dedication, inspiring locker room speeches, and other well-mined sports cliches. Based on a true story (of course). **108m/C DVD.** *US* Jeffrey Donovan, Samantha Mathis, Bruce Dern, Bob Gunton, Heather Matarazzo, Alicia Lagano; ***D:*** Robert Collector; ***W:*** Robert Collector; ***C:*** James L. Carter; ***M:*** David Torn.

The Believer 🦴🦴 **2001** Inspired by the true story of neo-Nazi Daniel Burros and the New York Times expose that revealed he was Jewish. In Bean's version, Danny Balint (Gosling) is a ferociously intelligent former yeshiva student whose personal identity crisis has led him to a fascist movement led by Curtis Zampf (Zane) and to virulent anti-Semitism. But even while leading his own band of skinheads, Danny discovers he can't easily leave his Jewish heritage behind. **98m/C VHS, DVD.** Ryan Gosling, Summer Phoenix, Billy Zane, Theresa Russell, Glenn Fitzgerald; ***D:*** Henry Bean; ***W:*** Henry Bean; ***C:*** Jim Denault; ***M:*** Joel Diamond.

The Believers 🦴🦴 **1/2 1987 (R)** Tense horror mystery set in New York city about a series of gruesome, unexplained murders. A widowed police psychologist investigating the deaths unwittingly discovers a powerful Santeria cult that believes in the sacrifice of children. Without warning he is drawn into the circle of the "Believers" and must free himself before his own son is the next sacrifice. Gripping (and grim), unrelenting horror. **114m/C VHS, DVD.** Martin Sheen, Helen Shaver, Malick Bowens, Harris Yulin, Robert Loggia, Jimmy Smits, Richard Masur, Harley Cross, Elizabeth Wilson, Lee Richardson, Carla Pinza; ***D:*** John Schlesinger; ***W:*** Mark Frost; ***C:*** Robby Muller; ***M:*** J. Peter Robinson.

Believers 🦴 **1/2 2007 (R)** Two paramedics (Messner, Huertas) are kidnapped by a doomsday cult that believes the end is at hand so they're going to commit mass suicide. Not quite sure why a suicidal cult wants paramedics in its midst, but it's a creepy story. **101m/C DVD.** Johnny Messner, Elizabeth Bogush, Daniel Benzali, Jon Huertas, John Farley, Deanna Russo; ***D:*** Daniel Myrick; ***W:*** Daniel Myrick; ***C:*** Andrew Huebscher; ***M:*** Kays Al-Atrakchi. **VIDEO**

Belizaire the Cajun 🦴🦴 **1/2 1986 (PG)** 19th-century Louisiana love story. White prejudice against the Cajuns is rampant and violent, but that doesn't stop sexy faith healer Assante from falling in love with the inaccessible Cajun wife (Youngs) of a rich local. Made with care on a tight budget. Worthwhile, though uneven. **103m/C VHS, DVD.** Armand Assante, Gail Youngs, Will Patton, Stephen McHattie, Michael Schoeffling, Robert Duvall, Nancy Barrett; ***D:*** Glen Pitre; ***W:*** Glen Pitre; ***C:*** Richard Bowen; ***M:*** Michael Doucet, Howard Shore.

Bell, Book and Candle 🦴🦴 **1/2 1958** Gillian Holroyd (Novak) is a beautiful modern-day witch (from a family of witches) who has made up her mind to refrain from using her powers. That is until Sheperd Henderson (Stewart) moves into her building and she decides to enchant him with a love spell. But spells have a way of backfiring on those who cast them. Lanchester is romantic Aunt Queenie and Lemmon is a standout as Gillian's jazz-loving, bongo-playing brother, Nicky. **106m/C VHS, DVD.** James Stewart, Kim Novak, Jack Lemmon, Elsa Lanchester, Ernie Kovacs, Hermione Gingold, Janice Rule; ***D:*** Richard Quine; ***W:*** Daniel Taradash; ***C:*** James Wong Howe; ***M:*** George Duning.

Bell from Hell 🦴🦴 **1974** A tale of insanity and revenge, wherein a young man, institutionalized since his mother's death, plots to kill his aunt and three cousins. **80m/C VHS, DVD.** Viveca Lindfors, Renaud Verley, Alfredo Mayo; ***D:*** Claudio Guerin Hill.

The Bell Jar 🦴 **1/2 1979 (R)** Based on poet Sylvia Plath's acclaimed semi-autobiographical novel, this is the story of a young woman who becomes the victim of mental illness. Not for the easily depressed and a disjointed and disappointing adaptation of Plath's work. **113m/C VHS, DVD.** Marilyn Hassett, Julie Harris, Barbara Barrie, Anne Bancroft, Robert Klein, Anne Jackson; ***D:*** Larry Peerce.

Bella 🦴🦴 **2006 (PG-13)** Saccharine storytelling, appealing leads. Jose (Verastegui) is the head chef at his brother Manny's (Perez) upscale Mexican restaurant in Manhattan. Intolerant of unprofessional behavior, Manny fires waitress Nina (Blanchard) when she's late for work. Jose discovers the reason is because the unmarried young woman has just learned she's pregnant, so he leaves as well. Jose then spends the day with Nina, trying to convince her to have the baby, with his motives slowly revealed through flashbacks. **91m/C DVD.** Eduardo Verastegui, Tammy Blanchard, Manny Perez, Angelica Aragon, Jamie Tirelli, Ali Landry, Ramon Rodriguez; ***D:*** Alejandro Monteverde; ***W:*** Patrick Million; ***C:*** Andrew Cadelago; ***M:*** Stephen Altman.

Bella Mafia 🦴🦴 **1/2 1997 (R)** Over-the-top trash and that's meant in the finest possible way. This lurid melodrama, originally a two-part miniseries, concerns the Sicilian mob family, the Lucianos, who have suffered the loss of father Roberto (Farina) and three sons. Widowed matriarch Graziella (Redgrave) decides to join with her three daughters-in-law, Sophia (Kinski), Teresa (Douglas), and Moyra (Tilly), and avenge their deaths. Oh yes, there's also Sophia's secret son Luca (Marsden), a killer who turns up to insinuates himself into family life. Adapted by La Plante from her novel. **117m/C VHS.** Vanessa Redgrave, Nastassja Kinski, Illeana Douglas, Jennifer Tilly, James Marsden, Peter Bogdanovich, Dennis Farina, Gina Philips; ***D:*** David Greene; ***W:*** Lynda La Plante. **TV**

Bellamy 🦴 **1981** Murderous madman massacres masseuses, and Bellamy is the cop out to get him. **92m/C VHS.** John Stanton, Timothy Elston, Sally Conabere; ***D:*** Gary Conway. **TV**

The Bellboy 🦴🦴 **1/2 1960** Lewis makes his directorial debut in this plotless but clever outing. He also stars as the eponymous character, a bellboy at Miami's Fountainbleau Hotel. Cameos from Berle and Winchell are highlights. **72m/B VHS, DVD.** Jerry Lewis, Alex Gerry, Bob Clayton, Sonny Sands, Bill Richmond, Larry Best, Maxie "Slapsie" Rosenbloom; ***Cameos:*** Milton Berle, Walter Winchell; ***D:*** Jerry Lewis; ***W:*** Jerry Lewis; ***C:*** Haskell Boggs; ***M:*** Walter Scharf.

The Bellboy and the Playgirls
WOOF! *The Playgirls and the Bellboy; Mit Eva Fing Die Sunde An* **1962** Early Coppola effort adds new film footage to a 1958 German movie. Stars Playboy playmate June "The Body" Wilkinson, with other centerfolds of the time. **93m/C VHS.** June Wilkinson, Donald Kenney, Karin Dor, Willy Fritsch, Michael Cramer, Louise Lawson, Ann Myers; ***D:*** Francis Ford Coppola; ***W:*** Francis Ford Coppola.

Belle Americaine 🦴🦴 *What a Chassis!* **1961** Title refers to the Cadillac car young Parisian factory worker Dhery buys at a suspiciously bargain price. Naturally, his deal is too good to be true and trouble follows. Dubbed in English. **97m/C VHS.** *FR* Robert Dhery, Louis de Funes, Collette Brosset, Alfred Adam, Bernard Lavelette, Annie Ducaux; ***D:*** Robert Dhery; ***W:*** Robert Dhery, Alfred Adam, Pierre Tchernia; ***C:*** Ghislan Cloquet; ***M:*** Gerard Calvi.

Belle de Jour 🦴🦴🦴 **1/2 1967 (R)** Based on Joseph Kessel's novel, one of director Bunuel's best movies has all his characteristic nuances: the hypocrisy of our society; eroticism; anti-religion. Deneuve plays Severine, a chic, frigid Parisian newlywed, who decides to become a daytime prostitute, unbeknownst to her husband. Bunuel blends reality with fantasy, and the viewer is never sure which is which in this finely crafted movie. French with subtitles. **100m/C VHS, DVD.** *FR* Catherine Deneuve, Jean Sorel, Genevieve Page, Michel Piccoli, Francisco Rabal, Pierre Clementi, Georges Marchal, Francoise Fabian; ***D:*** Luis Bunuel; ***W:*** Luis Bunuel, Jean-Claude Carriere; ***C:*** Sacha Vierny.

Belle Epoque 🦴🦴🦴 *The Age of Beauty* **1992 (R)** Young army deserter Fernando (Sanz) embarks on a personal voyage of discovery when he meets Manolo (Gomez), an eccentric old man, and father to four beautiful daughters. Fernando can't believe his luck—and the sisters share his interest, resulting in an amusing round of musical beds. Bittersweet tale set amidst the anarchy and war of 1930s Spain with a terrific screenplay that tastefully handles the material without stooping to the obvious leering possibilities. In addition to Oscar, won nine Spanish Goyas, including best picture, director, actress (Gil), and screenplay. Title ironically refers to the era at the end of the 19th century before the wars of the 20th century tore Europe apart. Spanish with English subtitles or dubbed. **108m/C VHS, DVD.** *SP* Jorge Sanz, Fernando Fernan-Gomez, Ariadna Gil, Maribel Verdu, Penelope Cruz, Miriam Diaz-Aroca, Mary Carmen Ramirez, Michel Galabru, Gabino Diego; ***D:*** Fernando Trueba; ***W:*** Rafael Azcona; ***C:*** Jose Luis Alcaine; ***M:*** Antoine Duhamel. Oscars '93: Foreign Film.

The Belle of New York 🦴🦴 **1952** A turn-of-the-century bachelor falls in love with a Salvation Army missionary in this standard musical. ♫ Naughty But Nice; Baby Doll; Oops; I Wanna Be a Dancin' Man; Seeing's Believing; Bachelor's Dinner Song; When I'm Out With the Belle of New York; Let a Little Love Come In. **82m/C VHS.** Fred Astaire, Vera-Ellen, Marjorie Main, Keenan Wynn, Alice Pearce, Gale Robbins, Clinton Sundberg; ***D:*** Charles Walters.

Belle of the Nineties 🦴🦴 **1/2** *It Ain't No Sin* **1934** West struts as a 1890s singer who gets involved with a boxer. Her trademark sexual innuendos were already being censored but such lines as "It's better to be looked over than overlooked," done in West style, get the point across. **73m/B VHS, DVD.** Mae West, Roger Pryor, Johnny Mack Brown, John Miljan, Katherine DeMille, Harry Woods, Edward (Ed) Gargan; ***D:*** Leo McCarey; ***W:*** Mae West; ***C:*** Karl Struss; ***M:*** Arthur Johnston.

Belle Starr 🦴 **1/2 1979** The career of Wild West outlaw Belle Starr is chronicled in this strange western pastiche about lawlessness and sexual agression. Wertmuller directed under the pseudonym Nathan Wich. Dubbed in English. **90m/C VHS.** *IT* Elsa Martinelli, George Eastman, Dan Harrison; ***D:*** Lina Wertmuller.

Belle Toujours 🦴🦴🦴 **2006** Thirty-nine years after "Belle de Jour" comes this sequel—or perhaps more of an homage—from Manoel de Oliveira. A chance meeting after so many years places Henri Husson (Piccoli) and Severine (Ogier) at a candlelit dinner table where they discuss the past, the intervening years, and thoughts of the future. Severine, now a widow worn down by years of carrying secrets and lies, seems to care little about reliving their sexually complicated past and in fact is prepared to retire to a convent. Henri, still feeling the dart of her rejection, wants to recount the sordid history they share. In the earlier film the young Severine supported herself and her disabled husband as a daytime prostitute, a secret she meticulously kept from her husband; Henri wanted a relationship with her that never happened. Paris sparkles in this beautifully crafted work. **68m/C DVD.** *FR PT* Michel Piccoli, Bulle Ogier, Ricardo Trepa, Leonor Baldaque, Julia Buisel; ***D:*** Manoel de Oliveira; ***W:*** Manoel de Oliveira; ***C:*** Sabine Lancelin.

The Belles of St. Trinian's 🦴🦴🦴 **1953** Sim is priceless in a dual role as the eccentric headmistress of a chaotic, bankrupt girls' school and her bookie twin brother who scheme the school into financial security. The first in a series of movies based on a popular British cartoon by Ronald Searles about a girls' school and its mischievous students. Followed by "Blue Murder at St. Trinian's," "The Pure Hell of St. Trinian's," and "The Great St. Trinian's Train Robbery." **86m/B VHS.** *GB* Alastair Sim, Joyce Grenfell, Hermione Baddeley, George Cole, Eric Pohlmann, Renee Houston, Beryl Reid, Balbina, Jill Braidwood, Annabelle Covey, Betty Ann Davies, Diana Day, Jack Doyle, Irene Handl, Arthur Howard, Sidney James, Lloyd Lamble, Jean Langston, Belinda Lee, Vivian Martin, Andree Melly, Mary Merrall, Guy Middleton, Joan Sims, Jerry Verno, Richard Wattis; ***D:*** Frank Launder; ***W:*** Frank Launder, Sidney Gilliat, Val Valentine; ***C:*** Stanley Pavey; ***M:*** Malcolm Arnold.

Belles on Their Toes 🦴🦴 **1952** Somewhat less charming sequel to 1950's "Cheaper by the Dozen" is big on nostalgia. Now widowed, Lillian Gilbreth (Loy) is struggling to support her large family, having to overcome women in the workplace prejudice. Using her industrial engineering degree, Lillian finally gets a job training young engineers, but this means eldest daughter Ann (Crain) must pick up the domestic slack. Which puts a crimp in Ann's budding romance with young Dr. Bob (Hunter). Based on the memoir by Gilbreth children Frank and Ernestine. **89m/C DVD.** Myrna Loy, Jeanne Crain, Debra Paget, Jeffrey Hunter, Edward Arnold, Hoagy Carmichael, Barbara Bates, Robert Arthur, Martin Milner, Verna Felton, Carole Nugent, Tommy "T.V." Ivo, Jimmy Hunt, Robert Easton, Cecil Weston; ***D:*** Henry Levin; ***W:*** Henry Ephron, Phoebe Ephron; ***C:*** Arthur E. Arling; ***M:*** Cyril Mockridge.

Bellissima 🦴🦴🦴 **1951** A woman living in an Italian tenement has unrealistic goals for her plain but endearing daughter when a famous director begins casting a role designed for a child. The mother's maternal fury and collision with reality highlight a poignant film. Italian with subtitles. **130m/B VHS, DVD.** *IT* Anna Magnani, Walter Chiari, Alessandro Blasetti, Tina Apicella, Gastone Renzelli; ***D:*** Luchino Visconti; ***W:*** Luchino Visconti, Cesare Zavattini, Francesco Rosi, Suso Cecchi D'Amico; ***C:*** Piero Portalupi, Paul Ronald.

Bellman and True 🦴🦴 **1/2 1988 (R)** Rewarding, but sometimes tedious character study of a mild mannered computer whiz who teams with a gang of bank robbers. Fine performances, especially subtle dangerous gang characters. **112m/C VHS.** *GB* Bernard Hill, Kieran O'Brien, Richard Hope, Frances Tomelty, Derek Newark, John Kavanagh, Ken Bones; ***D:*** Richard Loncraine; ***W:*** Desmond Lowden; ***C:*** Ken Westbury; ***M:*** Colin Towns.

The Bells 🦴🦴🦴 **1926** The mayor of an Alsatian village kills a wealthy merchant and steals his money. The murderer experiences pangs of guilt which are accentuated when a traveling mesmerist comes to town and claims to be able to discern a person's darkest secrets. Silent with music score. **67m/B VHS, DVD.** Lionel Barrymore, Boris Karloff, Gustav von Seyffertitz; ***D:*** James L. Young; ***W:*** James L. Young; ***C:*** L.W. O'Connell.

Bells Are Ringing 🦴🦴🦴 **1960** A girl who works for a telephone answering service can't help but take an interest in the lives of the clients, especially a playwright with an inferiority complex. Based on Adolph Green and Betty Comden's Broadway musical. ♫ Just in Time; The Party's Over; It's a Perfect Relationship; Do It Yourself; It's a Simple Little System; Better Than a Dream; I Met a Girl; Drop That Name; I'm Going Back. **126m/C VHS, DVD.** Judy Holliday, Dean Martin, Fred Clark, Eddie Foy Jr., Jean Stapleton; ***D:*** Vincente Minnelli; ***W:*** Betty Comden, Adolph Green; ***C:*** Milton Krasner; ***M:*** Andre Previn.

Bells of Capistrano 🦴 **1/2 1942** The last film Autry made before serving in the Army finds the singing star wanted as a crowd-drawing attraction for two rival rodeo companies. Gene chooses the one owned by the pretty girl, which causes problems with the competition. ♫ In Old Capistrano; Forgive Me; Don't Bite the Hand That's Feeding You; At Sundown. **73m/B VHS.** Gene Autry, Smiley Burnette, Virginia Grey, Lucien Littlefield; ***D:*** William M. Morgan; ***W:*** Lawrence Kimble; ***C:*** Reggie Lanning.

Bells of Coronado 🦴🦴 **1950** Rogers and Evans team up to expose the murderer of the owner of a profitable uranium mine. A gang of smugglers trying to trade the ore to foreign powers is thwarted. The usual thin storyline, but filled with action and riding stunts. **67m/B VHS, DVD.** Roy Rogers, Dale Evans, Pat Brady, Grant Withers; ***D:*** William Witney.

Bells of Death 1/2 *Dun Hun Ling* **1968** A young martial arts student infiltrates the gang that killed his family and kidnapped his sister, finishing them off one by one. **91m/C VHS, DVD.** *HK* Chun Ping, Chang Yi, Chao Hsin Yen; ***D:*** Yueh Fung.

Bells of Rosarita 1/2 **1945** Roy helps foil an evil plan to swindle Evans out of the circus she inherited. All-star western cast under the big top. **54m/B VHS, DVD.** Roy Rogers, Dale Evans, George "Gabby" Hayes, Sunset Carson, Adele Mara, Grant Withers, Roy Barcroft, Addison Richards; ***D:*** Frank McDonald.

The Bells of St. Mary's 1/2 **1945** An easy-going priest finds himself in a subtle battle of wits with the Mother Superior over how the children of St. Mary's school should be raised. It's the sequel to "Going My Way." Songs include the title tune and "Aren't You Glad You're You?" Also available in a colorized version. **126m/B VHS, DVD.** Bing Crosby, Ingrid Bergman, Henry Travers; ***D:*** Leo McCarey; ***W:*** Dudley Nichols; ***C:*** George Barnes; ***M:*** Robert Emmett Dolan, Johnny Burke, James Van Heusen. Oscars '45: Sound; Golden Globes '46: Actress—Drama (Bergman); N.Y. Film Critics '45: Actress (Bergman).

Bells of San Angelo **1947** Roy foils thieves' attempts to steal a girl's inherited ranch. **54m/C VHS, DVD.** Roy Rogers, Dale Evans; ***D:*** William Witney.

Bells of San Fernando **1947** An Irish seaman wanders into California during early Spanish rule and confronts a cruel overseer in this lackluster Western drama. Scripted by "Cisco Kid" Renaldo. **75m/B VHS, DVD.** Donald Woods, Gloria Warren, Byron Foulger; ***D:*** Terry Morse; ***W:*** Jack DeWitt, Duncan Renaldo.

Belly **1998 (R)** Inner-city crime tale preaches against crime, violence and drugs while it visually glorifies the opulent benefits of them. Childhood pals Tommy (Simmons) and Sincere (Jones) are successful criminals who head down different paths. Sincere dreams of turning legit and moving his family to Africa. Tommy gets deeper into the drug biz until he is caught by feds and forced to bring down innocent black leader Reverend Saviour (Muhammed). Although the movie ends with a plea for change, it may itself be part of the problem. **95m/C VHS, DVD.** Nas, DMX, Taral Hicks, Tionne "T-Boz" Watkins, Method Man, Tyrin Turner, Hassan Johnson, Power, Louie Rankin, Minister Benjamin F. Muhammed; ***D:*** Hype Williams; ***W:*** Nas, Hype Williams, Anthony Bodden; ***C:*** Malik Hassan Sayeed; ***M:*** Stephen Cullo.

The Belly of an Architect 1/2 **1991 (R)** A thespian feast for the larger-than-life Dennehy as blustering American architect whose personal life and health both crumble as he obsesssively readies an exhibition in Rome. A multi-tiered, carefully composed tragicomedy from the ideosyncratic filmmaker Greenaway, probably his most accessible work for general audiences. **119m/C VHS, DVD.** *GB IT* Brian Dennehy, Chloe Webb, Lambert Wilson, Sergio Fantoni, Geoffrey Copleston, Marino (Martin) Mase; ***D:*** Peter Greenaway; ***W:*** Peter Greenaway; ***C:*** Sacha Vierny; ***M:*** Glenn Branca, Wim Mertens.

Bellyfruit **1999** Film, which refers to pregnancy, was inspired by the real-life stories of teen mothers in L.A. 14-year-old Shanika is living in a home for troubled girls when she's taken in by the charms of Damon, equally young Christina witnesses her mother (who had Christina when she was a teen) drug and party and decides to follow her example, while 16-year-old Aracely becomes pregnant by her boyfriend Oscar. Although he stands by her, Aracely's traditional Latin father kicks her out of the house. And when they have their babies, the teens lives just get more confused. **95m/C VHS, DVD.** Kelly Vint, Tamara La Seon Bass, Tonatzin Mondragon, T.E. Russell, Michael Pena, Bonnie Dickenson, Kimberly Scott, James Dumant; ***D:*** Kerri Green; ***W:*** Kerri Green, Maria Bernhard, Suzannah Blinkoff, Janet Borrus; ***C:*** Peter Calvin.

Beloved 1/2 **1998 (R)** Sethe (Winfrey) is a middle-aged former slave in rural Ohio years after her emancipation from a Kentucky planation. She is haunted (literally) by the painful legacy of slavery in the form of a mud-covered feral child known as Beloved (Newton). Another reminder is Paul D (Glover), a former slave from the same Kentucky plantation, who stokes Sethe's embers. Metaphors abound as we wonder if Beloved really is the child Sethe killed years before. Oprah's pet project (she's owned the film rights for 10 years) is a faithful adaptation of Toni Morrison's Pulitzer Prize-winning novel. Unfortunately, the long-awaited feature can't fulfill the huge expectations. While performances are excellent, pic suffers from a sense of self-indulgence, which is accentuated by the three-hour running time. At times powerful and moving, but also slow and occasionally confusing. **172m/C VHS, DVD.** Oprah Winfrey, Thandie Newton, Danny Glover, Kimberly Elise, Lisa Gay Hamilton, Beah Richards, Irma P. Hall, Albert Hall, Jason Robards Jr., Jude Ciccolella; ***D:*** Jonathan Demme; ***W:*** Akosua Busia, Richard LaGravenese, Adam Brooks; ***C:*** Tak Fujimoto; ***M:*** Rachel Portman.

Beloved Enemy **1936** A romantic tragedy set in Civil War-torn Ireland in the 1920s. A rebel leader and a proper English lady struggle to overcome the war's interference with their burgeoning relationship. **86m/B VHS.** David Niven, Merle Oberon, Brian Aherne, Karen Morley, Donald Crisp; ***D:*** H.C. Potter; ***C:*** Gregg Toland.

Beloved/Friend *Amigo/Amado* **1999** Everybody wants something (or someone) they can't have. Jaume (Pou) is a middleaged gay college prof who pines for his student David (Selvas), a cold-hearted stud who hustles to pay his tuition. In fact, the only way Jaume can get attention from David is to buy his services (although David has something of a father figure complex). Then, Jaume's best friend Pere (Gas) discovers that David has gotten his daughter, Alba (Montala), pregnant. David seems to be a catalyst for a lot of soul-searching but nothing much gets resolved. Spanish with subtitles. **90m/C VHS, DVD.** *SP* Jose Maria Pou, David Selvas, Mario Gas, Irene Montala, Rosa Maria Sarda; ***D:*** Ventura Pons; ***W:*** Josep Maria Benet i Jornet; ***C:*** Jesus Escosa; ***M:*** Carles Cases.

Beloved Infidel 1/2 **1959** Sudsy, lavish romancer, based on the book by gossip queen Sheilah Graham, about her brief romance with novelist F. Scott Fitzgerald. Fitzgerald (a badly miscast Peck) was in Hollywood trying to write screenplays when he meets young, English, aspiring writer Graham (an equally miscast Kerr). She becomes his mistress, putting up with Fitzgerald's drinking and insults, while he interferes with her career. Story is slanted towards Graham nobly trying to rescue Fitzgerald from himself (he did actually die from a heart attack while with Graham). **123m/C VHS.** Gregory Peck, Deborah Kerr, Eddie Albert, Philip Ober, Herbert Rudley, John Sutton, Karin (Karen, Katharine) Booth; ***D:*** Henry King; ***W:*** Sy Bartlett; ***C:*** Leon Shamroy; ***M:*** Franz Waxman.

The Beloved Rogue **1927** Crosland—who gained a reputation for innovation by directing "Don Juan" and "The Jazz Singer"—mounted this well-designed and effects-laden medieval costumer with poetic license and typical excesses of the day. Barrymore is swashbuckling poet Francois Villon, who battles verbally with Louis XI (Veidt, in his first US role). Louis banishes him after a tiff with the evil Duke of Burgundy and Villon must uncover the Dukes's plans. Crosland plays fast and loose when the facts aren't fab enough, but it's great entertainment. **98m/B DVD.** John Barrymore, Conrad Veidt, Lawson Butt, Marceline Day, Henry Victor, Slim Summerville, Mack Swain; ***D:*** Alan Crosland Jr.; ***W:*** Paul Bern; ***C:*** Joseph August.

Below 1/2 **2002 (R)** Nothing is certain in director David Twohy's creepy submarine thriller. The captain of World War II sub U.S.S. Manta has died under dubious circumstances, and the crew is already on edge when they rescue three survivors of a torpedoed British hospital ship. When one of these survivors is a woman (Williams), allegedly unlucky on a sub, tensions run even higher. With the Germans tracking the sub, strange events begin to occur, which could be vengeful actions of the captain's ghost, a saboteur, hallucinations caused by lack of oxygen or some combination of the three. As the disasters pile up, the crew becomes divided between acting captain Brice (Greenwood) and rebellious ensign O'Dell (Davis), who has the strangely outspoken Claire on his side. Characters are a bit one-dimensional, but the effects and acting are above average for a B movie. **103m/C VHS, DVD.** *US* Bruce Greenwood, Matthew Davis, Olivia Williams, Holt McCallany, Scott Foley, Zach Galifianakis, Jason Flemyng, Dexter Fletcher, Nicholas Chinlund, Andrew Howard, Christopher Fairbank; ***D:*** David N. Twohy; ***W:*** David N. Twohy, Darren Aronofsky, Lucas Sussman; ***C:*** Ian Wilson; ***M:*** Graeme Revell.

Below the Belt **1980 (R)** Almost interesting tale of street-smart woman from New York City who becomes part of the blue-collar "circus" of lady wrestlers. Ex-wrestling champ Burke plays herself. **98m/C VHS, DVD.** Regina Baff, Mildred Burke, John C. Becher, Lenny Montana; ***D:*** Robert Fowler.

Below the Border 1/2 **1942** The Rough Riders go undercover to straighten out some cattle rustlers. **57m/B VHS, DVD.** Buck Jones, Tim McCoy, Raymond Hatton, Linda Brent, Roy Barcroft, Charles "Blackie" King; ***D:*** Howard Bretherton.

Below the Deadline **1929** A man framed for embezzlement is set free and allowed to clear his name by a sympathetic detective. **79m/B VHS.** Frank Leigh, Barbara Worth, Arthur (L.) Rankin, Walter Merrill; ***D:*** J(ohn) P(aterson) McGowan.

Belphegar: Phantom of the Louvre 1/2 *Belphegar: Le Fantome du Louvre* **2001** Gets the extra half-bone because Marceau is such a looker. Silly French horror (remake of a 1965 miniseries that was based on a pulp novel) about a sarcophagus discovered during a renovation of the museum. A demon is unleashed and poor Lisa (Marceau) becomes its unwitting host. British archeologist Glenda Spencer (Christie) tries to find out more about the mummy inside while retired police detective Verlac (Serrault) is called in to investigate the theft of items from the Egyptology wing, which is similar to an earlier unsolved case. French with subtitles. **97m/C DVD.** *FR* Sophie Marceau, Michel Serrault, Julie Christie, Jean-Francois Balmer, Patachou, Frederic Diefenthal; ***D:*** Jean-Paul Salome; ***W:*** Daniele Thompson, Jerome Tonnerre, Jean-Paul Salome; ***C:*** Jean-Francois Robin; ***M:*** Bruno Coulais.

The Belstone Fox **1973** Orphaned fox goes into hiding, and is hunted by the hound he has befriended and his former owner. **103m/C VHS.** Eric Porter, Rachel Roberts, Jeremy Kemp; ***D:*** James Hill.

Ben 1/2 **1972 (PG)** Sequel to "Willard" finds police Detective Kirtland still on the hunt for a killer rat pack led by Ben, king of the rodents. Title song by young Michael Jackson hit the top of the charts. **95m/C VHS.** Joseph Campanella, Lee Montgomery, Arthur O'Connell, Rosemary Murphy, Meredith Baxter, Norman Alden, Paul Carr, Kaz Garas, Kenneth Tobey, Richard Van Heet; ***D:*** Phil Karlson; ***W:*** Gilbert Ralston; ***C:*** Russell Metty; ***M:*** Walter Scharf. Golden Globes '73: Song ("Ben").

Ben-Hur **1926** Second film version of the renowned story of Jewish and Christian divisiveness in the time of Jesus. Battle scenes and chariot races still look good, in spite of age. Problems lingered on the set and at a cost of over $4,000,000 it was the most expensive film of its time and took years to finish. A hit at the boxoffice, it still stands as the all-time silent classic. In 1931, a shortened version was released. Based on the novel by Lewis Wallace. **148m/B VHS, DVD.** Ramon Novarro, Francis X. Bushman, May McAvoy, Betty Bronson, Claire McDowell, Carmel Myers, Nigel de Brulier, Ferdinand P. Earle; ***D:*** Fred Niblo; ***C:*** Clyde De Vinna. Natl. Film Reg. '97.

Ben-Hur **1959** The third film version of the Lew Wallace classic stars Heston in the role of a Palestinian Jew battling the Roman empire at the time of Christ. Won a record 11 Oscars. The breathtaking chariot race is still one of the best screen races today. Perhaps one of the greatest pictures of all time. Also available in letterbox format. **212m/C VHS, DVD.** Charlton Heston, Jack Hawkins, Stephen Boyd, Haya Harareet, Hugh Griffith, Martha Scott, Sam Jaffe, Cathy O'Donnell, Finlay Currie; ***D:*** William Wyler; ***W:*** Karl Tunberg; ***C:*** Robert L. Surtees; ***M:*** Miklos Rozsa. Oscars '59: Actor (Heston), Art Dir./Set Dec., Color, Color Cinematog., Costume Des. (C), Director (Wyler), Film Editing, Picture, Sound, Support. Actor (Griffith), Orig. Dramatic Score; AFI '98: Top 100; British Acad. '59: Film; Directors Guild '59: Director (Wyler); Golden Globes '60: Director (Wyler), Film—Drama, Support. Actor (Boyd), Natl. Film Reg. '04;; N.Y. Film Critics '59: Film.

Ben X **2007** Ben has Asperger's Syndrome, which makes social interactions difficult, so he is repeatedly bullied at his public high school. His only comfort is an online role-playing game where his alter ego Ben X can win the day. When the bullying becomes intolerable, Ben loses control and plans a way to get even with the aid of a fellow gamer he knows as Scarlite. Based on a true story; Flemish with subtitles. **93m/C DVD.** *BE* Greg Timmermans, Laura Verlinden, Titus De Voogdt, Maarten Claeyssens; ***D:*** Nic Balthazar; ***W:*** Nic Balthazar; ***C:*** Lou Berghmans; ***M:*** Praga Khan.

The Benchwarmers **2006 (PG-13)** Relentlessly stupid comedy with more than its share of gross-out moments. Gus (Schneider) was a bullied nerd in school, as were his two still-maladjusted pals, Richie (Spade) and Clark (Heder). Ex-bullied nerd-turned-billionaire Mel (a fun-loving Lovitz) offers a chance for sweet revenge by putting his trio of losers up against a Little League team of young terrors. Farting, vomiting, and booger jokes follow, and Reggie Jackson offers baseball advice. **81m/C DVD, Blu-ray Disc, UMD.** *US* Rob Schneider, David Spade, Jon Heder, Jon Lovitz, Molly Sims, Craig Kilborn, Tim Meadows, Nick Swardson, Amaury Nolasco, Dennis Dugan, Erinn Bartlett, Max Prado, Brooke Langton, Lochlyn Munro, Mary Jo Catlett, Blake Clark, Terry Crews; ***Cameos:*** Reggie Jackson; ***D:*** Dennis Dugan; ***W:*** Nick Swardson, Allen Covert; ***C:*** Thomas Ackerman; ***M:*** Waddy Wachtel; ***V:*** James Earl Jones.

Bend It Like Beckham **2002 (PG-13)** Sweet family comedy has girl power galore. Jesminder (Nagra) is the teenaged daughter of East Indian parents, living in a middle-class London suburb. They wish Jess would be more like her older sister Pinky (Panjabi), who is anticipating her traditional wedding. But what shy Jess wants is to play professional soccer—her hero is superstar player David Beckham—and she secretly joins a local team after befriending fellow player Juliette (Knightley). She impresses (and develops a crush on) her coach Joe (Rhys-Meyers) while trying to keep her activities from her disapproving parents. Of course, there has to be a big game, which will showcase Jess's talents. **112m/C VHS, DVD.** *GB GE* Parminder K. Nagra, Keira Knightley, Jonathan Rhys Meyers, Shaheen Khan, Anupam Kher, Archie Panjabi, Juliet Stevenson, Frank Harper, Shaznay Lewis; ***D:*** Gurinder Chadha; ***W:*** Gurinder Chadha, Paul Mayeda Berges, Guljit Bindra; ***C:*** Jong Lin; ***M:*** Craig Pruess.

Bend of the River *Where the River Bends* **1952** A haunted, hardened guide leads a wagon train through Oregon territory, pitting himself against Indians, the wilderness and a former comrade-turned-hijacker. **91m/C VHS, DVD.** James Stewart, Arthur Kennedy, Rock Hudson, Harry (Henry) Morgan, Royal Dano; ***D:*** Anthony Mann.

Beneath **2007 (R)** Convoluted and plodding story about creepy, depressed people having visions usually followed by someone ending up dead. Initial suspense stems from in-laws' eerie house complete with mysterious hatches, weird holes, and a monster inside the walls. Although intriguing, its eccentricities never get fully explained as the darkness and drab lead only to an anticlimatic snore. **81m/C DVD.** Nora Zehetner, Matthew Settle, Gabrielle Rose, Carly Pope, Don S. Davis, Jessica Amlee; ***D:*** Dagen Merrill; ***W:*** Dagen Merrill, Kevin Burke; ***C:*** Mike Southon; ***M:*** John (Gianni) Frizzell, Frederik Wiedmann. **VIDEO**

Beneath Loch Ness **2001** Laughable adventure tale finds paleontologist Case Howell (Wimmer) carrying on the work of his mentor, Professor Egan, who believed that Loch Ness was a breeding ground for ancient marine reptiles. Unfortunately, the prof disappeared while conducting research at the loch. But that isn't stopping Howell from leading another expedition to find Nessie. **95m/C VHS, DVD.** Brian Wimmer, Patrick Bergin, Lysette Anthony, Vernon Wells; ***D:*** Chuck Comisky; ***W:*** Justin Stanley, Chuck Comisky, Shane Bitterling; ***C:*** Philip Timme; ***M:*** Richard John Baker. **VIDEO**

Beneath the Bermuda Triangle ½½ **1998 (R)** Submarine commander Alan Deakins (Fahey) and his crew are cruising in dangerous waters when they unexpectedly enter a time portal that transports them to the future. As usual, it's ugly—a repressive, military government is in control and Deakins decides to join a rebel organization, that happens to be lead by his grandson (Fahey again). No-brain actioner. **84m/C VHS.** Jeff Fahey, Richard Tyson, Linda Hoffman, Jack Coleman; ***D:*** Scott Levy. **VIDEO**

Beneath the Planet of the Apes 1/2 **1970 (G)** In the first sequel, another Earth astronaut passes through the same warp and follows the same paths as Taylor, through Ape City and to the ruins of bomb-blasted New York's subway system, where warhead-worshipping human mutants are found. The strain of sequelling shows instantly, and gets worse through the next three films; followed by "Escape from the Planet of the Apes." **108m/C VHS, DVD.** James Franciscus, Kim Hunter, Maurice Evans, Charlton Heston, James Gregory, Natalie Trundy, Jeff Corey, Linda Harrison, Victor Buono, Paul (E.) Richards, David Watson, Thomas Gomez; ***D:*** Ted Post; ***W:*** Paul Dehn; ***C:*** Milton Krasner; ***M:*** Leonard Rosenman.

Beneath the 12-Mile Reef
1953 Two rival groups of divers compete for sponge beds off the Florida coast. Lightweight entertainment notable for underwater photography and early Cinemascope production, as well as Moore in a bathing suit. **102m/C VHS, DVD.** Angela (Clark) Clarke, Robert Wagner, Terry Moore, Gilbert Roland, Richard Boone, Peter Graves, J. Carrol Naish; ***D:*** Robert D. Webb; ***W:*** A(lbert) I(saac) Bezzerides; ***C:*** Edward Cronjager; ***M:*** Bernard Herrmann.

Beneath the Valley of the Ultra-Vixens **1979** Sex comedy retread directed by the man with an obsession for big. Scripted by Roger Ebert, who also scripted the cult classic "Beyond the Valley of the Dolls." Explicit nudity. **90m/C VHS, DVD.** Francesca "Kitten" Natividad, Ann Marie, Ken Kerr, Stuart Lancaster, Steve Tracy, Henry Rowland, DeForest Covan, Aram Katcher, Candy Samples, Robert Pearson; ***D:*** Russ Meyer; ***W:*** Roger Ebert, Russ Meyer; ***C:*** Russ Meyer.

Benedict Arnold: A Question of Honor **2003** By-the-numbers bio of Revolutionary War general turned British Loyalist, Benedict Arnold (Quinn). By 1776, Arnold was falling out of favor with Congress amidst accusations of incompetence, although he's still supported by his friend, George Washington (Grammer). But after meeting Margaret Shippen (Montgomery), the daughter of a loyalist sympathizer, the increasingly resentful Arnold, who also needs money to stave off bankruptcy, begins to sell information to the enemy and comes up with a plan to turn over West Point to the redcoats. **100m/C VHS, DVD.** Aidan Quinn, Kelsey Grammer, Flora Montgomery, John Light, John Kavanagh; ***D:*** Mikael Salomon; ***W:*** William Mastrosimone; ***C:*** Seamus Deasy; ***M:*** David Williams. **CABLE**

The Beneficiary **1997 (R)** Widow Haiduk is the primary suspect in her wealthy husband's death until she gives her inheritance to charity, thus eliminating her motive for murder. But detective Ashby, a friend of the husband, still decides to keep his eye (and maybe more) on the lady. **97m/C VHS.** Suzy Amis, Ron Silver, Linden Ashby, Stacy Haiduk, Robert Davi; ***D:*** Marc Bienstock; ***W:*** Vladimir Nemirovsky; ***C:*** Sead Muhtarevic. **CABLE**

Benefit of the Doubt **1993 (R)** Ex-con Sutherland, released from prison after 22 years, attempts to repaint his family a la Norman Rockwell. Grown-up daughter Irving, who testified against him in her mother's murder, wants to put a crimp in those plans since daddy's new vision of family fondness frankly makes her stomach turn. Aside from the sexual shenanigans, and the haunting Monument Valley backdrop, an extended chase scene would seem to be the film's only hope of salvation. Unfortunately, it fails to deliver, since it's both implausible and boring. Based on a story by Michael Lieber. **92m/C VHS.** Donald Sutherland, Amy Irving, Christopher McDonald, Rider Strong, Graham Greene, Theodore Bikel, Gisele Kovach, Ferdinand "Ferdy" Mayne; ***D:*** Jonathan Heap; ***W:*** Jeffrey Polman, Christopher Keyser; ***M:*** Hummie Mann.

The Bengali Night **1988** Slow-moving romantic drama was the first starring role for Grant who plays British engineer Allan, who works in Calcutta. When he becomes ill, his employer invites Allan to recuperate at his home and lets him stay on after his recovery. But when Allan and the Sens' eldest daughter Gayatri (Pathak) become romantically involved, the culture clash leads to heartbreak. Based on a true story. **111m/C DVD.** Hugh Grant, Shabana Azmi, Soumitra Chatterjee, John Hurt, Anne Brochet, Supriya Pathak; ***D:*** Nicolas Klotz; ***W:*** Nicolas Klotz; ***C:*** Jean-Claude Carriere; ***M:*** Emmanuel Machuel, Brij Narayan.

The Beniker Gang 1/2 **1983 (G)** Five orphans, supported by the eldest who writes a syndicated advice column, work together as a family. **87m/C VHS.** Andrew McCarthy, Jennifer (Jennie) Dundas Lowe, Danny Pintauro, Charlie (Charles) Fields; ***D:*** Ken Kwapis. **TV**

Benji **1974 (G)** In the loveable mutt's first feature-length movie, he falls in love with a female named Tiffany, and saves two young children from kidnappers. Kiddie classic that was a boxoffice hit when first released. Followed by "For the Love of Benji." **87m/C VHS, DVD.** Benji, Peter Breck, Christopher Connelly, Patsy Garrett, Deborah Walley, Cynthia Smith; ***D:*** Joe Camp; ***W:*** Joe Camp; ***C:*** Don Reddy; ***M:*** Euel Box. Golden Globes '75: Song ("I Feel Love").

Benji: Off the Leash! 1/2 **2004 (PG)** A generally amiable retro addition to the series that began in 1974. Colby's (Whitaker) nasty stepfather Hatchett (Kendrick) runs a puppy mill in their small Mississippi town. He plans to kill a mongrel pup, which Colby rescues and hides (and calls Puppy). Puppy (played by the latest version of Benji) befriends a smart stray named Lizard Tongue while avoiding a couple of inept dogcatchers (Newsome, Stephens) and trying to rescue his sickly mom from the mean breeder. The abuse themes (both animal and human) may scare the little ones but, of course, the dogs are cute and lovable. **97m/C VHS, DVD.** *US* Nick Whitaker, Nate Bynum, Chris Kendrick, Randall Newsome, Duane Stephens, Forrest Landis, Carleton Bluford, Neal Barth, Melinda Haynes, Kathleen Camp, Jeff Olson, Lincoln Hoppe, Joey Miyashima, Scott Wilkinson, Christy Summerhays; ***D:*** Joe Camp; ***W:*** Joe Camp; ***C:*** Don Reddy; ***M:*** Anthony DiLorenzo.

Benji the Hunted 1/2 **1987 (G)** The heroic canine, shipwrecked off the Oregon coast, discovers a litter of orphaned cougar cubs, and battles terrain and predators to bring them to safety. **89m/C VHS, DVD.** Benji, Red Steagall, Frank Inn; ***D:*** Joe Camp; ***W:*** Joe Camp; ***M:*** Euel Box.

Benny & Joon 1/2 **1993 (PG)** Depending on your tolerance for cute eccentrics and whimsy this will either charm you with sweetness or send you into sugar shock. Masterson is Joon, a mentally disturbed young woman who paints and has a habit of setting fires. She lives with overprotective brother Benny (Quinn). Sam (Depp) is the outsider who charms Joon, a dyslexic loner who impersonates his heroes Charlie Chaplin and Buster Keaton with eery accuracy. Depp is particularly fine with the physical demands of his role, but the film's easy dismissal of Joon's mental illness is a serious flaw. **98m/C VHS, DVD.** Johnny Depp, Mary Stuart Masterson, Aidan Quinn, Julianne Moore, Oliver Platt, CCH Pounder, Dan Hedaya, Joe Grifasi, William H. Macy, Eileen Ryan; ***D:*** Jeremiah S. Chechik; ***W:*** Barry Berman; ***C:*** Jason Schwartzman; ***M:*** Rachel Portman.

The Benny Goodman Story
1955 The life and music of Swing Era bandleader Benny Goodman is recounted in this popular bio-pic. Covering Benny's career from his child prodigy days to his monumental 1938 Carnegie Hall Jazz Concert, the movie's soggy plot machinations are redeemed by a non-stop music track featuring the real Benny and an all-star lineup. ♫ Don't Be That Way; Memories of You; Sing, Sing, Sing; Slipped Disc. **116m/C VHS, DVD.** Steve Allen, Donna Reed, Gene Krupa, Lionel Hampton, Kid Ory, Ben Pollack, Harry James, Stan Getz, Teddy Wilson, Martha Tilton; ***D:*** Valentine Davies; ***M:*** Henry Mancini.

Benny's Video 1/2 **1992** Teen Benny (Frisch) is obsessed with the violent videos he watches and makes, including the slaughter of a pig with a bolt gun, which Benny then uses in a very unfortunate manner. Heavy-handed message movie was Hanecke's second feature. German with subtitles. **105m/C DVD.** *GE* Arno Frisch, Angela Winkler, Ulrich Muhe, Ingrid Strassner; ***D:*** Michael Haneke; ***W:*** Michael Haneke.

Bent **1997 (NC-17)** Theatre director Mathias makes his film debut with Sherman's adaptation of his 1979 play. Gay playboy Max (Owen) is enjoying the nightlife in decadent Berlin—until the Nazi crackdown. Soon, Max is in a cattle car on his way to Dachau, where he passes himself off as Jewish, thinking he'll be treated better. However Horst (Bluteau), who befriended Max on the train, is openly part of the pink triangle prisoners. Still, Max gets Horst assigned to the same meaningless hard labor and the duo fall in love—without ever being allowed to touch. Good performances (with Jagger notable in a brief role as a drag star) but the lingering staginess is to the film's detriment. An R-rated version is also available. **104m/C VHS, DVD.** *GB* Clive Owen, Lothaire Bluteau, Ian McKellen, Brian Webber, Mick Jagger, Nikolaj Coster-Waldau, Paul Bettany; ***Cameos:*** Jude Law, Rupert Graves; ***D:*** Sean Mathias; ***W:*** Martin Sherman; ***C:*** Yorgos Arvanitis; ***M:*** Philip Glass.

Beowulf 1/2 **1998 (R)** Cheesy retelling of the dark ages Saxon saga that has seemingly time travelled to a vague post-apocalypse time. Wandering knight Beowulf (Lambert) battles beast Grendel, who comes each night to feed on those who live in the Outpost. Cult icon Mitra was one of the models for Lara Croft of "Tomb Raider" game fame. **92m/C VHS, DVD.** Christopher Lambert, Rhona Mitra, Oliver Cotton, Patricia Velasquez, Goetz Otto, Layla Roberts, Brent J. Lowe; ***D:*** Graham Baker; ***W:*** Mark Leahy, David Chappe; ***C:*** Christopher Faloona; ***M:*** Ben Watkins.

Beowulf **2007 (PG-13)** Not your father's epic poem! Director Zemeckis takes the Old English classic and turns it into both a highly stylized computer-generated swordfest and a satirical take on the lit class staple. Beowulf (Winstone) battles Grendel (Glover), gets sexy with Grendel's mom (Jolie), and fights a dragon on his way to eternal heroic glory. Purists may object to the liberties taken by writers Gaiman and Avery, but they do a good job of connecting and streamlining the source material's various storylines. While still resembling a video game, Zemeckis's second attempt at the "performance capture" digital style is a dramatic improvement over his previous attempt in the lifeless "The Polar Express." **114m/C DVD.** *US* ***D:*** Robert Zemeckis; ***W:*** Neil Gaiman, Roger Avary; ***C:*** Robert Presley; ***M:*** Alan Silvestri; ***V:*** Ray Winstone, Angelina Jolie, Crispin Glover, Anthony Hopkins, Robin Wright Penn, John Malkovich, Alison Lohman.

Beowulf & Grendel **2006 (R)** Live-action adaptation of the 1000-year-old Scandanavian poem retells the story of Beowulf (Butler), the Norse warrior who helps his pal, Danish King Hrothgar (Skarsgard), rid his land of the murderous troll Grendel (Sigurdsson). Tries to appeal to modern audiences with flashy fighting, lots of blood, and awkward comedic attempts, but succeeds only in showing how beautiful Iceland is (that's where it was filmed). **102m/C DVD, Blu-ray Disc.** *GB CA IC* Gerard Butler, Stellan Skarsgard, Sarah Polley, Eddie Marsan, Ingvar Sigurdsson, Tony Curran, Rory McCann, Ronan Vilbert, Martin Delaney, Olafur Darri Olafsson, Mark Lewis, Elva Osk Olafsdottir; ***D:*** Sturla Gunnarsson; ***W:*** Andrew Rai Berzins; ***C:*** Jan Kiesser; ***M:*** Hilmar Orn Hilmarsson.

Beretta's Island **1992 (R)** When Interpol operative Beretta comes out of retirement to track his friend's killer, the chase leads him back to his homeland of Sardinia, which has been overrun by drugs. **97m/C VHS.** Elizabeth Kaitan, Van Quattro, Jo Champa, Franco (Columbo) Columbu, Ken Kercheval; ***Cameos:*** Arnold Schwarzenegger; ***D:*** Michael Preece; ***C:*** Massimo Zeri; ***M:*** Cliff Magness.

Berkeley 1/2 **2005 (R)** In 1968, Ben Sweet (Nick Roth) enrolls at UC Berkeley mainly to avoid the draft and is introduced to political activism, drugs, and sex. The lead actor is the director's son and the film is based on Bobby Roth's own college days although the rambling nostalgia isn't as interesting as Roth seems to believe. **88m/C DVD.** Nick Roth, Henry Winkler, Sarah Carter, Laura Jordan, Bonnie Bedelia, Sebastian Tillinger, Jake Newton, Tom Morello; ***D:*** Bobby Roth; ***W:*** Bobby Roth; ***C:*** Steve Burns; ***M:*** Christopher Franke.

Berkeley Square 1/2 **1998** In 1902 London, three young women become nannies and grow to be friends. Tough and experienced East Ender Matty (Wilkie) goes to work for the well-bred St. Johns; country-raised Hannah (Smurfit) has an illegitimate child by her previous titled employer's son—a fact she keeps hidden from the neglectful Hutchinsons; and farm girl Lydia (Wady) is hired by the avant-garde Lamson-Scribeners, who believe in education even for servants. Naturally, the threesome become very involved in each other's lives and loves. On five cassettes. **500m/C VHS, DVD.** *GB* Victoria Smurfit, Tabitha Wady, Clare Wilkie, Rosemary Leach, Judy Parfitt; ***D:*** Leslie Manning, Richard Signy, Martin Hutchings, Richard Holthouse. **TV**

The Berlin Affair **1985 (R)** A sordid tale from "The Night Porter" director about a Japanese woman seducing various parties in pre-WWII Germany. **97m/C VHS.** *IT GE* Mio Takaki, Gudrun Landgrebe, Kevin McNally; ***D:*** Liliana Cavani; ***M:*** Pino Donaggio.

Berlin Alexanderplatz 1/2 **1980** Fassbinder's 15 1/2-hour epic follows the life, death, and resurrection of Franz Biberkof, a former transit worker who has just finished a lengthy prison term and must learn to adjust in the harsh social atmosphere of Berlin in the 1920s. Melodramatic parable with biblical overtones considered by some to be a masterpiece. Based on the novel by Alfred Doblin; originally aired as a miniseries on German TV. **930m/C VHS.** *GE* Gunter Lamprecht, Hanna Schygulla, Barbara Sukowa, Gottfried John, Elisabeth Trissenaar, Brigitte Mira, Karin Baal, Ivan Desny, Margit Carstensen; ***D:*** Rainer Werner Fassbinder; ***W:*** Rainer Werner Fassbinder; ***C:*** Xaver Schwarzenberger; ***M:*** Peer Raben. **TV**

Berlin Blues **1989 (PG-13)** A nightclub singer is torn between two men. **90m/C VHS.** Julia Migenes, Keith Baxter; ***D:*** Ricardo Franco.

The Berlin Conspiracy **1991 (R)** Espionage/action potboiler does an imaginative job of setting its action against the fall of the Berlin Wall and the end of the Cold War. A CIA agent forms a shaky alliance with his East German spymaster rival to prevent germ warfare technology from falling into terrorist hands. **83m/C VHS.** Marc Singer, Mary Crosby, Stephen Davies, Richard Lepartmentier, Terence Henry; ***D:*** Terence H. Winkless.

Berlin Express 1/2 **1948** Battle of wits ensues between the Allies and the Nazis who are seeking to keep Germans divided in post-WWII Germany. Espionage and intrigue factor heavily. **86m/B VHS.** Robert Ryan, Merle Oberon, Paul Lukas, Charles Korvin; ***D:*** Jacques Tourneur.

Berlin Tunnel 21 1/2 **1981** Based on the novel by Donald Lindquist in which five American soldiers attempt a daring Cold War rescue of a beautiful German girl. The plan is to construct a tunnel under the Berlin Wall. Better-than-average. **150m/C VHS.** Richard Thomas, Jose Ferrer, Horst Buchholz; ***D:*** Richard Michaels. **TV**

Berlinguer I Love You **WOOF!** *Berlinguer Ti Voglio Bene* **1977** Crude and disgustingly obnoxious comedy about a mama's-boy loser who is led to believe that his shrewish mother has died. When he returns home for her funeral, she is not happy to see him. Title refers to a popular politician of the era. Italian with subtitles. **95m/C DVD.** *IT* Roberto Benigni, Alida Valli, Carlo Monni; ***D:*** Giuseppe Bertolucci; ***W:*** Roberto Benigni,

Giuseppe Bertolucci; *C:* Renato Tafuri; *M:* Frank Coletta.

The Bermuda Depths ½ **1978** Made-for-TV fantasy horror involving the Bermuda Triangle, a giant sea turtle, a beautiful ghostly girl who apparently sold her soul for eternal youth, a troubled young man, and a couple of scientists. It's sorta goofy and watchable at the same time. **98m/C DVD.** Leigh McCloskey, Connie Sellecca, Burl Ives, Carl Weathers, Julie Woodson, Ruth Attaway; *D:* Tom Kotani; *W:* William Overgard; *C:* Jeri Sopanen; *M:* Maury Laws. **TV**

Bernadette ½ **1990** A French-made version of the legend of St. Bernadette, who endured persecution after claiming to have seen the Virgin Mary. Beautiful in its simplicity, but overly long. **120m/C VHS.** *FR* Sydney Penny, Roland LeSaffre, Michele Simonnet, Bernard Dheran, Arlette Didier; *D:* Jean Delannoy.

Bernard and Doris **2008** Doris (Sarandon) is eccentric, cynical, lonely, aging billionaire tobacco heiress Doris Duke. Bernard Lafferty (Fiennes) is her Irish, gay, alcoholic butler. They form a delightfully odd-couple partnership where the ever-more devoted Bernard protects Doris from hangers-on (and herself)—so much so that Duke made Lafferty the executor of her will (and when he died, he left everything to her trusts). Gets the bones for the Sarandon/Fiennes combo alone even if Sarandon looks waaaaay too good as the ravaged Duke. **109m/C DVD.** Susan Sarandon, Ralph Fiennes, James Rebhorn, Nick Rolfe; *D:* Bob Balaban; *W:* Hugh Costello; *C:* Mauricio Rubinstein; *M:* Alex Wurman. **CABLE**

Bernard and the Genie ½ **1991 (G)** It seems Bernard Bottle is not going to have a happy Christmas—he's been fired from his job and his girlfriend has left him. But things take a turn for the better when he discovers an antique lamp and its resident Genie. But with the Genie granting his every wish, Bernard's sudden wealth is causing some suspicions among both his greedy ex-employer and the police. Meanwhile, the Genie discovers the delights of modern-day England and poses as a department store Santa to truly fulfill a child's Christmas wish. Amusing family fare. **70m/C VHS.** *GB* Alan Cumming, Lenny Henry, Rowan Atkinson; *D:* Paul Weiland.

Berserk! ½ **1967** A seedy traveling circus is beset by a series of murders. Not heralded as one of Crawford's best pieces. **95m/C VHS.** Joan Crawford, Diana Dors, Judy Geeson, Ty Hardin; *D:* James O'Connolly.

Berserker **1987 (R)** Six camping college students are attacked by a bloodthirsty psychotic out of a Nordic myth, who takes the shape of a badder-than-the-average bear. **85m/C VHS.** Joseph Alan Johnson, Valerie Sheldon, Greg Dawson; *D:* Jefferson (Jeff) Richard.

Bert Rigby, You're a Fool ½ **1989 (R)** A starstruck British coal miner finds his way to Hollywood singing old showtunes, only to be rebuffed by a cynical industry. Available with Spanish subtitles. **94m/C VHS.** Robert Lindsay, Robbie Coltrane, Jackie Gayle, Bruno Kirby, Cathryn Bradshaw, Corbin Bernsen, Anne Bancroft; *D:* Carl Reiner; *W:* Carl Reiner; *C:* Jan De Bont; *M:* Ralph Burns.

Beshkempir the Adopted Son **1998** In a rural community in the Central Asian nation of Kyrgyzstan, a young teen lives a carefree existence getting into mild mischief with his buddies. Until one day, during an argument, he suddenly discovers he was adopted, which throws his world (at least temporarily) into rebellious turmoil. Kyrgyzstani with subtitles. **81m/B VHS, DVD.** *RU* Mirlan Abdykalykov; *D:* Aktan Abdykalykov; *W:* Aktan Abdykalykov, Avtandil Adikulov, Marat Sarulu; *C:* Khasan Kydyraliyev; *M:* Nurlan Nishanov.

Besieged ½ **1998 (R)** Fans of Bertolucci will enjoy this airy quasi-love story, but the slow pace and meandering plot will frustrate other viewers. Shandurai (Newton) moves to Rome after her husband becomes a political prisoner in Kenya. In order to put herself through medical school, she takes a job as a maid for an eccentric British musician (Thewlis). He begins to fall for his beautiful housekeeper, but she ignores his advances. To prove his love, he begins selling off his personal belongings so he can bribe officials to release her husband. **94m/C VHS, DVD.** *IT* David Thewlis, Thandie Newton, Claudio Santamaria; *D:* Bernardo Bertolucci; *W:* Bernardo Bertolucci, Clare Peploe; *C:* Fabio Cianchetti; *M:* Alessio Vlad.

Best Defense **1984 (R)** A U.S. Army tank operator is sent to Kuwait to test a new state-of-the-art tank in a combat situation. Although the cast is popular, the movie as a whole is not funny and the story frequently is hard to follow. **94m/C VHS, DVD.** Dudley Moore, Eddie Murphy, Kate Capshaw, George Dzundza, Helen Shaver; *D:* Willard Huyck; *W:* Willard Huyck, Gloria Katz.

Best Enemies ½ **1986** An English film about a man suffering the trials of the 1960s, including Vietnam, and how it affects his relationships with his friends and wife. **96m/C VHS.** *GB* Sigrid Thornton, Paul Williams, Judy Morris, Brandon Burke; *D:* David Baker.

Best Foot Forward ½ **1943** Vintage musical about a movie star who agrees to accompany a young cadet to a military ball. Based on the popular Broadway show. The film debuts of Walker, Allyson, and DeHaven. ♫Buckle Down, Winsocki; The Three B's (Barrelhouse, Boogie Woogie, and the Blues); Alive and Kicking; Two O'Clock Jump; Ev'ry Time; Three Men on a Date; Wish I May; Shady Lady; My First Promise. **95m/C VHS, DVD.** Lucille Ball, June Allyson, Tommy Dix, Nancy Walker, Virginia Weidler, Gloria De Haven, William Gaxton, Harry James; *D:* Edward Buzzell; *W:* Irving Brecher; *M:* George Bassman.

Best Friends **1982 (PG)** A pair of screenwriters decide to marry after years of living and working together. Story based on the lives of screenwriters Barry Levinson and Valerie Curtin. **109m/C VHS, DVD.** Goldie Hawn, Burt Reynolds, Jessica Tandy, Barnard Hughes, Audra Lindley, Keenan Wynn, Ron Silver; *D:* Norman Jewison; *W:* Valerie Curtin, Barry Levinson; *C:* Jordan Cronenweth.

Best in Show **2000 (PG-13)** Director Christopher Guest follows the successful "Waiting for Guffman" with another faux-documentary mixing improvisation and unique characters. This time, the subject is the snooty world of show dogs and the freaky, neurotic pooch-owners hoping to claim its greatest prize: Best in Show at the Mayflower Kennel Club Dog Show. The quirky dog-lovers include Meg (Posey) and Hamilton (Hitchcock), whose kinky sex life is giving their Weimaraner angst; doting gay Shih-Tzu owners Scott (Higgins) and Stefan (McKean); and seemingly tame suburbanites Gerry (Levy) and Cookie (O'Hara). Fred Willard steals the spotlight as Buck Laughlin, a sports announcer who has no knowledge of the event he's broadcasting. Worth a rental just for the bizarre one-liners fired off by the clueless commentator on such subjects as the dogs' anatomy and edibility. **89m/C VHS, DVD.** Christopher Guest, Michael McKean, Parker Posey, Eugene Levy, Catherine O'Hara, Fred Willard, Michael Hitchcock, John Michael Higgins, Jennifer Coolidge, Trevor Beckwith, Bob Balaban, Ed Begley Jr., Patrick Cranshaw, Don Lake, Larry Miller; *D:* Christopher Guest; *W:* Christopher Guest, Eugene Levy; *C:* Roberto Schaefer; *M:* C.J. Vanston.

The Best Intentions ½ **1992** Ingmar Bergman wrote the screenplay chronicling the early years of the stormy relationship of his parents. Set in Sweden at the turn of the century, the film focuses on the class differences that divide his mother and father, while portrayal of little Bergy is limited to a bundle under his mother's maternity dress. Inspired performances and directing illuminates the emotionally complex relationship, revealing truths about the universal human condition along the way. Six-hour version was shot for TV in Europe and Japan. Director August and actress August met and married during filming. In Swedish with English subtitles. **182m/C VHS.** *SW* Samuel Froler, Pernilla August, Max von Sydow, Ghita Norby, Mona Malm, Lena Endre, Bjorn Kjellman; *D:* Bille August; *W:* Ingmar Bergman; *C:* Jorgen Persson; *M:* Stefan Nilsson. Cannes '92: Actress (August), Film.

Best Kept Secrets ½ **1988** A feisty woman discovers corruption and blackmail in the police department where her husband is an officer. **104m/C VHS.** Patty Duke, Frederic Forrest, Peter Coyote; *D:* Jerrold Freedman.

Best Laid Plans **1999 (R)** Another contemporary noir where no one and nothing is as it seems (except the overly familiar plot). Nick (Nivola) and his bud, Bryce (Brolin), are bar hopping when Bryce picks up Lissa (Witherspoon). Later, a frantic Bryce calls Nick saying Lissa is underage and accusing him of rape. Nick offers to talk to Lissa and the story flashes back to the beginnings of an elaborate scam leading all concerned to a number of ill-considered decisions. **90m/C VHS, DVD.** Alessandro Nivola, Josh Brolin, Reese Witherspoon, Rocky Carroll, Michael G. (Mike) Hagerty, Jamie Marsh; *D:* Mike Barker; *W:* Ted Griffin; *C:* Ben Seresin; *M:* Craig Armstrong.

The Best Little Girl in the World **1981** Exceptional made-for-TV tale of an apparently perfect teenager (Leigh) suffering from anorexia. Slow starvation is her only cry for help. Fine performances from Durning and Saint. Look for Helen Hunt and Ally Sheedy as classmates. **96m/C VHS.** Charles Durning, Eva Marie Saint, Jennifer Jason Leigh, Melanie Mayron, Viveca Lindfors, Jason Miller, David Spielberg, Lisa Pelikan, Ally Sheedy, Helen Hunt; *D:* Sam O'Steen; *M:* Billy Goldenberg. **TV**

The Best Little Whorehouse in Texas **1982 (R)** Parton is the buxom owner of The Chicken Ranch, a house of ill-repute that may be closed down unless Sheriff-boyfriend Reynolds can think of a way out. Strong performances don't quite make up for the erratically comic script. Based on the long-running Broadway musical, in turn based on a story by Larry McMurtry. **115m/C VHS, DVD.** Dolly Parton, Burt Reynolds, Dom DeLuise, Charles Durning, Jim Nabors, Lois Nettleton; *D:* Colin Higgins.

The Best Man ½ **1964** An incisive, darkly satiric political tract, based on Gore Vidal's play, about two presidential contenders who vie for the endorsement of the aging ex-president, and trample political ethics in the process. **104m/B VHS.** Henry Fonda, Cliff Robertson, Lee Tracy, Margaret Leighton, Edie Adams, Kevin McCarthy, Ann Sothern, Gene Raymond, Shelley Berman, Mahalia Jackson; *D:* Franklin J. Schaffner; *W:* Gore Vidal; *C:* Haskell Wexler.

The Best Man ½ *Il Testimone dello Sposo* **1997 (PG)** It's 1899 in a small northern Italian town and beautiful Francesca (Sastre) must marry the lascivious older Edgardo Osti (Cantarelli) in order to solve her father's business problems. Francesca is revolted but does become smitten by the best man—Angelo (Abatantuono), who's returned from America, apparently with a fortune. Marriage or no, Francesca becomes obsessed with getting Angelo. Italian with subtitles. **99m/C VHS, DVD.** *IT* Ines Sastre, Diego Abatantuono, Dario Cantarelli, Valeria (Valerie Dobson) D'Obici, Mario Erpichini; *D:* Pupi Avati; *W:* Pupi Avati; *C:* Pasquale Rachini; *M:* Riz Ortolani.

The Best Man **1999 (R)** Writer/director Malcolm D. Lee, cousin of co-producer Spike Lee, makes an impressive debut in this ensemble piece that plays like a hipper "Big Chill." Novelist Harper (Diggs) heads to New York to attend the wedding of his best friend Lance (Chestnut) and the beautiful Mia (Calhoun). Unfortunately, his soon-to-be-released first novel is a thinly disguised autobiography which alludes to an affair between Harper and the bride-to-be. As other college buddies and old flames show up for the nuptials, past issues and romantic tensions come bubbling back up to the surface. The cast gives good performances across the board, with Howard as the wisecracking and womanizing Quentin standing out in particular. **120m/C VHS, DVD.** Taye Diggs, Monica Calhoun, Morris Chestnut, Nia Long, Melissa De Sousa, Harold Perrineau Jr., Terrence Howard, Sanaa Lathan, Victoria Dillard; *D:* Malcolm Lee; *W:* Malcolm Lee; *C:* Frank Prinzi; *M:* Stanley Clarke.

Best Men ½ *Independence* **1998 (R)** There's a wedding, there's a would-be bank heist, and there's five men caught in the siege at the bank of Independence in this kooky crime comedy/drama. Jesse (Wilson) is heading straight from prison to his wedding to Hope (Barrymore) with his four tuxedo-clad buddies. Billy (Flanery) needs some cash before the big event and persuades the boys to stop at the bank—only his withdrawal is the illegal kind. Soon Billy's dad (Ward), who happens to be the local sheriff, is trying to contain the situation when the feds show up as does the bewildered bride-to-be. **89m/C VHS, DVD.** Sean Patrick Flanery, Dean Cain, Luke Wilson, Andy Dick, Mitchell Whitfield, Drew Barrymore, Fred Ward, Raymond J. Barry, Brad Dourif, Art Edler Brown, Tracy Fraim; *D:* Tamra Davis; *W:* Art Edler Brown, Tracy Fraim; *C:* James Glennon; *M:* Mark Mothersbaugh.

The Best of Everything **1959** Trashy sexist soap opera about women seeking success and love in the publishing world of N.Y.C. Several stories take place, the best being Crawford's hard-nosed editor who's having an affair with a married man. Look for Evans as a philandering playboy (he went on to become the producer of "Chinatown," among others.) Based on the novel by Rona Jaffe. **121m/C VHS, DVD.** Hope Lange, Stephen Boyd, Suzy Parker, Diane Baker, Martha Hyer, Joan Crawford, Brian Aherne, Robert Evans, Louis Jourdan; *D:* Jean Negulesco; *W:* Edith Sommer, Mann Rubin; *C:* William Mellor; *M:* Alfred Newman.

Best of the Badmen ½ **1950** A whole bunch of outlaws, although seemingly quite nice, are brought together by an ex-Union general who is being framed. Too much talk, not enough action. **84m/B VHS.** Robert Ryan, Claire Trevor, Jack Buetel, Robert Preston, Walter Brennan, Bruce Cabot, John Archer, Lawrence Tierney; *D:* William D. Russell.

Best of the Best ½ **1989 (PG-13)** An interracial kick-boxing team strives to win a world championship. **95m/C VHS, DVD.** Edward (Eddie) Bunker, Eric Roberts, Sally Kirkland, Christopher Penn, Phillip Rhee, James Earl Jones, John P. Ryan, John Dye, David Agresta, Tom Everett, Louise Fletcher, Simon Rhee; *D:* Robert Radler.

Best of the Best 2 ½ **1993 (R)** The Coliseum is a notorious martial-arts venue owned by the champion fighter Brackus and his manager Weldon. No rules death matches are the norm and when their friend is killed Tommy and Alex set up a grudge match with Brackus. **100m/C VHS, DVD.** Edward (Eddie) Bunker, Eric Roberts, Phillip Rhee, Christopher Penn, Ralph (Ralf) Moeller, Wayne Newton, Edan Gross, Sonny Landham, Meg Foster, Simon Rhee, Claire Stansfield, Betty Carvalho; *D:* Robert Radler; *W:* John Allen Nelson, Max Strom; *M:* David Michael Frank.

Best of the Best 3: No Turning Back **1995 (R)** Asian-American Tommy Lee (Rhee) discovers a band of racist vigilantes are trying to take over the rural community of Liberty, where his sister lives. But with the help of his brother-in-law Jack (McDonald), who's also the sheriff, and school teacher Margo (Gershon), Tommy is going to fight back. **102m/C VHS, DVD.** Phillip Rhee, Gina Gershon, Christopher McDonald, Mark Rolston, Peter Simmons, Dee Wallace; *D:* Phillip Rhee; *W:* Deborah Scott; *C:* Jerry Watson; *M:* Barry Goldberg.

Best of the Best: Without Warning ½ **1998 (R)** It's Russian mobsters, counterfeit money, and high tech gadgets this time around as LAPD martial arts consultant Tommy Lee (Rhee) goes after the gang who killed his best friend's daughter. **90m/C VHS, DVD.** Phillip Rhee, Ernie Hudson, Tobin Bell, Thure Riefenstein, Chris Lemmon, Jessica Collins; *D:* Phillip Rhee; *C:* Michael D. Margulies; *M:* David Grant. **VIDEO**

The Best of Times **1986 (PG)** Slim story of two grown men who attempt to redress the failures of the past by reenacting a football game they lost in high school due to a single flubbed pass. With this cast, it should have been better. **105m/C VHS, DVD.** Robin Williams, Kurt Russell, M. Emmet Walsh, Pamela Reed, Holly Palance, Donald Moffat, Margaret Whitton, Kirk Cameron; *D:* Roger Spottiswoode; *W:* Ron Shelton; *C:* Charles F.

Wheeler; ***M:*** Arthur B. Rubinstein.

Best of Youth *La Meglio Gioventu* **2003 (R)** Sprawling modern-times epic spanning 40 years of Italy's tumultuous history through the eyes of two brothers. At close to six hours the film encapsulates the entire relationship between Nicola (Lo Cascio), an optimistic med student, wooing women worldwide before settling into a successful career as a psychiatrist, and his brother Matteo (Boni), a world-weary, brooding idealist who eventually joins the Italian police in hopes of righting the wrongs of an unfair society. History is seen with human eyes and expressed in striking passion, somehow never overindulging itself. Originally an Italian television miniseries, went on to win over the crowds and critics at Cannes. **383m/C DVD.** *IT* Luigi Lo Cascio, Adriana Asti, Alessio Boni, Jasmine Trinca, Sonia Bergamasco, Fabrizio Gifuni, Maya Sansa, Valentina Carnelutti, Andrea Tidona, Lidia Vitale, Camilla Filippi, Greta Cavuoti, Sara Pavoncello, Claudio Gioe; ***D:*** Marco Tullio Giordana; ***W:*** Sandro Petraglia, Stefano Rulli; ***C:*** Roberto Forza. **TV**

Best Revenge **1983 (R)** Two aging hippies engage in a Moroccan drug deal in order to free a kidnapped friend from a sleazy gangster. They get caught by the police, but escape, searching for the engineers of the frame-up. **92m/C VHS.** John Heard, Levon Helm, Alberta Watson, John Rhys-Davies, Moses Znaimer; ***D:*** John Trent; ***M:*** Keith Emerson.

Best Seller **1987 (R)** Interesting, subtext-laden thriller about a cop/bestselling author with writer's block, and the strange symbiotic relationship he forms with a slick hired killer, who wants his own story written. Dennehy is convincing as the jaded cop, and is paired well with the psychotic Woods. **112m/C VHS, DVD.** James Woods, Brian Dennehy, Victoria Tennant, Paul Shenar, Seymour Cassel, Allison Balson, George Coe, Anne Pitoniak; ***D:*** John Flynn; ***W:*** Larry Cohen; ***C:*** Fred Murphy; ***M:*** Jay Ferguson.

The Best Way 1/2 *The Best Way to Walk; La Meilleure Facon de Marcher* **1976** Two summer camp counselors discover they might be gay and desirous of each other. Miller's first film; in French with English subtitles. **85m/C VHS, DVD.** *FR* Patrick Dewaere, Patrick Bouchitey, Christine Pascal, Claude Pieplu; ***D:*** Claude Miller; ***W:*** Luc Beraud, Claude Miller; ***C:*** Bruno Nuytten; ***M:*** Alain Jomy.

The Best Years of Our Lives **1946** Three WWII vets return home to try to pick up the threads of their lives. A film that represented a large chunk of American society and helped it readjust to the modern postwar ambience is now considered an American classic. Supporting actor Russell, an actual veteran, holds a record for winning two Oscars for a single role. In addition to his Best Supporting Actor award, Russell was given a special Oscar for bringing hope and courage to fellow veterans. Based on the novella by MacKinlay Kantor. Remade for TV as "Returning Home" in 1975. **170m/B VHS, DVD.** Fredric March, Myrna Loy, Teresa Wright, Dana Andrews, Virginia Mayo, Harold Russell, Hoagy Carmichael, Gladys George, Roman Bohnen, Steve Cochran, Charles Halton, Cathy O'Donnell, Ray Collins, Victor Cutler, Minna Gombell, Walter Baldwin, Dorothy Adams, Don Beddoe, Ray Teal, Howland Chamberlain; ***D:*** William Wyler; ***W:*** Robert Sherwood; ***C:*** Gregg Toland; ***M:*** Hugo Friedhofer. Oscars '46: Actor (March), Director (Wyler), Film Editing, Picture, Screenplay, Support. Actor (Russell), Orig. Dramatic Score; AFI '98: Top 100; British Acad. '47: Film; Golden Globes '47: Film—Drama; Natl. Bd. of Review '46: Director (Wyler), Natl. Film Reg. '89;; N.Y. Film Critics '46: Director (Wyler), Film.

Bethune 1/2 **1977** The life story of a Canadian doctor who started a practice in Communist China. **88m/C VHS.** Donald Sutherland, Kate Nelligan, David Gardner, James Hong; ***D:*** Eric Till.

Betrayal **1974** Psycho-thriller pits an unhappy widow against her seemingly innocent hired companion. Seems this girl has a boyfriend who has a plan to murder the lonely lady for her money. Routine and predictable. **78m/C VHS.** Amanda Blake, Dick Haymes, Tisha Sterling, Sam Groom; ***D:*** Gordon Hessler; ***M:*** Ernest Gold.

Betrayal 1/2 **1978** Telefilm based on the book by Lucy Freeman and Julie Roy about a historic malpractice case involving a psychiatrist and one of his female patients. The doctor convinced the female patient that sex with him would serve as therapy. **95m/C VHS, DVD.** Lesley Ann Warren, Rip Torn, Ron Silver, Richard Masur, Stephen Elliott, John Hillerman, Peggy Ann Garner; ***D:*** Paul Wendkos.

Betrayal 1/2 **1983 (R)** An unusual adult drama, beginning at the end of a seven-year adulterous affair and working its way back in time to finally end at the start of the betrayal of a husband by his wife and his best friend. Kingsley and Irons make Pinter's adaptation of his own play work. **95m/C VHS.** *GB* Ben Kingsley, Patricia Hodge, Jeremy Irons; ***D:*** David Hugh Jones; ***W:*** Harold Pinter.

Betrayal from the East **1944** A carnival barker saves the Panama Canal from the vicious Japanese war machine in this rather silly wartime drama. **82m/B VHS.** Lee Tracy, Nancy Kelly, Richard Loo, Abner Biberman, Regis Toomey, Philip Ahn, Addison Richards, Victor Sen Yung, Drew Pearson; ***D:*** William Berke.

Betrayal of the Dove **1992 (R)** Slater stars as a divorced woman set-up on a blind date by best friend Le Brock. Zane is the dashing doctor who sweeps Slater off her feet but things are never quite what they seem. He may not be Mr. Right and the best friend has her own hidden agenda. **93m/C VHS.** Helen Slater, Kelly Le Brock, Billy Zane, Alan Thicke, Harvey Korman, Stuart Pankin, David Lander; ***D:*** Strathford Hamilton; ***W:*** Robby Benson.

Betrayed **1954** Bombshell Turner and strongman Gable star in this story of WWII intrigue. Suspected of being a Nazi informer, Turner is sent back to Holland for a last chance at redemption. Her cover as a sultry nightclub performer has the Nazis drooling and ogling (can you spell h-o-t?), but her act may be blown by an informant. Can luscious Lana get out of this one intact? **107m/C VHS.** Clark Gable, Lana Turner, Victor Mature, Louis Calhern, O.E. Hasse, Wilfrid Hyde-White, Ian Carmichael, Niall MacGinnis, Nora Swinburne, Roland Culver; ***D:*** Gottfried Reinhardt; ***C:*** Frederick A. (Freddie) Young.

Betrayed **1988 (R)** A rabid political film, dealing with an implausible FBI agent infiltrating a white supremacist organization via her love affair with a handsome farmer who turns out to be a murderous racist. Winger is memorable in her role as the FBI agent, despite the film's limitations, and admirers of Costa-Gavras's directorial work and political stances will want to see how the director botched this one. **112m/C VHS, DVD.** Tom Berenger, Debra Winger, John Mahoney, John Heard, Albert Hall, Jeffrey DeMunn; ***D:*** Constantin Costa-Gavras; ***W:*** Joe Eszterhas; ***C:*** Patrick Blossier.

The Betrayed 1/2 **2008** When Jamie (George), the married mom of a young son, regains consciousness after a car accident, she's being held captive in an isolated warehouse. Her captor says her husband has stolen millions from a crime syndicate and if Jamie wants to keep her son safe, she must kill her husband. **99m/C DVD.** Melissa George, Donald Adams, Christian Campbell, Scott Heindl, Ken Tremblett, Connor Christopher Levins, Roger Vernon, Blaine Anderson; ***D:*** Amanda Gusack; ***W:*** Amanda Gusack; ***M:*** Deborah Lurie. **VIDEO**

The Betsy *Harold Robbins' The Betsy* **1978 (R)** A story of romance, money, power, and mystery centering around the wealthy Hardeman family and their automobile manufacturing business. Loosely patterned after the life of Henry Ford as portrayed in the Harold Robbins' pulp-tome. Olivier is the redeeming feature. **132m/C VHS, DVD.** Laurence Olivier, Kathleen Beller, Robert Duvall, Lesley-Anne Down, Edward Herrmann, Tommy Lee Jones, Katharine Ross, Jane Alexander; ***D:*** Daniel Petrie; ***W:*** William Bast, Walter Bernstein; ***C:*** Mario Tosi; ***M:*** John Barry.

Betsy's Wedding 1/2 **1990 (R)** Betsy wants a simple wedding, but her father has other, grander ideas. Then there's the problem of paying for it, which Dad tries to take care of in a not-so-typical manner. Alda at his hilarious best. **94m/C VHS, DVD.** Alan Alda, Joey Bishop, Madeline Kahn, Molly Ringwald, Catherine O'Hara, Joe Pesci, Ally Sheedy, Burt Young, Anthony LaPaglia, Julie Bovasso, Nicolas Coster, Bibi Besch, Dylan Walsh, Samuel L. Jackson, Frankie Faison; ***D:*** Alan Alda; ***W:*** Alan Alda; ***C:*** Kelvin Pike; ***M:*** Bruce Broughton.

Better Dayz 1/2 **2002** High schooler Faye (Cargle) has her head turned by smoothie drug dealer Vaughn (Odell)—until she sees him kill a rival. When Vaughn threatens Faye, she turns to her hot-headed brother Johnny (Williams) to keep her safe. Technical flaws detract from what slowly becomes a dramatic story. **101m/C VHS, DVD.** Erik Williams, Shantel Cargle, Rich Odell; ***D:*** Norman C. Linton; ***W:*** Norman C. Linton; ***C:*** Brenden Flint. **VIDEO**

Better Late Than Never **1979** Fun TV tale of senior citizens in revolt at an old-age home. Fine characters portrayed by some of the best in the business. **100m/C VHS.** Harold Gould, Tyne Daly, Strother Martin, Harry (Henry) Morgan, Victor Buono, George Gobel, Lou Jacobi, Donald Pleasence, Larry Storch; ***D:*** Richard Crenna; ***M:*** Charles Fox. **TV**

Better Late Than Never 1/2 **1983** Two penniless old fools vie for the acceptance of a bratty 10-year-old millionairess, who must choose one as her guardian. Niven's last film. **95m/C VHS.** David Niven, Art Carney, Maggie Smith, Kimberly Partridge, Catherine Hicks, Melissa Prophet; ***D:*** Bryan Forbes; ***M:*** Henry Mancini.

Better Luck Tomorrow **2002 (R)** Controversial film about Asian-American teens gone wild. Overachieving students in a wealthy Orange County suburb, they outwardly conform to the stereotype of smart, well-behaved, ambitious kids. But their extracurricular activities involve drugs and criminal activities that escalate from the petty to the serious as events spin out of their control. **98m/C VHS, DVD.** *US* Parry Shen, Jason J. Tobin, Roger Fan, Sung Kang, John Cho, Karin Anna Cheung; ***D:*** Justin Lin; ***W:*** Justin Lin, Ernesto M. Foronda, Fabian Marquez; ***C:*** Patrice Lucien Cochet; ***M:*** Michael J. Gonzales.

Better Off Dead 1/2 **1985 (PG)** A compulsive teenager's girlfriend leaves him and he decides to end it all. After several abortive attempts, he decides instead to outski his ex-girlfriend's obnoxious new boyfriend. Uneven but funny. **97m/C VHS, DVD.** John Cusack, Curtis Armstrong, Diane Franklin, Kim Darby, David Ogden Stiers, Dan Schneider, Amanda Wyss, Taylor Negron, Vincent Schiavelli, Demian Slade, Scooter Stevens, Elizabeth (E.G. Dailey) Daily, Yano Ayana, Steven Williams; ***D:*** Savage Steve Holland; ***W:*** Savage Steve Holland; ***C:*** Isidore Mankofsky; ***M:*** Rupert Hine.

Better Off Dead 1/2 **1994** Preachy, manipulative TV movie redeemed by good performances. Kit (Winningham) is an unrepentant white-trash thief who kills a black police officer and is sentenced to death. Cutter Dubuque (Ferrell) is the ambitious black district attorney who prosecuted the case but comes to doubt the wisdom of the death penalty and slowly begins to try to help Kit. **91m/C VHS.** Mare Winningham, Tyra Ferrell, Kevin Tighe, Don Harvey; ***D:*** Neema Barnette; ***W:*** Marlane X. Meyer; ***C:*** Ueli Steiger; ***M:*** John Barnes.

The Better 'Ole 1/2 **1926** Cockney Old Bill (Chaplin) is a WWI private with the British infantry. Bill and his mate Alfie (Ackroyd) must find the traitor in their ranks who is responsible for a French town falling to the Germans. Based on cartoon characters created by Bruce Bairnsfather, with the title referring to a foxhole. Some of the humor is blunted by the passage of time, although the visual of Chaplin and Ackroyd in a horse's costume is still amusing. **97m/B DVD.** Sydney Chaplin, Jack Ackroyd, Edgar Kennedy, Charles Gerrard, Theodore Lorch, Harold Goodwin; ***D:*** Charles Reisner; ***W:*** Charles Reisner, Darryl F. Zanuck; ***C:*** Edwin DuPar.

Better Than Chocolate **1999 (R)** Sweetly touching romantic comedy follows college dropout Maggie (Dwyer), who's trying to establish her own identity, which isn't so easy when she hasn't told her flighty mother, Lila (Crewson), that she's a lesbian. But now mom is getting divorced and she and Maggie's brother Paul (Mundy) are temporarily moving in, with Maggie trying to pass off her lover Kim (Cox) as just a roommate. Meanwhile, naive Lila is confiding in Maggie's transseuxual friend, singer Judy (a stellar Outerbridge), and discovering the joys of sex toys. **101m/C VHS, DVD.** *CA* Karyn Dwyer, Wendy Crewson, Christina Cox, Peter Outerbridge, Ann-Marie MacDonald, Kevin Mundy, Marya Delver, Jay Brazeau, Tony Nappo; ***D:*** Anne Wheeler; ***W:*** Peggy Thompson; ***C:*** Gregory Middleton; ***M:*** Graeme Coleman.

Better Than Sex 1/2 **2000 (R)** Cin (Porter) meets Josh (Wenham) at a party and takes him home for the night. When things go exceptionally well, Cin agrees to Josh's staying on until he flies home to London in a couple of days. But amidst all the sex, little things like relationships, love, and commitment begin to creep in. Voiceovers from the twosome comment on the action and what they're really feeling rather than what they're telling each other. Porter and Wenham are attractive and there's (unsurprisingly) a lot of displayed skin. **85m/C VHS, DVD.** *AU FR* David Wenham, Susie Porter, Catherine McClements, Kris McQuade, Simon Bossell, Imelda Corcoran; ***D:*** Jonathan Teplitzky; ***W:*** Jonathan Teplitzky; ***C:*** Garry Phillips; ***M:*** David Hirschfelder. Australian Film Inst. '00: Director, Film, Score (Hirschfelder).

A Better Tomorrow, Part 1 1/2 *Ying Huang Boon Sik; Gangland Boss* **1986** Former hit men (Lung and Fat) team up to bring down the mob boss who double-crossed them and sent one to prison and the other to the streets. One of them also has to protect his younger brother, a cop, from the gang. Considered one of the best of Woo's Hong Kong efforts, there's plenty of his hallmark balletic action and an interesting story. In Cantonese with English subtitles. **95m/C VHS, DVD.** *CH HK* Chow Yun-Fat, Leslie Cheung, Ti Lung, Emily Chu, Waise Lee, John Woo; ***D:*** John Woo; ***W:*** John Woo; ***C:*** Wing-Hung Wong; ***M:*** Ka-Fai Koo.

A Better Tomorrow, Part 2 1/2 *Yinghung Bunsik 2* **1988** A smooth-talking gangster, who was killed in Part I, returns in Part II as the dead man's twin brother (unmentioned in Part I). He teams up with a cop and a reformed gangster to fight the forces of evil. In Cantonese with English subtitles. **100m/C VHS, DVD.** *HK* Chow Yun-Fat, Leslie Cheung; ***D:*** John Woo; ***W:*** John Woo; ***M:*** Joseph Koo.

A Better Tomorrow, Part 3 *Love and Death in Saigon* **1989** Prequel set in 1974 finds detective Mark Gor (Fat) and his cousin (Leung) seeking to escape from Saigon. Unfortunately, they both fall for the same sultry babe (Mui), who's also a gangster's moll. Mandarin with subtitles. **114m/C VHS, DVD.** *HK* Chow Yun-Fat, Tony Leung Ka-Fai, Anita (Yim-Fong) Mui; ***D:*** Tsui Hark.

A Better Way to Die **2000 (R)** An ex-cop heads home to try to start a new life but is instead mistaken for a government agent who has had a contract put out on his life by a Chicago mob boss. So the cop tries to get the feds to assist him before the wiseguys get to him first. **101m/C VHS, DVD.** Andre Braugher, Joe Pantoliano, Natasha Henstridge, Lou Diamond Phillips, Wayne Duvall, Scott Wiper; ***D:*** Scott Wiper; ***W:*** Scott Wiper. **VIDEO**

Betty **1992** Sulky, drunken Betty (Trintignant) is doing her best to destroy her bourgeois life, escaping from her marriage into adultery and debasement. She meets the concerned middle-aged widow Laure (Audran), who inexplicably takes her to her hotel room, cleans her up, and spends the remainder of the movie as Betty's sounding-board. Betty's passive personality offers little to explain her appeal to either Laure or the viewer. Based on the novel by Georges Simenon. French with subtitles. **103m/C VHS, DVD.** *FR* Marie Trintignant, Stephane Audran, Jean-Francoise Garreaud, Yves Lambrecht, Christiane Minazzoli, Pierre Vernier; ***D:*** Claude Chabrol; ***W:*** Claude Chabrol; ***M:*** Matthieu Chabrol.

Betty 1/2 **1997** Betty Monday (Pollak) is a well-known actress undergoing a breakdown. So she leaves Hollywood for Palm Springs and tries out a "normal" life—at least by movie star standards. Offbeat comedy has the potential to pleasantly surprise. **88m/C VHS, DVD.** Cheryl Pollak, Holland Taylor, Udo Kier, Ron Perlman, Stephen Gregory; ***D:*** Richard D. (R.D.) Murphy; ***W:*** Richard D. (R.D.) Murphy.

Betty Blue *37.2 le Matin; 37.2 Degrees in the Morning* **1986 (R)** A vivid, intensely erotic film about two young French lovers and how their inordinately strong passion for each other destroys them, leading to poverty, violence, and insanity. English subtitles. From the director of "Diva." Based on the novel "37.2 Le Matin" by Philippe Djian. **121m/C VHS, DVD.** *FR* Beatrice Dalle, Jean-Hugues Anglade, Gerard Darmon, Consuelo de Haviland, Clementine Celarie, Jacques Mathou, Vincent Lindon; ***D:*** Jean-Jacques Beineix; ***W:*** Jean-Jacques Beineix; ***C:*** Jean-Francois Robin; ***M:*** Gabriel Yared.

The Betty Ford Story **1987** Gena Rowlands deserved her Emmy for her strong portrayal of First Lady Betty Ford in this adaptation of Ford's autobiography "The Times of My Life." Ford earns national admiration for her candid reveal of her breast cancer and subsequent treatment but she hides her addictions to alcohol and prescription drugs. After her husband (Sommer) loses his 1976 reelection bid, her family intervenes and Betty gets clean, then decides to open her own center for substance abusers. **93m/C DVD.** Gena Rowlands, Josef Sommer, Nan Woods, Concetta Tomei, Brian McNamara, Bradley Whitford, Daniel McDonald, Ken Tigar; ***D:*** David Greene; ***W:*** Karen Hall; ***C:*** Dennis Dalzell; ***M:*** Arthur B. Rubinstein. **TV**

Between **2005** Allegedly spooky pic with a nonsensical plot and weak acting. Chicago lawyer Nadine Roberts (Montgomery) keeps having terrifying visions of her estranged sister Diane, who vanished in Tijuana. So Nadine heads south of the border to investigate but doesn't get much cooperation even as her nightmares worsen. Then people start calling Nadine by Diane's name and there's all this ridiculous symbolism before the surprise ending that isn't at all. **86m/C DVD.** Poppy Montgomery, Danny Pino, Adam Kaufman, Jose Yenque, Patricia Reyes Spindola; ***D:*** David Ocanas; ***W:*** Robert Nelms; ***C:*** Rob Sweeney; ***M:*** Joel J. Richard. **CABLE**

Between Fighting Men ½ **1932** The orphaned daughter of a shepherd is adopted by the cowpoke who caused her father's death. The cowpoke's sons fall in love with, and compete for, the love of the girl. **62m/B VHS.** Ken Maynard, Ruth Hall, Josephine Dunn, Wallace MacDonald; ***D:*** Forrest Sheldon.

Between Friends ½ **1983** Two women with only their respective divorces in common, meet and become fast friends. The rapport between Burnett and Taylor makes for a touching drama. Adapted from the book "Nobody Makes Me Cry," by Shelley List, one of the producers. **105m/C VHS.** Elizabeth Taylor, Carol Burnett; ***D:*** Lou Antonio; ***M:*** James Horner. **CABLE**

Between God, the Devil & a Winchester **1972** Violent western with plenty of shooting and dust. Lots of cowboys are hot on the trail of some stolen loot from a church but apparently God isn't on their side since the majority bite the dust and become a snack for the vultures. **98m/C VHS.** Gilbert Roland, Richard Harrison; ***D:*** Dario Silvester.

Between Heaven and Earth **1993** Maria (Maura) is an ambitious TV journalist, prone to surreal dreams, who becomes pregnant after a one-night stand. After witnessing a violent protest, Maria becomes convinced that she can communicate with her unborn baby and that the child is unwilling to be born into such a violent world. So Maria must try to convince her baby otherwise. In French with English subtitles. **80m/C VHS.** *BE FR SP* Carmen Maura, Jean-Pierre Cassel, Didier Bezace, Samuel Mussen, Andre Delvaux; ***D:*** Marion Hansel; ***W:*** Marion Hansel.

Between Heaven and Hell **1956** Prejudiced Southern gentleman Wagner finds how wrong his misconceptions are, as he attempts to survive WWII on a Pacific Island. Ebsen is exceptional, making this rather simplistic story a meaningful classic. **94m/C VHS, DVD.** Robert Wagner, Terry Moore, Broderick Crawford, Buddy Ebsen, Robert Keith, Brad Dexter, Mark Damon, Ken Clark, Harvey Lembeck, Frank Gorshin, Scatman Crothers, Carl "Alfalfa" Switzer, L.Q. Jones, Tod Andrews; ***D:*** Richard Fleischer; ***W:*** Harry Brown; ***C:*** Leo Tover; ***M:*** Hugo Friedhofer.

Between Love & Goodbye **2008** French citizen Marcel marries lesbian Sarah so he can get a green card to stay in New York with lover Kyle. Marcel and Kyle are living together when Kyle offers his troubled transgendered sister April a place to crash. Jealous of Kyle and Marcel's relationship, April sets out to break them up, which Kyle refuses to believe. The two lovers are so petulant and clueless that their romantic problems are more annoying than compelling. **87m/C DVD.** Robert Harmon, Justin Tensen, Simon Miller, Jane Elliott; ***D:*** Casper Andreas; ***W:*** Casper Andreas; ***C:*** Jon Fordham; ***M:*** Scott Starrett.

Between Men **1935** A father kills a man he believes killed his son and flees. Later in life, the son meets his father. For father and son, this causes some major concern. **59m/B VHS.** Johnny Mack Brown, Beth Marion, William Farnum, Earl Dwire, Lloyd Ingraham, Milburn (Milt) Morante; ***D:*** Robert North Bradbury.

Between Something & Nothing **2008** Small-town teen Joe gets into a prestigious big-city art school but he and fellow student/best friend Jennifer are constantly struggling to pay tuition and other living expenses. Then Joe meets hustler Ramon, who suggests his new bud try the sex-for-pay route and soon Joe is using his new life as inspiration for his art. **105m/C DVD.** Tim Swain, Julia Frey, Gil Bar-Sera; ***D:*** Todd Verow; ***W:*** Todd Verow, James Dwyer; ***C:*** Todd Verow; ***M:*** Colin Owens. **VIDEO**

Between Strangers **2002 (R)** Three Toronto women suffer personal crises and contemplate changing their lives. Housewife Olivia (Loren) is debating whether to leave her abusive invalid husband (Postlethwaite); war photographer Natalia (Sorvino) is burned out trying to live up to her father's reputation and contemplates a career change; and cellist Catherine (Unger) is upset over her father's (McDowell) recent release from prison for a crime that has haunted her since childhood. Ponti's debut and his mom Loren's 100th film. **97m/C VHS, DVD.** *US CA IT* Sophia Loren, Mira Sorvino, Deborah Kara Unger, Pete Postlethwaite, Malcolm McDowell, Klaus Maria Brandauer, Gerard Depardieu, Wendy Crewson, Andrew Tarbet; ***D:*** Edoardo Ponti; ***W:*** Edoardo Ponti; ***C:*** Gregory Middleton; ***M:*** Zbigniew Preisner.

Between the Lines ½ **1977 (R)** A witty, wonderfully realized ensemble comedy about the staff of a radical post-'60s newspaper always on the brink of folding, and its eventual sell-out. **101m/C VHS.** John Heard, Lindsay Crouse, Jeff Goldblum, Jill Eikenberry, Stephen Collins, Lewis J. Stadlen, Michael J. Pollard, Marilu Henner, Bruno Kirby; ***D:*** Joan Micklin Silver; ***W:*** Fred Barron; ***M:*** Michael Kamen.

Between Two Women **1986** A wife's relationship with her bossy mother-in-law is rocky until the latter has a stroke and needs care. Dewhurst won an Emmy for her portrayal of the mother-in-law. **95m/C VHS.** Farrah Fawcett, Michael Nouri, Colleen Dewhurst, Steven Hill, Bridgette Andersen, Danny Corkill; ***D:*** Jon Avnet. **TV**

Between Wars **1974** Young doctor in Australia's Medical Corps encounters conflict when he tries to introduce Freud's principles into his work. **97m/C VHS.** *AU* Corin Redgrave, Arthur Dignam, Judy Morris, Patricia Leehy, Gunter Meisner; ***D:*** Michael Thornhill.

Between Your Legs *Entre las Piernas* **1999** Provocatively titled sexual thriller. Receptionist Miranda (Abril) meets writer Javier (Bardem) at a group therapy session for sex addicts. He's addicted to phone sex and the married Miranda likes to have sex with strangers. While they get to know each other a murder occurs and the investigation is assigned to detective Felix (Gomez), who happens to be Miranda's husband. Soon, suspicions begins to point in Javier's direction. The triangle is strong but subplots are undeveloped and the film sinks into implausibility. Spanish with subtitles. **120m/C VHS, DVD.** *SP FR* Victoria Abril, Javier Bardem, Carmelo Gomez, Juan Diego, Sergi Lopez, Javier Albala; ***D:*** Manuel Gomez Pereira; ***W:*** Manuel Gomez Pereira, Joaquin Oristrell, Yolanda Garcia Serrano, Juan Luis Iborra; ***C:*** Juan Amoros; ***M:*** Bernardo Bonezzi.

Beulah Land ½ **1980** Miniseries about 45 years in the lives of a Southern family, including the Civil War. Based on the novels "Beulah Land" and "Look Away, Beulah Land" by Lonnie Coleman. **267m/C VHS, DVD.** Lesley Ann Warren, Michael Sarrazin, Don Johnson, Meredith Baxter, Dorian Harewood, Eddie Albert, Hope Lange, Paul Rudd; ***D:*** Virgil W. Vogel, Harry Falk. **TV**

The Beverly Hillbillies ½ **1993 (PG)** Big-screen transfer of the long-running TV show may appeal to fans. Ozark mountaineer Jed Clampett discovers oil, becomes an instant billionaire, and packs his backwoods clan off to the good life in California. Minimal plot finds dim-bulb nephew Jethro and daughter Elly May looking for a bride for Jed. Not that any of it matters. Everyone does fine by their impersonations, particularly Varney as the good-hearted Jed and Leachman as stubborn Granny. Ebsen, the original Jed, reprises another of his TV roles, detective Barnaby Jones. And yes, the familiar strains of the "Ballad of Jed Clampett" by Jerry Scoggins starts this one off, too. **93m/C VHS, DVD.** Jim Varney, Erika Eleniak, Diedrich Bader, Cloris Leachman, Dabney Coleman, Lily Tomlin, Lea Thompson, Rob Schneider, Linda Carlson, Penny Fuller, Kevin Connolly; ***Cameos:*** Buddy Ebsen, Zsa Zsa Gabor, Dolly Parton; ***D:*** Penelope Spheeris; ***W:*** Larry Konner, Mark Rosenthal, Jim Fisher, Jim Staahl; ***C:*** Robert Brinkmann; ***M:*** Lalo Schifrin.

Beverly Hills Bodysnatchers ½ **1989 (R)** A mad scientist and a greedy mortician plot to get rich, but their plan backfires when they bring a Mafia godfather back to life and he terrorizes Beverly Hills. **85m/C VHS.** Vic Tayback, Frank Gorshin, Brooke Bundy, Seth Jaffe, Art Metrano, Allison Barron, Rodney Eastman, Warren Selko, Keone Young; ***D:*** Jonathan Mostow.

Beverly Hills Brats **1989 (PG-13)** A spoiled, rich Hollywood brat hires a loser to kidnap him, in order to gain his parents' attention, only to have both of them kidnapped by real crooks. **90m/C VHS, DVD.** Martin Sheen, Burt Young, Peter Billingsley, Terry Moore; ***D:*** Dimitri Sotirakis; ***M:*** Barry Goldberg.

Beverly Hills Chihuahua **2008 (PG)** Chloe, a pampered Chihuahua living the good life in Beverly Hills, finds herself lost in Mexico with the spoiled pet-sitter during a weekend romp. Along the way Chloe must be rescued from the grips of Mexican dogfight wranglers and falls in love with Papi, a Chihuahua from the wrong side of the tracks. Light-hearted family affair with a strong Hispanic cast, as well as Barrymore as the voice of Chloe and Curtis as Chloe's wildly indulgent owner. Cute, tame, kind of lame. **86m/C DVD, Blu-ray Disc.** *US* Nick Zano, Piper Perabo, Manolo Cardona, Jose Maria Yazpik; ***D:*** Raja Gosnell; ***W:*** Jeffrey Bushell, Analisa LaBianco; ***C:*** Phil Mereaux; ***M:*** Hector Pereira; ***V:*** Drew Barrymore, Salma Hayek, George Lopez, Andy Garcia, Jamie Lee Curtis, Marguerite Moreau, Michael Urie, Richard "Cheech" Marin, Paul Rodriguez, Placido Domingo, Edward James Olmos, Loretta Devine, Luis Guzman.

Beverly Hills Cop ½ **1984 (R)** When a close friend of smooth-talking Detroit cop Axel Foley is brutally murdered, he traces the murderer to the posh streets of Beverly Hills. There he must stay on his toes to keep one step ahead of the killer and two steps ahead of the law. Better than average Murphy vehicle. **105m/C VHS, DVD.** Eddie Murphy, Judge Reinhold, John Ashton, Lisa Eilbacher, Ronny Cox, Steven Berkoff, James Russo, Jonathan Banks, Stephen Elliott, Bronson Pinchot, Paul Reiser, Damon Wayans, Rick Overton; ***D:*** Martin Brest; ***W:*** Danilo Bach, Daniel Petrie Jr.; ***C:*** Bruce Surtees; ***M:*** Harold Faltermeyer.

Beverly Hills Cop 2 ½ **1987 (R)** The highly successful sequel to the first profitable comedy, with essentially the same plot, this time deals with Foley infiltrating a band of international munitions smugglers. **103m/C VHS, DVD.** Eddie Murphy, Judge Reinhold, Jurgen Prochnow, Ronny Cox, John Ashton, Brigitte Nielsen, Allen (Goorwitz) Garfield, Paul Reiser, Dean Stockwell, Chris Rock, Gil Hill, Robert Ridgely, Gilbert Gottfried, Todd Susman, Robert Pastorelli, Tommy (Tiny) Lister, Paul Guilfoyle, Hugh Hefner; ***D:*** Tony Scott; ***W:*** Larry Ferguson, Warren Skaaren; ***C:*** Jeffrey L. Kimball; ***M:*** Harold Faltermeyer. Golden Raspberries '87: Worst Song ("I Want Your Sex").

Beverly Hills Cop 3 ½ **1994 (R)** Yes, Detroit cop Axel Foley (Murphy) just happens to find another case that takes him back to his friends on the Beverly Hills PD. This time he uncovers a criminal network fronting WonderWorld, an amusement park with a squeaky-clean image. Fast-paced action, lots of gunplay, and Eddie wisecracks his way through the slow spots. Reinhold returns as the still impossibly naive Rosewood, with Pinchot briefly reprising his role as Serge of the undeterminable accent. Critically panned boxoffice disappointment relies too heavily on formula and is another disappointing followup. **105m/C VHS, DVD.** Louis Lombardi, Eddie Murphy, Judge Reinhold, Hector Elizondo, Timothy Carhart, Stephen McHattie, Theresa Randle, John Saxon, Alan Young, Bronson Pinchot, Al Green, Gil Hill; ***D:*** John Landis; ***W:*** Steven E. de Souza; ***C:*** Mac Ahlberg; ***M:*** Nile Rodgers.

Beverly Hills Family Robinson **1997** Cooking show host Marsha Robinson decides to take her family on a yachting vacation in the South Seas. Naturally, they get hijacked by pirates and shipwrecked and must learn to survive on their not-quite-deserted island. And just how good is Marsha is at campfire cooking? **88m/C VHS.** Dyan Cannon, Martin Mull, Sarah Michelle Gellar, Josh Picker, Nique Needles, Ryan O'Donohue; ***D:*** Troy Miller. **TV**

Beverly Hills Madam **1986 (PG-13)** In this routine plot, a stable of elite call girls struggle with their lifestyle and their madam, played by Dunaway. **97m/C VHS.** Faye Dunaway, Louis Jourdan, Donna Dixon, Robin Givens, Marshall Colt, Melody Anderson, Terry Farrell; ***D:*** Harvey Hart. **TV**

Beverly Hills Ninja ½ **1996 (PG-13)** Farley plays Haru, a pathetically inept adopted son of a ninja, who is, nevertheless, sent to Beverly Hills on a rescue mission to break up an international counterfeiting ring. There, second-time spoof siren Sheridan hires the "great white ninja" to follow her no-good boyfriend and becomes the object of Haru's desire. Farley's extraordinary gift for physical comedy is exploited to the hilt, and the increase in Haru's tripping and stumbling (and in one harrowing scene, stripping) usually coincides with the fumbling of the plot. Rock's talents are squandered on a poorly conceived bellboy character. Farley's first feature sans fellow SNL alumni Spade suffers for his absence. Director Duggan, who also helmed Adam Sandler's "Happy Gilmore," might want to start screening his calls. **88m/C VHS, DVD.** Chris Farley, Nicolette Sheridan, Robin Shou, Nathaniel Parker, Chris Rock, Soon-Teck Oh, Francois Chau, Keith Cooke Hirabayashi; ***D:*** Dennis Dugan; ***W:*** Mark Feldberg, Mitch Klebenoff; ***C:*** Arthur Albert; ***M:*** George S. Clinton.

Beverly Hills Vamp **1988 (R)** A madame and her girls are really female vampires with a penchant for hot-blooded men. **88m/C VHS.** Britt Ekland, Eddie Deezen, Debra Lamb, Michelle (McClellan) Bauer, Brigitte Burdine, Tim Conway Jr., Jillian Kesner, Tom Shell; ***D:*** Fred Olen Ray; ***W:*** Ernest Farino; ***C:*** Stephen Blake; ***M:*** Chuck Cirino.

Beware ½ **1946** A black singer saves a college from bankruptcy and makes off with the gym teacher. The photography may be a bit harsh, but the all-black cast made this a pioneering but impressive film. **64m/B VHS, DVD.** Louis Jordan, Frank Wilson, Emory Richardson, Valerie Black, Milton Woods; ***D:*** Bud Pollard.

Beware! Children at Play **WOOF!** **1995 (R)** Cult leader kidnaps kids and introduces them to cannibalism. Bleech! As if this didn't sound grim enough, there's also an unrated version. **90m/C VHS, DVD.** Michael Robinson, Eric Tonken, Jamie Krause, Mik

Cribben, Danny McClaughlin; ***D:*** Mik Cribben; ***C:*** Mik Cribben.

Beware, My Lovely ½ **1952** Taut chiller. Lonely widow Lupino hires a new handy-man. He's great with screen doors and storm windows, but has a problem with sharp tools. Intense and gripping with fine performances. **77m/B VHS.** Ida Lupino, Robert Ryan, Taylor Holmes, O.Z. Whitehead, Barbara Whiting, Dee Pollock; ***D:*** Harry Horner.

Beware of a Holy Whore *Warnung Vor Einer Heiligen Nutte* **1970** German film crew sits around a Spanish resort—complaining, drinking, and making love—as they wait for financial support from Bonn. Provocative and self-indulgently honest look at filmmaking. Filmed on location in Sorrento, Italy; German with subtitles. **103m/C VHS, DVD.** *GE* Lou Castel, Eddie Constantine, Hanna Schygulla, Marquard Bohm, Ulli Lommel, Margarethe von Trotta, Kurt Raab, Ingrid Caven, Werner Schroeter, Rainer Werner Fassbinder; ***D:*** Rainer Werner Fassbinder; ***W:*** Rainer Werner Fassbinder; ***C:*** Michael Ballhaus; ***M:*** Peer Raben.

Beware of Pity ½ **1946** A crippled baroness thinks she's found true love with a military officer, but it turns out his marriage proposal grew out of pity for her, not passion. A quality but somber British-made historical drama, based on a novel by Stefan Zweig. **129m/B VHS.** Lilli Palmer, Albert Lieven, Cedric Hardwicke, Gladys Cooper, Ernest Thesiger, Freda Jackson, Linden Travers, Ralph Truman, Peter Cotes, Jenny Laird, Emrys Jones, Gerhard Kempinski, John Salew, Kenneth Warrington; ***D:*** Maurice Elvey; ***W:*** W.P. Lipscomb, Elizabeth Barron, Margaret Steen; ***C:*** Derick Williams.

Beware! The Blob *Son of Blob* **1972 (PG)** A scientist brings home a piece of frozen blob from the North Pole; his wife accidentally revives the dormant gray mass. It begins a rampage of terror by digesting nearly everyone within its reach. A host of recognizable faces make for fun viewing. Post-Jeannie, pre-Dallas Hagman directed this exercise in zaniness. **87m/C VHS, DVD.** Robert Walker Jr., Godfrey Cambridge, Carol Lynley, Shelley Berman, Larry Hagman, Burgess Meredith, Gerrit Graham, Dick Van Patten, Gwynne Gilford, Richard Stahl, Richard Webb, Cindy Williams; ***D:*** Larry Hagman; ***W:*** Jack Woods, Anthony Harris; ***C:*** Al Hamm; ***M:*** Mort Garson.

Bewitched **2005 (PG-13)** Instead of an actual remake of the 1964-72 hit TV show, the Ephron sisters opted for a behind-the-scenes parody. Down-and-out actor Jack Wyatt (Ferrell) hopes his new role as Darrin will magically revive his career. Not wanting to be upstaged, he picks a nose-wiggling—and unknown—Isabel (Kidman) for Samantha the witch, not knowing that she really IS one. Since she disavowed (sort of) her witchery to live a mortal life, she accepts and sees Jack as a potential worldly mate. Once his egomania becomes evident, she can't help but revert to a little voodoo to shake things up. Great cast but tale doesn't cast a spell. **100m/C DVD, UMD.** *US* Nicole Kidman, Will Ferrell, Shirley MacLaine, Michael Caine, Jason Schwartzman, Heather Burns, Jim Turner, David Alan Grier, Steve Carell, Amy Sedaris, Richard Kind, Stephen Colbert, Kristin Chenoweth, Michael Badalucco, Carol(e) Shelley, Kate Walsh; ***D:*** Nora Ephron; ***W:*** Nora Ephron, Delia Ephron; ***C:*** John Lindley; ***M:*** George Fenton.

The Beyond *Seven Doors of Death; E Tu Vivrai Nel Terrore—L'aldila* **1982 (R)** A young woman inherits a possessed hotel. Meanwhile, hellish zombies try to check out. Chilling Italian horror flick that Fulci directed under the alias "Louis Fuller." **88m/C VHS, DVD.** *IT* Al Cliver, Katherine (Katriona) MacColl, David Warbeck, Farah Keller, Tony St. John; ***D:*** Lucio Fulci; ***W:*** Lucio Fulci, Dardano Sacchetti, Giorgio Mariuzzo; ***C:*** Sergio Salvati.

Beyond a Reasonable Doubt **1956** In order to get a behind-the-scenes glimpse at the judicial system, a man plays the guilty party to a murder. Alas, when he tries to vindicate himself, he is the victim of his own folly. Not as interesting as it sounds on paper. **80m/B VHS.** Dana Andrews, Joan Fontaine, Sidney Blackmer, Philip Bourneuf, Barbara Nichols, Shepperd Strudwick, Arthur Franz, Edward Binns; ***D:*** Fritz Lang; ***W:*** Douglas S. Morrow.

Beyond a Reasonable Doubt **2009 (PG-13)** This remake of Fritz Lang's 1956 legal thriller gets an updated treatment but loses the pacing, suspense and intrigue of the original. The magnificently coifed Martin Hunter (Douglas) is a Louisiana DA suspected by newcomer TV reporter from New York, CJ Nichols (Metcalfe) of planting evidence to pad his conviction rate. To get the goods on the DA, Nichols acts the part of accused perp of an unsolved murder, thinking he'll trap Hunter while planting bogus evidence. Things don't quite work out as planned and the film never fully explores its chance to shine a light on judicial corruption, instead skimming the surface with car chases and Hunter's super-fine hairdo. **105m/C DVD.** *US* Michael Douglas, Jesse Metcalfe, Amber Tamblyn, Orlando Jones, Joel David Moore; ***D:*** Peter Hyams; ***W:*** Peter Hyams; ***C:*** Peter Hyams; ***M:*** David Shire.

Beyond Atlantis **WOOF!** **1973 (PG)** An ancient underwater tribe is discovered when it kidnaps land-lubbin' women with which to mate. **91m/C VHS, DVD.** *PH* John Ashley, Patrick Wayne, George Nader; ***D:*** Eddie Romero; ***W:*** Charles Johnson; ***C:*** Justo Paulino.

Beyond Borders ½ **2003 (R)** Decades-spanning romance between an overzealous doctor and a lovely do-gooder suffers from a too-earnest presentation and romantic cliches. Dashing doctor Nick (Owen) inspires American socialite Sarah (Jolie) to leave her stuffy British hubby (Roache) and really get involved in international aid relief rather than just writing a check. She follows the doc to Ethiopia and later to Cambodia and Checknya (film goes from 1984-1995), where the trouble-prone Nick has apparently been kidnapped. At least the film inspired Jolie personally since she became a goodwill ambassador for the United Nations High Commissioner for Refugees and adopted her son from Cambodia. **127m/C VHS, DVD.** *US* Angelina Jolie, Clive Owen, Teri Polo, Linus Roache, Yorick Van Wageningen, Noah Emmerich, Kate Ashfield, Jamie Bartlett, Timothy West, Kate Trotter, Burt Kwouk; ***D:*** Martin Campbell; ***W:*** Caspian Tredwell-Owen; ***C:*** Phil Meheux; ***M:*** James Horner.

Beyond Darkness ½ **1992 (R)** When Peter and his family move into their New England home they are immediately beset by some unknown terror. With the help of Father George, Peter learns his house was built upon the graves of 20 witches burned for heresy. The witches have decided to seek revenge by kidnapping Peter's young son and sacrificing him to an evil demon. Can Peter destroy the evil spirits before they destroy his son? **111m/C VHS.** Gene Le Brock, David Brandon, Barbara Bingham, Michael Stephenson, Stephen Brown; ***D:*** Clyde (Claudio Fragasso) Anderson.

Beyond Desire ½ **1994 (R)** Elvis Ray (Forsythe) is released after 14 years in prison and gets picked up by corvette-driving prison groupie and Las Vegas prostitute Rita (Wuhrer) but more than sex is on both their minds. **87m/C VHS.** William Forsythe, Kari Wuhrer, Leo Rossi, Sharon Farrell; ***D:*** Dominique Othenin-Girard; ***W:*** Dale Trevillion; ***C:*** Sven Kirsten; ***M:*** Mark Holden.

Beyond Dream's Door **1988** A young, All-American college student's childhood nightmares come back to haunt him, making dreams a horrifying reality. **86m/C VHS, DVD.** Nick Baldasare, Rick Kesler, Susan Pinsky, Norm Singer; ***D:*** Jay Woelfel.

Beyond Erotica **1979** After being cut out of his father's will, a sadistic young man takes out his rage on his mother and a peasant girl. **90m/C VHS.** David Hemmings, Alida Valli, Andrea Rau; ***D:*** Jose Maria Forque.

Beyond Evil **WOOF!** **1980 (R)** Relatively dim-witted newlywed couple moves into an old island mansion despite rumors that the house is haunted. Sure enough, wife George becomes possessed by the vengeful spirit of a woman murdered 200 years earlier, and a reign of pointless terror begins. Poor rip-off of hybrid Amityville/Exorcist paranormality. **98m/C VHS, DVD.** John Saxon, Lynda Day George, Michael Dante, Mario Milano; ***D:*** Herb Freed; ***W:*** Herb Freed; ***M:*** Pino Donaggio.

Beyond Fear ½ *Au-Dela de la Peur* **1975** Compelling drama about a man forced to aid a gang in robbery while they hold his wife and son captive. **92m/C VHS.** *FR IT* Michael Boquet, Michel Constantin, Marilu Tolo, Paul Crauchet, Michel Creton, Moustache, Jean-Pierre Darras; ***D:*** Yannick Andrei; ***W:*** Yannick Andrei; ***C:*** Pierre Petit; ***M:*** Alain Goraguer.

Beyond Fear ½ **1993 (R)** Tipper Taylor (Lesseos) is a wilderness tour guide who's also a martial arts expert. This is going to come in handy when her tour group is stalked by two men who are after a videotape innocently filmed by someone in Tipper's group. It seems the tape shows the men committing a murder. **84m/C VHS, DVD.** Mimi Lesseos; ***D:*** Robert F. Lyons; ***W:*** Robert F. Lyons, Mimi Lesseos; ***C:*** Bodo Holst; ***M:*** Miriam Cutler.

Beyond Forgiveness ½ **1994 (R)** Basic maverick cop goes after his brother's killers and winds up involved in an international black market in transplantable human organs. **95m/C VHS.** Thomas Ian Griffith, Rutger Hauer, John Rhys-Davies; ***D:*** Bob Misiorowski; ***W:*** Charles Cohen.

Beyond Honor **2005** Egyptian-American medical student Sahira tries to be a modern woman but her father Mohammad is a strict Muslim who dominates the family. When he discovers that Sahira has a boyfriend and is no longer a virgin, he enacts a brutal punishment for her dishonoring their family. **101m/C DVD.** Jason Smith, Ruth Osuna, Wadie Andrawis, Laurel Melegrano, Ryan Izay; ***D:*** Varun Khanna; ***W:*** Varun Khanna; ***C:*** Dinesh Kampani; ***M:*** David Mann.

Beyond Innocence **1987** A 17-year-old lusts after a mature married woman. Ostensibly based on Raymond Radiguet's "Devil in the Flesh." **87m/C VHS.** Keith Smith, Katia Caballero, John Morris; ***D:*** Scott Murray; ***C:*** Andrzej Bartkowiak.

Beyond Justice **1992 (PG-13)** High action-adventure with the prolific Hauer starring as an ex-CIA agent who is hired to rescue the kidnapped son of a beautiful executive. **113m/C VHS, DVD.** *IT* Rutger Hauer, Carol Alt, Omar Sharif, Elliott Gould, Kabir Bedi, David Flosi, Brett Halsey, Peter Sands; ***D:*** Duccio Tessari; ***W:*** Sergio Donati, Luigi Montefiore; ***C:*** Giorgio Di Battista; ***M:*** Ennio Morricone.

Beyond Justice *Lawless: Beyond Justice* **2001** New Zealand TV thriller with a modicum of action. Private detectives John Lawless (Smith) and Jodie Keane (Dotchin) are hired by widow Lana Vitale (Rubin) to investigate her husband's suspicious death. Lana's not exactly grieving since she's all too willing to get up close and personal with Lawless. Meanwhile, Jodie follows some clues that lead her to a porno ring. **95m/C VHS, DVD.** *NZ* Kevin Smith, Jennifer Rubin, Angela Dotchin, Bruce Hopkins, Dean O'Gorman; ***D:*** Geoffrey Cawthorn; ***W:*** Gavin Strawhan. **TV**

Beyond Obsession *Oltre la Porta* **1982** The strange relationship between a political prisioner, his daughter, and her obsession with a mysterious American is provocatively explored. **116m/C VHS, DVD.** *IT* Marcello Mastroianni, Elenora Giorgi, Tom Berenger, Michel Piccoli; ***D:*** Liliana Cavani; ***W:*** Liliana Cavani.

Beyond Rangoon ½ **1995 (R)** Sisters Laura (Arquette) and Andy (McDormand) Bowman travel to Burma to unwind, only to have political unrest and a repressive regime spoil the holiday. Dr. Laura (yeah, right) loses her passport and must flee from trigger-happy soldiers with a political dissident (Ko, a real-life exiled Burmese activist) who befriends her. The search for her passport soon becomes a imperiled trek of survival and self-discovery. Tense, well-crafted action sequences hint at a potential for excitement and intrigue; too bad Arquette isn't the least bit convincing. Filmed in Malaysia. **100m/C VHS.** Patricia Arquette, Frances McDormand, Spalding Gray, U Aung Ko, Victor Slezak; ***D:*** John Boorman; ***W:*** Alex Lasker, Bill Rubenstein; ***C:*** John Seale; ***M:*** Hans Zimmer.

Beyond Re-Animator **2003 (R)** Mad scientist Herbert West (Combs) has been in a maximum security prison for 15 years but has continued his experiments (this time on the rats in his cell). When idealistic young Howard Phillips (Barry) becomes the new prison doctor, he wants to aid West with his re-animation experiments. Of course, things still don't work out as planned and zombie mayhem ensues in this schlocky-but-fun third adventure. **95m/C DVD.** *US SP* Jeffrey Combs, Jason Barry, Simon Andreu, Elsa Pataky; ***D:*** Brian Yuzna; ***W:*** Jose Manuel Gomez; ***C:*** Andreu Rebes; ***M:*** Xavier Capellas.

Beyond Reason **1977** A psychologist uses unorthodox methods by treating the criminally insane with dignity and respect. **88m/C VHS.** Telly Savalas, Laura Johnson, Diana Muldaur, Marvin Laird, Priscilla Barnes; ***D:*** Telly Savalas; ***C:*** John A. Alonzo.

Beyond Reasonable Doubt ½ **1980** Chilling true-life murder mystery which shattered the peaceful quiet of a small New Zealand town and eventually divided the country. An innocent farmer (Hargreaves) was convicted of a grisly double murder based on evidence planted by a local cop (Hemmings, in a superb role). It wasn't until Yallop's book questioned the facts of the case that it was reopened. Yallop also wrote the screenplay. **127m/C VHS.** *NZ* David Hemmings, John Hargreaves, Martyn Sanderson, Grant Tilly, Diana Rowan, Ian Watkin; ***D:*** John Laing; ***W:*** David Yallop.

Beyond Redemption **1999 (R)** A serial killer goes after highly respected targets, crucifying his victims, and Detective Smith is in charge of catching the bad guy. It all hinges on faith—and whose is stronger. **97m/C VHS, DVD.** *CA* Andrew McCarthy, Michael Ironside, Jayne Heitmeyer, Suzy Joachim; ***D:*** Chris Angel. **VIDEO**

Beyond Sherwood Forest **2009** Apparently what's beyond Sherwood Forrest is the realm of stupid. Syfy cable version of the Robin Hood story has Robin (Dunne), the Merry Men, and Maid Marian (Durance) battling druids and some lame CGI dragon while Malcolm (Sands), the Sheriff of Nottingham, ineffectually hunts them down as usual. **93m/C DVD.** *CA* Robin Dunne, Erica Durance, Julian Sands, Richard Klerk de, David Richmond-Peck, Robert Lawrenson, Robert Lawrenson; ***D:*** Peter DeLuise; ***W:*** Chase Parker; ***M:*** Darren Fung. **CABLE**

Beyond Silence *Jenseits der Stille* **1996 (PG-13)** Lara (Trieb/Testud), the daughter of deaf parents, has been their guide to the outside world since childhood. When her Aunt Clarissa (Canonica) gives her a clarinet, it opens Lara's life to music and gives her the courage to move beyond the limits of her family. German with subtitles. **109m/C VHS, DVD.** *GE* Sylvie Testud, Tatjana Trieb, Howie Seago, Emmanuelle Laborit, Sibylle Canonica; ***D:*** Caroline Link; ***W:*** Caroline Link; ***C:*** Gernot Roll; ***M:*** Niki Reiser.

Beyond Suspicion ½ *Auggie Rose* **2000** John C. Nolan Jr. (Goldblum) is an insurance bigshot, who stops by the neighborhood liquor store and gets caught up in an armed robbery. The store clerk, Auggie Rose (Coates), gets killed and Nolan feels responsible. He learns Auggie is fresh out of prison and is expecting to meet his prison pen pal, Lucy (Heche). John meets Lucy instead and doesn't correct her assumption that he's Auggie. In fact, John decides to just give up his old life and take up with Lucy. Film's got an intriguing premise that never develops. **108m/C VHS, DVD.** Jeff Goldblum, Anne Heche, Timothy Olyphant, Nancy Travis, Richard T. Jones, Kim Coates, Joe Santos, Jack Kehler, Nicholas Chinlund; ***D:*** Matthew Tabak; ***W:*** Matthew Tabak; ***C:*** Adam Kimmel; ***M:*** Don Harper, Mark Mancina. **VIDEO**

Beyond the Bermuda Triangle ½ **1975** Unfortunate and flat TV flick. Businessman MacMurray, now retired, doesn't have enough to do. He begins an investigation of the mysterious geometric island area when his friends and fiancee disappear. Silly. **78m/C VHS.** Fred MacMurray, Sam Groom, Donna Mills, Suzanne Reed, Dana Plato, Woody Woodbury; ***D:*** William A. Graham. **TV**

Beyond the Call ½ **1996 (R)** Connecticut housewife Pam O'Brien (Spacek) learns from the paper that her high-school sweetheart Russell Cates (Strathairn) is on death row in South Carolina for killing a cop and his execution has been scheduled within weeks. Pam writes Russell and then hears from his sister Fran (Wright), who urges Pam to visit her brother and get him to apply for a clemency hearing. Husband Keith (Howard) becomes angry and alarmed as Pam gets more involved with Russell and his case, which hinges on Russell's Vietnam experiences and post-traumatic shock syndrome. **101m/C VHS, DVD.** David Strathairn, Sissy Spacek, Arliss Howard, Janet Wright; ***D:*** Tony Bill; ***W:*** Doug Magee; ***C:*** Jean Lepine; ***M:*** George S. Clinton. **CABLE**

Beyond the Call of Duty 1/2 **1992 (R)** Renegade U.S. Army Commander Len Jordan (Vincent) is after a particularly deadly Vietcong enemy. Aided by the head of a special forces naval unit he tracks his quarry through the notorious Mekong River Delta. But Jordan's mission may be hindered, both personally and professionally, by a beautiful American journalist after a hot story. **92m/C VHS, DVD.** Jan-Michael Vincent, Eb Lottimer, Jillian McWhirter; ***D:*** Cirio H. Santiago.

Beyond the Clouds 1/2 *Par-dela les Nuages* **1995** A wandering film director (Malkovich) muses on four stories of life and obsession, including unconsummated relationships, romantic triangles, and even violence. Based on sketches from Antonioni's book "That Bowling Alley on the Tiber." English, French, and Italian with subtitles. **109m/C VHS, DVD.** *IT GE FR* John Malkovich, Marcello Mastroianni, Sophie Marceau, Fanny Ardant, Vincent Perez, Jean Reno, Jeanne Moreau, Irene Jacob, Peter Weller, Chiara Caselli, Ines Sastre, Kim Rossi-Stuart; ***D:*** Michelangelo Antonioni, Wim Wenders; ***W:*** Michelangelo Antonioni, Wim Wenders, Tonino Guerra; ***C:*** Robby Muller, Alfio Contini; ***M:*** Van Morrison, Lucio Dalla, Laurent Petitgand.

Beyond the Door WOOF! *Beyond Obsession; Chi Sei; The Devil within Her* **1975 (R)** San Francisco woman finds herself pregnant with a demonic child. One of the first "Exorcist" ripoffs; skip this one and go right to the sequel, "Beyond the Door 2." In Italian; dubbed. **97m/C VHS, DVD.** *IT* Juliet Mills, Richard Johnson, David Colin Jr.; ***D:*** Richard Barrett, Ovidio G. Assonitis; ***W:*** Richard Barrett, Ovidio G. Assonitis.

Beyond the Door 3 WOOF! 1991 (R) Fool American students in Yugoslavia board a hellish locomotive which speeds them toward a satanic ritual. Demonic disaster-movie stuff (with poor miniatures) isn't as effective as the on-location filming; Serbian scenery and crazed peasants impart an eerie pagan aura. What this has to do with earlier "Beyond the Door" movies only the marketing boys can say. Some dialogue in Serbo-Croat with English subtitles. **94m/C VHS.** Mary Kohnert, Sarah Conway Ciminera, William Geiger, Renee Rancourt, Alex Vitale, Victoria Zinny, Savina Gersak, Bo Svenson; ***D:*** Jeff Kwitny.

Beyond the Forest 1/2 **1949** Camp diva Davis, in her last role for Warner Bros., really turns on the histrionics as a big-city gal married to a small-town guy (Cotten) and bored out of her mind. Although the most memorable line, "What a dump," has become larger-than-life, the film itself is rather small and muddled (interestingly, Vidor directed "The Fountainhead" the same year.) A trashy melodrama full of ennui, envy, unwanted pregnancy, and murder, it's definitely high on camp and low on art. **96m/B VHS.** Bette Davis, Joseph Cotten, David Brian, Ruth Roman, Minor Watson, Regis Toomey; ***D:*** King Vidor; ***C:*** Robert Burks; ***M:*** Max Steiner.

Beyond the Law *Bloodsilver; Al Di La Della Legge* **1968** Spaghetti western with Van Cleef as the too smart bad guy. He becomes sheriff, picks up the stack of silver at the depot, and disappears. Humorous and clever, with fine location photography. **91m/C VHS, DVD.** *IT* Lee Van Cleef, Antonio (Tony) Sabato, Lionel Stander, Bud Spencer, Gordon Mitchell, Ann Smyrner; ***D:*** Giorgio Stegani.

Beyond the Law 1/2 *Fixing the Shadow* **1992 (R)** Ex-undercover cop Danny Saxon (Sheen) is recruited by the FBI to infiltrate a biker gang involved in drugs and gun smuggling. But Saxon finds himself drawn too close into the unconventional biker lifestyle and into an uneasy friendship with leader Blood (Madsen). Clumsy and exploitative. **101m/C VHS, DVD.** Michael Berry, Charlie Sheen, Michael Madsen, Linda Fiorentino, Courtney B. Vance, Leon Rippy, Rip Torn; ***D:*** Larry Ferguson; ***W:*** Larry Ferguson; ***C:*** Robert M. Stevens; ***M:*** Cory Lerios, John D'Andrea.

Beyond the Limit 1/2 *The Honorary Consul* **1983 (R)** The story of an intense and darkly ominous love triangle which takes place in the South American coastal city of Corrientes. Based on Graham Greene's novel "The Honorary Consul." **103m/C VHS.** Michael Caine, Richard Gere, Bob Hoskins, Elpidia Carrillo; ***D:*** John MacKenzie; ***W:*** Christopher Hampton; ***C:*** Phil Meheux.

Beyond the Next Mountain **1987 (PG)** A missionary in China attempts to convert all those he meets. Thin plot and marginal acting will likely make viewers fall asleep. **97m/C VHS.** Alberto Isaac, Jon Lormer, Bennett Ohta, Richard Lineback, Edward Ashley, Barry Foster; ***D:*** James F. Collier, Rolf Forsberg.

Beyond the Poseidon Adventure **1979 (PG)** A sequel to the 1972 film in which salvage teams and ruthless looting vandals compete for access to the sunken ocean liner. Sinking ships should be abandoned. **115m/C VHS, DVD.** Michael Caine, Sally Field, Telly Savalas, Peter Boyle, Jack Warden, Slim Pickens, Shirley Knight, Shirley Jones, Karl Malden, Mark Harmon; ***D:*** Irwin Allen; ***C:*** Joseph Biroc.

Beyond the Rockies 1/2 **1932** Keene and a group of cowboys battle cattle rustlers in this action-packed sagebrush saga. Solid script with good direction by Allen. **55m/B VHS.** Tom Keene, Rochelle Hudson, Ernie Adams, Julian Rivero, Hank Bell, Tom London; ***D:*** Fred Allen; ***W:*** John P. McCarthy.

Beyond the Rocks 1/2 **1922** Sam Wood's 1922 silent film stars icons Rudolph Valentino and Gloria Swanson, and was until recently thought to have been lost forever. One surviving print was found in a Dutch archive, which has been given an impressive restoration and a new sound track. Zany rescues abound: Lord Bracondale (Valentino) rescues Theadora Fitzgerald (Swanson) after her rowboat capsizes off the British coast, and again later in the Swiss Alps after a mountaineering accident. Well worth seeing for the craft involved in creating early film. **81m/B DVD.** *US* Gloria Swanson, Rudolph Valentino, Edythe Chapman, Alec B. Francis, Gertrude Astor, Mabel van Buren, June Elvidge, Robert Bolder, Helen Dunbar, Raymond Blathwayt, F.R. Butler; ***D:*** Sam Wood; ***W:*** Jack Cunningham; ***C:*** Alfred Gilks.

Beyond the Sea **2004 (PG-13)** Energetic if superficial biography of Bobby Darin is the personal labor of love for director/star/producer Spacey—even if he's technically too old for the role (Darin died at 37 in 1973). His conceit is showcasing the older Darin in his own fantasy autobiography, beginning with his childhood self (Ullrich) and advancing confidently as Darin finds success crooning at the Copa, becomes a teen idol with the ditty "Splish Splash," and falls in love with teenaged golden girl actress Sandra Dee (Bosworth). This being showbiz, things eventually take a downward spiral for the insecure Darin as his smooth style becomes irrelevant in the hippie sixties before he attempts the inevitable comeback. It's Spacey's show (and he supplies his own more-than-adequate vocals) but supporting actors Hoskins, Blethyn, Aaron, and Goodman all run with their screen time. Title is taken from a 1960 Darin hit. **121m/C VHS, DVD.** *US* Kevin Spacey, Kate (Catherine) Bosworth, John Goodman, Bob Hoskins, Brenda Blethyn, Greta Scacchi, Caroline Aaron, Peter Cincotti, William Ullrich, Tayfun Bademsoy; ***D:*** Kevin Spacey; ***W:*** Kevin Spacey, Lewis Colick; ***C:*** Eduardo Serra; ***M:*** Christopher Slaski.

Beyond the Silhouette *Ultimate Desires* **1990** It starts out as another sleazy video sex thriller, as the lawyer heroine discovers her sensuality and poses a lot in her underclothes. Then in the third act it become a hyper-paranoid political-conspiracy assassination-o-rama. Pretty weird junk. **90m/C VHS.** *CA* Tracy Scoggins, Marc Singer, Brion James; ***D:*** Lloyd A. Simandl.

Beyond the Stars **1989** A sci-fi adventure directed by the author of "Cocoon," wherein a whiz-kid investigates the NASA cover-up of a deadly accident that occurred on the moon during the Apollo 11 landing. Unfortunately, the interesting cast can't make up for the script. **94m/C VHS, DVD.** Martin Sheen, Christian Slater, Olivia D'Abo, F. Murray Abraham, Robert Foxworth, Sharon Stone; ***D:*** David Saperstein.

Beyond the Time Barrier 1/2 **1960** Air Force test pilot gets more than he bargained for when his high speed plane carries him into the future. There he sees the ravages of an upcoming plague, to which he must return. **75m/B VHS.** Robert Clarke, Darlene Tompkins, Arianne Arden, Vladimir Sokoloff; ***D:*** Edgar G. Ulmer.

Beyond the Trail **1926** One of Bill Patton's most entertaining and funny films. In this comedic Western adventure he must face Black Mike and his gang and rescue Mary from their clutches. **50m/C VHS.** Bill(y) (William Patten) Patton, Sheldon Lewis, Stuart Holmes, Eric Wayne, Janet Dawn, Clara Horton, James F. Fulton; ***D:*** Al(bert) Herman.

Beyond the Valley of the Dolls 1/2 *Hollywood Vixens* **1970 (NC-17)** Sleazy, spirited non-sequel to "Valley of the Dolls." Meyer ("Faster, Pussycat! Kill! Kill!") directed this Hollywood parody ("BVD," as it came to be known) about an all-girl rock combo and their search for stardom. Labeled the first "exploitation horror camp musical"—how can you pass that up? Screenplay by film critic Ebert, from an original story by Ebert and Meyer. Mondo trasho. **109m/C VHS, DVD.** Dolly Reed, Cynthia Myers, Marcia McBroom, John Lazar, Michael Blodgett, David Gurian, Erica Gavin, Edy Williams, Phyllis E. Davis, Harrison Page, Duncan McLeod, James Iglehart, Charles Napier, Haji, Pam Grier; ***D:*** Russ Meyer; ***W:*** Roger Ebert; ***C:*** Fred W. Koenekamp; ***M:*** The Strawberry Alarm Clock, Stu Phillips.

Beyond the Wall of Sleep *H.P. Lovecraft's Beyond the Wall of Sleep* **2006 (R)** Ponderous, repetitive (and loose) adaptation of a Lovecraft story. In 1908, in New York's Catskill Mountains, deformed Joe Slaader (Sanderson) is confined to the Ulster County Asylum after murdering his family. But with Joe's arrival come sinister forces that seemingly infect the inmates and they begin to take over the madhouse. **84m/C DVD.** *US* William Sanderson, Tom Savini, Rick Dial, Fountain Yount; ***D:*** Barrett J. Leigh, Tom Maurer; ***W:*** Barrett J. Leigh, Tom Maurer; ***C:*** Bill Burton; ***M:*** Kaveh Cohen. **VIDEO**

Beyond the Walls 1/2 *Meachorei Hasoragim* **1984 (R)** The opposing factions of a hellish Israeli prison unite to beat the system. Brutal with good characterizations. Available in both subtitled and dubbed versions. **104m/C VHS.** *IS* Arnon Zadok, Muhamad Bakri; ***D:*** Uri Barbash; ***W:*** Benny Barbash. Venice Film Fest. '85: Film.

Beyond Therapy 1/2 **1986 (R)** A satire on modern psychotherapy, from the play by Christopher Durang, about a confused, crazily neurotic couple and their respective, and not any saner, analysts. Unfortunately, comes off as disjointed and confused. **93m/C VHS, DVD.** Jeff Goldblum, Tom Conti, Julie Hagerty, Glenda Jackson, Christopher Guest; ***D:*** Robert Altman; ***W:*** Robert Altman.

Beyond Tomorrow **1940** Young romance is guided from the spirit world during the Christmas season, as two "ghosts" come back to help young lovers. **84m/B VHS, DVD.** Richard Carlson, Sir C. Aubrey Smith, Jean Parker, Charles Winninger, Harry Carey Sr., Maria Ouspenskaya, Rod La Rocque; ***D:*** Edward Sutherland; ***W:*** Adele Comandini; ***C:*** Lester White.

Bhaji on the Beach 1/2 **1994 (R)** Amusing comedy-drama about a group of Indian women who organize a bus outing from Birmingham to the seaside resort town of Blackpool. They range from sari-clad elders to feminist Gen Xers and a couple of teenagers looking for romance. There's bonding and gossiping and secrets galore before the story is tidily wrapped up. **100m/C VHS.** *GB* Kim Vithana, Jimmi Harkishin, Sarita Khajuria, Mo Sesay, Lalita Ahmed, Shaheen Khan, Zohra Sehgal; ***D:*** Gurinder Chadha; ***W:*** Meera Syal, Gurinder Chadha; ***C:*** John Kenway; ***M:*** John Altman, Craig Pruess.

Bhowani Junction **1956** A half-Indian, half-English woman is torn between her country and the British officer she loves in post-colonial India. Great cinematography. Based on a book by John Masters. **110m/C VHS.** Ava Gardner, Stewart Granger, Bill Travers, Abraham Sofaer, Francis Matthews, Marne Maitland, Peter Illing, Edward Chapman, Freda Jackson, Lionel Jeffries; ***D:*** George Cukor; ***W:*** Ivan Moffat; ***C:*** Frederick A. (Freddie) Young; ***M:*** Miklos Rozsa.

The Bible **1966** Bloated, even by religious epic standards, Huston's drama covers the first 22 chapters of Genesis. So you get the Creation, Adam and Eve, Noah and the ark, the flood, the Tower of Babel, and Abraham, among other would-be spectacles. **174m/C VHS, DVD.** Michael Parks, Ulla Bergryd, Richard Harris, Stephen Boyd, George C. Scott, Ava Gardner, Peter O'Toole, Franco Nero, John Huston; ***D:*** John Huston; ***W:*** Christopher Fry, Vittorio Bonicelli; ***C:*** Giuseppe Rotunno; ***M:*** Toshiro Mayuzumi; ***Nar:*** John Huston.

The Bible and Gun Club **1996** Foul-mouthed look at the wasted lives of five middle age traveling salesmen who sell, you guessed it, bibles and guns. There's a turf war between the Anaheim, CA and the Las Vegas branches of the club, there's a sales convention, the salesmen try to sell their goods to the real-life denizens of a poor trailer park, there's a porn shoot. There's a number of shoot-outs and to say the least, the salesmen are not politically correct—they're racist, sexist losers. It's depressing and disturbing and highlighted by some spot-on acting. Harris' debut feature. **87m/B VHS.** Andy Kallok, Don Yanan, Julian Ott, Al Schuerman, Robert Blumenthal; ***D:*** Daniel J. Harris; ***W:*** Daniel J. Harris; ***C:*** Alex Vendler; ***M:*** Shawn Patterson.

Bicentennial Man 1/2 **1999 (PG)** Robin Williams is Andrew, a domestic robot of the near-future. When he's purchased by the Martin family, they notice that he's different than most robots. He exhibits compassion, as well as other human qualities. Led by Sir, the father (Niell) they help to further Andrew's growth. As time goes on, Andrew continues to develop past his programming, and eventually seeks his freedom and the pursuit of a more human form. The first hour deals mostly with a very leisurely character development, with some amusing moments. The problems occur when the film turns to the serious questions of immortality, defining humanity, and the rights of artificial entities. Director Columbus opts for sentiment and empty platitudes instead of exploring the questions the film raises. **131m/C VHS, DVD.** Robin Williams, Embeth Davidtz, Sam Neill, Wendy Crewson, Hallie Kate Eisenberg, Oliver Platt, Stephen (Steve) Root, Lynne Thigpen, Bradley Whitford, Kiersten Warren, John Michael Higgins, George D. Wallace; ***D:*** Chris Columbus; ***W:*** Nicholas Kazan; ***C:*** Phil Meheux; ***M:*** James Horner.

Bickford Shmeckler's Cool Ideas **2006 (R)** Bickford (Fugit) is a loner college student who spends his time filing a notebook with his revelatory philosophical theories and ideas. At a party, Sarah (Wilde) steals the book, sending Bick on a wild journey to get it back, finding out in the process that it has taken on a popularity of its own among the campus "intelligensia." Mixes more big ideas than you'd expect into your basic raunchy college romp. **80m/C DVD.** Patrick Fugit, Olivia Wilde, John Cho, Matthew Lillard, Cheryl Hines; ***D:*** Scott Lew; ***W:*** Scott Lew; ***C:*** Lowell Peterson; ***M:*** John Swihart. **VIDEO**

The Bicycle Thief *Ladri di Biciclette* **1948** A world classic and indisputable masterpiece about an Italian workman who finds a job, only to have the bike he needs for work stolen; he and his son search Rome for it. A simple story that seems to contain the whole of human experience, and the masterpiece of Italian neo-realism. Based on the book by Luigi Bartolini. In Italian with English subtitles. **90m/B VHS, DVD.** *IT* Lamberto Maggiorani, Lianella Carell, Enzo Staiola, Elena Altieri, Vittorio Antonucci, Gino Saltamerenda, Fausto Guerzoni; ***D:*** Vittorio De Sica; ***W:*** Vittorio De Sica, Cesare Zavattini; ***C:***

Carlo Montuori; **M:** Alessandro Cicognini. Oscars '49: Foreign Film; British Acad. '49: Film; Golden Globes '50: Foreign Film; Natl. Bd. of Review '49: Director (De Sica); N.Y. Film Critics '49: Foreign Film.

Big 1/2 **1988 (PG)** 13-year-old Josh makes a wish at a carnival fortune-teller to be "big." When he wakes up the next morning he finds that he suddenly won't fit into his clothes and his mother doesn't recognize him. Until he finds a cure, he must learn to live in the adult world—complete with job (in a toy firm), Manhattan apartment, and romance. Perkins is wonderful as a cynical fellow employee who warms to the new guy's naivete, while Hanks is totally believable as the little boy inside a man's body. Marshall directs with authority and the whole thing clicks from the beginning. **98m/C VHS, DVD.** Tom Hanks, Elizabeth Perkins, John Heard, Robert Loggia, Jared Rushton, David Moscow, Jon Lovitz, Mercedes Ruehl; **D:** Penny Marshall; **W:** Gary Ross; **C:** Michael Ballhaus; **M:** Howard Shore. Golden Globes '89: Actor—Mus./Comedy (Hanks); L.A. Film Critics '88: Actor (Hanks).

Big and Hairy 1/2 **1998** When Picasso Dewlap and his family move from Chicago to a small town, the kid has trouble making friends (no wonder with that name). Then he joins the school basketball team. However, Picasso sucks. But after he meets a teen bigfoot (nicknamed Ed) who just happens to be a natural at hoops, Picasso and his hairy friend become team heroes. Based on the book by Brian Daly. **94m/C VHS, DVD.** Richard Thomas, Donnelly Rhodes, Robert Karl Burke, Trevor Jones, Chilton Crane; **D:** Philip Spink; **C:** Peter Benison; **M:** Daryl Bennett, Jim Guttridge. **CABLE**

Big Bad John 1/2 **1990 (PG-13)** Some good ol' boys ride around in trucks as they get into a variety of shootouts. The soundtrack includes music by Willie Nelson, The Charlie Daniels Band, and others. **91m/C VHS, DVD.** Jimmy Dean, Ned Beatty, Jack Elam, Bo Hopkins, Romy Windsor, Doug English, John Dennis Johnston, Anne Lockhart, Jeffery Osterhage, Jerry Potter, Red Steagall; **D:** Burt Kennedy; **W:** Joseph Berry; **C:** Ken Lamkin; **M:** Ken Sutherland.

Big Bad Love **2002 (R)** Howard's ambitious directorial debut is an adaptation of the short stories of Larry Brown. Vietnam vet and would-be writer Leon Barlow's (Howard), obsession with writing about his constant melancholy and getting his stories published alienates him from everything around him, especially his family, which includes his terminally ill daughter. He seems to get away with his behavior through his wry wit and some past misfortunes. Howard gives in to his most poetic and literary impulses, which results in some breathtaking scenes alongside some annoyingly self-indulgent ones. Not surprisingly, film is uneven, with some quality performances lifting the proceedings. **111m/C VHS, DVD.** Arliss Howard, Debra Winger, Paul LeMat, Angie Dickinson, Rosanna Arquette, Michael Parks; **D:** Arliss Howard; **W:** Arliss Howard, Jim Howard; **C:** Paul Ryan; **M:** Tom Waits; **V:** Sigourney Weaver.

Big Bad Mama 1/2 **1974 (R)** Tough and sexy machine-gun toting mother moves her two nubile daughters out of Texas during the Depression, and they all turn to robbing banks as a means of support while creating sharp testosterone increases among the local men. "Wild Palm" Dickinson has notable nude scene with Captain Kirk. "Big Bad Mama 2" arrived some 13 years later. **83m/C VHS, DVD.** Angie Dickinson, William Shatner, Tom Skerritt, Susan Sennett, Robbie Lee, Sally Kirkland, Noble Willingham, Royal Dano, Dick Miller, Joan Prather, Tom Signorelli; **D:** Steve Carver; **W:** William W. Norton Sr., Frances Doel; **C:** Bruce Logan; **M:** David Grisman.

Big Bad Mama 2 1/2 **1987 (R)** Belated Depression-era sequel to the 1974 Roger Corman gangster film, where the pistol-packin' matriarch battles a crooked politician with the help of her two daughters. **85m/C VHS, DVD.** Angie Dickinson, Robert Culp, Danielle Brisebois, Julie McCullough, Bruce Glover, Jeff Yagher, Jacque Lynn Colton, Ebbe Roe Smith, Charles Cyphers; **D:** Jim Wynorski; **W:** Jim Wynorski, R.J. Robertson; **C:** Robert New; **M:** Chuck Cirino.

The Big Bad Swim 1/2 **2006** Needing some stress relief from work and marital problems, Amy (Brewster) decides to join an adult swim class held at a local community center. In a mixed and quirky group, Amy befriends Jordan (Weixler), a croupier and part-time stripper who has the hots for their hunky-but-insecure instructor Noah (Branson). Sharp comedy that focuses on characters rather than situations. **93m/C DVD.** Paget Brewster, Joanna Adler, Jeff Branson, Jess Weixler, Grant Aleksander, Raviv (Ricky) Ullman, Avi Setton, Todd Sussman, Michael Mosley; **D:** Ishai Setton; **W:** Daniel Schechter; **C:** Josh Silfen; **M:** Chad Kelly. **VIDEO**

Big Bear 1/2 **1998** In the 1880s, Cheif Big Bear (Tootoosis) refuses to surrender Cree ancestral lands to settlers for fear of the many broken promises made by the government. So Canadian army troops surround the Cree in order to starve them into submission. Cree warriors decide to stage an attack against the settlers that only brings the troops down on them. **190m/C VHS, DVD.** *CA* Tantoo Cardinal, Gordon Tootoosis, Ken Charlette; **D:** Gil Cardinal. **TV**

The Big Bet **1985 (R)** High school sex comedy about a guy who is challenged by the school bully to get the gorgeous new girl into bed. Energetic romp is for adults. **90m/C VHS, DVD.** Sylvia Kristel, Kimberly Evenson, Ron Thomas; **D:** Bert I. Gordon.

The Big Bird Cage *Women's Penitentiary 2* **1972 (R)** Prison spoof sequel to "The Big Doll House." Horny females incarcerated in a rural jail decide to defy their homosexual guards and plan an escape. They are aided by revolutionaries led by a Brooklynese expatriate and his lover. **93m/C VHS, DVD.** Pam Grier, Sid Haig, Anitra Ford, Candice Roman, Teda Bracci, Carol Speed, Karen McKevic, Vic Diaz; **D:** Jack Hill; **W:** Jack Hill; **C:** Felipe Sacdalan; **M:** William Allen Castleman, William Loose.

The Big Blue 1/2 *Le Grand Bleu* **1988 (PG)** Vapid, semi-true tale about competing free-divers, who descend deep into the big blue without the aid of any kind of breathing apparatus. Arquette is the ditz who makes them come up for air. **122m/C VHS, DVD.** Rosanna Arquette, Jean Reno, Jean-Marc Barr, Paul Shenar, Sergio Castellitto, Marc Duret, Griffin Dunne; **D:** Luc Besson; **W:** Luc Besson; **C:** Carlo Varini; **M:** Bill Conti. Cesar '89: Sound, Score.

Big Bluff *Worthy Deceivers* **1955** Disappointing result from an interesting premise; fatally ill woman finds love, but when she surprisingly recovers, her new husband decides to help her back along the path to death. Uneven and melodramatic. **70m/B VHS.** *SI* John Bromfield, Martha Vickers, Robert Hutton, Rosemary Bowe; **D:** W. Lee Wilder.

Big Boss 1/2 *Mr. Scarface* **1977 (R)** A hoodlum climbs to the top of a crime syndicate. An Italian film previously titled "Mr. Scarface." **90m/C DVD.** *IT* Jack Palance, Edmund Purdom, Al Cliver, Harry Baer, Gisela Hahn; **D:** Fernando Di Leo.

The Big Bounce **1969 (R)** First adaptation of Elmore Leonard's first crime novel after years of westerns is also Ryan O'Neal's first shot at leading man status. O'Neal shows his inexperience as well as glimpes of the boxoffice star he would become as Jack Ryan (not the CIA guy), a drifter who gets mixed up with dangerous woman Nancy (Taylor-Young, also very early in her career) and her plot to swindle her married lover, who happens to be his boss. Doesn't have the spark of Leonard's later crime capers, and the flat direction, disappointing finale, and overwhelming music don't help. But the obvious chemistry between O'Neal and Taylor-Young heats up the screen. **102m/C DVD.** Ryan O'Neal, Leigh Taylor-Young, Van Heflin, Lee Grant, James Daly, Robert Webber, Cynthia Eilbacher, Noam Pitlik; **D:** Alex March; **W:** Robert Dozier; **C:** Howard Schwartz; **M:** Michael Curb.

The Big Bounce **2004 (PG-13)** Second adaptation of Elmore Leonard's first crime novel. Owen Wilson plays Jack Ryan, a small time hood who gets mixed up with Ray Ritchie, a crooked developer. Meanwhile, Ritchie's mistress Nancy (Foster) wants Ryan to steal $200,000 from Ritchie. Of course, double-crosses and deceptions ensue. Tends to meander about and lose focus, but it's somewhat enjoyable if you don't think too hard. Disappointing, considering the solid cast and the source material. **89m/C DVD.** *US* Owen Wilson, Morgan Freeman, Gary Sinise, Vinnie Jones, Sara Foster, Willie Nelson, Bebe Neuwirth, Charlie Sheen, Harry Dean Stanton, Andrew Wilson, Steve Jones, Anahit Minasyan; **D:** George Armitage; **W:** Sebastian Gutierrez; **C:** Jeffrey L. Kimball; **M:** George S. Clinton.

Big Boy 1/2 **1930** Based on Jolson's stage hit with Al in blackface in the minstrel tradition. Wisecracking Kentucky stablehand Gus turns jockey to ride the Bedford's horse Big Boy to victory in the Kentucky Derby despite gamblers trying to get him fired. There's a coda where Al comes out (as himself) telling the audience a Jolson film needs to end with a song so he does 'Tomorrow's Another Day.' **68m/B DVD.** Al Jolson, Claudia Dell, Lloyd Hughes, Louise Closser Hale, Eddie (Edward) Phillips, Colin Campbell, Lew Harvey, Franklin Batie; **D:** Alan Crosland; **W:** William K. Wells, Perry Vekroff; **C:** Hal Mohr.

The Big Brass Ring 1/2 **1999 (R)** Murky political drama based on an unproduced screenplay by Orson Welles. Ambitious William Blake Pellarin (Hurt) is a candidate for governor of Missouri but his ultimate goal is the presidency. However, an ugly scandal threatens his campaign, thanks to the appearance of Dr. Kimball Mennaker (Hawthorne), who's a little too close to the Pellarin family and knows about some skeletons even William isn't aware of. **104m/C VHS, DVD.** William Hurt, Nigel Hawthorne, Miranda Richardson, Irene Jacob, Jefferson Mays, Ewan Stewart, Ron Livingston, Gregg Henry; **D:** George Hickenlooper; **W:** George Hickenlooper, F.X. Feeney; **C:** Kramer Morgenthau; **M:** Thomas Morse.

The Big Brawl 1/2 **1980 (R)** Chicago gangster recruits a martial arts expert to fight in a free-for-all match in Texas. **95m/C VHS, DVD.** Jackie Chan, Jose Ferrer, Mako, Rosalind Chao, Lenny Montana; **D:** Robert Clouse; **W:** Robert Clouse; **M:** Lalo Schifrin.

The Big Broadcast of 1938 1/2 **1938** Fields is the owner of an ocean liner which he enters in a race. Supposedly, the ship can convert the electricity from radio broadcasts into power for the propellers. No, it doesn't make sense, as it's just an excuse for various radio stars to show off their routines in the ship's entertainment room. Hope, in his first feature, gets to sing his Oscar-winning signature tune "Thanks for the Memories." **94m/B VHS, DVD.** W.C. Fields, Martha Raye, Dorothy Lamour, Shirley Ross, Russell Hicks, Bob Hope, Ben Blue, Leif Erickson; **D:** Mitchell Leisen; **W:** Walter DeLeon, Francis Martin; **C:** Harry Fischbeck; **M:** Boris Morros, Ralph Rainger, Leo Robin. Oscars '38: Song ("Thanks for the Memories").

Big Brother Trouble 1/2 **2000 (G)** Mitch (Suchenek) has always lived in the shadow of his big brother Sean (Hart), who's the star of the soccer team. But it's Mitch to the rescue when Sean is kidnapped to insure that his team loses the City Championship game. **88m/C VHS, DVD.** Michael Suchenek, Shad Hart, Lindsay Brooke, Mario Lopez, Bo Hopkins, Dick Van Patten; **D:** Ralph Portillo; **W:** Jeff Nimoy, Seth Walther; **C:** John Huneck; **M:** Steven Stern.

Big Brown Eyes **1936** Wisecracking hotel manicurist Eve (Bennett) is in love with detective Danny Barr (Grant). When Eve loses her job, she suddenly gets a new one working as a reporter and goes off to scope out a murder, which gets her in hot water. There's a lot of screwball complications, and the convoluted plot (which also involves a jewel heist) never does make much sense. **77m/B DVD.** Cary Grant, Joan Bennett, Walter Pidgeon, Lloyd Nolan, Alan Baxter, Marjorie Gateson, Isabel Jewell, Douglas Fowley, Henry (Kleinbach) Brandon; **D:** Raoul Walsh; **W:** Raoul Walsh, Bert Hanlon; **C:** George T. Clemens.

Big Bully **1995 (PG)** David Leary (Moranis) is an aspiring novelist who moves back to the town where he was picked on as a kid. His son immediately starts bullying a smaller child, whose father happens to be Roscoe "Fang" Bigger (Arnold), David's former tormentor. The timid hen-pecked Roscoe's sadistic streak is awakened with the reappearance of his old prey, leading to a barrage of wet willies and indian burns. The slapstick quickly escalates to danger before all is tied up in a syrupy sweet ending. With Moranis playing the nerdy bespectacled underdog and Arnold playing the loud obnoxious guy (although that might not be acting), it may be time to call the typecasting cops. Don Knotts (looking very un-Barney-like) makes an appearance as the high school principal. **93m/C VHS, DVD.** Tom Arnold, Rick Moranis, Julianne Phillips, Don Knotts, Carol Kane, Jeffrey Tambor, Curtis Armstrong, Faith Prince, Tony Pierce, Blake Bashoff; **D:** Steve Miner; **W:** Mark Steven Johnson; **C:** Daryn Okada; **M:** David Newman. Golden Raspberries '96: Worst Actor (Arnold).

The Big Bus **1976 (PG)** The wild adventures of the world's first nuclear-powered bus as it makes its maiden voyage from New York to Denver. Clumsy disaster-movie parody. **88m/C VHS, DVD.** Joseph Bologna, Stockard Channing, Ned Beatty, Ruth Gordon, Larry Hagman, John Beck, Jose Ferrer, Lynn Redgrave, Sally Kellerman, Stuart Margolin, Richard Mulligan, Howard Hesseman, Richard B. Shull, Rene Auberjonois, Bob (Robert) Dishy, Vic Tayback, Murphy Dunne; **D:** James Frawley; **W:** Lawrence J. Cohen, Fred Freeman; **C:** Harry Stradling Jr.; **M:** David Shire.

Big Business **1988 (PG)** Strained high-concept comedy about two sets of identical twins, each played by Tomlin and Midler, mismatched at birth by a near-sighted country nurse. The city set of twins intends to buy out the factory where the country set of twins work. So the country twins march up to the big city to stop the sale and destruction of their beloved home. Both set of twins stay in the Plaza Hotel and zany consequences ensue. Essentially a one-joke outing with some funny moments, but talented comediennes Midler and Tomlin are somewhat wasted. Great technical effects. **98m/C VHS, DVD.** Bette Midler, Lily Tomlin, Fred Ward, Edward Herrmann, Michele Placido, Barry Primus, Michael Gross, Mary Gross, Daniel Gerroll, Roy Brocksmith; **D:** Jim Abrahams; **C:** Dean Cundey.

Big Business Girl **1931** Less than remarkable comedy starring Young as a corporate climber who must dodge her boss' advances and save her troubled marriage when her jazz singer husband is called away to perform in Paris. Based on a story by Patricia Reilly and Harold N. Swanson. **72m/B VHS.** Loretta Young, Frank Albertson, Ricardo Cortez, Joan Blondell, Dorothy Christy; **D:** William A. Seiter; **W:** Robert Lord.

The Big Bust Out **WOOF!** **1973 (R)** Several female convicts escape from prison only to be sold into slavery and face additional torture. Nothing redeeming about this exploitative film. **75m/C VHS.** Vonetta McGee, Monica Taylor, Linda Fox, Karen Carter, Gordon Mitchell; **D:** Karen Carter.

Big Calibre **1935** A rancher is inches away from being lynched for his dad's murder before he is found to be innocent. **59m/B VHS.** Bob Steele, Bill Quinn, Earl Dwire, Peggy Campbell, John Elliott, Georgia O'Dell; **D:** Robert North Bradbury.

The Big Cat **1949** Mountain valley in Utah is ravaged by a cougar, while two ranchers fuss and feud. Big cat, bickering, help make okay adventure. **75m/C VHS, DVD.** Lon (Bud) McCallister, Peggy Ann Garner, Preston Foster, Forrest Tucker; **D:** Phil Karlson; **C:** William Howard Greene.

Big Chase **1954** A rookie cop chases down a mob of payroll thieves in this early action film. **60m/B VHS.** Glenn Langan, Adele Jergens, Douglas Kennedy, Jim Davis, Jack Daly, Phil Arnold, Wheaton Chambers, Lon Chaney Jr.; **D:** Arthur Hilton; **W:** Fred Freiberger.

The Big Chill 1/2 **1983 (R)** Seven former '60s radicals, now coming upon middle age and middle-class affluence, reunite following an eighth friend's suicide and use the occasion to re-examine their past relationships and commitments. A beautifully acted, immensely enjoyable ballad to both the counter-culture and its Yuppie descendants. Great period music. Kevin Costner is the dead man whose scenes never made it to the big screen. **108m/C VHS, DVD.** Tom Berenger, Glenn Close, Jeff Goldblum, William Hurt, Kevin Kline, Mary Kay Place, Meg Tilly, JoBeth Williams; *D:* Lawrence Kasdan; *W:* Lawrence Kasdan, Barbara Benedek; *C:* John Bailey. Writers Guild '83: Orig. Screenplay.

The Big Circus ½ **1959** Hank Twirling's (Mature) circus is failing and to get a bank loan he must put up with the presence of bank officer Sherman (Buttons) and Helen (Fleming), the publicist that Sherman hires to drum up business. But Hank has bigger problems since a saboteur is at work—letting the lions loose, starting a fire, and even causing a deadly train wreck. Fairly typical circus story featured many of the famous acts of the day. **108m/C DVD.** Victor Mature, Red Buttons, Rhonda Fleming, Gilbert Roland, Kathryn Grant, Vincent Price, Peter Lorre, David Nelson, Joseph M. Newman; *D:* Joseph M. Newman; *W:* Irwin Allen, Charles Bennett, Irving Wallace.

The Big City *Mahanagar* **1963** When debts threaten to overwhelm the Mazumdar family, Arati does the unthinkable and gets a job as a saleswoman. She soon begins to realize she not only likes to work but enjoys the freedom and respect her job brings. Bengali with subtitles. **131m/B VHS.** *IN* Anil Chatterjee, Madhabi Mukherjee, Vicky Redwood, Haren Chatterjee; *D:* Satyajit Ray; *W:* Satyajit Ray; *C:* Subrata Mitra; *M:* Satyajit Ray.

Big City Blues **1999 (R)** One long night in the lives of hit men Connor (Reynolds) and Hudson (Forsythe) as they get mixed up with the plans of a hooker (Cates). **94m/C VHS, DVD.** Burt Reynolds, William Forsythe, Georgina Cates, Giancarlo Esposito, Roger Floyd, Balthazar Getty, Arye Gross, Donovan Leitch, Roxana Zal, Amy Lyndon, Jad Mager; *D:* Clive Fleury; *W:* Clive Fleury; *C:* David Bridges; *M:* Tomas San Miguel.

The Big Clock **1948** George Stroud (Milland) is the editor of the successful Crimeways magazine, owned by tyrannical publisher Earl Janoth (Laughton). Forced to miss a vacation with his wife Georgette (O'Sullivan), George winds up spending time with lovely Pauline (Johnson), whom he inadvertently discovers is the boss' mistress. Pauline's murdered and George is quick to realize all the clues are deliberately pointed in his direction. Classic crime melodrama adapted from Kenneth Fearing's novel. Remade as "No Way Out" (1987). **95m/B VHS, DVD.** Ray Milland, Charles Laughton, Maureen O'Sullivan, George Macready, Rita Johnson, Dan Tobin, Elsa Lanchester, Harry (Henry) Morgan; *D:* John Farrow; *W:* Jonathan Latimer; *C:* John Seitz; *M:* Victor Young.

Big Combo **1955** A gangster's ex-girlfriend helps a cop to smash a crime syndicate. Focuses on the relationship between Wilde's cop and the gangster Conte in an effective film noir, with some scenes of torture that were ahead of their time. **87m/B VHS, DVD.** Cornel Wilde, Richard Conte, Jean Wallace, Brian Donlevy, Earl Holliman, Lee Van Cleef, Helen Walker; *D:* Joseph H. Lewis; *W:* Philip Yordan; *C:* John Alton; *M:* David Raksin.

The Big Country ½ **1958 (R)** Ex-sea captain Peck heads west to marry fiance Baker and live on her father's (Bickford) ranch. Peck immediately clashes with ranch foreman Heston and finds out there's a vicious feud with neighbor Ives. Then Peck decides he and Baker aren't meant to be and he falls for schoolmarm Simmons instead. It's too long but if you like sprawling western sagas, this one has its moments. **168m/C VHS, DVD.** Gregory Peck, Charlton Heston, Burl Ives, Jean Simmons, Carroll Baker, Chuck Connors, Charles Bickford; *D:* William Wyler; *W:* Jessamyn West, Robert Wyler, James R. Webb, Sy Bartlett, Robert Wilder; *C:* Franz Planer; *M:* Jerome Moross. Oscars '58: Support. Actor (Ives); Golden Globes '59: Support. Actor (Ives).

The Big Crimewave **1986** A cast of unknowns in a comedy about a loner who takes a bus to Kansas City (Kansas City?) to become a screenwriter, with comic adventures along the way. A feast of jabs at genre films. **80m/C VHS.** *CA* John Paizs, Eva Covacs, Darrel Baran; *D:* John Paizs.

Big Daddy **1999 (PG-13)** Critic-proof film for Sandler's fans—the rest won't find anything to tempt them. He's 32-year-old slacker law-school grad Sonny Koufax, who's got a big Peter Pan complex, since he's incapable of assuming any adult responsibility. However, he does want to impress women, so he decides to go for the "awww" factor by becoming the guardian of his travelling-in-China roommate Kevin's (Stewart) heretofore unknown son, five-year-old Julian (Sprouse). He teaches the kid a number of disgusting traits and winds up bonding with the tyke (they have the same emotional IQ—how hard can it be?). **95m/C VHS, DVD, UMD.** Adam Sandler, Cole Sprouse, Dylan Sprouse, Joey Lauren Adams, Jon Stewart, Leslie Mann, Josh Mostel, Rob Schneider, Kristy Swanson, Joseph Bologna, Steve Buscemi; *D:* Dennis Dugan; *W:* Steve Franks, Tim Herlihy, Adam Sandler; *C:* Theo van de Sande; *M:* Teddy Castellucci. MTV Movie Awards '00: Comedic Perf. (Sandler); Golden Raspberries '99: Worst Actor (Sandler).

The Big Day *We Met on the Vineyard* **1999 (R)** Sara (Margulies) is supposed to be getting married. She shows up at the church but groom John (Sergei) is a no-show after his knucklehead brother Zack (Rohner) confesses to an indiscretion that leaves John with big doubts about the marriage thing. So the family starts to panic and the wedding party tries to find the groom and it's chaos everywhere you go. **88m/C VHS, DVD.** Julianna Margulies, Ivan Sergei, Clayton Rohner, Dixie Carter, Kevin Tighe, Adrian Pasdar, Kathleen York, Andrew Buckley, Nancy Banks; *D:* Ian McCrudden; *W:* Andrew Buckley, Nancy Banks; *C:* Tony Cucchiari.

Big Deadly Game ½ *The Deadly Game; Third Party Risk* **1954** A vacationing American gets caught up in a complicated espionage plot by helping a mysterious wartime buddy. **63m/B VHS.** Lloyd Bridges, Simone Silva, Finlay Currie; *D:* Daniel Birt; *W:* Daniel Birt, Robert Dunbar; *C:* Walter J. (Jimmy W.) Harvey; *M:* Michael Krein.

Big Deal on Madonna Street ½ *The Usual Unidentified Thieves; I Soliti Ignoti; Persons Unknown* **1958** Peppe (Gassman) is a bungling thief who leads a band of equally inept crooks who plan to make themselves very rich when they attempt to rob a jewelry store on Madonna Street. Their elaborate plans cause numerous (and hilarious) disasters. Italian with subtitles. Remade in 1984 as "Crackers." **90m/B VHS, DVD.** *IT* Marcello Mastroianni, Vittorio Gassman, Claudia Cardinale, Renato Salvatori, Memmo Carotenuto, Toto, Rosanna Rory; *D:* Mario Monicelli; *W:* Mario Monicelli, Furio Scarpelli, Suso Cecchi D'Amico; *C:* Gianni Di Venanzo; *M:* Pierro Umiliani.

The Big Dis **1989** An interracial comedy about a young black soldier on a weekend pass who's looking for a willing sexual partner. His confidence is shattered when 12 possibilities turn him down. Feature debut of Eriksen and O'Brien. **88m/B VHS, DVD.** Gordon Eriksen, Heather Johnston, James Haig, Kevin Haig, Monica Sparrow; *D:* Gordon Eriksen, John O'Brien; *W:* Gordon Eriksen, John O'Brien; *C:* John O'Brien.

The Big Doll House *Women's Penitentiary 1; Women in Cages; Bamboo Dolls House* **1971 (R)** Roger Corman-produced prison drama about a group of tormented female convicts who decide to break out. Features vintage Grier, and a caliber of women's-prison sleaziness that isn't equalled in today's films. **93m/C VHS, DVD.** Judy (Judith) Brown, Roberta Collins, Pam Grier, Brooke Mills, Pat(ricia) Woodell, Sid Haig, Christiane Schmidtmer, Kathryn Loder, Jerry Frank, Charles Davis; *D:* Jack Hill; *W:* Don Spencer; *C:* Fred Conde; *M:* Les Baxter, Hall Daniels.

The Big Easy ½ **1987 (R)** A terrific thriller. Slick New Orleans detective Remy McSwain (Quaid, oozing charm and a cornball accent) uncovers a heroin-based mob war while romancing uptight assistant DA Anne Osborne (Barkin, all banked fire) who's investigating corruption on the police force. An easy, Cajun-flavored mystery, a fast-moving action-comedy, a very sexy romance, and a serious exploration of the dynamics of corruption. **101m/C VHS, DVD.** Dennis Quaid, Ellen Barkin, Ned Beatty, John Goodman, Ebbe Roe Smith, Charles Ludlam, Lisa Jane Persky, Tom O'Brien, Grace Zabriskie, Marc Lawrence; *D:* Jim McBride; *W:* Daniel Petrie Jr.; *C:* Alfonso Beato; *M:* Brad Fiedel. Ind. Spirit '88: Actor (Quaid).

Big Eden ½ **2000 (PG-13)** Sweet-natured gay romance says you can go home again. Henry Hart (Gross) is an artist, living in New York, who returns to the small Montana town of Big Eden when his grandfather Sam (Coe) has a stroke. Henry has never admitted to anyone in his hometown that he's gay although it's pretty clear to his quirky neighbors, including the guys who hang out at the post office/general store, which is run by shy Native American Pike Dexter (Schweig), who will display some hidden talents on Henry's behalf. Henry is thrilled to discover his first crush, Dean (DeKay), is also back in town but he's looking for love in the wrong person. A happy ending is a comforting thing. **118m/C VHS, DVD.** Arye Gross, Eric Schweig, George Coe, Tim DeKay, Louise Fletcher, Nan Martin, O'Neal Compton, Corinne Bohrer, Veanne Cox; *D:* Thomas Bezucha; *W:* Thomas Bezucha; *C:* Rob Sweeney; *M:* Joseph Conlan.

The Big Empty **1998** Lloyd Matthews (writer McManus) is a private eye who's burned out on divorce work when he's hired by a suspicious wife (Goldwasser) to find the truth about her too-good-to-be true husband (Bryan). Comparisons to Coppola's "The Conversation" are not out of place. This one's a solid sleeper. **93m/C VHS, DVD.** James McManus, Pablo Bryant, Ellen Goldwasser, H.M. Wynant; *D:* Jack Perez; *W:* James McManus; *C:* Shawn Maurer; *M:* Jean-Michael Michenaud.

The Big Empty **2004 (R)** Struggling actor John Person (Favreau) accepts an offer to deliver a suitcase to a cowboy in a desert town for $25,000. Along the way he meets a wacky band of characters, including a bartender (Hannah) and her nympho daughter (Cook), and space aliens. Solid cast who seem to be enjoying themselves, quirky and original story, and a great soundtrack add up to an entertaining timewaster. **94m/C VHS, DVD.** Jon Favreau, Bud Cort, Daryl Hannah, Jon(athan) Gries, Kelsey Grammer, Rachael Leigh Cook, Joey Lauren Adams, Adam Beach, Melora Walters, Sean Bean, Danny Trejo, Gary Farmer, Brent Briscoe; *D:* Steve Anderson; *W:* Steve Anderson; *C:* Chris Manley; *M:* Brian Tyler. **VIDEO**

The Big Fall **1996 (R)** L.A. private investigator Blaize Rybeck (Howell) is hired by mystery babe Emma (Ward) to find her brother, Kenny, a pilot. Blaize meets some of Kenny's thrill-seeking friends at the airfield and draws the suspicious interest of FBI agent Wilcox (Applegate). Seems Kenny was mixed up in some shady dealings that get both his sister and her nosy P.I. into trouble. **94m/C VHS, DVD.** C. Thomas Howell, Sophie Ward, Jeff Kober, Justin Lazard, Titus Welliver, William Applegate Jr.; *D:* C. Thomas Howell; *W:* William Applegate Jr.; *C:* Jurgen Baum.

Big Fan ½ **2009 (R)** Uncomfortably odd film about an isolated man who has nothing in his life but his obsession with the New York Giants. Bottom-rung Paul (Oswalt) listens to sports radio all day and offers call-in diatribes to his favorite radio show at night. He and loser pal Sal (Corrigan) can't afford tickets so they watch the Giants on TV from the Meadowlands parking lot. A chance encounter with linebacker Quantrell Bishop (Hamm) leads to a string of bad events. **86m/C DVD.** Patton Oswalt, Kevin Corrigan, Jonathan Hamm, Gino Cafarelli, Matt Servitto, Marcia Jean Kurtz, Michael Rapaport; *D:* Robert Siegel; *W:* Robert Siegel; *C:* Michael Simmonds; *M:* Philip Watts.

Big Fat Liar **2002 (PG)** The boy who cried wolf goes to Hollywood in search of Marty Wolf (Giamatti), the unscrupulous movie producer who stole his short story. As nobody believes his far-out tale of being ripped off by Hollywood, notorious liar Jason Shepherd (Muniz) also makes sure to bring along a witness to his pursuit, in the form of his friend Kaylee (Bynes). Pulling an array of inspired pranks, the teens zestfully set about dismantling the sanity of Wolf, to the delight, and sometimes with the aid of, some of his many enemies. Talented small-screen star Muniz and his co-star Bynes make this a likeable, though not especially inspired, broad comedy with Giamatti mugging up a storm. Their romp through Universal Studios, especially, lets you know who's really behind this mostly entertaining movie for the preteen set. **87m/C VHS, DVD.** *US* Frankie Muniz, Paul Giamatti, Amanda Bynes, Amanda Detmer, Donald Adeosun Faison, Lee Majors, Sandra Oh, Russell Hornsby, Christine Tucci, Sean O'Bryan, Amy Hill, Michael Bryan French; *D:* Shawn Levy; *W:* Dan Schneider; *C:* Jonathan Brown.

Big Fella ½ **1937** Musical drama starring Robeson as Joe, a Marseilles dockworker (a familiar film occupation for the actor), who's asked by the police to help find a young boy (Grant) missing from an ocean liner. When Joe locates the boy, he discovers the child ran away from his wealthy family and doesn't want to return. Joe takes the boy to his cafe singer girlfriend, Miranda (Welch), and the two become his surrogate parents. Loose adapatation of the 1929 novel, "Banjo," by Claude McKay. ♫Lazin'; Roll Up Sailorman; You Didn't Ought to Do Such Things; All God's Chillun Got a Robe; My Curly Headed Baby; River Steals My Folks from Me. **73m/B VHS, DVD.** *GB* Paul Robeson, Elisabeth Welch, Eldon Grant; *D:* J. Elder Wills; *W:* Ingram D'Abbes, Fenn Sherie; *C:* Cyril Bristow; *M:* Eric Ansell.

Big Fish **2003 (PG-13)** This is right up Burton's alley, as it's about a great storyteller prone to out-sized flights of fancy. Ed Bloom (Finney) is a man on his deathbed hoping to reconcile with the son (Crudup) he's alienated with the yarns he's spun about his life. When Will, who's become a journalist as a form of rebellion, returns and asks one last time for the truth, Ed again begins the familiar tall tale. This is where we learn of Ed's version of his courtship of wife Sandra, his battle with a huge catfish, his adventures with a giant in the circus, the Korean War, and an idyllic town where the residents seem content to walk around barefoot and happy. Burton is in his element with the flashback/yarn portion, but handles the delicate drama of the father-son scenes with aplomb as well. Cast is uniformly excellent, with Finney making the most of a largely sedentary role. **125m/C DVD, Blu-ray Disc.** *US* Ewan McGregor, Albert Finney, Billy Crudup, Jessica Lange, Alison Lohman, Helena Bonham Carter, Robert Guillaume, Steve Buscemi, Danny DeVito, Marion Cotillard, David Denman, Missi Pyle, Matthew McGrory, Loudon Wainwright III; *D:* Tim Burton; *W:* John August; *C:* Philippe Rousselot; *M:* Danny Elfman.

The Big Fix **1978 (PG)** Private investigator Moses Wine finds himself in an ironic situation: searching for a fugitive alongside whom he'd protested in the 60s. Based on a Roger Simon novel. **108m/C VHS.** Richard Dreyfuss, Susan Anspach, Bonnie Bedelia, John Lithgow, F. Murray Abraham, Fritz Weaver, Mandy Patinkin; *D:* Jeremy Paul Kagan; *M:* Bill Conti.

Big Foot **WOOF!** **1972** Even genre devotees will be disappointed with this one. Sasquatch, who has procreation on his mind, searches rather half-heartedly for a human mate. A horror flick that forgot to include the horror. **92m/C VHS.** Chris Mitchum, Joi Lansing, John Carradine, John Mitchum; *D:* Bob Slatzer.

The Big Gag **1987 (R)** An international group of comedians travel the world and pull gags on people. Lame. **84m/C VHS.** *IS* Yehuda Barkan, Cyril Green, Caroline Langford; *D:* Yehuda Barkan.

The Big Game ½ *Control Factor* **1972** It's about espionage not big game hunting but it's dull in any case. Prof. Handley (Milland) designs a mind control device for the U.S. military to brainwash soldiers into becoming fighting machines. For safety's sake, the contraption is being moved via a fishing boat but the bad guys know where it's headed and plan to steal it. **90m/C DVD.** Stephen Boyd, Cameron Mitchell, Ray Milland, France Nuyen, John Stacy, Brendon Boone, Michael Kirner; *D:* Robert Day; *W:* Robert Day, Stanley Norman, Ralph Anders; *C:* Mario Fioretti; *M:* Francesco De Masi.

Big Girls Don't Cry... They Get Even ½ **1992 (PG)** A teenage girl decides to run away from home after she's driven crazy by her eccentric new stepfamily. Comic confusion ensues as various family members set out to find her. Hackneyed script and annoying characters hinder this comedy. **98m/C VHS, DVD.** Hillary Wolf, Griffin Dunne, Margaret Whitton, David Strathairn, Ben Savage, Adrienne Shelly, Patricia Kalember; ***D:*** Joan Micklin Silver.

The Big Green 1/2 **1995 (PG)** British teacher Anna Montgomery (D'Abo) blows into a small Texas town determined to give the deprived kiddies a boost of self-esteem. With help from the town sheriff (Guttenberg), Anna organizes a soccer team that's supposed to give the kids a reason to live. Problems abound when the star player disappears just before the face-off with the biggest, nastiest team in the league. Sound familiar? This is the soccer version of "The Bad News Bears," "The Little Giants," and "The Mighty Ducks." The formula is less successful in this case, but some mildly amusing moments and a few fresh performances from the kids offer minor bright spots in this tired scenario. **100m/C VHS, DVD.** Olivia D'Abo, Steve Guttenberg, Jay O. Sanders, John Terry, Chauncey Leopardi, Patrick Renna, Billy L. Sullivan, Yareli Arizmendi, Bug Hall; ***D:*** Holly Goldberg Sloan; ***W:*** Holly Goldberg Sloan; ***C:*** Ralf Bode; ***M:*** Randy Edelman.

A Big Hand for the Little Lady 1/2 *Big Deal at Dodge City* **1966** Fonda and Woodward, playing two West-headed country bumpkins, get involved in a card game in Laredo against high rollers Robards and McCarthy. Fonda risks their savings, finds himself stuck with a losing hand, and has a bit of heart trouble; that's where the little lady comes in. Fine performances and a nifty twist ending don't entirely compensate for the overly padded script (which evolved from a 48-minute TV play drafted by Sydney Carroll). **95m/C VHS.** Henry Fonda, Joanne Woodward, Jason Robards Jr., Charles Bickford, Burgess Meredith, Kevin McCarthy; ***D:*** Fielder Cook; ***C:*** Lee Garmes.

The Big Hangover **1950** Odd story about a man whose allergy to alcohol makes him drunk at the most inopportune moments. Johnson stars as the attorney with the peculiar problem and Taylor plays the boss' daughter who helps him overcome the allergy. Good supporting cast can't help this otherwise boring and predictable film. **82m/B VHS.** Van Johnson, Elizabeth Taylor, Percy Waram, Fay Holden, Leon Ames, Edgar Buchanan, Selena Royle, Gene Lockhart; ***D:*** Norman Krasna; ***W:*** Norman Krasna; ***C:*** George J. Folsey.

The Big Heat 1/2 **1953** When detective Ford's wife (played by Jocelyn Brando, sister of Marlon) is killed in an explosion meant for him, he pursues the gangsters behind it and uncovers a police scandal. His appetite is whetted after this discovery and he pursues the criminals even more vigorously with the help of gangster moll Gloria Grahame. Definitive film noir. **90m/B VHS, DVD.** Glenn Ford, Lee Marvin, Gloria Grahame, Jocelyn Brando, Alexander Scourby, Carolyn Jones; ***D:*** Fritz Lang; ***W:*** Sydney (Sidney) Boehm; ***C:*** Charles B(ryant) Lang Jr.

The Big Hit 1/2 **1998 (R)** Combustible mixture of extravagent stunts, cartoon violence, hip-hop soundtrack, and a colorful cast serve up an intermittently funny look at organized crime. When not executing their skills as ruthless hitmen, Melvin, Cisco, Vince, and Crunch (Wahlberg, Phillips, Sabato, Jr., and Woodbine) are regular working Joes with regular problems. For Melvin, financial and female problems force him to partner with Cisco in the kidnapping of a Chinese heiress. Said heiress turns out to be the goddaughter of their own crime boss. Much hilarity ensues. Phillips brings gusto to his flamboyant homeboy character and Wahlberg is his equal as the sappy gun for hire with a heart of gold. Big plot holes and fickle storyline, but bigger laughs make you not care so much. American directorial debut of Hong Kong import Che-Kirk Wong. **91m/C VHS, DVD, Blu-ray Disc, UMD.** Mark Wahlberg, Lou Diamond Phillips, Bokeem Woodbine, Antonio Sabato Jr., Christina Applegate, Avery Brooks, China Chow, Lainie Kazan, Elliott Gould, Lela Rochon, Sab Shimono; ***D:*** Kirk Wong; ***W:*** Ben Ramsey; ***C:*** Danny Nowak; ***M:*** Graeme Revell.

The Big House **1930** Prison melodrama at its best follows top con Beery as he plans a big breakout—and is betrayed. Life in the pen is depicted as brutal and futile, with sadistic guards and a hapless warden. Spawned numerous imitators. **80m/B VHS.** Wallace Beery, Chester Morris, Robert Montgomery, Lewis Stone, Leila Hyams, George F. Marion Sr., Karl (Daen) Dane, DeWitt Jennings; ***D:*** George Hill; ***W:*** Frances Marion.

The Big Hurt 1/2 **1987 (R)** A reporter investigating a bizarre double murder discovers a secret government agency involved in torture and mind-control. **90m/C VHS.** *AU* David Bradshaw, Lian Lunson, Simon Chilvers, Nick Waters; ***D:*** Barry Peak.

Big Jake **1971 (PG)** An aging Texas cattle man who has outlived his time swings into action when outlaws kidnap his grandson and wound his son. He returns to his estranged family to help them in the search for Little Jake. O'Hara is once again paired up with Wayne and the chemistry is still there. **90m/C VHS, DVD.** Harry Carey Jr., John Wayne, Richard Boone, Maureen O'Hara, Patrick Wayne, Chris Mitchum, Bobby Vinton, John Agar; ***D:*** George Sherman; ***C:*** William Clothier; ***M:*** Elmer Bernstein.

Big Jim McLain **1952** Wayne and Arness are federal agents working on behalf of the House Un-American Activities Committee to eliminate communist terrorism in Hawaii. And there's a suspicious psychiatrist, too: Wayne falls for a babe whose boss is a shrink who doesn't quite seem on the level. Definitely not a highpoint in the Duke's career. **90m/C VHS, DVD.** John Wayne, Nancy Olson, James Arness, Veda Ann Borg; ***D:*** Edward Ludwig; ***C:*** Archie Stout.

The Big Kahuna 1/2 **2000 (R)** Spacey produced and stars as Larry, a loudly cynical industrial lubricants salesman at a convention in Kansas. He's there with Phil (DeVito), his burned-out collegue who's going through a divorce and looking for spirituality; and Bob (Facinelli), a newlywed, devout Christian research engineer who's new to the company. They spend the night in a hospitality suite waiting for a potential client—the Big Kahuna—and discussing how work, religion, ethics, and personal life coexist. Adapted from Rueff's play "Hospitality Suite" and it feels like it. The dialogue and setting is very stagey, but the performances are excellent, especially DeVito's. **90m/C VHS, DVD.** Kevin Spacey, Danny DeVito, Peter Facinelli; ***D:*** John Swanbeck; ***W:*** Roger Rueff; ***C:*** Anastas Michos; ***M:*** Christopher Young.

The Big Knife **1955** Palance plays a Hollywood superstar who refuses to renew his studio contract, which enrages studio boss Steiger. It seems Steiger knows a very damaging secret about the star and is willing to go to any lengths to have Palance re-sign or wind up destroying himself. A ruthless, emotional look at fame and power, with excellent performances by all. Based on the play by Clifford Odets. **113m/B DVD.** Jack Palance, Rod Steiger, Ida Lupino, Shelley Winters, Wendell Corey, Jean Hagen, Ilka Chase, Everett Sloane, Wesley Addy, Paul Langton; ***D:*** Robert Aldrich; ***C:*** Ernest Laszlo.

The Big Lebowski 1/2 **1997 (R)** Jeff Lebowski (Bridges), a stuck-in-the-'70s stoner who insists on being called "the Dude" and loves to go bowling, is mistaken for a wheelchair-bound millionaire of the same name, and suffers a beating at the hands of thugs who are after money owed by the rich Lebowski's slutty wife. Dude is drawn into kidnapping, the attempted scamming of payoff money, and more bowling. While this may seem like plot-a-plenty, it's mainly a showcase for the Coen brothers' unique texturing of style and quirky-but-deep characters. Goodman is loud and funny as a Vietnam vet who takes any opportunity to pull a gun or explode into DI-like obscenities. Turturro steals his scenes as a pervert rival bowler who loves skintight lilac jumpsuits and polishing his ball. The showpiece is an amazing musical-bowling-fantasy sequence that would've made Busby Berkeley proud. **117m/C VHS, DVD, HD DVD.** Jack Kehler, Jeff Bridges, John Goodman, Steve Buscemi, Julianne Moore, Peter Stormare, David Huddleston, Philip Seymour Hoffman, Flea, Leon Russom, Sam Elliott, John Turturro, David Thewlis, Ben Gazzara, Tara Reid; ***D:*** Joel Coen; ***W:*** Joel Coen, Ethan Coen; ***C:*** Roger Deakins; ***M:*** Carter Burwell.

The Big Lift 1/2 **1950** Two G.I.'s assigned to the Berlin airlift ally themselves in counter-intelligence when they discover that their mutual girlfriend is a spy. **119m/B VHS, DVD.** Montgomery Clift, Paul Douglas, Cornell Borchers, Bruni Lobel, O.E. Hasse; ***D:*** George Seaton.

The Big Man: Crossing the Line *Crossing the Line* **1991 (R)** Neeson shines as a down on his luck Scottish miner who loses his job during a union strike. Desperate for cash and unable to resolve his bitterness at being unable to support his family, he's enticed by a Glasgow hood to fight in an illegal bare-knuckled boxing match. What follows is an overlong and extremely brutal fight. Good performances from a talented cast overcome a rather preachy script that doesn't disguise its contempt for the Thatcher government, but also allows a glimpse into the tough times that many Brits suffered during the '80s. Based on the novel by William McIlvanney. **93m/C VHS, DVD.** *GB* Liam Neeson, Joanne Whalley, Ian Bannen, Billy Connolly, Hugh Grant, Maurice Roeves, Rob Affleck; ***D:*** David Leland; ***W:*** Don MacPherson; ***M:*** Ennio Morricone.

Big Man Japan 1/2 *Dai Nipponjin; Great Japanese* **2007 (PG-13)** Weird mockumentary about a Japanese superhero with bad press. Everyman Daisato works for the Defense Department where he is routinely turned humungous, thanks to a burst of electricity, so he can battle a variety of monsters that plague Tokyo. Since they regularly destroy the city, this doesn't make the citizens too happy. Japanese with subtitles. **113m/C DVD.** *JP* Riki Takeuchi, Ryunosuke Kamiki, Itsuji Itao, Hitoshi Matsumoto, Ua; ***D:*** Hitoshi Matsumoto; ***W:*** Hitoshi Matsumoto, Mitsuyoshi Yakasu; ***C:*** Hideo Yamamoto; ***M:*** Towa Tei.

Big Man on Campus **1989 (PG-13)** A modern-day Quasimodo makes his home in an affluent university's belltower. Of course he falls in love with one of the pretty young co-eds and races out of his tower only to be captured by the psychology department. Really, really bad. **102m/C VHS.** Tom Skerritt, Corey Parker, Allan Katz, Cindy Williams, Melora Hardin, Jessica Harper, Gerrit Graham; ***D:*** Jeremy Paul Kagan; ***W:*** Allan Katz; ***C:*** Bojan Bazelli; ***M:*** Joseph Vitarelli.

Big Meat Eater **1985** A musical gore-comedy about extraterrestrials using radioactive butcher's discards for ship fuel. Deliberate camp that is so bad its funny! **81m/C VHS, DVD.** *CA* George Dawson, Big Miller, Andrew Gillies, Stephen Dimopoulos, Georgina Hegedos, Ida Carnevali, Sharon Wahl; ***D:*** Chris Windsor; ***W:*** Chris Windsor, Phil Savath, Laurence Keane; ***C:*** Doug McKay.

Big Mo *Mauri* **1973 (G)** True story of the friendship that developed between Cincinnati Royals basketball stars Maurice Stokes and Jack Twyman after a strange paralysis hit Stokes. **110m/C VHS.** Bernie Casey, Bo Svenson, Stephanie Edwards, Janet MacLachlan; ***D:*** Daniel Mann.

Big Momma's House **2000 (PG-13)** FBI agent Lawrence is sent to Georgia to protect single mom Long and her son from her escaped con ex. Since he's a master of disguise, Lawrence passes himself off as her grandma, who's known as "Big Momma." Lawrence, like his pal Eddie Murphy, has plenty of experience with costumes, disguises, and multiple roles. So it's kind of disappointing that this isn't a better movie. Sporadic laughs are too often mined from toilet humor, and the plot doesn't allow for many quiet moments, which Lawrence needs to balance out the slapstick. **98m/C VHS, DVD.** Martin Lawrence, Nia Long, Paul Giamatti, Terrence Howard, Anthony Anderson, Carl Wright, Ella Mitchell, Jascha Washington, Starletta DuPois, Cedric the Entertainer; ***D:*** Raja Gosnell; ***W:*** Darryl Quarles, Don Rhymer; ***C:*** Michael D. O'Shea; ***M:*** Richard Gibbs.

Big Momma's House 2 **2006 (PG-13)** Hey, if you liked seeing Lawrence in a fat suit and a dress the first time, you'll probably think the sequel is okay. The plot, such as it is, has FBI agent Malcolm Turner's alter ego Hattie Mae Pierce posing as a nanny to investigate Tom Fuller (Moses), a computer expert who has created a worm that threatens national security. Long returns too, this time as Turner's suspicious pregnant missus. Be warned: the sight of Momma running along the beach in cornrows and a bright yellow bathing suit may scar the psyche for life. **98m/C DVD.** *US* Martin Lawrence, Nia Long, Emily Procter, Mark Moses, Kat Dennings, Chloe Grace Moretz, Marisol Nichols, Josh Flitter, Dan Lauria, Zachary Levi, Preston Shores, Trevor Shores, Lisa Arrindell Anderson; ***D:*** John Whitesell; ***W:*** Don Rhymer; ***C:*** Mark Irwin; ***M:*** George S. Clinton.

Big Mouth **1967** A dopey fisherman gets ahold of a treasure map and is pursued by cops and gangsters. Standard Lewis fare, with the requisite infantile histrionics; must be French to appreciate. **107m/C VHS.** Jerry Lewis, Jeannine Riley, Harold J. Stone, Charlie Callas, Buddy Lester, Susan Bay; ***D:*** Jerry Lewis; ***W:*** Jerry Lewis; ***M:*** Harry Betts.

Big News **1929** Based on the play "For Two Cents" by George S. Brooks, this early talkie uses sound to great advantage. Fired for going after a gangster who's a big advertiser (Hardy), reporter Armstrong nevertheless keeps after the crook. When the intrepid reporter pushes too far, murder enters the picture. **75m/B VHS.** Robert Armstrong, Carole Lombard, Tom Kennedy, Warner Richmond, Wade Boteler, Sam Hardy, Lew Ayres; ***D:*** Gregory La Cava.

Big Night 1/2 **1995 (R)** Set in '50s New Jersey, film provides an Old World/New World look at Italian brothers Primo (Shalhoub) and Secondo (Tucci) Pilaggi and their elegant but failing restaurant. Primo is the perfectionist chef who hates compromise while Secondo wants to Americanize the place in an effort to make it a success. (He knows the customer is always right even if they can't appreciate Primo's exquisitely authentic Italian dishes). In order to get attention, Secondo arranges a special night in honor of jazz great Louis Prima, with Primo out to cook the feast of a lifetime—if they can pull it off. Another food film guaranteed to make you hungry. **109m/C VHS, DVD.** Tony Shalhoub, Stanley Tucci, Ian Holm, Minnie Driver, Campbell Scott, Isabella Rossellini, Marc Anthony, Allison Janney, Dina Spybey; ***D:*** Stanley Tucci, Campbell Scott; ***W:*** Stanley Tucci, Joseph Tropiano; ***C:*** Ken Kelsch. Ind. Spirit '97: First Screenplay; Natl. Soc. Film Critics '96: Support. Actor (Shalhoub); Sundance '96: Screenplay.

Big Nothing 1/2 **2006** Now there's a title just leaving itself wide open. Well, it's more like "little nothing" anyway. Struggling writer Charlie (Schwimmer) takes a job at a call center. Co-worker Gus (Pegg) persuades Charlie to join him in blackmailing a preacher who likes kiddie-porn websites. They pick up a third partner in blonde babe Josie (Eve). **86m/C DVD.** *GB* David Schwimmer, Simon Pegg, Alice Eve, Mimi Rogers, Natascha (Natasha) McElhone, Jon Polito, Billy Asher, Mitchell Mullen; ***D:*** Jean-Baptiste Andrea; ***W:*** Jean-Baptiste Andrea; ***C:*** Richard Greatrex; ***M:*** Alan Anton. **VIDEO**

The Big One **1998 (PG-13)** Moore once again takes his populist, CEO-baiting act on the road in search of corporate evildoers, this time on Random House's dime. Documentary lovingly follows Moore on his 1996 book promo tour, as he highlights plant closings, verbally spars with Nike boss Phil Knight, plays pranks on his "handlers," and mugs for his adoring fans. His style is still the same as in "Roger & Me," but since he's joined the celebrity ranks, Moore isn't going to sneak up on anybody. To his credit, he doesn't try, but to his discredit, he ends up haranguing the very working people he claims to be standing up for, mostly exasperated receptionists and secretaries. Corporate greed and apathy are still squarely in Moore's crosshairs, but this time his own ego prevents him from getting a clear shot at his target. **90m/C VHS, DVD.** ***D:*** Michael Moore; ***Nar:*** Michael Moore.

The Big Parade **1925** Wonderful WWI silent, considered to be one of the best war flicks of all time. Gilbert and Adoree are exceptional as lovers torn apart by the conflict. Interesting and thoughtful picture of the trauma and trouble brought to men and their loved ones in wartime. Battle scenes are compelling and intense; Vidor's masterpiece. **141m/B VHS.** John Gilbert, Renee Adoree, Hobart Bosworth, Claire McDowell, Claire Adams, Karl (Daen) Dane, Robert Ober, Tom (Thomas E.) O'Brien, Rosita Marstini; ***D:*** King Vidor; ***W:*** Harry Behn; ***C:*** John Arnold; ***M:***

William Axt, David Mendoza. Natl. Film Reg. '92.

The Big Picture 1/2 **1989 (PG-13)** A hilarious, overlooked comedy by and starring a variety of Second City/National Lampoon alumni, about a young filmmaker who is contracted by a big studio, only to see his vision trampled by formula-minded producers, crazed agents, hungry starlets, and every other variety of Hollywood predator. **95m/C VHS, DVD.** Kevin Bacon, Jennifer Jason Leigh, Martin Short, Michael McKean, Emily Longstreth, J.T. Walsh, Eddie Albert, Richard Belzer, John Cleese, June Lockhart, Stephen Collins, Roddy McDowall, Kim Miyori, Teri Hatcher, Dan Schneider, Jason Gould, Tracy Brooks Swope; ***D:*** Christopher Guest; ***W:*** Michael Varhol, Michael McKean, Christopher Guest; ***M:*** David Nichtern.

The Big Push 1/2 *Timber Tramps* **1975 (PG)** Motley bunch of Alaskan lumberjacks get together to save a poor widow's logging camp from a pair of greedy mill owners. **98m/C VHS.** Joseph Cotten, Claude Akins, Cesar Romero, Tab Hunter, Roosevelt "Rosie" Grier, Leon Ames, Stubby Kaye, Patricia Medina; ***D:*** Tay Garnett.

Big Red 1/2 **1962** Set amid the spectacular beauty of Canada's Quebec Province, an orphan boy protects a dog which later saves him from a mountain lion. **89m/C VHS, DVD.** Walter Pidgeon, Gilles Payant; ***D:*** Norman Tokar; ***W:*** Louis Pelletier; ***C:*** Edward Colman; ***M:*** Oliver Wallace, Richard M. Sherman, Robert B. Sherman.

The Big Red One 1/2 **1980 (PG)** Fuller's harrowing, intense semi-autobiographical account of the U.S. Army's famous First Infantry Division in WWII, the "Big Red One." A rifle squad composed of four very young men, led by the grizzled Marvin, cut a fiery path of conquest from the landing in North Africa to the liberation of the concentration camp at Falkenau, Czechoslovakia. In part a tale of lost innocence, the film scores highest by bringing the raw terror of war down to the individual level. New restored version adds about 47 minutes and sports an "R" rating. **113m/C VHS, DVD.** Lee Marvin, Robert Carradine, Mark Hamill, Stephane Audran, Bobby DiCicco, Perry Lang, Kelly Ward, Siegfried Rauch, Serge Marquand, Charles Macaulay, Alain Doutey, Maurice Marsac, Colin Gilbert, Joseph Clark, Ken Campbell, Doug Werner, Marthe Villalonga; ***D:*** Samuel Fuller; ***W:*** Samuel Fuller; ***C:*** Adam Greenberg; ***M:*** Dana Kaproff.

The Big Scam 1/2 *A Nightingale Sang in Berkeley Square; The Mayfair Bank Caper* **1979** Criminal mastermind Niven recruits ex-con Jordan to pull off a massive bank heist. **102m/C DVD.** Richard Jordan, David Niven, Oliver Tobias, Elke Sommer, Gloria Grahame, Hugh Griffith, Richard Johnson, Joss Ackland, Alfred Molina; ***D:*** Ralph Thomas; ***W:*** Guy Elmes; ***C:*** John Coquillon; ***M:*** Stanley Myers.

Big Score **1983 (R)** When a policeman is falsely accused and dismissed from the Chicago Police Department, he goes after the men who really stole the money from a drug bust. Script was originally intended to be a Dirty Harry flick; too bad it wasn't. **88m/C VHS, DVD.** Fred Williamson, John Saxon, Richard Roundtree, Nancy Wilson, Ed Lauter, Ron Dean, D'Urville Martin, Michael Dante, Joe Spinell; ***D:*** Fred Williamson; ***C:*** Joao Fernandes.

Big Shot: Confessions of a Campus Bookie 1/2 **2002 (R)** Based on the true story of Brooklyn-born Benny Silman (Krumholtz) who undergoes culture shock when he begins attending Arizona State University. He takes frequent trips to Vegas and is soon running his own campus bookmaking operation but wants more. Then Benny meets hoops star Stevin Smith (Kittles) who isn't adverse to making some money on the side. So Benny hooks up with a big-time Vegas gambler (Turturro) to shave points in ASU games. **83m/C VHS, DVD.** David Krumholtz, Nicholas Turturro, Jenny (Jennifer) Morrison, Tory Kittles, Carmine D. Giovinazzo, Alex Rocco, James LeGros; ***D:*** Ernest R. Dickerson; ***W:*** Jason Keller; ***C:*** Steven Bernstein; ***M:*** Reinhold Heil, Johnny Klimek. **CABLE**

Big Shots **1987 (PG-13)** Two kids, one naive and white, the other black and streetwise, search for a stolen watch. **91m/C VHS.** Ricky Busker, Darius McCrary, Robert Joy, Paul Winfield, Robert Prosky, Jerzy Skolimowski; ***D:*** Robert Mandel; ***W:*** Joe Eszterhas; ***M:*** Bruce Broughton.

Big Shot's Funeral *Da Wan* **2001 (PG)** American director Don Tyler (Sutherland) is on location in Beijing when he suffers a serious health crisis and winds up in the hospital. He tells cameraman YoYo (Ge) that should he die, he wants a blow-out funeral, which YoYo promises to arrange. Since he has no money, YoYo auctions off advertising and sponsorships for the funeral but then Don begins to improve. Would-be comedy has very few laughs. English and Manderin with subtitles. **100m/C VHS, DVD.** *HK* Donald Sutherland, Ge You, Rosamund Kwan, Da(nniel) Ying, Paul Mazursky; ***D:*** Feng Xiao Gang; ***W:*** Feng Xiao Gang; ***C:*** Li Zhang; ***M:*** San Bao.

Big Show *Home in Oklahoma* **1937** A western adventure about the making of a western adventure. Autry jangles spurs aplenty in duel role. **54m/B VHS, DVD.** Gene Autry, Smiley Burnette; ***D:*** Mack V. Wright.

The Big Sky **1952** It's 1830, and a rowdy band of fur trappers embark upon a back breaking expedition up the uncharted Missouri River. Based on the A.B. Guthrie Jr. novel, it's an effortlessly enjoyable and levelheaded Hawksian American myth, with a streak of gentle gallows humor. Also available colorized. **122m/C VHS.** Kirk Douglas, Dewey Martin, Arthur Hunnicutt, Elizabeth Threatt, Buddy Baer, Steven Geray, Jim Davis; ***D:*** Howard Hawks.

The Big Sleep **1946** Private eye Philip Marlowe, hired to protect a young woman from her own indiscretions, falls in love with her older sister while uncovering murders galore. A dense, chaotic thriller that succeeded in defining and setting a standard for its genre. The very best Raymond Chandler on film combining a witty script with great performances, especially from Bogart and Bacall. **114m/B VHS, DVD.** Humphrey Bogart, Lauren Bacall, John Ridgely, Martha Vickers, Louis Jean Heydt, Regis Toomey, Peggy Knudsen, Dorothy Malone, Bob Steele, Elisha Cook Jr.; ***D:*** Howard Hawks; ***W:*** Jules Furthman, Leigh Brackett, William Faulkner; ***C:*** Sid Hickox; ***M:*** Max Steiner. Natl. Film Reg. '97.

The Big Sleep **1978 (R)** A tired remake of the Raymond Chandler potboiler about exhausted Los Angeles private dick Marlowe and his problems in protecting a wild young heiress from her own decadence and mob connections. Mitchum appears to need a rest. **99m/C VHS, DVD.** Robert Mitchum, Sarah Miles, Richard Boone, Candy Clark, Edward Fox, Joan Collins, John Mills, James Stewart, Oliver Reed, Harry Andrews, James Donald, Colin Blakely, Richard Todd; ***D:*** Michael Winner; ***W:*** Michael Winner.

The Big Slice 1/2 **1990 (R)** Two would-be crime novelists want to improve their fiction. One masquerades as a cop, the other as a crook, and they infiltrate the underworld from both ends. Clever comedy premise, but vaudeville-level jokes fall flat. **86m/C VHS, DVD.** Casey Siemaszko, Leslie Hope, Justin Louis, Heather Locklear, Kenneth Welsh, Nicholas (Nick) Campbell, Henry Ramer; ***D:*** John Bradshaw; ***W:*** John Bradshaw; ***M:*** Mychael Danna, Jeff Danna.

The Big Sombrero 1/2 **1949** Autry takes a stand against the marriage between an unsuspecting, wealthy Mexican girl and the fortune-seeking bridegroom who wants her land. **77m/C VHS, DVD.** Gene Autry, Elena Verdugo, Steve (Stephen) Dunne, George Lewis; ***D:*** Frank McDonald.

The Big Squeeze 1/2 **1996 (R)** Married bartender Tanya (Boyle) is displeased to find out her born-again hubby Henry (Bercovici) has been holding out a large wad of cash from an insurance settlement, apparently about to donate it to a local Spanish mission. Enter Benny (Dobson), a cocky con man willing to help Tanya get her share of the dough for his own cut; sweet bartender Jesse (Nucci), who's secretly in love in Tanya; and fellow barmaid Cece (Dispina), who catches Benny's wandering eye. All get caught up in the frantic double-dealing. **100m/C VHS, DVD.** Lara Flynn Boyle, Peter Dobson, Luca Bercovici, Danny Nucci, Teresa Dispina, Sam Vlahos, Valente Rodriguez; ***D:*** Marcus De Leon; ***W:*** Marcus De Leon; ***C:*** Jacques Haitkin; ***M:*** Mark Mothersbaugh.

Big Stakes **1922** Extremely rare Western feature that has a Texas cowboy falling for a Mexican senorita. Plenty of action as complications ensue. **61m/B VHS.** H.B. Warner, Elinor Fair, Les Bates; ***D:*** Clifford S. Elfelt; ***W:*** Frank Howard Clark.

The Big Stampede **1932** Twenty-five-year-old Wayne stars in this action-packed Western that was a remake of "Land Beyond the Law" from Ken Maynard's silent. Based on a story by Marion Jackson. **63m/B VHS, DVD.** John Wayne, Noah Beery Sr., Luis Alberni, Berton Churchill, Paul Hurst, Lafe (Lafayette) McKee, Frank Ellis, Hank Bell; ***D:*** Tenny Wright; ***W:*** Kurt Kempler.

Big Stan **2007 (R)** Surprisingly funny prison comedy from Schneider (who also directs) as long as you don't expect too much. Con man Stan (Schneider) gets convicted of fraud but the judge postpones his sentence for six months. Naturally worried about how he'll survive in the joint, the weakling enlists martial arts guru The Master (a deadpan Carradine) to teach him defensive skills. Stan's transformation leads to his becoming a leader among the inmates, much to the displeasure of crooked warden Gasque (Wilson). **105m/C DVD.** Rob Schneider, Scott Wilson, David Carradine, Jenny (Jennifer) Morrison, M. Emmet Walsh, Richard Kind, Henry Gibson, Sally Kirkland, Dan Haggerty, Marcia Wallace, Kevin Gage, Bob Sapp; ***D:*** Rob Schneider; ***W:*** Josh Lieb; ***C:*** Victor Hammer; ***M:*** John Hunter.

Big Steal **1949** An Army officer recovers a missing payroll and captures the thieves after a tumultuous chase through Mexico. **72m/B VHS, DVD.** Robert Mitchum, William Bendix, Jane Greer, Ramon Novarro, Patric Knowles, Don Alvarado, John Qualen; ***D:*** Donald Siegel; ***W:*** Daniel Mainwaring, Gerald Drayson Adams; ***C:*** Harry Wild; ***M:*** Leigh Harline.

Big Store 1/2 **1941** Late Marx Brothers in which they are detectives in a large metropolitan department store, foiling a hostile takeover and preventing a murder. Their last MGM effort, with some good moments between the Tony Martin song numbers which include "If It's You" and the immortal "Tenement Symphony." Groucho also leads the "Sing While You Sell" number. **96m/B VHS, DVD.** Groucho Marx, Harpo Marx, Chico Marx, Tony Martin, Margaret Dumont, Virginia Grey, Virginia O'Brien, Douglass Dumbrille, Marion Martin, Henry Armetta; ***D:*** Charles Reisner; ***W:*** Hal Fimberg, Ray Golden, Sid Kuller; ***C:*** Charles Lawton Jr.; ***M:*** George Bassman.

Big Street 1/2 **1942** A timid busboy, in love with a disinterested nightclub singer, gets to prove his devotion when she is crippled in a fall. Based on a Damon Runyon story, "Little Pinks." **88m/B VHS, DVD.** Henry Fonda, Lucille Ball, Agnes Moorehead, Louise Beavers, Barton MacLane, Eugene Pallette, Ozzie Nelson; ***D:*** Irving Reis.

The Big Sweat **1990** Maybe you've heard this one before: a man who has been framed by the mob escapes from prison and heads for Mexico. But first, he's got to get past the mobsters and police who are hot on his trail. And maybe you've seen some of it before: some of the same stock footage appears in Lommel's "Cold Heat." Not surprisingly, this one bypassed theatres and went straight to video. **85m/C VHS.** Robert Z'Dar, Steve Molone, Kevin McBride, William Roebuck, Cheri Caspari, David Rushing, Joanne Watkins, Ken Letner; ***D:*** Ulli Lommel; ***W:*** Max Bolt; ***M:*** John Massari. **VIDEO**

The Big Switch 1/2 *Strip Poker* **1970 (R)** Gambler is framed for murder and becomes embroiled in a plot to reinstate an old gangster kingpin. **68m/C VHS.** Sebastian Breaks, Virginia Wetherell, Erika Raffael; ***D:*** Pete Walker.

The Big Tease **1999 (R)** Gay Glasgow hairdresser Crawford Mackenzie (Ferguson) thinks he's being asked to compete in the prestigious World Freestyle Hairdressing Championship being held in Los Angeles. So he heads to Hollywood and discovers he's just been asked to observe. Blithely self-confident, Crawford simply decides he will not only find a way to enter but he will defeat his snippy Swedish rival, Stig (Rasche). Good-natured, campy fluff. **86m/C VHS, DVD.** *GB* Kevin Allen, Craig Ferguson, Frances Fisher, Chris Langham, Mary McCormack, Donal Logue, Larry Miller, David Rasche, Charles Napier, David Hasselhoff, Cathy Lee Crosby, Bruce Jenner, Isabella Aitken; ***D:*** Kevin Allen; ***W:*** Craig Ferguson, Sacha Gervasi; ***C:*** Seamus McGarvey; ***M:*** Mark Thomas.

Big Top Pee-wee **1988 (PG)** Pee-wee's second feature film following the success of "Pee-wee's Big Adventure." This time Pee-wee owns a farm, has a girlfriend (!) and lives the good life until a weird storm blows a traveling circus onto his property. Cute, but not the manic hilarity the first one was. **86m/C VHS, DVD.** Paul (Pee-wee Herman) Reubens, Kris Kristofferson, Susan Tyrrell, Penelope Ann Miller; ***D:*** Randal Kleiser; ***W:*** Paul (Pee-wee Herman) Reubens; ***C:*** Steven Poster; ***M:*** Danny Elfman.

Big Town *Guilty Assignment* **1947** A newspaper is saved by a new editor who brings integrity to the once scandalous paper. The editor and his reporters also solve a series of murders. Some action, but weak dialogue and direction hold it back. Based on the radio program of the same name. **59m/B VHS.** Philip Reed, Hillary Brooke, Robert Lowery, Byron Barr, Veda Ann Borg, Nana Bryant, Charles Arnt, John Dehner; ***D:*** William C. Thomas; ***W:*** Daniel Mainwaring, Maxwell Shane; ***C:*** Fred H. Jackman Jr.; ***M:*** Darrell Calker.

Big Town 1/2 **1987 (R)** A farmboy, lucky with dice, hits Chicago to claim his fortune where he meets floozies, criminals, and other streetlife. Standard '50s period underworld drama is elevated by exceptional cast's fine ensemble work. Look for Lane's strip number. **109m/C VHS, DVD.** Matt Dillon, Diane Lane, Tommy Lee Jones, Bruce Dern, Tom Skerritt, Lee Grant, Suzy Amis, David Marshall Grant, Don Francks, Del Close, Cherry Jones, David James Elliot, Don Lake, Diego Matamoros, Gary Farmer, Sarah Polley, Lolita (David) Davidovich; ***D:*** Ben Bolt, Harold Becker; ***W:*** Robert Roy Pool; ***C:*** Ralf Bode; ***M:*** Michael Melvoin.

Big Town After Dark *Underworld After Dark* **1947** Daring journalists search for the bottom-line story on a gang of criminals. They find themselves caught behind the firing lines when the sun goes down. Slightly better than average thriller based on the radio show "Big Town." **69m/B VHS, DVD.** Philip Reed, Hillary Brooke, Richard Travis, Ann Gillis, Vince Barnett, Joseph (Joe) Sawyer, Robert Kent, Charles Arnt; ***D:*** William C. Thomas; ***C:*** Ellis W. Carter; ***M:*** Darrell Calker.

Big Trail **1930** This pioneering effort in widescreen cinematography was Wayne's first feature film. A wagon train on the Oregon trail encounters Indians, buffalo, tough terrain, and romantic problems. **110m/B VHS, DVD.** John Wayne, Marguerite Churchill, El Brendel, Tully Marshall, Tyrone Power Sr., Ward Bond, Helen Parrish; ***D:*** Raoul Walsh. Natl. Film Reg. '06.

Big Trees **1952** A ruthless lumberman attempts a takeover of the California Redwood Timberlands that are owned by a group of peaceful homesteaders. **89m/C VHS, DVD.** Kirk Douglas, Patrice Wymore, Eve Miller, Alan Hale Jr., Edgar Buchanan; ***D:*** Felix Feist.

Big Trouble **1986 (R)** An insurance broker endeavors to send his three sons to Yale by conspiring with a crazy couple in a fraud scheme that goes awry in every possible manner. Look for the cameo by screenwriter Bergman as Warren Bogle. **93m/C VHS, DVD.** Alan Arkin, Peter Falk, Beverly D'Angelo, Charles Durning, Robert Stack, Paul Dooley, Valerie Curtin, Richard Libertini; ***Cameos:*** Andrew Bergman; ***D:*** John Cassavetes; ***W:*** Andrew Bergman; ***C:*** Bill Butler; ***M:*** Bill Conti.

Big Trouble **2002 (PG-13)** Fast-paced ensemble comedy based on the novel by Dave Barry packs a metric ton of narrative, not to mention characters, into a mere 84 minutes, most of which involve the clash of various characters tracking down a nuclear bomb in Miami. Suburban Anna (Russo) is trapped in a loveless marriage with unscrupulous businessman Arthur Herk (Tucci) who wants to buy a nuclear bomb, thus getting involved with some undesirable characters, most notably two hit men (Farina and Kehler). The plot kicks off when Matt (Foster), the son of divorced journalist Allen decides to snipe the Herk's daughter Jenny (Deschanel) with a high-powered squirt gun on the same night the hit men visit. Of the strong cast, Allen and Foster are the stand-outs. Cartoony, heavy-handed direction buries satire for which Barry is known. **84m/C VHS, DVD.** *US* Tim Allen, Rene Russo, Stanley Tucci, Tom Sizemore, Johnny Knoxville, Dennis Farina, Jack Kehler, Janeane Garofalo, Patrick Warburton, Ben Foster, Zooey Deschanel, Dwight "Heavy D" Myers, Omar Epps, Jason Lee, Andy Richter, Sofia Vergara; ***D:*** Barry Sonnenfeld; ***W:*** Robert Ramsey, Matthew Stone; ***C:*** Greg Gardiner; ***M:*** James Newton Howard.

Big Trouble in Little China 🦴🦴 1/2 **1986 (PG-13)** A trucker plunges beneath the streets of San Francisco's Chinatown to battle an army of spirits. An uproarious comic-book-film parody with plenty of action and a keen sense of sophomoric sarcasm. **99m/C VHS, DVD, UMD.** Kurt Russell, Suzee Pai, Dennis Dun, Kim Cattrall, James Hong, Victor Wong, Kate Burton; ***D:*** John Carpenter; ***W:*** David Weinstein, Gary Goldman, W.D. Richter; ***C:*** Dean Cundey; ***M:*** John Carpenter, Alan Howarth.

The Big Turnaround 🦴 1/2 *Turnaround* **1988** Drug-dealing punks push their goods into Mexico via a lowly southwest town but local do-gooders led by a struggling doctor (Cranston, whose father, Joseph, serves as director and producer) and a priest (Borgnine) boldly unite to save the day in this misguided effort. **98m/C VHS, DVD.** Mindi Miller, Michael J. Reynolds, Robert Axelrod, Robert V. Barron, Ernest Borgnine, Bryan Cranston, Luis Latino, Rick Le Fever, Ruben Castillo, Al Fleming, Stu Weltman; ***D:*** Joseph L. Cranston; ***W:*** Luis Johnston; ***C:*** Karen Grossman; ***M:*** Jasmin Larkin. **VIDEO**

Big Wednesday 🦴🦴 1/2 *Summer of Innocence* **1978 (PG)** Three California surfers from the early '60s get back together after the Vietnam war to reminisce about the good old days and take on the big wave. **120m/C VHS, DVD.** Jan-Michael Vincent, Gary Busey, William Katt, Lee Purcell, Patti D'Arbanville; ***D:*** John Milius; ***W:*** John Milius; ***M:*** Basil Poledouris.

The Big Wheel 🦴🦴 1/2 **1949** Old story retold fairly well. Rooney is young son determined to travel in his father's tracks as a race car driver, even when dad buys the farm on the oval. Good acting and direction keep this a cut above average. **92m/B VHS, DVD.** Mickey Rooney, Thomas Mitchell, Spring Byington, Mary Hatcher, Allen Jenkins, Michael O'Shea; ***D:*** Edward Ludwig.

The Big White 🦴 1/2 **2005 (R)** A waste of talent in a lame comedy. Alaska travel agent Paul Barnell (Williams) has money problems. Then he finds a frozen body in a dumpster. Paul hopes to pass the body off as his estranged brother Raymond (Harrelson) and collect the life insurance, but agent Ted (Ribisi) is suspicious. Add in Paul's troubled wife Margaret (Hunter), the sudden return of Raymond, and a couple of wannabe kidnapper/hitmen (Nelson, Brown) and Paul's got more complications than he can handle. **105m/C DVD.** *US CA NZ* Robin Williams, Holly Hunter, Woody Harrelson, Tim Blake Nelson, Giovanni Ribisi, W. Earl Brown, Alison Lohman; ***D:*** Mark Mylod; ***W:*** Collin Friesen; ***C:*** James Gleason; ***M:*** Mark Mothersbaugh.

Big Zapper 🦴 1/2 **1973** Violent P.I. Marlowe and masochistic assistant Rock work together in this British comic strip film. **94m/C VHS.** *GB* Linda Marlowe, Gary Hope, Sean Hewitt, Richard Monette, Penny Irving; ***D:*** Lindsay Shonteff.

The Bigamist 🦴 1/2 **1953** Have you heard the one about the traveling salesman in this movie? He has one wife in Los Angeles, another in San Francisco, and they inevitably find out about each other. A maudlin soap opera with a do-it-yourself ending, only shows why bigamy was done better as farce in the later "Micki and Maude." **79m/B VHS, DVD.** Edmond O'Brien, Joan Fontaine, Ida Lupino, Edmund Gwenn, Jane Darwell, Kenneth Tobey; ***D:*** Ida Lupino.

Bigfoot: The Unforgettable Encounter 🦴🦴 1/2 **1994 (PG)** Young boy heads off into the woods, comes face to face with Bigfoot, and sets off a media frenzy and a band of ruthless bounty hunters determined to capture his hairy friend. **89m/C VHS, DVD.** Zachery Ty Bryan, Matt McCoy, Barbara Willis Sweete, Clint Howard, Rance Howard, David Rasche; ***D:*** Corey Michael Eubanks; ***W:*** Corey Michael Eubanks; ***M:*** Shimon Arama.

Bigger Stronger Faster 🦴🦴 1/2 **2008 (PG-13)** Director Bell grew up in the mid 1980s, an era of steroid-enhanced wrestlers and bodybuilding actors, and his commentary on how America's obsession with winning might be destroying it is filled with ambivalence towards the fate of juiced athletes, including his two brothers. Much time is spent attempting to debunk the dangers of steroids, and the rest is devoted to the idea that the ideal of winning at any cost is the real danger. **107m/C DVD.** Chris Bell; ***D:*** Chris Bell; ***W:*** Chris Bell, Alexander Buono, Tamsin Rawady; ***C:*** Alexander Buono; ***M:*** Dave Porter. **VIDEO**

Bigger Than the Sky 🦴🦴 1/2 **2005 (PG-13)** Recently-dumped Peter (Thomas), stuck in a lousy dead-end job, decides he needs something new. He tries out for the community theatre and finds what he's looking for through company regulars Michael (Corbett) and Grace (Smart). A very mild romantic comedy that almost works. Anyone involve in small theatre will relish in the details. Features Patty Duke playing mother to her real-life son, Sean Astin. **106m/C VHS, DVD.** Marcus Thomas, John Corbett, Amy Smart, Sean Astin, Clare Higgins, Patty Duke, Allan Corduner, Matt Salinger, Greg Germann; ***D:*** Al Corley; ***W:*** Rodney Vaccaro; ***C:*** Christine Gentet; ***M:*** Rob Cairns. **VIDEO**

The Biggest Fan 🦴 1/2 **2002** Silly teen romance about a fan and a boy band. Shy high school sophomore Debbie (Amariah) is the number one fan of Dream Street. Disappointed at missing their local concert, Debbie wakes up the next morning to a huge shock—she finds lead singer Chris Trousdale (playing himself) passed out in her room! Loopy from cold medicine, Chris missed the concert and stumbled around until he found a convenient place to crash. Debbie agrees to hide the dreamboat, who needs a timeout from all that squealing and screaming, but what if her parents find out? **95m/C DVD.** *US* Marissa Tait, Richard Moll, Noriyuki "Pat" Morita, Michael Meyer, Kaila Amariah, Chris Trousdale, Morgan Brittany, Leslie Easterbrook, Jesse McCartney, Shanelle Workman, Cindy Williams; ***D:*** Michael Criscione; ***W:*** Michael Criscione, LeeAnn Kemp, Liz Sinclair; ***C:*** Wes Llewellyn. **VIDEO**

Biggles 🦴🦴 *Biggles: Adventures in Time* **1985 (PG)** Time-travel fantasy in which a young businessman from present-day New York City is inexplicably transferred into the identity of a 1917 WWI flying ace. He suddenly finds himself aboard a fighter plane over Europe during WWI. **100m/C VHS, DVD.** *GB* Neil Dickson, Alex Hyde-White, Peter Cushing; ***D:*** John Hough.

Biker Boyz 🦴🦴 1/2 **2003 (PG-13)** Kid (Luke) is the hotshot teenager biker who challenges Smoke (Fishburne) the long-time reigning "King of Cali." Often referred to as "The Fast and the Furious" on motorcycles, but doesn't achieve the same level of entertainment. Soap opera subplots and cliched dialogue don't help. Then again, "Furious" had the same problems and managed to make a boatload of cash. The actors, however, do a good job with a so-so script, and Luke is fast becoming an actor worth noticing. **111m/C VHS, DVD.** *US* Laurence Fishburne, Derek Luke, Orlando Jones, Djimon Hounsou, Lisa Bonet, Brendan Fehr, Larenz Tate, Kid Rock, Rick Gonzalez, Meagan Good, Salli Richardson, Vanessa Bell Calloway, Eriq La Salle, Titus Welliver, Kadeem Hardison, Terrence Howard, Tyson Beckford; ***D:*** Reggie Rock Bythewood; ***W:*** Reggie Rock Bythewood, Craig Ferandez; ***C:*** Greg Gardiner; ***M:*** Camara Kambon.

Bikini Beach 🦴🦴 1/2 **1964** Surfing teenagers of the "Beach Party" series follow up "Muscle Beach Party" with a third fling at the beach and welcome a visitor, British recording star "Potato Bug" (Avalon in a campy dual role). But, golly gee, wealthy Wynn wants to turn their sandy, surfin' shores into a retirement community. What to do? Sing a few songs, dance in your bathing suits, and have fun. Classic early '60s nostalgia is better than the first two efforts; followed by "Pajama Party." ♫Because You're You; Love's a Secret Weapon; Bikini Drag. **100m/C VHS, DVD.** Annette Funicello, Frankie Avalon, Martha Hyer, Harvey Lembeck, Don Rickles, Stevie Wonder, John Ashley, Keenan Wynn, Jody McCrea, Candy Johnson, Danielle Aubry, Meredith MacRae, Dolores Wells, Donna Loren, Timothy Carey, Boris Karloff; ***D:*** William Asher; ***W:*** William Asher, Leo Townsend, Robert Dillon; ***C:*** Floyd Crosby; ***M:*** Les Baxter.

Bikini Bistro 🦴 **1994 (R)** A boring vegetarian cafe gets turned into a gourmet restaurant but, faced with an eviction notice, the female owners decide to increase business by waitressing in bikinis. Also available in an unrated version at 84 minutes. **80m/C VHS, DVD.** Marilyn Chambers, Amy Lynn Baxter, Joan Gerardi, Isabelle Fortea, John Altamura, Joseph Pallister; ***D:*** Ernest G. Sauer; ***W:*** Matt Unger.

The Bikini Car Wash Company WOOF! *California Hot Wax* **1990 (R)** Babes in bikinis in Los Angeles. A young man is running his uncle's carwash when he meets a business major who persuades him to let her take over the business for a cut of the profits. She decides that a good gimmick would be to dress all the female employees in the tiniest bikinis possible. The story is of course secondary to the amount of flesh on display. Also available in an unrated version. **87m/C VHS, DVD.** Joe Dusic, Neriah Napaul, Sara Suzanne Brown, Kristie Ducati; ***D:*** Ed Hansen.

The Bikini Car Wash Company 2 🦴 **1992 (R)** Entrepreneur Melissa and the other lovely ladies of the Bikini Car Wash Co. find themselves a big success, so much so that a greedy businessman wants to buy them out. In order to get money to fight the takeover, the ladies take to the airwaves of a cable-access station. Their new business adventure involves selling sexy lingerie which means the flesh quotient is as great as ever. An unrated version is also available. **94m/C VHS, DVD.** Kristie Ducati, Sara Suzanne Brown, Neriah Napaul, Rikki Brando, Greg Raye, Larry De Russy; ***D:*** Gary Orona; ***W:*** Bart B. Gustis; ***M:*** Michael Smith.

Bikini Drive-In 🦴 1/2 **1994 (R)** Babe (Rhey) inherits grandad's decrepit drive-in, which is wanted by a mall mogul, but she refuses to sell. So to raise some cash, Rhey stages a B-movie marathon with in-person, bikini-clad scream queens. **85m/C VHS.** Ashlie Rhey, Richard Gabai, Ross Hagen, Sara Bellomo, Steve Barkett, Conrad Brooks; ***D:*** Fred Olen Ray.

Bikini House Calls 🦴 **1996** The students of Bikini Med School love anatomy as much as they love to party. In fact, combining both activities is their idea of a perfect time. **87m/C VHS, DVD.** Thomas Draper, Sean Abbananto, Kim (Kimberly Dawn) Dawson, Tamara Landry; ***D:*** Michael Paul Girard; ***W:*** Michael Paul Girard; ***C:*** Denis Maloney; ***M:*** Miriam Cutler. **VIDEO**

Bikini Island 🦴 **1991 (R)** Beautiful swimsuit models gather on a remote tropical island for a big photo shoot, each vying to be the next cover girl of the hottest swimsuit magazine. Before long, scantily clad lovelies are turning up dead and full out madness ensues. Will the mystery be solved before they run out of models, or will the magazine have no choice but to grace its cover with a bikinied cadaver? Low-budget trash that has few, if any, redeeming qualities. **85m/C VHS.** Holly Floria, Alicia Anne, Jackson Robinson, Shannon Stiles, Cyndi Pass, Sherry Johnson; ***D:*** Anthony Markes; ***W:*** Emerson Bixby; ***M:*** Marc David Decker.

Bikini Med School 🦴 **1998** So how do med students get rid of all that nasty tension? Why they party, of course! And practice playing doctor with all the nubile lovelies they can. **87m/C VHS, DVD.** Kim (Kimberly Dawn) Dawson, Tamara Landry, Thomas Draper, Sean Abbananto; ***D:*** Michael Paul Girard; ***W:*** Michael Paul Girard; ***C:*** Denis Maloney; ***M:*** Miriam Cutler. **VIDEO**

Bikini Summer 🦴 1/2 **1991** Laughs, music, and skin are the order of the day as two nutty guys and a few beautiful girls form an unlikely friendship on the beach. Konop was Julia Robert's "Pretty Woman" body double. Sort of the '90s version of the old '60s Frankie and Annette beach parties. **90m/C VHS, DVD.** David Millbern, Melinda Armstrong, Jason Clow, Shelley Michelle, Alex Smith, Kent Lipham, Kelly Konop, Carmen Santa Maria; ***D:*** Robert Veze; ***W:*** Robert Veze, Nick Stone; ***M:*** John Gonzalez.

Bikini Summer 2 🦴 **1992 (R)** An eccentric family decides to stage a bikini contest to raise money to help the homeless. **94m/C VHS, DVD.** Jeff Conaway, Jessica Hahn, Melinda Armstrong, Avalon Anders; ***D:*** Jeff Conaway; ***M:*** Jim Halfpenny.

Bikini Summer 3: South Beach Heat 🦴 **1997 (R)** Babes in bikinis frolic on Miami's fashionable South Beach for the chance to become the spokesmodel for Mermaid Body Splash. **84m/C VHS, DVD.** Heather-Elizabeth Parkhurst, Tiffany Turner; ***D:*** Ken Blakey.

Bilitis 🦴 1/2 **1977 (R)** A young girl from a private girls' school is initiated into the pleasures of sex and the unexpected demands of love. One of director Hamilton's exploitative meditations on nudity. **95m/C VHS, DVD.** *FR* Patti D'Arbanville, Bernard Giraudeau, Mona Kristensen; ***D:*** David Hamilton.

Bill 🦴🦴🦴 **1981** Based on a true story about a mentally retarded man who sets out to live independently after 44 years in an institution. Rooney gives an affecting performance as Bill and Quaid is strong as the filmmaker who befriends him. Awarded Emmys for Rooney's performance and the well written script. Followed by "Bill: On His Own." **97m/C VHS.** Mickey Rooney, Dennis Quaid, Largo Woodruff, Harry Goz; ***D:*** Anthony Page. **TV**

Bill & Ted's Bogus Journey 🦴🦴 **1991 (PG)** Big-budget sequel to B & T's first movie has better special effects but about the same quota of laughs. Slain by lookalike robot duplicates from the future, the airhead heroes pass through heaven and hell before tricking the Grim Reaper into bringing them back for a second duel with their heinous terminators. Most excellent closing-credit montage. Non-fans still won't think much of it. **98m/C VHS, DVD.** Keanu Reeves, Alex Winter, William Sadler, Joss Ackland, Pam Grier, George Carlin, Amy Stock-Poynton, Hal Landon Jr., Annette Azcuy, Sarah Trigger, Taj Mahal, Roy Brocksmith, William Shatner, Chelcie Ross; ***D:*** Peter Hewitt; ***W:*** Chris Matheson, Edward Solomon; ***C:*** Oliver Wood; ***M:*** David Newman.

Bill & Ted's Excellent Adventure 🦴🦴 1/2 **1989 (PG)** Excellent premise: when the entire future of the world rests on whether or not two '80s dudes pass their history final, Rufus comes to the rescue in his time-travelling telephone booth. Bill and Ted share an adventure through time as they meet and get to know some of history's most important figures. Lightweight but fun. **105m/C VHS, DVD, UMD.** Keanu Reeves, Alex Winter, George Carlin, Bernie Casey, Dan Shor, Robert V. Barron, Amy Stock-Poynton, Ted Steedman, Terry Camillieri, Rod Loomis, Al Leong, Tony Camilieri; ***D:*** Stephen Herek; ***W:*** Chris Matheson, Edward Solomon; ***C:*** Tim Suhrstedt; ***M:*** David Newman.

A Bill of Divorcement 🦴🦴 1/2 **1932** Hepburn's screen debut, as the daughter of a shell-shocked WWI vet, who requires her care after her mother decides to divorce him. Creaky early talker. **76m/B VHS.** John Barrymore, Katharine Hepburn, Billie Burke, Henry Stephenson, David Manners, Paul Cavanagh, Elizabeth Patterson; ***D:*** George Cukor; ***M:*** Max Steiner.

Bill: On His Own 🦴🦴🦴 **1983** Rooney is again exceptional in this sequel to the Emmy-winning TV movie "Bill." After 44 years in an institution, a mentally retarded man copes more and more successfully with the outside world. Fine supporting cast and direction control the melodramatic potential. **100m/C VHS.** Mickey Rooney, Helen Hunt, Teresa Wright, Dennis Quaid, Largo Woodruff, Paul Leiber, Harry Goz; ***D:*** Anthony Page.

Billboard Dad 🦴🦴 1/2 **1998 (G)** The Olsen twins decide it's time for their dad to remarry so they paint a personal ad on a billboard advertising his availability. Eventually, their Dad meets Brooke, who's a winner except for her bratty son who's the girls' rival. But nothing will stop the twins if it means making Dad happy. **90m/C VHS.** Ashley (Fuller) Olsen, Mary-Kate Olsen, Tom Amandes, Jessica Tuck, Sam Selatta, Carl Banks; ***D:*** Alan Metter; ***W:*** Maria Jacquemetton; ***C:*** Mauro Fiore; ***M:*** David Michael Frank. **VIDEO**

Billie & 1/2 **1965** Duke stars as a tomboy athlete who puts the boys' track team to shame. Some amusing but very predictable situations, plus a few songs from Miss Duke. Based on Ronald Alexander's play "Time Out for Ginger." **86m/C VHS, DVD.** Patty Duke, Jim Backus, Jane Greer, Warren Berlinger, Billy DeWolfe, Charles Lane, Dick Sargent, Susan Seaforth Hayes, Ted Bessell, Richard Deacon; ***D:*** Don Weis; ***W:*** Ronald Alexander.

Billion Dollar Brain && *Operation Espionage* **1967** The third of five films based on the Harry Palmer spy novels by Len Deighton, this one has Michael Caine repeating his performance as British agent Harry Palmer, now a down-on-his-luck private investigator. Forced back into the espionage game, he is sent to deliver a package to an old friend, only to find him now working for a rabid right-wing Texas oil billionaire who has made a super computer running a spy ring dedicated to perpetuating the cold war and destroying the Soviet Union. Confusing and full of triple crosses, it is fairly close to the source material. **111m/C DVD.** *GB* Michael Caine, Karl Malden, Ed Begley Jr., Oscar Homolka, Francoise Dorleac, Guy Doleman, Vladek Sheybal, Mark Elwes, John Brandon, Tony Harwood, Milo Sperber; ***D:*** Ken Russell; ***W:*** Len Deighton, John McGrath; ***C:*** Billy Williams; ***M:*** Richard Rodney Bennett.

The Billion Dollar Hobo & 1/2 **1978 (G)** Poor, unsuspecting heir of a multimillion dollar fortune must duplicate his benefactor's experience as a hobo during the Depression in order to collect his inheritance. Slow-moving family stuff. **96m/C VHS, DVD.** Tim Conway, Will Geer, Eric Weston, Sydney Lassick; ***D:*** Stuart E. McGowan.

A Billion for Boris && 1/2 **1990** Boris' TV gives a sneak preview of the future and Boris plans to make some money off of it. Zany comedy in the vein of "Let It Ride." **89m/C VHS, DVD.** Lee Grant, Tim Kazurinsky; ***D:*** Alex Grasshof; ***W:*** Mary Rogers.

Billionaire Boys Club && 1/2 **1987** Chilling look at greed in the '80s. Nelson plays Joe Hunt, who gets together with a group of rich, preppie friends to manipulate investments in the commodities markets. When a slick con man (Silver) gets in their way he's murdered to keep their schemes intact. Based on a true story and adapted from the book by Sue Horton. The video version is considerably pared down from the original TV broadcast. **94m/C VHS.** Judd Nelson, Frederic Lehne, Brian McNamara, Raphael Sbarge, John Stockwell, Barry Tubb, Stan Shaw, Jill Schoelen, Ron Silver, James Sloyan, James Karen, Dale Dye; ***D:*** Marvin J. Chomsky. **TV**

Billy Bathgate && 1/2 **1991 (R)** Uneven but well acted drama set in 1935 New York. A street-wise young man decides getting ahead during the Depression means gaining the attention of mobster Dutch Schultz and joining his gang. As Billy becomes the confidant of the racketeer he learns the criminal life is filled with suspicion and violence; in order to stay alive he must rely on every trick he's learned. Willis has a small role as a rival mobster who gets fitted for cement overshoes. Kidman does well as Dutch's girlfriend with Hill fine as the gang's number man. Based on the novel by E.L. Doctorow. **107m/C VHS, DVD.** Dustin Hoffman, Nicole Kidman, Loren Dean, Bruce Willis, Steven Hill, Steve Buscemi, Stanley Tucci, Tim Jerome, Billy Jaye, Katharine Houghton, Mike Starr, John A. Costelloe, Moira Kelly; ***D:*** Robert Benton; ***W:*** Tom Stoppard; ***C:*** Nestor Almendros; ***M:*** Mark Isham.

Billy Budd &&& **1962** The classic Melville good-evil allegory adapted to film, dealing with a British warship in the late 1700s, and its struggle between evil master-at-arms and innocent shipmate. Stamp's screen debut as the naive Billy who is tried for the murder of the sadistic first mate. Well directed and acted. **123m/B VHS, DVD.** *GB* Terence Stamp, Peter Ustinov, Robert Ryan, Melvyn Douglas, Paul Rogers, John Neville, Ronald Lewis, David McCallum, John Meillon; ***D:*** Peter Ustinov; ***W:*** Peter Ustinov, Robert Rossen; ***C:*** Robert Krasker.

Billy Elliot &&& *Dancer* **2000 (R)** Eleven-year-old Billy (Bell) is trying to survive in a Durham County town during the 1984 miners' strike that is affecting his family. His widowed dad (Lewis) wants Billy to take boxing lessons but the boy is more interested in the ballet class taught at the same gym by hard-living Mrs. Wilkinson (Walters), whose daughter Debbie (Blackwell) taunts Billy into trying to dance. Billy's natural talent is so great that Mrs. Wilkinson encourages him to audition for the Royal Ballet School in London. Of course, when his dad finds out what's been going on, there's trouble. The unfortunate rating is due to language but the film has all-around appeal and some fine performances. Stage director Daldry makes his film debut as does Bell. **111m/C VHS, DVD.** *GB* Jamie Bell, Julie Walters, Gary Lewis, Jamie Driven, Nicola Blackwell, Jean Heywood, Stuart Wells, Adam Cooper; ***D:*** Stephen Daldry; ***W:*** Lee Hall; ***C:*** Brian Tufano; ***M:*** Stephen Warbeck. British Acad. '00: Actor (Bell), Film, Support. Actress (Walters).

Billy Galvin && 1/2 **1986 (PG)** A bull-headed ironworker tries to straighten out the turbulent relationship he has with his rebellious son. **95m/C VHS.** Karl Malden, Lenny Von Dohlen, Joyce Van Patten, Toni Kalem, Keith Szarabajka, Alan North, Paul Guilfoyle, Barton Heyman; ***D:*** John Gray; ***W:*** John Gray; ***M:*** Joel Rosenbaum.

Billy Jack && **1971 (PG)** On an Arizona Indian reservation, a half-breed ex-Green Beret with pugnacious martial arts skills (Laughlin) stands between a rural town and a school for runaways. Laughlin stars with his real-life wife Taylor. Features the then-hit song "One Tin Soldier," sung by Coven. The movie and its marketing by Laughlin inspired a "Billy Jack" cult phenomenon. A Spanish-dubbed version of this film is also available. Followed by a sequel in 1974, "Trail of Billy Jack," which bombed. **112m/C VHS, DVD.** Tom Laughlin, Delores Taylor, Clark Howat, Bert Freed, Julie Webb, Victor Izay, Teresa Kelly, Lynn Baker, Stan Rice, Howard Hesseman; ***D:*** Tom Laughlin; ***W:*** Tom Laughlin, Delores Taylor; ***C:*** Fred W. Koenekamp, John Stephens; ***M:*** Mundell Lowe.

Billy Liar &&& **1963** A young Englishman dreams of escaping from his working class family and dead-end job as an undertaker's assistant. Parallels James Thurber's story, "The Secret Life of Walter Mitty." **94m/B VHS, DVD.** *GB* Tom Courtenay, Julie Christie, Finlay Currie; ***D:*** John Schlesinger; ***W:*** Willis Hall, Keith Waterhouse; ***C:*** Denys Coop; ***M:*** Richard Rodney Bennett.

Billy Madison & 1/2 **1994 (PG-13)** Wealthy slacker Billy (Sandler) must prove to Dad he is capable of running the family hotel business by undertaking the obvious challenge of repeating grades 1-12 in six months. Ponder a few bodily function gags, and you'll have exhausted the humor in this lame attempt at creating a feature-length movie out of what would barely pass as a Saturday Night Live sketch. For only the most diehard fans of Sandler's silly shtick. **90m/C VHS, DVD, HD DVD.** Adam Sandler, Darren McGavin, Bridgette Wilson-Sampras, Bradley Whitford, Josh Mostel, Norm MacDonald, Mark Beltzman, Larry Hankin, Theresa Merritt, Chris Farley, Steve Buscemi; ***D:*** Tamra Davis; ***W:*** Adam Sandler; ***C:*** Victor Hammer; ***M:*** Randy Edelman.

Billy: Portrait of a Street Kid && **1977** A ghetto youngster tries to pry himself up and out of his bleak surroundings through education, but complications arise when he gets his girlfriend pregnant. **96m/C VHS.** LeVar Burton, Tina Andrews, Ossie Davis, Michael Constantine; ***D:*** Steven Gethers. **TV**

Billy Rose's Jumbo &&& *Jumbo* **1962** Better-than-average update of the circus picture. Durante and Raye are terrific, as are the Rodgers and Hart songs. Fun, with lively production numbers in the inimitable Berkeley style. ♫ Over and Over Again; Circus on Parade; Why Can't I?; This Can't Be Love; The Most Beautiful Girl in the World; My Romance; Little Girl Blue; What is a Circus; Sawdust, Spangles and Dreams. **125m/C VHS, DVD.** Doris Day, Stephen Boyd, Jimmy Durante, Martha Raye, Dean Jagger; ***D:*** Charles Walters; ***W:*** Sidney Sheldon.

Billy the Kid && 1/2 **1941** Billy Bonney joins up with a group of outlaws in a Southwest town where he bumps into his old friend Jim Sherwood, now the marshal. Attempting to change his ways, he falls back into the life of a bandit when an outlaw friend is murdered. Although an entertaining western, the story bears no resemblance to the actual last days of Billy the Kid. Based on a story by Howard Emmett Rogers and Bradbury Foote, suggested by the book "The Saga of Billy the Kid" by Walter Noble Burns. **94m/C VHS.** Carl Pitti, Robert Taylor, Brian Donlevy, Ian Hunter, Mary Howard, Gene Lockhart, Lon Chaney Jr., Guinn "Big Boy" Williams, Cy Kendall, Henry O'Neill, Ted Adams, Frank Puglia, Mitchell Lewis, Dick Curtis, Grant Withers, Joe Yule, Eddie Dunn, Kermit Maynard, Chill Wills, Olive Blakeney; ***D:*** David Miller; ***W:*** Gene Fowler Sr.; ***C:*** William V. Skall, Leonard Smith; ***M:*** David Snell.

Billy the Kid in Santa Fe & 1/2 **1941** Steele's last outing as the outlaw finds Billy busting out of jail to clear his name of a murder he didn't commit. He and pals Jeff and Fuzzy travel to Santa Fe where Billy is determined to get a confession from the real killer. **61m/B DVD.** Bob Steele, Al "Fuzzy" St. John, Rex Lease, Dave O'Brien, Marin Sais, Dennis Moore, Karl Hackett; ***D:*** Sam Newfield; ***W:*** Joseph O'Donnell; ***C:*** Jack Greenhalgh.

Billy the Kid in Texas & 1/2 **1940** The famed outlaw takes on trouble and makes sure the Texans never forget that he has been there. **52m/B VHS.** Bob Steele, Al "Fuzzy" St. John, Carleton Young, John Merton; ***D:*** Sam Newfield; ***W:*** Joseph O'Donnell; ***C:*** Jack Greenhalgh; ***M:*** Lew Porter.

Billy the Kid Returns & 1/2 **1938** While trying to clean up a town of its criminal element, Rogers is mistaken for the legendary Billy. Complications ensue. **60m/B VHS, DVD.** Roy Rogers, George "Gabby" Hayes, Smiley Burnette, Lynne Roberts; ***D:*** Joseph Kane.

Billy the Kid Trapped & 1/2 **1942** Billy and his partner are rescued from hanging by an outlaw band. **59m/B VHS, DVD.** Buster Crabbe, Al "Fuzzy" St. John, Malcolm "Bud" McTaggart, Anne Jeffreys, Glenn Strange; ***D:*** Sam Newfield.

Billy the Kid Versus Dracula && **1966** The title says it all. Dracula travels to the Old West, anxious to put the bite on a pretty lady ranch owner. Her fiance, the legendary outlaw Billy the Kid, steps in to save his girl from becoming a vampire herself. A Carradine camp classic. **95m/C VHS, DVD.** Chuck Courtney, John Carradine, Melinda Plowman, Walter Janovitz, Harry Carey Jr., Roy Barcroft, Virginia Christine, Bing (Neil) Russell, Olive Carey, William Challee, William Forrest; ***D:*** William Beaudine; ***W:*** Carl K. Hittleman; ***C:*** Lothrop Worth; ***M:*** Raoul Kraushaar.

Billy Two Hats && 1/2 *The Lady and the Outlaw* **1974 (PG)** Grizzled Scottish bandit Deans (Peck) teams up with young half-breed Billy (Arnaz Jr.) to pull off a robbery that results in an accidental death and Billy's capture. Deans is shot while breaking the kid out of jail and must rely on Billy to get them through, while being pursued by the law. It ain't happy. Mainly notable as the first western shot in Israel. **139m/C VHS.** Gregory Peck, Desi Arnaz Jr., Jack Warden, Sian Barbara Allen, David Huddleston; ***D:*** Ted Kotcheff; ***W:*** Alan Sharp; ***C:*** Brian West; ***M:*** John Scott.

Billy's Holiday && 1/2 **1995 (R)** Excessively offbeat Australian musical lacks the highly polished look of Hollywood's best, but given the setting and subject matter, it is probably not meant to have it. The subject is Billy Apples (Cullen), hangdog hardware owner by day, hangdog jazz musician at night. His audiences regularly fall asleep, but Kate (McQuade), owner of the beauty shop down the street, still loves him. Then one night, Billy magically receives the ability to sing just like his idol, Billie Holiday. The main attractions are the likeably middle-aged stars and a soundtrack filled with big band tunes. **92m/C DVD.** *AU* Max Cullen, Kris McQuade, Tina Bursill, Drew Forsythe, Genevieve Lemon, Richard Roxburgh, Rachel Coopes; ***D:*** Richard Wherrett; ***W:*** Denis Whitburn; ***C:*** Roger Lanser.

Billy's Hollywood Screen Kiss && 1/2 **1998 (R)** Very gay Billy (Hayes) is an aspiring arts photographer in L.A. who's looking for romance. He thinks he's got a hot prospect in handsome-if-sexually-confused Gabriel (Rowe), a waiter/model. Billy's latest project is recreating great film romantic scenes with drag queens and he hires Gabriel to play the male lover. But it looks as if Billy is going to get his heart broken if he expects Gabriel to carry the role over into real life. Amusing feature debut for director O'Haver and a standout performance from the witty Hayes. **92m/C VHS, DVD.** Sean P. Hayes, Brad Rowe, Richard Ganoung, Meredith Scott Lynn, Paul Bartel, Armando Valdes-Kennedy; ***D:*** Tommy O'Haver; ***W:*** Tommy O'Haver; ***C:*** Mark Mervis; ***M:*** Alan Ari Lazar.

Biloxi Blues && 1/2 *Neil Simon's Biloxi Blues* **1988 (PG-13)** Eugene Morris Jerome has been drafted and sent to boot camp in Biloxi, Mississippi where he encounters a troubled drill sergeant, hostile recruits, and a skillful prostitute. Walken is the drill sergeant from hell. Some good laughs from the ever-wry Broderick. A sequel to Neil Simon's "Brighton Beach Memoirs" and adapted by Simon from his play. Followed by "Broadway Bound." **105m/C VHS, DVD.** Matthew Broderick, Christopher Walken, Casey Siemaszko, Matt Mulhern, Corey Parker, Penelope Ann Miller, Michael Dolan, Park Overall; ***D:*** Mike Nichols; ***W:*** Neil Simon; ***C:*** Bill Butler; ***M:*** Georges Delerue.

Bimini Code & **1984** Two female adventurers accept a dangerous mission where they wind up on Bimini Island in a showdown with the mysterious Madame X. **95m/C VHS.** Vickie Benson, Krista Richardson, Frank Alexander, Rosanna Simanaitis; ***D:*** Barry Clark.

Bingo && 1/2 **1991 (PG)** Mediocre spoof of hero-dog movies. The heroic title mutt roams from Denver to Green Bay in search of his absent-minded master, with numerous absurd adventures en route. Some cute moments, but sometimes Bingo is just lame-o. Good family fare. **90m/C VHS, DVD.** Cindy Williams, David Rasche, Robert J. Steinmiller Jr., David French, Kurt Fuller, Joe Guzaldo, Glenn Shadix; ***D:*** Matthew Robbins; ***W:*** Jim Strain; ***M:*** Richard Gibbs.

Bingo Long Traveling All-Stars & Motor Kings &&& **1976 (PG)** Set in 1939, this film follows the comedic adventures of a lively group of black ball players who have defected from the old Negro National League. The All-Stars travel the country challenging local white teams. **111m/C VHS, DVD.** Billy Dee Williams, James Earl Jones, Richard Pryor, Stan Shaw; ***D:*** John Badham; ***W:*** Matthew Robbins, Hal Barwood; ***C:*** Bill Butler; ***M:*** William Goldstein.

Bio-Dome & **1996 (PG-13)** Pauly Shore in a hermetically sealed environment separated from the rest of society? Great! Where do I sign? Unfortunately, it's only a movie, and a typically useless one, at that. Shore brings his lame schtick to a scientifically created "perfect environment" that he and his college (yeah, right) buddy Doyle (Baldwin) mistake for a mall and eventually destroy. In Bloom's not-too-auspicious directorial debut, bodily function jokes found in Jim Carrey's wastebasket masquerade as a script, while the supporting cast wanders aimlessly, perhaps pondering a switch in agents. **94m/C VHS, DVD.** Pauly Shore, Stephen Baldwin, William Atherton, Henry Gibson, Joey Lauren Adams, Teresa Hill, Kylie Minogue, Jack Black, Kevin West, Denise Dowse, Dara Tomanovich, Kyle Gass, Rose McGowan, Taylor Negron, Phil LaMarr; ***D:*** Jason Bloom; ***W:*** Scott Marcano, Kip Koenig; ***C:*** Phedon Papamichael; ***M:*** Andrew Gross. Golden Raspberries '96: Worst Actor (Shore).

Bio Hazard & **1985 (R)** A toxic monster needs human flesh to survive and consequently goes on a rampage. **84m/C VHS, DVD.** Angelique Pettyjohn, Carroll Borland, Richard Hench, Aldo Ray; ***D:*** Fred Olen Ray.

Biohazard: The Alien Force & 1/2 **1995 (R)** Reptilian mutant, the result of a genetic experiment gone awry, must be hunted down before it can reproduce.

Sounds like a rip-off of "Species." **88m/C VHS, DVD.** Steve Zurk, Chris Mitchum, Susan Fronsoe, Tom Ferguson, Patrick Moran, John Maynard; ***D:*** Steve Latshaw.

Bionic Ninja **1985** In one of the most confusing and obscure ninja films of all time, a CIA agent must personally take on and defeat a horde of KGB-sponsored ninjas (Russian ninjas?) to get back a stolen scientific discovery. Despite the name there are no cyborgs, or anything to do with bionics. It's actually several other ninja films with the same or similar actors spliced together into a bizarre mish-mash with new footage. **91m/C VHS.** *HK* Mike Abbott; ***D:*** Godfrey Ho; ***W:*** Godfrey Ho; ***C:*** Raymond Chang; ***M:*** Stephen Tsang.

The Bionic Woman **1975** Skydiving accident leaves tennis pro Jaimie Somers crippled and near death. Her bionic buddy, Steve Austin, gets his friends to rebuild her and make her better than she was before. Pilot for the TV series. **96m/C VHS.** Lindsay Wagner, Lee Majors, Richard Anderson, Alan Oppenheimer; ***D:*** Richard (Dick) Moder. **TV**

Bionicle 3: Web of Shadows **2005 (PG)** In this third animated toy commercial, the Toa return to the city of Metra Nui on a rescue mission, only to find it overrun by giant spider like fiends whose paralyzing webs transform their victims. Quickly subdued, the Toa are transformed into the Toa Hardika, odd mismatched-looking machines with new powers that will hopefully give them a chance of completing their mission. **76m/C DVD.** Brian Drummond, Scott McNeil; ***D:*** David Molina, Terry Shakespeare; ***W:*** Henry Gilroy, Bob Thompson, Bret Matthews; ***M:*** Nathan Furst; ***V:*** Kathleen Barr, Paul Dobson, Brian Drummond, Alessandro Juliani, Scott McNeil, Trevor Devall, Christopher Gaze, Tabitha St. Germain, French Tickner.

Biozombie 1/2 **1998** Playing as a mixture of "Mallrats" and "Dawn of the Dead," this Hong Kong import is aimed squarely at a Generation-X audience. The film introduces us to Woody (Jordan Chan) and Bee (Sam Lee), two slackers who work at a video store. While on an errand to pick up their boss's car, they hit a strange pedestrian and take him back to the mall. This stranger turns out to be a zombie, and he soon infects several others. With the mall locked up for the night, Woody and Bee must take it upon themselves to protect the few humans remaining...while doing the least amount of work possible. The film turns into a true rollercoaster ride, as we start with the comedic opening, then move into the action-horror, and finally, a very nihilistic ending. **94m/C DVD.** *HK* Jordan Chan, Sam Lee; ***D:*** Wilson (Wai-Shun) Yip.

The Birch Interval **1978 (PG)** A chronicle of a young Amish girl growing up and experiencing adult passions and fears when she visits her kin in their isolated Pennsylvania community. **104m/C VHS.** Eddie Albert, Rip Torn, Ann Wedgeworth; ***D:*** Delbert Mann; ***W:*** Joanna Crawford.

Bird **1988 (R)** The richly textured, though sadly one-sided biography of jazz sax great Charlie Parker, from his rise to stardom to his premature death via extended heroin use. A remarkably assured, deeply imagined film from Eastwood that never really shows the Bird's genius of creation. The soundtrack features Parker's own solos re-mastered from original recordings. **160m/C VHS, DVD.** Forest Whitaker, Diane Venora, Michael Zelniker, Samuel E. Wright, Keith David, Michael McGuire, James Handy, Damon Whitaker, Morgan Nagler, Peter Crook; ***D:*** Clint Eastwood; ***W:*** Joel Oliansky; ***C:*** Jack N. Green; ***M:*** Lennie Niehaus. Oscars '88: Sound; Cannes '88: Actor (Whitaker); Golden Globes '89: Director (Eastwood); N.Y. Film Critics '88: Support. Actress (Venora).

Bird of Paradise 1/2 **1932** An exotic South Seas romance in which an adventurer is cast onto a remote Polynesian island when his yacht haphazardly sails into a coral reef. There he becomes enamored of an exotic island girl, and nature seems to disapprove. **80m/B VHS, DVD.** Joel McCrea, Dolores Del Rio, Lon Chaney Jr.; ***D:*** King Vidor; ***M:*** Max Steiner.

Bird of Prey 1/2 **1995 (R)** Nick Milev (Milushev) has just been released from a Bulgarian prison for attacking Jonathan Griffith (Chamberlain), the drugs-and-arms dealer who was responsible for the death of Milev's policeman father. But Milev still wants revenge, though matters get complicated by Kily (Tilly), Griffith's naive daughter, with whom he falls in love. Plot's so-so but characters make up for some of the routiness. Filmed on location in Sofia, Bulgaria. **102m/C VHS.** Boyan Milushev, Jennifer Tilly, Richard Chamberlain, Lenny Von Dohlen, Robert Carradine, Lesley Ann Warren; ***D:*** Temistocles Lopez; ***W:*** Boyan Milushev; ***C:*** David Knaus.

Bird on a Wire **1990 (PG-13)** Disappointing action-comedy finds Gibson forced to emerge from a prolonged period under the Witness Protection Program, whereupon he and ex-girlfriend Hawn are pursued by old enemies. Too little action and too little comedy add up to surprisingly dull outing, considering the cast. **110m/C VHS, DVD.** Mel Gibson, Goldie Hawn, David Carradine, Bill Duke, Stephen Tobolowsky, Clyde Kusatsu, Joan Severance, Harry Caesar, John Pyper-Ferguson, Jeff Corey; ***D:*** John Badham; ***W:*** David Seltzer; ***C:*** Robert Primes; ***M:*** Hans Zimmer.

The Bird with the Crystal Plumage 1/2 *L'Ucello dalle Plume di Cristallo; The Phantom of Terror; The Bird with the Glass Feathers; The Gallery Murders* **1970 (PG)** An American writer living in Rome witnesses a murder. He becomes involved in the mystery when the alleged murderer is cleared because the woman believed to be his next victim is shown to be a psychopathic murderer. Vintage Argento mayhem. **98m/C VHS, DVD, Blu-ray Disc.** *IT GE* Tony Musante, Suzy Kendall, Eva Renzi, Enrico Maria Salerno, Mario Adorf, Renato Romano, Reggie Nalder, Werner Peters, Umberto Raho, Dario Argento; ***D:*** Dario Argento; ***W:*** Dario Argento; ***C:*** Vittorio Storaro; ***M:*** Ennio Morricone.

The Birdcage *Birds of a Feather* **1995 (R)** Somewhat overlong but well-played remake of "La Cage aux Folles" features Williams suppressing his usual manic schtick to portray Armand, the subdued half of a longtime gay couple living in Miami. His partner is the ever-hysterical-but-loving drag queen Albert (Lane), whose presence provides a distinct challenge when Armand's son Val (Futterman) announces his engagement to the daughter of family values, right-wing senator Kevin Keeley (Hackman). When the Senator and family arrive for dinner, Armand tries to play it straight while Albert opts for a matronly mom impersonation (think Barbara Bush). Highlights include Armand's initial attempts to teach Albert to be butch (walk like John Wayne) and Hackman congoing in drag. **120m/C VHS, DVD.** Robin Williams, Nathan Lane, Gene Hackman, Dianne Wiest, Hank Azaria, Dan Futterman, Christine Baranski, Calista Flockhart, Tom McGowan; ***D:*** Mike Nichols; ***W:*** Elaine May; ***C:*** Emmanuel Lubezki; ***M:*** Mark Mothersbaugh, Jonathan Tunick. Screen Actors Guild '96: Cast.

Birdman of Alcatraz **1962** Robert Stroud, convicted of two murders and sentenced to life imprisonment on the Island, becomes an internationally accepted authority on birds. Lovingly told, with stunning performance from Lancaster, and exceptionally fine work from the supporting cast. The confinement of Stroud's prison cell makes the film seem claustrophobic and tedious at times, just as the imprisonment must have been. Ritter played Stroud's mother, who never stops trying to get him out of prison. **143m/B VHS, DVD.** Burt Lancaster, Karl Malden, Thelma Ritter, Betty Field, Neville Brand, Edmond O'Brien, Hugh Marlowe, Telly Savalas; ***D:*** John Frankenheimer; ***W:*** Guy Trosper; ***C:*** Burnett Guffey, Robert Krasker; ***M:*** Elmer Bernstein. British Acad. '62: Actor (Lancaster).

The Birds 1/2 **1963 (PG-13)** Hitchcock attempted to top the success of "Psycho" with this terrifying tale of Man versus Nature, in which Nature alights, one by one, on the trees of Bodega Bay to stage a bloody act of revenge upon the civilized world. Only Hitchcock can twist the harmless into the horrific while avoiding the ridiculous; this is perhaps his most brutal film, and one of the cinema's purest, horrifying portraits of apocalypse. Based on a short story by Daphne Du Maurier; screenplay by novelist Evan Hunter (aka Ed McBain). **120m/C VHS, DVD.** Rod Taylor, Tippi Hedren, Jessica Tandy, Veronica Cartwright, Suzanne Pleshette, Ethel Griffies, Charles McGraw, Ruth McDevitt, Lonny (Lonnie) Chapman, Joe Mantell, Morgan Brittany, Alfred Hitchcock; ***D:*** Alfred Hitchcock; ***W:*** Evan Hunter; ***C:*** Robert Burks; ***M:*** Bernard Herrmann.

The Birds 2: Land's End **WOOF!** **1994 (R)** Unfortunate rip-off of the Hitchcock fright classic. Killer seagulls begin attacking the inhabitants of east coast Gull Island. Seems they're tired of being oil slick victims. Hedren's the town shopkeeper in a role that's nothing like the one she played in the original. Definitely for the birds—even the director refuses to acknowledge it by officially using the film industry pseudonym "Alan Smithee." Made for TV. **87m/C VHS.** Brad Johnson, Chelsea Field, Tippi Hedren, James Naughton, Jan Rubes, Megan Gallagher; ***D:*** Rick Rosenthal; ***W:*** Jim Wheat, Ken Wheat. **TV**

Birds & the Bees **1956** A millionaire falls in love with an alluring card shark, and then calls it all off when he learns of her profession, only to fall in love with her again when she disguises herself. A remake—and poor shade—of Preston Sturge's 1941 classic "The Lady Eve." **94m/C VHS.** Mitzi Gaynor, David Niven, George Gobel, Reginald Gardiner, Hans Conried; ***D:*** Norman Taurog; ***W:*** Sidney Sheldon.

Birds of America **2008 (R)** College prof Morrie Tanager (Perry) and his wife Betty (Graham) lead a highly controlled life in reaction to Morrie's family history of mental instability. Just as it seems that Morrie will achieve his dreams of tenure, he's forced back into caretaker mode by his depressed, homeless brother Jay (Foster) and his promiscuous, booze-swilling sister Ida (Goodwin), who both move in. Betty's tolerance is fraying and Morrie has to decide how he's going to live his life. **85m/C DVD.** Matthew Perry, Lauren Graham, Ben Foster, Ginnifer Goodwin, Gary Wilmes, Hilary Swank, Zoe Kravitz; ***D:*** Craig Lucas; ***W:*** Elyse Friedman; ***C:*** Yaron Orbach; ***M:*** Ahrin Mishan.

Birds of Prey **1972** Action film pits an ex-WWII army pilot against a group of kidnapping thieves in an airborne chopper chase. **81m/C VHS, DVD.** David Janssen, Ralph Meeker, Elayne Heilveil; ***D:*** William A. Graham; ***C:*** Jordan Cronenweth. **TV**

Birdy 1/2 **1984 (R)** An adaptation of the William Wharton novel about two Philadelphia youths, one with normal interests, the other obsessed with birds, and their eventual involvement in the Vietnam War, wrecking one physically and the other mentally. A hypnotic, evocative film, with a compelling Peter Gabriel soundtrack. **120m/C VHS, DVD.** Matthew Modine, Nicolas Cage, John Harkins, Sandy Baron, Karen Young, Bruno Kirby; ***D:*** Alan Parker; ***W:*** Jack Behr, Sandy Kroopf; ***M:*** Peter Gabriel. Cannes '85: Grand Jury Prize.

Birgitt Haas Must Be Killed 1/2 **1983** A ruthless secret agent (Noiret) plots to murder a German female terrorist and make it appear that her boyfriend was the killer. Never quite hits the mark, despite novel premise and strong cast. **105m/C VHS.** Philippe Noiret, Jean Rochefort, Elisabeth (Lisa) Kreuzer; ***D:*** Laurent Heynemann.

Birth **2004 (R)** Creepy psychological thriller finds widowed Anna (Kidman) finally making a commitment to marry Joseph (Huston) ten years after her husband Sean's death. That is until a strange 10-year-old, also named Sean (Bright), turns up insisting that Anna cannot remarry because he is her spouse. Sean is impervious to any suggestion otherwise and his very insistence comes to convince the emotionally fragile woman. None of this goes over well with Anna's imperious mother (Bacall) or the rest of her family, let alone her frustrated fiance. Various explanations are offered and director Glazer elegantly camouflages plot holes. Kidman, with her severe pixie haircut, somewhat resembles Mia Farrow in "Rosemary's Baby," but one thing you can be certain of is here, the devil didn't do it. **100m/C DVD.** *US* Nicole Kidman, Cameron Bright, Danny Huston, Lauren Bacall, Arliss Howard, Alison Elliot, Anne Heche, Peter Stormare, Ted Levine, Cara Seymour, Zoe Caldwell, Milo Addica; ***D:*** Jonathan Glazer; ***W:*** Milo Addica, Jonathan Glazer, Jean-Claude Carriere; ***C:*** Harris Savides; ***M:*** Alexandre Desplat.

The Birth of a Nation *The Clansman* **1915** Lavish Civil War epic in which Griffith virtually invented the basics of film grammar. Gish and Walthall have some of the most moving scenes ever filmed and the masterful battle choreography brought the art of cinematography to new heights. Griffith's positive attitude toward the KKK notwithstanding, this was the first feature length silent, and it brought credibility to an entire industry. Based on the play "The Clansman" and the book "The Leopard's Spots" by Thomas Dixon, it is still a rouser, and of great historical interest. Silent with music score. Also available in a 124-minute version. **175m/B VHS, DVD.** Lillian Gish, Mae Marsh, Henry B. Walthall, Ralph Lewis, Robert "Bobbie" Harron, George Siegmann, Joseph Henabery, Spottiswoode Aitken, George Beranger, Mary Alden, Josephine Crowell, Elmer Clifton, Walter Long, Howard Gaye, Miriam Cooper, John Ford, Sam De Grasse, Maxfield Stanley, Donald Crisp, Raoul Walsh, Erich von Stroheim, Eugene Pallette, Wallace Reid; ***D:*** D.W. Griffith; ***W:*** D.W. Griffith, Frank E. Woods; ***C:*** Billy (G.W.) Bitzer; ***M:*** D.W. Griffith. AFI '98: Top 100, Natl. Film Reg. '92.

Birth of the Blues 1/2 **1941** Songman Crosby starts a band in New Orleans in the midst of the jazz boom. Help from partner Martin and real-life trombonist Teagarden, with comic relief from Eddie "Rochester" Anderson, make for a fun-filled story. Plot is riddled with some unbelievable gangster scenes, but the music and laughs will keep you amused. In B&W with color segments. ♫ St. Louis Blues; St. James Infirmary; Melancholy Baby; Birth of the Blues. **76m/B VHS, DVD.** Bing Crosby, Mary Martin, Brian Donlevy, Eddie Anderson, J. Carrol Naish, Cecil Kellaway, Warren Hymer, Horace McMahon, Carolyn Lee, Jack Teagarden; ***D:*** Victor Schertzinger; ***W:*** Harry Tugend, Walter DeLeon; ***C:*** William Mellor; ***M:*** Robert Emmett Dolan.

Birthday Boy **1985** A cable comedy about a buffoonish salesman's 30th birthday, on which he takes an ill-fated business trip. Written by Belushi. **33m/C VHS.** James Belushi; ***D:*** Claude Conrad; ***W:*** James Belushi. **CABLE**

Birthday Girl **2002 (R)** Love story cum actioner stars Chaplin as a timid London bank clerk, John, and Kidman as Nadia, his mysterious and sexy online Russian mail-order bride with a secret. Nadia doesn't speak English, but the two begin to speak the international language anyway. Afraid, intrigued, then tickled with his Soviet missus who brings some color into his dull, drab life, John hardly has time to wallow in his new-found bliss when he's beset by Russian baddies (Frenchmen Kassovitz and Cassel) claiming to be Nadia's relatives, who show up on his doorstep one day. Kidman shows her range, however, and reportedly learned Russian for the film. Decent turn from the Butterworth clan, who also produced the hip debut film "Mojo." **93m/C VHS, DVD.** *US GB* Nicole Kidman, Ben Chaplin, Vincent Cassel, Mathieu Kassovitz, Kate Evans; ***D:*** Jez Butterworth; ***W:*** Jez Butterworth, Tom Butterworth; ***C:*** Oliver Stapleton; ***M:*** Stephen Warbeck.

The Bishop's Wife **1947** Episcopalian biship Henry (Niven) is praying to find the money to build a new church but his faith is shaky and his marriage to Julia (Young) even more so. But his prayers are answered (although Henry doesn't know it) in the form of angel Dudley (Grant), who's sent down to earth at Christmas to help work things out. Excellent performances by the cast make this an entertaining outing. Based on the novel by Robert Nathan. **109m/B VHS, DVD.** Cary Grant, Loretta Young, David Niven, Monty Woolley, Elsa Lanchester, James Gleason, Gladys Cooper, Regis Toomey; ***D:*** Henry Koster; ***W:*** Leonardo Bercovici, Robert Sherwood; ***C:*** Gregg Toland; ***M:*** Hugo Friedhofer. Oscars '47: Sound.

The Bitch **WOOF!** **1978 (R)** High-camp follies are the rule in this lustful continuation of "The Stud" as it follows the erotic adventures of a beautiful divorcee playing sex games for high stakes on the international playgrounds of high society. A collaborative effort by the sisters Collins: written by Jackie, with sister Joan well cast in the title role. **90m/C VHS, DVD.** *GB* Joan Collins, Kenneth Haigh, Michael Coby, Ian Hendry, Carolyn Seymour, Sue Lloyd, John Ratzenberger; ***D:*** Gerry O'Hara.

Bite the Bullet 1/2 **1975 (PG)** Moralistic western tells of a grueling 600-mile horse race where the participants reluctantly develop respect for one another. Unheralded upon release and shot in convincing epic style by Harry Stradling, Jr. Excellent cast. **131m/C VHS, DVD.** Gene Hackman, James Coburn, Candice Bergen, Dabney Coleman, Jan-Michael Vincent, Ben Johnson, Ian Bannen, Paul Stewart, Sally Kirkland, Mario Arteaga; ***D:*** Richard Brooks; ***W:*** Richard Brooks; ***C:*** Harry Stradling Jr.; ***M:*** Alex North.

Bitter Harvest **1981** Emmy-nominated TV movie concerning a dairy farmer frantically trying to discover what is mysteriously killing off his herd. Howard is excellent as the farmer battling the bureaucracy to find the truth. Based on a true story. **98m/C VHS.** Ron Howard, Art Carney, Tarah Nutter, Richard Dysart, Barry Corbin, Jim Haynie, David Knell; ***D:*** Roger Young. **TV**

Bitter Harvest **1993 (R)** Rubin and Kensit are the femme fatales who turn their considerable wiles on the innocent Baldwin. He's more than happy to be their lover but does he want to be their victim as well? **98m/C VHS.** Stephen Baldwin, Patsy Kensit, Jennifer Rubin, Adam Baldwin, M. Emmet Walsh; ***D:*** Duane Clark; ***W:*** Randall Fontana; ***C:*** Remi Adefarasin.

Bitter Moon **1992 (R)** Polanski effort looks promising, but ultimately disappoints. Bored British couple (Grant and Scott Thomas) meet up with sexual deviants (Coyote and Seigner, aka Mrs. Polanski) on a cruise and learn that passion and cruelty often share the same path to destruction. Masquerades as high class art, but whenever substance is lacking expect a silly, kinky sex scene. Needless to say, there isn't much substance, so erotic mischief abounds. Scott Thomas manages to hold her own, but Coyote is almost embarrassingly over the top. Based on the Pascal Bruckner novel "Lunes de Fiel." **139m/C VHS, DVD.** Peter Coyote, Emmanuelle Seigner, Hugh Grant, Kristin Scott Thomas, Stockard Channing, Victor Banerjee, Sophie Patel; ***D:*** Roman Polanski; ***W:*** Roman Polanski, Gerard Brach, John Brownjohn; ***C:*** Tonino Delli Colli; ***M:*** Vangelis.

Bitter Rice *Riso Amaro* **1949** Mangano became a star with her sultry performance about survival in postwar Italy. She scrapes by, working in the rice fields of the Po Valley, loved by the down-to-earth Vallone, who provides her with little excitement. Gassman is the rotten-to-the-core thief who meets up with Mangano while he's running from the police. He mistreats her, she steals his money and betrays her friends, and both destroy each other. In Italian with English subtitles. **96m/C VHS.** *IT* Silvana Mangano, Vittorio Gassman, Raf Vallone, Doris Dowling; ***D:*** Guiseppe de Santis; ***W:*** Guiseppe de Santis, Carlo Lizzani, Gianni Puccini; ***C:*** Otello Martelli; ***M:*** Goffredo Petrassi.

Bitter Sugar *Azucar Amarga* **1996** Young, idealistic communist Gustavo (Lavan) is a Havana university student who still believes that the Castro regime can make things better. His rock musician brother Bobby (Villanueva) is a radical, defying government policies, and his psychiatrist father Tomas (Gutierrez) makes more money playing piano at a tourist hotel than in his practice. But Gustavo's eyes are opened, not only by his family situtation, but when he falls in love with cynical dancer Yolanda (Vilan), who longs to escape to Miami. Serious politics bolstered by excellent performances and sharp cinematography. Spanish with subtitles. **102m/B VHS, DVD.** *CU* Rene Lavan, Mayte Vilan, Miguel Gutierrez, Larry Villanueva; ***D:*** Leon Ichaso; ***W:*** Leon Ichaso, Orestes Matacena; ***C:*** Claudio Chea; ***M:*** Manuel Tejada.

Bitter Sweet **1/2 1933** Tragic tale of a woman who finally marries the man she loves, only to find that he is a compulsive gambler. Written by Coward, adapted from his operetta. **76m/B VHS.** *GB* Anna Neagle, Fernand Gravey, Esme Percy, Clifford Heatherley, Hugh Williams; ***D:*** Herbert Wilcox; ***W:*** Noel Coward.

Bitter Sweet **1940** The second version of the Noel Coward operetta, about young romance in 1875 Vienna. Creaky and overrated, but the lush Technicolor and Coward standards help to compensate. ♫Ziguener; I'll See You Again. **94m/C VHS.** Jeanette MacDonald, Nelson Eddy, George Sanders, Felix Bressart, Ian Hunter, Sig Rumann, Herman Bing, Fay Holden, Curt Bois, Edward Ashley; ***D:*** Woodbridge S. Van Dyke; ***W:*** Lesser Samuels, Noel Coward.

Bitter Sweet **1998 (R)** Everhart spends four years in the big house after being tricked by her boyfriend into participating in a robbery. All she wants when she gets out is to get revenge on the lowlife and she gets the opportunity when approached by cop Russo, who's looking to bring down her ex-beau's gangster boss (Roberts). **96m/C VHS, DVD.** Angie Everhart, James Russo, Eric Roberts, Brian Wimmer; ***D:*** Luca Bercovici. **VIDEO**

The Bitter Tea of General Yen **1933** Stanwyck arrives in Shanghai to marry a missionary (Gordon) during the threatening days of China's civil war. Unexpectedly swept into the arms of an infamous warlord (Asher), she becomes fascinated, although his attempts to seduce her fail. She even remains with him while his enemies close in. Exotic and poetic, if melodramatic by today's standards. The interracial aspects were considered very daring for their time. Adapted from the book by Grace Zaring Stone. **89m/B VHS.** Barbara Stanwyck, Nils Asther, Gavin Gordon, Walter Connolly, Lucien Littlefield, Toshia Mori, Richard Loo, Clara Blandick; ***D:*** Frank Capra; ***W:*** Edward Paramore.

The Bitter Tears of Petra von Kant **1/2** *Die Bitteren Traenen der Petra von Kant* **1972** Dark German story of lesbian love, the fashion world, obsession and anger. Claustrophobic settings and slow pace may frustrate some viewers. In German with English subtitles. **124m/C VHS, DVD.** *GE* Margit Carstensen, Hanna Schygulla, Irm Hermann, Eva Mattes; ***D:*** Rainer Werner Fassbinder; ***W:*** Rainer Werner Fassbinder; ***C:*** Michael Ballhaus.

Bitter Vengeance **1994 (R)** Security guard Jack Westford (Greenwood) pulls off a bank heist with his lover Isabella (Hocking) and plans to frame his wife Annie (Madsen) for the crime. Only Annie finds out and sets out to get them before the police get her. **90m/C VHS.** Virginia Madsen, Bruce Greenwood, Kristen Dalton, Eddie Velez, Gordon Jump, Carlos Gomez, Tim Russ; ***D:*** Stuart Cooper; ***W:*** Pablo F. Fenjves; ***M:*** David Michael Frank. **CABLE**

Bittersweet Love **1/2 1976 (PG)** Two young people fall in love and marry, only to have the bride's mother and the groom's father confess a 30-year-old affair, disclosing that the two newlyweds are actually half-siblings. **92m/C VHS.** Lana Turner, Robert Lansing, Celeste Holm, Robert Alda, Meredith Baxter; ***D:*** David Miller.

Bix **1990** Based on the brief life of legendary Jazz Age cornetist Leon Bix Beiderbecke, who died at age 28. Story unfolds in flashbacks, through friend Joe Venuti memories of the dissipated genius and the music he created with Hoagy Carmichael, Pee Wee Russell, Paul Whiteman, and others. **100m/C VHS.** *IT* Bryant Weeks, Emile Levisetti, Mark Collver, Sally Groth; ***D:*** Pupi Avati; ***W:*** Pupi Avati, Antonio Avati, Lino Patruno.

Bizarre **1987** When a wife escapes her perverse, psychologically threatening marriage, she finds her husband still haunts her literally and figuratively, and plots psychological revenge. Dubbed. **93m/C VHS, DVD.** *IT* Florence Guerin, Luciano Bartoli, Robert Egon Spechtenhauser, Stefano Sabelli; ***D:*** Giuliana Gamba.

Bizarre Bizarre *Drole de Drama* **1939** A mystery writer is accused of murder and disappears, only to return in disguise to try to clear his name. Along the way, a number of French comedians are introduced with a revue of comedy-farce sketches that include slapstick, burlesque, black humor, and comedy of the absurd. In French with English subtitles. **90m/B VHS, DVD.** *FR* Louis Jouvet, Michel Simon, Francoise Rosay, Jean-Pierre Aumont, Nadine Vogel, Henri Guisol, Jenny Burnay; ***D:*** Marcel Carne; ***W:*** Jacques Prevert; ***C:*** Eugen Shuftan; ***M:*** Maurice Jaubert.

The Black Abbot **1963** A mysterious black-hooded figure is seen entering a ruined Abbey tower that leads to a country house with buried treasure. Based on an Edgar Wallace story. **95m/C VHS.** *GE* Joachim Fuchsberger, Dieter Borsche, Gritt Bottcher, Eva Scholtz, Franz Gottlieb; ***D:*** Franz Gottlieb.

Black and White **1999 (R)** Director Toback attempts to investigate white kids' facsination with black hip-hop culture by creating an intriguing combination of pseudo-documentary and urban melodrama, with cameos and performances by professional celebrities alongside professional actors. In the more effective part of the film, Shields is a documentary filmmaker asking rich white kids why they're into hip-hop. This section also includes Robert Downey as her gay husband hitting on Mike Tyson (playing himself in one of the film's strongest scenes). The part that doesn't work as well is the more conventional storyline (which seems added to satisfy studio executives looking for straight narrative) involving an undercover cop (Stiller) bribing college basketball star Dean (Houston) to throw a game in an attempt to get at Dean's best friend Rich (Power), a drug kingpin turned rap mogul. While the parts don't add up to an entirely satisfying whole, the journey is worth the interesting ride. **98m/C VHS, DVD.** Scott Caan, Robert Downey Jr., Stacy Edwards, Gaby Hoffman, Jared Leto, Marla Maples, Joe Pantoliano, Brooke Shields, Power, Claudia Schiffer, William Lee Scott, Ben Stiller, Eddie Kaye Thomas, Elijah Wood, Mike Tyson, James Toback, Allan Houston, Kidada Jones, Bijou Phillips, Raekwon; ***D:*** James Toback; ***W:*** James Toback; ***C:*** David Ferrara.

Black & White **1/2 1999 (R)** Rookie cop Chris O'Brien (Cochrane) is partnered with tough veteran female officer Nora Hugosian (Gershon), who's known for both her sexiness and her ruthless style. The two begin an affair while searching for a serial killer. And then the rookie comes across some evidence that seems to implicate his partner in the crimes. **97m/C VHS, DVD.** Gina Gershon, Rory Cochrane, Ron Silver, Alison Eastwood, Marshall Bell; ***D:*** Yuri Zeltser; ***W:*** Yuri Zeltser, Leon Zeltser; ***C:*** Phil Parmet.

Black and White As Day and Night **1978** A man's talent for the game of chess becomes a destructive obsession. In German with English subtitles. **103m/C VHS.** Bruno Ganz, Rene Deltgen, Ljuba Tadic, Gila von Weitershausen; ***D:*** Wolfgang Petersen; ***W:*** Jochen Wedegartner, Karl Heinz Willschrei; ***C:*** Jorg-Michael Baldenius; ***M:*** Klaus Doldinger.

Black and White in Color *La Victoire en Chantant* **1976 (PG)** Award-winning satire about a French soldier at an African outpost, who, upon hearing the news of the beginning of WWI, takes it upon himself to attack a neighboring German fort. Calamity ensues. In French, with English subtitles. **100m/C VHS, DVD.** *FR* Jean Carmet, Jacques Dufilho, Catherine Rouvel, Jacques Spiesser, Dora Doll, Jacques Perrin; ***D:*** Jean-Jacques Annaud; ***W:*** Georges Conchon, Jean-Jacques Annaud; ***M:*** Pierre Bachelet. Oscars '76: Foreign Film.

Black Angel **1946** Catherine Bennett (Vincent) tries to clear the name of estranged husband Kirk (Phillips), who's accused of murdering his lover, blackmailing chanteuse Mavis Marlowe (Dowling). Catherine enlists the aid of Mavis' husband, drunken songwriter Martin Blair (Duryea), whom she suspects actually did the deed. Another suspect is sleazy nightclub owner Marko (Lorre), where the duo get a job to check things out. Blair falls for Catherine and goes on another bender when she rejects him, as Kirk's execution day draws ever closer. Atmospheric noir is based on the novel by Cornell Woolrich. **80m/B VHS, DVD.** June Vincent, Dan Duryea, Peter Lorre, Broderick Crawford, John Phillips, Constance Dowling, Wallace Ford, Hobart Cavanaugh, Freddie (Fred) Steele; ***D:*** Roy William Neill; ***W:*** Roy Chanslor; ***C:*** Paul Ivano; ***M:*** Frank Skinner.

Black Arrow *Black Arrow Strikes* **1948** Original adventure film of the famous Robert Louis Stevenson novel. Upon return from 16th century's War of the Roses, a young man must avenge his father's murder by following a trail of clues in the form of black arrows. Well made and fun. **76m/B VHS, DVD.** Louis Hayward, Janet Blair, George Macready, Edgar Buchanan, Paul Cavanagh; ***D:*** Gordon Douglas.

The Black Arrow **1984** Exiled bowman returns to England to avenge the injustices of a villainous nobleman. Cable version of the Robert Louis Stevenson medieval romp is not as well done as the 1948 adaptation. **93m/C VHS.** Oliver Reed, Benedict Taylor, Georgia Slowe, Stephan Chase, Donald Pleasence; ***D:*** John Hough. **CABLE**

The Black Balloon **2009 (PG-13)** All Thomas wants is a normal adolescence. But when he and his oddball family, including his autistic brother, Charlie, move to a new neighborhood, his vulnerabilities and familial eccentricities are exposed, specifically to Jackie, the object of his kept affections. It isn't until swimming class and mandated mouth-to-mouth practice, that their mutual feelings are exposed. **97m/C DVD.** Luke Ford, Toni Collette, Erik Thomson, Rhys Wakefield; ***D:*** Elissa Down; ***W:*** Elissa Down, Jimmy Jack.

Black Beauty **1946** In this adaptation of Anna Sewell's familiar novel, a young girl develops a kindred relationship with an extraordinary horse. **74m/B VHS.** Mona Freeman, Richard Denning, Evelyn Ankers; ***D:*** Max Nosseck.

Black Beauty **1971 (G)** International remake of the classic horse story by Anna Sewell. **105m/C VHS, DVD.** *GB GE SP* Mark Lester, Walter Slezak; ***D:*** James Hill; ***C:*** Chris Menges; ***M:*** Lionel Bart.

Black Beauty **1994 (G)** Remake of the classic Anna Sewell children's novel about an oft-sold horse whose life has its shares of ups and downs. Timeless tale still brings children and adults to tears. Six-year-old quarterhorse named Justin gives a nuanced portrayal as the Black Beauty, recalling Olivier in "Hamlet." Directorial debut of "Secret Garden" screenwriter Thompson. **88m/C VHS, DVD.** Andrew Knott, Sean Bean, David Thewlis, Jim Carter, Alun Armstrong, Eleanor Bron, Peter Cook, Peter Davison, John McEnery, Nicholas Jones; ***D:*** Caroline Thompson; ***W:*** Caroline Thompson; ***C:*** Alex Thomson.

The Black Belly of the Tarantula *La Tarantola dal Ventre Nero* **1971** Inspector Tellini (Giannini) investigates a series of murders where the victims are first paralyzed with wasp venom before being cut open while they're still alive. And the connection between the victims seems to be a beauty spa. Italian with subtitles. **89m/C DVD.** *IT* Giancarlo Giannini, Claudine Auger, Barbara Bouchet, Stefania Sandrelli, Barbara Bach, Rossella Falk; ***D:*** Paolo Cavara; ***W:*** Marcello Danon, Lucille Laks; ***C:*** Marcello Gatti; ***M:*** Ennio Morricone.

Black Belt **1992 (R)** A private detective is hired to protect a rock star from a fanatic Vietnam vet. **80m/C VHS, DVD.** Don "The Dragon" Wilson, Richard Beymer, Alan Blumenfeld, Matthias Hues; ***D:*** Charles Philip Moore; ***W:*** Charles Philip Moore.

Black Belt **1/2** *Kuro-Obi* **2007** Set in Japan in the 1930s, presents a Karate dojo being dismantled by the Japanese military. The master dies before choosing a successor, and his top three students must face both the military and each other as they try to live up to the standards they believe in, and inherit their master's school. Unfortunately their philosophies are quite different, and a clash is inevitable. The main actors are all accomplished Karate practitioners, and the presentation of martial arts is far more realistic than recent wire fu efforts. **95m/C DVD.** *JP* Tatsuya Naka, Akihito Yagi, Yuji Suzuki; ***D:*** Shunich Nagasaki; ***W:*** Joji Iida; ***C:*** Masato Kaneko; ***M:*** Naoki Sato.

Black Belt Jones **1974 (R)** Martial arts expert fights the mob to save a school of self-defense in Los Angeles' Watts district. **87m/C VHS.** Jim Kelly, Gloria Hendry, Scatman Crothers; ***D:*** Robert Clouse.

Black Bikers from Hell **1/2** *Black Angels* **1970 (R)** Black gang-members infiltrate and wreak havoc on their rivals. Who can stop these brutal young men? Cast with real bikers and biker chicks. **87m/C VHS.** John King III, Des Roberts, Linda Jackson,

James Whitworth, James Young-El, Clancy Syrko, Beverly Gardner; *D:* Laurence Merrick; *W:* Laurence Merrick.

Black Bird **1975 (PG)** In this satiric "sequel" to "The Maltese Falcon," detective Sam Spade, Jr. searches for the mysterious black falcon statuette that caused his father such trouble. Features appearances by Elisha Cook Jr. and Lee Patrick, who starred in the 1941 classic "The Maltese Falcon" with Humphrey Bogart. **98m/C VHS.** George Segal, Stephane Audran, Lionel Stander, Lee Patrick, Elisha Cook Jr., Connie Kreski; *D:* David Giler.

Black Book 1/2 *Zwartboek* **2006 (R)** Wow—Verhoeven directs his first film in his native Netherlands in 20 years and comes up with an unsentimental WWII thriller with a compelling lead performance by van Houten. In 1944, Jewish Rachel has been hiding out in the country until she joins a Dutch resistance unit. After some cosmetic changes, and now renamed Ellis, she's assigned to bed Gestapo chief Ludwig Muentze (Koch) and ferret out some Nazi secrets. What Rachel/Ellis doesn't mean to do is fall in love. The story twists and turns (eventually ending up in Israel in 1956) but is definitely worth the journey. English, Dutch, German, and Hebrew with subtitles. **145m/C DVD, Blu-ray Disc.** *GB BE NL* Sebastian Koch, Thom Hoffman, Halina Reijn, Derek de Lint, Carice van Houten, Waldemar Kobus, Christian Berkel, Peter Blok; *D:* Paul Verhoeven; *W:* Paul Verhoeven, Gerard Soeteman; *C:* Karl Walter Lindenlaub; *M:* Anne Dudley.

Black Box Affair 1/2 **1966** An American secret agent must find a black box lost in a B-52 plane crash before it falls into the wrong hands. **95m/C VHS.** *IT SP* Craig Hill, Teresa Gimpera, Luis Martin, Jorge (George) Rigaud; *D:* James B. Harris.

Black Brigade *Carter's Army* **1969** Pryor and Williams star in this low budget movie as leaders of an all-black outfit assigned to a suicide mission behind Nazi lines during WWII. Their force wreaks havoc and earns them the respect of military higher-ups. Lots of action and climactic finish. **90m/C VHS, DVD.** Stephen Boyd, Robert Hooks, Susan Oliver, Roosevelt "Rosie" Grier, Moses Gunn, Richard Pryor, Billy Dee Williams; *D:* George McCowan; *W:* Aaron Spelling; *M:* Fred Steiner.

Black Cadillac **2003** A night of partying goes awry when a bum car strands three buddies in the frigid, lonely mountains. Their luck seems to change after a deputy sheriff rescues them, but relief turns to terror as they find a mysterious black Cadillac on their tail. Effective entry in the "mysterious spooky car" genre. **92m/C VHS, DVD.** Randy Quaid, Kiersten Warren, Shane Johnson, Josh Hammond, Jason Dohring, Adam Vernier; *D:* John Murlowski; *W:* John Murlowski, Will Aldis; *C:* S. Douglas Smith; *M:* Chris Bell. **VIDEO**

Black Caesar **1973 (R)** A small-time hood climbs the ladder to be the head of a Harlem crime syndicate. Music by James Brown. Followed by the sequel "Hell Up in Harlem." **92m/C VHS, DVD.** Fred Williamson, Julius W. Harris, Val Avery, Art Lund, Gloria Hendry, James Dixon; *D:* Larry Cohen; *W:* Larry Cohen; *C:* Fenton Hamilton, James Signorelli; *M:* James Brown.

The Black Camel **1931** In the 2nd Charlie Chan mystery, set (and filmed) in Honolulu, the detective (Oland) investigates the murder of movie starlet Sheila Fane. Lugosi plays a psychic. Based on the Earl Derr Bigger's novel. **71m/B DVD.** Warner Oland, Bela Lugosi, Robert Young, Victor Varconi, J.M. Kerrigan, Marjorie White, Sally Eilers, Dorothy Revier, Dwight Frye; *D:* Hamilton McFadden; *W:* Barry Connors, Philip Klein; *C:* Joseph August, Daniel B. Clark; *M:* Samuel Kaylin.

The Black Castle **1952** MacNally plays an 18th-century Austrian count whose guests tend to disappear after a visit. This happens to two of Greene's friends and he decides to investigate. Uninspired and melodramatic, not enough horror. Karloff doesn't have enough to do. **81m/B VHS.** Richard Greene, Boris Karloff, Stephen McNally, Rita (Paula) Corday, Lon Chaney Jr., John Hoyt; *D:* Nathan "Jerry" Juran.

The Black Cat 1/2 *House of Doom; Vanishing Body* **1934** The first of the Boris and Bela pairings stands up well years after release. Polished and taut, with fine sets and interesting acting. Confrontation between architect and devil worshipper acts as plot, with strange twists. Worth a look. **65m/B VHS, DVD.** Boris Karloff, Bela Lugosi, David Manners, Julie Bishop, Lucille Lund, Henry Armetta, Egon Brecher, Albert Conti, Harry Cording, John Carradine; *D:* Edgar G. Ulmer; *W:* Edgar G. Ulmer, Peter Ruric; *C:* John Mescall; *M:* Heinz Roemheld.

The Black Cat 1/2 **1941** Wealthy Henrietta Winslow (Loftus) has left her estate to her greedy grandchildren but only after her faithful housekeeper Abigail (Sondergaard) and all her beloved cats die. Naturally, strange and murderous events begin occurring. Not to be confused with the 1934 classic horror film of the same title. **71m/B VHS.** Basil Rathbone, Hugh Herbert, Gale Sondergaard, Broderick Crawford, Bela Lugosi, Gladys Cooper, Anne Gwynne, Cecilia Loftus, Claire Dodd, John Eldridge, Alan Ladd; *D:* Albert Rogell; *W:* Robert Lees, Frederic Rinaldo, Eric Taylor, Robert Neville; *C:* Stanley Cortez.

The Black Cat WOOF! *Il Gatto Nero* **1981** Spaghetti splatter-meister Fulci, best known for his unabashed ripoffs "Zombie" and "Gates of Hell," tones down the gore this time in a vaguely Poe-ish tale of a medium with some marbles loose (Magee) whose kitty provides the temporary habitat for spirits its master calls up. The dreary English village setting and the downright myopic camera work add up to an oppressive viewing experience. **92m/C VHS, DVD.** *IT GB* Patrick Magee, Mimsy Farmer, David Warbeck, Al Cliver, Dagmar Lassander, Geoffrey Copleston, Daniela Dorio; *D:* Lucio Fulci; *W:* Lucio Fulci, Biagio Proietti; *C:* Sergio Salvati; *M:* Pino Donaggio.

Black Cat 1/2 **1990** Filmmakers find lots of action in a haunted house. Chock full of references to the works of spaghetti horror dons Mario Bava and Dario Argento. **120m/C VHS.** *IT* Caroline Munro, Brett Halsey; *D:* Lewis (Luigi Cozzi) Coates; *W:* Lewis (Luigi Cozzi) Coates.

Black Cat Run **1998 (R)** Race car driver's girlfriend is abducted and then he gets involved with a psycho deputy. Lots of action. **88m/C VHS, DVD.** Patrick Muldoon, Amelia Heinle, Russell Means, Kevin J. O'Connor, Peter Greene, Jake Busey; *D:* D.J. Caruso; *W:* Frank Darabont, Douglas Venturelli; *C:* Bing Sokolsky; *M:* Jeff Rona. **CABLE**

Black Cat, White Cat **1998** Emir Kusturica's rambling tale of scheming Gypsies who live on the banks of the Danube river is a mixture of slapstick humor, folk tales and music. The cheesily dressed and mostly nonprofessional actors light up a plot involving a cargo of fuel, an arranged marriage, and a corpse on ice. Non-political (and much lighter) follow-up to Kusturica's Palme d'Or winning "Underground." Serbo-Croatian and Romany with subtitles. **129m/C VHS.** Bajram Severdzan, Florijan Ajdini, Salija Ibraimova, Branka Katic, Zabit Memedov, Sabri Sulejman, Jasar Destani, Srdan Todorovic, Ljubica Adzovic, Miki (Predrag) Manojlovic; *D:* Emir Kusturica; *W:* Gordan Mihic; *C:* Thierry Arbogast; *M:* D. Nele Karajilic, Vajislav Aralica, Dejo Sparavalo.

The Black Cauldron 1/2 **1985 (PG)** Disney's 25th full-length animated movie follows the adventures of pig-keeper Taran, who discovers his psychic pig Hen Wen is the key to keeping a magical cauldron out of the hands of the evil Horned King. Based on the "Chronicles of Prydain" novels by Lloyd Alexander. **82m/C VHS, DVD.** *D:* Ted Berman, Richard Rich; *W:* Ted Berman, Richard Rich; *M:* Elmer Bernstein; *V:* Grant Bardsley, Susan Sheridan, John Hurt, Freddie Jones, Nigel Hawthorne, John Byner, Arthur Malet; *Nar:* John Huston.

Black Christmas 1/2 *Silent Night, Evil Night; Stranger in the House* **1975 (R)** A college sorority is besieged by an axe-murderer over the holidays. **98m/C VHS, DVD.** *CA* Andrea Martin, Art Hindle, Olivia Hussey, Keir Dullea, Margot Kidder, John Saxon; *D:* Bob (Benjamin) Clark; *W:* Roy Moore; *C:* Reginald Morris; *M:* Carl Zittrer.

Black Christmas **2006 (R)** The 1974 original was an early entry in the slasher/dead teen genre. This weak remake, which takes itself way too seriously, ups the gore and adds lurid flashbacks for the killer, but so what? Sorority sisters (you may recognize a couple of faces) are stuck in their Alpha Kappa house at Christmas because of a blizzard, but the psycho killer (who lived in the sorority house when it was his family home) manages to escape the loony bin and hide out in the attic. He then terrorizes the gals before offing them, using handy holiday decorations for the most part. After seeing what he does with a cookie cutter, you may never eat Christmas cookies again. Writer/director Morgan deserves coal in his stocking. **84m/C DVD, HD DVD.** *US CA* Michelle Trachtenberg, Lacey Chabert, Mary Elizabeth Winstead, Andrea Martin, Katie Cassidy, Robert Mann, Oliver Hudson, Crystal Lowe, Kristen Cloke, Jessica Harmon, Dean Friss; *D:* Glen Morgan; *W:* Glen Morgan; *C:* Robert McLachlan; *M:* Shirley Walker.

Black Circle Boys 1/2 **1997 (R)** Depressed high schooler Kyle (Bairstow) is still trying to fit in at his new school. He makes the mistake of getting involved with the "Black Circle Boys"—a clique of losers involved with drugs and the occult that's led by Shane (Mabius). The Boys enjoy malicious pranks and Kyle begins to have qualms about his participation but Shane doesn't want to let him go. Murky script gets increasingly silly as pic progresses. **100m/C VHS, DVD.** Scott Bairstow, Eric Mabius, Heath Lourwood, Chad Lindberg, Tara Subkoff, Dee Wallace, Donnie Wahlberg, John Doe; *D:* Matthew Carnahan; *W:* Matthew Carnahan; *C:* Geary McLeod.

Black Cloud 1/2 **2004 (PG-13)** Schroder debuts as a writer/director in this formulaic but appealing drama about a Native American boxer. Black Cloud (Sparks) is an angry, out-of-control young boxer whose life outside the ring is marred by an alcoholic father, a dead mother, self-hatred, and racism. All he's got in his corner is his world-wise trainer Bud (Means) and his girlfriend Sammi (Jones). Black Cloud struggles with adversity in and out of the ring, but ultimately he's his own worst enemy. The story is strictly seen-it-before, but the strong performances (especially Sparks) balance out the predictability. **95m/C DVD.** *US* Eddie Spears, Russell Means, Wayne Knight, Peter Greene, Julia Jones, Rick Schroder, Nathaniel Arcand, Tim McGraw, Branscombe Richmond; *D:* Rick Schroder; *W:* Rick Schroder; *C:* Steve Gainer; *M:* John E. Nordstrom.

Black Cobra WOOF! **1983 (R)** A lesbian exacts revenge for her lover's snake-bite murder by trapping the guilty party with his own snakes. **97m/C VHS, DVD.** *IT* Laura Gemser, Jack Palance; *D:* Joe D'Amato.

The Black Cobra WOOF! *Cobra Nero* **1987 (R)** After photographing a psychopath in the process of killing someone, a beautiful photographer seeks the help of a tough police sergeant to protect her. The leader of the Black Cobras gang gives chase. **90m/C VHS, DVD.** *IT* Fred Williamson, Bruno Bilotta, Eva Grimaldi; *D:* Stelvio Massi.

Black Cobra 2 **1989 (R)** A mismatched team of investigators tracks a notorious terrorist. They find him holding a school full of children as hostage. **95m/C VHS, DVD.** *IT* Nicholas Hammond, Emma Hoagland, Najid Jadali, Fred Williamson; *D:* Stelvio Massi; *C:* Guglielmo Mancori; *M:* Aldo Salvi.

Black Cobra 3: The Manila Connection 1/2 **1990 (R)** Interpol turns to police lieutenant Robert Malone (Williamson) when a team of high-tech weapons thieves threatens the world. Malone attacks like a cyclone on the terrorists' jungle haven. They won't know what hit 'em! **92m/C VHS, DVD.** Fred Williamson, Forry Smith, Debra Ward; *D:* Don Edwards.

The Black Dahlia **2006 (R)** Adaptation of James Ellroy's novel about the lurid unsolved murder features director De Palma's feverish eye for noir. Great-looking, over-stuffed, and ultimately unsatisfying production has Hollywood wannabe Elizabeth Short's (Kirshner) mutilated body discovered in a vacant lot in LA in 1947. Detective Lee Blanchard (Eckhart) becomes obsessed with the case—to the detriment of his life with blonde babe lover, Kay Lake (Johansson). Meanwhile, Lee's callow partner Buck (Hartnett) is investigating wealthy brunette Madeleine's (Swank) involvement with Short, which leads him to her lunatic clan. Fedoras, red lipstick, and cigarette smoke abound, but the glam hides plenty of dirt and corruption. **121m/C DVD.** *US* Josh Hartnett, Scarlett Johansson, Aaron Eckhart, Hilary Swank, Mike Starr, Fiona Shaw, John Kavanagh, Rachel Miner, Mia Kirshner, Troy Evans, Gregg Henry, Rose McGowan, Jemima Rooper, William Finley, Kevin Dunn, Ian McNeice, Pepe Serna, Patrick Fischler; *D:* Brian De Palma; *W:* Josh Friedman; *C:* Vilmos Zsigmond; *M:* Mark Isham.

Black Dawn 1/2 **2005 (R)** Former CIA agent Jonathon Cold (Seagal) is working for himself now, and takes an assignment springing a terrorist from jail so he can infiltrate his group before they detonate a nuclear bomb in downtown LA. Seagal unfortunately is an action star past his prime using a stunt double that looks nothing like him to film all his fight scenes. **96m/C DVD.** Steven Seagal, Tamara Davies, John Pyper-Ferguson, Julian Stone, Nicholas Davidoff, Warren DeRosa, Don Franklin, Timothy Carhart, Eddie Velez, Matt Salinger, Ryan Bollman, Roman Varshavsky, Noa Hegesh, David St. James, Angela Gots; *D:* Alexander Grusynski; *W:* Darren O. Campbell, Martin Wheeler; *C:* Bruce McCleery; *M:* David Wurst, Eric Wurst.

Black Day Blue Night **1995 (R)** Rinda (Forbes) and Hallie (Sara) take a road trip from Utah to Phoenix and pick up the handsome Dodge (Bellows). Turns out he's being pursued by cop John Quinn (Walsh) as a suspect in a murder/robbery. Women-in-peril-who-help-themselves type story. **99m/C VHS.** Michelle Forbes, Mia Sara, Gil Bellows, J.T. Walsh, Tim Guinee, John Beck; *D:* J.S. Cardone; *W:* J.S. Cardone; *C:* Michael Cardone; *M:* Johnny Lee Schell, Joe Sublett.

Black Devil Doll from Hell **1984** This shot-on-video movie deals with a nasty little voodoo doll that likes to kill its owners. **70m/C VHS.** Shirley Jones, Rickey Roach, Marie Sainvilvs; *D:* Chester Turner.

The Black Devils of Kali *Mystery of the Black Jungle* **1955** Adventurers in the Indian jungle discover a lost race of idol-worshipping primitives. Racist garbage produced near the end of Republic Pictures' existence. Based on a novel by Emillio Salgari. **72m/B VHS.** Lex Barker, Jane Maxwell, Luigi Tosi, Paul Muller; *D:* Ralph Murphy.

Black Dog **1998 (PG-13)** Not since the '70s heyday of CBs and C.W. McCall have 18-wheelers been so lovingly portrayed. Too bad the rest of the characters weren't given the same attention. Swayze (resurrecting his sensitive butt-kicker persona from "Roadhouse") plays disgraced trucker Jack Crews, recently released from prison after a vehicular manslaughter rap. With no driver's license and an overdue mortgage, he agrees to an "off the books" run for his shady boss (Beckel). The cargo turns out to be guns, which attracts the attention of the FBI, ATF, and a scuzzy band of hijackers led by the Bible-quoting Red (Meatloaf). Of course, the paint-by-numbers plot puts Jack's family in harm's way, and gives him a soulful, country-croonin' ally (Travis). Avoid this mutt like three-day-old roadkill unless you're a big-rig fetishist. **88m/C VHS, DVD.** Patrick Swayze, Randy Travis, Meat Loaf Aday, Gabriel Casseus, Graham Beckel, Stephen Tobolowsky, Charles S. Dutton, Brian Vincent, Brenda Strong, Erin Broderick; *D:* Kevin Hooks; *W:* William Mickelberry, Dan Vining; *C:* Buzz Feitshans IV; *M:* George S. Clinton.

The Black Doll 1/2 **1938** Shady mine owner Nicholas Rood is murdered as revenge for killing his business partner. While local officials have things utterly confused, Rood's daughter's fiance, who happens to be a private detective, eventually pieces the clues together. Low-caliber installment of the "Crime Club" series. **66m/B VHS.** Donald Woods, Nan Grey, Edgar Kennedy, Doris Lloyd; *D:* Otis Garrett; *W:* Otis Buckley. **VIDEO**

The Black Dragons **1942** Weird and fairly stupid war drama involving sabotage by the Japanese. Lugosi is the plastic surgeon who deftly cuts and pastes Japanese face parts to permit agents to pass as Americans. Also available colorized. **62m/B VHS, DVD.** Bela Lugosi, Joan Barclay, George Pembroke, Clayton Moore; *D:* William Nigh.

Black Dynamite 1/2 **2009 (R)** Sly, satiric homage to 1970s blaxploitation films that finds heroic Black Dynamite (White) fighting all the way to Honky House (AKA Richard M. Nixon's White House) to avenge his brother's murder and prevent the destruction of his 'hood by The Man. The film looks and sounds deliberately garish with grainy film stock, a funk soundtrack, gratuitous female nudity, and a swaggering, jive-talking hero who carries a.44 Magnum and wields a mean nunchuck. These are all pluses since director/writer Sanders and writers White and Minns are complimentary to the genre rather than smug. **90m/C DVD.** *US* Michael Jai White, Byron Keith Minns, Kym E. Whitley, Obba Babatunde, Kevin Chapman, Tommy Davidson, Salli Richardson-Whitfield, Arsenio Hall, Cedric Yarbrough, Mykelti Williamson, Bokeem Woodbine, James McManus, Nicole Sullivan; ***D:*** Scott Sanders; ***W:*** Michael Jai White, Byron Keith Minns, Scott Sanders; ***C:*** Shawn Maurer.

Black Eagle **1988 (R)** Pre-Glasnost, anti-Soviet tale of two high-kicking spies. CIA and KGB agents race to recover innovative equipment in the Mediterranean. **93m/C VHS, DVD.** Bruce Doran, Jean-Claude Van Damme, Sho Kosugi; ***D:*** Eric Karson; ***W:*** Shimon Arama; ***M:*** Terry Plumeri.

Black Eliminator **1978** A black cop struggles to stop a maniacal secret agent who plans to destroy the world. **84m/C VHS, DVD.** Jim Kelly, George Lazenby, Harold Sakata, Bob Minor, Patch MacKenzie, Aldo Ray; ***D:*** Al Adamson.

Black Eyes 1/2 **1939** A lowly waiter, working in a Moscow restaurant, manages to overhear a number of stock tips from the wealthy patrons and makes a tidy pile of rubles to improve his daughter's life. The daughter already thinks he's a successful businessman and is disillusioned when she discovers dad's true profession. All comes out right in the end. **72m/B VHS.** *GB* Otto Kruger, Mary Maguire, Walter Rilla, George L. Baxt, Marie Wright; ***D:*** Herbert Brenon.

Black Force **1975** Brothers who fight crime with violent actions, are called for assistance in the recovery of an African artifact. Originally known as "Force Four." **82m/C VHS.** Malachi Lee, Warhawk Tanzania, Owen Watson, Judie Soriano; ***D:*** Michael Fink.

Black Force 2 **1978 (R)** The brothers are back on the scene in another violent, cartilage-shattering adventure. **90m/C VHS.** Terry Carter, James B. Sikking, Gwen Mitchell; ***D:*** Edward Lakso.

Black Fox: Blood Horse 1/2 **1994** Alan Johnson (Reeve) and Britt (Todd) try to maintain an uneasy peace with the local Kiowas until evil Ralph Holtz (Wiggins) tries to stir things up and have some vigilantes attack the tribe. The second episode in the three-part series. **90m/C VHS.** Christopher Reeve, Raoul Trujillo, Tony Todd, Chris Wiggins; ***D:*** Steven Hilliard Stern; ***C:*** Frank Tidy, Eric N. Robertson.

Black Fox: Good Men and Bad 1/2 **1994** Britt (Todd) accepts a job as a federal marshall while Alan (Reeve) goes after desperado Carl Glenn (Fox) and his gang. During a stagecoach robbery, the outlaws take Hallie (Rowan) hostage, thinking she's the wife of a tycoon and Alan manages to use her to get to Glenn. The third episode in the sagebrush series. **90m/C VHS, DVD.** Christopher Reeve, David Fox, Tony Todd, Kim Coates, Kelly Rowan; ***D:*** Steven Hilliard Stern; ***C:*** Frank Tidy; ***M:*** Eric N. Robertson.

Black Fox: The Price of Peace 1/2 **1994** Former plantation owner Alan Johnson (Reeve) and childhood friend Britt (Todd), whom he frees from slavery, try to forge a new life in 1860s Texas. But there's trouble when abusive bigot Ralph Holtz (Wiggins) threatens the peace between settlers and Indians when he goes after his wife delores (Holtz) who left him for a Kiowa warrior, Running Dog (Trujillo). Based on the novel by Matt Braun; made for TV. **90m/C VHS, DVD.** Christopher Reeve, Raoul Trujillo, Tony Todd, Chris Wiggins, Cynthia (Cyndy, Cindy) Preston; ***D:*** Steven Hilliard Stern; ***C:*** Frank Tidy; ***M:*** Eric N. Robertson. **TV**

Black Friday 1/2 **1940** Karloff is a surgeon who saves the life of his college professor friend (Ridges) by transplanting part of the brain of a gangster (involved in the same car crash) into the man's body. This results in a Jekyll/Hyde complex with the gangster's evil portion taking over and seeking revenge on rival mobster Lugosi. Horror stars Karloff and Lugosi never have any scenes together. **70m/B VHS, DVD.** Boris Karloff, Stanley Ridges, Bela Lugosi, Anne Nagel, Anne Gwynne, Paul Fix, Virginia Brissac, James Craig; ***D:*** Arthur Lubin; ***W:*** Curt Siodmak, Eric Taylor; ***C:*** Elwood "Woody" Bredell.

Black Fury **1935** A coal miner's efforts to protest working conditions earn him a beating by the company goons who also kill his friend. He draws national attention to this brutal plight of the workers when he barricades himself inside the mine. Muni's carefully detailed performance adds authenticity to this powerful drama, but it proved too depressing to command a big boxoffice. **95m/B VHS.** Paul Muni, Barton MacLane, Henry O'Neill, John Qualen, J. Carrol Naish; ***D:*** Michael Curtiz.

The Black Gate *The Darkening; Dark Encounters* **1995** Psychic investigator Scott Griffin's (Rector) vacation to a seemingly pleasant cliff-top inn is interrupted by horrific visions that lead him to an ancient object of great evil that could wreak havoc on Earth unless he can destroy it. More frightening than the lame ghost story are the poor visual effects. **81m/C VHS, DVD.** Jeff Rector, George Philip Saunders, Rebecca Kyler Downs, Red Montgomery, Brian Carlton; ***D:*** William Mesa; ***W:*** John G. Jones, Victoria Parker; ***C:*** William Mesa. **VIDEO**

Black Gestapo **WOOF!** **1975 (R)** Black-exploitation film about a vigilante army taking over a Los Angeles ghetto, first to help residents, but later to abuse them. Extremely violent. **89m/C VHS, DVD.** Rod Perry, Charles Robinson, Phil Hoover, Ed(ward) Cross, Angela Brent, Wes Bishop, Lee Frost, Charles Howerton, Uschi Digart; ***D:*** Lee Frost; ***W:*** Wes Bishop, Lee Frost; ***C:*** Derek Scott.

Black Girl *Une Noire de...; La Noire de...* **1966** The first feature-length film by Senegal's Ousmane Sembene tells the tragic, inevitable story of a young Senegalese maid's forced exile when her white employers want to use her as a servant at their home in the south of France. The film that is most often cited as marking the birth of the African cinema, it remains one of the most powerfully disturbing depictions of the dehumanizing power of racism in the history of cinema. Chilling and unforgettable. **65m/B DVD.** Robert Fontaine, Anne-Marie Jelinek, Therese N'Bissine Diop, Momar Nar Sene; ***D:*** Ousmane Sembene; ***W:*** Ousmane Sembene; ***C:*** Christian Lacoste.

Black Glove *Face the Music* **1954** A trumpet star defends himself against charges of murdering a Spanish singer by tracking down the real killer. **84m/B VHS, DVD.** *GB* Alex Nicol, John Salew, Arthur Lane, Eleanor Summerfield, Paul Carpenter, Geoffrey Keen, Martin Boddey, Fred Johnson; ***D:*** Terence Fisher; ***W:*** Ernest Borneman; ***C:*** Walter J. (Jimmy W.) Harvey.

Black God, White Devil *Deus e o Diabo na Terra do Sol* **1964** Another Brazilan socio-political commentary by Rocha, an oft-incendiary filmmaker whose left-leaning works are steeped in mysticism, obscure folklore, and powerful images. An impoverished man transforms from a religious zealot to a bandit, his tale underscored by conflict between poor masses and wealthy landowners. Portuguese with subtitles. **102m/C VHS.** *BR* Yona Magalhaes, Geraldo Del Rey, Othon Bastos, Mauricio Do Valle, Lidio Silva; ***D:*** Glauce Rocha; ***W:*** Glauce Rocha; ***C:*** Waldemar Lima.

Black Godfather **1974 (R)** The grueling story of a hood clawing his way to the top of a drug-selling mob. Features an all-black cast. **90m/C VHS, DVD.** Rod Perry, Damu King, Don Chastain, Jimmy Witherspoon, Diane Summerfield; ***D:*** John Evans; ***W:*** John Evans; ***C:*** Jack Steely.

Black Gold **1936** Oil field suspense thriller by "B" movie king Hopton. **57m/B VHS, DVD.** Frankie Darro, Leroy Mason; ***D:*** Russell Hopton.

Black Gunn 1/2 **1972 (R)** Early blaxploitation flick filled with car chases (one in a white Rolls Royce), fights, and explosions. L.A. nightclub owner Gunn (Brown) wants revenge on mobster Capelli (Landau) who order his brother Scott (Jefferson) killed. Of course, Scott was involved in ripping off a mobbed-up bookie joint to fund his militant activities but Gunn isn't cutting anyone any slack. **96m/C DVD.** Jim Brown, Martin Landau, Brenda Sykes, Bruce Glover, Luciana Paluzzi, Herbert Jefferson Jr., Bernie Casey, Gary Conway, Stephen McNally, Keefe Brasselle, Vida Blue; ***D:*** Robert Hartford-Davis; ***W:*** Franklin Coen; ***C:*** Richard H. Kline; ***M:*** Tony Osborne.

The Black Hand **1950** Kelly plays well against character in this atmospheric turn-of-the-century thriller. The evil society of the Black Hand murders his father, and he seeks revenge. Well-made drama. **93m/B VHS.** Gene Kelly, J. Carrol Naish, Teresa Celli, Marc Lawrence, Frank Puglia; ***D:*** Richard Thorpe; ***C:*** Paul Vogel.

Black Hand 1/2 **1973** Unemployed Italian immigrant is drawn into a web of murder and betrayal after he is attacked by an Irish gang. **90m/C VHS.** *IT* Lionel Stander, Michele Placido, Rosanna Fratello; ***D:*** Antonio Racciopi; ***C:*** Riccardo (Pallton) Pallottini; ***M:*** Carlo Rustichelli.

Black Hawk Down 1/2 **2001 (R)** Producer Bruckheimer and director Scott faithfully and superbly re-create the Battle of Mogadishu of October, 1993. U.S. Army Rangers and Delta Force units are sent to apprehend Somali warlord Muhammad Farah Aidid's top staff in an Aidid-controlled section of the city. When two Black Hawk helicopters are shot down, the focus of the mission changes to rescue and defense. The usual introduction of the troops is dispensed with fairly quickly, in favor of background on the Somalian situation, and details of the impending operation. No-frills setup works perfectly with the following action, which is fierce, intense, and non-stop. Once the fighting begins, Scott's brilliance with visuals really kicks in, but nothing that happens, no matter how gruesome, seems forced or exploitative. Fine ensemble cast is nominally led by Hartnett, but no one disappoints. Based on the book by Mark Bowden. **143m/C VHS, DVD, Blu-ray Disc, UMD.** *US* Josh Hartnett, Eric Bana, Ewan McGregor, Tom Sizemore, William Fichtner, Sam Shepard, Gabriel Casseus, Kim Coates, Hugh Dancy, Ron Eldard, Ioan Gruffudd, Tom Guiry, Charlie Hofheimer, Danny Hoch, Jason Isaacs, Zeljko Ivanek, Glenn Morshower, Jeremy Piven, Brendan Sexton III, Johnny Strong, Richard Tyson, Brian Van Holt, Steven Ford, Gregory Sporleder, Carmine D. Giovinazzo, Chris Beetem, George Harris, Ewen Bremner, Boyd Kestner, Nikolaj Coster-Waldau, Ian Virgo, Thomas (Tom) Hardy, Tac Fitzgerald, Matthew Marsden, Orlando Bloom, Kent Linville, Enrique Murciano, Michael Roof, Treva Etienne, Ty Burrell; ***D:*** Ridley Scott; ***W:*** Ken Nolan; ***C:*** Slawomir Idziak; ***M:*** Hans Zimmer. Oscars '01: Film Editing, Sound.

Black Heat 1/2 *Girls Hotel; The Murder Gang; U.S. Vice* **1976 (R)** 'Kicks' Carter (Brown) is a detective in L.A. attempting to stop a gang from using an all women's hotel as a prostitution ring. Possibly because he's supposed to be the film's hero, but equally possibly because his girlfriend of the moment happens to live there. Even as bad exploitation films go this one is pretty pointless, except for genre enthusiasts who like formulaic brutality. **90m/C DVD.** Timothy Brown, Russ Tamblyn, Geoffrey Land, Regina Carrol, Tanya Boyd, Al Richardson, Jana Bellan, Darlene Anders, Neal Furst, J.C. Wells; ***D:*** Al Adamson; ***W:*** John D'Amato, Sheldon Lee, Bud Donnelly; ***C:*** Gary Graver; ***M:*** Paul Lewinson.

Black Hills **1948** Dull oater with Dean and his sidekick Ates out to avenge the murder of a struggling ranch owner. **60m/B VHS, DVD.** Eddie Dean, Roscoe Ates, Shirley Patterson, Terry Frost, Nina Bara, William "Bill" Fawcett; ***D:*** Ray Taylor.

The Black Hole 1/2 **1979 (G)** A high-tech, computerized Disney space adventure dealing with a mad genius who attempts to pilot his craft directly into a black hole. Except for the top quality special effects, a pretty creaky vehicle. **97m/C VHS, DVD.** Maximilian Schell, Anthony Perkins, Ernest Borgnine, Yvette Mimieux, Joseph Bottoms, Robert Forster; ***D:*** Gary Nelson; ***W:*** Gerry Day; ***C:*** Frank Phillips; ***M:*** John Barry.

Black Horizon 1/2 *Stranded; On Eagle's Wings; Space Station* **2001 (R)** No matter what it's called, this flick is still a less-than-exciting space opera. A Russian space station is falling apart and an international team is sent aboard a space shuttle to rescue the inhabitants. While there, the station is struck by a meteor that knocks out all communication and causes an oxygen leak, which threatens the team and crew. And on Earth, a government agent discovers that some people don't want the team to ever return. **92m/C VHS, DVD.** Ice-T, Hannes Jaenicke, Michael Dudikoff, Yvette Nipar, Richard Gabai, Alex Veadov, Art Hindle, Larry Poindexter, Andrew Stevens; ***D:*** Fred Olen Ray; ***W:*** Steve Latshaw; ***C:*** Theo Angell. **VIDEO**

The Black House *Kuroi Ie* **2000** Insurance fraud is a problem in Japan, if this film is any indication. After her husband dies, a widow pesters her insurance company to pay up. An agent goes to meet her and discovers that the widow has already remarried a very odd man and her son has hanged himself. The loving parents are most interested as to when they will begin receiving insurance payments for the boy's death as well. So the insurance company has the agent meet with a psychiatrist at a strip club (of course) as a prelude to his investigation of what will be a very odd couple. **117m/C DVD.** *JP* Machiko Washio, Daikichi Sugawara, Katsunobu Ito, Kenichi Katsura, Chikako Yuri, Toshie Kobayashi, Asako Kobayashi; ***D:*** Ataru Oikawa; ***W:*** Ataru Oikawa, Kei Oishi, Takamasa Sato; ***C:*** Tokushu Kikomura; ***M:*** John Lissauer, Masako Miyoshi.

Black House *Geomeun jip* **2007** A Korean remake of a Japanese film of the same name, about an insurance agent investigating what may be a fraudulent claim. Jeon (Hwang Jeon-min) believes his client may have faked his son's suicide for insurance money, and believes he may be out to kill his wife as well. The Korean version drops much of the black humor of the Japanese original, and relies more on gore than story to provide frights (it's often compared to Hollywood remakes of successful Asian horror films). **103m/C DVD.** *KN* Shin-il Kang, Jeong-min Hwang, Seo-hyeong Kim, Seon Yu, Jeong-min Hwang, Yusuke Iseya, Kumiko Aso, Akira Terao, Fumiyo Kohinata, Hiroyuki Miyasako, Hidetoshi Nishijima, Susumu Terajima, Ryo, Tetsuji Tamayama, Hideji Otaki, Tatsuya Mihashi, Kanako Higuchi, Mayumi Sada, Jun Kaname, Mitsuhiro Oikawa, Toshiaki Karasawa; ***D:*** Terra Shin, Kazuaki Kiriya; ***W:*** Yusuke Kishi, Youngjong Lee, Sung-ho Kim, Kazuaki Kiriya, Dai Sato, Shotaru Suga, Tatsuo Yoshida; ***C:*** Ju-young Choi, Kazuaki Kiriya; ***M:*** Seung-hyun Choi, Shiroh Sagisu.

Black Ice **1992 (R)** After an affair with a popular politician ends violently, Vanessa (Pacula) realizes her boss set up his death—and she's next in line. She finds the nearest taxi and offers the driver plenty of cash if he can quickly get her out of the country. It's going to be the ride of her life. Also available in an unrated version. **90m/C VHS.** Michael Nouri, Michael Ironside, Joanna Pacula; ***D:*** Neill Fearnley; ***M:*** Amin Bhatia.

Black Irish 1/2 **2007 (R)** Familiar family drama buoyed by strong performances. Teenager Cole McKay (Angarano) is a promising high school baseball pitcher growing up in South Boston. His dad Desmond (Gleeson) is an unemployed drinker, his mother Margaret (Leo) holds to the illusion that they are a decent Catholic family, and his older sister Kathleen (Van Camp) is unmarried and pregnant. But the biggest problem for Cole is violent elder brother Terry (Guiry), who's drifted into drugs and crime and wants to drag Cole down with him. **95m/C DVD.** Michael Angarano, Brendan Gleeson, Tom Guiry, Melissa Leo, Emily Van Camp, Michael Rispoli, Francis Capra, Finn Curtin; ***D:*** Brad Gann; ***W:*** Brad Gann; ***C:*** Michael Fimognari; ***M:*** John (Gianni) Frizzell.

Black Jesus *Seduta Alla Sua Destra; Seated At His Right* **1968** Lalubi (Strode) is an African leader using passive resistance to save his people from a dictatorial regime that's supported by European colonialism. When he's betrayed by a follower, Lalubi's imprisoned and tortured, along with a thief who gains a greater understanding after contact with the leader. Film is a thinly disguised depiction of Zaire and its history. **100m/C VHS, DVD.** *IT* Woody Strode, Jean Servais; ***D:*** Valerio Zurlini.

The Black King 1/2 *Harlem Hot Shot* **1932** Prejudiced propaganda based on the life of Marcus Garvey, black leader of the '20s, who advocated black superiority and a return to Africa. A black con man takes advantage of fellow blacks by organizing a phony back-to-Africa movement, enriching himself in the process. When one man's girlfriend deserts him for the bogus leader, the jilted one blows the whistle. **70m/B VHS, DVD.** A.B. Comethiere, Vivianne Baber, Knolly Mitchell, Dan Michaels, Mike Jackson; ***D:*** Bud Pollard.

The Black Klansman *I Crossed the Line* **1966** A black man masquerades as a white extremist in order to infiltrate the KKK and avenge his daughter's murder. In the interest of racial harmony, he seduces the Klan leader's daughter. As bad as it sounds. **88m/B VHS.** Richard Gilden, Rima Kutner, Harry Lovejoy; ***D:*** Ted V. Mikels.

Black Knight **2001 (PG-13)** The utterly unoriginal title should be a clue. Another remake of "A Connecticut Yankee in King Arthur's Court," and a particularly bad and formulaic one at that. Lazy, selfish Jamal (Lawrence) is transported from his minimum-wage job at theme park Medieval World to 14th century England, the real medieval world, where some life lessons await. Obvious fish-out-of-water jokes ensue, as Jamal seeks to make sense of his new surroundings, knock boots with Nubian maidens and lead a revolution against an evil king. The film's few decent gags are swallowed by lots of inane humor, a tired script and Lawrence's desperate mugging. Ironically, the story's moral message about giving up selfishness for a cause is lost on its star, who acts as if he's the only person on screen. Ye olde bore. **95m/C VHS, DVD.** *US* Martin Lawrence, Tom Wilkinson, Vincent Regan, Marsha Thomason, Kevin Conway, Daryl (Chill) Mitchell, Jeannette Weegar, Michael Burgess, Isabell Monk, Helen Carey; ***D:*** Gil Junger; ***W:*** Darryl Quarles, Peter Gaulke, Gerry Swallow; ***C:*** Ueli Steiger; ***M:*** Randy Edelman.

The Black Lash **1952** Two lawmen go undercover to break a silver hijacking gang. **55m/B VHS.** Lash LaRue, Al "Fuzzy" St. John, Peggy Stewart, Kermit Maynard; ***D:*** Ron Ormond.

The Black Legion **1937** Social drama isn't as dated as we'd like to think. Auto worker Frank Taylor (Bogart) is angry at being passed over for an expected promotion that goes to a Polish immigrant. So he's easy pickings for a Klan-like secret society that practices hatred and Frank gets in deep, eventually losing his family. His best pal, Ed (Foran), tries to get Frank out but only tragedy follows. Very grim and one of Bogart's early unsympathetic starring roles. **83m/B VHS, DVD.** Humphrey Bogart, Dick Foran, Erin O'Brien-Moore, Helen Flint, Ann Sheridan, Henry (Kleinbach) Brandon, Robert Barrat, Joseph (Joe) Sawyer, Addison Richards, Samuel S. Hinds, John Litel, Eddie Acuff; ***D:*** Archie Mayo; ***W:*** Abem Finkel, William Wister Haines; ***C:*** George Barnes; ***M:*** Bernhard Kaun.

Black Lemons *E venne il giorno dei limoni neri* **1970** While in prison, a convict is stalked by the Mafia because of what he knows. He eventually spills the beans to the cops, putting himself in unavoidable jeopardy. **93m/C VHS.** *IT* Peter Carsten, Antonio (Tony) Sabato, Florinda Bolkan; ***D:*** Camillo Bazzoni.

Black Like Me 1/2 **1964** Based on John Howard Griffin's successful book about how Griffin turned his skin black with a drug and traveled the South to experience prejudice firsthand. Neither the production nor the direction enhance the material. **107m/B VHS, DVD.** James Whitmore, Roscoe Lee Browne, Will Geer, Walter Mason, John Marriott, Clifton James, Dan Priest; ***D:*** Carl Lerner; ***W:*** Carl Lerner, Gerda Lerner; ***C:*** Victor Lukens, Henry Mueller; ***M:*** Meyer Kupferman.

Black Limelight 1/2 **1938** Massey plays a fugitive from justice and Marion the loyal wife who clears her husband of the murder of his mistress. Distracting lead performance by Marion who insists on shouting her lines. Based on the play by Gordon Sherry. **60m/B VHS.** *GB* Raymond Massey, Joan Marion, Walter Hudd, Henry Oscar, Dan Tobin; ***D:*** Paul Stein; ***W:*** Walter Summers.

Black Listed 1/2 **2003 (R)** Fed-up lawyer Alan Chambers (Townsend) compiles a list of a dozen thugs who have escaped doing time thanks to legal loopholes. It's just a way to vent his anger, until some friends take the list and turn vigilante, dragging Alan into the mess. **94m/C DVD.** Robert Kevin Townsend, Harry J. Lennix, Vanessa Williams, Calvin Levels, Eugene "Porky" Lee, Dick Anthony Williams, Richard Lawson, Victoria Rowell, Heavy D; ***D:*** Robert Kevin Townsend; ***W:*** Robert Kevin Townsend; ***C:*** Charles Mills. **VIDEO**

Black Lizard *Kurotokage* **1968** A camp spectacle set in the Japanese underworld. The Lizard is the glamorous queen of Tokyo crime who plots to steal a famous diamond by first kidnapping the owner's daughter. Complications arise when she falls for a detective. The Lizard is played by female impersonator Maruyama. Mishima, who wrote the original drama and the screenplay, has a cameo as an embalmed corpse. Style is all. In Japanese with English subtitles. **112m/C VHS.** *JP* Akihiro Maruyama, Isao Kimura, Yukio Mishima, Kikko Matsuoka; ***D:*** Kinji Fukasaku; ***W:*** Yukio Mishima.

Black Magic 1/2 **1949** Cagliostro the magician becomes involved in a plot to supply a double for Marie Antoinette. **105m/B VHS.** Orson Welles, Akim Tamiroff, Nancy Guild, Raymond Burr; ***D:*** Gregory Ratoff; ***W:*** Charles Bennett.

Black Magic 1/2 **1992 (PG-13)** Insomniac Alex, haunted by the nightly appearances of his dead cousin Ross, goes to Ross's hometown to see if he can find a way to make the apparition disappear. On the way, he runs into his cousin's ex-girlfriend Lilian and falls in love. Problem is, Lilian's a witch, maybe. Lightweight cable fare. **94m/C VHS.** Rachel Ward, Judge Reinhold, Brion James, Anthony LaPaglia; ***D:*** Daniel Taplitz; ***W:*** Daniel Taplitz. **CABLE**

Black Magic Terror **1979** Jilted by her lover, the old queen of black magic has everybody under her spell. Trouble starts, however, when she turns her back on one of her subjects. **85m/C VHS, DVD.** *JP* Suzanna, W.D. Mochtar, Alan Nuary; ***D:*** L. Sudjio.

Black Magic Woman WOOF! **1991 (R)** An art gallery owner has an affair with a beautiful and exotic woman but starts to get cold feet when he's plagued by inexplicable phenomena. Seems that black magic woman has put a voodoo spell on him. Listless companion to director Warren's "Blood Spell" that gives away the ending, has a wretched script, and poor acting. **91m/C VHS.** Mark Hamill, Amanda Wyss, Apollonia, Abadah Viera, Larry Hankin, Victor Rivers, Bonnie Ebson; ***D:*** Deryn Warren; ***W:*** Gerry Daly; ***M:*** Randy Miller.

The Black Marble **1979 (PG)** A beautiful policewoman is paired with a policeman who drinks too much, is divorced, and is ready to retire. Surrounded by urban craziness and corruption, they eventually fall in love. Based on the Joseph Wambaugh novel. **110m/C VHS, DVD.** Paula Prentiss, Harry Dean Stanton, Robert Foxworth, James Woods, Michael Dudikoff, Barbara Babcock, John Hancock, Judy Landers, Anne Ramsey, Christopher Lloyd; ***D:*** Harold Becker; ***M:*** Maurice Jarre.

Black Market Rustlers 1/2 **1943** The Range Busters are at it again. This time they break up a cattle rustling syndicate. **60m/B VHS.** Ray Corrigan, Dennis Moore, Max Terhune; ***D:*** S. Roy Luby.

Black Mask 1/2 *Hak Hap* **1996 (R)** Hong Kong action star Jet Li (second only to Jackie Chan in Hong Kong boxoffice success) is Tsui, a mild-mannered librarian who used to be a member of a secret, biogenetically enhanced squad of super soldiers known as the "701 Squad." These commandos, who feel no fear or pain, are out to take over Hong Kong's underworld, and are killing the crime lords in grisly fashion. Tsui, aided by his detective buddy and dressed a lot like Kato from the "Green Hornet," goes into action to stop his ex-mates. Action may be a little bloody for those not used to the Hong Kong style, but Jet Li is an exciting performer who should break out big with this one after his impressive Stateside debut in "Lethal Weapon 4." Re-dubbed from the 1996 Hong Kong release. **95m/C VHS, DVD.** *HK* Jet Li, Karen Mok, Francoise Yip, Lau Ching Wan; ***D:*** Daniel Lee; ***W:*** Tsui Hark, Teddy Chen; ***C:*** Cheung Tung Leung; ***M:*** Ben Vaughn, Teddy Robin.

Black Mask 2: City of Masks 1/2 *Hak Hap 2; Hei xia 2* **2002 (R)** The Black Mask (Andy On) is consulting the world's leading geneticists seeking a cure for his inability to feel pain (a condition many would probably prefer). But the people he's asking for help are getting killed one by one, and he soon discovers it's being done by a group of mutant pro wrestlers whose superpowers were created by the same super computer that made him. Far more comic book-like than the original, it will appeal to fans of that genre. **101m/C DVD.** *HK* Tobin Bell, Tyler Mane, Andrew Bryniarski, Scott Adkins, Sean Marquette, Oris Erhuero, Michael Bailey Smith, Traci Lords, Andy On, Silvio Simac, John Polito, Teresa Herrera, Rob van Dam, Robert Allan Mukes, Terence Yin; ***D:*** Tsui Hark; ***W:*** Tsui Hark, Julien Carbon, Laurent Cortiaud, Charles Cain, Jeff Black; ***C:*** Wing-Hung Wong, William Yim; ***M:*** J.M. Logan.

Black Moon Rising 1/2 **1986 (R)** Based on an idea by John Carpenter dealing with the theft of a new jet-powered car and its involvement in an FBI investigation. Solid performances and steady action enhance this routine effort. **100m/C VHS, DVD.** Tommy Lee Jones, Linda Hamilton, Richard Jaeckel, Robert Vaughn; ***D:*** Harley Cokliss; ***W:*** John Carpenter; ***C:*** Misha (Mikhail) Suslov; ***M:*** Lalo Schifrin.

Black Narcissus 1/2 **1947** A group of Anglican nuns attempting to found a hospital and school in the Himalayas confront native distrust and human frailties amid beautiful scenery. Adapted from the novel by Rumer Godden. Stunning cinematography. Crucial scenes were cut from the American release by censors. **101m/C VHS, DVD.** *GB* Deborah Kerr, David Farrar, Sabu, Jean Simmons, Kathleen Byron, Flora Robson, Esmond Knight, Jenny Laird, Judith Furse, May Hallatt, Nancy Roberts; ***D:*** Michael Powell, Emeric Pressburger; ***W:*** Michael Powell, Emeric Pressburger; ***C:*** Jack Cardiff; ***M:*** Brian Easdale. Oscars '47: Art Dir./Set Dec., Color, Color Cinematog.; N.Y. Film Critics '47: Actress (Kerr).

Black Oak Conspiracy **1977 (R)** Based on a true story, this film deals with a mining company conspiracy discovered by an inquisitive stuntman. **92m/C VHS.** Jesse Vint, Karen Carlson, Albert Salmi, Seymour Cassel, Robert F. Lyons; ***D:*** Bob Kelljan.

Black Ops 1/2 *Deadwater* **2007 (R)** A WWII battleship is recommissioned and deployed to the Persian Gulf. When the ship falls into radio silence after a distress call, a Marine task force is sent in and finds most of the crew slaughtered. At first, they suspect terrorists but it turns out something else on the ship is responsible and it's so ridiculous, your jaw will drop open in disbelief. Henriksen does his usual professional job and Randolph is eye candy in a tiny tank top and a shower scene. **90m/C DVD.** Lance Henriksen, James Russo, Katherine Randolph, Gary Stretch, Jim Hanks, D.C. Douglas, Grant Mathis; ***D:*** Roel Reine; ***W:*** Roel Reine, Ethan Wiley; ***C:*** Roel Reine; ***M:*** Joseph Bauer. **VIDEO**

Black Orchid 1/2 **1959** A businessman and a crook's widow fall in love and try to persuade their children it can work out. **96m/B VHS, DVD.** Sophia Loren, Anthony Quinn, Ina Balin, Peter Mark Richman, Jimmy Baird; ***D:*** Martin Ritt; ***W:*** Joseph Stefano; ***C:*** Robert Burks.

Black Orpheus 1/2 *Orfeu Negro* **1958** The legend of Orpheus and Eurydice unfolds against the colorful background of the carnival in Rio de Janeiro. In the black section of the city, Orfeo (Mello) is a streetcar conductor and Eurydice (Dawn), a country girl fleeing from a stranger sworn to kill her. The man has followed her to Rio and disguised himself as the figure of Death. Dancing, incredible music, and black magic add to the beauty of this film. Based on the play "Orfeu da Conceica" by De Moraes. In Portuguese with English subtitles or dubbed. **103m/C VHS, DVD.** *BR FR PT* Breno Mello, Marpessa Dawn, Lea Garcia, Fausto Guerzoni, Lourdes De Oliveira, Adhemar Da Silva, Alexandro Constantino, Waldetar De Souza; ***D:*** Marcel Camus; ***W:*** Vinicius De Moraes, Jacques Viot; ***C:*** Jean (Yves, Georges) Bourgoin; ***M:*** Antonio Carlos Jobim, Luis Bonfa. Oscars '59: Foreign Film; Cannes '59: Film; Golden Globes '60: Foreign Film.

Black Out 1/2 **1996 (R)** John Grey (Bosworth), who's suffering from amnesia after a car crash, becomes desperate to remember his life after his wife (DuBois) is murdered. **98m/C VHS.** Brian Bosworth, Brad Dourif, Claire Yarlett, Marta DuBois; ***D:*** Allan Goldstein.

Black Panther 1/2 **1977** True story of psycho-killer Donald Neilson, who murdered heiress Lesley Whittle in England in the 1970s. **90m/C VHS.** Donald (Don) Sumpter, Debbie Farrington; ***D:*** Ian Merrick; ***W:*** Michael Armstrong.

Black Patch **1957** New Mexico marshal Clay Morgan (Montgomery) is nicknamed "Black Patch" because he lost an eye in the Civil War. When his old friend Hank Danner (Gordon) arrives in town, so does trouble, since Danner is married to Morgan's ex-love Helen (Brewster). Danner is also accused of bank robbery so Morgan tosses him in jail and he winds up dead after an escape. Now would-be gunslinger Carl (Pittman) thinks he should avenge his friend Danner's death. **82m/B DVD.** George Montgomery, Diane Brewster, Tom Pittman, Leo Gordon, House Peters Jr., Sebastian Cabot, Strother Martin; ***D:*** Allen Miner; ***W:*** Leo Gordon; ***C:*** Edward Colman; ***M:*** Jerry Goldsmith.

Black Peter 1/2 *Cerny Petr; Peter and Pavla* **1963** Director Forman's first feature offers a glimpse into the struggles of a young Czech man as he copes with an oppressive father, a menial grocery store job, and first-love jitters. In Czech, with subtitles. **85m/B VHS, DVD.** *CZ* Ladislav Jakim, Jan Vostrcil, Vladimir Pucholt, Pavla Martinkova, Pavel Sedlacek; ***D:*** Milos Forman; ***W:*** Milos Forman, Jaroslav Papousek; ***C:*** Jan Nemecek; ***M:*** Jiri Slitr.

The Black Pirate *Rage of the Buccaneers; The Black Buccaneer; Gordon il Pirata Nero* **1926** A shipwrecked mariner vows revenge on the pirates who destroyed his father's ship. Quintessential Fairbanks, this film features astounding athletic feats and exciting swordplay. Silent film with music score. Also available in color. **122m/B VHS, DVD.** *IT* Douglas Fairbanks Sr., Donald Crisp, Billie Dove; ***D:*** Albert Parker; ***W:*** Jack Cunningham, Douglas Fairbanks Sr.; ***C:*** Henry Sharp; ***M:*** Mortimer Wilson. Natl. Film Reg. '93.

Black Pit of Dr. M *Misterios del Ultratumba* **1947** The ghost of a doctor who has been unjustly executed for murder seeks revenge on employees of an insane asylum. The horror is not just confined to the asylum. **90m/B VHS, DVD.** *MX* Gaston Santos, Rafael Bertrand, Mapita Cortes; ***D:*** Fernando Mendez; ***W:*** Ramon Obon.

Black Point **2001 (R)** John Hawkins (Caruso) is a former Naval captain, down on his luck and living in the harbor town of Black Point. When he meets Natalie (Haskell), he thinks she's the woman of his dreams. He's wrong. **107m/C VHS, DVD.** *CA* David Caruso, Susan Haskell, Thomas Ian Griffith, Gordon Tootoosis, Alex Bruhanski; ***D:*** David Mackay; ***W:*** Thomas Ian Griffith, Greg Mellott; ***C:*** Stephen McNutt; ***M:*** Terry Frewer.

Black Rain *Kuroi Ame* **1988** Erstwhile Ozu assistant Imamura directs this powerful portrait of a post-Hiroshima family five years after the bombing. Tanaka plays a young woman who, having been caught in a shower of black rain (radioactive fallout) on an ill-timed visit to Hiroshima, returns to her village to find herself ostracized by her peers and no longer considered marriage-worthy. Winner of numerous awards (including five Japanese Academy Awards). In Japanese with English subtitles. **123m/B VHS, DVD.** *JP* Kazuo Kitamura, Yoshiko Tanaka, Etsuko Ichihara, Shoichi Ozawa, Norihei Miki, Keisuke

Ishida; *D:* Shohei Imamura; *W:* Shohei Imamura, Toshiro Ishido; *C:* Takashi Kawamata; *M:* Toru Takemitsu.

Black Rain 1/2 **1989 (R)** Douglas portrays a ruthless American cop chasing a Japanese murder suspect through gang-controlled Tokyo. Loads of action and stunning visuals from the man who brought you "Blade Runner." **125m/C VHS, DVD, Blu-ray Disc, HD DVD.** Stephen (Steve) Root, Michael Douglas, Andy Garcia, Kate Capshaw, Ken Takakura, Yusaku Matsuda, John Spencer, Shigeru Koyama; *D:* Ridley Scott; *W:* Craig Bolotin, Warren Lewis; *C:* Jan De Bont; *M:* Hans Zimmer.

Black Rainbow **1991 (R)** Surprisingly good thriller that's relatively unknown, haunted by a menacing mood. Robards and Arquette are a father/daughter duo who perform clairvoyance scams at carnival sideshows. Suddenly, without warning, Arquette's former cons become real: she sees murder victims—before their demise. Quirky sleeper filmed on location in North Carolina. **103m/C VHS, DVD.** Rosanna Arquette, Jason Robards Jr., Tom Hulce, Ron Rosenthal, John Bennes, Linda Pierce, Mark Joy; *D:* Mike Hodges; *W:* Mike Hodges.

The Black Raven 1/2 **1943** An action film that combines several plots into one. The Black Raven is an inn that sees more excitement than any other—not the least of which is murder! **64m/B VHS, DVD.** George Zucco, Wanda McKay, Glenn Strange, I. Stanford Jolley; *D:* Sam Newfield; *W:* Fred Myton; *C:* Robert E. Cline.

Black Robe 1/2 **1991 (R)** In 1634 young Jesuit priest Father Laforgue (Bluteau) journeys across the North American wilderness to bring the word of God to Canada's Huron Indians. The winter journey is brutal and perilous and he begins to question his mission after seeing the strength of the Indian's native ways. Stunning cinematography, a good script, and fine acting combine to make this superb. Portrays the Indians in a realistic manner, the only flaw being that Beresford portrays the white culture with very few redeeming qualities and as the only reason for the Indian's downfall. Moore adapted his own novel for the screen. **101m/C VHS, DVD.** *AU CA* Lothaire Bluteau, Aden Young, Sandrine Holt, August Schellenberg, Tantoo Cardinal, Billy Two Rivers, Lawrence Bayne, Harrison Liu, Marthe Tungeon; *D:* Bruce Beresford; *W:* Brian Moore; *C:* Peter James; *M:* Georges Delerue. Australian Film Inst. '92: Cinematog.; Genie '91: Director (Beresford), Film.

The Black Room **1935** As an evil count lures victims into his castle of terror, the count's twin brother returns to fulfill an ancient prophecy. Karloff is wonderful in his dual role as the twin brothers. **70m/B DVD.** Boris Karloff, Marian Marsh, Robert "Tex" Allen, Katherine DeMille, John Buckler, Thurston Hall; *D:* Roy William Neill; *W:* Henry Myers, Arthur Strawn; *C:* Allen Siegler.

The Black Room **1982 (R)** Couples are lured to a mysterious mansion where a brother and his sister promise to satisfy their sexual desires. Not much to recommend unless you're a fan of the vampire as psychology test case. **90m/C VHS, DVD.** Linnea Quigley, Stephen Knight, Cassandra Gaviola, Jim Stathis; *D:* Norman Thaddeus Vane.

The Black Rose 1/2 **1950** Technicolor action, set in the 13th century, as English Saxon Walter of Gurnie (Power) seeks to restore his fortunes by traveling in a caravan to the wilds of Cathay. Welles is the bizarre and brutal Tartan general Bayan, and pretty (and young) French actress Aubrey looks out of place as runaway concubine, Maryam, so the romance between her and Walter is sketchy at best. Based on the novel by Thomas B. Costain. **120m/C DVD.** Tyrone Power, Orson Welles, Cecile Aubry, Jack Hawkins, Finlay Currie, Herbert Lom, Michael Rennie, Robert (Bobby) Blake; *D:* Henry Hathaway; *W:* Talbot Jennings; *C:* Jack Cardiff; *M:* Richard Addinsell.

Black Roses **1988 (R)** A disgusting band of rockers shows up in a small town, and the local kids start turning into monsters. Coincidence? **90m/C VHS.** Carmine Appice, Sal Viviano, Carla Ferrigno, Julie Adams, Ken Swofford, John Martin; *D:* John Fasano.

Black Sabbath *I Tre Volti della Paura; Black Christmas; The Three Faces of Terror; The Three Faces of Fear; Les Trois Visages de la Peur* **1964** An omnibus horror film with three parts, climaxing with Karloff as a Wurdalak, a vampire who must kill those he loves. **99m/C VHS, DVD.** *IT FR* Boris Karloff, Jacqueline Pierreux, Michele Mercier, Lidia Alfonsi, Susy Andersen, Mark Damon, Rika Dialina, Glauco Onorato, Massimo Righi; *D:* Mario Bava; *W:* Mario Bava, Marcello Fondato, Alberto Bevilacqua; *C:* Ubaldo Terzano; *M:* Les Baxter.

Black Samurai **1977 (R)** When his girlfriend is held hostage, a martial arts warrior will stop at nothing to destroy the organization that abducted her. **84m/C VHS, DVD.** Marilyn Joi, Biff Yeager, Bill Roy, Roberto Contreras, Jim Kelly; *D:* Al Adamson; *W:* B. Readick; *C:* Louis Horvath.

The Black Scorpion 1/2 **1957** Two geologists in Mexico unearth a nest of giant scorpions living in a dead volcano. Eventually one of the oversized arachnids escapes to wreak havoc on Mexico City. **85m/B VHS, DVD.** Richard Denning, Mara Corday, Carlos Rivas; *D:* Edward Ludwig; *W:* Robert Blees.

Black Scorpion 1/2 *Roger Corman Presents: Black Scorpion* **1995 (R)** Darcy Walker (Severance) is an ex-cop-turned-superhero (the scorpion is her symbol), who dons a mask and fetching (and tight) black vinyl to fight crime and avenge her dad's death. She's got the prerequisite sidekick—an ex-chop shop operator (Morris)—and a supervillain—the asthmatic Breathtaker (Siemaszko) who threatens to annihilate the city with toxic gas. Campy, schlock fun. **92m/C VHS, DVD.** Joan Severance, Garrett Morris, Casey Siemaszko, Rick Rossovich; *D:* Jonathan Winfrey; *W:* Craig J. Nevius; *C:* Geoffrey George; *M:* Kevin Kiner. **CABLE**

Black Scorpion 2: Ground Zero *Black Scorpion 2: Aftershock* **1996 (R)** Fetching crimefighter Darcy Walker (Severance) returns to battle villains Gangster Prankster (Jackson) and AfterShock (Rose), who are set on destroying the City of Angels by earthquake. **85m/C VHS, DVD.** Joan Severance, Whip Hubley, Stoney Jackson, Sherrie Rose, Garrett Morris, Laura Elena Harring; *D:* Jonathan Winfrey; *W:* Craig J. Nevius; *C:* Mark Kohl; *M:* Kevin Kiner. **CABLE**

Black Shampoo WOOF! **1976** A black hairdresser on the Sunset Strip fights the mob with a chainsaw. **90m/C VHS, DVD.** John Daniels, Tanya Boyd, Joe Ortiz; *D:* Greydon Clark.

Black Sheep 1/2 **1996 (PG-13)** Isn't there a five-day waiting period for remakes? The previously viewed copies of "Tommy Boy" hadn't even hit the sale bin before Spade and Farley went in search of more property to destroy. The twist here? Spade is assigned to keep the oafish brother (not son) of a gubernatorial candidate (not auto parts dealer) out of trouble until after the election (not so he can save the family business). In an effort to provide humor, plot points, and character development, Farley falls out of, off of or onto every prop in sight while Spade smirks. **87m/C VHS, DVD.** Chris Farley, David Spade, Tim Matheson, Christine Ebersole, Gary Busey, Grant Heslov, Timothy Carhart, Bruce McGill, Fred Wolf; *D:* Penelope Spheeris; *W:* Fred Wolf; *C:* Daryn Okada; *M:* William Ross.

Black Sheep **2006** Cheery gorefest. Henry (Meister) returns to the family farm in rural New Zealand, hoping to cure his aversion to sheep and get a buyout from older brother Angus (Feeney). Only Angus has been doing some genetic experimenting on the woolies that turns the placid creatures into blood-thirsty killers! **87m/C DVD.** *NZ* Nathan Meister, Peter Feeney, Tandi Wright, Oliver Driver, Danielle Mason, Tammy Davis; *D:* Jonathan King; *W:* Jonathan King; *C:* Richard Buck; *M:* Victoria Kelly.

The Black Shield of Falworth 1/2 **1954** Typically silly '50s Technicolor swashbuckler with Curtis (and his New York accent) as Myles, the son of a disgraced knight, who's out to thwart a conspiracy against King Henry IV (Keith) and win the hand of fair maiden, Lady Anne (Leigh, Curtis' wife at the time). Loosely based on the Howard Pyle novel, "Men of Iron." **98m/C VHS.** Tony Curtis, Janet Leigh, Ian Keith, David Farrar, Barbara Rush, Herbert Marshall, Dan O'Herlihy, Rhys Williams, Torin Thatcher, Patrick O'Neal, Craig Hill; *D:* Rudolph Mate; *W:* Oscar Brodney; *C:* Irving Glassberg; *M:* Joseph Gershenson.

Black Sister's Revenge *Emma Mae* **1976** Poorly selected video title mars this intelligent drama about a young black woman's struggle to adjust to the big city after growing up in the deep South. **100m/C VHS, DVD.** Jerri Hayes, Ernest Williams II, Charles D. Brook III, Eddie Allen; *D:* Jamaa Fanaka; *W:* Jamaa Fanaka.

The Black Six **1974 (R)** Six black Vietnam veterans are out to punish the white gang who killed the brother of one of the black men. **91m/C VHS, DVD.** Gene Washington, Carl Eller, Lem Barney, Mercury Morris, Joe "Mean Joe" Greene, Willie Lanier, Rosalind Miles, John Isenbarger, Ben Davidson, Maury Wills, Mikel Angel, Fred Scott; *D:* Matt Cimber; *W:* George Theakos; *C:* William Swenning; *M:* David Moscoe.

The Black Sleep *Dr. Cadman's Secret* **1956** Mad scientist Dr. Cadman (Rathbone) invents a drug that causes a deathlike trance and uses it to perform brain surgery on unwilling patients. Needing an assistant, Cadman frames Dr. Ramsay (Rudley) for murder and uses the drug to rescue him from the gallows. Then some of Cadman's experiments get loose and want revenge. Over-the-top hokum that wastes a who's who of horror, including Lugosi (in nearly his last role) as a mute butler. **82m/B VHS.** Basil Rathbone, Herbert Rudley, Akim Tamiroff, Lon Chaney Jr., John Carradine, Bela Lugosi, Tor Johnson, Patricia Blake; *D:* Reginald LeBorg; *W:* John C. Higgins; *C:* Gordon Avil; *M:* Les Baxter.

Black Snake Moan **2007 (R)** Over-heated stew finds Jackson playing grizzled blues musician/farmer Lazarus, who's turned to religion to help him cope with his wife running off. So he's the one man ready to tackle the sex demons of abused white trash Rae (tiny Ricci in barely-there attire), even if it means chaining her inside his shack until she can control that nympho itch. Part sermon, part exploitation, wholly dull. **115m/C DVD, Blu-ray Disc, HD DVD.** *US* Samuel L. Jackson, Christina Ricci, Justin Timberlake, S. Epatha Merkerson, John Cothran Jr., Kim Richards, David Banner; *D:* Craig Brewer; *W:* Craig Brewer; *C:* Amy Vincent; *M:* Scott Bomar.

Black Snow 1/2 **1989** The mob is off on a violent search for 50 million bucks in cocaine. **90m/C VHS.** Jane Badler, Peter Sherayko, Julia Montgomery, Randy Brooks; *D:* Frank Patterson.

The Black Stallion **1979 (PG)** A young boy and a wild Arabian Stallion are the only survivors of a shipwreck, and they develop a deep affection for each other. When rescued, they begin training for an important race. Exceptionally beautiful first half. Rooney plays a horse trainer, again. Great for adults and kids. **120m/C VHS, DVD.** Kelly Reno, Mickey Rooney, Teri Garr, Clarence Muse, Hoyt Axton; *D:* Carroll Ballard; *W:* William D. Wittliff, Melissa Mathison, Jeanne Rosenberg; *C:* Caleb Deschanel; *M:* Carmine Coppola. Oscars '79: Sound FX Editing; L.A. Film Critics '79: Cinematog., Natl. Film Reg. '02;; Natl. Soc. Film Critics '79: Cinematog.

The Black Stallion Returns 1/2 **1983 (PG)** Sequel to "The Black Stallion" follows the adventures of young Alec as he travels to the Sahara to search for his beautiful horse, which was stolen by an Arab chieftain. Unfortunately lacks much of the charm that was present in the first film. Adapted from the stories by Walt Farley. **103m/C VHS, DVD.** Kelly Reno, Teri Garr, Vincent Spano, Angelo Infanti; *D:* Robert Dalva; *C:* Carlo Di Palma; *M:* Georges Delerue.

Black Starlet 1/2 *Black Gauntlet* **1974 (R)** A girl from the projects of Chicago travels to Hollywood in search of fame. She winds her way through a world of sleaze and drugs in order to make it to the top. **90m/C VHS.** Juanita Brown, Eric Mason, Rockne Tarkington, Damu King, Diane Holden; *D:* Chris Munger.

Black Sunday *La Maschera del Demonio; The Demon's Mask; House of Fright; Revenge of the Vampire; Mask of Satan* **1960** In 1630, witch Asa (Steele) who also happens to be a vampire, is executed along with her lover Juvato (Dominici) by her own brother. Two hundred years later, they are accidentally resurrected and in revenge, Asa goes after her descendents, including her look-alike, Katia. A must see for horror fans; firsts for Steele as star and Bava as director. **83m/B VHS, DVD.** *IT* Barbara Steele, John Richardson, Ivo Garrani, Andrea Checchi, Arturo Dominici, Antonio Pierfederici, Tino Bianchi, Clara Bindi, Enrico Olivieri, Germana Dominici; *D:* Mario Bava; *W:* Mario Bava, Ennio de Concini, Mario Serandrei; *C:* Mario Bava, Ubaldo Terzano; *M:* Les Baxter.

Black Sunday 1/2 **1977 (R)** An Arab terrorist group, with the help of a disgruntled Vietnam vet, plots to steal the Goodyear Blimp and load it with explosives. Their intent is to explode it over a Miami Super Bowl game to assassinate the U.S. president and to kill all the fans. Based on Thomas Harris' novel. **143m/C VHS, DVD.** Robert Shaw, Bruce Dern, Marthe Keller, Fritz Weaver, Steven Keats, Michael V. Gazzo, William Daniels, Clyde Kusatsu; *D:* John Frankenheimer; *W:* Ernest Lehman; *C:* John A. Alonzo; *M:* John Williams.

The Black Swan **1942** Swashbuckling pirate film, based on the novel by Rafael Sabatini, stars Power as James Waring, compatriot of notorious buccanneer Henry Morgan (Cregar). Morgan is pardoned and sent to Jamaica as its new governor—if he can prevent his from associates from continuing their criminal ways. He enlists Waring to help him fight the renegades; meanwhile Waring falls in love with former governor's daughter Margaret (O'Hara). Lots of derring do. **85m/C VHS, DVD.** Tyrone Power, Maureen O'Hara, Laird Cregar, Thomas Mitchell, George Sanders, Anthony Quinn, George Zucco, Edward Ashley, Fortunio Bonanova; *D:* Henry King; *W:* Ben Hecht, Seton I. Miller; *C:* Leon Shamroy; *M:* Alfred Newman. Oscars '42: Color Cinematog.

Black Swarm **2007** Cartoonish CGI wasps made for a very non-scary SciFi Channel creature feature. The sting of genetically engineered wasps creates mindless human drones of the folks of Black Stone. The wasps intend to use human innards for breeding purposes and even scientist Eli Giles (Englund) knows this is wrong. So he teams up with exterminator Devin Hall (Roberts) and sheriff Jane Kozik (Allen) to swat the flying pests permanently. **89m/C DVD.** Sebastien Roberts, Sarah Allen, Robert Englund, Jayne Heitmeyer, Rebecca Windheim, Robert Higden; *D:* David Winning; *W:* Todd Samovitz, Ethlie Ann Vare; *C:* Daniel Vincelette; *M:* Mario Sevigny. **CABLE**

Black Terrorist **1985** Terrorists take over a ranch and slay the inhabitants. They keep a young boy alive and the mother tries to rescue him. **81m/C VHS.** Allan Granville, Vera Jones; *D:* Neil Hetherington.

Black Thunder 1/2 **1998 (R)** An Air Force stealth jet, nicknamed "Black Thunder," is hijacked by a Libyan agent during testing. A top gun, Vince Connors (Dudikoff), is paired with hotdog pilot Rick Jannick (Hudson) to retrieve the jet. A standard actioner. **85m/C VHS, DVD.** Michael Dudikoff, Gary Hudson, Richard Norton, Rob Madrid, Nancy Valen, Michael Cavanaugh, Robert Miranda, Frederic Forrest; *D:* Rick Jacobson; *W:* William Martell; *C:* Michael G. Wojciechowski; *M:* Michael Clark. **VIDEO**

Black Tide *Stormy Crossing* **1958** Suspicions arise that a drowning may have actually been a murder. **69m/C VHS.** *GB* John Ireland, Derek Bond, Leslie Dwyer, Maureen Connell, Sheldon Lawrence, Jack Taylor, Joy Webster, Cameron Hall, Arthur Lowe, John Horsley; *D:* C.M. Pennington-Richards; *W:* Brock Williams; *C:* Geoffrey Faithfull; *M:* Stanley Black.

Black Tight Killers *Ore Ni Sawaru to Abunaize* **1966** Imagine a Japanese Matt Helm movie with an Elvis impersonator in the lead. That's essentially what's going on in this gonzo adventure/comedy from the mid-'60s. Hondo (Kobayashi) is a combat photographer just back from Vietnam. He and his stewardess girlfriend (Matsubara) become involved with various gangsters in a fast-moving plot filled with such bizarre devices as Ninja chewing gum bullets. **84m/C DVD.** *JP* Akira Kobayashi, Chieko Matsubara; ***D:*** Yasuharu Hasebe.

Black Tights ½ *Un, Deux, Trois, Quatre!* **1960** Chevalier introduces four stories told in dance by Roland Petit's Ballet de Paris company: "The Diamond Crusher," "Cyrano de Bergerac," "A Merry Mourning," and "Carmen." A keeper for dance fans. Shearer's Roxanne in "Cyrano" was her last performance before retirement. **120m/C VHS, DVD.** *FR* Cyd Charisse, Zizi Jeanmaire, Moira Shearer, Dirk Sanders, Roland Petit; ***D:*** Terence Young; ***Nar:*** Maurice Chevalier.

Black Tower **1950** An interesting murder mystery telling the story of a desperately impoverished medical student. **54m/B VHS.** Peter Cookson, Warren William, Anne Gwynne, Charles Calvert.

A Black Veil for Lisa **1968** A man attempts to exact revenge upon his unfaithful wife, but things go horribly awry. **87m/C VHS.** *IT GE* John Mills, Luciana Paluzzi, Robert Hoffman; ***D:*** Massimo Dallamano.

Black Venus **WOOF!** **1983 (R)** A soft-core epic, starring the former Miss Bahamas, Josephine Jacqueline Jones, about the 18th-century French aristocracy. Laughably based upon the stories of Balzac. European film dubbed in English. **80m/C VHS, DVD.** *SP* Josephine Jacqueline Jones, Emiliano Redondo, Jose Antonio Ceinos, Monique Gabrielle, Florence Guerin, Helga Line, Mandy Rice-Davies; ***D:*** Claude Mulot; ***W:*** Gregorio Garcia Segura, Harry Alan Towers; ***C:*** Jacques Assuerus, Julio Burgos.

Black Water ½ **1994** Tennessee fishing trip turns into a nightmare for an innocent man accused of murder. Based on the novel "Minnie" by Hans Werner Kettenbach. **105m/C VHS.** Julian Sands, Stacey Dash, Ned Beatty, Ed Lauter, Denise Crosby, William McNamara, Rod Steiger; ***D:*** Nicolas Gessner; ***W:*** Nicolas Gessner, Laird Koenig; ***M:*** Gabriel Yared.

Black Water **2007 (R)** You'll root for the crocs to get this trio of whiners as quickly as possible in this remarkably dull creature feature. Lee (Dermody) joins her sister Grace (Glenn) and brother-in-law Adam (Rodoreda) on an ill-fated boating trip into a northern Australian mangrove swamp. A croc eats their guide and the three hustle up a tree while they try to figure out how to get back into their boat without becoming dinner. **89m/C DVD.** *GB AU* Ben Oxenbould, Diana Glenn, Maeve Dermody, Andy Rodoreda; ***D:*** Andrew Traucki, David Nerlick; ***W:*** Andrew Traucki, David Nerlick; ***C:*** John Biggins; ***M:*** Rafael May.

Black Water Gold ½ **1969** TV movie about a search for sunken Spanish gold. **75m/C VHS, DVD.** Ricardo Montalban, Keir Dullea, Lana Wood, Bradford Dillman, France Nuyen; ***D:*** Alan Landsburg. **TV**

The Black Widow *Sombra, the Spider Woman* **1947** A fortune-teller plots to steal scientific secrets and take over the world. Serial in 13 episodes. **164m/B VHS.** Bruce Edwards, Carol Forman, Anthony Warde; ***D:*** Spencer Gordon Bennet.

Black Widow **1954** Rogers gets cast against type as heartless Broadway diva Lottie, who's mixed-up in the death of secretive aspiring writer Nanny (Garner). But since the gal died in the apartment of producer Peter (Heflin), he's suspect numero uno, according to Detective Bruce (Raft). And that doesn't make Peter's actress wife Iris (Tierney) too happy. **95m/C DVD.** Ginger Rogers, Van Heflin, Gene Tierney, George Raft, Peggy Ann Garner, Reginald Gardiner, Virginia Leith, Otto Kruger, Cathleen Nesbitt, Skip Homeier; ***D:*** Nunnally Johnson; ***W:*** Nunnally Johnson; ***C:*** Charles G. Clarke; ***M:*** Leigh Harline.

Black Widow **1987 (R)** A federal agent pursues a beautiful murderess who marries rich men and then kills them, making the deaths look natural. The agent herself becomes involved in the final seduction. The two women are enticing and the locations picturesque. **101m/C VHS, DVD.** Debra Winger, Theresa Russell, Sami Frey, Nicol Williamson, Terry O'Quinn, Dennis Hopper, D.W. Moffett, Lois Smith, Mary Woronov, Rutanya Alda, James Hong, Diane Ladd; ***Cameos:*** David Mamet; ***D:*** Bob Rafelson; ***W:*** Ronald Bass; ***C:*** Conrad L. Hall; ***M:*** Michael Small.

The Black Widow *Before It Had a Name* **2005** Upon the death of her lover, Eleanora (Colagrande) visits his eccentric estate known as the Rubber House, to discover more about this mysterious man. The caretaker (Defoe) is more than willing to help her discover a few secrets she herself has been hiding. Amateur attempts all around make for a directionless, awkwardly spoken tale. Dafoe might want to consider different writing partners. **99m/C DVD.** *US IT* Giada Colagrande, Willem Dafoe, Seymour Cassel, Claudio Botosso; ***D:*** Giada Colagrande; ***W:*** Giada Colagrande, Willem Dafoe; ***C:*** Ken Kelsch; ***M:*** Gyorgy Ligeti.

The Black Windmill ½ **1974 (PG)** An English spy is caught between his service and the kidnapping of his family by rival spies. **102m/C VHS.** Michael Caine, Donald Pleasence, Delphine Seyrig, Clive Revill, Janet Suzman, John Vernon; ***D:*** Donald Siegel.

Blackbeard the Pirate **1952** The 18th-century buccaneer is given the full-blooded, Hollywood treatment. **99m/C VHS, DVD.** Robert Newton, Linda Darnell, Keith Andes, William Bendix, Richard Egan; ***D:*** Raoul Walsh.

Blackbeard's Ghost **1967** Disney comedy in which the famed 18th-century pirate's spirit (Ustinov) is summoned to wreak havoc in order to prevent an old family home from being turned into a casino. **107m/C VHS, DVD.** Peter Ustinov, Dean Jones, Suzanne Pleshette, Elsa Lanchester, Richard Deacon, Joby Baker, Elliott Reid, Michael Conrad, Kelly Thordsen; ***D:*** Robert Stevenson; ***W:*** Bill Walsh, Don DaGradi; ***C:*** Edward Colman; ***M:*** Robert F. Brunner.

Blackbelt 2: Fatal Force ½ *Spyder* **1993 (R)** A man seeks to avenge his brother's murder by going after his killers. **83m/C VHS, DVD.** Blake Bahner, Roxanne Baird, Michael Vlastas; ***D:*** Joe Mari Avellana.

Blackboard Jungle ½ **1955** Well-remembered urban drama about an idealistic teacher in a slum area who fights doggedly to connect with his unruly students. Bill Hailey's "Rock Around the Clock" over the opening credits was the first use of rock music in a mainstream feature film. Based on Evan Hunter novel. **101m/B VHS, DVD.** Glenn Ford, Anne Francis, Louis Calhern, Sidney Poitier, Vic Morrow, Richard Kiley, Margaret (Maggie) Hayes, John Hoyt, Warner Anderson, Paul Mazursky, Jamie Farr, Richard Deacon, Emile Meyer; ***D:*** Richard Brooks; ***W:*** Richard Brooks; ***C:*** Russell Harlan; ***M:*** Charles Wolcott.

Blackenstein **WOOF!** *Black Frankenstein* **1973 (R)** Doctor into nouveau experimentation restores a man's arms and legs. But a jealous assistant gives our man a bogus injection, causing him to become "Blackenstein," a large African American with chip on hulking shoulder who enjoys killing people and otherwise causing big trouble. Ripe blaxploitation. **87m/C VHS, DVD.** John Hart, Ivory Stone, Andrea King, Liz Renay, Joe DeSue, Roosevelt Jackson, Nick Bolin; ***D:*** William A. Levey; ***W:*** Frank R. Saletri; ***C:*** Robert Caramico; ***M:*** Cardella Demilo, Lou Frohman.

Blackheart **1998 (R)** A pair of con artists have their scam down—the seductive Annette (Alonso) picks up wealthy men, then Ray (Grieco) steps in, roughs them up, and takes their cash. Things get messy when they learn of a young woman (Loewi) who has yet to learn of an enormous inheritance, and Ray steps into the role of seducer. Although the film runs out of steam in the last 20 minutes, Grieco and Loewi are likeable in the lead roles. **95m/C VHS, DVD.** Maria Conchita Alonso, Richard Grieco, Fiona Loewi, Christopher Plummer; ***D:*** Dominic Shiach; ***W:*** Brock Simpson, Brad Simpson; ***C:*** Ousama Rawi.

The Blackheath Poisonings ½ **1992** The Collards and the Vandervents are toy-making families who share more than a profession—they share Albert Villa in the London suburb of Blackheath in 1894. Unhappy adults, an illicit affair, a scheming stranger—everyone has something to hide. But when a gruesome murder is committed the ensuing police inquiry will rattle both families skeletons. Based on the novel by Julian Symons. **150m/C VHS, DVD.** *GB* Christine Kavanagh, Ian McNeice, Zoe Wanamaker, Judy Parfitt, James Faulkner, Christien Anholt, Julia St. John, Nicholas Woodeson, Ronald Fraser, Donald (Don) Sumpter; ***D:*** Stuart Orme; ***W:*** Simon Raven; ***C:*** Dick Pope; ***M:*** Colin Towns. **TV**

Blackjack **1978 (R)** Las Vegas is the scene for action and excitement as the mob puts the hit on tough guy William Smith! **104m/C VHS.** William (Bill) Smith, Tony Burton, Paris Earl, Damu King, Diane Summerfield, Angela May; ***D:*** John Evans.

Blackjack ½ **1997 (R)** Former U.S. Marshal Jack Devlin (Lundgren), who has a pathological fear of the color white, becomes the bodyguard of a young supermodel (Haskin) who's the target of a psycho killer (Mackenzie). To highlight Devlin's phobia, Woo sets one of his big action scenes in a dairy flooded with milk. **113m/C VHS, DVD.** *CA* Dolph Lundgren, Kam Haskin, Saul Rubinek, Fred Williamson, Phillip MacKenzie, Kate Vernon, Padraigin Murphy; ***D:*** John Woo; ***W:*** Peter Lance; ***C:*** Bill Wong; ***M:*** Micky Erbe. **VIDEO**

Blacklight **1998** Clairvoyant Sharon Avery (Welch) tried to help the police with a boy's abduction but it was too late and the child was found dead. In despair, Sharon gets into an auto accident and loses both her sight and, apparently, her gift. She later tries to drown herself, but suddenly sees images of another child kidnapping. Inspector Frank Shumann (Ironside) is reluctant to accept her help until a little girl is found murdered. Now Sharon is on a collison course with a child killer. **91m/C VHS.** Tahnee Welch, Michael Ironside, Currie Graham, Anne Marie Loder, Lori Hallier, Walter Mills, Billy Morton; ***D:*** Michael Storey; ***C:*** Michael Storey; ***M:*** Ken Harrison. **VIDEO**

Blackmail **1929** This first sound film for Great Britain and director Hitchcock features an early visualization of some typical Hitchcockian themes. The story follows the police investigation of a murder, and a detective's attempts to keep his girlfriend from being involved. Look for Hitchcock's screen cameo. Made as a silent, this was reworked to become a talkie. **86m/B VHS, DVD.** *GB* Anny Ondra, John Longden, Sara Allgood, Charles Paton, Cyril Ritchard, Donald Calthrop, Hannah Jones, Percy Parsons, Johnny Butt, Harvey Braban, Phyllis Monkman, Alfred Hitchcock; ***D:*** Alfred Hitchcock; ***W:*** Charles Bennett, Benn W. Levy, Garnett Weston, Alfred Hitchcock; ***C:*** Jack Cox.

Blackmail **1991 (R)** Familiar story is given new life in this suspenseful movie. Blakely is a lonely woman who succumbs to Midkiff's attentions. She doesn't suspect that he's conning her with the help of his lover, Toussaint. Engaging thriller adapted from a short story by Bill Crenshaw. **87m/C VHS.** Susan Blakely, Dale Midkiff, Beth Toussaint, John Saxon, Mac Davis; ***D:*** Ruben Preuss. **CABLE**

Blackmale ½ **1999 (R)** Small-time hustlers Jimmy (Woodbine) and Luther (Pierce) bet everything on a fixed fight and lose big. Now they owe $100,000 to a loan shark. So they decide to blackmail a doctor (Rees) with an incriminating videotape and discover that their would-be mark is more dangerous than they could have imagined. **89m/C VHS, DVD.** Bokeem Woodbine, Justin Pierce, Roger Rees, Sascha Knopf, Erik Todd Dellums; ***D:*** George Baluzy, Mike Baluzy. **VIDEO**

Blackout ½ **1950** Blind man recovers his sight and finds that the brother of his girlfriend, once thought dead, is actually alive and well and running a smuggling ring. Routine. **73m/B VHS.** *GB* Maxwell Reed, Dinah Sheridan, Patric Doonan, Eric Pohlmann; ***D:*** Robert S. Baker.

Blackout *Murder by Proxy* **1954** A drunken private eye is offered a murder case, and is subsequently framed for the crime. **87m/B VHS.** Dane Clark, Belinda Lee, Betty Ann Davies, Eleanor Summerfield, Andrew Osborn, Harold Lang, Jill Melford, Alfie Bass; ***D:*** Terence Fisher; ***W:*** Richard H. Landau; ***C:*** Walter J. (Jimmy W.) Harvey; ***M:*** Ivor Slaney.

Blackout **1978 (R)** Four killers terrorize an office building during the 1977 New York electrical blackout. Soon the police enter, confront them, and the fun starts. Comic touches provide some relief from the violence here. **86m/C VHS, DVD.** Jim Mitchum, Robert Carradine, Ray Milland, June Allyson, Jean-Pierre Aumont, Belinda J. Montgomery; ***D:*** Eddy Matalon; ***W:*** Joseph Stefano.

Blackout ½ **1985** Cable thriller in which an aging police chief suspects a disfigured amnesiac is responsible for past killings, in spite of the fact that he now leads a subdued family life. **99m/C VHS.** Richard Widmark, Keith Carradine, Kathleen Quinlan, Michael Beck, Gerald Hiken; ***D:*** Douglas Hickox; ***W:*** David Ambrose. **CABLE**

Blackout **1988 (R)** Strange memories from childhood come back to her as a woman fights for her life. **91m/C VHS.** Carol Lynley, Gail O'Grady, Michael Keys Hall, Joseph Gian, Joanna Miles; ***D:*** Doug Adams; ***C:*** Arledge Armenaki.

The Blackout **1997 (R)** Movie star Matty (Modine) has multiple addictions he indulges on a trip home to Miami. He proposes to pregnant girlfriend Annie (Dalle) but when he learns she's had an abortion, Matty goes on a binge and suffers a blackout. 18 months later in New York, Matty has kicked his addictions and found Susan (Schiffer) but his nightmares compel him back to Miami and the possibility that he committed murder. Sleazy and the symbolism is heavy-handed. **100m/C VHS, DVD.** Matthew Modine, Beatrice Dalle, Claudia Schiffer, Dennis Hopper, Sarah Lassez; ***D:*** Abel Ferrara; ***W:*** Abel Ferrara, Chris Zois, Marla Hanson; ***C:*** Ken Kelsch; ***M:*** Joe Delia.

Blackout ½ **2007 (R)** A psycho-thriller unfairly marketed as a horror flick. Three troubled strangers are trapped in an elevator in a nearly-deserted building because of a blackout. Naturally, one of the three turns out to be a killer. Lots of flashbacks set up the clues as to who and why. Too short to wear out its welcome but not as intense as you might expect. **74m/C DVD.** Amber Tamblyn, Aidan Gillen, Katie Stuart, Armie Hammer; ***D:*** Rigoberto Castaneda; ***W:*** Ed Dougherty; ***C:*** Alejandro Martinez; ***M:*** Reinhold Heil, Johnny Klimek. **VIDEO**

Blackrock **1997** Cliched though dramatic saga, inspired by a true story, and adapted by Enright from his play. Uncommunicative teenager Jared (Breuls) throws a bash upon the return to town of his best surfing bud Ricko (Lyndon). The party gets out of control and Jared witnesses a group of his mates beating and raping Tracey (Novakovitch), who's discovered dead the next morning. Her death attracts rabid media attention and divides the community while Jared is filled with guilt for doing nothing to stop the act. But his conflicts increase when he realizes the extent of Ricko's involvement and he tries to decide where his loyalties lie. **100m/C VHS, DVD.** *AU* Laurence Breuls, Simon Lyndon, Linda Cropper, Rebecca Smart, David Field, Chris Haywood, Boyana Novakovitch; ***D:*** Steven Vidler; ***W:*** Nick Enright; ***C:*** Martin McGrath, George Greenough; ***M:*** Steve Kilbey.

Blacksnake! **WOOF!** *Sweet Suzy; Dutchess of Doom; Slaves* **1973 (R)** Overheated sex and race tale, set in 1835, finds a British lord travelling to a Caribbean island in search of his brother. What he finds is his sadistic sister-in-law and her evil overseer using violence to keep the slaves in line. **83m/C VHS.** Milton McCollin, Anouska (Anoushka) Hempel, David Warbeck, Percy Herbert, David Prowse; ***D:*** Russ Meyer; ***W:*** Russ Meyer, Leonard Neubauer; ***C:*** Arthur Ornitz; ***M:*** William Loose, Al Teeter.

Blackwater Trail **1995 (R)** Novelist Matt Curran (Nelson) travels from L.A. to Michelton, Australia, to attend the funeral of his best friend Andy, a cop who supposedly committed suicide. But Andy's sister (and Matt's former lover) Cathy (Smart) thinks he was murdered because of a case involving a serial killer. Matt decides to snoop around and finds out the killer likes to leave behind body parts and biblical quotations. Contrived plotting but some good performances and some spectacular scenery. **100m/C VHS.** *AU* Judd Nelson, Dee Smart, Peter Phelps, Mark Lee, Brett Climo; ***D:*** Ian Barry; ***W:*** Andrew Russell; ***C:*** John Stokes; ***M:*** Stephen Rae.

Blackwoods **WOOF!** **2002 (R)** It's just like a M. Night Shyamalan movie... only much, much worse. Uwe Boll, Germany's answer to Ed Wood, directs this pointless thriller that apes every third-act twist cliche in the book. Matt (Muldoon) and Dawn (Tracy) drive up to the "Blackwoods" to visit Dawn's hillbilly family, but after checking into a creepy motel (staffed by Clint Howard, no less), Dawn disappears and crazy axe-wielding psychos start attacking Matt. It's all leading up to one big twist that's telegraphed further than a ten-meter cattle prod. Honestly, if you can't figure out the whole movie in the first five minutes, you should put down the airplane glue and move your trailer away from the power lines. **90m/C VHS, DVD.** *GE CA* Patrick Muldoon, Keegan Connor Tracy, Michael Pare, Clint Howard, Will Sanderson, Matthew (Matt) Walker, Anthony Harrison, Janet Wright, Sean Campbell, Ben Derrick; ***D:*** Uwe Boll; ***W:*** Robert Dean Klein, Uwe Boll; ***C:*** Mathias Neumann; ***M:*** Reinhard Besser.

Blacula **1972 (PG)** The African Prince Mamuwalde stalks the streets of Los Angeles trying to satisfy his insatiable desire for blood. Mildly successful melding of blaxploitation and horror that spawned a sequel, "Scream, Blacula, Scream." **92m/C VHS, DVD.** William Marshall, Thalmus Rasulala, Denise Nicholas, Vonetta McGee, Gordon Pinsent, Emily Yancy, Charles Macaulay, Ted Harris, Elisha Cook Jr., Lance Taylor; ***D:*** William Crain; ***W:*** Raymond Koenig, Joan Torres; ***C:*** John Stevens; ***M:*** Gene Page.

Blade **1972 (PG)** An honest cop challenges a dirty cover-up in killer-stalked New York. **79m/C VHS.** Steve Landesberg, John Schuck, Kathryn Walker; ***D:*** Ernest Pintoff.

Blade **1998 (R)** Action-packed gore-fest that provides for high-octane escapist entertainment, with some eye-catching visuals and a pulsating techno soundtrack. Blade (Snipes) is a half-vampire/half-human, who's intent on preventing evil, ambitious Deacon Frost (Dorff) from unleashing a vampire apocalypse upon humanity so he can take over. Helping out Blade are his grizzled mentor, vampire hunter Abraham Whistler (Kristofferson), and Dr. Karen Janson (Wright), who's searching for a cure for vampirism. Adapted from the Marvel comic book character. **91m/C VHS, DVD, UMD.** Wesley Snipes, Stephen Dorff, Kris Kristofferson, N'Bushe Wright, Donal Logue, Udo Kier, Traci Lords, Tim Guinee, Arly Jover, Sanaa Lathan; ***D:*** Stephen Norrington; ***W:*** David S. Goyer; ***C:*** Theo van de Sande; ***M:*** Mark Isham. MTV Movie Awards '99: Villain (Dorff).

Blade 2 **2002 (R)** Sequel takes the more, more, more approach—more vampires, more battles, more gore. Half-vampire, half-human daywalker Blade (Snipes at his coolest) first rescues mentor Whistler (Kristofferson) from the vamps who have been holding him prisoner. Then, he's offered a truce by vampire overload Damaskinos (Kretschmann) who needs Blade to hunt an even more deadly enemy. The rat-like Reapers feed on both humans and vampires and their bite turns their victims into insatiable bloodsuckers themselves. Of course, as Blade goes a-huntin', he discovers the situation isn't as clear-cut as it seems. **116m/C VHS, DVD.** *US* Wesley Snipes, Kris Kristofferson, Ron Perlman, Leonor Varela, Norman Reedus, Thomas Kretschmann, Luke Goss, Matt Schulze, Donnie Yen, Danny John Jules, Daz Crawford, Karel Roden, Tony Curran, Santiago Segura, Marit Velle Kile; ***D:*** Guillermo del Toro; ***W:*** David S. Goyer; ***C:*** Gabriel Beristain; ***M:*** Marco Beltrami, Danny Saber.

Blade Boxer *The Boxer* **1997** Police detectives go undercover to expose an illegal fight ring that has its combatants battling to the death, and equipped with deadly steel talons. **91m/C VHS, DVD.** Kevin King, Todd McKee, Andrew Martino, Cass Magda, Dana Plato; ***D:*** Bruce Reisman.

Blade in Hong Kong 1/2 **1985** Investigator travels to Hong Kong, finds trouble and romance in the underbelly of the city. Pilot for un-sold series. **100m/C VHS.** Terry Lester, Keye Luke, Mike (Michael) Preston, Jean-Marie Hon, Leslie Nielsen, Nancy Kwan, Anthony Newley, Ellen Regan; ***D:*** Reza Badiyi. **TV**

A Blade in the Dark *La Casa con la Scala Nel Buio; House of the Dark Stairway* **1983** A young man composing a score for a horror film moves into a secluded villa and is inspired and haunted by the mysterious murder he witnesses. **104m/C VHS, DVD.** Michele (Michael) Soavi, Fabiola Toledo, Valeria Cavalli, Lara Naszinsky, Andrea Occhipintl, Anny Papa; ***D:*** Lamberto Bava; ***W:*** Dardano Sacchetti; ***C:*** Gianlorenzo Battaglia; ***M:*** Guido de Angelis, Maurizio de Angelis.

Blade Master 1/2 *Ator the Invincible* **1984 (PG)** In this sequel to "Ator the Fighting Eagle," O'Keeffe as Ator is back as the Blade Master. Ator defends his people and his family name in a battle against the "Geometric Nucleus": a primitive bomb. His quest leads him and his small band of men to the castle of knowledge. D'Amato used the pseudonym David Hills. **92m/C VHS.** Miles O'Keeffe, Lisa Foster; ***D:*** Joe D'Amato.

Blade of the Ripper **WOOF!** *The Next Victim; Next!; Lo Strano Vizio della Signora Ward* **1970** A madman armed with a razor slashes his way through the lovelies of the international jet set. **90m/C VHS, DVD.** George Hilton, Edwige Fenech, Alberto De Mendoza, Ivan Rassimov; ***D:*** Sergio Martino; ***W:*** Ernesto Gastaldi, Eduardo Brochero.

Blade Runner 1/2 **1982 (R)** Los Angeles, the 21st century. World-weary cop tracks down a handful of renegade "replicants" (synthetically produced human slaves who, with only days left of life, search madly for some way to extend their prescribed lifetimes). Moody, beautifully photographed, dark thriller with sets from an architect's dream. Based on "Do Androids Dream of Electric Sheep" by Philip K. Dick. Director's cut, released at 117 minutes, removes Ford's narration and the last scene of the film, which Scott considered too "up," and inserts several short scenes, including a dream sequence. **122m/C VHS, DVD, Blu-ray Disc, HD DVD.** Harrison Ford, Rutger Hauer, Sean Young, Daryl Hannah, M. Emmet Walsh, Edward James Olmos, Joe Turkel, Brion James, Joanna Cassidy, William Sanderson; ***D:*** Ridley Scott; ***W:*** Hampton Fancher, David Peoples; ***C:*** Jordan Cronenweth; ***M:*** Vangelis. L.A. Film Critics '82: Cinematog., Natl. Film Reg. '93.

Blade: Trinity **2004 (R)** The last of the "Blade" trilogy (at least with the stoic Snipes), bloody actioner sticks to what it does best, this time with writer Goyer also taking on directing chores. Bitchy bloodsucker Danica (a gleeful Posey), who leads the Vampire Nation, decides to wake up Dracula, aka Drake (Purcell)—whose blood will allow them to walk in the daylight. Blade is busy doing his slaying thing when he gets involved—along with a couple of mouthy youngsters, dishy Abigail (Biel), who happens to be Whistler's (Kristofferson) daughter, and wisecracking recovered vamp Hannibal King (Reynolds). There is, of course, a final mano a mano battle between Blade and Drac, uh, Drake. The ending also leaves wiggle room for the younger actors to continue the bloodletting. **105m/C VHS, DVD.** *US* Wesley Snipes, Kris Kristofferson, Jessica Biel, Ryan Reynolds, Parker Posey, Dominic Purcell, John Michael Higgins, James Remar, Eric Bogosian, Patton Oswalt, Callum Keith Rennie, Natasha Lyonne, Mark Berry, Francoise Yip, Chris Heyerdahl, Paul Anthony; ***D:*** David S. Goyer; ***W:*** David S. Goyer; ***C:*** Gabriel Beristain; ***M:*** RZA, Ramin Djawadi.

Blades **1989 (R)** Another junk heap from Troma, dealing with the efforts of three golfers who try to stop a maniacal power mower that's been grinding duffers with regularity. **101m/C VHS, DVD.** Robert North, Jeremy Whelan, Victoria Scott, Jon McBride; ***D:*** Thomas R. Rondinella; ***W:*** William R. Pace; ***C:*** James Hayman; ***M:*** John Hodian.

Blades of Courage *Skate!* **1988** Biography of Olympic skater Lori Larouche. Choreographed by Debbi Wilkes. **98m/C VHS.** *CA* Lynn Nightingale, Christianne Hirt, Colm Feore, Rosemary Dunsmore; ***D:*** Randy Bradshaw. **TV**

Blades of Glory 1/2 **2007 (PG-13)** Lumpy Ferrell gets a mullet and stuffs himself into spandex and sparkles to play bad boy ice skater Chazz Michael Michaels, whose rival is wispy blonde peacock Jimmy MacElroy (Heder). After the two are banned from singles competition for public brawling, a loophole allows them to compete as the first male/male pairs skating team, much to the disgust of oh-so-close brother/sister skating champs, the Van Waldenbergs (real-life spouses Arnett and Poehler). The jokes are obvious, which doesn't necessarily mean they aren't funny. **93m/C DVD, Blu-ray Disc, HD DVD.** *US* Will Ferrell, Jon Heder, Amy Poehler, Will Arnett, Jenna Fischer, Craig T. Nelson, William Fichtner, Nick Swardson; ***D:*** Will Speck, Josh Gordon; ***W:*** Jeff Cox, Craig Cox, John Altschuler, Dave Krinsky; ***C:*** Stefan Czapsky; ***M:*** Theodore Shapiro.

The Blair Witch Project **1999 (R)** A Sundance Film Festival favorite, this low-budget horror film turned out to be the most successful indie ever, thanks to heavy (and savvy) market promotion. In 1994, a three-person film crew heads into the Black Hills region of Maryland to document a local legend about a demonic apparition. They vanish, but a year later their film footage is found and this amateurish, black and white footage makes up what the audience sees. Largely improvisational, the film manages a palpable sense of dread and claustrophobia, while being (deliberately) technically crude. However, the herky-jerky camera movements made a number of viewers physically sick and an equal number found the would-be theatrics boring. **87m/C VHS, DVD.** Michael Williams, Heather Donahue, Joshua Leonard; ***D:*** Eduardo Sanchez, Daniel Myrick; ***W:*** Eduardo Sanchez, Daniel Myrick; ***C:*** Neal Fredericks; ***M:*** Tony Cora. Golden Raspberries '99: Worst Actress (Donahue).

Blaise Pascal 1/2 **1971** Another of Rossellini's later historical portraits, detailing the life and times of the 17th-century philosopher, seen as a man whose scientific ideas conflicted with his own religious beliefs. Italian with subtitles. **131m/C VHS.** *IT* Pierre Arditti, Giuseppe Addobati, Christian de Sica, Rita Forzano; ***D:*** Roberto Rossellini; ***W:*** Roberto Rossellini; ***C:*** Mario Fioretti; ***M:*** Mario Nascimbene. **TV**

Blake of Scotland Yard 1/2 **1936** Blake, the former Scotland Yard inspector, battles against a villain who has constructed a murderous death ray. Condensed version of the 15 episode serial (originally at 180 minutes). **70m/B VHS, DVD.** Ralph Byrd, Herbert Rawlinson, Joan Barclay, Lloyd Hughes; ***D:*** Robert F. "Bob" Hill.

Blame It on Fidel 1/2 *La Faute a Fidel* **2006** Amusing and tender film told from the point of view of nine-year-old Anna (Kervel), who becomes increasingly upset when her bourgeois parents, Fernando (Accorsi) and Marie (Depardieu, daughter of Gerard), suddenly decide to devote their time and money to various political/activist causes (it's 1970 in Paris). She and her younger brother are moved from their comfortable home to a shabby apartment and are left in the care of oddball political refugees. Anna doesn't take well to all these changes and is confused about what she hears and is told to believe. Writer/director Gavras is the daughter of political filmmaker Costas-Gavras. French with subtitles. **100m/C DVD.** *FR IT* Julie Depardieu, Stefano Accorsi, Olivier Perrier, Nina Kremer, Benjamin Feuillet, Martine Chevallier, Marie Kremer, Marie-Noelle Bordeaux; ***D:*** Julie Gavras; ***W:*** Julie Gavras; ***C:*** Nathalie Durant; ***M:*** Armand Amar.

Blame It on Rio **1984 (R)** A middle-aged man has a ridiculous fling with his best friend's daughter while on vacation with them in Rio de Janeiro. Caine and Johnson are amusing, but the script is somewhat weak. Remake of the French film "One Wild Moment." **90m/C VHS, DVD.** Michael Caine, Joseph Bologna, Demi Moore, Michelle Johnson, Valerie Harper; ***D:*** Stanley Donen; ***W:*** Charlie Peters, Larry Gelbart; ***C:*** Reynaldo Villalobos; ***M:*** Kenneth Wannberg.

Blame It on the Bellboy 1/2 **1992 (PG-13)** Wild farce set in Venice about a hotel bellboy who confuses three similarly named visitors—sending the wrong ones to meet corporate bigwigs, date women, or even kill. The brisk pace loses it towards the end and devolves into chase scenes. **79m/C VHS, DVD.** Dudley Moore, Bryan Brown, Richard Griffiths, Andreas Katsulas, Patsy Kensit, Alison Steadman, Bronson Pinchot, Lindsay Anderson, Penelope Wilton; ***D:*** Mark Herman; ***W:*** Mark Herman; ***M:*** Trevor Jones.

Blame It on the Night **1984 (PG-13)** A rock star gets to take care of the military cadet son he never knew after the boy's mother suddenly dies. Mick Jagger helped write the story. Available in VHS and Beta Hi-Fi. **85m/C VHS.** Nick Mancuso, Byron Thames, Leslie Ackerman, Billy Preston, Merry Clayton; ***D:*** Gene Taft.

Blanche Fury 1/2 **1948** Governess Blanche (Hobson) marries her wealthy widowed cousin but the man she truly desires is the illegitimate Philip Thorn (Granger), who manages the estate for her husband. So Blanche decides to get rid of the man she doesn't love. Based on England's 19th-century Rush murder and adapted from the novel by Joseph Shearing. **95m/C VHS.** *GB* Valerie Hobson, Stewart Granger, Walter Fitzgerald, Michael Gough, Maurice Denham, Sybilla Binder; ***D:*** Marc Allegret; ***W:*** Hugh Mills; ***C:*** Guy Green, Geoffrey Unsworth; ***M:*** Clifton Parker.

Blank Check *Disney's Blank Check* **1993 (PG)** Parents may want to verify the whereabouts of their checkbooks after this one. Eleven-year-old Preston receives a blank check from a mobster on the run, cashes it for a million bucks, and goes on a spending orgy under an assumed name. Where are his parents? Apparently they don't have a problem with a shadowy benefactor taking their son under his wing. Sound familiar? And who thought it would be a good idea to have the little twerp mooning after a comely bank teller? Formula aside, this blatant rip-off of "Home Alone" tries to throw in an ending moral but probably won't fool the kids either. **93m/C VHS, DVD.** Brian Bonsall, Miguel Ferrer, Michael Lerner, Tone Loc, Ric(k) Ducommun, Karen Duffy; ***D:*** Rupert Wainwright; ***W:*** Colby Carr, Blake Snyder; ***M:*** Nicholas Pike.

Blankman **1994 (PG-13)** Self-appointed superhero (Wayans), who makes up in creativity what he lacks in superpowers, fights crime in his underwear and a cape made from his grandmother's bathrobe. Life is simple, until an ambitious TV reporter (Givens) finds out about him. Silly one-joke premise is carried a little too far; didn't similar "Meteor Man" crash? Gifted comedian Wayans tries, but can't make this guy fly. **96m/C VHS, DVD.** Damon Wayans, Robin Givens, David Alan Grier, Jason Alexander, Jon Polito, Nick(y) Corello; ***D:*** Mike Binder; ***W:*** J.F. Lawton, Damon Wayans; ***C:*** Newton Thomas (Tom) Sigel; ***M:*** Miles Goodman.

Blast **1996** Terrorists take a group of spectators hostage at the Atlanta Summer Olympics. **98m/C VHS.** Linden Ashby, Andrew Divoff, Rutger Hauer, Tim Thomerson; ***D:*** Albert Pyun.

Blast 1/2 **2004 (R)** Mercenaries try to detonate an electromagnetic bomb over the U.S using an oil rig. A tug boat captain (Griffin) teams with an FBI agent and computer expert in order to foil the plan. Griffin is surprisingly effective as an action hero, and the proceedings, while not breaking any new ground, provide the requisite excitement and wisecracks in the "Die Hard/Under Siege" mode. **91m/C DVD.** Eddie Griffin, Vinnie Jones, Breckin Meyer, Vivica A. Fox, Tommy (Tiny) Lister, Anthony Hickox; ***D:*** Anthony Hickox; ***W:*** Steven E. de Souza; ***C:*** Giulio Biccari; ***M:*** Danny Saber. **VIDEO**

Blast from the Past 1/2 **1998 (PG-13)** Mistaking a plane crash in his yard for an atomic bomb blast, paranoid scientist Calvin (Walken) and his pregnant wife Helen (Spacek) lock themselves in their bomb shelter. Fearful of radioactive fallout, they raise their son Adam (Fraser) in the shelter on a diet of canned goods, Perry Como music, and ballroom dancing. After 35 years, Adam is sent out for supplies and to find a nice, non-mutant wife. Plot degenerates into by-the-book romantic comedy mush after he meets cute with Eve (Silverstone), a thoroughly modern woman with a low opinion of modern men. **106m/C VHS, DVD.** Brendan Fraser, Alicia Silverstone, Christopher Walken, Sissy Spacek, Dave Foley, Joey Slotnick, Dale Raoul; ***D:*** Hugh Wilson; ***W:*** Hugh Wilson, Bill Kelly; ***C:*** Jose Luis Alcaine; ***M:*** Steve Dorff.

Blast of Silence **1961** Hard-boiled crime. Frank Bono (Baron) comes to Manhattan at Christmas for a contract hit for the mob. He follows his target and decides on the best place to make his shot, just waiting for the right time. When Frank makes a mistake and tries to get out of the contract, he realizes that he'll be next on the hit parade. **77m/B DVD.** Allen Baron, Peter Clune, Larry Tucker, Molly McCarthy; ***D:*** Allen Baron; ***W:*** Allen Baron; ***M:*** Meyer Kupferman; ***Nar:*** Lionel Stander.

Blast-Off Girls **1967** A scuzzball promoter sets out to avenge himself for being blacklisted by the rock 'n' roll industry. He discovers a fresh group, but without corporate backing he can only pay them with groovy clothes and mini-skirted girls. Trouble ensues when they unexpectedly hit the charts and want real money. **83m/C VHS, DVD.** Ray Sager, Dan Conway, Harland "Colonel" Sanders; ***D:*** Herschell Gordon Lewis; ***W:*** Herschell Gordon Lewis.

Blastfighter **WOOF!** **1985 (R)** After local hoodlums kill his daughter, an ex-con cop goes on a spree of violence and revenge. Director Bava uses the pseudonym "John Old, Jr.," as his father Mario Bava occasionally credited himself as John Old. Italian film shot in Atlanta. **93m/C VHS.** *IT* Michael Sopkiw, Valerie Blake, George Eastman; ***D:*** Lamberto Bava.

Blaze 1/2 **1989 (R)** The true story of Louisiana governor Earl Long who became involved with a stripper, Blaze Starr, causing a political scandal of major proportions. Robust, good-humored bio-pic featuring a fine character turn by Newman. **117m/C VHS, DVD.** Paul Newman, Lolita (David) Davidovich, Jerry Hardin, Robert Wuhl, Gailard Sartain, Jeffrey DeMunn, Richard Jenkins, Garland Bunting; ***D:*** Ron Shelton; ***W:*** Ron Shelton; ***C:*** Haskell Wexler.

Blazing Across the Pecos 1/2 **1948** The Durango Kid (Starrett) is after Pecos Flats mayor Ace Brockaway (Wilson), who's secretly selling guns to the local Indian tribe so they'll attack the supply wagons of his business rivals. **54m/B VHS, DVD.** Charles Starrett, Smiley Burnette, Charles C. Wilson, Chief Thundercloud; ***D:*** Ray Nazarro.

Blazing Guns *Marshal of Heldorado* **1950** A marshal, masquerading inexplicably as a tenderfoot, enters a lawless town and is immediately hired as a deputy. **54m/B VHS.** James Ellison, Russell Hayden, Raymond Hatton, Fuzzy Knight, Julie Adams; ***D:*** Thomas Carr.

Blazing Saddles 1/2 **1974 (R)** Wild, wacky spoof by Brooks of every cliche in the western film genre. Little is Black Bart, a convict offered a reprieve if he will become a sheriff and clean up a nasty frontier town; the previous recipients of this honor have all swiftly ended up in shallow graves. A crazy, silly film with a cast full of lovable loonies including comedy greats Wilder, Kahn, and Korman. Watch for the Count Basie Orchestra. A group writing effort, based on an original story by Bergman. Was the most-viewed movie in its first year of release on HBO cable. **90m/C VHS, DVD, Blu-ray Disc, HD DVD.** Cleavon Little, Harvey Korman, Madeline Kahn, Gene Wilder, Mel Brooks, John Hillerman, Alex Karras, Dom DeLuise, Liam Dunn, Slim Pickens, David Huddleston, Burton Gilliam, Count Basie; ***D:*** Mel Brooks; ***W:*** Norman Steinberg, Andrew Bergman, Richard Pryor, Alan Uger, Mel Brooks; ***C:*** Joseph Biroc; ***M:*** John Morris. Natl. Film Reg. '06;; Writers Guild '74: Orig. Screenplay.

Blazing Stewardesses **WOOF!** *Texas Layover* **1975 (R)** The Hound salutes the distributor for truth in advertising, as they stamped this as one of the world's worst videos. Lusty, busty stewardesses relax at a western guest ranch under siege from hooded riders and the aging gags of the Ritz Brothers. **95m/C VHS, DVD.** Yvonne De Carlo, Robert "Bob" Livingston, Donald (Don "Red") Barry, Regina Carrol, Connie Hoffman; ***Cameos:*** Harry Ritz, Jimmy Ritz; ***D:*** Al Adamson.

Bleak House 1/2 **1985** Miniseries adaptation of the Charles Dickens tome about an interminable lawsuit and the decadent, criminal ruling class of 19th-century England. **391m/C VHS, DVD.** *GB* Denholm Elliott, Diana Rigg, Philip Franks, Peter Vaughan, T.P. McKenna; ***D:*** Ross Devenish; ***M:*** Geoffrey Burgon. **TV**

Bleak House 1/2 **2005** Charles Dickens' serialized novel gets the BBC treatment in all its extended suffering. A long court case involving a disputed inheritance hides many secrets and many protagonists, including a fiendish lawyer, an icy aristocratic beauty, two innocents, and an illegitimate child, as well as obsession, madness, and murder. **510m/C DVD.** Gillian Anderson, Charles Dance, Denis Lawson, Patrick Kennedy, Anna Maxwell Martin, Timothy West, Nathaniel Parker, Carey Mulligan, Tom Georgeson; ***D:*** Justin Chadwick, Susanna White; ***W:*** Andrew Davies; ***C:*** Kieran McGuigan; ***M:*** John Lunn. **TV**

Bleak Moments *Loving Moments* **1971** Bored secretary Sylvia (Raitt) tries to work her flirtatious charms on a repressed teacher (Allan) and an eccentric musician (Bradwell) in order to escape the pressures of caring for a mentally retarded sister. **110m/C VHS, DVD.** *GB* Anne Raitt, Eric Allen, Mike Bradwell, Joolia Cappleman; ***D:*** Mike Leigh; ***W:*** Mike Leigh; ***C:*** Bahram Manocheri; ***M:*** Mike Bradwell.

Bleeders **WOOF!** *Hemoglobin* **1997 (R)** John Struass (Dupuis), suffering from a hereditary blood disease, travels to a remote Atlantic island to research his ancestors and discovers the descendants are a grotesque clan of incestuous malformed creatures, who only emerge from their catacombs to satisfy their need for human blood and flesh. **89m/C VHS, DVD.** *CA* Rutger Hauer, Roy Dupuis, Jackie Burroughs, Kristen Lehman, Joanna Noyes, John Dunn-Hill, Lisa Bronwyn Moore; ***D:*** Peter Svatek; ***W:*** Dan O'Bannon, Charles Adair, Ronald Shusett; ***C:*** Barry Gravelle; ***M:*** Alan Reeves. **VIDEO**

Bleeding Hearts 1/2 **1994** A liberal white professor falls in love with the teenaged black student he's tutoring and then becomes aware of the vast differences between them. Their problems increase when the young woman becomes pregnant. **95m/C VHS, DVD.** Gregory Hines, Mark Evan Jacobs, Ranjit (Chaudry) Chowdhry, Elliott Gould, Robert Levine, Peter Riegert, Lorraine Toussaint; ***D:*** Gregory Hines.

Bless the Beasts and Children 1/2 **1971 (PG)** A group of six teenage boys at a summer camp attempt to save a herd of buffalo from slaughter at a national preserve. Treacly Kramer backwater. Based on the novel by Glendon Swarthout. **109m/C VHS.** Billy Mumy, Barry Robins, Miles Chapin, Darel Glaser, Bob Kramer, Ken Swofford, Jesse White; ***D:*** Stanley Kramer; ***M:*** Perry Botkin.

Bless the Child **2000 (R)** Basinger doesn't even attempt to hide her boredom as Maggie, aunt and caretaker to a six-year-old with supernatural powers. Everyone drops the ball in this failed ripoff of "The ExorOmen's Baby's Sixth Sense." Satanist and self-help guru Stark (Sewell) wants to recruit the gifted tyke to work for the Devil, while Maggie gets an occult-expert FBI agent (Smits, perhaps making a mortgage payment) and a bunch of exposition cameos on her side. This movie's idea of thrills is showing kids getting kidnapped and later turning up dead. Not exactly the feel-good movie of the year. **110m/C VHS, DVD.** Kim Basinger, Jimmy Smits, Rufus Sewell, Holliston Coleman, Christina Ricci, Michael Gaston, Lumi Cavazos, Angela Bettis, Ian Holm, Eugene Lipinski, Anne Betancourt, Dimitra Arlys; ***D:*** Chuck Russell; ***W:*** Thomas (Tom) Rickman, Clifford Green, Ellen Green; ***C:*** Peter Menzies Jr.; ***M:*** Christopher Young.

Blessed Event **1932** Fast-moving, entertaining film about a Broadway gossip columnist with a poison pen. Tracy has the role of a lifetime as a Walter Winchell prototype who thinks no one is exempt from his juicy column. Powell makes film debut as a crooner after a brief career as a band singer. Based on a play by Manuel Seff and Forrest Wilson. **77m/B VHS.** Lee Tracy, Mary Brian, Dick Powell, Allen Jenkins, Ruth Donnelly, Emma Dunn, Walter Miller, Tom Dugan, Isabel Jewell; ***D:*** Roy Del Ruth; ***W:*** Howard J. Green.

Blessing **1994** It's an unhappy time down on the Wisconsin dairy farm in this tale of family life. Embittered patriarch Jack (Griffis) can barely make a go of it and takes his frustrations out by beating his cows and climbing to the top of the silo. Despairing wife Arlene (Glynn) enters newspaper lotteries and collects religious statues while daughter Randi (Griffis) keeps delaying leaving the farm because of a nagging sense of responsibility. Claustrophobic atmosphere. **94m/C VHS.** Guy Griffis, Carlin Glynn, Melora Griffis, Gareth Williams, Clovis Siemon; ***D:*** Paul Zehrer; ***W:*** Paul Zehrer; ***C:*** Stephen Kazmierski; ***M:*** Joseph S. DeBeasi.

Blind Ambition 1/2 **1979** Miniseries docudrama traces the career of John Dean, special counsel to President Richard M. Nixon. Focuses on his fractured personal life and touches on virtually all of the Watergate headlines. **95m/C VHS.** Martin Sheen, Rip Torn, Theresa Russell, Michael Callan, William Daniels, Ed Flanders, Christopher Guest, James Karen, Kip Niven, Gerald S. O'Loughlin, Alan Oppenheimer, Lawrence Pressman, John Randolph, Peter Mark Richman, William Schallert, William Windom; ***D:*** George Schaefer; ***W:*** Stanley R. Greenberg; ***C:*** Edward R. Brown; ***M:*** Walter Scharf. **TV**

Blind Date 1/2 **1984 (R)** Blind man agrees to have a visual computer implanted in his brain in order to help the police track down a psychopathic killer. Violent scenes may be disturbing to some. **100m/C VHS, DVD.** Joseph Bottoms, Kirstie Alley, Keir Dullea, James Daughton, Lana Clarkson, Marina Sirtis; ***D:*** Nico Mastorakis; ***W:*** Nico Mastorakis.

Blind Date **1987 (PG-13)** A blind date between a workaholic yuppie and a beautiful blonde starts off well, but when she drinks too much at dinner, things get out of hand. In addition to embarrassing her date and destroying the restaurant, she has a jealous ex-boyfriend who must be dealt with. **95m/C VHS, DVD.** Sab Shimono, Kim Basinger, Bruce Willis, John Larroquette, William Daniels, George Coe, Mark Blum, Phil Hartman, Stephanie Faracy, Alice Hirson, Graham Stark; ***D:*** Blake Edwards; ***W:*** Dale Launer; ***C:*** Harry Stradling Jr.; ***M:*** Henry Mancini.

Blind Date **2008** The games couples play. Estranged married couple Don (Tucci) and Janna (Clarkson) place personal ads for specific role-playing dates as they struggle to reconnect in the wake of their young daughter's tragic death. Loose but loyal interpretation of a film by Dutch director Theo van Gogh, who was murdered by a Muslim extremist in 2004. Tucci's version is not as developed as the original and is a thinly veiled attempt at an homage. Shot on a single set, it would have fared better as a play but instead is an awkward mix of tragedy, comedy, and romance. **80m/C DVD.** Stanley Tucci, Patricia Clarkson; ***C:*** Thomas Kist.

Blind Dating 1/2 **2006 (PG-13)** Danny (Pine) is a young blind man, trying to decide if he should have experimental surgery that might allow him to see. Since he has no romantic experience, his sleazy brother (Kaye) has been setting him up on a series of really bad—uh—blind dates. But Danny falls for his doctor's receptionist Leeza (Jay), an Indian woman who is in an arranged engagement. But neither can quite forget about the other. **95m/C DVD.** Chris Pine, Eddie Kaye Thomas, Jane Seymour, Anjali Jay; ***D:*** James Keach; ***W:*** Christopher Theo; ***C:*** Julio Macat; ***M:*** Hector Pereira.

Blind Eye 1/2 **2006 (R)** Volatile cop Nick Browning (Oliver) gets a call from his ex-wife when their daughter goes missing. Nick returns to his hometown, hoping to use his personal connections to get in on the investigation. When days pass without any leads, Nick realizes that something stinks and if he wants to find his daughter alive, his now-former friends are going down. **96m/C DVD.** Nick Mancuso, Roddy Piper, Levi Oliver, Tara Goudreau, Simone Randall, Phil Babcock, Shaun Hood, Joel Hookey; ***D:*** Mark McNabb; ***W:*** Virginia Carraway, Charlie Fitzgerald; ***C:*** Paul Dunlop; ***M:*** Iain Kelso. **VIDEO**

Blind Faith **1989 (R)** Action and adventure take a turn for the horrific when several men find themselves in captivity. **?m/C VHS.** Eric Gunn, Kevin Yon, Lynne Browne; ***D:*** Dean Wilson; ***W:*** Dean Wilson.

Blind Faith 1/2 **1998 (R)** In 1957, John Williams (Vance) is a struggling new lawyer, living with elder sibling Charles (Dutton) and his family in a Bronx neighborhood. The first black NYPD sergeant, Charles has an uneasy relationship with his eldest son, Charlie (Whitt). The family's shocked when Charlie's accused of murdering a white boy during a robbery attempt, especially when he confesses. John thinks the cops beat the confession out of the boy and becomes determined to defend him but he gradually becomes suspicious of the story Charlie is telling him. **122m/C VHS, DVD.** Courtney B. Vance, Charles S. Dutton, Garland Whitt, Kadeem Hardison, Lonette McKee, Karen Glave, Dan Lett; ***D:*** Ernest R. Dickerson; ***W:*** Frank Military; ***C:*** Rodney Charters; ***M:*** Ron Carter. **CABLE**

Blind Fear 1/2 **1989 (R)** A blind woman is stalked by three killers in an abandoned country inn. **98m/C VHS, DVD.** Shelley Hack, Jack Langedijk, Kim Coates, Jan Rubes, Heidi von Palleske; ***D:*** Tom Berry; ***W:*** Sergio D. Altieri.

Blind Fools 1/2 **1940** A scathing indictment of children neglected by ambitious parents. **66m/B VHS.** Herbert Rawlinson, Claire Whitney, Russell Hicks, Miriam Battista, Vinton (Hayworth) Haworth, Wesley Barry, Robert Emmett Keane; ***D:*** John Varley; ***W:*** Arthur Hoerl, Ivan Abramson; ***C:*** William J. Miller.

Blind Fury 1/2 **1990 (R)** A blind Vietnam vet enlists the aid of a Zen master and a sharpshooter to tackle the Mafia. Hauer works well in the lead, but unfortunately, the movie doesn't. **86m/C VHS, DVD.** Rutger Hauer, Terry O'Quinn, Brandon Call, Lisa Blount, Randall "Tex" Cobb, Noble Willingham, Meg Foster, Sho Kosugi, Nick Cassavetes, Charles Cooper, Rick Overton; ***D:*** Phillip Noyce; ***W:*** Charles Robert Carner; ***C:*** Don Burgess; ***M:*** J. Peter Robinson.

Blind Heat **2000 (R)** Unfaithful hubby Jeffrey Scott (Sapienza) takes wife Adriana (Alonso) on a business trip to Mexico where she gets kidnapped. Rather than pay the ransom, Scott hires negotiator Paul Burke (Fahey) to get his wife back by force. Meanwhile, kidnapper Victor (Peck) falls for Adriana and doesn't want to kill her when their plot turns sour. **95m/C VHS, DVD.** Maria Conchita Alonso, Jeff Fahey, J. Eddie Peck, Al Sapienza; ***D:*** Adolfo Martinez Solares; ***W:*** Adolfo Martinez Solares, Jeff O'Brien; ***C:*** Keith Holland. **VIDEO**

Blind Horizon 1/2 **2004 (R)** A head wound gives Frank Cavanaugh (Kilmer) a case of amnesia but he can't shake ominous flashbacks of a presidential assassination attempt—especially when he hears the president is about to visit. But trying to convince a local New Mexico sheriff (Shepard) of the imminent danger isn't so easy since he's distracted by his reelection bid. And Frank can't be sure that his fiancee Chloe (Campbell) is really who she claims to be. Subplots are overdone and memory loss is nothing new. It works well enough, though. Faye Dunaway gets a slick bit part. **99m/C VHS, DVD.** Amy Smart, Gil Bellows, Giancarlo Esposito, Faye Dunaway; ***D:*** Michael Haussman; ***W:*** F. Paul Benz, Steve Tomlin; ***C:*** Max Malkin. **VIDEO**

Blind Husbands 1/2 **1919** An Austrian officer is attracted to the pretty wife of a dull surgeon. Controversial in its day, this lurid, sumptuous melodrama instigated many stubborn Hollywood myths, including the stereotype of the brusque, jodhpur-clad Prussian officer. This was von Stroheim's first outing as director. **98m/B VHS, DVD.** Erich von Stroheim, Fay Wray; ***D:*** Erich von Stroheim.

Blind Justice **1986** An innocent man is identified as a rapist, and the accusation ruins his life. **94m/C VHS.** Tim Matheson, Lisa Eichhorn, Mimi Kuzyk, Philip Charles MacKenzie, Tom Atkins; ***D:*** Rod Holcomb; ***M:*** Miles Goodman. **TV**

Blind Justice 1/2 **1994 (R)** Gunfighter gets blinded in battle and rides into a small town where he's nursed back to health by an attractive lady doctor. While he recovers, he learns the town is trying to protect a cache of government silver from being stolen by bandits. **85m/C VHS, DVD.** Jack Black, Armand Assante, Elisabeth Shue, Robert Davi, Adam Baldwin; ***D:*** Richard Spence; ***W:*** Daniel Knauf; ***C:*** Jack Conroy; ***M:*** Richard Gibbs. **CABLE**

Blind Man's Bluff **1991 (PG-13)** A blind professor is accused of murdering his neighbor, but as he tries to solve the mystery, evidence points to his ex-girlfriend who may have framed him for the murder. Surprisingly suspenseful cable movie is hampered by a stock Hollywood ending. **86m/C VHS.** Robert Urich, Lisa Eilbacher, Patricia Clarkson, Ken Pogue, Ron Perlman; ***D:*** James Quinn; ***W:*** Joel Gross; ***M:*** Richard Bellis. **CABLE**

Blind Rage 🦴 **1978 (R)** When the United States government transports $15 million to the Philippines, five blind kung fu masters want a piece of the action. **81m/C VHS.** *PH* D'Urville Martin, Leo Fong, Tony Ferrer, Dick Adair, Darnell Garcia, Leila Hermosa, Fred Williamson; ***D:*** Efren C. Pinon.

Blind Side 🦴 1/2 **1993 (R)** DeMornay and Silver are a married couple whose Mexican vacation turns into trouble when they get into a hit-and-run accident which they don't report. Back home, they're frightened by the sudden appearance of Hauer, who's also just back from Mexico. They think he's after blackmail but he's really just a run-of-the-mill psycho intrigued by DeMornay, who at least keeps her character in control. Silver and Hauer have a great time chewing scenery. Also available in a 98-minute unrated version. **92m/C VHS, DVD.** Rebecca De Mornay, Ron Silver, Rutger Hauer; ***D:*** Geoff Murphy; ***W:*** John Carlen. **CABLE**

The Blind Side 🦴🦴 **2009 (PG-13)** Although based on the true story of NFL football player Michael Oher (Aaron), this feel-good sports tale is dominated by Bullock's portrayal of Leigh Anne Tuohy. She is the sassy Memphis belle in charge of the family that takes the disadvantaged young Michael off of the streets. She charms and wisecracks her way past her amiable husband (McGraw), her snooty friends and every other obstacle in her crusade to help Michael fulfill his potential. The not-so-subtle story is heartwarming, but a bit over the top. Based on the book by Michael Lewis. **128m/C DVD.** *US* Sandra Bullock, Tim McGraw, Quinton Aaron, Kathy Bates, Ray McKinnon; ***D:*** John Lee Hancock; ***W:*** John Lee Hancock; ***C:*** Alar Kivilo; ***M:*** Carter Burwell. Oscars '09: Actress (Bullock); Golden Globes '10: Actress—Drama (Bullock); Screen Actors Guild '09: Actress (Bullock).

Blind Spot 🦴🦴 1/2 **1993** Okay family drama which works because of the performances and not the script. Woodward stars as Nell Harrington, a take-charge U.S. Representative long married to Simon (Weaver). Her troubled, pregnant daughter Phoebe (Linney) is married to Nell's aide Charlie (Diamond). Charlie is killed and Phoebe injured in a car crash but the real tragedy is when Nell discovers what caused the accident—drugs—and that her daughter is a cocaine addict. Lots of suffering. **99m/C VHS.** Joanne Woodward, Laura Linney, Fritz Weaver, Reed Edward Diamond, Cynthia Martells, Patti Yasutake, Patti D'Arbanville; ***D:*** Michael Toshiyuki Uno; ***W:*** Nina Shengold; ***M:*** Patrick Williams. **TV**

Blind Vengeance 🦴🦴 1/2 **1990 (R)** A man whose son was murdered by white supremacists decides to take his own special revenge when they are acquited by the local jury. But this isn't your usual bloodbath; instead, he plays psychological games with the men, waiting for them to break. **93m/C VHS.** Gerald McRaney, Marg Helgenberger, Thalmus Rasulala, Lane Smith, Don Hood, Grand L. Bush; ***D:*** Lee Philips; ***W:*** Henri Simoun, Curt Allen. **CABLE**

Blind Vision 🦴 1/2 **1991** Von Dohlen stars as William Dalton, a mail clerk who is in love with his beautiful neighbor Leanne (Shelton). Suffering from extreme shyness, Dalton can only spy on her through a telephoto lens. Things start to get complicated for him when one of Leanne's boyfriends turns up dead outside her apartment. Soon afterwards, their landlady and a local police detective uncover a shocking sexual secret that forces Dalton into a deadly game of obsession and desire. **92m/C VHS.** Lenny Von Dohlen, Deborah Shelton, Ned Beatty, Robert Vaughn, Louise Fletcher; ***D:*** Shuki Levy.

Blind Witness 🦴🦴 1/2 **1989** Routine story about a blind woman who's the only witness to her husband's murder during a robbery. **92m/C VHS, DVD.** Victoria Principal, Paul LeMat, Stephen Macht, Matt Clark, Tim Choate; ***D:*** Richard A. Colla; ***M:*** Robert Alcivar. **TV**

Blind Woman's Curse 🦴🦴 *Kaidan nobori ryu; Black Cat's Revenge; Strange Tales of a Dragon Tattoo; The Tattooed Swordswoman* **1970** Akemi (Meiko Kaji, of "Lady Snowblood" fame) is a Yakuza, and head of a group of deadly swordswomen. Attempting to kill the leader of a rival clan she blinds his daughter when the girl throws herself in front of her father. The young blind girl and her freakishly deformed henchman devote themselves to destroying Akemi by any means necessary. **85m/C DVD.** *JP* Meiko Kaji, Makoto Sato, Toru Abe, Hideo Sunazuka, Ryohei Uchida, Hoki Tokuda, Yoshi Kato, Shiro Otsuji, Yoko Takagi; ***D:*** Teru Ishii; ***W:*** Teru Ishii, Chusei Sone; ***C:*** Shigeru Kiazumi; ***M:*** Hajime Kaburagi.

Blinded by the Light 🦴🦴 **1982** Young woman tries to save her brother from attachment to a quasi-religious cult, The Light of Salvation. Real-life brother and sister McNichol team up in this drama, one of the earlier examinations of cult behavior. **90m/C VHS.** Kristy McNichol, Jimmy (James Vincent) McNichol, Anne Jackson, Michael McGuire; ***D:*** John A. Alonzo. **TV**

Blindfold: Acts of Obsession 🦴🦴 **1994 (R)** Madeline's (Doherty) marriage is boring so she consults therapist Jennings (Nelson). He suggests a number of sexual fantasies Madeline plays out with hubby Woods only to have murder enter the picture. Then Madeline's older sister Chris (Alfonso) is assigned to investigate and lets out lots of family secrets. Shannen in the buff, murder, infidelity, deception, and sex. An unrated version is also available. **93m/C VHS.** Shannen Doherty, Judd Nelson, Michael Woods, Kristian Alfonso, Shell Danielson, Drew Snyder; ***D:*** Lawrence L. Simeone; ***W:*** Lawrence L. Simeone; ***M:*** Shuki Levy.

Blindness 🦴 1/2 **2008 (R)** An entire city's population is suddenly struck blind, degraded to lost souls wandering the streets, filthy, ruined, and dying. The only ones not affected by the epidemic are the inmates quarantined at prison, who descend into sheer madness from hunger, and an oppressive leader (Bernal) who wields a gun and newly-discovered sense of dictatorship. Much to her confusion, the local eye doctor's wife (Moore) also retains her vision, as well as her sense of order. The relentless allegorical suffering and way-too-artsy effects make it almost impossible to lay off the fast-forward button. Adapted from the novel by Jose Saramago. **118m/C DVD.** *BR CA* Julianne Moore, Mark Ruffalo, Danny Glover, Gael Garcia Bernal, Alice Braga, Maury Chaykin, Don McKellar; ***D:*** Fernando Meirelles; ***W:*** Don McKellar; ***C:*** Cesar Charlone; ***M:*** Marcus Antonio Guimaraes.

Blindside 🦴🦴 **1988 (R)** A surveillance hobbyist who owns a motel spies on his tenants until a murder involves him in a big-scale drug war. **98m/C VHS.** Harvey Keitel, Lori Hallier, Lolita (David) Davidovich, Alan Fawcett, Michael Rudder; ***D:*** Paul Lynch.

Blindsided 🦴🦴 1/2 **1993 (PG-13)** A former police officer temporarily loses his sight when he plays the middle man in a bank robbery. Sight improving, he falls for a woman who draws him into another crime. **93m/C VHS.** Jeff Fahey, Mia Sara, Rudy Ramos, Jack Kehler, Ben Gazzara; ***D:*** Thomas Michael Donnelly.

Blink 🦴🦴 1/2 **1993 (R)** Recent corneal transplants allow blind musician Emma (Stowe) to regain her sight, but until they "settle" what she sees may not register in her mind immediately, a phenomenon the script dubs "retroactive vision." This poses a problem for Chicago cop Quinn when he falls for Emma—the only one who can recognize a sadistic killer. Average thriller has been done better before, but adds two attractive leads, enough suspense, and a unique twist to the typical woman-in-jeopardy tale to keep things interesting. The distorted images in Stowe's blurry vision were created by computer. Stowe also learned fiddle for her place as the fictional member of the real-life Irish-American band, The Drovers. **106m/C VHS, DVD.** Madeleine Stowe, Aidan Quinn, Laurie Metcalf, James Remar, Bruce A. Young, Peter Friedman, Paul Dillon, Michael Kirkpatrick; ***D:*** Michael Apted; ***W:*** Dana Stevens; ***C:*** Dante Spinotti; ***M:*** Brad Fiedel.

Blink of an Eye 🦴 1/2 *Blink of an Eye* **1992 (R)** Special agent Sam Browning (Pare) must use his psychic powers and military skills against the terrorists who have kidnapped the CIA director's daughter. **90m/C VHS.** Michael Pare, Janis Lee, Uri Gavriel, Amos Lavi, Sasson Gabai, Jack Widerker; ***D:*** Bob Misiorowski; ***W:*** Edward Kovach; ***C:*** David Gurfinkel; ***M:*** Vladimir Horunzhy.

Bliss 🦴🦴🦴 1/2 **1985 (R)** A savage, surreal Australian comedy about an advertising executive who dies suddenly for a few minutes, and upon his awakening he finds the world maniacally, bizarrely changed. Based on the Peter Carey novel, and one of the most inspired absurdist films of the decade. **112m/C VHS.** *AU* Barry Otto, Lynette Curran, Helen Jones; ***D:*** Ray Lawrence; ***W:*** Peter Carey. Australian Film Inst. '85: Film.

Bliss 🦴 1/2 **1996 (R)** Creepy feature-length sex-ed lecture delves deeply into sexual problems in modern society. So deeply, in fact, that it could've been called "Ouch, You're on my Hair." Clueless yuppies Joseph (Sheffer) and Maria's (Lee) sexual dysfunctions lead her to seek aid from unconventional therapist Baltazar (Stamp), who does things like compare women to violins (hint: they're not really the same. Unless you REALLY like wood). Joseph has his doubts, but soon becomes a chanting tantric goofball. Too clinical to be sexy, but too sexy to be used as an Army training film. **103m/C VHS, DVD.** Sheryl Lee, Craig Sheffer, Terence Stamp, Casey Siemaszko, Spalding Gray, Leigh Taylor-Young, Lois Chiles, Blu Mankuma; ***D:*** Lance Young; ***W:*** Lance Young; ***C:*** Mike Molloy; ***M:*** Jan A.P. Kaczmarek.

The Bliss of Mrs. Blossom 🦴🦴🦴 **1968** Three's a crowd in this light-hearted romp through the machinations of a brassiere manufacturer (Attenborough) and his neglected wife (MacLaine). Mrs. Blossom finds sewing machine repairman Booth so appetizing that she hides him in the attic of the Blossom home. He reads books and redecorates, until, several plot twists later, Attenborough discovers the truth. Witty and wise, with fine supporting cast and excellent pacing. **93m/C** *GB* Shirley MacLaine, Richard Attenborough, James Booth, Freddie Jones, John Cleese; ***D:*** Joseph McGrath.

Blithe Spirit 🦴🦴🦴 1/2 **1945** Charming and funny adaptation of Coward's famed stage play. A man re-marries and finds his long-dead wife is unhappy enough about it to come back and haunt him. Clever supporting cast, with Rutherford exceptional as the medium. Received Oscar for its Special Effects. **96m/C VHS, DVD.** *GB* Rex Harrison, Constance Cummings, Kay Hammond, Margaret Rutherford, Hugh Wakefield, Joyce Carey, Jacqueline Clarke; ***D:*** David Lean; ***W:*** Noel Coward, Anthony Havelock-Allan; ***C:*** Ronald Neame; ***M:*** Richard Addinsell.

Blitz 🦴 1/2 *Killing Cars* **1985 (R)** A German car designer's pet project, a car that runs without gas, is halted by the influence of an Arab conglomerate. He nevertheless tries to complete it, and is hunted down. **104m/C VHS, DVD.** Jurgen Prochnow, Senta Berger, William Conrad, Agnes Soral; ***D:*** Michael Verhoeven; ***W:*** Michael Verhoeven; ***C:*** Jacques Steyn; ***M:*** Michael Landau.

The Blob 🦴🦴 1/2 **1958** Sci-fi thriller about a small town's fight against a slimy jello invader from space. Slightly rebellious McQueen (in his first starring role) redeems himself when he saves the town with quick action. Low-budget, horror/teen-fantasy became a camp classic. Other names considered included "The Glob," "The Glob that Girdled the Globe," "The Meteorite Monster," "The Molten Meteorite," and "The Night of the Creeping Dead." Followed by a worthless sequel in 1972, "Son of Blob," and a worthwhile remake in 1988. **83m/C VHS, DVD.** Steve McQueen, Aneta Corsaut, Olin Howlin, Earl Rowe, Alden "Steve" Chase, John Benson, Vincent Barbi; ***D:*** Irvin S. Yeaworth Jr.; ***W:*** Kate Phillips, Theodore Simonson; ***C:*** Thomas E. Spalding; ***M:*** Burt Bacharach, Hal David, Ralph Carmichael.

The Blob 🦴🦴🦴 **1988 (R)** A hi-tech remake of the 1958 camp classic about a small town beset by a fast-growing, man-eating mound of glop shot into space by scientists, irradiated into an unnatural being, and then returned to earth. Well-developed characters make this an excellent tribute to the first film. **92m/C VHS, DVD.** Kevin Dillon, Candy Clark, Joe Seneca, Shawnee Smith, Donovan Leitch, Jeffrey DeMunn, Ricky Paull Goldin, Del Close; ***D:*** Chuck Russell; ***W:*** Chuck Russell, Frank Darabont; ***C:*** Mark Irwin.

Block-heads 🦴🦴🦴 **1938** Twenty years after the end of WWI, soldier Stan is found, still in his foxhole, and brought back to America, where he moves in with old pal Ollie. Also includes a 1934 Charley Chase short "I'll Take Vanilla." **75m/B VHS, DVD.** Stan Laurel, Oliver Hardy, Billy Gilbert, Patricia Ellis, James Finlayson, Charley Chase; ***D:*** John Blystone.

Blockhouse **WOOF!** **1973** Four men are entombed in a subterranean stronghold for six years after the D-Day invasion of Normandy. Encourages claustrophobic feeling in viewer. Based on Jean Paul Cleberts' novel "Le Blockhaus." **88m/C VHS, DVD.** *GB* Peter Sellers, Charles Aznavour, Per Oscarsson, Peter Vaughan, Leon Lissek, Alfred Lynch, Jeremy Kemp; ***D:*** Clive Rees.

The Blonde 🦴🦴 *La Bionda* **1992** Tommaso (Rubini) is driving through the Milan streets when he knocks down a young blonde woman (Kinski). She loses her memory (apparently due to shock) and Tommaso agrees to help her—soon falling in love. One day her memory returns and Christina remembers she's involved with a drug dealer and other shady characters. She leaves Tommaso to protect him but he's got other ideas. Italian with subtitles. **100m/C VHS, DVD.** *IT* Sergio Rubini, Nastassja Kinski, Ennio Fantastichini, Umberto Raho, Veronica Lazar, Giacomo Piperno; ***D:*** Sergio Rubini; ***W:*** Sergio Rubini, Filippo Ascione, Umberto Marino; ***C:*** Alessio Gelsini Torresi; ***M:*** Jurgen Knieper.

Blonde 🦴🦴 1/2 **2001** Montgomery may not be as curvy as the real Marilyn Monroe, but she does well in this routine biopic about the bombshell who suffered from life-long problems with self-esteem and men. Based on the novel by Joyce Carol Oates, the miniseries covers Marilyn from her disturbing childhood/teenage Norma Jean Baker years to her transformation into a screen goddess, although it ends before her death. **240m/C DVD.** Poppy Montgomery, Skye McCole Bartusiak, Patricia Richardson, Ann-Margret, Kirstie Alley, Eric Bogosian, Wallace Shawn, Patrick Dempsey, Jensen Ackles, Titus Welliver, Griffin Dunne, Richard Roxburgh; ***D:*** Joyce Chopra; ***W:*** Joyce Eliason; ***C:*** James Glennon; ***M:*** Patrick Williams. **TV**

Blonde Ambition 🦴 1/2 **2007 (PG-13)** Simpson plays a clueless blonde (how's that for typecasting?) in this would-be comedy that at least has a couple of supporting performances to save it. Naive Katie heads to NY to see her boyfriend, discovers him cheating, but bucks up when she suddenly gets a job working for a bigshot CEO (Larry Miller) and begins dating Ben (a befuddled Wilson) from the mailroom. The job is a set-up by a couple of sleazy co-workers (Penelope Ann Miller, Dick) looking for a corporate takeover and the blonde must save the day. **93m/C DVD.** Jessica Simpson, Luke Wilson, Larry Miller, Penelope Ann Miller, Andy Dick, Rachael Leigh Cook, Drew Fuller, Willie Nelson; ***D:*** Scott Marshall; ***W:*** John Cohen; ***C:*** Mark Irwin.

Blonde and Blonder 🦴 **2007 (PG-13)** The distaff "Dumb and Dumber" with lots of pink. Dee (Anderson) and Dawn (Richards) witness a mob hit done by pro Kat (Vaugier) and associate Kit (Ory) and then, somehow, get mistaken for the hired killers. They are offered a contract to take out Chinese gangster Mr. Wong (Mann), naturally believing that "take out" means something much less lethal, thus leading to more comic misadventure. Both blondes are getting too old to play ditzy dames even when they're in on the joke. **95m/C DVD.** Pamela Anderson, Denise Richards, Byron Mann, Emmanuelle Vaugier, Meaghan Ory, John Farley, Kevin Farley; ***D:*** Dean Hamilton; ***W:*** Dean Hamilton, Rolfe Kanefsky, Gerry Anderson; ***C:*** C. Kim Miles; ***M:*** William Goodrum. **VIDEO**

Blonde Blackmailer 🦴 **1958** Boring story about an innocent man who serves time for the murder of a female blackmailer. When he's released, he searches for the real killer. **69m/B VHS.** *GB* Richard Arlen, Susan Shaw, Vincent Ball, Constance Leigh; ***D:*** Charles Deane; ***W:*** Charles Deane.

Blonde Comet 🦴 **1941** Betsy Blake (Vale) is a famous female European race car driver who decides to try her hand at racing in

America. She soon runs into a rival in the form of Jim Flynn (Kent), a racer trying to invent a new form of carburetor. The usual evil bad guy attempts to foil his inventing efforts and their budding romance. Despite Vale playing a female driver long before women drivers were allowed, don't expect her to portray a feminist—this was made in the 40s after all. **65m/B DVD.** Virginia Vale, Robert Kent, Barney Oldfield, Vince Barnett, William (Bill) Halligan, Joey Ray, Red Knight, Diane Hughes; ***D:*** William Beaudine; ***W:*** Phillip Juergens, Robin Daniels; ***C:*** Jack Greenhalgh; ***M:*** Andrew Keresztes.

Blonde Crazy 1/2 *Larceny Lane* **1931** A charming grifter hooks up with a gorgeous blonde as he works the territory of a big wheel criminal. Escapist fare, with fun performances from Cagney and Blondell. **81m/B VHS.** James Cagney, Joan Blondell, Louis Calhern, Ray Milland, Nat Pendleton; ***D:*** Roy Del Ruth.

Blonde for a Day 1/2 **1946** Private eye Michael Shayne (Beaumont) is on the case for a newspaper reporter who finds herself in trouble when she writes articles attacking the police department for failing to solve a string of murders. She's got info about a gambling ring and the crooks are none too happy about it. Shayne's got to help the reporter and bring the crooks to justice. **68m/B DVD.** Hugh Beaumont, Kathryn Adams, Cy Kendall, Marjorie Hoshelle, Richard Fraser; ***D:*** Sam Newfield; ***W:*** Brett Halliday, Fred Myton; ***C:*** Jack Greenhalgh.

Blonde in Black Leather 1/2 **1977** A bored Italian housewife takes up with a leather-clad lady biker, and together they cavort about. **88m/C VHS.** Claudia Cardinale, Monica Vitti; ***D:*** Carlo Di Palma.

Blonde Savage **1947** Charting African territories, an adventurer encounters a white jungle queen swinging amongst the vines. Essentially a cheap, distaff "Tarzan." **62m/B VHS, DVD.** Leif Erickson, Gale Sherwood, Veda Ann Borg, Douglass Dumbrille, Frank Jenks, Matt Willis, Ernest Whitman; ***D:*** Steve Sekely.

Blonde Venus 1/2 **1932** A German cafe singer marries an Englishman, but their marriage hits the skids when he contracts radiation poisoning and she gets a nightclub job to pay the bills. Sternberg's and Dietrich's fourth film together, and characteristically beautiful, though terribly strange. Dietrich's cabaret number "Hot Voodoo," in a gorilla suit and blonde afro, attains new heights in early Hollywood surrealism. **94m/B VHS, DVD.** Marlene Dietrich, Herbert Marshall, Cary Grant, Dickie Moore, Hattie McDaniel, Sidney Toler; ***D:*** Josef von Sternberg.

Blondes Have More Guns **1995 (R)** Very dumb detective Harry Bates (McGaharin) is investigating a chainsaw murder and falls for the mysterious Montana (Key), who's possibly a serial killer, or maybe it's her half-sister, Dakota (Lusiak). Spoof of "Basic Instinct" and others of that ilk, done in the usual Troma fashion. **90m/C VHS, DVD.** Michael McGahern, Elizabeth Key, Gloria Lusiak, Richard Neil, Bennie Buttner, Romana Lisa, Andre Brazeau; ***D:*** George Merriweather; ***W:*** George Merriweather, Dan Goodman, Mary Guthrie; ***C:*** Maximo Munzi; ***M:*** Joe Renzetti.

Blondie 1/2 **1938** Chic Young's famous comic strip debuted on the big screen with Singleton in the title role, Lake as the bumbling Dagwood, and Simms as Baby Dumpling (son Alexander, when he grows up). The couple are about to celebrate their 5th wedding anniversary when Dagwood loses his job and Blondie suspects him of infidelity. The series eventually contained 28 films. **68m/B VHS, DVD.** Penny Singleton, Arthur Lake, Larry Simms, Gene Lockhart, Ann Doran, Jonathan Hale, Gordon Oliver, Stanley Andrews, Dorothy Moore; ***D:*** Frank Strayer; ***W:*** Richard Flournoy; ***C:*** Henry Freulich.

Blondie Brings Up Baby **1939** Baby Dumpling is enrolled in school but on his first day he plays hooky to find Daisy who's been caught by the dogcatcher. But Blondie and Dagwood think the tyke has been kidnapped! **67m/B VHS, DVD.** Penny Singleton, Arthur Lake, Larry Simms, Jonathan Hale, Danny Mummert, Fay Helm, Peggy Ann Garner, Irving Bacon; ***D:*** Frank Strayer; ***W:*** Richard Flournoy, Gladys Lehman; ***C:*** Henry Freulich.

Blondie for Victory 1/2 **1942** As her personal contribution to the war effort, Blondie joins the Housewives of America who perform various home front duties. Only their husbands aren't very happy since they're left home tending to the kids and the household chores. **68m/B VHS.** Penny Singleton, Arthur Lake, Larry Simms, Jonathan Hale, Danny Mummert, Stuart Erwin, Irving Bacon; ***D:*** Frank Strayer; ***W:*** Connie Lee, Karen De Wolf; ***C:*** Henry Freulich.

Blondie Goes Latin **1942** Mr. Dithers invites the Bumsteads on a South American cruise and Dagwood winds up the drummer in the shipboard band while Singleton gets to show off her Broadway background in some musical numbers. **70m/B VHS, DVD.** Penny Singleton, Arthur Lake, Jonathan Hale, Larry Simms, Ruth Terry, Tito Guizar, Danny Mummert, Irving Bacon; ***D:*** Frank Strayer; ***W:*** Richard Flournoy, Karen De Wolf; ***C:*** Henry Freulich.

Blondie Goes to College **1942** Actually both Bumsteads enroll but decide to pass themselves off as single, which leads to complications. Blondie draws the attentions of the school's top athlete while Dagwood's joins the rowing team and turns the head of a pretty coed. **68m/B VHS, DVD.** Penny Singleton, Arthur Lake, Larry Simms, Jonathan Hale, Danny Mummert, Janet Blair, Larry Parks, Lloyd Bridges; ***D:*** Frank Strayer; ***W:*** Lou Breslow; ***C:*** Henry Freulich.

Blondie Has Trouble 1/2 *Blondie Has Servant Trouble* **1940** Mr. Dithers has a property he just can't sell because of rumors that the house is haunted. So he offers to let the Bumsteads stay in it to prove that the rumors are false. The Bumsteads also find the creepy mansion comes complete with two equally creepy servants. 6th film in the series. **70m/B VHS, DVD.** Penny Singleton, Arthur Lake, Larry Simms, Danny Mummert, Jonathan Hale, Arthur Hohl, Esther Dale, Irving Bacon; ***D:*** Frank Strayer; ***W:*** Richard Flournoy; ***C:*** Henry Freulich; ***M:*** Leigh Harline.

Blondie Hits the Jackpot 1/2 **1949** Dagwood is fired for the umpteenth time after he makes a mistake in a construction deal and tries frantically to get his job back. Meanwhile, Blondie wins the big prize on a radio quiz show. The 26th film in the series. **66m/B VHS.** Penny Singleton, Arthur Lake, Larry Simms, Marjorie Ann Mutchie, Jerome Cowan, Lloyd Corrigan, Danny Mummert, James Flavin; ***D:*** Edward L. Bernds; ***W:*** Jack Henley; ***C:*** Vincent Farrar; ***M:*** Mischa Bakaleinikoff.

Blondie in Society 1/2 **1941** A weak entry (the ninth) in the comedic series. Dagwood brings home a pedigreed Great Dane and Blondie decides to enter the pooch in the local dog show. Then an important client of Dagwood's decides he wants the dog. **77m/B VHS, DVD.** Penny Singleton, Arthur Lake, Larry Simms, William Frawley, Edgar Kennedy, Jonathan Hale, Danny Mummert, Chick Chandler; ***D:*** Frank Strayer; ***W:*** Karen De Wolf; ***C:*** Henry Freulich.

Blondie Knows Best 1/2 **1946** Dagwood impersonates his boss, Mr. Dithers, and causes all sorts of problems. Howard, one of the Three Stooges, has a cameo as a myopic process-server. The 18th film in the series. **66m/B VHS.** Penny Singleton, Arthur Lake, Larry Simms, Marjorie Ann Mutchie, Jonathan Hale, Steven Geray, Jerome Cowan, Danny Mummert; ***Cameos:*** Shemp Howard; ***D:*** Abby Berlin; ***W:*** Edward L. Bernds, Al Martin.

Blondie Meets the Boss **1939** Dagwood goes on a fishing trip and manages to get into trouble with Blondie when a photograph puts him in a comprising pose with another woman. Then, Blondie winds up at the office doing Dagwood's job (whatever that may be). Second in the series. **75m/B VHS, DVD.** Penny Singleton, Arthur Lake, Larry Simms, Jonathan Hale, Dorothy Moore, Don Beddoe, Stanley Brown, Danny Mummert, Irving Bacon; ***D:*** Frank Strayer; ***W:*** Richard Flournoy; ***C:*** Henry Freulich.

Blondie On a Budget **1940** Dagwood wins 200 bucks in a contest and enlists the aid of ex-girlfriend Joan (Hayworth) to buy Blondie the fur coat she's been wanting. But Blondie wants to use the money to get Dagwood into a fishing club and misinterprets the situation. **68m/B VHS, DVD.** Penny Singleton, Arthur Lake, Larry Simms, Rita Hayworth, Danny Mummert, Don Beddoe, Fay Helm, John Qualen, Irving Bacon; ***D:*** Frank Strayer; ***W:*** Richard Flournoy; ***C:*** Henry Freulich.

Blondie Plays Cupid **1940** The Bumsteads are traveling to visit relatives in the country when they happen across a young couple (Ford and Walters) trying to elope. So Blondie decides to help the youngsters out. **68m/B VHS, DVD.** Penny Singleton, Arthur Lake, Larry Simms, Jonathan Hale, Glenn Ford, Luana Walters, Danny Mummert, Irving Bacon; ***D:*** Frank Strayer; ***W:*** Richard Flournoy, Karen De Wolf; ***C:*** Henry Freulich.

Blondie Takes a Vacation 1/2 **1939** Third in the series of fluff films adapted from Chic Young's comic strip. After the Bumstead family is snubbed at a snobby mountain resort they move to a friendlier nearby hotel where they try to help out the owners who are in danger of losing their investment. Baby Dumpling does his bit by unleashing a skunk in the ventilation system of the competing hotel. **68m/B VHS, DVD.** Penny Singleton, Arthur Lake, Larry Simms, Danny Mummert, Donald Meek, Donald MacBride, Thomas Ross, Robert Wilcox, Irving Bacon; ***D:*** Frank Strayer; ***W:*** Richard Flournoy; ***C:*** Henry Freulich.

Blondie's Blessed Event 1/2 **1942** Cookie is born, causing even more chaos in the Bumstead household. Meanwhile, Dagwood gets into trouble at work when he hires a cynical playwright to write an important speech for him. 11th entry in series. **69m/B VHS.** Penny Singleton, Arthur Lake, Larry Simms, Norma Jean Wayne, Jonathan Hale, Danny Mummert, Hans Conried, Irving Bacon, Stanley Brown, Mary Wickes, Paul Harvey, Arthur O'Connell; ***D:*** Frank Strayer; ***W:*** Richard Flournoy, Karen De Wolf, Connie Lee; ***C:*** Henry Freulich.

Blood Alley **1955** A seasoned Merchant Marine captain takes on a cargo of refugee Chinese to smuggle through enemy territory. Middling, mid-career Wayne vehicle. **115m/C VHS, DVD.** John Wayne, Lauren Bacall, Paul Fix, Joy Kim, Berry Kroeger, Mike Mazurki, Anita Ekberg; ***D:*** William A. Wellman; ***C:*** William Clothier.

Blood and Black Lace *Fashion House of Death; Six Women for the Murderer; Sei Donne per l'Assassino* **1964** Beautiful models are being brutally murdered and an inspector is assigned to the case, but not before more gruesome killings occur. Bava is, as usual, violent and suspenseful. Horror fans will enjoy this flick. **90m/C VHS, DVD.** *IT FR GE* Cameron Mitchell, Eva Bartok, Mary Arden, Dante DiPaolo, Arianna Gorini, Lea Krugher, Harriet Medin, Giuliano Raffaelli, Thomas Reiner, Frank Ressel, Massimo Righi; ***D:*** Mario Bava; ***W:*** Mario Bava, Marcello Fondato, Joe Barilla; ***C:*** Ubaldo Terzano; ***M:*** Carlo Rustichelli.

Blood & Chocolate 1/2 **2007 (PG-13)** Interspecies dating. American Vivian (Bruckner) works in a Bucharest chocolate shop when not turning furry at the full moon. She falls for cute human artist Aiden (Dancy), who's obsessed with werewolves, but has a problem since she's betrothed to hot pack leader Gabriel (Martinez). What's a shapeshifting gal to do? Tame story from von Garnier based on the edgier teen novel by Annette Curtis Klause; the pic's ending goes for conventional romance as does the schmaltzy music. Special effects are minimal. **96m/C DVD, Blu-ray Disc.** *GB RO* Agnes Bruckner, Olivier Martinez, Hugh Dancy, Bryan Dick, Katja Riemann; ***D:*** Katja von Garnier; ***W:*** Ehren Kruger, Christopher Landon; ***C:*** Brendan Galvin; ***M:*** Johnny Klimek, Reinhold Heil.

Blood & Concrete: A Love Story **1990 (R)** Bizarre, violent and stylish film-noir spoof, definitely not for all tastes. The innocent hero gets drawn into a maelstrom of intrigue over a killer aphrodisiac drug. Beals, an addicted punk rocker, gets to perform a few songs. **97m/C VHS.** Billy Zane, Jennifer Beals, Darren McGavin, James LeGros, Nicholas Worth, Mark Pellegrino, Harry Shearer, Billy Bastiani; ***D:*** Jeff Reiner; ***W:*** Jeff Reiner, Richard LaBrie; ***C:*** Declan Quinn; ***M:*** Vinnie Golia.

Blood & Donuts **1995 (R)** Hungry vampire Boya (Currie) is looking for a rat snack when he stumbles across an all-night donut shop where pretty cashier Molly (Clarkson) and friendly cabbie Earl (Louis) seek his help with a local crime boss. Mild horror mixed with comedy and limited gore. **89m/C VHS.** *CA* Gordon Currie, Justin Louis, Helene Clarkson, Fiona Reid, Frank Moore; ***Cameos:*** David Cronenberg; ***D:*** Holly Dale; ***W:*** Andrew Rai Berzins; ***C:*** Paul Sarossy.

Blood and Guns 1/2 **1979 (R)** Romance, revenge, and action abound in post-revolutionary Mexico. **96m/C VHS.** Orson Welles, Tomas Milian, John Steiner; ***D:*** Giulio Petroni.

Blood and Roses *Et Mourir de Plaisir* **1961** A girl who is obsessed with her family's vampire background becomes possessed by a vampire and commits numerous murders. The photography is good, but the plot is hazy and only effective in certain parts. Based on the story "Carmilla" by Sheridan Le Fanu. Later remade as "The Vampire Lovers" and "The Blood-Spattered Bride." **74m/C VHS.** *FR IT* Mel Ferrer, Elsa Martinelli, Annette (Stroyberg) Vadim, Marc Allegret, Jacques-Rene Chauffard, Serge Marquand, Gabriella Farinon, Alberto Bonucci, Nathalie Le Foret; ***D:*** Roger Vadim; ***W:*** Roger Vadim, Claude Martin, Roger Vailand, Claude Brule; ***C:*** Claude Renoir; ***M:*** Jean Prodromides.

Blood and Sand 1/2 **1922** Vintage romance based on Vicente Blasco Ibanez's novel about the tragic rise and fall of a matador, and the women in his life. The film that made Valentino a star. Remade in 1941. Silent. **87m/B VHS, DVD.** Rudolph Valentino, Nita Naldi, Lila Lee, Walter Long; ***D:*** Fred Niblo; ***W:*** June Mathis; ***C:*** Alvin Wyckoff.

Blood and Sand **1941** Director Mamoulian "painted" this picture in the new technicolor technique, which makes it a veritable explosion of color and spectacle. Power is the matador who becomes famous and then falls when he is torn between two women, forsaking his first love, bullfighting. Based on the novel "Sangre y Arena" by Vicente Blasco Ibanez. This movie catapulted Hayworth to stardom, primarily for her dancing, but also for her sexiness and seductiveness (and of course, her acting). Remake of the 1922 silent classic; remade again in 1989. **123m/C VHS, DVD.** Tyrone Power, Linda Darnell, Rita Hayworth, Alla Nazimova, Anthony Quinn, J. Carrol Naish, John Carradine, George Reeves; ***D:*** Rouben Mamoulian; ***W:*** Jo Swerling; ***C:*** Ernest Palmer, Ray Rennahan; ***M:*** Alfred Newman. Oscars '41: Color Cinematog.

Blood and Sand **1989 (R)** A bullfighter on the verge of super-stardom risks it all when he falls under the spell of a sexy, seductive woman. Will she destroy his one opportunity for fame? Interesting for people who actually enjoy watching the "sport" of bullfighting. Originally made in 1922 and remade in 1941. **96m/C VHS, DVD.** Christopher Rydell, Sharon Stone, Ana Torrent, Jose-Luis De Villalonga, Simon Andreu; ***D:*** Javier Elorrieta; ***W:*** Rafael Azcona, Ricardo Franco, Thomas Fucci; ***C:*** Antonio Rios; ***M:*** Jesus Gluck.

Blood and Steel **1925** The railroad tycoon's daughter and the construction foreman wind up together on an exciting train ride. Silent. **?m/B VHS.** Helen Holmes, William Desmond; ***D:*** J(ohn) P(aterson) McGowan; ***W:*** George Plympton; ***C:*** Roland Price.

Blood & Wine 1/2 **1996 (R)** Miami wine merchant Alex (Nicholson) gets involved with terminally ill safecracker Victor (Caine) to steal a necklace worth a cool million. Meanwhile he must deal with his crumbling marriage to Suzanne (Davis) and the bitter relationship with his stepson Jason (Dorff), who has eyes for both the necklace and his Cuban mistress (Lopez). Characterizations and strong performances (particularly by Nicholson and Caine) haul the sometimes lumbering plot to its violent conclusion. Promoted as the third part of a "dysfunctional family trilogy" with "Five Easy Pieces" and "The King of Marvin's Gardens." Seventh time Nicholson has worked with director Rafelson. **100m/C VHS, DVD.** Jack Nicholson, Michael Caine, Judy Davis, Stephen Dorff, Jennifer Lopez, Harold Perrineau Jr.; ***D:*** Bob Rafelson; ***W:*** Nick Villiars, Allison Cross; ***C:*** Newton Thomas (Tom) Sigel; ***M:*** Stephen Cohen.

Blood Angels *Thralls* **2005 (R)** Ashley (Baruc) left her bad home life to hang with her big sis—who, it ends up, is part of a group of half-vampire, half-human gal pals. The girls fill their human blood quota by tempting men to a club run by their oppressive master, Mr. Jones (Lamas), who won't give them full vampire powers, so they decide to use Ashley to give him the boot. **98m/C VHS, DVD.** *CA* Lorenzo Lamas, Siri Baruc, Sonya Salomaa, Crystal Lowe, Leah Cairns, Fiona Scott, Lisa Marie Caruk, Monica Delain; ***D:*** Ron Oliver; ***W:*** Lisa Morton, Brett Thompson; ***C:*** David Pelletier. **VIDEO**

Blood at Sundown 1/2 **1988** Routine oater where man returns home after the Civil War to find his wife kidnapped by a group of Mexican outlaws who have also taken over his village. **92m/C VHS.** Giuliano Gemma, Hally Hamond, Nieves Navarro, Antonio Casas, Fernando (Fernand) Sancho, Pajarito, George Martin; ***D:*** Duccio Tessari.

Blood Beach **WOOF!** **1981 (R)** A group of teenagers are devoured by menacing sand, which keeps people from getting to the water by swallowing them whole. Weak parody with some humorous moments; more silly than scary. **92m/C VHS.** David Huffman, Marianna Hill, John Saxon, Burt Young, Otis Young, Pamela McMyler, Bobby Bass, Darrell Fetty, Stefan Gierasch, Harriet Medin, Lynn(e) Marta, Mary Jo Catlett; ***D:*** Jeffrey Bloom; ***W:*** Jeffrey Bloom; ***C:*** Steven Poster; ***M:*** Gil Melle.

Blood Beast Terror 1/2 *The Vampire-Beast Craves Blood; Deathshead Vampire* **1967** An entomologist transforms his own daughter into a Deathshead Moth and she proceeds to terrorize and drink innocent victims' blood. **81m/C VHS, DVD.** *GB* Peter Cushing, Robert Flemyng, Wanda Ventham, Vanessa Howard; ***D:*** Vernon Sewell; ***W:*** Peter Bryan; ***C:*** Stanley Long; ***M:*** Paul Ferris.

Blood Bride 1/2 **1980** A lonely young woman finally finds happiness with her new husband but her world comes crashing about her with soul-mangling ferocity when she discovers he is actually a bloodthirsty maniac. **90m/C VHS.** Ellen Barber, Philip English; ***D:*** Robert J. Avrech.

Blood Brothers **1974 (R)** A young man who dreams of becoming a lawyer is disturbed when he discovers that his family has mafia ties. **148m/C VHS.** *IT* Claudia Cardinale, Franco Nero, Lina Polito; ***D:*** Pasquale Squitieri.

Blood Brothers **1997** Darryl has always looked up to older brother Sylvester. And then one day he witnesses a gang murder and Sylvester is one of the killers. The District Attorney senses Darryl knows more than he's saying and the gang bangers want to shut him up permanently, so each brother must look to his conscience and decide how best to be his brother's keeper. **91m/C VHS, DVD.** Clark Johnson, Richard Chevolleau, Mia Korf, Richard Yearwood, Ron White, Amir Williams, Ndehru Roberts, Timothy Stickney, Bill Nunn; ***D:*** Bruce Pittman; ***W:*** Paris Qualles; ***M:*** Harold Wheeler.

Blood Brothers *Tian Tang Kou* **2007 (R)** Largely told in flashback, this sketchy underworld drama depicts three childhood buddies climbing the crime ladder in 1930s Shanghai. Feng (Wu) is the romantic, Gang (Liu) the muscle, and Gang's younger brother Hu (Yang) serves as backup. Through several coincidences, the trio begins working for kingpin Boss Hong (Sun). But eventually Kang makes his own bid for power. John Woo serves as a producer, which seems only right since director Tan was inspired by Woo's 1990 pic, "A Bullet in the Head." Chinese with subtitles. **95m/C DVD.** *CH HK TW* Daniel Wu, Ye Liu, Tony Yang, Honglei Sun, Qi Shu, Xiaolu "Lulu" Li, Chang Chen; ***D:*** Alexi Tan; ***W:*** Tony Chan, Alexi Tan, Dan Jiang; ***C:*** Michel Taburiaux; ***M:*** Daniel Belardinelli.

Blood Clan 1/2 **1991 (R)** Based on the true story of Katy Bane, daughter of notorious Scottish cult leader, Sawney Bane, in whose lair were found the remains of over 1000 killed and cannibalized followers. When found, Bane's entire family was sentenced to death with the exception of Katy, who left to make a new start in Canada. When a rash of mysterious deaths break out in Katy's new home, she must defend herself from rumors that her father's murderous cult is resurfacing. **91m/C VHS.** Gordon Pinsent, Michelle Little, Robert Wisden; ***D:*** Charles Wilkinson.

Blood Creek 1/2 *Town Creek* **2009 (R)** Splatter horror with some good visuals and really stupid plot elements. In 1936, Nazi occultist Richard Wirth (Fassbinder) travels to a West Virginia farmhouse owned by German immigrants to examine a rune stone's demonic abilities. Decades pass and EMT worker Evan Marshall (Cavill) is shocked when his missing brother Victor (Purcell) suddenly turns up horribly scarred, claiming he was held hostage at the same farmhouse and they must stop what is happening there. Which involves Wirth. **90m/C DVD.** Dominic Purcell, Henry Cavill, Michael Fassbender, Emma Booth, Rainer Winkelvoss; ***D:*** Joel Schumacher; ***W:*** David Kajganich; ***C:*** Darko Suvak; ***M:*** David Buckley. **VIDEO**

Blood Crime 1/2 **2002** No-brainer B movie. Seattle cop Daniel Pruitt (Schaech) and his wife Jessica (Lackey) take a camping trip into Oregon. While he's away, she gets attacked in the woods. When Jessica identifies her attacker, her husband beats him. Later, she changes her mind about who her assailant is but by then it's too late—the man, who turns out to be the no-good son of Sheriff McKenna (Caan)—has died. **128m/C VHS, DVD.** James Caan, Johnathon Schaech, Elizabeth Lackey, David Field; ***D:*** William A. Graham; ***W:*** Preston A. Whitmore II, Mark Lawrence Miller; ***C:*** Robert Steadman; ***M:*** Chris Boardman. **CABLE**

Blood Cult **1985 (R)** A bizarre series of murder-mutilations take place on a small midwestern campus. Contains graphic violence that is not for the squeamish. This film was created especially for the home video market. **89m/C VHS, DVD.** Chuck Ellis, Julie Andelman, Jim Vance, Joe Hardt; ***D:*** Christopher Lewis; ***M:*** Rod Slane. **VIDEO**

Blood Debts **1983** A father is out for revenge after he saves his daughter from some hunters who raped her and also killed her boyfriend. **91m/C VHS.** Richard Harrison, Mike Manty, Jim Gaines, Anne Jackson, Anne Milhench; ***D:*** Teddy Page.

Blood Diamond 1/2 **2006 (R)** Flawed, well-intentioned adventure-drama takes place in 1999, during the horrors of civil war in Sierra Leone. Rebels raid a village, committing mass murder and forcing the boys to become child soldiers while the men are slave labor in the diamond mines. These so-called "conflict stones" are then used to buy more weapons. Solomon Vandy (Hounsou) unearths and hides a valuable pink diamond in order to ransom his family after he escapes. But Vandy's find comes to the attention of Afrikaner smuggler Danny Archer (DiCaprio), who is looking to use the diamond to his own advantage. American journalist Maddy (Connelly) happens to be around to prick Danny's nearly non-existent conscience. The actors do well and the story is harrowing but director Zwick has a tendency to be a scold. **143m/C DVD, Blu-ray Disc, HD DVD.** *US* Leonardo DiCaprio, Djimon Hounsou, Jennifer Connelly, Arnold Vosloo, Kagiso Kuypers, Michael Sheen, Jimi Mistry, Stephen Collins, David Harewood, Anthony Coleman, Benu Mabhena, Basil Wallace; ***D:*** Edward Zwick; ***W:*** Charles Leavitt; ***C:*** Eduardo Serra; ***M:*** James Newton Howard.

Blood Diner **WOOF!** **1987** Two spirit-possessed, diner-owning brothers kill countless young girls for demonic rituals, and serve their corpses as gourmet food in their restaurant. Some funny moments mixed in with the requisite gore. Cult potential. **88m/C VHS.** Rick Burks, Carl Crew, Roger Dauer, Lisa Guggenheim, Roxanne Cybelle, Cynthia Baker; ***D:*** Jackie Kong; ***W:*** Michael Sonye; ***C:*** Jurg Walther; ***M:*** Don Preston.

Blood Feast *Feast of Flesh* **1963** The first of Lewis' gore-fests, in which a demented caterer butchers hapless young women to splice them together in order to bring back an Egyptian goddess. Dated, campy, and gross; reportedly shot in four days (it shows). **70m/C VHS, DVD.** Connie Mason, William Kerwin, Mal Arnold, Scott H. Hall, Lyn Bolton, Toni Calvert, Gene Courtier, Ashlyn Martin, Jerome (Jerry Stallion) Eden, David Friedman; ***D:*** Herschell Gordon Lewis; ***W:*** Allison Louise Downe; ***C:*** Herschell Gordon Lewis; ***M:*** Herschell Gordon Lewis.

Blood Feud *Revenge* **1979 (R)** In Italy preceding Europe's entry into WWII, a young widow is in mourning over the brutal murder of her husband by the Sicilian Mafia. In the meantime she must contend with the rivalry between Mastroianni as a lawyer and Giannini as a small-time crook both vying for her affections. Dubbed. **112m/C VHS.** *IT* Sophia Loren, Marcello Mastroianni, Giancarlo Giannini; ***D:*** Lina Wertmuller; ***W:*** Lina Wertmuller.

Blood for a Silver Dollar 1/2 *One Silver Dollar; Un Dollar Troue* **1966** Action-filled western, littered with murder, revenge and romance. **98m/C VHS.** *IT FR* Montgomery Wood, Evelyn Stewart, Pierre Cressoy; ***D:*** Giorgio Ferroni; ***M:*** Gianni Ferrio.

Blood for Blood 1/2 **1995 (R)** Cop must take up the martial arts skills he learned in childhood in order to protect his family from assassination. **93m/C VHS.** Lorenzo Lamas, James Lew, Mako, Eric Pierpoint, James Shigeta, James Callahan; ***D:*** John Weidner; ***M:*** Joel Goldsmith.

Blood Freak **WOOF!** *Blood Freaks* **1972** An absolutely insane anti-drug, Christian splatter film. A Floridian biker is introduced to drugs by a young woman and eventually turns into a poultry-monster who drinks the blood of junkies. Narrated by a chain smoker who has a coughing fit. Don't miss it. **86m/C VHS, DVD.** Steve Hawkes, Dana Cullivan, Randy Grinter Jr., Tina Anderson, Heather Hughes; ***D:*** Brad Grinter, Steve Hawkes.

Blood Frenzy **1987** Psychologist's patients take a therapeutic trip to the desert. The sun and heat take their toll, and everyone gets violent. This kind of therapy we don't need, and the movie's a waste, as well. Made for video. Loring was Wednesday on TV's "The Addams Family." **90m/C VHS.** John Montero, Lisa Loring, Hank Garrett, Wendy MacDonald; ***D:*** Hal Freeman. **VIDEO**

Blood from the Mummy's Tomb 1/2 **1971** The immortal spirit of Tera, Egyptian queen of evil, haunts Margaret (Leon), the daughter of an archaeologist who discovered her tomb. As a long-prophesied conjunction of stars begins to occur, Margaret finds herself enthralled by Tera's power and finds herself becoming possessed by Tera's spirit. This adaptation of Bram Stoker's "The Jewel of Seven Stars" begins well, with a wonderfully mysterious and moody first half, but it loses steam in the somewhat muddled (and tedious) second half. Coulouris (without the old age makeup) looks exactly like his Thatcher character in "Citizen Kane," 30 years earlier, but sadly is given not much to do other than roll his eyes and scream. Leon is a likable heroine but that wig and false eyelashes have got to go! Remade in post-"Omen" fashion as "The Awakening." **94m/C VHS, DVD.** *GB* Andrew Keir, Valerie Leon, James Villiers, Hugh Burden, George Coulouris, Mark Edwards; ***D:*** Seth Holt; ***W:*** Christopher Wicking; ***C:*** Arthur Grant; ***M:*** Tristram Cary.

Blood Games **WOOF!** **1990 (R)** Buxom baseball team bats 1000 against the home team and the winning babes find out just how poor losers can be. Diamonds aren't always a girl's best friend. **90m/C VHS.** Gregory Cummings, Laura Albert, Shelly Abblett, Luke Shay, Ross Hagen; ***D:*** Tanya Rosenberg.

Blood Gnome **2002 (R)** Evil, hungry gnomes attack patrons of the local dominatrix, with a crime scene photographer as the sole spectator to the carnage. Grisly and made on the cheap, and looks it. **87m/C VHS, DVD.** Vincent Bilancio, Stephanie Beaton, Julie Strain, Massimo Avidano, Melissa Pursley; ***D:*** John Lechago; ***W:*** John Lechago. **VIDEO**

Blood, Guts, Bullets and Octane **1999 (R)** Used-car salesmen Sid (Carnahan) and Bob (Leis) are trying to keep their failing business afloat when a broker offers then a quarter million to let a 1963 Pontiac Le Mans convertible (burgundy) stay on their lot for 48 hours. The FBI are after the car and its owners, who've left a bloody cross-country trail. And the motor-mouth duo decide to renege on the deal. Desperate lowlifes and vicious crime winds up looking very familiar. **87m/C VHS, DVD.** Joe Carnahan, Dan Leis, Ken Rudolph, James Salter, Dan Harlan; ***D:*** Joe Carnahan; ***W:*** Joe Carnahan; ***C:*** John A. Jimenez; ***M:*** Mark Priolo, Martin Burke.

Blood Hook 1/2 **1986** A self-parodying teenage-slasher film about kids running into a backwoods fishing tournament while on vacation, complete with ghouls, cannibalism and grotesquerie. **85m/C VHS, DVD.** Mark Jacobs, Lisa Todd, Patrick Danz; ***D:*** James "Jim" Mallon.

Blood In ... Blood Out: Bound by Honor 1/2 *Bound by Honor* **1993 (R)** Three-hour epic about Chicano gang culture focuses on three buddies whose lives evolve into a drug-addicted artist, a narc, and a prison regular. Written by acclaimed poet Baca, the film touches on issues such as poverty, racism, drugs, and violence as they pertain to Hispanic life. Unfortunately, the extreme violence (shootings, stabbings, and garrotings) completely overwhelms the rest of the story. Based on a story by Ross Thomas. **180m/C VHS, DVD.** Thomas F. Wilson, Damian Chapa, Jesse Borrego, Benjamin Bratt, Enrique Castillo, Victor Rivers, Delroy Lindo, Tom Towler; ***D:*** Taylor Hackford; ***W:*** Floyd Mutrux, Jimmy Santiago Baca, Jeremy Iacone; ***C:*** Gabriel Beristain; ***M:*** Bill Conti.

Blood Island *The Shuttered Room* **1968** A couple inherits an old house on a remote New England island where the woman grew up. They discover that this old house needs more than a paint job to make it livable; seems there's something evil in them there walls. Based on an H.P. Lovecraft story. Greene, who's best known for later directing "Godspell," and the solid cast fail to animate the inert script. **100m/C VHS.** *GB* Gig Young, Carol Lynley, Oliver Reed, Flora Robson; ***D:*** David Greene.

Blood Legacy *Legacy of Blood* **1973 (R)** Four heirs must survive a night in a lonely country estate to collect their money; what do you think happens? Average treatment of the haunted house theme. **77m/C VHS, DVD.** John Carradine, John Russell, Faith Domergue, Merry Anders, Richard (Dick) Davalos, Jeff Morrow, Roy Engle; ***D:*** Carl Monson; ***W:*** Eric Norden; ***C:*** Jack Beckett.

Blood Mania **1970 (R)** A retired surgeon's daughter decides to murder her father to collect her inheritance prematurely, but soon learns that crime doesn't pay as well as medicine. Low-budget, low-interest flick. **90m/C VHS, DVD.** Peter Carpenter, Maria de Aragon, Alex Rocco; ***D:*** Robert Vincent O'Neil.

Blood Money 1/2 **1980 (PG)** A dying ex-criminal returns to Australia to redeem his name and die with dignity. **64m/C VHS.** *AU* Bryan Brown, John Flaus, Chrissie James; ***D:*** Christopher Fitchett.

Blood Money *The Arrangement* **1998 (R)** Five dead bodies, $4 million, and one eye-witness, stripper Candy (Petty), are what remains of a drug deal gone south. Now, Detective Connor (Ironside) must protect his witness from Mob reprisals. **95m/C VHS, DVD.** Michael Ironside, Lori Petty, Currie Graham; ***D:*** Michael Ironside. **VIDEO**

Blood Money **1999 (R)** Tony Restrelli (Bloom) is the legit member of a mob family who made his money in the stock market. Now his financial knowledge is needed by his family to fend off would-be interlopers—and he can also avenge his brother's murder. **95m/C VHS, DVD.** Brian Bloom, Alan Arkin, Alicia Coppola, Jennifer Gatti, Bruce Kirby, Jonathan Scarfe, Gregory Sierra, Leonard Stone; ***D:*** Aaron Lipstadt. **CABLE**

Blood Money: The Story of Clinton and Nadine 1/2 *Clinton & Nadine* **1988** A confusing action/thriller with a good cast. Garcia is a small-time exotic bird smuggler whose gun-running brother has been murdered. He uses high-class hooker Barkin to get close to his brother's contacts, who turn out to be running guns to the Nicaraguan contras and involved in a dangerous government conspiracy. **95m/C VHS, DVD.** Andy Garcia, Ellen Barkin, Morgan Freeman; ***D:*** Jerry Schatzberg. **CABLE**

Blood Monkey **2007** Six American grad students arrive in Africa (Thailand substituted) to study apes with Professor Hamilton (Abraham). But his studies mean investigating local rumors of a tribe of killer chimpanzees. When the students witness the carnage first-hand, they want out but neither the professor nor the chimps are willing to let them go. Not much monkey action since the budget apparently didn't stretch too far. **90m/C DVD.** F. Murray Abraham, Amy Manson, Matt Reeves, Freishia Bomanbehram, Sebastian Armesto, Matt Ryan, Laura Aikman; ***D:*** Robert Young; ***W:*** George LaVoo, Gary Dauberman; ***C:*** Choochart Nantitanyatada; ***M:*** Charles Olins, Mark Ryder. **TV**

The Blood of a Poet 1/2 *Le Sang d'un Poete* **1930** Cocteau's first film, a practically formless piece of poetic cinema, detailing all manner of surreal events occurring in the instant a chimney falls. In French with English subtitles. **55m/B VHS, DVD.** Enrique Rivero, Feral Benga, Jean Desbordes; ***D:*** Jean Cocteau; ***W:*** Jean Cocteau; ***C:*** Georges Perinal; ***M:*** Georges Auric.

Blood of Dracula 1/2 *Blood Is My Heritage; Blood of the Demon* **1957** They don't make 1950s rock 'n' roll girls' school vampire movies like this anymore, for which we may be grateful. Hypnotism, an amulet, and a greasepaint makeup job turn a shy female student into a bloodsucker. **71m/B VHS.** Sandra Harrison, Louise Lewis, Gail Ganley, Jerry Blaine, Heather Ames, Malcolm Atterbury, Richard Devon, Thomas B(rowne). Henry, Don Devlin, Edna Holland; ***D:*** Herbert L. Strock; ***W:*** Aben Kandel; ***C:*** Monroe Askins; ***M:*** Paul Dunlap.

Blood of Dracula's Castle *Dracula's Castle; Castle of Dracula* **1969** Couple inherits an allegedly deserted castle, but upon moving in discover Mr. and Mrs. Dracula have settled there. The vampires keep young women chained in the dungeon for continual blood supply. Also present are a hunchback and a werewolf. Awesome Adamson production is highlighted by the presence of the gorgeous Volante. Early cinematography effort by the renowned Laszlo Kovacs. **84m/C VHS, DVD.** John Carradine, Alexander D'Arcy, Paula Raymond, Ray Young, Vicki Volante, Robert Dix, John Cardos, Ken Osborne; ***D:*** Jean Hewitt, Al Adamson; ***W:*** Rex Carlton; ***C:*** Laszlo Kovacs.

Blood of Ghastly Horror WOOF! *The Fiend with the Atomic Brain; Psycho a Go Go!; The Love Maniac; The Man with the Synthetic Brain; The Fiend with the Electronic Brain* **1972** A young man thinks he has a new lease on life when he is the happy recipient of a brain transplant, but his dreams are destroyed when he evolves into a rampaging killer. This movie is so awful it hides behind numerous but rather creative aliases. **87m/C VHS, DVD.** John Carradine, Kent Taylor, Tommy Kirk, Regina Carrol, Roy Morton, Tracey Robbins; ***D:*** Al Adamson; ***W:*** Chris Martino, Dick Poston; ***C:*** Vilmos Zsigmond.

The Blood of Heroes *The Salute of the Jugger* **1989 (R)** A post-apocalyptic action flick detailing the adventures of a battered team of "juggers," warriors who challenge small village teams to a brutal sport (involving dogs' heads on sticks) that's a cross between jousting and football. **97m/C VHS, DVD.** Rutger Hauer, Joan Chen, Vincent D'Onofrio, Anna (Katerina) Katarina; ***D:*** David Peoples; ***W:*** David Peoples; ***C:*** David Eggby; ***M:*** Todd Boekelheide.

Blood of Jesus **1941** A sinful husband accidentally shoots his newly baptized wife, causing an uproar in their rural town. Williams later starred as Andy on the "Amos 'n' Andy" TV series. **50m/C VHS, DVD.** Spencer Williams Jr., Cathryn Caviness; ***D:*** Spencer Williams Jr.; ***W:*** Spencer Williams Jr. Natl. Film Reg. '91.

The Blood of Others **1984** A driveling adaptation of the Simone de Beauvoir novel about a young French woman at the outbreak of WWII torn between her absent boyfriend in the Resistance and a kind, wealthy German. Made for French TV, it stars Jodie Foster and Michael Ontkean as the Gallic pair. **130m/C VHS.** *FR* Jodie Foster, Sam Neill, Michael Ontkean, Stephane Audran, Lambert Wilson, John Vernon, Kate Reid, Jean-Pierre Aumont; ***D:*** Claude Chabrol; ***W:*** Brian Moore. **TV**

Blood of the Hunter 1/2 **1994 (PG-13)** Psycho-killer holds postman's wife captive in a remote cabin in the Canadian wilderness. Turns out hubby and psycho share a mysterious past. **92m/C VHS.** Michael Biehn, Alexandra Vandernoot, Gabriel Arcand; ***D:*** Gilles Carle.

Blood of the Vampire 1/2 **1958** A Transylvanian doctor is executed for being a vampire and his hunchbacked assistant brings him back to life. **84m/C VHS, DVD.** *GB* Donald Wolfit, Vincent Ball, Barbara Shelley, Victor Maddern; ***D:*** Henry Cass; ***W:*** Jimmy Sangster.

The Blood on Satan's Claw *Satan's Skin; Satan's Claw* **1971** Graphic tale centering on the Devil himself. Townspeople in an English village circa 1670 find the spirit of Satan taking over their children, who begin to practice witchcraft. Well made with lots of attention to period details. Not for the faint-hearted. **90m/C VHS.** *GB* Patrick Wymark, Linda Hayden, Barry Andrews, Michele Dotrice, James Hayter, Avice Landon, Simon Williams, Tamara Ustinov; ***D:*** Piers Haggard; ***C:*** Dick Bush.

Blood on the Badge 1/2 **1992** Illegal arms have been stolen from a military arsenal and fall into the hands of Libyan Nationalists who begin a terrorist campaign. Detective Neal Farrow is assigned to stop them. **92m/C VHS.** Ramon Estevez, David Harrod, Rocky Patterson, Desiree Laforge, Dean Nolen, Melissa Deleon, Todd Everett; ***D:*** Bret McCormick.

Blood on the Moon 1/2 **1948** Well-acted film about a cowboy's involvement in a friend's underhanded schemes. Based on a Luke Short novel, this dark film revolves around a western land dispute between cattlemen and homesteaders. **88m/B VHS.** Robert Mitchum, Robert Preston, Walter Brennan, Barbara Bel Geddes; ***D:*** Robert Wise.

Blood on the Mountain **1988** After escaping from prison, Jim plots revenge against his accomplice, only to kill an innocent man instead. **71m/C VHS.** Stracker Edwards, Tim Jones, Paula Preston, Cliff Turknett, Rich Jury; ***D:*** Donald W. Thompson.

Blood on the Sun 1/2 **1945** Newspaperman in Japan uncovers plans for world dominance as propaganda, violence, and intrigue combine in this action-adventure. Also available colorized. **98m/B VHS, DVD.** James Cagney, Sylvia Sidney, Robert Armstrong, Wallace Ford; ***D:*** Frank Lloyd; ***W:*** Lester Cole, Nathaniel Curtis, Frank Melford; ***C:*** Theodor Sparkuhl; ***M:*** Miklos Rozsa.

The Blood Oranges 1/2 **1997 (R)** Pretentious film is set in the anything-goes '70s in a tropical backwater village. Bohemian marrieds Cyril (Dance) and Fiona (Lee) believe in fulfilling every sexual fantasy but their latest exchange of marital partners comes with unexpected complications. Fiona is attracted to photographer Hugh (Lane), who resists her charms for more deviant behavior, while Hugh's wife Catherine (Robins) is easily seduced by Cyril's courtship. Dialogue is laughable and the acting equally overblown. Based on the novel by John Hawkes. **93m/C VHS, DVD.** Charles Dance, Sheryl Lee, Colin Lane, Laila Robins, Rachael Bella; ***D:*** Philip Haas; ***W:*** Belinda Haas, Philip Haas; ***C:*** Bernard Zitzermann; ***M:*** Angelo Badalamenti.

Blood Orgy of the She-Devils **WOOF! 1974 (PG)** Exploitative gore nonsense about female demons, beautiful witches, and satanic worship. Some movies waste all their creative efforts on their titles. **73m/C VHS, DVD.** Lila Zaborin, Tom Pace, Leslie McRae, Ray Myles, Victor Izay, William Bagdad; ***D:*** Ted V. Mikels; ***W:*** Ted V. Mikels; ***C:*** Anthony Salinas.

Blood Pledge *A Blood Pledge: Broken Promise; Whispering Corridors 5: Suicide Pact; Yeogo goedam 5: Dong-ban-ja-sal* **2009** The fifth film in Korea's Whispering Corridors series is, as usual, set in an all girls' school for overachievers with malicious students and staff. Eon-joo (Jang Kyeong-ah) is found dead, an apparent suicide, and her younger sister is determined to find out why. Apparently there was a suicide pact between her and three other girls who are still alive, implying they may have been responsible for her demise. The usual ghost is not far behind. **88m/C DVD.** *KN* Son Eun-seo, Son Eun-seo, Song Min-jeong, Oh Yeon-seo, Yoo Shin-ae; ***D:*** Jong-yong Lee; ***W:*** Jong-yong Lee.

Blood Rage WOOF! *Nightmare at Shadow Woods* **1987 (R)** A maniacal twin goes on a murderous rampage through his brother's neighborhood. AKA "Nightmare at Shadow Woods." Only for die-hard "Mary Hartman" fans. **87m/C VHS, DVD.** Louise Lasser, Mike Soper; ***D:*** John Grissmer; ***M:*** Richard Einhorn.

Blood Rain *Hyeol-ui nu* **2005** Set in 1808 during Korea's Joseon dynasty, a local shaman collapses and seems to be possessed by the spirit of Lord Kang, a commissioner executed years ago for treason and practicing Catholicism. One by one all the informants in Kang's case begin dying, and investigator Won-kyu (Seung-won Cha) is sent to find out if there is a ghost at work, or simple human revenge. Not quite a detective mystery and not quite a slasher film. **115m/C DVD.** *KN* Seung-won Cha, Ji-na Choi, Seong Ji, Hyeon-kyeong Oh, Yong-woo Park, Ho-jin Jeon; ***D:*** Dae-seung Kim; ***W:*** Seong-jae Kim, Won-jae Lee; ***C:*** Yeong-hwon Choi; ***M:*** Yeong-wook Jo, Ji-Soo Lee.

Blood Red 1/2 **1988 (R)** In 1895 Northern California, an Italian immigrant and his family give bloody battle to a powerful industrialist who wants their land in wine-growing country. Watch for the scenes involving veteran Roberts and his then-newcomer sister, pretty woman Julia. **91m/C VHS.** Eric Roberts, Dennis Hopper, Giancarlo Giannini, Burt Young, Carlin Glynn, Lara Harris, Susan Anspach, Julia Roberts, Elias Koteas, Frank Campanella, Aldo Ray, Horton Foote Jr.; ***D:*** Peter Masterson; ***W:*** Ron Cutler.

Blood Relations 1/2 **1987 (R)** A woman is introduced to her fiance's family only to find out that they, as well as her fiance, are murdering, perverted weirdos competing for an inheritance. **88m/C VHS, DVD.** *CA* Jan Rubes, Ray Walston, Lydie Denier, Kevin Hicks, Lynne Adams, Sam Malkin, Steven Saylor, Carrie Leigh; ***D:*** Graeme Campbell.

Blood Relatives *Les Liens de Sang* **1977** Langlois admits she saw her brother kill her cousin, with whom he had been carrying on an incestuous relationship. But the discovery of the dead girl's diary by police inspector Sutherland reveals many more layers of intrigue than were initially evident. Based on a novel by Ed McBain. The French actors have been dubbed into English. **94m/C VHS.** *CA* Lisa Langlois, Donald Sutherland, Stephane Audran, David Hemmings, Donald Pleasence, Laurent Malet, Micheline Lanctot, Aude Landry; ***D:*** Claude Chabrol; ***W:*** Claude Chabrol.

Blood Relic 1/2 **2005 (R)** Pilot Hank Campbell (Christian) is possessed by a mysterious talisman, commits mass murder on a naval base, and winds up in the loony bin for 22 years. Upon his release, he heads back to the scene of the crime and discovers history buff Harry (Drago) is turning the base into a museum with the help of a bunch of handy young people (handy for slaughtering that is). Anyway, mayhem is likely since Campbell is determined to find his talisman again. **86m/C DVD.** John Christian, Billy Drago, Jennifer Grant, Debbie Rochon, Joshua Park, Kelly Ray; ***D:*** J. Christian Ingvordsen; ***W:*** J. Christian Ingvordsen, Matt Howe; ***C:*** Matt Howe; ***M:*** Timo Elliston. **VIDEO**

Blood Ring 1/2 **1993** When Sue's boxer husband goes missing she enlists old friend Max to help find him. They uncover a gambling ring run by drug lords where the kickboxing matches are to the death. Naturally, Max decides to use his expert kickboxing skills to get a violent revenge. **90m/C VHS.** Dale "Apollo" Cook, Andrea Lamatsch, Don Nakaya Neilsen, Steve Tartalia; ***D:*** Irvin Johnson; ***W:*** Ron Davies.

Blood Salvage *Mad Jake* **1990 (R)** A crazy junkman kidnaps beautiful girls, selling their organs to the highest bidder. He meets his match when a potential target refuses to become a victim in spite of her wheelchair. Interesting plot twists keep this Grade B thriller above average. **90m/C VHS.** Danny Nelson, Lori Birdsong, John Saxon, Ray Walston, Christian Hesler, Ralph Pruitt Vaughn, Laura Whyte, Evander Holyfield; ***D:*** Tucker Johnson; ***W:*** Tucker Johnson, Ken Sanders; ***C:*** Michael Karp.

Blood Screams WOOF! 1988 (R) Nosy people drop in on an old town in Mexico and attempt to uncover the secrets hidden there, but bizarre entities throw out the unwelcome mat and terrorize them. Lots of blood and screaming. **75m/C VHS.** Ran Sands, James Garnett, Ralph Navarro, Mario Almada, Alfredo Gutierrez, Stacey Shaffer, Russ Tamblyn, Isela Vega; ***D:*** Glenn Gebhard.

Blood Simple 1/2 **1985 (R)** A jealous husband hires a sleazy private eye to murder his adulterous wife and her lover. A dark, intricate, morbid morality tale that deviates imaginatively from the standard murder mystery thriller. First film scripted by the Coen brothers. **96m/C VHS, DVD.** John Getz, M. Emmet Walsh, Dan Hedaya, Frances McDormand, Samm-Art Williams, Van Brooks, Lauren Bivens, Holly Hunter; ***D:*** Joel Coen; ***W:*** Joel Coen, Ethan Coen; ***C:*** Barry Sonnenfeld; ***M:*** Carter Burwell. Ind. Spirit '86: Actor (Walsh), Director (Coen); Sundance '85: Grand Jury Prize.

Blood Sisters WOOF! 1986 (R) Sorority babes intend to spend a giggle-strewn night in a haunted house but end up decapitated, butchered, and cannibalized. **85m/C VHS, DVD.** Amy Brentano, Marla MacHart, Brigete Cossu, Randy Mooers; ***D:*** Roberta Findlay.

Blood Song *Dream Slayer* **1982** A patient (yester-decade teen throb Frankie Avalon) escapes into the night from a mental institution after murdering an attendant. He takes his only possession with him, a carved wooden flute. A young woman sees him burying his latest victim, and now he's on a hunt to play his "blood song" for her. Pretty bad, but fun to see Avalon play a less-than-squeaky-clean role. **90m/C VHS, DVD.** Frankie Avalon, Donna Wilkes, Richard Jaeckel, Dane Clark, Antoinette Bower, Lenny Montana; ***D:*** Alan J. Levi; ***W:*** Lenny Montana.

The Blood Spattered Bride *Blood Castle; La Novia Esangrentada; Bloody Fiance; Till Death Us Do Part* **1972** Newlywed couple honeymoons in a remote castle in southern Spain. They are visited by a mysterious young woman who begins to influence the bride in the ways of lesbian bloodsucking. O.K. '70s Euro-eroti-horror based on Sheridan Le Fanu's "Carmilla." **101m/C VHS, DVD.** *SP* Simon Andreu, Maribel Martin, Alexandra Bastedo, Dean Selmier, Rosa Ma Rodriguez, Montserrat Julio, Angel Lombarte; ***D:*** Vicente Aranda; ***W:*** Vicente Aranda; ***C:*** Fernando Arribas.

Blood Stained Tradewind 1/2 *Xue zai feng shang* **1990** Shing (Fong) and Hong (Lee) are brothers raised by a Triad Gang leader. When he decides Shing will be the new leader and refuses, he is tossed out, forced to go on the straight and narrow. Hong takes over and he and Shing are immediately accused by rivals of stealing from the gang. Blood and fists fly for the immediate future. **94m/C DVD.** *CH* Alex Fong, Shui-Fan Fung, Waise Lee, Carrie Ng, Fong Pao; ***D:*** Yuen Tat Chor; ***W:*** Philip Cheng.

Blood Surf *Crocodile* **2000 (R)** A filmmaker and her crew travel to Australia to do a documentary on the extreme sport of blood surfing where thrillseekers try to out surf sharks to shore. Only the sharks aren't the problem—a giant salt-water crocodile gets to the participants first. Very silly; your enjoyment will depend on your tolerance for the fake croc. **88m/C VHS, DVD.** Matt Borlenghi, Duncan Regehr, Kate Fischer, Taryn Reif, Joel West, Dax Miller; ***D:*** James D.R. Hickox; ***W:*** Sam Bernard, Robert L. Levy; ***C:*** Christopher Pearson; ***M:*** Jim Manzie. **VIDEO**

Blood: The Last Vampire 1/2 **2009 (R)** Tedious live-action adaptation of a 2001 anime flick that's heavy on the gore. Saya (Jeon) is a 400-year-old samurai, who looks like a 16-year-old schoolgirl (complete with kinky uniform) who is charged with hunting down the vampires and demons who plague Japan. She is ordered by a secret organization to protect the students at an American military base where her cover is blown when she must rescue general's daughter Alice (Miller) from a vampire attack. Then it all comes down to the ultimate battle between Saya and super-vamp Onigen (Koyuki).

91m/C DVD. *FR HK* Koyuki, Liam Cunningham, Larry Lamb, Ji-hyun Jeon, Allison Miller, Costanza Balduzzi, Yasuaka Kurata; ***D:*** Chris Nahon; ***W:*** Chris Chow, Yasuaka Kurata; ***C:*** Hang-Seng Poon; ***M:*** Clint Mansell.

Blood Thirst 🦴🦴 **1965** Obscure horror film about a woman who stays young by indulging in ritual killings and strange experiments. **73m/B VHS, DVD.** *PH* Robert Winston, Yvonne Nielson, Vic Diaz; ***D:*** Newton Arnold.

Blood Tide 🦴 *The Red Tide* **1982 (R)** A disgusting, flesh-eating monster disrupts a couple's vacation in the Greek isles. Beautiful scenery, good cast, bad movie. **82m/C VHS, DVD.** James Earl Jones, Jose Ferrer; ***D:*** Richard Jeffries; ***W:*** Nico Mastorakis.

Blood Ties 🦴 ½ **1987** An American naval engineer in Sicily gets involved with the Mob in order to save his father's life. **98m/C VHS.** *IT* Brad Davis, Tony LoBianco, Vincent Spano, Barbara DeRossi, Maria Conchita Alonso; ***D:*** Giacomo Battiato.

Blood Ties 🦴🦴 ½ **1992** Reporter Harry Martin belongs to an unusual family—modern-day vampires (who prefer to be known as Carpathian-Americans). But they have an age-old problem with a band of fanatical vampire hunters. This time around you'll root for the bloodsuckers. **90m/C VHS, DVD.** Harley Venton, Patrick Bauchau, Kim Johnston-Ulrich, Michelle Johnson, Jason London, Bo Hopkins, Grace Zabriskie, Salvator Xuereb; ***D:*** Jim McBride; ***W:*** Richard Shapiro. **TV**

Blood Tracks 🦴 ½ **1986** A woman kills her abusive husband, then hides out in the mountains with her kids until they turn into cannibalistic savages. Years later, people show up to shoot a music video. Blood runs in buckets. **82m/C** Jeff Harding, Michael Fitzpatrick, Naomi Kaneda, Angelo Infanti; ***D:*** Mike Jackson.

Blood Trails 🦴 ½ **2006 (R)** After a one-night stand with unstable bike cop Chris (Price), bike messenger Anne (Palmer) takes off with boyfriend Michael (Frederick) for a weekend of mountain biking. Guess who appears to stalk Anne? Basically a chase on two wheels and not particularly frightening. **87m/C DVD.** Rebecca Palmer, Ben Price, Tom Frederick; ***D:*** Robert Krause; ***W:*** Robert Krause, Florian Puchert; ***C:*** Ralf Noack; ***M:*** Ben Bartlett. **VIDEO**

Blood Vows: The Story of a Mafia Wife 🦴🦴 **1987** TV's Laura Ingalls (Gilbert) leaps from the prairie to modern-day mafia in this warped Cinderella story. She meets the man of her dreams, whom she slowly finds is her worst nightmare as she becomes trapped within the confines of her new-found "family." TV soaper is way over the top in terms of melodrama. **100m/C VHS.** Melissa Gilbert, Joe Penny, Eileen Brennan, Talia Shire, Anthony (Tony) Franciosa; ***D:*** Paul Wendkos; ***M:*** William Goldstein. **TV**

Blood Voyage **WOOF! 1977 (R)** A crewman aboard a pleasure yacht must find out who is killing off his passengers one by one. **80m/C VHS.** Jonathon Lippe, Laurie Rose, Midori, Mara Modair; ***D:*** Frank Mitchell.

Blood Warriors 🦴 ½ **1993** An ex-Marine finds out a old buddy is leading a private army of mercenaries. When he refuses to join up their friendship turns violent. **93m/C VHS.** David Bradley, Frank Zagarino; ***D:*** Sam Firstenberg; ***W:*** David Bradley.

Blood Wedding 🦴🦴🦴 *Bodas de Sangre* **1981** A wonderfully passionate dance film from Saura and choreographed by Gades, based on the play by famed author Federico Garcia Lorca. A young bride (Hoyos) runs off with her married lover (Gades) on her wedding day and her jilted husband (Jimenez) comes after them. The film is set-up at a dress rehearsal where the dancers, led by Gades, perform upon a bare stage. If you like flamenco, there are two more: "Carmen" and "El Amor Brujo." Spanish with subtitles. **71m/C VHS.** *SP* Antonio Gades, Cristina Hoyos, Marisol, Carmen Villena, Juan Antonio Jimenez; ***D:*** Carlos Saura; ***W:*** Carlos Saura, Antonio Gades; ***C:*** Teodoro Escamilla; ***M:*** Emillo De Diego.

Blood Work 🦴🦴 ½ **2002 (R)** Retired FBI profiler Terry McCaleb (Eastwood) has just had a heart transplant. But, while undergoing checkups, he's brought back to track a serial killer who apparently murdered the woman who became his donor. Clint can still do the loner detective to a T, the question is, should he? The evidence her points to "probably not." It's not that he's not good at it, it's that there's really nothing more he can do WITH it. The killer is easy to spot from a mile away, and thankfully McCaleb does, which leaves the how and when of catching him (in the gender-nonspecific sense) as the only suspense. Well done, but ultimately forgettable. Based on the novel by Michael Connelly. **111m/C VHS, DVD.** *US* Clint Eastwood, Anjelica Huston, Jeff Daniels, Wanda De Jesus, Paul Rodriguez, Tina Lifford, Dylan Walsh, Gerry Becker, Alix Koromzay, Mason Lucero, Rick Hoffman; ***D:*** Clint Eastwood; ***W:*** Brian Helgeland; ***C:*** Tom Stern; ***M:*** Lennie Niehaus.

Bloodbath 🦴🦴 *Sky is Falling* **1976** Drugs, sex and terrorism—Hopper is typecast as an American degenerate who, along with his expatriate friends, is persecuted by local religious cults who need sacrifices. **89m/C VHS, DVD.** Dennis Hopper, Carroll Baker, Richard Todd, Faith Brook, Win Wells; ***D:*** Silvio Narizzano.

Bloodbath 🦴 **1998** Detectives Tony Martin and Maggie Donovan are investigating a series of murders whose victims are all starlets. As they dig into the world of underground filmmaking, they find a literal bloodbath involving a group of movie-happy vampires. **90m/C VHS.** Susannah Devereux, Kathryn Cleasby, Anthony Martini, Jan Bryant, Charles Currier, Dana Fredsti; ***D:*** Dan Speaker, Anne Kimberly; ***W:*** Dana Fredsti; ***C:*** Joseph Raymond Garcia. **VIDEO**

Bloodbath at the House of Death 🦴🦴 **1985** Price and his compatriots fight a team of mad scientists in this parody of popular horror films. Fun to see Price spoofing his own genre; die-hard horror camp fans will be satisfied. Best line: "Wanna fork?" **92m/C VHS.** *GB* Kenny Everett, Pamela Stephenson, Vincent Price, Gareth Hunt, Sheila Steafel, John Fortune, Graham Stark, Cleo Rocos; ***D:*** Ray Cameron; ***W:*** Ray Cameron, Barry Cryer; ***C:*** Brian West, Dusty Miller; ***M:*** Mark London, Mike Moran.

Bloodbath in Psycho Town 🦴 **1989 (R)** A film crew is marked for death by a hooded man when it enters a remote little village. **87m/C VHS, DVD.** Ron Arragon, Donna Baltron, Dave Elliott; ***D:*** Allessandro DeGaetano; ***W:*** Allessandro DeGaetano.

Bloodbeat 🦴 **1985** A supernatural being terrorizes a family as they gather at their country home to celebrate Christmas. **84m/C VHS.** Helen Benton, Terry Brown, Claudia Peyton; ***D:*** Fabrice A. Zaphiratos.

Bloodbrothers 🦴🦴 ½ **1978 (R)** Portrayal of working-class Italian men's lives—if that's possible without the benefit of Italian writers, producers, or director. Still, lots of cussing and general intensity, as Gere's character struggles between staying in the family construction business and doing what he wants to do—work with children. Re-cut for TV and re-titled "A Father's Love." **120m/C VHS.** Richard Gere, Paul Sorvino, Tony LoBianco, Kenneth McMillan, Marilu Henner, Danny Aiello, Lelia Goldoni, Yvonne Wilder; ***D:*** Robert Mulligan; ***C:*** Robert L. Surtees; ***M:*** Elmer Bernstein.

Bloodfist 🦴🦴 **1989 (R)** A kickboxer tears through Manila searching for his brother's killer. A Roger Corman production. **85m/C VHS, DVD.** Don "The Dragon" Wilson, Rob Kaman, Billy Blanks, Kris Aguilar, Riley Bowman, Michael Shaner, Joe Mari Avellana, Marilyn Bautista; ***D:*** Terence H. Winkless; ***W:*** Robert King; ***C:*** Ricardo Jacques Gale; ***M:*** Sasha Matson.

Bloodfist 2 🦴🦴 ½ **1990 (R)** Six of the world's toughest martial artists find themselves kidnapped and forced to do the bidding of the evil Su. The mysterious recluse stages a series of incredible fights between the experts and his own army of drugged warriors. **85m/C VHS, DVD.** Don "The Dragon" Wilson, Maurice Smith, James Warring, Timothy Baker, Richard (Rick) Hill, Rina Reyes, Kris Aguilar, Joe Mari Avellana; ***D:*** Andy Blumenthal; ***W:*** Catherine Cyran; ***C:*** Bruce Dorfman; ***M:*** Nigel Holton.

Bloodfist 3: Forced to Fight 🦴 ½ **1992 (R)** Just as long as nobody's forced to watch, real-life world champion kickboxer Wilson thrashes his way through another showdown-at-the-arena plot. Better-than-average fight choreography. **90m/C VHS, DVD.** Don "The Dragon" Wilson, Richard Roundtree, Laura Stockman, Richard Paul, Rick Dean, Peter "Sugarfoot" Cunningham; ***D:*** Oley Sassone; ***W:*** Allison Burnett; ***C:*** Rick Bota; ***M:*** Nigel Holton.

Bloodfist 4: Die Trying 🦴 ½ **1992 (R)** To rescue his daughter, a fighter must do battle with the FBI, the CIA, and an international arms cartel. **86m/C VHS, DVD.** Don "The Dragon" Wilson, Catya (Cat) Sassoon, Amanda Wyss, James Tolkan, Liz Torres; ***D:*** Paul Ziller.

Bloodfist 5: Human Target 🦴 ½ **1993 (R)** When undercover FBI agent Jim Roth (Wilson) attempts to unravel an international arms deal he's found out and left for dead. He comes to with no memory only to find himself caught between the arms dealers and the FBI, who think he's turned double-agent. Both sides want Roth dead. **84m/C VHS, DVD.** Don "The Dragon" Wilson, Denice Duff, Yuji Okumoto, Don Stark, Danny Lopez, Steve James, Michael Yama; ***D:*** Jeff Yonis; ***W:*** Jeff Yonis; ***C:*** Michael G. Wojciechowski; ***M:*** David Wurst, Eric Wurst.

Bloodfist 6: Ground Zero 🦴 ½ **1994 (R)** Nick Corrigan (Wilson) must battle terrorists who have a nuclear missile aimed at New York City. **86m/C VHS, DVD.** Don "The Dragon" Wilson, Cat Sasson, Steve Garvey; ***D:*** Rick Jacobson; ***W:*** Brendan Broderick, Rob Kerchner; ***C:*** Michael Gallagher; ***M:*** John Graham.

Bloodfist 7: Manhunt 🦴🦴 **1995 (R)** Martial arts expert Jim Trudell is accused by corrupt cops of murder and is forced on the run while he tries to prove his innocence. **95m/C VHS, DVD.** Don "The Dragon" Wilson, Jonathan Penner, Jillian McWhirter, Stephen Davies, Cyril O'Reilly, Eb Lottimer, Steven Williams; ***D:*** Jonathan Winfrey; ***W:*** Brendan Broderick, Rob Kerchner; ***C:*** Michael Gallagher; ***M:*** Elliot Anders, Mike Elliot. **VIDEO**

Bloodfist 8: Hard Way Out 🦴 *Hard Way Out* **1996 (R)** Widowed teacher Rick Cowan (Wilson) turns out to have a lurid past when he and teen son Chris (White) are targeted for death. Dull dad is ex-CIA and someone is afraid their dirty secrets will get out if he's not eliminated. **78m/C VHS, DVD.** Don "The Dragon" Wilson, John Patrick White, Warren Burton, Richard Farrell; ***D:*** Barry Samson; ***W:*** Alex Simon; ***C:*** John Aronson; ***M:*** John Faulkner.

Bloodhounds 🦴🦴 **1996 (R)** Detective Nikki Cruz (Harnos), who's skilled in the martial arts, reluctantly agrees to team up with writer Harrison Coyle (Bernsen), whose specialty is criminal cases, to catch escaped serial killer, Charles Veasey (Baltz). **86m/C VHS.** Corbin Bernsen, Christina Harnos, Kirk Baltz, Gina Mastrogiacomo, James Pickens Jr., Marcus Flanagan; ***D:*** Michael Katleman; ***W:*** Pablo F. Fenjves; ***C:*** Fernando Arguelles. **CABLE**

Bloodhounds 2 🦴🦴 **1996 (PG-13)** True-crime writer Harrison Coyle (Bersen) teams up with PI Nikki Cruz (Peeples) to nab serial killer Matthew Standing (Tracey), who hunts down convicted rapists he thinks haven't been punished enough. Turns out the killer is also a fan of Coyle's and begins contacting him about them writing a book together. **89m/C VHS.** Corbin Bernsen, Nia Peeples, Ian Tracey, Amy Yasbeck, Jim Byrnes, Suki Kaiser, Tom Cavanagh; ***D:*** Stuart Cooper; ***W:*** Pablo F. Fenjves; ***C:*** Curtis Petersen; ***M:*** Charles Bernstein. **CABLE**

Bloodhounds of Broadway 🦴🦴 ½ **1952** New York bookie Numbers Foster (Brady) heads out of town to avoid a criminal investigation and winds up in backwoods Georgia where he meets talented Tessie (Gaynor), who convinces Numbers to take her back up north with him. She finds success on Broadway and finally persuades the bookie to turn himself in. Based on a story by Damon Runyon. **90m/C DVD.** Mitzi Gaynor, Scott Brady, Mitzie Green, Marguerite Chapman, Michael O'Shea, Wally Vernon; ***D:*** Harmon Jones; ***W:*** Sy Gomberg; ***C:*** Edward Cronjager; ***M:*** Lionel Newman.

Bloodhounds of Broadway 🦴🦴 ½ **1989 (PG)** A musical tribute to Damon Runyon, detailing the cliched adventures of an assortment of jazz-age crooks, flappers, chanteuses, and losers. **90m/C VHS, DVD.** Madonna, Rutger Hauer, Randy Quaid, Matt Dillon, Jennifer Grey, Julie Hagerty, Esai Morales, Anita Morris, Josef Sommer, William S. Burroughs, Ethan Phillips, Stephen McHattie, Dinah Manoff, Googy Gress, Tony Azito, Tony Longo, Madeleine Potter; ***D:*** Howard Brookner; ***W:*** Howard Brookner, Colman DeKay; ***C:*** Elliot Davis; ***M:*** Jonathan Sheffer.

Bloodknot 🦴🦴 **1995 (R)** The Reaves' are devastated when their son Martin is killed in a military accident. So they're an easy target when Kaye (Vernon) shows up, claiming to be Martin's girlfriend. Mom Evelyn (Kidder) and brother Tom (Dempsey) are only too eager to welcome Kaye into the family but it wouldn't be a thriller if devious Kaye didn't have some deadly ulterior motives. **98m/C VHS.** Patrick Dempsey, Kate Vernon, Margot Kidder, Craig Sheffer; ***D:*** Jorge Montesi; ***W:*** Randy Kornfield; ***C:*** Philip Linzey; ***M:*** Ian Thomas. **CABLE**

Bloodlines 🦴🦴 ½ **2005** Policewoman Justine Hopkin (Pierson) finds her mother's dead body just after her dad James (McNally) is released from prison (he was in on a murder rap). She believes he's innocent and now has to prove it. **137m/C DVD.** *GB* Kevin McNally, Robert Pugh, Kieran O'Brien, Jan Francis, Emma Pierson, Max Beesley; ***D:*** Philip Martin; ***W:*** Mike Cullen; ***C:*** Julian Court; ***M:*** Nicholas Hooper. **TV**

Bloodlink 🦴 ½ **1986 (R)** A well-to-do doctor has a recurring nightmare about killing an elderly woman. This prompts him to explore his past, discovering that he was separated at birth from a twin brother. Naturally, only by searching frantically for his long-lost sibling can the good doctor hope to solve the mystery of the recurring nightmare. A somnolent tale indeed. **98m/C VHS.** Michael Moriarty, Penelope Milford, Geraldine Fitzgerald, Cameron Mitchell, Sarah Langenfeld; ***D:*** Alberto De Martino.

Bloodlust 🦴 **1959** More teenagers fall prey to yet another mad scientist, who stores their dead bodies in glass tanks. Low-budget ripoff of "The Most Dangerous Game" and other such films. A must for Mike Brady (Robert Reed) fans though. **89m/B VHS, DVD.** Wilton Graff, June Kenney, Robert Reed, Lilyan Chauvin; ***D:*** Ralph Brooke; ***W:*** Ralph Brooke.

Bloodlust: Subspecies 3 🦴 ½ *Subspecies 3* **1993 (R)** Equally gory followup to "Bloodstone: Subspecies 2." Sadistic vampire Radu is still battling for Michelle's soul, this time against Michelle's sister Becky, aided by his disgusting Mummy and the demonic Subspecies. Castle Vladislas is awash is blood and Becky discovers more than Michelle's fate is at risk. **83m/C VHS.** Anders (Tofting) Hove, Kevin Blair Spirtas, Denice Duff, Pamela Gordon, Ion Haiduc, Michael DellaFemina; ***D:*** Ted Nicolaou; ***W:*** Ted Nicolaou.

Bloodmatch 🦴 **1991 (R)** A whodunit, martial-arts-style: the "sleuth" kidnaps all the suspects in a corruption case and kickboxes each to death until somebody confesses. Not exactly Agatha Christie, and artsy camera moves fail to exploit the fancy footwork. **85m/C VHS.** Thom Mathews, Michel Qissi, Benny "The Jet" Urquidez, Marianne Taylor, Hope Marie Carlton, Dale Jacoby, Thunder Wolf, Vincent Klyn, Peter "Sugarfoot" Cunningham, Hector Pena; ***D:*** Albert Pyun; ***W:*** K. Mannah; ***M:*** Tony Riparetti.

Bloodmoon **WOOF! 1990** The setting is Australia but the sleazy story's all too familiar: an insane killer employs knives and other sharp objects to prevent sex-crazed students from getting past third base. **104m/C VHS, DVD.** *AU* Leon Lissek, Christine Amor, Ian Patrick Williams, Helen Thomson, Hazel Howson, Craig Cronin, Anya Molina; ***D:*** Alec Mills; ***W:*** Richard Brennan; ***M:*** Brian May.

Bloodmoon 🦴 ½ **1997** A New York serial killer is quite a specialist—he only kills fighters, and he kills with his bare hands. So it's up to Ken O'Hara (Daniels), who specializes in tracking murderers, to find this guy before he kills again. A good display of martial arts skills keep this one interesting. **105m/C VHS, DVD.** Gary Daniels, Chuck Jeffreys, Darren Shahlavi, Nina Repeta, Frank Gorshin, Jeffrey Pillars, Joe Hess; ***D:*** Tony Leung Siu Hung; ***W:*** Keith W. Strandberg; ***C:*** Derek M.K. Wan; ***M:*** Richard Yuen.

BloodRayne WOOF! 2006 (R) There are moments in this painful period vampire "epic" where you honestly have to wonder if director Uwe Boll was aware that the camera was rolling. Whatever the excuse, Boll's latest video game movie proves that even sex, gore, and violence can be boring in the hands of the right director. Rayne (Loken) is a half-vampire, half-human warrior who's out to stop her illegitimate father, Kagin (Kingsley), the king of vampires, from... sigh, bored yet? You will be. Even the cast looks half-asleep. (Madsen and Kingsley take "phoning it in" to a new and scary level.) But nothing beats the barely rehearsed fight scenes. A community theatre production of "Braveheart" would have more convincing stage combat. **95m/C DVD.** *GE US* Kristanna Loken, Michael Madsen, Matthew Davis, Michelle Rodriguez, Ben Kingsley, Will Sanderson, Udo Kier, Meat Loaf Aday, Michael Pare, Billy Zane, Geraldine Chaplin; ***D:*** Uwe Boll; ***W:*** Guinevere Turner; ***C:*** Mathias Neumann; ***M:*** Henning Lohner.

BloodRayne 2: Deliverance WOOF! 2007 (R) Probably the worst vampire western ever made, and that's saying something. After the first "BloodRayne" bombed, Boll somehow got financing to produce this direct-to-DVD sequel. Set in the Old West, the "plot" revolves around vampire Billy the Kid (played by Scut Farkus from "A Christmas Story"), and his plans to use the railroad to help his cowboy vamp posse to take over America. (Seriously.) Enter the sexually-ambiguous warrior-woman Rayne (Malthe), a half-human/half-vampire, who fights in the name of justice with her fangs and bare midriff. Unfortunately, vampire John Ford doesn't show up to punish Boll for his crimes against the western. **95m/C DVD.** Natassia Malthe, Zack (Zach) Ward, Brendan Fletcher, Michael Pare, Christopher Coppola, Michael Eklund; ***D:*** Uwe Boll; ***W:*** Christopher Donaldson, Neil Every; ***M:*** Jessica de Rooij. **VIDEO**

Bloodspell ✗ **1987 (R)** A student with an evil power unleashes it on those who cross his path. **87m/C VHS, DVD.** Anthony Jenkins, Aaron Teich, Alexandra Kennedy, John Reno; ***D:*** Deryn Warren.

Bloodsport ✗ 1/2 **1988 (R)** American soldier Van Damme endeavors to win the deadly Kumite, an outlawed martial arts competition in Hong Kong. Lots of kick-boxing action and the sound of bones cracking. **92m/C VHS, DVD.** Jean-Claude Van Damme, Leah Ayres, Roy Chiao, Donald Gibb, Bolo Yeung, Norman Burton, Forest Whitaker; ***D:*** Newton Arnold; ***W:*** Christopher Cosby.

Bloodsport 2: The Next Kumite ✗ 1/2 **1995 (R)** Old-fashioned kickfest has Alex (Bernhardt) stealing antiquities in Thailand. He's left to take the fall by his partner in the theft of an ancient sword belonging to powerful businessman Leung (Morita) and is sent to a prison where sadistic head guard Demon (Han) takes an instant dislike to him. Alex learns about a sacred fighting competition, the Kumite, from wise prison sage Sun (Hong) and naturally, once Alex manages to get into the contest, his opponent is—you guessed it—Demon. **87m/C VHS.** Daniel Bernhardt, Ong Soo Han, Noriyuki "Pat" Morita, James Hong; ***D:*** Alan Mehrez.

Bloodsport 3 ✗ 1/2 **1997** Alex (Bernhardt) must avenge the death of his mentor (Hong) and regain the Kumite sword. **92m/C VHS.** Daniel Bernhardt, John Rhys-Davies, James Hong, Noriyuki "Pat" Morita; ***D:*** Alan Mehrez; ***W:*** James Williams; ***M:*** Stephen (Steve) Edwards.

Bloodsport 4: The Dark Kumite ✗ **1998 (R)** Undercover agent infiltrates a prison to find out why prisoners are disappearing and ends up forced to participate in a to-the-death tournament. Enjoyable if a steady dose of kicks to the head is your idea of intricate plotting. **100m/C VHS, DVD.** Daniel Bernhardt, Ivan Ivanov, Lisa Stothard, Elvis Restaino; ***D:*** Elvis Restaino; ***W:*** George Saunders; ***M:*** Alex Wurman. **VIDEO**

The Bloodstained Shadow ✗✗ *Solamente Nero; Only Blackness* **1978** Stefano (Capolicchio) decides to visit his priest brother Paolo (Hill), who lives on the island of Murano near Venice. He meets the mysterious Sandra (Casini) on his journey and then witnesses a midnight murder upon his arrival. More deaths follow as Paolo and Stefano investigate. Italian with subtitles. **109m/C DVD.** *IT* Lino Capolicchio, Craig Hill, Stefania Casini, Massimo Serato, Juliette Mayniel; ***D:*** Antonio Bido; ***W:*** Antonio Bido, Marisa Andalo, Domenico Malan; ***C:*** Mario Vulpiani; ***M:*** Stelvio Cipriani, The Goblins.

Bloodstalkers WOOF! 1976 Two vacationers in Florida meet up with a band of slaughtering, swamp-based lunatics. **91m/C VHS.** Kenny (Ken) Miller, Celea Ann Cole, Jerry Albert; ***D:*** Robert W. Morgan.

Bloodstone ✗✗ **1988 (PG-13)** A couple honeymooning in the Middle East unexpectedly become involved in a jewel heist when they discover a valuable ruby amongst their luggage. Non-stop action and humor. **90m/C VHS, DVD.** Charlie Brill, Christopher Neame, Jack Kehler, Brett Stimely, Anna Nicholas; ***D:*** Dwight Little; ***W:*** Nico Mastorakis, Curt Allen.

Bloodstone: Subspecies 2 ✗ 1/2 *Subspecies 2* **1992 (R)** A gory sequel to "Subspecies" finds Radu the vampire pursuing the luscious Michelle. Radu gets some help from his ghoulish mother and yucky demonic spawn. Filmed on location in Romania. **107m/C VHS.** Anders (Tofting) Hove, Denice Duff, Kevin Blair Spirtas, Michael Denish, Pamela Gordon, Ion Haiduc; ***D:*** Ted Nicolaou; ***W:*** Ted Nicolaou.

Bloodstorm: Subspecies 4 ✗ 1/2 *Subspecies 4; Subspecies 4: Bloodstorm—The Master's Revenge* **1998 (R)** Master vampire Radu Vladislas (Hove) has awakened with an agenda. He wants to reclaim his vast wealth and recapture fledgling vamp, Michelle (Duff). Meanwhile, Radu hangs around with former protege, Ash (Morris), and Michelle is taken in by a creepy doctor (Dinvale) who's after the bloodstone. If you liked the first three, this is just more of the same. **90m/C VHS, DVD.** Anders (Tofting) Hove, Denice Duff, Jonathan Morris, Mihai Dinvale, Floriella Grappini; ***D:*** Ted Nicolaou; ***W:*** Ted Nicolaou; ***C:*** Adolfo Bartoli; ***M:*** Richard Kosinski. **VIDEO**

Bloodstream WOOF! 2000 Convoluted plot first involves a worker who smuggles a mystery vial out of a genetics lab and then gets murdered. Now we switch to Pamela (Mills), who's come to hear her sister sing at open-mic night, only sis has gone missing. And it turns out she's been taken by a serial killer but...oh, who cares. Low-budget crap. **m/C VHS.** Meredith Mills, Eric Bunton, Joe Decker, Joey Day; ***D:*** Dennis Devine, Steve Jarvis; ***W:*** Dennis Devine, Steve Jarvis; ***C:*** Dennis Devine; ***M:*** Jonathan Price.

The Bloodsuckers ✗✗ *Incense for the Damned; Doctors Wear Scarlet; The Freedom Seekers* **1970** British horror tale set on a Greek Island. An Oxford don is seduced into an ancient vampire cult. Director Michael Burrowes replaces Hartford-Davis in the credits due to a dispute over post-production editing. **90m/C VHS, DVD.** *GB* Patrick Macnee, Peter Cushing, Patrick Mower, Edward Woodward, Alex Davion, Imogen Hassall, Madeline Hinde, Johnny Sekka; ***D:*** Robert Hartford-Davis; ***W:*** Julian More; ***C:*** Desmond Dickinson.

Bloodsuckers from Outer Space WOOF! 1983 Via an alien invasion, Texas farmers becoming bloodsucking zombies. **80m/C VHS.** Thom Meyer, Laura Ellis, Billie Keller, Kim Braden; ***D:*** Glenn Coburn.

Bloodsucking Freaks WOOF! *The Incredible Torture Show; The House of the Screaming Virgins* **1975 (R)** Virtually plotless Troma gagfest full of torture, cannibalistic dwarfs, and similar debaucheries, all played out on a Soho Grand Guignol stage (horror shows that allegedly contained real torture and death). Features "The Caged Sexoids," if that tells you anything (a cage of naked cannibal women tended by a dwarf). Not to mention the woman who has her brain sucked out through a straw. Filmed in "Ghoulovision" and originally rated X. Intolerable for most. **89m/C VHS, DVD.** Seamus O'Brian, Niles McMaster, Viju Krem, Alan Dellay, Dan Fauci; ***D:*** Joel M. Reed; ***W:*** Joel M. Reed; ***C:*** Gerry Toll; ***M:*** Michael Sahl.

Bloodsucking Pharoahs of Pittsburgh WOOF! *Picking up the Pieces* **1990 (R)** Pittsburgh is plagued by crazed cannibals who think eternal life is in Pennsylvania. Two detectives on the case are mystified. **89m/C VHS, DVD.** Jake Dengel, Joe Sharkey, Suzanne Fletcher, Beverly Penberthy, Shawn Elliott, Pat Logan, Jane (Veronica Hart) Hamilton; ***D:*** Dean Tschetter, Alan Smithee; ***W:*** Dean Tschetter; ***C:*** Peter Reniers; ***M:*** Michael Melvoin.

Bloody Avenger ✗ **1980** A trio of detectives search for a murderer in the streets of Philadelphia. **100m/C VHS.** Jack Palance, George Eastman, Jenny Tamburi; ***D:*** Al (Alfonso Brescia) Bradley.

Bloody Beach ✗ 1/2 *Haebyeoneuro gada* **2000** A group of teens from an Internet chat site decide to say goodbye to anonymity and meet at the beach for vacation, and sure enough a banned ex-member begins killing them off. Horror films aren't a staple of Korean cinema, so while this is probably new to Koreans it is an example of an old school American slasher film. **85m/C DVD.** *KN* Hyun-Jung Kim, Dong-Kun Yang, Seung-chae Lee, Jeong-jin Lee, Hyun-kyoon Lee, Tae-seong Jin, Se-eun Lee; ***D:*** In Soo Kim; ***W:*** Seung-jae Baek, Jin-soo Noh, Mi-young Park, Hae-won Shim, Kwang-soo Son; ***C:*** Yoon-soo Kim; ***M:*** Jun-Seok Bang, Young-ook Cho.

Bloody Birthday ✗ 1/2 *Creeps* **1980 (R)** Three youngsters, bound together by their eerie birth during an eclipse (you know what that means), kill everyone around them that ever gave them problems. Typical "and the fun continues" ending; standard fare. **92m/C VHS, DVD.** Susan Strasberg, Jose Ferrer, Lori Lethin, Melinda Cordell, Joe Penny, Ellen Geer, Julie Brown, Michael Dudikoff, Billy Jacoby, Elizabeth Hoy, Andy Freeman; ***D:*** Ed(ward) Hunt; ***W:*** Ed(ward) Hunt, Barry Pearson.

The Bloody Brood WOOF! 1959 Really bad flick about a drug-dealing beatnik gang who commit nasty crimes, like feeding messenger boys hamburgers filled with ground glass. Yuck. **80m/C VHS, DVD.** *CA* Jack Betts, Barbara Lord, Peter Falk, Robert Christie; ***D:*** Julian Hoffman.

Bloody Mama ✗✗ 1/2 **1970 (R)** Corman's violent, trashy story of the infamous Barker Gang of the 30s, led by the bloodthirsty and sex-crazed Ma Barker (Winters, can't you just picture it?) and backed by her four perverted sons. De Niro is the space cadet sibling, Walden the homosexual excon, Stroud the sadistic mama lover, and Kimbrough the lady killer. They're joined by Walden's prison lover, Dern, who also has a thing for Ma Barker. Winters is a riot in this perverse stew of crime, violence, and, of course, sentimental blood bonding (the family that slays together, stays together). First of the Corman-produced (and sometimes directed) mama movies, followed by "Big Bad Mama" and "Crazy Mama." **90m/C VHS.** Shelley Winters, Robert De Niro, Don Stroud, Pat Hingle, Bruce Dern, Diane Varsi, Robert Walden, Clinton Kimbrough, Scatman Crothers, Pamela Dunlap, Michael Fox, Stacy Harris; ***D:*** Roger Corman; ***W:*** Robert Thom; ***C:*** John A. Alonzo; ***M:*** Don Randi.

Bloody Moon WOOF! *Die Saege des Todes* **1983** Tourists are being brutally attacked and murdered during a small Spanish village's Festival of the Moon. **84m/C VHS.** *GE* Olivia Pascal, Christopher Brugger, Ann-Beate Engelke, Antonia Garcia, Nadja Gerganoff, Corinna Gillwald, Jasmin Losensky, Maria Rubio, Alexander Waechter; ***D:*** Jess (Jesus) Franco; ***W:*** Jess (Jesus) Franco, Rayo Casablanca; ***C:*** Juan Soler.

Bloody Murder WOOF! 1999 (R) Stupid teen campers in peril from maniac movie. This time the creepoid wears a hockey mask (sound familiar?) and has a chainsaw in place of his left arm. Ick. **90m/C VHS, DVD.** Michael Stone, Jessica Morris, Peter Guillemette, Patrick Cavanaugh, Christelle Ford, Tracy Pacheco, Justin Martin; ***D:*** Ralph Portillo; ***W:*** John R. Stevenson; ***C:*** Keith Holland; ***M:*** Steven Stern. **VIDEO**

Bloody Murder 2 WOOF! 2003 (R) The sequel is no improvement over the first stinker, which was your basic teen slasher flick. Trevor Moorehorse returns after five years to slaughter a new batch of camp counselors at Camp Placid Pines. **85m/C VHS, DVD.** Katy Woodruff, Kelly Gunning, Amanda Magarian, Lane Anderson, Benjamin Schneider; ***D:*** Robert Spera; ***C:*** David Trulli; ***M:*** Steven Stern. **VIDEO**

Bloody New Year ✗ *Time Warp Terror* **1987 (R)** Corpses stalk the living as a group of teens happen upon an impromptu New Year's Eve party on a deserted island. Auld acquaintance shouldn't be forgot, just this flick. **90m/C VHS, DVD.** Suzy Aitchison, Nikki Brooks, Colin Haeywood, Mark Powley, Catherine Roman, Julian Ronnie; ***D:*** Norman J. Warren; ***W:*** Frazer Pearce; ***C:*** John Shann; ***M:*** Nick Magnus.

The Bloody Pit of Horror ✗ 1/2 *Crimson Executioner; The Red Hangman; Il Boia Scarlatto* **1965** While wife Jayne Mansfield was in Italy filming "Primitive Love," bodybuilder Hargitay starred in this sado-horror epic. He owns a castle that is visited by a group of models for a special shoot. While in the dungeon, Hargitay becomes possessed by the castle's former owner, a sadist, and begins torturing the models. Supposedly based on the writings of the Marquis de Sade. **87m/B VHS, DVD.** *IT* Mickey Hargitay, Louise Barrett, Walter Brandi, Moa Thai, Ralph Zucker, Albert Gordon; ***D:*** Max (Massimo Pupillo) Hunter; ***W:*** Romano Migliorini, Roberto Natale; ***C:*** Luciano Trasatti; ***M:*** Gino Peguri.

Bloody Proof ✗✗✗ **1999** A serial killer is stalking well-to-do women in Mexico. Detective Ibarra (Bauer) is assigned to the case. Rookie tabloid reporter Estela (Arizmendi) finds an important clue. The resolution of the stereotypical premise runs true to form, but the characters are treated seriously and the film is stylishly made with a few moments of abrupt, shocking violence. **99m/C VHS, DVD.** Steven Bauer, Yareli Arizmendi, Olivia Hussey; ***D:*** Gabriel Beristain; ***W:*** M. Francesconi, Tim Hoy; ***C:*** Andres Leon Becker; ***M:*** Eduardo Gamboa.

Bloody Sunday ✗✗✗ **2001 (R)** Docudrama covers the January 30, 1972 civil rights march through Derry, Northern Ireland to protest the policy of British internment without trial. Although the majority of the marchers are Catholic, they are led by the area's Protestant MP Ivan Cooper (Nesbitt), who believes the situation can be handled peacefully. Maj. Gen. Robert Ford (Piggott-Smith) reiterates that the British Army has banned all such marches and that participants are subject to arrest. As the march splinters into factions, the Army fires on the crowd—27 civilians are wounded and 14 died. The re-creation of the event by director Greengrass is stunning at the very least. "Sunday Bloody Sunday" was eulogized in a song by U2. **110m/C VHS, DVD.** *IR GB* James Nesbitt, Tim Pigott-Smith, Nicholas Farrell, Gerard McSorley, Kathy Kiera Clarke, Allan Gildea, Gerard Crossan, Mary Moulds, Carmel McCallion, Declan Duddy, Simon Mann; ***D:*** Paul Greengrass; ***W:*** Paul Greengrass; ***C:*** Ivan Strasburg; ***M:*** Dominic Muldowney. Berlin Intl. Film Fest. '02: Film.

Bloody Trail ✗ **1972** A Union soldier who chooses the recently pummeled South as the venue for postwar R-and-R is, for some reason, pursued by Confederates. And his good ol' boy pursuers don't have a sudden change of heart when he teams up with a former slave. Lots of violence and nudity; little plot and entertainment. **91m/C VHS.** Paul Harper, Rance Howard, John Mitchum; ***D:*** Richard Robinson.

Bloody Wednesday ✗✗ 1/2 **1987** It's sanity check-out time when a hotel caretaker is driven mad by tormentors...or is he driving himself mad? What is it about vacant hotels that make men lose their minds? If you can remove "The Shining" from yours, this flick's worthwhile. **89m/C VHS, DVD.** Raymond Elmendorf, Pamela Baker, Navarre Perry; ***D:***

Mark Gilhuis; *W:* Philip Yordan; *M:* Albert Sendrey.

Bloom ✐✐ *Bl.m* **2003 (R)** Rookie director Walsh's drab take of James Joyce's revered 1922 "Ulysses" lays out the events of Leopold Bloom's (Rea) daylong journey on June 16th, 1904 in Dublin as he deals with his wife Molly's (Ball) affair and serves as young poet Stephen's (O'Conor) mentor. **108m/C VHS, DVD.** Stephen Rea, Angeline Ball, Hugh O'Conor, Neili Conroy, Eoin McCarthy, Britta Smith, Paul Ronan, Alan Devlin, Alvaro Lucchesi, Maria Hayden, Mark Huberman, Kenneth McDonnell, Andrew McGibney, Dan Colley, Des Braiden, Donncha Crowley, Howard Jones, Russell Smith, Jimmy Keogh, Donal O'Kelly, Phelim Drew, Ronan Wilmot, Sarah Jane Drummey, Dearbhla Molloy, Jenny Maher, Ruaidhri Finnegan, Eoin MacDonagh, Peter Gaynor, Rachael Pilkington, Jamie Baker, Maria Lennon, Steve Simmonds, Colman Hanley, Conor Delaney, Charlie Bonner, Alexander Downes, Eamon Rohan, Luke Hayden, Julie Hale, Caoileann Murphy, Ciaran O'Brien, Dermot Moore, Maurice Shanahan, Seamus Walsh, Adam Fox Clarke; *D:* Sean Walsh; *W:* James Joyce; *C:* Ciaran Tanham; *M:* David Kahne. **VIDEO**

Blossoms in the Dust ✐✐ **1941** The true story of Edna Gladney is told as she starts the Texas Children's Home and Aid Society of Fort Worth. Major league Garson tear-jerker. **100m/B VHS.** Greer Garson, Walter Pidgeon, Felix Bressart, Marsha Hunt, Fay Holden, Samuel S. Hinds, Kathleen Howard; *D:* Mervyn LeRoy.

Blossoms on Broadway ✐✐ **1937** Musical-comedy pre-World War II goofiness. A young con-woman (Ross) tries to bilk a mine owner out of his fortune, only he turns out to be as short on funds as everyone else. She's got a love interest, of course, but he turns out to be a detective. **88m/B VHS.** Edward Arnold, Shirley Ross, John Trent, William Frawley; *D:* Richard Wallace; *W:* Theodore Reeves.

The Blot ✐✐ **1921** A story about a poorly paid professor and his family, whose lifestyle contrasts with that of an affluent neighbor, a butcher. **55m/B VHS, DVD.** Louis Calhern, Claire Windsor; *D:* Lois Weber.

Blow ✐✐ ½ **2001 (R)** Memorable, visually stunning, true story of cocaine entrepreneur George Jung features, at its best, stellar performances (especially from Reubens, Cruz, and Depp), and at its worst, a "Goodfellas" meets "Traffic" familiarity. Epic follows Jung (Depp) from his humble New England beginnings through his California surfer-bum days, to his rise and fall as America's biggest cocaine pipeline of the '70s and '80s without judging him or his lifestyle, although it does tend to sympathize with his family issues with mom, dad, and his own child. **124m/C VHS, DVD.** *US* Johnny Depp, Penelope Cruz, Jordi Molla, Franka Potente, Rachel Griffiths, Ray Liotta, Ethan Suplee, Paul (Pee-wee Herman) Reubens, Max Perlich, Clifford Curtis, Miguel (Michael) Sandoval, Kevin Gage, Jesse James, Dan Ferro, Emma Roberts, Bob(cat) Goldthwait, Jaime (James) King; *D:* Ted (Edward) Demme; *W:* David McKenna, Nick Cassavetes; *C:* Ellen Kuras; *M:* Graeme Revell.

Blow Dry ✐✐ **2000 (R)** Comedic possibilities and family healing ensue when the National British Hairdressing Championships come to a sleepy English town. An odd assortment of Brits and Yanks populate this familiar tale, and even dependable Rickman can't save the film, whose destination is obvious from even the newspaper ads—take "The Full Monty," replace strippers with hairdressers and, voila: "Blow Dry." Written by Simon Beaufoy, author of (you guessed it) "The Full Monty." Director Breathnach fared better with his previous film, the Irish comedy "I Went Down." **91m/C VHS, DVD.** *GB US* Alan Rickman, Natasha Richardson, Rachel Griffiths, Rachael Leigh Cook, Josh Hartnett, Bill Nighy, Warren Clarke, Rosemary Harris, Hugh Bonneville, Peter McDonald, Heidi Klum, Michael McElhatton; *D:* Paddy Breathnach; *W:* Simon Beaufoy; *C:* Cian de Buitlear; *M:* Patrick Doyle.

Blow Out ✐✐✐ **1981 (R)** When a prominent governor and presidential candidate is killed in a car crash, a sound effects engineer becomes involved in political intrigue as he tries to expose a conspiracy with the evidence he has gathered. An intricate mystery and homage to Antonioni's "Blow-Up." **108m/C VHS, DVD.** John Travolta, Nancy Allen, John Lithgow, Dennis Franz; *D:* Brian De Palma; *W:* Brian De Palma; *C:* Vilmos Zsigmond; *M:* Pino Donaggio.

Blow-Up ✐✐✐ ½ **1966** A young London photographer takes some pictures of a couple in the park and finds out he may have recorded evidence of a murder. Though marred by badly dated 1960s modishness, this is Antonioni's most accessible film, a sophisticated treatise on perception and the film-consumer-as-voyeur, brilliantly assembled and wrought. **111m/C VHS, DVD.** *GB IT* David Hemmings, Vanessa Redgrave, Sarah Miles, Jane Birkin, Veruschka, Peter Bowles, John Castle, Gillian Hills, Julian Chagrin, Harry Hutchinson, The Yardbirds; *D:* Michelangelo Antonioni; *W:* Michelangelo Antonioni, Tonino Guerra; *C:* Carlo Di Palma; *M:* Herbie Hancock. Cannes '67: Film; Natl. Soc. Film Critics '66: Director (Antonioni), Film.

Blowback ✐✐ **1999 (R)** Police officer Don Morell (Van Peebles) witnesses the execution of serial killer Claude Whitman (Remar)—or does he? Former jury members are being murdered and Morell finds cryptic bible messages at the scenes—a Whitman hallmark. So has the killer come back from the grave or has someone conspired to keep Whitman alive for their own purposes? **93m/C VHS, DVD.** Mario Van Peebles, James Remar, Stephen Caffrey, David Groh; *D:* Mark L. Lester; *W:* Jeffrey Goldenberg, Bob Held, Randall Frakes; *C:* Jacques Haitkin; *M:* Sean Callery. **CABLE**

Blowin' Smoke ✐✐ *Freak Talks About Sex* **1999 (R)** Goofball stoner Freak (Zahn) lives his life (in his parents' basement) as the ultimate slacker. His best bud (besides the pot) is the equally unambitious Dave (Hamilton), who does at least have a job. Dave also has an ex-girlfriend who wants to see him again, a sweet high schooler who has a crush on him, and a family who wishes he would do something with his life. Well, at least Dave has Freak to turn to in times of stress. Based on the novel by co-writer Galvin. **88m/C VHS, DVD.** Steve Zahn, Josh Hamilton, Heather McComb, Arabella Field, David Kinney; *D:* Paul Todisco; *W:* Paul Todisco, Michael M.B. Galvin, Peter Speakman; *C:* Douglas W. Shannon; *M:* Pete Snell.

Blowing Wild ✐ ½ **1954** Filmed in Mexico, this Quinn-Stanwyck-Cooper love triangle, set in the early thirties, speaks of lust and vengeance, rashness and greed. Stanwyck, married to oil tycoon Quinn, lusts after one-time lover wildcatter Cooper. **92m/B VHS.** Gary Cooper, Barbara Stanwyck, Anthony Quinn, Ruth Roman, Ward Bond; *D:* Hugo Fregonese; *W:* Philip Yordan.

Blown Away ✐ **1990 (R)** A mafia wife goes up against her husband in order to retrieve her kidnapped child. **92m/C VHS.** Loni Anderson, John Heard, James Naughton; *D:* Michael Miller.

Blown Away ✐ ½ **1993 (R)** Haim and Feldman are brothers working at a ski resort where Haim falls for rich teenager Eggert. She's a young femme fatale who manages to get Haim all hot and bothered but she's actually using the unsuspecting dupe in a murder plot. Also available in an unrated version at 93 minutes. **91m/C VHS, DVD.** *CA* Nicole Eggert, Corey Haim, Corey Feldman, Jean LeClerc, Kathleen Robertson, Gary Farmer; *D:* Brenton Spencer; *W:* Robert Cooper; *M:* Paul Zaza.

Blown Away ✐✐ **1994 (R)** Boston Irish bomb-squad cop Jimmy Dove (Bridges) is after former compatriot Ryan Gaerity (Jones), an Irish radical who's taken his bombing expertise onto Jimmy's new turf. Meanwhile, Jimmy wants to keep his unsavory past from unsuspecting wife Amis. Real life dad Lloyd plays Jeff's uncle. While Jones seems adequately obsessed with making things go boom and Bridges significantly concerned that they don't, thriller moves on predictable path toward explosive climax. Special effects create the suspense, as everyday objects become lethal in Gaerity's knowledgeable hands. The final explosion was more than even the special effects coordinator desired—windows were unintentionally blown out in nearby buildings. **121m/C VHS, DVD.** Jeff Bridges, Tommy Lee Jones, Suzy Amis, Lloyd Bridges, Forest Whitaker; *D:* Stephen Hopkins; *W:* Joe Batteer, John Rice; *C:* Gregory McClatchy; *M:* Alan Silvestri.

Blue ✐ **1968** A dull western about an American boy (Stamp) raised by Mexicans who doesn't trust another living soul until he finds himself face to face with his former gang, led by his adoptive father (Montalban). **113m/C VHS, DVD.** Terence Stamp, Joanna Pettet, Karl Malden, Ricardo Montalban, Joe De Santis, Sally Kirkland; *D:* Silvio Narizzano; *W:* Ronald M. Cohen; *M:* Manos Hadjidakis.

Blue ✐✐ **1993 (R)** Meditation/memoir of director Jarman's deteriorating AIDS condition consists of narration and a soundtrack set against an unvaried blue screen. Jarman ponders the associations with the color blue (sky, ocean, blindness, heaven, eternity) and his own physical problems, alternately expressed with dreamy vagueness or incendiary contempt. Limited in appeal, depending highly on boredom tolerance and ability to suspend visual expectations. **76m/C VHS.** *GB D:* Derek Jarman; *W:* Derek Jarman; *M:* Simon Fisher Turner; *Nar:* John Quentin, Nigel Terry, Tilda Swinton, Derek Jarman.

The Blue and the Gray ✐✐ **1982** Epic miniseries about love and hate inflamed by the Civil War. Keach plays a Pinkerton's secret service agent in this loosely based historical romance. Available in uncut and 295-minute versions. **381m/C VHS, DVD.** Gregory Peck, Lloyd Bridges, Colleen Dewhurst, Stacy Keach, John Hammond, Sterling Hayden, Warren Oates; *D:* Andrew V. McLaglen; *M:* Bruce Broughton. **TV**

The Blue Angel ✐✐✐✐ *Der Blaue Engel* **1930** Tale of a man stripped of his dignity. A film classic filled with sensuality and decay, which made Dietrich a European star and led to her discovery in Hollywood. When a repressed professor (Jannings) goes to a nightclub hoping to catch some of his students in the wrong, he's taken by Lola, the sultry singer portrayed by Dietrich. After spending the night with her, losing his job, and then marrying her, he goes on tour with the troupe, peddling indiscreet photos of his wife. Versions were shot in both German and English, with the German version sporting English subtitles. ♫Falling in Love Again; They Call Me Wicked Lola. **90m/B VHS, DVD.** *GE* Marlene Dietrich, Emil Jannings, Kurt Gerron, Rosa Valetti, Hans Albers; *D:* Josef von Sternberg; *W:* Robert Liebmann, Carl Zuckmayer, Karl Vollmoller; *C:* Gunther Rittau; *M:* Frederick "Friedrich" Hollander.

The Blue Bird ✐✐✐ **1940 (G)** A weird, dark fantasy about two children who search for the blue bird of happiness in various fantasy lands, but find it eventually at home. Overlooked and impressively fatalistic. **98m/C VHS.** Shirley Temple, Gale Sondergaard, John Russell, Eddie Collins, Nigel Bruce, Jessie Ralph, Spring Byington, Sybil Jason; *D:* Walter Lang; *C:* Arthur C. Miller.

Blue Blazes Rawden ✐✐ **1918** Hart plays a lumberjack who gains control of a local saloon after shooting its villainous proprietor. **65m/B VHS.** William S. Hart, Robert McKim, Maud(e) (Ford) George, Jack Hoxie; *D:* William S. Hart.

Blue Blood ✐ **1973** A demonic butler inflicts nightmares upon a family to gain possession of its mansion. **90m/C VHS.** *GB* Oliver Reed, Derek Jacobi, Fiona Lewis; *D:* Andrew Sinclair.

Blue Blood ✐ ½ *If I Didn't Care* **2007** Predictable thriller with Scheider channeling Columbo. Trophy husband Davis (Sage) resides in the Hamptons while his wealthy lawyer wife Janice (Beck) works in the city. Davis is fooling around with real estate agent Hadley (Misner) and the two decide to bump off the missus, although Hadley is the one who must do the actual work. Only their plan is botched, which brings in suspicious PI Linus (Scheider). **74m/C DVD.** Bill Sage, Roy Scheider, Ronald Guttman, Susan Misner, Noelle Beck, Brian McQuillan; *D:* Benjamin Cummings, Orson Cummings; *W:* Benjamin Cummings, Orson Cummings; *C:* Bryan Pryzpek; *M:* Michael Tremante.

The Blue Butterfly ✐✐ **2004 (PG)** Based on a true story. Pete Carlton (Donato) is 10 and dying. His one wish is to capture the rare blue morpho butterfly. World-weary entomologist Alan Osborne (Hurt) is persuaded by Pete's mother, Teresa (Bussieres), to let them accompany his expedition into the rain forest of Costa Rica. Beautiful scenery but an overly-sappy saga. **97m/C DVD.** *CA* William Hurt, Marc Donato, Pascale Bussieres, Steve Adams; *D:* Lea Pool; *W:* Pete McCormack; *C:* Michel Arcand; *M:* Stephen Endelman.

Blue Canadian Rockies ✐ ½ **1952** Autry's employer sends him to Canada to discourage his daughter from marrying a fortune hunter. The daughter has turned the place into a dude ranch and wild game preserve. When Autry arrives, he encounters some mysterious killings. **58m/B VHS, DVD.** Gene Autry, Pat Buttram, Gail Davis, Ross Ford, Tom London; *D:* George Archainbaud.

Blue Car ✐✐✐ ½ **2003 (R)** Impressive directorial debut by Moncrieff tells the story of troubled teen Meg (Bruckner) and her sad, beaten-down English teacher Mr. Auster (Strathairn). Meg's life has been turned upside down with the divorce of her parents. Her mother is distant and overworked, and her sister (Arnold, in an excellent performance) is self-destructive. When she finds solace in poetry, Auster recognizes and encourages her talent, which leads to an awkwardly closer relationship, skulkingly engineered by the teacher. Excellent script and direction, as well as stellar performances by Bruckner and Strathairn, allow the film to explore the situation without exploiting or judging. The characters are well-rounded and real, as is the dialogue, which makes the unfolding events that much more disturbing. **96m/C VHS, DVD.** *US* Agnes Bruckner, David Strathairn, Margaret Colin, Regan Arnold, Frances Fisher, A.J. Buckley, Sarah Beuhler; *D:* Karen Moncrieff; *W:* Karen Moncrieff; *C:* Rob Sweeney; *M:* Stuart Spencer-Nash.

Blue Chips ✐✐ ½ **1994 (PG-13)** Nolte does Bobby Knight in this saga of Western U basketball coach Pete Bell, suffering through his first losing season. What follows is a tug of war between rich alumni who want to win at any cost and his ethics as he recruits for a new season. Larger than life hoopster O'Neal's film debut. McDonnell and Woodard are merely afterthoughts, but look for cameos from many real life b-ballers, including Dick Vitale and Larry Bird. Average script is bolstered by exciting game footage, shot during real games for authenticity. **108m/C VHS, DVD.** Nick Nolte, Shaquille O'Neal, Mary McDonnell, Ed O'Neill, J.T. Walsh, Alfre Woodard; *Cameos:* Larry Bird, Bobby Knight, Rick Pitino; *D:* William Friedkin; *W:* Ron Shelton; *M:* Nile Rodgers, Jeff Beck, Jed Leiber.

Blue City ✐ ½ **1986 (R)** A young man returns to his Florida hometown to find his father murdered, and subsequently vows to solve and avenge the matter. Based on a Ross MacDonald thriller. **83m/C VHS.** Judd Nelson, Ally Sheedy, Paul Winfield, Anita Morris, David Caruso, Julie Carmen, Scott Wilson; *D:* Michelle Manning; *W:* Walter Hill, Lukas Heller; *M:* Ry Cooder.

Blue Collar ✐✐✐ **1978 (R)** Funnyman Pryor (in one of his best film roles) offers most of the laughs in this very serious drama of how three Detroit auto assembly workers (Pryor, Kotto, and Keitel), feeling the strain of family life and inflation, hatch a plan to rob their corrupt union office only to stumble into a bigger crime that later costs them dearly. Schrader makes his directorial debut in this searing study of the working class and the robbing of the human spirit, which is made memorable by the strong performances of its three leads. Filmed entirely in Detroit and Kalamazoo, Michigan. **114m/C VHS, DVD.** Richard Pryor, Harvey Keitel, Yaphet Kotto, Ed Begley Jr., Lane Smith, Cliff DeYoung; *D:* Paul Schrader; *W:* Paul Schrader, Leonard Schrader; *C:* Bobby Byrne; *M:* Jack Nitzsche.

Blue Country ✐✐ ½ *Le Pays Bleu* **1977 (PG)** A joyful romantic comedy about a pair of free souls who leave their stagnant lives behind to seek out a more idyllic existence. Subtitled in English. **104m/C VHS.** *FR* Brigitte Fossey, Jacques Serres, Ginette Garcin, Armand Meffre, Ginette Mathieu, Roger Crouzet; *D:* Jean-Charles Tacchella; *W:* Jean-Charles Tacchella; *C:* Edmond Sechan; *M:* Gerard Anfosso.

Blue Crush ✐✐✐ **2002 (PG-13)** Director John Stockwell brings back the beach/surfing genre with a story about board riding women who would kick Gidget's narrow behind. Surfer girl Anne Marie (Bosworth) moves to Hawaii, determined to win the traditionally all-male Rip Masters competition. Aided by fellow surfers Eden (Rodriguez) and Lena (Lake), she tries to mentally recover from a near-fatal accident in time for the meet. Unfortunately, the distraction of new boyfriend Matt (Davis) may cause her dreams to wipe out. Both the ripped bodies and the surfing action seem a little enhanced by science, but both are very visually stimulating. **104m/C VHS, DVD.** *US* Kate (Catherine) Bosworth, Michelle Rodriguez, Matthew Davis, Sanoe Lake, Mika Boorem, Faizon Love, Chris Taloa, Kala Alexander; ***D:*** John Stockwell; ***W:*** John Stockwell, Elizabeth Weiss; ***C:*** David Hennings; ***M:*** Paul Haslinger.

The Blue Dahlia ½ **1946** Classic film noir finds Navy vet Johnny Morrison (Ladd) returning home to discover his wife Helen (Dowling) has been keeping the home fires burning—with Eddie Harwood (Da Silva), owner of the Blue Dahlia nightclub. After a nasty fight, Johnny takes off and is picked up by sultry blonde Joyce (Lake). The next day Johnny discovers he's wanted by the cops for the murder of his wife and decides to hide out until he can find the real killer, with Joyce's help. Very stylish and fast-paced with excellent performances; Chandler's first original screenplay. **100m/B VHS.** Alan Ladd, Veronica Lake, William Bendix, Howard da Silva, Doris Dowling, Tom Powers, Hugh Beaumont, Howard Freeman, Don Costello; ***D:*** George Marshall; ***W:*** Raymond Chandler; ***C:*** Lionel Lindon; ***M:*** Victor Young.

Blue De Ville **1986 (PG)** Two young women buy a '59 Cadillac and journey from St. Louis to New Mexico, having adventures on the way. The rambling, free-spirited movie was a pilot for a prospective series that never set sail—but when "Thelma & Louise" hit big this superficially similar item was hauled out on video. **96m/C VHS.** Jennifer Runyon, Kimberly Pistone, Mark Thomas Miller, Alan Autry, Robert Prescott; ***D:*** Jim Johnston. **TV**

Blue Desert **1991 (R)** Cox is strong in her performance as Lisa Roberts, a comic book artist who leaves New York City for small town Arizona life after surviving a traumatic rape. Once there, she's befriended by Sheffer and Sweeney, a local cop. Battersby does a good job of keeping the suspense level high (in his directorial debut) as Cox finds that there's danger in small towns, too. Fine performances keep this slightly above average. **98m/C VHS, DVD.** D.B. Sweeney, Courteney Cox, Craig Sheffer, Philip Baker Hall, Sandy Ward; ***D:*** Bradley Battersby; ***W:*** Bradley Battersby, Arthur Collis; ***M:*** Jerry Goldsmith.

Blue Fin **1978 (PG)** When their tuna boat is shipwrecked, and the crew disabled, a young boy and his father learn lessons of love and courage as the son tries to save the ship. **93m/C VHS, DVD.** *AU* Hardy Kruger, Greg Rowe; ***D:*** Carl Schultz; ***C:*** Geoff Burton.

Blue Fire Lady **1978** The heartwarming story of a young girl and her love of horses which endures even her father's disapproval. Good family fare. **96m/C VHS, DVD.** *AU* Cathryn Harrison, Mark Holden, Peter Cummins, Marion Edward, Anne Sutherland, Garry Waddell, John Wood, John Ewart; ***D:*** Ross Dimsey; ***C:*** Vincent Monton; ***M:*** Mike Brady.

Blue Flame **1993 (R)** Vigilante cop is hired to track down two humanoid aliens who have escaped captivity in futuristic L.A. They evade him by time-traveling through alternate realities, infiltrating the cop's mind, and using his fantasies against him. **88m/C VHS, DVD.** Brian Wimmer, Ian Buchanan, Kerri Green, Cecilia Peck, Jad Mager; ***D:*** Cassian Elwes; ***W:*** Cassian Elwes.

The Blue Gardenia ½ **1953** Seminal but rarely seen film noir. Norah Larkin (Baxter) wakes up one morning in the apartment of womanizing lout Harry Prebble (Burr). He's dead and she's labeled "The Blue Gardenia" murderess by newspaper columnist Casey Mayo (Conte). Required viewing for fans of vintage mysteries. **88m/B DVD.** Anne Baxter, Richard Conte, Ann Sothern, Raymond Burr, George Reeves, Nat King Cole, Jeff Donnell, Richard Erdman, Ray Walker, Ruth Storey; ***D:*** Fritz Lang; ***W:*** Charles Hoffman; ***C:*** Nicholas Musuraca; ***M:*** Raoul Kraushaar.

Blue Hawaii **1962 (PG)** A soldier, returning to his Hawaiian home, defies his parents by taking a job with a tourist agency. Presley sings "Can't Help Falling in Love." For Elvis fans. **101m/C VHS, DVD.** Pam(ela) Austin, Elvis Presley, Angela Lansbury, Joan Blackman, Roland Winters, Iris Adrian, John Archer, Steve Brodie; ***D:*** Norman Taurog; ***W:*** Hal Kanter.

Blue Heaven **1984** A couple struggles through problems with their marriage and alcohol abuse. **100m/C VHS.** Leslie Dennison, James Eckhouse; ***D:*** Kathleen Dowdey.

Blue Hill Avenue **2001 (R)** Four childhood friends in 1970's Boston are taken under the wing of a drug dealer and taught to be gangsters. One of them, Tristan (Payne) eventually decides he has had enough and makes the inevitable betrayal of his master before the equally inevitable ensuing bloodbath. Nothing new, but still well done. **120m/C DVD.** Allen Payne, Angelle Brooks, Michael "Bear" Taliferro, William L. Johnson, Aaron Spears, Andrew Divoff, Richard Lawson, Marlon Young, Dee Freeman, Anthony Sherwood, Gail Fulton Ross, Veronica Redd, Clarence Williams III, William Forsythe, Myquan Jackson, Latamara Smith, William Butler, Pooch Hall, Chris Thornton, William Springfield, Martin Roach, David Julian Hirsh, Anthony Nuncio, Nichole McLean, Linette Robinson, Kenny Robinson, Nadia-Leigh Nascimento; ***D:*** Craig Ross Jr.; ***W:*** Craig Ross Jr.; ***C:*** Carl F. Bartels; ***M:*** William L. Johnson, Aaron Spears, Cruel Timothy, Jan Poperans.

The Blue Hour **1991** Theo is a Berlin hustler whose business is so good he can pick his clients. Marie, his next-door neighbor, lives with her boyfriend Paul until he just walks out one day. Marie is shattered and refuses to leave her apartment until Theo takes an interest in her plight. Just when it seems that the improbable couple could find true love, Paul comes back. In German with English subtitles. **87m/C VHS, DVD.** *GE* Andreas Herder, Dina Leipzig, Cyrill Rey-Coquais; ***D:*** Marcel Gisler.

Blue Ice ½ **1992 (R)** Harry Anders (Caine) is an ex-spy with an eye for the ladies and a loyalty to his friends. When his friends start winding up dead, Harry decides to investigate—a very dangerous decision, especially when a mysterious woman (Young) takes an interest. **96m/C VHS, DVD.** Michael Caine, Sean Young, Ian Bannen, Bob Hoskins; ***D:*** Russell Mulcahy; ***W:*** Ron Hutchinson; ***M:*** Michael Kamen. **CABLE**

Blue Iguana **1988 (R)** An inept bounty hunter travels south of the border to recover millions from a crooked South American bank, and meets up with sexy women, murderous thugs, and corruption. **88m/C VHS, DVD.** Dylan McDermott, Jessica Harper, James Russo, Dean Stockwell, Pamela Gidley, Tovah Feldshuh; ***D:*** John Lafia.

Blue in the Face ½ **1995 (R)** Wang and Auster's immediate follow-up to "Smoke," shot in five days, recycles the same Brooklyn cigar shop setting and contains a dozen fast-paced, loosely scripted or wholly improvised scenes that they couldn't cram into "Smoke," led by Reed's deadpan riff on eyewear, New York, and smoking. The action again centers around Auggie (Keitel), the shop manager, who hangs out with the mostly eccentric, and sometimes famous clientele. Jarmusch idly waxes philosophic on smoking technique, while puffing on what he claims is his last. Scenes are woven together with videotaped interviews from actual Brooklyn residents, creating a tribute to life in the borough with a documentary feel. Improv lovers will enjoy watching what sometimes seems more like outtakes than finished performances. **83m/C VHS, DVD.** Harvey Keitel, Lou Reed, Michael J. Fox, Roseanne, Jim Jarmusch, Lily Tomlin, Mel Gorham, Jared Harris, Giancarlo Esposito, Victor Argo, Madonna, Keith David, Mira Sorvino, Malik Yoba, Michael Badalucco, Jose Zuniga, Stephen Gevedon, John Lurie, Sharif Rashed, RuPaul Charles; ***D:*** Wayne Wang, Paul Auster; ***W:*** Wayne Wang, Paul Auster.

Blue Jeans ½ **1978** A young French boy experiences sexual awakening and humiliation in a British school. In French with English subtitles. **80m/C VHS.** *FR* Gilles Budin, Michel Gibet, Daniel Very, Thierry Dolon; ***D:*** Hugues des Roziers; ***W:*** Hugues des Roziers; ***C:*** Jacques Assuerus; ***M:*** David MacNeil.

Blue Jeans and Dynamite **1976** A stuntman is hired to lift the "Golden Mask of the Duct Tomb" and is followed on land, water, and air. Great chase scenes and action-filled finale. **90m/C VHS.** Robert Vaughn, Simon Andreu, Katia Kristine; ***D:*** Gordon Hessler; ***W:*** Jose Maesso, Ricardo Ferrer; ***C:*** Julio Bragado; ***M:*** Adolfo Waitzman.

Blue Juice ½ **1995 (R)** Early work from several young actors who've gone on to bigger things. Billed as Britain's first surf picture, this comedy follows the escapades of nearly 30 JC (Pertwee), a local hero of the Cornish surfing community who can't commit to his more practical girlfriend, Chloe (Zeta-Jones). Then some of JC's London buddies, Dean (McGregor), Josh (Mackintosh), and Terry (Gunn), show up for a sort of last hurrah against the boredom of acting like adults. **90m/C VHS, DVD.** *GB* Sean Pertwee, Catherine Zeta-Jones, Ewan McGregor, Steven Mackintosh, Peter Gunn, Heathcote Williams; ***D:*** Carl Prechezer; ***W:*** Carl Prechezer, Peter Salmi; ***C:*** Richard Greatrex; ***M:*** Simon Davison.

The Blue Kite *Lan Feng Zheng* **1993** Fifteen years of political and cultural upheaval in China is shown through the eyes of young troublemaker Tietou, who certainly earns his nickname of "Iron Head" after his 1954 birth. Soon his father is sent to a labor reform camp and his mother remarries—only to be faced with more struggles as the years go by. The kite is Tietou's cherished toy, which keeps getting lost or destroyed but is always being rebuilt, offering one token of hope. Chinese with subtitles. **138m/C VHS, DVD.** *CH* Liping Lu, Zhang Wenyao, Pu Quanxin; ***D:*** Tian Zhuangzhuang; ***W:*** Xiao Mao; ***C:*** Yong Hou; ***M:*** Yoshihide Otomo.

The Blue Knight ½ **1975** Kennedy brings energy and care to this basically standard story. Policeman waiting for retirement searches for his partner's killer. Unexceptional treatment made palatable by actors. **72m/C VHS.** George Kennedy, Alex Rocco, Glynn Turman, Verna Bloom, Michael Margotta; ***D:*** J. Lee Thompson; ***C:*** Richard L. Rawlings. **TV**

The Blue Lagoon **WOOF! 1980 (R)** Useless remake of 1949 film of the same name. An adolescent boy and girl marooned on a desert isle discover love (read: sex) without the restraints of society. Not too explicit, but nonetheless intellectually offensive. Gorgeous photography of island paradise is wasted on this Shields vehicle. **105m/C VHS, DVD.** Brooke Shields, Christopher Atkins, Leo McKern, William Daniels; ***D:*** Randal Kleiser; ***W:*** Douglas Day Stewart; ***C:*** Nestor Almendros; ***M:*** Basil Poledouris. Golden Raspberries '80: Worst Actress (Shields).

The Blue Lamp **1949** Action-adventure fans familiar with the hoary plot where a cop must avenge the wrongful death of his partner will appreciate this suspenseful British detective effort. It's one of the very first in the genre to explore buddy cop revenge in a very British sort of way. Also sports a concluding chase scene which has stood the test of time. Led to the long-running British TV series "Dixon of Dock Green." **84m/B VHS.** *GB* Dirk Bogarde, Jimmy Hanley, Jack Warner, Bernard Lee, Robert Flemyng, Patric Doonan, Bruce Seton, Frederick Piper, Betty Ann Davies, Peggy Evans; ***D:*** Basil Dearden. British Acad. '50: Film.

The Blue Light *Das Blaue Licht* **1932** Fairy-tale love story, based on an Italian fable about a mysterious woman, thought to be a witch, and a painter. Riefenstahl's first film which brought her to the attention of Adolf Hitler, who requested she make films glorifying the Nazi Party. In German with English subtitles. **77m/B VHS.** *GE* Leni Riefenstahl, Matthias Wieman, Max Holsboer; ***D:*** Leni Riefenstahl; ***W:*** Bela Balazs, Leni Riefenstahl; ***C:*** Hans Schneeberger; ***M:*** Giuseppe Becce.

The Blue Lightning ½ **1986** Investigator Elliott travels to Australia to retrieve the priceless Blue Lightening gem. He must fight the crime lord in his Aussie encampment. Nice scenery, but unexceptional TV story. **95m/C VHS.** Sam Elliott, Rebecca Gilling, Robert Culp, John Meillon, Robert Coleby, Max Phipps; ***D:*** Lee Philips. **TV**

The Blue Max ½ **1966** During WWI a young German, fresh out of aviation training school, competes for the coveted "Blue Max" flying award with other members of a squadron of seasoned flyers from aristocratic backgrounds. Based on a novel by Jack D. Hunter. **155m/C VHS, DVD.** George Peppard, James Mason, Ursula Andress, Jeremy Kemp, Karl Michael Vogler, Anton Diffring, Harry Towb, Peter Woodthorpe, Derek Newark, Derren Nesbitt, Loni von Friedl; ***D:*** John Guillermin; ***W:*** Ben Barzman, Basilio Franchina, David Pursall, Jack Seddon, Gerald Hanley; ***C:*** Douglas Slocombe; ***M:*** Jerry Goldsmith.

Blue Money **1984** A wild, comedic caper film about a cab-driving nightclub impressionist who absconds with a briefcase packed with cash and is pursued by everyone, even the I.R.A. **82m/C VHS.** *GB* Tim Curry, Dabby Bishop, Billy Connolly, Frances Tomelty; ***D:*** Colin Bucksey. **TV**

Blue Monkey *Green Monkey* **1987 (R)** A mysterious alien plant impregnates a man, who gives birth to a huge, man-eating insect larva. It subsequently grows up into a giant bug, and roams around a quarantined hospital looking for patients to eat. What made you think it had anything to do with monkeys? **97m/C VHS.** Steve Railsback, Susan Anspach, Gwynyth Walsh, John Vernon, Joe Flaherty; ***D:*** William Fruet.

Blue Moon ½ **2000 (PG-13)** Marrieds Gazzara and Moreno take a trip to the Catskills and wish on the blue moon which, according to legend, will grant them a wish. Of course, exactly how that wish will come true may not be exactly as the couple would hope. **90m/C VHS, DVD.** Ben Gazzara, Rita Moreno, Alanna Ubach, Brian Vincent, Heather Matarazzo, Vincent Pastore, Burt Young, Victor Argo, Lillo Brancato; ***D:*** John A. Gallagher; ***W:*** John A. Gallagher, Steve Carducci; ***C:*** Craig DiBona; ***M:*** Stephen Endelman.

Blue Movies **WOOF! 1988 (R)** A couple of jerks try their hand at making porn films with predictable results. **92m/C VHS.** Larry Linville, Lucinda Crosby, Steve Levitt, Darien Mathias, Larry Poindexter, Christopher Stone, Don Calfa, Russell Johnson; ***D:*** Paul Koval, Ed Fitzgerald; ***W:*** Paul Koval, Ed Fitzgerald.

Blue Murder at St. Trinian's **1956** The second of the madcap British comedy series (based on cartoons by Ronald Searle) about an incredibly ferocious pack of schoolgirls. This time they travel to the European continent and make life miserable for a jewel thief. Highlight: fantasy sequence in ancient Rome showing the girls thrown to the lions—and scaring the lions. **86m/B VHS.** *GB* Joyce Grenfell, Terry-Thomas, George Cole, Alastair Sim, Lionel Jeffries, Thorley Walters; ***D:*** Frank Launder; ***M:*** Malcolm Arnold.

Blue Ridge Fall **1999 (R)** In the small town of Jefferson Creek, North Carolina, Danny (Facinelli) is the star high school quarterback who can do no wrong. He's befriended simple-minded Aaron (Eastman), who is driven to violent desperation by his abusive father. Danny enlists his buddies to cover up Aaron's crime but their plans quickly go wrong and things just get more desperate for them all. **99m/C VHS, DVD.** Peter Facinelli, Rodney Eastman, Will Estes, Jay R. Ferguson, Tom Arnold, Amy Irving, Chris Isaak, Brent Jennings, Heather Stephens, Garvin Funches; ***D:*** James Rowe; ***W:*** James Rowe; ***C:*** Chris Walling; ***M:*** Greg Edmonson.

Blue River ½ **1995 (PG-13)** Flashbacks highlight this saga of a troubled family. Successful doctor Edward Sellers (McDonough) is dismayed when his derelict older brother Lawrence (O'Connell), whom he hasn't seen in 15 years, suddenly appears on his doorstep. A gifted teenager, Lawrence once built his world around science and logic after their father deserted the family but his only purpose turns out to be getting even with everyone he feels has betrayed him. Young Edward (Stahl) tried to be the "good" son, while Mom (Dey) retreated into religion and an affair with self-righteously nasty school principal Henry Howland (Elliott). TV adaptation of the novel by Ethan Canin. **90m/C VHS, DVD.** Jerry O'Connell, Nick Stahl, Susan

Dey, Sam Elliott, Neal McDonough, Jean Marie Barnwell, Patrick Renna; *D:* Larry Elikann; *W:* Maria Nation; *C:* Eric Van Haren Noman; *M:* Lawrence Shragge.

Blue Skies **1946** Former dancer turned radio personality Astaire flashes back to his friendship with singer Crosby and the gal (Caulfield) that came between them. Flimsy plot is just an excuse for some 20 Irving Berlin songs and Astaire's split-screen dance number, "Puttin' on the Ritz." ♫ All By Myself; Always; Any Bonds Today?; Blue Skies; A Couple of Song and Dance Men; Everybody Step; Getting Nowhere; Heat Wave; I'll See You in C-U-B-A. **104m/C VHS, DVD.** Fred Astaire, Bing Crosby, Joan Caulfield, Billy DeWolfe, Olga San Juan, Frank Faylen; *D:* Stuart Heisler; *W:* Arthur Sheekman; *C:* Charles B(ryant) Lang Jr.

Blue Skies Again 1/2 **1983 (PG)** Spunky young woman determined to play major league baseball locks horns with the chauvinistic owner and the gruff manager of her favorite team. **91m/C VHS.** Robyn Barto, Harry Hamlin, Mimi Rogers, Kenneth McMillan, Dana Elcar, Andy Garcia; *D:* Richard Michaels.

Blue Sky **1991 (PG-13)** Carly Marshall (Lange) is an irrepressible beauty, long married to adoring but uptight military scientist Hank (Jones). Things are barely in control when they're stationed in Hawaii but after Hank's transfer to a backwater base in Alabama, Carly's emotional mood swings go wildly out of control. Hell truly breaks loose when Carly attracts the attention of the camp's commander (Boothe), who's only too willing to take advantage. Set in 1962, a nuclear radiation subplot (Hank's new project) proves a minor distraction. Exceptional performance by Lange with Jones providing a quiet counterpoint as a man still deeply in love with his disturbed wife. Director Richardson's final film. Release date was delayed to 1994 due to studio Orion's financial problems. **101m/C VHS, DVD.** Jessica Lange, Tommy Lee Jones, Powers Boothe, Carrie Snodgress, Amy Locane, Chris O'Donnell, Mitchell Ryan, Dale Dye, Richard Jones; *D:* Tony Richardson; *W:* Arlene Sarner, Jerry Leichtling, Rama Laurie Stagner; *C:* Steve Yaconelli; *M:* Jack Nitzsche. Oscars '94: Actress (Lange); Golden Globes '95: Actress—Drama (Lange); L.A. Film Critics '94: Actress (Lange).

Blue Smoke 1/2 *Nora Roberts' Blue Smoke* **2007** After her family's pizzeria is destroyed by fire when she's 11, Reena grows up to become an arson investigator. A neighborhood reunion leads her to romance with carpenter Bo, but Reena soon discovers that fire is following her. Seems an arsonist is targeting everything—and everyone—she holds dear. Lifetime original movie based on the novel by Nora Roberts. **90m/C DVD.** Alicia Witt, Matthew Settle, Scott Bakula, Talia Shire, John Henry Reardon, Eric Keenleyside, Chris Fassbender, Ben Ayres; *D:* David Carson; *W:* Ronni Kern; *C:* Nikos Evdemon; *M:* Chris P. Bacon, Stuart M. Thomas. **CABLE**

Blue State **2007 (R)** Fervently liberal John (Meyer) drunkenly proclaims that he'll move to Canada if Dubya is elected POTUS and then feels he must follow through. He finds a green card marriage website and decides to travel to Winnipeg. Needing someone to share the driving, John meets secretive Chloe (Paquin), who has her own reasons for leaving the country. Tends toward one-sided diatribes and its views on Canadians vs. Americans are stereotypical and condescending. **99m/C DVD.** Breckin Meyer, Anna Paquin, Richard Blackburn, Adriana O'Neill, Joyce Krenz; *D:* Marshall Lewy; *W:* Marshall Lewy; *C:* Phil Parmet; *M:* Nathan Johnson.

Blue Steel **1934** A young Wayne saves a town from financial ruin by leading the citizens to a gold strike. **59m/B VHS, DVD.** John Wayne, George "Gabby" Hayes; *D:* Robert North Bradbury.

Blue Steel **1990 (R)** Director Bigelow's much-heralded, proto-feminist cop thriller. A serious female rookie's gun falls into the hands of a Wall Street psycho who begins a killing spree. Action film made silly with over-anxious sub-text and patriarchy-directed rage. **102m/C VHS, DVD.** Jamie Lee Curtis, Ron Silver, Clancy Brown, Louise Fletcher, Philip Bosco, Elizabeth Pena, Tom Sizemore; *D:* Kathryn Bigelow; *W:* Kathryn Bigelow, Eric Red; *M:* Brad Fiedel.

Blue Streak **1999 (PG-13)** Only hardcore Martin Lawrence fans will enjoy this formulaic buddy-cop-with-a-twist action comedy. Lawrence plays jewel thief Miles Logan, who hides a gem from his latest heist at a construction site just before he's caught. Three years later and out of jail, Logan tries to retrieve his diamond only to discover the site is now a police station. While impersonating a detective in order to sneak in and grab the stash, he accidentally catches an escaping felon and is forced to continue the charade. He's saddled with rookie partner Carlson (Wilson) and begins using his criminal knowledge to catch other crooks, including his old crony Tulley (Chappelle). Lawrence gives a good effort but all of his frantic mugging can't save the lame material he's forced to work with, making this feel like a poor man's "Beverly Hills Cop." **94m/C VHS, DVD.** Martin Lawrence, Luke Wilson, Peter Greene, Dave Chappelle, William Forsythe, Graham Beckel, Tamala Jones, Nicole Ari Parker, Robert Miranda, Olek Krupa, Anne Marie Howard; *D:* Les Mayfield; *W:* Stephen Carpenter, Michael Berry, John Blumenthal; *C:* David Eggby.

Blue Sunshine 1/2 **1978 (R)** A certain brand of L.S.D. called Blue Sunshine starts to make its victims go insane. **94m/C VHS, DVD.** Zalman King, Deborah Winters, Mark Goddard, Robert Walden, Charles Siebert, Ann Cooper, Ray Young, Alice Ghostley, Richard Crystal, Bill Adler, Stefan Gierasch, Brion James; *D:* Jeff Lieberman; *W:* Jeff Lieberman; *M:* Charles Gross.

Blue Thunder 1/2 **1983 (R)** Police helicopter pilot Scheider is chosen to test an experimental high-tech chopper that can see through walls, record a whisper, and level a city block. Seems anti-terrorist supercopter is needed to ensure security during 1984 Olympics. Bothered by Vietnam flashbacks, Scheider then battles wacky McDowell in the skies over L.A. High-techy police drama with satisfying aerial combat scenes nearly crashes with story line. **110m/C VHS, DVD.** Roy Scheider, Daniel Stern, Malcolm McDowell, Candy Clark, Warren Oates; *D:* John Badham; *W:* Dan O'Bannon, Don Jakoby; *C:* John A. Alonzo.

Blue Tiger **1994 (R)** Gina Hayes (Madsen) is shopping with her young son when a masked gunman enters the store and opens fire. When Gina realizes her son has been killed she becomes obsessed with finding the assailant. Her one clue—a blue tiger tattoo. **88m/C VHS, DVD.** Virginia Madsen, Toru Nakamura, Harry Dean Stanton, Ryo Ishibashi; *D:* Norberto Barba; *W:* Joel Soisson.

The Blue Tooth Virgin **2009 (R)** Successful magazine editor David and aspiring screenwriter Sam have been friends for years. But when David gives a too-honest critique of Sam's latest work it causes problems that spread throughout their lives. **80m/C DVD.** *US* Austin Peck, Lauren Stamile, Bryce Johnson, Tom Gilroy, Roma Maffia, Amber Benson, Karen Black; *D:* Russell Brown; *W:* Russell Brown; *C:* Marco Fargnoli; *M:* Karen Black.

Blue Tornado **1990 (PG-13)** An eerie bright light, emitted from a mountain, makes supersonic jets disappear into thin air. A beautiful researcher and a cocky pilot set out to solve the mystery. Better-than-average aerial sequences don't make up for goofy story and ludicrous dialogue. **96m/C VHS.** Dirk Benedict, Patsy Kensit, Ted McGinley, David Warner; *D:* Tony B. Dobb.

Blue Valentine **2010** Cianfrance's flick traces the frustration, anger, and dissolution of the marriage of Dean (Gosling) and Cindy (Williams) while offering flashbacks to happier times. **120m/C DVD.** *US* Ryan Gosling, Michelle Williams, Mike Vogel, John Doman, Ben Shenkman, Faith Wladyka; *D:* Derek Cianfrance; *W:* Derek Cianfrance, Joey Curtis; *C:* Andrij Parekh.

Blue Velvet **1986 (R)** Disturbing, unique exploration of the dark side of American suburbia, involving an innocent college youth who discovers a severed ear in an empty lot, and is thrust into a turmoil of depravity, murder, and sexual deviance. Brutal, grotesque, and unmistakably Lynch; an immaculately made, fiercely imagined film that is unlike any other. Mood is enhanced by the Badalamenti soundtrack. Graced by splashes of Lynchian humor, most notably the movie's lumber theme. Hopper is riveting as the chief sadistic nutcase and Twin Peaks' MacLachlan is a study in loss of innocence. **121m/C VHS, DVD.** Kyle MacLachlan, Isabella Rossellini, Dennis Hopper, Laura Dern, Hope Lange, Jack Nance, Dean Stockwell, George Dickerson, Brad Dourif, Priscilla Pointer, Angelo Badalamenti; *D:* David Lynch; *W:* David Lynch; *C:* Frederick Elmes; *M:* Angelo Badalamenti. Ind. Spirit '87: Actress (Rossellini); L.A. Film Critics '86: Director (Lynch), Support. Actor (Hopper); Montreal World Film Fest. '86: Support. Actor (Hopper); Natl. Soc. Film Critics '86: Cinematog., Director (Lynch), Film, Support. Actor (Hopper).

Blue, White and Perfect 1/2 **1942** Shayne (Nolan) promises his marriage-minded girlfriend Merle (Hughes) that he'll leave the PI business behind and get a steady wartime job. Only the shamus soon finds himself mixed-up in the smuggling of industrial diamonds that has Shayne taking an ocean liner to Hawaii and discovering espionage and Nazis aboard ship. **74m/B DVD.** Lloyd Nolan, Mary Beth Hughes, George Reeves, Steven Geray, Helen Reynolds, Henry Victor, Curt Bois, Mae Marsh, Arthur Loft; *D:* Herbert I. Leeds; *W:* Samuel G. Engel; *C:* Glen MacWilliams.

The Blue Yonder 1/2 *Time Flyers* **1986** In this made-for-video feature, a young boy travels back in time to meet the grandfather he never knew, risking historical integrity. **89m/C VHS.** Art Carney, Peter Coyote, Huckleberry Fox; *D:* Mark Rosman.

Bluebeard 1/2 **1944** Tormented painter with a psychopathic urge to strangle his models is the basis for this effective, low-budget film. One of Carradine's best vehicles. **73m/B VHS, DVD.** John Carradine, Jean Parker, Nils Asther; *D:* Edgar G. Ulmer; *W:* Pierre Gendron; *C:* Jock Feindel.

Bluebeard *Landru* **1963** French biography of Henri-Desire Landru, who seduced and murdered 11 women and was subsequently beheaded. Dubbed into English. **108m/C VHS.** *FR* Charles Denner, Danielle Darrieux, Michele Morgan, Hildegarde Knef, Stephane Audran; *D:* Claude Chabrol.

Bluebeard 1/2 **1972 (R)** Lady killer Burton knocks off series of beautiful wives in soporific remake of the infamous story. **128m/C VHS, DVD.** Richard Burton, Raquel Welch, Joey Heatherton, Nathalie Delon, Virna Lisi, Sybil Danning; *D:* Edward Dmytryk; *W:* Edward Dmytryk, Ennio de Concini, Maria Pia Fusco; *C:* Gabor Pogany; *M:* Ennio Morricone.

Bluebeard's Eighth Wife **1938** Problematic comedy set on the French Riviera about a spoiled millionaire (Cooper) who's been married seven times and wants to go for eight with Colbert, the daughter of a destitute aristocrat. Good for a few laughs, but Coop seemed out of place in his role. Based on the play by Alfred Savoir, American version by Charlton Andrews. **86m/B VHS.** Claudette Colbert, Gary Cooper, David Niven, Edward Everett Horton, Elizabeth Patterson, Herman Bing, William Hymer, Franklin Pangborn; *D:* Ernst Lubitsch; *W:* Charles Brackett, Billy Wilder; *C:* Leo Tover; *M:* Werner R. Heymann, Frederick "Friedrich" Hollander.

Blueberry Hill 1/2 **1988 (R)** While her mother struggles with the grief over husband's death, a young girl in a small town learns about life, music, and her late father from a jazz singer. Good soundtrack. **93m/C VHS.** Jennifer Rubin, Carrie Snodgress, Margaret Avery; *D:* Strathford Hamilton.

A Blueprint for Murder 1/2 **1953** Low-budget but well-done noir thriller. Whitney "Cam" Cameron (Cotten) becomes suspicious of his brother's attractive widow Lynne (Peters) when his young niece dies under strange circumstances (as did his brother). An autopsy reveals poisoning and Cam is convinced that Lynne wants to become the sole inheritor to her husband's estate and is going after her stepson next. Cam chases after Lynne, who's off on an ocean voyage, in order to prove she's a cold-blooded killer despite his attraction to her. **77m/B DVD.** Joseph Cotten, Jean Peters, Freddy Ridgeway, Gary Merrill, Catherine McLeod, Jack Kruschen, Barney (Bernard) Phillips; *D:* Andrew L. Stone; *W:* Andrew L. Stone; *C:* Leo Tover; *M:* Lionel Newman.

The Blues Brothers **1980 (R)** As an excuse to run rampant on the city of Chicago, Jake (Belushi) and Elwood (Aykroyd) Blues attempt to raise $5,000 for their childhood orphanage by putting their old band back together. Good music, quotable dialogue, lots of wrecked cars, plenty of cameos. A classic. **133m/C VHS, DVD.** Murphy Dunne, John Belushi, Dan Aykroyd, James Brown, Cab Calloway, Ray Charles, Henry Gibson, Aretha Franklin, Carrie Fisher, John Candy, Kathleen Freeman, Steven Williams, Charles Napier, Stephen Bishop; ***Cameos:*** Frank Oz, Steven Spielberg, Twiggy, Paul (Pee-wee Herman) Reubens, Steve Lawrence, John Lee Hooker, John Landis, Chaka Khan; *D:* John Landis; *W:* John Landis, Dan Aykroyd; *C:* Stephen M. Katz; *M:* Ira Newborn, Elmer Bernstein.

Blues Brothers 2000 **1998 (PG-13)** Eighteen years after the original caper, Landis, Aykroyd, and most of the original cast return to the scene of the crime. Jake's died but Elwood's (Aykroyd) still around. He gets the band back together, recruits a Blues cousin (Goodman), a half-foster-brother (Morton), and an orphan (Bonifant) in need of mentoring, and heads for a battle of the bands between New Orleans and Chicago. The music, performed by the original Blues Brothers Band as well as a rock and blues all-star lineup, is the highlight. As for the rest of the flick, watch the original instead. Did Aykroyd learn nothing from "Caddyshack 2"? **123m/C VHS, DVD.** Paul Shaffer, Murphy Dunne, Dan Aykroyd, John Goodman, Joe Morton, Evan Bonifant, Nia Peeples, Kathleen Freeman, Frank Oz, Steve Lawrence, Aretha Franklin, B.B. King, James Brown, Erykah Badu, Darrell Hammond; *D:* John Landis; *W:* John Landis, Dan Aykroyd; *C:* David Herrington; *M:* Paul Shaffer.

Blues Busters 1/2 **1950** Another entry in the "Bowery Boys" series. When Sach emerges from a tonsillectomy with the velvety voice of a crooner, Slip cashes in by turning Louie's Sweet Shop into a nightclub, the better to showcase his buddy's talents. Sach's singing voice provided by John Lorenz. **68m/B VHS.** Leo Gorcey, Huntz Hall, Adele Jergens, Gabriel Dell, Craig Stevens, Phyllis Coates, Bernard Gorcey, David Gorcey; *D:* William Beaudine.

Blues in the Night **1941** Unusually downbeat story about struggling musicians. Jigger (Whorf) forms a jazz/blues group with pals Nickie (Kazan), Peppi (Halop), Leo (Carson), and Leo's wife Ginger (Lane), who's their singer. They're not making any dough touring so they accept the offer of gangster Del Davis (Nolan) to play at his New Jersey roadhouse, where they're also introduced to hard-boiled dame Kay (Field), who immediately causes trouble. Whorf and Kazan later became better-known as directors. Harold Arlen and Johnny Mercer wrote the Oscar-nominated title song. **89m/B DVD.** Richard Whorf, Priscilla Lane, Betty Field, Elia Kazan, Jack Carson, Lloyd Nolan, Billy Halop, Wallace Ford, Peter Whitney, Howard de Silva; *D:* Richard Whorf, Anatole Litvak; *W:* Elia Kazan, Robert Rossen; *C:* Ernest Haller; *M:* Heinz Roemheld.

Bluffing It **1987** TV movie about an older man who has been disguising his illiteracy for years. **120m/C VHS.** Dennis Weaver, Janet Carroll, Michelle Little, Robert Sean Leonard, Cleavant Derricks, Victoria Wauchope; *D:* James Sadwith; *M:* Brad Fiedel. **TV**

The Blum Affair **1948** In post-WWI Germany, a Jewish man is framed for the murder of an accountant and uncovers in his capture and prosecution a rat's nest of corruption and anti-Semitism. In German with English subtitles. **109m/B VHS.** *GE* Hans-Christian Blech, Gisela Trowe, Kurt Ehrhardt, Paul Bildt, Klaus Becker; *D:* Erich Engel.

Blume in Love **1973 (R)** An ironic comedy/drama about a man who falls hopelessly in love with his ex-wife who divorced him for cheating on her while they were married. **115m/C VHS.** George Segal, Susan Anspach, Kris Kristofferson, Shelley Winters, Marsha Mason; *D:* Paul Mazursky; *W:* Paul

Mazursky; ***C:*** Bruce Surtees; ***M:*** Bill Conti.

Blush *Hongfen* **1995** Shanghai prostitutes and friends Quiyi (Ji) and Xiao (Saifei) are stripped of their vocation by the communist takeover in 1949. Quiyi manages to take refuge with her favorite customer, wealthy Lao Pu (Zhiwen), while Xiao is re-educated and becomes a worker in a silk factory. Eventually thrown out of the house by Lao's disapproving mother, Quiyi learns to make her own way. Xiao meets Lao after his family has lost their money and winds up marrying him, unhappily since Lao continually pines for Quiyi. Based on the novel by Su Tong; Cantonese with subtitles. **119m/C VHS.** *CH* Wang Ji, Saifei He, Zhiwen Wang, Wang Rouli; ***D:*** Li Shaohong; ***W:*** Li Shaohong, Ni Zhen; ***C:*** Zeng Nianping; ***M:*** Guo Wenjing.

BMX Bandits **1983** Three adventurous Aussie teens put their BMX skills to the test when they witness a crime and are pursued by the criminals. Much big air. **92m/C VHS.** Nicole Kidman, David Argue, John Ley, Angelo D'Angelo; ***D:*** Brian Trenchard-Smith; ***W:*** Patrick Edgeworth.

Boa **2002 (R)** A prehistoric snake, 100 feet in length, makes a reappearance beneath a maximum security prison located in Antarctic. Warden Ryan (Wasson) calls for a rescue team, which includes paleontologists Robert (Cain) and his wife Jessica (Lackey). A handful of survivors try to make it from the prison to the plane but that's one hungry snake. **95m/C VHS, DVD.** Dean Cain, Elizabeth Lackey, Grand L. Bush, Craig Wasson, Mark A. Seppard; ***D:*** Phillip J. Roth; ***W:*** Phillip J. Roth, Terry Neish; ***C:*** Todd Barron; ***M:*** Rich McHugh. **VIDEO**

Boarding Gate **2007 (R)** It's not a good movie by any means but there's super-confident Argento in black undies, stiletto heels, and holding a gun to keep your interest. Bad girl Sandra used to be involved in a kinky sex and business relationship with shady American financier Miles (a menacing Madsen). She's now working for a shady import firm run by dragon lady Sue (Lin) and her husband Lester (Ng) and doing drug smuggling on the side for some quick cash. Sandra's also doing Lester and when he finds out about the drug deals, he pressures her into a murder-for-hire of Miles and a quick exit to Hong Kong. Why do these plans never go as expected? English, French and Chinese with subtitles. **93m/C DVD.** *FR* Asia Argento, Michael Madsen, Joana Preiss, Alex Descas, Kim Gordon, Kelly Lin, Carl Ng; ***D:*** Olivier Assayas; ***W:*** Olivier Assayas; ***C:*** Yorick Le Saux; ***M:*** Brian Eno.

Boarding House **1983 (R)** Residents of a boardinghouse discover sinister doings in the basement. It does not occur to any of them to move to another house. **90m/C VHS.** Hank Adly, Kalassu, Alexandra Day; ***D:*** John Wintergate.

Boarding School *The Passion Flower Hotel* **1983 (R)** Basic teen sex comedy about students at a proper Swiss boarding school for girls who devise a plan to seduce the boys at a nearby school by posing as prostitutes. Kinski stars as the American girl who masterminds the caper. **100m/C VHS, DVD.** *GE* Nastassja Kinski; ***D:*** Andre Farwagi.

Boardinghouse Blues **1948** A showbiz musical centered around a boarding house with tenant troubles. It's an excuse for popular black entertainers of the day to perform, including Lucky Millinder, Bull Moose Jackson, Una Mae Carlisle, and Stumpy and Stumpy. **90m/C VHS, DVD.** Dusty Fletcher, Moms (Jackie) Mabley; ***D:*** Josh Binney.

The Boat Is Full *Das Boot Ist Voll* **1981** A group of refugees pose as a family in order to escape from Nazi Germany as they seek asylum in Switzerland. Available in German with English subtitles or dubbed into English. **104m/C VHS, DVD.** *SI* Tina Engel, Curt Bois, Renate Steiger, Mathias Gnaedinger, Hans Diehl, Martin Walz, Gerd David; ***D:*** Markus Imhoof; ***W:*** Markus Imhoof; ***C:*** Hans Liechti. Berlin Intl. Film Fest. '81: Director (Imhoof).

Boat Trip WOOF! **2003 (R)** Isn't it about time for Gooding, Jr. to give back his Oscar? Or at least fire his agent? In this pathetic attempt at comedy, he's Jerry, a lovesick guy distraught over a failed relationship. To the rescue comes his buddy Nick (Sanz), a loudmouth skirt chaser who suggests a singles cruise. When Nick insults the travel agent, they're sent on a gay cruise, where Jerry falls for the ship's choreographer Gabrielle (Sanchez) and must pretend to be gay to win her. Yep, it's as crappy as it sounds. Gooding, Jr. tries hard, but he can't bail out this floater, which is aimed straight at the rocks of a cliche-ridden and spectacularly unfunny script and direction that wouldn't make the cut on a third-rate sitcom. **95m/C VHS, DVD, UMD.** *US* Cuba Gooding Jr., Horatio Sanz, Roselyn Sanchez, Vivica A. Fox, Maurice Godin, Roger Moore, Lin Shaye, Victoria Silvstedt, Richard Roundtree, Will Ferrell, Artie Lange, Bob Gunton, Jennifer Gareis; ***D:*** Mort Nathan; ***W:*** Mort Nathan, William Bigelow; ***C:*** Shawn Maurer; ***M:*** Robert Folk.

The Boatniks **1/2** **1970 (G)** An accident-prone Coast Guard ensign finds himself in charge of the "Times Square" of waterways: Newport Harbor. Adding to his already "titanic" problems is a gang of ocean-going jewel thieves who won't give up the ship! **99m/C VHS, DVD.** Robert Morse, Stefanie Powers, Phil Silvers, Norman Fell, Wally Cox, Don Ameche, Kelly Thordsen; ***D:*** Norman Tokar; ***M:*** Robert F. Brunner.

Bob & Carol & Ted & Alice **1/2** **1969 (R)** Two California couples have attended a trendy therapy session and, in an attempt to be more in touch with sexuality, resort to applauding one another's extramarital affairs and swinging. Wacky and well-written, this is a farce on free love and psycho-speak. Mazursky's directorial debut. **104m/C VHS, DVD.** Natalie Wood, Robert Culp, Dyan Cannon, Elliott Gould; ***D:*** Paul Mazursky; ***W:*** Paul Mazursky, Larry Tucker; ***C:*** Charles B(ryant) Lang Jr.; ***M:*** Quincy Jones. N.Y. Film Critics '69: Screenplay, Support. Actress (Cannon); Natl. Soc. Film Critics '69: Screenplay; Writers Guild '69: Orig. Screenplay.

Bob Funk **1/2** **2009 (R)** Overly-earnest comedy. Mrs. Funk (Zabriskie) demotes eldest son Bob (Campbell) to the family futon company's janitor because his booze and broads lifestyle interferes with his work. She then hires ad exec Ms. Thorne (Cook) and depressed Bob suddenly gets a spark of interest in turning his life around. **90m/C DVD.** Michael Leydon Campbell, Rachael Leigh Cook, Grace Zabriskie, Amy Ryan, Edward Jemison, Stephen (Steve) Root, Robert Canada, Lucy Davis; ***D:*** Craig Carlisle; ***W:*** Craig Carlisle; ***C:*** Lisa Wiegand; ***M:*** Tim Montijo. **VIDEO**

Bob le Flambeur *Bob the Gambler* **1955** Aging Bob (Duchesne) is a down-on-his-luck gambler who visits the Deauville Casino with his friend Roger (Garret), who just happens to know croupier Jean (Cerval). Informed that the casino safe is bursting with cash, Bob decides to have a final fling by robbing the casino. Low-budget, bittersweet crime comedy. French with subtitles. **97m/B VHS, DVD.** *FR* Roger Duchesne, Isabel Corey, Daniel Cauchy, Howard Vernon, Gerard Buhr, Guy Decomble; ***D:*** Jean-Pierre Melville; ***W:*** Jean-Pierre Melville, Auguste Le Breton; ***C:*** Henri Decae; ***M:*** Jean Boyer, Eddie Barclay.

Bob Roberts **1992 (R)** Excellent pseudo-documentary satire about a 1990 Pennsylvania senatorial race between Robbins' titular right-wing folk singer/entrepreneur versus Brickley Paiste's (Vidal) aging liberal incumbent. Roberts seems like a gee-whiz kinda guy but he'll stop at nothing to get elected and he knows a lot about political dirty tricks and, even more important, manipulating the media to get what he wants. Robbins directorial debut turned out to be very timely in view of the 1992 Clinton/Bush presidential campaign. Features a number of cameos. Line to remember: "Vote first. Ask questions later." **105m/C VHS, DVD.** Jack Black, Tom Atkins, Helen Hunt, Peter Gallagher, Lynne Thigpen, Bingo O'Malley, Kathleen Chalfant, Matthew Faber, Matt McGrath, Jeremy Piven, Steve Pink, Fisher Stevens, Bob Balaban, Allan Nicholls, June Stein, Adam Simon, Ned Bellamy, Robert Hegyes, Lee Arenberg, Natalie Strong, Merilee Dale, Tim Robbins, Giancarlo Esposito, Ray Wise, Rebecca Jenkins, Harry J. Lennix, John Ottavino, Robert Stanton, Alan Rickman, Gore Vidal, Brian Murray, Anita Gillette, David Strathairn, Susan Sarandon, James Spader, John Cusack, Fred Ward, Pamela Reed; ***D:*** Tim Robbins; ***W:*** Tim Robbins; ***C:*** Jean Lepine; ***M:*** David Robbins.

Bob the Butler **1/2** **2005 (PG)** Harmless fluff stars the usually obnoxious Green as perennial loser Bob Tree, who can't keep a job. His latest career attempt is attending butler school. His first placement is with neurotic Anne (Shields), who fired him when he was Bob the babysitter. Still, the single mom is desperate and hires Bob to look after her house and two exasperating children (Buechner, Smith), who decide the butler is better than mom's current boyfriend. **90m/C DVD.** *GB CA* Tom Green, Brooke Shields, Benjamin Smith, Simon Callow, Genevieve Buechner, Rob LeBelle; ***D:*** Gary Sinyor; ***W:*** Gary Sinyor, Jane Walker Wood, Steven Manners; ***C:*** Jason Lehel; ***M:*** David A. Hughes. **VIDEO**

Bobbie Jo and the Outlaw **1/2** **1976 (R)** Wonderwoman Carter is a bored carhop who yearns to be a country singer. She becomes involved with Marjoe, who fancies himself as a contemporary Billy the Kid. Together, they do their Bonnie and Clyde thing, to a significantly lesser dramatic effect than the original, though a glut of violence keeps the bodies dropping. **89m/C VHS.** Lynda Carter, Marjoe Gortner, Jesse Vint; ***D:*** Mark L. Lester.

Bobbie's Girl **2002** Meandering drama long on theatrics and short on sense. American Bailey (Peters) and her lover, Englishwoman Bobbie (Ward) run a pub in a seaside town near Dublin, assisted by Bailey's brother David (Silverman). Bobbie is diagnosed with breast cancer at the same time she learns that her estranged brother and his wife have died and their 10-year-old son, Alan (Sangster), is orphaned into Bobbie's care. Bobbie and Alan are naturally struggling to cope with their situations while eccentrics (they're both ex-actors) Bailey and David try to provide encouragement. **100m/C VHS, DVD.** Bernadette Peters, Rachel Ward, Jonathan Silverman, Thomas Sangster; ***D:*** Jeremy Paul Kagan; ***W:*** Samuel Bernstein; ***C:*** Ciaran Tanham; ***M:*** Bruce Broughton. **CABLE**

Bobby **1/2** **2006 (R)** Writer-director Emilio Estevez uses a star-studded cast to compare turbulent events of the '60s with modern problems, with mixed results. This homage to Robert F. Kennedy uses multiple storylines and characters that revolve around L.A.'s Ambassador Hotel on the day leading up to RFK's assassination. Estevez liberally sprinkles the stories of no less than twenty-two characters surrounding the imminent tragedy, including the hotel beautician (Stone), her cheating husband (Macy) and a couple soon to be married (Lohan, Wood). The characters aren't allowed to achieve much depth, and the performances are hit and miss. The impact of the assassination drives home the trivialities of the characters and reinforces the loss of RFK, who only appears in archival footage. **119m/C DVD.** *US* Anthony Hopkins, Harry Belafonte, William H. Macy, Sharon Stone, Christian Slater, Freddy Rodriguez, Laurence Fishburne, Demi Moore, Martin Sheen, Helen Hunt, Lindsay Lohan, Elijah Wood, Nick Cannon, Heather Graham, Ashton Kutcher, Shia LaBeouf, Brian Geraghty, Joshua Jackson, David Krumholtz, Emilio Estevez, Mary Elizabeth Winstead, Jacob Vargas, Joy Bryant, Svetlana Metkina; ***D:*** Emilio Estevez; ***W:*** Emilio Estevez; ***C:*** Michael Barrett; ***M:*** Mark Isham.

Bobby Deerfield **1977 (PG)** Cold-blooded Grand Prix driver comes face to face with death each time he races, but finally learns the meaning of life when he falls in love with a critically ill woman. Even with race cars, soap opera stalls. **124m/C VHS.** Al Pacino, Marthe Keller, Anny (Annie Legras) Duperey, Romolo Valli; ***D:*** Sydney Pollack; ***W:*** Alvin Sargent; ***C:*** Henri Decae; ***M:*** Dave Grusin.

Bobby Jones: Stroke of Genius **1/2** **2004 (PG)** Bloated homage to the late great golfer of the title starring a red-hot post-"Passion" Caviezel. Practically a natural, Jones, who still reigns as the only golfer to win all four major tournaments in a single calendar year, had to overcome a number of personal demons to become one of the greatest golfers in the world. An extremely moral man, Jones suffered from depression and sported a legendary temper that he battled in order to work his way to the top of golf world of the 1920s. After his Grand Slam coup, Jones was diagnosed with a spinal disorder and retired from golf at 28 to practice law and spend more time with wife Mary (Forlani). Historically faithful and elegant, with a fine performance by its star, but is hindered by sub-par script, formulaic plot, and undeveloped supports. **126m/C DVD.** *US* James (Jim) Caviezel, Claire Forlani, Jeremy Northam, Malcolm McDowell, Connie Ray, Brett Rice, Dan Albright, Larry Thompson, Paul Freeman, John Curran, Aidan Quinn, Alistair Begg, Kenny Alfonso, Tom Arcuragi, Devon Gearhart, Thomas Lewis, Hilton McCrae; ***D:*** Rowdy Herrington; ***W:*** Rowdy Herrington, Tony Depaul, Bill Pryor; ***C:*** Tom Stern; ***M:*** James Horner.

Bobby Z *Let's Kill Bobby Z; The Life and Death of Bobby Z* **2007 (R)** Lots of action and limited acting required. Con Tim Kearney (Walker) agrees to DEA agent Tad Gruszka's (Fishburne) plan to pass himself off as missing surfer/drug dealer Bobby Z in order to get paroled. Seems drug lords are holding Gruszka's partner hostage and they'll trade for Bobby. Things go wrong and Kearney goes on the lam with Bobby's ex-lover (Wilde) and his young son (Villareal). Based on "The Death and Life of Bobby Z" by Don Winslow. **97m/C DVD.** Paul Walker, Laurence Fishburne, Olivia Wilde, Joaquim Almeida, J.R. Villarreal, Jason Lewis, Jacob Vargas, Jason Flemyng, Keith Carradine, Chuck Liddell; ***D:*** John Herzfeld; ***W:*** Bob Krakower, Allen Lawrence; ***M:*** Tim Jones.

The Bobo **1/2** **1967** Lousy bullfighter tries to lure a gorgeous woman into romance. Filmed in Spain and Italy. **103m/C VHS.** *GB* Peter Sellers, Britt Ekland, Rossano Brazzi, Adolfo Celi; ***D:*** Robert Parrish; ***W:*** David R. Schwartz.

Boca **1994 (R)** American journalist J.J. (Chong) arrives in Rio during Carnival to investigate a story about random killings throughout the Brazilian streets. She gets stonewalled asking questions, until she meets an up-from-poverty crimelord named Boca De Ouro (Meira). Now, our noisy journalist may learn too much to keep her alive. Filmed in Rio de Janiero. **92m/C VHS.** Rae Dawn Chong, Martin Kemp, Tarcisio Meira, Martin Sheen; ***D:*** Sandra Werneck, Walter Avancini; ***W:*** Ed Silverstein.

Boccaccio '70 **1962** Three short bawdy/comedy/pageant-of-life films inspired by "The Decameron," each pertaining to ironically twisted sexual politics in middle class life. A fourth story, "Renzo and Luciana," by Mario Monicelli, has been cut. Dubbed. **145m/C VHS, DVD.** *IT* Anita Ekberg, Romy Schneider, Tomas Milian, Sophia Loren, Peppino de Filippo, Luigi Gillianni; ***D:*** Vittorio De Sica, Luchino Visconti, Federico Fellini; ***W:*** Luchino Visconti, Federico Fellini, Tullio Pinelli, Ennio Flaiano, Cesare Zavattini; ***C:*** Otello Martelli, Giuseppe Rotunno; ***M:*** Nino Rota, Armando Trovajoli.

Bodies, Rest & Motion **1993 (R)** Stagnant 20-something movie in which four young people basically do nothing in the sun-baked town of Enfield, Arizona. Similar to the movie "Singles," but without the Seattle grunge scene. The title's reference to Newton is fitting: "A body in rest or motion remains in that state unless acted upon by an outside force." Appealing cast is wasted in listless film that's content to just drift along. Based on the play by Roger Hedden. **94m/C VHS, DVD.** Phoebe Cates, Bridget Fonda, Tim Roth, Eric Stoltz, Scott Frederick, Scott Johnson, Alicia Witt, Rich Wheeler, Peter Fonda; ***D:*** Michael Steinberg; ***W:*** Roger Hedden; ***C:*** Bernd Heinl; ***M:*** Michael Convertino.

Bodily Harm **1995 (R)** By-the-numbers neo-noir features Fiorentino as Vegas detective Rita Cates, who's investigating the murders of two women with ties to ex-cop Sam McKeon (Baldwin), not incidentally Rita's former lover. She rekindles their lust but then begins to have second thoughts about Sam's innocence. Unconvincing despite the expert cast. **91m/C VHS.** Linda Fiorentino, Daniel Baldwin, Gregg Henry, Bill Smitrovich, Troy Evans, Joe Regalbuto, Millie Perkins, Todd Susman, Shannon Kenny; ***D:*** James (Momel) Lemmo; ***W:*** James (Momel) Lemmo, Joseph Whaley, Ronda Barendse; ***M:*** Robert Sprayberry.

The Body **2001 (PG-13)** Would-be religious thriller with wooden acting, laughable dialog, and clunky plot. In modern-day Jerusalem, Israeli archeologist Sharon Golban (Williams) checks out a tomb discovered beneath a shop and finds the skeleton of a crucified man. Could it be the remains of Jesus? When word reaches the Vatican, Cardinal Pesci (Wood) dispatches Father Matt Gutierrez (Banderas) to deal with the provocative situation. **108m/C VHS, DVD.** Antonio Banderas, Olivia Williams, John Wood, John Shrapnel, Derek Jacobi, Jason Flemyng, Makram Khoury, Vernon Dobtcheff, Ian McNeice; ***D:*** Jonas McCord; ***W:*** Jonas McCord; ***C:*** Vilmos Zsigmond; ***M:*** Serge Colbert.

Body and Soul 🦴🦴 **1924** The first screen appearance of Robeson has him cast in a dual role as a conniving preacher and his good brother. The preacher preys on the heroine, making her life a misery. Objections by censors to the preacher's character caused him to be redeemed and become worthy of the heroine's love. **102m/B VHS.** Paul Robeson, Julia Theresa Russell, Mercedes Gilbert; ***D:*** Oscar Micheaux.

Body and Soul 🦴🦴🦴 ½ *An Affair of the Heart* **1947** Charlie Davis (Garfield) is a Jewish boxer whose parents want him to quit the ring and get an education. Instead, he rises quickly to the top, thanks in part to gangster "protector" Roberts (Goff). After becoming a champ, Charlie starts the inevitable downward slide. One-time pro-welterweight Lee plays boxing rival Ben. A vintage '40s boxing film that defines the genre. Remade in 1981 with Leon Isaac Kennedy. **104m/B VHS, DVD.** John Garfield, Lilli Palmer, Hazel Brooks, Anne Revere, William Conrad, Canada Lee, Joseph Pevney, Lloyd Goff; ***D:*** Robert Rossen; ***W:*** Abraham Polonsky; ***C:*** James Wong Howe; ***M:*** Hugo Friedhofer. Oscars '47: Film Editing.

Body & Soul 🦴🦴 ½ **1981 (R)** Interesting remake of 1947 gem about a boxer who loses his perspective in the world of fame, fast cars, and women. **109m/C VHS, DVD.** Leon Isaac Kennedy, Jayne Kennedy, Peter Lawford, Muhammad Ali, Perry Lang; ***D:*** George Bowers.

Body & Soul 🦴🦴🦴 **1993** After spending 16 years as a cloistered nun in a Welsh convent, with vows of poverty, celibacy, and obedience, Anna Gibson (Scott Thomas) must return to the outside world. Following her brother's suicide, Anna is forced to deal with his pregnant widow (Redman) and two children and her family's failing Yorkshire mill. Anna suffers a crisis of faith as both the secular and the religious exert their strong influences and she's drawn as well to two very different men—younger Hal (Mavers), the mill's supervisor, and divorced bank manager Daniel Stern (Bowe). Based on the 1991 novel by Marcelle Bernstein; British TV miniseries. **312m/C VHS.** *GB* Kristin Scott Thomas, Amanda Redman, Gary Mavers, Anthony Valentine, Sandra Voe, John Bowe, Dorothy Tutin, Patrick Allen; ***D:*** Moira Armstrong; ***W:*** Paul Hines; ***C:*** Peter Middleton; ***M:*** Jim Parker.

Body and Soul 🦴🦴 **1998 (R)** Cliched remake of the familiar boxing saga that finds ambitious boxer Mancini and his manager Chiklis heading for a potential championship bout in Reno. Mancini might still have the boxing moves but he's certainly no amateur and his professionalism is actually a deterrent. **95m/C VHS, DVD.** Ray "Boom Boom" Mancini, Michael Chiklis, Rod Steiger, Joe Mantegna, Jennifer Beals, Tahnee Welch; ***D:*** Sam Henry Kass; ***W:*** Sam Henry Kass; ***C:*** Arturo Smith; ***M:*** David Waters. **CABLE**

Body Armor 🦴 ½ **1996 (R)** Special agent Conway (McColm) is recruited by an ex-girlfriend (Schofield) to find a missing scientist. This leads our hero to nutball virologist Dr. Krago (Perlman) who's using germ warfare for personal gain. For the action junkie (who doesn't mind a little eye candy as well). **95m/C VHS, DVD.** Matt McColm, Ron Perlman, Annabel Schofield, Carol Alt, Clint Howard, Morgan Brittany, Shauna O'Brien; ***D:*** Jack Gill; ***W:*** Jack Gill; ***C:*** Robert Hayes; ***M:*** Mark Holden. **VIDEO**

Body Armour 🦴 ½ **2007** Maybe it was a good excuse for the actors to enjoy the Spanish sunshine, because it's not much of a movie. Secret Service agent John's (Schweiger) career is ruined when the presidential nominee he's guarding gets blown up by a car bomb. Three years later, ex-agent John reluctantly accepts a bodyguard job in Barcelona and learns his client is the man responsible—international assassin Maxwell (Palminteri) who's turned on his associates and become a government witness. They want him dead (and so does John). **90m/C DVD.** Til Schweiger, Chazz Palminteri, Lluis Homar, Gustavo Salmeron, Cristina Brondo; ***D:*** Gerry Lively; ***W:*** Ken Lamplugh, John Weidner; ***C:*** Christof Wahl; ***M:*** Jose Mora. **VIDEO**

Body Bags 🦴🦴 ½ *John Carpenter Presents Body Bags* **1993 (R)** Three gory, though humorous, stories hosted by horrormeister Carpenter as your friendly local coroner. "The Gas Station" finds the young female overnight attendent menaced by a psycho. "Hair" is about a balding yuppie who'll do anything for a full head of hair. Then he meets the sinister Dr. Lock and his magical new-hair growth treatment. The grisly "Eye" concerns a ballplayer who loses the aforementioned appendage and finds that his transplanted eyeball, taken from an executed serial killer, is subject to ghastly visions. Several fellow horror directors have cameos. **95m/C VHS, DVD.** Alex Datcher, Robert Carradine, Stacy Keach, David Warner, Mark Hamill, Twiggy, John Agar, Deborah Harry, Sheena Easton, David Naughton, John Carpenter; ***Cameos:*** Wes Craven, Sam Raimi, Roger Corman, Tobe Hooper; ***D:*** Tobe Hooper, John Carpenter; ***W:*** Billy Brown, Dan Angel; ***M:*** John Carpenter, Jim Lang. **CABLE**

Body Beat 🦴🦴 *Dance Academy* **1988 (PG)** Wild jazz and rock dancers are integrated into a previously classical ballet academy. While the students become fast friends, the teachers break off into two rival factions. **90m/C VHS.** Tony Fields, Galyn Gorg, Scott Grossman, Eliska Krupka, Virgil Frye, Steve La Chance, Leonora Leal, Julie Newmar, Paula Nichols, Serge Rodnunsky; ***D:*** Ted Mather; ***W:*** Ted Mather; ***C:*** Dennis Peters; ***M:*** Guido de Angelis, Maurizio de Angelis.

The Body Beneath **WOOF!** *Vampire's Thirst* **1970** A living-dead ghoul survives on the blood of innocents and is still preying on victims today. **85m/C VHS, DVD.** Gavin Reed, Jackie Skarvellis, Susan Heard, Colin Gordon; ***D:*** Andy Milligan.

Body Chemistry 🦴 **1990 (R)** A married sexual-behavior researcher starts up a passionate affair with his lab partner. When he tries to end the relationship, his female associate becomes psychotic. You've seen it all before in "Fatal Attraction." And you'll see it again in "Body Chemistry 2." **84m/C VHS, DVD.** Marc Singer, Mary Crosby, Lisa Pescia, Joseph Campanella, David Kagen; ***D:*** Kristine Peterson; ***W:*** Jackson Barr, Thom Babbes; ***C:*** Phedon Papamichael; ***M:*** Terry Plumeri.

Body Chemistry 2: Voice of a Stranger 🦴 ½ **1991 (R)** An ex-cop (Harrison) obsessed with violent sex gets involved with a talk-radio psychologist (Pescia) whose advice could prove deadly in this erotic sequel. **84m/C VHS, DVD.** Gregory Harrison, Lisa Pescia, Morton Downey Jr., Robin Riker, Jeremy Piven, John Landis; ***D:*** Adam Simon; ***W:*** Jackson Barr, Christopher Wooden; ***C:*** Richard Michalak; ***M:*** Nigel Holton.

Body Chemistry 3: Point of Seduction 🦴🦴 **1993 (R)** TV producer Alan Clay (Stevens) finds himself caught in a business and sexual triangle when he okays the making of a movie about the life of a TV sex therapist (Shattuck). Seems the lady's lovers have a nasty habit of getting murdered which doesn't prevent Clay from getting personally involved. His actress wife (Fairchild), who wants to star in the movie, is not pleased. Lives up to its title. **90m/C VHS, DVD.** Andrew Stevens, Morgan Fairchild, Shari Shattuck; ***D:*** Jim Wynorski; ***W:*** Jackson Barr; ***C:*** Don E. Fauntleroy; ***M:*** Chuck Cirino.

Body Chemistry 4: Full Exposure 🦴 ½ **1995 (R)** When sex psychologist Claire Archer (Tweed) is accused of murder she hires Simon Mitchell (Poindexter), the best criminal defense attorney around. But Simon becomes just a little too closely involved with his possibly psycho client and it could cost him not only his career and marriage but his life. Also available unrated. **89m/C VHS, DVD.** Shannon Tweed, Larry Poindexter, Andrew Stevens, Chick Vennera, Larry Manetti, Stella Stevens; ***D:*** Jim Wynorski; ***W:*** Karen Kelly; ***C:*** Zoran Hochstatter; ***M:*** Paul Di Franco.

Body Count 🦴 ½ *The 11th Commandment* **1987** A weird and wealthy family will stop at nothing, including murder and cannibalism, to enhance their fortune. Rather than bodies, count the minutes 'til the movie's over. **90m/C VHS.** Marilyn Hassett, Dick Sargent, Steven Ford, Greg Mullavey, Thomas Ryan, Bernie (Bernard) White; ***D:*** Paul Leder.

Body Count 🦴 ½ **1995 (R)** Professional killer Makoto (Chiba) and his partner Sybil (Nielsen) seek revenge on the New Orleans cops who set them up. Opposing them are special crime unit partners, Eddie Cook (Davi) and Vinnie Rizzo (Bauer). Lots of shootouts and macho bravado. **93m/C VHS, DVD.** Sonny Chiba, Brigitte Nielsen, Robert Davi, Steven Bauer, Jan-Michael Vincent, Talun Hsu; ***D:*** Talun Hsu; ***W:*** Henry Madden; ***C:*** Blake T. Evans; ***M:*** Don Peake.

Body Count 🦴🦴 **1997 (R)** Fiorentino and Caruso are reteamed (after "Jade") in a crime saga about a heist gone bad. There is no honor among thieves as driver Hobbs (Caruso) learns when he plans a job with some unreliable associates at the Boston Museum of Fine Arts and things go very wrong. The gang decide to drive to Miami in order to sell their ill-gotten gains, squabbling all the way. Then mystery woman Natalie (Fiorentino) comes aboard, to cause more friction between the gun-happy boys. **84m/C VHS, DVD.** David Caruso, Linda Fiorentino, John Leguizamo, Ving Rhames, Donnie Wahlberg, Forest Whitaker; ***D:*** Robert Patton-Spruill; ***W:*** Theodore Witcher; ***C:*** Charles Mills; ***M:*** Curt Sobel. **VIDEO**

Body Count 🦴🦴 *Below Utopia* **1997 (R)** Daniel (Theroux) takes fiancee Suzanne (Milano) home to meet his wealthy family and they just happen to be out of the line of immediate mayhem when a gang of thieves (led by Ice-T) break in to steal the family art collection. Now, they're playing a very serious game of hide-and-seek in order to stay alive—only the situations isn't as clear as it seems. **88m/C VHS, DVD.** Ice-T, Alyssa Milano, Justin Theroux, Tommy (Tiny) Lister, Jeannette O'Connor, Nicholas Walker, Eric Saiet, Marta Kristen, Ron Harper, Robert Pine, Richard Danielson; ***D:*** Kurt Voss; ***W:*** David Diamond; ***C:*** Denis Maloney; ***M:*** Joseph Williams. **VIDEO**

Body Double 🦴🦴🦴 **1984 (R)** A voyeuristic unemployed actor peeps on a neighbor's nightly disrobing and sees more than he wants to. A grisly murder leads him into an obsessive quest through the world of pornographic films. **114m/C VHS, DVD.** Craig Wasson, Melanie Griffith, Gregg Henry, Deborah Shelton, Guy Boyd, Dennis Franz, David Haskell, Rebecca Stanley, Barbara Crampton, Mindi Miller; ***D:*** Brian De Palma; ***W:*** Brian De Palma, Robert J. Avrech; ***C:*** Stephen Burum; ***M:*** Pino Donaggio. Natl. Soc. Film Critics '84: Support. Actress (Griffith).

Body Heat 🦴🦴🦴 ½ **1981 (R)** During a Florida heat wave, a none-too-bright lawyer becomes involved in a steamy love affair with a mysterious woman and then in a plot to kill her husband. Hurt and Turner (in her film debut) became stars under Kasdan's direction (the three would reunite for "The Accidental Tourist"). Hot love scenes supplement a twisting mystery with a suprise ending. Rourke's arsonist and Danson's soft shoe shouldn't be missed. **113m/C VHS, DVD.** William Hurt, Kathleen Turner, Richard Crenna, Ted Danson, Mickey Rourke, J.A. Preston, Kim Zimmer, Jane Hallaren; ***D:*** Lawrence Kasdan; ***W:*** Lawrence Kasdan; ***C:*** Richard H. Kline; ***M:*** John Barry.

The Body in the Library 🦴 ½ *Agatha Christie's Miss Marple: The Body In the Library* **1984** A Miss Marple mystery, based on Agatha Christie's 1942 novel, involving the septuagenarian detective investigating the murder of a young woman in a wealthy British mansion. **155m/C VHS, DVD.** *GB* Gwen Watford, Valentine Dyall, Moray Watson, Frederick Jaeger, Raymond Francis, Joan Hickson; ***D:*** Silvio Narizzano; ***W:*** T.R. Bowen; ***C:*** John Walker; ***M:*** Alan Blaikley. **TV**

Body Language 🦴🦴 **1992 (R)** A successful businesswoman, with a man problem, hires a super secretary with answers to all life's questions—and a deadly agenda all her own. **93m/C VHS.** Heather Locklear, Linda Purl, Edward Albert, James Acheson; ***D:*** Arthur Allan Seidelman; ***W:*** Dan Gurskis, Brian Ross; ***C:*** Hanania Baer.

Body Language 🦴🦴 ½ **1995 (R)** Criminal defense attorney Gavin St. Claire (Berenger) falls for a topless dancer (Schanz), which leads him into all sorts of trouble, including murder. **95m/C VHS, DVD.** Tom Berenger, Heidi Schanz, Nancy Travis; ***D:*** George Case.

Body Melt 🦴🦴 ½ **1993** When a crazed doctor unleashes an experimental drug on an unsuspecting town, the residents begin to literally melt away. **82m/C VHS, DVD.** *AU* Gerard Kennedy, Andrew Daddo, Ian Smith, Vincent (Vince Gill) Gil, Regina Gaigalas; ***D:*** Philip Brophy; ***W:*** Philip Brophy, Rod Bishop; ***M:*** Philip Brophy.

Body Moves 🦴🦴 **1990 (PG-13)** Romantic entanglements heat up the competition when two couples enter a steamy dance contest. Not apt to move you. **98m/C VHS.** *IT* Kirk Rivera, Steve Messina, Dianne Granger, Linsley Allen, Philip Spruce, Nicole Kolman, Susan Gardner; ***D:*** Gerry Lively; ***W:*** Daniel Steel.

Body of Evidence **WOOF!** **1992 (R)** Bad movie with pretensions takes "Basic Instinct" a step further. Instead of an ice pick and sex, sex itself is used as the weapon in a murder trial featuring Madonna as the defendant, Dafoe as her lawyer, and Mantegna as the prosecutor. The plot is, of course, secondary to the S&M sex scenes with Dafoe which feature hot wax and broken glass. Madonna's lack of performance is the least of the film's problems since everyone seems to have forgotten any acting talent they possess. Director Edel fails to direct—the film even looks bad. "Body" was the subject of another NC-17 ratings flap but this film shouldn't be seen by anybody. An unrated version is also available. **99m/C VHS, DVD.** Madonna, Willem Dafoe, Joe Mantegna, Anne Archer, Michael Forest, Charles Hallahan, Mark Rolston, Richard Riehle, Julianne Moore, Frank Langella, Jurgen Prochnow, Stan Shaw; ***D:*** Uli Edel; ***W:*** Brad Mirman; ***C:*** Doug Milsome; ***M:*** Graeme Revell. Golden Raspberries '93: Worst Actress (Madonna).

Body of Influence 🦴🦴 **1993 (R)** A Beverly Hills psychiatrist gets overly involved with a beautiful female patient. But she not only wants his love—she wants his life. Also available in an unrated version. **96m/C VHS, DVD.** Nick Cassavetes, Shannon Whirry, Sandahl Bergman, Don Swayze, Anna Karin, Catherine Parks, Diana Barton, Richard Roundtree; ***D:*** Andrew Garroni; ***W:*** David Schreiber.

Body of Influence 2 🦴 **1996 (R)** Shrink Dr. Benson (Anderson) finds he's using his couch for more than professional purposes with his latest patient, Leza (Fisher), whose seductive charms prove more than the doc can handle. The unrated version is 94 minutes. **88m/C VHS, DVD.** Daniel Anderson, Jodie Fisher, Steve Poletti, Jonathan Goldstein, Pat Brennan; ***D:*** Brian J. Smith; ***W:*** Brian J. Smith; ***C:*** Azusa Ohno; ***M:*** Ron Sures.

Body of Lies 🦴🦴 ½ **2008 (R)** Crowe packed on the pounds and sports a southern-fried accent in another collaboration with director Scott, this time as veteran CIA operative Ed Hoffman, the stateside handler of field agent Roger Ferris (DiCaprio), who's hot on the trail of a terrorist leader in Jordan and plans to infiltrate his network. But Hoffman seems to have his own agenda, leaving Ferris to wonder whom he can trust. Fraught with formulaic post-9/11, Middle Eastern terrorist v. American spy genre cliches (satellite images, chases/explosions in the local bazaar, frantic yelling into cell phones), and elements of suspense feel manufactured by heavy doses of convoluted double-crosses. Crowe's convincing portrayal of amorality, however, props up what is an otherwise pointless rehash of the evening news. Based on the 2007 novel by David Ignatius. **129m/C DVD.** *US* Leonardo DiCaprio, Russell Crowe, Mark Strong, Carice van Houten, Golshifteh Farahani, Vince Colosimo, Michael Gaston, Oscar Isaac, Simon McBurney, Alon Aboutboul; ***D:*** Ridley Scott; ***W:*** William Monahan; ***C:*** Alexander Witt; ***M:*** Marc Streitenfeld.

Body Parts 🦴🦴 **1991 (R)** A crime psychologist loses his arm in an auto accident and receives a transplant from an executed murderer. Does the limb have an evil will of its own? Poorly paced horror goes off the deep end in gore with its third act. Based on the novel "Choice Cuts" by French writers Pierre Boileau and Thomas Narcejac, whose work inspired some of the greatest suspense films. **88m/C VHS, DVD.** Jeff Fahey, Kim Delaney, Lindsay Duncan, Peter Murnik, Brad Dourif, Zakes Mokae, James Kidnie, Paul Ben-Victor; ***D:*** Eric Red; ***W:*** Eric Red, Norman Snider, Patricia Herskovic; ***C:*** Theo van de Sande; ***M:*** Loek Dikker.

Body Parts 🦴 **1994** For fans of the demented dismemberer niche. Body Parts, a sleazy skin club, loses some of its star talent when the strippers start turning up in cameo video appearances. Seems there's a psycho killer on the loose who videotapes the dismemberment of his stripper-victims. The police decide they've got to meet this guy when he sends them a sample of his work. **90m/C VHS, DVD.** Teri Marlow, Clement von Franckenstein, Dick Monda, Johnny Mandel; ***D:*** Michael Paul Girard; ***W:*** Michael Paul Girard; ***M:*** Miriam Cutler.

Body Rock WOOF! 1984 (PG-13) Brooklyn breakdancer Lamas deserts his buddies to work at a chic Manhattan nightclub. Watching Lamas as the emcee/breakdancing fool is a hoot. ♫ Body Rock; Team Work; Why Do You Want to Break My Heart?; One Thing Leads to Another; Let Your Body Rock; Vanishing Point; Sharpshooter; The Jungle; Deliver. **93m/C VHS, DVD.** Lorenzo Lamas, Vicki Frederick, Cameron Dye, Michelle Nicastro, Ray Sharkey, Grace Zabriskie, Carole Ita White; ***D:*** Marcelo Epstein.

The Body Shop WOOF! *Doctor Gore* **1972** Unorthodox love story in which a man decides to patch up his relationship with his dead wife by piecing together her dismembered body. For lovers only. Under "Doctor Gore" title the film includes an intro by horror director Herschell Gordon Lewis. **91m/C VHS, DVD.** Pat Patterson, Jenny Driggers, Roy Mehaffey, Linda Faile, Candy Furr; ***D:*** Pat Patterson.

Body Shot 🦴🦴 **1/2 1993 (R)** Celebrity shutterbug Mickey Dane (Patrick) is fingered in the murder of a rock star after it turns out he did a kinky layout for a look-alike. When police find out he had an obsession for the dead woman, he employs his photographic expertise in the search for the real killer. Effective tension-builder with fast-paced chases through the seamy side of Los Angeles. **98m/C VHS, DVD.** Robert Patrick, Michelle Johnson, Ray Wise, Jonathan Banks, Kim Miyori, Kenneth Tobey, Charles Napier; ***D:*** Dimitri Logothetis; ***W:*** Robert Strauss; ***C:*** Nicholas Josef von Sternberg; ***M:*** Cliff Magness.

Body Shots 🦴 **1/2 1999 (R)** An ensemble cast of twentysomethings explores sex and dating while traversing L.A.'s nightlife. Eight friends come to reflect on their hedonistic lifestyles when Sara (Reid) accuses macho football player Michael (O'Connell) of date rape. During the ultimate "he said/she said" battle, wafer-thin declarations on love in the '90s are made by characters who are as appealing as root canal surgery. **102m/C VHS, DVD.** Sean Patrick Flanery, Jerry O'Connell, Amanda Peet, Tara Reid, Ron Livingston, Emily Procter, Brad Rowe, Sybil Temchen; ***D:*** Michael Cristofer; ***W:*** David McKenna; ***C:*** Rodrigo Garcia; ***M:*** Mark Isham.

Body Slam 🦴 **1/2 1987 (PG)** A small-time talent monger hits it big with a rock and roll/professional wrestling tour. Piper's debut; contains some violence and strong language. **100m/C VHS.** Roddy Piper, Captain Lou Albano, Dirk Benedict, Tanya Roberts, Billy Barty, Charles Nelson Reilly, John Astin, Wild Samoan, Tonga Kid, Barry J. Gordon; ***D:*** Hal Needham; ***W:*** Steven H. Burkow; ***M:*** John D'Andrea.

The Body Snatcher 🦴🦴🦴 **1/2 1945** Based on Robert Louis Stevenson's story about a grave robber who supplies corpses to research scientists. Set in Edinburgh in the 19th century, this Lewton production is superior. One of Karloff's best vehicles. **77m/B VHS, DVD.** Edith Atwater, Russell Wade, Rita (Paula) Corday, Boris Karloff, Bela Lugosi, Henry Daniell, Sharyn Moffett, Donna Lee; ***D:*** Robert Wise; ***W:*** Philip MacDonald, Val Lewton; ***C:*** Robert De Grasse.

Body Snatcher from Hell 🦴 **1/2** *Goke, Body Snatcher from Hell; Goke the Vampire; Kyuketsuki Gokemidoro* **1969** An airliner passes through a mysterious cloud and crashes in a desert. One by one, the passengers are turned into vampires. Some interesting special effects. **84m/C VHS.** *JP* Hideo Ko, Teruo Yoshida, Tomomi Sato, Eizo Kitamura, Masay Takahashi, Cathy Horlan, Kazuo Kato, Yuko Kusunoki; ***D:*** Hajime Sato.

Body Snatchers 🦴🦴 **1993 (R)** Yet another version of "Invasion of the Body Snatchers." An innocent family arrive at an Army base which turns out to be infested with pod people. This time around the heroine is angst-ridden teenager Marti (Anwar) and the pods have something to do with a mysterious toxic spill. The 1978 remake was well done; this so-so version takes advantage of the advances in special effects (particularly in Anwar's bathtub scene) and sound technology but is slow-paced with few jolts of terror. **87m/C VHS, DVD.** Gabrielle Anwar, Meg Tilly, Terry Kinney, Forest Whitaker, Billy Wirth, R. Lee Ermey, Reilly Murphy; ***D:*** Abel Ferrara; ***W:*** Stuart Gordon, Dennis Paoli, Nicholas St. John; ***C:*** Bojan Bazelli; ***M:*** Joe Delia.

Body Strokes 🦴 *Siren's Kiss* **1995** Blocked artist Leo Kessler (Johnston) is aroused by the wild fantasies of his beautiful models Beth (Knittle) and Claire (Weber). But it's just fantasy and it also helps get Leo's marriage back on track when manager/wife Karen (Beck) gets jealous. Also available unrated. **99m/C VHS, DVD.** Bobby Johnston, Dixie Beck, Kristen Knittle, Catherine Weber; ***D:*** Edward Holzman; ***W:*** April Moskowitz; ***C:*** Kim Haun; ***M:*** Richard Bronskill.

Body Trouble 🦴 **1/2** *Joker's Wild* **1992 (R)** After being attacked by sharks while vacationing in the Caribbean, a man washes ashore in Miami and then somehow makes his way to New York City. There he meets Vera Vin Rouge and her friends Cinnamon, Spice, Paprika, and Johnny Zero, a gangster. Zero decides he doesn't like the man, so he chases him back to the Caribbean. Supposedly this all happens in only one day. Hmmm... **98m/C VHS, DVD.** Dick Van Patten, Priscilla Barnes, Frank Gorshin, James Hong, Marty Rackham, Michael Unger, Jonathan Soloman, Brit Helfer, Leigh Clark, Patricia Cardell, Richie Barathy; ***D:*** Bill Milling; ***W:*** Bill Milling.

The Body Vanished 🦴🦴 **1939** Murder mystery featuring a corpse that disappears from the scene of the crime. **46m/B VHS, DVD.** *GB* Anthony Hulme, Ernest Sefton, C. Denier Warren; ***D:*** Walter Tennyson.

Body Waves 🦴 **1/2 1992 (R)** Beach comedy starring Calvert as a teenager who bets his father that he can raise money on his own. In typical teen movie fashion, he invents a sex cream that drives boys and girls wild. Brain candy featuring lots of skimpy bikinis. **80m/C VHS.** Bill Calvert, Leah Lail, Larry Linville, Dick Miller, Jim Wise; ***D:*** P.J. Pesce.

The Bodyguard 🦴 **1/2 1976 (R)** The Yakuza, Japan's mafia, and New York's big crime families face off in this martial arts extravaganza. **89m/C VHS, DVD.** *JP* Etsuko (Sue) Shihomi, Sonny Chiba, Aaron Banks, Bill Louie, Judy Lee; ***D:*** Maurice Sarli.

The Bodyguard 🦴🦴 **1992 (R)** Buttoned-down, ex-Secret Service agent turned private bodyguard reluctantly takes on a wildly successful singer/actress as a client. Houston, in her acting debut as the over-indulged diva, doesn't have to stretch too far but acquits herself well. Costner has really bad hair day but easily portrays the tightly wound Frank. Critically trashed, a boxoffice smash, and too long. Originally scripted by producer Kasdan over a decade ago, with Steve McQueen in mind. Predictable romantic melodrama is kept moving by the occasional sharp dialog and a few action pieces. Songs include the smash hit "I Will Always Love You," written and originally performed by Dolly Parton. **130m/C VHS, DVD.** Kevin Costner, Whitney Houston, Gary Kemp, Bill Cobbs, Ralph Waite, Tomas Arana, Michele Lamar Richards, Mike Starr, Christopher Birt, DeVaughn Nixon, Charles Keating, Robert Wuhl; ***Cameos:*** Debbie Reynolds; ***D:*** Mick Jackson; ***W:*** Lawrence Kasdan; ***C:*** Andrew Dunn; ***M:*** Alan Silvestri. MTV Movie Awards '93: Song ("I Will Always Love You").

The Bodyguard from Beijing 🦴🦴 **1/2** *The Defender; Zhong Nan Hai Bao Biao* **1994** Beijing bodyguard John Chang (Li) is hired to protect pampered rich girl Michelle (Chung), who's the witness to a murder. And John also has to deal with the revenge plans of an ex-soldier whose brother John has killed. Cantonese with subtitles. **90m/C VHS, DVD.** *HK* Jet Li, Christy Chung, Kent Cheng, Collin Chou; ***D:*** Corey Yuen; ***W:*** Gordon Chan, Kin-Chung Chan; ***C:*** Tom Lau.

Bodywork 🦴🦴 **1999 (R)** Virgil Guppy (Matheson) buys a second-hand Jaguar that gives him nothing but trouble, especially when he finds a dead prostitute in the trunk of the car. Virgil goes on the run and hides out with a young woman (Coleman) who's a professional car thief. British crime caper finally has too many twists for its own good. The Winslet who plays Virgil's girlfriend is the sister of actress Kate. **93m/C VHS, DVD.** *GB* Hans Matheson, Charlotte Coleman, Clive Russell, Beth Winslet; ***D:*** Gareth Rhys Jones; ***W:*** Gareth Rhys Jones; ***C:*** Thomas Wuthvich; ***M:*** Dusan Kojic, Srdjan Kurpjel.

Boeing Boeing 🦴🦴 **1/2 1965** A dated but still amusing sex farce about a bachelor newspaperman (Curtis) in Paris, his three stewardess girlfriends, and the elaborate plots he resorts to in trying to keep them from finding out about each other. When the new Boeing jet makes air travel faster all Curtis' schemes may come crashing down. Ritter is fun as the exasperated housekeeper and Lewis amazingly subdued as Curtis' business rival. **102m/C VHS.** Tony Curtis, Jerry Lewis, Dany Saval, Christiane Schmidtmer, Suzanna Leigh, Thelma Ritter; ***D:*** John Rich; ***W:*** Edward Anhalt.

Boesman & Lena 🦴🦴 **1/2 2000** Adaptation of the apartheid-era play by Athol Fugard follows the travails of downtrodden couple, Boesman (Glover) and Lena (Bassett). Their shanty town home in Cape Town has been bulldozed by the government so they take to the dusty road with their meager belongings, constantly bickering about their plight. The couple construct a makeshift abode for the night, which attracts the attention of an old man (Jonah) even lower on the economic ladder, whom Lena allows to stay to Boesman's displeasure. Performances are outstanding. Last film for director Berry. **86m/C VHS, DVD.** *FR* Danny Glover, Angela Bassett, Willie Jonah; ***D:*** John Berry; ***W:*** John Berry; ***C:*** Alain Choquart; ***M:*** Wally Badarou.

Bog 🦴 **1984 (PG)** Boggy beast from the Arctic north awakens to eat people. Scientists mount an anti-monster offensive. **90m/C VHS, DVD.** Gloria De Haven, Marshall Thompson, Leo Gordon, Aldo Ray, Glen Voros, Ed Clark, Carol Terry; ***D:*** Don Keeslar; ***W:*** Carl Kitt; ***C:*** Jack Willoughby; ***M:*** Bill Walker.

Boggy Creek II 🦴 **1/2** *The Barbaric Beast of Boggy Creek, Part II* **1983 (PG)** The continuing saga of the eight-foot-tall, 300 pound monster from Texarkana. Third in a series of low-budget movies including "The Legend of Boggy Creek" and "Return to Boggy Creek." **93m/C VHS, DVD.** Charles B. Pierce, Cindy Butler, Serene Hedin; ***D:*** Charles B. Pierce; ***W:*** Charles B. Pierce.

Bogie: The Last Hero 🦴 **1/2 1980** Biography of Humphrey Bogart, populated by almost-lookalikes who can almost act. **100m/C VHS.** Kevin J. O'Connor, Kathryn Harrold, Ann Wedgeworth, Patricia Barry, Alfred Ryder, Donald May, Richard Dysart, Arthur Franz; ***D:*** Vincent Sherman; ***M:*** Charles Bernstein. **TV**

Bogus 🦴🦴 **1996 (PG)** Aptly named fantasy-comedy has orphan Albert (Osment) sent to foster aunt Harriet (Goldberg) after his magician's assistant mom (Travis) dies in a car accident. He brings along an imaginary friend, the eponymous Bogus (Depardieu) to ease the transition. Harriet is your typical workaholic easterner and isn't too thrilled with the arrangement. Goldberg and Depardieu are fine, but predictability drains most of the magic. **112m/C VHS, DVD.** Whoopi Goldberg, Gerard Depardieu, Haley Joel Osment, Nancy Travis, Andrea Martin, Denis Mercier, Ute Lemper, Sheryl Lee Ralph, Al Waxman, Fiona Reid, Don Francks; ***D:*** Norman Jewison; ***W:*** Alvin Sargent; ***C:*** David Watkin; ***M:*** Marc Shaiman.

The Bogus Witch Project 🦴 **2000 (R)** In the long and ignoble history of cheap parodies, this is surely one of the cheapest. It's a series of short films—sketches and blackouts, really—that use the premise of the original "Blair Witch" film to poke fun at the movie biz. Here's the preface to one: "In August 1999, three out-of-work actors disappeared in the woods near Sherman Oaks, California, while looking for Blair Underwood to give him a script. Twenty-four hours later, their footage was found and turned into a vehicle for shameless self-promotion." The episode starring Pauly Shore is the weakest of the weak. Funnier bits appear between spoofs. **85m/C DVD.** Pauly Shore, Michael Ian Black; ***D:*** Victor Kargan; ***M:*** Carvin Knowles.

Bohachi Bushido: Code of the Forgotten Eight 🦴 **1/2** *Porno jidaigeki: Bohachi bushido* **1973** Written by Kazuo Koike, this is one of the author's more over-the-top series. Shiro (Tetsuro Tamba) is an assassin tired of living. Prevented from committing suicide by the Bohashi clan, they nurse him back to health and ask only that he dispose of their enemies in return for protecting him from the authorities that have pursued him all of his life. But the Bohashi are a clan of soulless monsters charged with filling Edo's brothels, which they do through kidnapping, slavery, and torture. **81m/C DVD.** *JP* Tetsuro Tamba; ***D:*** Teru Ishii; ***W:*** Kazuo Koike, San Kaji, Goseki Kojima; ***C:*** Jubei Suzuki; ***M:*** Hajime Kaburagi.

Bohemian Girl 🦴🦴🦴 **1936** The last of Laurel and Hardy's comic operettas finds them as guardians of a young orphan (Hood, famous for her roles in the Our Gang comedies), whom no one realizes is actually a kidnapped princess. **74m/B VHS.** Stan Laurel, Oliver Hardy, Mae Busch, Darla Hood, Julie Bishop, Thelma Todd, James Finlayson; ***D:*** James W. Horne.

Boiler Room 🦴🦴🦴 **2000 (R)** Basic plot about a greedy naive young man caught up in a situation that's out of his control gets the high testosterone treament. Seth (Ribisi) jumps at the chance to become a trainee at an up-and-coming brokerage firm filled with macho twentysomethings greedy for success. But what Seth eventually discovers is that the firm he's allied himself with runs an illegal stock-trading operation that's under investigation. Well-cast and stylish, with Affleck effective in a small role as the firm's strutting recruiter. **120m/C VHS, DVD.** Jon Abrahams, Kirk Acevedo, Giovanni Ribisi, Vin Diesel, Nicky Katt, Nia Long, Scott Caan, Ron Rifkin, Jamie Kennedy, Taylor Nichols, Tom Everett Scott, Ben Affleck; ***D:*** Ben Younger; ***W:*** Ben Younger; ***C:*** Enrique Chediak.

Boiling Point 🦴 **1/2 1932** Lawman proves once again that justice always triumphs. **67m/B VHS.** Hoot Gibson, Helen Foster, Wheeler Oakman, Skeeter Bill Robbins, Billy Bletcher, Lafe (Lafayette) McKee, Charles Bailey, George "Gabby" Hayes; ***D:*** George Melford; ***W:*** Donald W. Lee; ***C:*** Tom Galligan, Harry Neumann.

Boiling Point 🦴🦴 *3x Jugatsu* **1990** Masaki (Ono) is a young, inarticulate, misfit, loser gas-station attendent who even lets down his local baseball team when he tries to play ball. Then he makes the mistake of slugging a yakuza member, so he heads to Okinawa to buy a gun to defend himself and meets up with the ultimate Mr. Cool—Uehara (Kitano). Uehara is such a bad ass even the yakuza don't want anything to do with him, so who better than the master to teach Masaki how to survive. The Japanese title refers to a baseball score, which somehow seems more apt. Japanese with subtitles. **98m/C VHS, DVD.** *JP* Takeshi "Beat" Kitano, Masahiko Ono, Hisashi Igawa; ***D:*** Takeshi "Beat" Kitano; ***C:*** Katsumi Yanagishima.

Boiling Point 🦴🦴 **1/2 1993 (R)** Darkly flavored action drama delves into the personalities of its two main characters before setting up a final confrontation. Treasury agent Jimmy Mercer (Snipes) is trying to solve his partner's murder, relentlessly pursuing the murderers in cold and methodical fashion. Sleazy Red Diamond (Hopper), just out of prison, owes the mob and has one week to pay them back. Lawman and crook both come home to women, (Davidovich and Perrine) graduates of the Hollywood school of female martyrdom, selflessly supportive of their men. Grim but cliched. Adapted from the Gerald Petievich novel "Money Men." **93m/C VHS, DVD.** Wesley Snipes, Dennis Hopper,

Lolita (David) Davidovich, Viggo Mortensen, Dan Hedaya, Valerie Perrine, Seymour Cassel, Jonathan Banks, Tony LoBianco, Christine Elise, James Tolkan, Paul Gleason; *D:* James B. Harris; *W:* James B. Harris; *C:* King Baggot; *M:* Cory Lerios, John D'Andrea.

Bojangles 1/2 **2001** Made-for-cable biopic of Bill "Bojangles" Robinson is strictly a by-the-numbers affair from the beginning at the funeral to the various characters who turn and address the camera to explain what they thought of the contradictory man. Gregory Hines does his usual excellent job in the lead, and the film looks very good. **101m/C VHS, DVD.** Gregory Hines, Peter Riegert, Kimberly Elise, Savion Glover, Maria Ricossa; *D:* Joseph Sargent; *W:* Richard Wesley, Robert P. Johnson; *C:* Donald M. Morgan; *M:* Terence Blanchard. **CABLE**

The Bold Caballero 1/2 *The Bold Cavalier* **1936** Rebel chieftain Zorro overthrows oppressive Spanish rule in the days of early California. **69m/B VHS, DVD.** Robert "Bob" Livingston, Heather Angel, Sig Rumann, Robert Warwick; *D:* Wells Root.

The Boldest Job in the West *El Mas Fabulosi Golpe del Far West* **1971** Italian western about bankrobbers who meet to divide their spoils. Problem is, the guys with the loot don't show. Dubbed in English. **200m/C VHS.** *IT* Mark Edwards, Frank Sancho, Carmen Sevilla; *D:* Jose Antonio De La Loma.

Bolero 1/2 **1982** Beginning in 1936, this international epic traces the lives of four families across three continents and five decades, highlighting the music and dance that is central to their lives. **173m/C VHS, DVD.** James Caan, Geraldine Chaplin, Robert Hossein, Nicole Garcia, Jacques Villeret; *D:* Claude Lelouch; *W:* Claude Lelouch.

Bolero **WOOF!** *Bolero: An Adventure in Ecstasy* **1984 (R)** What sounds like a wet dream come true is really just a good snooze: Bo Derek plays a beautiful young woman who goes on a trip around the world in hopes of losing her virginity; in Spain, she meets a bullfighter who's willing to oblige. Too bad Bo cannot act as good as she looks. **106m/C VHS, DVD.** Bo Derek, George Kennedy, Andrea Occhipinti, Anna (Ana Garcia) Obregon, Olivia D'Abo; *D:* John Derek; *W:* John Derek; *M:* Peter Bernstein, Elmer Bernstein. Golden Raspberries '84: Worst Picture, Worst Actress (Derek), Worst Director (Derek), Worst Screenplay, Worst New Star (D'Abo).

Bollywood Hero 1/2 **2009** Kattan parodies himself and his acting career. Frustrated by his lack of leading roles, he impulsively agrees to travel to India to star in a Bollywood production for a brother-sister team who are trying to revive their father's film studio. The dance numbers are bright but Kattan's character is a whiner and the story lacks surprises. **168m/C DVD.** Chris Kattan, Pooja Kumar, Julian Sands, Ali Fazal, Rachna Shah, Neha Dhupia; *Cameos:* Maya Rudolph, Keanu Reeves; *D:* Bill Bennett, Ted Skillman; *W:* Laurie Parres, Benjamin Brand; *C:* Tobias Hochstein; *M:* David Bergeaud, Niels Bye Nielsen. **CABLE**

Bolt 1/2 **2008 (PG)** On his hit action TV series, German Shepherd Bolt (voiced by Travolta) has superpowers to crush his arch enemy, Dr. Calico, and save his owner, Penny (voiced by Cyrus). However, having spent his entire life on the studio lot, he doesn't realize that he's just another canine actor, and not a superhero. A series of accidents leaves Bolt homeless on the streets of New York, while Penny is back in Hollywood. Convinced that the evil Dr. Calico has kidnapped his owner, Bolt, along with his two new friends, the reluctant alley cat Mittens and overeager hamster Rhino, sets out for a journey across the country to save the day. The first Disney animated feature to come out since Pixar guru John Lasseter traded teams. He wisely blends smart jokes with Disney's classic animated storytelling traditions, rather than trying to one-up his former employer's spastic cool factor. **96m/C DVD.** *US* Malcolm McDowell, James Lipton, Greg Germann; *D:* Chris(topher) Williams, Byron Howard; *W:* Chris(topher) Williams, Dan Fogelman; *M:* John Powell; *V:* John Travolta, Susie Essman, Mark Walton, Miley Cyrus.

Boltneck 1/2 *Big Monster on Campus; Teen Monster* **1998** When school outcast Karl becomes the victim of a hazing by jocks, nerdy Frank Stein (get it?) decides to try an experiment in re-animating the dead. But unknown to Frank, the brain he's used (which he stole from his father's lab—how convenient) is that of a mass killer and the new Karl has developed quite an attitude. **92m/C VHS, DVD.** Justin Walker, Ryan Reynolds, Christine Lakin, Bianca Lawson, Kenny Blank, Judge Reinhold, Shelley Duvall, Charles Fleischer, Matthew Lawrence, Richard Moll; *D:* Mitch Marcus; *W:* Dave Payne; *M:* Roger Neill. **VIDEO**

Bomb at 10:10 **1967** An American pilot escapes from a German POW camp and plots to assassinate a camp commandant. **87m/C VHS.** George Montgomery, Rada Popovic, Peter Banicevic; *D:* Charles Damic.

Bomb Squad *Cold Night Into Dawn* **1997** Suicidal terrorist has a nuclear bomb small enough to fit into a suitcase and has decided to make Chicago his target. The Feds have 24-hours to find and defuse it. **91m/C VHS, DVD.** Anthony Michael Hall, Michael Ironside, Tony LoBianco; *D:* Serge Rodnunsky; *W:* Serge Rodnunsky. **VIDEO**

Bomb the System **WOOF!** **2005 (R)** A trio of young artists conduct nightly "bombings" in New York City, covering available spaces with their graffiti signatures. In sync with the subculture, their paint is always stolen, although they do pay for their drugs. One of the outlaws is continually nagged by his mother to take the art scholarship he was offered in San Francisco, but he's deaf to her pleadings. There are run-ins with the law, some girlfriend situations and self-righteous speeches thrown into the mix but one never feels much sympathy toward the rebel-with-a-cause premise because truly they're just low-life druggie vandals. **93m/C DVD.** *US* Mark Webber, Gano Grills, Jade Yorker, Jaclyn DeSantis, Joey Dedio, Stephan Buchanana, Bonz Malone, Donna Mitchell, Al Sapienza, Kumar Pallana; *D:* Adam Bhala Lough; *W:* Adam Bhala Lough; *C:* Ben Kutchins; *M:* El-P.

Bombardier 1/2 **1943** A group of cadet bombardiers discover the realities of war on raids over Japan during WWII. Also available colorized. **99m/B VHS.** Pat O'Brien, Randolph Scott, Robert Ryan, Eddie Albert, Anne Shirley, Barton MacLane; *D:* Richard Wallace.

Bombay Mail 1/2 **1934** A great example of a Universal Studio B movie, set on the train from Calcutta to Bombay and offering a multiple murder mystery with appearances of all the usual exotic suspects, from Indian mystics to eccentric scientists to larger than life opera singers, all with witty and adroit dialogue. **70m/B DVD.** Edmund Lowe, Shirley Grey, Onslow Stevens, Ralph Forbes, John Davidson; *D:* Edwin L. Marin; *W:* Tom Reed, Lawrence G. Blochman; *C:* Charles Stumar; *M:* Heinz Roemheld.

Bombay Talkie 1/2 **1970 (PG)** A bored British writer (Kendal) heads to India to gather "experiences" and becomes involved with an Indian movie actor (Kapoor). Early clash-of-cultures film from Merchant Ivory has it's dull spots; the behind-the-scenes look at the Indian film industry is more interesting than the romance. **110m/C VHS, DVD.** *IN* Jennifer Kendal, Shashi Kapoor, Zia Mohyeddin, Aparna Sen; *D:* James Ivory; *W:* Ruth Prawer Jhabvala.

Bombers B-52 **1957** Chuck Brennan (Malden) has worked 20 years as a ground-crew chief for the Air Force and his daughter Lois (Wood) is encouraging him to retire. While Chuck decides, he tries to discourage the budding romance between Lois and commanding officer Jim Herlihy (Zimbalist), whom he distrusts. Predictable plot is all a backdrop for the showcase of various planes, especially the B-52 Superfortress. **106m/C DVD.** Natalie Wood, Karl Malden, Efrem Zimbalist Jr., Marsha Hunt, Don Kelly, Nelson Leigh; *D:* Gordon Douglas; *W:* Irving Wallace; *C:* William Clothier; *M:* Leonard Rosenman.

Bombs Away! **1986** An atomic bomb is mistakenly shipped to a seedy war surplus store in Seattle, and causes much chicanery. **90m/C VHS.** Michael Huddleston, Pat McCormick; *D:* Bruce Wilson.

Bombshell *Blonde Bombshell* **1933** Wry insightful comedy into the Hollywood of the 1930s. Harlow plays a naive young actress manipulated by her adoring press agent. He thwarts her plans until she finally notices and begins to fall in love with him. Brilliant satire with Harlow turning in perhaps the best performance of her short career. **96m/B VHS.** Jean Harlow, Lee Tracy, Pat O'Brien, Una Merkel, Sir C. Aubrey Smith, Franchot Tone; *D:* Victor Fleming.

Bombshell **1997 (R)** Scientist Buck Hogan (Thomas) discovers a deadly flaw in the world's first cancer-killing drug, which he publicly reveals, much to the dismay of the manufacturer's head honcho Donald (James). But then Hogan and his girlfriend Angeline (Amick) are abducted by a terrorist group, and Buck's implanted with a device that will kill him unless he does as they say. **95m/C VHS.** Michael Jace, Henry Thomas, Frank Whaley, Madchen Amick, Brion James, Pamela Gidley, Shawnee Smith, Martin Hewitt; *D:* Paul Wynne; *W:* Paul Wynne.

Bon Cop Bad Cop **2006** A Canadian bilingual buddy cop movie that plays on the cultural differences between English and French-speakers. Quebec maverick David Bouchard (Huard) is paired with by-the-book Ontario detective Martin Ward (Feore) when a body is deliberately left straddling the border of the two provinces. The investigation soon involves a serial killer targeting the hockey community, and the bickering duo learns to work together and realizes what they have in common (they're both divorced but devoted dads). It's contrived and unsubtle but director Canuel seems to be clear that's the way he wanted it. **116m/C DVD.** *CA* Patrick Huard, Colm Feore, Lucie Laurier, Sarain Boylan, Pierre Lebeau, Sarah-Jeanne Labrosse, Louis-Jose Houde, Sylvain Marcel, Rick Mercer, Patrice Belanger; *D:* Erik Canuel; *W:* Kevin Tierney; *C:* Bruce Chun; *M:* Michael Corriveau.

Bon Voyage! 1/2 **1962** A family's long-awaited European "dream" vacation turns into a series of comic misadventures in this very Disney, very family, very predictable comedy. **131m/C VHS, DVD.** Fred MacMurray, Jane Wyman, Deborah Walley, Michael Callan, Tommy Kirk, Jessie Royce Landis; *D:* James Neilson.

Bon Voyage **2003 (PG-13)** Successful comedy-adventure mixes romance, espionage, murder, and melodrama amid the chaos of the Nazi occupation of France. In the role of a lifetime, Adjani is Viviane, an amoral movie star who's seeing government minister Beaufort (Depardieu) but gets humble former flame Frederic (Derangere) to do her bidding, including disposing of the body of a blackmailer (Vaude). Fred gets busted with the body, takes the rap, and winds up in jail only to escape with the help of resourceful criminal Raoul (Attal). Coyote does a turn as a spy posing as a journalist who also has a thing for the tres popular Viviane. The lives of all the characters intersect with interesting results in this not completely original but engaging and well-made romp. **114m/C DVD.** *FR* Isabelle Adjani, Gerard Depardieu, Virginie Ledoyen, Yvan Attal, Peter Coyote, Aurore Clement, Xavier De Guillebon, Edith Scob, Michel Vuillermoz, Gregori Derangere, Jean-Marc Stehle, Nicolas Pignon; *D:* Jean-Paul Rappeneau; *W:* Jean-Paul Rappeneau, Gilles Marchand, Patrick Modiano; *C:* Thierry Arbogast; *M:* Gabriel Yared.

Bon Voyage, Charlie Brown 1/2 **1980 (G)** The "Peanuts" comic strip gang are exchange students in Europe, led by Charlie Brown, Linus, Peppermint Patty, Marcie, and the irrepressible beagle, Snoopy. How can you go wrong with the "little round-headed kid" and his pals? **76m/C VHS.** *D:* Bill Melendez, Lee Mendelson; *W:* Charles M. Schulz; *M:* Ed Bogas; *V:* Arrin Skelley, Laura Planting, Casey Carlson, David Anderson, Annalisa Bartolin, Scott Beads.

Bonanno: A Godfather's Story *Youngest Godfather* **1999** Old-fashioned storytelling seems to fit the story of an old-fashioned New York mobster—Joseph Bonanno (Landau)—thought to be the inspiration for Mario Puzo's Don Vito Corleone. The elderly Bonanno reflects on his life and how he got into criminal activity back in the Prohibition days, drawing the attention of boss Salvatore Maranzano (Olmos). From there it's just a matter of time as Joe works his way up through the ranks. Based on the autobiography of Joseph Bonanno and the book written by his son Bill. **139m/C VHS, DVD.** Martin Landau, Bruce Ramsay, Costas Mandylor, Edward James Olmos, Tony Nardi, Zachary Bennett, Philip Bosco, Claudia Ferri, Robert Loggia, Patti LuPone; *D:* Michel Poulette; *W:* Thomas Michael Donnelly; *C:* Serge Ladouceur; *M:* Richard Gregoire. **CABLE**

Bonanza: The Return 1/2 **1993 (PG)** In 1905, the children of various members of the Cartwright clan work to see the Ponderosa is safe from an unscrupulous businessman. Lame update of the classic family western series. **96m/C VHS.** Michael Landon Jr., Dirk Blocker, Emily Warfield, Alistair MacDougall, Brian Leckner, Dean Stockwell, Ben Johnson, Richard Roundtree, Linda Gray, Jack Elam; *D:* Jerry Jameson; *W:* Michael McGreevey; *C:* Haskell Boggs. **TV**

Bonanza Town 1/2 **1951** Steve Ramsey (Starrett), aka The Durango Kid, and sidekick Smiley (Burnette) are hired to locate the loot stolen in a Dodge City hold-up. Marked money leads our heroes to Bonanza Town, where the Kid tracks down outlaws and corrupt officials. **56m/B VHS, DVD.** Charles Starrett, Smiley Burnette, Myron Healey, Fred F. Sears; *D:* Fred F. Sears; *C:* Henry Freulich.

Bond of Fear 1/2 **1956** Routine British programmer. John Sewell (Walsh) is packing up the car, caravan, wife and kids for a trip across the Channel to the south of France. Too bad they have an unexpected guest hiding out: escaped killer Terence Dewar (Colicos) who insists the Sewells take him to the port of Dover despite road blocks, hikers needing assistance, and other complications. **66m/B DVD.** *GB* Anthony Pavey, Marily Baker, Dermot Walsh, John Colicos, Jane Barrett, Alan MacNaughton, Jameson Clark; *D:* Henry Cass, John Gilling; *W:* John Gilling, Norman Hudis; *C:* Monty Berman; *M:* Stanley Black.

The Bone Collector 1/2 **1999 (R)** Lincoln Rhyme (Washington) is a brilliant NYPD detective and forensics expert who was left a quadriplegic after an on-the-job accident. His suicidal thoughts are distracted by the work of a serial killer with a gruesome MO and the admirable work of hotshot young policewoman, Amelia Donoghy (Jolie). Amelia soon becomes Rhyme's surrogate investigator. The situation comes to a climax in Rhyme's apartment as he lies helpless. Thriller turns out to be predictable but Washington, as usual, turns in a fine performance. Based on the 1997 novel by Jeffrey Deaver. **118m/C VHS, DVD, HD DVD.** Denzel Washington, Angelina Jolie, Queen Latifah, Ed O'Neill, Michael Rooker, Mike McGlone, Leland Orser, Luis Guzman, John Benjamin Hickey, Bobby Cannavale; *D:* Phillip Noyce; *W:* Jeremy Iacone; *C:* Dean Semler; *M:* Craig Armstrong.

Bone Daddy **1997 (R)** Former chief medical examiner William Palmer (Hauer) turns his experiences into a best-selling novel and excites the rage of a psychopathic killer. The surgical killer, who's nicknamed "Bone Daddy" because he likes to extract the bones of his victims, is busy at work and Palmer teams up with a reluctant detective (Williams) to track the looney down. **90m/C VHS.** Rutger Hauer, Barbara Williams, R.H. Thomson, Joseph Kell, Robin Gammell, Daniel Kash, Christopher Kelk; *D:* Mario Azzopardi; *W:* Thomas Szollosi; *C:* Danny Nowak; *M:* Christophe Beck.

Bone Dry **2007 (R)** Eddie (Goss) finds himself knocked out and left in the middle of the desert by a man named Jimmy (Hendriksen). Jimmy informs Eddie via walkie-talkie that he needs to head north, and should he go in any other direction a sniper rifle will put an end to him, and his wife and children will follow him into the ground quickly after. What follows is not pretty to watch. **100m/C DVD.** Lance Henriksen, Tommy (Tiny) Lister, Dee Wallace, Luke Goss; *D:* Brett Hart; *W:* Brett Hart; *C:* John Darbonne, Kevin G. Ellis; *M:* Scott Glasgow.

Bone Eater **2007** Native Americans are protesting at a construction site that's disturbing an ancient burial ground. The workers hit a pile of bones that assembles itself into the legendary Bone Eater, which promptly destroys the crew. Sheriff Evans (Boxleitner) shows up to investigate—more people disappear—corporate greed—blah,

blah, blah. It's good for a chuckle (the Bone Eater figure certainly isn't scary) but that's probably not what director Wynorski intended. **90m/C DVD.** Bruce Boxleitner, Clara Bryant, James Storm, Gil Gerard, Veronica Hamel, Adoni Maropis, Michael Horse, Roark Critchlow, Walter Koenig, William Katt, Tom Schmid; *D:* Jim Wynorski; *W:* Jim Wynorski; *M:* Chuck Cirino. **CABLE**

The Bone Yard ♂ **1990 (R)** A weird mortuary is the setting for strange goings on when a murder is investigated. **98m/C VHS, DVD.** Ed Nelson, Deborah Rose, Norman Fell, Jim Eustermann, Denise Young, Willie Stratford Jr., Phyllis Diller; *D:* James Cummins; *W:* James Cummins; *C:* Irl Dixon; *M:* Kathleen Ann Porter, John Lee Whitener.

Bones ♂♂ ½ **2001 (R)** Combining the best of blaxploitation and horror elements, Dickerson smartly reveals the story of benevolent pimp Jimmy Bones'(Snoop Dogg) disappearance and subsequent resurrection 22 years later as a vengeful spirit. When an entrepreneurial buppie (Kain) decides to open a dance hall in Jimmy's former digs, walls begin oozing, animals become abundant and mean, and old secrets are revealed, much to the chagrin of the kid's rich father (Davis), and a cop (Weiss). Grier shines as a neighborhood psychic, and Snoop adds miles of style and presence, keeping this one a notch above the standard-issue haunted house fare. **94m/C VHS, DVD.** Snoop Dogg, Pam Grier, Michael T. Weiss, Clifton Powell, Ricky Harris, Bianca Lawson, Khalil Kain, Katharine Isabelle, Merwin Mondesir, Sean Amsing; *D:* Ernest R. Dickerson; *W:* Adam Simon; *C:* Flavio Martinez Labiano; *M:* Elia Cmiral.

The Bonfire of the Vanities ♂ ½ **1990 (R)** If you liked Tom Wolfe's viciously satirical novel, chances are you won't like this version. If you didn't read the book, you probably still won't like it. Miscast and stripped of the book's gutsy look inside its characters, the film's sole attribute is Vilmos Zsigmond's photography. Hanks is all wrong as wealthy Wall Street trader Sherman McCoy who, lost in the back streets of the Bronx, panics and accidentally kills a young black kid. Willis' drunken journalist/narrator, Griffith's mistress, and Freeman's righteous judge are all awkward and thinly written. If you're still awake, look for F. Murray Abraham's cameo as the Bronx D.A. **126m/C VHS, DVD.** Tom Hanks, Melanie Griffith, Bruce Willis, Morgan Freeman, Alan King, Kim Cattrall, Saul Rubinek, Clifton James, Donald Moffat, Richard Libertini, Andre Gregory, Robert Stephens; *Cameos:* F. Murray Abraham; *D:* Brian De Palma; *W:* Michael Cristofer; *C:* Vilmos Zsigmond; *M:* Dave Grusin.

Bongwater ♂♂ **1998 (R)** David (Wilson) is a Portland pot dealer and aspiring artist who becomes roommates with Serena (Witt), although mixed signals prevents anything closer even if David is definitely lovesick. Thanks to a misunderstanding, Serena heads to New York, a bong ignites the house where David was living—burning it to the ground—and he is forced to rely on the kindness of his fellow pot buddies while Serena has her own problems in the Big Apple. However, you won't really care except Wilson is appealing in a goofy doper sort of way. **98m/C VHS, DVD.** Luke Wilson, Alicia Witt, Amy Locane, Brittany Murphy, Jack Black, Andy Dick, Jeremy Sisto, Jamie Kennedy, Scott Caan, Patricia Wettig; *D:* Richard Sears; *W:* Nora MacCoby, Eric Weiss; *C:* Richard Crudo; *M:* Mark Mothersbaugh, Josh Mancell.

Bonjour Monsieur Shlomi ♂♂♂ *Ha'Kohavim Shel Shlomi* **2003** Light-hearted human comedy about sixteen-year-old, Shlomi, a mildly slow-witted Jewish boy juggling school, love, and the family circus at home. Willing to put his own interests aside, Shlomi dedicates most of his life to caring for his senile grandfather, cooking elaborate meals for the family, and falling behind in school. His secret joys come from poetry, snooping through his older brother's explicit diary, and daydreaming about the girl next door. A surprisingly warm Israeli film that manages to avoid the usual melodramatic pitfalls of most American coming-of-age flicks. **94m/C DVD.** Esti Zakheim, Aya Koren, Assi Cohen, Oshri Cohen, Arie Elias, Yigal Naor, Albert Illouz, Jonathan Rozen, Rotem Abuhav, Rotem Zisman, Nisso Khavia, Aya Steinovitz; *D:* Shemi Zarhin; *W:* Shemi Zarhin; *C:* Itzik Portal; *M:* Jonathan Bar-Girora.

Bonjour Tristesse ♂♂♂ **1957** An amoral French girl (Seberg) conspires to break up her playboy father's (Niven) upcoming marriage to her stuffy godmother (Kerr) in order to maintain her decadent freedom. Preminger attempted, unsuccessfully, to use this soaper to catapult Seberg to stardom. Based on the novel by Francoise Sagan. **94m/B VHS, DVD.** *FR* Deborah Kerr, David Niven, Jean Seberg, Mylene Demongeot, Geoffrey Horne, Walter Chiari, Jean Kent; *D:* Otto Preminger; *W:* Arthur Laurents; *C:* Georges Perinal.

Bonneville ♂♂ **2006 (PG)** On a mission to spread the ashes of a dead husband, three middle-aged women hit the open road in a 1966 Bonneville, driving from Idaho to California. Along the way they laugh about the good old days, cry about car trouble, and connect all the dots required of a formulaic road trip flick. Bates, Lange, and Allen are excellent, but ultimately wasted on a script that's lacking surprise and running on fumes from the start. **93m/C DVD.** *US* Jessica Lange, Kathy Bates, Joan Allen, Christine Baranski, Victor Rasuk, Tom Amandes, Tom Wopat, Tom Skerritt; *D:* Christopher Rowley; *W:* Daniel Davis; *C:* Jeffrey L. Kimball; *M:* Jeff Cardoni.

Bonnie & Clyde ♂♂♂ ½ **1967** Based on the biographies of the violent careers of Bonnie Parker (Dunaway) and Clyde Barrow (Beatty), who roamed the Southwest robbing banks. In the Depression era, when any job, even an illegal one, was cherished, money, greed, and power created an unending cycle of violence and fury. Highly controversial and influential, with pronounced bloodshed (particularly the pairs balletic and bullet-ridden end) that spurred mainstream cinematic proliferation. Established Dunaway as a star; produced by Beatty in one of his best performances. **111m/C VHS, DVD, Blu-ray Disc.** Warren Beatty, Faye Dunaway, Michael J. Pollard, Gene Hackman, Estelle Parsons, Denver Pyle, Gene Wilder, Dub Taylor, Evans Evans; *D:* Arthur Penn; *W:* David Newman, Robert Benton; *C:* Burnett Guffey; *M:* Charles Strouse. Oscars '67: Cinematog., Support. Actress (Parsons); AFI '98: Top 100, Natl. Film Reg. '92;; N.Y. Film Critics '67: Screenplay; Natl. Soc. Film Critics '67: Screenplay, Support. Actor (Hackman); Writers Guild '67: Orig. Screenplay.

Bonnie Prince Charlie ♂♂ ½ **1948** Historical epic opening in 1745 and romanticizing the title pretender to the British throne, who united Scottish clans in a doomed campaign against King George. Talky and rather slow-moving except for stirring battle scenes. A notorious boxoffice flop in its native Britain, where the original running time was 140 minutes. **114m/C VHS.** *GB* David Niven, Margaret Leighton, Judy Campbell, Jack Hawkins, Morland Graham, Finlay Currie, Elwyn Brook-Jones, John Laurie; *D:* Anthony Kimmins.

Bonnie Scotland ♂♂ ½ **1935** Laurel & Hardy accidentally join an India-bound Scottish regiment. Laughs aplenty. **81m/B VHS, DVD.** Stan Laurel, Oliver Hardy, James Finlayson, Daphne Pollard, June Lang; *D:* James W. Horne.

Bonnie's Kids ♂ ½ **1973 (R)** Two sisters become involved in murder, sex, and stolen money. **107m/C VHS.** Tiffany Bolling, Robin Mattson, Scott Brady, Alex Rocco; *D:* Arthur Marks.

Boo! ♂♂ **2005** Five college students decide to check out the abandoned Santa Mira Hospital on Halloween to see if rumors about it being haunted are true. They discover a vengeful spirit that wants to make sure no one gets out alive. Low-budget but inventive and sufficiently creepy for a dark and stormy night. **100m/C DVD.** Dee Wallace, Trish Coren, M. Steven Felty, Josh Holt, Jilon Ghai, Nicole Rayburn, Michael Samluk, Dig Wayne; *D:* Anthony C. Ferrante; *W:* Anthony C. Ferrante; *C:* Carl F. Bartels. **VIDEO**

The Boob ♂♂ **1926** Farmhand Peter (Arthur) is in love with sweet Amy (Olmstead) who has fallen for the dubious charms of city slicker Harry (D'Algy). Peter is suspicious that Harry is a bootlegger so he becomes a revenue agent. He meets Jane (Crawford), a fellow agent, at Harry's club and she wonders if Peter is working the same undercover case she is—albeit for personal reasons. **64m/B DVD.** Gertrude (Olmstead) Olmsted, George K. Arthur, Joan Crawford, Charles Murray, Gertrude (Olmstead) Olmsted, George K. Arthur, Joan Crawford, Antonio 'Tony' D'Algy, Charles Murray, William A. Wellman; *D:* William A. Wellman, William A. Wellman; *W:* Katherine Hilliker, H. H. Caldwell, William A. Wellman, Katherine Hilliker, H. H. Caldwell; *C:* William H. Daniels, William H. Daniels.

The Boogey Man ♂♂ **1980 (R)** Through the reflection in a mirror, a girl witnesses her brother murder their mother's lover. Twenty years later this memory still haunts her; the mirror is now broken, revealing its special powers. Who will be next? Murder menagerie; see footage from this flick mirrored in "The Boogey Man 2." **93m/C VHS, DVD.** John Carradine, Suzanna Love, Ron James; *D:* Ulli Lommel; *W:* Ulli Lommel, Suzanna Love; *C:* Jochen Breitenstein, David Sperling; *M:* Tim Krog.

Boogey Man 2 **WOOF!** **1983** The story continues; same footage, new director but with Lommel, the director of the original "Boogey Man," co-writing the script and appearing in the film. **90m/C VHS, DVD.** John Carradine, Suzanna Love, Shannah Hall, Ulli Lommel, Sholto Von Douglas; *D:* Bruce Starr.

Boogeyman ♂ ½ **2005 (PG-13)** Weak horror flick about monsters in the closet. Tim (Watson) returns to his hometown for his mother's (Lawless) funeral and revisits the childhood home where his father was apparently sucked into young Tim's bedroom closet by the boogeyman and killed. Naturally, Tim has an aversion to closets. He wants to prove the boogeyman is all in his imagination like his shrink says; the boogeyman has other ideas. **86m/C DVD, UMD.** *US* Barry Watson, Emily Deschanel, Skye McCole Bartusiak, Lucy Lawless, Philip Gordon, Aaron Murphy, Robyn Malcolm, Victoria (Tory) Mussett, Andrew Glover, Charles Mesure, Jennifer Rucker; *D:* Stephen Kay; *C:* Bobby Bukowski; *M:* Joseph LoDuca.

Boogeyman 2 ♂ ½ **2007** When Laura (Savre) and her brother (Cohen) were children, they watched their father get slaughtered by the boogeyman. Naturally, this caused a lot of trauma, so Laura decides to check herself into a local mental hospital in hopes of getting past her continuing fear. But when patients start dying, it becomes clear the creature is trolling the hospital for his next victims. **93m/C DVD.** Tobin Bell, Renee O'Connor, Danielle Savre, Matt Cohen; *D:* Jeff Betancourt; *W:* Brian Sieve; *C:* Nelson Cragg. **VIDEO**

Boogeyman 3 ♂ ½ **2008** College sophomore Sarah Morris (Cahill) witnesses the alleged suicide of friend Audrey (Sanderson), who was terrified that the boogeyman was after her. Sarah tries to convince the other dorm inhabitants that evil does exist but they all think she's crazy until they become the next victims. A cut above most DTV horror sequels since the predictable plot does offer some scares. **92m/C DVD.** Mimi Michaels, Matt Rippy, Kate Maberly, Erin Cahill, Chuck Hittinger, Nikki Sanderson; *D:* Gary Jones; *W:* Brian Sieve; *C:* Lorenzo Senatore; *M:* Joseph LoDuca. **VIDEO**

Boogie Boy ♂ ½ **1998 (R)** Recently released from prison, Jesse (Dacascos) gets involved as muscle for a drug deal involving his ex-cellmate, the drug-addicted Larry (Woolvett), in order to get some quick cash. Naturally, the deal goes sour and they wind up on the lam. **110m/C VHS, DVD.** Mark Dacascos, Emily Lloyd, Jaimz Woolvett, Traci Lords, Frederic Forrest, Joan Jett, Ben Browder, James Lew, Linnea Quigley; *D:* Craig Hamann; *W:* Craig Hamann; *M:* Tim Truman.

The Boogie Man Will Get You ♂♂ ½ **1942** Crazy scientist Nathaniel Billings (Karloff) has been working on creating a race of supermen in his basement. He sells his home to Bill (Parks) and Winnie (Donnell), who are turning the place into a bed and breakfast, thinking that he can use their guests as fresh subjects. Lorre plays multiple roles, including a fellow nutcase. Karloff was unavailable to reprise his role in the film version of "Arsenic and Old Lace" so he did this similar comedy instead. **66m/B VHS.** Boris Karloff, Peter Lorre, Maxie "Slapsie" Rosenbloom, Larry Parks, Jeff Donnell, Maude Eburne; *D:* Lew Landers; *W:* Edwin Blum; *C:* Henry Freulich.

Boogie Nights ♂♂♂ ½ **1997 (R)** Epic tale covering the rise and fall of porn star Eddie Adams (Wahlberg). The protege of director Jack Horner (Reynolds), 17-year-old Eddie jumps in a hot tub at an industry bash, christens himself Dirk Diggler, and goes on to become the toast of the adult entertainment industry. Brilliantly spanning the decadent disco-era 70s and the excess of the 80s, 27-year-old writer/director Anderson boldly delves into fresh, albeit dangerous, territory most successfully in this lengthy sophomore outing. What Tarantino did for Travolta, Anderson does here for Reynolds, who plays the past-his-prime but touchingly ambitious auteur with a dream to make a legitimately legendary skin flick. Wahlberg proves himself a serious and seriously good actor in his turn, surrounded by equally fine performances of the ensemble cast. Details such as wardrobe, bits of dialogue, and music are deftly used, avoiding parody. Nonstop disco and early 80s music, often with a message, and energetic camera work make you shake your booty. **155m/C VHS, DVD.** Michael Penn, Mark Wahlberg, Burt Reynolds, Julianne Moore, Don Cheadle, William H. Macy, Heather Graham, John C. Reilly, Luis Guzman, Philip Seymour Hoffman, Alfred Molina, Philip Baker Hall, Robert Ridgely, Joanna Gleason, Thomas Jane, Ricky Jay, Nicole Ari Parker, Melora Walters, Michael Jace, Nina Hartley, John Doe, Laurel Holloman, Robert Downey; *D:* Paul Thomas Anderson; *W:* Paul Thomas Anderson; *C:* Robert Elswit; *M:* Michael Penn. Golden Globes '98: Support. Actor (Reynolds); L.A. Film Critics '97: Support. Actor (Reynolds), Support. Actress (Moore); MTV Movie Awards '98: Breakthrough Perf. (Graham); N.Y. Film Critics '97: Support. Actor (Reynolds); Natl. Soc. Film Critics '97: Support. Actor (Reynolds), Support. Actress (Moore).

Boogiepop and Others ♂ ½ *Boogiepop wa Wawaranai* **2000** Five young girls at the Shinyo academy try to piece together a mystery involving the appearance of a new street drug, the disappearance of some of their classmates, and an urban legend named Boogiepop who may be a personification of death itself. Originally a novel, then manga, with an anime series ("Boogiepop Phantom") as a sequel. Campy effects don't help, but it serves to set up the non-linear sequel. Deviates somewhat from the source material, but most audiences outside of Japan won't notice. **198m/C DVD.** *JP* Asumi Miwa, Tetsu Sawaki, Hassei Takano, Yukihiro Hotaru, Sayaka Yoshino, Maya Kurosu, Daijiro Kawaoka, Ayana Sakai, Mami Shimizu, Kai Hirohashi, Hideyuki Kasahara, Takako Baba, Erika Kuroishi, Kasumi Minagawa, Kaori Sakagami, Takeru Shibaki, Yasufumi Terawaki, Keiko Unno, Osamu Yagibashi, Ryoko Yasuda; *D:* Ryu Kaneda; *W:* Sadayuki Murai, Kouhei Kadono; *C:* Satoshi Maeda; *M:* Yuki Kajiura.

The Book of Eli ♂♂ ½ **2010 (R)** Star/producer Washington plays Eli, a wanderer in a post-apocalyptic desert landscape who guards a mysterious book he believes will redeem mankind. In his divinely inspired trek westward, Eli shoots and slices through thieves, murderers and cannibals. Eventually, he crosses paths with Carnegie (Oldman), a warlord in a small town who covets the book and its power. Caught between the two are Carnegie's minions Claudia (Beals) and her daughter Solara (Kunis). The religious themes and surprise ending earned both scorn and praise for the Hughes brothers. This effort marks the siblings' return to filmmaking after a ten-year hiatus. **117m/C DVD.** Denzel Washington, Gary Oldman, Mila Kunis, Ray Stevenson, Jennifer Beals, Malcolm McDowell, Michael Gambon; *D:* Allen Hughes, Albert Hughes; *W:* Gary Whitta, Anthony Peckham; *C:* Don Burgess; *M:* Atticus Ross, Leopold Ross, Claudia Sarne.

Book of Love ♂♂ **1991 (PG-13)** "Zany" hijinks as a teenager struggles with friendship, girls, and those all-important hormones when he moves to a new neighborhood in the mid-'50s. Average rehash of every '50s movie and TV show cliche in existence. Surprise! There's a classic rock 'n' roll soundtrack. Adapted by Kotzwinkle from his novel "Jack in the Box." **88m/C VHS, DVD.** Chris Young, Keith Coogan, Aeryk Egan, Josie Bissett, Tricia Leigh Fisher, Danny Nucci, Michael McKean, John Cameron Mitchell, Lewis

Arquette; ***D:*** Robert Shaye; ***W:*** William Kotzwinkle; ***M:*** Stanley Clarke.

Book of Love 1/2 **2004 (R)** David (Baker) and Elaine's (O'Connor) childless marriage hits a lull, so the couple befriends Chet (Smith)—David's 15-year-old student—to fill the void. Life for the happy wanna-be-family gets muddled up when David discovers that Chet and Elaine had a creepy and very illegal affair. **85m/C VHS, DVD.** Frances O'Connor, Simon Baker, Gregory Edward Smith, Bryce Dallas Howard, Joanna Adler, Ari Graynor; ***D:*** Alan Brown; ***W:*** Alan Brown; ***C:*** William Rexer. **VIDEO**

Book of Shadows: Blair Witch 2 1/2 *Blair Witch 2* **2000 (R)** Thankfully, they've gotten rid of the shaky-cam (which shook more than a few viewers' stomachs), that's one plus for this sequel that finds five followers of the Blair Witch myth heading back into the woods. Unfortunately, they've also gotten rid of the scares produced by mysterious offscreen witchy shenanigans and replaced them with buckets of fake blood. This group is led by Jeff (Donovan), a townie who's decided to cash in on the Blair Witch craze by organizing tours of the sites made famous in the first movie. Grad students Tristen (Skyler) and Stephen (Turner), practicing Wiccan Erica (Leerhsen) and goth-chick Kim (Director), have fun skewering the movie and its internet movement while partying on the first night. The next day they realize they've lost five hours of their lives. They try to discover what happened, and if it has anything to do with another tour group getting disemboweled. Disappointing fictional debut from documentary director Berlinger, who filmed the truly horrific (and true) "Paradise Lost: The Child Murders at Robin Hood Hills." The townspeople of Burkittsville, Maryland were so fed up with the first film that the second was filmed elsewhere. **90m/C VHS, DVD.** Jeffrey Donovan, Kim Director, Tristen Skylar, Stephen Barker Turner, Erica Leerhsen; ***D:*** Joe Berlinger; ***W:*** Joe Berlinger, Dick Beebe; ***C:*** Nancy Schreiber; ***M:*** Carter Burwell. Golden Raspberries '00: Worst Remake/Sequel.

The Book of Stars 1/2 **1999** Penny (Masterson) is the older sister and only support for teenaged Mary (Malone), who suffers from cystic fibrosis. Penny is a jaded, pill-popping hooker while Mary, however, refuses to give up her optomistic outlook on life. With the aid of cantankerous neighbor Professor (Lindo) and a couple of new friends, Mary is determined to change Penny's views as well. Manages to skirt the subject's inherent sentimentality with some winning performances. **98m/C VHS, DVD.** Mary Stuart Masterson, Jena Malone, Karl Geary, D.B. Sweeney, Delroy Lindo; ***D:*** Michael Miner; ***W:*** Tasca Shadix; ***C:*** James Whitaker; ***M:*** Richard Gibbs. **VIDEO**

Bookies **2003 (R)** Thinking they can strike it rich the easy way, three college pals set up shop as bookies. Naturally, their hot streak abruptly ends when the local syndicate takes issue with the amateurs cutting into their cash flow. **90m/C VHS, DVD.** Nick Stahl, Lukas Haas, Johnny Galecki, Rachael Leigh Cook, David Proval, John Diehl, Zuri Williams; ***D:*** Mark Illsley; ***W:*** Michael Bacall; ***C:*** Brendan Galvin; ***M:*** Christopher Tyng, Giuseppe Cristiano. **VIDEO**

Boom! 1/2 **1968 (PG)** Laughable adaptation of the Williams' play "The Milk Train Doesn't Stop Here Anymore" was a Hollywood star disaster. Flora Goforth (Taylor) is a dying millionairess living in isolated glory on an island near Sardinia. Chris Flanders (Burton) is a wandering poet, nicknamed the "Angel of Death," who shows up and becomes Flora's confidante. Does have pretty scenery. **113m/C VHS.** Elizabeth Taylor, Richard Burton, Noel Coward, Joanna Shimkus, Michael Dunn, Romolo Valli; ***D:*** Joseph Losey; ***W:*** Tennessee Williams; ***C:*** Douglas Slocombe; ***M:*** John Barry.

Boom in the Moon WOOF! *A Modern Bluebeard* **1946** Keaton fares poorly in this sci-fi comedy. He's trapped on a space ship to the moon. Poor production, with uneven direction and acting. **83m/C VHS.** Buster Keaton, Angel Garasa, Virginia Serret, Fernando Soto Mantequilla, Luis Barreiro; ***D:*** Jaime Salvador.

Boom Town 1/2 **1940** A lively vintage comedy/drama/romance about two oil-drilling buddies competing amid romantic mix-ups and fortunes gained and lost. **120m/B VHS, DVD.** Clark Gable, Spencer Tracy, Claudette Colbert, Hedy Lamarr, Frank Morgan, Lionel Atwill, Chill Wills, Curt Bois; ***D:*** Jack Conway; ***W:*** John Lee Mahin; ***C:*** Harold Rosson, Elwood "Woody" Bredell; ***M:*** Franz Waxman.

Boomerang **1947** Film noir based on actual events features the murder of a Connecticut clergyman and the quick arrest of vagrant John Waldron (Kennedy). Prosecuting attorney Henry Harvey (Andrews) is told by his political bosses to get an equally quick conviction to stem public outrage. The evidence seems overwhelming but Harvey begins his own investigation and suddenly switches to the defense to prove Waldron's innocence in dramatic courtroom style. Kazan filmed on location in Bridgeport, CT in a successful semi-documentary style that heightened the tension. **88m/B VHS, DVD.** Dana Andrews, Arthur Kennedy, Lee J. Cobb, Jane Wyatt, Cara Williams, Sam Levene, Ed Begley Sr., Karl Malden, Taylor Holmes, Robert Keith; ***D:*** Elia Kazan; ***W:*** Richard Murphy; ***C:*** Norbert Brodine; ***M:*** David Buttolph.

Boomerang 1/2 **1976** A father rescues his wrongly convicted son from prison. Dubbed. **101m/C VHS.** *IT* Alain Delon, Carla Gravina, Dora Doll; ***D:*** Jose Giovanni.

Boomerang **1992 (R)** Successful, womanizing marketing exec for a cosmetics company (Murphy) meets his match when he falls for a colleague (Givens) who is as vain and sexually predatory as he is. She treats him the way he treats women (as a sex object), and he's shocked into the arms of a nice girl (Berry). Although it's refreshing to see this sexual role reversal, the typical Murphy-style humor is in play with sexist jokes and a couple of vulgar female characters. Grier and Lawrence are great as Murphy's best friends. Blaustein and Sheffield are the same guys who wrote Murphy's "Coming to America." **118m/C VHS, DVD.** Eddie Murphy, Halle Berry, Robin Givens, David Alan Grier, Martin Lawrence, Grace Jones, Geoffrey Holder, Eartha Kitt, Chris Rock, Tisha Campbell, John Witherspoon, Melvin Van Peebles; ***D:*** Reginald (Reggie) Hudlin; ***W:*** Barry W. Blaustein, David Sheffield.

Boondock Saints **1999 (R)** Two Boston Irish-Catholic brothers, Connor (Flanery) and Murphy (Reedus) McManus, turn into unlikely local heroes after the self-defense killings of some Russian mobsters who were threatening to close down their local pub. They turn vigilante, believing they're doing God's work to rid the world of evil, which leads to more slaughter. Investigating the crimes is gay FBI agent Paul Smecker (Dafoe), who is shown reconstructing the carnage in a series of flashbacks. **110m/C VHS, DVD, Blu-ray Disc, UMD.** Sean Patrick Flanery, Norman Reedus, Willem Dafoe, David Della Rocco, Carlo Rota, Billy Connolly, David Ferry, Brian Mahoney, Ron Jeremy; ***D:*** Troy Duffy; ***W:*** Troy Duffy; ***C:*** Adam Kane; ***M:*** Jeff Danna.

The Boondock Saints II: All Saints Day 1/2 **2009 (R)** In this second installment, Flanery and Reedus return as twin brothers Connor and Murphy, forced out of exile when they are linked to a priest's murder. Even lower-grade Tarantino rip-off than the first, this one takes racist, homophobic jokes and impossible violence to a new level of absurdity. While writer/director Duffy's 10 years between films did improve his cinematography, it didn't hone his creativity—he overcompensates what is lacking by blasting metal and techno music. If not for the original's cult status, the Boston boys and their vigilante justice would have never been reunited. **118m/C DVD.** *US* Sean Patrick Flanery, Norman Reedus, Billy Connolly, Clifton (Gonzalez) Collins Jr., Julie Benz, Peter Fonda, Judd Nelson; ***D:*** Troy Duffy; ***W:*** Troy Duffy, Taylor Duffy; ***C:*** Miroslaw Baszak; ***M:*** Jeff Danna.

The Boost 1/2 **1988 (R)** A feverish, messy melodrama about a young couple's spiraling decline from yuppie-ish wealth in a haze of cocaine abuse. **95m/C VHS, DVD.** James Woods, Sean Young, John Kapelos, Steven Hill, Kelle Kerr, John Rothman, Amanda Blake, Grace Zabriskie; ***D:*** Harold Becker; ***W:*** Darryl Ponicsan; ***C:*** Howard Atherton.

Boot Hill 1/2 **1969 (PG)** Two guys mess with western baddies and wild women in spaghetti oater. **97m/C VHS, DVD.** *IT* Terence Hill, Bud Spencer, Woody Strode, Victor Buono, Lionel Stander; ***D:*** Giuseppe Colizzi.

Boot Hill Bandits 1/2 **1942** "Crash" Corrigan fights on the side of right in this classic western as he helps corral Wells Fargo bandits. **58m/B VHS, DVD.** Ray Corrigan, John "Dusty" King, Max Terhune, Jean Brooks, John Merton, Glenn Strange; ***D:*** S. Roy Luby.

Boothill Brigade **1937** Former footballer Brown rides to the rescue when criminals steal land from homesteaders. **58m/B VHS.** Johnny Mack Brown, Claire Rochelle, Dick Curtis, Horace Murphy, Frank LaRue, Edward Cassidy, Bobby Nelson, Frank Ball, Steve Clark; ***D:*** Sam Newfield.

Bootleg **1985** A detective is on a case that leads to crooked politics and espionage. **82m/C VHS.** John Flaus, Carmen Duncan, Ian Nimmo, Ray Meagher; ***D:*** John Prescott; ***W:*** John Prescott; ***C:*** Stephen Frost; ***M:*** Stephen Cronin.

Bootmen **2000 (R)** Young Sean must make his dance dreams come true despite a bitter, critical father and his working-class Australian surroundings. Director Dein Perry has turned his hit show "Tap Dogs" into a fictionalized and semi-autobiographical tale that combines some of the better qualities of "The Full Monty" and the standard twists and turns of so many other dance films. The "Let's put on a show" plot doesn't provide much sustenance to see the viewer through to some of the excellent choreography. Features several players from the original Tap Dogs company. **95m/C VHS, DVD.** *AU* Adam Garcia, Sophie Lee, William Zappa, Sam Worthington, Susie Porter; ***D:*** Dein Perry; ***W:*** Steve Worland; ***C:*** Steve Mason. Australian Film Inst. '00: Cinematog., Costume Des., Score.

Boots & Saddles 1/2 **1937** A young English lord wants to sell the ranch he has inherited but Autry is determined to make him a real Westerner. **54m/B VHS, DVD.** Gene Autry, Judith Allen, Smiley Burnette; ***D:*** Joseph Kane.

Boots Malone 1/2 **1952** An old down-on-his-luck gambling addict and a young, rich kid fascinated by the sordid atmosphere of the racetrack stumble upon one another and form a symbiotic relationship. All goes well for while, but there'd be no movie unless a collection of obstacles suddenly threatens their success, friendship, and even their lives. A rather melodramatic buddy tale, but Holden and Stewart hold interest. **103m/C VHS.** William Holden, John Stewart, Ed Begley Sr., Harry (Henry) Morgan, Whit Bissell; ***D:*** William Dieterle; ***W:*** Harold Buchman, Milton Holmes; ***M:*** Elmer Bernstein.

Boots of Destiny **1937** Cheap western with Maynard and his sidekick Barnett on the lam and coming to the aid of ranch owner Dell. Based on a story by E. Morton Hough. **59m/B VHS.** Ken Maynard, Claudia Dell, Vince Barnett, Edward Cassidy, Martin Garralaga; ***D:*** Arthur Rosson; ***W:*** Arthur Rosson.

Booty Call 1/2 **1996 (R)** Reserved Rushon (Davidson) and conservative Nikki (Jones) have been dating for a couple of months and Rushon's decided they should consummate their relationship. Nikki's more ambivalent and first sets up a double date with her vivacious best friend Lysterine (Fox) and Rushon's bragging buddy Bunz (Foxx). The duos do pair up but since the "no glove, no love" rule prevails, first the guys have to find some condoms. Raunch rules as might be expected but it's an appealing cast. **120m/C VHS, DVD.** Jamie Foxx, Tommy Davidson, Vivica A. Fox, Tamala Jones, Art Malik, Gedde Watanabe, Scott LaRose, Ammie Sin, Bernie Mac, David Hemblen; ***D:*** Jeff Pollack; ***W:*** Takashi Bufford; ***C:*** Ronald Orieux; ***M:*** Robert Folk.

Bopha! **1993 (PG-13)** Father-son strife set against the anti-apartheid movement. In the Senior township police officer Mikah takes pride in his peaceful community, particularly in light of the growing unrest in the other townships. Son Zweli has become an activist and wife Rosie must be the family peacemaker. Then a prominent freedom movement member is arrested and two officers of the secret police make their sinister appearance. Well acted; directorial debut of Freeman. Adapted from the play by Percy Mtwa, although the hopeful ending has been changed in the movie. The title, a Zulu word, stands for arrest or detention. Filmed on location in Zimbabwe. **121m/C VHS, DVD.** Danny Glover, Maynard Eziashi, Alfre Woodard, Malcolm McDowell, Marius Weyers, Malick Bowens, Robin Smith, Michael Chinyamurindi, Christopher John Hall, Grace Mahlaba; ***D:*** Morgan Freeman; ***W:*** Brian Bird, John Wierick; ***M:*** James Horner.

Borat: Cultural Learnings of America for Make Benefit Glorious Nation of Kazakhstan **2006 (R)** British comic Sacha Baron Cohen is outrageously funny as Borat, the cheerfully ignorant and prejudiced "sixth best known reporter in Kazakhstan." The plot follows Borat's travels through America in order to bring back to his homeland two things he feels strongly about: lessons on America and Pamela Anderson. The plot is just a frame to prop up the real aim of the moviefilm, which is to allow the American public to parody and incriminate itself. Viewers will simultaneously wince and laugh as Borat's seemingly innocent Third World anti-Semitism, homophobia and misogyny are reflected in unknowing victims from both jerkwater towns and cosmopolitan cities. Critically hailed upon its release, the film was dogged with numerous lawsuits and complaints from offended parties, particularly the Kazakh government. The humor is often crude (there is a credit for "Feces provided by") and disturbing (an extended scene of graphic "dudity" when Borat and producer Azamat (Davitian) wrestle over a magazine picture), but it is genuinely funny and unsettling. **82m/C DVD.** *US* Sacha Baron Cohen, Pamela Anderson, Ken Davitian, Pat Haggerty, Alan Keyes, Luenell; ***D:*** Larry Charles; ***W:*** Sacha Baron Cohen, Peter Baynham, Dan Mazer, Anthony Hines; ***C:*** Luke Geissbuhler, Anthony Hardwick; ***M:*** Erran Baron Cohen. Golden Globes '07: Actor—Mus./Comedy (Cohen).

Bordello **1979** Western spoof about cowboys and shady ladies. **90m/C VHS.** Chuck Connors, Michael Conrad, John Ireland, Isela Vega, Jorge (George) Rivero; ***D:*** Ray Fellows. **TV**

The Border **1982 (R)** A border guard faces corruption and violence within his department and tests his own sense of decency when the infant of a poor Mexican girl is kidnapped. Excellent cast, fine cinematography, unusual Nicholson performance. **107m/C VHS, DVD.** Jack Nicholson, Harvey Keitel, Valerie Perrine, Warren Oates, Elpidia Carrillo; ***D:*** Tony Richardson; ***W:*** Deric Washburn, Walon Green; ***M:*** Ry Cooder.

Border Badmen 1/2 **1945** It's just another tired old western, even if it does appropriate the classic mystery-thriller plot; following the reading of a silver baron's will, someone starts killing off the relatives. **59m/B VHS.** Buster Crabbe, Lorraine Miller, Charles "Blackie" King, Ray Bennett, Arch (Archie) Hall Sr., Budd Buster, Bud Osborne; ***D:*** Sam Newfield.

Border Bandits **1946** Plodding oater has Brown going after the bad guys. Not only is it a dirty job, but apparently pretty boring. **57m/B VHS.** Johnny Mack Brown, Raymond Hatton, John Merton, Frank LaRue, Steve Clark, Charles Stevens, Bud Osborne; ***D:*** Lambert Hillyer.

Border Blues 1/2 **2003 (R)** Ex-Russian cop who tries to sneak a woman and her daughter across the U.S.-Mexico border is the primary suspect in connection with an L.A. mail-bomb scare. Painful to watch Busey and Estrada in their law enforcement roles. **86m/C VHS, DVD.** Eric Roberts, Gary Busey, Yekaterina Rednikova, Lisa Gerstein, Erik Estrada, Rodion Nakhapetov; ***D:*** Rodion Nakhapetov; ***W:*** Rodion Nakhapetov; ***C:*** Sergei Kozlov; ***M:*** David G. Russell. **VIDEO**

Border Caballero 1/2 **1936** Western star McCoy and lady cowpoke January shoot out the skies in this lackluster McCoy vehicle.

Based on a story by Norman S. Hall. **57m/B VHS, DVD.** Tim McCoy, Lois January, Ralph Byrd, Ted Adams; ***D:*** Sam Newfield; ***W:*** Joseph O'Donnell.

Border Devils **1932** A boy is pursued by a ruthless gang of outlaws, until he is saved by the good guys. **60m/B VHS.** Harry Carey Sr., Art Mix, George "Gabby" Hayes; ***D:*** William Nigh.

Border Feud **1947** LaRue endeavors to prevent someone who, by instigating a family feud, will claim large gold mine rights. **54m/B VHS.** Lash LaRue, Al "Fuzzy" St. John, Bob Duncan; ***D:*** Ray Taylor.

Border Incident **1949** Average crime melodrama from director Mann in which federales on both sides of the border team up to prevent the exploitation and murder of illegal farm workers. Jack Bearnes (Murphy) has stolen work permits he's willing to sell to crooked rancher Owen Parkson (Da Silva) while Pablo Rodriguez (Montalban) poses as an illegal migrant, and both agents find themselves in grave danger. **94m/B DVD.** Ricardo Montalban, George Murphy, Howard da Silva, James Mitchell, Arnold Moss, Alfonso Bedoya, Teresa Celli, Charles McGraw, Jose Torvay, John Ridgely, Arthur Hunnicutt, Sig Rumann; ***D:*** Anthony Mann; ***W:*** John C. Higgins, George Zuckerman; ***C:*** John Alton.

Border Law 1/2 **1931** Jones plays a heroic Texas Ranger who goes undercover to find the man who killed his brother. One of Jones' finest outings and far better than most B westerns. **62m/B VHS.** Buck Jones, Lupita Tovar, James Mason, Frank Rice, Glenn Strange; ***D:*** Louis King; ***W:*** Stuart Anthony.

The Border Legion 1/2 *West of the Badlands* **1940** Sappy retelling of Grey's novel about an outlaw sacrificing himself for a pair of young lovers. This time Rogers is the outlaw with a heart of gold. Originally filmed in 1930 with Jack Holt, Richard Arlen, and Fay Wray. **58m/B VHS, DVD.** Roy Rogers, George "Gabby" Hayes, Carol Hughes, Joseph (Joe) Sawyer, Maude Eburne, Jay Novello; ***D:*** Joseph Kane; ***W:*** Olive Cooper, Louis Stevens.

Border Lost 1/2 **2008 (R)** Typical actioner. A U.S. task force works along the Mexican border to prevent bandoleros from preying upon illegal immigrants. When one the men is killed and his girlfriend kidnapped, the other agents defy orders to cross into Mexico on a mission of rescue and revenge. **105m/C DVD.** Chris Cleveland, Emilio Rossi, Protasio, Wes McGee, Marian Zapico, Daniel Ledesma, Kelly Noonan, Robert Vazquez; ***D:*** David Murphy, Scott Peck; ***W:*** David Murphy, Scott Peck; ***C:*** Scott Peck; ***M:*** Christopher Peck. **VIDEO**

Border Patrol **1943** Another installment in the Hopalong Cassidy series. This time there's a villainous owner of a silvermine to reckon with. A man so low he's abducting hapless Mexicans as they cross the border, forcing them to work his mines. Hoppy is saddled with the task of persuading him that the town ain't big enough for the both of them. Robert Mitchum makes his perfectly forgettable film debut as one of the bad guys. Not one of the best in the series, but plenty of action. **63m/B VHS, DVD.** William Boyd, Andy Clyde, Jay Kirby, Russell Simpson, Claudia Drake, George Reeves, Duncan Renaldo; ***D:*** Lesley Selander.

Border Patrol 1/2 **2001 (PG-13)** This Border Patrol is in charge of policing the realm of the dead, making sure sinners and the good get their proper punishment and rewards. Patrolman Numan is forced to break the rules and ask the help of a mortal Miami cop in order to stop vicious serial killer Dr. Helms from opening the gateway to other realms. **89m/C VHS.** Michael Delorenzo, Lewis Fitz-Gerald, Clayton Rohner, Kenny Ransom; ***D:*** Mark Haber; ***W:*** Miguel Tejada-Flores. **CABLE**

Border Phantom **1937** Steele (whom you might recognize as Canino in "The Big Sleep"), takes on a suave Chinese businessman who heads a mail order business: seems he's smuggling mail-order brides from Mexico in this vintage "B"-grade horse opera. **60m/B VHS, DVD.** Bob Steele, Harley Wood, Don Barclay, Karl Hackett, Horace Murphy, Miki Morita; ***D:*** S. Roy Luby.

Border Radio **WOOF!** **1988** A rock singer decides to steal a car and try to outrun some tough thugs hot on his trail. **88m/B VHS, DVD.** Chris D, Luana Anders; ***D:*** Allison Anders, Kurt Voss; ***W:*** Allison Anders, Kurt Voss; ***M:*** Dave Alvin.

Border Rangers **1950** A man joins the Rangers in order to avenge the murders of his brother and sister-in-law. **57m/B VHS.** Robert Lowery, Donald (Don "Red") Barry, Lyle Talbot, Pamela Blake; ***D:*** William Berke.

Border River 1/2 **1947** Mexican General Calleja (Armendariz) runs Zona Libre, a small enclave at the U.S.-Mexico border. For those running from the law—or the lawless—Zona Libre offers sanctuary, for a price. New arrival Confederate officer Clete Mattson (McCrea) shows up with a cool $2 million in gold, looking to buy guns for the Confederacy. Hot tamale Carmelita (De Carlo) fancies Mattson, but the General has dibs on her, and can Mattson trust these guys at Zona Libre, anyway? Either way, trouble's a brewin'. **80m/C DVD.** Joel McCrea, Yvonne De Carlo, Pedro Armendariz Sr., Howard Petrie, Erika Nordin, Alfonso Bedoya, Ivan Triesault, George Lewis, George D. Wallace, Lane Chandler, Charles Horvath, Nacho Galindo; ***D:*** George Sherman; ***W:*** William Sackheim, Louis Stevens.

Border Romance 1/2 **1930** Three Americans have their horses stolen by bandits while riding through Mexico. Trouble with the locals follows in this early sound western. **58m/B VHS.** Don Terry, Armida, Marjorie "Babe" Kane, Victor Potel, Nina Martan, J. Frank Glendon, Harry Von Meter, William Costello; ***D:*** Richard Thorpe; ***W:*** Jack Natteford; ***C:*** Harry Zech; ***M:*** Al Short.

Border Roundup **1941** The "Lone Rider" uncovers a gang of thieving crooks. **57m/B VHS.** George Houston, Al "Fuzzy" St. John, Dennis Moore; ***D:*** Sam Newfield.

Border Saddlemates **1952** U.S. government veterinarian Allen is asked to sub for the local doc in the Canadian border town of Pine Rock. But he learns that a gang is using silver fox pelts to smuggle illegal goods into the U.S. and it's up to Allen and the Rhythm Riders to stop them. **67m/B VHS.** Rex Allen, Mary Ellen Kay, Slim Pickens, Roy Barcroft, Forrest Taylor, Jimmy Moss, Zon Murray, Keith McConnell; ***D:*** William Witney; ***W:*** Albert DeMond; ***C:*** John MacBurnie; ***M:*** Stanley Wilson.

Border Shootout **1990 (PG)** A trigger-happy sheriff battles a rich young cattle rustler. **110m/C VHS, DVD.** Glenn Ford, Charlene Tilton, Jeff Kaake, Michael Horse, Russell Todd, Cody Glenn, Sergio Calderon, Michael Ansara; ***D:*** Chris T. McIntyre.

Border Vengeance 1/2 **1935** Reb is a member of a family of outlaws. He aims to improve himself and steer his family to the straight and narrow trail. **45m/B VHS, DVD.** Reb Russell, Mary Jane Carey, Kenneth MacDonald, Hank Bell, Glenn Strange, Norman Feusier, Charles "Slim" Whitaker; ***D:*** Ray Heinz.

Border Vigilantes **1941** Hoppy and pals try to rid a town of outlaws that even the vigilantes can't run off. The big surprise comes when they find out who the leader of the outlaws is. **61m/B VHS, DVD.** William Boyd, Russell Hayden, Andy Clyde, Victor Jory, Morris Ankrum, Frances Gifford, Ethel Wales, Hal Taliaferro; ***D:*** Derwin Abrahams.

Borderland 1/2 **1937** Hopalong Cassidy (Boyd) goes bad?! (He's mean to kids and drinks liquor.) Well no, he's just secretly after a bandit known as "The Fox." But the outlaw didn't get his nickname by being stupid, and he sets a trap when he realizes what Hoppy is up to. The ninth film in the series. **82m/B DVD.** William Boyd, George "Gabby" Hayes, James Ellison, Nora Lane, Morris Ankrum, Charlene Wyatt; ***D:*** Nate Watt; ***W:*** Harrison Jacobs; ***C:*** Archie Stout.

Borderland **2007** Super-creepy and bloody, and based on a true 1989 crime. Henry (Muxworthy), Phil (Strong), and Ed (Presley) take a road trip to party in a Mexican border town. Phil doesn't make it back to the hotel and the police are no help. Henry and Ed learn that kidnappings are common and tied to a cult lead by drug dealer Santillan (Cuevas). He's convinced his followers that ritual human sacrifices will make them invulnerable and though the locals (and the cops) know what's going on, they're too terrified to do anything about it. **105m/C DVD.** Brian Presley, Rider Strong, Jake Muxworthy, Martha Higareda, Sean Astin, Beto Cuevas, Marco Bacuzzi; ***D:*** Zev Berman; ***W:*** Zev Berman, Eric Poppen; ***C:*** Scott Kevan; ***M:*** Andres Levin.

Borderline **1950** MacMurray and Trevor play undercover agents trying to infiltrate a Mexican drug ring. With their real identities hidden, they fall for each other and make a run for the border. Although the leads work well together, they're hindered by an occasionally confusing script. Unfortunately, director Seiter never decides whether the material is of a comedic or dramatic nature. **88m/B VHS, DVD.** Fred MacMurray, Claire Trevor, Raymond Burr, Roy Roberts, Jose Torvay, Morris Ankrum, Charles Lane, Don Diamond, Nacho Galindo, Pepe Hern, Richard Irving; ***D:*** William A. Seiter; ***C:*** Lucien N. Andriot; ***M:*** Hans J. Salter.

Borderline **1980 (PG)** Bronson is a border patrol guard in pursuit of a murderer in this action flick. Meanwhile, he gets caught up in trying to help an illegal alien and her young child. **106m/C VHS, DVD.** Charles Bronson, Wilford Brimley, Bruno Kirby, Benito Morales, Ed Harris, Kenneth McMillan; ***D:*** Jerrold Freedman.

Borderline **2002 (R)** A good suspenser about obsession. Dr. Lila Colleti (Gershon) is a shrink for the criminally insane at the local prison, which may be why her ex got custody of their two daughters. Lily's troubles increase when one of her patients, Ed Baikman (Flanery), is released to a halfway house, despite his delusions that they are romantically involved. After murdering her ex on her behalf, Ed threatens Lily when she doesn't return his love and implicates her in his crime. Soon, even her detective boyfriend Macy Kobacek (Biehn) has doubts about Lily's innocence. **94m/C VHS, DVD.** Gina Gershon, Sean Patrick Flanery, Michael Biehn; ***D:*** Evelyn Purcell; ***W:*** David Loucka; ***C:*** Michael Brierley; ***M:*** Anthony Marinelli. **CABLE**

Bordertown **1935** Poor Mexican lawyer Johnny Ramirez (Muni) loses his first case and his temper, which results in his disbarment. He takes a job as a bouncer at a bordertown nightclub where owner Charlie's (Pallette) hot-to-trot missus, Marie (Davis), makes a play that gets rejected. Johnny is stupid over slumming society dame Dale (Lindsay), and Marie gets tragically desperate in trying to get Johnny's attention. The ending borders on the absurd and Davis' performance is scaled way over-the-top throughout although Muni does his best. **80m/B DVD.** Paul Muni, Bette Davis, Margaret Lindsay, Eugene Pallette, Gavin Gordon; ***D:*** Archie Mayo; ***W:*** Laird Doyle, Wallace Smith; ***C:*** Gaetano Antonio "Tony" Gaudio; ***M:*** Bernhard Haun.

Bordertown 1/2 **2006 (R)** Generic thriller based on a true story. Ambitious Chicago journalist Lauren (Lopez) is assigned to write about a series of rape/murders that have happened to young women in Juarez, Mexico. She hooks up with former colleague Alfonso (Banderas), whose persistence on covering the crimes has him in trouble with authorities. Lauren meets Eva (Zapata), who is in hiding after surviving her attack, and it is implied that the victims are all poor workers at factories making goods for the U.S. market. The politics muddies a story that, unfortunately, hasn't been compellingly told. **112m/C DVD.** Jennifer Lopez, Antonio Banderas, Maya Zapata, Sonia Braga, Martin Sheen; ***D:*** Gregory Nava; ***W:*** Gregory Nava; ***C:*** Reynaldo Villalobos; ***M:*** Graeme Revell.

Bordertown Gunfighters 1/2 **1943** A cowboy breaks up a vicious lottery racket and falls in love in the process. **56m/B VHS.** William (Wild Bill) Elliott, Anne Jeffreys, George "Gabby" Hayes, Ian Keith, Harry Woods, Edward Earle, Karl Hackett, Roy Barcroft, Bud Geary, Carl Sepulveda; ***D:*** Howard Bretherton; ***W:*** Norman S. Hall; ***C:*** Jack Marta.

Boricua's Bond **2000 (R)** First-time director Lik (at 21) debuts with an urban drama about Puerto Rican-born artist Tommy (Negron) who would rather paint than be an active part of the South Bronx street gangs that surround him. Then Anglo single mom Susan (Karp) and son Allen (played by Lik) move into the 'hood, where they are immediately hasseled. Tommy befriends Allen but there's a string of not entirely unexpected tragedies that change everyone's lives. **95m/C VHS.** Val Lik, Frankie Negron, Robyn Karp, Marco Sorisio, Kirk "Sticky Fingaz" Jones; ***D:*** Val Lik; ***W:*** Val Lik; ***C:*** Brendan Flynt.

Boris and Natasha: The Movie 1/2 **1992 (PG)** The two inept spies from the classic TV cartoon "The Adventures of Rocky and Bullwinkle" star in this mediocre live-action comedy. These nogoodniks are sent by "Fearless Leader" to America and encounter the usual misadventures. For true fun watch the original animated versions. Never released theatrically; it aired for the first time on cable TV. **88m/C VHS.** Sally Kellerman, Dave Thomas, Paxton Whitehead, Andrea Martin, Alex Rocco, Larry Cedar, Arye Gross, Christopher Neame, Anthony Newley; ***Cameos:*** John Candy, John Travolta, Charles Martin Smith; ***D:*** Charles Martin Smith.

B.O.R.N. 1/2 **1988 (R)** Hagen uncovers an underground network of doctors who kill people and sell the body parts and organs. **90m/C VHS.** Ross Hagen, P.J. Soles, William (Bill) Smith, Hoke Howell, Russ Tamblyn, Amanda Blake, Clint Howard, Rance Howard, Debra Lamb; ***D:*** Ross Hagen.

Born Again **1978** Adaptation of Watergate criminal Charles Colson's biography of his becoming a born again Christian. Standard TV biopic stuff. **110m/C VHS.** Dean Jones, Anne Francis, Dana Andrews, George Brent; ***D:*** Irving Rapper; ***W:*** Walter Bloch; ***C:*** Harry Stradling Jr.; ***M:*** Les Baxter.

Born American *Arctic Heat* **1986 (R)** Pre-Glasnost flick about teenagers vacationing in Finland who "accidentally" cross the Russian border. There they battle the Red Plague. Melodramatic and heavily politicized. Original release banned in Finland. **95m/C VHS, DVD.** Mike Norris, Steve Durham, David Coburn, Thalmus Rasulala, Albert Salmi; ***D:*** Renny Harlin.

Born Bad **1997 (R)** Teens bungle a bank robbery and hold up in the bank with hostages. The town sheriff wants to end the standoff calmly but the teens' hot-headed leader won't surrender. **84m/C VHS, DVD.** James Remar, Corey Feldman, Taylor Nichols, Justin Walker, Heidi Noelle Lenhardt; ***D:*** Jeff Yonis. **VIDEO**

Born Beautiful 1/2 **1982** Made for TV. Beautiful young women come to New York, hoping to strike it rich in the world of modeling. At the same time, a still beautiful, but older and overexposed model comes to grips with a change in her career. Well-told, but sugar-coated. **100m/C VHS.** Erin Gray, Ed Marinaro, Polly Bergen, Lori Singer, Ellen Barber, Judith Barcroft, Michael Higgins; ***D:*** Harvey Hart; ***M:*** Brad Fiedel. **TV**

Born for Hell *Naked Massacre* **1976** A maniac Vietnam vet kills nurses, leaving no clues for the police to follow. **90m/C VHS, DVD.** Matthieu Carriere, Carole Laure; ***D:*** Denis Heroux.

Born Free **1966** The touching story of a game warden in Kenya and his wife raising Elsa the orphaned lion cub. When the cub reaches maturity, they work to return her to life in the wild. Great family entertainment based on Joy Adamson's book. Theme song became a hit. ♫Born Free. **95m/C VHS, DVD.** Virginia McKenna, Bill Travers; ***D:*** James Hill; ***W:*** Lester Cole; ***M:*** John Barry. Oscars '66: Song ("Born Free"), Orig. Score.

Born in 68 *Nes en 68* **2008** Overstuffed epic traces the lives of a French family from the Paris student rebellions of 1968 to the gay rights movement in the late 1980s. Twenty-year-olds Catherine, Yves, and Herve are all involved in leftist student groups, although they eventually leave the city for a rural commune. Friendships fray and Herve tires of the pastoral life while Catherine and Yves stay to raise their two children, Boris and Ludmilla. French with subtitles. **166m/C DVD.** *FR* Laetitia Casta, Yannick Renier, Yann Tregouet, Theo Frilet, Edouard Collin, Sabrina Seyvecou, Marc Citti, Kate Moran; ***D:*** Jacques Martineau, Olivier Ducastel;

W: Jacques Martineau, Olivier Ducastel, Catherine Corsini, Guillaume Le Touze; *C:* Mathieu Poirot-Delpech; *M:* Philippe Miller.

Born in America *Dead Aim* **1990** A young orphan is adopted by an undertaker. The boy grows up enveloped by his guardian's business and, when things are slow, works to bring in business himself. **90m/C VHS.** James Westerfield, Glen Lee, Virgil Frye, Venetia Vianello; *D:* Jose Antonio Bolanos.

Born in East L.A. **1987 (R)** Marin brings his Bruce Springsteen-parody song to life as he plays a mistakenly deported illegal alien who struggles to return to the U.S. Suprisingly resolute effort by the usually self-exploiting Mexican-American. Stern is the American expatriate who helps him get back and Lopez is the love interest who stalls him. **85m/C VHS, DVD.** Richard "Cheech" Marin, Daniel Stern, Paul Rodriguez, Jan-Michael Vincent, Kamala Lopez, Tony Plana, Vic Trevino, A. Martinez; *D:* Richard "Cheech" Marin; *W:* Richard "Cheech" Marin; *C:* Alex Phillips Jr.; *M:* Lee Holdridge.

Born in '45 *Jahrgang '45* **1965** Auto mechanic Alfred and maternity nurse Lisa are newlyweds. However, they might not be wed much longer as they find marital adjustments (especially in their tiny apartment) difficult to make. Alfred goes wandering around Berlin, hoping to make some decisions, but the film ends with their future uncertain. German with subtitles. **94m/B DVD.** *GE* Monika Hilldebrand, Rolf Romer, Paul Eichbaum, Holger Mahlich; *D:* Jurgen Bottcher; *W:* Jurgen Bottcher; *C:* Roland Graf; *M:* Klaus Poche.

Born Innocent ½ **1974** As if "The Exorcist" weren't bad enough, Blair is back for more abuse-on-film, this time as a 14-year-old runaway from a dysfunctional family who lands in a reform school for girls. There, she must struggle to be as brutal as her peers in order to survive. Fairly tame by today's standards, but controversial at its made-for-TV premiere, chiefly due to a rape scene involving a broom handle. First trip up the river for Blair. **92m/C VHS, DVD.** Linda Blair, Joanna Miles, Kim Hunter, Richard Jaeckel, Janit Baldwin, Mitch Vogel; *D:* Donald Wrye; *M:* Fred Karlin. **TV**

Born Into Brothels: Calcutta's Red Light Kids **2004 (R)** Photojournalist Zana Briski presents the world of Calcutta prostitution through the eyes and pictures of the children who live it. Not only does she give them photography instruction as a means to help lift them from their current situation, she goes a step further in trying to place them in boarding school—much to the chagrin of the opposing parents. The subject is nothing new but her drive to make a change in these doomed lives is commendable and may hopefully inspire others. **85m/C DVD.** *US IN D:* Zana Briski, Ross Kauffman; *W:* Zana Briski, Ross Kauffman; *C:* Zana Briski, Ross Kauffman; *M:* John McDowell. Oscars '04: Feature Doc.

Born Killer ½ **1989** Teenagers in the woods meet up with murderous escaped convicts. **90m/C VHS.** Francine Lapensee, Fritz Matthews, Ted Prior, Adam Tucker; *D:* Kimberly Casey.

Born Killers *Piggy Banks* **2005 (R)** Grubby, flashback-heavy story about low-lifes. Brothers John (Muxworthy) and Michael (Mann) were raised by their sociopathic father (Sizemore), who made his living robbing and killing his victims. His sons follow in his footsteps, although Michael prefers to bed the young women who are his targets first, and he becomes fond of Archer (Garner) to the point of balking at killing her. John has his own dilemma when he discovers they have a half-sister Gertie (German), whom he immediately falls into reciprocated lust with. **87m/C DVD.** Jake Muxworthy, Gabriel Mann, Tom Sizemore, Kelli Garner, Lauren German; *D:* Morgan J. Freeman; *W:* Kendall Delcambre; *C:* Nancy Schreiber; *M:* Jim Lang.

Born Losers **1967 (PG)** The original "Billy Jack" film in which the Indian martial arts expert takes on a group of incorrigible bikers bothering some California babes and runs afoul of the law. Classic drive-in fare. **112m/C VHS, DVD.** Tom Laughlin, Elizabeth James, Jeremy Slate, William Wellman Jr., Robert Tessier, Jane Russell, Stuart Lancaster, Edwin Cook, Jeff Cooper; *D:* Tom Laughlin; *W:* E. James Lloyd, Tom Laughlin; *C:* Gregory Sandor.

Born of Fire ½ **1987 (R)** A flutist investigating his father's death seeks the Master Musician; his search leads him to the volcanic (and supernatural) mountains of Turkey. **84m/C VHS.** Peter Firth, Susan Crowley, Stephan Kalipha; *D:* Jamil Dehlavi; *M:* Colin Towns.

Born on the Fourth of July ½ **1989 (R)** A riveting meditation on American life affected by the Vietnam War, based on the real-life, bestselling experiences of Ron Kovic, though some facts are subtly changed. The film follows him as he develops from a naive recruit to an angry, wheelchair-bound paraplegic to an active antiwar protestor. Well-acted and generally lauded; Kovic co-wrote the screenplay and appears as a war veteran in the opening parade sequence. **145m/C VHS, DVD, HD DVD.** Bill Allen, Tom Cruise, Kyra Sedgwick, Raymond J. Barry, Jerry Levine, Tom Berenger, Willem Dafoe, Frank Whaley, John Getz, Caroline Kava, Bryan Larkin, Abbie Hoffman, Stephen Baldwin, Josh Evans, Dale Dye, William Baldwin, Don "The Dragon" Wilson, Vivica A. Fox, Holly Marie Combs, Tom Sizemore, Daniel Baldwin, Ron Kovic; *Cameos:* Oliver Stone; *D:* Oliver Stone; *W:* Oliver Stone; *C:* Robert Richardson; *M:* John Williams. Oscars '89: Director (Stone), Film Editing; Directors Guild '89: Director (Stone); Golden Globes '90: Actor—Drama (Cruise), Director (Stone), Film—Drama, Screenplay.

Born Reckless ½ **1959** Van Doren plays a singer working the rodeo circuit who falls for aging rider Richards. Not bad enough to be funny, however, Van Doren shows an incredible lack of talent while singing several tunes. ♫ Song of the Rodeo; Born Reckless; A Little Longer; Home Type Girl; Separate the Men from the Boys; Something to Dream About; You, Lovable You. **79m/B VHS.** Mamie Van Doren, Jeff Richards, Arthur Hunnicutt, Carol Ohmart, Donald (Don "Red") Barry, Nacho Galindo; *D:* Howard W. Koch.

Born Romantic **2000 (R)** Six lonely Londoners converge at a salsa club hoping to find a little romance. There's screwy Jocelyn (McCormack), no-nonsense Mo (Horrocks), uptight Eleanor (Williams), would-be Lothario Frank (Ferguson), awkward Eddie (Mistry), and lovelorn Fergus (Morrissey). Cabbie Jimmy (Lester) offers advice. Enjoyable (if predictable) romantic comedy. **97m/C VHS, DVD.** *GB* Craig Ferguson, Adrian Lester, Catherine McCormack, Jimi Mistry, David Morrissey, Olivia Williams, Jane Horrocks, Hermione Norris, Ian Hart, Kenneth Cranham, Paddy Considine; *D:* David Kane; *W:* David Kane; *C:* Robert Alazraki; *M:* Simon Boswell.

Born to Be Bad ½ **1950** Fontaine, an opportunistic woman who was b-b-born to be b-b-bad, attempts to steal a wealthy business man away from his wife while carrying on an affair with a novelist. Ray's direction (he's best known for "Rebel Without a Cause," filmed five years later) prevents the film from succumbing to standard Hollywood formula. **93m/B VHS.** Joan Fontaine, Robert Ryan, Zachary Scott, Joan Leslie, Mel Ferrer; *D:* Nicholas Ray.

Born to Be Wild **1938** A pair of truck drivers are commissioned to deliver a shipment of dynamite. The dynamite will be used to destroy a dam, preventing the surrounding land from falling into the hands of unscrupulous land barons. Good action picture thanks to the cast. **66m/B VHS, DVD.** Ralph Byrd, Doris Weston, Ward Bond, Robert Emmett Keane, Bentley Hewlett, Charles Williams; *D:* Joseph Kane.

Born to Be Wild ½ **1995 (PG)** Rebellious teenager Rick (Hornoff) befriends Katie, the three-year-old gorilla his behavioral scientist mom (Shaver) is studying. When Katie's owner (Boyle) decides she would make a better sideshow attraction than science project, Rick busts her out and they head for the Canadian border. Animal slapstick and bodily function jokes ensue as the chase continues. "Free Willy"-inspired plot and primate hijinks should keep young kids interested, but anyone over the age of nine probably won't be too impressed. **98m/C VHS, DVD.** Thomas F. Wilson, Wil Horneff, Helen Shaver, Peter Boyle, Jean Marie Barnwell, John C. McGinley, Marvin J. McIntyre; *D:* John Gray; *W:* John Bunzel, Paul Young; *C:* Donald M. Morgan.

Born to Boogie *Marc Bolan and T-Rex: Born to Boogie* **1972** A concert, a chronicle, and a tribute, "Born To Boogie" is about Marc Bolan and his band T. Rex. The film, which features concert footage from a 1972 concert at the Wembley Empire Pool in London, chronicles the glitter rock era and the next wave of British rock and roll, and pays tribute to Bolan, who died in 1977 just as he was starting a comeback. Ringo Starr and Elton John join T. Rex in the studio for "Children of the Revolution" and "Tutti-Frutti" as well as a psychadelic soiree where Bolan plays acoustic versions of his hits. This film was never released in the United States. **75m/C VHS, DVD.** Marc Bolan, Elton John, Ringo Starr; *D:* Ringo Starr.

Born to Dance ½ **1936** A quintessential MGM 1930s dance musical, wherein a beautiful dancer gets a sailor and a big break in a show. Great songs by Cole Porter sung in a less than great manner by a gangly Stewart. Powell's first starring vehicle. ♫ Love Me Love My Pekinese; I've Got You Under My Skin; Hey Babe Hey; Easy to Love; Rolling Home; Rap Tap on Wood; Entrance of Lucy James; Swingin' the Jinx Away. **108m/B VHS.** Eleanor Powell, James Stewart, Virginia Bruce, Una Merkel, Frances Langford, Sid Silvers, Raymond Walburn, Reginald Gardiner, Buddy Ebsen; *D:* Roy Del Ruth; *M:* Cole Porter, Cole Porter.

Born to Kill *Lady of Deceit* **1947** A ruthless killer marries a girl for her money. Minor tough-as-nails film noir exemplifying Tierney's stone-faced human-devil film persona. **92m/B VHS, DVD.** Lawrence Tierney, Claire Trevor, Walter Slezak, Elisha Cook Jr.; *D:* Robert Wise.

Born to Lose **1999** The Spoilers are an L.A. punk back led by singer Stevie Monroe (Rye). They're an underground success but can't break out of the music ghetto until public relations gal Lisa (Ashton) takes an interest in Stevie. Too bad she's a junkie who pulls the singer into a downward spiral that effectively destroys the band as well. Filmed in a mock-documentary style. **80m/C VHS, DVD.** Joseph Rye, Elyse Ashton, Francis Fallon; *D:* Doug Cawker; *W:* Doug Cawker, Howard Roth; *C:* John Rhode; *M:* Greg Kuehn.

Born to Race **1988 (R)** In the world of competitive auto racing, a beautiful engineer is kidnapped for her new controversial engine design. **95m/C VHS.** Joseph Bottoms, George Kennedy, Marc Singer, Marla Heasly; *D:* James Fargo.

Born to Ride **1991 (PG)** A biker rebel joins the Army prior to WWII in order to escape a prison term after a good ol' boy brush with the law. He shuns Army discipline, but proves himself in action as the leader of a scout troup for the Army's motorcycle cavalry brigade. Available with Spanish subtitles. **88m/C VHS.** John Stamos, John Stockwell, Teri Polo, Kris Kamm; *D:* Graham Baker.

Born to Run ½ **1993** Nicky Donatello (Grieco) is a Brooklyn street drag racer who gets mixed up with the mob while trying to rescue his no-account brother. But he still finds time to fall for an uptown model who also happens to be the mobster's girlfriend. **97m/C VHS.** Richard Grieco, Jay Acovone, Shelli Lether, Christian Campbell, Brent Stait, Martin Cummins, Wren Roberts, Joe Cortese; *D:* Albert Magnoli; *W:* Randall Badat. **TV**

Born to Win ½ *Addict* **1971 (R)** A New York hairdresser with an expensive drug habit struggles through life in this well-made comedy drama. Excellent acting from fine cast, and interestingly photographed. Not well received when first released, but worth a look. **90m/C VHS, DVD.** George Segal, Karen Black, Paula Prentiss, Hector Elizondo, Robert De Niro, Jay Fletcher; *D:* Ivan Passer; *W:* Ivan Passer, David Scott Milton; *C:* Jack Priestley; *M:* William S. Fisher.

Born Under Libra *Motevalede Mahe Mehr* **2001** In Tehran, Daniel falls in love with fellow university student Mahtab, whose father is pushing for segregated classes. Daniel associates with the religious while Mahtab sides with the reformers. Despite their differences, the romance blossoms but trouble has them fleeing the city. Farsi with subtitles. **94m/C DVD.** *IA* Mohammad Reza Forutan, Mitra Hajjar; *D:* Ahmad Reza Darvish; *W:* Ahmad Reza Darvish; *C:* Adam Herschman; *M:* Mohammad Reza Aligholi.

Born Wild ½ **1995 (PG)** Documentary filmmaker Christine Shaye (Shields) has just gotten her first important assignment from overbearing boss Dan Walker (Sheen), which is to capture the beauty of Africa. Christine arrives at the South African game preserve of Londolozi where she meets passionate conservationist John Varty (who plays himself). Varty has filmed one leopard family for 12 years but when the mother leopard is killed, he violates his own ethical code when he rescues her two orphaned cubs. **98m/C VHS.** Brooke Shields, Martin Sheen, John Varty, David Keith; *D:* Duncan McLachlan; *W:* Duncan McLachlan, Andrea Buck.

Born Yesterday ½ **1950** Ambitious junk dealer Harry Brock (Crawford) is in love with smart but uneducated Billie Dawn (Holliday). He hires newspaperman Paul Verrall (Holden) to teach her the finer points of etiquette. During their sessions, they fall in love and Billie realizes how she has been used by Brock. She retaliates against him and gets to deliver that now-famous line: "Do me a favor, drop dead." Holliday is a solid gold charmer as the not-so-dumb blonde, in the role she originated in Garson Kanin's Broadway play. Remade in 1993. **103m/B VHS, DVD.** Judy Holliday, Broderick Crawford, William Holden, Howard St. John, Frank Otto, Larry Oliver, Barbara Brown; *D:* George Cukor; *W:* Albert Mannheimer; *C:* Joseph Walker; *M:* Frederick "Friedrich" Hollander. Oscars '50: Actress (Holliday); Golden Globes '51: Actress—Mus./Comedy (Holliday).

Born Yesterday **1993 (PG)** Remake of the 1950 classic suffers in comparison, particularly Griffith, who has the thankless task of surpassing (or even meeting) Judy Holliday's Oscar-winning mark as not-so-dumb blonde Billie Dawn. Her intellectual inadequacies are glaring when she hits the political world of D.C. with obnoxious tycoon boyfriend Goodman. To save face, he hooks her up with a journalist (Johnson) willing to coach her in Savvy 101, a la Eliza Doolittle. What worked well in post-WWII America seems sadly outdated today; stick with the original. **102m/C VHS, DVD.** Melanie Griffith, John Goodman, Don Johnson, Edward Herrmann, Max Perlich, Fred Dalton Thompson, Nora Dunn, Benjamin C. Bradlee, Sally Quinn, Michael Ensign, William Frankfather, Celeste Yarnall, Meg Wittner; *D:* Luis Mandoki; *W:* Douglas McGrath; *C:* Lajos Koltai; *M:* George Fenton.

Borom Sarret **1966** One day in the life of a cart-driver in the bustling city of Dakar. As the small details and cumulative indignities of his life compound, the film achieves a haunting and precise sense of outrage that grows organically out of the near-documentary images. Doesn't aspire to the same richness and complexity that some of Sembene's later features reached, but it remains not only a pioneering work of African cinema, but an early example of the cinematic skills of a master. Available as part of the "Black Girl" DVD. **20m/B DVD.** *D:* Ousmane Sembene.

Borough of Kings **1998 (R)** Jimmy O'Conner (Stanek) is trying to get away from a life of crime in Brooklyn but the ties are hard to cut. Similar stories have been told dozens of times before. This little independent production has a strong spirit and commitment to the characters on its side, which outweigh its predictability. **95m/C DVD.** Philip Bosco, Jim Stanek, Kerry Butler, Joseph Lyle Taylor, Erik Jensen, Patrick Newall, Olympia Dukakis; *D:* Elyse Lewin; *W:* Patrick Newall; *C:* Nils Kenaston; *M:* Alan Elliott.

The Borrower **1989 (R)** An exiled unstable mutant insect alien serial killer (you know the type) must switch heads with human beings regularly to survive. This colorful, garish gorefest has humor and attitude, but never develops behind the basic grossout situation. **97m/C VHS.** Rae Dawn Chong, Don Gordon, Antonio Fargas, Tom Towler; ***D:*** John McNaughton.

The Borrowers 1993 Excellent TV adaptation of the May Norton children's classics "The Borrowers" and "The Borrowers Afield." This miniature family (about mouse-size) live beneath the floorboards of an English house and borrow what they need to survive from the normal-sized human inhabitants. Problems come when the teeny family are discovered and must make their way to a new home. Sweet and humorous. **199m/C VHS.** *GB* Ian Holm, Penelope Wilton, Rebecca Callard, Paul Cross, Sian Phillips, Tony Haygarth; ***D:*** John Henderson; ***W:*** Richard Carpenter; ***C:*** Clive Tickner; ***M:*** Howard Goodall. **TV**

The Borrowers 1/2 **1997 (PG)** Charming big-screen, big-budget tale about the little people who live under the floor. The British, elfin, and about four inch tall Clock family, headed by papa Pod (Broadbent) lives hidden in the walls of the home of the normal-sized American Lenders and exist by "borrowing" objects from their human's household. When an evil lawyer (Goodman), also American, threatens their happiness, the Borrowers bond with young Peter Lender (Pierce) who "discovers" them and volunteers to help them save their way of life. This remake focuses mainly on the impressive special effects, lending a modern look and appeal. Goodman is lovably evil in that wonderfully Snidely Whiplash way. Based on the children's books of Mary Norton. **86m/C VHS, DVD.** *GB* John Goodman, Hugh Laurie, Jim Broadbent, Mark Williams, Celia Imrie, Bradley Michael Pierce, Raymond Pickard, Aden (John) Gillett, Ruby Wax, Flora Newbigin, Tom Felton, Doon Mackichan; ***D:*** Peter Hewitt; ***W:*** John Kamps, Gavin Scott; ***C:*** John Fenner, Trevor Brooker; ***M:*** Harry Gregson-Williams.

Borsalino **1970 (R)** Delon and Belmondo are partners in crime in this seriocomic film about gang warfare in 1930s Marseilles. The costumes, settings, and music perfectly capture the mood of the period. Followed by a sequel "Borsalino and Co." Based on "The Bandits of Marseilles" by Eugene Saccomano. **124m/C VHS.** *FR* Jean-Paul Belmondo, Alain Delon, Michel Bouquet, Catherine Rouvel, Francoise Christophe, Corinne Marchand; ***D:*** Jacques Deray; ***W:*** Jacques Deray, Jean Cau, Claude Sautet, Jean-Claude Carriere; ***C:*** Jean-Jacques Tarbes; ***M:*** Claude Bolling.

Borstal Boy 1/2 **2000** Irish teen, IRA partisan, (and future writer) Brendan Behan (Hatosy) is caught smuggling dynamite into Britain and sent to reform school, known as a "borstal," in East Anglia in 1939. Naturally, he learns that all Brits aren't the devil incarnate as he befriends gay Cockney sailor Charlie (Millwall) and falls in love with fair-but-tough Warden Joyce's (York) daughter, Liz (Birthistle). Inspired by Behan's 1958 memoirs. **91m/C VHS, DVD.** *IR GB* Shawn Hatosy, Danny Dyer, Eva Birthistle, Michael York, Lee Ingleby, Robin Laing; ***D:*** Peter Sheridan; ***W:*** Peter Sheridan, Nye Heron; ***C:*** Ciaran Tanham; ***M:*** Stephen McKeon.

Boss 1/2 *The Black Bounty Killer; Boss Nigger; The Black Bounty Hunter* **1974 (PG)** Blaxploitation western parody with Williamson and Martin as a couple of bounty hunters tearing apart a town to find a fugitive. Relatively non-violent. **87m/C VHS.** Fred Williamson, D'Urville Martin, R.G. Armstrong, William (Bill) Smith, Carmen Hayworth, Barbara Leigh; ***D:*** Jack Arnold; ***W:*** Fred Williamson.

Boss Cowboy **1935** A cowboy shows who wears the chaps in his family when he kidnaps his girlfriend to prevent her from moving East. **51m/B VHS.** Buddy Roosevelt, Frances Morris, Sam Pierce, Fay McKenzie, Lafe (Lafayette) McKee; ***D:*** Victor Adamson.

The Boss Is Served *La Padrona e Servita* **1976** A mother (Berger) and three daughters, racked with debt, are forced to take in boarders. The lascivious man and teenage son want to be more than just boarders to the lovely Berger. In Italian with English subtitles. **95m/C VHS.** *IT* Senta Berger, Maurizio Arena, Bruno Zanin, Erika Blanc, Pina Cei, Angiolina Quinterno, Patrizia de Clara; ***D:*** Mario Lanfranchi; ***W:*** Mario Lanfranchi, Pupi Avati; ***C:*** Pasquale Fanetti; ***M:*** Stelvio Cipriani.

Boss of Big Town **1943** Gangsters try to infiltrate the milk industry in this standard crime drama. **65m/B VHS, DVD.** John Litel, Florence Rice, H.B. Warner, Jean Brooks, John Miljan, Mary Gordon, John Maxwell; ***D:*** Arthur Dreifuss.

Boss of Boomtown 1/2 **1944** Steve Hazard (Cameron) and Jim Ward (Tyler) are cavalry sergeants who go from friendly rivals to apparent enemies. Jim re-enlists but Steve has been persuaded by Treasury agent Cornwall (Flint) to help him investigate a stagecoach robbery of a mine payroll. Steve must pose as an outlaw but since Jim doesn't know he's working undercover, he jeopardizes the plan by arresting his former compatriot. **58m/B DVD.** Tom Tyler, Rod Cameron, Fuzzy Knight, Sam Flint, Vivian Austin, Jack Ingram, Robert V. Barron, Max Wagner; ***D:*** Ray Taylor; ***W:*** William Lively; ***C:*** William Sickner.

Boss of Bosses 1/2 **1999** Yet another in a long line of Mafia portrayals and betrayals but this one is flat and uninspired. Paul Castellano (Palminteri) takes organized crime into the white-collar level from the streets into legit businesses but the world is still violent, plagued by internal feuds and the feds sniffing around. Castellano wound up being the last public Mafia hit (arranged by John Gotti)—outside a New York steak house. **94m/C VHS, DVD.** Chazz Palminteri, Daniel Benzali, Jay O. Sanders, Clancy Brown, Al Ruscio, Steven Bauer, Angela Alvarado, Sonny Marinelli; ***D:*** Dwight Little; ***W:*** Jere P. Cunningham; ***C:*** Brian Reynolds; ***M:*** John Altman. **CABLE**

Boss of Bullion City 1/2 **1941** A crooked sheriff is exposed by Brown and sidekick Knight in this sagebrush saga. Based on a story by Arthur St. Claire. **61m/B VHS, DVD.** Johnny Mack Brown, Fuzzy Knight, Maria Montez, Earle Hodgins, Harry Woods; ***D:*** Ray Taylor; ***W:*** Victor McLeod, Arthur St. Claire.

The Boss of It All *Direktoren for Det Hele* **2006** Von Trier trades in polemics for a corporate comedy. Ravn (Gantzler), the director of an IT firm, decides to hire actor Kristoffer (Albinus) to portray the non-existent president of his company so he can sell out to a larger organization. But thanks to Kristoffer's overacting, the deal gets put on hold for a week and they must keep up the charade. The film was shot by Von Tier's experimental Automavision, a computer-controlled camera, and looks fairly awful. Danish with subtitles. **99m/C DVD.** *CZ FR IT SW* Peter Gantzler, Jens Albinus, Fridrik Thor Fridriksson, Iben Hjejle, Sofie Grabol, Benedikt Erlingsson; ***D:*** Lars von Trier; ***W:*** Lars von Trier.

Boss of Rawhide **1944** The Texas Rangers fight for law and order in the old west despite odds against them. **60m/B VHS.** Dave O'Brien, James Newill, Guy Wilkerson, Nell O'Day, Edward Cassidy, Jack Ingram, Billy Bletcher, Charles "Blackie" King, George Chesebro; ***D:*** Elmer Clifton; ***W:*** Elmer Clifton; ***C:*** Robert E. Cline; ***M:*** Lee Zahler, Oliver Drake, Herbert Myers, Dave O'Brien, James Newill.

Boss' Son **1978** Worthwhile coming-of-age tale about a young man who learns more than he bargained for about life when he goes to work for his father in the family carpet business. Dad feels he should work his way up through the ranks and makes him a delivery man. The young man meets reality head on and must deal with the injustices of the world around him. Independently filmed by director/writer Roth. **97m/C VHS.** Rita Moreno, James Darren, Asher Brauner, Rudy Solari, Henry Sanders, Richie Havens, Piper Laurie, Elena Verdugo; ***D:*** Bobby Roth; ***W:*** Bobby Roth; ***C:*** Alfonso Beato.

The Boss' Wife **1986 (R)** A young stockbroker attempts to fix what's wrong with his life by maneuvering sexually with the boss' wife, and complications set in. **83m/C VHS.** Daniel Stern, Arielle Dombasle, Christopher Plummer, Martin Mull, Melanie Mayron, Lou Jacobi; ***D:*** Ziggy Steinberg; ***M:*** Bill Conti.

Bossa Nova 1/2 **1999 (R)** Sexy romantic comedy set to the beat of sultry Brazil. Middleaged American widow Mary (Irivng) teaches English in Rio and catches the romantic eye of Pedro (Fagundes), an attorney who has been dumped by his wife. Meanwhile, Mary's soccer-playing pupil Acacio (Borges) is trying to become a teacher's pet before transferring his affections to Pedro's clerk Sharon (Antonelli), who just happens to be involved with Pedro's half-brother (Cardoso). And the romantic complications just keep building. Soundtrack is filled with the songs of bossa nova composer Antonio Carlos Jobim. Based on the novel "Miss Simpson" by Sergio Sant'Anna. **95m/C VHS, DVD.** *BR* Amy Irving, Antonio Fagundes, Alexandre Borges, Debora Bloch, Pedro Cardoso, Alberto De Mendoza, Stephen Tobolowsky, Drica Moraes, Giovanna Antonelli, Rogerio Cardoso; ***D:*** Bruno Barreto; ***W:*** Alexandre Machado, Fernanda Young; ***C:*** Pascal Rabaud; ***M:*** Eumir Deodato.

Boston Kickout **1995** A quartet of teenaged friends/losers struggle to grow up in a bleak concrete town outside London. There are neglected girlfriends, dysfunctional families, menial jobs, petty crime, emotional disasters—and some faint glimmer of hope for at least a couple of the lads. Title refers to a destructive game the boys play. **105m/C VHS, DVD.** *GB* John Simm, Andrew Lincoln, Richard Hanson, Nathan Valente, Emer McCourt, Marc Warren, Derek Martin, Vincent Phillips, Natalie Davies; ***D:*** Paul Hills; ***W:*** Paul Hills, Diane Whitley, Roberto Troni; ***C:*** Roger Bonnici; ***M:*** Robert Hartshorne.

The Boston Strangler 1/2 **1968** Based on Gerold Frank's bestselling factual book about the deranged killer who terrorized Boston for about a year and a half. Traces events from first killing to prosecution. Curtis, going against type, is compelling in title role. **116m/C VHS, DVD.** Tony Curtis, Henry Fonda, George Kennedy, Murray Hamilton, Mike Kellin, George Voskovec, William Hickey, James Brolin, Hurd Hatfield, William Marshall, Jeff Corey, Sally Kellerman; ***D:*** Richard Fleischer; ***W:*** Edward Anhalt.

The Boston Strangler: The Untold Story 1/2 **2008 (R)** Faustino stars as Albert De Salvo, a smalltime criminal who confesses to the serial sex killings that terrified Boston in the early 1960s. De Salvo decides to take credit for the murders while in jail on another conviction but Detective John Marsden (Divoff) isn't certain they've got the right perp or that the crimes were committed by just one man. **90m/C DVD.** David Faustino, Andrew Divoff, Corin "Corky" Nemec, Joe Torry, Kostas Sommer; ***D:*** Michael Feifer; ***W:*** Michael Feifer; ***C:*** Hank Baumert Jr.; ***M:*** Andres Boulton. **VIDEO**

The Bostonians 1/2 **1984 (PG)** A faith healer's daughter is forced to choose between the affections of a militant suffragette and a young lawyer in 19th Century Boston. Based on Henry James' classic novel. **120m/C VHS, DVD.** Christopher Reeve, Vanessa Redgrave, Madeleine Potter, Jessica Tandy, Nancy Marchand, Wesley Addy, Linda Hunt, Wallace Shawn; ***D:*** James Ivory; ***W:*** Ruth Prawer Jhabvala; ***C:*** Walter Lassally. Natl. Soc. Film Critics '84: Actress (Redgrave).

Botany Bay **1953** A rousing costumer about a convict ship in the 1700s that, after a trying voyage, lands in Australia, wherein a framed doctor conquers the local plague. From the novel by Charles Nordoff. **99m/C VHS.** Alan Ladd, James Mason, Patricia Medina, Cedric Hardwicke; ***D:*** John Farrow.

Botched 1/2 **2007** Odd and not particularly successful mix of horror, comedy, and crime. American Ritchie (Dorff) must be a lousy professional thief because his jobs keep going wrong. He's sent to Moscow to steal an antique cross that's kept in a bank building and is given a couple of inept locals for backup. Naturally their getaway gets screwed and they wind up with hostages and are diverted to the building's unused 13th floor. They find out it's been abandoned for a very good reason. **94m/C DVD.** Stephen Dorff, Sean Pertwee, Jamie Foreman, Russell Smith, Jaime Murray, Bronagh Gallagher, Edward Baker-Duly; ***D:*** Kit Ryan; ***W:*** Derek Boyle, Eamon Friel, Raymond Friel; ***C:*** Bryan Loftus; ***M:*** Tom Green. **VIDEO**

Bottle Rocket 1/2 **1995 (R)** A trio of inexperienced but aspiring criminals attempt to make their mark on the world in suburban Dallas. Newcomers Wilson, who plays the group's ambitious leader Dignan, and Anderson penned this smart ensemble piece first as a 13-minute black and white short. A subsequent showing at the Sundance Film Festival got the attention of producer James L. Brooks ("Broadcast News"). Film got the backing to go feature length with Anderson directing, and deservedly so, with its fresh dialogue and surprising warmth. **91m/C VHS, DVD, Blu-ray Disc.** Ned Dowd, Owen Wilson, Luke Wilson, Robert Musgrave, Lumi Cavazos, James Caan, Andrew Wilson, Jim Ponds; ***D:*** Wes Anderson; ***W:*** Wes Anderson, Owen Wilson; ***C:*** Robert Yeoman; ***M:*** Mark Mothersbaugh. MTV Movie Awards '96: New Filmmaker (Anderson).

Bottle Shock **2008 (PG-13)** A mostly-based-on-real-life story taken from an historic 1976 blind wine competition arranged by wine elitist Englishman Steven Spurrier (Rickman) and his struggling Parisian wine business, pitting French wines against the unsung vineyards of California's Napa Valley, including former lawyer Jim Barrett's (Pullman) Chateau Montelena. While Jim clashes with his surfer son Bo (Pine, sporting a disturbingly unrealistic wig), Bo vies with his friend and coworker Gustavo (Rodriguez) for the attention of intern Samantha (Taylor). Though the contest's outcome is expected and the general pace is slow, director Miller ably squeezes out some patriotism-inspired moments. **110m/C DVD.** *US* Alan Rickman, Bill Pullman, Chris Pine, Rachael Taylor, Freddy Rodriguez, Eliza Dushku, Dennis Farina, Miguel (Michael) Sandoval, Bradley Whitford, Joe Regalbuto; ***D:*** Randall Miller; ***W:*** Randall Miller, Jody Savin, Ross Schwartz; ***C:*** Michael Ozier; ***M:*** Mark Adler.

The Bottom of the Sea **2003** Dark comedic thriller has an obsessively jealous young architect stalking his girlfriend's secret lover on one fateful night. An unexpected climax and easy-on-the-eyes actors make this Argentinean endeavor cinematically satisfying. Subtitled. **95m/C DVD.** *AR* Dolores Fonzi, Daniel Hendler, Gustavo Garzon, Ramiro Aguero; ***D:*** Damien Szifron; ***W:*** Damien Szifron. **VIDEO**

Bottoms Up **WOOF!** **2006 (R)** Bottom of the barrel is more like it. Owen (Mewes) heads to L.A. to enter a bartending contest in hopes of using the winnings to save his dad's restaurant. Things don't exactly work out and Owen's uncle (Keith) gets him a job with actor Hayden (Hallisay) and his vapid girlfriend, Lisa (a typecast Hilton). When Owen learns a few tabloid-worthy secrets, he has to decide whether to sell out his new pals for the much-needed cash. Even Mewes can't work up much enthusiasm for this mess. **89m/C DVD.** Jason Mewes, Paris Hilton, David Keith, Phil Morris, Brian Hallisay, Jon Abrahams, Tim Thomerson; ***D:*** Erik MacArthur; ***W:*** Erik MacArthur, Nick Ballo; ***C:*** Massimo Zeri. **VIDEO**

Boudu Saved from Drowning 1/2 *Boudu Sauve des Eaux* **1932** A suicidal tramp completely disrupts the wealthy household of the man that saves him from drowning. A gentle but sardonic farce from the master filmmaker. Remade in 1986 as "Down and Out In Beverly Hills." **87m/B VHS, DVD.** *FR* Michel Simon, Charles Granval, Jean Daste, Marcelle Hainia, Severine Lerczinska, Jacques Becker; ***D:*** Jean Renoir; ***W:*** Jean Renoir; ***C:*** Marcel Lucien.

Bought and Sold **2003** Coming of age tale set in Jersey City. Ray Ray Morales (Sardina) is working for minimum wage at a shoe store but really wants to buy some pawnshop turntables so he can be a DJ. So he gets a second job with local loan shark Chunks (Grifasi), who wants him to keep an eye on elderly pawnshop owner Kutty (Margulies) who owes Chunks money. Soon Ray Ray is falling for Kutty's niece, Ruby (Neshat), and getting too involved. When Kutty can't meet his payments, Ray Ray has to make some decisions about what's really important to him. **92m/C** David Margulies, Joe Grifasi, Rafael Sardina, Marjan Neshat, Frank Harts, Christina Ablaza, Anthony Chisholm; ***D:*** Michael Tolajian; ***W:*** Michael Tolajian; ***C:*** Kip Bogdahn; ***M:*** Joe Delia.

Boulevard 1/2 **1994 (R)** Jennefer (Wuhrer) is forced to give her baby up for adoption, after escaping from an abusive husband, and make her way on the city's mean streets. She meets prostitute Ola (Chong), who decides to look after the naif and protect Jennefer from violent pimp Hassan (Phillips). But Ola gets into trouble with tough cop

Claren (Henriksen) and soon Jennefer must survive on her own—against both Hassan and her vengeful husband. Woman empowerment, complete with standard cliches. **96m/C VHS.** Kari Wuhrer, Rae Dawn Chong, Lou Diamond Phillips, Lance Henriksen, Joel Bissonnette; ***D:*** Penelope Buitenhuis; ***W:*** Rae Dawn Chong; ***M:*** Ian Thomas.

Boulevard Nights **1979 (R)** A young Latino man tries to escape his neighborhood's streetgang violence, while his older brother is sucked into it. Music by Schifrin, known for the "Mission: Impossible" theme. **102m/C VHS.** Richard Yniguez, Danny De La Paz, Marta DuBois, Carmen Zapata, Victor Millan; ***D:*** Michael Pressman; ***C:*** John Bailey; ***M:*** Lalo Schifrin.

Boulevard of Broken Dreams **1988 (PG-13)** Successful Hollywood screenwriter Tom Garfield (Waters) returns to his native Australia to figure out how his life got so screwed up. His estranged wife is living with someone else and his daughter barely remembers him. Affecting look at personal priorities versus success. **95m/C VHS.** *AU* John Waters, Kim Gyngell, Penelope Stewart; ***D:*** Pino Amenta.

Bounce 1/2 **2000 (PG-13)** Ad exec Affleck swaps his airline ticket with a stranger who's anxious to get home to his wife. But since no good deed goes unpunished, the plane crashes and the man is killed. The guilt-stricken Affleck visits the stranger's widow (Paltrow) and winds up falling in love with her, only she doesn't know about their unfortunate connection. Okay, the plot is contrived, predictable, and a little schmaltzy, but it somehow avoids maudlin, and takes pains to make the emotions real. In this, director Roos is aided greatly by Affleck, who turns in some of his best work to date, and Paltrow, who seems less actress-y in an understated, smart performance. The two leads were said to be an item during filming. **105m/C VHS, DVD.** Gwyneth Paltrow, Ben Affleck, Natasha Henstridge, Jennifer Grey, Tony Goldwyn, Joe Morton, David Paymer, Johnny Galecki, Alex D. Linz, Juan Garcia, Sam Robards, Julia Campbell, Michael Laskin, John Levin, David Dorfman; ***D:*** Don Roos; ***W:*** Don Roos; ***C:*** Robert Elswit; ***M:*** Mychael Danna.

Bound **1996 (R)** Ex-con Corky (Gershon) is busy fixing up her new apartment after serving five years for robbery. Her next-door neighbors are Caesar (Pantoliano), a neurotic, money-laundering mobster, and his sexy girlfriend, a seemingly dumb brunette named Violet (Tilly). The femme twosome hook up (in and out of bed) and hatch a plan to steal two million freshly laundered dollars from Caesar, who goes ballistic when he discovers the money gone. It's a flashy—but not substantive—thriller. Directorial debut for the brothers Wachowski. **107m/C VHS, DVD.** Gina Gershon, Jennifer Tilly, Joe Pantoliano, John P. Ryan, Barry Kivel, Christopher Meloni, Peter Spellos, Richard Sarafian, Mary Mara, Susie Bright, Ivan Kane, Kevin M. Richardson, Gene Borkan; ***D:*** Andy Wachowski, Larry Wachowski; ***W:*** Andy Wachowski, Larry Wachowski; ***C:*** Bill Pope; ***M:*** Don Davis.

Bound and Gagged: A Love Story **1993 (R)** For some reason, Elizabeth (Saltarelli), who is desperate for a husband, thinks that she might increase her chances of finding one if she kidnaps her friend Leslie (Allen) and goes on a weird wild goose chase through Minnesota with the hostage and her hopeless partner-in-crime, Cliff (Denton). Go figure. **96m/C VHS, DVD.** Ginger Lynn Allen, Karen Black, Chris Denton, Elizabeth Saltarelli, Mary Ella Ross, Chris Mulkey; ***D:*** Daniel Appleby; ***W:*** Daniel Appleby; ***C:*** Dean Lent; ***M:*** William Murphy.

Bound by Lies 1/2 **2005** Detectives Max Garrett (Baldwin) and Eddie Fulton (Whitfield) are assigned to protect Laura (Swanson)—a sexy photographer of erotic images—when a rash of serial murders linked to her work is uncovered. But Garrett puts himself in danger by falling for her. **85m/C VHS, DVD.** Kristy Swanson, Stephen Baldwin, Charles Malik Whitfield, Natassia Malthe, Kevin Chamberlin, Joel Brooks, Tracy Howe; ***D:*** Valerie Landsburg; ***W:*** D. Alvelo, Leland Zaitz; ***C:*** Maximo Munzi. **VIDEO**

Bound for Glory 1/2 **1976 (PG)** The award-winning biography of American folk singer Woody Guthrie set against the backdrop of the Depression. Superb portrayal of the spirit and feelings of the period featuring many of his songs encased in the incidents that inspired them. Haskell Wexler's award-winning camera work is superbly expressive. **149m/C VHS, DVD.** David Carradine, Ronny Cox, Melinda Dillon, Randy Quaid; ***D:*** Hal Ashby; ***W:*** Robert Getchell; ***C:*** Haskell Wexler. Oscars '76: Cinematog., Orig. Song Score and/or Adapt.; L.A. Film Critics '76: Cinematog.; Natl. Bd. of Review '76: Actor (Carradine); Natl. Soc. Film Critics '76: Cinematog.

The Bounty 1/2 **1984 (PG)** A new version of "Mutiny on the Bounty," with emphasis on a more realistic relationship between Fletcher Christian and Captain Bligh—and a more sympathetic portrayal of the captain, too. The sensuality of Christian's relationship with a Tahitian beauty also receives greater importance. **130m/C VHS, DVD.** Mel Gibson, Anthony Hopkins, Laurence Olivier, Edward Fox, Daniel Day-Lewis, Bernard Hill, Philip Davis, Liam Neeson; ***D:*** Roger Donaldson; ***W:*** Robert Bolt; ***C:*** Arthur Ibbetson; ***M:*** Vangelis.

The Bounty Hunter 1/2 *The Bounty* **2010 (PG-13)** This trite romantic comedy inflicts a predictable plot, grating dialogue, and a plodding pace—a multiple offender. Bounty hunter Milo (Butler) is overjoyed when he finds out his next assignment is to bring in his ex-wife Nicole (Aniston), a reporter who missed her court date to look into a suspicious suicide. The majority of the movie consists of the couple bickering and one-upping each other while evading goons trying to stop Nicole from discovering the truth. The two finally decide to work together and romance is rekindled, despite the fact that Aniston and Butler have less chemistry than a remedial science class. Watch the classic "His Girl Friday" to see how it's done correctly. **110m/C DVD.** Gerard Butler, Jennifer Aniston, Jason Sudeikis, Christine Baranski, Cathy Moriarty; ***D:*** Andy Tennant; ***W:*** Sarah Thorp; ***C:*** Oliver Bokelberg.

Bounty Hunter 2002 1/2 *2002: The Rape of Eden* **1994** A rogue virus kills most of the world's population and few of those remaining are completely immune. Slave trading in the capture and sale of immune survivors is a lucrative business and a bounty hunter's last assignment is to bring in a beautiful but deadly woman. **90m/C VHS.** Phil Nordell, Francine Lapensee, Vernon Wells, Jeff Conaway; ***D:*** Sam Auster; ***W:*** Sam Auster.

Bounty Hunters **1989 (R)** A man hunts down his friend's killer. **91m/C VHS.** Robert Ginty, Bo Hopkins, Loeta Waterdown; ***D:*** Robert Ginty.

Bounty Hunters **1996 (R)** Rival bounty hunters (and ex-lovers) Jersey Bellini (Dudikoff) and B.B. Mitchell (Howard) join forces to capture bail-jumping, stolen-car king Delmos (Ratner), who's also the target of mob hitmen. Gunplay and car chases. **98m/C VHS, DVD.** Michael Dudikoff, Lisa Howard, Benjamin Ratner; ***D:*** George Erschbamer; ***W:*** George Erschbamer; ***C:*** A.J. Vesak; ***M:*** Norman Orenstein.

Bounty Hunters 2: Hardball *Hardball* **1997 (R)** A bounty hunter and his female partner tick off the mob by foiling a heist and now must fend off hired killers looking for revenge. **97m/C VHS, DVD.** Michael Dudikoff, Lisa Howard, Steve Bacic, Tony Curtis; ***D:*** George Erschbamer; ***W:*** George Erschbamer, Jeff Barmash, Michael Ellis; ***C:*** Brian Pearson; ***M:*** Leon Aronson. **VIDEO**

The Bounty Man **1972** A bounty hunter brings an outlaw in, robbing him of his freedom and his girlfriend. **74m/C VHS.** Clint Walker, Richard Basehart, Margot Kidder, Arthur Hunnicutt, John Ericson, Gene Evans; ***D:*** John Llewellyn Moxey.

Bounty Tracker 1/2 **1993 (R)** Johnny Damone (Lamas) is a bounty-hunter in pursuit of the killer-for-hire who murdered his brother. This personal vendetta leads to an action-packed martial arts showdown between Johnny and his cold-blooded prey. **90m/C VHS.** Lorenzo Lamas, Matthias Hues, Eugene Robert Glazer, Cyndi Pass, Eric Mansker, Judd Omen, Eddie Frias, George Perez; ***D:*** Kurt Anderson.

Bouquet of Barbed Wire 1/2 **1976** Overlong soaper revolves around a weathly family and their hidden secrets: incest and infidelity. On three tapes. **330m/C VHS.** Frank Finlay, Susan Penhaligon, Deborah Grant, Sheila Allen, James Aubrey; ***D:*** Tom Wharmby.

The Bourne Identity **1988** Chamberlain stars as an amnesiac trying to piece together the fragments of his memory. Is he U.S. espionage agent Jason Bourne or an international terrorist? Aided by Smith (the kidnap victim who falls in love with her captor), the two traverse Europe trying to escape the spy network out to assassinate the mystery man who knows too little. Exciting miniseries adaptation of the Robert Ludlum thriller. **185m/C VHS, DVD.** Richard Chamberlain, Jaclyn Smith, Denholm Elliott, Anthony Quayle, Donald Moffat, Yorgo Voyagis; ***D:*** Roger Young; ***W:*** Carol Sobieski. **TV**

The Bourne Identity 1/2 **2002 (PG-13)** First-rate international espionage thriller loosely based on the first book (published in 1981) of Robert Ludlum's trilogy, previously filmed as a 1988 TV miniseries starring Richard Chamberlain. A young man (Damon) gets fished out of the ocean with a couple of bullet holes and amnesia—his only clue a numbered Swiss account. This reveals he has multiple identities, including that of Jason Bourne, who has an apartment in Paris. To get there, Bourne pays free-spirited Marie (Potente) for a ride. As Bourne tries to piece his past together, he learns he's a highly efficient assassin for a covert CIA operation and his boss (Cooper) considers him a rogue operative and is trying to kill him. **118m/C VHS, DVD, UMD, HD DVD.** *US* Matt Damon, Franka Potente, Chris Cooper, Brian Cox, Clive Owen, Julia Stiles, Gabriel Mann, Adewale Akinnuoye-Agbaje, Walton Goggins, Josh Hamilton, Tim Dutton; ***D:*** Doug Liman; ***W:*** Tony Gilroy, W(illiam) Blake Herron; ***C:*** Oliver Wood; ***M:*** John Powell.

The Bourne Supremacy **2004 (PG-13)** Warning! The easily-queasy should be wary of the hand-held camerawork and quick edits of the action sequences. Amnesiac CIA-trained assassin Jason Bourne (Damon) is now living quietly with girlfriend Marie (Potente) when he's targeted for death by Russian bad guys and made the patsy for a Berlin hit on a couple of agents. CIA officer Landy (Allen) and her boss (Cox) try to reel Bourne in while he tries to figure out just who wants him dead this time (and why). The non-stop action moves from India to Berlin to Amsterdam to Moscow, and while the plot eventually turns out to be simple enough, the chases are not. Damon once again proves adept as an action man while making Bourne an intelligent and oddly sympathetic character. Loosely adapted from the second book of Robert Ludlum's Bourne trilogy. **109m/C VHS, DVD, UMD, HD DVD.** *US* Matt Damon, Franka Potente, Joan Allen, Brian Cox, Marton Csokas, Gabriel Mann, Karel Roden, Julia Stiles, Karl Urban, Tomas Arana, Tim Griffin, Michelle Monaghan, Tom Gallop, John Bedford Lloyd, Ethan Sandler, Oksana Akinshina; ***D:*** Paul Greengrass; ***W:*** Tony Gilroy; ***C:*** Oliver Wood; ***M:*** John Powell.

The Bourne Ultimatum 1/2 **2007 (PG-13)** In this third (and final?) chapter Jason Bourne (Damon) continues his search for clues to to his past with Treadstone, the mothballed facility where he was trained. Now CIA official Vosen (Strathairn) wants to revive the project, and assigns agent Lundy (Allen) to eliminate Bourne. Meanwhile, Bourne is outmaneuvering cops, feds, spooks, and Interpol agents in Moscow, Paris, Madrid, Tangier, London, and New York. Smart, tense, and frenetic, with excellent performances from all involved. The only drawback is the confusion- and nausea-inducing camera work during the action sequences. **111m/C DVD, HD DVD.** *US* Matt Damon, Julia Stiles, Joan Allen, David Strathairn, Paddy Considine, Edgar Ramirez, Scott Glenn, Albert Finney, Tom Gallop, Corey Johnson, Daniel Bruhl, Colin Stinton, Joey Ansah; ***D:*** Paul Greengrass; ***W:*** Tony Gilroy, Scott Burns, George Nolfi; ***C:*** Oliver Wood; ***M:*** John Powell. Oscars '07: Film Editing, Sound, Sound FX Editing; British Acad. '07: Film Editing, Sound.

Boutique 1/2 **2004** Window dresser at a chic boutique in Tehran steals a pair of jeans for a girl he's interested in after she says she can't afford anything at the establishment. This is the beginning of a downward spiral in his life. Thoughtfully moving film makes startling observations of Iranian society. In Farsi with English subtitles. **113m/C DVD.** Mohammad Reza Golzar, Golshifteh Farahani, Reza Rooygari; ***D:*** Hamid Nematollah; ***W:*** Hamid Nematollah; ***C:*** Mahmoud Kalari; ***M:*** Fariborz Lachini. **VIDEO**

The Bowery **1933** Chuck Connors (Beery) owns a saloon on New York's Bowery in the 1890s and is a friendly rival to daredevil gambler Steve Brodie (Raft). Only things aren't so friendly when the men both fall for hard-luck dame Lucy (Wray). Connors proposes that Brodie jump off the Brooklyn Bridge (a feat he allegedly accomplished before) to impress Lucy and offers ownership of his saloon as added incentive. Cooper, who starred opposite Beery in 1931's "The Champ," plays streetwise orphan Swipes McGurk. **92m/B VHS.** Wallace Beery, George Raft, Fay Wray, Jackie Cooper, Pert Kelton; ***D:*** Raoul Walsh; ***W:*** Howard Estabrook; ***C:*** Barney McGill; ***M:*** Alfred Newman.

Bowery at Midnight 1/2 **1942** Lugosi plays a man who recycles criminals into zombies that commit crimes for his benefit. Bela and an intense mood can't quite save this pic. **60m/B VHS, DVD.** Bela Lugosi, Tom Neal, Dave O'Brien, Wanda McKay; ***D:*** Wallace Fox; ***W:*** Gerald Schnitzer; ***C:*** Mack Stengler; ***M:*** Edward Kay.

Bowery Blitzkrieg *Stand and Deliver* **1941** This lesser "East Side Kids" entry has Gorcey opting to enter the boxing ring rather than turn to crime. Needs more Huntz. **62m/B VHS, DVD.** Leo Gorcey, Huntz Hall, Bobby Jordan, Warren Hull, Charlotte Henry, Keye Luke; ***D:*** Wallace Fox.

Bowery Boys Meet the Monsters **1954** The infamous Bowery Boys display their usual hilarious hijinks in this comedy in which they confront a group of transplant-happy scientists. **65m/C VHS.** Leo Gorcey, Huntz Hall, Bernard Gorcey, Bennie Bartlett, Lloyd Corrigan; ***D:*** Edward L. Bernds.

Bowery Buckaroos **1947** The Bowery Boys take their act West in search of gold, meeting up with the usual amounts of goofy characters and hilarious misunderstandings. **66m/B VHS.** Leo Gorcey, Huntz Hall, Bobby Jordan, Gabriel Dell, William Benedict, David Gorcey, Julie Briggs, Bernard Gorcey, Chief Yowlachie, Iron Eyes Cody; ***D:*** William Beaudine.

Bowfinger *Bowfinger's Big Thing* **1999 (PG-13)** Martin stars as wannabe Hollywood player Bobby Bowfinger, who is desperate to break into the big time. His one hope is to convince action star Kit Ramsey (Murphy) to be in a cheesy sci-fi scare flick entitled "Chubby Rain." But Ramsey and his tyrannical New Age advisor Stricter (Stamp) want nothing to do with the movie. Bowfinger gets a crew together and stalks Ramsey through the streets of L.A., filming his every movement so that the material can be used in the movie. After his tactics send Ramsey to the "relaxation home," Bowfinger hires geeky lookalike Jiff (also Murphy) to take his place. The pairing of Martin and Murphy works well, and Frank Oz is an expert at directing offbeat comedies such as this. **96m/C VHS, DVD.** Steve Martin, Eddie Murphy, Christine Baranski, Heather Graham, Terence Stamp, Jamie Kennedy, Robert Downey Jr., Barry Newman; ***D:*** Frank Oz; ***W:*** Steve Martin; ***C:*** Ueli Steiger; ***M:*** David Newman.

Bowling for Columbine **2002 (R)** Moore takes on the trigger-happy American gun culture, as well as the media, the NRA, and Littleton, Colorado—the site of the Columbine High School killings—with his usual blend of satire and chutzpah. **120m/C VHS, DVD.** ***D:*** Michael Moore; ***W:*** Michael Moore. Oscars '02: Feature Doc.; Ind. Spirit '03: Feature Doc.; Writers Guild '02: Orig. Screenplay.

The Box 1/2 **2003 (R)** Ah, it must be true love when an ex-con and an ex-stripper hook up at the local diner. But problems plague the happy pair's future like his mob connections, her psycho ex-husband, and the thugs who want their big bag of loot.

99m/C VHS, DVD. James Russo, Theresa Russell, Brad Dourif, Steve Railsback, Jon Polito, Michael Rooker, Joe Palese, Lee Weaver; ***D:*** Richard Pepin; ***W:*** James Russo; ***M:*** Chris Anderson. **VIDEO**

The Box 2007 (R) Two homicide detectives question a thief and a victim of a robbery gone wrong. One detective has to face past mistakes, while the other gets an offer from the criminal behind the botched heist. **96m/C DVD.** Gabrielle Union, Giancarlo Esposito, A. J. Buckley, Jason George, Mia Maestro, James Madio, Yul Vazquez, Brett Donowho; ***D:*** A.J. Kparr; ***W:*** A.J. Kparr; ***C:*** Sion Michel; ***M:*** James T. Sale.

The Box 1/2 **2009 (PG-13)** A troubled married couple, Norma and Arthur (Diaz and Marsden), is given a mysterious wooden box by a stranger who tells them if they press the button to open the box they will be given $1 million. The downside is that a person unknown to them will be murdered and they have 24 hours to decide what to do. A preposterous premise stretched to its absolute limits, but done so smoothly that somehow logic never comes into question. Director Kelly, of "Donnie Darko" cult fame, brings his usual touch of controlled confusion, loved by many and hated by just as many. Based on the Richard Matheson short story "Button, Button," also made into a Twilight Zone episode in 1986. **115m/C DVD.** *US* Cameron Diaz, James Marsden, Frank Langella, Gillian Jacobs, James Rebhorn, Holmes Osborne, Sam Oz Stone; ***D:*** Richard Kelly; ***W:*** Richard Kelly; ***C:*** Steven Poster; ***M:*** Win Butler.

Box of Moonlight **1996 (R)** Hard-working, by-the-book electrical systems engineer Al Fountain (Turturo) feels mysteriously compelled to play hookey from his family and career while on an out-of-town business trip. Lost and confused, Al meets up with the Kid, a quirky recluse played with energy and appeal by Rockwell. Through a series of mix-ups, the nice-but-stuffy Al and the wild-but-well-meaning Kid end up spending the fourth of July weekend together. Al's inability to see the point of his journey long after the audience probably has makes the film a bit predictable and stale. DeCillo's third feature was six years in the making and financed by the success of his second feature, "Living in Oblivion." **111m/C VHS, DVD.** John Turturro, Sam Rockwell, Catherine Keener, Lisa Blount, Annie Corley, Dermot Mulroney, Alexander Goodwin; ***D:*** Tom DiCillo; ***W:*** Tom DiCillo; ***C:*** Paul Ryan; ***M:*** Jim Farmer.

Boxboarders! **2007 (PG-13)** Two goofy teen extreme sports enthusiasts with too much time on their hands find a refrigerator box in the trash and decide to mount it on a skateboard and see what happens. As they keep tinkering with their creation, they invent an unlikely new sport that draws somewhat overwhelming media attention (complete with racing footage) and unwelcome competition. **90m/C DVD.** Austin Basis, Melora Hardin, Stephen Tobolowsky, Julie Brown, Dale Midkiff, James Immekus, Mitch Eakins; ***D:*** Rob Heddon; ***W:*** Rob Heddon; ***C:*** Matthew Williams. **VIDEO**

Boxcar Bertha 1/2 **1972 (R)** Scorsese's vivid portrayal of the South during the 1930s' Depression casts Hershey as a woman who winds up in cahoots with an anti-establishment train robber. Based on the book "Sister of the Road" by Boxcar Bertha Thomson. **90m/C VHS, DVD.** Barbara Hershey, David Carradine, John Carradine, Barry Primus, Bernie Casey, Victor Argo, Martin Scorsese, John Stephens; ***D:*** Martin Scorsese; ***W:*** John W. Corrington, Joyce H. Corrington; ***C:*** John Stephens; ***M:*** Gib Guilbeau, Thad Maxwell.

Boxcar Blues **1990** Bird (Coufos) is a down and out fighter who decides to fight "The Man" (Ventura), a bare knuckle fighter who enjoys beating his opponents to death. On the way to the fight, in New Orleans, he meets up with his girl Casey (Langrick), along with some other shady characters, including a truck driving preacher. **96m/C VHS.** Paul Coufos, Margaret Langrick, Jesse Ventura, M. Emmet Walsh, Donny Lalonde; ***D:*** Damian Lee.

The Boxer 1/2 **1997 (R)** Affecting, if predictable, romance set in Ulster, Northern Ireland. Having served 14 years in prison Danny Flynn (Day-Lewis) wants nothing more to do with politics and violence. But his return to his old neighborhood—where he hopes to get back to his boxing career—finds him in the thick of both. Danny manages to persuade his ex-trainer, the alcoholic Ike (Stott), to help him re-open the local gym but resentment is high. Particularly from hardliner Harry (McSorley), who doesn't like Danny's live-and-let-live attitude and is incensed that he's interested in rekindling his lost-but-never-forgotten love for Maggie (Watson), who's the daughter of local IRA boss Joe (Cox), and the wife of another IRA prisoner. Things quickly turn ugly but the emotionally fragile Danny and Maggie continue to fight to be together against formidable odds. **113m/C VHS, DVD.** *GB IR* Daniel Day-Lewis, Emily Watson, Brian Cox, Gerard McSorley, Ken Stott, Ciaran Fitzgerald, Kenneth Cranham; ***Cameos:*** Tom Bell; ***D:*** Jim Sheridan; ***W:*** Jim Sheridan, Terry George; ***C:*** Chris Menges; ***M:*** Gavin Friday, Maurice Seezer.

The Boxer and Death **1963** A new-wave Czech film about a boxer in a Nazi concentration camp who interests the boxing-obsessed commandant in a match. In Czech with subtitles. **120m/B VHS.** Manfred Krug, Josef Kondrat, Valentina Thielova, Edwin Marian, Gerhard Rachold, Stefan Kvietik; ***D:*** Peter Solan; ***C:*** Tibor Biath; ***M:*** William Bukovy.

Boxing Helena **1993 (R)** Highly publicized as the film that cost Basinger almost $9 million in damages, the debut of director/writer Jennifer Lynch (daughter of David) explores the dark side of relationships between men and women. Sands is Dr. Nick Cavanaugh, a surgeon who becomes dangerously obsessed with the beautiful, yet unattainable Helena (Fenn). When she is hit by a car near his home, he performs emergency surgery and amputates her arms and legs, forcing her to be dependent on him. Metaphorically a situation, albeit an extreme one, that mirrors the power struggle in any sexual relationship. Problematic in some aspects, although equally fascinating as it is disturbing. **107m/C VHS, DVD.** Julian Sands, Sherilyn Fenn, Bill Paxton, Kurtwood Smith, Betsy Clark, Nicolette Scorsese, Art Garfunkel, Meg Register, Bryan Smith; ***D:*** Jennifer Lynch; ***W:*** Jennifer Lynch; ***C:*** Bojan Bazelli; ***M:*** Graeme Revell. Golden Raspberries '93: Worst Director (Lynch).

Boy A **2007 (R)** The 24-year-old, newly renamed Jack Burridge (Garfield) has gotten out of a Manchester prison after 14 years for his involvement in the brutal murder of another youngster. His dedicated caseworker Terry (Mullan) emphasizes that Jack must not reveal his previous identity or discuss his crime or jail time. Jack hesitantly reenters society and gets an apartment, a job, and a girlfriend (Lyons), but one act of heroism backfires when media attention leads to exposure about his past. **100m/C DVD.** *GB* Andrew Garfield, Peter Mullan, Shaun Evans, Katie Lyons, Taylor Doherty; ***D:*** John Crowley; ***W:*** Mark O'Rowe; ***C:*** Rob Hardy; ***M:*** Paddy Cunneen.

A Boy and His Dog 1/2 **1975 (R)** In the post-holocaust world of 2024, a young man (Johnson) and his telepathic canine (McIntire supplies narration of the dog's thoughts) cohort search for food and sex. They happen upon a community that drafts Johnson to repopulate their largely impotent race; Johnson is at first ready, willing, and able, until he discovers the mechanical methods they mean to employ. Based on a short story by Harlan Ellison. The dog was played by the late Tiger of "The Brady Bunch." **87m/C VHS, DVD.** Don Johnson, Susanne Benton, Jason Robards Jr., Charles McGraw, Alvy Moore, Helene Winston, Hal Baylor, L.Q. Jones; ***D:*** L.Q. Jones; ***W:*** L.Q. Jones; ***C:*** John Morrill; ***M:*** Tim McIntire; ***V:*** Tim McIntire.

A Boy Called Hate **1995 (R)** Troubled teen Steve (Caan)—whose nickname is "Hate" after his tattoo—lives with his divorced dad in an L.A. suburb. Steve's on a latenight motorcycle ride, taking potshots at billboards with his trusty handgun, when he stumbles onto what he thinks is an attempted rape. So Steve shoots at the rapist, Richard (Gould), and takes off with would-be victim Cindy (Crider). Turns out Richard is the assistant D.A. and he tells the cops he's been robbed, so the teen duo are now on the run. Familiar tale with some good twists and believable performances. Caan is the son of James (seen in a cameo as the dad). Debut for director Marcus. **98m/C VHS.** Scott Caan, Missy (Melissa) Crider, Elliott Gould, Adam Beach; ***Cameos:*** James Caan; ***D:*** Mitch Marcus; ***W:*** Mitch Marcus; ***C:*** Paul Holahan.

Boy Culture **2006** Money, desire, and emotional denial. X (Magyar) is a cynical hustler with a high-end and limited clientele of older men. His newest client, the urbane Gregory (Bachau), confuses X by paying for his company but refusing his sexual favors unless X is also emotionally involved. X can't even admit his attraction to his roommate Andrew (Stevens), who's unsure of his own sexuality, while their other roomie, twink Joey (Trent), openly lusts after X. Based on the novel by Matthew Rettenmund. **90m/C DVD.** Derek Magyar, Patrick Bauchau, Darryl Stephens, John Trent; ***D:*** Q. Allan Brocka; ***W:*** Q. Allan Brocka; ***C:*** Jerusha Hess; ***M:*** Ryan Beveridge.

Boy, Did I Get a Wrong Number! **1966** A real estate agent gets more than he bargained for when he accidentally dials a wrong number. Zany comedy persists as Hope gets entangled in the life of sexy starlet Sommer. **100m/C VHS.** Bob Hope, Phyllis Diller, Marjorie Lord, Elke Sommer, Cesare Danova, Kelly Thordsen; ***D:*** George Marshall; ***W:*** Albert Lewin, Burt Styler; ***C:*** Lionel Lindon; ***M:*** Richard LaSalle.

The Boy Friend **1971 (G)** Russell pays tribute to the Busby Berkeley Hollywood musical. Lots of charming dance numbers and clever parody of plotlines in this adaptation of Sandy Wilson's stage play. Fun! ♫ The Boy Friend; I Could Be Happy; Won't You Charleston With Me?; Fancy Forgetting; Sur La Plage; A Room in Bloomsbury; Safety in Numbers; It's Never Too Late to Fall in Love; Poor Little Pierette. **135m/C VHS.** *GB* Twiggy, Christopher Gable, Moyra Fraser, Max Adrian, Vladek Sheybal, Georgina Hale, Tommy Tune; ***D:*** Ken Russell; ***W:*** Ken Russell; ***C:*** David Watkin. Golden Globes '72: Actress—Mus./Comedy (Twiggy).

Boy in Blue 1/2 **1986 (R)** A "Rocky"-esque biography of Canadian speed-rower Ned Hanlan, who set aside lackluster pursuits to turn to rowing. **97m/C VHS, DVD.** *CA* Nicolas Cage, Christopher Plummer, David Naughton, Cynthia Dale, Melody Anderson, James B. Douglas; ***D:*** Charles Jarrott; ***W:*** Douglas Bowie; ***C:*** Pierre Mignot; ***M:*** Roger Webb.

The Boy in the Plastic Bubble 1/2 **1976** Well-made, sensitive drama about a young man born with immunity deficiencies who must grow up in a specially controlled plastic environment. Travolta is endearing as the boy in the bubble. **100m/C VHS, DVD.** John Travolta, Robert Reed, Glynnis O'Connor, Diana Hyland, Ralph Bellamy, Anne Ramsey, Vernee Watson-Johnson, P.J. Soles, John Friedrich; ***D:*** Randal Kleiser; ***W:*** Douglas Day Stewart; ***C:*** Arch R. Dalzell; ***M:*** Paul Williams, Mark Snow. **TV**

The Boy in the Striped Pajamas **2008 (PG-13)** In 1940's Germany, eight-year-old Bruno (Butterfield), the son of a Nazi prison camp commandant (Thewlis), and his family move from a comfortable home in Berlin out to the country where they will live on a "farm." Bruno questions his parents about the people working the fields he can see from his new bedroom window, wondering why they all wear striped pajamas. When his parents answers are inadequate, Bruno sneaks out to the far reaches of the farm, where he meets and befriends a boy his own age, Shmuel. Their circumstances seem equally confusing to both boys as they build a bond through the barbed wire fence. The story unfolds primarily from Bruno's perspective until the final scenes, which begin to switch to Shmuel's point of view. Poignant and timeless, the film is primarily directed at a young audience and serves to point out how easily people accept evil when they elevate some purpose above basic morality. Adapted from John Boyle's 2006 novel of the same name. **94m/C DVD.** *US GB* David Thewlis, Vera Farmiga, David Hayman, Rupert Friend, Bruno, Shmuel, Amber Beattie, Sheila Hancock, Richard Johnson, Jim Norton; ***D:*** Mark Herman; ***W:*** Mark Herman; ***C:*** Benoit Delhomme; ***M:*** James Horner.

Boy Meets Girl **1938** Cagney and O'Brien play screenwriters whose every film is a variation on the boy meets girl theme. Trouble is they're running out of ideas and their scripts get increasingly outlandish. A fading cowboy actor is supposed to star in the duo's next film—if they can ever settle down to work. Then they get the idea to feature their friend Wilson's baby in the movie—and guess who becomes a new star. Good satire on moviemaking and movie moguls, which made fine use of the Warner studio back lots, sound stages, and offices. Based on the play by Bella and Samuel Spewack who also wrote the screenplay. **86m/B VHS.** James Cagney, Pat O'Brien, Ralph Bellamy, Dick Foran, Marie Wilson, Frank McHugh, Bruce Lester, Ronald Reagan, Penny Singleton, James Stephenson; ***D:*** Lloyd Bacon; ***W:*** Bella Spewack, Samuel Spewack.

Boy Meets Girl **1984** Alex (Lavant), a French Holden Caulfield type character, cruises the seamier side of Paris in this acclaimed film. Carax's directoral debut at age 22. Alex will return in the Carax films "Bad Blood" (1986) and "The Lovers on the Bridge" (1991). French with subtitles. **100m/B VHS, DVD.** *FR* Denis Lavant, Mireille Perrier, Carroll Brooks, Anna Baldaccini; ***D:*** Leos Carax; ***W:*** Leos Carax; ***C:*** Jean-Yves Escoffier; ***M:*** Jacques Pinault.

Boy of Two Worlds 1/2 *Paws; Lure of the Jungle* **1959 (G)** Because he is of a lineage foreign to his late father's town, a boy is exiled to the life of a junior Robinson Crusoe. **103m/C VHS.** *DK* Jimmy Sternman, Edvin Adolphson; ***D:*** Astrid Henning Jensen.

Boy Takes Girl **1983** A little girl finds it hard adjusting to life on a farming cooperative during a summer recess. **93m/C VHS.** Gabi Eldor, Hillel Neeman, Dina Limon; ***D:*** Michal Bat-Adam.

Boy! What a Girl **1945** Moore (in drag) is mistaken for a woman, and is fought over by a couple of suitors. **60m/B VHS, DVD.** Tim Moore, Duke Williams, Sheila Guyse, Beth Mays, Elwood Smith; ***D:*** Arthur Leonard.

The Boy Who Could Fly **1986 (PG)** After a plane crash kills his parents, a boy withdraws into a fantasy land where he can fly. The young daughter of a troubled family makes friends with him and the fantasy becomes real. A sweet film for children, charming though melancholy for adults, too. Fine cast, including Savage, Dewhurst, and Bedelia keep this from becoming sappy. **120m/C VHS, DVD.** Lucy Deakins, Jay Underwood, Bonnie Bedelia, Colleen Dewhurst, Fred Savage, Fred Gwynne, Louise Fletcher, Jason Priestley; ***D:*** Nick Castle; ***W:*** Nick Castle; ***C:*** Steven Poster; ***M:*** Bruce Broughton.

The Boy Who Left Home to Find Out About the Shivers **1981** From "Faerie Tale Theatre" comes this tale about a boy who learns about fear. **60m/C VHS, DVD.** Peter MacNichol, Christopher Lee, David Warner, Dana Hill, Frank Zappa; ***D:*** Graeme Clifford; ***V:*** Vincent Price. **CABLE**

The Boy Who Loved Trolls **1984** Paul's fantastic dreams come true when he meets Ofoeti, a real, live troll. The only problem is Ofeoti only has a day to live, and Paul must find a way to save him. Aired on PBS as part of the "Wonderworks" series. **58m/C VHS.** Sam Waterston, Susan Anton, Matt Dill; ***D:*** Harvey Laidman.

The Boy with the Green Hair **1948** When he hears that his parents were killed in an air raid, a boy's hair turns green. The narrow-minded members of his community suddenly want nothing to do with him and he becomes an outcast. Thought-provoking social commentary. **82m/C VHS, DVD.** Pat O'Brien, Robert Ryan, Barbara Hale, Dean Stockwell; ***D:*** Joseph Losey.

Boycott 1/2 **2002** Superb HBO docudrama re-creates the Civil Rights movement's early days, from Rosa Parks's (Little-Thomas) refusal to give up her seat to a white man on a segregated Montgomery, Alabama, bus, through the subsequent boycott of the bus system by the city's black population, to the success of the boycott and the rise to prominence of Dr. Martin Luther King Jr. (Wright) as the movement's most eloquent and popular leader. Through the use and mix of many different visual styles, director Johnson uses artful touches to tell the story without overplaying his hand. Wright is fantastic as King, with other outstanding performances turned in by Howard as Ralph Abernathy and Pounder as boycott organizer Jo Anne Robinson. **112m/C VHS, DVD.** Jeffrey Wright, Terrence Howard, CCH Pounder, Carmen Ejogo, Reg E. Cathey, Brent Jennings, Shawn Michael Howard, Erik Todd Dellums, Iris Little-Thomas, Whitman Mayo, E. Roger Mitchell, Mike Hodge, Clark Johnson; ***D:*** Clark Johnson; ***W:*** Timothy J. Sexton, Herman Daniel Farrell III; ***C:*** David Hennings; ***M:*** Stephen James Taylor. **CABLE**

A Boyfriend for Christmas ☙☙ 1/2 **2004** When she was 12, Holly Grant asked Santa for a Christmas boyfriend and he promises her one—in 20 years. Now working for a nonprofit, Holly (Williams) is ticked at attorney Ryan (Muldoon), whom she's never met, when he misses an important appointment. When he turns up on her doorstep with a Christmas tree to make amends, Holly thinks he's someone else and he goes along with the charade so they can have a chance at romance. Her family thinks Holly's new guy is great but what will happen when the truth comes out? A Hallmark Channel original. **100m/C DVD.** Kelli Williams, Patrick Muldoon, Charles Durning, Shannon Wilcox, Martin Mull, Bruce Thomas, Maeve Quinlan, Bridget Ann White, David Starzyk; ***D:*** Kevin Connor; ***W:*** Roger Schroeder; ***C:*** Amit Bhattacharya; ***M:*** Charles Syndor. **CABLE**

Boyfriends ☙☙ **1996** Gay sexual roundelay that takes place over a weekend spent in the English countryside. Paul (Dreyfus) and Ben (Sands) are on the verge of splitting up after five years, orderly Matt's (Urwin) in love with philandering Owen (Ableson), and social worker Will (Coffey) wants more than a one-nighter with working-class pickup Adam (Petrucci). They all head to James's (McGrath) house and the sexual games begin. Low-budget first feature from Hunter and Hunsinger. **82m/C VHS, DVD.** *GB* James Dreyfus, Mark Sands, Andrew Ableson, Michael Urwin, David Coffey, Darren Petrucci, Michael McGrath, Russell Higgs; ***D:*** Neil Hunter, Tom Hunsinger; ***W:*** Neil Hunter, Tom Hunsinger; ***C:*** Richard Tisdall.

Boyfriends & Girlfriends ☙☙ 1/2 *My Girlfriend's Boyfriend; L'Ami de Mon Ami* **1988 (PG)** Another one of Rohmer's "Comedies and Proverbs," in which two girls with boyfriends fade in and out of interest with each, casually reshuffling their relationships. Typical, endless-talks-at-cafes Rohmer, the most happily consistent of the aging French New Wave. In French with subtitles. **102m/C VHS, DVD.** *FR* Emmanuelle Chaulet, Sophie Renoir, Eric Viellard, Francois-Eric Gendron, Anne-Laure Meury; ***D:*** Eric Rohmer; ***W:*** Eric Rohmer; ***C:*** Bernard Lutic; ***M:*** Jean-Louis Valero.

The Boynton Beach Club ☙☙ 1/2 *The Boynton Beach Bereavement Club* **2005 (R)** Aged lonely hearts find support and possibly love as members of a bereavement club at a Florida "active adult" community—an unlikely but surprisingly refreshing setting for a romantic comedy. Newly widowed Marilyn (Vaccarro) joins the group after a car backs over her husband. There she meets a range of characters more interested in romance and life beyond blue hair and early-bird specials. Hotties-of-a-certain-age Cannon and Kellerman mix with master casanova Bologna and his reluctant protege Cariou to show both the funny and tender sides of the senior dating game. Plays a little sitcom-y at times, but manages to keep things dignified and unpatronizing. Director Seidelman got the idea for the movie from her mother Florence, who received a producer's credit. **105m/C DVD.** *US* Dyan Cannon, Brenda Vaccaro, Sally Kellerman, Joseph Bologna, Len Cariou, Michael Nouri, Renee Taylor; ***D:*** Susan Seidelman; ***W:*** Susan Seidelman, Shelly Gitlow; ***C:*** Eric Moynier; ***M:*** Marcelo Zarvos.

Boys ☙ *The Girl You Want* **1995 (PG-13)** Seems like only yesterday we saw Haas as that big-eared, doe-eyed Amish kid from "Witness," but now, in this dry love story, he has grown into a big-eared, doe-eyed teenager lusting after older woman Ryder. John (Haas) saves Patty (Ryder) after a riding accident leaves her unconscious near his New England prep school. Immediately taken by her beauty and mystery, John decides to hide her in his dorm room and a romance blossoms between the unlikely pair. But John isn't the only one hiding something. Patty has a terrible secret from her past (gasp!), but when it's finally revealed, you'll be too bored to care. Based on the short story "Twenty Minutes" by James Salter. **86m/C VHS, DVD.** Winona Ryder, Lukas Haas, John C. Reilly, William Sage, Skeet Ulrich; ***D:*** Stacy Cochran; ***W:*** Stacy Cochran; ***C:*** Robert Elswit; ***M:*** Stewart Copeland.

The Boys ☙☙ 1/2 *Les Boys* **1997** Popular, simply plotted French-Canadian comedy about a group of ordinary guys who play in an amateur hockey league. "Les Boys" are sponsored by local tavern-owner Stan (Girard), who's got a gambling jones and is in debt to small-time mobster, Meo (Lebeau). Meo strikes a deal pitting Stan's ragtag hockey players against his own team of thugs. If Stan's team is defeated, he loses his bar. Dirty tricks abound on both sides. French with subtitles. **107m/C VHS, DVD.** *CA* Remy Girard, Marc Messier, Patrick Huard, Serge Theriault, Yvan Ponton, Dominic Philie, Patrick Labbe, Roc Lafortune, Pierre Lebeau, Paul Houde; ***D:*** Louis Saia; ***W:*** Christian Fournier; ***C:*** Sylvain Brault; ***M:*** Normand Corbeil.

The Boys ☙☙☙ **1998 (R)** After his release from prison on an assault charge, psychopathic Brett (Wenham), heads to the home of his mother Sandra (Curran) and younger brother Stevie (Hayes). His other brother Glenn (Polson) is now married to Jackie (Cronin) who wants him to stay out of trouble. Also greeting Brett is girlfriend Michelle (Collette) but the volatile duo are soon arguing furiously. As Brett gets drunker and more stoned, he also becomes more enraged, leading to a brutal crime. Chilling story with powerful performances; adapted from the 1991 play by Gordon Graham. **84m/C VHS.** *AU* David Wenham, Toni Collette, John Polson, Lynette Curran, Anthony Hayes, Jeanette Cronin, Anna Lise, Pete Smith; ***D:*** Rowan Woods; ***W:*** Stephen Sewell; ***C:*** Tristan Milani. Australian Film Inst. '98: Adapt. Screenplay, Director (Woods), Support. Actor (Polson), Support. Actress (Collette).

The Boys and Girl From County Clare ☙☙ 1/2 *The Boys From County Clare* **2003** Set in the 1960s, Liverpool businessman Jimmy (Meaney) returns to his home in Ireland after 24 years to compete in the annual Celli music festival, which brings him into direct conflict with his long-estranged older brother John Joe (Hill). Soon enough the brothers are fighting about music and Maisie (Bradley), who Jimmy deserted for life in Liverpool. Meanwhile their bands are doing everything they can to sabotage each other, and Jimmy's flutist (Evans) is falling for John Joe's fiddler (Corr). Lighthearted comedy/drama uses traditional Irish music as a backdrop for an appealing but routine sibling rivalry story. **90m/C DVD.** *GB IR GE* Bernard Hill, Colm Meaney, Charlotte Bradley, Stephen Brennan, Andrea Corr, Eamon Owens, Shaun Evans, Phil Barantini, Patrick Bergin; ***D:*** John Irvin; ***W:*** Nicholas Adams; ***C:*** Thomas Burstyn; ***M:*** Fiachra Trench.

Boys and Girls ☙☙ **2000 (PG-13)** Nondescript teen romance has lifelong acquaintances and most-time friends Ryan (Prinze Jr.) and Jennifer (Forlani) trying to decide if they love each other after their hormones get the better of them one night. And get this! They're complete opposites! She's carefree and live-for-the-moment. He's button-down, plan-every-second-precise. Biggs and Donahue, as the respective sidekicks, steal the movie from the leads whenever they show up. Sort of a young, poor man's "When Harry Met Sally," without the wit and insight. **94m/C VHS, DVD.** Freddie Prinze Jr., Claire Forlani, Jason Biggs, Heather Donahue, Alyson Hannigan, Amanda Detmer, Lisa Eichhorn; ***D:*** Robert Iscove; ***W:*** Andrew Lowery, Andrew Miller; ***C:*** Ralf Bode; ***M:*** Stewart Copeland.

The Boys Are Back ☙☙ 1/2 *The Boys are Back in Town* **2009 (PG-13)** When Aussie sports writer Joe Warr's (Owen) wife dies from cancer, he becomes a single dad to his two sons—a six-year-old and a rebellious teen—without much of a clue as to how to proceed. Joe's philosophy degenerates into a lack of rules, which constantly puts them all on the brink of family disaster. Owens' excellent performance, combining toughness and sensitivity, saves it from sinking into melodrama. Possibly a little too picturesque with its scenic South Australian vistas, the setting doesn't always jive with the story's angst. Similarly, the glib title doesn't do justice to the emotional hardship and redemption all principal characters experience. Based on Simon Carr's 2001 memoir. **104m/C DVD.** *AU* Clive Owen, George MacKay, Laura Fraser, Emma Booth, Erik Thomson, Nicholas McAnulty; ***D:*** Scott Hicks; ***W:*** Scott Hicks, Allan Cubitt; ***C:*** Greig Fraser; ***M:*** Hal Lindes.

The Boys Club ☙☙ **1996 (R)** Teens-in-trouble film is given a tough core by first time director Fawcett. Excitement-craving 14-year-olds Kyle (Zamprogna), Eric (Sawa), and Brad (Stone) spend all their free time at an abandoned shack at the outskirts of their small town. Only one day they discover it occupied by gun-pointing criminal Luke Cooper (Penn), who tells the boys he's actually a good cop who's been shot and is on the run from some bad cops. The boys are willing to buy into the story at first but Cooper is quick to show his psycho colors, taking Eric hostage, and precipitating a violent finale. **92m/C VHS, DVD.** *CA* Christopher Penn, Stuart Stone, Devon Sawa, Dominic Zamprogna, Nicholas (Nick) Campbell, Jarred Blanchard; ***D:*** John Fawcett; ***W:*** Peter Wellington; ***C:*** Thom Best; ***M:*** Michael Timmins.

Boys Don't Cry ☙☙☙ **1999 (R)** Falls under the truth is stranger than fiction category. Brandon Teena (heavily awarded Swank) moves from Lincoln, Nebraska, to the small town of Falls City hoping to start over and keep his past a secret. Brandon gets a girlfriend, Lana (Sevigny), and runs afoul of the reckless John (Sarsgaard). And then Brandon's secret is discovered—he is actually a girl and the gender revelation leads to tragic consequences. Based on a true story, which is also the subject of the documentary, "The Brandon Teena Story." Pierce's version, not unexpectedly, was subjected to the charges of dramatic license, but the story is still forceful. **116m/C VHS, DVD.** Hilary Swank, Chloe Sevigny, Peter Sarsgaard, Brendan Sexton III, Alison Folland, Alicia (Lecy) Goranson, Matt McGrath, Rob Campbell, Jeanetta Arnette; ***D:*** Kimberly Peirce; ***W:*** Kimberly Peirce, Andy Bienen; ***C:*** Jim Denault; ***M:*** Nathan Larson. Oscars '99: Actress (Swank); Golden Globes '00: Actress—Drama (Swank); Ind. Spirit '00: Actress (Swank), Support. Actress (Sevigny); L.A. Film Critics '99: Actress (Swank), Support. Actress (Sevigny); N.Y. Film Critics '99: Actress (Swank); Natl. Soc. Film Critics '99: Support. Actress (Sevigny); Broadcast Film Critics '99: Actress (Swank).

The Boys from Brazil ☙☙ 1/2 **1978 (R)** Based on Ira Levin's novel, a thriller about Dr. Josef Mengele endeavoring to reconstitute the Nazi movement from his Brazilian sanctuary by cloning a brood of boys from Hitler's genes. **123m/C VHS, DVD.** Gregory Peck, James Mason, Laurence Olivier, Uta Hagen, Steve Guttenberg, Denholm Elliott, Lilli Palmer; ***D:*** Franklin J. Schaffner; ***W:*** Heywood Gould; ***C:*** Henri Decae; ***M:*** Jerry Goldsmith. Natl. Bd. of Review '78: Actor (Olivier).

The Boys in Company C ☙☙ **1977 (R)** A frank, hard-hitting drama about five naive young men involved in the Vietnam War. **127m/C VHS.** Stan Shaw, Andrew Stevens, James Canning, Michael Lembeck, Craig Wasson, R. Lee Ermey, James Whitmore Jr., Scott Hylands, Noble Willingham, Santos Morales, Claude Wilson, Drew Michaels, Karen Hilger, Peggy O'Neal, Stan Johns; ***Cameos:*** Rick Natkin; ***D:*** Sidney J. Furie; ***W:*** Sidney J. Furie, Rick Natkin; ***C:*** Godfret A. Godar; ***M:*** Jaime Mendoza-Nava.

Boys in Love ☙☙ **1995** Four gay shorts about young men in love. "Death in Venice, CA" finds a repressed academic drawn to his landlady's stepson. The animated "Achilles" features the Greek heros Achilles and Petroclus at the battle of Troy. A young man becomes determined to conquer "My Polish Waiter" and a rejected Latin lover finds love again (with some help from a dog) in "Miguel, Ma Belle." **83m/C VHS.** ***D:*** Barry Purves, P. David Ebersole.

The Boys in the Band ☙☙ 1/2 **1970 (R)** A group of gay friends get together one night for a birthday party. A simple premise with a compelling depiction of friendship, expectations, and lifestyle. One of the first serious cinematic presentations to deal with the subject of homosexuality. The film was adapted from Mart Crowley's play using the original cast. **120m/C VHS, DVD.** Frederick Combs, Cliff Gorman, Laurence Luckinbill, Kenneth Nelson, Leonard Frey; ***D:*** William Friedkin; ***W:*** Matt Crowley.

Boys Life ☙☙ **1994** Three shorts about gay teenagers coming of age. "Pool Days" has 17-year-old Justin (Weinstein) taking a summer job as a lifeguard at a health spa. Still clueless as to his sexual preferences, Justin is flustered when cruised by a charming male swimmer but it does get him to thinking. "A Friend of Dorothy" finds NYU student Winston (O'Connell) seeking freedom in Greenwich Village as he looks for like-minded friends (and a little romance). "The Disco Years" takes place in California during the Nixon era as casually gay-bashing high-schooler Tom (Nolan) gradually realizes his true nature. **90m/C VHS, DVD.** Josh Weinstein, Nick Poletti, Kimberly Flynn, Richard Salamanca, Raoul O'Connell, Kevin McClatchy, Greg Lauren, Anne Zupa, Matt Nolan, Russell Scott Lewis, Gwen Welles, Dennis Christopher; ***D:*** Robert Lee King, Brian Sloan, Raoul O'Connell; ***W:*** Robert Lee King, Brian Sloan, Raoul O'Connell; ***C:*** W. Mott Hupfel III, Jonathan Schell, Greg Gardiner.

Boys Love ☙ **2006** This gooey confection fits into the popular Japanese genre of romantic manga (yaoi), primarily aimed at women, about young men in love. Magazine editor Taishin (Kotani) interviews popular teenaged model Noeru (Takumi), who takes their meeting to a new level by including sex. When the two fall in love, Noeru's childhood friend Chidori (Matsumoto), who harbors an unrequited passion, can't stand the competition—with tragic results. Japanese with subtitles. **90m/C DVD.** *JP* Yoshikazu Kotani, Saito Takumi, Hiroya Matsumoto; ***D:*** Kotaro Terauchi; ***W:*** Kotaro Terauchi; ***C:*** Chika Fujino. **VIDEO**

The Boys Next Door ☙☙ 1/2 **1985 (R)** Two California lads kill and go nuts during a weekend in Los Angeles. Sheen overacts as a budding psychotic, not an easy thing to do. Apparently is trying to show what a particular lifestyle can lead to. Violent. **90m/C VHS, DVD.** Maxwell Caulfield, Charlie Sheen, Christopher McDonald, Hank Garrett, Patti D'Arbanville, Moon Zappa; ***D:*** Penelope Spheeris; ***W:*** Glen Morgan, James Wong; ***C:*** Arthur Albert; ***M:*** George S. Clinton.

The Boys Next Door ☙☙ 1/2 **1996 (PG)** Gentle comedy/drama, based on Tom Griffin's play, about four mentally disabled men—Norman (Lane), Barry (Leonard), Arnold (Jeter), and Lucien (Vance)—who share a house under the supervision of too-dedicated social worker Jack (Goldwyn). In fact, Jack's devotion is causing enough problems in his marriage to have him consider changing careers, even as each of "the boys" struggle with their daily lives. TV movie is overly sweet but the performances are very good. **99m/C VHS.** Nathan Lane, Tony Goldwyn, Robert Sean Leonard, Michael Jeter, Courtney B. Vance, Mare Winningham, Jenny Robertson, Elizabeth Wilson, Richard Jenkins, Lynne Thigpen; ***D:*** John Erman; ***W:*** William Blinn; ***C:*** Frank Tidy; ***M:*** John Kander. **TV**

Boys' Night Out ☙☙☙ **1962** Amusing comedy about four businessmen who desperately want to escape the suburban doldrums by setting up an apartment equipped with plaything Novak. Little do they know, but Novak is a sociology student studying the American male, and they are merely her guinea pigs in an experiment beyond their control. Blair, Page, and Gabor provide comic relief. Based on a story by Marvin Worth and Arne Sultan. **113m/C VHS.** Kim Novak, James Garner, Tony Randall, Howard Duff, Janet Blair, Patti Page, Jessie Royce Landis, Oscar Homolka, Zsa Zsa Gabor; ***D:*** Michael Gordon; ***W:*** Ira Wallach.

The Boys of Baraka ☙☙ 1/2 **2005** Directors Ewing and Grady inform us that 76 percent of Baltimore's black male students do not graduate from high school. So, in 2002, 20 at-risk students are given scholarships to attend the progressive Baraka boarding school—in Kenya—which is run by American volunteers. They are supposed to stay two years, but a transformation is begun that cannot be completed when terrorists attack Nairobi and the school is forced to close. The film may not have the "feel good" ending viewers are expecting, although it seems the lives of several boys are changed for the better. **84m/C** *US*

The Boys of St. Vincent 🦴🦴🦴🦴 **1993** Outstanding, and heartbreaking, story of sexual abuse by Catholic clergy that was inspired by actual events. Divided into two segments, the drama begins in 1975 with 10-year-old Kevin Reevey (Morina) living at the St. Vincent orphanage in an eastern Canadian town. The orphanage is run by charismatic and terrifying Brother Lavin (Czerny), who it turns out has a special fondness for "his boy" Kevin. Nor is Brother Lavin alone—a fact eventually revealed by a police investigation, although the matter is hushed up by both the church and the government. Until 15 years later. In 1990, the case is reopened and Lavin, having married and fathered two sons, is returned to face charges. Now the young men must open wounds that have never truly healed and confront their tormentors in a court of law, amidst a blaze of publicity. Czerny gives a truly inspired performance as the self-loathing monster. The emotional agony is excruciating to watch and be forwarned that the depiction of the sexual abuse is unflinching. Made for Canadian TV; on two cassettes. **186m/C VHS, DVD.** *CA* Henry Czerny, Johnny Morina, Sebastian Spence, Brian Dodd, David Hewlett, Jonathan Lewis, Jeremy Keefe, Phillip Dinn, Brian Dooley, Greg Thomey, Michael Wade, Lise Roy, Timothy Webber, Kristine Demers, Ashley Billard, Sam Grana; ***D:*** John N. Smith; ***W:*** Sam Grana, John N. Smith, Des Walsh; ***C:*** Pierre Letarte; ***M:*** Neil Smolar. **TV**

The Boys of 2nd Street Park 🦴🦴🦴 **2003 (R)** Drawn together for this compelling documentary, childhood buddies frankly recount the life-changing events they've confronted over the years while pining for the simpler times growing up in Brighton Beach, NY, in the 1950s. **91m/C VHS, DVD.** ***D:*** Dan Klores, Ron Berger; ***C:*** Buddy Squires. **VIDEO**

Boys of the City 🦴🦴 *The Ghost Creeps* **1940** The East Side Kids run amuck in an eerie mansion while trying to solve the murder of a judge. **63m/B VHS, DVD.** Leo Gorcey, Bobby Jordan; ***D:*** Joseph H. Lewis.

Boys on the Side 🦴🦴 ½ **1994 (R)** It's "Thelma & Louise" come to "Terms of Endearment" by way of "Philadelphia." Goldberg is Jane, an unemployed lesbian singer, who connects with Ms. Priss real estate agent Robin (Parker) for a road trip to California. The two become a female version of the Odd Couple as Jane tags Robin as "the whitest woman in America." They stop off to pick up addle-brain friend Holly (Barrymore) who has just knocked her drug-crazed abusive beau in the head with a baseball bat. Holly's accident turns fatal and the threesome are on the run from cops. They bond like crazy glue and become a family as they face two huge setbacks—one's pregnant, another has AIDS. Strong performances by the lead actresses and a cool soundtrack may make up for this often trite movie of the week premise. **117m/C VHS, DVD.** James Remar, Anita Gillette, Matthew McConaughey, Whoopi Goldberg, Mary-Louise Parker, Drew Barrymore; ***D:*** Herbert Ross; ***W:*** Don Roos; ***C:*** Donald E. Thorin; ***M:*** David Newman.

Boy's Reformatory 🦴 ½ **1939** Brothers are framed. One takes the rap, goes to the title institution, breaks out, and hunts the real bad guys. Creaky and antiquated. **62m/B VHS, DVD.** Frankie Darro, Grant Withers, David Durand, Warren McCollum; ***D:*** Howard Bretherton.

Boys Town 🦴🦴🦴 ½ **1938** Righteous portrayal of Father Flanagan and the creation of Boys Town, home for juvenile soon-to-be-ex-delinquents. **93m/B VHS, DVD.** Spencer Tracy, Mickey Rooney, Henry Hull, Gene Reynolds, Sidney Miller, Frankie Thomas Jr.; ***D:*** Norman Taurog. Oscars '38: Actor (Tracy), Story.

Boys Will Be Boys 🦴🦴 ½ **1997 (PG)** With their parents away at a company party, Matt and Robbie are home alone for the first time. Expect chaos when the boys discover that their father's business rival has something nasty in store and the brothers will use anything around to defeat him. **89m/C VHS, DVD.** Randy Travis, Julie Hagerty, Jon Voight, Michael DeLuise, Catherine Oxenberg, Mickey Rooney, Ruth Buzzi, Dom DeLuise, Charles Nelson Reilly, James Williams, Drew Winget; ***D:*** Dom DeLuise; ***W:*** Gregory Poppon, Mark Dubas; ***C:*** Leonard Schway; ***M:*** Kristopher Carter. **VIDEO**

Boystown 🦴🦴 *Chuecatown* **2007** Who'd a thought you could have a cuddly couple involved in a serial killer story? Slimy Madrid realtor Victor kills little old ladies for their apartments in a gentrifying gay neighborhood. When Rey and Leo unexpectedly inherit their next-door neighbor's apartment, the police suspect them of the crimes. Things actually get worse when Rey's hateful mother Antonia, who wants to split the couple up, takes over the disputed apartment. Too bad for her since that really interferes with Victor's plans. Spanish with subtitles. **93m/C DVD.** *SP* Carlos Fuentes, Rosa Maria Sarda, Pablo Puyol, Pepon Nieto, Concha Valasco, Eduard Soto; ***D:*** Juan Flahn; ***W:*** Juan Flahn, Felix Sabroso, Dunia Ayaso; ***C:*** Juan Carlos Lausin; ***M:*** David San Jose, Joan Crossas.

Boyz N the Hood 🦴🦴🦴 ½ **1991 (R)** Singleton's debut as a writer and director is an astonishing picture of young black men, four high school students with different backgrounds, aims, and abilities trying to survive L.A. gangs and bigotry. Excellent acting throughout, with special nods to Fishburne and Gooding Jr. Violent outbreaks outside theatres where this ran only proves the urgency of its passionately nonviolent, pro-family message. Hopefully those viewers scared off at the time will give this a chance in the safety of their VCRs. Singleton was the youngest director ever nominated for an Oscar. **112m/C VHS, DVD, UMD.** Laurence Fishburne, Ice Cube, Cuba Gooding Jr., Nia Long, Morris Chestnut, Tyra Ferrell, Angela Bassett, Whitman Mayo; ***D:*** John Singleton; ***W:*** John Singleton; ***C:*** Charles Mills; ***M:*** Stanley Clarke. MTV Movie Awards '92: New Filmmaker (Singleton), Natl. Film Reg. '02.

Bra Boys 🦴 ½ **2007 (R)** Title is an Aussie diminutive for Sydney's Maroubra Beach and refers to a notorious local working-class surfer gang. Formed around Abberton brothers Koby, Jai, and director/writer Sunny, the Bra Boys are known to the cops for turf wars and scrapes with the law while locals in the poor suburb praise the surfers for their work with troubled youth. (Don't do as I do, do as I say?) There's also lengthy coverage of a murder trial involving Jai and Koby but it's a decidedly one-sided documentary. **86m/C DVD.** *AU* ***D:*** Sunny Abberton; ***W:*** Sunny Abberton; ***C:*** Macario De Souza, Brooke Silvester; ***M:*** Jamie Holt; ***V:*** Russell Crowe.

Braddock: Missing in Action 3 🦴 **1988 (R)** The battle-scarred, high-kicking 'Nam vet battles his way into the jungles once more, this time to rescue his long-lost Vietnamese family. A family effort, Chuck co-wrote the script; his brother directed. **104m/C VHS, DVD.** Chuck Norris, Aki Aleong, Roland Harrah III; ***D:*** Aaron Norris; ***W:*** Chuck Norris, James Bruner; ***C:*** Joao Fernandes.

The Brady Bunch Movie 🦴🦴🦴 **1995 (PG-13)** Grunge and CDs may be the norm in the '90s, but the Bradys still live in the eight-track world of the '70s, where Davy Jones rocks and every day is a sunshine day. Then greedy developer McKean schemes to cash in on Mike and Carol's financial woes. (Hawaii! The Grand Canyon! What were they thinking?) Great ensemble cast capably fills the white platform shoes of the originals—Cole sounds just like Mr. Brady, Cox hilariously channels Jan's tormented middle child angst, and Taylor's self-absorbed Marcia, Marcia, Marcia is dead-on, right down to the frosty pursed lips. Look for neat-o cameos from some original Bradys and most of the Monkees. Followed by "A Very Brady Sequel." **88m/C VHS, DVD.** Shelley Long, Gary Cole, Michael McKean, Jean Smart, Henriette Mantel, Christopher Daniel Barnes, Christine Taylor, Paul Sutera, Jennifer Elise Cox, Jesse Lee, Olivia Hack, David Graf, Jack Noseworthy, Shane Conrad, RuPaul Charles; ***Cameos:*** Ann B. Davis, Florence Henderson, Davy Jones, Barry Williams, Christopher Knight, Michael (Mike) Lookinland, Mickey Dolenz, Peter Tork; ***D:*** Betty Thomas; ***W:*** Bonnie Turner, Terry Turner, Laurice Elehwany, Rick Copp; ***C:*** Mac Ahlberg; ***M:*** Guy Moon.

Brady's Escape 🦴 ½ *The Long Ride* **1984** American WWII pilot is shot down in the Hungarian countryside and befriended by Hungarian csikos (cowboys). **92m/C VHS.** *HU* John Savage, Kelly Reno; ***D:*** Pal Gabor. **CABLE**

The Brain 🦴🦴 ½ *Vengeance* **1962** A scientist learns that a mind isn't always a terrible thing to waste when he finds himself being manipulated by the brain of a dead man he's trying to keep alive. Remake of "Donovan's Brain" (1953). **83m/B VHS.** *GB GE* Anne Heywood, Peter Van Eyck, Bernard Lee, Cecil Parker, Jack MacGowran; ***D:*** Freddie Francis.

The Brain 🦴🦴 *Le Cerveau* **1969 (G)** Run of the mill comedy caper has Niven planning to heist millions from a NATO train. The caper begins when lots of other crooks decide to rob the same train. The cast holds this one together. **100m/C VHS.** *FR* David Niven, Jean-Paul Belmondo, Andre Bourvil, Eli Wallach, Silvia Monti, Fernand Valois; ***D:*** Gerard Oury; ***M:*** Georges Delerue.

The Brain 🦴 ½ **1988 (R)** Dr. Blake, host of a popular TV talk-show, is in league with a power-hungry alien brain. Viewers of his show kill themselves and others in the midst of many special effects. The ratings go down. **94m/C VHS.** Tom Breznahan, Cynthia (Cyndy, Cindy) Preston, David Gale; ***D:*** Ed(ward) Hunt.

Brain Damage 🦴🦴 **1988 (R)** A tongue-in-bloody-cheek farce about a brain-sucking parasite. The parasite in question, Aylmer, addicts our dubious hero to the euphoria induced by the blue liquid the parasite injects into his brain, paving the way for the bloody mayhem that follows. Poor shadow of Henenlotter's far-superior "Basket Case." In fact, it even includes an inside-joke cameo by Van Hentenryck, reprising his "Basket Case" character; look for him on the subway. **89m/C VHS, DVD.** Rick Herbst, Gordon MacDonald, Jennifer Lowry, Theo Barnes, Lucille Saint Peter, Kevin Van Hentenryck, Beverly Bonner; ***D:*** Frank Henenlotter; ***W:*** Frank Henenlotter; ***C:*** Bruce Torbet; ***M:*** Gus Russo, Clutch Reiser; ***V:*** John Zacherle.

Brain Dead 🦴🦴🦴 ½ **1989 (R)** Low-budget but brilliantly assembled puzzle-film about a brain surgeon who agrees to perform experimental surgery on a psychotic to retrieve some corporately valuable data—his first mistake, which begins a seemingly endless cycle of nightmares and identity alterations. A mind-blowing sci-fi feast from ex-"Twilight Zone" writer Charles Beaumont. **85m/C VHS, DVD.** Bill Pullman, Bill Paxton, Bud Cort, Patricia Charbonneau, Nicholas Pryor, George Kennedy, Brian Brophy, Lee Arenberg, Andy Wood; ***D:*** Adam Simon; ***W:*** Adam Simon, Charles Beaumont; ***M:*** Peter Rotter.

Brain Donors 🦴🦴 ½ **1992 (PG)** Goofy, uneven film starring Turturro as a sleazy lawyer trying to take over the Oglethorpe Ballet Company by sweet-talking its aged patronness. He is helped by two eccentric friends, and together the three crack a lot of bad but witty jokes. The film culminates into a hilarious ballet scene featuring someone giving CPR to the ballerina playing the dying swan, an actor in a duck suit, duck hunters, and a pack of hounds. This trio reminds us of second-rate Marx Brothers (or the Three Stooges) but the movie has enough funny moments to be worth a watch. **79m/C VHS, DVD.** John Turturro, Bob Nelson, Mel Smith, Nancy Marchand, John Savident, George de la Pena, Juli Donald, Spike Alexander, Teri Copley; ***D:*** Dennis Dugan; ***W:*** Pat Proft; ***M:*** Ira Newborn.

Brain Drain 🦴🦴 **1998** Young Argentine street kids are thieves who specialize in car radios. Their dreams of a better life are at odds with their surroundings. Things go wrong when they make false accusations against a cop and he comes after them. **92m/C DVD.** Nicolas Cabre, Luis Quiroz, Enrique Liporace; ***D:*** Fernando Musa; ***W:*** Fernando Musa, Branko Andjic; ***C:*** Carlos Torlaschi; ***M:*** Luis Maria Serra.

The Brain Eaters 🦴🦴 **1958** A strange ship from inside the Earth invades a small town, and hairy monsters promptly attach themselves to people's necks in a daring bid to control the planet. The imaginative story compensates somewhat for the cheap special effects. Watch for Nimoy before he grew pointed ears. **60m/B VHS.** Edwin Nelson, Alan Frost, Jack Hill, Joanna Lee, Jody Fair, Leonard Nimoy; ***D:*** Bruno VeSota.

The Brain from Planet Arous 🦴 **1957** Lassie meets Alien when an evil alien brain appropriates the body of a scientist in order to take over planet Earth. His plans are thwarted, however, by a good alien brain that likewise inhabits the body of the scientist's dog. High camp and misdemeanors. **80m/B VHS, DVD.** John Agar, Joyce Meadows, Robert Fuller, Henry Travis, Bill Giorgio, Tim Graham, Thomas B(rowne). Henry, Ken Terrell; ***D:*** Nathan "Jerry" Juran; ***W:*** Ray Buffum; ***C:*** Jacques "Jack" Marquette; ***M:*** Walter Greene.

Brain of Blood **WOOF!** *The Creature's Revenge; Brain Damage* **1971** Deals with a scientist who transplants the brain of a politician into the body of a deformed idiot. The change is minimal. **107m/C VHS, DVD.** *PH* Kent Taylor, John Bloom, Regina Carrol, Angelo Rossitto, Grant Williams, Reed Hadley, Vicki Volante, Zandor Vorkov, Richard Smedley; ***D:*** Al Adamson; ***W:*** Joe Van Rogers; ***C:*** Louis Horvath.

Brain Smasher... A Love Story 🦴 **1993 (PG-13)** A bouncer and a super model become the targets of a gang of killer ninjas who want the mysterious blood-red lotus the model's been given. Of course they do. What's the lovely Hatcher doing in such a stupid movie? **88m/C VHS.** Andrew (Dice Clay) Silverstein, Teri Hatcher, Deanna (Dee) Booher, Deborah Van Valkenburgh, Brion James, Yuji Okumoto, Tim Thomerson, Charles Rocket, Nicholas Guest, Lin Shaye; ***D:*** Albert Pyun; ***W:*** Albert Pyun; ***C:*** George Mooradian; ***M:*** Tony Riparetti.

The Brain that Wouldn't Die 🦴🦴 ½ *The Head that Wouldn't Die* **1963** Love is a many-splattered thing when a brilliant surgeon keeps the decapitated head of his fiancee alive after an auto accident while he searches for a suitably stacked body onto which to transplant the head. Absurd and satiric (head talks so much that Doc tapes her/its mouth shut) adding up to major entry in trash film genre; much of the gore was slashed for the video, however. **92m/B VHS, DVD.** Herb Evers, Virginia Leith, Adele Lamont, Leslie Daniel, Bruce Brighton, Paula Maurice; ***D:*** Joseph Green; ***W:*** Joseph Green; ***C:*** Stephen Hajinal; ***M:*** Tony Restaino.

The Brainiac 🦴 ½ *El Baron del Terror; Baron of Terror* **1961** Sorcerer sentenced for black magic returns to strike dark deeds upon the descendants of those who judged him. He turns himself into a hideous monster, feeding on his victims' brains and blood. Yuck. **75m/B VHS, DVD.** *MX* Abel Salazar, Ariadne Welter, Mauricio Garces, Rosa Maria Gallardo, Ruben Rojo, German Robles; ***D:*** Chano Urueto; ***W:*** Frederick Curiel, Alfredo Torres Portillo; ***C:*** Jose Ortiz Ramos; ***M:*** Gustavo Cesar Carrion.

Brainscan 🦴 **1994 (R)** Teenage loner takes a trip in virtual reality and finds that murder is the first stop. Furlong ("Terminator 2") is the troubled youth whose voyage is led by Smith as Trickster, the Freddy Krueger meets David Bowie tour guide from virtual hell. Langella turns in a straight performance as a local cop hot on the trail. Hard-core horror fans will be disappointed by the lack of on-screen violence, and special effects buffs won't see anything new. Lame effort tries to appeal to a wide audience and is bland as a result. The end is left wide open, so expect a sequel or two or three. **96m/C VHS, DVD.** Edward Furlong, Frank Langella, T. Ryder Smith, David Hemblen, Amy Hargreaves, Jamie Marsh, Victor Ertmanis; ***D:*** John Flynn; ***W:*** Andrew Kevin Walker; ***M:*** George S. Clinton.

Brainstorm 🦴🦴 ½ **1983 (PG)** Husband-and-wife scientist team invents headphones that can record dreams, thoughts, and fantasies (VCR-style) and then allow other people to experience them by playing back the tape. Their marriage begins to crumble as the husband becomes more and more obsessed with pushing the limits of the technology; things get worse when the government wants to exploit their discovery. Special effects and interesting camera work punctuate this sci-fi flick. Wood's last film; in fact, she died before production was completed. **106m/C VHS, DVD.** Natalie Wood,

Christopher Walken, Cliff Robertson, Louise Fletcher; ***D:*** Douglas Trumbull; ***W:*** Bruce Joel Rubin; ***C:*** Richard Yuricich; ***M:*** James Horner.

Brainwashed *Die Schachnovelle; The Royal Game; Three Moves to Freedom* **1960** Austrian aristocrat Werner von Basil (Jurgens) is captured by the Nazis and interrogated to uncover military information. In order to keep his sanity, the prisoner concentrates on a chess book he keeps hidden in his cell. Based on the novel by Stefan Zweig. German with subtitles. **127m/C VHS.** *GE* Curt Jurgens, Claire Bloom, Hansjorg Felmy, Mario Adorf, Albert Lieven, Alan Gifford, Karel Stepanek; ***D:*** Gerd Oswald; ***W:*** Gerd Oswald, Harold Medford; ***C:*** Gunther Senftleben; ***M:*** Hans-Martin Majewski.

Brainwaves **1982 (R)** A young woman has disturbing flashbacks after her brain is electrically revived following a car accident. Curtis is the demented doctor who jump-starts her. **83m/C VHS, DVD.** Suzanna Love, Tony Curtis, Keir Dullea, Vera Miles, Eve Brent; ***D:*** Ulli Lommel; ***W:*** Ulli Lommel; ***C:*** Ulli Lommel, Jon Kranhouse; ***M:*** Robert O. Ragland.

Bram Stoker's Dracula *Dracula* **1992 (R)** Coppola's highly charged view of the vampire classic is visually stunning, heavy on eroticism and violence, and weak in plot and performance. Oldman, in a number of amazing transformations, portrays the deadly bloodsucker as a lonely soul determined to reunite with his lost love, the innocent Ryder. Hopkins cheerfully chews the scenery as nemesis Van Helsing, newcomer Frost is fetching, Reeves is lightweight, and Ryder goes way over the top. Musician Waits is great as bug-eating madman Renfield. Filmed entirely on soundstages with beautiful costumes and some amazing visual effects and sets. **128m/C VHS, DVD, Blu-ray Disc.** Monica Bellucci, Christina (Kristina) Fulton, Gary Oldman, Winona Ryder, Anthony Hopkins, Keanu Reeves, Richard E. Grant, Cary Elwes, Billy Campbell, Sadie Frost, Tom Waits; ***D:*** Francis Ford Coppola; ***W:*** James V. Hart; ***C:*** Michael Ballhaus. Oscars '92: Costume Des., Makeup, Sound FX Editing.

Bram Stoker's Shadowbuilder *Shadowbuilder* **1998 (R)** Silly update that apparently takes the title of the Bram Stoker short story but not much else. Shadowbuilder (Jackson) is a demonic creature that wants to unleash hell's power upon the unsuspecting town of Grand River. But he needs 12-year-old Chris (Zegers) for your basic satanic ritual, which doesn't go over well with the local priest (Rooker) and sheriff (Thompson). **101m/C VHS, DVD.** Michael Rooker, Leslie Hope, Andrew Jackson, Kevin Zegers, Shawn Thompson, Tony Todd, Richard McMillan; ***D:*** Jamie Dixon; ***W:*** Michael Stokes; ***C:*** David Pelletier; ***M:*** Eckart Seeber. **VIDEO**

Bram Stoker's The Mummy *The Mummy; Legend of the Mummy* **1997 (R)** Modern retelling of the horror tale focuses on the savage incident that left Egyptologist Abel Trelawny (Bochner) in a coma. Now his daughter, Margaret (Locane), seeks the help of her ex-lover, Robert (Lutes), to uncover the connection between Trewlawny and an Egyptian ritual to raise a queen from her tomb. Based on Stoker's book "The Jewel of the Seven Stars." **100m/C VHS, DVD.** Mary Jo Catlett, Amy Locane, Eric Lutes, Louis Gossett Jr., Victoria Tennant, Lloyd Bochner, Mark Lindsay Chapman, Richard Karn; ***D:*** Jeffrey Obrow; ***W:*** Jeffrey Obrow; ***C:*** Antonio Soriano; ***M:*** Rick Cox. **VIDEO**

Bram Stoker's Way of the Vampire **2005 (R)** Has absolutely nothing to do with Stoker's writings. Van Helsing (Giles) goes after Dracula (Logan), leaving his wife in the care of colleague Sebastian (Beckett). Only Sebastian is actually a blood-drinker, so no more missus. Van Helsing makes a deal with God to gain immortality until the last of Dracula's kin are dead. Which leads to a showdown in present-day LA between Van Helsing and Sebastian. **81m/C DVD.** Denise Boutte, Paul Logan, Rhett Giles, Brent Falco; ***D:*** Sara Nean Bruce, Eduardo Durao; ***W:*** Karrie Melendrez, Sherri Strain; ***C:*** Andreas Beckett, Zack Richard; ***M:*** Ralph Rieckermann.

The Bramble Bush **1/2 1960** Guy (Burton) is a doctor who returns to his New England hometown to care for a dying friend, Larry (Drake). Unfortunately, Guy falls for Larry's wife Mar (Rush) and they have an affair. When Guy pulls the plug on his friend's suffering, suspicious townspeople (who of course know what's going on) wonder just how "merciful" the doctor was really being and he's tried for murder. Tawdry "Peyton Place"-ish soap opera based on the novel by Charles Mergendahl. **104m/C VHS.** Richard Burton, Barbara Rush, Tom Drake, Jack Carson, Angie Dickinson, James Dunn, Henry Jones, Frank Conroy, Carl Benton Reid; ***D:*** Daniel Petrie; ***W:*** Philip Yordan.

Brand New Life **1972** A childless couple in their 40s are unexpectedly confronted by the wife's first pregnancy. Both have careers and well-ordered lives that promise to be disrupted. **74m/C VHS, DVD.** Cloris Leachman, Martin Balsam, Wilfrid Hyde-White, Mildred Dunnock; ***D:*** Sam O'Steen; ***M:*** Billy Goldenberg. **TV**

Brand of Fear **1/2 1949** Crooning cowpoke Wakely puts down his guitar long enough to chase rustlers off the land of an innocent lady in this average oater. **56m/B VHS.** Jimmy Wakely, Dub Taylor, Gail Davis, Tom London; ***D:*** Oliver Drake; ***W:*** Basil Dickey.

Brand of Hate **1934** A good cowboy rustles up a gang of rustlers. **61m/B VHS, DVD.** Bob Steele, George "Gabby" Hayes, Lucille Browne, James Flavin; ***D:*** Lewis D. Collins.

Brand of the Outlaws **1936** A cowboy becomes an unwitting aid to rustlers in this early western. **56m/B VHS.** Bob Steele, Margaret Marquis, Virginia True Boardman, Jack Rockwell; ***D:*** Robert North Bradbury.

Brand Upon the Brain! **2006 (R)** Like most of writer/director Guy Maddin's work, this requires a deliberate viewing. A silent film in black and white sets up primarily as a flashback, possibly to the director's youth, set on an island with a lighthouse that has served as an orphanage in the past. Film moves freely through images and recollections, revealing secret longings within an utterly absurd plot for which the film is not the least diminished. Make no mistake, this is a grandly indulgent art film. But what did you expect? Most enjoyable is the narration by Isabella Rossellini. **95m/C DVD.** *CA US* Erik Steffen Maahs, Sullivan Brown, Gretchen Krich, Maya Lawson, Todd Jefferson Moore, Katherine E. Scharhon; ***D:*** Guy Maddin; ***W:*** Guy Maddin, George Toles; ***C:*** Benjamin Kasulke; ***M:*** Jason Staczek; ***Nar:*** Isabella Rossellini.

Branded **1/2 1950** Ladd (pre-"Shane") impersonates the long-gone son of rich rancher Bickford, with unusual results. Nicely balanced action and love scenes makes this story a better-than-average western. Filmed in Technicolor. Based on the novel "Montana Rides" by Max Brand. **95m/C VHS, DVD.** Alan Ladd, Mona Freeman, Charles Bickford, Joseph Calleia, Milburn Stone; ***D:*** Rudolph Mate.

Branded a Bandit **1924** Yakima must avoid the sheriff while tracking down the killers of an old miner so that he can clear himself of the crime. **58m/C VHS.** Yakima Canutt; ***D:*** Paul Hurst.

Branded a Coward **1935** A man whose parents were killed seeks revenge via his trusty six-shooters. **56m/B VHS, DVD.** Johnny Mack Brown, Billie Seward, Yakima Canutt; ***D:*** Sam Newfield.

Branded Men **1931** A couple of oddballs become mixed up in a number of zany, western-type adventures. **60m/B VHS.** Ken Maynard, June Clyde, Irving Bacon, Billy Bletcher, Charles "Blackie" King, Donald Keith; ***D:*** Phil Rosen.

Branded to Kill *Koroshi no Rakuin* **1967** Visual tricks, including animated graphics, and a blues score highlight this gangster story, which follows No. 3 Killer, who's bungled his last hit. Now he's the target of No. 1 Killer. Japanese with subtitles. **91m/B VHS, DVD.** *JP* Joe Shishido, Mari Annu, Koji Nambara, Isao Tamagawa, Mariko Ogawa; ***D:*** Seijun Suzuki; ***W:*** Hachiro Guryu; ***C:*** Kazue Nagatsuka; ***M:*** Naozumi Yamamoto.

Brannigan **1/2 1975 (PG)** The Duke stars in the somewhat unfamiliar role of a rough and tumble Chicago police officer. He travels across the Atlantic to arrest a racketeer who has fled the States rather than face a grand jury indictment. Humor and action abound. **111m/C VHS, DVD.** John Wayne, John Vernon, Mel Ferrer, Daniel Pilon, James Booth, Ralph Meeker, Lesley-Anne Down, Richard Attenborough; ***D:*** Douglas Hickox; ***W:*** Michael Butler, William W. Norton Sr.; ***C:*** Gerry Fisher; ***M:*** Dominic Frontiere.

Brass **1/2 1985 (PG)** First post-Archie Bunker role for O'Connor, who plods through this average police drama at a snail's pace, dragging everything else down with him. Made-for-TV pilot for a series that never aired. **94m/C VHS.** Carroll O'Connor, Lois Nettleton, Jimmy Baio, Paul Shenar, Vincent Gardenia, Anita Gillette; ***D:*** Corey Allen. **TV**

The Brass Bottle **1/2 1963** Silly but amusing comedy that served as the inspiration for the TV series "I Dream of Jeannie," although Eden plays the girlfriend in this movie. Ives stars as jovial genie Fakrash, whose antique bottle is bought by architect Harold Ventimore (Randall). Fakrash wants nothing more than to make his new master happy but his efforts cause constant crises for the bewildered man, who'd prefer his life return to normal. Based on the novel by F. Anstey. **90m/C VHS.** Tony Randall, Burl Ives, Barbara Eden, Edward Andrews, Ann Doran, Kamala Devi, Howard Smith, Parley Baer; ***D:*** Harry Keller; ***W:*** Oscar Brodney; ***C:*** Clifford Stine; ***M:*** Bernard Green.

Brass Target **1/2 1978 (PG)** Hypothetical thriller about a plot to kill George Patton in the closing days of WWII for the sake of $250 million in Nazi gold stolen by his staff. Interesting cast can't find story. **111m/C VHS.** Sophia Loren, George Kennedy, Max von Sydow, John Cassavetes, Patrick McGoohan, Robert Vaughn, Bruce Davison, Edward Herrmann, Ed Bishop; ***D:*** John Hough; ***W:*** Alvin Boretz.

Brassed Off **1/2 1996 (R)** Bittersweet tale of despair and hope in the fictional coal mining town of Grimly in Yorkshire, England. Set in 1992, when sweeping closures of British coal mines devastated the area, the sole respite of these workers is playing in the pit's brass band. Secretly suffering from black lung disease, the band's leader (Postlethwaite) dreams of winning a competition in Albert Hall. Fitzgerald plays the flugelhorn-tooting vixen who returns to the small town, inspiring the music (and virility) of the formerly all male band. She resumes her relationship with former flame MacGregor, but all is on shaky ground with the imminent closure of the mine. Fine performances brighten the generally gloomy proceedings. The band is played by the real-life Grimethorpe Colliery Brass Band. **100m/C VHS, DVD.** *GB* Pete Postlethwaite, Ewan McGregor, Tara Fitzgerald, Jim Carter, Philip Jackson, Peter Martin, Stephen Tompkinson; ***D:*** Mark Herman; ***W:*** Mark Herman; ***C:*** Andy Collins; ***M:*** Trevor Jones. Cesar '98: Foreign Film.

Bratz **WOOF! 2007 (PG)** Four high school freshmen and best friends (Ramos, Browning, Parrish, and Shayne) find themselves at odds with the bossy student body president, who aims to split them up into (gasp!) separate social cliques. There's singing and dancing (like a big, long, pink, fluffy music video), and how sweetly cliche is it that these real-life Bratz are all from different ethnicities and socio-economic classes, yet still BFFs? At least these girls are (somewhat) real humans and not the creepy-faced, bubble-headed dolls (and animated characters) the movie is based on, but even your lip gloss-wearing 'tweener will roll her eyes at the mere suggestion of this film, which is cloying at best, intolerable at worst. **100m/C DVD.** *US* Skyler Shaye, Anneliese van der Pol, Jon Voight, Lainie Kazan, Nathalia Ramos, Janel Parrish, Logan Browning, Chelsea Staub, Stephen Lunsford, Ian Nelson; ***D:*** Sean McNamara; ***W:*** Susan Estelle Jansen; ***C:*** Christian Sebaldt; ***M:*** John Coda.

The Bravados **1958** A rough, distressing Western revenge tale, wherein a man is driven to find the four men who murdered his wife. In tracking the perpetrators, Peck realizes that he has been corrupted by his vengeance. **98m/C VHS, DVD.** Gregory Peck, Stephen Boyd, Joan Collins, Albert Salmi, Henry Silva, Lee Van Cleef, George Voskovec, Barry Coe; ***D:*** Henry King; ***W:*** Philip Yordan; ***C:*** Leon Shamroy. Natl. Bd. of Review '58: Support. Actor (Salmi).

The Brave Bunch **1/2 1970** A courageous Greek soldier tries to save his men and country during WWII. **110m/C VHS.** *GR* Peter Funk, Giannis Voglis; ***D:*** Costa Carayiannis.

Brave New Girl **1/2 2004 (PG-13)** Holly's got what it takes to get into the big-time music school and her poor-yet-resourceful mom won't let their lack of money stand in the way of her daughter's dream. But getting there is only half the ditty. Generically inspiring tale. Based on the novel "A Mother's Gift," by co-executive producers Britney and Lynne Spears. **90m/C VHS, DVD.** Virginia Madsen, Barbara Mamabolo, Aaron Ashmore, Lindsey Haun, Jackie Rosenbaum, Joanne Boland, Nick Roth; ***D:*** Bobby Roth; ***W:*** Britney Spears, Lynne Spears, Amy Talkington; ***C:*** Eric Van Haren Noman; ***M:*** Asher Ettinger. **TV**

The Brave One **1956** A love story between a Spanish boy and the bull who saves his life. The animal is later carted off to the bullring. Award-winning screenplay by the then-blacklisted Trumbo, credited as "Robert Rich." **100m/C VHS, DVD.** Michel Ray, Rodolfo Hoyos, Joi Lansing; ***D:*** Irving Rapper; ***W:*** Dalton Trumbo; ***C:*** Jack Cardiff; ***M:*** Victor Young. Oscars '56: Story.

The Brave One **1/2 2007 (R)** Erica Bain (Foster), the host of a radio show named "City Walk,", has spent years gushing about the wonders of life in her beloved New York City. She encounters a trio of thugs while walking with fiance David (Andrews) in Central Park. The two suffer a gruesome beating, which proves lethal for David and barely survivable for Erica, who, after months of recovery and in the throes of post-traumatic stress, acquires a hand gun. Erica suddenly and routinely witnesses violent criminal acts and begins to mete out street justice while forming a platonic relationship with Detective Mercer (Howard), who is investigating the series of vigilante-style slayings. Their interactions are a bright spot in an otherwise brutal story line. It may sound a bit (okay, a lot) like "Death Wish" but the distinction is Erica's inner turmoil, skillfully played out by Foster. Still, the overwhelming violence outweighs the attempt to humanize her character, and ultimately it fails as both an insightful psycho-thriller and as a vigilante shoot-'em-up. **119m/C DVD, HD DVD.** *US* Jodie Foster, Terrence Howard, Naveen Andrews, Carmen Ejogo, Nicky Katt, Mary Steenburgen, Lenny Venito, Lenny Kravitz; ***D:*** Neil Jordan; ***W:*** Roderick Taylor, Bruce Taylor, Cynthia Mort; ***C:*** Philippe Rousselot; ***M:*** Dario Marianelli.

Braveheart **1/2 1925** When a Native American adapts to the white man's world, he alienates his own people. He eventually chooses to renounce his love for a white woman, and returns to lead his people. Silent. **62m/B VHS.** Lillian Rich, Robert Edeson, Tyrone Power, Sally Rand, Arthur Housman, Rod La Rocque; ***D:*** Alan Hale; ***W:*** Mary O'Hara; ***C:*** Faxon M. Dean.

Braveheart **1/2 1995 (R)** Producer-director-star Gibson does it all in this bold, ferocious, reasonably accurate epic about the passion and cost of freedom. Charismatic 13th century Scottish folk hero William Wallace leads his desperate and outnumbered clansmen in revolt against British oppression. Sweeping, meticulous battle scenes fit suprisingly well with moments of stirring romance and snappy wit. Among the mostly unknown (in the States, anyway) cast, Marceau and McCormack are elegant as Wallace's lady loves, and McGoohan is positively hateful as King Edward I. Gory and excessively violent (as medieval warfare tends to be) and a bit too long (as historical epics tend to be), but rewarding entertainment for those who stick it out—where else can you see the king's army get mooned en masse? Script was based on 300 pages of rhyming verse attributed to a blind poet known as Blind Harry. Gibson put up $15 million of his own money to complete the film. **178m/C VHS, DVD.** Mel Gibson, Sophie Marceau, Patrick McGoohan, Catherine McCormack, Brendan Gleeson, James Cosmo, David O'Hara, Angus MacFadyen, Peter Hanly, Ian Bannen, Sean McGinley, Brian Cox, Stephen Billington, Barry McGovern, Alun Armstrong, Tommy Flanagan; ***D:*** Mel Gibson; ***W:*** Randall

Wallace; *C:* John Toll; *M:* James Horner. Oscars '95: Cinematog., Director (Gibson), Makeup, Picture; British Acad. '95: Cinematog.; Golden Globes '96: Director (Gibson); MTV Movie Awards '96: Action Seq.; Writers Guild '95: Orig. Screenplay; Broadcast Film Critics '95: Director (Gibson).

The Bravos 🦴🦴 **1972** U.S. Cavalry officer Harkness (Peppard) is in charge of remote outpost. He's trying to protect his fort and a wagon train from an Indian uprising while also searching for his missing son (Van Patten). Standard made-for-TV adventure with a familiar cast. **97m/C DVD.** George Peppard, Pernell Roberts, Belinda J. Montgomery, L.Q. Jones, Vincent Van Patten, George Murdock, Barry Brown, Dana Elcar, Bo Svenson; *D:* Ted Post; *W:* Christopher Knopf; *C:* Leonard Rosenman. **TV**

Brazil 🦴🦴🦴 ½ **1985 (R)** The acclaimed nightmare comedy about an Everyman trying to survive in a surreal paper-choked bureaucratic society. There are copious references to "1984" and "The Trial," fantastic mergings of glorious fantasy and stark reality, and astounding visual design. The DVD version has a 142-minute director's cut as well as a documentary. **131m/C VHS, DVD.** *GB* Jonathan Pryce, Robert De Niro, Michael Palin, Katherine Helmond, Kim Greist, Bob Hoskins, Ian Holm, Peter Vaughan, Ian Richardson; *D:* Terry Gilliam; *W:* Charles McKeown, Terry Gilliam, Tom Stoppard; *C:* Roger Pratt; *M:* Michael Kamen. L.A. Film Critics '85: Director (Gilliam), Film, Screenplay.

Breach 🦴🦴 ½ **2007 (PG-13)** Somber true story follows ambitious FBI agent Eric O'Neill (Phillippe), who's planted by tough boss Kate Burroughs (Linney) as the new assistant to veteran agent Robert Hanssen (Cooper). She says the bureau is worried because Hanssen is a perv, but he's actually been selling info to the Russians and the feds want to catch him in the act. Hanssen starts getting suspicious, which ratchets up the tension, but there's never any clear idea of why he turned traitor, although Cooper is a creepily effective enigma. **110m/C DVD, HD DVD.** *US* Chris Cooper, Ryan Phillippe, Laura Linney, Dennis Haysbert, Caroline Dhavernas, Gary Cole, Bruce Davison, Kathleen Quinlan; *D:* Billy Ray; *W:* Billy Ray, Adam Mazer, William Rotko; *C:* Tak Fujimoto; *M:* Mychael Danna.

Breach of Conduct 🦴 ½ **1994 (PG-13)** Col. Bill Case (Coyote) is the commander of the Fort Benton, Utah, Army base where Helen Lutz's (Thorne-Smith) husband Tom (Verica) has just been transferred. At first there's a mutual attraction between Helen and Case, but then hubby is assigned a mission off base and, when Helen refuses Case's overtures, things turn very nasty. **93m/C VHS.** Peter Coyote, Courtney Thorne-Smith, Tom Verica, Beth Toussaint; *D:* Tim Matheson; *W:* Scott Abbott; *C:* Gideon Porath. **CABLE**

Breach of Trust 🦴🦴 ½ **1995 (R)** Smalltime crook Casey (Biehn) winds up in big trouble when he steals a computer disc with access codes to millions in drug cartel money. He goes on the lam and meets Madeline (Ferrer), an undercover cop who thinks that some police are on the cartel's payroll. So the daring duo decide to take on the drug lords and the dirty cops. **96m/C VHS.** Michael Biehn, Matt Craven, Leilani Sarelle Ferrer, Miguel (Michael) Sandoval, Kim Coates, Ed Lauter; *D:* Charles Wilkinson; *W:* Gordon Basichis, Raul Inglis; *C:* Michael Slovis; *M:* Graeme Coleman.

Bread and Chocolate 🦴🦴🦴 *Pane e Cioccolata* **1973** Uneducated Italian immigrant Manfredi works a series of odd jobs in complacently bourgeois Switzerland and tries desperately to fit in and better himself (which he fails utterly to do). Culture clash satire, with an engaging everyman lead. Italian with subtitles. **110m/C VHS, DVD.** *IT* Nino Manfredi, Anna Karina, Johnny Dorelli, Paolo Turco; *D:* Franco Brusati; *W:* Nino Manfredi, Franco Brusati, Iaia Fiastri; *C:* Luciano Tovoli; *M:* Daniele Patrucchi. N.Y. Film Critics '78: Foreign Film.

Bread and Roses 🦴🦴 **2000 (R)** Typical Loach political polemic—this time about union organizing of janitors (many of them illegals) in Los Angeles. Maya (Padilla) is an illegal immigrant from Mexico who's working for an office cleaning company. She meets union organizer Sam (Brody) who convinces Maya to join with him, even though she not only risks her job but deportation. Things go from bad to worse for Maya but Loach never takes the easy road and his characters are flawed human beings rather than mere symbols. English and Spanish with subtitles. **106m/C VHS, DVD.** *GB* Adrien Brody, Elpidia Carrillo, Pilar Padilla, George Lopez, Jack McGee, Alonso Chavez; *D:* Ken Loach; *W:* Paul Laverty; *C:* Barry Ackroyd; *M:* George Fenton.

Bread and Tulips 🦴🦴🦴 *Pane e Tulipani* **2001 (PG-13)** Sweet Rosalba (Maglietta) is a much-neglected wife and mother who is accidentally left behind at a rest stop while the family is on vacation. Impulsively, Rosalba doesn't go home but hitches a ride to Venice, a city she has always longed to see. Although, she dutifully lets her husband Mimmo (Catania) know where she is, she delays her return, is befriended by waiter Fernando (Ganz), and finds a job working for a florist. Rosalba's idyll doesn't last as her loyalties pull her back to her old life but events don't work out as expected. Italian with subtitles. **105m/C VHS, DVD.** *IT SI* Licia Maglietta, Bruno Ganz, Marina Massironi, Guiseppe Battiston, Antonio Catania, Felice Andreasi, Vitalba Andrea; *D:* Silvio Soldini; *W:* Silvio Soldini, Doriana Leondeff; *C:* Luca Bigazzi; *M:* Giovanni Venosta.

Bread, Love and Dreams 🦴🦴 *Pane, Amore e Fantasia* **1953** Middle-aged Antonio (DeSica) is the new police chief in a small village who's looking to make sexy young Maria (Lollobrigida) his wife. But she's in love with one of his subordinates, and another woman (Merlini) is interested in Antonio instead. Followed by "Bread, Love and Jealousy" (1954). Italian with subtitles. **90m/B DVD.** *IT* Gina Lollobrigida, Roberto Risso, Vittorio DeSica, Marisa Merlini; *D:* Luigi Comencini; *W:* Luigi Comencini; *C:* Arturo Gallea; *M:* Alessandro Cicognini.

The Bread, My Sweet 🦴🦴 ½ *A Wedding for Bella* **2001 (PG-13)** Corporate exec Dominic (Baio) also helps his brothers, Eddie (Mott) and Pinio (Hensley), run a bakery in an old Italian neighborhood in Pittsburgh. Their landlords (and surrogate parents) are old-fashioned immigrants Massimo (Seitz) and Bella (Prinz), who confides to Dominic that she's dying. So Dominic impulsively decides to marry their free-spirited daughter Lucca (Minter), who goes along so her marriage-minded mother can die in peace. Naturally (and unsurprisingly) the cutie twosome develop real feelings for one another. **105m/C DVD.** *US* Scott Baio, Kristin Minter, Rosemary Prinz, John Seitz, Billy Mott, Shuler Hensley; *D:* Melissa Martin; *W:* Melissa Martin; *C:* Mark Knobil; *M:* Susan Hartford.

The Break 🦴🦴 **1995 (PG-13)** Clumsy teen tennis hopeful Ben (Jorgensen) refuses to give up his dreams even after his bookie dad Robbins (Sheen) hires washed-up player Nick Irons (Van Patten) as a coach to show Ben the error of his game. **104m/C VHS, DVD.** Vincent Van Patten, Martin Sheen, Ben Jorgensen, Rae Dawn Chong, Valerie Perrine, Betsy Russell; *D:* Lee H. Katzin; *W:* Dan Jenkins, Vincent Van Patten.

The Break 🦴🦴 ½ *A Further Gesture* **1997 (R)** Disillusioned IRA gunman Dowd (Rea) breaks out of prison and escapes to New York to find a new life. Instead, he befriends (and falls in love with one of) a group of Guatemalan refugees who plan to kill the dictator who persecuted them. Appalled by their inability, he agrees to help them. This is definitely Rea's film (it's based on an idea of his), mainly because his is the only character that's really fleshed out. Character study of a man who's lost whatever passion he had for the cause but can't give up the life doesn't delve into specific Irish or Guatemalan politics, and loses some impact as a result. **97m/C VHS.** Stephen Rea, Rosana Pastor, Brendan Gleeson, Pruitt Taylor Vince, Maria Doyle Kennedy, Jorge Sanz, Carolyn Seymour, Sean McGinley, Paul Giamatti; *D:* Robert Dornhelm, Alfred Molina; *W:* Ronan Bennett; *C:* Andrzej Sekula; *M:* John Keane.

Break 🦴 ½ **2009** Hitman Frank (Krueger) is hired by crime boss The Man (Everett), who has a terminal illness. Frank's okay with the contract until The Man insists Frank also kill his girlfriend (Thompson) so he won't die alone. Naturally the woman turns out to be Frank's long-lost love. Low-budget and kinda campy with its silly plot, but it does have a fair amount of action. **93m/C DVD.** Frank Krueger, Chad Everett, Sarah Thompson, Michael Madsen, David Carradine, Charles Durning, James Russo; *D:* Marc Clebanoff; *W:* Marc Clebanoff; *C:* Tim Otholt; *M:* Peter DiStefano. **VIDEO**

Break a Leg 🦴🦴 **2003 (R)** Struggling actor Max (John Cassini) has talent but keeps losing roles to bigger names and nepotism. So he decides to literally cripple the competition, only to find out that an undercover cop (Rivera) is taking an interest in the case. **98m/C DVD.** John Cassini, Molly Parker, Rene Rivera, Jennifer Beals, Kevin Corrigan, Sandra Oh, Danny Nucci, Eric Roberts, Frank Cassini; *D:* Monika Mitchell; *W:* John Cassini, Frank Cassini; *C:* Eric Goldstein; *M:* Roger Bellon.

Break of Dawn 🦴🦴 ½ **1988** Pedro J. Gonzalez (Chavez) is a veteran of Pancho Villa's army who takes his family and crosses into the U.S. Despite the Depression, he finds work at a radio station in L.A. and soon becomes a popular personality in the Latino community. But Gonzalez never leaves politics very far behind and his radical civil rights views lead to a political witchhunt that sends him to prison. **105m/C VHS, DVD.** Oscar Chavez, Maria Rojo, Tony Plana, Peter Henry Schroeder, Pepe Serna, Kamala Lopez-Dawson; *D:* Isaac Artenstein; *W:* Isaac Artenstein; *C:* Stephen Lighthill; *M:* Mark Adler. **TV**

Break of Hearts 🦴🦴 ½ **1935** Hepburn marries Boyer, who becomes an alcoholic, and then more troubles arise. Very soapy, but well-made. **78m/B VHS.** Katharine Hepburn, Charles Boyer, Jean Hersholt, John Beal, Sam Hardy; *D:* Philip Moeller; *W:* Victor Heerman; *M:* Max Steiner.

The Break Up 🦴🦴 ½ **1998 (R)** Predictable thriller finds Jimmy Dade (Fonda) awakening in the hospital to discover her abusive husband (Bochner) is dead and she is the prime suspect. **101m/C VHS, DVD.** Bridget Fonda, Kiefer Sutherland, Penelope Ann Miller, Steven Weber, Hart Bochner, Tippi Hedren; *D:* Paul Marcus; *W:* Anne Amanda Opotowsky.

The Break-Up 🦴🦴 **2006 (PG-13)** Gary (Vaughn) and Brooke (Aniston) are a completely incompatible couple (he's boorish, she's high-strung) who own a Chicago condo that comes into bitter dispute when they split. Since neither will willingly leave, they seek to drive the other crazy enough so they'll bail...as everyone else must watch and suffer. There's not much romance or comedy to be seen and it's definitely NOT a date movie—unless you're planning a break-up of your own. **106m/C DVD, HD DVD.** *US* Jennifer Aniston, Vince Vaughn, Joey Lauren Adams, Judy Davis, Cole Hauser, Jon Favreau, Ann-Margret, Justin Long, Vincent D'Onofrio, Jason Bateman, Peter Billingsley, John Michael Higgins, Ivan Sergei; *D:* Peyton Reed; *W:* Jeremy Garelick, Jay Lavender; *C:* Eric Alan Edwards; *M:* Jon Brion.

Breakaway 🦴 **1995 (R)** Myra (Thompson) decides to get away from her drop-woman job with $300,000 of mob money. Naturally, she's pursued by a hit man (Estevez) and then betrayed by a boyfriend (De Rose), who steals the cash and hides it in the apartment of the other woman he's seeing (Harding). Thompson does fine but to describe Harding's debut performance as wooden is to be very, very kind. **94m/C VHS.** Teri Thompson, Joe Estevez, Chris De Rose, Tonya Harding, Tony Noakes, Rick Beatty, Michael Garganese; *D:* Sean Dash; *W:* Sean Dash, Eric Gardner; *C:* Carlos Montaner; *M:* Robert Wait.

Breakaway 🦴 ½ *Christmas Rush* **2002 (R)** Poorly made rip-off of the "Die Hard" series. Set in a mall at Christmas, Cornelius Morgan (Cain)—suspended by the force—swings by to get his wife (Eleniak-Goglia) but a robbery/hostage situation unfolds. Strictly for those in need of a holiday explosion fix. **91m/C DVD.** Dean Cain, Erika Eleniak, Richard Yearwood, Roman Podhora, Bernard Browne, Santino Buda, Aleks Punovic, Angelo Tsarouchas, Eric Roberts, Jack Wallace, Christopher Benson, Larry Mannell, Rothaford Gray, Jessica Smith, Brooke Palsson, Trevor Toffan, Corinne Conley, Vicki Marentette, Patricia Harras, Ed Sutton, Ernesto Griffith, David (Dave) Brown, Tommy Chang, Vince Crestejo; *D:* Charles Robert Carner; *W:* Charles Robert Carner; *C:* Michael Goi; *M:* Louis Febre. **TV**

Breakdown 🦴 **1953** A boxer is set up by his girlfriend's father to take the rap for a murder. Lackluster effort. **76m/B VHS, DVD.** Ann Richards, William Bishop, Anne Gwynne, Sheldon Leonard, Wally Cassell, Richard Benedict; *D:* Edmond Angelo.

Breakdown 🦴🦴🦴 **1996 (R)** Jeff (Russell) and Amy (Quinlan) are high-falootin' Easterners on their way to San Diego when their car breaks down somewhere in the vast Southwest. When a trucker (Walsh) stops and offers to take Amy to the next stop while Jeff guards their yuppie treasure trove, they accept willingly. Inconvenience soon turns to terror when Jeff gets the car started, drives to meet his wife and finds her nowhere in sight. Spotting the truck by the side of the road, he confronts the trucker with the cops only to have him deny ever having seen them before. Thus begins the frantic hunt. Russell's descent from dismay to panic to resolve is grippingly played. You may know where it's going, but the fun is in getting there. **93m/C VHS, DVD.** Kurt Russell, Kathleen Quinlan, J.T. Walsh, M.C. Gainey, Jack Noseworthy, Rex Linn, Ritch Brinkley, Kim Robillard; *D:* Jonathan Mostow; *W:* Jonathan Mostow; *C:* Doug Milsome; *M:* Basil Poledouris.

Breaker! Breaker! 🦴 **1977 (PG)** Convoy of angry truck drivers launch an assault on the corrupt and sadistic locals of a small Texas town. Goofy entry in "mad or sex-crazed trucker armed with a CB radio" genre. **86m/C VHS, DVD.** Chuck Norris, George Murdock, Terry O'Connor, Don Gentry, Jack Nance; *D:* Don Hulette; *W:* Terry Chambers; *C:* Mario DiLeo; *M:* Don Hulette.

Breaker Morant 🦴🦴🦴 ½ **1980 (PG)** In 1901 South Africa, three Australian soldiers are put on trial for avenging the murder of several prisoners. Based on a true story which was then turned into a play by Kenneth Ross, this riveting, popular antiwar statement and courtroom drama heralded Australia's film renaissance. Rich performances by Woodward and Waters. **107m/C VHS, DVD, Blu-ray Disc.** *AU* Edward Woodward, Jack Thompson, John Waters, Bryan Brown, Charles "Bud" Tingwell, Terence Donovan, Vincent Ball, Ray Meagher, Chris Haywood, Lewis Fitz-Gerald, Rod Mullinar, Alan Cassell, Rob Steele; *D:* Bruce Beresford; *W:* Bruce Beresford, Jonathan Hardy, David Stevens; *C:* Donald McAlpine; *M:* Phil Cunneen. Australian Film Inst. '80: Actor (Thompson), Film.

Breakfast at Tiffany's 🦴🦴🦴 ½ **1961** Truman Capote's amusing story of an endearingly eccentric New York City playgirl and her shaky romance with a young writer. Hepburn lends Holly Golightly just the right combination of naivete and worldly wisdom with a dash of melancholy. A wonderfully offbeat romance. ♫Moon River. **114m/C VHS, DVD.** Audrey Hepburn, George Peppard, Patricia Neal, Buddy Ebsen, Mickey Rooney, Martin Balsam, John McGiver; *D:* Blake Edwards; *W:* George Axelrod; *C:* Franz Planer; *M:* Henry Mancini. Oscars '61: Song ("Moon River"), Orig. Dramatic Score.

The Breakfast Club 🦴🦴🦴 **1985 (R)** Five students from different cliques at a Chicago suburban high school spend a day together in detention. Rather well done teenage culture study; these characters delve a little deeper than the standard adult view of adolescent stereotypes. One of John Hughes' best movies. Soundtrack features Simple Minds and Wang Chung. **97m/C VHS, DVD, HD DVD.** Ally Sheedy, Molly Ringwald, Judd Nelson, Emilio Estevez, Anthony Michael Hall, Paul Gleason, John Kapelos; *D:* John Hughes; *W:* John Hughes; *C:* Thomas Del Ruth; *M:* Gary Chang, Keith Forsey.

Breakfast for Two 🦴🦴 ½ **1937** Snappy screwball comedy finds Texas heiress Valentine (Stanwyck) trying to get playboy Jonathan (Marshall) to take some responsibility for his failing steamship line. Valentine buys a controlling interest in the company to teach him a lesson, which only results in Jonathan deciding to marry his golddigger fiancee Carol (Farrell) when you just know who really suits him. Well, Butch (Blore) the valet is also smarter than his employer and that shipboard wedding runs into some problems. **68m/B DVD.** Barbara Stanwyck, Herbert Marshall, Glenda Farrell, Eric Blore, Etienne Girardot, Frank M. Thomas Sr., Donald Meek; ***D:*** Alfred Santell; ***W:*** Paul Yawitz, Charles Kaufman, Viola Brothers Shore; ***C:*** J. Roy Hunt; ***M:*** George Hively.

Breakfast in Hollywood 🦴 1/2 *The Mad Hatter* **1946** Movie about the popular morning radio show of the 1940s hosted by Tom Breneman, a coast-to-coast coffee klatch. **93m/B VHS, DVD.** Tom Breneman, Bonita Granville, Eddie Ryan, Beulah Bondi, Billie Burke, Zasu Pitts, Hedda Hopper, Spike Jones; ***D:*** Harold Schuster.

Breakfast in Paris 🦴 1/2 **1981** Two American professionals in Paris, both crushed from past failures in the love department, find each other. **85m/C VHS.** *AU* Rod Mullinar, Barbara Parkins, Jack Lenoir; ***D:*** John Lamond.

Breakfast of Champions 🦴 1/2 **1998 (R)** Messy adaptation of Kurt Vonnegut's 1973 satire on American greed and commercialism. Relentlessly upbeat salesman Dwayne Hoover (Willis) runs the most successful car dealership in middle America's Midland City. A leading citizen, who stars in his own garish TV commercials, Dwayne has alienated his tube-addicted wife, Celia (Hershey), and his aspiring lounge singer son, Bunny (Haas). Dwayne also thinks he's going nuts and his one hope for salvation lies with Kilgore Trout (Finney), an eccentric hack sci fi writer/philosopher. Oh yeah, and Nolte is around as Dwayne's sales manager Harry, who likes to wear women's lacy lingerie beneath his suits. **110m/C VHS, DVD.** Bruce Willis, Albert Finney, Nick Nolte, Barbara Hershey, Glenne Headly, Lukas Haas, Omar Epps, Buck Henry, Vicki Lewis, Ken H. Campbell, Will Patton, Chip Zien, Owen Wilson, Alison Eastwood, Shawnee Smith, Kurt Vonnegut Jr.; ***D:*** Alan Rudolph; ***W:*** Alan Rudolph; ***C:*** Elliot Davis; ***M:*** Mark Isham.

Breakheart Pass 🦴🦴 **1976 (PG)** A governor, his female companion, a band of cavalrymen, and a mysterious man travel on a train through the mountains of Idaho in 1870. The mystery man turns out to be a murderer. Based on a novel by Alistair MacLean. **92m/C VHS, DVD.** Charles Bronson, Ben Johnson, Richard Crenna, Jill Ireland, Charles Durning, Ed Lauter, Archie Moore, Sally Kirkland; ***D:*** Tom Gries; ***W:*** Alistair MacLean; ***C:*** Lucien Ballard; ***M:*** Jerry Goldsmith.

Breakin' 🦴🦴 *Breakdance* **1984 (PG)** Dance phenomenon break dancing along with the hit songs that accompanied the fad. ♫Tibetan Jam; Heart of the Beat; Breakin...There's No Stopping Us; Street People; Showdown; 99 1/2. **87m/C VHS, DVD.** Lucinda Dickey, Adolfo "Shabba Doo" Quinones, Michael "Boogaloo Shrimp" Chambers, Ben Lokey, Christopher McDonald, Phineas Newborn III; ***D:*** Joel Silberg; ***W:*** Allen N. DeBevoise; ***C:*** Hanania Baer; ***M:*** Michael Boyd.

Breakin' 2: Electric Boogaloo 🦴 *Breakdance 2: Electric Boogaloo; Electric Boogaloo "Breakin' 2"* **1984 (PG)** Breakdancers hold a benefit concert to preserve an urban community center. ♫Electric Boogaloo; Radiotron; Action; When I.C.U. **94m/C VHS, DVD.** Lucinda Dickey, Adolfo "Shabba Doo" Quinones, Michael "Boogaloo Shrimp" Chambers, Susie Bono; ***D:*** Sam Firstenberg; ***C:*** Hanania Baer.

Breakin' All The Rules 🦴🦴 1/2 **2004 (PG-13)** Predictable romantic comedy stars Foxx as L.A. men's magazine exec Quincy Watson, who gets dumped by his fiancee Helen (Lawson) the same day his timid boss Phillip (MacNicol) wants Quincy to lay off 15% of the mag's staff. Instead, Quincy axes himself and takes his frustrations and rejections out on paper, writing what turns out to be the best-selling "Breakup Handbook." Suddenly, Quincy is Mr. Advice for Phillip, who wants to know how to avoid the gold-digging Rita (Esposito), and Quincy's playa cousin Evan (Chestnut),who wants to dump his girlfriend Nicky (Union) before she dumps him. Complications ensue when Quincy unwittingly falls for Nicky and Rita goes after Evan thinking he's Quincy. It's contrived but well done, with Foxx smirking likeably and Union lovely as always. **85m/C VHS, DVD.** *US* Jamie Foxx, Gabrielle Union, Morris Chestnut, Peter MacNichol, Jennifer Esposito, Bianca Lawson, Jill Ritchie; ***Cameos:*** Heather Headley; ***D:*** Daniel Taplitz; ***W:*** Daniel Taplitz; ***C:*** David Hennings; ***M:*** Marcus Miller.

Breakin' Through 🦴 **1984** The choreographer of a troubled Broadway-bound musical decides to energize his shows with a troupe of street dancers. **73m/C VHS.** Ben Vereen, Donna McKechnie, Reid Shelton; ***D:*** Peter Medak.

Breaking All the Rules 🦴 1/2 **1985 (R)** Comedy about two teenage lovers who find themselves embroiled in a slapdash jewel robbery at an amusement park during the last day of summer break. **91m/C VHS.** *CA* Carolyn Dunn, Carl Marotte, Thor Bishopric, Rachel Hayward; ***D:*** James Orr; ***W:*** James Orr, Jim Cruickshank.

Breaking and Entering 🦴🦴 **2006 (R)** Landscape architect Will (Law) and his partner Sandy (Freeman) are pioneers in the urban renewal of the crime-ridden King's Cross area in North London. However, after their office is repeatedly broken into, Will finally manages to chase the young thief long enough to discover where he lives. The thief, Miro (Gavron), is a teenaged Bosnian refugee, living with his widowed seamstress mother, Amira (Binoche). Instead of immediately ratting Miro out, Will cozies up to his attractive mum since his own home life is lacking (Wright Penn plays his depressive live-in). Law's character is a polite cipher and the dicey situations resolve themselves a little too neatly in Minghella's slice of life drama. **116m/C DVD.** *GB* Jude Law, Juliette Binoche, Robin Wright Penn, Martin Freeman, Ray Winstone, Vera Farmiga, Juliet Stevenson, Rafi Gavron, Poppy Rogers; ***D:*** Anthony Minghella; ***W:*** Anthony Minghella; ***C:*** Benoit Delhomme; ***M:*** Gabriel Yared.

Breaking Away 🦴🦴🦴 1/2 **1979 (PG)** A lighthearted coming-of-age drama about a high school graduate's addiction to bicycle racing, whose dreams are tested against the realities of a crucial race. An honest, open look at present Americana with tremendous insight into the minds of average youth; shot on location at Indiana University. Great bike-racing photography. Quaid, Barrie, and Christopher give exceptional performances. Basis for a TV series. **100m/C VHS, DVD.** Dennis Christopher, Dennis Quaid, Daniel Stern, Jackie Earle Haley, Barbara Barrie, Paul Dooley, Amy Wright; ***D:*** Peter Yates; ***W:*** Steve Tesich; ***C:*** Matthew F. Leonetti; ***M:*** Patrick Williams. Oscars '79: Orig. Screenplay; Golden Globes '80: Film—Mus./Comedy; Natl. Bd. of Review '79: Support. Actor (Dooley); N.Y. Film Critics '79: Screenplay; Natl. Soc. Film Critics '79: Film, Screenplay; Writers Guild '79: Orig. Screenplay.

Breaking Free 🦴🦴 1/2 **1995 (PG)** Teenaged loser Rick Chilton (London) forms an unlikely friendship with bitter gymnast Lindsay (Phillips) who's been blinded and forced to give up her dreams. Mostly avoids the stickiness inherent in such stories thanks to some fine performances. **106m/C VHS.** Jeremy London, Gina Philips, Christine Taylor, Megan Gallagher, Nicolas Surovy, Adam Wylie, Brian Krause, Scott Coffey; ***D:*** David Mackay; ***C:*** Christopher Faloona; ***M:*** Steve Dorff.

Breaking Glass 🦴🦴 1/2 **1980 (PG)** A "New Wave" musical that gives an insight into the punk record business and at the same time tells of the rags-to-riches life of a punk rock star. **94m/C VHS, DVD.** *GB* Hazel O'Connor, Phil Daniels, Jon Finch, Jonathan Pryce; ***D:*** Brian Gibson.

Breaking Home Ties 🦴🦴 1/2 *Norman Rockwell's Breaking Home Ties* **1987** Norman Rockwell's illustration is the basis for this coming-of-age story set in a small Texas town. A young man is eager to be off to college and lessen his family ties but his mother's serious illness may prevent both. Good performances help overcome the sentimentality. **95m/C VHS.** Jason Robards Jr., Eva Marie Saint, Doug McKeon, Claire Trevor, Erin Gray; ***D:*** John Wilder; ***W:*** John Wilder. **TV**

Breaking In 🦴🦴🦴 **1989 (R)** A semi-acclaimed comedy about a professional thief who takes a young amateur under his wing and shows him the ropes. Under-estimated Reynolds is especially charming. Witty and innovative script, with intelligent direction from Forsyth. **95m/C VHS, DVD.** Burt Reynolds, Casey Siemaszko, Sheila Kelley, Lorraine Toussaint, Albert Salmi, Harry Carey Jr., Maury Chaykin, Stephen Tobolowsky, David Frishberg; ***D:*** Bill Forsyth; ***W:*** John Sayles; ***C:*** Michael Coulter; ***M:*** Michael Gibbs.

Breaking Loose 🦴 1/2 **1990 (R)** A surfer is on the run from a vicious motorcycle gang that kidnapped his girlfriend, but turns to fight eventually, board in hand. **88m/C VHS.** Peter Phelps, Vince Martin, Abigail, David Ngoombujarra; ***D:*** Rod Hay.

Breaking News 🦴🦴 *Daai Si Gin* **2004** Action director To starts off with a mesmerizing 7-minute scene that follows the camera along a Hong Kong street, culminating in a shootout between crooks and cops (cops lose). Since a TV news crew got the whole debacle on tape, the humiliated department lets ambitious Inspector Rebecca Fong (Chen) equip the cops with web cams that will allow the proper spin as they hunt for the hostage-taking thieves; too bad the criminals strike back with their own video ops. Cantonese with subtitles. **90m/C DVD.** *HK* Richie Jen, Kelly Chen, Nick Cheung, Hui Siu Hung, Lam Suet, Cheung Sui Fai, Simon Yam, You Yong, Ding Hai Feng, Le Hai Tao, Maggie Shiu; ***D:*** Johnny To; ***W:*** Chan Hing Kai, Ip Tin Shing; ***C:*** Cheng Siu Keung; ***M:*** Ben Cheung, Ching Chi Wing.

Breaking Point 🦴🦴 1/2 **1994 (R)** Excop Dwight Meadows (Busey) retired from the force when he was nearly killed by a scalpel-wielding mass murderer known as "The Surgeon." Now the psycho is back and Meadows returns to active duty, paired with relentless officer Dana Preston (Fluegel), who wants the killer caught—at any cost. Vancouver, British Columbia fills in for the Seattle, Washington setting. **95m/C VHS.** Gary Busey, Darlanne Fluegel, Jeff Griggs, Kim Cattrall; ***D:*** Paul Ziller; ***M:*** Graeme Coleman.

Breaking Point 🦴 1/2 **2009 (R)** One of the few reasons to watch this generic crime drama is the ferocious performance of Busta Rhymes as a murderous gangster. Former defense attorney Steven Luisi (Berenger) was brought low by drug addiction and personal tragedy. Trying to redeem himself by investigating a high-profile murder, Luisi finds his former dealer Al Bowen (Rhymnes) and corrupt DA Marty Berlin (Assante) behind the violence. **93m/C DVD.** Tom Berenger, Busta Rhymes, Armand Assante, Kirk "Sticky Fingaz" Jones, Musetta Vander, Frankie Faison, Robert Capelli Jr.; ***D:*** Jeff Celentano; ***W:*** Vincent Campanella; ***C:*** Emmanuel Vouniozos; ***M:*** Pinar Toprak. **VIDEO**

Breaking the Code 🦴🦴 1/2 **1995** Alan Turing (Jacobi) is a British mathematical genius whose work leads to the birth of the digital computer and who is instrumental in enabling the allies to crack the German WWII Enigma code. An active homosexual when homosexuality was illegal, Turing's personal behavior was tolerated because of the importance of his war work but after the gay spy scare of the '50s, Turing was regarded as a security risk and his life increasingly restricted. British TV adaptation based on the play by Hugh Whitemore (Jacobi also played the role on stage) and the book "Alan Turing: The Enigma" by Andrew Hodges. **90m/C VHS.** *GB* Derek Jacobi, Amanda Root, Prunella Scales, Harold Pinter, Julian Kerridge, Richard Johnson; ***D:*** Herbert Wise; ***W:*** Hugh Whitemore.

Breaking the Ice 🦴🦴 **1938** Unlikely mixture of Mennonites and a big city ice skating show. Young man leaves the farm to get a job singing at the rink. Musical numbers abound with backing by Victor Young and his Orchestra. **79m/B VHS.** Bobby Breen, Charlie Ruggles, Dolores Costello, Billy Gilbert, Margaret Hamilton, Jonathan Hale; ***D:*** Edward F. (Eddie) Cline; ***W:*** Mary C. McCall, Bernard Schubert, Manuel Seff; ***C:*** Jack MacKenzie; ***M:*** Victor Young.

Breaking the Rules 🦴🦴 1/2 **1992 (PG-13)** Predicatable buddy-road movie with a tearjerking premise and comedic overtones. Rob, Gene, and Phil were best buds growing up in Cleveland but young adulthood has separated them. They are reunited by Phil, who is dying of leukemia, and whose last wish is a cross-country road trip to California so he can appear as a contestant on "Jeopardy." Along the way they meet brassy waitress Mary, who impulsively decides to join them and winds up bringing the trio's shaky friendship back together. Potts does well as the big-haired, big-hearted Mary but the actors must work hard to maintain any dignity given the story's melodrama. **100m/C VHS.** Jason Bateman, C. Thomas Howell, Jonathan Silverman, Annie Potts, Kent Bateman, Shawn (Michael) Phelan; ***D:*** Neal Israel; ***W:*** Paul Shapiro; ***M:*** David Kitay.

Breaking the Surface: The Greg Louganis Story 🦴🦴 1/2 **1996** Trials and tribulations of the gold-medal winning Olympic diver, including his overbearing father, abusive lover, and his own HIV-positive status. Based on Louganis' autobiography; made for TV. **95m/C VHS, DVD.** Mario Lopez, Michael Murphy, Jeffrey Meek, Bruce Weitz, Rosemary Dunsmore; ***D:*** Steven Hilliard Stern; ***W:*** Alan Hines. **CABLE**

Breaking the Waves 🦴🦴🦴 **1995 (R)** Sacrifical journey of shy, religious Bess (Watson), who's living in an austere northern Scotland coastal village in the '70s. Bess, who regularly talks to God, marries Jan (Skarsgard), an adventurer working on a North Sea oil rig. It must be a case of opposites attracting but the couple are happy until Jan is paralyzed from the neck down in a rig accident. Bess, who blames herself, begins sleeping around, believing her actions can somehow help Jan, and slides ever deeper into mental instability. Powerful story is divided into seven chapters and an epilogue. **152m/C VHS, DVD.** *DK FR* Emily Watson, Stellan Skarsgard, Katrin Cartlidge, Adrian Rawlins, Jean-Marc Barr, Sandra Voe, Udo Kier, Mikkel Gaup; ***D:*** Lars von Trier; ***W:*** Lars von Trier; ***C:*** Robby Muller; ***M:*** Joachim Holbek. Cannes '96: Grand Jury Prize; Cesar '97: Foreign Film; N.Y. Film Critics '96: Actress (Watson), Cinematog., Director (von Trier); Natl. Soc. Film Critics '96: Actress (Watson), Cinematog., Director (von Trier), Film.

Breaking Up 🦴🦴 1/2 **1978** A woman fights to rediscover her personal identity after her 15-year marriage crumbles in this Emmy-nominated movie. **90m/C VHS.** Lee Remick, Granville Van Dusen, David Stambaugh; ***D:*** Delbert Mann. **TV**

Breaking Up 🦴 1/2 **1997 (R)** What steamy sheet action brings together, dreary day to day living easily pulls apart. That is the basic message of this bland romantic comedy that brings nothing new to the tired genre. Typical opposites attract but can't stay together (yet can't stay apart) plot finds photographer Crowe and teacher Hayek madly in lust and impulsively marrying. Hayek had more to work with when she played this role in "Fools Rush In," and Crowe seems uncomfortable as the lackluster boyfriend. Told in a chatty style with frequent asides to the audience by the main characters and a string of flashback sequences, director Greenwald's theatre background is apparent here. Clever camera work and editing are highlights. Adapted from Michael Cristofer's Pulitzer Prize-winning play. **90m/C VHS, DVD.** Salma Hayek, Russell Crowe; ***D:*** Robert Greenwald; ***W:*** Michael Cristofer; ***M:*** Mark Mothersbaugh.

Breaking Up Is Hard to Do 🦴 **1979** Six men leave their wives and shack up together on Malibu for a summer of partying and introspection. Made for television; edited down from its original 201 minute length. **96m/C VHS.** Billy Crystal, Bonnie Franklin, Ted Bessell, Jeff Conaway, Tony Musante, Robert Conrad, Trish Stewart, David Ogden Stiers, George Gaynes; ***D:*** Lou Antonio; ***M:*** Richard Bellis. **TV**

Breakout 🦴🦴 **1975 (PG)** The wife of a man imprisoned in Mexico hires a Texas bush pilot (Bronson) to help her husband (Duvall) escape. **96m/C VHS, DVD.** Charles Bronson, Jill Ireland, Robert Duvall, John Huston, Sheree North, Randy Quaid; ***D:*** Tom Gries; ***W:*** Howard B. Kreitsek, Marc Norman, Elliott Baker; ***C:*** Lucien Ballard; ***M:*** Jerry Goldsmith.

Breakout 🦴🦴 **1998** Zack (Carradine) has invented an environmentally friendly alternative energy source that makes him the scourge of the oil cartels. So the bad guys decide to kidnap Zack's son Joe (Bonifant) as a bargaining chip, only the kid turns out to be as smart as his old man. **86m/C VHS, UMD.** Robert Carradine, Evan Bonifant, James Hong, Chris Chinchilla; ***D:*** John Bradshaw; ***W:***

Naomi Jantzen; *C:* Edgar Egger; *M:* Gary Koftinoff. **VIDEO**

The Breaks **1999 (R)** White Irish kid gets adopted by a black family in South Central L.A. and naturally grows up to think of himself as a homeboy. But his adoptive mom is tired of his shenanigans and gives him one simple task to do—bring home a carton of milk by supper—or else. Why isn't this as easy as it sounds ('cause it certainly is as dumb). **86m/C VHS, DVD.** Mitch Mullany, Carl Anthony Payne II, Paula Jai Parker, Clifton Powell, Loretta Devine; *D:* Eric Meza; *W:* Mitch Mullany; *C:* Carlos Gonzalez; *M:* Adam Hirsh. **VIDEO**

Breakthrough *Sergeant Steiner* **1978 (PG)** German soldier, broken at the end of WWII, sets out to negotiate with the Allies. Average at best. **96m/C VHS.** Richard Burton, Robert Mitchum, Rod Steiger, Michael Parks, Curt Jurgens; *D:* Andrew V. McLaglen.

The Breakup Artist **1/2 2004 (R)** A rom-com from the male point of view. Jim (Taylor) is looking for love in the Big Apple, except he can't stay focused on just one girl (hence the title). Meanwhile, sweet coworker Teresa (Devicq) is engaged to a jerk. Of course, they're made for each other—if only Jim and Teresa can figure it out. **86m/C DVD.** Joseph Lyle Taylor, Paula DeVicq, Sarita Choudhury, Sabrina Lloyd, Ron Mongeluzzo; ***Cameos:*** Edward Burns, Regis Philbin, Bobby Cannavale; *D:* Vincent Rubino; *W:* Vincent Rubino; *C:* Nicholas Baratta; *M:* Thomas DeRenzo, Paul Conte.

Breast Men **1/2 1997 (R)** A campy fictional look into the lives and careers of the two doctors who invented the silicone breast implant in 1960s Texas. Struggling Kevin Saunders (Schwimmer) is an ambitious geek who works with grumpy plastic surgeon mentor, Dr. William Larson (Cooper), to develop a prosthetic breast, made from Dow-Corning's silicone gel. It's an immediate success and the doctors become rich, successful, and ever more obnoxious. Then come the lawsuits and life is suddenly no longer so sweet. And yes, you will see a lot of naked breasts. **95m/C VHS, DVD.** John Stockwell, Terry O'Quinn, Kathleen Wilhoite, Lisa Marie, David Schwimmer, Chris Cooper, Louise Fletcher, Emily Procter, Matt Frewer; *D:* Lawrence O'Neil; *W:* John Stockwell; *C:* Robert M. Stevens; *M:* Dennis McCarthy. **CABLE**

Breath of Scandal **1960** An American diplomat in Vienna rescues a princess when she is thrown off a horse; he falls for her like a ton o' bricks. Viennese politics complicate things. Based on a play by Molnar. **98m/C VHS, DVD.** Sophia Loren, John Gavin, Maurice Chevalier, Angela Lansbury; *D:* Michael Curtiz.

Breathing Fire **1991 (R)** A Vietnamese teenager and his American brother find out their ex-GI father is behind an armed bank robbery and murder. They join together to protect the only eyewitness—a young girl—against the ruthless gang of criminals and their own father. Lots of kickboxing action for martial arts fans. **86m/C VHS, DVD.** Bolo Yeung, Jonathan Ke Quan, Jerry Trimble; *D:* Lou Kennedy.

Breathing Lessons **1994 (PG)** Sweet look at a long-term marriage that renews itself on a road trip. Flighty Maggie and pragmatic Ira have been married for 28 squabbling but loving years. They're driving from their Baltimore home to a funeral in Pennsylvania and the road stops provide some small adventures and a great deal of conversation. Drama rests easily on the capable shoulders of the veteran performers. Based on the novel by Anne Tyler. Made for TV. **98m/C VHS.** James Garner, Joanne Woodward, Paul Winfield, Kathryn Erbe, Joyce Van Patten, Eileen Heckart, Tim Guinee, Henry Jones, Stephi Lineburg, Jean (Louisa) Kelly, John Considine; *D:* John Erman; *W:* Robert W. Lenski. **TV**

Breathing Room *'Til Christmas* **1996 (R)** New Yorker David (Futterman) has trouble with commitment to girlfriend Kathy (Floyd) and the duo break up again at Thanksgiving when he won't tell her he loves her. Kathy decides they need a break and refuses to see David until Christmas. She plays at seeing her boss, both get too much advice from friends and family, they attend the same holiday party—and the inevitable happens. Nothing new here. **90m/C VHS.** Dan Futterman, Susan Floyd, David Thornton; *D:* Jon Sherman; *W:* Jon Sherman, Tom Hughes; *C:* Jim Denault; *M:* Pat Irwin.

Breathless *A Bout de Souffle* **1959** Godard's first feature catapulted him to the vanguard of French filmmakers. Carefree Parisian crook, Michel (Belmondo), who emulates Humphrey Bogart, falls in love with gamine American student Patricia (Seberg) with tragic results. Wonderful scenes of Parisian life. Established Godard's Brechtian, experimental style. Belmondo's film debut. Mistitled "Breathless" for American release, the film's French title actually means "Out of Breath"; however, the fast-paced, erratic musical score leaves you breathless. French with English subtitles. Remade with Richard Gere in 1983 with far less intensity. **90m/B VHS, DVD.** *FR* Jean-Paul Belmondo, Jean Seberg, Daniel Boulanger, Jean-Pierre Melville, Liliane Robin; *D:* Jean-Luc Godard; *W:* Jean-Luc Godard; *C:* Raoul Coutard; *M:* Martial Solal. Berlin Intl. Film Fest. '60: Director (Godard).

Breathless **1983 (R)** Car thief turned cop killer has a torrid love affair with a French student studying in Los Angeles as the police slowly close in. Glossy, smarmy remake of the Godard classic that concentrates on the thin plot rather than any attempt at revitalizing the film syntax. **105m/C VHS, DVD.** Richard Gere, Valerie Kaprisky, Art Metrano, John P. Ryan, Lisa Jane Persky; *D:* Jim McBride; *W:* Jim McBride, L.M. Kit Carson; *M:* Jack Nitzsche.

Breathtaking **2000** Workaholic Dr. Caroline Henshaw (Whalley) is a psychologist with many mental problems of her own, stemming from her own past sexual abuse. But Caroline has managed to keep it together until she meets a new patient (Maitland)—a self-destructive masseuse who's being battered by her sicko hubby (Foreman). **105m/C VHS.** *GB* Joanne Whalley, Neil Dudgeon, Sandra Maitland, Jamie Foreman; *D:* David Green; *W:* Nicky Cowan; *C:* Gavin Finney; *M:* Robert (Rob) Lane.

The Breed **2001 (R)** Set in a noirish anytime, this horror film tells the story of an FBI agent Grant (a very stiff Woodbine), who starts out searching for a serial killer and ends up teamed with Aaron Grey (Paul), who turns out to be a vampire. Seems that the vampires who walk among us are ready to come out of the closet and join society, but a political dissident in the vampire ranks is trying to start a war...or is he? Could there be crosses and double crosses afoot? Grant, a black man, is less than thrilled at being teamed with a vampire, which results in not-too-subtle moral banter about racism and the Nazis to explain the vamps' fear of the humans and condemn the human sense of self preservation. It has moments of promise, but the poor acting and choppy editing and direction make everyone look uncomfortable amid the atmospheric scenery. **91m/C VHS, DVD.** Adrian Paul, Bai Ling, Bokeem Woodbine, Zen Gesner, Jake Eberle; *D:* Michael Oblowitz; *W:* Christos N. Gage, Ruth Fletcher. **VIDEO**

The Breed **2006 (R)** Bad doggie flick! Two brothers inherit their uncle's remote island and decide to fly three friends to join them in a party weekend. Too bad they didn't know their uncle rented part of the island to a special canine research unit and that the genetically-enhanced dogs have gone wild. Lots of plot holes, lots of genre cliches. **87m/C DVD.** Oliver Hudson, Hill Harper, Eric Lively, Michelle Rodriguez, Taryn Manning; *D:* Nick Mastandrea; *W:* Robert Conte, Peter Martin Wortmann; *C:* Giulio Biccari; *M:* Tom Mesmer. **VIDEO**

A Breed Apart **1984 (R)** An ongoing battle over a rare eagle's eggs strikes sparks between a reclusive conservationist and a scheming adventurer hired by a billionaire collector. **95m/C VHS.** Kathleen Turner, Rutger Hauer, Powers Boothe, Donald Pleasence, Brion James, John Dennis Johnston; *D:* Philippe Mora.

Breed of the Border *Speed Brent Wins* **1933** Tough-fisted cowboys must take the law into their own hands. **60m/B VHS, DVD.** Bob Steele, Marion Byron, George "Gabby" Hayes, Ernie Adams; *D:* Robert North Bradbury.

Breeders **1/2 1986 (R)** Ridiculous foam rubber monster attacks and impregnates women in New York. **77m/C VHS, DVD.** Teresa Farley, Frances Raines, Amy Brentano, Lance Lewman, Natalie O'Connell; *D:* Tim Kincaid; *W:* Tim Kincaid; *C:* Arthur Marks.

Breeders **WOOF! 1997 (R)** Alien on a mating mission terrorizes a Boston womens' college. Doesn't deliver on its exploitation premise, so don't bother. **92m/C VHS, DVD.** Todd Jensen, Samantha Janus, Kadamba Simmons, Oliver Tobias; *D:* Paul Matthews; *W:* Paul Matthews; *M:* Ben Heneghan.

Brenda Starr **1986 (PG)** Amateurish adaptation of the comic strip by Dale Messick. Shields stars as girl reporter Brenda Starr, who is once again risking her life to get the scoop. She finds herself in the jungles of South America searching for a mad scientist who is creating a rocket fuel that could destroy the world. The most entertaining thing about this film is the costumes designed by Bob Mackie. **94m/C VHS, DVD.** Brooke Shields, Timothy Dalton, Tony Peck, Diana Scarwid, Nestor Serrano, Jeffrey Tambor, June Gable, Charles Durning, Eddie Albert, Henry Gibson, Ed Nelson; *D:* Robert Ellis Miller; *W:* James David Buchanan; *C:* Freddie Francis; *M:* Johnny Mandel.

The Bretts **1988** Amusing two-part British miniseries follows the egos and eccentricities of the British theatrical dynasty, the Bretts. Part 1 is set in the '20s and introduces the family heads, Charles (Rodway) and Lydia (Murray), who enjoy performing off-stage almost as well as they enjoy performing on. Also introduced are their five children and loyal (if opinionated) servants. Part 2 follows the family into the '30s with son Edwin (Yelland) having become a film star, actress daughter Martha (Lang) falling for a politician, and son Tom (Winter) continuing to write his gloomy social dramas. Each part is on six cassettes. **600m/C VHS, DVD.** *GB* Barbara Murray, Norman Rodway, David Yelland, Belinda Lang, George Winter, Janet Maw, Tim Wylton, Bert Parnaby, Lysette Anthony, Clive Francis, Frank Middlemass, John Castle, Hugh Fraser, Patrick Ryecart, Sally Cookson, Billy Boyle; *W:* Rosemary Anne Sisson.

Brewster McCloud **1/2 1970 (R)** Altman's first picture after M*A*S*H reunites much of the cast and combines fantasy, black comedy, and satire in the story of a young man whose head is in the clouds or at least in the upper reaches of the Houston Astrodome. Brewster (Cort) lives covertly in the Dome and dreams of flying. He also has a guardian angel (Kellerman) who watches over him and may actually be killing people who give him a hard time. Murphy is a cop obsessed with catching the killer. And there's a circus allegory as well. Hard to figure what it all means and offbeat as they come, but for certain tastes, exquisite. **101m/C VHS.** Bud Cort, Sally Kellerman, Shelley Duvall, Michael Murphy, William Windom, Rene Auberjonois, Stacy Keach, John Schuck, Margaret Hamilton; *D:* Robert Altman; *W:* Doran William Cannon; *C:* Lamar Boren, Jordan Cronenweth; *M:* Gene Page.

Brewster's Millions **1/2 1945** If Brewster, an ex-GI, can spend $1 million in one year, he will inherit a substantially greater fortune. Originally a 1902 novel, this is the fifth of seven film adaptations. **79m/B VHS.** Dennis O'Keefe, June Havoc, Eddie Anderson, Helen Walker, Gail Patrick, Mischa Auer; *D:* Allan Dwan.

Brewster's Millions **1/2 1985 (PG)** An aging minor league baseball player must spend $30 million in order to collect an inheritance of $300 million. He may find that money can't buy happiness. Seventh remake of the story. **101m/C VHS, DVD.** Richard Pryor, John Candy, Lonette McKee, Stephen Collins, Jerry Orbach, Pat Hingle, Tovah Feldshuh, Hume Cronyn, Rick Moranis, Yakov Smirnoff, Joe Grifasi, Peter Jason, Grand L. Bush, Reni Santoni, Conrad Janis, Lin Shaye; *D:* Walter Hill; *W:* Herschel Weingrod, Timothy Harris; *C:* Ric Waite; *M:* Ry Cooder.

Brian's Song **1971 (G)** The story of the unique relationship between Gale Sayers, the Chicago Bears' star running back, and his teammate Brian Piccolo. The friendship between the Bears' first interracial roommates ended suddenly when Brian Piccolo lost his life to cancer. Incredibly well received in its time. **74m/C VHS, DVD.** James Caan, Billy Dee Williams, Jack Warden, Shelley Fabares, Judy Pace, Bernie Casey; *D:* Buzz Kulik; *W:* William Blinn; *C:* Joseph Biroc; *M:* Michel Legrand. **TV**

Brian's Song **2001** Unnecessary remake of the 1971 made-for-TV classic dealing with the friendship between Gale Sayers and Brian Piccolo, and Piccolo's fight against cancer heads right for the disease-of-the-week cliches with almost none of the original's charm or depth. Phifer, as Sayers, and Cale, as Joy Piccolo, along with a deeper understanding of the wives' point of view, are the main reasons to check it out. But it still can't compare to the original. **89m/C VHS, DVD.** Mekhi Phifer, Sean Maher, Paula Cale, Elise Neal, Ben Gazzara, Aidan Devine, Dean McDermott; *D:* John Gray; *W:* John Gray, Allen Clare, William Blinn; *C:* James Chressanthis; *M:* Richard (Rick) Marvin.

The Bribe **1/2 1948** Federal Agent Rigby (Taylor) is sent to a tropical isle off the coast of Central America to investigate a smuggling ring dealing in contraband war surplus airplane engines. It's run by playboy Carwood (Price) and sleazy Bealler (Laughton) along with former wartime pilot Tug (Hodiak). Tug's wife—torch singer Elizabeth (Gardner)—doesn't know about the scheme but when Rigby falls for the femme, the crooks try setting him up so Rigby will compromise his career so he can save her. **98m/B DVD.** Robert Taylor, Ava Gardner, Vincent Price, Charles Laughton, John Hodiak, Samuel S. Hinds; *D:* Robert Z. Leonard; *W:* Marguerite Roberts; *C:* Joseph Ruttenberg; *M:* Miklos Rozsa.

Brick **2006 (R)** Ever wonder what it would look like if Raymond Chandler wrote for the "Sweet Valley High" series? In his debut film, writer/director Johnson delivers one of the most impressive examples of hard-boiled noir in years, set, strangely enough, in a California high school. Gordon-Levitt brilliantly channels Humphrey Bogart as Brendan, a tough-as-nails teenaged shamus who's trying to locate his missing ex-girlfriend (de Ravin) in the seamy underbelly of drug-dealing jocks and cheerleader femme fatales. The mystery's a twisty one, peppered with Johnson's own brand of tough guy slang that will either delight or confound you. But you can't ignore the ambition of this "Miller's Crossing" meets "Breakfast Club" hybrid. **110m/C DVD.** *US* Joseph Gordon-Levitt, Lukas Haas, Noah Fleiss, Matt O'Leary, Nora Zehetner, Noah Segan, Meagan Good, Emilie de Ravin, Brian White, Richard Roundtree, Lucas Babin; *D:* Rian Johnson; *W:* Rian Johnson; *C:* Steve Yedlin; *M:* Nathan Johnson.

Bridal Fever **2008** Hallmark Channel movie about finding old-fashioned romance in the most cliched way possible. Single Gwen (Roth) has been singed once too often and is reluctant to change her marital status until she's hired by romance author Dahlia Merchant (Burke) to edit her autobiography. The much-married Dahlia has Gwen and her friend Sandra (Deines) doing some pre-wedding visualization before they go on a serious hubby hunt. **88m/C DVD.** Andrea Roth, Delta Burke, Gabriel Hogan, Melinda Deines, Vincent Walsh, Nigel Bennett, Richard Fitzpatrick; *D:* Ron Oliver; *W:* Karen McClellan; *C:* Gerald Packer. **CABLE**

The Bride **1/2 1985 (PG-13)** Re-telling of "The Bride of Frankenstein." Sting's Dr. Frankenstein has much more success in creating his second monster (Beals). She's pretty and intelligent and he may even be falling in love with her. When she begins to gain too much independence, though, the awful truth about her origins comes out. Fans of the two leads will want to see this one, but for a true classic see Elsa Lanchester's bride. **118m/C VHS, DVD.** *GB* Sting, Jennifer Beals, Anthony (Corlan) Higgins, David Rappaport, Geraldine Page, Clancy Brown, Phil Daniels, Veruschka, Quentin Crisp, Cary Elwes; *D:* Franc Roddam; *W:* Lloyd Fonvielle; *C:* Stephen Burum; *M:* Maurice Jarre.

Bride & Prejudice **2004 (PG-13)** Bollywood meets Jane Austen in Chandha's brightly-colored confection. Will Darcy

(Henderson) and chum Balraj (Andrews) arrive in Amritsar for a friend's wedding. A stuffy but wealthy businessman, Will finds himself drawn to the strikingly beautiful and headstrong Lalita (Rai) who's irritated by his arrogance. That they are meant for each other is obvious but the film must travel from India to London and L.A. and back again before it all plays out, amidst various musical numbers and family trials. **110m/C DVD.** *US* Aishwarya Rai, Martin Henderson, Anupam Kher, Naveen Andrews, Daniel Gillies, Indira Varma, Marsha Mason, Nadira Babbar, Namrala Shirodkar, Meghnaa, Peeya Rai Choudhuri; ***D:*** Gurinder Chadha; ***W:*** Gurinder Chadha, Paul Mayeda Berges; ***C:*** Santosh Sivan.

The Bride & the Beast WOOF! *Queen of the Gorillas* **1958** While on an African safari honeymoon, a big game hunter's new bride is carried off by a gorilla. Ludicrous jungle tale. **78m/B VHS, DVD.** Charlotte Austin, Lance Fuller, William Justine, Johnny Roth, Jeanne Gerson, Gilbert Frye, Slick Slavin, Bhogwan Singh; ***D:*** Adrian Weiss; ***W:*** Edward D. Wood Jr.; ***C:*** Roland Price; ***M:*** Les Baxter.

The Bride Came C.O.D. **1941** Rough 'n' tough pilot Cagney is hired by a rich Texas oil man to prevent his daughter (the one with the Bette Davis eyes) from marrying cheesy bandleader Carson. The payoff: $10 per pound if she's delivered unwed. What a surprise when Cagney faces the timeworn dilemma of having to choose between love and money. A contemporary issue of "Time" magazine trumpeted: "Screen's most talented tough guy roughhouses one of screen's best dramatic actresses." That tells you right there it's a romantic comedy. Cagney and Davis—a likely pairing, you'd think—are essentially fish out of water, bothered and bewildered by a weak script. **92m/B VHS, DVD.** Bette Davis, James Cagney, Stuart Erwin, Jack Carson, George Tobias, Eugene Pallette, William Frawley, Harry Davenport; ***D:*** William Keighley; ***W:*** Julius J. Epstein, Philip G. Epstein; ***C:*** Ernest Haller; ***M:*** Max Steiner.

The Bride Is Much Too Beautiful 1/2 *Her Bridal Night; La Mariee Est Trop Belle* **1958** French farm girl Bardot becomes a model with the help of some fashion magazine employees and then winds up posing as the bride in a fake marriage. Dubbed. **90m/C VHS.** *FR* Brigitte Bardot, Louis Jourdan, Micheline Presle, Marcel Amont; ***D:*** Pierre Gaspard-Huit; ***W:*** Odette Joyeux, Philippe Agostini; ***C:*** Louis Page; ***M:*** Norbert Glanzberg.

Bride of Chucky 1/2 **1998 (R)** Just when you thought you had seen the last of that creepy little doll, "Chucky" returns. This fourth installment in the "Child's Play" franchise finds Chucky back on the lam after being sprung from the pen by the ex-girlfriend of his former human incarnation, serial killer Charles Lee Ray. After killing his ex, Tiffany (Tilly), Chucky transforms her soul into an equally creepy girl doll. Together, they must make their way to the very spot where he was gunned down by police in order to transfer their souls back into human forms. Aside from Chucky and both incarnations of Tiffany, the rest of the characters are undeveloped and rather useless. Fortunately, the filmmakers knew not to take themselves too seriously, and managed a few funny moments. But its really only Tilly's excellent campy-vampy performance and an occasional clever jab from the Chuckster that lift this one above a woof. **89m/C VHS, DVD.** Jennifer Tilly, Katherine Heigl, Nick Stabile, John Ritter, Alexis Arquette, Gordon Michael Woolvett, Lawrence Dane, Michael Johnson, Kathy Najimy; ***D:*** Ronny Yu; ***W:*** Don Mancini; ***C:*** Peter Pau; ***M:*** Graeme Revell; ***V:*** Brad Dourif.

The Bride of Frank **1996** Former homeless man Frank has a temper and he's not afraid to use it on the belittling ladies who make the ill-fated gaffe of responding to his personals ad, which leads to their horrific, over-the-top, brutal demises. But, hey, he still has a sense of humor about it all. The viewer, however, might not. **89m/C VHS, DVD.** Frank Meyer, Johnny Horizon, Steve Ballot; ***D:*** Steve Ballot; ***W:*** Steve Ballot; ***C:*** Steve Ballot. **VIDEO**

The Bride of Frankenstein **1935** The classic sequel to the classic original in which Dr. F. seeks to build a mate for his monster. More humor than the first, but also more pathos, including the monster's famous but short-lived friendship with a blind hermit. Lanchester plays both the bride and Mary Shelley in the opening sequence. **75m/B VHS, DVD.** Boris Karloff, Elsa Lanchester, Ernest Thesiger, Colin Clive, Una O'Connor, Valerie Hobson, Dwight Frye, John Carradine, E.E. Clive, O.P. Heggie, Gavin Gordon, Douglas Walton, Billy Barty, Walter Brennan; ***D:*** James Whale; ***W:*** John Lloyd Balderston, William Hurlbut; ***C:*** John Mescall; ***M:*** Franz Waxman. Natl. Film Reg. '98.

Bride of Killer Nerd **1991** Harold Kunkel, left over from the original "Killer Nerd," finds his opposite sex nirvana in the person of Thelma, also a nerd in mind, body, and soul. They relentlessly pursue revenge on the rockers who humiliate them at a campus beer bash. **75m/C VHS, DVD.** Toby Radloff, Wayne A. Harold, Heidi Lohr; ***D:*** Mark Steven Bosko.

Bride of Re-Animator 1/2 *Re-Animator 2* **1989** Herbert West is back, and this time he not only re-animates life but creates life—sexy female life—in this sequel to the immensely popular "Re-Animator." High camp and blood curdling gore make this a standout in the sequel parade. Available in a R-rated version as well. **99m/C VHS, DVD.** Bruce Abbott, Claude Earl Jones, Fabiana Udenio, Jeffrey Combs, Kathleen Kinmont, David Gale, Mel Stewart, Irene Forrest; ***D:*** Brian Yuzna; ***W:*** Brian Yuzna, Rick Fry, Woody Keith; ***C:*** Rick Fichter; ***M:*** Richard Band.

Bride of the Gorilla **1951** Burr travels to the jungle where he finds a wife, a plantation, and a curse in this African twist on the werewolf legend. Chaney is the local policeman on his trail. Burr's physical changes are fun to watch. **76m/B VHS, DVD.** Raymond Burr, Barbara Payton, Lon Chaney Jr., Tom Conway, Paul Cavanagh; ***D:*** Curt Siodmak; ***W:*** Curt Siodmak.

Bride of the Monster WOOF! *Bride of the Atom* **1955** Lugosi stars as a mad scientist trying to create a race of giants. Classic Woodian badness. **68m/B VHS, DVD.** Bela Lugosi, Tor Johnson, Loretta King, Tony McCoy, Harvey B. Dunn, George Becwar, Paul Marco, William Benedict, Dolores Fuller, Don Nagel, Bud Osborne, Conrad Brooks; ***D:*** Edward D. Wood Jr.; ***W:*** Edward D. Wood Jr., Alex Gordon; ***C:*** William C. Thompson; ***M:*** Frank Worth.

Bride of the Wind 1/2 **2001 (R)** Dull biopic of Alma Mahler (Wynter), a 20th-century femme who put her own musical career aside to marry composer Gustav Mahler (Pryce) in old Vienna. Alma intrigues a number of famous men, including architect Walter Gropius (Verhoeven), artist Oskar Kokoschka (Perez), and others while her marriage to the stoic Gustav suffers. Unfortunately, it's neither titillating nor interesting despite the players. **99m/C VHS, DVD.** Sarah Wynter, Jonathan Pryce, Vincent Perez, Simon Verhoeven, August Schmolzer, Gregor Seberg, Dagmar Schwarz, Wolfgang Hubsch, Johannes Silberschneider; ***D:*** Bruce Beresford; ***W:*** Marilyn Levy; ***C:*** Peter James; ***M:*** Stephen Endelman.

The Bride Walks Out **1936** Newlywed crisis: a woman with rich taste learns how to adjust to living on her husband's poor salary, but not before she samples the life of the wealthy. Interesting in a sociological sort of way. **81m/B VHS.** Barbara Stanwyck, Gene Raymond, Robert Young, Ned Sparks, Willie Best, Helen Broderick, Hattie McDaniel; ***D:*** Leigh Jason.

Bride Wars 1/2 **2009 (PG)** Liv (Hudson) and Emma (Hathaway) are lifelong pals and soon-to-be brides who share the dream of being married at Manhattan's Plaza Hotel. But the sweet, charming women's plans of their same-season weddings hit a snag when their wedding planner's (Bergen) snafu results in the Plaza scheduling the big events on the same day. With no other openings in the schedule, the otherwise caring friends won't budge and become each other's bridezilla nightmare. Their sub-par sabotage stunts come off as childish, desperate, and downright mean, with characters that never feel real. Style over substance bittersweet confection is gorgeously shot with a beautiful cast that will likely cause producers to vow "I do" to a sequel. **90m/C DVD.** *US* Anne Hathaway, Kate Hudson, Kirsten Johnson, Bryan Greenberg, Steve Howey, Chris Pratt, Candice Bergen, John Pankow, Bruce Altman, Michael Arden; ***D:*** Gary Winick; ***W:*** Casey Wilson, June Raphael; ***C:*** Frederick Elmes; ***M:*** Ed Shearmur.

The Bride with White Hair *Jiang-Hu: Between Love and Glory* **1993** Operatic martial arts fable based on a novel by Leung Yu-Sang. A young warrior revives a beautiful witch (also a champion warrior) who was killed by jealous Siamese twins. Now the duo, who have fallen in love, must battle the evil twins who rule the corrupt Mo Dynasty. Available dubbed or in Chinese with subtitles. **92m/C VHS, DVD.** *HK* Leslie Cheung, Brigitte Lin, Nam Kit-Ying, Frances Ng, Elaine Lui; ***D:*** Ronny Yu; ***W:*** Ronny Yu, David Wu, Lan Kei-Tou, Tseng Pik-Yin; ***C:*** Peter Pau; ***M:*** Richard Yuen.

The Bride with White Hair 2 *Jiang-Hu: Between Love and Glory 2* **1993** The magic saga continues with the massacre of the followers of the Eight Lineages. Powerful and obsessed with vengeance, the Bride can only be stopped by the one man who loves her. Chinese with subtitles or dubbed. **80m/C VHS, DVD.** *HK* Brigitte Lin, Leslie Cheung, Christy Chung; ***D:*** David Wu, Ronny Yu; ***W:*** David Wu.

The Bride Wore Black *La Mariee Etait en Noir* **1968** Truffaut's homage to Hitchcock, complete with Bernard Herrmann score. Young bride Julie (Moreau) exacts brutal revenge on the five men who accidentally killed her husband on the steps of the church on their wedding day. Adapted from a novel by Cornell Woolrich. **107m/C VHS, DVD.** *FR* Jeanne Moreau, Claude Rich, Jean-Claude Brialy, Michel Bouquet, Michael (Michel) Lonsdale, Charles Denner, Daniel Boulanger; ***D:*** Francois Truffaut; ***W:*** Francois Truffaut, Jean-Louis Richard; ***C:*** Raoul Coutard; ***M:*** Bernard Herrmann.

The Bride Wore Red **1937** Crawford stars as a cabaret singer who masquerades as a socialite in an attempt to break into the upper crust. When a wealthy aristocrat invites her to spend two weeks at a posh resort in Tyrol, Crawford plays her part to the hilt, managing to charm both a rich gentleman and the village postman. Typical "love conquers all" melodrama. **103m/B VHS.** Joan Crawford, Franchot Tone, Robert Young, Billie Burke, Reginald Owen, Lynne Carver, George Zucco; ***D:*** Dorothy Arzner; ***C:*** George J. Folsey.

Brides of Christ 1/2 **1991** Set in the Australian Santo Spirito Convent during the Vatican II upheaval of the 1960s. Explores the tensions between old and new religious ideas by focusing on novices, older nuns, and the Reverend Mother of the convent as they try to cope with a changing world. TV miniseries. **300m/C VHS, DVD.** Brenda Fricker, Sandy Gore, Josephine Byrnes, Lisa Hensley, Naomi Watts, Kym Wilson, Melissa Thomas; ***D:*** Ken Cameron; ***W:*** John Alsop, Sue Smith.

The Brides of Dracula 1/2 **1960** A young French woman unknowingly frees a vampire. He wreaks havoc, sucking blood and creating more of the undead to carry out his evil deeds. One of the better Hammer vampire films. **86m/C VHS, DVD.** *GB* Peter Cushing, Martita Hunt, Yvonne Monlaur, Freda Jackson, David Peel, Mona Washbourne, Miles Malleson, Henry Oscar, Michael Ripper, Andree Melly; ***D:*** Terence Fisher; ***W:*** Peter Bryan, Edward Percy, Jimmy Sangster; ***C:*** Jack Asher.

Brides of Fu Manchu **1966** In Lee's second outing as the villainous character, Fu Manchu kidnaps the nubile daughters of various scientists so that they will be forced to build him a weapon to take over the world. Naturally, his Scotland Yard nemesis Nayland Smith (Wilmer) will stop him. Based on the characters created by Sax Rohmer. **93m/C DVD.** *GB* Christopher Lee, Douglas Wilmer, Tsai Chin, Joseph Furst, Marie Versini, Heinz Drache; ***D:*** Don Sharp; ***W:*** Harry Alan Towers; ***C:*** Ernest Steward; ***M:*** Bruce Montgomery.

Brides of the Beast WOOF! *Brides of Blood; Grave Desires; Island of the Living Horror* **1968** Filipino radiation monsters get their jollies by eating beautiful young naked women. Newly arrived research scientist and his bride oppose this custom. First in a series of "Blood Island" horrors. **85m/B VHS, DVD.** *PH* John Ashley, Kent Taylor, Beverly (Hills) Powers, Eva Darren, Mario Montenegro; ***D:*** Eddie Romero, Gerardo (Gerry) De Leon; ***W:*** Eddie Romero, Gerardo (Gerry) De Leon.

Brideshead Revisited **1981** The acclaimed British miniseries based on the Evelyn Waugh classic about an Edwardian young man who falls under the spell of a wealthy aristocratic family and struggles to retain his integrity and values. On six tapes. **540m/C VHS, DVD.** *GB* Jeremy Irons, Anthony Andrews, Diana Quick, Laurence Olivier, John Gielgud, Claire Bloom, Stephane Audran, Mona Washbourne, John Le Mesurier, Charles Keating; ***D:*** Charles Sturridge, Michael Lindsay-Hogg; ***M:*** Geoffrey Burgon. **TV**

Brideshead Revisited 1/2 **2008 (PG-13)** It's between the world wars in England, and middle-class Charles Ryder (Goode) is enamored by the snooty lifestyle of brother and sister Sebastian (Whishaw) and Julia (Atwell) at their Brideshead estate, where they live with their mother, the devout Catholic Lady Marchmain (Thompson). At first, Charles hooks up with the boozy Sebastian but later turns his amorous attention to Julia, fueling Sebastian's jealously and Lady Marchmain's ire. Despite the lush backdrop and Thompson's icy turn, it falls short of the acclaimed 1981 British miniseries version. Adapted from the 1945 novel by Evelyn Waugh. **135m/C DVD.** *US GB* Matthew Goode, Ben Whishaw, Hayley Atwell, Emma Thompson, Michael Gambon, Greta Scacchi, Jonathan Cake, Patrick Malahide; ***D:*** Julian Jarrold; ***W:*** Andrew Davies, Jeremy Brock; ***C:*** Jess Hall; ***M:*** Adrian Johnston.

The Bridesmaid *La Demoiselle d'Honneur* **2004** Creepy thriller based on a novel by Ruth Rendell. Hard-working Philippe (Magimel) lives with his flirtatious mother Christine (Clement) and his two younger siblings. At his sister's wedding, he meets sultry bridesmaid Senta (Smet), who likes a lot of drama in her life. She easily seduces the uptight Philippe, who turns out to have some dark inner urges and continually tests the limits of his love. Then Senta asks, would he kill for her? French with subtitles. **111m/C DVD.** *FR* Benoit Magimel, Laura Smet, Aurore Clement, Bernard Le Coq, Solene Bouten, Anna Mihalcea, Michel Duchaussoy, Eric Seigne, Pierre-Francois Dumeniaud; ***D:*** Claude Chabrol; ***W:*** Claude Chabrol, Peter Leccia; ***C:*** Eduardo Serra; ***M:*** Matthieu Chabrol.

The Bridge *Die Brucke* **1959** In 1945, two days before the end of WWII, seven German schoolboys are drafted to defend an unimportant bridge from American tanks. Emotional anti-war film based on the autobiographical novel of Manfred Gregor. German with subtitles. **102m/B VHS, DVD.** *GE* Fritz Wepper, Volker Bohnet, Frank Glaubrecht, Karl Michael Balzer, Gunther Hoffman, Michael Hinz, Cordula Trantow, Wolfgang Stumpf, Volker Lechtenbrink, Gunter Pfitzmann, Edith Schultze-Westrum, Ruth Hausmeister, Eva Vaitl; ***D:*** Bernhard Wicki; ***W:*** Bernhard Wicki, Michael Mansfield, Karl-Wilhelm Vivier; ***C:*** Gerd Von Bonen; ***M:*** Hans-Martin Majewski.

The Bridge **2000** In 1963, Mira (Bouquet) loves to go to the movies to watch "Jules et Jim" and "West Side Story." She has a 15-year-old son, but that doesn't stop her from entering into an affair with a visiting engineer (Berling) who's in her little town to build a bridge. Director Depardieu plays her husband, a builder who's working on the bridge. It's precisely the sort of material that the French handle so deftly and Depardieu proves that he's a competent craftsman behind the camera. **92m/C DVD.** *FR* Carole Bouquet, Gerard Depardieu, Charles Berling; ***D:*** Frederic Auburtin, Gerard Depardieu; ***W:*** Francois Bupeyron; ***C:*** Pascal Ridao; ***M:*** Frederic Auburtin.

The Bridge at Remagen 1/2 **1969 (PG)** Based on the true story of allied attempts to capture a vital bridge before retreating German troops destroy it. For war-film buffs. **115m/C VHS, DVD.** George Segal, Robert Vaughn, Ben Gazzara, Bradford Dillman, E.G. Marshall; ***D:*** John Guillermin; ***W:*** William Roberts; ***C:*** Stanley Cortez; ***M:*** Elmer Bernstein.

Bridge of Dragons **1999 (R)** Dictator Tagawa, having murdered the kingdom's rightful ruler, plots to marry the country's princess (Shane) to consolidate his power. But when the princess escapes to join the rebel forces, human killing machine Lundgren is sent to retrieve her. Only he decides to fight with her instead. Lots of explosions and high-tech gadgets. **91m/C VHS, DVD.** Dolph Lundgren, Cary-Hiroyuki Tagawa, Gary Hudson, Scott Schwartz, Rachel Shane; ***D:*** Isaac Florentine; ***W:*** Carlton Holder; ***C:*** Yossi Wein; ***M:*** Stephen (Steve) Edwards. **VIDEO**

The Bridge of San Luis Rey **1944** A priest investigates the famous bridge collapse in Lima, Peru that left five people dead. Based upon the novel by Thornton Wilder. **89m/B VHS, DVD.** Lynn Bari, Francis Lederer, Louis Calhern, Akim Tamiroff, Donald Woods, Alla Nazimova, Blanche Yurka; ***D:*** Rowland V. Lee; ***W:*** Howard Estabrook, Herman Weissman; ***C:*** John Boyle; ***M:*** Dimitri Tiomkin.

The Bridge of San Luis Rey **2005 (PG)** Thornton Wilder's moving, Pulitzer Prize-winning 1928 novel is disastrously adapted by director McGluckian, with stellar actors generally miscast in a stuffy costume drama. In colonial Peru in the early 18th century, Franciscan missionary Brother Juniper (Byrne) has been investigating five travelers who plunged to their deaths when the titular bridge collapsed. He's trying to determine if there's some common denominator to their fate and delivers his conclusions to a church court presided over by the Archbishop of Lima (De Niro). Flashbacks depict the lives of the victims and their survivors and the abrupt shifts in scene and character make for confusion. **120m/C DVD.** *SP GB FR* Robert De Niro, F. Murray Abraham, Kathy Bates, Gabriel Byrne, Geraldine Chaplin, Emilie Dequenne, Adriana Dominguez, Harvey Keitel, Pilar Lopez de Ayala, John Lynch, Mark Polish, Michael Polish; ***D:*** Mary McGuckian; ***C:*** Javier Aguirresarobe; ***M:*** Lalo Schifrin.

The Bridge on the River Kwai **1957** Award-winning adaptation of the Pierre Bouelle novel about the battle of wills between a Japanese POW camp commander and a British colonel over the construction of a rail bridge, and the parallel efforts by escaped prisoner Holden to destroy it. Holden's role was originally cast for Cary Grant. Memorable too for whistling "Colonel Bogey March." Because the writers were blacklisted, Bouelle (who spoke no English) was originally credited as the screenwriter. **161m/C VHS, DVD, Blu-ray Disc.** *GB* William Holden, Alec Guinness, Jack Hawkins, Sessue Hayakawa, James Donald, Geoffrey Horne, Andre Morell, Ann Sears, Peter Williams, John Boxer, Percy Herbert, Harold Goodwin, Henry Okawa, Keiichiro Katsumoto, M.R.B. Chakrabandhu; ***D:*** David Lean; ***W:*** Carl Foreman, Michael Wilson; ***C:*** Jack Hildyard; ***M:*** Malcolm Arnold. Oscars '57: Actor (Guinness), Adapt. Screenplay, Cinematog., Director (Lean), Film Editing, Picture, Orig. Song Score and/or Adapt.; AFI '98: Top 100; British Acad. '57: Actor (Guinness), Film, Screenplay; Directors Guild '57: Director (Lean); Golden Globes '58: Actor—Drama (Guinness), Director (Lean), Film—Drama; Natl. Bd. of Review '57: Actor (Guinness), Director (Lean), Support. Actor (Hayakawa), Natl. Film Reg. '97;; N.Y. Film Critics '57: Actor (Guinness), Director (Lean), Film.

Bridge to Hell 1/2 **1987** A group of allied P.O.W.s try to make their way to the American front during WWII in Yugoslavia. A heavily guarded bridge occupied by Nazi troops stands between them and freedom. A special introduction by Michael Dudikoff doing martial arts. **94m/C VHS, DVD.** Jeff Connors, Francis Ferre, Andy Forrest, Paky Valente; ***D:*** Umberto Lenzi.

The Bridge to Nowhere **1986** Five city kids go hunting and back-packing in the New Zealand wilderness, and are hunted by a maniacal backwoodsman. **82m/C VHS.** *NZ* Bruno Lawrence, Alison Routledge, Margaret Umbers, Philip Gordon; ***D:*** Ian Mune.

Bridge to Silence **1989** A young hearing-impaired mother's life begins to crumble following the death of her husband in a car crash. Her mother tries to get custody of her daughter and a friend applies romantic pressure. Melodrama features Matlin in her first TV speaking role. **95m/C VHS.** Marlee Matlin, Lee Remick, Josef Sommer, Michael O'Keefe, Allison Silva, Candice Brecker; ***D:*** Karen Arthur. **TV**

Bridge to Terabithia 1/2 **2007 (PG)** Katherine Paterson's popular 1977 novel isn't so much about a fantasy world (the film's CGI is limited) as it is about friendship and imagination. Jess (Hutcherson) is a bullied 10-year-old misfit with four sisters and a stern dad (Patrick). Adventurous new neighbor Leslie (Robb) turns out to be Jess' imaginative kindred soul and, between his drawings and her stories, they populate the nearby woods with their own world. For those not familiar with the book, beware—there's tragedy looming that will affect both kids and adults. **94m/C DVD, Blu-ray Disc.** *US* Josh Hutcherson, AnnaSophia Robb, Robert Patrick, Zooey Deschanel, Bailey Madison, Kate Butler, Lauren Clinton; ***D:*** Gabor Csupo; ***W:*** Jeff Stockwell, David Paterson; ***C:*** Michael Chapman; ***M:*** Aaron Zigman.

A Bridge Too Far **1977 (PG)** A meticulous re-creation of one of the most disastrous battles of WWII, the Allied defeat at Arnhem in 1944. Misinformation, adverse conditions, and overconfidence combined to prevent the Allies from capturing six bridges that connected Holland to the German border. **175m/C VHS, DVD, Blu-ray Disc.** *GB* Sean Connery, Robert Redford, James Caan, Michael Caine, Elliott Gould, Gene Hackman, Laurence Olivier, Ryan O'Neal, Liv Ullmann, Dirk Bogarde, Hardy Kruger, Arthur Hill, Edward Fox, Anthony Hopkins, Maximilian Schell, Denholm Elliott, Wolfgang Preiss, Nicholas (Nick) Campbell, Christopher Good, John Ratzenberger, Colin Farrell; ***D:*** Richard Attenborough; ***W:*** William Goldman; ***C:*** Geoffrey Unsworth; ***M:*** John Addison. British Acad. '77: Support. Actor (Fox); Natl. Soc. Film Critics '77: Support. Actor (Fox).

The Bridges at Toko-Ri 1/2 **1955** Based on the James A. Michener novel, the rousing war-epic about a lawyer being summoned by the Navy to fly bombing missions during the Korean War. A powerful anti-war statement. **103m/C VHS, DVD.** William Holden, Grace Kelly, Fredric March, Mickey Rooney, Robert Strauss, Earl Holliman, Keiko Awaji, Charles McGraw, Richard Shannon, Willis Bouchey; ***D:*** Mark Robson; ***W:*** Valentine Davies; ***C:*** Loyal Griggs; ***M:*** Lyn Murray.

The Bridges of Madison County **1995 (PG-13)** Robert Kincaid (Eastwood) is on assignment in 1965 Iowa to photograph Madison County's scenic covered bridges. Only problem is he gets lost and stops for directions at Francesca Johnson's (Streep) farmhouse. There's an immediate attraction between the repressed Italian war-bride-turned-farm-wife and the charismatic world traveler, which they act on in four short days. Much of the treacle from Robert James Waller's novel has been fortunately abandoned but the mature romance remains. 64-year-old Eastwood exudes lowkey sexiness while Streep (with a light Italian accent) is all earthy warmth. Fans of both book and stars should be pleased, though the leisurely paced film takes too long to get started. **135m/C VHS, DVD.** Clint Eastwood, Meryl Streep, Victor Slezak, Annie Corley, Jim Haynie; ***D:*** Clint Eastwood; ***W:*** Richard LaGravenese; ***C:*** Jack N. Green; ***M:*** Lennie Niehaus.

Bridget Jones: The Edge of Reason 1/2 **2004 (R)** The film sequel (loosely based on Fielding's book sequel) tries too hard to be endearingly kooky, but can't go that far wrong with Zellweger, who once again packed on the pounds to play the plumpish London singleton. When we last saw Bridget, she had finally chosen steady lawyer Mark Darcy (Firth), but her insecurities get the better of her. She trashes her relationship and is soon once again with sly cad Daniel (Grant), now the host of a TV travel show. This leads Bridget and Daniel to Thailand where, in an unfortunate plot contrivance, Bridget is thrown into a Thai jail. This only serves to teach Bridget that she really loves Mark. Zellweger is subjected to many pratfalls, which she handles with good spirit, and all the supporting roles are on the money. **108m/C VHS, DVD.** *US* Renee Zellweger, Hugh Grant, Colin Firth, Jim Broadbent, Gemma Jones, Jacinda Barrett, James Callis, Shirley Henderson, Sally Phillips, Neil Pearson, Jessica Stevenson, Paul Nicholls; ***D:*** Beeban Kidron; ***W:*** Andrew Davies, Helen Fielding, Richard Curtis, Adam Brooks; ***C:*** Adrian Biddle; ***M:*** Harry Gregson-Williams.

Bridget Jones's Diary **2001 (R)** So you've got this petite, sunny-faced Texan playing a "singleton" Brit who drinks and smokes and consumes too many calories and has man trouble and is the beloved heroine of Helen Fielding's novel. No wonder the English got a little upset—not, as it turns out, for any good reason since Zellweger is fab as Bridget tries to take control of her chaotic life. Of course having a romp with your caddish, clever boss Daniel Cleaver (Grant) and ignoring the handsome but apparently stuffy Mark Darcy (Firth) isn't a good start but Bridget—bless her—does try. The movie is truncated (to the detriment of Bridget's friendships) but it still works. **115m/C VHS, DVD.** Renee Zellweger, Hugh Grant, Colin Firth, Gemma Jones, Jim Broadbent, Embeth Davidtz, Shirley Henderson, James Callis, Sally Phillips, Lisa Barbuscia; ***D:*** Sharon Maguire; ***W:*** Richard Curtis, Andrew Davies, Helen Fielding; ***C:*** Stuart Dryburgh; ***M:*** Patrick Doyle.

Brief Encounter **1946** Based on Noel Coward's "Still Life" from "Tonight at 8:30," two middle-aged, middle-class people become involved in a short and bittersweet romance in WWII England. Intensely romantic, underscored with Rachmaninoff's Second Piano Concerto. **86m/B VHS, DVD.** *GB* Celia Johnson, Trevor Howard, Stanley Holloway, Cyril Raymond, Joyce Carey, Everley Gregg, Margaret Barton, Dennis Harkin, Valentine Dyall, Marjorie Mars, Irene Handl; ***D:*** David Lean; ***W:*** Noel Coward, David Lean, Ronald Neame, Anthony Havelock-Allan; ***C:*** Robert Krasker. N.Y. Film Critics '46: Actress (Johnson).

A Brief History of Time **1992 (G)** A stunning documentary about physicist Stephen Hawking, the author of the popular book "Brief History of Time." Crippled by Lou Gehrig's Disease, Hawking narrates the film in the computer-synthesized voice he uses to speak. Interviews with family, friends, and colleagues, bring Hawking's scientific theories to light. **85m/C VHS.** Stephen Hawking; ***D:*** Errol Morris; ***W:*** Stephen Hawking; ***C:*** John Bailey; ***M:*** Philip Glass. Sundance '92: Filmmakers Trophy.

Brief Interviews With Hideous Men 1/2 **2009** Brief drama based on the book by David Foster Wallace is the writing/directing debut of actor Krasinski, also featured as Ryan, who dumped Sara (Nicholson), who is now interviewing male subjects about private matters. The battle of the sexes monologues aren't terribly interesting for the most part and this seems more like a filmmaking exercise than a film. **78m/C DVD.** John Krasinski, Julianne Nicholson, Timothy Hutton, Max Minghella, Lou Taylor Pucci, Dominic Cooper, Ben Shenkman, Chris Messina, Will Arnett, Bobby Cannavale, Josh Charles; ***D:*** John Bailey; ***C:*** John Bailey.

The Brig **1964** A film by Jonas Mekas documenting the Living Theatre's infamous performance of Kenneth H. Brown's experimental play. Designed by Julian Beck. **65m/B VHS.** Adolfas Mekas, Jim Anderson, Warren Finnerty, Henry Howard, Tom Lillard, James Tiroff, Gene Lipton; ***D:*** John Mekas.

Brigadoon **1954** The story of a magical, 18th century Scottish village which awakens once every 100 years and the two modern-day vacationers who stumble upon it. Main highlight is the Lerner and Loewe score. ♫Brigadoon; Almost Like Being in Love; I'll Go Home With Bonnie Jean; Wedding Dance; From This Day On; Heather on the Hill; Waitin' For My Dearie; Once in the Highlands. **108m/C VHS, DVD.** Elaine Stewart, Barry Jones, Albert Sharpe, Gene Kelly, Van Johnson, Cyd Charisse; ***D:*** Vincente Minnelli; ***W:*** Alan Jay Lerner; ***C:*** Joseph Ruttenberg; ***M:*** Alan Jay Lerner, Frederick Loewe.

Brigham City 1/2 **2001 (PG-13)** Skillful murder-mystery set in the fictitious Brigham City, Utah. The townspeople mostly know each other and most are also members of the Mormon Church. Sheriff Wes Clayton (Dutcher) and his deputy Terry's (Brown) duties are usually mundane—until they discover the mutiliated body of a young female tourist at an abandoned homestead. Clayton is willing to defer to the FBI but then a second body is discovered and the media vultures descend on the formerly quiet community as their faith is all put to an unexpected test. **115m/C VHS, DVD.** Richard Dutcher, Wilford Brimley, Matthew A. Brown, Carrie Morgan, John Enos, Tayva Patch; ***D:*** Richard Dutcher; ***W:*** Richard Dutcher; ***C:*** Ken Glassing; ***M:*** Sam Cardon.

Brigham Young: Frontiersman **1940** Somewhat interesting story about the pioneering Mormons and their founding of Salt Lake City. Under the leadership of Brigham Young (Jagger), they set out across the plains, battling hardships and starvation along the way. An emphasis was placed on the historical rather than the religious in an effort not to scare off moviegoers, but the picture failed at the boxoffice anyway. Based on the story by Louis Bromfield. **114m/C VHS, DVD.** Tyrone Power, Linda Darnell, Dean Jagger, Brian Donlevy, John Carradine, Jane Darwell, Jean Rogers, Mary Astor, Vincent Price, Willard Robertson, Moroni Olsen, Marc Lawrence, Selmer Jackson, Stanley Andrews; ***D:*** Henry Hathaway; ***W:*** Lamar Trotti, Ann E. Todd; ***C:*** Arthur C. Miller; ***M:*** Cyril Mockridge, Alfred Newman.

Bright Angel 1/2 **1991 (R)** Road movie pairs an unconventional team: George wants to visit his aunt to see if she's heard from his mother who ran off with another man; Luey is a free-spirit trying to free her brother from jail. Good performances by Mulroney, Taylor, & Pullman. Ford adapted two of his short stories, "Childern" and "Great Falls" for the gritty and uncompromising script of life in the modern west. **94m/C VHS.** Dermot Mulroney, Lili Taylor, Sam Shepard, Valerie Perrine, Burt Young, Bill Pullman, Benjamin Bratt, Mary Kay Place, Delroy Lindo, Kevin Tighe, Sheila McCarthy; ***D:*** Michael Fields; ***W:*** Richard Ford; ***M:*** Christopher Young.

Bright Eyes **1934 (PG)** Shirley (Temple) lives with her widowed mother Mary (Wilson), who works as a maid for the snobbish Smythe family, where only wealthy, crochety Uncle Ned (Sellon) befriends the cutie. His niece Adele (Allen) is engaged to Shirley's godfather, flyboy Loop Merritt (Dunn), who wants the tyke to live with him when her mom is killed. But Uncle Ned also wants to adopt her and there's a battle over custody. Shirley warbles "On the Good Ship Lollipop" in her usual winsome way. **84m/B VHS, DVD.** Shirley Temple, James Dunn, Lois Wilson, Jane Withers, Judith Allen, Jane Darwell, Charles Sellon; ***D:*** David Butler; ***W:*** David Butler, Edwin Burke, William Conselman; ***C:*** Arthur C. Miller.

Bright Future *Akarui mirai* **2003** Mamoru and Yuji are best friends, co-workers, and roommates in an existentially cool and cold modern world. Dreamlike plot takes Mamoru to jail for a crime he didn't commit, but won't deny. He seems fine there, drifting in and out of reality, almost living vicariously through his pet jellyfish he entrusted with Yuji before hitting the slammer. Japanese director Kiyoshi Kurosawa's new-wave vision of art and horror are fascinating, yet alienating at once. Fans of bizarro Asian cinema will flip. Originally titled "Jellyfish Alert," a title somehow more accurately describing this movie than any review could. **92m/C DVD.** Tadanobu Asano, Tatsuya Fuji, Joe Odagiri, Marumi Shiraishi; ***D:*** Kiyoshi Kurosawa; ***W:*** Kiyoshi Kurosawa; ***C:*** Takahide Shibanushi; ***M:*** Pacific 231.

Bright Leaf 1/2 **1950** In 1894, Brant Royle (Cooper) returns to his Kingsmont hometown and gets smitten brothel owner Sonia (Bacall) to become an investor in his automated cigarette-making business. His success nearly bankrupts the local tobacco tycoons, including James Singleton (Crisp) who originally ran Brant out of town for courting his daughter, Margaret (Neal). But when Margaret tries to save her family Brant ends up being used. **110m/B DVD.** Gary Cooper, Lauren Bacall, Patricia Neal, Donald Crisp, Jack Carson, Jeff Corey, Gladys George; ***D:*** Michael Curtiz; ***W:*** Ranald MacDougall; ***C:*** Karl Freund; ***M:*** Victor Young.

Bright Lights, Big City **1988 (R)** Based on Jay McInerney's popular novel, Fox plays a contemporary yuppie working in Manhattan as a magazine journalist. As his world begins to fall apart, he embarks on an endless cycle of drugs and nightlife. Fox is poorly cast, and his character is hard to care for as he becomes more and more dissolute. Although McInerney wrote his own screenplay, the intellectual abstractness of the novel can't be captured on film. **110m/C VHS, DVD.** David Warrilow, Sam Robards, Kelly Lynch, Annabelle Gurwitch, Maria Pitillo, David Hyde Pierce, Jessica Lundy, Michael J. Fox, Kiefer Sutherland, Phoebe Cates, Frances Sternhagen, Swoosie Kurtz, Tracy Pollan, Jason Robards Jr., John Houseman, Dianne Wiest, Charlie Schlatter, William Hickey; ***D:*** James Bridges; ***C:*** Gordon Willis.

A Bright Shining Lie 1/2 **1998 (R)** Based on Neil Sheehan's 1988 Pulitzer Prize-winning book, which chronicles the Vietnam War as seen through the eyes of Lt. Col. John Paul Vann (Paxton). The brash Vann arrived as a military adviser to the Vietnamese Army in 1962 and eventually left that post to become part of the State Department's Civilian Aid Program, where he exposed falsified battle reports and other deceptions to newsman Steven Burnett (Logue). The complex and controversial Vann was killed in a chopper crash in 1972. **118m/C VHS, DVD.** Bill Paxton, Donal Logue, Kurtwood Smith, Eric Bogosian, Amy Madigan, Vivian Wu, Robert John Burke, James Rebhorn, Ed Lauter, Harve Presnell; ***D:*** Terry George; ***W:*** Terry George; ***C:*** Jack Conroy; ***M:*** Gary Chang. **CABLE**

Bright Star 1/2 **2009 (PG)** Oh to be young and in the throes of first love! In 1818, flirty 18-year-old Fanny Brawne (Cornish) and her family live next door to brooding 23-year-old romantic poet John Keats (Whishaw) and his friend and patron, Charles Brown (Schneider). Keats is poor (and terminally ill) and fashionable seamstress Fanny knows she must meet her family's expectations and make a respectable marriage. She becomes his muse and then the object of his passionate letters. No consummation is possible so director Campion wisely makes the most of every glance, touch, and word. Title refers to the poem Keats dedicated to Fanny. **119m/C DVD.** *GB AU* Paul Schneider, Thomas Sangster, Ben Whishaw, Abbie Cornish, Kerry Fox, Edie Martin, Gerard Monaco, Antonia Campbell-Hughes; ***D:*** Jane Campion; ***W:*** Jane Campion; ***C:*** Greig Fraser; ***M:*** Mark Bradshaw.

Bright Young Things 1/2 **2003 (R)** Actor/director/writer Stephen Fry tackles literary satire with his adaptation of Evelyn Waugh's 1930 novel, "Vile Bodies." And if not precisely vile, those bodies are wicked indeed as seen through the everyman eyes of Adam (Moore), a poor aspiring novelist-turned-gossip columnist who wishes to marry superficial party girl Nina (Mortimer). Fry breezily tackles the jaded, flapper milieu of upper-class London between the wars that lends itself to glitter and eccentricity, embodied by feckless social butterflies (Woolgar) and drug-taking peers (the gentlemanly 94-year-old Sir John Mills doing a little coke in a cameo). These bored young things are bright only in the way they briefly shine before drab reality takes over. They (and the viewer) may as well enjoy it while they can. **106m/C DVD.** Emily Mortimer, James McAvoy, Michael Sheen, David Tennant, Fenella Woolgar, Dan Aykroyd, Jim Broadbent, Simon Callow, Jim Carter, Stockard Channing, Richard E. Grant, Julia McKenzie, Peter O'Toole, Stephan Campbell Moore; ***D:*** Stephen Fry; ***W:*** Stephen Fry; ***C:*** Henry Braham; ***M:*** Anne Dudley.

Brighton Beach Memoirs 1/2 *Neil Simon's Brighton Beach Memoirs* **1986 (PG-13)** The film adaptation of the popular (and semiautobiographical) Neil Simon play. Poignant comedy/drama about a young Jewish boy's coming of age in Depression-era Brooklyn. Followed by "Biloxi Blues" and "Broadway Bound." **108m/C VHS, DVD.** Blythe Danner, Bob (Robert) Dishy, Judith Ivey, Jonathan Silverman, Brian Drillinger, Stacey Glick, Lisa Waltz, Jason Alexander; ***D:*** Gene Saks; ***W:*** Neil Simon; ***C:*** John Bailey; ***M:*** Michael Small.

Brighton Rock *Young Scarface* **1947** Sterling performances highlight this seamy look at the British underworld. Attenborough is Pinkie Brown, a small-time hood who ends up committing murder. He manipulates a waitress to get himself off the hook, but things don't go exactly as he plans. Based on the novel by Graham Greene. **92m/B VHS.** *GB* Richard Attenborough, Hermione Baddeley, William Hartnell, Carol Marsh, Nigel Stock, Wylie Watson, Alan Wheatley, George Carney, Reginald Purdell; ***D:*** John Boulting; ***W:*** Graham Greene.

Brighton Strangler **1945** An actor who plays a murderer assumes the role of the strangler after suffering from a concussion. Decent psychodrama. **67m/B VHS.** John Loder, June Duprez, Miles Mander; ***D:*** Max Nosseck.

Brighty of the Grand Canyon 1/2 **1967** The spunky donkey Brighty roams across the Grand Canyon in search of adventure. He finds friendship with a gold-digging old prospector who hits pay dirt. **90m/C VHS, DVD.** Joseph Cotten, Pat Conway, Dick Foran, Karl Swenson; ***D:*** Norman Foster.

A Brilliant Disguise 1/2 **1993 (R)** Sportswriter gets involved with an artist who turns out to have multiple personality disorder and a sinister psychiatrist. Then his friends start to turn up dead but things aren't exactly what they seem. **97m/C VHS.** Lysette Anthony, Anthony John (Tony) Denison, Corbin Bernsen, Gregory McKinney, Robert (Bobby Ray) Shafer; ***D:*** Nick Vallelonga; ***W:*** Nick Vallelonga.

Brilliant Lies 1/2 **1996** Susy Connor (Gia Carides) has brought an official complaint of sexual harassment against former boss Gary Fitzgerald (LaPaglia), who denies the charge. She claims her sister Katie (Zoe Carides) will substantiate her story, which she will, even though Katie knows it's a lie. As a matter of fact, Susy's a consummate liar though, in a way, she also turns out to be telling the truth. Fine performances from the Carides sisters, as well as LaPaglia (who's married to Gia) and Barrett, who plays the self-pitying Connor patriarch. Adapted from the play by David Williamson. **93m/C VHS.** *AU* Gia Carides, Anthony LaPaglia, Zoe Carides, Ray Barrett, Michael Veitch, Neil Melville, Catherine Wilkin, Grant Tilly; ***D:*** Richard Franklin; ***W:*** Richard Franklin, Peter Fitzpatrick; ***C:*** Geoff Burton; ***M:*** Nerida Tyson-Chew.

Brimstone & Treacle **1982 (R)** Weird, obsessive psychodrama in which a young rogue (who may or may not be an actual agent of the Devil) infiltrates the home of a staid British family caring for their comatose adult daughter. **85m/C VHS, DVD.** *GB* Sting, Denholm Elliott, Joan Plowright, Suzanna Hamilton; ***D:*** Richard Loncraine; ***W:*** Dennis Potter. Montreal World Film Fest. '82: Film.

Bring It On 1/2 **2000 (PG-13)** Bring on the guilty pleasure. Equal parts satire, exploitation, and earnest (if not totally successful) teen flick, the film follows cheerleader Torrence (Dunst) as she becomes captain of the Rancho Carne High Toros cheer squad, who soon after discovers her squad's championship moves have been lifted from another school, the East Compton High Clovers. All of this culminates in a showdown between the two squads, while interspersed throughout are standard teenage goings-on. No gem, by any means, but fun if you're in the mood (or spirit). But be advised: probably too raunchy for its intended young adult audience. **98m/C VHS, DVD.** Kirsten Dunst, Eliza Dushku, Jesse Bradford, Gabrielle Union, Clare Kramer, Nicole Bilderback, Tsianina Joelson, Rini Bell, Ian Roberts, Richard Hillman, Lindsay Sloane, Cody McMains; ***D:*** Peyton Reed; ***W:*** Jessica Bendinger; ***C:*** Shawn Maurer; ***M:*** Christophe Beck.

Bring It On Again **2003 (PG-13)** College freshman Whittier (Judson-Yager) proves to be a cheerleading rival that head pom-pom girl Tina (Turner) won't tolerate. So when Whittier is cut from the squad, she decides to form a new team and challenge Tina to a cheer off. **90m/C VHS, DVD.** Anne Judson-Yager, Bree Turner, Richard Lee Jackson, Faune A. Chambers, Kevin Cooney, Bryce Johnson; ***D:*** Damon Santostefano; ***W:*** Claudio Grazioso; ***C:*** Richard Crudo; ***M:*** Paul Haslinger. **VIDEO**

Bring It On: All or Nothing 1/2 **2006 (PG-13)** The plot hardly matters as long as the cheer routines astonish (which they do). Britney (Panettiere) was the cheer captain at her rich 'burb school but is just another wannabe after a move to a more urban setting. But she wins over leader Camille (Knowles-Smith) with some new routines and is ready to go up against her old squad. **99m/C DVD.** Hayden Panettiere, Jake McDorman, Solange Knowles-Smith, Gus Carr, Marcy Rylan; ***D:*** Steve Rash; ***W:*** Alyson Fouse. **VIDEO**

Bring It On: Fight to the Finish **2009 (PG-13)** Yet another cheerleading sequel. East L.A. high school cheer captain Lina Cruz (Milian) feels her squad is a lock to win the Spirit Championships until her mother remarries and they relocate to Malibu. Lina soon learns that the Malibu Vista High Sea Lions aren't winning material until she vows to whip them into shape to knock off the award-winning rival Jaguars and their trash-talking captain, Avery (Smith). Soon Lina notices just how darn cute Avery's brother Evan (Longo) is. **103m/C DVD.** Christina Milian, Rachele Brooke Smith, Cody Longo, Vanessa Born, Gabrielle Dennis, Nikki SooHoo, Meagan Holder, David Starzyk; ***D:*** Bille Woodruff; ***W:*** Elena Song, Alyson Fouse; ***C:*** David Claessen; ***M:*** Andrew Gross. **VIDEO**

Bring It On: In It to Win It 1/2 **2007 (PG-13)** It's the battle of the coastal babes as SoCal Carson (Benson) and Big Apple Brooke (Scerbo) and their cheer squads meet up at the national championships. Carson falls for Penn (Copon), who happens to be on Brooke's team, and Brooke challenges Carson to a personal cheer-off. This leads to a brawl and both teams are disqualified, but they're determined to get back into the finals. **90m/C DVD.** Adam Vernier, Ashley Benson, Cassie Scerbo, Michael Copon, Jennifer Tisdale, Kierstin Koppell, Noel Areizaga; ***D:*** Steve Rash; ***W:*** Alyson Fouse; ***C:*** Levie Isaacks. **VIDEO**

Bring Me the Head of Alfredo Garcia **1974 (R)** Peckinpah falters in this poorly paced outing. American piano player on tour in Mexico finds himself entwined with a gang of bloodthirsty bounty hunters. Bloody and confused. **112m/C VHS, DVD.** Warren Oates, Isela Vega, Gig Young, Robert Webber, Helmut Dantine, Emilio Fernandez, Kris Kristofferson; ***D:*** Sam Peckinpah; ***W:*** Gordon Dawson, Sam Peckinpah; ***C:*** Alex Phillips Jr.; ***M:*** Jerry Fielding.

Bringing Down the House **2003 (PG-13)** Straitlaced divorced lawyer Martin makes an online date and winds up with parolee Queen Latifah, who proceeds to turn his life upside-down in her quest to get him to help her prove her innocence. Moments of inspired comedy have everything to do with the talents of Martin and Latifah, and little to do with script or direction. Levy makes the most of his sidekick role. May play better on the small screen. **105m/C VHS, DVD.** *US* Steve Martin, Queen Latifah, Eugene Levy, Jean Smart, Angus T. Jones, Kimberly J. Brown, Joan Plowright, Missi Pyle, Steve Harris, Michael Rosenbaum, Betty White; ***D:*** Adam Shankman; ***W:*** Jason Filardi; ***C:*** Julio Macat; ***M:*** Lalo Schifrin.

Bringing Out the Dead 1/2 **1999 (R)** Cage hasn't looked this haggard since his boozehound role in "Leaving Las Vegas" which could be considered a dress rehearsal for this turn as burnt out New York City paramedic Frank Pierce. Aided by Scorsese's kinetic filmmaking style, Schrader's on-tempo script, and revved up performances by Rhames and Sizemore as Pierce's partners, movie successfully convey's the day-to-day stress of emergency units. Unfortunately, Cage's sleepwalking character is a bore, and a lack of chemistry with real-life spouse Arquette as Pierce's singular ray of hope only makes you yearn for Scorsese's similarly themed masterpiece "Taxi Driver." Based on the novel by Joe Connelly. **120m/C VHS, DVD.** Jon Abrahams, Nicolas Cage, John Goodman, Tom Sizemore, Ving Rhames, Patricia Arquette, Marc Anthony, Mary Beth Hurt, Clifford Curtis, Nestor Serrano, Aida Turturro, Afemo Omilami, Arthur J. Nascarelli, Cynthia Roman, Cullen Oliver Johnson; ***D:*** Martin Scorsese; ***W:*** Paul Schrader; ***C:*** Robert Richardson; ***M:*** Elmer Bernstein.

Bringing Up Baby **1938** The quintessential screwball comedy, featuring Hepburn as a giddy socialite with a "baby" leopard, and Grant as the unwitting object of her affections. One ridiculous situation after another adds up to high speed fun. Hepburn looks lovely, the supporting actors are in fine form, and director Hawks manages the perfect balance of control and mayhem. From a story by Hagar Wilde, who helped Nichols with the screenplay. Also available in a colorized version. **103m/B VHS, DVD.** Katharine Hepburn, Cary Grant, May Robson, Charlie Ruggles, Walter Catlett, Fritz Feld, Jonathan Hale, Barry Fitzgerald, Ward Bond; ***D:*** Howard Hawks; ***W:*** Dudley Nichols; ***C:*** Russell Metty. AFI '98: Top 100, Natl. Film Reg. '90.

Brink 1/2 **1998** Andy Brinker leads of group of in-line skaters who are dedicated to the sport. But Andy also needs money to help out his family and when a rival team offers him cash to join them on the circuit, Andy's forced into a hard choice. **88m/C VHS.** Christina Vidal, Erik von Detten, Patrick Levis, Asher Gold, Sam Horrigan; ***D:*** Greg Beeman. **CABLE**

Brink of Life 1/2 *Nara Livet* **1957** Three pregnant women in a hospital maternity ward await the impending births with mixed feelings. Early Bergman; in Swedish with English subtitles. **82m/B VHS.** *SW* Eva Dahlbeck, Bibi Andersson, Ingrid Thulin, Babro Ornas, Max von Sydow, Erland Josephson, Gunnar Sjoberg; ***D:*** Ingmar Bergman. Cannes '58: Actress (Dahlbeck), Actress (Andersson, Thulin), Director (Bergman).

Brink's Job **1978 (PG)** Re-creates the "crime of the century," Tony Pino's heist of $2.7 million from a Brink's truck. The action picks up five days before the statute of limitations is about to run out. **103m/C VHS.** Peter Falk, Peter Boyle, Warren Oates, Gena Rowlands, Paul Sorvino, Sheldon Leonard, Allen (Goorwitz) Garfield; ***D:*** William Friedkin; ***W:*** Walon Green; ***M:*** Richard Rodney Bennett.

Britannia Hospital 1/2 **1982 (R)** This is a portrait of a hospital at its most chaotic: the staff threatens to strike, demonstrators surround the hospital, a nosey BBC reporter pursues an anxious professor, and the eagerly anticipated royal visit degenerates into a total shambles. **111m/C VHS, DVD.** *GB* Malcolm McDowell, Leonard Rossiter, Graham Crowden, Joan Plowright, Mark Hamill, Alan Bates, Dave Atkins, Marsha A. Hunt; ***D:*** Lindsay Anderson; ***W:*** David Sherwin; ***C:*** Mike Flash; ***M:*** Alan Price.

Britannic **1999** The Brittanic, the Titanic's sister ship, was built as a luxury liner but when WWI began the ship was turned into a hospital transport after its launch in 1914. The ship did sink off the Greek coast in 1916 (probably due to a torpedo or mine) but the filmmakers haven't let any other facts of the story stand in the way of this poor man's "Titanic" with its class difference romance and other cliches. **96m/C VHS, DVD.** Edward Atterton, Jacqueline Bisset, John Rhys-Davies, Bruce Payne, Amanda Ryan, Ben Daniels; ***D:*** Brian Trenchard-Smith; ***W:*** Brian Trenchard-Smith, Brett Thompson, Dennis A. Pratt; ***C:*** Ivan Strasburg; ***M:*** Alan Parker. **CABLE**

British Intelligence 1/2 **1940** Silly American-made film about British espionage. Boris Karloff plays a butler (who is also a spy) trapped by an agent who visits the home of a British bureaucrat. Half-baked story that doesn't hold up. **62m/B VHS, DVD.** Boris Karloff, Margaret Lindsay, Maris Wrixon, Holmes Herbert, Leonard Mudie, Bruce Lester; ***D:*** Terry Morse.

Brittanic **2000** Talk about your lousy luck! The Britannic is the sister ocean liner to the infamous Titanic and guess what happens? Yes, indeedy, it sinks as well. But this one was being used as a hospital ship in WWI. **96m/C VHS, DVD.** Jacqueline Bisset, Edward Atterton, Amanda Ryan, Bruce Payne, John Rhys-Davies; ***D:*** Brian Trenchard-Smith. **CABLE**

A Brivele der Mamen *A Letter to Mother; A Letter to Mama* **1938** A Jewish mother does her best to hold her fragile family together, in spite of the ravages of war and poverty. Her travails take her and her family from the Polish Ukraine to New York City. In Yiddish with English subtitles. **90m/C VHS.** *PL* Berta Gersten, Lucy Gerhman, Misha Gerhman, Edmund Zayenda; ***D:*** Joseph Green.

Broadcast Bombshells **1995 (R)** TV station WSEX has a station manager who'll do anything to improve ratings, an ambitious associate producer after the weather girl's job, a sexaholic sportscaster, and lots of chaos involving a mad bomber. The barely there plot is just the excuse for a considerable display of T&A anyway. Also available unrated. **80m/C VHS, DVD.** Amy Lynn Baxter, Debbie Rochon, John Richardson, Elizabeth Heyman, Joseph Pallister; ***D:*** Ernest G. Sauer.

Broadcast News ♂♂♂ 1/2 **1987 (R)** The acclaimed, witty analysis of network news shows, dealing with the three-way romance between a driven career-woman producer, an ace nebbish reporter and a brainless, popular on-screen anchorman. Incisive and funny, though often simply idealistic. **132m/C VHS, DVD.** William Hurt, Albert Brooks, Holly Hunter, Jack Nicholson, Joan Cusack, Robert Prosky, Lois Chiles, John Cusack, Gennie James; ***D:*** James L. Brooks; ***W:*** James L. Brooks; ***C:*** Michael Ballhaus; ***M:*** Bill Conti, Michael Gore. L.A. Film Critics '87: Actress (Hunter); Natl. Bd. of Review '87: Actress (Hunter); N.Y. Film Critics '87: Actress (Hunter), Director (Brooks), Film, Screenplay.

Broadway ♂ 1/2 **1942 91m/B DVD.** George Raft, Pat O'Brien, Broderick Crawford, Janet Blair, Anne Gwynne, Marjorie Rambeau; ***D:*** William A. Seiter; ***W:*** John Bright, Felix Jackson; ***C:*** George Barnes; ***M:*** Charles Previn.

Broadway Bill ♂♂♂ *Strictly Confidential* **1934** A man decides to abandon his nagging wife and his job in her family's business for the questionable pleasures of owning a racehorse known as Broadway Bill. This racetrack comedy was also remade by Frank Capra in 1951 as "Riding High." **90m/C VHS, DVD.** Warner Baxter, Myrna Loy, Walter Connolly, Helen Vinson, Margaret Hamilton, Frankie Darro; ***D:*** Frank Capra.

Broadway Bound ♂♂ 1/2 *Neil Simon's Broadway Bound* **1992** The final film in Simon's trilogy (preceded by "Brighton Beach Memoirs" and "Biloxi Blues"), this one made for TV. The playwright's alter ego, Eugene Morris Jerome, is ready to leave Brooklyn for good, hoping to make it as a comedy writer for a radio show. Meanwhile, his mother decides what to do about his unfaithful father. **90m/C VHS.** Jonathan Silverman, Anne Bancroft, Jerry Orbach, Corey Parker, Hume Cronyn, Michele Lee; ***D:*** Paul Bogart; ***W:*** Neil Simon. **TV**

Broadway Damage ♂ 1/2 **1998** Amateurish gay comedy whose best asset is the shopaholic (and only female) character played by Hobel, as the typical overweight fag hag roomie of aspiring New York actor Marc (Lucas). Beyond-shallow Marc is looking for a lover and only a perfect 10 will do, which means he gets dumped a lot by narcissitic manipulators. Meanwhile, his plain best friend, Robert (Williams), pines for the twit to notice him in a romantic way. **110m/C VHS, DVD.** Michael Shawn Lucas, Aaron Williams, Mara Hobel, Hugh Panaro; ***D:*** Victor Mignatti; ***W:*** Victor Mignatti; ***C:*** Mike Mayers; ***M:*** Elliot Sokolov.

Broadway Danny Rose ♂♂♂ 1/2 **1984 (PG)** One of Woody Allen's best films, a hilarious, heart-rending anecdotal comedy about a third-rate talent agent involved in one of his client's infidelities. The film magically unfolds as show business veterans swap Danny Rose stories at a delicatessen. Allen's Danny Rose is pathetically lovable. **85m/B VHS, DVD.** Woody Allen, Mia Farrow, Nick Apollo Forte, Sandy Baron, Milton Berle, Howard Cosell; ***D:*** Woody Allen; ***W:*** Woody Allen; ***C:*** Gordon Willis. British Acad. '84: Orig. Screenplay; Writers Guild '84: Orig. Screenplay.

The Broadway Drifter ♂♂ **1927** A silent Jazz Age drama about a playboy who repents his decadent ways by opening a girls' health school. Complications ensue. **90m/B VHS.** George Walsh, Dorothy Hall, Bigelow Cooper, Arthur Donaldson; ***D:*** Bernard McEveety Sr.

Broadway Limited ♂♂ *The Baby Vanishes* **1941** Three aspiring actors head for the Great White Way with a baby to use as a prop. Thinking the baby kidnapped, the police make things tough for the trio. McLaglen was wasted on this one, which was apparently made to show off the considerable assets of Woodworth. **75m/B VHS, DVD.** Victor McLaglen, Marjorie Woodworth, Dennis O'Keefe, Patsy Kelly, Zasu Pitts, Leonid Kinskey, George E. Stone; ***D:*** Gordon Douglas.

Broadway Melody ♂♂ 1/2 **1929** Early musical in which two sisters hope for fame on Broadway, and encounter a wily song and dance man who traps both their hearts. Dated, but still charming, with a lovely score. Considered the great granddaddy of all MGM musicals; followed by three more melodies in 1935, 1937, and 1940. ♫ Broadway Melody; Give My Regards to Broadway; Truthful Parson Brown; The Wedding of the Painted Doll; The Boy Friend; You Were Meant For Me; Love Boat; Broadway Babies. **104m/B VHS, DVD.** Bessie Love, Anita Page, Charles King, Jed Prouty, Kenneth Thomson, Edward Dillon, Mary Doran; ***D:*** Harry Beaumont; ***M:*** Nacio Herb Brown, Arthur Freed. Oscars '29: Picture.

Broadway Melody of 1936 ♂♂♂ **1935** Exceptional musical comedy with delightful performances from Taylor and Powell. Benny is a headline-hungry columnist who tries to entrap Taylor by using Powell. ♫ Broadway Melody; Broadway Rhythm; You Are My Lucky Star; I've Got a Feeling You're Fooling; All I Do Is Dream of You; Sing Before Breakfast; On a Sunday Afternoon. **110m/B VHS.** Jack Benny, Eleanor Powell, Robert Taylor, Una Merkel, Sid Silvers, Buddy Ebsen; ***D:*** Roy Del Ruth; ***C:*** Charles Rosher; ***M:*** Nacio Herb Brown, Arthur Freed.

Broadway Melody of 1938 ♂♂ 1/2 **1937** Third entry in the melody series lacks the sparkle of "Broadway Melody of 1936" despite the all-star cast. Lots of singing and dancing without much charm. Two bright spots: a young Garland singing the now famous "Dear Mr. Gable" and the always lovely Powell's dance numbers. ♫ Broadway Rhythm; Dear Mr. Gable (You Made Me Love You); A New Pair of Shoes; Yours and Mine; I'm Feeling Like a Million; Everybody Sing; Follow in My Footsteps; Your Broadway and My Broadway; Sun Showers. **110m/B VHS.** Eleanor Powell, Sophie Tucker, George Murphy, Judy Garland, Robert Taylor, Buddy Ebsen, Binnie Barnes; ***D:*** Roy Del Ruth; ***C:*** William H. Daniels; ***M:*** Nacio Herb Brown, Arthur Freed.

Broadway Melody of 1940 ♂♂ 1/2 **1940** The last entry in the melody series features the only screen teaming of Astaire and Powell. The flimsy plot is just an excuse for a potent series of Cole Porter musical numbers. ♫ I Concentrate on You; I've Got My Eye on You; Begin the Beguine; I am the Captain; Please Don't Monkey With Broadway; Between You and Me; Il Bacio. **103m/B VHS, DVD.** Fred Astaire, Eleanor Powell, George Murphy, Frank Morgan, Ian Hunter; ***D:*** Norman Taurog.

Broadway Rhythm ♂♂ 1/2 **1944** A too-long look at Broadway behind-the-scenes. Murphy plays a Broadway producer who hopes to land a Hollywood star for his new show. She rejects his offer in favor of a show being produced by his father. Just a chance to showcase a number of popular vaudeville acts, songs, and the music of Tommy Dorsey and his orchestra. ♫ All the Things You Are; That Lucky Fellow; In Other Words; Seventeen; All In Fun; Brazilian Boogie; What Do You Think I Am?; Somebody Loves Me; Milkman Keep Those Bottles Quiet. **111m/C VHS.** George Murphy, Ginny Simms, Charles Winninger, Gloria De Haven, Nancy Walker, Ben Blue, Lena Horne, Eddie Anderson; ***D:*** Roy Del Ruth; ***W:*** Dorothy Kingsley, Harry Clork.

Broadway Serenade ♂♂ 1/2 **1939** Melodramatic musical in which a songwriter (Ayres) and his wife, singer MacDonald, make career choices that destroy their marriage. ♫ Broadway Serenade for the Lonely Heart; High Flyin'; One Look at You; Time Changes Everything; Un Bel Di; No Time to Argue; Italian Street Song; Les Filles de Cadiz; Musical Contract. **114m/B VHS, DVD.** Jeanette MacDonald, Lew Ayres, Ian Hunter, Frank Morgan, Wally Vernon, Rita Johnson, Virginia Grey, William Gargan; ***D:*** Robert Z. Leonard; ***W:*** Charles Lederer.

Broadway to Cheyenne ♂ *From Broadway to Cheyenne* **1932** A group of big city gangsters try to take over a small western town but are opposed by heroic cowboys. **53m/B VHS, DVD.** Rex Bell, George "Gabby" Hayes, Marceline Day, Robert Ellis, Alan Bridge, Matthew Betz; ***D:*** Harry Fraser.

Brokeback Mountain ♂♂♂ 1/2 **2005 (R)** Yes, it's primarily known as the movie that inspired a million "gay cowboy" jokes, but Lee's heartbreaking drama deserves so much better. In 1963, cowhands Ennis (Ledger) and Jack (Gyllenhaal) spend the summer watching over a herd of sheep on a Wyoming mountain range and falling deeply and inexplicably in love. Terrified to admit their feelings to the outside world, Ennis and Jack try to ignore their passions by getting married to aloof women (Williams and Hathaway) and only meeting for semi-annual fishing trips. The script blends the powerful western themes of "Lonesome Dove" with a classic tragic love tale, and Ledger's outstanding lead performance carries the picture. **134m/C DVD, HD DVD.** *US* Heath Ledger, Jake Gyllenhaal, Linda Cardellini, Anna Faris, Anne Hathaway, Michelle Williams, Randy Quaid, Graham Beckel, Scott Michael Campbell, Kate Mara, Roberta Maxwell, Peter McRobbie, David Harbour; ***D:*** Ang Lee; ***W:*** Larry McMurtry, Diana Ossana; ***C:*** Rodrigo Prieto; ***M:*** Gustavo Santaolalla. Oscars '05: Adapt. Screenplay, Director (Lee), Orig. Score; British Acad. '05: Adapt. Screenplay, Film, Support. Actor (Gyllenhaal); Directors Guild '05: Director (Lee); Golden Globes '06: Director (Lee), Film—Drama, Screenplay, Song ("A Love That Will Never Grow Old"); Ind. Spirit '06: Director (Lee), Film; L.A. Film Critics '05: Director (Lee), Film; Natl. Bd. of Review '05: Director (Lee), Support. Actor (Gyllenhaal); N.Y. Film Critics '05: Actor (Ledger), Director (Lee), Film; Writers Guild '05: Adapt. Screenplay.

Brokedown Palace ♂♂ 1/2 **1999 (PG-13)** Danes and Beckinsale take a trip to Thailand following their high school graduation and are targeted by a smooth-talking Australian drug dealer. After he invites the pair to Hong Kong, he hides heroin in their luggage and they're busted at the airport. Accused of drug trafficking, they are sentenced to 33 years in a Thai prison. Phillips is an unfriendly DEA official, while Pullman is the expatriate American lawyer who comes to their aid. The story focuses more on the girls' relationship as friends than on their legal nightmare, however. Nevertheless, the government of Thailand was none too pleased by the script, so most of the Thai scenes were actually shot in the Phillipines. **100m/C VHS, DVD.** Claire Danes, Kate Beckinsale, Bill Pullman, Daniel Lapaine, Lou Diamond Phillips, Jacqueline Kim, Tom Amandes, Aimee Graham, John Doe; ***D:*** Jonathan Kaplan; ***W:*** David Arata; ***C:*** Newton Thomas (Tom) Sigel; ***M:*** David Newman.

The Broken ♂ 1/2 **2008 (R)** The plot's broken too or maybe the director doesn't care that it doesn't make much sense. London radiologist Gina (Headey) glimpses her doppelganger on the street and gets obsessed. She also gets into a car crash, comes out of a coma, has flashbacks, and thinks her family and boyfriend are behaving strangely. She's paranoid at the very least. **88m/C DVD.** *GB* Lena Headey, Richard Jenkins, Melvil Poupaud, Ulrich Thomsen, Asier Newman, Michaelle Duncan; ***D:*** Sean Ellis; ***W:*** Sean Ellis; ***C:*** Angus Hudson; ***M:*** Guy Farley.

Broken Angel ♂ 1/2 **1988** Jamie seemed to be such a nice girl, with good looks and great grades—and membership in a notorious street gang. When Jamie disappears, her family discovers her secret activities and dad tries to find his wayward little girl. Melodramatic TV goo. **94m/C VHS.** William Shatner, Susan Blakely, Erika Eleniak, Roxann Biggs-Dawson; ***D:*** Richard T. Heffron. **TV**

Broken Arrow ♂♂ 1/2 **1950** A U.S. scout befriends Cochise and the Apaches, and helps settlers and Indians live in peace together in the 1870s. Acclaimed as the first Hollywood film to side with the Indians, and for Chandler's portrayal of Cochise. Based on the novel "Blood Brother" by Elliot Arnold. **93m/C VHS, DVD.** James Stewart, Jeff Chandler, Will Geer, Debra Paget, Basil Ruysdael, Arthur Hunnicutt, Jay Silverheels; ***D:*** Delmer Daves; ***W:*** Albert (John B. Sherry) Maltz; ***C:*** Ernest Palmer.

Broken Arrow ♂♂ **1995 (R)** Air Force pilot Vic Deakins (Travolta) rips off a couple of nuclear weapons during a routine exercise over the Utah desert. Deakins' ex-co-pilot Riley Hale (Slater), with help from spunky park ranger Terry Carmichael (Mathis), sets out to find and retrieve the warheads before the big bang. Hong Kong action king Woo once again tries his hand at the big-budget Hollywood action extravaganza, with mixed results. Triple script whammy of cheesy dialogue, continuity problems, and predictability undercuts, but doesn't obscure, his talent for choreographing mayhem. Travolta plays the All-American Boy as creepily charming psychotic to great effect. **108m/C VHS, DVD, Blu-ray Disc.** John Travolta, Christian Slater, Samantha Mathis, Delroy Lindo, Bob Gunton, Frank Whaley, Howie Long; ***D:*** John Woo; ***W:*** Graham Yost; ***C:*** Peter Levy; ***M:*** Hans Zimmer.

Broken Badge ♂♂♂ *The Rape of Richard Beck* **1985** Crenna stars as a macho, chauvinistic cop whose attitude towards rape victims changes dramatically after he himself is raped by a couple of thugs. Excellent TV movie. **100m/C VHS, DVD.** Richard Crenna, Meredith Baxter, Pat Hingle, Frances Lee McCain, Cotter Smith, George Dzundza, Joanna Kerns; ***D:*** Karen Arthur; ***W:*** James G. Hirsch; ***M:*** Peter Bernstein.

Broken Blossoms ♂♂♂ 1/2 **1919** One of Griffith's most widely acclaimed films, about a young Chinese man in London's squalid Limehouse district hoping to spread the peaceful philosophy of his Eastern religion. He befriends a pitiful street waif who is mistreated by her brutal father, resulting in tragedy. Silent. Revised edition contains introduction from Gish and a newly recorded score. **89m/B VHS, DVD.** Lillian Gish, Richard Barthelmess, Donald Crisp; ***D:*** D.W. Griffith; ***W:*** D.W. Griffith; ***C:*** Billy (G.W.) Bitzer; ***M:*** Louis F. Gottschalk. Natl. Film Reg. '96.

Broken Bridges ♂ 1/2 **2006 (PG-13)** Hard-drinking, washed-up country singer Bo Price returns to his Tennessee hometown when five soldiers are killed in a training accident. One is Bo's younger brother and another is the sibling of Angela Delton, whom Bo abandoned when she got pregnant. Angela returns with her 16-year-old daughter Dixie, but the Deltons prefer to keep their distance from Bo, who wants to make amends. **105m/C DVD.** Toby Keith, Kelly Preston, Lindsey Haun, Burt Reynolds, Tess Harper, Anna Maria Horsford; ***D:*** Steven Goldman; ***W:*** Cherie Bennett, Jeff Gottesfeld; ***C:*** Patrick Cady; ***M:*** Toby Keith. **CABLE**

The Broken Chain ♂♂ 1/2 **1993** In the mid 18th-century Joseph Brant (Schweig), a member of the Mohawk tribe, is sent away to be educated by the British. When he returns, his loyalties are divided between his Native American roots and his English mentor, Sir William Johnson (Brosnan). His boyhood friend Lohaheo (White Shirt) disdains Joseph's white man ways, leading to tragic consequences. Historical background features the French and Indian Wars, the splintering of the Iroquois Confederacy, and the coming of the American Revolution. Filmed on location in Virginia. **93m/C VHS.** Eric Schweig, Wes Studi, Buffy Saint Marie, Pierce Brosnan, J.C. White Shirt, Floyd "Red Crow" Westerman, Graham Greene, Elaine Bilstad, Kim Snyder; ***D:*** Lamont Johnson; ***W:*** Earl W. Wallace; ***M:*** Charles Fox. **TV**

Broken Embraces ♂♂♂ *Los Abrazos Rotos* **2009 (R)** Director Almodovar's twisting tale of filmmaking and revenge is bursting with colors that belie the darkness of the story. One-time film director Mateo Blanco (Homar) abandons his name and career after being blinded in a car crash. As Harry Caine, he is hired by the mysterious Ray X (Ochandiano) to write a screenplay about the life of movie producer Martel (Gomez), Mateo's former partner. The common thread linking all three men is Lena (Cruz), a beautiful starlet with a checkered past. Movies within the movie and characters who change names (and personas) lend extra dimension to the serpentine plot. Almodovar also uses many clever devices to reveal his opinions about the director and his role in the movie industry. In Spanish with subtitles. **128m/C DVD.** *SP* Penelope Cruz, Lluis Homar, Blanca Portillo, Jose Luis Gomez, Tamar Novas; ***D:*** Pedro Almodovar; ***W:*** Pedro Almodovar.

Broken English ♂♂ 1/2 **1996 (NC-17)** Ethnically diverse New Zealand is the setting for this story of young lovers and the parents who don't understand them. Croatian refugee Nina (Vujcic) and Maori cook Eddie (Arahanga) meet in the Chinese restaurant where they both work and quickly fall in love. Nina's menacing father Ivan (Serbedzija) objects to their passion, sometimes with a baseball bat. Film deals honestly with immigration and racial issues. Engaging debut for Vujcic, a Croatian refugee director Nicholas met in a bar. Also available in an R-rated version. **92m/C VHS.** *NZ* Aleksandra Vujcic, Julian (Sonny) Arahanga, Rade Serbedzija, Marton Csokas, Jing Zhao, Yang Li, Madeline McNamara; ***D:*** Gregor Nicholas; ***W:*** Gregor Nicholas, Johanna Pigott, Jim Salter; ***C:*** John Toon.

Broken English 1/2 **2007 (PG-13)** Nora (Posey) is a single, moderately neurotic New Yorker working a job for which she's over-qualified, while both she and her mother wonder why she's so unlucky at love. Enter charming and perfect Julien, who seems to look past Nora's insecurities and fears in exchange for a (mostly) perfect weekend. Posey shines and Cassavetes (daughter of legendary director John) shows insight into her characters, but it's not enough to completely transcend the well-worn lonely-hearts story. **97m/C DVD.** *US* Parker Posey, Melvil Poupaud, Drea De Matteo, Gena Rowlands, Justin Theroux, Tim Guinee, Josh Hamilton, Michael Panes; ***D:*** Zoe Cassavettes; ***W:*** Zoe Cassavettes; ***C:*** John Pirozzi; ***M:*** Scratch Massive.

Broken Flowers **2005 (R)** Quirky, if forlorn, comedy from Jarmusch. Murray does minimalism in his portrayal of confirmed, middle-aged bachelor Don Johnston whose orderly life becomes disarrayed when he learns he fathered a son from a long-ago liaison. Only there are four potential moms (a fifth has died), so Don reluctantly goes on a road trip to re-acquaint himself with Laura (Stone), Dora (Conroy), Carmen (Lange), and Penny (Swinton). His welcome varies—not much really happens—and Murray is more Don Quixote (with Wright as his stay-at-home Sancho Panza) than Don Juan. **105m/C DVD.** *FR US* Bill Murray, Jeffrey Wright, Sharon Stone, Frances Conroy, Jessica Lange, Tilda Swinton, Julie Delpy, Mark Webber, Chloe Sevigny, Christopher McDonald, Alexis Dziena, Larry Fessenden, Chris Bauer, Pell James, Heather Alicia Simms, Brea Frazier; ***D:*** Jim Jarmusch; ***W:*** Jim Jarmusch; ***C:*** Frederick Elmes.

Broken Glass 1/2 **1996** Set in Brooklyn in 1938 and adapted from a play by Arthur Miller. Jewish housewife, Sylvia Gellberg (Leicester), has been stricken by a mysterious paralysis and Dr. Harry Hyman (Patinkin) is called in to treat her. Her illness is apparently psychosomatic and Sylvia gradually reveals her anxiety about her unhappy marriage and her obsessive fears with newspaper reports concerning Jewish persecution in Germany. Hyman and his wife Margaret (McGovern) soon find themselves drawn in deeper than they could have imagined. Made for TV. **120m/C VHS.** Mandy Patinkin, Margot Leicester, Henry Goodman, Elizabeth McGovern; ***D:*** David Thacker; ***W:*** David Thacker, David Holman. **TV**

Broken Harvest 1/2 **1994** Jimmy O'Leary remembers his youth in rural 1950s Ireland when a poor wheat harvest led to his family's financial demise and a feud between his father (Lane) and neighbor Josie McCarthy (O'Brien) threatened to destroy their lives. The men fought side by side for Ireland's independence, but the friendship dissolved when they took different sides during the ensuing civil war, and fought over Jimmy's mother. Strong performances and the beautiful West Cork and Wicklow location shots provide a nice balance to the uneven narrative. The black and white scenes were actually filmed in the mid-'80s when the independently financed project was begun. Adapted from O'Callaghan's own story "The Shilling." **101m/C VHS, DVD.** *IR* Colin Lane, Niall O'Brien, Marian Quinn, Darren McHugh, Joy Florish, Joe Jeffers, Pete O'Reilly, Michael Crowley; ***D:*** Maurice O'Callaghan; ***W:*** Maurice O'Callaghan; ***C:*** Jack Conroy; ***M:*** Patrick Cassidy.

The Broken Hearts Club **2000 (R)** Talk can be cheap, but it's also what sustains the relationships in the lives of a group of gay friends in this chatty, likable film set in West Hollywood. Despite their mostly superficial (sex) conversations, the boys suspect there's more to life, and aim, hesitantly, to move beyond this dead-end topic. Witty and confident in his characters, writer/director Berlanti (co-creator of "Dawson's Creek") has put together a film about gay men that thankfully moves beyond the staleness of many of its predecessors. Good cast with notable performances by Cain (Superman in TV's "Lois and Clark") and Mahoney as the fatherly proprietor of the Broken Hearts restaurant. **94m/C VHS, DVD.** Dean Cain, John Mahoney, Timothy Olyphant, Andrew Keegan, Nia Long, Zach Braff, Matt McGrath, Billy Porter, Justin Theroux, Mary McCormack; ***D:*** Greg Berlanti; ***W:*** Greg Berlanti; ***C:*** Paul Elliott; ***M:*** Christophe Beck.

Broken Hearts of Broadway **1923** Stories of heartbreak and success along the Great White Way. **85m/B VHS.** Colleen Moore, Johnnie Walker, Alice Lake, Tully Marshall, Creighton Hale; ***D:*** Irving Cummings.

Broken Lance 1/2 **1954** Western remake of "House of Strangers" that details the dissolution of a despotic cattle baron's family. Beautifully photographed. **96m/C VHS, DVD.** Spencer Tracy, Richard Widmark, Robert Wagner, Jean Peters, Katy Jurado, Earl Holliman, Hugh O'Brian, E.G. Marshall; ***D:*** Edward Dmytryk; ***W:*** Philip Yordan; ***C:*** Joe MacDonald; ***M:*** Leigh Harline. Oscars '54: Story.

A Broken Life 1/2 **2007** When Max Walker (Sizemore) decides to commit suicide, he hires his struggling film student friend Bud (Sevier) to record his last days. Max lets his rage out, confronting his former boss and ex-wife, as well as doing some really stupid things. As his chosen end nears, Max is shown kindness by wheelchair-bound Melinda (Kosaka) and starts rethinking his plans. **97m/C DVD.** Tom Sizemore, Corey Sevier, Ving Rhames, Saul Rubinek, Cynthia Dale, Kris Holden-Ried, Grace Kosaka; ***D:*** Neil Coombs; ***W:*** Neil Coombs; ***C:*** Peter Benison; ***M:*** Christopher Dedrick. **VIDEO**

Broken Lullaby 1/2 **1994** Genealogist Jordan Kirkland (Harris) travels to Europe to research her orphaned Aunt Kitty's (Hyland) murky past at the time of the Russian Revolution. Her only clue is a photograph of a young girl holding a music box topped with a priceless Faberge egg. Jordan meets Hungarian art dealer Nick Rostov (Stewart), who has his own reasons for finding the same music box, but they're not the only ones searching for it. From the Harlequin Romance Series; adapted from the Laurel Pace novel. **91m/C DVD.** *CA* Mel Harris, Rob Stewart, Oliver Tobias, Jennifer Dale, Frances Hyland, Charmion King, Vivian Reis; ***D:*** Michael Kennedy; ***W:*** Jim Henshaw, Guy Mullaly; ***C:*** Nyika Jancso; ***M:*** Claude Desjardins, Eric N. Robertson. **TV**

The Broken Mask **1928** A doctor performs remarkable plastic surgery on a patient, but when the patient becomes attracted to his sweetheart, he throws the Hippocratic oath to the wind, and his patient's spiffy new look has got to go. A groundbreaker amid plastic surgery-gone-amok pieces. **58m/B VHS.** Cullen Landis, Barbara Bedford, Wheeler Oakman, James A. Marcus; ***D:*** James Hogan.

Broken Melody 1/2 *Vagabond Violinist* **1934** An opera singer sent to prison by mistake must escape in order to return to the woman of his dreams. **62m/B VHS, DVD.** *GB* John Garrick, Margot Grahame, Merle Oberon, Austin Trevor, Charles Carson, Harry Terry; ***D:*** Bernard Vorhaus.

Broken Mirrors 1/2 *Gebroken Spiegels* **1985** A disturbing film which intertwines two stories of violence against women: prostitutes go about their daily business in Amsterdam, while a twisted serial killer who imprisons, photographs, and ultimately destroys his victims, draws near. An independently made chiller with staunch feminist agenda. **110m/C VHS.** *NL* Lineke Rijxman, Henriette Tol, Edda Barends, Eddie Brugman, Coby Stunnenberg; ***D:*** Marleen Gorris; ***W:*** Marleen Gorris.

Broken Silence *Silencio Roto* **2001** Director Armendariz's engaging production is set in 1944 when 21-year-old Lucia (Jimenez) goes back to her homeland only to witness the dramatic and violent impact that the Spanish Civil War has had upon the people of her rustic village. Still, she finds love with Manuel (Botto), a blacksmith who is part of the resistance group, the Maquis. An uprising swells and Franco's fascist army shows up to squash it, forcing the young lovers to face the cruel realities inherent to the hostilities. In Spanish with subtitles. **110m/C VHS, DVD.** *SP* Juan Diego Botto, Mercedes Sampietro, Lucia Jimenez, Maria Botto, Andoni Erburu, Alvaro de Luna; ***D:*** Montxo Armendariz; ***W:*** Montxo Armendariz; ***C:*** Guillermo Navarro; ***M:*** Pascal Gaigne. **VIDEO**

Broken Strings **1940** All-black musical in which a concert violinist must come to terms with himself after an auto accident limits the use of his left hand. **50m/B VHS.** Clarence Muse, Sybil Lewis, William Washington, Matthew "Stymie" Beard; ***D:*** Bernard B. Ray.

Broken Trail **2006** In 1898, aging cowpoke Print Ritter (Duvall) is herding 500 horses from Oregon to Wyoming with the help of his estranged nephew Tom Harte (Church). During the trip they hire on Heck (Cooper) and rescue five Chinese girls who were sold to be prostitutes in a mining camp. But this puts the horse traders at odds with madam Big Rump Kate (Schwimmer), who sends sadistic Big Ears (Mulkey) after her property. Not having enough to deal with, Print also protects good-hearted whore Nola (Scacchi) on that long, dusty trail. But everyone's in very good company. **184m/C DVD, Blu-ray Disc.** *US* Robert Duvall, Thomas Haden Church, Greta Scacchi, Chris Mulkey, Rusty Schwimmer, James Russo, Scott Cooper, Gwendoline Yeo, Van Dyke Parks; ***D:*** Walter Hill; ***W:*** Alan Geoffrion; ***C:*** Lloyd Ahern II; ***M:*** David Mansfield. **CABLE**

Broken Trust **1993** Erica inherits her fabulously weathy uncle's estate but she has problems knowing who to trust now that she has all this money. Seems her husband is greedy and her sister resentful but just how far will they go to get what Erica has? **85m/C VHS.** Kimberly Foster, Nick Cassavetes, Kathryn Harris, Don Swayze, Edward Albert, Wendy MacDonald; ***D:*** Rafael Portillo.

Broken Trust 1/2 **1995** Municipal judge Timothy Nash (Selleck) is recruited for a sting operation, designed to ensnare fellow judges, by two slightly less-than-ethical feds (Atherton and McGovern). When Nash decides he doesn't like what's going on he discovers it's not going to be so easy to get out. Selleck's stoic, McGovern provides attractive ornamentation, and Atherton excels as the smarmy villain. From the novel "Court of Honor" by William P. Wood. **90m/C VHS.** Tom Selleck, Elizabeth McGovern, William Atherton, Fritz Weaver, Marsha Mason, Charles Haid, Stanley DeSantis, Cynthia Martells; ***D:*** Geoffrey Sax; ***W:*** Joan Didion, John Gregory Dunne; ***C:*** Ronald Orieux; ***M:*** Richard Horowitz. **CABLE**

Broken Vessels **1998 (R)** Rent this with "Bringing Out the Dead" and you'll have a double feature that will make you take 911 off the speed dial. Both movies were released in the same year, but Scorsese's movie depicts a paramedic demented by caring too much. The ambulance drivers in "Broken Vessels" become unhinged by a cold, drug-induced indifference. Tom (London) is pulled into a downward spiral by his crazed partner Jimmy (Field), who smokes heroin and feels up unconscious girls while on break from saving lives. Clearly, things are not destined to go well for the pair, not to mention those who end up in the back of their meat wagon. Excellent debut from producer-director Scott Ziehl. **90m/C VHS, DVD.** Todd Field, Jason London, Roxana Zal, Susan Traylor, James Hong, Patrick Cranshaw, William (Bill) Smith, Dave Baer; ***D:*** Scott Ziehl; ***W:*** Scott Ziehl, Dave Baer, John McMahon; ***C:*** Antonio Calvache.

Broken Vows 1/2 **1987** Thriller with Jones as ghetto priest Father Joseph, who has doubts about his calling. When he gives last rites to a murder victim, he decides to help the victim's girlfriend find his killers. Based on the novel "Where the Dark Secrets Go" by Dorothy Salisbury Davis. **95m/C VHS, DVD.** Tommy Lee Jones, Annette O'Toole, M. Emmet Walsh, Milo O'Shea, David Groh, Madeline Sherwood, Jean De Baer, David Strathairn; ***D:*** Jud Taylor; ***C:*** Thomas Burstyn. **TV**

Broken Wings *Knafayim Shvurot* **2002 (R)** Writer/director Bergman's touching feature debut about an Israeli family's inability to cope with the recent loss of patriarch David. Widow Dafna Ulman (Zilberschatz-Banai) takes up working odd shifts as a midwife for a local hospital, forcing 17-year-old daughter Maya (Maron) to put her music career on hold to care for younger siblings Ido (Daniel Magon) and Bahr (Eliana Magon). Faring little better is 16-year-old son Yair (Gvirtz), who has thrown away a potential basketball career by dropping out of school and now passes out leaflets in the subway dressed in a mouse costume. Things suddenly go from bad to worse, forcing the Ulmans into crisis mode. Simply told but very effective human drama. In Hebrew with subtitles. **83m/C DVD.** *IS* Orly Silbersatz Banai, Maya Maron, Nitai Gaviratz, Valdimir Friedman, Dana Ivgi, Danny Niv, Daniel Magon, Eliana Magon; ***D:*** Nir Bergman; ***W:*** Nir Bergman; ***C:*** Valentin Belonogov; ***M:*** Avi Bellili.

Bronco Billy 1/2 **1980 (PG)** Eastwood stars as a New Jersey shoe clerk who decides to fulfill his dream of being a cowboy hero by becoming the proprietor of a rag-tag wild west show. Locke's one-note performance as a spoiled rich girl who joins up is a problem and the film's charm is as ragged as the acts. Good if you want to see Eastwood in something other than a shoot-'em-up. **117m/C VHS, DVD.** Clint Eastwood, Sondra Locke, Bill McKinney, Scatman Crothers, Sam Bottoms, Geoffrey Lewis, Dan Vadis, Sierra Pecheur; ***D:*** Clint Eastwood; ***W:*** Dennis Hackin; ***C:*** David Worth; ***M:*** Steve Dorff.

Bronson **2009 (R)** Stylized Brit bio, with a ferocious performance by Hardy, about Michael Petersen, a young man jailed for armed robbery in 1974 who renames himself Charles Bronson after the tough guy American actor. Bronson eventually spends more than 30 years in solitary confinement thanks to his incorrigible glee in committing violent acts within the prison system itself. The lead in his own mental movie, Bronson speaks directly to the camera and is a media celebrity due to sheer outrageousness (the real Bronson has become an artist and writer behind bars and has published numerous books). But he's always a violent criminal, not a sympathetic character. **92m/C DVD.** *GB* Tom Hardy, Juliet Oldfield, Matt King, Hugh Ross, Jonathan Phillips, James Lance; ***D:*** Nicolas Winding Refn; ***W:*** Brock Norman Brock, Nicolas Winding Refn; ***C:*** Larry Smith.

Bronson's Revenge 1/2 *Condenados a Vivir; Cut-Throats Nine* **1972 (R)** Two frontier soldiers face constant danger as they attempt to transport death row prisoners, a large quantity of gold, and a stranded woman across the Rocky Mountains territory. **90m/C VHS.** *SP* Claudio Undari, Emma Cohen, Alberto Dalbes, Antonio Iranzo; ***D:*** Joaquin Luis Romero Marchent; ***W:*** Joaquin Luis Romero Marchent; ***C:*** Luis Cuadrado; ***M:*** Carmelo A. Bernaola.

The Brontes of Haworth 1/2 **1973** The bleak moorlands and the village of Haworth are the setting for a dramatic look at the lives of writers Charlotte, Emily, and Anne Bronte, their wastral brother Branwell, and the tragedies that haunted them all. On 4 cassettes. **270m/C VHS, DVD.** *GB* Ann Penfold, Michael Kitchen, Vickery Turner, Rosemary McHale, Alfred Burke; ***D:*** Marc Miller; ***W:*** Christopher Fry. **TV**

The Bronx Executioner **1986** Android, robot, and human interests clash in futuristic Manhattan and all martial arts hell breaks loose. Special introduction by martial arts star Michael Dudikoff. **88m/C VHS, DVD.** Rob Robinson, Margie Newton, Chuck Valenti, Gabriel Gori; ***D:*** Bob Collins.

The Bronx Is Burning 1/2 **2007** In 1977, New York City was paralyzed by a citywide blackout, political strife, and the Son of Sam killing spree. And then there were the New York Yankees, owned by bombastic George Steinbrenner (Platt), managed by volatile, hard-drinking Billy Martin (Turturro), and with egotistical Reggie Jackson (Sunjata) as their star hitter. Nostalgic miniseries shows how the city came together as the Yanks made their bid for the World Series. **360m/C DVD.** John Turturro, Oliver Platt, Daniel Sunjata, Erik Jensen, Michael Rispoli, Dan Lauria, Kevin Conway, Loren Dean, Charles S. Dutton, Alex Cranmer, Leonard Robinson; ***D:*** Jeremiah S. Chechik; ***W:*** James Solomon, Gordon Greisman; ***C:*** Douglas Koch; ***M:*** Tree Adams. **CABLE**

A Bronx Tale **1993 (R)** Vivid snapshot of a young Italian-American boy growing up in the '60s among neighborhood small-time wiseguys. As a nine-year-old

Calogero witnesses mobster Sonny kill a man but doesn't rat to the police, so Sonny takes the kid under his wing. His upright bus-driving father Lorenzo doesn't approve but the kid is drawn to Sonny's apparent glamor and power. At 17, he's gotten both an education in school and on the streets but he needs to make a choice. Good period detail and excellent performances. Palminteri shows both Sonny's charisma and violence and De Niro handles the less-showy father role with finesse. Based on Palminteri's one-man play; De Niro's directorial debut. **122m/C VHS, DVD.** Robert De Niro, Chazz Palminteri, Lillo Brancato, Francis Capra, Taral Hicks, Kathrine Narducci, Clem Caserta, Alfred Sauchelli Jr., Frank Pietrangolare, Joseph (Joe) D'Onofrio; ***Cameos:*** Joe Pesci; ***D:*** Robert De Niro; ***W:*** Chazz Palminteri; ***C:*** Reynaldo Villalobos; ***M:*** Butch Barbella.

The Bronx War 1990 **(R)** Rival gangs take to the streets in this film from the director of "Hangin' with the Homeboys." A malicious gang leader tricks his gang into going to war over a girl he wants. Very violent; an unrated version available. **91m/C VHS, DVD.** Joseph B. Vasquez, Fabio Urena, Charmaine Cruz, Andre Brown, Marlene Forte, Francis Colon, Miguel Sierra, Kim West; ***D:*** Joseph B. Vasquez.

Bronze Buckaroo 1939 Horse opera in which a cowpoke seeks revenge for his pa's death. Commendable performances from the all-black cast and crew. **57m/B VHS, DVD.** Herbert Jeffries, Artie Young, Rellie Hardin, Spencer Williams Jr., Clarence Brooks, F.E. (Flourney) Miller; ***D:*** Richard C. Kahn; ***W:*** Richard C. Kahn.

The Brood 1/2 1979 **(R)** Cronenberg's inimitable biological nightmares, involving an experimentally malformed woman who gives birth to murderous demon-children that kill every time she gets angry. Extremely graphic. Not for all tastes. **92m/C VHS, DVD.** *CA* Samantha Eggar, Oliver Reed, Art Hindle, Susan Hogan, Nuala Fitzgerald, Cindy Hinds, Robert A. Silverman, Gary McKeehan; ***D:*** David Cronenberg; ***W:*** David Cronenberg; ***C:*** Mark Irwin; ***M:*** Howard Shore.

The Brooklyn Heist *Capers* 2008 **(PG-13)** Crazy crime caricatures shot in three distinct styles with overlapping stories. Set in Brooklyn, three criminal gangs co-exist without knowing anything about each other: the Amateurs get their look and attitude from 1970s mob flicks; the Moolies are African-Americans caught up in bad rap/gangsta videos; and the Sputniks live in a literally black-and-white world from the 1950s where the cold war hasn't ended and they constantly try to buy nuclear materials. All three gangs share the same hatred for racist pawnshop owner Connie and when she dies all plan to crack her legendary safe and all decide to do it on the same night. **86m/C DVD.** Danny Masterson, Leon, Johnathan Hova, Dominique Swain, Aysan Celik, Michael Cecchi, Serena Reeder, Blanchard Ryan, Phyllis Somerville, Daniel Stewart Sherman; ***D:*** Julian mark Kheel; ***W:*** Julian mark Kheel, Brett Halsey; ***C:*** Carlo Scialla; ***M:*** David Poe.

Brooklyn Lobster 2005 Frank Giorgio (Aiello) is a hard-headed Sheepshead Bay lobster wholesaler whose business is about to be auctioned off and whose wife, Maureen (Curtin), has walked out on him. Son Michael (Sauli) comes home for the Christmas holidays to lend a hand, accompanied by his girlfriend Kerry (Burns), but her presence creates more problems. Aiello is especially impressive in a slice of life drama that was inspired by writer/director Jordan's own family. **90m/C DVD.** *US* Danny Aiello, Jane Curtin, Marisa Ryan, Heather Burns, Sam Freed, Daniel Serafini Sauli, Ian Kahn, Tom Mason, Barbara Garrick, John Rothman, Rick Aiello; ***D:*** Kevin Jordan; ***W:*** Kevin Jordan; ***C:*** David Tumblety; ***M:*** Craig Maher.

Brooklyn Rules 2007 **(R)** Mild coming of age pic about three lifelong buddies, set in 1985 Brooklyn. Michael (Prinze) leaves the 'hood behind to go to law school and date an uptown girl (Suvari). Easy-going Bobby (Ferrara) plans to get married and have a steady straight job. But slickster Carmine (Caan) wants to be part of local wiseguy Cesar's (Baldwin) crew. Naturally these differing aims pull the guys apart. **99m/C DVD.** Freddie Prinze Jr., Scott Caan, Mena Suvari, Alec Baldwin, Jerry Ferrara, Monica Keena, Robert Turano, Phyllis Kay; ***D:*** Michael Corrente; ***W:*** Terence Winter; ***C:*** Richard Crudo; ***M:*** Benny Rietveld.

A Brooklyn State of Mind 1997 **(R)** Al (Spano) works for shady real estate developer Frank Parente (Aiello) in Brooklyn. When his Aunt Rose (King) rents a room to beautiful Gabriella (Cucinotta), who says she's working on a documentary about the neighborhood, Al is quick to succumb to her charms. But he's also suspicious—and when he finds a dossier on Frank in Gabriella's room, Al learns her father's murder is tied to his own father's death and both involve Frank. **90m/C VHS.** Vincent Spano, Danny Aiello, Maria Grazia Cucinotta, Tony Danza, Morgana King, Abe Vigoda; ***D:*** Frank Rainone; ***W:*** Frank Rainone, Fred Stroppel; ***C:*** Ken Kelsch; ***M:*** Paul Zaza.

Brooklyn's Finest 1/2 2009 **(R)** Fuqua appears to be redoing his 2001 film "Training Day" with this continuously violent story of corruption and impending doom that centers around three policemen. Burned-out veteran beat cop Eddie (Gere), about to retire, drinks too much and plans for his suicide; crooked narc Sal (Hawke) will do anything (including murder) for a big score to help his ill wife; and undercover cop Tango (Cheadle) is a little too comfortable in the thug life while needing to ensnare former major player Caz (Snipes) in order to stay on the NYPD promotional fast track. **125m/C DVD.** *US* Richard Gere, Ethan Hawke, Don Cheadle, Wesley Snipes, Ellen Barkin, Will Patton, Brian F. O'Byrne, Vincent D'Onofrio, Michael K. Williams, Lili Taylor, Shannon Kane; ***D:*** Antoine Fuqua; ***W:*** Michael C. Martin; ***C:*** Patrick Murguia; ***M:*** Marcelo Zarvos.

Broth of a Boy 1/2 1959 A hungry British producer decides to film a birthday party of the oldest man in the world. The old Irishman wants a portion of the profits. Well made and thought provoking. **77m/B VHS.** *IR* Barry Fitzgerald, Harry Brogan, Tony Wright, June Thorburn, Eddie Golden; ***D:*** George Pollock.

Brother *Brat* 1997 Danila (Bodrov Jr.) has just gotten out of the army and needs a job so he decides to visit big brother Viktor (Sukhoroukov) in St. Petersburg. He discovers his bro is a contract killer for the Russian mob and hires on as Viktor's assistant. Danila successfully accomplishes his first assignment—the murder of a mob rival—but then has the other gangsters out for revenge. Fast-paced and gritty, with casual violence and crime the easiest options in a broken-down society. Russian with subtitles. **96m/C VHS.** *RU* Sergei Bodrov Jr., Viktor Sukhorukov, Svetlana Pismitchenko, Maria Joukova, Yuri Kouznetzov; ***D:*** Alexsei Balabanov; ***W:*** Alexsei Balabanov; ***C:*** Sergei Astakhov; ***M:*** Viatcheslav Boutoussov.

Brother 2000 **(R)** Kitano's films are something of an acquired taste. He mixes abrupt graphic (and usually brief) violence with prolonged scenes of introspection, and when it comes to expressing emotion, he seldom does more than twitch or take off his sunglasses. But the man is cool, and to those who accept his measured pace, his work has a hypnotic quality. In his first film set in America, he plays Yamamoto, an exiled Japanese yakuza who partners up with street hustler Denny (Epps) and takes on the local drug gangs. Yes, that's the stuff of hundreds of video premiere action flicks, but he transcends the cliches. English and Japanese dialog with subtitles. **118m/C VHS, DVD.** *JP* Takeshi "Beat" Kitano, Omar Epps, Kuroudo Maki, Masaya Kato, Susumu Terajima, James Shigeta; ***D:*** Takeshi "Beat" Kitano; ***W:*** Takeshi "Beat" Kitano; ***C:*** Katsumi Yanagishima; ***M:*** Joe Hisaishi.

Brother Bear 1/2 2003 **(G)** Rather grim but ultimately heartwarming coming-of-ager invoking the far superior "The Lion King," and "Bambi." Kenai (Phoenix) is a brash Native American youth living with his two brothers in the Pacific Northwest during the end of the Ice Age. After a bear attacks and kills his brother Sitka (Sweeney), Kenai is magically transformed into a bear himself. In his new hirsute form, Kenai learns some important lessons about nature with the help of orphaned bear cub Koda (Suarez). Much needed but underdeveloped comic relief comes from Thomas and Moranis as a pair of bickering moose. Largely hand-drawn animation is lushly beautiful but overshadowed by derivative plot and heavy-handed message. Lackluster score by soft pop-meister Phil Collins. **85m/C VHS, DVD.** *US* ***D:*** Aaron Blaise, Robert Walker; ***W:*** Tab Murphy, Lorne Cameron, David Hoselton, Steve Bencich, Ron J. Friedman; ***M:*** Phil Collins, Mark Mancina; ***V:*** Joaquin Rafael (Leaf) Phoenix, Jeremy Suarez, Jason Raize, Rick Moranis, Dave Thomas, D.B. Sweeney, Joan Copeland, Michael Clarke Duncan, Harold Gould, Estelle Harris.

Brother Bear 2 1/2 2006 **(G)** Animated Disney sequel based on the 2003 release. Nita had a strong bond with Kenai when they were children (before he was turned into a bear). But if she wants to marry, Nita has to break that bond. She is told by the shaman that she and Kenai must perform a certain ritual but Kenai thinks maybe he should ask the Great Spirit if he can become human again (which he refused to do in the first film). For pure comic relief, moose buddies Rutt and Tuke are back and chasing after some moosettes. **74m/C DVD.** *US* ***D:*** Ben Gluck; ***W:*** Rich Burns; ***M:*** Matthew Gerrard, Dave Metzger, Robbie Nevil; ***V:*** Patrick Dempsey, Mandy Moore, Jeremy Suarez, Rick Moranis, Dave Thomas, Wanda Sykes, Andrea Martin, Catherine O'Hara. **VIDEO**

The Brother from Another Planet 1984 A black alien escapes from his home planet and winds up in Harlem, where he's pursued by two alien bounty hunters. Independently made morality fable by John Sayles before he hit the big time; features Sayles in a cameo as an alien bounty hunter. **109m/C VHS, DVD.** Joe Morton, Dee Dee Bridgewater, Ren Woods, Steve James, Maggie Renzi, David Strathairn; ***Cameos:*** John Sayles; ***D:*** John Sayles; ***W:*** John Sayles; ***M:*** Mason Daring.

Brother Future 1991 T.J., a black, streetsmart city kid who thinks school and helping others is all a waste of time gets knocked out in a car accident. As he's lying unconscious, he is transported back in time to a slave auction block in the Old South. There the displaced urbanite is forced to work on a cotton plantation, and watch the stirrings of a slave revolt. T.J. sees the light and realizes how much opportunity he's been wasting in his own life. He comes to just a few moments later, but worlds away from who he was before. Part of the "Wonderworks" series. **110m/C VHS.** Phill Lewis, Frank Converse, Carl Lumbly, Vonetta McGee; ***D:*** Roy Campanella; ***W:*** Roy Campanella.

Brother John 1970 **(PG-13)** An early look at racial tensions and labor problems. An angel goes back to his hometown in Alabama to see how things are going. **94m/C VHS, DVD.** Sidney Poitier, Will Geer, Bradford Dillman, Beverly Todd, Paul Winfield; ***D:*** James Goldstone; ***M:*** Quincy Jones.

Brother of Sleep *Schlafes Bruder* 1995 **(R)** Elias (Eisermann), the illegitimate son of the local priest, is discovered to have perfect pitch, a beautiful voice, and a special symbiosis with nature. Which does nothing to endear him to the superstitious inhabitants of his 19th-century Austrian mountain village. Elias doesn't know whether his gift is a blessing or a curse but he'd give it up if he could win the love of his cousin Elspeth (Vavrova). Schneider scripted from his 1992 novel, which has previously been adapted as a ballet and opera. German with subtitles. **133m/C VHS, DVD.** *GE* Andre Eisermann, Dana Vavrova, Ben Becker; ***D:*** Joseph Vilsmaier; ***W:*** Robert Schneider; ***C:*** Joseph Vilsmaier; ***M:*** Norbert J. Schneider.

Brother Orchid 1940 Mobster puts a henchman in charge of his gang while he vacations in Europe. Upon his return, he is deposed and wounded in an assassination attempt. Hiding out in a monastary, he plots to regain control of the gang, leading to fish outta water episodes and a change in his outlook on life. Fine cast fans through farce intelligently. **87m/B VHS.** Edward G. Robinson, Humphrey Bogart, Ann Sothern, Donald Crisp, Ralph Bellamy, Allen Jenkins, Charles D. Brown, Cecil Kellaway; ***D:*** Lloyd Bacon; ***C:*** Gaetano Antonio "Tony" Gaudio.

Brother Sun, Sister Moon 1/2 1973 **(PG)** Post-'60s costume epic depicting the trials of St. Francis of Assisi as he evaluates his beliefs in Catholicism. **120m/C VHS, DVD.** Graham Faulkner, Judi Bowker, Alec Guinness, Leigh Lawson, Kenneth Cranham, Lee Montague, Valentina Cortese; ***D:*** Franco Zeffirelli; ***M:*** Donovan.

Brother to Brother 1/2 2004 Ambitious debut effort ties the personal plight of a modern African-American painter to the artistic turmoil of the Harlem Renaissance. Perry (Mackie) is thrown out of his house once his father discovers that he is homosexual. Embittered, Perry rails against the anti-gay hostility within the black community and his college classrooms. After he meets a homeless man, Bruce Nugent (Robinson), in a local shelter, Perry realizes that Bruce was once a noted poet during the Harlem Renaissance. We then flash back to the 1930s to witness Bruce interacting with such luminaries as Langston Hughes and Zora Neale Hurston. Evans effectively shows how issues of politics and sexuality transcend time, but the film lapses into didacticism once too often. **94m/C DVD.** *US* Anthony Mackie, Roger Robinson, Larry (Lawrence) Gilliard Jr., Aunjanue Ellis, Duane Boutte, Daniel Sunjata, Alex Burns; ***D:*** Rodney Evans; ***W:*** Rodney Evans; ***C:*** Harlan Bosmajian; ***M:*** Marc Anthony Thompson, Bill Coleman.

The Brotherhood 1/2 1968 Two hot-headed brothers in a Mafia syndicate clash over old vs. new methods and the changing of the Family's guard. **96m/C VHS, DVD.** Kirk Douglas, Alex Cord, Irene Papas, Luther Adler, Susan Strasberg, Murray Hamilton; ***D:*** Martin Ritt; ***W:*** Lewis John Carlino; ***C:*** Boris Kaufman; ***M:*** Lalo Schifrin.

Brotherhood 2: The Young Warlocks WOOF! 2001 Luke is a new kid at a private school who decides to recruit a group of fellow outcast kids for a coven he's starting. Laughably bad in all regards except that some of the cast are hotties. **85m/C VHS, DVD.** Sean Faris, Forrest Cochran, Stacey Scowley, Noah Frank, Julie Briggs, Justin Allen, C.J. Thomason; ***D:*** David DeCoteau. **VIDEO**

The Brotherhood 3: The Young Demons WOOF! 2002 Teenagers heavily into a role-playing wizard and warriors game gather every Friday to perform faux ceremonies complete with costumes and weaponry. When they find a real book of magic, they can't resist chanting a few spells, which conjures up some medieval horrors. **82m/C VHS, DVD.** Kristopher Turner, Paul Andrich, Ellen Wieser, Julie Pedersen; ***D:*** David DeCoteau. **VIDEO**

Brotherhood of Blood 1/2 2008 The world's best vampire slayer (a comely young blonde) has been captured by the King of Vampires and languishes in his dungeons while her compatriots attempt to find a way in to release her. Meanwhile the King must somehow figure out how to stop the coming of a vampiric demon, who may end up making the world a hell on earth. The team-up between himself and his imprisoned enemy to stop this is inevitable, and surprisingly not so exciting. **90m/C DVD.** Victoria Pratt, Sid Haig, Ken Foree, Jason Connery, Wes Ramsey, Jeremy James Kissner, Rachel Grant, William Snow; ***D:*** Michael Roesch, Peter Scheerer; ***W:*** Michael Roesch, Peter Scheerer; ***C:*** River O'Mahoney Hagg; ***M:*** Ralph Rieckermann, Tom Bimmerman. **VIDEO**

Brotherhood of Death 1/2 1976 **(R)** Three black Vietnam veterans return to their southern hometown to get even with the Klansmen who slaughtered all of the townspeople. **85m/C VHS, DVD.** Roy Jefferson, Larry Jones, Mike Bass, Le Tari, Haskell V. Anderson; ***D:*** Bill Berry.

Brotherhood of Justice 1986 Young men form a secret organization to rid their neighborhood of drug dealers and violence. As their power grows, their propriety weakens, until all are afraid of the "Brotherhood of Justice." **97m/C VHS, DVD.** Keanu Reeves, Kiefer Sutherland, Billy Zane, Joe Spano, Darren Dalton, Evan Mirand, Don Michael Paul; ***D:*** Charles Braverman; ***M:*** Brad Fiedel. **TV**

Brotherhood of Murder 1999 Based on the book by Thomas Martinez and John Gunther that depicts the rise and fall of the white supremacist group known as "The Order." Martinez (Baldwin) is a struglling family man who falls in with charismatic Bob Mathews (Gallagher) and his hate group—until the shooting starts. **93m/C VHS, DVD.** William Baldwin, Peter Gallagher, Kelly Lynch, Joel S. Keller, Zack (Zach) Ward, Vincent Gale; ***D:*** Martin Bell; ***W:*** Robert J. Avrech; ***C:*** James R. Bagdonas; ***M:*** Laura Karpman. **CABLE**

The Brotherhood of Satan ☙☙ 1/2 **1971 (PG)** In an isolated southern town, a satanic coven persuades children to join in their devil-may-care attitude. Worthwhile. **92m/C VHS, DVD.** Strother Martin, L.Q. Jones, Charles Bateman, Ahna Capri, Charles Robinson, Alvy Moore, Geri Reischl, Helene Winston; ***D:*** Bernard McEveety; ***W:*** William Welch; ***C:*** John Morrill.

The Brotherhood of the Rose ☙ 1/2 **1989 (PG-13)** Too many twists and turns mar the otherwise mediocre plot of this murky adaption of a book by David (First Blood) Morrell. Strauss and Morse are the C.I.A. agents marked for death and running for their lives after uncovering their boss's (Mitchum) plot of world domination. Though almost every scene takes place in a different country, the movie was in fact filmed entirely in New Zealand. Convoluted and frustratingly difficult to follow. **103m/C VHS.** Robert Mitchum, Peter Strauss, Connie Sellecca, James B. Sikking, David Morse, M. Emmet Walsh, James Hong; ***D:*** Marvin J. Chomsky.

Brotherhood of the Wolf ☙☙ *Le Pacte des Loups* **2001 (R)** Based on the French legend about the Beast of Gevaudan, a wolf-like creature that killed more than 100 people in the 1760s. In 1765, in a remote province, a mysterious creature is savagely killing women and children throughout the countryside. Naturalist Gregoire de Fronsac (Le Bihan) and his Iroquis blood brother Mani (Dacascos) are sent by King Louis XV to kill and stuff the beast for posterity. But what they finally discover is quite unexpected. Flamboyantly entertaining adventure. French with subtitles. **143m/C VHS, DVD.** *FR* Samuel Le Bihan, Mark Dacascos, Vincent Cassel, Emilie Dequenne, Jeremie Renier, Monica Bellucci, Jean Yanne, Edith Scob, Jean-Francois Stevenin, Hans Meyer, Jacques Perrin, Philippe Nahon, Eric Prat, Johan Leysen, Bernard Fresson, Bernard Farcy, Virginie Darmon; ***D:*** Christophe Gans; ***W:*** Christophe Gans, Stephane Cabel; ***C:*** Dan Laustsen; ***M:*** Joseph LoDuca.

Brotherly Love ☙ 1/2 **1985** Good twin/bad twin made-for-TV mystery about an escaped psychopath who's out to get his businessman twin brother (Hirsch in both roles). **94m/C VHS.** Judd Hirsch, Karen Carlson, George Dzundza, Barry Primus, Lori Lethin; ***D:*** Jeff Bleckner.

The Brothers ☙☙☙ **2001 (R)** A chain reaction of male introspection is set off as four successful, young African-American men navigate the tricky waters of serious relationships in modern Los Angeles. All the bases are covered: there is the womanizing lawyer, Brian (Bellamy); the one night standweary physician, Jackson (Chestnut); the just-engaged Terry (Shemar); and the unhappily married Derrick (Hughley). Not quite as strong as its female counterpart, the much-praised "Waiting to Exhale," but novelist Hardwick's first film is well managed and funny, and he never lets his capable comic actors veer too far away from the exploration of modern sexual politics. **101m/C VHS, DVD.** Morris Chestnut, D.L. Hughley, Bill Bellamy, Shemar Moore, Gabrielle Union, Tamala Jones, Susan Dalian, Angelle Brooks, Jenifer Lewis, Clifton Powell, Marla Gibbs, Tatyana Ali, Julie Benz; ***D:*** Gary Hardwick; ***W:*** Gary Hardwick; ***C:*** Alexander Grusynski.

Brothers ☙☙☙ *Brodre* **2004 (R)** Michael is a husband and father in the Danish military deployed to Afghanistan. When his helicopter crashes he is presumed dead. In his absence his younger "screw-up" brother steps up to the plate to help Michael's wife and children cope with life in his absence. However, Michael was not dead, but captured by guerrilla fighters and forced to commit a barbaric act. When he finally returns home he is a different man. Great narrative drive, emotionally explosive and brutally honest. In Danish with English subtitles. **110m/C DVD.** Connie Nielsen, Ulrich Thomsen, Nikolaj Lie Kaas; ***D:*** Suzanne (Susanne) Bier; ***W:*** Anders Thomas Jensen; ***C:*** Morten Soborg; ***M:*** Johan Soderqvist.

Brothers ☙☙ **2009 (R)** All-American Marine Capt. Sam Cahill (Maguire) is presumed dead during a tour of duty in Afghanistan, leaving a wife, Grace (Portman), and two young daughters. Trying to fill in for his responsibilities is his brother, Tommy (Gyllenhaal), a troubled ex-con. When Sam, held prisoner by the Taliban, finally returns, the trauma he's endured is made worse when it seems that the formerly unreliable Tommy has replaced him. A remake of Susanne Blier's 2004 Danish film, it occasionally rises to the original's depth but mostly misses the mark, opting for overstatement and melodrama instead. **110m/C DVD.** *US* Tobey Maguire, Jake Gyllenhaal, Natalie Portman, Sam Shepard, Mare Winningham, Patrick Flueger, Carey Mulligan; ***D:*** Jim Sheridan; ***W:*** David Benioff; ***C:*** Frederick Elmes; ***M:*** Thomas Newman.

The Brothers Bloom ☙☙ **2009 (PG-13)** Orphans Stephen (Ruffalo) and his younger brother Bloom (Brody) spent their troubled youth perfecting their natural-born con artist abilities. Now grown up, the moody Bloom decides he's had enough of the game but a persuasive Stephen gets him to do one last con. Enter eccentric heiress Penelope (Weisz) who's looking for a little excitement in life but of course Bloom complicates things by falling hard for their mark. A familiar farce that's still appealing enough, just as is its cast—Weisz, especially—with a gorgeous European backdrop. But writer/director Johnson makes it a little too hyper and witty for its own good. **109m/C DVD.** *US* Adrien Brody, Mark Ruffalo, Rachel Weisz, Maximilian Schell, Rinko Kikuchi, Robbie Coltrane, Ricky Jay; ***D:*** Rian Johnson; ***W:*** Rian Johnson; ***C:*** Steve Yedlin; ***M:*** Nathan Johnson; ***Nar:*** Ricky Jay.

The Brothers Grimm ☙ 1/2 **2005 (PG-13)** Rather grim indeed is this ill-conceived fairytale from Gilliam that had a rocky and delayed production (it was filmed in 2003). Wilhelm (Damon) and Jacob (Ledger) are 18th century German con men fleecing credulous country folk who believe in the supernatural. But in order to save their own skins, the brothers must investigate the disappearance of a number of young women who have vanished into a truly enchanted forest that is the domain of the Mirror Queen (Bellucci). The film looks good but it's really all an illusion. **118m/C DVD, Blu-ray Disc, UMD.** *US CZ* Matt Damon, Heath Ledger, Monica Bellucci, Jonathan Pryce, Lena Headey, Peter Stormare, Jan Unger; ***D:*** Terry Gilliam; ***W:*** Ehren Kruger; ***C:*** Newton Thomas (Tom) Sigel; ***M:*** Dario Marianelli.

Brothers in Arms ☙☙ **1988 (R)** Savage mountainmen have developed a weird religion that requires them to hunt down and mercilessly massacre human prey. **95m/C VHS.** Todd Allen, Jack Starrett, Dedee Pfeiffer, Mitch Pileggi; ***D:*** George J. Bloom III; ***W:*** Steve(n) Fisher.

Brothers in Law ☙☙ 1/2 **1957** Wry British humor in this tale of a rookie lawyer up against a veteran judge who forces him to sink or swim. **94m/B VHS.** *GB* Richard Attenborough, Ian Carmichael, Terry-Thomas, Miles Malleson, John Le Mesurier; ***D:*** Roy Boulting; ***W:*** Roy Boulting.

Brothers in Trouble ☙☙ **1995** Illegal Pakistani immigrants occupy a squalid boardinghouse in '60s Yorkshire, including newly arrived Amir (Malhotra). He settles in, befriending young student Sakib (Kumar), and learning the ropes from house leader Hossein Shah (Puri). But Shah brings unexpected problems to the group when his pregnant, white English girlfriend Mary (Ball) comes to stay and his nephew Irshad (Bhatti) arranges a paper marriage with the young woman. Based on the novel "Return Journey" by Abdullah Hussein. **104m/C VHS.** *GB* Om Puri, Pavan Malhotra, Pravesh Kumar, Angeline Ball, Ahsen Bhatti; ***D:*** Udayan Prasad; ***W:*** Robert Buckler; ***C:*** Alan Almond; ***M:*** Stephen Warbeck.

The Brothers Karamazov ☙☙☙ *Karamazov; The Murderer Dmitri Karamazov; Der Morder Dimitri Karamasoff* **1958** Hollywood adaptation of the classic novel by Dostoyevsky, in which four 19th-Century Russian brothers struggle with their desires for the same beautiful woman and with the father who brutalizes them. Incredible performances from every cast member, especially Cobb. Long and extremely intense, with fine direction from Brooks. Marilyn Monroe tried desperately to get Schell's part. **147m/C VHS.** Yul Brynner, Claire Bloom, Lee J. Cobb, William Shatner, Maria Schell, Richard Basehart; ***D:*** Richard Brooks; ***W:*** Richard Brooks; ***C:*** John Alton.

Brother's Keeper ☙☙☙ **1992** Filmmakers Berlinger and Sinofsky document the story of the eccentric and reclusive Ward brothers, four bachelor dairy farmers who shared the same two-room shack for more than 60 years in rural New York. When Bill Ward dies, brother Delbert is accused of murder and goes to trial. The film covers a year's span in preparation for the trial and how the media attention changed the Ward's lives. **104m/C VHS, DVD.** ***D:*** Joe Berlinger, Bruce Sinofsky; ***C:*** Douglas Cooper. Directors Guild '92: Feature Doc. (Berlinger), Feature Doc. (Sinofsky); Natl. Bd. of Review '92: Feature Doc.; N.Y. Film Critics '92: Feature Doc.; Sundance '92: Aud. Award.

Brother's Keeper ☙☙ *My Brother's Keeper* **2002 (R)** After police detective Lucinda Pond (Tripplehorn) screwed up and let a killer get away, she left the force to run a fishing boat and start drinking. Ex-partner/lover Travis (Orser) shows up when his current homicide case turns out to be identical to the incident that ended Lucinda's career. She unofficially agrees to help but solving the case may lead her close to home and her crazy brother Ellis (Nemec). **86m/C VHS, DVD.** Jeanne Tripplehorn, Corin "Corky" Nemec, Leland Orser, Evan Dexter Parke; ***D:*** John Badham; ***W:*** Steven Baigelman, Glen Gers; ***C:*** Ron Stannett; ***M:*** John Ottman, John Willett. **CABLE**

A Brother's Kiss ☙☙ **1997 (R)** Growing up in an East Harlem neighborhood with an alcoholic mother (Moriarty), two brothers are set on different paths that strain their brotherly love. Lex (Chinlund) is a never-was ex-basketball player with a bad marriage and an even worse drug problem. Mick (Raynor) is a tightly wound, obsessive, and sexually dysfunctional cop. Both of their problems stem from a childhood trauma that neither is able or willing to discuss with the other. Starts out strong but runs out of energy by the second half. Expanded from a one-act play by director Rosenfeld. **92m/C VHS, DVD.** Nicholas Chinlund, Michael Raynor, Justin Pierce, Cathy Moriarty, Rosie Perez, Marisa Tomei, Joshua Danowsky, John Leguizamo, Michael Rapaport, Frank Minucci, Adrian Pasdar; ***D:*** Seth Zvi Rosenfeld; ***W:*** Seth Zvi Rosenfeld; ***C:*** Fortunato Procopio; ***M:*** Frank London.

Brothers Lionheart ☙☙ 1/2 **1977 (G)** The Lion brothers fight for life, love and liberty during the Middle Ages. Based on a novel by Astrid Lindgren. **120m/C VHS.** *SW* Staffan Gotestam, Lars Soderdahl, Allan Edwall; ***D:*** Olle Hellbom.

The Brothers McMullen ☙☙☙ **1994 (R)** Slice of life drama finds three Irish-American brothers suddenly living under the same Long Island roof for the first time since childhood. Eldest brother Jack (Mulcahy) is a stolid high-school basketball coach married to teacher Molly (Britton) who's pressing him to have children. Cynical middle brother Barry (Burns), a writer, has just broken up with free-spirited Ann (McKay), and earnest young Patrick (McGlone) is engaged to Jewish girlfriend Susan (Albert). All three find their romantic relationships, as well as their belief in each other, tested. Generally good performances and dialogue, with Burns proving himself a triple threat as actor/writer/director. **98m/C VHS, DVD.** Edward Burns, Jack Mulcahy, Mike McGlone, Connie Britton, Shari Albert, Elizabeth P. McKay, Maxine Bahns, Jennifer Jostyn, Catharine Bolt, Peter Johansen; ***D:*** Edward Burns; ***W:*** Edward Burns; ***C:*** Dick Fisher; ***M:*** Seamus Egan. Ind. Spirit '96: First Feature; Sundance '95: Grand Jury Prize.

Brothers of the Head ☙☙ **2006 (R)** Bizzare mockumentary a la "This Is Spinal Tap," only without the humor, tells the fictional story of British conjoined twins who are sold by their father to an unsavory music promoter who turns them into a freak-show punk band. The flashback-documentary style shows the rapid rise and fall of the band due to the usual rock and roll excesses. Pic gets a half bone for recreating an authentic 1970s British art/rock scene that makes an otherwise creepy flick watchable. Based on the 1977 illustrated novel by Brian Aldiss. **120m/C DVD.** *GB* Sean Harris, Jonathan Pryce, John Simm, Jane Horrocks, Harry Treadway, Luke Treadway, Bryan Dick, Elizabeth Rider, Howard Attfield, Luke Wagner, Anna Nygh, Ed Hogg, Thomas Sturridge, Barbara Ewing; ***Cameos:*** Ken Russell; ***D:*** Keith Fulton, Louis Pepe; ***W:*** Tony Grisoni; ***C:*** Anthony Dod Mantle; ***M:*** Clive Langer.

Brothers of the West ☙ 1/2 **1937** Cowboy saves his brothers from being lynched by proving the guilt of the real outlaws. **56m/B VHS.** Tom Tyler, Bob Terry, Lois Wilde, Dorothy Short, Lafe (Lafayette) McKee, Dave O'Brien, Roger Williams; ***D:*** Sam Katzman; ***W:*** Basil Dickey; ***C:*** William (Bill) Hyer.

Brothers O'Toole ☙☙ **1973 (G)** The misadventures of a pair of slick drifters who, by chance, ride into a broken-down mining town in the 1890s. **94m/C VHS, DVD.** John Astin, Steve Carlson, Pat Carroll, Hans Conried, Lee Meriwether; ***D:*** Richard Erdman.

The Brothers Rico ☙☙ **1957** Eddie (Conte) left the mob life behind, got married, and has a successful business, but his two brothers remained in the rackets. Unbeknownst to Eddie, they are targeted by mob boss Kubik (Gates) who uses Eddie's family loyalty to track them down. When Eddie discovers his brothers have been rubbed out, he decides to turn informer. Based on a novella by Georges Simenon. **92m/B DVD.** Richard Conte, James Darren, Paul Picerni, Dianne Foster, Kathryn Grant, Larry Gates, Lamont Johnson, Argentina Brunetti; ***D:*** Phil Karlson; ***W:*** Lewis Meltzer, Ben L. Perry; ***C:*** Burnett Guffey; ***M:*** George Duning.

The Brothers Solomon ☙ 1/2 **2007 (R)** Dean (Forte) and John (Arnett) decide to grant their father's (Majors) last wish before he slipped into a coma: a grandchild. Unfortunately, they were raised in the Arctic, have no social skills, and are, well, idiots. Along comes surrogate Janine (Wiig), who is willing to bear the child for a price. Mostly, though, it's just a set up for an endless series of gags based on how stupid and out of touch the brothers are. Arnett and Forte's "even dumber than dumberer" act, as directed by Odenkirk, is exhausting and the occasional splashes of sweetness don't make up for what is basically a one-joke extended sketch comedy skit. **93m/C DVD.** *US* Will Arnett, Will Forte, Chi McBride, Jenna Fischer, Kristen Wiig, Malin Akerman, David Koechner, Lee Majors; ***D:*** Bob Odenkirk; ***W:*** Will Forte; ***C:*** Tim Suhrstedt; ***M:*** John Swihart.

Brothers Three ☙ 1/2 **2007 (R)** Dysfunctional family 101. College-educated businessman Peter (Wilson) receives an urgent message from his hot-tempered outdoorsman brother Rick (McDonough) to join him and their mentally-challenged younger brother Norman (Campbell) at the family's remote, run-down cabin. Once there, Peter learns that their shifty father (Heard) has recently died a violent death. The brothers then spend their time drinking and offering up confessions that reveal dark secrets (through some confusing flashbacks). **102m/C DVD.** Patrick Wilson, Neal McDonough, Scott Michael Campbell, John Heard, Melora Walters; ***D:*** Paul Kampf; ***W:*** Paul Kampf; ***C:*** Henryk Cymerman.

The Brown Bunny ☙☙ 1/2 **2003** After his film's trashing as the worst movie in the history of the Cannes Film Festival, director/writer/star Gallo slashed nearly a half-hour from this story of a forlorn motorcycle racer's long, lonely coast-to-coast journey from a New Hampshire competition to his home in L.A., where he eventually meets up with true love Daisy (Sevigny). An infamously graphic oral sex scene ensues, which leads to a funky final plot twist. Curiosity, about the Cannes hubbub and the sex scene, will be rewarded by an interesting, sometimes poignant, homage to the maverick filmmaking of the 1970s. **93m/C DVD.** Vincent Gallo, Chloe Sevigny, Cheryl Tiegs, Elizabeth Blake, Anna Vareschi, Mary Morasky; ***D:*** Vincent Gallo; ***W:*** Vincent Gallo; ***C:*** Vincent Gallo.

Brown Sugar ☙☙ 1/2 **2002 (PG-13)** Using the world of hip-hop music as its background, this romantic comedy succeeds in breathing life into a rather tired formula.

Record producer Dre (Diggs) and music journalist Sidney (Lathan) are childhood friends who are drawn together by their shared love of the music. Although they think that romance is out of the question for them, everyone else knows that they're wrong, especially Sidney's friend Francine (Latifah). Unfortunately, Sidney doesn't figure it out until Dre becomes engaged to lovely lawyer Reese (Parker). She rebounds with suave basketball player Kelby (Kodjoe). Mos Def steals scenes as the shy, rapping cabbie who has a crush on Francine. **109m/C VHS, DVD.** *US* Taye Diggs, Sanaa Lathan, Mos Def, Nicole Ari Parker, Queen Latifah, Wendell Pierce, Boris Kodjoe, Erik Weiner, Reggi Wyns; ***D:*** Rick Famuyiwa; ***W:*** Rick Famuyiwa, Michael Elliot; ***C:*** Enrique Chediak; ***M:*** Robert Hurst.

The Browning Version 1/2 **1951** A lonely, unemotional classics instructor at a British boarding school realizes his failure as a teacher and as a husband. From the play by Terrence Rattigan. **89m/B VHS, DVD.** *GB* Michael Redgrave, Jean Kent, Nigel Patrick, Wilfrid Hyde-White, Bill Travers; ***D:*** Anthony Asquith. Cannes '51: Actor (Redgrave).

The Browning Version 1/2 **1994 (R)** Mediocre remake of the Terence Rattigan play, previously filmed in 1951. Austere classics professor (Finney) at prestigious British boys school is disillusioned with both his floundering career and marriage. His emotional chill drives his younger wife (Scacchi) into an affair with a visiting American science teacher (Modine). Unfortunately updated to contemporary times, which can't hide apparent mustiness. Worth seeing for Finney's superb work as the out-of-touch prof. **97m/C VHS, DVD.** Albert Finney, Greta Scacchi, Matthew Modine, Michael Gambon, Julian Sands, Ben Silverstone, Maryam D'Abo; ***D:*** Mike Figgis; ***W:*** Ronald Harwood; ***M:*** Mark Isham.

Brown's Requiem 1/2 **1998 (R)** Ex-cop and ex-drunk Fritz Brown (Rooker) is a sometime L.A. private eye and repo man. He's hired by the aptly named Freddie "Fat Dog" Baker (Sasso) to check out Solly K (Gould), at whose manse Baker's kid sister Jane (Blair) is living. Solly's involved with ex-cop Cathcart (James), with whom Fritz has a longstanding beef, and the P.I. uncovers various lowlifes and a scam. Based on James Ellroy's Chandleresque detailed and dialogue-heavy first novel, which was published in 1981. **97m/C VHS, DVD.** Michael Rooker, Brion James, Harold Gould, Selma Blair, Kevin Corrigan, Tobin Bell, Jack Conley, Brad Dourif, Will Sasso, Valerie Perrine, Barry Newman; ***D:*** Jason Freedland; ***W:*** Jason Freedland; ***C:*** Sead Muhtarevic; ***M:*** Cynthia Millar.

Brubaker **1980 (R)** A sanctimonious drama about a reform warden who risks his life to replace brutality and corruption with humanity and integrity in a state prison farm. Powerful prison drama. **131m/C VHS, DVD.** Robert Redford, Jane Alexander, Yaphet Kotto, Murray Hamilton, David Keith, Morgan Freeman, Matt Clark, M. Emmet Walsh, Everett McGill; ***D:*** Stuart Rosenberg; ***W:*** W.D. Richter, Arthur Ross; ***M:*** Lalo Schifrin.

The Bruce 1/2 **1996** Based on the story of Scottish king, Robert the Bruce (Welch) and the battle at Bannockburn against English King Edward I's (Blessed) forces. Not blessed with the biggest budget and the actors tend to chew the scenery but not a bad bit of history. Robert the Bruce may also be familiar from the film "Braveheart." **110m/C VHS.** *GB* Sandy Welch, Oliver Reed, Brian Blessed, Michael Van Wijk, Pavel Douglas; ***D:*** Bob Carruthers, David McWhinnie; ***M:*** Paul Farrer.

Bruce Almighty 1/2 **2003 (PG-13)** No, it's not a Springsteen documentary, it's an enjoyable, if slight, Jim Carrey comedy. Carrey is Bruce Nolan, a TV reporter stuck with the fluff stories and longing to be taken seriously. He gets his chance when God (Freeman) decides to turn over the reins for a day and gives Bruce his divine powers. The comedy set-pieces are well done, and Carrey can do a lot with a little (at least in his comedies), but the overall effect is less laugh-out-loud funny than fans of the earlier Carrey-Shadyac pairings would expect. Aniston's not given much to do, but Carrell and Freeman stand out among the supporting cast. **101m/C VHS, DVD, HD DVD.** *US* Jim Carrey, Jennifer Aniston, Morgan Freeman, Lisa Ann Walter, Philip Baker Hall, Catherine Bell, Nora Dunn, Steve Carell; ***D:*** Tom Shadyac; ***W:*** Steve Oedekerk, Steve Koren, Mark O'Keefe; ***C:*** Dean Semler; ***M:*** John Debney.

Bruce Lee: Curse of the Dragon *The Curse of the Dragon* **1993** A behind the scenes look at the continuing mystery surrounding the life and untimely death of the martial arts superstar who died in 1973 at the age of 32. Highlights the spectacular fight sequences from Lee's movies as well as footage from his funeral and an interview with his son Brandon Lee, whose own death in 1993 raised further comment about a Lee family curse. **90m/C VHS.** ***D:*** Tom Kuhn, Fred Weintraub; ***W:*** Davis Miller; ***Nar:*** George Takei.

Bruce Lee Fights Back from the Grave **1976 (R)** Bruce Lee returns from the grave to fight the Black Angel of Death with his feet and to wreak vengeance on the evil ones who brought about his untimely demise. **84m/C VHS, DVD.** Bruce Le, Deborah Chaplin, Anthony Bronson; ***D:*** Umberto Lenzi.

Bruiser 1/2 **2000** First film from horror icon Romero in more than seven years offers a great central premise, but little else. Henry Creedlow (Flemyng) is a nice guy who gets used by everyone around him. His cheating wife, his overbearing boss, and his dishonest stock broker all push Henry around, but he never stands up for himself. That is, until the day that he wakes up to find that his face has been replaced by a blank white mask. Being "faceless" allows Henry to assert himself and get revenge. The film is boring and filled with many unlikable characters, the worst of which is Henry. The last act is simply absurd and one can't help but wonder what has happened to the once great Romero. **99m/C VHS, DVD.** Jason Flemyng, Peter Stormare, Leslie Hope, Nina Garbiras, Tom Atkins, Jeff Monahan; ***D:*** George A. Romero; ***W:*** George A. Romero; ***C:*** Adam Swica; ***M:*** Donald Rubinstein.

Bruno **2009 (R)** Really, did Baron Cohen actually think this character was funny or was he merely being smug and cynical? After "Borat," it's time to retire this shtick of a ridiculously stupid—or in this case, flamboyant and stupid—staged character intersecting with 'real' people and situations. Over-the-top gay Austrian fashionista Bruno heads to L.A. to become a 'superstar' though, like some reality TV show participant, he lacks any talent except that of relentless self-promotion. The sexual content is constantly crude rather than provocative. Erratic, nausea-inducing, and takes a turn for the nasty. **83m/C DVD.** *US* Sacha Baron Cohen; ***D:*** Larry Charles; ***W:*** Sacha Baron Cohen; ***M:*** Erran Baron Cohen.

Brush with Fate **2003** Mousy teacher Cornelia (Close) is in possession of a 300-year-old Dutch painting called "Girl in Hyacinth Blue." It's possibly a Vermeer but Cornelia is afraid to find out since she may not be the legal owner. Still Cornelia would like new art professor Richard (Gibson) to give her his opinion. But the painting's history (told in flashbacks) has caused its previous owners trouble as well. Based on the novel by Susan Vreeland. **100m/C VHS, DVD.** Glenn Close, Thomas Gibson, Ellen Burstyn, Phyllida Law, Kelly Macdonald, Patrick Bergin; ***D:*** Brent Shields; ***W:*** Richard Russo; ***C:*** Eric Van Haren Noman; ***M:*** Lawrence Shragge. **TV**

Brutal Fury **1992** Detective Molly Griffin goes undercover at a local high school and discovers a secret female vigilante group, called the "Fury," which goes after the drug dealers and rapists preying on the school's students. Teenagers with an attitude. **97m/C VHS.** Tom Campitelli, Lisa-Gabrielle Greene, Annette Gerbon, Karen Eppers, Jennifer Winder, Allen Arkus; ***D:*** Frederick P. Watkins.

Brutal Glory **1989** Set in New York City in 1918 and based on the true story of the boxer known as "The Real McCoy." Fascinating and detailed history of a period, a champion, and the man who made it happen. **96m/C VHS.** Robert Vaughn, Timothy Brantley, Leah K. Pinsent; ***D:*** Koos Roets.

Brutal Massacre: A Comedy **2007 (R)** Horror director Harry Penderecki's (Naughton) career has been plagued by box-office bombs and critical disdain and he hasn't had a money-maker in years. Harry's trying to shoot his low-budget comeback film, "Brutal Massacre," but the mishaps keep increasing, leaving him teetering on the edge while every move is being recorded by reporter Bert Campbell (Butta) for a behind-the-scenes documentary. **95m/C DVD.** David Naughton, Brian O'Halloran, Ellen Sandweiss, Ken Foree, Gunnar Hansen, Gerry Bednob, Vincent Butta; ***D:*** Stevan Mena; ***W:*** Stevan Mena; ***C:*** Brendan Flynt.

The Brutal Truth **1999 (R)** Group of high school friends get together for a 10-year reunion at a secluded mountain cabin for a weekend of fun, but then learn that one of the gang, Emily (Applegate), has committed suicide. This leads to arguments and secrets revealed. **89m/C VHS, DVD.** Christina Applegate, Justin Lazard, Johnathon Schaech, Moon Zappa, Paul Gleason, Molly Ringwald, Leslie Horan; ***D:*** Cameron Thor.

Brute 1/2 **1997** Schweiger is doing humanitarian work in Eastern Europe when he discovers a group of orphans who are being abused by institute director Postlethwaite. So he tries to come to their rescue. Based on a true story. English and Polish with subtitles. **90m/C DVD.** *GE PL* Til Schweiger, Pete Postlethwaite, John Hurt, Polly Walker, Ida Jablonska; ***D:*** Maciej Dejczer; ***W:*** Cezary Harasimowicz; ***C:*** Paul Prokop, Arthur Reinhart; ***M:*** Michael Lorenc.

Brute Force 1/2 **1947** Lancaster (in a star-making turn) is Joe, an inmate in an overcrowded prison lorded over by sadistic guard Munsey (Cronyn). When Munsey pushes the prisoners too far, Joe leads a daring prison break attempt. While some see this intense drama as heavy-handed (all of the inmates are victims of circumstance), the portrayals are compelling, and the story is first-rate noir. **102m/B DVD.** Burt Lancaster, Ann Blyth, Ella Raines, Yvonne De Carlo, Hume Cronyn, Charles Bickford, Whit Bissell, Howard Duff, Jeff Corey; ***D:*** Jules Dassin; ***W:*** Richard Brooks; ***C:*** William H. Daniels; ***M:*** Miklos Rozsa.

The Brute Man **1946** A young man who had been disfigured by his school mates goes out on a trail of revenge. Hatton is convincing in the title role, as in real life he was afflicted with acromegaly, an ailment that produces an enlargment of the bones in the face, hands, and feet. **62m/B VHS, DVD.** Rondo Hatton, Tom Neal, Jane Adams, Donald McBride, Peter Whitney; ***D:*** Jean Yarbrough; ***W:*** George Bricker, M. Coates Webster; ***C:*** Maury Gertsman; ***M:*** Hans J. Salter.

The Brylcreem Boys **1996 (PG-13)** In September, 1941, Canadian pilot Miles Keogh (Campbell) and his crew are forced to bail out of their plane. They land in neutral southern Ireland, where they're interned in the local POW camp run by Sean O'Brien (Byrne). The camp holds both Allies and Germans—separated by only a thin wire fence. Keogh figures it's his patriotic duty to try to escape as does German officer Rudolph von Stegenbeck (Macfadyen), and problems compound when both soldiers are let out on day-release passes and, naturally, fall for the same lovely local colleen, Mattie (Butler). It's pleasant but unmemorable. **105m/C VHS, DVD.** *GB* Billy Campbell, Angus MacFadyen, William McNamara, Gabriel Byrne, Jean Butler, Joe McGann, Oliver Tobias, Gordon John Sinclair; ***D:*** Terence Ryan; ***W:*** Terence Ryan, Jamie Brown; ***C:*** Gerry Lively; ***M:*** Richard Hartley.

BTK Killer **WOOF! 2006 (R)** Nonsensical and loathsome flick purportedly about Dennis Rader, the Wichita serial killer who wasn't caught for 30 years. The initials stand for Rader's methods: Bind. Torture. Kill. For some unknown reason, hack director Lommel pads things out by including non-related animal slaughter scenes. **82m/C DVD.** Gerard Griesbaum; ***D:*** Ulli Lommel; ***W:*** Ulli Lommel; ***C:*** Bianco Pacelli; ***M:*** Robert Walsh. **VIDEO**

Bubba Ho-Tep **2003 (R)** Elvis and JFK team up to battle the dark forces of Egypt, who threaten the residents of their East Texas convalescent home. Believable plot aside, director Coscarelli's delightfully wacky cult-concept comedy still manages to take the whole thing seriously, especially with an inspired performance from Campbell, playing it totally straight. In addition to the presumed-dead celebrities and world leaders, the small town of Mud Creek also attracts an Egyptian mummy known as Bubba Ho-Tep, who terrorizes the aged Texans. The feisty King and former Prez gleefully open a king-sized can of whoop-ass on the ancient terror. While flawed, it's still solid campy fun. Adapted from a short story by Joe Lansdale. **92m/C VHS, DVD.** *US* Bruce Campbell, Ossie Davis, Ella Joyce, Reggie Bannister, Bob Ivy, Larry Pennell, Heidi Marnhout; ***D:*** Don A. Coscarelli; ***W:*** Don A. Coscarelli; ***C:*** Adam Janeiro; ***M:*** Brian Tyler.

Bubble **2006 (R)** Soderbergh's uneven, low-budget experiment features a non-professional cast portraying blue-collar workers at a small Midwestern doll factory. Overweight, middle-aged Martha's (Doebereiner) life consists of caring for her sick, elderly father and fussing over young, shy co-worker Kyle (Ashley). The boring predictability of their lives is shaken by a new co-worker, outgoing single mom Rose (Wilkins), and Martha baby-sits when Rose asks Kyle out on a date. Then one of the three is murdered and there's an investigation. It's all as minimalist and banal as the lives it depicts. Besides directing, Soderbergh shot the film under the pseudonym Peter Andrews. **73m/C DVD.** *US* Debbie Doebereiner, Dustin Ashley, Misty Wilkins, K. Smith; ***D:*** Steven Soderbergh; ***W:*** Coleman Hough; ***C:*** Steven Soderbergh; ***M:*** Robert Pollard.

The Bubble *Ha Buah* **2006** The westernized district of Sheikin St. in Tel Aviv seems far removed from the racial and religious conflicts plaguing the area. Lulu (Wircer) shares her apartment (and life) with two gay men: Yali (Firedmann) and Noam (Knoller), who is in love with Palestinian Ashraf (Sweid). Ashraf is living and working in the city illegally and his abrupt return to his home in Nablus leads to a last act that strains credibility. Hebrew and Arabic with subtitles. **117m/C DVD.** *IS* Ohad Knoller, Yousef (Joe) Sweid, Alon Friedmann, Daniela Wircer, Roba Blal, Shredy Jabarin; ***D:*** Eytan Fox; ***W:*** Eytan Fox, Gal Uchovsky; ***C:*** Yaron Sharf; ***M:*** Ivri Lider.

Bubble Boy **2001 (PG-13)** Disney has finally jumped on the crude and offensive humor bandwagon, with a simplistic storyline involving the journey of Jimmy (Gyllenhaal), a naive guy born with an immune system deficiency that requires him to live in a germ-free environment, as he races across the country to stop his sweetheart (Shelton) from marrying a jerk. Jimmy constructs a mobile bubble and hits the road. Along the way, the alleged jokes manage to offend Christians, Hindus, Jews, Republicans, Latinos, Asians and circus freaks while still wallowing in boner humor. That'd be almost forgivable if the "humor" was actually funny. **84m/C VHS, DVD.** *US* Jake Gyllenhaal, Swoosie Kurtz, Marley Shelton, Danny Trejo, John Carroll Lynch, Stephen Spinella, Verne Troyer, Dave Sheridan, Brian George, Patrick Cranshaw, Fabio; ***D:*** Blair Hayes; ***W:*** Ken Daurio, Cinco Paul; ***C:*** Jerzy Zielinski; ***M:*** John Ottman.

The Buccaneer **1958** A swashbuckling version of the adventures of pirate Jean LaFitte and his association with President Andrew Jackson during the War of 1812. Remake of Cecille B. DeMille's 1938 production. **121m/C VHS, DVD.** Yul Brynner, Charlton Heston, Claire Bloom, Inger Stevens, Charles Boyer, Henry Hull, E.G. Marshall, Lorne Greene; ***D:*** Anthony Quinn; ***C:*** Loyal Griggs; ***M:*** Elmer Bernstein.

The Buccaneers **1995** Lavish adaptation of the Edith Wharton novel follows the adventures of four American girls in 1870s society. Nouveaux riche, the young ladies are unable to crack New York snobbery and, after vivacious Brazilian Conchita (Sorvino) manages to snag Lord Richard (Vibert), the others are encouraged by English governess Laura Testvalley (Lunghi) to try their luck in London. There, Virginia (Elliott), sister Nan (Gugino), their friend Lizzy (Kihlstedt), and Conchita all find hope and heartbreak among the English aristocracy. Wharton's novel was unfinished at her death and, though she left story notes, scripter Wadey concedes to changes. Made for TV. **288m/C VHS, DVD.** *GB* Carla Gugino, Mira Sorvino, Alison Elliott, Rya Kihlstedt, Cherie Lunghi, Connie Booth, Mark Tandy, Ronan Vibert, Jenny Agutter, Richard Huw, Greg Wise, James Frain, Michael Kitchen, Sheila Hancock, Rosemary Leach, Elizabeth Ashley, Conchata Ferrell, Peter Michael Goetz, James Rebhorn, E. Katherine Kerr; ***D:*** Philip Saville; ***W:*** Maggie Wadey; ***C:*** Maggie Wadey; ***M:*** Colin Towns. **TV**

Buccaneer's Girl 🦴🦴 1/2 **1950** Charming swashbuckler. Pirate Frederick Baptiste (Friend) only attacks the ships of evil Narbonne (Douglas) as revenge for his father's death. During one of his raids, New Orleans entertainer Deborah (De Carlo) stows away and falls for the sea-faring Robin Hood. However, hoping to marry into money, Deborah sets her sights on an aristocrat, only to figure out that Baptiste has been leading a double life. **77m/C DVD.** Yvonne De Carlo, Philip Friend, Robert Douglas, Elsa Lanchester, Andrea King, Norman Lloyd, Jay C. Flippen; ***D:*** Fred de Cordova; ***W:*** Joseph Hoffman, Harold Shumate; ***C:*** Russell Metty; ***M:*** Walter Scharf.

Buchanan Rides Alone 🦴🦴 1/2 **1958** Loner Buchanan (Scott) befriends young Mexican Juan (Rojas) in a California border town run by the bickering Agry family. Juan kills a bullying Agry in self-defense, but he and Buchanan both wind up in the pokey. However, Buchanan manages to pit the Agrys against each other. **89m/C DVD.** Randolph Scott, Craig Stevens, Barry Kelley, Peter Whitney, Manuel Rojas, Tol Avery, L.Q. Jones; ***D:*** Budd Boetticher; ***W:*** Charles Land; ***C:*** Lucien Ballard.

Buck and the Magic Bracelet 🦴🦴 1/2 **1997 (PG-13)** In the old west a teen and his dog escape an attack on their prospecting camp. They're aided in bringing the bad guys to justice by a shaman's magic bracelet. **99m/C VHS.** Matt McCoy, Abby Dalton, Felton Perry, Conrad Nichols; ***D:*** Tonino Ricci; ***W:*** Fabio Carpi; ***C:*** Giovanni Bergamini; ***M:*** Stefano Curti.

Buck and the Preacher 🦴🦴 1/2 **1972 (PG)** A trail guide and a con man preacher join forces to help a wagon train of former slaves who are seeking to homestead out West. Poitier's debut as a director. **102m/C VHS, DVD.** Sidney Poitier, Harry Belafonte, Ruby Dee, Cameron Mitchell, Denny Miller; ***D:*** Sidney Poitier.

Buck Benny Rides Again 🦴🦴 1/2 **1940** Radio performer Benny (playing himself) boasts he's a regular cowboy type with a ranch in Nevada—claims challenged by rival Fred Allen. So Benny is forced to travel west, where he makes a fool of himself before accidentally capturing two outlaws while romancing singer Joan (Drew). Rochester is there to assist as well as others from the Benny program. **82m/B DVD.** Jack Benny, Ellen Drew, Virginia Dale, Eddie Anderson, Andy Devine, Phil Harris, Dennis Day; ***D:*** Mark Sandrich; ***W:*** Edmund Beloin, William Morrow; ***C:*** Charles Lang.

Buck Privates 🦴🦴 1/2 *Rookies* **1941** Abbott and Costello star as two dim-witted tie salesmen, running from the law, who become buck privates during WWII. The duo's first great success, and the film that established the formula for each subsequent film. **84m/B VHS, DVD.** Bud Abbott, Lou Costello, Shemp Howard, Lee Bowman, Alan Curtis, The Andrews Sisters; ***D:*** Arthur Lubin; ***W:*** Arthur T. Horman, John Grant; ***C:*** Milton Krasner; ***M:*** Charles Previn.

Buck Privates Come Home 🦴🦴🦴 *Rookies Come Home* **1947** Abbott and Costello return to their "Buck Privates" roles as two soldiers trying to adjust to civilian life after the war. They also try to help a French girl sneak into the United States. Funny antics culminate into a wild chase scene. **77m/B VHS, DVD.** Bud Abbott, Lou Costello, Tom Brown, Joan Shawlee, Nat Pendleton, Beverly Simmons, Don Beddoe, Don Porter, Donald MacBride; ***D:*** Charles T. Barton; ***W:*** John Grant, Frederic Rinaldo, Robert Lees; ***C:*** Charles Van Enger; ***M:*** Walter Schumann.

Buck Rogers Conquers the Universe 🦴🦴 **1939** The story of Buck Rogers, written by Phil Nolan in 1928, was the first science-fiction story done in the modern superhero space genre. Many of the "inventions" seen in this movie have actually come into existence—spaceships, ray guns (lasers), anti-gravity belts—a testament to Nolan's almost psychic farsightedness. **91m/B VHS.** Buster Crabbe, Constance Moore, Jackie Moran; ***D:*** Ford Beebe, Saul Goodkind.

Buck Rogers in the 25th Century 🦴🦴 **1979 (PG)** An American astronaut, preserved in space for 500 years, is brought back to life by a passing Draconian flagship. Outer space adventures begin when he is accused of being a spy from Earth. Based on the classic movie serial. TV movie that began the popular series. Additional series episodes are available. **90m/C VHS, DVD.** Gil Gerard, Pamela Hensley, Erin Gray, Henry Silva; ***D:*** Daniel Haller; ***V:*** Mel Blanc. **TV**

The Bucket List 🦴 1/2 **2007 (PG-13)** Yes, that's as in "kick the bucket." Cliched sitcom finds cancer patients Edward Cole (Nicholson) and Carter Chambers (Freeman) getting the bad news that their time is very limited. Since Edward is a self-satisfied gazillionaire estranged from his family, he decides to indulge his every last whim and takes fellow patient Carter, a working-class married father, on their own buddy road trip 'round the world. Nicholson's crazy, Freeman's serious, and the scenery seems to be all computer-generated. **97m/C DVD, Blu-ray Disc.** *US* Jack Nicholson, Morgan Freeman, Sean P. Hayes, Beverly Todd, Alfonso Freeman, Rowena King, Rob Morrow; ***D:*** Rob Reiner; ***W:*** Justin Zackham; ***C:*** John Schwartzman; ***M:*** Marc Shaiman.

A Bucket of Blood 🦴🦴🦴 **1959** Cult favorite Dick Miller stars as a sculptor with a peculiar "talent" for lifelike artwork. Corman fans will see thematic similarities to his subsequent work, "Little Shop of Horrors" (1960). "Bucket of Blood" was made in just five days, while "Little Shop of Horrors" was made in a record breaking two days. Corman horror/spoof noted for its excellent beatnik atmosphere. **66m/B VHS, DVD.** Dick Miller, Barboura Morris, Antony Carbone, Julian Burton, Ed Nelson, Bert Convy, Judy Bamber, John Brinkley, Myrtle Domerel, John Herman Shaner, Bruno VeSota; ***D:*** Roger Corman; ***W:*** Charles B. Griffith; ***C:*** John Marquette; ***M:*** Fred Katz.

Buckeye and Blue 🦴 1/2 **1987 (PG)** A hero turned outlaw, his 14 year-old female sidekick, and a gang known as the McCoys are all on the lam from the law in this western adventure. **94m/C VHS.** Robin (Robyn) Lively, Jeffery Osterhage, Rick Gibbs, Will Hannah, Kenneth Jensen, Patrick Johnston, Stuart Rogers, Michael Horse; ***D:*** J.C. Compton.

Buckskin 🦴 1/2 **1968** Slowmoving western about a marshall protecting townspeople from a greedy, land-grabbing cattle baron. **98m/C VHS.** Barry Sullivan, Wendell Corey, Joan Caulfield, Lon Chaney Jr., John Russell, Barbara Hale, Barton MacLane, Bill Williams; ***D:*** Michael D. Moore.

Buckskin Frontier 🦴 1/2 **1943** Story is built around Western railroad construction and cattle empires in the 1860s. Cobb tries to stop the railroad from coming through by hiring Jory to do his dirty work. **75m/B VHS, DVD.** Richard Dix, Jane Wyatt, Lee J. Cobb, Albert Dekker, Victor Jory, Lola Lane, Max Baer Sr.; ***D:*** Lesley Selander.

Bucktown 🦴 1/2 **1975 (R)** A black man who reopens his murdered brother's bar fights off police corruption and racism in a Southern town. **95m/C VHS, DVD.** Fred Williamson, Pam Grier, Bernie Hamilton, Thalmus Rasulala, Art Lund, Robert (Skip) Burton, Carl Weathers; ***D:*** Arthur Marks; ***W:*** Bob Ellison; ***C:*** Robert Birchall; ***M:*** Johnny Pate.

Bud and Lou 🦴 1/2 **1978** Comedy/drama recounts Abbott & Costello's rise in Hollywood. While the story, based on the book by Bob Thomas, is interesting, the two funnymen in the leads can't pull off the old classic skits. **98m/C VHS.** Harvey Korman, Buddy Hackett, Michele Lee, Arte Johnson, Robert Reed; ***D:*** Robert C. Thompson.

The Buddha of Suburbia 🦴🦴🦴 **1992** Satire set in late '70s suburban London follows the coming of age adventures of Karim (Andrews), the handsome son of an Indian father and English mother. His gleeful father Haroon (Seth) exploits the vogue for eastern philosophies he knows nothing about with lectures to the upper-middle classes while he carries on with devotee Eva (Fleetwood). When his mother finds out, Karim and his father move into central London with Eva, where Karim decides to take up acting in fringe theatre and sex while his friend, Eva's son Charlie (Mackintosh), experiments with the punk music scene. TV miniseries adapted by Kureishi from his novel. **220m/C VHS.** *GB* Naveen Andrews, Roshan Seth, Susan Fleetwood, Steven Mackintosh, Brenda Blethyn, John McEnery, Janet Dale, David Bamber, Donald (Don) Sumpter, Jemma Redgrave, David Bradley; ***D:*** Roger Michell; ***W:*** Hanif Kureishi, Roger Michell; ***C:*** John McGlashan; ***M:*** David Bowie. **TV**

Buddy 🦴🦴 1/2 **1997 (PG)** Animals run amok in the Lintz household. Mother hen Gertrude Lintz (Russo) raises just about everything from mischievous chimps to impressionable parrots on her estate. A baby gorilla (named Buddy, short for Budha) becomes part of the family, but as he grows in size, so does the difficulty in caring for him. Amiable tale of one woman's motherly bond with a gorilla includes convincing performances by Russo and an animatronic gorilla courtesy of Jim Henson's Creature Shop. Well-paced and very touching at moments, children will definitely enjoy the zany animal antics, and adults should be moved by the unusual relationship. Based on the book by Lintz. **84m/C VHS, DVD.** Rene Russo, Robbie Coltrane, Irma P. Hall, Alan Cumming, Paul (Pee-wee Herman) Reubens; ***D:*** Caroline Thompson; ***W:*** Caroline Thompson; ***C:*** Steve Mason; ***M:*** Elmer Bernstein.

Buddy Boy 🦴🦴 1/2 **1999 (R)** Isolated by the need to care for his ailing mother (Tyrell), shy Francis (Gillen) begins a voyeuristic relationship with his sexy neighbor (Seigner). Strange but captivating film provides some gothic creepiness as well as commentary on the toll of enforced isolation. **105m/C DVD.** Aidan Gillen, Emmanuelle Seigner, Susan Tyrrell, Mark Boone Jr., Hector Elias, Harry Groener; ***D:*** Mark Hanlon; ***W:*** Mark Hanlon; ***C:*** Hubert Taczanowski; ***M:*** Graeme Revell, Brian Eno, Michael Brook.

Buddy Buddy 🦴🦴 1/2 **1981 (R)** A professional hitman's well-ordered arrangement to knock off a state's witness keeps being interrupted by the suicide attempts of a man in the next hotel room. **96m/C VHS.** Jack Lemmon, Walter Matthau, Paula Prentiss, Klaus Kinski; ***D:*** Billy Wilder; ***W:*** Billy Wilder, I.A.L. Diamond; ***C:*** Harry Stradling Jr.; ***M:*** Lalo Schifrin.

The Buddy Holly Story 🦴🦴🦴 1/2 **1978 (PG)** An acclaimed biography of the famed 1950s pop star, spanning the years from his meteoric career's beginnings in Lubbock to his tragic early death in the now famous plane crash of February 3, 1959. Busey performs Holly's hits himself. ♫ Rock Around the Ollie Vee; That'll Be the Day; Oh, Boy; It's So Easy; Well All Right; Chantilly Lace; Peggy Sue. **113m/C VHS, DVD.** Gary Busey, Don Stroud, Charles Martin Smith, Conrad Janis, William Jordan, Albert "Poppy" Popwell; ***D:*** Steve Rash; ***W:*** Robert Gittler; ***C:*** Stevan Larner; ***M:*** Joe Renzetti. Oscars '78: Orig. Song Score and/or Adapt.; Natl. Soc. Film Critics '78: Actor (Busey).

The Buddy System 🦴🦴 **1983 (PG)** A tale of contemporary love and the modern myths that outline the boundaries between lovers and friends. **110m/C VHS.** Richard Dreyfuss, Susan Sarandon, Jean Stapleton, Nancy Allen, Wil Wheaton, Edward Winter, Keene Curtis; ***D:*** Glenn Jordan; ***W:*** Mary Agnes Donoghue.

Buddy's Song 🦴🦴 **1991 (R)** A '60s coming of age tale, only in this case it's the father and not the son who needs to grow up. Dad (Daltrey) is more interested in hanging out with his no-account musician friends than in looking after his family. Although he's not above meddling in his teenage son's musical career, which could be the success his father's never was. Based on the novel by Nigel Hinton who also did the screenplay. British teen idol Hawkes (in his film debut) had a top ten hit song from the film with "The One and Only." **106m/C VHS.** *GB* Roger Daltrey, Chesney Hawkes, Sharon Duce, Michael Elphick, Douglas Hodge, Lee Ross, James Aubrey, Liza Walker; ***D:*** Claude Whatham; ***W:*** Nigel Hinton; ***C:*** John Hooper; ***M:*** John Grover, Roger Daltrey.

Buena Vista Social Club 🦴🦴🦴 **1999 (G)** American musician Ry Cooder assembled a number of aging Cuban musicians and singers, informally known as the Buena Vista Social Club, to record an album in Havana. The success of that 1997 venture led director Wenders to record this documentary as the group reunites for a concert tour that culminates in a 1998 performance at Carnegie Hall. **106m/C VHS, DVD.** Ry Cooder; ***D:*** Wim Wenders. L.A. Film Critics '99: Feature Doc.; Natl. Bd. of Review '99: Feature Doc.; N.Y. Film Critics '99: Feature Doc.; Natl. Soc. Film Critics '99: Feature Doc.

Buffalo Bill 🦴🦴 **1944** A light, fictionalized account of the life and career of Bill Cody, from frontier hunter to showman. **89m/C VHS, DVD.** Joel McCrea, Maureen O'Hara, Linda Darnell, Thomas Mitchell, Edgar Buchanan, Anthony Quinn, Moroni Olsen, Sidney Blackmer; ***D:*** William A. Wellman; ***C:*** Leon Shamroy.

Buffalo Bill & the Indians 🦴🦴🦴 *Sitting Bull's History Lesson* **1976 (PG)** A perennially underrated Robert Altman historical pastiche, portraying the famous Wild West character as a charlatan and shameless exemplar of encroaching imperialism. Great all-star cast amid Altman's signature mise-en-scene chaos. **135m/C VHS, DVD.** Paul Newman, Geraldine Chaplin, Joel Grey, Will Sampson, Harvey Keitel, Burt Lancaster, Kevin McCarthy; ***D:*** Robert Altman; ***W:*** Robert Altman, Alan Rudolph; ***M:*** Richard Baskin.

Buffalo Bill Rides Again 🦴 1/2 **1947** With an Indian uprising on the horizon, Buffalo Bill is called in. Mr. Bill finds land swindlers pitting natives against ranchers, but there's precious little action or interest here. **68m/C VHS.** Richard Arlen, Jennifer Holt, Edward Cassidy, Edmund Cobb, Charles Stevens; ***D:*** Bernard B. Ray; ***W:*** Barney A. Sarecky; ***C:*** Robert E. Cline.

Buffalo Boy 🦴🦴 *Mua Len Trau* **2004** Coming-of-age story set in 1940s Vietnam. Teenaged Kim is sent by his ill father Dinh to herd their two starving water buffalo to new pasture. Kim falls in with a tough group of buffalo herders, winds up with one buffalo, and tries to mend the rift with his father before the old man dies. Vietnamese with subtitles. **102m/C DVD.** *VT BE FR* Le the Lu, Nguyen Huu Thanj, Vo Hoang Nhan; ***D:*** Minh Nguyen-Vo; ***W:*** Minh Nguyen-Vo; ***C:*** Yves Cape; ***M:*** Ton That Tiet.

Buffalo Girls 🦴🦴 1/2 **1995** Western saga, set in the 1870s, tells of the lifelong friendship between hard-drinking, hard-living Calamity Jane (Huston—who's not exactly any plain Jane) and buxom, soft-hearted madam Dora DuFran (Griffith). Dora's in love (but refuses to marry) rancher Teddy Blue (Byrne) while Calamity has a daughter by Wild Bill Hickok (Elliott) that she gives up for adoption. There's lots of rambling and commiserating over the changing and civilizing of the west and various man trouble. Based on the novel by Larry McMurty; originally a two-part TV miniseries. **180m/C VHS, DVD.** Anjelica Huston, Melanie Griffith, Gabriel Byrne, Peter Coyote, Jack Palance, Sam Elliott, Reba McEntire, Floyd "Red Crow" Westerman, Tracey Walter, Russell Means, Charlaine Woodard, John Diehl, Liev Schreiber, Andrew Bicknell, Kathryn Witt; ***D:*** Rod Hardy; ***W:*** Cynthia Whitcomb; ***C:*** David Connell; ***M:*** Lee Holdridge.

Buffalo Jump 🦴🦴🦴 *Getting Married in Buffalo Jump* **1990** An independent woman, working as a lounge singer in Toronto, returns to her home in Alberta when her father dies. To her surprise he has left her the family ranch and, to the surprise of everyone else, she decides to stay and run it. She hires a good-looking local man to help her out and they both discover that they want more than a working relationship. However, the fireworks really start when he proposes a marriage of convenience. Engaging performances and beautiful scenery help raise this romantic tale of opposites above the average. **97m/C VHS, DVD.** *CA* Wendy Crewson, Paul Gross, Marion Gilsenan, Kyra Harper, Victoria Snow; ***D:*** Eric Till.

Buffalo Rider 🦴 1/2 **1978** An adventure film depicting the real-life experiences of C.J. "Buffalo" Jones who worked to save the American buffalo from extinction. **90m/C VHS.** Rick Guinn, John Freeman, Pricilla Lauris, George Sager, Rich Scheeland; ***D:*** George Lauris.

Buffalo 66 **1997** Billy Brown (Gallo) is a loser of epic proportions. He's named after the Buffalo Bills, notorious losers of Super Bowls. After he loses $10,000 on of those Super Bowls, he turns to a life of crime and promptly lands in prison. He gets out of jail as a man with a mission. Stumbling into a dance studio, Billy kidnaps the nubile Layla (Ricci) and forces her to pose as his wife for a visit to his parents. He had explained his five-year absence to them by saying that he was working for the CIA overseas with his new bride. His father Jimmy (Gazzara), a bitter ex-lounge singer, barely hides his disdain for Billy, and mother Janet (Huston) is so too obsessed with the Bills to interact with him. They both like Layla instantly, and she seems to take unexpected glee in playing her part. Former artist and rock musician Gallo also directed, co-wrote and composed the music for the film. **112m/C VHS, DVD.** Vincent Gallo, Christina Ricci, Anjelica Huston, Ben Gazzara, Kevin Corrigan, Mickey Rourke, Rosanna Arquette, Jan-Michael Vincent; ***D:*** Vincent Gallo; ***W:*** Alison Bagnall, Vincent Gallo; ***C:*** Lance Acord; ***M:*** Vincent Gallo. Natl. Bd. of Review '98: Support. Actress (Ricci).

Buffalo Soldiers **1997** Post-Civil War western concerns the all-black Cavalry troops, created by Congress in 1866 to patrol the west. They received their nickname from the Indians, who thought the black soldiers on horseback looked like buffalo. A former slave and by-the-book Army man, Sgt. Washington Wyatt (Glover) leads the chase for Apache warrior Victorio (Lowe) across the New Mexico Territory while trying tp deal with the common degradation suffered by his troops at the hands of white officers. Lots of cruelty and explicit violence. **120m/C VHS, DVD.** Danny Glover, Carl Lumbly, Bob Gunton, Tom Bower, Harrison Lowe, Glynn Turman, Michael Warren, Mykelti Williamson, Timothy Busfield, Gabriel Casseus; ***D:*** Charles Haid; ***W:*** Frank Military, Susan Rhinehart; ***C:*** William Wages; ***M:*** Joel McNeely. **CABLE**

Buffalo Soldiers 1/2 **2001 (R)** Darkly satiric look at the military revolves around a supply unit of an American Army base in 1989 Germany. Leader of the pack is the bored, amoral Elwood (Phoenix) who gets his kicks and a few extra bucks by dabbling in the black market, dealing in heroin and illegal weapons, and other equally illicit activities. Soon, the newly prosperous Elwood is basically running things at the base until a new Top Sergeant (Glenn) cracks down. Elwood retaliates by dating Sarge's daughter (Paquin) but finds he's actually falling for her. Premiered at the Toronto Film Festival in 2001, then waited for a more appropriate release date, which never actually came (it's not exactly complimentary to the military). Based on a novel by Robert O'Connor. **98m/C VHS, DVD.** *US GB GE* Joaquin Rafael (Leaf) Phoenix, Scott Glenn, Anna Paquin, Ed Harris, Leon Robinson, Dean Stockwell, Elizabeth McGovern, Gabriel Mann, Shiek Mahmud-Bey, Michael Pena, Glenn Fitzgerald, Brian Delate, Jimmie Ray Weeks; ***D:*** Gregor Jordan; ***W:*** Gregor Jordan, Eric Weiss, Nora MacCoby; ***C:*** Oliver Stapleton; ***M:*** David Holmes.

Buffalo Stampede **1933** Our heroes are involved in a plot to round up buffalo to sell for meat. **60m/B VHS, DVD.** Randolph Scott, Buster Crabbe, Harry Carey Sr., Noah Beery Sr., Raymond Hatton, Judith Allen, Blanche Frederici; ***D:*** Henry Hathaway.

Buffet Froid 1/2 **1979** Surreal black comedy about a group of bungling murderers. First rate acting and directing makes this film a hilarious treat. From the director of "Menage." In French with English subtitles. **95m/C VHS, DVD.** *FR* Gerard Depardieu, Bernard Blier, Jean Carmet, Genevieve Page, Denise Gence, Carole Bouquet, Jean Benguigui, Michel Serrault; ***D:*** Bertrand Blier; ***W:*** Bertrand Blier; ***C:*** Jean Penzer; ***M:*** Philippe Sarde. Cesar '80: Writing.

Buffy the Vampire Slayer **1992 (PG-13)** Funny, near-camp teen genre spoof. Buffy is a typical mall gal concerned with shopping and cheerleading, until the mysterious Sutherland proclaims it her destiny to slay the vampires who have suddenly infested Los Angeles. Like, really. Buffy requires some convincing, but eventually takes up the challenge, fighting off the vamps and their seductive leader Hauer, aided by perpetual guy-in-distress Perry. "Pee-wee" Reubens is unrecognizable and terribly amusing as the vampire king's sinister henchman, engaging in one of the longer death scenes of film history. Check out Cassandra (Wagner), Natalie Wood's daughter. **98m/C VHS, DVD.** Stephen (Steve) Root, Ben Affleck, Mark DeCarlo, Thomas Jane, Ricki Lake, Kristy Swanson, Donald Sutherland, Luke Perry, Paul (Peewee Herman) Reubens, Rutger Hauer, Michele Abrams, Randall Batinkoff, Hilary Swank, Paris Vaughan, David Arquette, Candy Clark, Natasha Gregson Wagner; ***D:*** Fran Rubel Kuzui; ***W:*** Joss Whedon; ***C:*** James Hayman; ***M:*** Carter Burwell.

Buford's Beach Bunnies **1992 (R)** Harry Buford has made a fortune selling barbecued rabbit sandwiches served by the sexiest waitresses around. Harry wants to leave the business to his son Jeeter—if Jeeter can overcome his overwhelming fear of women. So three of Harry's waitresses decide to show Jeeter a very good time. Lots of pretty girls in not much clothing. **90m/C VHS.** Jim Hanks, Rikki Brando, Monique Parent, Amy Page, Barrett Cooper, Ina Rogers, Charley Rossman, David Robinson; ***D:*** Mark Pirro; ***W:*** Mark Pirro.

Bug WOOF! *The Bug* **1975 (PG)** The city of Riverside is threatened with destruction after a massive earth tremor unleashes a super-race of ten-inch mega-cockroaches that belch fire, eat raw meat, and are virtually impervious to Raid. Produced by gimmick-king William Castle, who wanted to install windshield wiper-like devices under theatre seats that would brush against the patrons' feet as the cockroaches crawled across the screen; unfortunately, the idea was squashed flat. **100m/C VHS, DVD.** Bradford Dillman, Joanna Miles, Richard Gilliland, Jamie Smith-Jackson, Alan Fudge, Jesse Vint, Patty McCormack, Brendan Dillon Jr., Frederic Downs, William Castle; ***D:*** Jeannot Szwarc; ***W:*** Thomas Page, William Castle; ***C:*** Michael Hugo; ***M:*** Charles Fox.

Bug **2006 (R)** Girl (Judd) meets boy (Shannon). Girl and boy have one night stand. Boy goes insane and takes girl with him (maybe). Thriller based on a play and marketed as a horror film because its director is famous for "The Exorcist." If you like dark psychological movies shot almost entirely in one room where people talk and slowly lose their minds, this film is for you. If you were expecting a gory traditional horror movie, you will likely be disappointed. But you'll probably be somewhat happy that Ashley Judd briefly gets naked. **101m/C DVD.** *US* Ashley Judd, Michael Shannon, Harry Connick Jr., Lynn Collins, Brian F. O'Byrne; ***D:*** William Friedkin; ***W:*** Tracy Letts; ***C:*** Michael Grady; ***M:*** Brian Tyler.

Bug Buster **1999 (R)** The Griffins, dad (Kopell), mom (Lockhart) and daughter Shannon (Heigl) move to scenic Mountainview to flee the stress of city life. But they didn't bargain for the giant creature "unknown to science" that's attacking people and leaving giant bug larvae in 'em. Mutant insects overrun the town, leaving the survivors one last hope, in the form of ex-military man-turned-uberexterminator General George (Quaid). Plenty of gore and over-the-top acting, plus Scotty and Mr. Sulu, give this one late-night cult potential. **93m/C VHS, DVD.** Randy Quaid, Katherine Heigl, Meredith Salenger, Bernie Kopell, Anne Lockhart, George Takei, James Doohan, Ty O'Neal, Downtown Julie Brown, Brenda Doumani, David Lipper; ***D:*** Lorenzo Doumani; ***W:*** Malik Khoury; ***C:*** Hanania Baer; ***M:*** Sidney James.

Bugged! **1996 (PG-13)** Flesh-eating insects attack a beautiful homemaker and a group of bumbling exterminators are her only hope. **90m/C VHS, DVD.** Ronald K. Armstrong, Priscilla Basque, Jeff Lee, Derek C. Johnson, Billy Graham; ***D:*** Ronald K. Armstrong; ***W:*** Ronald K. Armstrong; ***C:*** S. Torriano Berry; ***M:*** Boris Elkis.

Bugles in the Afternoon **1952** Life in the army during Custer's last days, with a love triangle, revenge and the Little Big Horn for added spice. **85m/C VHS.** Ray Milland, Hugh Marlowe, Helena Carter, Forrest Tucker, Barton MacLane, George Reeves, James Millican, Gertrude Michael, Hugh Beaumont, Sheb Wooley; ***D:*** Roy Rowland; ***W:*** Daniel Mainwaring, Harry Brown; ***C:*** Wilfrid M. Cline; ***M:*** Dimitri Tiomkin.

Bugs **2003** A cop chasing a bad guy through an unfinished subway tunnel is eaten by a huge scorpion-like prehistoric insect whose nest he disturbed. FBI agent Matt Pollack (Sabato Jr.) and insect expert Emily Foster (Everhart) investigate, but they (along with a SWAT team) are soon trapped in the bug-infested tunnel. A Sci-Fi Channel original. **85m/C DVD.** Antonio Sabato Jr., Angie Everhart, R.H. Thomson, Karl Pruner, Duane Murray, Romano Orzari; ***D:*** Joseph Conti; ***W:*** Robinson Young, Patrick Doody, Chris Valenziano; ***C:*** Richard Wincenty; ***M:*** William T. Stromberg. **CABLE**

A Bug's Life **1998 (G)** Computer animated feature by Pixar, the makers of "Toy Story," takes a cutesy look into the world of insects. Flik (Foley) is an ant who must help defend his colony after he messes up a tribute to a bullying group of grasshoppers led by Hopper (Spacey). He recruits a crew of misfits from a flea circus, including a male ladybug with gender issues (Leary), a prissy stick bug (Pierce), and an obese caterpillar (Ranft). Together they form a plan to keep the grasshoppers away, but still must confront Hopper in order to ensure lasting peace. Amazing animation, from the blades of grass down to the facial expressions of the bugs, along with dozens of sight gags keep this family feature flying. Competed with fellow computer animated insect feature "Antz" on its release. **94m/C VHS, DVD.** ***D:*** John Lasseter, Andrew Stanton; ***W:*** Donald McEnery, Bob Shaw, Andrew Stanton, Joe Ranft; ***C:*** Sharon Calahan; ***M:*** Randy Newman; ***V:*** Dave Foley, Kevin Spacey, Julia Louis-Dreyfus, Phyllis Diller, Richard Kind, David Hyde Pierce, Joe Ranft, Denis Leary, Jonathan Harris, Madeline Kahn, Bonnie Hunt, Michael McShane, John Ratzenberger, Brad Garrett, Roddy McDowall, Edie McClurg, Hayden Panettiere, Alex Rocco, David Ossman.

Bugsy 1/2 **1991 (R)** Beatty is Benjamin "Bugsy" Siegel, the 40s gangster who built the Flamingo Hotel in Las Vegas when it was still a virtual desert, before it became a gambling mecca. Bening is perfect as Bugsy's moll, Virginia Hill, who inspired him to carry out his dream of building the Flamingo (which was her nickname). Beatty and Bening heat up the screen and their off-screen relationship was no different. Fans anticipated their seemingly imminent marriage almost as much as the release of this movie. Almost nothing mars this film which Toback adapted from a novel by Dean Jennings, "We Only Kill Each Other: The Life and Bad Times of Bugsy Siegel." **135m/C VHS, DVD.** Warren Beatty, Annette Bening, Harvey Keitel, Ben Kingsley, Elliott Gould, Joe Mantegna, Richard Sarafian, Bebe Neuwirth, Wendy Phillips, Robert Beltran, Bill Graham, Lewis Van Bergen, Debrah Farentino; ***D:*** Barry Levinson; ***W:*** James Toback; ***C:*** Allen Daviau; ***M:*** Ennio Morricone. Oscars '91: Art Dir./Set Dec., Costume Des.; Golden Globes '92: Film—Drama; L.A. Film Critics '91: Director (Levinson), Film, Screenplay; Natl. Bd. of Review '91: Actor (Beatty).

Bugsy Malone 1/2 **1976 (G)** Delightful musical features an all-children's cast highlighting this spoof of 1930s' gangster movies. **94m/C VHS, DVD.** *GB* Jodie Foster, Scott Baio, Florrie Augger, John Cassisi, Martin Lev; ***D:*** Alan Parker; ***W:*** Alan Parker; ***C:*** Peter Biziou; ***M:*** Paul Williams. British Acad. '76: Screenplay.

Bull Durham 1/2 **1988 (R)** Lovable American romantic comedy, dealing with a very minor minor-league team and three of its current constituents: aging baseball groupie Annie Savoy (Sarandon) who beds one player each season; a cocky, foolish new pitcher, Ebby Calvin "Nuke" LaLoosh (Robbins); and older, weary catcher Crash Davis (Costner), who's brought in to wise the rookie up. The scene in which Annie tries poetry out on the banal rookie (who has more earthly pleasures in mind) is a hoot. Highly acclaimed, the film sears with Sarandon and Costner's love scenes and some clever dialogue. **107m/C VHS, DVD.** Kevin Costner, Susan Sarandon, Tim Robbins, Trey Wilson, Robert Wuhl, Jenny Robertson; ***D:*** Ron Shelton; ***W:*** Ron Shelton; ***C:*** Bobby Byrne; ***M:*** Michael Convertino. L.A. Film Critics '88: Screenplay; N.Y. Film Critics '88: Screenplay; Natl. Soc. Film Critics '88: Screenplay; Writers Guild '88: Orig. Screenplay.

Bull of the West 1/2 **1971** Cattlemen battle for land in the wide open spaces of the old West. **90m/C VHS.** Charles Bronson, Lee J. Cobb, Brian Keith, George Kennedy, DeForest Kelley, Doug McClure, James Drury, Geraldine Brooks, Lois Nettleton, Ben Johnson, Gary Clarke; ***D:*** Jerry Hopper; ***W:*** Don Ingalls; ***C:*** Benjamin (Ben H.) Kline; ***M:*** Hal Mooney.

Bulldance *Forbidden Son* **1988** At a gymnastic school in Crete, a girl's obsession with Greek mythological ritual leads to murder. **105m/C VHS, DVD.** Lauren Hutton, Cliff DeYoung, Renee Estevez; ***D:*** Zelda Barron.

Bulldog Courage **1935** Young man is out to avenge his father's murder. **66m/B VHS, DVD.** Tim McCoy, Lois January, Joan Woodbury, John Elliott; ***D:*** Sam Newfield.

Bulldog Drummond 1/2 **1929** The Bulldog Drummond character, created by "Sapper" (Herman Cyril McNeile), underwent a number of different incarnations from 20s silents through the 40s, and even occassionally in the 50s and 60s. A suave ex-British officer (a precursor to the glib shaken-not-stirred gentleman-spy variety), Bulldog has been played by the likes of Colman, Ralph Richardson, and Tom Conway, among others. In this, the first installment in the long-standing series, a WWI vet, bored with civilian life, is enlisted by a beautiful woman to help her father in various adventures. **85m/B VHS.** Ronald Colman, Joan Bennett, Montagu Love, Lilyan Tashman, Lawrence Grant, Wilson Benge, Claud Allister, Adolph Milar, Charles Sellon, Tetsu Komai, Donald Novis; ***D:*** F. Richard Jones; ***W:*** Sidney Howard, Wallace Smith; ***C:*** George Barnes, Gregg Toland.

Bulldog Drummond at Bay **1937** Drummond searches for a group of foreign agents who are trying to steal the plans for a top-secret warplane. Poor British entry to the "Bulldog Drummond" series. **63m/B VHS, DVD.** *GB* John Lodge, Dorothy Mackaill, Victor Jory, Claud Allister, Hugh Miller; ***D:*** Norman Lee.

Bulldog Drummond Comes Back **1937** Drummond, aided by Colonel Nielson, rescues his fiancee from the hands of desperate kidnappers. **119m/B VHS, DVD.** John Howard, John Barrymore, Louise Campbell, Reginald Denny, Guy Standing; ***D:*** Louis King.

Bulldog Drummond Escapes **1937** Drummond, aided by his side-kick and valet, rescues a beautiful girl from spies. He then falls in love with her. **67m/B VHS, DVD.** Ray Milland, Heather Angel, Reginald Denny, Guy Standing, Porter Hall, E.E. Clive; ***D:*** James Hogan; ***W:*** Edward T. Lowe; ***C:*** Victor Milner.

Bulldog Drummond's Bride **1939** Ace detective Bulldog Drummond has to interrupt his honeymoon in order to pursue a gang of bank robbers across France and England. The last of the Bulldog Drummond film series. **69m/B VHS, DVD.** John Howard, Heather Angel, H.B. Warner, E.E. Clive, Reginald Denny, Eduardo Ciannelli, Elizabeth Patterson, John Sutton; ***D:*** James Hogan; ***W:*** Garnett Weston; ***C:*** Harry Fischbeck.

Bulldog Drummond's Peril **1938** Murder and robbery drag the adventurous Drummond away from his wedding and he pursues the villains until they are behind bars. One in the film series. **77m/B VHS, DVD.** John Barrymore, John Howard, Louise Campbell, Reginald Denny, E.E. Clive, Porter Hall; ***D:*** James Hogan.

Bulldog Drummond's Revenge 1/2 **1937** Bulldog's "Revenge" was made during the series' heyday and was the second to star Howard as Drummond; Barrymore revels in the character of Inspector Neilson of Scotland Yard, and Denny is Algy. In this typically fast-paced installment, suave sleuth Drummond stalks the master criminal responsible for stealing the formula to an explosive. **55m/B VHS, DVD.** John Howard, John Barrymore, Reginald Denny, Louise Campbell, Frank Puglia, Nydia Westman, Lucien Littlefield; ***D:*** Louis King.

Bulldog Drummond's Secret Police **1939** The 15th Drummond film, adapted from Herman Cyril McNeile's famed detective novels featuring a million-pound treasure stashed in the Drummond manor and the murderous endeavors to retrieve it. **54m/B VHS, DVD.** John Howard, Heather Angel, H.B. Warner, Reginald Denny, E.E. Clive, Leo G. Carroll; ***D:*** James Hogan; ***W:*** Garnett Weston; ***C:*** Merritt B. Gerstad.

Bulldog Edition **1936** Two newspapers engage in an all-out feud to be number one in the city, even going so far as to employ gangsters for purposes of sabotage. **57m/B VHS.** Ray Walker, Evalyn Knapp, Regis Toomey, Cy Kendall, William "Billy" Newell, Oscar Apfel, Betty Compson, Robert Warwick; ***D:*** Charles Lamont.

Bulldog Jack *Alias Bulldog Drummond* **1935** Fine entry in the series has Drummond's colleague battling it out with Richardson, the leader of gang of jewel thieves. **62m/B VHS.** *GB* Fay Wray, Jack Hulbert, Claude Hulbert, Ralph Richardson, Paul Graetz, Gibb McLaughlin; ***D:*** Walter Forde.

Bullet 1/2 **1994 (R)** Butch (Rourke) gets released from prison and immediately returns to his old drug and burglary ways on New York's mean streets. And he's got a score to settle with crazy drug kingpin Tank (Shakur). Has little to recommend it, except to those who like violence, with lackluster performances and a dull script. **96m/C VHS.** Mickey Rourke, Tupac Shakur, Ted Levine, Adrien Brody, John Enos; ***D:*** Julien Temple; ***W:*** Bruce Rubenstein; ***C:*** Crescenzo G.P. Notarile.

Bullet Code **1940** It's quick-shooting shenanigans when O'Brien chases a pack of angry rustlers off his neighbor's land. **56m/B VHS.** George O'Brien, Virginia Vale, Howard Hickman, Harry Woods, Charles "Slim" Whitaker; ***D:*** David Howard; ***W:*** Doris Schroeder.

Bullet Down Under *Signal One* **1994 (R)** Cop Atkins joins Australian police and gets involved with a crime syndicate and a female killer. **?m/C VHS.** *AU* Christopher Atkins, Mark "Jacko" Jackson, Virginia Hey; ***D:*** Rob Stewart; ***W:*** Karl Schiffman; ***C:*** Martin McGrath; ***M:*** Art Phillips.

A Bullet for Joey 1/2 **1955** Fifties red scare flick. American physicist Carl Macklin (Dolenz) is teaching in Montreal. Gangster Joey Victor (Raft) has been hired to kidnap Macklin, unaware that the commies are behind the snatch. A couple of murders bring Inspector Raoul Leduc (Robinson) onto the scene and he soon tags Joey, who turns patriotic when he discovers he's being used by reds. **85m/B DVD.** Edward G. Robinson, George Raft, Peter Van Eyck, Joseph (Joe) Vitale, George Dolenz, Audrey Trotter, Bill Bryant, John Cliff; ***D:*** Lewis Allen; ***W:*** Daniel Mainwaring, A(lbert) I(saac) Bezzerides; ***C:*** Harry Neuman; ***M:*** Harry Sukman.

Bullet for Sandoval **1970 (PG)** An ex-Confederate renegade loots and pillages the north Mexican countryside on his way to murder the grandfather of the woman he loves. **96m/C VHS, DVD.** *SP IT* Ernest Borgnine, George Hilton; ***D:*** Julio Buchs.

A Bullet for the General *Quien Sabe?* **1968** An American mercenary joins with rebel forces during the Mexican Revolution. **95m/C VHS, DVD.** *IT* Martine Beswick, Lou Castel, Gian Marie Volonte, Klaus Kinski; ***D:*** Damiano Damiani; ***W:*** Salvatore Laurani, Franco Solinas; ***C:*** Antonio Secchi; ***M:*** Luis Bacalov.

A Bullet in the Head *Die Xue Jie Tou* **1990** Violent (no surprise there) tale of friendship finds Frank (Cheung), Ben (Leung), and Paul (Lee) heading out of 1967 Hong Kong for Saigon, where they hope to make money selling contraband goods in the city. They wind up on the wrong side of the Vietnamese Army, steal a fortune in gold from a local crime lord, and end up the prisoners of the Viet Cong. There's betrayal and death and a final moral reckoning and—did we mention lots and lots of (over-the-top) violence? Chinese with subtitles. **85m/C VHS, DVD.** *HK* Tony Leung Chiu-Wai, Jacky Cheung, Waise Lee, Simon Yam, Fennie Yuen, Yolinda Yam, John Woo; ***D:*** John Woo; ***W:*** Janet Chun, Patrick Leung, John Woo; ***C:*** Wilson Chan, Ardy Lam, Chai Kittikum Som, Wing-Hung Wong; ***M:*** Romeo Diaz, James Wong.

A Bullet Is Waiting **1954** A diligent sheriff finally catches his man only to be trapped in a blinding snowstorm with the hardened criminal. **83m/C VHS.** Jean Simmons, Rory Calhoun, Stephen McNally, Brian Aherne; ***D:*** John Farrow.

Bullet to Beijing 1/2 *Len Deighton's Bullet to Beijing* **1995 (R)** After some 30 years, Caine returns to his role as intelligence agent Harry Palmer. Forced into retirement, Harry finds himself privately recruited by Russian businessman Alex (Gambon) to retrieve a stolen chemical weapon being transported on a train headed for China. Harry gets a little local help from Nicolai and Natasha (Connery and Sara) but treachery is all around. Follows "The Ipcress File," "Funeral in Berlin," and "Billion Dollar Brain"; based on the novel by Len Deighton. **105m/C VHS.** *GB* Michael Caine, Michael Gambon, Jason Connery, Mia Sara, Patrick Allen, Burt Kwouk, Michael Sarrazin, Sue Lloyd; ***D:*** George Mihalka; ***W:*** Harry Alan Towers; ***C:*** Terence Cole; ***M:*** Rick Wakeman.

Bulletproof **1988 (R)** An unstoppable ex-CIA agent battles to retrieve a high-tech nuclear tank from terrorist hands. **93m/C VHS, DVD.** Gary Busey, Darlanne Fluegel, Henry Silva, Thalmus Rasulala, L.Q. Jones, R.G. Armstrong, Rene Enriquez; ***D:*** Steve Carver; ***W:*** Steve Carver.

Bulletproof **1996 (R)** Desperately trying to be a male buddy bonding movie, "Bulletproof" fails miserably in every respect. Keats (Wayans) and Moses (Sandler) are an unlikely pair of car thieves with an equally unlikely bond to each other. Turns out Keats is really undercover cop Jack Carter, who is trying to infiltrate a drug cartel via his pal Moses. When the bust goes bad, Carter must bring Moses in unharmed to testify. Meanwhile the two rejuvenate their tainted relationship amid many homoerotic innuendoes. It's an embarrassment all around, especially for ex-Spike Lee cinematographer Dickerson on his first directing outing. **85m/C VHS, DVD, HD DVD.** Damon Wayans, Adam Sandler, James Caan, Kristen Wilson, James Farentino, Bill Nunn, Mark Roberts, Xander Berkeley, Allen Covert, Jeep Swenson, Larry McCoy; ***D:*** Ernest R. Dickerson; ***W:*** Joe Gayton, Lewis Colick; ***C:*** Steven Bernstein; ***M:*** Elmer Bernstein.

Bulletproof Heart *Killer* **1995 (R)** Mick (LaPaglia), a hit man with a severe case of burnout, is assigned to kill Fiona (Rogers), a beautiful socialite who, conveniently, wants to die. Despite being warned by his boss (Boyle) that Fiona has a habit of making men weak, he falls in love and can't bring himself to kill her. First-time director Malone takes great care to establish the noir look and feel, capitalizing on the all-in-one-night timeframe to raise the tension level. LaPaglia and Rogers turn in riveting performances, but can't stop the film from losing momentum when it becomes self-consciously melodramatic near the end. **95m/C VHS.** Anthony LaPaglia, Mimi Rogers, Peter Boyle, Matt Craven, Monica Schnarre, Joseph Maher; ***D:*** Mark Malone; ***W:*** Gordon Melbourne, Mark Malone; ***C:*** Tobias Schliessler; ***M:*** Graeme Coleman.

Bulletproof Monk 1/2 **2003 (PG-13)** Chow-Yun Fat is the monk with no name, chosen to protect The Scroll of the Ultimate, which gives the power to shape the world to the person who reads it aloud. Each monk can only protect the scroll for 60 years, so the new chosen one must be found. An unlikely candidate emerges in a New York pickpocket named Kar, after a chance meeting between the two. Adding a definite "Indiana Jones" vibe are Jade, a mysterious "bad girl" who catches Kar's eye, and the villains, a Nazi who tried to steal the scroll years earlier, and his icy granddaughter. Plot holes abound if you look too closely, but the action sequences are nicely timed to distract you from them, and Chow-Yun Fat's cool persona adds a touch of grace. Scott makes a nice first step from teen comedy doofus to action hero. **103m/C VHS, DVD, Blu-ray Disc.** *US* Chow Yun-Fat, Seann William Scott, Jaime (James) King, Karel Roden, Victoria Smurfit, Mako, Roger Yuan, Marcus Jean Pirae; ***D:*** Paul Hunter; ***W:*** Ethan Reiff, Cyrus Voris; ***C:*** Stefan Czapsky; ***M:*** Eric Serra.

Bullets or Ballots **1938** Tough New York cop goes undercover to join the mob in order to get the goods on them. Old-fashioned danger and intrigue follow, making for some action-packed thrills. **82m/B VHS, DVD.** Edward G. Robinson, Humphrey Bogart, Barton MacLane, Joan Blondell, Frank McHugh, Louise Beavers; ***D:*** William Keighley; ***W:*** Seton I. Miller; ***C:*** Hal Mohr.

Bullets over Broadway 1/2 **1994 (R)** Mediocre playwright David Shayne (Cusack, in the Allen role) talks up the virtues of artistic integrity to his pretentious hothouse contemporaries, then sells out to a gangster who agrees to finance his latest play provided his no-talent, brassy moll (Tilly) gets a part. And it's her hit-man bodyguard's (Palminteri) unexpected artistic touches that redeem Shayne's otherwise lousy work. Wiest as the eccentric diva, Ullman as the aging ingenue, Reiner as the Greenwich Village sage, and Broadbent as the increasingly plump matinee idol lead a collection of delicious, over-the-top performances in this smart and howlingly funny tribute to Jazz Age New York City that showcases Woody at his self-conscious best. **106m/C VHS, DVD.** Dianne Wiest, John Cusack, Jennifer Tilly, Rob Reiner, Chazz Palminteri, Tracey Ullman, Mary-Louise Parker, Joe (Johnny) Viterelli, Jack Warden, Jim Broadbent, Harvey Fierstein, Annie-Joe Edwards; ***D:*** Woody Allen; ***W:*** Woody Allen, Douglas McGrath; ***C:*** Carlo Di Palma. Oscars '94: Support. Actress (Wiest); Golden Globes '95: Support. Actress (Wiest); Ind. Spirit '95: Support. Actor (Palminteri), Support. Actress (Wiest); L.A. Film Critics '94: Support. Actress (Wiest); N.Y. Film Critics '94: Support. Actress (Wiest); Natl. Soc. Film Critics '94: Support. Actress (Wiest); Screen Actors Guild '94: Support. Actress (Wiest).

Bullfighter & the Lady 1/2 **1950** An American goes to Mexico to learn the fine art of bullfighting in order to impress a beautiful woman. **87m/B VHS.** Robert Stack, Gilbert Roland, Virginia Grey, Katy Jurado; ***D:*** Budd Boetticher.

Bullfighters **1945** Stan and Ollie are in hot pursuit of a dangerous criminal which leads them to Mexico where Stan winds up in a bull ring. **61m/B VHS.** Stan Laurel, Oliver Hardy, Margo Woode, Richard Lane; ***D:*** Malcolm St. Clair.

Bullies WOOF! **1986 (R)** A woodland-transplanted young man decides to fight back against an ornery mountain clan who have raped his mother, tortured his father, and beat up his girlfriend. Brutal and unpalatable. **96m/C VHS, DVD.** *CA* Janet-Laine Green, Dehl Berti, Stephen Hunter, Jonathan Crombie, Olivia D'Abo; ***D:*** Paul Lynch.

Bullitt **1968 (PG)** A detective assigned to protect a star witness for 48 hours senses danger; his worst fears are confirmed when his charge is murdered. Based on the novel, "Mute Witness" by Robert L. Pike, and featuring one of filmdom's most famous car chases. **105m/C VHS, DVD, Blu-ray Disc, HD DVD.** Steve McQueen, Robert Vaughn, Jacqueline Bisset, Don Gordon, Robert Duvall, Norman Fell, Simon Oakland; ***D:*** Peter Yates; ***W:*** Alan R. Trustman; ***C:*** William A. Fraker; ***M:*** Lalo Schifrin. Oscars '68: Film Editing, Natl. Film Reg. '07;; Natl. Soc. Film Critics '68: Cinematog.

Bullseye! 1/2 **1990 (PG-13)** Knockabout farce is a letdown considering the talents involved. Shady scientists (Moore and Caine) pursue/are pursued by lookalike con-artists (Caine and Moore), who are pursued in turn by international agents. Full of inside jokes and celebrity cameos, but nothing exceptional. **95m/C VHS.** Michael Caine, Roger Moore, Sally Kirkland, Patsy Kensit, Jenny Seagrove, John Cleese, Lee Patterson, Deborah Maria Moore, Mark Burns, Deborah Leng, Alexandra Pigg; ***Cameos:*** Lynn Nesbitt, Steffanie Pitt; ***D:*** Michael Winner; ***W:*** Michael Winner, Leslie Bricusse; ***M:*** John Du Prez.

Bullshot 1/2 **1983 (PG)** Zany English satire sends up the legendary Bulldog Drummond. In the face of mad professors, hapless heroines, devilish Huns and deadly enemies, our intrepid hero remains distinctly British. **84m/C VHS, DVD.** *GB* Alan Shearman, Diz White, Ron House, Frances Tomelty, Michael Aldridge, Ron Pember, Christopher Good; ***D:*** Dick Clement; ***M:*** John Du Prez.

Bullwhip **1958** A man falsely accused of murder saves himself from the hangman's noose by agreeing to a shotgun wedding. **80m/C VHS.** Guy Madison, Rhonda Fleming, James J. Griffith, Peter Adams; ***D:*** Harmon Jones.

Bully **2001** Director Clark continues his cinematic theme (announced in "Kids") of amoral and hedonistic young adults with this adaptation of the true story of a 1993 murder by a group of teens in Florida. Bobby (Stahl) is a dominating scumbag who pushes his best friend Marty (Renfro) around and pressures him into unwanted sexual and narcotic experimentation. When Marty meets and begins dating Lisa (Miner), Bobby forces himself into their sexual encounters. After Bobby rapes Lisa's friend Ali (Phillips), Lisa decides that the only solution is to kill Bobby. Inexperienced in such things, the homicidal posse gets some advice from a hit man (Fitzpatrick) who's barely older than they are. Filling the screen with graphic scenes of drug use and joyless sex, Clark doesn't seem to have any message other than "Look how bad these kids are. Now look at them naked." No psychological depth is given to the characters, although the actors do their best with what they've got. Also available in an R-rated version at 107 minutes. **113m/C VHS, DVD.** *US* Brad Renfro, Nick Stahl, Bijou Phillips, Rachel Miner, Michael Pitt, Kelli Garner, Daniel Franzese, Leo Fitzpatrick; ***Cameos:*** Larry Clark; ***D:*** Larry Clark; ***W:*** Zachary Long, Roger Pullis; ***C:*** Steve Gainer.

Bulworth **1998 (R)** No-holds barred look at the political process. Senator John Jay Bulworth (Beatty), bored and disillusioned by the banality of his own political career, hires a hitman to end his misery. During his last days on earth fufilling re-election duties, and with nothing to loose, he starts spewing the truth about politics and big business, much to the dismay of his constituents and assistants. Morphing into a hip-hop political phrophet, he becomes entranced and invigorated by beautiful South Central resident Nina (Berry). Beatty (in an engaging and funny performance) tackles his fiery subject matter of dwindling racial harmony and corporate deceit with a brazen and winning sense of humor lost in contemporary films. Fine script and enjoyable supporting performances by Platt as Bulworth's panic-stricken aide and Cheadle as an enterprising drug lord. **107m/C VHS, DVD.** Warren Beatty, Halle Berry, Oliver Platt, Paul Sorvino, Don Cheadle, Jack Warden, Christine Baranski, Isaiah Washington IV, Joshua Malina, Richard Sarafian, Amiri Baraka, Sean Astin, Laurie Metcalf, Wendell Pierce, Michele Morgan, Ariyan Johnson, Graham Beckel, Nora Dunn, Jackie Gayle; ***D:*** Warren Beatty; ***W:*** Jeremy Pikser, Warren Beatty; ***C:*** Vittorio Storaro; ***M:*** Ennio Morricone. L.A. Film Critics '98: Screenplay.

The Bumblebee Flies Anyway 1/2 **1998 (PG-13)** Amnesiac Barney Snow (Wood) is residing at a facility where all the other youths are terminally ill. As the doctors try to help Barney remember his past, Barney and the other patients go through the usual bonding rituals. Ordinary story at least has some winning performers to get past the maudlin aspects. Based on the novel by Robert Cormier. **95m/C VHS, DVD.** Elijah Wood, Janeane Garofalo, Rachael Leigh Cook, Roger Rees, Joe Perrino, George Gore III, Chris Petrizzo; ***D:*** Martin Duffy; ***W:*** Jennifer Sarja; ***C:*** Stephen Kazmierski; ***M:*** Christopher Tyng.

Bummer WOOF! **1973 (R)** Rock band's wild party turns into tragedy when the bass player goes too far with two groupies. It's a bad scene, man. **90m/C VHS, DVD.** Kipp Whitman, Dennis Burkley, Carol Speed, Connie Strickland; ***D:*** William Allen Castleman; ***W:*** Alvin L. Fast.

Bums **1993** Sergeant Andrew Holloman is a military officer in search of his long lost brother. It turns out his brother was homeless and is now dead at the hands of a skid row killer. Holloman recruits a platoon of other homeless people to help him track the killer but what he discovers is a multimillion conspiracy behind the murders. **94m/C VHS.** Christopher McDonald, Haskell Phillips, Dawn Evans; ***D:*** Andy Galler; ***W:*** Pat Allee, Ben Hurst.

Bunco **1977** Two policemen working for the Los Angeles Police Department's Bunco Squad discover a college for con artists complete with tape-recorded lessons and on-the-job training. **60m/C VHS.** Tom

Selleck, Robert Urich, Donna Mills, Will Geer, Arte Johnson, Alan Feinstein, James Hampton, Michael Sacks, Bobby Van, Diana Scarwid, Kenneth Mars; ***D:*** Alexander Singer.

Bundle of Joy 1/2 **1956** Salesgirl who saves an infant from falling off the steps of a foundling home is mistaken for the child's mother. Remake of 1939's "Bachelor Mother." ♫ Bundle of Joy; I Never Felt This Way Before; Lullaby in Blue; Worry About Tomorrow; All About Love; Someday Soon; What's So Good About Morning?; You're Perfect In Every Department. **98m/C VHS.** Debbie Reynolds, Eddie Fisher, Adolphe Menjou; ***D:*** Norman Taurog.

Bundy: A Legacy of Evil WOOF! *Bundy: An American Icon* **2008 (R)** Limp, low-budget serial killer flick hits all the usual points about Bundy's life of crime, which marginally improves when Ted gets to killing. The subsequent capture, trial, and Bundy's imprisonment are equally dull. **92m/C DVD.** Corin "Corky" Nemec, Jen Nikolaisen, David DeLuise, Shannon Pierce, Kane Hodder; ***D:*** Michael Feifer; ***C:*** Roberto Schein; ***M:*** Andres Boulton. **VIDEO**

Bunny Whipped **2006 (R)** Where's a killer rabbit when you need one? Bob (Powell) is looking to change his life and finds it when rapper Cracker Jack is murdered. Bob transforms himself into a cartoonish vigilante ("The Whip") and the media attention gets Bob a call from ex-girlfriend Ann (Adams), an animal rights activist, who wants Bob's help in saving some lab rabbits. But his rapper case doesn't go away as it seems Bob's suspect, rival rapper Kenny Kent (Alonso), doesn't want this goof poking into his business. Just all-around lame-but gets a bone for having honey Adams in the cast. **91m/C DVD.** Esteban Louis Powell, Joey Lauren Adams, Laz Alonso, Rebecca Gayheart, Amanda Noret, Brande Roderick; ***D:*** Rafael Riera; ***W:*** Rafael Riera; ***C:*** Bob Brill; ***M:*** Jessika Zen. **VIDEO**

A Bunny's Tale **1985** The story of Gloria Steinem's undercover journey into the Playboy Club as a fledgling journalist. It is here that she discovered her dedication as a feminist. Based on the book by Steinem. **97m/C VHS.** Kirstie Alley, Cotter Smith, Deborah Van Valkenburgh, Joanna Kerns, Delta Burke, Diana Scarwid; ***D:*** Karen Arthur.

Buona Sera, Mrs. Campbell 1/2 **1968** The lovely Lollobrigida and some fast-paced plot moves are the main highlights of this comedy. Mrs. Campbell convinced her three American WWII lovers that each of them had fathered her daughter. All three have supported mother and child through the years, unbeknowst to each other and their wives. When their 20-year reunion brings them back to Italy, Mrs. Campbell must do some fast-thinking and some quick-stepping to keep everyone happy. **113m/C VHS.** Gina Lollobrigida, Shelley Winters, Phil Silvers, Peter Lawford, Telly Savalas, Lee Grant, Janet Margolin, Marian Moses; ***D:*** Melvin Frank.

The 'Burbs 1/2 **1989 (PG)** A tepid satire about suburbanites suspecting their creepy new neighbors of murderous activities. Well-designed and sharp, but light on story. **101m/C VHS, DVD.** Tom Hanks, Carrie Fisher, Ric(k) Ducommun, Corey Feldman, Brother Theodore, Bruce Dern, Gale Gordon, Courtney Gains; ***D:*** Joe Dante; ***W:*** Dana Olsen; ***C:*** Robert M. Stevens; ***M:*** Jerry Goldsmith.

Burden of Dreams 1/2 **1982** The landmark documentary chronicling the berserk circumstances behind the scenes of Werner Herzog's epic "Fitzcarraldo." Stuck in the Peruvian jungles, the film crew was subjected to every disaster imaginable while executing Herzog's vision, including disease, horrendous accident, warring local tribes and the megalomaniacal director himself. Considered better than "Fitzcarraldo," although both films discuss a man's obsession. **94m/C VHS, DVD.** Klaus Kinski, Mick Jagger, Jason Robards Jr., Werner Herzog; ***D:*** Les Blank.

Bureau of Missing Persons 1/2 **1933** Comedy-drama about big-city bureau of missing persons, in which the hardened Stone is in charge. O'Brien plays a tough cop who is transferred to the bureau and Davis stars as the mystery woman with whom he gets involved. Although fast-paced and intriguing, the film is somewhat confusing and never stays in one direction for very long. **75m/B VHS.** Bette Davis, Lewis Stone, Pat O'Brien, Glenda Farrell, Allen Jenkins, Ruth Donnelly, Hugh Herbert; ***D:*** Roy Del Ruth; ***W:*** Robert Presnell Sr.; ***C:*** Barney McGill; ***M:*** Bernhard Kaun.

Burglar **1987 (R)** A cat burglar moves to the right side of the law when she tries to solve a murder case. Whoopi's always a treat, but this movie's best forgotten; Goldberg's fans should watch "Jumpin' Jack Flash" again instead. Co-star Goldthwait elevates the comedic level a bit. **103m/C VHS, DVD.** Whoopi Goldberg, Bob(cat) Goldthwait, Lesley Ann Warren, John Goodman, G.W. Bailey, James Handy, Anne DeSalvo; ***D:*** Hugh Wilson; ***W:*** Hugh Wilson; ***C:*** William A. Fraker; ***M:*** Sylvester Levay, Bernard Edwards.

Burglar *Vzlomschik* **1987** Not to be confused with the Whoopi Goldberg vehicle, this Russian film relates a story no less American than apple pie and teenage angst. Senka and would-be punk star Kostya are two neglected and disaffected brothers whose father is a drunken womanizer best known for absentee paternalism. When Howmuch, a serious heavy metalloid, pressures Kostya to steal a synthesizer, brother Senka steps in to steal the Community Center's property himself. In Russian with English subtitles, the solid performances hold their own against the heavy musical content. **89m/C VHS, DVD.** *RU* Konstantin Kinchev, Oleg Yelykomov; ***D:*** Valery Orgorodnikov.

Burial Ground **1985** A classically grisly splatter film in which the hungry dead rise and proceed to kill the weekend denizens of an isolated aristocratic mansion. **85m/C VHS, DVD.** Karen Well, Peter Bark; ***D:*** Andrea Bianchi.

Burial of the Rats 1/2 *Roger Corman Presents Burial of the Rats; Bram Stoker's Burial of the Rats* **1995 (R)** Based on a short story by Bram Stoker, this cable campiness features young Bram (Alber) himself being kidnapped while traveling in Eastern Europe. He's taken to the "Queen of Vermin" (Barbeau), who heads a bloodthirsty cult that hate men, worship rats, and live by violence. Fortunately, the Queen decides to spare Bram so he can write of their exploits and he falls for the fleshy charms of rat-woman Madeleine (Ford). **85m/C VHS, DVD.** Adrienne Barbeau, Maria Ford, Kevin Alber; ***D:*** Dan Golden.

Buried **2010** Paul Conroy (Reynolds) is a civilian truck driver whose convoy is ambushed by insurgents in Iraq. He's kidnapped, buried alive, and held for ransom. Conroy has a lighter, a pen, and a cell phone to contact the outside world (with his captors able to contact him) and finds neither his employer nor the State Department is willing to help. **93m/C DVD.** *SP* Ryan Reynolds, Stephen Tobolowsky, Samantha Mathis, Erik Palladino, Robert Paterson, Jose Luis Garcia-Perez; ***D:*** Rodrigo Cortes; ***W:*** Chris Sparling; ***C:*** Eduard Grau; ***M:*** Victor Reyes.

Buried Alive **1939** A man is sent to prison on trumped up charges. Only the prison nurse believes he is innocent as a crooked politician strives to keep him behind bars. **74m/B DVD.** Beverly Roberts, Robert Wilcox, George Pembroke, Ted Osborn, Paul McVey, Alden Chase; ***D:*** Victor Halperin.

Buried Alive **1981** Director d'Amato reaps his finest gore-fest to date, incorporating the well-established taxidermist gone loony motif in his repertoire of appalling bad taste. Not for the squeamish, this bloodier-than-thou spaghetti spooker is chock full of necrophilia, cannibalism, and more. **90m/C VHS, DVD.** *IT* Kieran Canter, Cinzia Monreale, Franca Stoppi; ***D:*** Joe D'Amato.

Buried Alive **1989 (R)** Once Ravenscroft Hall was an asylum for the incurably insane. Now, the isolated mansion is a school for troubled teenage girls, run by a charismatic psychiatrist. Captivated by his charm, a young woman joins the staff. Soon, she is tormented by nightmare visions of the long-dead victims of a nameless killer. When the students begin to disappear, she realizes he still lives...and she may be his next victim. Carradine's last role. **97m/C VHS, DVD.** Robert Vaughn, Donald Pleasence, Karen Witter, John Carradine, Ginger Lynn Allen; ***D:*** Gerard Kikoine.

Buried Alive 1/2 **1990 (PG-13)** One of the many horror flicks entitled "Buried Alive," this one is not bad, injecting a bit of levity into the time-worn genre. Schemestress Leigh and her paramour poison her husband. Or so they think, only to discover that he's not quite dead. **93m/C VHS.** Tim Matheson, Jennifer Jason Leigh, William Atherton, Hoyt Axton; ***D:*** Frank Darabont; ***W:*** Mark Patrick Carducci, Jake Clesi; ***M:*** Michel Colombier. **CABLE**

Buried Alive 2 1/2 **1997 (PG-13)** Randy (Caffrey) wants to get rid of rich wife Laura (Sheedy) so he and girlfriend Roxanne (Needham) can enjoy her cash. So he slips some blowfish venom into her wine and buries her. But the venom only simulated death and after clawing her way out of the grave, Laura is one angry gal. Clint Goodman (Matheson), who was buried in the first movie, shows up to help out the wronged wife. **92m/C VHS.** Ally Sheedy, Stephen Caffrey, Tracey Needham, Tim Matheson; ***D:*** Tim Matheson; ***W:*** Walter Klenhard. **CABLE**

Burke & Wills 1/2 **1985 (PG-13)** A lush, big-budgeted true story of the two men who first crossed Australia on foot, and explored its central region. Popular Australian film. **120m/C VHS.** *AU* Jack Thompson, Nigel Havers, Greta Scacchi, Ralph Cotterill, Drew Forsythe, Chris Haywood, Matthew Fargher; ***D:*** Graeme Clifford; ***W:*** Michael Thomas; ***C:*** Russell Boyd; ***M:*** Peter Sculthorpe.

Burlesque on Carmen **1916** A silent pastiche of the Bizet opera, with Charlie as Don Schmose. Interesting early work. **30m/B VHS, DVD.** Charlie Chaplin, Ben Turpin, Edna Purviance; ***D:*** Charlie Chaplin; ***W:*** Charlie Chaplin.

Burma Convoy 1/2 **1941** A truck driver on the Burma Road—a dangerous stretch of roadway in Asia used to hall munitions during World War II—sets out to uncover the mystery of his younger brother's death. **72m/B VHS.** Charles Bickford, Evelyn Ankers, Frank Albertson, Cecil Kellaway, Willie Fung, Keye Luke; ***D:*** Noel Mason Smith; ***W:*** Roy Chanslor, Stanley Rubin.

The Burmese Harp *Harp of Burma; Birumano Tategoto* **1956** At the end of WWII, a Japanese soldier is spiritually traumatized and becomes obsessed with burying the masses of war casualties. A searing, acclaimed anti-war statement, in Japanese with English subtitles. Remade by Ichikawa in 1985. **115m/B VHS, DVD.** *JP* Shoji Yasui, Rentaro Mikuni, Tatsuya Mihashi, Tanie Kitabayashi, Yunosuke Ito; ***D:*** Kon Ichikawa; ***W:*** Natto Wada; ***C:*** Minoru Yokoyama; ***M:*** Akira Ifukube.

Burn! 1/2 *Quemimada!* **1970 (PG)** An Italian-made indictment of imperialist control by guerrilla-filmmaker Pontecorvo, depicting the efforts of a 19th century British ambassador to put down a slave revolt on a Portuguese-run Caribbean island. Great Brando performance. **112m/C VHS, DVD.** *FR IT* Marlon Brando, Evarist Marquez, Renato Salvatori, Norman Hill, Dana Ghia, Giampiero Albertini, Tom Lyons; ***D:*** Gillo Pontecorvo; ***W:*** Giorgio Arlorio, Franco Solinas; ***C:*** Marcello Gatti; ***M:*** Ennio Morricone.

Burn After Reading 1/2 **2008 (R)** Two greedy and none-too-smart gym employees (Pitt, McDormand) attempt to sell a disk containing the memoirs of an ousted CIA agent (Malkovich) with unpleasant consequences. Swinton and Clooney, who are re-teamed after "Michael Clayton," play the agent's unhappy wife and her scheming lover. Swinton looks like she's still in that movie, while Clooney gets into Coen brothers mode effortlessly and is a highlight. Convoluted plot takes a back seat to excellent dialogue and pleasantly over the top characters. Pitt looks like he's having a blast with his dim-bulb workout junkie. Simmons and Jenkins shine in limited roles as bosses trying to figure out what the hell is going on. **96m/C DVD, Blu-ray Disc.** *US* Brad Pitt, George Clooney, John Malkovich, Tilda Swinton, Frances McDormand, Richard Jenkins, J.K. Simmons, David Rasche, Olek Krupa, Jeffrey DeMunn, Elizabeth Marvel; ***D:*** Joel Coen, Ethan Coen; ***W:*** Joel Coen, Ethan Coen; ***C:*** Emmanuel Lubezki; ***M:*** Carter Burwell.

Burn Witch, Burn! *Night of the Eagle* **1962** A college professor proudly finds himself rapidly rising in his profession. His pride turns to horror though when he discovers that his success is not due to his own abilities, but to the efforts of his witchcraft practicing wife. Excellent, atmospheric horror with a genuinely suspenseful climax. **87m/B VHS.** *GB* Peter Wyngarde, Janet Blair, Margaret Johnston, Anthony Nicholls, Colin Gordon, Kathleen Byron, Reginald Beckwith, Jessica Dunning, Norman Bird, Judith Scott; ***D:*** Sidney Hayers; ***W:*** Richard Matheson, Charles Beaumont, George L. Baxt; ***C:*** Reg Wyer.

Burndown **1989 (R)** Victims of a serial killer in a town with a large nuclear reactor are themselves radioactive, which leads the Police Chief and a beautiful reporter to the truth and the hidden conspiracy. **97m/C VHS.** Cathy Moriarty, Peter Firth; ***D:*** James Allen.

The Burning **1982 (R)** Story of macabre revenge set in the dark woods of a seemingly innocent summer camp. **90m/C VHS, DVD.** Brian Matthews, Leah Ayres, Brian Backer, Larry Joshua, Jason Alexander, Ned Eisenberg, Garrick Glenn, Carolyn Houlihan, Fisher Stevens, Lou David, Holly Hunter; ***D:*** Tony Maylam; ***W:*** Bob Weinstein, Peter Lawrence; ***C:*** Harvey Harrison; ***M:*** Rick Wakeman.

The Burning Bed 1/2 **1985** Dramatic expose (based on a true story) about wife-beating. Fawcett garnered accolades for her performance as the battered wife who couldn't take it anymore. Highly acclaimed and Emmy-nominated. **95m/C VHS, DVD.** Farrah Fawcett, Paul LeMat, Penelope Milford, Richard Masur; ***D:*** Robert Greenwald. **TV**

The Burning Court 1/2 *La Chambre Ardente* **1962** Unusual horror film involving occultism, possession, and family curses. Dubbed into English. Based on a story by John Dickson Carr. **102m/C VHS.** *IT FR* Nadja Tiller, Jean-Claude Brialy, Edith Scob, Perette Pradier, Claude Rich; ***D:*** Julien Duvivier.

Burning Daylight **1928** Alaskan real estate baron loses everything to a group of San Francisco sharpies. Based on the story by Jack London. **72m/B VHS.** Milton Sills, Arthur Stone, Doris Kenyon, Guinn "Big Boy" Williams; ***D:*** Richard A. Rowland.

Burning Down the House **2001 (R)** Desperate director Jake Selling (Savage) has his next story all lined up but no money to pursue his ambitions until he crosses paths with B-movie producer Arnie Green (Wilder). They figure out the only way to raise money is to burn down Jake's house for the insurance. Only Jake's ex—actress Brenda Goodman (Baron)—catches the scam on film and demands to be in the movie. And the insurance investigator turns out to be a wannabe actor as well whom they may also have to placate. **84m/C VHS, DVD.** John Savage, James Wilder, Joanne Baron, William Atherton, Arye Gross, Rene Auberjonois, Orson Bean, John Ales, C. Thomas Howell, Luca Bercovici, David Keith; ***Cameos:*** Mick Fleetwood; ***D:*** Philippe Mora; ***W:*** Michael Cole Dinelli; ***C:*** Dan Gillham; ***M:*** Jeff Marsh.

The Burning Hills 1/2 **1956** Unexceptional cow flick based on a Louis L'Amour novel. Hunter hides from cattle thieves in a barn and, eventually, in the arms of a half-breed Mexican girl (Wood). Tedious and unsurprising. **94m/C VHS.** Tab Hunter, Natalie Wood, Skip Homeier, Eduard Franz; ***D:*** Stuart Heisler.

Burning Life 1/2 **1994** In the eastern states of a recently reunified Germany, Anna and Lisa become punk folk heroines after a series of bank robberies. One of the most unbelievable aspects is that these not-too-bright amateurs continue to elude the efficient East German police, who are made to look like bumpkins. German with subtitles. **105m/C DVD.** *GE* Anna Thalbach, Maria Schrader, Max Tidof, Jaecki Schwarz, Andreas Hoppe, Dani Levy; ***D:*** Peter Welz; ***W:*** Stefan Kolditz; ***C:*** Michael Schaufert; ***M:*** Neil Quinton.

The Burning Plain 1/2 **2008 (R)** An elaborate mishmash of stories and characters that covers 20-some years and travels between Oregon and New Mexico before the inevitable reveal. Married New Mexico mom Gina (Basinger) has an affair with married father Nick (de Almeida) that ends in their deaths and haunts both their families. Twenty years later, unhappy, promiscuous Sylvia (Theron) is being pestered by Carlos (Yazpik) about the past. Then there's the plight of young Maria (La), whose father has just died and who was—not so coincidentally—a friend of Carlos' who takes Maria in until they can find her other relatives. **111m/C DVD.** *US* Charlize Theron, Kim Basinger, Joaquim de Almeida, Danny Pino, Jose Maria Yazpik, Brett Cullen, J.D. Pardo, John Corbett, Robin Tunney, Rachel Ticotin, Tessa Ia, Jennifer Lawrence; ***D:*** Guillermo Arriaga; ***W:*** Guillermo Arriaga; ***C:*** Robert Elswit; ***M:*** Hans Zimmer, Omar Rodrguez Lopez.

Burning Rage 🦴 **1984** A blazing, abandoned coal mine threatens to wreak havoc in the Appalachians. The government sends geologist Mandrell to help prevent a disaster. **100m/C VHS, DVD.** Barbara Mandrell, Tom Wopat, Bert Remsen, John Pleshette, Carol Kane, Eddie Albert; ***D:*** Gilbert Cates. **TV**

The Burning Season 🦴🦴🦴 **1994** In one of his last performances, Julia inspires as Chico Mendes, a socialist union leader who fought to protect the homes and land of Brazilian peasants in the western Amazon rain forest. With Mendes' help the peasants form a union and struggle to prevent the building of a road that will provide easy access to forest land for speculators and cattlemen. Naturally, they are violently opposed by corruption-ridden capitalist powers in the government. Julia provides a haunting portrayal of the heroic figure who was assassinated in 1990. Based in part on the book by Andrew Revkin. Filmed on location in Mexico. **123m/C VHS.** Raul Julia, Edward James Olmos, Sonia Braga, Luis Guzman, Nigel Havers, Kamala Dawson, Tomas Milian, Esai Morales, Tony Plana, Carmen Argenziano; ***D:*** John Frankenheimer; ***W:*** William Mastrosimone, Michael Tolkin, Ron Hutchinson; ***M:*** Gary Chang. **CABLE**

Burning Secret 🦴🦴 *Brennendes Geheimnis* **1989 (PG)** After WWI, a widow in Austria (Dunaway) meets a baron (Brandauer) who has befriended her son. Mutual seduction ensues but the sparks don't fly. Adapted from Stefan Zweig story. **107m/C VHS.** *GB* Faye Dunaway, Klaus Maria Brandauer, Ian Richardson, David Eberts; ***D:*** Andrew Birkin; ***W:*** Andrew Birkin; ***M:*** Hans Zimmer.

Burnt by the Sun 🦴🦴🦴 *Outomlionnye Solntsem* **1994 (R)** Masterful evocation of '30s Stalinist Russia, covering a day in the life of Soviet revolutionary hero Serguei (Mikhalkov) and his family, far from the purges and gulags. Enjoying a country existence with wife Moroussia (Dapkounaite) and daughter Nadia (played by Mikhalkov's daughter), his idyll is disturbed by mystery man Dimitri (Menchikov), and Serguei realizes their fates are bound by the difference between their Communist dreams and reality. Symbolism is a little heavy but film delivers emotionally. Russian with subtitles. **134m/C VHS, DVD.** *RU FR* Nikita Mikhalkov, Ingeborga Dapkounaite, Oleg Menshikov, Nadia Mikhalkov, Andre Oumansky, Viatcheslav Tikhonov, Svetlana Krioutchkova, Vladimir Ilyine; ***D:*** Nikita Mikhalkov; ***W:*** Nikita Mikhalkov, Rustam Ibragimbekov; ***C:*** Vilen Kalyuta; ***M:*** Eduard Artemyev. Oscars '94: Foreign Film; Cannes '94: Grand Jury Prize.

Burnt Money 🦴🦴 *Plata Quemada* **2000** Based on a 1965 true crime story set in Argentina and Uruguay. Twentysomething lovers Nene (Sbaraglia) and the unstable Angel (Noriega), nicknamed the Twins, are stickup men hired by veteran criminal Fontana (Bartis) for a big money heist in Buenos Aires. They're paired with young, pill-popping getaway driver Cuervo (Echarri) but things go wrong when the Twins become cop killers. The foursome flee with the money to a squalid apartment in Montevideo where they wait for new identity papers. The young trio begin to unravel amidst a lot of drinking, drugs (who knew cocaine was so popular in the '60s?), and boredom, leading to a lethal confrontation with authorities. Title refers to what happens to the heist cash. Spanish with subtitles. **125m/C VHS, DVD.** *AR* Leonardo Sbaraglia, Eduardo Noriega, Ricardo Bartis, Pablo Echarri, Leticia Bredice, Dolores Fonzi; ***D:*** Marcelo Pineyro; ***W:*** Marcelo Figueras; ***C:*** Alfredo Mayo; ***M:*** Osvaldo Montes.

Burnt Offerings 🦴🦴 **1976 (PG)** A family rents an old mansion for the summer and they become affected by evil forces that possess the house. Based on the novel by Robert Marasco. **116m/C VHS, DVD.** Oliver Reed, Karen Black, Bette Davis, Burgess Meredith; ***D:*** Dan Curtis; ***W:*** Dan Curtis.

Burnzy's Last Call 🦴🦴 **1995** Sal (McCaffrey) tends bar at Eppy's, a Manhattan joint where Burnzy (Gray), a retired newspaperman, is a regular. The film is an ensemble piece that focuses on the various colorful characters who drift in and out of the place. **88m/C VHS, DVD.** Sam Gray, David Johansen, James McCaffrey, Christopher Noth, Sherry Stringfield, Roger Robinson, Tony Todd; ***D:*** Michael de Avila; ***W:*** George Gilmore; ***C:*** Scott St. John.

Bury Me an Angel 🦴 **1971** A female biker sets out to seek revenge against the men who killed her brother. **85m/C VHS.** Dixie Peabody, Terry Mace, Clyde Ventura, Dan Haggerty, Stephen Whittaker, Gary Littlejohn, Dave Atkins, Marie Denn, Alan DeWitt; ***D:*** Barbara Peeters; ***C:*** Sven Walnum; ***M:*** Richard Hieronymous.

Bury Me Not on the Lone Prairie 🦴🦴 **1941** When his brother is murdered in cold blood by claim jumpers, mining engineer Brown goes to avenge the dead. Based on a story by Sherman Lowe. **57m/B VHS, DVD.** Johnny Mack Brown, Fuzzy Knight, Nell O'Day, Frank O'Connor, Kermit Maynard; ***D:*** Ray Taylor; ***W:*** Sherman Lowe, Victor McLeod.

Bury My Heart at Wounded Knee 🦴🦴 1/2 **2007** Loose adaptation of the 1970 Dee Brown book. This oversimplified version concentrates on the experiences of the Sioux from Little Big Horn to the Wounded Knee massacre. It follows Charles Eastman (Beach)—who's not in Brown's book, by the way—who grew up among the Sioux (he's a quarter white on his mother's side) until his Christianized father claims him. Eastman is educated in the East and becomes a doctor at Pine Ridge, aided by his white wife (Paquin). The story is given over to various confrontations and philosophical differences. **?m/C DVD.** Adam Beach, Aidan Quinn, Anna Paquin, August Schellenberg, J.K. Simmons, Shawn Johnston, Gordon Tootoosis, Wes Studi, Eric Schweig, Colm Feore, Fred Dalton Thompson; ***D:*** Yves Simoneau; ***W:*** Daniel Giat; ***C:*** David Franco; ***M:*** George S. Clinton. **CABLE**

Bus Stop 🦴🦴🦴 *The Wrong Kind of Girl* **1956** Murray plays a naive cowboy who falls in love with Monroe, a barroom singer, and decides to marry her without her permission. Considered by many to be the finest performance by Marilyn Monroe; she sings "That Old Black Magic" in this one. Very funny with good performances by all. Based on the William Inge play. **96m/C VHS, DVD.** Marilyn Monroe, Arthur O'Connell, Hope Lange, Don Murray, Betty Field, Max (Casey Adams) Showalter, Hans Conried, Eileen Heckart; ***D:*** Joshua Logan; ***W:*** George Axelrod; ***C:*** Milton Krasner; ***M:*** Cyril Mockridge, Alfred Newman.

Bush Pilot 🦴 1/2 **1947** Red North (Willis) has his own small business as a bush pilot in the Canadian north. Then his vindictive half-brother Paul (La Rue) decides to muscle in and steal Red's routes (and maybe his girl as well). **60m/B VHS, DVD.** *CA* Austin Willis, Jack La Rue Jr., Rochelle Hudson; ***D:*** Sterling Campbell; ***W:*** Scott Darling.

The Bushbaby 🦴 1/2 **1970** The young Brooks is given a tiny bushbaby while visiting Africa with her father. Because of her pet she misses her ship home and finds herself with former servant Gossett, who agrees to take her to a family friend. Unfortunately, the authorities think he's kidnapped the girl and the two, along with the trouble-causing pet, are pursued by the police. Simple-minded kiddie fare. **100m/C VHS.** Margaret Brooks, Louis Gossett Jr., Donald Houston, Laurence Naismith, Marne Maitland, Geoffrey Bayldon, Jack (Gwyllam) Gwillim; ***D:*** John Trent.

The Busher 🦴 1/2 **1919** All-American pitcher's romance is interrupted by a gratuitous Mr. Moneybags. Minor-league conflict with little real hardball. **54m/B VHS.** Charles Ray, Colleen Moore, John Gilbert, Margaret Livingston; ***D:*** Jerome Storm.

The Bushido Blade 🦴🦴 1/2 *The Bloody Bushido Blade* **1980** An action-packed samurai thriller of adventure and betrayal set in medieval Japan. **92m/C VHS, DVD.** *JP* Richard Boone, James Earl Jones, Frank Converse; ***D:*** Tom Kotani.

Bush's Brain 🦴🦴 **2004** Election year investigation of the role Karl Rove played in crafting Dubyah into a president. Yet another volley in the political documentary war of 2004. Interesting exploration of behind-the-scenes political dirty work. Though based largely on hearsay, film will surely outrage democrats everywhere. **80m/C VHS, DVD.** ***D:*** Michael Shoob, Joseph Mealey; ***C:*** Joseph Mealey; ***M:*** David Friedman, Michelle Shocked.

The Bushwackers 🦴 1/2 *The Rebel* **1952** Ireland plays a veteran of the Confederate army who wishes only to put his violent past behind him. He is forced to reconsider his vow when old-west bullies threaten his family. **70m/B VHS, DVD.** Dorothy Malone, John Ireland, Wayne Morris, Lawrence Tierney, Jack Elam, Lon Chaney Jr., Myrna Dell; ***D:*** Rod Amateau.

Bushwhacked 🦴🦴 1/2 *Tenderfoots; The Tenderfoot* **1995 (PG-13)** Crude, rude, dim-witted, kid-hating Max Grabelski (Stern) is falsely accused of murder and forced to become a fugitive. While not to be confused with Harrison Ford, he is mistaken for the leader of a group of Cub Scouts out on their maiden camping trip and soon finds himself in an unlikely partnership with the boys. Together they encounter everything from grizzly bears to whitewater rapids. Lighthearted, goofy comedy continues Stern's tendency toward kid-intensive, family-oriented fare in the "Rookie of the Year" vein. **85m/C VHS, DVD.** Daniel Stern, Jon Polito, Brad Sullivan, Ann Dowd, Anthony Heald, Tom Wood; ***D:*** Greg Beeman; ***W:*** Tommy Swerdlow, Michael Goldberg, John Jordan, Danny Byers; ***M:*** Bill Conti.

The Business 🦴🦴 **2005 (R)** The sunny, tacky setting makes this Cockney crime flick, set amid the conspicuous consumption of the 1980s, at least a little different though the plot is ordinary enough. Young Frankie (Dyer) heads to the criminal haven of Spain's Costa del Sol and gets a job driving for flashy Charlie (Hassan) and his psycho partner Sammy (Bell). Then Frankie starts running drugs for Charlie and multiple betrayals are set in motion. **92m/C DVD.** *GB* Danny Dyer, Tamer Hassan, Geoff Bell, Georgina Chapman, Linda Henry, Eddie Weber; ***D:*** Nick Love; ***W:*** Nick Love; ***C:*** Damian Bromley; ***M:*** Ivor Guest.

A Business Affair 🦴🦴 1/2 *D'Une Femme a L'Autre* **1993 (R)** Kate Swallow (the ravishing Bouquet), the neglected wife of tempermental author Alex Bolton (Pryce), begins an affair with his flamboyant American publisher Vanni Corso (Walken). While the men posture between themselves for her affections, Kate, who has literary aspirations, decides to strike out on her own. Based on the romantic triangle of British writers Barbara Skelton and Cyril Connolly and his publisher George Weidenfeld and taken from Skelton's memoirs "Tears Before Bedtime" and "Weep No More." **102m/C VHS, DVD.** Carole Bouquet, Jonathan Pryce, Christopher Walken, Sheila Hancock; ***D:*** Charlotte Brandstrom; ***W:*** William Stadiem; ***C:*** Willy Kurant; ***M:*** Didier Vasseur.

Business As Usual 🦴🦴 **1988 (PG)** A meek boutique manager in Liverpool defends a sexually harassed employee, is fired, fights back, and creates a national furor over her rights as a woman. **89m/C VHS.** Glenda Jackson, Cathy Tyson, John Thaw, Craig Charles, Eamon Boland; ***D:*** Lezli-Ann Barrett; ***W:*** Lezli-Ann Barrett; ***C:*** Ernest Vincze.

Business for Pleasure 🦴 1/2 **1996** Wealthy tycoon orchestrates a sexual triangle between himself, his closest assistant, and a beautiful exec in order to explore the wilder side of sex and fantasy. **97m/C VHS.** Gary Stretch, Joanna Pacula, Jeroen Krabbe, Caron Bernstein; ***D:*** Rafael Eisenman; ***W:*** Zalman King; ***C:*** Eagle Egilsson; ***M:*** George S. Clinton.

Business is Business 🦴 1/2 *Diary of a Hooker; Any Special Way* **1971** Verhoeven's first feature film (after his television work) is a sex comedy about a couple of prostitutes who are apartment neighbors in Amsterdam. Nel's got an abusive boyfriend she just can't shake despite the efforts of her friend Blonde Greet. BG decides they should become partners (she's got a lot of fetish clients) but she gets put-out when Nel finds a nice, boring guy who wants to marry her and take her out of the life. Especially since Blonde Greet's special guy is already hitched. A slight and surprisingly timid story considering Verhoeven's later work but everyone's gotta start somewhere. Dutch with subtitles. **89m/C DVD.** *NL* Ronnie Bierman, Sylvia De Leur, Piet Romer, Jules Hamel, Bernard Droog, Henk Molenberg, Albert Mol; ***D:*** Paul Verhoeven; ***W:*** Gerard Soeteman; ***C:*** Jan De Bont; ***M:*** Mulius Steffaro.

The Business of Fancydancing 🦴🦴 **2002** Seymour (Adams) is a gay Native American who has left the reservation, gone to college, and now uses his heritage to achieve literary fame as a poet. He hasn't been back to the rez in years but returns for the funeral of onetime friend Mouse (Kanim). Seymour's return is awkward as it triggers the frustrated resentment of another boyhood pal Aristotle (Tagaban) as well as a confrontation with his college girlfriend Agnes (St. John) who is now Aristotle's lover. **103m/C VHS, DVD.** *US* Evan Adams, Michelle St. John, Gene Tagaban, Swil Kanim, Rebecca Carroll, Cynthia Geary, Leo Rossi, Kevin Phillip, Elaine Miles; ***D:*** Sherman Alexie; ***W:*** Sherman Alexie; ***C:*** Holly Taylor.

The Business of Strangers 🦴🦴 **2001 (R)** Julie Styron (Channing) is a tough, middleaged executive for a software company who is having a bad day at an out-of-town meeting. She worries she's about to be fired and then fires her young assistant Paula (Stiles) for missing the meeting and ruining Julie's presentation. Instead, Julie gets a promotion and decides to rehire Paula after they diss men over drinks at the hotel bar. When Paula spots corporate headhunter Nick (Weller), she tells Julie that he raped a friend of hers and it's payback time. But since the two women have been playing mind games, is this the truth or not? **83m/C VHS, DVD.** *US* Stockard Channing, Julia Stiles, Frederick Weller, Marcus Giamatti; ***D:*** Patrick Stettner; ***W:*** Patrick Stettner; ***C:*** Teodoro Maniaci; ***M:*** Alexander Lasarenko.

B.U.S.T.E.D. 🦴🦴 *Everybody Loves Sunshine* **1999 (R)** Gangmates and cousins Terry (Goldie) and Ray (Goth) are just out of prison. Violent Terry is looking to re-take control from efficient Bernie (Bowie), who's been looking after the business. Ray decides he wants to go legit and falls for lovely Clare (Shelley). But Terry wants his coz with him and kidnaps Clare to force Ray's hand—a bad move since Ray decides love is thicker than blood. The leads are caricatures and American audiences will be hampered by the regional Brit slang but Bowie's cool intensity is worth watching. **97m/C VHS, DVD.** *GB* Clint Dyer, Sarah Shackleton, Goldie, Andrew Goth, David Bowie, Rachel Shelley; ***D:*** Andrew Goth; ***W:*** Andrew Goth; ***C:*** Julian Morson; ***M:*** Nicky Matthew.

Busted Up 🦴 **1986 (R)** A young, hard-luck urban street-fighter battles for the sake of his family and neighborhood against local crimelords. **93m/C VHS.** *CA* Irene Cara, Paul Coufos, Tony Rosato, Stan Shaw, Gordon Judges; ***D:*** Conrad Palmisano; ***M:*** Charles P. Barnett.

Buster 🦴🦴 1/2 **1988 (R)** The story of Buster Edwards, the one suspect in the 1963 Great Train Robbery who evaded being captured by police. Collins makes his screen debut as one of Britain's most infamous criminals. Collins also performs on the film's soundtrack, spawning two hit singles, "Two Hearts" and "Groovy Kind of Love." **102m/C VHS, DVD.** *GB* Phil Collins, Julie Walters, Larry Lamb, Stephanie Lawrence, Ellen Beaven, Michael Atwell, Ralph Brown, Christopher Ellison, Sheila Hancock, Martin Jarvis, Anthony Quayle; ***D:*** David Green; ***M:*** Anne Dudley.

Buster and Billie 🦴 1/2 **1974 (R)** Tragedy ensues when a popular high school student falls in love with the class tramp in rural Georgia in 1948. Serious, decently appointed period teen drama. **100m/C VHS.** Jan-Michael Vincent, Joan Goodfellow, Clifton James, Pamela Sue Martin, Robert Englund; ***D:*** Daniel Petrie.

Bustin' Loose **1981 (R)** A fast-talking ex-con reluctantly drives a bus load of misplaced kids and their keeper cross-country. **94m/C VHS, DVD.** Richard Pryor, Cicely Tyson, Robert Christian, George Coe, Bill Quinn; ***D:*** Oz Scott; ***W:*** Lonnie Elder III, Richard Pryor; ***C:*** Dennis Dalzell; ***M:*** Roberta Flack, Mark Davis.

Busting **1/2 1974 (R)** Gould and Blake play a pair of slightly off-the-wall L.A. cops. The pair are forced "to bust" local addicts and prostitutes instead of the real crime bosses because much of the police department is on the take. Plenty of comedy and action as well as highly realistic drama. **92m/C VHS.** Elliott Gould, Robert (Bobby) Blake, Allen (Goorwitz) Garfield, Antonio Fargas, Michael Lerner, Sid Haig, Cornelia Sharpe; ***D:*** Peter Hyams; ***W:*** Peter Hyams; ***M:*** Billy Goldenberg.

The Busy Body **1967** A plethora of sixties comedians enliven this mild flick from Castle, who's probably better-known for schlock film promotions. Bumbling smalltime crook George (Caesar) is suspected of pilfering mob money by his gangland boss Charley Baker (Ryan). If he doesn't want to wind up wearing cement overshoes, George had better find the real thief and the corpse that's buried in a suit lined with the stolen moolah. Adapted from a Donald E. Westlake novel. **102m/C DVD.** Sid Caesar, Robert Ryan, Anne Baxter, Kay Medford, Jan Murray, Richard Pryor, Bill Dana, Ben Blue, Dom DeLuise, Godfrey Cambridge, Marty Ingels, George Jessel, Charles McGraw, Arlene Golanka; ***D:*** William Castle; ***W:*** Ben Starr; ***C:*** Michael Reed, Harold E. Stine; ***M:*** Vic Mizzy.

But I'm a Cheerleader **1999 (R)** Broad satire falls flat. Megan (Lyonne) is a peppy high school cheerleader who is suspected of being a lesbian by her rigid parents, who send her off to a rehabilitation camp designed to turn adolescent homosexuals into straight members of society. Megan (who's naively unaware of her true nature) goes along with the program until she befriends rebellious Graham (DuVall) and discovers that, golly, she really does like girls. **81m/C VHS, DVD.** Natasha Lyonne, Clea DuVall, Cathy Moriarty, RuPaul Charles, Bud Cort, Mink Stole, Julie Delpy, Eddie Cibrian; ***D:*** Jamie Babbit; ***W:*** Jamie Babbit, Brian Wayne Peterson; ***C:*** Jules Labarthe; ***M:*** Pat Irwin.

But Not for Me **1/2 1959** Gable stars as a middled-aged entertainment executive who thinks he can forestall maturity by carrying on with his youthful secretary. **105m/B VHS.** Clark Gable, Carroll Baker, Lilli Palmer, Lee J. Cobb, Barry Coe, Thomas Gomez, Charles Lane; ***D:*** Walter Lang; ***W:*** John Michael Hayes; ***C:*** Robert Burks.

But Where Is Daniel Wax? **1974** At a class reunion, a doctor and a popular singing star reminisce about their youth and Daniel Wax, their one-time hero. Hebrew with English subtitles. **95m/C VHS.** Lior Yaeni, Michael Lipkin, Esther Zevko; ***D:*** Avram Heffner.

Butch and Sundance: The Early Days **1/2 1979 (PG)** Traces the origins of the famous outlaw duo. It contains the requisite shoot-outs, hold-ups, and escapes. A "prequel" to "Butch Cassidy and the Sundance Kid." **111m/C VHS, DVD.** Tom Berenger, William Katt, John Schuck, Jeff Corey, Jill Eikenberry, Brian Dennehy, Peter Weller; ***D:*** Richard Lester; ***W:*** Allan Burns.

Butch Cassidy and the Sundance Kid **1969 (PG)** Two legendary outlaws at the turn of the century take it on the lam with a beautiful, willing ex-school teacher. With a clever script, humanly fallible characters, and warm, witty dialogue, this film was destined to become a classic. Featured the hit song "Raindrops Keep Falling on My Head" and renewed the buddy film industry, as Newman and Redford trade insult for insult. Look for the great scene where Newman takes on giant Ted Cassidy in a fist fight. ♫ Raindrops Keep Fallin' on My Head; On a Bicycle Built for Joy. **110m/C VHS, DVD, Blu-ray Disc.** Paul Newman, Robert Redford, Katharine Ross, Jeff Corey, Strother Martin, Cloris Leachman, Kenneth Mars, Ted Cassidy, Henry Jones, George Furth, Sam Elliott; ***D:*** George Roy Hill; ***W:*** William Goldman; ***C:*** Conrad L. Hall; ***M:*** Burt Bacharach. Oscars '69: Cinematog., Song ("Raindrops Keep Fallin' on My Head"), Story & Screenplay, Orig. Score; AFI '98: Top 100; British Acad. '70: Actor (Redford), Actress (Ross), Director (Hill), Film, Screenplay; Golden Globes '70: Score, Natl. Film Reg. '03;; Writers Guild '69: Adapt. Screenplay.

The Butcher **1/2 2007** Mob enforcer Merle Hench (Roberts) is set-up to take the fall for a bigtime heist on a rival mob boss. Surviving the trap, and grabbing a piece of the take, Merle decides being betrayed after 20 years of loyalty deserves payback. **113m/C DVD.** Eric Roberts, Robert Davi, Keith David, Geoffrey Lewis, Michael Ironside, Bokeem Woodbine; ***D:*** Jesse Johnson; ***W:*** Jesse Johnson; ***C:*** Robert Hayes; ***M:*** Marcello De Francisci. **VIDEO**

The Butcher **2007** A group of snuff film producers kidnap four people (two of which are husband and wife), strap cameras to their heads, and then force them to endure inhumane punishments in a game designed to murder them as grotesquely as possible. **75m/C DVD, Blu-ray Disc.** *KN* Dong-Hun You, Sung-Il Kim; ***D:*** Jin-Won Kim; ***W:*** Jin-Won Kim; ***C:*** Sang-hyeon Lee.

The Butcher Boy **1997 (R)** Offbeat, black comedy takes a disturbing look into the madness of 12-year old Francie Brady (Owens) in Ireland in the 1960s. An alcoholic father and a mentally strained mother makes Francie escape into a world populated by voices in his head, comic books, and his one childhood friend. When his homelife becomes unbearable, Frankie's demons catapult him into a climatic and destructively criminal breakdown. Newcomer Owens is electrifying as the red-haired dynamo whose lost childhood turns him into a monster and Stephen Rea (a regular in any Jordan film) provides stern support as Francie's loser father and film's narrator. The rural Irish town is recreated with stunning detail, with light touches of kitsch that may put off some looking for a serious treatment of main character's plight. Still a daring movie, with pop star O'Connor as the Virgin Mary. Based on the novel by Peter McCabe. **105m/C VHS, DVD.** Eamon Owens, Stephen Rea, Fiona Shaw, Sinead O'Connor, Aisling O'Sullivan, Alan Boyle, Ian Hart, Andrew Fullerton, Patrick McCabe, Sean McGinley, Brendan Gleeson, Milo O'Shea; ***D:*** Neil Jordan; ***W:*** Neil Jordan, Patrick McCabe; ***C:*** Adrian Biddle; ***M:*** Elliot Goldenthal. L.A. Film Critics '98: Score.

The Butcher's Wife **1991 (PG-13)** Charming tale of a young psychic (Moore) who brings romance to a Greenwich Village neighborhood that never quite gets off the ground. Moore stars as the clairvoyant whose mystical powers bring magic into the lives of everyone around her, including the local psychiatrist (Daniels), who falls under her spell. Talented cast is virtually wasted with a script that is lightweight; excepting Steenburgen and Dzundza who shine. **107m/C VHS, DVD.** Demi Moore, Jeff Daniels, George Dzundza, Frances McDormand, Margaret Colin, Mary Steenburgen, Max Perlich, Miriam Margolyes, Christopher Durang, Diane Salinger; ***D:*** Terry Hughes; ***W:*** Ezra Litwack, Marjorie Schwartz; ***C:*** Frank Tidy; ***M:*** Michael Gore.

Butler's Dilemma **1943** A jewel thief and a playboy both claim the identity of a butler who never existed, with humorous results. **75m/B VHS.** *GB* Richard Hearne, Francis L. Sullivan, Hermione Gingold, Ian Fleming, Alf Goddard, Judy Kelly, Henry Kendall, Wally Patch, Frank Pettingell, Andre Randall, Marjorie Rhodes, Ronald Shiner, Ralph Truman; ***D:*** Leslie Hiscott; ***W:*** Michael Barringer; ***C:*** Erwin Hillier.

The Buttercup Chain **1/2 1970** First cousins France (Bennett) and Margaret (Asher) are fighting incestuous feelings so France decides they should both get involved with others: he chooses Swedish student Fred (Taube) for Margaret and free-spirited American Manny (Taylor-Young) for himself. But it's Manny and Fred who marry and move away; when France and Margaret eventually visit, they discover the marriage is unhappy. **95m/C DVD.** *GB* Hywel Bennett, Leigh Taylor-Young, Jane Asher, Sven-Bertil Taube, Clive Revill, Roy Dotrice; ***D:*** Robert Ellis Miller; ***W:*** Peter Draper; ***C:*** Douglas Slocombe; ***M:*** Richard Rodney Bennett.

Butterfield 8 **1960** A seedy film of the John O'Hara novel about a prostitute that wants to go straight and settle down. Taylor won an Oscar, perhaps because she was ill and had lost in the two previous years in more deserving roles. **108m/C VHS, DVD.** Elizabeth Taylor, Laurence Harvey, Eddie Fisher, Dina Merrill, Mildred Dunnock, Betty Field, Susan Oliver, Kay Medford; ***D:*** Daniel Mann; ***W:*** John Michael Hayes, Charles Schnee; ***C:*** Joseph Ruttenberg. Oscars '60: Actress (Taylor).

Butterflies Are Free **1972 (PG)** Fast-paced humor surrounds the Broadway play brought to the big screen. Blind youth Albert is determined to be self-sufficient. A next-door-neighbor actress helps him gain independence from his over-protective mother (Heckart). **109m/C VHS, DVD.** Goldie Hawn, Edward Albert, Eileen Heckart, Michael Glaser; ***D:*** Milton Katselas; ***C:*** Charles B(ryant) Lang Jr.; ***M:*** Robert Alcivar. Oscars '72: Support. Actress (Heckart).

Butterfly **1/2 1982 (R)** Based on James M. Cain's novel about an amoral young woman (Pia, who'd you think?) who uses her beauty and sensual appetite to manipulate the men in her life, including her father. Set in Nevada of the 1930s, father and daughter are drawn into a daring and forbidden love affair by their lust and desperation. **105m/C VHS.** Pia Zadora, Stacy Keach, Orson Welles, Edward Albert, James Franciscus, Lois Nettleton, Stuart Whitman, June Lockhart, Ed McMahon; ***D:*** Matt Cimber; ***W:*** Matt Cimber; ***M:*** Ennio Morricone. Golden Raspberries '82: Worst Actress (Zadora), Worst Support. Actor (McMahon), Worst New Star (Zadora).

Butterfly *La Lengua de las Mariposas; Butterfly's Tongue* **1998 (R)** Young Moncho (Lozano) grows up in 1935 Galicia, Spain and is guided by his leftist teacher Don Gregorio (Gomez). But their lives are soon torn apart by the politics of the Spanish Civil War. This kind of languidly paced coming-of-age story is almost never found in American theatrical releases these days. Europeans tend to treat the material with more seriousness. Director Jose Cuerda's work is solidly in the tradition of Fellini and Truffaut. Based on the stories of Manuel Riva; Spanish with subtitles. **94m/C VHS, DVD.** *SP* Fernando Fernan-Gomez, Manuel Lozano, Uxia Blanco; ***D:*** Jose Luis Cuerda; ***W:*** Rafael Azcona; ***C:*** Javier Salmones; ***M:*** Alejandro Amenabar.

The Butterfly *Le Papillon* **2002** Likeable tale of Julien—a lonely, grumpy old guy in Paris—who can't resist his spunky yet equally lonely eight-year-old neighbor, Elsa, who's working, single mom doesn't have time for her. When he sets off to the mountains in a quest to snag a rare butterfly, Elsa slyly tags along and the two connect amid the stunning scenery. Her unwitting mother notices she's missing, becomes despondent, and triggers an APB for her. In French with subtitles. **80m/C VHS, DVD.** Michel Serrault, Francoise Michaud, Dominique Marcas, Idwig Stephane, Francis Frappat, Francoise Dubois, Dominic Gould, Auriele Meriel, Claire Bouanich, Nade Dieu, Helene Hily, Pierre Poirot, Jacky Nercessian, Jacques Bouanich, Catherine Cyler, Jerry Lucas, Laurent Adrien, Gabrielle Arger, Fabien Behar, Alain Bert, Alain Blazquez, Magali Bonat, Christiane Bopp, Armand Chagot, Laurent Chouteau, Jerome Foucher, Phlippe LeDem, Gerard Maillet, Esther Perez-Pajares, Fabien Traverci; ***D:*** Philippe Muyl; ***W:*** Philippe Muyl; ***C:*** Nicolas Herdt; ***M:*** Nicolas Errera. **VIDEO**

Butterfly Affair **1/2 1971 (PG)** Beautiful singer, involved in a scheme to smuggle $2 million worth of gems, plots to double-cross her partners in crime. **75m/C VHS.** Claudia Cardinale, Henri Charriere, Stanley Baker; ***D:*** Jean Herman.

Butterfly Ball **1976** Retelling of the 19th century classic combines the rock music of Roger Glover, live action and animation by Halas and Batchelor. Only for the brain-cell depressed. **85m/C VHS, DVD.** *GB* Twiggy, Ian Gillian, David Coverdale; ***D:*** Tony Klinger; ***Nar:*** Vincent Price.

Butterfly Collectors **1999** While investigating a murder, DI John McKeown (Postlethwaite) develops an unlikely friendship with 17-year-old suspect Dex (Draven), who is raising his younger siblings. But as McKeown gets closer to the family, his suspicions grow, and not just about Dex's involvement in the original crime. **150m/C DVD.** *GB* Pete Postlethwaite, Crissy Rock, Jamie Draven, Alison Newman; ***D:*** Jean Stewart; ***W:*** Paul Abbott; ***C:*** Cinders Forshaw; ***M:*** Philip Appleby, Jocelyn Pook. **TV**

The Butterfly Effect **1/2 2004 (R)** Kutcher takes time out from his usual dumb pretty-boy roles and tries his hand at a thriller. He plays Evan Treborn, a college psych major with a troubled past. He discovers that he can go back in time and change childhood events, which he does, to save himself and a group of friends from childhood traumas. Unfortunately, when he returns to the present, he finds his actions have changed everything that has happened since then, and not always for the better. There's a strong "ick" factor, touching on several rather disturbing topics. Kutcher acquits himself admirably, but not enough to save this jumbled mess. **113m/C DVD, UMD.** *US* Ashton Kutcher, Amy Smart, Eric Stoltz, William Lee Scott, Elden (Ratliff) Henson, Logan Lerman, Irene Gorovaia, Jesse James, Melora Walters, Ethan Suplee, John Patrick Amedori, Kevin G. Schmidt; ***D:*** Eric Bress, J. Mackye Gruber; ***W:*** Eric Bress, J. Mackye Gruber; ***C:*** Matthew F. Leonetti; ***M:*** Michael Suby.

The Butterfly Effect 2 **1/2 2006 (R)** Nick (Lively) loses control of his car, resulting in an accident that kills his girlfriend Julie (Durance) and two friends. Still traumatized after a year, Nick realizes that he feels a power whenever he looks at the photos of their last trip and can actually travel back in time to that particular moment. But when Nick returns to the present, he doesn't always like the changes that occurred as he tries to save Julie's life. An overly-complicated execution ruins the suspense factor. **92m/C DVD.** Eric Lively, Gina Holden, J.R. Bourne, Erica Durance, Dustin Milligan; ***D:*** John R. Leonetti; ***W:*** Michael D. Weiss; ***C:*** Brian Pearson; ***M:*** Michael Suby. **VIDEO**

The Butterfly Effect 3: Revelation **2009 (R)** This low-budget DTV sequel is a cut above the last effort, thanks to Miner's fine performance as Jenna, jumper Sam's (Carmack) fragile sister. Sam is working with Detroit police, getting a paycheck by helping solve cold cases. When he time-travels back to ID his own girlfriend's killer, Sam changes his past and his efforts to fix one mistake result in him becoming the prime suspect in a series of murders. **90m/C DVD.** Chris Carmack, Rachel Miner, Richard Wilkinson; ***D:*** Seth Grossman; ***W:*** Holly Brix; ***C:*** Dan Stoloff; ***M:*** Adam Balzacs. **VIDEO**

Butterfly Kiss **1994** Strange psychodrama/road tale finds drifter Eunice (Plummer) wandering the motorways of northern England. At one service station she meets Miriam (Reeves)—the two, immediately drawn together, make love at Miriam's that night. When Eunice hitches a ride with a trucker next morning, Miriam decides to follow and discovers Eunice with the truck and the driver's dead body. It's soon not the only dead body Miriam encounters as she discovers Eunice is a serial killer—not that this seems to worry Miriam a great deal as she herself gets into the spirit of their crimes. Grim all the way 'round. **90m/C VHS, DVD.** *GB* Amanda Plummer, Saskia Reeves, Paul Bown, Des McAleer, Ricky Tomlinson; ***D:*** Michael Winterbottom; ***W:*** Frank Cottrell-Boyce; ***C:*** Seamus McGarvey; ***M:*** John Harle.

Butterfly Wings *Alas de Mariposa* **1991** The tragedy of a dysfunctional family. Pregnant Carmen longs for a boy to carry on her husband's name but she's afraid to tell her shy six-year-old daughter Ami about the baby. Maybe with reason, since the child's brith triggers a series of nightmarish events. Spanish with subtitles. **105m/C VHS.** *SP* Silvia Munt, Susan Garcia, Fernando Valverde; ***D:*** Juanma Bajo Ulloa; ***W:*** Juanma Bajo Ulloa; ***C:*** Aiter Mantxola; ***M:*** Bingen Mendizabal.

Buy & Cell **1/2 1989 (R)** A stockbroker attempts to set up a business while serving a prison sentence. An assortment of amusing inmates doesn't help matters much. Fans of Malcolm McDowell will enjoy his performance as the shady warden. **95m/C VHS.** Robert Carradine, Michael Winslow, Malcolm McDowell, Ben Vereen, Lise Cutter, Randall "Tex" Cobb, Roddy Piper; ***D:*** Robert Boris.

Buying the Cow 1/2 **2002 (R)** Commitment-phobe David (O'Connell) is being pressured by long-time girlfriend Sarah (Wilson) to get married. Cliched romantic comedy. **88m/C VHS, DVD.** Jerry O'Connell, Bridgette Wilson-Sampras, Ryan Reynolds, Bill Bellamy, Annabeth Gish, Ron Livingston; ***D:*** Walt Becker; ***W:*** Walt Becker, Peter W. Nelson; ***C:*** Nancy Schreiber; ***M:*** Andrew Gross.

Buying Time **1989 (R)** Two teenagers are arrested when they try to pry their money away from a dishonest bookie, and the police use their connections to solve a drug-related murder. **97m/C VHS.** Dean Stockwell, Jeff Schultz, Michael Rudder, Tony De Santis, Leslie Toth, Laura Cruickshank; ***D:*** Mitchell Gabourie.

Buzzy Rides the Range **1940** Average "B" western with a kid saving the day. **60m/C VHS.** Robert "Buzzy" Henry, Dave O'Brien, George Eldredge, Frank Marlo, George Morrell, Claire Rochelle; ***D:*** Richard C. Kahn.

By Dawn's Early Light **1989** Thriller about two Air Force pilots who must decide whether or not to drop the bombs that would begin WWIII. **100m/C VHS, DVD.** Powers Boothe, Rebecca De Mornay, James Earl Jones, Martin Landau, Rip Torn, Darren McGavin; ***D:*** Jack Sholder; ***M:*** Trevor Jones. **CABLE**

By Dawn's Early Light 1/2 **2000** Aging Colorado cowboy Ben (Crenna) is pleased when his grandson Mike (Olivero) comes to stay for the summer. Until he realizes that Mike is a sullen teen given to pranks that backfire. After one such episode, Ben decides Mike needs some discipline and decides they should go on an 800-mile trip—by horseback. **105m/C VHS, DVD.** Richard Crenna, Chris Olivero, David Carradine, Stella Stevens, Ben Cardinal; ***D:*** Arthur Allan Seidelman; ***W:*** Jacqueline Feather, David Seidler. **CABLE**

By Design **1982 (R)** Two cohabiting women want to have a baby, so they embark on a search for the perfect stud. Not one of Astin's better performances. **90m/C VHS.** *CA* Patty Duke, Sara Botsford; ***D:*** Claude Jutra.

By Love Possessed 1/2 **1961** Can a seemingly typical, quiet, New England town stay quiet when Lana Turner is your neighbor? Vintage romantic melodrama about an attorney who is drawn into an affair when he realizes his home life is not all it could be. **115m/C VHS.** Lana Turner, Efrem Zimbalist Jr., Jason Robards Jr., George Hamilton, Thomas Mitchell; ***D:*** John Sturges; ***C:*** Russell Metty; ***M:*** Elmer Bernstein.

By the Blood of Others **1973** In a small French town, a psycho holds two women hostage in a farmhouse, and the townspeople try to figure out a solution without getting anyone killed. In French with English subtitles. **90m/C VHS.** *FR* Yves Beneyton, Francis Blanche, Bernard Blier, Robert Castel, Mariangela Melato; ***D:*** Marc Simenon; ***W:*** Jean Max; ***C:*** Rene Verzier; ***M:*** Francis Lai.

By the Light of the Silvery Moon 1/2 **1953** The equally old-fashioned sequel to "On Moonlight Bay" finds Day engaged to MacRae, who's just returned from Army service in WWI. He wants to postpone their marriage until he gets financially secure and the waiting causes some jealous misunderstandings (naturally resolved by movie's end). Based on Booth Tarkington's "Penrod" stories. ♫ By the Light of the Silvery Moon; I'll Forget You; Your Eyes Have Told Me So; Be My Little Baby Bumble Bee; If You Were the Only Girl in the World; Ain't We Got Fun; King Chanticleer. **101m/C VHS, DVD.** Doris Day, Gordon MacRae, Leon Ames, Billy Gray, Rosemary DeCamp, Mary Wickes, Russell Arms, Maria Palmer; ***D:*** David Butler; ***W:*** Robert O'Brien, Irving Elinson; ***M:*** Max Steiner.

By the Sword 1/2 **1993 (R)** Maximilian Suba (Abraham) is a one-time fencing whiz who has spent the last 25 years in prison for the murder of his mentor during a fencing match. Upon his release, Suba heads back to his old fencing grounds to see what's become of the murdered man's now-grown son and discovers Alexander (Roberts) is as ruthless and ambitious as Suba once was. Incoherent plot leaves both actors and viewers in the dark. **91m/C VHS.** F. Murray Abraham, Eric Roberts, Mia Sara, Christopher Rydell; ***D:*** Jeremy Paul Kagan; ***W:*** John McDonald, James Donadio; ***C:*** Arthur Albert; ***M:*** Bill Conti.

By Way of the Stars 1/2 **1992 (PG)** Young man is pursued by a killer while he searches for his father on the 19th-century Canadian frontier. Made for TV. **150m/C VHS.** *CA* Zachary Bennett, Tantoo Cardinal, Gema Zamprogna, Jan Rubes, Michael Mahonen; ***D:*** Allan King. **TV**

Bye-Bye **1996** Ismael (Bouajila), 25, and his 14-year-old brother Mouloud (Embarek) are French-born Arabs whose parents have abruptly returned to their Tunisian homeland after a family tragedy. The brothers have travelled from Paris to stay with their uncle (Ahourari) and his family in the port city of Marseilles. Their cousin Rhida (Mammeri), a petty criminal involved with drugs, takes the innocent Mauloud under his wing and hides him away so the boy won't be sent back to his parents. Ismael desperately roams the city trying to find his brother while he also struggles to make a fresh start amidst much societal hostility. French and Arabic with subtitles. **105m/C VHS, DVD.** *FR* Sami Bouajila, Ouassini Embarek, Benhaissa Ahourari, Sofiane Mammeri, Jamila Darwich-Farah, Nozha Khouadra; ***D:*** Karim Dridi; ***W:*** Karim Dridi; ***C:*** John Mathieson; ***M:*** Jimmy Oihid, Steve Shehan.

Bye Bye Baby **1988 (R)** Two luscious young women cavort amid lusty Italian men on various Mediterranean beaches. **80m/C VHS, DVD.** *IT* Carol Alt, Brigitte Nielsen, Jason Connery, Luca Barbareschi; ***D:*** Enrico Oldoini; ***M:*** Manuel De Sica.

Bye, Bye, Birdie **1963** Energized and sweet film version of the Broadway musical about a teen rock and roll idol (Pearson doing Elvis) coming to a small town to see one of his fans before he leaves for the army. The film that made Ann-Margret a star. ♫ Bye Bye Birdie; The Telephone Hour; How Lovely to be a Woman; Honestly Sincere; One Boy; Put on a Happy Face; Kids; One Last Kiss; A Lot of Livin' to Do. **112m/C VHS, DVD.** Dick Van Dyke, Janet Leigh, Ann-Margret, Paul Lynde, Bobby Rydell, Maureen Stapleton, Ed Sullivan, Trudi Ames, Jesse Pearson; ***D:*** George Sidney; ***W:*** Irving Brecher; ***C:*** Joseph Biroc; ***M:*** Johnny Green.

Bye Bye Birdie 1/2 **1995 (G)** TV adaptation of the Broadway musical (previously filmed in 1963) about an Elvis-like singer, about to be inducted into the Army, who causes havoc when he visits fans in a small town. **135m/C VHS, DVD.** Jason Alexander, Vanessa L(ynne) Williams, Chynna Phillips, George Wendt, Tyne Daly, Marc Kudisch; ***D:*** Gene Saks. **TV**

Bye Bye Blues 1/2 **1989 (PG)** The lives of the Cooper family are disrupted when the husband is called to service during WWII and is then taken prisoner by the Japanese. In need of money, wife Daisy (Jenkins) joins a local swing band and begins charming all who watch her, especially the band's trombone player (Reilly). A sweet-spirited tale of love, loyalty, and the search for inner strength. Jenkins gives a strong performance as the shy wife who becomes an independent woman during her husband's absence. **110m/C VHS.** *CA* Rebecca Jenkins, Michael Ontkean, Luke Reilly, Stuart Margolin, Robyn Stevan, Kate Reid, Wayne Robson, Shiela Moore, Leon Pownall, Vincent Gale, Susan Sneath; ***D:*** Anne Wheeler; ***W:*** Anne Wheeler; ***C:*** Vic Sarin; ***M:*** George Blondheim. Genie '90: Actress (Jenkins), Support. Actress (Stevan).

Bye Bye Braverman 1/2 **1967** Cliched character study of four New York Jewish men, all of whom are writers, mourning the death of their friend Braverman. They attempt to travel from Greenwich Village to Brooklyn to attend his funeral but run into a number of delays. **95m/C DVD.** George Segal, Jack Warden, Joseph Wiseman, Jessica Walter, Phyllis Newman, Zohra Lampert, Godfrey Cambridge, Sorrell Booke; ***D:*** Sidney Lumet; ***W:*** Herbert Sergent; ***C:*** Boris Kaufman; ***M:*** Peter Matz.

Bye Bye Brazil 1/2 **1979** A changing Brazil is seen through the eyes of four wandering gypsy minstrels participating in a tent show traveling throughout the country. Lots of Brazilian charm. In Portuguese with English subtitles. **115m/C VHS.** *BR* Jose Wilker, Betty Faria, Fabio Junior, Zaira Zambello; ***D:*** Carlos Diegues; ***W:*** Carlos Diegues; ***M:*** Chico Buarque.

Bye Bye, Love 1/2 **1994 (PG-13)** Forty-eight hours in the lives of three divorced buddies starts at the local Mickey D's for the biweekly exchange of their kids. The dads don't offer any surprises: Donny (Reiser) still loves his ex, Vic (Quaid) hates his, and Dave (Modine) loves anything in a skirt. Sometimes witty, but just as often sadly poignant, the plot is as shallow as a TV sitcom, with an easy answer for every difficult question about divorce. The three leads are likeable enough, but Garofalo is the gem in an otherwise dull flick. She looks like she's having a blast, stealing scenes with abandon as Vic's blind date from hell. **107m/C VHS, DVD.** Matthew Modine, Randy Quaid, Paul Reiser, Rob Reiner, Janeane Garofalo, Ed Flanders, Lindsay Crouse, Johnny Whitworth, Maria Pitillo, Amy Brenneman, Ross Malinger, Eliza Dushku, Wendell Pierce, Cameron Boyd, Mae Whitman, Jayne Brook, Dana Wheeler-Nicholson, Amber Benson, Stephen (Steve) Root, Danny Masterson, Brad Hall, Jack Black; ***D:*** Sam Weisman; ***W:*** Gary David Goldberg, Brad Hall; ***M:*** J.A.C. Redford.

Byron 1/2 **2003** Byron as poet comes in second to Byron as scandalous lover in this BBC production that depicts the price of fame. Byron's (Miller) romantic style includes radical politics and adventure after the aristocrat becomes famous in 1812. His marriage to the pious Annabella (Cox) is a disaster and he's forced into exile when Byron's alleged love affair with half-sister Augusta (Little) becomes society gossip. Miller is both sympathetic and self-aware in the title role. **150m/C DVD.** *GB* Johnny Miller, Philip Glenister, Natasha Little, Vanessa Redgrave, Julie Cox, Camilla Power, Sally Hawkins, Oliver Dimsdale; ***D:*** Julian Farino; ***W:*** Nick Dear; ***C:*** David Odd; ***M:*** Adrian Johnston. **TV**

The C-Man **1949** Customs agent Jagger finds work isn't so dull after all. Murder and theft on an international scale make for a busy week as he follows jewel smugglers from Paris to New York. Docu-style though routine crime story. **75m/B VHS, DVD.** Dean Jagger, John Carradine, Harry Landers, Rene Paul; ***D:*** Joseph Lerner.

Cabaret 1/2 **1972 (PG)** Hitler is rising to power, racism and anti-Semitism are growing, and the best place to hide from it all is the Berlin cabaret. With dancing girls, an androgynous master of ceremonies (Grey), and American expatriate singer Sally Bowles (Minnelli), you can laugh and drink and pretend tomorrow will never come. Sally does just that. Face to face with the increasing horrors of Nazism, she persists in the belief that the "show must go on." Along for the ride is Englishman Brian Roberts (York, in a role based on Christopher Isherwood's own experiences), who serves both as participant and observer. Based on the John Kander's hit Broadway musical (and Isherwood's stories), the film is impressive, with excellent direction and cinematography. ♫ Cabaret; Wilkommen; Mein Herr; Maybe This Time; Two Ladies; Money, Money; Hieraten; Tomorrow Belongs to Me; If You Could See Her. **119m/C VHS, DVD.** Liza Minnelli, Joel Grey, Michael York, Marisa Berenson, Helmut Griem, Fritz Wepper, Elisabeth Neumann-Viertel; ***D:*** Bob Fosse; ***W:*** Jay Presson Allen; ***C:*** Geoffrey Unsworth; ***M:*** Ralph Burns. Oscars '72: Actress (Minnelli), Art Dir./Set Dec., Cinematog., Director (Fosse), Film Editing, Sound, Support. Actor (Grey), Orig. Song Score and/or Adapt.; British Acad. '72: Actress (Minnelli), Director (Fosse), Film; Golden Globes '73: Actress—Mus./Comedy (Minnelli), Film—Mus./Comedy, Support. Actor (Grey); Natl. Bd. of Review '72: Director (Fosse), Support. Actor (Grey), Support. Actress (Berenson), Natl. Film Reg. '95;; Natl. Soc. Film Critics '72: Support. Actor (Grey); Writers Guild '72: Adapt. Screenplay.

Cabaret Balkan ***The Powder Keg; Bure Baruta*** **1998 (R)** Acerbicly cruel and frequently physically brutal comedy is set in Belgrade one winter night and features characters whose stories turn out to be interrelated and are bookended by the comments of sneering nightclub M.C. Boris (Ristanovski). There are betrayals, feuds, random acts of violence, and various absurdities set in a war-torn country where the veneer of civilization has long-since disappeared. Based on the play "Bure Baruta" by Dukovski. Serbo-Croatian with subtitles. **102m/C VHS.** *YU* Miki (Predrag) Manojlovic, Nikola Ristanovski, Nebojsa Glogovac, Marko Urosevic, Bogdan Diklic; ***D:*** Goran Paskalyevic; ***W:*** Goran Paskalyevic, Dejan Dukovski; ***C:*** Milan Spasic; ***M:*** Zoran Simjanovic.

Cabeza de Vaca **1990 (R)** In 1528, a Spanish expedition shipwrecks in unknown territory off the Florida coast. Only survivor Cabeza de Vaca is captured by the Iguase Indian tribe and made a slave to their shaman. He's later freed, but leaves with respect for their culture. Spanish soldiers find him and want his help in capturing the natives, but he is outraged by their cruelty and must confront his own people. Strong visual style easily brings the audience deeply into this uncharted world. Based on Cabeza de Vaca's book "Naufragios." Director Echevarria's feature film debut. Spanish and Indian with subtitles. **111m/C VHS, DVD.** *MX SP* Juan Diego, Daniel Gimenez Cacho, Roberto Sosa, Carlos Castanon, Gerardo Villarreal, Roberto Cobo, Jose Flores, Ramon Barragan; ***D:*** Nicolas Echevarria; ***W:*** Guillermo Sheridan, Nicolas Echevarria; ***C:*** Guillermo Navarro; ***M:*** Mario Lavista.

Cabin Boy **WOOF! 1994 (PG-13)** Obnoxious "fancy lad" Elliott mistakenly boards the wrong boat and becomes the new cabin boy for a ridiculous bunch of mean, smelly sailors. Fish out of water saga is so bad it's—bad, a blundering attempt at parody that's just plain stupid. Surprisingly produced by Tim Burton, this effort will disappoint even diehard fans. Look for Chris' real life dad Bob as the lad's dad; good friend Letterman appears briefly as nasty "Old Salt," but uses the alias Earl Hofert in the final credits. As usual, the acerbic Letterman gets the best line, "Man, oh, man do I hate them fancy lads." We know how you feel, Dave. **80m/C VHS, DVD.** Andy Richter, Chris Elliott, Ann Magnuson, Ritch Brinkley, James Gammon, Brian Doyle-Murray, Russ Tamblyn, Brion James, Ricki Lake, Bob Elliott; ***Cameos:*** David Letterman; ***D:*** Adam Resnick; ***W:*** Adam Resnick; ***C:*** Amy Barrett; ***M:*** Steve Bartek.

Cabin by the Lake **2000** Screenwriter Stanley (Nelson) takes his work a little too seriously when he does research on a story about a serial killer who kidnaps and drowns his female victims. Stanley has his own garden of victims until one young woman escapes and a trap is laid for the killer. **91m/C VHS, DVD.** Judd Nelson, Hedy Burress, Michael Weatherly, Bernie Coulson, Susan Gibney; ***D:*** Po-Chih Leung; ***W:*** C. David Stephens; ***C:*** Philip Linzey; ***M:*** Frankie Blue, Daniel Licht. **CABLE**

Cabin Fever **2003 (R)** Scattershot horror/comedy with a twist has five teenagers rent a cabin in the woods for a week contend with a very deadly and very gross virus. A bloody man who appears in the woods is the harbinger of doom for the appropriately sex- and booze-crazed archetypical horror movie teens. They are soon knee-deep in local weirdos and rednecks as well as appropriate amounts of blood and gore. Though not outstanding, pic boasts enough gore to satisfy the most hard-core horror fans. **94m/C VHS, DVD, UMD.** *US* Jordan Ladd, Rider Strong, James DeBello, Cerina Vincent, Joey Kern, Arie Verveen, Giuseppe Andrews, Eli Roth; ***D:*** Eli Roth; ***W:*** Eli Roth, Randy Pearlstein; ***C:*** Scott Kevan; ***M:*** Nathan Marr.

The Cabin in the Cotton 1/2 **1932** Davis stars as a rich, ruthless Southern belle in this dated melodrama about sharecroppers. Barthelmess is cast as a poor sharecropper who is almost brought to ruin when he falls for the sexy Southern vamp. Contains Davis's most famous line, "Ah'd love t'kiss you, but ah jes washed mah hair." **77m/B VHS.** Bette Davis, Richard Barthelmess, Dorothy Jordan, Henry B. Walthall, Tully Marshall; ***D:*** Michael Curtiz; ***W:*** Paul Green.

Cabin in the Sky **1943** A poor woman fights to keep her husband's soul out of the devil's clutches. Based on a Broadway show and featuring an all-Black cast. Lively dance numbers and a musical score with contributions from Duke Ellington. Minnelli's first feature film. ♫Cabin in the Sky; Happiness Is Just a Thing Called Joe; Taking a Chance on Love; Life's Full of Consequence; Li'l Black Sheep; Shine; Honey in the Honeycomb. **99m/C VHS, DVD.** Ethel Waters, Eddie Anderson, Lena Horne, Rex Ingram, Louis Armstrong, Duke Ellington; ***D:*** Vincente Minnelli; ***M:*** Duke Ellington, Harold Arlen, E.Y. Harburg, George Bassman.

The Cabinet of Dr. Caligari 🦴🦴🦴🦴 *Das Cabinet des Dr. Caligari; Das Kabinett des Doktor Caligari* **1919** A pioneering film in the most extreme expressionistic style about a hypnotist in a carnival and a girl-snatching somnambulist. Highly influential in its approach to lighting, composition, design and acting. Much imitated. Silent. **92m/B VHS, DVD.** *GE* Conrad Veidt, Werner Krauss, Lil Dagover, Hans von Twardowski, Rudolf Klein-Rogge, Friedrich Feher, Rudolf Lettinger; ***D:*** Robert Wiene; ***W:*** Carl Mayer, Hans Janowitz; ***C:*** Willy Hameister.

Cabiria 🦴🦴 ½ **1914** The pioneering Italian epic about a Roman and a slave girl having a love affair in Rome during the Second Punic War. Immense sets and set-pieces; an important influence on Griffith and DeMille. Silent. **123m/B VHS, DVD.** *IT* Lidia Quaranta, Bartolomeo Pagano, Umberto Mozzato; ***D:*** Giovanni Pastrone; ***W:*** Giovanni Pastrone, Gabriele D'Annunzio; ***C:*** Segundo de Chomon.

The Cable Guy 🦴🦴 ½ **1996 (PG-13)** Carrey's first $20 million paycheck finds cable subscriber Broderick in for a comedic nightmare when he accepts the offer of free movie channels. The overeager installer (Carrey, naturally) turns his life upside down. A little darker humor than Carrey fans may be used to, and don't expect any bodily ventriloquism. Carrey (did we mention he's in it?) gets to act with real life people. Director Stiller does a nice job of reining in his more manic impulses when necessary. Broderick holds his own as the reluctant pal. Original scripter Holtz won a Writer's Guild arbitration for sole writing credit from producer-writer Judd Apatow. **95m/C VHS, DVD.** Jim Carrey, Matthew Broderick, Leslie Mann, George Segal, Diane Baker, Jack Black, Janeane Garofalo, Andy Dick, Charles Napier, Ben Stiller, Bob Odenkirk, David Cross, Owen Wilson, Joel Murray, Kathy Griffin, Sean M. Whalen, Annabelle Gurwitch, Conrad Janis, Alex D. Linz; ***D:*** Ben Stiller; ***W:*** Judd Apatow, Lou Holtz Jr.; ***C:*** Robert Brinkmann; ***M:*** John Ottman. MTV Movie Awards '97: Villain (Carrey), Comedic Perf. (Carrey).

Cabo Blanco 🦴🦴 **1981 (R)** A bartender and a variety of other characters, including an ex-Nazi and a French woman searching for her lover, assemble in Peru after WWII. Nazi Robards controls police chief Rey, while American Bronson runs the local watering hole and eyes French woman Sanda. Hey, this sounds familiar. Everyone shares a common interest: finding a missing treasure of gold, lost in a ship wreck. Remaking "Casablanca" via "The Treasure of Sierra Madre" is never easy. **87m/C VHS, DVD.** Charles Bronson, Jason Robards Jr., Dominique Sanda, Fernando Rey, Gilbert Roland, Simon MacCorkindale; ***D:*** J. Lee Thompson; ***W:*** Morton S. Fine, Milton S. Gelman; ***C:*** Alex Phillips Jr.; ***M:*** Jerry Goldsmith.

Cactus 🦴🦴 ½ **1986** Melodrama about a young French woman, separated from her husband, who faces the reality of losing her sight after a car accident. She experiences a growing relationship with a blind man and contemplates the thought of risky surgery which may improve her eyesight or cause complete blindness. Countering all that blindness and tangled romance is a camera that pans lush Australian landscapes and humorously focuses on the small telling details of daily life. **95m/C VHS, DVD.** *AU* Isabelle Huppert, Robert Menzies, Monica Maughan, Sheila Florance, Norman Kaye, Banduk Marika; ***D:*** Paul Cox; ***W:*** Norman Kaye, Paul Cox, Bob Ellis; ***C:*** Yuri Sokol; ***M:*** Giovanni Pergolese, Yannis Markopolous, Elsa Davis.

Cactus Flower 🦴🦴 **1969 (PG)** Good cast doesn't quite suffice to make this adaptation of a Broadway hit work. A middle-aged bachelor dentist gets involved with a kookie mistress, refusing to admit his real love for his prim and proper receptionist. Hawn's big leap to stardom. **103m/C VHS, DVD.** Walter Matthau, Goldie Hawn, Ingrid Bergman, Jack Weston, Rick Lenz; ***D:*** Gene Saks; ***W:*** I.A.L. Diamond; ***C:*** Charles B(ryant) Lang Jr.; ***M:*** Quincy Jones. Oscars '69: Support. Actress (Hawn); Golden Globes '70: Support. Actress (Hawn).

Cactus in the Snow 🦴 ½ **1972** A virginal Army private serving during the Vietnam War era tries to find sex on a 72-hour leave and instead discovers love. Some guys have all the luck. Melodrama never grabs where it ought to. **90m/C VHS.** Richard Thomas, Mary Layne, Lucille Benson; ***D:*** Martin Zweiback.

Caddie 🦴🦴 ½ **1976** Based on an autobiographical story of a woman who leaves her unfaithful husband in 1930s Australia. Struggling to raise her two children, she works as a waitress in a bar where she finds romance with one of the regulars. Average script bolstered by Morse's performance. **107m/C VHS.** *AU* Helen Morse, Jack Thompson, Takis Emmanuel, Jacki Weaver; ***D:*** Donald Crombie; ***W:*** Joan Long; ***C:*** Peter James; ***M:*** Patrick Flynn.

The Caddy 🦴🦴 **1953** Lewis plays frantic caddy prone to slapstick against Martin's smooth professional golfer with a bent toward singing. Mostly a series of Martin and Lewis sketches that frequently land in the rough. Introduces several songs, including a classic Martin and Lewis rendition of "That's Amore." Look for cameos by a host of professional golfers. **95m/C VHS.** Dean Martin, Jerry Lewis, Donna Reed, Barbara Bates, Joseph Calleia, Marshall Thompson, Fred Clark; ***Cameos:*** Ben Hogan, Sam Snead, Byron Nelson, Julius Boros, Jimmy Thomson, Harry E. Cooper; ***D:*** Norman Taurog; ***W:*** Danny Arnold.

Caddyshack 🦴🦴🦴 ½ **1980 (R)** Inspired performances by Murray and Dangerfield drive this sublimely moronic comedy onto the green. The action takes place at Bushwood Country Club, where caddy Danny (O'Keefe) is bucking to win the club's college scholarship. Characters involved in various sophomoric set pieces include obnoxious club president Judge Smails (Knight), playboy Ty Webb (Chase), who is too laid back to keep his score, loud, vulgar, and extremely rich Al Czernik (Dangerfield), and filthy gopher-hunting groundskeeper Carl (Murray). Occasional dry moments are followed by scenes of pure (and tasteless) anarchy, so watch with someone immature. Does for golf what "Major League" tried to do for baseball. **99m/C VHS, DVD, HD DVD.** Chevy Chase, Rodney Dangerfield, Ted (Edward) Knight, Michael O'Keefe, Bill Murray, Sarah Holcomb, Brian Doyle-Murray, Cindy Morgan, Scott Colomby, Dan Resin, Henry Wilcoxon, Elaine Aiken; ***D:*** Harold Ramis; ***W:*** Harold Ramis, Doug Kenney, Brian Doyle-Murray; ***C:*** Stevan Larner; ***M:*** Johnny Mandel.

Caddyshack 2 🦴 ½ **1988 (PG)** Obligatory sequel to "Caddyshack," minus Bill Murray, who wisely avoided further encroachment of gopher holes, and director Ramis who opted for the screenwriting chore. Mason is the star of the show as a crude self-made millionaire who tangles with the snobs at the country club. Although it occasionally earns a chuckle, "Shack 2" has significantly fewer guffaws than the original, proving once again that funny guys are always undone by lousy scripts and weak direction. **103m/C VHS, DVD.** Jackie Mason, Chevy Chase, Dan Aykroyd, Dyan Cannon, Robert Stack, Dina Merrill, Randy Quaid, Jessica Lundy, Jonathan Silverman, Chynna Phillips; ***D:*** Allan Arkush; ***W:*** Harold Ramis, Peter Torokvei; ***C:*** Harry Stradling Jr.; ***M:*** Ira Newborn. Golden Raspberries '88: Worst Support. Actor (Aykroyd), Worst Song ("Jack Fresh").

Cadence 🦴🦴 **1989 (PG-13)** The directorial debut of actor Martin Sheen, this fitful melodrama stars son Charlie as an unruly trooper on a 1960s army base. Placed in an all-black stockade for punishment, he bonds with his brother prisoners by defying the hardcase sergeant (played by Sheen the elder). Characters and situations are intriguing but not rendered effectively. Based on the novel "Count a Lonely Cadence" by Gordon Weaver. **97m/C VHS, DVD.** Charlie Sheen, Martin Sheen, Laurence Fishburne, Michael Beach, Ramon Estevez; ***D:*** Martin Sheen; ***M:*** Georges Delerue.

Cadillac Girls 🦴 ½ **1993** Page is a self-destructive teenager who is arrested for car theft. To avoid jail, Page is placed in her single mom's custody and moves to her family's straitlaced hometown in Nova Scotia. Mom isn't exactly good at parenting and Page's adolescent anger extends to putting the moves on mom's potential new beau. **99m/C VHS.** Jennifer Dale, Gregory Harrison, Mia Kirshner, Adam Beach; ***D:*** Nicholas (Nick) Kendall. Genie '93: Score.

Cadillac Man 🦴🦴 **1990 (R)** Williams is the quintessential low-life car salesman in this rather disjointed comedy. A lesser comedic talent might have stalled and been abandoned, but Williams manages to drive away despite the flat script and direction. One storyline follows his attempt to sell 12 cars in 12 days or lose his job, while another follows his confrontation with a gun-toting, mad-as-hell cuckolded husband. Williams and Robbins are often close to being funny in a hyperkinetic way, but the situations are dumb enough to rob most of the scenes of their comedy. Watch for a movie-stealing bit by the spunky waitress at the local Chinese restaurant. **95m/C VHS, DVD.** Robin Williams, Tim Robbins, Pamela Reed, Fran Drescher, Zack Norman, Annabella Sciorra, Lori Petty, Paul Guilfoyle, Tristen Skylar; ***D:*** Roger Donaldson; ***W:*** Ken Friedman; ***C:*** David Gribble; ***M:*** J. Peter Robinson.

Cadillac Ranch 🦴🦴 ½ **1996 (R)** CJ (Amis), Frances (Feeney), and Mary Katharine (Humphrey) Crowley are three squabbling Texas sisters who have reunited to celebrate Mary K.'s upcoming marriage. CJ works in a strip club owned by greedy ex-Texas Ranger Wood (Lloyd), who sent their long-gone daddy, Travis (Metzler), to prison for a heist Wood was involved in. When CJ gets fired, the threesome steal a key from Wood that will supposedly access money from the heist and the vengeful Wood goes after them. **104m/C VHS, DVD.** Suzy Amis, Renee Humphrey, Caroleen Feeney, Christopher Lloyd, Jim Metzler, Linden Ashby; ***D:*** Lisa Gottlieb; ***W:*** Jennifer Cecil; ***C:*** Bruce Douglas Johnson; ***M:*** Christopher Tyng.

Cadillac Records 🦴🦴🦴 **2008 (R)** Chronicles the rise and fall of legendary Chicago blues label Chess Records in the 1950s and 1960s, which began with Muddy Waters (Wright) and later featured Chuck Berry (Mos Def), Etta James (Knowles, also serving as executive producer), and Howlin' Wolf (Walker). Founded by brothers Leonard and Phil Chess, Polish immigrants who rose from poverty, the film ignores Phil and focuses only on Leonard (Brody). Packed with the great sounds of an era that led to the birth of rock and roll, writer-director Martin showcases the singers more than the story. The fact that the actors did their own performances gives it a natural feel though, led by Knowles, whose powerful voice captures the spirit of the passionate and troubled James. **108m/C DVD.** *US* Emmanuelle Chriqui, Adrien Brody, Gabrielle Union, Beyonce Knowles, Mos Def, Jeffrey Wright, Eamonn Walker, Cedric the Entertainer, Tammy Blanchard, Columbus Short, Eric Bogosian; ***D:*** Darnell Martin; ***W:*** Darnell Martin; ***C:*** Anastas Michos; ***M:*** Terence Blanchard.

Caesar and Cleopatra 🦴🦴 ½ **1946** Based on the classic George Bernard Shaw play. Caesar meets the beautiful Cleopatra in ancient Egypt and helps her gain control of her life. Remains surprisingly true to Shaw's adaptation, unlike many other historical films of the same era. **135m/C VHS, DVD.** *GB* Claude Rains, Vivien Leigh, Stewart Granger, Flora Robson, Francis L. Sullivan, Cecil Parker; ***D:*** Gabriel Pascal; ***C:*** Robert Krasker.

Caesar the Conqueror 🦴 *Giulio Cesare, il conquistatore delle Gallie* **1963** Based (incredibly loosely) on a book supposed to be Julius Caesar's autobiography, covers the Roman leader's battles against Gaul. Coincidentally, marketing this film probably also took incredible gall at the time. Disappointing even for diehard fans of Italian Sword and Sandal costume dramas from the 1960s. **103m/C DVD.** *IT* Cameron Mitchell, Rick (Rik) Battaglia, Dominique Wilms, Ivica Pajer, Raffaella Carra, Carlo Tamberlani, Giulio Donnini, Cesare Fontani, Carla Calo, Nerio Bernardi, Bruno Tocci, Aldo Pini, Lucia Randi, Enzo Petracca; ***D:*** Tanio Boccia; ***W:*** Gaius Julius Caesar, Nino Scolaro, Arpad DeRiso, George Higgins 2; ***C:*** Romolo Garroni; ***M:*** Guido Robuschi, Gian Stellari.

Cafe au Lait 🦴🦴🦴 *Metisse* **1994** Actor/director/writer Kassovitz scores in his debut feature about an interracial menage a trois. Beautiful mulatto Lola (Mauduech) is pregnant but she's not sure by which of her two contrasting lovers (who don't yet know about each other). It could be white, Jewish, easy-going bicycle messenger Felix (Kassovitz) or stuffy, wealthy, black Moslem student Jamal (Kounde). Both men desire the fatherhood role and both move in with Lola to share responsibility. This is not without complications. Generally light and frothy without ignoring racial tensions. French with subtitles. **94m/C VHS, DVD.** *FR* Mathieu Kassovitz, Julie Mauduech, Hubert Kounde, Vincent Cassel, Tadek Lokcinski, Jany Holt; ***D:*** Mathieu Kassovitz; ***W:*** Mathieu Kassovitz; ***C:*** Pierre Aim; ***M:*** Marie Daulne, Jean-Louis Daulne.

Cafe Express 🦴🦴 ½ **1983** A con artist (he sells coffee illegally aboard an Italian train) stays one step ahead of the law as he raises money to help his ailing son. As in "Bread and Chocolate," Manfredi is again the put-upon working class hero comedically attempting to find a better way of life in this bittersweet tale. **90m/C VHS, DVD.** *IT* Nino Manfredi, Gigi Reder, Adolfo Celi, Vittorio Mezzogiorno; ***D:*** Nanni Loy.

Cafe Lumiere 🦴 ½ *Kohi jikou* **2005** Taiwanese director Hou dedicates his homage to Japanese master Yasujiro Ozu with a narrative about loneliness, isolation, and modern urban life. In Tokyo, Yoko (pop star Hitoto in her debut) announces to her father and stepmother that she's pregnant but has no intention of marrying. Her best friend is bookseller Hijame (Asano). She is doing research on composer Jiang Wen-Ye (whose work is used on the soundtrack); he's doing a computer art project about the city's commuter trains, which mean you see a lot of the subway system. It's understated to the point of inertia. Japanese with subtitles. **104m/C DVD.** ***D:*** Hou Hsiao-Hsien; ***W:*** Chu Tien-Wen; ***C:*** Lee Ping-Bing; ***M:*** Jiang Wen.

Cafe Metropole 🦴🦴 **1937** Parisian restauranteur Victor Lombard (Menjou) gets into money trouble and thinks he's getting out when he wins at baccarat. Too bad the check he gets from impecunious American Alexander Brown (Power) is rubber. Lombard blackmails Brown into pretending to be Russian royalty to romance heiress Laura (Young). Naturally, Brown falls in love so Lombard then tells Laura's protective daddy that Brown is a fraud. It's a romantic comedy so things work out for practically everyone. **84m/B DVD.** Adolphe Menjou, Tyrone Power, Loretta Young, Charles Winninger, Gregory Ratoff, Helen Westley; ***D:*** Edward H. Griffith; ***W:*** Jacques Deval; ***C:*** Lucien N. Andriot; ***M:*** Louis Silvers.

Cafe Ole 🦴🦴 ½ **2000** Malcolm lives a happy, if somewhat lonely, existence in his Montreal neighborhood, working at a video store and passing time with neighbors at the local cafe. After a string of unsuccessful dates, mostly engineered by his matchmaker brother, Malcolm meets Alicia. He realizes she's the one for him, but she has a secret that will disrupt his heretofore uneventful life. Charming little romantic comedy, with the kick of some steamy love scenes. **97m/C VHS.** Andrew Tarbet, Laia Marull, Macha Grenon, Dino Tavarone, Stephanie Morgenstern; ***D:*** Richard Roy; ***W:*** Emil Sher. **VIDEO**

Cafe Romeo 🦴🦴 **1991 (R)** Tale of 20-something friendships forged in the neighborhood coffeehouse of a heavily Italian community. Lia (Stewart) is a waitress who dreams of becoming a fashion designer, but her marriage to a small time hood holds her back. Crombie, her cousin by marriage, is a dental student confused about his future, but very much in love with Lia. Quiet movie boasts average script that's helped along by strong performances. Originally broadcast on Canadian TV. **93m/C VHS.** *CA* Catherine Mary Stewart, Jonathan Crombie; ***D:*** Rex Bromfield.

Cafe Society 🦴🦴 ½ **1997 (R)** The fictional nightclub El Casbah is the setting for director De Felitta's debut take on a 1952

New York prostitution scandal. Wealthy young playboy Mickey Jelke (Whaley) prefers to mix with lowlifes rather than high society. Newcomer Jack Kale (Gallagher) is working the scene and turns out to be an undercover cop investigating a prostitution ring operating out of the clubs. Jack befriends both Mickey and his latest girlfriend, in-the-know Patricia Ward (Boyle), who's not above selling her favors. Then patsy Jelke gets indicted as a pimp and all cafe society's tawdriness is exposed. **104m/C VHS.** Peter Gallagher, Frank Whaley, Lara Flynn Boyle, John Spencer, Anna Thomson, David Patrick Kelly, Paul Guilfoyle; ***D:*** Raymond De Felitta; ***W:*** Raymond De Felitta; ***C:*** Mike Mayers; ***M:*** Chris Guardino.

Caffeine **2006** Intermittently amusing workplace comedy, set in London, about the denizens of the Black Cat Cafe. Manager Rachel fires boyfriend/chef Charlie for cheating on her and leaves ill-prepared waiter Tom in charge of the kitchen; waiter Dylan is waiting to hear if his novel is going to be published; waitress Vanessa must bring her crazy grandmother Lucy to work for the day; and the customers have an equal number of problems, including bad blind dates, jealous boyfriends, and cross-dressing secrets. **88m/C DVD.** Marsha Thomason, Callum Blue, Breckin Meyer, Mena Suvari, Mark Pellegrino, Katherine Heigl, Daz Crawford, Mike Vogel, Roz Witt, Andrew Lee Pitts, Sonya Walger, Orlando Seale; ***D:*** John Cosgrove; ***W:*** Dean Craig; ***C:*** Shawn Maurer; ***M:*** David Kitay.

The Cage **1989 (R)** Gangsters enlist a brain-damaged Vietnam vet played by Ferrigno to participate in illegal "cage fights," enclosed wrestling matches fought to the death. Crude and annoying. **101m/C VHS, DVD.** Lou Ferrigno, Reb Brown, Michael Dante, Mike Moroff, Marilyn Tokuda, James Shigeta, Al Ruscio; ***D:*** Hugh Kelley.

The Cage **1990** Sent to prison for murdering his girlfriend, Jive has no idea what the pen has in store for him. The inmates stage a mock trial, the defendant is found guilty and the sentence is too horrible to imagine. From a stage play by the San Quentin Drama Workshop and co-starring Hayes, author of "Midnight Express." **90m/C VHS, DVD.** Rick Cluchey, William Hayes; ***D:*** Rick Cluchey; ***W:*** Rick Cluchey.

Cage 2: The Arena of Death ½ **1994 (R)** Billy Thomas (Ferrigno) is kidnapped by a vicious mobster and forced to battle martial arts experts in a steel cage battle to the death. But his best friend (Brown) plans to infiltrate the show and put a stop to the carnage. **94m/C VHS.** Lou Ferrigno, Reb Brown; ***D:*** Lang Elliott.

Caged **1950** Innocent Marie Allen (Parker) is sent to prison as an accomlice to her husband's fatal armed robbery attempt because she was in the car. Once inside, the frightened, pregnant widow encounters reform-minded warden Benton (Moorehead) and vicious matron Harper (Emerson), who fight for her soul, along with a varied cast of fellow inmates. Harper's vicious treatment of the inmates eventually turns Allen into a hardened con. A classic, which shouldn't be lumped in with later exploitation examples of the genre. Excellent performances and scripting make it a fine representation of noir. **96m/B DVD.** Eleanor Parker, Agnes Moorehead, Hope Emerson, Ellen Corby, Betty Garde, Jan Sterling, Lee Patrick, Olive Deering, Sheila MacRae, Jane Darwell, Gertrude Michael, Don Beddoe, Edith Evanson, Gertrude Hoffman; ***D:*** John Cromwell; ***W:*** Bernard C. Schoenfeld, Virginia Kellogg; ***C:*** Carl Guthrie; ***M:*** Max Steiner.

Caged Fear ½ **1992 (R)** Young Krissie (Cloke) is mistakenly put behind bars in a brutal, high-security prison for a shootout caused by her outlaw husband Tommy (Keith) during their honeymoon. Tommy comes up with an outrageous scheme to rescue her. Not quite as bad as it sounds, but close. **94m/C VHS.** David Keith, Deborah May, Ray Sharkey, Loretta Devine, Karen Black, Kristen Cloke, Stanley DeSantis; ***D:*** Bobby Houston; ***W:*** Bobby Houston; ***C:*** Alan Caso.

Caged Fury **1980 (R)** American women being held captive in Southeast Asia are brainwashed into becoming walking time bombs. Yes, that dame's gonna blow. Made in the Philippines with the best of intentions. **90m/C VHS.** *PH* Bernadette Williams, Taaffe O'Connell, Jennifer Laine; ***D:*** Cirio H. Santiago.

Caged Fury **1990** Two Los Angeles women allegedly commit sexual crimes and are sent to prison. Cheap, exploitive women's prison rehash. **85m/C VHS.** Erik Estrada, Richie Barathy, Roxanna Michaels, Paul Smith, James Hong, Greg Cummins, Mindi Miller; ***D:*** Bill Milling.

Caged Hearts **1995 (R)** Chicks-behind-bars flick finds Kate (Genzel) and Sharon (McClure) framed for murder by a shady organization called "The Shield." Cliches abound. **87m/C VHS, DVD.** Tane McClure, Carrie Genzel, Taylor Leigh, Nick Wilder; ***D:*** Henri Charr.

Caged Heat *Renegade Girls; Caged Females* **1974 (R)** Low-budget babes-behind-bars film touted as the best sexploitation film of the day. Demme's directorial debut is a genre-altering installment in Roger Corman's formulaic cellblock Cinderella cycle. Recycled plot—innocent woman is put behind bars, where she loses some of her innocence—boasts an updated treatment. These babes may wear hot pants and gratuitously bare their midriffs, but they're not brainless bimbos. They're strong individuals who work together to liberate themselves. Reached cult status. Cult diva Steele returned to the big screen after six years to play the wheelchair-ridden prison warden, written specifically for her. **83m/C VHS, DVD.** Juanita Brown, Erica Gavin, Roberta Collins, Barbara Steele, Ella Reid, Cheryl "Rainbeaux" Smith, John Aprea, Amy Barrett, Gary Goetzman; ***D:*** Jonathan Demme; ***W:*** Jonathan Demme; ***C:*** Tak Fujimoto; ***M:*** John Cale.

Caged Heat 2: Stripped of Freedom ½ **1994 (R)** Women-in-prison formula with a princess thrown into the pen following a political coup. CIA agent is sent undercover as an inmate to bust her out. Usual sadistic guards, rape, and revenge scenes. From Roger Corman's direct-to-video factory. **84m/C VHS.** Jewel Shepard, Chanel Akiko Hirai, Pamella D'Pella, Vic Diaz; ***D:*** Cirio H. Santiago.

Caged Heat 3000 **1995 (R)** Yes, it's a sci-fi chicks-in-prison movie! Innocent Kira Murphy (Leigh) is wrongly condemned to an underground prison located 45 lightyears from Earth where there are lots of racial tensions and evil prison officials. Prerequisite shower scenes and sadistic guards also add to the standard exploitation. **84m/C VHS.** Cassandra Leigh, Kena Land, Debra Beatty; ***D:*** Cirio H. Santiago; ***W:*** Paul Ziller.

Caged in Paradiso ½ **1989 (R)** A convicted criminal and his wife are dumped onto a remote prisoner's isle to live out their lives. When Cara loses contact with her husband, she must fend for herself. Survival tale boringly told. **90m/C VHS.** Irene Cara; ***D:*** Michael Snyder.

Caged Terror **WOOF!** **1972** Two urbanites hit the countryside for a weekend and meet a band of crazy rapists who ravage the wife and set the husband raging with bloodthirsty revenge. Squalid stroll through the ruins. **76m/C VHS, DVD.** Percy Harkness, Elizabeth Suzuki, Leon Morenzie; ***D:*** Barry McLean.

Caged Women *Women's Penitentiary 4* **1984 (R)** Undercover journalist enters a women's prison and gets the usual eyeful. Mattei used the pseudonym Vincent Dawn. **97m/C VHS, DVD.** *FR IT* Laura Gemser, Gabriele Tinti, Lorraine (De Sette) De Selle, Maria Romano; ***D:*** Bruno Mattei.

Cahill: United States Marshal **1973 (PG)** The aging Duke in one of his lesser moments, portraying a marshal who comes to the aid of his sons. The boys are mixed up with a gang of outlaws, proving that no matter how good a parent you are, sometimes the kids just lean toward the wayward. Turns out, though, that the boys harbor a grudge against the old man due to years of workaholic neglect. Will Duke see the error of his ways and reconcile with the delinquent boys? Will he catch the outlaw leader? Will he go on to star in other Duke vehicles? **103m/C VHS, DVD.** John Wayne, Gary Grimes, George Kennedy, Neville Brand, Marie Windsor, Harry Carey Jr., Clay O'Brien; ***D:*** Andrew V. McLaglen; ***M:*** Elmer Bernstein.

Cain and Mabel ½ **1936** Would-be musical comedy star (and ex-waitress) Mabel O'Dare (Davies) and heavyweight boxer Larry Cain (Gable) are promoted as a couple to boost their careers although they can't stand each other. Of course that changes but when the duo decide to ditch their time in the limelight for marriage and regular jobs it causes consternation among their handlers. Davies, a little too mature for such naivety, did best with the comedic portion of her role while Gable is most notable for being mustache-less per director Bacon's insistence. **89m/B DVD.** Marion Davies, Clark Gable, Allen Jenkins, Roscoe Karns, Walter Catlett, Ruth Donnelly, Pert Kelton, Robert Paige, Hobart Cavanaugh; ***D:*** Lloyd Bacon; ***W:*** Laird Doyle; ***C:*** George Barnes.

The Caine Mutiny **1954** A group of naval officers revolt against a captain they consider mentally unfit. Bogart is masterful as Captain Queeg, obsessed with cleanliness while onboard and later a study in mental meltdown during the court-martial of a crew member who participated in the mutiny. Based on the Pulitzer-winning novel by Herman Wouk, the drama takes a close look at the pressure-filled life aboard ship during WWII. **125m/C VHS, DVD.** Humphrey Bogart, Jose Ferrer, Van Johnson, Fred MacMurray, Lee Marvin, Claude Akins, E.G. Marshall, Robert Francis, May Wynn, Tom Tully, Arthur Franz, Warner Anderson, Katherine Warren, Jerry Paris, Steve Brodie, Whit Bissell, Robert Bray, Ted Cooper; ***D:*** Edward Dmytryk; ***W:*** Stanley Roberts, Michael Blankfort; ***C:*** Franz Planer; ***M:*** Max Steiner.

The Caine Mutiny Court Martial **1988 (PG)** A young lieutenant is up for a court-martial after taking control of the USS Caine in the midst of a typhoon. In order to save him, his lawyer must discredit the paranoid Commander Queeg. As the events of the mutiny unfold, it becomes clear that Queeg's obsession with discipline had become a threat to everyone aboard. Good performances, particularly by Bogosian as the lawyer. Based on the novel by Pulitzer prize-winner Herman Wouk. **100m/C VHS.** Jeff Daniels, Eric Bogosian, Brad Davis, Peter Gallagher, Michael Murphy, Kevin J. O'Connor, Daniel H. Jenkins; ***D:*** Robert Altman. **TV**

Cain's Cutthroats *Cain's Way; The Blood Seekers; Justice Cain* **1971 (R)** A former Confederate army captain and a bounty hunting preacher team up to settle the score with soldiers on a gang-raping, murdering spree. **87m/C VHS.** Scott Brady, John Carradine, Robert Dix, Don Epperson, Adair Jamison, Darwin Joston, Bruce (Kemp) Kimball, Russ McCubbin, Valda Hansen; ***D:*** Kent Osborne; ***W:*** Wilton Denmark; ***C:*** Ralph Waldo; ***M:*** Harley Hatcher.

Cairo **1942** War correspondent Young lands in Cairo where he is supposed to pass along classified information to a Nazi spy posing as a Brit. He meets and falls in love with American movie queen thought to be enemy agent (MacDonald) and a race across the desert follows when Young is trapped in a pyramid. Catchy tunes can't save this cheesy WWII spy spoof that marked the end of MacDonald's MGM contract. **101m/B VHS.** Jeanette MacDonald, Robert Young, Ethel Waters, Reginald Owen, Grant Mitchell, Lionel Atwill, Eduardo Ciannelli, Mitchell Lewis; ***D:*** Woodbridge S. Van Dyke; ***W:*** John McClain; ***M:*** Herbert Stothart.

Cairo Time **2009** Old-fashioned romance about a middle-aged woman set free by her experiences in Cairo (both with the city and a particular man). Juliette (Clarkson) travels to Egypt to spend some time with her hubby Mark (McCamus) who's working at a Gaza refugee camp. But when he can't get away, Mark asks former colleague Tareq (Siddig) to serve as Juliette's tour guide, which leads to a certain attraction between the two. **88m/C DVD.** *CA IR* Patricia Clarkson, Alexander Siddig, Tom McCamus, Elena Anaya, Ruba Nadda; ***D:*** Ruba Nadda; ***W:*** Ruba Nadda; ***C:*** Luc Montpellier; ***M:*** Niall Byrne.

Cake **2005 (R)** Happily single with no interest in married life, travel writer Pippa (Graham) is thrown for a loop when her ill publisher father puts her in charge of his wedding publication. As her day-to-day work causes her to face her marital phobias, her fling with her usual studly-type guy (Diggs) is complicated by her feelings for her more grounded mentor (Sutcliffe)at the magazine. **94m/C DVD.** Heather Graham, David Sutcliffe, Taye Diggs, Sandra Oh, Cheryl Hines, Sarah Chalke, Reagan Pasternak, Kate Kelton, Bruce Grey, Sabrina Grdevich, Suzanne Cyr; ***D:*** Nisha Ganatra; ***W:*** Tassie Cameron; ***C:*** Gregory Middleton; ***M:*** Andrew Lockington. **VIDEO**

The Cake Eaters ½ **2007 (R)** It's not a happy family reunion. Unsuccessful indie rocker Guy (Bartok) is in the doghouse with younger bro Beagle (Stanford) when he finally returns home after their mother's death. With his dad Easy (Dern) abdicating responsibility, Beagle was forced into being the family caretaker. Now he's attracted to terminally ill but fiercely determined teen Georgia (Stewart), whose family is more closely involved with Beagle's than he realizes. Meanwhile Guy has decided to make a play for ex-fiancee Stephanie (Shor) who's involved with another guy. Directorial debut of Masterson. **86m/C DVD.** Aaron Stanford, Kristen Stewart, Jayce Bartok, Bruce Dern, Talia Balsam, Elizabeth Ashley, Melissa Leo, Miriam Shor, Jesse L. Martin; ***D:*** Mary Stuart Masterson; ***W:*** Jayce Bartok; ***C:*** Peter Masterson; ***M:*** Duncan Sheik.

Cal **1984 (R)** Cal (Lynch), a young Catholic man, is reluctantly recruited into the Irish Republican Army. He falls in love with the older Marcella (Mirren), the widow of a Protestant policeman whom he helped kill while acting as the get-away driver for his fellow Republicans. Thoughtful and tragic, with excellent performances; set in Northern Ireland. **104m/C VHS.** *IR* Helen Mirren, John Lynch, Donal McCann, Kitty Gibson, Ray McAnally, John Kavanagh; ***D:*** Pat O'Connor; ***W:*** Bernard MacLaverty; ***M:*** Mark Knopfler. Cannes '84: Actress (Mirren).

The Calamari Wrestler **WOOF!** *Ika resuraa* **2004** A surreal satire of "Rocky" (and similar sports films) and the Buddhist concept of Reincarnation, a former champion pro wrestler is comes back as a giant squid and retakes his former championship while trying to rekindle his romance with his human girlfriend. Various rivals reincarnate themselves as sea life as well, and rubber monster fights abound. **86m/C DVD.** *JP* Kana Ishida, Osamu Nishimura, Miho Shiraishi, Yoshihiro Takayama; ***D:*** Minoru Kawasaki; ***W:*** Minoru Kawasaki, Masakazu Migita.

Calamity Jane **1953** In one of her best Warner musicals, Day stars as the rip-snortin', gun-totin' Calamity Jane of Western lore, in an on-again, off-again romance with Wild Bill Hickok. ♫Secret Love; Just Blew in From the Windy City; The Black Hills of Dakota; The Deadwood Stage (Whip-Crack-Away!). **101m/C VHS, DVD.** Doris Day, Howard Keel, Allyn Ann McLerie, Dick Wesson; ***D:*** David Butler; ***W:*** James O'Hanlon; ***C:*** Wilfrid M. Cline; ***M:*** Sammy Fain, Paul Francis Webster. Oscars '53: Song ("Secret Love").

Calamity Jane ½ **1982** A biography of the famous lady crack shot. Alexander is cast as the tough-as-nails woman who considered herself on a par with any man. **96m/C VHS.** Jane Alexander, Frederic Forrest, Ken Kercheval, Talia Balsam, David Hemmings; ***D:*** James Goldstone. **TV**

Calcutta ½ **1947** Pals Neale Gordon (Ladd) and Pedro Blake (Bendix) are cargo pilots routing flights between Chungking and Calcutta. When their pal Bill is murdered, they become suspicious of his former fiancee, Virginia. **83m/B DVD.** Alan Ladd, Gail Russell, William Bendix, June Duprez, Lowell Gilmore; ***D:*** John Farrow; ***W:*** Seton I. Miller.

Calendar **1993** A Canadian photographer (Egoyan) is hired to take pictures of ancient Armenian churches for a calendar. His wife (Egoyan's real-life spouse Khanjian) accompanies him, serving as a translator, and they hire a driver (Adamian) who turns out to be an architectural expert. Told in flashback, the film gradually reveals a romantic triangle—with the photographer becoming so caught up in his work that he fails to realize his wife, increasingly drawn to her ethnic heritage, and their driver are having an affair. This romantic puzzle also includes the photographer, having returned to Canada wifeless and apparently seeking a replacement, having dinner with a series of women he's meet through the personals. In English and Armenian. **73m/C VHS, DVD.** *CA* Atom Egoyan, Arsinee Khanjian, Ashot Adamian; ***D:*** Atom Egoyan; ***W:*** Atom Egoyan; ***C:*** Norayr Kasper.

Calendar Girl 1/2 **1993 (PG-13)** In 1962 three high-school best friends borrow a convertible and travel from their Nevada homes to Hollywood to meet their pinup idol, Marilyn Monroe. Roy's (Priestley) a rebel, Ned's (Olds, in his film debut) sensitive, and Scott's (O'Connell) just a nice guy. They stay with Roy's Uncle Harvey (Pantoliano), an aspiring actor, and work to meet their dream girl. Which they finally do, in a notably weak sequence which fits in with this notably uninspired film. The three actors at least have enough comradery to make realistic buddies—one of the few true touches in the film. **86m/C VHS.** Jason Priestley, Gabriel Olds, Jerry O'Connell, Joe Pantoliano, Stephen Tobolowsky, Kurt Fuller, Steve Railsback, Emily Warfield, Stephanie Anderson; ***Cameos:*** Chubby Checker; ***D:*** John Whitesell; ***W:*** Paul Shapiro; ***M:*** Hans Zimmer.

Calendar Girl Murders 1/2 **1984** Minor mystery about the murder of some girlie magazine pinups. **104m/C VHS, DVD.** Robert Culp, Tom Skerritt, Barbara Parkins, Sharon Stone; ***D:*** William A. Graham; ***M:*** Brad Fiedel. **TV**

Calendar Girls 1/2 **2003 (PG-13)** The local members of the Women's Institute club in Yorkshire decide to pose nude for a calendar in order to raise money for leukemia research. The calendar, surprisingly, is a hit, even though the models are a little older than your usual calendar pinup girls. Enjoyable for the right audience (read: fans of veddy understated British humor that is secondary to the drama), but starts losing cohesiveness near the end. Loosely based on a true story. **108m/C VHS, DVD.** *GB* Helen Mirren, Julie Walters, John Alderton, Linda Bassett, Annette Crosbie, Philip Glenister, Ciaran Hinds, Celia Imrie, Geraldine James, Penelope Wilton, George Costigan, Graham Crowden, John Fortune; ***Cameos:*** Jay Leno; ***D:*** Nigel Cole; ***W:*** Juliette Towhidi, Tim Firth; ***C:*** Ashley Rowe; ***M:*** Patrick Doyle.

California Casanova WOOF! 1989 (R) Mirthless, semi-musical farce about a nerdy stagehand learning to be a great lover to win a beautiful singer's heart who's being blackmailed by a cruel gangster. Nice cast; nobody's home. **94m/C VHS.** Jerry Orbach, Audrey Landers, Tyrone Power Jr., Bryan Genesse, Ken Kercheval, Ted Davis, Joyce Blair; ***D:*** Nathaniel Christian; ***W:*** Nathaniel Christian.

California Dreaming **1979 (R)** Nerdy young man heads west to California where he tries to fit in with the local beach crowd. Reminiscent of the popular beach movies of the '60s. **93m/C VHS.** Dennis Christopher, Tanya Roberts, Glynnis O'Connor, John Calvin, Seymour Cassel; ***D:*** John Hancock.

California Dreaming *Out of Omaha* **2007 (PG)** Stu (Foley) and Ginger (Thompson) Gainer seem like the typical married suburban couple: they have jobs, they have a house, they have two kids and a dog. Control freak Ginger thinks it would be fun to rent an RV and take a family vacation from their Omaha home to California. Naturally, it's the road trip from heck (the pic is rated PG after all). **?m/C DVD.** Dave Foley, Lea Thompson, Patricia Richardson, Ethan Phillips, Vicki Lewis, Lindsay Seim, David Kalis, Melissa Jarecke, Nicholas Fackler, Ethan Philips; ***D:*** Linda Voorhees; ***W:*** Linda Voorhees; ***C:*** James Bartle.

California Girls **1984** Radio station stages a beauty contest and three sexy ladies prove to be tough competition. Features women in little swimsuits, minimal plot, and a soundtrack by the Police, Kool & the Gang, Blondie, Queen, and 10cc. **83m/C VHS, DVD.** Al Music, Mary McKinley, Alicia Allen, Lantz Douglas, Barbara Parks; ***D:*** Rick Wallace; ***C:*** Gil Hubbs.

California Gold Rush **1981** Hays portrays young aspiring writer, Bret Harte, who, in search of adventure in 1849, arrives in Sutter's Fort and takes on a job at the local sawmill. When gold is found, Sutter's Fort is soon overrun with fortune hunters whose greed, violence, and corruption threaten to tear apart the peaceful community. **100m/C VHS.** Robert Hays, John Dehner, Dan Haggerty, Ken Curtis; ***D:*** Jack B. Hively. **TV**

California Joe **1943** California is being eyed by Confederate sympathizers and also by their leader, who wants it for his own plans. Enter California Joe, a Union officer in disguise, who will save the day. Standard western. **55m/B VHS.** Donald (Don "Red") Barry, Lynn Merrick, Helen Talbot, Wally Vernon, Twinkle Watts, Brian O'Hara, Terry Frost, Leroy Mason, Edward Earle, Charles "Blackie" King; ***D:*** Spencer Gordon Bennet; ***W:*** Norman S. Hall; ***C:*** Ernest Miller.

The California Kid **1974** A sadistic small town sheriff (Morrow) deals with speeders by ramming their car and sending them over a cliff. Eventually a relative of one of his victims (Sheen) shows up to find out what happened to his brother. He is unhappy to say the least. And what better way to show your unhappiness than to challenge the sheriff to a deadly mountain race? **75m/C DVD.** Martin Sheen, Vic Morrow, Michelle Phillips, Nick Nolte, Janit Baldwin, Gary Morgan, Frederic Downs, Don Mantooth, Joe Estevez, Britt Leach, Norman Bartold, Barbara Collentine, Gavan O'Herlihy, Michael Richardson, Jack McCulloch, Ken Johnson, Monika Henreid, Sandy Brown Wyeth; ***D:*** Richard T. Heffron; ***W:*** Richard Compton; ***C:*** Terry Meade; ***M:*** Luchi De Jesus.

California Straight Ahead **1925** Denny—whose niche in the '20s was silent action comedies, and who had teamed with director Pollard earlier in the decade to produce "The Leatherpushers" series—stars in this silent actioner which features a cross-country road trip, zoo animals-on-a-rampage, and a car-racing conclusion (sounds like an action formula ahead of its time). Audiences didn't realize until the talkies that the All-American manly man was in fact played by a Brit. For those who revel in trivia, Denny appeared in the 1961 "Batman." **77m/B VHS.** Reginald Denny, Gertrude (Olmstead) Olmsted, Tom Wilson, Lucille Ward, John Steppling; ***D:*** Harry A. Pollard.

California Straight Ahead! **1937** Not a John Wayne western. The small trucking company run by Biff (Wayne) and Charlie (Treacy) is taking work away from rival Padula (Mason) with tragic consequences for Charlie. Biff wants revenge so he hires on with Corrigan (McWade) who is involved in a cross-country race with Padula and his new boss, railroad magnate Gifford (von Eltz), to prove which transport delivery method is faster. **57m/B DVD.** John Wayne, Louise Latimer, Robert McWade, Theodore von Eltz, Leroy Mason, Emerson Treacy, Tully Marshall; ***D:*** Arthur Lubin; ***W:*** W. Scott Darling; ***C:*** Harry Neumann.

California Suite **1978 (PG)** The posh Beverly Hills Hotel is the setting for four unrelated Neil Simon skits, ranging from a battling husband and wife to feuding friends. Smith is notable as a neurotic English actress in town for the Oscar awards while Caine is effectively low-key in the role of her bisexual husband. Simonized dialogue is crisp and funny. **103m/C VHS, DVD.** Alan Alda, Michael Caine, Bill Cosby, Jane Fonda, Walter Matthau, Richard Pryor, Maggie Smith, Elaine May; ***D:*** Herbert Ross; ***W:*** Neil Simon; ***C:*** David M. Walsh; ***M:*** Claude Bolling. Oscars '78: Support. Actress (Smith); Golden Globes '79: Actress—Mus./Comedy (Smith).

The California Trail 1/2 **1933** The corrupt mayor of La Loma, California, is attempting to force the peons to deed over their land by starving them out with the help of his brother, the commander of the local troops. Santa Fe Stewart is hired to bring in food relief and gets into big trouble with the crooked authorities. **65m/B DVD.** Buck Jones, George Humbert, Luis Alberni, Helen Mack, Chris-Pin (Ethier Crispin Martini) Martin, Charles Stevens, Carlos Villarias, Emile Chautard; ***D:*** Lambert Hillyer; ***W:*** Lambert Hillyer; ***C:*** Benjamin (Ben H.) Kline.

Caligula WOOF! 1980 Infamous, expensive, extremely graphic, and sexually explicit adaptation of the life of the mad Roman emperor, Caligula. Scenes of decapitation, necrophilia, rape, bestiality, and sadomasochism abound. Biggest question is why Gielgud, O'Toole, and McDowell lent their talents to this monumentally abhorred film (not to mention Gore Vidal on the writing end, who didn't want the credit). Adult magazine publisher Bob Guccione coproduced and didn't particularly want to release it. Also available in a censored, "R" rated version. **143m/C VHS, DVD.** *IT* Malcolm McDowell, John Gielgud, Peter O'Toole, Helen Mirren, Theresa-Ann Savoy, John Steiner, Paolo Bonacelli, Adriana Asti; ***D:*** Tinto Brass; ***W:*** Gore Vidal; ***C:*** Tinto Brass, Silvano Ippoliti; ***M:*** Paul Clemente.

Call Him Mr. Shatter *Shatter* **1974 (R)** A hired killer stalks a tottering Third World president and becomes embroiled in international political intrigue. **90m/C VHS, DVD.** *GB* Stuart Whitman, Peter Cushing, Anton Diffring; ***D:*** Michael Carreras.

Call It a Day 1/2 **1937** The first day of spring makes everyone in the conservative British Hilton family go a little silly in strange ways, including having several unexpected romantic dalliances thwarted. De Havilland gets top billing as the family's lovesick daughter although she has a smaller role than Hunter and Inescort, who play her parents. **89m/B DVD.** Olivia de Havilland, Ian Hunter, Frieda Inescort, Anita Louise, Alice Brady, Roland Young, Bonita Granville, Peter Willes, Walter Woolf King, Peggy Wood, Marcia Ralston; ***D:*** Archie Mayo; ***W:*** Casey Robinson; ***C:*** Ernest Haller.

Call Me **1988 (R)** Psycho-drama about a lusty young woman who responds positively to an obscene telephone caller until she witnesses him murder another person. Doubt creeps into the relationship. **98m/C VHS.** Patricia Charbonneau, Patti D'Arbanville, Sam Freed, Boyd Gaines, Stephen McHattie; ***D:*** Sollace Mitchell.

Call Me Bwana 1/2 **1963** Pure cornpone with Hope as a bumbling explorer sent with CIA agent Adams to track down a lost American space capsule in deepest Africa. Enemy agents Ekberg and Jeffries try to make things difficult. **103m/C VHS.** Bob Hope, Edie Adams, Anita Ekberg, Lionel Jeffries, Percy Herbert, Paul Carpenter, Orlando Martins; ***D:*** Gordon Douglas; ***W:*** Nate Monaster, Johanna Harwood.

Call Me Claus **2001** Goldberg mugs her way through her role as a TV shopping network producer with Scrooge-like tendencies. Hawthorne is the good-natured St. Nick who wants to retire and have her replace him at the yuletide gig. Might rate a few chuckles if you've seen all the good Christmas movies twice already. **90m/C VHS, DVD.** Whoopi Goldberg, Nigel Hawthorne, Taylor Negron, Brian Stokes Mitchell, Victor Garber, Gregory Bernstein, Brian Bird; ***D:*** Peter Werner; ***W:*** Sarah Bernstein; ***M:*** Garth Brooks. **TV**

Call Me: The Rise and Fall of Heidi Fleiss 1/2 **2004** Stale made-for-TV flick follows the real story of Heidi Fleiss (DiScala) as she leaves behind her posh family life to take over a call-girl business for the rich and famous Hollywood crowd. Her time to revel in the excess is cut short, and Tinseltown's movers-and-shakers fear exposure from the publicity of Heidi's little black book. Interestingly, DiScala is said to have shunned most of the sex scenes. **84m/C VHS, DVD.** Jamie-Lynn Sigler, Saul Rubinek, Emmanuelle Vaugier, Ian Tracey, Natassia Malthe, Corbin Bernsen, Brenda Fricker, Robert Davi, Lisa Marie Caruk, Missy Peregrym; ***D:*** Charles McDougall; ***W:*** Norman Snider; ***C:*** David Franco; ***M:*** Ryan Shore. **VIDEO**

Call Northside 777 1/2 *Calling Northside 777* **1948** Hard-boiled Chicago reporter McNeal (Stewart) finds himself in the crux of a decade-old murder investigation when he follows up a newspaper ad offering $5,000 for any information leading to the arrest and conviction of a police killer. The cunning reporter discovers police coverups and missing evidence pointing to an imprisoned man's innocence. Powerful performance from Stewart directs this docu-drama based on the real-life story of Chicago's Joe Majczek, unjustly imprisoned for 11 years, and the Pulitzer Prize winning reporter Jim McGuire who, through a clever investigation, found enough evidence to have the case re-opened. **111m/B VHS, DVD.** James Stewart, Richard Conte, Lee J. Cobb, Helen Walker, Betty Garde, Moroni Olsen, E.G. Marshall, Howard Smith, John McIntire, Paul Harvey, George Tyne, Michael Chapin, Addison Richards, Richard Rober, Eddie Dunn, Charles Lane, Walter Greaza, William Post Jr., George Melford, Charles F. Miller, Lionel Stander, Jonathan Hale, Freddie (Fred) Steele; ***D:*** Henry Hathaway; ***W:*** Jerome Cady, Jay Dratler; ***C:*** Joe MacDonald; ***M:*** Alfred Newman.

Call of the Canyon 1/2 **1942** A crooked agent for a local meat packer won't pay a fair price, so Gene goes off to talk to the head man to set him straight. **71m/B VHS, DVD.** Gene Autry, Smiley Burnette, Ruth Terry, Thurston Hall, Pat Brady; ***D:*** Joseph Santley.

Call of the Forest 1/2 **1949** Bobby makes friends with a beautiful wild black stallion which is captured and tamed by his father. The father has found a goldmine, also desired by an villain, and Bobby and his horse must come to his father's aid. Black Diamond (the horse) has the best role. **74m/B VHS.** Robert Lowery, Ken Curtis, Martha Sherrill, Chief Thundercloud, Charles Hughes; ***D:*** John F. Link.

Call of the Rockies **1944** Action-packed oater in which Carson and Burnette ride across country to save Placer City's mine from crooked townsmen. **54m/B VHS.** Sunset Carson, Smiley Burnette; ***D:*** Lesley Selander.

Call of the Wild **1972 (PG)** Jack London's famous story about a man whose survival depends upon his knowledge of the Alaskan wilderness almost comes to life. Filmed in Finland. **105m/C VHS, DVD.** Charlton Heston, Michele Mercier, George Eastman; ***D:*** Ken Annakin; ***W:*** Harry Alan Towers, Hubert Frank; ***C:*** John Cabrera; ***M:*** Carlo Rustichelli.

Call of the Wild 1/2 **1993** Another of Jack London's survival tales is dramatized for TV. John Thornton (Schroder) is a rich greenhorn seeking adventure during the 1897 Klondike gold rush. Buck is a German shepherd, sold as a sled dog, who finds adventures of his own in the frozen North until man and dog are united to search for a legendary gold mine. The book is more exciting but the film is more violent. Filmed on location in British Columbia. **97m/C VHS.** *IT* Rick Schroder, Gordon Tootoosis, Mia Sara, Duncan Fraser, Richard Newman, Brent Stait, Allan Lysell, Tom Heaton, Eric McCormack, Vince Metcalfe; ***D:*** Alan Smithee, Michael Toshiyuki Uno; ***C:*** David Geddes; ***M:*** Lee Holdridge. **TV**

Call of the Wild 1/2 *Jack London's Call of the Wild* **2004** Filmed for the Animal Planet network, and based very loosely on the novel, this is the first film in a series. Fifteen-year-old Miles Challenger (Meier) has his life change after meeting a heroic dog named Buck. Very family-oriented, and not quite as dark as the novel. **100m/C DVD.** Shane Meier, Nick Mancuso, Rachel Hayward, Kathleen Duborg, Mark Hildreth, Crystal Buble, Harvey Dumansky, George Josef; ***D:*** Brenton Spencer, David Winning, Zale Dalen, Jorge Montesi; ***W:*** David Fallon, Tim John, David Assael, Michael Sloan, Madeline Sunshine; ***C:*** Wade Ferley, Stephen McNutt, Tony Westman; ***M:*** Hal Beckett.

Call of the Yukon 1/2 **1938** A female writer and her various animal companions travel to a remote Alaskan Eskimo village in search of inspiration for her new novel. Unfortunately the Eskimos are fleeing the oncoming winter, and the leader of a vicious wolf pack named Swift Lightning. When winter sets in, the entire group gets trapped in a cabin and love triangles among humans and animals ensue. Likeable for diehard fans of 1930s cinema but tedious otherwise. **70m/B DVD.** Richard Arlen, Beverly Roberts, Lyle Talbot, Mala, Garry Owen, Ivan Miller, Al "Fuzzy" St. John; ***D:*** John T. Coyle, B. Reeves Eason; ***W:*** Gertrude Orr, Bill Peet; ***C:*** Ernest Miller; ***M:*** Alberto Colombo.

Call Out the Marines **1942** A group of army buddies re-enlist to break up a spy ring. Two of the guys fall in love with the same girl, not realizing that she's one of the spies. McLaglen and Lowe's last comedy together. Mediocre outing isn't redeemed by below average musical numbers. ♫ Call Out the Marines; Zana Zaranda; The Light of My Life; Beware; Hands Across the Border. **67m/B VHS.** Edmund Lowe, Victor McLaglen, Binnie Barnes, Paul Kelly, Dorothy Lovett, Franklin Pangborn; ***D:*** Frank Ryan; ***W:*** Frank Ryan, William Hamilton; ***C:*** J. Roy Hunt, Nicholas Musuraca.

Call the Mesquiteers 🦴 ½ **1938** Thieves steal the silk shipments from the Desert Express train and then make their getaway by hijacking the Three Mesquiteers truck and holding them hostage. When the trio do free themselves, the Mesquiteers find the authorities suspect them of committing the robberies and they must clear their names. The thirteenth film in the series. **55m/B DVD.** Ray Corrigan, Robert "Bob" Livingston, Max Terhune, Lynne Roberts, Earle Hodgins, Eddy (Eddie, Ed) Waller, Sammy McKim, Maston Williams; ***D:*** John English; ***W:*** Lucille Ward; ***C:*** William Nobles.

Call to Glory 🦴🦴 ½ **1984** Pilot for the critically praised TV series. An Air Force pilot and his family face turbulent times during the Cuban missile crisis. **96m/C VHS.** Craig T. Nelson, Cindy Pickett, Gabriel Damon, Keenan Wynn, Elisabeth Shue, G.D. Spradlin, David Hollander, Kathleen Lloyd; ***D:*** Thomas Carter. **TV**

A Call to Remember 🦴🦴 ½ **1997 (R)** Paula Rubinek (Danner) and David Tobias (Mantegna) are concentration camp survivors who both had their spouses and children killed by the Nazis. They've married, moved to America, and are living in the suburbs with their two sons and trying to forget the past, which causes problems for their children. But Paula's quiet world explodes when she receives a phone call notifying her that a son she thought died in the war has in fact survived. Writer Eisenberg based this drama on his parents' history. **105m/C VHS.** Blythe Danner, Joe Mantegna, David Lascher, Kevin Zegers, Joe Spano, Kevin McNulty, Blu Mankuma; ***D:*** Jack Bender; ***W:*** Max Eisenberg; ***C:*** David Geddes. **CABLE**

Callas Forever 🦴🦴 **2002** Cinematic tribute by Zeffirelli to his longtime friend, opera diva Maria Callas who died in 1977. His own alter ego is British impresario Larry Kelly (Irons), Callas's former manager. Callas (Ardant) is living in isolation in her Paris apartment, mourning the loss of both her voice and her great love, Aristotle Onassis. Kelly and journalist friend Sarah (Plowright) persuade the singer to come out of retirement to lip-synch to a film version of "Carmen," one of her best roles. She agrees and the film shoot revives her but what happens when the filming stops? Ardant may not resemble the real Callas but she has a commanding charisma that enhances her portrayal. **108m/C DVD.** Fanny Ardant, Jeremy Irons, Joan Plowright, Jay Rodan, Gabriel Garko; ***D:*** Franco Zeffirelli; ***W:*** Franco Zeffirelli, Martin Sherman; ***C:*** Ennio Guarnieri; ***M:*** Alessio Vlad.

The Caller 🦴 **1987 (R)** A strange man enters the house of a lone woman and sets off a long night of suspense and an almost longer evening of inept movie-making. **90m/C VHS.** Malcolm McDowell, Madolyn Smith; ***D:*** Arthur Allan Seidelman; ***M:*** Richard Band.

The Caller 🦴 ½ **2008 (PG-13)** Distancing and talky drama that goes nowhere. Jimmy (Langella), an exec at an international energy firm, blows the whistle on their illegal practices and knows he's now a target. So he secretly hires PI Frank (Gould) to document his every move over a two-week period before his probable murder. Frank doesn't realize the guy he's shadowing is the guy who hired him. There's also something about Jimmy wanting to make peace with some childhood trauma that took place in 1940s France. **92m/C DVD.** Frank Langella, Elliott Gould, Laura Elena Harring, Anabel Sosa; ***D:*** Richard Ledes; ***W:*** Richard Ledes; ***C:*** Stephen Kazmierski; ***M:*** Robert Miller.

Callie and Son 🦴🦴 *Rags to Riches* **1981** Details the sordid story of a waitress who works her way up to become a Dallas socialite and her obsessive relationship with her illegitimate son. **97m/C VHS, VHS, DVD.** Lindsay Wagner, Dabney Coleman, Jameson Parker, Andrew Prine, James Sloyan, Michelle Pfeiffer; ***D:*** Waris Hussein; ***M:*** Billy Goldenberg.

Calling Dr. Death 🦴🦴 ½ **1943** In 1943's "Calling Dr. Death," Chaney plays a neurologist with an unfaithful wife who gets herself murdered. Naturally, Chaney's the primary suspect. Based on radio's "Inner Sanctum" mysteries. **63m/B VHS.** Lon Chaney Jr., Patricia Morison, J. Carrol Naish, David Bruce, Ramsay Ames, Fay Helm, Holmes Herbert, Mary Hale; ***D:*** Reginald LeBorg; ***W:*** Edward Dein; ***C:*** Virgil Miller; ***M:*** Paul Sawtell.

Calling Paul Temple 🦴 ½ **1948** The wealthy patients of a nerve doctor have been dying and a detective is called in to investigate. **92m/B VHS.** *GB* John Bentley, Dinah Sheridan, Margaretta Scott, Abraham Sofaer, Celia Lipton, Alan Wheatley, Wally Patch; ***D:*** Maclean Rogers.

Calling Wild Bill Elliott 🦴 ½ **1943** The crooked territorial governor is exposed by hero Elliott and sidekick Hayes and justice is restored in this typical B-western. Elliott's first film for Republic; he went on to star in 16 Red Ryder films as well as other westerns for the studio. **55m/B VHS.** William (Wild Bill) Elliott, George "Gabby" Hayes, Herbert (Hayes) Heyes, Anne Jeffreys, Fred Kohler Jr., Roy Barcroft, Yakima Canutt; ***D:*** Spencer Gordon Bennet.

Calm at Sunset 🦴🦴 ½ **1996 (PG)** James Pfeiffer (Facinelli) drops out of college to pursue his dream of becoming a commercial fisherman, much to the dismay of his parents (Moriarty, Nelligan) who already know how rough that life can be. But James gets his chance when he rescues seaman Kelly Dobbs (Conway) and the two become partners. Still, James must deal with secrets, a tragedy, and some hard decisions. TV drama with some solid performances. Based on the novel "Calm at Sunset, Calm at Dawn" by Paul Watkins. **98m/C VHS.** Peter Facinelli, Michael Moriarty, Kate Nelligan, Kevin Conway, Gretchen Mol, Melvin Van Peebles; ***D:*** Daniel Petrie; ***W:*** Pamela Gray, John Kent Harrison, David Young; ***C:*** Glen MacPherson; ***M:*** Ernest Troost. **TV**

Cambridge Spies 🦴🦴 ½ **2003** Semi-fictional and romanticized account of the friendship of longtime British spies Harold Philby (Stephens), Guy Burgess (Hollander), Anthony Blunt (West), and Donald Maclean (Penry-Jones), which began in the 1930s while the quartet was at Cambridge University and continued for more than 30 years (Philby defected to Moscow in 1964). **240m/C DVD.** *GB* Toby Stephens, Samuel West, Tom Hollander, Rupert Penry-Jones, Anthony Andrews, Imelda Staunton, Stuart Laing, Patrick Kennedy, James Fox, Anna-Louise Plowman, John Light; ***D:*** Tim Fywell; ***W:*** Peter Moffatt; ***C:*** David Higgs; ***M:*** John Lunn. **TV**

Came a Hot Friday 🦴🦴 **1985 (PG)** Two cheap conmen arrive in a 1949 southern New Zealand town, run various scams and pursue women. **101m/C VHS.** *NZ* Peter Bland, Philip Gordon, Billy T. James; ***D:*** Ian Mune; ***C:*** Alun Bollinger.

Camel Boy 🦴 ½ **1984** True story of a young Arabian boy who befriends a camel and their treacherous trek across the desert. **78m/C VHS.** *AU* ***D:*** Yoram Gross; ***V:*** Michael Pate, Ron Haddrick, John Meillon.

Camelot 🦴🦴 **1967** The long-running Lerner and Loewe Broadway musical about King Arthur, Guinevere, and Lancelot was adapted from T.H. White's book, "The Once and Future King." Redgrave and Nero have chemistry as the illicit lovers, Harris is strong as the king struggling to hold together his dream, but muddled direction undermines the effort. ♫ I Wonder What the King is Doing Tonight; The Simple Joys of Maidenhood; Camelot; C'est Moi; The Lusty Month of May; Follow Me; How To Handle a Woman; Then You May Take Me to the Fair; If Ever I Would Leave You. **150m/C VHS, DVD.** Richard Harris, Vanessa Redgrave, David Hemmings, Franco Nero, Lionel Jeffries; ***D:*** Joshua Logan; ***W:*** Alan Jay Lerner; ***C:*** Richard H. Kline; ***M:*** Frederick Loewe, Alan Jay Lerner. Oscars '67: Adapt. Score, Art Dir./Set Dec., Costume Des.; Golden Globes '68: Actor—Mus./Comedy (Harris), Song ("If Ever I Should Leave You"), Score.

Camera Buff 🦴🦴 *Amator* **1979** Satire on bureaucracy finds a factory worker buying a home-movie camera to film his new baby but becoming obsessed with his new toy. So he begins recording everything he sees—even things the authorities don't want shown. Polish with subtitles. **108m/C VHS, DVD.** *PL* Jerzy Stuhr, Malgorzata Zajaczkowska, Ewa Pokas, Krzysztof Zanussi; ***D:*** Krzysztof Kieslowski; ***W:*** Jerzy Stuhr, Krzysztof Kieslowski; ***M:*** Krzysztof Knittel.

The Cameraman 🦴🦴🦴🦴 **1928** After moving to MGM, Keaton made his first feature with a major studio, giving up the artistic control he had enjoyed in his previous films. Spared from the vilification of studio politics (not the case with later Keaton films) "The Cameraman" enjoyed both critical and popular success. Keaton's inept tintype portrait-maker has a heart that pitter-patters for an MGM office girl. He hopes to impress her by joining the ranks of the newsreel photographers. Fortuitously poised to grab a photo scoop on a Chinese tong war, he is forced to return empty-handed when an organ-grinder's monkey absconds with his firsthand footage. Silent with a musical score. **78m/B VHS, DVD.** Buster Keaton, Marceline Day, Harold Goodwin, Harry Gribbon, Sidney Bracy, Edward Brophy, Vernon Dent, William Irving; ***D:*** Edward Sedgwick. Natl. Film Reg. '05.

Cameron's Closet 🦴 ½ **1989 (R)** Every child's nightmare comes true. A young boy is convinced that a monster lives in his closet due to his perverse father's psychological tortures. Only this time the monster is real! **86m/C VHS, DVD.** Cotter Smith, Mel Harris, Scott Curtis, Chuck McCann, Leigh McCloskey, Kim Lankford, Tab Hunter; ***D:*** Armand Mastroianni; ***W:*** Gary Brandner; ***C:*** Russell Carpenter.

Camila 🦴🦴🦴 **1984** The true story of the tragic romance between an Argentinean socialite and a Jesuit priest in 1847. The two lovers escape to a small provincial village where they live together as man and wife. Eventually they are recognized and condemned to death. Available in Spanish with English subtitles or dubbed into English. **105m/C VHS, DVD.** *AR SP* Susu Pecoraro, Imanol Arias, Hector Alterio, Elena Tasisto; ***D:*** Maria-Luisa Bemberg.

Camilla 🦴🦴 ½ **1994 (PG-13)** Tandy is delightful in her last starring role as a former violinist on the run with frustrated musician Fonda. Oafish son (Chaykin) and insensitive husband (Koteas) just don't understand, so its time to head to Toronto, site of a fondly, if perhaps incorrectly, remembered triumph. Sort of a May-December female-bonding roadtrip with lots of conversation and comic asides. An inevitably poignant pairing of Tandy and real-life husband Cronyn offers the chance to experience one of America's greatest acting teams one last time. Lack of stereotyping and fairly novel twist on the road movie keep this one on the highway. **91m/C VHS, DVD.** Jessica Tandy, Bridget Fonda, Hume Cronyn, Elias Koteas, Maury Chaykin, Graham Greene; ***D:*** Deepa Mehta; ***W:*** Paul Quarrington; ***M:*** Daniel Lanois.

Camille 🦴🦴 **1921** Dying courtesan falls in love with innocent young man in the Dumas classic. Valentino in his prime. **55m/B VHS.** Rudolph Valentino, Alla Nazimova; ***D:*** Fred Niblo.

Camille 🦴🦴🦴 ½ **1936** Marguerite (Garbo) has found success as Parisian courtesan "La Dame aux Camille" but has never found love. Until she unwisely falls for a handsome but innocent, young aristocrat, Armand (Taylor). Still, Camille agrees to give him up, realizing her scandalous past will jeopardize his future. Oh yes, then she contracts TB and fades away beautifully in gowns by Adrian. This classic Alexandre Dumas story somehow manages to escape the cliches and stands as one of the most telling monuments to Garbo's unique magic and presence on film. **108m/B VHS, DVD.** Greta Garbo, Robert Taylor, Lionel Barrymore, Henry Daniell, Elizabeth Allan, Rex O'Malley, Lenore Ulric, Laura Hope Crews; ***D:*** George Cukor; ***W:*** Frances Marion, James Hilton, Zoe Akins; ***C:*** William H. Daniels; ***M:*** Herbert Stothart. N.Y. Film Critics '37: Actress (Garbo).

Camille Claudel 🦴🦴🦴 **1989 (R)** A lushly romantic version of the art world in the late 19th century, when art was exploding in new forms and independence for women was unheard of. Young sculptor Claudel's (Adjani) tragic love for art, Auguste Rodin (the larger-than-life Depardieu), and independence clash, costing her sanity and her confinement to an insitution for the last 30 years of her life. Very long, it requires an attentive and thoughtful viewing. In French with English subtitles. **149m/C VHS, DVD.** *FR* Isabelle Adjani, Gerard Depardieu, Laurent Grevill, Alain Cuny, Madeleine Robinson, Katrine Boorman, Daniele Lebrun; ***D:*** Bruno Nuytten; ***W:*** Bruno Nuytten, Marilyn Goldin; ***C:*** Pierre Lhomme; ***M:*** Gabriel Yared. Cesar '89: Actress (Adjani), Art Dir./Set Dec., Cinematog., Costume Des., Film.

Camille 2000 🦴 ½ **1969** Dumas meets Debbie Does Rome in this artier than thou mess. Unreasonably well endowed Marguerite (Gaubert) spends much horizontal time with Rome's decadent society denizens while pining pitifully for tru luv Armand (Castelnuovo). She dies a horrible death in the end, but her disease's initials aren't TB. **115m/C VHS, DVD.** Silvana Venturelli, Massimo Serato, Daniele Gaubert, Nino Castelnuovo, Eleanora Rossi-Drago; ***D:*** Radley Metzger; ***W:*** Michael DeForrest; ***C:*** Ennio Guarnieri; ***M:*** Piero Piccioni.

The Camomile Lawn 🦴🦴 ½ **1992** In August 1939, various young cousins gather at their uncle's house on the Cornish coast for a last holiday before the inevitable war changes all their lives. Thirty years later, they return to the house for a funeral and the chance to look back on their frequently risque behavior. Naughty adaptation of the novel by Mary Wesley. **264m/C DVD.** *GB* Jennifer Ehle, Tara Fitzgerald, Toby Stephens, Felicity Kendal, Rebecca Hall, Paul Eddington, Oliver Cotton, Claire Bloom, Rosemary Harris, Richard Johnson, Virginia McKenna, Nicholas Le Prevost; ***D:*** Peter Hall; ***W:*** Kenneth Taylor; ***C:*** Ernest Vincze; ***M:*** Stephen (Steve) Edwards. **TV**

Camorra: The Naples Connection 🦴🦴 *Un Complicato Intrigo Di Donne, Vicoli E Delitti* **1985 (R)** A prostitute and an American drug dealer find themselves embroiled in the murders of Neapolitan Mafia heads. Violent, overblown, minor Wertmuller. **94m/C VHS.** *IT* Harvey Keitel, Angela Molina, Lorraine Bracco, Francisco Rabal; ***D:*** Lina Wertmuller; ***W:*** Lina Wertmuller.

Camouflage 🦴🦴 ½ **2000 (R)** Dumb, blond but likeable actor Marty Mackenzie (Munro) wants to perfect his tough-guy persona so he decides to apprentice with old-timer PI Jack Potter (Nielsen). But the routine surveillance case that Jack assigns Marty to turns out to be the tip of a deadly iceberg. It's a goof but don't expect "Naked Gun" type humor. **98m/C VHS, DVD.** Leslie Nielsen, Lochlyn Munro, Vanessa Angel, William Forsythe; ***D:*** James Keach; ***W:*** Tom Epperson, Billy Bob Thornton; ***C:*** Glen MacPherson. **VIDEO**

Camp 🦴🦴 ½ **2003 (PG-13)** Wanna-be teenage thesps flock to Camp Ovation-the summertime equivalent of the "Fame" school—where they can sing, dance and generally be nerdy to their heart's content. First-time director/writer Graff, who in real life was a counselor at a performing arts camp, assembles a cast of typical misfit kids drawn to the stage: budding transvestite Michael (de Jesus), tomboy Ellen (Chilcoat), and the good-looking, seemingly straight Vlad (Letterle), shepherded into adult theaterhood by the cynical, alcoholic musical-theater pro (Dixon). Story follows the ups and downs of these hopefuls, as well as other fringe characters but especially focuses on the sexual preference of Vlad. Despite uneven acting and stereotypical scenarios, flick is an indie with integrity and heart, while also boasting some rousing musical numbers. **114m/C VHS, DVD.** *US* Daniel Letterle, Joanna Chilcoat, Robin De Jesus, Tiffany Taylor, Sasha Allen, Alana Allen, Anna Kendrick, Don Dixon; ***D:*** Todd Graff; ***W:*** Todd Graff; ***C:*** Kip Bogdahn; ***M:*** Stephen Trask.

Camp Cucamonga: How I Spent My Summer Vacation 🦴 **1990** Zany antics at summer camp abound when Camp Cucamonga's owner mistakes the new handyman for the camp inspector. Well-known stars from TV's "Cheers," "The Jeffersons," "The Wonder Years," and "The Love Boat" are featured in this silly flick. **100m/C VHS, DVD.** John Ratzenberger, Sherman Hemsley, Josh Saviano, Danica McKellar, Chad Allen, Dorothy Lyman, Lauren Tewes, G. Gordon Liddy; ***D:*** Roger Duchowny. **TV**

Camp Nowhere 🦴🦴 **1994 (PG)** Video fodder for the juniors in the household as kids turn tables on parents. Instead of trudging off to summer camp for the umpteenth time, a group of upscale kids create their own with the help of laid-off drama teacher Lloyd, who must first con their parents into believing that Camp Nowhere is legit. What follows is that very special summer camp in the Hollywood tradition with lots of junk food, video games galore, and of course, no rules. Camp be-serko formula good for a few laughs. **106m/C VHS, DVD.** Christopher Lloyd, Wendy Makkena, M. Emmet Walsh, Peter Scolari, Peter Onorati, Ray Baker, Kate Mulgrew, Jonathan Jackson, Romy Walthall, Maryedith Burrell, Thomas F. Wilson, Nathan Cavaleri, Andrew Keegan, Melody Kay, Joshua Gibran Mayweather, John Putch, Devin Oatway, Burgess Meredith, Marne Patterson, Jessica Alba; ***D:*** Jonathan Prince; ***W:*** Andrew Kurtzman, Eliot Wald; ***C:*** Sandi Sissel.

Camp Rock 1/2 **2008** Think Cinderella as a wannabe pop star in this Disney Channel original. Bubbly teenager Mitchie (Lovato) is desperate to attend a prestigious rock camp her family can't afford. So her mom gets a job as the camp cook, which means Mitchie can be a student if she works part-time in the kitchen. Embarrassed, Mitchie pretends to be as wealthy and popular as her new friends. Then she's overheard singing (but not seen) by celebrity camp instructor and troubled teen heartthrob Shane Gray (Joe Jonas), who wants to know who the voice belongs to. But can Mitchie come clean about her deception? Jonas brothers Nick and Kevin also appear. Filmed at Kilcoo Camp in Ontario. **90m/C DVD.** Alyson Stoner, Demi Lovato, Joe Jonas, Maria Canals-Barrera, Meaghan Jette Martin, Jasmine Richards, Anna Maria Perez de Tagle; ***D:*** Matthew Diamond; ***W:*** Karin Gist, Regina Hicks. **CABLE**

Campfire Tales 1998 (R) Four teens get lost in the woods and are terrorized by a maniac. **103m/C VHS, DVD.** James Marsden, Kim Murphy, Christine Taylor, Jay R. Ferguson, Christopher K. Masterson, Ron Livingston, Jennifer MacDonald, Hawthorne James, Alex McKenna, Glenn Quinn, Erick Fleeks, Amy Smart, Rick Lawrence, Suzanne Goddard; ***D:*** David Semel, Martin Kunert, Matt Cooper; ***W:*** Martin Kunert, Matt Cooper, Eric Manes; ***C:*** John Peters; ***M:*** Andrew Rose.

Campus Confessions **1938** Son of the college dean, Wayne Atterbury (Henry) struggles to be an ace student and top jock in this campus-set romantic comedy so that Joyce (Grable) will notice him. So he joins the basketball team, hoping to win the championship game (teammates include All-American star player Hank Luisetti). **67m/B VHS.** William Henry, Betty Grable, Richard Denning, Fritz Feld, Thurston Hall, Roy Gordon, Eleanore Whitney, John Arledge; ***D:*** George Archainbaud; ***W:*** Lloyd Corrigan; ***C:*** Henry Sharp; ***M:*** John Leipold, Stephan Pasternacki.

The Campus Corpse **1977 (PG)** Young man stumbles into deadly college frat hazing and discovers he and rest of cast are utterly devoid of acting ability. **92m/C VHS.** Charles Martin Smith, Jeff East, Brad Davis; ***D:*** Douglas Curtis.

Campus Knights **1929** If you're a serious student of the campus caper film, this is one of the earliest (though not one of the best) of the genre (if such a distinction can be made). The story involves twin brothers—one a tweedy high-browed professor, the other a bon vivant man about town—who wreak fraternal chaos on the quads. **70m/B VHS.** Raymond (Ray) McKee, Shirley Palmer, Marie Quillen, Jean Laverty, Sybil Grove; ***D:*** Albert Kelley.

Campus Man **1987 (PG)** An entrepreneurial college student markets a beefcake calendar featuring his best friend, until the calendar's sales threaten his friend's amateur athletic status. **94m/C VHS, DVD.** John Dye, Steve Lyon, Kim Delaney, Miles O'Keeffe, Morgan Fairchild, Kathleen Wilhoite; ***D:*** Ron Casden; ***W:*** Geoffrey Baere; ***M:*** James Newton Howard.

Can-Can **1960** Lackluster screen adaptation of the Cole Porter musical bears little resemblance to the stage version. MacLaine is a cafe owner who goes to court to try and get the "Can-Can," a dance considered risque in gay Paree at the end of the 19th century, made legal. Love interest Sinatra happens to be a lawyer. ♫ C'est Manifique; Let's Do It; I Love Paris; You Do Something to Me; It's All Right With Me; Live and Let Live; Come Along With Me; Just One of Those Things. **131m/C VHS, DVD.** Frank Sinatra, Shirley MacLaine, Maurice Chevalier, Louis Jourdan, Juliet Prowse, Marcel Dalio, Leon Belasco; ***D:*** Walter Lang; ***C:*** William H. Daniels.

Can I Do It... Till I Need Glasses?
WOOF! 1977 More to the point, can you stay awake till the end? Prurient juvenile junk. Brief Williams footage was grafted to this mess during 15 minutes of Mork fame. **72m/C VHS.** Robin Williams, Roger Behr, Debra Klose, Moose Carlson, Walter Olkewicz; ***D:*** I. Robert Levy.

Can of Worms 1/2 **2000** When young Mike Pillsbury's science project goes wrong, he sends a message into outer space to be rescued from his dismal life on Earth. But he certainly isn't expecting aliens to hear his plea and come to his aid. **88m/C VHS.** Malcolm McDowell, Adam Wylie, Michael Schulman, Erika Christensen, Lee Garlington, Brighton Hertford, Terry David Mulligan; ***D:*** Paul Schneider. **CABLE**

Can She Bake a Cherry Pie?
1983 Two offbeat characters meet and fall in love in an odd sort of way. Slow-moving and talky but somewhat rewarding. One of Black's better performances. **90m/C VHS, DVD.** Karen Black, Michael Emil, Michael Margotta, Frances Fisher, Martin Frydberg; ***D:*** Henry Jaglom; ***W:*** Henry Jaglom; ***M:*** Karen Black.

Can You Feel Me Dancing?
1985 Family-happy lightweight entertainment coproduced by Kent Bateman and starring Bateman progeny Jason and Justine as brother and sister, a novel premise that only a father could love. A blind independence-impaired teenager tries to liberate herself from her overbearing family, and finds the secret to conquering her fears and to standing up for herself when she falls in love. Written by spouse-team Steven and J. Miyoko Hensley. **95m/C VHS.** Jason Bateman, Justine Bateman; ***D:*** Michael Miller; ***W:*** Steven Hensley, J. Miyoko Hensley.

Can You Hear the Laughter? The Story of Freddie Prinze
1979 Heartstring tugging biography of the late Puerto Rican comedian whose troubled life lead to suicide in spite of his apparent success. He was most noted for his starring role in "Chico and the Man." **100m/C VHS.** Ira Angustain, Kevin Hooks, Randee Heller, Devon Ericson, Julie Carmen, Stephen Elliott; ***D:*** Burt Brinckerhoff.

Canada's Sweetheart: The Saga of Hal C. Banks *Sweetheart!* **1985** True story of Banks, hired by the Canadian government to break up a strike among the communist-led seaman's union which had put a stranglehold on Canadian commerce, and who was eventually convicted of strong-arm tactics. **115m/C VHS.** *CA* Maury Chaykin, Colin Fox, R.H. Thomson, Sean McCann; ***D:*** Donald Brittain; ***W:*** Donald Brittain; ***C:*** Andreas Poulsson; ***M:*** Eldon Rathburn; ***Nar:*** Donald Brittain. Toronto-City '85: Canadian Feature Film.

Canadian Bacon 1/2 **1994 (PG)** Regrettably amateurish satire (with some sharp observations) serves as the feature film debut for Moore, who irritated many with "Roger & Me." Title refers to the military code name for a campaign to whip up anti-Canadian hysteria and justify a U.S. invasion of its neighbor to the north. Evil political advisor Pollak convinces well-meaning but inept President Alda that it's just the thing to get the presidential popularity up and those defense industries humming. Ugly Americans abound, at expense of polite Canadians, eh? Filmed in Toronto, which is shown to good advantage. Candy in one of last roles is the superpatriotic sheriff of Niagara Falls, New York. **110m/C VHS, DVD.** Alan Alda, Kevin Pollak, John Candy, Rhea Perlman, Rip Torn, Bill Nunn, Kevin J. O'Connor, Steven Wright, G.D. Spradlin, James Belushi, Wallace Shawn, Dan Aykroyd; ***Cameos:*** Michael Moore; ***D:*** Michael Moore; ***W:*** Michael Moore; ***C:*** Haskell Wexler; ***M:*** Elmer Bernstein, Peter Bernstein.

Cancel My Reservation **1972 (G)** New York talk show host Hope sets out for a vacation on an Arizona ranch, but winds up in trouble due to a mysterious corpse, a rich rancher, and an enigmatic mystic. Even more muddled than it sounds. Based on the novel "Broken Gun" by Louis L'Amour, with pointless cameos by Crosby, Wayne, and Wilson. **99m/C VHS.** Bob Hope, Eva Marie Saint, Ralph Bellamy, Anne Archer, Forrest Tucker, Keenan Wynn, Flip Wilson, Noriyuki "Pat" Morita, Chief Dan George; ***Cameos:*** John Wayne, Bing Crosby, Doodles Weaver; ***D:*** Paul Bogart; ***W:*** Arthur Marx; ***C:*** Russell Metty.

The Candidate **1972 (PG)** Realistic, satirical look at politics and political campaigning. Bill McKay (Redford) is a telegenic, idealistic lawyer whose father (Douglas) was once governor of California. Uninterested in politics, Bill is eventually persuaded to run for the Senate against bluff incumbent Jarman (Porter). Bill refuses to follow the party line but discovers the lure of political power when he begins to gain in the polls. Director Ritchie also worked with Redford on "Downhill Racer." **105m/C VHS, DVD.** Robert Redford, Peter Boyle, Don Porter, Allen (Goorwitz) Garfield, Karen Carlson, Melvyn Douglas, Michael Lerner; ***D:*** Michael Ritchie; ***W:*** Jeremy Larner; ***C:*** John Korty, Victor Kemper; ***M:*** John Rubinstein. Oscars '72: Story & Screenplay; Writers Guild '72: Orig. Screenplay.

Candles at Nine 1/2 **1944** An innocent showgirl must spend a month in her late uncle's creepy mansion in order to inherit it, much to the malevolent chagrin of the rest of the family who want the place and the loot for themselves. Uninspired. **84m/B VHS.** *GB* Jessie Matthews, John Stuart, Reginald Purdell; ***D:*** John Harlow.

Candleshoe **1978 (G)** A Los Angeles street urchin poses as an English matron's long lost granddaughter in order to steal a fortune hidden in Candleshoe, her country estate, where Niven butlers. Somewhat slapschticky Disney fare. **101m/C VHS, DVD.** Vivian Pickles, Helen Hayes, David Niven, Jodie Foster, Leo McKern; ***D:*** Norman Tokar; ***W:*** Rosemary Anne Sisson, David Swift; ***C:*** Paul Beeson; ***M:*** Ronald Goodwin.

Candy **1968 (R)** Sexual satire, based on the book by Terry Southern and Mason Hoffenberg, can't sustain its simple premise. The teenaged nubile, blonde, and naive title character (Aulin) sets out to discover her sexual awakening and gets chased by every kook she meets, including guru Brando, alcoholic poet Burton, gardener Starr, general Matthau, hunchback Aznavour, surgeon Coburn, and even her own dad, Astin. Very much of part of its psychedelic age. **124m/C VHS, DVD.** *FR IT* Ewa Aulin, Marlon Brando, Charles Aznavour, Richard Burton, Ringo Starr, James Coburn, Walter Matthau, John Huston, John Astin, Elsa Martinelli, Anita Pallenberg, "Sugar Ray" Robinson; ***D:*** Christian Marquand; ***W:*** Buck Henry; ***C:*** Giuseppe Rotunno.

Candy **2006 (R)** Heroin chic. Handsome Dan (Ledger) is a would-be poet wooing lovely artist Candy (Cornish). He's already shooting heroin and Candy (who sniffs the stuff) demands he let her needle up. A near-overdose doesn't dim Candy's enthusiasm, especially when their fatherly dealer Casper (Rush) is such a reliable supplier. Pic naturally descents into druggie hell as the two turn to crime to help pay for their habits, with intermittent efforts to get clean. Typical junkie fare, although much less harrowing than a lot of addiction flicks. **108m/C DVD.** *AU* Heath Ledger, Abbie Cornish, Geoffrey Rush, Tony (Anthony) Martin, Noni Hazlehurst; ***W:*** Neil Armfield, Luke Davies; ***C:*** Garry Phillips; ***M:*** Paul Charlier.

Candy Mountain **1987 (R)** Guitar playin' O'Connor roadtrips across America and Canada in search of a legendary guitar maker Yulin. Occasional interest derives from musician cameos from the likes of Buster Poindexter, Dr. John and Redbone. **90m/C VHS.** *FR SI CA* Kevin J. O'Connor, Harris Yulin, Tom Waits, Bulle Ogier, David Johansen, Leon Redbone, Joe Strummer, Roberts Blossom; ***Cameos:*** Rita MacNeil, Laurie Metcalf; ***D:*** Robert Frank; ***W:*** Rudy Wurlitzer.

Candy Stripe Nurses *Sweet Candy* **1974 (R)** Even hard-core Roger Corman fans might find his final installment in the nursing comedy pentad to be a lethargic exercise in gratuitous "sexual situations." Bet those uniforms don't meet hospital standards. The previous films in the series are: "The Student Nurses," "Private Duty Nurses," "Night Call Nurses," and "The Young Nurses." **80m/C VHS, DVD.** Candice Rialson, Robin Mattson, Maria Rojo, Kimberly Hyde, Dick Miller, Stanley Ralph Ross, Monte Landis, Tom Baker, Don Keefer, Sally Kirkland, Rick Gates; ***D:*** Allan Holleb.

Candy Tangerine Man **1975** Respectable businessman leads a double life as loving father and LA pimp. **88m/C VHS.** John Daniels, Tom Hankerson, Eli Haines, Marva Farmer, George "Buck" Flower; ***D:*** Matt Cimber.

Candyman **1992 (R)** Terrifying tale from horror maven Clive Barker is an effective combination of American gothic, academia, and urban squalor. A search for dissertation material leads graduate student Helen Lyle (Madsen) into gang-infested housing. There she encounters the urban myth of Candyman, the son of a former slave who was lynched and is now back with a hook and a vendetta. Filled with the appropriate amount of yucky stuff, yet successfully employs subtle scare tactics and plausible characters. **98m/C VHS, DVD.** Virginia Madsen, Tony Todd, Xander Berkeley, Kasi Lemmons, Vanessa L(ynne) Williams, DeJuan Guy, Michael Culkin, Gilbert Lewis, Stanley DeSantis, Mark Daniels; ***D:*** Bernard Rose; ***W:*** Bernard Rose; ***C:*** Anthony B. Richmond; ***M:*** Philip Glass.

Candyman 2: Farewell to the Flesh **1994 (R)** Explains the origins of the urban bogeyman called Candyman—the man, the hook, and the bees. Rehashes the same old scare tactics from previous and better horror movies and uses cheesy special effects. The sensual background of New Orleans during Mardi Gras can't help this stale sequel. Embrace this "Farewell" from a distance. Based on stories by Clive Barker. **99m/C VHS, DVD.** Tony Todd, Kelly Rowan, Veronica Cartwright, Timothy Carhart, William O'Leary, Bill Nunn, Fay Hauser, Joshua Gibran Mayweather; ***D:*** Bill Condon; ***W:*** Rand Ravich, Mark Kruger; ***C:*** Tobias Schliessler; ***M:*** Philip Glass.

Candyman 3: Day of the Dead **1998 (R)** The Candyman (Todd) haunts an L.A. descendent (D'Errico), framing her for murder, in the hopes that she will join him. **93m/C VHS, DVD.** Tony Todd, Donna D'Errico, Jsu Garcia, Lupe Ontiveros; ***D:*** Turi Meyer; ***W:*** Turi Meyer, Al Septien; ***C:*** Michael G. Wojciechowski. **VIDEO**

Cannery Row 1/2 **1982 (PG)** Baseball has-been Nolte lives anonymously among the downtrodden in the seamy part of town and carries on with working girl girlfriend Winger. Based on John Steinbeck's "Cannery Row" and "Sweet Thursday." **120m/C VHS.** Nick Nolte, Debra Winger, Audra Lindley, M. Emmet Walsh, Frank McRae, James Keane, Lloyd "Sunshine" Parker; ***D:*** David S. Ward; ***W:*** David S. Ward; ***C:*** Sven Nykvist; ***M:*** Jack Nitzsche; ***Nar:*** John Huston.

Cannes Man **1996 (R)** Features legendary Hollywood producer Sy Lerner (Cassel), who vows to make unknown cabbie/screenwriter Frank Rhinoslavsky (Quinn) a star, all while being schmoozed at Cannes by stars who want to be in his latest epic, while he tries to find backers for his unwritten script. **88m/C VHS, DVD.** Seymour Cassel, Francesco Quinn, Rebecca Broussand; ***D:*** Richard Martini.

Cannibal Apocalypse WOOF! *Cannibals in the Streets; Savage Apocalypse; The Slaughterers; Cannibals in the City; Virus; Invasion of the Flesh Hunters* **1980** Group of tortured Vietnam veterans returns home carrying a cannibalistic curse with them. Smorgasbord of gore and sensationalism is not for discriminating tastes. **96m/C VHS, DVD.** *IT* John Saxon, Elizabeth Turner, Giovanni Lombardo Radice, Tony King; ***D:*** Anthony M. Dawson; ***W:*** Anthony M. Dawson, Dardano Sacchetti, Jimmy Gould; ***C:*** Fernando Arribas; ***M:*** Alexander Blonksteiner.

Cannibal Campout **1988** Crazed orphans with eating disorders make square meal of coed babes getting back to nature. **89m/C VHS, DVD.** Carrie Lindell, Richard Marcus, Amy Chludzinski, Jon McBride; ***D:*** Jon McBride, Tom Fisher.

Cannibal Holocaust 🦴🦴 *Ruggero Deodato's Cannibal Holocaust* **1980** Ostensibly a social commentary on the evils of mass media, one of the most brutal films ever made follows a scholar's trek into the jungle a year after a group of celebrity documentary filmmakers have disappeared. He finds their cameras, and the lost footage is infinitely disturbing: apparently his predecessors, unable to find anything interesting to film (except a tribe of cannibals), massacred most of the village to film the aftermath and have something "newsworthy." The tribe's revenge isn't pretty. **96m/C DVD.** Robert Kerman, Luca Barbareschi, Salvatore Basile, Francesca Ciardi, Perry Pirkanen, Ricardo Fuentes, Carl Gabriel Yorke; ***D:*** Ruggero Deodato; ***W:*** Gianfranco Clerici; ***C:*** Sergio d'Offizi; ***M:*** Riz Ortolani. **VIDEO**

Cannibal Man 🦴🦴 *The Apartment on the 13 Floor; La Semana del Asesino; Week of the Killer* **1971** Slaughterhouse worker Marcos (Parra) accidentally kills a man in a fight and then covers up the incident with more killings. Then he's got to get rid of all those dead bodies and what better place than at the butcher's where he works. **98m/C VHS, DVD.** *SP* Vicente Parra, Emma Cohen, Eusebio Poncela; ***D:*** Eloy De La Iglesia; ***W:*** Eloy De La Iglesia.

Cannibal! The Musical 🦴 **1996 (R)** Only those wacky people at Troma could offer a horror/musical about a group of 1883 gold miners who get lost in the Colorado Rockies, have some strange adventures, and eventually wind up as dinner to cannibal Alferd Packer (who's telling his version of the story to a female reporter while in prison). Seven rather tedious musical numbers lead up to the gore-splashed finale. From director Trey Parker, who also repulses (and amuses us) with TV's "South Park." **105m/C VHS, DVD, UMD.** Ian Hardin, Jason McHugh, Matt Stone, Trey Parker, Juan Schwartz; ***D:*** Trey Parker; ***W:*** Trey Parker.

Cannibal Women in the Avocado Jungle of Death 🦴🦴 ½ **1989 (PG-13)** Tongue-in-cheek cult classic features erstwhile playmate Tweed as feminist anthropologist who searches with ditzy student and mucho macho male guide for lost tribe of cannibal women who dine on their mates. Lawton directed under the alias "J.D. Athens." **90m/C VHS, DVD.** Shannon Tweed, Adrienne Barbeau, Karen Mistal, Barry Primus, Bill Maher, Jim MacKrell, Brett Stimely, Paul Ross; ***D:*** J.F. Lawton, J.D. Athens; ***W:*** J.F. Lawton, J.D. Athens; ***C:*** Robert Knouse; ***M:*** Carl Dante.

Cannonball 🦴🦴 *Carquake* **1976 (PG)** Assorted ruthless people leave patches of rubber across the country competing for grand prize in less than legal auto race. Not top drawer New World but nonetheless a cult fave. Inferior to Bartel's previous cult classic, "Death Race 2000." Most interesting for plethora of cult cameos, including Scorsese, Dante, and grandmaster Corman. **93m/C VHS, DVD.** *HK* Martin Scorsese, Roger Corman, Joe Dante, Paul Bartel, David Carradine, Bill McKinney, Veronica Hamel, Gerrit Graham, Robert Carradine, Jonathan Kaplan, Belinda Balaski, Judy Canova, Carl Gottlieb, Archie Hahn, Sylvester Stallone, Dick Miller, Mary Woronov; ***D:*** Paul Bartel; ***W:*** Paul Bartel, Donald Stewart; ***C:*** Tak Fujimoto; ***M:*** David A. Axelrod.

Cannonball Run 🦴 ½ **1981 (PG)** So many stars, so little plot. Reynolds and sidekick DeLuise disguise themselves as paramedics to foil cops while they compete in cross-country Cannonball race. Shows no sign of having been directed by an ex-stuntman. One of 1981's top grossers—go figure. Followed by equally languid sequel "Cannonball Run II." **95m/C VHS, DVD.** Burt Reynolds, Farrah Fawcett, Roger Moore, Dom DeLuise, Dean Martin, Sammy Davis Jr., Jack Elam, Adrienne Barbeau, Peter Fonda, Molly Picon, Bert Convy, Jamie Farr; ***D:*** Hal Needham; ***W:*** Brock Yates; ***C:*** Michael C. Butler; ***M:*** Al Capps.

Cannonball Run 2 🦴 **1984 (PG)** More mindless cross-country wheel spinning with gratuitous star cameos. Director Needham apparently subscribes to the two wrongs make a right school of sequels. **109m/C VHS, DVD.** Burt Reynolds, Dom DeLuise, Jamie Farr, Marilu Henner, Shirley MacLaine, Jim Nabors, Frank Sinatra, Sammy Davis Jr., Dean Martin, Telly Savalas, Susan Anton, Catherine Bach, Jack Elam, Sid Caesar, Ricardo Montalban, Charles Nelson Reilly, Henry Silva, Tim Conway, Don Knotts, Molly Picon, Jackie Chan; ***D:*** Hal Needham; ***W:*** Harvey Miller; ***C:*** Nick McLean; ***M:*** Steve Dorff.

Cannonball Run Europe: The Great Escape 🦴 ½ **2005** Documentary following legendary Cannonball racer Tim 'Maverick' Porter, as he and his fellow Cannonballers begin in London and set out to race across Europe. More notable for the cast of incredibly eccentric driving teams than racing action (after all they can't really film most of the illegal stuff). **135m/C DVD.** *GB* ***D:*** Rupert Bryan.

Can't Buy Me Love 🦴 ½ **1987 (PG-13)** Unpopular high school nerd Dempsey buys a month of dates with teen babe Peterson for $1000 in order to win friends and influence people. Semi-amusing and earnest in a John Hughes Lite kind of way. Previously known as "Boy Rents Girl." **94m/C VHS, DVD.** Patrick Dempsey, Amanda Peterson, Dennis Dugan, Courtney Gains, Seth Green, Katrina Caspary, Sharon Farrell, Darcy Demoss, Devin Devasquez, Eric Bruskotter, Gerardo Mejia, Ami Dolenz, Max Perlich; ***D:*** Steve Rash; ***W:*** Michael Swerdlick; ***C:*** Peter Lyons Collister; ***M:*** Robert Folk.

Can't Hardly Wait 🦴🦴 *The Party* **1998 (PG-13)** Writer-directors Kaplan and Elfont attempt to reheat the John Hughes 80s teen-party-and-angst casserole for the kids of the 90s. Unfortunately, it's lost its flavor. All of your favorite high school cardboard cut-ups are here. Jock-jerk Mike (Facinelli) dumps teen queen Amanda (Hewitt) on the eve of a graduation blowout. Shy, sensitive Preston (Embry), who believes himself linked to Amanda by fate and their mutual love of toaster pastry, decides this is his opportunity to finally tell her how he feels. Frolicking in the background are your stereotypical foreign exchange students, stoners, geeks, metal heads, jocks and bimbos herded around by the ever-present Girl Whose Party It Is. Wavers between (unsuccessfully) trying to be thoughtful like "American Graffiti" and thoughtless like "Animal House." **101m/C VHS, DVD, Blu-ray Disc.** Ethan (Randall) Embry, Jennifer Love Hewitt, Peter Facinelli, Charlie Korsmo, Seth Green, Jerry O'Connell, Lauren Ambrose, Jenna Elfman, Michelle Brookhurst, Erik Palladino, Steve Monroe; ***D:*** Harry Elfont, Deborah Kaplan; ***W:*** Harry Elfont, Deborah Kaplan; ***C:*** Lloyd Ahern II; ***M:*** David Kitay, Matthew Sweet.

Can't Help Singing 🦴🦴 ½ **1945** In 1849, willful heiress Caroline (Durbin) ignores her senator father's (Collins) wishes and heads west to marry her Army sweetheart (Bruce). But on the wagon train she falls for wagon master Lawlor (Paige), who's a better guy anyway. Durbin's first color musical. **90m/C VHS, DVD.** Deanna Durbin, Robert Paige, David Bruce, Akim Tamiroff, Leonid Kinskey, Ray Collins, June Vincent, Thomas Gomez; ***D:*** Frank Ryan; ***W:*** Frank Ryan, Lewis R. Foster; ***C:*** Elwood "Woody" Bredell, William Howard Greene; ***M:*** Hans J. Salter, Jerome Kern, E.Y. Harburg.

Can't Stop the Music WOOF! 1980 (PG) Retired model invites friends from Greenwich Village to a party to help the career of her roommate, an aspiring composer. Disco inferno that nearly reaches heights of surreal ineptness. Put it in a time capsule and let the people of the future decide what the heck was going on in the '70s. Features two of the top hits by the Village People. ♫Y.M.C.A.; Macho Man; Give Me a Break; The Sound of the City; Samantha; I'm a Singing Juggler; Sophistication; Liberation; I Love You to Death. **120m/C VHS, DVD.** Valerie Perrine, Bruce Jenner, Steve Guttenberg, Paul Sand, Leigh Taylor-Young, Village People; ***D:*** Nancy Walker; ***W:*** Bronte Woodard, Allan Carr; ***C:*** Bill Butler; ***M:*** Jacques Morali. Golden Raspberries '80: Worst Picture, Worst Screenplay.

A Canterbury Tale 🦴🦴🦴 **1944** Writer-director team Powell and Pressburger have loosely modeled a retelling of Chaucer's famous tale of a pilgrimage to the cathedral in Canterbury. Set in Nazi-threatened Britain in 1944, the story follows the pilgrimage of three Brits and an American GI to the eponymous cathedral. Strange, effective, worth looking at. The 95-minute American version, with added footage of Kim Hunter, is inferior to the 124-minute original. **124m/B VHS, DVD.** *GB* Eric Portman, Sheila Sim, Dennis Price, Esmond Knight, Charles Hawtrey, Hay Petrie; ***D:*** Michael Powell, Emeric Pressburger.

The Canterbury Tales 🦴🦴 *I Racconti di Canterbury* **1971** Four Chaucer tales, most notably "The Merchant's Tale" and "The Wife of Bath," are recounted by travelers, with director Pasolini as the bawdy poet. Deemed obscene by the Italian courts, it's the second entry in Pasolini's medieval "Trilogy of Life," preceded by "The Decameron" and followed by "The Arabian Nights." In Italian with English subtitles. **109m/C VHS, DVD.** *IT* Laura Betti, Ninetto Davoli, Pier Paolo Pasolini, Hugh Griffith, Josephine Chaplin, Michael Balfour, Jenny Runacre; ***D:*** Pier Paolo Pasolini; ***W:*** Pier Paolo Pasolini; ***C:*** Tonino Delli Colli; ***M:*** Ennio Morricone. Berlin Intl. Film Fest. '72: Golden Berlin Bear.

The Canterville Ghost 🦴🦴 ½ **1944** Laughton, a 300-year-old ghost with a yellow streak, is sentenced to spook a castle until he proves he's not afraid of his own shadow. American troops stay at the castle during WWII, and, as luck would have it, soldier Young is distantly related to spunky young keeper of the castle O'Brien, ghost Laughton's descendant. Once Young is acquainted with his cowardly ancestor, he begins to fear a congenital yellow streak, and both struggle to be brave despite themselves. Vaguely derived from an Oscar Wilde tale. **95m/B VHS.** Charles Laughton, Robert Young, Margaret O'Brien, William Gargan, Reginald Owen, Rags Ragland, Una O'Connor, Peter Lawford, Mike Mazurki; ***D:*** Jules Dassin; ***W:*** Edwin Blum; ***M:*** George Bassman.

The Canterville Ghost 1991 During a family's vacation in an old English manor, they run into a ghost who is doomed to haunt the place until he can overcome his fears. Problems start when the family tries to scare him away. From the "Wonderworks" family movie series. **58m/C VHS, DVD.** Richard Kiley, Mary Wickes, Shelley Fabares; ***D:*** William Claxton.

The Canterville Ghost 🦴🦴 ½ **1996 (PG)** Stewart is the highlight of this updated TV version of the Oscar Wilde short story. He's the cursed Elizabethan spirit of Sir Simon de Canterville, doomed to haunt the family mansion until a prophecy is fulfilled. But he's not happy with a family of American intruders, until teenager Virginia (Campbell) discovers Sir Simon and realizes she may hold the key to freeing the unhappy ghost. **91m/C VHS, DVD.** Patrick Stewart, Neve Campbell, Ed Wiley, Cherie Lunghi, Donald Sinden, Joan Sims, Leslie Phillips, Ciaran Fitzgerald, Daniel Betts, Raymond Pickard; ***D:*** Syd Macartney; ***W:*** Robert Benedetti; ***C:*** Denis Lewiston; ***M:*** Ernest Troost.

The Cantor's Son 🦴 ½ *Dem Khann's Zindl* **1937** Real-life story based on Moishe Oysher's life, vaguely influenced by Jolson's "Jazz Singer." Runaway Oysher joins troupe of performers as a youth, travels to the shores of America, and finds fame once his beautiful voice is discovered. Returning to his mother country to celebrate his parents' golden anniversary, he encounters his childhood sweetheart and falls in love, but another woman is written into the plot to complicate matters. Poorly acted, laughable staging. In Yiddish with English subtitles. **90m/B VHS.** Judith Abarbanel, Florence Weiss, Moishe Oysher, Isadore Cashier; ***D:*** Ilya Motyleff.

Canvas 🦴🦴 ½ **2006 (PG-13)** Convincing performances help out a somewhat familiar plot about mental illness. Ten-year-old Chris (Gearhart) returns home after a stay with relatives. His mom, Mary (Harden), was hospitalized for schizophrenia and her sanity is still in question, despite the best efforts of hard-working hubby John (Pantoliano). Countless problems inundate their lives as Mary becomes more disruptive and an embarrassment Chris finds hard to bear. **101m/C DVD.** William Morrissey, Marcia Gay Harden, Joe Pantoliano, Devon Gearhart, Marcus Johns, Sophia Bairley; ***D:*** Joseph Greco; ***W:*** Joseph Greco; ***C:*** Rob Sweeney; ***M:*** Joel Goodman.

Canvas: The Fine Art of Crime 🦴🦴 **1992 (R)** A ruthless, underhanded art gallery owner recruits a desperate young artist into his art stealing schemes. The artist learns how to steal, but decides he wants out after his burglary partner has a brush with death. The gallery owner, however, wants one last job completed. **94m/C VHS.** Gary Busey, John Rhys-Davies, Vittorio Rossi, Nick Cavaiola, Cary Lawrence; ***D:*** Alain Zaloum.

Canyon Passage 🦴🦴🦴 **1946** Rip-roarin' western set in the Oregon Territory in 1856. Stuart (Andrews) is a former scout turned store owner who falls for Lucy (Hayward), who happens to be the fiancee of banker/gambler Camrose (Donlevy). Camrose gets into money troubles, there's a villain named Bragg (Bond), and a pretty spectacular Indian attack. Carmichael serves as the wandering minstrel to the action, singing four songs. Director Tourneur was best known for his horror films. **92m/C VHS, DVD.** Dana Andrews, Brian Donlevy, Susan Hayward, Ward Bond, Hoagy Carmichael, Lloyd Bridges, Andy Devine, Patricia Roc; ***D:*** Jacques Tourneur; ***W:*** Ernest Pascal; ***C:*** Edward Cronjager; ***M:*** Frank Skinner.

Canyon River 🦴🦴 ½ **1956** Typical oater has Wyoming rancher Steve Patrick (Montgomery) and his foreman Bob Andrews (Graves) traveling to Oregon to bring back some breeding stock to improve his herd. Too bad Andrews has plotted with rancher Maddox (Sande) to kill Patrick and steal the herd instead. **80m/C DVD.** George Montgomery, Peter Graves, Walter Sande, Marcia Henderson, Richard Eyer, Robert J. Wilke, Alan Hale Jr.; ***D:*** Harmon Jones; ***W:*** Daniel Ullman; ***C:*** Ellsworth Fredricks; ***M:*** Marlin Skiles.

Cape Fear 🦴🦴🦴 ½ **1961** Former prosecutor turned small-town lawyer Peck and his family are plagued by the sadistic attentions of criminal Mitchum, who just finished a six year sabbatical at the state pen courtesy of prosecutor Peck. Taut and creepy; Mitchum's a consummate psychopath. Based on (and far superior to) John MacDonald's "The Executioners." Don't pass this one up in favor of the Scorsese remake. **106m/B VHS, DVD.** Gregory Peck, Robert Mitchum, Polly Bergen, Martin Balsam, Telly Savalas, Jack Kruschen, Lori Martin; ***D:*** J. Lee Thompson; ***C:*** Sam Leavitt; ***M:*** Bernard Herrmann.

Cape Fear 🦴🦴🦴 **1991 (R)** Scorsese takes on this terrifying tale of brutality and manipulation (previously filmed in 1961) and cranks it up a notch as a paroled convict haunts the lawyer who put him away. Great cast, a rollercoaster of suspense. Note the cameos by Mitchum, Peck, and Balsam, stars of the first version. Original source material was "The Executioners" by John D. MacDonald. Breath-taking rollercoaster of a film. Elmer Bernstein adapted the original score by Bernard Herrmann. **128m/C VHS, DVD.** Robert Mitchum, Gregory Peck, Martin Balsam, Robert De Niro, Nick Nolte, Jessica Lange, Juliette Lewis, Joe Don Baker, Illeana Douglas, Fred Dalton Thompson; ***D:*** Martin Scorsese; ***W:*** Wesley Strick; ***C:*** Freddie Francis; ***M:*** Elmer Bernstein.

Cape of Good Hope 🦴🦴 ½ **2004 (PG-13)** A Cape Town animal rescue shelter is the link for numerous characters and their stories. Kate (Brown) runs the shelter and is the object of attraction for a shy vet (Visser). She befriends young Thabo (Masilo), whose widowed mother, Lindiwe (Moshesh), is being pressured to marry an elderly, wealthy minister, but refugee Jean Claude (Ebouaney), who works at the shelter, loves her. Meanwhile, Kate's friend and co-worker Sharifa (Adams) is having marital trouble. Director Bamford doesn't ignore poverty and racism in a post-apartheid South Africa but his focus remains on how this group deals with ordinary, everyday life. **107m/C DVD.** *US* Eriq Ebouaney, Nthati Moshesh, David Isaacs, Nick Boraine, Debbie Brown, Morne Visser, Quanita Adams, Kamo Masilo; ***D:*** Mark Bamford; ***W:*** Mark Bamford, Suzanne Kay; ***C:*** Larry Fong; ***M:*** J.B. Eckl.

Caper of the Golden Bulls 🦴 *Carnival of Thieves* **1967** Former bank robber Boyd is blackmailed into joining a group of safecrackers who plan to assault the Royal Bank of Spain during the annual Santa Maria bull run. More like siesta of the golden bulls. **104m/C VHS.** Stephen Boyd, Yvette Mimieux, Giovanna

Ralli, Walter Slezak, Vito Scotti; *D:* Russell Rouse.

Capitaine Conan *Captain Conan* **1996** On the Bulgarian border in 1918, during the last clashes of WWI, Conan (Torreton) is a fearless, impulsive warrior, reserving his respect only for his men. Although armistice is finally declared, the troops stationed in the Balkans are not demobilized and become increasingly fractious. This causes a rift between Conan and his educated friend Norbert (Le Bihan), who's been appointed a military legal representative. They are warily reunited in defense of a soldier (Val) charged with desertion, while still dealing with the ravages of the long conflict. Adapted from the book by Roger Vercel; French with subtitles. **129m/C VHS, DVD.** *FR* Philippe Torreton, Samuel Le Bihan, Bernard Le Coq, Francois Berleand, Claude Rich, Catherine Rich, Pierre Val; *D:* Bertrand Tavernier; *W:* Bertrand Tavernier, Jean Cosmos; *C:* Alain Choquart; *M:* Oswald D'Andrea. Cesar '97: Actor (Torreton), Director (Tavernier), Film.

Capital Punishment 1/2 **1996** Martial arts expert James Thayer (Daniels) is recruited by the DEA to go undercover and stop Nakata (Yamashita), the supplier of a new illegal drug. His operation turns up a corrupt police chief (Carradine), who frames him for murder, and lots of action. **90m/C VHS, DVD.** Gary Daniels, Tadashi Yamashita, David Carradine, Mel Novak, Ian Jacklin, Ava Fabian; *D:* David Hue; *W:* David Hue; *C:* David Swett.

Capitalism: A Love Story 1/2 **2009 (R)** Loud-mouthed provocateur Moore's documentary on the global financial crisis and the meltdown of the U.S. economy during the transition from the Bush to the Obama administrations. Moore's belief is that capitalism rewards greed and that corporations and financial institutions exploit (and deliberately confuse) the majority of Americans with their practices. Moore likes to grandstand but he's not afraid to tackle big subjects that can (and should) be up for debate. **120m/C DVD.** *US* Michael Moore; *D:* Michael Moore; *W:* Michael Moore; *C:* Jayme Roy, Daniel Marracino; *M:* Jeff Gibbs.

The Capitol Conspiracy 1/2 **1999 (R)** CIA agents Jarrid Maddox (Wilson) and Vicki Taylor (Keith) uncover evidence that links government officials with illegal mind-control experiments. The duo become targets of a hit squad determined to keep the information secret. Very familiar actioner. **83m/C VHS, DVD.** Don "The Dragon" Wilson, Alexander Keith, Paul Michael Robinson, Arthur Roberts, Barbara Steele; *D:* Fred Olen Ray; *C:* Gary Graver. **VIDEO**

Capone 1/2 *The Revenge of Al Capone* **1989 (R)** Story of the gangster after Elliot Ness put him in a Chicago jail. That didn't stop Capone from running his crime empire until a single FBI agent worked to sent the crime boss to Alcatraz, where his power would be useless. Exuberant performances from Sharkey and Carradine. **96m/C VHS, DVD.** Ray Sharkey, Keith Carradine, Debrah Farentino, Jayne Atkinson, Bradford English, Marc Figueroa, Neil Giuntoli, Charles Haid, Nicholas Mele, Scott Paulin, Alan Rosenberg; *D:* Michael Pressman; *W:* Tracy Keenan Wynn; *C:* Tim Suhrstedt; *M:* Craig Safan. **TV**

Capote **2005 (R)** Based on the book "Capote" by Gerald Clark. Enigmatic Truman Capote (an outstanding Hoffman) was a celebrated author and a member of elite New York society. Biopic sheds light on Capote's obsessive research into the killers behind the startling murders of a Kansas family, which formed the groundwork for his "In Cold Blood," an obsession that ultimately led to Capote's own demise, spiraling into obesity, alcoholism and ouster from the intellectual elite. Hoffman nails his portrayal of the self-absorbed man at his manipulative best. **114m/C DVD.** *US* Philip Seymour Hoffman, Catherine Keener, Chris Cooper, Bruce Greenwood, Bob Balaban, Amy Ryan, Mark Pellegrino, Clifton (Gonzalez) Collins Jr.; *D:* Bennett Miller; *W:* Dan Futterman; *C:* Adam Kimmel; *M:* Mychael Danna. Oscars '05: Actor (Hoffman); British Acad. '05: Actor (Hoffman); Golden Globes '06: Actor—Drama (Hoffman); Ind. Spirit '06: Actor (Hoffman), Screenplay; L.A. Film Critics '05: Actor (Hoffman), Screenplay, Support. Actress (Keener); Natl. Bd. of Review '05: Actor (Hoffman); N.Y. Film Critics '05: First Feature; Natl. Soc. Film Critics '05: Actor (Hoffman), Film; Screen Actors Guild '05: Actor (Hoffman); Broadcast Film Critics '05: Actor (Hoffman).

Caprica 1/2 **2009** Prequel to the "Battlestar Galatica" series, set 58 years before those events, and intended as the pilot episode for another series. Robotics expert Daniel Graystone (Stoltz) is disturbed by his failing marriage and his rebellious daughter Zoe (Toressani). A robotics whiz herself, Zoe has created a virtual world (and a virtual avatar) where she and her friends can discuss their monotheistic beliefs vs. Caprica's polytheistic society. When Zoe is killed in a terrorist bombing, Daniel discovers he can use her avatar to create an artificial life and thus the Cylons are born. Daniel isn't the only one to suffer: mobbed-up lawyer Joseph Adama (Morales), an immigrant from the Tauron colony, has lost his wife and daughter and is raising son William alone, but he regards Daniel's experiment as an abomination. **93m/C DVD.** Eric Stoltz, Esai Morales, Paula Malcomson, Polly Walker, Alessandra Toressani, Magda Apanowicz, Sasha Roiz; *D:* Jeff Reiner; *W:* Ronald D. Moore; *C:* Joel Ransom; *M:* Bear McCreary. **CABLE**

Caprice **1967** Truly awful comedy, best left to Day fans only. The middle-aged actress is still playing wide-eyed and primly sunny, even as industrial spy Patricia Fowler. Pat is trying to get something on a rival cosmetics company, which leads her to mystery man Christopher White (Harris), her would-be rescuer and love interest. Actually, the only interesting thing is how Day's costumes are frequently coordinated to their settings. With material like this, no wonder she retired from movies in 1968. **98m/C DVD.** Doris Day, Richard Harris, Ray Walston, Jack Kruschen, Edward Mulhare, Lilia Skala, Michael J. Pollard, Irene Tsu; *D:* Frank Tashlin; *W:* Frank Tashlin; *C:* Leon Shamroy; *M:* Frank DeVol.

Capricorn One **1978 (R)** Astronauts Brolin, Simpson and Waterston follow Mission Controller Holbrook's instructions to fake a Mars landing on a soundstage when their ship is discovered to be defective. When they find out they're supposed to expire in outer space so that the NASA scam won't become public knowledge, they flee to the desert, while reporter Gould sniffs out the cover up. Based on a pseudonymous novel by Ken Follett. **123m/C VHS, DVD.** Elliott Gould, James Brolin, Brenda Vaccaro, O.J. Simpson, Hal Holbrook, Sam Waterston, Karen Black, Telly Savalas; *D:* Peter Hyams; *W:* Peter Hyams; *C:* Bill Butler; *M:* Jerry Goldsmith.

Captain America *The Return of Captain America* **1944** Captain America battles a mad scientist in this 15-episode serial based on the comic book character. **240m/B VHS.** Dick Purcell, Adrian Booth, Lionel Atwill; *D:* John English; *W:* Elmer Clifton.

Captain America 1/2 **1979** Marvel Comic character steps into feature film and flounders. The patriotic superhero son of WWII hero fights bad guy with contraband nuclear weapon. **98m/C VHS.** Reb Brown, Len Birman, Heather Menzies, Steve Forrest, Robin Mattson, Joseph Ruskin, Michael McManus; *D:* Rod Holcomb. **TV**

Captain America 1/2 **1989 (PG-13)** Based on the Marvel Comics superhero. It's 1941 and Steve Rogers has just been recruited to join a top secret experimental government program after flunking his army physical. Injected with a serum, Steve becomes super strong, fast, and smart but is matched in all three by an evil Nazi counterpart, Red Skull. The two battle to a WWII standstill and while Red Skull goes on with his evil plots, the next 40 years finds Captain America fast frozen in the Alaskan tundra. Finally, our hero is thawed in time to do a final battle with his evil nemesis. This one is ridiculous even by comic book standards but it may amuse the kids. **103m/C VHS.** Matt Salinger, Scott Paulin, Ronny Cox, Ned Beatty, Darren McGavin, Melinda Dillon; *D:* Albert Pyun; *W:* Stephen Tolkin.

Captain America 2: Death Too Soon **1979** Terrorists hit America where it hurts, threatening to use age accelerating drug. Sequelized superhero fights chronic crow lines and series dies slow, painful death. **98m/C VHS.** Reb Brown, Connie Sellecca, Len Birman, Christopher Lee, Katherine Justice, Lana Wood, Christopher Carey; *D:* Ivan Nagy. **TV**

Captain Apache **1971** Union intelligence officer Van Cleef investigates murder of Indian commissioner and discovers fake Indian war landscam. As clever as the title. **95m/C VHS, DVD.** Lee Van Cleef, Carroll Baker, Stuart Whitman; *D:* Alexander Singer; *W:* Philip Yordan.

Captain Blackjack *Black Jack* **1951** All-star cast craps out in wanna-be thriller about drug smuggling on the French Riviera. Social butterfly Moorehead directs drug traffic, detective Marshall undercovers as doctor, and Sanders looks bored in a British sort of way. **90m/B VHS.** *FR* George Sanders, Herbert Marshall, Agnes Moorehead, Patricia Roc, Marcel Dalio; *D:* Julien Duvivier.

Captain Blood 1/2 **1935** Sabatini adventure story launched then unknown 26-year-old Flynn and 19-year-old De Havilland to fame in perhaps the best pirate story ever. Exiled into slavery by a tyrannical governor, Irish physician Peter Blood is forced into piracy but ultimately earns a pardon for his swashbuckling ways. Love interest De Havilland would go on to appear in seven more features with Flynn, who took the part Robert Donat declined for health reasons. Cleverly budgeted using ship shots from silents, and miniature sets when possible. First original film score by composer Korngold. Also available colorized. **120m/B VHS, DVD.** Errol Flynn, Olivia de Havilland, Basil Rathbone, J. Carrol Naish, Guy Kibbee, Lionel Atwill, Ross Alexander; *D:* Michael Curtiz; *W:* Casey Robinson; *C:* Hal Mohr; *M:* Erich Wolfgang Korngold.

Captain Boycott 1/2 **1947** In 1880 Ireland, Boycott (Parker) is the despised rent collector for an aristocratic English landlord. When the poor tenant farmers can't pay, he's quick to throw them off the land. The farmers then band together to get rid of Boycott. Granger and Ryan are the prerequisite young lovers. Adapted from the novel by Philip Rooney. **94m/B VHS.** *GB* Cecil Parker, Stewart Granger, Kathleen Ryan, Niall MacGinnis, Robert Donat, Mervyn Johns, Alastair Sim, Noel Purcell, Maurice Denham; *D:* Frank Launder; *W:* Frank Launder, Wolfgang Wilhelm; *C:* Wilkie Cooper, Oswald Morris; *M:* William Alwyn.

Captain Calamity 1/2 *Captain Hurricane* **1936** Bill Jones (Houston) is known better as 'Captain Calamity' due to his penchant for getting into fights and trouble. When he pays for his supplies in gold the locals assume he's found a hidden treasure somewhere, and the local pirates immediately begin to chase him down. Pretty much bad news for Bill and the young woman whose mission of revenge he has just agreed to help. It's not quite as good as the plot sounds really. **65m/B DVD.** George Houston, Marion (Marian) Nixon, Vince Barnett, Juan Torena, Movita, Crane Wilbur, George Lewis, Roy D'Arcy, Matthew Irving, Barry Norton, Louis Natheaux, Lloyd Ingraham, Alberto Gandero, Harold Howard, Charles Moyer; *D:* John Reinhardt; *W:* Gordon Ray Young, Crane Wilbur; *C:* Mack Stengler.

Captain Caution **1940** Young girl throws caution to the wind when dad dies during the War of 1812, assisting young Mature to take over the old man's ship to do battle with the British. Watch for then unknown sailor Ladd. **84m/B VHS.** Victor Mature, Louise Platt, Bruce Cabot, Alan Ladd, Robert Barrat, Vivienne Osborne; *D:* Richard Wallace.

Captain Corelli's Mandolin **2001 (R)** Based on the novel by Louis de Bernieres, the film is set on the Greek island of Cephallonia during the early days of WWII. After numerous scenes of hearty Greek peasant life, the island is occupied by an aria-singing Italian army troop, led by mandolin strumming Captain Corelli (Cage). He moves into the local doctor's (Hurt) place and quickly falls for his daughter Pelagia (Cruz). The problem is that she's engaged to fisherman Mandras (Bale), a Greek partisan. Cage's over-done accent makes him sound like he's trying to sell you a pizza, but it matches the overwrought tone. Director Madden was signed late in pre-production after scheduled director Roger Michell suffered a heart attack. **127m/C VHS, DVD.** *GB US* Nicolas Cage, Penelope Cruz, Christian Bale, John Hurt, David Morrissey, Irene Papas, Patrick Malahide; *D:* John Madden; *W:* Shawn Slovo; *C:* John Toll; *M:* Stephen Warbeck.

Captain from Castile **1947** Exciting saga finds 16th-century Spanish nobleman Pedro De Vargas (Power) forced to flee the wrath of Inquisition chief De Silva (Sutton). He takes peasant girl Cantana (Peters), who's helped him, and joins Cortez's expedition to Mexico and the search for Aztec riches. Lots of adventures and old-fashioned pageantry. Peters' screen debut. **141m/C VHS, DVD.** Tyrone Power, Jean Peters, Cesar Romero, Lee J. Cobb, John Sutton, Antonio Moreno, Thomas Gomez, Alan Mowbray; *D:* Henry King; *W:* Lamar Trotti; *C:* Charles G. Clarke, Arthur E. Arling; *M:* Alfred Newman.

The Captain from Koepenick 1/2 *Der Hauptmann von Koepenick* **1956** Popular true life comedy about a Berlin cobbler in 1906 who rebels against military bureaucracy by impersonating a Prussian officer and wreaking havoc on his town, arresting authorities and capturing soldiers, only to enjoy folk herodom when his ruse is discovered. Remake of Richard Oswald's 1931 classic. In German with subtitles. **93m/B VHS.** *GE* Heinz Ruhmann, Hannelore Schroth, Martin Held, Erich Schellow; *D:* Helmut Kautner.

Captain Horatio Hornblower **1951** A colorful drama about the life and loves of the British sea captain during the Napoleonic wars. Peck is rather out of his element as the courageous, swashbuckling hero (Errol Flynn was originally cast) but there's enough fast-paced derring-do to make this a satisfying saga. Based on the novel by C.S. Forester. **117m/C VHS, DVD.** *GB* Gregory Peck, Virginia Mayo, Robert Beatty, Denis O'Dea, Christopher Lee; *D:* Raoul Walsh; *W:* Ivan Goff; *C:* Guy Green.

Captain Jack 1/2 *An Inch Over the Horizon* **1998** Sentimental, old-fashioned story about eccentric sea captain Jack (Hoskin) who dreams of sailing the same journey as Captain Scoresby made in 1791—from Whitby in northern England to the Arctic. But his misfit crew is a group of novices and his vessel is deemed unseaworthy by authorities. Nevertheless, Jack and his group set sail. **96m/C VHS, DVD.** *GB* Bob Hoskins, Peter McDonald, Sadie Frost, Gemma Jones, Anna Massey, Maureen Lipman, Robert Addie, Trevor Bannister; *D:* Robert M. Young; *W:* Jack Rosenthal; *C:* John McGlashan; *M:* Richard Harvey.

Captain January 1/2 **1936 (G)** Crusty old lighthouse keeper rescues little orphan girl with curly hair from drowning and everyone breaks into cutesy song and dance, interrupted only when the authorities try to separate the two. Also available colorized. ♫At the Codfish Ball; Early Bird; The Right Somebody to Love. **81m/B VHS, DVD.** Shirley Temple, Guy Kibbee, Buddy Ebsen, Slim Summerville, Jane Darwell, June Lang, George Irving, Si Jenks; *D:* David Butler.

Captain Kidd 1/2 **1945** Laughton huffs and puffs and searches for treasure on the high seas, finds himself held captive with rest of cast in anemic swashbuckler. **83m/B VHS, DVD.** Charles Laughton, John Carradine, Randolph Scott, Reginald Owen, Gilbert Roland, Barbara Britton, John Qualen, Sheldon Leonard; *D:* Rowland V. Lee; *W:* Norman Reilly Raine; *C:* Archie Stout.

Captain Kronos: Vampire Hunter *Kronos; Vampire Castle* **1974 (R)** Captain Kronos fences thirsty foes in Hammer horror hybrid. Artsy, atmospheric and atypical, it's written and directed with tongue firmly in cheek by Clemens, who penned many an "Avengers" episode. **91m/C VHS, DVD.** *GB* Horst Janson, John Carson, Caroline Munro, Ian Hendry, Shane Briant, Wanda Ventham, John Cater, Lois Daine, William Hobbs, Robert James, Elizabeth Dear; *D:* Brian Clemens; *W:* Brian Clemens; *C:* Ian Wilson; *M:* Laurie Johnson.

Captain Nemo and the Underwater City 1/2 **1969** A dull use of the Jules Verne characters in this would-be adventure story. Capt. Nemo (Ryan) uses his submarine the Nautilus to rescue the survivors of a sinking sailing ship. He takes them to his fabulous domed underwater city of Templemer but then doesn't want to let them go, fearing they'll reveal his secrets to the world and destroy his utopia. Naturally, they still plan an escape. **105m/C DVD.** *GB* Robert Ryan, Chuck Connors, Nanette Newman, Luciana Paluzzi, Bill Fraser, Kenneth Connor, John Turner; ***D:*** James Hill; ***W:*** Robert W(right) Campbell, Jane Barker, Pip Barker; ***C:*** Alan Hume; ***M:*** Angela Morley.

Captain Newman, M.D. ½ **1963** Three army guys visit stiff shrink Peck during the final months of WWII in VA ward for the mentally disturbed. Much guilt and agonizing, with comic relief courtesy of Curtis. Peck is sub par, the direction flounders and there's something unsettling about quicksilver shifts from pathos to parody. Nonetheless touching with fine performance from Darin as guilt ridden hero. Based on the novel by Leo Rosten. **126m/C VHS.** Gregory Peck, Bobby Darin, Tony Curtis, Angie Dickinson, Eddie Albert, James Gregory, Jane Withers, Larry Storch, Robert Duvall; ***D:*** David Miller.

Captain Nuke and the Bomber Boys ½ *Demolition Day* **1995 (PG)** Three teenagers, who've stumbled across an atomic bomb, decide to use the device to get school called off. Instead, they wind up with the FBI and a couple of crooks after them. **90m/C VHS.** Joe Mantegna, Martin Sheen, Joe Piscopo, Joanna Pacula, Rod Steiger, Kate Mulgrew; ***D:*** Charles Gale; ***W:*** Charles Gale.

Captain Ron ½ **1992 (PG-13)** Harried couple Short and Place inherit a large boat and, with their two smart-mouthed kids, go to the Caribbean to sail the boat back to the U.S. Of course they know nothing about sailing, so they hire Captain Ron (Russell), a one-eyed, Long John Silver-talking boat captain. From there, numerous mishaps occur. Amusing sounding premise sinks like a stone. Russell looks great in his teeny-weeny bikini, and the scenery is beautiful, but that's about it. **104m/C VHS, DVD.** Kurt Russell, Martin Short, Mary Kay Place, Meadow Sisto, Benjamin Salisbury, Dan E. Butler; ***D:*** Thom Eberhardt; ***W:*** Thom Eberhardt.

Captain Scarlett ½ **1953** Formulaic swashbuckler has nobleman Greene and highway guy Young fighting nasty French Royalists who've been putting the pressure on impecunious peasants. Runaway Spanish damsel in distress courtesy of Amar. Most novel aspect of the production is that the post-Napoleon French terrain has that vaguely south of the border feel. **75m/C VHS, DVD.** Richard Greene, Leonora Amar, Isobel Del Puerto, Nedrick Young, Manolo Fabregas; ***D:*** Thomas Carr.

Captain Sinbad ½ **1963** Captain Sinbad must destroy the evil El Kerim, but first he must tackle a many-headed ogre, man-eating fish and crocodiles, a large fist clad in a spiked glove, an invisible monster, and more. To kill the villain, Sinbad must destroy his heart, which is kept in a tower with no entrance. A huge, witty, epic production with lots of special effects. This one is fun. **85m/C VHS.** Guy Williams, Heidi Bruhl, Pedro Armendariz Sr., Abraham Sofaer, Bernie Hamilton, Helmuth Schneider; ***D:*** Byron Haskin; ***W:*** Ian McLellan Hunter, Guy Endore.

Captain Swagger ½ **1925** A man on the brink of thievery experiences some changes that keep him on the right side of the law. **50m/B VHS.** Rod La Rocque, Sue Carol, Richard Tucker, Victor Potel, Ullrich Haupt; ***D:*** Edward H. Griffith.

Captains Courageous **1937** Rich brat Bartholomew takes a dip sans life jacket while leaning over an ocean liner railing to relieve himself of the half dozen ice cream sodas imprudently consumed at sea. Picked up by a Portugese fishing boat, he at first treats his mandatory three month voyage as an unscheduled cab ride, but eventually, through a deepening friendship with crewman Tracy, develops a hitherto unheralded work ethic. The boy's filial bond with Tracy, of course, requires that the seaman meet with watery disaster. Based on the Rudyard Kipling novel. Director Fleming went on to "Gone With the Wind" and "The Wizard of Oz." **116m/B VHS, DVD.** Spencer Tracy, Lionel Barrymore, Freddie Bartholomew, Mickey Rooney, Melvyn Douglas, Charley Grapewin, John Carradine, Bobby Watson, Jack La Rue; ***D:*** Victor Fleming. Oscars '37: Actor (Tracy).

Captains Courageous ½ **1995** TV adaptation of the 1897 novel by Rudyard Kipling finds pampered rich kid Vadas learning to become a man at the hands of stalwart sea captain Urich. **93m/C VHS, DVD.** Robert Urich, Kenny Vadas, Kaj-Erik Eriksen, Robert Wisden, Duncan Fraser; ***D:*** Michael Anderson Jr.; ***W:*** John McGreevey; ***C:*** Glen MacPherson; ***M:*** Eric N. Robertson, Claude Desjardins.

Captains of the Clouds ½ **1942** Unabashedly patriotic film starring Cagney as a daredevil, independent Canadian bush pilot who makes his own flying rules. When WWII begins he joins the Royal Canadian Air Force but washes out when he can't follow orders. However, he finds a way to prove himself a hero as a civilian pilot ferrying a bomber to England. Cagney's first Technicolor film. **113m/C VHS, DVD.** James Cagney, Dennis Morgan, Brenda Marshall, Alan Hale, George Tobias, Reginald Gardiner, Reginald Denny, Russell Arms, Paul Cavanagh, Charles Halton; ***D:*** Michael Curtiz; ***M:*** Max Steiner.

Captain's Paradise **1953** Golden Fleece captain Guinness chugs between wives in Gibraltar and North Africa, much to the adulation of chief officer Goldner. While Gibraltar's little woman Johnson is homegrown homebody, little woman de Carlo is paint the town red type, allowing Guinness to have cake and eat it too, it seems, except that he's inconveniently positioned in front of a firing squad at movie's start. **89m/B VHS, DVD.** *GB* Alec Guinness, Yvonne De Carlo, Celia Johnson, Miles Malleson, Nicholas Phipps, Ferdinand "Ferdy" Mayne, Sebastian Cabot; ***D:*** Anthony Kimmins; ***W:*** Alec Coppel, Nicholas Phipps; ***C:*** Edward Scaife; ***M:*** Malcolm Arnold.

The Captain's Table **1960** Former cargo vessel captain Gregson is given luxury liner to command, and fails to revise his cargo captain style to fit new crew and clientele. British cast saves unremarkable script from mediocrity. **90m/C VHS.** *GB* John Gregson, Peggy Cummins, Donald Sinden, Nadia Gray; ***D:*** Jack Lee.

Captive ½ **1987 (R)** Spoiled heiress is kidnapped by terrorist trio and brainwashed into anti-establishment Hearst-like creature. **98m/C VHS.** Oliver Reed, Irina Brook, Xavier DeLuc, Hirofumi Arai; ***D:*** Paul Mayersberg.

Captive ½ **1997** New bride Samantha Hoffman's (Eleniak) husband is murdered on their wedding night. Blaming herself, Samantha attempts suicide and then voluntarily commits herself to a mental institution at her brother-in-law's suggestion. But Samantha soon discovers she can't leave. What's worse is she finds that she's the pawn in a plot involving her husband's death. **93m/C VHS.** *CA* Erika Eleniak, Michael Ironside, Catherine Colvey, Stewart Bick; ***D:*** Rodney Gibbons; ***W:*** Rodney Gibbons, Richard Stanford; ***C:*** Bruno Philip; ***M:*** David Findlay. **VIDEO**

Captive Heart **1947** Czech soldier Redgrave assumes the identity of a dead British officer in order to evade Nazis in WWII. Captured and imprisoned in camp reserved for British POWs, his stalagmates think they smell a spy, but he manages to convince them he's an OK Joe. Meanwhile, he's been writing letters home to the little missus, which means he's got a little explaining to do when he's released from prison. Especially fine Redgrave performance. **86m/B VHS.** *GB* Michael Redgrave, Basil Radford, Jack Warner, Jimmy Hanley, Rachel Kempson, Mervyn Johns; ***D:*** Basil Dearden.

Captive Hearts **1987 (PG)** Well frayed story holds cast captive in sushi romance. Two American flyers are shot down and taken prisoner in isolated Japanese mountain village, and one is shot by Cupid's arrow. **97m/C VHS.** Noriyuki "Pat" Morita, Michael Sarrazin, Chris Makepeace; ***D:*** Paul Almond; ***M:*** David Benoit.

A Captive in the Land ½ **1991 (PG)** Routine survival pic pits two strangers against the frozen Arctic tundra. Potapov is a Soviet airman who's too injured to walk when he's discovered by American meteorologist Waterston. When a rescue seems unlikely, the two are forced to try for a trek to civilization. Based on the novel by James Aldridge. **96m/C VHS.** Sam Waterston, Alexander Potapov; ***D:*** John Berry; ***M:*** Bill Conti, Lee Gold.

Captive Planet **1978** Bargain basement FX and really atrocious acting hold audience captive in routine earth on the verge of obliteration yarn. **95m/C VHS, DVD.** Sharon Baker, Chris Auram, Anthony Newcastle; ***D:*** Al (Alfonso Brescia) Bradley.

Captive Rage **1988 (R)** South American general Reed hijacks planeful of girlies to encourage US to release his son, who's in trouble because he swaps money for white powder. Violence lives up to title, all else disappoints. **99m/C VHS.** Oliver Reed, Robert Vaughn, Claudia Udy; ***D:*** Cedric Sundstrom.

The Captive: The Longest Drive 2 *The Quest* **1976 (PG-13)** Matheson and Russell play two recently reunited brothers in search of their sister, whom they believe is still a captive of the Cheyenne Indians who also raised Russell. Along the way the two come to the aid of a pioneer woman and her young son. This western was actually a brief TV series known as "The Quest," and is a continuation of the pilot episode released on video as "The Longest Drive." **80m/C VHS.** Kurt Russell, Tim Matheson; ***D:*** Lee H. Katzin. **TV**

Captive Wild Woman ½ **1943** Mad scientist Dr. Sigmund Walters (Carradine) transforms an ape into the beautiful Paula Depress (Aquanetta), who promptly joins the circus as a mysterious animal trainer. Unfortunately, she falls in love with fellow trainer Fred (Stone), who already has a gal, bringing back the beast in the pretty Paula. Sequelled by "Jungle Captive" and "Jungle Woman." **61m/B VHS.** Acquanetta, John Carradine, Milburn Stone, Evelyn Ankers, Lloyd Corrigan, Vince Barnett, Paul Fix; ***D:*** Edward Dmytryk; ***W:*** Griffin Jay, Henry Sucher.

Captives ½ **1994 (R)** Middle-class dentist Rachel Clifford (Ormond), recently separated from her husband, takes a part-time job at a local prison where she becomes attracted to her patient, Cockney charmer Philip Chaney (Roth). He's coming to the end of a 10-year sentence and the lusty duo manage to consummate their relationship during one of Philip's day-releases. Only problem is fellow con Towler (Salmon) notices what's happening and blackmails and threatens Rachel—leading to a violent confrontation. Roth and Ormond click believably as opposites-attract partners though the script has some weak elements. **100m/C VHS, DVD.** *GB* Tim Roth, Julia Ormond, Colin Salmon, Keith Allen, Siobhan Redmond, Peter Capaldi, Richard Hawley, Annette Badland, Jeff Nuttal; ***D:*** Angela Pope; ***W:*** Frank Deasy; ***C:*** Remi Adefarasin; ***M:*** Colin Towns.

Captivity **WOOF!** **2007 (R)** The kazillionth contribution to the relatively new subgenre known as torture-porn. Yeah, they keep coming—only by now anything shocking, original, or smart has been milked. Generic fashion model Jennifer (Cuthbert) has been drugged and abducted for the purpose of sporting torture and mutilation. Forced by her captor to endure one indignity after another as she pleads for her life, Jennifer somehow strikes up an unlikely romance with dungeon mate and hot guy Gillies. Way too grisly to sit through, not even the pretty people can save it. **85m/C DVD.** *US RU* Elisha Cuthbert, Daniel Gillies, Laz Alonso, Pruitt Taylor Vince, Michael Harney; ***D:*** Roland Joffe; ***W:*** Larry Cohen, Joseph Tura; ***C:*** Daniel Pearl; ***M:*** Marco Beltrami.

The Capture **1950** Above-average story told in flashback has Ayres hiding out in Mexico because he thought he killed an innocent man. He seeks out the widow to question her about him and they wind up marrying. When he finds the real culprit, the man is killed and the evidence points to Ayres. Ayres and Wright are great, as is the native Mexican musical score. **67m/B VHS, DVD.** Lew Ayres, Teresa Wright, Victor Jory, Jacqueline White, Jimmy Hunt, Duncan Renaldo, William "Billy" Bakewell; ***D:*** John Sturges.

The Capture of Bigfoot **1979 (PG)** Barefoot monster tracks footprints around town after 25 years of peace, and evil businessman attempts to capture creature for personal gain. **92m/C VHS.** Stafford Morgan, Katherine Hopkins, Richard Kennedy, Otis Young, George "Buck" Flower, John Goff; ***D:*** Bill Rebane.

The Capture of Grizzly Adams ½ **1982** Framed for murder, Adams and his ever-faithful companion Ben the bear must not only clear his name but outwit a band of outlaws who are holding his young daughter captive. **96m/C VHS.** Dan Haggerty, Chuck Connors, June Lockhart, Kim Darby, Noah Beery Jr., Keenan Wynn, Sydney Penny, G.W. Bailey, Todd Everett; ***D:*** Don Keeslar. **TV**

Captured **1999 (R)** Car thief picks the wrong auto to boost when he gets locked inside a special high-tech Porsche, which is maneuvered by a remote control in the hands of its sadistic owner. Who decides the thief needs to be taught a lesson. **95m/C VHS, DVD.** Andrew Divoff, Nick Mancuso, Linda Hoffman, Michael Mahonen; ***D:*** Peter Paul Liapis. **VIDEO**

Captured in Chinatown **1935** Dog chases bad guys in Chinatown. Bow wow. **53m/B VHS.** Marion Shilling, Charles Delaney, Philo (Philip, P.H., P.M.) McCullough, Robert Ellis; ***D:*** Elmer Clifton.

Capturing the Friedmans **2003** Disturbing documentary follows the lives of the Friedman family of Great Neck, Long Island. On Thanksgiving of 1987, police raid the Friedman home and find child pornography belonging to father Arthur, who's a high school science and computer teacher. The police allege that Arthur and youngest son, Jesse (then 18), molested dozens of boys. There is a rash of conflicting testimony as the case goes to trial (both are convicted, though Jesse's guilt is called into question). Shows excerpts from some 50 hours of home movies, much of which eldest son David filmed, and which the family permitted director Jarecki to use. He also conducted present-day interviews with a number of figures involved in the case. **107m/C DVD.** *US* ***D:*** Andrew Jarecki; ***C:*** Adolfo Doring; ***M:*** Andrea Morricone. Sundance '03: Feature Doc.

The Car **1977 (PG)** Driverless black sedan appears out of nowhere to terrorize the residents of a small New Mexico town. And it's up to Sheriff Wade Parent (Brolin) to stop the demonic auto. **96m/C VHS, DVD.** James Brolin, Kathleen Lloyd, John Marley, Ronny Cox, John Rubinstein, R.G. Armstrong, Elizabeth Thompson, Roy Jenson, Robert Phillips; ***D:*** Elliot Silverstein; ***W:*** Dennis Shryack, Michael Butler; ***C:*** Gerald Hirschfeld; ***M:*** Leonard Rosenman.

Car Babes **2006 (PG-13)** A very misleading title since you're probably expecting a flick about scantily-clad ladies purring over automobiles. Wrong kind of comedy. Owing his dad money, recent college grad Ford Davis (Savage) must take a job at the family's used car lot and figures out it means more than just a paycheck. He makes friends with the usual group of wacky salesmen and then is forced into action when the business is threatened by a rival dealership. **90m/C DVD.** Ben Savage, Carolina Garcia, Jon(athan) Gries, Marshall Manesh, Blake Clarke, Kevan Blackton, Donnell Rawlings, David Shackelford, John Campo; ***D:*** Christopher Wolf, Nick Fumia; ***W:*** Christopher Wolf, Nick Fumia, Blake Dirickson; ***C:*** Oden Roberts; ***M:*** Dino Campanella. **VIDEO**

Car Crash **1980** Organized crime hits stock car racing head on to produce crashing bore. **103m/C VHS.** Joey Travolta, Anna (Ana Garcia) Obregon, Vittorio Mezzogiorno; ***D:*** Antonio Margheriti; ***W:*** Massimo De Rita, Mario Giordano; ***C:*** Hans Burman; ***M:*** Giosy Capuano, Mario Cupuano.

Car 54, Where Are You? **1994 (PG-13)** Exceedingly lame remake of the exceedingly lame TV series, which ran for only two seasons, 1961-63. This time, Toody (Johansen) and Muldoon (McGinley) are protecting a mafia stool pigeon (Piven), while vampy Velma Velour (Drescher) sets her sights on Muldoon. Not many laughs and a waste of a talented cast. Sat on the shelf at Orion for three years (with good reason).

89m/C VHS, DVD. David Johansen, Fran Drescher, Rosie O'Donnell, John C. McGinley, Nipsey Russell, Al Lewis, Daniel Baldwin, Jeremy Piven; ***D:*** Bill Fishman; ***W:*** Ebbe Roe Smith, Erik Tarloff, Peter McCarthy, Peter Crabbe; ***M:*** Bernie Worrell, Pray for Rain. Golden Raspberries '94: Worst Support. Actress (O'Donnell).

Car Trouble 1/2 **1985** Dull Gerald Spong loves his new Jaguar much more than his neglected wife Jacqueline. When Jacqueline borrows the car, she accidentally gets trapped in the two-seater with an amorous car salesman, resulting in the police having to cut apart the Jag to free them. An incensed Gerald decides only Jacqueline's death will now satisfy him. **93m/C DVD.** Ian Charleston, Julie Walters, Stratford Johns, Hazel O'Connor, Vincent Riotta; ***D:*** David Green; ***W:*** A.J Tipping, James Whaley; ***C:*** Mike Garfath.

Car Trouble 1/2 **1986 (R)** Young English husband buys new Jaguar and wife's not so minor car trouble causes major marital trouble. Funnybone-tickling pairing of Walters and Charleson. **93m/C VHS.** *GB* Julie Walters, Ian Charleson; ***D:*** David Green; ***M:*** Meat Loaf Aday.

Car Wash 1/2 **1976 (PG)** L.A. carwash provides a soap-opera setting for disjointed comic bits about owners of dirty cars and people who hose them down for a living. Econo budget and lite plot, but serious comic talent. A sort of disco carwash version of "Grand Hotel." **97m/C VHS, DVD.** Franklin Ajaye, Sully Boyar, Richard Brestoff, George Carlin, Richard Pryor, Melanie Mayron, Ivan Dixon, Antonio Fargas; ***D:*** Michael A. Schultz; ***W:*** Joel Schumacher; ***C:*** Frank Stanley; ***M:*** Norman Whitfield.

Caracara *The Last Witness* **2000 (R)** Ornithologist Rachel Sutherland (Henstridge) agrees to allow the FBI to use her apartment for a stakeout and falls for agent David MacMillan (Schaech). Then she learns she's been duped—her "guests" are actually assassins planning to kill Nelson Mandela. **93m/C VHS, DVD.** Natasha Henstridge, Johnathon Schaech, David McIlwraith, Lauren Hutton; ***D:*** Graeme Clifford; ***W:*** Craig Smith; ***C:*** Bill Wong. **CABLE**

Caramel *Sukkar Banat* **2007 (PG)** Modernity collides with custom as five women, portrayed mostly by local nonprofessionals, lament on issues involving sex, religion, and family at a beauty salon in Beirut, Lebanon (where apparently the titular sticky-sweet treat is used to remove unwanted hair). Even when it gets a bit soapy, actor/writer/director Labaki (a stunner both in front of and behind the camera) deftly winds the personal and cultural impact of each woman's dilemma into a story of universal sisterhood. The result is a cut above most Western chick-flickery, with a refreshing lack of Hollywood gloss. **95m/C DVD.** *FR* Nadine Labaki, Yasmine Al Masri, Joanna Moukarzel, Gisele Aouad, Sihame Haddad, Aziza Semaan; ***D:*** Nadine Labaki; ***W:*** Nadine Labaki, Jihad Hojeily, Rodney Al Haddad; ***C:*** Yves Schnaoui; ***M:*** Khaled Mouzanar.

Carandiru **2003 (R)** Hellish fact-based prison drama based on events leading up to the 1992 San Paolo massacre in which 111 inmates died. A nameless doctor (Vasconcelos) arrives at the city's infamous House of Detention because of an AIDS epidemic. As he tests and treats the inmates of the severely overcrowded facility, he learns about their lives on the outside (shown in flashbacks) and about the prison's codes, which are enforced by the inmates and not the guards or warden. Viewers are lulled into a false sense of normalcy before the horror begins. Based on "Carandiru Station," the fictionalized account of Dr. Drauzio Varella's experiences. Portuguese with subtitles. **148m/C DVD.** *BR* Luiz Carlos Vasconcelos, Milhem Cortaz, Milton Goncalves, Ivan de Almeida, Ailton Graca, Maria Luisa Mendonca, Aida Lerner, Rodrigo Santoro, Gero Camilo, Caio Blat, Wagner Moura; ***D:*** Hector Babenco; ***W:*** Hector Babenco, Victor Nava, Fernando Bonassi; ***C:*** Walter Carvalho; ***M:*** Andre Abujarrura.

Caravaggio **1986** Controversial biography of late Renaissance painter Caravaggio (Terry), famous for his bisexuality, fondness for prostitute models, violence and depravity. The painter divides his time between two street models, Ranuccio (Bean) and his lover Lena (Swinton), the decadent cardinals who commission his religious works, and Caravaggio's young assistant (Leigh), who cares for the artist as he lies dying. Photography by Gabriel Beristain reproduces the artist's visual style. **97m/C VHS.** *GB* Spencer Leigh, Michael Gough, Nigel Davenport, Robbie Coltrane, Jack Birkett, Nigel Terry, Sean Bean, Tilda Swinton; ***D:*** Derek Jarman; ***W:*** Derek Jarman; ***C:*** Gabriel Beristain; ***M:*** Simon Fisher.

Caravan to Vaccares **1974 (PG)** French Duke hires young American to sneak Eastern European scientist into the States, and little suspense ensues. Based on Alistair MacLean novel. **98m/C VHS.** David Birney, Charlotte Rampling; ***D:*** Geoffrey Reeve.

The Caravan Trail **1946** A cowboy becomes marshal in order to bring to justice those who have stolen land and murdered his friend. This was shot in color, which was rare for the 1940s. **53m/C VHS.** Eddie Dean, Lash LaRue, Emmett Lynn, Jean Carlin, Charles "Blackie" King, Bob (Robert) Barron, Lloyd Ingraham, Bud Osborne; ***D:*** Robert Emmett Tansey.

Carbide and Sorrel 1/2 *Karbid und Sauerampfer* **1963** To rebuild a Dresden cigarette factory destroyed by bombing in WWII, workers need carbide for welding torches. So Kalle travels to Wittenberg to buy seven barrels of the rationed material and then must find a way to get them home while dodging Soviet soldiers, mines, and other various hazards. German with subtitles. **80m/B DVD.** *GE* Erwin Geschonneck, Marita Bohme, Kurt Rackelmann, Margot Busse; ***D:*** Frank Beyer; ***W:*** Frank Beyer, Hans Oliva; ***C:*** Gunter Marczinkowski; ***M:*** Joachim Werzlau.

Carbon Copy *Time of the Wolves; The Last Shot; The Heist; Le Temps des Loups; Dillinger 70* **1969** A criminal with a split personality (Hossein) has renamed himself Dillinger because he patterns his crimes after the legendary gangster. As he and his gang strike, an Inspector (Aznavour) tries to bring him down. Dubbed. **105m/C VHS, DVD.** *FR IT* Robert Hossein, Charles Aznavour, Virna Lisi, Marcel Bozzuffi; ***D:*** Sergio Gobbi; ***W:*** Andre Tabet, Sergio Gobbi; ***C:*** Daniel Diot; ***M:*** Georges Garvarentz.

Carbon Copy **1981 (PG)** Successful white executive has life turned inside out when his 17-year-old illegitimate son, who happens to be black, decides it's time to look up dear old dad. Typical comedy-with-a-moral. **92m/C VHS, DVD.** George Segal, Susan St. James, Jack Warden, Paul Winfield, Dick Martin, Vicky Dawson, Tom Poston, Denzel Washington; ***D:*** Michael A. Schultz; ***W:*** Stanley Shapiro; ***M:*** Bill Conti.

Cardiac Arrest **1974 (PG)** Lunatic eviscerates victims in trolley town. They left their hearts in San Francisco. **95m/C VHS, DVD.** Garry Goodrow, Mike Chan, Max Gail; ***D:*** Murray Mintz.

The Cardinal 1/2 **1963** Priestly young Tryon rises through ecclesiastical ranks to become Cardinal, struggling through a plethora of tests of faith, none so taxing as the test of the audience's patience. Had Preminger excised some 60 minutes of footage, he might have had a compelling portrait of faith under fire, but as it stands, the cleric's life is epic confusion. Fine acting, even from Tryon, who later went on to bookish fame, and from Huston who's normally on the other side of the camera. McNamara's final performance. Based on the Henry Morton Robinson novel. **175m/C VHS, DVD.** Tom Tryon, Carol Lynley, Dorothy Gish, Maggie McNamara, Cecil Kellaway, John Huston, John Saxon, Burgess Meredith; ***D:*** Otto Preminger; ***C:*** Leon Shamroy. Golden Globes '64: Film—Drama, Support. Actor (Huston).

Career 1/2 **1959** An overwrought, depressing drama about the trials and tribulations of an actor trying to make it on Broadway. He'll try anything to succeed. Good direction, but so-so acting. **105m/B VHS.** Dean Martin, Anthony (Tony) Franciosa, Shirley MacLaine, Carolyn Jones, Joan Blackman, Robert Middleton, Donna Douglas; ***D:*** Joseph Anthony; ***C:*** Joseph LaShelle. Golden Globes '60: Actor—Drama (Franciosa).

Career Girls **1997 (R)** Two young women, the caustic acid-tongued Hannah (Cartlidge) and shy eczema-scarred Annie (Steadman), are introduced in a flashback sequence as they meet and become college roommates. They reunite for a weekend visit six years after they graduate. Both have become career women and have smoothed out their rough edges. In their wanders around London, they coincidentally run into people they knew back in the day, including a smarmy real estate agent (Tucker) who dated them both and a despondent schizophrenic (Benton) who pursued Annie. Excellent performances from a largely unknown cast. **87m/C VHS, DVD.** Katrin Cartlidge, Lynda Steadman, Kate Byers, Mark Benton, Andy Serkis, Joe Tucker, Margo Stanley, Michael Healy; ***D:*** Mike Leigh; ***W:*** Mike Leigh; ***C:*** Dick Pope; ***M:*** Marianne Jean-Baptiste, Tony Remy.

Career Opportunities 1/2 **1991 (PG-13)** "Home Alone" clone for teenagers from John Hughes' factory. Whaley is an unsuccessful con-artist who finally gets a job as the night janitor of the local department store. He fools around at company expense until he finds the town's beauty (Connelly) asleep in a dressing room. The pair then play make-believe until its time to thwart some small-time thieves. Unexciting and unrealistic in the worst way; no wonder Candy isn't billed—he probably didn't want to be. **83m/C VHS, DVD.** Frank Whaley, Jennifer Connelly, Dermot Mulroney, Kieran Mulroney, John M. Jackson, Jenny O'Hara, Noble Willingham, Barry Corbin, Denise Galik, William Forsythe, John Candy; ***D:*** Bryan Gordon; ***W:*** John Hughes; ***C:*** Donald McAlpine; ***M:*** Thomas Newman.

Carefree **1938** Dizzy radio singer Rogers can't make up her mind about beau Bellamy, so he sends her to analyst Astaire. Seems she can't even dream a little dream until shrink Astaire prescribes that she ingest some funny food, which causes her to dream she's in love with the Fredman. Au contraire, says he, it's a Freudian thing, and he hypnotically suggests that she really loves Bellamy. The two line up to march down the aisle together, and Fred stops dancing just long enough to realize he's in love with Ginger. A screwball comedy with music. ♫ I Used to be Colorblind; The Night is Filled With Music; Change Partners; The Yam. **83m/B VHS, DVD.** Fred Astaire, Ginger Rogers, Ralph Bellamy, Jack Carson, Franklin Pangborn, Hattie McDaniel; ***D:*** Mark Sandrich; ***M:*** Irving Berlin.

Careful **1992** Butler-in-training Neale courts Neville in an alpine mountain village where silence is golden, or at least being quiet will lessen the chance of an avalanche. Dig a little deeper and you find incest, repression and other nasty things. Highly individualistic black comedy parodies German Expressionism and Freudian psychology to the point of absurdity, dealing with snow, sex, sleep, spirits, and obsessive/compulsive personality disorders. Third film from Canadian cult director Maddin is awash in vivid primary colors when it suits the scene's mood and employs between-scenes titles in a homage to cinematic antiquity. **100m/C VHS, DVD.** Kyle McCulloch, Gosia Dobrowolska, Jackie Burroughs, Sarah Neville, Brent Neale, Paul Cox, Victor Cowie, Michael O'Sullivan, Vince Rimmer, Katya Gardner; ***D:*** Guy Maddin; ***W:*** Guy Maddin, George Toles; ***C:*** Guy Maddin; ***M:*** John McCulloch.

Careful, He Might Hear You **1984 (PG)** Abandoned by his father, six-year-old P.S. becomes a pawn between his dead mother's two sisters, one working class and the other wealthy, and his worldview is further overturned by the sudden reappearance of his prodigal father. Set in Depression-era Australia, Schultz's vision is touching and keenly observed, and manages a sort of child's eye sense of proportion. Based on a novel by Sumner Locke Elliott. **113m/C VHS, DVD.** *AU* Nicholas Gledhill, Wendy Hughes, Robyn Nevin, John Hargreaves; ***D:*** Carl Schultz; ***W:*** Michael Jenkins; ***C:*** John Seale; ***M:*** Ray Cook. Australian Film Inst. '83: Actress (Hughes), Film.

Careless 1/2 **2007 (R)** Meandering dramedy that only fitfully maintains interest. Mild-mannered mystery bookstore employee Wiley Roth (Hanks) is shocked to find a severed finger on his kitchen floor. He stows the digit in the freezer and enlists his oddball father (Shalhoub) and best bud Mitch (Kranz) to track down the finger's owner. When Wiley meets Rachel (Blanchard) at a party, he can't help noticing her bandaged hand but she doesn't want to talk about her injury. **90m/C DVD.** Colin Hanks, Tony Shalhoub, Fran Kranz, Rachel Blanchard; ***D:*** Peter Spears; ***W:*** Eric Laster; ***C:*** Byron Shah; ***M:*** John (Gianni) Frizzell.

Caresses *Caricies* **1997** Eleven short scenes confront the lack of tenderness in the restless lives of a big city's inhabitants over the course of one night, until the film circles back to where it began—with the domestic argument between a young man and woman who no longer love each other. Adaptation of Belbel's play. Spanish with subtitles. **94m/C VHS, DVD.** *SP* Julieta Serrano, Augustin Gonzalez, Sergi Lopez, David Selvas, Laura Conejero, Montserrat Salvador, Naim Thomas, Merce Pons, Jordi Dauder, Roger Coma, Rosa Maria Sarda; ***D:*** Ventura Pons; ***W:*** Ventura Pons, Sergi Belbel; ***C:*** Jesus Escosa; ***M:*** Carles Cases.

Caribe 1/2 **1987** Caribbean travelogue masquerades as spy thriller. Arms smuggling goes awry, and neither voodoo nor bikinied blondes can prevent audience from dozing. Never released theatrically. **96m/C VHS, DVD.** John Savage, Kara Glover, Stephen McHattie, Sam Malkin; ***D:*** Michael Kennedy.

The Cariboo Trail **1950** Two prospecting men seek their fortune in British Columbia, the golden West of Canada in the 1890s. But they find themselves opposed by a ruthless rancher and claim-jumpers. Actually filmed in Colorado with excellent cinematography and solid performances from some big names, it's still a run-of-the-mill entry. Made the same year that the Gabby Hayes' show first aired. **80m/C VHS.** Randolph Scott, George "Gabby" Hayes, Bill Williams, Victor Jory; ***D:*** Edwin L. Marin.

Carla's Song **1997** Left-leaning director Loach sets his sometimes gripping, sometimes over-bearing political/love story in war torn Nicaragua in the late 1980s. George (Carlyle) is a Glasgow bus driver who helps out passenger Carla (Cabezas), a Nicaraguan emigre who raises money for the Sandanista cause. George falls in love with Carla and decides that the only way she can get on with her life is to confront her former lover Antonio, who was maimed by the contras and has disappeared. The two lovers go to Nicaragua, where George is totally out of his environment. Shot (with great difficulty) on location in Nicaragua. **127m/C VHS, DVD.** Robert Carlyle, Oyanka Cabezas, Gary Lewis, Scott Glenn, Subash Sing Pall; ***D:*** Ken Loach; ***W:*** Paul Laverty; ***C:*** Barry Ackroyd; ***M:*** George Fenton.

Carlito's Way **1993 (R)** Puerto Rican crime czar Carlito Brigante (Pacino) has just gotten out of jail and wants to go straight. But his drug underworld cohorts don't believe he can do it. Penn (barely recognizable) is great as a sleazy coked-out lawyer who's way out of his league. Remarkably subdued violence given DePalma's previous rep—it's effective without being gratuitous, especially the final shootout set in Grand Central Station. Pacino's performance is equally subdued, with controlled tension and lots of eye contact rather than grandiose emotions. Based on the novels "Carlito's Way" and "After Hours" by Edwin Torres. Pacino and DePalma previously teamed up for "Scarface." **145m/C VHS, DVD, HD DVD.** Al Pacino, Sean Penn, Penelope Ann Miller, Luis Guzman, John Leguizamo, Ingrid Rogers, James Rebhorn, Viggo Mortensen, Jorge Porcel, Joseph Siravo, Adrian Pasdar, Jon Seda, Vincent Pastore; ***D:*** Brian De Palma; ***W:*** David Koepp; ***C:*** Stephen Burum; ***M:*** Patrick Doyle.

Carlito's Way: Rise to Power **2005 (R)** Depicts the early years of Puerto Rican drug dealer Carlito Brigante (Hernandez), who wants to become the crime kingpin of New York's Spanish Harlem in the '70s. Carlito is drawn into an alliance with numbers runner Earl (Van Peebles) and mobster Rocco (Kelly) despite Harlem boss Hollywood Nicky (Combs) and various crooked cops. Hernandez does what he can with Pacino's shadow looming over him but this is familiar territory. Adapted from a book by Edwin Torres. **100m/C DVD, UMD, HD DVD.** Jay Hernandez, Mario Van Peebles, Sean (Puffy, Puff Daddy, P. Diddy) Combs, Michael Kelly, Luis Guzman, Jaclyn DeSantis, Giancarlo Esposito, Burt Young, Domenick Lombardozzi, Juan Carlos Hernandez, Mtume Gant, Tony Cucci; ***D:*** Michael Scott Bregman; ***W:*** Michael Scott Bregman; ***C:***

Adam Holender; *M:* Joe Delia. **VIDEO**

Carlton Browne of the F.O. 🦴🦴 ½ *Man in a Cocked Hat* **1959** Bumbling Brit diplomat Thomas visits tiny Pacific island of Gallardia, forgotten by the mother country for some 50 years, to insure tenuous international agreement after the island's king dies. Not sterling Sellers but some shining moments. **88m/C VHS, DVD.** *GB* Peter Sellers, Terry-Thomas, Luciana Paluzzi, Ian Bannen; *D:* Roy Boulting, Jeffrey Dell; *W:* Roy Boulting; *M:* John Addison.

Carmen 🦴🦴🦴 **1983 (R)** Choreographer casts Carmen and finds life imitates art when he falls under the spell of the hotblooded Latin siren. Bizet's opera lends itself to erotically charged flamenco context. Well acted, impressive scenes including cigarette girls' dance fight and romance between Carmen and Don Jose. In Spanish with English subtitles. **99m/C VHS.** *SP* Antonio Gades, Laura Del Sol, Paco de Lucia, Cristina Hoyos; *D:* Carlos Saura; *W:* Antonio Gades, Carlos Saura; *C:* Teodoro Escamilla. British Acad. '84: Foreign Film.

Carmen 🦴🦴 **2003** The screenwriters use Prosper Merimee's original 1845 novel rather than George Bizet's 1875 opera, although the plot is certainly familiar. Sultry gypsy Carmen (Vega) toys with the affections of military officer Jose (Sbaraglia) until his obsession leads to disgrace, murder, and execution. This version is told by Jose to Prospero (Benedict) in flashbacks. Vega is a looker (and not shy about disrobing) but she doesn't have a lot of chemistry with the various actors in the lurid story. **119m/C DVD.** *SP GB IT* Paz Vega, Leonardo Sbaraglia, Jay Benedict, Antonio Dechent, Joan Crosas, Joe Mackay, Josep Linuesa; *D:* Vicente Aranda; *W:* Vicente Aranda, Joaquin Jorda; *C:* Paco Femenia; *M:* Jose Nieto.

Carmen: A Hip Hopera 🦴🦴 ½ **2001 (PG-13)** Modernized and urban set version of Bizet's tragic opera, originally made for MTV. Carmen (Knowles) is the femme fatale who seduces straight-laced cop Derek Hill (Phifer) to keep herself out of jail. He abandons everything to follow her to California, where, naturally, Carmen wants to break into show biz. But she tires of Derek's devotion and becomes interested in an up-and-coming rapper. Surprisingly effective and the cast does a fine job. **88m/C VHS, DVD.** Beyonce Knowles, Mekhi Phifer, Mos Def, Rah Digga, Bow Wow, Nelust Wyclef Jean, Troy Winbush; *D:* Robert Kevin Townsend; *W:* Michael Elliot; *C:* Geary McLeod; *M:* Kip Collins; *Nar:* Da Brat. **CABLE**

Carmen, Baby 🦴 ½ **1966** Metzger's erotic modern update of Bizet's opera "Carmen." Spanish prostitute Carmen (Levka) becomes the object of obsession for a local cop (Ringer) and things wind up badly because of his jealousy. **90m/C VHS, DVD.** Uta Levka, Claus Ringer, Barbara Valentin, Walter Wilz; *D:* Radley Metzger; *W:* Jesse Vogel; *C:* Hans Jura; *M:* Daniel Hart.

Carmen Jones 🦴🦴🦴 **1954** Bizet's tale of fickle femme fatale Carmen heads South with an all black cast and new lyrics by Hammerstein II. Soldier Belafonte falls big time for factory working belle Dandridge during the war, and runs off with miss thang after he kills his C.O. and quits the army. Tired of prettyboy Belafonte, Dandridge's eye wanders upon prize pugilist Escamillo, inspiring ex-soldier beau to wring her throaty little neck. Film debuts of Carroll and Peters. More than a little racist undertone to the direction. Actors' singing is dubbed. ♫Dat's Love; Dere's a Cafe on de Corner; Beat Out Dat Rhythm on a Drum; You Talk Just Like My Maw; Stand Up and Fight; Dis Flower; My Joe. **105m/C VHS, DVD.** Dorothy Dandridge, Harry Belafonte, Pearl Bailey, Roy Glenn, Diahann Carroll, Brock Peters; *D:* Otto Preminger; *W:* Harry Kleiner; *C:* Sam Leavitt; *M:* Oscar Hammerstein, Georges Bizet. Golden Globes '55: Film—Mus./Comedy, Natl. Film Reg. '92.

Carnage 🦴 **1984** Hungry house consumes inhabitants. **91m/C VHS.** Leslie Den Dooven, Michael Chiodo, Deeann Veeder; *D:* Andy Milligan.

Carnage 🦴🦴 **2002** Okay, this film is about a dead bull and its various body parts. Said bull gores a matador during a bullfight and is subsequently killed and butchered. It's various parts go to various people throughout Spain and France, including a young girl named Winnie who gets a bull bone for her Great Dane, a taxidermist who gets the animal's horns, steaks that wind up in a restaurant, etc. There's a lot of obscure symbolism about how life and death are connected. You may not care. Spanish and French with subtitles. **130m/C VHS, DVD.** *FR SP BE SI* Chiara Mastroianni, Angela Molina, Lucia Sanchez, Bernard Sens, Esther Gorintin, Jacques Gamblin, Feodor Atkine, Marilyne Even, Clovis Cornillac, Raphaelle Molinier, Lio; *D:* Delphine Gleize; *W:* Delphine Gleize; *C:* Crystal Fournier; *M:* Eric Neveux.

Carnal Crimes 🦴 ½ **1991 (R)** Well-acted upscale softcore trash about a sensuous woman, ignored by her middle-aged lawyer husband and drawn to a young stud photographer with a shady past and S&M tendencies. Available in a sexy unrated version also. **103m/C VHS, DVD.** Martin Hewitt, Linda Carol, Rich Crater, Alex Kubik, Yvette Stefens, Paula Trickey; *D:* Alexander Gregory (Gregory Dark) Hippolyte; *W:* Jon Robert Samsel; *C:* Paul Desatoff; *M:* Matthew Ross, Jeff Fishman.

Carnal Knowledge 🦴🦴🦴 **1971 (R)** Carnal knowledge of the me generation. Three decades in the sex-saturated lives of college buddies Nicholson and Garfunkel, chronicled through girlfriends, affairs, and marriages. Controversial upon release, it's not a flattering anatomy of Y-chromosome carriers. Originally written as a play. Kane's debut. **96m/C VHS, DVD.** Jack Nicholson, Candice Bergen, Art Garfunkel, Ann-Margret, Rita Moreno, Carol Kane; *D:* Mike Nichols; *W:* Jules Feiffer; *C:* Giuseppe Rotunno. Golden Globes '72: Support. Actress (Ann-Margret).

Carnegie Hall 🦴🦴 ½ **1947** Widowed Irish-American Nora (Hunt) gets a job at Carnegie Hall and raises her son Tony to be a talented pianist. But the adult Tony (Prince) develops an interest in jazz and popular music that his ma despises. They have a rift, Tony goes on the road with a band, marries singer Ruth (O'Drsicoll), and becomes a famous jazz pianist. After years pass, Ruth decides it's about time to reunite mother and son and Carnegie Hall plays a big part in her scheme. Schmaltzy story showcases a number of big musical stars of the day. **134m/B VHS, DVD.** Marsha Hunt, William Prince, Martha O'Driscoll, Frank McHugh; *D:* Edgar G. Ulmer; *W:* Karl Kamb; *C:* William J. Miller.

Carnera: The Walking Mountain 🦴 ½ **2008 (R)** Standard biopic about Italian heavyweight boxing legend Prima Carnera (Iaia). Moving from his impoverished childhood, bellicose Carnera becomes a circus strongman and goes into boxing with shady promoters Leon See (Abraham) and Lou Soresi (Young) as Martinelli twists the facts to serve his dully-presented situations. Italian with subtitles or dubbed. **125m/C DVD.** *IT* Andrea Iaia, Burt Young, F. Murray Abraham, Anna Valle, Paolo Seganti, Antonio Cupo, Kasia Smutniak; *D:* Renzo Martinelli; *W:* Renzo Martinelli, Alessandro Gassman, Franco Ferrini; *C:* Saverio Guarna; *M:* Pivio de Scalzi, Aldo De Scalzi.

Carnival in Flanders 🦴🦴🦴 ½ *La Kermesse Heroique* **1935** When Spanish invaders enter a small 17th century Flemish village they discover all the men have diappeared. So it's up to the women to save the town from destruction—and they decide to do it by seducing the invaders. Classic French costume farce with a witty script and fine performances. In French with English subtitles. **90m/B VHS.** *FR* Francoise Rosay, Louis Jouvet, Jean Murat, Andre Aleme, Micheline Cheirel; *D:* Jacques Feyder; *C:* Harry Stradling Sr.; *M:* Louis Beydts. N.Y. Film Critics '36: Foreign Film; Venice Film Fest. '36: Director (Feyder).

Carnival Lady 🦴 **1933** Silver spooner Vincent is scheduled to tie the knot until little lady-to-be discovers he's a bit out of pocket after the stock market takes a wee dip. Jilted and impecunious, he heads for the big top, where he horns in on the high diver's turf, and it's all downhill from there. **66m/B VHS.** Patricia "Boots" Mallory, Allen Vincent, Gertrude Astor, Kit Guard, Donald (Don) Kerr, Rollo Lloyd, Jason Robards Sr.; *D:* Howard Higgin; *W:* Harold Tarshis; *C:* Edward Kull.

Carnival of Blood 🦴 *Death Rides a Carousel* **1971 (PG)** Boring talky scenes punctuated by Coney Island murder mayhem followed by more boring talky scenes. Young's debut, not released for five years. The question's not why they delayed release, but why they bothered at all. A carnival of cliches. **80m/C VHS, DVD.** Earle Edgerton, Judith Resnick, Martin Barlosky, John Harris, Burt Young, Kaly Mills, Gloria Spivak; *D:* Leonard Kirtman; *W:* Leonard Kirtman; *C:* David Howe.

Carnival of Souls 🦴🦴🦴 **1962** Cult-followed zero budget zombie opera has young Hilligoss and girlfriends take wrong turn off bridge into river. Mysteriously unscathed, Hilligoss rents room and takes job as church organist, but she keeps running into dancing dead people, led by director Harvey. Spooky, very spooky. **72m/B VHS, DVD.** Candace Hilligoss, Sidney Berger, Frances Feist, Stan Levitt, Art Ellison, Bill de Jarnette, Steve Boozer, Pamela Ballard, Harold (Herk) Harvey; *D:* Harold (Herk) Harvey; *W:* John Clifford; *C:* Maurice Prather; *M:* Gene Moore.

Carnival of Souls WOOF! *Wes Craven Presents Carnival of Souls* **1998 (R)** A young girl witnesses the brutal murder of her mother by a circus clown. As an adult she has nightmares about the circus, which intensify when the carnival hits town. Craven's "remake" has nothing much in common with the original except the title. Boring, disjointed waste of time. **87m/C VHS, DVD.** Bobbie Phillips, Larry Miller, Paul Johansson, Cleavant Derricks, Sidney Berger, Shawnee Smith; *D:* Adam Grossman; *W:* Adam Grossman; *M:* Andrew Rose.

Carnival of Wolves 🦴 ½ **1996** Four friends who have only their unemployed status in common decide that it would be a good idea to rob the local casino. Which happens to be owned by the easily angered boss of a Chinese Triad (who is a Caucasian male in a bit of a weird moment). Unfortunately the casino has security cameras (oops!), and the guys very soon have a large problem. **103m/C DVD.** Mike Norris, Stoney Jackson, Forrest Montegomery; *D:* Takeshi Watanabe; *W:* Eric P. Sherman; *C:* Kaz Tanaka, Kazunari Tanaka.

Carnival Rock 🦴 ½ **1957** Story of love triangular in seedy nightclub. Club owner Stewart loves chanteuse Cabot who loves card playin' Hutton. Who cares? Maybe hardcore Corman devotees. Good tunes from the Platters, the Blockbusters, Bob Luman, and David Houston. **80m/B VHS.** Susan Cabot, Brian Hutton, David J. Stewart, Dick Miller, Iris Adrian, Jonathan Haze, Ed Nelson, Bob Luman, Frankie Ray, Bruno VeSota; *D:* Roger Corman; *W:* Leo Lieberman; *C:* Floyd Crosby; *M:* Buck Ram.

Carnival Story 🦴 ½ **1954** Yet another melodramatic cliche about love triangular under the big top. German girl joins American-owned carnival and two guys start acting out unbecoming territorial behavior. Filmed in Germany. **94m/C VHS, DVD.** Anne Baxter, Steve Cochran, Lyle Bettger, George Nader; *D:* Kurt Neumann.

Carnosaur 🦴🦴 **1993 (R)** Straight from the Corman film factory, this exploitive quickie about dinosaurs harkens back to '50s-style monster epics. Predictable plot with extremely cheap effects. Genetic scientist Dr. Jane Tiptree (Ladd) is hatching diabolic experiments with chickens when things go awry. The experiments result in a bunch of lethal prehistoric creatures wrecking havoc among the community. **82m/C VHS, DVD.** Diane Ladd, Raphael Sbarge, Jennifer Runyon, Harrison Page, Clint Howard, Ned Bellamy; *D:* Adam Simon; *W:* Adam Simon; *C:* Keith Holland; *M:* Nigel Holton.

Carnosaur 2 🦴 ½ **1994 (R)** Technicians investigating a power shortage at a secret military mining facility encounter deadly dinos. Entertaining schlock. **90m/C VHS, DVD.** John Savage, Cliff DeYoung, Arabella Holzbog, Ryan Thomas Johnson; *D:* Louis Morneau; *C:* John Aronson; *M:* Ed Tomney, Michael Palmer.

Carnosaur 3: Primal Species 🦴 ½ **1996** Terrorists get big surprise when the cargo they hijack turns out to be three very hungry dinos who make snacks of them all. Then it's up to commando Valentine, scientist Gunn, and some soldiers to get rid of the beasts. **82m/C VHS, DVD.** Scott Valentine, Janet Gunn, Rick Dean, Rodger Halston, Tony Peck; *D:* Jonathan Winfrey; *C:* Andrea V. Rossotto; *M:* Kevin Kiner.

Carny 🦴🦴🦴 **1980 (R)** Hothead carnival bozo Busey and peacemaker Robertson experience friendship difficulties when runaway Foster rolls in hay with one and then other. Originally conceived as a documentary by "Derby" filmmaker Kaylor, it's a candid, unsavory, behind-the-scenes anatomy. Co-written by "The Band" member Robertson. **102m/C VHS, DVD.** Gary Busey, Robbie Robertson, Jodie Foster, Meg Foster, Kenneth McMillan, Elisha Cook Jr., Craig Wasson; *D:* Robert Kaylor; *W:* Robbie Robertson, Thomas Baum; *C:* Harry Stradling Jr.; *M:* Alex North.

Caro Diario 🦴🦴🦴 *Dear Diary* **1993** Three offbeat chapters from director Moretti's own life. "On My Vespa" has the director taking off on a personal tour of Rome, including its cinemas and their influence on him. In "Islands" Moretti and friend Gerardo travel to a series of island communities, including Salina, dominated by only children to whom their parents defer obsessively. "Doctors" finds Moretti experiencing a misdiagnosed medical crisis. Lots of charm and a certain shameless romanticism. Italian with subtitles. **100m/C VHS.** *IT* Nanni Moretti, Renato Carpentieri; *D:* Nanni Moretti; *W:* Nanni Moretti; *C:* Giuseppe Lanci; *M:* Nicola Piovani. Cannes '94: Director (Moretti).

Carolina 🦴 ½ **2003 (PG-13)** Carolina (Stiles) and her two sisters, Georgia (Skye) and Maine (Boorem), were raised by their eccentric grandma (McLaine) since dad (Quaid) kept skipping out of their lives. Carolina works for a reality matchmaking TV show in L.A. though, naturally, she doesn't have a love-life of her own since she doesn't realize her longtime best friend Albert (Nivola) is actually in love with her but too shy to make a move. **98m/C DVD.** Julia Stiles, Shirley MacLaine, Alessandro Nivola, Edward Atterton, Randy Quaid, Azura Skye, Mika Boorem, Jennifer Coolidge, Alan Thicke; *D:* Marleen Gorris; *W:* Katherine Fugate; *C:* John Peters; *M:* Steve Bartek.

Carolina Cannonball 🦴 ½ **1955** Slapstick comedy stars yodeling singer Canova as herself. Judy and Grandpa Canova run a trolley between a train depot and a Nevada ghost town. Meanwhile, three spies are tracking a stray atomic missile, which has crashed nearby. When the trolley breaks down, Judy and Grandpa unwittingly use the engine from the missile to make repairs. Much lowbrow hilarity ensues. **73m/B VHS.** Judy Canova, Andy Clyde, Ross Elliott, Emil Sitka, Sig Rumann, Jack Kruschen, Frank Wilcox, Leon Aksin; *D:* Charles Lamont, Charles Lamont; *W:* Barry Shipman; *C:* Reggie Lanning; *M:* Donald Kahn.

Carolina Moon 🦴🦴 ½ *Nora Roberts' Carolina Moon* **2007** Psychic Tory returns to her hometown to confront the terrible memories of her past—the night her friend Hope was murdered. But Tory discovers that Hope's was only the first in a series of deaths and that the killer has been waiting patiently for Tory's return. Can Hope's older brother Cade help Tory save herself before she becomes the next victim? Lifetime original movie based on the novel by Nora Roberts. **90m/C DVD.** Claire Forlani, Oliver Hudson, Jacqueline Bisset, Jonathan Scarfe, Josie Davis, Chad Willet, Greg Lawson; *D:* Stephen Tolkin; *W:* Stephen Tolkin; *C:* Derick Underschultz; *M:* Steve Porcaro. **CABLE**

Carolina Skeletons 🦴🦴 **1992 (R)** As a child in a small southern town, Gossett watched as his brother was accused of a vicious double murder and quickly tried and executed. Thirty years later, the ex-Green Beret returns home to find the real killer and clear his brother's name. But there are those in the town who will do anything to stop their secrets from being revealed. **94m/C VHS, DVD.** Louis Gossett Jr., Bruce Dern, Melissa Leo, Paul Roebling, G.D. Spradlin, Bill Cobbs, Henderson Forsythe, Clifton James; *D:* John Erman; *W:* Tracy Keenan Wynn; *C:* Tony Imi; *M:* John Morris.

Caroline? 🦴🦴🦴 **1990 (PG)** A wealthy young woman is presumed dead in a plane crash. Now 15 years later a stranger appears at the family home claiming to be Caroline—and wanting her inheritance. Is it possible that what she says is true or is it all an elaborate ruse? An especially good performance by Zimbalist. A a "Hallmark Hall of Fame" presentation. Based on the novel "Father's Arcane Daughter" by E.L. Konigsburg. **100m/C VHS.** Stephanie Zimbalist, Pamela Reed, George Grizzard, Dorothy McGuire, Patricia Neal, Shawn (Michael) Phelan, Jenny Jacobs; ***D:*** Joseph Sargent; ***M:*** Charles Bernstein. **TV**

Caroline at Midnight **1993 (R)** After a reporter's former girlfriend, Caroline, dies in a mysterious auto accident he winds up falling for her girlfriend Victoria. Then he discovers both women are connected to drug-dealing cops. Good cast in this atmospheric erotic thriller with plenty of puzzles. **92m/C VHS.** Clayton Rohner, Mia Sara, Timothy Daly, Judd Nelson, Virginia Madsen, Zach Galligan, Thomas F. Wilson, Stacey Travis; ***D:*** Scott McGinnis.

Carousel **1956** Much-loved Rodgers & Hammerstein musical based on Ferenc Molnar's play "Liliom" (filmed by Fritz Lang in 1935) about a swaggering carnival barker (MacRae) who tries to change his life after he falls in love with a good woman. Killed during a robbery he was reluctantly involved in, he begs his heavenly hosts for the chance to return to the mortal realm just long enough to set things straight with his teenage daughter. Now indisputably a classic, the film lost $2 million when it was released. ♫If I Loved You; Soliloquy; You'll Never Walk Alone; What's the Use of Wond'rin; When I Marry Mister Snow; When the Children Are Asleep; A Real Nice Clambake; Carousel Ballet; Carousel Waltz. **128m/C VHS, DVD.** Gordon MacRae, Shirley Jones, Cameron Mitchell, Gene Lockhart, Barbara Ruick, Robert Rounseville, Richard Deacon, Tor Johnson; ***D:*** Henry King; ***W:*** Henry Ephron, Phoebe Ephron; ***C:*** Charles G. Clarke; ***M:*** Richard Rodgers, Oscar Hammerstein.

The Carpathian Eagle **1981** Police wonder why murdered victims have hearts ripped out while audience wonders what weird title has to do with anything. Routine evisceration fest, part of Elvira's Thriller Video. **60m/C VHS, DVD.** Suzanne Danielle, Sian Phillips, Pierce Brosnan, Anthony Valentine; ***D:*** Francis Megahy.

The Carpenter **1989 (R)** Post-nervous breakdown woman receives nightly visits from guy who builds stuff with wood. Very scary stuff. Also available in slightly longer unrated version. **85m/C VHS.** *CA* Wings Hauser, Lynne Adams, Pierce Lenoir, Barbara Ann Jones, Beverly Murray; ***D:*** David Wellington; ***W:*** Doug Taylor; ***C:*** David Franco.

Carpet of Horror **1964** The city of London is terrorized by a small ball emitting poison gas in this schlock horror film. Death results when the ball is rolled into the living rooms of intended victims. **93m/C VHS.** *GE* Joachim Fuchsberger, Carl Lange, Karin Dor; ***D:*** Harald Reinl.

The Carpetbaggers **1964 (PG)** Uncannily Howard Hughesian Peppard wallows in wealth and women in Hollywood in the 1920s and 1930s. Spayed version of the Harold Robbins novel. Ladd's final appearance. Followed by the prequel "Nevada Smith." Introduced by Joan Collins. **150m/C VHS, DVD.** George Peppard, Carroll Baker, Alan Ladd, Elizabeth Ashley, Lew Ayres, Martha Hyer, Martin Balsam, Robert Cummings, Archie Moore, Audrey Totter, Leif Erickson, Tom Lowell; ***D:*** Edward Dmytryk; ***W:*** John Michael Hayes; ***C:*** Joe MacDonald; ***M:*** Elmer Bernstein. Natl. Bd. of Review '64: Support. Actor (Balsam).

Carpool **1996 (PG)** Dumb but amiable comedy finds harried dad Daniel Miller stuck driving a minivan filled with kids to school. Too bad he gets sidetracked and hijacked by bumbling would-be bank robber Franklin Laszlo (Arnold) who takes them hostage and on a really wild ride through the streets and shopping malls of Seattle (except it's filmed in Vancouver). **92m/C VHS, DVD.** Tom Arnold, David Paymer, Rhea Perlman, Rod Steiger, Kim Coates, Rachael Leigh Cook, Mikey Kovar, Micah Gardener, Blake Warkol; ***D:*** Arthur Hiller; ***W:*** Don Rhymer; ***C:*** David M. Walsh; ***M:*** John Debney. Golden Raspberries '96: Worst Actor (Arnold).

Carpool Guy **1/2 2005 (PG-13)** If you're a soap opera fan, your pleasure may derive from seeing familiar actors in other roles 'cause there's not much else to recommend this comedy. Ad exec Joel (Hearst) wants that newly-vacated corner office but may lose out because he's always late for work thanks to L.A.'s horrendous traffic. So he hires homeless guy Oliver (Geary) to ride with him, making Joel eligible to drive in the carpool lane. But Oliver also has some unexpected business smarts that Joel can use. **118m/C DVD.** Rick Hearst, Anthony Geary, Sean Kanan, Kristoff St. John, Lauralee Bell, Jeanne Cooper, Corbin Bernsen; ***D:*** Corbin Bernsen; ***W:*** Pete Soldinger; ***C:*** Mike Jones; ***M:*** Adam Barber. **VIDEO**

Carrie **1952** In a part turned down by Cary Grant, Olivier plays a married American who self destructs as the woman he loves scales the heights to fame and fortune. The manager of a posh epicurean mecca, Olivier deserts wife Hopkins and steals big bucks from his boss to head east with paramour Jones, a country bumpkin transplanted to Chicago. Once en route to thespian fame in the Big Apple, Jones abandons her erstwhile beau, who crumbles pathetically. Adapted from Theodore Dreiser's "Sister Carrie," it's mega melodrama, but the performances are above reproach. **118m/B VHS, DVD.** Laurence Olivier, Jennifer Jones, Miriam Hopkins, Eddie Albert, Basil Ruysdael, Ray Teal, Barry Kelley, Sara Berner, William Reynolds, Mary Murphy, Charles Halton; ***D:*** William Wyler; ***C:*** Victor Milner.

Carrie **1976 (R)** Overprotected by religious fanatic mother Laurie and mocked by the in-crowd, shy, withdrawn high school girl Carrie White is asked to the prom. Realizing she's been made the butt of a joke, she unleashes her considerable telekinetic talents. Travolta, Allen, and Irving are teenagers who get what they deserve. Based on the Stephen King novel. **98m/C VHS, DVD.** Sissy Spacek, Piper Laurie, John Travolta, William Katt, Amy Irving, Nancy Allen, Edie McClurg, Betty Buckley, P.J. Soles, Sydney Lassick, Stefan Gierasch; ***D:*** Brian De Palma; ***W:*** Lawrence D. Cohen; ***C:*** Mario Tosi; ***M:*** Pino Donaggio. Natl. Soc. Film Critics '76: Actress (Spacek).

Carrie **1/2 2002** This remake (broadcast on NBC) of King's first novel was stretched to three hours (with commercials) by introducing new characters and using flashbacks. Face it, what you want to see is the outcast Carrie (Bettis) getting her telekinetic revenge on all her tormentors at the high school prom. That's about the last half-hour, so just fast-forward to the good stuff. **132m/C VHS, DVD.** Angela Bettis, Patricia Clarkson, Rena Sofer, Tobias Mehler, Kandyse McClure, Emilie de Ravin, Katharine Isabelle, David Keith, Jasmine Guy; ***D:*** David Carson; ***W:*** Bryan Fuller; ***C:*** Victor Goss; ***M:*** Laura Karpman. **TV**

Carried Away **1/2** *Acts of Love* **1995 (R)** Exposing his middle-aged bod, as well as the myth that he can play only psycho toughs, Hopper, as the Midwestern teacher Joseph, is seduced by a 17-year-old student (Locane) in their small conservative town. Based on Harrison's novel "Farmer," it's a sexually active slice of life with the injured Joseph limping through the care of his dying mother, the fate of the small country school where he teaches and his relationship with longtime lover Rosealee (Amy Irving). Hopper's not the only one playing against type, as Irving turns in a fine performance as the widowed schoolmarm. Director Barreto (and Irving's husband) pushes the envelope with full frontal nudity. **107m/C VHS, DVD.** Dennis Hopper, Amy Irving, Amy Locane, Gary Busey, Julie Harris, Hal Holbrook, Christopher Pettiet, Priscilla Pointer, Gail Cronauer; ***D:*** Bruno Barreto; ***W:*** Ed Jones; ***C:*** Declan Quinn; ***M:*** Bruce Broughton.

The Carrier **1987 (R)** Smalltown Sleepy Rock is ideal family-raising turf until plague mysteriously blights inhabitants, and townspeople are out to exterminate all potential carriers. Silverman is standout as local spiritual leader; well-orchestrated crowd scenes. Best park your IQ before watching. Filmed on location in Manchester, Michigan. **99m/C VHS.** Gregory Fortescue, Steve Dixon, Paul Silverman, Paul Urbanski, Patrick Butler; ***D:*** Nathan J. White; ***W:*** Nathan J. White; ***C:*** Peter Deming; ***M:*** Joseph LoDuca.

Carriers **1/2 2009 (PG-13)** An unspecified plague that turns infected citizens into red-faced ghouls leaves some tough survivors, including four in the rural Southwest: Brian (Pine), Bobby (Perabo), Danny (Pucci), and Kate (VanCamp). When a man (Meloni) asks for help for his apparently infected daughter (Shipka), Brian initially refuses but of course the story doesn't end there with a nasty twist to come. Rating means there's more chills than outright grossness but that's definitely in the flick's favor. **84m/C DVD.** Chris Pine, Piper Perabo, Christopher Meloni, Lou Taylor Pucci, Emily VanCamp, Kiernan Shipka; ***D:*** Alex Pastor, David Pastor; ***W:*** Alex Pastor, David Pastor; ***C:*** Benoit Debie; ***M:*** Peter Nashel, Brick Garner.

Carrie's War **1/2 2004** 14-year-old Carrie (Fawcett) and her younger brother Nick (Stanley) are sent to live in the country to escape the London bombings during WWII. Naturally, they must cope with a variety of characters both pleasant and strict. Based on the Nina Bawden novel. **90m/C DVD.** *GB* Jack Stanley, Lesley Sharp, Alun Armstrong, Geraldine McEwan, Keeley Fawcett, Pauline Quirke, Eddie Cooper, Jamie Boddard; ***D:*** Coky Giedroyc; ***W:*** Michael Crompton; ***C:*** Julian Court; ***M:*** Nick Bicat. **TV**

Carrington **1/2 1995 (R)** England's artistic Bloomsbury group is examined through the eccentric relationship of artist Dora Carrington (Thompson) and her love for homosexual Lytton Strachey (Pryce), celebrated author of "Eminent Victorians." There's many a menage as the duo live together with Carrington's husband (Waddington), on whom Strachey has a crush, and both their various amours (though Carrington's heart is reserved for Lytton). Film is distractingly divided into titled segments (from 1915 to 1932) and, while Pryce gives a bravura performance, Thompson is merely enigmatic. Based on Michael Holroyd's biography "Lytton Strachey." Hampton's directorial debut. **120m/C VHS, DVD.** *FR GB* Emma Thompson, Jonathan Pryce, Steven Waddington, Samuel West, Rufus Sewell, Penelope Wilton, Jeremy Northam, Peter Blythe, Janet McTeer, Alex Kingston, Sebastian Harcombe, Richard Clifford; ***D:*** Christopher Hampton; ***W:*** Christopher Hampton; ***C:*** Denis Lenoir; ***M:*** Michael Nyman. Cannes '95: Special Jury Prize, Actor (Pryce); Natl. Bd. of Review '95: Actress (Thompson).

Carrington, V.C. *Court Martial* **1954** British army major Niven is brought up for a court-martial on embezzlement charges because he arranges, without official permission, to be reimbursed for money owed to him. A former war hero, he decides to defend himself in court, and, once an affair comes to light, his vindictive wife joins the opposition. Good cast, superlative Niven performance. **100m/B VHS.** *GB* David Niven, Margaret Leighton, Noelle Middleton, Laurence Naismith; ***D:*** Anthony Asquith.

Carry Me Back **1/2 1982** Two brothers carry dead dad back to Australian ranch in order to inherit mucho dinero. **93m/C VHS.** *NZ* Grant Tilly, Kelly Johnson, Dorothy McKegg, Derek Hardwick, Joanne Mildehall, Alex Trousdell, Frank Edwards; ***D:*** John Reid; ***W:*** John Reid, Keith Aberdein, Derek Morton; ***C:*** Graeme Cowley; ***M:*** James Hall.

Carry Me Home **2004 (PG-13)** As Harriet (Miller) suffers through the loss of her husband from his WWII tour of duty, her tomboy daughter Carrie (Orr) deals with the pain by angrily shutting her mom out, particularly when Harriet moves on with the high-brow Bernard (Basche) causing Carrie to seek comfort from Charlie (Anderson), a mentally-challenged and troubled local farmhand. Showtime cable coming-of-age drama feels more like a tearjerker-of-the-week Lifetime channel show. **97m/C VHS, DVD.** Penelope Ann Miller, Kevin Anderson, David Alan Basche, Ashley Rose Orr, Jane Alexander, Leo Burmester, Nicholas Braun; ***D:*** Jace Alexander; ***W:*** Christopher Fay; ***C:*** David Herrington; ***M:*** Bill Elliott. **CABLE**

Carry On Abroad **1/2 1972** British tourists arrive for a cheap packaged holiday at the Spanish town of Elsbels to find the weather is terrible, the hotel is unfinished, and apparently there is only one person on staff. The 23rd entry in the series. **89m/C DVD.** *GB* Kenneth Williams, Sidney James, Joan Sims, Charles Hawtrey, Bernard Bresslaw, Peter Butterworth, Kenneth Connor, Barbara Windsor, June Whitfield, Hattie Jacques; ***D:*** Gerald Thomas; ***W:*** Talbot Rothwell; ***C:*** Alan Hume; ***M:*** Eric Rogers.

Carry On Admiral **1/2** *The Ship was Loaded* **1957** Weak British comedy about two friends who get drunk and decide it would be fun to switch identities. One has an easy job as a public relations exec but the other is supposedly the captain of a ship. His lack of sea knowledge causes wacky catastrophes. Unrelated to the "Carry On" series of comedies. **85m/B VHS.** *GB* David Tomlinson, Brian Reece, Peggy Cummins, Eunice Gayson, A.E. Matthews, Lionel Murton, Joan Sims; ***D:*** Val Guest; ***W:*** Val Guest.

Carry On Again Doctor **1969** Disgraced doctor Jimmy Nookey (Dale) leaves England to practice medicine on a remote tropical isle. Fellow worker Gladstone Screwer (James) has learned how to make a native weight-loss potion, and Nookey takes the formula back to England, where he establishes a successful weight-loss clinic, but some of his fellow doctors want him taken down a peg. The 18th film in the series follows the usual pattern of innuendo and slapstick. **86m/C DVD.** *GB* Jim Dale, Sidney James, Kenneth Williams, Charles Hawtrey, Joan Sims, Barbara Windsor, Hattie Jacques, Patsy Rowlands; ***D:*** Gerald Thomas; ***W:*** Talbot Rothwell; ***C:*** Ernest Steward; ***M:*** Eric Rogers.

Carry On at Your Convenience **1/2** *Carry On 'Round the Bend* **1971** Williams, who played in the original ("Carry On Sergeant"), and Carry On regulars (charpei-mugged James and ever-zaftig Jacques) go 'round the bend in yet another installment of the British spoof in and around a toilet factory. **86m/C VHS.** *GB* Sidney James, Kenneth Williams, Charles Hawtrey, Joan Sims, Kenneth Cope, Hattie Jacques; ***D:*** Gerald Thomas.

Carry On Behind **1975** "Carry On" crew heads for archeological dig and find themselves sharing site with holiday caravan. **95m/C VHS.** *GB* Sidney James, Kenneth Williams, Elke Sommer, Joan Sims; ***D:*** Gerald Thomas.

Carry On Cabby **1963** The seventh entry in the series is a little sharper-edged than usual. Charlie Hawkins (James) is so busy running the Speedee Cab Company that he forgets his wedding anniversary. In retaliation, neglected wife Peggy (Jacques) starts Glamcabs, where all the drivers are beautiful women in skimpy uniforms. Charlie is upset about losing business to his new rival (not knowing his wife is the boss) and vows to get even. **91m/B DVD.** *GB* Sidney James, Hattie Jacques, Kenneth Connor, Charles Hawtrey, Esma Cannon, Oscar Karlweis, Bill Owen, Milo O'Shea, Jim Dale; ***D:*** Gerald Thomas; ***W:*** Talbot Rothwell; ***C:*** Alan Hume; ***M:*** Eric Rogers.

Carry On Camping **1/2 1971** Another entry in the silly series finds James and Bresslaw trying to persuade their girlfriends to go on a camping trip to what the men hope is a nudist colony. They don't find nudists but they do find a group of sex-starved schoolgirls. **88m/C VHS.** *GB* Sidney James, Bernard Bresslaw, Kenneth Williams, Joan Sims, Charles Hawtrey, Barbara Windsor; ***D:*** Gerald Thomas; ***W:*** Talbot Rothwell.

Carry On Cleo **1/2 1965** "Carry On" spoof of Shakespeare's "Antony and Cleopatra." The film used some of the sets from the budget-busting 1963 disaster "Cleopatra." **91m/C VHS, DVD.** *GB* Sidney James, Amanda Barrie, Kenneth Williams, Kenneth Connor, Jim Dale, Charles Hawtrey, Joan Sims; ***D:*** Gerald Thomas.

Carry On Columbus **1992** A lame effort to revive the franchise after 1978's "Carry on Emmannuelle." This 30th entry finds a befuddled Christopher Columbus (Dale) searching for a new route to India in order to bypass the greedy Sultan of Turkey (Mayall) and winding up in the Americas, where the natives speak with Brooklyn accents and call him Columbo. **91m/C DVD.** *GB* Jim Dale, Bernard Cribbins, Rik Mayall, Leslie Phillips, June Whitfield, Maureen Lipman, Peter Richardson, Larry Miller, Charles Fleischer,

Alexei Sayle, Sara Crowe; ***D:*** Gerald Thomas; ***W:*** David Freeman; ***C:*** Alan Hume; ***M:*** John Du Prez.

Carry On Constable **1960** In the fourth film of the series a flu epidemic results in no-nonsense Sgt. Frank Wilkins (James) having to work with a trio of oddball new recruits who bumble every assignment. Then they have to track down and arrest a criminal gang who robbed a payroll truck without mucking it up. **86m/B DVD.** *GB* Sidney James, Leslie Phillips, Kenneth Williams, Kenneth Connor, Charles Hawtrey, Hattie Jacques, Eric Barker, Shirley Eaton, Joan Sims, Joan Hickson; ***D:*** Gerald Thomas; ***W:*** Norman Hudis; ***C:*** Edward Scaife; ***M:*** Bruce Montgomery.

Carry On Cowboy *Rumpo Kid* **1966** "Carry On" Western parody of "High Noon." **91m/C VHS, DVD.** *GB* Sidney James, Kenneth Williams, Jim Dale, Joan Sims, Charles Hawtrey, Angela Douglas, Peter Butterworth, Bernard Bresslaw, Percy Herbert, Davy Kaye; ***D:*** Gerald Thomas; ***W:*** Talbot Rothwell; ***C:*** Alan Hume; ***M:*** Eric Rogers.

Carry On Cruising **1962** "Carry On" gang attacks sailing world with low humor and raunchiness. **89m/C VHS, DVD.** Sidney James, Kenneth Williams, Liz Fraser; ***D:*** Gerald Thomas.

Carry On Dick **1975** What made the seemingly endless "Carry On" series of super-low-budget British farces such a hit is a mystery not to be solved. Low production values, scripts that peter out midway, and manifest humor don't normally a classic make; and yet the gang has its following. "Dick," a spoof on highwayman Dick Turpin, was preceded by some 20-odd carryings on; suffice it to say that the series, which began in 1958 with "Carry on Sergeant," has not improved with age in subsequent incarnations. **95m/C VHS.** *GB* Sidney James, Joan Sims; ***D:*** Gerald Thomas.

Carry On Doctor **1968** British series continues as characters of questionable competence join the medical profession. **95m/C VHS.** *GB* Frankie Howerd, Kenneth Williams, Jim Dale, Barbara Windsor; ***D:*** Gerald Thomas.

Carry On Emmanuelle **1978** Emmanuelle, the wife of the French Ambassador to England, uses bedroom diplomacy to foster international relations. Part of the British "Carry On" series. **104m/C VHS.** *GB* Suzanne Danielle, Kenneth O'Connor, Kenneth Williams, Beryl Reid; ***D:*** Gerald Thomas.

Carry On England **1976** Mercifully, the gang didn't carry on much beyond this entry, in which a WWII anti-aircraft gun battery crew bumbles through the usual pranks and imbroglios. **89m/C VHS.** *GB* Kenneth Connor, Patrick Mower, Judy Geeson; ***D:*** Gerald Thomas.

Carry On Henry VIII 1/2 **1971** Slapstick sex humor with Henry marrying the French Marie of Normandie and having to deal with both her addiction to garlic and the fact that she's pregnant by her lover. **88m/C VHS.** *GB* Sidney James, Kenneth Williams, Joan Sims, Charles Hawtrey, Barbara Windsor, Kenneth Connor, Julian Holloway; ***D:*** Gerald Thomas; ***W:*** Talbot Rothwell.

Carry On Jack *Carry On Venus* **1963** The eighth in the film series is a spoof of seafaring/Horatio Hornblower yarns with innocent Midshipman Albert Poop-Decker (Cribbins) losing his uniform to sultry Sally (Mills) and sailing with sea-hating, misnamed Captain Fearless (Williams), battling pirates and mutineers ala "Mutiny on the Bounty." **91m/C DVD.** *GB* Bernard Cribbins, Juliet Mills, Percy Herbert, Cecil Parker, Kenneth Williams, Charles Hawtrey, Donald Huston, Jim Dale; ***D:*** Gerald Thomas; ***W:*** Talbot Rothwell; ***C:*** Alan Hume; ***M:*** Eric Rogers.

Carry On Loving 1/2 **1970** The 20th entry is rife with the usual sight gags and sexual innuendo as Sidney Bliss (James) runs a fake lonely hearts agency designed to unite the love-starved in a series of bumbling blind dates. **90m/C DVD.** *GB* Sidney James, Hattie Jacques, Kenneth Williams, Charles Hawtrey, Joan Sims, Terry Scott, Joan Hickson; ***D:*** Gerald Thomas; ***W:*** Talbot Rothwell; ***C:*** Ernest Steward; ***M:*** Eric Rogers.

Carry On Matron 1/2 **1972** In the 24th entry in the series (another hospital spoof), a group of thieves plan to steal a shipment of contraceptive pills from Finisham Maternity Hospital. But they are continually thwarted by oblivious head doctor Cutting (Williams) and Matron (Jacques). **89m/C DVD.** *GB* Kenneth Williams, Hattie Jacques, Terry Scott, Charles Hawtrey, Barbara Windsor, Joan Sims, Kenneth Connor, Sidney James, Bernard Bresslaw, Kenneth Cope; ***D:*** Gerald Thomas; ***W:*** Talbot Rothwell; ***C:*** Ernest Steward; ***M:*** Eric Rogers.

Carry On Nurse **1959** Men's ward in a British hospital declares war on nurses and the rest of the hospital. The second of the "Carry On" series. **86m/B VHS, DVD.** *GB* Shirley Eaton, Kenneth Connor, Hattie Jacques, Wilfrid Hyde-White; ***D:*** Gerald Thomas.

Carry On Regardless **1961** A series of slapstick sketches tied together with the flimsiest of plots. Bert Handy (James) hires a bunch of incompetents for his employment agency to work a variety of odd jobs, including baby-sitters, bouncers, models, and house cleaners (or wreckers in this case). Fifth in the series. **90m/B DVD.** *GB* Sidney James, Kenneth Connor, Charles Hawtrey, Joan Sims, Kenneth Williams, Liz Fraser, Bill Owen, Esma Cannon, Joan Hickson, Stanley Unwin; ***D:*** Gerald Thomas, Ralph L. (R.L.) Thomas; ***W:*** Tony Lo Bianco; ***C:*** Alan Hume; ***M:*** Bruce Montgomery.

Carry On Screaming **1966** "Carry On" does horror. A pair of goofy detectives trail monsters suspected in kidnapping. **97m/C VHS, DVD.** *GB* Harry H. Corbett, Kenneth Williams, Fenella Fielding, Joan Sims, Charles Hawtrey, Jim Dale, Angela Douglas, Jon Pertwee; ***D:*** Gerald Thomas.

Carry On Sergeant **1958** The first in the long-running comedy series chronicles the misadventures of Sergeant Grimshawe (Hartnett) and his latest batch of recruits doing their National Service. Grimshawe is due to retire and wants to leave a success so he takes the bet of rival Sgt. O'Brien (Scott) that he will have the championship platoon. Then he meets the bumblers he must whip into shape. Based on the book "The Bull Boys" by R.F. Delderfield. The title was deliberately used to cash in on the success of 1957's "Carry On Admiral," which had nothing to do with the subsequent films. **81m/B DVD.** *GB* William Hartnell, Kenneth Williams, Eric Barker, Charles Hawtrey, Terence Longdon, Norman Rossington, Kenneth Connor, Hattie Jacques, Terry Scott, Bob Monkhouse, Shirley Eaton, Terry Scott; ***D:*** Gerald Thomas; ***W:*** Peter Hennessy; ***C:*** Norman Hudis; ***M:*** Bruce Montgomery.

Carry On Spying **1964** The "Carry On" gang does a spoof of spy films with their silly names, villains, and gadgets. Top-secret chemical Formula X has been stolen by STENCH and it's up to gullible, inexperienced Desmond (Williams), an agent of BOSH, to get it back, assisted by toothsome Daphne Honeybutt (Windsor). The ninth in the series. **87m/C DVD.** *GB* Kenneth Williams, Barbara Windsor, Eric Pohlmann, Bernard Cribbins, Charles Hawtrey, Judith Furse, Eric Barker, Jim Dale, Victor Maddern; ***D:*** Gerald Thomas; ***W:*** Sid Colin, Talbot Rothwell; ***C:*** Alan Hume; ***M:*** Eric Rogers.

Carry On Up the Jungle 1/2 **1970** The 19th entry in the series is in the intrepid explorer/Tarzan mode as ornithologist Inigo Tinkle (Howerd) searches for a rare bird while Lady Bagley (Sims) looks for her long-lost son. Meanwhile, they're beset by cannibals, a female tribe from Aphrodisia looking for mates, and an amorous gorilla. **89m/C DVD.** *GB* Frankie Howerd, Sidney James, Joan Sims, Charles Hawtrey, Terry Scott, Kenneth Connor, Bernard Bresslaw; ***D:*** Gerald Thomas; ***W:*** Talbot Rothwell; ***C:*** Ernest Steward; ***M:*** Eric Rogers.

Carry On Up the Khyber 1/2 **1968** In this 16th entry, the gang mangles the heroic "Brits defending the Empire" epic. The men of the Third Foot and Mouth regiment are sent to the Khyber Pass to prevent the revolting Burpas, led by Khasi of Kalabar (Williams), from discovering what's beneath the kilts of the fearsome Scottish Devil's Regiment. (Hint: it's not regulation wear.) **87m/C DVD.** *GB* Sidney James, Kenneth Williams, Charles Hawtrey, Joan Sims, Bernard Bresslaw, Terry Scott, Roy Castle, Angela Douglas, Peter Butterworth; ***D:*** Gerald Thomas; ***W:*** Talbot Rothwell; ***C:*** Ernest Steward; ***M:*** Eric Rogers.

Cars **2006 (G)** Brightly-colored animated adventure from those Pixar folks about automobiles. Arrogant rookie racecar Lightning McQueen (Wilson) is detoured to the sleepy town of Radiator Springs on his way to a big race. Forced to perform community service, Lightning gets a lesson in humility and figures out that fame isn't everything, thanks to such new friends as Sally Carrera (Hunt), a hot 2002 Porsche 911; gruff Doc (Newman), the 1951 Hudson Hornet; and Mater (Larry the Cable Guy), a goofy, good-natured tow truck. Just as heartwarming and funny as you'd expect a Pixar feature to be. **118m/C DVD, Blu-ray Disc.** *US* Larry the Cable Guy; ***D:*** John Lasseter; ***W:*** Joe Ranft, John Lasseter, Dan Fogelman, Kiel Murray, Phil Lorin, Jorgen Klubien; ***C:*** Jean-Claude Kalache; ***M:*** Randy Newman; ***V:*** Owen Wilson, Paul Newman, Bonnie Hunt, Paul Dooley, Joe Ranft, George Carlin, Katherine Helmond, Michael Keaton, Richard "Cheech" Marin, John Ratzenberger, Tony Shalhoub, Richard Petty, Guido Quaroni, Jenifer Lewis, Michael Wallis. Golden Globes '07: Animated Film.

The Cars That Ate Paris *The Cars That Eat People* **1974 (PG)** Parasitic town in the Parisian (Australia) outback preys on car and body parts generated by deliberate accidents inflicted by wreck-driving wreckless youths. Weir's first film released internationally, about a small Australian town that survives economically via deliberately contriving car accidents and selling the wrecks' scrap parts. A broad, bitter black comedy with some horror touches. **91m/C VHS, DVD.** *AU* Terry Camillieri, Kevin Miles, John Meillon, Melissa Jaffer; ***D:*** Peter Weir; ***W:*** Peter Weir; ***M:*** Bruce Smeaton.

Carson City 1/2 **1952** Silent Jeff Kincaid (Scott) is a construction engineer hired by Carson City banker William Sloan (Keating) to build a railway line between Carson City and Virginia City, Nevada. Sloan is tired of the stagecoach being constantly robbed but the locals (and the bandits) try to prevent the rail line from going through. The bandits cause a landslide (which results in several deaths) and then steal a shipment of gold bullion until Jeff can set things right. **87m/C DVD.** Randolph Scott, Raymond Massey, Richard Webb, James Millican, Lucille Norman, Larry Keating, George Cleveland, Don Beddoe; ***D:*** Andre de Toth; ***W:*** Winston Miller, Sloan Nibley, Eric Jonsson; ***C:*** John Boyle; ***M:*** David Buttolph.

Carson City Kid 1/2 **1940** Typical western which has Rogers trying to exact revenge on the man who killed his brother. **54m/B VHS, DVD.** Roy Rogers, George "Gabby" Hayes, Bob Steele, Noah Beery Jr., Pauline Moore, Francis McDonald, Wally Wales, Arthur Loft, George Rosener, Chester Gan; ***D:*** Joseph Kane; ***W:*** Gerald Geraghty, Robert Yost; ***C:*** William Nobles; ***M:*** Cy Feuer, Peter Tinturin.

Cartel **WOOF!** **1990 (R)** O'Keeffe, "B" actor extraordinaire, plays the wrong man to pick on in this rancid dope opera. Hounded by drug lord Stroud and framed for murder, pilot O'Keeffe decides the syndicate has gone too doggone far when they kill his sister. Exploitive and otherwise very bad. **106m/C VHS, DVD.** Miles O'Keeffe, Don Stroud, Crystal Carson, William (Bill) Smith; ***D:*** John Stewart; ***W:*** Moshe Hadar; ***C:*** Thomas Callaway; ***M:*** Rick Krizman.

Carthage in Flames *Cartagine in Fiamme; Carthage en Flammes* **1960** A graphic portrayal of the destruction of ancient Carthage in a blood and guts battle for domination of the known world. A tender love story is a welcome aside in this colorful Italian-made epic. **96m/C VHS, DVD.** *IT* Anne Heywood, Jose Suarez, Pierre Brasseur; ***D:*** Carmine Gallone.

Cartier Affair **1984** A beautiful TV actress unwittingly falls in love with the man who wants to steal her jewels. Collins designed her own wardrobe. **120m/C VHS, DVD.** Joan Collins, David Hasselhoff, Telly Savalas, Ed Lauter, Joe La Due; ***D:*** Rod Holcomb; ***C:*** Hanania Baer. **TV**

Cartouche *Swords of Blood* **1962** A swashbuckling action-comedy set in 18th-century France. Belmondo plays a charming thief who takes over a Paris gang, aided by the lovely Cardinale. When he is captured, she sacrifices her life to save him and Belmondo and his cohorts vow to have their revenge. Based on a French legend and a well-acted combination of tragedy, action, and farce. In French with English subtitles. **115m/C VHS, DVD.** *FR IT* Jean-Paul Belmondo, Claudia Cardinale, Odile Versois, Philippe Lemaire; ***D:*** Philippe de Broca; ***W:*** Philippe de Broca; ***M:*** Georges Delerue.

Carve Her Name with Pride 1/2 **1958** The true story of Violette Szabo who at age 19 became a secret agent with the French Resistance in WWII. **119m/B VHS.** *GB* Virginia McKenna, Paul Scofield, Jack Warner, Denise Grey, Alan Saury, Maurice Ronet, Anne Leon, Nicole Stephane, Sydney Tafler, Avice Landone; ***D:*** Lewis Gilbert; ***W:*** Lewis Gilbert, Vernon Harris; ***C:*** John Wilcox; ***M:*** William Alwyn.

Carved *Kuchisake-onna; Slit-Mouthed Woman* **2007** Urban legend has the spirit of a woman grotesquely disfigured by her jealous husband roaming the streets of a suburban town terrorizing young victims. Children are coming up missing, but as teachers and officials desperately investigate, panic rises and dark secrets are revealed. Remake does not add any depth or height to an already well used premise. Japanese with subtitles. **90m/C DVD.** *JP* Eric Sato, Haruhiko Kato, Miki Mizuno, Chihauro Kawai, Rie Kuwana, Kazuyuki Matsuzawa, Saaya Irie; ***D:*** Kohi Shiraishi; ***W:*** Kohi Shiraishi, Naoyuki Yokota; ***C:*** Shozo Morishita; ***M:*** Fujino Chika, Wano Gen.

Carver's Gate **1996** Thanks to an environmental disaster, earth is in big trouble and its inhabitants take refuge in a virtual reality game called Afterlife. But when an engineer tries to improve the game by heightening its reality, the game's computer-generated demons get loose and it's up to cybercop Pare to stop them by traveling between virtual reality and the actual world. **97m/C VHS, DVD.** Michael Pare, Kevin Stapleton, Marian Skretas, Tara Maria Manuel, Peter Wylde, Pamela Keyes; ***D:*** Sheldon Inkol; ***W:*** Sheldon Inkol; ***C:*** Jonathan Freeman; ***M:*** Donald Quan.

Casa de los Babys **2003 (R)** Sayles's quiet, insightful look at adoption, poverty, politics and international trade as five diverse American women wait (and wait) at a local motel nicknamed Casa de Los Babys to adopt children in an unnamed South American country. Each has a particular reason for adoption: Fitness freak Skipper (Hannah) has had three miscarriages while Jennifer (Gyllenhaal) hopes adoption will help her ailing marriage. Rounding out the gang of expectant mothers are the hardened single-mom to be Leslie (Taylor); Steenburgen's alcoholic Gayle; and the extremely disagreeable Nan (Harden), Memorably poignant scene as the Irish Eileen and the Latina Asuncion (Lynch and Martinez, respectively) bond over heartfelt exchanges in a language that neither can understand. **95m/C VHS, DVD.** *US* Maggie Gyllenhaal, Marcia Gay Harden, Daryl Hannah, Susan Lynch, Mary Steenburgen, Lili Taylor, Rita Moreno, Vanessa Martinez; ***D:*** John Sayles; ***W:*** John Sayles; ***C:*** Mauricio Rubinstein; ***M:*** Mason Daring.

Casablanca **1942 (PG)** Can you see George Raft as Rick? Jack Warner did, but producer Hal Wallis wanted Bogart. Considered by many to be the best film ever made and one of the most quoted movies of all time, it rocketed Bogart from gangster roles to romantic leads as he and Bergman (who never looked lovelier) sizzle on screen. Bogart runs a gin joint in Morocco during the Nazi occupation, and meets up with Bergman, an old flame, but romance and politics do not mix, especially in Nazi-occupied French Morocco. Greenstreet, Lorre, and Rains all create memorable characters, as does Wilson, the piano player to whom Bergman says the oft-misquoted, "Play it, Sam." Without a doubt, the best closing scene ever written; it was scripted on the fly during the end of shooting, and actually shot several ways. Written from an unproduced play. See it in the original black and white. 50th Anniversary Edition contains a restored and remastered print, the original 1942 theatrical trailer, a film documentary narrated by Lauren Bacall, and a booklet. **102m/B VHS, DVD, Blu-ray Disc, HD DVD.** Humphrey Bogart, Ingrid Bergman, Paul Henreid, Claude Rains, Peter Lorre, Sydney Greenstreet, Conrad Veidt, S.Z. Sakall, Dooley Wilson, Marcel Dalio, John Qualen, Helmut Dantine, Madeleine LeBeau, Joy Page, Leonid Kinskey, Curt Bois, Oliver Blake, Monte Blue, Martin Garralaga, Ilka Gruning, Ludwig Stossel, Frank Puglia; ***D:*** Michael Curtiz; ***W:*** Julius J. Epstein, Philip G. Epstein, Howard Koch; ***C:*** Arthur Edeson; ***M:*** Max Steiner. Oscars '43: Director (Curtiz), Picture, Screenplay; AFI '98: Top 100, Natl. Film Reg. '89.

Casablanca Express **1989** Nazi commandos hijack Churchill's train in this action-adventure drama. **90m/C VHS, DVD.** Glenn Ford, Donald Pleasence, Jason Connery; ***D:*** Sergio Martino.

Casanova **1987 (PG-13)** A comedic romp through the bedrooms of 18th-century Europe with Chamberlain as the legendary lover. Lots of lovely ladies and hammy performances. **122m/C VHS.** Richard Chamberlain, Faye Dunaway, Sylvia Kristel, Ornella Muti, Hanna Schygulla, Sophie Ward, Frank Finlay, Kenneth Colley; ***D:*** Simon Langton; ***W:*** George MacDonald Fraser; ***C:*** Giuseppe Rotunno. **TV**

Casanova **2005 (R)** Set in Venice and loosely based on the legendary life of the 18th century womanizer. Casanova (Ledger) is running from the Roman Inquisitor Pucci (Irons) who wants to try him for heresy, which sets up an excuse for drama and disguise resulting in an unlikely clandestine relationship with Francesca (Miller), who may be Venice's first feminist writer. Don't look for a naughty glimpse of the legendary exploits of Casanova. Here he is forced posthumously to figure out that a woman's true value is her intellect...um...et tu, Casanova? If you love romantic costume comedies set in Venice and you're house-bound for the weekend, you could do worse. **108m/C DVD.** *US* Heath Ledger, Sienna Miller, Jeremy Irons, Oliver Platt, Lena Olin, Omid Djalili, Stephen Greif, Ken Stott, Charlie Cox, Tim (McInnerny) McInnery, Phil Davies, Paddy Ward, Helen McCrory, Leigh Lawson, Natalie Dormer; ***D:*** Lasse Hallstrom; ***W:*** Jeffrey Hatcher, Kimberly Simi; ***C:*** Oliver Stapleton; ***M:*** Alexandre Desplat.

Casanova **2005** The elderly Giacomo Casanova (O'Toole) has been exiled from Venice and is working as a librarian in a crumbling castle. Depressed, he finds new vigor relating his lustful adventures as a young man to his maid, Edith (Byrne). The younger Casanova (Tennant) was a reckless bon vivant willing to risk everything, especially for the love of noblewoman Henriette (Fraser). Wonderful romp; both O'Toole and Tennant sparkle. **182m/C DVD.** *GB* Peter O'Toole, David Tennant, Rose Byrne, Laura Fraser, Rupert Penry-Jones, Nina Sosanya, Nickolas Grace; ***D:*** Sheree Folkson; ***W:*** Russell T. Davies; ***C:*** Anthony Radcliffe; ***M:*** Murray Gold. **TV**

Casanova Brown 1/2 **1944** Lighthearted comedy about a shy English professor (Cooper) who learns that his recent ex-wife (Wright) has had a baby (guess whose). When Cooper learns Wright has decided to give their daughter up for adoption he kidnaps the tyke and attempts fatherhood in a hotel room. When Wright finds out where he is, the twosome (who have really been in love all along) decide to remarry and be a family. Cooper, with baby and surrounded by diapers, makes a comedic sight. Based on the play "The Little Accident" by Floyd Dell and Thomas Mitchell. **94m/B VHS, DVD.** Gary Cooper, Teresa Wright, Frank Morgan, Anita Louise, Patricia Collinge, Edmund Breon, Jill Esmond, Emory Parnell, Isobel Elsom, Mary Treen, Halliwell Hobbes; ***D:*** Sam Wood; ***W:*** Nunnally Johnson; ***M:*** Arthur Lange.

Casanova '70 1/2 **1965** Mastroianni plays a handsome soldier who has a knack for enticing liberated women in this comic rendition of the much-cinematized legendary yarn. Trouble is, he's in the mood only when he believes that he's in imminent danger. In Italian with English subtitles. **113m/C VHS.** *IT* Marcello Mastroianni, Virna Lisi, Michele Mercier, Guido Alberti, Margaret Lee, Bernard Blier, Liana Orfei; ***D:*** Mario Monicelli; ***W:*** Tonino Guerra.

Casanova's Big Night 1/2 **1954** Classic slapstick comedy stars Hope masquerading as Casanova to test Fontaine's virtue before her marriage to a duke. The all-star cast provides one hilarious scene after another in this dated film. Price has a cameo as the "real" Casanova. Based on a story by Aubrey Wisberg. **85m/C VHS, DVD.** Bob Hope, Joan Fontaine, Audrey Dalton, Basil Rathbone, Hugh Marlowe, Vincent Price, John Carradine, Raymond Burr; ***D:*** Norman Z. McLeod; ***W:*** Hal Kanter, Edmund Hartmann; ***C:*** Lionel Lindon.

Casbah **1948** Fine musical remake of the 1937 French film "Pepe Le Moko" and its American counterpart, 1938's "Algiers." Criminal Pepe (Martin) is safe as long as he hides out in the Casbah—outside lurks patient policeman Slimmane (Lorre), who's determined to capture him. Of course, it's l'amour that trips Pepe up when he falls for tourist Gaby (Toren), who's leaving Algiers. If Pepe had any brains, he would have stuck with hot local number, Inez (De Carlo), instead. **94m/B VHS.** Tony Martin, Peter Lorre, Yvonne De Carlo, Marta Toren, Douglas Dick, Hugo Haas, Thomas Gomez, Katherine Dunham; ***D:*** John Berry; ***W:*** Arnold Manoff; ***C:*** Irving Glassberg; ***M:*** Walter Scharf.

A Case for Murder 1/2 **1993 (R)** Jack Hammet has just become the youngest full partner ever at his Chicago law firm, with a knack for winning impossible cases. His next one's a beaut. Seems an envious colleague has gotten himself murdered and his estranged wife is the prime suspect. Jack decides to work with newly arrived lawyer Kate Weldon but as the two become personally involved, Kate begins to question Jack's ethics. Seems the evidence is more than a little shady and Jack isn't telling all. **94m/C VHS.** Peter Berg, Jennifer Grey, Belinda Bauer; ***D:*** Duncan Gibbins; ***W:*** Duncan Gibbins, Pablo F. Fenjves.

A Case of Deadly Force **1986** Based on the true story of a black man wrongfully killed by Boston's Tactical Police Force who mistook him for a robber. The police investigation calls it self-defense but the family and the attorney they hire fight to change the verdict. Excellent cast, great dramatic story. **95m/C VHS.** Richard Crenna, John Shea, Lorraine Toussaint, Francis X. (Frank) McCarthy, Tom Isbell; ***D:*** Michael Miller. **TV**

A Case of Libel 1/2 **1983** Dramatization based on attorney Louis Nizer's account of Quentin Reynolds's libel suit against columnist Westbrook Pegler. **90m/C VHS.** Daniel J. Travanti, Ed Asner; ***D:*** Eric Till. **TV**

The Case of the Bloody Iris *Perche Quelle Strane Gocce di Sangre sul Corpo di Jennifer?; Whare Are Those Strange Drops of Blood on the Body of Jennifer?* **1972** Models and friends Jennifer (French) and Marilyn (Quattrini) move into an apartment building where two women have already been killed. The police suspect Andrea Barto (Hilton), who not only owns the apartment building but a modeling agency, and who knew both women. Soon, Jennifer realizes she is being stalked but there are several candidates, including her estranged husband who belongs to a weird sex cult. Italian with subtitles. **94m/C DVD.** *IT* Edwige Fenech, George Hilton, Giampiero Albertini, Paola Quattrini, Jorge (George) Rigaud; ***D:*** Giuliano Carnimeo; ***W:*** Ernesto Gastaldi; ***C:*** Stelvio Massi; ***M:*** Bruno Nicolai.

The Case of the Frightened Lady *The Frightened Lady* **1939** A homicidal family does its collective best to keep its dark past a secret in order to collect some inheritance money. Watch, if you're still awake, for the surprise ending. **80m/B VHS, DVD.** *GB* Marius Goring, Helen Haye, Penelope Dudley Ward, Felix Aylmer, Patrick Barr; ***D:*** George King.

The Case of the Lucky Legs 1/2 **1935** Yes, there was a Perry Mason before Raymond Burr. Erle Stanley Gardner's sleuthing litigator's first appearance was 1934's "The Case of the Howling Dog," which initiated Warner Bros' "A"-grade (but soon-to-be "B"-grade) series. More akin to Nick Charles than to Gardner's character or to his later TV incarnation, the "Lucky Legs" Perry is a high-living, interminably hungover tippler who winces and wisecracks as he unravels the case of the corpse of a crooked con man. William, who left shortly after the series was downgraded to "B" status, plays the esquire; Tobin plays his smart-mouthed secretary, and Ellis is the tomato suspected of murder. **76m/B VHS.** Warren William, Genevieve Tobin, Patricia Ellis, Lyle Talbot, Allen Jenkins, Barton MacLane, Peggy Shannon, Porter Hall; ***D:*** Archie Mayo.

The Case of the Scorpion's Tail *La Coda dello Scorpione* **1971** A series of murders follows a million-dollar insurance settlement, which brings investigator Peter Lynch (Hilton) looking into the situation. Reporter Cleo Dupont (Strindberg) helps out and becomes a potential victim. Set in Athens. Italian with subtitles. **90m/C DVD.** *IT* George Hilton, Anita Strindberg, Alberto De Mendoza, Ida Galli, Janine Reynaud, Luigi Pistilli; ***D:*** Sergio Martino; ***W:*** Ernesto Gastaldi, Sauro Scavolini, Eduardo Brochero; ***C:*** Emilio Foriscot; ***M:*** Bruno Nicolai.

Case 39 **2010 (R)** Social worker Emily Jenkins needs a foster care family for troubled 10-year-old Lilith after her parents try to kill her. But they obviously know more about the little horror than Emily does. **109m/C DVD.** Renee Zellweger, Jodelle Ferland, Ian McShane, Bradley Cooper, Callum Keith Rennie, Adrian Lester, Cynthia Stevenson, Georgia Craig, Kerry O'Malley; ***D:*** Christian Alvart; ***W:*** Christian Alvart, Ray Wright; ***C:*** Hagen Bogdanski; ***M:*** Michi Britsch, John Willett.

Casey's Shadow **1978 (PG)** The eight-year-old son of an impoverished horse trainer raises a quarter horse and enters it in the world's richest horse race. **116m/C VHS, DVD.** Walter Matthau, Alexis Smith, Robert Webber, Murray Hamilton; ***D:*** Martin Ritt; ***C:*** John A. Alonzo.

Cash Crop 1/2 *Harvest* **2001 (R)** Kids try to protect their farmer parents who decided to grow marijuana in order to pay off big debts. The DEA shows up, coming into conflict with the local sheriff, who's sympathetic to the farmers' plight. Fairly even-handed treatment, confounding expectations of an easy stoner comedy. **96m/C VHS, DVD.** Mary McCormack, John Slattery, James Van Der Beek, Jeffrey DeMunn, Wil Horneff, Frederick Weller, Paula Garces, Julianne Nicholson, Lisa Emery, Josh(ua) Lucas, Evan Handler; ***D:*** Stuart Burkin; ***W:*** Stuart Burkin, James Biederman, David A. Korn; ***C:*** Oliver Bokelberg; ***M:*** Paul Rabjohns. **VIDEO**

Cash McCall 1/2 **1960** McCall (Garner) is a corporate raider who just loves making money. But problems come in when he falls for the lovely daughter (Wood) of his latest takeover target, failing businessman Jagger. Based on the novel by Cameron Hawley. **116m/C VHS.** James Garner, Natalie Wood, Dean Jagger, Nina Foch, E.G. Marshall, Henry Jones, Otto Kruger, Roland Winters, Parley Baer, Dabbs Greer; ***D:*** Joseph Pevney; ***W:*** Lenore Coffee, Marion Hargrove; ***C:*** George J. Folsey; ***M:*** Max Steiner.

Cashback **2006 (R)** After a painful break-up, art student Ben Willis develops insomnia. So he decides to get a job working the late shift at the supermarket, where he becomes interested in checkout girl Sharon. Ben can freeze time—so he does, and wanders around the store, mostly stripping down unsuspecting women, drawing them, and then re-dressing them. It sounds sleazier than it actually is, but still. Ick. **90m/C DVD.** *GB* Sean Biggerstaff, Emilia Fox, Shaun Evans, Michael Dixon, Michelle Ryan, Stuart Goodman, Marc Pickering, Michael Lambourne; ***D:*** Sean Ellis; ***W:*** Sean Ellis; ***C:*** Angus Hudson; ***M:*** Guy Farley.

Casino 1/2 **1980** Thriller about backstabbings and ritzy romance aboard a high-priced gambling liner. **100m/C VHS.** Mike Connors, Lynda Day George, Bo Hopkins, Gary Burghoff, Joseph Cotten, Robert Reed, Barry Sullivan; ***D:*** Don Chaffey. **TV**

Casino **1995 (R)** Final part of the Scorsese underworld crime trilogy that began with "Mean Streets" and continued in "GoodFellas." Casino boss Sam "Ace" Rothstein (De Niro), his ex-hustler wife Ginger (Stone), and his loose-cannon enforcer pal Nicky (Pesci) are the principals in this lengthy, fictionalized account of how the mob lost Las Vegas in a haze of drugs, sex, coincidence, and betrayal. Flashy, intricate, and unflinchingly violent account of mob-run '70s Vegas clicks when exploring the inner workings of a major casino and its hierarchy. Although Stone shines as a hedonistic money chaser, visuals are great and the soundtrack is a killer, storyline suffers from deja vu. Pileggi again adapted the screenplay from his own book. **177m/C VHS, DVD, HD DVD.** Robert De Niro, Joe Pesci, Sharon Stone, James Woods, Don Rickles, Alan King, Kevin Pollak, L.Q. Jones, Dick Smothers, John (Joe Bob Briggs) Bloom, Frankie Avalon, Steve Allen, Jayne Meadows, Jerry Vale; ***D:*** Martin Scorsese; ***W:*** Nicholas Pileggi, Martin Scorsese; ***C:*** Robert Richardson. Golden Globes '96: Actress—Drama (Stone).

The Casino Job **2008 (R)** Scumbag casino owner Barry Kaylin (Mauro) rents four strippers for an evening and forces himself on one of them. The police won't arrest him, so the strippers plot revenge by stealing his money. Described by some as 'a porn film without the sex,' the movie is somewhat impressive given its incredibly low budget. **81m/C DVD.** Amylia Joiner, Dean Munro, Iisa Martinez, Jay Anthony Franke, Irina Voronina, Curtis Joe Walker, Deanna Minerva, Julia Beatty, Mokis Zavros, Warren Thomas, Barry Sharp, Kerry M. Shahan, Paul Joseph, Ken Kupstis, Brian H. Scott, Clint Wilder, Christopher J. Buzzell; ***D:*** Christoper Robin Hood; ***W:*** Nick Murphy; ***C:*** Jeffrey Mahon; ***M:*** George Dare.

Casino Royale **1967** The product of five directors, three writers and a mismatched cast of dozens, this virtually plotless spoof of James Bond films can stand as one of the low-water marks for 1960s comedy. And yet, there are some marvelous bits within, scenes of bizarre hilarity. Welles and Sellers literally couldn't stand the sight of one another, and their scenes together were filmed separately, with stand-ins. **130m/C VHS, DVD.** David Niven, Woody Allen, Peter Sellers, Ursula Andress, Orson Welles, Jacqueline Bisset, Deborah Kerr, Peter O'Toole, Jean-Paul Belmondo, Charles Boyer, Joanna Pettet, John Huston, William Holden, George Raft, Kurt Kasznar, Terence Cooper, Barbara Bouchet, Anna Quayle, Geoffrey Bayldon, Duncan MacRae, Burt Kwouk, David Prowse, Caroline Munro; ***D:*** John Huston, Ken Hughes, Robert Parrish, Val Guest, Joseph McGrath; ***W:*** Wolf Mankowitz, John Law, Michael Sayers; ***C:*** Jack Hildyard; ***M:*** Burt Bacharach.

Casino Royale **2006 (PG-13)** Bond is back and Craig does not destroy the franchise as the whiners would have you believe. Based on Fleming's first (1953) novel, Bond has just achieved 007 status and is still learning his way. He may be blond(ish) but he's brutal, ruthless, and arrogant (and he bleeds). Story revolves around a high-stakes poker game with a Eurotrash banker (Mikkelsen) to terrorists and the Bond babe is Vesper Lynd (Green), a sexy, cool accountant. Dench returns as M, and she and Bond share some of the best moments as she tries to keep her "blunt instrument" in line. It's a little too long but Craig proves he can wear a tux, say "Bond...James Bond," and kill, which is what true aficionados require. **144m/C DVD, Blu-ray Disc.** *GB US CZ GE* Daniel Craig, Eva Green, Mads Mikkelsen, Judi Dench, Jeffrey Wright, Giancarlo Giannini, Caterina Murino, Isaach de Bankole, Simon Abkarian, Ivana Milicevic, Tobias Menzies, Claudio Santamaria, Jesper Christensen, Sebastien Foucan; ***D:*** Martin Campbell; ***W:*** Paul Haggis, Neal Purvis, Robert Wade; ***C:*** Phil Meheux; ***M:*** David Arnold. British Acad. '06: Sound.

Casper **1995 (PG)** World's friendliest ghost appears on the big screen with outstanding visual trickery (from Industrial Light and Magic) and a lively, if hokey, story. Evilish Carrigan Crittenden (Moriarty) inherits ghost-infested Whipstaff Manor and hires scatterbrained "ghost therapist" Dr. Harvey (Pullman) to get rid of its unwanted occupants. His daughter Kat (Ricci) is soon the object of Casper's friendly attention while the good doc must contend with Casper's mischievous uncles—Stinkie, Fatso, and Stretch. Exec producer Spielberg shows his influence with numerous topical gags and screen references that help amuse the adults while the ghosts work their magic on the kiddies. Silberling's directorial debut; based on the comic-book and TV cartoon character created more than 30 years ago. **95m/C VHS, DVD.** Christina Ricci, Bill Pullman, Cathy Moriarty, Eric Idle, Amy Brenneman, Ben Stein; ***Cameos:*** Don Novello, Rodney Dangerfield, Clint Eastwood, Mel Gibson, Dan Aykroyd; ***D:*** Brad Silberling; ***W:*** Sherri Stoner, Deanna Oliver; ***C:*** Dean Cundey; ***M:*** James Horner; ***V:*** Malachi Pearson, Joe Nipote, Joe Alaskey, Brad Garrett.

Casque d'Or *Golden Marie* **1952** Crime passionnel in turn-of-the-century Paris as an honest carpenter (Reggiani) gets drawn into the netherworld of pimps and thieves. He's finally driven to murder—all for love of gangster's moll Marie (a very sultry Signoret). French with subtitles. **96m/B VHS, DVD.** *FR* Serge Reggiani, Simone Signoret, Claude Dauphin, Raymond Bussieres, Gaston Modot; ***D:*** Jacques Becker; ***W:*** Jacques Becker, Jacques Companeez; ***C:*** Robert Lefebvre; ***M:*** Georges Van Parys.

Cass **1978** Disenchanted filmmaker returns home to Australia to experiment with alternative lifestyles. **90m/C VHS.** *AU* Michelle Fawden, John Waters, Judy Morris, Peter Carroll, Peter Whitford; ***D:*** Chris Noonan; ***W:*** Laura Jones; ***C:*** Mick von Bornemann; ***M:*** Rory O'Donoghue.

Cass Timberlane 1/2 **1947** Scandalous story of a May-December romance set in a small Midwestern town. Tracy stars as Cass Timberlane, a widowed judge who falls for a voluptuous young girl from the wrong side of the tracks (Turner). They marry and experience problems when she is shunned by his snobbish friends. Good performances, especially from the supporting cast, dominate this fairly predictable film. Based on the novel by Sinclair Lewis. **119m/B VHS.** Spencer Tracy, Lana Turner, Zachary Scott, Tom Drake, Mary Astor, Albert Dekker, Margaret Lindsay, John Litel, Mona Barrie, Josephine Hutchinson, Rose Hobart, Selena Royle; ***Cameos:*** Walter Pidgeon; ***D:*** George Sidney; ***W:*** Donald Ogden Stewart.

Cassandra **1987 (R)** A fragile young woman has dreams that foretell the future—specifically, a series of grisly murders. **94m/C VHS.** Shane Briant, Briony Behets, Tessa Humphries, Kit Taylor, Lee James; ***D:*** Colin Eggleston.

The Cassandra Crossing 1/2 **1976 (R)** A terrorist with the plague causes havoc on a transcontinental luxury train. Turgid adventure filmed in France and Italy. **129m/C VHS, DVD.** *GB* Sophia Loren, Richard Harris, Ava Gardner, Burt Lancaster, Martin Sheen, Ingrid Thulin, Lee Strasberg, John Phillip Law, Lionel Stander, O.J. Simpson, Ann Turkel, Alida Valli; ***D:*** George P. Cosmatos; ***W:*** George P. Cosmatos, Tom Mankiewicz; ***C:*** Ennio Guarnieri; ***M:*** Jerry Goldsmith.

Cassandra's Dream 1/2 **2007 (PG-13)** Not a comedy and not in New York? Woody Allen fortunately breaks form again with this decidedly unfunny crime drama set in London. A tale of two brothers, ambitious Ian (McGregor) is stuck in the family restaurant; Terry (Farrell) is a mechanic, gambler, and addict. On a winning streak at the dog races, the pair buy a yacht and name it "Cassandra's Dream," the name of the winning pooch. Things are looking up, but Ian finds love in a dangerous woman and Terry's gambling luck dries up. They both turn to elusive and wealthy Uncle Howard (Wilkinson), and their already tenuous lives really begin to unravel. Turns out Uncle Howard is in his own trouble, and his help will come at a cost. Like many of Allen's serious films, moral ties are tested and individual choices have far-reaching and devastating consequences, and the characters are smart and multilayered. **108m/C DVD.** *FR US* Ewan McGregor, Colin Farrell, Hayley Atwell, Sally Hawkins, Tom Wilkinson, John Benfield, Clare Higgins, Tom Fisher; ***D:*** Woody Allen; ***W:*** Woody Allen; ***C:*** Vilmos Zsigmond; ***M:*** Philip Glass.

Cassie *Up 'n Coming* **1983 (R)** Follows the rise of Cassie, a successful country and western singer, and documents all her trials along the way. **75m/C VHS.** Lisa De Leeux, Herschel Savage, Richard Pacheco, Marilyn Chambers; ***D:*** Stu Segall; ***C:*** Jacques Remy; ***M:*** Mike Lyman.

Cast a Dark Shadow **1955** Bogarde is the charmer who decides to reap his reward by marrying and murdering elderly women for their fortunes. But Bogarde meets his match when he plots against his latest intended (Lockwood). Tidy thriller with effective performances. Based on the play "Murder Mistaken" by Janet Green. **82m/B VHS, DVD.** *GB* Dirk Bogarde, Margaret Lockwood, Mona Washbourne, Kay Walsh, Kathleen Harrison, Robert Flemyng, Walter Hudd; ***D:*** Lewis Gilbert; ***W:*** John Cresswell.

Cast a Deadly Spell **1991 (R)** A bubbly, flavorful witch's brew of private-eye and horror cliches, set in a fantasy version of 1948 Los Angeles where sorcery and voodoo abound, but gumshoe Harry P. Lovecraft uses street smarts instead of magic to track down a stolen Necronomicon—and if you know what that is you'll want to watch. Wild creatures and f/x wizardry complement this cable-TV trick and treat. **93m/C VHS.** Fred Ward, David Warner, Julianne Moore, Clancy Brown, Alexandra Powers; ***D:*** Martin Campbell; ***W:*** Joseph Dougherty, Dave Edison. **CABLE**

Cast a Giant Shadow **1966** Follows the career of Col. David "Mickey" Marcus, an American Jew and WWII hero who helped turn Israel's army into a formidable fighting force during the 1947-48 struggle for independence. **138m/C VHS, DVD.** Kirk Douglas, Senta Berger, Angie Dickinson, John Wayne, James Donald, Chaim Topol, Frank Sinatra, Yul Brynner; ***D:*** Melville Shavelson; ***W:*** Melville Shavelson; ***C:*** Aldo Tonti; ***M:*** Elmer Bernstein.

Cast Away 1/2 **2000 (PG-13)** Hanks first gained, and then lost, 40 pounds for his role as FedEx employee Chuck Noland, who gets marooned on a South Pacific island for four years. He does an excellent job of showing Chuck's desperation, isolation, and finally, resignation, and for a good chunk of the movie, does it without saying a single word (although later he does get to "talk" to a volleyball named Wilson). Zemeckis does his part with amazing visuals and a restrained approach to the score, which he uses sparingly. **143m/C VHS, DVD, Blu-ray Disc.** Tom Hanks, Helen Hunt, Nick Searcy, Michael Forest, Viveka Davis, Christopher Noth, Geoffrey Blake, Jenifer Lewis, David Allan Brooks, Nan Martin, Steve Monroe; ***D:*** Robert Zemeckis; ***W:*** William Broyles Jr.; ***C:*** Don Burgess; ***M:*** Alan Silvestri.

Cast the First Stone **1989** Made for TV soaper based on the true story of a former nun who becomes a small town schoolteacher. After being raped, Diane Martin discovers she's pregnant and when she decides to keep the baby the school board dismisses her. The plot centers around her fight to regain her job and dignity—while trying to convince everybody that she doesn't deserve to lose her job simply because she is an unwed mother. Eikenberry gives a strong performance, but it can't carry this lackluster film. **94m/C VHS.** Jill Eikenberry, Richard Masur, Joe Spano, Lew Ayres, Holly Palance; ***D:*** John Korty; ***M:*** Ira Newborn. **TV**

Castaway 1/2 **1987 (R)** Based on the factual account by Lucy Irvine. The story of Michael Wilmington, who placed an ad for a young woman to spend a year on a Pacific atoll with him, and the battle of the sexes that followed. **118m/C VHS.** *GB* Oliver Reed, Amanda Donohoe, Tony Rickards, Georgina Hale, Frances Barber, Todd Rippon; ***D:*** Nicolas Roeg; ***W:*** Allan Scott; ***C:*** Harvey Harrison; ***M:*** Stanley Myers.

The Castaway Cowboy **1974 (G)** Shanghaied Texas cowboy Lincoln Costain (Garner) jumps ship in Hawaii and becomes partners with widowed Henrieatta MacAvoy (Miles) when she turns her potato farm into a cattle ranch. That means turning the islanders into cowpokes and dealing with both a local witch doctor and Henrieatta's suitor. **91m/C VHS, DVD.** James Garner, Robert Culp, Vera Miles; ***D:*** Vincent McEveety; ***M:*** Robert F. Brunner.

The Castilian 1/2 *Valley of the Swords* **1963** Some very odd casting in this historical tale of heroism and swordplay about a Spanish nobleman who leads his followers against the invading Moors and their evil king (Crawford). Based on a 13th century poem. **128m/C VHS.** Cesar Romero, Broderick Crawford, Alida Valli, Frankie Avalon, Espartaco (Spartaco) Santoni, Fernando Rey, Jorge (George) Rigaud; ***D:*** Javier Seto; ***W:*** Sidney W. Pink.

The Castle *Das Schloss* **1968** A man is summoned by the seemingly invisible occupants of a castle to their village. All his efforts to meet with those inhabiting the castle are futile and the task gradually becomes his obsession. Both wonderfully acted and shot, this is a well-executed adaptation of Franz Kafka's novel. **90m/C VHS.** *GE SI* Maximilian Schell, Cordula Trantow, Trudik Daniel, Helmut Qualtinger; ***D:*** Rudolf Noelte.

The Castle **1997 (R)** The Kerrigans are a working class clan who happily live directly adjacent to Melbourne's Tullamarine airport. But when the airport decides to expand, their house is subject to a compulsory acquisition order. However, Daryl Kerrigan (Caton) decides to fight and takes their case all the way to the High Court in Canberra. It's a David vs. Goliath comedy with an Aussie disdain for authority figures. Cultural references may not travel overseas but the film was a hit on its home turf. **93m/C VHS, DVD.** *AU* Michael Caton, Charles "Bud" Tingwell, Sophie Lee, Anne Tenney, Eric Bana, Stephen Curry, Anthony Simcoe, Wayne Hope, Tiriel Mora; ***D:*** Rob Sitch; ***W:*** Rob Sitch, Santo Cilauro, Tom Gleisner, Jane Kennedy; ***C:*** Miriana Marusic; ***M:*** Craig Harnath. Australian Film Inst. '97: Orig. Screenplay.

Castle Freak **1995 (R)** Italian countess leaves her creepy haunted castle to her American nephew and his family. They find an unwelcome surprise lurking in the cellar. **90m/C VHS, DVD.** Jeffrey Combs, Barbara Crampton, Jonathan Fuller, Jessica Dollarhide; ***D:*** Stuart Gordon; ***W:*** Dennis Paoli; ***C:*** Mario Vulpiani; ***M:*** Richard Band.

Castle in the Desert 1/2 **1942** Charlie Chan (Toler) is called in to investigate the poisoning death of one of the weekend guests at a house party given by wealthy Paul Manderley (Dumbrille). He and his wife (Lane) live in a mock medieval castle in the Mojave Desert and Chan discovers all outside communications have been suspiciously cut off. The 27th film in the series was the last to be made by 20th Century-Fox. **62m/B DVD.** Sidney Toler, Victor Sen Yung, Douglass Dumbrille, Lenita Lane, Arleen Whelan, Richard Derr, Henry Daniell, Edmund MacDonald, Ethel Griffies, Milton Parsons; ***D:*** Harry Lachman; ***W:*** John Larkin; ***C:*** Virgil Miller.

Castle Keep **1969** One of the most bizarre war films ever made. Eight battle-weary American soldiers, led by a randy one-eyed major (Lancaster), make a defiant last stand in a fairytale medieval castle against the German assault on the Ardennes in WWII. Loopy surreal parable pushes past every boundary of good taste and stays enjoyable to the end. Full of great memorable characters and silly over-the top moments that almost always work, such as an impotent count (Aumont) pimping out his wife to German and American alike to keep the dynasty going, and a soldier (Falk) who takes over the local village bakery, waxing poetically about the superiority of bread to war. The whole film is absurdly done up in full sixties regalia and topped off with a loungy Michel Legrand soundtrack. A forgotten camp treasure. **105m/C VHS, DVD.** Burt Lancaster, Patrick O'Neal, Jean-Pierre Aumont, Peter Falk, Astrid Heeren, Scott Wilson, Tony Bill, Bruce Dern, Al Freeman Jr., James Patterson, Michael Conrad, Caterina Boratto, Olga Bisera, Harry Baird, Ernest Clark; ***D:*** Sydney Pollack; ***W:*** David Rayfiel, Daniel Taradash; ***C:*** Henri Decae; ***M:*** Michel Legrand.

Castle of Blood *Castle of Terror; Coffin of Terror; Danza Macabra; Dimensions in Death; Terrore* **1964** Staying overnight in a haunted castle, a poet is forced to deal with a number of creepy encounters. Cult favorite Steele enhances this atmospheric chiller. Dubbed in English. **85m/B VHS, DVD.** *IT FR* Barbara Steele, George Riviere, Margrete Robsahm, Henry Kruger, Silvano Tranquilli, Sylvia Sorente; ***D:*** Anthony M. Dawson; ***W:*** Jean (Giovanni Grimaldi) Grimaud; ***C:*** Riccardo (Pallton) Pallottini; ***M:*** Riz Ortolani.

The Castle of Cagliostro **1980** Animated Japanese adventure tale featuring a hero named Wolf, who's a thief. Wolf infiltrates the suspicious country of Cagliostro, whose one industry is conterfeiting money, and winds up rescuing a princess. Lots of violence to go with the action. In Japanese with English subtitles. **100m/C VHS, DVD.** *JP* ***D:*** Hayao Miyazaki; ***C:*** Hirokata Takahashi; ***M:*** Yuji Ono; ***V:*** David Hayter, Bridget Hoffman, Dorothy Elias-Fahn, Kirk Thornton.

Castle of Evil WOOF! **1966** Group of heirs gathers on a deserted isle to hear the reading of the will of your basic mad scientist. One by one, they fall victim to a humanoid created by the loony doc in his own image. Inspired moments of unintentional fun. **81m/C VHS.** Scott Brady, Virginia Mayo, Lisa Gaye, David Brian, Hugh Marlowe, William Thourlby, Shelley Morrison; ***D:*** Francis D. Lyon.

The Castle of Fu Manchu *Assignment: Istanbul; Die Folterkammer des Dr. Fu Manchu* **1968 (PG)** The final chapter in a series starring Lee as the wicked doctor. This time, Lee has developed a gadget which will put the earth into a deep freeze, and at his mercy. To fine tune this contraption, he enlists the help of a gifted scientist by abducting him. However, the helper/hostage has a bad ticker, so Lee must abduct a heart surgeon to save his life, and thus, the freezer project. Most critics felt this was the weakest installment in the series. **92m/C VHS, DVD.** *GE SP IT GB* Christopher Lee, Richard Greene, Howard Marion-Crawford, Tsai Chin, Gunther Stoll, Rosalba Neri, Maria Perschy, Werner Abrolat, Jose Martin; ***D:*** Jess (Jesus) Franco; ***W:*** Harry Alan Towers; ***C:*** Manuel Merino; ***M:*** Gert Wilden.

Castle of the Creeping Flesh WOOF! **1968** A surgeon's daughter is brutally murdered. Vowing to bring her back he begins ripping out the organs of innocent people and transplanting them into her body. Has the dubious honor of being one of the few movies to sport actual open heart surgery footage. So bad it's...just bad. **85m/C VHS.** Adrian Hoven, Janine Reynaud, Howard Vernon; ***D:*** Percy G. Parker.

Castle of the Living Dead *Il Castello de Morti Vivi* **1964** Evil Count Drago's hobbies include mummifying a traveling circus group visiting his castle. Lee is as evil as ever, but be sure to look for Sutherland's screen debut. In a dual role, he plays not only the bumbling inspector, but also a witch, in drag. **90m/B VHS, DVD.** *IT FR* Christopher Lee, Gaia Germani, Phillippe LeRoy, Jacques Stanislawsky, Donald Sutherland; ***D:*** Herbert Wise.

Castle on the Hudson **1940** **71m/B DVD.** John Garfield, Ann Sheridan, Pat O'Brien, Jerome Cowan, Burgess Meredith, Guinn "Big Boy" Williams, Henry O'Neill, John Litel; ***D:*** Anatole Litvak; ***W:*** Brown Holmes, Seton I. Miller, Courtney Terrett; ***C:*** Arthur Edeson.

Casual Sex? 1/2 **1988 (R)** Two young women, looking for love and commitment, take a vacation at a posh resort where they are confronted by men with nothing on their minds but sex, be it casual or the more formal black-tie variety. Supposedly an examination of safe sex in a lightly comedic vein, though the comic is too light and the morality too limp. Adapted from the play by Wendy Goldman and Judy Toll. **87m/C VHS, DVD.** Lea Thompson, Victoria Jackson, Stephen Shellen, Jerry Levine, Mary Gross, Andrew (Dice Clay) Silverstein; ***D:*** Genevieve Robert; ***W:*** William Goldman, Judy Toll; ***C:*** Rolf Kestermann; ***M:*** Van Dyke Parks.

Casualties **1997 (R)** Annie's (Goodall) got very unfortunate luck with men. Her abusive husband Bill's (Gries) a cop and she can't safely get away from home. Then she meets a seemingly nice guy, Tommy (Harmon), at her cooking class, who offers to help Annie out. But when Tommy's behavior becomes erratic (turns out he's a hitman), Annie figures she just has to rely on herself. **86m/C VHS.** Mark Harmon, Caroline Goodall, Michael Beach, Jon(athan) Gries, John Diehl; ***D:*** Alex Graves; ***W:*** Alex Graves.

Casualties of Love: The "Long Island Lolita" Story **1993 (PG-13)** Told from the Buttafuoco's point of view, Amy Fisher was nothing but a wacko fatally attracted teenager who misunderstood Joey's harmless flirtations and deliberately went after his wife with a gun. The Buttafuocos received $300,000 from CBS to tell their side of the story which features Milano, who resembles Amy not in the least, as the lead. One of three competing network TV versions of the sordid story. See also: "The Amy Fisher Story" and "Lethal Lolita—Amy Fisher: My Story." **94m/C VHS.** Jack Scalia, Alyssa Milano, Phyllis Lyons, Jack Kehler, Michael Bowen, J.E. Freeman, Nick(y) Corello, Lawrence Tierney, Peter Van Norden, Anne DeSalvo, Leo Rossi; ***D:*** John Herzfeld; ***W:*** John Herzfeld; ***C:*** Karl Walter Lindenlaub; ***M:*** David Michael Frank. **TV**

Casualties of War **1989 (R)** A Vietnam war morality play about army private Fox in the bush who refuses to let his fellow soldiers and commanding sergeant (Penn) skirt responsibility for the rape and murder of a native woman. Fox achieves his dramatic breakthrough. Based on the true story by Daniel Lang. **120m/C VHS, DVD.** Sean Penn, Michael J. Fox, Don Harvey, Thuy Thu Le, John Leguizamo, Sam Robards, John C. Reilly, Erik King, Dale Dye; ***D:*** Brian De Palma; ***W:*** David Rabe; ***C:*** Stephen Burum; ***M:*** Ennio Morricone.

A Casualty of War 1/2 **1990 (R)** Made-for-TV adaptation of Frederick Forsyth's thriller about modern-day arms smuggling (Libya to Ireland) and espionage. Well-acted, with the exception of Hack. **96m/C VHS.** Shelley Hack, David Threlfall, Richard Hope, Alan Howard, Clarke Peters; ***D:*** Tom Clegg; ***W:*** Frederick Forsyth.

The Cat **1966** A boy and a tamed mountain lion become friends on the run from a murderous poacher. **95m/C VHS.** Peggy Ann Garner, Roger Perry, Barry Coe; ***D:*** Ellis Kadison.

Cat and Mouse 1/2 *Le Chat et la Souris* **1978 (PG)** A very unorthodox police inspector is assigned to investigate a millionaire's mysterious death. Who done it? French dialogue with English subtitles. **107m/C VHS.** *FR* Michele Morgan, Serge Reggiani, Jean-Pierre Aumont, Philippe Labro, Philippe Leotard, Valerie Lagrange, Michel Perelon, Christine Laurent; ***D:*** Claude Lelouch; ***W:*** Claude Lelouch; ***C:*** Andre Perlstein; ***M:*** Francis Lai.

The Cat and the Canary
1927 A group of greedy relatives gather on a stormy night in a creepy mansion for the reading of a 20-year-old will. But before anyone can claim the money, they must spend the night in the manor—and an escaped lunatic is at large! Remade twice, once in 1939 and again in 1979. **81m/B VHS, DVD.** Laura La Plante, Creighton Hale, Tully Marshall, Gertrude Astor, Arthur Edmund Carewe, Lucien Littlefield; ***D:*** Paul Leni; ***W:*** Robert F. "Bob" Hill, Alfred A. Cohn; ***C:*** Gilbert Warrenton.

The Cat and the Canary **1979 (PG)** A stormy night, a gloomy mansion, and a mysterious will combine to create an atmosphere for murder. An entertaining remake of the 1927 silent film. **96m/C VHS, DVD.** *GB* Carol Lynley, Michael Callan, Wendy Hiller, Olivia Hussey, Daniel Massey, Honor Blackman, Edward Fox, Wilfrid Hyde-White, Beatrix Lehmann, Peter McEnery; ***D:*** Radley Metzger; ***W:*** Radley Metzger; ***C:*** Alex Thomson.

The Cat and the Fiddle **1934** Lovely Jerome Kern-Oscar Hammerstein operetta in which Novarro plays a struggling composer who forces his affections on MacDonald. She sings in response to his romantic proposals. The final sequence is in color. ♫ The Night Was Made for Love; She Didn't Say 'Yes'; A New Love is Old; Try to Forget; One Moment Alone; Don't Ask Us Not To Sing; I Watch the Love Parade; The Breeze Kissed Your Hair; Impressions in a Harlem Flat. **90m/B VHS.** Ramon Novarro, Jeanette MacDonald, Frank Morgan, Charles Butterworth, Jean Hersholt, Vivienne Segal, Frank Conroy, Henry Armetta, Adrienne D'Ambricourt, Joseph Cawthorn; ***D:*** William K. Howard; ***W:*** Bella Spewack, Samuel Spewack, Jerome Kern; ***C:*** Charles G. Clarke, Ray Rennahan, Harold Rosson; ***M:*** Herbert Stothart, Jerome Kern.

Cat Ballou 1/2 **1965** At the turn of the century, a schoolmarm turns outlaw with the help of a drunken gunman. Marvin played Kid Shelleen and his silver-nosed evil twin Tim Strawn in this cheery spoof of westerns. Cole and Kaye sing the narration in a one of a kind Greek chorus. **96m/C VHS, DVD.** Jane Fonda, Lee Marvin, Michael Callan, Dwayne Hickman, Reginald Denny, Nat King Cole, Stubby Kaye, Robert Phillips; ***D:*** Elliot Silverstein; ***W:*** Frank Pierson; ***C:*** Jack Marta; ***M:*** Frank DeVol. Oscars '65: Actor (Marvin); Berlin Intl. Film Fest. '65: Actor (Marvin); British Acad. '65: Actor (Marvin); Golden Globes '66: Actor—Mus./Comedy (Marvin); Natl. Bd. of Review '65: Actor (Marvin).

Cat Chaser **1990** Weller walks listlessly through the role of an ex-soldier in Miami who has an affair with the wife of an exiled—but still lethal—military dictator. Surprisingly low-key, sometimes effective thriller that saves its energy for sex scenes, also available in a less steamy, 90-minute "R" rated version. Based on an Elmore Leonard novel. **97m/C VHS, DVD.** Kelly McGillis, Peter Weller, Charles Durning, Frederic Forrest, Tomas Milian, Juan Fernandez; ***D:*** Abel Ferrara; ***W:*** Elmore Leonard, Jim Borrelli; ***M:*** Chick Corea.

The Cat from Outer Space
1978 (G) An extraterrestrial cat named Jake crashes his spaceship on Earth and leads a group of people on endless escapades. Enjoyable Disney fare. **103m/C VHS, DVD.** Ken Berry, Sandy Duncan, Harry (Henry) Morgan, Roddy McDowall, McLean Stevenson; ***D:*** Norman Tokar; ***W:*** Ted Key; ***C:*** Charles F. Wheeler; ***M:*** Lalo Schifrin.

Cat Girl **1957** A young bride on her honeymoon finds she has inherited the family curse—she has a psychic link to a ferocious leopard. Numerous murders ensue. Poor production value and a weak script, despite Shelley's fine acting, add up to an unworthy film. **69m/B VHS.** Barbara Shelley, Robert Ayres, Kay Callard, Paddy Webster, Ernest Milton; ***D:*** Alfred Shaughnessy; ***W:*** Lou Rusoff; ***C:*** Peter Hennessy.

Cat in the Cage 1/2 **1968** A young man finds many things have changed at home while he was in a mental institution. Dad has remarried, the housekeeper is practicing witchcraft, the chauffeur is after his mistress, and the cat is gone. So where'd that cat go? **96m/C VHS, DVD.** Colleen Camp, Sybil Danning, Mel Novak, Frank De Kova; ***D:*** Tony Zarin Dast.

The Cat o' Nine Tails **1971 (PG)** A blind detective and a newsman team up to find a sadistic killer. A gory murder mystery. **112m/C VHS, DVD.** *GE FR IT* Karl Malden, James Franciscus, Catherine Spaak, Cinzia de Carolis, Carlo Alighiero; ***D:*** Dario Argento; ***W:*** Dario Argento; ***C:*** Erico Menczer; ***M:*** Ennio Morricone.

Cat on a Hot Tin Roof 1/2
1958 Tennessee Williams' powerful play about greed and deception in a patriarchal Southern family. Big Daddy (Ives) is dying. Members of the family greedily attempt to capture his inheritance, tearing the family apart. Taylor is a sensual wonder as Maggie the Cat, though the more controversial elements of the play were toned down for the film version. Intense, believable performances from Ives and Newman. **108m/C VHS, DVD.** Paul Newman, Burl Ives, Elizabeth Taylor, Jack Carson, Judith Anderson; ***D:*** Richard Brooks; ***W:*** Richard Brooks, James Poe; ***C:*** William H. Daniels.

Cat on a Hot Tin Roof 1/2 **1984** Showtime/PBS co-production of the Tennesse Williams classic about alcoholic ex-jock Brick (Jones) and his sultry wife Maggie (Lange) and their desires. This version uses a script revised by Williams to revive some of the sexual frankness watered down in other productions. **122m/C VHS, DVD.** Tommy Lee Jones, Jessica Lange, Rip Torn, Kim Stanley, David Dukes, Penny Fuller; ***D:*** Jack Hofsiss; ***W:*** Tennessee Williams. **TV**

Cat People **1942** Irena (Simon) is an immigrant from the Balkans who believes in a curse that will change her into a deadly panther who must kill to survive. So she won't consummate her marriage to Oliver (Smith). When he confides her troubles to co-worker Alice (Randolph), Irena's jealousy precipitates her transformation as she stalks Alice. A classic among the horror genre with unrelenting terror from beginning to end, especially since the metamorphosis is only suggested. First horror film from RKO producer Val Lewton. **73m/B VHS, DVD.** Simone Simon, Kent Smith, Jane Randolph, Jack Holt, Elizabeth Russell, Alan Napier, Tom Conway; ***D:*** Jacques Tourneur; ***W:*** DeWitt Bodeen; ***C:*** Nicholas Musuraca; ***M:*** Roy Webb. Natl. Film Reg. '93.

Cat People 1/2 **1982 (R)** A beautiful young woman learns that she has inherited a strange family trait—she turns into a vicious panther when sexually aroused. The only person with whom she can safely mate is her brother, a victim of the same genetic heritage. Kinski is mesmerizing as the innocent, sensual woman. Remake of the 1942 film. **118m/C VHS, DVD, HD DVD.** Nastassja Kinski, Malcolm McDowell, John Heard, Annette O'Toole, Ruby Dee, Ed Begley Jr., John Larroquette; ***D:*** Paul Schrader; ***W:*** Alan Ormsby; ***C:*** John Bailey; ***M:*** Giorgio Moroder.

Cat Women of the Moon *Rocket to the Moon* **1953** Scientists land on the moon and encounter an Amazon-like force of skimpily attired female chauvinists. Remade as "Missile to the Moon." Featuring the Hollywood Cover Girls as various cat women. Available in its original 3-D format. **65m/B VHS, DVD.** Sonny Tufts, Victor Jory, Marie Windsor, Bill Phipps, Douglas Fowley, Carol Brewster, Suzanne Alexander, Susan Morrow, Ellye Marshall, Bette Arlen, Judy W, Roxann Delman; ***D:*** Arthur Hilton; ***W:*** Roy Hamilton; ***C:*** William F. Whitley; ***M:*** Elmer Bernstein.

Cataclysm 1/2 *Satan's Supper* **1981 (R)** A swell flick about a sadistic demon who spends his time either finding people willing to join him or killing the people who won't. **94m/C VHS, DVD.** Cameron Mitchell, Marc Lawrence, Faith Clift, Charles Moll; ***D:*** Tom McGowan, Gregg Tallas, Philip Marshak.

Catacombs **1989 (R)** An investigative monk and a beautiful photographer stumble across a mysterious, centuries-old evil power. **112m/C VHS.** Timothy Van Patten, Laura Schaefer, Ian Abercrombie, Jeremy West; ***D:*** David Schmoeller; ***W:*** C. Courtney Joyner; ***M:*** Pino Donaggio.

Catacombs **2007** The running and screaming turns out to be remarkably boring. Nervous Victoria (Sossamon) heads to Paris to visit her naughty sister Caroline (Moore) who insists on taking her to a secret rave held in the catacombs, the limestone tunnels that run for miles under the city and that house the bones of the dead. Carolyn's friends scare Victoria with a legend about a satanic cult and a flesh-eating beast and when she's separated from the group, Victoria's convinced something is stalking her. **92m/C DVD.** Shannyn Sossamon, Alicia Moore, Emil Hostina, Mihai Stanescu, Sandi Dragoi, Cabral Ibacka, Cain Manoli; ***D:*** Tomm Coker; ***W:*** David Elliot, Tomm Coker; ***C:*** Maxime Alexandre; ***M:*** Yoshiki Hayashi. **VIDEO**

The Catamount Killing 1/2 **1974 (PG)** The story of a small town bank manager and his lover. They decide to rob the bank and run for greener pastures only to find their escape befuddled at every turn. **82m/C VHS.** *GE* Horst Buchholz, Ann Wedgeworth; ***D:*** Krzysztof Zanussi.

Catch a Fire 1/2 **2006 (PG-13)** Fierce political drama centering on the Apartheid-era terrorism in South Africa during the early '80s. Patrick Chamusso (Luke) is an unassuming oil refinery foreman wrongly accused, imprisoned, and tortured for a plant bombing. The injustice transforms the apolitical worker into a radicalized insurgent, who then carries out his own successful sabotage mission. Robbins plays the Security Branch Colonel on Chamusso's case. A decent script and good performances, but the dated material lacks a sense of urgency and importance. **101m/C DVD.** *US GB SA* Derek Luke, Tim Robbins, Bonnie Henna, Mncedisi Shabangu, Malcolm Purkey; ***D:*** Phillip Noyce; ***W:*** Shawn Slovo; ***C:*** Ron Fortunato, Garry Phillips; ***M:*** Philip Miller.

Catch and Release **2007 (PG-13)** Kevin Smith is cuddly. But fortunately, he's not the rebound romance for the ever-appealing Garner because that would really make heads spin. Garner plays Gray, a one-of-the-guys kinda gal whose fiance Grady died before the wedding. Crushed, Gray (who seems to have no family or girlfriends) becomes roomies with his buds Sam (Smith) and Dennis (Jaeger), who was also Grady's partner in a fly-fishing venture. Frisky Fritz (Olyphant), will eventually console Gray, who finds out some secrets about Grady that involve a ditzy single mom, played too weirdly by Lewis. Grant's directorial debut veers uncertainly between tragedy and comedy. **110m/C DVD, Blu-ray Disc.** *US* Jennifer Garner, Timothy Olyphant, Kevin Smith, Juliette Lewis, Sam Jaeger, Fiona Shaw, Joshua Friesen; ***D:*** Susannah Grant; ***W:*** Susannah Grant; ***C:*** John Lindley; ***M:*** BT (Brian Transeau), Tommy Stinson.

Catch as Catch Can *Lo Scatenato* **1968** An Italian male model is comically besieged by animals of every type, making a mess of his life and career. Dubbed. **95m/C VHS.** *IT* Vittorio Gassman, Martha Hyer, Gila Golan; ***D:*** Franco Indovina; ***M:*** Luis Bacalov.

Catch Me a Spy 1/2 *To Catch a Spy* **1971** A foreign agent attempts to lure an innocent man into becoming part of a swap for an imprisoned Russian spy. **94m/C VHS, DVD.** *GB FR* Kirk Douglas, Tom Courtenay, Trevor Howard, Marlene Jobert, Bernard Blier, Patrick Mower, Bernadette LaFont; ***D:*** Dick Clement; ***W:*** Dick Clement, Ian La Frenais; ***M:*** Claude Bolling.

Catch Me... If You Can **1989 (PG)** High school class president Melissa doesn't want to see the school torn down. To raise fast cash, she teams up with a drag racer and the fun begins. **105m/C VHS.** Matt Lattanzi, Loryn Locklin, M. Emmet Walsh, Geoffrey Lewis; ***D:*** Stephen Sommers.

Catch Me If You Can 1/2 **2002 (PG-13)** Spielberg's lightweight, entertaining, but overly lengthy flick follows the exploits of Frank Abagnale Jr. (DiCaprio), who, starting at age 16, eluded the FBI (in the person of Carl Hanratty, played by Hanks) while passing bad checks in the guise of airline pilot, doctor, lawyer, and college professor in the early '60s. Frank's journey starts when his perfect suburban life is turned upside-down by the divorce of his parents and his dad's (Walken) trouble with the IRS. DiCaprio is chameleon-like in his portrayal of Frank, as befits the role, but takes it further by looking every age he's supposed to be. Hanks make the most of what could've been a thankless role as Frank's workaholic pursuer/father figure, but Walken stands out as the broken father who, with more chutzpah and luck, might've been what Junior became. Based on the real Frank Abagnale, Jr's memoirs. **140m/C VHS, DVD.** *US* Leonardo DiCaprio, Tom Hanks, Christopher Walken, Nathalie Baye, Martin Sheen, Amy Adams, James Brolin, Jennifer Garner, Frank John Hughes, Steve Eastin, Chris Ellis, John Finn, Brian Howe; ***D:*** Steven Spielberg; ***W:*** Jeff Nathanson; ***C:*** Janusz Kaminski; ***M:*** John Williams. British Acad. '02: Support. Actor (Walken); Natl. Soc. Film Critics '02: Support. Actor (Walken); Screen Actors Guild '02: Support. Actor (Walken).

Catch That Kid **2004 (PG)** One part kid caper to one part heist movie, equals a real klunky movie. Maddy (Stewart), a 12-year-old adventurous (and apparently morally flexible) tomboy, decides to pull off a $250,000 bank robbery so the family can afford an operation for her father (Robards), who is paralyzed. The worst crime here is the lackluster writing and uninspired direction. Adapted from the Danish film "Klatretosen." **92m/C VHS, DVD.** *US* Kristen Stewart, Corbin Bleu, Max Thieriot, Jennifer Beals, Sam Robards, John Carroll Lynch, James LeGros, Michael Des Barres, Kevin G. Schmidt, Stark Sands, Grant Hayden Scott, Shane Avery Scott; ***D:*** Bart Freundlich; ***W:*** Michael Brandt, Derek Haas; ***C:*** Julio Macat; ***M:*** George S. Clinton.

Catch the Heat *Feel the Heat* **1987 (R)** Alexandra is an undercover narcotics agent sent to infiltrate Steiger's South American drug operation. **90m/C VHS, DVD.** Tiana Alexandra, David Dukes, Rod Steiger; ***D:*** Joel Silberg; ***W:*** Stirling Silliphant; ***M:*** Tom Chase, Steve Rucker.

Catch-22 **1970 (R)** Buck Henry's adaptation of Joseph Heller's black comedy about a group of fliers in the Mediterranean during WWII. A biting anti-war satire portraying the insanity of the situation in both a humorous and disturbing manner. Perhaps too literal to the book's masterfully chaotic structure, causing occasional problems in the "are you following along department?" Arkin heads a fine and colorful cast. **121m/C VHS, DVD.** Richard Libertini, Bruce Kirby, Elizabeth

Wilson, Liam Dunn, Alan Arkin, Martin Balsam, Art Garfunkel, Jon Voight, Richard Benjamin, Buck Henry, Bob Newhart, Paula Prentiss, Martin Sheen, Charles Grodin, Anthony Perkins, Orson Welles, Jack Gilford, Bob Balaban, Susanne Benton, Norman Fell, Austin Pendleton, Peter Bonerz, Jon Korkes, Collin Wilcox-Paxton, John Brent; *D:* Mike Nichols; *W:* Buck Henry; *C:* David Watkin.

The Catcher ½ **1998** After being released from an insane asylum, a man returns to the ballfield where he murdered his father and begins hanging around the minor-league stadium in order to finish off various players and managers. **90m/C VHS.** David Heavener, Monique Parent, Joe Estevez, Sean Dillingham; *D:* Guy Crawford, Yvette Hoffman. **VIDEO**

Category 7 : The End of the World **2005** Delightfully inept disaster pic finds FEMA head Judith Carr (sexy Gershon) trying to pinpoint the cause of deadly weather that's causing worldwide havoc. She turns to ex-beau and discredited scientist Ross (Daddo) for answers while fighting the bureaucrats. Meanwhile, scientist Faith (Doherty) teams up with Tornado Tommy (Quaid) to track the storms up close and personal. The subplots are especially lame, although Brolin as an evangelist is a hoot. **169m/C DVD.** *US* Gina Gershon, Cameron Daddo, Shannen Doherty, Randy Quaid, James Brolin, Swoosie Kurtz, Robert Wagner, Sebastian Spence, Nicholas Lea, Tom Skerritt, James Kirk; *D:* Dick Lowry; *W:* Christian Ford, Roger Soffer; *C:* Neil Roach; *M:* Joseph Williams. **TV**

Category 6 : Day of Destruction **2004** Amusingly cheesy disaster flick with lots of predictable subplots and bad CGI. Hackers shut down the Chicago power company's computers during a heatwave, just as a super tornado is heading to that toddlin' town to make one major headache for all involved. Followed by "Category 7: The End of the World." **174m/C DVD.** Thomas Gibson, Nancy McKeon, Chandra West, Brian Markinson, Nancy Sakovich, Randy Quaid, Dianne Wiest, Brian Dennehy, Andrew Jackson, Christopher Shyer, Ari Cohen; *D:* Dick Lowry; *W:* Matt Dorff; *C:* Neil Roach; *M:* Jeff Rona, Joseph Williams. **TV**

The Catered Affair *Wedding Breakfast* **1956** Davis, anti-typecast as a Bronx housewife, and Borgnine, as her taxi-driving husband, play the determined parents of soon-to-be-wed Reynolds set on giving her away in a style to which she is not accustomed. Based on Paddy Chayefsky's teleplay, the catered affair turns into a familial trial, sharing the true-to-life poignancy that marked "Marty," the Oscar-winning Chayefsky drama of the previous year. **92m/B VHS.** Bette Davis, Ernest Borgnine, Debbie Reynolds, Barry Fitzgerald, Rod Taylor, Robert F. Simon; *D:* Richard Brooks; *W:* Gore Vidal; *C:* John Alton; *M:* Andre Previn.

Caterina in the Big City *Caterina va in citta* **2003** Caterina (Teghil) is a small town teenager who experiences a nasty case of culture shock when her family moves to Rome. Frustrated, ambitious school teacher dad Giancarlo (Castellitto) is glad to be out of the sticks and back to the big city but Caterina is soon pulled between two high school cliques—lead by rebellious bohemian Margherita (Iaquaniello) and spoiled debutante Daniela (Sbrenna). Meant to be seen (in a cynical comedic way) as a microcosm of Italian society with the middle-class caught between the strident, communist left and the elitist, conservative right. Italian with subtitles. **106m/C DVD.** *IT* Alice Teghil, Sergio Castellitto, Margherita Buy, Carolina Iaquaniello, Federica Sbrenna, Claudio Amendola; *D:* Paolo Virzi; *W:* Paolo Virzi, Francesco Bruni; *C:* Arnaldo Catinari; *M:* Paolo Virzi.

Catfish **2010** What happens when a user gets too involved with an online posting on a social network? Yaniv 'Nev' Schulman, 24, has a photo published in the "New York Sun" and suddenly starts receiving paintings from a young girl named Abby Pierce. Then, Nev goes on Facebook where Abby's 19-year-old sister Megan posts her party girl pictures; Nev's interest is more than a little naive. **86m/C DVD.** *US D:* Ariel Schulman, Henry Joost; *C:* Ariel Schulman, Henry Joost, Yaniv Schulman.

Catfish in Black Bean Sauce ½ **2000 (PG-13)** While serving in Vietnam, African-American Harold Williams (Winfield) saved the lives of Vietnamese Mai (Tom) and her young brother Dwayne (Lo) and he and wife Dolores (Alice) adopted the duo. Dwayne acts black and has a black girlfriend, Nina (Lathan), but married Mai has never forgotten her roots and announces to the stunned family that she has located her birth mother, Thanh (Chinh), and the woman is coming not only to visit but to live with her. But Thanh turns out to be a critical schemer, unreasonably jealous of the Williams', and determined to reclaim her grown children, no matter what the cost. **111m/C VHS, DVD.** Chi Muoi Lo, Lauren Tom, Kieu Chinh, Paul Winfield, Mary Alice, Sanaa Lathan, Tzi Ma, Tyler Christopher; *D:* Chi Muoi Lo; *W:* Chi Muoi Lo; *C:* Dean Lent; *M:* Stanley A. Smith.

Catherine & Co. ½ **1976 (R)** Lonely, penniless girl arrives in Paris and "opens shop" on the streets of Paris. As business booms, she takes a cue from the big corporations and sells stock in herself. **91m/C VHS.** *FR IT* Jane Birkin, Patrick Dewaere, Jean-Pierre Aumont, Jean-Claude Brialy; *D:* Michel Boisrond.

Catherine Cookson's Colour Blind ½ *Colour Blind* **1998** In post-WWI England, Bridget McQueen comes to stay with her sprawling, poor family with her new husband and their baby daughter. But Bridget has neglected to tell her family that her husband is black. This not only stirs up a lot of trouble but more tribulations follow as Bridget's mixed-race daughter grows up. On two cassettes. **150m/C VHS.** *GB* Niamh Cusack, Carmen Ejogo, Art Malik, Tony Armatrading; *D:* Alan Grint; *W:* Gordon Hann. **TV**

Catherine Cookson's The Black Candle ½ **1992** Mill owner is caught up in a murder case that involves the father of her child, her husband (not the same guy), her husband's brother, and many aristocratic machinations. Well-done story boasts an excellent cast. Based on the novel by Catherine Cookson; made for British TV. **103m/C VHS, DVD.** *GB* Nathaniel Parker, James Gaddas, Bob Smeaton, Brian Hogg, Cathy Sandford, Samantha Bond, Tara Fitzgerald, Denholm Elliott; *D:* Roy Battersby; *W:* Gordon Hann; *C:* Ken Morgan; *M:* Dominic Muldowney. **TV**

Catherine Cookson's The Black Velvet Gown ½ *The Black Velvet Gown* **1992** Riah Millican (McTeer) is a poor miner's widow living in rural 1834 England with her three children. She finds work as a housekeeper to the reclusive Miller (Peck), who agrees to educate her children and even gives Riah the titular gown, which was once his mother's. Now educated out of their working-class, the Millican's lives provide unexpected love and tragedy for all concerned. Based on the novel by Catherine Cookson; made for British TV. **103m/C VHS, DVD.** *GB* Janet McTeer, Bob Peck, Geraldine Somerville; *D:* Norman Stone; *W:* Gordon Hann; *C:* Ken Westbury; *M:* Carl Davis. **TV**

Catherine Cookson's The Cinder Path ½ *The Cinder Path* **1994** Coming-of-age story begins in 1913 with unassuming Charlie MacFell (Owen) forced to take over the family farm. Charlie (who needs a spine transplant) also goes along with an arranged marriage to local lovely Victoria (Zeta-Jones), a disaster since she's little more than a well-bred tart and it's her younger sister Nellie (Miles) who's really in love with Charlie anyway. As if Charlie didn't have enough to cope with, he's soon an army soldier as WWI begins and up against vindictive Ginger (Byrne), a former farmhand who resents the monied classes Charlie represents. Based on the novel by Catherine Cookson. **145m/C VHS, DVD.** *GB* Lloyd Owen, Catherine Zeta-Jones, Maria Miles, Antony Byrne, Tom Bell; *D:* Simon Langton; *W:* Alan Seymour; *M:* Barrington Pheloung. **TV**

Catherine Cookson's The Dwelling Place ½ *The Dwelling Place* **1994** Sixteen-year-old Cissie (Whitwell) struggles to hold her family together after the death of their parents in 1830's England. But her situation turns tragic when she's raped and left pregnant but drunken young aristocrat Clive (Rawle-Hicks), eventually giving the baby to be raised by Clive's father (Fox). Based on a novel by Catherine Cookson. **145m/C VHS, DVD.** *GB* Tracy Whitwell, James Fox, Edward Rawle-Hicks; *D:* Gavin Millar; *W:* Gordon Hann; *C:* John Hooper; *M:* Colin Towns. **TV**

Catherine Cookson's The Fifteen Streets ½ *The Fifteen Streets* **1990** Kind-hearted dock worker John O'Brien (Teale) is the quiet one in a boozing, brawling Irish family living in near poverty in late-Victorian England. He meets well-bred schoolteacher Mary Llewellyn (Holman) and the two fall in love but bigotry, scandal, and tragedy challenge their chances at happiness. Based on a novel by Catherine Cookson. **108m/C VHS, DVD.** *GB* Owen Teale, Clare Holman, Sean Bean, Billie Whitelaw, Ian Bannen, Jane Horrocks, Anny Tobin, Leslie Schofield; *D:* David Wheatley; *W:* Rob Bettinson; *C:* Ken Morgan; *M:* Colin Towns. **TV**

Catherine Cookson's The Gambling Man ½ *The Gambling Man* **1998** Rent collector Rory O'Connor is ambitious to escape his humble past and his talent at gambling leads him to winning a fortune. But a lie and a tragedy return to haunt him. Based on a book by Catherine Cookson. **150m/C VHS, DVD.** *GB* Robson Green, Sylvestria Le Touzel, Bernard Hill, Stephanie Putson, Anne Kent; *D:* Norman Stone; *W:* T.R. Bowen; *C:* Doug Hallows; *M:* David Ferguson. **TV**

Catherine Cookson's The Girl ½ *The Girl* **1996** Illegitimate Hannah Boyle is simply called "The Girl" by her jealous stepmother, who forces her into a disastrous marriage. But Hannah is willing to fight to regain her freedom and the man she truly loves. TV adaptation of the novel by Catherine Cookson. **148m/C VHS, DVD.** *GB* Siobhan Flynn, Malcolm Stoddard, Jonathan Cake, Jill Baker, Mark Benton; *D:* David Wheatley; *W:* Gordon Hann; *C:* Doug Hallows; *M:* Colin Towns. **TV**

Catherine Cookson's The Glass Virgin ½ *The Glass Virgin* **1995** In 1859, young Annabella Lagrange (Mortimer) discovers that her spendthrift father, Edmund (Haver), has been hiding the secrets surrounding her birth. These revelations force Annabella to find her own way in a new life. Based on a novel by Catherine Cookson. **150m/C VHS, DVD.** *GB* Emily Mortimer, Nigel Havers, Brendan Coyle, Christine Kavanagh, Sylvia Syms, Samantha Glenn, Jan Graveson; *D:* Sarah Hellings; *W:* Alan Seymour; *C:* Doug Hallows; *M:* Christopher Gunning. **TV**

Catherine Cookson's The Man Who Cried ½ *The Man Who Cried* **1993** Abel Mason (Hinds) is an unhappily married man with a vindictive wife (Walsh) and a young son he's desperate to provide for. When an affair with a married woman ends in murder, Mason and his son travel in search of a new life. Desperate for a home, Mason enters into a bigamous marriage with a widow—only to find himself falling in love with her sister. Based on the novel by Catherine Cookson. Set in the years between England's depression and WW2. **156m/C VHS, DVD.** *GB* Ciaran Hinds, Amanda Root, Kate Buffery, Angela Walsh, Daniel Massey; *D:* Michael Whyte; *W:* Gordon Hann; *C:* Fred Tammes; *M:* Richard Hartley. **TV**

Catherine Cookson's The Moth ½ *The Moth* **1996** Robert Bradley leaves the shipyards to work in his uncle's furniture business but soon finds himself at odds with the old man. So he becomes a servant for the destructive Thormans, and falls for the lady of the house, Sarah. But in 1913 this upstairs/downstairs romance can only lead to disaster. TV movie based on the novel by Catherine Cookson. **150m/C VHS, DVD.** *GB* Jack Davenport, Juliet Aubrey, David Bradley, Justine Waddell; *D:* Roy Battersby; *W:* Gordon Hann; *C:* Alec Mills; *M:* Colin Towns. **TV**

Catherine Cookson's The Rag Nymph ½ *The Rag Nymph* **1996** Aggie Winkowski finds 10-year-old Millie Forrester abandoned on the streets. Knowing how dangerous the child's life could become, Aggie decides to take Millie in. TV movie based on the novel by Catherine Cookson. **150m/C VHS, DVD.** *GB* Honeysuckle Weeks, Val McLane, Perdita Weeks, Alec Newman, Crispin Bonham Carter; *D:* David Wheatley; *W:* T.R. Bowen; *C:* Alec Mills; *M:* Colin Towns. **TV**

Catherine Cookson's The Round Tower ½ *The Round Tower* **1998** Post-WWII Britain finds 17-year-old Vanessa Radcliffe pregnant. Her wealthy, socially conscious parents are appalled, especially when they think the father is the son of their housekeeper, Angus Cotten. He's not but winds up marrying Vanessa anyway—this unlikely circumstance putting Angus on the road to success. **150m/C VHS.** *GB* Emilia Fox, Keith Barron, Jan Harvey, Ben Miles, Denis Lawson; *D:* Alan Grint; *W:* T.R. Bowen; *C:* Robin Vidgeon. **TV**

Catherine Cookson's The Secret *The Secret* **2000** Complex historical thriller is based on Catherine Cookson's "The Harrogate Secret." In 19th-century England, Freddie Musgrave (Buchanan) has to work through secrets hidden in his own past as a runner and messenger for criminals. Anonymous letters, diamonds, and the like are involved. **156m/C DVD.** *GB* Colin Buchanan, June Whitfield, Stephen Moyer, Hannah Yelland, Clare Higgins; *D:* Alan Grint; *W:* T.R. Bowen; *C:* Allan Pyrah; *M:* Colin Towns. **TV**

Catherine Cookson's The Tide of Life ½ *The Tide of Life* **1996** TV adaptation of Catherine Cookson's novel finds young Emily Kennedy entering service as a maid to the McGilby family and weathering various tragedies, romantic and otherwise. **156m/C VHS, DVD.** *GB* Gillian Kearney, Ray Stevenson, John Bowler, James Purefoy, Diana Hardcastle; *D:* David Wheatley; *W:* Gordon Hann; *C:* Doug Hallows; *M:* Colin Towns.

Catherine Cookson's The Wingless Bird ½ *The Wingless Bird* **1997** Agnes Conway (Skinner) is the strong-minded daughter of a Newcastle shop-owner in class-conscious England in December, 1913. Managing her unhappy father's store, Claire waits on two members of the wealthy Farrier family and is soon drawn into their lives when the younger Farrier son, Charles (Atterton), falls in love with her, despite their class differences. But the Conway's have their own class problems—Agnes' younger sister Jessie becomes pregnant by a lower-class lad and her father's fury is murderous. Still as Agnes' love for Charlie grows, she must also deal with the outbreak of WWI, which will bring changes for all concerned. **156m/C VHS, DVD.** *GB* Claire Skinner, Edward Atterton, Julian Wadham, Frank Grimes, Moira Redmond, Elspet Gray, Dinsdale Landen, Anne Reid; *D:* David Wheatley; *W:* Alan Seymour; *M:* Colin Towns. **TV**

Catherine Cookson's Tilly Trotter ½ *Tilly Trotter* **1999** Tilly lives in rural England in the 1830s where the young woman is envied for her beauty by the local ladies and lusted after because of that same beauty by the local gentlemen. Accused of witchcraft, Tilly is rescued by a married farmer but there's another romance on the horizon as well. **210m/C VHS.** *GB* Carli Norris, Simon Shepherd, Gavin Abbott, Madelaine Newton, Rosemary Leach, Basil Moss, Amelia Bullmore, Richard Dempsey; *D:* Alan Grint; *W:* Ray Marshall; *C:* Robin Vidgeon; *M:* Colin Towns. **TV**

Catherine the Great ½ *The Rise of Catherine the Great* **1934** Slow but lavish and engrossing British dramatization of the tortured and doomed love affair between Catherine, Empress of Russia, and her irrational, drunken husband Peter. **88m/B VHS, DVD.** *GB* Douglas Fairbanks Jr., Elisabeth Bergner, Flora Robson; *D:* Paul Czinner; *C:* Georges Perinal.

Catherine the Great ½ **1995** Teenaged German princess Sophia (Zeta-Jones) marries into Russian royalty in 1744 when she weds Peter (Jaenicke), nephew of the Empress Elizabeth (Moreau), and has a name change when she's crowned Catherine II. The marriage is a disaster and with the help of her lover Gregory Orlov (McGann), Catherine eventually gets rid of Peter and is crowned Empress and Czarina of all the Russias as she struggles to drag her medieval empire into the modern world. Typically lavish and simplistic historical retelling. Originally released as a two-part miniseries. **100m/C VHS, DVD.** *GE* Catherine Zeta-Jones, Paul McGann, Ian Richardson, Jeanne Moreau, Mark McGann, Hannes Jaenicke, Mel Ferrer, Omar Sharif, John Rhys-Davies, Brian Blessed; ***D:*** Marvin J. Chomsky; ***W:*** John Goldsmith; ***C:*** Elemer Ragalyi; ***M:*** Laurence Rosenthal. **TV**

Catherine's Grove 1/2 **1998 (R)** Miami detective Jack Doyle (Fahey) is tracking down a serial killer while moonlighting as a P.I. Along with girlfriend Charley (Alonso), Jack's investigating the disappearance of rich girl Catherine, who may be involved with her creepy Uncle Joe (Madsen). So, do you think Doyle's two cases could possibly be connected? **91m/C VHS.** Michael Madsen, Jeff Fahey, Maria Conchita Alonso, Priscilla Barnes, Jeffrey Donovan; ***D:*** Rick King; ***W:*** Tony DiTocco; ***C:*** Bart Tau; ***M:*** Harry Manfredini. **VIDEO**

Catholics *The Conflict* **1973** A sensitive exploration of contemporary mores and changing attitudes within the Roman Catholic church. Sheen is sent by the Pope to Ireland to reform some priests. Based on Brian Moore's short novel. **86m/C VHS, DVD.** Martin Sheen, Trevor Howard; ***D:*** Jack Gold; ***M:*** Carl Davis. **TV**

Cathy's Curse *Cauchemares* **1977** The spirit of her aunt, who died as a child, possesses a young girl in this Canadian-French collaboration. Tries to capitalize on the popularity of "The Exorcist," but falls seriously short. **90m/C VHS, DVD.** *FR CA* Alan Scarfe, Beverly Murray; ***D:*** Eddy Matalon.

Catlow 1/2 **1971 (PG-13)** A comedic western with Brynner aiming to steal $2 million in gold from under the nose of his friend, lawman Crenna. Based on the novel by Louis L'Amour. **103m/C VHS.** Yul Brynner, Richard Crenna, Leonard Nimoy, JoAnn Pflug, Jeff Corey, Michael Delano, David Ladd, Bessie Love; ***D:*** Sam Wanamaker; ***W:*** Scot (Scott) Finch, J.J. Griffith.

Cats & Dogs **2001 (PG)** Mix of live-action and animatronics as the secret war between cats and dogs is exposed in your neighborhood. It seems the latest cat plot is to destroy a vaccine that would prevent all human allergies to dogs and the dogs, of course, must keep that from happening. The human actors are upstaged at every turn (naturally) and the plot showcases some inconsistent pacing, but the kids should enjoy it (unless they like cats) and adults won't hate it until, say, the sixth or seventh viewing. **87m/C VHS, DVD.** *US* Jeff Goldblum, Elizabeth Perkins, Miriam Margolyes, Alexander Pollock; ***D:*** Lawrence (Larry) Guterman; ***W:*** John Requa, Glenn Ficarra; ***C:*** Julio Macat; ***M:*** John Debney; ***V:*** Glenn Ficarra, Tobey Maguire, Sean P. Hayes, Alec Baldwin, Joe Pantoliano, Susan Sarandon, Michael Clarke Duncan, Jon Lovitz, Charlton Heston, Salome Jens.

Cats & Dogs: The Revenge of Kitty Galore **2010** In this sorta sequel to the 2001 pic, Kitty Galore (voiced by Midler) has gone rogue from spy organization MEOW and now wants to take down her cat comrades as well as her canine enemies. So cats, dogs, and their humans must band together to overcome the threat. Live action, animation, and puppetry combo. **m/C DVD.** *US* Chris O'Donnell, Jack McBrayer, Paul Rodriguez, Roger Moore; ***D:*** Brad Peyton; ***W:*** Ron J. Friedman, Steve Bencich; ***C:*** Steven Poster; ***M:*** Christopher Lennertz; ***V:*** Bette Midler, Michael Clarke Duncan, Joe Pantoliano, Alec Baldwin.

Cats Don't Dance **1997 (G)** Animated musical/comedy finds Danny (Bakula) a hoofer wanna-be trying to break into '30s Hollywood. Only problem is that he's a cat and can't understand why he only gets parts playing animals. He gets into trouble with bratty human star Darla Dimple (Peldon) and nearly sees his chance at a career vanish. Combines "Singin' in the Rain" and "Who Framed Roger Rabbit," with some showbiz cynicism from "The Player" to create a cartoon that will most likely sail over the heads of its target audience. Most of the time, as in the old Warner Bros. classics, that's a good thing. Not in this case, however. **77m/C VHS, DVD.** ***D:*** Mark Dindal; ***W:*** Cliff Ruby, Roberts Gannaway, Elana Lesser, Theresa Pettengill; ***M:*** Steve Goldstein, Randy Newman; ***V:*** Scott Bakula, Jasmine Guy, Ashley Peldon, Kathy Najimy, John Rhys-Davies, George Kennedy, Rene Auberjonois, Hal Holbrook, Don Knotts, Frank Welker, David Johansen, Natalie Cole.

Cat's Eye *Stephen King's Cat's Eye* **1985 (PG-13)** An anthology of three Stephen King short stories connected by a stray cat who wanders through each tale. **94m/C VHS, DVD.** Drew Barrymore, James Woods, Alan King, Robert Hays, Candy Clark, Kenneth McMillan, James Naughton, Charles S. Dutton; ***D:*** Lewis Teague; ***W:*** Stephen King; ***C:*** Jack Cardiff; ***M:*** Alan Silvestri.

The Cat's Meow 1/2 **2001 (PG-13)** Bogdanovich takes on an old Hollywood scandal in this period drama. In 1924 publishing tycoon William Randolph Hearst (Herrmann) and his much-younger mistress, actress Marion Davies (Dunst), invite a group of partygoers aboard Hearst's yacht for a weekend. Producer/director Thomas Ince (Elwes) dies—but how is in question (heart attack? murder?)—and there's a coverup. Did Hearst mistakenly kill Ince while aiming for guest Charlie Chaplin (Izzard), whom Hearst suspected of carrying on with Davies? Film looks terrific, has a talented cast, and the story shows that little has changed in Hollywood regarding sex, scandal, ambition, and power. **112m/C VHS, DVD.** *GB GE* Edward Herrmann, Kirsten Dunst, Cary Elwes, Eddie Izzard, Joanna Lumley, Jennifer Tilly, Victor Slezak, James Laurenson, Ronan Vibert, Claudia Harrison; ***D:*** Peter Bogdanovich; ***W:*** Steven Peros; ***C:*** Bruno Delbonnel.

Cat's Play *Mascskajatek* **1974** A widowed music teacher makes a ceremonial occasion of a weekly dinner with an old flame. Then an old friend from her youth suddenly reappears and begins an affair with the gentleman, causing self-destructive passions to explode. In Hungarian with English subtitles. **115m/C VHS, DVD.** *HU* Margit Dayka, Margit Makay, Elma Bulla; ***D:*** Karoly Makk.

Cattle Queen of Montana 1/2 **1954** Reagan stars as an undercover federal agent investigating livestock rustlings and Indian uprisings. **88m/C VHS, DVD.** Ronald Reagan, Barbara Stanwyck, Jack Elam, Gene Evans, Lance Fuller, Anthony Caruso; ***D:*** Allan Dwan; ***W:*** Robert Blees.

Cattle Town 1/2 **1952** Texas ranchers are displaced by nesters when Northerner Judd Hastings (Teal) starts buying up their grazing land in the post-Civil War depression. Mike McCann (Morgan) is sent in by the governor to play peacemaker between the two groups although there's a stampede before order is restored. Morgan does find the time to sing four forgettable ditties in between the action. **70m/B DVD.** Dennis Morgan, Ray Teal, Amanda Blake, Phil Carey, Rita Moreno, Paul Picerni, Jay Novello, George O'Hanlon, Robert J. Wilke, Charles Meredith; ***D:*** Noel Mason Smith; ***W:*** Tom Blackburn; ***C:*** Ted D. McCord; ***M:*** William Lava.

Catwoman **2004 (PG-13)** Halle Berry is Patience Phillips, an artist in the ad department of a cosmetics company who overhears a discussion about side effects of their newest product. Soon she and the scientist who discovered the problem are disposed of. Luckily, a few cats are around to revive our heroine and dress her in a tight leather catsuit to take her revenge. Unfortunately, Berry's talents and wardrobe are not enough to carry a movie that, while it will undoubtedly have an extended shelf-life as a camp classic, is a mess. Director Pitof saturates every frame with his presence and revels in drawing attention to flamboyant visuals and frenetic editing rather than focusing on characterization or good, old-fashioned storytelling. Wooden characters and a laughable storyline make this arguably one of the worst comic book adaptations ever made. **91m/C VHS, DVD.** Halle Berry, Sharon Stone, Benjamin Bratt, Lambert Wilson, Alex Borstein, John Cassini, Frances Conroy, Byron Mann, Michael Massee, Kim Smith, Chris Heyerdahl, Peter Wingfield; ***D:*** Pitof; ***W:*** John Brancato, Michael Ferris, John Rogers; ***C:*** Thierry Arbogast; ***M:*** Klaus Badelt. Golden Raspberries '04: Worst Picture, Worst Actress (Berry), Worst Director (Pitof), Worst Screenplay.

Caught **1949** A woman marries for wealth and security and is desperately unhappy. She runs away and takes a job with a struggling physician, and falls in love with him. Her husband finds her, forcing her to decide between a life of security or love. **90m/B VHS.** James Mason, Barbara Bel Geddes, Robert Ryan, Curt Bois, Natalie Schafer, Art Smith; ***D:*** Max Ophuls; ***C:*** Lee Garmes.

Caught **1996 (R)** Homeless Irishman Nick (Verveen) winds up in the New Jersey fish shop run by Joe (Olmos) and his wife Betty (Alonso). Betty takes a liking to the good-looking young man and encourages Joe to offer him a job and even invites Nick to stay with them in departed son Danny's (Schub) old room. Soon, room and board isn't all the spicy Betty is offering and Nick's willing to please, especially since Joe turns a blind eye. Too bad cocaine-addicted Danny, a failed comedian, returns home and immediately becomes jealous of the interloper. He's also too willing to drag secrets out into the open, whatever the cost. Based on Pomerantz's novel "Into It." **109m/C VHS, DVD.** Joseph (Joe) D'Onofrio, Edward James Olmos, Maria Conchita Alonso, Arie Verveen, Steven Schub, Bitty Schram, Shawn Elliot; ***D:*** Robert M. Young; ***W:*** Edward Pomerantz; ***C:*** Michael Barrow; ***M:*** Chris Botti.

Caught in the Act 1/2 **1993 (PG-13)** Scott McNally (Harrison) is an out-of-work actor who teaches acting classes to make a buck. Into one of his classes walks the sultry Rachel (Hope) and they start a hot affair. Then Rachel calls Scott, claiming to be kidnapped, he suddenly finds $10 million in his bank account, and his landlord is murdered. Scott finds himself the pawn in an embezzlement scheme and framed for murder. But this is one role Scott doesn't want and he intends to work with a new script of his own devise. **93m/C VHS.** Gregory Harrison, Leslie Hope, Patricia Clarkson, Kevin Tighe; ***D:*** Deborah Reinisch; ***W:*** Ken Hixon. **CABLE**

Caught in the Draft **1941** Hope's funniest role has him as a Hollywood star trying to evade the draft in WW II, but he ends up accidentally enlisting himself. Lamour plays the daughter of a colonel in the Army whom Hope plans to marry, thinking it will get him out of the service. Very funny military comedy and one of Hope's best. Based on a story by Harry Tugend. **82m/B VHS, DVD.** Bob Hope, Dorothy Lamour, Lynne Overman, Eddie Bracken, Clarence (C. William) Kolb, Paul Hurst, Ferike Boros, Irving Bacon; ***D:*** David Butler; ***W:*** Harry Tugend.

Caught Up **1998 (R)** Directorial debut for Darin Scott follows the luckless path of ex-con Daryl (Woodbine). After serving five years as an unwitting accomplice to a bank robbery, he meets Vanessa (Williams) who is a dead ringer for his ex-girlfriend. She gets him a job as a limo driver that caters to thugs and gangsters. Unfortunately for Daryl, Vanessa has stolen some diamonds from a Rastafarian, so Daryl gets tangled up violence and deceit. He is also tangled in a plot that twists and turns a little too much for its own good. Director Scott tries a few too many fancy tricks, although some of them work reasonably well. Cameos from Snoop Doggy Dog and LL Cool J. **95m/C VHS, DVD.** Bokeem Woodbine, Cynda Williams, Snoop Dogg, Joseph Lindsey, Clifton Powell, Basil Wallace, Tony Todd, LL Cool J, Jeffrey Combs, Damon Saleem, Shedric Hunter Jr.; ***D:*** Darin Scott; ***W:*** Darin Scott; ***C:*** Thomas Callaway; ***M:*** Marc Bonilla.

Cauldron of Blood 1/2 *Blind Man's Bluff; El Coleccionista de Cadaveres* **1967 (PG)** Blind sculptor Karloff unwittingly uses human skeletons supplied by his crazed wife Lindfors as the framework of his art pieces. **95m/C VHS.** *SP* Boris Karloff, Viveca Lindfors, Jean-Pierre Aumont, Rosenda Monteros, Ruben Rojo, Dianik Zurakowska; ***D:*** Edward Andrew (Santos Alcocer) Mann; ***W:*** Edward Andrew (Santos Alcocer) Mann.

Cause Celebre **1987** Absorbing true crime drama set in Britain during the '30s. Alma Rattenbury (Mirren) is in a dull marriage to an aging and ill husband (Andrews) and is beset by financial and domestic difficulties. Then Alma hires 18-year-old George Bowman (Morrissey) as a family servant/chauffeur and, despite their age difference, the two are soon lovers. When her husband is bludgeoned to death, both Alma and George are swiftly arrested and on trial. But just who committed the crime and who is covering up? **105m/C VHS, DVD.** *GB* Helen Mirren, David Morrissey, David Suchet, Harry Andrews, Norma West, Oliver Ford Davies, Geoffrey Bayldon, Gillian Martell; ***D:*** John Gorrie; ***W:*** Kenneth Taylor; ***C:*** Malcolm Harrison, Trevor Vaisey; ***M:*** Richard Harvey. **TV**

Cause for Alarm 1/2 **1951** A jealous husband recovering from a heart attack begins to lose his mind. He wrongly accuses his wife of having an affair and attempts to frame her for his own murder. A fast-paced thriller with a nifty surprise ending. **74m/B VHS, DVD.** Loretta Young, Barry Sullivan, Bruce Cowling, Margalo Gillmore, Irving Bacon, Carl "Alfalfa" Switzer; ***D:*** Tay Garnett; ***M:*** Andre Previn.

Cause of Death 1/2 **1990 (R)** After the accidental death of his brother, Colombian drug lord Manuel Ramirez is lured to L.A. to collect his millions in blood money. **90m/C VHS, DVD.** Michael Barak, Sydney Coale Phillips, Daniel Martine; ***D:*** Philip Jones.

Cause of Death **2000 (R)** Taylor Lewis (Bergin) is a prosecutor in Baltimore, who is assigned to a seemingly open-and-shut murder in which Angela Carter (Severance) has murdered her corrupt businessman husband to collect on his large insurance policy. But Lewis is cautious because of a past mistake and then he starts getting very close to the beautiful widow. Is Angela guilty or is someone in power pulling the strings? **95m/C VHS, DVD.** Patrick Bergin, Joan Severance, Maxim Roy, Michael Ironside, Larry Day; ***D:*** Marc S. Grenier; ***W:*** Les Weldon; ***C:*** Yves Belanger. **VIDEO**

Cavalcade **1933** Traces the lives of the British Marryot family from the death of Queen Victoria, through WWI, the Jazz Age, and the Depression. A wistful adaptation of the hit play by Noel Coward with its touching portrayal of one family trying to weather good times and bad together. **110m/B VHS.** Diana Wynyard, Clive Brook, Herbert Mundin, Una O'Connor, Ursula Jeans, Beryl Mercer, Merle Tottenham, Frank Lawton, John Warburton, Margaret Lindsay, Billy Bevan; ***D:*** Frank Lloyd; ***C:*** Ernest Palmer. Oscars '33: Director (Lloyd), Picture.

Cavalcade of the West **1936** Typical western with two brothers, separated by a kidnapping, growing up on opposite sides of the law. Much later they meet, and the question is: will the outlaw be reformed and reunited with his happy family? **70m/B VHS, DVD.** Hoot Gibson, Rex Lease, Marion Shilling, Earl Dwire; ***D:*** Harry Fraser.

Cavalier of the West **1931** An Army captain is the only negotiating force between the white man and a primitive Indian tribe. **66m/B VHS.** Harry Carey Sr., Kane Richmond, George "Gabby" Hayes; ***D:*** John P. McCarthy.

Cavalry 1/2 **1936** A Union Army Lieutenant is reunited with his family after the Civil War, bringing them happiness and joy. **60m/B VHS.** Bob Steele, Frances Grant, Karl Hackett, Hal Price; ***D:*** Robert North Bradbury.

Cavalry Charge 1/2 *The Last Outpost* **1951** Vance Britton (Reagan) is the captain of a brigade of Confederate troops wreaking havoc on Union outposts. His brother Jeb (Bennett) is a Union soldier sent to the western frontier to take care of the Confederate problem. Vance's former fiance Julie (Fleming) is also living in the territories with her new husband. All three converge when the Union fort, where Julie is living and Jeb is defending, is attacked by Apaches. Brother Vance rides to the rescue. Lots of action. **72m/C VHS, DVD.** Ronald Reagan, Bruce Bennett, Rhonda Fleming, Noah Beery Jr., Bill Williams, Peter Hansen, Hugh Beaumont, John Ridgely, Lloyd Corrigan, James Burke, Richard Crane, Ewing Mitchell; ***D:*** Lewis R. Foster; ***W:*** Daniel Mainwaring, George Worthing Yates, Winston Miller; ***C:*** Loyal Griggs.

Cavalry Command 1/2 *Cavalleria Commandos* **1963** Good will and integrity characterize the U.S. soldiers called into a small village to quiet a guerrilla rebellion. **77m/C VHS, DVD.** John Agar, Richard Arlen, Myron Healey, Alicia Vergel, William Phipps, Eddie Infante; ***D:*** Eddie Romero; ***W:*** Eddie Romero.

The Cave **2005 (PG-13)** Cut from the same cloth as the hundred or so other films you've seen that were called "The (insert scary place or thing here)." All of the essential stereotypes are present, so everyone gets a character to relate to, hate, or both. Explorers Jack (Hauser) and Tyler (Cibrian) assemble a team of cavers, divers and scientists to explore a massive network of caves beneath a medieval Romanian church. As they descend into the cave it becomes clear that they have company in the form of hideous flying monsters. **97m/C DVD, UMD.** *US* Cole Hauser, Morris Chestnut, Eddie Cibrian, Marcel Iures, Daniel Dae Kim, Lena Headey, Piper Perabo, Rick Ravanello, Kieran Darcy-Smith; ***D:*** Bruce Hunt; ***W:*** Michael Steinberg, Tegan West; ***C:*** Emery Ross; ***M:*** Johnny Klimek, Reinhold Heil.

Cave Girl WOOF! *Cavegirl* **1985 (R)** After falling through a time-warp during a high-school field trip, a social pariah makes a hit with a pre-historic honey. Sexist teen exploitation film, with few original ideas and a not-so-hot cast. **85m/C VHS, DVD.** Daniel Roebuck, Cindy Ann Thompson, Saba Moor, Jeff Chayette; ***D:*** David Oliver; ***W:*** David Oliver; ***C:*** David Oliver; ***M:*** Jon St. James.

Cave of the Living Dead WOOF! *Der Fluch Der Gruenen Augen; Night of the Vampire; The Curse of Green Eyes* **1965** Mad professor with a past is up to something in a cave under castle. Villagers summon Inspector Doren of Interpol to solve a rash of nasty murders that they've blamed on green-eyed, cave-dwelling vampires. A challenge to watch till the end. Filmed in Sepiatone. **87m/B VHS, DVD.** *GE YU* Adrian Hoven, Erika Remberg, Carl Mohner, Wolfgang Preiss, Karin (Karen) Field, John Kitzmiller, Akos Von Rathony; ***D:*** Akos Von Rathony; ***W:*** C.V. Rock; ***C:*** Hrvoje Saric.

The Cave of the Silken Web ½ *Pan si dong; Pun see dung* **1967** In the late 1960s the Shaw Brothers did a series of four films based on the Chinese epic fable "Journey to the West" about the Monkey King (also inspiration for the anime series "Dragon Ball"). In this third film in the series, the Seven Spider Sisters kidnap the Tang Monk as he journeys to India, intending to devour him to gain immortality. Working to save him are the Monkey King, Pig, and Sand. Unintentional comedy, martial arts choreography, and flamboyant costumed dance numbers abound. **82m/C DVD.** *HK* Chien Yu, Liang Hua Liu, Fan Ho, Peng Peng, Lung Chang Chou, Shun Tien, Ekin Cheng, Josie Ho, George Lam, Candy Lo, Bey Logan, Shawn Tam, Chapman To, Kenneth Tsang, Andy Hui, Yi Huang, Clarence Hui, Kar Yan Lam, Hacken Lee; ***D:*** Meng Hua Ho, Chun-Chun Wong; ***W:*** Kang Cheng, Chun-Chun Wong, Lawrence Cheng, Cindy Tang; ***C:*** Kuo-Hsiang Lin; ***M:*** Fu-ling Wang, Ken Chan.

Caveman **1981 (PG)** Starr stars in this prehistoric spoof about a group of cavemen banished from different tribes who band together to form a tribe called "The Misfits." **92m/C VHS, DVD.** Ringo Starr, Barbara Bach, John Matuszak, Dennis Quaid, Jack Gilford, Shelley Long, Cork Hubbert, Avery Schreiber; ***D:*** Carl Gottlieb; ***W:*** Carl Gottlieb, Rudy DeLuca; ***C:*** Alan Hume; ***M:*** Lalo Schifrin.

The Caveman's Valentine ½ **2001 (R)** Jackson plays a homeless schizophrenic who finds a dead body outside his cave in Central Park and must pull his faltering mental faculties together enough to play Sherlock Holmes and solve the who-done-it. Plot points stretch well beyond the bounds of believability and venture into the territory of the ridiculous as the Caveman conveniently infiltrates every realm of society he wishes in order to follow up on his suspicions. Granted, he used to be a master pianist before his mental downfall, but come on. Director Lemmons's second feature film, the first being "Eve's Bayou." Based on the Edgar Award-winning 1994 novel by George Dawes Green. **105m/C VHS, DVD.** Samuel L. Jackson, Aunjanue Ellis, Colm Feore, Ann Magnuson, Rodney Eastman, Tamara Tunie, Anthony Michael Hall, Jay Rodan; ***D:*** Kasi Lemmons; ***W:*** George Dawes Green; ***C:*** Amy Vincent; ***M:*** Terence Blanchard.

The Cavern ½ *Within* **2005 (R)** An eight-person team exploring a newly discovered cavern in Kyzl Kum Desert in Central Asia run into big trouble when they find themselves trapped. Too familiar story and not very frightening. **81m/C DVD.** *AU* Sybil Temtchine, Mustafa Shakir, Ogy Durham, Andrew Caple-Shaw, Danny A. Jacobs, Andres Saenz-Hudson, Johnnie Colter, Neno Pervan; ***D:*** Olatunde Osunsanmi; ***W:*** Olatunde Osunsanmi; ***C:*** Yasu Tanida; ***M:*** Bryan Galvez.

Cavite ½ **2005** No-budget thriller set and filmed in the Philippines. Adam (Gamazon) is summoned to Manila to attend his father's funeral but his mother and sister aren't at the airport to meet him. Instead, Adam gets a cell phone call informing him that they have been kidnapped and he must not only retrieve money his father had stashed but also carry out a terrorist mission if Adam wants to keep his family alive. All the while, the jeering caller sends Adam running throughout the poor city of Cavite, doing his bidding. English and Tagalog with subtitles. **80m/C DVD.** Ian Gamazon, Dominique Gonzalez, Jeffrey Lagna; ***D:*** Ian Gamazon, Neill Dela Llana; ***W:*** Ian Gamazon, Neill Dela Llana; ***C:*** Neill Dela Llana.

CB4: The Movie ½ **1993 (R)** Falling somewhere between a serious attempt and parody, CB4 tries to do both and succeeds at neither. Written in the key of "Wayne's World" by "Saturday Night Live's" Rock, it starts out as a "rockumentary" (please refer to "This is Spinal Tap"), but quickly turns into a sitcom after two gangsta rap friends assume the identity of a local club owner when he is in jail. Hartman, also of SNL, appears as a right-wing city councilman. Chock full of violence, sexism, and profanity tucked into a wandering plot. **83m/C VHS, DVD.** Chris Rock, Allen Payne, Deezer D, Phil Hartman, Charlie (Charles Q.) Murphy, Khandi Alexander, Art Evans, Chris Elliott, Willard Pugh, Theresa Randle; ***D:*** Tamra Davis; ***W:*** Chris Rock, Nelson George, Robert Locash; ***M:*** John Barnes.

C.C. & Company *Chrome Hearts* **1970 (R)** Rebel biker rescues a buxom gal from a fate worse than death, than vies for control of the gang. Laughable, with Namath hopeless in his film debut. Redeemed only by Ann-Margret in continual disarray. **91m/C VHS, DVD.** Joe Namath, Ann-Margret, William (Bill) Smith, Jennifer Billingsley, Teda Bracci, Greg Mullavey, Sid Haig, Bruce Glover; ***D:*** Seymour Robbie; ***W:*** Roger Smith; ***C:*** Charles F. Wheeler; ***M:*** Lenny Stack.

Cease Fire **1985 (R)** The story of a troubled Vietnam vet who finds solace in a veterans' therapy group. Adapted from the play by George Fernandez. **97m/C VHS.** Don Johnson, Robert F. Lyons, Lisa Blount; ***D:*** David Nutter; ***M:*** Gary Fry.

Cecil B. Demented ½ **2000 (R)** Waters returns to a more hard-edged satire with this indictment against the studio system. Dorff is Cecil B. Demented, indie auteur who, along with his band of cinema terrorists, wreack havoc on Hollywood. They kidnap A-list actress Honey Whitlock (Griffith) and force her to appear in their film—in doing so, making her the poster child for their cause. Punish bad film! No English-language remakes of foreign film! Death to those who are cinematically incorrect! Will appeal more to fans of Waters's very early work than to those who enjoyed "Serial Mom" or "Hairspray." **88m/C VHS, DVD.** Stephen Dorff, Melanie Griffith, Jack Noseworthy, Alicia Witt, Larry (Lawrence) Gilliard Jr., Adrian Grenier, Patty (Patricia Campbell) Hearst, Ricki Lake, Mink Stole, Maggie Gyllenhaal, Eric M. Barry, Zenzele Uzoma, Erika Lynn Rupli, Harriet Dodge, Eric Roberts; ***D:*** John Waters; ***W:*** John Waters; ***C:*** Robert M. Stevens; ***M:*** Basil Poledouris, Zoe Poledouris.

Ceiling Zero **1935** Cagney is an irrepressible pilot who does as he pleases and loves to aggravate his soft-hearted boss O'Brien. He falls for aviatrix Travis and neglects his duties to woo her, which leads to tragedy. Naturally, this sobers Cagney up and he volunteers for a dangerous test flight. Lots of fast-paced action and Cagney is at his swaggering best. Based on a play by Frank Wead, who also wrote the screenplay. Remade in 1941 as "International Squadron." **95m/B VHS.** James Cagney, Pat O'Brien, June Travis, Stuart Erwin, Henry Wadsworth, Isabel Jewell, Barton MacLane; ***D:*** Howard Hawks; ***W:*** Frank Wead.

The Celebration *Festen* **1998 (R)** Danish patriarch Helge (Moritzen) is turning 60 and a black-tie bash is being given to celebrate the event. But the celebration turns into a rancid display when all the family skeletons coming rattling out of their closets. Everyone's got a score to settle and is more than happy to air the family's dirty linen. Danish with subtitles. The film was shot with a hand-held video camera in available light and sound according to the tenets of Dogma 95—a Danish filmmaking collective Vinterberg belongs to. **105m/C VHS, DVD.** *DK* Henning Moritzen, Ulrich Thomsen, Thomas Bo Larsen, Paprika Steen, Lene Laub Olsen, Helle Dolleris, Gbatokai Dakinah; ***D:*** Thomas Vinterberg; ***W:*** Thomas Vinterberg, Mogens Rukov; ***C:*** Anthony Dod Mantle. Ind. Spirit '99: Foreign Film; L.A. Film Critics '98: Foreign Film; N.Y. Film Critics '98: Foreign Film.

Celebrity ½ **1985** A tragic childhood secret must be confronted by three friends when one is charged with murder. Based on the Thomas Thompson novel. **313m/C VHS.** Michael Beck, Ben Masters, Joseph Bottoms; ***D:*** Paul Wendkos. **TV**

Celebrity **1998 (R)** Woody examines the phenomenon of celebrity with his usual sarcastic and semi-autobiographical perspective. Lee Simon (Branaugh) is a hack celebrity journalist who attempts to enter the glitz and glam world of the famous people he follows and writes about. In true Allen fashion, bitter irony abounds as Simon loses sight of his pathetic reality while those around him acquire what he so desperately seeks. DiCaprio steals his 15 minutes of screen time playing a hedonistic, hotel-trashing, spoiled young film star with amazing ease and conviction (Coincidence? Perhaps...). The writing is among Allen's best, but watching Branaugh, and Judy Davis as Lee's estranged wife, do their best Woody Allen impressions grates on the nerves. Although it's redundant, nobody plays Woody like Woody. **113m/B VHS, DVD.** Kenneth Branagh, Judy Davis, Hank Azaria, Leonardo DiCaprio, Joe Mantegna, Famke Janssen, Winona Ryder, Melanie Griffith, Michael Lerner, Charlize Theron, Bebe Neuwirth, Dylan Baker, Patti D'Arbanville, Kate Burton, Gretchen Mol, Allison Janney, Aida Turturro, Jeffrey Wright, J.K. Simmons, Polly Adams; ***Cameos:*** Greg Mottola, Isaac Mizrahi, Andre Gregory, Donald Trump; ***D:*** Woody Allen; ***W:*** Woody Allen; ***C:*** Sven Nykvist.

Celeste **1981** Adlon (who later made the offbeat comedy "Sugarbaby") directed this longish but finely detailed and beautifully photographed biographical look at French writer Marcel (Remembrance of Things Past) Proust. Based on the memoirs of Proust's housekeeper, Celeste Albaret, an uneducated farmgirl, portraying the woman's devoted relationship ('til death did them part) with the middle-aged, homosexual author. It does so with wit, poignancy, and insight, but is not entirely successful in its attempt to render Proust's verbal literary style into a visual medium. In German with English subtitles. **107m/C VHS.** *GE* Eva Mattes, Jurgen Arndt, Norbert Wartha, Wolf Euba; ***D:*** Percy Adlon; ***W:*** Percy Adlon; ***C:*** Jurgen Martin.

Celestial Clockwork ½ *Mecaniques Celestes* **1994** Runaway Venezuelan bride Ana (Gil), an aspiring opera singer, takes off for Paris clutching her Maria Callas poster. God must protect the innocent because she meets a friendly cabbie, immediately finds a place to live, and gets the perfect singing teacher, a cranky Russian emigre named Grigorief (Debrane). In fact, the only problem in this Cinderella's life is jealous would-be star Celeste (Dombasle), who wants the same lead theatrical role that Ana is also interested in. French with subtitles. **85m/C VHS, DVD.** *FR* Ariadna Gil, Arielle Dombasle, Evelyne Didi, Frederic Longbois, Lluis Homar, Michel Debrane; ***D:*** Fina Torres; ***W:*** Fina Torres; ***C:*** Ricardo Aronovich; ***M:*** Michel Musseau, Francois Farrugia.

The Celestine Prophecy **2006 (PG)** Pure hokum and clumsy in narrative, dialog, and character development. John Woodson (Settle) impulsively travels to Peru after a friend alerts him to the discovery of ancient scrolls said to reveal universal life truths. But when John arrives he discovers that both the church and the government want to suppress the find and stop those involved from talking. Based on the metaphysical novel by James Redfield, who co-scripted. **99m/C DVD.** Matthew Settle, Thomas Kretschmann, Annabeth Gish, Hector Elizondo, Sarah Wayne Callies, Jurgen Prochnow, Obba Babatunde, Joaquim Almeida; ***D:*** Armand Mastroianni; ***W:*** Dan Gordon, James Redfield, Barnet Bain; ***C:*** R. Michael Givens; ***M:*** Nuno Malo.

Celia: Child of Terror **1989** Set in the 1950s, this film deals with the awful results of a young girl's inability to handle disappointment. **110m/C VHS.** *AU* Rebecca Smart, Nicholas Eadie, Victoria Longley, Mary-Anne Fahey; ***D:*** Ann Turner; ***C:*** Geoffrey Simpson.

Celine **2008 (PG-13)** Riddled with errors and dull to boot. This unauthorized bio of Canadian super-singer Celine Dion starts with her childhood in Quebec (although basically ignoring the fact that she's French-Canadian and started her career singing in French) and then marches through her climb up the showbiz ladder, including her meeting with manager Rene Angelil. In what passes for scandal, Dion has to hide her romantic involvement with the married Rene until he gets a divorce; after that, the flick hurries through various career highlights including her successful showcase in Las Vegas. **90m/C DVD.** *CA* Jodelle Ferland, Enrico Colantoni, Grant Nickalls, Peter MacNeill, Christine Ghawi, Louis Pitre; ***D:*** Jeff Woolnough; ***W:*** Donald Martin; ***C:*** Miroslaw Baszak; ***M:*** Jack Lenz. **CABLE**

Celine and Julie Go Boating **1974** Strange fantasy follows magician Celine (Berto) and her librarian friend, Julie (Labourier). Celine sometimes works as a governess for a little girl who lives with her widowed father in a possibly haunted house. Two women are in love with the father but he'd promised his wife never to remarry as long as their invalid daughter was still alive. Celine and Julie become worried for the little girl and decide to rescue her. An adaptation of the Henry James story "A Romance of Certain Old Clothes." French with subtitles. **193m/C VHS.** Juliet Berto, Dominique Labourier, Bulle Ogier, Marie-France Pisier, Barbet Schroeder, Philippe Clevenot, Nathalie Asnor; ***D:*** Jacques Rivette; ***W:*** Jacques Rivette, Eduardo Di Gregorio; ***C:*** Jacques Renard; ***M:*** Jean-Marie Senia.

The Cell ½ **2000 (R)** Psychotherapist Catherine (Lopez) is involved in breakthrough research that allows her access into a patient's mind. Desperate FBI agent Novak (Vaughn) asks her to invade the mind of a comatose serial killer (D'Onofrio) in order to save his latest victim. As you'd expect, the mind of a serial killer is not an exactly pleasant place to be, and Catherine (and the audience) encounters some pretty creepy and disturbing stuff. Feature debut of music video director Tarsem (REM's "Losing My Religion") is long on dazzling visual effects, trippy images, and style, but short on real suspense and cohesive plotting. Narrative is not the main focus here, however, so the faint of heart and the plot-dependent are forewarned. **110m/C VHS, DVD.** Jennifer Lopez, Vince Vaughn, Vincent D'Onofrio, Marianne Jean-Baptiste, Dylan Baker, Jake Weber, Patrick Bauchau, James Gammon, Tara Subkoff, Gareth Williams, Colton James, Catherine Sutherland, Dean Norris, Pruitt Taylor Vince; ***D:*** Tarsem; ***W:*** Mark Protosevich; ***C:*** Paul Laufer; ***M:*** Howard Shore.

The Cell 2 **2009 (R)** Another one of those in-name-only sequels. Serial killer "The Cusp" tortures his victims by letting them flatline and then reviving them over and over again. His first victim, Maya (Santiago), managed to escape and developed psychic powers after recovering from her ordeal. Now she's recruited by the FBI to get the madman. **94m/C DVD.** Chris Bruno, Frank Whaley, Bart Johnson, Tessie Santiago; ***D:*** Tim Iacofano; ***W:*** Lawrence Silverstein, Alex Barder; ***C:*** Geno Salvatori; ***M:*** John Massari. **VIDEO**

The Cellar ½ **1990 (PG-13)** A young boy finds an ancient Comanche monster spirit in the basement of his home. His parents, as usual, don't believe him, so he must battle the monster alone. **90m/C VHS.** Patrick Kilpatrick, Suzanne Savoy, Chris Miller, Ford Rainey; ***D:*** Kevin S. Tenney.

Cellar Dweller WOOF! 1987 A cartoonist moves into an old house and soon discovers it's haunted by a demonic cartoonist who killed himself 30 years earlier. What a coincidence. Low-budget scare-'em-upper filmed on one set and lit by a floodlamp. **78m/C**

VHS. Pamela Bellwood, Deborah Muldowney, Brian Robbins, Vince Edwards, Jeffrey Combs, Yvonne De Carlo; ***D:*** John Carl Buechler.

Cellblock Sisters: Banished Behind Bars 1/2 **1995 (R)** Biker babe Harris reunites with college girl sis Wood to off their disgusting stepfather who separately sold them to adoptive families after killing their junkie mom. Harris does the crime but Wood does the time—until her guilty sibling deliberately gets thrown behind bars in order to protect her. Has all the standard jail chicks elements. **95m/C VHS, DVD.** Gail Harris, Annie Wood, Ace Ross; ***D:*** Henri Charr.

Cello 1/2 **2005 (R)** Confusing Korean ghost story—or maybe the main character is just nuts. Cello teacher Mi-Ju (Seong) barely survived a car accident that ruined her professional career and killed her best friend. Now Mi-Ju is being threatened by one of her students and thinks she's haunted by a ghost. Korean with subtitles. **93m/C DVD.** *KN* Heyon-a Seong, Ho-bin Jeong, Da-an Park; ***D:*** Woo-cheol Lee; ***W:*** Woo-cheol Lee.

Cellular 1/2 **2004 (PG-13)** Efficient little thriller wastes no time. Science teacher Jessica Martin (Basinger) is kidnapped and locked in a grungy attic. Head bad guy Ethan (Statham) smashes the wall phone but Jessica hears a dial tone and manages to connect the wires and randomly gets the cell phone of beach bum Ryan (Evans), who naturally thinks it's a prank. Finally convinced, Ryan also figures out if he loses the call, the lady is lost, which leads to a number of realistic obstacles as he races to warn her husband and son, who are also targets. Veteran actor Macy plays veteran LAPD desk sergeant Mooney, who's about to retire when this case lands in his lap. The story is by Larry Cohen, who was also into phones as the screenwriter of 2002's "Phone Booth." **94m/C VHS, DVD.** *US* Kim Basinger, Chris Evans, Jason Statham, Eric Christian Olsen, Matt McColm, Noah Emmerich, William H. Macy, Brendan Kelly, Caroline Aaron, Richard Burgi, Rick Hoffman, Eric Etebari, Adam Taylor Gordon, Jessica Biel; ***D:*** David R. Ellis; ***W:*** Larry Cohen, Chris Morgan; ***C:*** Gary Capo; ***M:*** John Ottman.

The Celluloid Closet 1/2 **1995 (R)** Terrific documentary on how Hollywood films have depicted homosexual characters, subliminally and otherwise. Working chronologically and in an historical context, beginning with silent films, there are clips from more than 100 films, along with interviews from writers and actors. (Notable is writer Gore Vidal's comments on the gay subtext in 1959's "Ben-Hur"). Based on Vito Russo's 1981 book. **102m/C VHS, DVD.** ***D:*** Robert Epstein, Jeffrey Friedman; ***W:*** Armistead Maupin; ***C:*** Nancy Schreiber; ***M:*** Carter Burwell; ***Nar:*** Lily Tomlin.

Celtic Pride **1996 (PG-13)** Mike O'Hara (Stern) and Jimmy Flaherty (Aykroyd) are the worst kind of crazy. They're sports nuts. They are so consumed with passion for their beloved Celtics that they kidnap foul-mouthed superstar Lewis Scott (Wayans) of the Utah Jazz before game seven of the NBA finals. If this sounds far fetched, well..it is, unless you have an ESPN junkie in your life. There's not as much court action as you would expect, since most of the story revolves around intermittent trash-talking and escape attempts. If you're a Celtic hater, stick around for the end, when the Boston Garden is demolished using special effects. **90m/C VHS, DVD.** Damon Wayans, Daniel Stern, Dan Aykroyd, Gail O'Grady, Christopher McDonald, Paul Guilfoyle, Adam Hendershott, Deion Sanders, Gus Williams, Ted Rooney, Vladimir Cuk, Darrell Hammond; ***Cameos:*** Larry Bird, Bill Walton; ***D:*** Tom DeCerchio; ***W:*** Judd Apatow; ***C:*** Oliver Wood; ***M:*** Basil Poledouris.

Cement 1/2 **1999 (R)** Intense performances in a nasty crime story told via flashbacks. Hollywood vice detectives Holt (Penn) and Nin (Wright) have crossed the line between the cops and the criminals. When violent Holt catches his gal (Fenn) with a local wiseguy (DeSando), he buries him in a cement freeway and the mob is out for revenge. Pasdar's directorial debut. **100m/C VHS, DVD.** Christopher Penn, Jeffrey Wright, Sherilyn Fenn, Anthony De Sando, Henry Czerny; ***D:*** Adrian Pasdar; ***W:*** Justin Monjo; ***C:*** Geary McLeod; ***M:*** Doug Caldwell.

The Cement Garden **1993** Fatherless 15-year-old Jack (Robertson) and 16-year-old sister Julie (Gainsbourg) are afraid that they and their two younger siblings Sue (Coulthard) and Tom (Birkin) will be taken into foster care after their mother dies at home. So to keep their secret, they bury her in the basement and try to assume a normal family life. Not that this works for long—Jack and Julie give into an incestuous fascination and the household slowly sinks into chaotic squalor around them. Gainsbourg is the director's niece and the young Birkin is his son. Based on Ian McEwan's 1978 novel. **105m/C VHS, DVD.** *FR GE GB* Charlotte Gainsbourg, Andrew Robertson, Alice Coulthard, Ned Birkin, Sinead Cusack, Hanns Zischler, Jochen Horst; ***D:*** Andrew Birkin; ***W:*** Andrew Birkin; ***C:*** Stephen Blackman; ***M:*** Ed Shearmur.

The Cemetery Club 1/2 **1993 (PG-13)** Story of three Jewish widows who make weekly visits to their husband's graves while attempting to cope with their lives. Doris (Dukakis) is loyal to the memory of her husband and acts as the moral conscience of the trio. Lucille (Ladd) is a merry widow who wears clothes more suitable for younger women, but she also harbors a painful secret. Esther (Burstyn) struggles with her loneliness until a widowed cab driver begins to woo her. Commendably, the characters are given more dimension than Hollywood usually grants women of a certain age. Based on the play "The Cemetary Club" by Menchell, who also wrote the screenplay. **114m/C VHS, DVD.** Ellen Burstyn, Olympia Dukakis, Diane Ladd, Danny Aiello, Lainie Kazan, Christina Ricci, Bernie Casey, Alan Mason, Sam Schwartz, Jeff Howell, Robert Costanzo, Wallace Shawn, Louis Guss; ***D:*** Bill Duke; ***W:*** Ivan Menchell; ***C:*** Steven Poster; ***M:*** Elmer Bernstein.

Cemetery High **1989** Beautiful high school girls decide to lure the local boys into a trap and kill them. **80m/C VHS, DVD.** Debi Thibeault, Karen Nielsen, Lisa Schmidt, Ruth (Coreen) Collins, Simone, Tony Kruk, David Coughlin, Frank Stewart; ***D:*** Gorman Bechard; ***W:*** Gorman Bechard, Carmine Capobianco.

Cemetery Man *Dellamorte Dellamore; Of Death, of Love* **1995 (R)** Grotesque little saga about zombies and necrophilia set in a small Italian cemetery. Thanks to a weird post-death plague the corpses refuse to stay quietly in their graves, forcing watchman Francisco Dellamorte (Everett) and mute gravedigger Gnaghi (Hadji-Lazaro) to split their heads open. But when Francisco's dead sweetheart (Falchi) rises from her grave, he's a little slow to rebury the still-active corpse. Based on the Italian graphic novel "Dellamorte Dellamore," from the "Dylan Dog" series by Tiziano Sclavi. **100m/C VHS, DVD.** *IT* Rupert Everett, Anna Falchi, Francois Hadji-Lazaro, Mickey Knox; ***D:*** Michele (Michael) Soavi; ***W:*** Gianni Romoli; ***C:*** Mauro Marchetti; ***M:*** Manuel De Sica.

Centennial **1978** Epic 12-part TV miniseries, based on the 1974 novel by James Michener, about the building of the Rocky Mountain town of Centennial, Colorado, from 1795 to the present. There are trappers and Indians, immigrants and cattlemen, soldiers, conservationists, and politicians all with their own stories to tell. **1258m/C VHS.** Robert Conrad, Richard Chamberlain, Raymond Burr, Sally Kellerman, Barbara Carrera, Michael Ansara, Gregory Harrison, Stephanie Zimbalist, Christina Raines, Stephen McHattie, Kario Salem, Chad Everett, Alex Karras, Mark Harmon, Dennis Weaver, Timothy Dalton, Richard Crenna, Cliff DeYoung, Glynn Turman, Brian Keith, Les Lannom, Rafael Campos, Anthony Zerbe, Doug McKeon, Lynn Redgrave, William Atherton, A. Martinez, Lois Nettleton, David Janssen, Robert Vaughn, Andy Griffith, Sharon Gless; ***D:*** Virgil W. Vogel, Harry Falk, Paul Krasny, Bernard McEveety; ***W:*** John Wilder.

Center of the Web **1992 (R)** John Phillips is a victim of mistaken identity—someone thinks he's a professional hit man. After surviving an apparent mob attempt on his life, Phillips is persuaded by a CIA operative to go along with the deception in order to capture a potential political assassin. At least that's what Phillips is told, but he soon realizes that the deeper he gets into his new role, the deadlier the plot becomes. Davi is one of the best bad guys around and the fast-paced stunts and plot twists make this watchable. **88m/C VHS.** Ted Prior, Robert Davi, Tony Curtis, Charlene Tilton, Bo Hopkins, Charles Napier; ***D:*** David A. Prior.

The Center of the World **2001** Put this one strongly in the love it or hate it category. Richard (Sarsgaard) is a wealthy dot.com geek who offers stripper Florence (Parker) a lot of dough to spend a few days with him in Vegas. She makes some strict rules about what she will and won't do for him—which she promptly breaks. They're both immature and vulnerable and inclined to play humiliating mind games with each other. The sex show turns out to be nothing to get hot and bothered about and the leads give as credible performances as the narrowness of their characters allow. Shot in digital video; the screenwriters used the pseud. "Ellen Benjamin Wong." **86m/C VHS, DVD.** Peter Sarsgaard, Molly Parker, Carla Gugino, Balthazar Getty, Mel Gorham; ***D:*** Wayne Wang; ***W:*** Wayne Wang; ***C:*** Mauro Fiore.

Center Stage **2000 (PG-13)** How familar does this sound? Newcomers enrolled at the American Ballet Academy vie for places in the professional company. Meanwhile, former dancer/company director Jonathan (Gallagher) has to contend with his insolent star dancer Cooper (Stiefel), whose ambitions are growing by leaps and bounds. There's also the usual love connections to be made (and unmade). The professional dancers in the cast have limited acting ability and aren't served particularly well by most of the choreography. **116m/C VHS, DVD.** Peter Gallagher, Ethan Stiefel, Amanda Schull, Sascha Radetsky, Susan May Pratt, Ilia Kulik, Donna Murphy, Zoe Saldana, Debra Monk, Julie Kent, Eion Bailey, Shakiem Evans, Victor Anthony, Elizabeth Hubbard, Priscilla Lopez; ***D:*** Nicholas Hytner; ***W:*** Carol Heikkinen; ***C:*** Geoffrey Simpson; ***M:*** George Fenton.

Center Stage: Turn It Up 1/2 **2008 (PG-13)** A predictable but fun "fight for your dreams" flick. Self-taught dancer Kate heads to New York to audition for the American Academy of Ballet. No big surprise when she doesn't meet the school's rigid and traditional standards, but Kate isn't giving up. She spends some time working on her moves at a popular hip-hop club, partnered with Tommy, an ex-hockey player turned dancer. (Now there's a career change.) **95m/C DVD.** Peter Gallagher, Ethan Stiefel, Rachele Brooke Smith, Kenny Wormald, Sarah Jayne Jensen; ***D:*** Steven Jacobson; ***W:*** Karen Bloch; ***C:*** Dino Parks; ***M:*** Laura Karpman. **VIDEO**

The Centerfold Girls **WOOF! 1974 (R)** Microscopic story line involves a deranged man who is determined to kill all the voluptuous young women who have posed nude for a centerfold. **93m/C VHS.** Andrew Prine, Tiffany Bolling, Aldo Ray, Jeremy Slate, Ray Danton, Francine York; ***D:*** John Peyser.

Centipede **WOOF! 2005 (PG-13)** A party of spelunkers encounter, yup, you guessed it, killer centipedes. But the caves are so dark that the actors and centipedes are rarely seen. When the creatures do show up, they look like killer sock-puppets. Too goofy and takes itself too seriously. **90m/C DVD.** George Foster, Larry Casey, Margaret Cash, Trevor Murphy, Matthew Pohlson, Danielle Kirlin, Steve Herd; ***D:*** Gregory Gieras; ***W:*** Gregory Gieras; ***C:*** Ajayan Vincent; ***M:*** Tom Batoy, Franco Tortora. **CABLE**

Central Station *Central Do Brasil* **1998 (R)** Dora (Montenegro) is a bitter, aging woman who makes a living writing letters for the illiterate at a stand located in Rio de Janeiro's central railway station. One of her customers sends letters to her 9-year-old son Josue's (de Oliveira) father, who lives in northern Brazil and who has never seen the boy. When Josue's mother is killed in an accident, Dora reluctantly takes the homeless boy in and reluctantly decides they must locate his father. Their road trip turns out to have some unexpected consequences. Portuguese with subtitles. **110m/C VHS, DVD.** *BR* Fernanda Montenegro, Vinicius de Oliveira, Marilia Pera, Othon Bastos; ***D:*** Walter Salles; ***W:*** Joao Emmanuel Carneiro, Marcos Bernstein; ***C:*** Walter Carvalho; ***M:*** Antonio Pinto, Jaques Morelembaum. British Acad. '98: Foreign Film; Golden Globes '99: Foreign Film; L.A. Film Critics '98: Actress (Montenegro); Natl. Bd. of Review '98: Actress (Montenegro), Foreign Film.

Century **1994 (R)** Ambitious young doctor Paul Reisner (Owen), the son of a prosperous Jewish father (Stephens), gets a position at a London research hospital headed by the charismatic Professor Mandry (Dance). Paul manages to disgrace himself by provoking Mandry and is dismissed but finds out some disturbing information and is determined to discredit his former mentor. Anti-Semitism lurks as does the change from Victorian mores to the challenging dawn of the 20th century. Complex performances are somewhat undermined by the static direction. **112m/C VHS.** *GB* Clive Owen, Charles Dance, Miranda Richardson, Robert Stephens, Joan Hickson, Lena Headey, Neil Stuke; ***D:*** Stephen Poliakoff; ***W:*** Stephen Poliakoff; ***C:*** Witold Stok; ***M:*** Michael Gibbs.

Cerberus 1/2 **2005 (R)** In this nonsensical effort from the SciFi Channel, Attila the Hun makes a pact with Satan that causes whoever holds his sword to be invincible. Surprisingly somehow Attila still dies, and the monster Cerberus becomes his guardian. Fast forward to the modern day when an Asian nutcase with a stockpile of nukes hires unsuspecting Americans to steal Attila's breastplate in order to get the sword because he needs it to threaten the world. **88m/C DVD.** Garret Sato, Bodan Uritescu, Greg Evigan; ***D:*** John Terlesky; ***W:*** Raul Inglis; ***C:*** Viorel Sergovici Jr.; ***M:*** Aldo Shllaku, Neal Acree.

Certain Fury **1985 (R)** Two timid women go on the lam when they are mistaken for escaped prostitutes who shot up a courthouse. The sooner they get caught, the better. **88m/C VHS.** Tatum O'Neal, Irene Cara, Peter Fonda, Nicholas (Nick) Campbell, Moses Gunn; ***D:*** Stephen Gyllenhaal.

A Certain Justice 1/2 **1999** Adam Dalgleish's (Marsden) latest case of murder involves barrister Venetia Aldridge (Downie), who is found bizarrely costumed and stabbed to death in her chambers. It turns out a number of people had a reason to dislike Venetia and prying the truth from a group of lawyers proves to be a challenge even for Scotland Yard's eminent Commander. **180m/C VHS, DVD.** *GB* Roy Marsden, Penny Downie, Ricci Harnett, Flora Montgomery, Frederick Treves, Matthew Marsh, Ian McNeice, Sarah Winman, Richard Huw, Ken Jones, Britta Smith, Miles Anderson, Philip Stone; ***D:*** Ross Devenish; ***W:*** Michael Russell. **TV**

Certain Sacrifice **1980** Nineteen-year-old Madonna expresses herself in her film debut. Seeking revenge on the man who raped her, she murders him in a strange ritualistic manner underneath the Brooklyn Bridge. Poor is the man whose pleasures depend on the permission of another? **60m/C VHS.** Madonna, Jeremy Pattnosh, Charles Kurtz; ***D:*** Stephen Lewicki.

Cesar **1936** This is the third and most bittersweet part of Pagnol's famed trilogy based on his play depicting the lives and loves of the people of Provence, France. Marius returns after a 20-year absence to his beloved Fanny and his now-grown son, Cesariot. The first two parts of the trilogy are "Marius" and "Fanny" and were directed by Alexander Korda and Marc Allegret respectively. In French with English subtitles. **117m/B VHS, DVD.** *FR* Raimu, Pierre Fresnay, Orane Demazis, Charpin, Andre Fouche, Alida Rouffe; ***D:*** Marcel Pagnol; ***W:*** Marcel Pagnol; ***M:*** Vincent Scotto.

Cesar & Rosalie **1972 (PG)** Acclaimed French comedy depicts the love triangle between a beautiful divorcee, her aging live-in companion and a younger man. Engaging portrait of how their relationship evolves over time. In French with English subtitles. **110m/C VHS, DVD.** *FR* Romy Schneider, Yves Montand, Sami Frey, Umberto Orsini; ***D:*** Claude Sautet; ***W:*** Jean-Loup Dabadie, Claude Neron, Claude Sautet; ***C:*** Jean Boffety; ***M:*** Philippe Sarde.

Cesare Borgia **1923** Veidt stars in this bloodthirsty saga as the ruthless son of Pope Alexander VI who'll let nothing come between him and his desires. **83m/B VHS.** *GE* Conrad Veidt; ***D:*** Richard Oswald.

Chain Gang Girls *Kuga no ori: Nami dai-42 zakkyobo* **2008** Yet another women-in-prison film, this one re-using the set from "Female Prisoner Sigma." Nami (Yuka Kosaka) is framed for the murder of her boyfriend's pregnant significant other—even worse, he's a prosecutor with jurisdiction over the prison she's sent to and tells the warden to make life hell for her. The prisoners outnumber the guards 100 to 1, making the odds of a riot higher with each passing day. **75m/C DVD.** *JP* Jeong-min Hwang, Jaeyong Lee, Ju-hyeon Lee, Ju-Bong Gi, Yun-shik Baek; ***D:*** Sasuke Sasuga; ***W:*** Bakuto Ijuin.

Chain Gang Killings **1980** Pair of shackled prisoners, one black, the other white, escape from a truck transporting them to prison. **99m/C VHS.** Ian Yule, Ken Gampu; ***D:*** Clive Harding; ***W:*** Ian Yule; ***C:*** Vincent Cox; ***M:*** Paul Nissen.

Chain Gang Women WOOF! 1972 (R) Sordid violence. Two escaped convicts plunder, rob, and rape until a victim's husband comes looking for revenge. **85m/C VHS, DVD.** Robert Lott, Barbara Mills, Michael Stearns, Linda York, Wes Bishop, Phil Hoover, Chuck Wells; ***D:*** Lee Frost.

Chain Lightning **1950** Bogart stars as a bomber pilot who falls in love with a Red Cross worker (Parker) while fighting in Europe in 1943. They lose touch after the war until Bogie goes to work as a test pilot for the same shady airplane manufacturer (Massey) where Parker works. He is given the chance to test a new plane, which has already cost the life of one of his friends. Bogart has more success, along with rekindling the flames of romance. Average script but the flying sequences are well-done. **94m/B VHS.** Humphrey Bogart, Eleanor Parker, Raymond Massey, Richard Whorf; ***D:*** Stuart Heisler; ***W:*** Liam O'Brien, Vincent B. Evans.

Chain Link **1/2 2008** In this first time effort by director Dylan Reynolds, Anthony (Irvingsen) is a con just released from prison struggling to make ends meet, get a job, and bond with his son without having to resort to his old habits to survive. Not quite as cliche as it sounds, since it doesn't portray the lead as a misunderstood guy. **98m/C DVD.** Mark Irvingsen, Jody Jaress, David Kallaway, Peter Looney, Luciano Rauso, Jim Round, Jim Storm, Yassmin Alers, Lelia Goldoni; ***D:*** Dylan Reynolds; ***W:*** Jim Storm; ***C:*** Matt Gulley.

Chain of Command **1995 (R)** Anti-terrorist agent Merrill Ross (Dudikoff) goes up against hired mercenaries trying to overthrow the government of the oil-rich Republic of Qumir. Then Ross realizes he's being manipulated and it could be by any number of players. **97m/C VHS, DVD.** Todd Curtis, Keren Tishman, Michael Dudikoff, R. Lee Ermey; ***D:*** David Worth; ***W:*** Christopher Applegate, Ben Jonson Handy; ***C:*** Avi Koren; ***M:*** Gregory King.

Chain of Command **2000 (R)** Agent Mike Connelly (Muldoon) must protect the President's (Scheider) briefcase-sized computer that holds the nuclear codes. But when one of Connelly's colleagues betrays them, a nuclear winter could be as close as a madman's command. **96m/C VHS, DVD.** Patrick Muldoon, Roy Scheider, Michael Biehn, Maria Conchita Alonso, Ric Young, William R. Moses, Michael Mantell, Pat Skipper; ***D:*** John Terlesky. **VIDEO**

Chain of Desire **1993** Nightclub inside Manhattan's Chrysler Building is the spot for numerous folk to have lot of meaningless sexual encounters and look at the emptiness of their lives. **107m/C VHS.** Linda Fiorentino, Elias Koteas, Malcolm McDowell, Grace Zabriskie, Tim Guinee, Assumpta Serna, Patrick Bauchau, Seymour Cassel, Kevin Conroy, Angel Aviles, Holly Marie Combs, Jamie Harrold, Dewey Weber, Suzzanne Douglass; ***D:*** Temistocles Lopez; ***W:*** Temistocles Lopez; ***C:*** Nancy Schreiber; ***M:*** Nathan Birnbaum.

Chain of Fools **1/2 2000 (R)** Suicidal barber Zahn comes into possession of a stolen treasure and falls for detective Hayek, who's assigned to the case. Director Traktor is actually a six-person Swedish filmmaking collective. **98m/C DVD.** Steve Zahn, Salma Hayek, Jeff Goldblum, Elijah Wood, David Cross, Tom Wilkinson, Orlando Jones, Kevin Corrigan, David Hyde Pierce, Lara Flynn Boyle, Michael Rapaport, Craig Ferguson, John Cassini; ***D:*** Traktor.

Chain of Souls WOOF! 2000 Cult finds self-fulfillment through murder, luring wannabe actresses to fake auditions. One victim has a sister who worries when she doesn't hear from her sibling so she hightails it to Hollywood to find out what happened. Sound familiar? **105m/C VHS, DVD.** Joe Decker, Eric Chaikin, Denise Gossett, Suzanne Talhouk, Deborah Joy Vinall, Stephanie Kane; ***D:*** Steve Jarvis; ***W:*** Dennis Devine; ***C:*** Dennis Devine; ***M:*** Michael Kelley. **VIDEO**

Chain Reaction **1/2** *Nuclear Run* **1980** When a nuclear scientist is exposed to radiation after an accident at an atomic power plant, he must escape to warn the public of the danger. **87m/C VHS, DVD.** Steve Bisley, Ross Thompson; ***D:*** Ian Barry; ***C:*** Russell Boyd.

Chain Reaction **1/2** *Dead Drop* **1996 (PG-13)** Government/scientific conspiracy chase story finds Chicago lab tech Eddie Kasalivich (Reeves) a member of a research team that's discovered the formula for cheap, pollution-free energy. This doesn't sit well with someone since the team's leader is murdered and the lab destroyed in an explosion. Eddie and scientist Lily Sinclair (Weisz) become prime suspects and are pursued by the feds as they try to find the real culprits. Old pro Freeman, as money man Paul Shannon, is the best reason to watch (as usual). Davis did "The Fugitive," so he knows his tension-filled chases but this is just more same old-same old. **107m/C VHS, DVD, Blu-ray Disc, UMD.** Keanu Reeves, Morgan Freeman, Rachel Weisz, Fred Ward, Brian Cox, Kevin Dunn, Joanna Cassidy, Chelcie Ross, Tzi Ma, Nicholas Rudall, Peter J. D'Noto; ***D:*** Andrew Davis; ***W:*** J.F. Lawton, Michael Bortman; ***C:*** Frank Tidy; ***M:*** Jerry Goldsmith.

Chained **1/2 1934** Crawford and Gable star in this love triangle that somehow never sizzles. Crawford, in love with married businessman Kruger, takes a South American cruise to get away from it all, meets Gable, and of course falls in love. Seems simple enough, but wait! Crawford goes back to New York City and marries Kruger (his wife grants him a divorce) and is miserable. But then Gable shows up, further complicating matters. Choices, choices. Predictable script was not helped by half-hearted performances. **73m/B VHS.** Joan Crawford, Clark Gable, Otto Kruger, Stuart Erwin, Una O'Connor; ***D:*** Clarence Brown; ***C:*** George J. Folsey.

Chained for Life WOOF! 1951 Daisy and Violet Hilton, real life Siamese twins, star in this old-fashioned "freak" show. When a gigolo deserts one twin on their wedding night, the other twin shoots him dead. The twins go on trial and the judge asks the viewer to hand down the verdict. Exploitative and embarrassing to watch. **81m/B VHS, DVD.** Daisy Hilton, Violet Hilton, Allen Jenkins, Sheldon Leonard; ***D:*** Harry Fraser; ***W:*** Nat Tanchuck.

Chained Heat **1983 (R)** Seamy tale of the vicious reality of life for women behind bars. Naive Blair is imprisoned again (after another bad jailhouse gig in "Born Innocent") and has usual assortment of negative experiences with domineering prisoners, degenerative guards, and the creepy warden who maintains a prison bachelor pad equipped with hot tub. Needless to say, she grows up in a hurry. Trashifying, archetypal women-in-prison effort that aims to satisfy full range of low-quality audience demands. Sequel to 1982 "Concrete Jungle." **97m/C VHS, DVD.** *GE* Linda Blair, Stella Stevens, Sybil Danning, Tamara Dobson, Henry Silva, John Vernon, Nita Talbot, Louisa Moritz, Sharon Hughes, Robert Miano, Kendal Kaldwell; ***D:*** Paul Nicholas; ***W:*** Paul Nicholas, Vincent Mongol; ***C:*** Mac Ahlberg; ***M:*** Joseph Conlan. Golden Raspberries '83: Worst Support. Actress (Danning).

Chained Heat 2 **1/2 1992 (R)** Another sordid tale of women behind bars. Nielsen stars as the psychotic stiletto-heeled warden of an infamous prison, complete with sadistic heroin-smuggling guards. This drug ring also deals in prostitution, which results in two imprisoned sisters (innocent, naturally) being separated from one another. One sister is determined to find true justice. **98m/C VHS, DVD.** Brigitte Nielsen, Paul Koslo, Kari Whitman, Kimberley Kates; ***D:*** Lloyd A. Simandl; ***W:*** Chris Hyde.

Chained Heat 3: Hell Mountain **1/2** *Chained Heat 3: The Horror of Hell Mountain; Chained Heat 3* **1998 (R)** Future Earth is a barren wasteland where survivors are forced to work in the mines of overlord Stryker. Each year, young women are taken to the mines on Hell Mountain but this time Kal is determined to save his girlfriend and destroy Stryker. **97m/C VHS, DVD.** Bentley Mitchum, Kate Rodger, Christopher Clarke, Karel Augusta, Noelle Balfour, Jack Scalia, Sarah Douglas; ***D:*** Mike Rohl; ***W:*** Chris Hyde; ***C:*** David Frazee; ***M:*** Peter Allen. **VIDEO**

Chains **1989 (R)** A Chicago gangland feud entraps two couples in its web, and the innocents must take care of themselves when the situation goes from bad to worse. **93m/C VHS.** Jimi Jourdan, Michael Dixon, John L. Eves; ***D:*** Roger J. Barski.

Chains of Gold **1992 (R)** Kind social worker (Travolta) befriends teen who wants to get out of the crack-dealing gang in which he's involved. He infiltrates the gang and risks his life helping the boy get out. **95m/C VHS, DVD.** John Travolta, Marilu Henner, Bernie Casey, Hector Elizondo, Joey Lawrence; ***D:*** Rod Holcomb; ***M:*** Trevor Jones. **CABLE**

The Chair *Hot Seat* **1987 (R)** The penitentiary where an evil superintendent was fried in his own electric chair during an inmate uprising is reopened after two decades. The new warden (Benedict), who used to be a subordinate to the dead man, believes in rigid control of the inmates and locks horns with the big-house shrink (Coco), who on the surface is an intelligent humanitarian, but may have a darker side. This acrimonious dispute takes a back seat, when it appears that the spirit of the late warden has come back to make the inmates pay for his untimely death. **90m/C VHS.** James Coco, Paul Benedict, Stephen Geoffreys, Trini Alvarado, Gary McCleery, Paul Calderon; ***D:*** Waldemar Korzeniowsky; ***C:*** Steven J. Ross.

The Chairman *Most Dangerous Man in the World* **1969 (PG)** Typically bizarre 60s spy thriller involving a scientist unknowingly carrying a bomb in his head trying to steal crop research from China. A relic of cold-war paranoia that will seem odd to modern audiences (its title is a reference to Mao Zedong), it's still interesting to watch Gregory Peck in the lead. **102m/C DVD.** *GB* Gregory Peck, Anne Heywood, Arthur Hill, Alan Dobie, Conrad Yama, Zienia Merton, Eric Young, Francesca Tu, Ori Levy, Burt Kwouk, Keye Luke, Helen Horton, J. Lee Thompson; ***D:*** J. Lee Thompson; ***W:*** J. Lee Thompson, Ben Maddow, Jay Richard Kennedy; ***C:*** John Wilcox, Ted Moore; ***M:*** Jerry Goldsmith.

Chairman of the Board WOOF! 1997 (PG-13) Some studio executive decided to take a bad prop comic named after a vegetable and give him a major motion picture. If this movie accomplishes one thing, it may be the abolition of Friday afternoon 12-martini lunches in Hollywood. Carrot Top plays Edison, a wacky surfer/inventor who befriends an old eccentric man. After the old guy heads for the big wave in the sky, it turns out that he was fabulously wealthy and left his company to Edison. This doesn't sit well with the conniving Bradford (Miller). Courtney Thorne-Smith plays Natalie (although this does not stop Mr. Top from calling her Courtney in one scene) as the standard love interest. Also appearing are Jack Warden, Raquel Welch and M. Emmet Walsh. Why? That's what they're asking their agents. Rent it only if every single video, including the instructional mime section, is already out. **95m/C VHS, DVD.** Carrot Top, Courtney Thorne-Smith, Larry Miller, Raquel Welch, Jack Warden, Estelle Harris, Bill Erwin, M. Emmet Walsh, Jack McGee, Glenn Shadix, Fred Stoller, Mystro Clark, Jack Plotnick; ***D:*** Alex Zamm; ***W:*** Al Septien, Turi Meyer, Alex Zamm; ***C:*** David Lewis; ***M:*** Chris Hajian.

Chalk **1/2 2006 (PG-13)** Dark comedic look at the frustrations endured by a group of high school teachers over a typical school year. Assistant principal Reddell (Haragan) finds administrative duties are even worse than teaching; vain Mr. Stroope (Mass) is determined to be popular with his students so he can be named teacher of the year; tough gym coach Ms. Webb (J. Schremmer) is tired of everyone assuming she's a lesbian; and shy rookie Mr. Lowrey (T. Schremmer) can't manage his unruly students. **84m/C DVD.** Chris Mass, Shannon Haragan, Janelle Schremmer, Troy Schremmer; ***D:*** Mike Akel; ***W:*** Chris Mass, Mike Akel; ***C:*** Steven Schaefer; ***M:*** Chris Jagich.

The Chalk Garden **1964** A woman with a mysterious past takes on the job of governess for an unruly 14-year-old girl, with unforseen consequences. An excellent adaptation of the Enid Bagnold play although not as suspenseful as the stage production. **106m/C VHS.** *GB* Deborah Kerr, Hayley Mills, Edith Evans, John Mills, Elizabeth Sellars, Felix Aylmer; ***D:*** Ronald Neame; ***W:*** John Michael Hayes; ***M:*** Malcolm Arnold. Natl. Bd. of Review '64: Support. Actress (Evans).

The Challenge **1938** Story of the courageous party of explorers who conquered the Matterhorn. Incredible avalanche scenes. **77m/B VHS.** *GB* Luis Trenker, Robert Douglas, Joan Gardner, Mary Clare, Frank Birch, Geoffrey Wardwell, Lyonel (Lionel) Watts, Fred Groves, Lawrence (Laurence) Baskcomb, Ralph Truman; ***D:*** Milton Rosmer, Luis Trenker; ***W:*** Milton Rosmer, Patrick Kirwan; ***C:*** Albert Benitz, Georges Perinal; ***M:*** Allan Gray, Muir Mathieson.

Challenge WOOF! 1974 (PG) When his entire family is killed, dad decides to seek revenge with his shotgun. Very bloody and violent and very nearly plotless. **90m/C VHS.** Earl Owensby, William T. Hicks, Katheryn Thompson, Johnny Popwell; ***D:*** Martin Beck.

The Challenge **1/2 1982 (R)** A contemporary action spectacle which combines modern swordplay with the mysticism and fantasy of ancient Samurai legends. **108m/C VHS.** Scott Glenn, Toshiro Mifune; ***D:*** John Frankenheimer; ***W:*** John Sayles, Richard Maxwell; ***M:*** Jerry Goldsmith.

The Challenge *Kampfansage* **2005** In the year 2050 economic devastation and natural disasters have combined to nearly wipe out mankind, now ruled by feuding warlords. A street urchin named Jonas (Landwehr) is one of the last surviving heirs to an ancient form of martial arts, which the local warlord has decided to eradicate as being a danger to his control over the area. Predictable revenge plot ensues. **103m/C DVD.** *GE* Mathis Landwehr, Volkram Zschiesche, Christian Monz, Esther Schweins, Bela B. Felsenheimer, Ron Matz, The Anh Ngo, Tippy Walker, Sinta Weisz, Wolfgang Stegemann; ***D:*** Johannes Jaeger; ***W:*** Johannes Jaeger; ***C:*** Marcus Stotz; ***M:*** Marco Jovic, Alex Pfeffer.

A Challenge for Robin Hood **1/2 1968** Innocuous and poorly done children's adventure tale about the daring 12th-century nobleman-turned-bandit, Robin Hood (Ingham), and his usual gang in Sherwood Forest. This time Robin has been framed for murder by his evil cousin, Roger (Blythe), and must prove his innocence. **96m/C VHS.** *GB* Barrie Ingham, Peter Blythe, James Hayter, John Arnatt, Leon Greene, Gay Hamilton; ***D:*** C.M. Pennington-Richards; ***W:*** Peter Bryan; ***C:*** Arthur Grant; ***M:*** Gary Hughes.

Challenge of a Lifetime **1/2 1985** Marshall stars as a divorcee whose dream is to compete in the Hawaiian Ironman Triathlon. Cult favorite; Woronov has a substantial supporting role. **100m/C VHS.** Penny Marshall, Richard Gilliland, Jonathan Silverman, Mary Woronov, Paul Gleason, Mark Spitz, Cathy Rigby; ***D:*** Russ Mayberry.

Challenge of McKenna **1970** Run-of-the-prairie horse opera has drifter Ireland stumble upon danger and intrigue when he enters a mysterious town. **90m/C VHS.** *IT SP* Annabella Incontrera, Roberto Camardiel, John Ireland, Robert Woods; ***D:*** Leon Klimovsky; ***W:*** Leon Klimovsky; ***C:*** Francisco Sanchez; ***M:*** Francesco De Masi.

Challenge of the Gladiator *Il Gladiatore che Sfido l'Impero* **1965** Typically bad dubbing and nonsensical plot. Evil Roman senator Quintilius (Serato) journeys to Thrace in search of a legendary treasure. He has ex-gladiator Terenzius (Barnes) posing as the Emperor Nero so the locals won't be any trouble, but that plan backfires when word comes that the real Nero has died back in Rome. Local governor Metellus (Lulli) is peeved and joins with rebellious Spartacus (Lupus using the wonderful nom de film "Rock Stevens") to defeat the traitors. **90m/C DVD.** *IT* Peter Lupus, Massimo Serato, Pierro Lulli, Walter Barnes, Livio Lorenzon, Maria Fie; ***D:*** Domenico Paolella; ***W:*** Domenico Paolella; ***C:*** Raffaele Masciocchi; ***M:*** Giuseppe Piccillo.

Challenge of the Masters **1989** A young Kung-Fu artist wins a new tutor in a contest. Soon he's fighting for a friend to protect his family's honor. **97m/C VHS, DVD.** Liu Chia Hui, Liu Chia-Yung, Chen Kuan-Tai, Chiang Yang; ***D:*** Liu Chia-Liang.

Challenge To Be Free *Mad Trapper of the Yukon* **1976 (G)** Action adventure geared toward a young audience depicting the struggles of a man being pursued by 12 men and 100 dogs across a thousand miles of frozen wilderness. The last film directed by Garnett, who has a cameo as Marshal McGee. Produced in 1972, the release wasn't until 1976. **90m/C VHS, DVD.** Mike Mazurki, Jimmy Kane; ***Cameos:*** Tay Garnett; ***D:*** Tay Garnett.

Challenge to Lassie 1/2 **1949 (G)** When Lassie's Scottish master dies, the faithful pup remains at his grave. An unsympathetic policeman orders Lassie to leave the premises, inspiring a debate among the townsfolk as to the dog's fate. Based on a true story (although the original hero was a Skye Terrier); remade as "Greyfriar's Bobby." **76m/C VHS.** Edmund Gwenn, Donald Crisp, Geraldine Brooks, Reginald Owen, Alan Webb, Henry Stephenson, Alan Napier, Sara Allgood; ***D:*** Richard Thorpe; ***M:*** Andre Previn.

Challenge to White Fang 1/2 **1986 (PG)** A courageous dog prevents a scheming businessman from taking over an old man's gold mine. **89m/C VHS.** Harry Carey Jr., Franco Nero; ***D:*** Lucio Fulci.

The Challengers 1/2 **1989** Young Mackie wants to join local rock band The Challengers, only to discover their main rule is no girls. So Mackie disguises herself as her male cousin Mac—getting ever more confused as she tries to juggle her dual identities. Then she gets found out. **97m/C VHS.** Gema Zamprogna, Gwynyth Walsh, Eric Christmas, Eric Till; ***W:*** Clive Endersby.

The Chamber **1996 (R)** Dull retelling of yet another John Grisham legal thriller fails to engross. White supremacist Sam Cahall (Hackman) is on Mississippi's death row for killing two Jewish boys in a 1967 bombing. Young Chicago lawyer Adam Hall (O'Donnell), looking to find out more about his family's odious past, volunteers to work on his grandfather's case and win a stay of execution. Sam's an unrepentent racist but there's some question about whether he was the only culprit. Hackman and Dunaway (as his alcoholic daughter) are their usual professional selves while the charming O'Donnell seems out of his depth. Co-screenwriter Robinson used the pen name Chris Reese. **113m/C VHS, DVD.** Gene Hackman, Chris O'Donnell, Faye Dunaway, Lela Rochon, Robert Prosky, Raymond J. Barry, Bo Jackson, David Marshall Grant, Millie Perkins; ***D:*** James Foley; ***W:*** Phil Alden Robinson, William Goldman; ***C:*** Ian Baker; ***M:*** Carter Burwell.

Chamber of Horrors 1/2 *The Door with Seven Locks* **1940** A family is brought together at an English castle to claim a fortune left by an aristocrat. However, there's a catch—seven keys may open the vault with the fortune, or leave the key turner dead. Based on the work by Edgar Wallace. **80m/B VHS, DVD.** *GB* Leslie Banks, Lilli Palmer; ***D:*** Norman Lee.

The Chambermaid on the Titanic *La Femme de Chambre du Titanic; The Chambermaid* **1997** French foundry worker Horty (Martinez) wins a strongman contest and his prize is a trip to Southampton to see the launch of the Titanic. There he (platonically) shares a hotel room with maid Maria (Sanchez-Gijon), who says she has a job aboard the ship. After returning home and learning about the Titanic's sinking, Horty regales his friends with stories of his night with Maria—gradually beginning to believe his own lies about his passionate escapade. Based on the novel by Didier Decoin. French with subtitles. **96m/C VHS.** *FR SP* Olivier Martinez, Aitana Sanchez-Gijon, Romane Bohringer, Didier Bezace, Aldo Maccione; ***D:*** Bigas Luna; ***W:*** Bigas Luna, Cuca Canals; ***C:*** Patrick Blossier; ***M:*** Alberto Iglesias.

Chameleon **1995 (R)** Undercover agent, and master of disguise, Willie Serling (LaPaglia), had his wife and daughter murdered by drug smuggler Alberto Cortese (Mandola) and he naturally wants revenge. Willie poses as a bank auditor to learn if Cortese is behind a money-laundering scheme and things get increasingly complex. Talky thriller with lots of cliches. **108m/C VHS.** Anthony LaPaglia, Kevin Pollak, Melora Hardin, Wayne Knight, Tony Mandola, Derek McGrath, Andy Romano, Robin Thomas, Richard Brooks; ***D:*** Michael Pavone; ***W:*** Michael Pavone; ***C:*** Ross Berryman; ***M:*** John Debney.

Chameleon **1998 (R)** Phillips is a genetically engineered hit woman who can literally blend into any background (hence the title). Her evil creator/employers send her to dispose of a ragtag band of malcontent scientists whose leader has invented a dangerous microchip. But she develops unexpected maternal feelings towards the now-orphaned young son (Lloyd) of the group's leader and vows to protect him. **90m/C VHS.** Bobbie Phillips, Eric Lloyd, Philip Casnoff; ***D:*** Stuart Cooper. **TV**

Chameleon 2: Death Match **1999** Kam (Phillips), the genetically engineered ultimate hunter, returns and her assignment is to infiltrate an exclusive nightclub where a terrorist is holding a bunch of execs hostage. **87m/C VHS.** Bobbie Phillips, Casey Siemaszko, Tasha Smith, Kara Zediker, Simon Westaway, Mark Lee; ***D:*** Russell King; ***W:*** Bennett Cohen; ***C:*** David Connell; ***M:*** Roger Neill. **TV**

Chameleon 3: Dark Angel **2000** Genetically engineered Kam (Phillips), who's working for the International Bureau of Investigation, is called upon to protect a sullen, suspicious young woman who knows how to control an energy matter device that was stolen from a government facility. But Kam's assignment is threatened by her evil counterpart—her own genetically engineered brother, Kane (Kuzelicki). **87m/C VHS.** Bobbie Phillips, Suzi Dougherty, Alex Kuzelicki, Teal Redmann, Doug Penty; ***D:*** John Lafia; ***W:*** Ronnie Christensen; ***C:*** David Foreman; ***M:*** Joel Goldsmith. **TV**

Chameleon Street **1989 (R)** Entertaining fact-based account of William Douglas Street, a Detroit man who successfully impersonated, among others, a Time magazine reporter and a surgeon until he was caught and sent to prison. He escaped and went to Yale, faked his identity as a student, and then returned to Michigan to impersonate a lawyer for the Detroit Human Rights Commission. Harris wrote and directed this insightful look into the man who fooled many people, including the mayor of Detroit, Coleman A. Young, who appears briefly as himself. **95m/C VHS.** Wendell B. Harris Jr., Angela Leslie, Amina Fakir, Paula McGee, Mano Breckenridge, David Kiley, Anthony Ennis; ***Cameos:*** Coleman A. Young; ***D:*** Wendell B. Harris Jr.; ***W:*** Wendell B. Harris Jr.; ***C:*** Daniel S. Noga; ***M:*** Peter S. Moore. Sundance '90: Grand Jury Prize.

The Champ **1932** A washed up boxer dreams of making a comeback and receives support from no one but his devoted son. Minor classic most notorious for jerking the tears and soiling the hankies, this was the first of three Beery/Cooper screen teamings. **87m/B VHS, DVD.** Wallace Beery, Jackie Cooper, Irene Rich, Roscoe Ates, Edward Brophy, Hale Hamilton, Jesse Scott, Marcia Mae Jones; ***D:*** King Vidor; ***W:*** Frances Marion. Oscars '32: Actor (Beery), Story.

The Champ 1/2 **1979 (PG)** An ex-fighter with a weakness for gambling and drinking is forced to return to the ring in an attempt to keep custody of his son. Excessive sentiment may cause cringing. Remake of the 1931 classic. **121m/C VHS, DVD.** Jon Voight, Faye Dunaway, Rick Schroder, Jack Warden, Arthur Hill, Strother Martin, Joan Blondell, Elisha Cook Jr.; ***D:*** Franco Zeffirelli; ***C:*** Fred W. Koenekamp; ***M:*** Dave Grusin.

Champagne **1928** A socialite's father fakes bankruptcy to teach his irresponsible daughter a lesson. Early, silent endeavor from Hitchcock is brilliantly photographed. **93m/B VHS, DVD.** *GB* Betty Balfour, Gordon Harker, Ferdinand von Alten, Clifford Heatherley, Jack Trevor; ***D:*** Alfred Hitchcock; ***W:*** Alfred Hitchcock.

Champagne for Breakfast **1935 (R)** Sex comedy follows the fun-filled adventures of "Champagne," a free-spirited beauty living life to the fullest. **69m/B VHS.** Mary Carlisle, Hardie Albright, Joan Marsh, Lila Lee, Sidney Toler, Bradley Page, Emerson Treacy; ***D:*** Melville Brown.

Champagne for Caesar **1950** The laughs keep coming in this comedy about a self-proclaimed genius-on-every-subject who goes on a TV quiz show and proceeds to win everything in sight. The program's sponsor, in desperation, hires a femme fatale to distract the contestant before the final program. Wonderful spoof of the game-show industry. **99m/B VHS, DVD.** Ronald Colman, Celeste Holm, Vincent Price, Art Linkletter, Barbara Britton; ***D:*** Richard Whorf.

Champion 1/2 **1949** An ambitious prizefighter alienates the people around him as he desperately fights his way to the top. When he finally reaches his goal, he is forced to question the cost of his success. From a story by Ring Lardner. Certainly one of the best films ever made about boxing, with less sentiment than "Rocky" but concerned with sociological correctness. **99m/B VHS, DVD.** Kirk Douglas, Arthur Kennedy, Marilyn Maxwell, Ruth Roman, Lola Albright, Paul Stewart; ***D:*** Mark Robson; ***W:*** Carl Foreman; ***C:*** Franz Planer; ***M:*** Dimitri Tiomkin. Oscars '49: Film Editing.

Champions **1984** Moving but cliched story of Bob Champion, a leading jockey who overcame cancer to win England's Grand National Steeplechase. A true story, no less. **113m/C VHS, DVD.** *GB* John Hurt, Gregory Jones, Mick Dillon, Ann Bell, Jan Francis, Peter Barkworth, Edward Woodward, Ben Johnson, Kirstie Alley, Alison Steadman; ***D:*** John Irvin; ***W:*** Evan Jones; ***M:*** Carl Davis.

Chan Is Missing **1982** Two cab drivers try to find the man who stole their life savings. Wry, low-budget comedy filmed in San Francisco's Chinatown was an art-house smash. The first full-length American film produced exclusively by an Asian-American cast and crew. **80m/B VHS, DVD.** Wood Moy, Marc Hayashi, Laureen Chew, Judy Mihei, Peter Wang, Presco Tabios, Frankie Allarcon, Virginia Cerenio, Roy Chan, George Woo, Emily Yamasaki, Ellen Yeung; ***D:*** Wayne Wang; ***W:*** Wayne Wang, Terrel Seltzer, Isaac Cronin; ***C:*** Michael G. Chin; ***M:*** Robert Kikuchi-Yngojo. Natl. Film Reg. '95.

Chance 1/2 **1989** With over $1 million in diamonds missing, Haggerty and Jacobs throw out all the stops to recover them in this action thriller. **90m/C VHS, DVD.** Dan Haggerty, Lawrence-Hilton Jacobs, Addison Randall, Roger Rudd, Charles Gries, Pamela Dixon; ***D:*** Addison Randall, Charles Kanganis.

Chances Are **1989 (PG)** After her loving husband dies in a chance accident, a pregnant woman remains unmarried, keeping her husband's best friend as her only close male companion. Years later, her now teenage daughter brings a friend home for dinner, but due to an error in heaven, the young man begins to realize that this may not be the first time he and this family have met. A wonderful love-story hampered only minimally by the unbelievable plot. **108m/C VHS, DVD.** Cybill Shepherd, Robert Downey Jr., Ryan O'Neal, Mary Stuart Masterson, Josef Sommer, Christopher McDonald, Joe Grifasi, James Noble, Susan Ruttan, Fran Ryan; ***D:*** Emile Ardolino; ***W:*** Randy Howze, Perry Howze; ***C:*** William A. Fraker; ***M:*** Maurice Jarre.

Chandni Chowk to China 1/2 **2009 (PG-13)** This comedic mishmash of genres probably won't convert anyone not already of fan of extended Bollywood productions. Simple Delhi cook Sidhu works in the Chandni Chowk market. He is mistaken for the reincarnation of a Chinese warrior, who's needed to defeat a local bad guy terrorizing peasants in the countryside. Sidhu's really unclear about what's going on so he keeps reassuring himself by talking to a potato that he thinks bears the likeness of heroic Lord Ganesh. There's also singing, dancing, and lots of martial arts action but none of it makes much sense. Hindi and Chinese with subtitles. **155m/C DVD.** *IN* Gordon (Chia Hui) Liu, Roger Yuan, Akshay Kumar, Deepika Padukone, Mithun Chakraborty, Ranvir Shorey; ***D:*** Nikhil Advani; ***W:*** Shridhar Raghavan; ***C:*** Himman Dhamija.

Chandu on the Magic Island **1934** Chandu the Magician takes his powers of the occult to the mysterious lost island of Lemuri to battle the evil cult of Ubasti. Sequel to "Chandu the Magician" and just as campy. **67m/B VHS, DVD.** Bela Lugosi, Maria Alba, Clara Kimball Young; ***D:*** Ray Taylor.

Chandu the Magician **1932** Bad guy searches desperately for the secret of a powerful death ray so he can (surprise!) destroy civilization. Not well received in its day, but makes for great high-camp fun now. One of Lugosi's most melodramatic performances. **70m/B VHS.** Edmund Lowe, Bela Lugosi, Irene Ware, Henry B. Walthall; ***D:*** William Cameron Menzies, Marcel Varnel; ***C:*** James Wong Howe.

Chanel Solitaire **1981 (R)** Uninspiring biography follows the fabulous (simply fabulous) career of dress designer Gabrielle "Coco" Chanel. Ah, go sew something. **124m/C VHS.** Marie-France Pisier, Rutger Hauer, Timothy Dalton, Karen Black, Brigitte Fossey; ***D:*** George Kaczender.

Chang: A Drama of the Wilderness 1/2 **1927** A farmer and his family has settled a small patch of ground on the edge of the jungle and must struggle for survival against numerous wild animals. The climatic elephant stampede is still thrilling. Shot on location in Siam. **67m/B VHS, DVD.** ***D:*** Merian C. Cooper, Ernest B. Schoedsack; ***W:*** Merian C. Cooper, Ernest B. Schoedsack; ***C:*** Ernest B. Schoedsack.

Change My Life *Change Moi Ma Vie* **2001** Nina is a middle-aged actress who has long been unemployed. In despair, she takes an overdose of tranquilizers and collapses on a Paris street, where she is found by a passerby. Algerian immigrant Sami saves Nina and she is determined to find and thank him. When she does, Nina discovers Sami working as a transvestite prostitute and the two lonely souls vow to support each other and make changes in their lives. French with subtitles. **101m/C DVD.** *FR* Fanny Ardant, Roschdy Zem, Fanny Cottencon, Sami Bouajila, Olivier Cruveiller; ***D:*** Liria Begeja; ***W:*** Jerome Beaujour, Francois Olivier Rousseau, Liria Begeja; ***C:*** Laurent Machuel.

Change of Habit **1969 (G)** Three novitiates undertake to learn about the world before becoming full-fledged nuns. While working at a ghetto clinic a young doctor forms a strong, affectionate relationship with one of them. Presley's last feature film. ♫Change of Habit; Let Us Pray; Rubberneckin'. **93m/C VHS, DVD.** Elvis Presley, Mary Tyler Moore, Barbara McNair, Ed Asner, Ruth McDevitt, Regis Toomey, Jane Elliot, Leora Dana, Robert Emhardt, Richard Carlson, William (Bill) Elliott; ***D:*** William A. Graham; ***W:*** Eric Bercovici, John Joseph; ***C:*** Russell Metty; ***M:*** Billy Goldenberg.

Change of Heart 1/2 **1998** Smart is always good in wronged woman roles and she's got a doozy in this weepie. Elaine Marshall (Smart) thinks she and husband Jim (Terry) are doing okay marriage-wise. They've been together 20 years, have a couple of kids, two good careers, and apparent happiness. Then Elaine realizes Jim's having an affair. The real shocker for Elaine comes when she finds out her husband's lover is another man. **?m/C VHS.** Jean Smart, John Terry, Gretchen Corbett, Phillip Geoffrey Hough, Shawna Waldron, Dorian Harewood; ***D:*** Arvin Brown; ***W:*** Aaron Mendelsohn; ***C:*** John Campbell; ***M:*** Patrick Williams. **CABLE**

A Change of Place 1/2 **1994** Identical twins Kate and Kim (Roth) lead completely different lives. Kate is known as fashion model Domenique in Paris wile Kim is a shy grad student. Kate is also a drunk and when Kim checks her into rehab, Kate pleads with her sister to take her place at the fashion house. Too bad Kate didn't warn Kim that she is suspected of stealing designs by Philippe (Springfield). Can Kim quietly clear her sister's name or should she reveal the truth to the man she's falling in love with? From the Harlequin Romance Series; adapted from the Tracy Sinclair novel. **91m/C DVD.** *CA* Andrea Roth, Rick Springfield, Stephanie Beacham, Geordie Johnson, Ian Richardson; ***D:*** Donna Deitch; ***W:*** Jim Henshaw, Rosemary Anne Sissons; ***C:*** Nyika Jancso; ***M:*** Brent Barkman, Carl Lennox. **TV**

A Change of Seasons 🦴🦴 **1980 (R)** One of them so-called sophisticated comedies that look at the contemporary relationships and values of middle-class, middle-aged people who should know better. The wife of a college professor learns of her husband's affair with a seductive student and decides to have a fling with a younger man. The situation reaches absurdity when the couples decide to vacation together. **102m/C VHS, DVD.** Shirley MacLaine, Bo Derek, Anthony Hopkins, Michael Brandon, Mary Beth Hurt; ***D:*** Richard Lang; ***W:*** Erich Segal; ***M:*** Henry Mancini.

The Changeling 🦴🦴 ½ **1980 (R)** A music teacher moves into an old house and discovers that a young boy's ghostly spirit is his housemate. The ghost wants revenge against the being that replaced him upon his death. Scary ghost story with some less than logical leaps of script. **114m/C VHS, DVD.** *CA* George C. Scott, Trish Van Devere, John Russell, Melvyn Douglas, Jean Marsh, John Colicos, Barry Morse, Roberta Maxwell, James B. Douglas; ***D:*** Peter Medak; ***W:*** William Gray, Diana Maddox; ***C:*** John Coquillon. Genie '80: Film.

Changeling 🦴🦴🦴 ½ **2008 (R)** In 1928, single mother Christine Collins (Jolie) comes home from work to discover her 10-year-old son Walter missing. When the LAPD returns a boy to her months later, Christine insists that he's not her son—and she's not the only one to say so, as political and police corruption and cover-ups lead down some very disturbing paths. Eastwood creates another superb film in yet another genre (horror for adults), showcasing an Oscar-worthy performance by Jolie, who flaunts her acting chops more than her beauty, while Malkovich is typically intense and captivating, further elevating this harrowing story to the cinematic stratosphere. Loosely based on the crimes known as the "Wineville Chicken Murders." **141m/C DVD.** *US* Angelina Jolie, John Malkovich, Jeffrey Donovan, Michael Kelly, Colm Feore, Jason Butler Harner, Eddie Alderson, Amy Ryan, Denis O'Hare, Peter Gerety, Gattlin Griffith; ***D:*** Clint Eastwood; ***W:*** J. Michael Straczynski; ***C:*** Tom Stern; ***M:*** Clint Eastwood.

Changes 🦴 **1969 (PG)** A young man leaves home and thumbs across the California coast in order to find himself. On the road again. **103m/C VHS.** Kent Lane, Michele Carey, Jack Albertson, Marcia Strassman, Tony Giorgio; ***D:*** Hall Bartlett.

Changing Habits 🦴 ½ **1996 (R)** Starving artist Soosh (Kelly) moves into a nunnery, in exchange for doing chores, in order to save money. She's so broke, she's taken to stealing art supplies, but salesman Felix (Walsh) is more interested in romancing Soosh than turning her in. Dull, dull, dull, and a waste of a talented cast. **92m/C VHS, DVD.** Moira Kelly, Christopher Lloyd, Teri Garr, Shelley Duvall, Dylan Walsh, Marissa Ribisi, Frances Bay, Bob Gunton, Anne Haney, Eileen Brennan; ***D:*** Lynn Roth; ***W:*** Scott Davis Jones; ***C:*** Mike Mayers; ***M:*** David McHugh.

Changing Lanes 🦴🦴🦴 **2002 (R)** A fender-bender on the FDR pits two harried New Yorkers in an escalating battle of revenge. Banek (Affleck), a privileged Wall Street lawyer, and Gipson (Jackson), a recovering-alcoholic insurance man, both need to get to court on time. Banek to file documents crucial to his firm's success, and Gipson, to prove he's fit to retain joint custody of his two kids. Because of the accident, neither gets quite what he wants. When Gipson finds that he has the the vital document, after having been stranded by Banek (and subsequently late to the custody hearing), he begins the battle. Throughout the back and forth, the plot (and many of its excesses), gives way to a fully realized character study and thoughtful pondering of motivations, corruption, and desperation, powered by dialogue not usually seen in a "revenge" flick. Michell deftly brings out the best in every member of a talented cast. **98m/C VHS, DVD.** *US* Ben Affleck, Samuel L. Jackson, Toni Collette, Sydney Pollack, William Hurt, Amanda Peet, Richard Jenkins, Kim Staunton, John Benjamin Hickey, Jennifer (Jennie) Dundas Lowe, Dylan Baker, Matt Malloy, Pamela Hart; ***D:*** Roger Michell; ***W:*** Michael Tolkin, Chap Taylor; ***C:*** Salvatore Totino; ***M:*** David Arnold.

Changing Times 🦴🦴 *Les Temps Qui Changent* **2004** Sucessful engineer Antoine (Depardieu) has spent the last three decades pining for Cecile (Deneuve), the love of his life, who left France for Morocco more than 30 years ago, and has since moved on with her life. Antoine volunteers for a job in Tangiers and promptly tracks down Cecile (and her much younger doctor-husband) in order to win her back, as he informs them both. Layers of heady complications follow, including the appearance of Cecile's son, who drops by with his girlfriend despite his being gay, Cecile's own deteriorating marriage, and cultural clashes between French and Moroccan characters and their values. Pic is a reunion of French legends Deneuve, Depardieu and director Andre Techine and will appeal to Francophiles and probably few others. **98m/C DVD.** *FR* Catherine Deneuve, Gerard Depardieu, Gilbert Melki, Malik Zidi, Lubna Azabal, Tanya Lopert, Nabila Baraka, Idir Elomri, Nadem Rachati, Jabir Elomri; ***D:*** Andre Techine; ***W:*** Andre Techine, Pascal Bonitzer, Laurent Guyot; ***C:*** Julien Hirsch; ***M:*** Juliette Garrigues.

The Channeler 🦴 **1989** The traditional dopey students probe an old Colorado mine and encounter black-robed, demon whazzits. A spunky cast and nice scenery didn't stop the Hound from switching channels on this one. **90m/C VHS.** Dan Haggerty, Richard Harrison, Jay Richardson, David Homb, Oliver Darrow, Robin Sims, Charles Solomon; ***D:*** Grant Austin Waldman.

The Chant of Jimmie Blacksmith 🦴🦴🦴 **1978 (R)** Intense, ultrviolent true story set in 19th century Australia follows aborigine Jimmie as he is brutalized by white civilization and reponds in kind. Shocking violence perpetrated by and to Jimmie is not for the faint of heart, and is not softened in the least by the superb performances by the excellent cast. **120m/C VHS, DVD.** *AU* Tommy (Tom E.) Lewis, Bryan Brown, Ray Barrett, Elizabeth (Liz) Alexander, Jack Thompson, Peter Carroll, Liddy Clark, Ruth Cracknell, Arthur Dignam, Ian Gilmour, John Jarratt, Ray Meagher, Kevin Miles, Robyn Nevin, Angela Punch McGregor, Peter Sumner; ***D:*** Fred Schepisi; ***W:*** Fred Schepisi; ***C:*** Ian Baker; ***M:*** Bruce Smeaton.

Chantilly Lace 🦴🦴 ½ **1993 (R)** Ensemble cast tries hard in this story of modern American women and friendship in the '90s. Val (Eikenberry) gathers a group of seven close friends at her new house in Sundance. Turns out trying to "have it all" is causing some emotional crises to surface, which are explored over the course of a year. Actresses improvised their dialogue from basic character information. Lots of weeping and bonding. **102m/C VHS.** Jill Eikenberry, Ally Sheedy, Helen Slater, Lindsay Crouse, JoBeth Williams, Martha Plimpton, Talia Shire; ***D:*** Linda Yellen; ***W:*** Linda Yellen, Rosanne Ehrlich; ***M:*** Patrick Seymour. **CABLE**

Chaos 🦴🦴 **2001** Workaholic Parisian businessman Paul (Lindon) and his wife Helene (Frot) are driving to dinner when a frantic young Algerian immigrant, Noemie (Brakni), begs them to let her in as thugs grab and beat her before their eyes. Paul refuses to get involved and abandons the girl, which sets in motion a domestic crisis for Helene. Guilt-ridden and disgusted by her husband's indifference, Helene tracks the severly-injured Noemie to a hospital and abandons her family to assume responsibility for Noemie and her rehabilitation, which includes protecting her from her abusers. French with subtitles. **109m/C VHS, DVD.** *FR* Catherine Frot, Vincent Lindon, Rachida Brakni, Line Renaud, Wojciech Pszoniak, Aurelien Wilk; ***D:*** Coline Serreau; ***W:*** Coline Serreau; ***C:*** Jean-Francois Robin; ***M:*** Ludovic Navarre.

Chaos WOOF! **2005 (NC-17)** Repulsive, exploitative horror flick features a group of psycho-sickos, led by the Manson-like Chaos (Gage), who torture and finally murder two female college students. Atrocious in every imaginable way. **78m/C DVD.** *US* Kevin Gage, Sage Stallone, Kelly K. C. Quann, Stephen Wozniak; ***D:*** David DeFalco; ***W:*** David DeFalco; ***C:*** Brandon Trost.

Chaos & Cadavers 🦴🦴 ½ **2003** Newlyweds Edward (Moran) and Samantha (Hawes) have their honeymoon at a remote hotel disrupted by rowdy conventioneers attending an undertakers' conference. But when the head of the funeral director's association is found dead under suspicious circumstances, they decide to find out whodunit. **90m/C DVD.** *GB* Nick Moran, Keeley Hawes, Steve Huison, John Bennett, Ian McNeice, Hugh Fraser, Rick Mayall; ***D:*** Niklaus Hilber; ***W:*** Niklaus Hilber, Drew Bird; ***C:*** Tony Imi; ***M:*** Warren Bennett.

The Chaos Experiment 🦴 ½ *The Steam Experiment* **2009 (R)** Crazy ex-professor James Pettis (Kilmer) wants to prove his theory of the effects of global warming so he traps six people in a Tampa bathhouse. He vows to turn up the heat on his hostages until his theories get published on the front page of the newspaper. This isn't torture porn so the steambath stuff quickly gets dull and it may be all a delusion on Pettis' part, which is what Detective Mancini (Assante) has to figure out. **96m/C DVD.** Val Kilmer, Armand Assante, Eric Roberts, Patrick Muldoon, Megan Brown, Eve Mauro, Quinn Duffy, Cordelia Reynolds; ***D:*** Philippe Martinez; ***W:*** Robert Malkani; ***C:*** Erik Curtis; ***M:*** Don MacDonald. **VIDEO**

Chaos Factor 🦴🦴 **2000 (R)** Jack Poynt (Sabato Jr.) is an Army Intelligence officer working in Cambodia. He discovers evidence linking the death of American soldiers to high-ranking officials and becomes the target of a deadly coverup by the Defense Department. **102m/C VHS, DVD.** Antonio Sabato Jr., Fred Ward, Kelly Rutherford, Sean Kanan, R. Lee Ermey; ***D:*** Terry Cunningham. **VIDEO**

Chaos Theory 🦴🦴 **2008 (PG-13)** Motivational speaker and efficiency expert Frank Allen (Reynolds) has driven wife Susan (Mortimer) nuts with their micromanaged lifestyle. (Frank really lives what he preaches.) Susan resets their clocks, making Frank late for a conference and throwing his organized world into chaos, which he decides to embrace when he can't seem to get it back under control. But his new attitude leads to Frank and Susan splitting up and just causing a whole different set of problems. Reynolds is likeable (Mortimer less so) but it's a rather odd rom-com entry until it heads into happy ending territory. **86m/C DVD.** *US* Ryan Reynolds, Emily Mortimer, Stuart Townsend, Sarah Chalke, Mike Erwin, Constance Zimmer, Elisabeth Harnois, Damon, Jocelyne Loewen; ***D:*** Marcos Siega; ***W:*** Daniel Taplitz; ***C:*** Ramsay Nickell; ***M:*** Gilad Benamram.

Chapayev 🦴🦴🦴 **1934** Striking propagandist drama dealing with the exploits of a legendary Red Army commander during the 1919 battle with the White Russians. Stunning, and carefully choreographed, battle scenes. Adapted from a biographical novel by Dmitri Furmanov. In Russian with English subtitles. **101m/B VHS.** *RU* Boris Babochkin, Leonid Kmit, Boris Chirkov, Varvara Myasnikova, Illarian Pevzov, Stephan Shkurat, Boris Blinov, Vyacheslav Volkov, Nikolai Simonov, Georgi Zhzhenov; ***D:*** Sergei Vassiliev, Georgy Vassiliev; ***W:*** Sergei Vassiliev, Georgy Vassiliev; ***C:*** Aleksander Sigayev, Alexander Xenofontov; ***M:*** Gavriil Popov.

Chaplin 🦴🦴🦴 **1992 (PG-13)** The life and career of "The Little Tramp" is chronicled by director Attenborough and brilliantly portrayed by Downey, Jr, as Chaplin. A flashback format traces his life from its poverty-stricken Dickensian origins in the London slums through his directing and acting career, to his honorary Oscar in 1972. Slow-moving at parts, but captures Chaplin's devotion to his art and also his penchant towards jailbait. In a clever casting choice, Chaplin's own daughter from his fourth marriage to Oona O'Neill, Geraldine Chaplin, plays her own grandmother who goes mad. **135m/C VHS, DVD.** *GB* Robert Downey Jr., Dan Aykroyd, Geraldine Chaplin, Kevin Dunn, Anthony Hopkins, Milla Jovovich, Moira Kelly, Kevin Kline, Diane Lane, Penelope Ann Miller, Paul Rhys, John Thaw, Marisa Tomei, Nancy Travis, James Woods, David Duchovny, Deborah Maria Moore, Bill Paterson, John Standing, Robert Stephens, Peter Crook; ***D:*** Richard Attenborough; ***W:*** Bryan Forbes, William Boyd, William Goldman; ***C:*** Sven Nykvist; ***M:*** John Barry. British Acad. '92: Actor (Downey).

The Chaplin Revue 🦴🦴 ½ **1958** The "Revue," put together by Chaplin in 1958, consists of three of his best shorts: "A Dog's Life" (1918), the WWI comedy "Shoulder Arms" (1918), and "The Pilgrim," in which a convict hides out in a clerical guise (1922). Chaplin added self-composed score, narration, and some documentary on-the-set material. **121m/B VHS, DVD.** Charlie Chaplin, Edna Purviance, Sydney Chaplin, Mack Swain; ***D:*** Charlie Chaplin.

Chapter 27 🦴 ½ **2007 (R)** Leto gained more than 60 pounds for this?! Well, he's starring as tubby, delusional Mark David Chapman, the killer of John Lennon. Writer/director Schafer covers the three days leading up to the murder, from Chapman's arrival in New York from Hawaii to his staking out the Dakota. There's not much room for anyone else in the story (although Lohan pops up as Beatles fan Jude) but there's nothing particularly new to view. **84m/C DVD.** Jared Leto, Lindsay Lohan, Judah Friedlander, Ursula Abbott; ***D:*** Jarrett Schaefer; ***W:*** Jarrett Schaefer; ***C:*** Tom Richmond; ***M:*** Anthony Marinelli.

Chapter Two 🦴🦴 **1979 (PG)** Loosely based on Neil Simon's marriage to Mason and his Broadway hit of the same name. A writer, grief-stricken over the death of his first wife, meets the woman who will become his second. Witty dialogue in first half deteriorates when guilt strikes. **124m/C VHS.** James Caan, Marsha Mason, Valerie Harper, Joseph Bologna; ***D:*** Robert Moore; ***W:*** Neil Simon.

Character 🦴🦴 *Karakter* **1997 (R)** Based on the 1938 novel by F. Bordewijk, which follows the troubled relationship of young lawyer Jacob Willem Katadreuffe (van Huet) and his overbearing father in 1920s Rotterdam. Dreverhaven (Decleir) is a powerful baliff who has an illegitimate son with his servant, Joba (Schuurman), who turns down his marriage proposal. Still, Dreverhaven is determined to control his son's life, even if it means ruining him first. No wonder the old man gets murdered. Dark and unsentimental. Dutch with subtitles. **114m/C VHS, DVD.** *NL* Fedja Van Huet, Jan Decleir, Betty Schuurman, Victor Low, Tamar van den Dop, Hans Kestig; ***D:*** Mike van Diem; ***W:*** Mike van Diem; ***C:*** Rogier Stoffers; ***M:*** Paleis Van Boem. Oscars '97: Foreign Film.

Charade 🦴🦴 **1953** Mason and wife Pamela star in this trilogy of love and violence. "Portrait of a Murderer" has a young artist sketching the picture of the man who—unknown to her—has just murdered her girlfriend. "Duel at Dawn" concerns an 1880s Austrian officer who steals a woman from another officer and is then challenged to a duel. "The Midas Touch" revolves around a successful but dissatisfied man who abandons his riches to find the meaning of life. Mason himself had said he hoped "this curiosity" would disappear. **83m/B VHS, DVD.** James Mason, Pamela Mason, Scott Forbes, Paul Cavanagh, Bruce Lester, Sean McClory, Vince Barnett; ***D:*** Roy Kellino.

Charade 🦴🦴🦴 ½ **1963** After her husband is murdered, a young woman finds herself on the run from crooks and double agents who want the $250,000 her husband stole during WWII. Hepburn and Grant are charming and sophisticated as usual in this stylish intrigue filmed in Paris. Based on the story "The Unsuspecting Wife" by Marc Behm and Peter Stone. **113m/C VHS, DVD.** Cary Grant, Audrey Hepburn, Walter Matthau, James Coburn, George Kennedy; ***D:*** Stanley Donen; ***W:*** Peter Stone; ***C:*** Charles B(ryant) Lang Jr.; ***M:*** Henry Mancini. British Acad. '64: Actress (Hepburn).

The Charge of the Light Brigade 🦴🦴🦴 **1936 (PG-13)** A British army officer stationed in India deliberately starts the Balaclava charge to even an old score with Surat Khan, who's on the other side. Still an exciting film, though it's hardly historically accurate. De Havilland is along to provide the requisite romance with Flynn. Also available colorized. **115m/B VHS, DVD.** Errol Flynn, Olivia de Havilland, David Niven, Nigel Bruce, Patric Knowles, Donald Crisp, C.

Henry Gordon, J. Carrol Naish, Henry Stephenson, E.E. Clive, Scotty Beckett, G.P. (Tim) Huntley Jr., Robert Barrat, Spring Byington, George Regas; *D:* Michael Curtiz; *W:* Michael Jacoby, Rowland Leigh; *C:* Sol Polito; *M:* Max Steiner.

The Charge of the Light Brigade 1/2 **1968 (PG-13)** Political indictment of imperialistic England in this revisionist retelling of the notorious British defeat by the Russians at Balaclava. Battle scenes are secondary to this look at the stupidity of war. Fine cast; notable animation sequences by Richard Williams. **130m/C VHS, DVD.** *GB* Trevor Howard, John Gielgud, David Hemmings, Vanessa Redgrave, Harry Andrews, Jill Bennett, Peter Bowles, Mark Burns, Alan Dobie, T.P. McKenna, Corin Redgrave, Norman Rossington, Rachel Kempson, Donald Wolfit, Howard Marion-Crawford, Mark Dignam, Ben Aris, Peter Woodthorpe, Roger Mutton, Joely Richardson; *D:* Tony Richardson; *W:* Charles Wood; *C:* David Watkin; *M:* John Addison.

Charge of the Model T's 1/2 **1976 (G)** Comedy about a WWI German spy who tries to infiltrate the U.S. army. **90m/C VHS.** Louis Nye, John David Carson, Herb Edelman, Carol Bagdasarian, Arte Johnson; *D:* Jim McCullough Sr.; *W:* Jim McCullough Sr.

Chariots of Fire 1/2 **1981 (PG)** A lush telling of the parallel stories of Harold Abraham and Eric Liddell, English runners who competed in the 1924 Paris Olympics. One was compelled by a hatred of anti-Semitism, the other by the love of God. Outstanding performances by the entire cast. **123m/C VHS, DVD.** *GB* Ben Cross, Ian Charleson, Nigel Havers, Ian Holm, Alice Krige, Brad Davis, Dennis Christopher, Patrick Magee, Cheryl Campbell, John Gielgud, Lindsay Anderson, Nigel Davenport; *D:* Hugh Hudson; *W:* Colin Welland; *C:* David Watkin; *M:* Vangelis. Oscars '81: Costume Des., Orig. Screenplay, Picture, Orig. Score; British Acad. '81: Film, Support. Actor (Holm); Golden Globes '82: Foreign Film; N.Y. Film Critics '81: Cinematog.

Charisma *Karisuma* **1999** Detective Goro (Koji Yakusho) is a burned-out hostage negotiator on forced vacation in the forest after botching a hostage situation that ends up with everyone dying. Confronting him there are the locals feuding over a tree named Charisma which some claim is slowly poisoning the forest and rivers. **104m/C DVD.** *JP* Koji Yakusho, Ren Osugi, Yoriko Douguchi, Jun Fubuki, Hiroyuki Ikeuchi, Yutaka Matsushige, Masayuki Shionoya, Yoji Tanaka, Akira Otaka, Sachiko Meguro, Atsushi Nishida; *D:* Kiyoshi Kurosawa; *W:* Kiyoshi Kurosawa; *C:* Junichiro Hayashi; *M:* Gary Hashiya.

The Charlatan **1929** Peter Dwight's (Herbert) wife Florence (Livingston) takes their baby daughter and walks out on their marriage to be with her lover. Adopting the disguise of fortune teller Count Merlin, Dwight eventually tracks Florence down and disturbs her by revealing so much of her past. Things go horribly wrong for the promiscuous Florence though and Peter might be to blame. **63m/B DVD.** Holmes Herbert, Margaret Livingston, Rockliffe Fellowes, Crauford Kent, Philo (Philip, P.H., P.M.) McCullough, Fred MacKaye; *D:* George Melford; *W:* J.G. Hawks, Robert N. Lee; *C:* George Robinson.

Charlemagne 1/2 **1995** British miniseries follows the life of the royal conqueror who civilized western Europe and ruled as emperor from 800-814. On five cassettes. **250m/C VHS.** *GB* Christian Brendel, Anny (Annie Legras) Duperey; *D:* Clive Donner.

Charles & Diana: A Palace Divided 1/2 **1993** Trashy scandalous tale of the disintegration of the fairytale romance and marriage of Prince Charles and Princess Diana. Oxenberg stars as Princess Di, a role she played a decade ago in "The Royal Romance of Charles and Diana," and Rees does a fine job playing the conservative Prince Charles. Although the film covers all of the couple's highly publicized troubles, it's such a quick superficial treatment that it's often hard to follow. Nonetheless, it's a flashingly inviting look into the privileged House of Windsor. **92m/C VHS, DVD.** Roger Rees, Catherine Oxenberg, Benedict Taylor, Tracy Brabin, Amanda Walker, David Quilter, Jane How; *D:* John Power.

Charles: Dead or Alive *Charles: Mort ou Vif* **1969** Aging Charles De (Simon) has always lead an ordinary life when he suddenly drops out and re-emerges as a madman, who lives only on his own terms. His family becomes so upset by his bizarre behavior that they commit him to an asylum. First feature film by Tanner. French with subtitles. **93m/B VHS.** *SI* Francois Simon; *D:* Alain Tanner; *W:* Alain Tanner; *C:* Renato Berta.

Charles et Lucie **1979** A has-been couple are ripped off, pursued, persecuted, and saddled with very bad luck in the South of France. Essentially a character study; semi-acclaimed. In French with subtitles. **96m/C VHS.** *FR* Daniel Ceccaldi, Ginette Garcin, Jean-Marie Proslier, Samson Fainsilber; *D:* Nelly Kaplan.

Charleston **1926** Renoir's third film, a simple erotic dance fantasy that caused much controversy in its day. Silent, with jazz score and historical introduction. **30m/B VHS.** Catherine Hessling; *D:* Jean Renoir.

Charley and the Angel 1/2 **1973 (G)** Touching story of a man who changes his cold ways with his family when informed by an angel that he hasn't much time to live. Amusing Disney movie set in the Great Depression. **93m/C VHS.** Fred MacMurray, Cloris Leachman, Harry (Henry) Morgan, Kurt Russell, Vincent Van Patten, Kathleen (Kathy) Cody, Kelly Thordsen; *D:* Vincent McEveety.

Charley Varrick **1973 (PG)** Matthau, a small-town hood, robs a bank only to find out that one of its depositors is the Mob. Baker's the vicious hit-man assigned the job of getting the loot back. A well-paced, on-the-mark thriller. **111m/C VHS, DVD.** Walter Matthau, Joe Don Baker, Felicia Farr, John Vernon, Sheree North, Norman Fell, Andrew (Andy) Robinson, Jacqueline Scott, Albert "Poppy" Popwell; *D:* Donald Siegel; *W:* Dean Riesner; *M:* Lalo Schifrin.

Charley's Aunt 1/2 **1925** Amusing Victorian farce in which two young male students convince an older fellow student to dress up as their female chaperon so they can pitch woo to two local lovelies. Fun performances and well-paced direction by Sidney. Based on the Brandon Thomas farce, the movie was remade in 1930, starring Charles Ruggles, and again in 1941, with Jack Benny. **75m/B VHS.** Sydney Chaplin, Ethel Shannon, Lucien Littlefield, Alec B. Francis, Mary Akin, Priscilla Bonner, Jimmy Harrison, David James, Eulalie Jensen, James E. Page, Phillips Smalley; *D:* Scott Sidney; *W:* F. McGrew Willis, Joe Farnham; *C:* Gus Peterson, Paul Garnett.

Charley's Aunt **1941** Benny's at his comedic best in this amusing farce. Lord Fancourt "Babbs" Babberly (Benny) and his Oxford roommates Jack Chesney (Ellison) and Charley Wyckeham (Haydn in his film debut) must find a proper escort so their lady friends (Whelan, Baxter) will agree to visit. Babbs dons drag to impersonate Charley's maiden aunt (from Brazil—where the nuts come from) but finds himself fending off the romantic overtures of a couple of codgers (Cregar, Gwenn). Based on the play by Brandon Thomas. **80m/B VHS.** Jack Benny, Kay Francis, James Ellison, Richard Haydn, Arleen Whelan, Anne Baxter, Laird Cregar, Edmund Gwenn, Reginald Owen; *D:* Archie Mayo; *W:* George Seaton; *C:* J. Peverell Marley; *M:* Alfred Newman.

Charlie **2004 (R)** Based on the actual events of South London's "Torture Gang" leader Charlie Richardson's (Goss) barbaric 1960s underworld reign. Dramatizes the gang's 1966 trial after Richardson is caught doing shady deals with a South African diamond baron. Director Needs' dizzying flashbacks are intense but also question whether the group was really to blame. **94m/C DVD.** Luke Goss, Steven Berkoff, Marius Weyers, Anita Dobson, Leslie Grantham; *D:* Malcolm Needs; *W:* Malcolm Needs. **VIDEO**

Charlie & Me **2008** Keep the tissues handy for this sentimental family drama from the Hallmark Channel. Aging jazz aficionado Charlie Baker (Bosley) is felled by a heart attack, which makes him more determined to bond with his feisty 12-year-old granddaughter Casey (Benattar) and her widowed father, Charlie's workaholic son, Jeffrey (Gallanders). **88m/C DVD.** Tom Bosley, Jordy Benattar, James Gallanders, Barclay Hope, Hannah Fleming, Tyler Stentiford; *D:* David Weaver; *W:* Karen Struck; *C:* Francois Dagenais; *M:* Ron Ramin. **CABLE**

Charlie and the Chocolate Factory **2005 (PG)** Unlike 1971's "Willy Wonka & the Chocolate Factory," this is not a musical, although the Oompa Loompas still sing. And Burton does a more faithful adaptation of the 1964 book by Roald Dahl. Poor boy Charlie Bucket (Highmore) is one of five winners of a golden ticket that allows him to tour the mysterious Willy Wonka's (Depp) chocolate factory. Fans of the original may have qualms, but this one has a little more depth and heart, great visuals, and the cooperation of Dahl's widow, an exec producer. Depp is brilliantly quirky and Highmore shines. **115m/C DVD, Blu-ray Disc, UMD, HD DVD.** *US GB* Johnny Depp, Freddie Highmore, David Kelly, Anna-Sophia Robb, Deep Roy, Christopher Lee, Helena Bonham Carter, Noah Taylor, James Fox, Missi Pyle, Julia Winter, Jordan Fry, Philip Wiegratz, Franziska Troegner, Harry Taylor, Adam Godley, Eileen Essell, Liz Smith, David Morris; *D:* Tim Burton; *W:* John August; *C:* Philippe Rousselot; *M:* Danny Elfman; *Nar:* Geoffrey Holder.

Charlie and the Great Balloon Chase **1982** When a grandfather takes his grandson on a cross-country balloon trip, they are hotly pursued by the boy's mother, her stuffy fiance (who wants the boy in military school), the FBI, a reporter, and the Mafia. **98m/C VHS.** Jack Albertson, Adrienne Barbeau, Slim Pickens, Moosie Drier; *D:* Larry Elikann. **TV**

Charlie Bartlett **2007 (R)** Troubled teen Charlie (Yelchin) is forced to attend the local public high school after getting the boot from a private academy, and he soon realizes his years of therapy will serve him well with his new mixed-up, angst-ridden school mates. Before long he's set up shop in the boys room handing out sage advice along with fistfulls of the meds his psychs dispense to him. Charlie begins to work his docs for all manner of drugs, and the line to the bathroom grows exponentially with his popularity, much to the chagrin of school officials, especially Principal Gardner (Downey Jr.), whose daughter (Dennings) is Charlie's new galpal. Newcomer Yelchin is super charming, and the film puts the whole pop psych Dr. Phil culture on a humorous skewer while calling to mind classic John Hughes teen flicks. Smart viewing. **96m/C DVD.** *US* Anton Yelchin, Kat Dennings, Robert Downey Jr., Hope Davis, Tyler Hilton, Mark Rendall, Jake Epstein, Megan Park, Ishan Dave, Jonathan Malen; *D:* Jon Poll; *W:* Gustin Nash; *C:* Paul Sarossy; *M:* Christophe Beck.

Charlie Boy 1/2 **1981** The new owner of an ancient African idol enters the world of the supernatural when he casts a death spell on six people. **60m/C VHS, DVD.** Leigh Lawson, Angela Bruce, Marius Goring; *D:* Robert M. Young.

Charlie Bravo **1980 (R)** A commando group is commanded to rescue a captured nurse in Vietnam. Dubbed. **94m/C VHS.** *FR* Bruno Pradal, Karen Verlier, Jean-Francois Poron; *D:* Rene Demoulin.

Charlie Chan and the Curse of the Dragon Queen 1/2 **1981 (PG)** The famed Oriental sleuth confronts his old enemy the Dragon Queen, and reveals the true identity of a killer. **97m/C VHS, DVD.** Peter Ustinov, Lee Grant, Angie Dickinson, Richard Hatch, Brian Keith, Roddy McDowall, Michelle Pfeiffer, Rachel Roberts; *D:* Clive Donner; *W:* David Axelrod, Stanley Burns.

Charlie Chan at Monte Carlo **1937** Chan (Oland) is gambling in Monaco when two murders occur. One is a two-bit gangster working as a hotel bartender and the other is a casino messenger who was traveling to Paris with a million bucks in bonds that has disappeared. Now Chan has to tie the cases together to solve the crimes. A good portion of the dialog is in French and much is made of the language difficulties of Chan and company. This was Oland's last appearance as the sleuth; he died in 1938. 16th in the series. **71m/B DVD.** Warner Oland, Keye Luke, Virginia Field, Sidney Blackmer, Harold Huber, Kay Linaker, Robert Kent; *D:* Eugene Forde; *W:* Jerome Cady, Charles Belden; *C:* Daniel B. Clark; *M:* Samuel Kaylin.

Charlie Chan at the Circus 1/2 **1936** On vacation, Chan takes his wife and 12 (!) children to the circus. When one of the owners is murdered, Chan investigates with the help of some of the performers. Filmed at the Al G. Barnes Circus. 11th in the series. **72m/B DVD.** Warner Oland, Keye Luke, Shirley Deane, John McGuire, Francis Ford, J. Carrol Naish, George Brasno, Olive Brasno, Maxine Reiner, Drue Leyton; *D:* Harry Lachman; *W:* Robert Ellis, Helen Logan; *C:* Daniel B. Clark; *M:* Samuel Kaylin.

Charlie Chan at the Olympics 1/2 **1937** Chan's (Oland) son Lee (Luke) is a member of the American swim team at the Berlin Olympics. When an experimental auto pilot device is stolen, Chan is called in (arriving by blimp) and suspects German spies. Since Lee is busy training, Charlie Chan Jr. (Tom Jr.) steps in to help his pop, but when Lee is kidnapped they may have to stop their investigation to save his life. Newsreel shots of the actual 1936 Olympics add to the atmosphere. 14th in the series. **71m/B DVD.** Warner Oland, Keye Luke, Katherine DeMille, Pauline Moore, Layne Tom Jr., Allan "Rocky" Lane, C. Henry Gordon; *D:* Tom Krause; *W:* Robert Ellis, Helen Logan; *C:* Daniel B. Clark; *M:* Samuel Kaylin.

Charlie Chan at the Opera **1936** The great detective investigates an amnesiac opera star (Karloff) who may have committed murder. Considered one of the best of the series. Interesting even to those not familiar with Charlie Chan. **66m/B VHS, DVD.** Warner Oland, Boris Karloff, Keye Luke, Charlotte Henry, Thomas Beck, Nedda Harrigan, William Demarest; *D:* H. Bruce Humberstone.

Charlie Chan at the Race Track **1936** Chan (Oland) is traveling by ship from Honolulu to L.A. with some racehorses after his friend, the owner of a champion, is murdered. He and number one son Lee (Luke) tie the death into the Santa Anita race track where Chan figures out that gamblers have substituted a nag for a winning horse in order to cash in on the betting action. 12th in the series. **70m/B DVD.** Warner Oland, Keye Luke, Helen Wood, Thomas Beck, Alan Dinehart, Gavin Muir; *D:* H. Bruce Humberstone; *W:* Robert Ellis, Helen Logan, Edward T. Lowe; *C:* Harry Jackson; *M:* Samuel Kaylin.

Charlie Chan at the Wax Museum 1/2 **1940** Charlie and number one son must find a criminal hiding out in a wax museum. Chills abound when the fugitive heads for the chamber of horrors. **63m/B VHS.** Sidney Toler, Victor Sen Yung, C. Henry Gordon, Marc Lawrence, Joan Valerie, Marguerite Chapman, Ted Osborn, Michael Visaroff; *D:* Lynn Shores.

Charlie Chan at Treasure Island **1939** Chan (Toler) investigates the alleged suicide of a writer friend, aided by Fred Radini (Romero), an illusionist at the Treasure Island theater at the San Francisco International Exposition. The trail leads them to phony mystic Dr. Zodiac (Mohr), whose predictions always involve blackmail. 19th entry in series. **72m/B DVD.** Sidney Toler, Victor Young, Cesar Romero, Gerald Mohr, Pauline Moore, Douglas Fowley, June Gale, Douglass Dumbrille, Sally Blane, Louis Jean Heydt, Donald MacBride; *D:* Norman Foster; *W:* John Larkin; *C:* Virgil Miller; *M:* Samuel Kaylin.

Charlie Chan in City of Darkness 1/2 **1939** Chan (Toler) travels to Paris for a reunion of his WWI buddies and finds himself investigating the murder of a munitions manufacturer (Dumbrille) with unsavory clients. Notably preachy entry that reflects the distrust of appeasement and the Munich pact. 20th entry in series. **75m/B DVD.** Sidney Toler, Lynn Bari, Richard Clarke, Douglass Dumbrille, Harold Huber, Leo G. Carroll, Lon Chaney Jr., C. Henry Gordon, Dorothy Tree, Noel Madison, Pedro de Cordoba; *D:* Herbert I. Leeds; *W:* Helen

Logan, Robert Ellis; *C:* Virgil Miller.

Charlie Chan in Egypt ♪♪ **1935** Charlie Chan (Oland) is at a dig in Egypt where an archeologist has disappeared. An X-ray reveals that the body in a pharaoh's sarcophagus is that of the missing man. Is there a curse on the team for desecrating the ruler's tomb? 8th in the series. **72m/B DVD.** Warner Oland, Thomas Beck, Rita Hayworth, James Thomas, Pat Paterson, Frank M. Thomas Sr., Stepin Fetchit; *D:* Louis King; *W:* Robert Ellis, Helen Logan; *C:* Daniel B. Clark; *M:* Samuel Kaylin.

Charlie Chan in Honolulu ♪♪ **1938** Toler makes his first appearance as Chan, who discovers a murder aboard a cruise ship docked at Honolulu and refuses to let the liner leave until the case is solved. Sons Jimmy (Yung) and Willie (Tom Jr.) try to help out. 17th entry in the series. **67m/B DVD.** Sidney Toler, Phyllis Brooks, Victor Young, Layne Tom Jr., Eddie Collins, John "Dusty" King, Claire Dodd, George Zucco, Robert Barrat; *D:* H. Bruce Humberstone; *W:* Charles Belden; *C:* Charles G. Clarke.

Charlie Chan in London ♪♪ **1934** Pamela (Leyton) pleads with Chan (Oland) to help her brother Paul (Walton), who is about to be hanged for murder. Chan follows Pamela to the country home of Geoffrey Richmond (Mowbray) and tries to reconstruct the crime, nearly getting himself killed in the process. 6th in the series. **72m/B DVD.** Warner Oland, Alan Mowbray, Douglas Walton, Ray Milland, Drue Leyton, Mona Barrie; *D:* Eugene Forde; *W:* Philip MacDonald; *C:* L.W. O'Connell; *M:* Samuel Kaylin.

Charlie Chan in Paris ♪♪ ½ **1935** Chan scours the city of lights to track down a trio of counterfeiters. Top-notch plot and plenty of suspense will please all. **72m/B VHS.** Warner Oland, Mary Brian, Thomas Beck, Erik Rhodes, John Miljan, Minor Watson, John Qualen, Keye Luke, Henry Kolker; *D:* Lewis Seiler.

Charlie Chan in Rio ♪♪ **1941** Local police call on Chan to help solve a double murder. One of the series' weaker entries but with fine setting and music. **60m/B VHS.** Sidney Toler, Mary Beth Hughes, Cobina Wright Jr., Ted North, Victor Jory, Harold Huber, Victor Sen Yung; *D:* Harry Lachman.

Charlie Chan in Shanghai ♪♪ **1935** Chan (Oland) is called in by the Chinese government to investigate a murder that is tied to an opium ring and he's aided by number one son Lee (Luke). Pretty standard fare is ninth in the series. **70m/B DVD.** Warner Oland, Keye Luke, Irene Hervey, Jon Hall, Russell Hicks, Halliwell Hobbes; *D:* James Tinling; *W:* Edward T. Lowe, Gerald Fairlie; *C:* Barney McGill; *M:* Samuel Kaylin.

Charlie Chan in the Secret Service ♪ ½ **1944** Toler's Chan is now a government agent who is assigned to find the killer of an inventor. Moreland joins up as Chan's taxi-driving, constantly terrified sidekick. The series moved from 20th-century Fox to low-budget Monogram Pictures with this entry, with an ensuing drop in production quality. **64m/B VHS, DVD.** Sidney Toler, Mantan Moreland, Gwen Kenyon, Arthur Loft, Marianne Quon, Lela Tyler, Benson Fong; *D:* Phil Rosen.

Charlie Chan on Broadway ♪♪ **1937** Fellow ocean liner passenger Billie Bronson (Henry) hides her diary in Chan's (Oland) luggage for safekeeping. Seems Billie is wanted as a material witness in a gangster scandal (the diary names names) and upon her return to New York, she's soon murdered. The diary disappears and Chan has to hit the city's nightspots to investigate. 15th entry in the series. **68m/B DVD.** Warner Oland, Keye Luke, Joan Marsh, J. Edward Bromberg, Louise Henry, Douglas Fowley, Harold Huber, Leon Ames, Joan Woodbury, Jerome Cady; *D:* Eugene Forde; *W:* Charles Belden; *C:* Harry Jackson; *M:* Samuel Kaylin.

Charlie Chan's Murder Cruise ♪ ½ **1940** Scotland Yard Inspector Duff is strangled before revealing to his friend Charlie Chan (Toler) how he intended to trap a killer aboard a cruise ship heading from Honolulu to San Francisco. Chan joins the cruise and tries to unmask the killer before too many passengers also die. 21st in the series. **70m/B DVD.** Sidney Toler, Victor Sen Yung, Marjorie Weaver, Lionel Atwill, Cora Witherspoon, Robert Lowery, Don Beddoe, Leo G. Carroll, Kay Linaker, Leonard Mudie; *D:* Eugene Forde; *W:* Lester Ziffren, Robertson White; *C:* Virgil Miller.

Charlie Chan's Secret ♪♪ **1935** Chan must solve the murder of the heir to a huge fortune. A good, logical script with plenty of suspects to keep you guessing. **72m/B VHS.** Warner Oland, Rosina Lawrence, Charles Quigley, Henrietta Crosman, Edward Trevor, Astrid Allwyn; *D:* Gordon Wiles.

Charlie Chaplin: Night at the Show **1915** Chaplin plays two different mugs, both out for a night on the town. Mr. Pest, a sharp-dressed upper-cruster, clings to his disgusting habits, and Mr. Rowdy is his working-class doppleganger. Both obnoxious Chaplins-in-disguise collaborate to wreak havoc on a local theatre. Contains original organ score. **?m/B VHS.** Charlie Chaplin, Edna Purviance; *D:* Charlie Chaplin; *W:* Charlie Chaplin.

Charlie Chaplin ... Our Hero! ♪♪♪ **1915** Two shorts from 1915 written and directed by Chaplin, "Night at the Show" and "In the Park," as well as a 1914 film, "Hot Finish," in which Charlie plays the villain. **58m/B VHS.** Charlie Chaplin, Edna Purviance, Lloyd Bacon, Mabel Normand, Chester Conklin, Mack Sennett; *D:* Charlie Chaplin.

Charlie Grant's War ♪♪ **1980** The true story of a Canadian businessman who hears of Nazi brutality and determines to save European Jews from persecution during the Holocaust. Not among the more distinguished works of its kind. **130m/C VHS.** *GB* Jan Rubes, R.H. Thomson, Joan Orenstein; *D:* Martin Lavut.

Charlie McCarthy, Detective WOOF! **1939** Crooked newspaper editor with mob ties is murdered, and Charlie McCarthy shows up to not really help solve much of anything. Doesn't really work as a mystery or a comedy. **65m/B VHS.** Edgar Bergen, Robert Cummings, Constance Moore, John Sutton, Louis Calhern, Edgar Kennedy, Samuel S. Hinds; *D:* Frank Tuttle; *W:* Harold Shumate, Edward Eliscu, Richard Mack; *C:* George Robinson. **VIDEO**

Charlie Muffin ♪♪ *A Deadly Game* **1979** East-West intrigue prior to the fall of the Berlin Wall finds a Western operative returning from a dangerous mission, only to walk into a trap set by his own side. **104m/C VHS.** *GB* David Hemmings, Sam Wanamaker, Jennie Linden, Pinkas Braun, Ian Richardson, Ralph Richardson, Shane Rimmer, Donald Churchill, Clive Revill, Frederick Treves; *D:* Jack Gold; *W:* Keith Waterhouse; *C:* Ousama Rawi; *M:* Christopher Gunning.

Charlie the Lonesome Cougar ♪♪ ½ **1967** A classic Disney family movie filmed in the style of a wilderness documentary, this is the story of Jess Bradley (Brown) who adopts an orphaned baby cougar that quickly becomes the mascot of his logging camp. But as the cat grows older, his behavior begins to cause problems, and it quickly becomes apparent he will have to be reintroduced to the wild. **75m/C DVD.** Ron Brown, Brian Russell; *D:* Rex Allen; *W:* Winston Hibler; *C:* William W. Bacon III, Lloyd Beebe, Charles L. Draper; *M:* Franklyn Marks; *Nar:* Rex Allen.

Charlie White WOOF! **2004** Charlie White is a self-destructive party boy with more money than brains, trying to get noticed on the London scene. Charlie takes it badly when someone else steals the limelight but you won't care at all about these upper-class twits. Big yawn. **85m/C DVD.** *GB* Alex McGettigan, Danny George, Alex Besley, Lucy McCall, Hamish Jenkinson; *D:* Samuel P. Abrahams; *W:* Samuel P. Abrahams; *C:* Samuel P. Abrahams, Oliver Campbell; *M:* Philip Zikking.

Charlie Wilson's War ♪♪ **2007 (R)** In the "truth is stranger than fiction" category, Charlie Wilson (Hanks) is a hard-drinking, pleasure-loving Democratic congressman from East Texas who's also resourceful and interested in foreign affairs. Houston socialite Joanne Herring (Roberts in big hair) is a power broker who convinces Charlie that they can help end the cold war by arming the Afghan mujahideen so they can defeat the invading Russkies. (It's set in the 1980s.) Charlie heads off to Afghanistan to check things out and is given assistance by renegade CIA op Gust Avrakotos (Hoffman), which leads back to some D.C. maneuvering. A big story (based on the bestseller by George Crile) that's packed into a brief running time, so things seem just a little hurried, with Hanks and Hoffman vying to see who can steal the picture. **97m/C DVD.** *US* Tom Hanks, Julia Roberts, Philip Seymour Hoffman, Amy Adams, Ned Beatty, Emily Blunt, Om Puri, Ken Stott, John Slattery, Denis O'Hare, Peter Gerety, Brian Markinson; *D:* Mike Nichols; *W:* Aaron Sorkin; *C:* Stephen Goldblatt; *M:* James Newton Howard.

Charlie's Angels ♪♪ ½ **2000 (PG-13)** Seventies TV jigglefest finally gets a belated big screen treatment that has the trio (Barrymore, Diaz, Liu) saving Charlie (Forsythe reprises his voice role) from assassination and thwarting bad guy Roger Corwin (Curry). Merchant-Ivory it ain't (yay!), but it is everything a summer movie's supposed to be: loud, flashy, and fun. Matt LeBlanc, Tom Green, and Luke Wilson are around as nominal romantic interests but it's the women who run the show. Everyone seems to be having a good time, especially Murray as Bosley and Diaz as "perky" angel, Natalie. **99m/C VHS, DVD, UMD.** Drew Barrymore, Cameron Diaz, Lucy Liu, Bill Murray, Tim Curry, Sam Rockwell, Kelly Lynch, Crispin Glover, Matt LeBlanc, LL Cool J, Tom Green, Luke Wilson, Sean M. Whalen, Alex Trebek, Michael (Mike) Papajohn; *D:* McG; *W:* John August, Ryan Rowe, Ed Soloman; *C:* Russell Carpenter; *M:* Ed Shearmur; *V:* John Forsythe.

Charlie's Angels: Full Throttle ♪♪ **2003 (PG-13)** The Angels investigate murders linked to the theft of a Witness Protection database. Enough about plot. Murray's been replaced by Bernie Mac, Demi Moore returns to the screen as a former Angel gone bad, and a good time is still had by all. McG and the girls amp up the "boom" quotient, but some of the breezy fun of the original feels a bit forced this time around. **105m/C VHS, DVD.** *US* Drew Barrymore, Cameron Diaz, Lucy Liu, Bernie Mac, Demi Moore, Luke Wilson, Matt LeBlanc, Crispin Glover, Robert Patrick, John Cleese, Shia LaBeouf, Jaclyn Smith, Justin Theroux, Rodrigo Santoro, Ja'net DuBois, Robert Forster, Eric Bogosian, Carrie Fisher; *Cameos:* Pink, Ashley (Fuller) Olsen, Mary-Kate Olsen; *D:* McG; *W:* John August, Marianne S. Wibberley, Cormac Wibberley; *C:* Russell Carpenter; *M:* Ed Shearmur; *V:* John Forsythe. Golden Raspberries '03: Worst Remake/Sequel, Worst Support. Actress (Moore).

Charlie's Ghost: The Secret of Coronado ♪♪ ½ *Charlie's Ghost Story* **1994 (PG)** Kid who has trouble fitting in is befriended by the ghost of a Spanish conquistador. **92m/C VHS, DVD.** Richard "Cheech" Marin, Trenton Knight, Anthony Edwards, Linda Fiorentino, Daphne Zuniga; *D:* Anthony Edwards.

Charlotte Forten's Mission: Experiment in Freedom ♪♪♪ *Half Slave, Half Free 2* **1985** Fact-based story, set during the Civil War. A wealthy, educated black woman, determined to prove to President Lincoln that blacks are equal to whites, journeys to a remote island off the coast of Georgia. There she teaches freed slaves to read and write. Part of the "American Playhouse" series on PBS. Preceded by "Solomon Northrup's Odyssey." **120m/C VHS.** Melba Moore, Mary Alice, Ned Beatty, Carla Borelli, Micki Grant, Moses Gunn, Anna Maria Horsford, Bruce McGill, Glynn Turman, Roderick Wimberly; *D:* Barry Crane; *W:* Samm-Art Williams.

Charlotte Gray ♪♪ **2001 (PG-13)** Uninvolving WWII romantic drama based on the 1998 novel by Sebastian Faulks. Scottish Charlotte (Blanchett) is living in London when she meets dashing RAF pilot Peter Gregory (Penry-Jones). After learning that Peter has been shot down over France, Charlotte (who speaks perfect French) volunteers for British Special Operations and is sent to work with the Resistance in Vichy. Charlotte's contacts are Levade (Gambon) and his handsome son Julian (Crudup). Naturally, there are supposed to be sparks between the two but the romance fizzles rather than sizzles as does the film itself. Chameleon Blanchett and gruff Gambon are the main reasons to watch. **118m/C VHS, DVD.** *GB AU* Cate Blanchett, Billy Crudup, Michael Gambon, Rupert Penry-Jones, Anton Lesser, James Fleet, Ron Cook, Jack Shepherd, Nicholas Farrell, Helen McCrory, Abigail Cruttenden, Charlie Condou, David Birkin; *D:* Gillian Armstrong; *W:* Jeremy Brock; *C:* Dion Beebe; *M:* Stephen Warbeck.

Charlotte Sometimes ♪♪ ½ **2002 (R)** Michael manages his Aunt Margie's (Hoshi) duplex and runs the family auto repair business. He has a crush on tenant Lori (Yuan), who has a boyfriend, Justin (Westmore), although she frequently turns to the diffident Michael for friendly companionship. Then Michael meets the mysterious Darcy (Kim) at the local bar. She is sexually agressive, while insisting that she's only in town for a few days. But Darcy seems overly interested in the relationship between Michael and Lori and it turns out the two women have a history than neither wants Michael to discover. **85m/C VHS, DVD.** Michael Idemoto, Jacqueline Kim, Eugenia Yuan, Matt Westmore, Shizuko Hoshi, Kimberly Rose; *D:* Eric Byler; *W:* Eric Byler; *C:* Robert Humphreys; *M:* Michael Brook.

Charlotte's Web ♪♪ ½ **1973 (G)** E.B. White's classic story of a friendship between a spider and a pig is handled only adequately by Hanna-Barbera studios. Some okay songs. **94m/C VHS, DVD.** *D:* Charles A. Nichols, Iwao Takamoto; *W:* Earl Hamner; *M:* Irwin Kostal; *V:* Pamelyn Ferdin, Danny Bonaduce, Debbie Reynolds, Agnes Moorehead, Paul Lynde, Henry Gibson; *Nar:* Rex Allan.

Charlotte's Web ♪♪♪ **2006 (G)** Faithful to E.B. White's timeless 1952 children's novel about a young girl, Fern (played graciously by Fanning, just barely young enough for the role), who rescues runt pig Wilbur from the smokehouse. Wilbur is later aided by Charlotte, a sophisticated spider (Roberts) whose "some pig" artwork awes the masses. Though the animals' mouths move thanks to CG effects, the animals and action are the real deal, as are the appealing gaggle of celebrities. Sticks to the book's gentle nature, but things get a bit sluggish at times. **96m/C DVD.** *US* Dakota Fanning, Kevin Anderson, Essie Davis, Gary Basaraba, Siobhan Fallon Hogan, Beau Bridges; *D:* Gary Winick; *W:* Susannah Grant, Karey Kirkpatrick; *C:* Seamus McGarvey; *M:* Danny Elfman; *V:* Julia Roberts, Steve Buscemi, John Cleese, Dominic Scott Kay, Oprah Winfrey, Cedric the Entertainer, Kathy Bates, Reba McEntire, Robert Redford, Thomas Haden Church, Andre Benjamin, Sam Shepard, Abraham Benrubi.

Charly ♪♪♪ **1968** A retarded man becomes intelligent after brain surgery, then romances a kindly caseworker before slipping back into retardation. Moving account is well served by leads Robertson and Bloom. Adapted from the Daniel Keyes novel "Flowers for Algernon." **103m/C VHS, DVD.** Cliff Robertson, Claire Bloom, Lilia Skala, Leon Janney, Dick Van Patten, William Dwyer; *D:* Ralph Nelson; *W:* Stirling Silliphant. Oscars '68: Actor (Robertson); Golden Globes '69: Screenplay; Natl. Bd. of Review '68: Actor (Robertson).

Charm of La Boheme ♪♪ ½ **1936** A vintage German musical based on the Puccini opera. With English subtitles. **90m/B VHS, DVD.** *GE* Jan Kiepura, Martha Eggerth, Paul Kemp; *D:* Geza von Bolvary.

The Charmer ♪♪ ½ **1987** Havers stars as Ralph Gorse, a charming but amoral con man who uses any means to get what he wants. This includes using the affection (and money) of an older woman, blackmail, and even murder. Set in the late '30s. Made for British TV miniseries. **312m/C VHS, DVD.** *GB* Nigel Havers, Rosemary Leach, Bernard Hepton, Fiona Fullerton, Abigail McKern, George Baker, Judy Parfitt; *D:* Alan Gibson; *W:* Allan Prior. **TV**

Charming Billy ♪♪ **1998** Living a life of quiet desperation finally proves to be too much for Billy Starkman (Hayden) and he goes postal—sniping at passersby from the top of a rural water tower. Flashbacks show how Billy got to that desperate point in his life. **80m/C VHS, DVD.** Michael Hayden, Sally Murphy, Tony Mockus Sr., Chelcie Ross; ***D:*** William R. Pace; ***W:*** William R. Pace; ***C:*** William Newell; ***M:*** David Barkley.

Charms for the Easy Life ½ **2002** Southern matriarch and holistic healer, Miss Charlie Kate (Rowlands) has definite opinions—she loathes her no-account son-in-law and won't set foot in her daughter Sophie's (Rogers) house. Fortunately, he eventually dies and Miss Charlie moves in to help look after granddaughter Margaret (Pratt). Miss Charlie has a generally low opinion of men since her husband ran off but the more fragile Sophie is pleased to have a suitor (Johnson) and teen Margaret also finds a boy (Mitchell) who thinks she's neat. Set in the mid-1940s; based on Kaye Gibbon's 1993 novel. Graceful and charming and all three actresses keep the sentimental excess to a minimum. **111m/C VHS, DVD.** Gena Rowlands, Mimi Rogers, Susan May Pratt, Geordie Johnson, Kenneth Mitchell; ***D:*** Joan Micklin Silver; ***W:*** Angela Shelton; ***C:*** Jean Lepine; ***M:*** Van Dyke Parks. **CABLE**

Charro! **1969 (G)** Presley in a straight role as a reformed bandit hounded by former gang members. Western fails on nearly all accounts, with Presley hopelessly acting outside the bounds of his talent. Furthermore, he sings only one song. **98m/C VHS, DVD.** Elvis Presley, Ina Balin, Victor French, Lynn Kellogg, Barbara Werle, Paul Brinegar, James B. Sikking; ***D:*** Charles Marquis Warren; ***W:*** Charles Marquis Warren; ***M:*** Hugo Montenegro.

Charulata *The Lonely Wife* **1964** Charulata is a loyal and dutiful wife taken for granted by her husband. But when his young cousin Amal comes to live with them, Charulata glimpses what true love could be. Adapted from the novella by Rabindranath Tagore. Bengali with subtitles. **117m/B VHS, DVD.** *IN* Shailan Mukherjee, Shyamal Ghoshal, Gitali Roy, Bholanath Koyal, Suku Mukherjee, Dilip Bose, Joydeb, Bankim Ghosh, Subrata Sensharma, Madhabi Mukherjee, Soumitra Chatterjee; ***D:*** Satyajit Ray; ***W:*** Satyajit Ray; ***C:*** Subrata Mitra; ***M:*** Satyajit Ray, Rabindranath Tagore.

The Chase ½ **1946** Not realizing that his boss-to-be is a mobster, Cummings takes a job as a chauffeur. Naturally, he falls in love with the gangster's wife (Morgan), and the two plan to elope. Somewhat miffed, the cuckolded mafioso and his bodyguard (Lorre) pursue the elusive couple as they head for Havana. The performances are up to snuff, but the story's as unimaginative as the title, with intermittent bouts of suspense. **86m/B VHS, DVD.** Robert Cummings, Michele Morgan, Peter Lorre, Steve Cochran, Lloyd Corrigan, Jack Holt, Don Wilson; ***D:*** Arthur Ripley; ***W:*** Philip Yordan.

The Chase ½ **1966** Southern community is undone when rumors circulate of a former member's prison escape and return home. Excellent cast only partially shines. Brando is outstanding as the beleaguered, honorable sheriff, and Duvall makes a splash in the more showy role of a cuckold who fears the escapee is returning home to avenge a childhood incident. Reliable Dickinson also makes the most of her role as Brando's loving wife. Fonda, however, was not yet capable of fashioning complex characterizations, and Redford is under-utilized as the escapee. Adapted from the play by Horton Foote. Notorious conflicts among producer, director, and writer kept it from being a winner. **135m/C VHS, DVD.** Marlon Brando, Robert Redford, Angie Dickinson, E.G. Marshall, Jane Fonda, James Fox, Janice Rule, Robert Duvall, Miriam Hopkins, Martha Hyer; ***D:*** Arthur Penn; ***W:*** Lillian Hellman, Horton Foote; ***M:*** John Barry.

Chase ½ **1985** A big-city lawyer returns to her small hometown to defend a killer and ends up at odds with the town, including an ex-lover. Routine drama. **104m/C VHS.** Jennifer O'Neill, Robert Woods, Richard Farnsworth, Michael Parks; ***D:*** Rod Holcomb; ***M:*** Charles Bernstein. **TV**

The Chase **1991 (PG-13)** Routine actioner in which an ex-con killer leads a ruthless cop and a TV news team on a wild chase. Loosely based on a true story. **93m/C VHS, DVD.** Ben Johnson, Casey Siemaszko, Gerry Bamman, Robert Beltran, Barry Corbin, Ricki Lake, Megan Follows, Sheila Kelley, Gailard Sartain; ***D:*** Paul Wendkos; ***W:*** Guerdon (Gordon) Trueblood; ***C:*** Chuck (Charles G.) Arnold; ***M:*** W.G. Snuffy Walden. **TV**

The Chase ½ **1993 (PG-13)** Heiress Natalie Voss (Swanson) is in the wrong place at the wrong time when she's carjacked by escaped con Jack Hammond (Sheen) who uses a Butterfinger for his weapon. Frantic chases ensues as it turns out that Daddy Voss is a media hungry millionaire and he's followed by not only the cops but the media as well. One-dimensional characters aren't helped by a one-dimensional script, but slick filmmaking and a little charm helps. Skewers the media hype that surrounds crime, taking on news programs that offer immediate coverage and reality based shows with glee. **87m/C VHS, DVD.** Joao Fernandes, Kristy Swanson, Charlie Sheen, Josh Mostel, Ray Wise, Henry Rollins, Flea; ***D:*** Adam Rifkin; ***W:*** Adam Rifkin; ***M:*** Richard Gibbs.

Chasers **1994 (R)** Gruff Navy petty officer Rock Reilly (Berenger) and his conniving partner Eddie Devane (McNamara) are stuck escorting maximum security prisoner Toni Johnson (Eleniak) to a Charleston naval base. Imagine their surprise when Toni turns out to be a beautiful blonde whose one purpose is to escape her jail-sentence for going AWOL. Considering how dumb her jailers are this shouldn't be too difficult. Lots of sneering, leering, and macho posturing. **100m/C VHS, DVD.** Tom Berenger, William McNamara, Erika Eleniak, Gary Busey, Crispin Glover, Dean Stockwell, Seymour Cassel, Frederic Forrest, Marilu Henner, Dennis Hopper; ***D:*** Dennis Hopper; ***W:*** Joe Batteer, John Rice, Dan Gilroy; ***C:*** Ueli Steiger; ***M:*** Dwight Yoakam, Pete Anderson.

Chasing Amy ½ **1997 (R)** Holden (Affleck) and best friend Banky (Lee), New Jersey comic book artists, attend a convention in New York where Holden is immediately attracted to fellow artist Alyssa (Adams). His ego is quickly deflated when Alyssa lets him know she's a lesbian. They try for friendship, head into a rocky romance, and then Holden discovers Alyssa's had a wild (and heterosexual) past, which pushes all his emotional buttons. Writer/director Smith supplies his trademark sharp dialogue, and the leads all contribute fine performances. Jay (Mewes) and Silent Bob (Smith), from Smith's earlier pics, make another appearance and supply the story that gives the film its title. **113m/C VHS, DVD.** Ben Affleck, Joey Lauren Adams, Jason Lee, Dwight Ewell, Jason Mewes, Kevin Smith, Matt Damon, Carmen (Lee) Llywelyn, Ethan Suplee, Brian O'Halloran, Guinevere Turner; ***D:*** Kevin Smith; ***W:*** Kevin Smith; ***C:*** David Klein; ***M:*** David Pirner. Ind. Spirit '97: Screenplay, Support. Actor (Lee).

Chasing Butterflies *La Chasse aux Papillons* **1994** Society's decline is represented by a once-grand, now-decaying chateau, located in a small French village, and its equally decaying inhabitants. Marie-Agnes, confined to a wheelchair, is attended to by her cousin Solange and sullen maid Valerie. When Marie-Agnes suddenly dies, the greedy relatives descend, as well as untrustworthy antiques dealers, and Japanese businessmen interested in acquiring foreign real estate. The film is also an acquired taste. French with subtitles. **115m/C VHS.** *FR* Thamar Tarassachvili, Narda Blanchet, Pierrette Pompom Bailhache, Alexandre Tcherkassoff; ***D:*** Otar Iosseliani; ***W:*** Otar Iosseliani.

Chasing Christmas **2005 (PG)** Bahhumbug. Bitter divorcee Jack Cameron (Arnold) is a holiday Scrooge who comes to the attention of the Bureau of Yuletide Affairs. It's decided to "Dickens" him with the ghosts of Christmas Past, Present, and Future, only when peevish Past (Jordan) takes Jack back to his 1965 boyhood, he decides to take a sudden vacation and leaves Jack stranded. This means Present (Roth) has to fix the timeline and get Jack to see the error of his ways. Lame holiday humor, although seeing Arnold tied to a chair with Christmas lights is kinda funny. **90m/C DVD.** Tom Arnold, Andrea Roth, Leslie Jordan, Jed Rees, Brittney Wilson; ***D:*** Ron Oliver; ***W:*** Todd Berger; ***C:*** C. Kim Miles; ***M:*** John Sereda. **CABLE**

Chasing Destiny ½ **2000 (PG-13)** Once famous as a '60s rock 'n' roller, Jet James (Lloyd) is in debt and has a collector (Van Dien) at his door. But when his pretty daughter (Graham) comes to visit, Jet thinks getting the two young people together could be his way out of financial crisis. **90m/C VHS, DVD.** Christopher Lloyd, Casper Van Dien, Lauren Graham, Roger Daltrey, Justin Henry, Stuart Pankin, Deborah Van Valkenburgh; ***D:*** Tim Boxell. **VIDEO**

Chasing Dreams ½ **1981 (PG)** Sickly melodrama about a farmboy who finds fulfillment as a baseball player. Lame film promoted as Costner baseball vehicle, but the star of "Bull Durham" and "Field of Dreams" appears only briefly in a secondary role. **96m/C VHS.** David G. Brown, John Fife, Jim Shane, Lisa Kingston, Matt Clark, Kevin Costner; ***D:*** Sean Roche, Therese Conte.

Chasing Freedom ½ **2004** After escaping the brutal Taliban rule in Afghanistan in 2004, Meena (Alizada) must battle to remain in the United States or face death in her native country if deported. Pro bono lawyer Libby (Lewis), a cocky corporate counselor is been ordered to take on her case. An original drama by cable channel Court TV. **89m/C VHS, DVD.** Juliette Lewis, Brian Markinson, Bruce Gray, Layla Alizada, Gail Hanrahan; ***D:*** Don McBrearty; ***W:*** Barbara Samuels. **CABLE**

Chasing Ghosts ½ **2005** Derivative cop caper. Kevin Harrison (Madsen) is about to retire and is trying to get through a complicated murder case while breaking in new partner Davies (Large). But Harrison is also guilt-ridden over the death of cop Mark Spencer (Rooker), which happened because Harrison has been bought and paid for by mobster Alfiri (Busey). Soon the investigation is leading in directions Harrison doesn't want it to go. **114m/C DVD.** Michael Madsen, Michael Rooker, Meat Loaf Aday, Gary Busey, Corey Large, Shannyn Sossamon, Lochlyn Munro, Sean M. Whalen, Danny Trejo, James Duval; ***D:*** Kyle Dean Jackson; ***W:*** Alan Pao; ***C:*** Andrew Huebscher; ***M:*** Scott Glasgow. **VIDEO**

Chasing Holden ½ **2001 (R)** Cliched teen angst comedy/drama does refer to Holden Caulfield of "Catcher in the Rye." 19-year-old Neal (Qualls) is back at prep school after a two-year stay in a mental hospital. His English teacher Alex (Kanan) assigns his students an essay on what happened to Holden after the end of the Salinger novel. Neal decides the best way to find out is to visit the reclusive author—accompanied by his one friend, T.J. (Blanchard). **101m/C VHS, DVD.** DJ Qualls, Rachel Blanchard, Sean Kanan; ***D:*** Malcolm Clarke; ***W:*** Sean Kanan. **VIDEO**

Chasing Liberty ½ **2004 (PG-13)** Singer Moore is restless and rebellious First Daughter Anna, who chafes under the scrutiny of the Secret Service. Mayhem and romance ensues when Anna tags along on a friend's travels across Europe and meets up with a cutie Brit (Goode). While Moore has better acting chops than your average pop singer turned movie actor, this isn't much more than a decaffeinated version of "Roman Holiday." Even so, it should please its target audience of pre-adolescent girls. **110m/C DVD.** *US* Mandy Moore, Matthew Goode, Mark Harmon, Caroline Goodall, Jeremy Piven, Annabella Sciorra, Stark Sands, Miriam Margolyes, Beatrice Rosen(blatt); ***D:*** Andy Cadiff; ***W:*** Derek Guiley, David Schneiderman; ***C:*** Ashley Rowe; ***M:*** Christian Henson.

Chasing Papi **2003 (PG-13)** Hottie L.A. ad exec Tomas Fuentes (Verastegui) travels a lot for his work and makes friends wherever he goes—girlfriends, that is. There's dancer Cici (Vergara) in Miami, attorney Lorena (Sanchez) in Chicago, and heiress Patricia in New York (Velasquez). But the pressure is getting to this lothario and his doctor (Gomez) prescribes tranquilizers and abstinence. Then, Tomas's three ladies all decide to pay him surprise visits. Naturally, the surprise is on them. There's an odd subplot about stolen money and an FBI agent (Vidal) but it's what the threesome discover about themselves—girl power!—that's important. Everyone involved is very, very attractive. **92m/C VHS, DVD.** *US* Eduardo Verastegui, Roselyn Sanchez, Sofia Vergara, Jaci Velasquez, Lisa Vidal, Freddy Rodriguez, D.L. Hughley, Maria Conchita Alonso, Ian Gomez; ***D:*** Linda Mendoza; ***W:*** Steve Antin, Laura Angelica Simon, Alison Balian, Elizabeth Sarnoff; ***C:*** Xavier Perez Grobet; ***M:*** Emilio Estefan Jr.

Chasing Sleep **2000 (R)** College prof. Ed Saxon (Daniels) worries when his wife doesn't return from work. The cops find her car but that's all. Meanwhile, pill-popping insomniac Ed discovers his wife's diary, which reveals she was having an affair with a neighbor. Then he keeps having to deal with strange household plumbing problems. Ed becomes increasinly disoriented, so is he hallucinating the whole thing or has something terrible really happened? Daniels gives an effective off-center performance but the story loses its momentum. **104m/C VHS, DVD.** Jeff Daniels, Emily Bergl, Gil Bellows, Zach Grenier, Julian McMahon, Ben Shenkman, Molly Price; ***D:*** Michael Walker; ***W:*** Michael Walker; ***C:*** Jim Denault.

Chasing the Deer **1994** In 1745, Scotland's Bonnie Prince Charlie (Carrara) has returned from France intent on resurrecting the Jacobite cause and regaining the English throne. Reluctant Alistair Campbell (Zajac) joins the army only to protect his son Euan (Rae), who's supposedly being held prisoner for shooting a Highlander. Euan's actually fallen into the hands of a sympathetic Englishman, Major Elliot (Blessed), advisor to the government's troops. The Jacobites begin their march south until that fateful day on Culloden Moor, which will determine all their futures. **92m/C VHS.** *GB* Brian Blessed, Matthew Zajac, Iain Cuthbertson, Lewis Rae, Dominique Carrara, Fish; ***D:*** Graham Holloway; ***W:*** Jerome Vincent, Bob Carruthers, Steve Gillham; ***C:*** Alan M. Trow; ***M:*** John Wetton.

Chasing the Green ½ **2009** In the 1990s, twenty-something entrepreneur Ross gets his brother Andy to go into partnership in the transaction-credit card processing industry through their marketing of electronic terminals. The brothers become rich but their lack of business experience shows when they ignore Federal Trade Commission warnings. The FTC starts investigating alleged complaints but something stinks since the Commission gets involved at the behest of the brothers' industry competitors. Andy finds solace from their corporate woes through his golf obsession while Ross tries to keep their business from collapsing. Based on a true story. **102m/C DVD.** Jeremy London, Ryan Hurst, Heather McComb, William Devane, Robert Picardo, Larry Pine, Dan Grimaldi; ***D:*** Russ Emanuel; ***W:*** Craig Frankel, Emilio Iasiello; ***C:*** Seth Melnick; ***M:*** Jason Lively, Neil Agro. **VIDEO**

The Chateau ½ **2001 (R)** Naif geek Graham (Rudd) and his black entrepreneurial adoptive brother Allen (Malco) unexpectedly inherit a crumbling chateau in the French countryside. The servants seemed surprised by their arrival and even more shocked when the brothers say they intend to sell the property. They conspire to make the sale as difficult as possible until they can outsmart (which isn't hard) these uncouth Americans and save their home and jobs. English and French with subtitles. **92m/C VHS, DVD.** *US* Paul Rudd, Romany Malco, Sylvie Testud, Didier Flamand, Philippe Nahon, Maria Verdi, Nathalie Jouen, Donal Logue; ***D:*** Jesse Peretz; ***W:*** Jesse Peretz, Thomas Bidegain; ***C:*** Tom Richmond; ***M:*** Nathan Larson, Patrik Bartosch, Nina Persson.

Chato's Land ½ **1971 (PG)** An Indian is tracked by a posse eager to resolve a lawman's death. Conventional violent Bronson vehicle is bolstered by presence of masterful Palance. **100m/C VHS, DVD.** Charles Bronson, Jack Palance, Richard Basehart, James Whitmore, Simon Oakland, Richard Jordan, Ralph Waite, Victor French, Lee Patterson; ***D:*** Michael Winner; ***W:*** Gerald Wilson; ***C:*** Robert Paynter; ***M:*** Jerry Fielding.

Chattahoochee ½ **1989** A man suffering from post-combat syndrome lands in a horrifying institution. Strong cast, with Oldman fine in the lead, and Hopper memorable in extended cameo. Fact-based film is, unfortunately, rather conventionally rendered. **97m/C VHS, DVD.** Gary Oldman, Dennis Hopper, Frances McDormand, Pamela Reed, Ned Beatty, M. Emmet Walsh, William De Acutis, Lee Wilkof, Matt Craven, Gary Klar; ***D:*** Mick Jackson; ***W:*** James Cresson.

Chattanooga Choo Choo ½ **1984 (PG)** A football team owner must restore the Chattanooga Choo Choo and make a 24-

hour run from Chattanooga to New York in order to collect $1 million left to him in a will. The train never leaves the station. **102m/C VHS.** Barbara Eden, George Kennedy, Melissa Sue Anderson, Joe Namath, Bridget Hanley, Christopher McDonald, Clu Gulager, Tony Azito; ***D:*** Bruce Bilson.

Chatterbox 𝒮𝒮 **1976** A starlet's life and career are severely altered when her sex organs begin speaking. So why didn't they warn her about movies like this? Plenty of B-queen Rialson on view. Good double bill with "Me and Him." **73m/C VHS.** Candice Rialson, Larry Gelman, Jean Kean, Perry Bullington; ***D:*** Tom De Simone.

The Chatterley Affair 𝒮𝒮 **1/2 2006** In October of 1960, D.H. Lawrence's scandalous novel "Lady Chatterley's Lover" is brought before a British jury in a famous (and landmark) obscenity trial. But jurors Keith (Spall) and Helena (Delamere) soon find themselves more enthralled with each other than the court proceedings. **90m/C DVD.** *GB* Rafe Spall, Louise Delamere, Karl Johnson, Kenneth Cranham, Mary Healey, Claire Bloom; ***D:*** James Hawes; ***W:*** Andrew Davies; ***C:*** James Aspinall; ***M:*** Nicholas Hooper. **TV**

Che 𝒮𝒮 **2008** Soderbergh's ambitious, generally straightforward, and overlong biography of iconic revolutionary, Argentinian-born Ernesto "Che" Guevara. It starts with Che (Del Toro) meeting Fidel Castro (Bichir) in 1955 and then moves through the Cuban revolution, Che's speech at the United Nations, his desire to spread Marxism in Central and South America, and his fatal misadventures in Bolivia. Released as both a single film (with an intermission) and in two parts: "The Argentine" and "Guerrilla." Soderbergh seems determined not to be overly-dramatic, but instead he's boring and Del Toro's Che (though a fine performance) seems almost a bystander to his own story. English and Spanish with subtitles. **258m/C DVD.** *US* Benicio Del Toro, Demian Bichir, Santiago Cabrera, Elvira Minguez, Jorge Perugorria, Edgar Ramirez, Victor Rasuk, Catalina Sandino Moreno, Rodrigo Santoro, Carlos Bardem, Joaquim de Almeida, Jordi Molla, Julia Ormond, Lou Diamond Phillips, Franka Potente, Armando Riesco; ***Cameos:*** Matt Damon; ***D:*** Steven Soderbergh; ***W:*** Peter Buchman; ***C:*** Steven Soderbergh; ***M:*** Alberto Iglesias.

The Cheap Detective 𝒮𝒮𝒮 **1978 (PG)** Neil Simon's parody of the "Maltese Falcon" gloriously exploits the resourceful Falk in a Bogart-like role. Vast supporting cast—notable Brennan, DeLuise, and Kahn—equally game for fun in this consistently amusing venture. **92m/C VHS, DVD.** Peter Falk, Ann-Margret, Eileen Brennan, Sid Caesar, Stockard Channing, James Coco, Dom DeLuise, Louise Fletcher, John Houseman, Madeline Kahn, Fernando Lamas, Marsha Mason, Phil Silvers, Vic Tayback, Abe Vigoda, Paul Williams, Nicol Williamson; ***D:*** Robert Moore; ***W:*** Neil Simon; ***C:*** John A. Alonzo.

Cheap Shots 𝒮 **1/2 1991 (PG-13)** Cheap best describes this. Two guys running a sleazy New York State resort motel plot to videotape patrons having sex, but capture an apparent mob murder instead. More of a character study than sexploitation, but who needs these characters? Not a stellar writing/directing debut for Ureles and Stoeffhaas. **90m/C VHS.** Louis Zorich, David Patrick Kelly, Mary Louise Wilson, Michael Twaine, Patience Moore; ***D:*** Jeff Ureles; ***W:*** Jeff Ureles, Jerry Stoeffhaas; ***M:*** Jeff Beal.

Cheaper by the Dozen 𝒮𝒮𝒮 **1950** Turn-of-the-century family comedy based on the book by Frank B. Gilbreth Jr., and Ernestine Gilbreth Carey, which chronicled life in the expansive Gilbreth household—12 children, efficiency expert father Frank (Webb), and psychologist mother Lillian (Loy). Stern dad likes to test his theories on the family (and have everything his own way) while nuturing mom easily manages him as well as their large household. There are various family crises (times 12) but it's all very heartwarming. Followed by "Belles on Their Toes." **85m/C VHS, DVD.** Clifton Webb, Myrna Loy, Jeanne Crain, Edgar Buchanan, Mildred Natwick, Sara Allgood, Betty Lynn, Barbara Bates, Norman Ollestad; ***D:*** Walter Lang; ***W:*** Lamar Trotti; ***C:*** Leon Shamroy; ***M:*** Cyril Mockridge.

Cheaper by the Dozen 𝒮𝒮 **1/2 2003 (PG)** Has little in common with the 1950 original, except the title and the number of kids. Mom (Hunt) and Dad (Martin) and the 12 kids have to cope with moving to Chicago while Mom goes on a book tour and Dad ponders a higher-profile coaching gig. A rather perky, old-fashioned lot, this is a brood for which the term "family values" was presumably invented. Cute in a harmless, antiseptic kind of way. Martin adds his usual bemused charm, and the kids should enjoy the sibling-induced highjinks. **98m/C VHS, DVD, UMD.** *US* Steve Martin, Bonnie Hunt, Piper Perabo, Tom Welling, Hilary Duff, Ashton Kutcher, Kevin J. Edelman, Alyson Stoner, Jacob Smith, Liliana Mumy, Paula Marshall, Alan Ruck, Richard Jenkins, Holmes Osborne, Vanessa Bell Calloway, Rex Linn, Amy Hill, Morgan York, Forrest Landis, Blake Woodruff, Brent Kinsman, Shane Kinsman, Steven Anthony Lawrence; ***Cameos:*** Regis Philbin, Kelly Ripa; ***D:*** Shawn Levy; ***W:*** Sam Harper, Joel Cohen, Alec Sokolow; ***C:*** Jonathan Brown; ***M:*** Christophe Beck.

Cheaper by the Dozen 2 𝒮𝒮 **2005 (PG)** Another in the rather endless string of lazy, mediocre family slapstick comedies. Dad Tom Baker (Martin) and wife Kate (Hunt) are still trying to manage their motley crew, but now a few are older and about to leave the family nest. The solution? One last family vacation to Lake Winnetka, Wisconsin. Only the beloved lakefront property is a bit decrepit, and Baker's arch-rival (Levy)—who has eight kids of his own AND a hot new wife (Electra)—has built a mansion across the lake. Lots of harmless silliness. Martin, Levy, and Hunt have all done much better work elsewhere, and they're obviously just picking up a paycheck. **94m/C DVD.** *US* Steve Martin, Eugene Levy, Bonnie Hunt, Tom Welling, Piper Perabo, Carmen Electra, Jaime (James) King, Hilary Duff, Alyson Stoner, Jonathan Bennett, Jacob Smith, Liliana Mumy, Morgan York, Kevin G. Schmidt, Forrest Landis, Taylor Lautner; ***D:*** Adam Shankman; ***W:*** Sam Harper; ***C:*** Peter James; ***M:*** John Debney.

Cheaper to Keep Her **WOOF! 1980 (R)** Alleged comedy about a private detective hired to track likely alimony dodgers. Loathsome, repellent fare, with Davis hopeless in the lead. **92m/C VHS.** Mac Davis, Tovah Feldshuh, Jack Gilford, Rose Marie; ***D:*** Ken Annakin; ***W:*** Herschel Weingrod, Timothy Harris.

The Cheat 𝒮𝒮𝒮 **1915** Ward plays a frivolous socialite heavily indebted to Hayakawa as the Japanese money lender. Hayakawa makes Ward pay with her honor and her flesh by branding her. A dark and captivating drama. Silent with piano score. **55m/B VHS, DVD.** Jack Dean, James Neill, Dana Ong, Hazel Childers, Fannie Ward, Sessue Hayakawa; ***D:*** Cecil B. DeMille; ***W:*** Alvin Wyckoff, Hector Turnbull. Natl. Film Reg. '93.

The Cheat 𝒮𝒮 **1931** Elsa (Bankhead) loses a fortune gambling and tries to keep the news from her husband Jeffrey (Stephens) by embezzling money from a charity fund and speculating on the stock market. When Elsa loses that too, she accepts dough from sleazy admirer Livingston (Pichel), but she's not willing to accept his repayment terms. There's a courtroom climax. Remake of a 1915 silent. **65m/B DVD.** Tallulah Bankhead, Harvey Stephens, Irving Pichel, Williard Dashiell, Edward (Ed Kean, Keene) Keane, Robert Strange, Jay Fassett; ***D:*** George Abbott; ***W:*** Harry Hervey; ***C:*** George J. Folsey.

The Cheaters 𝒮𝒮𝒮 **1945** A well-to-do family has a fabulous idea to impress their friends for the holidays, they take in a down-and-out actor who has recently tried to commit suicide. Unsurprisingly they get more than they bargained for and learn some valuable lessons about what's really important in life. Great family classic. **87m/B VHS.** Joseph Schildkraut, Billie Burke, Eugene Pallette, Robert "Bob" Livingston; ***D:*** Joseph Kane; ***W:*** Frances Hyland. **VIDEO**

The Cheaters 𝒮 **1976 (R)** A young gambler runs away with his boss's son's girlfriend, and is pursued therein. **91m/C VHS, DVD.** *IT* Dayle Haddon, Luc Merenda, Lino Troisi, Enrico Maria Salerno; ***D:*** Sergio Martino.

Cheaters 𝒮 **1/2 1984** Two middle class couples are having affairs with each other's spouses. Complications arise when their respective children decide to marry each other. **103m/C VHS, DVD.** Peggy Cass, Jack Kruschen.

Cheaters 𝒮𝒮 **1/2 2000 (R)** Students at Chicago's run-down Steinmetz High School don't have a prayer of winning the state Academic Decathalon championship until they stumble across a copy of the test and decide that winning is everything—encouraged by their teacher/coach Gerald Plecki (Daniels), who helps them cheat, believing his intentions are good. Based on a true story. **106m/C VHS, DVD.** Jeff Daniels, Jena Malone, Paul Sorvino, Luke Edwards, Blake Heron; ***D:*** John Stockwell; ***W:*** John Stockwell; ***C:*** David Hennings; ***M:*** Paul Haslinger. **CABLE**

Cheatin' Hearts 𝒮𝒮 **1/2 1993 (R)** Kirkland is a woman beset by woe: she's about to lose her house, her philandering husband (Brolin) wanders back to town with his latest bimbo in tow, and her daughter's getting married. This should be a good thing, except hubby makes a fool of himself at the wedding and nearly ruins everything. Well, at least local rancher Kristofferson is around to lift a woman's spirits. And yes, there's a (predictably) happy ending. **88m/C VHS, DVD.** Sally Kirkland, James Brolin, Kris Kristofferson, Pamela Gidley, Laura Johnson; ***D:*** Rod McCall.

Check & Double Check 𝒮 **1930** Radio's original Amos 'n' Andy (a couple of black-faced white guys) help solve a lover's triangle in this film version of the popular radio series. Interesting only as a novelty. Duke Ellington's band plays "Old Man Blues" and "Three Little Words." **85m/B VHS, DVD.** Freeman Gosden, Charles Correll, Duke Ellington; ***D:*** Melville Brown; ***M:*** Max Steiner.

Check Is in the Mail 𝒮 **1/2 1985 (R)** Lame comedy about a financier determined to make his home entirely independent from the rat-race of capitalist society. Dependables Dennehy and Archer are wasted. **83m/C VHS.** Brian Dennehy, Anne Archer, Dick Shawn; ***D:*** Joan Darling.

Check Your Guns 𝒮𝒮 **1948** A crooked judge and a gang of outlaws team up to prey on law-abiding folk and cause headaches for the new sheriff, who's pushing an unsuccessful Old West version of gun control. Nothing really noteworthy here. **55m/B VHS.** Eddie Dean, Roscoe Ates, Nancy Gates, George Chesebro, I. Stanford Jolley, Mikel Conrad, William "Bill" Fawcett; ***D:*** Ray Taylor.

The Checkered Flag 𝒮 **1963** Lame auto-racing drama about an aging, millionaire race car driver with an alcoholic wife who would like nothing more than to see him dead. She talks a young rookie into helping her dispose of hubby. Plans go awry—with horrifying results. Racing scenes overshadow incredibly weak script and performances. **110m/C VHS.** "Miami" Joe Morrison, Evelyn King, Charles G. Martin, Peggy Vendig; ***D:*** William Grefe; ***W:*** William Grefe.

Checking Out 𝒮 **1/2 1989 (R)** Black comedy about a manic hypochondriac who is convinced that his demise will soon occur. You'll pray that he's right. Daniels can't make it work, and supporters Mayron and Magnuson also have little chance in poorly conceived roles. **95m/C VHS, DVD.** Jeff Daniels, Melanie Mayron, Michael Tucker, Kathleen York, Ann Magnuson, Allan Havey, Jo Harvey Allen, Felton Perry, Alan Wolfe; ***D:*** David Leland; ***W:*** Joe Eszterhas; ***M:*** Carter Burwell.

Cheech and Chong: Still Smokin' 𝒮 **1/2** *Still Smokin'* **1983 (R)** Not really. More like still trying to make a buck. Veteran marijuana-dazed comedy duo travel to Amsterdam to raise funds for a bankrupt film festival group by hosting a dope-a-thon. Lots of concert footage used in an attempt to hold the slim plot together. Only for serious fans of the dopin' duo. **91m/C VHS, DVD.** Richard "Cheech" Marin, Thomas Chong; ***D:*** Thomas Chong; ***W:*** Richard "Cheech" Marin, Thomas Chong; ***C:*** Harvey Harrison; ***M:*** George S. Clinton.

Cheech and Chong: Things Are Tough All Over 𝒮𝒮 **1982 (R)** Stoner comedy team are hired by two rich Arab brothers (also played by Cheech and Chong in acting stretch) and unwittingly drive a car loaded with money from Chicago to Las Vegas. Tired fourth in the series. **87m/C VHS, DVD.** Richard "Cheech" Marin, Thomas Chong, Shelby Fiddis, Rikki Marin, Evelyn Guerrero, Rip Taylor; ***D:*** Tom Avildsen; ***W:*** Richard "Cheech" Marin, Thomas Chong.

Cheech and Chong's Next Movie 𝒮𝒮 **1980 (R)** A pair of messed-up bumblers adventure into a welfare office, massage parlor, nightclub, and flying saucer, while always living in fear of the cops. Kinda funny, like. Sequel to "Up in Smoke." **95m/C VHS, DVD.** Richard "Cheech" Marin, Thomas Chong, Evelyn Guerrero, Edie McClurg, Paul (Pee-wee Herman) Reubens, Phil Hartman; ***D:*** Thomas Chong; ***W:*** Richard "Cheech" Marin, Thomas Chong.

Cheech and Chong's Nice Dreams 𝒮𝒮 **1981 (R)** The spaced-out duo are selling their own "specially mixed" ice cream to make cash and realize their dreams. Third in the series. **97m/C VHS, DVD.** Sab Shimono, Sandra Bernhard, Linnea Quigley, Michael Winslow, Richard "Cheech" Marin, Thomas Chong, Evelyn Guerrero, Stacy Keach, Paul (Pee-wee Herman) Reubens; ***Cameos:*** Timothy Leary; ***D:*** Thomas Chong; ***W:*** Richard "Cheech" Marin, Thomas Chong; ***C:*** Charles Correll; ***M:*** Harry Betts.

Cheech and Chong's The Corsican Brothers **WOOF! 1984 (PG)** Wretched swashbuckler features the minimally talented duo in a variety of worthless roles. Dumas would vomit in his casket if he knew about this. Fifth in the series. **91m/C VHS, DVD.** Richard "Cheech" Marin, Thomas Chong, Roy Dotrice, Rae Dawn Chong, Shelby Fiddis, Rikki Marin, Edie McClurg; ***D:*** Thomas Chong; ***W:*** Richard "Cheech" Marin, Thomas Chong; ***C:*** Harvey Harrison.

Cheech and Chong's Up in Smoke 𝒮𝒮 **1/2** *Up in Smoke* **1979 (R)** A pair of free-spirited burn-outs team up for a tongue-in-cheek spoof of sex, drugs, and rock and roll. First and probably the best of the dopey duo's cinematic adventures. A boxoffice bonanza when released and still a cult favorite. **87m/C VHS, DVD.** Richard "Cheech" Marin, Thomas Chong, Stacy Keach, Edie Adams, Strother Martin, Cheryl "Rainbeaux" Smith; ***D:*** Lou Adler; ***W:*** Richard "Cheech" Marin, Thomas Chong; ***C:*** Gene Polito.

The Cheerful Fraud 𝒮𝒮 **1/2 1927** Denny, who appeared in some two hundred-odd films in his career, masquerades as a butler to be near the girl he loves. A fool for love is a cheerful fraud. A zanily romantic silent comedy. **64m/B VHS.** Reginald Denny, Gertrude (Olmstead) Olmsted, Emily Fitzroy, Gertrude Astor; ***D:*** William A. Seiter.

Cheering Section **WOOF! 1973 (R)** High school football teams compete for the grand prize—the privilege of ravishing the losing school's cheerleaders. Rah, rah, rah. **84m/C VHS.** Rhonda Foxx, Tom Leindecker, Gregg D'Jah, Patricia Michelle, Jeff Laine; ***D:*** Harry Kerwin.

Cheerleader Camp **WOOF!** *Bloody Pom Poms* **1988 (R)** Nubile gals are stalked by a psychopath while they cavort semi-clad at summer camp. **89m/C VHS, DVD.** Betsy Russell, Leif Garrett, Lucinda Dickey, Lorie Griffin, George "Buck" Flower, Teri Weigel, Rebecca Ferratti, Travis McKenna, Kathryn Litton; ***D:*** John Quinn; ***W:*** David Lee Fein, R.L. O'Keefe; ***C:*** Bryan England; ***M:*** Joel Hamilton, Muriel Hodler-Hamilton.

The Cheerleaders **WOOF! 1972 (R)** Dim-witted exploitation effort has the usual suspects—moronic jocks and lamebrained gals—cavorting exuberantly. Followed by "Revenge of the Cheerleaders." **84m/C VHS, DVD.** Stephanie Fondue, Denise Dillaway, Jovita Bush, Debbie Lowe, Sandy Evans; ***D:*** Paul Glickler.

Cheerleaders' Wild Weekend **WOOF! 1985 (R)** Group of cheerleaders are held captive by a disgruntled former football star. Pom poms wave. **87m/C VHS.** Jason Williams, Kristine DeBell; ***D:*** Jeff Werner.

Cheers for Miss Bishop 𝒮𝒮 **1/2 1941** The story of a woman who graduates from college then teaches at the same institution for the next 50 years. Somewhat moving. Based on Bess Streeter Aldrich's novel. **95m/B VHS, DVD.** Martha Scott, William Gargan, Edmund Gwenn, Sterling Holloway, Rosemary DeCamp; ***D:*** Tay Garnett; ***M:*** Edward Ward.

Cheetah **1989 (G)** Two California kids visiting their parents in Kenya embark on the adventure of their lives when, with the help of a young Masai, they adopt and care for an orphaned cheetah. Usual Disney kids and animals story. **80m/C VHS, DVD.** Keith Coogan, Lucy Deakins, Collin Mothupi; ***D:*** Jeff Blyth; ***W:*** John Cotter; ***C:*** Thomas Burstyn.

The Cheetah Girls 1/2 **2003 (G)** This Disney Channel original is made for undiscriminating tween girls. New York teens Galleria (Raven-Symone), Chanel (Bailon), Aqua (Williams), and Dorinda (Bryan) form a pop group for the school talent show. They get a professional chance when record producer Jackal Johnson (Corazza) hears their music, but Jackal's aptly named when he wants to give them a makeover. However, the girls have another problem when their success turns Galleria into a diva, which isn't "cheetah-licious." (Yes, they have their own catch phrase.) **93m/C DVD.** Raven, Vincent Corazza, Lynn Whitfield, Kyle Schmid, Sandra Caldwell, Adrienne Bailon, Kiely Williams, Sabrina Bryan; ***D:*** Oz Scott; ***W:*** Alison Taylor; ***C:*** Derick Underschultz; ***M:*** John Van Tongeren. **CABLE**

The Cheetah Girls 2 1/2 **2006 (G)** In this Disney Channel sequel, Galleria (Raven-Symone) enters the Cheetah Girls in a talent competition/music festival being held in Barcelona, Spain. When the girls arrive, they're so interested in everything else going on (boys, sightseeing, shopping) that they neglect their music, which frustrates Galleria because they have a real rival in local teen queen Marisol (Peregrin). **96m/C DVD.** Raven, Adrienne Bailon, Sabrina Bryan, Kiely Williams, Abel Folk, Lynn Whitfield, Belinda Peregrin, Lori Alter, Golan Yosef, Kim Manning; ***D:*** Kenny Ortega; ***W:*** Alison Taylor, Bethesda Brown; ***C:*** Daniel Aranyo; ***M:*** David Lawrence. **CABLE**

The Cheetah Girls: One World 1/2 **2008 (G)** Galleria is off to college so only Chanel, Dorinda, and Aqua appear in this third colorful music extravaganza. The girls head to India after being cast in a Bollywood flick only to learn the producer actually wants just one of them and they will have to compete for the part. But are the Cheetah Girls willing to risk their friendships or can they find a way to make the situation work? **88m/C DVD.** Adrienne Bailon, Sabrina Bryan, Kiely Williams, Roshan Seth, Michael Steger, Kunal Sharma, Rupak Ginn, Deepti Daryanani; ***D:*** Paul Hoen; ***W:*** Nisha Ganatra; ***C:*** Donald Duncan; ***M:*** David Lawrence. **CABLE**

A Chef in Love *Les Mille et Une Recettes du Cuisinier Amoureux; The Cook in Love* **1996 (PG-13)** In 1920, Parisian Pascal Ishac (Richard) meets Georgian Princess Cecilia (Kirtadze) while travelling and decides to stay and open a French restaurant in the capital of Tbilisi. When the capital is invaded by the Red Army in 1921, communist leader Zigmund (Kahmhadze) forces Cecilia to marry him and shuts down Pascal's eatery. With his great love and his restaurant both gone, Pascal writes a master cookbook and memoir that is later discovered and translated by Cecilia's son Anton (Gautier), who also discovers that Pascal is his father. French, Russian and Georgian with subtitles. **95m/C VHS, DVD.** ***FR*** Pierre Richard, Nino Kirtadze, Temur Kahmhadze, Jean-Yves Gautier, Micheline Presle; ***D:*** Nana Dzhordzadze; ***W:*** Irakli Kvirikadze; ***C:*** Georgi Beridze; ***M:*** Goran Bregovic.

Chef's Special *Fuera de Carta* **2008** Overwhelmed Madrid chef Maxi is trying to keep his restaurant afloat while waiting for an important review that could make his career. Then his personal life implodes when his ex-wife dies and the self-absorbed man is forced to raise his two estranged children. And find romance with the gorgeous soccer superstar who just came out of the closet (and moved into an apartment down the hall). Lots of silly situations. Spanish with subtitles. **111m/C DVD.** ***SP*** Javier Camara, Lola Duenas, Fernando Tejero, Benjamin Vicuna, Chus (Maria Jesus) Lampreave, Luis Varela; ***D:*** Nacho G. Velilla; ***W:*** Nacho G. Velilla, Antonia Sanchez, David Sanchez, Oriol Capel; ***C:*** David Omedes; ***M:*** Juanjo Javierre.

Chelsea Walls **2001 (R)** Hawke's directorial debut features wife Thurman as one of the would-be artists living at the legendary (and seedy) Chelsea Hotel. There's a variety of struggling writers, musicians, and artists who all have romantic dilemmas and substance abuse problems as well. Lots of chatter and atmosphere but the characters are all walking cliches. **108m/C VHS, DVD.** ***US*** Kris Kristofferson, Uma Thurman, Vincent D'Onofrio, Natasha Richardson, Tuesday Weld, Rosario Dawson, Mark Webber, Kevin Corrigan, Robert Sean Leonard, Steve Zahn, Frank Whaley; ***D:*** Ethan Hawke; ***W:*** Nicole Burdette; ***C:*** Tom Richmond; ***M:*** Jeff Tweedy.

Cheri **2009 (R)** Exquisite-looking, if bloodless, melodrama about doomed love. Lea (Pfeiffer) is a still beautiful, middle-aged courtesan in Belle Epoque Paris, now retired from her very successful career. She exchanges barbs and gossip with former colleague Charlotte (Bates), who has a louche teenaged son nicknamed Cheri (Friend), and Charlotte decides Lea should give him some seasoning. Six years later the mismatched lovers are still together, refusing to recognize any of the deep emotions they have for each other. Then Charlotte makes other plans for Cheri's future, and Lea plays at not caring. Based on two novels by Colette. **92m/C DVD.** ***GB FR GE*** Michelle Pfeiffer, Kathy Bates, Rupert Friend, Felicity Jones, Iben Hjejle, Bette Bourne, Anita Pallenberg, Frances Tomelty, Harriet Walter, Nichola McAuliffe; ***D:*** Stephen Frears; ***W:*** Christopher Hampton; ***C:*** Darius Khondji; ***M:*** Alexandre Desplat; ***Nar:*** Stephen Frears.

Cherish **2002 (R)** Zoe (Tunney) is a nervous San Francisco dot.commer who, under convoluted circumstances, winds up accused of vehicular manslaughter while driving under the influence. She winds up under house arrest wearing an electronic surveillance anklet with deputy Daly (Blake) to check up on her. She gets to make friends with her neighbors and convinces Daly to help her find the stalker who's the cause of all her misery. Confusing blend of genres with a good soundtrack. **99m/C VHS, DVD.** ***US*** Robin Tunney, Tim Blake Nelson, Jason Priestley, Nora Dunn, Brad Hunt, Liz Phair, Lindsay Crouse, Stephen Polk, Ricardo Gil, Kenny Kwong; ***D:*** Finn Taylor; ***W:*** Finn Taylor; ***C:*** Barry Stone; ***M:*** Mark De Gil Antoni.

The Cherokee Kid 1/2 **1996 (PG-13)** Western/comedy about a novice gunslinger (Sinbad) avenging his family. There's a corrupt banker (Coburn), a bounty hunter (Hines), a Mexican freedom fighter (Martinez), and a gang of bankrobbing nuns to keep things interesting while the Kid learns his outlaw ways. **91m/C VHS, DVD.** Sinbad, James Coburn, Burt Reynolds, Gregory Hines, A. Martinez, Ernie Hudson; ***D:*** Paris Barclay; ***W:*** Tim Kazurinsky, Denise DeClue; ***M:*** Stanley Clarke. **CABLE**

Cherry Blossoms *Cherry Blossoms: Hanami; Kirschbluesten-Hanami* **2008** Hausfrau Trudi (Elsner) is fascinated by Japan and wants her overbearing husband Rudi (Wepper) to agree to visit their son who has a job in Tokyo. Instead, Rudi insists they see their other children who live nearby in Berlin. Trudi dies suddenly and the aimless widower decides to honor his wife by finally visiting Japan, where he meets a teenage Butoh dancer in Tokyo and makes a pilgrimage to Mount Fuji. Unhurried drama about loss and acceptance. German and Japanese with subtitles. **127m/C DVD.** ***GE*** Hannelore Elsner, Nadja Uhl, Maximilian Bruckner, Birgit Minichmayr, Felix Eitner, Floriane Daniel, Elmar Wepper, Aya Irizuki; ***D:*** Doris Doerrie; ***W:*** Doris Doerrie; ***C:*** Hanno Lentz; ***M:*** Claus Bantzer.

Cherry Crush 1/2 **2007 (R)** Dull noir wannabe. Prep school student Jordan Wells (Tucker) is expelled after taking naughty pics of female classmates. Now enrolled in public school, Jordan is putty for wrong side of the tracks Shay (Reed), even when things turn deadly. Reed's more petulant than provocative. **89m/C DVD.** Jonathan Tucker, Nikki Reed, Frank Whaley, Michael O'Keefe, Julie Gonzalo, Dennis Boutsikaris, Haviland (Haylie) Morris; ***D:*** Nicholas DiBella; ***W:*** Nicholas DiBella, Paul Root; ***C:*** Tim Wainwright; ***M:*** Joe Kaltenbach. **VIDEO**

Cherry Falls 1/2 **2000 (R)** The small town of Cherry Falls is plagued by a serial killer who only kills teenaged virgins, so naturally every teen there is out to do it and save themselves. However Sheriff Marken (Biehn) has no intention of letting daughter Jody (Murphy) go to such extremes. This one is an amusing parody of slasher flicks, teen sex comedies, and suburban nightmares. **100m/C VHS, DVD.** Jay Mohr, Michael Biehn, Brittany Murphy, Candy Clark, Gabriel Mann, Keram Malicki-Sanchez, Jesse Bradford; ***D:*** Geoffrey Wright; ***W:*** Ken Selden; ***C:*** Anthony B. Richmond; ***M:*** Walter Werzowa.

Cherry Hill High WOOF! **1976 (R)** Five teen girls compete for former-virgin status. Pass on this one. **92m/C VHS.** Linda McInerney, Carrie Olsen, Nina Carson, Lynn Hastings, Gloria Upson, Stephanie Lawlor; ***D:*** Alex E. Goiten.

Cherry 2000 **1988 (PG-13)** Futuristic flick concerns a man who short-circuits his sex-toy robots and embarks on a search for replacement parts across treacherous territory, only to meet a real female—Griffith. Offbeat, occasionally funny. **94m/C VHS, DVD.** Melanie Griffith, David Andrews, Ben Johnson, Tim Thomerson, Michael C. Gwynne, Pamela Gidley; ***D:*** Steve DeJarnatt; ***W:*** Michael Almereyda; ***C:*** Jacques Haitkin; ***M:*** Basil Poledouris.

The Chess Player *Le Joueur d'Echecs* **1927** In 1776, Polish nobleman Boleslas Vorowski heads a secret movement to free his country from Russian control. When Vorowski is wounded in battle, his mentor, inventor Baron von Kempelen, constructs a chess-playing automaton named Turk that conceals Vorowski in order to smuggle him to safety. When Catherine the Great learns of Turk's chess prowess, she commands the automaton be brought to Russia for a royal match. From the novel by Henri Dupuy-Mazuel, which is based on the real 18th-century machine. **133m/B VHS, DVD.** ***FR*** Pierre Blanchar, Edith Jehanne, Charles Dullin, Camille Bert, Pierre Batcheff; ***D:*** Raymond Bernard; ***W:*** Raymond Bernard; ***C:*** Joseph-Louis Mundwiller, Willy, Marc Bujard; ***M:*** Henri Rabaud.

Chesty Anderson USN *Anderson's Angels* **1976** Ultra-lame sexploitation about female naval recruits. Minimal nudity. **90m/C VHS, DVD.** Shari Eubank, Dorri Thompson, Rosanne Katon, Marcie Barkin, Scatman Crothers, Frank Campanella, Fred Willard; ***D:*** Ed Forsyth.

Cheyenne Autumn 1/2 **1964** The newly restored version of the ambitious, ultimately hit-and-miss western epic about three hundred Cheyenne Indians who migrate from Oklahoma to their Wyoming homeland in 1878. The cavalry, for once, are not the good guys. Widmark is strong in the lead. Stewart is memorable in his comic cameo as Wyatt Earp. Last film from genre master Ford, capturing the usual rugged panoramas. Based on a true story as told in the Mari Sandoz novel. **156m/C VHS, DVD.** Richard Widmark, Carroll Baker, Karl Malden, Dolores Del Rio, Sal Mineo, Edward G. Robinson, Ricardo Montalban, Gilbert Roland, Arthur Kennedy, John Carradine, Victor Jory, Mike Mazurki, George O'Brien, John Qualen; ***Cameos:*** James Stewart; ***D:*** John Ford; ***C:*** William Clothier; ***M:*** Alex North.

Cheyenne Kid 1/2 **1933** Determined bronco buster is up against a gang of bad guys. **40m/B VHS.** Tom Keene, Mary Mason, Roscoe Ates, Alan Bridge, Otto Hoffman, Anderson Lawler, Alan Roscoe; ***D:*** Robert F. "Bob" Hill; ***W:*** Jack Curtis; ***C:*** Nicholas Musuraca; ***M:*** Max Steiner.

Cheyenne Rides Again 1/2 **1938** Cheyenne poses as an outlaw to hunt a gang of rustlers. **60m/B VHS.** Tom Tyler, Lucille Browne, Lon Chaney Jr., Roger Williams, Charles "Slim" Whitaker; ***D:*** Robert F. "Bob" Hill.

The Cheyenne Social Club **1970 (PG)** Stewart inherits a brothel and Fonda helps him operate it. Kelly directs, sort of. Some laughs, but this effort is beneath this trio. **103m/C VHS, DVD.** Henry Fonda, James Stewart, Shirley Jones, Sue Ane Langdon, Elaine Devry, Arch Johnson, Dabbs Greer, Jackie Joseph, Richard Collier, Charles Tyner, Robert J. Wilke, Warren Kemmerling, John Dehner, James Lee Barrett; ***D:*** Gene Kelly; ***C:*** William Clothier; ***M:*** Walter Scharf.

Cheyenne Takes Over **1947** Lash sniffs out the bad guy in the case of a murdered ranch heir. **56m/B VHS.** Lash LaRue, Al "Fuzzy" St. John, George Chesebro; ***D:*** Ray Taylor.

Cheyenne Warrior 1/2 **1994 (PG)** Pregnant young bride Rebecca heads west with a husband who soons winds up dead, leaving her stranded at an isolated trading post. She takes in a wounded Cheyenne warrior, nurses him back to health, and he tries to convince her to let his tribe care for her. Respectable performances if unexciting. **90m/C VHS, DVD.** Kelly Preston, Pato Hoffmann, Bo Hopkins, Dan Haggerty, Charles Powell, Rick Dean, Clint Howard; ***D:*** Mark Griffiths; ***W:*** Michael B. Druxman.

Chicago 1/2 **2002 (R)** The first Oscar-winning musical since the 1970s celebrates the unlikely themes of murder, adultery and greed with winning results. Heroine Roxie Hart (Zellweger) in jail for offing her two-timing boyfriend, finally finds the fame she craved. Ditto for Zeta-Jones' Velma Kelly, who's also in stir for popping her old man. The hot-headed beauties share the same slick lawyer, Billy Flynn (Gere). Reilly is Zellweger's simpleton husband, the sole spot of earnestness in an otherwise cynical film. Deftly directed, with musical numbers done as fantasy segments. Zeta-Jones and Latifah are the ones with the pipes for the genre, while lesser singer/dancers Gere and Zellweger score with appealing performances. Big-screen version of the award-winning musical by John Kander, Fred Ebb, and Bob Fosse. **113m/C VHS, DVD.** ***US*** Renee Zellweger, Catherine Zeta-Jones, Richard Gere, Queen Latifah, John C. Reilly, Christine Baranski, Lucy Liu, Taye Diggs, Colm Feore, Dominic West; ***D:*** Rob Marshall; ***W:*** Bill Condon; ***C:*** Dion Beebe; ***M:*** Danny Elfman, John Kander, Fred Ebb. Oscars '02: Art Dir./Set Dec., Costume Des., Film, Film Editing, Sound, Support. Actress (Zeta-Jones); British Acad. '02: Support. Actress (Zeta-Jones); British Acad. '03: Sound; Directors Guild '02: Director (Marshall); Golden Globes '03: Actor—Mus./Comedy (Gere), Actress—Mus./Comedy (Zellweger), Film—Mus./Comedy; Screen Actors Guild '02: Actress (Zellweger), Support. Actress (Zeta-Jones), Cast.

Chicago Cab *Hellcab* **1998 (R)** This checkered sketch piece about a cab driver (Dillon) and the assorted passengers he picks up during a "normal" day never really pulls away from the curb. Despite cameos from actors such as John Cusack, Gillian Anderson and Laurie Metcalf, the passengers are nasty obnoxious stereotypes drawn to prove the point that other people are irritating. Will Kern adapted the screenplay from his original play "Hellcab." **96m/C VHS.** Paul Dillon, Gillian Anderson, John Cusack, Julianne Moore, Michael Ironside, John C. Reilly, Laurie Metcalf, Matt Roth, Shulle Cowen, Philip Van Lear, Michael Shannon; ***D:*** Mary Cybulski, John Tintori; ***W:*** Will Kern; ***C:*** Hubert Taczanowski; ***M:*** Page Hamilton.

Chicago Joe & the Showgirl **1990 (R)** A London-based GI befriends a loopy showgirl and helps her in various crimes during WWII. Appealing Lloyd overwhelms Sutherland, who shows only limited acting ability here. Kensit and Pigg are fine in smaller roles. **105m/C VHS, DVD.** ***GB*** Emily Lloyd, Kiefer Sutherland, Patsy Kensit, Keith Allen, Liz Fraser, Alexandra Pigg, Ralph Nossek, Colin Bruce; ***D:*** Bernard Rose; ***M:*** Hans Zimmer.

Chicago 10 1/2 **2007 (R)** A unique blend of archival footage, vocal reenactment, and rotoscope animation recounts the infamous trial of eight anti-war protesters following the 1968 Democratic National Convention, along with the chaos surrounding the case. An unconventional and fresh take on the documentary form, almost as radical as its subjects. Rather than being set to the music of the heroes of the day, like Dylan or CSN, contemporary artists provide the soundtrack, going as far as having Rage Against the Machine covering "Kick Out the Jams" during footage of the MC5 performing the original live during the protests. **103m/C DVD.** ***US D:*** Brett Morgen; ***W:*** Brett Morgen; ***M:*** Jeff Danna; ***V:*** Hank Azaria, Dylan Baker, Nick Nolte, Mark Ruffalo, Roy Scheider, Liev Schreiber, Jeffrey Wright, Amy Ryan, Debra Eisenstadt.

The Chicken Chronicles **1977 (PG)** An affluent high school dude longs to get horizontal with his dream girl. Set in the

1960s. First feature film appearance for Guttenberg. **94m/C VHS.** Phil Silvers, Ed Lauter, Steve Guttenberg, Lisa Reeves, Meridith Baer; ***D:*** Francis Simon.

Chicken Little ½ **2005 (G)** Disney's first solo (without Pixar) foray into CG animation won't please everyone, but the intended audience of grade-schoolers probably won't notice. Chicken Little (Braff) causes a panic and big trouble for himself when he thinks the sky is falling and sounds the alarm. He spends most of his time trying to live the incident down and build a good relationship with his pop (Marshall) a former athletic hero. When a piece of the "sky" falls on him again, it's up to him and his pals to convince everyone that it really happened, especially when an alien kid gets stranded in town, almost prompting an invasion. Lacks the originality, verve, and adult-pleasing inside humor of the Pixar collaborations, but not a bad first try. **82m/C DVD, Blu-ray Disc.** *US* ***D:*** Mark Dindal; ***W:*** Steve Bencich, Ron J. Friedman, Ron Anderson; ***M:*** John Debney; ***V:*** Zach Braff, Garry Marshall, Joan Cusack, Steve Zahn, Amy Sedaris, Don Knotts, Harry Shearer, Patrick Stewart, Wallace Shawn, Fred Willard, Catherine O'Hara, Adam West, Patrick Warburton.

Chicken Run ½ **2000 (G)** It's a prisoner-of-war escape movie with chickens. This Claymation wonder is a comedy set on a failing 1950s Yorkshire chicken farm, where the hens realize their necks are literally on the chopping block when greedy farm wife, Mrs. Tweedy (Richardson), decides to go into the chicken pie business. So chicken leader, Ginger (Sawalha), tries to find a workable mass escape plan. And then daredevil Yankee rooster Rocky (Gibson) literally drops into the barnyard and Ginger believes he can teach all the hens to fly out. Chickens are just funny and you'll be amazed at what the animators have managed to make them do and how expressive they are. **86m/C VHS, DVD.** *GB* ***D:*** Nick Park, Peter Lord; ***W:*** Karey Kirkpatrick; ***M:*** John Powell, Harry Gregson-Williams; ***V:*** Mel Gibson, Julia Sawalha, Miranda Richardson, Jane Horrocks, Tony Haygarth, Timothy Spall, Imelda Staunton, Phil Daniels, Benjamin Whitrow, Lynn Ferguson.

Chicken Tikka Masala **2005** Jimi Chopra (Bisson) is from an Anglo-Hindi family and is expected to go along with his arranged marriage to Simran (Mahal). Except he's gay and living with his boyfriend Jack (Ash), though obviously Jimi hasn't the courage to tell his family. So he tries to convince them that he's already involved with Jack's sister Vanessa (Bankes). The ruse is hopeless as is the entire film, with its weak script, timid storytelling, and risible acting. **92m/C DVD.** *GB* Chris Bisson, Saeed Jaffrey, Zohra Sehgal, Sally Bankes, Peter Ash, Jinder Mahal, Jamila Massey; ***D:*** Hormage Singh Kalirai; ***W:*** Roopesh Parekh; ***C:*** Mike Muschamp.

Chicks, Man **1999** Boring, man. Rod and Jack are a couple of clueless, mopey Gen-Xers who don't understand the ladies. Jack gets dumped and then tries rebound dating while Rod macks on Heather at a party and is later beaten up by Heather's boyfriend for taking liberties. There's much whining—not least by unwary viewers of this tedious pic. **93m/C DVD.** Aaron Priest, Robia LaMorte, Krista Gano, Nick Wechsler, Scott Roberts, Renee Humphrey; ***D:*** Jeremy Wagener; ***W:*** Jeremy Wagener; ***C:*** Michael J. Bruggemeyer; ***M:*** David Stout.

Chiefs **1983** A police chief in a Southern town discovers a series of murders concealed by town big wigs. Made for TV film boasts a surprisingly strong cast, but provides otherwise conventional entertainment. **200m/C VHS.** Charlton Heston, Paul Sorvino, Keith Carradine, Brad Davis, Billy Dee Williams, Wayne Rogers, Stephen Collins, Tess Harper, Victoria Tennant; ***D:*** Jerry London. **TV**

The Child *Kill and Go Hide* **1976 (R)** Low-budget horror-quickie combining elements of "The Bad Seed," "The Omen," and "Night of the Living Dead," that attempts to cash in on the fright-film craze of the early '70s. What we get is a poorly dubbed film that makes little sense, but does offer some interesting shocks. A young woman returns to her hometown to be the nanny for a disturbed girl, Rosalie (Cole), who has a bad habit of killing neighbors and talking to zombies in the local graveyard, all the way harping on her mother's mysterious death. This is one of those movies where everyone acts very eccentric, but said behavior doesn't add anything to the plot. The finale offers some excitement, but overall the film is more of a curiosity than a "must-see." **95m/C VHS, DVD.** Laurel Barnett, Rosalie Cole, Frank Janson, Richard Hanners, Ruth Ballan; ***D:*** Robert Voskanian; ***W:*** Ralph Lucas; ***C:*** Mori Alavi; ***M:*** Rob Wallace.

The Child *L'Enfant* **2005 (R)** Amoral, 20-year-old petty criminal Bruno (Renier) and his younger girlfriend Sonia (Francois) have just had a baby boy. Unprepared for fatherhood, he casually sells the child to a black market adoption ring. Bruno discovers his thoughtless actions have consequences when Sonia becomes hysterical and wants her son back. This turns out to be less easy than the original transaction. French with subtitles. **95m/C DVD.** *BE FR* Jeremie Renier, Fabrizio Rongione, Olivier Gourmet, Deborah Francois, Jeremie Segard, Samuel de Ryck, Mireille Bailly; ***D:*** Jean-Pierre Dardenne, Luc Dardenne; ***W:*** Jean-Pierre Dardenne, Luc Dardenne; ***C:*** Alain Marcoen.

Child Bride of Short Creek ½ **1981** A young Korean war veteran returns to his community where polygamy is allowed, to find that his father intends to marry again, this time to a 15-year-old. Conflict ensues. Based on an actual event that occurred in the 1950s. **100m/C VHS, DVD.** Diane Lane, Conrad Bain, Christopher Atkins, Kiel Martin, Helen Hunt; ***D:*** Robert Lewis. **TV**

Child in the Night **1990 (R)** A shaken eight-year-old boy is a witness to murder in his family, and a psychologist with plenty of her own problems must get him to testify. First film for Wood. Middling TV-movie suspense. **93m/C VHS.** Tom Skerritt, JoBeth Williams, Darren McGavin, Season Hubley, Elijah Wood; ***D:*** Mike Robe.

A Child Is Waiting **1963** Poignant and provocative story of teachers in an institution for the mentally retarded. Fine performances include Lancaster as the institution's administrator and Garland as a teacher who cares too much for everyone's good. Cassavetes incorporates footage using handicapped children as extras—not entirely seamlessly—providing a sensitive and candid edge. **105m/B VHS.** Burt Lancaster, Judy Garland, Gena Rowlands, Steven Hill, Bruce Ritchey; ***D:*** John Cassavetes; ***W:*** Abby Mann; ***M:*** Ernest Gold.

Child of Darkness, Child of Light ½ **1991 (PG-13)** A priest is sent to investigate two virgin pregnancies and discovers that one child will be a savior and the other the Anti-Christ. Totally mindless brain candy resembling the "Omen" movies and "Rosemary's Baby." Adapted from James Patterson's book "Virgin." **85m/C VHS.** Anthony John (Tony) Denison, Brad Davis, Paxton Whitehead, Claudette Nevins, Sydney Penny, Kristin Dattilo-Hayward, Viveca Lindfors, Sela Ward, Alan Oppenheimer, Eric Christmas; ***D:*** Marina Sargenti; ***W:*** Brian Taggert. **CABLE**

Child of Glass **1978 (G)** A young boy's family moves into a huge New Orleans mansion, and soon after encounters a young girl's ghost and lost treasure from the Civil War. A Disney made for TV movie. **93m/C VHS.** Barbara Barrie, Biff McGuire, Anthony Zerbe, Nina Foch, Steve (Steven) Shaw, Katy Kurtzman, Olivia Barash; ***D:*** John Erman. **TV**

Child of the Prairie **1918** An early Mix film about a young cowboy and his city-loving wife down on their luck in a western town. Silent with music score. **63m/B VHS.** Tom Mix; ***D:*** Tom Mix; ***W:*** Tom Mix.

Child Star: The Shirley Temple Story ½ **2001** TV biopic that charts the rise to Depression-era fame of little Shirley Temple (with an entertaining performance by Orr). Shirley's mom Gertrude (Britton) is around to see that big bad studio mogul Darryl Zanuck (Vidler) doesn't take advantage of her little darling. The best parts are the faithful re-creations of some of Temple's most famous song-and-dance numbers, including those with Bill (Bojangles) Robinson, here played by Battle. **88m/C VHS, DVD.** Ashley Rose Orr, Connie Britton, Steven Vidler, Colin Friels, Emily Anne Hart, Hinton Battle; ***D:*** Nadia Tass; ***W:*** Joe Wiesenfeld; ***C:*** David Parker; ***M:*** Bill Elliot. **TV**

The Children WOOF! **1980 (R)** Familiar nuclear leak leads to monster mutants done to a novel (though extremely low-budget) turn: after a school bus passes through radioactive fog, the kiddies inside assume the ability to incinerate whoever they hug. They also assume a certain zombie-like demeanor and sport black fingernails. None of this is noted by their uncaring and less-than-observant parents, many of whom are enticed into a very warm hug. This may be intended as social satire. Not only are the little microwaves extremely dangerous, the only way to kill them is to chop off their hands, leading to a wild limbless finale. **89m/C VHS, DVD.** Martin Shaker, Gale Garnett, Gil Rogers; ***D:*** Max Kalmanowicz.

The Children ½ **1990** Kingsley stars as a middle-aged engineer who finds himself caring for seven children in this touching love story from novelist Edith Wharton. Shot on location in Venice, the cinematography is excellent and the cast is superb, but the film lags in places. A remake of "The Marriage Playground." **90m/C VHS.** *GB GE* Ben Kingsley, Kim Novak, Siri Neal, Geraldine Chaplin, Joe Don Baker, Britt Ekland, Donald Sinden, Karen Black, Robert Stephens, Rupert Graves, Rosemary Leach; ***D:*** Tony Palmer.

The Children Are Watching Us *The Little Martyr; I Bambini Ci Guardano* **1944** Sobering drama of a family dissolution as seen by a child. A four-year-old boy drifts unloved by his suicidal father and by his mother, who's only interested in her own love affair. Worthy example of Italian neo-realism marks the first collaboration between Zavattini and De Sica. In Italian with subtitles. **92m/B VHS, DVD.** *IT* Luciano de Ambrosis, Isa Pola, Emilio Cigoli; ***D:*** Vittorio De Sica; ***W:*** Cesare Zavattini, Vittorio De Sica.

Children in the Crossfire ½ **1984** When youngsters from war-torn Northern Ireland spend a summer in America with children from the Republic of Ireland, both sides find their nationalistic prejudices falling away. But a great challenge awaits them when they return home from their summer of fun. Nicely done drama. **96m/C VHS, DVD.** Charles Haid, Karen Valentine, Julia Duffy, David Hoffman; ***D:*** George Schaefer; ***M:*** Brad Fiedel. **TV**

Children of a Lesser God ½ **1986 (R)** Based upon the play by Mark Medoff, this sensitive, intelligent film deals with an unorthodox speech teacher at a school for the deaf, who falls in love with a beautiful and rebellious ex-student. Inarguably romantic; the original stage production won the Best Play Tony in 1980. Hurt and Matlin reportedly continued their romance off-screen as well. **119m/C VHS, DVD.** William Hurt, Marlee Matlin, Piper Laurie, Philip Bosco, E. Katherine Kerr; ***D:*** Randa Haines; ***W:*** Hesper Anderson, Mark Medoff; ***C:*** John Seale; ***M:*** Michael Convertino. Oscars '86: Actress (Matlin); Golden Globes '87: Actress—Drama (Matlin).

The Children of An Lac ½ **1980** Three women attempt to rescue hundreds of Vietnamese orphans before Saigon falls to the communists. The film derives from actress Balin's actual wartime experience. **100m/C VHS.** Shirley Jones, Ina Balin, Beulah Quo, Alan Fudge, Ben Piazza, Lee Paul, Kieu Chinh, Vic Diaz; ***D:*** John Llewellyn Moxey; ***M:*** Paul Chihara. **TV**

Children of Divorce ½ **1980** TV drama shows divorce from the children's point of view. Standard fare. **96m/C VHS.** Barbara Feldon, Lance Kerwin, Stacey Nelkin, Billy Dee Williams; ***D:*** Joanna Lee; ***M:*** Minette Alton. **TV**

Children of Dune **2003** The continuation of the 2000 miniseries "Dune" is based on the second and third novels of Frank Herbert's series and may be confusing to the uninitiated. It's now 12 years since Paul Atreides (Newman) has become emperor of Arrakis, which has a monopoly on the precious commodity Spice, but his ascension to the throne has caused a holy war across the universe. It has also caused rivalry with the deposed royal family led by scheming Princess Wensicia (Sarandon). Paul's children, Leto (McAvoy) and Ghanima (Brooks), who are being groomed to rule, soon come to realize they must destroy their father's legacy in order to save their world. **266m/C VHS, DVD.** Alec Newman, Susan Sarandon, James McAvoy, Jessica Brooks, Alice Krige, Edward Atterton, Steven Berkoff, Julie Cox, Barbara Kodetova, Ian McNeice, P. H. Moriarty; ***D:*** Greg Yaitanes; ***W:*** John Harrison; ***C:*** Arthur Reinhart; ***M:*** Brian Tyler. **CABLE**

Children of Fury *In the Line of Duty: Siege at Marion* **1994 (PG-13)** Fact-based TV movie covers the death (at police hands) of self-proclaimed prophet, Utah polygamist John Singer (Weisser), whose wife Vickie (Harper) and children vow revenge. When fundamentalist Addam Swapp (Secor) joins their group, he soon begins intimidating the locals and bombs a building in the town of Marion. Authorities call in the FBI and chief agent Bill Bryant (Franz) sets up a siege of the property. **85m/C VHS.** Kyle Secor, Tess Harper, Dennis Franz, Ed Begley Jr., Paul LeMat, Norbert Weisser, William H. Macy, Rex Linn; ***D:*** Charles Haid; ***W:*** Rich Husky; ***C:*** William Wages; ***M:*** Gary Chang. **TV**

Children of Hannibal *Figli de Annibale* **1998** Unemployed sad-sack Domenico (Orlando) decides to rob a Turin bank and head north to Switzerland, but he bungles the job and winds up with businessman Tommaso (Abatantuono) as a hostage. However, Tommaso has his own money troubles—nearly bankrupt, he persuades Domenico to head south with the loot and get help from Tommaso's friend, Orfeo (Insinni), who just happens to be a cop and Tommaso's lover. Then, Tommaso's daughter Rita (Cervi) decides to join their strange road trip. Italian with subtitles. **93m/C VHS, DVD.** *IT* Diego Abatantuono, Silvio Orlando, Valentina Cervi, Flavio Insinna, Ugo Conti; ***D:*** Davide Ferrario; ***W:*** Davide Ferrario; ***C:*** Giovanni Cavallini; ***M:*** Damiano Rota.

Children of Heaven ½ **1998 (PG)** When nine-year-old Ali (Hashemian) discovers that his younger sister Zahra's (Seddiqi) shoes have somehow been lost, he keeps the information from his parents who are already desperately struggling to provide for them. They share Ali's tattered sneakers so that both children can still go to school. Then Ali learns of a race where one of the prizes is a pair of running shoes and he becomes determined to win them. Story is simple enough that kids may enjoy watching other kids even in a foreign film. Farsi with subtitles. **88m/C VHS, DVD.** *IA* Mir Farrokh Hashemian, Bahareh Seddiqi, Amir Naji; ***D:*** Majid Majidi; ***W:*** Majid Majidi; ***C:*** Parviz Malek-zadeh; ***M:*** Keivan Jahan-shahi.

The Children of Huang Shi **2008 (R)** A humanitarian wartime adventure weepie based on the story of British reporter George Hogg (Rhys-Meyers). He's reporting on the Sino-Japanese War and the Japanese invasion of Nanking in 1937 when he's wounded and taken by Australian nurse Lee (Mitchell) to recover in a remote orphanage for boys. It's not remote enough, however, to escape the war. As the Japanese army approaches, George, Lee, and Communist rebel Chen (Chow) lead 60 boys on a 700-mile trip across the mountains to a safer haven. English, Chinese, and Japanese with subtitles. **114m/C DVD.** *AU CH GE* Jonathan Rhys Meyers, Radha Mitchell, Yun-Fat Chow, Michelle Yeoh, David Wenham, Li Guang; ***D:*** Roger Spottiswoode; ***W:*** James MacManus, Jane Hawksley; ***C:*** Xiaoding Zhao; ***M:*** David Hirschfelder.

Children of Men **2006 (R)** The future's never fun. It's 2027 and there's global infertility and worldwide chaos, which doesn't matter much to British bureaucratic drone Theo Faron (Owen), until he's pulled into an activist group headed by his ex, Julian (Moore). Seems she needs Faron to take illegal refugee Kee (Ashitay), who's pregnant with the first child conceived in 18 years, to safety. This involves a long, strange, and dangerous trip—and a stop at Theo's pothead friend Jasper's (a raucous Caine) cottage. Dark and dreary yet oddly fascinating. Loosely based on the 1993 novel by P.D. James. **108m/C DVD, HD DVD.** *US* Clive Owen, Julianne Moore, Michael Caine, Chiwetel

Ejiofor, Charlie Hunnam, Pam Ferris, Danny Huston, Peter Mullan, Clare-Hope Ashitey; ***D:*** Alfonso Cuaron; ***W:*** Alfonso Cuaron, Timothy J. Sexton; ***C:*** Emmanuel Lubezki. British Acad. '06: Cinematog.

Children of Nature 1/2 *Born Natturunnar* **1991** A 78-year-old man unwillingly enters a nursing home where he meets a long-ago sweetheart. The two fall in love again and decide to escape from the home and return to their childhood village. Sweet love story about late-blooming passions laced with fantasy and humor. Iceland's first Academy Award nomination. In Icelandic with English subtitles. **85m/C VHS.** *IC* Gisli Halldorsson, Sigridur Hagalin, Bruno Ganz; ***D:*** Fridrik Thor Fridriksson; ***W:*** Fridrik Thor Fridriksson, Einar Mar Gudmundsson; ***M:*** Hilmar Orn Hilmarsson.

The Children of Noisy Village 1/2 *The Children of Bullerby Village; Alla vi barn i Bullerby* **1986** Noisy Village is a small town in the Swedish countryside consisting of three red frame houses. In the town, a group of adventurous children discover a multitude of fantasy lands right in their own backyard—their backyard being the beautiful pastures, ponds, and fields of Sweden. Based on the stories of Astrid "Pippi Longstocking" Lindgren. Dubbed. **88m/C VHS.** *SW* Linda Bergstrom, Anna Sahlin, Ellem Demerus, Harsald Lonnbro; ***D:*** Lasse Hallstrom.

Children of Paradise *Les Enfants du Paradis* **1944** Considered by many to be the greatest film ever made, certainly one of the most beautiful. In the Parisian theatre district of the 1800s an actor falls in love with a seemingly unattainable woman. Although circumstances keep them apart, their love never dies. Produced in France during WWII right under the noses of Nazi occupiers; many of the talent (including the writer, poet Jacques Prevert) were active resistance fighters. In French with English subtitles. **188m/B VHS, DVD.** *FR* Jean-Louis Barrault, Arletty, Pierre Brasseur, Maria Casares, Albert Remy, Leon Larive, Marcel Herrand, Pierre Renoir, Gaston Modot, Jane (Jeanne) Marken, Louis Salou; ***D:*** Marcel Carne; ***W:*** Jacques Prevert; ***C:*** Roger Hubert; ***M:*** Maurice Thiriet, Joseph Kosma.

Children of Rage 1/2 **1975 (PG)** High-minded and long-winded drama dealing with the Israeli/Palestinian war and terrorism from the viewpoint of an Israeli doctor yearning for peace. **106m/C VHS.** *GB IS* Simon Ward, Cyril Cusack, Helmut Griem, Olga Georges-Picot; ***D:*** Arthur Allan Seidelman; ***W:*** Richard Alfieri.

Children of Sanchez **1979 (PG)** Mexican man attempts to provide for his family with very little except faith and love. U.S./Mexican production based on Oscar Lewis' novel. **103m/C VHS, DVD.** *MX* Anthony Quinn, Dolores Del Rio, Katy Jurado, Lupita Ferrer; ***D:*** Hall Bartlett; ***W:*** Hall Bartlett; ***M:*** Chuck Mangione.

Children of the Century *Les Enfants du Siecle* **1999** Antenuated costumer depicting the volatile affair between the Baroness Dudevant, soon to be known as writer George Sand (Binoche), and the younger (and dissolute) poet, Alfred de Musset (Magimel). To escape his wealthy family's disapproval, the lovers travel to Venice where Alfred's continued dissipation leads to illness and the services of Dr. Pagello (Dionisi), with whom a fed-up Sands soon begins a romance. Musset returns to Paris and when Sands follow later, the duo try to rekindle their romantic ardor. Musset's fictionized version of their affair was entitled "Confessions of a Child of the Century." French with subtitles. **137m/C VHS, DVD.** *FR* Juliette Binoche, Benoit Magimel, Stefano Dionisi, Robin Renucci, Karin Viard, Isabelle Carre, Denis Podalydes; ***D:*** Diane Kurys; ***W:*** Diane Kurys, Murray Head, Francois Olivier Rousseau; ***C:*** Vilko Filac; ***M:*** Luis Bacalov.

Children of the Corn 1/2 **1984 (R)** Young couple lands in a small Iowa town where children appease a demon by murderously sacrificing adults. Time to move or dispense with some major spankings. Infrequently scary. Another feeble attempt to translate the horror of a Stephen King book to film. **93m/C VHS, DVD, UMD.** Peter Horton, Linda Hamilton, R.G. Armstrong, John Franklin, Courtney Gains, Robbie Kiger; ***D:*** Fritz Kiersch; ***W:*** George Goldsmith; ***C:*** Raoul Lomas; ***M:*** Jonathan Elias.

Children of the Corn 2: The Final Sacrifice 1/2 **1992 (R)** Reporter working for a tabloid paper gets more than he bargained for when he decides to do a story on the adults murdered in the town of Gatlin, Nebraska. Gatlin's surviving children, who killed their parents in the first film, are now living in a neighboring town and free to kill again. This youthful satanic cult does in authority figures in a number of sacrifical ways, working ever more smartly to create the prime attraction—blood flow. Not based on anything written by Stephen King. **93m/C VHS.** Terence Knox, Paul Scherrer, Rosalind Allen, Christie Clark, Ned Romero, Ryan Bollman, Ted Travelstead; ***D:*** David F. Price; ***W:*** Gilbert Adler, A.L. Katz.

Children of the Corn 3: Urban Harvest **1995 (R)** Joshua (Melendez) and younger brother Eli (Cerny) are adopted by a wealthy couple and transplanted from Nebraska to Chicago's suburbia. But when Eli grows a corn patch that resurrects an evil force, only Joshua can stop his reign of terror. Contrived premise but lots of nifty special effects. **103m/C VHS, DVD.** Daniel Cerny, Ron Melendez, Mari Morrow, Duke Stroud, Jim Metzler, Nancy Lee Grahn; ***D:*** James D.R. Hickox; ***W:*** Dode Levenson; ***M:*** Daniel Licht.

Children of the Corn 4: The Gathering *Deadly Harvest* **1996 (R)** Medical student Grace Rhodes (Watts) seeks to free the children of her Nebraska hometown from a mysterious plague and a shadowy figure. **85m/C VHS, DVD.** Naomi Watts, Brent Jennings, Jamie Renee Smith, William Windom, Karen Black; ***D:*** Greg Spence; ***W:*** Stephen Berger, Greg Spence; ***C:*** Richard Clabaugh; ***M:*** David Williams.

Children of the Corn 5: Fields of Terror 1/2 **1998 (R)** Alison (Galina), Greg (Arquette), Tyrus (Vaughan), and Kir (Mendez) have traveled to Divinity Falls to bury the cremated remains of Kir's recently deceased boyfriend. That's when they run into the local cult of murderous children and Alison realizes that her long-lost brother, Jacob (Buzzotta), is one of them. She's determined to get him away but the evil force that leads the children has other ideas. **85m/C VHS, DVD.** Alexis Arquette, Greg Vaughan, Stacy Galina, Eva Mendes, Adam Wylie, Dave Buzzotta, David Carradine, Fred Williamson; ***D:*** Ethan Wiley; ***W:*** Ethan Wiley; ***C:*** David Lewis; ***M:*** Paul Rabjohns. **VIDEO**

Children of the Corn: Revelation **2001** Jamie (Mink) is looking for her missing grandma at the condemned Hampton Arms where the remaining residents are meeting grisly fates. She and detective Armbrister (Cassie) are informed by a mysterious priest (Ironside) that the condos were built on the site of a tent revival fire that killed a number of children. Of course the kids turn out to be the Gatlin killer-kiddie cult and they return to reclaim their land. Some decent shockers in this 7th installment of the series. **81m/C VHS, DVD.** Claudette Mink, Michael Ironside, Troy Yorke, Sean Smith, Kyle Cassie, Michael Rogers, Taylor Hobbs, Jeff(rey) Ballard, Crystal Lowe; ***D:*** Guy Magar. **VIDEO**

Children of the Corn 666: Isaac's Return 1/2 **1999 (R)** Hannah Martin (Ramsey) is traveling to Nebraska in search of her birth mother but when she arrives in the small town of Gatlin, she finds the residents want to keep their secrets. **82m/C VHS, DVD.** Natalie Ramsey, John Franklin, Stacy Keach, Alix Koromzay, Nancy Allen; ***D:*** Keri Skogland. **VIDEO**

Children of the Damned **1963** Six children, who are a sample of what man will evolve to in a million years, are born all around the world with genius IQs; ray-gun eyes, and murderous dispositions. Two investigators bring the children together, and while they are being examined by scientists they escape. The children hide out in a church, but they are doomed because their destiny is to be destroyed to teach a lesson to modern man. A sequel to "Village of the Damned" based loosely on the novel "The Midwich Cuckoos" by John Wyndham. **90m/B VHS, DVD.** *GB* Ian Hendry, Alan Badel, Barbara Ferris, Alfred Burke, Sheila Allen, Clive Powell, Frank Summerscales, Mahdu Mathen, Gerald Delsol, Roberta Rex, Franchesca Lee, Harold Goldblatt, Ralph Michael, Martin Miller, Lee Yoke-Moon; ***D:*** Anton Leader; ***W:*** John Briley; ***C:*** Davis Boulton.

Children of the Full Moon **1984** A young couple find themselves lost in a forest that is the home of a family of werewolves. Earns praise only for brevity. Even bad movie aficionados will want to skip this howler. **60m/C VHS, DVD.** *GB* Christopher Cazenove, Celia Gregory, Diana Dors, Jacof Witken, Robert Urquhart; ***D:*** Tom Clegg.

Children of the Living Dead **WOOF! 2000 (R)** Standard "...of the Living Dead" fare has only producer John Russo as a connection to the original. One of the worst of these seemingly endless low-budget horrors. The voice dubbing sounds exceptionally unnatural; lighting is amateurish with the odd flash when someone behind the camera mishandles a mirror; acting is poor. Story is the same old same old. **90m/C DVD.** Tom Savini, A. Barrett Worland, Jamie McCoy; ***D:*** Tor Ramsey; ***W:*** Karen Wolf.

Children of the Night 1/2 **1992 (R)** Allburg seems like a typically quiet small town far removed from any danger—until a vampire is released from an underground crypt and decides to make the town his bloodthirsty target. When a teacher, whose girlfriend is visiting Allburg, learns of the supernatural goings on he decides to investigate, which may be a deadly mistake. **92m/C VHS, DVD.** Peter DeLuise, Karen Black, Ami Dolenz, Maya McLaughlin, Evan Mackenzie, David Sawyer, Garrett Morris; ***D:*** Tony Randel; ***W:*** Nicolas Falacci; ***C:*** Richard Michalak.

Children of the Revolution **1995 (R)** Mockumentary covering 45 years of Australian history and politics, beginning in 1951 when the conservative Prime Minister attempts to ban the Australian Communist Party. Party member (and Stalin admirer) Joan Fraser (Davis) helps to prevent the ban, bringing her to the Russian leader's attention, and she's invited to Moscow. There, Joan winds up in bed with Stalin (Abraham) and comes home pregnant. Eventually, son Joe (Rush) makes an entry into the Australian political scene, resulting in chaos. There's almost too much more for the film to handle, although the actors don't seem to have any problems. **101m/C VHS, DVD.** *AU* Judy Davis, Sam Neill, Richard Roxburgh, Rachel Griffiths, Geoffrey Rush, F. Murray Abraham; ***D:*** Peter Duncan; ***W:*** Peter Duncan; ***C:*** Martin McGrath; ***M:*** Nigel Westlake. Australian Film Inst. '96: Actress (Davis), Art Dir./Set Dec., Costume Des.

Children of the Wild 1/2 *Killers of the Wild* **1937** Adventure story about a pack of dogs surviving in the Rocky Mountain wilderness. Splendid scenery and some interesting sequences. **65m/B VHS.** Joan Valerie, James Bush, Leroy Mason, Patsy Moran; ***D:*** Charles (Hutchison) Hutchinson, Vin Moore; ***W:*** Hilda May Young; ***C:*** Robert Doran; ***M:*** Edward Kilenyi.

The Children of Theatre Street **1977** Absorbing documentary follows three children attending the renowned Kirov Ballet School. A show for all ages that may be especially enjoyed by kids who are interested in ballet. Kelly's last film appearance. **92m/C VHS, DVD.** *RU* Angelina Armeiskaya, Alec Timoushin, Lena Voronzova, Michaela Cerna, Galina Messenzeva, Konstantin Zaklinsky; ***D:*** Robert Dornhelm; ***W:*** Beth Gutcheon; ***C:*** Karl Kofler; ***Nar:*** Grace Kelly.

The Children of Times Square **1986** A mother pursues her son who has fled home and joined a gang of drug dealers in N.Y.C.'s seedy Times Square. Ordinary film despite strong casting of Cassidy and Rollins. **95m/C VHS.** Joanna Cassidy, Howard E. Rollins Jr., Brandon Douglas, David Ackroyd, Griffin O'Neal, Danny Nucci, Larry B. Scott, Jacob Vargas, De'voreaux White, Joe Spinell, Jason Bernard, R.D. Call, John Capodice, Ami Dolenz, Courtney Gains; ***D:*** Curtis Hanson; ***W:*** Curtis Hanson; ***M:*** Patrick Gleeson. **TV**

Children On Their Birthdays 1/2 **2002 (PG)** Based on a short story by Truman Capote and set in small Medda, Alabama in 1947, which is where 13-year-old Billy Bob Murphy (Pichler) lives with his widowed mother Elinore (Lee). His best bud is Preacher (Plemons) but the two are soon vying for the affections of the new girl in town—Lilly Jane Bobbit (Raymonde). Meanwhile, romance is in the air for Elinore and sheriff/mechanic Speedy (McDonald) to Billy Bob's dismay. And there's even more excitement over the shady dealings of smooth-talking Lionel Quince (Arnold). **102m/C VHS, DVD.** Joe Pichler, Jesse Plemons, Sheryl Lee, Tania Raymonde, Phyllis Frelich, Christopher McDonald, Tom Arnold; ***D:*** Mark Medoff; ***W:*** Douglas J. Sloan; ***C:*** Steve (Steven) Shaw; ***M:*** James D. Hinton, Ross Vannelli.

Children Shouldn't Play with Dead Things 1/2 *Revenge of the Living Dead* **1972** A band of foolhardy hippie filmmakers on an island cemetary skimp on special effects by using witchcraft to revive the dead. The plan works. Soon the crew has an island full of hungry ghouls to contend with. Film strives for yucks, frequently succeeds. A late night fave, sporting some excellent dead rising from their grave scenes as well as a selection of groovy fashions. Screenwriter/star Ormsby went on to write the remake of "Cat People," while director Clark would eventually helm "Porky's." **85m/C VHS, DVD.** Alan Ormsby, Valerie Mamches, Jeff Gillen, Anya Ormsby, Paul Cronin, Jane Daly, Roy Engelman, Robert Philip, Bruce Solomon, Alecs Baird, Seth Sklarey; ***D:*** Bob (Benjamin) Clark; ***W:*** Bob (Benjamin) Clark, Alan Ormsby; ***C:*** Jack McGowan; ***M:*** Carl Zittrer.

Children Underground **2003** A disturbing documentary about homeless street children in Bucharest, and their daily life of despair and pain. **104m/C DVD.**

The Children's Hour *The Loudest Whisper* **1961** The teaching careers of two women are ruined when girls begin circulating vicious rumors. Only an occasionally taut drama despite forceful handling of a lesbian theme. Updated version of Lillian Hellman's play (adapted by Hellman) is more explicit, but less suspenseful in spite of excellent performances from the talented cast. Remake of Wyler's own "These Three." **107m/C VHS, DVD.** Shirley MacLaine, Audrey Hepburn, James Garner, Miriam Hopkins, Veronica Cartwright, Fay Bainter; ***D:*** William Wyler; ***W:*** John Michael Hayes; ***M:*** Alex North.

Child's Play 1/2 **1988 (R)** A boy discovers that his new doll named Chucky is actually the embodiment of a deranged killer. His initially skeptical mom and a police officer come around after various killings. Exciting, if somewhat moronic, fare, with fine special effects. Followed by "Child's Play 2." **95m/C VHS, DVD.** Catherine Hicks, Alex Vincent, Chris Sarandon, Dinah Manoff, Brad Dourif, Tommy Swerdlow, Jack Colvin; ***D:*** Tom Holland; ***W:*** Tom Holland, Don Mancini, John Lafia; ***C:*** Bill Butler; ***M:*** Joe Renzetti.

Child's Play 2 **WOOF! 1990 (R)** Chucky lives. Basic doll-on-a-rampage story, a metaphor for the Reagan years, lives on in the sequel (you remember: somehow guy-doll Chucky made it past the quality control people with a highly inflammable temper). A little dotty from playing with dolls, young Vincent finds himself fostered by two new parents, and plagued by an obnoxious and very animated doll that fosters ill will toward all. What's worse is the doll is transmigratory, craving the boy's body as his next address. Chef d'effects Kevin Yagher's new toy is bad, real bad, and so are the other part two FX. Little Chucky's saga, however grows a tad tiresome. A bad example for small children. **84m/C VHS, DVD.** Alex Vincent, Jenny Agutter, Gerrit Graham, Christine Elise, Grace Zabriskie; ***D:*** John Lafia; ***W:*** Don Mancini; ***C:*** Stefan Czapsky; ***M:*** Graeme Revell; ***V:*** Brad Dourif.

Child's Play 3 **1991 (R)** Possessed doll Chucky returns to life again in search of a new child to control, and luckily finds his old pal (Whalin) at a military school filled with the usual stereotypes. Gory sequel in a mostly awful series. "Don't F— with the Chuck" was its catch phrase; that should indicate the level of this junk. **89m/C VHS, DVD.** Justin Whalin, Perrey Reeves, Jeremy Sylvers, Peter Haskell, Dakin Matthews, Travis Fine, Dean Jacobson, Matthew (Matt) Walker, Andrew (Andy) Robinson; ***D:*** Jack Bender; ***W:*** Don Mancini; ***M:*** Cory Lerios, John D'Andrea; ***V:*** Brad Dourif.

Chill 🦴 1/2 **2006 (R)** Struggling writer Sam (Calabro) takes a job at a small L.A. grocery store to pay the bills. The owner, Dr. Munoz (Kurtz), is a former scientist who claims that his strange skin condition requires freezing temperatures but Sam discovers that Munoz has been dead a long time and has made an occult pact to keep going. Now he expects Sam to help him or become his next victim. Based on the H.P. Lovecraft story "Cool Air." **86m/C DVD.** Thomas Calabro, Ashley Laurence, James Russo, Shaun Kurtz; ***D:*** Serge Rodnunsky; ***W:*** Serge Rodnunsky; ***C:*** Serge Rodnunsky. **VIDEO**

Chill Factor 🦴🦴 **1990 (R)** A TV reporter for an investigative news show uncovers evidence of an international conspiracy. Plot twists abound. **95m/C VHS, DVD.** Paul Williams, Patrick Macnee, Andrew Prine, Carrie Snodgress, Patrick Wayne, Gary Crosby; ***D:*** David L. Stanton.

Chill Factor 🦴 1/2 **1999 (R)** Stealing every plot device and cliche in the action thriller genre, this is indeed one unoriginal cold turkey. After accidentally blowing up a platoon of soldiers while testing a chemical weapon codenamed "Elvis" and pinning the blame on cranky general Brynner (Firth), scientist Dr. Long (Paymer) moves to Montana to take up fly-fishing while continuing his research. He befriends diner clerk Tim (Ulrich), but only until the general is released from prison with a grudge to settle. The general has plans to sell the weapon to the highest bidder, but Long manages to get Elvis out of the building. The canister can't get hotter than 50 degrees, or Elvis will become a hunka hunka burnin' Armageddon. Tim hijacks an ice cream truck and its driver Arlo (Gooding), and the pair are chased and shot at until the movie is mercifully over. **102m/C VHS, DVD.** Skeet Ulrich, Cuba Gooding Jr., Peter Firth, David Paymer, Daniel Hugh-Kelly, Kevin J. O'Connor, Judson Mills, Hudson (Heidi) Leick, Jim Grimshaw; ***D:*** Hugh Johnson; ***W:*** Drew Gitlin, Mike Cheda; ***C:*** David Gribble; ***M:*** Hans Zimmer, John Powell.

Chillers 🦴 **1988** Travellers waiting for a bus are besieged by carnivorous zombies and voracious vampires. How this is different from the standard bus trip is unclear. **90m/C VHS, DVD.** Jesse Emery, Marjorie Fitzsimmons, Laurie Pennington, Jim Wolfe, David Wohl; ***D:*** Daniel Boyd; ***W:*** Daniel Boyd.

The Chilling WOOF! *Gamma 693* **1989 (R)** Corpses preserved in a deep freeze come alive and plague Kansas City as flesh-chomping zombies. Utterly worthless film doesn't even provide convincing effects. **91m/C VHS, DVD.** Linda Blair, Dan Haggerty, Troy Donahue, Jack A. De Rieux, Ron Vincent; ***D:*** Deland Nuse, Jack A. Sunseri.

Chilly Dogs WOOF! *Kevin of the North* **2001 (PG-13)** A woofer that deserves to be buried. Slacker Kevin Manley (Ulrich) learns he's inherited land in Alaska from his grandfather. But in order to collect he must compete in the 1,000 mile dog sled race between Anchorage and Nome, Alaska. Babe Bonnie (Nestridge) is willing to help the tenderfoot out while sneaky lawyer Thornton (Nielsen) is among those trying to undermine Kevin's every chance. At least the similarly themed "Snow Dogs" had a certain amount of kiddie humor to sustain it. **102m/C VHS, DVD.** *CA* Skeet Ulrich, Natasha Henstridge, Leslie Nielsen, Rik Mayall, Lochlyn Munro, Jay Brazeau; ***D:*** Bob Spiers; ***W:*** William Osborne; ***M:*** Harvey Summers.

Chilly Scenes of Winter 🦴🦴 1/2 *Head Over Heels* **1979 (PG)** Quirky comedy with a cult following about a man obsessed with regaining the love of a former girlfriend who is now married. He must also deal with an insane mom and various other problems. Strong, subtle performances from Heard and Riegert. Hurt is somewhat less satisfying as the supposedly fascinating woman. Released with a different, inferior ending as "Head Over Heels." Adapted by Joan Micklin Silver from Ann Beattie's first novel. Watch for Beattie's cameo as a waitress. **96m/C VHS.** John Heard, Mary Beth Hurt, Peter Riegert, Kenneth McMillan, Gloria Grahame, Nora Heflin, Griffin Dunne; ***Cameos:*** Ann Beattie; ***D:*** Joan Micklin Silver; ***W:*** Joan Micklin Silver.

Chimes at Midnight 🦴🦴🦴🦴 *Falstaff; Campanadas a Medianoche* **1967** Classic tragedy—derived by Welles from five Shakespeare plays—about a corpulent blowhard and his friendship with a prince. Crammed with classic sequences, including a battle that is both realistic and funny. The love scene between massive Welles and a nonetheless willing Moreau also manages to be both sad and amusing. Great performances all around, but Welles understandably dominates. The film's few flaws (due to budget problems) are inconsequential before considerable strengths. This one ranks among Welles', and thus the entire cinema's, very best. **115m/B VHS.** *SP SI* Orson Welles, Jeanne Moreau, Margaret Rutherford, John Gielgud, Marina Vlady, Keith Baxter, Fernando Rey, Norman Rodway; ***D:*** Orson Welles; ***W:*** Orson Welles; ***C:*** Edmond Richard; ***M:*** Angelo Francesco Lavagnino; ***Nar:*** Ralph Richardson.

China 🦴🦴 1/2 **1943** David Jones (Ladd) is an unfeeling profiteer who's making money off the Japanese invading China (it's 1941). But he and buddy Johnny Sparrow (Bendix) have their truck hijacked by a group of Chinese guerrillas, lead by China-born American teacher Carolyn Grant (Young), who need a group of schoolgirls driven to safety through enemy lines. Naturally, Jones has a change of heart (and sides) and battles the Japanese troops. Typically fervent propaganda film. Based on the play by Archibald Forbes. **79m/B VHS.** Alan Ladd, Loretta Young, William Bendix, Philip Ahn, Victor Sen Yung, Marianne Quon, Richard Loo; ***D:*** John Farrow; ***W:*** Frank Butler; ***C:*** Leo Tover.

China Beach 🦴🦴🦴 **1988** TV movie/pilot launched the acclaimed series about American military women behind the lines during the chaos of the Vietnam War. Nurse McMurphy has only seven days left on her first tour of duty, and in spite of her hate of the brutality of the war, she has mixed feelings about leaving her friends and her work. A USO singer on a one week tour finds her search for men brings the war too close for comfort. Cherry, a new Red Cross volunteer, shows up at the Beach. Skillfully introduces the viewer to all the characters, their problems and joys, without melodrama or redundancy. **95m/C VHS.** Dana Delany, Chloe Webb, Robert Picardo, Nan Woods, Michael Boatman, Marg Helgenberger, Tim Ryan, Concetta Tomei, Jeff Kober, Brian Wimmer; ***D:*** Rod Holcomb; ***W:*** John Sacret Young. **TV**

China Cry 🦴🦴 1/2 **1991 (PG-13)** Based on the true story of Sung Negn Yee who escaped from Communist China to the freedom of Hong Kong in the early '60s. Fine portrayal of the young woman from a privileged background who witnessed some of the atrocities of Mao's government policies. **103m/C VHS, DVD.** Julia Nickson-Soul, Russell Wong, James Shigeta, France Nuyen; ***D:*** James F. Collier.

China Gate 🦴🦴🦴 **1957** A band of multi-national troops follows a French officer against a communist stronghold in Indochina. Conventional fare bolstered considerably by director Fuller's flair for action. Weak male leads, but Dickinson shines. **97m/B VHS.** Gene Barry, Angie Dickinson, Nat King Cole, Paul Dubov, Lee Van Cleef, George Givot, Marcel Dalio, Gerald Milton, Neyle Morrow, Maurice Marsac, Warren Hsieh, Paul Busch, Sasha Hardin, James Hong, Walter Soo Hoo, Weaver Levy; ***D:*** Samuel Fuller; ***W:*** Samuel Fuller; ***C:*** Joseph Biroc; ***M:*** Max Steiner, Victor Young.

China Girl 🦴🦴 1/2 **1987 (R)** An Italian-American boy and a Chinese-American girl romance despite a war between gangs in their respective NYC communities. This often violent drama is enriched by director Ferrara's slick, high-energy approach. **90m/C VHS.** Richard Panebianco, James Russo, Sari Chang, Russell Wong, David Caruso, Joey Chin; ***D:*** Abel Ferrara; ***W:*** Nicholas St. John; ***C:*** Bojan Bazelli; ***M:*** Joe Delia.

China Heat 🦴 1/2 *Zhing hua jing hua* **1990** Captain Tie Hua (Hu) leads a three-woman Chinese police task force en route to New York City to track down an infamous drug lord fleeing mainland China. Cheesy acting, bizarre stunts, and pretty decent kung fu ensue. Cheesy B-movie with some good fights and lots of "what the...!" moments. **90m/C DVD.** *CH* Michael Depasquale Jr., Sibelle Hu; ***D:*** William Cheung, Yang Yang.

The China Lake Murders 🦴🦴 1/2 **1990 (PG-13)** Crazy-cop-on-the-loose fable in which a serial killer disguised as a highway patrolman practices population control on the inhabitants of a small town in the Mojave desert. Meanwhile the local sheriff (Skerritt), unwittingly befriends the killer-patrolman. **100m/C VHS.** Tom Skerritt, Michael Parks, Nancy Everhard, Lauren Tewes, Bill McKinney, Lonny (Lonnie) Chapman; ***D:*** Alan Metzger; ***W:*** Nevin Schreiner. **CABLE**

China Moon 🦴🦴 1/2 **1991 (R)** Convoluted police thriller, set in Florida, about beautiful Rachel (Stowe), who's married to rich-but-abusive Rupert (Dance). Kyle (Harris) is the lonely homicide detective who's besotted by Rachel and conveniently helps her dispose of her murdered husband's body. Kyle's problems increase when his rookie partner (Del Toro) turns out to be smarter than anyone thinks. Good performances but the suspense is only average. **99m/C VHS, DVD.** Ed Harris, Madeleine Stowe, Benicio Del Toro, Charles Dance; ***D:*** John Bailey; ***W:*** Roy Carlson; ***C:*** Willy Kurant; ***M:*** George Fenton.

China, My Sorrow 🦴🦴 1/2 *Chine, Ma Douleur* **1989** Thirteen-year-old "Little Four Eyes" is sent to a Chinese re-education camp for the crime of playing a love song to a girl. There he befriends another enemy of the revolution and a Buddhist monk who help him maintain his familial traditions and identity. Tragi-comic look at how freedom's spirit survived the Cultural Revolution. Mandarin with subtitles. **86m/C VHS.** *CH* Guo Yiang Yi, Tieu Quan Nghieu, Vong Han Lai, Chi-Vy Sam, Chang Cheung Siang; ***D:*** Dai Sijie; ***W:*** Dai Sijie, Shan Yuan Zhu; ***M:*** Chen Qi Gang.

China O'Brien 🦴 1/2 **1988 (R)** Gorgeous police officer with martial arts expertise returns home for a little R&R, but finds she has to kick some major butt instead. Violent, dim-witted action drama proves only that cleavage can be macho too. **90m/C VHS, DVD.** Cynthia Rothrock, Richard Norton, Patrick Adamson, David Blackwell, Steven Kerby, Robert Tiller, Lainie Watts, Keith Cooke; ***D:*** Robert Clouse; ***W:*** Robert Clouse; ***C:*** Kent Wakeford; ***M:*** Paul Antonelli.

China O'Brien 2 🦴 1/2 **1989 (R)** The unbreakable China, now a sheriff, battles the standard-issue Vietnam-vet druglord who invades her little town. Made back-to-back with the first film (note that both pics' bad guys have the same gang of henchman!), and in both films Rothrock is basically invincible, so there's no suspense. **85m/C VHS.** Cynthia Rothrock, Richard Norton, Keith Cooke; ***D:*** Robert Clouse.

China Seas 🦴🦴🦴 **1935** The captain of a commercial steamship on the China route has to fight off murderous Malay pirates, a spurned woman, and a raging typhoon to reach port safely. Fast-moving romantic action taken from Crosbie Garstin's novel. **89m/B VHS, DVD.** Clark Gable, Jean Harlow, Wallace Beery, Rosalind Russell, Lewis Stone, Sir C. Aubrey Smith, Dudley Digges, Robert Benchley, William Henry, Lillian Bond, Edward Brophy, Hattie McDaniel, Akim Tamiroff; ***D:*** Tay Garnett; ***W:*** Jules Furthman, James Kevin McGuinness; ***C:*** Ray June; ***M:*** Herbert Stothart.

China Sky 🦴🦴 **1944** An American doctor fights alongside Chinese guerillas against the Japanese during WWII. Drama, to its credit, often opts for character conflict instead of warfare, but this makes it merely dull instead of cliched. Adapted from a Pearl S. Buck novel. **78m/B VHS.** Randolph Scott, Ellen Drew, Ruth Warrick, Anthony Quinn, Carol Thurston, Richard Loo, Philip Ahn; ***D:*** Ray Enright.

The China Syndrome 🦴🦴🦴 1/2 **1979 (PG)** A somewhat unstable executive at a nuclear plant uncovers evidence of a concealed accident and takes drastic steps to publicize the incident. Lemmon is excellent as the anxious exec, while Fonda and Douglas are scarcely less distinguished as a sympathetic TV journalist and camera operator, respectively. Tense, prophetic thriller that ironically preceded the Three Mile Island accident by just a few months. Produced by Douglas. **123m/C VHS, DVD.** Jane Fonda, Jack Lemmon, Michael Douglas, Scott Brady, James Hampton, Peter Donat, Wilford Brimley, James Karen; ***D:*** James Bridges; ***W:*** James Bridges, Mike Gray, T.S. Cook; ***C:*** James A. Crabe. British Acad. '79: Actor (Lemmon), Actress (Fonda); Cannes '79: Actor (Lemmon); Writers Guild '79: Orig. Screenplay.

China White **1991 (R)** Violence erupts in the streets of Paris, Amsterdam, and Bangkok, when international drug cartels battle over the ownership of China White—premium heroin, its sources and its outlets. Rousing, realistic action. **99m/C VHS.** Billy Drago, Russell Wong, Lisa Schrage, Steven Leigh; ***D:*** Ronny Yu.

Chinatown 🦴🦴🦴🦴 **1974 (R)** Private detective Jake Gittes (Nicholson) finds himself overwhelmed in a scandalous case involving the rich and powerful of Los Angeles. Gripping, atmospheric mystery excels in virtually every aspect, with strong narrative drive and outstanding performances from Nicholson, Dunaway, and Huston. Director Polanski also appears in a suitable unsettling cameo. Fabulous. A sneaky, snaking delight filled with seedy characters and plots-within-plots. Followed more than 15 years later by "The Two Jakes." **131m/C VHS, DVD.** Roman Polanski, Jack Nicholson, Faye Dunaway, John Huston, Diane Ladd, John Hillerman, Burt Young, Perry Lopez, Darrell Zwerling, Joe Mantell; ***D:*** Roman Polanski; ***W:*** Robert Towne; ***C:*** John A. Alonzo; ***M:*** Jerry Goldsmith. Oscars '74: Orig. Screenplay; AFI '98: Top 100; British Acad. '74: Actor (Nicholson), Director (Polanski), Screenplay; Golden Globes '75: Actor—Drama (Nicholson), Director (Polanski), Film—Drama, Screenplay, Natl. Film Reg. '91;; N.Y. Film Critics '74: Actor (Nicholson); Natl. Soc. Film Critics '74: Actor (Nicholson); Writers Guild '74: Orig. Screenplay.

Chinatown After Dark 🦴 **1931** Ludicrous, inane melodrama about a white girl raised by the Chinese. **50m/B VHS, DVD.** Rex Lease, Barbara Kent, Carmel Myers; ***D:*** Stuart Paton.

Chinatown Connection 🦴 **1990 (R)** For some inexplicable reason, local drug dealers start selling poisoned cocaine. Two renegade cops discover the super-secret organization doing the poisoning, arm themselves heavily, and kill lots of people while putting an end to the poisonings. Violent, foolish film with dull performances. **94m/C VHS.** Bruce Ly, Lee Majors, Pat McCormick, Art Camacho, Susan Frailey, Scott Richards; ***D:*** Jean-Paul Ouellette.

The Chinatown Kid 🦴 **1978** Tan Tung escapes from Red China on a ship bound for San Francisco. There he becomes involved in a local extortion racket and he'll need all his martial arts skills to overcome the two gangs fighting for power. **115m/C VHS, DVD.** Alexander Fu Sheng, Sun Chein, Shirley Yu, Shaw Yin-Yin; ***D:*** Chen Chen.

The Chinatown Murders: Man against the Mob 🦴🦴 *Man Against the Mob: The Chinatown Murders* **1989 (R)** A tough cop is up against the Chinese mafia and his own corrupt police force as he tries to stay alive and find some justice. **96m/C VHS, DVD.** George Peppard, Charles Haid, Richard Bradford, Ursula Andress, Jason Beghe, Julia Nickson-Soul, James Pax, Sandy Ward; ***D:*** Michael Pressman; ***C:*** Tim Suhrstedt.

Chinese Box 🦴🦴 1/2 **1997** Hong Kong's return to Chinese rule is the backdrop for Wang's story of a dying British journalist (Irons) and a former bar girl turned nightclub owner (Li). In the months before the 1997 handover, business writer John learns he is dying of leukemia and decides to pursue Vivian, the woman he has secretly loved for some time. He also sets out to discover the "meaning" of Hong Kong itself. This quest is personified by Jean (Cheung), a street hustler with stories to tell. Metaphors abound as Wang tries to convey the everyday chaos and impenetrability of Hong Kong life. Striking visuals provide cues and clues to the not-always-subtle symbolism. Mandarin and English dialogue. **109m/C VHS, DVD.** *FR JP* Jeremy Irons, Gong Li, Maggie Cheung, Ruben

Blades, Michael Hui; *D:* Wayne Wang; *W:* Wayne Wang, Jean-Claude Carriere, Larry Gross, Paul Theroux; *C:* Vilko Filac; *M:* Graeme Revell.

Chinese Boxes 🦴🦴 1/2 **1984** An American man in Berlin is framed in a murder and becomes caught in an international web of crime and intrigue. Low budget but interesting thriller. **87m/C VHS.** *GE GB* Will Patton, Adelheid Arndt, Robbie Coltrane; *D:* Christopher Petit; *W:* L.M. Kit Carson.

The Chinese Cat 🦴 **1944** Poorly scripted formula mystery has the younger Chan smitten with a girl who needs the elder Chan's detective skills in finding her father's killer. **65m/B VHS, DVD.** Sidney Toler, Benson Fong, Mantan Moreland, Weldon Heyburn, Joan Woodbury, Ian Keith, Sam Flint; *D:* Phil Rosen.

Chinese Connection 🦴🦴 1/2 *Fist of Fury; The Iron Hand; Jing Wu Men* **1973 (R)** A martial arts expert tracks sadistic brutes who slew his instructor. Wild action sequences provide a breathtaking view of Lee's skill. Dubbed. **90m/C VHS, DVD.** *HK* Bruce Lee, James Tien, Robert Baker; *D:* Lo Wei; *W:* Lo Wei; *C:* Chen Ching Chu; *M:* Fu-ling Wang.

Chinese Connection 2 🦴 *Fistful of the Dragon; Fists of Fury 2; Jie Quan Ying Zhao Gong* **1977 (R)** A martial-arts expert learns that the school where he trained is now run by an unappealing master. Conflict ensues. Bruce Li is not Bruce Lee (who, to make things more confusing, is shown in flashbacks since he started in the first film), but he is fairly good in action portions of this otherwise dull, sloppy venture. **96m/C VHS, DVD.** *HK* Bruce Li, Bruce Lee, Lieh Lo, Quin Lee; *D:* Tso Nam Lee.

Chinese Roulette 🦴🦴 1/2 **1986** A host of unappealing characters convene at a country house for sexual shenanigans and a cruel game masterminded by a sadistic crippled girl. Cold effort from German master Fassbinder. In German with English subtitles. **82m/C VHS, DVD.** *GE* Anna Karina, Margit Carstensen, Ulli Lommel, Brigitte Mira, Macha Meril, Andrea Schober, Volker Spengler; *D:* Rainer Werner Fassbinder; *W:* Rainer Werner Fassbinder; *C:* Michael Ballhaus.

Chinese Web 🦴 **1978** Spiderman adventure in which Spidey becomes entwined in international intrigue and corrupt officials. **95m/C VHS.** Nicholas Hammond, Robert F. Simon, Rosalind Chao, Ted Danson; *D:* Donald McDougall.

Chino 🦴🦴 *Valdez the Half Breed; The Valdez Horses* **1975 (PG)** A half-Indian horse rancher struggles to maintain his livelihood in this spaghetti western. Not among Bronson's stronger—that is, more viscerally effective—films. Adapted from Lee Hoffman's novel. **97m/C VHS, DVD.** *IT* Charles Bronson, Jill Ireland, Vincent Van Patten; *D:* John Sturges; *W:* Massimo De Rita, Clair Huffaker, Arduino (Dino) Maiuri; *C:* Armando Nannuzzi; *M:* Guido de Angelis, Maurizio de Angelis.

Chip of the Flying U 🦴 1/2 **1939** Margaret Whitmore, the new owner of the Flying U ranch, is led to believe that her foreman Chip Bennett is guilty of bank robbery. To prove his innocence, Chip and his pal Weary go after the real criminals—enemy agents who are smuggling munitions along the coast line that borders the ranch. **55m/B DVD.** Johnny Mack Brown, Fuzzy Knight, Bob Baker, Doris Weston, Forrest Taylor, Anthony Warde; *D:* Ralph Straub; *W:* Andrew Bennison, Larry Rhine; *C:* William Sickner.

Chips, the War Dog 🦴🦴 1/2 **1990** A WWII Army recruit, who's scared of dogs, is assigned to train a German shepherd for duty. **90m/C VHS.** Brandon Douglas, Ned Vaughn, Paxton Whitehead, Ellie Cornell, Robert Miranda, William Devane; *D:* Ed Kaplan. **CABLE**

The Chisholms 🦴🦴 1/2 **1979** If you're into oaters, here's a high fiber six-hour serial: Chisolm (Preston) leads the family as they head west and find trouble with a capital "T" en route from Virginia to Californ-i-a. Originally a network miniseries, it's now a two-cassette rentable; adapted by Evan Hunter from his novel. **300m/C VHS,** Robert Preston, Rosemary Harris, Brian Keith, Ben Murphy, Charles Frank; *D:* Mel Stuart; *M:* Elmer Bernstein.

Chisum 🦴 1/2 **1970 (G)** Cattle baron faces various conflicts, including a confrontation with Billy the Kid. Lame Wayne vehicle contributes nothing to exhausted western genre. **111m/C VHS, DVD.** John Agar, John Wayne, Forrest Tucker, Geoffrey Deuel, Christopher George, Ben Johnson, Bruce Cabot, Patric Knowles, Richard Jaeckel, Glenn Corbett; *D:* Andrew V. McLaglen; *W:* Andrew J. Fenady; *C:* William Clothier.

Chitty Chitty Bang Bang 🦴🦴 **1968 (G)** An eccentric inventor spruces up an old car and, in fantasy, takes his children to a land where the evil rulers have forbidden children. Poor special effects and forgettable score stall effort. Loosely adapted by Roald Dahl and Hughes from an Ian Fleming story. ♫ Chitty Chitty Bang Bang; Hushabye Mountain; Truly Scrumptious; You Two; Toot Sweet; Me Ol' Bam-Boo; Lovely Lonely Man; Posh; The Roses of Success. **142m/C VHS, DVD.** *GB* Dick Van Dyke, Sally Ann Howes, Lionel Jeffries, Gert Frobe, Anna Quayle, Benny Hill; *D:* Ken Hughes; *W:* Ken Hughes, Roald Dahl; *C:* Christopher Challis; *M:* Richard M. Sherman, Robert B. Sherman.

Chloe **2009** Catherine (Moore) suspects her popular college professor husband David (Neeson) may be cheating so she hires escort Chloe (Seyfied) to try to seduce him. Only Chloe is a liar, spinning tales of her encounters that have Catherine becoming increasingly volatile. Remake of Anne Fontaine's 2003 film "Nathalie." **99m/C DVD.** *CA FR* Julianne Moore, Liam Neeson, Amanda Seyfried, Max Thieriot, R.H. Thomson, Nina Dobrev; *D:* Atom Egoyan; *W:* Erin Cressida Wilson; *C:* Paul Sarossy; *M:* Mychael Danna.

Chloe in the Afternoon 🦴🦴🦴 *L'Amour l'Apres-midi* **1972 (R)** A married man finds himself inexplicably drawn to an ungainly young woman. Sixth of the "Moral Tales" series is typical of director Rohmer's talky approach. Not for all tastes, but rewarding for those who are drawn to this sort of thing. In French with English subtitles. **97m/C VHS, DVD.** *FR* Bernard Verley, Zouzou, Francoise Verley, Daniel Ceccaldi, Malvina Penne, Babette Ferrier, Suze Randall, Marie-Christine Barrault; *D:* Eric Rohmer; *W:* Eric Rohmer; *C:* Nestor Almendros; *M:* Arie Dzierlatka.

Chocolat 🦴🦴🦴 1/2 **1988 (PG-13)** A woman recalls her childhood spent in French West Africa and the unfulfilled sexual tension between her mother and black servant. Vivid film provides a host of intriguing characters and offers splendid panoramas of rugged desert landscapes. Profound, if somewhat personal filmmaking from novice director Denis. In French with English subtitles. **105m/C VHS, DVD.** Mireille Perrier, Emmet Judson Williamson, Cecile Ducasse, Giulia Boschi, Francois Cluzet, Isaach de Bankole, Kenneth Cranham; *D:* Claire Denis; *W:* Claire Denis, Jean-Pol Fargeau.

Chocolat 🦴🦴🦴 **2000 (PG-13)** Free-spirited Vianne (Binoche) and her young daughter Anouk (Thivisol) are literally blown into the dull French town of Lansquenet in the late 1950s. Before the scandalized eyes of the Comte de Reynaud (Molina), the community's moral arbitrator, the unmarried hussy opens a chocolaterie—during Lent! While the Comte tries to rally the residents to boycott the establishment, Vianne's delicacies are setting the townspeople's pulses racing, as she becomes intrigued by gypsy vagabond Roux (Depp). Sweetly predictable if overly chastising against religion and conventional morality. Binoche is radiant as usual (and have some chocolate handy when you watch). Based on the novel by Joanne Harris. **121m/C VHS, DVD.** *FR* Juliette Binoche, Victorie Thivisol, Johnny Depp, Alfred Molina, Judi Dench, Lena Olin, Peter Stormare, Carrie-Anne Moss, John Wood, Hugh O'Conor, Leslie Caron, Aurelien Parent Koenig; *D:* Lasse Hallstrom; *W:* Robert Nelson Jacobs; *C:* Roger Pratt; *M:* Rachel Portman. Screen Actors Guild '00: Support. Actress (Dench).

The Chocolate Soldier 🦴 **1941** Dull musical in which an opera star tests his wife's fidelity. Lovers of the musical genre will find that this one has too much talking, not enough singing. Lovers of fine films will realize that more singing would hardly improve things. Based loosely on Molnar's play "The Guardsman." **102m/B VHS.** Nelson Eddy, Rise Stevens, Nigel Bruce, Florence Bates, Dorothy Gilmore, Nydia Westman; *D:* Roy Del Ruth; *C:* Karl Freund.

The Chocolate War 🦴🦴🦴 **1988 (R)** An idealistic student and a hardline headmaster butt heads at a Catholic boys' school over an unofficial candy business in this tense, unsettling drama. Glover is notable in his familiar villain role, and Gordon is effective in his first effort as director. Based on the Robert Cormier novel. **95m/C VHS, DVD.** John Glover, Jenny Wright, Wallace (Wally) Langham, Bud Cort, Ilan Mitchell-Smith, Adam Baldwin; *D:* Keith Gordon; *W:* Keith Gordon.

The Choice 🦴🦴 **1981** A young woman must make the choice between aborting or keeping her baby in this fairly insipid drama. **96m/C VHS.** Susan Clark, Jennifer Warren, Mitchell Ryan, Largo Woodruff; *D:* David Greene. **TV**

Choice of Arms 🦴🦴 1/2 **1983** A gangster's rural retirement is undone by a dim-witted criminal in this sometimes-gripping drama. Montand and Deneuve are serviceable in undemanding roles of the gangster and his glamorous wife; Depardieu is more impressive as the trouble-making punk. In French with English subtitles. **114m/C VHS.** *FR* Gerard Depardieu, Catherine Deneuve, Yves Montand; *D:* Alain Corneau.

Choice of Weapons 🦴🦴 *A Dirty Knight's Work; Trial by Combat* **1976** Ex-cop trying to solve murders focuses on a curious group of 20th-century men who live within a 12th-century fantasy—jousting for sport and chivalrous honor. Offbeat lance thruster notable for incongruity and all-star cast. **88m/C VHS.** *GB* David Birney, Peter Cushing, Donald Pleasence, Barbara Hershey, John Mills, Margaret Leighton; *D:* Kevin Connor; *W:* Julian Bond.

Choices 🦴 1/2 **1981** A hearing-impaired athlete suffers alienation when banned from the football squad. What? Controversial covergirl Moore is a supporting player in this, her first film. **90m/C VHS, DVD.** Paul Carafotes, Victor French, Lelia Goldoni, Val Avery, Dennis Patrick, Demi Moore; *D:* Rami Alon; *W:* Rami Alon; *C:* Hanania Baer; *M:* Christopher Stone.

Choices 🦴🦴 1/2 **1986** Scott is a 62-year-old man with a lovely second wife (Bisset) and a rebellious grown daughter (Gilbert), who announces she's pregnant and is getting an abortion. Meanwhile, his wife also discovers she's pregnant and wants the child, although Scott is adamantly opposed to raising a second family at his age. Family strife carried by fine performances. **95m/C VHS, DVD.** George C. Scott, Jacqueline Bisset, Melissa Gilbert; *D:* David Lowell Rich. **TV**

The Choir 🦴🦴🦴 **1995** Crisis has overtaken Aldminster Cathedral and its famed boys' choir, which was begun more than 400 years before. Expensive repairs are needed on the building and ambitious dean, Hugh Cavendish (Fox), is ready to sacrifice the choir if it will get funding and blunt city council criticism about what some see as an expensive frill. Opposing are King's School headmaster Alexander Troy (Warner) and music master Leo Beckford (Farrell)—who just happens to be having an affair with his top choirster's mother (Harrison). Religion, politics, music, and sex all provide for some interesting drama. Based on the novel by Joanna Trollope. **?m/C VHS.** *GB* James Fox, David Warner, Nicholas Farrell, Cathryn Harrison, Jane Asher, Anthony Way, Peter Vaughan, Richenda Carey, Oliver Milburn, Claire Cox, John Standing, Robert Flemyng; *D:* Ferdinand Fairfax; *W:* Ian Curteis. **TV**

The Choirboys 🦴 **1977 (R)** Thoroughly mediocre production about overbearing L.A. cops and their off-hours handling of job stress. Few of the strong cast emerge unscathed. Based on the Joseph Wambaugh novel. **120m/C VHS.** Charles Durning, Louis Gossett Jr., Perry King, Clyde Kusatsu, Stephen Macht, Tim McIntire, Randy Quaid, Chuck Sacci, Don Stroud, James Woods, Burt Young, Robert Webber, Barbara Rhoades, Vic Tayback, Blair Brown, Charles Haid, Jim Davis; *D:* Robert Aldrich; *C:* Joseph Biroc.

Choke 🦴 1/2 **2000 (R)** Weak thriller with dumb dialogue. Shady businessman Harry (Hopper) is trying to cover up his daughter's deadly drunken hit-and-run accident when he's threatened by a con man who knows about the crime. Then Harry just makes the situation worse by accepting the help of a killer (Madsen) who knows how to get rid of troublesome bodies. **95m/C VHS, DVD.** Dennis Hopper, Michael Madsen, L.P. Brown III, Chelsy Reynolds, Roy Tate; *D:* John Sjogren. **VIDEO**

Choke 🦴🦴 1/2 **2008 (R)** Sex addict Victor Mancini (Rockwell) supplements his modest income as a historical re-enactor at a colonial village theme park by conning upscale restaurant patrons into believing he is choking and then preying on their sympathies and fat wallets, a scam that helps him keep his crazy mother Ida (Huston) in an expensive private mental hospital. His vacant life takes a turn when, in a rare lucid moment, his mother reveals his father's shocking identity, giving him cause to reflect on his pathetic, single-track life. Graphic sex scenes border on gratuitous, but Rockwell makes an otherwise detestable character somewhat sympathetic and likeable while pitching black dark comedy. Will either strongly offend or greatly entertain, depending on a tolerance of Oedipal complexes and kink as comedy. Based on the novel by "Fight Club" author Chuck Palahniuk, and directorial debut of Gregg, who also has a role. **89m/C DVD.** *US* Sam Rockwell, Anjelica Huston, Kelly Macdonald, Bijou Phillips, Brad William Henke, Clark Gregg, Gillian Jacobs; *D:* Clark Gregg; *W:* Clark Gregg; *C:* Tim Orr; *M:* Nathan Larson.

Choke Canyon 🦴🦴 **1986 (PG)** An environmentalist thwarts the henchmen of an industrialist eager to coverup a nuclear dump in a picturesque canyon. Good intentions do not necessarily make for a good movie. **95m/C VHS.** Stephen Collins, Bo Svenson, Lance Henriksen; *D:* Charles "Chuck" Bail.

C.H.O.M.P.S. 🦴 1/2 **1979 (PG)** Comedy in which a youthful inventor and a popular robot guard dog become the target of a business takeover. Harmless but unfunny and unfun. **90m/C VHS, DVD.** Jim Backus, Valerie Bertinelli, Wesley Eure, Conrad Bain, Chuck McCann, Red Buttons; *D:* Don Chaffey.

Choose Connor 🦴🦴 **2007** Idealistic 15-year-old Owen Norris (Linz) gets a summer job working on the senate campaign of Congressman Connor (Weber), who's eager to use Owen as his youth spokesman. However, Owen is soon disillusioned by how self-serving and corrupt politics can be. There's also a disturbing subplot involving Connor's adopted teenaged nephew, Caleb (Holloway), who has both physical and emotional scars, and his burgeoning relationship to Owen. **109m/C DVD.** Alex D. Linz, Steven Weber, Diane Delano, John Rubinstein, Erik Avari, Christopher Marquette, Escher Holloway; *D:* Luke Eberl; *W:* Luke Eberl; *C:* Jim Timperman; *M:* Kazimir Boyle.

Choose Me 🦴🦴🦴 1/2 **1984 (R)** Comedy-drama about sad, lonely, and often quirky characters linked to an unlikely L.A. radio sex therapist. Moody, memorable fare features especially strong playing from Bujold as a sexually inexperienced sex therapist and Warren as one of her regular listeners. Typically eccentric fare from director Rudolph. **106m/C VHS, DVD.** Keith Carradine, Genevieve Bujold, Lesley Ann Warren, Rae Dawn Chong, John Larroquette, John Considine, Patrick Bauchau; *D:* Alan Rudolph; *W:* Alan Rudolph; *C:* Jan Kiesser; *M:* Phil Woods.

Chopper 🦴🦴 1/2 **2000** Biopic of famous Aussie criminal Mark "Chopper" Read is highlighted by Bana's extraordinary performance in the title role. Dominik's directorial debut follows Read's career from prison, where he murders one inmate, forces another to cut off his ears, and generally makes hardened criminal fear for their lives, to his old haunts, where he seeks revenge for past wrongs. Full of gore and ultraviolence, it's not for the sqeamish, but it does make its point about society's preoccupation with the "celebrity criminal." Read didn't participate in the production, but it was based on his nine bestsellers, and he did suggest Bana for the lead. **94m/C DVD.** *AU* Eric Bana, Vince Colosimo, Simon Lyndon, David Field, Daniel Wyllie, Bill Young, Garry Waddell, Kate Beahan, Kenny Graham; *D:* Andrew Dominik; *W:* Andrew Dominik; *C:* Geoffrey Hall; *M:* Mick Harvey. Australian Film Inst. '00: Actor (Bana), Director

(Dominik), Support. Actor (Lyndon).

Chopper Chicks in Zombietown 🦴🦴 **1991 (R)** Tough but sexy Chopper Chicks show up in that American vacation mecca, Zombietown, for a little rest and relaxation. Little do they know that a mad mortician has designs on turning our hot heroines into mindless zombie slaves. Can the buxom biker babes thwart the evil embalmer before it's too late, or will they abandon their Harleys to shuffle about in search of human flesh? From the Troma Team, featuring Oscar-winner Billy Bob Thornton as "Donny." **86m/C VHS, DVD.** Jamie Rose, Catherine Carlen, Lycia Naff, Vicki Frederick, Kristina Loggia, Gretchen Palmer, Whitney Reis, Nina Peterson, Ed Gale, David Knell, Billy Bob Thornton, Don Calfa, Martha Quinn; ***D:*** Dan Hoskins; ***W:*** Dan Hoskins; ***C:*** Tom Fraser; ***M:*** Daniel May.

The Choppers 🦴 **1961** Naw, not a fable about false teeth. Teen punk Hall operates a car theft ring made up of fellow punksters. Rock'n'roll tunes by the Hall-meister include the much-overlooked "Monkey in my Hatband." **66m/B VHS, DVD.** Arch Hall Jr., Marianne Gaba, Robert Paget, Tom Brown, Rex Holman, Bruno VeSota; ***D:*** Leigh Jason; ***W:*** Arch (Archie) Hall Sr.; ***C:*** Clark Ramsey; ***M:*** Al Pellegrini.

Chopping Mall 🦴 1/2 *Killbots* **1986 (R)** A freak electric storm unleashes killer security robots on a band of teens trapped inside the mall. Nobody shops. Premise undone by obscure humor, lack of flair, action, or horror. Updated imitation of the 1973 TV movie "Trapped." **77m/C VHS, DVD.** Kelli Maroney, Tony O'Dell, Suzee Slater, Russell Todd, Paul Bartel, Mary Woronov, Dick Miller, Karrie Emerson, Barbara Crampton, Nick Segal, John Terlesky, Gerrit Graham, Mel Welles; ***D:*** Jim Wynorski; ***W:*** Jim Wynorski, Steve Mitchell; ***C:*** Tom Richmond; ***M:*** Chuck Cirino.

The Chorus 🦴🦴 *Les Choristes* **2004 (PG-13)** Two childhood friends, drawn together again by personal tragedy, reflect on the role of an old mentor who elevated their lives through song. Story of saintly teacher is told in flashback from his point of view. Very schmaltzy retread that has been made so many times before. Tired and predictably inspiring. **95m/C DVD.** Gerard Jugnot, Francois Berleand, Jacques Perrin, Marie Bunel, Kad Merad, Jean-Baptiste Maunier, Didier Flamand, Jean-Paul Bonnaire, Phillippe Du Janerand, Maxence Perrin; ***D:*** Christophe Barratier; ***W:*** Christophe Barratier, Philippe Lopes-Curval; ***C:*** Carlo Varini; ***M:*** Bruno Coulais.

A Chorus Line 🦴🦴 **1985 (PG-13)** A range of performers reveal their insecurities and aspirations while auditioning before a hardnosed director in this adaptation of the popular, overblown Broadway musical. Singing and dancing is rarely rousing. Director Attenborough probably wasn't the right choice for this one. ♫Dance 10, Looks 3; What I Did for Love; At the Ballet; I Can Do That; Let Me Dance For You; I Hope I Get It; Nothing; The Music and the Mirror; And. **118m/C VHS, DVD.** Michael Douglas, Audrey Landers, Gregg Burge, Alyson Reed, Janet Jones, Michael Blevins, Terrence Mann, Cameron English, Vicki Frederick, Nicole Fosse, Michelle Johnson; ***D:*** Richard Attenborough; ***W:*** Arnold Schulman; ***M:*** Marvin Hamlisch, Ralph Burns.

A Chorus of Disapproval 🦴 1/2 **1989 (PG)** Adaptation of prolific Alan Ayckbourn's play about a withdrawn, somewhat dim-witted British widower who attempts social interaction by joining community theatre, then finds himself embroiled in romantic shenanigans and theatrical intrigue. Irons is fine in the lead, but Hopkins sparkles in the more spectacular role of the musical production's demanding but beleaguered director. Seagrove is impressive as an amoral sexpot. Sharper focus from director Winner would have improved this one, but the film is fun even when it isn't particularly funny. **105m/C VHS.** *GB* Jeremy Irons, Anthony Hopkins, Jenny Seagrove, Lionel Jeffries, Patsy Kensit, Gareth Hunt, Prunella Scales, Sylvia Syms, Richard Briers, Barbara Ferris; ***D:*** Michael Winner; ***W:*** Michael Winner, Alan Ayckbourn; ***M:*** John Du Prez.

The Chosen **WOOF!** *Holocaust 2000* **1977 (R)** Executive of a nuclear power facility located in the Sahara Desert realizes that his son is the Anti-Christ bent on the world's destruction. This truly horrible film provides nothing in terms of entertainment. It's rarely even laughably bad. **102m/C VHS.** Kirk Douglas, Simon Ward, Agostina Belli, Anthony Quayle, Virginia McKenna, Alexander Knox; ***D:*** Alberto De Martino; ***M:*** Ennio Morricone.

The Chosen 🦴🦴🦴 **1981** Set in 1940s Brooklyn about the friendship between two teenagers—Benson, the Hassidic son of a rabbi, and Miller, whose father is a Zionist professor. Based on the novel by Chaim Potok. **108m/C VHS, DVD.** Robby Benson, Barry Miller, Maximilian Schell, Rod Steiger, Hildy Brooks, Ron Rifkin, Val Avery; ***D:*** Jeremy Paul Kagan; ***M:*** Elmer Bernstein.

The Chosen One: Legend of the Raven 🦴🦴 **1998 (R)** McKenna Ray ("Baywatch" babe Electra) wants payback after her sister is murdered and is transformed into a superheroine avenger (guided by her shaman father) so she can rid the world of scum. Electra has a provocative costume but the nude scenes are courtesy of a body-double. **105m/C VHS, DVD.** Carmen Electra, Michael Stadvec, Dave Oliver, Shauna Sand; ***D:*** Lawrence Lanoff; ***W:*** Sam Rappaport, Khara Bromiley; ***C:*** Robert New; ***M:*** Keith Arem.

Christ Stopped at Eboli 🦴🦴🦴🦴 *Eboli; Cristo si e fermato a Eboli* **1979** Subdued work about an anti-Fascist writer exiled to rural Italy in the 1930s. Excellent performances from the lead Volonte and supporting players Papas and Cuny. Slow, contemplative film is probably director Rosi's masterpiece. Adapted from Carlo Levi's book. In Italian with English subtitles. **118m/C VHS, DVD.** *IT FR* Gian Marie Volonte, Irene Papas, Paolo Bonacelli, Francois Simon, Alain Cuny, Lea Massari; ***D:*** Francesco Rosi; ***W:*** Francesco Rosi; ***C:*** Pasqualino De Santis. British Acad. '82: Foreign Film.

Christabel 🦴🦴 **1989** Condensed version of the BBC miniseries based on the true-life WWII exploits of Christabel Bielenberg, a British woman who battled to save her German husband from the horrors of the Ravensbruck concentration camp. **148m/C VHS.** *GB* Elizabeth Hurley, Stephen (Dillon) Dillane, Nigel le Vaillant, Geoffrey Palmer, Ann Bell, Ralph Brown, John Burgess, Suzan Crowley, Eileen Maciejewska, Hugh Simon, Nicola Wright; ***D:*** Adrian Shergold; ***W:*** Dennis Potter; ***C:*** Remi Adefarasin; ***M:*** Stanley Myers. **TV**

Christian the Lion 🦴🦴 1/2 **1976 (G)** The true story of Christian, a lion cub raised in a London zoo, who is transported to Africa to learn to live with other lions. With the principals from "Born Free." **87m/C VHS, DVD.** *GB* Virginia McKenna, Bill Travers, George Adamson, James Hill; ***D:*** Bill Travers.

Christiane F. 🦴🦴🦴 **1982 (R)** Gripping, visually impressive story of a bored German girl's decline into drug use and prostitution. Based on a West German magazine article. Sobering and dismal look at a milieu in which innocence and youth have run amok. The film's impact is only somewhat undermined by poor dubbing. Bowie appears in a concert sequence. **120m/C VHS, DVD.** *GE* Natja Brunkhorst, Thomas Haustein, David Bowie; ***D:*** Uli Edel; ***M:*** David Bowie.

Christie's Revenge 🦴 1/2 **2007** In this Lifetime cable movie, 16-year-old Christie Colton (Kind) comes home to discover her father has committed suicide. As Christie remembers it, he badly needed a loan and was refused by his doctor brother Ray (Shipp). Three years later, with her mother remarried, Christie finagles her way into living with Uncle Ray and his family, determined to destroy his life as her father's was destroyed. But is what Christie remembers what actually happened? **90m/C DVD.** Danielle Kind, John Wesley Shipp, Cynthia Gibb, James McGowan, Annie Bovaird, Anastasia Phillips; ***D:*** Douglas Jackson; ***W:*** Christine Conradt; ***C:*** Bert Tougas; ***M:*** Steve Gurevitch. **CABLE**

Christina 🦴🦴 1/2 **1974 (PG)** Gloomy suspense fare in which a beautiful woman pays a forlorn fellow $25,000 to marry her, then disappears as he begins to actually fall in love with her. His search takes him to various gothic settings. Intriguing, but not really fulfilling. Parkins, however, is appropriately mysterious in the lead. **95m/C VHS.** *CA* Barbara Parkins, Peter Haskell; ***D:*** Paul Krasny.

Christina's House 🦴🦴 **1999** Teen learns she's likely to be the next victim of a murderous stalker who's hiding within her own home. **97m/C VHS, DVD.** *CA* Brendan Fehr, Brad Rowe, John Savage, Allison Lange, Lorne Stewart; ***D:*** Gavin Wilding. **VIDEO**

Christine 🦴🦴 1/2 **1984 (R)** Unassuming teen gains posession of a classic auto equipped with a murderous will. Then it's the car doing the possessing. The car more than returns the care and consideration its owner provides it. Are you listening GMC? Better than average treatment of Stephen King's work features a creepy performance by Gordon. **110m/C VHS, DVD.** Keith Gordon, John Stockwell, Alexandra Paul, Robert Prosky, Harry Dean Stanton, Kelly Preston, Christine Belford, Roberts Blossom, William Ostrander, David Spielberg, Robert Darnell; ***D:*** John Carpenter; ***W:*** Bill Phillips; ***C:*** Donald M. Morgan; ***M:*** John Carpenter, Alan Howarth.

Christmas at Water's Edge 🦴🦴 1/2 **2004** Leila Turner is from a wealthy family but she helps out at a home for troubled teens. However, the building is about to be demolished, thanks to one of her father's development projects. Leila and her friend Tre discover some of the teens can sing and they decide to hold a fund-raising concert that's helped by some heavenly influence. **87m/C DVD.** Keisha Knight Pulliam, Richard Lawson, Tom Bosley, Earl Billings, Pooch Hall, Ray J. Norwood; ***D:*** Lee Davis, Janet Hubert; ***W:*** Riley Weston, Mike Watts. **CABLE**

The Christmas Blessing 🦴🦴 1/2 **2005** Weepy, heartfelt sequel to "The Christmas Shoes." The now grown-up Nathan Andrews (Harris) is a medical resident, but when a young patient dies, he's in crisis and decides to move back home to think things over. Volunteering at the local school, Nathan falls for teacher Meagan (Gayheart) but he needs a Christmas miracle when both her life and that of a young boy (Jones) are in danger. **90m/C DVD.** Neil Patrick Harris, Rebecca Gayheart, Angus T. Jones, Rob Lowe, Hugh Thompson, Wanda Cannon, Shaun Johnston; ***D:*** Karen Arthur; ***W:*** Wesley Bishop; ***M:*** Lawrence Shragge. **TV**

The Christmas Box 🦴🦴 1/2 **1995** Tearjerking Christmas drama based on Richard Paul Evans' surprising 1992 bestseller, which started out as a story for the author's children. Richard (Thomas) and Keri (O'Toole) Evans have money troubles so they and their five-year-old daughter Jenna (Mulrooney) move into the mansion of elderly widow Mary Parkin (O'Hara) as caretakers. Richard keeps seeing an angel in a recurring dream and hears a familiar tune—all of which leads to a music box hidden in the attic, a series of love letters, and Mary's unhappy past. **92m/C VHS, DVD.** Maureen O'Hara, Richard Thomas, Annette O'Toole, Kelsey Mulrooney; ***D:*** Marcus Cole; ***W:*** Greg Taylor; ***C:*** John Newby.

Christmas Caper 🦴🦴 **2007 (PG)** Typical "true meaning of Christmas" cable comedy. Thief Cate Dove (Doherty) hides out in her quaint hometown of Comfort, Connecticut, when her partner Clive (Coates) double-crosses her. Since her sister (Salomaa) and brother-in-law (Lewis) are delayed out of town, Cate the grinch is left caring for her niece and nephew and uses the time to plan her next heist for Christmas Eve. But the season softens even the hardest heart, especially since Cate's hunky ex-beau Hank (Olsson), now the town's sheriff, is taking an interest. **88m/C DVD.** Shannen Doherty, Ty Olsson, Conrad Coates, Stefanie von Pfetten, Sonya Salomaa, David Lewis, Natasha Calis, Josh Hayden; ***D:*** David Winkler; ***W:*** April Blair. **CABLE**

The Christmas Card 🦴🦴 1/2 **2006** Career solider Cody Cullen (Newton) is touched by the strangers who have sent Christmas cards to his unit in Afghanistan. He saves one special card from Faith Spelman (Evans) and when Cody gets leave, he impulsively decides to visit her small hometown. Faith and her father (Asner) welcome Cody and he soon feels part of their family but as Cody and Faith get closer, he needs to decide where his future lies. **84m/C DVD.** Alice Evans, Ed Asner, Lois Nettleton, Peter Jason, Ben Weber; ***D:*** Stephen Bridgewater; ***W:*** Joany Kane; ***C:*** Maximo Munzi, John Newton; ***M:*** Roger Bellon, Brian Robinson. **CABLE**

A Christmas Carol 🦴🦴🦴 **1938** An early version of Dickens' classic tale about miser Scrooge, who is instilled with the Christmas spirit after a grim evening with some ghosts. Good playing from Owen as Scrooge and Lockhart as the hapless Bob Cratchit. Scary graveyard sequence too. **70m/B VHS, DVD.** Reginald Owen, Gene Lockhart, Terence (Terry) Kilburn, Leo G. Carroll, Lynne Carver, Ann Rutherford; ***D:*** Edwin L. Marin.

A Christmas Carol 🦴🦴🦴🦴 *Scrooge* **1951** A fine retelling of the classic tale about a penny-pinching holiday hater who learns appreciation of Christmas following a frightful, revealing evening with supernatural visitors. Perhaps the best rendering of the Dickens classic. "And God bless Tiny Tim!" **86m/B VHS, DVD.** *GB* Alastair Sim, Kathleen Harrison, Jack Warner, Michael Hordern, Patrick Macnee, Mervyn Johns, Hermione Baddeley, Clifford Mollison, George Cole, Carol Marsh, Miles Malleson, Ernest Thesiger, Hattie Jacques, Peter Bull, Hugh Dempster; ***D:*** Brian Desmond Hurst; ***W:*** Noel Langley; ***C:*** C.M. Pennington-Richards; ***M:*** Richard Addinsell.

A Christmas Carol 🦴🦴 **1954** Musical version of the Dickens' classic about a stingy old man who is visited by three ghosts on Christmas Eve. **54m/B VHS.** Fredric March, Basil Rathbone, Ray Middleton, Bob Sweeney, Christopher Cook; ***D:*** Ralph Levy; ***W:*** Maxwell Anderson; ***M:*** Bernard Herrmann.

A Christmas Carol 🦴🦴🦴 **1984 (PG)** Excellent TV adaptation of the Dickens Christmas classic features a memorable Scott as miserly misanthrope Ebenezer Scrooge, who gets a scary look at his life thanks to a Christmas Eve visit from the ghosts of Christmas Past, Present, and Future. Terrific supporting cast; filmed on location in Shrewsbury, England. **100m/C VHS, DVD.** George C. Scott, Nigel Davenport, Edward Woodward, Frank Finlay, Lucy Gutteridge, Angela Pleasence, Roger Rees, David Warner, Susannah York; ***D:*** Clive Donner; ***W:*** Roger O. Hirson; ***C:*** Tony Imi; ***M:*** Nick Bicat.

A Christmas Carol 🦴🦴 1/2 **1999** Oft-told tale does have the advantage of Stewart (who has a one-man stage production of the Dickens saga as well as recording an audio-book) as the miserly Scrooge. It also has a strong supporting cast and special effects that enhance but don't overwhelm. **120m/C VHS, DVD.** Patrick Stewart, Richard E. Grant, Joel Grey, Saskia Reeves, Desmond Barrit, Bernard Lloyd, Tim Potter, Ben Tibber, Dominic West, Trevor Peacock, Liz Smith, Elizabeth Spriggs, Laura Fraser, Celia Imrie; ***D:*** David Hugh Jones; ***W:*** Peter Barnes; ***C:*** Ian Wilson; ***M:*** Stephen Warbeck. **CABLE**

A Christmas Carol *Disney's A Christmas Carol* **2009** Animated 3-D version of the Dickens Christmas classic with Carrey as the voice of miser Ebenezer Scrooge (as well as the three Ghosts who help show him the true meaning of the season). **m/C DVD.** ***D:*** Robert Zemeckis; ***W:*** Robert Zemeckis; ***C:*** Robert Presley; ***M:*** Alan Silvestri; ***V:*** Jim Carrey, Gary Oldman, Colin Firth, Bob Hoskins, Robin Wright Penn, Lesley Manville.

Christmas Child 🦴🦴 **2003** Typical seasonal heart-tugger based on a short story by Max Lucado. Troubled journalist Jack (Moses) is on his way to Dallas when a mystery photo catches his eye and detours him to the small town of Clearwater. He's intrigued by the town's living nativity scene and finds out his Christmas birthday is somehow related to the annual celebration. **96m/C DVD.** William R. Moses, Megan Follows, Steve Chapman, Tonya Bordeaux, Vicki Taylor Ross; ***D:*** William Ewing; ***W:*** Andrea Jobe, Eric Newman; ***C:*** Fernando Argelles; ***M:*** Phil Marshall. **CABLE**

The Christmas Choir 🦴🦴 1/2 **2008** Hallmark Channel holiday fare about workaholic accountant Peter Brockman (Gedrick) who finds unexpected rewards when he decides to volunteer at a men's homeless shelter run by cantankerous Sister Agatha (Perlman). After hearing some of the musical talents of the guys, Peter's encouraged to form a choir. **85m/C DVD.** Jason Gedrick, Rhea Perlman, Michael Sarrazin, Tyrone Benskin, Luis Oliva, Marianne Farley, Claudia Ferri, Cindy Sampson; ***D:*** Peter Svatek; ***W:*** Donald Martin; ***C:*** Eric Cayla; ***M:*** James Gelfand. **CABLE**

The Christmas Coal Mine Miracle 🦴 ½ *Christmas Miracle in Caulfield, U.S.A* **1977** Syrupy story about miners struggling for survival in a collapsed mine on Christmas Eve. **98m/C VHS.** Mitchell Ryan, Kurt Russell, Andrew Prine, John Carradine, Barbara Babcock, Melissa Gilbert, Don Porter, Shelby Leverington; ***D:*** Jud Taylor. **TV**

Christmas Comes to Willow Creek 🦴🦴 **1987** Mutually antagonistic brothers are enlisted to deliver Christmas gifts to an isolated Alaskan community. Can brotherly love be far off? Two leads played together in the rowdy TV series "Dukes of Hazzard." This is hardly an improvement. **96m/C VHS, DVD.** John Schneider, Tom Wopat, Hoyt Axton, Zachary Ansley, Kim Delaney; ***D:*** Richard Lang; ***M:*** Charles Fox.

The Christmas Cottage 🦴🦴 *Thomas Kinkade's The Christmas Cottage; Thomas Kinkade's Home for Christmas* **2008 (PG)** How the inspirational artist got his start. College student Thomas Kinkade (Padalecki) comes home for Christmas and discovers the family home is about to go into foreclosure. So with the help of mentor Glenn (O'Toole), Thomas accepts a commission to paint a mural of his hometown and realizes his true calling. **96m/C DVD.** Jared Padalecki, Marcia Gay Harden, Peter O'Toole, Kiersten Warren, Gina Holden, Aaron Ashmore, Richard Burgi, Richard Moll; ***D:*** Michael Campus; ***W:*** Ken LaZebnik; ***C:*** Robert Brinkmann. **VIDEO**

Christmas Do-Over 🦴 ½ **2006** Think "Groundhog Day" only at Christmas. Grumpy Kevin (Mohr) isn't happy to be spending the holiday with his ex-wife Jill (Zuniga) and his in-laws but he does want to see his cute-as-a-button son Ben (Grove). Ben wishes to have Christmas every day and Kevin is stuck reliving the holiday until he understands this is his last chance to get his old life back. Except Kevin is such a selfish whiner you know why Jill dumped him, which spoils the whole fantasy. **90m/C DVD.** Jay Mohr, Daphne Zuniga, Adrienne Barbeau, Logan Grove, Tim Thomerson, David Millbern, Ruta Lee; ***D:*** Catherine Cyran; ***W:*** Trevor Reed Cristow, Jacqueline David; ***C:*** Ken Blakey; ***M:*** Andrew Gross. **CABLE**

Christmas Eve 🦴 ½ **1947** When a conniving nephew tries to deem his spinster aunt unfit so he can control her estate, she rallies together her three adopted sons, a globe-trotting playboy, a shady criminal type and a wayward cowboy to help. Involves some cute adventures but rather poor acting. Story culminates on Christmas Eve, but it's not a holiday tale. **90m/B VHS.** George Raft, George Brent, Randolph Scott, Joan Blondell, Virginia Field; ***D:*** Edwin L. Marin; ***W:*** Laurence Stallings. **VIDEO**

Christmas Evil 🦴 ½ *Terror in Toyland; You Better Watch Out* **1980 (R)** Once again a knife-wielding lunatic dresses as Santa Claus to strike terror and death into the hearts of children. **92m/C VHS, DVD.** Brandon Maggart, Jeffrey DeMunn, Dianne Hull, Scott McKay, Peter Friedman, Joe Jamrog, Rutanya Alda, Raymond J. Barry, Andy Fenwick, Sam Gray, Patricia Richardson; ***D:*** Lewis Jackson; ***W:*** Lewis Jackson; ***C:*** Ricardo Aronovich.

Christmas in Connecticut 🦴🦴🦴 *Indiscretion* **1945** Lightweight comedy about a housekeeping magazine's successful columnist who isn't quite the expert homemaker she presents herself to be. When a war veteran is invited to her home as part of a publicity gimmick, she must master the ways of housekeeping or reveal her incompetence. Stanwyck is winning in the lead role. Also available in a colorized version. **101m/B VHS, DVD.** Barbara Stanwyck, Reginald Gardiner, Sydney Greenstreet, Dennis Morgan, S.Z. Sakall, Una O'Connor, Robert Shayne, Joyce Compton; ***D:*** Peter Godfrey.

Christmas in Connecticut 🦴🦴 **1992** Cannon hosts a weekly TV show as America's favorite homemaker/hostess. A local forest ranger (Kristofferson) becomes a hero by saving a little boy's life and her network stages a media event by inviting him to her home for a traditional Christmas dinner. There's only one problem: she can't cook. Schwarzenegger's directorial debut lacks challenge in this fluffy remake. See the original instead. **93m/C VHS, DVD.** Dyan Cannon, Kris Kristofferson, Tony Curtis, Richard Roundtree, Kelly Cinnante, Gene Lithgow, Vivian Bonnell; ***D:*** Arnold Schwarzenegger; ***W:*** Janet Brownell. **CABLE**

Christmas in July 🦴🦴🦴 ½ **1940** A young man goes on a spending spree when he thinks he's won a sweepstakes. Things take a turn for the worse when he finds out that it was all a practical joke. Powell provides a winning performance in this second film from comic master Sturges. **67m/B VHS, DVD.** Dick Powell, Ellen Drew, Raymond Walburn, William Demarest, Franklin Pangborn; ***D:*** Preston Sturges.

Christmas in the Clouds 🦴🦴 ½ **2001 (PG)** Fun, screwball comedy set in a very upscale Native-American owned resort. The main characters all seem to bring a peculiar little twist to the story line. A writer from a prestigious travel guide publication is expected to make a surprise visit. Joe Clouds on Fire (Vlhos) has secretly been writing love letters to a pen pal, Tina (Tosca), who shows up to spy on her suitor only to be mistaken for the hotel critic. The actual critic, Stu O'Malley (Walsh), is a disheveled half-drunk grouch, and is shuffled to a small, cramped room. Very funny farce filmed in Utah's Sundance Resort. **97m/C DVD.** *US* Sam Vlahos, M. Emmet Walsh, Graham Greene, Sheila Tousey, Rosalind Ayres, Tim Vahle, MariAna Tosca, Jonathan Joss; ***D:*** Kate Montgomery; ***W:*** Kate Montgomery; ***C:*** Steven Bernstein; ***M:*** Rita Coolidge.

Christmas in Wonderland 🦴🦴 **2007 (PG)** The Saunders family has just moved to a new city and have no money, no friends, and no Christmas spirit. Then 12-year-old Brian and 6-year-old Mary find a bag of money at the mall and go on a shopping spree. Only the cash is counterfeit and the crooks want it back. **70m/C DVD.** Patrick Swayze, Tim Curry, Chris Kattan, Carmen Electra, Preston Lacey, Matthew Knight, Amy Schlagel, Zoe Schlagel; ***D:*** James Orr; ***W:*** James Orr, Jim Cruickshank; ***C:*** Duane Manwiller; ***M:*** Terry Frewer. **VIDEO**

The Christmas Kid 🦴 ½ **1968** A desperado struggles to determine his true identity while stopping in a frontier town. Gunplay ensues. Don't bother with this one. **87m/C VHS.** *SP* Jeffrey Hunter, Louis Hayward, Gustavo Rojo, Perla Cristal, Luis Prendes; ***D:*** Sidney W. Pink.

Christmas Lilies of the Field 🦴🦴 ½ **1984** Sequel to "Lilies of the Field" follows an ex-soldier who returns to the church he helped build. This time he sets out to build an orphanage. **98m/C VHS.** Billy Dee Williams, Maria Schell, Fay Hauser, Judith Piquet; ***D:*** Ralph Nelson. **TV**

The Christmas Miracle of Jonathan Toomey 🦴🦴 ½ **2007** Reclusive woodcarver Jonathan Toomey (Berenger) is hired by widowed Susan McDowell (Richardson) to carve a replica of a nativity set (now lost) that was given to her son Thomas (Ward-Wilkinson) by his late father. But the work and the approaching holiday bring up painful memories for everyone that they must overcome in order to find hope in the season. **97m/C DVD.** *GB* Tom Berenger, Joely Richardson, Ronald Pickup, Saoirse Ronan, Luke Ward-Wilinson; ***D:*** Bill Clark; ***W:*** Bill Clark; ***C:*** Emmanuel (Manu) Kadosh; ***M:*** Guy Farley. **VIDEO**

A Christmas Proposal 🦴🦴 **2008 (PG)** Two lawyers fight over a proposal to turn a quaint mountain ski community into an all-year resort. Then they discover they were childhood sweethearts and when big city lawyer Rick has a car accident and is forced to stick around, the small town plus Lisa's presence finds him changing his mind about his current case. **90m/C DVD.** Nicole Eggert, David O'Donnell, Tom Arnold, David DeLuise, Shannon Sturges, Sarah Thompson, Patty McCormack; ***D:*** Michael Feifer; ***W:*** Peter Sullivan; ***C:*** Mark Ritchie; ***M:*** Andres Boulton. **VIDEO**

A Christmas Reunion 🦴🦴 ½ **1993 (PG)** Young boy, still trying to adjust to his parents' death, runs away from his grandfather's house. But they're reunited thanks to street corner Santa and an enchanted book. **92m/C VHS.** James Coburn, Edward Woodward, Meredith Edwards; ***D:*** David Hemmings.

The Christmas Shoes 🦴🦴 ½ **2002** Lawyer Robert Layton (Lowe) isn't feeling any Christmas cheer as his work commitments keep him from his family, including daughter Lily's (Marshall) choir concerts. Choir director Maggie Andrews (Williams) is terminally ill and her son Nathan (Morrow) wants to buy his mother a special pair of red shoes. Naturally, Robert and Nathan's lives will overlap to make the spirit of the season meaningful for them all. Still, this is a flick about a dying mom so it may be too sad for the youngest members of the family to view. Based on the novel by Donna Van Lieve. **100m/C DVD.** Rob Lowe, Kimberly Williams, Max Morrow, Maria Del Mar, Hugh Thompson, Dorian Harewood, Shirley Douglas, Amber Marshall; ***D:*** Andy Wolk; ***W:*** Wesley Bishop; ***C:*** John Berrie; ***M:*** Lawrence Shragge. **TV**

A Christmas Story 🦴🦴🦴🦴 **1983 (PG)** Unlikely but winning comedy of Ralphie's (Billingsley) single-minded obsession to acquire a Red Ryder BB-gun for Christmas, and the obstacles that everyday life in 1940s Indiana can throw his way. Particularly great sequence involving an impatient department-store Santa. Fun for everyone. Based on "In God We Trust, All Others Pay Cash," an autobiographical story by Shepherd. Followed by "My Summer Story" in 1994, also from Shepherd's book. **95m/C VHS, DVD, Blu-ray Disc, HD DVD.** *CA US* Peter Billingsley, Darren McGavin, Melinda Dillon, Ian Petrella, Bob (Benjamin) Clark, Zack (Zach) Ward, Leslie (Les) Carlson, Scott Schwartz, R.D. Robb, Tedde Moore, Yano Ayana; ***Cameos:*** Jean Shepherd; ***D:*** Bob (Benjamin) Clark; ***W:*** Bob (Benjamin) Clark, Leigh Brown, Jean Shepherd; ***C:*** Reginald Morris; ***M:*** Paul Zaza, Carl Zittrer; ***Nar:*** Jean Shepherd. Genie '84: Director (Clark).

A Christmas Tale 🦴🦴🦴 *Un Conte de Noel* **2008** When matriarch Junon is diagnosed with leukemia she uses the opportunity of the Christmas holiday to invite her bickering family home for a reunion in hopes one of them will be a match for a bone marrow transplant. Not exactly your typical warm and fuzzy American holiday fare; that's because it's French and is as dark as it sounds. Despite the premise, pic is buoyed by wit, humor (albeit dark) and excellent performances, namely from the legendary Deneuve. French with subtitles. **150m/C DVD.** *FR* Catherine Deneuve, Jean-Paul Roussillon, Mathieu Amalric, Chiara Mastroianni, Hippolyte Girardot, Anne Consigny, Melvil Poupaud, Emmanuelle Devos, Francoise Bertin, Emile Berling, Laurent Capelluto; ***D:*** Arnaud Desplechin; ***W:*** Arnaud Desplechin, Emmanuel Bourdieu; ***C:*** Eric Gautier; ***M:*** Gregoire Hetzel.

The Christmas That Almost Wasn't 🦴 ½ *Il Natale Che Quasi Non Fu* **1966 (G)** Loathsome humbug decides to destroy Christmas forever by removing Santa Claus from the North Pole. Crude Italian-made children's film nonetheless remembered fondly by a generation of kids. ♫The Christmas That Almost Wasn't; Christmas is Coming; Hustle Bustle; I'm Bad; Kids Get All the Breaks; The Name of the Song is Prune; Nothing to do But Wait; Santa Claus; Time For Christmas. **95m/C VHS, DVD.** *IT* Rossano Brazzi, Paul Tripp, Lidia Brazzi, Sonny Fox, Mischa Auer; ***D:*** Rossano Brazzi.

A Christmas to Remember 🦴🦴 ½ **1978 (G)** Depression-era Minnesota farmer who has lost his son in WWI brings his city-bred grandson to the farm for a holiday visit. Somber, occasionally poignant film buoyed by Robards presence, and Saint's as well. **96m/C VHS.** Jason Robards Jr., Eva Marie Saint, Joanne Woodward; ***D:*** George Englund. **TV**

Christmas Town 🦴🦴 **2008 (G)** A week before Christmas, no-nonsense single mom Liz and her 9-year-old son Mason visit her estranged father who lives in a holiday-bedecked town that's amped up with the Christmas spirit. Her former banker dad is surprisingly working as a cook at the local cafe that's owned by Kevin, who seems to have been chosen by the community to be Liz's special gift. Meanwhile, Mason insists that Santa is actually living inside the local Christmas-themed corporation, North Pole, Inc., and he's determined to see the workshop, the elves, and Santa himself. **90m/C DVD.** Nikki de Boer, Patrick Muldoon, Gig Morton, Garry Chalk; ***D:*** George Erschbamer; ***W:*** Ron McGee; ***M:*** Peter Allen. **VIDEO**

The Christmas Wife 🦴🦴 ½ **1988** A lonely man pays a woman to be his holiday companion at a mountain retreat. Sturdy performances by Robards and Harris manage to keep this one from going to the dogs. Based on a story by Helen Norris. **73m/C VHS, DVD.** Jason Robards Jr., Julie Harris, Don Francks, Patricia Hamilton, Deborah Grover, James Eckhouse; ***D:*** David Hugh Jones. **CABLE**

Christmas With the Kranks 🦴 **2004 (PG)** After the two "Santa Clause" movies, Allen sticks with the holiday in this crass, slapstick comedy based on John Grisham's 2001 novel "Skipping Christmas." That is what Luther (a game Allen) and wife Nora (the ill-used Curtis) intend to do when their only daughter, Blair (Gonzalo), announces she won't be coming home to suburban Chicago for the holiday. Mr. Krank decides a nice Caribbean cruise is in order, but the duo find themselves the recipients of neighborhood scorn when they refuse to get in the seasonal spirit. That changes when Blair suddenly decides to return, accompanied by her brand-new fiance, and the Kranks cave in to Christmas commercialism with zealous glee. Pic is dedicated to the late Alan King, who was cast in a small role as Allen's boss. **98m/C VHS, DVD, UMD.** *US* Tim Allen, Jamie Lee Curtis, Dan Aykroyd, Erik Per Sullivan, Jake Busey, M. Emmet Walsh, Elizabeth Franz, Rene Lavan, Austin Pendleton, Patrick Breen, Felicity Huffman, Julie Gonzalo, Richard "Cheech" Marin, Kevin Chamberlain, Caroline Rhea, Arden Myrin; ***D:*** Joe Roth; ***W:*** Chris Columbus; ***C:*** Don Burgess; ***M:*** John Debney.

A Christmas Without Snow 🦴🦴 ½ **1980** A lonely divorced woman finds communal happiness within a local church choir led by a crusty choir master. **96m/C VHS, DVD.** Michael Learned, John Houseman, Ramon Bieri, James Cromwell, Valerie Curtin, Ruth Nelson, Beah Richards, Calvin Levels; ***D:*** John Korty; ***M:*** Ed Bogas. **TV**

Christopher Columbus 🦴🦴 ½ **1949** Step-by-step biography of the 15th-century explorer, his discovery of America, the fame that first greeted him, and his last days. **103m/C VHS.** *GB* Fredric March, Florence Eldridge, Francis L. Sullivan; ***D:*** David MacDonald.

Christopher Columbus 🦴🦴 ½ **1985** The man who explored the New World is shown in all his flawed complexity in this film that takes a contemporary approach to the discoveries and character of Christopher Columbus. Shot on location in Spain, Malta, and the Dominican Republic, the film features an exact replica of Columbus's flagship, the Santa Maria. Originally aired as a six-hour TV miniseries. **128m/C VHS.** Gabriel Byrne, Faye Dunaway, Oliver Reed, Max von Sydow, Eli Wallach, Nicol Williamson, Jose Ferrer, Virna Lisi, Raf Vallone; ***D:*** Alberto Lattuada. **TV**

Christopher Columbus: The Discovery 🦴 **1992 (PG-13)** The 500th anniversary of Columbus' voyage brought this lame excursion in historical biography to the screen briefly. Columbus is portrayed as a swashbuckling adventurer who finally gets the Queen of Spain to agree to finance his voyage of discovery (which primarily consists of discovering a lot of bare-breasted native women). Story is secondary to the banality of the entire production, including the acting. Brando is briefly seen as Torquemada—another film in which he took his substantial paycheck and ran. **120m/C VHS.** Georges Corraface, Rachel Ward, Tom Selleck, Marlon Brando, Robert Davi, Oliver Cotton, Benicio Del Toro, Catherine Zeta-Jones, Matthieu Carriere, Nigel Terry, Branscombe Richmond; ***D:*** John Glen; ***W:*** John Briley, Mario Puzo, Cary Bates; ***M:*** Cliff Eidelman. Golden Raspberries '92: Worst Support. Actor (Selleck).

Christopher Strong 🦴🦴 ½ **1933** Interesting Hepburn turn as a daredevil aviatrix who falls in love with a married British statesman. **77m/B VHS.** Katharine Hepburn, Billie Burke, Colin Clive, Helen Chandler; ***D:*** Dorothy Arzner; ***M:*** Max Steiner.

Christy 1/2 **1994** Pilot movie for the TV series finds 19-year-old Christy Huddleston (Martin) leaving her privileged Southern life to teach school in the Great Smoky Mountains. It's 1912 in Cutter Gap, Tennessee, and her students are literally dirt poor, with ignorance and supersitition the norm. Christy's inspiration in Miss Alice (Daly), a middle-aged Quaker who runs the mission school. And Christy needs encouragement as she struggles to cope with her new life and responsibilities. Based on the novel by Catherine Marshall, which is a fictional biography of her mother. **90m/C VHS.** Kellie Martin, Tyne Daly, Tess Harper, Randall Batinkoff, Annabelle Price, Stewart Finlay-McLennan; ***D:*** Michael Rhodes; ***M:*** Ron Ramin. **TV**

Chrome and Hot Leather 1/2 **1971 (PG)** A Green Beret is out for revenge after vicious bikers kill his fiance. Conventional, tasteless genre fare notable only as Gaye's first film. **91m/C VHS, DVD.** William (Bill) Smith, Tony Young, Michael Haynes, Peter Brown, Marvin Gaye, Michael Stearns, Kathrine Baumann, Wes Bishop, Herbert Jeffries; ***D:*** Lee Frost.

Chrome Soldiers **1992** Five Vietnam veterans come together to avenge a friend's murder in a town controlled by drug dealers. Busey, as the murdered man's brother, leads the "Chrome Soldiers" in their battle to expose the killers and end local corruption. **92m/C VHS.** Gary Busey, Ray Sharkey, William Atherton, Yaphet Kotto, Nicholas Guest, Kim Robillard, Norman Skaggs, D. David Morin; ***D:*** Thomas J. Wright; ***W:*** Nick Randall; ***C:*** Billy Dickson.

Chronically Unfeasible *Cronicamente Inviavel* **2000** Social satire takes on the Brazilian middleclass as six disparate characters meet in a restaurant in Sao Paulo, struggling with political, class, sexual, and economic issues. Portuguese with subtitles. **101m/C VHS, DVD.** *BR* Patrick Alencar, Leonardo Vieira, Umberto Magnani, Betty Gofman, Daniel Dantas, Dira Paes, Dan Stulbach, Cecil Thire; ***D:*** Sergio Bianchi; ***W:*** Sergio Bianchi, Gustavo Steinberg; ***C:*** Marcelo Coutinho, Antonio Penido.

Chronicle of a Boy Alone *Chronicle of a Lonely Child; Cronica de un Nino Solo* **1964** Eleven-year-old Polin is abandoned by his family and sent to live in a state-run orphanage where well-meaning administrators succeed in destroying the childrens' lives. Spanish with subtitles. **86m/C VHS.** *AR* Oscar Espindola, Beto Gianola, Victoriano Moreira, Leonardo Favio; ***D:*** Leonardo Favio; ***W:*** Leonardo Favio; ***C:*** Ignacio Souto.

Chronicle of a Disappearance **1996** Born in Nazareth in 1960, Suleiman has been living in New York in self-imposed exile for 12 years. He finally decides to return to the Middle East and explore his roots as a Palestinian and the problems that political instability have caused his people and their identity. Arabic with subtitles. **88m/C VHS, DVD.** Elia Suleiman; ***D:*** Elia Suleiman; ***W:*** Elia Suleiman; ***C:*** Marc Andre Batigne.

Chronicle of an Escape *Cronica de una Fuga; Buenos Aires, 1977* **2006 (R)** This brutal look at Argentina's "dirty war" is based on a true story. Soccer player Claudio Tamburrini (de la Serna) is falsely accused of being part of a liberal activist underground. Kidnapped off the streets in Buenos Aires by military thugs, he's taken to a secret government facility that holds dozens of people suspected of anti-government activities. Interrogated and tortured, Claudio realizes his death is a certainty unless he can escape. Spanish with subtitles. **104m/C DVD.** *AR* Rodrigo de la Serna, Pablo Echarri, Nazareno Casero, Martin Urruty, Lautaro Delgado, Matias Marmorato; ***D:*** Adrian Caetano; ***W:*** Adrian Caetano, Esteban Student, Julian Loyola; ***C:*** Julian Apezteguia; ***M:*** Ivan Wyszogrod.

Chronicle of the Raven *Jennifer's Shadow* **2004 (R)** Fairly atmospheric horror flick finds Jennifer (Phillips) traveling to Buenos Aires after she inherits the house of her recently deceased twin. Her sinister grandmother, Mary Ellen (a theatrical Dunaway), who also lives there, doesn't want Jennifer to sell the place. Suddenly, Jennifer begins having nightmares about being attacked by flesh-eating ravens and discovers strange wounds when she wakes up. Seems Granny isn't above killing her kin to get her way. **90m/C DVD.** *US AR* Gina Philips, Faye Dunaway, Duilio Marzio, Hilda Bernard, Nicolas Pauls; ***D:*** Daniel De La Vega, Pablo Pares; ***W:*** Daniel De La Vega, Pablo Pares; ***C:*** Monty Rowan, Robin Melhuish; ***M:*** Micha Liberman.

The Chronicles of Narnia **1989** Exceptional BBC production of the C.S. Lewis fantasy about four brave children who battle evil in a mythical land where the animals talk and strange creatures roam the countryside. In three volumes; aired on PBS as part of the "Wonderworks" family movie series. **180m/C VHS, DVD.** *GB* Barbara Kellerman, Jeffrey S. (Jeff) Perry, Richard Dempsey, Sophie Cook, Jonathan Scott, Sophie Wilcox, David Thwaites, Tom Baker; ***D:*** Alex Kirby.

The Chronicles of Narnia: Prince Caspian **2008 (PG)** As is often the case with sequels, this one is darker and more conventional. The Pevensie siblings (Henley, Keynes, Moseley, Popplewell) are transported from war-torn 1940s London to war-torn Narnia some 1300 years after they left. They discover that the Telmarines have conquered the original Narnians and their ruthless ruler, King Miraz (Castellitto), has driven the survivors, including his nephew, Prince Caspian (Barnes), the rightful heir, into the woods. Caspian and the sibs rally the denizens, and some big (albeit PG-rated) battles ensue, while lion Aslan (voiced by Neeson) turns up, offering bits of wise counsel. The series' religious allegories have been toned down even farther and the CGI visual effects heightened while events are set up for the next installment. **140m/C DVD, Blu-ray Disc.** *US* Georgie Henley, Skander Keynes, William Moseley, Anna Popplewell, Sergio Castellitto, Pierfrancesco Favino, Peter Dinklage, Warwick Davis, Ben Barnes, Tilda Swinton; ***D:*** Andrew Adamson; ***W:*** Andrew Adamson, Christopher Markus, Stephen McFeely; ***C:*** Karl Walter Lindenlaub; ***M:*** Harry Gregson-Williams; ***V:*** Liam Neeson, Eddie Izzard.

The Chronicles of Narnia: The Lion, the Witch and the Wardrobe 1/2 **2005 (PG)** "Shrek" director Adamson turns C.S. Lewis' children's classic into a "Lord of the Rings" meets "Veggie Tales" adventure-allegory for kids. The four Pevensie siblings stumble into a magical wardrobe that transports them to the wonderful world of Narnia, a fairy tale kingdom torn between the evil White Witch (Swinton, in the film's best role) and the messianic lion Aslan (Neeson). Adamson stays faithful to the book, but bolsters the eye candy factor with lots of PG-friendly battles between fauns, unicorns, and giants. Fun stuff for seven-year-olds, but if you're a grown-up, you'll be rolling your eyes at the heavy-handed religious allusions and cutrate CGI effects. **139m/C DVD, Blu-ray Disc, UMD.** *US* Tilda Swinton, Anna Popplewell, James McAvoy, Jim Broadbent, James Cosmo, Judy McIntosh, Elizabeth Hawthorne, Georgie Henley, Skander Keynes, William Moseley, Kiran Shah; ***D:*** Andrew Adamson; ***W:*** Andrew Adamson, Ann Peacock, Christopher Markus, Stephen McFeely; ***C:*** Donald McAlpine; ***M:*** Harry Gregson-Williams; ***V:*** Liam Neeson, Ray Winstone, Dawn French, Rupert Everett, Sim Evan-Jones, Cameron Rhodes, Philip Steuer, Jim May. Oscars '05: Makeup; British Acad. '05: Makeup.

The Chronicles of Riddick *Pitch Black 2: Chronicles of Riddick* **2004 (PG-13)** Riddick (of "Pitch Black" fame) is back in this overstuffed compilation of cliched space shenanigans. The fascist Necromongers, led by Lord Marshall (Feore), have one edict: join us or we destroy your planet. Dame Judi Dench goes slumming as an ethereal prophetess named Aereon, who predicts that Riddick (Diesel again) will once again (if reluctantly) be a big hero. Diesel scowls a lot and then goes about saving the galaxy with a lot of big battles but not much gore given the MPAA rating. All acting is subordinate to the action anyway, but Newton swans about nicely as a devious wife who thinks her hubby (Urban) should be head creep. **119m/C VHS, DVD, UMD, HD DVD.** *US* Vin Diesel, Judi Dench, Thandie Newton, Colm Feore, Karl Urban, Linus Roache, Nicholas Chinlund, Keith David, Alexa Davalos, Yorick Van Wageningen; ***D:*** David N. Twohy; ***W:*** David N. Twohy; ***C:*** Hugh Johnson; ***M:*** Graeme Revell.

Chrysalis **2007 (PG-13)** Hard-boiled French Police Detective David Hoffman (Dupontel) watches as his wife and partner are killed by notorious human trafficker Dimitry Nikolov (Figlarz). Years later while investigating the death of an illegal immigrant, he is led to the doors of a plastic surgery clinic whose lead surgeon is researching human memory and identity. He also has links to Dimitry, and Detective Hoffman finds there are worse things than simple human trafficking as he begins his quest for revenge. **91m/C DVD.** *FR* Albert Dupontel, Marie Guillard, Marthe Keller, Melanie Thierry, Claude Peron, Alain Figlarz, Smadi Wolfman, Patrick Bauchau, Guy Lecluyse, Cyril Lecomte, Francis Renaud, Manon Chevallier, Estelle Lefebure; ***D:*** Julien Leclercq; ***W:*** Franck Phillipon; ***C:*** Thomas Hardmeier; ***M:*** Jean-Jacques Hertz, Francois Roy.

Chu Chu & the Philly Flash **WOOF!** **1981 (PG)** A has-been baseball player and a lame dance teacher meet while hustling the same corner; he sells hot watches, she's a one-woman band. A briefcase full of government secrets soon involves them with the feds, the mob, and a motley collection of back-alley bums. Insipid comedy is actually worse than its title, with Burnett and Arkin both trying too hard. Supporters Warden, Aiello, and Glover don't help either. **102m/C VHS.** Alan Arkin, Carol Burnett, Jack Warden, Danny Aiello, Ruth Buzzi, Danny Glover, Lou Jacobi; ***D:*** David Lowell Rich; ***W:*** Barbara Dana.

Chuck & Buck 1/2 **2000 (R)** In the mood for a pseudo-comedy about a stalking homosexual idiot man-child? Buck (White), the childhood friend from hell, attempts to latch back onto former pal Chuck (Chris Weitz) after a reunion at the funeral of Buck's mother. Apparently, Chuck and Buck shared a furtive moment of experimental sexuality as kids, and Buck never advanced emotionally beyond this point. So when Chuck (who, being an adult, prefers being called Charles) and his fiancee Carlyn (Colt) casually invite Buck to their home in L.A., he drops everything in order to rekindle his imagined affair with the poor guy. After Chuck tells him to stay away, Buck writes and produces an uncomfortably transparent play titled "Hank & Frank" about their relationship, hiring a Chuck look-alike (Paul Weitz, brother of the lead) as his love interest. White manages to keep a sense of innocence in portraying Buck, but the overwhelming creepiness of the plot overrides any sense of subtlety in the performances. **99m/C VHS, DVD.** Mike White, Chris Weitz, Paul Weitz, Lupe Ontiveros, Paul Sand, Beth Colt, Maya Rudolph, Mary Wigmore, Gino Buccola; ***D:*** Miguel Arteta; ***W:*** Mike White; ***C:*** Chuy Chavez; ***M:*** Joey Waronker. Natl. Bd. of Review '00: Support. Actress (Ontiveros).

Chuck Berry: Hail! Hail! Rock 'n' Roll **1987 (PG)** Engaging, energetic portrait of one of rock's founding fathers, via interviews, behind-the-scenes footage and performance clips of Berry at 60. Songs featured: "Johnny B. Goode," "Roll Over Beethoven," "Maybelline," and more. Appearances by Eric Clapton, Etta James, John and Julian Lennon, Roy Orbison, Linda Ronstadt, Bo Diddley and Bruce Springsteen among others. **121m/C VHS, DVD.** Chuck Berry, Eric Clapton, Etta James, Robert Cray, Julian Lennon, Keith Richards, Linda Ronstadt, John Lennon, Roy Orbison, Bo Diddley, Jerry Lee Lewis, Bruce Springsteen, Kareem Abdul-Jabbar; ***D:*** Taylor Hackford.

C.H.U.D. **WOOF!** **1984 (R)** Cannibalistic Humanoid Underground Dwellers are what it's about. Exposed to toxic wastes, a race of flesh-craving, sewer-dwelling monstrosities goes food shopping on the streets of New York. Don't be fooled by the presence of real actors, this one is inexcusable. Followed by a sequel. **90m/C VHS, DVD.** John Heard, Daniel Stern, Christopher Curry, Kim Greist, John Goodman, Jay Thomas, Eddie Jones, Sam McMurray, Justin Hall, Cordis Heard, Michael O'Hare, Vic Polizos; ***D:*** Douglas Cheek; ***W:*** Parnell Hall; ***C:*** Peter Stein; ***M:*** David A. Hughes.

C.H.U.D. 2: Bud the Chud **WOOF!** **1989 (R)** Asinine teens steal a corpse that is actually a zombie cannibal capable of passing the trait to anyone it bites (but doesn't eat entirely). Graham excels as the kidnapped corpse, but this horror-comedy is consistently repellent. Contains one of Jagger's few film appearances, a situation of no despair. **84m/C VHS.** Brian Robbins, Bill Calvert, Gerrit Graham, Tricia Leigh Fisher, Bianca Jagger, Robert Vaughn, Larry Cedar; ***D:*** David Irving.

Chuka 1/2 **1967** A gunfighter tries to resolve a conflict between Indians and unlikeable troops while simultaneously romancing the fort's beautiful occupant. Pedestrian western features convincing playing from the always reliable Taylor. **105m/C VHS, DVD.** Rod Taylor, Ernest Borgnine, John Mills, Luciana Paluzzi, James Whitmore, Angela Dorian, Louis Hayward, Michael Cole, Hugh Reilly; ***D:*** Gordon Douglas.

A Chump at Oxford 1/2 **1940** Two street cleaners foil a bank robbery and receive an all-expenses-paid education at Oxford as their reward. This loopy Laurel and Hardy vehicle provides regular amusement in detailing the duo's exploits in Britain. **63m/B VHS.** Stan Laurel, Oliver Hardy, James Finlayson, Wilfrid Lucas, Peter Cushing, Charlie Hall; ***D:*** Alfred Goulding.

The Chumscrubber 1/2 **2005 (R)** The unfortunate title refers to a videogame avenger who appears a la the creepy rabbit in "Donnie Darko" throughout this smug satire. Brooding SoCal teen Dean (Bell)—yes, think James—fails to tell anyone that his best friend, Troy (Janowicz), has hung himself in his bedroom. Problem is, Troy was the local drug supplier and when word does get out, his fellow high school scuzzballs expect Dean to find Troy's stash or else. Depiction of self-satisfied suburbia and teen angst has been better told elsewhere. **102m/C DVD.** *US* Jamie Bell, Camilla Belle, Justin Chatwin, Glenn Close, Rory Culkin, Tim DeKay, William Fichtner, Ralph Fiennes, Caroline Goodall, John Heard, Lauren Holly, Jason Isaacs, Allison Janney, Carrie-Anne Moss, Lou Taylor Pucci, Rita Wilson, Thomas Curtis, Richard Gleason, Josh Janowicz; ***D:*** Arie Posin; ***W:*** Zac Stanford; ***C:*** Lawrence Sher; ***M:*** James Horner.

Chungking Express *Hong Kong Express; Chongqing Senlin* **1995 (PG-13)** Director Kar-wai presents two quirky tales of loneliness and love, loosely linked by a snack bar in the tourist section of Hong Kong. Cops and drugs are still a part of the storyline, but this is no chop-socky action movie. Both male protagonists are cops, identified only by their badge numbers, who have recently been dumped by their girlfriends. One has a fixation for canned pineapple and expiration dates, the other talks to the inanimate objects in his apartment. The women they eventually fall for are a blonde-wigged heroin dealer and a shy counter girl who bops to "California Dreaming" after breaking in and cleaning the cop's apartment without his knowledge. Shot commando-style in 23 days during the hiatus of Wong's "Ashes of Time" without permits or professional lighting. The high energy is reflected in the pacing and acting performances. Chosen by Quentin Tarantino as the first release of his Miramax-backed Rolling Thunder imprint. **102m/C VHS, DVD, Blu-ray Disc.** *HK* Brigitte Lin, Takeshi Kaneshiro, Tony Leung Chiu-Wai, Faye Wong, Valerie Chow, Piggy Chan; ***D:*** Wong Kar-Wai; ***W:*** Wong Kar-Wai; ***C:*** Christopher Doyle, Lau Wai-Keung; ***M:*** Frankie Chan, Roel A. Garcia.

Chunhyang 1/2 **2000** Romance based on a 13th-century folktale of forbidden love. Chunhyang (Lee) is the educated daughter of a courtesan who is expected to be a plaything for wealthy gentlemen. Instead, she falls in love and secretly marries the higher-caste Mongryong (Cho), who leaves his bride to complete his studies in Seoul. Chunhyang is soon beset by advances from the new governor and, when she refuses, he sentences her to death. Korean with subtitles. **120m/C VHS, DVD.** *KN* Hyo Jung Lee, Seung Woo Cho, Jung Hun Lee, Sung Nyu Kim; ***D:*** Kwon Taek Im; ***W:*** Myoung Kon Kim; ***C:*** Il Sung Jung; ***M:*** Jung Gil Kim.

Chupacabra Terror 1/2 *Chupacabra: Dark Seas* **2005 (R)** A mythical beast, the Chupacabra, is caught in the Caribbean by cryptozoologist Dr. Pena, who somehow figures that transporting the evil brute on a cruise ship is a good idea. Carnage ensues for everyone on-board upon its escape. **88m/C VHS, DVD.** John Rhys-Davies, Giancarlo Esposito, Dylan Neal, Paula Shaw, Chelan Simmons, David Millbern, Steve Jankowski; ***D:*** John Shepphird; ***W:*** John Shepphird, Steve Jankowski. **VIDEO**

The Church *La Chiesa* **1998** Italian thrill-meister Argento scripted and produced this ecclesiastical gorefest. A gargoyle-glutted gothic cathedral which happens to stand on the site of a gruesome mass murder is renovated, and the kirk-cleaning turns into a special-effects loaded demonic epiphany. It'll have you muttering your pater noster. Unrated, it's also available in an R-rated version. **102m/C VHS, DVD.** *IT* Tomas Arana, Hugh Quarshie, Feodor Chaliapin Jr., Barbara Cupisti, Antonella Vitale, Asia Argento; ***D:*** Michele (Michael) Soavi; ***W:*** Dario Argento, Michele (Michael) Soavi, Franco Ferrini; ***C:*** Renato Tafuri; ***M:*** Keith Emerson.

The Church Mouse 1/2 **1934** Lively British comedy with a Cinderella plot. Betty Miller (La Plante) is hired by prominent banker Jonathan Steele (Hunter) as his secretary because she's efficient but dowdy and he tends to fall for his female staff. But eventually Betty gets a makeover and oh, my! **75m/B DVD.** *GB* Laura La Plante, Ian Hunter, Jane Carr, Edward Chapman, Clifford Heatherley, Montague (Monty) Banks, John Batten; ***D:*** Montague (Monty) Banks; ***W:*** Scott Darling, Tom Geraghty; ***C:*** Basil Emmett.

Churchill and the Generals **1981** The true story of how Winston Churchill led England away from the bleak Dunkirk battle and rallied the Allied generals to a D-Day victory. Based upon Churchill's memoirs. **180m/C VHS.** Timothy West, Joseph Cotten, Arthur Hill, Eric Porter, Richard Dysart; ***D:*** Alan Gibson; ***Nar:*** Eric Sevareid.

Chutney Popcorn 1/2 **1999** Amusing and touching comedy about family ties and cultural differences. Reena (Ganatra) is a New York photographer from a very traditional East Indian immigrant family. Her mother Meenu (Jaffrey) is already upset because her daughter is a lesbian but Reena has a chance to get in her good graces when she impulsively agrees to act as a surrogate for her married older sister Sarita (Jaffrey), who is infertile. But the plan upsets Reena's girlfriend Lisa (Hennessy) and then Sarita has her own change of heart, even though Reena is now pregnant. **93m/C VHS, DVD.** Nisha Ganatra, Jill(ian) Hennessey, Madhur Jaffrey, Sakina Jaffrey, Nicholas Chinlund, Cara Buono, Ajay Naidu, Priscilla Lopez; ***D:*** Nisha Ganatra; ***W:*** Susan Carnival, Nisha Ganatra; ***C:*** Erin King; ***M:*** Karsh Kale.

C.I.A.: Code Name Alexa 1/2 **1992 (R)** Alexa is the beautiful and deadly protege of Victor, who heads an international crime ring. A CIA agent decides the best way to stop Victor is to turn Alexa against her boss. Lots of action and violence. **93m/C VHS, DVD.** Kathleen Kinmont, Lorenzo Lamas, Alex Cord, O.J. Simpson, Stephen Quadros, Pamela Dixon, Michael Smith; ***D:*** Joseph Merhi.

C.I.A. 2: Target Alexa **1994** When a nuclear guidance system is stolen from a government facility CIA agent Mark Graver (Lamas) reteams with former terrorist Alexa (Kinmont) to retrieve the system from international terrorist Franz Klug (Savage). Complicating things are ex-CIA agent Straker (Ryan), who now heads his own commando army and wants to sell the device to the highest bidder. **90m/C VHS, DVD.** Lorenzo Lamas, Kathleen Kinmont, John Savage, John P. Ryan, Pamela Dixon, Larry Manetti; ***D:*** Lorenzo Lamas; ***W:*** Michael January.

Ciao Federico! Fellini Directs Satyricon 1/2 **1969** A documentary of Frederico Fellini's filming of Petronius' "Satyricon." Portrays the Italian filmmaker's larger-than-life directorial approach and relationship with his actors. In English and Italian, with English subtitles. **60m/C VHS.** Federico Fellini, Martin Potter, Hiram Keller, Roman Polanski, Sharon Tate; ***D:*** Gideon Bachmann.

Ciao, Professore! 1/2 *Io Speriamo Che Me La Cavo* **1994 (R)** Okay comedy about conventional teacher Marco Sperelli (Villaggio), from northern Italy, who is mistakenly sent to a ramshackle village school in Naples, populated by poor, wily, unruly students. Both, of course, manage to learn from each other. Humor derived from northern vs. southern Italian culture clash may bypass most viewers although the cast of amateur kid actors provide charm. Italian with subtitles. **91m/C VHS, DVD.** *IT* Paolo Villaggio, Isa Danieli, Ciro Esposito; ***D:*** Lina Wertmuller; ***W:*** Leonardo Benvenuti, Piero De Bernardi, Alessandro Bencivenni, Domenico Saverni, Lina Wertmuller.

The Cider House Rules **1999 (PG-13)** Homer Wells (Maguire) grows up in the St. Clouds, Maine orphanage, with his mentor, Dr. Larch (Caine), teaching Homer everything about caring for the children, delivering babies, and performing (illegal) abortions (which Homer refuses to do). But, in 1943, when flyboy Wally (Rudd) shows up with girlfriend Candy (Theron), Homer gets his chance to see something of the world. He winds up as an apple picker and, when Wally returns to the war, Candy's new beau. But Homer has a lot of lessons to learn about making—and living by—your own rules. Irving wrote his first screenplay from his novel. Old-fashioned, coming of age story with excellent performances. **125m/C VHS, DVD.** Evan Dexter Parke, Tobey Maguire, Charlize Theron, Michael Caine, Delroy Lindo, Paul Rudd, Erykah Badu, Kathy Baker, Jane Alexander, Kieran Culkin, Kate Nelligan, K. Todd Freeman, Dwight "Heavy D" Myers, J.K. Simmons, Erik Per Sullivan; ***Cameos:*** John Irving; ***D:*** Lasse Hallstrom; ***W:*** John Irving; ***C:*** Oliver Stapleton; ***M:*** Rachel Portman. Oscars '99: Adapt. Screenplay, Support. Actor (Caine); Screen Actors Guild '99: Support. Actor (Caine).

Cider with Rosie 1/2 **1999** Adaptation of Laurie Lee's 1959 story about his Cotswolds childhood. Set in 1918, in the Slad Valley, disorganized Annie Lee (Stevenson) has been left to raise nine children on her own. Laurie's childhood consists of school, church, village festivals, eccentric relations and neighbors, and the usual childhood tribulations. Lee himself provided narration before his death at 82 in 1997. **120m/C VHS, DVD.** *GB* Juliet Stevenson, Emily Mortimer, Joe Roberts, Dashiell Reece, David Troughton, Robert Lang, Hugh Lloyd; ***D:*** Charles Beeson; ***W:*** John Mortimer; ***C:*** Rex Maidment; ***M:*** Geoffrey Burgon. **TV**

The Cigarette Girl of Mosselprom 1/2 **1924** A lowly cigarette girl is thrust into the world of moviemaking in this sharp Russian satire. Silent with orchestral score. **78m/B VHS.** *RU* Yulia Solntseva, Igor Ilyinsky, Nikolai Tsereteli, Anna Dmokhovskaya, Leonid Baratov, M. Tsybulsky; ***D:*** Yuri Zhelyabuzhsky; ***W:*** Aleksey Fajko, Fyodor Otsep; ***C:*** Yuri Zhelyabuzhsky.

Cimarron **1931** Hopelessly overblown saga of an American frontier family from 1890 to 1915. Hokey, cliched, with only sporadic liveliness. How did this one win an Oscar? An adaptation of Edna Ferber's novel, featuring Dunne in an early major role. Remade in 1960. **130m/B VHS, DVD.** Richard Dix, Irene Dunne, Estelle Taylor, Nance O'Neil, William "Buster" Collier Jr., Roscoe Ates, George E. Stone, Stanley Fields, Edna May Oliver, Dennis O'Keefe; ***D:*** Wesley Ruggles; ***M:*** Max Steiner. Oscars '31: Adapt. Screenplay, Picture.

Cimarron 1/2 **1960** Director Mann's remake of the 1931 Academy Award-winning film about frontier life in Oklahoma. This version features Ford as a carefree survivor of the Old West with an extreme case of wanderlust. Schell plays his civilizing wife. Based on Edna Ferber's novel. **140m/C VHS.** Glenn Ford, Maria Schell, Anne Baxter, Arthur O'Connell, Russ Tamblyn, Mercedes McCambridge, Vic Morrow, Robert Keith, Charles McGraw; ***D:*** Anthony Mann; ***W:*** Arnold Schulman; ***M:*** Franz Waxman.

The Cincinnati Kid 1/2 **1965** Gambler "The Cincinnati Kid" (McQueen) is hustling card games in New Orleans when he comes up against the veteran cardshark Lancey Howard (Robinson). During a marathon card game, Kid notices dealer Shooter (Malden) is throwing the game his way but he only wants to win fair and square. Conventional fare, with Ann-Margaret around for some conventional romance, helped along by serviceable performances and some stunning cinematography. **104m/C VHS, DVD.** Steve McQueen, Edward G. Robinson, Ann-Margret, Tuesday Weld, Karl Malden, Joan Blondell, Rip Torn, Jack Weston, Cab Calloway; ***D:*** Norman Jewison; ***W:*** Ring Lardner Jr., Terry Southern; ***C:*** Philip Lathrop; ***M:*** Lalo Schifrin. Natl. Bd. of Review '65: Support. Actress (Blondell).

Cinderella 1/2 **1950** Classic Disney animated fairytale about the slighted beauty who outshines her evil stepsisters at a royal ball, then returns to her grim existence before the handsome prince finds her again. Engaging film, with a wicked stepmother, kindly fairy godmother, and singing mice. ♫ Cinderella; Bibbidy-Bobbidi-Boo; So This Is Love; A Dream Is a Wish Your Heart Makes; The Work Song; Oh Sing, Sweet Nightingale. **76m/C VHS, DVD.** ***D:*** Wilfred Jackson; ***V:*** Ilene Woods, William Phipps, Verna Felton, James MacDonald. Venice Film Fest. '50: Special Jury Prize.

Cinderella 1/2 **1964** Charming musical version of the fairy tale as scored by Rodgers and Hammerstein. Warren is lovely as Cinderella, Damon is a handsome prince, and Holm is a perfect fairy godmother. **83m/C VHS, DVD.** Lesley Ann Warren, Ginger Rogers, Walter Pidgeon, Stuart Damon, Celeste Holm; ***D:*** Charles S. Dubin; ***W:*** Joseph Schrank; ***M:*** Richard Rodgers. **TV**

Cinderella **1984** From the "Faerie Tale Theatre" comes the classic tale of a poor girl who goes to a ball to meet the man of her dreams, despite her nasty stepmother and stepsisters. **60m/C VHS, DVD.** Jennifer Beals, Jean Stapleton, Matthew Broderick, Eve Arden; ***D:*** Mark Cullingham. **CABLE**

Cinderella 1/2 *Rodgers & Hammerstein's Cinderella* **1997** Disney does some multiracial casting in this lavish, latest TV version of the fairytale. Norwood is sweetly sincere in the title role, with Houston as her diva-like Fairy Godmother. Peters camps as wicked stepmama, Goldberg's the Prince's mother, and the Prince is handsome newcomer Montalban. And Alexander gets the role of comic relief as the princely confidante, Lionel. The Rodgers and Hammerstein score, written for the 1957 TV version, has been augmented with other Richard Rodgers tunes. ♫ The Sweetest Sounds; Impossible; Do I Love You Because You're Beautiful?; Falling in Love with Love. **92m/C VHS, DVD.** Brandy Norwood, Whitney Houston, Paolo Montalban, Jason Alexander, Bernadette Peters, Whoopi Goldberg, Victor Garber; ***D:*** Robert Iscove; ***W:*** Robert Freedman. **TV**

Cinderella Liberty **1973 (R)** Bittersweet romance in which a kindly sailor falls for a brash hooker with a son. Sometimes funny, sometimes moving, with sometimes crude direction overcome by truly compelling performances from Caan and Mason. Story written by Darryl Ponicsan from his novel. **117m/C VHS, DVD.** James Caan, Marsha Mason, Eli Wallach, Kirk Calloway, Burt Young, Bruno Kirby, Dabney Coleman, Sally Kirkland, Allyn Ann McLerie, Allan Arbus, David Proval, Don Calfa; ***D:*** Mark Rydell; ***W:*** Darryl Ponicsan; ***C:*** Vilmos Zsigmond; ***M:*** John Williams. Golden Globes '74: Actress—Drama (Mason).

Cinderella Man 1/2 **2005 (PG-13)** Taken from the true story of heavyweight boxer Jim Braddock (Crowe) whose promising career was stalled by an injury, winless streak, and a revoked license. Despite his fall from glory, wife Mae (Zellweger) and their children remain unwavering in their devotion while Braddock labors on the Jersey docks during the Depression. Out of shape after a year, he finds himself back in the ring and winning again, which leads to a title bout in 1935 against the (fictitiously) vicious Max Baer (well-played by Bierko). Just as in the Oscar-winning "A Beautiful Mind," Crowe and Howard connect, with Crowe pounding out another stellar portrayal while Howard easily blends the fierceness of the boxing ring with the plain-spoken goodness of family-man Braddock. **144m/C DVD, HD DVD.** *US* Russell Crowe, Renee Zellweger, Paul Giamatti, Craig Bierko, Paddy Considine, Bruce McGill, Ron Canada, David Huband, Connor Price, Ariel Waller, Patrick Louis, Rosemarie DeWitt, Linda Kash, Nicholas (Nick) Campbell, Gene Pyrz; ***D:*** Ron Howard; ***W:*** Cliff Hollingsworth, Akiva Goldsman; ***C:*** Salvatore Totino; ***M:*** Thomas Newman. Screen Actors Guild '05: Support. Actor (Giamatti); Broadcast Film Critics '05: Support. Actor (Giamatti).

A Cinderella Story **2004 (PG)** A movie designed for tweenies who worship the chirpy Duff. This trifle finds Valley teen Samantha (Duff) bereft after the death of her father and stuck slaving for pea-brained stepmom Fiona (Coolidge) and her vicious twin daughters. Sam's only consolation is an email flirtation with a poetic soul who's actually the school's hottie football star Austin (Murray). Thanks to fairy godmother Rhonda (King), the cute twosome hook up at the Halloween dance but, alas, Sam slips out before revealing her true identity to hunk boy (although she does leave behind her cell phone). Of course, it's all so sugary that anyone who's not a 12-and-under girl will probably gag. **96m/C VHS, DVD.** *US* Hilary Duff, Jennifer Coolidge, Chad Michael Murray, Dan Byrd, Regina King, Julie Gonzalo, Lin Shaye, Madeline Zima, Andrea Avery, Mary Pat Gleason, Paul Rodriguez, Whip Hubley, Kevin Kilner, Erica Hubbard, Simon Helberg, Brad Bufanda, J.D. Pardo, Kady Kole, Hannah Robinson; ***D:*** Mark Rosman; ***W:*** Leigh Dunlap; ***C:*** Anthony B. Richmond; ***M:*** Christophe Beck.

Cinderella 2000 **1978 (R)** Softcore musical version of the classic fairy tale. It's the year 2047 and sex is outlawed, except by computer. Strains of Sugarman's score, including "Doin' Without" and "We All Need Love," set the stage for Erhardt's Cinderella to meet her Prince Charming at that conventional single prince romance venue, a sex orgy. Trouble is, it wasn't a shoe Cinderella lost before she fled, and the charming one must interface, as it were, with the local pretenders to the throne in order to find his lost princess. Touching. **86m/C VHS, DVD.** Catharine Erhardt, Jay B. Larson, Vaughn Armstrong; ***D:*** Al Adamson; ***M:*** Sparky Sugarman.

Cinderfella 1/2 **1960** This twist on the classic children's fairy tale features Lewis as the hapless buffoon guided by his fairy godfather. Somewhat overdone, with extended talking sequences and gratuitous musical interludes. Lewis, though, mugs effectively. **88m/C VHS, DVD.** Jerry Lewis, Ed Wynn, Judith Anderson, Anna Maria Alberghetti, Henry Silva, Count Basie, Robert Hutton; ***D:*** Frank Tashlin; ***W:*** Frank Tashlin.

Cinema Paradiso *Nuovo Cinema Paradiso* **1988** Memoir of a boy's life working at a movie theatre in small-town Italy after WWII. Film aspires to both majestic sweep and stirring poignancy, but only occasionally hits its target. Still manages to move the viewer, and it features a suitably low-key performance by the masterful Noiret. Autobiographically inspired script written by Tornatore. The version shown in America is approximately a half-hour shorter than the original Italian form. **123m/C VHS, DVD.** *IT* Philippe Noiret, Jacques Perrin, Salvatore Cascio, Marco Leonardi, Agnes Nano, Leopoldo Trieste; ***D:*** Giuseppe Tornatore; ***W:*** Giuseppe Tornatore; ***C:*** Blasco Giurato; ***M:*** Ennio Morricone. Oscars '89: Foreign Film; British Acad. '90: Actor (Noiret), Foreign Film, Orig. Screenplay, Support. Actor (Cascio); Cannes '89: Grand Jury Prize; Golden Globes '90: Foreign Film.

Circadian Rhythm 1/2 **2005** Killer babe in lingerie. Sarah (Miner) wakes up in a bare room with no idea where she is or—more importantly—who she is. Soon she's wondering why people are trying to kill her and how she knows how to defend herself. Of course, it's one of those government conspiracy plots. **82m/C DVD.** Rachel Miner, Seymour Cassel, Sarah Wynter, David Anders, Robert Berson; ***D:*** Rene Besson; ***W:*** James Portolese; ***C:*** Nick Hay; ***M:*** Jason Nesmith. **VIDEO**

The Circle *Dayereh* **2000** Arezou (Almani) and Nargess (Mamizadeh) have just been released from an Iranian prison. Arezou apparently prostitutes herself (you don't see anything) in order to get the money for Nargess to travel back to her village, only because of Iranian law the girl can't travel without permission from a male. Nargress leads to two other former inmates who suffer because of their female identity and eventually everything circles back to the prison again. The film was banned in Iran because it makes the ceaseless difficulties of being born female in such a society very clear. Farsi with subtitles. **91m/C VHS, DVD.** *IA* Mariam Palvin Almani, Nargess Mamizadeh, Fereshteh Sadr Orfani, Fatemeh Naghavi, Monir Arab, Elham Saboktakin, Mojhan Faramarzi; ***D:*** Jafar Panahi; ***W:*** Kambuzia Partovi; ***C:*** Bahram Badakhshami. Venice Film Fest. '00: Film.

Circle Canyon ✓ **1933** In a remote canyon two opposing outlaw gangs battle to the death. **48m/B VHS.** Buddy Roosevelt, Allen Holbrook, Clyde McClary, Ernest Scott, John Tyke, Bob Williamson; ***D:*** Victor Adamson; ***W:*** Burl R. Tuttle.

Circle Man ✓ *Last Man Standing* **1987** A made-for-video action drama about the underground sporting phenomenon, bare-knuckle fighting. **90m/C VHS.** Vernon Wells, Michael Copeman, Real Andrews, Franco (Columbo) Columbu, William Sanderson; ***D:*** Damian Lee; ***W:*** Damian Lee, David Mitchell; ***C:*** Ludek Bogner; ***M:*** Charles P. Barnett.

Circle of Death ✓ 1/2 **1936** Average formula western about a white boy who is raised as an Indian. Later he falls in love with a white girl and leaves the tribe. **55m/B VHS.** Monte Montana, Yakima Canutt, Henry Hall, Ben (Benny) Corbett; ***D:*** J. Frank Glendon; ***W:*** Roy Claire; ***C:*** James Diamond.

Circle of Deceit ✓✓ 1/2 **1994** SAS officer John Neil (Waterman) is called back into service in Belfast two years after his wife and child were killed by terrorists. His assignment is to assume the identity of recently deceased IRA soldier Jackie O'Connell and learn about an arms shipment headed for Northern Ireland. But can his disguise hold against local IRA commander Liam McAuley (Vaughan)? Made for British TV. **103m/C VHS, DVD.** *GB* Dennis Waterman, Peter Vaughan, Derek Jacobi, Clare Higgins; ***W:*** Jean-Claude Carriere. **TV**

Circle of Fear ✓ 1/2 **1989 (R)** An ex-hitman who worked for the Mob upends the black market for sex and drugs in the Philippines while looking for his daughter who was sold into a sex slave ring. El cheapo exploiter. **90m/C VHS, DVD.** *PH* Patrick Dollaghan, Welsey Pfenning, Joey Aresco, Vernon Wells; ***D:*** Clark Henderson.

Circle of Friends ✓✓ 1/2 **1994 (PG-13)** Nostalgic Irish coming-of-ager focuses on three friends and the trials and tribulations they face when hearts and hormones conflict with a strict Catholic upbringing. Small-town teenager Benny (Driver), overweight and slightly awkward, reunites with her friends at university in Dublin. Benny begins a romance with gentle, doe-eyed Jack Foley (O'Donnell) and endures the humorous but sometimes painful passage from adolescence to womanhood. Sentimental moments can be too sticky-sweet at times, but humor, disappointment, and small triumphs are convincingly portrayed, offering a universal appeal. Adapted from the Maeve Binchy novel. **96m/C VHS, DVD.** Chris O'Donnell, Minnie Driver, Geraldine O'Rawe, Saffron Burrows, Colin Firth, Alan Cumming, Aidan Gillen, Mick (Michael) Lally; ***D:*** Pat O'Connor; ***W:*** Andrew Davies; ***C:*** Kenneth Macmillan; ***M:*** Michael Kamen.

Circle of Iron ✓✓ 1/2 *The Silent Flute* **1978 (R)** Plenty of action and martial arts combat abound in this story of one man's eternal quest for truth. Originally co-written by and intended for Bruce Lee as a rib-crunching vehicle, until he died before production began and was replaced by Kung-Fu Carradine. A cut above most chop-socky actioners. Filmed in Israel. **102m/C VHS, DVD.** *GB* Jeff Cooper, David Carradine, Roddy McDowall, Eli Wallach, Christopher Lee; ***D:*** Richard Moore; ***W:*** Bruce Lee, James Coburn, Stirling Silliphant; ***M:*** Bruce Smeaton.

Circle of Love ✓✓ **1964** Episodic melodrama drifts from romance to romance in contemporary Paris. A somewhat pretentious remake of Ophuls classic "La Ronde," which was in turn adapted from Arthur Schnitzler's play. Credible performers are undone by Vadim's strained direction. **110m/C VHS, DVD.** *FR* Jane Fonda, Francine Berge, Marie DuBois, Jean-Claude Brialy, Catherine Spaak, Claude Giraud; ***D:*** Roger Vadim; ***W:*** Jean Anouilh.

Circle of Passion ✓✓ *Never Ever* **1997 (R)** Devoted hubby Thomas Murray (Finch) works for his father-in-law at a London bank. But when Thomas is transferred to Paris and his socialite wife (March) refuses to go with him, devotion falls by the wayside when he falls in love with the free-spirited Katherine (Bonnaire). Now Thomas has to choose between money and love. **94m/C VHS.** Charles Finch, Sandrine Bonnaire, Jane March, Julian Sands, James Fox; ***D:*** Charles Finch.

Circle of Power ✓ 1/2 *Brainwash; The Naked Weekend; Mystique* **1983 (R)** Mimieux must cure various business men of their problems (homosexuality, alcoholism and the like) to help them become better executives. Intriguing and somewhat disturbing, supposedly based on a true story. **103m/C VHS.** *GB* Yvette Mimieux, John Considine, Terence Knox, Cindy Pickett, Christopher Allport; ***D:*** Bobby Roth; ***W:*** Stephen F. Bello; ***C:*** Alfonso Beato.

Circle of Two ✓✓ **1980 (PG)** A platonic friendship between an aging artist and a young girl is misunderstood by others. Well, of course they do meet in a porno theatre. Pedestrian fare adapted from a story by Marie Therese Baird. **90m/C VHS, DVD.** *CA* Richard Burton, Tatum O'Neal, Kate Reid; ***D:*** Jules Dassin.

Circonstances Attenuantes ✓✓ 1/2 *Extenuating Circumstances* **1936** French classic about a retired judge who moves to the outskirts of Paris with his wife and attempts to convert the locals from disreputable to law-abiding citizens. Also available dubbed. **90m/B VHS.** *FR* Michel Simon, Arletty; ***D:*** Jean Boyer.

Circuit ✓ 1/2 **2002** Sexual hedonism is alive and well in West Hollywood in this would-be cautionary tale of a small town Midwesterner who comes to the big, bad city. John (Drahos) gets introduced to the party circuit of casual gay sex and lots of drugs but vows to keep his distance. This doesn't last and John sinks ever deeper into the self-destructive pursuit of pleasure. **90m/C VHS, DVD.** Jonathan Wade Drahos, Daniel Kucan, Andre Khabbazi, Brian Lane Green, Kiersten Warren, William Katt; ***D:*** Dirk Shafer; ***W:*** Dirk Shafer, Gregory Hinton; ***C:*** Joaquin Sedilb; ***M:*** Tony Moran.

The Circuit ✓✓ 1/2 **2008** ABC Family movie finds pro racecar track circuit driver Al Shines (Campbell) getting fired by his shady sponsor Robin Cates (Rae). While Al tries to start his own team, Cates hires Al's resentful, inexperienced daughter Kylie (Trachtenberg) in a marketing ploy. Kylie sets out to prove herself to her widowed dad as well as reigning champ Kid Walker (Fuller) with whom she begins a troublesome romance. **89m/C DVD.** Michelle Trachtenberg, Billy Campbell, Drew Fuller, Paul Rae, Tommy Lioutas, Maurice Dean Wint; ***D:*** Peter Werner; ***W:*** Bill Hanley, Quinton Peeples; ***C:*** Neil Roach; ***M:*** Danny Lux. **CABLE**

Circuitry Man ✓✓ 1/2 **1990 (R)** Post-apocolyptic saga of future American life as a woman tries to deliver a briefcase full of computer chips to the underground Big Apple. Along the way she runs into Plughead, a humanoid with electrical outlets that allow him to "plug in" to other people's fantasies. Intelligent retelling of a standard tale with an inspired soundtrack by Deborah Holland. Witty and original. **85m/C VHS, DVD.** Jim Metzler, Dana Wheeler-Nicholson, Lu Leonard, Vernon Wells, Barbara Alyn Woods, Dennis Christopher; ***D:*** Steven Lovy; ***W:*** Robert Lovy, Steven Lovy; ***C:*** Jamie Thompson; ***M:*** Deborah Holland.

Circumstances Unknown ✓ 1/2 **1995 (R)** Paul Kinsey (Nelson) is a serial killer who drowns his victims, including a woman who happens to be the fiance of his friend Tim (Moses). Years later, Tim has married and Paul decides to stalk him and wife Deena (Glasser). Too many loose ends since you never know why Paul kills. Based on the novel by Jonellen Heckler. **91m/C VHS.** Judd Nelson, Isabel Glasser, William R. Moses; ***D:*** Robert Lewis; ***W:*** Thomas Hood, Emily Shoemaker; ***C:*** Bruce Worrall.

Circumstantial Evidence ✓✓ **1935** Newspaper reporter (Chandler) goes to extremes for a story and nearly dies as a result. Chandler sets it up to look like he's murdered a colleague, and he's tried and convicted on, you guessed it, circumstantial evidence. The colleague's then supposed to come forward but there's a problem. **69m/B VHS, DVD.** Chick Chandler, Shirley Grey, Dorothy Revier, Arthur Vinton; ***D:*** Charles Lamont; ***W:*** Ewart Adamson.

The Circus ✓✓✓ 1/2 **1919** Classic comedy silent details the tramp's exploits as a member of a traveling circus, including a romance with the bareback rider. Hilarious, less sentimental than most of Chaplin's feature films. Chaplin won a special Academy Award for "versatility and genius in writing, acting, directing and producing" for this one. Outrageous final scenes. **105m/B VHS, DVD.** Charlie Chaplin, Merna Kennedy, Allan Garcia; ***D:*** Charlie Chaplin; ***W:*** Charlie Chaplin; ***C:*** Roland H. Totheroh; ***M:*** Charlie Chaplin.

Circus ✓✓ **2000 (R)** British gambler/con man Leo Garfield (Hannah) is being pressured by gang boss Bruno (Conley) to manage his Brighton casino. But Leo and his equally shady American wife Lily (Janssen) have some double-crossing ideas of their own, involving Bruno's brother Caspar (Burfield), his accountant Julius (Stormare), Julius' unfaithful wife Gloria (Donohue), and well, things get even more complicated but the film doesn't have the flair to pull off all the plots. It does make an interesting attempt, though. **95m/C VHS, DVD.** *GB* John Hannah, Famke Janssen, Peter Stormare, Brian Conley, Eddie Izzard, Fred Ward, Amanda Donohoe, Ian Burfield, Tommy (Tiny) Lister, Neil Stuke; ***D:*** Rob Walker; ***W:*** David Logan; ***C:*** Ben Seresin; ***M:*** Simon Boswell.

Circus Angel ✓✓✓ **1965** The renowned director of "The Red Balloon" creates a fantasy about a klutzy burglar transformed by a found nightgown into an angel. He begins to serve the dreams and actions of an odd lot of characters. Subtitled in English. **80m/B VHS.** *FR* Philippe Avron, Mirielle Negre; ***D:*** Albert Lamorisse.

Circus Girl ✓ 1/2 **1937** Big top romance with Bob (Livingston) and Charles (Cook) vying for the affections of trapeze artist Kay (Travis). **64m/B DVD.** Robert "Bob" Livingston, Donald Cook, Betty Compson, Kay Rogers, Charlie Murray; ***D:*** John H. Auer; ***W:*** Bradford Ropes, Adele Buffington; ***C:*** Jack Marta.

Circus of Fear ✓ 1/2 *Psycho-Circus* **1967** A travelling troupe is stalked by a murderer. The unedited version is occasionally scary. **92m/C VHS, DVD.** *GB GE* Christopher Lee, Leo Genn, Anthony Newlands, Heinz Drache, Eddi Arent, Klaus Kinski, Margaret Lee, Suzy Kendall; ***D:*** John Llewellyn Moxey.

Circus of Horrors ✓✓ 1/2 **1960** Nip 'n' tuck horror about a plastic surgeon who takes over a circus to escape a disfigured patient bent on revenge. The circus is staffed by former patients with new faces who, one by one, fall victim in fine circus style. A bloody one-ring extravaganza. **92m/C VHS, DVD.** *GB* Donald Pleasence, Anton Diffring, Erika Remberg, Yvonne Monlaur, Jane Hylton, Kenneth Griffith, Colette Wilde, Charla Challoner; ***D:*** Sidney Hayers; ***W:*** George L. Baxt; ***C:*** Douglas Slocombe; ***M:*** Muir Mathieson.

Circus World ✓✓ 1/2 *The Magnificent Showman* **1964** A circus boss tries to navigate a reckless, romancing crew through a European tour while searching for aerialist he loved 15 years before and whose daughter he has reared. Too long and too familiar, but nonetheless well done with an excellent finale. **132m/C VHS, DVD.** John Wayne, Rita Hayworth, Claudia Cardinale, Lloyd Nolan, Richard Conte; ***D:*** Henry Hathaway; ***W:*** Ben Hecht, James Edward Grant, Julian Zimet; ***C:*** Jack Hildyard. Golden Globes '65: Song ("Circus World").

Cirque du Freak: The Vampire's Assistant ✓ 1/2 *The Vampire's Assistant* **2009 (PG-13)** Static and muddled adaptation of the young adult fantasy series by Darren Shan that features a teenager named—wait for it—Darren Shan (a disappointingly bland Massoglia). Darren and rebellious best friend Steve (Hutcherson) meet florid Larten Crepsley (Reilly) at a freak show. Darren is sure Crepsley is a vampire and, thanks to youthful bad judgment and the theft of a spider, Darren is soon a half-vampire, joining the Cirque du Freak on the road after unwittingly breaking a 200-year-old truce between warring vampire factions. **108m/C DVD.** *US* Chris Massoglia, Josh Hutcherson, Salma Hayek, John C. Reilly, Jane Krakowski, Ray Stevenson, Patrick Fugit, Ken(saku) Watanabe, Orlando Jones, Frankie Faison, Willem Dafoe, Michael Cerveris, Jessica Carlson; ***D:*** Paul Weitz; ***W:*** Paul Weitz, Brian Helgeland; ***C:*** J.(James) Michael Muro; ***M:*** Stephen Trask.

The Cisco Kid ✓✓ 1/2 **1994** The Cisco Kid and his sidekick Pancho went from O. Henry's short story, to silent movies, talkies, a '50s TV series, and now this made for TV movie. Benito Juarez is leading an uprising to overthrow the French-backed Emperor Maximilian in 1867 Mexico. Cisco's (Smits) supplying the rebels with guns while carrying on romantic escapades (watch for the tango). Meanwhile, true-believer Pancho tries to convince his friend to become a revolutionary. Light-hearted with pedestrian action shots. Filmed on location in Mexico. **96m/C VHS.** Jimmy Smits, Richard "Cheech" Marin, Sadie Frost, Tim Thomerson, Bruce Payne; ***D:*** Luis Valdez; ***W:*** Michael Kane, Luis Valdez. **TV**

The Citadel ✓✓✓ **1938** From the A.J. Cronin novel, the intelligent and honest Hollywood drama about a young British doctor who is morally corrupted by his move from a poor mining village to a well-off practice treating wealthy hypochondriacs. Somewhat hokey but still consistently entertaining, with Donat fine in the lead. **114m/C VHS.** *GB* Robert Donat, Rosalind Russell, Rex Harrison, Ralph Richardson, Emlyn Williams, Penelope Dudley Ward; ***D:*** King Vidor; ***C:*** Harry Stradling Sr. N.Y. Film Critics '38: Film.

Citizen Cohn ✓✓ **1992 (R)** An appallingly fascinating look at a human monster. Told in hallucinatory flashbacks, as he lays dying from AIDS, Roy Cohn is a lawyer and power broker, probably best-remembered as the malevolent sidekick to Communist-hunting Senator Joseph McCarthy. But his contempt also extended to antisemitism and gay-bashing (though Cohn was both homosexual and Jewish), and his past comes, literally, back to haunt him. Woods does an exceptional job in bringing this sociopathic heel to wretched life. Adapted from the biography by Nicholas von Hoffman. **112m/C VHS, DVD.** James Woods, Joe Don Baker, Joseph Bologna, Ed Flanders, Frederic Forrest, Lee Grant, Pat Hingle; ***D:*** Frank Pierson; ***W:*** David Franzoni; ***C:*** Paul Elliott. **CABLE**

Citizen Kane ✓✓✓✓ **1941** Extraordinary film is an American tragedy of a newspaper tycoon (based loosely on William Randolph Hearst) from his humble beginnings to the solitude of his final years. One of the greatest films ever made—a stunning tour-de-force in virtually every aspect, from the fragmented narration to breathtaking, deep-focus cinematography; from a vivid soundtrack to fabulous ensemble acting. Welles was only 25 when he co-wrote, directed, and starred in this masterpiece. Watch for Ladd and O'Connell as reporters. **119m/B VHS, DVD.** Orson Welles, Joseph Cotten, Everett Sloane, Dorothy Comingore, Ruth Warrick, George Coulouris, Ray Collins, William Alland, Paul Stewart, Erskine Sanford, Agnes Moorehead, Alan Ladd, Gus Schilling, Philip Van Zandt, Harry Shannon, Sonny Bupp, Arthur O'Connell; ***D:*** Orson Welles; ***W:*** Orson Welles, Herman J. Mankiewicz; ***C:*** Gregg Toland; ***M:*** Bernard Herrmann. Oscars '41: Orig. Screenplay; AFI '98: Top 100, Natl. Film Reg. '89;; N.Y. Film Critics '41: Film.

Citizen Ruth ✓✓ 1/2 *Precious; Meet Ruth Stoops* **1996 (R)** Glue-sniffing, pregnant Ruth Stoops (Dern) has already borne four children and been declared an unfit mother. In trouble again, Ruth's quietly told it's in her best interests to get an abortion but a couple (Smith and Place) from the pro-life community bail her out and give her a place to stay, while the group uses her as a propaganda symbol. Added to the commotion is a smarmy televangelist (Reynolds) and tough pro-choice Diane (Kurtz), who manages to get Ruth to stay with her while Ruth ineffectually tries to get some control over her wayward life. Doesn't take sides—both the pro-choice and pro-life camps are tweaked, with neither willing to compromise. **104m/C VHS, DVD.** Laura Dern, Swoosie Kurtz, Mary Kay Place, Kurtwood Smith, Kelly Preston, Burt Reynolds, M.C. Gainey, Kenneth Mars, Kathleen Noone, David Graf, Tippi Hedren, Alicia Witt,

Diane Ladd; *D:* Alexander Payne; *W:* Alexander Payne, Jim Taylor; *C:* James Glennon; *M:* Rolfe Kent. Montreal World Film Fest. '95: Actress (Dern).

Citizen Toxie: The Toxic Avenger 4 WOOF! **2001** As gleefully offensive as always, this sequel comes 12 years after part 3. An explosion in Tromaville creates a parallel universe in which Toxie and his evil twin, Noxie AKA Noxious Offender (who lives in Amortville), change places. Noxie promptly terrorizes the community while Toxie goes on with his good deeds in his new dimension. Meanwhile, a coalition of other superheroes try to eliminate the evil Noxie from their midst. **100m/C DVD.** David Mattey, Heidi Sjursen, Paul Kyrmse, Dan Snow; *D:* Lloyd Kaufman; *W:* Lloyd Kaufman, Gabriel Friedman, Trent Haaga; *C:* Brendan Flynt; *M:* Wesly Nagy.

Citizen X **1995 (R)** Based on the true story of '80s Russian serial killer Andrei Chikatilo (DeMunn) and his 52 victims. Viktor Burakov (Rea) is a beleagured rural forensics expert who is blatantly told by party officials that the Soviet state does not have serial killers—in spite of a rising body count. His only ally is Col. Fetisov (Sutherland), who's adept at political maneuvering, but it takes the duo eight frustrating years to bring the grisly killer to justice. Fine performances highlight a literate script from Robert Cullen's book "The Killer Department." Filmed on location in Budapest, Hungary. **100m/C VHS, DVD.** Stephen Rea, Donald Sutherland, Jeffrey DeMunn, John Wood, Joss Ackland, Max von Sydow, Ralph Nossek, Imelda Staunton, Radu Amzulrescu, Czeskaw Grocholski, Ion Caramitru, Andras Balint, Tusse Silberg; *D:* Chris Gerolmo; *W:* Chris Gerolmo; *C:* Robert Fraisse; *M:* Randy Edelman. **CABLE**

Citizens Band *Handle With Care* **1977 (PG)** Episodic, low-key comedy about people united by their CB use in a midwestern community. Notable performance from Clark as a soft-voiced guide for truckers passing through. Demme's first comedy is characteristically idiosyncratic. **98m/C VHS.** Paul LeMat, Candy Clark, Ann Wedgeworth, Roberts Blossom, Charles Napier, Marcia Rodd, Bruce McGill, Ed Begley Jr., Alix Elias; *D:* Jonathan Demme; *W:* Paul Brickman; *C:* Jordan Cronenweth; *M:* Bill Conti. Natl. Soc. Film Critics '77: Support. Actress (Wedgeworth).

The City **1976** Police desperately search for a psychotic determined to kill a country singer. He shouldn't be too hard to find. **78m/C VHS.** Don Johnson, Robert Forster, Ward (Edward) Costello, Jimmy Dean, Mark Hamill; *D:* Harvey Hart. **TV**

The City and the Dogs *La Ciudad y los Perros* **1985** A brutal, cynical adaptation of Mario Vargas Llosa's novel. A young military recruit rebels against the authority establishments around him. In Spanish with English subtitles. **135m/C VHS.** *SP* Pablo Serra, Gustavo Bueno, Juan Manuel Ochoa, Pili Flores-Guerra, Eduardo Ardianzen; *D:* Francisco J. Lombardi Pery; *W:* Jose Watanabe; *C:* Enrique Iturriaga.

City Beneath the Sea 1/2 **1971** Irwin Allen TV pilot movie has Admiral Mike Matthews (Whitman) forced to return to his former command in the undersea city of Pacifica where his old crew doesn't trust him. The city is about to store a highly-unstable radioactive explosive, which must be surrounded by the USA's gold reserves for safety's sake. Naturally, an asteroid is headed towards earth and thieves want to get to the gold when Matthews' orders an evacuation of the city. **93m/C DVD.** Stuart Whitman, Robert Colbert, Robert Wagner, Rosemary Forsyth, Susan Miranda, Richard Basehart, Joseph Cotten, James Darren, Whit Bissell, Burr de Benning; *D:* Irwin Allen; *W:* John Meredyth Lucas; *C:* Kenneth Peach Sr.; *M:* Richard LaSalle. **TV**

City Boy **1993** At the turn of the century the orphaned Nick makes his way from Chicago to the Pacific Northwest in search of his natural father. He takes a job guarding Limberlost, a valuable old-growth forest, from thieves and is torn between the ideals of two new friends. His mentor Tom sees the forest as timber that will build homes and provide jobs, while Angelica sees the forest as an irreplaceable sanctuary. Filmed on location in Vancouver, British Columbia. Adaptation of "Freckles" by Gene Stratton Porter. **120m/C VHS.** *GB CA* Christian Campbell, James Brolin, Sarah Chalke, Wendel Meldrum, Christopher Bolton; *D:* John Kent Harrison; *W:* John Kent Harrison.

City by the Sea 1/2 **2002 (R)** Pitch-black drama starring De Niro as NYC homicide detective La Marca, an absentee father trying to find his son Joey (Franco), a junkie on the lam for murder. Though he's not exactly a model son, La Marco is convinced Joey is not the perp who popped a loathsome drug dealer. Events force him to revisit the title's run-down Long Island city, where he must confront his bitter ex (LuPone) and the troubled past he fled 14 years ago. McDormand appears as La Marca's trusty some-time-girlfriend. Suffers from overwrought, lengthy exposition, mostly via De Niro (not exactly his specialty). Overacting only exposes a depressing, overcooked script. Loosely based on a true story. **108m/C VHS, DVD.** *US* Robert De Niro, James Franco, Frances McDormand, Eliza Dushku, William Forsythe, George Dzundza, Patti LuPone, Anson Mount, John Doman, Brian Tarantina, Nestor Serrano, Leo Burmester; *D:* Michael Caton-Jones; *W:* Ken Hixon; *C:* Karl Walter Lindenlaub; *M:* John Murphy.

City for Conquest **1940** Two lovers go their separate ways to pursue individual careers. He attempts to become a boxing champ, but is blinded in the ring and ends up selling newspapers. She takes a shot at a dancing career but hooks up with an unscrupulous partner. Will the ill-fated pair find happiness again? **101m/B VHS, DVD.** James Cagney, Ann Sheridan, Frank Craven, Donald Crisp, Arthur Kennedy, Frank McHugh, George Tobias, Anthony Quinn, Blanche Yurka, Elia Kazan, Bob Steele; *D:* Anatole Litvak; *W:* John Wexley; *C:* James Wong Howe; *M:* Max Steiner.

City Girl 1/2 *Our Daily Bread* **1930** Friedrich Murnau, who directed the silent vampire classic "Nosferatu," was removed from the director's chair before "City Girl" was completed and it shows. But so do the marks of his inimitable camera direction. The story concerns a Minnesota grain grower who visits the Windy City and returns with a waitress as his wife. Frustratingly inconsistent, leading you to wonder what could have been had Murnau remained behind the camera (he died the following year). Silent. **90m/B VHS.** Charles Farrell, Mary Duncan; *D:* F.W. Murnau.

City Hall **1995 (R)** Investigating the deaths of a heroic cop, a drug dealer, and six-year old boy in a shoot-out, idealistic deputy mayor Cusack uncovers a web of corruption and deceit in the Big Apple. Pacino excels as charismatic mayor John Pappas by showing the crafty string-puller behind the glossy image of the modern politico. Supporting cast is also strong, including Aiello as a Rodgers and Hammerstein-loving Brooklyn boss, and Fonda as the police union lawyer and standard issue love interest. Screenplay was conceived by Ken Lipper, who was once deputy mayor under Ed Koch, but the involvement of three other scripters causes confusion over what type of picture it's aiming to be. Cash-strapped New York rented its actual city hall out for filming at a price of $50,000. **111m/C VHS, DVD.** Al Pacino, John Cusack, Bridget Fonda, Danny Aiello, David Paymer, Martin Landau, Anthony (Tony) Franciosa, Lindsay Duncan, Nestor Serrano, Mel Winkler, Richard Schiff; *D:* Harold Becker; *W:* Paul Schrader, Nicholas Pileggi, Bo Goldman, Ken Lipper; *C:* Michael Seresin; *M:* Jerry Goldsmith.

City Heat 1/2 **1984 (PG)** A hard-nosed cop and a plucky private eye berate each other while opposing the mob in this overdone comedy. Both Eastwood and Reynolds spoof their screen personas, but the results are only slightly satisfactory. Good back-up, though, from Alexander and Kahn as the dames. Screenplay written by Blake Edwards under the pseudonym Sam O. Brown. **98m/C VHS, DVD.** Clint Eastwood, Burt Reynolds, Jane Alexander, Irene Cara, Madeline Kahn, Richard Roundtree, Rip Torn, Tony LoBianco, William Sanderson; *D:* Richard Benjamin; *W:* Blake Edwards; *M:* Lennie Niehaus.

City in Fear **1980** Stellar cast lights up a drama about a tired newspaper columnist (Janssen) who communicates directly with a murdering psychotic (Rourke), as publisher Vaughn applauds and hypes. Rourke's first role, Janssen's last, and Smithee is actually Jud Taylor. **135m/C VHS.** David Janssen, Robert Vaughn, Mickey Rourke, William Daniels, Perry King, Susan Sullivan, William Prince; *D:* Alan Smithee. **TV**

City in Panic **1986** A detective and radio talk show host try to catch a psychotic mass murderer busy offing homosexuals throughout the city. Violent with no redeeming social qualities. **85m/C VHS.** Dave Adamson, Ed Chester, Leeann Westegard; *D:* Robert Bouvier.

City Killer **1987** A lunatic tries to blackmail the girl he loves into going out on a few dates by committing huge destructive acts of inner-city terrorism (flowers won't do). **120m/C VHS.** Heather Locklear, Gerald McRaney, Terence Knox, Peter Mark Richman, John Harkins; *D:* Robert Lewis. **TV**

City Lights **1931** Masterpiece that was Chaplin's last silent film. The "Little Tramp" falls in love with a blind flower seller. A series of lucky accidents permits him to get the money she needs for a sight-restoring surgery. One of the most eloquent movies ever filmed, due to Chaplin's keen balance between comedy and tragedy. **86m/B VHS, DVD.** Charlie Chaplin, Virginia Cherrill, Florence Lee, Hank Mann, Harry C. (Henry) Myers, Henry Bergman, Jean Harlow; *D:* Charlie Chaplin; *W:* Charlie Chaplin; *C:* Roland H. Totheroh, Gordon Pollock; *M:* Alfred Newman, Charlie Chaplin. AFI '98: Top 100, Natl. Film Reg. '91.

City Limits **1985 (PG-13)** In a post-apocalyptic city, gangs of young people on choppers clash. **85m/C VHS.** John Stockwell, Kim Cattrall, Darrell Larson, Rae Dawn Chong, Robby Benson, James Earl Jones, Jennifer Balgobin; *D:* Aaron Lipstadt.

City of Angels 1/2 **1998 (PG-13)** Weepy American remake of Wim Wenders' "Wings of Desire" finds guardian angel Seth (Cage) falling in love with heart surgeon Maggie (Ryan) and then trying to decide whether he wants to become mortal in order to join her. Subtle, it is not. Cage does his doe-eyed best to convey Seth's longing and innocence to earthly ways, and the chemistry with Ryan really clicks. Overly sappy and sentimental, especially near the end, but that won't stop the intended audience from loving it. Big Hollywood flick that wears its art-house aspirations on its sleeve. **117m/C VHS, DVD.** Nicolas Cage, Meg Ryan, Andre Braugher, Dennis Franz, Colm Feore, Robin Bartlett, Joanna Merlin; *D:* Brad Silberling; *W:* Dana Stevens; *C:* John Seale; *M:* Gabriel Yared.

City of Blood 1/2 **1988 (R)** A South African doctor is embroiled in mystery with racial overtones when prostitutes are being killed with a spiked club. Packaged as a horror film, this movie actually deals with the questions of South African racial tensions in a sophisticated, ultimately tragic manner. **96m/C VHS.** *SA* Joe Stewardson, Ian Yule, Susan Coetzer; *D:* Darrell Roodt.

City of Ember 1/2 **2008 (PG)** The end of humanity, death of a civilization, dwindling resources, a race against time and corrupt authorities—all in a family-friendly fantasy setting! Imperiled humans built the underground city of Ember to provide a safe haven for 200 years. But time is up, and the generator that powers the city has broken. Now, teenagers Lina and Doon are on a secret mission to save the inhabitants from certain death. Original and visually impressive, with a relevant "green" theme, but the funhouse-like setting and general weirdness detract from the story. **95m/C DVD.** *US* Saoirse Ronan, Harry Treadway, Bill Murray, Tim Robbins, Martin Landau, Mackenzie Crook, Mary Kay Place, Toby Jones, Marianne Jean-Baptiste; *D:* Gil Kenan; *W:* Caroline Thompson; *C:* Xavier Perez Grobet; *M:* Andrew Lockington.

City of Fear 1/2 **1959** Escaping from a prison hospital, con Ryker (Edwards) steals a canister he thinks contains pharmaceutical heroin. Instead, it's radioactive material (in powdered form) and the container is leaking. The authorities rush to capture Ryker even as he's dying of radiation poisoning. **75m/B DVD.** Vince Edwards, Lyle Talbot, John Archer, Patricia Blair, Steven Ritch; *D:* Irving Lerner; *W:* Steven Ritch, Robert Dillon; *C:* Lucien Ballard; *M:* Jerry Goldsmith.

City of Ghosts 1/2 **2003 (R)** Dillon makes his directorial debut (as well as starring and co-writing the screenplay) with this overly-ambitious effort. Jimmy Creemins (Dillon) works for a shady New York insurance agency. His boss (and Jimmy's mentor), Marvin (Caan), has cleaned out the firm's offshore accounts and the feds think Jimmy was in on the scam. Jimmy discovers Marvin is holed up in Phnom Penh and he heads to Cambodia to join him at the Belleville Hotel, the usual sort of seedy Euro-dive, which is run by Frenchman Emile (Depardieu). Soon Jimmy is caught up in further unsavory activities, with various unsavory characters, a damsel-in-distress (McElhone), and more sideline plots. **117m/C VHS, DVD.** *US* Matt Dillon, James Caan, Natascha (Natasha) McElhone, Gerard Depardieu, Sereyvuth Kem, Chalee Sankhavesa, Stellan Skarsgard, Rose Byrne, Christopher Curry, Shawn Andrews; *D:* Matt Dillon; *W:* Matt Dillon, Barry Gifford; *C:* Jim Denault; *M:* Tyler Bates.

City of God 1/2 *Cidade de Deus* **2002 (R)** A long and generally lively chronicle (covering the late sixties to the early eighties) of the drug trade and gang warfare in the slums of Rio. Taken from Paulo Lins novel, the narrator is budding photographer Rocket (Rodrigues), a kid from the projects observing the violence and trying to stay out of its grip. He observes the rise to gang power of the ruthless Little Ze (da Hora), who will eventually go up against his rival, amateur boxer Knockout Ned (Jorge), who has a personal as well as professional grudge. Portuguese with subtitles. **130m/C DVD.** *BR* Alexandre Rodriques, Leandro Firmino da Hora, Phelipe Haagensen, Matheus Nachtergaele, Seu Jorge, Johnathan Haagensen; *D:* Fernando Meirelles, Katia Lund; *W:* Braulio Mantovani; *C:* Cesar Charlone; *M:* Antonio Pinto, Ed Cortes. N.Y. Film Critics '03: Foreign Film.

City of Hope **1991 (R)** The picture that "Bonfire of the Vanities" wanted to be, an eventful few days in the fictional metropolis of Hudson: an ugly racial incident threatens to snowball, the corrupt mayor pushes a shady real-estate deal, and a botched robbery has profound implications. Some of the subplots resolve too easily, but this cynical, crazy-quilt of urban life is worthy of comparison with "American Graffiti" and "Nashville" as pure Americana. **132m/C VHS.** Vincent Spano, Tony LoBianco, Joe Morton, Todd Graff, David Strathairn, Anthony John (Tony) Denison, Barbara Williams, Angela Bassett, Gloria Foster, Lawrence Tierney, John Sayles, Maggie Renzi, Kevin Tighe, Chris Cooper, Jace Alexander, Frankie Faison, Michael Mantell, Josh Mostel, Joe Grifasi, Louis Zorich, Gina Gershon, Rose Gregorio, Bill Raymond, Maeve Kinkead, Ray Aranha; *D:* John Sayles; *W:* John Sayles; *C:* Robert Richardson; *M:* Mason Daring. Ind. Spirit '92: Support. Actor (Strathairn).

City of Industry **1996 (R)** Efficient contemporary noir that doesn't always live up to its promise. Old pro thief Roy Egan (Keitel), now retired, is drawn into the final jewel heist of his younger brother, Lee (Hutton), who's also vowed to get out of the game. Unfortunately for him, Lee's picked one wrong partner in volatile wheelman Skip Kovich (Dorff). When the violent Skip decides he doesn't want to share the goods it starts an elaborate cat-and-mouse hunt through the seedier sides of L.A. **97m/C VHS, DVD.** Harvey Keitel, Stephen Dorff, Famke Janssen, Timothy Hutton, Michael Jai White, Wade Dominguez, Reno Wilson, Lucy Liu, Dana Barron, Elliott Gould; *D:* John Irvin; *W:* Ken Solarz; *C:* Thomas Burstyn; *M:* Stephen Endelman.

City of Joy **1992 (PG-13)** Disillusioned American heart surgeon Swayze flees to India after losing a patient. In Calcutta he is beaten by a street gang and loses his money and passport, but finds help from a farmer (Puri) who takes him to a nearby clinic in the City of Joy, one of Calcutta's poorest areas. Collins runs the clinic and recruits the reluctant doctor, who undergoes a life-changing transformation. The squalor of Calcutta is shown, but the city's portrayal as a magical place where problems miraculously disappear is unrealistic. Swayze lacks the emotional range for his part, but Collins and Puri are excellent in their roles. Adapted from the book by Dominique Lapierre. **134m/C VHS,**

DVD. *GB FR* Patrick Swayze, Pauline Collins, Om Puri, Shabana Azmi, Art Malik, Ayesha Dharker, Santu Chowdhury, Imran Badsah Khan, Shyamanand Jalan; ***Cameos:*** Sam Wanamaker; ***D:*** Roland Joffe; ***W:*** Mark Medoff; ***C:*** Peter Biziou; ***M:*** Ennio Morricone.

The City of Lost Children *La Cite des Enfants Perdus* **1995 (R)** Weird not-for-the-kiddies fairytale finds crazed inventor Krank (Emilfork) getting his evil one-eyed minions, the appropriately named Cyclops, to kidnap local children so that he can steal their dreams (because Krank himself is incapable of dreaming). The latest victim is young Denree (Lucien), the adopted brother of sideshow strongman One (Perlman), who single-mindedly pursues a way to get Denree back—aided by nine-year-old feral child Miette (Vittet) and a band of orphan thieves. Freaks galore with avant-garde designer Jean-Paul Gaultier in charge of costumes. French with subtitles or dubbed. **114m/C VHS, DVD.** *FR* Marc Caro, Ron Perlman, Daniel Emilfork, Joseph Lucien, Judith Vittet, Dominique Pinon, Jean-Claude Dreyfus, Odile Mallet, Genevieve Brunet, Mireille Mosse; ***D:*** Jean-Pierre Jeunet, Marc Caro; ***W:*** Jean-Pierre Jeunet, Marc Caro, Gilles Adrien; ***C:*** Darius Khondji; ***M:*** Angelo Badalamenti; ***V:*** Jean-Louis Trintignant. Cesar '96: Art Dir./Set Dec.

City of M *Ciudad de M* **2001** M (Magill) lives on the streets and has no job prospects, but he's happy enough since he can still party with his girlfriend and the guys. Then, he's offered the chance to become a drug courier to Miami. It's the only opportunity he's got but is the risk worth his future? Spanish with subtitles. **102m/C VHS, DVD.** *PV* Santiago Magill, Christian Meier, Vanessa Robbiano; ***D:*** Felipe Degregori; ***W:*** Giovanna Pollarolo; ***C:*** Micaela Cajhuaringa.

City of Men 1/2 *Cidade des Homens* **2007 (R)** Two teenage friends, Ace and Wallace, struggle to grow up in a gang-ridden Brazilian shantytown, where much of their thoughts drift to the idea of fatherhood. Ace's father was gunned down at an early age, and he's now become a new father himself. Wallace, about to turn 18 and needing an ID card, must track down his long-lost deadbeat dad to get a necessary signature. The fight to connect with his father is touching and plagued with danger as the two friends scurry from the neighborhood to neighborhood, dodging gang warfare along the way. Based on the Brazilian television series of the same name, and loosely follows Meirelles' earlier gangster epic "City of God," using some of the same actors, but taking a more emotional and mature approach to the themes. **110m/C DVD.** *BR* Douglas Silva, Darlan Cunha, Johnathan Haagensen, Camila Monteiro, Rodrigo dos Santos, Eduardo BR Piranha; ***D:*** Paulo Morelli; ***W:*** Elena Soarez; ***C:*** Adriano Goldman; ***M:*** Antonio Pinto.

City of Shadows **1986 (R)** Twins separated at birth are reunited by a criminal mind with evil intentions. Double trouble? **97m/C VHS.** John P. Ryan, Paul Coufos, Tony Rosato; ***D:*** David Mitchell; ***M:*** Tangerine Dream.

City of the Walking Dead *Nightmare City; Nightmare; Incubo Sulla Citta Contaminata* **1980** Eco-misery as a community must contend with prowling, radiation-zapped zombies who enjoy chewing through human flesh. **92m/C VHS, DVD.** *IT SP* Mel Ferrer, Hugo Stiglitz, Laura Trotter, Francisco Rabal; ***D:*** Umberto Lenzi; ***W:*** Antonio Corti, Luis Maria Delgado, Piero Regnoli; ***C:*** Hans Burman; ***M:*** Stelvio Cipriani.

The City of Violence 1/2 *Jjakpae* **2006** Tae-su (Doo-hong Jung) returns to his hometown to attend the funeral of an old friend who has been murdered. Being a cop, Tae-su is a little suspicious of events, and soon discovers an old acquaintance is responsible for the assassination, and he and his old partner decide to get revenge personally. It's a style-over-substance film, but the fights and musical score do well to make up for its shortcomings in plot. Besides, it's a revenge movie with the prerequisite amounts of massive butt kickin'. **92m/C DVD.** *KN* Doo-hong Jung, Seung-wan Ryoo, Kil-Kang Ahn, Seok-yong Jeng, Beom-su Lee; ***D:*** Seung-wan Ryoo; ***W:*** Seung-wan Ryoo, Jeong-min Kim, Won-jae Lee; ***C:*** Yeong-cheol Kim; ***M:*** Jun-Seok Bang.

City of Women *La Citte delle Donne* **1981 (R)** Visually stunning, but otherwise thin fantasy/drama about a man smothered with women. A journalist wanders through a feminist theme park replete with a roller rink and screening room. Some worthwhile adventures are mixed in with rather dull stretches. Not among the best from either Mastroianni, who is under utilized, or Fellini, who here seems incapable of separating good ideas from bad. Plenty of buxom babes, but otherwise undistinguished. In Italian with English subtitles. **140m/C VHS, DVD.** *IT* Marcello Mastroianni, Ettore Manni, Anna Prucnal, Bernice Stegers; ***D:*** Federico Fellini; ***W:*** Federico Fellini; ***C:*** Giuseppe Rotunno; ***M:*** Luis Bacalov.

City on Fire **WOOF!** **1978 (R)** Arguably the worst of Hollywood's disaster epics, this stinker came at the end of the cycle. The plot borrows heavily from such boxoffice heavyweights as "The Towering Inferno" and "The Poseidon Adventure." A cast of second-magnitude stars (with the exception of Henry Fonda) deals with civic corruption, an enraged pyromaniac, political ambitions, blackmail, and assorted hanky-panky. Several stuntmen are set afire, but the titular blaze is handled with unimpressive effects. The rest is choppy editing, cliched situations, and flat characters. **101m/C VHS.** *CA* Barry Newman, Susan Clark, Shelley Winters, Leslie Nielsen, Henry Fonda, Ava Gardner; ***D:*** Alvin Rakoff.

City on Fire 1/2 **1987** Ko Chow (Chow Yun-Fat) is an undercover cop who just wants out so he can marry his girl and forget about his past. He agrees to do one more job for his uncle, an aging inspector being forced out by an ambitious newcomer. He infiltrates a violent crew (one that's already killed a cop who had gotten in with them) that's planning a jewel heist. Like most Hong Kong cops-and-gangs flicks, it goes heavy on the action, but it also delves into Chow's character, sometimes to the detriment of the pacing. Most people know this as the inspiration for Tarantino's "Reservior Dogs." **98m/C VHS, DVD.** *HK* Chow Yun-Fat, Sun Yueh, Danny Lee, Carrie Ng, Roy Cheung; ***D:*** Ringo Lam; ***W:*** Ringo Lam, Tommy Sham; ***C:*** Wai Keung (Andrew) Lau; ***M:*** Teddy Robin Kwan.

City Slickers **1991 (PG-13)** Three men with mid-life crises leave New York City for a cattle-ranch vacation that turns into an arduous, character-building stint. Many funny moments supplied by leads Crystal, Stern, and Kirby, but Palance steals the film as a salty, wise cowpoke. Slater is fetching as the lone gal vacationer on the cattle drive. Boxoffice winner notable for a realistic calf birthing scene, one of few in cinema history. From an idea by Crystal, who also produced. Palance stole the show from Oscar ceremonies host Crystal a second time when he accepted his award and suddenly started doing one-arm pushups, startling the audience into laughter. **114m/C VHS, DVD.** Billy Crystal, Daniel Stern, Bruno Kirby, Patricia Wettig, Helen Slater, Jack Palance, Noble Willingham, Tracey Walter, Josh Mostel, David Paymer, Bill Henderson, Jeffrey Tambor, Phill Lewis, Kyle Secor, Yeardley Smith, Jayne Meadows; ***D:*** Ron Underwood; ***W:*** Lowell Ganz, Babaloo Mandel; ***C:*** Dean Semler; ***M:*** Marc Shaiman. Oscars '91: Support. Actor (Palance); Golden Globes '92: Support. Actor (Palance); MTV Movie Awards '92: Comedic Perf. (Crystal).

City Slickers 2: The Legend of Curly's Gold 1/2 **1994 (PG-13)** Mid-life crisis meets the wild west, part deux. Crystal and his fellow urban dudes discover a treasure map in the hat of departed trail boss Curly and decide to go a-huntin'. Palance is back as Curly's seafarin,' equally cantankerous, twin brother. Lovitz occupies the screen as Crystal's ne'er-do-well brother, replacing sidekick Bruno Kirby. A bit of a rehash, formulaic and occasionally straining for a punchline, it's still pretty darn funny, especially when the boys start to improvise. **116m/C VHS, DVD.** Billy Crystal, Daniel Stern, Jon Lovitz, Jack Palance, Patricia Wettig, Pruitt Taylor Vince, Bill McKinney, Lindsay Crystal, Noble Willingham, David Paymer, Josh Mostel; ***D:*** Paul Weiland; ***W:*** Billy Crystal, Lowell Ganz, Babaloo Mandel; ***M:*** Marc Shaiman.

City That Never Sleeps 1/2 **1953** A Chicago cop must decide whether or not to run off with an entertainer, or continue his life with his family. Decisions, decisions. Moody but dated melodrama that's finely acted and indecisively directed, with good use of dim city lights. Nothing new here. **90m/B VHS.** Gig Young, Mala Powers, Edward Arnold, Paula Raymond, Chill Wills, Marie Windsor; ***D:*** John H. Auer.

City Unplugged *Darkness in Tallinn* **1995** Heist film with some twists. $970 million in gold, in Paris for safekeeping since WWII, has been returned to the treasury in the newly independent Republic of Estonia. The thieves, who belong to the Russian mob, plan to cut all electricity in the capital city of Tallinn, break into the bank, and move the gold to a nearby cigarette factory where it can be melted down and repackaged as cigarettes. The mob's use of local electrician Toivo proves to be their undoing in a comedy of errors. Estonian with subtitles. **99m/C VHS.** Peter Oja, Ivo Uukkivi, Milena Gulbe, Monika Mager; ***D:*** Ilkka Jarvilaturi; ***W:*** Paul Kolsby; ***C:*** Rein Kotov.

City Without Men 1/2 **1943** Melodramatic story about a boarding house near a prison where the women tenants await the release of their imprisoned men. Little plot, no suspense. **75m/B VHS, DVD.** Linda Darnell, Sara Allgood, Michael Duane, Edgar Buchanan, Leslie Brooks, Glenda Farrell, Margaret Hamilton, Sheldon Leonard; ***D:*** Sidney Salkow.

The City's Edge 1/2 **1983** A young man becomes involved with the mysterious residents of a boarding house on the edge of the ocean. **86m/C VHS.** *AU* Mark Lee; ***D:*** Ken Quinnell.

Civic Duty 1/2 **2006 (R)** Terry Allen (Krause) has lost his job, and now spends his days at home while his wife goes to work. Eventually he begins obsessing over a middle-eastern looking neighbor who he begins to believe is a terrorist. Soon he's driving off his wife, annoying the FBI, and watching media hype about the 'terrorist threat' to our country. And stalking his neighbor, who may or may not be what he seems. Take it seriously and you may begin to wonder what those gophers in your yard are up to... **98m/C DVD.** *US* Peter Krause, Richard Schiff, Kari Matchett, Ian Tracey, Khaled Abol Naga, Mark Brandon, Val Cole, Brenda Crichlow, Agam Darshi, P. Lynn Johnson; ***D:*** Jeff Renfroe; ***W:*** Andrew Joiner; ***C:*** Dylan MacLeod; ***M:*** Terry Huud, Eli Krantzberg.

A Civil Action 1/2 **1998 (PG-13)** Low-key courtroom thriller doesn't contain many thrills. Travolta is Jan Schlichtmann, a flashy lawyer who freely admits that he's an ambulance chasing weasel. When a grieving mother (Quinlan) approaches him with a case accusing two corporate conglomerates of causing an outbreak of leukemia among children, Jan smells a big payoff. As the case drags on (and his firm falls deeper into debt pursuing it), his perspective changes and he begins to seek justice for the lost children. Robert Duvall steals the show as the homespun Harvard lawyer representing one of the companies. Based on a true story. **115m/C VHS, DVD.** James Gandolfini, John Travolta, Robert Duvall, Kathleen Quinlan, Tony Shalhoub, Zeljko Ivanek, John Lithgow, William H. Macy, Bruce Norris, Sydney Pollack, Peter Jacobson; ***D:*** Steven Zaillian; ***W:*** Steven Zaillian; ***C:*** Conrad L. Hall; ***M:*** Danny Elfman. Screen Actors Guild '98: Support. Actor (Duvall).

Civil Brand 1/2 **2002 (R)** Minority inmates stage a bloody revolt against abuse and exploitation. Melodrama quickly boils over the top and doesn't lose its charge. Notable performances by rappers MC Lite, Da Brat, and Mos Def. Neema Barnette makes good use of her low budget but scrimps on attention to pertinent civil issues. **95m/C DVD.** *US* LisaRaye, Mos Def, N'Bushe Wright, Monica Calhoun, Da Brat, M.C. Lyte, Clifton Powell, Lark Voorhies, Tichina Arnold, Reed McCants; ***D:*** Neema Barnette; ***W:*** Joyce Renee Lewis, Preston A. Whitmore II; ***C:*** Yuri Neyman; ***M:*** Mandrill.

Civil War Diary *Across Five Aprils* **1990** Too young to go to war, a young man struggles for the survival of his family amidst harsh winters, the devastation of the Civil War and his own personal nightmares. Winner of the International Heritage Award in 1990. Based on the Newberry Award winning young people's novel "Across Five Aprils." **82m/C VHS.** Miriam Byrd-Nethery, Todd Duffey, Hollis McCarthy; ***D:*** Kevin Meyer; ***W:*** Kevin Meyer.

Civilization **1916** A silent epic about the horrors and immorality of war as envisioned by the ground-breaking film pioneer Ince, who was later murdered. Famous scene involves Christ walking through body-ridden battlefields. **80m/B VHS.** Howard Hickman, Enid Markey, Lola May; ***D:*** Thomas Ince, Reginald Barker, Raymond B. West. Natl. Film Reg. '99.

Cjamango 1/2 **1967** Gunslinger Cjamango was robbed of his fortune in gold and left for dead. He tracks his money to a town controlled by bandit El Tigre and steals it back but El Tigre learns that Cjamango's weakness is a young orphan he's caring for and demands the gold be returned. Dubbed spaghetti western. **90m/C DVD.** *IT* Ivan Rassimov, Mickey Hargitay, Pierro Lulli, Livio Lorenzon, Helene Chanel, Ignazio Spalla, Giusva (Gilda) Fioravanti; ***D:*** Edoardo Mulargia; ***W:*** Fabio Piccioni; ***C:*** Vitaliano Natalucci; ***M:*** Felice Di Stefano.

The Claim 1/2 **2000 (R)** Winterbottom, who already adapted Thomas Hardy's "Jude the Obscure," takes on Hardy's "The Mayor of Casterbridge," transporting the story to California during the gold rush. Miner Dillon (Mullan) sells his wife Elena (Kinski) and baby daughter for gold and uses the money to establish his own town. But his sins come back to haunt him when his dying wife and grown daughter Hope (Polley) arrive, as does railway surveyor Dalglish (Bentley). Now Dillon's very future is threatened. There's more than the winter weather that's chilly about the film, which never reaches the tragic dimensions it should. **120m/C VHS, DVD.** *GB CA* Peter Mullan, Nastassja Kinski, Sarah Polley, Wes Bentley, Milla Jovovich, Sean McGinley, Julian Richings; ***D:*** Michael Winterbottom; ***W:*** Frank Cottrell-Boyce; ***C:*** Alwin Kuchler; ***M:*** Michael Nyman.

Claire Dolan **1997** Irish immigrant Claire (Cartlidge), a hooker, decides to relocate after her mother dies and she leaves town owing her pimp, Roland (Meaney), a lot of money. She moves to Newark, gets a job as a beautician, and begins a romance with Elton (D'Onofrio). Then Roland finds her and forces Claire back into business to pay off her debt. Bleak but well-acted. **95m/C VHS.** Katrin Cartlidge, Vincent D'Onofrio, Colm Meaney; ***D:*** Lodge Kerrigan; ***W:*** Lodge Kerrigan; ***C:*** Teodoro Maniaci; ***M:*** Simon Fisher Turner.

Claire of the Moon **1992** Famous satirist Claire goes to a women writers retreat in the Pacific Northwest where she's assigned a room with Noel, a solemn sex therapist. Noel's recovering from a disasterous love affair while Claire is promiscuous and unwilling to commit. Inspite of their differences, the two women find themselves drawn together. Too many philosophical debates slow the story down but the gentle romance works well. **102m/C VHS, DVD.** Trisha Todd, Karen Trumbo, Faith McDevitt, Damon Craig; ***D:*** Nicole Conn; ***W:*** Nicole Conn; ***M:*** Michael Allen Harrison.

Claire's Knee 1/2 *Le Genou de Claire* **1971** A grown man about to be married goes on a holiday and develops a fixation on a young girl's knee. Another of Rohmer's Moral Tales exploring sexual and erotic obsessions. Lots of talk, little else. You'll either find it fascinating or fail to watch more than 10 minutes. Most, however, consider it a classic. Sophisticated dialogue, lovely visions of summer on Lake Geneva. In French with English subtitles. **105m/C VHS, DVD.** *FR* Jean-Claude Brialy, Aurora Cornu, Beatrice Romand, Laurence De Monaghan, Gerard Falconetti; ***D:*** Eric Rohmer; ***W:*** Eric Rohmer; ***C:*** Nestor Almendros. Natl. Soc. Film Critics '71: Film.

Clambake **1967** Noxious Elvis vehicle about a rich man's son who wants success on his own terms, so he trades places with a water-skiing teacher. Inane, even in comparison to other Elvis ventures. ♫Clambake; The Girl I Never Loved; Hey, Hey, Hey; Confidence; Who Needs Money?; A House That Has Everything. **98m/C VHS, DVD.** Elvis Presley, Shelley Fabares, Bill Bixby, James Gregory, Gary Merrill, Will Hutchins, Harold (Hal) Peary, Suzie Kaye, Angelique Pettyjohn; ***D:***

Arthur Nadel; *W:* Arthur Browne Jr.; *C:* William Margulies; *M:* Jeff Alexander.

The Clan of the Cave Bear 🦴 1/2 **1986 (R)** A scrawny cavegirl is taken in by Neanderthals after her own parents are killed. Hannah is lifeless as a primitive gamine, and the film is similarly DOA. Ponderous and only unintentionally funny. Based on the popular novel by Jean M. Auel. **100m/C VHS, DVD.** Daryl Hannah, James Remar, Pamela Reed, John Doolittle, Thomas G. Waites; *D:* Michael Chapman; *W:* John Sayles; *C:* Jan De Bont; *M:* Alan Silvestri.

Clancy Street Boys 🦴 1/2 **1943** Muggs McGinnis (Gorcey) recruits his pals to pose as his siblings to fool wealthy Pete, a visiting friend of his late father's, who has been giving the family financial aid under the mistaken impression the McGinnis' had seven children. But a local thug hears about the scam and tries to horn in. Part of the "East Side Kids" series. **89m/B DVD.** Leo Gorcey, Huntz Hall, Bobby Jordan, Amelita Ward, Noah Beery Sr., Martha Wentworth, Bennie Bartlett; *D:* William Beaudine; *W:* Harvey Gates; *C:* Mack Stengler.

Clara's Heart 🦴 **1988 (PG-13)** A Jamaican maid enriches the lives of her insufferable, bourgeois employers and their particularly repellent son. A kinder, gentler waste of film and Goldberg; sentimental clap-trap which occasionally lapses into comedy. **108m/C VHS.** Whoopi Goldberg, Michael Ontkean, Kathleen Quinlan, Neil Patrick Harris, Spalding Gray, Beverly Todd, Hattie Winston; *D:* Robert Mulligan; *W:* Mark Medoff; *M:* Dave Grusin.

Clarence 🦴🦴 1/2 **1991 (G)** Clarence, the benevolent angel from the classic "It's a Wonderful Life," is back, risking his wings for a beautiful young woman. **92m/C VHS.** Robert Carradine, Kate Trotter; *D:* Eric Till; *W:* Lorne Cameron. **CABLE**

Clarence, the Cross-eyed Lion 🦴🦴🦴 **1965** Follows the many adventures of a cross-eyed lion and his human compatriots. Great family viewing from the creator of "Flipper." **98m/C VHS.** Marshall Thompson, Betsy Drake, Richard Haydn, Cheryl Miller, Rockne Tarkington, Maurice Marsac; *D:* Andrew Marton; *W:* Alan Caillou.

Clarissa 🦴🦴🦴 1/2 **1991** Clarissa Harlowe (Wickham) is a wealthy heiress famed for her virtue who is badgered by her family to marry a nobleman, which leads her to rebellion and into the arms of the handsome rake Lovelace (Bean). His seductive tactics are foiled by Clarissa's strength of character and his own heart, leading him down a path of self-destruction. Fabulous period costumes, gorgeous settings and stellar acting. **156m/C DVD.** Saskia Wickham, Sean Bean, Lynsey Baxter, Sean Pertwee, Jonathan Phillips, Jeffrey Wickham, Cathryn Harrison, Shirley Henderson; *D:* Robert Bierman; *W:* Janet Barron, David Nokes; *C:* John McGlashan; *M:* Colin Towns. **VIDEO**

Clash by Night 🦴🦴🦴 1/2 **1952** A wayward woman marries a fisherman, then beds his best friend. Seamy story line is exploited to the hilt by master filmmaker Lang. An utterly unflinching melodrama. Early Monroe shines in a supporting role too. Based on the Clifford Odets play. **105m/B VHS, DVD.** Barbara Stanwyck, Paul Douglas, Marilyn Monroe, Robert Ryan, J. Carrol Naish; *D:* Fritz Lang.

Clash of the Ninja 🦴 1/2 **1986** Evil Occidental ninja runs medical smuggling operation. Interpol ninja sets out to stop him. Wild ninja nonsense includes ninja with rotating head and exploding ninja. Dubbed poorly. **90m/C VHS.** *HK* Paul Torcha, Louis Roth, Eric Neff, Bernie Junker, Joe Redner, Klaus Mutter, Eddie Chan, Max Kwan, Tom Allen, Stanley Tong; *D:* Wallace Chan; *W:* Kurt Spielberg.

Clash of the Titans WOOF! 1981 (PG) Mind-numbing fantasy derived from Greek legends about heroic Perseus, who slays the snake-haired Medusa and rescues a semi-clad maiden from the monstrous Kraken. Wooden Hamlin plays Perseus and fares better than more accomplished Olivier and Smith, who seem in need of enemas as they lurch about Mt. Olympus. Only Bloom seems truly godlike in a supporting role. Some good, some wretched special effects from pioneer Harryhausen. **118m/C VHS, DVD.** *GB* Laurence Olivier, Maggie Smith, Claire Bloom, Ursula Andress, Burgess Meredith, Harry Hamlin, Sian Phillips, Judi Bowker; *D:* Desmond Davis; *W:* Beverley Cross; *C:* Ted Moore.

Clash of the Titans 2010 Remake of the campy 1981 fantasy-adventure. Perseus must embrace his own destiny as the son of an Olympic god (though he was raised as a man) when vengeful Hades tries usurping Zeus' power to unleash hell on earth. **m/C DVD.** Sam Worthington, Liam Neeson, Ralph Fiennes, Danny Huston, Izabella Miko, Mads Mikkelsen, Jason Flemyng; *D:* Louis Leterrier; *W:* Phil Hay, Matt Manfredi; *C:* Peter Menzies Jr.; *M:* Craig Armstrong, Mike Higham.

Class 🦴🦴 **1983 (R)** A prep school student discovers that his mother is the lover whom his roommate has bragged about. Lowe is serviceable as the stunned son of sexy Bisset, who woos McCarthy, even in an elevator. Too ludicrous to be enjoyed, but you may watch just to see what happens next. **98m/C VHS, DVD.** Jacqueline Bisset, Rob Lowe, Andrew McCarthy, Cliff Robertson, John Cusack, Stuart Margolin, Casey Siemaszko; *D:* Lewis John Carlino; *W:* Jim Kouf, David Greenwalt; *C:* Ric Waite; *M:* Elmer Bernstein.

The Class 🦴🦴 1/2 *Entre les Murs; Between the Walls* **2008 (PG-13)** A school year in the life of the 14- and 15-year-old students and their teacher in one high school classroom in Paris. Based on his own 2006 novel, Begaudeau plays a variation of himself—humorous, self-aware, dedicated teacher Francois Marin. His classroom is a cultural and intellectual mix of the diligent and the troubled with director Cantet rejecting a clear narrative in favor of fly-on-the-wall dialogue and situations. French with subtitles. **128m/C DVD.** *FR* Francois Begaudeau, Esmeralda Oeurtaini, Rachel Regulier, Franck Keita, Wei Huang; *D:* Laurent Cantet; *W:* Laurent Cantet, Robin Campillo, Francois Begaudeau; *C:* Pierre Milon, Catherine Pujol, Georgi Lazarevski. Ind. Spirit '09: Foreign Film.

Class Act 🦴🦴 1/2 **1991 (PG-13)** Rappers Kid 'N' Play team up once again in this role reversal comedy. A straight-laced brain and a partying, macho bully find their school records and identifications switched when they enroll in a new high school. This turns out to be good for the character of both young men, as the egghead learns to loosen up and the bully learns what it feels like to be respected for his ideas rather than a fierce reputation. Comedy is very uneven but the duo are energetic and likable. **98m/C VHS.** Christopher Reid, Christopher Martin, Meshach Taylor, Karyn Parsons, Doug E. Doug, Ric(k) Ducommun, Rhea Perlman; *D:* Randall Miller; *M:* Vassal Benford.

Class Action 🦴🦴🦴 **1991 (R)** 1960s versus 1990s ethics clash when a father and daughter, both lawyers, wind up on opposing sides of a litigation against an auto manufacturer. Hackman and Mastrantonio give intense, exciting performances, almost surmounting the melodramatic script. **110m/C VHS, DVD.** Mary Elizabeth Mastrantonio, Gene Hackman, Joanna Merlin, Colin Friels, Laurence Fishburne, Donald Moffat, Jan Rubes, Matt Clark, Fred Dalton Thompson, Jonathan Silverman, Dan Hicks; *D:* Michael Apted; *W:* Samantha Shad, Christopher Ames; *M:* James Horner.

Class of Fear 🦴 1/2 *Monday Morning* **1991 (R)** The new kid in school is having a particularly rough time. He's been framed for murdering a teacher and must prove his innocence before he winds up in prison. **105m/C VHS.** Julianne McNamara, Noah Blake, Brandon Hooper, Karl Wiedergott; *D:* Donald Murphy; *C:* John Aronson; *M:* Bill Johnson.

Class of '44 🦴 1/2 **1973 (PG)** The sequel to "Summer of '42" finds insufferable boys becoming insufferable men at miltary school. Worse than its predecessor, and notable only in that it is Candy's film debut. **95m/C VHS.** Gary Grimes, Jerry Houser, Oliver Conant, Deborah Winters, William Atherton, Sam Bottoms, John Candy; *D:* Paul Bogart; *M:* David Shire.

The Class of Miss MacMichael 🦴🦴 **1978 (R)** A dedicated instructor inherits and ultimately inspires a class of high school misfits and malcontents. Derivative venture is beneath considerable talents of Jackson. Based on a novel by Sandy Hutson. **95m/C VHS.** *GB* Glenda Jackson, Oliver Reed, Michael Murphy, Rosalind Cash; *D:* Silvio Narizzano; *W:* Judd Bernard.

Class of 1984 WOOF! 1982 (R) Teacher King must face a motley crew of teenagers in the classroom. Ring leader and student psychopath Van Patten leads his groupies on a reign of terror through the high school halls, stopping to gang rape King's wife. Teacher attempts revenge. Bloody and thoughtless update of "Blackboard Jungle." Early Fox appearance. Followed by "Class of 1999." **93m/C VHS, DVD.** *CA* Perry King, Roddy McDowall, Timothy Van Patten, Michael J. Fox, Merrie Lynn Ross, Stefan Arngrim, Al Waxman, Lisa Langlois; *D:* Mark L. Lester; *W:* Mark L. Lester, Tom Holland; *C:* Albert J. Dunk; *M:* Lalo Schifrin.

Class of 1999 🦴 **1990 (R)** Freewheeling sci-fi set in the near future where teen gangs terrorize seemingly the entire country. A high school principal determines to enforce law and order by installing human-like robots with rocket launchers for arms. Violent, crude entertainment. Class dismissed. Sequel to "Class of 1984" and available in an unrated version. **98m/C VHS.** Bradley Gregg, Traci Lind, Malcolm McDowell, Stacy Keach, Patrick Kilpatrick, Pam Grier, John P. Ryan, Darren E. Burrows, Joshua John Miller; *D:* Mark L. Lester; *W:* C. Courtney Joyner.

Class of 1999 2: The Substitute 🦴 1/2 **1993 (R)** High school in 1999 is filled with violent gangs who murder at random. Enter substitute teacher John Bolen, who has his own ideas of discipline—leading to an even higher body count. John just doesn't seem human and when a CIA agent starts investigating, school may never be the same. **90m/C VHS.** Sasha Mitchell, Nick Cassavetes, Caitlin Dulany, Jack Knight, Gregory West, Richard (Rick) Hill; *D:* Spiro Razatos; *W:* Mark Sevi.

Class of Nuke 'Em High 🦴 1/2 **1986 (R)** Team Troma once again experiments with the chemicals, with violent results. Jersey high school becomes a hotbed of mutants and maniacs after a nuclear spill occurs. Good teens Chrissy and Warren succumb, the school blows, life goes on. High camp, low budget, heavy gore. Followed by "Class of Nuke 'Em High Part 2." **84m/C VHS, DVD.** Janelle Brady, Gilbert Brenton, Robert Prichard, R.L. Ryan, Theo Cohan, Diana De Vries, Brad Dunker, Gary Schneider; *D:* Richard W. Haines, Lloyd Kaufman; *W:* Richard W. Haines, Lloyd Kaufman, Mark Rudnitsky, Stuart Strutin.

Class of Nuke 'Em High 2: Subhumanoid Meltdown 🦴 **1991 (R)** The Troma team brings us back into the world of the strange. In this adventure, the evil Nukamama Corporation holds secret experiments at their "college" and create subhumanoids as slave labor, swelling unemployment and wrecking the economy. This does not fare too well with the rest of society, including our heroes Roger the reporter, Professor Holt, and the scantily clad sub-humanoid Victoria. **96m/C VHS, DVD.** Lisa Gaye, Brick Bronsky, Leesa Rowland, Michael Kurtz, Scott Resnick; *D:* Eric Louzil; *W:* Eric Louzil, Lloyd Kaufman; *C:* Ron Chapman; *M:* Bob Mithoff.

Class of Nuke 'Em High 3: The Good, the Bad and the Subhumanoid WOOF! 1994 (R) Revisit Tromie the nuclear rodent and the other disaster-prone denizens of Tromaville, USA. Admire the classic good twin vs. evil subhumanoid twin plot as they battle against each other, aided by chicks with guns and tin undergarments. Supposedly inspired by Shakespeare's "Comedy of Errors." Tip: stick to the BBC production for your senior thesis. **95m/C VHS, DVD.** Brick Bronsky, Lisa Gaye, Lisa Star, John Tallman, Albert Rear, Phil Rivo; *D:* Eric Louzil; *W:* Lloyd Kaufman; *C:* Ron Chapman; *M:* Bob Mithoff.

Class of '61 🦴🦴 1/2 **1992** 1861, that is, as this class of West Point cadets prepares for the outbreak of war. Three close friends find themselves on opposing sides and with romantic entanglements, as well. Illustrated history, complete with voiceover passages from soldiers' letters, tend to slow the action, although the battles scenes are well done. **95m/C VHS.** Dan Futterman, Clive Owen, Josh(ua) Lucas, Sophie Ward, Laura Linney, Andre Braugher, Len Cariou, Dana Ivey, Scott Burkholder, Niall O'Brien, Christien Anholt, Paul Guilfoyle, Beverly Todd, Ed Wiley, Sue-Ann Leeds; *D:* Gregory Hoblit; *W:* Jonas McCord; *C:* Janusz Kaminski. **TV**

Class of '63 🦴🦴 **1973** An unfulfilled woman finally discovers the lover she lost nearly ten years ago at her college reunion. Nearly average. **74m/C VHS.** James Brolin, Joan Hackett, Cliff Gorman, Ed Lauter; *D:* John Korty. **TV**

Class Reunion WOOF! 1972 Sexual highjinks are the order of the day at a 10-year high school reunion. Insipid softcore effort. It's cheaper just to cut out heads from yearbooks and paste 'em to skin mags torsos. Not to be confused with "National Lampoon's Class Reunion," equally bad but nonetheless distinct. **90m/C VHS.** Marsha Jordan, Renee Bond, Terry Johnson; *D:* Stephen C. Apostolof; *W:* Edward D. Wood Jr.; *C:* Allen Stone.

Class Reunion Massacre WOOF! *The Redeemer* **1977 (R)** Typically lame-brained horror about the mysterious deaths of former school jerks who've reconvened for the 10-year reunion. Worthless flick stars someone named Finkbinder. Contains graphic violence that is not for the squeamish. **87m/C VHS.** T.K. Finkbinder, Damien Knight, Nick Carter, Jeanetta Arnette, Christopher Flint; *D:* Constantine S. Gochis; *W:* William Vernick.

Classe Tous Risque 🦴🦴🦴 *The Big Risk* **1960** Classic crime thriller deserves to be rediscovered. Aging French gangster Abel Davos (Ventura) has been hiding out in Italy for years with his wife and sons. Deciding he wants to move back to Paris, Davos agrees to pull off a payroll heist with an old pal in order to finance his return, but the getaway is botched. So Davos tries calling in some favors from his former gang, who are reluctant to disturb their own lives. Instead, they hire Erik (Belmondo) to handle things, though Davos is wary of the respectful new kid. French and Italian with subtitles. **100m/B DVD.** *FR IT* Lino Ventura, Jean-Paul Belmondo, Marcel Dalio, Sandra Milo, Claude Cerval, Michele Meritz, Michel Ardan, Simone France, Stan Krol; *D:* Claude Sautet; *W:* Claude Sautet, Jose Giovanni, Pascal Jardin; *C:* Ghislan Cloquet; *M:* Georges Delerue.

Claudia 🦴🦴 **1985 (R)** A wealthy woman who's part of London's high society falls for a lowly musician while trying to escape her dominating husband. Melodramatic meanderings not likely to move you. **88m/C VHS.** Deborah Raffin, Nicholas Ball; *D:* Anwar Kawadri.

The Claw 🦴🦴 **1927** A young British profligate goes to Africa to prove his manhood to the woman who rejected him. Silent. **54m/B VHS.** Claire Windsor, Norman Kerry; *D:* Sidney Olcott; *C:* John Stumar.

Clawed: The Legend of Sasquatch 🦴 1/2 *The Unknown* **2005 (R)** A group of bear poachers are found brutally mauled on Echo Mountain and many in the nearby town of Pine Creek believe a grizzly was to blame—or maybe the mountain's lurid legend has resurfaced. A Native American forest ranger sets out to investigate and so do four teen campers. **90m/C DVD.** Miles O'Keeffe, Nathaniel Arcand, Jack Conley, Chelsea Hobbs, Dylan Purcell, Brandon Henschell, David "Shark" Fralick, Casey LaBow; *D:* Karl Kozak; *W:* Karl Kozak, Don J. Rearden; *C:* Victor Lou; *M:* Lawrence Nash Groupe. **VIDEO**

Claws 🦴 **1977 (PG)** A woodsman, a game commissioner, and an Indian band together to stop a grizzly bear who is killing residents of a small Alaskan town. **100m/C VHS.** Leon Ames, Jason Evers, Anthony Caruso, Glenn Sipes, Carla Layton, Myron Healey; *D:* Richard Bansbach, R.E. Pierson.

Claws WOOF! 1985 A lone farmboy is subjected to repeated attacks by feline mutants. Meow, baby. **84m/C VHS.** Jason Roberts, Brian O'Shaughnessy, Sandra Prinsloo; ***D:*** Alan Nathanson.

The Clay Bird *Matir Moina* **2002** Anu (Bablu) is sent to a strict Islamic religious school where he befriends outcast Rokon (Farazi). Times are troubled in East Pakistan (it's the late 1960s) as the residents wish to create an independent state, which is causing problems with the Muslim rulers in West Pakistan. As Anu's family gets more politically involved, life becomes more dangerous. (Bangladesh was formed in 1971.) Bengali with subtitles. **98m/C DVD.** Nurul Islam Bablu, Russell Farazi, Jayanto Chattopadhyay, Rokeya Prachy, Soaeb Islam; ***D:*** Tareque Masud; ***W:*** Tareque Masud, Catherine Masud; ***C:*** Sudhir Palsane; ***M:*** Moushumi Bhowmik.

The Clay Pigeon 1/2 **1949** Seaman comes to in the hospital after a long coma and discovers he's about to be court-martialed for treason and murder. Effective suspense as he goes after the man who incriminated him. **63m/B VHS.** Bill Williams, Barbara Hale, Richard Loo, Richard Quine, Frank Fenton, Frank Wilcox, Robert Bray, Martha Hyer, Ann Doran, Mary(a) Marco; ***D:*** Richard Fleischer; ***W:*** Carl Foreman; ***C:*** Robert De Grasse; ***M:*** Paul Sawtell.

Clay Pigeons 1/2 **1998 (R)** Bodies are mysteriously piling up in a sleepy Montana town after strange cowboy trucker Lester (Vaughn) shows up. Clay Birdwell (Phoenix) finds himself a prime suspect after a series of bizarre twists stemming from his affair with his best friend's wife. After crossing paths, Clay and Lester quickly become best buddies. When they discover a body while fishing, Clay begins to link unsolved murders elsewhere in the state to his new pal. Problem is, the FBI has just shown up to investigate the disappearance of Clay's best friend and his wife, while Lester has disappeared, leaving Clay to take the heat. Features outstanding performances by Phoenix and Vaughn. Vaughn is given free reign, and goes near, but never over, the top. Second half is slower and less fun than the first half. Still, the original story and clever twists keep it interesting. **104m/C VHS, DVD.** Vince Vaughn, Joaquin Rafael (Leaf) Phoenix, Janeane Garofalo, Scott Wilson, Georgina Cates, Phil Morris, Vince Vieluf, Nikki Arlyn, Monica Moench, Joseph D. Reitman, Gregory Sporleder; ***D:*** David Dobkin; ***W:*** Matthew Healy; ***C:*** Eric Alan Edwards; ***M:*** John Lurie.

Clayton County Line **1978** Plucky buddies decide to end a cruel sheriff's reign of terror. Derivative and unredeeming. **80m/C VHS.** Kelly Bradish, Vince Csapos, Michael Heinz, Donald Kenney, Kathy Kenney, Gregg Schultz, Dan Quine, Steve Szilagyi, Dean Wilson; ***D:*** Dean Wilson.

Clean **2004 (R)** Emily (Cheung) and her common-law husband Lee Hauser (Johnston) are heroin addicts who abandoned their young son to Lee's parents. Lee, a faded 80s rocker, dies of an overdose, and Emily is sent to jail, where she tries to get clean. After her release, Emily wants to reconnect with her son, but grandma Rosemary (Henry) hates her; grandpa Albrecht (Nolte) is more willing to give Emily a chance. Emily struggles to keep off drugs while attempting to find work and mend fences but the character is so prickly and self-centered that she garners little sympathy. **110m/C VHS, DVD.** *CA GB FR* Maggie Cheung, Nick Nolte, Beatrice Dalle, Jeanne Balibar, Don McKellar, Martha Henry, James Johnston, Remi Martin, James Dennis, Laetitia Spigarelli; ***Cameos:*** David Roback; ***D:*** Olivier Assayas; ***W:*** Olivier Assayas; ***C:*** Eric Gautier; ***M:*** David Roback, Brian Eno.

Clean and Sober 1/2 **1988 (R)** A drug addict hides out at a rehabilitation clinic and actually undergoes treatment. A serious, subtle, and realistic look at the physical/emotional detoxification of an obnoxious, substance-abusing real estate broker; unpredictable and powerful without moralizing. Keaton is fine in unsympathetic lead, with both Baker and Freeman excelling in lesser roles. Not for all tastes, but it's certainly a worthwhile work. Caron, creator of TV's "Moonlighting," debuts here as director. **124m/C VHS, DVD.** Michael Keaton, Kathy Baker, Morgan Freeman, M. Emmet Walsh, Claudia Christian, Pat Quinn, Ben Piazza, Brian Benben, Luca Bercovici, Tate Donovan, Henry Judd Baker, Mary Catherine Martin; ***D:*** Glenn Gordon Caron; ***W:*** Tod Carroll; ***C:*** Jan Kiesser; ***M:*** Gabriel Yared. Natl. Soc. Film Critics '88: Actor (Keaton).

Clean, Shaven **1993** Schizophrenic Peter Winter (Greene in a stunning performance) is searching bleak Miscou Island, off the New Brunswick coast, for the young daughter his mother put up for adoption after Peter was institutionalized and his wife died. Peter's being tailed by Detective McNally (Albert), who suspects him of a child's murder, and his tenuous hold on reality slowly disintegrates into torment and self-mutilation. Debut for director/writer Kerrigan. **80m/C VHS, DVD.** Peter Greene, Robert Albert, Jennifer MacDonald, Megan Owen, Molly Castelloe; ***D:*** Lodge Kerrigan; ***W:*** Lodge Kerrigan; ***C:*** Teodoro Maniaci; ***M:*** Hahn Rowe.

Clean Slate **1994 (PG-13)** Private-eye Maurice Pogue (Carvey) sustains injuries that cause a rare type of amnesia making every day seem like the first day of his life. As the only witness to a crime, he bumbles through mix-ups with the mob and his job as a bodyguard. Lightweight comedy fare is good for a few yuks but doesn't work as well as the similar "Groundhog Day." Barkley the sight-impaired dog steals nearly every scene he's in. **106m/C VHS, DVD.** Bob Odenkirk, Dana Carvey, Valeria Golino, James Earl Jones, Kevin Pollak, Michael Murphy, Michael Gambon, Jayne Brook, Vyto Ruginis, Olivia D'Abo, Peter Crook; ***D:*** Mick Jackson; ***W:*** Robert King; ***M:*** Alan Silvestri.

Cleaner **2007 (R)** Disappointingly lackluster thriller. Former New Jersey cop Tom Carver (Jackson) now makes his living cleaning up crime scenes. But Tom is shocked to discover that his recent clean-up of a shooting has erased evidence, which points to a cover-up and maybe Tom becoming the fall guy for murder. **91m/C DVD.** Samuel L. Jackson, Ed Harris, Robert Forster, Luis Guzman, Marc Macaulay, Eva Mendes, Keke Palmer, Jose Pablo Cantillo, Maggie Lawson; ***D:*** Renny Harlin; ***W:*** Matthew Aldrich; ***C:*** Scott Kevan; ***M:*** Richard Gibbs. **VIDEO**

Clear and Present Danger 1/2 **1994 (PG-13)** Ford returns for a second go at CIA agent Jack Ryan in the third installment of Tom Clancy's bestselling adventures. With the Cold War over, the U.S. government is the bad guy as Ryan discovers a link between a South American drug cartel and a Presidential advisor. Viewers will also finally get an answer to that nagging question at the end of "Patriot Games:" is it a boy or a girl? Archer's back as Ryan's annoying wife, and Birch and Jones also return. Keep alert for complex plot twists in lieu of tons of action, though there's enough to keep action fans happy. **141m/C VHS, DVD.** Harrison Ford, Anne Archer, James Earl Jones, Willem Dafoe, Thora Birch, Henry Czerny, Harris Yulin, Raymond Cruz, Joaquim de Almeida, Miguel (Michael) Sandoval, Donald Moffat, Theodore (Ted) Raimi, Dean Jones; ***D:*** Phillip Noyce; ***W:*** John Milius, Donald Stewart, Steven Zaillian; ***C:*** Donald McAlpine; ***M:*** James Horner. Blockbuster '95: Action Actor, T. (Ford); Blockbuster '96: Action Actor, V. (Ford).

Clearcut 1/2 **1992 (R)** Progressive lawyer finds his liberalism and his survival skills tested among modern Canadian Indians, when a militant native resorts to kidnapping the businessman who threatens their land. Well-acted, brutal drama that asks tough questions; it includes what purports to be the first authentic sweat-lodge ceremony ever filmed. **98m/C VHS.** *CA* Graham Greene, Ron Lea, Michael Hogan, Floyd "Red Crow" Westerman, Rebecca Jenkins; ***D:*** Richard Bugajski.

The Clearing **2004 (R)** Rich businessman Redford is kidnapped from his driveway by frustrated former employee Dafoe. As Dafoe leads Redford through the woods towards an appointed meeting spot with the other kidnappers, Redford tries to talk Dafoe into letting him go free. His wife (Mirren), meanwhile, finally notices his prolonged absence and calls in family and FBI. Redford talks to Dafoe about his wife; Mirren talks to an understanding agent about her husband. As the tension builds around them, the two reflect upon their importance to one another. Quietly suspenseful and full of interesting, fully fleshed characters, with a deliberate pace, beautiful acting, and a rewarding twist at the end. **91m/C DVD.** *US* Robert Redford, Willem Dafoe, Helen Mirren, Matt Craven, Alessandro Nivola, Melissa Sagemiller, Wendy Crewson, Larry Pine, Diana Scarwid, Elizabeth Ruscio; ***D:*** Pieter Jan Brugge; ***W:*** Justin Haythe; ***C:*** Denis Lenoir; ***M:*** Craig Armstrong.

Clearing the Range 1/2 **1931** Hoot wants the bad guy who knocked off his brother so he poses as a cringing coward in the hopes of uncovering the villain. Eilers is the love interest as well as his real-life wife. **64m/B VHS.** Hoot Gibson, Sally Eilers, Hooper Atchley; ***D:*** Otto Brower.

Cleo from 5 to 7 1/2 *Cleo de 5 a 7* **1961** A singer strolls through Paris for 90 minutes, and reconsiders her life while awaiting the results of medical tests for cancer. Typical documentary-like effort from innovative filmmaker Varda, who constructed the film in real time. Look for a brief appearance of master director Jean-Luc Godard. In French with English subtitles. **90m/B VHS, DVD.** *FR* Corinne Marchand, Antoine Bourseiller, Dorothee Blanck, Michel Legrand, Jean-Claude Brialy, Jean-Luc Godard, Anna Karina, Eddie Constantine, Sami Frey; ***D:*** Agnes Varda; ***W:*** Agnes Varda; ***C:*** Jean Rabier; ***M:*** Michel Legrand.

Cleo/Leo **1989 (R)** Crude and sexist jerk Leo gets chased into the East River by a gun-toting feminist. Reincarnated, Leo returns as Cleo and endures the same Neanderthal remarks and attitudes that "he" used to dish out. Tasteless, exploitive comedy only cynically explores the sex reversal theme. **94m/C VHS.** Jane (Veronica Hart) Hamilton, Scott Thompson Baker, Kevin Thomas, Alan Naggar, Ginger Lynn Allen; ***D:*** Chuck Vincent.

Cleopatra **1934** Early Hollywood DeMille version of the Egyptian temptress's lust for Marc Antony after Julius Caesar's death. Intermittently interesting extravaganza. Colbert seems to be enjoying herself in the lead role in this hokey, overdone epic. Includes the original theatrical trailer on laser-track 2. Remade in 1963. **100m/B VHS, DVD.** Claudette Colbert, Henry Wilcoxon, Warren William, Gertrude Michael, Joseph Schildkraut, Sir C. Aubrey Smith; ***D:*** Cecil B. DeMille; ***C:*** Victor Milner. Oscars '34: Cinematog.

Cleopatra **1963** And we thought DeMille's version was extravagant. After the death of Julius Caesar, Cleopatra, Queen of Egypt, becomes infatuated with Mark Antony. Costly four-hour epic functions like a blimp-sized, multi-colored sleeping tablet. Historical characters are utterly dwarfed by the film's massive scope, and audiences are benumbed by a spectacle of crowd scenes and opulent, grotesque interiors. Taylor looks and often acts like a sex bomb ruler, while Harrison has some notion of Caesar's majesty. Burton, however, is hopelessly wooden. Hard to believe this came from director Mankiewicz. **246m/C VHS, DVD.** Elizabeth Taylor, Richard Burton, Rex Harrison, Roddy McDowall, Martin Landau, Pamela Brown, Michael Hordern, Kenneth Haigh, Andrew Keir, Hume Cronyn, Carroll O'Connor; ***D:*** Joseph L. Mankiewicz; ***W:*** Joseph L. Mankiewicz; ***C:*** Leon Shamroy; ***M:*** Alex North. Oscars '63: Art Dir./Set Dec., Color, Color Cinematog., Costume Des. (C), Visual FX; Natl. Bd. of Review '63: Actor (Harrison).

Cleopatra **1999** Lavishly trashy TV miniseries about the infamous Egyptian queen and her Roman lovers. Young royal, Cleopatra (Varela), wants to rule Egypt but she needs the power of Rome to make things happen. When Julius Caesar (Dalton) comes to Egypt, she seduces the conqueror to gain a kingdom. But after Caesar's murder, Cleopatra pins her hopes on rash Marc Antony (Zane) and things don't turn out so well. Based on the book by Margaret George. **139m/C VHS, DVD.** Leonor Varela, Timothy Dalton, Billy Zane, Rupert Graves, Art Malik, John Bowe, Nadim Sawalha, Owen Teale, Daragh O'Malley, Sean Pertwee, Bruce Payne, Caroline Langrishe; ***D:*** Franc Roddam; ***W:*** Stephen Harrigan, Anton Diether; ***C:*** David Connell; ***M:*** Trevor Jones. **TV**

Cleopatra Jones **1973 (PG)** Lean and lethal government agent with considerable martial arts prowess takes on loathsome drug lords. Dobson is fetching as the lead performer in this fast-paced, violent flick. Followed by "Cleopatra Jones and the Casino of Gold." **89m/C VHS, DVD.** Tamara Dobson, Shelley Winters, Bernie Casey, Brenda Sykes, Albert "Poppy" Popwell; ***D:*** Jack Starrett; ***W:*** Max Julien, Sheldon Keller; ***C:*** David M. Walsh; ***M:*** J.J. Johnson.

Cleopatra Jones & the Casino of Gold **1975 (R)** Dobson returns as the lethal, physically imposing federal agent to Hong Kong to take on a powerful druglord in this sequel to "Cleopatra Jones." Watch for sexy Stevens as the Dragon Lady. **96m/C VHS.** Tamara Dobson, Stella Stevens, Norman Fell, Albert "Poppy" Popwell; ***D:*** Charles "Chuck" Bail.

Cleopatra's Second Husband **2000 (R)** Let's play master and servant. Whiny, selfish yuppie couple Robert (Hipp) and Hallie (Schram) Marrs go on vacation and need housesitters for their fabulous L.A. pad. They accept a recommendation from friends to employ sexy Zack (Kestner) and Sophie (Mitchell). Some friends—when the Marrs return early, their housesitters ask to stay on a little longer and proceed to take over. Hallie takes off after Robert gets it on with Sophie but the sexual/mind games are just beginning. **92m/C VHS, DVD.** Paul Hipp, Boyd Kestner, Radha Mitchell, Bitty Schram, Alexis Arquette, Jonathan Penner; ***D:*** Jonathan Reiss; ***W:*** Jonathan Reiss; ***C:*** Matt Faw; ***M:*** Cary Berger.

Clerks **1994 (R)** "What kind of convenience store do you run here?" Day in the life of a convenience store clerk is an often hilarious lesson in the profane from first time writer/director Smith (who has a cameo as Silent Bob). Twenty-two-year-old Dante Hicks (O'Halloran) is a disaffected New Jersey Quick Stop employee who spends most of his time bored and dealing with borderline crazies. The next-door video store is clerked by his best friend Randal (Anderson), who derives equal delight from tormenting his customers and debating absolutely anything (especially anything sexual). Nothing much actually happens but the very low-budget ($27,575) production has a decidedly scuzzy charm and a cult following. Based on the director's four years of clerking at the Quick Stop and shot on location. **89m/B VHS, DVD, UMD.** Brian O'Halloran, Jeff Anderson, Marilyn Ghigliotti, Lisa Spoonhauer, Jason Mewes; ***Cameos:*** Kevin Smith; ***D:*** Kevin Smith; ***W:*** Kevin Smith; ***C:*** David Klein; ***M:*** Scott Angley. Sundance '94: Filmmakers Trophy.

Clerks 2 **2006 (R)** Writer/director/actor Kevin Smith revisits the New Jersey suburban landscape that put him and his recurring characters on the map 12 years ago. Little has changed in the lives or ambitions of clerks Dante (Brian O'Halloran) and Randal (Jeff Anerson)—they still pass the time with Smith's signature debates and diatribes on such topics as beastiality, "The Man," and the virtues of "Star Wars" vs. "Lord of the Rings"—while harassing the occasional, unfortunate customer. The same semi-professional, low-budget charm of its predecessor makes for a strong follow-up. Simply put, if you liked "Clerks," you'll like "Clerks II"; if you were offended by the first, you'll be horrified by this one. **98m/C DVD, HD DVD.** *US US* Brian O'Halloran, Jeff Anderson, Jason Mewes, Rosario Dawson, Kevin Smith, Jennifer Schwalbach Smith, Jason Lee, Ethan Suplee, Trevor Fehrman, Kevin Weisman, Wanda Sykes; ***Cameos:*** Ben Affleck; ***D:*** Kevin Smith; ***W:*** Kevin Smith; ***C:*** David Klein; ***M:*** James L. Venable.

Click **2006 (PG-13)** Workaholic family man Michael Newman (Sandler) needs a universal remote to simplify at least one thing in his life. Salesclerk Morty (Walken) hands over a special device that allows Michael to pause, mute, fast-forward, and rewind his actual life. Naturally, this is not the blessing that Michael first imagines it to be. Sandler does some more of his disgruntled man-child shtick, Walken is benignly crazy, and Beckinsale is nagging and hot. **98m/C DVD, Blu-ray Disc.** *US* Adam Sandler, Kate Beckinsale, Christopher Walken, Sean Astin, David Hasselhoff, Henry Winkler, Julie Kavner, Jennifer Coolidge, Lorraine Nicholson, Jonah Hill, Rob Schneider, Rachel Dratch, Katie Cassidy, Nick Swardson, Tatum McCann; ***D:*** Frank Coraci; ***W:*** Mark O'Keefe, Steve Koren; ***C:*** Dean Semler; ***M:*** Rupert Gregson-Williams.

The Client ✓✓ 1/2 **1994 (PG-13)** Another legal thriller from the Grisham factory. Reggie Love (Sarandon) is a troubled attorney hired by 11-year-old Mark (Renfro), who witnessed the suicide of a Mafia attorney and now knows more than he should. Ambitious federal prosecutor Foltrigg's (Jones) willing to risk the boy's life in exchange for career advancement. Lacks the mega-big Hollywood names of "The Firm" and "The Pelican Brief" but gains solid acting in return with Renfro a find in his film debut. No frills, near-faithful adaptation by Schumacher basically travels down the path of least resistance. Filmed on location in Memphis. **121m/C VHS, DVD.** Ron Dean, Susan Sarandon, Tommy Lee Jones, Brad Renfro, Mary-Louise Parker, Anthony LaPaglia, Bradley Whitford, Anthony Edwards, Ossie Davis, Walter Olkewicz, J.T. Walsh, Will Patton, Anthony Heald, William H. Macy; ***D:*** Joel Schumacher; ***W:*** Robert Getchell, Akiva Goldsman; ***C:*** Tony Pierce-Roberts; ***M:*** Howard Shore. British Acad. '94: Actress (Sarandon).

Cliffhanger ✓✓✓ **1993 (R)** Action-packed thriller. Expert climber Gabe Walker (Stallone) faces his greatest challenge when criminal mastermind Lithgow and his henchman appear on the scene. Turner plays fellow climber and love interest. Lithgow makes a particularly convincing, if not downright chilling, murderous thief. Filmed in the Italian Alps with a budget of $70 million-plus; boasts stunning cinematography and breathtaking footage of the Dolomite mountain range. Harlin's expert pacing and direction combine to produce maximum thrills and suspense. The hit Stallone's been waiting for, placing eighth on the list of top 1993 boxoffice grossers. **113m/C VHS, DVD.** Sylvester Stallone, John Lithgow, Michael Rooker, Janine Turner, Rex Linn, Caroline Goodall, Leon, Paul Winfield, Ralph Waite, Craig Fairbrass, Michelle Joyner, Max Perlich; ***D:*** Renny Harlin; ***W:*** Sylvester Stallone, Michael France; ***C:*** Alex Thomson; ***M:*** Trevor Jones.

Clifford WOOF! **1992 (PG)** Short plays a 10-year-old in an effort delayed by Orion's financial crisis. Creepy little Clifford's uncle Martin (Grodin) rues the day he volunteered to babysit his nephew to prove to his girlfriend (Steenburgen) how much he likes kids. Clifford terrorizes Grodin in surprisingly nasty ways when their plans for visiting Dinosaurworld fall through, although Grodin sees to well-deserved revenge. Not just bad in the conventional sense, but bad in a bizarre sort of alien fashion that raises questions about who was controlling the bodies of the producers. To create the effect of Short really being short, other actors stood on boxes and sets were built slightly larger. **90m/C VHS, DVD.** Martin Short, Charles Grodin, Mary Steenburgen, Dabney Coleman, Sonia Jackson; ***D:*** Paul Flaherty; ***W:*** Bobby Von Hayes, Jay Dee Rock, Steven Kampmann, Will Aldis; ***C:*** John A. Alonzo; ***M:*** Richard Gibbs.

Clifford's Really Big Movie ✓✓ 1/2 **2004 (G)** Animated tale of TV's lovably oversized canine hero, Clifford (Ritter), and normal-sized friends Cleo the poodle (Summer) and T-Bone the mutt (Mitchell) who take to the road after the Big Red Dog mistakenly thinks his large appetite is causing his owners to go broke. The trio join up with a traveling carnival populated by plenty of child-delighting characters. Clifford revives the struggling show and becomes a star, all in the hope that the act will help him win a lifetime supply of his fave snack Tummy Yummies. Mildly evil doggie-treat tycoon (Goodman) has other plans for Clifford, however, and plots to kidnap the dog. Extremely gentle story and nice message especially suitable for younger viewers; older watchers won't find much here. **73m/C VHS, DVD.** ***D:*** Robert Ramirez; ***W:*** Robert Ramirez, Rhett Reese; ***M:*** Jody Gray; ***V:*** John Ritter, Wayne Brady, Jenna Elfman, John Goodman, Kel Mitchell, Judge Reinhold, Kath Soucie, Cree Summer, Grey DeLisle, Wilmer Valderrama, Earl Boen, Teresa Ganzel, Jess Harnell, Ernie Hudson, Oren Williams, Cam(eron) Clarke.

A Climate for Killing ✓✓ 1/2 **1991 (R)** Arizona police are baffled when a woman murdered 16 years earlier is again found dead. Case open? Hunks Bauer and Beck are earnest in leads, and Ross and Sara are foxy. Passable entertainment. **104m/C VHS.** Steven Bauer, John Beck, Katharine Ross, Mia Sara, John Diehl, Phil Brock, Dedee Pfeiffer, Lu Leonard, Jack Dodson, Eloy Casados; ***D:*** J.S. Cardone; ***W:*** J.S. Cardone; ***M:*** Robert Folk.

Climates ✓✓✓ *Iklimler* **2006** A Turkish couple's decision to call things off spans not only their native countryside but also several seasons. Beginning in summer, the distant 40ish professor Isa and his much-younger TV art director girlfriend Bahar break up, though the reasons are never given. In fact, not much is said throughout, though their feelings are usually obvious. Moving along to fall, Isa has a manic sex encounter with Serap (Kesal)—a possible culprit in Isa and Bahar's troubles—even though, in winter, Serap tells Isa where to find Bahar. Writer-director-lead actor Nuri Bilge Ceylan (Isa) is the real-life husband of Ebru Ceylan (Bahar). In Turkish with subtitles. **97m/C DVD.** *FR TU* Nuri Bilge Ceylan, Ebru Ceylan, Nazan Kirilmis, Mehmet Eryilmaz, Arif Asci, Can Ozbatur; ***D:*** Nuri Bilge Ceylan; ***W:*** Nuri Bilge Ceylan; ***C:*** Gokhan Tiryaki.

The Climax ✓✓ 1/2 **1944** Technicolor highlights this horror saga of obsession. House physician for Vienna's Royal Theatre, Dr. Hohner (Karloff) kills opera singer Marcellina (Vincent) when she rejects him. Twenty years later, Hohner hears the beautiful voice of Angela (Foster), a near duplicate of Marcellina's, and hypnotizes her to prevent her singing. Now, it's up to Angela's composer friend Franz (Bey) to overcome the doctor's evil influence. Adapted from a play by Edward Locke. Waggner directed this "The Phantom of the Opera" clone using the same sets as the 1943 "Phantom" remake. **86m/C VHS, DVD.** Boris Karloff, Susanna Foster, Turhan Bey, Gale Sondergaard, Thomas Gomez, June Vincent, Jane Farrar, Scotty Beckett; ***D:*** George Waggner; ***W:*** Curt Siodmak, Lynn Starling; ***C:*** Hal Mohr, William Howard Greene; ***M:*** Edward Ward.

The Climb ✓✓ 1/2 **1987 (PG)** German mountain climbers attempt to conquer the Himalayan Nanga Parbat, the world's fifth highest peak. Sometimes compelling film based on 1953 expedition in which only one member succeeded in reaching the summit. **90m/C VHS.** Bruce Greenwood, James Hurdle, Kenneth Welsh; ***D:*** Donald Shebib; ***W:*** Donald Shebib; ***M:*** Peter Jermyn.

The Climb ✓✓ 1/2 **1997 (PG-13)** In late '50s Baltimore, 12-year-old Danny (Smith) is the target of bullies and humiliated by the fact that his dad Earl (Strathairn) is accused of cowardice because he's not a vet. So Danny decides to prove his own courage by climbing the local, soon-to-be-demolished 203-foot radio tower. Danny is unexpected aided by his crochety neighbor, Chuck Langer (Hurt), a hard-drinking grump dying of cancer. But when Danny gets into trouble, it's his dad who comes to the rescue. Nostalgic family fare. **94m/C VHS, DVD.** *FR NZ* Gregory Edward Smith, John Hurt, David Strathairn, Stephen McHattie, Seth Smith, Sarah Buxton; ***D:*** Bob Swaim; ***W:*** Vince McKewin; ***C:*** Allen Guilford; ***M:*** Greco Casadeus.

Clipped Wings ✓✓ 1/2 **1953** The Bowery Boys are at their best as they inadvertantly join the army while visiting a friend; in the process of their usual bumblings, they uncover a Nazi plot. **62m/B VHS.** Leo Gorcey, Huntz Hall, Bernard Gorcey, David Condon, Bennie Bartlett, June Vincent, Mary Treen, Philip Van Zandt, Elaine Riley, Jeanne Dean, Lyle Talbot; ***D:*** Edward L. Bernds.

The Clique ✓✓ 1/2 **2008 (PG)** Based on the book series by Lisa Harrison for tweens too young for "Gossip Girl." Gawky Claire Lyons has just moved with her family to New York City from Florida. She's starting classes at Octavian Country Day school and it's obvious Claire doesn't fit in with the popular clique of mean girls. But will she let them bully her or change her? **87m/C DVD.** Ellen Marlow, Elizabeth McLaughlin, Samantha Boscarino, Sophie Anna Everhard, Bridgit Mendler, Elizabeth Keifer, Neal Matarazzo; ***D:*** Michael Lembeck; ***W:*** Liz Tigelaar; ***C:*** Michael Weaver; ***M:*** George S. Clinton. **VIDEO**

Clive Barker's Book of Blood ✓✓ *Book of Blood* **2008 (R)** Adapted from two 1984 framing stories by Barker: "Book of Blood" and "On Jerusalem Street." Paranormal investigator Mary Florescu (Ward) and her skeptic partner Reg Fuller (Blair) examine an old gothic Edinburgh mansion that Mary believes is used as an intersecting road for transporting souls into the afterlife. Mary recruits her student Simon (Armstrong) to assist with dire consequences. **100m/C DVD.** Sophie Ward, Paul Blair, Jonas Armstrong, Doug Bradley, Romana Abercromby, Simon Bramford; ***D:*** John Harrison; ***W:*** John Harrison, Darin Silverman; ***C:*** Philip Robertson; ***M:*** Guy Farley. **VIDEO**

Cloak and Dagger ✓✓ **1946** An American physicist joins the secret service during WWII and infiltrates Nazi territory to release a kidnapped scientist who is being forced to build a nuclear bomb. Disappointing spy show with muted anti-nuclear tone. **106m/B VHS, DVD.** Gary Cooper, Lilli Palmer, Robert Alda, James Flavin, Vladimir Sokoloff, J. Edward Bromberg, Marc Lawrence, Ludwig Stossel; ***D:*** Fritz Lang; ***W:*** Ring Lardner Jr., Albert (John B. Sherry) Maltz; ***M:*** Max Steiner.

Cloak & Dagger ✓✓ 1/2 **1984 (PG)** A young boy, last seen befriending E.T., depends upon his imaginary super-friend to help him out when some real-life agents are after his video game. Coleman is particularly fun as both dad and fantasy hero in an interesting family adventure. **101m/C VHS, DVD.** Dabney Coleman, Henry Thomas, Michael Murphy, John McIntire, Jeannette Nolan; ***D:*** Richard Franklin; ***W:*** Tom Holland; ***M:*** Brian May.

The Clock ✓✓✓ *Under the Clock* **1945** Appealing romance about an office worker who meets and falls in love with a soldier on two-day leave in NYC. Charismatic Walker and likeable Garland make a fine screen couple, and Wynn is memorable as the drunk. **91m/B VHS, DVD.** Judy Garland, Robert Walker, James Gleason, Marshall Thompson, Keenan Wynn; ***D:*** Vincente Minnelli; ***C:*** George J. Folsey; ***M:*** George Bassman.

Clockers ✓✓✓ **1995 (R)** Strike (Phifer), leader of a group of bottom-feeding drug dealers ("clockers"), engages in a power struggle with his boss (Lindo), his do-the-right-thing brother Victor (Washington), and his own conscience. He's also suspected of murder by relentless narcotics cop Rocco Klein (Keitel). Supported by an excellent cast, first-timer Phifer surprises with a fierce and powerful performance. Lindo, in particular, stands out as the paternally evil Rodney. Aggressively edited, with Turturro's performance mostly lost on the cutting room floor. Critically lauded cinematography is marred by the occasional boom shot. Poignant and compelling street drama is based on the Richard Price novel. Lee took over after Scorsese and De Niro dropped out to make "Casino." **128m/C VHS, DVD.** Mekhi Phifer, Harvey Keitel, John Turturro, Delroy Lindo, Keith David, Isaiah Washington IV, Lisa Arrindell Anderson, Kirk "Sticky Fingaz" Jones; ***D:*** Spike Lee; ***W:*** Spike Lee, Richard Price; ***C:*** Malik Hassan Sayeed; ***M:*** Terence Blanchard.

The Clockmaker ✓✓✓ 1/2 *L'Horloger de Saint-Paul* **1973** Contemplative drama about a clockmaker whose life is shattered when his son is arrested as a political assassin. Tavernier regular Noiret excels in the lead. In French with English subtitles. **105m/C VHS, DVD.** *FR* Philippe Noiret, Jean Rochefort, Jacques Denis, William Sabatier, Christine Pascal; ***D:*** Bertrand Tavernier; ***W:*** Bertrand Tavernier, Jean Aurenche, Pierre Bost; ***C:*** Sylvain Rougerie; ***M:*** Philippe Sarde.

Clockstoppers ✓✓ 1/2 **2002 (PG)** Amusing kid fare has heroes Zak (Bradford) and Venezuelan exchange student Francesca (Garces) zipping around in speeded-up "hypertime" to rescue Zak's scientists dad Dr. Gibbs (Thomas) from time-traveling baddies, headed by corporate bigwig Henry Gates (Biehn). It seems the wristwatch/time machine Gibbs invented needs tweaking, so Gibbs and top grad student Dopler (Stewart) are kidnaped to fix the snag by the evil QT corporation, which wants to use the device to, what else, conquer the world. The teen duo must do their rescuing, however, before they all prematurely age in hypertime (one of the snags). No stranger to sci-fi, director Frakes (Riker on "Star Trek: Next Generation") makes the most of the inherent FX. **94m/C VHS, DVD.** *US* Jesse Bradford, French Stewart, Michael Biehn, Paula Garces, Robin Thomas, Julia Sweeney, Linda Kim, Garikayi Mutambirwa; ***D:*** Jonathan Frakes; ***W:*** Rob Hedden, J. David Stem, David N. Weiss; ***C:*** Tim Suhrstedt; ***M:*** Jamshield Sharifi.

Clockwatchers ✓ 1/2 **1997 (PG-13)** Decent cast gets wasted in a slice of life story that goes nowhere. Meek temp Iris's (Collette) new assignment is at a big, faceless credit company. Iris is taken in hand by fellow temps Margaret (Posey), Paula (Kudrow), and Jane (Ubach), who like to complain about how badly they're treated by management. Things gets worse when the company makes an announcement about a rash of petty thefts and the temps get blamed. That's it. **105m/C VHS, DVD.** Toni Collette, Parker Posey, Lisa Kudrow, Alanna Ubach, Stanley DeSantis, Jamie Kennedy, David James Elliott, Kevin Cooney, Bob Balaban, Paul Dooley; ***D:*** Jill Sprecher; ***W:*** Jill Sprecher, Karen Sprecher; ***C:*** Jim Denault.

Clockwise ✓✓ 1/2 **1986 (PG)** Monty Python regular Cleese is a teacher preoccupied by punctuality. His neurosis proves his undoing when he falls victim to misadventure while traveling to deliver a speech. Cleese is acceptable, dialogue and story is less so, though sprinkled with a fair amount of humor. **96m/C VHS, DVD.** *GB* John Cleese, Penelope Wilton, Alison Steadman, Stephen Moore, Sharon Maiden; ***D:*** Christopher Morahan; ***W:*** Michael Frayn; ***C:*** John Coquillon; ***M:*** George Fenton.

A Clockwork Orange ✓✓✓✓ **1971 (R)** In the Britain of the near future, a sadistic punk leads a gang on nightly rape and murder sprees, then is captured and becomes the subject of a grim experiment to eradicate his violent tendencies in this extraordinary adaptation of Anthony Burgess's controversial novel. The film is an exhilarating experience, with an outstanding performance by McDowell as the funny, fierce psychopath. Many memorable, disturbing sequences, including a rape conducted while assailant McDowell belts "Singing in the Rain." Truly outstanding, provocative work from master filmmaker Kubrick. **137m/C VHS, DVD, Blu-ray Disc, HD DVD.** *GB* Malcolm McDowell, Patrick Magee, Adrienne Corri, Michael Bates, Warren Clarke, Aubrey Morris, James Marcus, Steven Berkoff, David Prowse, John Clive, Carl Duering, Miriam Karlin; ***D:*** Stanley Kubrick; ***W:*** Stanley Kubrick; ***C:*** John Alcott; ***M:*** Walter (Wendy) Carlos. AFI '98: Top 100; N.Y. Film Critics '71: Director (Kubrick), Film.

Clodhopper ✓✓ **1917** A farmboy decides to head out for New York where he achieves fame on Broadway for his dance number, the "Clophooper Glide." He stays true to his hometown girl, however, and returns to save his father's farm from financial ruin. **47m/B VHS.** Charles Ray, Margery Wilson; ***D:*** Victor Schertzinger.

The Clones ✓✓ **1973 (PG)** A doctor discovers a government experiment engineered to murder him with a perfect clone. **90m/C VHS.** Michael Greene, Gregory Sierra; ***D:*** Paul Hunt, Lamar Card.

Clones of Bruce Lee ✓✓ **1980 (R)** It's a martial arts free-for-all as bold masters from throughout the world duel for supremacy in the realm of self defense. If you like martial arts movies, you'll probably like this one. If you don't know if you like martial arts movies, find out with one of the actual Bruce Lee's flicks. **87m/C VHS, DVD.** Dragon Lee, Bruce Le, Bruce Lai, Bruce Thai; ***D:*** Joseph Kong.

The Clonus Horror ✓ 1/2 *Parts: The Clonus Horror* **1979** A scientist discovers a government plot to clone the population by freezing bodies alive and using their parts in surgery. **90m/C VHS, DVD.** Tim Donnelly, Keenan Wynn, Peter Graves, Dick Sargent, Paulette Breen; ***D:*** Robert S. Fiveson.

Close Encounters of the Third Kind ✓✓✓✓ **1977 (PG)** Middle-American strangers become involved in the attempts of benevolent aliens to contact earthlings. Despite the sometimes mundane nature of the characters, this Spielberg epic is a stirring achievement. Studded with classic sequences; the ending is an exhilarating experience of special effects and peace-on-earth feelings. Dreyfuss and Dillon excel as friends who are at once bewildered and obsessed by the alien presence, and French filmmaker Truffaut is also strong as the stern, ultimately kind scientist. **152m/C VHS, DVD, Blu-ray Disc.** Richard Dreyfuss, Teri Garr,

Melinda Dillon, Francois Truffaut, Bob Balaban, Cary Guffey, J. Patrick McNamara; *D:* Steven Spielberg; *W:* Steven Spielberg; *C:* Vilmos Zsigmond; *M:* John Williams. Oscars '77: Cinematog., Sound FX Editing; AFI '98: Top 100, Natl. Film Reg. '07.

Close My Eyes 1991 **(R)** Insecure Natalie (Reeves) is newly married to wealthy and garrulous entrepreneur Sinclair (Rickman) when she reunites with her long-estranged younger brother, Richard (Owen). Richard has just taken a job as a city planner in London and is suddenly Natalie's confidante and soon much more. The simmering sexual tension between the two finally explodes into a volatile relationship that becomes an obsession to Richard. And when Natalie decides to break off their affair, he's determined to stop her. Reeves's character is somewhat whiny and unappealing so it's up to the men to carry the movie, which they do with aplomb. **105m/C VHS, DVD.** *GB* Alan Rickman, Clive Owen, Saskia Reeves, Karl Johnson, Lesley Sharp; *D:* Stephen Poliakoff; *W:* Stephen Poliakoff; *C:* Witold Stok; *M:* Michael Gibbs.

Close to Eden *Urga* **1990 (PG)** A peasant couple living in inner Mongolia with their three children are prevented by strict Chinese law from having a fourth. The husband sets out from his village to obtain birth control from the nearby town. While on his way, the farmer (Bayaertu) saves a Russian truck driver (Gostukhin) after he drives into a lake. Sergei is introduced to another way of life when he's taken home by his rescuer to meet the family and becomes accustomed to the tranquility of farm life in the rural Mongolian steppe. Essentially a story about the changes modern civilization can bring to a rural way of life. Filmed in Mongolia. In Russian with English subtitles. **109m/C VHS.** *RU* Baoyinhexige, Badema, Nikita Mikhalkov; *D:* Nikita Mikhalkov; *W:* Rustam Ibragimbekov; *M:* Eduard Artemyev. Venice Film Fest. '91: Film.

Close to Home 1986 A runaway fleeing a home life of abuse and neglect befriends a TV journalist doing a story on similar girls. She turns to him for support after she is arrested and returned home. Merely mediocre. **93m/C VHS.** *CA* Daniel Allman, Jillian Fargey, Anne Petrie; *D:* Rick Beairsto.

Close to Leo *Tout Contre Leo* **2002** Uneven-but-intimate family drama finds 20-year-old Leo (Mignard), the eldest of four sons, revealing to his family that he is HIV-positive. His parents decide that their youngest, 12-year-old Marcel (Lespert), is too young to hear the news, although the kid is bright enough to realize something serious is going on and resentful that he is being left out. Honore adapted and directed from his own 1996 novel. French with subtitles. **90m/C DVD.** *FR* Pierre Mignard, Yannis Lespert, Marie Bunel, Dominic Gould, Rodolphe Pauly, Jeremie Lippmann; *D:* Christophe Honore; *W:* Christophe Honore, Diasteme; *C:* Remy Chevrin; *M:* Alexandre Beaupain. **TV**

Close to My Heart 1/2 **1951** Family melodrama. Newspaperman Brad Sheridan (Milland) and his wife Midge (Tierney) are dismayed by the long adoption process so when Brad learns a baby has been abandoned at the police station, he and Midge offer to care for the tyke. Brad gets obsessed with finding out about the boy's parentage, which doesn't put him in a good light with adoption supervisor Mrs. Morrow (Bainter) and Midge may lose the baby she's come to love. **90m/B DVD.** Ray Milland, Gene Tierney, Fay Bainter, Howard St. John, Mary Beth Hughes, James Seay, Ann Morrison; *D:* William Keighley; *W:* James R. Webb; *C:* Robert Burks; *M:* Max Steiner.

Close Your Eyes 1/2 *Hypnotic; Dr. Sleep* **2002 (R)** Psychic hypnotist Michael Strother (Visnjic) has limited himself to curing smokers after an unsavory event in the U.S. caused him to flee to the UK. When Janet (Henderson), who also happens to be a British cop, comes to Michael hoping to kick her cigarette habit, Michael has a vision which reluctantly brings about his involvement in the highly publicized "tattoo murderer" case and the serial killer's only living victim, Heather. After hypnotizing the now-mute Heather to find some answers, Michael is knee deep in the case against the wishes of his pregnant wife (Otto). He teams up with Janet, who bucks traditional police methods to go with her gut. Not quite a horror film, this overly elaborate, stale supernatural thriller boasts interesting locales, suitably moody climate, and decent performances. **108m/C DVD.** *GB* Goran Visnjic, Shirley Henderson, Miranda Otto, Paddy Considine, Claire Rushbrook, Fiona Shaw, Corin Redgrave, Sophie Stuckey; *D:* Nick Willing; *W:* Nick Willing, William Brookfield; *C:* Peter Sova; *M:* Simon Boswell.

Closely Watched Trains 1/2 *Ostre Sledovane Vlaky* **1966** A novice train dispatcher attempts to gain sexual experience in German-occupied Czechoslovakia during WWII. Many funny scenes in this film regarded by some as a classic. Based upon the Czech novel by Bohumil Hrabal. In Czech with English subtitles. **89m/B VHS, DVD.** *CZ* Vaclav Neckar, Jitka Bendova, Vladimir Valenta, Josef Somr; *D:* Jiri Menzel; *W:* Jiri Menzel; *C:* Jaromir Sofr; *M:* Jiri Sust. Oscars '67: Foreign Film.

The Closer 1/2 **1991 (R)** Aiello is "The Closer," a high-powered salesman whose world is falling apart. Somewhere between the money and the power, he's lost touch with his family and the truly important things in life. Is it too late to get them back? **87m/C VHS.** Danny Aiello, Michael Pare, Joe Cortese, Justine Bateman, Diane Baker, James Karen, Rick Aiello, Michael Lerner; *D:* Dimitri Logothetis; *W:* Robert Keats, Louis LaRusso II; *M:* Al Kasha.

Closer **2004 (R)** Love stinks. Especially in this caustic adaptation by Marber of his 1997 drama. Waifish stripper Alice (Portman) enchants writer Dan (Law) after they meet cute in London. Dan later writes a novel about his life with Alice and indulges in a flirtation with successful photographer Anna (Roberts). Dan then decides to impersonate Anna during an Internet sex chat and arranges to meet dermatologist Larry (a ferocious performance by Owen), who does meet, and eventually marries, the real Anna. Dan has an affair with Anna, which Larry finds out about (in a laceratingly brutal verbal scene), and Larry meets the abandoned Alice without knowing about their secondhand connection. Marber changed Alice's fate from his play and made both female characters American to accommodate his leads. Owen played the role of Dan in the original National Theatre production. **101m/C DVD, HD DVD.** *US* Julia Roberts, Jude Law, Natalie Portman, Clive Owen; *D:* Mike Nichols; *W:* Patrick Marber; *C:* Stephen Goldblatt; *M:* Steven Patrick Morrissey. British Acad. '04: Support. Actor (Owen); Golden Globes '05: Support. Actor (Owen), Support. Actress (Portman).

Closer and Closer 1/2 **1996** Cable thriller finds author Kate Sander (Delaney) paralyzed after being stalked by someone resembling the stalker character in her last book "Gargoyle." Kate works with wheelchair-bound personal trainer B.J. Connors (York) to regain her strength, which she'll need as she writes "Gargoyle 2." This time Kate's decided to kill off her stalker/serial killer and soon real murders begin to occur. **93m/C VHS, DVD.** Kim Delaney, John J. York, Peter Outerbridge, Peter MacNeill, Scott Craft, Anthony Sherwood; *D:* Fred Gerber; *W:* Matt Dorff. **CABLE**

The Closet 1/2 *Le Placard* **2000 (R)** Francois Pignon (Auteuil) is a dull everyguy accountant who learns he's about to be fired after 20 years (from his job at a condom factory). His new (gay) neighbor Belone (Aumont) makes a unique suggestion—he will send doctored photos, showing Pignon at a gay bar, to Pignon's company and they will be forced to back down or be accused of sexual discrimination. Francois protests he can't pass as gay but he doesn't have to—his bosses and co-workers believe the rumors and make their own assumptions, including the homophobic personnel director Felix (Depardieu) who fears for his own job if he's not especially nice to Francois. Balances neatly between slapstick and sentiment. French with subtitles. **86m/C VHS, DVD.** *FR* Daniel Auteuil, Gerard Depardieu, Thierry Lhermitte, Michel Aumont, Michele Laroque, Jean Rochefort, Alexandra Vandernoot; *D:* Francis Veber; *W:* Francis Veber; *C:* Luciano Tovoli; *M:* Vladimir Cosma.

Closet Land 1/2 **1990 (R)** Severe, stylized political allegory aims high but fails to convincingly distill totalitarian repression into just two characters—a government inquisitor and his captive, a woman subjected to hideous mental and physical torture. Child-molesting emerges as an ill-advised subtheme. A better video on the same subject: "Interrogation," from Poland. **95m/C VHS.** Madeleine Stowe, Alan Rickman; *D:* Radha Bharadwaj; *W:* Radha Bharadwaj; *C:* Bill Pope; *M:* Richard Einhorn.

Closing the Ring **2007 (R)** Schmaltzy drama begins in the 1990s with Ethel (MacLaine) burying her unloved husband. She's surprised when their old friend Jack (Plummer) comes to the funeral. Meanwhile in Ireland, Quinlan (Postlethwaite) digs around a WWII B-17 bomber crash site and finds a ring engraved with the names Ethel and Teddy. Flashbacks lead to the 1940s romance of Ethel (Barton) and her first husband Teddy (Amell), which also involved his best friends Chuck (Alpay) and Jack (Smith). **118m/C DVD.** *CA GB* Shirley MacLaine, Christopher Plummer, Pete Postlethwaite, Mischa Barton, Gregory Edward Smith, David Alpay, Neve Campbell, Martin McCann, Brenda Fricker, Stephen Amell; *D:* Richard Attenborough; *W:* Peter Woodward; *C:* Roger Pratt; *M:* Jeff Danna.

Closure WOOF! *Straightheads* **2007 (R)** Cheap, violent, and nasty. Alice and Adam are brutally attacked by a group of hunters while driving home from a country party. A chance meeting leads Alice to the identity of the attackers and she forces the guilt-ridden Adam to go along with her plan for revenge. **80m/C DVD.** *GB* Gillian Anderson, Danny Dyer, Ralph Brown; *D:* Dan Reed; *W:* Dan Reed; *C:* Chris Seager; *M:* Ilan Eshkeri.

Cloud Dancer **1980 (PG)** A self-absorbed acrobat uses and abuses those around him, including his girlfriend. Carradine and O'Neill fail to distinguish themselves in this mediocre film. **107m/C VHS.** David Carradine, Jennifer O'Neill, Joseph Bottoms, Colleen Camp; *D:* Barry Brown; *W:* William Goodhart.

Cloud Waltzing 1/2 **1987** The screen version of a Harlequin romance about a journalist who arrives in France to interview a vintner and finds romance and danger. Melodrama bolstered by the presence of photogenic Beller. **103m/C VHS.** Kathleen Beller, Francois-Eric Gendron, Paul Maxwell, Therese Liotard, Claude Gensac, David Baxt; *D:* Gordon Flemyng.

The Clouded Yellow **1951** Young, lovely, and a little unstable, Sophie Malraux (Simmons) is accused of murdering the handyman who worked for her guardians (Jones and Dresdel). Ex-British Secret Service agent David Somers (Howard), who's in love with Sophie, helps her escape from jail and the two head for Liverpool and a ship to Mexico. But the police (hoping to find the real killer) are hot on their trail. Romantic suspense with good lead pairing. **95m/B VHS.** *GB* Jean Simmons, Trevor Howard, Sonia Dresdel, Barry Jones, Maxwell Reed, Kenneth More, Andre Morell, Geoffrey Keen; *D:* Ralph Thomas; *W:* Eric Ambler; *C:* Geoffrey Unsworth.

Clouds over Europe *Q Planes* **1939** A test pilot and a man from Scotland Yard team up to find out why new bomber planes are disappearing. **82m/B VHS.** Laurence Olivier, Valerie Hobson, Ralph Richardson, George Curzon, George Merritt, Gus McNaughton, David Tree, Sandra Storme, Hay Petrie, Frank Fox, Gordon McLeod, John Longden, Reginald Purdell, John Laurie, Pat Aherne; *D:* Tim Whelan; *W:* Ian Dalrymple; *C:* Harry Stradling Sr.

Cloudy with a Chance of Meatballs 1/2 **2009 (PG)** Wildly irreverent 3D animated fantasy based on the children's book by Judi and Ron Barrett. Would-be inventor Flint Lockwood's gadgets tend not to work as planned but he's still hoping to impress his dad by helping the depressed economy of their island home of Swallow Falls by turning water into food. It turns out to be gigantic food that falls from the sky (orange juice showers, mashed potato snow...) that has the mayor changing the town's name to Chew and Swallow and making it a tourist destination. But it isn't as much fun as you might think (and quite messy) when the weather takes a turn for the worse. **81m/C DVD.** *US* *D:* Chris Miller, Phil Lord; *W:* Judi Barrett, Ron Barrett; *M:* Mark Mothersbaugh; *V:* Bill Hader, Anna Faris, Andy Samberg, Mr. T, Tracy Morgan, James Caan, Bruce Campbell.

Cloverfield 1/2 **2008 (PG-13)** Rob (Stahl-David) and friends are enjoying his going-away party in Manhattan on the night before he is to leave for Japan. Pal Hud (Miller) is filming the party, complete with mushy goodbyes and confessions of things undone—and one might get drowsy here if not for the dizzying effect of Hud's camerawork—when there's a terrifying rattle. Thinking an earthquake hit, the friends rush to the roof only to realize it's no earthquake and the city's in total chaos, evidenced by screams and fireballs and Lady Liberty's head (yes, the statue) rolling down a city street. Not to spoil the fun, but it's an old-fashioned monster movie. The "Blair Witch" generation will be nonplussed by the jumpy, hyperactive filming (the unfolding tragedy is all captured courtesy of Hud's digital video cam), and others will appreciate the nod to monster flicks of the past. A fun romp with a scary monster and a little love story tossed in—mix up and enjoy. **90m/C DVD, Blu-ray Disc.** *US* Lizzy Caplan, Jessica Lucas, Michael Stahl-David, Mike Vogel, T.J. Miller, Odette Yustman; *D:* Matt Reeves; *W:* Drew Goddard; *C:* Michael Bonvillain.

Clown 1/2 **1953** A broken-down funny man with a worshipful son obtains one last career opportunity. This "Champ"-derived tearjerker features credible playing from Skelton and Considine as father and son, respectively. **91m/B VHS.** Red Skelton, Jane Greer, Tim Considine, Steve Forrest; *D:* Robert Z. Leonard; *C:* Paul Vogel.

Clown Murders 1/2 **1983** Posh Halloween party is undone when a cruel group fakes a kidnapping to ruin a too-prosperous pal's business deal. Awkward thriller boasts little suspense. Candy plays it straight, mostly, in this one. **94m/C VHS, DVD.** John Candy, Al Waxman, Susan Keller, Lawrence Dane; *D:* Martyn Burke.

Clownhouse **1988 (R)** Young brothers are stalked in their home by three murderous clowns. **95m/C VHS, DVD.** Nathan Forrest Winters, Brian McHugh, Sam Rockwell, Viletta Skillman, Timothy Enos, Tree; *D:* Victor Salva.

Clowning Around 1/2 **1992** Simon, who has lived in foster homes all his life, dreams of becoming a famous circus clown. When he's sent to a new home, his new foster parents think his idea is silly, so he runs away and joins the circus. There he meets Anatole, a European clown has-been who can no longer perform because of injuries. Simon believes Anatole can teach him about clowning, so he follows Anatole to Paris to help make his dream come true. Part of the "Wonderworks" series. **165m/C VHS.** *AU* Clayton Williamson, Jean-Michel Dagory, Ernie Dingo; *D:* George Whaley.

Clowning Around 2 1/2 **1993** The continuing story of Sim, whose dream is to become a world-famous clown. Now a member of the Winter Circus in Paris, he is still training with his mentor Anatole. But Sim is dissatisfied and when he befriends Eve, another young clown, he learns an experimental style of clowning which gets them both fired. He first follows Eve to her home in Montreal but then returns to his own home in Australia where he has been left the co-owner of a less-than-successful circus by a former employer. Filmed on location in Paris, France and Perth, Australia. **120m/C VHS.** *AU* Clayton Williamson, Jean-Michel Dagory, Ernie Dingo, Frederique Fouche; *D:* George Whaley.

The Clowns 1/2 **1971 (G)** An idiosyncratic documentary about circus clowns. Director Fellini has fashioned an homage that is sincere, entertaining, and personal. Contains some truly poignant sequences. Made for Italian TV with English subtitles. **90m/C VHS.** *IT* *D:* Federico Fellini; *W:* Federico Fellini, Barnardino Zapponi; *C:* Dario Di Palma; *M:* Nino Rota. **TV**

The Club *Players* **1981 (PG)** A soccer coach tries to train and motivate a mediocre squad into one worth playing for—and perhaps even winning—the league cup. Conventional sports story is significantly improved by Thompson's rendering of the coach. **99m/C VHS, DVD.** *AU* Jack Thompson, Graham Kennedy, John Howard, Alan Cassell; ***D:*** Bruce Beresford; ***W:*** David Williamson.

The Club **1994 (R)** Typical teens-in-peril flick finds the high school prom held in a mysterious old castle with ghouls out to get the unfortunate seniors. Visuals are decent but frights are tepid. **88m/C VHS.** Kim Coates, Joel Wyner, Andrea Roth, Rino Romano, Zack (Zach) Ward, Kelli Taylor, Matthew Ferguson; ***D:*** Brenton Spencer; ***W:*** Robert Cooper; ***M:*** Paul Zaza.

Club Dread *Broken Lizard's Club Dread* **2004 (R)** Fresh off spoofing highway patrolmen in Super Troopers, the Broken Lizard crew takes on beach vacation slasher movies, to lousy results. There's a killer on the loose at an island resort run by Jimmy Buffet wanna-be Coconut Pete (Paxton), interrupting the party. Stupidity ensues. Plot takes a backseat to lame gags, nudity, and slasher pic gore. Vacation elsewhere, because this club is a waste of time. **103m/C DVD.** *US* Bill Paxton, Jay Chandrasekhar, Kevin Heffernan, M.C. Gainey, Jordan Ladd, Lindsay Price, Michael Weaver, Samm Levine, Dan Montgomery Jr., Steve Lemme, Paul Soter, Erik Stolhanske, Brittany Daniel, Nat Faxon, Elena Lyons, Tanja (Tanya) Reichert; ***D:*** Jay Chandrasekhar; ***W:*** Jay Chandrasekhar, Kevin Heffernan, Steve Lemme, Paul Soter, Erik Stolhanske; ***C:*** Lawrence Sher; ***M:*** Nathan Barr.

Club Extinction ½ *Docteur M* **1989 (R)** A near-future thriller in which Berlin is plagued by a wave of suicides. An investigator suspects a spa representative and a media tycoon of being involved. Features a fine international cast, but the film is a lesser venture from prolific master Chabrol. **105m/C VHS.** *GE* Alan Bates, Andrew McCarthy, Jennifer Beals, Jan Niklas, Hanns Zischler, Benoit Regent, Peter Fitz, Wolfgang Preiss, Isolde Barth; ***D:*** Claude Chabrol.

Club Fed ½ **1990 (PG-13)** A rigid prison warden's plot to impose greater discipline is undone by inmate highjinks. Crude laughs and one-dimensional play from a cast of recognizable names and faces. **93m/C VHS, DVD.** Judy Landers, Sherman Hemsley, Karen Black, Burt Young, Rick Schmidt, Allen (Goorwitz) Garfield, Joseph Campanella, Lyle Alzado, Mary Woronov, Debbie Lee Carrington; ***D:*** Nathaniel Christian; ***C:*** Arledge Armenaki.

Club Havana ½ **1946** A benevolent nightclub owner tries to save one of his singers from the depths of despair by reuniting her with her boyfriend. Minor musical with minor musical numbers. ♫ Besame Mucho; Tico Tico. **62m/B VHS.** Tom Neal, Margaret Lindsay, Donald "Don" Douglas, Isabelita, Dorothy Morris, Ernest Truex; ***D:*** Edgar G. Ulmer.

Club Land ½ **2001 (R)** Stuey Walters (Weber) is an unhappy talent agent, working for his hard-driving, abrasive father Willie (Alda) in the 1950s. When their biggest client, comic Lou Montana (Garrett) fires Willie, Stuey doesn't know how to break it to his old man that he doesn't want to continue in the business. **107m/C VHS.** Steven Weber, Alan Alda, Brad Garrett, Jenna Byrne, Louise Lasser, David Deblinger, Eugene Levy; ***D:*** Saul Rubinek; ***W:*** Steven Weber; ***C:*** Rene Ohashi; ***M:*** David Buchbinder. **CABLE**

Club Life **1986 (R)** A hardened biker finds sex, drugs, and violence on the Hollywood streets. What did he expect? Peace, love, and understanding? **93m/C VHS.** Tony Curtis, Dee Wallace, Tom Parsekian, Michael Parks, Jamie Barrett; ***D:*** Norman Thaddeus Vane.

Club Med **1983 (PG)** An insecure comedian and his goofy friend try to make the most of a ski vacation. Perhaps your only chance to see Thicke, Killy, and Coolidge together. **60m/C VHS, DVD.** Alan Thicke, Jim Carrey, Jean-Claude Killy, Rita Coolidge, Ronnie Hawkins; ***D:*** David Mitchell, Bob Giraldi; ***M:*** Peter Bernstein.

Club Paradise ½ **1986 (PG-13)** A Chicago fireman flees the big city for a faltering tropical resort and tries to develop some night life. Somewhat disappointing with Williams largely playing the straight man. Most laughs provided by Martin, particularly when she is assaulted by a shower, and Moranis, who gets lost while windsurfing. **96m/C VHS, DVD.** Robin Williams, Peter O'Toole, Rick Moranis, Andrea Martin, Jimmy Cliff, Brian Doyle-Murray, Twiggy, Eugene Levy, Adolph Caesar, Joanna Cassidy, Mary Gross, Carey Lowell, Robin Duke, Simon Jones; ***D:*** Harold Ramis; ***W:*** Harold Ramis, Brian Doyle-Murray; ***M:*** David Mansfield, Van Dyke Parks.

Club Vampire **1998 (R)** Vampire Zero (Savage) wants to bite stripper Corri (Andreff) but Laura (Frank) gets there first and Corri starts to transform. Vampire leader Aiko (Parris) doesn't want any new converts and sends Zero to kill her. But Zero has other plans. A bore. **77m/C VHS, DVD.** John Savage, Starr Andreeff, Diana Frank, Michael J. Anderson, Marriam Parris, Ross Malinger; ***D:*** Andy Ruben; ***W:*** Andy Ruben; ***C:*** Steve Gainer; ***M:*** Michael Elliott. **VIDEO**

Clubhouse Detectives ½ **1996 (PG)** When Billy witnesses a crime at a neighbor's no one believes him—except his friends, so the clubhouse detectives decide to investigate. **85m/C VHS, DVD.** Michael Ballem, Michael Galeota, Jimmy Galeota, Suzanne Barnes; ***D:*** Eric Hendershot.

Clue ½ **1985 (PG)** The popular boardgame's characters must unravel a night of murder at a spooky Victorian mansion. The entire cast seems to be subsisting on sugar, with wild eyes and frantic movements the order of the day. Butler Curry best survives the uneven script and direction. Warren is appealing too. The theatrical version played with three alternative endings, and the video version shows all three successively. **96m/C VHS, DVD.** Lesley Ann Warren, Tim Curry, Martin Mull, Madeline Kahn, Michael McKean, Christopher Lloyd, Eileen Brennan, Howard Hesseman, Lee Ving, Jane Wiedlin, Colleen Camp, Bill Henderson; ***D:*** Jonathan Lynn; ***W:*** John Landis, Jonathan Lynn; ***C:*** Victor Kemper; ***M:*** John Morris.

Clueless *I Was a Teenage Teenager; No Worries* **1995 (PG-13)** Watch out "Beverly Hills 90210," here comes Cher. No, not the singer Cher, but ultra-filthy-rich brat Cher, who's out to make over her classmates and teachers, specifically flannel-shirted transfer student Tai (Murphy). Aerosmith vamp Silverstone stars as the teenage manipulator who knows all too well how to spend her trust fund. The only person who can match her wits is disapproving stepbrother Josh (Rudd). (Ah, love.) Loosely based on Jane Austen's "Emma," Heckerling, of "Fast Times at Ridgemont High" fame, knows this territory and directs a bright, surprisingly satirical romp. **113m/C VHS, DVD.** Alicia Silverstone, Stacey Dash, Paul Rudd, Brittany Murphy, Donald Adeosun Faison, Julie Brown, Jeremy Sisto, Dan Hedaya, Wallace Shawn, Breckin Meyer, Elisa Donovan, Aida Linares; ***D:*** Amy Heckerling; ***W:*** Amy Heckerling; ***C:*** Bill Pope; ***M:*** David Kitay. MTV Movie Awards '96: Female Perf. (Silverstone), Most Desirable Female (Silverstone); Natl. Soc. Film Critics '95: Screenplay; Blockbuster '96: Female Newcomer, T. (Silverstone).

The Clutching Hand **1936** The Clutching Hand seeks a formula that will turn metal into gold and detective Craig Kennedy is out to prevent him from doing so. A serial in 15 chapters on three cassettes. **268m/B VHS, DVD.** Jack Mulhall, Rex Lease, Mae Busch, William Farnum, Robert Frazer, Reed Howes, Marion Shilling; ***D:*** Al(bert) Herman.

Coach ½ **1978 (PG)** Sexy woman is unintentionally hired to coach a high school basketball team and mold rookies into lusty young champions. Low-grade roundball fever. **100m/C VHS, DVD.** Cathy Lee Crosby, Michael Biehn, Keenan Wynn, Sidney Wicks; ***D:*** Bud Townsend.

Coach Carter **2005 (PG-13)** Based on a true story of a coach who benched his entire team until their grades improved. Coach Carter (Jackson) is a self-made sporting goods businessman who decides to take a basketball coaching job at his alma mater Richmond High. Carter is a strict disciplinarian and makes it clear that the boys must follow a certain set of rules to play for him, and each student is required to sign a contract to maintain a grade point average of 2.3. Despite the familiar plot of inspirational teacher making a difference, the movie rises above due to a good supporting cast and a great performance by Jackson, making excellent use of his commanding screen presence. **137m/C DVD, Blu-ray Disc, UMD.** *US* Samuel L. Jackson, Robert Ri'chard, Debbi (Deborah) Morgan, Rick Gonzalez, Antwon Tanner, Denise Dowse, Rob Brown, Ashanti, Nana Gbewonyo, Channing Tatum, Texas Battle; ***D:*** Thomas Carter; ***W:*** Mark Schwahn, John Gatins; ***C:*** Sharon Meir; ***M:*** Trevor Rabin.

Coal Miner's Daughter **1980 (PG)** A strong bio of country singer Loretta Lynn, who rose from Appalachian poverty to Nashville riches. Spacek is perfect in the lead, and she even provides acceptable rendering of Lynn's tunes. Band drummer Helm shines as Lynn's father, and Jones is strong as Lynn's downhome husband. Uneven melodrama toward the end, but the film is still a good one. ♫ Coal Miner's Daughter; Sweet Dreams of You; I'm a Honky-Tonk Girl; You're Lookin' at Country; One's On the Way; You Ain't Woman Enough to Take My Man; Back in My Baby's Arms. **125m/C VHS, DVD.** Sissy Spacek, Tommy Lee Jones, Levon Helm, Beverly D'Angelo; ***D:*** Michael Apted; ***C:*** Ralf Bode. Oscars '80: Actress (Spacek); Golden Globes '81: Actress—Mus./Comedy (Spacek), Film—Mus./Comedy; L.A. Film Critics '80: Actress (Spacek); Natl. Bd. of Review '80: Actress (Spacek); N.Y. Film Critics '80: Actress (Spacek); Natl. Soc. Film Critics '80: Actress (Spacek).

Coast of Skeletons ½ **1963** Insurance investigator Sanders learns unscrupulous Magnus is looting sunken ships whose contents belong to Sanders' employers. Barely passable reworking of Edgar Wallace novel "Sanders of the Rivers." **90m/C DVD.** *GB* Richard Todd, Dale Robertson, Heinz Drache, Elga Andersen, Marianne Koch, Derek Nimmo; ***D:*** Robert Lynn; ***W:*** Anthony Scott Veitch; ***C:*** Stephen Dade; ***M:*** Christopher Whelen.

The Coast Patrol ½ **1925** B. Reeves Eason, responsible for the chariot scene in the silent "Ben Hur" and the action scenes in "The Charge of the Light Brigade," directed Fay in one of her earliest parts, eight years before the role that prompted her to say "I didn't realize that King Kong and I were going to be together for the rest of our lives, and longer... " Much Eason-style high action when smugglers meet the coast patrol. **63m/B VHS.** Kenneth McDonald, Claire De Lorez, Fay Wray; ***D:*** Bud Barsky.

Coast to Coast **1980 (PG)** A wacky woman escapes from a mental institution and teams with a pugnacious trucker for a cross-country spree. Ostensibly freewheeling comedy is only occasionally worthwhile despite appropriate playing from leads Cannon and Blake, who deserve better. **95m/C VHS.** Dyan Cannon, Robert (Bobby) Blake, Quinn (K.) Redeker, Michael Lerner, Maxine Stuart, William Lucking; ***D:*** Joseph Sargent; ***M:*** Charles Bernstein.

Coast to Coast **2004 (R)** An older married couple isn't sure they want to stay together anymore but luckily they have loads of time to figure things out cruising from Connecticut to L.A. to see their son tie the knot. **107m/C VHS, DVD.** Richard Dreyfuss, Judy Davis, Selma Blair, Maximilian Schell, Fred Ward, Saul Rubinek, John Salley, Paul Mazursky, Kate Lynch, Richard Fitzpatrick, Clare Coulter, Catherine Disher, James Kee, Nancy Sakovich, David Julian Hirsh, Owen Rotharmel, Rick Mota, Angela Asher, Catherine Burdon, Lyssa J. Caster, Laura Catalano, Paul Essiembre, Dominic Fung, Paula Garrido, Chris Gillett, Carolyn Goff, Lindsay Leese, Richard Partington, Les Porter, Krista Sutton, Joreen Todd; ***D:*** Paul Mazursky; ***W:*** Frederic Raphael; ***C:*** Jean Lepine; ***M:*** Bill Conti. **TV**

Coastlines **2002 (R)** Pulp noir in the Florida panhandle. Sonny (Olyphant) took the fall for his drug partners Fred (Forsythe) and Eddie (Lucas) Vance. Out of prison, he wants the $200K they owe him and to be left alone. The Vances would like Sonny gone permanently, which brings in Sonny's best bud, Dave (Brolin), who's the local sheriff, and his unsatisfied wife Ann (Wynter), immediately leading to a familiar and not very exciting triangle. Unfortunately, this is a mix of crime and sex that never successfully meshes together. **110m/C DVD.** *US* Timothy Olyphant, Josh Brolin, Sarah Wynter, Scott Wilson, Angela Bettis, Josh(ua) Lucas, Robert Wisdom, Daniel von Bargen, Blake Lindsley, Bob Glaudini, Edwin Hodge, Abigail Mavity, Elizabeth Caity; ***D:*** Victor Nunez; ***W:*** Victor Nunez; ***C:*** Virgil Marcus Mirano; ***M:*** Charles Engstrom.

Cobb **1994 (R)** Biography of Ty Cobb (Jones), the universally acknowledged "most hated man in baseball" who, near the end of his life, realizes he doesn't want to be remembered in that way. So he hires sportswriter Al Stump (Wuhl) to ghostwrite (read: sugarcoat) his life story. As seen through Stump's eyes, Cobb is an unrelenting, petty, bigoted, hateful, paranoid, drunken, and yet compelling man. They form an uneasy bond as Stump duly records the fiction Cobb is feeding him, secretly deciding to write the truth after the legend's death. Jones is at his scene-chewing, antagonistic best, while Wuhl seems both overwhelmed and overshadowed as the embattled Stump. Shelton has something to say about American hero worship and a celebrity's desire for posterity, but with the focus intent on portraying Cobb's meanness, it's hard to say what. Surprisingly little baseball action for a baseball bio. Based on Stump's "Cobb: A Biography." **128m/C VHS, DVD.** Tommy Lee Jones, Robert Wuhl, Lolita (David) Davidovich; ***D:*** Ron Shelton; ***W:*** Ron Shelton; ***C:*** Russell Boyd.

Cobra **1925** To pay off the debts incurred by his profligate playboyance, Valentino takes a job with an antique dealer, falls for the dealer's secretary and arranges an assignation with the dealer's wife, who is inconveniently killed at the designated rendezvous. Complications abound as Valentino finds himself Sheik out of luck. Lesser Valentino effort was released a year before the famous heartthrob's untimely death and enjoyed a rather acrid critical reception. Which isn't to say the public didn't flock to see the Italian stallion flare his nostrils. **75m/B VHS, DVD.** Rudolph Valentino, Nita Naldi, Casson Ferguson, Gertrude (Olmstead) Olmsted; ***D:*** Joseph Henabery.

The Cobra *Il Cobra; El Cobra* **1968** A tightlipped U.S. agent ogles a voluptuous siren when not fighting opium smugglers from the Middle East. A must for all admirers of Ekberg. **93m/C VHS.** Dana Andrews, Anita Ekberg; ***D:*** Mario Sequi.

Cobra ½ *Le Sant de l'Ange* **1971** A hired killer destroys most of a mob family and becomes the target of revenge for the lone survivor. Moody thriller boasts an international cast. **93m/C VHS.** *FR IT* Sterling Hayden, Senta Berger, Jean Yanne; ***D:*** Yves Boisset.

Cobra **1986 (R)** A cold-blooded cop protects a model from a gang of deranged killers. Low-brow, manipulative action fare void of feeling. Truly exploitive, with little expression from the leads. Highlight is the extended chase sequence. Based on the Paula Gosling novel "Fair Game," which was remade under the book's title (and in a more faithful adaptation) in 1995. **87m/C VHS, DVD.** Sylvester Stallone, Reni Santoni, Brigitte Nielsen, Andrew (Andy) Robinson; ***D:*** George P. Cosmatos; ***W:*** Sylvester Stallone; ***C:*** Ric Waite; ***M:*** Sylvester Levay.

The Cobra Strikes ½ **1948** Nosey thief gets more than he bargained for when he works his way through an inventor's studio. Low-budget and unexceptional. **62m/B VHS.** Sheila Ryan, Richard Fraser, Leslie Brooks, Herbert (Hayes) Heyes; ***D:*** Charles Reisner.

Cobra Verde *Slave Coast* **1988** Even by Herzog/Kinski standards, their last collaboration was one wild trip. Kinski is a 19th-century Brazilian bandit, known as Cobra Verde, who finds work as a slave overseer on a sugar plantation. When he impregnates all three of the owner's daughters, he's sent on an impossible mission to re-open the slave trade with a mad African king. Discovering he's being cheated, Cobra Verde trains an army of women to overthrow the king, so he can control the slave trade himself. Based on the novel "The Viceroy of Ouidah" by Bruce Chatwin. German with subtitles. **110m/C VHS, DVD.** *GE* Klaus Kinski, Peter Berling, Jose Lewgoy, Salvatore Basile; ***D:*** Werner Herzog; ***W:*** Werner Herzog; ***C:*** Viktor Ruzicka; ***M:*** Popul Vuh.

Cobra Woman ✐✐ ½ **1944** Technicolor adventure fantasy about the jungle queen (Montez) of a cobra-worshipping cult and her evil twin sister who wants the throne for herself. **70m/C VHS.** Maria Montez, Jon Hall, Sabu, Edgar Barrier, Lois Collier, Lon Chaney Jr., Mary Nash, Samuel S. Hinds, Moroni Olsen; ***D:*** Robert Siodmak; ***W:*** Richard Brooks, Gene Lewis; ***C:*** William Howard Greene; ***M:*** Edward Ward.

The Cobweb ✐✐ **1955** Shady goings on are uncovered at a psychiatric ward run by a bunch of neurotic administrators. A strong cast, director and producer do not add much to this dull outing. **125m/C** Lauren Bacall, Richard Widmark, Gloria Grahame, Charles Boyer, Lillian Gish, John Kerr, Susan Strasberg, Oscar Levant, Tommy Rettig, Paul Stewart, Adele Jergens, Bert Freed, Sandy Descher, Fay Wray, Virginia Christine; ***D:*** Vincente Minnelli; ***C:*** George J. Folsey.

The Coca-Cola Kid ✐✐✐ ½ **1984 (R)** Smug U.S. sales exec Becker (Roberts) treks to Australia to improve regional sales and becomes embroiled in sexual and professional shenanigans. He gets involved with free-spirited secretary Terri (sexy Scacchi) and discovers that a soft drink locally brewed by eccenric McDowall (Kerr) is his determined competition. Roberts is strong in the difficult lead role, and Scacchi is compelling in an awkwardly constructed part. Ambitious satire is somewhat scattershot, with more storylines than it needs. Still, filmmaker Makavejev is usually capable of juggling the entire enterprise. **94m/C VHS, DVD.** *AU* Eric Roberts, Greta Scacchi, Bill Kerr, Chris Haywood, Kris McQuade, Max Gilles; ***D:*** Dusan Makavejev; ***W:*** Frank Moorhouse; ***C:*** Dean Semler; ***M:*** William Motzing.

Cocaine Cowboys ✐ ½ **1979 (R)** Lame rockers support themselves between gigs by peddling drugs then find out they've run afoul of the mob. Palance is the only worthwhile aspect of this rambling venture produced at Andy Warhol's home. **90m/C VHS, DVD.** Jack Palance, Andy Warhol, Tom Sullivan, Suzanna Love, Richard Young; ***D:*** Ulli Lommel; ***W:*** Ulli Lommel, Victor Bockris, Tom Sullivan; ***C:*** Jochen Breitenstein; ***M:*** Elliot Goldenthal.

Cocaine Fiends ✐✐ *The Pace That Kills* **1936** Drug use leads siblings into a squalid life of addiction, crime, prostitution, and eventually suicide. Ostensibly straight morality tale functions better as loopy camp. Features memorable slang. **74m/B VHS, DVD.** Lois January, Noel Madison, Willy Castello, Dean Benton, Lois Lindsay, Sheila (Manors) Mannors; ***D:*** William A. O'Connor.

Cocaine: One Man's Seduction ✐✐ ½ **1983** Documents one man's degeneration into drug addiction. Weaver snorts convincingly in lead. **97m/C VHS.** Dennis Weaver, Karen Grassle, Pamela Bellwood, David Ackroyd; ***D:*** Paul Wendkos; ***M:*** Brad Fiedel. **TV**

Cocaine Wars ✐ **1986 (R)** An undercover U.S. agent kills dozens while trying to rescue his kidnapped girlfriend from an evil South American drug tycoon. Violent, but otherwise unaffecting. **82m/C VHS.** John Schneider, Kathryn Witt, Royal Dano; ***D:*** Hector Olivera.

Cock & Bull Story ✐✐ *Southside* **2003** Gritty examination of the machismo world of boxing and homophobia in a depressed working-class environment. Up-and-coming boxer Travis (Roberts) is the last hope for aging manager/trainer Pascoe (Mullavey). Pascoe (and everyone else) disapproves of the inseparable friendship between Travis and unemployed screw-up Jacko (Green). Rumors begin to circulate about Travis's sexuality and Jacko's own volatility makes matters worse. Of course, on the night of Travis's biggest fight, matters come to a head between the two men. Adapted from the play by Richard Crowe and Richard Zajdlic. **102m/C DVD.** Bret Roberts, Brian Austin Green, Greg Mullavey, Wendy Fowler, Darin Heames; ***D:*** Billy Hayes; ***W:*** Billy Hayes; ***C:*** Ben Kufrin; ***M:*** Pierpaolo Tiano.

Cockeyed Cavaliers ✐✐ **1934** Wheeler and Woolsey are stockaded for stealing the Duke's horses and carriage. To escape jail they swap clothes with some drunken royalty. **70m/B VHS.** Bert Wheeler, Robert Woolsey, Dorothy Lee, Thelma Todd; ***D:*** Mark Sandrich.

Cockfighter ✐✐✐ *Gamblin' Man; Born to Kill; Wild Drifters* **1974 (R)** A unique, grim portrait of a cockfighting trainer. Oates, in the lead, provides voiceover narrations, but the film otherwise remains silent until the end. Strong support from Stanton. Interesting, violent fare. **84m/C VHS, DVD.** Warren Oates, Harry Dean Stanton, Richard B. Shull, Troy Donahue, Millie Perkins, Robert Earl Jones, Warren Finnerty, Ed Begley Jr., Charles Willeford; ***D:*** Monte Hellman; ***W:*** Charles Willeford; ***C:*** Nestor Almendros; ***M:*** Michael Franks.

Cocktail ✐✐ ½ **1988 (R)** A smug young man finds fame and fortune as a proficient, flashy bartender, charming the ladies with his bottle and glass juggling act. Slick, superficial film boasts a busy soundtrack and serviceable exchanges between male leads Cruise and Brown. There's less chemistry between Cruise and love interest Shue. Filmed in a high-tech rock video style. **103m/C VHS, DVD.** Tom Cruise, Bryan Brown, Elisabeth Shue, Lisa Banes, Laurence Luckinbill, Kelly Lynch, Gina Gershon, Ron Dean, Paul Benedict; ***D:*** Roger Donaldson; ***W:*** Heywood Gould; ***C:*** Dean Semler; ***M:*** J. Peter Robinson. Golden Raspberries '88: Worst Picture, Worst Screenplay.

Coco Before Chanel ✐✐ *Coco avant Chanel* **2009 (PG-13)** Biopic of French fashion designer Gabrielle "Coco" Chanel from her humble upbringing to the height of the international fashion world and popular culture. The orphaned Gabrielle (Tautou) is working as a seamstress and cabaret singer when she meets millionaire roue Etienne Balsan (Poelvoorde), who makes her his mistress. Given the time, money, and opportunity, Chanel begins to experiment with simplifying the era's overly-fussy clothing and making herself both financially and sexually independent. Too much of the focus is wasted on a dull romance, giving little insight into Chanel's business savvy approach to becoming the icon of her day. Tautou's performance, unfortunately, takes a back seat to the extravagant fashions on parade. French with subtitles. **105m/C DVD.** *FR* Audrey Tautou, Benoit Poelvoorde, Alessandro Nivola, Marie Gillain, Emmanuelle Devos; ***D:*** Anne Fontaine; ***W:*** Anne Fontaine, Camille Fontaine, Christopher Gore; ***C:*** Christophe Beaucarne; ***M:*** Alexandre Desplat.

Coco Chanel ✐✐ **2008** Lavish—if melodramatic—biopic of the French fashion designer (played by Boblova and MacLaine). Story begins in 1954 with the aged Chanel seemingly irrelevant after a disastrous comeback attempt. Then it flashes back to the 1910s when the young Coco leaves the orphanage for work as a seamstress. Brashly appealing, Chanel is soon persuading her wealthy male admirers to fund her fashion ambitions as she negotiates two world wars and various romantic dilemmas. **139m/C DVD.** Shirley MacLaine, Barbara Bobulova, Sagamore Stevenin, Olivier Sitruk, Malcolm McDowell, Valetino Lodovini; ***D:*** Christian Duguay; ***W:*** Enrico Medioli; ***C:*** Fabrizio Lucci; ***M:*** Andrea Guerra. **CABLE**

Coco Chanel & Igor Stravinksy **2009** Depicts the brief 1920s affair between the married composer (with the ailing, jealous wife) and the diva fashion designer, who becomes his benefactor. Mouglalis began working as a Chanel model in 2002. **118m/C DVD.** *FR* Mads Mikkelsen, Anna Mouglalis, Elena Morozova, Anatole Taubman; ***D:*** Jan Kounen; ***W:*** Jan Kounen, Carol de Boutiny, Chris Greenhalgh, David Ungaro; ***M:*** Gabriel Yared.

The Cocoanuts ✐✐ ½ **1929** In their film debut, the Marx Brothers create their trademark, indescribable mayhem. Stagey, technically crude comedy nonetheless delights with zany, free-for-all exchanges, antics. Includes famous "viaduct" exchange. **96m/B VHS, DVD.** Groucho Marx, Chico Marx, Harpo Marx, Zeppo Marx, Margaret Dumont, Kay Francis, Oscar Shaw, Mary Eaton, Cyril Ring, Basil Ruysdael; ***D:*** Robert Florey, Joseph Santley; ***W:*** George S. Kaufman, Morrie Ryskind; ***C:*** George J. Folsey; ***M:*** Irving Berlin.

Cocoon ✐✐✐ **1985 (PG-13)** Humanist fantasy in which senior citizens discover their fountain of youth is actually a breeding ground for aliens. Heartwarming, one-of-a kind drama showcases elderly greats Ameche, Brimley, Gilford, Cronyn, and Tandy. A commendable, recommendable venture. Based on David Saperstein's novel and followed by "Cocoon: The Return." **117m/C VHS, DVD.** Wilford Brimley, Brian Dennehy, Steve Guttenberg, Don Ameche, Tahnee Welch, Jack Gilford, Hume Cronyn, Jessica Tandy, Gwen Verdon, Maureen Stapleton, Tyrone Power Jr., Barret Oliver, Linda Harrison, Herta Ware, Clint Howard; ***D:*** Ron Howard; ***W:*** Tom Benedek; ***M:*** James Horner. Oscars '85: Support. Actor (Ameche), Visual FX.

Cocoon: The Return ✐✐ **1988 (PG)** Old timers who left with aliens in "Cocoon" return to earth and face grave problems. Less compelling sequel misses guiding hand of earlier film's director, Ron Howard. Still, most of cast from the original is on board here, and the film has its moments. **116m/C VHS, DVD.** Don Ameche, Wilford Brimley, Steve Guttenberg, Maureen Stapleton, Hume Cronyn, Jessica Tandy, Gwen Verdon, Jack Gilford, Tahnee Welch, Courteney Cox, Brian Dennehy, Barret Oliver; ***D:*** Daniel Petrie; ***C:*** Tak Fujimoto; ***M:*** James Horner.

C.O.D. ✐ **1983 (PG)** Bosom buddies must develop advertising campaign for brassiere producer or find their careers are bust. Premise milked for all its worth, so you may want to keep abreast of this one. On the other hand, you may not give a hoot. Oh well, tit for tat. **96m/C VHS.** Chris Lemmon, Olivia Pascal, Jennifer Richards, Corinne Alphen, Teresa Ganzel, Carole (Raphaelle) Davis; ***D:*** Chuck Vincent; ***W:*** R.J. Marx.

The Code ✐ ½ *Thick as Thieves* **2009 (R)** Bad heist movie that telegraphs its twists. Ripley (Freeman), a criminal indebted to the Russian mob, recruits thief Jack (Banderas) to help him pull off a heist of Faberge eggs. Only things aren't what they seem—except for the actors not being very interested in what's going on. **103m/C DVD.** Morgan Freeman, Antonio Banderas, Robert Forster, Radha Mitchell, Rade Serbedzija; ***D:*** Mimi Leder; ***W:*** Ted Humphrey; ***C:*** Julio Macat; ***M:*** Atli Orvarsson. **VIDEO**

Code 46 ✐✐ ½ **2003 (R)** Stylish, sci-fi noir explores the not-too-distant future where, in order to travel from city to cloistered city, people need "papelles," a combination visa, passport and genetic ID code. Evidently, excessive cloning has led to DNA protected zones that require strict policing. Robbins is William Geld, an investigator who has been infected with an empathy virus that enables him to read minds. Geld is tracking forged papelles, which leads him to Shanghai and the suspect Maria (Morton), a Shanghai factory worker. Geld, however falls for Maria and they enter into an intense love affair. Some provocative ideas and good premise are compromised by lack of chemistry between Robbins and Morton. **92m/C DVD.** *GB* Tim Robbins, Samantha Morton, Jeanne Balibar, Om Puri, Essie Davis, Shelley King, David Fahm; ***D:*** Michael Winterbottom; ***W:*** Frank Cottrell-Boyce; ***C:*** Alwin Kuchler, Marcel Zyskind; ***M:*** David Holmes.

Code Name Alpha ✐✐ *Red Dragon; A-009 Missione Hong Kong* **1967** You don't have to have a federal case of intelligence to figure out where this FBI story's going and how it's going to get there. Someone's smuggling sophisticated electrical components to the communists, and a team of intelligence agents, including Granger and Schiaffino, hike over to Hong Kong to break up the party. Based on the story "Le Riviere des Trois Jonques" by Georges Godefroy. **89m/C VHS.** *IT GE* Stewart Granger, Rosanna Schiaffino, Harald Juhnke, Paul Klinger, Helga Sommerfeld, Horst Frank; ***D:*** Ernest Hofbauer.

Code Name: Chaos ✐✐ *Spies, Lies, and Alibis* **1990 (R)** A political spoof featuring a group of renegade spies trying to come up with a get-rich-quick scheme. It involves inventing a global crisis in a small Asian country but the plan comes under the scrutiny of a CIA agent who's not in on the scheme. **96m/C VHS.** Robert Loggia, Diane Ladd, David Warner, Alice Krige, Brian Kerwin; ***D:*** Antony Thomas.

Code Name: Dancer ✐✐ *Her Secret Life* **1987** A retired spy leaves her peaceful life, husband, and family to take care of business in Cuba. **93m/C VHS, DVD.** Kate Capshaw, Jeroen Krabbe, Gregory Sierra, Cliff DeYoung, Valerie Mahaffey, James Sloyan; ***D:*** Buzz Kulik; ***M:*** Georges Delerue. **TV**

Code Name: Diamond Head ✐ **1977** In Hawaii, a secret agent is assigned to retrieve a deadly chemical that has been hidden by a master of disguises. **78m/C VHS.** Roy Thinnes, France Nuyen, Zulu, Ian McShane; ***D:*** Jeannot Szwarc. **TV**

Code Name: Emerald ✐ **1985 (PG)** WWII drama in which an American agent must stop an enemy spy with knowledge of impending D-Day invasion. Conventional TV fare boasts a fine performance by von Sydow, but Stolz is hopelessly miscast as an adult. Perhaps the only film featuring both Buchholz and Berger. First feature film by NBC-TV network. **95m/C VHS.** Ed Harris, Max von Sydow, Eric Stoltz, Horst Buchholz, Helmut Berger, Cyrielle Claire, Patrick Stewart, Graham Crowden; ***D:*** Jonathan Sanger; ***W:*** Ronald Bass; ***M:*** John Addison.

Code Name: The Cleaner ✐ ½ **2007 (PG-13)** Low-brow action-comedy for Mr. The Entertainer's fans. Jake wakes up in a hotel room with no memory, next to a dead FBI agent and a lot of cash. Va-voomish Diane (Sheridan) picks him up, says they're married, and takes Jake to a grandiose mansion. Jake has flashbacks that convince him he's a secret agent and Diane is after a computer chip. When Jake runs into waitress Gina (Liu), she tells him he's actually a janitor and head trauma is causing his delusions. Ah, but there's more to the story (a lot of it extremely silly). Still, Liu is sexy in leather and the pic is nothing if not good-natured. **91m/C DVD.** *US* Cedric the Entertainer, Lucy Liu, Nicolette Sheridan, Mark Dacascos, Callum Keith Rennie, Niecy Nash, Will Patton, DeRay David; ***D:*** Les Mayfield; ***W:*** Robert Adetuyi, George Gallo; ***C:*** David Franco; ***M:*** George S. Clinton.

Code Name: Zebra ✐ ½ **1984** The Zebra Force helps the cops put bad guys away. When the bad guys get out, they want revenge. The result: lots of violence and action. Wasn't released theatrically. **96m/C VHS, DVD.** Jim Mitchum, Mike Lane, Timothy Brown, Joe Dante, Deana Jurgens, Frank Sinatra Jr., Robert Z'Dar; ***D:*** Joe Tornatore.

Code of Honor ✐ *Kill Squad* **1982** Prominent businessman embarks on mission of revenge when police fail to apprehend his wife's rapist. No surprise here. You either enjoy this sort of thing or you lead a reasonably fulfilling life. **90m/C VHS, DVD.** Frank Ramirez, Jeff Risk, Jean Glaude, Jerry Johnson, Cameron Mitchell, Mark Sabin; ***D:*** Patrick G. Donahue; ***W:*** Patrick G. Donahue; ***C:*** Christopher W. Strattan; ***M:*** Joseph Conlan.

Code of Honor ✐✐ ½ *Sweet Revenge* **1984** A young woman vows revenge on the military commanders who caused her brother's demise. Neatly made psychological thriller is surprisingly good for a TV movie. **105m/C VHS, DVD.** Kevin Dobson, Wings Hauser, Alec Baldwin, Merritt Butrick, Kelly McGillis, Alfre Woodard, Savannah Smith, Helen Hunt, Dana Elcar; ***D:*** David Green.

Code of Silence ✐✐ **1985 (R)** A police loner must contend with both a gang war and police department corruption. Hectic, violent action-drama with some wild stunts. **100m/C VHS, DVD.** Chuck Norris, Henry Silva, Bert Remsen, Molly Hagan, Nathan Davis, Dennis Farina; ***D:*** Andrew Davis; ***W:*** Michael Butler, Mike Gray.

Code of the Fearless ✐ **1939** A cowboy wins the heart of a beautiful maiden while bringing evildoers to justice. **56m/B VHS.** Fred Scott, Claire Rochelle, John Merton, Harry Harvey, Walter McGrail, Roger Williams; ***D:*** Bernard B. Ray.

Code of the Outlaw ✐ ½ **1942** Young Tim is the son of a bandit and has promised his father he'll never snitch. The Three Mesquiteers are after the men who stole the payroll from the Wells Fargo office and kill Tim's father during a chase. They take the boy in, hoping he'll tell them about the other gang members, but the gangs want to get to Tim before he can do that. The 42nd film in the series. **55m/B DVD.** Bob Steele, Tom Tyler, Rufe Davis, Bennie Bartlett, Weldon Heyburn, Donald Curtis, Linda Leighton, John Ince, Bob Steele, Tom Tyler, Rufe Davis, Bennie Bartlett, Weldon Heyburn, Donald Curtis, Linda Leighton, John Ince; ***D:*** John English, John English; ***W:*** Barry Shipman, Barry Shipman; ***C:*** Reggie Lanning, Reggie Lanning.

Code Unknown *Code Unknown: Incomplete Tales of Several Journeys; Code Inconnu: Recit Incomplet De Divers Voyages* **2000** Teeanger Jean (Hamidi) has run away from the farm work his father (Bierbichler) expects from him. He goes to see his brother Georges (Neuvic), a war photographer, in Paris. Although Georges is frequently away, Jean stays with Georges' lover Anne (Binoche) in their apartment. On the street, Jean insults Romanian beggar Maria (Gheorghiu) and gets into a scuffle with young black teacher Amadou (Yenke) over Jean's lack of respect. The characters lives continue to interact in random ways. French and Romanian with subtitles. **118m/C VHS, DVD.** *FR* Juliette Binoche, Alexandre Hamidi, Thierry Neuvic, Sepp Bierbichler, Ona Lu Yenke, Luminita Gheorghiu; ***D:*** Michael Haneke; ***W:*** Michael Haneke; ***C:*** Jurgen Jurges; ***M:*** Giba Concalves.

Codename: Foxfire *Slay It Again, Sam* **1985** An attractive secret agent is framed for wrongdoing and must clear her name by tracking the enemy spy lurking within the intelligence network. Always interesting Cassidy is an asset, but this by-the-numbers TV film is otherwise a misappropriation of the term "intelligence" in relation to espionage. **99m/C VHS.** Joanna Cassidy, John McCook, Sheryl Lee Ralph, Henry Jones, Luke Andreas; ***D:*** Corey Allen.

Codename: Icarus **1985** A young mathematical genius, enrolled at a special school for accelerated study, uncovers evil government plots to use the students for espionage. **106m/C VHS, DVD.** *GB* Barry Angel, Jack Galloway; ***D:*** Marilyn Fox. **TV**

Codename: Jaguar **½ 2000 (R)** Innocent Stuart Dempsey (Nucci) has just moved to New York when he is mistaken for an international assassin by both the CIA and the FBI. The assassin, codenamed Jaguar, is in town to kill the visiting Russian prez. But is innocent Stuart really that innocent after all? **93m/C VHS, DVD.** Danny Nucci, David Carradine, Victoria Sanchez, Jack Langedijk; ***D:*** John Hamilton; ***W:*** Tim Kring; ***C:*** Bert Tougas. **VIDEO**

Codename Kyril **½ 1991 (R)** Woodward plays a British spy pitted against Soviet assassin Kyril (Charleson) who's been sent to England by the KGB to rout out a double agent. Turns out there's more to it than Kyril knows, and nobody loves an assassin. Based on John Trenhaile's "A Man Called Kyril," the script is slow from the gun, but eventually builds something akin to momentum. **115m/C VHS.** Edward Woodward, Ian Charleson, Denholm Elliott, Joss Ackland, Richard E. Grant, Sven-Bertil Taube, Catherine Nielson, John McEnery, Peter Vaughan, James Laurenson; ***D:*** Ian Sharp; ***W:*** John Hopkins. **CABLE**

Codename: Terminate **½ 1990** Title says it all in this tender exploration of the human condition. Jungle-trained mercenaries grab their guns and go after an American pilot shot down behind enemy lines. **84m/C VHS.** Robert Mason, Jim Gaines.

Codename: Vengeance **1987 (R)** A macho fellow tries to stop a killer holding the shah's wife and son hostage. Dated. **97m/C VHS.** Robert Ginty, Cameron Mitchell, Shannon Tweed; ***D:*** David Winters.

Codename: Wildgeese **½** *Geheimecode Wildganse* **1984 (R)** The big-name cast of this meandering mercenary macho-rama probably wish they'd been credited under code names; solid histrionics cannot a silly script save. A troop of commandos-for-hire are engaged by the Drug Enforcement Administration to obliterate an opium operation in Asia's infamous Golden Triangle, and much mindless agitation ensues. **101m/C VHS, DVD.** *IT GE* Lewis Collins, Lee Van Cleef, Ernest Borgnine, Klaus Kinski, Mimsy Farmer; ***D:*** Anthony M. Dawson.

Cody **1977** A former bronco buster wants his son to "take it like a man" when the boy's dog dies. Then a mystical goose arrives to mellow the old man. That's really the plot. **82m/C VHS.** Tony Becker, Terry Evans; ***D:*** William D. Blackburn.

Coffee and Cigarettes **2003 (R)** Director/writer Jarmusch returns after a five-year absence with these 11 short films inspired by or having to do with the two addictions of the title. Shot in black and white, the short vignettes feature a wide range of talent from Cate Blanchett to Steven Wright. Jarmusch filmed the shorts over a period of 17 years between projects, and while some of the episodes are better than others there are more hits than misses. The highlight is "Somewhere in California" featuring Tom Waits and Iggy Pop. Jarmusch again demonstrates why he is the king of independent film makers today. **96m/B DVD.** *US* Iggy Pop, Tom Waits, Cate Blanchett, Steve Buscemi, Alfred Molina, RZA, Steve Coogan, Jack White, Roberto Benigni, Joie Lee, Steven Wright, Cinque Lee, Alex Descas, Isaach de Bankole, Michael Hogan, Meg White, Joe Rigano, Vinnie Vella, Vinnie Vella Jr., Renee French, E.J. Rodriguez, Bill Rice, Taylor Mead, Katy Hansz, GZA; ***Cameos:*** Bill Murray; ***D:*** Jim Jarmusch; ***W:*** Jim Jarmusch; ***C:*** Tom DiCillo, Frederick Elmes, Ellen Kuras, Robby Muller.

Coffee Date **2006** Generally sweet romantic comedy has straight-laced Todd's (Bray) loser brother Barry (Silverman) decides to hook him up with an online date. Only Barry places the ad in the "men seeking men" section. Todd chats with Kelly (Cruz) online, they arrange to meet for coffee, and—whoops—Kelly's a guy! The two become friends and everyone assumes divorced Todd is gay—and maybe Todd isn't quite as upset as he thinks he should be. **93m/C DVD.** Wilson Cruz, Jonathan Silverman, Sally Kirkland, Leigh Taylor-Young, Jonathan Bray, Jason Stuart, Elaine Hendrix, Deborah Gibson; ***D:*** Stuart Wade; ***W:*** Stuart Wade; ***C:*** Howard Wexler; ***M:*** Eban Schletter.

Coffy **1973 (R)** A beautiful woman feigns drug addiction to discover and destroy the evil dealers responsible for her sister's death. Grier is everything in this exploitative flick full of violence and nudity. **91m/C VHS, DVD.** William (Bill) Elliott, Sid Haig, Pam Grier, Booker Bradshaw, Robert DoQui, Allan Arbus; ***D:*** Jack Hill; ***W:*** Jack Hill; ***C:*** Paul Lohmann; ***M:*** Roy Ayers.

Cohen and Tate **1988 (R)** Two antagonistic mob hitmen kidnap a nine-year-old who witnessed his parent's recent murder by the mob. In order to survive, the boy begins to play one psycho off the other. **113m/C VHS.** Roy Scheider, Adam Baldwin, Harley Cross, Cooper Huckabee; ***D:*** Eric Red; ***W:*** Eric Red; ***M:*** Bill Conti.

Cold and Dark **½ 2005** Muddled Brit frightener finds young copper John Dark (Goss) being mentored by experienced detective Mortimer Shade (Howarth) as they investigate a series of strange murders. Dark eventually realizes that his partner is committing the crimes; having been taken over by an alien parasite, Shade needs fresh blood to survive. But Dark worries (as well he should!) when he realizes that Shade is becoming more monster and less human each time he kills. **94m/C DVD.** *GB* Luke Goss, Kevin Howarth, Cassandra Bell, Michael Culkin, Matt Lucas, Carly Jane Turnbull, Steven Elder; ***D:*** Andrew Goth; ***W:*** Joanne Reay; ***C:*** Sam McCurdy; ***M:*** Lauren Yason.

Cold Around the Heart **1997 (R)** Familiar crime/road movie finds sensitive jewel thief Ned (Caruso) partnering up (both in and out of the sack) with tough cookie Jude (Lynch). Only in their latest heist, Jude takes off with the diamonds and Ned's in pursuit across the southwest but, nice guy that Ned is, he stops to help out pregnant, black hitchhiker Bec (Dash). If you don't expect much, you won't be disappointed. **96m/C VHS, DVD.** David Caruso, Kelly Lynch, Stacey Dash, Christopher Noth, John Spencer; ***D:*** John Ridley; ***W:*** John Ridley; ***C:*** Malik Hassan Sayeed; ***M:*** Mason Daring.

Cold Blood **½** *Das Amulett des Todes* **1975 (R)** A pair of kidnap victims turn the tables on their captors. **90m/C VHS, DVD.** *GE* Rutger Hauer, Vera Tschechowa, Horst Frank, Gunther Stoll; ***D:*** Ralf Gregan, Gunter Vaessen; ***W:*** Gunter Vaessen; ***C:*** Michael Ballhaus; ***M:*** Rolf Bauer.

Cold Blooded **2000 (R)** Reporter suspects a cover-up when the police dismiss the death of a young woman as a suicide. He thinks she's another victim of a serial killer who has already killed 12 and isn't done yet. **94m/C VHS, DVD.** Michael Moriarty, Patti LuPone, John Kapelos, Gloria Reuben; ***D:*** Randy Bradshaw; ***W:*** Ian Adams; ***C:*** Dean Bennett; ***M:*** Tim McCauley. **VIDEO**

Cold Comfort **½ 1990 (R)** A father arranges his teen daughter's romance, but finds his plans going awry in this Canadian thriller. Nominated for several Canadian TV awards, including Best Actress, Best Actor, Best Picture and Best Musical Score. **90m/C VHS.** *CA* Margaret Langrick, Maury Chaykin, Paul Gross; ***D:*** Vic Sarin; ***W:*** Richard Beattie, Elliot L. Sims; ***C:*** Vic Sarin. **TV**

Cold Comfort Farm **½ 1971** The original BBC production of Stella Gibbon's satiric novel. Orphaned London sophisticate Flora Poste (Badel) is forced to rely on the kindness of her dotty country cousins, the Starkadders, when she needs somewhere to live. But Flora is determined to set things right with the peculiar clan. **135m/C VHS.** *GB* Sarah Badel, Brian Blessed, Fay Compton, Rosalie Crutchley, Alastair Sim, Peter Egan, Fionnula Flanagan, Freddie Jones, Sharon Gurney; ***D:*** Peter Hammond; ***W:*** David Turner. **TV**

Cold Comfort Farm **1994 (PG)** Stella Gibbons classic 1932 comedic novel is brought to life in this TV adaptation, which finds orphaned London lass Flora Poste (Beckinsdale) trying to take charge of the lives of her very odd country cousins, the Starkadders. The rowdy family and their dilapidated farm are putty in practical Flora's hands as she works to make everybody happy (including herself). Terrific ensemble cast, with a fast pace and wicked humor. **104m/C VHS, DVD.** *GB* Kate Beckinsale, Eileen Atkins, Ian McKellen, Sheila Burrell, Rufus Sewell, Maria Miles, Freddie Jones, Ivan Kaye, Miriam Margolyes, Joanna Lumley, Stephen Fry, Christopher Bowen; ***D:*** John Schlesinger; ***W:*** Malcolm Bradbury; ***C:*** Chris Seager; ***M:*** Robert Lockhart.

Cold Creek Manor **½ 2003 (R)** How is it that Michael Douglas isn't involved with this? This is just the kind of yuppie nightmare thriller for which he was the go-to guy for much of the 1980s and '90s. Quaid does an admirable job filling his shoes, however, as an NYC-based documentary filmmaker who, along with his business hotshot wife (Stone), decides to chuck the rat race of the city for a nice, quiet life in the country. Oops. They buy a big, creepy house "for a steal" and find it comes with some secrets, and a redneck caretaker (Dorff) who strangely attracts the missus, but creeps out the kids, especially daughter Kristen. Not much new is brought to the genre, but it has some truly creepy moments, and Figgis ads some much-needed subtle satire. Top-notch cast helps, as well. **118m/C VHS, DVD.** *US* Dennis Quaid, Sharon Stone, Stephen Dorff, Juliette Lewis, Kristen Stewart, Christopher Plummer, Ryan Wilson, Dana Eskelson; ***D:*** Mike Figgis; ***W:*** Richard Jefferies; ***C:*** Declan Quinn; ***M:*** Mike Figgis.

Cold Days **½ 1966** Four men await execution for their part in the WWII massacre of Jews and Serbs. Their reminiscences and justifications, if any, are examined. Stunning cinematography and unusual theme for 1960s Hungarian political climate. **102m/C VHS.** *HU* Zoltan Latonovits, Ivan Darvas, Tibor Szilagyi, Adam Szirtes; ***D:*** Andras Kovacs; ***W:*** Andras Kovacs; ***C:*** Ferenc Szecsenyi.

Cold Eyes of Fear **1970** A man and his girlfriend are besieged by a raving convict whom his uncle, a judge, had put away years before. Shades of "Cape Fear" on a low budget. **88m/C VHS, DVD.** Fernando Rey, Frank Wolfe, Karin Schubert; ***D:*** Enzo G. Castellari; ***W:*** Enzo G. Castellari, Tito Carpi, Leo Anchoriz; ***C:*** Antonio Ballesteros; ***M:*** Ennio Morricone.

Cold Feet **½ 1984 (PG)** Light romantic comedy about a TV director just recovering from a failed marriage and his fall for a lab researcher who just went through a break-up herself. **96m/C VHS.** Griffin Dunne, Marissa Chibas, Blanche Baker, Mark Cronogue; ***D:*** Bruce Van Dusen.

Cold Feet **½ 1989 (R)** Modern-day western in which a trio of loopy desperados smuggle jewels inside a racehorse's stomach. Quirky comedy offers wild performances from Waits and sex-bomb Kirkland, but could use a few more laughs. Filmed largely on McGuane's ranch. **94m/C VHS, DVD.** Keith Carradine, Tom Waits, Sally Kirkland, Rip Torn, Kathleen York, Bill Pullman, Vincent Schiavelli, Jeff Bridges; ***D:*** Robert Dornhelm; ***W:*** Thomas McGuane, Jim Harrison; ***C:*** Bryan Duggan; ***M:*** Tom Bahler.

Cold Fever **1995** Japanese yuppie Atsushi Hirata (Nagase) is expecting to vacation in the tropical paradise of Hawaii not the frozen reaches of Iceland. But instead he must perform a memorial ritual on the remote Icelandic spot where his parents died some time before. He arrives in a blizzard and things just go downhill from there. Some quirky characters but the film loses focus. **85m/C VHS.** *IC* Masatoshi Nagase, Gisli Halldorsson, Lili Taylor, Fisher Stevens; ***D:*** Fridrik Thor Fridriksson; ***W:*** Fridrik Thor Fridriksson, Jim Stark; ***M:*** Hilmar Orn Hilmarsson.

Cold Front **½ 1989 (R)** A hired assassin turned serial killer is hunted by two dedicated cops. **94m/C VHS.** *CA* Martin Sheen, Michael Ontkean, Beverly D'Angelo, Kim Coates; ***D:*** Allan Goldstein; ***C:*** Thomas Burstyn.

Cold Harvest **1998 (R)** A comet strikes the earth, killing a great portion of the population and then disaster strikes again when a deadly disease runs unchecked, killing those who become infected. A bounty hunter and his partner seek to find one of the seven people who carry the antibody to the disease. **93m/C VHS, DVD.** Gary Daniels, Barbara Crampton, Bryan Genesse; ***D:*** Isaac Florentine; ***W:*** Frank Dietz; ***C:*** David Varod; ***M:*** Stephen (Steve) Edwards. **VIDEO**

Cold Hearts **½ 1999** Charles is the head of a group of young vampires who take over a small New Jersey town. But best friends Viktoria and Alicia want to escape from Charles' influence and turn to a stranger for help. Low-budget vamp flick is surprisingly professional and watchable. **88m/C VHS, DVD.** Marisa Ryan, Amy Jo Johnson, Christopher Wiehl, Robert Floyd; ***D:*** Robert Masciantonio. **VIDEO**

Cold Heat **1990** When a custody battle rocks a crime boss' world, he pulls out all the stops in the war against his wife. **85m/C VHS.** John Phillip Law, Britt Ekland, Robert Sacchi, Roy Summerset, Joanne Watkins, Chance Michael Corbitt; ***D:*** Ulli Lommel.

Cold Heaven **½ 1992 (R)** Alex and Marie Davenport are on vacation when an accident occurs and Alex dies—or does he? The next day his body disappears and his unfaithful wife begins to have paranoid delusions that he is returning to exact retribution for her affair. But these aren't her only visions, for during the past year Marie has also had religious visions she believes are part of a personal battle with God. Harmon does what he can with his role as the alleged corpse but Russell is uncharacteristically whiny and bland. Convoluted story of marriage, death, and spirituality; doesn't pan out on any accounts. Based on a novel by Brian Moore. **103m/C VHS.** Theresa Russell, Mark Harmon, James Russo, Talia Shire, Will Patton, Richard Bradford; ***D:*** Nicolas Roeg; ***W:*** Allan Scott.

Cold Justice **1989 (R)** An ex-prizefighter (Daltrey) and his friends welcome an English priest into their tough south-side Chicago neighborhood. The good father seems too good to be true as he befriends the locals—even raising funds for the children's hospital. When the funds never make it to the hospital and the neighborhood begins to experience a number of violent tragedies, the residents decide to take their own revenge. **106m/C VHS.** Dennis Waterman, Roger Daltrey, Penelope Milford, Ron Dean, Bert Rosario; ***D:*** Terry Green; ***W:*** Terry Green.

Cold Light of Day **1995** Police officer Victor Marek (Grant) is hunting a serial killer of young children in the English countryside—and he'll do anything, including using a young girl as bait. Marek seduces single mother Milena (Baxter) to use her young daughter to set a trap for the killer but can he catch the madman before it's too late? **101m/C VHS.** *GB* Richard E. Grant, Lynsey Baxter, Simon Cadell, Perdita Weeks, James Laurenson, Heathcote Williams; ***D:*** Rudolf Van Den Berg; ***W:*** Doug Magee.

Cold Mountain 🦴🦴🦴1/2 **2003 (R)** Minghella's excellent adaptation of Charles Frazier's dense and challenging novel has Inman (Law) attempting to return home, "Odyssey"-style, to North Carolina after his friends are all killed in the disastrous battle at Petersburg, Virginia in 1864. Inman sees no point in continuing the fight and begins his journey so he can continue the brief, chaste, tentative courtship he had begun with the sophisticated Ada (Kidman) before the war. Ada has also seen hardship during their separation. Her father has died, leaving her unprepared to tend the farm until neighbor Ruby (Zellweger) is sent to help.All the actors are superb, with Zellweger stealing every scene she's in, and Minghella strikes the perfect balance between the two stories, thanks to some expert editing. **155m/C DVD.** *GB RO IT* Jude Law, Nicole Kidman, Renee Zellweger, Donald Sutherland, Eileen Atkins, Brendan Gleeson, Philip Seymour Hoffman, Natalie Portman, Giovanni Ribisi, Ray Winstone, Kathy Baker, James Gammon, Charlie Hunnam, Jack White, Ethan Suplee, Jena Malone, Melora Walters, Lucas Black, Taryn Manning, Tom Aldredge, James Rebhorn; ***D:*** Anthony Minghella; ***W:*** Anthony Minghella; ***C:*** John Seale; ***M:*** Gabriel Yared. Oscars '03: Support. Actress (Zellweger); British Acad. '03: Support. Actress (Zellweger), Score; Golden Globes '04: Support. Actress (Zellweger); Screen Actors Guild '03: Support. Actress (Zellweger).

Cold River 🦴🦴 1/2 **1981 (PG)** An experienced guide takes his two children on an extended trip through the Adirondacks. For the children, it's a fantasy vacation until their father succumbs to a heart attack in the chilly mountains. "Cold River" is a journey of survival, and an exploration of human relationships. **94m/C VHS, DVD.** Robert Earl Jones, Pat Petersen, Richard Jaeckel, Suzanne Weber, Brad Sullivan, Elizabeth Hubbard, Augusta Dabney; ***D:*** Fred G. Sullivan.

Cold Room 🦴1/2 *The Prisoner* **1984** College student on vacation with her father in East Berlin discovers the horrors hidden in an antiquated hotel room next to hers. From the novel by Jeffrey Caine. **95m/C VHS.** George Segal, Renee Soutendijk, Amanda Pays, Warren Clarke, Anthony (Corlan) Higgins; ***D:*** James Dearden; ***M:*** Michael Nyman. **CABLE**

Cold Sassy Tree 🦴🦴🦴1/2 **1989** Endearing romance of a scandalous May-December marriage as perceived by the younger woman's teenage son. Dunaway and Widmark shine, and small-town pettiness is vividly rendered. Adapted from the books by Olive Ann Burns. A superior made-for-cable production. **95m/C VHS.** Faye Dunaway, Richard Widmark, Neil Patrick Harris, Frances Fisher, Lee Garlington, John M. Jackson; ***D:*** Joan Tewkesbury; ***W:*** Joan Tewkesbury; ***M:*** Brad Fiedel. **CABLE**

Cold Showers 🦴🦴 *Doches Froides* **2005** Mickael (Libereau) is 17 and proud of his judo skills and hot squeeze Vanessa (Stevenin). He becomes friends with judo-club member Clement (Perrier) and the trio briefly become a menage although Mickael's jealousy soon surfaces. Slight story includes nudity and sex scenes (remember it's French). French with subtitles. **102m/C DVD.** *FR* Salome Stevenin, Florence Thomassin, Jean-Philippe Ecoffey, Johan Libereau, Pierre Perrier; ***D:*** Anthony Cordier; ***W:*** Anthony Cordier; ***C:*** Nicolas Gaurin; ***M:*** Nicolas Lemercier.

Cold Souls 🦴🦴 **2009 (PG-13)** Paul Giamatti plays an anxiety-ridden version of himself as the actor struggles with his stage role in Chekov's "Uncle Vanya." A magazine article offers a solution: Dr. Flintstein (Strathairn) specializes in 'soul storage,' which temporarily removes the soul and its emotional burdens. The only problem is that without his soul, Giametti can't act and so Flintstein loans him the soul of a Russian poet. Complications ensue when Russian Nina (Korzun), who deals in black-market souls, borrows Giamatti's stored soul, which then sends the actor to St. Petersburg so he can get it back. **101m/C DVD.** *US* Paul Giamatti, Dina Korzun, Katheryn Winnick, David Strathrain, Emily Watson, Lauren Ambrose, Boris Kievsky; ***D:*** Sophie Barthes; ***W:*** Sophie Barthes; ***C:*** Andrij Parekh; ***M:*** Dickon Hinchliffe.

Cold Steel 🦴1/2 **1987 (R)** Standard revenge drama about a hardnosed Los Angeles cop tracking his father's disfigured psycho-killer. Cast includes the always intense Davis, ex-pop star Ant, and screen scorchstress Stone. Still it's predictable, low-grade fare. **91m/C VHS, DVD.** Brad Davis, Jonathan Banks, Adam Ant, Sharon Stone; ***D:*** Dorothy Ann Puzo.

Cold Steel for Tortuga 🦴 **1965** An Italian epic about a mercenary rescuing his woman and his gold from an evil governor. Dubbed. **95m/C VHS.** *IT* Guy Madison, Rick (Rik) Battaglia, Ingeborg (Inge) Schoener; ***D:*** Luigi Capuano.

Cold Sweat 🦴🦴 *L'Uomo Dalle Due Ombre; De la Part des Copains* **1971 (PG)** A brutal drug trader takes his ultra-violent revenge after his wife is captured by a drug boss' moronic henchmen. Typical Bronson flick boasts superior supporting cast of Ullmann and Mason. Writing and direction, however, are mediocre. **94m/C VHS, DVD.** *IT FR* Charles Bronson, Jill Ireland, Liv Ullmann, James Mason; ***D:*** Terence Young; ***W:*** Albert Simonin, Shimon Wincelberg; ***C:*** Jean Rabier; ***M:*** Michel Magne.

Cold Sweat 🦴🦴 **1993 (R)** A professional hit man (Cross) is literally haunted by the ghost of his last victim (who happens to be female and usually appears naked), so he decides his next assignment will be his last. A ruthless businessman suspects his very sexy wife (Tweed) has been unfaithful but she has lots of other secrets to hide. **93m/C VHS.** Ben Cross, Shannon Tweed, Adam Baldwin, Dave Thomas; ***D:*** Gail Harvey; ***W:*** Richard Beattie.

Cold Turkey 🦴🦴🦴 **1971 (PG)** Often witty satire about what happens when an entire town tries to stop smoking for a contest. Van Dyke is fine as the anti-smoking minister; newscasters Bob and Ray are riotous; oldtimer Horton's swansong. Wholesome, somewhat tame fare. **99m/C VHS.** Dick Van Dyke, Pippa Scott, Tom Poston, Bob Newhart, Vincent Gardenia, Barnard Hughes, Jean Stapleton, Graham Jarvis, Edward Everett Horton; ***D:*** Norman Lear; ***W:*** Norman Lear; ***M:*** Randy Newman.

Cold War Killers 🦴1/2 **1986 (PG)** Soviet and British agents vie for control of prized cargo plane recently retrieved from the sea floor. **85m/C VHS, DVD.** *GB* Mike Lane, Robin Sachs, Peter Ivatts, Martin Dale, Terence Stamp; ***D:*** William Brayne; ***W:*** Murray Smith; ***C:*** Mike Blakely; ***M:*** Christopher Gunning.

Coldblooded 🦴1/2 **1994 (R)** Minor mob flunky (and dim bulb) Cosmo (Priestley) is unwillingly promoted to the position of hit man by his mobster boss. He's tutored by the organization's primo professional (Riegert) and finds out he has a real knack for murder. More sophomoric than satiric and a waste of Riegert's talents; Williams is attractive as Priestley's clueless girlfriend. Directorial debut of Wolodarsky. **92m/C VHS.** Jason Priestley, Peter Riegert, Kimberly Williams, Robert Loggia, Janeane Garofalo, Josh Charles, David Anthony Higgens, Doris Grau; ***Cameos:*** Talia Balsam, Michael J. Fox; ***D:*** M. Wallace Wolodarsky; ***W:*** M. Wallace Wolodarsky; ***C:*** Robert Yeoman; ***M:*** Steve Bartek.

Coldfire 🦴1/2 **1990** Two rookie cops work to undo the havoc unleashed on the streets of LA because of a deadly new drug sought for its powerful high. Not many surprises here. **90m/C VHS, DVD.** Wings Hauser, Kamar De Los Reyes, Robert Viharo, Gary Swanson; ***D:*** Wings Hauser.

The Colditz Story 🦴🦴 1/2 **1955** Prisoners of war from the Allied countries join together in an attempt to escape from Colditz, an allegedly escape-proof castle-prison deep within the Third Reich. **93m/B VHS, DVD.** John Mills, Eric Portman, Lionel Jeffries, Bryan Forbes, Ian Carmichael, Anton Diffring; ***D:*** Guy Hamilton.

Cole Justice 🦴🦴 **1989** An older man, haunted by the memory of his girlfriend's rape and murder 35 years earlier, takes to the streets to protect innocent citizens from lowlife criminals. Somewhat unusual revenge pic filmed in and around Tulsa, Oklahoma. **90m/C VHS.** Carl Bartholomew, Keith Andrews, Mike Wiles, Nick Zickefoose; ***D:*** Carl Bartholomew.

Collapse 🦴🦴 **2009** Talking-head analysis from independent writer and researcher Michael Ruppert who spreads his doomsday scenario that our industrial civilization is collapsing and global capitalism is finished. In 2006, Ruppert predicted the 2009 economic collapse in his self-published newsletter. Director Smith intersperses Ruppert's conversation with archival footage. **82m/C DVD.** *US* Michael Ruppert; ***D:*** Chris Smith; ***C:*** Max Malkin, Edward Lachman; ***M:*** Didier Leplae, Joe Wong.

Collateral 🦴🦴🦴 **2004 (R)** Vincent (Cruise) is a contract killer as cool and sleek as his gray-haired, gray-suited appearance suggests. He's got a busy schedule to keep in nighttime L.A.—five hits and out on the 6 A.M. flight. Fortunately, he's got the perfect cabbie, 12-year veteran Max (Foxx), who can get anywhere in the least possible time. Naturally, there's time to talk, and as Vincent shares his advice on how to adapt and improvise, Max gets some ideas on how he's going to survive. It's basically a two-handed drama and both actors give nuanced performances; Mann is also at the top of his game. Also notable is the high-def digital video of cinematographers Beebe and Cameron that makes the city another character in the drama. **119m/C DVD.** *US* Tom Cruise, Jamie Foxx, Mark Ruffalo, Irma P. Hall, Jada Pinkett Smith, Bruce McGill, Bodhi (Pine) Elfman, Javier Bardem, Peter Berg, Barry (Shabaka) Henley, Debi Mazar; ***D:*** Michael Mann; ***W:*** Stuart Beattie; ***C:*** Dion Beebe, Paul Cameron; ***M:*** James Newton Howard, Antonio Pinto, Tom Rothrock. British Acad. '04: Cinematog.

Collateral Damage 🦴🦴 **2002 (R)** Revenge drama pits Ah-nuld against the Columbian terrorists whose actions caused the death of his wife and child. When investigators come up short, nothing-left-to-lose fireman Gordy Brewer (Schwarzenegger) takes matters into his own hands and sets out to catch "The Wolf," the rebel leader of Columbia's civil war and the one responsible for his family's demise. In Columbia, he meets Selena (Neri) and her son Mauro (Posey) and his instinct to protect and serve them kicks into action, giving him renewed purpose. Highlights are Leguizamo as Felix, the Columbian drug producer, and Turturro as an exiled Canadian working as a mechanic. Mexico subs for Columbia in this unbelievable and formulaic actioner for genre and Arnold fans only. **109m/C VHS, DVD.** *US* Arnold Schwarzenegger, Elias Koteas, Francesca Neri, Clifford Curtis, John Leguizamo, John Turturro, Miguel (Michael) Sandoval, Harry J. Lennix, Lindsay Frost, Jsu Garcia; ***D:*** Andrew Davis; ***W:*** David Griffiths, Peter Griffiths; ***C:*** Adam Greenberg; ***M:*** Graeme Revell.

Collected Stories 🦴🦴🦴 **2002** Fine two-character study based on the 1997 play by Margulies, who adapted for this PBS presentation. Ruth Steiner (Lanvin) is a respected writer and teacher in her mid-50s who lives comfortably in her Greenwich Village apartment. It's there that Ruth agrees that ambitious graduate student and aspiring writer Lisa Morrison (Mathis) will become her assistant. Over six years, their relationship evolves into a friendship, which Lisa betrays when she turns the scandalous details of Ruth's life into a best-selling novel. **120m/C VHS.** Linda Lavin, Samantha Mathis; ***D:*** Gilbert Cates; ***W:*** Donald Margulies; ***C:*** Johnny (John W.) Simmons; ***M:*** Charles Fox. **TV**

The Collector 🦴🦴🦴1/2 **1965** Compelling adaptation of the John Fowles novel about a withdrawn butterfly collector who decides to add to his collection by kidnapping a beautiful girl he admires. He locks her in his cellar hoping she will fall in love with him. Chilling, unsettling drama with Stamp unnerving, yet sympathetic in lead. **119m/C VHS, DVD.** *GB* Terence Stamp, Samantha Eggar, Maurice Dallimore, Mona Washbourne; ***D:*** William Wyler; ***W:*** John Kohn, Stanley Mann; ***C:*** Robert Krasker, Robert L. Surtees; ***M:*** Maurice Jarre. Cannes '65: Actor (Stamp), Actress (Eggar); Golden Globes '66: Actress—Drama (Eggar).

The Collector 🦴 **2009 (R)** Seen "Saw"? Then you've seen this, since Dunstan and Melton were also writers of some of that franchise's lamer sequels. Ex-jewel thief turned handyman Arkin (Stewart) is trying to go straight, but only after he robs the home of the Chase family (he's got a good reason, of course). The family is supposed to be on vacation, but Arkin finds the house has been booby-trapped by a masked sicko and the family is unfortunately at home. Various cringe-making tortures abound. **88m/C DVD.** *US* Josh Stewart, Michael Reilly Burke, Andrea Roth, Karley Scott Collins, Madeline Zima, Juan Fernandez; ***D:*** Marcus Dunstan; ***W:*** Marcus Dunstan, Patrick Melton; ***C:*** Brandon Cox; ***M:*** Jerome Dillon.

The Collectors 🦴🦴 **1999 (R)** Mob boss sends hit men Ray (Van Dien) and A.K. (Fox) to collect a big debt that's owed but they would rather take the payoff and get out of New York—preferably alive. **97m/C VHS, DVD.** Casper Van Dien, Rick Fox, Catherine Oxenberg, Daniel Pilon; ***D:*** Sidney J. Furie. **VIDEO**

Collector's Item 🦴🦴🦴 **1989** Two lovers reunite after 16 years and a flurry of memories temporarily rekindles their passion, which comes dangerously close to obsession. Casting of the physically bountiful Antonelli helps this effective erotic drama. **99m/C VHS, DVD.** *IT* Tony Musante, Laura Antonelli, Florinda Bolkan; ***D:*** Giuseppe Patroni-Griffi.

Colleen 🦴🦴 **1936** The final collaboration between Powell and Keeler is a weak musical romance. Wealthy eccentric Cedric Ames (Herbert) buys gold-digging Minnie (Blondell) a dress shop where Colleen Reilly (Keeler) is also working. Cedric's suspicious nephew Donald (Powell) eventually persuades him to close the shop, even though Donald has fallen for Colleen. The family lawyer pays off Minnie but Colleen doesn't want their dough and gets a job on an ocean liner bound for Europe. Guess who turns out to be a passenger? **89m/B DVD.** Dick Powell, Ruby Keeler, Joan Blondell, Hugh Herbert, Jack Oakie, Addison Richard, Louise Fazenda; ***D:*** Alfred E. Green; ***W:*** F. Hugh Herbert, Sid Herzig, Peter Milne; ***C:*** Byron Haskin, Sol Polito.

College 🦴🦴🦴1/2 **1927** A high school valedictorian tries out for every sport in college, hoping to win the girl. Vintage Keaton antics, including disaster as a soda jerk, an attempt to be a track star, and the pole vault through a window to rescue the damsel in distress. **60m/B VHS, DVD.** Buster Keaton, Anne Cornwall, Harold Goodwin; ***D:*** James W. Horne; ***W:*** Brian Foy, Carl Harbaugh; ***C:*** Bert Haines; ***M:*** John Muri.

College WOOF! **2008 (R)** After being dumped by his girlfriend, a high school senior nerd and his two nerdier friends head to the college in an attempt to escape their otherwise pathetic lives and party like, well, freshmen. Attempts to rise to the stratospheric heights of such cinematic masterpieces as "Porky's," "Revenge of the Nerds," and even "American Pie," but offers little more than a deluge of low-brow, gross-out, t & a humor as the dorks get smashed, hit on hot girls way out of their league, and vomit. Not even an appearance by thespian Troyer can salvage a passing grade. **94m/C DVD.** *US* Drake Bell, Andrew Caldwell, Haley Bennett, Nick Zano, Ryan Pinkston, Verne Troyer, Kevin Covais, Camille Mana, Nathalie Walker, Alona Tal; ***D:*** Deb Hagan; ***W:*** Dan Callahan, Adam Ellison; ***C:*** Dan Stoloff; ***M:*** Transcenders.

College Humor 🦴🦴 1/2 **1933** Early musical comedy for Crosby finds him a college prof, Frederick Danvers, who attracts the attentions of pretty coed Barbara (Carlisle). Only Barbara's crush is leaving her football star boyfriend Mondrake (Arlen) in a jealous rage just before the big game. Fortunately, Barbara's brother Barney (Oakie) fills in. Burns and Allen appear as caterers. **80m/B VHS.** Bing Crosby, Jack Oakie, Richard Arlen, Mary Carlisle, Mary Kornman, Joseph (Joe) Sawyer, George Burns; ***D:*** Wesley Ruggles; ***W:*** Claude Binyon, Frank Butler; ***C:*** Leo Tover; ***M:*** Arthur Johnston, Sam Coslow.

College Road Trip 🦴 **2008 (G)** The good news is that a G rating ensures worry-free family viewing. The bad news is that instead of eliciting the universal road trip lament, "Are we there yet?" most parents will be asking, "Is it over yet?" Suburban Chicago police chief and over-protective dad James Porter (Lawrence) and high-school senior daughter Melanie (Symone) clash about her choice of colleges, so they set off on a road trip to visit the campus. Even with the cute little brother (Draper) and pet pig along for the ride, the overdone gags fall flat, especially the multiple encounters with another college-bound girl and her Cheez-Wiz dad Doug (Osmond). Sorry, Disney: creepily overprotective dads just aren't funny. **83m/C DVD, Blu-ray Disc.** *US* Martin Lawrence, Raven-Symone, Donny Osmond, Brenda Song, Will Sasso, Kym E. Whitley, Margo Harshman, Eshaya Draper, Vincent Pastore, Lucas Grabeel; ***D:*** Roger Kumble; ***W:*** Ken Daurio; ***C:*** Theo van de Sande; ***M:*** Ed Shearmur, Lisa Brown.

College Swing ♪ 1/2 *Swing, Teacher, Swing* **1938** Lightweight, lackluster musical about Allen inheriting a small town college which she turns into a hangout for her vaudeville pals. Top cast is basically wasted performing many forgettable songs and familiar routines. Based on an adaptation by Frederick Hazlitt Brennan from a story by Ted Lesser. ♫College Swing; What Did Romeo Say to Juliet?; I Fall In Love With You Every Day; You're a Natural; The Old School Bell; Moments Like This; How D'ja Like to Love Me?; What a Rumba Does to Romance. **86m/B VHS, DVD.** George Burns, Gracie Allen, Martha Raye, Bob Hope, Edward Everett Horton, Ben Blue, Betty Grable, Jackie Coogan, John Payne; ***D:*** Raoul Walsh; ***W:*** Walter DeLeon, Francis Martin; ***C:*** Victor Milner; ***M:*** Boris Morros, Hoagy Carmichael, Burton Lane, Frank Loesser.

Collier & Co.: Hot Pursuit ♪♪ 1/2 **2006 (PG)** Down-on-his-luck J.R. Collier (Schneider) wants to go legit and start his own car dealership to win back his estranged wife and daughter. He decides to sell the cars he wins street racing but a Dodge Charger has something in its glovebox that some goofy bad guys want back. Harmless family fun and a family affair since Schneider cast his own wife and daughter as his onscreen family too. He also cast The General Lee from his "Dukes of Hazzard" days, although not with the signature paint job. **107m/C DVD.** John Schneider, Rex Smith, Karis Schneider, Elly Castle; ***D:*** John Schneider; ***W:*** John Schneider; ***M:*** Bob Boykin. **VIDEO**

Collision Course ♪ **1989 (PG)** A wise-cracking cop from Detroit teams up with Japan's best detective to nail a ruthless gang leader. Release was delayed until 1992 due to a lawsuit, but it was resolved in time to coordinate the release with Leno's debut as the host of "The Tonight Show." Pretty marginal, but diehard fans of Leno may appreciate it. Filmed on location in Detroit. **99m/C VHS, DVD.** Noriyuki "Pat" Morita, Jay Leno, Chris Sarandon, Al Waxman; ***D:*** Lewis Teague.

The Colombian Connection ♪ 1/2 **1991** America's best undercover agent battles a powerful cocaine empire deep in the jungles of the Amazon, where slave labor and political corruption abound. **90m/C VHS.** Miles O'Keeffe, Henry Silva; ***D:*** Michael Lemick.

Colombian Love ♪♪ 1/2 *Ahava Colombianit* **2004** Light-hearted Israeli romantic comedy about three buddies coping with adulthood and amore. Womanizing Zydane is surprised when he begins obsessing over his Colombian ex-girlfriend; Omer is newly married and already having problems handling his added responsibilities; and Uri is caught between his independent girlfriend Tali and his domineering father. Hebrew with subtitles. **96m/C DVD.** *IS* Assi Cohen, Mili Avital, Nir Levy, Italy Barnea, Elinor Ben Haim, Shmil Ben Ari, Osnat Hakim; ***D:*** Shai Kannot; ***W:*** Regev Levy, Reshef Levy; ***C:*** Ofer Harari; ***M:*** Asaf Amdurski.

Colonel Chabert ♪♪ **1994** In the 1807 Battle of Eylau, French officer Chabert (Depardieu) is thought dead and stripped of all he possesses. After 10 years of imprisonment, a man shows up in the office of Paris lawyer Derville (Luchini), claiming to be the dead Chabert. His remarried wife (Ardant), now the Countess Ferraud, has used his fortune to bolster the political aspirations of her second husband (Dussollier) and refuses to acknowledge this stranger's claims. Is Chabert a fraud? And what exactly are the motives of all the players? Based on the novel by Honore de Balzac. Directorial debut of Angelo. French with subtitles. **111m/C VHS.** *FR* Gerard Depardieu, Fanny Ardant, Fabrice Luchini, Andre Dussollier; ***D:*** Yves Angelo; ***W:*** Yves Angelo, Jean Cosmos, Veronique Lagrange; ***C:*** Bernard Lutic.

Colonel Effingham's Raid ♪♪ 1/2 *Man of the Hour* **1945** A retired army colonel uses military tactics to keep an old historical courthouse open, while defeating some crooked politicians in the process. **70m/B VHS, DVD.** Joan Bennett, Charles Coburn, William Eythe, Donald Meek, Allyn Joslyn, Elizabeth Patterson, Frank Craven, Thurston Hall, Cora Witherspoon, Emory Parnell, Henry Armetta, Steve (Stephen) Dunne, Roy Roberts, Charles Trowbridge; ***D:*** Irving Pichel; ***W:*** Kathryn Scola; ***C:*** Edward Cronjager; ***M:*** Cyril Mockridge.

Colonel Redl ♪♪♪♪ **1984 (R)** Absorbing, intricately rendered psychological study of an ambitious officer's rise and fall in pre-WWI Austria. Brandauer is excellent as the vain, insecure homosexual ultimately undone by his own ambition and his superior officer's smug loathing. Muller-Stahl and Landgrebe are particularly distinguished among the supporting players. The second in the Szabo/Brandauer trilogy, after "Mephisto" and before "Hanussen." In German with English subtitles. **142m/C VHS, DVD.** *GE HU* Klaus Maria Brandauer, Armin Mueller-Stahl, Gudrun Landgrebe, Jan Niklas, Hans-Christian Blech, Laszlo Mensaros, Andras Balint; ***D:*** Laszlo Szabo; ***W:*** Laszlo Szabo, Peter Dobai; ***C:*** Lajos Koltai; ***M:*** Zdenko Tamassy. British Acad. '85: Foreign Film; Cannes '85: Special Jury Prize.

Colonel Wolodyjowski ♪♪ 1/2 **1969** An adaptation of the monumental novels by Henryk Sinkiewicz chronicling the attack on Poland's eastern border by the Turks in 1668. In Polish with English subtitles. **160m/C VHS, DVD.** *PL* Tadeusz Lomnicki, Magdalena Zawadzka, Daniel Olbrychski; ***D:*** Jerzy Hoffman.

The Colony ♪♪ 1/2 **1995 (PG-13)** "The Colony" is a luxurious and exclusive gated community owned by secretive billionaire developer Phillip Denning (Linden). Newest residents, security expert Rick Knowlton (Ritter), wife Leslie (Keller) and their two children, find out things are just too good to be true—and that trying to leave could be the very last thing they'll ever do. **93m/C VHS, DVD.** John Ritter, Hal Linden, Mary Page Keller, Marshall Teague, Frank Bonner, Michelle Scarabelli, June Lockhart, Todd Jeffries, Alexandra Picatto, Cody Dorkin; ***D:*** Rob Hedden; ***W:*** Rob Hedden; ***C:*** David Geddes.

The Colony ♪ 1/2 **1998 (R)** Aliens planning an earth invasion decide to test humankind by abducting four people and observing their survival skills. **94m/C VHS, DVD.** Isabella Hofmann, Michael Weatherly, Cristi Conaway, Eric Allen Kramer, Jeff Kober, James Avery, Clare Salstrom; ***D:*** Peter Geiger; ***W:*** Peter Geiger, Richard Kletter; ***C:*** Zoltan David; ***M:*** Paul Rabjohns. **CABLE**

Color Me Blood Red **WOOF!** *Model Massacre* **1964** Artist decides that the red in his paintings is best rendered with human blood. He even manages to continue his art career—when not busy stabbing and mutilating the unsuspecting citizenry. Short and shoddy. **74m/C VHS, DVD.** Don Joseph, Candi Conder, Elyn Warner, Scott H. Hall, Jerome (Jerry Stallion) Eden, Patricia Lee, James Jackel; ***D:*** Herschell Gordon Lewis; ***W:*** Herschell Gordon Lewis; ***C:*** Herschell Gordon Lewis.

Color Me Dead ♪ 1/2 **1969 (R)** A victim of an extremely slow-acting poison frantically spends his final days trying to uncover his killer. Another inferior remake of B-thriller "D.O.A." Rent that one instead. **97m/C VHS.** *AU* Tom Tryon, Carolyn Jones, Rick Jason, Patricia Connolly, Tony Ward; ***D:*** Eddie Davis.

Color Me Kubrick ♪ 1/2 **2005** Malkovich swans about in outrageous attire and attitude as con man Alan Conway, who made his way to London in the early 1990s and passed himself off as reclusive director Stanley Kubrick despite knowing nothing about filmmaking. The con man was after money and sex, which he was given by the flattered and gullible who were too embarrassed to press charges when they'd discovered they'd been had (much to the real Kubrick's frustration). A bit of silly fluff. **86m/C DVD.** *GB FR* John Malkovich, Jim Davidson, Richard E. Grant, Luke Mably, Terence Rigby, James Dreyfus, Peter Bowles, Leslie Phillips, William Hootkins; ***D:*** Brian Cook; ***W:*** Anthony Frewin; ***C:*** Howard Atherton; ***M:*** Bryan Adams.

Color of a Brisk and Leaping Day ♪♪ **1995** While living in L.A. at the end of WWII, Chinese-American John Lee (Alexander) learns that the Yosemite Valley Railroad is being scrapped and he becomes determined to save it—in part as a homage to his grandfather who emigrated to work as a railroad laborer. A romantic train fanatic himself, Lee arranges financing from wealthy businessman Pinchot (Diehl) but must make the railroad pay within a year—unlikely as the automobile rapidly takes over as preferred transportation. Well-captures a '40s atmosphere but pacing and dialogue are uneven. **87m/B VHS, DVD.** Peter Alexander, Jeri Arredondo, Henry Gibson, Michael Stipe, John Diehl, David Chung, Diana Larkin, Bok Yun Chon; ***D:*** Christopher Munch; ***W:*** Christopher Munch; ***C:*** Rob Sweeney. Sundance '96: Cinematog.

The Color of Courage ♪♪ 1/2 **1998 (PG)** Anna Sipes (Hamilton) is pleased to welcome Minnie McGhee (Whitfield) to her Detroit neighborhood in 1944. But not every one feels the same, since the McGhees are black. The community (including Anna's husband) wants to force an eviction but since Anna and Minnie have become friends, they are equally determined that the McGhees will remain where they are. Based on the landmark civil rights case, Sipes vs. McGhee. **92m/C VHS.** Linda Hamilton, Lynn Whitfield, Bruce Greenwood, Roger Guenveur Smith; ***D:*** Lee Rose; ***W:*** Kathleen McGhee-Anderson; ***C:*** Eric Van Haren Noman; ***M:*** Terence Blanchard. **CABLE**

The Color of Evening ♪♪ **1995** Aging painter Landau tries to regain his youth by pursuing his young model Skye, but it's the older Burstyn who really inspires his imagination. **90m/C VHS.** Kyle Chandler, Bill Erwin, Roddy McDowall, Martin Landau, Ellen Burstyn, Ione Skye; ***D:*** Stephen Stafford; ***W:*** Tamara Lynn Roth; ***C:*** Berhard Salzmann; ***M:*** Leonard Rosenman.

The Color of Freedom ♪ 1/2 *Goodbye Bafana* **2007 (R)** In 1968, Afrikaaner James Gregory (Fiennes) takes a job at Robben Island where Nelson Mandela (Haysbert) is a political prisoner. A firm believer in apartheid, Gregory becomes one of Mandela's principal guards because he can speak Xhosa and thus censor his prisoner's communications. But over a 20-year period, Gregory begins to change his views. Static storytelling, adapted from Gregory's memoirs, that's too noble to retain interest. **118m/C DVD.** *GB SA* Joseph Fiennes, Dennis Haysbert, Diane Kruger; ***D:*** Bille August; ***W:*** Greg Latter; ***C:*** Robert Fraisse; ***M:*** Dario Marianelli.

Color of Justice ♪♪ **1997** A political circus ensues after a suburban white woman is killed by four black teens. Betty Gainer (Pelikan) is forced to stop behind a stolen car and is killed by the teens in the struggle that follows. Manhattan D.A. Jim Sullivan (Abraham) insists on trying the four as adults, while court-appointed attorney Sam Lind (Hirsch) blames the cops, and media savvy black minister Walton (Hines) plays the race card. Meanwhile, Gainer's husband Frank (Davison) becomes increasingly frustrated as his wife's death seems to be forgotten. **95m/C VHS.** F. Murray Abraham, Judd Hirsch, Gregory Hines, Bruce Davison, Lisa Pelikan, Saul Rubinek, Mark L. Taylor, Gloria Carlin, Mia Korf, Dule Hill, Eugene Byrd, Malcolm Goodwin; ***D:*** Jeremy Paul Kagan; ***W:*** Lionel Chetwynd; ***C:*** Steven Poster; ***M:*** Michel Colombier. **CABLE**

The Color of Magic ♪♪ 1/2 *Terry Pratchett's The Color of Magic* **2008** Based on the first two books in Pratchett's Discworld fantasy series. Discworld is supported on the backs of four elephants that stand on the back of the Great A'Tuin (a giant turtle) that floats through space. Only the turtle has suddenly decided to move towards a fiery red star that will cause Discworld's destruction. In order to save the day, naive tourist Twoflower (Astin) and incompetent wizard Rinceweed (Jason) must collect eight spells that are all part of an elaborate game. **137m/C DVD.** *GB* Sean Astin, David Jason, Tim Curry, Jeremy Irons, David Bradley, James Cosmo, Janet Suzman, Karen Shenaz David; ***D:*** Vadim Jean; ***W:*** Vadim Jean; ***C:*** Gavin Finney; ***M:*** Paul Francis, David A. Hughes; ***V:*** Christopher Lee; ***Nar:*** Brian Cox. **TV**

The Color of Money ♪♪♪ 1/2 **1986 (R)** Flashy, gripping drama about former pool hustler Fast Eddie Felsen (Newman) who, after years off the circuit, takes a brilliant but immature pool shark (Cruise) under his wing. Strong performances by Newman as the grizzled veteran, Cruise as the showboating youth, and Mastrantonio and Shaver as the men's worldly girlfriends. Worthy sequel to "The Hustler." **119m/C VHS, DVD.** Paul Newman, Tom Cruise, Mary Elizabeth Mastrantonio, Helen Shaver, John Turturro, Forest Whitaker; ***D:*** Martin Scorsese; ***W:*** Richard Price; ***C:*** Michael Ballhaus; ***M:*** Robbie Robertson. Oscars '86: Actor (Newman); Natl. Bd. of Review '86: Actor (Newman).

Color of Night ♪ 1/2 **1994 (R)** Psychologist Dr. Bill Capa (Willis) takes over a murdered colleague's therapy group hoping to find out the killer's identity. Then he meets temptress Rose (March) and gets involved in a hot affair, but she's not what she seems—nor is anyone else. Preposterous thriller fails to deliver necessary suspense although the eroticism could spark some interest, particularly in the director's cut, which puts the sex back in the sex scenes between Willis and March (and is 15 minutes longer than the theatrical release). **136m/C VHS, DVD.** Bruce Willis, Jane March, Scott Bakula, Ruben Blades, Lesley Ann Warren, Lance Henriksen, Kevin J. O'Connor, Andrew Lowery, Brad Dourif, Eriq La Salle, Jeff Corey, Shirley Knight, Kathleen Wilhoite; ***D:*** Richard Rush; ***W:*** Matthew Chapman, Billy Ray, Richard Rush; ***C:*** Dietrich Lohmann; ***M:*** Dominic Frontiere. Golden Raspberries '94: Worst Picture.

The Color of Paradise ♪♪ *Rang-e Khoda* **1999 (PG)** Mohammad is an eight-year-old blind boy who is regarded as a burden by his recently widowed and hard-working father. His father hopes to remarry but thinks his son will be an obstacle and sends him to live with a carpenter, who is also blind, so that the boy can learn a trade. Of course, it is the father who must truly learn to see, since Mohammad already appreciates everything surrounding him. Farsi with subtitles. **90m/C VHS, DVD.** *IA* Mohsen Ramezani, Hossein Mahjoub; ***D:*** Majid Majidi; ***W:*** Majid Majidi; ***C:*** Mohammad Davudi; ***M:*** Alireza Kohandairy.

The Color of Pomegranates ♪♪♪ *Sayat Nova; Tsvet Granata* **1969** Paradjanov's depiction of the life of Armenian poet Arutiun Sayadin, known as Sayat Nova, who rises from carpet weaver to court minstrel to archbishop. Eloquent imagery and symbols are derived from Armenian paintings, poetry and history. In Armenian with English subtitles. Also includes "Hagop Hovnatanian," a 12-minute short on the artist. **80m/C VHS, DVD.** *RU* Sofiko Chiaureli, M. Aleksanian, V. Galstian; ***D:*** Sergei Paradjanov; ***W:*** Sergei Paradjanov; ***C:*** A. Samvelyan.

The Color Purple ♪♪♪ 1/2 **1985 (PG-13)** Celie is a poor black girl who fights for her self-esteem when she is separated from her sister and forced into a brutal marriage. Spanning 1909 to 1947 in a small Georgia town, the movie chronicles the joys, pains, and people in her life. Adaptation of Alice Walker's acclaimed book features strong lead from Goldberg (her screen debut), Glover, Avery, and talk-show host Winfrey (also her film debut). It's hard to see director Spielberg as the most suited for this one, but he acquits himself nicely, avoiding the facileness that sometimes flaws his pics. Brilliant photography by Allen Daviau and musical score by Jones (who co-produced) compliment this strong film. **154m/C VHS, DVD.** Whoopi Goldberg, Danny Glover, Oprah Winfrey, Margaret Avery, Adolph Caesar, Rae Dawn Chong, Willard Pugh, Akosua Busia; ***D:*** Steven Spielberg; ***W:*** Menno Meyjes; ***C:*** Allen Daviau; ***M:*** Chris Boardman, Quincy Jones. Directors Guild '85: Director (Spielberg); Golden Globes '86: Actress—Drama (Goldberg); Natl. Bd. of Review '85: Actress (Goldberg).

Colorado ♪ 1/2 **1940** Roy tries to find his brother, a Union deserter, during the Civil War. **54m/B VHS, DVD.** Roy Rogers, George "Gabby" Hayes, Milburn Stone; ***D:*** Joseph Kane.

Colorado Serenade ♪♪ **1946** Standard oater has Dean, Sharpe and Ates trying to prevent a young outlaw from bullying the local citizenry. Sharpe shows off his athletic prowess, and King provides some laughs. Other than that, it's pretty routine stuff. **68m/C VHS, DVD.** Eddie Dean, David Sharpe, Roscoe Ates, Forrest Taylor, Dennis Moore, Warner Richmond, Bob Duncan, Charles "Blackie" King; *D:* Robert Emmett Tansey.

Colorado Sundown **1952** A conniving brother and sister attempt to cheat a man out of his inheritance. **67m/B VHS, DVD.** Rex Allen, Mary Ellen Kay, Slim Pickens, June Vincent, Koko; *D:* William Witney.

Colorado Territory ½ **1949** Outlaw Wes McQueen (McCrea) breaks out of jail, vowing to go straight. Instead, he winds up back with his old partner Rickard (Ruysdael). He agrees to a last job railroad heist with Rickard's new gang, which includes former dance-hall dame Colorado (Mayo), and the chivalrous Wes decides to protect Colorado from his shifty cohorts. **94m/B DVD.** Joel McCrea, Virginia Mayo, Dorothy Malone, Henry Hull, Basil Ruysdael, John Archer, James Mitchell, Harry Woods, Morris Ankrum; *D:* Morris Ankrum, Raoul Walsh; *W:* Edmund H. North, John Twist; *C:* Sid Hickox; *M:* David Buttolph.

Colors ½ **1988 (R)** Vivid, realistic cop drama pairs sympathetic veteran Duvall and trigger-tempered rookie Penn on the gang-infested streets of East Los Angeles. Fine play from leads is one of the many assets in this controversial, unsettling depiction of deadly streetlife. Colorful, freewheeling direction from the underrated Hopper. Rattling rap soundtrack too. Additional footage has been added for video release. **120m/C VHS, DVD.** Glenn Plummer, Sy Richardson, Damon Wayans, Fred Asparagus, Sherman Augustus, R.D. Call, Seymour Cassel, Nick(y) Corello, Virgil Frye, Courtney Gains, Clark Johnson, Leon, Tina Lifford, Micole Mercurio, Jack Nance, Tony Todd, Gerardo Mejia, Sean Penn, Robert Duvall, Maria Conchita Alonso, Trinidad Silva, Randi Brooks, Grand L. Bush, Don Cheadle, Rudy Ramos; *D:* Dennis Hopper; *W:* Michael Schiffer; *C:* Haskell Wexler; *M:* Herbie Hancock.

Colorz of Rage ½ **1997** Story of an interracial relationship between Tony (Resteghini) and Debbie (Richards) covers familiar ground, but the New York locations have a gritty feel that's accentuated by the rough production values. **91m/C DVD.** Dale Resteghini, Nicki Richards, Cheryl "Pepsii" Riley, Don Wallace; *D:* Dale Resteghini; *W:* Dale Resteghini; *C:* Martin Ahlgren; *M:* Tony Prendatt.

Colossus and the Amazon Queen ½ *Colossus and the Amazons; La Regina delle Amazzoni* **1964** Idle gladiators are unwillingly recruited for service to Amazons. Doesn't seem like the worst way to make a living. But lead actor Taylor—so notable in comedies, thrillers, and action flicks—is too good for this sort of thing. Dubbed. **94m/C VHS, DVD.** *IT* Rod Taylor, Dorian Gray, Ed Fury, Gianna Maria Canale; *D:* Vittorio Sala.

Colossus of the Arena *Maciste, Il Gladiatore piu Forte del Monte* **1962** In 4th century Rome, Forest plays a mighty gladiator who uncovers a plot to imprison a beautiful princess. Through an incredible series of feats and combats, he exposes an evil duke as a traitor. **98m/C VHS.** *IT* Mark Forest, Scilla Gabel; *D:* Michele Lupo; *W:* Lionello De Felice, Ernesto Guida; *M:* Francesco De Masi.

Colossus: The Forbin Project *The Forbin Project* **1970** A computer designed to manage U.S. defense systems teams instead with its Soviet equal and they attempt world domination. Wire-tight, suspenseful film seems at once dated yet timely. Based on the novel by D.F. Jones. **100m/C VHS, DVD.** Eric (Hans Gudegast) Braeden, Susan Clark, Gordon Pinsent, William Schallert, Georg Stanford Brown; *D:* Joseph Sargent; *W:* James Bridges; *C:* Gene Polito; *M:* Michel Colombier.

Colt Comrades **1943** A bad guy's monopoly on water rights is jeopardized when Boyd and Clyde strike water while drilling for oil. Nothing really notable here, except for Bob (Robert) Mitchum and George ("Superman") Reeves in minor roles. **67m/B VHS, DVD.** William Boyd, Andy Clyde, Jay Kirby, George Reeves, Gayle Lord, Earle Hodgins, Victor Jory, Douglas Fowley, Herbert Rawlinson, Robert Mitchum; *D:* Lesley Selander.

Columbo: Murder by the Book ½ **1971** The rumpled, cigar-smoking TV detective investigates the killing of a mystery writer. Scripted by Bochco of "Hill Street Blues" and "L.A. Law" fame. **79m/C VHS, DVD.** Peter Falk, Jack Cassidy, Rosemary Forsyth, Martin Milner; *D:* Steven Spielberg; *W:* Steven Bochco.

Columbo: Prescription Murder **1967** Falk's debut as the raincoat-clad lieutenant who always has just one more question. In the TV series pilot he investigates the death of a psychiatrist's wife. Rich with subplots. Good mystery fare. **99m/C VHS.** Peter Falk, Gene Barry, Katherine Justice, William Windom, Nina Foch, Anthony James, Virginia Gregg; *D:* Richard Irving; *W:* Richard Levinson, William Link. **TV**

Columbus Day ½ **2008 (R)** Thief John Cologne (Kilmer) is determined to go straight so he can reunite with his ex-wife and daughter. He pulls off one last job—involving a briefcase full of diamonds—and has to fence the goods ASAP, which is how he winds up in a public park on Columbus Day yakking with some kid (Thompson). Garbled story. **90m/C DVD.** Val Kilmer, Ashley Johnson, Bobb'e J. Thompson, Wilmer Valderrama, Marg Helgenberger, Lobo Sebastian, Richard Edson, Michael Muhney; *D:* Charles Burmeister; *W:* Charles Burmeister; *C:* Julio Macat; *M:* Michael A. Levine.

Coma **1978 (PG)** A doctor discovers murder and corpse-nabbing at her Boston hospital, defies her male bosses, and determines to find out what's going on before more patients die. Exciting, suspenseful fare, with Bujold impressive in lead. Based on the novel by Robin Cook. **113m/C VHS, DVD.** Genevieve Bujold, Michael Douglas, Elizabeth Ashley, Rip Torn, Richard Widmark, Lois Chiles, Hari Rhodes, Tom Selleck, Ed Harris; *D:* Michael Crichton; *W:* Michael Crichton; *C:* Victor Kemper, Gerald Hirschfeld; *M:* Jerry Goldsmith.

Comanche Moon ½ **2008** Disappointing adaptation of McMurtry's 1997 novel, which falls second in terms of "The Lonesome Dove" timeframe, set mostly in the 1850s. Best friends Gus (Zahn) and Call (Urban) are Texas Rangers hunting Comanches, including leader Buffalo Hump (Studi). When their eccentric captain, Inish Scully (Kilmer), goes after a horse thief, they are left in charge. Kilmer spends a lot of time stuck in a pit and going crazy after Inish is captured by a Mexican bandito (Lopez). Back in town, Gus pines for Clara (Cardellini) while Call struggles with his feelings for Maggie (Banks), and Inish's wife Inez (Griffiths) spreads her charms amongst the Rangers. Oh yeah, and the Comanches attack. Disjointed storyline, stilted dialogue, and poor (miscast) performances doom this effort. **284m/C DVD.** Steve Zahn, Karl Urban, Val Kilmer, Linda Cardellini, Elizabeth Banks, Rachel Griffiths, Wes Studi, Sal Lopez, Ryan Merriman, Adam Beach, James Rebhorn, Jake Busey, Melanie Lynskey, Floyd "Red Crow" Westerman; *D:* Simon Wincer; *W:* Larry McMurtry, Diana Ossana; *C:* Alan Caso; *M:* Lennie Niehaus. **TV**

Comanche Station ½ **1960** Loner Jefferson Cody (Scott) agrees to rescue Mrs. Lowe (Gates), a senator's wife who's been captured by the Comanches. After Cody achieves her rescue, they fall in with outlaw Ben Lane (Akins) and his two young proteges, who insist on accompanying them back to the Lowe homestead, saying that they'll need additional protection. But Cody soon realizes that Lane is after the reward money and is planning an ambush. **73m/C VHS.** Randolph Scott, Nancy Gates, Claude Akins, Skip Homeier, Richard Rust, Rand Brooks; *D:* Budd Boetticher; *W:* Burt Kennedy; *C:* Charles Lawton Jr.

Comanche Territory **1950** Western frontiersman Jim Bowie travels to Comanche country and helps the Indians save their land from settlers. Routine oater. Based on a story by Meltzer. **76m/C VHS.** Maureen O'Hara, MacDonald Carey, Will Geer, Charles Drake; *D:* George Sherman; *W:* Oscar Brodney, Lewis Meltzer.

The Comancheros **1961** Texas Ranger Wayne and his prisoner fight with the Comancheros, an outlaw gang who is supplying guns and liquor to the dreaded Comanche Indians. Musical score adds flavor. Last film by Curtiz. **108m/C VHS, DVD.** John Wayne, Ina Balin, Stuart Whitman, Nehemiah Persoff, Lee Marvin, Bruce Cabot; *D:* Michael Curtiz; *C:* William Clothier; *M:* Elmer Bernstein.

Combat Academy **1986** Weak comedy about two goofballs sent to a military academy to straighten out, but instead turn the academy on its ear with their antics. Unremarkable. **96m/C VHS.** Keith Gordon, Jamie Farr, Sherman Hemsley, John Ratzenberger, Bernie Kopell, Charles Moll, George Clooney; *D:* Neal Israel.

Combat Killers **1968** A WWII Army captain grabs for individual glory on the battlefield, and jeopardizes the lives of his platoon. **96m/C VHS.** Paul Edwards, Marlene Dauden, Claude Wilson; *D:* Ken Loring; *W:* Ken Loring.

Combat Shock *American Nightmares* **1984 (R)** A Vietnam veteran returns home and can't cope with the stresses of modern life, including the lowlifes who have been taking over the streets. So he goes after some scum who have been trying to kill him, succeeds, but things don't end well. Familiar plot handled in a conventional manner. **85m/C VHS, DVD.** Ricky Giovinazzo, Nick Nasta, Veronica Stork, Mitch Maglio, Aspah Livni; *D:* Buddy Giovinazzo; *W:* Buddy Giovinazzo; *C:* Stella Varveris; *M:* Ricky Giovinazzo.

Combination Platter ½ **1993** Anxious young immigrant Robert (Lau), newly arrived from Hong Kong, becomes a waiter at the Szechuan Inn in Queens, New York, where he gets a crash course in American culture and romance (as well as tipping). Gentle comedy works best with little details that ring true: overheard customer conversations, staff banter, the kitchen scenes. Lau's earnest, but effort feels like a series of small vignettes rather than a complete story. Still, a worthy first effort for the then 24-year-old Chan, who directed on a $250,000 budget, using his parents restaurant after hours for a set. **84m/C VHS, DVD.** Jeff Lau, Coleen O'Brien, Lester Chan, Thomas S. Hsiung, David Chung, Colin Mitchell, Kenneth Lu, Eleonara Khilberg, James DuMont; *D:* Tony Chan; *W:* Tony Chan, Edwin Baker; *C:* Yoshifumi Hosoya; *M:* Brian Tibbs. Sundance '93: Screenplay.

Come Along with Me ½ **1984** TV adaptation of Shirley Jackson's unfinished novel about a woman who sells all and leaves her hometown when her husband dies, determined to start a new career as a seer. **60m/C VHS, DVD.** Estelle Parsons, Barbara Baxley, Sylvia Sidney; *D:* Joanne Woodward. **TV**

Come and Get It *Roaring Timber* **1936** A classic adaptation of the Edna Ferber novel about a lumber king battling against his son for the love of a woman. Farmer's most important Hollywood role. **99m/B VHS, DVD.** Frances Farmer, Edward Arnold, Joel McCrea, Walter Brennan, Andrea Leeds, Charles Halton; *D:* William Wyler, Howard Hawks; *W:* Jules Furthman, Jane Murfin; *C:* Rudolph Mate, Gregg Toland; *M:* Alfred Newman. Oscars '36: Support. Actor (Brennan).

Come and See *Idi i Smotri; Go and See* **1985** Harrowing, unnerving epic which depicts the horrors of war as a boy soldier roams the Russian countryside during the Nazi invasion. Some overwhelming sequences, including tracer-bullets flashing across an open field. War has rarely been rendered in such a vivid, utterly grim manner. Outstanding achievement from Soviet director Klimov. In Russian with English subtitles. **137m/C VHS, DVD.** *RU* Alexei Kravchenko, Olga Mironova, Lubomiras Lauciavicus, Vladas Bagdonas, Viktor Lorents, Juris Lumiste, Kazimir Rabetsky, Yevgeni Tilicheyev; *D:* Elem Klimov; *W:* Elem Klimov, Alex Adamovich; *C:* Alexei Rodionov; *M:* Oleg Yanchenko.

Come as You Are ½ **2005** Quickly sinking dotcom entrepreneur Craig (Sterling) hosts a reunion for his old college chums so they can meet Kellie (Fixx), his knockout fiancee. Little do they know, their buddy is desperately launching a new business. After a series of contrived events occur, a hostile porn director, crew, and cast show up to the rental house to start filming a sex video, causing Craig to fess up to his new smut-meister gig. Mostly unknown cast plays out matters of the heart and groin commendably. **83m/C DVD.** Maury Sterling, James Russo, Michelle Harrison, James Marshall, Barbara Fixx; *D:* Chuck Rose; *W:* Chuck Rose; *C:* Lawrence Schweich; *M:* Nathan Wang, John Abella. **VIDEO**

Come Back, Little Sheba ½ **1952** Unsettling drama about a worn-out housewife, her abusive, alcoholic husband and a comely boarder who causes further marital tension. The title refers to the housewife's despairing search for her lost dog. Booth, Lancaster, and Moore are all excellent. Based on the play by William Inge, this film still packs an emotional wallop. **99m/B VHS, DVD.** Burt Lancaster, Shirley Booth, Terry Moore, Richard Jaeckel, Philip Ober, Lisa Golm, Walter Kelley; *D:* Daniel Mann; *C:* James Wong Howe. Oscars '52: Actress (Booth); Cannes '53: Actress (Booth); Golden Globes '53: Actress—Drama (Booth); N.Y. Film Critics '52: Actress (Booth).

Come Back to the Five & Dime Jimmy Dean, Jimmy Dean **1982 (PG)** Five women convene at a run-down Texas drugstore for a 20-year reunion of a local James Dean fan club. The women recall earlier times and make some stunning revelations. Altman's filming of Ed Graczyk's sometimes funny, sometimes wrenching play proves fine vehicle for the actresses. Cher is probably the most impressive, but Dennis and Black are also memorable. **109m/C VHS.** Sandy Dennis, Cher, Karen Black, Kathy Bates, Sudie Bond, Marta Heflin; *D:* Robert Altman.

Come Blow Your Horn **1963** Neil Simon's first major Broadway success is a little less successful in its celluloid wrapper, suffering a bit from a familiar script. Sinatra's a playboy who blows his horn all over town, causing his close-knit New York Jewish family to warp a bit. Dad's not keen on his son's pledge of allegiance to the good life, and kid brother Bill would like to be his sibling's understudy in playboyhood. **115m/C VHS.** Frank Sinatra, Lee J. Cobb, Tony Bill, Molly Picon, Barbara Rush, Jill St. John; *D:* Bud Yorkin; *W:* Norman Lear; *C:* William H. Daniels.

Come Drink with Me *Da zui xia; Great Drunken Hero* **1965** Credited with inspiring both "Kill Bill" and "Crouching Tiger, Hidden Dragon" and directed by veteran filmmaker King Hu for the Shaw Brothers, this flick features equally legendary Chinese actress Cheng Pei-Pei as Golden Swallow, a female warrior disguised as a man hired to find the governor's kidnapped son. After a bar fight, she is joined in her quest by a kung fu master called the Drunken Cat, who has business of his own with the kidnappers. While it isn't the nonstop action film many classic kung fu movies are, Cheng Pei-Pei is a far more accomplished martial artist than some actors of the time. **91m/C DVD.** *CH* Jackie Chan, Pei-pei Ching, Hua Yueh, Hung Lieh Chen, Yunzhong Li, Chih-Ching Yang; *D:* King Hu; *W:* King Hu, Yang Erh; *C:* Tadashi Nishimoto; *M:* Lan-Ping Chow.

Come Early Morning ½ **2006 (R)** Lucy Fowler (Judd) lives two lives in her Arkansas community: she's very efficient at her day contractor job while raising hell as a hard-drinking, one-night-stand kinda gal in the evening. Maybe she's just emulating her womanizing, alcoholic pop (Wilson). Courtly newcomer Cal (Donovan) refuses to let her use him and leave, but even Cal may not be able to overcome Lucy's self-destructiveness. Adams does well with her slice-of-life tale—her writing/directing debut—as does surrogate Judd (Adams once intended to play the lead herself). **97m/C DVD.** *US* Ashley Judd, Jeffrey Donovan, Tim Blake Nelson, Laura Prepon, Stacy Keach, Scott Wilson, Diane Ladd, Pat Corley; *D:* Joey Lauren Adams; *W:* Joey Lauren Adams; *C:* Tim Orr; *M:* Alan Brewer.

Come on, Cowboys ½ **1937** The Three Mesquiteers rescue an old circus friend from certain death. Part of "The Three Mesquiteers" series. **54m/B VHS.** Robert "Bob" Livingston, Ray Corrigan, Max Terhune, Maxine Doyle, Willie Fung, Edward Peil Jr., Horace Murphy; *D:* Joseph Kane; *W:* Betty Burbridge; *C:* Ernest Miller.

Come on Danger! ½ **1932** Keene makes his "B" Western debut, out to avenge the death of his brother and battle an outlaw gang. Haydon is forced into a life of crime in order to save her ranch from villain Ellis and only Texas Ranger Keene can set her free. **60m/B VHS.** Tom Keene, Julie Haydon, Roscoe Ates, Robert Ellis, Wade Boteler; ***D:*** Robert F. "Bob" Hill; ***W:*** Bennett Cohen.

Come on Rangers *Come On Ranger* **1938** Rogers and his friends go to Texas to avenge the death of a comrade. **54m/B VHS.** Roy Rogers, George "Gabby" Hayes, Lynne Roberts, Raymond Hatton, J. Farrell MacDonald, Purnell Pratt, Harry Woods; ***D:*** Joseph Kane; ***W:*** Gerald Geraghty, Jack Natteford; ***C:*** Al Wilson; ***M:*** Cy Feuer.

Come on Tarzan 1/2 **1932** Maynard and his trusty horse Tarzan save wild horses from the bad guys who want to turn them into dog food. **60m/B VHS.** Ken Maynard, Merna Kennedy, Niles Welch, Roy Stewart, Kate Campbell, Robert F. (Bob) Kortman, Nelson McDowell, Jack Rockwell; ***D:*** Alan James; ***W:*** Alan James.

Come See the Paradise **1990 (R)** Jack McGurn (Quaid) takes a job at a movie theatre in Los Angeles' Little Tokyo and falls for owner's daughter Lily (Tomita). They marry, but after the bombing of Pearl Harbor all Japanese-Americans are interned. Told in flashback, the story offers a candid look at the racism implicit in the relocations and the hypocrisy that often lurks beneath the surface of the pursuit of liberty and justice for all. Sometimes melodramatic script indulges a bit too much in the obvious, but the subject is worthwhile, one that has not yet been cast into the vast bin of Hollywood cliches. The cast, apart from Quaid's misguided attempt at seriousness, is excellent. **135m/C VHS, DVD.** Dennis Quaid, Tamlyn Tomita, Sab Shimono, Shizuko Hoshi, Stan(ford) Egi, Ronald Yamamoto, Akemi Nishino, Naomi Nakano, Brady Tsurutani, Pruitt Taylor Vince, Joe Lisi; ***D:*** Alan Parker; ***W:*** Alan Parker; ***M:*** Randy Edelman.

Come September 1/2 **1961** American business tycoon Robert Talbot (Hudson) maintains a holiday villa on the Italian Riveria. But the only time he uses the place is the month of September, so when Talbot arrives in July he discovers his enterprising major domo Maurice (Slezak) has been managing the place as a hotel the rest of the year. Talbot finds his home filled with tourists and, to make matters worse, discovers his Italian lover Lisa (Lollobrigida) about to get married. Darin and Dee are the film's romantic ingenues and wound up getting married after filming wrapped; his screen debut. **114m/C VHS, DVD.** Rock Hudson, Gina Lollobrigida, Sandra Dee, Bobby Darin, Walter Slezak, Joel Grey, Brenda de Banzie; ***D:*** Robert Mulligan; ***W:*** Stanley Shapiro, Maurice Richlin; ***C:*** William H. Daniels; ***M:*** Hans J. Salter.

Come to the Stable **1949** Warm, delightful story about two French nuns, Young and Holm, who arrive in New England and set about building a children's hospital. Although Catholic in intent, pic demonstrates that faith and tenacity can move mountains. (This film must have been Fox's response to Paramount's "Going My Way" and "The Bells of Saint Mary's.") Based on a story by Clare Boothe Luce. **94m/B VHS.** Loretta Young, Celeste Holm, Hugh Marlowe, Elsa Lanchester, Regis Toomey, Mike Mazurki; ***D:*** Henry Koster; ***W:*** Oscar Millard, Sally Benson; ***C:*** Joseph LaShelle; ***M:*** Cyril Mockridge.

Come Undone *Presque Rien* **2000** A matter of fact coming of age tale about a French teenager, Mathieu (Elkaim), who acknowledges his sexuality when he falls in love with the slightly older Cedric (Rideau). Mathieu and his younger sister Sarah (Legrix) are stuck at their summer house in a coastal resort town with their depressed mother (Reymond) and their aunt (Matheron) who's serving as a nurse/housekeeper. The emotional Mathieu finds sex and solace with the volatile Cedric but their affair doesn't work out as expected. Film is non-linear and the viewer must piece together what has happened from the various scenes, which can be confusing. French with subtitles. **98m/C VHS, DVD.** *FR* Jeremie Elkaim, Stephane Rideau, Marie Matheron, Laetitia Legrix, Dominique Reymond, Nils Ohlund, Rejane Kerdaffrec, Guy Houssier; ***D:*** Sabastian Lifshitz; ***W:*** Sabastian Lifshitz, Stephane Bouquet; ***C:*** Pascal Paoucet; ***M:*** Perry Blake.

The Comeback *The Day the Screaming Stopped* **1977** A singer attempting a comeback in England finds his wife murdered. **100m/C VHS, DVD.** *GB* Jack Jones, Pamela Stephenson, David Doyle, Bill Owen, Sheila Keith, Richard Johnson; ***D:*** Pete Walker.

Comeback 1/2 **1983** The story of a disillusioned rock star, played by Eric Burdon (the lead singer of the Animals), who gives up his life in the fast lane and tries to go back to his roots. **105m/C VHS, DVD.** Eric Burdon; ***D:*** Christel Bushmann; ***M:*** Eric Burdon.

Comeback Kid **1980** An ex-big league baseball player is conned into coaching an urban team of smarmy street youths, and falls for their playground supervisor. **97m/C VHS.** John Ritter, Susan Dey; ***D:*** Peter Levin. **TV**

The Comebacks **2007 (PG-13)** Truly lame spoof of sports flicks. Losing football coach Lambeau Fields (Koechner) gets a last chance when he's hired at Heartland State U. So he moves his family, including limber hottie daughter Michelle (Nevin), to Texas to whip a bunch of losers into shape. The climatic game is called the Toilet Bowl—yea, those are the jokes, folks, in another "spoof everything and something might be funny" outing. **84m/C DVD.** *US* David Koechner, Melora Hardin, Brooke Nevin, Carl Weathers, Matthew Lawrence, Nick Searcy, Jermaine Williams, Jesse Garcia, George Back, Eric Christian Olsen, Will Arnett, Bradley Cooper, Dax Shepard, Jackie Long, Robert Ri'chard, Martin Spanjers, Jon(athan) Gries, Andy Dick, Kerri Kenney, Dennis Rodman, Frank Caliendo, Finesse Mitchell, Noureen DeWulf; ***Cameos:*** John Salley, Lawrence Taylor, Eric Dickerson, Michael Irvin; ***D:*** Tom Brady; ***W:*** Ed Yeager, Joey Gutierrez; ***C:*** Anthony B. Richmond; ***M:*** Christopher Lennertz.

The Comedians 1/2 **1967** Disturbing and powerful drama of political intrigue set against the murderous dictatorship of "Papa Doc" Duvalier. Burton plays the cynical owner of a resort hotel with Taylor as his German mistress. Ustinov is great as he does his usual scene-stealing in his role as a South American ambassador married to Taylor. Excellent cast was somewhat held back by sluggish direction and an uninspired script. Based on the novel of the same name by Graham Greene. **148m/C VHS.** Elizabeth Taylor, Richard Burton, Alec Guinness, Peter Ustinov, Paul Ford, Lillian Gish, Raymond St. Jacques, Zakes Mokae; ***D:*** Peter Glenville; ***W:*** Graham Greene. Natl. Bd. of Review '67: Support. Actor (Ford).

Comedy of Innocence *Comedie de L'Innocence* **2000** Nine-year-old Camille (Hugon) is addicted to videotaping everything that happens in his life. During a visit to the park, Camille insists that Ariane (Huppert) isn't his real mother and gives her an address that he says is his real home. When they visit, Ariane learns that the owner, Isabelle (Balibar), had a son Camille's age who drowned. Isabelle is later institutionalized, but escapes and Camille also runs away. Ariane watches Camille's videotapes to get clues to what's happened to her son. Adapted from the novel "Il Figlio di Due Madre" by Massimo Bontempelli. French with subtitles. **98m/C DVD.** *FR* Isabelle Huppert, Jeanne Balibar, Charles Berling, Nils Hugon, Edith Scob, Denis Podalydes; ***D:*** Raul Ruiz; ***W:*** Raul Ruiz, Francoise Dumas; ***C:*** Jacques Bouquin; ***M:*** Jorge Arriagada.

Comedy of Power *L'Ivresse du Pouvoir* **2006** The comedy comes from the self-important behavior of the characters. Huppert grimaces her way through her seventh collaboration with Chabrol, playing zealous, incorruptible examining magistrate Jeanne Charmant-Killman. She's looking into a corporate embezzlement scandal (based on a true incident) that has serious political implications for the government. Meanwhile, her neglected hubby, Philippe (Renucci), becomes even more unhappy when the case brings Jeanne a lot of attention. But she's breaking unspoken social codes among what is still a very male-dominated world. French with subtitles. **110m/C DVD.** *FR GE* Isabelle Huppert, Francois Berleand, Thomas Chabrol, Robin Renucci, Patrick Bruel, Marilyne Canto, Jean-Francois Balmer; ***D:*** Claude Chabrol; ***W:*** Claude Chabrol, Odile Barski; ***C:*** Eduardo Serra; ***M:*** Matthieu Chabrol.

The Comedy of Terrors *The Graveside Story* **1964** Comedy in which some deranged undertakers take a hands-on approach to insuring their continued employment. Much fun is supplied by the quartet of Price, Lorre, Karloff, and Rathbone, all veterans of the horror genre. **84m/C VHS, DVD.** Vincent Price, Peter Lorre, Boris Karloff, Basil Rathbone, Joe E. Brown, Joyce Jameson, Beverly (Hills) Powers, Buddy Mason; ***D:*** Jacques Tourneur; ***W:*** Richard Matheson; ***C:*** Floyd Crosby; ***M:*** Les Baxter.

Comes a Horseman 1/2 **1978 (PG)** Robards is a cattle baron, attempting to gobble up all the oil-rich land his neighbor owns. Neighbor Fonda has the courage to stand up to him, with the help of a WWII veteran and the local old timer Farnsworth, in this slow-moving but intriguing western drama. **119m/C VHS, DVD.** James Caan, Jane Fonda, Jason Robards Jr., George Grizzard, Richard Farnsworth, Jim Davis, Mark Harmon; ***D:*** Alan J. Pakula; ***W:*** Dennis Lynton Clark; ***C:*** Gordon Willis; ***M:*** Michael Small. Natl. Bd. of Review '78: Support. Actor (Farnsworth); Natl. Soc. Film Critics '78: Support. Actor (Farnsworth).

Comfort and Joy 1/2 **1984 (PG)** After his kleptomaniac girlfriend deserts him, a Scottish disc jockey is forced to reevaluate his life. He becomes involved in an underworld battle between two mob-owned local ice cream companies. Another odd comedy gem from Forsyth, who did "Gregory's Girl" and "Local Hero." Music by Dire Straits guitarist Knopfler. **93m/C VHS.** *GB* Bill Paterson, Eleanor David, Clare Grogan, Alex Norton, Patrick Malahide, Rikki Fulton, Roberto Berrardi; ***D:*** Bill Forsyth; ***W:*** Bill Forsyth; ***C:*** Chris Menges; ***M:*** Mark Knopfler. Natl. Soc. Film Critics '84: Cinematog.

The Comfort of Strangers **1991 (R)** Atmospheric psychological thriller. Mary and Colin (Richardson and Everett), a handsome young British couple, take a Venetian holiday to rediscover the passion in their relationship. Lost in the city, they chance, it seems, upon Robert (Walken), a sort of Virgil in an Italian suit. He later reappears, and, abetted by his wife Caroline (Mirren), gradually leads the couple on an eerie tour of urbane decadence that hints at danger. Psychologically tantalizing and horrifyingly erotic, the movie's based on Ian McEwan's novel. **102m/C VHS, DVD.** Christopher Walken, Natasha Richardson, Rupert Everett, Helen Mirren; ***D:*** Paul Schrader; ***W:*** Harold Pinter; ***C:*** Dante Spinotti; ***M:*** Angelo Badalamenti.

The Comic **1969 (PG)** Van Dyke is terrific as a silent screen comedian (a composite of several real-life screen comics) whose ego destroys his career. Recreations of silent films, and the blend of comedy and pathos, are especially effective. **96m/C VHS.** Dick Van Dyke, Mickey Rooney, Michele Lee, Cornel Wilde, Nina Wayne, Pert Kelton, Jeannine Riley; ***D:*** Carl Reiner; ***W:*** Carl Reiner.

The Comic **1985** In a future police state, a young comedian kills the star and takes his place in the show. His future rises, but who cares? **90m/C VHS.** Steve Munroe, Bernard Plant, Jeff Pirie; ***D:*** Richard Driscoll.

Comic Act **1998** The world of London stand-up comedy is the setting for a surprisingly sexy look at life beyond the microphone. Gus (Schneider) and Jay (Mullarkey) are struggling until Alex (Webster) joins their act. Her combination of intelligence and unembarrassed sexuality makes them a hit with audiences, and with that come all the temptations (and all the cliches) of show business. Yes, the same story has been told countless times, but this version is fresh and energetic. **107m/C VHS, DVD.** Stephen Moyer, Neil Mullarkey, David Schneider, Suki Webster, Magnus Hastings; ***D:*** Jack Hazan; ***W:*** Jack Hazan, David Mingay; ***C:*** Richard Branczik; ***M:*** Patrick Gowers.

Comic Book Kids 1/2 **1982 (G)** Two youngsters enjoy visiting their friend's comic strip studio, since they have the power to project themselves into the cartoon stories. Viewers will be less impressed. **90m/C VHS.** Joseph Campanella, Billy Barty, Robyn Finn, Jim Engelhardt, Fay De Witt, Anjelica Huston; ***D:*** Gene Weed; ***W:*** Jim Engelhardt.

Comic Book: The Movie **2004 (PG-13)** Donald Swan (director Hamill) is a teacher and comic book fan who has been hired as a technical consultant by a Hollywood studio that's adapting his favorite character into a big-budget movie. He soon learns that the studio plans on transforming the character from a wholesome WWII-era Nazi-fighter into a vengeful anti-terrorist vigilante, and begins a crusade to prevent the change. Hamill has a deep well of knowledge and affection for the comics industry and its fans, not to mention the rhythms of the fan convention. He uses it all to good effect here, capturing, but not making fun of the attitudes of everyone involved. Much of the dialogue seems ad-libbed, and that also works to the movie's advantage. **106m/C DVD.** Mark Hamill, Scott LaRose, Roger Rose, Arleen (Arlene) Sorkin, Tom Kenny, Billy West, Debi Derryberry, Donna D'Errico, Jonathan Winters, Sid Caesar, Lori Alan; ***Cameos:*** Jim (Jonah) Cummings, Stan Lee, Peter David, Kevin Smith, Ray Harryhausen, Bruce Campbell, Phil Morris, Chase Masterson, J.J. (Jeffrey) Abrams, Paul Dini, Billy Mumy, Ron Perlman, Peter Mayhew, David Prowse, Hugh Hefner; ***D:*** Mark Hamill; ***C:*** Jason Cooley; ***M:*** Billy West. **VIDEO**

Comic Book Villains **2002 (R)** Raymond (Logue) owns a comic book store for the love of the genre while Norman (Rapaport) and his wife Judy (Lyonne) are in it for the money. Both learn that a local collector has just died but find out that the man's mother (Brennan) refuses to sell his valuable collection. This doesn't stop either Raymond or Norman from planning ways to acquire the goods—although unexpected third-party Carter (Elwes) decides he'll just steal them. **93m/C VHS, DVD.** Donal Logue, Michael Rapaport, Natasha Lyonne, DJ Qualls, Cary Elwes, James Duval, Danny Masterson, Monet Mazur; ***D:*** James Dale Robinson; ***W:*** James Dale Robinson; ***C:*** Blake T. Evans; ***M:*** Joseph (Joey) Altruda.

Comin' Round the Mountain 1/2 **1951** The duo are caught in a Kentucky family feud while seeking a fortune in gold. Funniest bit has backwoods witch Hamilton squaring off with Costello when he refuses to pay for the love potion she's made him. **77m/B VHS, DVD.** Bud Abbott, Lou Costello, Dorothy Shay, Kirby Grant, Joseph (Joe) Sawyer, Margaret Hamilton, Glenn Strange, Guy Wilkerson; ***D:*** Charles Lamont; ***W:*** John Grant, Robert Lees, Frederic Rinaldo.

Coming Apart **1969** Free-love was never really very free as shrink Torn finds when he secretly films his sexual escapades with a variety of women, which lead to his own nervous breakdown. Avant-garde, sexually daring, and over-the-top. **111m/B VHS, DVD.** Rip Torn, Sally Kirkland, Viveca Lindfors; ***D:*** Milton Moses Ginsberg; ***W:*** Milton Moses Ginsberg; ***C:*** Jack Yager.

Coming Home 1/2 **1978 (R)** Looks at the effect of the Vietnam War on home front. The wife of a gung-ho Marine officer volunteers as an aide in a Veteran's Hospital, befriends and eventually falls in love with a Vietnam vet, paralyzed from war injuries. His attitudes, pain, and first-hand knowledge of the war force her to re-examine her previously automatic responses. Honest look at the everyday life of disabled veterans, unusual vision of the possibilities of simple friendship between men and women. Fonda and Voight are great; Dern's character suffers from weak scriptwriting late in the film. Critically acclaimed. Compelling score from late '60s music. **130m/C VHS, DVD.** Jane Fonda, Jon Voight, Bruce Dern, Penelope Milford, Robert Carradine, Robert Ginty, Mary Gregory, Kathleen Miller, Beeson Carroll, Willie Tyler, Charles Cyphers, Olivia Cole, Tresa Hughes, Bruce French, Richard Lawson, Rita Taggart, Pat Corley; ***D:*** Hal Ashby; ***W:*** Robert C. Jones; ***C:*** Haskell Wexler. Oscars '78: Actor (Voight), Actress (Fonda), Orig. Screenplay; Cannes '78: Actor (Voight); Golden Globes '79: Actor—Drama (Voight), Actress—Drama (Fonda); L.A. Film Critics '78: Actor (Voight), Actress (Fonda), Film; N.Y. Film Critics '78: Actor (Voight); Writers Guild '78: Orig. Screenplay.

Coming Home 1/2 *Rosamunde Pilcher's Coming Home* **1998** It's 1935, and Judith Dunbar is left behind in a British boarding school when her mother and sister travel to Singapore to join Judith's father. A school friendship with Loveday Carey-Lewis introduces Judith to the eccentric world of British aristocracy but the coming of WWII proves to be her coming of age. Based on the book by Rosamunde Pilcher. Made for German TV. **205m/C VHS, DVD.** *GE* Peter O'Toole, Joanna Lumley, David McCallum, Emily Mortimer, Katie Ryder Richardson, Paul Bettany, Susan Hampshire, Penelope Keith, Patrick Ryecart, Malcolm Stoddard; ***D:*** Giles Foster; ***W:*** John Goldsmith. **TV**

The Coming of Amos **1925** A wonderful send-up of all those Fairbanks-style melodramas, with La Rocque as an Aussie on vacation on the French Riviera falling for and eventually rescuing Goudal, as the Russian princess held captive by the lustful Beery. **60m/B VHS.** Rod La Rocque, Jetta Goudal, Noah Beery Sr., Florence Vidor; ***D:*** Paul Sloane.

Coming Out **1989** The first film produced by East Germany to deal with homosexuality. Ambivalent Philip (Freihof) is a popular high school educator, who has been involved with another teacher, Tanja (Manzel), who has just learned she's pregnant. But Philip has just admitted to himself that his attraction to the younger Matthias (Kummer) is more erotic than friendly. Philip, however, is an emotional coward—he's worried about prejudice and can't be honest with either lover, leading to a painful confrontation. German with subtitles. **113m/C VHS, DVD.** *GE* Matthias Freihof, Dagmar Manzel, Dirk Kummer; ***D:*** Heiner Carow; ***W:*** Wolfram Witt; ***C:*** Martin Schlesinger; ***M:*** Stefan Carow.

Coming Out Alive **½ 1984** Tense thriller about a woman and her hired mercenary who try to rescue her kidnapped son from his estranged father—a radical is involved in an assassination plot. Hylands is especially compelling. **73m/C VHS.** *CA* Helen Shaver, Scott Hylands, Michael Ironside, Monica Parker; ***D:*** Don McBrearty.

Coming Out of the Ice **1982 (PG)** Engrossing true story of Victor Herman, an outstanding American athlete who worked in Russia in the 1930s. He was imprisoned in Siberia (for 38 years!) for refusing to renounce his American citizenship. **100m/C VHS.** John Savage, Willie Nelson, Ben Cross, Francesca Annis, Peter Vaughan; ***D:*** Waris Hussein; ***M:*** Maurice Jarre. **TV**

Coming Soon **½ 1999 (R)** Three Manhattan prep school seniors deal with their sexual coming of age as well as college admission. Nell (Vessey), Stream (Root), and Jenny (Hoffman) discuss orgasms and try to find just the right guy. The unrated version clocks in at 96 minutes. **90m/C VHS, DVD.** Gaby Hoffman, Tricia Vessey, Ryan Reynolds, Bonnie Root, James Roday, Spalding Gray, Mia Farrow, Ryan O'Neal, Peter Bogdanovich, Leslie Lyles, Yasmine Bleeth; ***D:*** Colette Burson; ***W:*** Colette Burson, Kate Robin; ***C:*** Joaquin Baca-Asay.

Coming Through **½ 1985** Writer D.H. Lawrence meets the married Frieda von Richthofer and begins a scandalous affair which intertwines with his own writings, and the life of a young man in the present day. British TV production lacks passion. **78m/C VHS, DVD.** *GB* Kenneth Branagh, Helen Mirren, Alison Steadman, Philip Martin Brown, Norman Rodway; ***D:*** Peter Barber-Fleming; ***W:*** Alan Plater. **TV**

Coming to America **1988 (R)** An African prince (Murphy) decides to come to America in search of a suitable bride. He lands in Queens, and quickly finds American women to be more confusing than he imagined. Sometimes overly cute entertainment relieved by clever costume cameos by Murphy and Hall. Later lawsuit resulted in columnist Art Buchwald being given credit for story. **116m/C VHS, DVD, Blu-ray Disc, HD DVD.** Eddie Murphy, Arsenio Hall, James Earl Jones, John Amos, Madge Sinclair, Shari Headley, Don Ameche, Louie Anderson, Paul Bates, Allison Dean, Eriq La Salle, Calvin Lockhart, Samuel L. Jackson, Cuba Gooding Jr., Vanessa Bell Calloway, Frankie Faison, Vondie Curtis-Hall; ***D:*** John Landis; ***W:*** David Sheffield, Barry W. Blaustein; ***C:*** Woody Omens; ***M:*** Nile Rodgers.

Coming Up Roses **½** *Rhosyn A Rhith* **1987 (PG)** Pleasant comedy about the residents of a small mining village in the South of Wales who fight to keep their local movie house from being shut down. In Welsh with English subtitles. **95m/C VHS.** *GB* Dafydd Hywel, Iola Gregory, Olive Michael, Mari Emlyn, Bill Paterson; ***D:*** Stephen Bayly; ***W:*** Ruth Carter; ***M:*** Michael Storey.

The Command **½ 1954** Warner Bros. first film in CinemaScope, which at least makes the big Indians vs. the wagon train battle interesting. Inexperienced Army medical officer Capt. MacClaw (Madison) must take command when his senior officer is killed. This puts him in charge of escorting the wagon train through hostile territory and earning the respect of the men in his command, including skeptical Sgt. Elliott (Whitmore). **94m/C DVD.** Guy Madison, James Whitmore, Joan Weldon, Carl Benton Reid, Harvey Lembeck, Ray Teal; ***D:*** David Butler; ***W:*** Russell S. Hughes.

Command Decision **½ 1948** Upon realizing he must send his men on missions-of-no-return to destroy German jet production, Gable's WWII flight commander becomes tactically at odds with his political superior, Pidgeon (who's not keen to have his precision bombing plans placed in an unflattering light). Based on the stage hit by William Wister Haines, it's a late war pic by Wood, who earlier directed such diverse efforts as "A Night at the Opera," "The Devil and Miss Jones," and "Our Town." Vintage war-is-hell actioner. **112m/B VHS, DVD.** Clark Gable, Walter Pidgeon, Van Johnson, Brian Donlevy, Charles Bickford, John Hodiak, Ray Collins, Edward Earle, Sam Flint, Warner Anderson, Don Haggerty, Henry Hall, Alvin Hammer, Holmes Herbert; ***D:*** Sam Wood; ***W:*** George Froeschel, William Wister Haines, William R. Laidlaw; ***C:*** Harold Rosson; ***M:*** Miklos Rozsa.

Command Performance **½ 2009 (R)** Generic B-actioner. Drummer Joe (Lundgren) and his band are in Moscow for a charity concert with headliner Venus (Smith). Terrorists storm the arena and take hostages, including Venus, the Russian president and his two daughters, and the American ambassador. Naturally Joe, accompanied by Russian agent Mikhail (Baharov), must save the day. **93m/C DVD.** Dolph Lundgren, Melissaa Ann Smith, Dave Legano, Zahary Baharov, Hristo Naumov Shopov, Clement von Franckenstein, Ida Lundgren, Robin Dobson; ***D:*** Dolph Lundgren; ***W:*** Dolph Lundgren, Steve Latshaw; ***C:*** Marc Windon; ***M:*** Adam Norden. **VIDEO**

Commandments **1996 (R)** When Seth Warner (Quinn) loses his wife (Going), job, and even his dog, he finds no solace in faith and decides to test why God would make a good man suffer by breaking every one of the 10 commandments. Rachel (Cox), his wife's sister, persuades him to move in with her and her jerk husband Harry (LaPaglia), who can't really be bothered by Seth's problems. The three leads certainly have presence but given the ambivalence of the material, the movie doesn't hang together. **92m/C VHS, DVD.** Aidan Quinn, Courteney Cox, Anthony LaPaglia, Louis Zorich, Pat McNamara, Tom Aldredge, Pamela Gray, Alice Drummond, Jack Gilpin; ***Cameos:*** Joanna Going; ***D:*** Daniel Taplitz; ***W:*** Daniel Taplitz; ***C:*** Slawomir Idziak; ***M:*** Joseph Vitarelli.

Commando **1985 (R)** An ex-commando leader's daughter is kidnapped in a blackmail scheme to make him depose a South American president. He fights instead, and proceeds to rescue his daughter amid a torrential flow of falling bodies. Violent action spiced with throwaway comic lines. **90m/C VHS, DVD, Blu-ray Disc.** Chelsea Field, Bill Paxton, Arnold Schwarzenegger, Rae Dawn Chong, Dan Hedaya, Vernon Wells, James Olson, David Patrick Kelly, Alyssa Milano, Bill Duke; ***D:*** Mark L. Lester; ***W:*** Steven E. de Souza; ***C:*** Matthew F. Leonetti; ***M:*** James Horner.

Commando Attack **½ 1967** A tough sergeant leads a group of misfit soldiers to blow up a German radio transmitter the day before D-Day. **90m/C VHS.** Michael Rennie, Monica Randall, Bob Sullivan; ***D:*** Leon Klimovsky.

Commando Invasion **1987** When an army captain is accused of murder, he hunts down the man he knows is responsible for the crime. Jungle revenge mayhem is confusing. Set in Vietnam. **90m/C VHS.** Jim Gaines, Michael James, Gordon Mitchell, Carol Roberts, Pat Vance, Ken(saku) Watanabe; ***D:*** John Gale.

Commando Squad **1976 (R)** During WWII, soldiers go to battle to prevent the development of a device that re-animates flesh. The script stays dead. **82m/C VHS.** Chuck Alford, Peter Owen, April Adams; ***D:*** Charles Nizet.

Commando Squad **1987 (R)** Story of drug agents undercover in Mexico, and a female agent who rescues her kidnapped lover. Firepower is wasted, but Shower is a former "Playboy" Playmate of the Year. **90m/C VHS.** Brian Thompson, William (Bill) Smith, Kathy Shower, Sid Haig, Robert Quarry, Ross Hagen, Mel Welles, Marie Windsor, Russ Tamblyn; ***D:*** Fred Olen Ray.

Commandos **½** *Sullivan's Marauders* **1973 (PG)** Commando operation against Rommel's forces in North Africa during WWII. Too much said, not enough action. **100m/C VHS, DVD.** *GE IT* Lee Van Cleef, Jack Kelly, Giampiero Albertini, Marilu Tolo; ***D:*** Armando Crispino; ***W:*** Armando Crispino, Lucio Battistrada, Dario Argento, Stefano Strucchi; ***C:*** Benito Frattari; ***M:*** Mario Nascimbene.

Commandos Strike at Dawn **½ 1943** Norwegian villagers, including Muni, fight the invading Nazis, and eventually help the British Navy battle them over an Arctic supply line. Okay script helped along by veteran actors Muni and Gish. Based on a C.S. Forester story. **100m/B VHS, DVD.** Paul Muni, Lillian Gish, Cedric Hardwicke, Anna Lee, Ray Collins, Robert Coote, Alexander Knox, Rosemary DeCamp; ***D:*** John Farrow; ***W:*** Irwin Shaw; ***C:*** William Mellor.

Comment Ca Va? *How Is It Going?* **1976** The boss and workers in a Communist publishing house decide to make a simple film about how information is manufactured. But Odette, one of the workers, has some strange ideas about filmmaking. In French with English subtitles. **76m/C VHS.** *FR* Michel Marot, Anne-Marie Mieville; ***D:*** Anne-Marie Mieville, Jean-Luc Godard; ***W:*** Anne-Marie Mieville, Jean-Luc Godard; ***C:*** William Lubtchansky; ***M:*** Jean Schwarz.

The Commies Are Coming, the Commies Are Coming *Red Nightmare* **1957** Cult classic will leave viewers red from laughing in disbelief. Webb narrates this anti-communist movie about the Russians taking over the United States. Filmed in a documentary style, it captures the paranoia of the times. Re-released in 1984, just before the Evil Empire collapsed. **60m/B VHS.** Jack Webb, Jack Kelly, Jeanne Cooper, Peter Brown, Pat(ricia) Woodell, Andrew Duggan, Peter Breck, Robert Conrad; ***D:*** George Waggner; ***W:*** Vincent Fotre; ***C:*** Robert Hoffman; ***M:*** William Lara.

Commissar *Komissar* **1968** Before the Soviet Union ended up in the ashcan of history, this film was labeled as "treason" and shelved in Red Russia. Now, even Americans can view the story of a female Soviet soldier who becomes pregnant during the civil war of 1922. The Soviet military has no policy regarding pregnancy, so the woman is dumped on a family of outcast Jews to complete her pregnancy. This film makes the strong statement that women were just as discriminated against in the U.S.S.R. as were many races or creeds, especially Jews. In Russian with English subtitles. Released in the U.S. in 1988. **105m/B VHS, DVD.** *RU* Nonna Mordyukova, Rolan Bykov, Raisa Nedashkovskaya, Vasily Shukshin, Pavlik Levin, Ludmilla Volinskaya; ***D:*** Alexander Askoldov; ***W:*** Alexander Askoldov; ***C:*** Valery Ginsberg; ***M:*** Alfred Schnittke.

The Commitments **1991 (R)** Convinced that they can bring soul music to Dublin, a group of working-class youth form a band. High-energy production paints an interesting, unromanticized picture of modern Ireland and refuses to follow standard showbiz cliches, even though its lack of resolution hurts. Honest, whimsical dialogue laced with poetic obscenities, delivered by a cast of mostly unknowns. Very successful soundtrack features the music of Wilson Pickett, James Brown, Otis Redding, Aretha Franklin, Percy Sledge, and others, and received a Grammy nomination. Based on the book "The Commitments" by Roddy Doyle, part of a trilogy which includes "The Snapper" and "The Van." **116m/C VHS, DVD.** *IR* Andrew Strong, Bronagh Gallagher, Glen Hansard, Michael Aberne, Dick Massey, Ken McCluskey, Robert Arkins, Dave Finnegan, Johnny Murphy, Angeline Ball, Felim Gormley, Maria Doyle Kennedy, Colm Meaney; ***D:*** Alan Parker; ***W:*** Dick Clement, Roddy Doyle, Ian La Frenais; ***C:*** Gale Tattersall; ***M:*** Paul Bushnell. British Acad. '91: Adapt. Screenplay, Director (Parker), Film.

Committed **½ 1991 (R)** Schlockmeister Levey's latest directorial effort is a step above his earlier "Slumber Party" and "Happy Hooker Goes to Washington," a statement ringing with the faintest of praise. Thinking she's applying for a job at an asylum, a nurse discovers she has committed herself. Try as she may, not even a committed nurse can snake her way out of the pit of madness they call "The Institute." **93m/C VHS.** Jennifer O'Neill, William Windom, Robert Forster, Ron Palillo, Sydney Lassick; ***D:*** William A. Levey.

Committed **½ 1999 (R)** Joline (Graham) is the madly devoted wife of Carl (Wilson) who, two years after their marriage, decides he should leave their New York home to take a job in the Southwest—alone. Joline soon decides to track him down and heads out on the usual misadventurous road trip, accompanied by her brother (Affleck) and a handsome neighbor (Visnjic). Of course, when she does find Carl there's quite a lot that needs to be resolved. **98m/C VHS, DVD.** Heather Graham, Luke Wilson, Casey Affleck, Goran Visnjic, Patricia Velasquez, Alfonso Arau, Mark Ruffalo, Kim Dickens, Clea DuVall; ***D:*** Lisa Krueger; ***W:*** Lisa Krueger; ***C:*** Tom Krueger. Sundance '00: Cinematog.

Common Bonds **½ 1991 (PG)** After being put together in an experimental outreach program, two mismatched partners struggle to break free from a system that threatens to destroy them both. **109m/C VHS.** Rae Dawn Chong, Michael Ironside, Brad Dourif; ***D:*** Allan Goldstein; ***M:*** Graeme Coleman.

Common Ground **½ 2000** Three stories dealing with homosexuality in America from the 1950s to the present in the same small town of Homer, Connecticut. Vogel's "A Friend of Dorothy" finds Dorothy (Murphy) returning home after being dishonorably discharged from the Navy after being caught at a gay bar. McNally's "Mr. Roberts" focuses on the 70s and confused high school senior Toby Anderson (Thomas). Toby reaches out for some understanding from his closeted French teacher (Weber), only to be rejected. Fierstein's "Andy and Amos" takes place in 2000, with Amos (Le Gros) having the jitters over his commitment ceremony to lover Andy (Airlie). But it's his conservative dad Ira (Asner) who turns out to be an unexpected booster. **105m/C VHS.** Brittany Murphy, Margot Kidder, Brian Kerwin, Mimi Rogers, Jason Priestley, Joanne Vannicola, Helen Shaver, Jonathan Taylor Thomas, Steven Weber, Dan Lauria, Ed Asner, James LeGros, Andrew Airlie, Harvey Fierstein, Beau Bridges, Eric Stoltz; ***D:*** Donna Deitch; ***W:*** Harvey Fierstein, Terrance McNally, Paula Vogel; ***C:*** Jacek Laskus. **CABLE**

Common Law Wife **1963 (R)** Made-for-the-drive-in flick about a man whose common law marriage is threatened by his niece, who wants his money. Murder and mayhem abound when the man's moonshine is poisoned. Cheap and exploitative. **81m/B VHS, DVD.** Lacy Kelly, Shugfoot Rainey, Annabelle Lee, Jody Works, Anne MacAdams, George Edgely; ***D:*** Eric Sayers.

Common Threads: Stories from the Quilt **1989** Heavily awarded, made-for-cable-TV documentary about the Quilt: an immense 14-acre blanket created by the survivors of AIDS victims as a monument to their loved ones' premature deaths. All proceeds go to the NAMES Project Foundation in support of the Quilt and AIDS service providers. **79m/C VHS.** ***D:*** Robert Epstein, Jeffrey Friedman; ***Nar:*** Dustin Hoffman. Oscars '89: Feature Doc.

Communion **1989 (R)** A serious adaptation of the purportedly nonfictional bestseller by Whitley Strieber about his family's abduction by extraterrestrials. Spacey new age story is overlong and hard to swallow. **103m/C VHS, DVD.** Christopher Walken, Lindsay Crouse, Frances Sternhagen, Joel Carlson, Andreas Katsulas, Basil Hoffman; ***D:*** Philippe Mora; ***M:*** Eric Clapton.

Companeros 1/2 **1970 (R)** The Mexican revolution. Shoeshine boy Vasco (Milian) kills a federale officer and is made a lieutenant by General Mongo (Bodalo), one of many warring revolutionary warlords. Vasco and Swedish gun salesman Yodlof Pederson (Nero) become unlikely companions when MonMongo sends them to Yuma, to liberate authentic revolutionary Xantos (Rey), a pre-Gandhi preacher of nonviolence imprisoned by American oil interests in the hope of extorting oil leases from him. The conflict is a simple one between virtuous Communists and oppressive generals and capitalists. Director Corbucci's mood is less cynical, and more inclined toward comedy. The comedy direction is broader than broad, and obvious to the point of playing to juveniles. There is plenty of action in the film, guaranteeing a shootout or stunt every few minutes. **118m/C DVD.** *IT SP GE* Franco Nero, Tomas Milian, Jack Palance, Fernando Rey, Iris Berben, Francisco Bodalo; ***D:*** Sergio Corbucci; ***W:*** Sergio Corbucci, Massimo De Rita, Arduino (Dino) Maiuri, Fritz Ebert; ***C:*** Alejandro Ulloa; ***M:*** Ennio Morricone.

The Companion **1994 (R)** In 2015 romance novelist Gillian Tanner (Harrold) decides to hide out at a remote mountain cabin to get over a broken love affair. For safety's sake, Gillian takes along custom-designed android companion Geoffrey (Greenwood). But then Gillian decides to tinker with Geoffrey's programming, turning him from domestic guardian to devoted lover. Unfortunately, Geoffrey doesn't understand the difference between fantasy and reality (especially since he's getting his ideas from Gillian's romance novels) and becomes lethally obsessed. **94m/C VHS.** Kathryn Harrold, Bruce Greenwood, Talia Balsam, Brion James, Bryan Cranston, Joely Fisher; ***D:*** Gary Fleder; ***W:*** Ian Seeberg, Valerie Bennett; ***C:*** Rick Bota; ***M:*** David Shire. **VIDEO**

The Company **2003 (PG-13)** Altman delivers another fine ensemble work, this time dealing with the inner workings of the Joffrey Ballet of Chicago. Campbell stars as Ry, an up and coming ballerina struggling to establish herself. But even her story takes a backseat to the dancing and the behind-the-scenes business of creating a ballet. Strong cast, most of whom are dancers and not actors, makes for compelling viewing. Campbell, who once studied ballet before turning to acting, collaborated on the story as a personal project. **112m/C DVD.** *US GE* Neve Campbell, Malcolm McDowell, James Franco, Barbara Robertson, Susie Cusack, William Dick, Marilyn Dodds Frank; ***D:*** Robert Altman; ***W:*** Barbara Turner; ***C:*** Andrew Dunn; ***M:*** Van Dyke Parks.

The Company 1/2 **2007** Miniseries about the Cold War and the CIA based on the Robert Littell novel. Jack McAuliffe (O'Connell) is recruited to join the Agency fresh out of Yale, mentored by cynical expert Harry Torriti (Molina). In postwar Berlin, it's spy vs. spy with the KGB as the CIA tries to find a mole in their midst. McAuliffe is on hand for the 1956 Hungarian uprising—and gets involved with local freedom fighter Elizabet (McElhone)—and eventually is drawn into the fiasco that was the Bay of Pigs. Overstuffs a plot that spans decades and has to rush to tie up its loose ends. **286m/C DVD, Blu-ray Disc.** Chris O'Donnell, Alfred Molina, Michael Keaton, Rory Cochrane, Alessandro Nivola, Ulrich Thomsen, Natascha (Natasha) McElhone, Tom Hollander, Alexandra Maria Lara, Raoul Bova, Ted Atherton; ***D:*** Mikael Salomon; ***W:*** Ken Nolan; ***C:*** Ben Nott; ***M:*** Jeff Beal. **CABLE**

Company Business 1/2 **1991 (PG-13)** Sam Boyd is a retired CIA agent who's brought back to swap Pyiotr Grushenko (Baryshnikov), a Russian mole in the State Department, for a U-2 pilot being held in Moscow. The swap is to be made in Berlin and also involves $2 million of what turns out be to Colombian drug money. When things inevitably go wrong (both intelligence agencies would like them out of the way permanently) the two men find they must depend on each other if they want to stay alive. An unimaginative plot wastes a stalwart cast in this old-fashioned spy drama. **104m/C VHS, DVD.** Gene Hackman, Mikhail Baryshnikov, Kurtwood Smith, Terry O'Quinn; ***D:*** Nicholas Meyer; ***W:*** Nicholas Meyer.

Company Man **2000 (PG-13)** Goofy satire about the Bay of Pigs invasion co-written and co-directed by McGrath, who also stars as a wimpy grammar teacher who, through some bizarre coincidences, manages, unwittingly, to cause the Cold War debacle. Though the big name cast seems to be having fun, absurdity abounds and eventually topples this romping, madcap throwback. Woody Allen makes an appearance as a CIA veteran in Cuba. **81m/C VHS, DVD.** Douglas McGrath, Sigourney Weaver, John Turturro, Anthony LaPaglia, Ryan Phillippe, Denis Leary, Alan Cumming, Woody Allen, Heather Matarazzo, Jeffrey Jones; ***D:*** Douglas McGrath, Peter Askin; ***W:*** Douglas McGrath, Peter Askin; ***C:*** Russell Boyd; ***M:*** David Lawrence.

The Company of Wolves **1985 (R)** Thirteen-year-old Rosaleen (Patterson) lives with her parents (Warner, Silberg) on the outskirts of a forbidding forest. The girl, who's on the verge of womanhood, listens to her grandmother (Lansbury) tell fairy tales and dreams of a medieval fantasy world inhabited by men who turn into wolves. An adult "Little Red Riding Hood" that's heavy on dreamy visuals and Freudian symbolism. **95m/C VHS, DVD.** Angela Lansbury, David Warner, Stephen Rea, Tusse Silberg, Sarah Patterson, Brian Glover, Danielle Dax, Graham Crowden, Micha Bergese, Kathryn Pogson, Georgia Slowe; ***D:*** Neil Jordan; ***W:*** Neil Jordan, Angela Carter; ***C:*** Bryan Loftus; ***M:*** George Fenton.

The Competition **1980 (PG)** Two virtuoso pianists meet at an international competition and fall in love. Will they stay together if one of them wins? Can they have a performance career and love too? Is he trying to distract her with sex, so he can win? Dreyfuss and Irving are fine (they practiced for four months to look like they were actually playing the pianos), and Remick's character has some interesting insights into the world of art. **125m/C VHS.** Richard Dreyfuss, Amy Irving, Lee Remick, Sam Wanamaker, Joseph Cali, Ty Henderson, Priscilla Pointer, James B. Sikking; ***D:*** Joel Oliansky; ***M:*** Lalo Schifrin.

Complex World 1/2 **1992 (R)** The Heartbreak Hotel is a notorious rock club which may not be around much longer. It seems the young owner's father is an ex-CIA redneck who is running for President and his son's profession is a political liability. Meanwhile, the town's mayor wants to replace the club with a shopping mall. A bomb is planted in the club's basement, terrorists lurk, and a gang of bikers is spoiling for a fight but the crowd at the Heartbreak just rocks on. **81m/C VHS.** Dan Welch, Bob Owczarek, Jay Charbonneau, Tilman Gandy Jr., David P.B. Stephens, Captain Lou Albano, Stanley Matis; ***D:*** James Wolpaw; ***W:*** James Wolpaw.

Compromising Positions **1985 (R)** A philandering dentist is killed on Long Island, and a bored housewife begins to investigate, uncovering scandal after scandal. Black comedy mixed unevenly with mystery makes for unsatisfying brew. However, Ivey is a standout as Sarandon's best friend. Screenplay was written by Susan Isaacs, based on her novel of the same title. **99m/C VHS.** Susan Sarandon, Raul Julia, Edward Herrmann, Judith Ivey, Mary Beth Hurt, Joe Mantegna, Josh Mostel, Anne DeSalvo; ***D:*** Frank Perry; ***M:*** Brad Fiedel.

Compulsion 1/2 **1959** Artie Strauss (Dillman) is a mother-dominated sadist who, along with submissive friend Judd Steiner (Stockwell), plan and execute a cold-blooded murder. Flamboyant lawyer Jonathan Wilk (brilliantly portrayed by Welles) knows he has no defense so he attacks the system and establishment, seeking to at least save his clients from death. A suspenseful shocker with taut direction and a tight script. Based on the notorious 1924 Leopold and Loeb murder trial, also filmed as "Rope" and "Swoon." **103m/B VHS, DVD.** Orson Welles, Bradford Dillman, Dean Stockwell, Diane Varsi, E.G. Marshall, Martin Milner, Richard Anderson, Robert F. Simon, Edward Binns, Robert Burton, Wilton Graff, Gavin MacLeod, Wendell Holmes; ***D:*** Richard Fleischer; ***W:*** Richard Murphy; ***C:*** William Mellor.

Computer Beach Party **1988** A couple of surf-head college computer hackers foil their mayor's plans to develop their favorite beach. The title, at least, is original. **97m/C VHS.** Hank Amigo, Stacey Nemour, Andre Chimene; ***D:*** Gary A. Troy.

Computer Wizard **1977 (G)** Boy genius builds a powerful electronic device. His intentions are good, but the invention disrupts the town and lands him in big trouble. Not the "Thomas Edison Story." **91m/C VHS.** Henry Darrow, Kate Woodville, Guy Madison, Marc Gilpin; ***D:*** John Florea.

The Computer Wore Tennis Shoes 1/2 **1969 (G)** Disney comedy (strictly for the kids) about a slow-witted college student who turns into a genius after a "shocking" encounter with the campus computer. His new brains give the local gangster headaches. Sequel: "Now You See Him, Now You Don't." **87m/C VHS, DVD.** Kurt Russell, Cesar Romero, Joe Flynn, William Schallert, Alan Hewitt, Richard Bakalyan; ***D:*** Robert Butler; ***M:*** Robert F. Brunner.

Comrade X 1/2 **1940** Gable is an American correspondent in Moscow who is blackmailed into marrying die-hard Communist Lamarr in this comedic spinoff of "Ninotchka." The two stars failed to create any sparks as a love duo, although their previous film "Boom Town" was a hit. Based on a story by Walter Reisch. **87m/B VHS.** Clark Gable, Hedy Lamarr, Oscar Homolka, Felix Bressart, Eve Arden, Sig Rumann, Natasha Lytess, Vladimir Sokoloff; ***D:*** King Vidor; ***W:*** Ben Hecht, Charles Lederer.

Comrades in Arms 1/2 **1991 (R)** When an international drug cartel threatens to take over the world, the United States and Russia must set their differences aside and team up to stop them. **91m/C VHS.** Lyle Alzado, Rick Washburne, John Christian, Lance Henriksen; ***D:*** J. Christian Ingvordsen; ***W:*** J. Christian Ingvordsen.

The Comrades of Summer 1/2 **1992 (R)** Mantegna plays big-league baseball coach Sparky Smith, whose fiery temper gets him into big trouble. Out of a job, he discovers the only team willing to take a chance on him happens to be Russian. Sparky finds the players of the Russian National team need a lot of help—and not just with their English. **90m/C VHS.** Joe Mantegna, Natalia (Natalya) Negoda, Mark Rolston, John Fleck, Eric Allen Kramer, Michael Lerner, Ian Tracey; ***D:*** Tommy Lee Wallace; ***W:*** Robert Rodat; ***M:*** William Olvis. **CABLE**

The Con 1/2 **1998 (PG-13)** Barbara (De Mornay) is willing to do anything to get the money to pay off her loanshark, including marry small town Mississippi mechanic Bobby Sommersdinger (Macy), who doesn't know he's about to inherit a lot of money. But Bobby isn't quite the dim-wit he first appears to be, even as he succumbs to Barbara's charms. **92m/C VHS.** Rebecca De Mornay, William H. Macy, Frances Sternhagen, Angela Paton, Don Harvey; ***D:*** Steven Schachter; ***W:*** William H. Macy, Steven Schachter; ***C:*** Peter Stein; ***M:*** Peter Manning Robinson. **CABLE**

Con Air **1997 (R)** Producer Bruckheimer flies solo for the first time, and has a very successful flight. Cage re-ups as former Ranger Cameron Poe, jailed for manslaughter, who gets paroled just in time to catch a ride home aboard a plane filled with the worst of America's criminals. Led by Cyrus "The Virus" Grissom (Malkovich), the first-class psycho passengers take over the plane, and Cameron must save the day. Among the snappy one-liners, chases, shoot-outs, and stuff blowin' up real good, comes Federal Marshal Larkin (Cusack) to help Poe from the ground. Cusack can't shake his indie-film, quirky-kid image enough to really pass as an action hero, but he gives it his all. Flick supplies everything you'd expect from a summer blockbuster actioner, but it's best seen on a big-screen with surround sound to get the full effect. **105m/C VHS, DVD, Blu-ray Disc.** Nicolas Cage, John Malkovich, John Cusack, Mykelti Williamson, Ving Rhames, Steve Buscemi, Colm Meaney, Rachel Ticotin, Dave Chappelle, M.C. Gainey, Danny Trejo, Nicholas Chinlund, Jesse Borrego, Angela Featherstone, Monica Potter, John Roselius, Renoly, Landry Allbright, Jose Zuniga; ***D:*** Simon West; ***W:*** Scott Rosenberg; ***C:*** David Tattersall; ***M:*** Mark Mancina, Trevor Rabin.

The Con Artists 1/2 *The Con Man* **1980** After con man Quinn is sprung from prison, he and his protege set up a sting operation against the beautiful Capucine. Not clever or witty enough for the caper to capture interest. **86m/C VHS, DVD.** *IT* Anthony Quinn, Adriano Celentano, Capucine, Corinne Clery; ***D:*** Sergio Corbucci.

Con Games 1/2 **2002 (R)** John Woodrow (Thomas) goes undercover in a maximum security California prison to investigate the murder of a senator's grandson. The prison is ruled by corrupt guard Hopkins (Roberts) and Woodrow's life expectency takes a nosedive when Hopkins learns his true identity. **90m/C VHS, DVD.** Eric Roberts, Martin Kove, Tommy Lee Thomas, Jody Nolan; ***D:*** Jefferson Edward Donald; ***W:*** Tommy Lee Thomas, Jefferson Edward Donald; ***C:*** John Lazear. **VIDEO**

Conagher 1/2 *Louis L'Amour's Conagher* **1991** A lyrical, if poorly plotted Western about a veteran cowboy who takes the whole movie to decide to end up in the arms of the pretty widow lady. Cable adaptation of Louis L'Amour's novel doesn't have much intensity, though Elliott captures his character well. **94m/C VHS, DVD.** Sam Elliott, Katharine Ross, Barry Corbin, Buck Taylor, Dub Taylor, Daniel Quinn, Anndi McAfee, Billy Green Bush, Ken Curtis; ***D:*** Reynaldo Villalobos. **CABLE**

Conan the Barbarian **1982 (R)** A fine sword and sorcery tale featuring brutality, excellent production values, and a rousing score. Conan's (Arnie, who else) parents are killed and he's enslaved. But hardship makes him strong, so when he is set free he can avenge their murder and retrieve the sword bequeathed him by his father. Sandahl Bergman is great as The Queen of Thieves, and Schwarzenegger maintains an admirable sense of humor throughout. Jones is dandy, as always, this time as bad guy Thulsa Doom. Based on the character created by Robert E. Howard. Sequel: "Conan the Destroyer." **115m/C VHS, DVD.** Arnold Schwarzenegger, James Earl Jones, Max von Sydow, Sandahl Bergman, Mako, Ben Davidson, Valerie Quennessen, Cassandra Gaviola, William (Bill) Smith; ***D:*** John Milius; ***W:*** John Milius, Oliver Stone; ***C:*** Duke Callaghan, John Cabrera; ***M:*** Basil Poledouris.

Conan the Destroyer 1/2 **1984 (PG)** Conan is manipulated by Queen Tamaris into searching for a treasure. In return she'll bring Conan's love Valeria back to life. On his trip he meets Jones and Chamberlain, who later give him a hand. Excellent special effects, good humor, camp fun, somewhat silly finale. Sequel to the better "Conan the Barbarian." **101m/C VHS, DVD.** Arnold Schwarzenegger, Grace Jones, Wilt Chamberlain, Sarah Douglas, Mako, Jeff Corey, Olivia D'Abo, Tracey Walter; ***D:*** Richard Fleischer; ***W:*** Stanley Mann; ***C:*** Jack Cardiff; ***M:*** Basil Poledouris. Golden Raspberries '84: Worst New Star (D'Abo).

Concealed Weapon 1/2 **1994 (R)** A struggling actor gets the part of a lifetime but then becomes the prime suspect in a brutal crime. **80m/C VHS, DVD.** Daryl Haney, Suzanne Wouk, Monica Simpson, Mark Driscoll, Karen Stone; ***D:*** Dave Payne, Milan Zivkovich.

Conceiving Ada **1997** Experimental film is a homage to Lady Ada Lovelace (Swinton), daughter of Lord Byron, a 19th-century mathematician who developed what is now considered the first computer programming language. Ada is regarded by contemporary computer scientist Amy Coer (Faridany) as her spiritual mentor and Amy becomes obsessed with devising a method to actually communicate with the long-deceased Ada, whose life uncannily paralells her own. **85m/C VHS, DVD.** Tilda Swinton, Francesca Faridany, Karen Black, John E. O'Keefe, J.D. Wolfe, Timothy Leary, John Perry Barlow, Owen Murphy; ***D:*** Lynn Hershman Leeson; ***W:*** Lynn Hershman Leeson, Eileen Jones; ***C:*** Hiro Narita.

The Concentratin' Kid **1930** An unusual horse opera sans shootouts and fisticuffs. Hoot's fiancee is kidnapped and taken to the range so that the renegade cowpokes can, uh, benefit from a female perspective on home decorating. Despite being outnumbered, Hoot concentrates and sets the rescue in motion, taking on the gang of rustlers without firing a shot. **54m/B VHS.** Hoot Gibson, Kathryn Crawford, Duke Lee, Robert E. Homans, James Mason; ***D:*** Arthur Rosson.

The Concorde: Airport '79 ♪ *Airport '79* **1979 (PG)** A supersonic film in the "Airport" tradition has the Concorde chased by missiles and fighter aircraft before it crashes in the Alps. Incredibly far-fetched nonsense with an all-star cast doesn't fly. **103m/C VHS, DVD.** Alain Delon, Susan Blakely, Robert Wagner, Sylvia Kristel, John Davidson, Charo, Sybil Danning, Jimmie Walker, Eddie Albert, Bibi Andersson, Monica Lewis, Andrea Marcovicci, Martha Raye, Cicely Tyson, Mercedes McCambridge, George Kennedy, David Warner; ***D:*** David Lowell Rich; ***W:*** Eric Roth; ***M:*** Lalo Schifrin.

Concrete Angels ♪ **1987 (R)** A poignant glimpse at the influence of rock music in its infancy. A group of deprived teens in Toronto form a band and audition to open for the Beatles. Lack of nostalgia is refreshing, but too much of this is amateurish. **97m/C VHS.** *CA* Joseph Dimambro, Luke McKeehan, Omie Craden, Dean Bosacki; ***D:*** Carlo Liconti.

Concrete Beat ♪ 1/2 **1984** A newspaper reporter simultaneously searches for a murderer, tries to win his ex-wife back, and writes front page stories for his editor/ex-father-in-law. Tough assignment. **74m/C VHS.** Kenneth McMillan, John Getz, Darlanne Fluegel, Rhoda Gemignani; ***D:*** Robert Butler. **TV**

The Concrete Cowboys ♪ 1/2 *Ramblin' Man* **1979** Two bumbling cowboys from Montana come to the metropolis of Nashville and promptly turn detective to foil a blackmail scheme and locate a missing singer. Barbara Mandrell and Roy Acuff play themselves. Silly made-for-TV pilot of short-lived series. **100m/C VHS, DVD.** Jerry Reed, Tom Selleck, Morgan Fairchild, Claude Akins, Gene Evans, Roy Acuff, Barbara Mandrell; ***D:*** Burt Kennedy. **TV**

The Concrete Jungle ♪♪ *The Criminal* **1982 (R)** After being set up by her no-good boyfriend, Bregman is sent to a correctional facility for drug smuggling. There she must learn to fend for herself (or else). Typical prison for gals fare with cute babes in revealing outfits, a topless riot, the bad warden, and a concerned social worker. Followed by "Chained Heat." **106m/C VHS.** Tracy Bregman, Jill St. John, Barbara Luna, Peter Brown, Aimee (Amy) Eccles, Nita Talbot, Sondra Currie; ***D:*** Tom De Simone; ***W:*** Alan J. Adler.

Condemned ♪♪ 1/2 **1929** Colman's second talkie finds his character, Michel, sent to Devil's Island for theft. Michel makes life easier for himself by getting into the warden's (Diggs) good graces and into the heart of the warden's unhappy wife (Harding). Adapted from the novel "Condemned to Devil's Island" by Blair Niles. **86m/B VHS.** Ronald Colman, Ann Harding, Dudley Digges, Louis Wolheim; ***D:*** Wesley Ruggles; ***W:*** Sidney Howard; ***C:*** George Barnes, Gregg Toland; ***M:*** Jack Meskill, Pete Wendling.

The Condemned ♪ **2007 (R)** Violent grade-D actioner does exactly what it's supposed to and no more. Media slime Ian (Mammone) hits on a new reality concept: drop ten death-row inmates onto a remote island and tell them that the last survivor earns freedom and a paycheck while Internet subscribers pay to watch a live feed. Probably the only recognizable faces are former WWE wrestler Austin and Brit soccer star turned screen villain Jones but everyone is pretty much dead meat. **113m/C DVD, Blu-ray Disc.** *US* Steve Austin, Vinnie Jones, Robert Mammone, Victoria (Tory) Mussett, Masa Yamaguchi, Manu Bennett, Marcus Johnson, Christopher Baker, Rick Hoffman, Luke Pegler, Samantha Healy, Madeleine West, Emelia Burns, Nathan Jones, Angie Milliken; ***D:*** Scott Wiper; ***W:*** Scott Wiper, Rob Hedden; ***C:*** Ross Emery.

Condemned to Hell WOOF! *Atrapadas* **1984** A tough-as-iron street punk gets thrown into a women's prison, where she must fight for her existence. Low-brow violence galore. **97m/C VHS.** *AR* Camila Perisse, Betiana Blum, Cristina Murta, Leonor Benedetto; ***D:*** Anibal Di Salvo; ***W:*** Anibal Di Salvo; ***C:*** Carlos Torlaschi; ***M:*** Luis Maria Serra.

Condemned to Live ♪♪ **1935** Mild-mannered doctor Ralph Morgan and his fiancee Maxine Doyle seem like your average early 20th Century Middle-European couple-...but the doctor's hunchbacked servant Mischa Auer is a tipoff that this is a horror movie of some sort. Like many men, the doctor has suffered from a vampire curse all his life. And, like many men, he is unaware of his blood-sucking habit, thanks to the concealment efforts of his loyal (hunchback) servant. Doyle discovers her fiance's sanguine secret, but not before she finds out she really loves Gleason, anyway. Answers the question: just how do you jilt a vampire? **68m/B VHS, DVD.** Ralph Morgan, Maxine Doyle, Russell Gleason, Pedro de Cordoba, Mischa Auer, Lucy Beaumont, Carl Stockdale; ***D:*** Frank Strayer.

Condition Red ♪♪ **1995 (R)** Philadelphia prison guard Dan Capelli's (Russo) illicit involvement with inmate Gidell (Williams) turns into big trouble and double-crosses thanks to her drug-dealing boyfriend Angel (Calderon). **85m/C VHS.** James Russo, Cynda Williams, Paul Calderon; ***D:*** Mika Kaurismaki; ***W:*** Andre Degas; ***C:*** Ken Kelsch; ***M:*** Mauri Sumen.

Condorman ♪♪ 1/2 **1981 (PG)** Woody Wilkins, an inventive comic book writer, adopts the identity of his own character, Condorman, in order to help a beautiful Russian spy defect. A Disney film, strictly for the small fry. **90m/C VHS, DVD.** Michael Crawford, Oliver Reed, Barbara Carrera, James Hampton, Jean-Pierre Kalfon, Dana Elcar; ***D:*** Charles Jarrott; ***W:*** Glenn Gordon Caron; ***C:*** Charles F. Wheeler; ***M:*** Henry Mancini.

Conduct Unbecoming ♪♪ 1/2 **1975 (PG)** Late 19th-century India is the setting for a trial involving the possible assault of a British officer's wife. Ambitious production based on a British stage play suffers from claustrophobic atmosphere but is greatly redeemed by the first rate cast. **107m/C VHS, DVD.** *GB* Michael York, Richard Attenborough, Trevor Howard, Stacy Keach, Christopher Plummer, Susannah York, James Faulkner, Michael Culver, Persis Khambatta; ***D:*** Michael Anderson Sr.

The Conductor ♪♪ *Dyrygent* **1980** A famous Polish-born conductor (Gielgud) returns to his birthplace after 50 years of living in the U.S. A dying man, he decides to work with a struggling provincial orchestra, much to the dismay of their own conductor. But the conductor finds himself being used in government schemes to take advantage of his return. In English and Polish with subtitles. **101m/C VHS.** *PL* John Gielgud, Krystyna Janda, Andrzej Seweryn, Jan Ciercierski, Tadeusz Czechowski; ***D:*** Andrzej Wajda; ***W:*** Andrzej Kijowski.

Coneheads ♪♪ 1/2 **1993 (PG)** Comedy inspired by once popular characters from "Saturday Night Live" coasts in on the coattails of "Wayne's World." Aykroyd and Curtin reprise their roles as Beldar and Prymaat, the couple from the planet Remulak who are just trying to fit in on Earth. Newman, who created the role of teenage daughter Connie, appears as Beldar's sister, while Thomas takes over as Connie (toddler Connie is Aykroyd's daughter, in her film debut). One-joke premise is a decade late and a dime short, though cast of comedy all-stars provides a lift. **86m/C VHS, DVD.** Dan Aykroyd, Jane Curtin, Laraine Newman, Jason Alexander, Michelle Rene Thomas, Chris Farley, Michael Richards, Lisa Jane Persky, Sinbad, Shishir Kurup, Michael McKean, Phil Hartman, David Spade, Dave Thomas, Jan Hooks, Chris Rock, Adam Sandler, Julia Sweeney, Danielle Aykroyd; ***D:*** Steven Barron; ***W:*** Tom Davis, Bonnie Turner, Terry Turner, Dan Aykroyd; ***C:*** Francis Kenny; ***M:*** David Newman.

Confess ♪♪ **2005 (R)** Former hacker Terell (Byrd) is ticked off when the surveillance technology he developed is stolen, so he takes compromising footage (via spycams) of those who slighted him and puts it on the Internet. Then Terrell decides to go big-time and he and accomplice Olivia (Larter) start targeting CEOs, politicians, and others of the power elite. He becomes a front-page anti-hero but the feds are calling Terrell a cyber-terrorist and want him brought to justice. Terrell's got bigger problems when imitators take his idea to a violent extreme. **87m/C DVD.** Eugene Byrd, Ali Larter, William Sadler, Melissa Leo, Glenn Fitzgerald; ***D:*** Stefan C. Schaefer; ***W:*** Stefan C. Schaefer; ***C:*** Leland Krane; ***M:*** Scott Jacoby. **VIDEO**

Confessing to Laura ♪♪ *Confesion a Laura* **1990** Set in Colombia after the 1948 assassination of liberal leader Jorge Elieser Gaitain, which begets a violent civil war. Two people are trapped at Laura's house by the riots—setting up a night of volatile emotion. Spanish with subtitles. **90m/C VHS.** *CO* ***D:*** Jaime Osorio Gomez.

The Confession ♪♪ 1/2 **1920** A priest hears a killer's confession and must protect the oath of confidentiality, even as his own brother is being convicted of the murder. **78m/B VHS.** Henry B. Walthall, Francis McDonald, William H. Clifford, Margaret McWade, Margaret Landis; ***D:*** Bertram Bracken.

The Confession ♪♪ 1/2 **1998 (R)** Slick lawyer Roy Bleakie (Baldwin) suffers a crisis of conscience with his latest case—the one he expects will hand him the District Attorney's office. Harry Fertig (Kingsley) has killed the three people he regards as responsible for the death of his young son. He's confessed to the crime and wants to plead guilty and accept responsiblity—for his own ambitions Roy wants Harry to plead temporary insanity. But it turns out there's more to the case than even Roy knows. Good performances in what could be just another courtroom melodrama. **114m/C VHS, DVD.** Alec Baldwin, Ben Kingsley, Amy Irving, Jay O. Sanders, Kevin Conway, Anne Twomey, Christopher Lawford, Boyd Gaines, Christopher Noth; ***D:*** David Hugh Jones; ***W:*** David Black; ***C:*** Mike Fash; ***M:*** Mychael Danna.

The Confessional ♪ *House of Mortal Sin* **1975 (R)** A mad priest unleashes a monster from his confessional to wreak havoc upon the world. Pray for your VCR. **108m/C VHS, DVD.** *GB* Anthony Sharp, Susan Penhaligon, Stephanie Beacham, Norman Eshley, Sheila Keith; ***D:*** Pete Walker.

The Confessional ♪♪♪ *Le Confessionnal* **1995** Ambiguous psychological drama that's, in part, a homage to Alfred Hitchcock's 1952 film "I Confess," which was filmed in the same Quebec City locations. Pierre (Bluteau) returns to Quebec in 1989 for his father's funeral and to reunite with his adoptive brother Marc (Goyette). Marc's mother Rachel (who committed suicide shortly after his birth) refused to name his father, thought to be a priest, perhaps at the church where Hitchcock filmed his movie. Flashbacks depict the rotund director (Burrage) and his assistant (Scott Thomas) and their production. Lots of intriguing visuals, thanks to director Lepage's innovative stage background. French with subtitles. **100m/C VHS.** *CA FR GB* Lothaire Bluteau, Patrick Goyette, Jean-Louis Millette, Kristin Scott Thomas, Ron Burrage, Richard Frechette, Francois Papineau, Marie Gignac, Anne-Marie Cadieux, Normand Daneau, Suzanne Clement, Lynda Lepage-Beaulieu; ***D:*** Robert Lepage; ***W:*** Robert Lepage; ***C:*** Alan Dostie; ***M:*** Sacha Puttnam. Genie '95: Art Dir./Set Dec., Director (Lepage), Film.

Confessions of a Dangerous Mind ♪♪ 1/2 **2002 (R)** Clooney makes his directorial debut in this uneven but ultimately enjoyable biopic of TV game show producer Chuck Barris (Rockwell), who claimed in his "unauthorized" biography to be a CIA assassin during the height of his success. Clooney sometimes gets a little self-consciously "arty," but doesn't go overboard, and it actually fits with the absurdist tone of Kaufman's script. It's Rockwell who stands out here, with a breakout performance that showcases his range. **113m/C VHS, DVD.** *US* Sam Rockwell, Drew Barrymore, Rutger Hauer, George Clooney, Julia Roberts, Maggie Gyllenhaal, Kristen Wilson, Jennifer Hall; ***Cameos:*** Chuck Barris, Brad Pitt, Matt Damon, Jaye P. Morgan; ***D:*** George Clooney; ***W:*** Charlie Kaufman; ***C:*** Newton Thomas (Tom) Sigel; ***M:*** Alex Wurman. Natl. Bd. of Review '02: Screenplay.

Confessions of a Hit Man ♪♪ **1994 (R)** Nephew who stole millions from his mobster uncle must amend his sordid past. **93m/C VHS.** James Remar, Michael Wright, Emily Longstreth; ***D:*** Larry Leahy; ***W:*** Tony Cinciripini, Larry Leahy; ***M:*** Billy Talbot.

Confessions of a Nazi Spy ♪♪ **1939** Propaganda film from Warner Bros. based on the 1937 trials of several German-American Nazi sympathizers who were arrested for espionage. British intelligence uncovers a Nazi spy network that extends into New York and informs the FBI, who send agent Ed Renard (Robinson) to ferret out its members. Actual newsreel footage is included, which enhances director Litvak's semi-documentary film style. **89m/B DVD.** Edward G. Robinson, Francis Lederer, George Sanders, Paul Lukas, Dorothy Tree, Lya Lys, Joseph (Joe) Sawyer, Henry O'Neill; ***D:*** Anatole Litvak; ***W:*** John Wexley, Milton Krims; ***C:*** Sol Polito; ***M:*** Max Steiner.

Confessions of a Pit Fighter ♪ 1/2 **2005 (R)** Ex-con Eddie is struggling to go straight but then his younger brother is murdered during a bout at an illegal fight club and Eddie wants revenge. **99m/C DVD.** Armand Assante, James Russo, John Savage, Hector Echavarria, Flavor Flav, Richard Medina Jr.; ***D:*** Art Camacho; ***W:*** Art Camacho, R. Ellis Frazier; ***C:*** Curtis Petersen; ***M:*** Geoff Levin. **VIDEO**

Confessions of a Police Captain ♪♪ **1972 (PG)** A dedicated police captain tries to wipe out the bureaucratic corruption that is infecting his city. Balsam gives a fine performance in a heavy-going tale. **104m/C VHS, DVD.** *IT* Martin Balsam, Franco Nero, Marilu Tolo; ***D:*** Damiano Damiani; ***W:*** Damiano Damiani, Salvatore Laurani; ***C:*** Claudio Ragona; ***M:*** Riz Ortolani.

Confessions of a Serial Killer ♪♪ **1987** True story based on the life of Henry Lee Lucas, one of the nation's most vicious killers. Burns plays Lucas in this grisly account of his most violent murders. Shocking realistic look inside the mind of a serial killer. **85m/C VHS.** Robert A. Burns, Dennis Hill; ***D:*** Mark Blair.

Confessions of a Shopaholic ♪♪ **2009 (PG)** Spendthrift, debt-ridden fashionista New Yorker Rebecca Bloomwood (Fisher) ironically becomes a celebrity after getting a job as the advice columnist for a new financial magazine. But her intemperate ways threaten both her new career and new romance. It doesn't bode well for a pic to be on the losing end of a comparison to *Sex and the City*, but that about sums up this popcorn puff piece. A mindless chick-flick that banks on unbridled, inconspicuous spending as humor would be a tough sell on a good day but during a recession it's downright insulting. Fisher is easy on the eyes but everything else is utterly painful. Based on the chick lit series by Sophie Kinsella. **104m/C DVD.** *US* Isla Fisher, Hugh Dancy, Krysten Ritter, Joan Cusack, John Goodman, Kristin Scott Thomas, Leslie Bibb, Lynn Redgrave, Julie Hagerty, Wendie Malick, Clea Lewis, Christine Ebersole, John Lithgow, Fred Armisen, Robert Stanton; ***D:*** P.J. Hogan; ***W:*** Tim Firth, Tracey Jackson, Kayla Alpert; ***C:*** Jo Willems; ***M:*** James Newton Howard.

Confessions of a Sociopathic Social Climber ♪♪ **2005 (R)** Katya Livingston (Hewitt) is a bad girl—a bitchy, self-serving but successful ad exec who is desperate to be invited to the San Francisco social event of the year. Unfortunately for her, Katya previously insulted the hostess. But that won't stop her angling for an invite, even if it causes problems for her dreamboat beau, Charles (Ferguson). **85m/C DVD.** Jennifer Love Hewitt, Colin Ferguson, Natassia Malthe, Daniel Roebuck, Joseph Lawrence, James Kirk; ***D:*** Dana Lustig; ***W:*** Eric Charmelo, Nicole Snyder; ***C:*** Luc Montpellier; ***M:*** Phil Marshall. **CABLE**

Confessions of a Teenage Drama Queen ♪♪ **2004 (PG)** Hip 15-year-old Lola (Lohan)—who decides her real name, Mary, isn't cool enough—is totally bumming when her divorced mom (Headly) grows weary of Manhattan's big city lifestyle and banishes her to a quaint New Jersey suburb. To make matters worse she is snubbed by the popular set at her new high school and decides to take action, which includes vying against ultra-popular Carla (Fox) for the lead in the school play. Along the way there's ample opportunity to witness the self-absorbed, shallow, and materialistic behaviors that drown out any positive messages for the 'tweener target group. Mediocre Disney production is based on Dyan Sheldon's successful book. **89m/C VHS, DVD.** *US* Lindsay Lohan, Adam Garcia, Glenne Headly, Alison Pill, Carol Kane, Eli Marienthal, Sheila McCarthy, Tom McCamus, Megan Fox, Richard Fitzpatrick; ***D:*** Sara Sugarman; ***W:*** Gail Parent; ***C:*** Stephen Burum; ***M:*** Mark Mothersbaugh.

Confessions of a Vice Baron 🦴 **1942** Vice Baron Lombardo makes it big as a drug dealer and flesh peddler, then loses it all when he falls in love. Sleazy exploitation. **70m/B VHS, DVD.** Willy Castello; ***D:*** John Melville.

Confessions of Sorority Girls 🦴🦴 ½ **1994 (PG-13)** Sometime in the early '60s, wicked Sabrina (Luner) shows up at college and takes it by storm. Will she steal Rita's (Milano) beau? That's the least of her schemes. The villainy is played strictly for campy laughs and the film is never as trashy as its title suggests. Originally made as part of Showtime's "Rebel Highway" series and a remake of Roger Corman's 1957 "Sorority Girl." **83m/C VHS, DVD.** Jamie Luner, Alyssa Milano, Bette Rae, Brian Bloom, Natalija Nogulich; ***D:*** Uli Edel; ***C:*** Jean De Segonzac. **CABLE**

Confessions of Tom Harris 🦴 *Tale of the Cock; Childish Things* **1972 (PG)** Somewhere between all the prize-fighting, leg-breaking for the mob, and jail terms for rape, Tom Harris finds time for a life-changing encounter with love. Based on true story. **90m/C VHS.** Don Murray, Linda Evans, David Brian, Gary Clarke, Logan Ramsey, Angelique Pettyjohn; ***D:*** John Derek, David Nelson; ***W:*** Don Murray.

The Confessor 🦴 ½ *The Good Shepherd* **2004 (PG-13)** Worldly Father Daniel Clemens (Slater) is shocked when a parish priest (Flores) is arrested for the murder of a young street hustler and apparently commits suicide in jail. Clemens is convinced the priest was innocent and sets out to find out whodunit with the aid of journalist (and ex-flame) Madeline (Parker). Predictable story with huge plot holes. **90m/C DVD.** *CA* Christian Slater, Molly Parker, Stephen Rea, Gordon Pinsent, Von Flores, Nancy Beatty; ***D:*** Lewin Webb; ***W:*** Brad Mirman; ***C:*** Curtis Petersen; ***M:*** Gary Koftinoff. **VIDEO**

Confetti 🦴🦴 **2006 (R)** Over the top Brit romantic comedy about three would-be weddings. Bridal magazine Confetti is sponsoring a contest for the year's most original wedding. The three finalists are: competitive yuppies Josef (Mangan) and Isabelle (MacNeill) who choose a tennis theme; Matt (Freeman) and Sam (Stevenson) who want a musical extravaganza, though neither of them can sing or dance; and nudists Michael (Webb) and Joanna (Colman) who want a clothes-free ceremony, to the consternation of Confetti editor Vivien (Montagu). Meltdowns occur as the big finale approaches for one overwhelmed couple. **100m/C DVD.** *GB* Martin Freeman, Jessica Stevenson, Robert Webb, Stephen Mangan, Meredith MacNeill, Olivia Colman, Marc Wootton, Vincent Franklin, Jason Watkins; ***D:*** Debbie Isitt; ***C:*** Dewald Aukema; ***M:*** Paul Englishby.

Confidence 🦴🦴 ½ **2003 (R)** That would be "confidence" as in manner and game. Jake Vig (Burns) and his cronies are smalltime con artists who scam the wrong man—an accountant for L.A. crime boss King (Hoffman). To forestall any further unpleasantness, Jake goes to King and agrees to repayment by performing an elaborate con on King's rival. Let's just say that there's always another scam and things are hardly ever what they seem. Hoffman, with king-sized tics and quirks, veers into territory usually reserved for Walken or Pacino, but at least he's having fun. The movie could use a little more of that. Gritty and dark at times, this one's still an enjoyable entry in the scam/heist genre. **98m/C VHS, DVD.** *US* Edward Burns, Dustin Hoffman, Rachel Weisz, Andy Garcia, Paul Giamatti, Donal Logue, Luis Guzman, Brian Van Holt, Franky G., Morris Chestnut, Robert Forster, Leland Orser, Louis Lombardi, Tommy (Tiny) Lister, John Carroll Lynch; ***D:*** James Foley; ***W:*** Doug Jung; ***C:*** Juan Ruiz-Anchia.

Confidential 🦴🦴 ½ **1935** A G-man goes under cover to infiltrate a crime ring. Well made and full of action, fun array of character actors. Naish particularly good as nasty killer. **67m/B VHS.** Donald Cook, Evalyn Knapp, Warren Hymer, J. Carrol Naish, Herbert Rawlinson, Morgan Wallace, Kane Richmond, Theodore von Eltz, Reed Howes; ***D:*** Edward L. Cahn.

Confidential **WOOF! 1986 (R)** A '40s detective tries to solve a decades-old axe murder, only to disappear himself. Horrible fare from our friends north of the border. **95m/C VHS.** *CA* Neil Munro, August Schellenberg, Chapelle Jaffe, Tom Butler; ***D:*** Bruce Pittman.

Confidentially Yours 🦴🦴🦴 *Vivement Dimanche!; Finally, Sunday* **1983 (PG)** Truffaut's homage to Hitchcock, based on Charles Williams' "The Long Saturday Night." A hapless small-town real estate agent is framed for a rash of murders and his secretary, who is secretly in love with him, tries to clear his name. Truffaut's last film is stylish and entertaining. In French with English subtitles. **110m/B VHS, DVD.** *FR* Fanny Ardant, Jean-Louis Trintignant, Philippe Morier-Genoud, Philippe Laudenbach, Caroline Sihol; ***D:*** Francois Truffaut; ***W:*** Francois Truffaut, Suzanne Schiffman, Jean Aurel; ***C:*** Nestor Almendros; ***M:*** Georges Delerue.

Conflict 🦴🦴🦴 **1945** Bogart falls for his sister-in-law and asks his wife for a divorce. She refuses, he plots her murder, and thinks up the alibi. When the police fail to notify him of her death, Bogart is forced to report his wife missing. But is she dead? Her guilty husband smells her perfume, sees her walking down the street, and discovers the body is missing from the scene of the crime. Suspenseful thriller also features Greenstreet as a psychologist/family friend who suspects Bogart knows more than he's telling. **86m/B VHS.** Humphrey Bogart, Alexis Smith, Sydney Greenstreet, Rose Hobart, Charles Drake, Grant Mitchell; ***D:*** Curtis Bernhardt.

Conflict of Interest 🦴 ½ **1992 (R)** Gideon (Nelson) is a thug who runs stolen cars, drugs, and women from his heavy-metal club on the wrong side of town. Mickey Flannery (McDonald) is the new cop determined to get Gideon behind bars, especially after Gideon kills Mickey's wife, sets up his son on a phony murder rap, and kidnaps his son's girlfriend. Now it's personal and Mickey will stop at nothing to get his revenge. Over-the-top performance by Nelson will have the viewer hoping he gets it soon and puts the film out of its misery. **88m/C VHS.** Judd Nelson, Christopher McDonald, Alyssa Milano, Dey Young, Gregory Alan Harris; ***D:*** Gary Davis; ***W:*** Gregory Miller, Michael Angeli; ***C:*** Bryan England.

The Conformist 🦴🦴🦴🦴 *Il Conformista* **1971 (R)** Character study of young Italian fascist, plagued by homosexual feelings, who must prove his loyalty by killing his old professor. Decadent and engrossing story is brilliantly acted. Based on the novel by Alberto Moravia. **108m/C VHS, DVD.** *IT FR GE* Jean-Louis Trintignant, Stefania Sandrelli, Dominique Sanda, Pierre Clementi, Gastone Moschin, Pasquale Fortunato; ***D:*** Bernardo Bertolucci; ***W:*** Bernardo Bertolucci; ***C:*** Vittorio Storaro; ***M:*** Georges Delerue. Natl. Soc. Film Critics '71: Cinematog. (Storaro), Director (Bertolucci).

Confusion of Genders 🦴🦴 *La Confusion des Genres* **2000** Bisexual fortyish lawyer Alain (Greggory) wallows in various sexual relationships without committing emotionally to anyone in this provocative but ultimately tiresome farce, whose characters are all slick surface. The narcissist has a vague interest in having a family and has reluctantly agreed to marry longtime law partner Laurence (Richard), who is pregnant by him. Meanwhile, there's the lustful teenage brother, Christophe (Thouvenin), of one of Alain's ex-girlfriends and Alain's own interest in one of his incarcerated clients, Marc (Martinez). Marc is willing to trade sex with Alain for a jailhouse meeting with his girlfriend Babette (Gayet), whom Alain also gets involved with. And so it continues. French with subtitles. **94m/C DVD.** *FR* Pascal Greggory, Nathalie Richard, Julie Gayet, Vincent Martinez, Cyrille Thouvenin, Alain Bashung; ***D:*** Ilan Duran Cohen; ***W:*** Ilan Duran Cohen, Philippe Lasry; ***C:*** Jeanne Lapoirie; ***M:*** Jay-Jay Johanson.

Congo 🦴🦴 **1995 (PG-13)** Communications company supervisor jets off to the African jungle along with a primatologist to search for a lost city's priceless diamonds, and to return Amy, a gorilla who communicates with sign language to her natural habitat. Why she would want to return to volcanoes and bloodthirsty mutant gray gorillas is anybody's guess. This appropriately technology-laden adaptation of Michael Crichton's novel delivers all the cliches of the old B-movie jungle flicks, but none of the thrills or fun of other Crichton adaptations. **109m/C VHS, DVD.** Mary Ellen Trainor, Dylan Walsh, Laura Linney, Ernie Hudson, Tim Curry, Grant Heslov, Joe Don Baker; ***D:*** Frank Marshall; ***W:*** John Patrick Shanley; ***C:*** Allen Daviau; ***M:*** Jerry Goldsmith.

Congress Dances 🦴🦴 *Der Kongress Tanzt* **1931** A rare German musical about a romance in old Vienna. Popular in its day, it was subsequently banned by the Nazis in 1937. In German with English subtitles. **92m/B VHS.** *GE* Lilian Harvey, Conrad Veidt, Willy Fritsch; ***D:*** Erik Charell.

Conjurer 🦴 ½ **2008 (PG-13)** Shawn (Bowen) and his wife Helen (Bahns) move into her brother Frank's (Schneider) old farmhouse after suffering a tragedy. Helen feels at home but Shawn is uneasy, especially when he's around an old cabin on the property that has a nasty legend about a conjurer (witch) and a curse. Shawn becomes convinced that the place is haunted and ghosts are out to destroy his family but it may be all in his troubled mind. **88m/C DVD.** Andrew Bowen, Maxine Bahns, John Schneider, Tom Nowicki, Brett Rice; ***D:*** Clint Hutchison; ***W:*** Clint Hutchison,; ***C:*** Ken Blakey; ***M:*** Dana Niu. **VIDEO**

A Connecticut Yankee 🦴🦴🦴 **1931** A charming, if somewhat dated, version of the popular Mark Twain story, "A Connecticut Yankee in King Arthur's Court." Rogers is a radio shop owner who dreams his way back to the Knights of the Round Table. Story rewritten to fit Rogers' amiable style and to make then-current wisecracks. Great cast overcomes weak points in the script. **96m/B VHS.** Will Rogers, Myrna Loy, Maureen O'Sullivan, William Farnum, Frank Albertson; ***D:*** David Butler.

A Connecticut Yankee in King Arthur's Court 🦴🦴 ½ *A Yankee in King Arthur's Court* **1949** A pleasant version of the famous Mark Twain story about a 20th century man transported to Camelot and mistaken for a dangerous wizard. This was the third film version of the classic, which was later remade as "Unidentified Flying Oddball," a TV movie, and an animated feature. ♫ Once and For Always; Busy Doin' Nothin'; If You Stub Your Toe on the Moon; When Is Sometime?; Twixt Myself and Me. **108m/C VHS, DVD.** Bing Crosby, Rhonda Fleming, William Bendix, Cedric Hardwicke, Henry Wilcoxon, Murvyn Vye, Virginia Field; ***D:*** Tay Garnett; ***C:*** Ray Rennahan.

A Connecticut Yankee in King Arthur's Court 🦴🦴 ½ **1989** The Mark Twain classic has had a gender switch in this TV version, with Pulliam as the time-travelling heroine who winds up in the royal court. **100m/C VHS.** Keisha Knight Pulliam, Jean Marsh, Rene Auberjonois, Emma Samms, Whip Hubley, Michael Gross; ***D:*** Mel Damski; ***W:*** Paul Zindel. **TV**

The Connection 🦴🦴🦴 ½ **1961** The Living Theatre's ground-breaking performance of Jack Gelber's play about heroin addicts waiting for their connection to arrive, while a documentary filmmaker hovers nearby with his camera. **105m/B VHS, DVD.** Warren Finnerty, Carl Lee, William Redfield, Roscoe Lee Browne, Garry Goodrow, James Anderson, Jackie McLean; ***D:*** Shirley Clarke.

The Connection 🦴🦴 ½ **1973** Durning steps in to work a deal between hotel jewel thieves and the insurance company. Complex plot handled deftly by all concerned. **74m/C VHS.** Charles Durning, Ronny Cox, Dennis Cole, Zohra Lampert, Heather MacRae, Dana Wynter; ***D:*** Tom Gries. **TV**

Connie and Carla 🦴 ½ **2004 (PG-13)** "Victor/Victoria" meets "Some Like it Hot" in this train wreck. Writer Vardalos and Colette are Connie and Carla, who have been a singing team since childhood and who perform medleys in an airport lounge where, despite being has-beens that never were, the two still dream of stardom. In an unlikely turn of events, the two witness a mob hit and are forced to go on the lam to L.A., where they pretend to be female impersonators. The girls pretending to be boys pretending to be girls act is a surprise hit, allowing minor celebrity and close calls with the mob to ensue. Duchovney is the inferior sub-plot love interest who adds nothing to this unfunny, forced comedy filled with extremely cliched, stereotypical gay humor. **98m/C DVD.** *US* Nia Vardalos, Toni Collette, David Duchovny, Stephen Spinella, Ian Gomez, Nick Sandow, Dash Mihok, Robert John Burke, Alec Mapa, Chris(topher) Logan, Robert Kaiser, Boris McGiver, Babz Chula, Linda Darlow; ***Cameos:*** Debbie Reynolds; ***D:*** Michael Lembeck; ***W:*** Nia Vardalos; ***C:*** Richard Greatrex; ***M:*** Randy Edelman.

Connor's War 🦴 ½ **2006 (R)** After CIA special agent Connors (Treach) is blinded during a mission, he asks hot doctor Amanda (Peeples) to help him out while he takes down his former boss, Brooks (Mankuma), who's gone rogue. Treach does well in this routine actioner. **90m/C DVD.** Treach, Nia Peeples, Blu Mankuma; ***D:*** Nick Castle; ***W:*** D. Kyle Johnson; ***C:*** Suki Medencevic. **VIDEO**

The Conqueror **WOOF!** *Conqueror of the Desert* **1956** Wayne in pointed helmet and goatee is convincingly miscast as Genghis Khan in this woeful tale of the warlord's early life and involvement with the kidnapped daughter of a powerful enemy. Rife with stilted, unintentionally funny dialogue, Oriental western was very expensive to make (with backing by Howard Hughes), and is now listed in the "Fifty Worst Films of All Time." No matter; it's surreal enough to enable viewer to approximate an out-of-body experience. Even those on the set suffered; filming took place near a nuclear test site in Utah and many members of the cast and crew eventually developed cancer. **111m/C VHS, DVD.** John Wayne, Susan Hayward, William Conrad, Agnes Moorehead, Lee Van Cleef, Pedro Armendariz Sr., Thomas Gomez, John Hoyt, Ted de Corsia, Leslie Bradley, Peter Mamakos; ***D:*** Dick Powell; ***W:*** Oscar Millard; ***C:*** Joseph LaShelle, William E. Snyder, Leo Tover, Harry Wild; ***M:*** Victor Young.

The Conqueror & the Empress **WOOF!** *Sandokan alla Riscossa* **1964** Low-budget tale of English explorers who roust an island prince from his throne, motivating him to engage in inspired blood-letting. **89m/C VHS.** *IT* Guy Madison, Ray Danton, Mario Petri, Alberto (Albert Farley) Farnese; ***D:*** Luigi Capuano; ***W:*** Luigi Capuano.

The Conqueror Worm 🦴🦴🦴 *Witchfinder General; Edgar Allan Poe's Conqueror Worm* **1968** Price turns in a fine performance portraying the sinister Matthew Hopkins, a real-life 17th-century witchhunter. No "ham" in this low-budget, underrated thriller, based on Ronald Bassett's novel. The last of three films from director Reeves, who died from an accidental overdose in 1969. **95m/C VHS.** *GB* Vincent Price, Ian Ogilvy, Hilary Dwyer, Rupert Davies, Robert Russell, Patrick Wymark, Wilfrid Brambell, Nicky Henson, Bernard Kay, Tony Selby; ***D:*** Michael Reeves; ***W:*** Michael Reeves, Louis M. Heyward, Tom Baker; ***C:*** John Coquillon; ***M:*** Paul Ferris.

Conquest 🦴🦴🦴 *Marie Walewska* **1937** Garbo, as the Polish countess Marie Walewska, tries to persuade Napoleon (Boyer) to free her native Poland from the Russian Tsar. Garbo, Boyer, and Ouspenskaya are outstanding, while the beautiful costumes and lavish production help, but the script is occasionally weak. A boxoffice flop in the U.S., which ended up costing MGM more than any movie it had made up until that time. **115m/B VHS.** Greta Garbo, Charles Boyer, Reginald Owen, Alan Marshal, Henry Stephenson, Leif Erickson, May Whitty, Maria Ouspenskaya, Vladimir Sokoloff, Scotty Beckett; ***D:*** Clarence Brown; ***C:*** Karl Freund.

Conquest 🦴 ½ **1983 (R)** Sword and sorcery tale of two mighty warriors against an evil sorceress who seeks world domination. Excellent score. **92m/C VHS, DVD.** *IT SP*

MX Jorge (George) Rivero, Andrea Occhipinti, Violeta Cela, Sabrina Siani; ***D:*** Lucio Fulci; ***M:*** Claudio Simonetti.

Conquest 1/2 **1998** Pincer Bedier moves back to Conquest, the dying prairie town of his childhood, to run the local bank. Most of the town's aging citizens think he's crazy for trying to revitalize its boarded-up businesses. But Pincer's unexpectedly aided in his mission by Daisy MacDonald, a determined English lass who doesn't have the money to repair the car that stranded her in Conquest. She agrees to help out Bedier and they wind up falling in love. And then the town's other residents begin to believe in Bedier's maybe not-so-impossible dream. **90m/C VHS.** *CA GB* Lothaire Bluteau, Tara Fitzgerald, Monique Mercure, David Fox; ***D:*** Piers Haggard; ***W:*** Rob Forsyth; ***C:*** Gerald Packer; ***M:*** Ron Sures. Genie '98: Support. Actress (Mercure).

Conquest of Cochise **1953** Mediocre oater about a cavalry officer who must stop the war between the Apache and Comanche tribes and a group of Mexicans in the Southwest of the 1850s. **70m/C VHS.** John Hodiak, Robert Stack, Joy Page; ***D:*** William Castle.

Conquest of Mycene 1/2 *Ercole Contro Molock; Hercules vs. the Moloch* **1963** The Prince of Mycene (who becomes Hercules thanks to dubbing) battles evil queen Neri and her equally evil son, Moloch. Typical muscleman fodder. **102m/C VHS, DVD.** *IT FR* Gordon Scott, Rosalba Neri, Jany Clair, Alessandra Panaro, Michel Lemoine; ***D:*** Giorgio Ferroni; ***W:*** Giorgio Ferroni, Remigio del Grosso; ***C:*** Augusto Tiezzi; ***M:*** Carlo Rustichelli.

Conquest of Space 1/2 **1955** A spaceship sets off to explore Mars in spite of the commander's attempts to sabotage the voyage. He believes the flight is an heretical attempt to reach God. An uneasy mixture of religion and space exploration detracts from the nifty special effects which are the only reason to watch. **81m/C VHS, DVD.** Walter Brooke, Eric Fleming, Mickey Shaughnessy, Phil Foster, William Redfield, William Hopper, Benson Fong, Ross Martin; ***D:*** Byron Haskin; ***C:*** Lionel Lindon.

Conquest of the Normans *Normanni, I; Attack of the Normans* **1962** During the Norman invasion of England, Oliver is accused of kidnapping the King. To save his life, Oliver must find the true identity of the abductors. With so much plot, there should have been some suspense. **83m/C VHS, DVD.** *IT* Cameron Mitchell; ***D:*** Giuseppe Vari; ***W:*** Nino Stresa.

Conquest of the Planet of the Apes 1/2 **1972 (PG)** The apes turn the tables on the human Earth population when they lead a revolt against their cruel masters in the distant year of 1990. Sure, there's plenty of cliches—but the story drags you along. The 4th film in the series. Followed by "Battle for the Planet of the Apes." **87m/C VHS, DVD.** Roddy McDowall, Don Murray, Ricardo Montalban, Natalie Trundy, Severn Darden, Hari Rhodes, Asa Maynor, Gordon Jump, John Randolph, H.M. Wynant, Lou Wagner; ***D:*** J. Lee Thompson; ***W:*** Paul Dehn; ***C:*** Bruce Surtees; ***M:*** Tom Scott.

Conrack **1974 (PG)** The true story of Pat Conroy, who tried to teach a group of illiterate Black children in South Carolina by using common-sense teaching techniques to inspire their interest. Voight is convincing as the earnest teacher. Based on Conroy's novel "The Water Is Wide." **111m/C VHS.** Jon Voight, Paul Winfield, Madge Sinclair, Hume Cronyn, Martin Ritt; ***D:*** Martin Ritt; ***W:*** Harriet Frank Jr., Irving Ravetch; ***C:*** John A. Alonzo; ***M:*** John Williams.

The Conrad Boys **2006** After his mother dies, 19-year-old Charlie Conrad (Lo) must put off his own plans in order to care for his young brother Ben (Stewart). Their alcoholic father (Shay) has been out of the picture for years but suddenly re-enters their lives, sober and wanting to make amends. Charlie has more troubles than just his family—he's succumbed to drifter Jordan (Bartzen), who has charmed his way into the Conrad home and Charlie's bed. Lo's ambitious and the gay aspects are taken matter-of-factly but the story seems overly familiar. **93m/C DVD.** Boo Boo Stewart, Barry Shay, Nick Bartzen, Justin Lo; ***D:*** Justin Lo; ***W:*** Justin Lo; ***C:*** Oktay Ortabasi; ***M:*** Charles A. Lo.

Conseil de Famille **1986** Hallyday returns to his family from a five-year prison stint, ready to resume his safe-cracking career. Then he discovers the real talent lies with his son Francois (Martin), whose expertise raises the family to middleclass prosperity. But just as dad decides to affiliate with a bigger crime organization, Francois decides to get a straight job because he's fallen in love. Based on a novel by Francis Ryck. French with subtitles. **111m/C VHS.** *FR* Johnny Hallyday, Remi Martin, Fanny Ardant, Guy Marchand; ***D:*** Constantin Costa-Gavras; ***W:*** Constantin Costa-Gavras; ***C:*** Robert Alazraki; ***M:*** Georges Delerue.

Consenting Adult 1/2 **1985** A distressed family comes to terms with a favorite son's homosexuality. Restrained exploration of the controversial subject. Based on Laura Z. Hobson's novel. **100m/C VHS.** Marlo Thomas, Martin Sheen, Barry Tubb, Talia Balsam, Ben Piazza, Corinne Michaels; ***D:*** Gilbert Cates; ***W:*** John McGreevey. **TV**

Consenting Adults **1992 (R)** Cookie-cutter thriller capitalizes on popular "psycho-destroys-your-normal-life" theme. Average yuppie couple (Kline and Mastrantonio) are startled and then seduced by the couple moving in next door (Spacey and Miller), who conduct a considerably less-restrained lifestyle. Wife-swapping leads to murder and an innocent man is framed. Plot and characters are underdeveloped yet manage to hold interest through decent performances. **100m/C VHS, DVD.** Kevin Kline, Mary Elizabeth Mastrantonio, Kevin Spacey, Rebecca Miller, Forest Whitaker, E.G. Marshall, Billie Neal; ***D:*** Alan J. Pakula; ***W:*** Matthew Chapman.

Consolation Marriage 1/2 *Married in Haste* **1931** A couple meet and marry after being jilted by others, then must make a choice when their old flames return. Dunne and O'Brien make a charming couple in this early talkie. One of Dunne's early starring roles. **82m/B VHS.** Irene Dunne, Pat O'Brien, John Halliday, Matt Moore, Myrna Loy, Lester Vail; ***D:*** Paul Sloane.

Conspiracy **1989 (R)** Defense Secretary William Baine is haunted by a past sexual encounter, and a top secret team moves in to avert any hint of what could become a "sex scandal." Based on a true story. **87m/C VHS.** James Wilby, Kate Hardie, Glyn Houston; ***D:*** Christopher Barnard.

Conspiracy 1/2 **2001 (R)** Another in HBO's long line of excellent movies based on real-life events. This one covers the January, 1942 meeting of high-ranking Nazi SS and civilian government leaders to decide what to do about "the Jewish question." Led by SS Geneal Reinhard Heydrich (Branagh, in a riveting performance) and set up by SS Col. Adolf Eichmann (Tucci), this conference was conducted like a board meeting, and that's where the power of the movie comes from, because the outcome of the conference was implementation of the "final solution," the attempted extermination of the Jewish population of Europe. While every man in the room is a villain, they aren't the kind of Nazi villain we're used to. They are bureaucrats who offer administrative and logistical objections, but only token moral dissent (which is dispensed with rather quickly and completely). **96m/C VHS, DVD.** Stanley Tucci, Kenneth Branagh, Colin Firth, Barnaby Kay, Ben Daniels, David Threlfall, Jonathan Coy, Brendan Coyle, Ian McNeice, Owen Teale, Nicholas Woodeson, Ewan Stewart, Kevin McNally, Brian Pettifer; ***D:*** Frank Pierson; ***W:*** Loring Mandel; ***C:*** Stephen Goldblatt. **CABLE**

Conspiracy **2008 (R)** William Macpherson was forced to retire as a sniper after an injury. Bored with civilian life, he's eager to help out fellow Iraq War vet Miguel Silva with his new ranch in Lukeville, Arizona. Except when Macpherson arrives, Silva has disappeared and no one in town will admit to knowing anything. Macpherson discovers the town is controlled by ruthless John Rhodes, but Rhodes learns that Macpherson can't be intimidated. **90m/C DVD.** Val Kilmer, Gary Cole, Jennifer Esposito, Greg Serano, Bob Rumnock, Adam Marcus, Jay Jablonski; ***D:*** Debra Sullivan; ***W:*** Debra Sullivan; ***C:*** Ben Weinstein; ***M:*** Sujin Nam. **VIDEO**

Conspiracy of Fear **1996 (R)** After his father's strange death, Chris discovers he's being followed by a sadistic stalker and double agents who believe he has a package that everybody wants. Chris teams with a thief to solve both the mystery of the package and his father's death. **112m/C VHS.** Christopher Plummer, Geraint Wyn Davies, Leslie Hope, Andrew Lowery, Ken Walsh, Don Francks; ***D:*** John Eyres; ***W:*** Roy Sallows; ***C:*** Peter Benison; ***M:*** Stephen (Steve) Edwards.

Conspiracy of Hearts **1960** A convent of nuns hide Jewish children in 1943 Italy despite threats to their personal safety. Suspenseful tale despite the familiar plot. **113m/B VHS.** *GB* Lilli Palmer, Yvonne Mitchell, Sylvia Syms, Ronald Lewis; ***D:*** Ralph Thomas; ***W:*** Robert Presnell Jr.

A Conspiracy of Love **1987** Three generations of a divorce-torn family try to pull itself back together. Sugary domestic tale tries to be uplifting, succeeds in being cliche-ridden. **93m/C VHS.** Robert Young, Drew Barrymore, Glynnis O'Connor, Elizabeth Wilson, Mitchell Laurance, John Fujioka, Alan Fawcett; ***D:*** Noel Black. **TV**

Conspiracy of Silence 1/2 **2003** A desperately unbiased Irish drama about the troubles arising from priests required to take the vow of celibacy. Director John Deery is very obviously claiming that these otherwise good men are forced into a life of quiet lust and despair, leading to suicide and disturbing homosexual relations. Although well-acted, Deery's characters are presented in such sharp black or white, good or bad, friend or enemy, that it's kind of like watching a man argue with himself. **84m/C DVD.** *GB* Jason Barry, Brenda Fricker, Hugh Bonneville, John Lynch, Jim Norton, Sean McGinley, James Ellis, Hugh Quarshie, Fintan McKeown, Jonathan Forbes, Catherine Cusack, Catherine Walker, Patrick Casey, Owen McDonnell; ***Cameos:*** Gay Byrne; ***D:*** John Deery; ***W:*** John Deery; ***C:*** Jason Lehel; ***M:*** Stephen Parsons, Francis Haines.

Conspiracy of Terror **1975** Married detectives investigate a series of murders and unearth a grisly cult in a quiet suburb. Standard fare with a few too cute lines concerning the leads' mixed-faith marriage. **78m/C VHS.** Michael Constantine, Barbara Rhoades, Mariclare Costello, Roger Perry, David Opatoshu, Logan Ramsey; ***D:*** John Llewellyn Moxey. **TV**

Conspiracy: The Trial of the Chicago Eight **1987** Courtroom drama focuses on the rambunctious trial of the Chicago Eight radicals, charged with inciting a riot at the Democratic National Convention of 1968. Dramatized footage mixed with interviews with the defendants. Imaginative reconstruction of history. **118m/C VHS, DVD.** Peter Boyle, Elliott Gould, Robert Carradine, Martin Sheen, David Clennon, David Kagen, Michael Lembeck, Robert Loggia; ***D:*** Jeremy Paul Kagan.

Conspiracy Theory **1997 (R)** Whacked-out New York cabbie Jerry Fletcher (Gibson) writes a newsletter on conspiracy theories, which he finds in every possible place and situation. Naturally, he doesn't keep his thoughts to himself and exasperated Justice Department attorney Alice Sutton (Roberts) is stuck listening to the love-struck fool. But as the saying goes just because you're paranoid doesn't mean they're not out to get you. Sure enough, one of Jerry's conspiracies turns out to be true and suddenly he and Alice are being pursued by CIA shrink Dr. Jonas (Stewart), who's not what he seems to be either. Gibson's more geek than hero but appealing regardless, as is heroine Roberts. Another successful, enjoyable, and highly profitable, teaming of Donner, Gibson and producer Joel Silver. **135m/C VHS, DVD.** Terry Alexander, Mel Gibson, Julia Roberts, Patrick Stewart, Cylk Cozart; ***D:*** Richard Donner; ***W:*** Brian Helgeland; ***C:*** John Schwartzman; ***M:*** Carter Burwell.

Conspirator 1/2 **1949** Somewhat engrossing drama about a beautiful young girl who discovers that her new husband, a British army officer, is working with the Communists. Elizabeth Taylor stars as the naive American wife and Robert Taylor plays her Russkie agent husband. Although madly in love with his wife, he is given orders to kill her. Picture falls apart at end due to weak script. Based on the novel by Humphrey Slater. **85m/B VHS.** *GB* Robert Taylor, Elizabeth Taylor, Robert Flemyng, Harold Warrender, Honor Blackman, Marjorie Fielding, Thora Hird; ***D:*** Victor Saville; ***W:*** Sally Benson, Gerald Fairlie; ***C:*** Frederick A. (Freddie) Young.

The Constant Gardener **2005 (R)** Multi-faceted, multi-layered tale hits all the buttons of a great thriller: sex, love, murder, intrigue, exotic (if underprivileged) locale, and international politics, all mixed with a topical bent ripped from today's headlines. Justin (Fiennes) and Tessa (Weisz) plunge headfirst from passion into marriage, hardly knowing a thing about each other. He's an official in the British government; she's an activist; together they end up in Kenya where she witnesses foul play by drug companies who use the locals as guinea pigs for drug testing. The film starts with Tessa's brutal murder, and we follow along with Justin as he uncovers the mysteries of her life and death. Adapted from the 2001 novel by John le Carre. **129m/C DVD.** *GB* Ralph Fiennes, Rachel Weisz, Danny Huston, Bill Nighy, Pete Postlethwaite, Richard McCabe, Donald (Don) Sumpter, Juliet Aubrey, Hubert Kounde, Archie Panjabi, Gerard McSorley; ***D:*** Fernando Meirelles; ***W:*** Jeffrey Caine; ***C:*** Cesar Charlone; ***M:*** Alberto Iglesias. Oscars '05: Support. Actress (Weisz); British Acad. '05: Film Editing; Golden Globes '06: Support. Actress (Weisz); Screen Actors Guild '05: Support. Actress (Weisz).

Constantine 1/2 **2005 (R)** Freelance exorcist and all-around surly loner John Constantine (Reeves) stalks the divide between good and evil, playing the forces of Heaven and Hell against themselves, all for his own benefit. When a policewoman, Angela (Weisz), seeks out the chain-smoking ghostbuster to help solve her twin sister's mysterious suicide, Constantine acts as her guide into LA's supernatural underworld, revealing a plot involving the Spear of Destiny, rogue angels, and a scheme to unleash Hell on earth. Director Lawrence creates a nifty neo-noir atmosphere, but confusing exposition and an over-reliance on CGI scares hurts the final product. Based on DC's "Hellblazer" comic. **120m/C VHS, DVD, Blu-ray Disc, UMD, HD DVD.** *US* Keanu Reeves, Rachel Weisz, Djimon Hounsou, Max Baker, Pruitt Taylor Vince, Tilda Swinton, Peter Stormare, Shia LaBeouf, Gavin Rossdale, Jose Zuniga, Larry Cedar; ***D:*** Francis Lawrence; ***W:*** Kevin Brodbin, Frank Cappello; ***C:*** Philippe Rousselot; ***M:*** Brian Tyler, Klaus Badelt.

Consuming Passions 1/2 **1988 (R)** A ribald, food-obsessed English comedy about a young idiot who rises within the hierarchy of a chocolate company via murder. You'll never guess what the secret ingredient in his wonderful chocolate is. Based on a play by Michael Palin and Terry Jones (better known as part of the Monty Python troupe), the film is sometimes funny, more often gross, and takes a single joke far beyond its limit. **95m/C VHS.** *GB* Vanessa Redgrave, Jonathan Pryce, Tyler Butterworth, Freddie Jones, Prunella Scales, Sammi Davis, Thora Hird, John Wells, William Rushton, Timothy West; ***D:*** Giles Foster; ***W:*** Michael Palin, Andrew Davies, Paul Zimmerman.

Contact 1/2 **1997 (PG)** Thought-provoking (if overlong) drama rather than sci-fi spectacular (though it has its fair share of special effects). Radio astronomer Dr. Ellie Arroway (Foster) discovers signals being transmitted from the distant star Vega. When they're deciphered, the signals turn out to be blueprints for a craft that will take its occupant into space and a first meeting with aliens. Ellie fights to become that first spokesperson for Earth's inhabitants. More philosophical than the usual sci-fi alien encounter epic, but the excellent cast, led by Foster, pulls it off nicely. Based on the novel by Carl Sagan. **150m/C VHS, DVD.** Jodie Foster, Matthew McConaughey, James Woods, Tom Skerritt, Angela Bassett, John Hurt, David Morse, Rob Lowe, Jake Busey, William Fichtner, Geoffrey Blake, Jena Malone; ***D:*** Robert Zemeckis; ***W:*** Michael Goldenberg; ***C:*** Don Burgess; ***M:*** Alan Silvestri.

Contagion 1/2 **1987** Innocent real estate agent meets a reclusive, eccentric millionaire who offers him unlimited wealth and beautiful women, but only if he kills someone. Interesting ethical premise loses its philosophic purity. **90m/C VHS.** *AU* John (Roy Slaven) Doyle, Nicola Bartlett, Roy Barrett, Nathy Gaffney, Pamela Hawksford; ***D:*** Karl Zwicky.

Contagious 🦴🦴 1/2 **1996 (PG-13)** Epidemiologist Hanna (Wagner) discovers that passengers aboard a flight from Latin American have been exposed to cholera and could cause an epidemic. She teams with Detective Lou (Pena), who's tracking an infected drug smuggler, to find the source of the disease. **90m/C VHS.** Lindsay Wagner, Elizabeth Pena, Tom Wopat, Alexandra Purvis, Matt Hill, Brendan Fletcher; ***D:*** Joe Napolitano; ***W:*** Sandy Kroopf; ***C:*** Andreas Poulsson; ***M:*** Stephen Graziano. **CABLE**

The Contaminated Man 🦴 **2001 (R)** An infectious disease expert (Hurt) loses his family to an unknown disease. Now some years later at an "infectious disease laboratory" in a vaguely defined Russia, disgruntled security guard Muller (Weller) has been infected with a deadly pathogen, where one drop of his blood will now kill a person in matter of seconds. The disease expert is called in to investigate and teams up with an American reporter, as Muller is determined to get home to see his wife and son, even if it means infecting the entire Russian population. TV movie dull beyond belief. Peter Weller getting to do an eccentric Olivier-like turn as the Russian-accented, bald Muller is the only fun in the whole film. **98m/C DVD.** William Hurt, Natascha (Natasha) McElhone, Peter Weller, Katja Woywood, Michael Brandon; ***D:*** Anthony Hickox; ***W:*** John Penney; ***C:*** Bruce Douglas Johnson; ***M:*** Michael Hoenig. **TV**

Contempt 🦴🦴🦴 1/2 *Le Mepris; Il Disprezzo* **1964** A film about the filming of a new version of "The Odyssey," and the rival visions of how to tell the story. Amusing look at the film business features Fritz Lang playing himself, Godard as his assistant. Bardot is pleasant scenery. Adapted from Moravia's "A Ghost at Noon." **102m/C VHS, DVD.** *IT FR* Brigitte Bardot, Jack Palance, Fritz Lang, Georgia Moll, Michel Piccoli, Jean-Luc Godard, Linda Veras; ***D:*** Jean-Luc Godard; ***W:*** Jean-Luc Godard; ***C:*** Raoul Coutard; ***M:*** Georges Delerue.

The Contender 🦴🦴 1/2 **2000 (R)** An excellent cast propels this political potboiler, although the plot contains some hot air. After the sitting Veep dies, downhome Prez Evans (Bridges) nominates Sen. Laine Hanson (Allen) for the post. Although principled and experienced, she also happens to be a woman with a past. Evans's oily conservative rival Runyon (Oldman) takes advantage by digging up photos of the senator being the life of a college fraternity party. Hanson refuses to answer questions about her youthful indiscretions, arguing that her sexual history is nobody's business. As in real politics, much speechifying ensues and not much is accomplished. Allen shines in a role that was written expressly for her. Reports filtered out after the film's release that exec producer Oldman, a conservative himself, was unhappy about the editing and portrayal of his character, who he thought was the hero of the movie. **127m/C VHS, DVD.** Joan Allen, Gary Oldman, Jeff Bridges, Sam Elliott, Christian Slater, William L. Petersen, Philip Baker Hall, Saul Rubinek; ***D:*** Rod Lurie; ***W:*** Rod Lurie; ***C:*** Denis Maloney; ***M:*** Lawrence Nash Groupe.

Continental Divide 🦴🦴 **1981 (PG)** A hard-nosed political columnist takes off for the Colorado Rockies on an "easy assignment"—interviewing a reclusive ornithologist, with whom he instantly falls in love. A city slicker, he first alienates her, but she eventually falls for him, too. But it's not exactly a match made in heaven. Story meanders to a conclusion of sorts. Probably the most normal Belushi ever was on screen. **103m/C VHS, DVD.** John Belushi, Blair Brown, Allen (Goorwitz) Garfield, Carlin Glynn, Val Avery, Tony Ganios, Tim Kazurinsky; ***D:*** Michael Apted; ***W:*** Lawrence Kasdan; ***C:*** John Bailey.

Contraband 🦴🦴 1/2 *Blackout* **1940** Danish sea captain Andersen (Veidt) and the mysterious Mrs. Sorenson (Hobson) are kidnapped by a cell of Nazi spies operating in London in the early days of WWII. They manage to turn the tables on the bad guys. Story takes place under blackout conditions lending a lot of atmosphere to this early thriller. **88m/B VHS, DVD.** *GB* Conrad Veidt, Valerie Hobson, Esmond Knight, Hay Petrie, Raymond Lovell, Harold Warrender, Charles Victor; ***D:*** Michael Powell; ***W:*** Michael Powell; ***C:*** Frederick A. (Freddie) Young.

Contraband 🦴 1/2 *Luca il Contrabbandiere* **1980** The leader of a smuggling gang escapes from an ambush in which his brother was murdered. He searches for a haven of safety while his cronies seek brutal revenge. Average crime yarn lacks much excitement. Dubbed into English. **95m/C VHS, DVD.** *IT* Fabio Testi, Ivana Monti; ***D:*** Lucio Fulci; ***W:*** Gianni Di Chiara, Ettore Sanzo; ***C:*** Sergio Salvati; ***M:*** Fabio Frizzi.

Contract 🦴🦴🦴 1/2 **1980** A marriage ceremony between the children of two important families gets disrupted when the friends and relatives in attendance can't get along, and the bride can't seem to commit. Provides a biting social commentary against dirty politicians and unethical entrepreneurs. Polish with subtitles. **111m/C VHS.** *PL* Maja Komorowska, Tadeusz Lomnicki, Magda Jaroszowna, Leslie Caron, Ignacy Machowski; ***D:*** Krzysztof Zanussi; ***W:*** Krzysztof Zanussi; ***C:*** Slawomir Idziak; ***M:*** Wojciech Kilar.

The Contract 🦴🦴 **1998 (R)** Former black ops specialist Luc (Imbault) is now making a living as a pro assassin and is teaching the trade to daughter Hannah (Black). When dad gets killed in a set-up, Hannah wants revenge against the man behind the deed. It's Presidential candidate J. Harmon (Williams), who wants his own black ops past to stay hidden—but Hannah has other ideas. **90m/C VHS, DVD.** Billy Dee Williams, Johanna Black, Laurent Imbault; ***D:*** K.C. Bascombe. **VIDEO**

The Contract 🦴🦴 **2007 (R)** Frank Carden (Freeman) is a freelance hitman who gets arrested by some Washington state cops and is turned over to the feds for transport. Carden escapes into the woods with the help of some cronies, only to be re-captured by Ray Keene (Cusack), a former cop who is hiking with his teenaged son Chris (Anderson). Keene forces Carden to hike towards the authorities while his guntoting associates come searching. **96m/C DVD, Blu-ray Disc, HD DVD.** Morgan Freeman, John Cusack, Jamie Anderson, Alice Krige, Megan Dodds, Corey Johnson, Jonathan Hyde, Bill Smitrovich, Ned Bellamy; ***D:*** Bruce Beresford; ***W:*** Stephen Katz, John Darrouzet; ***C:*** Dante Spinotti; ***M:*** Normand Corbeil. **VIDEO**

Contract Killers 🦴 1/2 **2008** CIA assassin Jane plans to retire but her unhappy employers try framing her for the murder of her husband. However, they picked the wrong femme to mess with as Jane discovers a rogue CIA plot to ruin the Federal Reserve and decides to shut it down to get even. **86m/C DVD.** Frida Show, Nick Mancuso, Rhett Giles, Christian Willis; ***D:*** Justin B. Rhodes; ***W:*** Justin B. Rhodes; ***C:*** Andre Lascaris; ***M:*** Michael Mouracade. **VIDEO**

The Contractor 🦴 **2007 (R)** Routine would-be thriller has retired CIA assassin James Dial (Snipes) called in for one last job. Suddenly he's on the lam when the killing of a terrorist mastermind in London leads to a double-cross. James is befriended by 12-year-old Emma (Bennett), a witness who wants to help him prove his innocence. **105m/C DVD.** Wesley Snipes, Lena Headey, Eliza Bennett, Charles Dance, Ralph Brown, Gemma Jones; ***D:*** Josef Rusnak; ***W:*** Robert Foster, Joshua Michael Stern; ***C:*** Wendigo von Schultzendorff; ***M:*** Nicholas Pike. **VIDEO**

Control 🦴 1/2 **1987** Tedious tale of 15 volunteers for a 20-day fallout shelter habitation experiment who become trapped when a real nuclear emergency occurs. Filmed in Rome. **83m/C VHS.** *IT* Burt Lancaster, Kate Nelligan, Ben Gazzara, Andrea Ferreol, Lavinia Segurini, Andrea Occhipinti, Cyrielle Claire, Jean Benguigui, Kate Reid, Erland Josephson, Ingrid Thulin; ***D:*** Guiliano Montaldo. **CABLE**

Control 🦴🦴 **2007 (R)** Corbijn makes his directorial debut in this compelling B&W bio of Ian Curtis (Riley), frontman for British post-punk band "Joy Division." Epileptic and suffering from depression, Curtis is torn between a conventional life—a teenage marriage, child, and steady job—and the excitement and temptations of the music world. Although Curtis committed suicide in 1980 at the age of 23 this isn't the typical live fast/die young rock fantasy, but a thoughtful depiction of a young man who couldn't reconcile competing impulses. Based on the memoir "Touching from the Distance" by Deborah Curtis. **121m/B DVD.** *GB AU JP* Samantha Morton, Alexandra Maria Lara, Joe Anderson, James Anthony Pearson, Sam Riley, Craig Parkinson, Toby Kebbell, Harry Treadway, Andrew Sheridan, Robert Shelly; ***D:*** Anton Corbijn; ***W:*** Matt Greenhalgh, Deborah Curtis; ***C:*** Martin Ruhe; ***M:*** New Order.

Control Room 🦴🦴🦴 **2004** Shot days prior to the Iraq War, director Noujaim provides a fly on the wall account of the goings on at Al Jazeera, the leading news service for Arab-speaking viewers and also at Centcom, a makeshift media village set up by the U.S. military for the purpose of holding and briefing journalists from around the world. Your certainties will be scrambled and your assumptions shaken, if you think you can believe everything you hear on your news broadcasts. Presented in a surprisingly unbiased manner, provocative critique strongly questions the notion of journalistic objectivity. **85m/C VHS, DVD.** ***D:*** Jehane Noujaim; ***W:*** Jehane Noujaim, Julia Bacha; ***C:*** Jehane Noujaim; ***M:*** Hani Salama, Thomas DeRenzo.

The Convent 🦴🦴 **1995** Idiosyncratic saga of Paris-based American scholar Michael Padovic (Malkovich) and his French wife Helene (Deneuve) who travel to an ancient Portuguese monastery so Michael may do research at their library. The convent's guardian is the charming and sinister Baltar (Cintra), who flirts with neglected Helene, while playing Mephistopheles to Michael's Faust. Lots of mysticism and religious iconography. Portuguese, French, and English dialogue. **90m/C VHS, DVD.** *PT FR* John Malkovich, Catherine Deneuve, Luis Miguel Cintra, Leonor Silveira; ***D:*** Manoel de Oliveira; ***W:*** Manoel de Oliveira; ***C:*** Mario Barroso.

The Convent 🦴🦴 **2000 (R)** In 1960, a young woman enters a church, shoots several nuns and a priest, and then torches the place. Jump ahead to the present, as a group of college kids enter the now-condemned convent to perform a fraternity prank. Elsewhere in the dilapidated convent, amateur Satanists perform a ritual, releasing the evil spirits held captive in the sanctuary. From this point on, the movie becomes a monster mash, as each character is either possessed, killed, or both. The only hope for the trapped youngsters is the now-grown girl who started all of this in 1960. The film is creatively shot by director Mendez, and the demon makeup is unusual, but the action owes too much to "Night of the Demons 2," "The Church," and the "Goth Talk" skit from "Saturday Night Live." Horror aficionados will feel as if they've seen it all before. **79m/C VHS, DVD.** Adrienne Barbeau, Coolio, Bill Moseley, Joanna Canton, Megahn Perry, Dax Miller, David Gunn; ***D:*** Mike Mendez; ***W:*** Chaton Anderson; ***C:*** Jason Lowe; ***M:*** Joseph Bishara.

Convention Girl 🦴 1/2 *Atlantic City Romance* **1935** Cynthia "Babe" Laval (Hobart) is an aging lady of the evening who has become Atlantic City's most influential madam, controlling almost every call girl in town. Her real aim is to meet the man of her dreams, but she's caught between her desire for Wade Hollister (Rawlinson), a dull soap company executive, and the decidedly more dangerous Bill Bradley (Heyburn), who runs an illicit gambling joint. The two suitors clash, and Bradley gets nasty when he thinks he may be cut out of Babe's future plans. The plot is thin but classic Atlantic City attractions play a co-starring role. **66m/B DVD.** Rose Hobart, Weldon Heyburn, Sally O'Neil, Herbert Rawlinson, Shemp Howard; ***D:*** Luther Reed; ***W:*** George Boyle; ***C:*** Nick Rogelli.

The Conversation 🦴🦴🦴 1/2 **1974 (PG)** Freelance surveillance expert Harry Caul (Hackman) is becoming increasingly uneasy about his current job for a powerful businessman (Duvall). He and assistant Stan (Cazale) are watching a young couple (Williams, Forrest) when Harry begins to suspect that they are murder targets. Powerful statement about privacy, responsibility and guilt. One of the best movies of the '70s. **113m/C VHS, DVD.** Gene Hackman, John Cazale, Frederic Forrest, Allen (Goorwitz) Garfield, Cindy Williams, Robert Duvall, Teri Garr, Michael Higgins, Elizabeth McRae, Harrison Ford; ***D:*** Francis Ford Coppola; ***W:*** Francis Ford Coppola; ***C:*** Bill Butler; ***M:*** David Shire. Cannes '74: Film; Natl. Bd. of Review '74: Actor (Hackman), Director (Coppola), Natl. Film Reg. '95;; Natl. Soc. Film Critics '74: Director (Coppola).

Conversation Piece 🦴🦴🦴 *Violence et Passion; Gruppo di Famiglia in un Interno* **1975 (R)** An aging art historian's life is turned upside down when a Countess and her daughters rent out the penthouse in his estate. Sometimes-talky examination of scholarly pretensions. **112m/C VHS.** *IT FR* Burt Lancaster, Silvana Mangano, Helmut Berger, Claudia Cardinale, Claudia Marsani; ***D:*** Luchino Visconti; ***W:*** Luchino Visconti, Suso Cecchi D'Amico, Enrico Medioli; ***C:*** Pasqualino De Santis; ***M:*** Franco Mannino.

Conversations with Other Women 🦴🦴 1/2 **2005 (R)** Arty romantic-suspenser in which a man (Eckhart) and a woman (Bonham Carter) meet at a wedding reception and end up in bed, but as the night progresses it's revealed that they are possibly not strangers. Clever split-screen style shows each character separately navigating their encounter over the course of the evening, a technique that provides both emotional weight and insight to their backstory and motives as much as it illustrates the theme of perception-is-reality. Chemistry and fine acting turn a he said/she said one-night stand story into an examination of the passage of time, regret, and knowing better. **84m/C DVD.** *US* Helena Bonham Carter, Aaron Eckhart, Brian Geraghty, Olivia Wilde, Brianna Brown, Thomas Lennon, Nora Zehetner; ***D:*** Hans Canosa; ***W:*** Gabrielle Zevin; ***C:*** Steve Yedlin; ***M:*** Star Parodi, Jeff Eden Fair.

Convict Cowboy 🦴🦴 1/2 **1995 (R)** Hardbitten professional rodeo cowboy Ry Weston (Voight) killed a man and now works the Montana prison rodeo circuit. Newcomer greenhorn Clay Treyton (Chandler) wants to get out of kitchen duty and decides Ry is the perfect ridin' and ropin' teacher. Only Ry isn't interested in wasting his time (at first). It's a predictable bonding experience in a melodramatic movie. **106m/C VHS.** Jon Voight, Kyle Chandler, Ben Gazzara, Marcia Gay Harden, Glenn Plummer, Stephen McHattie; ***D:*** Rod Holcomb; ***C:*** James L. Carter. **CABLE**

Convict 762 🦴🦴 1/2 **1998 (R)** Zagarino and Drago are survivors of a remote penal colony who are rescued by the all-female crew of a cargo ship. But it turns out one of the duo is a murderer who begins to kill again. **100m/C VHS, DVD.** Frank Zagarino, Billy Drago, Shannon Sturges; ***D:*** Luca Bercovici; ***W:*** J. Reifel; ***C:*** Steven Wacks. **VIDEO**

Convicted 🦴🦴 1/2 **1932** Lean thriller about a woman cleared of a murder charge, but only when a second, identical murder occurs while she is jailed. **57m/B VHS.** Aileen Pringle, Jameson Thomas, Harry C. (Henry) Myers, Dorothy Christy, Richard Tucker; ***D:*** Christy Cabanne.

Convicted 🦴🦴 1/2 **1986** Solid story of innocent man imprisoned for rape, and his wife's determined efforts to free him. Larroquette does well in unexpected role. Based on a true story. **94m/C VHS.** John Larroquette, Carroll O'Connor, Lindsay Wagner; ***D:*** David Lowell Rich; ***M:*** Steve Dorff. **TV**

Convicted 🦴🦴 1/2 *Return to Sender* **2004 (R)** A deceitful former attorney (Quinn) makes some quick bucks selling off his letters with death row prisoners until he falls for convicted child killer Charlotte (Nielsen) and struggles to help clear her once new evidence surfaces. Decent as a message movie but stoops to stale action-movie-type twists toward the end. **108m/C VHS, DVD.** Connie Nielsen, Kelly Preston, Aidan Quinn, Timothy Daly, Mark Holton; ***D:*** Bille August; ***W:*** Neal Purvis, Robert Wade; ***C:*** Dirk Bruel; ***M:*** Harry Gregson-Williams. **VIDEO**

Convicted: A Mother's Story 🦴 **1987** Jillian embezzles cash from her employer, all for the sake of a bum of a boyfriend, and goes to jail. Odd casting hinders a ho-hum plot. **95m/C VHS.** Ann Jillian, Kiel Martin, Fred Savage, Gloria Loring, Christa Denton; ***D:*** Richard T. Heffron; ***M:*** David Shire. **TV**

Conviction 🦴🦴 **2002 (R)** Philadelphia-born Carl Upchurch (Epps) drops out of school at nine and into a life of crime that leads to various prison sentences. A man with a violent temper, he's no one to mess with but he also wants more from his life. This leads to his mentoring by Quaker prison instructor Martha (Delany) and Carl's goal to save other inner-city youth from a life of violence and imprisonment. Based on Upchurch's autobiography. **100m/C VHS, DVD.** Omar Epps, Dana Delany, Charles S. Dutton, Treach, Bentley Mitchum; ***D:*** Kevin Rodney Sullivan; ***W:*** Jon Huffman, Carl Upchurch; ***C:*** Miroslaw Baszak; ***M:*** Jeff Beal. **CABLE**

Convicts at Large 1938 An escaped convict steals the clothes of a inept architect. Left with only prison duds, the architect stumbles into the bad side of town and gets involved with the mob. Inane. **58m/B VHS, DVD.** Ralph Forbes, Paula Stone; ***D:*** Scott E. Beal; ***W:*** Scott E. Beal.

Convoy 1/2 **1940** Life aboard a convoy ship in the North Sea during WWII. The small cruiser is picked on by a German U-Boat. Will a rescuer appear? Noted for technical production values. **95m/B VHS.** Clive Brook, John Clements, Edward Chapman, Judy Campbell, Edward Rigby, Stewart Granger, Michael Wilding, George Benson; ***D:*** Pen Tennyson.

Convoy **1978 (R)** A defiant trucker leads an indestructible truck convoy to Mexico to protect high gasoline prices. Lightweight stuff was inspired by the song "Convoy" by C.W. McCall. **106m/C VHS, DVD.** Kris Kristofferson, Ali MacGraw, Ernest Borgnine, Burt Young, Madge Sinclair, Franklin Ajaye, Cassie Yates; ***D:*** Sam Peckinpah; ***C:*** Harry Stradling Jr.

Coogan's Bluff **1968 (PG)** An Arizona deputy sheriff (Eastwood) travels to New York in order to track down a killer on the loose. First Eastwood/Siegel teaming is tense actioner. The TV series "McCloud" was based on this film. **100m/C VHS, DVD.** Clint Eastwood, Lee J. Cobb, Tisha Sterling, Don Stroud, Betty Field, Susan Clark, Tom Tully, Albert "Poppy" Popwell; ***D:*** Donald Siegel; ***W:*** Dean Riesner; ***M:*** Lalo Schifrin.

The Cook, the Thief, His Wife & Her Lover 1/2 **1990 (R)** An exclusive restaurant houses four disturbing characters. Greenaway's powerful vision of greed, love, and violence may be too strong for some tastes. Available in several different versions: the standard unrated theatrical release, the unrated version in a letterboxed format, and an R-rated cut which runs half an hour shorter. **123m/C VHS, DVD.** *GB* Richard Bohringer, Michael Gambon, Helen Mirren, Alan Howard, Tim Roth; ***D:*** Peter Greenaway; ***W:*** Peter Greenaway; ***C:*** Sacha Vierny; ***M:*** Michael Nyman.

Cookie 1/2 **1989 (R)** Light comedy about a Mafia don's daughter trying to smart mouth her way into the mob's good graces. A character-driven vehicle, this plot takes a backseat to casting. Wiest is superb as Falk's moll. **93m/C VHS.** Emily Lloyd, Peter Falk, Dianne Wiest, Jerry Lewis, Brenda Vaccaro, Ricki Lake, Lionel Stander, Michael V. Gazzo, Adrian Pasdar, Bob Gunton, Rockets Redglare, G. Anthony "Tony" Sirico; ***D:*** Susan Seidelman; ***W:*** Alice Arlen, Nora Ephron; ***M:*** Thomas Newman.

Cookie's Fortune 1/2 **1999 (PG-13)** Neal is Jewel Mae "Cookie" Orcutt, the matriarch of a Mississippi family with its share of female eccentrics. When Cookie offs herself to join her deceased husband, her officious, scandal-fearing spinster neice Camille (Close) destroys the suicide note, setting up the family's loyal, good-natured handyman (Dutton) for the fall. At the same time, she's directing practically the whole town in a church performance of "Salome." Excellent script by Rapp allows more characterization than usual for Altman, as well as a pleasantly leisurely pace. Flawless ensemble work (another Altman hallmark) is highlighted by the performances of Neal, Close, and Dutton. **118m/C VHS, DVD.** Charles S. Dutton, Glenn Close, Patricia Neal, Liv Tyler, Chris O'Donnell, Julianne Moore, Ned Beatty, Courtney B. Vance, Donald Moffat, Lyle Lovett, Matt Malloy, Rufus Thomas, Danny Darst, Randle Mell, Niecy Nash, Ruby Wilson, Preston Strobel; ***D:*** Robert Altman; ***W:*** Anne Rapp; ***C:*** Toyomichi Kurita; ***M:*** David A. Stewart. Natl. Bd. of Review '99: Support. Actress (Moore).

Cooking Up Trouble *Three of a Kind* **1944** The crazy trio become foster dads in this "Stooge" type comedy. **60m/B VHS.** Shemp Howard, Billy Gilbert, Maxie "Slapsie" Rosenbloom; ***D:*** David Ross Lederman; ***W:*** Earle Snell.

The Cookout **2004 (PG-13)** Low-brow, slack-paced comedy debut from Rivera is filled with stereotypes. Todd Anderson (Storm P) takes advantage of being the NBA's No. 1 draft pick by letting his greedy girlfriend Brittany (Good) talk him into buying an ostentatious mansion in a gated community, among other perks. His distrustful mom (Lewis) insists he keep to his down-home ways by hosting the big annual cookout for family and friends, which brings all the hangers-on into the backyard. Queen Latifah has what's basically an extended cameo as a zealous community security guard. **88m/C VHS, DVD.** *US* Tim Meadows, Jenifer Lewis, Meagan Good, Jonathan Silverman, Ja Rule, Storm P, Farrah Fawcett, Frankie Faison, Eve, Danny Glover, Rita Owens, Marci Reed, Ruperto Vanderpool, Queen Latifah; ***Cameos:*** Marv Albert, Elton Brand, Baron Davis, Mark Cuban; ***D:*** Lance Rivera; ***W:*** Laurie B. Tuner, Ramsey Gbelawoe, Jeffrey Brian Holmes; ***C:*** Tom Houghton; ***M:*** Camara Kambon, Keir Gist.

Cool and the Crazy **1994 (R)** High school sweethearts Michael (Leto) and Roslyn (Silverstone) are now in a troubled marriage. Apparently dissatisfied by hubby's sexual performance, Roslyn decides to take a walk on the wide side with hoodlum Joey (Flint). Michael finds out and decides to have his own extramarital fling with a beatnik coworker (it's set in the 50s). But there's even more trouble ahead. Rather than "cool" and "crazy," it's amateurish and nonsensical. **90m/C VHS, DVD.** Alicia Silverstone, Jared Leto, Jennifer Blanc, Matthew Flint, Bradford Tatum, Christina Harnos, Tuesday Knight; ***D:*** Ralph Bakshi; ***W:*** Ralph Bakshi; ***C:*** Roberto Schaefer; ***M:*** Hummie Mann. **CABLE**

Cool As Ice **1991 (PG)** "Rapper" Vanilla Ice makes his feature film debut as a rebel with an eye for the ladies, who motors into a small, conservative town. Several so-so musical segments. For teenage girls only. **92m/C VHS.** Vanilla Ice, Kristin Minter, Michael Gross, Sydney Lassick, Dody Goodman, Naomi Campbell, Candy Clark; ***D:*** David Kellogg; ***C:*** Janusz Kaminski; ***M:*** Stanley Clarke. Golden Raspberries '91: Worst New Star (Vanilla Ice).

Cool Blue 1/2 **1988 (R)** An unsuccessful painter meets the woman of his dreams, has a brief affair, then tries to locate her in the greater Los Angeles metro area. Good luck. Watch for Penn's cameo. **93m/C VHS.** Woody Harrelson, Hank Azaria, Ely Pouget, John Diehl; ***Cameos:*** Sean Penn; ***D:*** Mark Mullin, Richard Shepard.

A Cool, Dry Place 1/2 **1998 (PG-13)** Basically a variation on "Kramer vs. Kramer." Russ Durrell (Vaughn) was a hot-shot Chicago lawyer with a five-year old son, Calvin (Moat), when wife Kate (Potter) took a hike. So Russ moves to small town Kansas to make a go of single fatherhood in a slower-paced world. Eventually, he begins dating Beth (Adams) and when things start to get serious, guess who turns up and decides she wants back into her son's life? Vaughn does fine as the dad but Potter is stuck with a dopey, inarticulate character. **97m/C VHS, DVD.** Vince Vaughn, Monica Potter, Joey Lauren Adams, Bobby Moat, Devon Sawa; ***D:*** John N. Smith; ***W:*** Matthew McDuffie; ***C:*** Jean Lepine; ***M:*** Curt Sobel.

Cool Hand Luke 1/2 **1967** One of the last great men-in-chains films. A man (Newman) sentenced to sweat out a term on a prison farm refuses to compromise with authority. Martin shines in his supporting role as the oily warden, uttering that now-famous phrase, "What we have here is a failure to communicate." Kennedy's performance as leader of the chain gang won him an Oscar. Based on the novel by Donn Pearce. **126m/C VHS, DVD, Blu-ray Disc.** Paul Newman, George Kennedy, J.D. Cannon, Strother Martin, Dennis Hopper, Anthony Zerbe, Lou Antonio, Wayne Rogers, Harry Dean Stanton, Ralph Waite, Joe Don Baker, Richard (Dick) Davalos, Jo Van Fleet, Robert Drivas, Clifton James, Morgan Woodward, Luke Askew, Robert Donner, Warren Finnerty, James Gammon, Rance Howard, Buck Kartalian, John McLiam, Charles Tyner, Donn Pearce, Marc Cavell, Charles Hicks, James Jeter, Robert Luster, John Pearce, Eddie Rosson; ***D:*** Stuart Rosenberg; ***W:*** Frank Pierson, Donn Pearce; ***C:*** Conrad L. Hall; ***M:*** Lalo Schifrin. Oscars '67: Support. Actor (Kennedy), Natl. Film Reg. '05.

Cool Mikado **1963** A jazzy modernization of the Gilbert-Sullivan operetta, in which an American soldier is kidnapped by the gangster fiance of the Japanese girl he loves. **81m/C VHS.** *GB* Stubby Kaye, Frankie Howerd, Dennis Price; ***D:*** Michael Winner.

Cool Runnings 1/2 **1993 (PG)** Bright, slapstick comedy based on the true story of the Jamaican bobsled team's quest to enter the 1988 Winter Olympics in Calgary. Candy is recruited to coach four unlikely athletes who don't quite exemplify the spirit of the Games. He accepts the challenge not only because of its inherent difficulty but because he needs to reconcile himself to past failures as a former sledder. When our heroes leave their sunny training ground for Calgary, their mettle is tested by serious sledders from more frigid climes who pursue the competition with a stern sense of mission. An upbeat story which will appeal to children, its target audience. **98m/C VHS, DVD.** Leon, Doug E. Doug, John Candy, Marco Brambilla, Malik Yoba, Rawle Lewis, Raymond J. Barry, Peter Outerbridge, Larry Gilman, Paul Coeur; ***D:*** Jon Turteltaub; ***W:*** Tommy Swerdlow, Lynn Siefert, Michael Goldberg; ***C:*** Phedon Papamichael; ***M:*** Hans Zimmer.

The Cool Surface **1992 (R)** Sex and ambition, Hollywood style. Dani, a wannbe actress, and Jarvis, an aspiring screenwriter become lovers. Jarvis turns their hot affair into a sizzling novel and then a script. Dani may have inspired the lead role but that doesn't mean she'll get the part. But it won't be for lack of trying (anything). **88m/C VHS, DVD.** Robert Patrick, Teri Hatcher, Matt McCoy, Cyril O'Reilly, Ian Buchanan; ***D:*** Erik Anjou; ***W:*** Erik Anjou; ***M:*** Dave Kopplin.

The Cool World 1/2 **1963** Tough-talking docudrama, set on the streets of Harlem, focuses on a 15-year-old black youth whose one ambition in life is to own a gun and lead his gang. **107m/B VHS.** Gloria Foster, Hampton Clanton, Carl Lee; ***D:*** Shirley Clarke. Natl. Film Reg. '94.

Cool World **1992 (PG-13)** Underground cartoonist Jack Deebs enters his own adult cartoon "Cool World," lured by his sex-kitten character "Holli Would," who needs him to leave her animated world and become human. Holli's plan is opposed by the only other human to occupy Cool World, a slick detective whose main job is to prevent noids (humans) and doodles (cartoons) from having sex and destroying the balance between the two existences. A mixture of live-action and wild animation. Director Bakshi's creations are not intended for children but this is less explicit than usual, which may be one of the problems. Little humor and a flat script leave this film too uninvolving. **101m/C VHS, DVD.** Gabriel Byrne, Kim Basinger, Brad Pitt, Michele Abrams, Deirdre O'Connell, Carrie Hamilton, Frank Sinatra Jr., Michael David Lally, William Frankfather; ***D:*** Ralph Bakshi; ***W:*** Michael Grais, Mark Victor; ***C:*** John A. Alonzo; ***M:*** Mark Isham.

The Cooler **2003 (R)** Bernie Lootz (Macy) is a Las Vegas gambler with a nasty losing streak. After getting into debt to casino manager Shelly Kaplow (Baldwin), Bernie finds himself indentured as a "cooler," a walking bad luck charm sent to cool off the winning streaks simply by sitting next to the gamblers. Bernie's luck begins to change about a week before he's finished paying off. He meets and falls for Natalie (Bello), a casino waitress, and it seems his perennial bad luck begins to disappear (but of course, there are complications). Great cast provides sterling performances all around. Most notable is Macy, who hits the jackpot playing a loser. **101m/C VHS, DVD.** *US* William H. Macy, Alec Baldwin, Maria Bello, Shawn Hatosy, Ron Livingston, Paul Sorvino, Estella Warren, Arthur J. Nascarelli, M.C. Gainey, Ellen Greene, Joey Fatone, Tony Longo; ***D:*** Wayne Kramer; ***W:*** Wayne Kramer, Frank Hannah; ***C:*** James Whitaker; ***M:*** Mark Isham. Natl. Bd. of Review '03: Support. Actor (Baldwin).

A Cooler Climate 1/2 **1999 (R)** Iris (Fields) is a middleaged married woman who divorces her husband (refusing any settlement) after she falls in love with another man. When her lover leaves her, Iris has no money and no job skills except her homemaking abilities. Those allow her to become the live-in housekeeper for the wealthy Tanners. But brittle Paula Tanner (Davis) soon finds herself on the rocky road to divorce and unable to cope while Iris discovers her self-esteem in her independence. The men are strictly cardboard but Fields and Davis are worth a watch. Based on a novel by Zena Collier. **100m/C VHS.** Sally Field, Judy Davis, Winston Rekert, Jerry Wasserman, Jessalyn Gilsig, Gerard Plunkett, Carly Pope, Peter Yunker; ***D:*** Susan Seidelman; ***W:*** Marsha Norman; ***C:*** John Bartley; ***M:*** Patrick Williams. **CABLE**

Cooley High **1975 (PG)** Black high school students in Chicago go through the rites of passage in their senior year during the '60s. Film is funny, smart, and much acclaimed. Great soundtrack featuring Motown hits of the era is a highlight. Basis for the TV series "What's Happening." **107m/C VHS, DVD.** Glynn Turman, Lawrence-Hilton Jacobs, Garrett Morris, Cynthia Davis; ***D:*** Michael A. Schultz; ***W:*** Eric Monte.

Cooperstown 1/2 **1993** Harry (Arkin) is a former major-league pitcher who now works as a baseball scout in Florida. He's been angry for 30 years over giving up a home-run pitch that kept his team (the ficitional Chicago Barons) out of the World Series. Harry's feels this error cost him his chance at induction into the Baseball Hall of Fame in Cooperstown, New York, and he's always blamed ex-friend and former catcher Raymond (Greene), who's just had the gall to be elected. Only Raymond's just died—but his ghostly figure visits Harry and urges him to take a road trip not only to the baseball shrine but into his past. **100m/C VHS.** Alan Arkin, Graham Greene, Hope Lange, Josh Charles, Ed Begley Jr., Maria Pitillo, Ann Wedgeworth, Paul Dooley, Joanna Miles, Charles Haid; ***D:*** Charles Haid; ***W:*** Lee Blessing. **CABLE**

Cop 1/2 **1988 (R)** Left by his wife and child, a ruthless and work-obsessed detective goes after a twisted serial killer. Woods' exceptional ability to play sympathetic weirdos is diluted by a script—based on James Ellroys's novel "Blood on the Moon"—that warps the feminist theme, is violent, and depends too heavily on coincidence. **110m/C VHS, DVD.** James Woods, Lesley Ann Warren, Charles Durning, Charles Haid, Raymond J. Barry, Randi Brooks, Annie McEnroe, Victoria Wauchope; ***D:*** James B. Harris; ***W:*** James B. Harris; ***M:*** Michel Colombier.

Cop and a Half 1/2 **1993 (PG)** Streetwise eight-year-old (Golden) accidentally witnesses a murder and then bullies police into letting him join the force (for a day) when he withholds key information. Enter his partner for the day—hard-edged detective Reynolds, who claims to hate kids, but who we know will learn to love them. Meanwhile, the outlaw (Sharkey) knows Devon saw him and is trying to silence him permanently. Predictable fantasy may appeal to kids, but will make most adults yawn. One of Sharkey's last roles. **87m/C VHS, DVD.** Norman D. Golden II, Burt Reynolds, Ruby Dee, Ray Sharkey, Holland Taylor, Frank Sivero, Marc Macaulay, Rocky Giordani, Sammy Hernandez; ***D:*** Henry Winkler; ***W:*** Arne Olsen; ***C:*** Bill Butler; ***M:*** Alan Silvestri. Golden Raspberries '93: Worst Actor (Reynolds).

The Cop & the Girl **1986** A cop falls for a teenage runaway, ends up on the lam. Confused story overpowered by camera work. Lots of violence and strong language. Dubbed. **94m/C VHS.** *GE* Jurgen Prochnow, Annette Von Klier; ***D:*** Peter Keglevic.

Cop Au Vin 1/2 *Poulet au Vinaigre* **1985** Chabrol's crime thriller is set in a corrupt provincial town. Possessive wheelchair-bound widow Madame Cuno (Audran) and her bullied son, postman Louis (Belvaux), are in danger of losing their home to local land speculators who won't take Madame's refusal to sell for an answer. Thanks to Louis reading their mail, the Cunos find out some dirty secrets and people go missing and then turn up dead. This shifts the focus and brings in cynical detective Levardin (Poiret) to investigate. French with subtitles. **100m/C DVD.** *FR* Stephane Audran, Jean Poiret, Lucas Belvaux, Jean Topart, Michel Bouquet, Caroline Cellier, Pauline Lafont, Jean-Claude Bouillaud; *D:* Claude Chabrol; *W:* Claude Chabrol; *C:* Jean Rabier; *M:* Matthieu Chabrol.

Cop in Blue Jeans 🦴 **1978** Undercover cop goes after a mob kingpin in this violent, badly dubbed crime yarn. **92m/C VHS, DVD.** Tomas Milian, Jack Palance, Maria Rosaria Omaggio, Guido Mannari; *D:* Bruno Corbucci.

Cop Killers WOOF! 1973 (R) Two men desperate for an easy way to make money embark on a murderous shooting spree. Mostly blanks. **93m/C VHS, DVD.** Jason Williams, Bill Osco; *D:* Walter R. Cichy; *W:* Walter R. Cichy; *C:* Howard Ziehm; *M:* Hal Yoergler.

Cop Land 🦴🦴🦴 *Copland* **1997 (R)** Partially deaf sheriff (Stallone), whose small New Jersey town is home to a number of New York cops, has divided loyalties when a criminal investigation could implicate his department and the cops he idolizes. Stallone wanted to put "actor" back on his resume, and made the ultimate sacrifice of his physique for the role by gaining some 35 pounds and letting his muscles go. Writer-director Mangold, who grew up in an upstate New York town populated by NYC cops and firemen, pairs his earnest morality tale with a Western feel to provide the excellent cast a chance to do what they do best. Welcome departure from the usual summer bombast. **105m/C VHS, DVD.** Sylvester Stallone, Robert De Niro, Annabella Sciorra, Harvey Keitel, Peter Berg, Janeane Garofalo, Michael Rapaport, Ray Liotta, Cathy Moriarty, Robert Patrick, Noah Emmerich, John Spencer, Malik Yoba, Frank Vincent, Arthur J. Nascarelli, Edie Falco, Deborah Harry; *D:* James Mangold; *W:* James Mangold; *C:* Eric Alan Edwards; *M:* Howard Shore.

Cop-Out 🦴🦴 *Stranger in the House* **1967** John Sawyer (Mason) is an alcoholic retired attorney who has lived in seclusion since his wife left him. His estranged daughter, Angela (Chaplin), runs with a swinging crowd and her boyfriend, Jo (Bertoya), is accused of killing another member of their group. So daddy comes to the rescue to defend him and expose the real killer. Mason is the only reason to watch this mishmash. Based on the Georges Simenon's novel "Stranger in the House" and previously filmed in 1942. **95m/C VHS.** *GB* James Mason, Geraldine Chaplin, Paul Bertoya, Bobby Darin, Ian Ogilvy, Clive Morton, James Hayter, Moira Lister; *D:* Pierre Rouve; *W:* Pierre Rouve; *C:* Ken Higgins; *M:* Patrick John Scott.

Cop-Out 🦴🦴 **1991** A cop is framed. His brother is mad. Teamed up with a sexy lawyer, he exposes the filth that is corrupting the city. Okay melodrama. **102m/C VHS.** David Buff, Kathryn Luster, Dan Ranger, Reggie DeMorton, Lawrence L. Simeone; *D:* Lawrence L. Simeone; *W:* Lawrence L. Simeone.

Cop Out 🦴 *A Couple of Dicks* **2010 (R)** Two awkwardly paired cops (Willis and Morgan) track down a stolen baseball card, rescue a babe, and deal with gangsters and laundered drug money in this send-up of cop buddy movies that manages to be worse than the movies it is trying to mock. Not entirely without laughs, but the sheer number of failed jokes—most of the poo-poo variety—more than overshadows the successes. Notable for being the first movie Smith directed that he did not also write, there are occasional signs of his unique wit but he shows little skill at working with someone else's material. **107m/C DVD.** *W:* Marc Cullen.

Copacabana 🦴🦴 **1947** A shady theatrical agent (Groucho) books a nightclub singer into two shows at the same time at New York's ritzy nightclub. Lots of energy spent trying to enliven a routine script. Also available colorized. ♫Tico Tico; Stranger Things Have Happened; Je Vous Amie; My Heart Was Doing a Bolero; Let's Do the Copacabana; I Haven't Got a Thing to Sell; We've Come to Copa. **91m/B VHS, DVD.** Groucho Marx, Carmen Miranda, Steve Cochran, Gloria Jean, Andy Russell; ***Cameos:*** Earl Wilson; *D:* Alfred E. Green; *W:* Allen Boretz, Laszlo Vadnay; *C:* Bert Glennon.

Copper Canyon 🦴🦴 **1/2 1950** Milland plays a Confederate Army officer who heads West after the Civil War, meets up with Lamarr, and sparks a romance. Good chemistry between the leads in this otherwise standard western. **84m/B VHS, DVD.** Ray Milland, Hedy Lamarr, MacDonald Carey, Mona Freeman, Harry Carey Jr., Frank Faylen, Taylor Holmes, Peggy Knudsen; *D:* John Farrow.

Copperhead 🦴 **1984 (R)** A group of copperhead snakes attack a family who possess a stolen Incan gold necklace. This one bites. **90m/C VHS.** Jack Renner, Gretta Ratliff, David Fritts, Cheryl Nickerson; *D:* Leland Payton; *W:* Leland Payton.

Cops and Robbers 🦴🦴 **1/2 1973 (PG)** Two cops use a Wall Street parade for returning astronauts as a cover for a multi-million dollar heist. Exceptional caper film thanks to the likable leads and genuine suspense. **89m/C VHS, DVD.** Joseph Bologna, Dick Ward, Shepperd Strudwick, John P. Ryan, Ellen Holly, Dolph Sweet, Joe Spinell, Cliff Gorman; *D:* Aram Avakian; *W:* Donald E. Westlake.

Cops and Robbersons 🦴 **1994 (PG)** Bored, dim-witted dad Chase, a TV cop-show junkie, wishes his life had a little more danger and excitement. How lucky for him when hard-nosed cop Palance sets up a command post in his house to stake out the mobster living next door (Davi). Predictable plot isn't funny and drags Chase's bumbling idiot persona on for too long; Wiest and Davi are two bright spots, but their talents are wasted, while Palance does little more than reincarnate his "City Slickers" character. Poor effort for otherwise notable director Ritchie. **93m/C VHS, DVD.** Jack Kehler, Chevy Chase, Jack Palance, Dianne Wiest, Robert Davi, Jason James Richter, Fay Masterson, Miko Hughes, Richard Romanus, David Barry Gray; *D:* Michael Ritchie; *W:* Bernie Somers; *C:* Gerry Fisher; *M:* William Ross.

Copycat 🦴🦴 **1995 (R)** Crowded serial killer genre yields crooner Connick as southern psychopath stuck on murder. Soon he's in jail, advising the police in their hunt for another serial killer who imitates the murders of other infamous serial killers. Agoraphobic, boozing criminal psychologist Helen Hudson (Weaver), still suffering the after effects of an attack by sicko subject Darryl Lee Cullum (Connick), is enlisted to help detective M.J. Monahan (Hunter) catch the homage specialist. Weaver and Hunter bring sparks to the usually testosterone-laden formula, helping mask the preponderance of serial killer cliches and giant holes in the script. Connick's turn as a nut-job killer won't make you forget Anthony Hopkins, or even Frank Sinatra. Exploitative and imitative, and always faithful to the formula. **124m/C VHS, DVD.** Sigourney Weaver, Holly Hunter, Dermot Mulroney, Harry Connick Jr., William McNamara, Will Patton, John Rothman, David Michael Silverman; *D:* Jon Amiel; *W:* Ann Biderman, David Madsen; *C:* Laszlo Kovacs; *M:* Christopher Young.

Coquette 🦴🦴 **1/2 1929** Pickford's first talkie portrays her as a flirtatious flapper from a well-to-do family who falls in love with a poor man her father despises. So much in fact that daddy kills the young man and then commits suicide, leaving his daughter to face the world alone. Pickford and Brown get to share a melodramatic death scene and audiences flocked to hear "America's Sweetheart" speak onscreen. Based on a play by George Abbott and Anne Preston. **75m/B VHS.** Mary Pickford, Johnny Mack Brown, Matt Moore, John St. Polis, Henry Kolker, George Irving, Louise Beavers, William Janney; *D:* Sam Taylor; *C:* Karl Struss. Oscars '29: Actress (Pickford).

Cora Unashamed 🦴🦴 **1/2 2000** Adaptation of the Langston Hughes short story that finds racism and tragedy in a small Iowa town in the 1930s. Cora Jenkins (Taylor) and her mother (Pounder) are the only blacks in the community. Cora works as a housekeeper for the Studevant family and becomes strongly attached to the family's daughter, Jessie (Graham). This bond is resented by Jessie's mother, selfish and cold Lizbeth (Jones), whose exaggerated sense of propriety brings about disaster. **95m/C VHS, DVD.** Regina Taylor, Cherry Jones, CCH Pounder, Michael Gaston, Arlen Dean Snyder, Molly Graham, Ellen Muth, Koh1 Sudduth; *D:* Deborah Pratt; *W:* Ann Peacock; *C:* Ernest Holzman; *M:* Patrice Rushen. **TV**

Coraline 🦴🦴🦴 **2009 (PG)** A stop-motion animated fantasy based on the novel by Neil Gaiman. Young Coraline Jones (Fanning), not a particularly nice little girl, discovers a secret door in her family's new home that leads to a bizarre, alternate version of her own life. Threatened by her new, strange parents to trap her in this "Alice in Wonderland" nightmare forever, she must then plan her escape. Director Selick suggests this creepy chiller is intended for "brave children." Shot in stereoscopic 3-D, which unfortunately doesn't translate well off the big screen. **100m/C DVD.** *US D:* Henry Selick; *W:* Henry Selick; *C:* Pete Kozachik; *M:* Bruno Coulais; *V:* Dakota Fanning, Teri Hatcher, Ian McShane, Keith David, Jennifer Saunders, Dawn French, John Hodgman, Robert Bailey Jr.

The Core 🦴🦴 **1/2 2003 (PG-13)** The molten-hot magma goo at the Earth's core has stopped spinning (?!), bringing about the end of the world...unless a team of scientists and pilots can drill to the center of the planet and detonate an atomic device to get it going again in this unabashedly silly popcorn flick. Led by scruffy geophysicist Josh Keyes (Eckard), the multi-ethnic, multi-talented crew sets off on their preposterous mission, knowing full-well that the whole thing is ridiculous. This self knowledge, agreeing that it's all absurd, and not taking itself to seriously, is what gets this disaster flick by. Everybody has a good time playing their characters' assigned quirks, especially Tucci as a smug, smarmy geophysicist. **135m/C VHS, DVD.** *US* Aaron Eckhart, Hilary Swank, Delroy Lindo, Stanley Tucci, DJ Qualls, Richard Jenkins, Tcheky Karyo, Bruce Greenwood, Alfre Woodard; *D:* Jon Amiel; *W:* John Rogers, Cooper Layne; *C:* John Lindley; *M:* Christopher Young.

Coriolanus, Man without a Country 🦴 **1964** When the Romans begin to abuse their rights, the Plebians call upon the brave and mighty Coriolanus to lead them into battle against their oppressors. Predictable muscle man outing. **96m/C VHS.** *IT* Gordon Scott, Alberto Lupo, Lilla Brignone; *D:* Giorgio Ferroni; *W:* Remigio del Grosso.

Corky of Gasoline Alley 🦴 **1/2 1951** Hope's drifter cousin Elwood shows up to mooch off her and Corky, causing havoc at home and work and for their friends as well. The second in the film series following "Gasoline Alley." Based on the Frank O. King comic strip. **80m/B DVD.** Scotty Beckett, Susan Morrow, Gordon Jones, Don Beddoe, James Lydon, Dick Wessel, Pat Brady; *D:* Edward L. Bernds; *W:* Edward L. Bernds; *C:* Henry Freulich.

Corky Romano 🦴 **2001 (PG-13)** Remember when ex-SNL cast members made good movies? Yeah, neither do they. Kattan is the title character—a spastic, twitchy veterinary assistant, estranged from his mob family, who's so naive, he thinks his Pops (Falk) is actually a landscaping mogul. He is talked into infiltrating the FBI to retrieve evidence against the family by gruff henchman Leo (Ward), the actual stool pigeon talking to the feds. His frantic bumbling is mistaken for genius by his FBI superior Schuster (Roundtree) and hottie special agent Kate (Shaw). The plot is just dressing for Kattan's "funny-looking rubbery guy knocks everything over" routine, and he plays it like Jerry Lewis without the subtlety. First "Night at the Roxbury," then "Monkeybone" and now this? Can someone get Kattan a script consultant? Please? **85m/C VHS, DVD.** *US* Chris Kattan, Vinessa Shaw, Peter Falk, Peter Berg, Christopher Penn, Fred Ward, Richard Roundtree, Matthew Glave, Dave Sheridan, Roger Fan; *D:* Rob Pritts; *W:* David Garrett, Jason Ward; *C:* Steven Bernstein; *M:* Randy Edelman.

Corleone 🦴 **1979 (R)** Limp tale about two boyhood friends who grow up to fight the evil landowners who dominate Italy. To accomplish this, one becomes a mobster, the other a politician. **115m/C VHS.** *IT* Claudia Cardinale, Giuliano Gemma; *D:* Pasquale Squitieri. Montreal World Film Fest. '79: Actor (Gemma).

Corn 🦴🦴 **2002 (PG)** The locals don't put much stock in Emily's word when the unmarried, pregnant college dropout starts carrying on about the dangers of some "genetically enhanced" corn crops even though a bunch of folks suddenly aren't feeling so good. What is it about corn that makes small towns go all crazy in the movies, anyway? **97m/C VHS, DVD.** Jena Malone, Pamela Gray, Peter McRobbie, Jamie Harrold, Libby Langdon, Don Harvey, John Hartmann, Brian Dykstra, David Matthew Feldman, Denise Grayson, John Quincy Lee, Rick Lyon, Adrian Martinez; *D:* Dave Silver; *W:* Dave Silver; *C:* H. Michael Otano; *M:* Craig Snyder. **VIDEO**

The Corn Is Green 🦴🦴🦴 **1945** Touching story of a school teacher in a poor Welsh village who eventually sends her pet student to Oxford. Davis makes a fine teacher, though a little young, while the on-site photography provides atmosphere. Based on the play by Emlyn Williams. Remade in 1979. **115m/B VHS.** Bette Davis, John Dall, Nigel Bruce, Joan Lorring, Arthur Shields, Mildred Dunnock, Rhys Williams, Rosalind Ivan; *D:* Irving Rapper; *M:* Max Steiner.

The Corn Is Green 🦴🦴🦴 **1979** Excellent TV adaptation of the Emlyn Willimas play has Hepburn as dedicated teacher Lilly Moffat, determined to bring education to a small Welsh mining village. She finds and mentors a student she believes can escape the mines with the power of his intellect. Cukor overcomes the limitations of television in his last collaboration with Hepburn. **93m/C VHS, DVD.** Katharine Hepburn, Bill Fraser, Anna Massey, Patricia Hayes, Dorothy Phillips; *D:* George Cukor; *W:* Ivan Davis; *M:* John Barry. **TV**

Cornbread, Earl & Me 🦴🦴 **1975 (R)** A high school basketball star from the ghetto is mistaken for a murderer by cops and shot, causing a subsequent furor of protest and racial hatred. Superficial melodrama. **95m/C VHS, DVD.** Moses Gunn, Rosalind Cash, Bernie Casey, Tierre Turner, Madge Sinclair, Keith Wilkes, Antonio Fargas, Laurence Fishburne; *D:* Joseph Manduke; *W:* Leonard Lamensdorf; *C:* Jules Brenner; *M:* Donald Byrd.

The Corner 🦴🦴 **1/2 2000** This HBO miniseries was adapted from reporter David Simon's book "The Corner: A Year in the Life of an Inner-City Neighborhood" that neighborhood being Fayette Street in Baltimore. This corner is the local hub of drug activity that draws in members of the same family: Fran Boyd (Alexander) and Gary McCullough (Carter), who are both addicts, as well as their 15-year-old son DeAndre (Nelson). His parents are losing the battle to keep DeAndre away from drugs, gangs, and other trouble but when Fran learns that DeAndre's equally young girlfriend is pregnant, it spurs her into rehab and the hope of making something right. **376m/C DVD.** Khandi Alexander, T.K. Carter, Sean Nelson, Glenn Plummer, Clarke Peters, Tyra Ferrell, Tasha Smith, Toy Connor; *D:* Charles S. Dutton; *W:* David Mills; *C:* Ivan Strasburg; *M:* Henry Butler, Corey Harris. **CABLE**

Cornered 🦴 **1932** McCoy is a sheriff, chasing bad guys, whose life is saved by Welch. Basically boring. **62m/B VHS.** Tim McCoy, Niles Welch, Raymond Hatton, Noah Beery Sr., Shirley Grey, Walter Long; *D:* B. Reeves Eason.

Cornered 🦴🦴🦴 **1945** Tough Powell plays an airman released from a German prison camp who pursues a Nazi war criminal to avenge the death of his wife and child. **102m/B VHS.** Dick Powell, Walter Slezak, Micheline Cheirel, Luther Adler; *D:* Edward Dmytryk.

The Coroner 🦴🦴 **1998 (R)** Dr. Leon Urasky (St. Louis) is both a coroner and a serial killer. He chooses lawyer Emma Santiago (Longenecker) as a victim, but she is no pushover. Horror/thriller has some humor, a few nice moments, but mostly tedious. **75m/C DVD.** Jane Longenecker, Dean St. Louis, Rebecca Gray; *D:* Juan A. Mas; *W:* Geralyn Ruane; *C:* Charles "Chip" Schneer.

Coroner Creek 🦴🦴 **1/2 1948** Chris Danning's (Scott) fiancee commits suicide after being held hostage during an Indian attack on her stagecoach and a payroll robbery. Danning sets out to trace the loot and exact his revenge. A superior production, notable for being one of the first westerns with an adult theme. **89m/B VHS.** Randolph Scott, Marguerite Chapman, George Macready, Sally Eilers, Edgar Buchanan, Wallace Ford, Forrest Tucker, William Bishop, Joe DeRita, Joseph (Joe) Sawyer, Russell Simpson; *D:* Ray Enright; *W:* Kenneth Gamet; *C:* Fred H. Jackman

Jr.; *M:* Rudolph (Rudy) Schrager.

Corporate Affairs 1990 **(R)** A ruthless business woman climbing her way to the top literally seduces her boss to death. **92m/C VHS, DVD.** Peter Scolari, Mary Crosby, Chris Lemmon, Ken Kercheval; *D:* Terence H. Winkless; *W:* Terence H. Winkless, Geoffrey Baere.

Corporate Affairs 2007 **(R)** Lame flick that can't make up its mind whether to be a morality tale or an office sex comedy. Ted (Meyer) is married to Cassie (Harris) and they live in the 'burbs with their kids. Ted enjoys being a computer programmer for a software company but can't turn down a big promotion to management because the pay is too good, but unfortunately Ted's a techno geek, not a schmoozer of clients. He starts to travel a lot for business and soon realizes that managers employ hookers as perks (for themselves and the clients), and Ted isn't man enough to resist. **99m/C DVD.** Breckin Meyer, Laura Harris, George Coe, Bess Armstrong, Adam Scott, Monica Keena, Melinda Page Hamilton; *D:* Dan Cohen; *W:* Dan Cohen; *C:* Ian Mcglocklin. **VIDEO**

The Corporate Ladder 1997 **(R)** Matt Taylor is looking for the perfect executive assistant and his choice is Nicole—she's beautiful, bright, and devoted. It's no wonder that soon Matt and Nicole are having an affair. Too bad that Nicole would much rather run the company than take dictation—and she has a lethal way of implementing her business plan. Unfortunately, everthing about this film is boringly predictable. **112m/C VHS.** Anthony John (Tony) Denison, Kathleen Kinmont, Talisa Soto, Jennifer O'Neill, Ben Cross; *D:* Nick Vallelonga; *W:* Nick Vallelonga; *M:* Jan Hammer.

The Corporation ½ *Subliminal Seduction; Roger Corman Presents Subliminal Seduction* **1996 (R)** Darrin Danver (Ziering), the new exec at a computer game company, discovers the games are controlling their users with powerful, subliminal messages. So he tries to expose his employers' lethal manipulations before they can kill him. Standard-issue made-for-TV movie doesn't bring anything new new to the "evil company" genre. Shot on location in L.A. and Las Vegas. **82m/C VHS.** Ian Ziering, Andrew Stevens, Katherine Kelly Lang, Dee Wallace, Larry Manetti, Kim Morgan Greene, Kin Shriner, Stella Stevens; *D:* Andrew Stevens; *W:* Karen Kelly; *C:* Gary Graver; *M:* Terry Plumeri. **VIDEO**

The Corpse Grinders WOOF! 1971 (R) Low-budget bad movie classic in which a cardboard corpse-grinding machine makes nasty cat food that makes cats nasty. Sets are cheap, gore effects silly, and cat attacks ridiculous. **73m/C VHS, DVD.** Sean Kenney, Monika Kelly, Sandford Mitchell, Byron J. Foster, Warren Ball, Ann Noble; *D:* Ted V. Mikels; *W:* Ted V. Mikels, Arch Hall Jr., Joseph L. Cranston; *C:* Bill Anneman.

The Corpse Vanishes ½ **1942** Lugosi at his chilling best as a diabolical scientist who snatches young brides and drains their blood in an effort to keep his 70-year-old wife eternally youthful. Not for newlyweds! **64m/B VHS, DVD.** Bela Lugosi, Luana Walters, Tristram Coffin, Elizabeth Russell, Vince Barnett, Joan Barclay, Angelo Rossitto; *D:* Wallace Fox.

Corregidor 1943 A love triangle develops between doctors treating the wounded during the WWII battle. A poor propaganda piece which contains only shaky stock footage for its "action" sequences. **73m/B VHS, DVD.** Otto Kruger, Elissa Landi, Donald Woods, Rick Vallin, Frank Jenks, Wanda McKay, Ian Keith; *D:* William Nigh.

Corridors of Blood ½ *The Doctor from Seven Dials* **1958** Karloff is a doctor, in search of a viable anesthetic, who accidently becomes addicted to drugs, then turns to grave robbers to support his habit. Karloff plays usual threatening doctor to perfection. **86m/C VHS, DVD.** *GB* Boris Karloff, Betta St. John, Finlay Currie, Christopher Lee, Francis Matthews, Adrienne Corri, Nigel Green; *D:* Robert Day; *W:* Jean Scott Rogers; *C:* Geoffrey Faithfull; *M:* Buxton Orr.

Corrina, Corrina ½ **1994 (PG)** Newly widowed jingle-writer Liotta needs someone to care for his withdrawn eight-year-old daughter. Enter Whoopi, as housekeeper and eventual love interest. Sweet, nostalgic romance set in the 1950s. Goldberg also found off-screen romance (again), this time with the film's union organizer Lyle Trachtenberg. Last role for Ameche. **115m/C VHS, DVD.** Whoopi Goldberg, Ray Liotta, Don Ameche, Tina Majorino, Wendy Crewson, Jenifer Lewis, Larry Miller, Erica Yohn, Anita Baker; *D:* Jessie Nelson; *W:* Jessie Nelson; *C:* Bruce Surtees; *M:* Rick Cox, Thomas Newman.

Corrupt *Order of Death; Cop Killers* **1984 (PG)** Bad narcotics cop goes after murderer, but mysterious Lydon gets in the way. An acquired taste, best if you appreciate Lydon, better known as Johnny Rotten of the Sex Pistols. **99m/C VHS, DVD.** *IT* Harvey Keitel, John (Johnny Rotten) Lydon, Sylvia Sidney, Nicole Garcia, Leonard Mann; *D:* Roberto Faenza; *W:* Roberto Faenza, Ennio de Concini, Hugh Fleetwood; *C:* Guiseppe Pinori; *M:* Ennio Morricone.

Corrupt ½ **1999 (R)** Corrupt (Ice-T) is the drug lord who holds the South Bronx but he has would-be competition from some up-and-coming homeboys. However, one ex-gang banger (Silkk the Shocker) wants out of the 'hood to make a new life for himself and his girl. Only Corrupt and his posse stand in the way. **72m/C VHS, DVD.** Ice-T, Ernie Hudson, silkk the Shocker, Karen Dyer; *D:* Albert Pyun. **VIDEO**

The Corrupt Ones ½ *Il Sigillo de Pechino; Die Holle von Macao; Les Corrompus; The Peking Medallion; Hell to Macao* **1967** Everyone's after a photographer who has a medallion that will lead to buried treasure in China. Great characters hampered by pedestrian script. **87m/C VHS.** Robert Stack, Elke Sommer, Nancy Kwan, Christian Marquand, Werner Peters; *D:* James Hill; *W:* Brian Clemens.

Corruption WOOF! *Sweet Trash* **1970 (R)** Mostly soft-porn. Alleged plot: The Mob is interested in having Shea work for them, and makes it worth his while. **80m/C VHS.** Mary McGee, Patrick Shea; *D:* John Hayes; *W:* John Hayes; *C:* Paul Hipp.

The Corruptor 1999 **(R)** Slick crime thriller starring Wahlberg as Danny, a young Caucasian cop assigned to New York's Chinatown precinct and partnered with shrewd veteran Chen (Chow Yun-Fat). The two men are drawn into a web of deception and betrayal as they try to stop a war between rival underworld factions. Chow finally receives a Hollywood role that showcases the talents that made him an international star in Asia, although the action segments suffer in comparison to his work with John Woo. The plot and performances are excellent, and there's enough shoot-'em-up to satisfy the average appetite for destruction. **110m/C VHS, DVD.** Chow Yun-Fat, Mark Wahlberg, Ric Young, Paul Ben-Victor, Brian Cox, Byron Mann, Kim Chan, Tovah Feldshuh, Jon Kit Lee, Andrew Pang, Elizabeth Lindsey, Bill MacDonald, Susie Trinh; *D:* James Foley; *W:* Robert Pucci; *C:* Juan Ruiz-Anchia; *M:* Carter Burwell.

Corsair 1931 Actioner about a gorgeous debutante and a handsome gangster who find themselves caught up with a gang of bootlegging pirates. Todd is always worth watching. **73m/B VHS, DVD.** Chester Morris, Thelma Todd, Frank McHugh, Ned Sparks, Mayo Methot; *D:* Roland West.

The Corsican Brothers ½ **1942** Siamese-twins Mario and Lucien are separated by Dr. Paoli (Warner) shortly before their parents are murdered by evil Colonna (Tamiroff). One boy is sent to Paris and the other grows up in the Corsican mountains. Reunited as adults (and dashingly played by Faribanks Jr.), the twins plot revenge. Entertaining swashbuckler based on a novel by Alexandre Dumas. **111m/B VHS.** Douglas Fairbanks Jr., Akim Tamiroff, Ruth Warrick, J. Carrol Naish, H.B. Warner, Henry Wilcoxon, Veda Ann Borg; *D:* Gregory Ratoff; *W:* George Bruce; *C:* Harry Stradling Sr.; *M:* Dimitri Tiomkin.

Corvette Summer *The Hot One* **1978 (PG)** After spending a semester restoring a Corvette in his high school shop class, an L.A. student must journey to Las Vegas to recover the car when it is stolen. There he meets a prostitute, falls in love, and steps into the "real world" for the first time. Potts is intriguing as the low-life love interest, but she can't save this one. **104m/C VHS, DVD.** Mark Hamill, Annie Potts, Eugene Roche, Kim Milford, Richard McKenzie, William (Bill) Bryant; *D:* Matthew Robbins; *W:* Matthew Robbins, Hal Barwood.

Cosh Boy WOOF! *The Slasher; Killer's Delight* **1952** Vicious male youths stalk women on the streets of London in this low-budget Jack the Ripper rip-off. **90m/B VHS.** *GB* Joan Collins, James Kennedy, Hermione Baddeley; *D:* Lewis Gilbert; *W:* Lewis Gilbert.

Cosi *Caught in the Act* **1995 (R)** Amiable Lewis (Mendelsohn) is hired to help with drama therapy at the local Sydney mental institution. Pressured by long-term patient Roy (Otto), Lewis finds himself agreeing to stage a production of Mozart's opera "Cosi Fan Tutte" though none of the patients can speak Italian or sing. Rehearsals prove a challenge, there are numerous setbacks, and then it's show time. Fine ensemble cast delivers; adapted from Nowra's play. Friels stepped into the role of security guard Errol when Bruno Lawrence died before filming was completed; pic is dedicated to Lawrence. **100m/C VHS, DVD.** *AU* Ben Mendelsohn, Barry Otto, Aden Young, Toni Collette, Rachel Griffiths, Colin Friels, Paul Chubb, Pamela Rabe, Jacki Weaver, David Wenham, Colin Hay, Tony Llewellyn-Jones, Kerry Walker; ***Cameos:*** Greta Scacchi, Paul Mercurio; *D:* Mark Joffe; *W:* Louis Nowra; *C:* Ellery Ryan; *M:* Stephen Endelman. Australian Film Inst. '96: Adapt. Screenplay, Support. Actress (Collette).

The Cosmic Eye 1971 Animated tale of three musicians from outer space who come to earth to spread the message of worldwide peace and harmony. A variety of cultural perspectives about the origins and destiny of the Earth are offered. Rather moralizing but the animation is impressive. **71m/C VHS, DVD.** *D:* Faith Hubley; *V:* Dizzy Gillespie, Maureen Stapleton, Benny Carter.

The Cosmic Man ½ **1959** An alien arrives on Earth with a message of peace and restraint. He is regarded with suspicion by us nasty Earthlings. Essentially "The Day the Earth Stood Still" without the budget, but interesting nonetheless. **72m/B VHS, DVD.** Bruce Bennett, John Carradine, Angela Greene, Paul Langton, Scotty Morrow; *D:* Herbert Greene; *W:* Arthur C. Pierce; *C:* John F. Warren; *M:* Paul Sawtell, Bert Shefter.

The Cosmic Monsters ½ *The Strange World of Planet X* **1958** Scientist accidentally pops a hole in the ionosphere during a magnetism experiment. Then huge, mean insects arrive to plague mankind. Coincidence? You figure it out. **75m/B VHS.** Forrest Tucker, Gaby Andre, Alec Mango, Hugh Latimer, Martin Benson; *D:* Gilbert Gunn.

Cosmic Slop 1994 **(R)** Three-part anthology. "Space Traders," based on a story by Derrick Bell, finds a fleet of aliens offering to solve all of U.S. society's most pressing social ills if they can have the entire black population in return (for what purpose is never explained). "The First Commandment" features a Catholic priest in a Latino parish who comes up against his parishoners pagan beliefs in Santeria. "Tang," based on a story by Chester Himes, finds a poor, desperately unhappy married couple dreaming about what they'll do with the rifle mysteriously delivered in a flower carton to their door. **87m/C VHS.** Robert Guillaume, Jason Bernard, Nicholas Turturro, Richard Herd, Paula Jai Parker, Chi McBride; *D:* Reginald (Reggie) Hudlin, Warrington Hudlin, Kevin Sullivan; *W:* Warrington Hudlin, Trey Ellis, Kyle Baker; *C:* Peter Deming.

Cosmos: War of the Planets WOOF! *Cosmo 2000: Planet Without a Name; War of the Planets* **1980 (PG)** The ultimate battle for survival is fought in outer space, though not very well and on a small budget. Special effects especially laughable. **90m/C VHS, DVD.** *IT* Katia Christine, West Buchanan, John Richardson, Yanti Somer; *D:* Al (Alfonso Brescia) Bradley.

Cote d'Azur *Crustaces et Coquillages; Cockles and Muscles* **2005** Silly sex farce set on the sunny French Riviera. Marrieds Beatrix and Marc take their daughter Laura, son Charly, and Charly's best pal Martin for a summer beach holiday. Laura promptly disappears with a new beau and Charly has his own reasons for not correcting his parents' misconception that he and the openly gay Martin are sexually involved. Meanwhile, Beatrix's city lover shows up to surprise her and Marc has a secret involving boyhood friend Didier. French with subtitles. **93m/C DVD.** *FR* Valeria Bruni-Tedeschi, Gilbert Melki, Jean-Marc Barr, Jacques Bonnaffe, Romain, Edouard Collin, Sabrina Seyvecou; *D:* Olivier Ducastel, Jacques Martineau; *W:* Olivier Ducastel, Jacques Martineau; *C:* Mathieu Poirot-Delpech; *M:* Philippe Miller.

Cottage to Let ½ *Bombsight Stolen* **1941** Propaganda thriller about a Nazi plot to kidnap the inventor of a new bombsight. Focused cast struggles with lackluster script. **90m/B VHS.** *GB* Leslie Banks, Alastair Sim, John Mills, Jeanne de Casalis, Carla Lehmann, George Cole, Michael Wilding, Frank Cellier, Wally Patch, Catherine Lacey; *D:* Anthony Asquith.

Cotter 1972 A Native American rodeo clown feels responsible for a cowboy's death, returns home to reflect on his life. Fair story, best at the small town feeling. **94m/C VHS, DVD.** Don Murray, Carol Lynley, Rip Torn, Sherry Jackson, Christopher Knight; *D:* Paul Stanley; *W:* William D. Gordon; *C:* Alan Stensvold.

Cotton Candy 1982 Follows the faintly interesting trials and tribulations of a high school senior who tries to form a rock band. At first he meets failure, but is ultimately successful with the band and romance. Joint script-writing venture by brothers Clint and Ron Howard. **97m/C VHS.** Charles Martin Smith, Clint Howard, Leslie King; *D:* Ron Howard; *W:* Clint Howard, Ron Howard. **TV**

The Cotton Club 1984 **(R)** With $50 million in his pocket, Francis reaches for an epic and delivers: handsome production, lots of dance, bit of singing, confused plot, uneven performances, tad too long. A musician playing at The Cotton Club falls in love with gangster Dutch Schultz's girlfriend. A black tap dancer falls in love with a member of the chorus line who can pass for white. These two love stories are told against a background of mob violence and music. Excellent performances by Hoskins and Gwynne. ♫Minnie the Moocher; Ill Wind; The Mooch; Ring Dem Bells; Drop Me Off in Harlem; Cotton Club Stomp; Truckin; Mood Indigo; Copper Colored Gal. **121m/C VHS, DVD.** Diane Lane, Richard Gere, Gregory Hines, Lonette McKee, Bob Hoskins, Fred Gwynne, James Remar, Nicolas Cage, Lisa Jane Persky, Allen (Goorwitz) Garfield, Gwen Verdon, Joe Dallesandro, Jennifer Grey, Tom Waits, Diane Venora, Robert Earl Jones; *D:* Francis Ford Coppola; *W:* Francis Ford Coppola, William Kennedy, Mario Puzo; *C:* Stephen Goldblatt; *M:* John Barry.

Cotton Comes to Harlem **1970 (R)** Cambridge and St. Jacques star as Harlem plainclothes detectives Grave Digger Jones and Coffin Ed Johnson in this successful mix of crime and comedy. They're investigating a suspicious preacher's back-to-Africa scheme which they suspect is a swindle. Directorial debut of Davis. Filmed on location in Harlem, New York. Based on the novel by Chester Himes. Followed by a weak sequel, "Come Back, Charleston Blue." **97m/C VHS, DVD.** Godfrey Cambridge, Raymond St. Jacques, Calvin Lockhart, Judy Pace, Redd Foxx, John Anderson, Emily Yancy, J.D. Cannon, Teddy Wilson, Eugene Roche, Cleavon Little, Lou Jacobi; *D:* Ossie Davis; *W:* Ossie Davis; *C:* Gerald Hirschfeld; *M:* Galt MacDermot.

Cotton Mary 1999 **(R)** Lily (Scacchi) is the lonely wife of reporter John (Wilby), living in India in 1954. She cannot nurse her newborn daughter and turns to the ministrations of bossy Anglo-Indian nurse Mary (Jaffrey), who is soon living in their household and having the child fed by her own sister, Blossom (Gupta). Meanwhile, the philandering John eyes Mary's niece, Rosie (Sakina Jaffrey), while Lily sinks into depression, and an increasingly mad Mary ruthlessly takes over their home. **124m/C VHS, DVD.** *GB* Madhur Jaffrey, Greta Scacchi, James Wilby, Neena Gupta, Sakina Jaffrey, Gemma Jones, Sarah Badel, Joanna David, Riyu Bajaj, Prayag Raj; *D:* Ismail Merchant; *W:* Alexandra

Viets; *C:* Pierre Lhomme; *M:* Richard Robbins.

Cotton Queen 🦴 ½ *Crying Out Loud* **1937** Romance and light intrigue plague the children of two rival textile mill owners. **80m/B VHS.** Will Fyffe, Stanley Holloway; *D:* Bernard Vorhaus.

A Couch in New York 🦴🦴 *Un Divan a New York* **1995 (R)** Limp romantic comedy features that old standby—opposites attracting. French dancer Beatrice (Binoche) responds to an ad for a temporary Paris-New York apartment switch placed by a stuffy psychoanalyst, Henry Harriston (Hurt). Henry's patients presume Beatrice is his replacement (he works at home) and the free-spirit begins giving them ad hoc advice. Meanwhile in Paris, Henry's plagued by all Beatrice's heartsick boyfriends and decides to come back early. When he arrives unannounced, she assumes he's a new patient and he's intrigued enough to go along. Lots of yakking, not too many sparks, and a strained artificiality make for a dull mix. **104m/C VHS, DVD.** *FR BE GE* William Hurt, Juliette Binoche, Paul Guilfoyle, Stephanie Buttle, Richard Jenkins, Kent Broadhurst, Henry Bean, Barbara Garrick; *D:* Chantal Akerman; *W:* Chantal Akerman, Jean-Louis Benoit; *C:* Dietrich Lohmann; *M:* Paolo Conte, Sonia Atherton.

The Couch Trip 🦴 ½ **1987 (R)** Aykroyd is an escapee from a mental institution who passes himself off as a radio psychologist and becomes a media sensation. There are a few laughs and some funny characters but for the most part this one falls flat. **98m/C VHS, DVD.** Dan Aykroyd, Walter Matthau, Charles Grodin, Donna Dixon, Richard Romanus, Arye Gross, David Clennon, Mary Gross; *D:* Michael Ritchie; *W:* Will Aldis, Steven Kampmann; *M:* Michel Colombier.

Cougar Club 🦴 ½ **2007** Usual sex comedy about horny guys. Two recent college grads are dismayed to find that their dream jobs at an upscale law firm consist of menial and demeaning tasks. So they decide to open an exclusive dating club for young men like themselves who are interested in fulfilling their fantasies with experienced older women. Soon their day jobs and their nighttime escapades are overlapping. **99m/C DVD.** Joe Mantegna, Kaley Cuoco, Izabela Scorupco, Joanie Laurer, Jason Jurman, Warren Kole, Jon Polito, Loretta Devine; ***Cameos:*** Faye Dunaway, Carrie Fisher; *D:* Christopher Duddy; *W:* Chris Mancuso; *C:* Dennis Laine; *M:* Steve Porcaro.

Could It Happen Here? 🦴 *Italia ultimo atto* **1977** A lurid Italian spectacle about a metropolis thrown into a state of chaotic martial law by terrorism. Dubbed. **90m/C VHS.** *IT* Luc Merenda, Marcella Michelangeli; *D:* Massimo Pirri.

Counsellor-at-Law 🦴🦴🦴 **1933** One of Barrymore's best. He stars as Jewish lawyer George Simon, who has climbed to the top of his profession in New York from a poverty-stricken past that continues to haunt him. His constant struggles in the elitist law community are taking their toll and his personal life is no better when George discovers that his gentile wife Cora (Kenyon) has been unfaithful. But his secretary Regina (Daniels), who has always loved him, remains loyal. Rice adapted from his own play. Director Wyler dumped the musical score except for what's heard over the opening and closing credits. **80m/B VHS, DVD.** John Barrymore, Bebe Daniels, Doris Kenyon, Onslow Stevens, Isabel Jewell, Melvyn Douglas, Thelma Todd, Mayo Methot; *D:* William Wyler; *W:* Elmer Rice; *C:* Norbert Brodine.

The Count 🦴🦴 ½ **1916** Chaplin pretends to be the secretary of his boss, who in turn is posing as a count. Silent with musical soundtrack added. **20m/B VHS, DVD.** Charlie Chaplin; *D:* Charlie Chaplin.

Count Dracula 🦴🦴 ½ *Bram Stoker's Count Dracula; Il Conte Dracula; Dracula 71; Nachts wenn Dracula Erwacht; The Nights of Dracula* **1971 (R)** Passable version of the Dracula legend (based on the novel by Bram Stoker) has Lee as the thirsty count on the prowl for fresh blood. Starts out as one of the most faithful adaptations, but loses momentum because Franco was running out of money. **90m/C VHS, DVD.** *SP GE IT* Christopher Lee, Herbert Lom, Klaus Kinski, Frederick Williams, Maria Rohm, Soledad Miranda, Paul Muller; *D:* Jess (Jesus) Franco; *W:* Jess (Jesus) Franco, Augusto Finochi, Harry Alan Towers, Milo G. Cuccia, Carlo Fadda; *C:* Manuel Merino.

Count Dracula 🦴🦴 ½ **1977** Three-part BBC adaptation of the Bram Stoker novel with French actor Jourdan naturally seductive and aloof in the vampire role. The pace is leisurely and there's more plot development but it's still not a completely faithful accounting, although only purists will probably be annoyed. **150m/C DVD.** *GB* Louis Jourdan, Judi Bowker, Bosco Hogan, Frank Finlay, Susan Penhaligon, Mark Burns, Richard Barnes, Jack Shepherd; *D:* Philip Saville; *W:* Gerald Savory; *C:* Peter Hall; *M:* Kenyon Emrys Roberts. **TV**

The Count of Monte Cristo 🦴🦴 ½ **1912** One of the first full-length features starring popular stage stars of the day. The first truly American feature, it was based on the classic tale of revenge by Alexander Dumas. Silent. Remade many times. Lead actor O'Neill was the father of famed American playwright, Eugene O'Neill, who covered his father's success in this role in his own family drama "Long Day's Journey Into Night." **90m/B VHS.** James O'Neill; *D:* Edwin S. Porter.

The Count of Monte Cristo 🦴🦴🦴 **1934** A true swashbuckling revenge tale about Edmond Dantes (Donat), who unjustly spends years in prison. After escaping and retrieving a pirate treasure from the island of Monte Cristo, he gains ever so sweet and served quite cold revenge. Adaptation of the Alexandre Dumas classic. **114m/B VHS.** Robert Donat, Elissa Landi, Louis Calhern, Sidney Blackmer, Irene Hervey, Raymond Walburn, O.P. Heggie; *D:* Rowland V. Lee; *W:* Rowland V. Lee, Philip Dunne; *C:* J. Peverell Marley; *M:* Alfred Newman.

The Count of Monte Cristo 🦴🦴 ½ **1974** The Alexander Dumas classic about an innocent man (Chamberlain) who is imprisoned, escapes, and finds the treasure of Monte Cristo, which he uses to bring down those who wronged him. Good version of the historical costumer. Originally shown in theatres in Europe, but broadcast on TV in the U.S. **104m/C VHS.** *GB* Richard Chamberlain, Kate Nelligan, Donald Pleasence, Alessio Orano, Tony Curtis, Louis Jourdan, Trevor Howard, Taryn Power, Angelo Infanti; *D:* David Greene.

The Count of Monte Cristo 🦴🦴 ½ *Le Comte de Monte Cristo* **1999** It seems only fitting that French TV produced this zestful miniseries version of the 1844 novel by Dumas pere. Depardieu obviously is enjoying himself in the lead role of Edmond Dantes, who is unjustly imprisoned for 20 years. After his escape, he discovers a fortune and uses it to get revenge as he adopts a fictional identity as the Count of Monte Cristo. Overwrought, over-the-top and lots of fun. Depardieu's daughter Julie and son Guillaume both have roles. French with subtitles. **480m/C VHS, DVD.** *FR* Gerard Depardieu, Ornella Muti, Sergio Rubini, Guillaume Depardieu, Pierre Arditti, Jean Rochefort, Florence Darel, Julie Depardieu, Naike Rivelli, Jean-Claude Brialy, Ines Sastre, Helene Vincent, Christopher Thompson, Stanislas Merhar, Constanze Engelbrecht, Georges Moustaki; *D:* Josee Dayan; *W:* Didier Decoin; *C:* Willy Stassen; *M:* Bruno Coulais. **TV**

The Count of Monte Cristo 🦴🦴 ½ **2002 (PG-13)** Yet another remake of the Dumas classic revenge tale with some beautiful cinematography by Dunn to distinguish it. Hero Edmond Dantes (Caviezel) is betrayed by best friend Fernand Mondego (Pearce), who wants his girlfriend Mercedes (Dominczyk) among other things, and unjustly imprisoned. Dantes learns of a great treasure from fellow inmate Abbe Faria (Harris), eventually escapes, finds said treasure, and seeks his revenge under the disguise of—well, you know. Pearce has fun as the foppish villain and Caviezel is suitably heroic. **131m/C VHS, DVD.** *US* James (Jim) Caviezel, Guy Pearce, Richard Harris, Dagmara Dominczyk, Luis Guzman, James Frain, Albie Woodington, Henry Cavill, Michael Wincott, Alex Norton, Freddie Jones; *D:* Kevin Reynolds; *W:* Jay Wolpert; *C:* Andrew Dunn; *M:* Ed Shearmur.

The Count of the Old Town 🦴🦴 *Munkbrogreven* **1934** Feisty townsfolk settle the score after a gang of booze smugglers trick them out of their money. Bergman's film debut as a maid swept off her feet by a mysterious young stranger. Adapted from the play "Greven fran Gamla Sta'n" by Arthur and Sigfried Fischer. In Swedish with English subtitles. **90m/B VHS.** *SW* Edvin Adolphson, Ingrid Bergman, Sigurd Wallen, Valdemar Dahlquist; *D:* Edvin Adolphson, Sigurd Wallen; *W:* Gosta Stevens.

Count Yorga, Vampire 🦴🦴 ½ *The Loves of Count Yorga, Vampire* **1970 (PG-13)** The vampire Count Yorga is practicing his trade in Los Angeles, setting up a coven and conducting seances. Good update of the traditional character, with Quarry suitably solemn and menacing. Followed by "The Return of Count Yorga." **93m/C VHS, DVD.** Robert Quarry, Roger Perry, Michael Murphy, Michael Macready, Donna Anders, Judith Lang, Marsha Jordan, Julie Conners, Paul Hansen; *D:* Bob Kelljan; *W:* Bob Kelljan; *C:* Arch Archambault; *M:* Bill Marx.

Countdown 🦴🦴 ½ **1968** Documentary-type fictional look at the first moon mission and its toll on the astronauts and their families. Timely because the U.S. was trying to send a man to the moon in 1968. Interesting as a look at the developing Altman style. **102m/C VHS.** James Caan, Robert Duvall, Michael Murphy, Ted (Edward) Knight, Joanna Moore, Barbara Baxley, Charles Aidman, Steve Ihnat, Robert Altman; *D:* Robert Altman.

Counter Attack 🦴 ½ **1984** Story of murder and insurance fraud takes place on the back lots of the Hong Kong film industry. As good as these get. **105m/C VHS, DVD.** Bruce Li, Dan Inosanto, John Ladalski, Young Kong; *D:* Bruce Li.

Counter Measures 🦴 **1985** A helicopter pilot stumbles on to a bizarre chain of crimes and disasters. **98m/C VHS.** Norman Forsey, Martin Howells, David Weatherley, Monte Markham; *D:* Gerban Ceth.

Counter Measures 🦴🦴 **1999 (R)** Zach Silver (Dudikoff) and the USS Springfield are deployed to hunt the Odessa, a Russian nuclear submarine that's been hijacked by terrorists. **93m/C VHS, DVD.** Michael Dudikoff, James Horan, Alexander Keith, Scott Marlowe, Tracy Brooks Swope, Cliff (Potter) Potts, Robert F. Lyons; *D:* Fred Ray Olen; *W:* Steve Latshaw; *C:* Thomas Callaway; *M:* Eric Wurst, David Wurst. **VIDEO**

Counter Punch 🦴🦴 ½ *Ripped Off; The Boxer; Uomo Dalla Pelle Dura; Murder in the Ring; Tough Guy* **1971 (R)** Blake is a boxer framed for the murder of his manager who sets out to clear his name by finding the killers. Fair rendition of a familiar plot. **72m/C VHS, DVD.** *IT* Robert (Bobby) Blake, Ernest Borgnine, Gabriele Ferzetti, Catherine Spaak, Tomas Milian; *D:* Franco Prosperi.

Counterblast 🦴🦴 *The Devil's Plot* **1948** A Nazi spy assumes the role of a British scientist in order to gain classified information for the Fatherland. The trouble begins when he refuses to carry out an order to execute a pretty young assistant. Appealing performances distract from the somewhat confusing plot. **99m/B VHS.** *GB* Robert Beatty, Mervyn Johns, Nova Pilbeam, Margaretta Scott, Sybilla Binder, Marie Lohr, Karel Stepanek, Alan Wheatley; *D:* Paul Stein.

The Counterfeit Traitor 🦴🦴🦴 ½ **1962** Suspense thriller with Holden playing a double agent in Europe during WWII. Based on the true adventures of Eric Erickson, the top Allied spy of WW II, who was captured by the Gestapo but escaped. **140m/C VHS, DVD.** William Holden, Lilli Palmer, Hugh Griffith, Werner Peters, Eva Dahlbeck; *D:* George Seaton; *W:* George Seaton; *C:* Jean (Yves, Georges) Bourgoin.

The Counterfeiters 🦴🦴🦴 ½ *Die Falscher* **2007 (R)** Russian-Jewish counterfeiter Salomon "Sally" Sorowitsch (Markovics) is arrested and winds up in a concentration camp in 1944 Berlin, where he's not only marked as Jewish, but designated as a habitual criminal, alienating him from the general prisoner population. There he's placed in charge of a secret counterfeiting unit with other prisoners, all of whom are afforded special privileges like clean sheets and cigarettes. Even with the "luxuries," there's no doubt about where they are—the screams penetrate the walls and their new clothes are from the victims. Sally and the others are forced to confront the morality of their situation (aid those who imprison them or rebel at the ultimate cost) as well as confronting their individual demons. Darkly provocative alternative to the more common heroic stories of camp survivorship. In German with subtitles. **98m/C DVD.** *AT GE* Karl Markovics, August Diehl, August Zirner, Marie Baumer, Dolores Chaplin, David Striesow, Martin Zirner; *D:* Stefan Ruzowitzky; *W:* Stefan Ruzowitzky; *C:* Benedict Neuenfels; *M:* Marius Ruhland. Oscars '07: Foreign Film.

Counterforce 🦴 *Escuadron* **1987 (R)** A rough group of mercenaries is hired to guard a Mideastern leader being chased by his country's ruling despot. Mild action with predictable story. **98m/C VHS.** Jorge (George) Rivero, George Kennedy, Andrew Stevens, Isaac Hayes, Louis Jourdan, Kevin Bernhardt, Hugo Stiglitz, Robert Forster, Susana Dosamantes; *D:* Jose Antonio De La Loma.

Counterspy Meets Scotland Yard 🦴 **1950** Sleuth David Harding (St. John) wants to track down the killer of one of his agents so he teams up with Scotland Yard detective Simon Langton (Randell), who poses as the dead man. Based on the radio series. **67m/B DVD.** Howard St. John, Ron Randell, Amanda Blake, June Vincent, Fred F. Sears, John Dehner; *D:* Seymour Friedman; *W:* Harold Greene; *C:* Philip Tannura.

Counterstrike 🦴🦴 ½ **2003 (PG-13)** Typical escapist cable fare finds a couple of secret service-type brothers (Estes, Lando) called into action when a group of Taiwanese nationalists decide to press their claim for independence from China by threatening to assassinate the presidents of the U.S. and China unless their demand is met by the U.N. Of course, the two heads of state just happen to be aboard the QE2 for a series of summit talks to make things easy. **96m/C DVD.** Robert Estes, Joe Lando, Marie Matiko, Carmen Duncan, Rachel Blakely, Christopher Lawford, Ron Lee; *D:* Jerry London; *W:* J.B. White; *C:* Ben Nott. **CABLE**

A Countess from Hong Kong 🦴 **1967 (G)** Very bad romantic comedy features impoverished Russian countess Natasha (would you believe Loren is Russian?) stowing away in the luxury liner suite of stuffy American diplomat Ogden Mears (equally miscast Brando). The ship is sailing from Hong Kong to Honolulu and Natasha has until then to persuade Ogden to assist her. Chaplin's final film. **108m/C VHS, DVD.** Marlon Brando, Sophia Loren, Sydney Chaplin, Tippi Hedren, Patrick Cargill, Michael Medwin, Oliver Johnston, Margaret Rutherford; *D:* Charlie Chaplin; *W:* Charlie Chaplin; *C:* Arthur Ibbetson; *M:* Charlie Chaplin.

Country 🦴🦴🦴 **1984 (PG)** Strong story of a farm family in crisis when the government attempts to foreclose on their land. Good performances all around and an excellent portrayal of the wife by Lange. "The River" and "Places in the Heart," both released in 1984, also dramatized the plight of many American farm families in the early 1980s. **109m/C VHS, DVD.** Jessica Lange, Sam Shepard, Wilford Brimley, Matt Clark, Therese Graham, Levi L. Knebel; *D:* Richard Pearce; *W:* William D. Wittliff.

The Country Bears 🦴🦴 **2002 (G)** Fresh out of new ideas, Disney apparently saw gold in a few of their amusement park rides and decided to make movies out of them. This tale of talking, singing bears is the first installment. When Beary (voice of Osment) finds out that he's adopted, and not actually part of the human family that raised him, he decides to take a journey to visit Country Bear Hall in order to find his roots. Unfortunately, the hall is slated for demolition by evil banker Reed Thimple (Walken). Beary attempts to reunite the Country Bears, the legendary band that made the hall famous, in order to save it. Standard Disney fare, which means nothing objectionable except the attempt to make you buy more of their toys. **88m/C VHS, DVD.** *US* Christopher Walken, Daryl (Chill) Mitchell, Diedrich Bader, Alex Rocco, Stephen Tobolowsky, M.C. Gainey, Meagen Fay, Eli Marienthal, Queen Latifah; *D:* Peter Hastings; *W:* Mark Perez; *C:* C. Mitchell Anderson; *M:* Christopher Young, John Hiatt; *V:* Diedrich

Bader, Haley Joel Osment, James Gammon, Brad Garrett, Candy Ford, Toby Huss, Kevin M. Richardson, Stephen (Steve) Root.

Country Gentlemen 🦴🦴 **1936** Vaudeville team, Olsen and Johnson, play fast-talking conmen who sell shares in a worthless oil field to a bunch of WWI veterans. What a surprise when oil is actually found there. Not one of the duo's better performances. **54m/B VHS, DVD.** Ole Olsen, Chic Johnson, Joyce Compton, Lila Lee, Ray Corrigan, Donald Kirke, Pierre Watkin; ***D:*** Ralph Staub.

Country Girl 🦴🦴🦴 1/2 **1954** In the role that completely de-glamorized her (and won her an Oscar), Kelly plays the wife of alcoholic singer Crosby who tries to make a comeback with the help of director Holden. One of Crosby's four dramatic parts, undoubtedly one of his best. Seaton won an Oscar for his adaptation of the Clifford Odets play. Remade in 1982. ♫ The Search is Through; Dissertation on the State of Bliss; It's Mine, It's Yours; The Land Around Us. **104m/B VHS, DVD.** Bing Crosby, Grace Kelly, William Holden, Gene Reynolds, Anthony Ross; ***D:*** George Seaton; ***W:*** George Seaton. Oscars '54: Actress (Kelly), Screenplay; Golden Globes '55: Actress—Drama (Kelly); Natl. Bd. of Review '54: Actress (Kelly); N.Y. Film Critics '54: Actress (Kelly).

Country Girl 🦴 **1982** Aging, alcoholic actor is desperate for a comeback. His director blames his fiercely loving wife for the downfall. Poor cable TV remake of 1954 version with Bing Crosby. **137m/C VHS.** Dick Van Dyke, Faye Dunaway, Ken Howard; ***D:*** Gary Halvorson. **CABLE**

The Country Kid 🦴🦴🦴 **1923** A freckle-faced teenager and his two brothers are beset by a wicked uncle out to steal their inheritance. One of Barry's best-remembered films. **60m/B VHS.** Wesley Barry, "Spec" (Walter) O'Donnell, Bruce Guerin, Kate Toncray, Helen Jerome Eddy, George Nicholls Jr.; ***D:*** William Beaudine.

Country Life 🦴🦴 **1995 (PG-13)** Down Under adaptation of Chekov's "Uncle Vanya," has Blakemore returning to Aussie farm roots after 22-year stint as unsuccessful London theatre critic. His bored young wife (Scacchi) upsets the business-as-usual life of her husband's brother-in-law (Hargreaves) and abandoned daughter, Sally (Fox), who is also jealous of the attention paid the beautiful Deborah by both her uncle and longtime crush, Dr. Askey (Neill). Exchanges Chekov's emotional exploration for a light comedy of manners and a message of Australian independence from England. **107m/C VHS, DVD.** *AU* Sam Neill, Greta Scacchi, Kerry Fox, John Hargreaves, Googie Withers, Patricia Kennedy, Michael Blakemore; ***D:*** Michael Blakemore; ***W:*** Michael Blakemore; ***C:*** Stephen Windon; ***M:*** Peter Best.

The Country Teacher 🦴🦴 *Venkovsky Ucitel* **2008** Shy, closeted teacher Petr leaves Prague hoping to find a new life by taking a job at a small school in the country. Despite the conservative community, Petr is soon accepted, especially by widow Marie who offers Petr a room at her farm. She believes her romantic overtures are rejected because she is older than Petr but little does she suspect that Petr has developed a crush on Marie's straight, 17-year-old son Lada. Problems occur when Petr's boorish ex-boyfriend makes a surprise appearance. Czech with subtitles. **113m/C DVD.** *CZ* Pavel Liska, Marek Daniel, Zuzana Bydzovska, Ladislav Sedivy; ***D:*** Bohdan Slama; ***W:*** Bohdan Slama; ***C:*** Divis Marek; ***M:*** Vladimir Godar.

Countryman 🦴🦴 **1983 (R)** A dope-smuggling woman crashes her plane in Jamaica and is rescued by Countryman, a rasta super hero. Not very good, but at least there's great music by Bob Marley and others. **103m/C VHS, DVD.** Hiram Keller, Kristine Sinclair; ***D:*** Dickie Jobson.

County Fair 🦴🦴 **1920** This early silent film is an adaptation of Neil Burgess' play about life in New England. **60m/B VHS.** Helen Jerome Eddy, David Butler; ***D:*** Edmund Mortimer, Maurice Tourneur; ***W:*** J. Grubb Alexander.

Coup de Grace 🦴🦴 1/2 **1978** Engaging political satire about a wealthy aristocratic woman in Latvia during the 1919-20 Civil War, and how she attempts to maintain her lifestyle as German soldiers are housed on her estate. Her unrequited love for a German officer adds to her troubles. In German with English subtitles. Co-written by von Trotta and based on the novel by Marguerite Yourcenar. **96m/B DVD.** *GE FR* Margarethe von Trotta, Matthias Habich, Rudiger Kirschstein, Matthieu Carriere; ***D:*** Volker Schlondorff; ***W:*** Margarethe von Trotta.

Coup de Torchon 🦴🦴🦴 *Clean Slate* **1981** Set in 1938 French West Africa, Noiret plays corrupt police chief Lucien Cordier who is consistently harrassed by his community, particularly by the town pimp. He usually overlooks the pimp's crimes, but when Cordier catches him and a friend shooting at plague victims' bodies floating down the river he decides to murder them in cold blood. Based on the novel "POP 1280" by Jim Thompson. In French with English subtitles. **128m/C VHS, DVD.** *FR* Philippe Noiret, Isabelle Huppert, Guy Marchand, Stephane Audran, Eddy Mitchell, Jean-Pierre Marielle, Irene Skobline; ***D:*** Bertrand Tavernier; ***W:*** Bertrand Tavernier; ***C:*** Pierre William Glenn; ***M:*** Philippe Sarde.

Coupe de Ville 🦴🦴 1/2 **1990 (PG-13)** Three brothers are forced by their father to drive mom's birthday present from Detroit to Florida in the summer of '63. Period concerns and music keep it interesting. **98m/C VHS.** Patrick Dempsey, Daniel Stern, Arye Gross, Joseph Bologna, Alan Arkin, Annabeth Gish, Rita Taggart, James Gammon; ***D:*** Joe Roth; ***W:*** Mike Binder; ***M:*** James Newton Howard.

Couples Retreat 🦴 1/2 **2009 (PG-13)** Troubled Midwestern marrieds Jason (Bateman) and Cynthia (Bell) persuade three pairs of friends to join them at the Eden Resort in Bora Bora where they can work on their relationship in a series of workshops while the others have fun in the sun. Upon arrival, their couples counselor Marcel (Reno) informs them that all four couples must participate (willingly or not—mostly not), leading to generally mainstream comedic moments. The scenery impresses more than the script or the acting, which are both bland. **107m/C DVD.** *US* Vince Vaughn, Jon Favreau, Jason Bateman, Faizon Love, Kristin Davis, Malin Akerman, Kristen Bell, Kali Hawk, Jean Reno, Ken Jeong, Temuera Morrison, Tasha Smith, Carlos Ponce, John Michael Higgins, Amy Hill, Charlotte Cornwell; ***D:*** Peter Billingsley; ***W:*** Vince Vaughn, Jon Favreau, Dana Fox; ***C:*** Eric Alan Edwards; ***M:*** A.R. Rahman.

Courage 🦴🦴🦴 **1986** Based on fact, about a Hispanic mother in NYC who, motivated by her drug-troubled children, goes undercover and exposes a multimillion-dollar drug ring. Loren is great in a decidedly non-glamorous role. **141m/C VHS, DVD.** Sophia Loren, Billy Dee Williams, Hector Elizondo, Val Avery, Dan Hedaya, Ron Rifkin, Jose Perez; ***D:*** Jeremy Paul Kagan. **TV**

Courage Mountain 🦴 **1989 (PG)** If you're looking for a good sequel to Johanna Spyri's classic "Heidi" this isn't it. Europe is on the brink of WWI when teenage Heidi leaves her beloved mountain for an exclusive boarding school in Italy. Not surprisingly in a war zone, the military takes over and the kids are sent to an orphanage run by nasties (see also "Oliver!"). The girls escape to the mountains and are saved by none other than Sheen as Heidi's pal Peter (who cast the 20-something Sheen as a teenager? Bad mistake.) Ridiculous sequel to the classic tale will appeal to kids despite what the critics say. **92m/C VHS, DVD.** Juliette Caton, Joanna Clarke, Nicola Stapleton, Charlie Sheen, Jan Rubes, Leslie Caron, Jade Magri, Kathryn Ludlow, Yorgo Voyagis, Laura Betti; ***D:*** Christopher Leitch; ***W:*** Weaver Webb; ***M:*** Sylvester Levay.

Courage of Black Beauty 🦴 1/2 **1957** Another version of the perennial heart warmer about a boy and his horse. **80m/C VHS.** Johnny Crawford, Mimi Gibson, John Bryant, Diane Brewster, J. Pat O'Malley; ***D:*** Harold Schuster.

Courage of Lassie 🦴🦴 1/2 *Blue Sierra* **1946 (G)** Fourteen-year-old Taylor is the heroine in this girl loves dog tale. In this case, the dog is actually called Bill, not Lassie, in spite of the film's title. Bill is found wounded by Taylor and she nurses him back to health. He proves to be loving, loyal, and useful, so much so that, through a complicated plotline, he winds up in the Army's K-9 division and returns home with the doggie version of shell-shock. Taylor's still there to nurse him back to his old kind self again. **93m/C VHS, DVD.** Elizabeth Taylor, Frank Morgan, Tom Drake, Selena Royle, Harry Davenport, Arthur Walsh; ***D:*** Fred M. Wilcox.

Courage of Rin Tin Tin 🦴🦴 *The Challenge of Rin Tin Tin* **1957** Rusty and his faithful dog Rin Tin Tin help the cavalry soldiers of Fort Apache keep law and order in a small Arizona town. The perennial kid-pleasing German Shepherd comes through again. **90m/C VHS.** James Brown, Lee Aaker; ***D:*** Robert G. Walker; ***W:*** John O'Dea.

Courage of the North 🦴 1/2 **1935** The Mounties break up a fur-stealing ring with the help of Captain Dog and Dynamite Horse. Bound to set your hair on end. **55m/B VHS.** John Preston, June Love, William Desmond, Tom London, Jimmy Aubrey; ***D:*** Robert Emmett Tansey; ***W:*** Robert Emmett Tansey.

The Courage to Love 🦴🦴 1/2 **2000 (PG-13)** Real-life portrayal of Henriette Dellille who, as the product of an affair between a white plantation owner and an African-American woman, shunned family and societal pressures to devote her life to caring for the underprivileged through her group the Sisters of the Holy Family in 19th-century New Orleans. **90m/C VHS, DVD.** Vanessa L(ynne) Williams, Gil Bellows, Lisa Bronwyn Moore, David La Haye, Cynda Williams, Diahann Carroll, Stacy Keach, Eddie Bo Smith Jr., Kevin Jubinville, Jean-Louis Roux, Lise Roy, Mariah Inger, Paul-Antoine Taillefer, Chris(topher) Williams, Karen Williams, Graeme Somerville, Susannah Hoffman, Raven Dauda, Sylvia Stewart, Heather Hale; ***D:*** Keri Skogland; ***W:*** Toni Johnson; ***C:*** Jonathan Freeman; ***M:*** Christopher Dedrick. **TV**

Courage Under Fire 🦴🦴🦴 **1996 (R)** Army Lt. Col. Nat Serling (Washington) is unexpectedly assigned to review the candidacy of Capt. Karen Emma Walden (Ryan, seen only in flashbacks) to receive the posthumous Medal of Honor for bravery in combat. A Gulf War Medevac pilot, Walden would be the first woman awarded the honor if Serling can figure out the truth from her surviving crew's wildly conflicting reports. Ironically, Serling's dealing with a guilt complex since four members of his tank unit died in the war under friendly fire. Stellar performances, including a frightening one by Phillips. Based on the novel by Duncan, who also did the screenplay; Washington and director Zwick previously worked together on "Glory." **120m/C VHS, DVD, Blu-ray Disc.** Denzel Washington, Meg Ryan, Matt Damon, Lou Diamond Phillips, Michael Moriarty, Scott Glenn, Bronson Pinchot, Seth Gilliam, Sean Astin, Regina Taylor, Tim Guinee, Ken Jenkins, Kathleen Widdoes, Zeljko Ivanek, Tim Ransom, Ned Vaughn; ***D:*** Edward Zwick; ***W:*** Patrick Sheane Duncan; ***C:*** Roger Deakins; ***M:*** James Horner.

Courageous Avenger 🦴 **1935** A sheriff brings a treacherous ore mine foreman to justice. **59m/B VHS.** Johnny Mack Brown; ***D:*** Robert North Bradbury; ***W:*** Charles Francis Royal.

Courageous Dr. Christian 🦴🦴 **1940** Dr. Christian is faced with an epidemic of meningitis among the inhabitants of a shanty town. Typical entry in the "Dr. Christian" series. **66m/B VHS, DVD.** Jean Hersholt, Dorothy Lovett, Tom Neal, Robert Baldwin, Maude Eburne; ***D:*** Bernard Vorhaus; ***C:*** John Alton.

The Courageous Heart of Irena Sendler 🦴🦴🦴 **2009** Another excellent Hallmark Hall of Fame production based on the book "The Mother of the Holocaust Children" by Anna Mieszkowskia. By 1941, the Jewish population has been sequestered in Poland's Warsaw ghetto. Realizing there's something sinister about the work camps to which the Jews are being sent, Catholic social worker Irena Sendler (Paquin) works with the families to smuggle children out of the ghetto and secretly place them with Christian families for safety. So that everything doesn't appear bleak, there's a modest romance between Irena and her former schoolmate Stefan (Visnjic). **90m/C DVD.** Anna Paquin, Goran Visnjic, Marcia Gay Harden, Paul Freeman, Leigh Lawson, Michelle Dockery; ***D:*** John Kent Harrison; ***W:*** John Kent Harrison, Lawrence John Spagnola; ***C:*** Jerzy Zielinski; ***M:*** Jan A.P. Kaczmarek. **TV**

The Courageous Mr. Penn 🦴🦴 *Penn of Pennsylvania* **1941** Slow-moving British film, outlining the achievements of William Penn, the Quaker founder of Pennsylvania. **79m/B VHS.** *GB* Clifford Evans, Deborah Kerr, Dennis Arundell, Aubrey Mallalieu, D.J. Williams, O.B. Clarence, Charles Carson, Henry Oscar, J.H. Roberts; ***D:*** Lance Comfort.

The Courier 🦴🦴 **1988 (R)** A former drug addict seeks revenge on the dealers who killed his friend. Only thing that saves it are the songs by U2, The Pogues, and Hothouse Flowers. Musical score by Elvis Costello. **85m/C VHS.** *IR* Gabriel Byrne, Ian Bannen, Padraig O'Loingsigh, Cait O'Riordan, Patrick Bergin; ***D:*** Frank Deasy, Joe Lee; ***M:*** Elvis Costello.

Courier of Death 🦴 **1984** A courier is embroiled in a mob war/struggle over a locked briefcase with mysterious contents. **77m/C VHS.** Joey Johnson, Barbara Garrison; ***D:*** Tom Shaw.

Court Jester 🦴🦴🦴 1/2 **1956** Swashbuckling comedy stars Danny Kaye as a former circus clown who teams up with a band of outlaws trying to dethrone a tyrant king. Kaye poses as the court jester so he can learn of the evil king's intentions. Filled with more color, more song, and more truly funny lines than any three comedies put together, this is Kaye's best performance. ♫ They'll Never Outfox the Fox; Baby, Let Me Take You Dreaming; My Heart Knows a Lovely Song; The Maladjusted Jester. **101m/C VHS, DVD.** Danny Kaye, Glynis Johns, Basil Rathbone, Angela Lansbury, Cecil Parker, John Carradine, Mildred Natwick, Robert Middleton; ***D:*** Melvin Frank, Norman Panama; ***W:*** Norman Panama; ***C:*** Ray June; ***M:*** Sammy Cahn, Sylvia Fine, Vic Schoen. Natl. Film Reg. '04.

The Court Martial of Billy Mitchell 🦴🦴🦴 *One-Man Mutiny* **1955** Terrific courtroom drama depicts the secret trial of Billy Mitchell, head of the Army Air Service in the 1920s, who predicted the role of airpower in subsequent warfare and the danger of war with Japan. Mitchell incurred the wrath of the military by publicly faulting the lack of U.S. preparedness for invasion. Steiger is outstanding as the attorney; Cooper is great as Mitchell. Debut for Montgomery. **100m/C VHS, DVD.** Gary Cooper, Charles Bickford, Ralph Bellamy, Rod Steiger, Elizabeth Montgomery, Fred Clark, James Daly, Jack Lord, Peter Graves, Darren McGavin, Robert F. Simon, Jack Perrin, Charles Dingle; ***D:*** Otto Preminger; ***C:*** Sam Leavitt.

The Court Martial of Jackie Robinson 🦴🦴🦴 1/2 **1990 (R)** True story of a little-known chapter in the life of the famous athlete. During his stint in the Army, Robinson refused to take a back seat on a bus and subsequently faced the possibility of court martial. **94m/C VHS.** Andre Braugher, Daniel Stern, Ruby Dee, Stan Shaw, Paul Dooley, Bruce Dern, Dale Dye; ***D:*** Larry Peerce; ***W:*** Dennis Lynton Clark; ***C:*** Don Burgess. **CABLE**

The Courtesans of Bombay 🦴🦴🦴 **1985** Gritty docudrama, set in Pavanpul, the poverty-stricken brothel section of Bombay, looks at how the impoverished women support themselves through a combination of prostitution and performing. **74m/C VHS, DVD.** *GB* Kareem Samar, Zohra Sehgal, Saeed Jaffrey; ***D:*** Ismail Merchant, James Ivory, Ruth Prawer Jhabvala. **TV**

Courtin' Wildcats 🦴 1/2 **1929** Early Gibson programmer in which he plays a frail eastern college boy who was sent west by his father to toughen up. Once there, he meets Gilbert and ends up marrying her. **56m/B VHS.** Hoot Gibson, Eugenia Gilbert, Monte Montague; ***D:*** Jerome Storm.

The Courtney Affair 🦴🦴 1/2 *The Courtneys of Curzon Street* **1947** An aristocratic young Britisher causes a stir when he marries an Irish maid. As a result, the couple must face terrific social ostracism. Classy soap opera family saga was a big money maker in England. **112m/B VHS.** *GB* Anna Neagle, Michael Wilding, Gladys Young, Michael Medwin, Coral Browne, Jack Watling, Bernard Lee; ***D:*** Herbert Wilcox.

Courtship ♪♪♪ **1987** From renowned playwright Horton Foote comes this touching story about a sheltered, upper-crust young girl who shocks her family and friends by eloping with a traveling salesman. **84m/C VHS, DVD.** Hallie Foote, William Converse-Roberts, Amanda Plummer, Rochelle Oliver, Michael Higgins; ***D:*** Howard Cummings. **TV**

The Courtship of Eddie's Father ♪♪♪ **1962** A clever nine-year-old boy plays matchmaker for his widowed dad in this rewarding family comedy-drama (the inspiration for the TV series). Some plot elements are outdated, but young Howard's performance is terrific; he would later excel at direction. Based on the novel by Mark Toby. **117m/C VHS, DVD.** Glenn Ford, Shirley Jones, Stella Stevens, Dina Merrill, Ron Howard, Jerry Van Dyke, Roberta Sherwood; ***D:*** Vincente Minnelli; ***W:*** John Gay; ***C:*** Milton Krasner.

The Courtyard ♪♪ **1995 (R)** Jonathan Hoffman (McCarthy) seems to have the perfect life—a great job, great girl, great California apartment. But then his apartment complex is bedeviled by a series of sinister crimes and Jonathan becomes the prime suspect. **103m/C VHS.** Andrew McCarthy, Madchen Amick, Richard "Cheech" Marin, Vincent Schiavelli; ***D:*** Fred Walton; ***W:*** Christopher Hawthorne.

Cousin Bette ♪♪ ½ **1997 (R)** Lange plays a mean game of Old Maid in this adaptation of Honore Balzac's novel, set in 1840s Paris. Always outshone by her more beautiful cousin Adeline (Chaplin), Bette is considered plain and not very bright by her aristocratic family. When Adeline's husband Hector (Laurie) asks her to become his housekeeper instead of his wife after Adeline dies, there is no doubt what she means when she hisses she will "take care of everyone." She uses her family's own baser instincts to bring about their downfall. Lange's performance as the cold and manipulative Bette is worth the price of a rental by itself. Big screen debut for theatrical director McAnuff. **112m/C VHS, DVD.** Jessica Lange, Elisabeth Shue, Aden Young, Bob Hoskins, Kelly Macdonald, Hugh Laurie, Geraldine Chaplin, Toby Stephens, John Sessions; ***D:*** Des McAnuff; ***W:*** Lynn Siefert, Susan Tarr; ***C:*** Andrzej Sekula; ***M:*** Simon Boswell.

Cousin, Cousine ♪♪♪ ½ **1976 (R)** Pleasant French comedy about distant cousins who meet at a round of family parties, funerals, and weddings and become friends, but their relationship soon becomes more than platonic. Remade in the U.S. in 1989 as "Cousins." In French with English subtitles. **95m/C VHS.** *FR* Marie-Christine Barrault, Marie-France Pisier, Victor Lanoux, Guy Marchand, Ginette Garcin, Sybil Maas; ***D:*** Jean-Charles Tacchella; ***W:*** Jean-Charles Tacchella; ***C:*** Georges Lendi; ***M:*** Gerard Anfosso. Cesar '76: Support. Actress (Pisier).

The Cousins ♪♪♪ *Les Cousins* **1959** Set against the backdrop of Parisian student life, two very different cousins (one twisted, the other saintly) vie for the hand of Mayniel. This country mouse, city mouse adult fable ultimately depicts the survival of the fittest. Chabrol's lovely but sad second directorial effort. **112m/B VHS.** *FR* Jean-Claude Brialy, Gerard Blain, Juliette Mayniel, Claude Cerval, Genevieve Cluny, Stephane Audran; ***D:*** Claude Chabrol; ***W:*** Claude Chabrol.

Cousins ♪♪♪ ½ **1989 (PG-13)** An American remake of "Cousin, Cousine," in which two distant cousins-by-marriage meet at a wedding and, due to their respective spouses' infidelities, fall into each other's arms. A gentle love story with a humorous and biting look at the foibles of extended families. **110m/C VHS, DVD.** Isabella Rossellini, Sean Young, Ted Danson, William L. Petersen, Norma Aleandro, Lloyd Bridges, Keith Coogan; ***D:*** Joel Schumacher; ***W:*** Stephen Metcalfe; ***C:*** Ralf Bode; ***M:*** Angelo Badalamenti.

The Cove ♪♪ **2009 (PG-13)** Richard O'Barry went from 1960s dolphin trainer on the "Flipper" TV show to dolphin rescuer. O'Barry is especially incensed by the mass harpooning of dolphins by fishermen that occurs in the port town of Tajii, Japan, where dolphins are lured into the titular cove. O'Barry has been arrested for trying to free the captive dolphins and barred from entering the cove. All photography and recording is banned so activists and divers must slip past security to plant cameras for their disturbing night footage in this compelling documentary. **92m/C DVD.** *US* Hayden Panettiere, Richard O'Barry, Louie Psihoyos; ***D:*** Louie Psihoyos; ***W:*** Mark Monroe; ***C:*** Brook Aitken; ***M:*** J. Ralph. Oscars '09: Feature Doc.; Writers Guild '09: Feature Doc.

The Covenant ♪ **2006 (PG-13)** Dull and dopey horror story focuses on the sons of Ipswich, four young studs who attend private Spenser Academy and have inherited supernatural powers from their spooky Massachusetts ancestors. Caleb (Strait) will come into his full powers on his 18th birthday but the more he uses them, the faster he'll age. This will be a problem since new transfer student Chase (Stan) is challenging Caleb for top warlock status. Can't even be considered cheesy fun, although the spider scene is pretty nasty. **97m/C DVD, Blu-ray Disc.** *US* Steven Strait, Laura Ramsey, Wendy Crewson, Sebastian Stan, Taylor Kitsch, Toby Hemingway, Jessica Lucas, Chace Crawford; ***D:*** Renny Harlin; ***W:*** J.S. Cardone; ***C:*** Pierre Gill; ***M:*** Tomandandy.

Cover ♪ **2008 (PG-13)** Screechy and simplistic morality tale. Church-going wife and mother Valerie (Ellis) is outraged when she's questioned about a murder. The problem stems from her family's recent move to Philly and hubby Dutch's (Adoti) taking up with some old college friends. Shady goings-on and infidelity turn out to be the least of the problems. **98m/C DVD.** Aunjanue Ellis, Louis Gossett Jr., Raz Adoti, Roger Guenveur Smith, Leon, Clifton Davis, Paula Jai Parker, Vivica A. Fox, Mya, Patti LaBelle, Obba Babatunde; ***D:*** Bill Duke; ***W:*** Aaron Rashaan Thomas; ***C:*** Francis Kenny; ***M:*** Kurt Farquhar.

Cover Girl ♪♪♪ **1944** A vintage wartime musical about a girl who must decide between a nightclub career and a future as a cover model. Hayworth is beautiful, Kelly dances like a dream, and Silvers and Arden are hilarious. ♫ Cover Girl; Sure Thing; Make Way For Tomorrow; Put Me to the Test; Long Ago and Far Away; That's the Best of All; The Show Must Go On; Who's Complaining?; Poor John. **107m/C VHS, DVD.** Rita Hayworth, Gene Kelly, Phil Silvers, Otto Kruger, Lee Bowman, Jinx Falkenberg, Eve Arden, Edward Brophy, Anita Colby; ***D:*** Charles Vidor; ***C:*** Rudolph Mate; ***M:*** Ira Gershwin, Jerome Kern. Oscars '44: Orig. Dramatic Score.

Cover Girl Models ♪ **1975** An action-packed '70s adventure in which beautiful models are forced to fight for survival. **82m/C VHS, DVD.** Lindsay Bloom, Pat Anderson, John Kramer, Rhonda Leigh Hopkins, Mary Woronov; ***D:*** Cirio H. Santiago.

The Cover Girl Murders ♪♪ ½ **1993 (PG-13)** Six beautiful models have been brought together on a remote island to shoot a magazine's popular swimsuit issue. Each one wants to be the cover model—but someone is willing to kill to get the job. **87m/C VHS.** Lee Majors, Jennifer O'Neill, Adrian Paul, Beverly Johnson, Vanessa Angel; ***D:*** James A. Contner; ***W:*** Douglas Barr, Bernard Maybeck; ***M:*** Rick Marotta.

Cover Me ♪♪ **1995 (R)** When beautiful models turn up dead, L.A. detectives Bobby Colter (Rossovich) and J.J. Davis (Sorvino) discover they were all on the cover of L.A. Erotica magazine. So detective Holly Jacobsen, Colter's girlfriend, (Taylor) goes undercover at the magazine and learns more about the seamy sex underworld than the killer wants her to know. **94m/C VHS.** Courtney Taylor, Rick Rossovich, Paul Sorvino, Elliott Gould, Corbin Bernsen; ***D:*** Michael Schroeder; ***W:*** Steve Johnson.

Cover Story ♪ ½ **1993** Journalist Matt McKendree falls in love with a mystery woman whose story he's investigating. Too bad she's dead—or is she. **93m/C VHS.** William Wallace, Tuesday Knight, Robert Forster, Christopher McDonald; ***D:*** Gregg Smith; ***W:*** Gregg Smith.

Cover-Up ♪ ½ **1991 (R)** Terrorist attacks on U.S. military bases in Israel are just a smokescreen for a greater threat. The below-par actioner stands out only for the hokey religious symbolism in its Good Friday climax. **89m/C VHS, DVD.** Dolph Lundgren, Louis Gossett Jr., John Finn; ***D:*** Manny Coto.

The Covered Wagon ♪♪ ½ **1923** Prototypical silent Western began the genre. Wagon train moves cross-country, battling weather and wild Indians. By today's standards, somewhat bucolic and uneventful, but the location photography holds up quite well. Big budget film in its day, and enormously popular. **98m/B VHS.** Warren Kerigan, Lois Wilson, Alan Hale, Ernest Torrence; ***D:*** James Cruze.

Covered Wagon Days ♪♪ **1940** The Three Mesquiteers set out after silver smugglers who have framed Rico's brother for murder. **54m/B VHS.** Robert "Bob" Livingston, Raymond Hatton, Duncan Renaldo, John Merton, Reed Howes; ***D:*** George Sherman.

Covered Wagon Trails ♪ **1940** Substandard Western has good guy Randall dealing with the shifty cattleman's association and making the West safe for the hardworking locals. Future Frankenstein monster Strange plays the hired muscle. **52m/B VHS.** Addison "Jack" Randall, Sally Cairns, David Sharpe, Lafe (Lafayette) McKee, Budd Buster, Glenn Strange; ***D:*** Bernard B. Ray; ***W:*** Tom Gibson.

Covergirl ♪ ½ *Dreamworld* **1983 (R)** Wealthy man decides to relieve his boredom by molding a young woman into a supermodel. She finds the glamorous life isn't always what it's cracked up to be. TV-type melodrama. **98m/C VHS.** *CA* Jeff Conaway, Irena Ferris, Cathie Shirriff, Roberta Leighton, Deborah Wakeham; ***D:*** Jean-Claude Lord.

Covert Action ♪ ½ **1988** A drug kingpin who desires to protect his business tries to frame a captain for a crime he did not commit. **85m/C VHS.** Rick Washburne, John Christian, Stuart Garrison Day, Amanda Zinsser, Johnny Stumper; ***D:*** J. Christian Ingvordsen.

Covert Assassin ♪♪ **1994 (R)** Anti-terrorist specialist is hired by wealthy widow to avenge her husband's murder. Adapted from the novel "Wild Justice" by Wilbur Smith. **114m/C VHS, DVD.** Roy Scheider, Sam Wanamaker, Ted McGinley, Christopher Buchholz; ***D:*** Tony Wharmby.

The Cow ♪♪ **1993** Adam (Holub) is the simple-minded son of the local prostitute in a remote mountain village. With his mother dying, Adam sells his beloved cow to pay for her morphine but after her death he sinks into further poverty and despair until the beautiful Rosa (Mihulova) takes pity on him. Bleak but powerful; Czech with subtitles. **86m/C VHS.** *CZ* Radek Holub, Alena Mihulova; ***D:*** Karel Kachyna; ***W:*** Karel Cabradek, Karel Kachyna.

Cow Belles ♪♪ ½ **2006 (G)** Frothy tween fare from the Disney Channel. Teen sisters Courtney and Taylor are well-provided for thanks to daddy's dairy business. But the girls have grown up selfish and irresponsible, so their fed-up father makes them work in the dairy over the summer. The girls get their "a-ha!" moment when dad is out of the country and the company's finances are suddenly in big trouble, which means the sisters must figure out a way to save the family business. **90m/C DVD.** Jack Coleman, Sheila McCarthy, Alyson Michalka, Amanda Michalka, Michael Trevino; ***D:*** Francine McDougall; ***W:*** Stu Krieger; ***C:*** Tony Westman; ***M:*** Kenneth Burgomaster. **CABLE**

Cow Town ♪♪ **1950** A range war results when ranchers begin fencing in their land to prevent cattle rustling. Autry's 72nd film has some good songs and a dependable cast. **70m/B VHS, DVD.** Gene Autry, Gail Davis, Jock Mahoney, Harry Shannon; ***D:*** John English.

The Coward ♪♪ **1962** A schoolteacher and his wife are living in a remote Slovak village during the last days of WWII. The wife supports the anti-Nazi partisans while her husband collaborates with the Germans that occupy the village. Eventually, he finds the courage to save some innocent victims of the Nazi purge. Czech with subtitles. **113m/C VHS.** *CZ* Daniel Smutna, Ladislav Chudik, Oleg Strizhenov, Willem Koch-Hooge; ***D:*** Jiri Weiss; ***W:*** Jiri Weiss; ***C:*** Josef Strecha; ***M:*** Jiri Srnka.

Coward of the County ♪♪ ½ **1981** A devout pacifist is put to the test when his girlfriend is raped. Good performances by all concerned. Based on the lyrics of Kenny Rogers's hit song of the same name. **115m/C VHS.** Kenny Rogers, Frederic Lehne, Largo Woodruff, Mariclare Costello, Ana Alicia, Noble Willingham; ***D:*** Dick Lowry. **TV**

Cowboy ♪♪♪ **1958** Western roundup based on the memoirs of tenderfoot-turned-cowpoke Frank Harris. Harris (Lemmon) is a Chicago hotel clerk who meets cattle boss Tom Reece (Ford) who's in the city on business. Losing his money in a poker game, Reece reluctantly accepts a loan from Harris in exchange for a piece of his cattle business. So Harris and Reece hit the dusty trail on a cattle drive that takes them into Mexico where Harris falls in love with Maria (Kashfi), the daughter of a wealthy rancher, and gradually turns from city slicker into hardened trail boss. Good cast, no fuss. From the book "Reminiscences As a Cowboy" by Harris. **92m/C VHS, DVD.** Jack Lemmon, Glenn Ford, Anna Kashfi, Brian Donlevy, Dick York, Victor Manuel Mendoza, Richard Jaeckel, King Donovan; ***D:*** Delmer Daves; ***W:*** Edmund H. North; ***C:*** Charles Lawton Jr.; ***M:*** George Duning.

The Cowboy & the Ballerina ♪♪ **1984** An aging rodeo star falls in love with a petite ballerina defecting from a Russian Dance Company. Good cast makes it watchable. **96m/C VHS.** Lee Majors, Leslie Wing, Christopher Lloyd, Anjelica Huston, George de la Pena; ***D:*** Jerry Jameson; ***M:*** Bruce Broughton. **TV**

Cowboy & the Bandit ♪ **1935** A cowboy comes to the aid of a widow being victimized by outlaws. **58m/B VHS.** Rex Lease, Bobby Nelson, William Desmond; ***D:*** Al(bert) Herman.

The Cowboy and the Lady ♪♪ ½ **1938** Oberon plays a madcap heiress who is deposited by her politician father on their Florida estate to keep her out of trouble while he seeks the Presidential nomination. She is bored and decides to go to a local rodeo where she meets cowboy Cooper. Both are instantly smitten and marry on impulse. Cooper doesn't know about her wealth and when her father finds out about the marriage he's appalled that his daughter has married beneath her. Since this is a comedy all comes out right in the end. Good cast, weak story. **91m/B VHS.** Gary Cooper, Merle Oberon, Patsy Kelly, Walter Brennan, Fuzzy Knight, Mabel Todd, Henry Kolker, Harry Davenport; ***D:*** H.C. Potter; ***C:*** Gregg Toland. Oscars '38: Sound.

Cowboy & the Senorita ♪♪ **1944** A cowboy solves the mystery of a missing girl and wins her lovely cousin. The first film that paired Rogers and Evans, who went on to become a winning team, on and offscreen. **56m/B VHS, DVD.** Roy Rogers, John Hubbard, Dale Evans; ***D:*** Joseph Kane; ***W:*** Gordon Kahn.

Cowboy Commandos ♪ ½ **1943** Improbable plot has cowboys riding out after Nazi spies, who want to steal valuable ore. **53m/B VHS.** Ray Corrigan, Dennis Moore, Max Terhune, Budd Buster, John Merton; ***D:*** S. Roy Luby.

Cowboy Counselor ♪ **1933** Cowboy Hoot Gibson helps an enchanting girl clear her innocent brother's name. **60m/B VHS.** Hoot Gibson, Sheila (Manors) Mannors, Skeeter Bill Robbins, Alan Bridge, Bobby Nelson, Merrill McCormick; ***D:*** George Melford; ***W:*** Jack Natteford.

Cowboy Millionaire ♪♪ ½ **1935** An Englishwoman comes to an American dude ranch and falls in love with one of the ranch hands. Entertaining Western comedy. **65m/B VHS.** George O'Brien, Evalyn Bostock, Edgar Kennedy, Alden Chase; ***D:*** Edward F. (Eddie) Cline.

Cowboy Up ♪♪ *Ring of Fire* **2000 (PG-13)** Hank (Sutherland) is a rodeo clown while younger brother Ely (Thomas) is a bullrider. They clash when barrel rider Celia (Hannah) comes into the picture, which causes Ely to take some dangerous chances to win a bull-riding championship. The film's original title, which was changed for the video release, comes from the Johnny Cash song. **105m/C VHS, DVD.** Kiefer Sutherland, Marcus Thomas, Daryl Hannah, Melinda Dillon, Molly Ringwald, Russell Means, Bo Hopkins, Pete Postlethwaite, Al Corley; ***D:*** Xavier Koller; ***W:*** James Redford; ***C:*** Andrew Dintenfass; ***M:*** Daniel Licht.

The Cowboy Way 1/2 **1994 (PG-13)** A mess from start to finish made somewhat watchable by cowpoke charm of the leads and one good horse chase. Two rodeo stars (Harrelson and Sutherland) from New Mexico ride into New York City to avenge a buddy's death, with Hudson as a mounted NYC cop who always yearned to be a cowboy. Great premise is overcome by tasteless humor and a patched-up plot shot full of holes. Good for a gander is the 90-foot Times Square billboard of Harrelson's character as a Calvin Klein underwear model, which stopped traffic even in jaded New York. **106m/C VHS, DVD.** Woody Harrelson, Kiefer Sutherland, Dylan McDermott, Ernie Hudson, Cara Buono, Marg Helgenberger, Tomas Milian, Joaquin Martinez; ***Cameos:*** Travis Tritt; ***D:*** Gregg Champion; ***W:*** William D. Wittliff, Rob Thompson; ***C:*** Dean Semler; ***M:*** David Newman.

The Cowboys **1972 (PG)** Wayne stars as a cattle rancher who is forced to hire 11 schoolboys to help him drive his cattle 400 miles to market. Clever script makes this one of Wayne's better Westerns. Carradine's film debut. Inspired the TV series. **128m/C VHS, DVD, Blu-ray Disc, HD DVD.** John Wayne, Roscoe Lee Browne, A. Martinez, Bruce Dern, Colleen Dewhurst, Slim Pickens, Robert Carradine, Clay O'Brien, Nicolas Beauvy; ***D:*** Mark Rydell; ***W:*** Harriet Frank Jr., Irving Ravetch; ***C:*** Robert L. Surtees; ***M:*** John Williams.

Cowboys and Angels 1/2 **2000 (PG)** Danny (Trese) gets dumped by his fiancee on the eve of their wedding (in favor of his best friend) and isn't sure he'll ever love again. So Danny decides to make some changes—he'll follow his dream of becoming a cowboy. Then, the bubbly Jo Jo (Mitchell) comes into his life. However, Jo Jo has a secret (let's put it this way—she's the second half of the title) and tries to steer Danny's affections in the direction of the receptive Candace (Kirshner). **97m/C VHS, DVD.** Adam Trese, Radha Mitchell, Mia Kirshner, Hamilton von Watts, Carmen (Lee) Llywelyn; ***D:*** Gregory C. Haynes; ***W:*** Gregory C. Haynes; ***C:*** Kramer Morgenthau; ***M:*** Stephen (Steve) Edwards.

Cowboys & Angels **2004 (PG)** Shane (Legge), a straight-laced 20-year-old decides to break away from his family and move to the city on his own. He takes an apartment with Vincent (Leech), a charismatic gay art student. They strike up a friendship, and Shane develops the confidence to create a new life for himself, with its fresh possibilities and dangers. Hip, appealing Irish coming-of-age film with a great, unknown cast. Notable for its portrait of a healthy gay/straight friendship. **90m/C DVD.** Michael Legge, Allen Leech, Frank Kelly, David Murray, Amy Shiels; ***D:*** David Gleeson; ***W:*** David Gleeson; ***C:*** Volker Tittel; ***M:*** Stephen McKeon.

Cowboys Don't Cry **1988** When a modern cowboy's wife is killed in an automobile accident, he must change his immature ways and build a solid future with his teenage son or perish in loneliness. **96m/C VHS.** Rebecca Jenkins, Ron White, Janet-Laine Green; ***D:*** Anne Wheeler.

Cowboys from Texas 1/2 **1939** The Three Mesquiteers bring about a peaceful settlement to a fight between cattlemen and homesteaders. Part of "The Three Mesquiteers" series. **54m/B VHS.** Robert "Bob" Livingston, Raymond Hatton, Duncan Renaldo, Carole Landis; ***D:*** George Sherman; ***W:*** Oliver Drake; ***C:*** Ernest Miller.

Coyote Summer **1996 (G)** Troubled teen girl tries to help an untamed horse. **93m/C VHS.** Cindy Pickett, Ed Lauter, Gordon Tootoosis, Michelle St. John, Vinessa Shaw, Adam Beach, Bruce Weitz; ***D:*** Matias Alvarez; ***W:*** Karen Krenis; ***C:*** Brian Sullivan; ***M:*** Steve Dorff.

Coyote Trails 1/2 **1935** Standard western adventure has cowboy Tyler helping a damsel in distress. **68m/B VHS, UMD.** Tom Tyler, Ben (Benny) Corbett; ***D:*** Bernard B. Ray; ***W:*** Rose Gordon.

Coyote Ugly 1/2 **2000 (PG-13)** Producer Bruckheimer revisits the "Flashdance" formula for this tale of a young innocent songwriter (Perabo) who ends up slingin' drinks and barin' her navel in the eponymous bar while seeking fame and fortune in New York. The plot is as naive and wide-eyed as the main character, leaving no room for surprise twists, but allowing for a movie-saving performance by John Goodman as the concerned dad and a discovery in Aussie Garcia as the love interest. The rest of the cast consists of jiggly window dressing, but the PG-13 rating guarentees disappointment for a large segment of the audience. It's bad, but not in a career-destroying, "Showgirls" kind of way. **94m/C VHS, DVD, UMD.** Piper Perabo, Maria Bello, Tyra Banks, John Goodman, Melanie Lynskey, Ellen Cleghorne, Bud Cort, Izabella Miko, Bridget Moynahan, Adam Garcia, Del Pentacost, Michael Weston; ***D:*** David McNally; ***W:*** Todd Graff, Kevin Smith, Gina Wendkos; ***C:*** Amir M. Mokri; ***M:*** Trevor Horn.

Coyote Waits 1/2 **2003** Another adaptation of a Tony Hillerman novel, following "Skinwalker," about Navaho policemen Jim Chee (Beach) and Joe Leaphorn (Studi). Chee discovers the dead body of a fellow officer near some caves and finds drunken suspect Ashie Pinto (Herman) wandering the roads with a bottle and a gun. Since Leaphorn's wife Emma (Tousey) and Pinto are kin, she requests her husband investigate while Chee also has some questions. Pinto told legends involving Butch Cassidy to a local professor, who believed the outlaw survived Bolivia, only to die on the Navaho reservation. A Vietnamese immigrant with ties to the CIA and Native American mysticism all play their part but the slow-paced story is sometimes confusing. **105m/C VHS, DVD.** Wes Studi, Adam Beach, Sheila Tousey, Jimmy Herman, Keith Carradine, Graham Greene, Alex Rice, Bodhi (Pine) Elfman, Long Nguyen; ***D:*** Jan Egleson; ***W:*** Lucky Gold; ***C:*** Roy Wagner; ***M:*** B.C. Smith. **TV**

CQ **2001 (R)** It's 1969 and film editor Paul (Davies) is in Paris working on an arty futuristic thriller for egotistical director Andrezej (Depardieu) while filming his own black and white personal documentary. When the film's producer, Enzo (Giannini), fires the director, Paul winds up with the gig and has to come up with the slam-bang ending Enzo is demanding. Also demanding is leading lady Valentine (Lindvall), who is paying extra attention to her new director, which distracts Paul from the film and his French girlfriend Marlene (Bouchoz). Paul's a dull character and the film suffers for it but it's not bad for a first effort from Coppola (son of Francis and brother of Sofia). **92m/C VHS, DVD.** *US* Jeremy Davies, Elodie Bouchez, Angela Lindvall, Gerard Depardieu, Giancarlo Giannini, Massimo Ghini, Jason Schwartzman, Billy Zane, John Phillip Law, Dean Stockwell; ***D:*** Roman Coppola; ***W:*** Roman Coppola; ***C:*** Robert Yeoman.

Crack House **1989 (R)** A man seeks revenge for the murder of a relative by drug dealers. Average exploitation flick. **91m/C VHS, DVD.** Jim Brown, Richard Roundtree, Anthony Geary, Angel Tompkins, Greg Gomez Thomsen, Clyde Jones, Cheryl Kay; ***D:*** Michael Fischa; ***C:*** Arledge Armenaki.

A Crack in the Floor 1/2 **2000 (R)** Three couples go on a weekend hiking trip in the mountains and run into the deranged local folk. But their nightmare really begins when they make camp in a seemingly abandoned cabin that's not so empty after all. **90m/C VHS, DVD.** Gary Busey, David Naughton, Mario Lopez, Tracy Scoggins, Bo Hopkins, Rance Howard, Justine Priestley; ***D:*** Sean Stanek, Corbin Timbrook; ***W:*** Sean Stanek. **VIDEO**

Crack Shadow Boxers **1979** Through a series of misadventures, Wu Lung and Chu San battle to protect the inhabitants of a small village from the onslaught of relentless bandits. **91m/C VHS, DVD.** *HK* Ku Feng, Chou Li Lung, Han Guo Gai; ***D:*** Weng Yao Hai.

Crack-Up 1/2 **1946** Largely ignored at the time of its release, this tense tale is now regarded as a minor classic of film noir. An art expert suffers a blackout while investigating a possible forgery and must piece together the missing hours to uncover a criminal conspiracy. **70m/B VHS.** Pat O'Brien, Claire Trevor, Herbert Marshall, Ray Collins, Wallace Ford, Damian O'Flynn, Erskine Sanford; ***D:*** Irving Reis.

Crack Up **1997** Three buddies hit a losing streak and decide they can improve their lives by ripping off a drug house. They wind up with more than half a million in cash without the dealers having a clue as to who committed the crime. That is, until two newscasters decide to focus on the story—each tidbit of information leading the drug dealers closer to the guys' hideout and a deadly confrontation. **90m/C VHS.** John Sayre, Mike Terner, Steven Saucedo, Guilanno Bele, Gregg Madsen, Jenny Royar; ***D:*** Jeff Leroy; ***W:*** Jeff Leroy, Marc Lutz; ***M:*** Jeffrey Alan Jones. **VIDEO**

Cracked Nuts 1/2 **1941** Small town young man (Erwin) wins some dough and heads to New York to propose to his gal (Merkel). However, he gets mixed up with a shyster lawyer and a couple of con men with a fake robot. **61m/B VHS.** Stuart Erwin, Una Merkel, Mischa Auer, William Frawley, Shemp Howard, Mantan Moreland, Astrid Allwyn; ***D:*** Edward F. (Eddie) Cline; ***W:*** Scott Darling, Erna Lazarus; ***C:*** Charles Van Enger.

Cracker: Best Boys **1995** Typically involving psycho-mystery actually finds Fitz (Coltrane) on the wrong track. A murder precipitates a crime spree and Fitz originally beieves a man and woman are involved. Of course the viewer already knows repressed factory foreman Grady (Cunningham) has befriended troubled teenaged apprentice Bill (Simm) who's turned shockingly violent. Meanwhile, Judith (Flynn) has gone into an emotional tailspin, leaving Fitz to cope with the new baby. **?m/C VHS.** *GB* Robbie Coltrane, Liam Cunningham, John Simm, Ricky Tomlinson, Geraldine Somerville, Barbara Flynn; ***D:*** Tim Fywell; ***W:*** Paul Abbott.

Cracker: Brotherly Love **1995** Everyone carries lots of emotional baggage in this entry of the British series. Detective Jane Penhaligon (Somerville) is still suffering from the aftereffects of rape, which she believes was by colleague Jimmy Beck (Cranitch), who's just returned to duty following a breakdown. Meanwhile, Fitz's (Coltrane) mother has died bringing him into contact with his stodgy brother Danny (Russell). And yes, there are murders to investigate—a killer who likes prostitutes to dress up as little girls. **150m/C VHS.** *GB* Robbie Coltrane, Geraldine Somerville, Lorcan Cranitch, Ricky Tomlinson, Barbara Flynn, Clive Russell, Kieran O'Brien, Tessa Thompson, Brid Brennan, David Calder, Mark Lambert; ***D:*** Roy Battersby; ***W:*** Jimmy McGovern. **TV**

The Cracker Factory 1/2 **1979** Wood is impressive as a woman committed to a mental institution who attempts to charm her way out of treatment. **90m/C VHS.** Natalie Wood, Perry King, Shelley Long, Vivian Blaine, Juliet Mills, Peter Haskell; ***D:*** Burt Brinckerhoff; ***M:*** Billy Goldenberg. **TV**

Cracker: Men Should Weep 1/2 **1994** Fitz's skills are called into play when he must deal with a serial rapist (Aggrey). However, things become personal when Detective Jane Penhaligon (Somerville) is raped. **150m/C VHS, DVD.** *GB* Robbie Coltrane, Geraldine Somerville, Lorcan Cranitch, Graham Aggrey; ***D:*** Jean Stewart; ***W:*** Jimmy McGovern. **TV**

Cracker: The Big Crunch 1/2 **1994** The leader of a Christian fundamentalist sect has an affair with a schoolgirl and then plots her murder to avoid a scandal. But what he can't avoid is Fitz (Coltrane). **150m/C VHS, DVD.** *GB* Robbie Coltrane, Jim Carter, Samantha Morton, James Fleet, Cherith Mellor; ***D:*** Julian Jarrold; ***W:*** Jimmy McGovern, Ted Whitehead. **TV**

Cracker: To Be a Somebody **1994** The murder of an Asian shopkeeper first prompts the Manchester police to look for their suspect in the violent world of skinheads. But when the professor helping to profile the killer is murdered, the cops are forced to call in irascible forensic psychologist "Fitz" Fitzgerald (Coltrane) to aid in their investigation. Made for TV. **150m/C VHS, DVD.** *GB* Robbie Coltrane, Robert Carlyle, Barbara Flynn, Christopher Eccleston, Geraldine Somerville, Lorcan Cranitch; ***D:*** Tim Fywell; ***W:*** Jimmy McGovern. **TV**

Cracker: True Romance **1995** Fitz (Coltrane) becomes the target of obsessive romantic Janice (Joyce) who sends him love letters and begins killing young men to get his attention. But when his son Mark (O'Brien) is placed in danger it will take all Fitz's psychological skills to discover the truth before it's too late. Meanwhile, Judith (Flynn) finds a good listener in Fitz's brother Danny (Russell) and the two edge towards more than friendship. **?m/C VHS.** *GB* Robbie Coltrane, Ricky Tomlinson, Geraldine Somerville, Barbara Flynn, Kieran O'Brien, Robert Cavanah, Wilbert Johnson, Rosemary Martin, Clive Russell, Emily Joyce; ***D:*** Tim Fywell; ***W:*** Paul Abbott.

Crackerjack **1994 (R)** Chicago cop Jack Wild (Griffith) agrees to join his brother's family at a vacation resort in the Rocky Mountains. Coincidentally, a team of mercenaries are determined to hijack $50 million in diamonds from the resort and it's up to Jack to stop them. **96m/C VHS.** Thomas Ian Griffith, Nastassja Kinski, Christopher Plummer; ***D:*** Michael Mazo; ***W:*** Jonas Quastel, Michael Bafaro; ***C:*** Danny Nowak; ***M:*** Peter Allen.

Crackerjack 2 1/2 *Hostage Train; Crackerjack 2: Hostage Train* **1997 (R)** Cop Jack Wild (Reinhold) discovers that the train carrying his girlfriend, financial analyst Dana Townsend (Alt), and several of her wealthy clients has been hijacked by terrorists. The train is trapped by an explosion in a tunnel in the Rockies and Jack must rescue the passengers before the rest of the terrorists' plan goes into motion. **98m/C VHS.** Karel Roden, Judge Reinhold, Carol Alt, Michael Sarrazin; ***D:*** Robert Lee; ***W:*** Chris Hyde; ***C:*** John Herzog; ***M:*** Peter Allen.

Crackerjack 3 **2000 (PG-13)** Jack Thorn (Svenson) is an ex-Navy S.E.A.L. and the current director of the CIA's covert ops. He's planning to retire when he discovers his would-be replacement, Marcus Clay (Gruner), wants to cause a worldwide economic catastrophe. So Jack gathers together some fellow old-timers and tries to cope with high tech in order to save the world. **97m/C VHS, DVD.** Bo Svenson, Olivier Gruner, Leo Rossi, Amy Weber; ***D:*** Lloyd A. Simandl; ***M:*** Peter Allen. **VIDEO**

Crackers **1984 (PG)** The offbeat story of two bumbling thieves who round up a gang of equally inept neighbors and go on the wildest crime spree you have ever seen. A would-be comic remake of "Big Deal on Madonna Street." **92m/C VHS.** Donald Sutherland, Jack Warden, Sean Penn, Wallace Shawn, Larry Riley, Trinidad Silva, Christine Baranski, Charlaine Woodard, Tasia Valenza; ***D:*** Louis Malle.

Cracking Up 1/2 *Smorgasbord* **1983 (PG)** Accident-prone misfit's mishaps on the road to recovery create chaos for everyone he meets. Lewis plays a dozen characters in this overboard comedy with few laughs. **91m/C VHS.** Jerry Lewis, Herb Edelman, Foster Brooks, Milton Berle, Sammy Davis Jr., Zane Buzby, Dick Butkus, Buddy Lester; ***D:*** Jerry Lewis.

The Cradle 1/2 **2006** Frank (Haas) is hoping a change of scene will help the postpartum depression of his wife Julie (Hampshire) so he moves them to an isolated new home. Too bad the house comes with its own ghost—the vengeful spirit of a murdered child—and soon Frank is having hallucinations about danger for his infant son Sam. **107m/C DVD.** Lukas Haas, Emily Hampshire, Amanda Smith; ***D:*** Timothy Brown; ***W:*** Timothy Brown; ***C:*** Paul Nelson; ***M:*** Marcus Elliott. **VIDEO**

The Cradle of Courage **1920** Crook-turned-soldier Square Kelly (Maynard) returns from WWI to his San Francisco hometown and becomes a cop. This miffs his old gang and leader Tierney (Santschi) shoots Kelly's brother Jim (Thorwald) so Kelly tries to get revenge through legal means. **67m/B DVD.** William S. Hart, Thomas Santschi, Ann Little, Francis (Frank) Thorwald, Gertrude Claire; ***D:*** William S. Hart, Lambert Hillyer; ***W:*** Lambert Hillyer; ***C:*** Joseph August.

Cradle 2 the Grave 1/2 **2003 (R)** Jewel theif Fait (DMX) steals some black diamonds that draw attention from many factions, including Li's Taiwanese government agent Su and some oily, world-domination types led by Su's former partner and friend Ling (Dacascos), who isn't above kidnapping Fait's daughter to get what he wants. DMX is pretty good at looking all cool and bad-ass, but runs into trouble when acting is called for. Li, the only real reason to bother with this flick, provides all the martial arts action you'd expect, but looks kinda bored doing it. Anderson and Arnold are around for comic relief (take that info as warning or praise, depending on your tolerance for both). **100m/C VHS, DVD.** *US* Jet Li, DMX, Anthony Anderson, Kelly Hu, Tom Arnold, Mark Dacascos, Gabrielle Union, Michael Jace, Chi McBride, Paolo Seganti, Drag-On, Paige Hurd; ***D:*** Andrzej Bartkowiak; ***W:*** John O'Brien; ***C:*** Daryn Okada; ***M:*** John (Gianni) Frizzell, Damon Blackman.

The Cradle Will Fall WOOF! 1983 Adaptation of the pulpy bestselling mystery by Mary Higgins Clark about a woman who cannot convince anyone she witnessed a murder. The cast of "The Guiding Light" appear. Poor script and poor direction do not a thriller make. **103m/C VHS.** Lauren Hutton, Ben Murphy, James Farentino, Charita Bauer, Peter Simon; ***D:*** John Llewellyn Moxey. **TV**

The Cradle Will Rock 1/2 **1999 (R)** An exuberant if not always successful attempt by Robbins to capture the artistic/political fervor of New York in the '30s. Theatrical collaborators Orson Welles (Macfadyen) and John Houseman (Elwes) agree to produce Marc Blitzstein's (Azaria) new political musical "The Cradle Will Rock" for their Federal Theater company in 1937. Right-wing political interference closes the theater on opening night but Welles leads his company to another venue in Manhattan where the actors (because of their union) must perform the piece from the audience—the dramatic circumstances offering a unique success and a place in theatre history. **133m/C VHS, DVD.** Angus MacFadyen, Cary Elwes, Hank Azaria, Cherry Jones, Ruben Blades, Joan Cusack, John Cusack, Philip Baker Hall, Bill Murray, Vanessa Redgrave, Susan Sarandon, Jamey Sheridan, John Turturro, Emily Watson, Bob Balaban, Paul Giamatti, Barnard Hughes, Barbara Sukowa, John Carpenter, Gretchen Mol, Harris Yulin, Dominic Chianese, Jack Black, Kyle Gass, Lee Arenberg, Daniel H. Jenkins, Peter Jacobson; ***D:*** Tim Robbins; ***W:*** Tim Robbins; ***C:*** Jean-Yves Escoffier; ***M:*** David Robbins.

The Craft 1/2 **1996 (R)** Call it "Heathers" with hexes. Troubled 17-year-old Sarah (Tunney) moves to L.A. and begins her senior year at St. Benedict's Academy. She takes up with three rebels—Nancy (Balk), Bonnie (Campbell), and Rochelle (True)—who like to dabble in witchcraft. Now, with the addition of would-be witch Sarah, these black magic women start slinging spells at their uppity classmates. Works best when concentrating on the girls and their problems, but degenerates into a special effects barrage toward the end. Alas, no one is turned into a newt. **100m/C VHS, DVD.** Robin Tunney, Fairuza Balk, Neve Campbell, Rachel True, Skeet Ulrich, Helen Shaver, Cliff DeYoung, Christine Taylor, Assumpta Serna; ***D:*** Andrew Fleming; ***W:*** Andrew Fleming, Peter Filardi; ***C:*** Alexander Grusynski; ***M:*** Graeme Revell. MTV Movie Awards '97: Fight (Fairuza Balk/Robin Tunney).

Craig's Wife **1936** A classic soap opera about a pitiful woman driven to total ruin by her desire for social acceptance and material wealth. Russell makes her surprisingly sympathetic. Based on a Pulitzer Prize-winning George Kelly play. Remake of a silent film, was also remade as "Harriet Craig." **75m/B VHS.** Rosalind Russell, John Boles, Alma Kruger, Jane Darwell, Billie Burke; ***D:*** Dorothy Arzner.

Crainquebille **1923** The classic satire based on the Anatole France story about a street merchant in Paris unfairly imprisoned and eventually surviving peacefully as a tramp. Silent. **50m/B VHS, DVD.** *FR* Maurice Feraudy; ***D:*** Jacques Feyder.

The Cranes Are Flying 1/2 *Letyat Zhuravit* **1957** When her lover goes off to fight during WWII, a girl is seduced by his cousin. Touching love story is free of politics. Filmed in Russia; English subtitles. **91m/B VHS, DVD.** *RU* Tatyana Samoilova, Alexei Batalov, Vasily Merkuryev, A. Shvorin; ***D:*** Mikhail Kalatozov; ***W:*** Viktor Rozov; ***C:*** Sergei Urusevsky; ***M:*** Moisej Vajnberg. Cannes '58: Film.

Cranford 1/2 **2008** Cranford is a seemingly quaint and quiet English village in 1842 that's about to undergo a profound upheaval, thanks to the expansion of the railroad. Its society is held in check by the local widows and spinsters who know everyone and gossip about everything. There's a number of accidents, deaths, would-be romances, engagements, misunderstandings, financial hardships, and societal changes for everyone to endure and overcome as at least some of the inhabitants find longed-for happiness. Based on the novel by Elizabeth Gaskell. **295m/C DVD.** *GB* Judi Dench, Simon Woods, Imelda Staunton, Julia McKenzie, Barbara Flynn, Francesca Annis, Julia Sawalha, Emma Fielding, Philip Glenister, Jim Carter, John Bowe, Greg Wise, Joseph McFadden, Michael Gambon, Eileen Atkins, Lisa Dillon, Kimberly Nixon, Alex Etel, Alex Jennings; ***D:*** Simon Curtis, Steve Hudson; ***W:*** Heidi Thomas; ***C:*** Ben Smithard; ***M:*** Carl Davis. **TV**

Crank 1/2 **2006 (R)** Mindlessly enjoyable "B" pic and proud of it. Freelance assassin Chev Chelios (Statham) learns his rival Ricky (Cantillo) has injected him with a toxin that kills if his heart rate drops too low. The only way Chev can fight the toxin is to continuously pump up his adrenaline, which leads him to rampage through LA in search of revenge, an antidote, and thrills of any kind. The premise is a variation on the 1950 noir "D.O.A." and it actually works if you don't think about it. **87m/C DVD, Blu-ray Disc.** *US* Jose Pablo Cantillo, Jason Statham, Amy Smart, Efren Ramirez, Dwight Yoakam, Carlos Sanz, Reno Wilson; ***D:*** Mark Neveldine, Brian Taylor; ***W:*** Mark Neveldine, Brian Taylor; ***C:*** Adam Biddle; ***M:*** Paul Haslinger.

Crank: High Voltage *Crank 2: High Voltage* **2009 (R)** Picking up right where the first movie left off, Chev (Statham) survives a climactic plunge to his most certain death on the streets of Los Angeles, only to be kidnapped by a mysterious Chinese mobster. Three months later, he wakes up to discover his nearly indestructible heart has been surgically removed and replaced with a battery-operated ticker that requires regular jolts of electricity in order to work. While he attends to that, he's also on a chase through L.A. to get his heart back. Takes over-the-top to a new level, as only the narrowest of target audiences will find the unrelenting violence, blood, nudity, and impossible action sequences the least bit entertaining. **96m/C DVD.** *US* Jason Statham, Corey Haim, Amy Smart, Bai Ling, Efren Ramirez, Dwight Yoakam, Clifton (Gonzalez) Collins Jr.; ***D:*** Mark Neveldine, Brian Taylor; ***W:*** Brian Taylor; ***C:*** Brandon Trost.

Crash **1995 (NC-17)** You can always expect surreal kinkiness from Cronenberg and this film, awarded a Special Jury Prize at Cannes for "daring, originality, and audacity," won't prove the exception. It's "auto" erotica taken to the max, with car crashes and bodily injury turned into fetishes. James (Spader) lands in the hospital after an accident, which injured Helen (Hunter), a passenger in the other car. Helen and James' shared experience soon leads to a sexual relationship, which doesn't bother James' wife, Catherine (Unger). Then there's Vaughan (Koteas) and his group, who like to reenact famous auto crashes (like those of James Dean and Jayne Mansfield). Oh yes, there's lots more sex (in various combinations). Based on J.G. Ballard's 1973 cult novel. An R-rated version clocks in at 90 minutes. **98m/C VHS, DVD.** *CA* James Spader, Holly Hunter, Elias Koteas, Deborah Kara Unger, Rosanna Arquette, Peter MacNeill; ***D:*** David Cronenberg; ***W:*** David Cronenberg; ***C:*** Peter Suschitzky; ***M:*** Howard Shore. Cannes '96: Special Jury Prize; Genie '96: Adapt. Screenplay, Cinematog., Director (Cronenberg), Film Editing.

Crash 1/2 **2005 (R)** From the writer of "Million Dollar Baby" comes this racially charged ensemble piece, which follows numerous lives intersecting over a 36-hour period in the volatile melting pot of L.A. Opening with a car-jacking, a central event that connects most of the characters, Haggis' drama meditates on the levels of class conflict between cops, criminals, showbiz types, and various ethnic and racial groups. A bit preachy at times, but the cast is so uniformly strong and the characters so multi-layered, you won't care. Cheadle, as always, stands out, but even the ensemble's typically bland Hollywood actors (Bullock, Fraser, Phillippe) acquit themselves nicely. **100m/C DVD, Blu-ray Disc, UMD.** *US* Ludacris, Sandra Bullock, Don Cheadle, Matt Dillon, Jennifer Esposito, William Fichtner, Brendan Fraser, Terrence Howard, Thandie Newton, Ryan Phillippe, Larenz Tate, Nona Gaye, Michael Pena, Beverly Todd, Keith David, Shaun Toub, Loretta Devine; ***D:*** Paul Haggis; ***W:*** Paul Haggis, Robert Moresco; ***C:*** J.(James) Michael Muro; ***M:*** Mark Isham. Oscars '05: Film, Film Editing, Orig. Screenplay; British Acad. '05: Orig. Screenplay, Support. Actress (Newton); Ind. Spirit '06: First Feature, Support. Actor (Dillon); Natl. Bd. of Review '05: Breakthrough Perf. (Howard); Screen Actors Guild '05: Cast; Writers Guild '05: Orig. Screenplay.

Crash and Burn 1/2 **1990 (R)** Rebels in a repressive future police state reactivate a huge, long-dormant robot to battle the establishment's army of powerful androids. Special effects by David Allen make the mayhem interesting. **85m/C VHS, DVD.** Ralph Waite, Paul Ganus, Eva LaRue, Bill Moseley, Jack McGee; ***D:*** Charles Band; ***W:*** J.S. Cardone; ***M:*** Richard Band.

Crash and Burn 1/2 **2007** Pretty much what this dull crime actioner does. Car thief Kevin (Palladino) delivers his latest ride to L.A. choppers Hill (Moscow) and Winston (Jason), who work for crime boss Vincent (Madsen). Kevin runs into ex-squeeze Penny (Marsden), who's unhappy Kev's still a criminal. But really Kevin is working undercover for the FBI, not only to bust Vincent but a rival gang of 'jackers who have turned to murder to protect their turf. **85m/C DVD.** Erik Palladino, Michael Madsen, Heather Marie Marsden, David Moscow, Peter Jason, Lobo Sebastian, Anthony John (Tony) Denison, Owen Beckman, Tom O'Keefe; ***D:*** Russell Mulcahy; ***W:*** Frank Hannah, Jack LoGiudice; ***C:*** Maximo Munzi; ***M:*** Jeff Rona. **TV**

Crash & Byrnes 1/2 **1999** Jack "Crash" Riley (Larson) is a retired CIA agent who is reluctantly called back into service to bring down a bioterrorist. A by-the-book kinda guy, Crash is, of course, paired with loose cannon DEA agent Roman Byrnes (Ellis). If the two can ever figure out a way to work together, they may just accomplish their mission. Standard fare in the wannabe "Lethal Weapon" mold. **92m/C VHS, DVD.** *CA* Wolf Larson, Greg Ellis, Joanna Pacula, Steven Williams, Sandra Lindquist, Terry Chen, Melanie Angel; ***D:*** Jon Hess; ***W:*** Wolf Larson; ***C:*** Anthony C. Metchie; ***M:*** Ken Williams.

Crash Course 1/2 *A Mother's Fight for Justice* **2000** Terry Stone's (Baxter) college student son Terry (Lively) is critically injured in a car crash and suffers from severe brain trauma. Since the accident was caused by a drunk driver, Terry seeks justice while Andrew struggles to regain his life. Based on a true story. **91m/C VHS, DVD.** Meredith Baxter, Alan Rosenberg, Eric Lively; ***D:*** Thomas (Tom) Rickman. **CABLE**

Crash Dive 1/2 **1943** WWII glory film provides comic relief in the form of romance. Second-in-command Power falls hopelessly in love with school teacher Baxter, only to find out later that she is Lt. Commander Andrews' fiance. Once this little tidbit of information is disclosed, the two officers embark on a mission to destroy a Nazi U-Boat responsible for laying mines in the North Atlantic. Fantastic special effects and sound. Based on the story by W.R. Burnett. **105m/B VHS, DVD.** Tyrone Power, Anne Baxter, Dana Andrews, James Gleason, May Whitty, Harry (Henry) Morgan, Ben Carter, Frank Conroy, Florence Lake, John Archer, Minor Watson, Kathleen Howard, Stanley Andrews, Thurston Hall, Trudy Marshall, Charles Tannen, Chester Gan; ***D:*** Archie Mayo; ***W:*** Jo Swerling, W.R. Burnett; ***C:*** Leon Shamroy; ***M:*** David Buttolph.

Crash Dive **1996 (R)** An atomic submarine is taken hostage by Richter (Schone) and his band of terrorists, who demand $1 billion in gold or Washington D.C. will become a nuclear disaster. Naturally, there's one hero—sub designer James Carter (Dudikoff)—who manages to sneak aboard and plots to save the day. Fast pace and top special effects make this one watchable. **90m/C VHS, DVD.** Michael Dudikoff, Reiner Schone, Frederic Forrest, Jay Acovone; ***D:*** Andrew Stevens; ***W:*** William Martell; ***C:*** Michael Slovis; ***M:*** Eric Wurst, David Wurst. **VIDEO**

The Crash of Flight 401 1/2 **1978** A plane, full of recognizable TV stars, crashes in the Florida Everglades. "Airport" for a smaller screen. Based on a real event. **97m/C VHS.** William Shatner, Adrienne Barbeau, Eddie Albert, Brooke Bundy, Christopher Connelly, Lorraine Gary, Ron Glass, Sharon Gless, Brett Halsey, George Maharis, Gerald S. O'Loughlin; ***D:*** Barry Shear. **TV**

Crashing **2007 (R)** Richard McMurray (Scott) was once a successful writer with a trophy wife and a house in Malibu. Now he's middle-aged, divorced, homeless, and suffering from extended writer's block. While guest-lecturing in a college writing class, he casually mentions his lack of a bed and is offered the couch in lithesome Jacqueline's (Caplan) and Kristin's (Miko) tiny apartment. Soon they're involved in a breezy ménage a trois and all are using their new arrangement to ignite their literary aspirations. No one seems conflicted, which makes a nice change from angsty musings on morality and sex. **80m/C DVD.** Campbell Scott, Lizzy Caplan, Izabella Miko, Alex Kingston; ***D:*** Gary Walkow; ***W:*** Gary Walkow; ***C:*** Andrew Huebscher; ***M:*** Ernest Troost.

Crashout 1/2 **1955** Six men break out of prison in this entertaining melodrama. Bendix plays the gang's leader to nasty perfection. **88m/B VHS.** William Bendix, Gene Evans, Arthur Kennedy, Luther Adler, William Talman, Marshall Thompson, Beverly Michaels, Gloria Talbott, Adam Williams, Percy Helton, Melinda Markey, Morris Ankrum; ***D:*** Lewis R. Foster; ***W:*** Hal E. Chester; ***C:*** Russell Metty; ***M:*** Leith Stevens.

The Crater Lake Monster WOOF! 1977 (PG) The dormant egg of a prehistoric creature hatches after a meteor rudely awakens the dozing dino. He's understandably miffed and begins a revenge campaign. Prehistoric yawner. **85m/C VHS, DVD.** Richard Cardella, Glenn Roberts, Mark Siegel, Bob Hyman, Kacey Cobb; ***D:*** William R. Stromberg; ***W:*** Richard Cardella; ***C:*** Paul Gentry.

The Craving *Return of the Wolfman; El Retorno del Hombre-Lobo* **1980 (R)** Naschy (AKA Jacinto Molina) returns as El Hombre Lobo for the umpteenth time and once again battles a female vampire (see "Werewolf vs. the Vampire Woman"). Although continental Europe's biggest horror star, this film was such a boxoffice disaster that Naschy went bankrupt. He was then forced to turn to Japan for financing (see "The Human Beasts"). Naschy/Molina directed under the pseudonym "Jack" Molina. **93m/C VHS.** *SP* Paul Naschy, Julie Saly, Silvia Aguilar, Azucena Hernandez, Beatriz Elorietta, Pilar Alcon; ***D:*** Paul Naschy.

Cravings *Daddy's Girl* **2006 (R)** Disturbing Brit psycho-horror. Widowed shrink Stephen (whose own wife committed suicide by slashing her wrists) gets a new patient in disturbed teen Nina, who cut her wrists and then drank the blood. Her mother, Liz, thinks Stephen treating Nina isn't a good idea since she's easily fixated. Stephen and Liz soon become sexually involved. **90m/C DVD.** *GB* Richard Harrington, Jaime Winstone, Louise Delamere, Ifan Huw Dafydd, Mark Lewis Jones, Katie Owen; ***D:*** D.J. Evans; ***W:*** D.J. Evans; ***C:*** Jonathan Bloom; ***M:*** Owen Powell, Rob Reed.

The Crawlers **1993 (R)** Illegal radioactive dumping has caused a living, lethal organism to invade in a small western town. Seems the local sheriff and the nuclear plant manager were partners in a toxic dumping scheme that went awry and two teenagers are the only ones willing to expose the truth. More to the point—scary monster attacks woman with artistically enhanced cleavage. Laurenti used the pseudonym Martin Newlin. **94m/C VHS.** Jason Saucier, Mary Sellers; ***D:*** Fabrizio Laurenti; ***W:*** Dan Price, Fabrizio Laurenti.

The Crawling Eye 🦴🦴 *The Trollenberg Terror* **1958** Hidden in a radioactive fog on a mountaintop, the crawling eye decapitates its victims and returns these humans to Earth to threaten mankind. Average acting, but particularly awful special effects. Based on a British TV series. **87m/B VHS, DVD.** *GB* Forrest Tucker, Laurence Payne, Janet Munro, Jennifer Jayne, Warren Mitchell; ***D:*** Quentin Lawrence; ***W:*** Jimmy Sangster; ***M:*** Stanley Black.

The Crawling Hand WOOF! 1963 An astronaut's hand takes off without him on an unearthly spree of stranglings. Silly stuff is a hands-down loser. **98m/B VHS, DVD.** Kent Taylor, Peter Breck, Rod Lauren, Sirry Steffen, Alan Hale Jr., Richard Arlen, Allison Hayes, Arline Judge; ***D:*** Herbert L. Strock; ***W:*** Herbert L. Strock; ***C:*** Willard Van der Veer.

Crawlspace 🦴 **1986 (R)** Beautiful girls lease rooms from a murdering, perverted doctor who spies on them, then kills. You may find Kinski amusing but not terrifying. **86m/C VHS, DVD.** Klaus Kinski, Talia Balsam, Joyce Van Patten, Sally Brown, Barbara Whinnery; ***D:*** David Schmoeller; ***W:*** David Schmoeller; ***M:*** Pino Donaggio.

Craze 🦴🦴 *The Infernal Idol; Demon Master* **1974 (R)** Toungue-in-cheek tale of a crazed antique dealer who slays a number of women as sacrifices to an African idol named Chuku. **96m/C VHS, DVD.** Jack Palance, Diana Dors, Julie Ege, Suzy Kendall, Michael Jayston, Edith Evans, Hugh Griffith, Trevor Howard; ***D:*** Freddie Francis.

Crazed WOOF! 1982 Dull plodder about a psychopath who keeps a dead girl's body in his boarding house and kills all intruders to keep his secret. **88m/C VHS.** Laszlo Papas, Belle Mitchell, Beverly Ross; ***D:*** Richard Cassidy.

Crazed Cop 🦴 *One Way Out* **1988** A man's mind snaps when his wife is found raped and murdered, and nothing will stop him on his quest for revenge. Low budget and violent. **85m/C VHS.** Ivan Rogers, Sandy Brooke, Rich Sutherlin, Doug Irk, Abdulah the Great; ***D:*** Paul Kyriazi.

The Crazies 🦴🦴 *Code Name: Trixie* **1973 (R)** A poisoned water supply makes the residents of a small town go on a chaotic, murderous rampage. When the army is called into to quell the anarchy, a small war breaks out. Message film about the military is muddled and derivative. **103m/C VHS, DVD.** Lane Carroll, Will MacMillan, Harold W. Jones, Lloyd Hollar, Lynn Lowry, Richard France, Richard Liberty, Will Disney, Harry Spillman; ***D:*** George A. Romero; ***W:*** George A. Romero; ***C:*** Bill (William Heinzman) Hinzman; ***M:*** Bruce Roberts.

The Crazies 🦴🦴 **2009 (R)** A biological weapon makes its way into the water supply of a small town, causing the townsfolk to lose their minds in a violent rage and die. Sheriff Dutton (Olyphant) and crew must defend themselves from the crazed masses, while the government responds by shutting the town off from the rest of the world. A remake of the George Romero classic, the movie offers up great screams, thrills, and other key elements of the horror genre, but misses Romero's social satire and mistrust of authority that provided the original such unique tension. **101m/C DVD.** *US* Timothy Olyphant, Radha Mitchell, Joe Reegan; ***D:*** Breck Eisner; ***W:*** Ray Wright, Scott Kosar; ***C:*** Maxime Alexandre.

Crazy as Hell 🦴🦴 ½ **2002 (R)** Eriq La Salle makes his feature directorial debut in this uneven swirl of psychiatric and metaphysical themes. Renowned psychiatrist Dr. Adams (Beach) arrives at a mental hospital to treat a group of patients using his controversial methods. Fueling his already robust superiority complex, his efforts are being filmed by weaselly documentary maker Parker (McGinley). When a seemingly rational man admits himself into the hospital claiming to be Satan (La Salle), Adams begins to lose control of his patients and his own sanity. Worthwhile for La Salle's performance but seems to drag when he's not on screen. **113m/C VHS, DVD.** Eriq La Salle, Michael Beach, Ronny Cox, John C. McGinley, Tia Texada, Sinbad, Tracy Pettit; ***D:*** Eriq La Salle; ***W:*** Erik Jendresen, Jeremy Leven, Butch Robinson; ***C:*** George Mooradian; ***M:*** Billy Childs.

crazy/beautiful 🦴🦴 ½ **2001 (PG-13)** Cultural clash and teen relationship troubles all set in the affluent neighborhood of Pacific Palisades. Latino Carlos (Hernandez), from the wrong-side-of-the tracks in East L.A., is going to the rich high school in order to better himself. Nicole (Dunst) is the self-destructive wealthy chick (and congressman's daughter) who shows him that money doesn't buy happiness because she's got troubles, man. Familiar teen flick redeemed somewhat by the lead performances with handsome newcomer Hernandez appealing as a decent guy who's intrigued by willful, misunderstood hottie Dunst. **99m/C VHS, DVD.** *US* Kirsten Dunst, Jay Hernandez, Taryn Manning, Rolando Molina, Bruce Davison, Lucinda Jenney, Soledad St. Hilaire; ***D:*** John Stockwell; ***W:*** Phil Hay, Matt Manfredi; ***C:*** Shane Hurlbut; ***M:*** Paul Haslinger.

Crazy Eights 🦴 **2006 (R)** You don't expect Oscar-caliber work in a cheap horror flick but it would be nice if the plot was at least semi-coherent. Six childhood friends reunite after 20 years for a friend's funeral. In his will said friend requests that they open the trunk they buried as kids. In the trunk, they find the decayed corpse of a young girl. Somehow the group then becomes trapped in an abandoned psychiatric hospital where the girl's ghost starts killing them off. So they have to figure out their past connection to the hospital and the dead girl. **80m/C DVD.** Traci Lords, Dina Meyer, Gabrielle Anwar, Frank Whaley, George Newbern, Dan DeLuca; ***D:*** James Koya Jones; ***W:*** Dan DeLuca, James Koya Jones; ***C:*** Stephen M. Lyons; ***M:*** Olivier Glissant.

Crazy Fat Ethel II WOOF! 1985 A fat, hungry, homicidal female psychopath gets released from the asylum and goes on a cannabilistic rampage. Offensive junk. Sequel to "Criminally Insane." **90m/C VHS.** Priscilla Alden, Michael Flood, Robert Copple; ***D:*** Nick (Steve Millard) Phillips.

Crazy for Love 🦴🦴 ½ *Le Trou Normand* **1952** A village idiot stands to inherit the town inn if he can get a diploma within a year. With English subtitles. **80m/B VHS.** *FR* Brigitte Bardot, Andre Bourvil, Jane (Jeanne) Marken, Nadine Basile; ***D:*** Jean Boyer; ***W:*** Arlette De Pitray; ***M:*** Paul Misraki.

Crazy from the Heart 🦴🦴🦴 **1991** Sweet cable romance finds Charlotte Bain (Lahti), the straitlaced high school principal in a small south Texas town, changing her ways. Charlotte surprises herself by agreeing to a date with the school's new janitor, Ernesto (Blades), and what's even more shocking to them both is how much they enjoy each other's company over one wild weekend. Strong, nuanced performances from Lahti and Blades make this chestnut of a story work beautifully, with able help from supporting actors. **104m/C VHS.** Christine Lahti, Ruben Blades, Mary Kay Place, Brent Spiner, William Russ, Louise Latham, Tommy Muntz, Robin (Robyn) Lively, Bibi Besch, Kamala Lopez; ***D:*** Thomas Schlamme; ***W:*** Linda Voorhees. **CABLE**

Crazy Heart 🦴🦴 ½ **2009 (R)** The plot is a country & western cliche but Bridges' vanity-free performance elevates the film above it. A physical and financial wreck, Bad Blake still has the charm and loves the music but he's a has-been reduced to croaking at bowling alley venues thanks to too much hard living. Sympathetic—and much younger—Santa Fe journalist/single mom Jean Craddock (Gyllenhaal) offers an unexpected lifeline as does Bad's very successful protege Tommy Sweet (Farrell) who gives him an opening act gig and the push to write some new songs. And yep, Bridges and Farrell are solid doing their own singing. Based on the 1987 novel by Thomas Cobb. **112m/C DVD.** *US* Jeff Bridges, Maggie Gyllenhaal, Robert Duvall, Colin Farrell, Tom Bower, James Keane, William Marquez; ***D:*** Scott Cooper; ***W:*** Scott Cooper; ***C:*** Barry Markowitz; ***M:*** T-Bone Burnett, Stephen Bruton. Oscars '09: Actor (Bridges), Song ("The Weary Kind"); Golden Globes '10: Actor—Drama (Bridges), Song ("The Weary Kind"); Ind. Spirit '10: Actor (Bridges), First Feature; Screen Actors Guild '09: Actor (Bridges).

Crazy Horse 🦴🦴🦴 **1996** TV bio of the Oglala Sioux warrior (Greyeyes) whose home in the Black Hills of South Dakota was threatened by western expansion and the constant breaking of government treaties. As war chief, Crazy Horse, along with Teton Sioux leader Sitting Bull (Schellenberg), lead the Cheyenne and Sioux against Custer (Horton) at the battle of Little Bighorn. They elude capture but constant harassment by troops lead to Crazy Horse's surrender and death in 1877, betrayed by both the whites and some of his own people. Gripping story with a fine cast. **120m/C VHS.** Michael Greyeyes, Jimmy Herman, Wes Studi, Irene Bedard, Peter Horton, John Finn, Steve Reevis, Gordon Tootoosis, August Schellenberg, Sheldon Peters Wolfchild, Ned Beatty; ***D:*** John Irvin; ***W:*** Robert Schenkkan; ***C:*** Thomas Burstyn; ***M:*** Lennie Niehaus.

Crazy Horse and Custer: "The Untold Story" 🦴 **1990 (R)** Long before Little Big Horn, two legendary enemies find themselves trapped together in deadly Blackfoot territory. George Armstrong Custer and Crazy Horse are forced to form a volatile alliance in their life-or-death struggle against the murderous Blackfoot Tribe. History takes a back seat to Hollywood scriptwriting. **120m/C VHS, DVD.** Slim Pickens, Wayne Maunder, Mary Ann Mobley, Michael Dante; ***D:*** Norman Foster; ***C:*** Harold E. Stine; ***M:*** Leith Stevens.

Crazy House 🦴🦴 ½ **1943** Olsen and Johnson have a fabulous follow up to their 'Hellzapoppin' feature but get refused by every studio in town, leading them to try and shoot the picture themselves. Much slapstick and great cameos ensue, including Shemp Howard, Count Basie, plus Basil Rathbone and Nigel Bruce as their famous sleuths. **80m/B VHS.** Ole Olsen, Chic Johnson, Martha O'Driscoll; ***Cameos:*** Cass Daley; ***D:*** Edward F. (Eddie) Cline, Frederic Rinaldo; ***W:*** Robert Lees. **VIDEO**

Crazy in Alabama 🦴 ½ **1999 (PG-13)** If they greenlighted this southern fried mess, they're crazy in Hollywood, too. Lucille (Griffith) is an unbalanced aging southern belle who decapitates her husband and heads off to fulfill her dream of becoming a Hollywood star. She also takes his severed noggin with her, although it is a little talkative. Woven through this bizarre storyline is another that focuses on Lucille's nephew Peejoe back home in Alabama as he stands up to a bigoted sheriff, helps protest for civil rights and meets Martin Luther King. Banderas' directoral debut is fine technically, but veers wildly all over the road as far as content goes. **111m/C VHS, DVD.** Melanie Griffith, David Morse, Lucas Black, Cathy Moriarty, Meat Loaf Aday, Rod Steiger, Richard Schiff, John Beasley, Robert Wagner, Noah Emmerich, Sandra Seacat, Paul Ben-Victor, Brad Beyer, Fannie Flagg, Elizabeth Perkins, Linda Hart, Paul Mazursky, William Converse-Roberts, Holmes Osborne, David Speck; ***D:*** Antonio Banderas; ***W:*** Mark Childress; ***C:*** Julio Macat; ***M:*** Mark Snow.

Crazy in Love 🦴🦴 ½ **1992** Three generations of women live on an island in the home that has been in their family for years. Hunter is wildly in love with her husband, but misses (and doesn't quite trust) him when he is away on business. Enter Sands, who showers her with affection and fills the void in her life. The supporting cast fleshes out the story nicely and illustrates the reasons behind Hunter's insecurity. Enjoyable romantic comedy doesn't throw out anything heavy. Adapted from the novel by Luanne Rice. **93m/C VHS.** Holly Hunter, Gena Rowlands, Bill Pullman, Julian Sands, Frances McDormand, Herta Ware, Joanne Baron; ***D:*** Martha Coolidge; ***W:*** Gerald Ayres. **TV**

Crazy Like a Fox 🦴 ½ **2004 (PG-13)** No, just crazy. Irresponsible Nat Banks (Rees) is the 8th generation to live on his now-impoverished family farm in Virginia. Forced to sell, Nat makes what he thinks is a deal with some northern land speculators to save the property and allow him and his family to continue to live on it. Instead, the Yankee carpetbaggers plan to turn the farm into a subdivision. So Nat retaliates by putting on a (no doubt original) Confederate uniform, hiding out in a cave, and practicing some guerilla warfare. Probably plays best south of the Mason-Dixon line. **99m/C DVD.** Roger Rees, Mary McDonnell, Robert Wisdom, Mark Joy, Paul Fitzgerald, Christina Rouner; ***D:*** Richard Squires; ***W:*** Richard Squires; ***C:*** Gary Grieg; ***M:*** David Kane, Richard Squires.

Crazy Little Thing 🦴🦴 ½ *The Perfect You* **2002 (R)** That "thing" would be love, of course. But reporter Whitney (McCarthy), newly arrived in New York, tells her friend Dee (de Matteo) that she's only looking for sex. So Dee sends her to a certain bar where Whitney can hire a male escort for the evening. Meanwhile, waiter Jimmy (Eigeman) is also hoping to get lucky and happens to turn up at the same bar. Whitney thinks Jimmy knows the score but after a night of wild sex, Jimmy turns out to want more than a one-night stand. **90m/C VHS, DVD.** Christopher Eigeman, Jenny McCarthy, Drea De Matteo, Paul Dooley, Alanna Ubach; ***D:*** Matthew Miller; ***W:*** Matthew Miller; ***C:*** Michael Barrett; ***M:*** Adam Dorn.

Crazy Love 🦴🦴🦴 **2007 (PG-13)** Documentary tells of the bizarre romance of Bronx-born ambulance-chasing attorney Burt Pugach and a stunning younger woman, Linda Riss, who breaks things off when she discovers he is married. Her departure pushes the obsessive Pugach over the edge, and he contracts three wiseguys to throw acid in her face, disfiguring and partially blinding her. Somehow the strength of attraction wins out, unthinkably bringing Burt and Linda together again. The film includes interviews with the couple, old friends, and reporters who covered the case as well as news footage and photographs. This is way too weird to be made up. **92m/C DVD.** *US* Burt Pugach, Lisa Riss Pugach; ***D:*** Dan Klores; ***C:*** Wolfgang Held; ***M:*** Douglas J. Cuomo. Ind. Spirit '08: Feature Doc.

Crazy Mama 🦴🦴 ½ **1975 (PG)** Three women go on a crime spree from California to Arkansas, picking up men and having a hoot. Crime and comedy in a campy romp. Set in the 1950s and loaded with period kitsch. **81m/C VHS, DVD.** Cloris Leachman, Stuart Whitman, Ann Sothern, Jim Backus, Linda Purl, Donny Most, Sally Kirkland, Dick Miller, Bill Paxton; ***D:*** Jonathan Demme; ***W:*** Robert Thom; ***C:*** Bruce Logan.

Crazy Moon 🦴🦴 ½ *Huggers* **1987 (PG-13)** A rich high school nerd falls in love with a deaf girl, and must struggle against his domineering father's and older brother's prejudices. The viewer must struggle against the romantic cliches and heavy-handed message to enjoy a basically tender tale of romance. **89m/C VHS.** Kiefer Sutherland, Vanessa Vaughan, Peter Spence, Ken Pogue, Eve Napier; ***D:*** Allan Eastman; ***W:*** Tom Berry, Stefan Wodoslowsky; ***M:*** Lou Forestieri.

Crazy on the Outside 🦴 ½ **2010 (PG-13)** Unfortunately, Allen's directorial debut (in which he also stars) is a weak and generic comedy that doesn't appear worthy of a big screen. Tommy (Allen) was in the big house for video piracy. After being released, the ex-con moves in with his over-protective sister Vicky (Weaver) and her skeptical husband Ed (Simmons) and tries to start over. First he gets a job in a pirate-themed fast food joint, then he meets up with former flame Christy (Bowen), and then Tommy finds that he's actually attracted to his single-mom parole officer, Angela (Tripplehorn). Too bad his old partner-in-crime Gray (Liotta) wants Tommy in on his latest scheme. The female roles are mostly one-note and some of the acting gets sitcom cartoonish. **96m/C DVD.** *US* Tim Allen, Julie Bowen, Sigourney Weaver, Ray Liotta, Jeanne Tripplehorn, Kelsey Grammer, J.K. Simmons, Jon(athan) Gries, Helen Slayton-Hughes; ***D:*** Tim Allen; ***W:*** Judd Pillot, John Peaslee; ***C:*** Robbie Greenberg; ***M:*** David Newman.

Crazy People 🦴 ½ **1990 (R)** Advertising exec Emory Leeston (Moore) writes commercials that describe products with complete honesty, and is committed to a mental hospital as a result. He meets a variety of characters at the hospital, including Hannah, with whom he falls in love. Tepid boxoffice blunder sounds funnier than it is. We give half a bone for the ad slogans, the funniest part of the movie. Our favorite: "Most of our passengers arrive alive" for an airline. **91m/C VHS, DVD.** Dudley Moore, Daryl Hannah, Paul Reiser, Mercedes Ruehl, J.T. Walsh, Ben Hammer, Richard (Dick) Cusack, Alan North, David Paymer, Danton Stone, Doug Yasuda, Bill Smitrovich, Paul Bates, Floyd Vivino; ***D:*** Tony Bill; ***W:*** Mitch Markowitz; ***M:*** Cliff Eidelman.

The Crazy Ray 🦴🦴🦴 *Paris Qui Dort* **1922** The classic silent fantasy about a mad scientist who endeavors to put the whole population of Paris in a trance. Vintage Clair nonsense. **60m/B VHS.** *FR* Henri Rollan, Albert Prejean, Marcel Vallee, Madeleine Rodrigue; ***D:*** Rene Clair.

Crazy Six 🦴 ½ **1998 (R)** In a futuristic Europe, organized crime families vie for control of the underground arms trade and the black market. **94m/C VHS, DVD.** Rob Lowe, Burt Reynolds, Ice-T, Mario Van Peebles; ***D:*** Albert Pyun.

The Crazy Stranger 🦴🦴 *Gadjo Dilo* **1998** The third film in director Gatlif's Gypsy trilogy following "Latcho Drom" and "Mondo." In order to honor his late father, Parisian Stephane (Duris) travels to Romania to track down and record the music of his father's favorite Gypsy singer. He's taken in by village headman, Isidor (Serban), whose own son has just been sent to prison. Isidor and the villagers make their living as musicians and Stephane is drawn ever deeper into their lives until tragedy forces him to make a choice. In French and Romany with subtitles. **97m/C VHS, DVD.** *FR* Romain Duris, Isidor Serban, Rona Hartner, Florin Moldovan; ***D:*** Tony Gatlif; ***W:*** Tony Gatlif; ***C:*** Eric Guichard; ***M:*** Tony Gatlif.

Crazylove 🦴🦴 **2005 (R)** Letty Mayer is happy with her teaching job, happy with her attorney boyfriend, and happy about her sister's upcoming wedding. But stress and her need for perfection drive Letty into a nervous breakdown and a stay in a mental institution. There she meets charming schizophrenic Michael. They decide to pursue their newfound passion when both are released, although Letty seems purposefully unaware of the severity of Michael's condition, especially when he's off his meds. **99m/C DVD.** Reiko Aylesworth, Bruno Campos, Marla Sokoloff, Meat Loaf Aday, JoBeth Williams, David Alan Basche, Greg Germann, K. Callan; ***D:*** Ellie Kanner; ***W:*** Carol Watson; ***C:*** Matthew Heckerling; ***M:*** Brad Segal.

The Crazysitter 🦴🦴 ½ **1994 (PG-13)** Edie (D'Angelo), a petty thief recently released from jail, is hired as a sitter to the twins-from-hell. So, she decides to sell the little monsters. **92m/C VHS, DVD.** Beverly D'Angelo, Ed Begley Jr., Carol Kane, Phil Hartman, Brady Bluhm, Rachel Duncan, Nell Carter, Steve Landesberg; ***D:*** Michael James McDonald; ***W:*** Michael James McDonald; ***C:*** Christopher Baffa; ***M:*** David Wurst, Eric Wurst.

Creation 🦴🦴 **2009 (PG-13)** Amiel's melodrama about Charles Darwin focuses not on the intellectual aspects of his writing but on his spiritual and personal consequences. Set in 1858, Darwin (Bettany) has been writing for 20 years but is still hesitant to complete and publish his work, "The Origin of Species," since he's reluctant to deal with the controversy he knows it will cause. Constantly brooding over the death of his favorite child Annie, Darwin is also unwilling to further upset his devout Christian wife Emma (Connelly) while his friends encourage him to publish for the sake of science. **108m/C DVD.** *GB* Paul Bettany, Jennifer Connelly, Jeremy Northam, Toby Jones, Benedict Cumberbatch, Jim Carter, Martha West; ***D:*** Jon Amiel; ***W:*** John Collee; ***C:*** Jess Hall; ***M:*** Christopher Young.

Creation of Adam 🦴🦴 **1993** Weirdly mystical Russian drama finds Andrey's marriage in trouble because his wife thinks he's gay. She may be right because during a business meeting, Andrey is drawn to the charasmatic Philip, who, it turns out, is some sort of angelic messenger whose mission seems to be to give Andrey confidence in love. Good performances although the plot lacks coherence and is not helped by the poor subtitling. Russian with subtitles. **93m/C VHS.** *RU* Alexander Strizhenov, Anzhelika Nevolina, Saulus Balandis, Serghei Vinogradov, Irina Metlitshkaya; ***D:*** Yuri Pavlov.

The Creation of the Humanoids WOOF! 1962 Set in the familiar post-holocaust future, this is a tale of humans outnumbered by androids and the resulting struggle for survival. Slow and silly low-budget sets. For some reason, Andy Warhol was reported to love this film. **84m/C VHS, DVD.** Don Megowan, Frances McCann, Erica Elliot, Don Doolittle, Dudley Manlove; ***D:*** Wesley Barry.

Creator 🦴🦴 **1985 (R)** A Frankenstein-like scientist plans to clone a being based on his wife, who died 30 years ago. As his experiments begin to show positive results, his romantic attention turns towards his beautiful lab assistant. O'Toole as the deranged scientist almost saves this one. Based on a novel by Jeremy Leven. **108m/C VHS, DVD.** Peter O'Toole, Mariel Hemingway, Vincent Spano, Virginia Madsen, David Ogden Stiers, John Dehner, Karen Kopins, Jeff Corey; ***D:*** Ivan Passer; ***W:*** Jeremy Leven; ***C:*** Robbie Greenberg; ***M:*** Sylvester Levay.

Creature 🦴 *Titan Find* **1985 (R)** A two thousand-year-old alien life form is killing off astronauts exploring the planet Titan. "Alien" rip-off has its moments, but not enough of them. Kinski provides some laughs. **97m/C VHS, DVD.** Klaus Kinski, Stan Ivar, Wendy Schaal, Lyman Ward, Annette McCarthy, Diane Salinger; ***D:*** William Malone; ***M:*** Tom Chase, Steve Rucker.

Creature from Black Lake 🦴 **1976 (PG)** Two anthropology students from Chicago travel to the Louisiana swamps searching for the creature from Black Lake. Predictably, they find him. McClenny, incidentally, is Morgan Fairchild's sister. **95m/C VHS, DVD.** Jack Elam, Dub Taylor, Dennis Fimple, John David Carson, Bill (Billy) Thurman, Catherine McClenny; ***D:*** Joy Houck Jr.; ***W:*** Jim McCullough Jr.

Creature from the Black Lagoon 🦴🦴🦴 **1954** An anthropological expedition in the Amazon stumbles upon the Gill-Man, a prehistoric humanoid fish monster who takes a fancy to fetching Adams, a coed majoring in "science," but the humans will have none of it. Originally filmed in 3-D, this was one of the first movies to sport top-of-the-line underwater photography and remains one of the most enjoyable monster movies ever made. Sequels: "Revenge of the Creature" and "The Creature Walks Among Us." **79m/B VHS, DVD.** Richard Carlson, Julie Adams, Richard Denning, Antonio Moreno, Whit Bissell, Nestor Paiva, Ricou Browning, Ben Chapman, Bernie Gozier; ***D:*** Jack Arnold; ***W:*** Arthur Ross, Harry Essex; ***C:*** William E. Snyder, Charles S. Welbourne; ***M:*** Hans J. Salter, Henry Mancini.

Creature from the Haunted Sea 🦴🦴 **1960** Monster movie satire set in Cuba shortly after the revolution and centering around an elaborate plan to loot the Treasury and put the blame on a strange sea monster. Corman comedy is predictably low budget but entertaining. "Wain" is really Robert Towne, winner of an Oscar for screenwriting. Remake of "Naked Paradise." **76m/B VHS, DVD.** Antony Carbone, Betsy Jones-Moreland, Beach Dickerson, Edward (Robert Towne) Wain, Edmundo Rivera Alvarez, Robert Bean, Sonya Noemi Gonzalez; ***Cameos:*** Roger Corman; ***D:*** Roger Corman, Monte Hellman; ***W:*** Charles B. Griffith; ***C:*** Jacques "Jack" Marquette; ***M:*** Fred Katz.

Creature of Destruction 🦴 **1967** A beautiful young woman is hypnotized and inadvertently reverted to her past life as a hideous sea monster. Buchanan's remake of his own 1956 production, "The She Creature." **80m/B VHS.** Les Tremayne, Aron Kincaid, Pat Delaney, Neil Fletcher, Ann McAdams, Scott McKay; ***D:*** Larry Buchanan; ***C:*** Robert C. Jessup.

Creature of the Walking Dead 🦴 ½ *La Marca del Muerto* **1960** Scientist brings his grandfather back to life with horrifying results for the cast and the audience. Made cheaply and quickly in Mexico in 1960, then released with added footage directed by Warren. **74m/B VHS.** *MX* Ann Wells, George Todd, Willard Gross, Bruno VeSota, Rosa Maria Gallardo, Katherine Victor; ***D:*** Fernando Cortes, Jerry Warren; ***W:*** Fernando Cortes, Alfredo Varela; ***C:*** Jose Ortiz Ramos.

The Creature Walks among Us 🦴 ½ **1956** Sequel to "Revenge of the Creature" has the Gill-Man once again being captured by scientists for studying purposes. Through an accidental lab fire, the creature's gills are burned off and he undergoes surgery in an attempt to live out of water. Final entry in the Creature series has little magic of the original. Also shot in 3-D. **79m/B VHS, DVD.** Jeff Morrow, Rex Reason, Leigh Snowden, Gregg (Hunter) Palmer, Ricou Browning, Don Megowan, Maurice Manson, Frank Chase, Larry Hudson, Paul Fierro; ***D:*** John Sherwood; ***W:*** Arthur Ross; ***C:*** Maury Gertsman; ***M:*** Henry Mancini, Joseph Gershenson.

The Creature Wasn't Nice 🦴 *Spaceship; Naked Space* **1981 (PG)** Spacecraft Vertigo ventures into outer space to an uncharted planet where a fast-growing, human-eating, song-singing creature snacks on the ship's crew. Nielsen stars in another genre spoof. **88m/C VHS, DVD.** Cindy Williams, Leslie Nielsen, Bruce Kimmel, Gerrit Graham, Patrick Macnee, Paul Brinegar, Cheri(e) Steinkellner, Ron Kurowski; ***D:*** Bruce Kimmel; ***W:*** Bruce Kimmel; ***C:*** Denny Lavil; ***M:*** Bruce Kimmel, David Spear. **VIDEO**

Creature with the Blue Hand 🦴🦴 **1970** A German horror film based on a passable Edgar Wallace story about a man unjustly convicted of murders actually committed by a lunatic. Dubbed. **92m/C VHS, DVD.** *GE* Klaus Kinski, Harald Leopold, Hermann Leschau, Diana Kerner, Carl Lange, Ilse Page; ***D:*** Alfred Vohrer.

Creatures from the Abyss 🦴🦴 ½ *Plankton* **1994** After being stranded on a raft, five young people board an abandoned yacht, which is actually an oceanographic research vessel where very strange fish were being studied. The youngsters decide to make the yacht their party-place, but things get nasty once they realize that killer fish are running wild on board the ship. As if that weren't bad enough, exposure to these aquatic nasties causes humans to mutate into monsters! On the surface (?!), this looks like the average Italian thriller, with bad acting, atrocious dubbing, and lackluster pacing, but the odd plot concerning mutant plankton and the fact that the movie consistently crosses the line with its disturbing special effects make it stand out. The timid will find the last act revolting, but those looking for a throwback to the gore-soaked '80s will love it. **86m/C DVD.** *IT*

Creatures from the Pink Lagoon 🦴🦴 **2007** B-movie spoof that sets-up '50s monsters and gay stereotypes. A group of gay friends gather at a beach cottage for a birthday party in 1967. They learn a nearby lagoon is overrun with zombies, who are man-eaters in more ways than one. **71m/B DVD.** Phillip Clarke, Nick Garrison, Lowell Deo, Evan Mosher, Vincent Kovar; ***D:*** Chris Diani; ***W:*** Chris Diani; ***C:*** Peter Torr; ***M:*** David Moddux. **VIDEO**

Creatures the World Forgot WOOF! 1970 A British-made bomb about two tribes of cavemen warring over power and a cavewoman. No special effects, dinosaurs, or dialogue. **96m/C VHS.** Julie Ege, Robert John, Tony Bonner, Rosalie Crutchley, Sue Wilson; ***D:*** Don Chaffey; ***W:*** Michael Carreras.

The Creeper 🦴🦴 **1948** After experimenting with a variety of serums, a doctor turns into a murderous monster with feline paws. **65m/B VHS.** Eduardo Ciannelli, Onslow Stevens, June Vincent, Ralph Morgan; ***D:*** Jean Yarbrough.

Creepers 🦴🦴 ½ *Phenomena* **1985 (R)** A young girl talks to bugs and gets them to follow her instructions, which comes in handy when she battles the lunatic who is killing her school chums. Argento weirdness—and graphic gore—may not be for all tastes. **82m/C VHS, DVD.** *IT* Jennifer Connelly, Donald Pleasence, Daria Nicolodi, Elenora Giorgi, Dalia di Lazzaro, Patrick Bauchau, Fiore Argento, Federica Mastroianni, Michele (Michael) Soavi, Gavin Friday; ***D:*** Dario Argento; ***W:*** Dario Argento, Franco Ferrini; ***C:*** Romano Albani; ***M:*** Simon Boswell.

The Creeping Flesh 🦴🦴 ½ **1972 (PG)** A scientist decides he can cure evil by injecting his patients with a serum derived from the blood of an ancient corpse. Some truly chilling moments will get your flesh creeping. **89m/C VHS, DVD.** *GB* Peter Cushing, Christopher Lee, Lorna Heilbron, George Benson, Kenneth J. Warren, Duncan Lamont, Harry Locke, Hedger Wallace, Michael Ripper, Jenny Runacre; ***D:*** Freddie Francis; ***W:*** Peter Spenceley, Jonathan Rumbold; ***C:*** Norman Warwick.

Creeping Terror WOOF! *The Crawling Monster; Dangerous Charter* **1964** Gigantic alien carpet monster (look for the tennis shoes sticking out underneath) devours slow-moving teenagers. Partially narrated because some of the original soundtrack was lost, with lots of bad acting, a worse script, laughable sets, and a ridiculous monster. Beware of the thermometer scene. **81m/B VHS.** Vic Savage, Shannon O'Neal, William Thourlby, Louise Lawson, Robin James, Byrd Holland, Jack King, Art J. Nelson; ***D:*** Art J. Nelson; ***W:*** Robert Silliphant; ***C:*** Andrew Janczak.

Creepozoids 🦴 **1987** In the near future, a monster at an abandoned science complex stalks army deserters hiding out there. Violent nonsense done better by others. **72m/C DVD.** Linnea Quigley, Ken Abraham, Michael Aranda; ***D:*** David DeCoteau.

The Creeps 🦴🦴 **1997 (PG-13)** A horror-film obsessed scientist, Dr. Winston Berber, steals the original manuscript of Mary Shelley's "Frankenstein" and librarian Anna (Griffin) hires detective David Rawley (Lauer) to get it back. Then Berber returns to steal Bram Stoker's original "Dracula" and kidnaps Anna to use in his wacky experiment as well. He decides to reanimate his four favorite movie monsters but when David rescues Anna before the experiment is complete, Dracula (Fondacaro), the Mummy (Smith), the Wolfman (Simanton), and Frankenstein's Monster (Wellington) wind up only three feet tall. Not pleased by their diminutive size, the creeps work to restore themselves to the proper height (and cause a little mayhem as well). **80m/C VHS, DVD.** Phil Fondacaro, Rhonda Griffin, Justin Lauer, Bill Moynihan, Kristin Norton, Jon Simanton, Joe Smith, Thomas Wellington; ***D:*** Charles Band; ***W:*** Benjamin Carr; ***C:*** Adolfo Bartoli; ***M:*** Carl Dante. **VIDEO**

Creepshow 🦴🦴 ½ **1982 (R)** Stephen King's tribute to E.C. Comics, those pulp horror comic books of the 1950s that delighted in grisly, grotesque, and morbid humor. The film tells five horror tales, and features King himself in one segment, as a none-too-bright farmer who unknowingly cultivates a strange, alien-origin moss. With despicable heroes and gory monsters, this is sure to delight all fans of the horror vein. Those easily repulsed by cockroaches beware! **120m/C VHS, DVD.** Hal Holbrook, Adrienne Barbeau, Viveca Lindfors, E.G. Marshall, Stephen King, Leslie Nielsen, Carrie Nye, Fritz Weaver, Ted Danson, Ed Harris, John Amplas, Tom Savini; ***D:*** George A. Romero; ***W:*** Stephen King; ***C:*** Michael Gornick; ***M:*** John Harrison.

Creepshow 2 🦴 ½ **1987 (R)** Romero adapted three Stephen King stories for this horror anthology which presents gruesome looks at a hit-and-run driver, a wooden Indian, and a vacation gone wrong. Gory and childish stuff from two masters of the genre. Look for King as a truck driver. **92m/C VHS, DVD.** Lois Chiles, George Kennedy, Dorothy Lamour, Tom Savini, Domenick John, Frank S. Salsedo, Holt McCallany, David Holbrook, Page Hannah, Daniel Beer, Stephen King, Paul Satterfield, Jeremy Green, Tom Wright; ***D:*** Michael Gornick; ***W:*** George A. Romero; ***C:*** Richard Hart, Tom Hurwitz; ***M:*** Les Reed, Rick Wakeman.

Cremains 🦴🦴🦴 **2000** Anthology centers on a mortician (Chester Delacruz) who is being investigated for cremating two bodies at once. As he is questioned by an unseen panel of inquisitors, he relates three stories. In the first, a young woman (Plimmer) makes the mistake of driving through a small town famous for its ritual sacrifices. In the next story, a serial killer (Williams) captures a hitchhiker and then the mind-games begin. The third story features a woman (Cole) who seeks out the help of a horror author (Smith), as she's convinced that a female vampire is after her. The final segment returns to the mortician and the macabre results of his double-cremation. The stories are good; while they aren't incredibly original, they all have that "urban legend" feel, which makes them accessible. Howeverm the film is way too long, and all of the segments feel padded. Not perfect, but actually better than some studio horror films released lately. **107m/C DVD.** Chester Delacruz, Wanda Plimmer, Chris(topher) Williams, Kimberly Lynn Cole, R.W. Smith; ***D:*** Steve Sessions; ***W:*** Steve Sessions. **VIDEO**

The Cremators WOOF! 1972 A meteorite carrying an alien lands at a seaside resort and everyone begins bursting into flames.

Low budget effort from the scripter of "It Came from Outer Space." **90m/C VHS, DVD.** Marvin Howard, Maria de Aragon; ***D:*** Harry Essex.

Crescendo 1969 Generally unimpressive Hammer psycho-thriller. American student Susan (Powers) is writing her thesis on a recently deceased composer and travels to the south of France where she is invited to stay in the creepy family mansion by his widow (Scott). Everyone is crazy, including the composer's wheelchair-bound, drug addict son (Olson), the hired help, and whoever is confined to the attic. **95m/C DVD.** *GB* Stefanie Powers, James Olson, Margaretta Scott, Jane Lapotaire, Joss Ackland; ***D:*** Alan Gibson; ***W:*** Jimmy Sangster, Alfred Shaughnessy; ***C:*** Paul Beeson; ***M:*** Malcolm Williamson.

The Crew 1995 **(R)** Sometimes it doesn't pay to be a good samaritan—as a boatload of pleasure cruisers discover when they rescue two psychopaths from a burning boat in the Bahamas. **99m/C VHS.** Viggo Mortensen, Jeremy Sisto, Pamela Gidley, Donal Logue, Laura Del Sol, Grace Zabriskie, John Philbin; ***D:*** Carl Colpaert; ***W:*** Carl Colpaert.

The Crew 2000 **(PG-13)** Dreyfuss, Hedaya, Reynolds, and Cassel are a quartet of retired wiseguys who hatch a plan to save their South Beach Miami retirement home with a fake mob hit. Complications arise when the body turns out to be a South American druglord's missing father. Occasionally funny but overly plotted script was written by former "Golden Girls" writer Fanaro, and the sitcom lineage is obvious. **88m/C VHS, DVD.** Richard Dreyfuss, Burt Reynolds, Dan Hedaya, Seymour Cassel, Carrie-Anne Moss, Jennifer Tilly, Lainie Kazan, Miguel (Michael) Sandoval, Jeremy Piven, Casey Siemaszko, Matt Borlenghi, Jeremy Ratchford, Mike Moroff, Billy Jayne Young, Jose Zuniga, Louis Lombardi, Allan Nicholls, Ron Karabatsos, Frank Vincent, Fyvush Finkel; ***D:*** Michael Dinner; ***W:*** Barry Fanaro; ***C:*** Juan Ruiz-Anchia; ***M:*** Steve Bartek.

The Crew 2008 British gangster flick set in Liverpool. Old-fashioned gang leader Ged wants to invest in a legit property development scheme but he needs to do one last job to get enough money. Meanwhile, his ambitious younger bro Ratter is working in the drug trade (to Ged's disgust) while other baddies try muscling in on Ged's action. Adapted from Kevin Sampson's 2001 novel "Outlaws." **100m/C DVD.** *GB* Kenny Doughty, Cordelia Bugeja, Rosie Fellner, Scot Williams, Raza Jaffrey, Rory McCann, Stephen Graham; ***D:*** Adrian Vitoria; ***W:*** Adrian Vitoria, Ian Brady; ***C:*** Mark Hamilton; ***M:*** James Edward Barker.

Cria *Cria Cuervos; Raise Ravens* **1976 (PG)** The award-winning story of a nine-year-old girl's struggle for maturity in a hostile adult world. In Spanish with English subtitles. **115m/C VHS.** *SP* Geraldine Chaplin, Ana Torrent, Conchita Perez, Maite Sanchez; ***D:*** Carlos Saura; ***W:*** Carlos Saura; ***C:*** Teodoro Escamilla; ***M:*** Federico Mompoll. Cannes '76: Grand Jury Prize.

Cria Cuervos 1/2 **1976** Moving freely between reality and fantasy, Saura portrays the complexities of childhood emotions through the grief of 8-year-old Ana (Torrent), who lives in Madrid and conjures her mother's ghost (Chaplin), as well as the struggles of Spain's middle class under fascist rule. Well-scripted, beautifully written and acted, the title is derived from the Spanish proverb: "Raise ravens and they'll peck out your eyes." Spanish with subtitles. **109m/C DVD.** *SP* Sydney Chaplin, Monica Randall, Ana Torrent, Florinda Chico, Hector Alterio, German Cobos, Mirta Miller; ***D:*** Carlos Saura; ***W:*** Carlos Saura; ***C:*** Teodoro Escamilla; ***M:*** Federico Mompou.

Cricket on the Hearth 1923 An adaptation of Charles Dickens' short story about a mail carrier and his bride, who find the symbol of good luck, a cricket on the hearth, when they enter their new home. Silent with organ score. **68m/B VHS.** Paul Gerson, Virginia Brown Faire, Paul Moore, Joan Standing, Lorimer Johnston; ***D:*** Lorimer Johnston; ***W:*** Caroline Francis Cooke.

Cries and Whispers *Viskingar Och Rop* **1972 (R)** As a woman dies slowly of tuberculosis, three women care for her: her two sisters, one sexually repressed, the other promiscuous, and her servant. The sisters remember family love and closeness, but are too afraid to look death in the face to aid their sister. Only the servant can touch her in her dying and only the servant believes in God and his will. Beautiful imagery, focused through a nervous camera, which lingers on the meaningless and whisks away from the meaningful. Absolute mastery of cinematic art by Bergman. **91m/C VHS, DVD.** *SW* Harriet Andersson, Ingrid Thulin, Liv Ullmann, Kari Sylway, Erland Josephson, Henning Moritzen; ***D:*** Ingmar Bergman; ***W:*** Ingmar Bergman; ***C:*** Sven Nykvist. Oscars '73: Cinematog.; Natl. Bd. of Review '73: Director (Bergman); N.Y. Film Critics '72: Actress (Ullmann), Director (Bergman), Film, Screenplay; Natl. Soc. Film Critics '72: Cinematog., Screenplay.

Cries of Silence 1997 In 1969 a teenaged girl (Buchanan) is found along a remote Mississippi island shore in the aftermath of Hurricane Camille. Young doctor Dorrie Walsh (York) brings the girl to her mother's (Black) home after the locals swear they don't know who she is and the girl herself is mute from trauma. Dorrie calls her Camille and struggles to communicate with her in the face of community opposition. It seems learning Camille's identity could reveal the truth behind more than one local secret. **109m/C VHS.** Kathleen York, Karen Black, Erin Buchanan, Ed Nelson, Ellen Crawford, Guy Boyd; ***D:*** Avery Crounse; ***W:*** Avery Crounse; ***C:*** Michael Barnard; ***M:*** Nigel Holton.

Crime & Passion 1/2 **1975 (R)** Two scheming lovers plan to get rich by having the woman marry a multimillionaire and sue for a quick divorce. The multimillionaire is no patsy, however, and seeks a deadly revenge. Three scripts by six writers were combined to create this story. That explains the many problems. **92m/C VHS, DVD.** Omar Sharif, Karen Black, Joseph Bottoms, Bernhard Wicki; ***D:*** Ivan Passer.

Crime and Punishment *Crime et Chatiment* **1935** Original French production (preceding the American version by just one week) of Dostoyevski's novel, the tale of a young murderer, his crime, and ultimately, his confession. Generally considered better than the American version, the French throw out all that is not dramatic, keeping the psychology and suspense. Remade in 1958. French with subtitles. **110m/B VHS.** Harry Baur, Pierre Blanchar, Madeleine Ozeray, Marcelle Geniat, Lucienne Lemarchand; ***D:*** Pierre Chenal; ***W:*** Marcel Ayme, Chenal, Christian Stengel, Wladimir Strijewski; ***M:*** Arthur Honegger.

Crime and Punishment **1935** Pared down but well-executed version of the Dostoyevski novel. Lorre is superb as Raskolnikov, who robs and murders an elderly pawnbroker. Believing he has committed the perfect murder, he accepts the invitation of police inspector Porfiry (Arnold) to observe the investigation. Gradually Raskolnikov's conscience begins to overwhelm him as Porfiry slowly works to wring a confession from the killer. Von Sternberg's subdued directorial approach worked well to explore the psychological aspects of guilt, although the melodramatic French film version (released at the same time) scored better with the critics. **88m/B VHS.** Peter Lorre, Edward Arnold, Marian Marsh, Tala Birell, Elisabeth Risdon, Robert "Tex" Allen, Douglass Dumbrille, Gene Lockhart; ***D:*** Josef von Sternberg; ***W:*** S.K. Lauren, Joseph Anthony.

Crime and Punishment **1970** Ponderous, excruciatingly long adaptation of the Dostoyevski classic involving a haunted murderer and the relentless policeman who seeks to prove him guilty. In Russian with English subtitles. **200m/B VHS, DVD.** *RU* Georgi Taratorkin, Victoria Fyodorova; ***D:*** Lev Kulijanov; ***W:*** Lev Kulijanov.

Crime and Punishment in Suburbia 1/2 **2000 (R)** Dostoyevsky heads to the mall in this suburban gloomfest very loosely based on the classic Russian novel. Roseanne (Keena) is a pretty, popular teen whose family life is screwed up beyond repair. Her father Fred (Ironside) is an abusive monster and her mother Maggie (Barkin) is a drunken floozy. She hopes that she can endure the situation until she graduates, but Fred's reaction to an affair by Maggie causes her to contemplate killing her father. With the help of her boyfriend Jimmy (DeBello), Roseanne murders her old man. When her mother is arrested for the crime and she becomes an outcast at school, she turns to mysterious classmate Vincent (Kartheiser) for solace, not knowing he's been lurking in the shadows and observing everything. The themes explored in this grim view of suburbia were better served up in "American Beauty." **98m/C VHS, DVD.** Monica Keena, Vincent Kartheiser, Ellen Barkin, Michael Ironside, Jeffrey Wright, James DeBello, Conchata Ferrell, Marshall Teague, Brad Greenquist, Lucinda Jenney; ***D:*** Rob Schmidt; ***W:*** Larry Gross; ***C:*** Bobby Bukowski; ***M:*** Michael Brook.

Crime and Punishment, USA 1/2 **1959** Modern update of the Dostoyevsky novel set in a seedy Southern California milieu. Law student Robert Cole (Hamilton) murders a pawnbroker and comes under the suspicious gaze of Lt. Porter (Silvera). **96m/B DVD.** George Hamilton, Frank Silvera, Mary Murphy, Marian Seldes, John Harding; ***D:*** Denis Sanders; ***W:*** Walter Newman; ***C:*** Floyd Crosby; ***M:*** Herschel Burke Gilbert.

Crime Broker 1994 A respected judge (Bisset) decides to experience life on the other side of the bench for a change. So she hooks up with a handsome partner to execute a series of high-profile robberies of bank vaults and museums. Implied sex so don't look for this under erotic thrillers. **93m/C VHS, DVD.** Jacqueline Bisset, Masaya Kato, Gary Day; ***D:*** Ian Barry; ***W:*** Tony Morphett; ***C:*** Dan Burstall; ***M:*** Roger Mason.

Crime Busters 1/2 **1978 (PG)** Two guys attempt to pull off a bank heist but accidentally join the Miami police force instead. Hill and Spencer are enjoyable as usual but the film suffers from poor dubbing. Remake of "Two Supercops." **114m/C VHS.** *IT* Terence Hill, Bud Spencer, Laura Gemser, Luciano Catenacci, David Huddleston; ***D:*** E.B. (Enzo Barboni) Clucher.

Crime Killer 1985 Confusing shenanigans about an explosive ex-CIA agent enlisted by the FBI to battle a brutal crime syndicate shipping guns to nasty Arabs. **90m/C VHS.** George Pan-Andreas, Leo Morrell, Althan Karras; ***D:*** George Pan-Andreas; ***C:*** Arledge Armenaki.

Crime Lords 1991 **(R)** When a pair of cops are suspended from the force for committing a blunder, they travel to Hong Kong to continue their investigation. Little do they know their sleuthing has drawn then into a confrontation with one of largest crime syndicates in the world. Lots of action, beautiful women, and exotic locations keep this basic buddy plot moving well. **96m/C VHS.** Wayne Crawford, Martin Hewitt, Susan Byun, Mel Castelo, James Hong; ***D:*** Wayne Crawford.

The Crime of Dr. Crespi 1935 A doctor takes his revenge on a man who is after his girlfriend by injecting him with suspended animation serum. Extremely campy performance from von Stroheim; Frye's biggest role in terms of screen time. **64m/B VHS.** Erich von Stroheim, Dwight Frye, Paul Guilfoyle, Harriett Russell, John Bohn; ***D:*** John H. Auer.

The Crime of Father Amaro *El Crimen del Padre Amaro* **2002 (R)** Eca de Queiroz's 1875 Portuguese novel is transplanted to modern-day Mexico, confronting a number of controversies surrounding the Catholic Church, including abortion, celibacy, and corruption. Young cleric Padre Amaro (Bernal) is the protege of Bishop Ernesto (Gomez Cruz) who sends him to the provinces to learn church politics from the seasoned Padre Benito (Gracia). Benito has had a longtime affair with Sanjuanera (Aragon) whose beautiful young daughter Amelia (Talancon) becomes infatuated with the handsome young priest. Amaro is soon learning to justify his less than priestly behavior with Amelia, which leads him down increasingly precarious moral paths. Spanish with subtitles. **120m/C VHS, DVD.** *MX* Gael Garcia Bernal, Sancho Gracia, Ana Claudia Talancon, Damian Alcazar, Angelica Aragon, Pedro Armendariz Jr., Luisa Huertas, Ernesto Gomez Cruz; ***D:*** Carlos Carrera; ***W:*** Vicente Lenero; ***C:*** Guillermo Granillo; ***M:*** Rosino Serrano.

Crime of Honor 1985 A European executive goes public with his company's corruption, and his family suffers predictable ruin as a result. Based on a true story. **95m/C VHS.** Maria Schneider, David Suchet; ***D:*** John Goldschmidt.

The Crime of Monsieur Lange *Le Crime de Monsieur Lange* **1936** Charming French socialist fantasy where workers at a publishing company turn the business into a thriving cooperative while their evil boss is gone. When he returns, worker Lefevre plots to kill him. Rather talky, but humorous. In French with subtitles. French script booklet also available. **90m/B VHS.** *FR* Rene Lefevre, Jules Berry, Florelle, Sylvia Bataille, Jean Daste, Nadia Sibirskaia, Henri Guisol; ***D:*** Jean Renoir; ***W:*** Jean Renoir, Jacques Prevert; ***C:*** Jean Bachelet; ***M:*** Jean Wiener, Joseph Kosma.

Crime of Passion 1/2 **1957** Stanwyck plays a femme fatale whose ambitions for detective hubby lead to murder. Good performances from Stanwyck, Hayden, and Burr make this an above-average, although outlandish, crime-drama. **85m/B VHS, DVD.** Barbara Stanwyck, Sterling Hayden, Raymond Burr, Fay Wray, Royal Dano, Virginia Grey, Dennis Cross, Robert E. (Bob) Griffin, Jay Adler, Malcolm Atterbury, S. John Launer, Brad Trumbull, Skipper McNally, Jean Howell, Peg La Centra, Nancy Reynolds, Marjorie Owens, Robert Quarry, Joe Conley, Stuart Whitman; ***D:*** Gerd Oswald; ***W:*** Jo Eisinger; ***C:*** Joseph LaShelle; ***M:*** Paul Dunlap.

Crime of the Century 1/2 **1996 (PG-13)** Another look at the 1932 kidnapping and death of Charles Lindbergh's 18-month-old son. Based on the 1985 book "The Airman and the Carpenter" by Ludovic Kennedy, it's clear the author regards Bruno Richard Hauptmann (Rea), who was executed in 1936, as an innocent scapegoat essentially railroaded thanks to media and political pressures. **116m/C VHS.** Stephen Rea, J.T. Walsh, David Paymer, John Harkins, Michael Moriarty, Isabella Rossellini, Bert Remsen, Allen (Goorwitz) Garfield, Don Harvey, Gerald S. O'Loughlin, Barry Primus; ***D:*** Mark Rydell; ***W:*** William Nicholson; ***C:*** Toyomichi Kurita; ***M:*** John (Gianni) Frizzell. **CABLE**

Crime School 1/2 **1938** Underwhelming Dead End Kids entry with the juvies ending up in reformatory hell thanks to a corrupt and brutal warden. When deputy corrections commissioner Braden (Bogart) makes a surprise inspection things turn around and the Kids return the favor when Braden lands in political hot water. **90m/B DVD.** Billy Halop, Bobby Jordan, Huntz Hall, Leo Gorcey, Bernard Punsley, Gabriel Dell, Humphrey Bogart, Gale Page, Charles Trowbridge, Crane Wilbur; ***D:*** Lewis Seiler, Vincent Sherman, Crane Wilbur, Terry Morse; ***W:*** Crane Wilbur; ***C:*** Arthur L. Todd; ***M:*** Max Steiner.

Crime Spree 1/2 *Wanted* **2003 (R)** After bungling a Paris heist, Daniel (Depardieu), Julien (Freiss), and Raymond (Dray) are sent by their boss, Laurent (Bohringer), to Chicago for a diamond heist. Joined by Marcel (Hallyday), Zero (Renaud), and Sami (Taghmaoui), the group manages to rob the wrong house—that of Chicago hood Frankie Zammeti (Keitel). Frankie has been staked out by the FBI, who want an audio cassette the French hoods have also taken, which incriminates his boss Giancarlo (Vigoda). Equal opportunity stereotypes abound with the bad guys—French, Italian, Latino, and blacks—but this aging buddy cast is so self-confident that they can carry this caper a long way. English and some French with subtitles. **99m/C VHS, DVD.** *CA GB* Gerard Depardieu, Johnny Hallyday, Renaud, Harvey Keitel, Richard Bohringer, Said Taghmaoui, Stephane Freiss, Albert Dray, Abe Vigoda; ***D:*** Brad Mirman; ***W:*** Brad Mirman; ***C:*** Derek Rogers; ***M:*** Rupert Gregson-Williams.

Crime Story *Hard to Die* **1993 (R)** Police Inspector Eddie Chan (Chan) tries to crack a kidnapping case and discovers his partner, Detective Hung (Cheng), is not on the up-and-up. Usual arobatic stunts from Chan and company. Cantonese with subtitles. **104m/C VHS, DVD.** *HK* Jackie Chan, Kent Cheng, Law Hang Kang, Christine Ng; ***D:*** Kirk Wong; ***C:*** Arthur Wong Ngok Tai, Ardy Lam.

Crime Wave 1954 Cons break out of San Q and then botch a gas-station robbery. They head for the home of ex-cellmate

Steve Lacey (Nelson), who's married Ellen (Kirk), gone straight, and doesn't want the trouble landing at his door. Steve's willing to cooperate with hard-boiled detective Sims (Hayden) but Penny (de Corsia) and Hastings (Bronson) take Ellen hostage and threaten Steve unless he helps them in a bank job. Nelson was better known as a song-and-dance man, but he's good in this noir role, and the toothpick-chewing Hayden can snarl with the best of them. **73m/B DVD.** Sterling Hayden, Gene Nelson, Phyllis Kirk, Ted de Corsia, Charles Bronson, Jay Novello, Nedrick Young, Timothy Carey; ***D:*** Andre de Toth; ***W:*** Bernard Gordon, Crane Wilbur, Richard Wormser; ***C:*** Bert Glennon; ***M:*** David Buttolph.

Crime Zone 🦴🦴 1/2 **1988 (R)** In a totalitarian, repressive, future society, two young lovers try to beat the system and make it on their own. A well-made, if occasionally muddled, low-budget film shot in Peru, of all places. **96m/C VHS.** David Carradine, Peter Nelson, Sherilyn Fenn, Orlando Sacha, Don Manor, Michael Shaner; ***D:*** Luis Llosa; ***W:*** Daryl Haney; ***M:*** Rick Conrad.

Crimebroker 🦴🦴 **1993 (R)** Australian judge Holly McPhee (Bisset) has a sideline—she devises criminal blueprints and then anonymously hires the rabbles that come before the bench to carry out the crime. But things get complicated when Japanese criminologist Jin Okazaki (Kato) figures out what's going on. **93m/C DVD.** *AU JP* Jacqueline Bisset, Masaya Kato, John Bach, Ralph Cotterill; ***D:*** Ian Barry; ***W:*** Tony Morphett; ***C:*** Dan Burstall; ***M:*** Roger Mason.

Crimebusters 🦴 1/2 **1979 (PG)** A man exacts revenge against a government conspiracy that kidnapped his loved ones. **90m/C VHS, DVD.** Henry Silva, Antonio (Tony) Sabato; ***D:*** Michael Tarantini.

Crimes & Misdemeanors 🦴🦴🦴 **1989 (PG-13)** One of Allen's most mature films, exploring a whole range of moral ambiguities through the parallel and eventually interlocking stories of a nebbish filmmaker—who agrees to make a profile of a smug Hollywood TV comic and then sabotages it—and an esteemed ophthalmologist who is being threatened with exposure by his neurotic mistress. Intriguing mix of drama and comedy few directors could pull off. Look for Daryl Hannah in an unbilled cameo. **104m/C VHS, DVD.** Martin Landau, Woody Allen, Alan Alda, Mia Farrow, Joanna Gleason, Anjelica Huston, Jerry Orbach, Sam Waterston, Claire Bloom, Jenny Nichols, Caroline Aaron, Daryl Hannah, Nora Ephron, Jerry Zaks; ***D:*** Woody Allen; ***W:*** Woody Allen; ***C:*** Sven Nykvist. Natl. Bd. of Review '89: Support. Actor (Alda); N.Y. Film Critics '89: Support. Actor (Alda); Writers Guild '89: Orig. Screenplay.

Crimes at the Dark House 🦴🦴🦴 **1939** In this campy, melodramatic adaptation of Wilkie Collins's novel "The Woman in White," a man kills his rich wife and puts a disguised mental patient in her place. Later remade using the book's title. **69m/B VHS, DVD.** *GB* David Keir, David Horne, Rita Grant, Margaret Yarde, Tod Slaughter, Hilary Eaves, Sylvia Marriott, Hay Petrie, Geoffrey Wardwell, Elsie Wagstaff; ***D:*** George King; ***W:*** Frederick Hayward, Edward Dryhurst, H.F. Maltby; ***C:*** Hone Glendinning.

Crimes of Dr. Mabuse 🦴🦴🦴 1/2 *The Testament of Dr. Mabuse; The Last Will of Dr. Mabuse* **1932** Supernatural horror classic about the evil Dr. Mabuse controlling an underworld empire while confined to an insane asylum. The third, and only sound, Mabuse film by Lang. German with subtitles. **120m/B VHS, DVD.** *GE* Rudolf Klein-Rogge, Otto Wernicke, Gustav Diesl, Karl Meixner; ***D:*** Fritz Lang.

Crimes of Passion 🦴🦴🦴 **1984** Vintage whacked-out Russell, not intended for the kiddies. A business-like fashion designer becomes a kinky prostitute at night. A disturbed street preacher makes her the heroine of his erotic fantasies. A dark terrifying vision of the underground sex world and moral hypocrisy. Sexually explicit and violent, with an extremely black comedic center. Turner's portrayal is honest and believable, Perkins overacts until he nearly gets a nosebleed, but it's all for good effect. Cut for "R" rating to get it in the theatres; this version restores some excised footage. Also available in rated version. **101m/C VHS, DVD.** Kathleen Turner, Anthony Perkins, Annie Potts, John Laughlin, Bruce Davison, Norman Burton, Ian Petrella, Gerald S. O'Loughlin; ***D:*** Ken Russell; ***W:*** Barry Sandler; ***C:*** Dick Bush; ***M:*** Rick Wakeman. L.A. Film Critics '84: Actress (Turner).

The Crimes of Stephen Hawke 🦴🦴 *Strangler's Morgue* **1936** The world knows Stephen Hawke as a big-hearted money lender. What they don't know is his favorite hobby is breaking peoples' spines. An entertaining thriller set in the 1800s. **65m/B VHS.** *GB* Tod Slaughter, Marjorie Taylor, D.J. Williams, Eric Portman, Ben Soutten; ***D:*** George King.

Crimes of the Heart 🦴🦴 1/2 **1986 (PG-13)** Based on Beth Henley's acclaimed play. A few days in the lives of three very strange Southern sisters, one of whom has just been arrested for calmly shooting her husband after he chased her black lover out of town. Spacek as the suicidal sister is a lark. A tart, black comedy that works better as a play than a film. **105m/C VHS, DVD.** Sissy Spacek, Diane Keaton, Jessica Lange, Sam Shepard, Tess Harper, Hurd Hatfield; ***D:*** Bruce Beresford; ***W:*** Beth Henley; ***C:*** Dante Spinotti; ***M:*** Georges Delerue. Golden Globes '87: Actress—Mus./Comedy (Spacek); N.Y. Film Critics '86: Actress (Spacek).

Crimetime 🦴 1/2 **1996 (R)** Silly thriller has actor Bobby (Baldwin) finding unexpected success portraying a serial killer in a crime re-enactment TV show called "Crimetime." Meanwhile, Sydney (Postlethwaite), who's the real killer Bobby's character is based on, becomes seduced by the media frenzy surrounding the crimes and seeing them re-enacted on television. He goes on killing, so the show can literally go on. **118m/C VHS, DVD.** Stephen Baldwin, Pete Postlethwaite, Sadie Frost, Geraldine Chaplin, Karen Black, James Faulkner; ***Cameos:*** Marianne Faithfull; ***D:*** George Sluizer; ***W:*** Brendan Somers; ***C:*** Jules Van Den Steenhoven.

Crimewave 🦴🦴 *The XYZ Murders; Broken Hearts and Noses* **1985 (PG-13)** Zany spoof about serial killers set in Detroit (director Raimi's hometown). A rhapsody to comic book style, short on plot and long on style. With such credentials you expect more. **83m/C VHS.** Louise Lasser, Paul Smith, Brion James, Bruce Campbell, Reed Birney, Sheree J. Wilson, Edward R. Pressman, Julius W. Harris, Antonio Fargas, Sean Farley, Frances McDormand, Theodore (Ted) Raimi; ***D:*** Sam Raimi; ***W:*** Ethan Coen, Joel Coen, Sam Raimi; ***C:*** Robert Primes; ***M:*** Joseph LoDuca, Arlon Ober.

The Criminal 🦴🦴 **2000 (R)** Unemployed musician Jasper (Mackintosh) thinks he's gotten lucky when he meets sultry Sarah (Little) at the pub and she agrees to go home with him. But before anything intimate happens, Sarah's killed by intruders in Jasper's flat. A grumpy detective (Hill) and his smart woman partner (Aird) are certain of Jasper's guilt while Jasper tries to elude both the cops and Sarah's killers. **96m/C VHS, DVD.** *GB* Steven Mackintosh, Natasha Little, Bernard Hill, Holly Aird, Eddie Izzard, Yvan Attal, Andrew Tiernan; ***D:*** Julian Simpson; ***W:*** Julian Simpson; ***C:*** Nic Morris; ***M:*** Tolga Kashif, Mark Sayer-Wade.

Criminal 🦴🦴 1/2 **2004 (R)** Experienced con man takes a novice under his wing to help bilk a rich collector. But like most con/heist flicks, everything is not what it seems. Complex and enjoyable remake of Argentine filmmaker Fabian Bielinski's "Nine Queens." Reilly and Luna give great performances, as do Gyllenhaal and Mullan. Fun in the vein of "Matchstick Men", full of twists and turns with a terrific payoff. **87m/C DVD.** *US* John C. Reilly, Diego Luna, Maggie Gyllenhaal, Jonathan Tucker, Peter Mullan; ***D:*** Gregory Jacobs; ***W:*** Gregory Jacobs, Steven Soderbergh; ***C:*** Chris Menges; ***M:*** Alex Wurman.

Criminal Act 🦴 1/2 *Tunnels* **1988** A newspaper editor hits the street to prove she's still a tough reporter, but uncovers a dangerous scandal in the process. **94m/C VHS, DVD.** Catherine Bach, Charlene Dallas, Nicholas Guest, John Saxon, Vic Tayback; ***D:*** Mark Byers.

Criminal Code 🦴🦴 1/2 **1931** Aging melodrama about a young man who's jailed for killing in self-defense. His life worsens at the hands of a prison warden when the head guy's daughter falls for him. Remade as "Penitentiary" and "Convicted." **98m/B VHS.** Walter Huston, Phillips Holmes, Boris Karloff, Constance Cummings, Mary Doran, DeWitt Jennings, John Sheehan; ***D:*** Howard Hawks.

Criminal Court 🦴🦴 **1946** A man accused of murdering his blackmailer hires the real killer as his attorney. Hard to follow, with an interesting premise that turns flat. **63m/B VHS.** Tom Conway, Martha O'Driscoll, Robert Armstrong, Addison Richards, June Clayworth, Pat Gleason, Steve Brodie; ***D:*** Robert Wise.

Criminal Hearts 🦴🦴 **1995 (R)** Keli (Locane) is driving to Phoenix when she picks up the hitchhiking Rafe (Dillon), who's just robbed a gas station. Turns out the stations are laundering mob drug money and when the store owners are killed, Rafe gets the blame for the murders as well. The killers are actually corrupt FBI agents Martin (Walsh) and Tierney (McDonald) who are soon of the trail of the twosome. **92m/C VHS.** Kevin Dillon, Amy Locane, Morgan Fairchild, M. Emmet Walsh, Michael James McDonald, Don Stroud; ***D:*** Dave Payne; ***W:*** Dave Payne; ***C:*** Christopher Baffa.

Criminal Justice 🦴🦴🦴 **1990 (R)** A black man is accused of a crime by a woman with whom he was involved. Is it justice or revenge? Strong cast in important story. **92m/C VHS.** Forest Whitaker, Jennifer Grey, Rosie Perez, Anthony LaPaglia, Tony Todd; ***D:*** Andy Wolk; ***W:*** Andy Wolk; ***C:*** Steven Fierberg. **CABLE**

Criminal Justice 🦴🦴 **2008** British miniseries. Young Ben Coulter is in prison, awaiting trial for a murder he very likely didn't commit (heavy drinking, sex with a stranger, and waking up next to a dead body is suspicious though). He's assigned a slovenly lawyer who seems rather cavalier about Ben's predicament, although the detective in charge of the investigation questions Ben's guilt as well. But being accused of a crime may be the least of Ben's troubles. **285m/C DVD.** *GB* ***D:*** Luke Watson; ***W:*** Peter Moffatt; ***C:*** Eric Maddison; ***M:*** John Lunn. **TV**

Criminal Law 🦴🦴 **1989 (R)** An ambitious young Boston lawyer gets a man acquitted for murder, only to find out after the trial that the man is guilty and renewing his killing spree. Realizing he's the only one privy to the killer's trust, the lawyer decides to stop him himself. A white-knuckled thriller burdened by a weak script. **113m/C VHS.** Kevin Bacon, Gary Oldman, Karen Young, Joe Don Baker, Tess Harper; ***D:*** Martin Campbell; ***W:*** Mark Kassen; ***C:*** Phil Meheux; ***M:*** Jerry Goldsmith.

The Criminal Life of Archibaldo de la Cruz 🦴🦴🦴 *Ensayo de un Crimen; Rehearsal for a Crime* **1955** Seeing the death of his governess has a lasting effect on a boy. He grows up to be a demented cretin whose failure with women leads him to conspire to kill every one he meets, a task at which he also fails. Hilarious, bitter Bunuelian diatribe. In Spanish with English subtitles. **95m/B VHS.** *MX SP* Ernesto Alonso, Ariadne Welter, Rita Macedo, Rodolfo Landa, Andrea Palma, Miroslava Stern; ***D:*** Luis Bunuel; ***W:*** Luis Bunuel; ***C:*** Augustin Jimenez; ***M:*** Jorge Perez.

Criminal Lovers 🦴🦴 *Les Amants Criminels* **1999** Aggressive 17-year-old Alice (Regnier) persuades her ambivalent boyfriend Luc (Renier) to kill their classmate Said, after telling Luc that Said got his friends to rape her. They drive the body into the woods to bury it but then become lost and seek refuge in a ramshackle cottage that happens to belong to a hermit (Manojlovic) who witnessed the burial. He tosses them in his cellar but soon releases Luc to satisfy his own pleasures (and those of the sexually confused boy). Eventually the duo escape, only to find the police on their trail. French with subtitles. **96m/C VHS, DVD.** *FR* Natacha Regnier, Jeremie Renier, Miki (Predrag) Manojlovic, Salim Kechiouche; ***D:*** Francois Ozon; ***W:*** Francois Ozon; ***C:*** Pierre Stoeber; ***M:*** Philippe Rombi.

The Criminal Mind 🦴🦴 **1993 (R)** L.A. District Attorney Nick August (Rossi) reunites with his long-lost brother (Cross), whom he discovers is very familiar with the other side of the law. Tied up with the mob, Cross forces his bro to watch a hit and then Rossi winds up the next target for a group of assassins and some corrupt cops. **93m/C VHS.** Ben Cross, Frank Rossi, Tahnee Welch, Lance Henriksen, Joseph Ruskin, Lynn-Holly Johnson; ***D:*** Joseph Vittorie; ***W:*** Sam A. Scribner.

Criminal Ways 🦴 1/2 *The Wannabes* **2003 (R)** Danny dreams of a showbiz career while teaching dance classes. He's hired by thug Marcus and his crew to show them how to entertain at a kiddie birthday party, not realizing the crooks plan to rob the place. Through a series of silly circumstances, Danny joins in, the job gets bungled, but the 'entertainers' are a hit as a children's musical group and find themselves on the road to stardom. Broadly-done Australian farce. **92m/C DVD.** *AU* Isla Fisher, Tony Nikolakopoulos, Ryan Thomas Johnson, Nick Giannopoulos, Russell Dykstra, Costas Kilias, Michael Carmen, Lena Cruz; ***W:*** Chris Anastassiades, Ray Boseley; ***C:*** Dan Burstall; ***M:*** David Hirschfelder.

Criminally Insane 🦴 **1975** Authorities release 250 pounds of cleaver-wielding maniacal fury from the loony bin. She seeks food and human blood. They should have known better. Followed by "Crazy Fat Ethel II." **61m/C VHS, DVD.** Priscilla Alden, Michael Flood; ***D:*** Nick (Steve Millard) Phillips.

Criminals Within 🦴 *Army Mystery* **1941** A scientist working on a top secret formula is murdered and a detective tries to nail the spy ring responsible. Very confusing, poor usage of some fine female cast members. **67m/B VHS, DVD.** Eric Linden, Ann Doran, Constance Worth, Donald Curtis, Weldon Heyburn, Ben Alexander; ***D:*** Joseph H. Lewis.

The Crimson Code 🦴 1/2 **1999 (R)** FBI agents Chandler (Muldoon) and Dobson (Moriarty) discover a serial killer who goes after other serial killers. Then Chandler is offered a chance to circumvent that pesky legal thing by joining a covert ops that takes retribution as it sees fit. Just one cliche after another. **90m/C VHS, DVD.** Patrick Muldoon, Cathy Moriarty, C. Thomas Howell, Fred Ward, Tim Thomerson; ***D:*** Jeremy Haft; ***W:*** Alex Metcalf; ***C:*** Ian Elkin; ***M:*** Ken Williams. **VIDEO**

The Crimson Cult 🦴 *The Crimson Altar; Curse of the Crimson Altar* **1968 (PG)** Eden and his girlfriend are invited to a mysterious mansion. They discover that Lee is out to enact revenge as his ancestor was burned for witchcraft by Eden's. An all-star horror disaster. Karloff was 80 and confined to a wheelchair. Despite ads claiming this as his last film, he made four more in Mexico. Highlights include the scantily clad Steele in sado-masochistic sequences and a psychedelic party with strippers and body painters. **87m/C VHS.** *GB* Boris Karloff, Christopher Lee, Mark Eden, Barbara Steele, Virginia Wetherell, Michael Gough, Rupert Davies; ***D:*** Vernon Sewell.

Crimson Force 🦴 **2005** How many ways can you deride yet another lame, low-budget Sci-Fi Channel original? The crew of the first manned mission to Mars has traveled to the big red planet in order to locate a new source of energy to use at home. What they discover is a Martian civilization in the midst of a civil war and the winners intend to invade Earth next. **90m/C DVD.** C. Thomas Howell, David Chokachi, Tony Amendola, Julia Rose, Terasa Livingstone, Jeff Gimble, Richard Gnolfo; ***D:*** David Flores; ***W:*** Rob Mecarini; ***C:*** Lorenzo Senatore; ***M:*** Chris Walden, Matthias Weber. **CABLE**

Crimson Gold 🦴🦴 1/2 *Talaye Sorgh* **2003** Hussein (Emadeddin) is a simple, war-veteran-turned-pizza-deliveryman, but the opening sequence shows him in the midst of a botched jewelry-store robbery that ends abruptly and grimly—resulting in tragedy. What follows are flashbacks (compelling yet often slow-paced) that attempt to define his behavior and the social rejection that led him down his destructive path. Set in Tehran and based on a true story, this has—like other Panahi films—been banned in Iran. Farsi with subtitles. **95m/C DVD.** *IA* Hossain Emadeddin, Kamyar Sheisi, Azita Rayeji, Shahram Vaziri, Ehsan Amani, Pourang Nakhael, Kaveh Najmabadi, Saber Safael; ***D:*** Jafar Panahi; ***W:*** Abbas Kiarostami; ***C:*** Hossain Djafarian; ***M:*** Peyman Yazdanian.

The Crimson Kimono 🦴🦴 **1959** Fuller's look at interracial romance and jealousy is tied up in a not-too-interesting murder investigation. Friends since the Korean War, Bancroft (Corbett) and Kojaku (Shigeta) work homicide in L.A. They're assigned a stripper's murder, which is how they meet artist Christine (Shaw) and both fall for her. She prefers gentlemanly Kojaku and Bancroft gets jealous although they set aside their differences for the sake of the case, which takes them into Little Tokyo. **81m/B DVD.** Glenn Corbett, James Shigeta, Victoria Shaw, Anna Lee, Paul Dubov, Neyle Morrow, Jaclynne Greene, Gloria Pall; ***D:*** Samuel Fuller; ***W:*** Samuel Fuller; ***C:*** Sam Leavitt; ***M:*** Harry Sukman.

Crimson Pirate ½ **1952** An 18th-century buccaneer pits his wits and brawn against the might of a ruthless Spanish nobleman. Considered by many to be one of the best swashbucklers, laced with humor and enthusiastically paced. Showcase for Lancaster and Cravat's acrobatic talents. **104m/C VHS, DVD.** *GB* Charles Farrell, Burt Lancaster, Eva Bartok, Torin Thatcher, Christopher Lee, Nick Cravat; ***D:*** Robert Siodmak.

The Crimson Rivers *Les Rivieres Pourpres* **2001 (R)** Audacious and gruesome thriller set in the French Alps. A librarian from the local private university is found horribly mutilated on a mountain slope and Parisian investigator Pierre Niemans (Reno) is called in. Before long, there's more than one victim, all of whom have ties to the university, and Niemans has a young, aggressive partner in provincial policeman Max Kerkerian (Cassel). French with subtitles or dubbed. **105m/C VHS, DVD.** *FR* Jean Reno, Vincent Cassel, Nadia Fares, Dominique Sanda, Laurent Avare, Jean-Pierre Cassel, Didier Flamand; ***D:*** Mathieu Kassovitz; ***W:*** Mathieu Kassovitz, Jean-Christophe Grange; ***C:*** Thierry Arbogast; ***M:*** Bruno Coulais.

Crimson Rivers 2: Angels of the Apocalypse ½ *Les Rivieres Pourpres II: Les Anges de L'apocalypse* **2005** A series of religious-related murders puts Parisian detective Pierre Niemans (Reno) on the case. He's paired with police captain Reda (Magimel)—who has stumbled upon a man resembling Jesus Christ—to solve the mystery and contend with a dark, deadly organization bent on razing Europe. Fans of the original should be pleased, though the story needs an oar and compass to find its way to shore. In French, with English subtitles or dubbed. **99m/C VHS, DVD.** *FR GB IT* Jean Reno, Benoit Magimel, Christopher Lee, Johnny Hallyday, Camille Natta, Augustin Legrand; ***D:*** Olivier Dahan; ***W:*** Jean-Christophe Grange, Luc Besson; ***C:*** Alex Lamarque; ***M:*** Colin Towns. **VIDEO**

Crimson Romance **1934** Two unemployed American pilots in Europe decide to join the German airforce for want of anything better to do. Conflicts revolve around a warmongering Commandant and his pilot. **70m/B VHS, DVD.** Ben Lyon, Sari Maritza, James Bush, Erich von Stroheim, Jason Robards Sr., Herman Bing, Vince Barnett; ***D:*** David Howard.

Crimson Tide **1995 (R)** Mutiny erupts aboard the submarine USS Alabama as Captain Ramsey (Hackman) and his Executive Officer Hunter (Washington) clash over the validity of orders to launch the sub's missiles. Ramsey, who wants to fire the missiles, and Hunter, who refuses to comply until the message is verified, battle for control of the sub. Suspenseful and well-paced thriller lets Hackman and Washington show off their considerable screen presence, while Bruckheimer, Simpson, and Scott show that they haven't lost any of their trademark big-budget, testosterone-laden flash. Original screenplay went under the knife of a number of script doctors, most notably Quentin Tarantino. **116m/C VHS, DVD, Blu-ray Disc, UMD.** Gene Hackman, Denzel Washington, George Dzundza, Viggo Mortensen, James Gandolfini, Matt Craven, Lillo Brancato, Danny Nucci, Steve Zahn, Rick Schroder, Vanessa Bell Calloway, Rocky Carroll; ***Cameos:*** Jason Robards Jr.; ***D:*** Tony Scott; ***W:*** Michael Schiffer, Richard P. Henrick; ***C:*** Darius Wolski; ***M:*** Hans Zimmer.

The Crimson Trail ½ **1935** Buck believes his uncle may be involved in cattle rustling. Lots of action, minimal plot. **56m/B VHS.** Buck Jones, Polly Ann Young, Carl Stockdale, Charles French, Ward Bond, Robert F. (Bob) Kortman, Bud Osborne, Charles Brinley, Robert Walker; ***D:*** Al Raboch; ***W:*** Jack Natteford.

The Crippled Masters **1982 (R)** After Li Ho's (Shum) arms are cut off by an evil warlord, he wanders the countryside facing ridicule until he teams up with disfigured Dax Oh Jen (Conn). Helped by an elderly yoga master, the duo unite to seek revenge. Features kung-fu masters with real-life disabilities. **90m/C VHS, DVD.** Frankie Shum, Jack Conn; ***D:*** Joe Law.

Crisis ½ **1950** Heavy-handed and dull political melodrama. Brain surgeon Eugene Ferguson (Grant) and his wife Helen (Raymond) are vacationing in some South American country that's suddenly beset by a revolution. However, dictator Farrago (Ferrer) needs an operation and makes sure the Fergusons can't leave. Revolutionary leader Gonzalez (Roland) wants Ferguson to botch the operation and holds Helen as a hostage for leverage. **95m/B DVD.** Cary Grant, Jose Ferrer, Paula Raymond, Gilbert Roland, Signe Hasso, Ramon Novarro, Leon Ames; ***D:*** Richard Brooks; ***W:*** Richard Brooks; ***C:*** Ray June; ***M:*** Miklos Rozsa.

Crisis at Central High **1980** A dramatic re-creation of the events leading up to the 1957 integration of Central High in Little Rock, Arkansas. Based on teacher Elizabeth Huckaby's journal. Emmy-nominated performance by Woodward as Huckaby. **120m/C VHS.** Joanne Woodward, Charles Durning, William Ross, Henderson Forsythe; ***D:*** Lamont Johnson; ***M:*** Billy Goldenberg. **TV**

Criss Cross **1948** A classic grade-B film noir, in which an armored car driver is suckered into a burglary by his ex-wife and her hoodlum husband. Multiple back-stabbings and double-crossings ensue. **98m/B VHS, DVD.** Burt Lancaster, Yvonne De Carlo, Dan Duryea, Stephen McNally, Richard Long, Tony Curtis, Alan Napier; ***D:*** Robert Siodmak; ***W:*** Daniel Fuchs; ***C:*** Franz Planer; ***M:*** Miklos Rozsa.

Crisscross ½ *Alone Together* **1992 (R)** It's 1969 and Tracy Cross is a divorced mom whose ex-husband is a traumatized Vietnam vet who has left her alone to raise their 12 year-old son Chris during some hard times. She works two jobs, as a waitress and, unbeknownst to her son, as a stripper in a local club. When Chris sneaks into the club and sees her act he takes drastic measures to help out—by selling drugs. Film is sluggish and relies too much on voice-overs to explain thoughts but Hawn gives a convincing and restrained performance as the mother. **107m/C VHS, DVD.** Goldie Hawn, David Arnott, Arliss Howard, James Gammon, Keith Carradine, J.C. Quinn, Steve Buscemi, Paul Calderon; ***D:*** Chris Menges; ***M:*** Trevor Jones.

Critical Care ½ **1997 (R)** Spader is a doctor in a high-tech intensive care unit dealing with the ethics of modern health care, such as insurance scams, euthanasia, and a drunken administrator (Brooks) whose only concern is the hospital's profits. Two sisters (Sedgwick and Martindale) fight over the fate of their terminally ill, near-vegetable father. Spader finds his career on the line after bedding Sedgwick and backing her attempts to pull the plug. Given the meatiness of the subject, director Lumet could have made a much more scathing satire. Schwartz's script is lame even for a first-time effort, and the usually interesting Shawn falls horribly flat with an embarrassing bit of dialogue. Occasional laughs (this was supposed to be a dark comedy) and good performances from Brooks and Mirren can't keep this one from flatlining. Watch an episode of "ER" instead. **105m/C VHS, DVD.** James Spader, Albert Brooks, Kyra Sedgwick, Helen Mirren, Margo Martindale, Jeffrey Wright, Wallace Shawn, Anne Bancroft, Philip Bosco, Edward Herrmann, Colm Feore, James Lally, Al Waxman, Harvey Atkin; ***D:*** Sidney Lumet; ***W:*** Steven S. Schwartz; ***C:*** David Watkin; ***M:*** Michael Convertino.

Critical Choices **1997 (R)** The Women's Health Clinic in Milwaukee, Wisconsin, provides safe and legal abortions. Run by Dr. Margaret Ludlow (Buckley) and her pro-choice supporter, Diana Johnson (Scarwid), the clinic becomes the focal point for right-wing evangelist Bobby Ray Flood (Kerwin) and his supporters, including Arlene Dickens (Reed). Tensions mount and violence erupts as everyone believes they're doing the right thing. **88m/C VHS.** Betty Buckley, Pamela Reed, Diana Scarwid, Terry Kinney, Brian Kerwin; ***D:*** Claudia Weill; ***W:*** Susan Cuscuna, Robin Green, Mitchell Burgess; ***M:*** Patrick Seymour. **CABLE**

Critical Condition **1986 (R)** During a blackout, a criminal masquerades as a doctor in a city hospital. Limp comedy embarrassing for Pryor. **99m/C VHS, DVD.** Richard Pryor, Rachel Ticotin, Ruben Blades, Joe Mantegna, Kate McGregor-Stewart; ***D:*** Michael Apted; ***C:*** Ralf Bode; ***M:*** Alan Silvestri.

Critical Mass **2000 (R)** This one will seem very familiar. Terrorist Samson (Kier) and his crew steal nuclear material and retreat to a deserted nuclear power plant in southern California in order to build a bomb. Only the power plant isn't so deserted and security guard Mike (Williams), aided by babe Janine (Loughlin), work to thwart Samson's nefarious plan. **95m/C VHS, DVD.** Treat Williams, Udo Kier, Lori Loughlin, Blake Clark, Andrew Prine; ***D:*** Fred Olen Ray; ***C:*** Theo Angell; ***M:*** Neal Acree. **VIDEO**

Critic's Choice **1963** Tedious adaptation of Ira Levin's insider play that's likely to only be appreciated by Ball and/or Hope fans. Angela Ballantine (Ball) is an aspiring playwright whose first effort is about to open on Broadway. And it's going to be reviewed by her theater critic husband, Parker (Hope), who would rather be doing anything else. Like having a few drinks with his consoling ex-wife Ivy (Maxwell). Parker stumbles into the theater, drunk and the center of unwelcome attention, especially from the current Mrs. Ballantine, who's not pleased. Edith Head did the costumes. **100m/C DVD.** Bob Hope, Lucille Ball, Marilyn Maxwell, Rip Torn, Jessie Royce Landis, John Dehner, Jim Backus, Rick Kelman, Marie Windsor, Joseph (Joe) Gallison, Richard Deacon, Jerome Cowan, Donald Losby, Soupy Sales; ***D:*** Don Weis; ***W:*** Jack Sher; ***C:*** Charles B(ryant) Lang Jr.; ***M:*** George Duning.

Critters ½ **1986 (PG-13)** A gang of furry, razor-toothed aliens escapes from its prison ship to Earth with their bounty hunters right behind them. They make it to a small town in Kansas where they begin to attack anything that moves. Not just a thrill-kill epic, but a sarcastic other-worldly thrill-kill epic. **86m/C VHS, DVD.** Dee Wallace, M. Emmet Walsh, Billy Green Bush, Scott Grimes, Nadine Van Der Velde, Terrence Mann, Billy Zane, Don Opper; ***D:*** Stephen Herek; ***W:*** Stephen Herek, Dominic Muir; ***C:*** Tim Suhrstedt; ***M:*** David Newman.

Critters 2: The Main Course **1988 (PG-13)** Sequel to the hit horror-comedy, wherein the voracious alien furballs return in full force to Grovers Bend, Kansas, from eggs planted two years before. Occasionally inspired "Gremlins" rip. **93m/C VHS, DVD.** Scott Grimes, Liane (Alexandra) Curtis, Don Opper, Barry Corbin, Terrence Mann; ***D:*** Mick Garris; ***W:*** Mick Garris, David N. Twohy; ***C:*** Russell Carpenter.

Critters 3 **1991 (PG-13)** The not-so-loveable critters are back, terrorizing the occupants of a tenement building. **86m/C VHS, DVD.** Frances Bay, Aimee Brooks, Leonardo DiCaprio, Don Opper; ***D:*** Kristine Peterson; ***W:*** David J. Schow.

Critters 4 **1991 (PG-13)** The ghoulish critters are back, and this time a strain of genetically engineered mutant critters (what's the difference?) wants to take over the universe. **94m/C VHS, DVD.** Don Opper, Paul Whitthorne, Angela Bassett, Brad Dourif, Terrence Mann; ***D:*** Rupert Harvey; ***W:*** David J. Schow.

Croc ½ **2007** There's a lot of unnecessary story added to this killer croc movie but here goes: ex-pat American Jack McQuade (Tuinstra) has a failing croc attraction at a Thai beach resort. His land is coveted by his competition so when locals go missing, Jack gets blamed since his star attraction, Delilah, is also absent. Jack and his pals decide to track Delilah, which means venturing into the most dangerous swampland in the area. **90m/C DVD.** Michael Madsen, Elizabeth Healey, Peter Tuinstra, Tawon Sawtang, Sherry Phungprasert; ***D:*** Stewart Raffill; ***W:*** Ken Solarz; ***C:*** Choochart Nantitanyatada; ***M:*** Charles Olins, Mark Ryder. **TV**

Crocodile WOOF! **1981 (R)** Giant crocodile attacks a beach town, killing and devouring dozens of people. The locals sit around trying to figure a way to stop the critter. Special effects include rear-projected croc. Lots of blood but lacking humor of "Alligator." Filmed in Thailand and Korea. **95m/C VHS, DVD.** *KN* Nat Puvanai, Tany Tim, Angela Wells, Kirk Warren; ***D:*** Sompote Sands.

Crocodile ½ **2000 (R)** Cheesy special effects doom this low-budget horror. College students spend spring break on a houseboat and are terrorized by a giant crocodile who regards them as a new snack food. **94m/C VHS, DVD.** Chris Solari, Mark McLaughlin, Caitlin Martin, Julie Mintz, Sommer Knight; ***D:*** Tobe Hooper; ***W:*** Michael D. Weiss, Adam Gierasch, Jace Anderson; ***C:*** Eliot Rockett. **VIDEO**

Crocodile 2: Death Swamp WOOF! **2001 (R)** Airliner crashes into a Mexican swamp and the survivors get picked off by big hungry crocodile. This one is too boring to even be bad fun. **90m/C VHS, DVD.** Heidi Lenhart, Steve Moreno, Joe Sklaroff, Martin Kove, Darryl Theirse; ***D:*** Gary Jones; ***W:*** Jace Anderson, Adam Gierasch; ***C:*** Rasool Ellore; ***M:*** Bill Wandel. **VIDEO**

Crocodile Dundee ½ **1986 (PG-13)** New York reporter Sue Charlton (Kozlowski) is assigned to the Outback to interview living legend Mike Dundee (Hogan). When she finally locates the man, she is so taken with him that she brings him back to New York with her. There, the naive Aussie wanders about, amazed at the wonders of the city and unwittingly charming everyone he comes in contact with, from high-society transvestites to street hookers. One of the surprise hits of 1986. **98m/C VHS, DVD.** *AU* Paul Hogan, Linda Kozlowski, John Meillon, David Gulpilil, Mark Blum; ***D:*** Peter Faiman; ***W:*** John Cornell, Paul Hogan; ***C:*** Russell Boyd; ***M:*** Peter Best. Golden Globes '87: Actor—Mus./Comedy (Hogan).

Crocodile Dundee 2 ½ **1988 (PG)** In this sequel Mike Dundee, the loveable rube, returns to his native Australia looking for new adventure, having "conquered" New York City. He finds trouble when Colombian drug lords kidnap his woman (Kozlowski again) and later track the couple to the Australian Outback. Lacks the charm and freshness of the first film. **110m/C VHS, DVD.** Stephen (Steve) Root, Jace Alexander, Luis Guzman, Colin Quinn, Paul Hogan, Linda Kozlowski, Kenneth Welsh, John Meillon, Ernie Dingo, Juan Fernandez, Charles S. Dutton; ***D:*** John Cornell; ***W:*** Paul Hogan; ***C:*** Russell Boyd; ***M:*** Peter Best.

Crocodile Dundee in Los Angeles ½ **2001 (PG)** Mick is back, for no good reason other than Hogan and Kozlowski probably needed the dough. The happy couple return to the States so Sue (Kozlowski) can investigate a movie studio that may be involved in a smuggling ring and, even worse, keeps cranking out dumb sequels. Where DO they come up with these ideas? Meanwhile, Dundee introduces their son (Cockburn) to life in the big city while working as an extra on the suspicious studio lot. It looks and feels like a real movie, but something's missing. What is it? Hmmmmm......Oh, yeah! A point! Unless the previous two installments left too many unanswered questions, you can probably skip this one. **95m/C VHS, DVD.** Paul Hogan, Linda Kozlowski, Jere Burns, Jonathan Banks, Paul Rodriguez, Alec Wilson, Serge Cockburn, Aida Turturro, Kaitlin Hopkins; ***Cameos:*** Mike Tyson; ***D:*** Simon Wincer; ***W:*** Matthew Berry, Eric Abrams; ***C:*** David Burr; ***M:*** Basil Poledouris.

The Crocodile Hunter: Collision Course ½ **2002 (PG)** Nature show hosts Steve Irwin and his wife Terri take their "The Crocodile Hunter" TV shtick to the big screen in this far-fetched story about a croc who swallows a top secret U.S. satellite beacon. Irwin attempts to protect the animal from a gun-toting farmer and some secret agents he mistakes for poachers. The story is just an excuse for Irwin to round up and irritate some of the world's most dangerous animals, presumably while Terri is checking his life insurance coverage. Kids who like the show will love the movie. **89m/C VHS, DVD.** *AU US* Steve Irwin, Terri Irwin, Magda Szubanski, David Wenham, Aden Young, Kenny Ransom, Lachy Hulme, Kate Beahan, Steven Vidler, Steve Bastoni; ***D:*** John Stainton; ***W:*** Holly Goldberg Sloan; ***C:*** David Burr; ***M:*** Mark McDuff.

Crocodile Tears 1998 Gay art teacher Simon (Sod) makes a devil's bargain (literally) when he learns he's HIV-positive. Sinister Mr. Cheseboro (Salyers) offers the gift of health if Simon will become a straight stand-up comic who specializes in racist, sexist, and homophobic humor. Simon becomes a huge success but can he live with the consequences? Outrageous if heavy-handed. **84m/C VHS, DVD.** Ted Sod, William Salyers, Dan Savage, Jeanne L. Klein; ***D:*** Ann Coppel; ***W:*** Ted Sod.

Crocodiles in Amsterdam *Krokodillen in Amsterdam* 1989 Lunatic girl-meets-girl movie about flighty Gino and would-be terrorist Nina who team up to rob Gino's rich uncle. Dutch with subtitles. **88m/C VHS.** *NL* Joan Nederlof, Yolanda Entius; ***D:*** Annette Apon; ***W:*** Yolanda Entius, Annette Apon.

Cromwell 1/2 1970 (G) A lavish British-made spectacle about the conflict between Oliver Cromwell and Charles I, and the British Civil War. History is twisted as Cromwell becomes the liberator of the oppressed. Harris gives a commanding performance and the battle scenes are stunners. **139m/C VHS, DVD.** *GB* Richard Harris, Alec Guinness, Robert Morley, Frank Finlay, Patrick Magee, Timothy Dalton; ***D:*** Ken Hughes; ***W:*** Ken Hughes; ***C:*** Geoffrey Unsworth. Oscars '70: Costume Des.

Cronicas 2004 (R) Manolo Bonilla (Leguizamo) is an ambitious Miami TV tabloid reporter who heads to an Ecuadorian village that has been targeted by a serial child rapist and killer. Bible salesman Vinicio (Alcazar) accidentally runs over a victim's brother, is set upon by a mob, and saved by Bonilla. In return, Vinicio promises to reveal the killer's identity, claiming they met on his travels. But is Vinicio, himself, the killer or is he stringing Manolo along in order to stay alive? And just how far will Manolo go to get his story? Runs out of steam but Leguizamo gives an intense performance. **111m/C DVD.** *MX* John Leguizamo, Leonor Watling, Damian Alcazar, Alfred Molina, Jose Maria Yazpik; ***D:*** Sebastian Cordero; ***W:*** Sebastian Cordero; ***C:*** Enrique Chediak; ***M:*** Antonio Pinto.

Cronos *Chronos* 1994 (R) Stylish Mexican variation of the vampire tale. Aged antiques dealer Jesus Gris (Luppi) comes across the mysterious title object—a 14th century golden egg possessing magical powers to grant eternal life. But can its possessor stand the consequences, which include a developing taste for blood? Another problem is Gris isn't the only one to know about the device. First feature for writer/director del Toro. Spanish with subtitles. **92m/C VHS, DVD.** *MX* Federico Luppi, Ron Perlman, Claudio Brook, Tamara Shanath, Margarita Isabel; ***D:*** Guillermo del Toro; ***W:*** Guillermo del Toro; ***C:*** Guillermo Navarro; ***M:*** Javier Alvarez.

The Crooked Circle 1/2 1932 More comedy than mystery as slapstick policeman Gleason goes under cover as a swami. Not helped at all by a weak script and poor photography. **68m/B VHS, DVD.** Ben Lyon, Zasu Pitts, James Gleason, C. Henry Gordon, Raymond Hatton, Roscoe Karns; ***D:*** H. Bruce Humberstone.

Crooked Hearts 1991 (R) Dysfunctional family drama means well but lays it on too thick, as a father/son rivalry threatens to sunder the tight-knit Warrens. Based on a novel by Robert Boswell. **113m/C VHS, DVD.** Peter Coyote, Jennifer Jason Leigh, Peter Berg, Cindy Pickett, Vincent D'Onofrio, Noah Wyle, Juliette Lewis, Wendy Gazelle, Marg Helgenberger; ***D:*** Michael Bortman; ***W:*** Michael Bortman; ***C:*** Tak Fujimoto; ***M:*** Mark Isham.

Crooked Trail 1936 A lawman and bad guy become friends. **58m/B VHS.** Johnny Mack Brown, John Merton, Lucille Browne; ***D:*** S. Roy Luby; ***W:*** George Plympton.

Crooklyn 1994 (PG-13) Director Lee turns from the life of Malcolm X to the early lives of Generation X in this profile of an African-American middle-class family growing up in 1970s Brooklyn. Lee's least politically charged film to date is a joint effort between him and sibs Joie and Cinque, and profiles the only girl in a family of five children coming of age. Tender and real performances from all, especially newcomer Harris, propel the sometimes messy, music-laden trip to nostalgia land. **112m/C VHS, DVD.** Alfre Woodard, Delroy Lindo, Zelda Harris, David Patrick Kelly, Carlton Williams, Sharif Rashed, Tse-March Washington, Christopher Knowings, Jose Zuniga, Isaiah Washington IV, Ivelka Reyes, N. Jeremi Duru, Frances Foster, Norman Matlock, Patriece Nelson, Joie Lee, Vondie Curtis-Hall, Tiasha Reyes, Spike Lee, RuPaul Charles; ***D:*** Spike Lee; ***W:*** Joie Lee, Cinque Lee; ***C:*** Arthur Jaffa; ***M:*** Terence Blanchard.

Crooks & Coronets 1/2 *Sophie's Place* 1969 (PG) Two-bit crooks plot to rob the country estate of an eccentric British dowager. **106m/C VHS.** *GB* Cesar Romero, Telly Savalas, Warren Oates, Edith Evans; ***D:*** James O'Connolly.

The Cross & the Switchblade 1/2 1972 (PG) An idealistic priest tries to bring the message of religion to the members of a vicious street gang. They don't wanna listen. Spanish language version available. **105m/C VHS, DVD.** Pat Boone, Erik Estrada, Jackie Giroux, Jo-Ann Robinson; ***D:*** Don Murray.

Cross Country 1/2 1983 (R) Action revolves around the brutal murder of a call girl, with initial suspicion falling on a TV advertising director involved with the woman. The story twists and turns from the suspect to investigating detective Ironside without becoming particularly interesting. **95m/C VHS.** *CA* Richard Beymer, Nina Axelrod, Michael Ironside; ***D:*** Paul Lynch; ***W:*** Logan N. Danforth.

Cross Creek 1/2 1983 (PG) Based on the life of Marjorie Kinnan Rawlings, author of "The Yearling," who, after 10 years as a frustrated reporter/writer, moves to the remote and untamed Everglades. There she meets colorful local characters and receives the inspiration to write numerous bestsellers. Well acted though overtly sentimental at times. **120m/C VHS, DVD.** Mary Steenburgen, Rip Torn, Peter Coyote, Dana Hill, Alfre Woodard, Malcolm McDowell; ***D:*** Martin Ritt; ***W:*** Dalene Young; ***C:*** John A. Alonzo; ***M:*** Leonard Rosenman.

Cross Examination 1/2 1932 A boy is charged with his father's murder, and a defense attorney struggles to acquit him. **61m/B VHS.** H.B. Warner, Sally Blane, Sarah Padden; ***D:*** Richard Thorpe; ***W:*** Arthur Hoerl; ***C:*** M.A. Anderson.

Cross Mission 1989 (R) Predictable actioner about a photographer and a soldier who are captured by the enemy. Packed with a bit of ninja, ammo, and occult. **90m/C VHS.** Richard Randall; ***D:*** Al (Alfonso Brescia) Bradley.

Cross My Heart 1988 (R) Light comedy about two single people with complicated, post-divorce lives who go on a date and suffer accordingly. Will true love prevail? **91m/C VHS.** Martin Short, Annette O'Toole, Paul Reiser, Joanna Kerns; ***D:*** Armyan Bernstein; ***W:*** Armyan Bernstein; ***M:*** Bruce Broughton.

Cross My Heart *La Fracture du Myocarde* 1991 A group of school children conspire to hide the death of their fellow student Martin's mother. This will prevent his placement in the state orphanage. Interesting premise is blandly treated by Fansten. Child actors don't seem realistic, photography is without flair. In French with English subtitles. **105m/C VHS.** *FR* Sylvain Copans, Nicolas Pardi, Cecilia Rouaud, Delphine Gouttman, Lucie Blossier; ***D:*** Jacques Fansten; ***W:*** Jacques Fansten; ***C:*** Jean-Claude Saillier; ***M:*** Jean-Marie Senia.

Cross My Heart and Hope to Die *Ti Kniver I Hjertet* 1994 Young Otto (Garfalk) is an average misfit kid until he comes to the attention of the mischief-making Frank (Kornstad), who is the catalyst for Otto to get into all kinds of trouble. Based on the novel by Lars Saaby Christensen. Norwegian with subtitles. **96m/C VHS, DVD.** *NO* Martin Dahl Garfalk, Jan Devo Kornstad; ***D:*** Marius Holst; ***W:*** Marius Holst; ***C:*** Philip Ogaard; ***M:*** Kjetil Bjerkestrand, Magne Furuholmen.

Cross of Iron 1/2 *Steiner—Das Eiserne Kreuz* 1976 (R) During WWII, two antagonistic German officers clash over personal ideals as well as strategy in combatting the relentless Russian attack. Followed by "Breakthrough." **120m/C VHS, DVD.** *GB GE* James Coburn, Maximilian Schell, James Mason, David Warner, Senta Berger, Klaus Lowitsch, Vadim Glowna, Roger Fritz, Dieter Schidor, Burkhard Driest, Fred Stillkrauth, Michael Nowka, Veronique Vendell, Arthur Brauss; ***D:*** Sam Peckinpah; ***W:*** Julius J. Epstein, Walter Kelley, James Hamilton; ***C:*** John Coquillon; ***M:*** Ernest Gold.

Crossbar 1979 Aaron Kornylo is determined to reach Olympic qualifications in the high jump despite having only one leg. Inspired by a true story, this program dramatically shows how far determination and work can take a person. **77m/C VHS.** John Ireland, Brent Carver, Kate Reid; ***D:*** John Trent.

Crosscut 1995 (R) Mob hitman Martin Niconi (Mandylor) makes a mistake that could cost him his life when a barroom brawl leads him to shooting the son of a Mafia don. He escapes to a small California logging town, changes his identity, and falls for single mom Anna (Gallagher) but the mob manages to track him down. Big shootout. **90m/C VHS.** Costas Mandylor, Megan Gallagher, Casey Sander, Allen (Culter) Cutler, Zack Norman, George Murdock; ***D:*** Paul Raimondi; ***W:*** Paul Raimondi, David Masiel, Scott Phillips; ***C:*** David Bridges; ***M:*** Christopher Tyng.

Crossfire 1/2 1947 A Jewish hotel guest is murdered and three soldiers just back from Europe are suspected of the crime. The first Hollywood film that explored racial bigotry. Due to the radical nature of its plot, the director and the producer were eventually black-listed for promoting "un-American" themes. Loosely based on Richard Brooks' "The Brick Foxhole." **86m/B VHS, DVD.** Robert Young, Robert Mitchum, Robert Ryan, Gloria Grahame, Paul Kelly; ***D:*** Edward Dmytryk.

Crossfire 1989 (R) A rescue team heads to Vietnam to pick up their MIA comrades. With no help from the government and the enemy at every turn, can they possibly succeed? **99m/C VHS.** Richard Norton, Michael Meyer, Daniel Dietrich, Don Pemrick, Eric Hahn, Wren Brown, Steve Young; ***D:*** Anthony Maharaj; ***W:*** Noah Blough.

Crossfire 1998 (R) Dekova wants revenge for the accidental death of his family and decides to use his wealth to hire terrorists to destroy the Statue of Liberty. Assassin Pike is visiting the site for professional reasons when he figures out something's going on and he might be in for a change of plans. **90m/C VHS.** Andrew Divoff, Mitchell Cox, Tim Thomerson, Yancey Arias; ***D:*** Gary S. Lipsky, Joe Zimmerman; ***W:*** Gary S. Lipsky, Joe Zimmerman; ***C:*** Ronald Vidor; ***M:*** Jose J. Herring. **VIDEO**

Crossfire Trail 2001 Cowboy Rafe Covington (Selleck) promises his dying friend that he will look out for the man's wife, Ann (Madsen), and their Wyoming spread. Rafe heads to town with his sidekicks (Brimley, O'Hara, Kane) and discovers the widow is already being courted by ruthless Bruce Barkow (Harmon), who wants the ranch since there's oil on the land. Naturally, Barkow has a hired gun (Johnson) and the sheriff (Corbin) in his pocket. Accomplished cast, straight forward direction, lush scenery (it's Calgary, Alberta), and a little humor. Based on Louis L'Amour's 1954 novel. **100m/C VHS, DVD.** Tom Selleck, Virginia Madsen, Mark Harmon, Wilford Brimley, David O'Hara, Christian Kane, Barry Corbin, Brad Johnson, William Sanderson, Joanna Miles, Ken Pogue, Rex Linn; ***D:*** Simon Wincer; ***W:*** Charles Robert Carner; ***C:*** David Eggby; ***M:*** Eric Colvin. **CABLE**

The Crossing 1992 (R) Powerful coming-of-age story in which Meg, a sheltered young woman, falls in love with an ambitious artist named Sam. When he decides to leave their small town to pursue his career, she turns to his best friend for comfort and companionship. However, when Sam unexpectedly returns, Meg is forced to make a choice that could drastically change all of their lives. **92m/C VHS.** *AU* Russell Crowe, Danielle Spencer, Robert Mammone; ***D:*** George Ogilvie; ***W:*** Ranald Allan; ***C:*** Jeff Darling; ***M:*** Martin Armiger.

The Crossing 1/2 2000 No, General George Washington did not cross the Delaware river standing in his boat as Emanuel Leutze's famous painting shows. But this historical story is still pretty darn exciting. On Christmas Day in 1776, it seems the American Revolution is destined for failure. Washington (Daniels) has only 2000 troops left and the Continental Army has continually been defeated by the British. But Washington wants to make a final push—a surprise attack on the Hessian garrison at Trenton. Adapted by Howard Fast from his novel. **100m/C VHS, DVD.** Jeff Daniels, Roger Rees, Sebastien Roche, Steven McCarthy, John Henry Canavan, Ned Vukovic; ***D:*** Robert Harmon; ***W:*** Howard Fast. **CABLE**

Crossing Delancey 1988 (PG) Jewish woman (Bozyk), in old world style, plays matchmaker to her independent 30-something granddaughter. Charming modern-day New York City fairy tale deftly manipulates cliches and stereotypes. Lovely performance from Irving as the woman whose heart surprises her. Riegert is swell playing the gentle but never wimpy suitor. Perfectly cast Bozyk was a star on the Yiddish vaudeville stage; this is her film debut. Appealing music by the Roches, with Suzzy Roche giving a credible performance as Irving's friend. Adapted for the big screen by Sandler from her play of the same name. **97m/C VHS, DVD.** Amy Irving, Reizl Bozyk, Peter Riegert, Jeroen Krabbe, Sylvia Miles, Suzzy Roche, George Martin, John Bedford Lloyd, Rosemary Harris, Amy Wright, Claudia Silver, David Hyde Pierce; ***D:*** Joan Micklin Silver; ***W:*** Susan Sandler.

The Crossing Guard 1994 (R) Nicholson headlines as Freddy Gale, a revenge-minded father who hunts down a drunk driver (Morse), who killed his daughter five years previous. Story focuses on dual emotions of the two men: Gale seeks an end to his grief and rage; Booth attempts to deal with guilt and regret. Writer Penn pairs one-time lovers Nicholson and Huston (playing ex-spouses here) in his sophomore directorial effort with explosive results. Focus is, accordingly, on emotional performances while narrative and directorial finesse take a back seat. Dedicated to the late chronicler of the curbside, Charles Bukowski. **111m/C VHS, DVD.** Jack Nicholson, Anjelica Huston, David Morse, Robin Wright Penn, Robbie Robertson, Piper Laurie, Richard Bradford, John Savage, Priscilla Barnes, Kari Wuhrer, Jennifer Leigh Warren, Richard Sarafian, Jeff Morris, Joe (Johnny) Viterelli, Eileen Ryan, Ryo Ishibashi, Michael Ryan, Nicky Blair, Gene Kirkwood, Jason Kristofer, Hadda Brooks; ***D:*** Sean Penn; ***W:*** Sean Penn; ***C:*** Vilmos Zsigmond; ***M:*** Jack Nitzsche.

Crossing Over 1/2 2009 (R) Bland multi-narrative melodrama about various U.S. immigration cases. Brit Gavin Kossef (Sturgess) and Aussie Claire Sheperd (Eve) have outstayed their visas; he keeps his status secret at his new job and she decides to trade sex with sleazy Cole Frankel (Liotta) for a chance at a green card. Meanwhile, Cole's wife Denise (Judd) is an immigration attorney who wants to adopt a Nigerian orphan. Ford's a good-guy immigration agent who takes a paternal interest in a young Mexican mother who's about to be deported and there's also a couple of subplots involving a Bangladeshi teenager writing a naive essay on terrorism and a Korean teen caught up in gang life. The coincidences seem forced and director Kramer wraps things up tidily—unlike real life. **140m/C DVD.** *US* Harrison Ford, Clifford Curtis, Ashley Judd, Sean Penn, Ray Liotta, Alice Braga, Alice Eve, Jim Sturgess, Summer Bishil, Justin Chon, Hamid Baraheri; ***D:*** Wayne Kramer; ***W:*** Wayne Kramer; ***C:*** James Whitaker; ***M:*** John Murphy, Mark Isham.

Crossing the Bridge 1992 (R) An after high-school tale of three buddies and their restless lives as they take their uncertain steps towards adulthood. It's 1975 in Detroit and Mort, Danny, and Tim cling to high-school memories as they pass time on petty jobs, drinking, and cruising across the Ambassador Bridge to check out the Canadian strip joints. Their big moment—for better or worse—comes when they are offered the chance to make a lot of quick cash if they'll smuggle hash from Toronto to Detroit. Directorial debut of Binder. **105m/C VHS, DVD.** Josh Charles, Jason Gedrick, Stephen Baldwin, Cheryl Pollak, Jeffrey Tambor; ***D:*** Mike Binder; ***W:*** Mike Binder.

Crossing the Line 1990 (R) Two motocross racers battle it out for the championship. **90m/C VHS, DVD.** Jon Stafford, Rick Hearst, Paul Smith, Cameron Mitchell, Vernon Wells, Colleen Morris, John Saxon; ***D:*** Gary Graver.

Crossover 1/2 **1982 (R)** A devoted male nurse works the graveyard shift in the psychiatric ward and neglects his personal life. **96m/C VHS.** James Coburn, Kate Nelligan; ***D:*** John Guillermin.

Crossover **2006 (PG-13)** So why are streetballers playing their game in an abandoned Detroit train station? Too cold outside? Not enough grunge atmosphere? A dopey and cliched sports soap opera, with very few actual basketball sequences, which has studious Cruise (Jonathan) getting a b-ball scholarship to an LA college while his best bud, dropout Tech (Mackie), just wants to beat local rival Jewelz (Champion). There's also a slick wannabe sports agent (Brady) and a couple of hotties (one good and one a gold-digger). This amateur night don't got game. **95m/C DVD.** *US* Anthony Mackie, Wesley Jonathan, Wayne Brady, Kristen Wilson, Lil' J.J., Phillip Champion, Eva Pigford, Alecia Fears; ***D:*** Preston A. Whitmore II; ***W:*** Preston A. Whitmore II; ***C:*** Christian Sebaldt; ***M:*** Matthias Weber.

Crossover Dreams 1/2 **1985** Actor and musician Blades moves this old story along. Sure that he has at last made the international Big Time, a salsa artist becomes a self-important back-stabber after cutting an album. Great music. Blades's first film. ♫Good For Baby; Liz's Theme; Sin Fe; Todos Vuelven; Libra Timbero; Elegua; Merecumbe; Judy, Part 2; Yiri Yiri Bon. **86m/C VHS, DVD.** Ruben Blades, Shawn Elliott, Elizabeth Pena, Virgilio Marti, Tom Signorelli, Frank Robles, Joel Diamond, Amanda Barber, John Hammil; ***D:*** Leon Ichaso; ***W:*** Ruben Blades, Leon Ichaso, Manuel Arce; ***M:*** Mauricio Smith.

Crossroads **1942** David Talbot (Powell) is a rising French diplomat, living in 1935 Paris with his bride Lucienne (Lamarr). David suddenly starts receiving blackmail letters, accusing him of being wanted criminal Jean Pelletier. The bewildered man goes to the police who trap Carlos Le Duc (Sokloff) who's then put on trial. When Henri Sarrou (Rathbone) testifies on David's behalf, David finds his intentions are insincere leaving him baffled. Hollywood remake of the 1938 French thriller "Carrefour." **84m/B DVD.** William Powell, Hedy Lamarr, Basil Rathbone, Claire Trevor, Felix Bressart, Sig Rugman, Vladimir Sokoloff, Margaret Wycherly; ***D:*** Jack Conway; ***W:*** Guy Trosper; ***C:*** Joseph Ruttenberg; ***M:*** Bronislau Kaper.

Crossroads 1/2 **1986 (R)** A blues-loving young white man, classically trained at Juilliard, befriends an aging black blues-master. After helping the old man escape from the nursing home, the two hop trains to the South where it's literally a duel with the devil. Fine performances by Macchio, Gertz, Seneca, and Morton. Wonderful score by Ry Cooder, with some help from Steve Vai in the final showdown. **100m/C VHS, DVD.** Ralph Macchio, Joe Seneca, Jami Gertz, Joe Morton, Robert Judd, Harry Carey Jr., Steve Vai; ***D:*** Walter Hill; ***W:*** John Fusco; ***C:*** John Bailey; ***M:*** Ry Cooder, Steve Vai.

Crossroads 1/2 **2002 (PG-13)** Underwhelming teen buddy road pic has pop tart Spears debut as Lucy, a virginal, small-town high school senior who hits the road to L.A. with childhood buds Kit (Saldana) and Mimi (Manning), with depressing results. Lucy's searching for her real mom (Cattrall); Kit, a no-good boyfriend; and Mimi trying to get to an open audition as a singer. Convenient cute love interest for Lucy is driver Ben (Mount), who may harbor a dangerous secret. Most laughable scene features Lucy scribbling "poetry" (actually lyrics to one of her soundtrack songs) while Ben "composes" the music for it. Spears is likeable and harmless while Manning is the real stand-out. One notch up from "Glitter," quality competed with quantity (of wardrobe) as lowest priority. **94m/C VHS, DVD.** *US* Britney Spears, Taryn Manning, Zoe Saldana, Anson Mount, Kim Cattrall, Dan Aykroyd, Justin Long, Beverly Johnson, Kool Moe Dee, Richard Voll; ***D:*** Tamra Davis; ***W:*** Shonda Rhimes; ***C:*** Eric Alan Edwards; ***M:*** Trevor Jones. Golden Raspberries '02: Worst Actress (Spears), Worst Song ("I'm Not a Girl, Not Yet a Woman").

Crossworlds **1996 (PG-13)** All dimensions of the universe collide in the mystical valley of Crossworlds. When alien night riders attack Joe Talbolt (Charles), he escapes with girlfriend Laura (Roth) and they meet up with mercenary A.T. (Hauer). Turns out the crystal pendant Joe's father left him is one of the keys that unlock the boundaries between the worlds. Along with a scepter, they give the owner unlimited power. So the trio enter Crossworlds to fight a battle between good and evil. **91m/C VHS, DVD.** Jack Black, Rutger Hauer, Josh Charles, Andrea Roth, Stuart Wilson; ***D:*** Krishna Rao; ***W:*** Raman Rao, Krishna Rao; ***C:*** Chris Walling; ***M:*** Christophe Beck. **CABLE**

Crouching Tiger, Hidden Dragon 1/2 **2000** Two veteran Wudan fighters (Yun-Fat and Yeoh) in 19th-century China recognize their passion for each other while tracking down a vengeful master criminal (Pei-Pei) and her protege (the exciting Ziyi). A martial arts love story that satisfies on both accounts. The emotional impact of the romance is as real and true as the choreographed fight scenes are spectacular and graceful. The film's overt feminism flies (literally) in the face of its patriarchal setting, yet doesn't seem a bit out of place. The extraordinary battle scenes were choreographed by Yuen Wo-Ping, who performed the same duties for "The Matrix." Mandarin with subtitles. **120m/C VHS, DVD, UMD.** Chow Yun-Fat, Michelle Yeoh, Zhang Ziyi, Chang Chen, Cheng Pei-Pei, Sihung Lung; ***D:*** Ang Lee; ***W:*** James Schamus, Wang Hui Ling, Tsai Kuo Jung; ***C:*** Peter Pau; ***M:*** Tan Dun. Oscars '00: Art Dir./Set Dec., Cinematog., Foreign Film, Orig. Score; Australian Film Inst. '01: Foreign Film; British Acad. '00: Director (Lee), Foreign Film, Score; Directors Guild '00: Director (Lee); Golden Globes '01: Director (Lee), Foreign Film; Ind. Spirit '01: Director (Lee), Film, Support. Actress (Ziyi); L.A. Film Critics '00: Cinematog., Film, Score; Natl. Bd. of Review '00: Foreign Film; N.Y. Film Critics '00: Cinematog.; Broadcast Film Critics '00: Foreign Film.

Croupier **1997** Director Hodges scored a hit with the 1971 British crime thriller "Get Carter." And after some rocky followups, he scores another with this cool casino neo-noir. A cynical South African, now living in London, Jack Manfred (Owen) is trying to escape the reach of his con man dad. The would-be writer (his detective character Jake does the film's narrative) takes a job as a casino dealer where he can observe life at his preferred distance—that is until a fellow South African, sulty gambling beauty Jani (Kingston), talks him into a shady scheme that provides fodder for Jack's writing. Owen is especially watchable in the title role. **91m/C VHS, DVD.** *GB* Clive Owen, Alex Kingston, Kate Hardie, Gina McKee, Nicholas Ball, Nick Reding; ***D:*** Mike Hodges; ***W:*** Paul Mayersberg; ***C:*** Mike Garfath; ***M:*** Simon Fisher Turner.

The Crow 1/2 **1993 (R)** Revenge-fantasy finds Eric Draven (Lee) resurrected on Devil's Night, a year after his death, in order to avenge his own murder and that of his girlfriend. 90% of the scenes are at night, in the rain, or both, and it's not easy to tell what's going on (a blessing considering the violence level). Very dark, but with good performances, particularly from Lee, in his last role before an unfortunate on set accident caused his death. That footage has been destroyed, but use of a stunt double and camera trickery allowed for the movie's completion. Film was dedicated to Lee and his fiance Eliza. Based on the comic strip by James O'Barr. The video release includes Brandon Lee's final interview. **100m/C VHS, DVD, UMD.** Brandon Lee, Ernie Hudson, Michael Wincott, David Patrick Kelly, Rochelle Davis, Angel David, Michael Massee, Bai Ling, Laurence Mason, Bill Raymond, Marco Rodriguez, Anna Thomson, Sofia Shinas, Jon Polito, Tony Todd; ***D:*** Alex Proyas; ***W:*** David J. Schow, John Shirley; ***C:*** Darius Wolski; ***M:*** Graeme Revell. MTV Movie Awards '95: Song ("Big Empty").

The Crow 2: City of Angels **1996 (R)** James O'Barr's cult graphic-novel "hero" returns in a new incarnation. It's eight years later (in film time) and the setting's changed from Detroit to L.A. but the horror remains. Ashe (Perez) and his young son witness a murder and are killed themselves by scumbags working for drug lord Judah (Brooks). So the Crow brings back Ashe to get revenge. Also involved is Sarah (Kirshner), who retains her role as story narrator but is now a grown-up tattoo artist who falls in love with Ashe. Lots of kink and flash—no substance—and confusing as well. The eerie sepia-toned look is created with sodium lighting. **93m/C VHS, DVD.** Vincent Perez, Mia Kirshner, Iggy Pop, Richard Brooks, Ian Dury, Thuy Trang, Thomas Jane, Vincent Castellanos, Tracey Ellis; ***D:*** Tim Pope; ***W:*** David S. Goyer; ***C:*** Jean-Yves Escoffier; ***M:*** Graeme Revell.

Crow Hollow **1952** A Victorian mansion inhabited by three whacko sisters is the site of a murder committed in an attempt to cash in on an inheritance. When a young woman investigates, eyebrows are raised. **69m/B VHS.** *GB* Donald Houston, Natasha Parry, Nora Nicholson, Esma Cannon, Melissa Stribling; ***D:*** Michael McCarthy.

The Crow Road **1996** Prentice Hogan comes back to his hometown for his grandmother's funeral. Old conflicts surface and Prentice becomes determined to solve the disappearance of his Uncle Rory, who's been missing seven years. As he reads his uncle's unpublished novel, Prentice discovers some very disturbing family secrets. Based on the novel by Iain Banks. **210m/C DVD.** *GB* Joseph McFadden, Peter Capaldi, Dougray Scott, Bill Paterson, Stella Gonet, Valerie Edmond, David Robb; ***D:*** Gavin Millar; ***W:*** Bryan Eisley; ***C:*** John Else; ***M:*** Colin Towns. **TV**

The Crow: Salvation **2000 (R)** Third in the series of films based on James O'Barr's comic book finds Alex Corvis (Mabius) wrongly convicted of murdering girlfriend Lauren Randall (O'Keefe). He's executed on his 21st birthday but returns as the Crow to seek revenge on those who wronged him. Alex convinces Erin (Dunst), Lauren's teenaged sister, of his innocence and they team up. Rather than revitalizing the franchise, this one basically got dumped by the studio, although the performances and the production are worth your time. **102m/C VHS, DVD.** Eric Mabius, Kirsten Dunst, Fred Ward, Jodi Lyn O'Keefe, William Atherton, Dale Midkiff, Grant Shaud; ***D:*** Bharat Nalluri; ***W:*** Chip Johannessen; ***C:*** Carolyn Chen; ***M:*** Marco Beltrami.

The Crow: Wicked Prayer **2005 (R)** A satanic gang murders a juvenile delinquent (Furlong) and his mystical girlfriend (Chriqui) so that their leader (Boreanaz) can become a powerful demon. Instead, the kid becomes The Crow and returns for vengeance against the gang. Not a whole lot to recommend to non-fans of the franchise, although Hopper scores in his campy cameo. **m/C DVD.** Edward Furlong, Emmanuelle Chriqui, David Boreanaz, Tara Reid, Dennis Hopper, Macy Gray, Danny Trejo, Marcus Chong, Yuji Okumoto; ***D:*** Lance Mungia; ***W:*** Lance Mungia, Sean Hood; ***C:*** Kurt Brabbee; ***M:*** Jason Christopherson. **VIDEO**

The Crowd **1928** A look at the day-to-day trials of a working-class family set against the backdrop of wealthy society. True-to-life, it's peppered with some happy moments, too. One of the best silent films. **104m/B VHS.** Eleanor Boardman, James Murray, Bert Roach, Daniel G. Tomlinson, Dell Henderson, Lucy Beaumont; ***D:*** King Vidor. Natl. Film Reg. '89.

The Crowded Sky **1960** A commercial jet and a Navy plane with defective navigation equipment and no radio are on a collision course. Flashbacks depict personal moments of the crew and passengers of the airliner who don't realize they're in imminent danger, unlike the Naval pilot who must make a terrible choice. **105m/C DVD.** Dana Andrews, Efrem Zimbalist Jr., Troy Donahue, Rhonda Fleming, John Kerr, Anne Francis, Keenan Wynn, Patsy Kelly; ***D:*** Joseph Pevney; ***W:*** Charles Schnee; ***C:*** Harry Stradling Sr.; ***M:*** Leonard Rosenman.

Crown Heights 1/2 **2002 (R)** An orthodox Rabbi and an African-American community leader join forces to save their racially-fractured neighborhood from more violence. Inspired by real-life events after the 1991 Brooklyn riots that were triggered by a Jewish man accidentally running down a black child. **93m/C VHS, DVD.** Jeremy Blackman, Jason Blicker, Daniel Kash, Judah Katz, Mpho Koaho, Michael Yarmush; ***D:*** Jeremy Paul Kagan; ***W:*** Michael D'Antonio, Toni Johnson; ***C:*** Rudolf Blahacek; ***M:*** Aaron Zigman. **TV**

The Crown Prince 1/2 *Kronprinz Rudolf* **2006** In the late 1880s, Crown Prince Rudolf, heir to the Austro-Hungarian Empire, enters into an unhappy marriage of convenience to try to please his controlling father, Emperor Franz-Joseph. Progressive for his time, Rudolf finds his suggestions for political alliances and reforms shunned and he seemingly has nothing better to do than fall obsessively in love with the beautiful Baroness Mary Vetsera, whom he takes to his castle at Mayerling. Rudolf's father does not approve; things don't end well. Based on a true story that has been filmed before, notably as 1969's "Mayerling." **181m/C DVD.** *AT GE* Omar Sharif, Christian Clavier, Klaus Maria Brandauer, Sandra Ceccarelli, Max von Thun, Victoria Puccini, Alexandra Vandernoot, Birgit Minichmayr; ***D:*** Robert Dornhelm; ***W:*** Didier Decoin, Klaus Lintschinger; ***C:*** Michael Riebl; ***M:*** Ludwig Eckmann, Joerg Magnus Pfeil. **TV**

Crows *Wrony* **1994** Emotionally neglected by her single mother, a nine-year-old nameless girl, known scornfully as The Crow (Ostrozna), desperately wants a family of her own. So she kidnaps a three-year-old to serve as her make-believe daughter and convinces the young child that they are going on a fairytale adventure to the end of the world. Polish with subtitles. **66m/C VHS.** *PL* Karolina Ostrozna, Kasia Szczepanik, Malgorzata Hajewska; ***D:*** Dorota Kedzierzawska; ***W:*** Dorota Kedzierzawska; ***C:*** Arthur Reinhart; ***M:*** Wlodek Pawlik.

Crows and Sparrows *Wuya Yu Maque* **1949** Poor tenants of a Shanghai boardinghouse are about to lose their home when their greedy landlord decides to sell and move to Taiwan. But the advancing Red Army causes a change in plans and they're saved! Sounds politically turgid but isn't, thanks to naturalistic acting and dialog. Completed just before the revolution, the film was censored by the Nationalist Kuomintang government but cuts were restored when the Communists came to power. Mandarin with subtitles. **108m/B VHS.** *CH* Zhao Dan, Wu Yin, Wei Heling, Daolin Sun, Li Tianji, Ouyang Yunzhu; ***D:*** Zheng Junli; ***W:*** Zhao Dan, Zheng Junli; ***C:*** Miao Zhenhua, Hu Zhenhua; ***M:*** Wang Yunjie.

The Crucible *The Witches of Salem; Les Sorcieres de Salem* **1957** Signoret is outstanding in this version of Arthur Miller's play about the Salem witch trials in 17th-century New England. Miller's depiction of witch hunts was written as a searing commentary on McCarthyism and the anti-communist panic that swept America in the 1950s. Film was made in France because Miller was blacklisted in America and blackballed by Hollywood at the time. In French with English subtitles. **135m/B VHS.** *FR* Raymond Rouleau, Simone Signoret, Yves Montand, Mylene Demongeot, Jean Debucourt, Jean Gaven, Jeanne Fusier-Gir; ***D:*** Raymond Rouleau; ***W:*** Jean-Paul Sartre; ***C:*** Claude Renoir; ***M:*** Georges Auric.

The Crucible **1996 (PG-13)** Mass hysteria reigns in 17th century Salem, Mass., when a group of teenaged girls, caught performing heathen rituals in the woods, concoct an elaborate story to exonerate themselves by whipping the town into a witch-hunting frenzy. Chief liar is Abigail Williams (Ryder), who was cast aside by married farmer John Proctor (Day-Lewis), for whom she still lusts. The deranged lass puts her dubious talents into getting Proctor's wife (Allen) out of the picture. Director Hytner demanded authentic period reproduction, down to the finest detail. Impressive cast does justice to the story, especially Scofield's delightfully odious Judge Danforth. Based on Miller's 1953 play which, not so coincidently, opened during the communist witch hunts of the early 1950s. Screenwriter Miller willingly slashed dialogue from his original work for cinematic purposes. Filmed at the remote wildlife sanctuary of Hog Island, Massachusetts. **123m/C VHS, DVD.** Daniel Day-Lewis, Winona Ryder, Paul Scofield, Joan Allen, Bruce Davison, Jeffrey Jones, Rob Campbell, Peter Vaughan, Karron Graves, Charlaine Woodard, Frances Conroy, Elizabeth Lawrence, George Gaynes; ***D:*** Nicholas Hytner; ***W:*** Arthur Miller; ***C:*** Andrew Dunn; ***M:*** George Fenton. British Acad. '96: Support. Actor (Scofield); Broadcast Film Critics '96: Support. Actress (Allen).

Crucible of Horror *Velvet House; The Corpse* **1969** Chilling story of a terrorized wife, who, along with her daughter, plots to murder her sadistic husband to end his abusive treatment of them. However, he isn't yet ready to die and comes back to drive them mad. **91m/C VHS, DVD.** *GB* Michael Gough, Yvonne Mitchell, Sharon Gurney, David Butler, Simon Gough, Nicholas Jones, Olaf Pooley, Mary Hignett; ***D:*** Viktors Ritelis; ***W:*** Olaf Pooley; ***C:*** John Mackey.

Crucible of Terror WOOF! 1972 Mad sculptor covers beautiful models with hot wax, then imprisons them in a mold of bronze. **95m/C VHS, DVD.** *GB* Mike Raven, Mary Maude, James Bolam, John Arnatt, Ronald Lacey, Judy Matheson, Me Me Lai, Melissa Stribling, Beth Morris; ***D:*** Ted Hooker; ***W:*** Ted Hooker, Tom Parkinson; ***C:*** Peter Newbrook.

The Crucifer of Blood ½ **1991** A disappointing Sherlock Holmes yarn. Heston is adequate as the Baker Street sleuth, but the mystery—about two retired British soldiers who share an accursed secret and a vengeful comrade—unreels clumsily in the form of flashbacks that give away most of the puzzle from the start. Interesting only in that Dr. Watson has a love affair, more or less. Adapted from a play (and looking like it) by Paul Giovanni, inspired by Arthur Conan Doyle's "The Sign of Four." **105m/C VHS.** Charlton Heston, Richard Johnson, Susannah Harker, John Castle, Clive Wood, Simon Callow, Edward Fox; ***D:*** Fraser Heston. **CABLE**

The Crucified Lovers ½ *Chikamatsu Monogatari* **1954** A shy scrollmaker falls in love with his master's wife. Excellent Japanese tragedy with fine performances all around. **100m/B VHS.** *JP* Kazuo Hasegawa, Kyoko Kagawa, Yoko Minamida, Eitaro Shindo, Shigehiro (Sakae) Ozawa; ***D:*** Kenji Mizoguchi.

The Crude Oasis ½ **1995 (R)** Shot in 14 days on a $25,000 budget, producer/writer/director Graves' debut is an aggressively moody suspenser. Karen (Taylor) is a neglected, suicidal Kansas housewife who is haunted by dreams of a mystery man. He turns up in the form of Shields, the pump jockey at a local gas station. Obsessed by the stranger, Karen begins following him, leading to situations paralleling her dream. Adept at setting up an atmosphere of small-town menace and constructing a plot with surprising twists and turns, Graves can't quite deliver the payoff required. **82m/C VHS.** Jennifer Taylor, Aaron Shields, Robert Peterson, Mussef Sibay, Lynn Bieler, Roberta Eaton; ***D:*** Alex Graves; ***W:*** Alex Graves; ***C:*** Steven Quale.

Cruel and Unusual *Watchtower* **2001 (R)** Adam Turrell (Berenger) comes to stay in a quiet Oregon fishing town, introducing himself as an English professor working on a first novel. He befriends sister and brother Kate (Hayward) and Mike (Runyan) O'Connor whose father has recently died. But their friendship takes a terrifying turn since Adam isn't at all what he seems. **100m/C VHS, DVD.** Tom Berenger, Rachel Hayward, Tygh Runyan, Mitchell Kosterman; ***D:*** George Mihalka; ***W:*** Robert Geoffrion, Rod Browning, Dan Witt; ***C:*** Peter Benison; ***M:*** Michel Cusson. **VIDEO**

Cruel Intentions ½ **1998 (R)** Fourth film adaptation of Choderlos de Loclos's 1782 novel "Les Liaisons Dangereuses" takes the tale of seduction and intrigue from the 18th century French court to a modern Manhattan prep school. Think "I Know Who You Did Last Summer." Gellar plays teen vamp Kathryn, who bets her stepbrother Sebastian (Phillipe) a night of passion against his car that he can't deflower the virginal Annette (Witherspoon). The overall effect is like the characters' lives: full of guilty pleasures. **95m/C VHS, DVD, Blu-ray Disc, UMD.** Sarah Michelle Gellar, Ryan Phillippe, Reese Witherspoon, Selma Blair, Joshua Jackson, Eric Mabius, Louise Fletcher, Swoosie Kurtz, Christine Baranski, Sean Patrick Thomas; ***D:*** Roger Kumble; ***W:*** Roger Kumble; ***C:*** Theo van de Sande; ***M:*** Ed Shearmur. MTV Movie Awards '00: Female Perf. (Gellar), Kiss (Sarah Michelle Gellar/Selma Blair).

Cruel Intentions 2 *Manchester Prep* **1999 (R)** A prequel to the 1998 release finds a rather precocious 16-year-old Sebastian deciding to become a one-woman guy—in this case to naive Danielle, the high school headmaster's daughter. However, his new stepsister Katherine has other adventures in mind. This was intended as the pilot to a TV series (based on the film) that was cancelled before it aired. **87m/C VHS, DVD.** Amy Adams, Mimi Rogers, Robin Dunne, Sarah Thompson, Keri Lynn Pratt, David McIlwraith; ***D:*** Roger Kumble; ***W:*** Roger Kumble; ***C:*** James R. Bagdonas. **TV**

Cruel Intentions 3 ½ **2004 (R)** Gratuitous, rehashed third version in which the scene has shifted to an exclusive southern California college. All-new fiendish players Cassidy (Anapau), Jason (Smith), and Patrick (Wetherington) use their considerable free time plotting and pursuing sexual conquests with others and among themselves. **85m/C VHS, DVD.** Kerr Smith, Natalie Ramsey, Tom Parker, Kristina Anapau, Nathan Wetherington, Melissa Yvonne Lewis; ***D:*** Scott Ziehl; ***W:*** Rhett Reese; ***C:*** Thomas Callaway; ***M:*** David Reynolds. **VIDEO**

Cruel Restaurant *Zankoku Hoten* **2008** Ms. Lin's (Mihiro Taniguchi) dumpling restaurant is the darling of the town and people will do anything to get them. When people start dying or going nuts, the local restaurant reviewer and cops think she's behind the murders and that the secret ingredient is actually people. Despite sounding like a horror mystery, it's actually supposed to be something of an erotic comedy and the female lead is naked for most of the film. **75m/C DVD.** Mihiro, Sakae Yamazaki, Katsuya Naruse, Yusuke Iwata, Miho Funatsu, Toshiyuki Teranaka, Chihiro Koganezaki, Kesuke; ***D:*** Koji Kawano; ***W:*** Satoshi Owada, Koji Kawano.

The Cruel Sea **1953** Well-made documentary-like account of a Royal Navy corvette on convoy duty in the Atlantic during WWII. **121m/B VHS, DVD.** *GB* Jack Hawkins, Stanley Baker, Denholm Elliott, Virginia McKenna; ***D:*** Charles Frend; ***W:*** Eric Ambler.

The Cruel Story of Youth *Seishun Zanoku Monogatari; Naked Youth; A Story of the Cruelties of Youth* **1960** A teenage girl and her criminal boyfriend use sex to get money out of rich, middle-aged men in this controversial look at the disillusionment of youth and the breaking of old values and traditions in Japan after WWII. In Japanese with English subtitles. **96m/C VHS.** *JP* Yusuke Kawazu, Miyuki Kuwano, Yoshiko Kuga; ***D:*** Nagisa Oshima; ***W:*** Nagisa Oshima.

Cruel World WOOF! 2005 (R) Grubby and stupid. Philip (Furlong) goes psycho over being dumped by Catherine (Pressly in an extended cameo) on the finale of their reality TV show. So he decides to create his own show, using an isolated mansion and enticing a group of college kids who don't realize that the elimination round is literal and permanent. **92m/C DVD, Blu-ray Disc.** Edward Furlong, Andrew Keegan, Susan Ward, Joel Michaely, Sanoe Lake, Brian Geraghty, Daniel Franzese, Laura Ramsey, Jaime Pressly; ***D:*** Kelsey T. Howard; ***W:*** Eugene Hess, Paul Lawrence, Paul T. Murray; ***C:*** Ward Russell. **VIDEO**

Cruise into Terror WOOF! 1978 A sarcophagus brought aboard a pleasure cruise ship unleashes an evil force that slowly starts to kill off the ship's passengers, most of whom likely thought they were on the Love Boat. **100m/C VHS.** Ray Milland, Hugh O'Brian, John Forsythe, Christopher George, Dirk Benedict, Frank Converse, Lynda Day George, Stella Stevens; ***D:*** Bruce Kessler. **TV**

Cruise Missile **1978** Unique task force is on a mission to keep the world from nuclear holocaust. **100m/C VHS.** Peter Graves, Curt Jurgens, Michael Dante; ***D:*** Ted V. Mikels.

The Cruise of the Jasper B **1926** The descendent of a pirate, Jerry (La Rocque) must marry aboard the Jasper B by his 25th birthday or lose his inheritance. He finds the perfect bride in Agatha (Harris) but problems arise before they can say 'I do.' Produced by Cecil B. DeMille. **63m/B DVD.** Rod La Rocque, Mildred Harris, Snitz Edwards, Jack Ackroyd, Otto Lederer; ***D:*** James W. Horne; ***W:*** Tay Garnett; ***C:*** Lucien N. Andriot.

Cruisin' High *Cat Murkil and the Silks* **1975 (R)** Two city street gangs battle it out. **109m/C VHS.** David Kyle, Kelly Yaegermann, Rhodes Reason; ***D:*** John Bushelman; ***W:*** William C. Thomas.

Cruising **1980 (R)** Rookie cop Pacino is deep undercover investigating the bizarre murders of homosexuals in New York's West Village. Sexually explicit but less than suspenseful mystery. Release was sensationalized, with many gay rights groups voicing loud disapproval of the sordid gay characterization, while others feared copycat crimes. Excellent NYC cinematography. **102m/C VHS, DVD.** Al Pacino, Paul Sorvino, Karen Allen, Powers Boothe, Richard Cox, Don Scardino, Joe Spinell, Ed O'Neill, James Remar, William Russ, Barton Heyman, Mike Starr; ***D:*** William Friedkin; ***W:*** William Friedkin; ***C:*** James A. Contner; ***M:*** Jack Nitzsche.

Crumb **1994 (R)** Countercultural documentary looking at the life of underground cartoonist Robert Crumb—'60s satirist and social misfit who created such drug and sex characters as Fritz the Cat and Mr. Natural. Crumb's extraordinarily dysfunctional family play a significant role, with his mother and two brothers, elder brother Charles and younger brother Max, also interviewed as well as Crumb's friends and current and former wives. The dead abusive father also plays a part. Director Zwigoff spent six years filming his material, and gained wider distribution for his work after taking the Grand Jury prize at Sundance. **119m/C VHS, DVD.** Robert Crumb; ***D:*** Terry Zwigoff; ***C:*** Maryse Alberti. Directors Guild '95: Feature Doc. (Zwigoff); Natl. Soc. Film Critics '95: Feature Doc.; Sundance '95: Cinematog., Grand Jury Prize.

Crusade: A March through Time *Crusade in Jeans* **2006 (PG)** Fifteen-year-old Dolf Vega's (Flynn) mother (Watson) works at a research center testing an actual time machine. When Dolf blows his soccer team's championship by missing a goal, Dolf thinks it would be easy to go back a few hours for a do-over. Oopsy! An error sends him back to the year 1212 instead! Dolf is rescued from bandits by Jenne (Leonidas), who is part of the Children's Crusade to Jerusalem, but a betrayal will put the pilgrimage in danger. **100m/C DVD.** *GE* Joe Flynn, Stephanie Leonidas, Emily Watson, Michael Culkin, Benno Furmann; ***D:*** Ben Sombogaart; ***W:*** Bill Haney; ***C:*** Reinier van Brummelen; ***M:*** Jurre Haanstra.

The Crusader ½ **1932** The title character is crusading District Attorney Phillip Brandon (Warner), who's giving the local crooks fits. They first try blackmail because Brandon's wife Tess (Brent) is a woman with a past. When a murder is committed, Tess's ex-sweetheart, bootlegger Jimmie (Cody), unexpectedly comes to the rescue. Creaky early talkie is pre-Production Code with a liberal use of salty language. **65m/B DVD.** H.B. Warner, Evelyn Brent, Marceline Day, Lew Cody, Ned Sparks, Walter Byron; ***D:*** Frank Strayer; ***W:*** Edward T. Lowe.

The Crusades ½ **1935** Typical DeMille extravaganza, loosely based on the Third Crusade, which finds Richard the Lionheart (Wilcoxon) and the armies of Europe battling Saladin and the Mahammedan horde in order to reclaim Jerusalem. Meanwhile, Richard marries by proxy in order to gain supplies for his men—something that enrages his bride Berengaria (Young). Once he realizes how beautiful she is, Richard tries to win her love. Obviously, not historically accurate and it's all secondary to the battle scenes, anyway. Based on the Harold Lamb book "The Crusade: Iron Men and Saints." **126m/B VHS, DVD.** Henry Wilcoxon, Loretta Young, Sir C. Aubrey Smith, Ian Keith, Katherine DeMille, Joseph Schildkraut, Alan Hale, C. Henry Gordon, George Barbier, Lumsden Hare, William Farnum, Hobart Bosworth, Montagu Love, Pedro de Cordoba, Mischa Auer; ***D:*** Cecil B. DeMille; ***W:*** Waldemar Young, Dudley Nichols, Harold Lamb; ***C:*** Victor Milner; ***M:*** Rudolph Kopp.

Crush **1993** Christina is a local New Zealand literary critic on her way to interview Colin, a reclusive novelist. Along for the ride is her seductive American friend Lane who manages to crash the car but walk away with hardly a scratch. Christina appears to be dead and Lane abandons her, finding her way to the home Colin shares with his teenage daughter Angela. Lane promptly sets out to seduce Colin, making Angela jealous, (oh, and Christina's not dead after all). Poor script finds the characters actions baffling and why Lane is so wildly attractive is never apparent. **97m/C VHS, DVD.** *NZ* Marcia Gay Harden, Donough Rees, William Zappa, Caitlin Bossley; ***D:*** Alison Maclean; ***W:*** Alison Maclean, Anne Kennedy; ***C:*** Dion Beebe.

The Crush ½ **1993 (R)** Wealthy 14-year-old temptress Silverstone (in her debut) develops an obsessive crush on handsome 28-year-old Elwes, who rents her family's guest house. In an attempt to win his heart, she rewrites his poorly composed magazine articles. This doesn't convince him they should mate for life, so she sabotages his apartment to vent her rage. Sound familiar? The plot's lifted right out of "Fatal Attraction" and Shapiro doesn't offer viewers anything inventively different. He does manage to substitute new methods for the spurned lover to snare her prey. Limp plot would have been exciting if we hadn't seen it so many times before. **89m/C VHS, DVD.** Cary Elwes, Alicia Silverstone, Jennifer Rubin, Kurtwood Smith, Gwynyth Walsh, Amber Benson; ***D:*** Alan Shapiro; ***W:*** Alan Shapiro; ***C:*** Bruce Surtees; ***M:*** Graeme Revell. MTV Movie Awards '94: Breakthrough Perf. (Silverstone), Villain (Silverstone).

Crush **2002 (R)** A "with friends like these, who needs enemies" movie that leaves a sour aftertaste. Kate (MacDowell), Janine (Staunton), and Molly (Chancellor) are three professional women in their 40s who live in a small English town and meet weekly to drink and commiserate about their lousy love lives. That is, until sexily repressed American headmistress Kate sets off sparks with hottie twentysomething Jed (Doughty), an organist and former pupil. Her friends are outraged and turn distinctly nasty trying to break up the happy twosome. Maybe they're jealous that Kate is having great sex and they're not. **115m/C VHS, DVD.** *GB* Andie MacDowell, Imelda Staunton, Anna Chancellor, Kenny Doughty, Bill Paterson; ***D:*** John McKay; ***W:*** John McKay; ***C:*** Henry Braham; ***M:*** Kevin Sargent.

Crusoe ½ **1989 (PG-13)** A lushly photographed version of the Daniel Defoe classic. Crusoe is an arrogant slave trader stranded on a desert island populated by unfriendly natives. Themes of prejudice, fear, and choice appear in this never-padded, thoughtful film. Quinn gives an excellent performance as the stranded slave-trader. **94m/C VHS.** Aidan Quinn, Ade Sapara, Jimmy Nail, Timothy Spall, Colin Bruce, Michael Higgins, Shane Rimmer, Hepburn Grahame; ***D:*** Caleb Deschanel; ***W:*** Walon Green, Christopher Logue; ***M:*** Michael Kamen.

Crutch ½ **2004 (R)** Sixteen-year-old David (Gordon) must deal with his alcoholic mom Katie (Walsh), who's forced into rehab after an accident. This leaves David vulnerable to the predatory desires of his 30-something drama teacher, Kenny (Moretti), who also introduces the impulsive, lonely teen to drugs. Unsettling story based on Moretti's own experiences. **88m/C DVD.** Rob Moretti, Eben Gordon, Juanita Walsh, James Earley; ***D:*** Rob Moretti; ***W:*** Rob Moretti, Paul Jacks; ***C:*** Brian Fass; ***M:*** Ben Goldberg.

Cry-Baby **1990 (PG-13)** An homage and spoof of '50s teen-rock melodramas by the doyen of cinematic Bad Taste, involving a terminal bad-boy high schooler who goes with a square blond and starts an inter-class rumble. Musical numbers, throwaway gags and plenty of knee-bending to Elvis, with a weak story supported by offbeat celeb appearances. **85m/C VHS, DVD.** Johnny Depp, Amy Locane, Polly Bergen, Traci Lords, Ricki Lake, Iggy Pop, Susan Tyrrell, Patty (Patricia Campbell) Hearst, Kim McGuire, Darren E. Burrows, Troy Donahue, Willem Dafoe, David Nelson, Mink Stole, Joe Dallesandro, Joey Heatherton, Robert Walsh, Mary Vivian Pearce; ***D:*** John Waters; ***W:*** John Waters; ***C:*** David Insley; ***M:*** Patrick Williams.

Cry Blood, Apache **1970 (R)** An old man (Joel McCrae) remembers when, as a young man (Jody McCrae), he and his sadistic friends massacred a group of Apaches and were hunted by the husband of one of their victims. It's violent but not as sadistic as some. **90m/C DVD.** Joel McCrea,

Jody McCrea, Robert Tessier, Marie Gahva, Don Henley; *D:* Jack Starrett; *W:* Sean McGregor; *C:* Bruce Scott; *M:* Elliot Kaplan.

Cry Danger 1951 A falsely imprisoned man is released from jail, and he searches for those who framed him. **80m/B VHS.** Dick Powell, Rhonda Fleming, William Conrad, Richard Erdman; *D:* Robert Parrish; *C:* Joseph Biroc.

A Cry for Love 1980 An amphetamine addict and an alcoholic meet, fall in love, and help each other recover. Based on the best seller by Jill Schary Robinson, "Bedtime Story." **96m/C VHS.** Susan Blakely, Powers Boothe, Gene Barry, Charles Siebert, Herb Edelman, Fern Fitzgerald, Lainie Kazan; *D:* Paul Wendkos.

Cry Freedom 1/2 **1987 (PG)** A romantic look at the short life of South African activist Steven Biko, and his friendship with the white news editor, Donald Woods. The film focuses on Woods' escape from Africa while struggling to bring Biko's message to the world. Based on a true story. **157m/C VHS, DVD.** Kevin Kline, Denzel Washington, Penelope Wilton, Kevin McNally, John Thaw, Timothy West, John Hargreaves, Alec McCowen, Zakes Mokae, Ian Richardson, Juanita Waterman; *D:* Richard Attenborough; *W:* John Briley; *C:* Ronnie Taylor; *M:* George Fenton, Jonas Gwangwa.

A Cry from the Mountain 1985 **(PG)** Heavily religious film about a father and son who go on a kayak trip through Alaska's wilderness so the father can break the news of his impending divorce. A series of events occurs that change their lives, and they meet a mysterious mountain man who relies on his faith in God to get by in the wilderness. Features an appearance by Rev. Billy Graham. **78m/C VHS.** James Cavan, Wes Parker, Rita Walter, Chris Kidd, Coleen Gray, Jerry Ballew, Allison Argo, Glen Alsworth, Myrna Kidd; *D:* James F. Collier.

A Cry from the Streets 1957 Drama about the plight of orphan children and dedicated social workers in England. **100m/C VHS.** *GB* Max Bygraves, Barbara Murray, Kathleen Harrison, Colin Petersen; *D:* Lewis Gilbert; *M:* Larry Adler.

A Cry in the Dark 1/2 *Evil Angels* **1988 (PG-13)** Tight film story of the infamous Australian murder trial of Lindy Chamberlain (Streep), who was accused of killing her own baby, mostly because of the intensely adverse public opinion, aroused by vicious press, that surrounded the case. Chamberlain blamed the death on a wild dingo dog, which dragged off the baby from where the family was camped. Near-documentary style, with Streep excellent as the religious, unknowable mother. Based on the book "Evil Angels" by John Bryson. This case was also detailed in the film "Who Killed Baby Azaria?" **120m/C VHS, DVD.** *AU* Meryl Streep, Sam Neill, Bruce Myles, Charles "Bud" Tingwell, Nick (Nicholas) Tate, Neil Fitzpatrick, Maurice Fields, Lewis Fitz-Gerald, Tony (Anthony) Martin; *D:* Fred Schepisi; *W:* Fred Schepisi, Robert Caswell; *C:* Ian Baker; *M:* Bruce Smeaton. Australian Film Inst. '89: Actor (Neill), Actress (Streep), Film; Cannes '89: Actress (Streep); N.Y. Film Critics '88: Actress (Streep).

A Cry in the Night 1/2 **1993 (PG-13)** After Jenny (Higgins Clark) marries an internationally acclaimed artist, she thinks her life is complete. However, once she and her two daughters move into his country estate, her life takes a tragic turn as she's haunted by the mysterious deaths of her ex-husband and newborn child. King plays the new husband who turns out to have a few psychological quirks of his own. Actress Higgins Clark is the daughter of bestselling novelist Mary Higgins Clark, upon whose work the story is based. **99m/C VHS.** Perry King, Carol Higgins Clark; *D:* Robin Spry; *W:* Robin Spry. **TV**

A Cry in the Wild **1990 (PG)** A 14-year-old boy must find his way back to civilization when he's the lone survivor of an airplane crash. Strong acting from Rushton, excellent nature photography make this well used story work again. **93m/C VHS, DVD.** Jared Rushton, Ned Beatty, Pamela Sue Martin, Stephen Meadows; *D:* Mark Griffiths; *W:* Catherine Cyran; *C:* Gregg Heschong; *M:* Arthur Kempel.

The Cry: La Llorona 1/2 **2007 (R)** Overly-ambitious horror story that's a retelling of the Mexican folktale about a woman who drowns her children and then haunts other mothers to do the same. The story is relocated to NYC where detectives Scott (Carmargo) and Perez (Leon) are assigned to a series of child murders and disappearances. Scott is also still dealing with the trauma of his own son being drowned by his late wife. Meanwhile, single mom Maria (Dominguez) has visions and keeps sketching pictures of the missing kids. Afraid for her own son, she whisks him off to Central Park after leaving a cryptic message for the detectives. The various strands of the story don't come together very well and the plot falls completely apart in the last act. **80m/C DVD.** Carlos Leon, Adriana Dominguez, Miriam Colon, Christian Carmargo; *D:* Bernadine Santistevan; *W:* Bernadine Santistevan, Monique Salazar; *C:* Richard Lopez; *M:* Dean Parker. **VIDEO**

Cry of a Prostitute: Love Kills **1972 (R)** Former prostitute joins with a professional assassin in an effort to pacify rival gangsters in Italy. **86m/C VHS, DVD.** Henry Silva, Barbara Bouchet; *D:* Andrea Bianchi.

Cry of Battle 1/2 *To Be a Man* **1963** Anxious for the challenges of manhood, a well-heeled young man joins a guerrilla militia in the Philippines. **99m/B VHS, DVD.** Van Heflin, Rita Moreno, James MacArthur; *D:* Irving Lerner.

Cry of the Banshee 1/2 **1970 (PG)** Witch-hunter Price and family are tormented by Satanic powers seeking revenge. Superior horror period piece. **87m/C VHS, DVD.** *GB* Vincent Price, Elisabeth Bergner, Essy Persson, Hugh Griffith, Hilary Dwyer, Sally Geeson, Patrick Mower, Marshall Jones, Michael Elphick, Pamela Fairbrother, Robert Hutton; *D:* Gordon Hessler; *W:* Christopher Wicking, Tim Kelly; *C:* John Coquillon; *M:* Les Baxter.

Cry of the Innocent 1980 An action-packed thriller about a Vietnam veteran who is out to find a group of Irish terrorists that killed his family. **93m/C VHS, DVD.** Cyril Cusack, Alexander Knox, Rod Taylor, Joanna Pettet, Nigel Davenport; *D:* Michael O'Herlihy.

The Cry of the Owl *Le Cri du Hibou* **1987** Robert (Malavoy) has divorced the dreadful Veronique (Thevenet) and struck up a friendship with Juliette (May). He admires the way her life seems so satisfied and orderly but Juliette decides she doesn't like this idea of herself and impulsively drops her swinish fiance Patrick (Penot) and pursues Robert instead. But Robert is only interested in friendship, leading to some very twisted revenge plots. Suspenseful look at what obsessions can drive people to do. Adapted from the novel by Patricia Highsmith. In French with English subtitles. **102m/C VHS, DVD.** *FR IT* Christophe MaLavoy, Mathilda May, Virginie Thevenet, Jacques Penot, Jean-Pierre Kalfon, Patrice Kerbrat; *D:* Claude Chabrol; *W:* Claude Chabrol, Odile Barski; *C:* Jean Rabier; *M:* Matthieu Chabrol.

Cry of the Penguins 1/2 *Mr. Forbush and the Penguins* **1971** Womanizing biologist Forbush (Hurt) heads off on an Antartic expedition to study penguins when his would-be romance with Tara (Mills) comes to naught. Beautiful photography, shallow story. Adapted from the novel "Mr. Forbush and the Penguins" by Graham Billing. Note the similarities with "Never Cry Wolf." **105m/C VHS, DVD.** *GB* John Hurt, Hayley Mills, Dudley Sutton, Tony Britton, Thorley Walters, Judy Campbell, Joss Ackland, Nicholas Pennell; *D:* Albert T. Viola; *W:* Anthony Shaffer; *M:* John Addison.

Cry of the Werewolf 1944 A beautiful New Orleans gypsy protects her mother's mummified remains by periodically turning into a werewolf and killing people. **63m/B VHS.** Nina Foch, Stephen Crane, Osa Massen, Blanche Yurka, Barton MacLane, Ivan Triesault, John Abbott, Fritz Leiber; *D:* Henry Levin; *W:* Charles "Blackie" O'Neal.

Cry Panic 1974 A man is thrown into a strange series of events after accidentally running down a man on a highway. **74m/C VHS, DVD.** John Forsythe, Anne Francis, Earl Holliman, Claudia McNeil, Ralph Meeker; *D:* James Goldstone. **TV**

Cry Terror *Kill Two Birds; Thriller: Kill Two Birds* **1976** Two escaped convicts take two beautiful women hostage hoping to gain their own freedom. Only a quick-thinking undercover police officer can save the girls. **71m/C VHS.** *GB* Bob Hoskins, Susan Hampshire, Gabrielle Drake; *D:* Robert Tronson; *W:* Brian Clemens. **TV**

Cry, the Beloved Country 1/2 *African Fury* **1951** A black country minister travels to Johannesberg to be with his son after the youth is accused of killing a white man. Through the events of the trial, the horror, oppression, and destruction of South Africa's apartheid system are exposed. Startling and moving, the first entertainment feature set against the backdrop of apartheid. Still trenchant; based on the novel by Alan Paton. **111m/B VHS.** *GB* Canada Lee, Charles Carson, Sidney Poitier, Joyce Carey, Geoffrey Keen; *D:* Zoltan Korda; *W:* John Howard Lawson, Alan Paton; *C:* Robert Krasker.

Cry, the Beloved Country **1995 (PG-13)** Alan Paton's classic South African apartheid novel (first filmed in 1951) depicts a Zulu Christian pastor and a wealthy white farmer finding common ground through personal loss—both of their sons were killed in regional violence. Rural black minister Stephen Kumalo (Jones), travels to Johannesburg only to discover his sister (Kente) is a prostitute, his younger brother John (Dutton) no longer believes in Christianity and his son is in prison for the murder of a white man. That man turns out to be the son of rich farmer James Jarvis (Harris), from Kumalo's own village. Both Jones and Harris turn in wonderfully understated performances in this hopeful tale of potential racial harmony. **120m/C VHS, DVD.** *SA* James Earl Jones, Richard Harris, Charles S. Dutton, Leleti Khumalo, Dambisa Kente, Vusi Kuriene, Eric Miyeni, Ian Robers; *D:* Darrell Roodt; *W:* Ronald Atwood; *C:* Paul Gilpin; *M:* John Barry.

Cry Uncle 1/2 **1971 (R)** Comic account of a private eye who investigates a blackmailing case involving a film of orgies in which, much to his chagrin, he participated. **85m/C VHS, DVD.** Allen (Goorwitz) Garfield, Paul Sorvino, Devin Goldenberg, Madeleine Le Roux; *D:* John G. Avildsen; *W:* David Odell; *C:* John G. Avildsen; *M:* Harper Mckay.

Cry Vengeance 1/2 **1954** A falsely imprisoned detective gets out of jail and searches for the people who framed him and killed his family. **83m/B VHS.** Mark Stevens, Joan Vohs, Martha Hyer, Skip Homeier; *D:* Mark Stevens.

Cry Wolf 1947 Weak mystery thriller places Stanwyck in creepy environs when she goes to claim her inheritance from her late husband's estate. Based on the novel by Marjorie Carleton. **83m/B VHS.** Errol Flynn, Barbara Stanwyck, Richard Basehart, Geraldine Brooks, Jerome Cowan, John Ridgely, Patricia Barry; *D:* Peter Godfrey; *W:* Catherine Turney.

The Crying Child 1/2 **1996 (PG-13)** Madeline Jeffreys (Hemingway) and her husband Ran (DelHoyo) retreat to their 19th-century island vacation cottage after the stillbirth of their first child. Madeline begins to hear a child crying in the house and sees a ghostly apparition—now she has to discover what the spirit wants (and convince everyone she's not just going crazy). TV movie based on the novel by Barbara Michaels. **93m/C VHS.** Mariel Hemingway, George DelHoyo, Finola Hughes, Kin Shriner, Collin Wilcox-Paxton; *D:* Robert Lewis; *W:* Rob Gilmer; *C:* Stephen Lighthill; *M:* Shirley Walker.

The Crying Game 1/2 **1992 (R)** PR lesson in how to launch a small movie into the hypersphere and ensure critical silence on salient characterization. Jordan's gritty drama is on par with his best, a complex blend of violence, love, betrayal, guilt, and redemption and is not about what it seems to be about much of the time. Wonderful performances by all, including Rea as the appealing, conscience-stricken Fergus; Richardson as the cold, violent IRA moll Jude; and Davidson, in a film debut, as the needy, charismatic Dil. Whitaker is terrific in his 15 minutes of intense screen time. Filled with definite surprises and unexpected pleasures. Title is taken from a top-5 British hit of 1964, three versions of which are heard. **112m/C VHS, DVD.** *IR* Stephen Rea, Jaye Davidson, Miranda Richardson, Forest Whitaker, Adrian Dunbar, Jim Broadbent, Ralph Brown, Breffini McKenna, Joe Savino, Birdy Sweeney, Andre Bernard; *D:* Neil Jordan; *W:* Neil Jordan; *C:* Ian Wilson; *M:* Anne Dudley. Oscars '92: Orig. Screenplay; Australian Film Inst. '93: Foreign Film; Ind. Spirit '93: Foreign Film; L.A. Film Critics '92: Foreign Film; N.Y. Film Critics '92: Screenplay, Support. Actress (Richardson); Natl. Soc. Film Critics '92: Actor (Rea); Writers Guild '92: Orig. Screenplay.

Crypt of Dark Secrets **1976 (R)** Vietnam veteran recovering from wounds in the Louisiana swamps encounters a friendly Indian spirit who saves him from death. **100m/C VHS, DVD.** Maureen Chan, Ronald Tanet, Wayne Mack, Herbert G. Jahncke; *D:* Jack Weis.

Crypt of the Living Dead **WOOF!** **1973 (PG)** An undead woman from the 13th century makes life miserable for visitors on Vampire Island. **75m/C VHS, DVD.** Andrew Prine, Mark Damon, Teresa Gimpera, Patty (Patti) Shepard, Francisco (Frank) Brana; *D:* Ray Danton.

Crystal Heart **1987 (R)** A medically isolated songwriter with an incurable disease falls in love with a lovely rock singer. **103m/C VHS.** Lee Curreri, Tawny Kitaen, Lloyd Bochner; *D:* Gil Bettman; *M:* Joel Goldsmith.

Crystal River 1/2 2008 Doesn't take the obvious road when examining love and friendship. Davie Nance (Carpenter) is a sweet, respected member of her community with a charitable heart, which is why she looks out for her crotchety elderly neighbor Olin Arrendal (Manson). However, after Davie suffers her fourth miscarriage, she feels lost and estranged from her husband Paul (Pralgo). When Olin's grandson Clay (Flanery), fleeing his own disappointments, comes to stay, Davie finds him easy to talk to, but their budding friendship causes town tongues to wag. **102m/C DVD.** Sean Patrick Flanery, Ted Manson, Karla Droege, Emily Carpenter, Robert Pralgo, Daniel Burnley, Brandon O'Dell; *D:* Brett Levner; *C:* Edwin Myers; *M:* Woody Pak.

Crystal's Diary 1999 Small town Emmanuel Crystal moves to Hollywood and winds up sharing a place with free-spirited Tabetha. The twosome make their cash lap dancing until Emmanuel makes the mistake of falling for a client and things just go downhill from there. **90m/C VHS.** Shelly Gurvitz, Monique Albers, David Alan, Vincent Bilancio, John Sayre; *D:* Jeff Leroy; *W:* Jeff Leroy; *M:* Larry Washington. **VIDEO**

Crystalstone **1988 (PG)** A wooden cross leads a pair of orphans on a dangerous search for the legendary Crystalstone. **103m/C VHS.** Frank Grimes, Kamlesh Gupta, Laura Jane Goodwin, Sydney Bromley; *D:* Antonio Pelaez.

Cry_Wolf **2005 (PG-13)** Bored trust-funders at a boarding school start up an internet game of spreading stories and rumors. The game turns serious when someone makes up a story about a serial killer and people start turning up dead. Twisty plot goes for sleight-of-hand and visceral thrills, and doesn't completely fail. But it's all only mildly effective. Typical slasher fare might keep you entertained but won't register past the final credits. **90m/C DVD.** *US* Lindy Booth, Jared Padalecki, Kristy Wu, Paul James, Julian Morris, Sandra McCoy, Jon Bon Jovi, Gary Cole, Jesse Janzen, Anna Deavere Smith; *D:* Jeff Wadlow; *W:* Jeff Wadlow, Beau Bauman; *C:* Romeo Tirone; *M:* Michael Wandmacher.

CSA: The Confederate States of America 1/2 **2004** Mockumentary ponders the history of the past 150 years had the Confederacy won the Civil War and slavery endured. Told via a faux British public network Ken Burns-type series and presented by Spike Lee. Purposely unsettling, with images like a black-faced Lincoln in hiding as Harriet Tubman helps him to escape to Canada, the picky attention to historical details falls short by presuming such modern events as JFK's presidency and assassination, and the Vietnam War would have really took place in such a world. **89m/C DVD.** *US* Charles Frank, Evamarii Johnson, Rupert Pate, Larry J. Peterson; ***C:*** Matthew Jacobson; ***M:*** Kelly Werts.

Cthulhu **2008 (R)** An unpronounceable title is just the first problem with this feeble supernatural thriller based on the works of H.P. Lovecraft. Russell March returns to his island home for his mother's funeral. His family consists of various crackpots, including his religious father whose cult-like church believes saving mankind means returning to the sea. Russell's also gay and there are some subplots about an old flame and a female friend, both with sexual designs on Russ, but the whole production is fairly unhinged. **109m/C DVD.** Cara Buono, Tori Spelling, Greg Michaels, Jason Cottle, Scott Patrick, Dennis Kleinsmith, Nancy Stark, Ian Geoghegan; ***D:*** Daniel Gildark; ***W:*** Grant Cogswell; ***C:*** Sean Kirby; ***M:*** Willy Greer.

Cthulhu Mansion **WOOF!** **1991 (R)** The oldest-looking juvenile delinquents you've ever seen release evil spirits when they take over a magician's estate. Not very special effects and abominable dialogue; it claims to be based on H.P. Lovecraft stories, but that's a load of dung. **95m/C VHS.** Frank Finlay, Marcia Layton, Brad Fisher, Melanie Shatner, Luis Fernando Alves, Kaethe Cherney, Paul Birchard, Francisco (Frank) Brana; ***D:*** J(uan) Piquer Simon; ***W:*** J(uan) Piquer Simon.

Cuba **1979 (R)** Cynical, satirical adventure/love story. Mercenary soldier rekindles an old affair during the Castro revolution. Charismatic cast and good direction make for an entertaining, if overlooked, Connery vehicle. **121m/C VHS, DVD.** Sean Connery, Brooke Adams, Jack Weston, Hector Elizondo, Denholm Elliott, Chris Sarandon, Lonette McKee; ***D:*** Richard Lester; ***W:*** Charles Wood; ***C:*** David Watkin; ***M:*** Patrick Williams.

Cuban Blood 1/2 *Dreaming of Julia* **2003 (PG-13)** Director Gerard's nostalgic semi-autobiographical tale centers around a nameless 8-year-old boy (Mendez) who lives in the town of Holguin, Cuba, in 1958. The boy loves the movies but in the middle of watching the thriller "Julie" (with Doris Day), guerrillas cut the power, foreshadowing the revolution about to take place. This situation eventually leads to a meeting between the boy and a beautiful blonde American woman (Hjejle) who has some unexpected ties to his grandfather, Che (Keitel). **109m/C DVD.** Harvey Keitel, Iben Hjejle, Gael Garcia Bernal, Andhy Mendez, Diana Bracho; ***D:*** Juan Gerard; ***W:*** Juan Gerard, Letvia Arza-Goderich; ***C:*** Kramer Morgenthau; ***M:*** Jose Padilla, Edesio Alejandro; ***V:*** Tony Plana.

Cube 1/2 **1998 (R)** Claustrophobic sci-fi thriller about six people who inexplicably wake up chained together in a bare room attached to other bare rooms that are fiendishly booby-trapped. They are forced to work together in order to escape. The fact that the bizarro force holding these people hostage is never explained may escape you; since your senses will be dulled by the bad acting and lack of plot. Not as much fun as spending an hour and a half in a refrigerator box. **90m/C VHS, DVD.** *CA* Maurice Dean Wint, Nikki de Boer, David Hewlett, Wayne Robson, Andrew Miller, Nicky Guadagni, Julian Richings; ***D:*** Vincenzo Natali; ***W:*** Graeme Manson, Vincenzo Natali, Andre Bijelic; ***C:*** Derek Rogers; ***M:*** Mark Korven.

Cube 2: Hypercube 1/2 *Hypercube* **2002 (R)** The sequel's basically a carbon copy of the first film with a couple more hostages. This time eight people find themselves trapped in a paranormal cube made up of deadly chambers. They struggle to escape and discover their would-be leader, Kate (Matchett), has her own agenda. Yawn. **94m/C VHS, DVD.** *CA* Kari Matchett, Geraint Wyn Davies, Matthew Ferguson, Neil Crone, Barbara Gordon, Lindsey Connell, Grace Lynn King, Greer Kent; ***D:*** Andrzej Sekula; ***W:*** Sean Hood; ***M:*** Norman Orenstein.

Cube: Zero 1/2 **2004 (R)** Third flick in the series is actually a story prequel that stays pretty close to the formula. Cube tech Wynn (Bennett) falls for Rain (Moore), an unwilling prisoner of the maze. Since Wynn has some idea of what's happening—and is a rebel—he enters the cube to try and rescue her. **94m/C DVD.** *CA* Zachary Bennett, Stephanie Moore, David Huband, Martin Roach, Michael Riley, Richard McMillan; ***D:*** Ernie Barbarash; ***W:*** Ernie Barbarash; ***C:*** Francois Dagenais; ***M:*** Norman Orenstein.

The Cuckoo 1/2 *Kushka* **2002 (PG-13)** It's not a joke but the film does have its humorous moments: a Russian, a Finn, and a Lapp are drawn together in 1944. That was the year the Nazis, who occupied Finland, pulled out, leaving behind Finns who had been pressed into service against the advancing Russians. One of these Finns is reluctant sniper Veiko (Haapasalo). The Russian is Ivan (Bychkov), wounded and found by the Lapp—young war widow Anni (Juuso)—who is caring for him in her hut. Veiko also stumbles upon the hut. None speak the other's language, which doesn't prevent a lot of conversation and misunderstandings as well as desire. In Finnish, Russian, and Sami (the Lapp language) with subtitles. **104m/C DVD.** *RU* Willie Haapsalo, Anni-Kristina Usso, Vikter Bychkov; ***D:*** Alexander Rogozhkin; ***W:*** Alexander Rogozhkin; ***C:*** Andrei Zhegalov; ***M:*** Dmitri Pavlov.

Cujo **1983 (R)** Bad doggie!! A rabid St. Bernard goes berserk and attacks mom Donna (Wallace Stone) and her five-year-old son Tad (Pintauro), who are trapped inside a broken-down Pinto. Frighteningly realistic film is based on Stephen King's bestseller. **94m/C VHS, DVD.** Dee Wallace, Daniel Hugh-Kelly, Danny Pintauro, Ed Lauter, Christopher Stone, Kaiulani Lee, Mills Watson, Jerry Hardin, Billy Jacoby, Sandy Ward; ***D:*** Lewis Teague; ***W:*** Lauren Currier, Don Carlos Dunaway; ***C:*** Jan De Bont; ***M:*** Charles Bernstein.

Cul de Sac **1966** A macabre, psychological thriller set in a dreary castle on a small island off the British coast. Pleasence is an eccentric, middle-aged hermit living acrimoniously with his young, nympho wife (Dorleac) when their home is invaded by two wounded gangsters (Stander and MacGowran), who proceed to hold the couple hostage. MacGowran soon dies of his wounds, leaving Stander and Pleasence to fight it out, encouraged by the luscious Dorleac, who finds her fun where she can. A bleak, sinister film considered one of Polanski's best. **111m/C VHS.** *GB* Donald Pleasence, Francoise Dorleac, Lionel Stander, Jack MacGowran, Jacqueline Bisset; ***D:*** Roman Polanski; ***W:*** Roman Polanski, Gerard Brach.

Culpepper Cattle Co. 1/2 **1972 (PG)** A young, starry-eyed yokel wants to be a cowboy and gets himself enlisted in a cattle drive, where he learns the harsh reality of the West. **92m/C VHS, DVD.** Gary Grimes, Billy Green Bush, Bo Hopkins, Charles Martin Smith, Geoffrey Lewis; ***D:*** Dick Richards; ***M:*** Jerry Goldsmith.

Cult 1/2 **2007** Dumb college horror. While researching a class project, co-ed Mindy (Miner) becomes obsessed with a Chinese legend about a murdered young girl who took a magical jade amulet to her grave. The amulet has been recovered by a cult leader who is using ritual sacrifice to harness its power. **90m/C DVD.** Rachel Miner, Taryn Manning, Joel Michaely, Glenn Dunk, Myke Michaels; ***D:*** Joe Knee; ***W:*** Benjamin Oren; ***C:*** Dave McFarland; ***M:*** Tung Thanh Tran. **VIDEO**

Cult of the Cobra **1955** Mysterious horror film that became minor camp classic. It seems ex-servicemen are being killed by exotic snake-lady Domergue. Cheesy film that can be fun. Based on a story by Jerry Davis. **75m/B VHS.** Faith Domergue, Richard Long, Marshall Thompson, William Reynolds, Jack Kelly, Kathleen Hughes; ***D:*** Francis D. Lyon; ***W:*** Jerry Davis.

The Cup 1/2 *Phorpa* **1999 (G)** Tibetan teenager Orgyen arrives at a monastery in the Himalayan foothills where he is to join the religious life. But Orgyen is soccer-mad and obsessed with the World Cup (he wears a soccer shirt under his robes) and sneaks out to watch the games. Eventually, the monastery's abbott agrees to allow the monks to have a satellite dish to watch the finals—if they can raise the money to obtain it. Bhutanese with subtitles. **94m/C VHS, DVD.** *AU* Jamyang Lodro, Orgyen Tobgyal, Lama Chonjor; ***D:*** Khyentse Norbu; ***W:*** Khyentse Norbu; ***C:*** Paul Warren; ***M:*** Douglas Mills.

Cup Final 1/2 *G'mar Giviya* **1992** The similarities and contraditions in war and sports, where passions and competition run high, are depicted in this emotional drama. Set in 1982 during Israel's invasion of Lebanon. Cohen is an Israeli soldier passionately interested in the World Cup soccer tournament. When he is taken prisoner by the PLO he discovers his captor Ziad shares his interest in the Italian national team. This common interest brings the two antagonists reluctantly together. In Hebrew and Arabic with English subtitles. **107m/C VHS, DVD.** *IS* Moshe Ivgi, Muhamad Bakri, Suheil Haddad; ***D:*** Eran Riklis; ***W:*** Eyal Halfon; ***M:*** Raviv Gazil.

Cupid 1/2 **1996 (R)** Eric (Galligan) develops a deadly obsession for beautiful Jennifer (Laurence), who discovers that Jack and his equally crazy sister Dana (Crosby) have a nasty habit of killing the women that don't measure up to Jack's fantasies. **94m/C VHS.** Zach Galligan, Ashley Laurence, Mary Crosby, Joseph Kell, Michael Bowen; ***D:*** Doug Campbell; ***W:*** David Benullo; ***C:*** M. David Mullen.

Cupid & Cate 1/2 **2000** Cate De Angelo (Parker) is the quirky owner of a failing D.C. vintage clothing store. The youngest in a large Italian/Irish American family, Cate is still trying to deal with her alcoholic mother's death and an ongoing feud with her overbearing father, Dominic (Bosco). She has a reliable relationship with dull Philip (Lansbury) but doesn't realize the passion she's been missing until she meets handsome Harry (Gallagher) the lawyer. Stereotypes abound as do too many subplots but the leads are endearing. Based on Christina Bartolomeo's novel "Cupid and Diana." **95m/C VHS, DVD.** Mary-Louise Parker, Peter Gallagher, Philip Bosco, David Lansbury, Bebe Neuwirth, Joanna Going, Brenda Fricker, Kurt McKinney, Rebecca Luker; ***D:*** Brent Shields; ***W:*** Jennifer Miller, Ron Raley; ***C:*** Kees Van Oostrum; ***M:*** Mark Adler. **TV**

Cupid's Mistake **2001** No-budget video feature about unrequited love that's set in Venice Beach. Actress Susan is in love with aspiring filmmaker Gil who's in love with Korean-American model Toya who's in love with Japanese-American bodybuilder Ken—and they are all so self-absorbed that you won't care about any of them. **70m/C DVD.** Susan Petry, Everardo Gil, Toya Cho, Ken Yasuda; ***D:*** Young Man Kang; ***W:*** Young Man Kang; ***C:*** Doo H. Lee; ***M:*** Oliver Lyons.

Curdled 1/2 **1995 (R)** And you thought your job sucked. Tarantino-funded dark comedy arouses interest with that tag line alone. Gore-obsessed Gabriela (Jones) gets her dream job cleaning up blood and guts with the Post-Forensic Cleaning Service and becomes obsessed with serial killer to the rich Paul (Baldwin), who is keeping her company hopping with one beheading after another. Cultishly violent pic culminates in a tango by the gruesome twosome around a murder scene. Tarantino spotted Jones, starring in Braddock's original student short, while touring with "Reservoir Dogs" and borrowed her for "Pulp Fiction," only to return the favor by exec producing this interesting feature debut. Soundtrack adds spice to the formaldehyde flavor. **87m/C VHS, DVD.** Angela Jones, William Baldwin, Mel Gorham, Barry Corbin, Bruce Ramsay, Daisy Fuentes, Lois Chiles, Carmen Lopez; ***D:*** Reb Braddock; ***W:*** John Maass, Reb Braddock; ***C:*** Steven Bernstein; ***M:*** Joseph Julian Gonzalez.

The Cure **1917** Chaplin arrives at a spa to take a rest cure, accompanied by a trunk full of liquor that somehow gets dumped into the water at the resort. Silent with music track. **20m/B VHS, DVD.** Charlie Chaplin, Edna Purviance, Eric Campbell, Albert Austin; ***D:*** Charlie Chaplin.

The Cure 1/2 **1995 (PG-13)** Erik (Renfro), the neighborhood bad kid, befriends Dexter (Mazzello), a boy with AIDS. As Dexter's health weakens, Erik decides they must go on a quest for a cure, Huck Finn style, by floating along the Mississippi River to New Orleans. Despite film's preposterous plot, the performances of the two young leads do inspire a level of sentiment. **99m/C VHS, DVD.** Renee Humphrey, Brad Renfro, Joseph Mazzello, Annabella Sciorra, Diana Scarwid, Bruce Davison; ***D:*** Peter Horton; ***W:*** Robert Kuhn; ***C:*** Andrew Dintenfass; ***M:*** Dave Grusin.

Cure 1/2 *The Cure; Kyua* **1997** A detective must solve a series of murders that all end with the victims having an "X" slashed in their throat. Eventually he discovers a young drifter who has no memory or self-identity, but somehow seems able to bring out the worst repressed desires in anyone he meets (they all end up killing people). **111m/C DVD.** *JP* Koji Yakusho, Masato Hagiwara, Anna Nakagawa, Yoriko Douguchi, Tsuyoshi Ujiki, Yukihiro Hotaru, Denden, Ren Osugi, Shin Nakazawa, Shogo Suzuki, Masahiro Toda, Akira Otaka; ***D:*** Kiyoshi Kurosawa; ***W:*** Kiyoshi Kurosawa; ***C:*** Tokusho Kikumura; ***M:*** Gary Hashiya.

Curfew **1988 (R)** A young woman rushes home so she doesn't break her curfew, only to find two killers with time on their hands waiting for her. Violent. **86m/C VHS, DVD.** John Putch, Kyle Richards, William Wellman Jr., Bert Remsen; ***D:*** Gary Winick.

The Curfew Breakers **1957** Dim teen-exploitation/message-movie finds a pair of community workers investigating the murder of a gas station attendent by a drug-crazed youth. **78m/B VHS, DVD.** Regis Toomey, Paul Kelly, Cathy Downs, Marilyn Madison, Sheila Urban; ***D:*** Alex Wells.

Curiosity Kills 1/2 **1990 (R)** Young people find more than they bargained for when they begin to investigate the death of a fellow tenant. Tense made-for-cable thriller. **86m/C VHS.** Rae Dawn Chong, C. Thomas Howell, Courteney Cox, Paul Guilfoyle, Jeff Fahey; ***D:*** Colin Bucksey; ***W:*** Joe Batteer, John Rice; ***C:*** Bojan Bazelli. **CABLE**

The Curiosity of Chance 1/2 **2006** Inspired by John Hughes' teen flicks, this deliberately campy comedy/drama finds openly gay teen and army brat Chance Marquis (Hilgenbrink) the new kid at yet another school (this one in some unnamed place in Europe). Chance (who wears a top hat and bow tie) is immediately persecuted by jock Brad (Maes) and befriended by a couple of fellow outcasts. He gets some good advice from a drag queen, so Chance decides to be himself (and go after the hunk next door). **99m/C DVD.** Tad Hilgenbrink, Brett Chukerman, Chris Mulkey, Maxim Maes, Aldevina Da Silva, Pieter van Nieuwenhuyze, Magali Uytterhaegen; ***D:*** Russell P. Marleau; ***W:*** Russell P. Marleau; ***C:*** Jack Messitt; ***M:*** Willie Aron, Josef Peters. **VIDEO**

The Curious Case of Benjamin Button 1/2 **2008 (PG-13)** As Hurricane Katrina bears down on New Orleans in 2005, daughter Caroline (Ormond) reads from her mother Daisy's (Blanchett) book as she lay dying, not realizing it's the story of Daisy's life, and of Benjamin Button (Pitt)—a man who was born a wrinkly-skinned senior citizen who goes through life aging backwards. Raised by Queenie (Henson) after being abandoned as a newborn by his father Thomas (Flemyng) in 1918, Benjamin sees the other old-timers who surround him at the old folks' home where his adoptive mother works pass on while he becomes more virile. While many adventures ensue, the focus is on Daisy and Benjamin's relationship, which begins while both are "young" (with Fanning as Daisy), even though Benjamin looks old and their friendship inappropriate but later blossoms when the pair meet in their prime. Loosely taken from F. Scott Fitzgerald's 1922 fantasy short story of the same name, the lead actors are golden in this endearing, though lengthy, tale. **167m/C DVD.** *US* Brad Pitt, Cate Blanchett, Tilda Swinton, Julia Ormond, Taraji P. Henson, Elias Koteas, Jason Flemyng, Jared Harris, Mahershalhashbaz Ali, Phyllis Somerville, Elle Fanning, Madisen Beaty; ***D:*** David Fincher; ***W:*** Eric Roth; ***C:*** Claudio Miranda; ***M:*** Alexandre Desplat. Oscars '08: Art Dir./Set Dec., Makeup, Visual FX; British Acad. '08: Makeup, Visual FX.

The Curious Dr. Humpp **1970** A mad scientist (Barbero) kidnaps exotic dancers and extracts their libidos to preserve his youth. Under the guise of research, he encourages his victims to engage in trysts so that their carnal energies will increase. Everything is hunky dory until a reporter (Bauleo) starts snooping around the laboratory, discovering Dr. Humpp observing multiple couplings via closed-circuit TV. Boldly exploitative, the American distributor added about 10 minutes of raunchy hard-core footage of exotic dance routines. **87m/B VHS, DVD.** *AR* Gloria Prat, Susan Beltran, Ricardo Bauleo, Aldo Barbero; ***D:*** Emilio Vieyra; ***W:*** Emilio Vieyra, Raul Zorrilla; ***C:*** Anibal Gonzalez Paz; ***M:*** Victor Buchino.

Curious George 🦴🦴 ½ **2006 (G)** The cute, mischievous chimp and The Man in the Yellow Hat (Ferrell) take a pleasant trip to the big screen. The New York museum where TMitYH works is having financial trouble, so he ventures to Africa to find a lost idol that will bring in the crowds. Along the way he meets George, who has been having fun with his jungle playmates. George takes a liking to The Man after a game of peek-a-boo and manages to follow him back to NYC. George's playful and curious nature gets The Man in trouble with the museum owner's son, who wants to close the museum and build a parking garage. The animation and story are simplistic, but that's just fine with the target audience of pre-schoolers and elementary-agers. The adults will find a few chuckle-worthy gags here and there, as well. **86m/C DVD.** *US* ***D:*** Matthew O'Callaghan; ***W:*** Ken Kaufman; ***C:*** Julie Rogers; ***M:*** Hector Pereira; ***V:*** Will Ferrell, Drew Barrymore, David Cross, Eugene Levy, Dick Van Dyke, Frank Welker, Joan Plowright, Clint Howard, Ed O'Ross.

Curley 🦴🦴 **1947** High-spirited youngsters play pranks on their schoolteacher. A part of the Hal Roach Comedy Carnival. **53m/C VHS.** Larry Olsen, Frances Rafferty, Eilene Janssen, Walter Abel; ***D:*** Bernard Carr.

Curly Sue 🦴🦴 **1991 (PG)** Adorable, homeless waif Porter and her scheming, adoptive father Belushi plot to rip off single, career-minded female attorney Lynch in order to take in some extra cash. Trouble is, all three heartstrings are tugged, and the trio develop a warm, caring relationship. A throwback to the Depression era's Shirley Temple formula films met with mixed reviews. Undiscriminating younger audiences should have a good time, though. **102m/C VHS, DVD.** James Belushi, Kelly Lynch, Alison Porter, John Getz, Fred Dalton Thompson; ***D:*** John Hughes; ***W:*** John Hughes; ***M:*** Georges Delerue.

Curly Top 🦴🦴 ½ **1935 (G)** Orphan Temple helps land a husband for her beautiful sister. Along the way, she sings "Animal Crackers in My Soup." Remake of the silent "Daddy Long Legs," which was remade again in 1955. **74m/B VHS, DVD.** Shirley Temple, John Boles, Rochelle Hudson, Jane Darwell, Esther Dale, Arthur Treacher, Rafaela (Rafael, Raphaella) Ottiano; ***D:*** Irving Cummings.

The Curse 🦴 *The Farm* **1987 (R)** After a meteorite lands near a small farming community and contaminates the area, a young boy tries to prevent residents from turning into slime-oozing mutants. Remake of "Die, Monster, Die." **92m/C VHS.** Wil Wheaton, Claude Akins, Malcolm Danare, Cooper Huckabee, John Schneider, David Keith, Amy Wheaton, David Chaskin, Kathleen Jordan Gregory; ***D:*** David Keith; ***W:*** David Chaskin; ***C:*** Robert D. Forges.

Curse 2: The Bite 🦴 **1988 (R)** Radiation affected snakes are transformed into deadly vipers whose bites change their unsuspecting victims into horrible creatures. **97m/C VHS, DVD.** Jill Schoelen, J. Eddie Peck, Jamie Farr, Savina Gersak, Bo Svenson, Sydney Lassick, Marianne Muellerleile, Terrence Evans; ***D:*** Fred Goodwin; ***W:*** Fred Goodwin, Susan Zelouf; ***C:*** Roberto D'Ettorre Piazzoli.

Curse 3: Blood Sacrifice 🦴 ½ *Panga* **1990 (R)** An African sugar cane plantation becomes host to a horrible nightmare when a voodoo curse is placed on the owners. The monstrous God of the Sea is summoned to avenge the accidental death of a baby, and the hellish journey into insanity begins. **91m/C VHS.** Christopher Lee, Jenilee Harrison, Henry Cele; ***D:*** Sean Barton.

Curse 4: The Ultimate Sacrifice 🦴 ½ *Catacombs* **1990 (R)** Beneath the monastery at San Pietro lies buried the beast of the Apocalypse. For 400 years the secret has been kept and then an American priest and a lovely school teacher unwittingly break the seal and unleash the cursed beast upon an unsuspecting world. **84m/C VHS.** Timothy Van Patten, Laura Schaefer, Jeremy West, Ian Abercrombie; ***D:*** David Schmoeller.

The Curse of Frankenstein 🦴🦴 ½ **1957** Young Victor Frankenstein reenacts his father's experiments with creating life from the dead resulting in a terrifying, hideous creature. The first in Hammer's Frankenstein series and followed by "Revenge of Frankenstein." From the Shelley story. Make-up by Jack Pierce, who also created the famous make-up for Universal's Frankenstein monster. **83m/C VHS, DVD.** *GB* Peter Cushing, Christopher Lee, Hazel Court, Robert Urquhart, Valerie Gaunt, Noel Hood; ***D:*** Terence Fisher; ***W:*** Jimmy Sangster; ***C:*** Jack Asher; ***M:*** James Bernard.

The Curse of Inferno 🦴 ½ **1996 (R)** Dumb-as-posts bankrobbers Shore and Perlich get mixed up in a sting operation to flush out the head of a money-laundering operation. **87m/C VHS.** Pauly Shore, Max Perlich, Janine Turner, Ned Beatty, John Pleshette, Stephen Tobolowsky, Edward "Blue" Deckert; ***D:*** John Warren; ***W:*** John Warren; ***C:*** Nancy Schreiber.

The Curse of King Tut's Tomb 🦴 ½ **1980** In 1922, archaeologists have just opened Tutankhamen's tomb. The curse of the boy king is unleashed as tragic events bring the adventurers uncommon gloom. Oh boy. **98m/C VHS.** Robin Ellis, Harry Andrews, Eva Marie Saint, Raymond Burr, Wendy Hiller; ***D:*** Philip Leacock; ***Nar:*** Paul Scofield. **TV**

Curse of Nostradamus 🦴🦴 *The Monster Demolisher; Genie of Darkness* **1960** The descendent of Nostradamus is a vampire, thus causing havoc for many townsfolk. Edited from a Mexican serial. **77m/B VHS, DVD.** *MX* German Robles; ***D:*** Frederick Curiel.

The Curse of the Aztec Mummy **WOOF!** *La Maldicion de la Momia Azteca* **1959** A mad scientist schemes to rob a Mayan pyramid of its treasure but the resident mummy will have none of it. Sequels are "Robot vs. the Aztec Mummy" and "Wrestling Women vs. the Aztec Mummy." **65m/B VHS, DVD.** *MX* Ramon Gay, Rosita (Rosa) Arenas, Crox Alvarado; ***D:*** Rafael Portillo.

Curse of the Black Widow 🦴🦴 *Love Trap* **1977** An investigator follows a trail of brutal murders to the lair of a supernatural gigantic spider in the middle of Los Angeles. **100m/C VHS.** Patty Duke, Anthony (Tony) Franciosa, Donna Mills, June Lockhart, Sid Caesar, Vic Morrow, June Allyson, Roz Kelly, Jeff Corey; ***D:*** Dan Curtis. **TV**

Curse of the Blue Lights **WOOF!** **1988 (R)** Mysterious lights begin appearing at the local romantic spot. Little do the young lovers know, it hails the arrival of a ghoul, intent on raising the dead. Also available in an unedited version. Unfortunately, nothing can resurrect this film. **93m/C VHS.** Brent Ritter, Bettina Julius, Kent E. Fritzell, Willard Hall; ***D:*** John H. Johnson; ***W:*** John H. Johnson.

Curse of the Cat People 🦴🦴🦴 **1944** A young sensitive girl is guided by the vision of her dead mother and bonds with an eccentric neighbor with family issues of her own. Dad and new wife Alice are understandably concerned. Sequel to "Cat People" doesn't come close to measuring up to the original. Available in a colorized version. **70m/B VHS, DVD.** Simone Simon, Kent Smith, Jane Randolph, Elizabeth Russell, Ann Carter; ***D:*** Robert Wise, Gunther Von Fritsch.

The Curse of the Crying Woman 🦴 ½ *La Maldicion de a Llorona; La Casa Embrujada* **1961** Unknowing descendant of a witch is lured to her aunt's home to perform the act that will revive the monstrous crying woman and renew a reign of evil. **74m/B VHS, DVD.** *MX* Rosita (Rosa) Arenas, Abel Salazar, Rita Macedo; ***D:*** Rafael Baledon Sr.; ***W:*** Rafael Baledon Sr., Fernando Galiana; ***C:*** Jose Ortiz Ramos.

Curse of the Crystal Eye 🦴🦴 **1993 (PG-13)** A gunrunner tries to get the treasure of Ali Baba aided by the requisite lovely lady and opposed by your usual bad guys. **90m/C VHS.** Jameson Parker, Cynthia Rhodes, Mike Lane, David Sherwood, Andre Jacobs; ***D:*** Joe Tornatore.

Curse of the Demon 🦴🦴🦴 ½ *Night of the Demon; The Haunted* **1957** A famous psychologist investigates a colleague's mysterious death and enters a world of demonology and the occult, climaxing in a confrontation with a cult's patron demon. Superb thriller based upon the story "Casting the Runes" by M.R. James. **81m/B VHS, DVD.** *GB* Dana Andrews, Peggy Cummins, Niall MacGinnis, Maurice Denham, Athene Seyler, Liam Redmond, Reginald Beckwith, Ewan Roberts, Peter Elliott, Brian Wilde, Rosamund Greenwood; ***D:*** Jacques Tourneur; ***W:*** Charles Bennett, Hal E. Chester; ***C:*** Edward Scaife; ***M:*** Clifton Parker.

Curse of the Devil 🦴 ½ *El Retorno de la Walpurgis* **1973 (R)** This time Naschy is turned into a werewolf by annoyed gypsies whose ancestors were slain by his. **73m/C VHS, DVD.** *MX SP* Paul Naschy, Maria Silva, Patty (Patti) Shepard, Fay Falcon, Fabiola Falcon, Mariano Vidal Molina, Ines Morales; ***D:*** Carlos Aured; ***W:*** Paul Naschy; ***C:*** Francisco Sanchez.

Curse of the Golden Flower 🦴🦴 *Man Cheng Jin Dai Huang Jin Jia* **2006 (R)** Zhang's tale, set in the 10th-century Tang Dynasty, is a sumptuous, convoluted saga of family mayhem. The Emperor (Chow) has returned home from a long battle, just before the annual chrysanthemum festival (the flower of the title). The emperor is having the royal doctor poison his unloved empress (Gong), who is having an affair with Crown Prince Wan, her stepson, who is actually in love with the doctor's daughter, Chan. The doctor's wife warns the empress about the poison; she turns out to be the emperor's ex-wife, and the mother of Wan (who thought she was dead) and Chan. There's some martial arts stuff between the imperial factions and it's all very operatic, including the elaborate corseted, bosom-lifting costumes the empress wears. Mandarin with subtitles. **114m/C DVD, Blu-ray Disc.** *CH* Gong Li, Liu Ye, Chow Yun-Fat, Jay Chou, Qin Junjie, Man Li, Ni Dahong, Chen Jin; ***D:*** Yimou Zhang; ***W:*** Yimou Zhang, Wu Nan, Bian Zhihong; ***C:*** Xiaoding Zhao; ***M:*** Shingeru Umebayashi.

Curse of the Headless Horseman **1972** The headless horseman rides again, bringing terror to all who cross his path! **80m/C VHS, DVD.** Don Carrara, Claudia Dean, B.G. Fisher, Margo Dean, Lee Byers, Joe Cody; ***D:*** John Kirkland.

The Curse of the Jade Scorpion 🦴🦴 ½ **2001 (PG-13)** Where can a 65-year-old guy who looks like Woody Allen bag a babe like Helen Hunt? In a Woody Allen movie, that's where. Hunt plays efficiency expert Betty Ann Fitzgerald, who's hired to update the offices of a Manhattan insurance agency where C.W. Briggs (Allen) is the chief investigator, so he and "Fitz" develop an immediate mutual dislike. After several increasingly tedious games of verbal darts, the two are mesmerized by nightclub hypnotist Voltan (Stiers) into believing that they're in love. He also uses hypnotic cues to have C.W. unknowingly pull off jewel heists of his own clients. After a mystery woman (Theron) shows up, C.W. begins to question where he's been and who he's been with late at night and enlists the help of the Coopersmith Brothers (Mulheren and Linari) to help crack the case. Lighter and shallower than most of Allen's work, it's still mostly fun to watch. Soundtrack is chock full of Allen's beloved 40s era jazz and Big Band tunes. **103m/C VHS, DVD.** *US* Woody Allen, Helen Hunt, Dan Aykroyd, Elizabeth Berkley, Charlize Theron, Wallace Shawn, David Ogden Stiers, John Schuck, Brian Markinson, Michael Mulheren, Peter Linari, Prof. Irwin Corey, Peter Gerety; ***D:*** Woody Allen; ***W:*** Woody Allen; ***C:*** Fei Zhao.

Curse of the Living Corpse 🦴 **1964** A millionaire comes back to rotting life to kill his negligent relatives. Scheider's first film. **84m/C VHS, DVD.** Candace Hilligoss, Roy Scheider, Helen Warren, Margot Hartman; ***D:*** Del Tenney.

Curse of the Pink Panther 🦴🦴 **1983 (PG)** Clifton Sleigh, an inept New York City detective played by Wass, is assigned to find the missing Inspector Clouseau. His efforts are complicated by an assortment of gangsters and aristocrats who cross paths with the detective. So-so attempt to keep popular series going after Seller's death. Niven's last film. **110m/C VHS, DVD.** Ed Parker, Ted Wass, David Niven, Robert Wagner, Herbert Lom, Joanna Lumley, Capucine, Robert Loggia, Harvey Korman, Leslie Ash, Denise Crosby; ***D:*** Blake Edwards; ***W:*** Blake Edwards; ***C:*** Dick Bush; ***M:*** Henry Mancini.

Curse of the Puppet Master: The Human Experiment 🦴 ½ **1998 (R)** The little guys have been taking a break since 1994's "Puppet Master 5" but they're baaaack. This time they're trying to prevent their new master, evil Dr. Magrew, from transforming more victims into living dolls. The director, "Victoria Sloan," is actually DeCoteau. **90m/C VHS, DVD.** George Peck, Emily Harrison, Michael Guerin, Robert Donovan; ***D:*** David DeCoteau; ***W:*** Benjamin Carr; ***C:*** Howard Wexler; ***M:*** Richard Band. **VIDEO**

Curse of the Queerwolf 🦴🦴 **1987** A man is bitten on the butt by gay werewolf and transforms into the title character. Filmed in Santa Barbara in 8mm; some funny moments. From the director of "A Polish Vampire in Burbank." **90m/C VHS, DVD.** Michael Palazzolo, Kent Butler, Taylor Whitney, Darwyn Carson, Sergio Bandera, Mark Pirro, Forrest J Ackerman, Conrad Brooks; ***D:*** Mark Pirro; ***W:*** Mark Pirro; ***M:*** Gregg Gross.

Curse of the Starving Class 🦴🦴 **1994 (R)** Ineffective adaptation of Sam Shepard's 1977 play exploring family disintegration. Weston (Woods) is the alcoholic, irresponsible patriarch of a decaying farm. His unhappy wife, Ella (Bates), wants to sell out to land speculator Taylor (Quaid) and move to Paris while rebellious teenager Emma (Fiorella) plans to run off to Mexico and sullen older brother Wesley (Thomas) desires to stay and make a go of things. One-dimensional characterizations don't translate well from stage to screen. **102m/C VHS.** James Woods, Kathy Bates, Henry Thomas, Kristin Fiorella, Randy Quaid, Louis Gossett Jr.; ***D:*** Michael McClary; ***W:*** Bruce Beresford; ***C:*** Dick Quinlan.

Curse of the Stone Hand **WOOF!** **1964** A pair of stone hands causes folks to do suicidal things. A mutation of a Mexican and a Chilean horror film, each purchased and monster-mashed into one by Warren. **72m/B VHS.** *MX* John Carradine, Ernest Walch, Sheila Bon, Katherine Victor, Lloyd Nelson; ***D:*** Jerry Warren.

Curse of the Swamp Creature 🦴 **1966** A mad scientist in the Everglades attempts to create half human/half alligator monsters. In turn, a geologic expeditionary force attempts to stop his experimentation. Low budget thrills courtesy of Larry Buchanan. **80m/C VHS, DVD.** John Agar, Francine York, Shirley McLine, Bill (Billy) Thurman, Jeff Alexander; ***D:*** Larry Buchanan.

Curse of the Undead 🦴 ½ *Affairs of the Vampire; Mark of the West; Mark of the Beast; The Invisible Killer; Le Teur Invisible; Les Griffes du Vampire; The Grip of the Vampire* **1959** Mediocre vampire western finds a small town suffering from the deaths of several young women—all with small wounds in the neck. Suspicions fall on gunslinger Drake Robey (Pate) and it's up to preacher Dan Young (Fleming) to take care of the blood-sucking miscreant. **89m/B VHS.** Eric Fleming, Michael Pate, Kathleen Crowley, John Hoyt, Bruce Gordon, Edward Binns, Jimmy Murphy, Jay Adler; ***D:*** Edward Dein; ***W:*** Edward Dein, Mildred Dein; ***C:*** Ellis W. Carter; ***M:*** Irving Gertz.

The Curse of the Werewolf 🦴🦴 ½ **1961** Horror film about a 19th-century European werewolf that is renowned for its ferocious departure from the stereotypical portrait of the beast. **91m/C VHS, DVD.** *GB* Oliver Reed, Clifford Evans, Yvonne Romain, Catherine Feller, Anthony Dawson, Michael Ripper, Peter Sallis; ***D:*** Terence Fisher; ***W:*** John (Anthony Hinds) Elder; ***C:*** Arthur Grant.

Curse of the Yellow Snake 🦴🦴 **1963** Voluminous yarn features a running battle over an ancient Chinese artifact, with crazed Chinese cultists running through foggy London streets. **98m/C VHS.** *GE* Joachim Fuchsberger, Werner Peters; ***D:*** Franz Gottlieb.

Cursed 1/2 **2004 (PG-13)** Writer Williamson and director Craven were much more successful with their "Scream" franchise than with this obvious werewolf horror. Los Angelenos Ellie (Ricci) and her geeky brother Jimmy (Eisenberg) encounter a nasty beastie after a car accident. They get bitten and start developing werewolf-like tendencies. Ellie doesn't want to accept the truth as her girlfriends are becoming beastie fodder. Rick Baker did better effects back in 1981 with "An American Werewolf in London." Film lives up to its title as it was rewritten, recast, reshot, and recut before it finally making it into the multiplex. **97m/C VHS, DVD.** *US* Christina Ricci, Joshua Jackson, Jesse Eisenberg, Judy Greer, Milo Ventimiglia, Kristina Anapau, Portia de Rossi, Shannon Elizabeth, Mya, Michelle Krusiec; ***Cameos:*** Scott Baio; ***D:*** Wes Craven; ***W:*** Kevin Williamson; ***C:*** Robert McLachlan; ***M:*** Marco Beltrami.

Cursed 1/2 *Jumon; Cho kowai hanashi A: yami no karasu* **2004** A perky young Japanese woman works at a convenience store, where the boss is a sadist and his wife is a deranged lunatic obsessed with watching the security camera in the back room. The register keeps ringing up 666, all of the customers die, crows keep doing ominous things, the night clerk is possessed, and the backyard smells like death himself has pooped there. Horror movie fun! **80m/C DVD.** *JP* Susumu Terajima, Osamu Takahashi, Kyoko Akiba, Takaaki Iwao, Hiroko Sato, Etsuyo Mitani; ***D:*** Yoshihiro Hoshino; ***W:*** Hirohoshi Kobayashi, Yoshihiro Hoshino, Yumeaki Hirayama; ***C:*** Masahiro Taniai; ***M:*** Kuniyuki Morohashi.

The Cursed Mountain Mystery 1/2 **1993 (R)** Two petty thieves steal a legendary precious gem rumored to cursed. The immortal warrior supposed to guard the gem lures the crooks to Sher Mountain, where he intends to eliminate them and return the stone to its keeper. **87m/C VHS.** Phillip Avalon, Tom Richards, Joe Bugner; ***D:*** Vince Martin; ***W:*** Denis Whitburn.

Curtain at Eight **1933** An elderly detective has a lot of suspects when an unpopular stage actor is murdered although it's clear to see whodunit. Unfortunately, it's not the monkey (who's part of the play's cast). **90m/B DVD.** Dorothy Mackaill, Sir C. Aubrey Smith, Paul Cavanagh, Sam Hardy, Russell Hopton, Marion Shilling; ***D:*** E. Mason Hopper; ***W:*** Edward T. Lowe; ***C:*** Ira Morgan.

Curtain Call **1997 (PG-13)** Publishing exec Stevenson Lowe (Spader) movies into a brownstone that is haunted by the ghosts of bickering theatrical marrieds Max (Caine) and Lily (Smith). Unfortunately for him, Stevenson is the only one who can see the duo, so his girlfriend Julia (Walker) thinks he's nuts. She has a problem with her commitment-phobe beau anyway and it's up to Max and Lily to see the duo stay together. **94m/C VHS, DVD.** James Spader, Polly Walker, Michael Caine, Maggie Smith, Buck Henry, Sam Shepard, Todd Alcott, Susan Berman, Marcia Gay Harden, Valerie Perrine, Frances Sternhagen, Frank Whaley; ***D:*** Peter Yates; ***W:*** Todd Alcott; ***C:*** Sven Nykvist; ***M:*** Richard Hartley. **VIDEO**

Curtain Up **1953** "Little theatre" dramatics and the exasperating temperaments of amateur theatricals are exposed in this adaptation of the play "On Monday Next," by Philip King. **82m/C VHS.** *GB* Robert Morley, Margaret Rutherford, Olive Sloane; ***D:*** Ralph Smart; ***W:*** Jack Davies; ***M:*** Malcolm Arnold.

Curtains **WOOF! 1983 (R)** Director has a clash of wills with a film star that spells "Curtains" for a group of aspiring actresses gathered together at a haunted house for an audition. Hamfest with no thrills, chills, gore, or gratuitous skin. No wonder why director Richard Ciupka hides behind pseudonym Stryker. **90m/C VHS.** *CA* John Vernon, Samantha Eggar; ***D:*** Jonathan Stryker; ***W:*** Robert Guza Jr.

Curtis's Charm 1/2 **1996** Thanks to his drug paranoia, crack addict Curtis (Wint) believes his wife Cookie (Crawford) and mother-in-law (Barnes-Hopkins) have put a voodoo spell on him. His friend Jim (Callum Rennie), a former addict, tries to help Curtis by coming up with some magic of his own, intended to convince the addled druggie that it will protect him. Lots of narration does little to make the character's friendship convincing. Based on a short story by Jim Carroll. **74m/B VHS.** *CA* Maurice Dean Wint, Callum Keith Rennie, Rachael Crawford, Barbara Barnes-Hopkins; ***D:*** John L'Ecuyer; ***W:*** James Dennis (Jim) Carroll, John L'Ecuyer; ***C:*** Harald Bachmann; ***M:*** Mark Korven. Genie '96: Score.

The Curve *Dead Man's Curve* **1997 (R)** Think "Dead Man on Campus" since you've got basically the same premise. College roomies Tim (Lillard), Rand (Batinkoff), and Chris (Vartan) learn that student myth is true at their small university. Should a roomie commit suicide, the survivors receive an automatic 4.0 for the semester. So Tim offs Rand and has Chris help him cover things up. Naturally this doesn't work out entirely as expected. Not nearly as clever as it tries to be. **90m/C VHS, DVD.** Matthew Lillard, Michael Vartan, Randall Batinkoff, Keri Russell, Dana Delany, Tamara Craig Thomas, Anthony Griffin, Bo Dietle, Kevin Huff, Henry Strozier; ***D:*** Dan Rosen; ***W:*** Dan Rosen; ***C:*** Joey Forsyte.

Custer's Last Fight 1/2 **1912** Contains the earliest surviving film of Custer's last stand. This 1925 re-release version of the original 1912 Thomas Ince production, filmed on location at the original battlefield, hosts a cast of real American Indians who claim to have taken part in the actual battle. Provides an authentic re-creation of the original battle. Comes with a copy of the original production pamphlet. **50m/B VHS.** ***D:*** Francis Ford.

Custer's Last Stand 1/2 **1936** Feature-length version of the Mascot serial recounting the last days of the famous General. **70m/B VHS, DVD.** Frank McGlynn, Rex Lease, Nancy Caseell, Lona Andre, William Farnum, Reed Howes, Jack Mulhall, Josef Swickard, Ruth Mix; ***D:*** Elmer Clifton.

The Custodian **1994 (R)** Honest cop must battle corruption of Australian police precinct while dealing with numerous personal problems. Good cast goes a long way in routine story. **110m/C VHS.** *AU* Anthony LaPaglia, Hugo Weaving, Barry Otto, Bill Hunter, Kelly Dingwall, Gosia Dobrowolska, Naomi Watts; ***D:*** John Dingwall.

Cut **2000 (R)** In this instance the title can be taken literally since a killer is knocking off those involved in a low-budget horror film. It seems that a group of film students want to finish a film that was shut down 15 years earlier after it's female director (Minogue) was murdered on the set. The students manage to get Vanessa (Ringwald), the star of the original, to reprise her role but is the film cursed or is someone giving their efforts a critical thumbs down? **82m/C VHS, DVD.** *AU* Molly Ringwald, Jessica Napier, Simon Bossell, Sarah Kants, Stephen Curry, Geoff Revell, Frank Roberts, Sam Lewis; ***Cameos:*** Kylie Minogue; ***D:*** Kimble Rendall; ***W:*** Dave Warner; ***C:*** David Foreman; ***M:*** Guy Gross. **VIDEO**

Cut and Run *Inferno in Diretta; Amazon: Savage Adventure; Straight to Hell* **1985 (R)** Two journalists follow a lead to the former South American home of Jim Jones, and are instantly captured by local guerrillas. **91m/C VHS, DVD.** *IT* Lisa Blount, Leonard Mann, Willie Aames, Richard Lynch, Michael Berryman, Karen Black, Eriq La Salle; ***D:*** Ruggero Deodato; ***W:*** Cesare Frugoni; ***C:*** Alberto Spagnoli; ***M:*** Claudio Simonetti.

The Cut Throats *She Devils of the S.S* **1969 (R)** Americans stumble upon an isolated Nazi outpost stocked with gold and beautiful women. Exploitation at its worst. **80m/C VHS.** Jay Scott, Joanne Douglas, Jeff Letham, Pat Michaels, Barbara Lane; ***D:*** John Hayes; ***W:*** John Hayes.

Cutaway 1/2 **2000 (R)** Vic Cooper (Baldwin) is a customs agent who goes undercover to infiltrate a group of drug dealers who deliver their goods via skydiving. He discovers the sport gives him a bigger adrenaline rush than his job, so which one will he choose? **104m/C VHS, DVD.** Tom Berenger, Stephen Baldwin, Dennis Rodman, Maxine Bahns, Casper Van Dien, Ron Silver; ***D:*** Guy Manos; ***W:*** Guy Manos, Greg Manos; ***C:*** Gerry Lively. **VIDEO**

Cutter's Way 1/2 *Cutter and Bone* **1981 (R)** An embittered and alcoholic disabled Vietnam vet and his small-time crook/gigolo friend wrestle with justice and morality when the drifter uncovers a murder but declines to get involved. An unusually cynical mystery from the novel by Newton Thorburg. **105m/C VHS, DVD.** Jeff Bridges, John Heard, Lisa Eichhorn, Ann Dusenberry, Stephen Elliott, Nina Van Pallandt, George Dickerson; ***D:*** Ivan Passer; ***W:*** Jeffrey Alladin Fiskin; ***C:*** Jordan Cronenweth; ***M:*** Jack Nitzsche.

Cutthroat Island 1/2 **1995 (PG-13)** Big-budget swashbuckling adventure—long on action and short on plot and character. Female pirate captain Morgan Adams (Davis) is left part of a treasure map by her father and "persuades" educated slave/thief William Shaw (Modine), who has lots of charm and no morals, to assist her. Her scurvy Uncle Dawg (despically well-played by Langella) also has a portion of the map and is willing to let Morgan find the treasure—on Cutthroat Island—before taking it for himself. Director Harlin likes lots of big, noisy explosions (when he doesn't know what else to do) but Davis' exuberance for her pirate queen role is appealing. **123m/C VHS, DVD.** Geena Davis, Matthew Modine, Frank Langella, Patrick Malahide, Stan Shaw, Maury Chaykin, Harris Yulin, George Murcell; ***D:*** Renny Harlin; ***W:*** Robert King, Marc Norman; ***C:*** Peter Levy; ***M:*** John Debney.

Cutting Class **1989 (R)** Murders proliferate in a high school, where a student with a history of mental illness is number one on the suspect list. Tongue-in-cheek mayhem. **91m/C VHS.** Jill Schoelen, Roddy McDowall, Donovan Leitch, Martin Mull, Brad Pitt; ***D:*** Rospo Pallenberg.

The Cutting Edge 1/2 **1992 (PG)** Spoiled figure skater's lifelong quest for Olympic gold is seriously hampered by her inability to be nice to her partners. In a final effort to snag the medal she teams up with a cocky guy who thinks the only sport on ice is hockey, but whose own dreams of NHL stardom were cut short by an injury. Saddled with a predictable and thin plot, it sometimes looks and feels like a TV movie. So why bother? Because the chemistry between photogenic leads Kelly and Sweeney is terrific. Add half a bone for the flying sparks and snappy dialogue, sit back, and enjoy. **101m/C VHS, DVD.** D.B. Sweeney, Moira Kelly, Roy Dotrice, Terry O'Quinn, Dwier Brown, Rachelle Ottley, Jo Jo Starbuck; ***D:*** Paul Michael Glaser; ***W:*** Tony Gilroy; ***C:*** Elliot Davis; ***M:*** Patrick Williams.

The Cutting Edge 3: Chasing the Dream **2008 (PG-13)** Same basic plot only with a role reversal. Medal-winning figure skater Zack Conroy (Lanter) drops his partner (literally) and her injury takes her out of competition. Needing a replacement in a hurry, Zack heads to the ice rink and recruits feisty amateur hockey player Alexandra Delgado (Raisa). There's the usual training montage, jeering rivals, and misunderstandings that all lead up to the big championship moment. At least Lanter and Raisa are cute eye candy. **92m/C DVD.** Christy Carlson Romano, Alycia Purrott, Matt Lanter, Francia Raisa, Sarah Gordon, Luis Oliva, Stefan Colacitti, Ben Hollingsworth; ***D:*** Stuart Gillard; ***W:*** Randall Badat; ***C:*** Pierre Jodoin; ***M:*** Robert Duncan. **CABLE**

The Cutting Edge: Going for the Gold 1/2 *The Cutting Edge 2: Going for the Gold* **2005 (PG-13)** Kate (Kramer) and Doug (Thompson) got married and their baby girl Jackie (Romano) is now a teenager following in their skate tracks as a promising figure skater who—like her mom way back when—is forced to pair up with a new partner, inline skater Alex (Thomas), and they face the same problems that Jackie's folks had. Major point deductions for the lifeless banter of this sequel, which might explain why original cast members Sweeney and Kelly decided to skip it. **99m/C DVD.** Christy Carlson Romano, Ross Thomas, Scott Thompson Baker, Stephanie Kramer, Kim Kindrick; ***D:*** Sean McNamara; ***W:*** Tony Gilroy, Daniel Berendsen. **VIDEO**

Cyber Bandits 1/2 **1994 (R)** In a future society, navigator Jack Morris (Kemp) has just sailed a pleasure craft to the island city of Pacifica. His passengers included wealthy Morgan Wells (Hays), whose scientists have developed a deadly virtual reality weapon, and Wells' mistress Rebecca (Paul). Rebecca steals the plans for the weapon and seduces Jack into having the data digitally transferred onto his back in the form of a tattoo. Then Rebecca disappears and Jack finds himself in big trouble. **86m/C VHS, DVD.** Martin Kemp, Alexandra Paul, Robert Hays, Adam Ant, Grace Jones; ***D:*** Erik Fleming; ***W:*** James Robinson, Winston Beard; ***M:*** Steve Hunter.

Cyber Ninja 1/2 *Mirai Ninja; Future Ninja; Robo Ninja* **1994** Warrior princess Saki is captured by the Dark Overlord, who plans to sacrifice her. It's up to a mercenary to come to her rescue. Lightweight, action-oriented Japanese mix of samurais and science fiction. Dubbed. **80m/C VHS.** *JP* Hanbel Kawai, Hiroki Ida; ***D:*** Keito Amamiya; ***W:*** Keito Amamiya.

Cyber-Tracker 1/2 **1993 (R)** In the judicial system of the future androids hunt down vicious criminals and execute them immediately. When secret service agent Eric Phillips is framed for murder, he's also marked for death. His only chance is to link up with rebels fighting the mechanized monsters. **91m/C VHS, DVD.** Don "The Dragon" Wilson, Richard Norton, Joseph Ruskin, Abby Dalton, John Aprea; ***D:*** Richard Pepin; ***W:*** Jacobsen Hart; ***C:*** Ken Blakey; ***M:*** Bill Montei, Lisa Popeil.

Cyber-Tracker 2 1/2 **1995 (R)** An international weapons dealer has gotten control of the cybertracker technology and created cyborg lookalikes of secret agent Eric Phillips (Wilson) and his newscaster wife Connie (Foster). When the cyborgs commit murder on live TV, the human duo become fugitives who must expose the real killers. **97m/C VHS, DVD.** Don "The Dragon" Wilson, Stacie Foster, Steve (Stephen) Burton; ***D:*** Richard Pepin; ***W:*** Richard Preston Jr.

Cybercity 1/2 **1999 (R)** When mercenary Howell's family is murdered by virtual prophet Piper, who's trying to take over the world, Howell tries for revenge with the aid of assassin von Palleske. **86m/C VHS, DVD.** C. Thomas Howell, Roddy Piper, Heidi von Palleske, David Carradine; ***D:*** Peter Hayman; ***W:*** Nehu Ghiran; ***C:*** Graeme Mears; ***M:*** Donald Quan. **VIDEO**

Cybermutt *Rex: Le cyber chien* **2002 (PG)** Eccentric scientist Nelson implants a computer chip into the dog that saved him from a car accident. The chip enables the dog to communicate with other computers and draws the attention of technospies who naturally want to use the bionic pup for their own nefarious purposes. Of course a boy who has befriended the dog is enperiled long the way. Adults won't find much worth sitting through, but kids will enjoy the feats of the canine star. **86m/C VHS, DVD.** *CA* Judd Nelson, Michelle Nolden, Ryan Cooley, Paulina Mielech, Tonio Arango; ***D:*** George Miller; ***W:*** Kevin Commins, Gerald Sanford; ***C:*** Gerald R. Goozie. **TV**

Cyberstalker 1/2 *The Digital Prophet* **1996** Detective twosome must track down a serial killer who uses the Internet to select his victims. **96m/C VHS, DVD.** Blake Bahner, Jeffrey Combs, Annie Biggs, Schnele Wilson; ***D:*** Christopher Romero; ***W:*** Tony Brownrigg, Annie Biggs.

Cyberzone 1/2 *Droid Gunner* **1995 (R)** Intergalactic investigator pursues four dangerous androids who are hiding on earth. **95m/C VHS.** Marc Singer, Matthias Hues, Rochelle Swanson, Robin Clarke, Kin Shriner, Brinke Stevens; ***D:*** Fred Olen Ray; ***W:*** William Martell.

Cyborg **1989 (R)** In a deathly, dirty, post-holocaust urban world, an able cyborg battles a horde of evil mutant thugs. Poorly made action flick. **85m/C VHS, DVD.** Jean-Claude Van Damme, Deborah Richter, Vincent Klyn, Dayle Haddon, Alex Daniels, Terrie Batson, Janice Graser, Jackson "Rock" Pinckney; ***D:*** Albert Pyun; ***W:*** Kitty Chalmers; ***C:*** Philip Alan Waters; ***M:*** Kevin Bassinson.

Cyborg 2 *Cyborg 2: Glass Shadow* **1993 (R)** In the year 2074 cyborgs have replaced humans at all levels. A devious company which manufactures cyborgs decides to get rid of its chief competition by literally killing them off. They plan to inject cyborg Cash Reese (Jolie) with a liquid explosive that will detonate her and everything else in sight. Tech-master Mercy (Palance) clues Cash in and she escapes with the help of the human Colton (Koteas) but they've become prey to a group of ruthless hunters. **99m/C VHS, DVD.** Angelina Jolie, Elias Koteas, Jack Palance, Billy Drago; *D:* Michael Schroeder; *W:* Michael Schroeder, Mark Geldman, Ron Yanover; *C:* Jamie Thompson; *M:* Peter Allen.

Cyborg 3: The Recycler **1995 (R)** Female cyborg has been programmed to become a creator—essentially making mankind useless. **90m/C VHS.** Khrystyne Haje, Zach Galligan, Andrew Bryniarski, Richard Lynch, Malcolm McDowell; *D:* Michael Schroeder; *W:* Barry Victor, Troy Bolotnick.

Cyborg Cop 1/2 **1993 (R)** DEA agent Phillip (Jenson) is captured during a foreign drug raid and is turned into a half-man, half-machine by mad scientist Kessel (Rhys-Davies), who wants to sell his cyborgs as unstoppable hitmen. Phillip's brother Jack (Bradley) tries to come to his rescue. Lots of stunts and car chases and even a minor romantic subplot with Jack and a tough reporter (Shaw). **97m/C VHS.** David Bradley, John Rhys-Davies, Todd Jensen, Alonna Shaw; *D:* Sam Firstenberg; *W:* Glenn A. Bruce, Greg Latter; *C:* Yossi Wein.

Cyborg Soldier 1/2 *Cyborg Cop 2* **1994 (R)** Loose cannon cop Jack Ryan (Bradley) is up against psycho killer Starkraven (Hunter) who gets turned into a new-model cyborg by your basic suspicious government agency. But when the cyborg decides to go on an unplanned human killing spree, Ryan gets to break out the heavy artillery to mow him down. Also available in an unrated version. **96m/C VHS.** David Bradley, Morgan Hunter, Jill Pierce; *D:* Sam Firstenberg; *W:* Jon Stevens.

Cyborg Soldier 1/2 *Weapon* **2008 (PG-13)** Isaac (Franklin) takes border patrol agent Lindsey Rearden (Thiessen) hostage after escaping from a military research facility. The former death row inmate was used as a scientific experiment and genetically reconstructed by robotics engineer Simon Hart (Greenwood) as a prototype super-weapon. Isaac wants to expose the military group behind the program and expects Lindsey to help him do that. **84m/C DVD.** Tiffani(-Amber) Thiessen, Richard Franklin, Bruce Greenwood, Aaron Abrams, Jim Annan, Wendy Anderson; *D:* John Stead; *W:* Christopher Warre Smets, John Flock; *C:* David Mitchell. **VIDEO**

Cycle Psycho **WOOF!** *Numbered Days; Savage Abduction* **1972 (R)** Serial killer blackmails the businessman whose wife he was contracted to kill into bringing him young girls to slaughter. The businessman hires out the job to sleazy motorcycle gang. **80m/C VHS, DVD.** Joe Turkel, Tom Drake, Stephen Oliver; *D:* John Lawrence; *W:* John Lawrence.

Cycle Vixens **WOOF!** *The Young Cycle Girls* **1979 (R)** Three girls jump on their hogs and head from Colorado to California. Much leather, motor revving and other obligatory motorcycle-trash trimmings. **90m/C VHS.** Loraine Ferris, Daphne Lawrence, Deborah Marcus, Lonnie Pense, Kevin O'Neill, Bee Lechat, Billy Bullet; *D:* Peter Perry.

Cyclo *Xich Lo* **1995** An orphaned 18-year-old (Van Loc), known only by by his profession of cyclo (pedal-taxi) driver, struggles on the streets of Ho Chi Minh City. When his vehicle is stolen, he's forced by his boss to repay its value and takes small-time jobs from local crime boss, The Poet (Leung), who, unbeknownst to the cyclo, is also his sister's (Yen-Khe) pimp. The deeper the young man gets into the criminal world, the closer he also gets to tragedy. Vietnamese with subtitles. **123m/C VHS, DVD.** *VT* Le Van Loc, Tran Nu Yen-Khe, Tony Leung Chiu-Wai, Nguyen Nhu Quynh; *D:* Tran Anh Hung; *W:* Tran Anh Hung; *C:* Benoit Delhomme; *M:* Ton That Tiet.

Cyclone **1987 (R)** The girlfriend of a murdered scientist must deliver a secretly devised motorcycle into righteous government hands, much to the dismay of evil agents and corrupt officials. Good fun, sparked by a stellar "B" cast. **89m/C VHS, DVD.** Heather Thomas, Jeffrey Combs, Ashley Ferrare, Dar Robinson, Martine Beswick, Robert Quarry, Martin Landau, Huntz Hall, Troy Donahue, Michael Reagan, Dawn Wildsmith, Bruce Fairbairn, Russ Tamblyn; *D:* Fred Olen Ray; *C:* Paul Elliott.

Cyclone Cavalier **1925** A dauntless hero travels through Central America on an adventurous spree. **58m/B VHS.** Carmelita Geraghty, Wilfrid Lucas, Jack Mower, Eric Mayne, Reed Howes; *D:* Albert Rogell; *W:* Burke Jenkins, Krag Johnson; *C:* H. Lyman Broening.

Cyclone of the Saddle **1935** Typical Western about a range war. **53m/B VHS.** Rex Lease, Bobby Nelson, William Desmond, Yakima Canutt; *D:* Elmer Clifton.

Cyclops **1956** When an expedition party searches throughout Mexico for a woman's long lost fiance, they are shocked when they find out that radiation has turned him into a one-eyed monster. **72m/B VHS, DVD.** Tom Drake, Gloria Talbott, Lon Chaney Jr., James Craig; *D:* Bert I. Gordon.

Cyclops **2008** Evil Roman Emperor Tiberius (Roberts) sends centurion Marcus (a bland Stapleton) to capture the Cyclops terrorizing the countryside. When the monster is safely in the dungeons, Marcus becomes embroiled in a slave revolt and is declared a traitor. He's forced into the arena to fight the Cyclops but they become allies to overthrow Tiberius instead. Cheese from the Sci-Fi Channel that comes across as a throwback to those old Italian-made gladiator flicks. **88m/C DVD.** Eric Roberts, Kevin Stapleton, Frida Show, Craig Archibald, Mike Straub; *D:* Declan O'Brien; *W:* Frances Doel; *C:* Emil Topuzov; *M:* Tom Hiel. **CABLE**

Cyclotrode "X" 1/2 *The Crimson Ghost* **1946** The Crimson Ghost attempts to kidnap the inventor of the title machine, which would enable him to rule the world. Moore (The Lone Ranger) plays a bad guy. Serial in 12 episodes. Also available in a 93-minute colorized edition. **100m/B VHS.** Charles Quigley, Linda Stirling, I. Stanford Jolley, Clayton Moore, Kenne Duncan; *D:* William Witney, Fred Brannon; *W:* Albert DeMond.

Cynthia 1/2 **1947** Trifle starring teen Elizabeth Taylor in the title role. Fifteen-year-old Cynthia has always been considered frail by her over-protective parents but the young woman is tired of sitting on the sidelines. She joins the high school choir (Taylor's singing voice is dubbed), starts a chaste romance with fellow student Ricky (Lydon) who gives Cynthia her first kiss, and goes to the prom while her parents struggle to get used to her newfound independence. **98m/B DVD.** Elizabeth Taylor, Mary Astor, George Murphy, James Lydon, S.Z. Sakall, Gene Lockhart, Spring Byington; *D:* Robert Z. Leonard; *W:* Charles Kaufman, Harold Buchman; *C:* Charles E. Schoenbaum; *M:* Bronislau Kaper.

Cypher **2002 (R)** Somewhat convoluted but intriguing sci-fi thriller. Milquetoast businessman Morgan Sullivan (Northam) hopes for a more exciting life when he applies for a job at multinational Digicorp. He's put to work as a corporate spy under the alias Jack Thursby and sent to a number of conventions to record the speeches that are made. Morgan/Jack doesn't understand the purpose of this until he meets mystery femme Rita (Liu), who informs Morgan that he has been brainwashed. She convinces him to turn double-agent and work for rival Sunway Systems but this only makes his life more confusing until a final assignment and shocking revelation. **96m/C DVD.** Jeremy Northam, Lucy Liu, Nigel Bennett, Timothy Webber, David Hewlett, Kari Matchett; *D:* Vincenzo Natali; *W:* Brian King; *C:* Derek Rogers; *M:* Michael Andrews.

Cypress Edge 1/2 **1999 (R)** The murder of Louisiana Senator Woodrow McCammon's (Steiger) daughter brings her estranged family back together. The motive is clear—an $18 million estate—and the benefactors are the usual suspects. **90m/C VHS, DVD.** Rod Steiger, Damian Chapa, Brad Dourif, Ashley Laurence, Charles Napier; *D:* Serge Rodnunsky; *W:* Serge Rodnunsky; *M:* Carl Dante.

Cyrano de Bergerac **1925** Silent version of Edmond Rostand's novel about romantic Cyrano who fears to reveal his love to Roxanne because he feels his enormous nose makes him unattractive. So, he serves as a surrogate lover by encouraging another man's attentions to her. Color-tinted. **114m/C VHS, DVD.** *IT FR* Pierre Magnier, Linda Moglia, Angelo Ferrari; *D:* Augusto Genina; *M:* Carlo Moser.

Cyrano de Bergerac **1950** Edmund Rostand's famous story of a large-nosed yet poetic cavalier, who finds himself too ugly to be loved. He bears the pain of his devotion to Roxanne from afar, and helps the handsome but tongue-tied Christian to romance her. Ferrer became famous for this role, which won him an Oscar. Based on Brian Hooke's translation of the play. Also available colorized. **113m/B VHS, DVD.** Jose Ferrer, Mala Powers, William Prince, Elena Verdugo, Morris Carnovsky; *D:* Michael Gordon; *W:* Carl Foreman; *C:* Franz Planer; *M:* Dimitri Tiomkin. Oscars '50: Actor (Ferrer); Golden Globes '51: Actor—Drama (Ferrer).

Cyrano de Bergerac 1/2 **1985** Edmond Rostand's gallant poet and swordsman, with the extraordinary nose, is well-portrayed by Jacobi in this Royal Shakespeare Company production. Translated and adapted by Anthony Burgess. **177m/C VHS.** *GB* Derek Jacobi, Sinead Cusack; *D:* Michael A. Simpson, Terry Hands; *W:* Anthony Burgess.

Cyrano de Bergerac **1990 (PG)** Depardieu brings to exhilarating life Rostand's well-loved play about the brilliant but grotesque-looking swordsman/poet, afraid of nothing—except declaring his love to the beautiful Roxanne (Brochet). But Cyrano expresses his own feelings by helping handsome (but tongue-tied) fellow soldier Christian (Perez) woo Roxanne instead. One of France's costliest modern productions, a multi-award winner for its cast, costumes, music and sets. English subtitles (by Anthony Burgess) are designed to capture the intricate rhymes of the original French dialogue. **135m/C VHS, DVD.** *FR* Gerard Depardieu, Jacques Weber, Anne Brochet, Vincent Perez, Roland Bertin, Josiane Stoleru, Philippe Volter, Philippe Morier-Genoud, Pierre Maguelon; *D:* Jean-Paul Rappeneau; *W:* Jean-Claude Carriere, Jean-Paul Rappeneau; *C:* Pierre Lhomme; *M:* Jean-Claude Petit. Oscars '90: Costume Des.; Cannes '90: Actor (Depardieu); Cesar '91: Actor (Depardieu), Art Dir./Set Dec., Cinematog., Costume Des., Director (Rappeneau), Film, Sound, Support. Actor (Weber), Score; Golden Globes '91: Foreign Film.

Cyrus **2010 (R)** Middle-aged and divorced, John (Reilly) meets cute with vibrant single mom Molly (Tomei) whose baggage is 21-year-old son Cyrus (Hill). The duo have a very close (crossing into queasy) relationship and Cyrus is deeply resentful that John is taking any of his mom's attention away. **91m/C DVD.** *US* Jonah Hill, John C. Reilly, Marisa Tomei, Catherine Keener, Matt Walsh, Tim Guinee; *D:* Jay Duplass, Mark Duplass; *W:* Jay Duplass, Mark Duplass; *C:* Jas Shelton; *M:* Michael Andrews.

Cyxork 7 **2006** The title refers to the name of the tired sci-fi franchise and its last gasp sequel currently being filmed by ambitious director Angela LaSalle (Smith). She has some artistic pretensions that clash with Rex Anderson (Wise), the aging actor typecast in the lead role who's just after a paycheck. When their arguments lead to the plug getting pulled, the two decide to brazen it out and finish the shoot, using a predicted L.A. earthquake to cheaply film their special effects shots and as a publicity hook. A Troma release. **93m/C DVD.** Ray Wise, Beata Pozniak, Joseph Culp, Paget Brewster, Greg Proops, Cassandra Creech, Rebecca Corry; *D:* John Huff; *W:* John Huff, Andreas Kossak; *C:* Michael Negrin. **VIDEO**

D-Day on Mars **1945** Alien invader the Purple Monster is bent on taking over Earth. Originally a 15-part Republic serial titled "The Purple Monster Strikes." **100m/B VHS.** Dennis Moore, Linda Stirling, Roy Barcroft, James Craven, Bud Geary, Mary Moore; *D:* Spencer Gordon Bennet, Fred Brannon.

D-Day, the Sixth of June *The Sixth of June* **1956** An American soldier has an affair with a Englishwoman weeks before D-Day, where he unhappily finds himself fighting side by side with her husband. Based on the novel by Lionel Shapiro. **106m/C VHS, DVD.** Richard Todd, Dana Wynter, Robert Taylor, Edmond O'Brien, John Williams, Jerry Paris, Richard Stapley; *D:* Henry Koster; *C:* Lee Garmes.

Da 1/2 **1988 (PG)** A middle-aged man returns to Ireland for his father's funeral. As he sorts out his father's belongings, his father returns as a ghostly presence to chat with him about life, death, and their own relationship. Based on the Hugh Leonard play with Hughes recreating his Tony-award winning role. **102m/C VHS.** Barnard Hughes, Martin Sheen, William Hickey, Hugh O'Conor; *D:* Matt Clark; *W:* Hugh Leonard; *M:* Elmer Bernstein.

Da Hip Hop Witch **2000 (R)** Not so much a parody of "Blair Witch Project" as a collection of rap artists' unscripted monologues about a woman who is doing terrible things to them. It also marks the return to the screen of Vanilla Ice, last seen in the abominable "Cool As Ice." **93m/C VHS, DVD.** Stacii Jae Johnson, Dale Resteghini, Pras, Killah Priest, Spliff Star, Mobb Deep, Eminem, Rock, Colleen (Ann) Fitzpatrick; *D:* Dale Resteghini; *W:* Dale Resteghini.

The Da Vinci Code **2006 (PG-13)** Dan Brown's controversial mega-best-seller hits the big screen with Howard and Hanks reuniting for their first feature since "Apollo 13." The murder of a Louvre curator leads to a conspiracy and a secret that has been protected by the Catholic Church since its beginnings. Cryptologist Sophie Neveu (Tautou) and Harvard symbiologist Robert Langdon (Hanks) team up to puzzle out the clues that are hidden in the works of Leonardo Da Vinci. Naturally, there are those who will protect the secret from being revealed at any cost. Solid performances by great cast generally overcomes Howard's faithful re-creation of the novel's talkiness, which doesn't always make for an abundance of thrills. **149m/C DVD.** *US* Tom Hanks, Audrey Tautou, Ian McKellen, Alfred Molina, Paul Bettany, Jean Reno, Jurgen Prochnow, Etienne Chicot, Jean-Pierre Marielle; *D:* Ron Howard; *W:* Akiva Goldsman; *C:* Salvatore Totino; *M:* Hans Zimmer.

Dad 1/2 **1989 (PG)** Hoping to make up for lost time, a busy executive rushes home to take care of his father who has just had a heart attack. What could have easily become sappy is made bittersweet by the convincing performances of Lemmon and Danson. Based on the novel by William Wharton. **117m/C VHS, DVD.** Jack Lemmon, Ted Danson, Ethan Hawke, Olympia Dukakis, Kathy Baker, Zakes Mokae, J.T. Walsh, Kevin Spacey, Chris Lemmon; *D:* Gary David Goldberg; *W:* Gary David Goldberg; *M:* James Horner.

Dad On the Run *Cours Toujours* **2000** In the summer of 1997, the Pope's visit to Paris has the city in an uproar, which makes things even more chaotic for new Jewish father Jonas (Sibony). Custom demands that after their son's bris, Jonas bury the foreskin within three days. He suffers a series of complications in his task, involving religious pilgrims and a truck filled with fish. French with subtitles. **92m/C VHS, DVD.** *FR* Clement Sibony, Rona Hartner, Isaac Sharry, Marie Desgranges, Emmanuelle Devos, Gilbert Levy, Francois Chattot, Francoise Bertin; *D:* Dante Desarthe; *W:* Dante Desarthe, Agnes Desarthe, Fabrice Guez; *C:* Laurent Machuel; *M:* Krishna Levy.

Dad Savage **1997 (R)** Strange British crime pic told in flashbacks. Dad Savage (Stewart) is an East Anglia gangster who grows tulips and has a fondness for country music and dressing like a cowboy. His son Sav (Wood) works for him and his right-hand man is H (McKidd). H tells fellow criminals Vic (Warren) and Bob (McFadden) that Dad has a stash of cash buried in a deserted house in the nearby woods. Dad finds out his workers are double-crossing him and there's hell to pay for everyone concerned. **104m/C VHS.** *GB* Patrick Stewart, Kevin McKidd, Joseph McFadden, Jake Wood, Marc Warren, Helen McCrory; *D:* Betsan Morris-Evans; *W:* Steven Williams; *C:* Gavin Finney; *M:* Simon Boswell.

Daddy & Them 1/2 **1999 (R)** Part romance, part dysfunctional family comedy, Thornton's followup to "Sling Blade" is set in Little Rock, Arkansas. Claude (Thornton) and wife Ruby (Dern) decide to head back home after they learn that Claude's Uncle Hazel (Varney) is in jail, convicted of a petty crime. But the homecoming with Claude's extended family is chaotic to say the least. The constant family bickering gets annoying and the film's minimal charm tires quickly. **101m/C VHS, DVD.** Billy Bob Thornton, Laura Dern, Ben Affleck, Jamie Lee Curtis, Kelly Preston, Diane Ladd, Brenda Blethyn, Andy Griffith, Jim Varney, Walton Goggins; ***D:*** Billy Bob Thornton; ***W:*** Billy Bob Thornton; ***C:*** Barry Markowitz; ***M:*** Marty Stuart.

Daddy Day Camp 🦴 **2007 (PG)** Is it still a sequel if the cast is nearly all new? In this sequel to "Daddy Day Care," Charlie Hinton (Gooding, Jr.) and buddy Phil (Rae) have finished their second year as owners of Daddy Day Care. Charlie's son Ben (Bridges) is about to attend summer day camp, but Charlie's trauma from his own childhood camp experience makes him put the kibosh on Ben's plans for uber-cool Camp Canola. Yep, Ben will relive his dad's past at scrappy Camp Driftwood—except the long-neglected Driftwood is about to be put to rest. It's daddies to the rescue as Camp Driftwood is resurrected (sort-of) and the bumbling pops try not to make a flop of their kids' summers (trying equally hard not to kill anyone in the process). Embarrassing and dreadfully predictable. **93m/C DVD, Blu-ray Disc.** *US* Cuba Gooding Jr., Lochlyn Munro, Richard Gant, Spencir Bridges, Paul Rae, Josh McLerran, Tamala Jones, Brian Doyle-Murray, Talon G. Ackerman; ***D:*** Fred Savage; ***W:*** David N. Weiss, Geoff Rodkey, J. David Stern; ***C:*** Geno Salvatori; ***M:*** James Dooley. Golden Raspberries '07: Worst Sequel/Prequel.

Daddy Day Care 🦴 **2003 (PG)** Laid-off coworkers (Murphy, Garlin) become stay-at-home dads and caregivers and come up with the idea of opening their own unconventional day-care center. This puts them in direct competition with the director (Huston) of the expensive Chapman Academy. The new Murphy's Law seems to be that for every success, he'll have four disasters. This one is definitely one of the latter, as even in his usually-successful family-friendly mode, he merely mugs amid the chaos. The script is ridiculous and unfunny, and the talented adult cast is wasted as foils for the ankle-biter inmates running the asylum. Sure they're cute, but it shouldn't be their job to carry an Eddie Murphy vehicle. Pre-school set may be amused by the antics of their on-screen peers, but their parents won't enjoy anything but the 93 minutes of quiet while their progeny zone out. **92m/C VHS, DVD, UMD.** *US* Eddie Murphy, Steve Zahn, Jeff Garlin, Regina King, Anjelica Huston, Lacey Chabert, Sloane Momsen, Kevin Nealon, Jonathan Katz, Khamani Griffin, Michelle Krusiec; ***D:*** Steve Carr; ***W:*** Geoff Rodkey; ***C:*** Steven Poster; ***M:*** David Newman.

Daddy Long Legs 🦴🦴 **1/2 1919** Judy (Pickford), the eldest inhabitant of a dreary orphanage, comes to the attention of a mysterious benefactor who sends her to college. She eventually discovers the identity of her guardian, falls in love, and marries him. Based on a play by Jean Webster. **94m/B VHS, DVD.** Mary Pickford, Milla Davenport, Mahlon Hamilton, Lillian Langdon, Marshall Neilan; ***D:*** Marshall Neilan; ***W:*** Agnes Christine Johnston; ***C:*** Charles Rosher, Henry Cronjager.

Daddy Long Legs 🦴🦴🦴 **1955** Far from the great musicals, but enjoyable. An eccentric millionaire glimpses a French orphan and becomes her anonymous benefactor. Her musing over his identity spawns some surreal (often inexplicable) dance numbers, but love conquers all, even lesser Johnny Mercer songs. From a story by Jean Webster, also done in 1919 with Mary Pickford, 1931 with Janet Gaynor and 1935 with Shirley Temple as "Curly Top." ♫ Daddy Long Legs; Something's Got To Give; Sluefoot; Dream; History of the Beat; C-A-T Spells Cat; Welcome Egghead. **126m/C VHS, DVD.** Fred Astaire, Leslie Caron, Terry Moore, Thelma Ritter, Fred Clark, Charlotte Austin, Larry Keating; ***D:*** Jean Negulesco; ***C:*** Leon Shamroy; ***M:*** Alex North.

Daddy Nostalgia 🦴🦴🦴 *These Foolish Things; Daddy Nostalgie* **1990** Birkin plays the estranged daughter of Bogarde, who rushes from her home in England to France to be with her seriously ill father. She must come to terms with her feelings for him just as Bogarde must deal with his own mortality. Wonderful performances, with Bogarde a charming and dominating presence. In French with English subtitles. **105m/C VHS, DVD.** *FR* Dirk Bogarde, Jane Birkin, Odette Laure; ***D:*** Bertrand Tavernier; ***W:*** Colo Tavernier O'Hagan; ***C:*** Denis Lenoir; ***M:*** Antoine Duhamel.

Daddy-O 🦴 *Out on Probation* **1959** Drag racer Daddy-O traps the killers of his best friend and lands the blonde bombshell Jana. It might seem bad since it's dated, but, hey, it may have been bad in 1959, too! **74m/B VHS.** Dick Contino, Sandra Giles; ***D:*** Lou Place; ***W:*** David Moessinger.

Daddy's Boys 🦴 **1/2 1987 (R)** Since farming during the Depression is a rather low-paying endeavor, this family turns to thieving instead. But all-for-one and one-for-all is not the credo for one of the sons who decides to branch out on his own. Produced by Roger Corman. **90m/C VHS.** Daryl Haney, Laura Burkett, Raymond J. Barry, Dan Shor, Robert V. Barron; ***D:*** Joe Minion; ***W:*** Daryl Haney; ***C:*** David G. Stump; ***M:*** Sasha Matson.

Daddy's Dyin'... Who's Got the Will? 🦴🦴 **1/2 1990 (PG-13)** Based on the critically acclaimed play, this bittersweet comedy stars Bridges and D'Angelo as two members of the spiteful Turnover clan. When Daddy is on his deathbed, the entire family uses the opportunity to stab each other in the back. Non-stop humor and deep-hearted honesty carries this delightful adaptation quickly from beginning to end. **95m/C VHS, DVD.** Beau Bridges, Beverly D'Angelo, Tess Harper, Judge Reinhold, Amy Wright, Keith Carradine, Patrika Darbo, Molly McClure, Bert Remsen; ***D:*** Jack Fisk; ***W:*** Del Shores; ***C:*** Paul Elliott; ***M:*** David McHugh.

Daddy's Girl 🦴 **1/2 1996 (R)** When adopted Jody's new family is threatened she'll stop at nothing to protect herself and them. **95m/C VHS.** William Katt, Michele Greene, Roxana Zal, Mimi (Meyer) Craven, Whip Hubley, Gabrielle Boni; ***D:*** Martin Kitrosser; ***W:*** Steve Pesce.

Daddy's Gone A-Hunting 🦴🦴🦴 **1969 (PG)** It's an eye for an eye, a baby for a baby in this well-done psychological thriller. A happily married woman is stalked by her deranged ex-boyfriend, whose baby she aborted years before. Now he wants the life of her child as just compensation for the loss of his. **108m/C VHS.** Carol White, Paul Burke, Scott Hylands, Rachel Ames, Mala Powers, James B. Sikking; ***D:*** Mark Robson; ***W:*** Larry Cohen; ***C:*** Ernest Laszlo; ***M:*** John Williams.

Daddy's Little Girls 🦴🦴 **1/2** *Tyler Perry's Daddy's Little Girls* **2007 (PG-13)** This isn't really about the little girls as much as it is about Monty (Elba) overcoming all obstacles to be a good father. He's a hard-working mechanic who loses custody to his greedy ex (Smith), thanks to some problems in his own past. This also leads to trouble in his growing relationship with his uptown lawyer, Julia (Union). Perry's characters tend to be two-dimensional but he's never less than sincere, and it's an uplifting story. **95m/C DVD, Blu-ray Disc.** *US* Idris Elba, Gabrielle Union, Louis Gossett Jr., Tasha Smith, Malinda Williams, Tracee Ellis Ross, Gary Sturgis, Sierra McClain, China McClain, Lauryn McClain, Craig Robinson; ***D:*** Tyler Perry; ***W:*** Tyler Perry; ***C:*** Toyomichi Jurita; ***M:*** Brian McKnight.

Daens 🦴🦴 **1/2 1992** Looks at the disparity between rich and poor at the turn of the century. Daens, a priest, returns home to Flanders to find desperate poverty among the Flemish-speaking workers of the local textile mill. The French-speaking mill owners are supported by the local Catholic church while Daens believes in the rights of the workers. Decleir makes his priest a complex and troubled man, who must choose between his conscience and social reform and the dictates of his church. Marred by somewhat cardboard villains and a complex political/social situation that isn't adequately explained. Based on the novel by Louis Paul Boon. Flemish and French with English subtitles. **134m/C VHS.** *FR BE NL* Jan Decleir, Gerard Desarthe, Antje De Boeck, Michael Pas, Johan Leysen, Idwig Stephane, Linda Van Dijck, Wim Meuwissen; ***D:*** Stijn Coninx; ***W:*** Francois Chevallier, Stijn Coninx; ***M:*** Dirk Brosse.

Dagger Eyes 🦴 **1/2** *Mystere; Murder Near Perfect* **1983** A political assassin at work is inadvertently captured on film by a photographer. The assassin's mob employers will go to any lengths to destroy the film. Say cheeeeeese! **84m/C VHS.** Carole Bouquet, Philip Coccioletti, John Steiner; ***D:*** Carlo Vanzina.

The Dagger of Kamui 🦴🦴🦴 *Kamui No Ken; Revenge of the Ninja Warrior* **1985** The only family Jiro has ever known is killed and he is accused of the crime. The evil Tenkai promises to take him to the real killer, but Jiro does not realize until later how cruelly he has been tricked. Then Jiro goes on a quest to find his past, all the while being manipulated by a vast and complex political machine. Watching this and Jiro's reactions make this anime more than a simple adventure or coming of age story. Whatever their motivations, Jiro's travels take him as far as America and into the paths of some characters as familiar to Western viewers as the historical figures in his homeland are to anyone knowledgeable of Japanese history. Based on the novels by Tetsu Yano. **132m/C VHS, DVD.** *JP* Michio Hazama; ***D:*** Taro Rin.

Dagora, the Space Monster WOOF! *Dagora; Space Monster Dagora; Uchudai Dogora; Uchu Daikaiiju Dogora* **1965** Giant, slimy, pulsating mass from space lands on Earth and begins eating everything in sight. Scientists join together in a massive effort to destroy the creature. Believe it or not, it's sillier than most of the Japanese sci-fi genre. **80m/C VHS, DVD.** *JP* Yosuke Natsuki, Yoko Fujiyama, Akiko Wakabayashi, Hiroshi Koizumi; ***D:*** Inoshiro Honda; ***W:*** Shinichi Sekizawa; ***C:*** Hajime Koizumi.

Dahmer 🦴🦴 **2002 (R)** That would be Dahmer as in serial killer Jeffrey who murdered, dismembered, and even munched on some 15 young men whom he killed in his Milwaukee, Wisconsin apartment. Although the story is sensationalistic, the film is surprisingly restrained and Renner gives a spooky performance as a psycho whose psychosis can never be explained. **101m/C VHS, DVD.** Jeremy Renner, Artel Kayaru, Bruce Davison, Matt Newton; ***D:*** David Jacobson; ***W:*** David Jacobson; ***C:*** Chris Manley.

Daimajin 🦴🦴 **1/2** *Majin; The Giant Majin* **1966** The peasants of a Japanese mountain village pray daily that the vengeful god Daimajin remains locked in the gigantic statue that serves as his prison. Unfortunately their lord's chamberlain decides prayer time is perfect for staging his long planned coup. His first act as the village's new dictator for life is to, of course, forbid their religion. Their first act is to basically inform him "you gonna get stomped by the statue someday." This ticks him off and he orders said statue destroyed. He is unsuccessful, and eventually the statue wakes up and begins destroying everyone, including the good guys. Because apparently helping those in need without stomping a few of them too means he's going soft or something. **90m/C DVD.** *JP* Miwa Takada, Yoshihiko Aoyama, Jun Fujimaki, Yutaro Gomi, Tatsuo Endo, Riki Hashimoto; ***D:*** Kimiyoshi Yasuda; ***W:*** Tetsuro Yoshida; ***C:*** Fujio Morita; ***M:*** Akira Ifukube.

The Dain Curse 🦴🦴 *Dashiell Hammett's The Dain Curse* **1978** In 1928, private eye Hamilton Nash must recover stolen diamonds, solve a millionaire's suicide, avoid being murdered, and end a family curse. Miniseries based on the novel by Dashiell Hammett. **138m/C VHS, DVD.** James Coburn, Jason Miller, Jean Simmons, Beatrice Straight, Hector Elizondo, Nancy Addison; ***D:*** E.W. Swackhamer. **TV**

Daisy Kenyon 🦴🦴 **1/2 1947** Daisy (Crawford) finally gets fed up when married lover Dan (Andrews) keeps breaking his promises. She decides to move on with kind war vet Peter (Fonda) and they get married. Despite this, Dan stays in touch with Daisy, and his wife (Warwick) finally figures things out and gets a divorce. Now a free man, Dan wants Daisy for himself but does she go to him or stay with the decent guy? Crawford can suffer with the best of 'em but Andrews' character is pretty much a heel. **99m/C DVD.** Joan Crawford, Dana Andrews, Henry Fonda, Peggy Ann Garner, Ruth Warwick, Martha Stewart, Connie Marshall, Nicholas Joy; ***D:*** Otto Preminger; ***W:*** David Hertz; ***C:*** Leon Shamroy; ***M:*** David Raskin.

Daisy Miller 🦴🦴 **1/2 1974 (G)** Shepherd portrays the title character in this adaptation of the Henry James novella about a naive young American woman travelling through Europe and getting a taste of the Continent during the late 19th century. Though it is intelligently written and has a good supporting cast, the film seems strangely flat, due in large part to Shepherd's hollow performance. **93m/C VHS, DVD.** Cybill Shepherd, Eileen Brennan, Cloris Leachman, Mildred Natwick; ***D:*** Peter Bogdanovich; ***W:*** Frederic Raphael.

Dakota 🦴🦴 **1945** Fine cast becomes embroiled in railroad land dispute. In the meantime, love strikes The Duke. Standard Wayne western saga never quite gets on track. **82m/B DVD.** John Wayne, Vera Hruba Ralston, Walter Brennan, Ward Bond, Ona Munson; ***D:*** Joseph Kane.

Dakota 🦴🦴 **1988 (PG)** A troubled half-breed teenager works for a rancher, romances his daughter, and befriends his crippled 12-year-old son. A well-meaning, but predictable drama. **96m/C VHS, DVD.** Lou Diamond Phillips, Dee Dee Norton, Eli Cummins, Herta Ware, Jordan Burton; ***D:*** Fred Holmes; ***C:*** James W. Wrenn.

Dakota Incident 🦴🦴 **1956** Decent western about stagecoach passengers travelling through Dakota Territory who must defend themselves against an Indian attack. **88m/C VHS.** Dale Robertson, Ward Bond, Linda Darnell, John Lund; ***D:*** Lewis R. Foster.

Daleks—Invasion Earth 2150 A.D. 🦴🦴 **1/2** *Invasion Earth 2150 A.D* **1966** A sequel to "Dr. Who and the Daleks," wherein the popular British character endeavors to save the Earth from a robotic threat. **81m/C VHS, DVD.** *GB* Peter Cushing, Andrew Keir, Jill Curzon, Ray Brooks; ***D:*** Gordon Flemyng.

Dallas 362 🦴🦴 **2003 (R)** Rusty (Hatosy) and Dallas (Caan) waste away their lives in a cycle of drinking, bar fights, and minor arrests—always to be bailed out by Rusty's mother Mary (Lynch). Mary puts her son in therapy and through unconventional methods he starts to see a better life for himself, though Dallas hurtles further toward the dark side. The subplot romance between the mother and therapist (Goldblum) is engaging but lacks depth. Conclusion provides a surprise emotional tug. **100m/C DVD.** *US* Scott Caan, Jeff Goldblum, Shawn Hatosy, Kelly Lynch, Dwight "Heavy D" Myers, Bob Gunton, Marley Shelton, Selma Blair, Isla Fisher, Freddy Rodriguez, James Caan; ***D:*** Scott Caan; ***W:*** Scott Caan; ***C:*** Phil Parmet.

The Dallas Connection 🦴 **1994 (R)** Three of the four scientists working on a satellite weapons system are assassinated by a trio of sexy but lethal females. Now the remaining scientist is under federal protection in Dallas while he continues his work. Lots of T&A. **90m/C VHS, DVD.** Julie Strain, Samantha (Sam) Phillips, Julie K. Smith, Wendy Hamilton; ***D:*** Andy Sidaris.

Daltry Calhoun 🦴 **2005 (PG-13)** Debut feature from Bronson stars Knoxville as the slick sod salesman of the title. Daltry hightailed it out of Ducktown, Tennessee, leaving behind his teenaged girlfriend and baby daughter. Fourteen years later, May (Banks) is dying of some mystery illness and needs Daltry to take responsibility for June (Traub). There are quirky townsfolk and quirky situations and quirky, annoying narration from June. And an intrusive soundtrack. **100m/C DVD.** *US* Johnny Knoxville, Juliette Lewis, Elizabeth Banks, Kick (Christopher) Gurry, David Koechner, Sophie Traub, Andrew Prine; ***D:*** Katrina Holden Bronson; ***W:*** Katrina Holden Bronson; ***C:*** Matthew Irving; ***M:*** John Swihart.

Dalva 🦴 **1/2 1995** Dull TV movie finds restless Dalva Northridge (Fawccett) deciding to search for the son she was forced to give up for adoption some 20 years before. But she gets sidetracked juggling two love affairs—with Sam Creekmouth (Boothe), whose Indian heritage is tied to Dalva's family, and alcoholic university professor Michael (Coyote) who wants the Northridge family diaries for his research on the Great Plains. Based on the novel by Jim Harrison. **96m/C VHS, DVD.** Farrah Fawcett, Powers Boothe, Peter Coyote, Rod Steiger, Carroll Baker; ***D:*** Ken

Cameron; ***W:*** Jim Harrison; ***C:*** Tony Imi. **TV**

Dam Busters 1/2 **1955** Well-done and exciting film details the efforts of British scientists trying to devise a method of destroying a strategic dam in Nazi Germany during WWII. Definitely one of the better in the war movie genre. **119m/B VHS, DVD.** *GB* Michael Redgrave, Richard Todd, Ursula Jeans, Basil Sydney, Frank Phillips; ***D:*** Michael Anderson Sr.

Dam Street *Hong Yan; Rouge Face* **2005** In 1983, 16-year-old Xiaoyun (Yi Liu) finds out she's pregnant by fellow student Wang Feng (Rui Liu). Disgraced, Wang leaves her and Xiaoyun is told her baby died, although the boy is secretly put up for adoption. Ten years later, Xiaoyun is still shunned and makes a meager living working as a singer. By chance, she befriends young Xiaoyong (Huang), who's supposedly the son of Wang's elder sister. But any story revelations can be seen for miles. Chinese with subtitles. **93m/C DVD.** *CH* Yi Liu, Xingrao Huang, Kechun Li, Yizhu Wang, Rui Lu; ***D:*** Yi Lu; ***W:*** Yi Lu, Li Fang; ***C:*** Wei Wang; ***M:*** Sijun Liu.

Damage **1992 (R)** The elegant Irons portrays Stephen, a middle-aged, married British politican who has always been completely in control of his life, especially where his feelings are concerned. Then he meets Anna (Binoche), his son's less-than-innocent fiance, and immediately begins an obsessive, wildly sexual affair with her. Stephen should have listened to Anna's warning about herself "Damaged people are dangerous, they know they can survive," because their passion leads to betrayal and tragedy. Binoche is more icon than human being but the film still hypnotizes as an exploration of passion. Based on the novel by Josephine Hart. An unrated version is also available. **111m/C VHS, DVD.** *GB FR* Jeremy Irons, Juliette Binoche, Rupert Graves, Miranda Richardson, Ian Bannen, Leslie Caron, Peter Stormare, Gemma Clark, Julian Fellowes; ***D:*** Louis Malle; ***W:*** David Hare; ***C:*** Peter Biziou; ***M:*** Zbigniew Preisner. British Acad. '92: Support. Actress (Richardson); L.A. Film Critics '92: Score.

Dames **1934** A millionaire with fanatically religious beliefs tries to stop the opening of a Broadway show. In the last of the grand budget-breaking spectacles before the "production code" came into being, distinguished choreographer Busby Berkeley took his imagination to the limit: watch for the dancing clothes on an ironing board and dancing girls with puzzle pieces on their backs which form the real Keeler. ♫ Dames; I Only Have Eyes For You; When You Were a Smile on Your Mother's Lips and a Twinkle in Your Father's Eye; Try To See It My Way; The Girl at the Ironing Board. **95m/B VHS, DVD.** Dick Powell, Joan Blondell, Ruby Keeler, Zasu Pitts, Guy Kibbee, Busby Berkeley; ***D:*** Ray Enright; ***W:*** Delmer Daves; ***C:*** George Barnes.

Dames Ahoy **1930** Three sailors on shore leave try to find the blonde who tricked one of them out of his pay. This is the original silent version with a piano score. **52m/B VHS.** Glenn Tryon, Otis Harlan, Eddie Gribbon, Helen Wright, Gertrude Astor; ***D:*** William James Craft.

Damien: Omen 2 **1978 (R)** Sequel to "The Omen" about Damien, a young boy possessed with mysterious demonic powers, who kills those people who anger him. Followed by "The Final Conflict." **110m/C VHS, DVD.** William Holden, Lee Grant, Lew Ayres, Robert Foxworth, Sylvia Sidney, Lance Henriksen, Jonathan Scott-Taylor, Nicholas Pryor, Allan Arbus, Meshach Taylor; ***D:*** Don Taylor; ***W:*** Mike Hodges; ***C:*** Bill Butler; ***M:*** Jerry Goldsmith.

Damien: The Leper Priest *Father Damien: The Leper Priest* **1980** True story of a Roman Catholic priest who doomed himself by voluntarily serving on a leper colony 100 years ago. Somewhat disappointing considering the dramatic material. Originally a vehicle for David Janssen, who died prior to filming. **100m/C VHS.** Ken Howard, Mike Farrell, Wilfrid Hyde-White, William Daniels, David Ogden Stiers; ***D:*** Steven Gethers. **TV**

Damn the Defiant *HMS Defiant* **1962** Adventure abounds when Guinness, as captain of the HMS Defiant during the Napoleonic wars, finds himself up against not only the French but his cruel second-in-command (Bogarde) and a mutinous crew as well. In the end, both a fleet-wide mutiny and a French invasion of England are avoided. Much attention is paid to period detail in this well-crafted film. **101m/C VHS, DVD.** *GB* Alec Guinness, Dirk Bogarde, Maurice Denham, Anthony Quayle; ***D:*** Lewis Gilbert; ***W:*** Nigel Kneale, Edmund H. North; ***C:*** Christopher Challis; ***M:*** Clifton Parker.

Damn Yankees *What Lola Wants* **1958** Musical feature adapted from the Broadway hit. A baseball fan frustrated by his team's lack of success makes a pact with the devil to become the team's new star. Verdon is dynamite as the devil's accomplice. Great Bob Fosse choreography. ♫ Whatever Lola Wants; (You Gotta Have) Heart; Shoeless Joe From Hannibal Mo; Goodbye, Old Girl; A Little Brains, a Little Talent; Who's Got the Pain; Two Lost Souls; There's Something About an Empty Chair; Those Were the Good Old Days. **110m/C VHS, DVD.** Gwen Verdon, Ray Walston, Tab Hunter, Jean Stapleton, Russ Brown; ***D:*** George Abbott, Stanley Donen.

Damnation Alley 1/2 **1977 (PG)** A warrior, an artist, and a biker jump in tank and set off in search of civilization after Armageddon. They go to Albany instead. So-so attempt to revive the post-nuclear holocaust genre which was more successfully accomplished by the "Mad Max" series. Adapted from Roger Zelazny's novel. **87m/C VHS, DVD.** George Peppard, Jan-Michael Vincent, Paul Winfield, Dominique Sanda, Jackie Earle Haley; ***D:*** Jack Smight; ***W:*** Alan Sharp, Lukas Heller; ***C:*** Harry Stradling Jr.; ***M:*** Jerry Goldsmith.

The Damned 1/2 **1969 (R)** Depicts the Nazi takeover of a German industrialist family and their descent into greed, lust, and madness. Comes in dubbed or subtitled formats. **146m/C VHS, DVD.** *IT GE* Dirk Bogarde, Ingrid Thulin, Helmut Griem, Charlotte Rampling, Helmut Berger; ***D:*** Luchino Visconti; ***M:*** Maurice Jarre.

The Damned **2006 (R)** Cheap, dull urban horror (with a thankfully brief runtime) about some Latino vampires moving into the 'hood. The guys next door discover their new neighbors are bloodsuckers and team up with a weary PI (Bridges) to get rid of the fanged threat. **76m/C DVD.** Todd Bridges, Elias Castillo, Victor Zaragoza, Chris Angelo, Raul Martinez, Jose Roseto; ***D:*** Eduardo Quiroz, Jose Quiroz; ***W:*** Eduardo Quiroz, Jose Quiroz; ***C:*** Eduardo Quiroz, Jose Quiroz; ***M:*** Eduardo Quiroz. **VIDEO**

The Damned Don't Cry 1/2 **1950** Crawford is a small-town girl who leaves her family to climb the social ladder to the top of organized crime as a boss's moll by using her looks and guile. Melodrama, in the vein of Crawford's "Mildred Pierce," mixes with a noirish atmosphere to create an interesting crime drama/character study. **103m/C DVD.** Joan Crawford, David Brian, Steve Cochran, Kent Smith, Hugh Sanders, Selena Royle, Jacqueline DeWit, Morris Ankrum, Edith Evanson, Richard Egan, Jimmy Moss, Eddie Marr; ***D:*** Vincent Sherman; ***W:*** Harold Medford; ***C:*** Ted D. McCord; ***M:*** Daniele Amfitheatrof.

Damned River 1/2 **1989 (R)** Four friends take a guided tour down Zimbabwe's Zambezi River, only to find midway down that their guide is a murderous psycho. Survival becomes a priority. **93m/C VHS.** Stephen Shellen, Lisa Aliff, John Terlesky, Marc Poppel, Bradford Bancroft; ***D:*** Michael Schroeder; ***W:*** John Crowther.

The Damned United 1/2 **2009 (R)** Fact and fiction mix in Hooper's bio of 70s-era football team manager Brian Clough (Sheen) who goes from successfully remaking Derby County into a winner to lead their archrivals Leeds United, where he quickly alienates both players and management. Follows typical rise-and-fall-of-the-rebel theme but Sheen kicks it up a notch (in fact, the role was reportedly written for him). More focused on Clough's hyper-competitive personality than the actual sport. **97m/C DVD.** *GB* Michael Sheen, Timothy Spall, Colm Meaney, Henry Goodman, Maurice Roeves, Jim Broadbent, Stephen Graham, Brian McCardie; ***D:*** Tom Hooper; ***W:*** Peter Morgan; ***C:*** Ben Smithard; ***M:*** Rob Lane.

A Damsel in Distress **1937** Astaire falls for an upper-class British girl, whose family wants her to have nothing to do with him. Features memorable songs from the Gershwins. ♫ A Foggy Day in Londontown; Nice Work If You Can Get It; Stiff Upper Lip; Put Me to the Test; I Can't Be Bothered Now; The Jolly Tar and the Milkmaid; Things Are Looking Up; Sing of Spring; Ah Che a Voi Perdoni Iddio. **101m/B VHS.** Fred Astaire, Joan Fontaine, George Burns, Gracie Allen, Ray Noble, Montagu Love, Reginald Gardiner; ***D:*** George Stevens; ***M:*** George Gershwin, George Bassman, Ira Gershwin.

Dan Candy's Law 1/2 *Alien Thunder* **1973** A Canadian mountie becomes a driven hunter, and then desperate prey, when he tries to track down the Indian who killed his partner. **90m/C VHS, DVD.** *CA* Donald Sutherland, Gordon Tootoosis, Chief Dan George, Kevin McCarthy; ***D:*** Claude Fournier; ***M:*** Georges Delerue.

Dan in Real Life 1/2 **2007 (PG-13)** Gee, a romantic comedy that features age-appropriate adults who actually act like grown-ups! Who knew? Likeable (if baffled) widower Dan (Carell) is trying to raise three daughters and write his family advice newspaper column (of course none of his advice works for him). Dan's not even thinking about dating until he takes his brood to a family reunion and meets beautiful, friendly Marie (Binoche), who happens to be his younger bro Mitch's (Cook) new love. Dan tries to suppress his feelings, which results in a number of amusing moments for Carell that don't go over the top. Engaging if predictable. **98m/C DVD.** *US* Steve Carell, Juliette Binoche, Dane Cook, Dianne Wiest, John Mahoney, Emily Blunt, Alison Pill, Brittany Robertson, Marlene Lawston, Norbert Lee Butz, Amy Ryan; ***D:*** Peter Hedges; ***W:*** Peter Hedges, Pierce Gardner; ***C:*** Lawrence Sher; ***M:*** Sondre Lerche.

Dance 1/2 **1990** Two ballet dancers struggle to find love amidst the backstage treacheries and demanding schedules of their profession. **90m/C VHS.** John Revall, Ellen Troy, Carlton Wilborn, Charlene Campbell; ***D:*** Robin Murray.

Dance Flick 1/2 **2009 (PG-13)** Clumsy genre spoof of teen/dance flicks from the Wayans brothers with ballet meeting hip-hop. Suburban white girl Megan (Bush) is rejected by Juilliard but finds Thomas (Wayans Jr.), the most non-threatening gangbanger in existence. He's also the brother of Megan's new bestie at Music High School, single mom Charity (Atkins). Thomas and his street dance crew owe money to super-size bad guy Sugar Bear (Grier, hilarious in a fat suit) and a dance-off is the answer to his woes. **83m/C DVD.** *US* Marlon Wayans, Shawn Wayans, Keenen Ivory Wayans, Amy Sedaris, Christina Murphy, Essence Atkins, David Alan Grier, Chris Elliott, Shoshana Bush, Damon Wayans Jr., Brennan Hillard, Craig Wayans; ***D:*** Damien Dante Wayans; ***W:*** Marlon Wayans, Shawn Wayans, Keenen Ivory Wayans, Damien Dante Wayans, Craig Wayans; ***C:*** Mark Irwin.

Dance Fools Dance **1931** Fast-paced drama has Crawford and Bakewell as a pair of spoiled rich kids who are forced to face poverty when the stock market crashes. He meets up with Gable, who's producing liquor illegally, while she gets a job at a newspaper. When Gable arranges something akin to the St. Valentine's Day Massacre, Bakewell's investigative reporting of the situation produces fatal results. The Hays Office had a problem with Crawford and friends appearing in their underwear. Cast notes: Gable was just starting out at MGM, which is why he was billed sixth; the William Holden here is not THE William Holden, and Edwards went on to provide the voice of Jiminy Cricket in "Pinocchio." **82m/B VHS.** Joan Crawford, Lester Vail, Cliff Edwards, William "Billy" Bakewell, Clark Gable; ***D:*** Harry Beaumont; ***C:*** Charles Rosher.

Dance, Girl, Dance **1940** The private lives and romances of a wartime nightclub dance troupe. Standard Hollywood potpourri of dance, drama, comedy. ♫ Mother, What Do I Do Now?; Jitterbug Bite; Morning Star. **88m/B VHS, DVD.** Maureen O'Hara, Louis Hayward, Lucille Ball, Virginia Field, Ralph Bellamy, Maria Ouspenskaya, Mary Carlisle, Katherine Alexander, Edward Brophy, Walter Abel, Harold Huber; ***D:*** Dorothy Arzner; ***W:*** Frank Davis, Tess Slesinger; ***C:*** Russell Metty; ***M:*** Edward Ward. Natl. Film Reg. '07.

The Dance Goes On **1992** After the death of an uncle, Keach and his estranged son Almond reunite at the old Quebec family farm left to them. The father is country-bred and appreciates the property but his Los Angeles-reared son wants to sell for a quick profit. Director Almond cast his own son in the starring role as well as ex-wife Bujold, who plays the ambitious showbiz mother. **104m/C VHS.** James Keach, Matt Almond, Genevieve Bujold, Cary Lawrence; ***D:*** Paul Almond; ***W:*** Paul Almond.

Dance Hall 1/2 **1941** A Pennsylvania dance hall owner is propelled into romantic confusion with the introduction of a sultry blond dancer into his club. **73m/B VHS.** Cesar Romero, Carole Landis, William Henry, June Storey, Charles Halton; ***D:*** Irving Pichel.

Dance Hall Racket **1958** A sleazy, stilted expose of dance hall vice featuring a brief appearance by Bruce and his wife, Harlow. **60m/B VHS, DVD.** Lenny Bruce, Honey Harlow; ***D:*** Phil Tucker.

Dance Macabre **1991 (R)** Englund takes on a dual role as a man with a split personality—one of whom is deadly. Jessica, an American ballerina, enrolls in a Russian dance academy and meets mesmerizing choreographer, Anthony. Unfortunately for Jessica she happens to look exactly like Anthony's long-dead lover and he becomes obsessed with her. Also, her fellow dancers are being brutally murdered. Are the events connected? **97m/C VHS.** Robert Englund, Michelle Zeitlin, Marianna Moen, Julene Renee, Alexander Sergeyev; ***D:*** Greydon Clark; ***W:*** Greydon Clark.

Dance Me Outside 1/2 **1995 (R)** Native Canadian teens look for some excitement on their Northern Ontario reservation and find themselves cut off from their tradition-bound parents in this slice of life drama. Friends Silas and Blackie plot revenge against a white who murdered a native girl while Silas' sister Illianna comes to visit from Toronto, with her Yuppie lawyer husband, just as her ex-boyfriend returns from a prison stint. Based on the novel by W.P. Kinsella. **91m/C VHS.** *CA* Ryan Black, Adam Beach, Michael Greyeyes, Lisa Lacroix; ***D:*** Bruce McDonald; ***W:*** Bruce McDonald, Don McKellar, John Frizzell. Genie '95: Film Editing.

Dance Me to My Song **1998** Very difficult movie to watch provides its own rewards thanks to the skills of filmmaker de Heer and lead Rose. Julia (Rose) suffers from severe cerebral palsy, is wheelchair-bound, and can only speak through a voice synthesizer. Although she lives alone, she is dependent on the daily caregivers supplied by the health department. Her latest is the short-tempered Madelaine (Kennedy), who is neglectful and ill-suited to her demanding work. What makes the situation more difficult is Julia's amible friend Eddie (Brumpton), whom Madelaine jealously decides is the ideal man. **103m/C VHS.** *AU* Heather Rose, Joey Kennedy, John Brumpton, Rena Owen; ***D:*** Rolf de Heer; ***W:*** Rolf de Heer, Frederick Stahl, Heather Rose; ***C:*** Tony Clark; ***M:*** Graham Tardif.

Dance of Death **WOOF!** *House of Evil; Macabre Serenade* **1968** Just before his death, Karloff agreed to appear in footage for four Mexican cheapies that were practically thrown together (Karloff actually filmed his scenes in Los Angeles). If they had mixed the footage instead of matched it, the flicks couldn't be any worse. This one concerns a lunatic toy-maker whose toys kill and maim his heirs. **89m/C VHS, DVD.** *MX* Boris Karloff, Julissa, Andres Garcia, Jack Hill; ***D:*** Juan Ibanez.

Dance of Life 1/2 **1929** A look at the backstage goings-on at a burlesque theatre. A successful entertainer's life goes down the tubes when he hits the bottle. His wife leaves him because of his philandering, but returns when she sees how much he really needs her. One scene of the Ziegfeld Follies uses two-tone Technicolor technology. This was re-made twice: as "Swing High, Swing Low" in 1937 and as "When My Baby Smiles at Me" in 1948. Carroll replaced the stage lead, who was said to have no "name recognition"—Barbara Stanwyck. ♫ True Blue Lou; King of Jazzmania; Cuddlesome Baby; Flip-pity Flop; Ladies of the Dance; The Mightiest Matador; Sweet Rosie O'Grady; In the Gloaming; Sam, the Accordion Man. **115m/B VHS.** Nancy Carroll, Hal Skelly, Ralph Theadore, Charles D. Brown, Dorothy Revier, Al "Fuzzy" St. John, Oscar Levant; *D:* John Cromwell.

Dance of the Damned ♪♪ **1988 (R)** A case where low-budget isn't synonymous with bomb. Fascinating noir-ish plot concerning a vampire who wants to learn more about the life of his next victim, a deep-thinking stripper, who has lost the will to live it. Surprisingly well-done and acted; above-par for this genre. **83m/C VHS.** Cyril O'Reilly, Starr Andreeff, Deborah Ann Nassar, Maria Ford; *D:* Katt Shea; *W:* Katt Shea, Andy Ruben; *C:* Phedon Papamichael; *M:* Gary Stockdale.

Dance of the Dead ♪♪ **2008** The obstacles of a good prom night are many: Getting the money for the dress, tux, and limo. Scoring the booze. Getting your date buzzed enough to agree to give it up. And, of course, escaping the hordes of flesh-eating zombies running down the street at top speed, kicking butt and stealing cars as they go. Oh, to be a teenager again, spending time gleefully shooting the undead while trying to seduce cheerleaders. **95m/C DVD.** Jared Kusnitx, Greyson Chadwick, Chandler Darby, Carissa Capobianco, Randy McDowell, Michael V. Mammoliti, Mark Lynch, Justin Welborn, Mark Oliver, Blair Redford, Lucas Till, Hunter Pierce, Jonathon Spencer, Stephen Caudill, J. Jacob Adelman; *D:* Gregg Bishop; *W:* Joe Ballarini; *C:* George Feucht; *M:* Kristopher Carter. **VIDEO**

Dance or Die ♪ **1987** Just goes to show that in Las Vegas you can't have your dance and drugs too, because if the Mob doesn't get you, the Feds will. Made for video (though maybe it shouldn't have been made at all). In HiFi Stereo. **90m/C VHS.** Ray Kieffer, Rebecca Barrington; *D:* Richard W. Munchkin. **VIDEO**

A Dance to the Music of Time ♪♪ ½ **1997** Explores the social, political, and artistic fortunes and foibles of upper-class Brits from the 1920s through the '60s from the viewpoint of everyman Nicholas Jenkins (D'Arcy and Purefoy) and his journey from schooldays to old age. Richardson is sexy man-eater Pamela Flitton and Beale is the unremarkable but ambitious and lucky Widmerpool among a cast of hundreds. Based on Anthony Powell's 12-volume series. **480m/C DVD.** *GB* James Purefoy, Miranda Richardson, Simon Russell Beale, James D'Arcy, Paul Rhys, Jonathan Cake, Claire Skinner, Alan Bennett, John Gielgud, Zoe Wanamaker, Edward Fox, Michael Williams, Eileen Atkins; *D:* Alvin Rakoff, Christopher Morhan; *W:* Hugh Whitemore; *C:* Chris Seager; *M:* Carl Davis. **TV**

Dance with a Stranger ♪♪♪ ½ **1985 (R)** The engrossing and factual story of Ruth Ellis (Richardson) who gained notoriety as the last woman hanged in Great Britain in 1955. This emotional and sometimes violent film mirrors the sensationalism and class conflicts of 1950s British society. The film follows single mom Ellis's pre-trial life as a tawdry nighclub hostess, struggling to maintain her independence, while becoming obsessively involved with immature cas/upper-class playboy David Blakely (Everett) whom she murders when he finally rejects her. **101m/C VHS, DVD.** *GB* Miranda Richardson, Rupert Everett, Ian Holm, Joanne Whalley, Matthew Carroll, Tom Chadbon, Jane Bertish, David Troughton, Paul Mooney, Stratford Johns, Susan Kyd, Lesley Manville, Sallie-Anne Field, Martin Murphy, Michael Jenn, Daniel Massey; *D:* Mike Newell; *W:* Shelagh Delaney; *C:* Peter Hannan; *M:* Richard Hartley. Cannes '85: Film.

Dance with Death ♪ **1991 (R)** When strippers turn up brutally murdered, a young journalist goes undercover to solve the case. **90m/C VHS, DVD.** Maxwell Caulfield, Barbara Alyn Jones, Martin Mull, Drew Snyder, Catya (Cat) Sassoon; *D:* Charles Philip Moore.

Dance with Me ♪♪ ½ *Shut Up and Dance* **1998 (PG)** Cuban emigre Rafael (Chayanne) winds up in Houston, teaching at the fading Excelsior Dance Studio, which is owned by a friend of his late mother's, John Burnett (Kristofferson). Instructor (and single mom) Ruby (Williams) is looking for a partner who can help her enter the competitive ballroom dance world but she's not looking for love. But at the World Open Dance Championships in Las Vegas, she may find both. Hot salsa music and dancing, as well as the charm of the two leads, make this one worth watching for any dancer fever fan. **126m/C VHS, DVD.** Vanessa L(ynne) Williams, Chayanne, Kris Kristofferson, Joan Plowright, Jane Krakowski, Beth Grant; *D:* Randa Haines; *W:* Daryl Matthews; *C:* Fred Murphy; *M:* Michael Convertino.

Dance with Me, Henry ♪ ½ **1956** When Lou becomes involved with Bud's gambling debts and the local district attorney turns up dead, Lou's not only wanted by the law, but by the mafia as well. This was the great comedy duo's last picture together and it's clear the pair are not happy about working with each other, even on this mediocre effort. **90m/B VHS, DVD.** Bud Abbott, Lou Costello, Gigi Perreau, Rusty Hamer, Mary Wickes, Ted de Corsia; *D:* Charles T. Barton.

Dance with the Devil ♪♪ *Perdita Durango* **1997 (R)** Prostitute Perdita (Perez) and witch doctor/drug dealer Romeo (Bardem) meet at the Mexican border and soon become lovers and criminal partners. They get a kinky job hijacking human fetuses for a Vegas mob boss and, since Romeo believes in human sacrifice before starting a new endeavor, they kidnap a cute teen couple as the victims. Then Romeo discovers his ex-partner, Shorty (Segura), isn't so ex—and there's lots more that's very weird and bloody. Based on the novel "59 and Raining: The Story of Perdita Durango" by Barry Gifford. **126m/C VHS, DVD.** *MX SP* Rosie Perez, Javier Bardem, Harley Cross, Aimee Graham, Don Stroud, James Gandolfini, Santiago Segura, Screamin' Jay Hawkins, Alex Cox, Carlos Bardem; *D:* Alex de la Iglesia; *W:* Alex de la Iglesia, Barry Gifford, Jorge Guerricaechevarria, David Trueba; *C:* Flavio Martinez Labiano; *M:* Simon Boswell.

Dancehall Queen ♪♪ **1997** Single mom Marcia is barely scraping together a living as a Kingston street vendor. So she decides to disguise herself and enter a dancehall contest to try to win some cash as well as solve some other personal problems. **96m/C DVD.** *JM* Audrey Reid, Carl Davis, Paul Campbell, Cherine Anderson; *D:* Don Letts, Rick Elgood; *W:* Suzanne Fenn, Don Letts; *C:* Louis Mulvey; *M:* Wally Badarou.

Dancer in the Dark ♪♪ **1999 (R)** A love it or hate it production from Danish provocateur Von Trier. Czech immigrant Selma (Bjork) is a single mom working in a small factory, where her best friend is another immigrant, Kathy (Deneuve). Selma is also close to her landlords Bill and Jean (Morse, Seymour) but tells no one that she's going blind, a fate her son will also suffer unless he gets an expensive operation. Then the money Selma has been saving is stolen and she accuses the bankrupt Bill, leading to tragedy. It sounds clear enough but mixed up in the story is Selma's participation in an amateur production of "The Sound of Music" and her numerous musical fantasies. Exteriors were filmed in Sweden and interiors in a Danish studio, although it's set in rural America. **141m/C VHS, DVD.** *DK SW FR* Bjork, Catherine Deneuve, David Morse, Peter Stormare, Cara Seymour, Joel Grey, Vincent Paterson, Vladica Kostic, Jean-Marc Barr, Udo Kier, Zeljko Ivanek; *D:* Lars von Trier; *W:* Lars von Trier; *C:* Robby Muller; *M:* Bjork. Cannes '00: Actress (Bjork), Film; Ind. Spirit '01: Foreign Film.

Dancer, Texas—Pop. 81 ♪♪♪ **1998 (PG)** Four buddies have to decide if they're going to fulfill the pact they made when they were 11 to leave the eponymous town upon graduating from high school. Each one has a reason to consider sticking around: Keller (Meyer) tkaes care of his widowed grandfather; Terrell Lee (Facinelli) is expected to join the family's failing oil business; Squirrel (Embry) thinks he should care for his alcoholic father; and John (Mills) is a natural at cattle ranching. Coming-of-age comedy deals in honest emotion and humor, and doesn't resort to syrupy sentiment or small-town stereotyping. Texas-born writer-director McCanlies' feature debut. **95m/C VHS, DVD.** Breckin Meyer, Peter Facinelli, Eddie Mills, Ethan (Randall) Embry, Ashley Johnson, Patricia Wettig, Michael O'Neill, Eddie Jones, Alexandra Holden; *D:* Tim McCanlies; *W:* Tim McCanlies; *C:* Andrew Dintenfass; *M:* Steve Dorff.

The Dancer Upstairs ♪♪ ½ **2002 (R)** Politics and romance once again make strange bedfellows in this adaptation of Shakespeare's 1995 novel. In an unidentified Latin American country (filmed in Ecuador), idealistic lawyer Agustin Rejas (Bardem) abandons the law to pursue justice by joining the police. He's been assigned to track down Ezequiel (Folk), a terrorist who's behind a series of executions of government leaders. Rejas dotes on his young daughter, who takes ballet lessons from the lovely Yolanda (Morante), with whom he becomes infatuated. But his interest leads to him learning of a connection between the teacher and his quarry. Malkovich's directorial debut. **128m/C VHS, DVD.** *US SP* Javier Bardem, Laura Morante, Juan Diego Botto, Elvira Minguez, Oliver Cotton, Luis Miguel Cintra, Abel Folk, Alexandra Lencastre; *D:* John Malkovich; *W:* Nicholas Shakespeare; *C:* Jose Luis Alcaine; *M:* Alberto Iglesias.

Dancers ♪ ½ **1987 (PG)** During the filming of the ballet "Giselle" in Italy, a famous, almost-over-the-hill dancer (Baryshnikov, ten years after his role in "The Turning Point") coaches a young, inexperienced starlet. He hopes to revitalize his life and his dancing. Features dancers from the Baryshnikov-led American Ballet Theatre. **99m/C VHS.** Mikhail Baryshnikov, Leslie Browne, Julie Kent, Mariangela Melato, Alessandra Ferri, Lynn Seymour, Victor Barbee, Tommy (Thomas) Rall; *D:* Herbert Ross; *M:* Pino Donaggio.

Dances with Wolves ♪♪♪ ½ **1990 (PG-13)** The story of a U.S. Army soldier, circa 1870, whose heroism in battle allows him his pick of posts. His choice, to see the West before it disappears, changes his life. He meets, understands and eventually becomes a member of a Lakota Sioux tribe in the Dakotas. Costner's first directorial attempt proves him a talent of vision and intelligence. This sometimes too objective movie lacks a sense of definitive character, undermining its gorgeous scenery and interesting perspective on the plight of Native Americans. Lovely music and epic proportions. Adapted by Blake from his novel. **181m/C VHS, DVD.** Kevin Costner, Mary McDonnell, Graham Greene, Rodney A. Grant, Floyd "Red Crow" Westerman, Tantoo Cardinal, Robert Pastorelli, Charles Rocket, Maury Chaykin, Jimmy Herman, Nathan Lee Chasing His Horse, Wes Studi; *D:* Kevin Costner; *W:* Michael Blake; *C:* Dean Semler; *M:* John Barry. Oscars '90: Adapt. Screenplay, Cinematog., Director (Costner), Film Editing, Picture, Sound, Orig. Score; AFI '98: Top 100; Directors Guild '90: Director (Costner); Golden Globes '91: Director (Costner), Film—Drama, Screenplay; Natl. Bd. of Review '90: Director (Costner), Natl. Film Reg. '07;; Writers Guild '90: Adapt. Screenplay.

Dancing at Lughnasa ♪♪ **1998 (PG-13)** Kate (Streep) is the eldest of five lonely unwed sisters living together on a farm in 1930s Ireland. Their brother Father Jack (Gambon) returns home, fresh from a stint as a missionary in Africa, and Gerry (Ifans), who fathered a son with sister Christina, turns up as well. The reunion and resulting emotions are the main elements in this anecdotal tale, but unfortunately most of the episodes are lacking energy and fun. Streep gives her usual impeccably accented performance, McCormack is sensual as Christina, but it's Ifans who delivers the only gusto as he readies to go to war in Spain. Adapted from the Tony Award-winning stage play by Brian Friels. Title refers to a pagan ritual the town engages in annually, and one would think just the dance alone should have led to a more energetic outing. **92m/C VHS, DVD.** *IR GB* Meryl Streep, Michael Gambon, Catherine McCormack, Rhys Ifans, Brid Brennan, Kathy Burke, Sophie Thompson, Lorcan Cranitch, Darrell Johnston, Peter Gowen, Dawn Bradfield, Marie Mullen; *D:* Pat O'Connor; *W:* Frank McGuinness; *C:* Kenneth Macmillan; *M:* Bill Whelan.

Dancing at the Blue Iguana ♪♪ ½ **2000 (R)** These "dancers" are strippers at the titular San Fernando Valley club and their interwoven stories comprise the plot. Stormy (Kelley) is the tough veteran with the questionable past; Angel (Hannah) is sweet but dumb; Jo (Tilly) must deal with an unplanned pregnancy; Jasmine (Oh) is an aspiring poet; and Jesse (Ayanna) is an over-eager newcomer. Eddie (Wisdom) presides over the establishment and has his own demons. Much of the film was improvised in workshops and rehearsals. **123m/C VHS, DVD.** Sheila Kelley, Daryl Hannah, Sandra Oh, Jennifer Tilly, Charlotte Ayanna, Robert Wisdom, Elias Koteas, Vladimir Mashkov, W. Earl Brown, Chris Hogan, Rodney Rowland, Kristin Bauer; *D:* Michael Radford; *W:* David Linter, Michael Radford; *C:* Ericson Core; *M:* Tal Bergman, Renato Neto.

Dancing in September ♪♪ ½ **2000 (R)** Black writer Tomasina "Tommy" Crawford (Parker) has just lost her job on a sitcom so she has nothing to lose by pitching a black issues comedy to George (Washington), a slick exec looking to make a name for himself at a startup network. Tommy also discovers the show's lead—former gangbanger and single dad James (Shannon). The three gain success but come under fire from the black community for being sellouts as they re-evaluate their personal and professional aspirations. **106m/C VHS, DVD.** Nicole Ari Parker, Isaiah Washington IV, Vicellous Shannon, Malinda Williams, Jay Underwood, Michael Cavanaugh, Chi McBride, James Avery, LeVar Burton, Peter Onorati, Kadeem Hardison, Jenifer Lewis, Anna Maria Horsford; *D:* Reggie Rock Bythewood; *W:* Reggie Rock Bythewood; *C:* Bill Dill. **CABLE**

Dancing in the Dark ♪♪ ½ **1986 (PG-13)** An interesting but slow-moving Canadian film about the perfect housewife who learns that after 20 years of devotion to him, her spouse has been unfaithful. Realizing how her life has been wasted she murders her husband and, in the end, suffers a mental breakdown. **93m/C VHS, DVD.** *CA* Martha Henry, Neil Munro, Rosemary Dunsmore, Richard Monette; *D:* Leon Marr; *W:* Leon Marr. Genie '87: Actress (Henry).

Dancing in Twilight ♪♪ **2005 (PG-13)** Houston businessman Madhav Singh (Evari) can barely function after the unexpected death of his wife (Patel). His loneliness is amplified when his estranged son Sam (Penn) comes home for a visit, accompanied by his girlfriend (Sheth). Now Madhav realizes he must make a decision about moving on with his life. **90m/C DVD.** Erik Avari, Kal Penn, Mimi Rogers, Louise Fletcher, Sheetal Sheth, Artee Patel; *D:* Bob Rose; *W:* Rishi Vij; *C:* Robert Steadman; *M:* Scott Szabo.

Dancing Lady ♪♪ ½ **1933** Rarely seen film is MGM's answer to "42nd Street," with Crawford as a small-time hoofer trying to break into Broadway. The screen debuts of Astaire and Eddy. Look for none other than the Three Stooges as stage hands. ♫ Everything I Have Is Yours; Heigh-Ho! The Gang's All Here; Hold Your Man; That's the Rhythm of the Day; My Dancing Lady; Let's Go Bavarian; Hey Young Fella. **93m/B VHS, DVD.** Clark Gable, Joan Crawford, Fred Astaire, Franchot Tone, Nelson Eddy, Ted Healy, Moe Howard, Curly Howard, Larry Fine, May Robson, Robert Benchley, Eve Arden; *D:* Robert Z. Leonard; *W:* P.J. Wolfson, Allen Rivkin, Zelda Sears; *C:* Oliver Marsh; *M:* Richard Rodgers, Burton Lane, Jimmy McHugh.

Dancing Man ♪ ½ **1933** A gigolo romances both mother and daughter and winds up implicated in murder as a result. Dismissable. **65m/B VHS.** Judith Allen, Reginald Denny, Natalie Moorhead; *D:* Albert Ray.

Dancing Mothers ♪♪ ½ **1926** A fast-living woman becomes involved with her mother's roguish boyfriend in this silent film with accompanying musical score. **85m/B VHS.** Clara Bow, Alice Joyce, Conway Tearle, Donald Keith; *D:* Herbert Brenon; *W:* Forrest Halsey; *C:* J. Roy Hunt.

Dancing Pirate ♪♪ **1936** A Boston dance instructor is kidnapped by pirates and jumps ship in Mexico, where he romances a mayor's daughter. The silly story boasts some Rodgers and Hart tunes, plus the early use of Technicolor, exploited here for all it was worth and then some. ♫ Are You My Love?; When You're Dancing the Waltz. **83m/C VHS.** Charles Collins, Frank Morgan, Steffi Duna, Luis Alberni, Victor Varconi, Jack La Rue; *D:* Lloyd Corrigan.

The Dancing Princesses ♪♪♪ **1984** When five naughty princesses wear the soles of their slippers out every night, their father the King must foot the bill. He soon tires of this expense and offers a reward to the person who can discover how this happens. A handsome prince becomes invisible to follow the lovely ladies and discover their secret. From the "Faerie Tale Theatre" series. **60m/C VHS, DVD.** Lesley Ann Warren, Peter Weller, Sachi (MacLaine) Parker, Roy Dotrice; ***D:*** Peter Medak. **CABLE**

Dancing with Danger 1/2 **1993 (PG-13)** A private investigator is hired to find out why a taxi dancer's customers all end up dead. Soon the PI's employer is the next victim of a serial killer whose ultimate target is the dancer herself. **90m/C VHS.** Cheryl Ladd, Ed Marinaro, Miguel (Michael) Sandoval, Pat Skipper; ***D:*** Stuart Cooper; ***W:*** Elisa Bell. **TV**

Dandelions **1974** German soft-core flick starring Hauer in an early role as a man jilted by his wife. To make himself feel better he decides to explore the sleazier side of life. Meaningless film evokes no sympathy but some may appreciate the titillation. Dubbed. **92m/C VHS.** *GE* Rutger Hauer, Dagmar Lassander; ***D:*** Adrian Hoven.

Dandy in Aspic 1/2 **1968 (R)** A double-agent is assigned to kill himself in this hard to follow British spy drama. The film is based on Derek Marlowe's novel. Mann died midway through shooting and Harvey finished direction. **107m/C VHS.** *GB* Laurence Harvey, Tom Courtenay, Lionel Stander, Mia Farrow, Harry Andrews, Peter Cook, Per Oscarsson; ***D:*** Anthony Mann; ***M:*** Quincy Jones.

Danger Ahead **1940** Newill stars again as Renfrew of the Mounties—this time he tries to rid the north woods of the baddies who are trying to take over. **57m/B VHS.** James Newill, Dorothea Kent, Guy Usher, Dave O'Brien, Bob Terry; ***D:*** Ralph Staub.

Danger Beneath the Sea **2002** What appears to be a made-for-TV adventure trots out every known submarine movie cliche. The massively jawed Van Dien is Capt. Sheffield, who's been given command of the Lansing, much to the dismay of many of the boat's officers. A nuclear incident occurs while the sub is in the China Sea, and he must deal with uncertainties about a possible war and a mutinous crew. The pace moves along nicely and production values are on the high side. **93m/C VHS, DVD.** Casper Van Dien, Gerald McRaney, Shane Daly, Stewart Bick; ***D:*** Jon Cassar; ***W:*** Lucien K. Truscott IV; ***C:*** Derick Underschultz; ***M:*** Norman Orenstein.

Danger: Diabolik *Diabolik* **1968 (PG-13)** A superthief called Diabolik (Law) continuously evades the law while performing his criminal antics. **99m/C VHS, DVD.** *IT* John Phillip Law, Marisa Mell, Michel Piccoli, Terry-Thomas, Adolfo Celi; ***D:*** Mario Bava; ***W:*** Mario Bava, Arduino (Dino) Maiuri, Adriano Barracio, Brian Degas, Tudor Gates; ***C:*** Antonio Rinaldi; ***M:*** Ennio Morricone.

Danger in the Skies 1/2 *The Pilot* **1979 (PG)** An alcoholic airline pilot tries to straighten out his life when he nearly loses everything while drinking on the job. **99m/C VHS.** Cliff Robertson, Diane Baker, Dana Andrews, Gordon MacRae, Milo O'Shea, Frank Converse, Edward Binns; ***D:*** Cliff Robertson; ***C:*** Walter Lassally. **CABLE**

Danger Lights 1/2 **1930** Depicts the railroads and the railroad men's dedication to each other and their trains. **73m/B VHS.** Jean Arthur, Louis Wolheim, Robert Armstrong; ***D:*** George B. Seitz.

Danger of Love 1/2 **1995 (R)** Married teacher Michael Carlin (Penny) has an affair with seductive colleague Carolyn Warmus (Robertson) but when he's about to end it, his wife is murdered. The detective (Bologna) thinks Michael is guilty but it's Carolyn who's hiding all the secrets. Based on a true story; made for TV. **95m/C VHS.** Joe Penny, Jenny Robertson, Joseph Bologna, Richard Lewis, Fairuza Balk, Deborah Benson, Sydney Walsh; ***D:*** Joyce Chopra. **TV**

Danger on the Air **1938** A radio program sponsor—a much-despised misogynist—is murdered, and the sound engineer attempts to solve the mystery. Features Cobb in one of his earliest roles; Garrett also directed "Lady in the Morgue" that year. **70m/B VHS.** Donald Woods, Nan Grey, Berton Churchill, Jed Prouty, William Lundigan, Richard "Skeets" Gallagher, Edward Van Sloan, George Meeker, Lee J. Cobb, Johnny Arthur, Linda Hayes, Louise Stanley; ***D:*** Otis Garrett.

Danger Trails 1/2 **1935** Rehashed western programmer. Features the hero who must save the rancher's honor as well as the ranch, while fighting detestable hombres with the traditional fare as an arsenal. **55m/B VHS.** Guinn "Big Boy" Williams, Marjorie Gordon, Wally Wales, John Elliott, Ace Cain, Edmund Cobb; ***D:*** Robert F. "Bob" Hill.

Danger UXB 1/2 **1981** During the 1940 London blitz, "Danger UXB" was scrawled wherever there was—or thought to be—an unexploded German bomb. This miniseries covers the exploits of the Royal Engineers whose job it was, with little training and lots of nerve, to defuse the bombs. Based on the memoirs of Major A.B. Hartley of the Royal Engineers. **660m/C VHS.** *GB* Anthony Andrews, Judy Geeson, Maurice Roeves, Kenneth Cranham, Jeremy Sinden, Iain Cuthbertson, George Innes, Norman Chappell, Kenneth Farrington, Gordon Kane, Ken Kitson, Robert Longden, Robert Pugh, Deborah Watling; ***D:*** Roy Ward Baker, Douglas Camfield, Ferdinand Fairfax, Henry Herbert, Simon Langton, Jeremy Summers. **TV**

Danger Zone **1951** A man is hired to bid for a saxophone at an auction and then has the instrument stolen from him. He discovers it contained stolen jewelry and tries to recover it. **56m/B VHS.** Hugh Beaumont, Tom Neal, Richard Travis, Virginia Dale; ***D:*** William Burke; ***W:*** Julian Harmon; ***C:*** Jack Greenhalgh.

Danger Zone WOOF! **1987 (R)** A low-budget, low-brow flick about an all-female rock band whose bus breaks down in the middle of the desert, leaving the girls to defend themselves against a merciless motorcycle gang. You'll wish this one was a mirage. **90m/C VHS.** Robert Canada, Jason Williams, Kriss Braxton, Dana Dowell, Jamie Ferreira; ***D:*** Henry Vernon.

Danger Zone **1995 (R)** American mining expert Rick Morgan (Zane) uncovers a worldwide nuclear plot when he's lured to East Africa to supposedly contain a toxic spill. Instead, he's being used to recover a load of plutonium. **92m/C VHS.** Billy Zane, Ron Silver, Robert Downey Jr., Cary-Hiroyuki Tagawa; ***D:*** Allan Eastman; ***W:*** Jeff Albert; ***C:*** Yossi Wein.

Danger Zone 2 **1989 (R)** A pernicious biker is released from prison on a technicality and decides to pay a social call to the undercover cop who set him up. **95m/C VHS.** Jason Williams, Robert Random; ***D:*** Geoffrey G. Bowers; ***W:*** Dulany Ross Clements.

Danger Zone 3: Steel Horse War **1990 (R)** The "Danger Zone" dude is back and this time he's taken on a bevy of biker-types in a most gruesome battle to make our deserts safe. **91m/C VHS.** Jason Williams, Robert Random, Barne Suboski, Juanita Ranney, Rusty Cooper, Giles Ashford; ***D:*** Douglas Bronco.

Dangerous 1/2 **1935** Davis won her first Oscar for her rather overdone portrayal of a has-been alcoholic actress reformed by a smitten architect who recognizes her from her days as a star. **72m/B VHS.** Bette Davis, Franchot Tone, Margaret Lindsay, Alison Skipworth, John Eldridge, Dick Foran; ***D:*** Alfred E. Green. Oscars '35: Actress (Davis).

The Dangerous 1/2 **1995 (R)** New Orleans' seamy underworld is the setting for a hot-headed cop (Pare), a mystery man (Davi), and the beauty (Barbieri) they're both interested in. Also available unrated. **96m/C VHS.** Robert Davi, Michael Pare, Paula Barbieri, Elliott Gould, John Savage, Joel Grey; ***D:*** Maria Dante, Rod Hewitt; ***W:*** Rod Hewitt.

A Dangerous Age 1/2 **1957** A young girl, hoping to marry her lover, runs away from boarding school. **70m/C VHS.** Ben Piazza, Ann Pearson; ***D:*** Sidney J. Furie; ***W:*** Sidney J. Furie; ***C:*** Herbert S. Alpert.

Dangerous Appointment *One in a Million* **1934** Story of an innocent store clerk accused of theft and attempted murder. **66m/B VHS.** Charles Starrett, Dorothy Wilson, Guinn "Big Boy" Williams, Holmes Herbert; ***D:*** Frank Strayer; ***W:*** Karl Brown, Robert Ellis; ***C:*** M.A. Anderson.

Dangerous Beauty *The Honest Courtesan; Indiscretion; Venice; Courtesan* **1998 (R)** In 16th-century Venice, poor but beautiful Veronica (McCormack) gains wealth and power by becoming a sought after courtesan. The bewigged, bewitched and bewildered heads of state fall as hard for the comely courtesan as victims to the plague that strikes Venice later in the film. The one man she wants, however, Marco Venier (Sewell), comes from a wealthy family that looks down on the common Veronica. Director Herskovitz mixes the strong feminist messages with humor and a modern sensibility that sometimes make you forget you're watching a period film. Based on the biography of the real Veronica Franco by Margaret Rosenthal. **112m/C VHS, DVD.** Catherine McCormack, Rufus Sewell, Moira Kelly, Jacqueline Bisset, Oliver Platt, Fred Ward, Naomi Watts, Jeroen Krabbe, Joanna Cassidy, Daniel Lapaine, Jake Weber, Simon Dutton, Michael Culkin, Peter Eyre; ***D:*** Marshall Herskovitz; ***W:*** Jeannine Dominy; ***C:*** Bojan Bazelli; ***M:*** George Fenton.

Dangerous Charter 1/2 **1962** A group of fishermen discover a deserted yacht and man its helm. But their good fortune takes a decided turn for the worst as they become caught in mob-propelled danger. **76m/C VHS.** Chris Warfield, Sally Fraser, Richard Foote, Peter Foster, Wright King; ***D:*** Robert Gottschalk.

Dangerous Child 1/2 **2001** Sixteen-year-old Jack Cambridge (Merriman) is one angry kid. He lives with his divorced mom Sally (Burke), who tries to make allowances for his temper, even when he starts hitting her, because she doesn't want Jack taken away from her. But it's only a matter of time before the situation gets worse. Scarily good performance by Merriman. **95m/C VHS, DVD.** Delta Burke, Ryan Merriman, Marc Donato; ***D:*** Graeme Campbell; ***W:*** Karen Stillman; ***C:*** Nikos Evdemon. **CABLE**

Dangerous Corner **1934** Adaptation of J.B. Priestley's play captures a seance after the suicide of the prime suspect in a theft of government bonds. Those closest to the deceased share inner secrets that reveal truths about the heist. Great twists, well cast, a film much ahead of its time. **66m/B VHS.** Virginia Bruce, Conrad Nagel, Melvyn Douglas; ***D:*** Phil Rosen; ***W:*** J.B. Priestley, Anne Morrison Chapman, Madeleine Ruthman. **VIDEO**

Dangerous Crossing **1953** Crain's lovely but this is a B-list film noir. Ruth Bowman (Crain) is enjoying her transatlantic honeymoon cruise until her new spouse John (Betz) disappears. The only problem is the passenger list says Ruth is traveling alone and no one admits to seeing the couple together. Only sympathetic ship's doctor Paul Manning (Rennie) is willing to help out the bewildered bride. **75m/B DVD.** Jeanne Crain, Michael Rennie, Carl Betz, Max (Casey Adams) Showalter, Mary Anderson, Willis Bouchey, Yvonne Peattie, Marjorie Hoshelle; ***D:*** Joseph M. Newman; ***W:*** Leo Townsend; ***C:*** Joseph LaShelle; ***M:*** Lionel Newman.

Dangerous Curves 1/2 **1988 (PG)** Two friends are assigned to deliver a new Porsche to a billionaire's daughter—one of them talks the other into taking a little detour, and the trouble begins. **93m/C VHS.** Robert Stack, Tate Donovan, Danielle von Zerneck, Robert Klein, Elizabeth Ashley, Leslie Nielsen; ***D:*** David Lewis. **VIDEO**

Dangerous Curves **1999 (R)** Handsome attorney decides to track down a former lover. This is always a mistake. **85m/C VHS, DVD.** Robert Carradine, David Carradine, Maxine Bahns, Marina Carradine; ***D:*** Jeremiah Cullinane; ***W:*** Christopher Wood; ***C:*** Laurence Manly; ***M:*** Siobhan Cleary. **VIDEO**

Dangerous Evidence: The Lori Jackson Story 1/2 **1999** Whitfield stars in this true story as Lori Jackson, a 1980s civil rights activist who takes on the case of Marine Corporal Lindsay Scott (Yearwood), the only black in the battalion, who is falsely accused of raping a white officer's wife. When he is convicted on circumstantial evidence, Jackson secures a new trial, which exacts a high price on her own life. Based on the book "Dangerous Evidence" by Ellis A. Cohen. **90m/C VHS, DVD.** Lynn Whitfield, Richard Lineback, Richard Yearwood, Peter MacNeill, Erica Luttrell, Barbara Mamabolo, Geordie Johnson, Bruce Gray; ***D:*** Sturla Gunnarsson; ***W:*** Sterling Anderson; ***M:*** Jonathan Goldsmith. **CABLE**

Dangerous Game 1/2 **1990 (R)** A computer hacker leads his friends through a department store's security system, only to find they can't get out until morning. They soon discover they are not alone when one of the group turns up dead. **102m/C VHS, DVD.** Miles Buchanan, Sandy Lillingston, Kathryn Walker, John Polson; ***D:*** Stephen Hopkins.

Dangerous Game *Snake Eyes* **1993 (R)** Abrasive filmmaker Eddie Israel's (Keitel) new movie is about a couple's disintegrating marriage turning violent. Stars Sarah (Madonna) and Francis (Russo) find the on-camera violence spilling over into their tangled private lives while Eddie finds his personal traumas intruding more and more into the fictional material. Very raw movie within a movie features volatile Keitel (who also worked with Ferrera on "Bad Lieutenant") and suitably histrionic Russo; Madonna manages to hold her own in the least showy role, a cinematic first. Eddie's betrayed and bewildered wife is sympathetically portrayed by Ferrara, director Abel's wife. Also available in an unrated version. **107m/C VHS, DVD.** Harvey Keitel, James Russo, Madonna, Nancy Ferrara; ***D:*** Abel Ferrara; ***W:*** Nicholas St. John.

Dangerous Ground **1996 (R)** Hackneyed thriller has expatriate South African Vusi (Cube) returning to his homeland to find his younger brother Steven, who has double-crossed the head of a drug cartel. Since Vusi's departure 12 years ago, apartheid's been replaced by gangs and drugs, and while combing the dangerous streets of Johannesburg, the graduate student implausibly turns into a gun-wielding hero. Rhames's sinister drug lord Muki is pic's best character. Lead Cube shows just how limited his acting ability is while Hurley displays the picture's clearly limited wardrobe budget. Interracial relationships are glossed over, while South Africa's sociological problems are used as plot devices and then ignored. Filmed on location in South Africa, this shoot-em-up's locale could easily be Anytown, USA. **92m/C VHS, DVD.** Ice Cube, Elizabeth Hurley, Ving Rhames, Eric Miyeni, Sechaba Morojele; ***D:*** Darrell Roodt; ***W:*** Darrell Roodt, Greg Latter; ***C:*** Paul Gilpin; ***M:*** Stanley Clarke.

Dangerous Heart **1993 (R)** A crooked undercover cop steals a bundle from a drug dealer and gets himself killed for his troubles. Only the dealer doesn't know where the money is. So he decides to befriend the cop's widow, get romantically involved, and see what she knows. **93m/C VHS.** Timothy Daly, Lauren Holly, Jeffrey Nordling, Alice Carter, Joe Pantoliano; ***D:*** Michael Scott; ***W:*** Patrick Cirillo.

Dangerous Holiday **1937** A young violin prodigy would rather be just "one of the boys" than be forced to practice all the time. He decides to run away but has everyone in an uproar thinking he's been kidnapped. **54m/B VHS.** Hedda Hopper, Guinn "Big Boy" Williams, Jack La Rue, Franklin Pangborn, Grady Sutton; ***D:*** Nicholas T. Barrows; ***W:*** Nicholas T. Barrows; ***C:*** William Nobles; ***M:*** Alberto Colombo.

Dangerous Hours **1919** An anti-communist propaganda film with Hughes as the innocent young college boy who gets duped by the evil Marxists until he realizes the truth of his all-American upbringing. Silent with original organ score. **88m/B VHS.** Lloyd Hughes; ***D:*** Fred Niblo; ***C:*** George Barnes.

Dangerous Indiscretion **1994 (R)** Ad exec finds his girlfriend is actually a woman married to a very powerful man, who's not going to be happy to find out about their liaison. **81m/C VHS.** Joan Severance, C. Thomas Howell, Malcolm McDowell; ***D:*** Richard Kletter; ***W:*** Richard Kletter, Jack Tarpon; ***M:*** Richard Gibbs.

Dangerous Liaisons *Les Liaisons Dangereuses; Dangerous Love Affairs* **1960** A couple take each other to the brink of destruction via their insatiable desire for extra-marital affairs. Vadim attempted to repeat his success with Brigitte Bardot by featuring wife Annette as a new sex goddess, but lightning didn't strike twice. **111m/B VHS, DVD.** *FR IT* Gerard Philipe, Jeanne Moreau, Jeanne Valerie, Annette (Stroyberg) Vadim, Simone Renant, Jean-Louis Trintignant, Nicolas Vogel; ***D:*** Roger Vadim; ***W:*** Roger Vadim; ***C:*** Marcel Grignon.

Dangerous Liaisons **1988 (R)** Stylish and absorbing, this adaptation of the Laclos novel and the Christopher Hampton play centers around the relationship of two decadent members of 18th-century French nobility. The Marquise de Merteuil (Close) and the Vicomte de Valmont (Malkovich) spend their time testing and manipulating the loves of others. Merteuil wishes Valmont to deflower teenager Cecile (Thurman) while Valmont himself is after the virtuous married Madame de Tourvel (Pfeiffer). They find love often has a will of its own. Interesting to comparison-view with director Milos Forman's version of this story, 1989's "Valmont." **120m/C VHS, DVD.** John Malkovich, Glenn Close, Michelle Pfeiffer, Uma Thurman, Keanu Reeves, Swoosie Kurtz, Mildred Natwick, Peter Capaldi; ***D:*** Stephen Frears; ***W:*** Christopher Hampton; ***C:*** Philippe Rousselot; ***M:*** George Fenton. Oscars '88: Adapt. Screenplay, Art Dir./Set Dec., Costume Des.; British Acad. '89: Adapt. Screenplay, Support. Actress (Pfeiffer); Cesar '90: Foreign Film; Writers Guild '88: Adapt. Screenplay.

Dangerous Liaisons 1/2 *Les Liaisons dangereuses* **2003** French miniseries of the oft-remade story moves the treachery to 1960s Paris high society. Deneuve and Everett head a fine cast, and they all perform well in the luscious, if overdone, adaptation. **200m/C DVD.** *FR* Catherine Deneuve, Rupert Everett, Nastassja Kinski, Leelee Sobieski, Danielle Darrieux, Francoise Brion, Cyrille Thouvenin, Andrzej Zulawski, Lynne Adams; ***D:*** Josee Dayan; ***W:*** Eric-Emmanuel Schmitt; ***M:*** Angelo Badalamenti. **TV**

Dangerous Life **1989** Explosive drama brings to the screen the story of the Philippine uprising. It shows the horrible events that lead to the fall of Marcos and permitted the rise of Corazon Aquino. **163m/C VHS.** Gary Busey, Ruben Rustia, Cris Vertido; ***D:*** Robert Markowitz; ***W:*** David Williamson.

The Dangerous Lives of Altar Boys **2002 (R)** Don't let the title keep you away from this innovative coming-of-ager set in the '70s. Rebellious Catholic schoolmates Francis (Hirsch) and Tim (Culkin) seek love and chaos, respectively, while attending St. Agatha Parochial school, run by iron-fisted, wooden-legged nun Foster and hard-drinking priest D'Onofrio. While Francis falls for a girl with a secret past (Malone), Tim fantasizes about staging a coup against the sadistic Sister. The boys channel their boredom into increasingly dangerous pranks and a sacrilegious comic book called "The Atomic Trinity," which stars motorcycle-riding witch Nunzilla (Foster's nun rides a moped). Inventive directorial debut by Care with animated fantasy segments deftly directed by Spawn creator Todd McFarlane. Based on the 1994 novel by Chris Fuhrman. **105m/C VHS, DVD.** *US* Kieran Culkin, Emile Hirsch, Jena Malone, Jodie Foster, Vincent D'Onofrio, Jake Richardson, Tyler Long; ***D:*** Peter Care; ***W:*** Jeff Stockwell, Michael Petroni; ***C:*** Lance Acord; ***M:*** Marco Beltrami, Joshua Homme. Ind. Spirit '03: First Feature.

Dangerous Love **WOOF!** **1987** Advice to the lovelorn: Avoid this one. Female members of a video dating service are being filmed in a death scene—their own. **87m/C VHS.** Lawrence Monoson, Brenda Bakke, Peter Marc, Elliott Gould, Anthony Geary; ***D:*** Marty Ollstein.

A Dangerous Man: Lawrence after Arabia **1991** At the 1919 Paris Peace Conference, T.E. Lawrence serves as the liaison to the Hashemite delegation in an effort to have the Allies agree to Arab independence. He finds the diplomatic fields more treacherous than anything he encountered during WWI. Fiennes does well in the difficult role of the reluctant, ambivalent hero. **104m/C VHS, DVD.** *GB* Ralph Fiennes, Denis Quilley, Alexander Siddig, Nicholas Jones, Roger Hammond, Peter Copley, Paul Freeman, Polly Walker; ***D:*** Christopher Menaul; ***W:*** Tim Rose Price. **TV**

Dangerous Minds 1/2 *My Posse Don't Do Homework* **1995 (R)** Based on the autobiography of LouAnne Johnson (Pfeiffer), a 10-year Marine turned inspirational inner-city high school English teacher. Naturally, Johnson has to take on the establishment educational system to fight for her kids. If you can buy Pfeiffer as an ex-jarhead, a tough teacher should be no problem. A subplot romance involving Pfeiffer and Andy Garcia was cut from the film to focus on the teacher/student byplay (which seems a real shame); Elaine May did a uncredited script rewrite. Kinda squishy and surprisingly successful. **99m/C VHS, DVD.** Michelle Pfeiffer, George Dzundza, Courtney B. Vance, Robin Bartlett, Renoly Santiago, Lorraine Toussaint, John Neville; ***D:*** John N. Smith; ***W:*** Ronald Bass; ***C:*** Pierre Letarte. Blockbuster '96: Drama Actress, T. (Pfeiffer).

Dangerous Mission 1/2 **1954** A young woman witnesses a mob murder in New York and flees to the Midwest, pursued by killers and the police. Good cast couldn't do much with this one. **75m/B VHS.** Victor Mature, Piper Laurie, Vincent Price, William Bendix; ***D:*** Louis King; ***W:*** W.R. Burnett, Charles Bennett.

Dangerous Moonlight *Suicide Squadron* **1941** Polish concert pianist becomes a bomber pilot for the British in WWII, though his wife wants him to stay at the piano. Great battle and music sequences; the piece "Warsaw Concerto" became a soundtrack hit. **97m/B VHS.** *GB* Anton Walbrook, Sally Gray, Derrick DeMarney, Cecil Parker, Percy Parsons, Kenneth Kent, Guy Middleton, John Laurie, Frederick Valk; ***D:*** Brian Desmond Hurst; ***W:*** Rodney Ackland, Terence Young; ***C:*** Georges Perinal; ***M:*** Richard Addinsell.

Dangerous Moves *La Diagonale du Fou* **1984 (PG)** A drama built around the World Chess championship competition between a renowned Russian master and a young, rebellious dissident. The chess game serves as both metaphor and background for the social and political tensions it produces. With English subtitles. **96m/C VHS, DVD.** *SI* Liv Ullmann, Michel Piccoli, Leslie Caron, Alexandre Arbatt; ***D:*** Richard Dembo; ***W:*** Richard Dembo; ***C:*** Raoul Coutard. Oscars '84: Foreign Film.

Dangerous Obsession *Divine Obsession; Mortal Sins* **1988 (R)** A woman kidnaps the doctor she blames for her boyfriend's death and instead of exacting revenge, she makes him her personal sex slave. In the case of this flick, it's really a fate worse than death. **81m/C VHS.** *IT* Corinne Clery, Brett Halsey; ***D:*** Lucio Fulci; ***M:*** Simon Boswell.

Dangerous Orphans 1/2 **1986 (R)** Not completely awful tale of three brothers, orphaned as boys when their father is murdered before their very eyes, and the vendetta they have against the killer. **90m/C VHS, DVD.** *NZ* Peter Stevens, Peter Bland, Ian Mune, Ross Girven, Jennifer Ward-Lealand; ***D:*** John Laing.

Dangerous Passage **1944** A ne'er-do-well inherits 200 grand but gets in trouble before he can collect it. He ends up falling in with assorted misfits aboard a tramp steamer. **60m/B VHS, DVD.** Robert Lowery, Phyllis Brooks, Jack La Rue, Victor Kilian, Charles Arnt, John Eldridge; ***D:*** William Berke; ***W:*** Daniel Mainwaring; ***C:*** Fred H. Jackman Jr.; ***M:*** Alexander Laszlo.

Dangerous Passion 1/2 **1995** Ruthless Lou (Williams) kills an intruder and tries to force his mechanic, Kyle (Weathers), to take the fall for him. But instead Kyle escapes with Lou's mistreated wife (and Kyle's lover) Meg (McKee), with Lou's henchman Frank (Boswell) on their tail. **94m/C VHS, DVD.** Billy Dee Williams, Carl Weathers, Lonette McKee, Charles Boswell, Elpidia Carrillo, Tony DiBenedetto, Dan Ziskie; ***D:*** Michael Miller; ***W:*** Brian Taggert; ***C:*** Steve (Steven) Shaw; ***M:*** Rob Mounsey.

A Dangerous Place 1/2 **1994 (R)** Teenaged Ethan (Roberts) joins a karate team to prove his older brother's death was not a suicide. But the Scorpion's leader (Feldman) has a definite mean streak. **97m/C VHS, DVD.** Ted Jan Roberts, Corey Feldman, Mako, Erin Gray, Dick Van Patten; ***D:*** Jerry P. Jacobs.

Dangerous Prey 1/2 **1995 (R)** Young woman, looking for adventure while vacationing in Europe, gets more than she bargained for when she gets mixed up with a high-tech training school for female mercenaries. **93m/C VHS.** Shannon Whirry, Ciara Hunter; ***D:*** Lloyd A. Simandl; ***M:*** Peter Allen.

Dangerous Pursuit **1989** A woman discovers that a man she slept with years ago is an assassin. Knowing too much, she finds herself next on his hit list. Decent psycho-thriller that was never released theatrically. **95m/C VHS.** Gregory Harrison, Alexandra Powers, Scott Valentine, Brian Wimmer, Elena Stiteler; ***D:*** Sandor Stern.

Dangerous Relations 1/2 *Father & Son: Dangerous Relations* **1993 (PG-13)** Made-for-TV drama with Gossett as a tough convict at the end of 15-year prison sentence whose authority is challenged by young punk prisoner Underwood. Imagine his surprise when the old con realizes the punk is the son he hasn't seen since he started his time behind bars. Things don't improve (well, not at first) when they are paroled into each other's custody. **93m/C VHS, DVD.** Louis Gossett Jr., Blair Underwood, Rae Dawn Chong, Clarence Williams III, Rigg Kennedy; ***D:*** Georg Stanford Brown; ***W:*** Walter Halsey Davis; ***C:*** James Chressanthis. **TV**

Dangerous Summer *The Burning Man* **1982** In Australia, an American businessman building a resort is the victim of elaborate arson/murder insurance schemes. **100m/C VHS, DVD.** *AU* Tom Skerritt, James Mason, Ian Gilmour, Wendy Hughes; ***D:*** Quentin Masters; ***W:*** David Ambrose; ***C:*** Peter Hannan.

Dangerous Touch 1/2 **1994 (R)** A very charming sociopath seduces a radio host/therapist into a willing, if kinky, sexual relationship. But everything she values is put at risk when he threatens to show an incriminating video tape if she doesn't continue to do as he demands. An unrated version is also available. **101m/C VHS, DVD.** Lou Diamond Phillips, Kate Vernon; ***D:*** Lou Diamond Phillips.

Dangerous When Wet **1953** A typical Williams water-musical. A farm girl dreams of fame by swimming the English Channel. One famous number pairs Williams with cartoon characters Tom & Jerry in an underwater frolic. ♫ I Got Out of Bed on the Right Side; Ain't Nature Grand; I Like Men; Fifi; In My Wildest Dreams. **96m/C VHS, DVD.** Esther Williams, Fernando Lamas, Charlotte Greenwood, William Demarest, Jack Carson; ***D:*** Charles Walters; ***M:*** Arthur Schwartz, Johnny Mercer.

A Dangerous Woman **1993 (R)** No, this isn't the femme fatale romance the word "dangerous" suggests. Instead, the eponymous character is a mildly retarded woman, Martha (Winger), whose simplistic view on life places her in ethically compromising positions. When a hunky Irish handyman (Byrne) comes on the scene and seduces both her and the aunt with whom she lives (Hershey), Martha awakens to feelings she has never experienced. Winger's performance is both sensitive and provocative, but is wasted in a film filled with two-dimensional characters, and really, not too much of a point. Adapted from a novel by Mary McGarry Morris. Screenplay by Foner, wife of director Gyllenhaal. **101m/C VHS.** Debra Winger, Barbara Hershey, Gabriel Byrne, David Strathairn, Chloe Webb, John Terry, Jan Hooks, Paul Dooley, Viveka Davis, Richard Riehle, Laurie Metcalf; ***D:*** Stephen Gyllenhaal; ***W:*** Naomi Foner; ***C:*** Robert Elswit; ***M:*** Carter Burwell.

Dangerous Youth *These Dangerous Years* **1958** Would-be Liverpool rocker Vaughan is drafted into the army where he becomes a man. He gets into trouble, goes AWOL, but manages to set things right. The Brit version of the troubled-teen exploitation flick. **97m/B VHS.** *GB* Frankie Vaughan, George Baker, Carole Lesley, Jackie Lane, Eddie Byrne, Thora Hird; ***D:*** Herbert Wilcox; ***W:*** Jack Trevor Story.

Dangerously Close 1/2 **1986 (R)** A group of anti-crime high school students organize a hall monitoring gang that becomes a group of neo-fascist disciplinarian elite. **96m/C VHS.** John Stockwell, Carey Lowell, J. Eddie Peck; ***D:*** Albert Pyun; ***C:*** Walt Lloyd.

Daniel 1/2 **1983 (R)** The children of a couple who were executed for espionage (patterned after the Rosenbergs) struggle with their past in the dissident 1960s. So-so adaptation of E.L. Doctorow's "The Book of Daniel." **130m/C VHS.** Timothy Hutton, Amanda Plummer, Mandy Patinkin, Lindsay Crouse, Ed Asner, Ellen Barkin; ***D:*** Sidney Lumet; ***C:*** Andrzej Bartkowiak.

Daniel Boone 1/2 **1934** Daniel Boone guides a party of settlers from North Carolina to the fertile valleys of Kentucky, facing Indians, food shortages and bad weather along the way. O'Brien turns in a fine performance as the early American frontier hero. **75m/B VHS, DVD.** George O'Brien, Heather Angel, John Carradine; ***D:*** David Howard.

Daniel Boone: Trail Blazer 1/2 **1956** Low-budget, though surprisingly well-acted rendition of the frontiersman's heroics, filmed in Mexico. **75m/B VHS, DVD.** Bruce Bennett, Lon Chaney Jr., Faron Young, Damian O'Flynn, Fred Kohler Jr., Claudio Brook, Kem Dibbs; ***D:*** Ismael Rodriguez, Albert C. Gannaway; ***W:*** Tom Hubbard, John Patrick; ***C:*** Jack Draper; ***M:*** Raul Lavista.

Daniel Deronda 1/2 **2002** Daniel Deronda (Dancy) is the handsome, upright young ward of Sir Hugo Malinger (Fox), who dreams of doing something with his life in 1875 Victorian England. Two women will influence his decisions. The first is the headstrong Gwendolen Harleth (Garai), who will make a devil's bargain when she agrees to marry the wealthy and possessive Henleigh Grandcourt (Bonneville) to rescue her family from penury. The second is Jewess Mira Lapidoth (May), whom Daniel saves from drowning. He aids her singing career and helps her search for her family—a search that will lead to revelations about Daniel's own past. Last novel by George Eliot. **210m/C VHS, DVD.** *GB* Hugh Dancy, Romola Garai, Hugh Bonneville, Jodhi May, Edward Fox, Barbara Hershey, Amanda Root, Greta Scacchi, Celia Imrie, David Bamber, Daniel Evans, Allan Corduner, Jamie Bamber; ***D:*** Tom Hooper; ***W:*** Andrew Davies; ***M:*** Robert (Rob) Lane. **TV**

Daniel Takes a Train *Szerencses Daniel* **1983** Daniel (Rudolf) and his friend Gyuri (Zsoter) take a train to a small town on the Austrian border, seeking to escape Hungary after the 1956 uprising. Gyuri is a soldier who has deserted and is anxious to get away, but Daniel refuses to leave his missing girlfriend Mariann (Szerb) behind. Hungarian with subtitles. **92m/C VHS.** *HU* Mari Torocsik, Peter Rudolf, Sandor Zsoter, Kati Szerb, Dezso Garas; ***D:*** Pal Sandor; ***W:*** Zsuzsa Toth; ***C:*** Elemer Ragalyi; ***M:*** Gyorgy Selmeczi.

Daniella by Night **1961** French model Daniella (Sommer) gets a contract to work for an Italian fashion house in Rome and she's soon attracting a lot of attention, including some that involves a spy plot. This leads to a chase through a Paris cabaret and a nude scene of Sommer, so how much does the story really matter, anyway. French with subtitles. **83m/B VHS, DVD.** *FR* Elke Sommer, Ivan Desny; ***D:*** Max Pecas; ***W:*** Grisha Dabat, Wolfgang Steinhardt; ***C:*** Andre Germain; ***M:*** Charles Aznavour, Georges Garvarentz.

Danielle Steel's Changes 1/2 *Changes* **1991** Ladd is a successful, divorced New York TV anchorwoman who turns her life upside-down when she marries an equally successful, widowed Los Angeles surgeon (Nouri). Can they overcome their bicoastal careers to make things work? What do you think? **96m/C VHS, DVD.** Cheryl Ladd, Michael Nouri, Christopher Gartin, Randee Heller, Charles Frank, James Sloyan, Cynthia Bain; ***D:*** Charles Jarrott. **TV**

Danielle Steel's Daddy 1/2 *Daddy* **1991** Ad exec Oliver Watson (Duffy) is happily married to Sarah (Mulgrew) and living the good life with their three kids—or so he thinks. Then Sarah announces she's leaving and Oliver's left to cope with family crisis as a single parent. A move to a new job in LA finds Oliver falling for an actress (Carter) and wondering if his family can ever be put back together again. **95m/C VHS, DVD.** Patrick Duffy, Lynda Carter, Kate Mulgrew; ***D:*** Michael Miller. **TV**

Danielle Steel's Fine Things 🦴🦴 1/2 *Fine Things* **1990** Bernie Fine thinks everything will be dandy now that he has a beautiful new bride and a cute stepdaughter. Then his wife dies and his stepdaughter's unreliable father wants sole custody. What's a nice guy to do? Based on the novel by Danielle Steel. **145m/C VHS, DVD.** D.W. Moffett, Tracy Pollan, Judith Hoag, Cloris Leachman, Noley Thornton; ***D:*** Tom (Thomas R.) Moore; ***W:*** Peter Lefcourt. **TV**

Danielle Steel's Heartbeat 🦴🦴 1/2 *Heartbeat* **1993** Shameless soap opera with Draper as Adrian Townsend, an L.A. TV-news producer with a self-involved ad-exec hubby (Kilner) who never wants children because of his own lousy childhood. When Adrian gets preggers the louse dumps her and she's left to weep prettily. That is until lovable divorced dad Bill Grant (Ritter) comes along to dry her eyes. Predictable and glossy adaptation of the Steel best-seller. **95m/C VHS, DVD.** Polly Draper, John Ritter, Kevin Kilner, Michael Lembeck, Nancy Morgan, Victor Dimattia, Christian Cousins; ***D:*** Michael Miller; ***W:*** Jan Worthington. **TV**

Danielle Steel's Kaleidoscope 🦴🦴 1/2 *Kaleidoscope* **1990** Three sisters are separated in childhood, after the mysterious deaths of their parents. Then a detective is hired to reunite the adult siblings. But Hilary, the eldest, has secrets she doesn't want her sisters to share. **96m/C VHS, DVD.** Jaclyn Smith, Perry King, Colleen Dewhurst, Donald Moffat; ***D:*** Jud Taylor. **TV**

Danielle Steel's Palomino 🦴🦴 1/2 *Palomino* **1991** Bittersweet romance with Frost as an ambitious photojournalist who gets involved with a headstrong cowboy (Horsley). Their differences drive them apart and tragedy strikes when Frost becomes a paraplegic after a horse-riding accident. This leads her to new goals and the eventual return of her old flame. Between the palomino's blond mane and the equally impressive blond locks of Frost, there's a lot of streaming in the wind hair shots. Horsley's merely tall, dark, and handsome. **90m/C VHS, DVD.** Lindsay Frost, Lee Horsley, Eva Marie Saint, Rod Taylor, Michele Greene, Beau Gravitte; ***D:*** Michael Miller; ***W:*** Karol Ann Hoeffner; ***C:*** Lloyd Ahern II; ***M:*** Dominic Frontiere. **TV**

Danielle Steel's Star 🦴 1/2 *Star* **1993** Garth is the country girl with big dreams of a singing career but an unhappy love life. She falls for an idealist lawyer (Bierko) but their romance is put on hold by career ambitions. She goes to Hollywood and gets discovered, becoming a singing/acting sensation who's under the thumb of her increasingly obsessed manager, Wass. Meanwhile, Bierko's trapped in a miserable marriage to the wealthy, influential Farrell. Do the true lovers get together? (Take a guess.) Although the story spans 15 years and lots of tribulations the young Garth never ages a day. **90m/C VHS, DVD.** Jennie Garth, Craig Bierko, Ted Wass, Terry Farrell, Penny Fuller, Mitchell Ryan, Jim Haynie; ***D:*** Michael Miller; ***W:*** Claire Labine. **TV**

Daniel's Daughter 🦴🦴 **2008** In this Hallmark Channel flick, successful magazine editor Cate (Leighton) returns to her tiny Massachusetts hometown after her father's death. She's still resentful over being sent away as a child after her mother died, but a chance to reexamine the past and then meeting a handsome attorney (Spence) bring some unexpected compensations. **88m/C DVD.** Laura Leighton, Sebastian Spence, Barry Flatman, Derek McGrath, Martin Doyle, Kelli Fox, Brandon Firla, Brad Borbridge; ***D:*** Neill Fearnley; ***W:*** Tracy Rosen; ***C:*** Francois Dagenais; ***M:*** Ian Thomas. **CABLE**

Danny 🦴🦴 1/2 **1979 (G)** Charming story of a lonely young girl who receives an injured horse that was no longer fit for the spoiled daughter of the rich owners. **90m/C VHS.** Rebecca Page, Janet Zarish, Barbara Jean Earhardt, Gloria Maddox, George Luce; ***D:*** Gene Feldman.

Danny Boy 🦴 1/2 **1946** Veteran dog, returning from the war, has difficulty adjusting to life back home. Things get worse for him and his young master when Danny Boy is assumed to be shell-shocked and dangerous. One of the few shell-shocked dog stories ever filmed. **67m/B VHS.** Robert "Buzzy" Henry, Ralph Lewis, Sybil Merritt; ***D:*** Terry Morse; ***W:*** Raymond L. Schrock; ***C:*** Jack Greenhalgh; ***M:*** Walter Greene.

Danny Boy 🦴🦴🦴 *Angel* **1982 (R)** Takes place in Ireland where a young saxaphonist witnesses a murder and, in an effort to understand it, sets out to find the killer. Thought-provoking film is meant to highlight the continuing struggles in Ireland. **92m/C VHS.** *IR* Stephen Rea, Veronica Quilligan, Honor Heffernan, Alan Devlin, Peter Caffrey, Ray McAnally; ***D:*** Neil Jordan; ***W:*** Neil Jordan; ***C:*** Chris Menges.

Danny Deckchair 🦴🦴 **2003 (PG-13)** Danny Morgan (Ifans), an eccentric dreamer and cement-truck driver, has just discovered his realtor girlfriend Trudy (Clarke) is dating one of her clients. Well, as any young man faced with this knowledge would do, he attaches giant helium balloons to a lawn chair and flies away. Faster than you can say "99 Luftballoons" he crashes in the backyard of Glenda (Otto), a small town parking cop who is lonely and frustrated with love. Typical of such premises, they fall in love in an endearing fashion. Despite unoriginal script and enormous plot holes, Aussie comedy is mainly watchable due to its two romantic leads. **99m/C VHS, DVD.** *AU* Rhys Ifans, Miranda Otto, Justine Clarke, Rhys Muldoon, Rod Zuanic, Maggie Dence, Jeanette Cronin, Frank Magree, Andrew Phelan, Andrew Batchelor, Jules Sobotta, Alan Flower, Michelle Boyle, Jane Beddows, Alex Mann; ***D:*** Jeff Balsmeyer; ***W:*** Jeff Balsmeyer; ***C:*** Martin McGrath; ***M:*** David Donaldson, Janet Roddick, Steve Roche.

Danny Roane: First Time Director 🦴 1/2 **2006 (R)** One-time sitcom star Danny Roane (Dick) has been blacklisted in Hollywood because of his infamous partying. After sobering up, Danny tries to make a comeback by directing his own autobiographical movie. But after Danny goes on a bender, he decides to suddenly turn his production into a musical and winds up in deep trouble. Your tolerance for Dick's antics will determine if you enjoy the flick. **83m/C DVD.** Andy Dick, Michael Hitchcock, Bob Odenkirk, Anthony Rapp, James Van Der Beek, Maura Tierney, Jack Black, Mo Collins, Danny Trejo, Sara Rue, Kevin Farley, Paul Henderson; ***Cameos:*** Ben Stiller; ***D:*** Andy Dick; ***W:*** Andy Dick; ***C:*** Ben Gamble; ***M:*** Jason Miller. **CABLE**

Dante 01 🦴🦴 **2008 (R)** Dank and disturbing space hell (yes, the title symbolism is deliberate). A shuttle delivers prisoner Saint Georges (Lambert) and new doctor Elisa (Pham) to the prison space station. Since the station is controlled by a pharmaceutical company, the violent inmates are used as guinea pigs in new technology trials. However, Saint Georges is apparently possessed by an alien entity that allows him to miraculously cure the inmates and a prison revolt is started. French with subtitles. **82m/C DVD.** *FR* Lambert Wilson, Linh Dan Pham, Dominique Pinon, Francois Levantal, Simona Maicanescu, Gerald Laroche; ***D:*** Marc Caro; ***W:*** Pierre Bordage; ***C:*** Jean Poissoon; ***M:*** Raphael Elig, Eric Wenger.

Dante's Inferno 🦴🦴🦴 **1924** Abandon all hope you who watch this film. A one-time friend sends his ruthless capitalist nemesis a copy of Dante's "Inferno," and the man reads the book and dreams he's gone to hell (would that be the dress circle?) A silent film that was controversial in its day: the body-stockinged actors were believed to be nude (which would have made it the first nudie Comedy). **54m/B VHS.** Lawson Butt, Howard Gaye, Ralph Lewis, Pauline Starke, Josef Swickard; ***D:*** Henry Otto.

Dante's Inferno: Life of Dante Gabriel Rossetti 🦴🦴 **1969** The flamboyant life of mid-19th century English Pre-Raphaelite artist/poet Dante Gabriel Rossetti is depicted with the usual Russell flair. The drunken, drug-taking, womanizing Rossetti was part of the leading intellectual group of his age, which included Swinburne, Morris, Ruskin, and Rossetti's sister, the poet Christina Rossetti. **90m/B VHS.** *GB* Oliver Reed; ***D:*** Ken Russell.

Dante's Peak 🦴🦴 1/2 **1997 (PG-13)** Northwest volcano serves up a smorgasbord of molten disaster in the second most desirable town in the U.S.—the titular Dante's Peak. Brosnan is the intuitive scientist who comes to Washington to match wits with the conical adversary and joins forces with the town's tres femme mayor Wando (Hamilton). Ashes fall like snow in January, computer generated lava flows profusely, poisonous gases leak out and water turns to acid, all with desired nail-biting effect. Wando's two kids, dog and grandma lend folksy charm and the requisite loved-ones-in-grave-danger, but this heated disaster flick is not exactly for the whole family. Cliched and predictable, flick runs the Disaster Movie Playbook page by page as plot takes a backseat to nonstop action. **112m/C VHS, DVD, HD DVD.** Pierce Brosnan, Linda Hamilton, Charles Hallahan, Grant Heslov, Elizabeth Hoffman, Jamie Renee Smith, Arabella Field, Tzi Ma, Jeremy Foley, Brian Reddy, Kirk Trutner; ***D:*** Roger Donaldson; ***W:*** Leslie Bohem; ***C:*** Andrzej Bartkowiak; ***M:*** John (Gianni) Frizzell.

Danton 🦴🦴🦴🦴 **1982 (PG)** A sweeping account of the reign of terror following the French Revolution. Focuses on the title character (wonderfully portrayed by Depardieu) and is directed with searching parallels to modern-day Poland by that country's premier filmmaker, Andrzej Wajda. Well-done period sets round out a memorable film. In French with English subtitles. **136m/C VHS, DVD.** *PL FR* Gerard Depardieu, Wojciech Pszoniak, Patrice Chereau, Angela Winkler, Boguslaw Linda; ***D:*** Andrzej Wajda; ***W:*** Jean-Claude Carriere, Agnieszka Holland, Boleslaw Michalek, Jacek Gasiorowski, Andrzej Wajda. British Acad. '83: Foreign Film; Cesar '83: Director (Wajda); Montreal World Film Fest. '83: Actor (Depardieu).

Danzon 🦴🦴🦴 1/2 **1991 (PG)** Julia (Rojo), a single, working-class mom escapes the drudgery of her simple existence by going to a Mexico City dance hall every Wednesday. There she loses herself to the movement of the danzon, a dance with Haitian roots, popular in Mexico for over 100 years. When her partner of six years, Carmelo (Rergis), doesn't show up one night, her life is turned upside down. So begins a search for Carmelo—and herself. Quiet and restrained, like the ballroom-style danzon at the center of the plot. Applauded at Cannes. In Spanish with English subtitles. **103m/C VHS.** *SP* Maria Rojo, Carmen Salinas, Blanca Guerra, Tito Vasconcelos, Victor Carpinteiro, Victor Vasconcelos; ***D:*** Maria Novaro; ***W:*** Maria Novaro, Betriz Novaro.

Daphne 🦴 1/2 **2007** Lifeless look at a seven-year period in the 1940s that depicts the two great loves of English author Daphne Du Maurier. Repressing her sexuality for marriage and motherhood, Daphne (Somerville) fell into an unrequited romance with Ellen (McGovern), the wife of her publisher Nelson Doubleday (Malcolm). This leads to her writing about forbidden longing in the play "September Tide," which introduces Daphne to bisexual actress Gertrude Lawrence (McTeer). Director Beavan used Du Maurier's letters and memoirs but it's still dull. **88m/C DVD.** *GB* Geraldine Somerville, Elizabeth McGovern, Janet McTeer, Christopher Malcolm; ***D:*** Clare Beavan; ***W:*** Amy Jenkins; ***C:*** Christopher Titus King. **TV**

Darby O'Gill & the Little People 🦴🦴🦴 1/2 **1959 (G)** Set in Ireland, roguish old story teller Darby O'Gill (Sharpe), whose also the caretaker of a large estate, tumbles into a well and visits the land of leprechauns who give him three wishes in order to rearrange his life. When he tries to tell his friends what happened, they think that it is only another one of his stories. Connery plays the youhg man who takes Darby's job and courts his daughter (Munro) as well. A wonderful Disney production (despite its disappointing boxoffice performance) with wit, charm and an ounce or two of terror. **93m/C VHS, DVD.** Albert Sharpe, Janet Munro, Sean Connery, Estelle Winwood, Kieron Moore, Jimmy O'Dea; ***D:*** Robert Stevenson; ***W:*** Lawrence Edward Watkin; ***C:*** Winton C. Hoch.

Darby's Rangers 🦴🦴 1/2 *Young Invaders* **1958** WWII pot-boiler with Garner as the leader of a commando team put together for covert operations in North Africa and Italy. Successful battle sequences combine with slow-paced romantic scenes as the soldiers chase women when not chasing the enemy. **122m/B VHS.** James Garner, Jack Warden, Edd Byrnes, Peter Brown, Stuart Whitman, David Janssen, Etchika Choureau, Venetia Stevenson, Torin Thatcher, Joan Elan, Corey Allen, Murray Hamilton; ***D:*** William A. Wellman; ***W:*** Guy Trosper; ***C:*** William Clothier; ***M:*** Max Steiner.

Dare 🦴🦴 **2009** This sexually charged coming-of-age tale takes the standard Hollywood teen comedy in unexpected directions. Alexa (Rossum) is a good-girl drama student who seduces popular jock Johnny (Gilford) after being ripped as inexperienced by a local actor (Cumming). Meanwhile, her sexually confused childhood friend Ben (Springer) is also making moves on Johnny. The story unfolds in three sections featuring each member of the triangle, with Gilford standing out as the surprisingly sensitive Johnny. Good performances all the way around help roughen the edges of this story that seems aimed at the art house crowd. **90m/C DVD.** *US* Ashley Springer, Rooney Mara, Emmy Rossum, Zach Gilford, Ana Gasteyer, Sandra Bernhard, Alan Cumming, Cady Huffman; ***D:*** Adam Salky; ***W:*** David Brind; ***C:*** Michael Fimognari; ***M:*** Poe David, Duncan Sheik.

Daredevil 🦴🦴 **2003 (PG-13)** Daredevil made his appearance in Marvel Comics in 1964. Having lost his sight in an industrial accident when he was a kid, his remaining senses are enhanced but he's basically still human. Too bad the movie isn't. It's flashy and loud but uninvolving. Lawyer Matt Murdock (Affleck) turns vigilante and dons red leather and a goofy mask when one too many criminals goes free. The big (literally) bad guy is Kingpin (an avuncular Duncan) who keeps flashy assassin Bullseye (Farrell) on the payroll. Meanwhile, Matt is trying to make time with heiress Electra (Garner) who thinks Daredevil killed her father—putting a crimp in the potential romance. Garner looks great in leather and refines the butt-kicking skills she uses in her TV series "Alias" to good effect. Affleck's sorta lightweight since Daredevil has lots of issues; he's better at sarcasm than angst. **114m/C VHS, DVD, Blu-ray Disc.** *US* Ben Affleck, Jennifer Garner, Michael Clarke Duncan, Colin Farrell, Joe Pantoliano, Jon Favreau, David Keith, Erik Avari, Paul Ben-Victor, Derrick O'Connor, Leland Orser, Scott Terra, Kevin Smith; ***Cameos:*** Stan Lee; ***D:*** Mark Steven Johnson; ***W:*** Mark Steven Johnson; ***C:*** Ericson Core; ***M:*** Graeme Revell. Golden Raspberries '03: Worst Actor (Affleck).

Daredevils of the Red Circle 🦴🦴 **1938** Three young men set out to free a man held prisoner by an escaped convict. A serial in 12 chapters. **195m/B VHS.** Charles Quigley, Bruce Bennett, Carole Landis; ***D:*** John English, William Witney.

Darfur Now 🦴🦴 1/2 **2007 (PG)** Documentary attempts to bring the complex, tribal-based Darfur (Sudan) conflict and its accompanying genocide to American audiences. Director Braun focuses on six individuals—three in the midst of the horror (a refugee camp leader, a mother who joins a guerilla group after the death of her son, and a food aid worker), and three trying to affect change from the outside (an activist advocating divestment of Sudanese stock, the UN prosecutor preparing a case against those responsible for the genocide, and actor Cheadle, who is committed to raising awareness about the conflict). Cheadle and fellow American Sterling are noble, but their stories are significantly less interesting than the others, especially Argentinian-born prosecutor Moreno-Ocampo, who has already lived through a brutal dictatorship in his homeland, and is committed to bringing justice to Darfur. **99m/C DVD.** *US* ***D:*** Theodore Braun; ***W:*** Theodore Braun; ***C:*** Kirsten Johnson; ***M:*** Graeme Revell.

Daring Danger 🦴 1/2 **1932** McCoy is nearly killed in a fight with the villainous Alexander. When he recovers he finds Alexander has joined forces with a rustler (Ellis), so McCoy battles both of them—while his horse goes for help. **58m/B VHS.** Tim McCoy, Richard Alexander, Robert Ellis, Alberta Vaughn, Wallace MacDonald, Murdock MacQuarrie, Max

Davidson; ***D:*** David Ross Lederman.

Daring Daughters ½ **1933** New York gold-digger Terry (Marian Marsh) gets a visit from her naive sister Betty (Joan Marsh) who wants to see what big city life is all about. Money and men, honey! And Terry doesn't want Betty corrupted by either. **63m/B DVD.** Marian Marsh, Joan Marsh, Kenneth Thomson, Bert Roach, Allen Vincent, Lita Chevret; ***D:*** Christy Cabanne; ***W:*** Barry Barringer, Frederick Hugh Herbert; ***C:*** Harry Forbes.

Daring Dobermans **1973 (PG)** In this sequel to "The Doberman Gang," the barking bank-robbers have a new set of crime-planning masters. A young Indian boy who loves the dogs enters the picture and may thwart their perfect crime. **88m/C VHS.** Charles Robinson, Tim Considine, David Moses, Claudio Martinez, Joan Caulfield; ***D:*** Byron Ross Chudnow.

Daring Game **1968** A group of scuba divers nicknamed the Flying Fish attempt to rescue a woman's husband and daughter from an island dictatorship. Failed series pilot by producer Ivan Tors, better known for "Sea Hunt" and "Flipper." **100m/C VHS.** Lloyd Bridges, Brock Peters, Michael Ansara, Joan Blackman, Michael Walker; ***D:*** Laszlo Benedek; ***M:*** George Bruns. **TV**

Dario Argento's Trauma *Trauma* **1993 (R)** When a teenage girl's parents are decapitated, she and an artist friend start following the clues to a psychotic killer known as "The Headhunter." Trademark horror work for Italian cult director Argento with high suspense quotient and equally high gore. An unrated version is also available. **106m/C VHS, DVD.** Christopher Rydell, Asia Argento, Laura Johnson, James Russo, Brad Dourif, Frederic Forrest, Piper Laurie; ***D:*** Dario Argento; ***W:*** T.E.D. Klein, Dario Argento.

The Darjeeling Limited **2007 (R)** Brothers Francis (Wilson), Peter (Brody), and Jack (Schwartzman) seek spiritual healing after their father's death on a cross-Asia trip aboard the Darjeeling Limited. Along the way, the three men struggle with each other and their own problems, including a (possibly intentional) accident that's left Francis's head in bandages, Peter's desertion of his pregnant wife, and Jack's recent breakup (chronicled in the companion short film "Hotel Chevalier"), until Francis reveals that their trip is taking them to their estranged mother (Huston), now a nun living in India. Anderson manages to capture the absurdity and humanity of the brothers while exploring the crises that have shaped their individual struggles for meaning and purpose, while infusing the film with his traditional detail-obsessed style. He and co-screenwriters Schwartzman and Coppola penned the film while traveling across India by, of course, train. **91m/C DVD.** *US* Owen Wilson, Adrien Brody, Jason Schwartzman, Amara Karan, Wally Wolodarsky, Anjelica Huston; ***D:*** Wes Anderson; ***W:*** Jason Schwartzman, Wes Anderson, Roman Coppola; ***C:*** Robert Yeoman.

The Dark ½ *The Mutilator* **1979 (R)** A supernatural beast commits a string of gruesome murders. **92m/C VHS, DVD.** William Devane, Cathy Lee Crosby, Richard Jaeckel, Keenan Wynn, Vivian Blaine, Biff (Elliott) Elliot, Warren Kemmerling, Casey Kasem, John Bloom; ***D:*** John Cardos; ***W:*** Stanford Whitmore; ***C:*** John Morrill.

The Dark ½ **1994 (R)** Cop and scientist seek a mysterious graveyard creature who holds both the power to heal and destroy. One man wants to kill it, one man wants to save it, and they race to be the first to find it. **90m/C VHS.** Brion James, Jaimz Woolvett, Cynthia Belliveau, Stephen McHattie, Dennis O'Connor, Neve Campbell, Christopher Bondy, William Lynn; ***D:*** Craig Pryce; ***W:*** Robert Cooper.

A Dark Adapted Eye **1993** Sinister TV mystery adapted from the psychological thriller by Ruth Rendell (writing as Barbara Vine). In 1951 Vera Hillyard (Imrie) is hung for murdering her younger sister Eden (Ward)—an act that has profound effects on the family, including young niece Faith (Bonham Carter). Long haunted by the "why" of the crime, Faith later begins an investigation into her family's past—and discovers very dark and disturbing secrets dating back to WWII. Title refers to a vision problem caused by remaining in darkness too long. **150m/C VHS.** *GB* Helena Bonham Carter, Celia Imrie, Sophie Ward, Robin Ellis, Ciaran Hinds, Pip Torrens, William Gaminara, Polly Adams, Bernice Stegers, Steven Mackintosh, Jason Durr; ***D:*** Tim Fywell; ***W:*** Sandy Welch; ***C:*** Rex Maidment; ***M:*** David Ferguson.

Dark Age ½ **1988 (R)** An Australian conservationist must track down a rampaging, giant, semi-mythical alligator before it is killed by bounty hunters. Based on the novel (and Aboriginal legend) "Numunwari." **90m/C VHS.** *AU* John Jarratt, David Gulpilil, Max Phipps, Ray Meagher, Nikki Coghill, Burnam Burnam; ***D:*** Arch Nicholson.

The Dark Angel ½ **1935** Kitty Vane (Oberon) loves both Alan Trent (March) and his best friend Gerald Shannon (Marshall) who are going off to fight in WWI. However, Kitty accepts Alan's marriage proposal. A misunderstanding leads to trouble and Alan is presumed dead. Actually, he's been blinded and decides not to return to Kitty after the war, so Alan changes his name and tries to make a new life. Meanwhile, Kitty has agreed to marry Gerald, although he knows she's still pining. Naturally, everyone finds out the truth in this sentimental weepie that got Oberon an Oscar nomination. **108m/B VHS.** Merle Oberon, Fredric March, Herbert Marshall, Janet Beecher, John Halliday, Claud Allister, Henrietta Crosman, Frieda Inescort; ***D:*** Sidney Franklin; ***W:*** Lillian Hellman, Mordaunt Shairp; ***C:*** Gregg Toland; ***M:*** Alfred Newman. Oscars '36: Art Dir./Set Dec.

The Dark Angel **1991** Maud is the young and innocent heiress to a fortune in this gothic mystery of creeping unease. She is intrigued by the romantic portrait of her youthful and unknown Uncle Silas. But her mysterious uncle is no longer the Byronic hero. What secret wickedness does his ravaged face hide? And what about Maud's drug-addicted governess and the brutish young man in the cemetary? Does Uncle Silas just want Maud's fortune or Maud herself? Excellent performances by O'Toole as the decadent uncle and Edney as the innocent-but-not-stupid Maud. Based on the novel "Uncle Silas" by Sheridan Le Fanu. Made for British TV. **150m/C VHS.** *GB* Peter O'Toole, Beatie Edney, Jane Lapotaire, Tim Woodward, Alan MacNaughton, Barbara Shelley, Guy Rolfe; ***D:*** Peter Hammond. **TV**

Dark Angel: The Ascent ½ **1994 (R)** She-devil gets tired of hell and decides to get a look at the world upstairs. She also decides to turn vigilante and dispatch some bad guy souls to her former home. **80m/C VHS.** Charlotte Stewart, Daniel Markel, Michael C. Mahon, Nicholas Worth, Milton James, Angela Featherstone; ***D:*** Linda Hassani; ***W:*** Matthew Bright; ***M:*** Fuzzbee Morse.

Dark Asylum **2001 (R)** Shrink Maggie Bleham (Porizkova) is called on to examined a serial killer (Drake) who's so dangerous that authorities have brought him to an abandoned asylum to be evaluated. Naturally, the nutball gets loose and kills his guards with the doc next on his list. Only she's got other ideas. **96m/C VHS, DVD.** Paulina Porizkova, Larry Drake, Judd Nelson, Jurgen Prochnow; ***D:*** Gregory Gieras; ***W:*** Gregory Gieras; ***C:*** Viorel Sergovici Jr. **VIDEO**

Dark August **1976 (PG)** A New Yorker drops out and transplants to rural Vermont, where he accidentally kills a young girl and then suffers numerous horrors as a result of a curse put on him by the girl's grandfather. **87m/C VHS.** J.J. Barry, Carole Shelyne, Kim Hunter, William Robertson; ***D:*** Martin Goldman.

The Dark Backward ½ **1991 (R)** A dark, subversive comedy about a garbage man who dreams of making it big in show biz as a stand-up comedian. He's terrible until a third arm starts growing out of his back and the sheer grotesqueness of his situation makes him a temporary star. Caan and Newton are interestingly cast, but young, first-time director Rifkin's foray into David Lynch territory was not well received by critics. **97m/C VHS, DVD.** Judd Nelson, Bill Paxton, Wayne Newton, Lara Flynn Boyle, James Caan, Rob Lowe, Claudia Christian, King Moody, Adam Rifkin; ***D:*** Adam Rifkin; ***W:*** Adam Rifkin; ***C:*** Joey Forsyte; ***M:*** Marc David Decker.

Dark Before Dawn ½ **1989 (R)** American farmers and Vietnam veterans team up against corrupt government officials and ruthless businessmen in this violent film about the plight of the underdog. **95m/C VHS.** Doug McClure, Sonny Gibson, Ben Johnson, Billy Drago, Rance Howard, Morgan Woodward, Buck Henry, Jeffery Osterhage, Red Steagall, John Martin, Gary Cooper; ***D:*** Robert Totten.

Dark Blue **2003 (R)** Another James Ellroy L.A. cop novel comes to life in this powerful tale of deep-seated corruption set against the Rodney King verdict and its aftermath. Veteran cop Eldon Perry (Russell) is part of the elite Special Investigations Squad, a brutal, corrupt, and racist unit run by Jack Van Meter (Gleeson). Partnered with Van Meter's green nephew Bobby (Speedman), Eldon is assigned to steer a homicide investigation away from the two snitches who did it. Standing in his way is the black deputy chief (Rhames) who has vowed to shut down the SIS. Russell's outstanding performance anchors the proceedings, which gets somewhat muddled by the pairing of Ayers's hard-boiled script with Shelton's more reflective bent. Ellroy's original first draft was set against the 1965 Watts riots, and Ayers wrote "Training Day" at about the same time he was adapting "Blue." **116m/C VHS, DVD.** *US* Kurt Russell, Ving Rhames, Scott Speedman, Brendan Gleeson, Michael Michele, Lolita (David) Davidovich, Dash Mihok, Kurupt, Khandi Alexander, Master P; ***D:*** Ron Shelton; ***W:*** David Ayer; ***C:*** Barry Peterson; ***M:*** Terence Blanchard.

Dark Blue Almost Black ½ *Azulo Scuro Casi Negro* **2006** Overstuffed debut drama about personal ambition vs. responsibility and family obligation. Jorge is forced to put his life on hold after his father suffers a severe stroke. He takes over his father's janitorial job while continuing his studies at night and coping with other personal issues, including an imprisoned brother and a gay best friend. Spanish with subtitles. **105m/C DVD.** *SP* Quim Gutierrez, Antonio de la Torre, Hector Colome, Marta Etura, Raul Arevalo, Eva Pallares; ***D:*** Daniel Sanchez Arevalo; ***W:*** Daniel Sanchez Arevalo; ***C:*** Juan Carlos Gomez; ***M:*** Pascal Gaigne.

Dark Blue World ½ *Trmavomodry Svet* **2001 (R)** Told in flashbacks, this is an old-fashioned WWII epic about heroism and romance. In 1950 in Czechoslovakia, Franta (Vetchy) is imprisoned by the Communists who fear the war hero's previous contacts with democracy. After the Nazis invaded his country in 1939, Franta fled to England, where he joins the RAF and befriends younger Czech pilot Karel (Hadek). But the duo have a falling out over a local woman, Susan (Fizgerald), who favors the mature Franta. Czech, German, and English dialogue. **115m/C VHS, DVD.** *CZ GB* Ondrej Vetchy, Tara Fitzgerald, Krystof Hadek, Oldrich Kaiser, Charles Dance, Linda Rybova, Hans-Jorg Assmann, Anna Massey; ***D:*** Jan Sverak; ***W:*** Zdenek Sverak; ***C:*** Vladimir Smutny; ***M:*** Ondrej Soukup.

Dark Breed **1996 (R)** Ewww, yuck, it's sci-fi infestation time once again as Nick Saxon (Scalia) is assigned to find the bodies of six astronauts whose top secret space craft has mysteriously crashed. He discovers that the bodies are playing host to reptilian parasites with designs on world domination. **104m/C VHS, DVD.** Jack Scalia, Jonathan Banks, Robin Curtis, Donna W. Scott; ***D:*** Richard Pepin.

Dark City *Dark Empire; Dark World* **1997 (R)** Brooding city of gloom floats in a sunless world, with skylines nightmarishly changing as its residents sleep. The city seems to belong to no era, looking at times like a neo-goth music video and at others like a work of German expressionism. Sometimes it just looks like '60s Cleveland. Director Proyas seems to have wanted to make a futuristic film noir like "Blade Runner," but gets lost somewhere along the way. He does however, keep the style. Disfigured Dr. Schreber (Sutherland) is forced by a dying race of pasty-faced long-coated aliens to use humans as guinea pigs in an attempt to find out what makes them tick. John Murdoch (Sewell) wakes up in a hotel room with a dead body and no memory of his life. Searching for his past, he wanders through one incredible set after another, but is it real or is it hypodermically injected? Hurt is a detective who only wants to stop the grisly murders. Garbled story rewards persistence at the end. **103m/C VHS, DVD, Blu-ray Disc.** Kiefer Sutherland, William Hurt, Rufus Sewell, Richard O'Brien, Jennifer Connelly, Ian Richardson, Colin Friels, Frank Gallacher, Bruce Spence, John Bluthal, Mitchell Butel, Melissa George; ***D:*** Alex Proyas; ***W:*** Alex Proyas, Lem Dobbs, David S. Goyer; ***C:*** Darius Wolski; ***M:*** Trevor Jones.

Dark Command **1940** The story of Quantrell's Raiders who terrorized the Kansas territory during the Civil War until one man came along to put a stop to it. Colorful and talented cast add depth to the script. Also available colorized. **95m/B VHS, DVD.** John Wayne, Walter Pidgeon, Claire Trevor, Roy Rogers, Marjorie Main, George "Gabby" Hayes; ***D:*** Raoul Walsh.

Dark Corner **1946** Private detective Bradford Galt (Stevens) is framed and suspects his ex-partner Jardine (Kreuger) is the culprit. But then Jardine winds up dead. Then there's a guy in a white suit (Bendix) who keeps dogging him and sinister wealthy art dealer Hardy Cathcart (Webb) seems to be pulling everyone's strings. It's a good thing Galt's loyal secretary Kathleen (Ball) believes in the lug. Gripping, intricate film noir. **99m/B VHS, DVD.** Mark Stevens, Clifton Webb, William Bendix, Lucille Ball, Cathy Downs, Reed Hadley, Constance Collier, Kurt Kreuger; ***D:*** Henry Hathaway; ***W:*** Jay Dratler, Bernard C. Schoenfeld, Leo Rosten; ***C:*** Joe MacDonald; ***M:*** Cyril Mockridge.

Dark Corners **2006** Writer/director Gower plays mind games with his audience and then leaves us confused and dissatisfied. Karen Clark (Birch), a suburban housewife undergoing fertility treatments, begins having horrific nightmares about a woman who looks just like her. Disturbed mortuary assistant Susan Hamilton (yep, Birch again) has blackouts. Both women learn that people they know are victims of a serial killer. Ah, if only the plot were actually that simple. **92m/C DVD.** *GB* Thora Birch, Christien Anholt, Toby Stephens, Oliver Price, Ray Charleson, Joanna Hole; ***D:*** Ray Gower; ***W:*** Ray Gower; ***C:*** Paul Sadourian; ***M:*** Andrew Pearce. **VIDEO**

Dark Country **2009 (R)** Richard (Jane) and Gina (German) impulsively married in Vegas and are now driving through a nighttime Nevada desert to begin their honeymoon. They spot an unconscious man injured in a car accident and decide to take him to a hospital. The man suddenly awakens but tragedy occurs. Then the newlyweds realize they are lost and left in unimaginable circumstances. Jane's directorial debut. **88m/C DVD.** Lauren German, Ron Perlman, Thomas Jane; ***D:*** Tab Murphy; ***W:*** Tab Murphy; ***C:*** Geoff Boyle; ***M:*** Eric Lewis. **VIDEO**

The Dark Crystal **1982 (PG)** Jen and Kira, two of the last surviving Gelflings, attempt to return a crystal shard (discovered with the help of a sorceress) to the castle where the Dark Crystal lies, guarded by the cruel and evil Skeksis. Designed by Brian Froud. From the creators of the Muppets. **93m/C VHS, DVD, UMD.** ***D:*** Jim Henson, Frank Oz; ***W:*** David Odell; ***C:*** Oswald Morris; ***M:*** Trevor Jones; ***V:*** Jim Henson, Frank Oz, Kathryn Mullen, Dave Goetz.

The Dark Dancer ½ **1995 (R)** Psychology prof Maggie (Tweed), who authors books on feminine sexual behavior, gets her experience first-hand by working in a strip club. Now, she's also the target of a police investigation. Also available unrated. **98m/C VHS.** Shannon Tweed, Jason Carter, Lisa Pescia, Francesco Quinn; ***D:*** Robert Burge; ***W:*** Robert Burge, Terry Chambers; ***C:*** Eric Scott; ***M:*** David Connor.

The Dark Dealer **1995** Three terror tales find the Devil's assistant dealing a deadly game of blackjack to a trio in limbo, with the cards propelling each man into a horrific adventure. Provides some real scares along with effective (if low-budget) special effects. **85m/C VHS.** Mark Fickert, Richard Hull, Vincent Gaskins, Rocky Patterson, Gordon Fox; ***D:*** Tom Alexander.

Dark Eyes ½ *Les Yeux Noirs; Oci Ciornie* **1987** An acclaimed Italian film based on a several short stories by Anton Chekov. Mastroianni is a weak-willed Italian, trapped in a marriage of convenience, who falls in love with a mysterious, also married, Russian beauty he meets in a health spa. He embarks on a journey to find her and, perhaps, his lost ideals. Hailed as Mastroianni's consummate performance. In Italian with English subtitles. **118m/C VHS.** *IT* Marcello Mastroianni, Silvana Mangano, Elena Sofonova, Marthe Keller; ***D:*** Nikita Mikhalkov; ***C:*** Franco Di Giacomo. Cannes '87: Actor (Mastroianni).

Dark Forces 🦴🦴 *Harlequin* **1983 (PG)** A faith-healer promises to help a senator's dying son and finds the politician's wife also desires his assistance. This Australian film is uneven and predictable. Though rated "PG," beware of two rather brief, but explicit, nudity scenes. **96m/C VHS, DVD.** *AU* Robert Powell, David Hemmings, Broderick Crawford, Carmen Duncan; ***D:*** Simon Wincer.

Dark Habits 🦴🦴 1/2 *Entre Tinieblas* **1984** An early Almodovar farce about already-demented nuns in a failing convent trying to raise funds with the help of a nightclub singer who is on the run. Although certainly irreverant, it doesn't quite have the zing of his later work. In Spanish with subtitles. **116m/C VHS, DVD.** *SP* Carmen Maura, Christina Pascual, Julieta Serrano, Marisa Paredes; ***D:*** Pedro Almodovar; ***W:*** Pedro Almodovar; ***C:*** Angel Luis Fernandez.

The Dark Half 🦴🦴 **1991 (R)** Flawed chiller based on a Stephen King novel. Thad Beaumont's serious novels have been failures, but writing as George Stark, he's had phenomenal success with grisly horror stories. In a publicity stunt Thad kills off and publicly buries George (who doesn't want to stay dead). Soon everyone who's crossed Thad is brutally murdered. Hutton acquits himself well in a change of pace dual role. Otherwise, the psychological thrills are few and the gore is plentiful. Pittsburgh serves as location double for King's usual New England territory. Film's release was delayed due to Orion's bankruptcy problems. **122m/C VHS, DVD.** Timothy Hutton, Amy Madigan, Michael Rooker, Julie Harris, Robert Joy, Kent Broadhurst, Beth Grant, Rutanya Alda, Tom Mardirosian, Chelsea Field, Royal Dano; ***D:*** George A. Romero; ***W:*** George A. Romero; ***C:*** Tony Pierce-Roberts; ***M:*** Christopher Young.

Dark Harbor 🦴🦴 **1998 (R)** A wealthy married couple, traveling to their vacation home off the coast of Maine, stop to help an injured young man. A series of coincidences leads the threesome to spend the weekend together in the couple's isolated retreat, where sexual attraction makes the situation very volatile. **89m/C VHS, DVD.** Alan Rickman, Polly Walker, Norman Reedus; ***D:*** Adam Coleman Howard; ***W:*** Adam Coleman Howard, Justin Lazard; ***C:*** Walt Lloyd; ***M:*** David Mansfield.

Dark Heart 🦴 1/2 **2006 (R)** Matt Taylor (Joelson) returns to his economically depressed mill hometown after a tour in Iraq. Swapping lies at a bar with old friend Bobby (Howe), Matt tells him a (probably apocryphal) story about an outfit that found millions in U.S. dollars hidden in Baghdad. The tale catches the attention of four desperate mill workers and they kidnap Matt, taking him to a remote cabin in hopes he'll confess to where the money is. **100m/C DVD.** R.D. Call, Brian Howe, Huntley Ritter, Sam Scarber, Greg Joelson, Darcy Halsey, William Dennis Hurley, Larry Weissman, Mageina Tovah; ***D:*** Kevin Lewis; ***W:*** Kevin Lewis; ***C:*** Marco Cappetta; ***M:*** Michael P. Bondies, Dax Pierson. **VIDEO**

Dark Honeymoon 🦴 1/2 **2008** Paul (Cornish) apparently marries Kathryn (Booth) because of the great sex even though he doesn't really know anything about her. When they honeymoon along the Oregon coast, he finds out a lot about his bride he probably doesn't want to know. Like why there seems to be dead bodies wherever she's been. **94m/C DVD.** Nick Cornish, Lindy Booth, Roy Scheider, Tia Carrere, Daryl Hannah, Eric Roberts, Wes Ramsey; ***D:*** David O'Malley; ***W:*** David O'Malley; ***C:*** Matt Molitor; ***M:*** Juan J. Colomer. **VIDEO**

Dark Horse 🦴🦴 1/2 **1992 (PG)** Meyers is a young woman distraught over the death of her mother. She gets into trouble and is assigned to do community service work at a horse farm where she finds herself caring for a prize-winning horse. **98m/C VHS.** Ari Meyers, Mimi Rogers, Ed Begley Jr., Donovan Leitch, Samantha Eggar; ***D:*** David Hemmings.

The Dark Hour 🦴 1/2 **1936** Two detectives team up to solve a murder in which multiple suspects are involved. Based on Sinclair Gluck's "The Last Trap." **72m/B VHS, DVD.** Ray Walker, Irene Ware, Berton Churchill, Hedda Hopper, Hobart Bosworth, E.E. Clive; ***D:*** Charles Lamont.

Dark Journey 🦴🦴🦴 *The Anxious Years* **1937** WWI Stockholm is the setting for a love story between a double agent and the head of German Intelligence. Clever, sophisticated production; Leigh is stunning. **82m/B VHS, DVD.** *GB* Vivien Leigh, Conrad Veidt, Joan Gardner, Anthony Bushell, Ursula Jeans; ***D:*** Victor Saville.

Dark Justice 🦴🦴 1/2 **1991** Judge by day, avenger by night, in this actioner created from three episodes of the late-night TV series. Judge Nicholas Marshall is disgusted by the criminals sprung on legal loopholes and backroom deals, so he decides to take justice into his own hands. **99m/C VHS, DVD.** Ramy Zada, Dick O'Neill, Clayton Prince, Begona Plaza. **TV**

Dark Justice 🦴🦴 *Yup-Yup Man* **2000** Thirty years after Robert (Bumiller) sees his homeless dad murdered on the LA streets, he's still traumatized—wandering around and muttering to himself (hence the alternate film title). Robert's personal hero is vigilante comic book star Dark Justice. In fact, he decides to emulate his hero by taking on real street criminals, except Robert kills them instead of turning them in to the cops. **89m/C DVD.** William Bumiller, David Bowe, Jocelyn Seagrave, Matt Gallini, Chase Mackenzie Bebak; ***D:*** Glenn Klinker; ***W:*** Glenn Klinker; ***C:*** Yoram Astrakhan; ***M:*** Sharon Farber.

The Dark Knight 🦴🦴🦴🦴 **2008 (PG-13)** Batman (Bale), along with Lt. Gordon (Oldman) has been cleaning up the streets of Gotham, and the criminal underworld wants him gone, along with crusading DA Harvey Dent (Eckhard). Along comes the grotesque and psychotic Joker (Ledger, in a tour de force performance, his last) to wreak havok for the pure sport of it. Nolan's masterpiece destroys the preconceptions of what a superhero movie can be, presenting a deep, thoughtful, action-packed, and VERY dark film. He also stretches the limits of the PG-13 rating to the breaking point. The cast is uniformly excellent (including Gyllenhaal, taking over the Rachel Dawes role from Katie Holmes), but Ledger surpasses them all in what should be an Oscar-winning performance. **152m/C DVD, Blu-ray Disc.** Christian Bale, Heath Ledger, Aaron Eckhart, Maggie Gyllenhaal, Gary Oldman, Michael Caine, Eric Roberts, Cillian Murphy, Morgan Freeman, Anthony Michael Hall, Monique Gabriela Curnen, Nestor Carbonell, Michael Jai White, Melinda McGraw, William Fichtner, Joshua Harto, Colin McFarlane, Ron Dean, Ritchie Coster, Nathan Gamble, Tommy (Tiny) Lister, Chin Han; ***D:*** Christopher Nolan; ***W:*** Christopher Nolan, Jonathan Nolan; ***C:*** Wally Pfister; ***M:*** Hans Zimmer, James Newton Howard. Oscars '08: Sound FX Editing, Support. Actor (Ledger); British Acad. '08: Support. Actor (Ledger); Screen Actors Guild '08: Support. Actor (Ledger).

Dark Matter 🦴🦴 **2007 (R)** Based on a true story that happened at the University of Iowa in 1991. Ambitious Chinese student Xing Liu (Liu) is honored to be studying for his PhD in America, especially when he becomes the protege of cosmology prof Jacob Reiser (Quinn). However, when Liu challenges Reiser's own ideas about dark matter, he's betrayed by school politics and it leads him to violence. Streep plays a university patron enamored of Chinese culture. Structured in five acts in accordance to the five elements of energy in Chinese philosophy. **90m/C DVD.** Ye Liu, Aidan Quinn, Meryl Streep, Erik Avari, Blair Brown; ***D:*** Shi-Zheng Chen; ***W:*** Billy Shebar; ***C:*** Oliver Bokelberg; ***M:*** Van Dyke Parks.

Dark Mirror 🦴🦴🦴 **1946** A psychologist and a detective struggle to determine which twin sister murdered a prominent physician. Good and evil siblings finely acted by de Havilland. **85m/B VHS, DVD.** Olivia de Havilland, Lew Ayres, Thomas Mitchell, Garry Owen; ***D:*** Robert Siodmak; ***C:*** Milton Krasner.

Dark Mirror 🦴🦴 **2007** Truly haunted house or truly haunted mind? Photographer Deborah (Vidal), her husband Jim (Chisum), and their young son Ian (Pelegrin) move into a creepy house that's filled with glass panels and mirrors. Deborah comes to believe that everyone she sees in the glass—or photographs—dies but maybe she's just going crazy. **89m/C DVD.** Lisa Vidal, David Chisum, Joshua Pelegrin, Christine Lakin, Lupe Ontiveros, Jim Storm; ***D:*** Pablo Proenza; ***W:*** Pablo Proenza, Matthew Reynolds; ***C:*** Armando Salas; ***M:*** Pieter A. Schlosser, Isaac Sprintis.

Dark Mountain 🦴 1/2 **1944** A forest ranger rescues his gal from the clutches of a hardened criminal. **56m/B VHS, DVD.** Robert Lowery, Ellen Drew, Regis Toomey, Eddie Quillan, Elisha Cook Jr.; ***D:*** William Berke, William C. Thomas; ***W:*** Maxwell Shane; ***C:*** Fred H. Jackman Jr.; ***M:*** Willy Stahl.

Dark Night of the Scarecrow 🦴🦴 1/2 **1981** Thriller with a moral. Prejudiced townspeople execute a retarded man who was innocently befriended by a young girl. After his death unusual things begin to happen. Slow to start but effective. **100m/C VHS.** Charles Durning, Tanya Crowe, Larry Drake; ***D:*** Frank De Felitta. **TV**

Dark Obsession 🦴🦴 *Diamond Skulls* **1990 (R)** Byrne portrays a husband who lives out his dark erotic fantasies with his wife (Donohoe), and is involved in a hit-and-run accident. Driven by guilt, madness slowly begins to take him. Ugly and depressing. Based on a true scandal. Available in an "NC-17" rated version. **87m/C VHS, DVD.** Peter Allen, Gabriel Byrne, Amanda Donohoe, Michael Hordern, Judy Parfitt, Douglas Hodge, Sadie Frost, Ian Carmichael; ***D:*** Nick Broomfield; ***W:*** Tim Rose Price; ***C:*** Michael Coulter; ***M:*** Hans Zimmer.

Dark Odyssey 🦴🦴 **1957** Metzger's first feature tells the tragic tale of a young Greek seaman who jumps ship in New York in order to avenge his sister's rape. He finds himself conflicted between his masculine sense of family honor and love when he falls for a Greek-American woman. Director's cut includes the original theatrical trailer. **85m/B VHS, DVD.** David Hooks, Edward Brazier, Jeanne Jerrems; ***D:*** William Kyriakis, Radley Metzger; ***W:*** William Kyriakis, Radley Metzger; ***C:*** Peter Erik Winkler; ***M:*** Laurence Rosenthal.

Dark of the Night 🦴🦴 1/2 *Mr. Wrong* **1985** A young woman, new to the city, purchases a used Jaguar and finds she must share it with the car's former owner—a woman murdered inside the Jag. Decent psycho-thriller with some suspenseful and amusing moments. **88m/C VHS.** *NZ* Heather Bolton, David Letch, Gary Stalker, Michael Haigh, Danny Mulheron, Kate Harcourt; ***D:*** Gaylene Preston; ***W:*** Gaylene Preston, Geoff Murphy, Graham Tetley; ***C:*** Thomas Burstyn; ***M:*** Jonathan Crayford.

Dark of the Sun 🦴🦴 1/2 *The Mercenaries* **1968 (PG)** Lots of action; routine plot. Taylor is a tough mercenary hired to retrieve a supply of uncut diamonds from a beseiged town in the Congo during the 1950s rebellion. Oh, and if he can help out the town's inhabitants, that's okay too. Based on the novel by Wilbur A. Smith. **101m/C VHS.** *GB* Rod Taylor, Jim Brown, Yvette Mimieux, Kenneth More, Peter Carsten, Calvin Lockhart, Andre Morell; ***D:*** Jack Cardiff; ***W:*** Quentin Werty, Adrian Spies; ***M:*** Jacques Loussier.

Dark Passage 🦴🦴 1/2 **1947** Bogart plays a convict who escapes from San Quentin to prove he was framed for the murder of his wife. He undergoes plastic surgery and is hidden and aided by Bacall as he tries to find the real killer. Stars can't quite compensate for a far-fetched script and so-so direction. **107m/B VHS, DVD.** Humphrey Bogart, Lauren Bacall, Agnes Moorehead, Bruce Bennett, Tom D'Andrea; ***D:*** Delmer Daves.

The Dark Past 🦴🦴🦴 **1949** A crazy, escaped convict holds a psychologist and his family hostage, and the two men engage in psychological cat-and-mouse combat. An underrated thriller with off-beat casting. **75m/B VHS.** William Holden, Lee J. Cobb, Nina Foch, Adele Jergens; ***D:*** Rudolph Mate; ***M:*** George Duning.

Dark Places 🦴🦴 **1973 (PG)** Masquerading as a hospital administrator, a former mental patient inherits the ruined mansion of a man who had killed his wife and children and died insane. As he lives in the house, the spirit of its former owner seems to overcome him with a need to repeat the crime. Meanwhile, Lee, Collins, and Lom think the nut is hiding money they would like to get their collective hands on. Low-budget but fairly effective. **91m/C VHS.** *GB* Joan Collins, Christopher Lee, Robert Hardy; ***D:*** Don Sharp.

Dark Planet 🦴🦴 **1997 (R)** In the year 2636 Earth is in the middle of WW6 and it's up to rebel commander Hawke (Mercurio) to search for the Dark Planet and complete a secret assignment that is humanity's last hope. **99m/C VHS, DVD.** Paul Mercurio, Harley Jane Kozak, Michael York, Maria Ford, Ed O'Ross; ***D:*** Albert Magnoli; ***W:*** S.O. Lee; ***C:*** William MacCollum.

The Dark Power 🦴 **1985** Ex-cowboy LaRue and his trusty whip provide this flick with its only excitement. As sheriff, he must deal with the dead Mexican warriors who rise to wreak havoc when a house is built on their burial ground. **87m/C VHS, DVD.** Lash LaRue, Anna Lane Tatum; ***D:*** Phil Smoot.

Dark Remains 🦴🦴 **2005 (R)** Scary little indie horror flick. Allen and Julie are devastated when their young daughter Emma is murdered in her bed. They rent a remote mountain cabin hoping the distance will help them heal, but photographer Julie sees Emma's ghostly image in the pictures she's taking. Seems the cabin has been the spot of numerous suicides and Emma is trying to warn her parents to get out. **91m/C DVD.** Greg Thompson, Cheri Christian, Rachel Jordan, Jeff Evans, Scott Hodges; ***D:*** Brian Avenet-Bradley; ***W:*** Brian Avenet-Bradley; ***C:*** Laurence Avenet-Bradley; ***M:*** Benedikt Bryden.

The Dark Ride 🦴 1/2 *Killer's Delight* **1978** Lunatic picks up women with the intention of raping and killing them. Ugly thriller based on the evil deeds of serial murderer Ted Bundy. **83m/C VHS.** James Luisi, Susan Sullivan, Martin Speer; ***D:*** Jeremy Hoenack.

Dark Rider **1991** Dark Rider is a mysterious, motorcycle riding hero who comes to the rescue of a small town. Besieged by a gangster who buys up all their land, the townspeople must abandon their homes and indeed, their very dreams. That is until Dark Rider rolls into to town to enact his own unique brand of vengeance. **94m/C VHS.** Joe Estevez, Doug Shanklin, Alicia Kowalski, David "Shark" Fralick, Chuck Williams; ***D:*** Bob Ivy; ***W:*** Bob Ivy, Chuck Williams; ***C:*** Mark W. Gray; ***M:*** Brad Scott Gish.

Dark River: A Father's Revenge 🦴🦴 **1990** When his daughter is killed in a toxic waste dump accident, a man begins revenge on the company and its managers. Tense, with important message. **95m/C VHS.** Helen Hunt, Mike Farrell, Tess Harper, Philip Baker Hall; ***D:*** Michael Pressman. **TV**

Dark Sanity **WOOF!** *Straight Jacket* **1982** Uninvolving attempt at horror has a recently de-institutionalized woman envisioning death and destruction (something you'll wish the film would do) while everyone else just thinks she's losing her marbles. Problem is we don't really care. **89m/C VHS.** Aldo Ray, Kory Clark, Andy Gwyn, Bobby Holt; ***D:*** Martin Greene.

The Dark Secret of Harvest Home 🦴🦴 1/2 **1978** An urban couple confront a pagan cult in the New England town into which they've moved. Based upon the Thomas Tryon novel. **118m/C VHS.** Bette Davis, Rosanna Arquette, David Ackroyd, Rene Auberjonois, Michael O'Keefe, Joanna Miles; ***D:*** Leo Penn; ***W:*** Jennifer Miller, Jack Guss; ***Nar:*** Donald Pleasence. **TV**

Dark Secrets 🦴 **1995 (R)** Reporter Claire (Parent) wants to get a hot story on sex club mogul Justin DeVille (Carroll) and winds up falling prey to his charms. But Justin's not the trusting kind and sets up some loyalty tests for Claire. The unrated version is 99 minutes. **90m/C VHS, DVD.** Monique Parent, Julie Strain, Justin Carroll; ***D:***

John Bowen; ***W:*** Steve Tymon; ***C:*** Keith Holland; ***M:*** Efrem Bergman.

Dark Side *Darkness Falling* **2002 (R)** While investigating the suicide of her twin sister Jane, corporate lawyer Megan (Kidder) discovers that Jane was involved with the lurid underworld of kinky sex and a mysterious lover. **85m/C VHS, DVD.** *CA GB* Janet Kidder, Jason Priestley, Patsy Kensit, Paul Johansson; ***D:*** Dominic Shiach; ***W:*** Sheldon Inkol; ***C:*** Harry Makin.

Dark Side of Genius **1994 (R)** Jennifer Cole (Hughes), a reporter for an L.A. arts weekly, tries to get the story on artist Julian Jons (Fraser), who's just been paroled after being imprisoned for the murder of his model. Now his lurid new paintings of a sultry nude model hint at some obsessive behavior and Jennifer's reporter instincts may be the death of her. **86m/C VHS.** Finola Hughes, Brendan Fraser, Glenn Shadix, Moon Zappa, Patrick Richwood, Seymour Cassel; ***D:*** Phedon Papamichael; ***W:*** Fred Stroppel; ***C:*** Phedon Papamichael; ***M:*** Tom Hiel.

The Dark Side of Love ½ **1979** A young girl gets involved with the rougher side of New Orleans society, gets pregnant, and realizes how she's been degraded. **94m/C VHS.** James Stacy, Glynnis O'Connor, Jan Sterling, Mickey Rooney; ***D:*** Sam Wanamaker; ***C:*** Michael D. Margulies. **TV**

Dark Side of Midnight ½ *The Creeper* **1986 (R)** A super-detective tracks down a psychopathic killer. **108m/C VHS, DVD.** James Moore, Wes Olsen, Sandy Schemmel, Dave Bowling; ***D:*** Wes Olsen; ***W:*** Wes Olsen; ***C:*** Wes Olsen.

The Dark Side of the Heart *El Lado Oscuro del Corazon* **1992** Magic realism features in this story of struggling Buenos Aires poet Oliverio (Grandinetti) who falls in love with prostitute Ana (Ballesteros). She wants to keep things businesslike but when a man finds a woman whose lovemaking causes them to actually levitate, he's not about to make things easy. Spanish with subtitles. **127m/C VHS, DVD.** *CA AR* Dario Grandinetti, Sandra Ballesteros, Nacha Guevara; ***D:*** Eliseo Subiela; ***W:*** Eliseo Subiela; ***C:*** Hugo Colace; ***M:*** Osvaldo Montes. Montreal World Film Fest. '92: Film.

Dark Side of the Moon **1990 (R)** Members of a space ship sent on a routine mission to the far side of the moon, discover an unknown force that feeds on human emotion and consumes the soul. Lukewarm science fiction/horror. **96m/C VHS.** William Bledsoe, Alan Blumenfeld, John Diehl, Robert Sampson, Wendy MacDonald, Camilla More, Joe Turkel; ***D:*** D.J. Webster.

The Dark Side of the Sun **1988 (R)** Pitt stars as a dying young man, traveling the world in search of a cure, who meets the woman of his dreams. Pitt's feature film debut. **107m/C VHS.** Brad Pitt, Cheryl Pollak, Guy Boyd.

Dark Star **1974 (G)** John Carpenter's directorial debut is a low-budget, sci-fi satire which focuses on a group of scientists whose mission is to destroy unstable planets. During their journey, they battle their alien mascot (who closely resembles a walking beach ball), as well as a "sensitive" and intelligent bombing device which starts to question the meaning of its existence. Enjoyable early feature from John "Halloween" Carpenter and Dan "Aliens" O'Bannon. Fun, weird, and unpredictable. **95m/C VHS, DVD.** Dan O'Bannon, Brian Narelle, Dre Pahich, Cal Duniholm; ***D:*** John Carpenter; ***W:*** John Carpenter, Dan O'Bannon; ***C:*** Douglas Knapp; ***M:*** John Carpenter.

Dark Streets **2008 (R)** Musical film noir turns out to be an unsuccessful mix that's not helped by the wooden acting (although the elaborate production numbers are well-staged). Set in the 1930s, nightclub owner Chaz Davenport (Mann) is having financial woes (he owes money to the mob) and dumps his singer girlfriend (Phillips) for another talented babe (Miko). Then there's some stuff about Davenport's dad, who maybe didn't commit suicide, and corporate corruption with the family firm but it doesn't add up to much. Based on the 2004 stage musical "The City Club" by Glenn M. Stewart. **83m/C DVD.** *US* Gabriel Mann, Bijou Phillips, Izabella Miko, Elias Koteas, Michael Fairman, Toledo Diamond; ***D:*** Rachel Samuels; ***W:*** Wallace King; ***C:*** Sharon Meir; ***M:*** George Acogny.

Dark Tide **1993 (R)** Erotic action thriller about a pair of deep sea divers whose love life is disturbed when their boat captain becomes sexually fixated on the woman. Also available in an uncut, unrated version. **92m/C VHS.** Brigitte Bako, Richard Tyson, Chris Sarandon; ***D:*** Luca Bercovici.

Dark Tower **1987 (R)** Decent cast is wasted in yet another inept attempt at horror. An architect is dismayed to learn that an evil force is inhabiting her building and it might just be the ghost of her dearly departed husband. **91m/C VHS.** Michael Moriarty, Jenny Agutter, Theodore Bikel, Carol Lynley, Anne Lockhart, Kevin McCarthy; ***D:*** Ken Barnett, Freddie Francis, Ken Wiederhorn; ***W:*** Robert J. Avrech, Ken Blackwell.

Dark Town **2004 (R)** Low-budget vampire flick that rarely makes sense although it really doesn't need a plot. A slumlord gets turned into a bloodsucker, goes homes to the 'burbs, and infects his family during a convenient blackout. Apparently, the only two not to succumb are a lesbian daughter (yeah, there's some gratuitous girl-on-girl action) and a black gang banger who wants revenge on the slumlord. Or something. Lots of blood and gore. **88m/C DVD.** Joe King, Janet Martin, Delpano Willis, Sarah Horvath, Meghan Stansfield, Curtis Nysmith; ***D:*** Desi Scarpone; ***W:*** David J. Burke; ***C:*** Adam Tash; ***M:*** Mark Fontana. **VIDEO**

Dark Universe ½ **1993 (R)** An alien terror wants to conquer the Earth and make its inhabitants their new food source. **83m/C VHS, DVD.** Blake Pickett, Cherie Scott, Bently Tittle, John Maynard, Paul Austin Saunders, Tom Ferguson, Steve Barkett, Joe Estevez, Patrick Moran; ***D:*** Steve Latshaw; ***W:*** Patrick Moran.

Dark Victory ½ **1939** A spoiled young heiress discovers she is dying from a brain tumor. She attempts to pack a lifetime of parties into a few months, but is rescued by her doctor, with whom she falls in love. Classic final scene with Davis at the top of her form. Bogart plays an Irish stable hand, but not especially well. Also available in a colorized version. **106m/B VHS, DVD.** Bette Davis, George Brent, Geraldine Fitzgerald, Humphrey Bogart, Ronald Reagan, Henry Travers; ***D:*** Edmund Goulding; ***W:*** Casey Robinson; ***C:*** Ernest Haller; ***M:*** Max Steiner.

Dark Water *Honogurai mizu no soko kara* **2002 (PG-13)** Yoshimi Matsubara is in the middle of a brutal divorce and custody battle. Normally the case would weigh heavily in her favor because of the Japanese Court's preference for letting children be raised by the mother. But Yoshimi has a history of mental imbalance due to a problematic childhood. The stress of the divorce and her conversion to a working single mother is weighing on her heavily. When she moves into a new apartment with her young daughter, bizarre frightening occurrences begin; she initially believes her husband is trying to make her crack to get sole custody. But then a small girl begins appearing and disappearing inside the apartment. **100m/C DVD.** *JP* Hitomi Kuroki, Fumiyo Kohinata, Yu Tokui, Isao Yatsu, Kiriko Shimizu, Rio Kanno, Mirei Oguchi, Asami Mizukawa, Shigemitsu Ogi, Maiko Asano, Yukiko Ikari, Shinji Nomura, Teruko Hanahara, Youko Yatsuda, Kono Tarou Suwa, Shichiro Gou, Sachiko Hara, Toru Shinagawa, Chihiro Otsuka, Takashige Ichise, Yoshihiro Nakamura; ***D:*** Hideo Nakata; ***W:*** Hideo Nakata, Koji Suzuki, Kenichi Suzuki; ***C:*** Junichiro Hayashi; ***M:*** Kenji Kawai, Shikao Suga.

Dark Water **2002 (PG-13)** Dahlia Williams' (Connelly) soon-to-be ex-husband tells her she's nuts and she wonders if he might be right when she moves with her five-year-old daughter Ceci (Gabe) into a dilapidated and perhaps, yes, haunted Roosevelt Island apartment that is plagued by creepy noises from a supposedly vacant flat upstairs. Then there's that little-but-quickly-expanding water stain on the ceiling that seems a little...alive. Tries to be spooky but is just all wet. Based on Hideo Nakata's 2002 Japanese horror film of the same name. **120m/C DVD, Blu-ray Disc, UMD.** *US* Ariel Gade, Jennifer Connelly, John C. Reilly, Tim Roth, Pete Postlethwaite, Dougray Scott, Camryn Manheim, Perla Haney-Jardine, Debra Monk, Elina Lowensohn, Jennifer Baxter; ***D:*** Walter Salles; ***W:*** Rafael Yglesias; ***C:*** Alfonso Beato; ***M:*** Angelo Badalamenti.

Dark Waters **1944** The drowning death of her parents has left a young woman mentally unstable. She returns to her family home in the backwaters of Louisiana with her peculiar aunt and uncle to serve as guardians. It eventually becomes apparent that someone is trying to drive her insane. This one tends to be rather murky and it's not simply due to the plentiful scenes of misty swampland. **93m/B VHS, DVD.** Merle Oberon, Franchot Tone, Thomas Mitchell, Fay Bainter, Elisha Cook Jr., John Qualen, Rex Ingram; ***D:*** Andre de Toth; ***W:*** Joan Harrison, Marian Cockrell; ***C:*** Archie Stout, John Mescall; ***M:*** Miklos Rozsa.

The Dark Wind ½ **1991 (R)** The first of Tony Hillerman's popular Native American mysteries comes to the screen in a lame adaptation. Phillips stars as the Navaho cop investigating a murder on a New Mexico Indian reservation. Since the Navaho believe a "dark wind" enters a man's soul when he does evil, expect some "spirited" goings-on as well. **111m/C VHS, DVD.** Lou Diamond Phillips; ***D:*** Errol Morris; ***W:*** Eric Bergren.

Dark World ½ **2008 (R)** The ex factor. Ex-L.A. cop Harry Boyd (Pare) teams up with his ex-partner Bob (Berg) to solve a series of missing person cases. Then Grace (Graham), the niece of Harry's ex-wife Nicole (Russell), goes missing, so Nicole and her boyfriend Rick (Bauer) travel from Vegas to help out. And soon everyone is suspected of something. **90m/C DVD.** Michael Pare, Theresa Russell, Steven Bauer, Julie St. Claire, Charles Arthur Berg, James Russo, Jen Graham, Trevor Stevens; ***D:*** Zia Mojabi; ***W:*** Zia Mojabi; ***C:*** Tom Hejda; ***M:*** P. Daniel Newman. **VIDEO**

Darkdrive ½ **1998 (R)** In the near future, the Zircon Corporation has created a virtual prison where the minds of criminals are held in isolation. Naturally, something's gone wrong and it's up to special operations officer Steven Falcon (Olandt) to risk his mind and solve the problem. **100m/C VHS, DVD.** Ken Olandt, Julie Benz, Claire Stansfield, Carlo Scandiuzzi; ***D:*** Phillip J. Roth; ***W:*** Alec Carlin; ***C:*** Andres Garreton; ***M:*** Jim Goodwin. **VIDEO**

Darker than Amber **1970 (R)** John D. MacDonald's houseboat-dwelling detective Travis McGee (Taylor) rescues a girl (Kendall) he's fallen for, and soon discovers that the mugs who thugged her were part of a collection racket. A violent action melodrama upgraded from its original "R" rating. **96m/C VHS.** Rod Taylor, Suzy Kendall, Theodore Bikel, Jane Russell, James Booth, Janet MacLachlan, William (Bill) Smith, Ahna Capri, Chris Robinson; ***D:*** Robert Clouse.

Darkest Africa *Batmen of Africa; King of the Jungleland* **1936** Legendary animal trainer Beatty is the hero of this 15 episode cliffhanger serial as he vies with beasts—both animal and human. **270m/B VHS.** Edmund Cobb, Clyde Beatty, Manuel King, Elaine Shepard; ***D:*** Joseph Kane, B. Reeves Eason; ***W:*** Barney A. Sarecky.

Darklight **2004 (R)** Really, waifish Shiri Appleby as some kind of formerly evil immortal? No wonder it's claptrap (from the Sci-Fi Channel of course). Lilith was the first woman created but is damned after rejecting God. One of those secret religious societies subdues her, wipes her memory, and has her living as a human. A disillusioned member of the society transforms himself into some creature called Demonicus and only Lilith, using her previously-hidden Darklight power, can stop the apocalypse. **89m/C DVD.** Shiri Appleby, David Hewlett, Richard Burgi, John de Lancie, Ross Manarchy; ***D:*** Bill Platt; ***W:*** Bill Platt, Chris Regina; ***C:*** Lorenzo Senatore; ***M:*** John Dickson. **CABLE**

Darkman **1990 (R)** Raimi's disfigured-man-seeks-revenge suspenser is comicbook kitsch cross-pollinated with a strain of gothic horror. Neeson plays a scientist who's on the verge of discovering the key to cloning body parts; brutally attacked by the henchmen of a crooked politico, his lab is destroyed and he's left for dead. Turns out he's not dead—just horribly disfigured and a wee bit chafed—and he stalks his deserving victims from the shadows, using his lab know-how to disguise his rugged bad looks. Exquisitely violent. Montage by Pablo Ferro. **96m/C VHS, DVD, HD DVD.** Liam Neeson, Frances McDormand, Larry Drake, Colin Friels, Nelson Mashita, Jenny Agutter, Rafael H. Robledo, Nicholas Worth, Theodore (Ted) Raimi, John Landis, William Lustig, Scott Spiegel, Bruce Campbell; ***D:*** Sam Raimi; ***W:*** Sam Raimi, Ivan Raimi, Daniel Goldin, Joshua Goldin, Chuck Pfarrer; ***C:*** Bill Pope; ***M:*** Danny Elfman.

Darkman 2: The Return of Durant ½ **1994 (R)** The first in a series of direct-to-video adventures about disfigured scientist Peyton "Darkman" Westlake (now played by Vosloo), who's continuing his liquid skin research in the hopes of transforming his grotesque appearance. He finds an ally in scientist David Brinkman but Westlake's nemesis, crime boss Robert G. Durant (Drake), wants the property where Brinkman's lab is located. And what Durant wants, he takes. Sam Raimi, who directed the original film, is one of the series producers. **93m/C VHS, DVD.** Arnold Vosloo, Larry Drake, Kim Delaney, Renee O'Connor, Rod Wilson; ***D:*** Bradford May; ***W:*** Steven McKay, Chuck Pfarrer; ***C:*** Bradford May; ***M:*** Randy Miller. **VIDEO**

Darkman 3: Die Darkman Die ½ **1995 (R)** The second direct-to-video Darkman saga finds Dr. Peyton Westlake (Vosloo) disrupting the drug-dealing activities of underworld boss Peter Rooker (Fahey). The obsessed Rooker is determined to figure out the secret to Darkman's enormous strength, employing the feminine wiles of his mistress, Dr. Bridget Thorne (Fluegel). Then Westlake/Darkman finds himself drawn to Rooker's neglected wife and young daughter. Our hero suffers a lot (as usual) and there's lots of action (as usual). **87m/C VHS.** Arnold Vosloo, Jeff Fahey, Darlanne Fluegel, Nigel Bennett, Roxann Biggs-Dawson; ***D:*** Bradford May; ***W:*** Mike Werb, Michael Colleary; ***C:*** Bradford May; ***M:*** Randy Miller.

Darkness **2002 (PG-13)** Spanish director Balaguero follows up his debut feature, "The Nameless," with a haunted house chiller that fails its fright quotient. Americans Mark (Glen), his wife Maria (Olin), and their kids Regina (Paquin) and Paul (Enquist) relocate to a rural house somewhere in Spain. Various paranormal experiences begin to occur, which Regina's parents ignore. Her little brother develops unexplained bruises and becomes afraid of the dark. Regina finds out the house has a disturbing history involving children who disappeared. Should have been more scary. **102m/C DVD.** *US* Lena Olin, Iain Glen, Giancarlo Giannini, Fele Martinez, Anna Paquin, Fermi Rexach, Stephen Enquist; ***D:*** Jaume Balaguero; ***W:*** Jaume Balaguero, Fernando de Felipe; ***C:*** Xavi Gimenez; ***M:*** Carles Cases.

Darkness Falls **1998 (R)** John Barrett (Winstone) is looking for revenge. His adulterous wife Jane (McCaffrey) was critically injured in a car crash from which her lover escaped. So John goes to the Driscoll home and decides to terrorize Jane's boyfriend Mark (Dutton) and his unsuspecting wife Sally (Fenn). Filmed on the Isle of Man, which may be the most interesting thing about this routine thriller. **91m/C VHS, DVD.** Sherilyn Fenn, Ray Winstone, Tim Dutton, Robin McCaffrey, Oliver Tobias, Michael Praed; ***D:*** Gerry Lively; ***W:*** John Howlett; ***C:*** Adam Santelli; ***M:*** Guy Farley.

Darkness Falls ½ **2003 (PG-13)** In the small New England town of Darkness Falls (aren't you asking for trouble when you name a town that?), young Kyle Walsh witnesses his mother's murder by a ghost who was wrongfully hanged 150 years earlier. Known as the Tooth Fairy, the spirit takes her revenge on the children of the town after they lose the last of their baby teeth. Twelve years later, Kyle is living in Las Vegas, psychologically scarred and paranoid from his encounter. Knowing that the ghost only comes in the dark, he surrounds himself with light. Caitlin (Caulfield), his childhood girlfriend, asks him to come back and help her younger brother, who's starting to have the same nightmares that Kyle use to have. Genuinely scary moments overcome some obvious plot devices.

Wisely, the movie is restrained and delivers on spooky atmosphere. **85m/C VHS, DVD.** *US* Chaney Kley, Emma Caulfield, Lee Cormie, Grant Piro, Sullivan Stapleton, Steve Mouzakis, Peter Curtin; *D:* Jonathan Liebesman; *W:* John Fasano, James Vanderbilt, Joe Harris; *C:* Dan Laustsen; *M:* Brian Tyler.

Darkroom ✐ 1/2 **1990** An unstable young man devises a scheme to photograph his father in bed with his mistress, and then use the pics to blackmail dear ol' dad. **90m/C VHS, DVD.** Jill Pierce, Jeffrey Allen Arbaugh, Sara Lee Wade, Aaron Teich; *D:* Terrence O'Hara. **VIDEO**

The Darkside ✐ 1/2 **1987 (R)** In this frightening drama, a young prostitute and an innocent cabbie attempt to escape the clutches of a maniacal film producer with a secret he won't let them reveal. **95m/C VHS, DVD.** Tony Galati, Cynthia (Cyndy, Cindy) Preston; *D:* Constantino Magnatta.

Darktown Strutters ✐ *Get Down and Boogie* **1974 (PG)** Effort to satirize racial stereotypes is humorless and ineffective. Black female motorcycle gang searches for the kidnapped mother of one of the members. **85m/C VHS.** Trina Parks, Roger E. Mosley, Shirley Washington; *D:* William Witney.

Darkwolf ✐ 1/2 **2003 (R)** A werewolf (Hodder) is stalking Los Angeles in search of newbie Josie (Armstrong) so they can mate and perpetuate the species. Detective Steve Turley (Alosio) wants to protect her from the big bad beast. Limited special effects and an overly confusing plot for the genre. **94m/C VHS, DVD.** Samaire Armstrong, Kane Hodder, Ryan Alosio, Tippi Hedren, Steven Williams, Jaime Bergman, Alexis Cruz; *D:* Richard Friedman; *W:* Geoffrey Alan Holliday; *C:* Stuart Asbjornsen; *M:* Geoff Levin. **VIDEO**

Darling ✐✐✐ 1/2 **1965** Amoral young model Diana Scott (Christie) tries to hold boredom at bay by having a number of love affairs. She moves from intellectual Robert (Bogarde) to playboy Miles (Harvey) and eventually joins the international jet set and manages to reach the top of European society by marrying a prince. Diana then learns what an empty life she has. Christie won an Oscar for her portrayal of the disillusioned, cynical young woman. **122m/B VHS, DVD.** *GB* Julie Christie, Dirk Bogarde, Laurence Harvey, Jose-Luis De Villalonga, Roland Curram; *D:* John Schlesinger; *W:* Frederic Raphael; *C:* Ken Higgins; *M:* John Dankworth. Oscars '65: Actress (Christie), Costume Des. (B&W), Story & Screenplay; British Acad. '65: Actor (Bogarde), Actress (Christie), Screenplay; Golden Globes '66: Foreign Film; Natl. Bd. of Review '65: Actress (Christie), Director (Schlesinger); N.Y. Film Critics '65: Actress (Christie), Director (Schlesinger), Film.

Darling Lili ✐✐ 1/2 **1970** Big-budget WWI spy comedy/musical with Andrews as a German agent posing as an English music hall performer, who falls in love with squadron leader Hudson and finds she can't betray him. A critical flop when first released, film has its charms though director Edwards did much better for Andrews in "Victor/Victoria." ♫ Whistling Away the Dark; The Girl In No Man's Land; Smile Away Each Rainy Day; I'll Give You Three Guesses; Your Good Will Ambassador; Darling Lili; The Little Birds. **136m/C VHS, DVD.** Julie Andrews, Rock Hudson, Jeremy Kemp, Jacques Marin, Michael Witney, Vernon Dobtcheff; *D:* Blake Edwards; *W:* Blake Edwards, William Peter Blatty; *M:* Henry Mancini, Johnny Mercer. Golden Globes '71: Song ("Whistling Away the Dark").

Darlings of the Gods ✐✐ 1/2 **1990** The glittering marriage of actors Sir Laurence Olivier and Vivien Leigh is just as dramatic as anything on stage or screen as Olivier's devotion to work and Leigh's fragile mental and physical health put their relationship on a star-crossed path. **180m/C VHS.** *GB* Anthony (Corlan) Higgins, Mel Martin, Jerome Ehlers, Rhys McConnochie, Lindy Davies, Shane Briant, Anthony Hawkins, Jackie Kelleher; *D:* Catherine Millar; *W:* Roger Simpson, Graeme Farmer; *M:* Brian May. **TV**

The Darwin Awards ✐ 1/2 **2006 (R)** Lumpy, leaden comedy. The Darwin Awards are given (posthumously) to those who die in the most stupid and preventable ways. Michael (Fiennes), a former San Francisco forensic detective-turned-insurance profiler, is paired up with claims investigator Siri (Ryder) and a film student (Valderrama) who's taping their investigations as they try to identify possible victims and prevent their demise (thus saving the insurance firm lots of pay-outs). There's also a serial killer (Nelson), who previously escaped Michael, that figures in the plot. Last role for Chris Penn. **90m/C DVD.** Joseph Fiennes, Winona Ryder, Wilmer Valderrama, Tim Blake Nelson, David Arquette, Ty Burrell, Alessandro Nivola, Tom Hollander, Julianna Margulies, Christopher Penn, David Perlich; *D:* Finn Taylor; *W:* Finn Taylor; *C:* Hiro Narita; *M:* David Kitay.

The Darwin Conspiracy WOOF! **1999 (PG)** Scientist uncovers a plot to conduct radical experiments in human intelligence using his retarded brother and a prehistoric body. Inept execution of a half-baked idea. **90m/C VHS.** Kevin Tighe, Jason Brooks, Robert Floyd, Stacy Haiduk; *D:* Winrich (Rich) Kolbe; *W:* Glen Larson; *C:* Mark Melville; *M:* Rob Walsh.

Darwin's Darkest Hour ✐✐ **2009** Charles Darwin (Cusick) has been writing his evolutionary opus "On the Origins of Species" for 20 years, fretting over completing his controversial work. But in 1858, Darwin receives a letter from naturalist Alfred Russell Wallace (Bevan-John) that shows similar conclusions. So Darwin must decide whether to publish—and knowingly take on religious opposition—or let others present their theories first. **104m/C DVD.** *GB* Henry Ian Cusick, Frances O'Connor, Alfred Russell Wallace; *D:* John Bradshaw; *W:* John Goldsmith; *C:* Christopher Ball; *M:* Charles Bernstein. **TV**

Darwin's Nightmare ✐✐✐ 1/2 **2004** Compelling documentary probing the traumatic economic and social effects on the people of Tanzania by the 1960s introduction of the non-native Nile perch fish to Lake Victoria, which has since depleted the lake of over 200 natural species. Without the guidance of voiceovers, director/writer Sauper depicts the local citizens' poor living conditions, as they don't benefit from the country's Nile perch industry—in fact, most struggle to survive on little food (the fish are too costly) and small wages (even with the highly hazardous nature of fishing on Victoria) despite the great profits that perch shipments to Europe and Russia bring to the government. **107m/C DVD.** *D:* Hubert Sauper; *W:* Hubert Sauper; *C:* Hubert Sauper.

D.A.R.Y.L. ✐✐ **1985 (PG)** The little boy found by the side of the road is too polite, too honest and too smart. His friend explains to him the necessity of imperfection (If you don't want the grown-ups to bother you too much) and he begins to become more like a real little boy. But the American military has a top-secret interest in this child, since he is in fact the combination of a cloned body and a computer brain. More interesting when it's involved with the human beings and less so when it focuses on science. **100m/C VHS, DVD.** Mary Beth Hurt, Michael McKean, Barret Oliver, Colleen Camp, Danny Corkill; *D:* Simon Wincer; *W:* David Ambrose, Allan Scott; *M:* Marvin Hamlisch.

Das Boot ✐✐✐✐ *The Boat* **1981 (R)** Superb detailing of life in a German U-boat during WWII. Intense, claustrophobic atmosphere complemented by nail-biting action provides a realistic portrait of the stressful conditions that were endured on these submarines. Excellent performances, especially from Prochnow. In German with subtitles. From the novel by Lothar-Guenther Buccheim. Originally a six-hour special made for German TV. **210m/C VHS, DVD.** *GE* Jurgen Prochnow, Herbert Gronemeyer, Klaus Wennemann, Hubertus Bengsch, Martin Semmelrogge, Bernd Tauber, Erwin Leder, Martin May, Heinz Honig, Uwe Ochsenknecht, Claude-Oliver Rudolph, Jan Fedder, Ralph Richer, Joachim Bernhard, Oliver Stritzel, Konrad Becker, Lutz Schnell, Martin Hemme, Rita Cadillac; *D:* Wolfgang Petersen; *W:* Wolfgang Petersen; *C:* Jost Vacano; *M:* Klaus Doldinger. **TV**

Dash and Lilly ✐✐ 1/2 **1999** Depicts the 30-year love affair between hard-drinking, promiscuous writers Dashiell Hammett (Shepard) and Lillian Hellman (Davis). Meeting in the 1930s, the successful Hammett becomes the up-and-coming Hellman's mentor. Though both are married, they also begin an affair. Eventually, their positions are reversed as Hammett's career declines and, after serving in WWII, he becomes increasingly plagued by ill health. Meanwhile, playwright Hellman has her own trials when she's blacklisted in the '50s during the Red Scare. **100m/C VHS.** Sam Shepard, Judy Davis, David Paymer, Bebe Neuwirth, Laurence Luckinbill, Zeljko Ivanek, Ned Eisenberg, Mark Zimmerman; *D:* Kathy Bates; *W:* Jerry Ludwig; *C:* Bruce Surtees; *M:* Laura Karpman. **CABLE**

Date Bait ✐ **1960** When a teen couple decides—much to their parents' chagrin—to elope, they find themselves on a date with danger when their post-nuptuals are plagued by pushers and assorted other bad guys. **71m/B VHS, DVD.** Gary Clarke, Marlo Ryan, Richard Gering, Danny Logan; *D:* O'Dale Ireland.

Date Movie ✐ 1/2 **2006 (PG-13)** Shameless mockery of romantic movies such as "My Big Fat Greek Wedding" and "Meet the Fockers" can't make it to first base. Obese Julia (Hannigan) is looking for love and freedom from her overbearing African-American "Greek" dad (Griffin) when she meets handsome Brit Grant Funckyerdoder and seeks the aid of a "Hitch"-like date doctor (Cox) to shape up. Penned by two of the "Scary Movie" series writers. **83m/C DVD, UMD.** *US* Alyson Hannigan, Eddie Griffin, Fred Willard, Jennifer Coolidge, Adam Campbell, Sophie Monk, Meera Simhan, Marie Matiko, Judah Friedlander, Carmen Electra, Tony Cox, Valery Ortiz; *D:* Aaron Seltzer; *W:* Aaron Seltzer, Jason Friedberg; *C:* Shawn Maurer; *M:* David Kitay. Golden Raspberries '06: Worst Support. Actress (Electra).

Date Night **2010** A married couple's usual dinner-and-a-movie date night turns into an adventure thanks to a case of mistaken identity, a con man, a cop, and a securities expert. **m/C DVD.** Tina Fey, Mark Ruffalo, James Franco, Leighton Meester, Taraji P. Henson, Kristen Wiig, Ray Liotta, Mila Kunis, Common, Steve Carrell; *D:* Shawn Levy, Josh Klausner; *W:* Tina Fey, Josh Klausner; *C:* Dean Semler; *M:* Christophe Beck.

Date with an Angel ✐ 1/2 **1987 (PG)** When aspiring musician Knight fishes a beautiful angel out of the swimming pool, he is just trying to rescue her. But the beauty of the angel overwhelms him and he finds himself questioning his upcoming wedding to Cates, a cosmetic mogul's daughter. Sickeningly cute and way too sentimental, though Beart's beauty is other-wordly. **105m/C VHS, DVD.** Charles Lane, Emmanuelle Beart, Michael E. Knight, Phoebe Cates, David Dukes, Bibi Besch, Albert Macklin, David Hunt, Michael Goodwin; *D:* Tom McLoughlin; *W:* Tom McLoughlin; *C:* Alex Thomson; *M:* Randy Kerber.

A Date with Judy ✐✐ **1948** Standard post-war musical dealing with teenage mix-ups in and around a big high school dance. Choreography by Stanley Donen. ♫ Cuanto La Gusto; Strictly on the Corny Side; It's a Most Unusual Day; Judaline; I've Got a Date with Judy; I'm Gonna Meet My Mary; Temptation; Mulligatawny. **114m/C VHS.** Jane Powell, Elizabeth Taylor, Carmen Miranda, Wallace Beery, Robert Stack, Xavier Cugat, Selena Royle, Leon Ames; *D:* Richard Thorpe; *C:* Robert L. Surtees.

Dating the Enemy ✐✐ **1995** War between the sexes comedy about two instantaneous lovers who have nothing in common. Tash (Karvan) is a serious journalist who falls for easy-going Brett (Pearce), the host of a musicvideo program. After a year of togetherness, Tash wishes macho Brett could understand what it's like to be a woman. Surprise! The duo mysteriously switch bodies and find their new sexual (and job) roles aren't easy. **104m/C VHS.** *AU* Claudia Karvan, Guy Pearce, Matt(hew) Day, Lisa Hensley, Pippa Grandison, John Howard; *D:* Megan Simpson; *W:* Megan Simpson; *C:* Steve Arnold; *M:* David Hirschfelder.

Daughter of Darkness ✐✐ 1/2 **1989 (R)** A young woman goes to Hungary in search of her family tree, only to discover vampires nestled there. **93m/C VHS.** Mia Sara, Anthony Perkins, Robert Reynolds, Jack Coleman; *D:* Stuart Gordon.

Daughter of Death ✐ *Julie Darling* **1982 (R)** A little mentally off-center since she witnessed the gruesome rape and murder of her mother, a teenage girl doesn't bond well with her new mom when dad remarries. **100m/C VHS, DVD.** *CA GE* Anthony (Tony) Franciosa, Isabelle Mejias, Sybil Danning, Cindy Girling, Paul Hubbard, Benjamin Schmoll; *D:* Paul Nicholas.

The Daughter of Dr. Jekyll ✐ 1/2 **1957** The doc's daughter believes she may have inherited her father's evil curse when several of the locals are found dead. Originally released in theaters on a double bill with "Dr. Cyclops." **71m/B VHS, DVD.** John Agar, Arthur Shields, John Dierkes, Gloria Talbott; *D:* Edgar G. Ulmer; *W:* Jack Pollexfen; *C:* John F. Warren; *M:* Melvyn Lenard.

Daughter of Don Q ✐✐ 1/2 **1946** Delores' father is very rich with a huge real estate empire and she is his only heir. Greedy cousin Carlos would like to change that—by killing Delores. Delores must dodge speeding cars, hurling harpoons, and more to escape Carlos' evil plot. Part of "The Cliffhanger Serials" series. **166m/B VHS.** Adrian Booth, Kirk Alyn, Leroy Mason; *D:* Fred Brannon, Spencer Gordon Bennet; *W:* Albert DeMond, Basil Dickey, Jesse Duffy, Lynn Perkins.

Daughter of Horror ✐✐ *Dementia* **1955** A young woman finds herself involved with a porcine mobster who resembles her abusive father. Trouble is, Dad's dead, and daughter dearest abetted his departure. Obscure venture into expressionism that was initially banned by the New York State Board of Censors. Shot on a low budget (how low was it? So low that McMahon narrated because shooting with sound was too expensive). The 55 minutes tend to lag, although the film should be intriguing to genre enthusiasts and to fans of things pseudo-Freudian. **60m/B VHS, DVD.** Adrienne Barrett, Ben Roseman, Richard Barron, Ed Hinkle, Lucille Howland, Angelo Rossitto, Bruno VeSota; *D:* John Parker; *W:* John Parker; *C:* William C. Thompson; *M:* George Antheil; *V:* Marni Nixon; *Nar:* Ed McMahon.

Daughter of Keltoum ✐✐ **2001** Rallia is 19 and has been raised by adoptive parents in Switzerland. She returns to her birthplace, a remote Berber settlement in Algeria, in order to learn from her mother Keltoum why she was abandoned as a baby. But when Rallia discovers that Keltoum is working in a luxury hotel in the city, she decides to travel there, accompanied by her Aunt Nedjma. The road trip opens Rallia's eyes to the harshness of Algerian life and finally meeting her mother leads to other revelations. French and Arabic with subtitles. **101m/C DVD.** *FR TU* Cylia Malki, Baya Belal, Deborah Lamy, Brahim Ben Salah; *D:* Mehdi Charef; *W:* Mehdi Charef; *C:* Alain Levent; *M:* Bernardo Sandoval.

Daughter of the Dragon ✐✐ **1931** Fu Manchu is again on the prowl, this time sending his daughter to murder Fletcher to avenge the death of his wife and son during China's Boxer Rebellion. Based on a Sax Rohmer story. **70m/B VHS.** Anna May Wong, Warner Oland, Sessue Hayakawa, Bramwell Fletcher, Holmes Herbert; *D:* Lloyd Corrigan.

Daughter of the Tong ✐ **1939** FBI agent gets tong twisted when he tries to put a lid on a smuggling ring headed by a woman (who's beautiful, of course). Something that resembles acting is wasted in a mess of a movie. **56m/B VHS, DVD.** Evelyn Brent, Grant Withers, Dorothy Short, Dave O'Brien; *D:* Bernard B. Ray.

Daughters of Darkness ✐✐✐ *Le Rouge aux Levres; Blut an den Lippen; Erzebeth; The Promise of Red Lips; The Red Lips* **1971 (R)** Newlyweds on their way to England stop at a posh French hotel. There they meet a beautiful woman whom the hotel owner swears had been there 40 years ago, even though she hasn't aged a bit. When she introduces herself as Countess of Bathory (the woman who bathed in the blood of virgins to stay young) folks begin to wonder. A really superb erotic vampire film charged with sensuality and a sense of dread. **87m/C VHS, DVD.** *BE GE IT FR* Delphine Seyrig, John Karlen, Daniele Ouimet, Andrea Rau, Paul Esser, Georges Jamin, Joris Collet, Fons Rademakers; *D:* Harry Kumel; *W:* Harry Kumel, Pierre Drouot, Jean Ferry; *C:* Eddy van der Enden; *M:* Francois de Roubaix.

Daughters of Satan 🦴🦴 **1972 (R)** Selleck, in an early role as a virile museum buyer, antagonizes a coven of witches when he purchases a painting. His wife, played by Grant, becomes a target of the witches' revenge and salacious shenanigans ensue. **96m/C VHS, DVD.** Tom Selleck, Barra Grant, Paraluman, Tani Phelps Guthrie; ***D:*** Hollingsworth Morse.

Daughters of the Dust 🦴🦴🦴 1/2 **1991** Five women of a Gullah family living on the Sea Islands off the Georgia coast in 1902 contemplate moving to the mainland in this emotional tale of change. The Gullah are descendants of West African slaves and their isolation has kept their superstitions and native dialect (a mixture of Western African, Creole, and English) intact. Family bonds and memories are celebrated with a quiet narrative and beautiful cinematography in Dash's feature-film directorial debut. **113m/C VHS, DVD.** Cora Lee Day, Barbara O, Alva Rogers, Kaycee Moore, Cheryl Lynn Bruce, Adisa Anderson, Eartha D. Robinson, Bahni Turpin, Tommy Redmond Hicks, Malik Farrakhan, Cornell (Kofi) Royal, Vertamae Crosvenor, Umar Abdurrahman, Sherry Jackson, Rev. Ervin Green; ***D:*** Julie Dash; ***W:*** Julie Dash; ***C:*** A. Jafa Fielder; ***M:*** John Barnes. Natl. Film Reg. '04;; Sundance '91: Cinematog.

Daughters of the Sun 🦴🦴 *Dakhtaran-e Khorshid* **2000** Amanagol (Taghani) is the eldest of six daughters from a poor rural family. In order to get money to support them and help her ill mother, Amanagol's father cuts her hair and disguises her as a boy named Aman, sending her to a distant village as an apprentice weaver. But her employer is dishonest—keeping her earnings instead of sending them to Aman's family. Then Aman learns her mother has died because of her employer's deception. Persian with subtitles. **92m/C VHS, DVD.** *IA* Altinay Ghelich Taghani; ***D:*** Mariam Shahriar; ***W:*** Mariam Shahriar; ***C:*** Homayun Payvar; ***M:*** Hosein Ali-Zadeh.

Dave 🦴🦴🦴 **1993 (PG-13)** Regular guy Dave Kovic (Kline) is a dead ringer for the President, launching him into the White House after the prez suffers a stroke in embarrassing circumstances. Seamless comedy prompts lots of hearty laughs and the feel-good faith that despite the overwhelming odds, everything will turn out just fine. Political cameos abound: look for real-life Senators Alan Simpson, Paul Simon, Howard Metzenbaum, Tom Harkin, and Christopher Dodd as well as the commentators from TV's "The McLaughlin Group," and Stone, poking fun at himself on "Larry King Live," as he tries to convince the public there's a conspiracy going on. **110m/C VHS, DVD.** Stephen (Steve) Root, Dan E. Butler, Bonnie Bartlett, Kevin Kline, Sigourney Weaver, Frank Langella, Kevin Dunn, Ving Rhames, Ben Kingsley, Charles Grodin, Faith Prince, Laura Linney, Bonnie Hunt, Parley Baer, Stefan Gierasch, Anna Deavere Smith, Bonnie Bartlett, Ben Stein; ***Cameos:*** Jay Leno, Larry King, Oliver Stone, Arnold Schwarzenegger; ***D:*** Ivan Reitman; ***W:*** Gary Ross; ***C:*** Adam Greenberg; ***M:*** James Newton Howard.

Dave Chappelle's Block Party 🦴🦴🦴 **2006 (R)** Comedian Chapelle is followed from his Ohio home to the free all-day concert he stages on a Brooklyn street on September 18, 2004. He impulsively hands out tickets and buses to the concertgoers while keeping the lineup a secret until such performers as Kanye West, Mos Def, the reunited Fugees, Dead Prez, Erykah Badu, Jill Scott, and Ohio's Central State University marching band take the stage. **100m/C DVD.** *US* Dave Chappelle; ***D:*** Michel Gondry; ***C:*** Ellen Kuras.

David 🦴🦴🦴 1/2 **1979** A haunting portrait of the survival of a Jewish teenager in Berlin during the Nazi reign of terror, based on the novel by Joel Koenig. Universally acclaimed, this was the first film about the Holocaust made in Germany by a German Jew. In German with English subtitles. **106m/C VHS.** *GE* Mario Fischel, Walter Taub, Irene Vrkijan, Torsten Hentes, Eva Mattes; ***D:*** Peter Lilienthal. Berlin Intl. Film Fest. '79: Golden Berlin Bear.

David 🦴🦴 1/2 **1997** TNT's Old Testament biblical series continues with the story of shepherd boy David (Turner) who succeeds Saul (Pryce) to become king over the tribes of Israel. When King David (Parker) becomes smitten with the married Bathsheba (Lee), he sends her husband into battle, soon leaving her a comely widow (although not for long). And there's also subplots involving three of David's children: Absalom (Rowan), Amnon (Hall), and Tamar (Bellar). Lots of action. **190m/C VHS, DVD.** Nathaniel Parker, Sheryl Lee, Jonathan Pryce, Leonard Nimoy, Dominic Rowan, Edward Hall, Clara Bellar, Marco Leonardi, Franco Nero, Ben Daniels, Maurice Roeves, Gina Bellman, Gideon Turner; ***D:*** Robert Markowitz; ***W:*** Larry Gross; ***C:*** Raffaele Mertes; ***M:*** Carlo Siliotto. **CABLE**

David and Bathsheba 🦴🦴🦴 **1951** The Bible story comes alive in this lush and colorful Fox production. Peck and Hayward are great together and Peck is properly concerned about the wrath of God over his transgressions. Terrific costumes and special effects, lovely music and a fine supporting cast keep this a notch above other Biblical epics. **116m/C VHS, DVD.** Gregory Peck, Susan Hayward, Raymond Massey, Kieron Moore, James Robertson Justice, Jayne Meadows, John Sutton, Dennis Hoey, Francis X. Bushman, George Zucco; ***D:*** Henry King; ***W:*** Philip Dunne; ***C:*** Leon Shamroy.

David and Lisa 🦴🦴🦴 **1962** Director Perry was given an Oscar for this sensitive independently produced film. Adapted from Theodore Isaac Rubin's true case history novel concerning a young man and woman who fall in love while institutionalized for mental illness. Dullea and Margolin are excellent in the title roles of this sleeper. **94m/B VHS, DVD.** Keir Dullea, Janet Margolin, Howard da Silva, Neva Patterson, Clifton James; ***D:*** Frank Perry; ***W:*** Eleanor Perry; ***C:*** Leonard Hirschfield; ***M:*** Mark Laurence.

David Copperfield 🦴🦴🦴🦴 **1935** Superior adaptation of Charles Dickens' great novel. An orphan grows to manhood in Victorian England with a wide variety of help and harm. Terrific acting by Bartholomew, Fields, Rathbone, and all the rest. Lavish production, lovingly filmed. **132m/B VHS, DVD.** Lionel Barrymore, W.C. Fields, Freddie Bartholomew, Maureen O'Sullivan, Basil Rathbone, Lewis Stone, Frank Lawton, Madge Evans, Roland Young, Edna May Oliver, Lennox Pawle, Elsa Lanchester, Una O'Connor, Arthur Treacher; ***D:*** George Cukor; ***W:*** Howard Estabrook, Hugh Walpole; ***M:*** Herbert Stothart.

David Copperfield 🦴🦴 1/2 **1970** This British made-for-TV production is more faithful to the Dickens classic than any of its predecessors. The added material, however, fails to highlight any one character as had the successful 1935 MGM version. Still, the exceptional (and largely stage-trained) cast do much to redeem the production. **118m/C VHS, DVD.** Richard Attenborough, Cyril Cusack, Edith Evans, Pamela Franklin, Susan Hampshire, Wendy Hiller, Ron Moody, Laurence Olivier, Robin Phillips; ***D:*** Delbert Mann; ***M:*** Malcolm Arnold. **TV**

David Copperfield 🦴🦴 1/2 **1999** Lavish and traditional retelling of the Dickens saga, which concerns the hard-knock life, from birth to maturity, of the title character. Hoskins' Mr. Micawber and Smith's Aunt Betsey Trotwood are particular standouts in a large cast. **210m/C VHS, DVD.** *GB* Daniel Radcliffe, Ciaran McMenamin, Bob Hoskins, Maggie Smith, Ian McKellen, Nicholas Lyndhurst, Pauline Quirke, Emilia Fox, Trevor Eve, Zoe Wanamaker, Alun Armstrong, Imelda Staunton, Amanda Ryan, Ian McNeice, Joanna Page; ***D:*** Simon Curtis; ***W:*** Adrian Hodges; ***C:*** Andy Collins; ***M:*** Robert (Rob) Lane; ***Nar:*** Tom Wilkinson. **TV**

David Harding, Counterspy 🦴 1/2 **1950** Covert spymaster David Harding sends Naval officer Jerry Baldwin into a munitions factory to protect torpedo plans. Harding suspects the plant has been infiltrated by enemy agents, who killed Baldwin's predecessor. Set in WWII. Based on the radio series. **71m/B DVD.** Howard St. John, Willard Parker, Audrey Long, Raymond Greenleaf, Alex Gerry; ***D:*** Ray Nazarro; ***W:*** Tom Reed, Clint Johnson; ***C:*** George E. Diskant.

David Harum 🦴🦴 1/2 **1934** Rogers plays the philosophical title character, a small-town banker, confirmed bachelor, and horse trader in the 1890s. Young bank teller John (Taylor) places a large bet on a horse race so he can afford to marry rich girl Ann (Venable) and Harum provides encouragement. **83m/B DVD.** Will Rogers, Louise Dresser, Kent Taylor, Evelyn Venable, Stepin Fetchit, Noah Beery Sr., Roger Imhof, Charles Middleton, Frank Melton; ***D:*** James Cruze; ***W:*** Walter Woods; ***C:*** Hal Mohr.

David Holzman's Diary 🦴🦴🦴 **1967** Director McBride helmed this fake underground movie, a legendary put-on focusing on film student pretensions. Holzman is a sincere geek who seeks the meaning of life by filming his own existence in oh-so-chic grainy black-and-white verite. He learns reality is more important than film. Drolly captures the state of the art in late '60s America. **71m/B VHS.** L.M. Kit Carson; ***D:*** Jim McBride; ***W:*** L.M. Kit Carson, Jim McBride. Natl. Film Reg. '91.

David Searching 🦴🦴 **1997** Aspiring documentary filmmaker David (Rapp) is broke and boyfriendless in his two-bedroom apartment. He needs a roomie to help with the rent and comes up with newly separated Gwen (Mannheim). She's equally in search of romance (or sex, as the case may be). Oh, and David stills needs to find that elusive job. Series of vignettes do feature some talented actors but the film never goes anywhere. **103m/C VHS.** Anthony Rapp, Camryn Manheim, Joseph Fuqua, Julie Halston, Stephen Spinella, John Cameron Mitchell, David Drake, Kathleen Chalfant, David Courier; ***D:*** Leslie L. Smith; ***W:*** Leslie L. Smith; ***C:*** John P. Scholz.

DaVinci's War 🦴🦴 **1992 (R)** Frank DaVinci's sister is murdered and he wants revenge. So he hooks up with a professional killer and a bunch of Vietnam vets and gets the firepower he needs to blow the bad guys away. **94m/C VHS, DVD.** Joey Travolta, Michael Nouri, Vanity, Richard Foronjy, Branscombe Richmond, Sam Jones, Jack Bannon, Brian Robbins, James Russo, Kamar De Los Reyes; ***D:*** Raymond Martino; ***W:*** Raymond Martino; ***M:*** Jeff Lass.

Davy Crockett and the River Pirates 🦴🦴 1/2 **1956 (G)** Another Disney splice and dice of two episodes from the TV series, chronicling the further adventures of our frontier hero. Davy meets up with Mike Fink, the King of the Ohio River, and the two engage in a furious keelboat race, and then unite to track down a group of thieves masquerading as Indians and threatening the peace. **81m/C VHS, DVD.** Fess Parker, Buddy Ebsen, Jeff York; ***D:*** Norman Foster; ***M:*** George Bruns.

Davy Crockett, King of the Wild Frontier 🦴🦴🦴 **1955 (PG)** Three episodes of the popular Disney TV series are blended together here to present the life and some of the adventures of Davy Crockett, including his days as an Indian fighter and his gallant stand in defense of the Alamo. Well-done by a splendid cast, the film helped to spread Davy-mania among the children of the 1950s. **93m/C VHS, DVD.** Fess Parker, Buddy Ebsen, Hans Conried, Ray Whiteside, Pat Hogan, William "Billy" Bakewell, Basil Ruysdael, Kenneth Tobey; ***D:*** Norman Foster; ***M:*** George Bruns. **TV**

Dawg 🦴🦴 *Bad Boy* **2002 (R)** Following 2001's "Double Whammy," Leary and Hurley also teamed up for this romantic comedy. The aptly named Doug "Dawg" Munford (Leary) stands to inherit a fortune but only if the love 'em and leave 'em lothario finds and apologizes to the many women he's used and dumped. And they have to forgive him. Estate attorney Anna Lockheart (Hurley) will tag along to make sure Dawg doesn't make a mess. **83m/C VHS, DVD.** Denis Leary, Elizabeth Hurley, Vanessa Bell Calloway, Alex Borstein, Mia Cottet; ***D:*** Victoria Hochberg; ***W:*** Ken Hastings; ***C:*** Steven Finestone; ***M:*** Jason Frederick.

Dawn! 🦴🦴 **1983** True story of Dawn Fraser, an Olympic champion swimmer and an unfulfilled woman willing to fight for her happiness. **114m/C VHS.** Bronwyn MacKay-Payne, Tom Richards, Bunny Brooke, Ron Haddrick; ***D:*** Ken Hannam; ***W:*** Joy Cavill; ***C:*** Russell Boyd.

Dawn Express 🦴 1/2 **1942** Nazi spies infiltrate the U.S. in search of a secret formula designed to enhance the power of gasoline. Another film made to contribute to the war effort that doesn't make much sense. **63m/B VHS.** Michael Whalen, Anne Nagel, William "Billy" Bakewell, Constance Worth, Hans von Twardowski, Jack Mulhall, George Pembroke, Kenneth Harlan, Robert Frazer; ***D:*** Al(bert) Herman.

Dawn of the Dead 🦴🦴🦴 1/2 *Zombi; Zombie; Zombies* **1978** Romero's gruesome sequel to his "Night of the Living Dead." A mysterious plague causes the recently dead to rise from their graves and scour the countryside for living flesh. Very violent, gory, graphic, and shocking, yet not without humor. Gives interesting consideration to the violence created by the living humans in their efforts to save themselves. **126m/C VHS, DVD, Blu-ray Disc.** David Emge, Ken Foree, Gaylen Ross, Scott H. Reiniger, David Crawford, David Early, Daniel Dietrich, Richard France, Tom Savini, Howard K. Smith, George A. Romero; ***D:*** George A. Romero; ***W:*** George A. Romero; ***C:*** Michael Gornick; ***M:*** Dario Argento, The Goblins.

Dawn of the Dead 🦴🦴🦴 **2004 (R)** The dead are rising from their graves yet again in this remake of the 1978 classic, except now the zombies move around much faster (no waddling allowed!). To level the playing field, Snyder (making his feature film directorial debut) includes more survivors to fight 'em off. The result is still lots of gory fun, but the biting humor so vital to the original is lacking. **100m/C DVD, Blu-ray Disc, UMD, HD DVD.** *US* Sarah Polley, Ving Rhames, Jake Weber, Mekhi Phifer, Ty Burrell, Michael Kelly, Kevin Zegers, Michael Barry, Lindy Booth, Jayne (Jane) Eastwood, Boyd Banks, Matt Frewer, R.D. Reid, Justin Louis, Kim Poirier, Tom Savini; ***D:*** Zack Snyder; ***W:*** James Gunn; ***C:*** Matthew F. Leonetti; ***M:*** Tyler Bates.

Dawn of the Mummy WOOF! **1982** Lousy plot and bad acting—not to mention gore galore—do this one in. A photographer and a bevy of young fashion models travel to Egypt for a special shoot. They unwittingly stumble upon an ancient tomb, teeming with vengeance-minded mummies. **93m/C VHS, DVD.** Brenda King, Barry Sattels, George Peck, Joan Levy; ***D:*** Frank Agrama.

Dawn on the Great Divide 🦴🦴 1/2 **1942** Jones' last film before his tragic and untimely death trying to save people from a fire at the Coconut Grove in Boston. Wagon train has to battle not only Indians, but bad guys as well. Plot provides more depth than the usual western fare. **57m/B VHS, DVD.** Buck Jones, Tim McCoy, Raymond Hatton, Mona Barrie, Robert Lowery, Betty Blythe, Jan Wiley, Harry Woods, Roy Barcroft; ***D:*** Howard Bretherton.

Dawn Patrol 🦴🦴🦴 **1938** Flynn plays a flight commander whose nerves are shot in this story of the British Royal Flying Corps during WWI. The focus is on the effects that the pressures and deaths have on all those concerned. Fine performances from all in this well-done remake of the 1930 film. **103m/B VHS, DVD.** Errol Flynn, David Niven, Basil Rathbone, Donald Crisp, Barry Fitzgerald, Melville Cooper, Carl Esmond, Peter Willes, Morton Lowry, Michael Brooke, James Burke, Stuart Hall; ***D:*** Edmund Goulding; ***W:*** Seton I. Miller, Dan Totheroh; ***C:*** Gaetano Antonio "Tony" Gaudio; ***M:*** Max Steiner.

Dawn Rider 🦴🦴 **1935** Formula western has all the right ingredients: Wayne as a cowboy out to get revenge on the gang that murdered his father. Features stuntman Canutt in rare acting role. **60m/B VHS, DVD.** John Wayne, Marion Burns, Yakima Canutt; ***D:*** Robert North Bradbury.

The Dawn Trail 🦴🦴 **1930** Larry Williams (Jones) is the sheriff of Osage county, which is in the middle of a range war between cattlemen and sheepmen over water rights. Williams tries to broker a truce but is put in a tough spot when his pal Mart (Morton) kills one of the sheepmen. But when he arrests Mart the cattlemen plot to free him. **60m/B DVD.** Buck Jones, Miriam Seegar, Charles Morton, Erville Alderson, Ed LeSaint, Hank Mann, Charles King; ***D:*** Christy Cabanne; ***W:*** John Thomas "Jack" Neville; ***C:*** Ted D. McCord.

The Dawning 🦴🦴 1/2 **1988** An Irish revolutionary in the 1920s draws a young woman into his dangerous world of romance, intrigue, and death. Howard's last film. Based on the novel "Old Jest" by Jennifer Johnston. **97m/C VHS, DVD.** *GB* Anthony Hopkins, Jean Simmons, Trevor Howard, Rebecca Pidgeon, Hugh Grant, Tara MacGowran; ***D:*** Robert Knights.

The Dawson Patrol 🦴 1/2 **1978** Royal Canadian Mountie dog-sled race turns into a dramatic battle for survival. **75m/C VHS.** George R. Robinson, Tim Henry, Neil Dainaro, James B. Douglas; ***D:*** Peter Kelly.

The Day After 🦴🦴🦴 **1983** Powerful drama graphically depicts the nuclear bombing of a midwestern city and its after-effects on the survivors. Made for TV, and very controversial when first shown, gathering huge ratings and vast media coverage. **122m/C VHS, DVD.** Jason Robards Jr., JoBeth Williams, John Lithgow, Steve Guttenberg, John Cullum; ***D:*** Nicholas Meyer. **TV**

The Day After Tomorrow 🦴🦴 1/2 **2004 (PG-13)** It was more fun watching the good guys battle aliens in Emmerich's "Independence Day" than this bunch of mopes who try to survive global warming. Paleoclimatologist Jack Hall (Quaid) predicts a new ice age and, sure enough, there's suddenly softball-sized hail blanketing Tokyo, L.A. gets leveled by tornadoes, New York is buried under ice and snow, and most of the northern hemisphere is wiped out just for fun. Jack's intrepid son Sam (Gyllenhaal)is trapped in Manhattan, riding out the weather with some friends in the New York Public Library and flirting with classmate Laura (Rossum). Meanwhile, Dad decides to snowshoe it from D.C. to NYC to rescue his boy. If you like watching familiar monuments destroyed (poor Lady Liberty), this special effects melodrama is for you. **123m/C DVD, Blu-ray Disc, UMD.** *US* Dennis Quaid, Jake Gyllenhaal, Sela Ward, Emmy Rossum, Ian Holm, Dash Mihok, Jay O. Sanders, Tamlyn Tomita, Austin Nichols, Arjay Smith, Kenneth Welsh, Glenn Plummer, Nestor Serrano, Adrian Lester, Sheila McCarthy, Perry King; ***D:*** Roland Emmerich; ***W:*** Roland Emmerich, Jeffrey Nachmanoff; ***C:*** Ueli Steiger; ***M:*** Harald Kloser. British Acad. '04: Visual FX.

The Day and the Hour 🦴🦴 1/2 *Today We Live; Le Jour et L'Heure; Il Giorno e L'Ora; Viviamo Oggi* **1963** A woman becomes accidentally involved in the resistance movement during the Nazi occupation of France in WWII. **110m/C VHS.** *FR JP IT* Simone Signoret, Stuart Whitman, Genevieve Page, Michel Piccoli, Reggie Nalder, Pierre Dux, Billy Kearns; ***D:*** Rene Clement; ***M:*** Claude Bolling.

Day at the Beach 🦴🦴 1/2 **1998** Jimmy (Veronis) works in a mob-fronted New York ravioli factory while trying to make a film—a gangster movie that features his fellow pasta workers. But when one of his buddies, John (Fitzgerald), tosses a briefcase over a river bridge for a scene, the heavy case accidently kills a passing fisherman. Now Jimmy's got a guilt-racked John to deal with and numerous other problems—all eventually leading to the palatial home of wealthy (and connected) Antonio Gintolini (Ragno). **93m/C VHS, DVD.** Nick Veronis, Patrick Fitzgerald, Neal Jones, Robert Maisonett, Catherine Kellner, Jane Adams, Joe Ragno, Ed Setrakian; ***D:*** Nick Veronis; ***W:*** Nick Veronis; ***C:*** Nils Kenaston; ***M:*** Tony Saracene.

A Day at the Races 🦴🦴🦴 1/2 **1937** Though it seems labored at times, the brilliance of the brothers Marx still comes through in this rather weak tale of a patient in a sanitorium who convinces horse doctor Groucho to take on running the place. ♫ A Message from the Man in the Moon; On Blue Venetian Waters; Tomorrow Is Another Day; All God's Chillun Got Rhythm. **111m/B VHS, DVD.** Groucho Marx, Harpo Marx, Chico Marx, Sig Rumann, Douglass Dumbrille, Margaret Dumont, Allan Jones, Maureen O'Sullivan, Leonard Ceeley, Esther Muir; ***D:*** Sam Wood; ***W:*** Robert Pirosh, George Seaton, George Oppenheimer; ***C:*** Joseph Ruttenberg; ***M:*** George Bassman, Bronislau Kaper, Walter Jurmann.

Day for Night 🦴🦴🦴🦴 *La Nuit Americaine* **1973 (PG)** Director Ferrand (Truffaut) is working on a mediocre romantic melodrama with sullen actor Alphonse (Leaud) who falls for his married co-star Julie (Bisset) in just one of the off-screen stories that's more interesting than what's being filmed. A wryly affectionate look at the profession of moviemaking—its craft, character, and the personalities that interact against the performances commanded by the camera. In French with English subtitles. **116m/C VHS, DVD.** *FR* Francois Truffaut, Jean-Pierre Leaud, Jacqueline Bisset, Jean-Pierre Aumont, Valentina Cortese, Alexandra Stewart, Dani, Nathalie Baye; ***D:*** Francois Truffaut; ***W:*** Suzanne Schiffman, Jean-Louis Richard, Francois Truffaut; ***C:*** Pierre William Glenn; ***M:*** Georges Delerue. Oscars '73: Foreign Film; British Acad. '73: Director (Truffaut), Film, Support. Actress (Cortese); N.Y. Film Critics '73: Director (Truffaut), Film, Support. Actress (Cortese); Natl. Soc. Film Critics '73: Director (Truffaut), Film, Support. Actress (Cortese).

A Day for Thanks on Walton's Mountain 🦴🦴 **1982** Many of the original television-show cast members returned for this sentimental Thanksgiving reunion on Walton's Mountain. **97m/C VHS.** Ralph Waite, Ellen Corby, Judy Norton-Taylor, Eric Scott, Jon Walmsley, Robert Wightman, Mary (Elizabeth) McDonough, David W. Harper, Kami Cotler, Joe Conley, Ronnie Clair Edwards, Richard Gilliland, Melinda Naud; ***D:*** Harry Harris; ***Nar:*** Earl Hamner. **TV**

A Day in October 🦴🦴 1/2 **1992 (PG-13)** 1943, Copenhagen, Denmark. There are signs the Jewish population is in danger from occupying Nazi officials and the resistance movement is active. Wounded resistance fighter Sweeney is rescued by the Jewish Sara (Wolf), and their relationship deepens as the realities of WWII change their lives. Based on historical fact, but there's little explanation of the politics or the fierce nationalism and intense loyalty most Danes felt towards their fellow countrymen, a loyalty that ultimately saved most of the Danish Jews from the Holocaust. Good performances, particularly Benzali as Sara's father, help overcome the script weaknesses. Filmed on location in Denmark. **96m/C VHS, DVD.** D.B. Sweeney, Kelly Wolf, Tovah Feldshuh, Daniel Benzali, Ole Lemmeke, Kim Romer, Anders Peter Bro, Lars Oluf Larsen; ***D:*** Kenneth Madsen; ***W:*** Damian F. Slattery; ***M:*** Jens Lysdal.

A Day in the Country 🦴🦴🦴 1/2 *Une Partie de Campagne* **1946** The son of the famed painter gives us the moving tale of a young woman's sudden and intense love for a man she meets while on a picnic with her family. Beautifully adapted from a story by Guy de Maupassant. Renowned photographer Henri Cartier-Bresson contributed to the wonderful cinematography. Subtitled. **40m/B VHS.** *FR* Sylvia Bataille, Georges Darnoux, Jane (Jeanne) Marken, Paul Temps; ***D:*** Jean Renoir; ***C:*** Henri Cartier-Bresson.

A Day in the Death of Joe Egg 🦴🦴🦴 **1971 (R)** Based on the Peter Nichols play, an unlikely black comedy about a British couple trying to care for their retarded/autistic child, nearly destroying their marriage in the process. They begin to contemplate euthanasia as a solution. Well-acted, but potentially offensive to some. **106m/C VHS.** *GB* Alan Bates, Janet Suzman, Elizabeth Robillard, Peter Bowles, Joan Hickson, Sheila Gish; ***D:*** Peter Medak; ***W:*** David Deutsch.

A Day in the Life 🦴 1/2 **2009 (R)** Stick is part of the New York gangsta life but wants to go straight for the sake of his girlfriend. Then his family is targeted by rivals and he gets pulled back in. All the dialogue is rapped rather than spoken. **90m/C DVD.** Kirk "Sticky Fingaz" Jones, Mekhi Phifer, Omar Epps, Faizon Love, Michael Rapaport, Fredro Starr, Malinda Williams, Michael K. Williams, Bokeem Woodbine, Ray J; ***D:*** Kirk "Sticky Fingaz" Jones; ***W:*** Kirk "Sticky Fingaz" Jones; ***C:*** Erik Voake; ***M:*** Kirk "Sticky Fingaz" Jones. **VIDEO**

The Day It Came to Earth WOOF! **1977 (PG)** Completely silly and unbelievable sci-fi flick has meteor crashing into the watery grave of a mobster. The decomposed corpse is revived by the radiation and plots to take revenge on those who fitted him with cement shoes. **89m/C VHS, DVD.** Roger Manning, Wink Roberts, Bob Ginnaven, Rita Wilson, Delight de Bruine; ***D:*** Harry Z. Thomason.

The Day My Parents Ran Away 🦴🦴 1/2 **1993 (PG)** Rebellious 16-year-old gets a tough lesson in responsibility when his parents get tired of his antics and decide to leave home in search of a new life. He finds out things aren't so easy on your own. **95m/C VHS, DVD.** Matt Frewer, Bobby Jacoby, Brigid Brannah, Blair Brown, Martin Mull; ***D:*** Martin Nicholson; ***W:*** Handel Glassberg; ***M:*** J. Peter Robinson.

Day Night Day Night 🦴🦴🦴 **2006** Luisa Williams plays a nameless young woman who at the story's outset is holed up in a shabby motel receiving instruction from black-hooded men. While few clues are given about her motivation, her intention is clearly to become a suicide bomber in Times Square. Once on the streets of New York, her scenes are filmed with handheld cameras in daylight amid the unwitting masses of Manhattan. The film raises many issues, leaving most unresolved and leaving viewers to contemplate the very real possibility of terrorism close to home. **94m/C DVD.** *US GE* Luisa Williams; ***D:*** Julia Loktev; ***W:*** Julia Loktev; ***C:*** Benoit Debie.

Day of Atonement 🦴🦴 1/2 **1993 (R)** It's a war for power between rival druglords when Hanin is released from prison and finds out his son and cousin are battling over turf. Then Walken is dragged into the fracas. Beals is the government agent trying to regain some control of the dangerous situation. **127m/C VHS.** *FR* Christopher Walken, Jennifer Beals, Jill Clayburgh, Roger Hanin, Richard Berry; ***D:*** Alexandre Arcady; ***W:*** Alexandre Arcady, Daniel Saint Hamont; ***C:*** Willy Kurant.

Day of Judgment 🦴 1/2 **1981** A mysterious stranger arrives in a town to slaughter those people who violate the Ten Commandments. **101m/C VHS.** William T. Hicks, Harris Bloodworth, Brownlee Davis; ***D:*** C.D.H. Reynolds.

Day of the Animals 🦴 *Something Is Out There* **1977 (PG)** Nature gone wild. It seems a depleted ozone layer has exposed the animals to the sun's radiation, turning Bambi and Bugs into brutal killers. A group of backpackers trek in the Sierras, unaware of the transformation. Far-fetched and silly (we hope). **95m/C VHS, DVD.** Christopher George, Leslie Nielsen, Lynda Day George, Richard Jaeckel, Michael Ansara, Ruth Roman, Jon Cedar, Susan Backlinie, Andrew Stevens, Gil Lamb; ***D:*** William Girdler; ***W:*** William W. Norton Sr.; ***C:*** Robert Sorrentino; ***M:*** Lalo Schifrin.

Day of the Assassin 🦴 **1981** A Mideast shah's yacht explodes, sending a huge fortune to the bottom of a murky bay. This sets off a rampage of treasure hunting by a variety of ruthless mercenaries. **94m/C VHS.** Glenn Ford, Chuck Connors, Richard Roundtree, Henry Silva, Jorge (George) Rivero; ***D:*** Brian Trenchard-Smith.

The Day of the Beast 🦴🦴 **1995 (R)** Lurid horror/melodrama concerns Father Angel (Angula), whose study of the Apocrypha has convinced him that the Antichrist will be born in Madrid on Christmas, which is only a few hours away. He enlists a couple of unlikely companions in his search for the infant. There's a lot of mayhem for all involved. Spanish with subtitles. **104m/C VHS.** *SP* Alex Angulo, Armando de Razza, Santiago Segura, Terele Pavez, Maria Grazia Cucinotta, Nathalie Sesena; ***D:*** Alex de la Iglesia; ***W:*** Jorge Guerricaechevarria, Alex de la Iglesia; ***C:*** Flavio Martinez Labiano; ***M:*** Battista Lena.

Day of the Cobra 🦴 1/2 **1984** A corrupt narcotics bureau official hires an ex-cop to find a heroin kingpin on the back streets of Genoa, Italy. **95m/C VHS, DVD.** *IT* Franco Nero, Sybil Danning, Mario Maranzana, Licinia Lentini, William Berger; ***D:*** Enzo G. Castellari.

Day of the Dead 🦴 1/2 **1985** The third in Romero's trilogy of films about flesh-eating zombies taking over the world. Romero hasn't thought up anything new for the ghouls to do, and the humans are too nasty to care about this time around. For adult audiences. **91m/C VHS, DVD, Blu-ray Disc.** Lori Cardille, Terry Alexander, Joe Pilato, Jarlath Conroy, Richard Liberty; ***D:*** George A. Romero; ***W:*** George A. Romero; ***C:*** Michael Gornick; ***M:*** John Harrison.

The Day of the Dolphin 🦴🦴 **1973 (PG)** Research scientist, after successfully working out a means of teaching dolphins to talk, finds his animals kidnapped; espionage and assassination are involved. Dolphin voices by Henry, who also wrote the screenplay. **104m/C VHS, DVD.** George C. Scott, Trish Van Devere, Paul Sorvino, Fritz Weaver, Jon Korkes, John Dehner, Edward Herrmann, Severn Darden; ***D:*** Mike Nichols; ***W:*** Buck Henry; ***M:*** Georges Delerue; ***V:*** Buck Henry.

The Day of the Jackal 🦴🦴🦴 1/2 **1973 (PG)** Frederick Forsyth's best-selling novel of political intrigue is splendidly brought to the screen by Zinnemann. A brilliant and ruthless assassin hired to kill Charles de Gaulle skirts the international intelligence pool, while intuitive police work try to stop him. Tense, suspenseful, beautiful location photography. Excellent acting by Fox, Cusack and Britton. **142m/C VHS, DVD.** Edward Fox, Alan Badel, Tony Britton, Derek Jacobi, Cyril Cusack, Olga Georges-Picot, Michael (Michel) Lonsdale; ***D:*** Fred Zinnemann; ***W:*** Kenneth Ross; ***C:*** Jean Tournier; ***M:*** Georges Delerue.

The Day of the Locust 🦴🦴🦴 1/2 **1975 (R)** Compelling adaptation of Nathaniel West's novel concerning the dark side of 1930s' Hollywood. A no-talent amoral actress's affair with a meek accountant leads to tragedy and destruction. Told from the view of a cynical art director wise to the ways of Hollywood. **140m/C VHS, DVD.** Donald Sutherland, Karen Black, Burgess Meredith, William Atherton, Billy Barty, Bo Hopkins, Richard Dysart, Geraldine Page; ***D:*** John Schlesinger; ***C:*** Conrad L. Hall; ***M:*** John Barry.

Day of the Maniac 🦴 1/2 **1977 (R)** Psychotic drug addict will stop at nothing to support his growing habit. **89m/C VHS, DVD.** George Hilton, Nieves Navarro; ***D:*** Sergio Martino.

The Day of the Outlaw 🦴🦴 1/2 **1959** Bleak wintry western. Wounded Jack Bruhn (Ives) and his gang take over the remote town of Bitter, Wyoming. Cattleman Blaise Starrett (Ryan) ignores the town's plight since he's upset that the settlers are stringing up barbed wire and his young love Helen (Louise) has married another. But finally Starrett's decency gets the better of him and he decides to take a stand against Bruhn. **92m/B DVD.** Robert Ryan, Burl Ives, Tina Louise, Alan Marshal, Nehemiah Persoff, Jack Lambert, Venetia Stevenson, David Nelson, Elisha Cook Jr., Dabbs Greer; ***D:*** Andre de Toth; ***W:*** Philip Yordan; ***C:*** Russell Harlan; ***M:*** Alexander Courage.

Day of the Panther 🦴 1/2 **1988** The Panthers—the world's most formidable martial artists—are mighty torqued when panther-Linda is pithed, and they're not known to turn the other cheek. Much chop-socky kicking and shrilling. **86m/C VHS, DVD.** John Stanton, Eddie Stazak; ***D:*** Brian Trenchard-Smith.

Day of the Triffids 🦴🦴🦴 **1963** The majority of Earth's population is blinded by a meteor shower which also causes plant spores to mutate into giant carnivores. Well-done adaptation of John Wyndham's science fiction classic; Philip Yordan acknowledged "fronting" for blacklisted screenwriter Gordon, who finally received credit in 1996. **94m/C VHS, DVD.** *GB* Howard Keel, Janette Scott, Nicole Maurey, Kieron Moore, Mervyn Johns, Alison Leggatt, Ewan Roberts, Janina Faye, Gilgi Hauser, Carol Ann Ford; ***D:*** Steve Sekely, Freddie Francis; ***W:*** Bernard Gordon, Philip Yordan; ***C:*** Ted Moore.

Day of the Warrior 🦴🦴 **1996 (R)** Babes who belong to a paramilitary law-and-order group infiltrate crime lord, the Warrior's, smuggling operations, strip joints and porn palaces. **96m/C VHS, DVD.** Julie Strain, Marcus Bagwell; ***D:*** Andy Sidaris; ***W:*** Andy Sidaris.

The Day of the Wolves 🦴 1/2 **1971** Seven nameless, bearded criminals are hired to loot an isolated town by first cutting off all outside communication. The town's former sheriff tries to stop them. There's a not-bad twist at the end but otherwise it's strictly a low-budget B-movie. **95m/C DVD.** Richard Egan, Martha Hyer, Jan Murray, Frankie Randall, Andre Marquis, Rick Jason, Zaldy Zschornack, Henry Capps, Smokey Roberts; ***D:*** Ferde Grofe Jr.; ***W:*** Ferde Grofe Jr.; ***C:*** Ric Waite; ***M:*** Sean Bonniwell.

Day of Triumph **1954** A dynamic version of the life of Christ as seen through the eyes of the apostles Andrew and Zadok, the leaders of the Zealot underground. **110m/C VHS.** Lee J. Cobb, Robert Wilson, Ralph Freud; ***D:*** Irving Pichel.

Day of Wrath *Vredens Dag* **1943** An involving psychological thriller based on records of witch trials from the early 1600s. Young Anne (Movin) is married to the much older and puritannical widower, Absalon (Roose) but falls in love with his son Martin (Lerdorff). She wishes aloud for her husband's death and when he does dies, Anne is accused of witchcraft. Grim and unrelentingly pessimistic, moving from one horrific scene to another, director Dreyer creates a masterpiece of terror. Based on a play by Hans Wiers Jenssen. In Danish with English subtitles. **110m/B VHS, DVD.** *DK* Thorkild Roose, Sigrid Neiiendam, Lisbeth Movin, Preben Lerdorff, Anna Svierker; ***D:*** Carl Theodor Dreyer; ***W:*** Carl Theodor Dreyer; ***C:*** Karl Andersson; ***M:*** Poul Schierbeck.

Day of Wrath ½ **2006 (R)** Pretty much of a snorer. 16th-century sheriff Ruy de Mendoza (Lambert) investigates the gruesome murders of several nobles during the Spanish Inquisition, only to discover family ties that put his life in peril. **101m/C DVD.** *GB HU* Christopher Lambert, Brian Blessed, James Faulkner, Phyllida Law, Blanca Marsillach, Ben O'Brien; ***D:*** Adrian Rudomin; ***W:*** Adrian Rudomin; ***C:*** Tamas Lajos; ***M:*** David Schweitzer. **VIDEO**

Day One **1989** Vivid re-creation of one of the most turbulent periods of American history—the WWII race to build the atomic bomb. Chronicles the two year top-secret efforts of the Manhattan Project, with General Leslie Groves (Dennehy) having to supervise the project and contain the scientific rivalries. Outstanding cast, with Strathairn notable as physicist J. Robert Oppenheimer. Adapted from "Day One: Before Hiroshima and After" by Peter Wyden. **141m/C VHS.** Brian Dennehy, David Strathairn, Michael Tucker, Hume Cronyn, Richard Dysart, Barnard Hughes, Hal Holbrook, David Ogden Stiers, John McMartin; ***D:*** Joseph Sargent; ***W:*** David W. Rintels; ***M:*** Mason Daring. **TV**

The Day Reagan Was Shot **2001 (R)** Recalls March 30, 1981 when President Reagan (Crenna) lay critically wounded in George Washington University hospital after having been shot by John W. Hinckley Jr. The administration is in chaos and power struggles break out between Secretary of State Alexander Haig (Dreyfuss) and Secretary of Defense Caspar Weinberger (Feore). Cable drama seems to be more satire than fact. **95m/C VHS, DVD.** Richard Crenna, Richard Dreyfuss, Colm Feore, Holland Taylor, Kenneth Welsh, Leon Pownall, Michael Murphy, Jack Jessop; ***D:*** Cyrus Nowrasteh; ***W:*** Cyrus Nowrasteh; ***C:*** Michael McMurray. **CABLE**

The Day Silence Died *El Dia Que Murio el Silencio* **1998** Into the sleepy, provincial town of Villaserena, Bolivia, comes Abelardo. This charismatic stranger calls himself a "radio operator" and he installs four public loudspeakers in the town square where he plays music and broadcasts the news. He also offers to sell airtime to the local residents, which results in the airing of much private and dirty laundry, causing a good deal of turmoil within the community. And just who are they going to blame? Spanish with subtitles. **108m/C VHS.** Dario Grandinetti, Gustavo Angarita, Elias Serrano, Guillermo Granda, Maria Laura Garcia, Blanca Morisson; ***D:*** Paolo Agazzi; ***W:*** Paolo Agazzi, Guillermo Aguirre; ***C:*** Livio Delgado, Guillermo Medrano.

The Day That Shook the World **1978 (R)** Slow-moving but intriguing account of events surrounding the assassination of Archduke Ferdinand of Austria that triggered WWI. Garnered an R-rating due to some disturbingly graphic scenes. **111m/C VHS.** Christopher Plummer, Florinda Bolkan, Maximilian Schell; ***D:*** Veljko Bulajic.

Day the Bookies Wept **1939** Decent yarn about cabbies tricked into buying a "racehorse." Turns out she's old as the hills and hooked on alcohol to boot, but they enter her in the big race anyway. **50m/B VHS.** Betty Grable, Joe Penner, Tom Kennedy, Richard Lane; ***D:*** Leslie Goodwins.

The Day the Earth Caught Fire ½ **1961** The earth is knocked out of orbit and sent hurtling toward the sun when nuclear testing is done simultaneously at both the North and South Poles. Realistic and suspenseful, this is one of the best of the sci-fi genre. **95m/B VHS, DVD.** Janet Munro, Edward Judd, Leo McKern; ***D:*** Val Guest; ***W:*** Wolf Mankowitz, Val Guest; ***C:*** Harry Waxman; ***M:*** Stanley Black. British Acad. '61: Screenplay.

The Day the Earth Froze **1959** Witch steals the sun because she couldn't have a magical mill that produced grain, salt, and gold. Everything on Earth freezes. Based on a Finnish epic poem. **67m/B VHS, DVD.** *FI RU* Nina Anderson, Jon Powers, Ingrid Elhardt, Paul Sorenson; ***D:*** Gregg Sebelious; ***Nar:*** Marvin Miller.

The Day the Earth Stood Still ½ **1951** A gentle alien lands on Earth to deliver a message of peace and a warning against experimenting with nuclear power. He finds his views echoed by a majority of the population, but not the ones who are in control. In this account based loosely on the story of Christ, Rennie is the visitor backed by the mighty robot Gort. One of the greatest science fiction films of all time. **92m/B VHS, DVD, Blu-ray Disc.** Michael Rennie, Patricia Neal, Hugh Marlowe, Sam Jaffe, Frances Bavier, Lock Martin, Billy Gray, Edith Evanson, Frank Conroy, Drew Pearson; ***D:*** Robert Wise; ***W:*** Edmund H. North; ***C:*** Leo Tover; ***M:*** Bernard Herrmann. Natl. Film Reg. '95.

The Day the Earth Stood Still **2008 (PG-13)** Subpar and bland reworking of the 1951 sci-fi classic is not out of this world, but maybe should be sent there. Alien Klaatu (Reeves) arrives in Central Park with another warning for earthlings—humankind must change the way they treat the environment or else be doomed. Klaatu's companion metal robot Gort is inexplicably less mighty than in the original, a poor excuse given the technology available. Wasted are the talents of: Connelly as microbiologist Helen Benson who is among a group of scientists the government forcibly gathers; Bates of the U.S. Department of Defense; and Cleese, an "Important Scientist." **103m/C DVD.** *US* Keanu Reeves, Jennifer Connelly, Jon Hamm, John Cleese, Jaden Smith, Kathy Bates, Kyle Chandler, Robert Knepper, James Hong; ***D:*** Scott Derrickson; ***W:*** David Scarpa; ***C:*** David Tattersall; ***M:*** Tyler Bates.

The Day the Sky Exploded ½ *Death From Outer Space; La Morte Viene Dalla Spazio; Le Danger Vient de l'Escape* **1957** Sci-fi disaster drama doesn't live up to the grandiose title, as a runaway rocket ship hits the sun, unleashing an asteroid shower that threatens Earth with tidal waves, earthquakes, heat waves and terrible dialogue. The highlight of this Franco-Italian effort is the cinematography by horror director Mario Bava. **80m/B VHS, DVD.** *FR IT* Paul (Christian) Hubschmid, Madeleine Fischer, Fiorella Mari, Ivo Garrani, Dario Michaelis; ***D:*** Richard Benson; ***C:*** Mario Bava.

The Day the Sun Turned Cold *Tianguo Niezi* **1994** In an apparent crisis of conscience a young man (Zhong Hua) enters a police station and tries to convince a weary captain (Hu) that his mother (Gowa) murdered his cruel father (Jingwu) 10 years before in order to marry another man. The detective eventually concludes he should investigate the supposed crime, which happened in a remote village, but Zhong Hua's accusations naturally stir up a great deal of resentment and anger. There's lots of questions about guilt, innocence, and motives—on everybody's part. Mandarin with subtitles. **99m/C VHS.** *HK* Siqin Gaowa, Tuo Zhong Hua, Wai Zhi, Ma Jingwu, Li Hu; ***D:*** Yim Ho; ***W:*** Yim Ho; ***C:*** Hou Yong; ***M:*** Yoshihide Otomo.

The Day the Women Got Even ½ **1980** Four suburban homemakers take up the life of vigilantes to save unsuspecting actresses from a talent agent's blackmail scheme. **98m/C VHS.** JoAnn Pflug, Tina Louise, Georgia Engel, Barbara Rhoades, Julie Hagerty, Ed O'Neill; ***D:*** Burt Brinckerhoff; ***M:*** Brad Fiedel. **TV**

Day the World Ended **1955** The first science-fiction film of exploitation director Roger Corman. Five survivors of nuclear holocaust discover a desert ranch house fortress owned by a survivalist (Birch) and his daughter (Nelson). With relatively abundant supplies, they fatuously wallow in false misery until a disfigured visitor, wasting away from radiation, stumbles into their paradise. His mutation into an alien being confronts them with the horror that lurks outside. **79m/B VHS, DVD.** Paul Birch, Lori Nelson, Adele Jergens, Raymond Hatton, Paul Dubov, Richard Denning, Mike Connors, Paul Blaisdell, Jonathan Haze; ***D:*** Roger Corman; ***W:*** Lou Rusoff; ***C:*** Jockey A. Feindel; ***M:*** Ronald Stein.

The Day the World Ended ½ **2001 (R)** Shrink Dr. Jennifer Stillman (Kinski) leaves New York for a small town as the school district's new therapist. Her first patient, Ben (Edner), is a young outsider whose adoptive father is the town doctor (Quaid). Jennifer realizes Ben is hiding something about his mother's mysterious death, which involves a coverup by the town. When several locals are brutally murdered, Jennifer becomes a suspect but Ben blames his biological father—a space alien. This cable remake has nothing to do with the 1955 original and even the title seems off. **90m/C VHS, DVD.** Nastassja Kinski, Randy Quaid, Debra Christofferson, Bobby Edner, Stephen Tobolowsky, Lee DeBroux, David Getz, Alexander Gould; ***D:*** Terence Gross; ***W:*** Annie de Young, Max Enscoe; ***C:*** Mark Vargo; ***M:*** Charles Bernstein. **CABLE**

Day Time Ended *Vortex; Timewarp* **1980** A pair of glowing UFO's streaking across the sky and an alien mechanical device with long menacing appendages are only two of the bizarre phenomena witnessed from a lone house in the desert. Good special effects. Also released as "Time Warp" (1978). **80m/C VHS, DVD.** Chris Mitchum, Jim Davis, Dorothy Malone; ***D:*** John Cardos; ***W:*** David Schmoeller, J. Larry Carroll; ***M:*** Richard Band.

Day-Time Wife **1939** Some questionable moral choices managed to sneak past the Hays Production Code in this marital drama. Exec Ken Norton (Power) calls his beautiful wife Jane (Darnell) and tells her he's working late and he's going to miss their second anniversary. He's working alright—making time with secretary Kitty (Barrie). Jane suspects and decides she wants to know why men fall for their secretaries so she takes a job (without Ken knowing) with womanizing architect Bernard Dexter (William). While out to dinner with Dexter, Jane spies Ken with Kitty. Will this married couple ever decide who they're meant to be with? **71m/B DVD.** Tyrone Power, Linda Darnell, Warren William, Wendy Barrie, Binnie Barnes, Joan Valerie, Joan Davis, Leonid Kinskey; ***D:*** Gregory Ratoff; ***W:*** Art Arthur, Robert Harari; ***C:*** J. Peverell Marley; ***M:*** Cyril Mockridge.

Day Watch *Dnevnoi Dozor: Mel Sudbi* **2006 (R)** Vampires, chases, explosions, "Matrix"-style fight scenes, and just a touch of post-Communist allegory make this an incoherent but fun ride. Two factions of Moscow vampires ("Darks" and "Lights") struggle to manage an uneasy truce as an inevitable conflict rises. Good-guy vamp Anton (Khabensky) is torn between two rising powers: his lover Svetlana (Poroshina) on one side and his increasingly evil son Yegor (Martynov) on the other. Non-stop action sequences make up for the thin plot but what really stands out is the creative characterization and innovative direction. Sequel to 2004's "Night Watch." **132m/C DVD.** *RU* Konstantin Khabensky, Maria Poroshina, Vladimir Menshov, Viktor Verzhbitsky, Galina Tyunina, Alexsei Chadov, Dima Martinov, Valery Zolotukhin; ***D:*** Timur Bekmambetov; ***W:*** Timur Bekmambetov, Sergei Lukyanenko, Aleksandr Talal; ***C:*** Sergei Trofimov; ***M:*** Yuri Potyeyenko.

The Day Will Dawn *The Avengers* **1942** Suspenseful British-made WWII thriller about a reporter and a young Norwegian girl who plot to sabotage a secret Nazi U-boat base near the girl's town. **100m/B VHS.** *GB* Deborah Kerr, Hugh Williams, Niall MacGinnis, Ralph Richardson, Francis L. Sullivan, Roland Culver, Finlay Currie, Patricia Medina; ***D:*** Harold French; ***W:*** Terence Rattigan.

A Day Without a Mexican ½ *Un dia sin mexicanos* **2004 (R)** One morning, the state of California wakes up to find the entire Latino population has disappeared. The consequences are huge. Fields remain unharvested, cars are abandoned, schools are closed and the poor Anglos are left holding the bag. Without cheap laborers and migrant workers, the economy falls into a hopeless shambles. The lone Latino survivor is Lila Rodriguez (Arizmendi, who also co-scripted), a reporter who becomes the center of intense scrutiny. Amusingly shot as a mockumentary, but what could have been a biting critique suffers from lack of focus and overly broad scope. **97m/C VHS, DVD.** *US MX* Yareli Arizmendi, John Getz, Maureen Flannigan, Muse Watson, Caroline Aaron, Melinda Allen, Eduardo Palomo, Bru Muller, Rick Najera; ***D:*** Sergio Arau; ***W:*** Yareli Arizmendi, Sergio Arau, Sergio Guerrero; ***C:*** Alan Caudillo; ***M:*** Juan J. Colomer.

Day Zero ½ **2007 (R)** In this slightly futuristic fare, the U.S. military draft has been reinstated because of increasing terrorist acts. Three New York friends are called up and react to the news in different ways: lawyer George (Klein) asks his wealthy dad to help him wriggle out; insecure writer Aaron (Wood) thinks the military can make him a man; and cabdriver James (Bernthal) is patriotic and willing to serve. Overly self-important and formulaic. **96m/C DVD.** Chris Klein, Elijah Wood, Ginnifer Goodwin, Elisabeth (Elissabeth, Elizabeth, Liz) Moss, Jon Bernthal, Ally Sheedy, Sofia Vassilieva; ***D:*** Bryan Gunnar Cole; ***W:*** Rob Makani; ***C:*** Matthew Clark; ***M:*** Erin O'Hara.

Daybreak ½ **1993 (R)** In the near future America has been decimated by a nameless, sexually transmitted disease (read AIDS parable) and public policy is to quarantine the infected in concentration camp-like prisons. This leads to a quasi-official group of green-shirted thugs roaming the streets and imprisoning or killing anyone they suspect has the disease. A small resistance movement is lead by Torch (Gooding Jr.), who happens to fall in love with Blue (Kelly), the sister of one of the fascist leaders. Based on Alan Bowne's play "Beirut, Daybreak." **91m/C VHS, DVD.** Cuba Gooding Jr., Moira Kelly, Omar Epps, Martha Plimpton, Alice Drummond, David Eigenberg, John Savage; ***Cameos:*** Phil Hartman; ***D:*** Stephen Tolkin; ***W:*** Stephen Tolkin. **CABLE**

Daybreak ½ **2001 (R)** A throwback to the cheesy disaster flicks of the '70s, which isn't necessarily a bad thing. An L.A. subway train is stuck in a tunnel after an earthquake and it's up to subway supervisor Dillan Johansen (McGinley) to find a way to save himself and the passengers from fire, water, and toxic chemicals. **93m/C VHS, DVD.** Ted McGinley, Roy Scheider, Adam Wylie, Ursula Brooks, Jaime Bergman; ***D:*** Jean Pellerin. **VIDEO**

Daybreakers **2009 (R)** In 2017, a plague has turned most humans into vampires, and blood's running out. As the vampire society slowly declines into a world where the rich get blood and the poor turn into rabid, starving animals, researcher Edward (Hawke) works to develop a blood substitute for a nasty corporate CEO (Neill). When he meets human rebel Elvis (an energetically over-the-top Dafoe), who claims to have found a cure for vampirism, Edward has to figure out where his loyalties lie with the future of humanity in his hands. Creates a beautifully realized, detailed world of vampire society and serves up some early thrills, but the story quickly settles into standard horror film gear and never aspires to aim higher than big explosions and corny dialogue. Fun, but fails to live up to its wickedly smart premise. **98m/C DVD.** *US AU* Willem Dafoe, Ethan Hawke, Sam Neill, Vince Colosimo, Claudia Karvan, Isabel Lucas, Isabel Lucas; ***D:*** Michael Spierig, Peter Spierig; ***W:*** Michael Spierig, Peter Spierig; ***C:*** Ben Nott; ***M:*** Christopher Gordon.

The Daydreamer ½ *Absent-Minded; Le Distrait* **1975** Actor/director/writer Richard stars as a bumbling fool let loose in the French corporate world with comical results. In French with subtitles. **90m/C VHS.** *FR* Pierre Richard, Bernard Blier, Maria Pacome, Marie-Christine Barrault; ***D:*** Pierre Richard; ***W:*** Pierre Richard; ***M:*** Vladimir Cosma.

Daylight **1996 (PG-13)** After a massive explosion seals both ends of New York's Holland Tunnel (The Tunneling Inferno?), a small band of stock disaster flick survivors are trapped under the waters of the Hudson River. Fortunately, a cab driver with a really square jaw who, conveniently, is an ex-emergency rescue worker AND who knows the entire layout of the tunnel happens to be driving toward the tunnel at the exact moment of the disaster. Coincidence? Nope, just Hollywood. Kit Latura (Stallone) leads the survivors through cave-ins, floods, fire, rats, and poison gas (The Poison-Hiding Adventure!) only to discover to their dismay that they have emerged in New Jersey. Long on special effects but short on character development, this nod to the catastrophe movies of the '70s is still enjoyable for those who like to watch things go boom. **109m/C VHS, DVD, HD DVD.** Sylvester Stallone, Viggo Mortensen, Amy Brenneman, Stan Shaw, Claire Bloom, Renoly Santiago, Sage Stallone, Dan Hedaya, Jay O. Sanders, Karen Young, Vanessa Bell Calloway, Colin Fox, Danielle Harris, Jo Anderson, Mark Rolston, Rosemary Forsyth, Barry Newman; ***D:*** Rob Cohen; ***W:*** Leslie Bohem; ***C:*** David Eggby; ***M:*** Randy Edelman.

Days 1/2 *Giorni* **2002** Caludio (Trabacchi) is a workaholic mid-30s bank exec in Rome. HIV-positive, he's stayed healthy with a rigid regime of drugs and exercise. Claudio also has a longtime lover, Andrea (Salerno), and they are supposed to be moving to Milan together. Except Claudio is suddenly reluctant—could this have anything to do with his encounter with handsome young waiter Dario (Bechini)? (What do you think.) Suddenly, uptight Claudio is acting very recklessly. He begins an affair with Dario, goes off his meds, sloughs off his job, and can't make up his mind about either man. Claudio's not the most likeable guy around but he's very, very real and you'll even understand why both his lovers still around to see what happens next. Italian with subtitles. **90m/C VHS, DVD.** *IT* Thomas Trabacchi, Riccardo Salerno, Davide Bechini; ***D:*** Laura Muscardin; ***W:*** Laura Muscardin, Francesco Montini, David Oserio, Jane Ruhm; ***C:*** Sabrina Varani; ***M:*** Ivan Iusco.

Days and Clouds *Giorni e Nuvole* **2007** Elsa is fulfilling her dream of getting an advanced degree in art restoration. After she graduates, her husband Michele confesses that he lost his job months ago and has been unsuccessful finding employment so they will have to drastically downsize their lives. Elsa goes into crisis mode and finds an office job to support them while Michele's apathy and depression get the best of him and their 20-year-old daughter Alice remains resolutely oblivious to the family's problems. Italian with subtitles. **115m/C DVD.** *IT* Margherita Buy, Antonio Albanese, Alba Rohrwacher, Guiseppe Battiston, Carla Signoris, Fabio Troiano; ***D:*** Silvio Soldini; ***W:*** Silvio Soldini, Doriana Leondeff, Francesco Piccolo, Federica Pontremoli; ***C:*** Ramiro Civita; ***M:*** Giovanni Venosta.

Days and Nights in the Forest 1/2 *Aranyer Din Ratri* **1970** Four men living in Calcutta decide to leave the city for a brief vacation. Each has a different emotional experience which will change him forever, including a brief love affair and finding true romance. In Bengali with English subtitles. **120m/C VHS.** *IN* Soumitra Chatterjee, Sharmila Tagore, Shubhendu Chatterjee, Samit Bhanja; ***D:*** Satyajit Ray; ***W:*** Satyajit Ray; ***C:*** Soumendu Roy; ***M:*** Satyajit Ray.

Days of Being Wild *A Fei jing juen; A Fei zheng zhuan; Ah Fei's Story* **1991** Yuddy (Leslie Cheung) learns his mom is an ex-prostitute who raised him when he was abandoned by his real mother. He is so stunned by the revelation he can't even make a decision between the two women fighting for him, even though they have other men fighting for them as well. When his adopted mother won't confess the identity of his real mother, Yuddy goes in search of her. Winner of many trophies at the Hong Kong Film Awards. **89m/C DVD.** *HK* Leslie Cheung, Maggie Cheung, Andy Lau, Carina Lau, Rebecca Pan, Jacky Cheung, Tony Leung Chiu-wai, Mei-Mei Hung; ***D:*** Kar-Wai Wong; ***W:*** Kar-Wai Wong; ***C:*** Christopher Doyle.

Days of Glory 1/2 **1943** Peck's screen debut finds him as a Russian peasant bravely fighting the Nazi blitzkrieg almost single-handedly. **86m/B VHS.** Tamara Toumanova, Gregory Peck, Alan Reed, Maria Palmer, Lowell Gilmore, Hugo Haas; ***D:*** Jacques Tourneur; ***C:*** Gaetano Antonio "Tony" Gaudio.

Days of Glory *Indigenes* **2006 (R)** Issue-based WWII drama caused a furor as it brought up the shabby treatment received by North African colonial recruits who fought for France as second-class citizens. Poorly trained, they bravely battle on while being unjustly treated and degraded by their superior officers. The Moroccans are more mouthpieces than individuals but the actors work well as an ensemble, and director Bouchareb keeps his drama to human scale. French and Arabic with subtitles. **123m/C DVD.** *AL BE FR* Jamel Debbouze, Roschdy Zem, Sami Bouajila, Mathieu Simonet, Samy Naceri, Bernard Blancan, Benoit Giros; ***D:*** Rachid Bouchareb; ***W:*** Rachid Bouchareb, Olivier Morelle; ***C:*** Patrick Blossier; ***M:*** Armand Amar.

Days of Heaven 1/2 **1978 (PG)** Drifter Gere, his younger sister, and a woman he claims is his sister become involved with a Texas sharecropper. Told through the eyes of the younger girl, this is a sweeping vision of the U.S. before WWI. Loss and loneliness, deception, frustration, and anger haunt these people as they struggle to make the land their own. Deservedly awarded an Oscar for breathtaking cinematography. **95m/C VHS, DVD.** Richard Gere, Brooke Adams, Sam Shepard, Linda Manz, Stuart Margolin; ***D:*** Terrence Malick; ***W:*** Terrence Malick; ***C:*** Nestor Almendros; ***M:*** Ennio Morricone. Oscars '78: Cinematog.; Cannes '79: Director (Malick); L.A. Film Critics '78: Cinematog., Natl. Film Reg. '07;; N.Y. Film Critics '78: Director (Malick); Natl. Soc. Film Critics '78: Cinematog., Director (Malick), Film.

Days of Hell *I Giorni Dell'Inferno* **1984** Forgettable tale of four mercenaries who are hired to rescue a doctor and his daughter held captive by guerrillas somewhere in Afghanistan only to find out they're pawns in an even bigger scheme. **90m/C VHS.** Conrad Nichols, Ottaviano Dell'Acqua, Stephen Elliott, Kiwako Harada; ***D:*** Anthony Richmond.

Days of Jesse James **1939** Roy is a member of a detective agency who joins the James gang incognito in order to prove that they didn't rob the Northfield bank. Roy figures out that bank officials actually planned the whole scheme. **63m/B VHS.** Roy Rogers, George "Gabby" Hayes, Donald (Don "Red") Barry, Harry Woods, Pauline Moore, Mike Worth, Glenn Strange; ***D:*** Joseph Kane; ***W:*** Earle Snell; ***C:*** Reggie Lanning.

Days of Thrills and Laughter 1/2 **1961** Delightful compilation of clips from the era of silent films, showcasing the talents of the great comics as well as daring stuntman. **93m/B VHS.** Buster Keaton, Charlie Chaplin, Harold Lloyd, Stan Laurel, Oliver Hardy; ***D:*** Robert Youngson.

Days of Thunder **1990 (PG-13)** "Top Gun" in race cars! Cruise follows the same formula he has followed for several years now (with the notable exception of "Born on the Fourth of July.") Cruise and Towne co-wrote the screenplay concerning a young kid bursting with talent and raw energy who must learn to deal with his mentor, his girlfriend, and eventually the bad guy. First film that featured cameras that were actually on the race cars. If you like Cruise or race cars then this is the movie for you. **108m/C VHS, DVD.** Tom Cruise, Robert Duvall, Randy Quaid, Nicole Kidman, Cary Elwes, Michael Rooker, Fred Dalton Thompson, John C. Reilly; ***D:*** Tony Scott; ***W:*** Tom Cruise, Robert Towne; ***C:*** Ward Russell; ***M:*** Hans Zimmer.

Days of Wine and Roses 1/2 **1958** The original "Playhouse 90" TV version of J.P. Miller's story which was adapted for the big screen in 1962. An executive on the fast track and his young wife, initially only social drinkers, find themselves degenerating into alcoholism. A well-acted, stirring drama. **89m/B VHS, DVD.** Cliff Robertson, Piper Laurie; ***D:*** John Frankenheimer. **TV**

Days of Wine and Roses 1/2 **1962** A harrowing tale of an alcoholic advertising man who gradually drags his wife down with him into a life of booze. Big screen adaptation of the play originally shown on TV. ♫ Days of Wine and Roses. **138m/B VHS, DVD.** Jack Lemmon, Lee Remick, Charles Bickford, Jack Klugman, Jack Albertson; ***D:*** Blake Edwards; ***W:*** J(ames) P(inckney) Miller; ***M:*** Henry Mancini, Johnny Mercer. Oscars '62: Song ("Days of Wine and Roses").

Dayton's Devils **1968** Nielsen is the leader of a motley crew of losers who plan to rob a military base bank in this action-packed heist flick. **107m/C VHS.** Rory Calhoun, Leslie Nielsen, Lainie Kazan, Eric (Hans Gudegast) Braeden, Georg Stanford Brown, Rigg Kennedy; ***D:*** Jack Shea.

The Daytrippers 1/2 **1996** Happily married Eliza D'Amico is living on Long Island while husband Louis (Tucci) goes to work in Manhattan. That is she's happy until she finds what appears to be a love letter addressed to her husband. Frantic, Eliza runs to aggressive mom Rita (Meara), who decides that her daughter should immediately confront her possibly erring husband at his office. So Eliza, her mom and dad (McNamara), sarcastic younger sister Jo (Posey), and Jo's pretentious boyfriend Carl (Schreiber) all pile into the family station wagon and head into the city. Only Louis isn't at his office and they scour Manhattan to track him down. **88m/C VHS, DVD.** Hope Davis, Anne Meara, Parker Posey, Liev Schreiber, Pat McNamara, Stanley Tucci, Campbell Scott, Marcia Gay Harden, Andy Brown; ***D:*** Greg Mottola; ***W:*** Greg Mottola; ***C:*** John Inwood.

Dazed and Confused **1993 (R)** A day in the life of a bunch of high schoolers should prove to be a trip back in time for those coming of age in the '70s. Eight seniors facing life after high school have one last year long hurrah, as they search for Aerosmith tickets and haze the incoming freshmen. Keen characterization by writer/director Linklater captures the spirit of a generation shaped by Watergate, the Vietnam War, feminism, and marijuana. Groovy soundtrack features Alice Cooper, Deep Purple, KISS, and Foghat. **97m/C VHS, DVD, HD DVD.** Jason London, Rory Cochrane, Sasha Jenson, Wiley Wiggins, Michelle Rene Thomas, Adam Goldberg, Anthony Rapp, Marissa Ribisi, Parker Posey, Joey Lauren Adams, Ben Affleck, Milla Jovovich, Cole Hauser, Matthew McConaughey, Kristin Hinojosa; ***D:*** Richard Linklater; ***W:*** Richard Linklater; ***C:*** Lee Daniel.

DC 9/11: Time of Crisis *The Big Dance* **2004 (R)** Retelling of the horrific terrorist attacks in New York City and Washington D.C. while providing a supposed behind-the-scenes view of the reaction of President Bush (played by Bottoms) and his administration. Undoubtedly will cause debates between those who see this as a vehicle to inflate the president's image and combat Michael Moore's flogging in "Fahrenheit 9/11" and others who consider it as fact. Let's remember it's a made for TV flick. **127m/C VHS, DVD.** Timothy Bottoms, John Cunningham, James Carroll, Greg Ellwand, Lawrence Pressman, Stephen Macht, Gregory Itzin, Penny Johnson, Myron Natwick, Andrew Gillies, Bobby Johnston, Debra McGrath, David McIlwraith, Brian Rhodes, Allan Royal, Greg Spottiswood, George Takei, Roger Barnes, Geoffrey Bowes, Dom(enico) Fiore, Chris Gillet, Thomas Hauff, Howard Jerome, Doug Lennox, Gerry Mendicino, Mary Gordon Murray, David Wolos-Fonteno; ***D:*** Brian Trenchard-Smith; ***W:*** Lionel Chetwynd; ***C:*** Ousama Rawi; ***M:*** Lawrence Shragge. **TV**

D.C. Cab 1/2 **1984 (R)** A rag-tag group of Washington, D.C. cabbies learn a lesson in self-respect in this endearing comedy. Though not without flaws, it's charming all the same. **100m/C VHS, DVD.** Mr. T, Leif Erickson, Adam Baldwin, Charlie Barnett, Irene Cara, Anne DeSalvo, Max Gail, Gloria Gifford, Gary Busey, Jill Schoelen, Marsha Warfield; ***D:*** Joel Schumacher; ***W:*** Joel Schumacher, Topper Carew; ***C:*** Dean Cundey.

De-Lovely *She's De Lovely* **2004 (PG-13)** Biopic of songwriter Cole Porter (Kline) is played as if Porter himself were directing a musical about his life. Focuses on his adultery-ridden marriage to put-upon wife Linda (Judd), who puts up with everything for as long she can. Dreary film is brightened by oddly updated covers of his tunes done by contemporary pop stars such as Elvis Costello, Alanis Morissette, and Sheryl Crow, but the story contains no real nods to Porter's artistic genius or creative struggles. Contrived staging is stolen from better films like "All That Jazz" and "Cabaret." Solid cast is very good, especially Judd, but story is deadly dull and glum. **125m/C DVD.** Kevin Kline, Ashley Judd, Jonathan Pryce, Keith Allen, Natalie Cole, Elvis Costello, Kevin McNally, Allan Corduner, Sandra Nelson, James Wilby, Kevin McKidd, Richard Dillane, Peter Polycarpou, Edward Baker-Duly; ***D:*** Irwin Winkler; ***W:*** Jay Cocks; ***C:*** Tony Pierce-Roberts.

De Mayerling a Sarajevo 1/2 *Mayerling to Sarajevo; Sarajevo* **1940** Looks at the romance and marriage, as well as royal pomp and circumstance, of the Countess Sophie (Feuillere) and the Archduke Franz-Ferdinand (Lodge). The assassination of these innocuous rulers at Sarajevo would lead to the outbreak of WWI. French with subtitles. **89m/B VHS.** *FR* Edwige Feuillere, John Lodge, Aime Clariond, Gabrielle Dorziat; ***D:*** Max Ophuls; ***W:*** Kurt Alexander; ***C:*** Curt Courant, Otto Heller; ***M:*** Oscar Straus.

Deacon Brodie **1998** William Deacon Brodie (Connolly) is one of Edinburgh's most respected citizens in 1788. So his trial and conviction for defrauding the city is doubly shocking—until his secret life of gambling, drinking, and wenching is exposed. **90m/C VHS, DVD.** *GB* Billy Connolly, Patrick Malahide, Catherine McCormack, Lorcan Cranitch; ***D:*** Philip Saville; ***W:*** Simon Donald; ***C:*** Ivan Strasburg; ***M:*** Simon Boswell. **TV**

The Dead 1/2 **1987 (PG)** The poignant final film by Huston, based on James Joyce's short story from "Dubliners." At a Christmas dinner party in 1904 Dublin, Gabriel Conroy (McCann) discovers how little he knows about his wife Gretta (Angelica Huston) when a song reminds her of a cherished lost love. Beautifully captures the spirit of the story while providing Huston an opportunity to create a last lament on the fickle nature of time and life. **82m/C VHS.** *GB* Anjelica Huston, Donal McCann, Marie Kean, Donal Donnelly, Dan O'Herlihy, Helen Carroll, Frank Patterson; ***D:*** John Huston; ***W:*** Tony (Walter Anthony) Huston; ***C:*** Fred Murphy; ***M:*** Alex North. Ind. Spirit '88: Director (Huston), Support. Actress (Huston); Natl. Soc. Film Critics '87: Film.

Dead Again 1/2 **1991 (R)** Branagh's first film since his brilliant debut as the director/star of "Henry V" again proves him a visionary force on and off camera. Smart, cynical L.A. detective Mike Church (Branagh) is hired to discover the identity of a beautiful but mute woman (Thompson) whom he calls Grace. With the help of hypnotist Franklyn Madson (Jacobi) Mike finds that he's apparently trapped in a nightmarish cycle of murder begun years before, involving a jealous conductor and his concert pianist wife. Literate, lovely to look at, suspenseful, with a sense of humor to match its high style. **107m/C VHS, DVD.** Kenneth Branagh, Emma Thompson, Andy Garcia, Lois Hall, Richard Easton, Derek Jacobi, Hanna Schygulla, Campbell Scott, Wayne Knight, Christine Ebersole; ***Cameos:*** Robin Williams; ***D:*** Kenneth Branagh; ***W:*** Scott Frank; ***C:*** Matthew F. Leonetti; ***M:*** Patrick Doyle.

Dead Ahead **1996 (PG-13)** Skilled archer Maura Loch (Zimbalist) is enjoying a camping trip with her family until four bankrobbers on the lam stumble across them and take Maura's son hostage. Armed with her bow, Maura tracks the criminals to save her child. **92m/C VHS.** Stephanie Zimbalist, Sarah Chalke, Tom Butler, Brendan Fletcher, Peter Onorati, John Tench, Michael Tayles, Douglas Arthurs; ***D:*** Stuart Cooper; ***W:*** David Alexander; ***C:*** Curtis Petersen; ***M:*** Charles Bernstein. **CABLE**

Dead Ahead: The Exxon Valdez Disaster *Disaster at Valdez* **1992 (PG-13)** Focuses on the first crucial days after the March 24, 1989, oil spill when the Exxon Valdez ran aground off Alaska in Prince William Sound. Portrays the inadequate precautions, incompetence, greed, and petty bureaucracy that made an appalling situation even worse. Lloyd stars as Exxon official Frank Iarossi, in charge of the official cleanup, caught between onsite confusion and corporate bungling while Heard is outraged environmentalist Dan Lawn. News and home videotapes of the actual spill are used to enhance the dramatization. Filmed in Vancouver, British Columbia. **90m/C VHS.** Christopher Lloyd, John Heard, Rip Torn, Michael Murphy, Don S. Davies, Kenneth Welsh, Bob Gunton, Mark Metcalf, Paul Guilfoyle, David Morse, Jackson Davies; ***D:*** Paul Seed; ***W:***

Michael Baker; ***M:*** David Ferguson. **CABLE**

Dead Aim WOOF! 1987 (R) A dud about Soviet spies who introduce even more drugs into New York City, ostensibly to bring about the downfall of the U.S. Obviously a completely far-fetched plot. **91m/C VHS.** Ed Marinaro, Isaac Hayes, Corbin Bernsen; ***D:*** William Vanderkloot.

Dead Air 🦴🦴 **1994 (PG-13)** Atmospheric murder mystery finds radio deejay Hines getting calls from a mystery woman who says she knows him well and has kidnapped his new girlfriend. Meanwhile, a woman claiming to be a reporter wants to interview him and things around the radio station start looking decidedly sinister. **91m/C VHS.** Gregory Hines, Debrah Farentino, Gloria Reuben, Beau Starr, Laura Harrington, Michael (M.K.) Harris, W. Earl Brown, Veronica Cartwright; ***D:*** Fred Walton; ***W:*** David Amann; ***M:*** Dana Kaproff.

Dead Alive 🦴🦴 *Braindead* **1993** This outrageously over-the-top horror flick from New Zealand is a gore aficionado's delight (think "Evil Dead" movies for comparison). Set in 1957 and satirizing the bland times, the "plot" has the mom of a nerdy son getting bitten by an exotic monkey, which promptly turns her into a particularly nasty ghoul. This condition is apparently contagious (except for her son who tries to hide the fact mom is literally a monster) and calls for lots of spurting blood and body parts which take on lives of their own. For those with strong stomachs and senses of humor. Also available in an 85-minute R-rated version. **97m/C VHS, DVD.** *NZ* Timothy Balme, Elizabeth Moody, Diana Penalver, Ian Watkin, Breanda Kendall, Stuart Devenie, Peter Jackson, Forrest J Ackerman; ***D:*** Peter Jackson; ***W:*** Fran Walsh, Stephen Sinclair, Peter Jackson; ***C:*** Murray Milne; ***M:*** Peter Dasent.

Dead and Buried 🦴🦴 **½ 1981 (R)** Farentino is the sheriff who can't understand why the victims of some pretty grisly murders seem to be coming back to life. Eerily suspenseful. **95m/C VHS, DVD, Blu-ray Disc.** James Farentino, Jack Albertson, Melody Anderson, Lisa Blount, Bill Quinn, Michael Pataki, Robert Englund, Barry Corbin, Lisa Marie; ***D:*** Gary Sherman; ***W:*** Dan O'Bannon, Ronald Shusett; ***C:*** Steven Poster; ***M:*** Joe Renzetti.

Dead Are Alive 🦴🦴 **½ 1972** Alcoholic archaeologist Jason (Cord) has come to Italy to search for Etruscan ruins near the home of orchestral conductor Nicos (John Marley) and his wife Myra (Samantha Eggar), Jason's ex-lover. Soon after he opens an Etruscan tomb, a series of violent murders begin. The above-average giallo shocker and is much better than director Crispino's more popular "Autopsy." **103m/C DVD.** *IT* Alex Cord, Samantha Eggar, John Marley, Nadja Tiller, Horst Frank, Enzo Tarascio; ***D:*** Armando Crispino; ***W:*** Armando Crispino, Lucio Battistrada; ***C:*** Erico Menczer; ***M:*** Riz Ortolani.

Dead As a Doorman 🦴 **½ 1985** A young writer takes a part-time post as a doorman and becomes the target of a murderous lunatic. **83m/C VHS.** Bradley Whitford, Sharon Schlarth, Bruce Taylor; ***D:*** Gary Youngman.

Dead Badge 🦴🦴 **½ 1994 (R)** An honest cop is reassigned to a corrupt precinct and becomes targeted for death. **95m/C VHS.** Brian Wimmer, Olympia Dukakis, Yaphet Kotto, M. Emmet Walsh, James B. Sikking, Marta DuBois; ***D:*** Douglas Barr; ***W:*** Douglas Barr; ***M:*** Mark Snow.

Dead Bang 🦴🦴 **½ 1989 (R)** A frustrated cop uncovers a murderous white supremacist conspiracy in L.A. Frankenheimer's deft directorial hand shapes a somewhat conventional cop plot into an effective vehicle for Johnson. **102m/C VHS, DVD.** Don Johnson, Bob Balaban, William Forsythe, Penelope Ann Miller, Tim Reid, Frank Military, Michael Higgins, Michael Jeter, Evans Evans, Tate Donovan; ***D:*** John Frankenheimer; ***W:*** Robert Foster; ***C:*** Gerry Fisher; ***M:*** Gary Chang, Michael Kamen.

Dead Beat 🦴🦴 **½ 1994 (R)** Teen love and lust—and murder—all set in Albuquerque, New Mexico, circa 1965. Womanizer Kit (Ramsey) will use any tale to score with his dates—and is happy to pass on tips to adoring disciple Rudy (Getty). When Kit meets up with rebellious rich girl Kirsten (Wagner), she demands proof of his love and he confides he once murdered a girl. Kirsten tries to tighten her stranglehold on Kit with this info and force Rudy from his life but Kit's dark side doesn't stay hidden either. **94m/C VHS.** Bruce Ramsay, Natasha Gregson Wagner, Balthazar Getty, Meredith Salenger, Sara Gilbert, Deborah Harry, Max Perlich, Alex Cox; ***D:*** Adam Dubov; ***W:*** Adam Dubov.

Dead Birds 🦴🦴 **2004 (R)** In 1863 Alabama, a group of Confederate soldiers, led by William (Thomas), rob a bank of its gold bullion—leaving a lot of dead bodies behind—and plan to head to Mexico. But first, they spend the night in an abandoned plantation house that apparently isn't so abandoned. They hear noises, see strange creatures, and start to get very spooked indeed. **91m/C DVD.** Henry Thomas, Patrick Fugit, Nicki Aycox, Michael Shannon, Muse Watson, Mark Boone Jr., Isaiah Washington IV; ***D:*** Alex Turner; ***W:*** Simon Barrett; ***C:*** Steve Yedlin; ***M:*** Peter Lopez.

Dead Bodies 🦴 **½ 2003** Premise strains credulity. After an argument, slacker Tommy (Scott) discovers that whiny ex-girlfriend Jean (Davis) has accidentally died. So Tommy decides to bury the body in the woods, only to find the one patch of dirt that already contains a dead body—a woman missing for 8 years. So the police find 2 dead bodies and Tommy is in deep muck. **84m/C DVD.** *IR* Andrew Scott, Kelly Reilly, Sean McGinley, Gerard McSorley, Darren Healy, Katy Davis; ***D:*** Robert Quinn; ***W:*** Derek Landy; ***C:*** Donal Gilligan; ***M:*** Ray Harman.

Dead Boyz Can't Fly 🦴🦴 **1993 (R)** Disturbing look at urban violence. Dysfunctional punk leads his equally amoral cohorts on a looting spree in a near-empty highrise in revenge against a patronizing businessman. The unrated version contains 10 more minutes of violence. **92m/C VHS.** Delia Sheppard, Sheila Kennedy, Ruth (Coreen) Collins, Mark McCulley, Brad Friedman; ***D:*** Howard Winters.

Dead Broke 🦴🦴 **1999 (R)** Lying witnesses make it hard for detective Sam (Glover) to solve a murder that happens outside a Brooklyn debt collection agency, whose employees are all suspicious characters. Hits all the film noir cliches but you're never quite sure if this is intended as a spoof or not. **98m/C DVD.** John Glover, Paul Sorvino, Jill(ian) Hennessey, Tony Roberts, Justin Theroux, Patricia Scanlon, Nela Wagman, Cheryl Rogers; ***D:*** Edward Vilga; ***W:*** Edward Vilga; ***C:*** Joaquin Baca-Asay; ***M:*** Edward Bilous.

A Dead Calling 🦴 **½ 2006 (R)** Familiar horror storyline has a few frights. Reporter Rachel (Holden) has returned home after a personal tragedy and joined the local TV station. She's given a fluff assignment to investigate the town's historic homes but runs into trouble with the Sullivan place. That's where Frank Sullivan (Oman) butchered his family and escaped custody. And when Rachel enters the house, the ghosts of the slain family plead for her help to find their eternal rest. Except Frank has other ideas. **90m/C DVD.** Alexandra Holden, Bill Moseley, Sid Haig, Leslie Easterbrook, Timothy Oman, John Burke, Caia Coley; ***D:*** Michael Feifer; ***W:*** Michael Feifer; ***C:*** Hank Beaumert Jr.; ***M:*** Glenn Morrisette. **VIDEO**

Dead Calm 🦴🦴🦴 **1989 (R)** A taut Australian thriller based on a novel by Charles Williams. A young married couple is yachting on the open seas when they happen upon the lone survivor of a sinking ship. They take him on board only to discover he's a homicidal maniac. Makes for some pretty suspenseful moments that somewhat make up for the weak ending. **97m/C VHS, DVD.** *AU* Sam Neill, Billy Zane, Nicole Kidman, Rod Mullinar; ***D:*** Phillip Noyce; ***W:*** Terry Hayes; ***C:*** Dean Semler; ***M:*** Graeme Revell.

Dead Center 🦴🦴 *Crazy Joe* **1994 (R)** Street punk gets trained as assassin by secret government agency that frames him for the murder of a U.S. senator. So now he has to stay alive long enough to prove his innocence. **90m/C VHS.** Justin Lazard, Eb Lottimer, Rachel York; ***D:*** Steve Carver.

Dead Certain 🦴 **1992 (R)** A "Silence of the Lambs" rip-off. Dourif (again specializing in weirdos) is the jailed serial killer providing tantalizing clues to the identity of a new killer on the loose. **93m/C VHS.** Brad Dourif, Francesco Quinn, Karen Russell, Joel Kaiser; ***D:*** Anders Palm; ***W:*** Anders Palm.

Dead Cold 🦴🦴 **½ 1996 (R)** Screenwriter Eric Thornsen (Mulkey) decides he and wife Alicia (Anthony) need a second honeymoon at a remote cabin. But their privacy is disturbed by homicidal fugitive Kale (Dobson), who drugs and dumps Eric's body down a ravine. But of course Eric's not really dead. Decent thriller is slow to start but picks up speed in the second half. **91m/C VHS.** Lysette Anthony, Chris Mulkey, Peter Dobson, Alina Thompson, Michael Champion; ***D:*** Kurt Anderson; ***W:*** Richard Brandes; ***C:*** M. David Mullen; ***M:*** Richard Bowers.

Dead Connection 🦴🦴 **1994 (R)** Beautiful reporter Bonet is in cahoots with cop Madsen to see justice brought the "phone sex killer" who is terrorizing Los Angeles. **93m/C VHS.** Michael Madsen, Lisa Bonet, Gary Stretch; ***D:*** Nigel Dick; ***W:*** Larry Grolin; ***M:*** Rolfe Kent.

Dead Cool 🦴🦴 **2004 (R)** Self-absorbed 15-year-old David (Geller) has yet to come to terms with his father Josh's (Callis) death and frequently talks to his ghost. He and his younger brother (Johnson) are upset when their mother Henny (Stubbs) decides to move them in with her divorced boyfriend Mark (Calf). To complicate the situation further, Mark's ex-wife Deirdre (Arquette), a self-help author, lives around the corner with the couple's two daughters. Since Deirdre has just written a book about stepfamilies, she decides they should all practice what she's preached. **103m/C DVD.** *GB* Stephen Geller, Imogen Stubbs, Anthony Calf, Rosanna Arquette, James Callis, Aaron Johnson, Liz Smith, Gemma Lawrence, Olivia Wedderburn; ***D:*** David Cohen; ***W:*** David Cohen; ***C:*** Jean-Paul Seresin; ***M:*** Andy Richards, Mike Higham.

Dead Creatures 🦴 **2001** A close-knit group of British twentysomething women travels around the dingy areas outside of London satiating their need for human flesh with saran-wrapped body parts they carry in their luggage. The girls are all suffering from a kind of zombie-disease that is inflicted by a bite and eventually results in the victim's literal decomposition. The dreary tone of the film echoes that of lower-class British TV dramas: heavy grainy images, squalid locations with minimal lighting and makeup. Parkinson directs this low-key horror drama without the usual female nudity prevalent in today's micro-budgeted horror films, but the lack of a thriller element or traditional genre structure works against it. Without anywhere to go with the story, this one peters out around the halfway mark. The gore effects, though used minimally, are repugnant and truly nauseating. **89m/C DVD.** Beverly Wilson, Antonia Beamish, Brendan Gregory; ***D:*** Andrew Parkinson; ***W:*** Andrew Parkinson; ***C:*** Jack Shepherd; ***M:*** Andrew Parkinson.

Dead Dog 🦴🦴 **2000** Tom and Perri's dog gets mowed down by a hit-and-run driver on the streets of NYC. Tormented, Tom's life unravels causing Perri to worry about the possible fallout from his urge for vengeance. **90m/C VHS, DVD.** Jeremy Sisto, Paige Turco, Emily Cline, Julianne Nicholson, Lisa Bowman, Christopher Cousins, Jay O. Sanders, Adrienne Shelly, David Thornton; ***D:*** Christopher Goode; ***W:*** Grant Morris; ***C:*** Eric Schmidt; ***M:*** John M. Davis. **VIDEO**

The Dead Don't Die 🦴 **1975** Unbelievable plot set in the 1930s has Hamilton as a detective trying to prove his brother was wrongly executed for murder. He ultimately clashes with the madman who wants to rule the world with an army of zombies. Perhaps if they had cast Hamilton as Master of the Zombies. **74m/C VHS.** George Hamilton, Ray Milland, Linda Cristal, Ralph Meeker, Joan Blondell, James McEachin; ***D:*** Curtis Harrington. **TV**

Dead Easy 🦴🦴 **1982** Livin' ain't easy for a Sydney sleaze-club owner, his working-girl girlfriend, and a slandered cop when they're caught between machete-wielding enemy gangs (it seems somebody made the crime boss REALLY mad). The three flee in that quintessential escape vehicle—a two-ton truck—to qualify the effort as an Australian contender for greatest chase scene ever (heavy chassis category). **92m/C VHS.** *AU* Scott Burgess, Rosemary Paul; ***D:*** Bert Deling.

Dead End 🦴🦴🦴 **½** *Cradle of Crime* **1937** Sidney Kingsley play, adapted for the big screen by Lillian Hellman, traces the lives of various inhabitants of the slums on New York's Lower East Side as they try to overcome their surroundings. Gritty drama saved from melodrama status by some genuinely funny moments. Film launched the Dead End Kids. **92m/B VHS, DVD.** Sylvia Sidney, Joel McCrea, Humphrey Bogart, Wendy Barrie, Claire Trevor, Allen Jenkins, Marjorie Main, Billy Halop, Huntz Hall, Bobby Jordan, Gabriel Dell, Leo Gorcey, Charles Halton, Bernard Punsley, Minor Watson, James Burke; ***D:*** William Wyler; ***W:*** Lillian Hellman; ***C:*** Gregg Toland; ***M:*** Alfred Newman.

Dead End 🦴🦴 **½ 1998 (R)** Police sargeant Henry Smolenski (Roberts) gains custody of his troubled 16-year-old son Adam (Tierney) after his ex-wife's death. Then he learns that the death is being investigated as a murder and Adam is the primary suspect. When Adam takes off, Henry searches for him and winds up becoming a suspect himself. Soon the estranged father and son are teaming up to discover who's out to frame them. Roberts gets to play a likable, caring character for a change of pace. **93m/C VHS, DVD.** *CA* Eric Roberts, Jacob Tierney, Jayne Heitmeyer, Eliza Roberts, Jack Langedijk, Frank Schorpion; ***D:*** Douglas Jackson; ***W:*** Karl Schiffman; ***C:*** Georges Archambault; ***M:*** Milan Kymlicka. **VIDEO**

Dead End City 🦴 **½ 1988** Street-wise resident of L.A. organizes fellow citizens into a vigilante force to fight the gangs for control of the city. **88m/C VHS.** Dennis Cole, Gregory Scott Cummins, Christine Lunde, Robert Z'Dar, Darrell Nelson, Alena Downs; ***D:*** Peter Yuval; ***W:*** Michael Bogert.

Dead End Drive-In 🦴🦴 **1986 (R)** In a surreal, grim future a man is trapped at a drive-in theatre-cum-government-run concentration camp, where those considered to be less than desirable members of society are incarcerated. **92m/C VHS, DVD.** *AU* Ned Manning, Natalie McCurry, Peter Whitford; ***D:*** Brian Trenchard-Smith.

Dead End Street 🦴 **½** *Kvish L'Lo Motzah* **1983** Young prostitute attempts to change her self-destructive lifestyle. It's not easy. **86m/C VHS, DVD.** *IS* Anat Atzmon, Yehoram Gaon; ***D:*** Yaky Yosha; ***W:*** Yaky Yosha, Eli Tavor.

Dead Evidence 🦴🦴 *Lawless: Dead Evidence* **2000 (R)** Young P.I. Jodie Keane (Dotchin) teams up with ex-cop John Lawless (Smith) to track a serial killer by offering herself as the next potential victim. **94m/C VHS, DVD.** *NZ* Kevin Smith, Angela Dotchin, C. Thomas Howell, Bruce Hopkins, Geoff Dolan, Andrew Binns; ***D:*** Charlie Haskell; ***W:*** Gavin Strawhan; ***C:*** Mark Olsen; ***M:*** Peter Blake. **TV**

Dead Eyes of London 🦴🦴 **½** *Dark Eyes of London; Die Toten Augen von London* **1961** Blind old German men are dying to lower their premiums in this geriatric thriller: someone (perhaps the director of the home for the blind?) is killing off the clientele for their insurance money, and a Scotland Yard inspector aims to expose the scam. Relatively early vintage Kinski, it's a remake of the eerie 1939 Lugosi vehicle, "The Human Monster" (originally titled "Dark Eyes of London"), adapted from Edgar Wallace's "The Testament of Gordon Stuart." **95m/B VHS, DVD.** *GE* Joachim Fuchsberger, Karin Baal, Dieter Borsche, Ady Berber, Klaus Kinski, Eddi Arent, Wolfgang Lukschy; ***D:*** Alfred Vohrer.

Dead Fire 🦴🦴 **1998** A space substation has been in orbit around earth for the past 50 years trying to regenerate the planet's poisoned atmosphere. But now a shipboard traitor is trying to destroy the operation. **105m/C VHS.** Matt Frewer, C. Thomas Howell, Monica Schnarre; ***D:*** Robert Lee; ***M:*** Peter Allen. **VIDEO**

Dead Fish 🦴 **2004 (R)** Despite the cast, it stinks like week-old dead fish too. Contract killer Lynch (Oldman) runs into trouble when he helps out Abe (Potts) and his pregnant girlfriend Mimi (Anaya) with a would-be thief. His and Abe's cell phones accidentally get switched and Lynch falls inexplicably and instantly in love with Mimi despite the fact that he's on the way to his next hit. **94m/C DVD.** *GB* Gary Oldman, Elena Anaya, Robert Carlyle, Karel Roden, Terence Stamp, Andrew Lee Potts, Billy Zane, Jimi Mistry; ***D:*** Charley Stadler; ***W:*** David Mitchell, Adam Kreutner; ***C:*** Fraser Taggart; ***M:*** Andrew Cato.

Dead for a Dollar 1/2 *T'ammazzo! Raccomandati a Dio* **1970** A Colonel, a con man, and a mysterious woman team up in the Old West to search for the $200,000 they stole from a local bank. **92m/C VHS.** John Ireland, George Hilton, Piero Vida, Sandra Milo; ***D:*** Osvaldo Civirani.

Dead Funny **1994 (R)** Vivian (Pena) returns to her Manhattan walk-up to find boyfriend Reggie (McCarthy) dead on her kitchen table, skewered by a Samurai sword. Instead of calling the police, Viv gets gal pal Louise (Turco) to come over to figure out who did Reg in. Instead, they get drunk and discuss Reggie's (who seen in flashbacks) immaturity and penchent for practical jokes. Good performances, twist ending, but situation runs out of steam. **91m/C VHS.** Elizabeth Pena, Andrew McCarthy, Paige Turco, Blanche Baker, Lisa Jane Persky, Michael Mantell; ***D:*** John Feldman; ***W:*** John Feldman; ***M:*** Sheila Silver.

The Dead Girl **2006 (R)** Moncrieff's troubling drama showcases one victim of a serial killer from five female perspectives. The title character is runaway druggie hooker Krista (Murphy), whose body is found by downtrodden Arden (Collette). Forensic student Leah (Byrne) first thinks the body is that of her missing sister, while enabling wife Ruth (Hurt) suspects her husband (Searcy) is the killer. Then Melora (Harden) rounds out the story when Krista is identified and the grieving mom is forced to confront how her daughter was living. **93m/C DVD.** *US* Toni Collette, Rose Byrne, Mary Beth Hurt, Marcia Gay Harden, Brittany Murphy, Kerry Washington, Giovanni Ribisi, Nick Searcy, Piper Laurie, Josh Brolin, James Franco, Mary Steenburgen, Bruce Davison; ***D:*** Karen Moncrieff; ***W:*** Karen Moncrieff; ***C:*** Michael Grady; ***M:*** Adam Gorgoni.

Dead Girls **1990 (R)** A rock group whose lyrics focus on suicide goes on vacation. The members find themselves stalked by a serial killer who decides to take matters out of the musicians' hands and into his own. Graphic violence. **105m/C VHS.** Diana Karanikas, Angela Eads; ***D:*** Dennis Devine; ***W:*** Steve Jarvis; ***C:*** Aaron Schneider.

Dead Gorgeous 1/2 **2002** Antonia Ashton (McCrory) is a brazen hussy and a consummate schemer. She's married to boring business tycoon Hector (Cook) while carrying on with hunky professor Vic (Owen). She wants out of her marriage—by murder if necessary. Mousy Rose Bell (Ripley) wishes she could get rid of her drunken, philandering spouse as well. Antonia and Rose—old friends from the war—meet again in a gray 1946 London. Antonia has a plan—she'll see that Rose's husband has an "accident" and Rose will do the same with Hector. Antonia carries through but a grateful Rose is more cautious. Some unexpected twists in this variation of "Strangers on a Train." From the 1989 novel, "On the Edge," by Peter Lovesey. **100m/C VHS, DVD.** *GB* Fay Ripley, Helen McCrory, Ron Cook, Lloyd Owen, Jonathan Phillips, Dermot Crowley, Michael Mueller; ***D:*** Sarah Harding; ***W:*** Andrew Payne; ***C:*** Simon Kossoff; ***M:*** Jennie Muskett. **TV**

The Dead Hate the Living **1999 (R)** Young filmmakers sneak into an abandoned medical research facility to make a low-budget horror feature about a scientist who raises the dead to be his zombie slaves. Little do they know that the facility was abandoned after a scientist's experiments to revive the dead through alchemical means went horribly wrong. When they discover the scientist's body, they decide to go use what they've found to add to the film's production value and accidentally manage to open a rift into the dimension of the dead. The script is a patchwork of influences. Effects are impressive, with many spectacular (and gruesome) zombies. **90m/C DVD.** Eric Clawson, Jamie Donahue, Brett Beardslee, Wendy Speake; ***D:*** Dave Parker; ***W:*** Dave Parker; ***C:*** Tom Calloway; ***M:*** Jared DePasquale.

Dead Heart **1996** Culture clash story set in the 1930s is highlighted by a terrific lead performance by Brown. He's cop Ray Lorkin, whose territory is the tiny community of Wala Wala in Australia's outback. This remote spot just happens to be a focal point for the local aboriginals, who regard the area as a spiritual place. Trouble erupts when an aboriginal prisoner (Pederson), who just happened to be having an affair with the schoolteacher's white wife (Mikkiken) is found hanged in his cell. Tradition demands revenge—from there every other situation in the community just gets worse. First-timer Parsons directs from his stage play. **106m/C VHS, DVD.** *AU* Bryan Brown, Ernie Dingo, Angie Milliken, Aasron Pedersen, Lewis Fitz-Gerald, John Jarratt, Anne Tenney, Gnarnayarrahe Waitaire, Lafe Charlton; ***D:*** Nick Parsons; ***W:*** Nick Parsons; ***C:*** James Bartle; ***M:*** Stephen Rae.

Dead Heat 1/2 **1988 (R)** Some acting talent and a few funny moments unfortunately don't add up to a fine film, though they do save it from being a complete woofer. In this one even the cops are zombies when one of them is resurrected from the dead to help his partner solve his murder and rid the city of the rest of the undead. **86m/C VHS, DVD.** Joe Piscopo, Treat Williams, Lindsay Frost, Darren McGavin, Vincent Price, Keye Luke, Clare Kirkconnell; ***D:*** Mark Goldblatt; ***W:*** Terry Black; ***C:*** Robert Yeoman; ***M:*** Ernest Troost.

Dead Heat 1/2 *I Fought the Law* **2001 (R)** Pally Lamarr (Sutherland) is a suicidal ex-cop with a drinking problem. His shady stepbrother Ray (LaPaglia) persuades Pally to purchase a long-shot racehorse with a jockey (Bluteau) who's an ex-con gambling addict. Things get even worse when a mobster (Benzali), who also wanted the horse, gets involved. Plot has too many holes but the two leads are worth watching. **97m/C VHS, DVD.** *CA* Kiefer Sutherland, Anthony LaPaglia, Radha Mitchell, Lothaire Bluteau, Daniel Benzali; ***D:*** Mark Malone; ***W:*** Mark Malone; ***M:*** Patric Caird.

Dead Heat on a Merry-Go-Round **1966 (R)** Coburn turns in a great performance as the ex-con who masterminds the heist of an airport safe. Intricately woven plot provides suspense and surprises. The film is also notable for the debut of Ford in a bit part (he has one line as a hotel messenger). **108m/C VHS, DVD.** James Coburn, Camilla Sparv, Aldo Ray, Nina Wayne, Robert Webber, Rose Marie, Todd Armstrong, Marian Moses, Severn Darden, Harrison Ford, Vic Tayback; ***D:*** Bernard Girard; ***W:*** Bernard Girard; ***C:*** Lionel Lindon; ***M:*** Stu Phillips.

Dead Heist 1/2 **2007** Four friends pick the wrong night for a bank heist and end up trapped by vampire zombie townsfolk. Were it not for Hunter (Kane), a mysteriously shady bloke familiar with creature extermination, they might never get away with their loot or their lives. A giddy attempt, seriously lacking in horror. **80m/C DVD.** Big Daddy Kane, D.J. Naylor, E-40, Bone Crusher; ***D:*** Bo Webb; ***W:*** Anghus Houvouras, Eric Tomosunas; ***C:*** Matt Malloy, Patrick Borowiak; ***M:*** Jim McKeever. **VIDEO**

Dead Husbands **1998 (PG-13)** Alex (Sheridan) is the beautiful wife of slick Dr. Carter Elston (Ritter), the best-selling author of relationship books. When Carter decides he wants to give everything up for smalltown life, horrified pampered spouse Alex meets a group of wives who offer her a unique solution (much more permanent than divorce). You see, the wives have a list of husbands to be gotten rid of—Alex kills the hubby at the top of the list and then adds Carter's name. Eventually, a fellow member will return the favor and off her annoying mate. But what happen when Dr. Elston finds the list? **90m/C VHS.** Nicolette Sheridan, John Ritter, Amy Yasbeck, Donna Pescow, Wendie Malick; ***D:*** Paul Shapiro. **CABLE**

Dead in a Heartbeat **2002** Veteran bomb squad cop Royko (Reinhold) teams up with heart surgeon Dr. Hayes (Miller) to find the mad bomber who's blowing people up via their pacemakers. Mediocre TV movie features a cliched plot that telegraphs all the twists. The leads do what they can with what they're given. **91m/C VHS, DVD.** *CA* Judge Reinhold, Penelope Ann Miller, Fulvio Cecere, Timothy Busfield, Matthew (Matt) Walker, Jeff(rey) Ballard, Sarah Jane Redmond; ***D:*** Paul Antier; ***W:*** Mark Rosman, Richard Ades; ***C:*** Danny Nowak; ***M:*** Louis Febre. **TV**

Dead in the Water 1/2 **1991 (PG-13)** Brown is Charlie Deegan, a big-time lawyer with a rich wife that he'd rather see dead. Charlie and his mistress plot the perfect murder to dispose of his spouse and collect her money. When plans go awry, he ends up as a suspect for the wrong murder in this story of infidelity and greed. **90m/C VHS.** Bryan Brown, Teri Hatcher, Anne DeSalvo, Veronica Cartwright; ***D:*** Bill Condon; ***W:*** Eleanor Gaver, Robert Seidenberg, Walter Klenhard.

Dead in the Water **2001 (R)** Wealthy hot babe Gloria (Swain) takes her boyfriend (Bairstow), their buddy (Thomas), and Marcos, the son of her father's business partner on the family cabin cruiser for a day of fun. Only tensions rise and violence erupts when Gloria gets too involved with the wrong guy. **89m/C VHS, DVD.** Dominique Swain, Henry Thomas, Scott Bairstow, Renata Fronzi, Sebastian DeVincente; ***D:*** Gustavo Lipzstein. **VIDEO**

Dead in the Water **2006 (R)** Arriving for a weekend retreat at the family cabin, Tiffany, Jen and their boyfriends find the cabin void of parents, cell phone reception, or a running vehicle. As night falls, zombies begin their attack. Instead of running like deer through the woods, the foursome decides to seek refuge in a boat out on the lake. Bad move, fairly decent movie. **78m/C DVD.** Alissa Bailey, Megan Renne Burgess, Mike Parrish, Bill Zasadil; ***D:*** Marc Buhmann; ***W:*** David Moore; ***C:*** Fred Miller; ***M:*** Piernicola Di Muro. **VIDEO**

Dead Leaves 1/2 **1998** After a young girl falls to her death her unstable boyfriend steals the body and embarks on a trip from New York to West Virginia, stopping along the way to perform strange rituals to preserve her beauty. As she increasingly decays physically so does he emotionally and mentally. Art-house flick has hypnotic music, long frames of rainy highways, deserted hotels, gloomy urban landscapes topped with narratives of dark poetry to portray the mood and feeling of a mad love. Not much in the way of dialogue, as the conversations tend to be a little one-sided. **80m/C DVD, UMD.** Haim Abramsky, Beth Gondek; ***D:*** Constantin Werner; ***W:*** Constantin Werner; ***C:*** Mindaugas Blaudziunas. **VIDEO**

Dead Lenny 1/2 **2006** Low-level LA mobster Lenny Long (Bauer) goes missing, along with the five million bucks he was supposed to deliver to NY wiseguy Tony Thick (Assante). Thick sends associate Shady (Baker) to straighten things out, only he finds a lot of crazy people who want a cut of any cash that turns up. Unsatisfying mob comedy. **89m/C DVD.** Armand Assante, Nicole Eggert, Stephen Baker, Steven Bauer, John Heard, Joe Piscopo, Whitney Able; ***D:*** Serge Rodnunsky; ***W:*** Serge Rodnunsky; ***C:*** Serge Rodnunsky; ***M:*** Greg Manning. **VIDEO**

Dead Letter Office 1/2 **1998** Lonely Alice (Otto) gets a job at the dead letter office of the postal system. Her boss is Frank (DelHoyo), a political refugee from Chile, who lost his family to the junta. Frank and Alice seem destined to hit it off but not before a few obstacles get in their path. Otto's father Barry has a brief scene as Alice's irresponsible dad. More distinctive than the story might indicate, thanks to the performances and tart comedy. **95m/C VHS.** *AU* Miranda Otto, George DelHoyo, Nicholas Bell, Syd Brisbane, Georgina Naidu, Vanessa Steele, Barry Otto; ***D:*** John Ruane; ***W:*** Deb Cox; ***C:*** Ellery Ryan; ***M:*** Roger Mason.

Dead Lucky 1/2 **1960** A novice tries gambling and wins a fortune, but his luck leads him into an entanglement with an assassin, a scam artist, and a beautiful woman. Based on the novel "Lake of Darkness." **91m/B VHS.** *GB* Vincent Ball, Betty McDowall, John Le Mesurier, Alfred Burke, Michael Ripper; ***D:*** Montgomery Tully.

Dead Man **1995 (R)** Depp wanders throughs the 19th-century American west as William Blake, an Ohio accountant who runs afoul of the law. Hooking up with a Native American named Nobody (Farmer), who envisions Blake as the famous English poet, the two try to stay one step ahead of the hired guns and lawmen out to get them. Action is sporadic and pace is all over the road in this offbeat and long-winded western, while Farmer's performance and Jarmusch's polished visuals are high points. **121m/B VHS, DVD.** Johnny Depp, Gary Farmer, Lance Henriksen, Michael Wincott, Mili Avital, Crispin Glover, Gabriel Byrne, Iggy Pop, Billy Bob Thornton, Jared Harris, Jimmie Ray Weeks, Mark Bringleson, John Hurt, Alfred Molina, Robert Mitchum; ***D:*** Jim Jarmusch; ***W:*** Jim Jarmusch; ***C:*** Robby Muller; ***M:*** Neil Young. N.Y. Film Critics '96: Cinematog.; Natl. Soc. Film Critics '96: Cinematog.

Dead Man on Campus **1997 (R)** Failing college freshmen Scott and Gosselaar learn that if your roomie commits suicide, you get a straight-A average for the year. So they decide to find a new roommate who's on the edge and make certain to push him over. Anyone who's ever done time in the dorms has heard this rumor, so it was only a matter of time before someone turned it into a screenplay. The wait wasn't long enough. One-joke premise can't sustain a whole movie, and Gosselaar goes a long way toward duplicating "Saved By the Bell" co-star Elizabeth Berkley's "Showgirls" um, success. **94m/C VHS, DVD.** Tom Everett Scott, Mark Paul Gosselaar, Alyson Hannigan, Poppy Montgomery, Lochlyn Munro, Randy Pearlstein, Mari Morrow, Jason Segel, Linda Cardellini, John Aprea; ***D:*** Alan Cohn; ***W:*** Michael Traeger, Mike White; ***C:*** John Thomas; ***M:*** Mark Mothersbaugh.

Dead Man Out **1989** Both Glover and Blades turn in exceptional performances in this thought-provoking drama. A convict on Death Row (Blades) goes insane and therefore cannot be executed. The state calls in a psychiatrist (Glover) to review the case and determine whether he can be cured so that the sentence can be carried out. Powerful and riveting morality check. **87m/C VHS.** Danny Glover, Ruben Blades, Tom Atkins, Larry Block, Samuel L. Jackson, Maria Ricossa; ***D:*** Richard Pearce; ***M:*** Cliff Eidelman.

Dead Man Walking **1988 (R)** In a post-holocaust future, half the population has been stricken with a deadly plague. Hauser is a mercenary, dying from the disease, who is hired to rescue a young woman who was kidnapped and is being held in the plague zone. **90m/C VHS.** Wings Hauser, Brion James, Pamela Ludwig, Sy Richardson, Leland Crooke, Jeffrey Combs; ***D:*** Gregory Brown; ***W:*** R.J. Marx.

Dead Man Walking 1/2 **1995 (R)** True story of a nun whose anti-death penalty beliefs put her in moral crisis with grieving victims when she becomes the spiritual advisor to a death-row murderer. Based on the book by Sister Helen Prejean, Sarandon stars as the nun who develops a relationship of understanding with inmate Poncelet (Penn), unwavering in her Christian beliefs even though Penn's character shows little or no remorse for the two young lovers he was accused of murdering. Penn offers one of the best performances (but worst hair-dos) of his career, while writer/director Robbins presents both sides of the death-penalty issue mingled with simple human compassion. **122m/C VHS, DVD.** Jon Abrahams, Jack Black, Susan Sarandon, Sean Penn, Robert Prosky, Raymond J. Barry, R. Lee Ermey, Celia Weston, Lois Smith, Scott Wilson, Roberta Maxwell, Margo Martindale, Barton Heyman, Larry Pine; ***D:*** Tim Robbins; ***W:*** Tim Robbins; ***C:*** Roger Deakins; ***M:*** David Robbins. Oscars '95: Actress (Sarandon); Ind. Spirit '96: Actor (Penn); Screen Actors Guild '95: Actress (Sarandon).

Dead Man's Bounty 1/2 *Summer Love* **2006 (R)** A Polish-made art house spaghetti western that's big on visuals but not much else. A nameless stranger rides into town with a dead outlaw. After collecting the bounty, he loses all the money in a card game with the sheriff and then considers reclaiming the body. Kilmer plays the dead guy. **94m/C DVD.** *PL* Boguslaw Linda, Karel Roden, Kasia (Katarzyna) Figura, Val Kilmer; ***D:*** Piotr Uklanski; ***W:*** Piotr Uklanski; ***C:*** Jacek Petrycki.

Dead Man's Eyes 1/2 **1944** Artist Chaney is accidentally blinded but may get a second chance through an eye operation.

His father-in-law offers his own eyes after he dies—and then he's murdered. Based on radio's "The Inner Sanctum Mysteries." **130m/B VHS, DVD.** Acquanetta, J. Edward Bromberg, Rosalind Ivan, Wilton Graff, Bernard B. Thomas, Lon Chaney Jr., Brenda Joyce, George Cleveland, Clara Blandick, Paul Kelly, Jean Parker, George Meeker; *D:* Wallace Fox, Reginald LeBorg; *W:* George Bricker, Dwight V. Babcock.

Dead Man's Revenge ♂♂ 1/2 **1993 (PG-13)** Ruthless railroad mogul Payton McCay (Dern) doesn't let anyone stand in his way—even if it means framing innocent homesteader Hatcher (Ironside) in order to get his land. Hatcher escapes from jail and goes after McCay, trailed by bounty hunter Bodeen (Coulouris). But Bodeen's not what he seems and has his own plans on getting even with the villainous McCay. **92m/C VHS.** Bruce Dern, Michael Ironside, Keith Coulouris, Randy Travis; *D:* Alan J. Levi; *W:* Jim Byrnes, David Chisholm.

Dead Man's Shoes ♂♂ **2004** Grungy revenge thriller has disturbed ex-soldier Richard (Considine) returning to his hometown in England's Midlands to get payback on the yabbos who tormented his mentally retarded younger brother Anthony (Kebbell). Things get quite bloody. **86m/C DVD.** *GB* Paddy Considine, Gary Stretch, Toby Kebbell; *D:* Shane Meadows; *W:* Shane Meadows; *C:* Danny Cohen.

Dead Mate ♂ **1988** A woman marries a mortician after a whirlwind romance only to discover that, to her husband, being an undertaker is not just a job, it's a way of life. **93m/C VHS.** Elizabeth Mannino, David Gregory, Lawrence Bockus, Adam Wahl; *D:* Straw Weisman.

Dead Men Can't Dance ♂♂ **1997 (R)** CIA agent Victoria Ellis (York) gets sent to South Korea to train with a women-only group of Army Rangers. Meanwhile, Vic's boyfriend Hart (Biehn) and his buddy Shooter (Paul) are in the demilitertized zone where Hart learns Shooter is out to steal nuclear detonators on behalf of crazy Senator Fowler (Ermey), who wants to revive the Cold War. Things go bad and the women are forced to take things into their own more than capable hands. Lots of action. **97m/C VHS.** Kathleen York, Michael Biehn, Adrian Paul, R. Lee Ermey, Grace Zabriskie; *D:* Steve (Stephen M.) Anderson; *W:* Mark Sevi, Bill Kerby, Paul Sinor; *C:* Levie Isaacks; *M:* Richard (Rick) Marvin.

Dead Men Don't Die ♂ 1/2 **1991 (PG-13)** An anchorman is slain by criminals but resurrected as a shambling voodoo zombie. Few viewers notice the difference in this inoffensive but repetitious farce. The living-dead Gould appears to be having a lot of fun. **94m/C VHS, DVD.** Elliott Gould, Melissa Anderson, Mark Moses, Philip Bruns, Jack Betts, Mabel King; *D:* Malcolm Marmorstein; *W:* Malcolm Marmorstein.

Dead Men Don't Wear Plaid ♂♂ 1/2 **1982 (PG)** Martin is hilarious as a private detective who encounters a bizarre assortment of suspects while trying to find out the truth about a scientist's death. Ingeniously interspliced with clips from old Warner Bros. films. Features Humphrey Bogart, Bette Davis, Alan Ladd, Burt Lancaster, Ava Gardner, Barbara Stanwyck, Ray Milland, and others. Its only flaw is that the joke loses momentum by the end of the film. **89m/B VHS, DVD.** Steve Martin, Rachel Ward, Reni Santoni, George Gaynes, Francis X. (Frank) McCarthy, Carl Reiner; *D:* Carl Reiner; *W:* Steve Martin, Carl Reiner; *C:* Michael Chapman; *M:* Miklos Rozsa.

Dead Men Tell ♂ 1/2 **1941** Eccentric Patience Nodbury (Griffies) believes she has discovered the whereabouts of a pirate ancestor's treasure. However, she dies mysteriously just after distributing portions of a map and hiring a boat to take her and several others exploring. Now it's up to Charlie Chan (Toler) to investigate (a talking parrot helps him out). 26th in the series. **61m/B DVD.** Sidney Toler, Victor Sen Yung, Sheila Ryan, Robert Weldon, George Reeves, Donald "Don" Douglas, Ethel Griffies, Milton Parsons, Truman Bradley; *D:* Harry Lachman; *W:* John Larkin; *C:* Charles G. Clarke.

Dead Men Walk ♂♂ *Creatures of the Devil* **1943** A decent, albeit low budget, chiller about twin brothers (Zucco in a dual role); one a nice, well-adjusted member of society, the other a vampire who wants to suck his bro's blood. Sibling rivalry with a bite. **65m/B VHS, DVD.** George Zucco, Mary Carlisle, Dwight Frye, Nedrick Young, Al "Fuzzy" St. John, Fern Emmett, Robert Strange; *D:* Sam Newfield; *W:* Fred Myton; *C:* Jack Greenhalgh; *M:* Leo Erdody.

The Dead Next Door ♂ **1989** Eerily reminiscent of "Night of the Living Dead." A scientist manufactures a virus which inhabits corpses and multiplies while replacing the former cells with its own. But the newly living corpses need human flesh to survive. In response, the government creates "The Zombie Squad" who do heroic battle with the stiffs. When a bizarre cult whose goal is the eradication of the human race befriend the dead, the battle gets ugly. **84m/C VHS, DVD.** Pete Ferry, Bogdan Pecic, Michael Grossi, Len Kowalewich, Jolie Jackunas, Robert Kokai, Scott Spiegel, J.R. Bookwalter; *D:* J.R. Bookwalter; *W:* J.R. Bookwalter; *M:* J.R. Bookwalter.

Dead of Night ♂♂♂♂ **1945** The template for episodic horror films, this suspense classic, set in a remote country house, follows the individual nightmares of five houseguests. Redgrave turns in a chillingly convincing performance as a ventriloquist terrorized by a demonic dummy. Not recommended for light-sleepers. Truly spine-tingling. **102m/B VHS, DVD.** *GB* Michael Redgrave, Mervyn Johns, Sally Ann Howes, Basil Radford, Naunton Wayne, Roland Culver, Googie Withers, Frederick Valk, Antony Baird, Judy Kelly, Miles Malleson, Ralph Michael, Mary Merrall, Renee Gadd, Michael Allan, Robert Wyndham, Esme Percy, Peggy Bryan, Hartley Power, Elisabeth Welch, Magda Kun, Garry Marsh; *D:* Alberto Cavalcanti, Charles Crichton, Basil Dearden, Robert Hamer; *W:* T.E.B. Clarke, John Baines, Angus MacPhail; *C:* Stanley Pavey, Douglas Slocombe; *M:* Georges Auric.

Dead of Night ♂ 1/2 **1977** This trilogy features Richard Matheson's tales of the Supernatural: "Second Chance," "Bobby," and "No Such Thing As a Vampire," all served up by your hostess, Elvira. **76m/C VHS.** Joan Hackett, Ed Begley Jr., Patrick Macnee, Anjanette Comer; *D:* Dan Curtis.

Dead of Night ♂ *Lighthouse* **1999 (R)** Leo Rook (Adamson) is a psycho who collects the severed heads of his victims as trophies. He's aboard the prison ship Hyperion, which is transporting criminals to a remote island off the northern English coast. Leo steals a lifeboat and escapes to desolate Gehenna Rocks just before the ship runs aground. Then the few survivors are subjected to Leo's stalking and slashing. Crude and gory. **95m/C VHS, DVD.** *GB* Chris(topher) Adamson, James Purefoy, Rachel Shelley, Paul Brooke, Don Warrington, Chris Dunne, Bob Goody, Pat Kelman; *D:* Simon Hunter; *W:* Simon Hunter; *C:* Tony Imi; *M:* Debbie Wiseman.

Dead of Winter ♂♂♂ **1987 (R)** A young actress is suckered into a private screen test for a crippled old director, only to find she is actually being remodeled in the guise of a murdered woman. Edge-of-your-seat suspense as the plot twists. **100m/C VHS, DVD.** Mary Steenburgen, Roddy McDowall, Jan Rubes, Ken Pogue, William Russ; *D:* Arthur Penn; *W:* Mark Shmuger, Mark Malone; *M:* Richard Einhorn.

Dead On ♂ 1/2 **1993 (R)** Illicit lovers want to get rid of their inconvenient spouses so they can be together always. But their perfect plan doesn't work out as expected. Also available in an unrated version. **87m/C VHS.** Matt McCoy, Shari Shattuck, David Ackroyd, Tracy Scoggins, Thomas Wagner; *D:* Ralph Hemecker; *W:* April Wayne.

Dead on Sight ♂♂ 1/2 **1994 (R)** A college student dreams of a masked man, a knife, a bound woman, and other terrors. Too bad her nightmares match the actions of a serial killer. **96m/C VHS.** Jennifer Beals, Daniel Baldwin, Kurtwood Smith, William H. Macy; *D:* Ruben Preuss; *W:* Lewis Green; *M:* Harry Manfredini.

Dead on the Money ♂♂ 1/2 **1991** Adequate made for TV suspenser about a woman who believes her lover plots a dire fate for her cousin. But nothing is what it seems here. Confusing, droopy in spots, but fun. **92m/C VHS.** Corbin Bernsen, Amanda Pays, John Glover, Eleanor Parker, Kevin McCarthy; *D:* Mark Cullingham; *W:* Gavin Lambert. **TV**

The Dead One ♂♂ **2007 (PG-13)** Diego (Valderrama) outfits himself in a zombie mariachi costume for the Mexican Day of the Dead parties but he's killed before he gets to do any celebrating. His restless spirit becomes a slave to the Atzec god of death, who has captured his soul. Diego is returned to the living to battle the death god for the soul of his girlfriend Maria (Cepeda) among others. Flashy-looking and fairly mild horror (note the rating) based on the comic book, "El Muerto." **88m/C DVD.** Wilmer Valderrama, Joel David Moore, Tony Plana, Maria Conchita Alonso, Angie Cepeda, Michael Parks, Tony Amendola, Billy Drago; *D:* Brian Cox; *W:* Brian Cox; *C:* Steve Yedlin; *M:* Tony Humecke. **VIDEO**

Dead or Alive ♂ 1/2 **1944** Tex and the Texas Rangers pretend to be outlaws in order to join a gang terrorizing a town. **54m/B VHS, DVD.** Tex Ritter, Dave O'Brien, Guy Wilkerson, Charles "Blackie" King, Bud Osborne, Reed Howes; *D:* Elmer Clifton.

Dead or Alive ♂ **2002** Parris Bally is a bounty hunter who alone can defeat an international terrorist, but his wife wants him to quit the business. Standard "one-last-job" actioner. **90m/C DVD.** Lowry Brooks Jr., Simeon Ndi, Gregory Dorsey, Veronica Pitts, Linda Floyd, Brian Horsey; *D:* Lowry Brooks Jr.; *W:* Lowry Brooks Jr.; *C:* Dominic Desantis; *M:* Gabriel Holden. **VIDEO**

Dead Pet ♂♂ 1/2 **2001** Kevin Coetteleer follows in the footsteps of Adam Sandler as a likeable, slightly geeky nice guy. He plays Jake Thompson who comes home from college to find that his repulsive parents have forgotten to pick him up at the airport and they've spent the rest of his education fund on an operation for their beloved poodle. From there, the comedy is nicely deadpan and inventive. **93m/C DVD.** Kevin Cotteleer, Gina Doctor, Brian Sostek; *D:* Kevin Cotteleer; *W:* Kevin Cotteleer; *C:* Dan Ming.

Dead Pigeon on Beethoven Street ♂♂ 1/2 **1972 (PG)** Sandy (Corbett) is a detective whose partner gets murdered while investigating blackmailers who take compromising pictures of international big-wigs. So Sandy goes undercover and joins the gang. Cheeky paranoia from Fuller. **92m/C VHS, DVD.** *GE* Glenn Corbett, Christa Lang, Anton Diffring, Alexander D'Arcy; *D:* Samuel Fuller; *W:* Samuel Fuller; *C:* Jerzy Lipman.

Dead Pit WOOF! **1989 (R)** Leave this one in the pit it crawled out of. Twenty years ago a mad scientist was killed as a result of horrible experiments he was conducting on mentally ill patients at an asylum. A young woman stumbles across his experiments, awakening him from the dead. **90m/C VHS.** Jeremy Slate, Steffen Gregory Foster; *D:* Brett Leonard.

Dead Poets Society ♂♂♂ 1/2 **1989 (PG)** An idealistic English teacher inspires a group of boys in a 1950s' prep school to pursue individuality and creative endeavor, resulting in clashes with school and parental authorities. Williams shows he can master the serious roles as well as the comic with his portrayal of the unorthodox educator. Big boxoffice hit occasionally scripted with a heavy hand in order to elevate the message. The ensemble cast is excellent. **128m/C VHS, DVD.** Robin Williams, Ethan Hawke, Robert Sean Leonard, Josh Charles, Gale Hansen, Kurtwood Smith, James Waterson, Dylan Kussman, Lara Flynn Boyle, Melora Hardin, Alexandra Powers; *D:* Peter Weir; *W:* Tom Schulman; *C:* John Seale; *M:* Maurice Jarre. Oscars '89: Orig. Screenplay; British Acad. '89: Film; Cesar '91: Foreign Film.

The Dead Pool ♂ 1/2 **1988 (R)** Dirty Harry Number Five features a new twist on the sports pool: a list of celebrities is distributed and bets are placed on who will be first to cross the finish line, literally. Unfortunately someone seems to be hedging their bet by offing the celebs themselves. When Harry's name appears on the list, he decides to throw the game. **92m/C VHS, DVD, Blu-ray Disc.** Clint Eastwood, Liam Neeson, Patricia Clarkson, Evan C. Kim, David Hunt, Michael Currie, Michael Goodwin, Jim Carrey, Louis Giambalvo, Justin Whalin; *D:* Buddy Van Horn; *M:* Lalo Schifrin.

Dead Presidents ♂♂ 1/2 **1995 (R)** Sophomore release for the Hughes brothers falls short of impact of "Menace II Society," but not for lack of ambition. Combination coming of age tale, war story, period piece and caper film follows Anthony ("Menace" veteran Tate) from his Bronx neighborhood in 1968 to Vietnam (for "Platoon" adventures in the wilds of Florida) and then back to the 'hood, where his life continues to spiral downward. Desperate to escape, he becomes involved in an armoured car heist to grab some cash (the "dead presidents"). Supported by hard-edged and effective acting, the Hughes continue to develop their control of cinematic imagery, displaying genius for staging violent, confrontational scenes. But the script, based on a story by the brothers, fails to live up to the vision, with characterization and dialogue lagging. Pounding period soundtrack with contributions by Curtis Mayfield, James Brown, and Marvin Gaye keeps things humming. **120m/C VHS, DVD.** Larenz Tate, Keith David, Chris Tucker, Freddy Rodriguez, N'Bushe Wright, Bokeem Woodbine, Rose Jackson, Clifton Powell, Kirk "Sticky Fingaz" Jones; *D:* Albert Hughes, Allen Hughes; *W:* Michael Henry Brown; *C:* Lisa Rinzler; *M:* Danny Elfman.

Dead Reckoning ♂♂♂ **1947** Bogart and Prince are two WWII veterans en route to Washington when Prince disappears. Bogart trails Prince to his Southern hometown and discovers he's been murdered. Blackmail and more murders follow as Bogie tries to uncover the truth. Suspenseful with good performances from all, especially Bogart. **100m/B VHS, DVD.** Matthew "Stymie" Beard, William Forrest, Humphrey Bogart, Lizabeth Scott, Morris Carnovsky, Charles Cane, Wallace Ford, William Prince, Marvin Miller; *D:* John Cromwell; *W:* Steve Fisher, Allen Rivkin, Oliver H.P. Garrett; *C:* Leo Tover; *M:* Marlin Skiles, Hugo Friedhofer.

Dead Reckoning ♂ 1/2 **1989 (R)** A plastic surgeon and his lovely wife embark on a cruise aboard his new luxury yacht. The intrigue begins with a storm, an isolated island, and the discovery that the captain is the wife's former lover. **95m/C VHS.** Cliff Robertson, Susan Blakely, Rick Springfield; *D:* Robert Lewis.

Dead Right ♂ 1/2 *If He Hollers, Let Him Go* **1968** A black man is unjustly put into prison in the Deep South. He manages to escape in order to try and prove his innocence. **111m/C VHS.** Raymond St. Jacques, Dana Wynter, Kevin McCarthy, Barbara McNair; *D:* Charles Martin; *W:* Charles Martin.

Dead Ringer ♂♂ 1/2 **1964** Bette Davis plays twins; Margaret, who's rich and recently widowed, and Edith, who's poor and feels that Margaret won her hubby unfairly (they were rivals for his affection). Edith kills Margaret and takes over her life, only to discover that the grass isn't always greener. Solid thriller showcases Davis in one of the better of her mystery/suspense roles of the 1960s. **115m/B VHS, DVD.** Bette Davis, Karl Malden, Peter Lawford, Phil Carey, Jean Hagen, George Macready, Estelle Winwood, George Chandler, Cyril Delevanti, Bert Remsen, Monika Henreid; *D:* Paul Henreid; *W:* Albert Beich, Oscar Millard; *C:* Ernest Haller; *M:* Andre Previn.

Dead Ringers ♂♂♂ **1988 (R)** A stunning, unsettling chiller, based loosely on a real case and the bestseller by Bari Wood and Jack Geasland. Irons, in an excellent dual role, is effectively disturbing as the twin gynecologists who descend into madness when they can no longer handle the fame, fortune, drugs, and women in their lives. Bujold is the actress/patient bedded by both brothers but jealously loved by Beverly. Acutely upsetting film made all the more so due to its graphic images and basis in fact. **117m/C VHS, DVD.** *CA* Jeremy Irons, Genevieve Bujold, Heidi von Palleske, Barbara Gordon, Shirley Douglas, Stephen Lack, Nick Nichols; *D:* David Cronenberg; *W:* David Cronenberg, Norman Snider; *C:* Peter Suschitzky; *M:* Howard Shore. Genie '89: Actor (Irons), Director (Cronenberg), Film; L.A. Film Critics '88: Director (Cronenberg), Support. Actress (Bujold); N.Y. Film Critics '88: Actor (Irons).

Dead Sexy ♂ 1/2 **2001 (R)** Detective Kate McBain (Tweed) is investigating the murders of four L.A. high-price hookers. Of course, she becomes more than a little interested in one of her suspects, charming Blue (Enos), but is Kate willing to die to find out the truth? **89m/C VHS, DVD.** Shannon Tweed, John Enos, Kenneth White, Sam Jones, Eric Keith; ***D:*** Robert Angelo; ***W:*** Anthony Laurence Greene, Elroy Canton; ***C:*** Kazuo Minami; ***M:*** Nicholas Rivera. **VIDEO**

Dead Silence **1990 (R)** Screenwriter Cliff Morgan has written a classic film noir screenplay... with the money, it seems all Cliff's problems are solved... or are they? **92m/C VHS.** Clete Keith, Doris Anne Soyka, Joseph Scott, Craig Fleming; ***D:*** Harrison Ellenshaw.

Dead Silence 1/2 **1996 (R)** Three escaped convicts, including ruthless Ted Handy (Coates), have hijacked a busload of deaf children and their teacher (Matlin) and are holding them hostage in an abandoned slaughterhouse. Veteran FBI agent John Cooper (Garner) is called in but he not only has to deal with a tense and possibly tragic situation but with a grandstanding politician (Smith) who's criticizing his every action and the last-minute arrival of another hostage negotiator (Davidovich). Based on the novel "A Maiden's Grave" by Jeffery Deaver. **105m/C VHS, DVD.** Gary Basaraba, Vanessa Vaughan, Blu Mankuma, Mimi Kuzyk, Scott Speedman, John Bourgeois, Barry Pepper, James Garner, Kim Coates, Marlee Matlin, Charles Martin Smith, Lolita (David) Davidovich, Kenneth Welsh, James Villemaire; ***D:*** Daniel Petrie Jr.; ***W:*** Donald Stewart; ***C:*** Thomas Burstyn; ***M:*** Jonathan Goldsmith. **CABLE**

Dead Silence 1/2 *Wilbur Falls* **1998** Renata (Edwards) decides on a simple plan of revenge against Jeff (Newmark) who humiliated her at their junior-high prom five years before. Only her plans backfire and he accidentally dies. That should be the plot but it's surrounded by so many other storylines that it gets lost in the telling, which is a shame since Edwards does a good job. **95m/C VHS, DVD.** Shanee Edwards, Danny Aiello, Sally Kirkland, Suzanne Cryer, Charles Newmark; ***Cameos:*** Maureen Stapleton; ***D:*** Juliane Glantz; ***W:*** Juliane Glantz; ***C:*** Kurt Brabbee; ***M:*** Jim Halfpenny.

Dead Silence 1/2 **2007 (R)** Did you know that automatonophobia is the fear of ventriloquist dummies? Well, they're usually pretty creepy even though this retro-looking flick isn't. Jamie (Kwanten) receives a vintage wooden dummy in the mail and then his wife gets murdered. He actually realizes that there's a connection between the two events and travels to his hometown of Ravens Fair, where ventriloquist Mary Shaw (Roberts) was murdered and her dummies buried with her. Except they're not staying in the ground and Mary's using them to get her revenge. **90m/C DVD, HD DVD.** *US* Ryan Kwanten, Donnie Wahlberg, Amber Valletta, Michael Fairman, Bob Gunton, Judith Roberts, Laura Regan, Joan Heney; ***D:*** James Wan; ***W:*** Leigh Whannell; ***C:*** John R. Leonetti; ***M:*** Charlie Clouser.

Dead Silent **1999 (R)** Doctor Julia Kerrbridge (Stewart) must care for her traumatized young niece whose parents were killed by the mob. But the girl, who has become mute, also has information that the bad guys will do anything to keep secret. Then there's Julia's new neighbor Kevin Finney (Lowe)—is he really a nice guy? Or a potential killer? **95m/C VHS, DVD.** Catherine Mary Stewart, Rob Lowe, Peter Colvey, Larry Day, Sean Devine, Allen Altman, Mark Camacho; ***D:*** Roger Cardinal; ***W:*** Ed Fitzgerald, Paul Koval; ***C:*** Bruno Philip; ***M:*** David Findlay. **VIDEO**

Dead Simple *Viva Las Nowhere* **2001 (R)** Frank Jacobs (Stern) and his nagging wife Helen (Richardson) owe a failing motel in dusty nowhere Kansas. Frank dreams of being a C&W singer and he hooks up with lounge performer Julie (Kohl), who has an abusive manager, has-been Roy Baker (Caan). Then there's Helen's twin sister Wanda (Richardson again), barmaid Marguerite (Stringfield), and the motel's garden, which gets a lot of unexpected fertilizer. Black comedy can't sustain its edge. **98m/C VHS, DVD.** Daniel Stern, James Caan, Patricia Richardson, Sherry Stringfield, Lacey Kohl, Tim Abell; ***D:*** Jason Bloom; ***W:*** Richard Uhlig, Steve Seitz; ***C:*** James Glennon; ***M:*** Andrew Gross.

Dead Sleep **1991 (R)** A nurse discovers that comatose patients at a private clinic have been used as guinea pigs by an overzealous doctor. This minor-league chiller from Down Under is said to have been inspired by an actual medical scandal. **95m/C VHS, DVD.** Linda Blair, Tony Bonner; ***D:*** Alec Mills.

Dead Snow **2009** Frozen Nazi zombies. Over their Easter break, seven medical students travel to a friend's remote cabin in northern Norway and are warned of evil in the woods. Turns out the area's one-time Nazi occupiers never left, they just became (hungry) zombies instead. Lots of gore and played for horror humor. Norwegian with subtitles. **91m/C DVD.** *NO* Bjorn Sundquist, Vegar Hoel, Stig Frode Henriksen, Charlotte Frogner, Jenny Skavlan, Jeppe Laursen, Lasse Valdal, Evy Kasseth Rosten, Orjan Gamst, Ane Dahl Torp, Tommy Wirkola; ***D:*** Tommy Wirkola; ***W:*** Tommy Wirkola; ***C:*** Matthew Weston; ***M:*** Christian Wibe.

Dead Solid Perfect **1988** Quaid stars as a golf pro whose life on the PGA tour is handicapped by his taste for scotch and his eye for the ladies. Based on the book by Dan Jenkins. **97m/C VHS.** Randy Quaid, Kathryn Harrold, Jack Warden, Larry Riley, Brett Cullen, Corinne Bohrer; ***D:*** Bobby Roth; ***W:*** Dan Jenkins, Bobby Roth.

Dead Space **1990 (R)** Dead space lay between the ears of whoever thought we needed this remake of 1982's "Forbidden World." At a lab on a hostile planet an experimental vaccine mutates into a prickly puppet monster who menaces the medicos. Needed: a vaccine against cheapo "Alien" ripoffs. **72m/C VHS.** Marc Singer, Laura Tate, Bryan Cranston, Judith Chapman; ***D:*** Fred Gallo.

Dead Tides **1997 (R)** Former Navy SEAL Mick (Piper) is hired by Nola (Kitaen) to pilot a sailboat from California to Mexico. But Mick soon realizes that Nola's the wife of a powerful drug dealer and he's in more trouble than he can imagine. **100m/C VHS.** Roddy Piper, Tawny Kitaen, Trevor Goddard, Miles O'Keeffe, Juan Fernandez; ***D:*** Serge Rodnunsky; ***W:*** Serge Rodnunsky. **VIDEO**

Dead to Rights 1/2 *Donato and Daughter* **1993 (R)** TV movie finds veteran LAPD cop Donato (Bronson) on the trail of a serial killer along with his new partner—who's not only his daughter but his superior officer. Based on the novel by Jack Early. **90m/C VHS.** Charles Bronson, Dana Delany, Xander Berkeley, Bonnie Bartlett, Jenette Goldstein, Louis Giambalvo; ***D:*** Rod Holcomb; ***W:*** Robert Roy Pool; ***C:*** Thomas Del Ruth; ***M:*** Sylvester Levay.

Dead Waters *Dark Waters* **1994** Elizabeth (Salter) travels to a remote Russian island to visit her sister, Theresa (Phipps), who resides at the convent there. But Theresa is murdered after witnessing an occult ritual and Elizabeth finds strange references to "The Beast" in the convent library and realizes the nuns are trying to raise the demonic creature. **94m/C VHS, DVD.** *IT RU GB* Louise Salter, Venera Simmons, Maria Kapnist, Anna Rose Phipps; ***D:*** Mariano Baino; ***W:*** Mariano Baino, Andrew Bark; ***C:*** Alex Howe; ***M:*** Igor Clark.

Dead Weekend **1995 (R)** Lt. Weed (Baldwin) is given the task of finding and destroying a seductively dangerous female alien. Turns out she has the ability to physically change into a number of different women—all of whom attract the willing-and-eager soldier. **82m/C VHS.** Richard Speight Jr., Stephen Baldwin, David Rasche, Alexis Arquette, Bai Ling, Tom Kenny, Jennifer MacDonald, Barbara Alyn Woods; ***D:*** Amos Poe; ***W:*** Joel Rose; ***C:*** Gary Tieche; ***M:*** Steve Hunter. **CABLE**

Dead Women in Lingerie WOOF! **1990 (R)** When beautiful models are turning up dead, a detective is called in to solve the mystery. Perhaps they committed suicide to avoid being in this picture any longer than necessary. Title sounds like the next episode of "Geraldo." **87m/C VHS, DVD.** June Lockhart, Lyle Waggoner, John Romo, Jerry Orbach, Maura Tierney, Laura Elena Harring; ***D:*** Erika Fox.

Dead Wrong 1/2 **1983** Undercover agent falls in love with the drug smuggler she's supposed to bring to justice. **93m/C VHS.** Britt Ekland, Winston Rekert, Jackson Davies; ***D:*** Len Kowalewich; ***W:*** Len Kowalewich.

Dead Zone **1983 (R)** Diffident teacher Johnny Smith (Walken) gains extraordinary psychic powers following a near-fatal car accident and a five-year coma. He has developed the ability to foresee a person's future by touching their hands—and when he shakes the hand of presidential candidate Greg Stillson (Sheen), he foresees a holocaust. So Johnny decides to use his "gift" to save mankind from impending evil. A good adaptation of the Stephen King thriller. **104m/C VHS, DVD.** Christopher Walken, Brooke Adams, Tom Skerritt, Martin Sheen, Herbert Lom, Anthony Zerbe, Colleen Dewhurst; ***D:*** David Cronenberg; ***W:*** Jeffrey Boam; ***C:*** Mark Irwin; ***M:*** Michael Kamen.

The Dead Zone 1/2 **2002 (R)** Pilot film for the cable series, which is based on the characters and story from the Stephen King novel. Johnny Smith (Hall) was in a coma for six years after a car crash. When he regains consciousness, he discovers he has psychic abilities that allow him to see into the lives of those he touches. **87m/C VHS, DVD.** Anthony Michael Hall, Nikki de Boer, David Ogden Stiers, Chris Bruno; ***D:*** Robert Lieberman; ***W:*** Michael Piller. **CABLE**

The Deadbeat Club **2004** Misfit teens in a small Texas town try to help a man whose family died in a fire. The actors look too old for their teen roles and virtue turns out to be really boring. **113m/C DVD.** *US* Daphne Khoury, Brandon Dixon, Jennifer Wetter, Nicole Cook, Jason Magee; ***D:*** Israel Luna; ***W:*** Israel Luna; ***C:*** Brad Walker; ***M:*** Philip Kappaz.

Deadbolt **1992 (R)** Divorced med student Marty Hiller (Bateman) desperately needs a roommate and Alec Danz (Baldwin) seems perfect. Soon they're sharing more than the rent, until Danz kills her friends and imprisons her in the apartment (equipped of course with soundproof walls and bulletproof glass—one wonders why she doesn't bang on the floor to gain attention.) Predictable and silly would-be thriller attempts to capitalize on the roommate-from-hell theme that started with "Single White Female," but isn't nearly as effective. Went straight to video and showed up on network TV several months later. **95m/C VHS.** Justine Bateman, Adam Baldwin, Michelle Scarabelli, Chris Mulkey, Cyndi Pass, Isabelle Truchon; ***D:*** Douglas Jackson. **VIDEO**

Deadfall 1/2 **1993 (R)** Father/son grifters plan an elaborate scam that goes wrong when son Joe (Biehn) inadvertently kills dear old dad (Coburn). When Joe is going through his father's effects he finds out about an unknown twin uncle, who also turns out to be a racketeer. Along with Uncle Lou's mistrustful henchman Eddie (Cage), they plan another con but swindles and vendettas abound. **99m/C VHS, DVD.** Michael Biehn, Sarah Trigger, Nicolas Cage, James Coburn, Charlie Sheen, Peter Fonda; ***D:*** Christopher Coppola; ***W:*** Christopher Coppola, David Peoples; ***C:*** Maryse Alberti; ***M:*** Jim Fox.

Deadlier Than the Male **1967** In this swinging '60s update on the '20s British hero, Bulldog Drummond (Johnson) is now a suave London insurance investigator after industrialist Carl Petersen (Green). It seems Petersen uses his own sexy assassins, Irma (Sommer) and Penelope (Koscina), to get rid of business partners and the competition. Gadgetry, exotic locations, and bikinied babes in a James Bond knockoff. **95m/C VHS, DVD.** *GB* Richard Johnson, Nigel Green, Elke Sommer, Sylva Koscina, Suzanna Leigh, Steve Carlson; ***D:*** Ralph Thomas; ***W:*** Jimmy Sangster, Liz Charles-Williams, David Osborn; ***C:*** Ernest Steward; ***M:*** Malcolm Lockyer.

Deadline 1/2 **1981** Journalist must find out the truth behind a minor earthquake in Australia. **94m/C VHS.** Barry Newman, Trisha Noble, Bill Kerr; ***D:*** Arch Nicholson; ***W:*** Walter Halsey Davis.

Deadline **1982** Eerie tale of horror writer's life as it begins to reflect his latest story in this play on the "truth is stranger than fiction" adage. **85m/C VHS.** Stephen Young, Sharon Masters, Cindy Hinds, Phillip Leonard; ***D:*** Mario Azzopardi.

Deadline **1987 (R)** Walken is a cynical American journalist assigned to cover the warring factions in Beirut. He finds himself becoming more and more involved in the events he's supposed to report when he falls in love with a German nurse who is aiding the rebel forces. Tense, though sometimes murky drama. **110m/C VHS, DVD.** *GE* Christopher Walken, Hywel Bennett, Marita Marschall; ***D:*** Nathaniel Gutman.

Deadline **2000 (R)** The publisher of a leading Chicago newspaper is murdered following his hostile takeover of said paper and the leading suspect is the paper's editor (but he's the wrong guy). Formulaic thriller. **94m/C VHS, DVD.** Patrick Bergin, Bruce Dinsmore, Annie Dufresne, Alex Ivonovic, Edward Yankie; ***D:*** Robbie Ditchburn; ***W:*** Ron Base, Michael Stokes; ***C:*** Daniel Valdilleneuve. **VIDEO**

Deadline **2009 (R)** After suffering a breakdown, writer Alice retreats to a remote Victorian house to concentrate on finishing her screenplay so she can meet her deadline. Hearing and seeing strange things, Alice fears her imagination is in overdrive until she explores the house's creepy attic and discovers a box of videotapes that have her investigating what became of the couple shown on them. **89m/C DVD.** Brittany Murphy, Thora Birch, Marc Blucas, Tammy Blanchard; ***D:*** Sean McConville; ***W:*** Sean McConville; ***C:*** Ross Richardson; ***M:*** Carlos Alvarez. **VIDEO**

Deadline Assault 1/2 *Act of Violence* **1990 (R)** Kate McSweeny is a beautiful young reporter who is brutally attacked and raped by a gang of savage youths. Kate must now face the unsettling facts; they're still on the streets and they may be stalking her again. **90m/C VHS.** Elizabeth Montgomery, James Sloyan, Sean Frye, Biff McGuire, Michael Goodwin, Linden Chiles; ***D:*** Paul Wendkos.

Deadline at Dawn **1946** Hayward is an aspiring actress who tries to help a sailor (Williams) prove that he is innocent of murder. Based on a novel by Cornell Woolrich. **82m/B VHS.** Bill Williams, Susan Hayward, Lola Lane, Paul Lukas, Joseph Calleia; ***D:*** Harold Clurman; ***W:*** Clifford Odets.

Deadline Auto Theft **1983** A fun lovin' guy drives fast cars and meets beautiful women. Nudge, nudge, wink, wink. **90m/C VHS.** H.B. Halicki, Hoyt Axton, Marion Busia, George Cole, Judi Gibbs, Lang Jeffries; ***D:*** H.B. Halicki.

Deadlock 1/2 **1991 (R)** Hauer and Rogers star as inmates in a prison of the future. This prison has no walls, no fences and no guards—and no one EVER escapes. Each prisoner wears an explosive collar that is tuned to the same frequency as one of the other prisoner's. Should the two separate by more than 100 yards, the collars explode. When Rogers convinces Hauer that they are on the same frequency, the two escape. Trouble is, they are being pursued not only by the police, but by Hauer's former partners in crime as well. Can the two find the freedom they are looking for—without losing their heads? **103m/C VHS, DVD.** Rutger Hauer, Mimi Rogers, Joan Chen, James Remar, Stephen Tobolowsky, Basil Wallace; ***D:*** Lewis Teague. **CABLE**

Deadlock 2 *Deadlocked: Escape from Zone 14* **1994 (R)** Same basic plot as in the first TV movie. Tony Archer (Morales) and Allie Thompson (Peeples), two strangers who have been set up by the same corrupt businessman, are being held in a violent correctional facility. Inmates wear electronic collars programmed to explode if they venture too far apart. But Tony figures a way around this trap only to discover he and Allie are caught in another. **120m/C VHS.** Esai Morales, Nia Peeples, Stephen McHattie, Jon Cuthbert; ***D:*** Graeme Campbell.

Deadlocked **2000** Demond Doyle (Jonz) is convicted of rape and murder and prosecutor Ned Stark (Caruso) wants the death penalty. Demond's father, Jacob (Dutton), is convinced that his son is innocent, so he takes the jury hostage. He tells Stark that he has 24 hours to find the evidence that will clear his son or the captives start dying. Compelling leads in a contrived story. **100m/C VHS.** David Caruso, Charles S. Dutton, John Finn, Jo D. Jonz, Malcolm Stewart, Tom Butler, Diego Wallraff, Michael Tomlinson; ***D:*** Michael Watkins; ***W:*** David Rosenfelt, Erik Jendresen; ***C:*** Thomas Burstyn; ***M:*** B.C. Smith. **CABLE**

Deadly Advice **1993 (R)** Meek bookseller Jodie (Horrocks) and her sister are constantly humiliated by their overbearing mother (Fricker), who also objects to Jodie's romance with the local doctor (Pryce). As life becomes increasingly unbearable, Jodie discovers a book on infamous killers and is visited by their ghosts, including Jack the Ripper, who is happy to suggest ways to get rid of mom. **91m/C VHS, DVD.** Jane Horrocks, Imelda Staunton, Brenda Fricker, Jonathan Pryce; ***D:*** Mandie Fletcher.

Deadly Alliance **1978** Two impecunious filmmakers (who happen to be hunks) and a babe (for good measure) poke their noses in where they're not wanted (in the shady business of an international oil cartel). "Deadly Dull" would be a more appropriate moniker. **90m/C VHS.** Kathleen Arc, Tony de Fonte, Michele Marsh, Walter Prince; ***D:*** Paul S. Parco.

The Deadly and the Beautiful *Wonder Women* **1973 (PG)** Dr. Tsu sends her "deadly but beautiful" task force to kidnap the world's prime male athletes for use in her private business enterprise. **82m/C VHS.** *PH* Nancy Kwan, Ross Hagen, Maria de Aragon, Roberta Collins, Tony Lorea, Sid Haig, Vic Diaz, Shirley Washington, Gale Hansen; ***D:*** Robert Vincent O'Neil.

Deadly Bet **1/2** **1991 (R)** A made-for-video saga of a kickboxer who loses his money and his girl when he loses the big match. Lots of fight sequences as he works to regain his career. **93m/C VHS.** Jeff Wincott, Charlene Tilton, Steven Leigh; ***D:*** Richard W. Munchkin.

Deadly Blessing **1981 (R)** A young, recently widowed woman is visited in her rural Pennsylvania home by some friends from the city. Something's not quite right about this country life and they become especially suspicious after meeting their friend's very religious in-laws. **104m/C VHS.** Maren Jensen, Susan Buckner, Sharon Stone, Ernest Borgnine, Jeff East, Lisa Hartman Black, Lois Nettleton, Colleen Riley, Douglas Barr, Michael Berryman; ***D:*** Wes Craven; ***W:*** Wes Craven, Glenn Benest, Matthew F. Barr; ***C:*** Robert C. Jessup; ***M:*** James Horner.

Deadly Breed **1/2** **1989** Beware your friendly neighborhood cop. A band of white supremacists has infiltrated the local police force, intent on causing violence, not keeping the peace. **90m/C VHS, DVD.** William (Bill) Smith, Addison Randall, Blake Bahner, Joe Vance; ***D:*** Charles Kanganis.

Deadly Business **1/2** *Skip Tracer* **1977** Hard-nosed collection man for a lethal loan shark finds he is the one with the debt to pay as he's stalked through the city street by hit men. **95m/C VHS.** David Peterson, John Lazarus; ***D:*** Zale Dalen; ***W:*** Zale Dalen.

Deadly Business **1986** The true story of a man who turned from crime to become a government informant. As a garbage man, he works to stop the illegal dumping of chemicals in New Jersey. An interesting made-for-televison drama. **100m/C VHS.** Alan Arkin, Armand Assante, Michael Learned, Jon Polito, George Morfogen, James Rebhorn; ***D:*** John Korty.

Deadly Companions **1/2** **1961** Keith is an ex-gunslinger who agrees to escort O'Hara through Apache territory in order to make up for inadvertenly killing her son. Director Peckinpah's first feature film. **90m/C VHS, DVD.** Maureen O'Hara, Brian Keith, Chill Wills, Steve Cochran; ***D:*** Sam Peckinpah; ***C:*** William Clothier.

Deadly Conspiracy **1991 (R)** Saxon plays a corrupt businessman who kills an employee about to blow the whistle on his shady dealings. Hauser is the good cop, with the bad personal life, who makes it his mission to bring Saxon to justice. The prolific Hauser brings some fast-paced action to this routine story. **92m/C VHS.** Wings Hauser, John Saxon, Frances Fisher, Patti D'Arbanville, Margaux Hemingway, Greg Mullavey; ***D:*** Paul Leder.

Deadly Currents **1993 (R)** Scott plays a former sea captain who owns a bar on the island of Curacao and enjoys regaling his patrons with his sea-going tales. Petersen is the exiled CIA agent stuck as the security officer of the American consulate. The dangerous pasts of both men catch them up and find them caught in a web of international intrigue. Based on the novel "The Prince of Malta" by James David Buchanan. **93m/C VHS.** George C. Scott, William L. Petersen, Julie Carmen, Alexei Sayle, Trish Van Devere, Philip Anglim, Maria Ellingsen; ***D:*** Carl Schultz; ***W:*** James David Buchanan.

Deadly Dancer **1/2** **1990** It's up to a lone cop to find out who's been offing the hoofers in L.A. **88m/C VHS.** Adolfo "Shabba Doo" Quinones, Smith Wordes, Walter W. Cox, Steve Jonson; ***D:*** Kimberly Casey; ***W:*** David A. Prior.

Deadly Daphne's Revenge **1/2** **1993** Gory story of rape and revenge from the Troma Team. Hitchhiker Cindy is beaten and raped by Charlie Johnson. When she seeks justice via the local police, Johnson makes plans to have her snuffed out. Meantime, another of his victims escapes from the asylum she's been in and comes looking for him with murder on her mind. **98m/C VHS, DVD.** Anthony Holt, Laurie Tait Partridge, John Suttle, Alan Levy, Richard Harding Gardner; ***D:*** Richard Harding Gardner; ***W:*** Tim Bennett, Richard Harding Gardner; ***C:*** Vern Virlene; ***M:*** John Banning.

Deadly Darling **WOOF!** **1985** Muddled, completely awful tale centering on two different rapes with no discernible attempt made to link the two or establish a plot. **91m/C VHS.** Fonda Lynn, Warren Chan, Bernard Tsui, Cherry Kwok; ***D:*** Karen Young.

Deadly Desire **1991 (R)** Seduced by the beautiful Harrold, security guard Scalia finds himself putting his life on the line when Harrold asks him to help cheat her husband out of millions in an insurance scam. Trouble ensues when they try to outsmart Harrold's powerful entrepreneurial husband. **93m/C VHS.** Jack Scalia, Kathryn Harrold, Will Patton, Joe Santos; ***D:*** Charles Correll.

Deadly Diamonds **1/2** **1991** Cop is on the trail of diamond smugglers who leave a trail of death in their wake. **90m/C VHS.** Dan Haggerty, Troy Donahue, Eli Rich, Kathleen Kane, Kenna Grob, Nicholas Mercer; ***D:*** Thomas Atcheson; ***W:*** Ron Herbst.

Deadly Dreams **1988 (R)** A young boy's parents are killed by a maniac who then commits suicide. Years later, he dreams that he is being stalked anew by the same killer. Nightmares turn into reality in this decent horror/suspense flick. **79m/C VHS.** Mitchell Anderson, Xander Berkeley, Thom Babbes, Juliette Cummins; ***D:*** Kristine Peterson; ***W:*** Thom Babbes.

Deadly Embrace **WOOF!** **1988 (R)** Sordid tale of wealthy man (Vincent) who wants to get rid of his wife—permanantly. He enlists the aid of a beautiful young coed. Soft-core sleaze with nary a redeemable quality. **82m/C VHS.** Jan-Michael Vincent, Jack Carter, Mindi Miller, Linnea Quigley, Michelle (McClellan) Bauer, Ken Abraham; ***D:*** David DeCoteau.

Deadly Encounter **1972** Thrilling actioner in which Hagman portrays a helicopter pilot—a former war ace—who allows an old flame to talk him into helping her escape from the mobsters on her trail. Terrific edge-of-your-seat aerial action. **90m/C VHS, DVD.** Larry Hagman, Susan Anspach, James Gammon; ***D:*** William A. Graham.

Deadly Exposure **1993 (R)** Benson stars as a burned-out journalist doing his own investigation of the right-wing extremist group that killed his father. Aspiring reporter Johnson helps out and turns up a conspiracy between the extremists, the government, and a plot to assassinate a U.S. senator. Also available in an unrated version. **100m/C VHS.** Robby Benson, Laura Johnson, Paul Hampton, Andrew Prine, Bentley Mitchum, Isaac Hayes; ***D:*** Lawrence Mortorff; ***W:*** Asher Brauner.

Deadly Eyes **1/2** *The Rats* **1982 (R)** After eating grain laced with steroids a group of rats grows to mammoth proportions (dachshunds in rat drag were used). Their appetites grow accordingly—now they crave humans. Amid the nibbling by the giant ratdogs, romance blooms. Silly adaptation by Charles Eglee of Frank Herbert's "The Rats." **93m/C VHS.** Sam Groom, Sara Botsford, Scatman Crothers, Lisa Langlois, Cec Linder; ***D:*** Robert Clouse.

Deadly Fieldtrip **1/2** **1974** Four female students and their teacher are abducted by a biker gang and held hostage on a deserted farm. **91m/C VHS, DVD.** Zalman King, Brenda Fogarty, Robert Porter; ***D:*** Earl Barton.

Deadly Force **1/2** **1983 (R)** Ex-cop turned private detective stalks a killer in Los Angeles who has left an "X" carved in the forehead of each of his 17 victims. If he had just signed his name, things could have been tidied up much earlier. **95m/C VHS.** Wings Hauser, Joyce Ingalls, Paul Shenar, Al Ruscio, Arlen Dean Snyder, Lincoln Kilpatrick; ***D:*** Paul Aaron; ***W:*** Robert Vincent O'Neil, Barry Schneider.

Deadly Friend **1986 (R)** A well-meaning horror flick? That's what Wes Craven has tried to provide for us. When the girlfriend of a lonely teenage genius is accidentally killed, he decides to insert his robot's "brain" in her body, though the results aren't entirely successful. The same can be said for the film which was based on Diana Henstell's more effective novel "Friend." **91m/C VHS.** Matthew Laborteaux, Kristy Swanson, Michael Sharrett, Anne Twomey, Richard Marcus, Anne Ramsey; ***D:*** Wes Craven; ***W:*** Bruce Joel Rubin; ***C:*** Philip Lathrop; ***M:*** Charles Bernstein.

Deadly Game **1977** Griffith reprises his role from 1977's "The Girl in the Empty Grave" as resort town police chief Abel Marsh. A dangerous chemical spill by an Army convoy traveling through the community may not have been an accident. Filmed on location in Big Bear, CA. **90m/C DVD.** Andy Griffith, James Cromwell, Dan O'Herlihy, Morgan Woodward, Rebecca Balding, Sharon Spelman, Fran Ryan, Eddie Foy Jr., Mitzi Hoag; ***D:*** Lane Slate; ***W:*** Lane Slate; ***C:*** Gayne Rescher; ***M:*** Mundell Lowe. **TV**

Deadly Game **1982 (R)** A reunion at a remote hotel leads to an ordeal of psychological terror and murderous intrigue. **108m/C VHS.** George Segal, Robert Morley, Trevor Howard, Emlyn Williams, Alan Webb; ***D:*** George Schaefer.

Deadly Game **1/2** **1983** Much-maligned and preyed-upon witness is protected by a weary cop, who speaks with the use of English subtitles. **90m/C VHS.** *GE* Mel Ferrer, Helmut Berger, Barbara Sukowa; ***D:*** Karoly Makk, Dieter Geissler.

Deadly Game **1/2** **1991 (R)** Horribly burned, a vengeful millionaire invites seven people he believes have wronged him to spend the weekend on his isolated island. He has promised them each a reward for their good deeds, but instead plans to have a big-game hunt with his "guests" as the prey. **93m/C VHS.** Roddy McDowall, Jenny Seagrove, Marc Singer, Michael Beck; ***D:*** Thomas J. Wright; ***W:*** Wes Claridge.

Deadly Game *Catch Me If You Can* **1998** Nathan is a 12-year-old runaway with an attitude who witnesses some mob business and winds up stealing a lot of mob cash. He decides to live it up on his ill-gotten gains until a down-on-his-luck cop (Matheson) catches up with Nathan and tries to protect him from the goons' revenge. **120m/C VHS, DVD.** Tim Matheson, Carol Alt, William Katt, Ryan DeBoer, Catherine Oxenberg, Ed Marinaro, Eddie Mekka; ***D:*** Jeff Reiner; ***W:*** Lorne Cameron, David Hoselton; ***C:*** Jonathan Freeman; ***M:*** Christopher Brady. **TV**

Deadly Games **1/2** **1980** Ineffective plot involving a series of murders in a small town is seemingly played out by the principal characters in a horror board game. Film is saved from being a complete waste by Groom's good performance as the local cop. **94m/C VHS.** Sam Groom, Jo Ann Harris, Steve Railsback, Dick Butkus, June Lockhart, Colleen Camp; ***D:*** Scott Mansfield.

Deadly Harvest **1972 (PG)** Scientists' worst fears have been realized—due to ecological abuse and over-development of the land, food has become extremely scarce. This in turn has caused people to become a bit savage. They are particularly nasty to a farmer and his family. Not a bad plot, but a poorly acted film. **86m/C VHS, DVD.** Clint Walker, Nehemiah Persoff, Kim Cattrall, David G. Brown, Gary Davies; ***D:*** Timothy Bond.

Deadly Hero **1975 (R)** Gripping tale of a young woman who becomes the prey of a New York City cop after questioning the brutal methods he employed while saving her from being assaulted, ultimately killing her attacker. Williams makes film debut in this chilling suspenser. **102m/C VHS.** Don Murray, James Earl Jones, Diahn Williams, Lilia Skala, Conchata Ferrell, George S. Irving, Treat Williams, Josh Mostel; ***D:*** Ivan Nagy; ***C:*** Andrzej Bartkowiak; ***M:*** Brad Fiedel.

Deadly Heroes **1996 (R)** Terrorists highjack an American plane at Athens International Airport with the demand that their leader, Carlos (Drago), who's jailed in Miami, be delivered to them. CIA agent and ex-Navy SEAL, Captain Cody Grant (Vincent), is forced to take Carlos to Athens but having captured Carlos once, Grant is determined that the terrorist and his associates won't be free for long. **104m/C VHS.** Jan-Michael Vincent, Billy Drago, Michael Pare, Claudette Mink; ***D:*** Menahem Golan; ***W:*** Damian Lee, Gregory Lee. **VIDEO**

Deadly Illusion *Love You to Death* **1987 (R)** Williams is a private detective who manages to get himself tangled in a complex web of intrigue and winds up framed for murder. Decent outing for all. **95m/C VHS.** Billy Dee Williams, Morgan Fairchild, Vanity, John Beck, Joe Cortese; ***D:*** William (Bill) Tannen, Larry Cohen; ***W:*** Larry Cohen; ***M:*** Patrick Gleeson.

Deadly Impact **1/2** **1984** Las Vegas casinos are targeted for rip-off by means of a computer. Svenson and Williamson give good performances, but that's not enough to save this one. De Angelis used the pseudonym Larry Ludman. **90m/C VHS, DVD.** *IT* Bo Svenson, Fred Williamson, Marcia Clingan, Giovanni Lambardo Radice, Vincent Conti; ***D:*** Fabrizio de Angelis.

Deadly Innocence **1/2** **1988 (R)** A shy, lonely girl works at an isolated gas station. After her father's death, she takes in a boarder—a mysterious woman being chased by her past. **90m/C VHS.** Mary Crosby, Andrew Stevens, Amanda Wyss; ***D:*** John D. Patterson, Hugh Parks.

Deadly Intent **1988** The widow of a murdered archeologist becomes the target of fortune hunters when they try to get their hands on the priceless jewel her husband brought back from a dig. **83m/C VHS.** Lisa Eilbacher, Steve Railsback, Maud Adams, Lance Henriksen, Fred Williamson, Persis Khambatta; ***D:*** Nigel Dick.

Deadly Intruder **1/2** **1984** Quiet vacation spot is being terrorized by an escapee from a mental institution. So much for a little R and R. **86m/C VHS.** Chris Holder, Molly Creek, Tony Crupi; ***D:*** John McCauley; ***W:*** Tony Crupi.

Deadly Lessons **1994** Misfit Ann gets shunned by the college "in" crowd but then a childhood friend comes to her aid and decides to take revenge on the nasty students. **90m/C VHS.** Andrea Gall, Mat McGinnis, Dana Wise; ***D:*** Leslie Delano.

The Deadly Mantis **1/2** *The Incredible Praying Mantis* **1957** A gigantic praying mantis lies in a million-year-old sleep in the frozen reaches of the Arctic. Then a volcanic eruption releases the critter and the flying beastie does it's destructive best on Washington, D.C., and New York City until the military can gas it into oblivion. Typically silly '50s sci-fi with decent special effects. **79m/B VHS.** Craig Stevens, William Hopper, Alix Talton, Pat Conway, Donald Randolph; ***D:*** Nathan "Jerry" Juran; ***W:*** Martin Berkeley.

Deadly Mission **1/2** *Quel Maledetto Treno Blindato* **1978 (R)** Five soldiers in WWII France are convicted of crimes against the Army, only to escape from lock-up and become focal points in a decisive battle. **99m/C VHS.** *IT* Bo Svenson, Peter Hooten, Fred Williamson; ***D:*** Enzo G. Castellari; ***W:***

Alessandro Continenza, Sergio Grieco, Romano Migliorini, Laura Toscano, Franco Marotta.

Deadly Neighbor 1991 New neighbor moves in, dead neighborhood housewives move out. Another neighbor becomes suspicious and investigates. **90m/C VHS, DVD.** Don Leifert, George Stover, Lydia Laurans; ***D:*** Donald M. Dohler.

Deadly Obsession 1/2 **1988 (R)** A disfigured lunatic stalks a young co-ed hoping to extort $1 million from the wealthy dean of the school. **93m/C VHS.** Jeffrey R. Iorio; ***D:*** Jeno Hodi; ***W:*** Brian Cox.

Deadly Outbreak 1996 (R) A chemical weapons facility is taken over by a renegade colonel who threatens to unleash a deadly plague. Now it's up to one man (Speakman) to free the hostage scientist who knows the formula for the antidote. **94m/C VHS.** Jeff Speakman, Ron Silver, Rochelle Swanson, Jonathan Sagalle; ***D:*** Rick Avery; ***M:*** Harvey W. Mason.

Deadly Passion 1/2 **1985 (R)** A James Cain-like thriller about a private eye getting carnally involved with a beautiful and treacherous woman who is manipulating her late husband's estate through murder and double-crossing. **100m/C VHS.** *SA* Brent Huff, Ingrid Boulting, Harrison Coburn, Lynn Maree; ***D:*** Larry Larson.

Deadly Past 1/2 **1995 (R)** Predictable story finds dumb ex-con bartender (Marquette) making the mistake of getting involved with a femme fatale (Alt) from his past. Also available in an unrated version. **90m/C VHS.** Ron Marquette, Carol Alt, Dedee Pfeiffer, Mark Dacascos; ***D:*** Tibor Takacs; ***W:*** Steven Iyama; ***C:*** Berhard Salzmann; ***M:*** K. Alexander (Alex) Wilkinson.

Deadly Possession **1988** A college student plays amateur detective when she tries to clear her ex-husband's name after he is accused of the horrible murder of a fellow student. **99m/C VHS.** *AU* Penny Cook, Anna-Maria Winchester, Liddy Clark, Olivia Hamnett; ***D:*** Craig Lahiff.

Deadly Prey WOOF! **1987 (R)** Prior is up against a fully outfitted army of bloodthirsty mercenaries who are using innocent people as "live targets" at their secret bootcamp. Plot lifted from "The Most Dangerous Game" has more than its share of gruesome violence. **87m/C VHS.** Cameron Mitchell, Troy Donahue, Ted Prior, Fritz Matthews; ***D:*** David A. Prior; ***W:*** David A. Prior.

Deadly Reactor **1989** In a post-nuclear future a lone preacher turns into an armed vigilante to protect the people of a town being terrorized by a vicious motorcycle gang. **88m/C VHS.** David Heavener, Stuart Whitman, Darwyn Swalve, Allyson Davis; ***D:*** David Heavener.

Deadly Recruits 1/2 **1986** The Russians did it! The Russians did it! Stamp is convinced that the downfall of several top students at Oxford, amid scandal and rumor, is due to a KGB conspiracy. **92m/C VHS, DVD.** *GB* Terence Stamp, Michael Culver, Carmen (De Sautoy) Du Sautoy, Robin Sachs; ***D:*** Roger Tucker.

Deadly Revenge **1983 (R)** Action-adventure pic with not much adventure and even less action. Small-town reporter finds himself up against a mob boss when he takes over the nightclub business of a friend killed by the mobsters. Dubbed. **90m/C VHS.** *IT* Rodolfo Ranni, Julio de Grazia, Silvia Montanari, Fred Commoner; ***D:*** Juan Carlos Sesanzo.

Deadly Rivals **1992 (R)** Stevens plays a laser specialist in Miami for a top-secret weapons conference. A beauty takes a interest in him but then she's first accused of being a spy and then mistaken for a courier in the pay of a ruthless crime boss. Can Stevens find the truth? **93m/C VHS.** Andrew Stevens, Cela Wise, Joseph Bologna, Margaux Hemingway, Richard Roundtree, Francesco Quinn, Randi Ingerman; ***D:*** James Dodson; ***W:*** Redge Mahaffey; ***M:*** Ashley Irwin.

Deadly Sanctuary WOOF! **1968** Censors stopped production of this film several times. The Marquis de Sade's writings provided the inspiration (though there's nothing inspired about it) for this tale of two recently orphaned young women who get caught up in prostitution, an S&M club, and murder. **92m/C VHS, DVD.** Jack Palance, Mercedes McCambridge, Sylva Koscina, Klaus Kinski, Akim Tamiroff, Romina Power; ***D:*** Jess (Jesus) Franco.

The Deadly Secret **1994** Randall Parks is a successful real estate agent with a past he has managed to hide for 20 years. When he is blackmailed, he decides to take matters into his own hands and track down his accusers. **98m/C VHS.** Joe Estevez, Tracy Spaulding, Reggie Cale, Douglas Stalgren; ***D:*** Jason Hammond; ***W:*** Douglas Stalgren; ***M:*** Erik Hansen.

Deadly Sins 1/2 **1995 (R)** Deputy sheriff Jack Gates (Keith) hooks up with P.I. Christina Herrera (Milano) to investigate a murder in a Catholic girls school. Christina poses as a student and uncovers sinister secrets. **98m/C VHS.** David Keith, Alyssa Milano, Terry David Mulligan, Corrie Clark; ***D:*** Michael Robison; ***W:*** John Langley, Malcolm Barbour.

Deadly Spygames **1989** A special agent for the United States Special Operations Bureau finds himself in deep trouble. **86m/C VHS.** Troy Donahue, Tippi Hedren; ***D:*** Jack M. Sell; ***W:*** Jack M. Sell.

Deadly Sting 1/2 *L'Insolent; The Killer* **1973** Silva devises an intricate scheme to gain revenge on the men who cheated him out of his share of a gold bullion heist. **90m/C VHS.** *FR* Henry Silva, Philip Clay, Andre Pousse; ***D:*** Jean-Claude Roy; ***W:*** Jacques Risser; ***C:*** Claude Saunier; ***M:*** Bernard Gerard, Max Gazzola.

Deadly Stranger *Border Heat* **1988** Fluegel's talents could have been put to much better use than as the selfish mistress of a plantation owner who is taking advantage of the migrant workers toiling on his land. Moore is a drifter and hired hand who rallies the workers to stand up to the owner. **93m/C VHS.** Darlanne Fluegel, Michael J. Moore, John Vernon, Ted White; ***D:*** Max Kleven.

Deadly Strangers **1982** Two people meet up on the road and decide to share a ride. We discover that one of them is an insane killer who's escaped from a mental institution. Suspense builds nicely, but the ending is flawed. **89m/C VHS.** *GB* Hayley Mills, Simon Ward, Sterling Hayden, Ken Hutchison; ***D:*** Sidney Hayers.

Deadly Sunday 1/2 **1982** A family's weekly Sunday drive turns terrifying when desperate jewel thieves detour them and hold them hostage. **85m/C VHS.** Dennis Ely, Henry Sanders, Gylian Roland, Douglas Alexander; ***D:*** Donald M. Jones.

Deadly Surveillance **1991 (R)** Two tough policemen investigate a series of drug-related murders and stake out a possible suspect—a beautiful woman who's the lover of one of the lawmen. Tension in this Canadian-made cop opera evaporates in the third act for a standard buddy-buddy action finale. **92m/C VHS.** Michael Ironside, Christopher Bondy, Susan Almgren, Vlasta Vrana, David Carradine; ***D:*** Paul Ziller. **TV**

Deadly Target 1/2 **1994 (R)** Detective Charles Prince (Daniels) is sent to L.A. to return a notorious Chinese gangster to Hong Kong for trial. But Prince finds out his would-be prisoner's escaped and soon he's involved in martial arts mayhem. **90m/C VHS, DVD.** Gary Daniels, Kenneth McLeod, Max Gail, Susan Byun; ***D:*** Charla Driver; ***W:*** Michael January, James Adelstein; ***C:*** Richard Pepin; ***M:*** Michael Lewis.

Deadly Thief *Shalimar* **1978** A former jewel thief comes out of retirement to challenge those who are now tops in the profession to try and steal the world's most precious ruby from him. Of course all they have to lose is their lives. What could have been an exciting adventure is made curiously boring. **90m/C VHS, DVD.** *IN* Rex Harrison, John Saxon, Sylvia Miles, Dharmendra, Zenat Aman, Shammi Kapoor; ***D:*** Krishna Shah.

The Deadly Trackers **1973 (PG)** If gorey oaters are your thing, this one's definitely for you; if not, make tracks. Harris plays a spiteful sheriff who heads south of the border to get his pound of flesh from the outlaws who slew his family in a bank robbery. Overlong revenge-o-rama based on Samuel Fuller's short story, "Riata"; might have been bearable if Fuller hadn't been bumped from the director's chair (as it is, he and other contributors refused to be listed in the credits). **104m/C VHS.** Richard Harris, Rod Taylor, Al Lettieri, Neville Brand, William (Bill) Smith, Paul Benjamin, Pedro Armendariz Jr.; ***D:*** Barry Shear.

The Deadly Trap *Death Scream* **1971 (PG)** Confusing thriller that couldn't. Dunaway is the mentally unstable wife of an ex-spy. His former employers have targeted him with plans to use her and her fragile state-of-mind to their advantage. **96m/C VHS.** *FR IT* Faye Dunaway, Frank Langella, Barbara Parkins, Maurice Ronet; ***D:*** Rene Clement.

Deadly Twins WOOF! **1985** After being beaten and gang-raped, twin sister singers are out to get revenge. Nothing new here; don't waste your time. **87m/C VHS.** Audrey Landers, Judy Landers, Ellie Russell, Wayne Allison; ***D:*** Joe Oaks.

Deadly Vengeance **1981** It's strictly low budget as the mob kills Jones's boyfriend, forcing her to mount a vengeful but inexpensive offensive against the crime syndicate's bigwigs. **84m/C VHS.** Grace Jones, Alan Marlowe, Arthur Roberts; ***D:*** Amin Qamar Chaudhri.

Deadly Voyage 1/2 **1996 (R)** In 1992, nine Ghanaian dockworkers are discovered hiding aboard a Ukrainian freighter bound for New York. Since each stowaway would cost the shipping company a hefty fine, sadistic first officer Ion (Pertwee) orders them killed. Only one, Kingsley (Epps), manages to survive and reveal the truth. **92m/C VHS.** Omar Epps, Sean Pertwee, Joss Ackland, David Suchet, Jean LaMarre, Andrew Divoff; ***D:*** John MacKenzie; ***C:*** Stuart Urban; ***M:*** John Scott. **CABLE**

Deadly Weapon **1988 (PG-13)** It's a bit of nerdish wish fulfillment when 15-year-old geek Eastman finds a secret anti-matter weapon conveniently lost by the military in an Arizona stream. You won't like the kid any more than you'll like the story of this low rent boy-gets-back-at-bullies sci fi fiasco. **89m/C VHS.** Rodney Eastman, Gary Frank, Michael Horse, Ed Nelson, Kim Walker; ***D:*** Michael Miner; ***W:*** Michael Miner; ***C:*** James L. Carter.

Deadly Weapons **1970 (R)** Chesty Morgan, she of the 73-inch bustline, takes on the mob using only her God-given abilities. One of Joe Bob Brigg's "Sleaziest Movies in the History of the World" series, and he is welcome to it. **90m/C VHS, DVD.** Chesty Morgan, Harry (Herbert Streicher) Reems, Greg Reynolds, Saul Meth, Phillip Stahl, Mitchell Fredericks, Denise Purcell, John McMohon; ***D:*** Doris Wishman; ***W:*** J.J. Kendall; ***C:*** Juan Fernandez.

Deadman's Curve **1978** Decent bio pic detailing the lives of Jan Berry and Dean Torrence who, as Jan and Dean, started the surf music wave only to wipe out after an almost-fatal car wreck. Shows how they deal with and recover from the tragedy. **100m/C VHS.** Richard Hatch, Bruce Davison, Pamela Bellwood, Susan Sullivan, Dick Clark, Wolfman Jack; ***D:*** Richard Compton. **TV**

Deadtime Stories 1/2 **1986** Mother Goose it's not. Fairy tales "Little Red Riding Hood" and "Goldilocks and the Three Bears," among others, are presented like you've never before seen them—as low-budget horror tales. **93m/C VHS, DVD.** Michael Mesmer, Brian DePersia, Scott Valentine, Phyllis Craig, Melissa Leo, Nicole Picard; ***D:*** Jeffrey Delman.

Deadwood 1/2 **1965** In the untamed West, a young cowboy is mistaken for the notorious Billy the Kid. **100m/C VHS, DVD.** Arch Hall Jr., Jack Lester, Liz Renay, Robert Dix; ***D:*** James Landis; ***C:*** Vilmos Zsigmond.

Deadwood Pass **1933** Below-standard fare has Tyler rescuing Monti more times than seems reasonable. Monti was once an all-around helper to W.C. Fields. **62m/B VHS, DVD.** Tom Tyler, Alice Dahl, Wally Wales, Buffalo Bill Jr., Lafe (Lafayette) McKee, Bud Osborne, Charles "Slim" Whitaker, Charlotte (Carlotta) Monti; ***D:*** J(ohn) P(aterson) McGowan.

The Deal **2005 (R)** It's the near future, the U.S. is at war with the 'Confederation of Arab States' and gas is $6 a gallon and rising. A Wall Street hotshot, Tom Grover (Slater), is called in to help seal a $20-billion deal with a Russian oil conglomerate called Black Star which is most likely a Russian Mafia 'oil-laundering' operation. Young Harvard grad, and new hire (Blair) acts as Grover's investigative partner and lust interest. Early portions of Epstein's script contain copious amounts of intriguing industrial data but once Angie Harmon enters the scene with her laughable Russian accent it becomes a corporate espionage thriller spoof. **107m/C DVD.** *US* Christian Slater, Selma Blair, John Heard, Angie Harmon, Kevin Tighe, Francoise Yip, Colm Feore, Robert Loggia, Philip Granger, Jim Thorburn, Ruth Epstein; ***D:*** Harvey Kahn; ***C:*** Adam Sliwinski; ***M:*** Christopher Lennertz.

The Deal 1/2 **2008 (R)** This is one deal you won't have any trouble passing up. Suicidal Hollywood producer Charlie Berns (Macy) decides to play the system, turning a snoozer script into a buzzworthy go project set to shoot in South Africa. Development exec Deidre Hearn (Ryan) sees the scam but goes along with the studio deal—at least until demanding lead actor Bobby Mason (LL Cool J) gets kidnapped; then Charlie and Deirdre are all about covering their assets. **98m/C DVD, Blu-ray Disc.** William H. Macy, Meg Ryan, LL Cool J, Elliott Gould, Jason Ritter; ***D:*** Steven Schachter; ***W:*** Steven Schachter; ***C:*** Paul Sarossy; ***M:*** Jeff Beal.

Deal 1/2 **2008 (PG-13)** Alex (Harrison) taught himself poker via online tournaments and he attracts the attention of retired pro Tommy (Reynolds), who offers to teach Alex the details that will get him into big money games. When Alex hits the World Poker Tournament in Vegas, their partnership falters and Tommy winds up across the table from his former protege. Reynolds projects the right air of world-weariness but Harrison is too callow a foil and there's nothing about the plot that'll be a surprise. **86m/C DVD.** Burt Reynolds, Bret Harrison, Shannon Elizabeth, Charles Durning, Jennifer Tilly, Gary Grubbs, Maria Mason; ***D:*** Gil Cates Jr.; ***W:*** Gil Cates Jr., Marc Weinstock; ***C:*** Thomas M. Harting; ***M:*** Peter Rafelson.

Deal of a Lifetime **1999 (PG)** It's a deal that's too good to be true, of course. Loser teen Henry (Goorjian) is tempted to sell his soul to the Devil's agent, Jerry (Pollak), in order to get a date with the school's most popular babe (Appleby). **95m/C VHS, DVD.** Kevin Pollak, Michael Goorjian, Shiri Appleby, Jennifer Rubin; ***D:*** Paul Levine; ***W:*** Katharine R. Sloan; ***C:*** Denise Brassard; ***M:*** Amotz Plessner. **VIDEO**

Deal of the Century **1983 (PG)** A first-rate hustler and his cohorts sell second-rate weapons to third-world nations; unfortunately, their latest deal threatens to blow up in their faces—literally. **99m/C VHS, DVD.** Chevy Chase, Sigourney Weaver, Gregory Hines, Richard Libertini, Wallace Shawn; ***D:*** William Friedkin; ***W:*** Paul Brickman.

Dealers 1/2 **1989 (R)** Two money-hungry stock traders mix business and pleasure, then set their sights on one final all or nothing score. **92m/C VHS, DVD.** *GB* Paul Guilfoyle, Rebecca De Mornay, Paul McGann, Derrick O'Connor; ***D:*** Colin Bucksey; ***W:*** Andrew Maclear; ***C:*** Peter Sinclair.

Dealing: Or the Berkeley-to-Boston Forty-Brick Lost-Bag Blues **1972** Counterculture time-capsule about hippies, drugs, and the Ivy League. Harvard Law student Peter (Lyons) goes to Berkeley to buy pot to bring back to Boston and falls for hippie chick Susan (Hershey). Peter convinces campus drug dealer John (Lithgow) to let Susan bring in another shipment but she gets busted by corrupt cop Murphy (Durning) and there's more trouble involving Cuban mobsters. Uh, yeah, the drug dealers are the good guys. **88m/C DVD.** John Lithgow, Ellen Barber; ***D:*** Paul Williams; ***W:*** David Odell.

Dean Koontz's Black River *Black River* **2001 (PG)** Novelist/screenwriter Bo Aikens (Mohr) is in need of a little creative inspiration and leaves Hollywood for the bucolic friendliness of the small town of Black River. Then Bo discovers the town is monitored by video cameras and he begins to get weird phone calls and notices an SUV tailing him. He can't escape unless he figures out the community's sinister secrets (which unfortunately turn out to be lame-o). **87m/C VHS, DVD.** Jay Mohr, Lisa Edelstein, Ann Cusack, Ron Canada, Stephen Tobolowsky; ***D:*** Jeff Bleckner; ***W:*** Daniel Taplitz; ***C:*** John Bartley. **TV**

Dean Koontz's Mr. Murder *Mr. Murder* **1998 (R)** Marty Stillwater (Baldwin) is a successful mystery writer and family man who discovers that he has a killer clone. Seems industrialist Drew Oslett Jr. (Church) managed to screwup in the biotech lab and now there's a bloodthirsty Marty lookalike named Alfie, who decides he wants Marty's life. Meanwhile, everyone thinks Marty is going crazy. **132m/C VHS, DVD.** Stephen Baldwin, Thomas Haden Church, Julie Warner, Bill Smitrovich, James Coburn, Don Hood, Dan Lauria; ***D:*** Dick Lowry; ***W:*** Stephen Tolkin; ***C:*** Greg Gardiner; ***M:*** Louis Febre. **TV**

Dear Boys **1980** A stylized film of sexual fantasies and romance between a moody writer and a carefree young man who relentlessly pursues excitement. Based on the novel by Gerald Reve. **90m/C VHS.** *NL* Hugo Netsers, Hans Dagelet, Bill Van Dijk, Albert Mol; ***D:*** Paul de Lussanet.

Dear Brigitte **1965** A young American kid ("Lost in Space" tyke Mumy) writes a love letter to Brigitte Bardot and travels to Paris to meet her in person. Based on the novel "Erasmus with Freckles" by John Haase. **100m/C VHS.** James Stewart, Billy Mumy, Glynis Johns, Fabian, Cindy Carol, John Williams, Jack Kruschen, Brigitte Bardot, Ed Wynn, Alice Pearce; ***D:*** Henry Koster; ***W:*** Hal Kanter.

Dear Dead Delilah **1/2 1972** Moorehead is Delilah, the matriarch of a southern family, who is on her deathbed. Her heirs are fighting to the bitter—and bloody—end to be the first to find Delilah's money, buried somewhere on her land. **90m/C VHS, DVD.** Agnes Moorehead, Will Geer, Michael Ansara, Patricia Carmichael, Dennis Patrick; ***D:*** John Farris.

Dear Detective *Dear Inspector; Tendre Poulet* **1977** Comedy/thriller/romance finds female police inspector (Girandot) investigating a murder while romancing a somewhat pompous professor of Greek (Noiret). French with subtitles. **105m/C VHS.** *FR* Annie Girardot, Philippe Noiret, Catherine Alric, Guy Marchand, Simone Renant; ***D:*** Philippe de Broca; ***W:*** Philippe de Broca, Michel Audiard; ***M:*** Georges Delerue.

Dear Detective **1978** Vaccaro is the head of the police homicide unit who is trying to track down the killer of several politicians. In the midst of her investigation, she falls for an old friend, a professor of Greek language. Based on a French TV series. **90m/C VHS.** Brenda Vaccaro, Arlen Dean Snyder, Michael MacRae, John Dennis Johnston, Jack Ging, Stephen McNally, M. Emmet Walsh, Constance Forslund, R.G. Armstrong; ***D:*** Dean Hargrove; ***M:*** Georges Delerue. **TV**

Dear Frankie **2004 (PG-13)** Scottish tearjerker about a woman, her deaf son, and the guy she pays to pretend to be Dad. Lizzie (Mortimer) has raised 9-year-old Frankie (McElhone) to believe that the father he doesn't remember is a member of a cargo ship crew, when in reality he was an abusive jerk that Lizzie left years ago. Of course, this means that she has to come up with a fake father on the spot, and finds a stranger (Butler) to fill the role, with the standard mom-falls-for-fake-dad, fake-dad-learns-to-like-his-fake-family results. Solid performances by all fail to make up for a bland, manipulative story. **102m/C DVD.** *GB* Emily Mortimer, Jack McElhone, Sharon Small, Cal Macaninch, Mary Riggans, Sophie Main, Katy Murphy, Gerard Butler; ***D:*** Shona Auerbach; ***W:*** Andrea Gibb; ***M:*** Alex Heffes.

Dear God **1996 (PG)** TV vets Marshall (director) and Kinnear team up for a sappy and predictable "Miracle on Melrose," a little piece of Capra-corn that feels like it lodged in your tooth. Cynical con man Tom (Kinnear) goes to work for the post office and gets stuck with a group of misfits at the Dead Letter Office, sorting mail for the likes of Elvis, Santa, and God. Even though he's merely working the ultimate angle for easy cash, the oddball team of postal workers think he's on a mission from the Lord and joins him in aiding the needy. Most unbelievable is the premise that single mom and love interest Gloria (Pitillo) can give the hardened criminal an instant psychological makeover. Broadly characterized supporting cast, including Conway and Metcalf, suffer at the hands of script. Strictly a star vehicle for Kinnear's budding movie career, it won't help. It also won't do anything for Marshall's downward-spiraling reputation. Ironic cameo from Christopher Darden as a reporter outside the courtroom, and Marshall himself as Postmaster General. **112m/C VHS.** Greg Kinnear, Laurie Metcalf, Maria Pitillo, Hector Elizondo, Tim Conway, Roscoe Lee Browne, Jon Seda, Anna Maria Horsford, Donal Logue, Nancy Marchand, Larry Miller, Rue McClanahan, Toby Huss, Jack Klugman; ***Cameos:*** Garry Marshall; ***D:*** Garry Marshall; ***W:*** Ed Kaplan, Warren Leight; ***C:*** Charles Minsky.

Dear John **2010 (PG-13)** Anyone who has read a Nicholas Sparks novel (or knows what the term "Dear John letter" means) knows that this tearjerker likely won't end well. John (Tatum) is a soldier on leave who meets the vacationing Savannah (Seyfried) in the spring of 2001. They immediately fall in love, as tragic romantics are prone to do. They promise to write each other letters until they can reunite. After the 9/11 attacks, John is compelled to re-enlist over and over. Plot lines involving autism and cancer are also thrown in just in case things aren't sad enough for the viewer. Tatum and Seyfried perform well, but this is really only for those looking for a good cry. **105m/C DVD.** Channing Tatum, Amanda Seyfried, Henry Thomas, Keith D. Robinson, Richard Jenkins, D.J. Cotrona, Cullen Moss, Gavin McCulley; ***D:*** Lasse Hallstrom; ***W:*** Jamie Linden; ***C:*** Terry Stacey; ***M:*** Deborah Lurie.

Dear Me: A Blogger's Tale **2008** Samantha suffers from a social anxiety disorder that has prevented her from her dream job in advertising. Then she discovers blogging and conveying her anxieties online helps put her in control and obtain a copywriting job. Samantha then falls for VP Desmond and everything is going well until a jealous coworker discovers her blog and it becomes an office sensation—unbeknownst to Samantha. **97m/C DVD.** Sarah Thompson, David O'Donnell, David DeLuise, Felecia Day, Dan Lauria, Michael Bowen, Jessica Anderson, Caia Coley, Zach Roerig; ***D:*** Michael Feifer; ***W:*** David Hirschmann, Steven Weiss-Smith; ***C:*** Matt Steinauer; ***M:*** Evan Beigel. **VIDEO**

Dear Murderer **1947** A husband suspects his wife of having an affair, and devises an ingenious, if complicated, trap for her. Inspired performances from the leads, but the plot is grim and confusing. **94m/B VHS.** *GB* Eric Portman, Greta Gynt, Dennis Price, Jack Warner, Maxwell Reed, Hazel Court, Andrew Crawford, Jane Hylton; ***D:*** Arthur Crabtree.

Dear Wendy **2005** A misfit gang of teens form, call themselves the Dandies, meet in a dingy mine with their guns and profess their vows of non-violence. Dick thinks Wendy is a toy gun at first, but she's not—and she's got some kind of hold on him. As if things aren't odd enough from the start, the only African American member of the Dandies has a thing for Wendy, making Dick jealous. Is all this going anywhere? Um-...Sure. It all leads to pacifist misfit teens brandishing their beloved handguns. Artsy, unraveling presentation of bizarre images and lost messages. **100m/C DVD.** *DK FR GE GB* Jamie Bell, Bill Pullman, Michael Angarano, Novella Nelson, Chris Owen, Alison Pill, Mark Webber, Danso Gordon; ***D:*** Thomas Vinterberg; ***W:*** Lars von Trier; ***C:*** Anthony Dod Mantle; ***M:*** Benjamin Wallfisch.

Dear Wife **1/2 1949** Comedy about those ties that bind. Even though her father is runnning for reelection to the State Senate, Freeman wants her brother-in-law (Holden) to run against him. Sequel to "Dear Ruth." **88m/B VHS.** William Holden, Joan Caulfield, Edward Arnold, Billy DeWolfe, Mona Freeman; ***D:*** Richard Haydn.

Death and Desire *Illicit Dreams 2* **1997 (R)** Fashion photographer Jeff Reed isn't tempted by the beautiful models he shoots because he's happily married. But when his wife is killed in an accident, the vulnerable Jeff becomes the target of fashion mag editor, Lynn, who desperately wants to offer him comfort. Too desperately. Soon Lynn's obsessed and Jeff's fighting for his life. Unrated version runs 88 minutes. **84m/C VHS, DVD.** Tane McClure, Tim Abell, Jennifer Burton; ***D:*** Fred Olen Ray; ***W:*** Steve Armogida; ***C:*** Gary Graver; ***M:*** Bob Kulick. **VIDEO**

Death and the Maiden **1994 (R)** Former political prisoner and torture victim (Weaver) turns the tables on the man she believes was her tormentor 15 years before. Pressing her civil rights lawyer husband (Wilson) into duty as defense attorney, she becomes prosecutor, judge, and jury. The accused (Kingsley) learns the dangers of picking up stranded motorists, as he is bound, gagged, and roughed up by the now empowered and vengeful Paulina. Tense, claustrophobic political thriller features a talented ensemble both on screen and behind the scenes. From the Ariel Dorfman play. **103m/C VHS, DVD.** Sigourney Weaver, Ben Kingsley, Stuart Wilson; ***D:*** Roman Polanski; ***W:*** Rafael Yglesias, Ariel Dorfman; ***C:*** Tonino Delli Colli; ***M:*** Wojciech Kilar.

The Death Artist **1/2 1995 (R)** Struggling busboy and would-be artist Walter Paisley (Hall) finds fame creating sculptures from dead bodies. Gruesome plot is a remake of Corman's 1960 "A Bucket of Blood" but the same premise was done much better with Vincent Price in 1953's "House of Wax." **79m/C VHS.** Anthony Michael Hall, Darcy Demoss, Shadoe Stevens, Paul Bartel, Mink Stole; ***D:*** Michael James McDonald; ***W:*** Michael James McDonald, Brendan Broderick; ***C:*** Christopher Baffa; ***M:*** David Wurst, Eric Wurst.

Death at a Funeral **2007 (R)** Ridiculous situations arise at the funeral of the patriarch of a dysfunctional British family, which brings about a reunion of estranged brothers Daniel (Macfayden) and Robert (Graves). They are also confronted by a blackmailer who's determined to give the family's dirty laundry a good airing, unless they can find a way to stop him. Not yet reviewed. **90m/C DVD.** *US NL GE* Rupert Graves, Peter Dinklage, Alan Tudyk, Daisy Donovan, Matthew Macfayden, Ewen Bremner, Peter Vaughan, Keeley Hawes, Andy Nyman, Jane Asher, Kris Marshall, Peter Egan; ***D:*** Frank Oz; ***W:*** Dean Craig; ***C:*** Oliver Curtis; ***M:*** Murray Gold.

Death at a Funeral **2010** American remake of the 2007 British flick about a funeral that exposes shocking family secrets and leads to blackmail and missing corpses. **m/C DVD.** Chris Rock, Tracy Morgan, Martin Lawrence, Loretta Devine, Ron Glass, Danny Glover, Regina Hall, James Marsden, Zoe Saldana, Columbus Short, Kevin Hart, Luke Wilson, Peter Dinklage; ***D:*** Neil LaBute; ***W:*** Dean Craig; ***C:*** Rogier Stoffers.

Death at Love House **1/2 1975** A screenwriter becomes obsessed when he is hired to write the life story of a long dead silent movie queen. Filmed at the Harold Lloyd estate. **74m/C VHS, DVD.** Robert Wagner, Kate Jackson, Sylvia Sidney, Joan Blondell, John Carradine; ***D:*** E.W. Swackhamer. **TV**

Death Be Not Proud **1975** Based on the book by John Gunther detailing the valiant battle fought by his son against the brain tumor that took his life at the age of 17. Wonderfully acted by the three principals, especially Alexander, this film leaves us feeling hopeful despite its subject. **74m/C VHS.** Arthur Hill, Robby Benson, Jane Alexander, Linden Chiles, Wendy Phillips; ***D:*** Donald Wrye. **TV**

Death Becomes Her **1992 (PG-13)** Aging actress Streep will do anything to stay young and beautiful, especially when childhood rival Hawn shows up, 200 pounds lighter and out to regain the loss of her fiance, Streep's henpecked hubby. Doing anything arrives in the form of a potion that stops the aging process (and keeps her alive forever). Watch for the hilarious party filled with dead celebrities who all look as good as the day they died. Great special effects and fun performances by Streep and Hawn playing their glamour-girl roles to the hilt add merit to this biting commentary on Hollywood's obsession with beauty and youth. **105m/C VHS, DVD.** Meryl Streep, Bruce Willis, Goldie Hawn, Isabella Rossellini, Sydney Pollack, Michael Caine, Ian Ogilvy, Adam Storke, Nancy Fish, Alaina Reed Hall, Michelle Johnson, Mimi Kennedy, Jonathan Silverman, Mary Ellen Trainor; ***Cameos:*** Fabio; ***D:*** Robert Zemeckis; ***W:*** Martin Donovan, David Koepp; ***C:*** Dean Cundey; ***M:*** Alan Silvestri. Oscars '92: Visual FX.

Death Before Dishonor **1/2 1987 (R)** Formula actioner stars Dryer as a tough Marine sergeant who battles ruthless Middle Eastern terrorists after they slaughter his men and kidnap his commanding officer (Keith). **95m/C VHS, DVD.** Fred (John F.) Dryer, Brian Keith, Joanna Pacula, Paul Winfield; ***D:*** Terry J. Leonard; ***W:*** John Gatliff; ***C:*** Don Burgess; ***M:*** Brian May.

Death Benefit **1/2 1996 (PG-13)** Corporate attorney Steven Keeney (Horton) takes on the case of Lou Anne Wilkins (Ruscio), who's having trouble getting her insurance company to cover the funeral expenses for her teenaged daughter Melissa, who died in a fall. The more Steven investigates, the more suspicious Melissa's death becomes—and he discovers money is the root of all evil. Based on the book "Death Benefit" by David Heilbroner. **89m/C VHS.** Jack Kehler, Peter Horton, Carrie Snodgress, Wendy Makkena, Elizabeth Ruscio, Belita Morena, Lee DeBroux; ***D:*** Mark Piznarski; ***W:*** Philip Rosenberg; ***C:*** Christopher Taylor. **CABLE**

Death Blow **1/2 1987 (R)** The victims of a violent rapist team together to stop the criminal after he repeatedly skirts conviction. **90m/C VHS, DVD.** Martin Landau, Frank Stallone, Jerry Van Dyke, Terry Moore, Henry Darrow, Jack Carter, Peter Lapis, Don Swayze, Donna Denton; ***D:*** Raphael Nussbaum.

Death by Dialogue **1988 (R)** Muddled story of some teenagers who discover an old film script from a project never produced because it was haunted by tragic accidents. **90m/C VHS.** Laura Albert, Ken Sagoes; ***D:*** Tom Dewier.

Death by Prescription **1/2 1986** After adjusting his patients' wills to benefit himself, an evil physician sees to their mysterious deaths. **75m/C VHS.** James Villiers, Jean Anderson, Timothy West, Nigel Davenport; ***D:*** Richard Stroud; ***W:*** Richard Gordon; ***C:*** Andrew Dunn.

Death Challenge **1/2 1980** Gangs battle without weapons, motive or discretion in this kung fu extravaganza. **94m/C VHS.** Steve Leving, Susan Wong.

Death Chase **1/2 1987** An average Joe, just jogging down the street, is thrown into a desperate game of cat-and-mouse when a body lands at his feet. **86m/C VHS.** William Zipp, Paul Smith, Jack Starrett, Bainbridge Scott; ***D:*** David A. Prior.

Death Collector **1/2 1989 (R)** In the future when insurance companies run the world, if you don't pay your premium, you die. **90m/C VHS.** Daniel Chapman, Ruth (Coreen) Collins; ***D:*** Tom Gniazdowski.

Death Cruise **1/2 1974** The six winners of a free cruise find that there is a fatal catch to the prize in this made-for-TV movie. **74m/C VHS.** Kate Jackson, Celeste Holm, Tom Bosley, Edward Albert, Polly Bergen, Michael Constantine, Richard Long; ***D:*** Ralph Senensky.

The Death Curse of Tartu **WOOF!** **1966** Another aspiring cult classic. (Read: A low-budget flick so bad it's funny). Students accidentally disturb the burial ground of an Indian medicine man who comes to zombie-like life with a deadly prescription. **84m/C VHS, DVD.** Fred Pinero, Doug Hobart, Babette Sherrill, Mayra Christine, Bill Marcos, Sherman Hayes, Gary Holtz, Frank Weed; ***D:*** William Grefe; ***W:*** William Grefe; ***C:*** Julio Chavez; ***M:*** Al Greene, Al Jacobs.

Death Defying Acts **1/2 2007 (PG)** Famed magician Harry Houdini (Pearce) is touring Edinburgh in 1926, offering a large monetary incentive to any medium who can channel his late mother. Mary McGarvie (Zeta-Jones) and her tomboy daughter Benji (Ronan) fake a music-hall psychic act and she wants the dough, despite knowing Houdini is an expert at exposing fakes. However, Harry becomes romantically interested in the attractive Mary and she starts developing a conscience. The leads look good but don't have much romantic chemistry. **97m/C DVD.** *GB AU* Guy Pearce, Catherine Zeta-Jones, Saoirse Ronan, Timothy Spall, Timothy Spall; ***D:*** Gillian Armstrong; ***W:*** Tony Grisoni, Brian Ward; ***C:*** Haris Zambarloukos; ***M:*** Cezary Skubiszewski.

Death Dreams **1992** Crista thinks she has a perfect life with her wealth, beautiful daughter Jennie, and handsome new husband George. Then Jennie tragically drowns. It appears to be an accident until Jennie contacts her mother from beyond the grave to tell what really happened. Is the tragedy turning Crista's mind or is there truly something sinister going on—something that involves George? Based on the novel by William Katz. **94m/C VHS.** Marg Helgenberger, Christopher Reeve, Fionnula Flanagan; ***D:*** Martin Donovan; ***W:*** Robert Glass. **CABLE**

Death Driver 1/2 **1978** In order to make a comeback, a stuntman attempts to do a stunt that was responsible for ending his career ten years earlier. Obviously brave but none too smart. **93m/C VHS.** Earl Owensby, Mike Allen, Patty Shaw, Mary Ann Hearn; ***D:*** Jimmy Huston.

Death Drug 1/2 **1983** Cliched alarmist film about a talented musician ruining his career by becoming addicted to the drug angel dust. **73m/C VHS.** Philip Michael Thomas, Vernee Watson-Johnson, Rosalind Cash; ***D:*** Oscar Williams.

Death Feud **1989** A man tries to save the woman he loves from the man who would destroy her and her former pimp. **98m/C VHS.** Karen Mayo-Chandler, Chris Mitchum, Frank Stallone; ***D:*** Carl Monson.

Death Force 1/2 **1978 (R)** When a Vietnam veteran comes to New York City, he becomes a hitman for the Mafia. **90m/C VHS, DVD.** Jayne Kennedy, Leon Isaac Kennedy, James Iglehart, Carmen Argenziano; ***D:*** Cirio H. Santiago.

Death from a Distance 1/2 **1936** A reporter and a detective put the moves on a group of astronomers who may be responsible for a murder. **73m/B VHS, DVD.** Russell Hopton, Lola Lane, George F. Marion Sr., John St. Polis, Lee Kohlmar, Lew Kelly, Wheeler Oakman, Robert Frazer, Cornelius Keefe; ***D:*** Frank Strayer.

Death Games 1/2 *Final Cut* **1980** Two young men shooting a documentary about an influential music promoter ask too many wrong questions, causing the powers-that-be to want them out of the picture for good. **78m/C VHS.** Lou Brown, David Clendenning, Jennifer Cluff; ***D:*** Ross Dimsey; ***W:*** Ross Dimsey; ***C:*** Ron Johanson; ***M:*** Howard J. Davidson.

Death Goes to School **1953** A strangler is loose in a girl's school, and the music teacher has a hunch as to who it is. **65m/B VHS.** *GB* Barbara Murray, Gordon Jackson, Pamela Allan, Jane Aird, Beatrice Varley; ***D:*** Stephen Clarkson.

Death House 1/2 **1988** Derek Keillor is on Death Row at Townsend State Prison when he discovers a plot to use inmates for scientific experiments in biological warfare. He decides the best way to get out is to volunteer, which means convincing the man who put him in prison that they're now on the same side. **92m/C VHS, DVD.** Dennis Cole, Anthony (Tony) Franciosa, Michael Pataki, John Saxon; ***D:*** John Saxon.

Death Hunt **1981 (R)** A man unjustly accused of murder pits his knowledge of the wilderness against the superior numbers of his pursuers. **98m/C VHS, DVD.** Charles Bronson, Lee Marvin, Ed Lauter, Andrew Stevens, Carl Weathers, Angie Dickinson; ***D:*** Peter Hunt; ***W:*** Mark Victor, Michael Grais.

Death in Brunswick *Nothing to Lose* **1990 (R)** Carl Fitzgerald (Neill) seems to be one of life's born losers—his wife's left him, his mother nags him, his house is falling apart, and he's unemployed. At least until he gets a job as a chef in a sleazy rock 'n' roll club and finds Sophie (Carides), the lovely barmaid, who just happens to be engaged to the club's owner. Of course, with Carl's luck, things go from bad to downright dangerous. Based on the novel by Boyd Oxlade. **106m/C VHS.** *AU* Sam Neill, Zoe Carides, Yvonne Lawley, Boris Brkic, John Clarke; ***D:*** John Ruane; ***W:*** John Ruane, Boyd Oxlade; ***C:*** Ellery Ryan.

Death in Deep Water **1974** A sensuous woman lures a man into a plot to kill her incredibly rich husband. **71m/C VHS.** Bradford Dillman, Suzan Farmer; ***D:*** James Ormerod; ***W:*** Brian Clemens. **TV**

A Death in the Family 1/2 **2002** Adaptation of James Agee's Pulitzer Prize-winning novel, set in Knoxville in 1915. Title tells you the tragedy that's about the befall the loving family of May (Gish) and Jay (Slattery) Follet when Jay is killed in an auto accident. It's up to the grieving May to cope and to tell their 7-year-old son Rufus (Wolff) that his father is dead. **90m/C VHS, DVD.** Annabeth Gish, John Slattery, James Cromwell, Austin Wolff, Kathleen Chalfant, Bill Raymond, David Alford, Christopher Strand; ***D:*** Gilbert Cates; ***W:*** Robert W. Lenski; ***C:*** Stephen M. Katz; ***M:*** Charles Fox. **TV**

Death in the Garden *La Mort en Ce Jardin; Evil Eden* **1956** Surreal film, filled with symbolism, about a group of French people, living in a South American settlement, who must flee a riot between soldiers and striking miners. Local adventurer, Chark (Marchal), agrees to lead them to safety but their trek through the jungle is fraught with peril (and not just from the animal life). French with subtitles. **90m/C VHS.** *MX FR* Georges Marchal, Simone Signoret, Charles Vanel, Michele Girardon, Michel Piccoli, Tito Junco; ***D:*** Luis Bunuel; ***W:*** Luis Bunuel, Luis Alcoriza, Raymond Queneau; ***C:*** Jorge Stahl Jr.; ***M:*** Paul Misraki.

Death in Venice 1/2 *Morte a Venezia* **1971 (PG)** A lush, decadent adaptation of the Thomas Mann novella about a aging, jaded, and dying composer Gustav von Aschenbach (Bogarde)—here suggested to be Gustav Mahler—who is plagued by fears that he can no longer feel anything. Instead, he becomes tragically obsessed with ideal beauty as personified in the young boy, Tadzio (Andresen). Visconti uses Mahler's 3rd and 5th symphonies to haunting effect. **124m/C VHS, DVD.** *IT* Dirk Bogarde, Mark Burns, Bjorn Andresen, Marisa Berenson, Silvana Mangano; ***D:*** Luchino Visconti; ***W:*** Luchino Visconti, Nicola Badalucco; ***C:*** Pasqualino De Santis.

Death Is Called Engelchen 1/2 *For We Too Do Not Forgive* **1963** An influential, important work of the Czech new wave. A survivor of WWII remembers his experiences with the SS leader Engelchen in a series of flashbacks. In Czech with subtitles. **111m/B VHS.** *CZ* Jan Kacer, Eva Polakova, Martin Ruzek, Blazena Holisova, Otto Lackovic q; ***D:*** Jan Kadar, Elmar Klos; ***W:*** Milos Faber; ***C:*** Rudolf Milic; ***M:*** Zdenek Liska.

Death Journey 1/2 **1976 (R)** Producer and director Williamson portrays private eye Jesse Crowder, hired by the New York D.A. to escort a key witness cross-country. A regular Williamsonfest. **90m/C VHS, DVD.** Fred Williamson, D'Urville Martin, Bernie Kuby, Heidi Dobbs, Stephanie Faulkner; ***D:*** Fred Williamson.

The Death Kiss 1/2 **1933** Creepy thriller about eerie doings at a major Hollywood film studio where a sinister killer does away with his victims while a cast-of-thousands movie spectacular is in production. **72m/B VHS, DVD.** Bela Lugosi, David Manners, Adrienne Ames, Edward Van Sloan, Vince Barnett; ***D:*** Edwin L. Marin.

Death Kiss 1/2 **1974 (R)** When a man hires a psychopath to murder his wife, his plan doesn't proceed exactly as expected. **90m/C VHS.** *GR* Larry Daniels, Dorothy Moore; ***D:*** Costas Karagiannis.

Death Machine 1/2 **1995 (R)** New company exec Hayden Cale (Pouget) uncovers questionable scientific project at weapons technology company and scientist in charge Jack Dante (Dourif) decides to get even by testing his death machine, which works by sensing fear, in corporate headquarters. **99m/C VHS, DVD.** Brad Dourif, Ely Pouget, William Hootkins; ***D:*** Stephen Norrington; ***W:*** Stephen Norrington; ***C:*** John de Borman.

Death Machines 1/2 **1976 (R)** Young karate student must face the "Death Machines," a team of deadly assassins who are trained to kill on command. **93m/C VHS, DVD.** Ron Marchini, Michael Chong, Joshua Johnson; ***D:*** Paul Kyriazi.

Death Magic 1/2 **1992** A group of five ceremonial magicians performs a spell to bring someone back from the dead, but the man they bring back, a soldier from the Civil War, decides to go on a vicious murdering spree to kill the descendants of the people who convicted him of murder in 1875. A suspensful first entry from director Clinco. **93m/C VHS.** Anne Coffrey, Keith DeGreen, Jack Dunlap, Danielle Frons, Norman Stone; ***D:*** Paul E. Clinco; ***W:*** Paul E. Clinco.

Death Mask 1/2 **1998** Screenwriter, executive producer, and star James Best plays Wilbur Johnson, a vengeful carnival worker who was abused and disfigured as a child. He becomes friends with Angel (Linnea Quigley), a sideshow dancer. After hearing Wilbur's story, she takes him to the swamp, where he meets a witch (Brigitte Hill), who gives him the titular "Death Mask." It causes violent and painful death to Wilbur's enemies when he dons the mask, so Wilbur goes on a killing spree. Then it's up to Angel to convince him to stop. Best hams it up in every scene and Quigley proves that she's still willing to take her clothes off whenever necessary. The film doesn't aim to be anything more than campy fun, and on that point, it delivers. **97m/C DVD.** James Best, Linnea Quigley, Brigitte Hill; ***D:*** Steve Latshaw; ***W:*** James Best.

Death Match **1994 (R)** John Larson gives up kickboxing after a tragedy but when his friend disappears, John is forced into a fighting bout with no rules and only one outcome. **90m/C VHS.** Matthias Hues, Martin Kove, Ian Jacklin, Nick (Nicholas, Niko) Hill, Renee Griffin; ***D:*** Joe Coppoletta.

The Death Merchant **1991** Foundering attempt at a nuclear thriller. A modern mad man hopes to sell a computer chip to third world countries but is thwarted by a secret agent. Confusing, illogical plot highlighted by mediocre performances. **90m/C VHS.** Lawrence Tierney, Martina Castle, Melody Munyan, Monica Schnarre; ***D:*** James R. Winburn; ***W:*** Kari Holman.

Death Note *Desu Noto* **2006** The God of Death has become bored with eternal existence, and has given the Death Note (a book that kills anyone whose name is written in it) to a mortal boy named Light Yagami (Fujiwara). An aspiring law student, Light immediately goes off the deep-end and uses the book to kill all the criminals in the world, earning him the displeasure of the police. They use a detective code named L (Ken'ichi Matsuyama) to track him down, hoping that he can find out who Light is before Light discovers L's true identity. **125m/C DVD.** *JP* Tatsuya Fujiwara, Ken'ichi Matsuyama, Asako Seto, Shigeki Hosokawa, Erika Toda, Shunji Fujimura, Takeshi Kaga, Yu Kashii; ***W:*** Tsugumi Oba, Takeshi Obata, Tetsuya Oishi; ***C:*** Hiroshi Takase; ***M:*** Kenji Kawai; ***V:*** Shusuke (Shu) Kaneko, Shiro Nakamura.

Death Note 2: The Last Name 1/2 *Death Note The Last Name; Desu Noto: The Last Name* **2007** Set directly after the events of the first movie, Light (Fujiwara) slides into darkness, using the Death Note to kill whomever he pleases as opposed to criminals. Even worse, another Death God has appeared and given a second Death Note to an emotionally unstable television personality who happens to be a fan of his killings, and she has volunteered to help him find L once and for all. Purists will be upset that this film deviates from the manga and anime a bit. **139m/C DVD.** *JP* Shin Shimizu, Shigeki Hosokawa, Tatsuya Fujiwara, Ken'ichi Matsuyama, Erika Toda, Takeshi Kaga; ***D:*** Shusuke (Shu) Kaneko; ***W:*** Tsugumi Oba, Takeshi Obata, Tetsuya Oishi; ***C:*** Kenji Takama; ***M:*** Kenji Kawai; ***V:*** Shiro Nakamura, Shiro Nakamura.

Death Note 3: L, Change the World 1/2 *L, Change the World* **2008** Detective L (Matsuyama) has finally solved his case, but as a result of events in the second film, his time has grown short. He has a mere 23 days to stop a bio-terrorist from destroying the world by unleashing a horrible virus. It's a departure from the Death Note comics and anime storyline, and unfortunately not a good one though it's also not a stand-alone storyline, so viewers who haven't seen the first two films will be lost. **129m/C DVD.** *JP* Tatsuya Fujiwara, Ken'ichi Matsuyama, Asako Seto, Shigeki Hosokawa, Erika Toda, Takeshi Kaga, Shunji Fujimura, Sota Aoyama, Hirohoshi Kobayashi; ***D:*** Hideo Nakata; ***W:*** Tsugumi Oba, Hideo Nakata, Takeshi Obata, Kiyomi Fujii, Hirohoshi Kobayashi; ***C:*** Tokusho Kikumura; ***M:*** Kenji Kawai; ***V:*** Shiro Nakamura.

Death Nurse **1987** Fresh from "Crazy Fat Ethel II," aspiring Queen of Camp Alden takes takes up residence in a health care establishment, much to the dismay of the patients who give up their lives in exchange for their money. **80m/C VHS.** Priscilla Alden, Michael Flood; ***D:*** Nick (Steve Millard) Phillips.

Death of a Bureaucrat *La Muerte de un Burocrata* **1966** A Cuban hero dies, and in tribute, the Communist government buries him with his union card. His widow, however, needs the card in order to collect a pension, and she enlists her nephew's help to retrieve it. The nephew soon finds himself buried in red tape, and digs himself in ever-deeper as he seeks to disinter his late uncle. A wry satire of the communist bureaucracy in Cuba, brimming with comedic tributes to Harold Lloyd, Buster Keaton and Laurel & Hardy. Alea's film was only briefly released in 1966 and was promptly banned, eventually finding its way to the U.S. in 1979. In Spanish with English subtitles. **87m/B VHS.** *CU* Salvador Wood, Silvia Planas, Manuel Estanillo, Gaspar de Santelices, Carlos Ruiz de la Tejera, Omar Alfonso, Ricardo Suarez, Luis Romay, Elsa Montero; ***D:*** Tomas Gutierrez Alea; ***W:*** Tomas Gutierrez Alea, Ramon Suarez; ***C:*** Ramon Suarez; ***M:*** Leo Brouwer.

Death of a Centerfold **1981** Drama based on the life and tragic death of Playboy model and actress Dorothy Stratten. More effectively handled in Bob Fosse's "Star 80." **96m/C VHS.** Jamie Lee Curtis, Bruce Weitz, Robert Reed, Mitchell Ryan, Bibi Besch; ***D:*** Gabrielle Beaumont.

Death of a Gunfighter **1969 (PG)** A western town courting eastern investors and bankers seeks a way to kill their ex-gunslinger sheriff. **94m/C VHS.** Richard Widmark, Lena Horne, Carroll O'Connor, John Saxon, Larry Gates, David Opatoshu, Kent Smith, Dub Taylor, Jacqueline Scott, Darlene Carr, Morgan Woodward, Michael McGreevey, Royal Dano, Kathleen Freeman, Harry Carey Jr., Victor French; ***D:*** Robert Totten, Donald Siegel; ***W:*** Joseph Calvelli; ***C:*** Andrew Jackson.

Death of a Salesman **1951** Screen adaptation of Arthur Miller's Pulitzer Prize-winning play has Fredric March superbly playing the failure and lament of Loman along with a first-rate supporting cast. Classic must see cinema. **115m/B VHS, DVD.** Fredric March, Mildred Dunnock, Kevin McCarthy, Cameron Mitchell; ***D:*** Laszlo Benedek; ***W:*** Stanley Roberts; ***C:*** Franz Planer; ***M:*** Alex North. **VIDEO**

Death of a Salesman 1/2 **1986** A powerful adaptation of the famous Arthur Miller play. Hoffman won an Emmy (as did Malkovich) for his stirring portrayal of Willy Loman, the aging salesman who realizes he's past his prime and tries to come to grips with the life he's wasted and the family he's neglected. Reid also turns in a fine performance as his long-suffering wife. **135m/C VHS, DVD.** Dustin Hoffman, John Malkovich, Charles Durning, Stephen Lang, Kate Reid, Louis Zorich; ***D:*** Volker Schlondorff; ***C:*** Michael Ballhaus; ***M:*** Alex North. **TV**

Death of a Scoundrel 1/2 *Loves of a Scoundrel* **1956** A womanizing entrepreneur is murdered and the culprit could be any one of his many jealous romantic conquests. **119m/B VHS.** George Sanders, Zsa Zsa Gabor, Yvonne De Carlo, Victor Jory; ***D:*** Charles Martin; ***M:*** Max Steiner.

Death of a Soldier 1985 (R) During WWII, the uneasy U.S.-Australian alliance explodes when a psychotic American soldier murders three Melbourne women. The lawyer hired to defend him has to fight political as well as legal influences. Based on a true story. **93m/C VHS.** *AU* James Coburn, Reb Brown, Maurie Field, Belinda Darey; ***D:*** Philippe Mora.

The Death of Adolf Hitler 1/2 **1984** Depicts Hitler's last ten days in an underground bunker. Drug-addled, suicidal, and Eva Braun-haunted, he receives the news of the fall of the Third Reich. While the film avoids cliche, it lacks emotional depth. **107m/C VHS.** *GB* Frank Finlay, Caroline Mortimer; ***D:*** Rex Firlin. **TV**

Death of an Angel 1/2 **1986** When her crippled daughter runs away to join a cult in Mexico, a recently ordained priest (Bedelia) follows her, only to become caught up herself with the leader of the group. **95m/C VHS.** Bonnie Bedelia, Nick Mancuso, Pamela Ludwig, Alex Colon; ***D:*** Petru Popescu.

The Death of Mr. Lazarescu *Moartea Domnului Lazarescu* **2005 (R)** The title character (Fiscutenau) is a grubby 62-year-old widower living in a shabby apartment with a lot of cats. After suffering head and stomach pains all day, he finally calls for help. Medic Mioara (Gheorghiu) and the ambulance driver eventually arrive and the dying man is trundled from one over-crowded hospital to another to be seen by one over-worked and/or indifferent doctor after another. He gets sicker and weaker until someone finally pays attention. This all takes a very, very long time and the message seems to be don't get seriously sick in Bucharest. Inspired by an actual 1997 incident; Romanian with subtitles. **154m/C DVD.** *RO* Luminita Gheorghiu, Ion Fiscuteanu, Gabriel Spahiu, Doru Ana, Dana Dogaru, Florin Zamfirescu; ***D:*** Cristi Puiu; ***W:*** Cristi Puiu, Razvan Radulescu; ***C:*** Oleg Mutu; ***M:*** Andreea Paduraru.

The Death of Richie *Richie* **1976** Gazzara does a fine job as a father driven to kill his drug-addicted teenage son, portrayed by Benson. Occasionally lapses into melodrama, but all-in-all a decent adaptation of Thomas Thompson's book "Richie," which was based on a true story. **97m/C VHS, DVD.** Ben Gazzara, Robby Benson, Eileen Brennan, Clint Howard; ***D:*** Paul Wendkos. **TV**

Death of the Incredible Hulk 1/2 **1990** Scientist David Banner's new job just may provide the clues for stopping his transformation into the monstrous Incredible Hulk. But first there are terrorists after the Hulk who need to be defeated and Banner's new romance to contend with. **96m/C VHS, DVD.** Bill Bixby, Lou Ferrigno, Elizabeth (Ward) Gracen, Philip Sterling; ***D:*** Bill Bixby. **TV**

Death on the Nile 1/2 **1978 (PG)** Agatha Christie's fictional detective, Hercule Poirot, is called upon to interrupt his vacation to uncover who killed an heiress aboard a steamer cruising down the Nile. Ustinov's first stint as the Belgian sleuth. Anthony Powell's costume design won an Oscar. **135m/C VHS, DVD.** *GB* Peter Ustinov, Jane Birkin, Lois Chiles, Bette Davis, Mia Farrow, David Niven, Olivia Hussey, Angela Lansbury, Jack Warden, Maggie Smith, George Kennedy, Simon MacCorkindale, Harry Andrews, Jon Finch; ***D:*** John Guillermin; ***W:*** Anthony Shaffer; ***C:*** Jack Cardiff; ***M:*** Nino Rota. Oscars '78: Costume Des.; Natl. Bd. of Review '78: Support. Actress (Lansbury).

Death on the Set 1/2 **1935** Complicated B-thriller. Gangster Cayley Morden (Kendall) is posing as his double, alcoholic film director Charlie Marsh, in order to commit crimes. When Inspector Burford (Marsh) gets too close, Morden murders Marsh and pins the crime on Lady Blanche (Stuart), Marsh's ex-lover whom Morden has been blackmailing over incriminating love letters. The plan goes bad when Morden's moll Laura (Gray) is strangled and Burford is ready to arrest the hood. **72m/B DVD.** *GB* Henry Kendall, Garry Marsh, Eve Gray, Jeanne Stuart, Adrienne Wilkinson, Robert Nainby; ***D:*** Leslie Hiscott; ***W:*** Michael Barringer; ***C:*** William Luff, Ernest Palmer.

Death Promise **1978 (R)** Ho-hum excuse for a horror flick has murderous landlord trying to evict his tenants using whatever means are necessary. **90m/C VHS.** Charles Bonet; ***D:*** Robert Warmflash; ***W:*** Norbert Albertson Jr.

Death Proof 1/2 *Quentin Tarantino's Death Proof; Grindhouse: Death Proof* **2007** Tarantino's half of the "Grindhouse" double bill features the best and worst of his creative impulses. Q creepily indulges foot and cheerleader fetishes, and overdoses on the dialogue-heavy scenes that have become his stock-in-trade, but in this instance just delay the action that everyone came to see. He pays homage to the slasher drive-in flicks of his youth with this tale of Stuntman Mike (Russell), who stalks his (always female) victims using his souped-up and reinforced muscle cars. The extended, and exciting chase scene that closes the film comes ohsoclose to making up for Tarantino's transgressions that led up to it. It is, in fact, one of the best car chase sequences put to film. **120m/C DVD, Blu-ray Disc.** *US* Kurt Russell, Rosario Dawson, Vanessa Ferlito, Sydney Tamiia Poitier, Zoe Bell, Tracie Thoms, Rose McGowan, Jordan Ladd, Mary Elizabeth Winstead, Eli Roth, Omar Doom, Michael Bacall, Jonathan Loughran, Melissa Arcaro, Michael Parks, James Parks, Marley Shelton, Nicky Katt, Quentin Tarantino; ***D:*** Quentin Tarantino; ***W:*** Quentin Tarantino; ***C:*** Quentin Tarantino.

Death Race 1/2 **2008 (R)** Contrary to its title and theme, not quite a remake of the 1975 cult classic "Death Race 2000,"—which was great campy, popcorn fun. This time around, in the grim future of 2012, ex-racecar driver and steelworker Jenson Aimes (Statham) is wrongly accused of murdering his wife and is ultimately sentenced to a Death Race, a race to win his freedom or die trying, in which each participant drives souped-up assault vehicles around the prison yard, trying to take out the other guy and avoid booby traps along the way. Looks like a video game, feels like a video game, and surprise, surprise, directed by video-game-to-screen veteran Anderson. The non-stop action would be fun if it weren't so serious. **105m/C DVD, Blu-ray Disc.** *US* Jason Statham, Tyrese Gibson, Ian McShane, Joan Allen, Nathalia Martinez, Max Ryan, Jason Clarke, Frederick Koehler, Jacob Vargas, Justin Mader, Robert LaSardo; ***D:*** Paul W.S. Anderson; ***W:*** Paul W.S. Anderson; ***C:*** Scott Kevan.

Death Race 2000 1/2 **1975 (R)** In the 21st century, five racing car contenders challenge the national champion of a cross country race in which drivers score points by killing pedestrians. Gory fun. Based on the 1956 story by Ib Melchior, and followed by "Deathsport." **80m/C VHS, DVD, UMD.** David Carradine, Simone Griffeth, Sylvester Stallone, Mary Woronov, Roberta Collins, Martin Kove, Louisa Moritz, John Landis, Don Steele; ***D:*** Paul Bartel; ***W:*** Charles B. Griffith, Robert Thom; ***C:*** Tak Fujimoto; ***M:*** Paul Chihara. **TV**

Death Rage 1/2 **1977 (R)** A hitman comes out of retirement to handle the toughest assignment he has ever faced: search for and kill the man who murdered his brother. He finds out he's the victim of a Mafia double-cross. **92m/C VHS, DVD.** *IT* Yul Brynner, Martin Balsam; ***D:*** Anthony M. Dawson.

Death Ray WOOF! **1967** It's a race to the finish as terrorists threaten to unleash the world's most powerful weapon. A very poor James Bond rip-off. Baldanello used the pseudonym Frank G. Carroll. **93m/C VHS.** *IT SP* Massimo Righi, Maureen Delphy, Nello Pazzafini, Gordon Scott; ***D:*** Gianfranco Baldanello; ***W:*** Juan Antonio Cabezas; ***C:*** Manuel Hernandez Sanjuan; ***M:*** James Anderson.

Death Ray 2000 1/2 *T.R. Sloane* **1981** Bondian superspy T.R. Sloane must search out the whereabouts of a stolen military device that could kill all life on Earth. TV pilot for the series "A Man Called Sloane." **100m/C VHS, DVD.** Robert F. Logan, Ann Turkel, Maggie Cooper, Dan O'Herlihy; ***D:*** Lee H. Katzin. **TV**

Death Rides the Plains **1944** Western with a twist. A man lures prospective buyers to his ranch, kills them, and steals their money. It's up to our heroes to ride to the rescue. **53m/B VHS, DVD.** Robert "Bob" Livingston, Al "Fuzzy" St. John, Nica Doret, Ray Bennett; ***D:*** Sam Newfield.

Death Rides the Range 1/2 **1940** Russian spies start a range war as a cover for an operation to pipe helium off a ranch and over the border. Maynard, an undercover FBI agent posing as a cowboy, is out to stop them. **58m/B VHS, DVD.** Ken Maynard, Fay McKenzie, Ralph Peters, Julian Rivero, Charles "Blackie" King, John Elliott, Bud Osborne; ***D:*** Sam Newfield.

Death Ring **1993 (R)** Basic action/martial arts tale about three men who must battle the bad guys to ensure their own survival. **91m/C VHS.** Mike Norris, Chad McQueen, Don Swayze, Billy Drago, Isabel Glasser; ***D:*** Robert J. Kizer; ***W:*** George T. LeBrun.

Death Row Diner 1/2 **1988** A movie mogul, executed for a crime he didn't commit, is brought back to life by a freak electrical storm. Nothing will stop him from exacting revenge. **90m/C VHS.** Jay Richardson, Michelle (McClellan) Bauer, John Content, Tom Schell, Dennis Mooney, Frank Sarcinello Sr., Dana Mason; ***D:*** B. Dennis Wood.

Death Row Girls 1/2 *Kuga no Shiro: Joshu 1316* **2008** The Japanese government needs an anti-terrorist unit, so to get a force of loyal fighters they put the absolute worst of the worst of their female prisoners in a prison/training facility/death camp, and brutalize them day after day. Those who refuse are buried in mass graves while those who succeed are supposed to become an elite, loyal fighting force. **83m/C DVD.** *JP* Aki Hoshino, Ami Natsui, David Ito; ***D:*** Sadaaki Haginiwa; ***W:*** Bun Kitizawa, Keita Oki.

Death Scream *Street Kill* **1975** Drama based on the New York murder of Kitty Genovese, whose cries for help while being assaulted went ignored by her neighbors. Good casting but the pacing deteriorates. **100m/C VHS.** Raul Julia, John P. Ryan, Lucie Arnaz, Ed Asner, Art Carney, Diahann Carroll, Kate Jackson, Cloris Leachman, Tina Louise, Nancy Walker, Eric (Hans Gudegast) Braeden, Allyn Ann McLerie, Tony Dow, Sally Kirkland, Helen Hunt; ***D:*** Richard T. Heffron; ***W:*** Stirling Silliphant. **TV**

Death Screams **1983 (R)** Attractive college coeds have a party and get hacked to pieces for their troubles by a machete-wielding maniac. **88m/C VHS.** Susan Kiger, Jennifer Chase, Jody Kay, William T. Hicks, Martin Tucker; ***D:*** David Nelson; ***W:*** Paul Elliot; ***M:*** Dee Barton.

Death Sentence 1/2 *Murder One* **1974** When a woman juror on a murder case finds out that the wrong man is on trial, she is stalked by the real killer. **74m/C VHS, DVD.** Cloris Leachman, Laurence Luckinbill, Nick Nolte, William Schallert; ***D:*** E.W. Swackhamer; ***M:*** Laurence Rosenthal. **TV**

Death Sentence 1/2 **2007 (R)** Nick Hume (Bacon) is a suited exec with a seemingly picture-perfect life: beautiful wife (Preston), two sons, comfortable suburban digs. Out for an evening hockey game, Nick and oldest son Brendan (Lafferty) stop for gas in a seedy neighborhood and, in the blink of an eye, find themselves part of a gang initiation that ends in Brendan's brutal murder at the hands of gangbanger wannabe Joe Darly (O'Leary). Joe's caught, but Nick has his own idea of justice for Joe and his gang, and it doesn't involve a jail cell. Unfortunately the film can't decide if it wants to be a thoughtful melodrama or an overly-violent action thriller, so it misses both targets. Missed opportunities for redemption and social commentary make this just another vigilante shoot-em-up. **105m/C DVD.** *US* Kevin Bacon, Garrett Hedlund, Kelly Preston, Aisha Tyler, John Goodman, Matt O'Leary, Jordan Garrett, Stuart Lafferty; ***D:*** James Wan; ***W:*** Ian Mackenzie Jeffers; ***C:*** John R. Leonetti; ***M:*** Charlie Clouser.

Death Ship **1980 (R)** A luxury liner is destroyed by an ancient, mysterious freighter on open seas, leaving the survivors to confront the ghost ship's inherent evil in this slow-going horror flick. **91m/C VHS.** *GB CA* George Kennedy, Richard Crenna, Nick Mancuso, Sally Ann Howes, Saul Rubinek, Kate Reid, Victoria Burgoyne, Danny Higham, Jennifer McKinney; ***D:*** Alvin Rakoff; ***W:*** John Robins; ***C:*** Rene Verzier; ***M:*** Ivor Slaney.

Death Shot **1973** Two plainclothes detectives (who seem just as sleazy as the criminals they're trying to bust) try to break up a drug ring and find that, with a little coercion, their best sources of information are the pimps and junkies they want to stop. Senseless attempt to make an action pic. **90m/C VHS.** Richard C. Watt, Frank Himes; ***D:*** Mitch Brown.

Death Spa WOOF! **1987 (R)** A health club is possessed by the spirit of a vengeful woman. The fitness craze takes on a campy new twist. **87m/C VHS.** William Bumiller, Brenda Bakke, Merritt Butrick; ***D:*** Michael Fischa.

Death Sport **1978 (R)** Another offering from Corman and Carradine follows, but isn't really a sequel of "Death Race 2000." Carradine is Kaz Oshay, leading a band of rebels against organized society. Upon capture Kaz participates in Death Sport, resulting in a show of fighting and motorcycle stunt work. Doesn't live up to the cult hit, but seems to fit into the genre. **83m/C VHS, DVD.** David Carradine, Claudia Jennings, Richard Lynch, William (Bill) Smithers, Will Walker, David McLean, Jesse Vint; ***D:*** Allan Arkush, Nicholas Niciphor; ***W:*** Donald Stewart, Nicholas Niciphor; ***C:*** Gary Graver; ***M:*** Andrew Stein.

The Death Squad 1/2 **1973** A police commissioner hires an ex-cop to find a group of vigilante cops who are behind a series of gangland-style executions. Good cast, though that's about all this flick has got going for it. **74m/C VHS.** Robert Forster, Melvyn Douglas, Michelle Phillips, Mark Goddard, Bert Remsen, Claude Akins; ***D:*** Harry Falk. **TV**

Death Stalk 1/2 **1974** Dream vacation turns nightmarish for two couples when the wives are taken hostage by several escaped convicts. **90m/C VHS.** Vince Edwards, Vic Morrow, Anjanette Comer, Robert Webber, Carol Lynley, Neville Brand, Norman Fell; ***D:*** Robert Day. **TV**

Death Takes a Holiday **1934** Death (March) is bored and wonders why humans fear him so much. He takes on human form, pretending to be the handsome Prince Sirki, and becomes a guest of Italian nobleman, Duke Lambert (Standing). He bewilders most, except the lovely Grazia (Venable), who falls in love with him. And when she does, nothing dies because Death is also in love and not attending to business. But Death is also afraid to reveal his true self for fear of repelling her. Based on Alberto Casella's play and the inspiration for the bloated "Meet Joe Black." **79m/B VHS.** Fredric March, Evelyn Venable, Guy Standing, Katherine Alexander, Gail Patrick, Helen Westley, Kent Taylor, Edward Van Sloan; ***D:*** Mitchell Leisen; ***W:*** Maxwell Anderson, Gladys Lehman, Walter Ferris; ***C:*** Charles B(ryant) Lang Jr.

Death Target 1/2 **1983** Three former mercenaries team up for one last mission that gets sidetracked when one of the soldiers-of-fortune falls for a worker with a habit. **72m/C VHS.** Jorge Montesi, Elaine Lakeman; ***D:*** Peter Hyams.

Death Tide **1958** Hoodlums pirate a ship full of diamonds in this story of death and crime on the high seas. **?m/B VHS.** Frank Silvera, Joan Alexander; ***D:*** Victor Komow.

Death to Smoochy **2002 (R)** DeVito-directed dark comedy follows a clash of the clowns: one good and one evil. Rainbow Randolph (Williams), is the corrupt, alcoholic star of a kiddie show fired over a bribery scandal and replaced by his polar opposite: Barney-esque purple rhino good-guy, Smoochy (Norton). Keener is the ruthless Kidsnet exec who takes orders from her fetid network boss (Stewart). Director DeVito doubles as a loathsome agent. Although Norton is proficient as the cloying, wide-eyed kiddie magnet and Williams clearly revels in ranting, this over-the-top to the point of ugliness revenge comedy's one note joke wears thin and behind the scenes kiddie show satire is way less subtle than it needs to be. **109m/C VHS, DVD.** *US* Robin Williams, Edward Norton, Catherine Keener, Danny DeVito, Jon Stewart, Harvey Fierstein, Michael Rispoli, Pam Ferris, Danny Woodburn, Vincent Schiavelli; ***D:*** Danny DeVito; ***W:*** Adam Resnick; ***C:*** Anastas Michos; ***M:*** David Newman.

Death Train 1/2 **1979** Dead man seems to have been struck by a train, but clueless investigator can't figure out where the train came from. **96m/C VHS.** Hugh Keays-Byrne, Ingrid Mason, Max Meldrum; ***D:*** Igor Auzins.

Death Trance 🦴🦴 ½ **2005 (R)** In an "unknown place and time" (it appears to be feudal Japan but people have bazookas and motorcycles) a master swordsman searches for the ultimate battle, as no one appears to be able to challenge him anymore. He hears tales of a mysterious coffin holding the body of the Goddess of Destruction who will bring about the Armageddon if she is released. Intrigued, he swipes the coffin, and it quickly becomes a free-for-all as everyone tries to take it from him while he tries to figure out how to open it. You'd think the whole concept of Armageddon would make everyone think twice, but sadly they seem oblivious. **90m/C DVD, Blu-ray Disc.** *JP* Tak Sakaguchi, Yuko Takeuchi, Yoko Fujita, Kentaro Seagal, Takamasa Suga, Osamu Takahashi; ***D:*** Yuji Shimomura; ***W:*** Yuji Shimomura, Seiji Chiba, Shinichi Fujita, Junya Kato; ***M:*** Rui Ogawa.

Death Tunnel 🦴 ½ **2005 (R)** A college freshman initiation gag goes horribly wrong for five women when they are trapped inside a deserted—and haunted—asylum with the only route to safety being an underground tunnel through which scores of deceased patients had once traveled. Filmed at the actual site of the Waverly Hills Sanatorium, which was built in the early 1900s and housed patients suffering from tuberculosis; many local residents were offended about the content of the film. **97m/C DVD.** Steffany Huckaby, Melanie Lewis, Yolanda Pecoraro, Kristin Novak, Annie Burgstede; ***D:*** Philip Adrian Booth; ***W:*** Philip Adrian Booth, Christopher Saint Booth. **VIDEO**

Death Valley 🦴 ½ **1946** Greed turns gold prospectors in Death Valley against each other. **70m/C VHS.** Robert Lowery, Helen Gilbert, Sterling Holloway; ***D:*** Lew Landers.

Death Valley 🦴 ½ **1981 (R)** Good cast, lousy plot. Youngster (Billingsley) gets caught up with a psycho cowpoke while visiting mom in Arizona. **90m/C VHS, DVD.** Paul LeMat, Catherine Hicks, Peter Billingsley, Wilford Brimley, Edward Herrmann, Stephen McHattie; ***D:*** Dick Richards; ***C:*** Stephen Burum.

Death Valley 🦴 ½ *Mojave* **2004 (R)** Mindless badass action. Josh (Olsen) is talked into going to a weekend techno rave in the desert by three buddies. But the pals manage to get on the wrong side of the local biker gang and its odious leader Dom (Mihok) and Josh seems to be the only one with the cojones to survive. **95m/C DVD.** Eric Christian Olsen, Rider Strong, Dash Mihok, Vince Vieluf, Bumper Robinson, Brendan Fletcher, Genevieve Cortese, Wayne Young; ***D:*** David Kebo, Rudi Liden; ***W:*** David Kebo, Rudi Liden; ***C:*** Thomas M. Harting; ***M:*** Nathan Barr.

Death Valley Manhunt 🦴🦴 **1943** A marshal hired to protect a man's oil wells discovers that the company manager is keeping the profits for himself. **55m/B VHS.** William (Wild Bill) Elliott, George "Gabby" Hayes, Anne Jeffreys; ***D:*** John English.

Death Valley Rangers 🦴 ½ **1944** The hero pretends to be an outlaw to expose a gang robbing gold-laden stagecoaches. **59m/B VHS.** Ken Maynard, Hoot Gibson, Bob Steele, Linda Brent, Kenneth Harlan; ***D:*** Robert Emmett Tansey.

Death Valley: The Revenge of Bloody Bill 🦴 **2004 (R)** Several college students on a road trip are carjacked by drug dealer Earl (Bastien) who takes them to the ghost town of Sunset Valley in search of his missing partner. Seems the town is haunted by the spirit of vengeful Confederate soldier "Bloody Bill" Anderson (Bouvet), who uses zombies to make his guests feel at home. **88m/C DVD.** Scott Carson, Chelsea Jean, Jeremy Bouvet, Gregory Bastien, Denise Boutte, Matt Marraccini, Steven Glinn, Kandis Erickson; ***D:*** Byron Werner; ***W:*** John Yuan, Matt Yuan; ***C:*** Byron Werner; ***M:*** Ralph Rieckermann.

Death Warmed Up 🦴 ½ **1985** A crazed brain surgeon turns ordinary people into bloodthirsty mutants, and a small group of young people travel to his secluded island to stop him. **83m/C VHS.** Michael Hurst, Margaret Umbers, David Letch; ***D:*** David Blyth.

Death Warrant 🦴🦴 **1990 (R)** Van Damme whams and bams a little less than usual in this cop-undercover-in-prison testosterone fest. As a Royal Canadian Mountie undercover in prison—where inmates are perishing under mysterious circumstances—the pectoral-perfect Muscles from Brussels is on the brink of adding two plus two when an inmate transferee threatens his cover. Contains the requisite gratuitous violence, prison bromide, and miscellaneous other Van Dammages. **111m/C VHS, DVD.** Jean-Claude Van Damme, Robert Guillaume, Cynthia Gibb, George Dickerson, Patrick Kilpatrick; ***D:*** Deran Sarafian; ***W:*** David S. Goyer; ***C:*** Russell Carpenter; ***M:*** Gary Chang.

Death Watch 🦴🦴🦴 **1980 (R)** In the future, media abuse is taken to an all time high as a terminally ill woman's last days are secretly filmed by a man with a camera in his head. Intelligent, adult science fiction with an excellent cast. **128m/C VHS.** *FR GE* Romy Schneider, Harvey Keitel, Harry Dean Stanton, Max von Sydow; ***D:*** Bertrand Tavernier; ***W:*** Bertrand Tavernier, David Rayfiel.

Death Weekend 🦴 ½ *House by the Lake* **1976** A woman is stalked by a trio of murderous, drunken hoodlums who seek to spoil her weekend. **89m/C VHS.** *CA* Brenda Vaccaro, Don Stroud, Chuck Shamata, Richard Ayres, Kyle Edwards; ***D:*** William Fruet.

Death Wish 🦴🦴 ½ **1974 (R)** Paul Kersey (Bronson) is a middle-aged businessman who turns vigilante after his wife and daughter are raped and left for dead by a gang of hoodlums (one is Goldblum in his film debut). He stalks the streets of New York seeking revenge on other muggers, pimps, and crooks, making the neighborhood safer for those less macho. Brosnan's his usual stoic self and the violence could be deemed excessive—certainly Brian Garfield, whose novel the film is based on, thought so. **93m/C VHS, DVD.** Charles Bronson, Vincent Gardenia, William Redfield, Hope Lange, Jeff Goldblum, Stuart Margolin, Olympia Dukakis; ***D:*** Michael Winner; ***W:*** Wendell Mayes; ***C:*** Arthur Ornitz; ***M:*** Herbie Hancock.

Death Wish 2 **WOOF!** **1982 (R)** Bronson re-creates the role of Paul Kersey, an architect who takes the law into his own hands when his family is victimized once again. Extremely violent sequel to the successful 1974 movie. Followed by "Death Wish 3" (1985) and 4 (1987) in which Bronson continues to torture the street scum and the viewers as well. **89m/C VHS, DVD.** Charles Bronson, J.D. Cannon, Jill Ireland, Vincent Gardenia, Anthony (Tony) Franciosa, Laurence Fishburne; ***D:*** Michael Winner; ***C:*** Richard H. Kline; ***M:*** Jimmy Page.

Death Wish 3 🦴 ½ **1985 (R)** Once again, Charles Bronson blows away the low lifes who have killed those who were dear to him and were spared in the first two films. **100m/C VHS, DVD.** Charles Bronson, Martin Balsam, Deborah Raffin, Ed Lauter, Alex Winter, Marina Sirtis; ***D:*** Michael Winner; ***M:*** Jimmy Page.

Death Wish 4: The Crackdown 🦴 **1987 (R)** The four-times-weary urban vigilante hits crack dealers this time, hard. **100m/C VHS, DVD.** Charles Bronson, John P. Ryan, Kay Lenz, Danny (Daniel) Webb; ***D:*** J. Lee Thompson.

Death Wish 5: The Face of Death **WOOF!** **1994 (R)** Paul Kersey (Bronson) returns to vigilantism when his clothing manufacturer fiancee Olivia (Downs) has her business threatened by mobsters, one of whom turns out to be her sadistic ex (Parks). Bronson looks bored with the rehashed material. Lots of explicit and grisly violence. **95m/C VHS, DVD.** Charles Bronson, Lesley-Anne Down, Michael Parks, Kenneth Welsh; ***D:*** Allan Goldstein; ***W:*** Allan Goldstein; ***C:*** Curtis Petersen; ***M:*** Terry Plumeri.

Death Wish Club 🦴 ½ *Carnival of Fools* **1983** Young woman gets involved in a club with an unusual mission—suicide. **93m/C VHS.** Meridith Haze, Rick Barns, J. Martin Sellers, Ann Fairchild; ***D:*** John Carr.

Deathcheaters 🦴 ½ **1976 (G)** Australian Secret Service offers two stuntmen a top secret mission in the Philippines. **96m/C VHS.** John Hargreaves, Grant Page, Noel Ferrer; ***D:*** Brian Trenchard-Smith; ***W:*** Michael Cove.

Deathdream 🦴🦴 ½ *Dead of Night; Night Walk; The Veteran; The Night Andy Came Home* **1972** In this reworking of the "Monkey's Paw" tale, a mother wishes her dead son would return from Vietnam. He does, but he's not quite the person he used to be. Gripping plot gives new meaning to the saying, "Be careful what you wish for—it might come true." One of Tom Savini's earliest F/X assignments. **98m/C VHS, DVD.** *CA* John Marley, Richard Backus, Lynn Carlin, Alan Ormsby; ***D:*** Bob (Benjamin) Clark; ***W:*** Alan Ormsby; ***C:*** Jack McGowan; ***M:*** Carl Zittrer.

Deathfight 🦴 ½ **1993 (R)** Let's face it, no one watches these movies because they have a plot. This is a fast-paced B-grade martial arts flick with numerous butts getting kicked. Oh, all right, if you insist on a plot—Norton's evil half-brother (Guerrero) is trying to turn their legitimate family business into a criminal front by framing Norton for murder. **92m/C VHS.** Richard Norton, Franco Guerrero, Karen Moncrieff, Chuck Jeffreys, Ron Vreeken, Tetchie Agbayani, Joe Mari Avellana; ***D:*** Anthony Maharaj; ***W:*** Tom Huckabee.

Deathhead Virgin 🦴 ½ **1974 (R)** An evil virgin spirit is waiting to possess one of two men eager to find a sunken fortune. The fate of the fortunate one is only death! **94m/C VHS.** Jock Gaynor, Larry Ward, Diane McBain, Vic Diaz; ***D:*** Norman Foster; ***W:*** Jock Gaynor, Larry Ward; ***C:*** Fred Conde; ***M:*** Richard LaSalle.

Deathlands: Homeward Bound 🦴 ½ **2003** By 2084 the Earth has been decimated by war and disaster and civilization has devolved into feudal states, with the USA simply called the Deathlands. Eyepatch-wearing Ryan Cawdor (Spano) leads a band of nomadic scavengers. Ryan decides it's time to return to his home in Front Royale, which has been ruled by his evil brother (Peterson) and his evil stepmother (Lords) ever since they offed his pops and took control. Ryan wants revenge. Sci-Fi Channel flick is adapted from the fifth book in James Axler's "Deathlands" series. **86m/C DVD.** Vincent Spano, Traci Lords, Jenya Lano, Alan C. Peterson, Colin Fox, Cliff Saunders, Nathan Carter; ***D:*** Joshua Butler; ***W:*** Gabrielle Stanton, Harry Werksman Jr.; ***C:*** Bruce Worrall; ***M:*** Christopher Lennertz. **CABLE**

Deathmask 🦴🦴 **1969** A four-year-old boy's corpse is found buried in a cardboard box, and a medical examiner—whose daughter met a similar fate—investigates the murder. Could've been done more tastefully. **102m/C VHS.** Farley Granger, Ruth Warrick, Danny Aiello; ***D:*** Richard Friedman.

Deathmoon 🦴 ½ **1978** A businessman plagued by recurring werewolf nightmares goes on a Hawaiian vacation to try to forget his troubles. Made for television. **90m/C VHS.** Robert Foxworth, Joe Penny, Debralee Scott, Dolph Sweet, Charles Haid; ***D:*** Bruce Kessler. **TV**

Deathrow Gameshow 🦴 ½ **1988** Condemned criminals can either win their freedom or die in front of millions on a new TV show that doesn't win the host many friends. **78m/C VHS.** John McCafferty, Robin Bluthe, Beano, Mark Lasky; ***D:*** Mark Pirro; ***W:*** Mark Pirro.

The Deaths of Ian Stone 🦴 ½ **2007 (R)** Ian Stone (Vogel) is hunted by demons who kill him over and over and then watch as he's resurrected into a new life. His stalkers feed off of human fear but why did they choose Ian to die? The character isn't so compelling that you'll care but there are a few good frights. **87m/C DVD.** *GB* Mike Vogel, Jaime Murray, Christina Cole, Michael Feast, Michael Dixon, Charlie Anson; ***D:*** Dario Piana; ***W:*** Brendan William Hood; ***C:*** Stefano Morcaldo; ***M:*** Elia Cmiral.

Deathstalker **WOOF!** *El Cazador de la Muerte* **1983 (R)** Deathstalker sets his sights on seizing the evil wizard Munkar's magic amulet so he can take over Munkar's castle. The only excuse for making such an idiotic film seems to have been to fill it with half-naked women. Filmed in Argentina and followed by two sequels that were an improvement. **80m/C VHS, DVD.** Richard (Rick) Hill, Barbi Benton, Richard Brooker, Victor Bo, Lana Clarkson; ***D:*** John Watson; ***W:*** Howard R. Cohen; ***C:*** Leonardo Solis; ***M:*** Oscar Cardozo Ocampo.

Deathstalker 2: Duel of the Titans 🦴🦴 **1987 (R)** Campy fantasy comically pits the lead character against an evil wizard. Sword-and-sorcery spoof doesn't take itself too seriously. **85m/C VHS, DVD.** John Terlesky, Monique Gabrielle, John Lazar, Toni Naples, Maria Socas, Deanna (Dee) Booher; ***D:*** Jim Wynorski; ***W:*** Jim Wynorski; ***C:*** Leonardo Solis; ***M:*** Chuck Cirino.

Deathstalker 3 🦴 ½ *Deathstalker 3: The Warriors From Hell* **1989 (R)** Another humorous entry in the Deathstalker saga. This time there's action, romance, magic and the Warriors From Hell. **85m/C VHS.** John Allen Nelson, Carla Herd, Terri Treas, Thom Christopher; ***D:*** Alfonso Corona; ***W:*** Howard R. Cohen.

Deathstalker 4: Match of Titans 🦴 **1992 (R)** The sword and sorcery epic continues, with our hero revealing yet more musculature in his efforts to defeat an evil queen and her legion of stone warriors. **85m/C VHS, DVD.** Richard (Rick) Hill, Maria Ford, Michelle Moffett, Brett (Baxter) Clark; ***D:*** Howard R. Cohen.

Deathtrap 🦴🦴 **1982 (PG)** A creatively blocked playwright, his ailing rich wife, and a former student who has written a sure-fire hit worth killing for, are the principals in this compelling comedy-mystery. Cross and double-cross are explored in this film based on the Broadway hit by Ira Levin. **118m/C VHS, DVD.** Henry Jones, Michael Caine, Christopher Reeve, Dyan Cannon, Irene Worth; ***D:*** Sidney Lumet; ***W:*** Jay Presson Allen; ***C:*** Andrzej Bartkowiak; ***M:*** Johnny Mandel.

Deathwatch 🦴🦴 ½ **2002 (R)** After an intensely bloody World War I battle, nine soldiers get off-track inside a massive labyrinth of deserted German trenches filled with mounds of the deceased and packed with a mother lode of rats. Further complicating matters is a deadly unearthly force that pits the men against one another while picking them off one at a time. Bassett nicely blends frightful atmosphere with a disturbingly realistic backdrop that somewhat atones for the uninspired dialogue. **95m/C VHS, DVD.** Jamie Bell, Ruaidhri Conroy, Laurence Fox, Dean Lennox Kelly, Kris Marshall, Hans Matheson, Hugh O'Conor, Matthew Rhys, Andy Serkis, Hugo Speer, Mike Downey, Roman Horak; ***D:*** Michael J. Bassett; ***W:*** Michael J. Bassett; ***C:*** Hubert Taczanowski; ***M:*** Curt Cress, Chris Weller. **VIDEO**

D.E.B.S. 🦴 ½ **2004 (PG-13)** Low-budget riot grrl send-up of "Charlie's Angels" begs the question "Why parody something that never took itself seriously in the first place?" A secret government agency known as the D.E.B.S. recruits nubile teenage girls through trick questions in the S.A.T. that identify their willingness to lie, cheat, and kill. After the team monitors supervillian Lucy Diamond (Brewster) during her blind date with assassin Ninotchka (Cauffiel), leader Amy (Foster) gets a crush on Lucy, which jeopardizes the whole team. Even with the lesbianism added for extra taboo, Robinson can't elevate her material beyond its one-joke premise. Pretty anemic comedy, but plenty for schoolgirl fetishists to be happy about. **91m/C DVD.** *US* Sara Foster, Jordana Brewster, Meagan Good, Devon Aoki, Jill Ritchie, Holland Taylor, Michael Clarke Duncan, Jimmi Simpson, Jessica Cauffiel, Geoff Stults; ***D:*** Angela Robinson; ***W:*** Angela Robinson; ***C:*** M. David Mullen; ***M:*** Steven Stern.

The Debt 🦴🦴 *Back to Even* **1998 (R)** Printing press operator Mitch's (Lamas) gambling problems get him deeply in debt to local wiseguy Danny Boyle (Pare) who gets Mitch to help him in a counterfeiting operation. Usual gangster cliches but the action moves along. **92m/C VHS, DVD.** Lorenzo Lamas, Michael Pare, Heidi Thomas, Angela Jones, Herb Mitchell; ***D:*** Rod Hewitt; ***W:*** Rod Hewitt; ***C:*** Garrett Fisher. **VIDEO**

The Debt 🦴🦴 ½ **2003** Safecracker Geoff Dresner (Clarke) has left his criminal past behind until his stupid son-in-law Terry (Freeman) fails to repay a dangerous loan shark. In order to protect his family, Geoff agrees to do one last job, which goes horribly wrong. **110m/C DVD.** Warren Clarke, Martin Freeman, Hugo Speer, Lee Williams, Orla Brady, Barbara Marten, Amanda Abbington; ***D:*** Jon Jones; ***W:*** Richard McBrien; ***C:*** John Pardue; ***M:*** Martin Phipps. **TV**

A Decade Under the Influence 1/2 **2002 (R)** Filmmakers LaGravenese and Demme chronicle the rise of new, independent filmmakers from the ashes of the old Hollywood studio system, beginning in 1967 with such films as "The Graduate" and "Bonnie & Clyde" and ending in 1977 with "Star Wars." Contains extensive film clips and interviews with diretors, actors, writers, and producers. Originally a three-part series shown on the Independent Film Channel; a theatrical version was released at 108 minutes. **180m/C DVD.** *US* ***D:*** Richard LaGravenese, Ted (Edward) Demme; ***C:*** Clyde Smith, Anthony Janelli; ***M:*** John Kimbrough.

The Decalogue 1/2 **1988** Originally produced for Polish TV, Kieslowski's 10-hour epic offers moments from the lives of residents of a late-Communist era Warsaw apartment complex. Each of the segments is a modern retelling of the Ten Commandments as the individuals confront morality, ethics, betrayal, and a variety of human frailities and crises. Polish with subtitles. **584m/C VHS, DVD.** *PL* Krystyna Janda, Aleksander Bardini, Maja Komorowska, Daniel Olbrychski, Janusz Gajos, Maria Pakulnis, Jerzy Stuhr, Zbigniew Zamachowski, Boguslaw Linda, Artur Barcis, Henryk Baranowski; ***D:*** Krzysztof Kieslowski; ***W:*** Krzysztof Kieslowski, Krzysztof Piesiewicz; ***C:*** Wieslaw Zdort, Edward Klosinski, Krysztof Pakulski, Slawomir Idziak, Witold Adamek, Dariusz Kuc, Andrzej Jaroszewicz, Piotr Sobocinski, Jacek Blawut; ***M:*** Zbigniew Preisner. **TV**

The Decameron 1/2 *Il Decameron* **1970 (R)** Pasolini's first epic pageant in his "Trilogy of Life" series. An acclaimed, sexually explicit adaptation of a handful of the Boccaccio tales. In Italian with English subtitles. **111m/C VHS, DVD.** *FR IT GE* Franco Citti, Ninetto Davoli, Angela Luce, Patrizia Capparelli, Jovan Jovanovich, Silvana Mangano, Pier Paolo Pasolini; ***D:*** Pier Paolo Pasolini; ***W:*** Pier Paolo Pasolini; ***C:*** Tonino Delli Colli; ***M:*** Ennio Morricone. Berlin Intl. Film Fest. '71: Silver Prize.

Decameron Nights 1/2 **1953** Story of Boccaccio's pursuit of a recently widowed young women is interwoven amongst the three of the 14th century Italian writer's bawdy tales. **87m/C VHS.** *GB* Louis Jourdan, Joan Fontaine, Binnie Barnes, Joan Collins, Marjorie Rhodes; ***D:*** Hugo Fregonese.

Decay WOOF! 1998 Katherine (Davies) is bored by dentist hubby Richard (Brock) and takes up with sleazy nightclub owner Ronnie (Storti), who offers to set up a hit on her spouse. But the hit man turns out to be a serial killer who specializes in strippers and—unbeknownst to his wife—the dentist has mob ties. The plot's actually more convoluted and not worth your time and effort. **86m/C VHS.** Tamara Davies, Raymond Storti, Robert Z'Dar, Brian Brock, Ron von Gober; ***D:*** Jason Robert Stephens; ***W:*** Jason Robert Stephens; ***C:*** Dennis Devine; ***M:*** Jonathan Price.

Deceit **1989 (R)** A sci-fi sex comedy with an environmental premise. Bailey and Brick are two aliens working for their planet's Environmental Protection Agency, whose idea of protection is to vaporize polluter planets. Guess which planet is next on their hit list. But before they get down to business, our two alien studs want to do the horizontal bop with two of the local lovelies, who decide that isn't how they want to spend their last moments on earth. It has a happy ending. **92m/C VHS.** Scott Paulin, Norbert Weisser, Samantha (Sam) Phillips; ***D:*** Albert Pyun; ***W:*** Kitty Chalmers.

Deceit **2006** Dave (Long), his best friend Brian (Mably), and Brian's girlfriend Emily (Chriqui) are recent college grads. Before Dave heads to law school, he and Emily have an alcohol-influenced one-nighter. Five years later, Brian is a millionaire and he and Emily are unhappily married. Dave returns home to settle his dad's estate and finds himself drawn to Emily again, which is not a good idea. **92m/C DVD.** Emmanuelle Chriqui, Matt Long, Luke Mably, Pell James, Jon Abrahams, Joe Pantoliano; ***D:*** Michael Cole Weiss; ***W:*** Michael Cole Weiss; ***C:*** Ruben O'Malley; ***M:*** Dan Silver. **CABLE**

Deceived 1/2 **1991 (PG-13)** A successful career woman with a passionate husband and a young daughter feels she has it all until her husband is apparently killed in a bizarre tragedy. But just how well did she know the man she married? Who was he really and what secrets are hidden in his past? As she struggles to solve these mysteries, her own life becomes endangered in this psychological thriller. **115m/C VHS, DVD.** Goldie Hawn, John Heard, Ashley Peldon, Jan Rubes, Amy Wright, Maia Filar, Robin Bartlett, Tom Irwin, Beatrice Straight, Kate Reid; ***D:*** Damian Harris; ***W:*** Mary Agnes Donoghue, Derek Saunders; ***C:*** Jack N. Green; ***M:*** Thomas Newman.

Deceiver *Liar* **1997 (R)** Contrived psychological thriller starts out with the requisite dead prostitute (Zellwegger, in a questionable career move) and the rounding up of the usual suspects, settling on disturbed but brainy Princeton grad Wayland (indie film icon Roth). Wayland uses his superior I.Q. and penchant for mind games to send head detectives Kennesaw and Braxton (Rooker and Penn) into a tailspin of deceit and lies, turning the investigation around on the gritty cops. Flashy camera work only adds to the tangled mayhem. Fine performances from talented cast bring this up a notch. Twin directors Jonas and Joshua Pate's convoluted spin on a noirish murder mystery follows up their 1996 debut, "Grave." **102m/C VHS, DVD.** Renee Zellweger, Tim Roth, Christopher Penn, Michael Rooker, Ellen Burstyn, Rosanna Arquette; ***D:*** Jonas Pate, Josh Pate; ***W:*** Jonas Pate, Josh Pate; ***C:*** Bill Butler; ***M:*** Harry Gregson-Williams.

The Deceivers **1988 (PG-13)** Brosnan stars as a British officer sent on a dangerous unercover mission in 1820s India. He's to infiltrate the notorious Thuggee cult, known for robbing and murdering unwary travelers. Interesting premise falters due to slow pacing and Brosnan's lack of believability. **112m/C VHS, DVD.** *IN GB* Pierce Brosnan, Saeed Jaffrey, Shashi Kapoor, Keith Michell; ***D:*** Nicholas Meyer; ***C:*** Walter Lassally.

December **1991 (PG)** Four prep-school students in New Hampshire must confront the reality of war when the Japanese bomb Pearl Harbor. A touching story of courage and friendship that takes place in one night during the suprise-attack. **92m/C VHS, DVD.** Wil Wheaton, Chris Young, Brian Krause, Balthazar Getty, Jason London; ***D:*** Gabe Torres; ***W:*** Gabe Torres.

December Boys 1/2 **2007 (PG-13)** The four "December Boys"— named so because they were all born in December—Sparks (Byers), Spit (Fraser), Misty (Cormie) and Maps (Radcliffe—yep, Harry Potter) are tight friends, and all orphans in Australia in the 60s. The teens get to leave the orphanage for a seaside holiday on the coast, where they learn that a couple down the beach may be interested in adopting one of them. Three of the four jostle for the attention of the would-be parents while Maps, having given up ever having his own family, pursues the local hot girl (Palmer). The boys get to live it up on the outside of the orphanage, but there's just nothing special in this uninspired and occasionally sappy plot. The breathtaking scenery of Australia's south coast, with its shoreline, caves, and rock formations, is interesting. **105m/C DVD.** Daniel Radcliffe, Lee Cormie, Teresa Palmer, Victoria Hill, Christin Byers, James Fraser, Sullivan Stapleton, Jack Thompson, Kris McQuade, Frank Gallacher; ***D:*** Rod Hardy; ***W:*** Marc Rosenberg; ***C:*** David Connell; ***M:*** Carlo Giacco.

December Bride 1/2 **1991** Determined young woman (Reeves) becomes the housekeeper to two taciturn Irish farmer/brothers (Hinds and McCann) and proceeds to bully them into prosperity in early 20th century rural Ireland. She also scandalizes the community by sleeping with both men and refusing to marry either—even after she becomes pregnant. Based on the novel by Sam Hanna Bell. **88m/C VHS.** *IR* Saskia Reeves, Ciaran Hinds, Donal McCann, Patrick Malahide, Brenda Bruce; ***D:*** Thaddeus O'Sullivan; ***W:*** David Rudkin; ***C:*** Bruno de Keyzer; ***M:*** Jurgen Knieper.

December Flower 1/2 **1984** A young woman arrives at her aunt's estate so she can nurse her back to health, but she finds her aunt a bit down in the mouth: seems someone is trying to kill her, and she could be next in line. **65m/C VHS.** Jean Simmons, Mona Washbourne, Bryan Forbes; ***D:*** Stephen Frears; ***M:*** Richard Hartley.

December 7th: The Movie 1/2 **1991** Banned for 50 years by the U.S. Government, this planned Hollywood explanation to wartime audiences of the Pearl Harbor debacle offers such "offensive" images as blacks fighting heroically alongside whites, loyal Japanese-Americans, and Uncle Sam asleep on the morning of the attack. The Chief of Naval Operations confiscated the original film, claiming it demeaned the Navy. The battle scenes were so realistic they fooled even documentarians. This isn't the most incisive video on the event—just an unforgettable snapshot. **82m/B VHS, DVD.** Walter Huston, Harry Davenport; ***D:*** John Ford; ***M:*** Alfred Newman.

Deception **1946** Davis is a pianist torn between two loves: her intensely jealous sponsor (Rains) and her cellist boyfriend (Henreid). Plot in danger of going over the melodramatic edge is saved by the very effective performances of the stars. **112m/B VHS.** Bette Davis, Paul Henreid, Claude Rains, John Abbott, Benson Fong; ***D:*** Irving Rapper.

Deception 1/2 *Ruby Cairo* **1992 (PG-13)** Talented cast is wasted in an old-fashioned mystery that lacks a coherent script. MacDowell is married to Mortensen, the owner of an aircraft salvage company. He's supposedly killed in a plane crash but she thinks he's just pulled a fast one and sets off to find him. Tracking her hubby's secret bank accounts takes her all over the world, and finally to Cairo, Egypt where she meets Neeson. Together they discover Mortensen's scam involves smuggling poison gas and the duo then try to outwit the hoods on their trail. Film was originally released at 110 minutes. **90m/C VHS.** Andie MacDowell, Liam Neeson, Viggo Mortensen, Jack Thompson, Jeff Corey, Miriam Reed, Luis Cortes, Paco Mauri; ***D:*** Graeme Clifford; ***W:*** Robert Dillon, Michael Thomas; ***M:*** John Barry.

Deception 1/2 **2008 (R)** McGregor is a milquetoast accountant, Jackman is a silky snake, and Williams is a blonde seductress. If you can buy the leads in these roles you may possibly find some enjoyment in this transparent thriller. Corporate numbers-cruncher Jonathan (McGregor) is led on a journey into NYC's anonymous sex underground by lawyer Wyatt (Jackman). Among the women Jonathan meets is the mysterious S (Williams), who soon disappears. The sex is all a set-up for something much more dangerous but—as the title blatantly proclaims—nothing is what it seems. **108m/C DVD, Blu-ray Disc.** *US* Ewan McGregor, Hugh Jackman, Michelle Williams, Maggie Q, Rachael Taylor, Natasha Henstridge, Lisa Gay Hamilton, Charlotte Rampling, Margaret Colin, Paz de la Huerta; ***D:*** Marcel Langenegger; ***W:*** Mark Bomback; ***C:*** Dante Spinotti; ***M:*** Ramin Djawadi.

Deceptions **1990 (R)** A risque, semi-erotic thriller about a wealthy society woman (Sheridan) who kills her husband. Sheridan claims that she acted in self-defense, but macho cop Hamlin has a different view. He interrogates her, grows increasingly attracted, and is drawn into her web of seduction. **105m/C VHS.** Harry Hamlin, Nicolette Sheridan; ***D:*** Ruben Preuss; ***W:*** Richard G. Taylor.

Deceptions 2: Edge of Deception 1/2 **1994 (R)** Voyeur detective becomes obsessed with his comely neighbor, leading to unpleasant consequences. **100m/C VHS.** Mariel Hemingway, Jennifer Rubin, Stephen Shellen; ***D:*** George Mihalka.

Decision at Sundown 1/2 **1957** Gunman Bart Allison (Scott) is obsessed with killing Tate Kimbrough (Carroll), whom he blames for the suicide of his wife Mary after she was seduced by Kimbrough. He gets in a lot of trouble after riding into a town controlled by Kimbrough and remains true to his deadly intentions even after learning the truth about his missus. But the final showdown doesn't go exactly as expected. **77m/C DVD.** Randolph Scott, John Carroll, Karen Steele, Valerie French, Noah Beery Jr., Andrew Duggan, John Archer; ***D:*** Budd Boetticher; ***W:*** Charles B(ryant) Lang Jr.; ***C:*** Burnett Guffey; ***M:*** Heinz Roemheld.

Deck the Halls 1/2 **2006 (PG)** Joyless holiday fare pumped out by the studio to scrooge a few dollars from the Christmas mall crowd. Steven (Broderick) is the smug, self-appointed "Christmas guy" of a sleepy New England town, making sure the holidays are celebrated tastefully. His crass neighbor Buddy (DeVito) wants to put enough lights on his house so that it can be seen from space. A war of childish pranks erupts between the two until a forced lesson on the "true meaning of Christmas" is tacked onto the ending. File this one in the Bastard Children of "Christmas Vacation" folder. **93m/C DVD.** *US* Danny DeVito, Matthew Broderick, Kristin Davis, Kristin Chenoweth, Alia Shawkat, Jorge Garcia, Dylan Blue, Kelly Aldridge, Sabrina Aldridge; ***D:*** John Whitesell; ***W:*** Don Rhymer, Matt Corman, Chris Ord; ***C:*** Mark Irwin; ***M:*** George S. Clinton.

The Decline of the American Empire 1/2 *Le Declin De L'Empire Americain* **1986 (R)** The critically acclaimed French-Canadian film about eight academic intellectuals who spend a weekend shedding their sophistication and engaging in intertwining sexual affairs. Examines the differing attitudes of men and women in regards to sex and sexuality. In French with English subtitles. **102m/C VHS, DVD.** *CA* Dominique Michel, Dorothee Berryman, Louise Portal, Genevieve Rioux; ***D:*** Denys Arcand; ***W:*** Denys Arcand. Genie '87: Director (Arcand), Film, Support. Actor (Arcand), Support. Actress (Portal); N.Y. Film Critics '86: Foreign Film; Toronto-City '86: Canadian Feature Film.

Decline of Western Civilization 1 **1981** The L.A. hard core punk scene. Music by X, Circle Jerks, Black Flag, Fear and more. **100m/C VHS.** ***D:*** Penelope Spheeris.

Decline of Western Civilization 2: The Metal Years **1988 (R)** Following Spheeris's first documentary about hardcore punk, she in turn delves into the world of heavy metal rock. We are given a look at some of the early rockers, as well as some of the smaller bands still playing L.A. clubs. Features appearances by Alice Cooper, Ozzy Osbourne, Poison, Gene Simmons, and Megadeth. **90m/C VHS.** Alice Cooper, Ozzy Osbourne, Gene Simmons, Lizzie Borden; ***D:*** Penelope Spheeris.

Deconstructing Harry 1/2 **1997 (R)** Interesting idea has Allen as a successful author, Harry Block, whose thinly veiled autobiographical fiction spills the beans on his ex-wives, lovers, friends, and family, thereby pissing them all off. Toggles back and forth between Harry's "real" life and scenes from his books, giving characters and situations two versions: one slanted to suit Harry and one more real than Harry wants or knows how to deal with. Infidelity, divorce, and art all get their usual treatment. Another not bad, but not great project by Allen that may be too self-absorbed for most. Features an elaborate, star-studded cast, mostly delegated to minor roles. **96m/C VHS, DVD.** Woody Allen, Billy Crystal, Judy Davis, Elisabeth Shue, Kirstie Alley, Caroline Aaron, Bob Balaban, Richard Benjamin, Eric Bogosian, Mariel Hemingway, Amy Irving, Julie Kavner, Eric Lloyd, Julia Louis-Dreyfus, Tobey Maguire, Demi Moore, Stanley Tucci, Robin Williams, Philip Bosco, Gene Saks, Hazelle Goodman; ***D:*** Woody Allen; ***W:*** Woody Allen; ***C:*** Carlo Di Palma.

Deconstructing Sarah **1994 (R)** Sarah Vincent (Ticotin) is a high-powered but bored ad exec who assumes an alter-ego, Ruth, when she heads for the wrong side of the tracks in her pursuit of casual sex. Her secret life is discovered when Sarah is murdered and best friend Elizabeth (Kelley) begins to turn up some likely suspects. Fast-paced whodunnit with good cast work. **120m/C VHS.** Rachel Ticotin, Sheila Kelley, A. Martinez, David Andrews, John Vickery, Jenifer Lewis, Dwier Brown, Peter Jason; ***D:*** Craig R.

Baxley; ***W:*** Lee Rose; ***C:*** Joao Fernandes; ***M:*** Tom Scott. **CABLE**

Decoration Day ♪♪♪ **1990 (PG)** Garner plays reclusive retired Southern judge Albert Sidney Finch who aids an angry black childhood friend, Gee (Cobbs), who has refused to accept his long-overdue Medal of Honor. Investigating the past leads to a decades-old mystery and a tragic secret that has repercussions for everyone involved. Based on the novel by John William Corrington. A Hallmark Hall of Fame presentation. **99m/C VHS, DVD.** James Garner, Bill Cobbs, Judith Ivey, Ruby Dee, Laurence Fishburne, Jo Anderson; ***D:*** Robert Markowitz; ***W:*** Robert W. Lenski. **TV**

Decoy ♪♪ ½ **1946** Ooooooh—bad girl flick! Margot (Gillie) is the heartless moll of death row gangster Olins (Armstrong) who won't reveal where he hid $400K. So Margot gets rival gangster Vincent (Norris) to agree to help her remove Olin's body from the gas chamber and force prison doc Craig (Rudley) to revive him with a special drug. The plan works—sorta—Olin revives, hands Margot a map, Vincent kills him for real, and they take the doc hostage as they go for the dough. But Margot doesn't want to split the loot, see, so she just happens to run over Vincent several times. There's also a prime double cross as Margot relates her "crime doesn't pay" tale to a cop (Leonard). **76m/B DVD.** Edward Norris, Herbert Rudley, Robert Armstrong, Sheldon Leonard, Jean Gillie, Philip Van Zandt; ***D:*** Jack Bernhard; ***W:*** Nedrick Young; ***C:*** L.W. O'Connell; ***M:*** Edward Kay.

Decoy ♪♪ ½ **1995 (R)** Two ex-government operatives, Baxter (Weller) and Travis (Patrick), are hired by their former commanding officer, Wellington (Breck), to protect his daughter Diana (Vogel) from business rival Jensen (Hylands) who's got a grudge against dad. But then it turns out the job's a set up, and Wellington and Jensen have their own deadly agenda. **98m/C VHS.** Peter Weller, Robert Patrick, Darlene Vogel, Charlotte Lewis, Peter Breck, Scott Hylands; ***D:*** Victor Rambaldi; ***W:*** Robert Sarno; ***C:*** Jon Kranhouse; ***M:*** Mark Adler.

Decoys ♪ ½ **2004 (R)** Goofy Canadian combo of a teen sex comedy with sci-fi horror. College freshman roommates Luke (Sevier) and Roger (Toufexis) are looking to get laid, preferably by their blonde bombshell neighbors Lilly (von Pfetten) and Constance (Poirier). Then a drunken Luke happens to witness the gals sprouting tentacles and comes to the conclusion that these alien babes are responsible for the flash-freezing deaths of horny frat boys. Naturally, everyone thinks Luke has had one too many brewskis. **96m/C DVD.** *CA* Corey Sevier, Kim Poirier, Stefanie von Pfetten, Meaghan Ory, Nicole Eggert, Elias Toufexis, Ennis Esmer; ***D:*** Matthew Hastings; ***W:*** Tom Berry, Matthew Hastings; ***C:*** Daniel Villeneuve; ***M:*** Daryl Bennett, Jim Guttridge.

Decoys: The Second Seduction ♪ *Decoys 2: Alien Seduction* **2007 (R)** Takes a dip on the ole quality meter although it's essentially the same movie. Grad student Luke (Sevier) has moved on to a new university but hasn't escaped his old alien babe problem since Constance (Poirier) has also returned. She's posing as a doctor in charge of student health services so she and her slutty cohorts have first pick of lusty lads for mating purposes. Have sex and die seems to be the alien way. **94m/C DVD.** *CA* Corey Sevier, Kim Poirier, Dina Meyer, Tobin Bell, Sam Easton, Tyler Johnston, Kailin See; ***D:*** Jeffrey Scott Lando; ***W:*** Miguel Tejada-Flores; ***C:*** John Spooner; ***M:*** Steve London. **VIDEO**

Dedee d'Anvers ♪♪ ½ *Dedee; Woman of Antwerp* **1949** A gritty dockside melodrama about a drunken prostitute abused by her pimp. A sailor and a local barkeep don't like it. In French with subtitles. **95m/B VHS.** Simone Signoret, Marcel Dalio, Bernard Blier, Marcel Pagliero, Jane (Jeanne) Marken; ***D:*** Yves Allegret; ***C:*** Jean (Yves, Georges) Bourgoin.

A Dedicated Man **1986** A lonely woman agrees to act as a wife for a businessman to lend him credibility. A British "Romance Theater" presentation. **60m/C VHS.** *GB* Alec McCowen, Joan Plowright; ***D:*** Robert Knights.

Dedication ♪ **2007 (R)** Henry Roth (Crudup), the most neurotic, compulsive children's book writer on the planet, finds himself without an illustrator after his collaborator Rudy (Wilkinson) dies suddenly. Henry and Rudy have had one big success together entitled "Marty the Beaver," and now Henry's editor forces a new illustrator, Lucy Reilly (Moore), on him to complete a "Marty" follow-up. Not easily accommodating change, Henry hates her, which isn't a surprise since he hates nearly everything. But wait, this is a romantic comedy, so of course his tune changes. Complications ensue in the forms of Rudy's ghost and Lucy's ex-lover, as well as her kooky mother. Worth a whirl if you can't get enough of the rom-com formula. **111m/C DVD.** *US* Billy Crudup, Mandy Moore, Tom Wilkinson, Bob Balaban, Dianne Wiest, Bobby Cannavale, Christine Taylor, Peter Bogdanovich, Martin Freeman; ***D:*** Justin Theroux; ***W:*** David Bromberg; ***C:*** Stephen Kazmierski; ***M:*** Ed Shearmur.

Dee Snider's Strangeland WOOF! *Strangeland* **1998 (R)** Former Twisted Sister singer Dee Snider proves that he can fail at movie-making worse than he can fail as a musician. He wrote, produced and starred in this dud that proves it's possible to be stupid, disgusting and boring at the same time. Snider plays Captain Howdy, an internet chat room sicko who lures young girls into a dungeon and tortures them by involuntarily piercing them and trying to act in front of them. Gage plays the dim detective trying to find the hair-sculpting madman. Only proves that Snider with a movie camera is more dangerous than the internet. **90m/C VHS, DVD.** Dee Snider, Kevin Gage, Brett Harrelson, Elizabeth Pena, Robert Englund, Amy Smart, Linda Cardellini; ***D:*** John Pieplow; ***W:*** Dee Snider; ***C:*** Goran Paviceric; ***M:*** Anton Sanko.

The Deep ♪♪ **1977 (PG)** An innocent couple get involved in an underwater search for a shipwreck, and they quickly find themselves in over their heads. Gorgeous photography manages to keep this slow mover afloat. Famous for Bisset's wet T-shirt scene. Based on the novel by Peter Benchley. **123m/C VHS, DVD.** Nick Nolte, Jacqueline Bisset, Robert Shaw, Louis Gossett Jr., Eli Wallach; ***D:*** Peter Yates; ***W:*** Peter Benchley, Tracy Keenan Wynn; ***C:*** Christopher Challis; ***M:*** John Barry.

Deep Blue ♪♪♪ ½ **2003 (G)** British documentary from the creators of the BBC TV series "The Blue Planet" about (what else) ocean life, which was shot in some 250 locations worldwide. Killer whales, gray whales, dolphins, sea lions, sharks, penguins, and polar bears as well as sea horses, jellyfish, and a variety of other strange deep sea dwellers are shown going about their daily struggle to survive. All accompanied by some stunning cinematography and a lush score. **90m/C DVD.** *GB GE* ***D:*** Alastair Fothergill; ***W:*** Alastair Fothergill, Andy Byatt, Tim Ecott; ***C:*** Doug Allan, Peter Scoones; ***M:*** George Fenton; ***Nar:*** Michael Gambon.

Deep Blue Sea ♪ ½ **1999 (R)** It's no longer safe to go back in the water. Marine biologist Susan McAlester (Burrows) is obsessed with finding a cure for Alzheimer's and has genetically enhanced the brains of a group of test sharks at a floating research facility off the Baja coast. Oh, and she didn't bother to tell anyone else in her group about these smarter-than-the-average sharks. But they soon learn, when the research facility suffers several accidents, begins to flood, and the sharks get loose—and looking for snacks. It's not a bomb but it's also nothing that you haven't seen before. And the fake sharks look, well, fake (and hokey). **105m/C VHS, DVD.** Saffron Burrows, Samuel L. Jackson, Thomas Jane, LL Cool J, Jacqueline McKenzie, Michael Rapaport, Stellan Skarsgard, Aida Turturro; ***D:*** Renny Harlin; ***W:*** Duncan Kennedy, Donna Powers, Wayne Powers; ***C:*** Stephen Windon; ***M:*** Trevor Rabin.

Deep Core ♪♪ **2000 (PG-13)** A rupture deep in the Earth's core causes a chain of natural disasters and could destroy the planet unless scientist Brian Goodman (Sheffer) can find a way to stop the geological threat. **90m/C VHS, DVD.** Craig Sheffer, James Russo, Terry Farrell, James Lew, Wil Wheaton, Bruce McGill; ***D:*** Rodney McDonald; ***W:*** Martin Lazarus; ***C:*** Richard Clabaugh. **VIDEO**

Deep Cover ♪ ½ **1988 (R)** A man dares to go beyond the walls of a mysterious English manor in order to expose the secrets that lie within the manor. **81m/C VHS.** Tom Conti, Donald Pleasence, Denholm Elliott, Kika Markham, Phoebe Nicholls; ***D:*** Richard Loncraine.

Deep Cover ♪♪ ½ **1992 (R)** Fishburne plays Russell Stevens Jr., a straight-arrow cop who goes undercover to infiltrate a Latin American cocaine cartel. While undercover, he becomes partners with drug dealer David Jason (Goldblum), and undergoes an inner transformation until he realizes he is betraying his cause. Confusing and commercial, yet marked with a moral rage. **107m/C VHS, DVD.** Laurence Fishburne, Jeff Goldblum, Victoria Dillard, Charles Martin Smith, Sydney Lassick, Clarence Williams III, Gregory Sierra, Roger Guenveur Smith, Cory Curtis, Glynn Turman, Def Jef; ***D:*** Bill Duke; ***W:*** Michael Tolkin, Henry Bean; ***C:*** Bojan Bazelli; ***M:*** Michel Colombier.

Deep Crimson ♪♪ *Profundo Carmesi* **1996** In 1949 Mexico, overweight nurse and willful romantic Coral (Orozco), impulsively answers a lonely hearts ad placed by Nicolas (Gimenez Cacho), who turns out to be a seedy con man. Coral, however, is certain she's found her true love and is obsessive in her devotion. So much so that she decides to help him with his swindling of vulnerable widows. But Coral's uncontrolled jealousy leads to murder. Based on the same true crime story that inspired the 1969 film, "The Honeymoon Killers." Spanish with subtitles. **109m/C VHS.** *MX SP* Regina Orozco, Daniel Gimenez Cacho, Marisa Paredes; ***D:*** Arturo Ripstein; ***W:*** Paz Alicia Garciadiego; ***C:*** Guillermo Granillo; ***M:*** David Mansfield.

Deep Down ♪ ½ **1994 (R)** When young Andy (Young) moves into a new apartment, he discovers his neighbor (Roberts) is a gorgeous married woman just looking for a little fun on the side. Too bad her husband (Segal) is a violent psychopath, totally suspicious of his wife's fidelity. Just how far will everyone go to get what they want? Also available in an unrated version. **86m/C VHS.** Tanya Roberts, Chris Young, George Segal; ***D:*** John Travers; ***W:*** John Travers, Alice Horrigan.

Deep End ♪♪♪ *Na Samyn Dnie* **1970** A 15-year-old boy working as an attendant in a bath house falls in love with a 20-year-old woman in this tragic tale of a young man obsessed. Good British cast and music by Cat Stevens. **88m/C VHS.** *GB GE* Jane Asher, John Moulder-Brown, Diana Dors, Karl Michael Vogler, Christopher Sandord; ***D:*** Jerzy Skolimowski; ***W:*** Jerzy Skolimowski, Jerry Gruza, Bloeslav Sulik; ***C:*** Charly Steinberger; ***M:*** Cat Stevens.

The Deep End ♪♪♪ **2001 (R)** Moms are used to cleaning up their kids' messes and Margaret Hall (Swinton) is no different, even if her situation is. Margaret lives with her three kids and cranky father-in-law in a quiet Lake Tahoe community. Her naval husband is away, which means when Margaret learns that teenaged son Beau (Tucker) is gay and involved with sleazy older bar owner, Darby (Lucas), she has no one to turn to. Things get tricky when Darby turns up dead on the beach and mom thinks son did the deed. She gets rid of the body but is soon being blackmailed by slick stranger Alek (Visnjic). Swinton is amazing as the woman who has no limits when it comes to maternal care. Based on Elizabeth Sanxay Holding's 1947 novel "The Blank Wall," which was previously filmed by Max Ophuls in 1949 as "The Reckless Moment." **99m/C VHS, DVD.** *US* Tilda Swinton, Goran Visnjic, Jonathan Tucker, Raymond J. Barry, Josh(ua) Lucas, Peter Donat, Tamara Hope, Jordan Dorrance; ***D:*** Scott McGehee, David Siegel; ***W:*** Scott McGehee, David Siegel; ***C:*** Giles Nuttgens; ***M:*** Peter Nashel. Sundance '01: Cinematog. (Nuttgens).

The Deep End of the Ocean ♪♪ **1998 (PG-13)** Beth (Pfeiffer) and husband Pat (Williams) live the ideal life in the suburbs, with a nice home and three beautiful kids. All of that is shattered when three-year-old Ben is abducted while Beth is distracted at a hotel. Shows the tortuous road of depression that Beth travels, and the effect it has on her family. Suddenly, nine years later Ben shows up at her doorstep, now named Sam, and offers to cut the lawn. Beth and detective Candy (Goldberg) determine that he is the lost boy, and painful choices must be made by all. Glosses over the story behind the child's abduction and wraps everything up a bit too easily. **105m/C VHS, DVD.** Michelle Pfeiffer, Treat Williams, John Kapelos, Jonathan Jackson, Ryan Merriman, Whoopi Goldberg, Michael McGrady, Brenda Strong, Alexa Vega, Tony Musante; ***D:*** Ulu Grosbard; ***W:*** Stephen Schiff; ***C:*** Stephen Goldblatt; ***M:*** Elmer Bernstein.

Deep Impact ♪♪ ½ **1998 (PG-13)** Poor Morgan Freeman. He gets a chance to play the President of the United States only to have his term shortened by a dastardly comet the size of the Grand Canyon. Although his presidency would have been more interesting, the destruction's the star of this show, as well as the touchy-feely interaction of various two-dimensional characters. There's the astronauts (led by Duvall) sent into space to nuke the thing; ordinary teenager Leo (Wood) who initially discovered the rock; and career-conscious news anchor (Leoni), who first breaks the story. The all-star cast is underused, but lend the film a sense of gravity by their presence. The remaining stick figure characters evoke more yawns than tears. Good thing the comet comes along to, ironically, inject a little life into the flick. The special effects are the best in recent film history, and worth the long, laborious wait. **120m/C VHS, DVD.** Morgan Freeman, Robert Duvall, Tea Leoni, Elijah Wood, Vanessa Redgrave, Maximilian Schell, James Cromwell, Blair Underwood, Ron Eldard, Jon Favreau, Leelee Sobieski, Mary McCormack, Dougray Scott, Alexander Baluyev, Charles Martin Smith, Richard Schiff, Gary Werntz, Bruce Weitz, Betsy Brantley, O'Neal Compton, Rya Kihlstedt, Denise Crosby, Laura Innes; ***D:*** Mimi Leder; ***W:*** Michael Tolkin, Bruce Joel Rubin; ***C:*** Dietrich Lohmann; ***M:*** James Horner.

Deep in My Heart ♪♪ ½ **1954** A musical biography of the life and times of composer Sigmund Romberg, with guest appearances by many MGM stars. ♫ Leg of Mutton; You Will Remember Vienna; Softly, as in a Morning Sunrise; Mr. & Mrs.; I Love to Go Swimmin' with Wimmin; The Road to Paradise; Will You Remember; It; Serenade. **132m/C VHS.** Jose Ferrer, Merle Oberon, Paul Henreid, Walter Pidgeon, Helen Traubel, Rosemary Clooney, Jane Powell, Howard Keel, Cyd Charisse, Gene Kelly, Ann Miller; ***D:*** Stanley Donen; ***C:*** George J. Folsey.

Deep in the Heart ♪♪ *Handgun* **1983 (R)** When a young teacher is raped at gunpoint on a second date, she takes the law into her own hands. Just-off-the-target film tries to take a stand against the proliferation of guns in the U.S. Thought-provoking all the same. **99m/C VHS, DVD.** *GB* Karen Young, Clayton Day, Ben Jones, Suzie Humphreys; ***D:*** Tony Garnett; ***W:*** Tony Garnett.

Deep in the Heart (of Texas) ♪♪ **1998** Two British documentary filmmakers, Robert (Cranham) and his wife Kate (Root), take an assignment for British TV to interview Texans. They choose the capital of Austin and the eccentric locals provide the requisite color but the couple are undergoing their own personal crisis that keeps interfering with their work. **90m/C VHS, DVD.** Kenneth Cranham, Amanda Root; ***D:*** Stephen Purvis; ***W:*** Tom Huckabee, Stephen Purvis, Jesse Sublett; ***C:*** Thomas Flores Alcala; ***M:*** Joe Ellen Doering, George Doering.

Deep in the Woods ♪♪ *Promenons Nous dans les Bois* **2000 (R)** Isolated castle, mute little boy, and a psycho-rapist on the loose as five actors are hired to give a performance of "Little Red Riding Hood." Then they begin to die at the paws of someone wearing the wolf costume. Gruesome creeper; French with subtitles. **88m/C VHS, DVD.** *FR* Clotilde Courau, Clement Sibony, Vincent Lecoeur, Alexia Stresi, Maud Buquet; ***D:*** Lionel Delplanque; ***W:*** Annabelle Perrichon; ***C:*** Denis Rouden; ***M:*** Jerome Coullet.

Deep Red ♪♪ **1994 (R)** When a young girl has an encounter with an extra-terrestrial spacecraft her blood chemistry is mysteriously altered. Now the proteins her body manufactures can lead to immortality and ruthless scientist Newmeyer wants to take advantage of the fact—any way he can. **85m/C VHS, DVD.** Michael Biehn, Joanna Pacula, John de Lancie; ***D:*** Craig R. Baxley; ***W:*** D. Brent Mote.

Deep Red: Hatchet Murders 🦴🦴 ½ *The Hatchet Murders; Profundo Rosso; Dripping Deep Red; The Sabre Tooth Tiger; Deep Red* **1975** A stylish but gruesome rock music-driven tale of a composer who reads a book on the occult which happens to relate to the sadistic, sangfroid murder of his neighbor. When he visits the book's author, he discovers that she has been horribly murdered as well. **100m/C VHS, DVD.** *IT* David Hemmings, Daria Nicolodi, Gabriele Lavia, Macha Meril, Eros Pagni, Guiliana Calandra, Erykah Badu, Clara Calamai, Nicoletta Elmi, Glauco Mauri; ***D:*** Dario Argento; ***W:*** Dario Argento, Barnardino Zapponi; ***C:*** Luigi Kuveiller; ***M:*** Giorgio Gaslini, The Goblins.

Deep Rising 🦴🦴 ½ **1998 (R)** Huge sea serpents cause massive destruction to the cruise ship Argonautica and put major dinks in the plans of mercenaries, led by Finnegan (Williams), who board the ship for greedy motives. Sticks to a reliable action-horror formula with the good sense to not take its characters or slimy creatures too seriously. Sea critters have inventive ways of disposing of extraneous cast members, resulting in gore aplenty. Slacker humor provided by Finnegan's sidekick Pantucci (Kevin J. O'Connor) injects the film with a certain goofiness. Typical B-movie fare that leans more toward guilty pleasure than quality entertainment. **106m/C VHS, DVD.** Treat Williams, Famke Janssen, Anthony Heald, Kevin J. O'Connor, Wes Studi, Derrick O'Connor, Jason Flemyng, Djimon Hounsou; ***D:*** Stephen Sommers; ***W:*** Stephen Sommers; ***C:*** Howard Atherton; ***M:*** Jerry Goldsmith.

Deep Six 🦴🦴 ½ **1958** A WWII drama that examines the conflict between pacifism and loyalty. A staunch Quaker is called to active duty as a lieutenant in the U.S. Navy, where his beliefs put him into disfavor with shipmates. **110m/C VHS.** Alan Ladd, William Bendix, James Whitmore, Keenan Wynn, Efrem Zimbalist Jr., Joey Bishop; ***D:*** Rudolph Mate.

Deep Space 🦴 ½ **1987** A flesh-eating alien lands on earth and, after devouring a cop, is stalked by his partner. An "Alien" rip-off. Some humorous moments keep us from thinking too hard about how much the monster resembles our friend from "Alien." **90m/C VHS.** Charles Napier, Ann Turkel, Ron Glass, Bo Svenson, Julie Newmar; ***D:*** Fred Olen Ray.

Deep Trouble 🦴 ½ **2001** It's strictly amateur hour in this hip-hip urban drama. New York drug kingpin Perry (Stovall) decides that the world of organized crime simply isn't enough, and decides to overtake the business of Star (Scarborough), an entertainment manager who represents up-and-coming actress Diana (Horsford), as well as several stand-up comics. Star and Diana decide that they aren't going to be pushed around by this bully, so they take a stand and the "trouble" begins. Filled with bad acting and amateurish special effects (several characters get shot in the head, which is represented by a simple trickle of blood). The film is very poorly paced, having more scenes of pointless dialogue than action. **102m/C DVD.** Count Stovall, Janel C. Scarborough, Alyah Horsford; ***D:*** Juney Smith; ***W:*** Juney Smith.

Deep Winter 🦴 ½ **2008 (PG-13)** Good snow action and scenery, lame plot. Rebellious downhill racer Tyler Crowe (Lively) reunites with equally risk-taking snowboard buddy Mark Rider (Lutz), whose sister Elisa (List) has a thing for Ty. The guys decide to head to Alaska on a sporting adventure where they'll attempt the most daring snow descent ever captured on film. Things go wrong. **96m/C DVD.** Eric Lively, Kellan Lutz, Peyton List, Michael Madsen, Robert Carradine, Luke Goss; ***D:*** Mikey Hilb; ***W:*** John Protass; ***C:*** Patrick Reddish; ***M:*** Gerald Brunskill. **VIDEO**

Deeply 🦴🦴 ½ **1999** Fiona McKay (Watson) takes her teenaged daughter Claire (Dunst) to her childhood home on an island off the coast of Nova Scotia. Claire's been traumatized by the sudden death of her boyfriend and is susceptible to the stories told by elderly neighbor, Claire (Redgrave), who has some dark secrets. **102m/C VHS, DVD.** *CA* Alberta Watson, Lynn Redgrave, Kirsten Dunst, Julia Brendler, Brent Carver; ***D:*** Sheri Elwood; ***W:*** Sheri Elwood; ***M:*** Micki Meuser.

Deepstar Six 🦴 ½ **1989 (R)** When futuristic scientists try to set up an undersea research and missile lab, a group of subterranean monsters get in the way. **97m/C VHS, DVD.** Taurean Blacque, Nancy Everhard, Greg Evigan, Miguel Ferrer, Matt McCoy, Nia Peeples, Cindy Pickett, Marius Weyers, Thom Bray, Elya Baskin; ***D:*** Sean S. Cunningham; ***W:*** Lewis Abernathy, Geof Miller; ***C:*** Mac Ahlberg; ***M:*** Harry Manfredini.

Deepwater 🦴🦴 **2005 (R)** Neo-noir. Young Nat (Black) is just out of rehab and drifting around when he rescues Finch (Coyote) from a road accident and is rewarded by a job in the man's rundown motel. Finch has a lot of shady local interests and his wife Iris (Maestro) is a hot young tease. Nat's not the most reliable narrator so the plot confusion deepens, leading to an unexpected twist. Adapted from the Matthew F. Jones novel. **93m/C DVD.** Lucas Black, Peter Coyote, Mia Maestro, Lesley Ann Warren, Michael Ironside, Kristen Bell, Ben Cardinal, Xander Berkeley; ***D:*** David S. Marfield; ***W:*** David S. Marfield; ***C:*** Scott Kevan; ***M:*** Charlie Clouser.

The Deer Hunter 🦴🦴🦴🦴 **1978 (R)** A powerful and vivid portrait of Middle America with three steel-working friends who leave home to face the Vietnam War. Controversial, brutal sequences in Vietnam are among the most wrenching ever filmed; the rhythms and rituals of home are just as purely captured. Neither pro- nor anti-war, but rather the perfect evocation of how totally and forever altered these people are by the war. Emotionally shattering; not to be missed. **183m/C VHS, DVD, HD DVD.** Robert De Niro, Christopher Walken, Meryl Streep, John Savage, George Dzundza, John Cazale, Chuck Aspegren, Rutanya Alda, Shirley Stoler, Amy Wright, Mady Kaplan, Mary Ann Haenel, Richard Kuss, Pierre Segui, Joe Grifasi, Christopher Colombi Jr., Joe Strnad, Paul D'Amato; ***D:*** Michael Cimino; ***W:*** Michael Cimino, Deric Washburn, Louis Garfinkle; ***C:*** Vilmos Zsigmond; ***M:*** John Williams, Stanley Myers. Oscars '78: Director (Cimino), Film Editing, Picture, Sound, Support. Actor (Walken); AFI '98: Top 100; Directors Guild '78: Director (Cimino); Golden Globes '79: Director (Cimino); L.A. Film Critics '78: Director (Cimino), Natl. Film Reg. '96;; N.Y. Film Critics '78: Film, Support. Actor (Walken); Natl. Soc. Film Critics '78: Support. Actress (Streep).

The Deerslayer 🦴 ½ **1978** Low-budget snoozer based on the classic novel by James Fenimore Cooper. Frontiersman Hawkeye and his Indian companion Chingachgook set out to rescue a beautiful Indian maiden and must fight bands of hostile Indians and Frenchmen along the way. **98m/C VHS.** Steve Forrest, Ned Romero, John Anderson, Joan Prather; ***D:*** Richard Friedenberg; ***M:*** Andrew Belling.

Def by Temptation 🦴🦴 **1990 (R)** A potent horror fantasy about a young black theology student who travels to New York in search of an old friend. There he meets an evil woman who is determined to seduce him and force him to give in to temptation. Great soundtrack. **95m/C VHS, DVD.** James Bond III, Kadeem Hardison, Bill Nunn, Samuel L. Jackson, Minnie Gentry, Rony Clanton, Cynthia Bond, John Canada Terrell; ***D:*** James Bond III; ***W:*** James Bond III; ***C:*** Ernest R. Dickerson; ***M:*** Paul Lawrence.

Def-Con 4 🦴 ½ **1985 (R)** Three marooned space travelers return to a holocaust-shaken Earth to try to start again, but some heavy-duty slimeballs are in charge and they don't want to give it up. Good special effects bolster a weak script. **85m/C VHS, DVD.** Maury Chaykin, Kate Lynch, Tim Choate; ***D:*** Paul Donovan.

Def Jam's How to Be a Player 🦴 *How to Be a Player* **1997 (R)** Dray (Bellamy) thinks that monogamy is a wood used to build furniture. Although he has steady girlfriend Lisa (Voorhies), he also has several other ladies in waiting. He is, in fact, a player. He even teaches others to play. What he needs, however, is a screenplay. His sister Jenny (Desselle), who has been hurt in love, cracks the numerical code to his organizer, and invites all of Dray's harem to one party. The result of this booty intervention is Dray's abandonment of his promiscuous ways. The stand-up comedy roots of much of the cast translate into clunky performances, and the direction is pretty played out, too. **93m/C VHS, DVD.** Bill Bellamy, Natalie Desselle, Mari Morrow, Jermaine "Huggy" Hopkins, A.J. (Anthony) Johnson, Max Julien, Beverly Johnson, Gilbert Gottfried, Bernie Mac, Elise Neal, Amber Smith, Lark Voorhies; ***D:*** Lionel C. Martin; ***W:*** Mark Brown, Demetria Johnson; ***M:*** Darren Floyd.

The Defector 🦴🦴 **1966** Cold War spy thriller with a fragile Clift starring in his last role as American scientist James Bower. While visiting East Germany, Bower is contacted by CIA agent Adam (McDowell) to help a defecting Russian scientist smuggle out some microfilm. The plan is discovered by Russian agent Heinzman (Kruger) who then tries to get Bower to defect to the East. **99m/C DVD.** *FR GE* Montgomery Clift, Hardy Kruger, Roddy McDowall, Macha Meril, David Opatoshu, Hannes Messemer; ***D:*** Raoul Levy; ***W:*** Raoul Levy, Robert Guenette, Peter Francke, Lewis Gannet; ***C:*** Raoul Coutard; ***M:*** Serge Gainsbourg.

Defenders of the Law 🦴🦴 **1931** Early action talkie concerned with gang warfare and law enforcement. **64m/B VHS.** John Holland, Mae Busch, Alan Cooke, Joseph Girard, Edmund Breese, Catherine Dale Owen, Robert Gleckler; ***D:*** Joseph Levering.

The Defenders: Payback 🦴🦴 ½ **1997 (R)** E.G. Marshall returns to the lawyer role of Lawrence Preston that he played in the CBS series from 1961-1965. This time around, Preston has his granddaughter, M.J. (Plimpton), joining the family firm along with son Don (Bridges). Their first case together is a doozy—unrepentent Michael Lane (Laroquette) has confessed to killing the recently paroled man who had gone to prison for raping Lane's young daughter. **95m/C VHS.** E.G. Marshall, Beau Bridges, Martha Plimpton, John Larroquette, Yaphet Kotto, Roma Maffia, Rachael Leigh Cook, Mimi Kuzyk, Clea DuVall, Nicholas Kilbertus; ***D:*** Andy Wolk; ***W:*** Andy Wolk, Peter Wolk; ***C:*** John Newby; ***M:*** Mark Isham. **CABLE**

The Defenders: Taking the First 🦴🦴 ½ **1998 (R)** Don (Bridges) and M.J. (Plimpton) defend a student accused of beating a Latino to death. Their client claims he was incited by white supremist leader, John Walker (Casnoff), and agrees to a plea bargain. This enrages the victim's brother, who files a wrongful death suit against Walker and chooses Don to represent the case. Now the team must try to prove Walker's culpability without disputing his First Amendment rights to free speech. **96m/C VHS.** Beau Bridges, Martha Plimpton, Philip Casnoff, Jeremy London; ***D:*** Andy Wolk; ***W:*** Andy Wolk, Peter Wolk; ***C:*** John Newby; ***M:*** Mark Isham. **CABLE**

Defending Your Life 🦴🦴🦴 **1991 (PG)** Brooks' cock-eyed way of looking at the world travels to the afterlife in this uneven comedy/romance. In Judgment City, where everyone goes after death, past lives are examined and judged. If you were a good enough person you get to stay in heaven (where you wear funny robes and eat all you want without getting fat). If not, it's back to earth for another go-round. Brooks plays an L.A. advertising executive who crashes his new BMW and finds himself defending his life. When he meets and falls in love with Streep, his interest in staying in heaven multiplies. Occasionally charming, seldom out-right hilarious. **112m/C VHS, DVD.** Albert Brooks, Meryl Streep, Rip Torn, Lee Grant, Buck Henry, George D. Wallace, Lillian Lehman, Peter Schuck, Susan Walters; ***D:*** Albert Brooks; ***W:*** Albert Brooks; ***C:*** Allen Daviau; ***M:*** Michael Gore.

Defendor **2009** Delusional social misfit Arthur (Harrelson) is the wannabe superhero of the title who decides to go after a dangerous mobster. **101m/C DVD.** *CA* Woody Harrelson, Elias Koteas, Michael Kelly, Kat Dennings, Sandra Oh, Lisa Ray, Peter Stebbings; ***D:*** Peter Stebbings; ***W:*** Peter Stebbings; ***C:*** David (Robert) A. Greene; ***M:*** John Rowley.

Defense of the Realm 🦴🦴🦴 ½ **1985 (PG)** A British politician is accused of selling secrets to the KGB through his mistress and only a pair of dedicated newspapermen believe he is innocent. In the course of finding the answers they discover a national cover-up conspiracy. An acclaimed, taut thriller. **96m/C VHS, DVD.** *GB* Gabriel Byrne, Greta Scacchi, Denholm Elliott, Ian Bannen, Bill Paterson, Fulton Mackay, Robbie Coltrane; ***D:*** David Drury; ***C:*** Roger Deakins. British Acad. '85: Support. Actor (Elliott).

Defense Play 🦴 ½ **1988 (PG)** Two teenagers are unwittingly stuck in the middle of a Soviet plot to steal the plans that created a technologically advanced helicopter. **95m/C VHS.** David Oliver, Susan Ursitti, Monte Markham, William Frankfather, Patch MacKenzie; ***D:*** Monte Markham.

Defenseless 🦴🦴 **1991 (R)** Hershey tries hard in an unplayable part as a giddy attorney who finds herself trapped in a love-affair/legal case that turns murderous. Good cast and interesting twists contend with a sexist sub-text, which proves a woman can't "have it all." **106m/C VHS, DVD.** Barbara Hershey, Sam Shepard, Mary Beth Hurt, J.T. Walsh, Sheree North; ***D:*** Martin Campbell; ***W:*** James Cresson; ***M:*** Trevor Jones.

Defiance 🦴🦴 **1979 (PG)** A former merchant seaman moves into a tenement in a run-down area of New York City. When a local street gang begins terrorizing the neighborhood, he decides to take a stand. Familiar plotline handled well in this thoughtful film. **101m/C VHS.** Jan-Michael Vincent, Art Carney, Theresa Saldana, Danny Aiello, Lenny Montana; ***D:*** John Flynn; ***W:*** Thomas Michael Donnelly; ***M:*** Basil Poledouris, John Beal.

Defiance 🦴🦴 ½ **2008 (R)** Based on the true story of the Bielski brothers, Jews who led a resistance movement against the Nazis in Belarus. Tuvia (Craig) is the stoic planner; Zus (Schreiber), the hothead who joins Russian partisans so he can fight more; and naive, young Asael (Bell) who has to grow up in a hurry. In 1941, they establish an unlikely community of refugees deep in the forest while using guerilla tactics to survive. Zwick alternates (not too successfully) between action and sentimentality (the brothers all find wives among the new community) but much will still seem like standard fare seen in countless wartime flicks. Based on the nonfiction book "Defiance: The Bielski Partisans" by Nechama Tec. **136m/C DVD.** Daniel Craig, Liev Schreiber, Jamie Bell, Mia Wasikowska, Alexa Davalos, Jodhi May, Mark Feuerstein, Tomas Arana, Allan Corduner, Iben Hjejle; ***D:*** Edward Zwick; ***W:*** Edward Zwick, Clayton Frohman; ***C:*** Eduardo Serra; ***M:*** James Newton Howard.

Defiant 🦴 ½ *The Wild Pack; The Sandpit Generals* **1970** Two rival street gangs clash when one admits a young orphan girl. **93m/C VHS.** Kent Lane, John Rubinstein, Tisha Sterling; ***D:*** Hall Bartlett.

The Defiant Ones 🦴🦴🦴 ½ **1958** Thought-provoking story about racism revolves around two escaped prisoners (one black, one white) from a chain gang in the rural South. Their societal conditioning to hate each other dissolves as they face constant peril together. Critically acclaimed. **97m/B VHS, DVD.** Tony Curtis, Sidney Poitier, Theodore Bikel, Lon Chaney Jr., Charles McGraw, Cara Williams; ***D:*** Stanley Kramer; ***W:*** Nedrick Young, Harold Jacob Smith; ***C:*** Sam Leavitt; ***M:*** Steve Dorff. Oscars '58: B&W Cinematog., Story & Screenplay; British Acad. '58: Actor (Poitier); Golden Globes '59: Film—Drama; N.Y. Film Critics '58: Director (Kramer), Film, Screenplay.

The Defilers 🦴 **1965 (R)** Disturbing, low-budget J.D. movie in which two thugs imprison a young girl in a basement and force her to be their love slave. **69m/B VHS, DVD.** Byron Mabe, Jerome (Jerry Stallion) Eden, Mai Jansson; ***D:*** David Friedman.

Definitely, Maybe 🦴🦴🦴 **2008 (PG-13)** Almost divorced dad Will Hayes (Reynolds), at daughter Maya's (Breslin) request, recounts the great loves that led him to marry her mother in the first place. As a young, idealistic 1992 Clinton campaign worker, Will has a long distance relationship with college girlfriend Emily (Banks), but soon becomes interested in both journalist Summer (Weisz) and free-spirit campaign worker April (Fisher, in a standout performance). Both Will's love life and career have their ups and downs as he tries to figure out what he wants in his life, learning some tough and often hilarious lessons on the way, and of course, the flick keeps you guessing as to which woman is actually Mom. Bittersweet, smart, above-average romantic comedy with excellent performances from its leads. **111m/C DVD.** *GB US* Ryan Reynolds, Abigail Breslin, Isla Fisher, Elizabeth Banks, Rachel Weisz, Derek Luke, Kevin Kline, Nestor Serrano, Annie Parisse, Liane Balaban, Kevin Corrigan, Adam Ferrara; ***D:*** Adam Brooks; ***W:*** Adam Brooks; ***C:*** Florian Ballhaus; ***M:*** Clint Mansell.

Defying Gravity **1999** Frat boy John Griffiths (Chilson) is hiding a secret from his fellow brothers—he's gay and even has a boyfriend, Pete (Handfield), who's sick of John's lying. Pete is gay-bashed and John agonizes over going to the cops with information if it means his off-campus activities could get out. Good intentions but director/writer Keitel's inexperience (this is his first film) shows in a slow pace and amateurishness. **101m/C VHS, DVD.** Daniel Chilson, Niklaus Lange, Don Handfield, Linna Carter, Seabass Diamond, Lesley Tesh; ***D:*** John Keitel; ***W:*** John Keitel; ***C:*** Thomas M. Harting; ***M:*** Tim Westergren.

Degree of Guilt **1/2 1995** Good miniseries adaptation of Richard Lloyd Patterson's novels "Eyes of a Child" and "Degree of Guilt." Lawyer Chris Paget (Elliott) makes the mistake of falling for associate Teresa Perlita (Zuniga), who's going through a bad divorce from Richie (Ventresca), a loser who wants custody of their daughter and a lot of money from Teresa. Meanwhile, he's taking on the defense of murder suspect Mary Carelli (Lawrence), who's also Chris's ex-lover and the mother of his son. However, this turns out not to be the only murder investigation going when Richie winds up dead and Chris becomes the prime suspect. **180m/C VHS, DVD.** David James Elliott, Daphne Zuniga, Sharon Lawrence, Nigel Bennett, Don Francks, Patricia Kalember; ***D:*** Mike Robe; ***W:*** Cynthia Whitcomb; ***C:*** Kees Van Oostrum; ***M:*** Craig Safan. **TV**

Deja Vu **1984 (R)** A lame romantic thriller about the tragic deaths of two lovers and their supposed reincarnation 50 years later. **95m/C VHS, DVD.** *GB* Jaclyn Smith, Nigel Terry, Claire Bloom, Shelley Winters; ***D:*** Anthony Richmond; ***W:*** Ezra D. Rappaport; ***M:*** Pino Donaggio.

Deja Vu **1989** Thriller set in 1925 and moving between Chicago and Odessa. A Chicago hitman is hired by the mob to kill a traitor who has fled to Odessa. Niczypur, the traitor, has been using the newly opened Chicago-Constantinople-Odessa shipping line for his own smuggling operation. Filled with shoot-outs, brawls, and chases. In English, Russian, and Polish with English subtitles. **108m/C VHS.** *PL* Jerzy Stuhr, Galina Pietrowa, Nikolai Karaczencow, Wladimir Golowin; ***D:*** Juliusz Machulski.

Deja Vu **1/2 1998 (PG-13)** After Dana (Foyt) has an encounter with a mysterious woman in Israel, she is led on a roundabout way to England's White Cliffs of Dover. There she meets Sean (Dillane), and they quickly fall in love, since they have so much in common, such as being married to other people. This proves to be no problem, for destiny, coincidence and director/screenwriter Jaglom conspire to have the two couples share a house for the weekend. Unfortunately, it's hard to detect the true love, since the two leads have as much chemistry as remedial science class. Vanessa Redgrave and her mother Rachel Kempson appear together for the first time as the sister and mother of the host, played by '60s pop singer Neil Harrison. **115m/C VHS.** Victoria Foyt, Stephen (Dillon) Dillane, Vanessa Redgrave, Glynis Barber, Michael Brandon, Vernon Dobtcheff, Noel Harrison, Rachel Kempson, Anna Massey; ***D:*** Henry Jaglom; ***W:*** Henry Jaglom, Victoria Foyt; ***C:*** Hanania Baer; ***M:*** Gaili Schoen.

Deja Vu **1/2 2006 (PG-13)** In their third outing, Scott and Washington tackle action and wormholes and bring pic to as logical a conclusion as can be expected. ATF agent Doug Carlin (Washington) is called to New Orleans when a ferry carrying U.S. sailors is blown up. Carlin discovers victim Claire (Patton) had actually died beforehand and must have some connection to the bomber. Carlin gets pulled in by FBI agent Pryzwarra (Kilmer), who tells him about a high-tech project that re-creates images from days earlier, so they can see Claire prior to the tragedy. Since Claire is a babe, Doug would naturally like to save her, and thanks to this time window, he now has a chance of getting to the bomber first. Scott has always known how to move things along and he sets a brisk pace throughout. **126m/C DVD, Blu-ray Disc, HD DVD.** *US* Denzel Washington, Val Kilmer, Paula Patton, Bruce Greenwood, Adam Goldberg, James (Jim) Caviezel, Elden (Ratliff) Henson, Erika Alexander; ***D:*** Tony Scott; ***W:*** Terry Rossio, Bill Marsilii; ***C:*** Paul Cameron; ***M:*** Harry Gregson-Williams.

Delgo **2008 (PG)** Computer animated sci-fi feature set in ancient times pits the winged Nohrin race against the kinetically-powered Lockni. The reign of Nohrin's king (Gossett Jr.) is threatened by his sinister sister Sedessa (the late Bancroft, in her final role) thus triggering a war that gets in the way of true love between Lockni teen Delgo (Prinze Jr.) and Nohrin princess Kyla (Love Hewitt). Little surprise that Kyla is kidnapped, thanks to Sedessa, and Delgo and his annoying pal Filo (Kattan) must save the day, along with Nohrin general Bogardus (Kilmer). Total rip-off of stories from "Star Wars" to "Romeo and Juliet" and is only spared a "woof" 'cuz it's pretty to look at. **89m/C DVD.** *US* ***D:*** Marc Adler, Jason Maurer; ***W:*** Patrick Cowan, Carl Dream, Jennifer A. Jones; ***C:*** Herb Kossover; ***M:*** Geoff Zanelli; ***V:*** Freddie Prinze Jr., Chris Kattan, Anne Bancroft, Val Kilmer, Jennifer Love Hewitt, Kelly Ripa, Eric Idle, Michael Clarke Duncan, Louis Gossett Jr., Malcolm McDowell, Burt Reynolds; ***Nar:*** Sally Kellerman.

The Deli **1997** Johnny Amico (Starr) runs a New York deli, has a bad gambling habit and a big debt to mobster Tommy Tomatoes (Vincent), an outspoken Mama (Malina), and a colorful clientele. Not much happens, the budget is small, but the actors charm. **98m/C VHS, DVD.** Joseph (Joe) D'Onofrio, Mike Starr, Judith Malina, Matt Keeslar, Frank Vincent, Ice-T, Heather Matarazzo, Iman, Jerry Stiller; ***D:*** John A. Gallagher; ***W:*** John A. Gallagher, John Dorrian; ***C:*** Robert Lechterman; ***M:*** Ernie Mannix.

Deliberate Intent **1/2 2001** Well-done fact-based drama follows the case of a triple murder-for-hire and the First Amendment issues the case raised. When Lawrence Horn (McDaniel) hires a man (Johnson) to kill his family, it's discovered that said killer used a book called "Hot Man: A Technical Manual for Independent Contractors" to plan the crime. Lawyer Siegel (Rifkin) brings in First Amendment expert Rod Smolla (Hutton) to sue the publisher for abetting the murder. **120m/C VHS, DVD.** Timothy Hutton, Ron Rifkin, James McDaniel, Clark Johnson, Penny Johnson, Cliff DeYoung, Kenneth Welsh; ***D:*** Andy Wolk; ***C:*** Ron Garcia. **CABLE**

The Deliberate Stranger **1986** Harmon is engrossing as charismatic serial killer Ted Bundy, sentenced to death for several Florida murders and suspected in the killings of a least 25 women in several states. After eluding police for five years Bundy was finally arrested in Florida in 1979. His case became a cause celebre on capital punishment as it dragged on for nine years. Bundy was finally executed in 1989. Based on the book "Bundy: The Deliberate Stranger" by Richard W. Larsen. **188m/C VHS.** Mark Harmon, M. Emmet Walsh, Frederic Forrest, John Ashton, George Grizzard, Ben Masters, Glynnis O'Connor, Bonnie Bartlett, Billy Green Bush, Lawrence Pressman; ***D:*** Marvin J. Chomsky. **TV**

The Delicate Delinquent **1/2 1956** Lewis's first movie without Dean Martin finds him in the role of delinquent who manages to become a policeman with just the right amount of slapstick. **101m/B VHS, DVD.** Jerry Lewis, Darren McGavin, Martha Hyer, Robert Ivers, Horace McMahon; ***D:*** Don McGuire; ***W:*** Don McGuire.

Delicatessen **1992 (R)** Set in 21st-century Paris, this hilarious debut from directors Jeunet and Caro focuses on the lives of the oddball tenants of an apartment building over a butcher shop. Although there is a famine, the butcher shop is always stocked with fresh meat—made from the building's tenants. Part comedy, part horror, part romance, this film merges a cacophony of sights and sounds with intriguing results. Watch for the scene involving a symphony of creaking bed springs, a squeaky bicycle pump, a cello, and clicking knitting needles. In French with English subtitles. **95m/C VHS, DVD.** *FR* Marie-Laure Dougnac, Dominique Pinon, Karin Viard, Jean-Claude Dreyfus, Ticky Holgado, Anne Marie Pisani, Edith Ker, Patrick Paroux, Jean-Luc Caron; ***D:*** Jean-Pierre Jeunet, Marc Caro; ***W:*** Gilles Adrien, Jean-Pierre Jeunet, Marc Caro; ***C:*** Darius Khondji; ***M:*** Carlos D'Alessi. Cesar '92: Art Dir./Set Dec., Writing.

Delightfully Dangerous **1945** Often Deadly Dull. A farfetched musical rooted in yesteryear about mismatched sisters, one a 15-year-old farm girl, the other a New York burlesque dancer, in competition on Broadway. ♫I'm Only Teasin'; In a Shower of Stars; Mynah Bird; Through Your Eyes to Your Heart; Delightfully Dangerous; Once Upon a Song. **92m/B VHS, DVD.** Jane Powell, Ralph Bellamy, Constance Moore, Arthur Treacher, Louise Beavers; ***D:*** Arthur Lubin.

Delinquent Daughters **1/2 1944** Slow-paced drama about a high school girl who commits suicide and the cop and reporter who try to find out why so darn many kids are getting into trouble. **71m/B VHS, DVD.** June Carlson, Fifi d'Orsay, Teala Loring; ***D:*** Al(bert) Herman.

Delinquent Girl Boss: Blossoming Night Dreams *Zubeko bancho: yume wa yoru hiraku; Tokyo Bad Girls* **1970** The first of four Pinky violence films directed by Kazuhiko Yamaguchi and starring Reiko Oshida. Rika (Reiko Oshida) has been in and out of reform school all her life. Trying to get a fresh start she joins some of her reform school friends at a nightclub (run by exploitation star Junko Miyazono), where she runs afoul of a Yakuza Boss who wants the land the nightclub sits on. **87m/C DVD.** *JP* Reiko Oshida; ***D:*** Kazuhiko Yamaguchi.

Delinquent Parents **1/2 1938** A wayward girl gives up her baby for adoption. She turns her life around and becomes a juvenile court judge. Years later, who should come up before her for misdeeds but her long-lost daughter. The Hound cannot improve on a contemporary critic who renamed this "Delinquent Producers." **62m/B VHS, DVD.** Doris Weston, Maurice Murphy, Helen MacKellar, Terry Walker, Richard Tucker, Morgan Wallace; ***D:*** Nick Grinde.

Delinquent School Girls **WOOF!** *Bad Girls* **1984 (R)** Three escapees from an asylum get more than they bargained for when they visit a Female Correctional Institute to fulfill their sexual fantasies. Buys into just about every conceivable stereotype. **89m/C VHS.** Michael Pataki, Bob Minos, Stephen Stucker; ***D:*** Gregory Corarito.

Delirious **1/2 1991 (PG)** A writer for a TV soap opera wakes from a bash on the head to find himself inside the story where murder and mayhem are brewing. Can he write himself back to safety, and find romance along the way? Somehow Candy just isn't believeable as a romantic lead and the film has few laughs. **96m/C VHS, DVD.** John Candy, Mariel Hemingway, Emma Samms, Raymond Burr, David Rasche, Dylan Baker, Charles Rocket, Jerry Orbach, Renee Taylor, Robert Wagner; ***D:*** Tom Mankiewicz; ***W:*** Lawrence J. Cohen; ***M:*** Cliff Eidelman.

Delirious **1/2 2006** Smalltime New York paparazzo Les Galantine (the perfectly cast Buscemi) doesn't like to admit to being lonely but when homeless wannabe actor Toby (Pitt) starts hanging around, Les offers him odd jobs and a place to crash. Toby may just prove to be Les's money shot when the handsome young man catches the eye of pop phenom K'Harma (Lohman) but Toby is smarter and more ambitious than he first appears, meaning Les may be left scrambling in the crowd once again. **107m/C DVD.** Steve Buscemi, Michael Pitt, Gina Gershon, Callie (Calliope) Thorne, Kevin Corrigan, K'Harma Leeds, Richard Short; ***D:*** Tom DiCillo; ***W:*** Tom DiCillo; ***C:*** Frank DeMarco; ***M:*** Anton Sanko.

Delirium **WOOF!** *Psycho Puppet* **1977** Homicidal maniac goes on a killing spree and has just one thing in mind—women. Angry group of citizens inadvertently includes the demonic villain in their vigilante club. Nothing redeeming here. **94m/C VHS.** Turk Cekovsky, Debi Shanley, Terry Ten Broeck; ***D:*** Peter Maris.

Deliver Us from Eva **1/2 2003 (R)** Eva (Union) is the overbearing, self-righteous eldest of the four Dandridge sisters. After their parents' untimely death, Eva took on the role of the surrogate mother and since then has become an overpowering influence in their lives. Her sisters' significant others, tired of their lives being dictated by Eva, decide to hire Ray (LL Cool J), a noted ladies man, to woo her out of their lives. The attraction turns real though, and complications arise. Plot is predictable, (it's yet another updating of Shakespeare's "Taming of the Shrew") but you don't mind due to great chemistry between the two solid leads. **105m/C VHS, DVD.** *US* Gabrielle Union, LL Cool J, Duane Martin, Essence Atkins, Robine Lee, Meagan Good, Mel Jackson, Dartanyan Edmonds, Kym E. Whitley, Royale Watkins, Matt Winston, Ruben Paul, Dorian Gregory; ***D:*** Gary Hardwick; ***W:*** Gary Hardwick, James Iver Mattson, B.E. Brauner; ***C:*** Alexander Grusynski; ***M:*** Marcus Miller.

Deliverance **1972 (R)** Terrifying exploration of the primal nature of man and his alienation from nature, based on the novel by James Dickey, which he adapted for the film (he also makes an appearance as a sheriff). Four urban professionals, hoping to get away from it all for the weekend, canoe down a southern river, encounter crazed backwoodsmen, and end up battling for survival. Excellent performances all around, especially by Voight. Debuts for Beatty and Cox. Watch for O'Neill as a sheriff, and director Boorman's son Charley as Voight's son. "Dueling Banjos" scene and tune are memorable as is scene where the backwoods boys promise to make the fellows squeal like pigs. **109m/C VHS, DVD, Blu-ray Disc, HD DVD.** Jon Voight, Burt Reynolds, Ronny Cox, Ned Beatty, James Dickey, Bill McKinney, Ed O'Neill, Charley Boorman; ***D:*** John Boorman; ***W:*** James Dickey; ***C:*** Vilmos Zsigmond; ***M:*** Eric Weissburg. Natl. Film Reg. '08.

Delivered *Death by Pizza* **1998 (R)** Pizza deliveryman Will Sherman (Strickland) is the unfortunate witness to a murder by serial killer Reed (Eldard). When Reed realizes Will saw him, he goes after him but the cops have come to the conclusion that it's Will who's the killer—so he has to evade the cops and Reed as well. It's all played for laughs. **90m/C VHS, DVD.** David Strickland, Ron Eldard, Leslie Stefanson, Scott Bairstow, Nicky Katt, Jillian Armenante, Bob Morrisey, Mark Berry; ***D:*** Guy Ferland; ***W:*** Andrew Liotta, Lawrence Trilling; ***C:*** Shane Kelly; ***M:*** Nicholas Pike.

The Delivery **1999 (R)** Euro-thriller finds buddies Guy (Douglas) and Alfred (van Huet) so desperate for money that they agree to do a job for a crime boss. Seems he needs them to deliver a large shipment of Ecstasy from Barcelona to Amsterdam. Added into the mix is the prerequisite tough babe—in this case, Loulou (Meriel). Drugs, chases, sex, and violence. **100m/C VHS, DVD.** *NL BE* Fedja Van Huet, Freddy Douglas, Auriele Meriel, Rik Launspach, Esmee De La Bretoniere, Jonathan Harvey, Hidde Maas, Christopher Simon; ***D:*** Roel Reine; ***W:*** David Hilton; ***C:*** Jan van den Nieuwenhuyzen.

Delivery Boys **1/2 1984 (R)** The "Delivery Boys," three breakdancers aiming to win the $10,000 New York City Break-Off, find unusual perils that may keep them from competing. **94m/C VHS.** Joss Marcano, Tom Sierchio, Jim Soriero, Mario Van Peebles, Samantha Fox; ***D:*** Ken Handley.

Delos Adventure **1986 (R)** A geological expedition in South America stumbles upon covert Russian activities and must battle to survive in this overly violent actioner. **98m/C VHS, DVD.** Roger Kern, Jenny Neumann, Kevin Brophy; ***D:*** Joseph Purcell.

The Delta **1997** White, middleclass Memphis teenager Lincoln Bloom (Gray) is leading a double life. He parties with his girlfriend Monica (Huss) and macho buddies but also sneaks off to cruise the city's gay pick-up spots. Which is where he meets the older John (Chan), an Amerasian immigrant from Vietnam, whose unknown father was a black soldier. The two have a brief romantic idyll but while the openly gay John is desperate for love, Lincoln is still uncertain about his sexual identity and the disparity between their lives. Feature debut for both Sachs and his two lead actors. **85m/C VHS, DVD.** Shayne Gray, Thang Chan, Rachel Zan Huss, Ricky Little; ***D:*** Ira Sachs; ***W:*** Ira Sachs; ***C:***

Benjamin P. Speth; *M:* Michael Rohatyn.

Delta Farce 🦴 **2007 (PG-13)** Watching a Larry movie is like dressing squirrels in little ballet outfits. It might seem like a good idea when you're drunk, but you aren't certain you'd like your friends and neighbors to see you doing it, and you'll probably feel bad about yourself when you're done. Three idiotic weekend warriors fall asleep in a cargo plane bound for Iraq. Due to weather problems, the pilot has to dump the cargo (and them) over Mexico, which does not happen to be between the US and Iraq on any map currently in print. They immediately begin to try to 'spread freedom and democracy' by helping a village in trouble, and can't even tell the difference between Mexicans and Iraqis. Ineptly done and poorly funded, at least it does its best to insult anyone who isn't white, male, straight, drunk, and stupid. **89m/C DVD, Blu-ray Disc.** *US* Larry the Cable Guy, DJ Qualls, Marisol Nichols, Danny Trejo, Bill Engvall, Keith David, Glenn Morshower, Christina Moore, Lisa Lampanelli, Ed O'Ross; *D:* C.B. Harding; *W:* Bear Aderhold, Thomas F.X. Sullivan; *C:* Tom Priestley; *M:* James Levine.

Delta Force 🦴🦴 **1986 (R)** Based on the true hijacking of a TWA plane in June 1985. Arab terrorists take over an airliner; the Delta Force, led by Lee Marvin and featuring Norris as its best fighter, rescue the passengers in ways that cater directly to our nationalistic revenge fantasies. Average thriller, exciting and tense at times, with fine work from Marvin, Norris, and Forster. **125m/C VHS, DVD.** Lee Marvin, Chuck Norris, Shelley Winters, Martin Balsam, George Kennedy, Hanna Schygulla, Susan Strasberg, Bo Svenson, Joey Bishop, Lainie Kazan, Robert Forster, Robert Vaughn, Kim Delaney; *D:* Menahem Golan; *W:* James Bruner; *C:* David Gurfinkel; *M:* Alan Silvestri.

Delta Force 2: Operation Stranglehold 🦴 1/2 **1990 (R)** Delta Force is back with martial artist and military technician Norris at the helm. Action-packed and tense. **110m/C VHS, DVD.** John P. Ryan, Chuck Norris, Billy Drago, Richard Jaeckel, Paul Perri; *D:* Aaron Norris; *W:* Lee Reynolds; *C:* Joao Fernandes; *M:* Frederic Talgorn.

Delta Force 3: The Killing Game 🦴 1/2 *Young Commandos* **1991 (R)** A terrorist mastermind plants an atomic bomb in an American city, and the President has only one choice...call in the Delta Force. The leading men in this lackluster thriller are the sons of some of Hollywood's biggest stars. **97m/C VHS, DVD.** Nick Cassavetes, Eric Douglas, Mike Norris, Matthew Penn, John P. Ryan, Sandy Ward; *D:* Sam Firstenberg; *W:* Boaz Davidson.

Delta Force Commando 🦴 1/2 **1987 (R)** Two U.S. Fighter pilots fight against terrorism in the deadly Nicaraguan jungle. **90m/C VHS, DVD.** *IT* Fred Williamson, Bo Svenson; *D:* Frank (Pierluigi Ciriaci) Valenti.

Delta Force Commando 2 🦴 *Priority Red One* **1990 (R)** The celluloid was hardly dry on the first "Delta Force Commando" before the resourceful Italians began grinding out this follow-up, with the lead commando getting the Force entangled in a deadly international conspiracy. **100m/C VHS.** *IT* Richard Hatch, Fred Williamson, Giannina Facio, Van Johnson; *D:* Frank (Pierluigi Ciriaci) Valenti.

Delta Fox 🦴🦴 **1977** Delta Fox is carrying $1 million for the mob, but the mob is carrying a grudge and the chase is on. **90m/C VHS.** Priscilla Barnes, Richard Lynch, Stuart Whitman, John Ireland; *D:* Beverly Sebastian, Ferd Sebastian.

Delta Heat 🦴🦴 **1992 (R)** A new designer drug hits L.A. and detective Mike Bishop (Edwards) follows his partner to the drug's source in Louisiana. When Bishop arrives he discovers his partner has been tortured and murdered in order to keep the drug lord's foes in line. Bishop must then save himself and find justice in the steamy streets of New Orleans. Routine lone guy vs. bad guys actioner. **91m/C VHS, DVD.** Anthony Edwards, Lance Henriksen, Betsy Russell, Linda Dona, Rod Masterson, John McConnell, Clyde Jones; *D:* Michael Fischa.

Delta of Venus 🦴 1/2 **1995 (R)** Paris, 1940—beautiful young American Elena (England), an aspiring author, falls for handsome Lawrence (Mandylor), a writer of dirty books. But she finds out Lawrence isn't faithful and winds up supporting herself as a nude model and writing her own erotic tales. Lots of sex scenes and an equal amount of pretensions. Based on the erotic novel "Delta of Venus" by Anais Nin. Prague substitutes for Paris as the film location. Also availble unrated; the theatrical version came out as NC-17. **100m/C VHS, DVD.** Audie England, Costas Mandylor, Erick Da Silva, Raven Snow; *D:* Zalman King; *W:* Patricia Louisianna Knop, Elisa Rothstein; *C:* Eagle Egilsson; *M:* George S. Clinton.

Deluge 🦴🦴 **1933** Tidal waves causd by earthquakes have destroyed most of New York (though some may think this is no great loss) in this early sci-fi pic. **72m/B VHS.** Edward Van Sloan, Peggy Shannon, Sidney Blackmer, Fred Kohler Sr., Matt Moore, Samuel S. Hinds, Lane Chandler; *D:* Felix Feist.

The Deluge 🦴🦴 *Potop* **1973** Romance woven around the Polish-Swedish war in the 17th century. Adapted from the 1886 novel by Nobel prize-winning author Henryk Sienkiewicz, and filmed largely on location in authentic castles of the era. Polish with subtitles. **185m/C VHS, DVD.** *PL* Daniel Olbrychski, Malgorzata Braunek, Wladyslaw Hancza, Leszek Herdegen, Andrzej Lapicki; *D:* Jerzy Hoffman; *C:* Jerzy Wojcik; *M:* Kazimierz Serocki.

Delusion 🦴 1/2 *The House Where Death Lives* **1980 (R)** Gothic thriller in which invalid Cotten and family are harassed by a possibly supernatural killer as told by Cotten's nurse. Filmed in 1980. Ending is a let-down. **93m/C VHS.** Patricia Pearcy, David Hayward, John Dukakis, Joseph Cotten, Simone Griffeth; *D:* Alan Beattie.

Delusion 🦴🦴 1/2 **1991 (R)** A yuppie with an embezzled fortune is held up in the Nevada desert by a psycho hood with a showgirl lover. But who's really in charge here? The snappy, hip, film-noir thriller takes a few unlikely twists and has an open Lady-or-the-Tiger finale that may infuriate. **100m/C VHS.** Jim Metzler, Jennifer Rubin, Kyle Secor, Robert Costanzo, Tracey Walter, Jerry Orbach; *D:* Carl Colpaert; *W:* Carl Colpaert, Kurt Voss; *C:* Geza Sinkovics; *M:* Barry Adamson.

Delusions of Grandeur 🦴🦴 1/2 *La Folle des Grandeurs* **1976** A French comedy of court intrigue set in 17th-century Spain. In French with English subtitles. Based loosely on Victor Hugo's "Ruy Blas." **85m/C VHS, DVD.** *FR* Yves Montand, Louis de Funes, Alice Sapritch, Karin Schubert, Gabriele Tinti; *D:* Gerard Oury.

Demented 🦴 **1980 (R)** Beautiful and talented woman is brutally gang-raped by four men, but her revenge is sweet and deadly as she entices each to bed and gives them a big dose of their own medicine. All-too-familiar plot offers nothing new. **92m/C VHS.** Sallee Elyse, Bruce Gilchrist; *D:* Arthur Jeffreys, Alex Rebar; *W:* Alex Rebar.

Dementia 🦴🦴 1/2 **1998** Wild-eyed sexual thriller owes a bit to "Diabolique." Recovering from a breakdown, wealthy Kathrine (Bursel) becomes friendly with her outpatient nurse Luisa (Sanchez). Then Luisa's smarmy ex-husband Sonny (Schulze) shows up and things get twisty. Production values are not top drawer and the cast is not well known, but director Keith keeps things moving nicely. **85m/C DVD.** Marisol Padilla Sanchez, Patricia Bursiel, Matt Schulze, Azura Skye, Matthew Sullivan, Jesus Nebot, Susan Davis; *D:* Woody Keith; *W:* Woody Keith, R.G. Fry; *C:* David Trulli; *M:* Karl Preusser.

Dementia 13 🦴🦴 1/2 *The Haunted and the Hunted* **1963** This eerie thriller, set in a creepy castle, is an early Coppola film about the members of an Irish family who are being offed by an axe murderer one by one. **75m/B VHS, DVD.** William Campbell, Luana Anders, Bart Patton, Patrick Magee, Barbara Dowling, Ethne Dunn, Mary Mitchell, Karl Schanzer; *D:* Francis Ford Coppola; *W:* Francis Ford Coppola; *C:* Charles Hannawalt; *M:* Ronald Stein.

Demetrius and the Gladiators 🦴🦴 1/2 **1954** A sequel to "The Robe," wherein the holy-robe-carrying slave is enlisted as one of Caligula's gladiators and mixes with the trampy empress Messalina. **101m/C VHS, DVD.** Victor Mature, Susan Hayward, Michael Rennie, Debra Paget, Anne Bancroft, Jay Robinson, Barry Jones, Richard Egan, William Marshall, Ernest Borgnine; *D:* Delmer Daves; *W:* Philip Dunne; *C:* Milton Krasner.

The Demi-Paradise 🦴🦴🦴 *Adventure for Two* **1943** Tongue-in-cheek look at people's perceptions of foreigners has Olivier as a Russian inventor (?!) who comes to England with some trepidation. Though the Brits are plenty quirky, he manages to find romance with Ward in this charming look at British life. **110m/B VHS.** *GB* Laurence Olivier, Penelope Dudley Ward, Margaret Rutherford, Marjorie Fielding, Felix Aylmer, Guy Middleton, Michael Shepley; *D:* Anthony Asquith.

Demolition 🦴 1/2 **1977** Ex-international courier finds that the "simple" task he has consented to do for his old employers is deceptively hazardous. **90m/C VHS.** John Waters, Belinda Giblin, Fred Steele, Vincent Ball; *D:* Kevin James Dobson.

Demolition High 🦴🦴 1/2 **1995 (R)** Standard actioner finds New York kid Lenny (Haim) having problems adjusting to his new California high school, where he's labeled a troublemaker. But real trouble comes along when a group of terrorists, fleeing police after a robbery, take over the school and hold the teachers and students as hostages. Fortunately, Lenny is able to lead a secret counterattact. **85m/C VHS.** Corey Haim, Alan Thicke, Jeff Kober, Dick Van Patten; *D:* Jim Wynorski; *W:* Steve Jankowski; *C:* Zoran Hochstatter; *M:* Kevin Kiner.

Demolition Man 🦴🦴 **1993 (R)** No-brain sci-fier rests on the action skills of Stallone and Snipes. Psychovillain Snipes (sporting a Dennis Rodman 'do) is pursued by equally violent cop Stallone in the late 1990s. Then they're cryogenically frozen, defrosted in 2032, and back to their old tricks. One problem. This is not a fun future: virtual reality sex is the only kind allowed and puritan ethics and political correctness are enforced to the max. Cop and bad guy get to show this highly orderly society some really violent times. Implausible plot and minimal acting, but lots of action and violence for fans. **115m/C VHS, DVD.** Jack Black, Steve Kahan, Grand L. Bush, Bill Cobbs, Dan Cortese, Rob Schneider, Jesse Ventura, Sylvester Stallone, Wesley Snipes, Sandra Bullock, Nigel Hawthorne, Benjamin Bratt, Bob Gunton, Glenn Shadix, Denis Leary; *D:* Marco Brambilla; *W:* Daniel Waters, Robert Reneau, Peter M. Lenkov; *C:* Alex Thomson; *M:* Elliot Goldenthal.

The Demolitionist 🦴🦴 **1995 (R)** Tough undercover cop Alyssa Lloyd (Eggert) is killed by crimelord Mad Dog Burne (Grieco) and then resurrected by scientist Jack Crowley (Abbott) as a hard-hitting futuristic superheroine who's out to save Metro City from evil. **100m/C VHS, DVD.** Nicole Eggert, Richard Grieco, Bruce Abbott, Susan Tyrrell, Peter Jason, Sarah Douglas, Andras Jones, Heather Langenkamp, David Anthony Marshall, Jack Nance, Tom Savini; *D:* Robert Kurtzman; *W:* Brian DiMuccio, Dino Vindeni; *C:* Marcus Hahn; *M:* Shawn Patterson.

The Demon 🦴 1/2 **1981 (R)** A small town may be doomed to extinction, courtesy of a monster's thirst for the blood of its inhabitants. **94m/C VHS, DVD.** *SA* Cameron Mitchell, Jennifer Holmes; *D:* Percival Rubens; *W:* Percival Rubens; *C:* Vincent Cox.

Demon Barber of Fleet Street 🦴🦴 1/2 *Sweeney Todd: The Demon Barber of Fleet Street* **1936** Loosely based on an actual event, this film inspired the 1978 smash play "Sweeney Todd." Slaughter stars as a mad barber who doesn't just cut his client's hair. He happens to have a deal cooked up with the baker to provide him with some nice 'juicy' filling for his meat pies. Manages to be creepy and funny at the same time. **68m/B VHS, DVD.** *GB* Tod Slaughter, Eve Lister, Bruce Seton; *D:* George King.

Demon for Trouble 🦴 **1934** Outlaws are murdering land buyers in this routine western. **58m/B VHS, DVD.** Bob Steele, Don Alvarado, Gloria Shea, Nick Stuart; *D:* Robert F. "Bob" Hill; *W:* Jack Natteford; *C:* William C. Thompson.

Demon Hunter 🦴 1/2 **1988** Terror reigns while a deranged killer stalks his next victim. **90m/C VHS.** George Ellis, Erin Fleming, Marrianne Gordon; *D:* Massey Cramer; *W:* Bob Corley.

A Demon in My View 🦴🦴 1/2 **1992 (R)** In a role similar to his infamous Norman Bates in "Psycho," Perkins stars as a man who hides a terrible secret—he is a former serial killer. When a fellow tenant in his apartment house accidentally destroys his doll, Perkins' tenuous sanity is shaken and he begins killing again. A smart thriller. Perkins last big-screen role. **98m/C VHS.** Anthony Perkins, Sophie Ward, Stratford Johns; *D:* Petra Haffter; *W:* Petra Haffter.

The Demon Lover WOOF! *Devil Master; Master of Evil* **1977 (R)** Leader of a satanic cult calls forth the devil when he doesn't get his way. Poorly acted and badly produced. Features comic book artists Val "Howard the Duck" Mayerick and Gunnar "Leatherface" Hansen. **87m/C VHS.** Christmas Robbins, Val Mayerick, Gunnar Hansen, Tom Hutton, David Howard; *D:* Donald G. Jackson, Jerry Younkins; *W:* Donald G. Jackson, Jerry Younkins.

Demon Lust 🦴🦴 **2001** "The Sopranos" meet "Dracula" in this ultra low-budget New Jersey independent production. Nick (Teller) and Tony (Vincent) owe $5,000 to a mobster who has sent a thug (Savini) to collect. After some allegedly comic bits, the two guys find themselves hooked up with Amanda (Stevens), a beautiful babe who's really a monster. Most of the lead roles are well acted. **??m/C DVD.** Edward Lee Vincent, Zander Teller, Brinke Stevens, Tom Savini; *D:* David A. Goldberg; *W:* Coven Balfour; *C:* Joseph Robert Jobe; *M:* Coven Balfour.

Demon of Paradise WOOF! **1987 (R)** Dynamite fishing off the coast of Hawaii unearths an ancient, man-eating lizard-man. Unveven, unexciting horror attempt. **84m/C VHS.** Kathryn Witt, William (Bill) Steis, Leslie Huntly, Laura Banks, Frederick Bailey; *D:* Cirio H. Santiago; *W:* Frederick Bailey; *C:* Ricardo Remías.

Demon Possessed 🦴 1/2 **1993 (R)** When Tom is critically injured in a snowmobile race in a remote woods, he and his friends find shelter in a deserted children's camp. It turns out the camp was run by a secret religious cult that practiced occult murder and the demon that haunted the place has never left. When Tom dies this satanic spirit finds the perfect host to return to human form and continue its bloody work. **97m/C VHS.** Dawn Laurrie, Aaron Kjenass, David Fields, Eve Montgomery; *D:* Christopher Webster; *W:* Julian Weaver; *M:* John Tatgenhorst.

Demon Queen 🦴 **1980** A vampirish woman seduces, then murders, many men. **70m/C VHS.** Mary Fanaro, Dennis Stewart, Cliff Dance; *D:* Donald Farmer.

Demon Rage 🦴 1/2 *Satan's Mistress; Fury of the Succubus; Dark Eyes* **1982 (R)** Neglected housewife drifts under the spell of a phantom lover. **98m/C VHS, DVD.** Britt Ekland, Lana Wood, Kabir Bedi, Don Galloway, John Carradine, Sherry Scott; *D:* James Polakof.

Demon Seed 🦴🦴🦴 **1977 (R)** When a scientist (Weaver) and his wife (Christie) separate so he can work on "Proteus," a somewhat biological supercomputer, the terminal within his computer-controlled home allows Proteus to infiltrate, taking over the house and his wife. Proteus' intent? To procreate. Bizarre and taut; based on a Dean Koontz novel. **97m/C VHS, DVD.** Julie Christie, Fritz Weaver, Gerrit Graham, Berry Kroeger, Ron Hays, Lisa Lu, Larry J. Blake; *D:* Donald Cammell; *W:* Robert Jaffe, Roger O. Hirson; *C:* Bill Butler; *V:* Robert Vaughn.

Demon Wind 🦴 1/2 **1990 (R)** A gateway to Hell opens up on a secluded farm and various heroic types try to close it. Meanwhile, demons attempt to possess those humans in their midst. Zombies abound in this near-woof. **97m/C VHS.** Eric Larson, Francine Lapensee, Rufus Norris; *D:* Charles Philip Moore.

Demon with a Glass Hand ✐ 1/2 **1964** In the vein of "The Terminator," a man goes back two hundred years in time to escape the evil race that rules the planet. **63m/B VHS.** Robert Culp, Arlene Martel, Abraham Sofaer; *D:* Byron Haskin; *W:* Harlan Ellison; *C:* Kenneth Peach Sr.; *M:* Harry Lubin.

Demonia WOOF! **1990** Archaeologists digging in Sicily uncover a sealed convent where five nuns were crucified in the 15th century. This discovery unleashes an ancient evil and bizarre murders begin to take place. Unfortunately, that's about it as far as the plot goes. Even by Fulci's standards, "Demonia" is slow and pondering, with many scenes taking place twice, once in reality and then again in a dream (nightmare?). Fulci's trademark gore is scant and the special effects are laughable. Even die-hard Fulci fans will be disappointed. **90m/C DVD.** *IT* Brett Halsey, Meg Register, Carla Cassola, Al Cliver, Lucio Fulci; *D:* Lucio Fulci; *W:* Lucio Fulci, Piero Regnoli; *C:* Luis Ciccarese.

Demonic Toys ✐ 1/2 **1990 (R)** The possessed play-things attack a bunch of unfortunates in a warehouse, and pumped-up lady cop Scoggins deserves an award for keeping a straight face. Skimpily scripted gore from the horror assembly-line at Full Moon Productions. Far more entertaining are the multiple behind-the-scenes featurettes on the tape. **86m/C VHS, DVD.** Richard Speight Jr., Tracy Scoggins, Bentley Mitchum, Michael Russo, Jeff Weston, Daniel Cerny, PeteR Schrum; *D:* Peter Manoogian.

Demonlover ✐✐ **2002** Big business meets the high-stakes game of high tech Internet pornography and results in a confusing, unnecessarily violent thriller. Nielsen plays Diane, a corporate spy acting as an assistant to Henri-Pierre Volf (Malartre), the head of multinational conglomerate VolfGroup. VolfGroup threatens to take over TokyoAnime, producers of revolutionary, animated 3-D smut, which sparks rival companies Mangatronics and Demonlover to get nasty. Nasty pretty much sums up just about all the characters and the rest of the action throughout, led by the particularly immoral Diane. Characters are totally devoid of sympathy while the plot begins to totally unravel halfway through. **120m/C VHS, DVD.** *FR* Connie Nielsen, Charles Berling, Chloe Sevigny, Gina Gershon, Dominique Reymond, Jean-Baptiste Malartre; *D:* Olivier Assayas; *W:* Olivier Assayas; *C:* Denis Lenoir; *M:* Sonic Youth.

Demonoid, Messenger of Death ✐ *Macabra* **1981 (R)** Discovery of an ancient temple of Satan worship drastically changes the lives of a young couple when the husband becomes possessed by the Demonoid, which initially takes on the form of a severed hand. Poor script needs hand, producing a number of unintentionally laughable moments. **85m/C VHS, DVD.** Samantha Eggar, Stuart Whitman, Roy Cameron Jenson; *D:* Alfredo Zacharias.

The Demons ✐ *Les Demons; Los Demonios* **1974 (R)** As she slips into death, a tortured woman curses her torturers. **116m/C VHS.** *FR PT* Anne Libert, Britt Nichols, Doris Thomas, Howard Vernon, Karin (Karen) Field, Luis Barboo; *D:* Jess (Jesus) Franco, Clifford Brown; *W:* Jess (Jesus) Franco.

Demons ✐ 1/2 *Demoni* **1986 (R)** A horror film in a Berlin theatre is so involving that its viewers become the demons they are seeing. The new monsters turn on the other audience members. Virtually plotless, very explicit. Rock soundtrack by Accept, Go West, Motley Crue, and others. Revered in some circles, blasted in others. Followed by "Demons 2." **89m/C VHS, DVD.** *IT* Urbano Barberini, Natasha Hovey, Paolo Cozza, Karl Zinny, Fiore Argento, Fabiola Toledo, Nicoletta Elmi, Michele (Michael) Soavi; *D:* Lamberto Bava; *W:* Lamberto Bava, Dario Argento, Franco Ferrini, Dardano Sacchetti; *C:* Gianlorenzo Battaglia; *M:* Claudio Simonetti.

Demons 2 ✐ 1/2 **1987 (R)** Inferior sequel to "Demons." The son of horror-meister Mario Bava, Lamberto collaborated with Italian auteur Argento (who co-wrote and produced) to create an improbable sequel (storywise) which seems to have been edited by some kind of crazed cutting room slasher with equally hackneyed dubbing. Residents of a chi-chi high rise watching a documentary about the events of "Demons"—a sort of high-tech play-within-a-play ploy—when a demon emerges from the TV, spreads his creepy cooties, and causes the tenants to sprout fangs and claws and nasty tempers. Lots of blood drips from ceilings, plumbing fixtures, and various body parts. **88m/C VHS, DVD.** *IT* David Edwin Knight, Nancy Brill, Coralina Cataldi-Tassoni, Bobby Rhodes, Asia Argento, Virginia Bryant; *D:* Lamberto Bava; *W:* Dario Argento, Lamberto Bava; *C:* Gianlorenzo Battaglia; *M:* Simon Boswell.

Demons from Her Past ✐ 1/2 **2007** Despite the lurid cover art, this Lifetime effort is not a horror movie (although it is rather horrible). At 18, Allison was wrongly convicted of vehicular homicide and sent to prison. Upon her release, she moved to Paris and made a new life for herself, but years later her grandmother's funeral brings Allison home. Knowing she was framed, Allison is determined to get revenge on the men responsible, but they have no intention of letting her reveal the truth. **93m/C DVD.** Alexandra Paul, Cynthia Gibb, Michael Woods, Rob Stewart, John Ralston, Kevin Jubinville, Sophie Gendron; *D:* Douglas Jackson; *W:* Christine Conradt; *C:* Bert Tougas; *M:* Steve Gurevitch. **CABLE**

Demons in the Garden ✐✐✐ *Demonios En El Jardin* **1982 (R)** Centers on the disintegration of a family after the end of the Spanish Civil War, due to sibling rivalries and a variety of indiscretions. Problems mount as two brothers become involved with their stepsister. Story takes on poignancy in its narration by a young boy. Beautiful cinematography. In Spanish with English subtitles. **100m/C VHS.** *SP* Angela Molina, Ana Belen, Encarna Paso, Imanol Arias; *D:* Manuel Gutierrez Aragon; *C:* Jose Luis Alcaine.

Demons of Ludlow ✐ **1975** Demons attend a small town's bicentennial celebration intent on raising a little hell of their own. **83m/C VHS, DVD.** Paul von Hauser, Stephanie Cushna, James Robinson, Carol Perry; *D:* Steven Kuether.

Demons of the Mind ✐✐ *Blood Evil; Blood Will Have Blood* **1972 (R)** A sordid psychological horror film about a baron in 19th century Austria who imprisons his children, fearing that mental illness is a family trait. **85m/C VHS, DVD.** *GB* Michael Hordern, Patrick Magee, Yvonne Mitchell, Robert Hardy, Gillian Hills, Virginia Wetherell, Shane Briant, Paul Jones, Thomas Heathcote, Kenneth J. Warren; *D:* Peter Sykes; *W:* Christopher Wicking; *C:* Arthur Grant.

Demonstone ✐ *Heartstone* **1989 (R)** A TV reporter becomes possessed by a Filipino demon and carries out an ancient curse against the family of a corrupt government official. **90m/C VHS, DVD.** R. Lee Ermey, Jan-Michael Vincent, Nancy Everhard; *D:* Andrew Prowse.

Demonstrator ✐✐ 1/2 **1971** A father and son are at odds when dad heads an Asian military coalition and junior protests. Notable for being one of the first major Australian films to use an entirely native cast. **82m/C VHS.** *AU* Joe James, Irene Inescort, Gerard Maguire, Wendy Lingham, Harold Hopkins; *D:* Warwick Freeman.

Demonwarp WOOF! **1987** A vengeance-minded hunter journeys into an evil, primeval forest to kill the monsters that abducted his daughter. **91m/C VHS.** George Kennedy, Pamela Gilbert; *D:* Emmett Alston; *W:* Bruce Akiyama.

Dempsey ✐✐ **1983** In this film, based on Jack Dempsey's autobiography, Williams plays the role of the famed world heavyweight champ. His rise through the boxing ranks as well as his personal life are chronicled. A bit slow-moving considering the pounding fists and other action. **110m/C VHS, DVD.** Treat Williams, Sam Waterston, Sally Kellerman, Victoria Tennant, Peter Mark Richman, Jesse Vint, Bonnie Bartlett, James Noble; *D:* Gus Trikonis; *M:* Billy Goldenberg. **TV**

Denial: The Dark Side of Passion ✐✐ **1991 (R)** A strong-willed woman tries to put a destructive love affair behind her—but if she succeeded there'd be no movie. Torrid stuff with a watchable cast. **103m/C VHS.** Robin Wright Penn, Jason Patric, Barry Primus, Christina Harnos, Rae Dawn Chong; *D:* Erin Dignam; *W:* Erin Dignam.

Denise Calls Up ✐✐ 1/2 **1995 (PG-13)** Comedy about futility and complications of urban relationships among overworked professionals. A group of six work-at-home city friends socialize, romance, and date entirely via phone, fax, and computer without ever meeting or leaving their homes, even for a close friend's funeral (who dies, oddly enough, while on the phone). Subplot involves title character, Denise (Ubach) tracking down sperm donor Martin (Gunther) and eventually giving birth, with the help of her cellular coaches. Funny premise is executed well, but doesn't hold up over a (barely) feature length film. **79m/C VHS.** Timothy Daly, Dana Wheeler-Nicholson, Caroleen Feeney, Liev Schreiber, Dan Gunther, Aida Turturro, Alanna Ubach, Sylvia Miles; *D:* Hal Salwen; *W:* Hal Salwen; *C:* Mike Mayers; *M:* Lynne Geller.

Dennis the Menace ✐✐ 1/2 **1993 (PG)** Straight from the Hughes kiddie farm comes Kevin McAllister—oops!—Dennis Mitchell (newcomer Gamble), curious, crafty, and blond five-year-old. He dreams and schemes, but everything he does manages to be a threat to the physical and mental well being of hot-head neighbor Mr. Wilson (Matthau, perfectly cast as the grump). Lloyd is very nasty as protagonist Switchblade Sam; Plowright, Thompson, and Stanton round out the cast as Mrs. Wilson and the Mitchell parents, respectively. Sure to please young kids, but parents may be less enthralled with this adaptation of the popular '50s comic strip and subsequent TV series. **96m/C VHS, DVD.** Walter Matthau, Mason Gamble, Joan Plowright, Christopher Lloyd, Lea Thompson, Robert Stanton, Billie Bird, Paul Winfield, Amy Sakasitz, Kellen Hathaway, Arnold Stang; *D:* Nick Castle; *W:* John Hughes; *C:* Thomas Ackerman; *M:* Jerry Goldsmith.

A Dennis the Menace Christmas ✐✐ **2007** In yet another variation of "A Christmas Carol," cutie neighborhood nuisance Dennis Mitchell (Cotton) tries to help grouchy Mr. Wilson (Wagner) learn the true meaning of Christmas. **?m/C DVD.** Robert Wagner, Louise Fletcher, George Newbern, Jack Noseworthy, Maxwell Perry Cotton, Kim Schraner; *D:* Ron Oliver; *W:* Kathleen Laccinole; *C:* C. Kim Miles; *M:* Peter Allen. **VIDEO**

Dennis the Menace: Dinosaur Hunter ✐✐ 1/2 **1993 (G)** Another version of Hank Ketchum's mischievious cartoon character brought to life to have adventures and disturb his neighbor Mr. Wilson. This time Dennis discovers a huge, primitive bone in his backyard and when an archaeologist declares it's a dinosaur bone, news crews, tourists, and scientists are suddenly everywhere. This badly disturbs Mr. Wilson's retirement and Dennis and his friends must save the day (and their neighborhood). **118m/C VHS.** Victor Dimattia, William Windom, Pat Estrin, Jim Jansen, Patsy Garrett; *D:* Doug Rogers.

Dennis the Menace Strikes Again ✐✐ 1/2 **1998 (G)** Direct-to-video sequel finds hyperactive Dennis (Cooper) trying to save curmudgeonly Mr. Wilson (Rickles) from a pair of con men. **75m/C VHS, DVD.** Justin Cooper, Don Rickles, George Kennedy, Betty White, Brian Doyle-Murray, Carrot Top; *D:* Charles Kanganis; *W:* Tim McCanlies; *C:* Christopher Faloona; *M:* Graeme Revell. **VIDEO**

The Dentist ✐✐✐ 1/2 **1932** Fields treats several oddball patients in his office. After watching the infamous tooth-pulling scene, viewers will be sure to brush regularly. **22m/B VHS, DVD.** W.C. Fields, Elise Cavanna, Marjorie "Babe" Kane, Bud Jamison, Zedna Farley, Dorothy Granger, Arnold Gray; *D:* Leslie Pearce, Monte Brice; *W:* W.C. Fields.

The Dentist ✐ 1/2 **1996 (R)** After seeing this movie, you may never want to sit in that dental chair again. When his marriage falls apart, L.A. dental specialist Dr. Alan Feinstone (Bernsen) takes to pill popping and psychotic behavior, including demonic drilling and particularly bloody oral surgery. **93m/C VHS, DVD.** Corbin Bernsen, Ken Foree, Linda Hoffman, Michael Stadvec; *D:* Brian Yuzna; *W:* Charles Finch, Stuart Gordon, Dennis Paoli; *C:* Levie Isaacks; *M:* Alan Howarth.

The Dentist 2: Brace Yourself ✐ **1998 (R)** Allan Feinstone (Bernsen) has escaped from the asylum to which he was sent in the first film. He's settled in a rural community and set up another practice. This is one guy who doesn't claim to be painless. **99m/C VHS, DVD.** Corbin Bernsen, Jillian McWhirter, Linda Hoffman; *D:* Brian Yuzna; *W:* Brian Yuzna; *C:* Jurgen Baum; *M:* Alan Howarth. **VIDEO**

Dentist In the Chair ✐ 1/2 **1960** Dumb Brit comedy about dental students David (Monkhouse) and Brian (Stevens) who inadvertantly get involved with smalltime crook Sam Field (Connor) who gives them a load of expensive dental equipment. But they have to get rid of the goods before they're accused of theft. **87m/B VHS.** *GB* Bob Monkhouse, Ronnie Stevens, Kenneth Connor, Peggy Cummins, Eric Barker, Stuart Saunders; *D:* Don Chaffey; *W:* Val Guest, Bob Monkhouse; *C:* Reg Wyer; *M:* Kenneth V. Jones.

The Denver & Rio Grande ✐✐ 1/2 **1951** Action-packed western about two rival railroads competing to be the first to complete a line through the Royal Gorge. Plot is predictable, but the scene featuring two trains crashing into each other is worth it (Haskin used actual trains for this stunt). **89m/C VHS.** Edmond O'Brien, Sterling Hayden, Dean Jagger, Zasu Pitts, J. Carrol Naish; *D:* Byron Haskin.

The Departed ✐✐✐ 1/2 **2006 (R)** Scorsese goes back to the mob (Irish and in Boston this time) for a complicated and violent tale of identity and betrayal based on the Hong Kong flick "Infernal Affairs." Colin (a strong Damon) is a state police officer who's actually a mole for crazy kingpin Frank Costello (Nicholson, nuttier than ever) while jittery Billy (an equally strong DiCaprio) is the cop who's infiltrated Costello's gang at the behest of his tough bosses Queenan (Sheen) and Dignam (Wahlberg). Both younger men are involved—in different ways—with lone femme, shrink Madolyn (Farmiga). Tension builds, insults and bullets fly, and the truth will out—with some unexpected consequences. Scorsese's at his best (if in familiar territory). **150m/C DVD, Blu-ray Disc, HD DVD.** *US* Leonardo DiCaprio, Matt Damon, Jack Nicholson, Mark Wahlberg, Martin Sheen, Ray Winstone, Vera Farmiga, Anthony Anderson, Alec Baldwin, James Badge Dale, Mark Rolston, Kevin Corrigan, James Dale, Kristen Dalton; *D:* Martin Scorsese; *W:* William Monahan; *C:* Michael Ballhaus; *M:* Howard Shore. Oscars '06: Adapt. Screenplay, Director (Scorsese), Film, Film Editing; Directors Guild '06: Director (Scorsese); Golden Globes '07: Director (Scorsese); Writers Guild '06: Adapt. Screenplay.

Department Store ✐ *Bargain Basement* **1935** Confusing crime-drama involving a store manager who mistakes an ex-convict for his employer's heir. Based on a story by H. F. Maltby. **65m/B VHS.** *GB* Garry Marsh, Eve Gray, Sebastian Shaw, Geraldine Fitzgerald, Jack Melford; *D:* Leslie Hiscott; *C:* William Luff.

Departures ✐✐ *Okuribito* **2008** Cellist Daigo Kobayashi (Motoki) is crushed when his Tokyo orchestra breaks up and he is jobless. Diago and his wife Mika (Hirosue) return to his hometown so they can start over and he responds to a job ad thinking it's for a travel agency. Only in this case 'preparing for departures' is a niche market for morticians which means ritually preparing bodies for cremation and working with grieving families. Although shocked at first, Daigo finds he has a natural affinity for the job, much to his wife's dismay. It gets a little sappy and it's too long but Motoki has an eccentric charm. Japanese with subtitles. **130m/C DVD.** *JP* Masahiro Motoki, Ryoko Hirosue, Tsutomu Yamazaki; *D:* Yojiro Takita; *W:* Kundo Koyama; *C:* Takashi Hamada; *M:* Joe Hisaishi. Oscars '08: Foreign Film.

Depraved ✐ 1/2 **1998** Opella and Dan spice up their sex lives by acting out their fantasies. But they start to go too far for Dan and he has a fight with his fiance, who storms out. Only the next morning Dan discovers

Opella's dead body. Naturally, instead of calling the cops, Dan calls his brother, and they decide to dispose of the body and come up with an alibi. Can you spell trouble? **90m/C VHS, DVD.** Seidy Lopez, Antonio Garcia Guzman, Mario Lopez, Barbara Niven; ***D:*** Rogelio Lobato. **VIDEO**

Depth Charge **2008** A familiar submarine actioner that borrows from other, better movies. Renegade Commander Krieg (Roberts) and his henchmen take over a nuclear sub and make ransom demands to U.S. President Taylor (Bostwick). The sub's doctor, Ellers (Gedrick), has remained aboard as has a young crewman (Warren Jr.) and they try to avoid getting killed while coming up with a heroic plan to save the day. **85m/C DVD.** Jason Gedrick, Eric Roberts, Barry Bostwick, Bridget Ann White, Chris Warren Jr., Corbin Bernsen; ***D:*** Terrence O'Hara; ***W:*** Dennis Pratt; ***C:*** Dane Peterson; ***M:*** Stephen Graziano. **VIDEO**

The Deputy Drummer **½ 1935** Second-rate early British musical, notable as a later vehicle for silent-era star Lane. He plays a penniless composer who impersonates an aristocrat to attend a party, and catches jewel robbers in the act. **71m/B VHS.** *GB* Lupino Lane, Jean Denis, Kathleen Kelly, Wallace Lupino, Margaret Yarde, Syd Crossley; ***D:*** Henry W. George; ***W:*** Reginald Long.

Deputy Marshal **½ 1950** Hall trails a pair of bankrobbers, fights off landgrabbers, and finds romance as well. **75m/B VHS.** Jon Hall, Frances Langford, Dick Foran; ***D:*** William Berke; ***W:*** William Berke.

Der Purimshpiler **½** *The Purim Player; The Jester; The Jewish Jester* **1937** A drifter embarks on a quest for happiness, which takes him to various small towns. In one, he meets and falls in love with a shoemaker's daughter. In Yiddish with English subtitles. **90m/B VHS.** *PL* Miriam Kressyn, Zygmund Turkow, Hymie Jacobsen; ***D:*** Joseph Green.

Der Todesking **½** *The Death King* **1989** From the man who gave us "Nekromantik" comes this story of a chain letter that brings suicide to seven unfortunates, on seven successive days of one week. Each suicide is separated by the image of a naked, progressively decomposing man's body. In German with confusing English subtitles. **80m/C VHS.** *GE* Herman Kopp, Heinrich Ebber, Michael Krause, Eva M. Kurz, Angelika Hock, Nicholas Petche, Jorg Buttgereit, Manfred O. Jelinski; ***D:*** Jorg Buttgereit; ***W:*** Franz Rodenkirchen, Jorg Buttgereit; ***C:*** Manfred O. Jelinski; ***M:*** Daktari Lorenz, Herman Kopp.

Derailed **2002 (R)** Spy Jacques Kristoff (Van Damme) has never told his family what he does for a living, which is a problem when they decide to surprise him on one of his "business trips." It's really bad timing since they're on the same Munich-bound train as thief Galina (Harring) who is carrying vials of mutated smallpox, which is wanted by international criminal Mason Cole (Arana), who hijacks the train. Low-budget but lots of action. **89m/C VHS, DVD.** Jean-Claude Van Damme, Laura Elena Harring, Tomas Arana, Susan Gibney, Jessica Bowman, Lucy Jenner; ***D:*** Bob Misiorowski; ***W:*** Adam Gierasch, Jace Anderson; ***C:*** Ross Clarkson; ***M:*** Serge Colbert. **VIDEO**

Derailed **½ 2005 (R)** Disappointing thriller has Owen as Charles Schine, unhappily married, in the midst of a midlife crisis, and more than willing to be enthralled by the charms of equally unhappy Lucinda (Aniston). However, while in their seedy hotel room, the couple is attacked by psycho-thief Laroche (Cassel), who then threatens to reveal their affair unless they pay him off. Since Owen can't convincingly play a wimp (though he tries), you wait for him to mop the floor with this sleazy Frenchman. First English-language feature for Swedish director Hafstrom; adapted from the James Siegel novel. **110m/C DVD, HD DVD.** *US* Clive Owen, Jennifer Aniston, Vincent Cassel, Melissa George, Giancarlo Esposito, David Morrissey, Georgina Chapman, Denis O'Hare, Tom Conti, Addison Timlin, Xzibit, RZA; ***D:*** Mikael Hafstrom; ***W:*** Stuart Beattie.

Deranged **1974 (R)** Of the numerous movies based on the cannibalistic exploits of Ed Gein ("Psycho," "The Texas Chainsaw Massacre," etc.), this is the most accurate. A dead-on performance by Blossom and a twisted sense of humor help move things along nicely. The two directors, Gillen and Ormsby, previously worked together on the classic "Children Shouldn't Play with Dead Things." An added attraction is the early special effect work of gore wizard Tom Savini. **82m/C VHS, DVD.** *CA* Roberts Blossom, Cosette Lee, Robert Warner, Marcia Diamond, Brian Sneagle, Leslie (Les) Carlson, Marion Waldman, Micki Moore, Pat Orr, Robert McHeady; ***D:*** Jeff Gillen, Alan Ormsby; ***W:*** Jeff Gillen, Alan Ormsby; ***C:*** Jack McGowan; ***M:*** Carl Zittrer.

Deranged **½ 1987 (R)** A mentally unstable, pregnant woman is attacked in her apartment after her husband leaves town. She spends the rest of the movie engaged in psychotic encounters, real and imagined. Technically not bad, but extremely violent and grim. Not to be confused with 1974 movie of the same name. **85m/C VHS, DVD.** Jane (Veronica Hart) Hamilton, Paul Siederman, Jennifer Delora, James Gillis, Jill Cumer, Gary Goldman; ***D:*** Chuck Vincent.

Deranged **½** *Anacardium* **2001** Ultra talky thriller dealing with the conversations between renter and landlord. Soon talk of revenge and a husband out for blood creep into play. Sounds ridiculous? Somehow pulled off through decent acting and a tight script. Awarded best picture at the New York Independent Film Festival. **125m/C DVD.** Frank John Hughes, Richard Ruccolo, Sean Masterson, Bob Rumnock, Laura Cayouette; ***D:*** Scott Thomas; ***W:*** Scott Thomas; ***C:*** Carl F. Bartels; ***M:*** Lars Anderson. **VIDEO**

Derby **1971 (R)** The documentary story of the rise to fame of roller-derby stars on the big rink. **91m/C VHS.** Charlie O'Connell, Lydia Gray, Janet Earp, Ann Colvello, Mike Snell; ***D:*** Robert Kaylor.

The Derby Stallion **½ 2005** No, it's not a good movie but it's got horses and Efron is as cute as heck, so you think tweener girls will care? Teenager Patrick (Efron) discovers his calling when he befriends alcoholic Houston Jones (Cobbs), who offers to train him to ride in the statewide steeplechase race. But Patrick's father (Moses), a former big leaguer, is pressuring him to stick with baseball. **98m/C DVD.** Zac Efron, Bill Cobbs, William R. Moses, Colton James, Tonja Walker, Michael Nardini, Sarah Blackman, Crystal Hunt, Rob Pinkston; ***D:*** Craig Clyde; ***W:*** Kimberly Gough; ***C:*** John Gunselman; ***M:*** Billy Preston. **VIDEO**

Dersu Uzala **½ 1975** An acclaimed, photographically breathtaking film about a Russian surveyor in Siberia who befriends a crusty, resourceful Mongolian. They begin to teach each other about their respective worlds. Produced in Russia; one of Kurosawa's stranger films. **140m/C VHS, DVD.** *JP RU* Yuri Solomin, Maxim Munzuk; ***D:*** Akira Kurosawa; ***W:*** Akira Kurosawa, Yuri Nagibin; ***C:*** Asakazu Nakai, Yuri Gantman, Fyodor Dobronravov; ***M:*** Isaak Shvarts. Oscars '75: Foreign Film.

Descending Angel **1990 (R)** The premise is familiar: a swastika-friendly collaborator is forced out of the closet. But the cast and scripting make this cable there's-a-Nazi-in the-woodwork suspenser better than average, despite its flawed finale. Scott plays a well-respected Romanian refugee—active in the community, in the church, and in Romanian-American activities—whose daughter's fiance (Roberts) suspects him of Nazi collusion. **96m/C VHS, DVD.** George C. Scott, Diane Lane, Eric Roberts, Mark Margolis, Vyto Ruginis, Amy Aquino, Richard Jenkins, Jan Rubes; ***D:*** George C. Scott, Jeremy Paul Kagan; ***W:*** George C. Scott. **CABLE**

The Descent **½ 2005 (R)** Six adventure-junkie galpals go spelunking in Appalachia and find their vacation ruined by a pack of creepy humanoids who are none too happy to have guests in their cave. So much for the trip serving to distract poor Sarah (MacDonald) from her grief over the deaths of her family. Smart, nerve-jangling terror ensues as the friends battle personal demons and each other while fending off the slimy subterranean creatures. The effects aren't always very special, but horror fans will still dig both the gory splatter and the mental tension. Original ending shown in the film's U.K. version was slightly changed for its U.S. release. **99m/C DVD, Blu-ray Disc.** *GB* Shauna Macdonald, Natalie Mendoza, Alex Reid, Nora-Jane Noone, Saskia Mulder, Oliver Milburn, MyAnna Buring, Molly Kayall; ***D:*** Neil Marshall; ***W:*** Neil Marshall; ***C:*** Sam McCurdy; ***M:*** David Julyan.

Descent **½ 2007 (NC-17)** Feminist empowerment or just revenge fantasy exploitation? College grad school student Maya (Dawson) is brutally raped by date Jared (Faust) in an attack that she doesn't report and that leaves her a basket case. She seems to get back some equilibrium by hitting the clubs and getting interested in dominating DJ Adrian (Patrick), which also appears to get Maya focused on planning revenge on Jared. Dawson's worth watching but the film is only so-so. Also available in an R-rated version. **104m/C DVD.** Rosario Dawson, Chad Faust, Marcus Patrick; ***D:*** Talia Lugacy; ***W:*** Talia Lugacy, Brian Priest; ***C:*** Christopher La Vasseur, Jonathan Furmanski; ***M:*** Alex Moulton.

Desert Bloom **1986 (PG)** On the eve of a nearby nuclear bomb test, a beleaguered alcoholic veteran and his family struggle through tensions brought on by a promiscuous visiting aunt and the chaotic, rapidly changing world. Gish shines as the teenage daughter through whose eyes the story unfolds. From a story by Corr and Linda Ramy. **103m/C VHS, DVD.** Jon Voight, JoBeth Williams, Ellen Barkin, Annabeth Gish, Allen (Goorwitz) Garfield, Jay Underwood; ***D:*** Eugene Corr; ***W:*** Eugene Corr; ***C:*** Reynaldo Villalobos; ***M:*** Brad Fiedel.

Desert Blue **1998 (R)** Baxter, California is a tiny (pop. 87) desert town whose one claim to fame is a towering re-creation of an ice cream cone that has drawn the attention of pop culture prof Lance (Heard). Lance has come to Baxter with his snooty teen TV star daughter, Skye (Hudson), and the duo are trapped in town when it's quarantined by a toxic spill. Skye eventually connects to the town's disaffected teens, including Blue (Sexton), Pete (Affleck), and Ely (Ricci). **87m/C VHS, DVD.** Brendan Sexton III, Kate Hudson, John Heard, Christina Ricci, Casey Affleck, Sara Gilbert, Ethan Suplee, Lucinda Jenney; ***D:*** Morgan J. Freeman; ***W:*** Morgan J. Freeman; ***C:*** Enrique Chediak; ***M:*** Vytas Nagisetty.

Desert Commandos **1967** When the Allies appear to be winning WWII, the Nazis devise a plan to eliminate all of the opposing forces' leaders at once. **96m/C VHS, DVD.** *IT GE FR* Ken Clark, Horst Frank, Jeanne Valerie, Carlo Hinterman, Gianni Rizzo; ***D:*** Umberto Lenzi; ***W:*** Umberto Lenzi.

The Desert Fox *Rommel—Desert Fox* **1951** Big-budgeted portrait of German Army Field Marshal Rommel, played by Mason, focuses on the soldier's defeat in Africa during WWII and his subsequent, disillusioned return to Hitler's Germany. Mason played Rommel again in 1953's "Desert Rats." **87m/B VHS, DVD.** James Mason, Cedric Hardwicke, Jessica Tandy, Luther Adler; ***D:*** Henry Hathaway.

Desert Gold **½ 1936** A fierce Indian chief battles a horde of greedy white men over his tribe's gold mine. Based on a novel by Zane Grey. **58m/B VHS, DVD.** Buster Crabbe, Robert Cummings, Marsha Hunt, Tom Keene, Raymond Hatton, Monte Blue, Leif Erickson; ***D:*** Charles T. Barton.

Desert Hearts **1986 (R)** An upstanding professional woman travels to Reno, Nevada in 1959 to obtain a quick divorce, and slowly becomes involved in a lesbian relationship with a free-spirited casino waitress. **93m/C VHS, DVD.** Helen Shaver, Audra Lindley, Patricia Charbonneau, Andra Akers, Dean Butler, Jeffrey Tambor, Denise Crosby, Gwen Welles; ***D:*** Donna Deitch; ***W:*** Natalie Cooper; ***C:*** Robert Elswit.

Desert Heat *Inferno; Coyote Moon* **1999 (R)** Loner Eddie Lomax (Van Damme) is left for dead at an abandoned highway stop in the Mojave Desert after a gang steals his motorcycle. An unexpected rescue by an old friend leaves Eddie with one thought—revenge. **95m/C VHS, DVD.** Jean-Claude Van Damme, Noriyuki "Pat" Morita, Danny Trejo, Gabrielle Fitzpatrick, Larry Drake, Vincent Schiavelli; ***D:*** Danny Mulroon; ***W:*** Tom O'Rourke; ***C:*** Ross A. Maehl; ***M:*** Bill Conti. **VIDEO**

Desert Kickboxer **1992 (R)** A border guard takes on a cocaine dealer and his henchmen, fighting for gold and, of course, a beautiful woman. Lots of kickboxing action. **86m/C VHS.** John Haymes Newton, Judie Aronson, Sam DeFrancisco, Paul Smith; ***D:*** Isaac Florentine.

Desert Nights **½ 1929** Gilbert's last starring role in a silent film is a not particularly good adventure story with continuity problems (apparently the original release was 80 minutes). Hugh Rand (Gilbert), the manager of a South African diamond mine, makes nice when Lord Stonehill (Torrence) and his daughter Diana (Nolan) visit. Only the two are imposters who rob the office of diamonds and take Hugh hostage. But the thieves can't survive in the desert without his expert help since water is much more precious than gems. **62m/B DVD.** John Gilbert, Ernest Torrence, William Nigh, John Gilbert, Ernest Torrence, Mary Nolan, Mary Ainslee; ***D:*** Mary Nolan, William Nigh, Cedric Gibbons; ***W:*** Mary Ainslee, Mary Ainslee, Ruth Cummings; ***C:*** James Wong Howe, James Wong Howe.

Desert of the Lost **½ 1927** Wales flees to Mexico after shooting a man in self-defense. He's aided by Montgomery and, in turn, helps save her from a forced marriage. **58m/B VHS.** Wally Wales, Peggy Montgomery, William J. Dyer, Edward Cecil, Richard Neill, Kelly Cafford, Ray Murro, George Magrill, Charles "Slim" Whitaker; ***D:*** Richard Thorpe.

The Desert of the Tartars *Le Desert des Tartares; Il Deserto dei Tartari* **1976 (PG)** Story of a young soldier who dreams of war and discovers that the real battle for him is with time. **140m/C VHS, DVD.** *FR IT IA* Vittorio Gassman, Giuliano Gemma, Helmut Griem, Philippe Noiret, Jacques Perrin, Fernando Rey, Jean-Louis Trintignant, Max von Sydow; ***D:*** Valerio Zurlini; ***W:*** Jean-Louis Bertucelli, Andre G. Brunelin; ***C:*** Luciano Tovoli; ***M:*** Ennio Morricone.

Desert Phantom **½ 1936** Villains threaten to rob a woman of her ranch until a stranger rescues her. **66m/B VHS, DVD.** Johnny Mack Brown, Sheila (Manors) Mannors, Charles "Blackie" King, Ted Adams, Hal Price, Nelson McDowell; ***D:*** S. Roy Luby.

The Desert Rats **1953** A crusty British captain (Burton) takes charge of an Australian division during WWII. Thinking they are inferior to his own British troops, he is stiff and uncaring to the Aussies until a kind-hearted drunk and the courage of the division win him over. Crack direction from Wise and Newton's performance (as the wag) simply steal the movie. Mason reprises his role as Germany Army Field Marshal Rommel from "The Desert Fox." **88m/B VHS, DVD.** Richard Burton, Robert Newton, Robert Douglas, Torin Thatcher, Chips Rafferty, Charles "Bud" Tingwell, James Mason; ***D:*** Robert Wise.

Desert Saints **2001 (R)** Hit man Banks (Sutherland) picks up hitchhiker Bennie (Walters) and impulsively decides to use her assistance in his next job. But Bennie turns out to be an FBI agent assigned to hunt Banks down—or maybe she isn't. **88m/C VHS, DVD.** Kiefer Sutherland, Melora Walters, Rachel Ticotin, Jamey Sheridan, Leslie Stefanson, William Sage; ***D:*** Richard Greenberg; ***W:*** Richard Greenberg, Wally Nichols; ***C:*** John Newby; ***M:*** Richard (Rick) Marvin.

Desert Snow **1989 (R)** Here's a non-formulaic dope opera oater: cowboys 'n' drug runners battle it out for an out-of-the-way, underpopulated western town. About as clever as the title. **90m/C VHS.** Frank Capizzi, Flint Carney, Shelley Hinkle, Sam Incorvia, Carolyn Jacobs; ***D:*** Paul DeGruccio.

The Desert Song **½ 1953** MacRae secretly leads a band of do-gooders against the evil forces of a dastardly sheik. Grayson is the general's daughter who falls in love with our disguised hero. Third filmed version of the Sigmund Romberg operetta creaks along with the talents of MacRae and Grayson rising about the hackneyed plot. ♫The Desert Song; Gay Parisienne; Long Live the Night; One Alone; One Flower; The

Riff Song; Romance. **96m/C VHS.** Gordon MacRae, Kathryn Grayson, Raymond Massey, Steve Cochran, Dick Wesson, Allyn Ann McLerie, Ray Collins, William Conrad; ***D:*** H. Bruce Humberstone; ***W:*** Roland Kibbee; ***C:*** Robert Burks; ***M:*** Max Steiner.

Desert Steel 1/2 **1994 (PG)** Rival racers risk their lives in the big off-road race. **89m/C VHS.** David Naughton, Brian Skinner, Amanda Wyss, Russ Tamblyn; ***D:*** Glenn Gebhard.

Desert Thunder **1999 (R)** Lee Miller (Baldwin) is a retired Air Force pilot who rejoins the action when he's called to lead a commando mission to defeat an Iraqi terrorist threat. Low-budget still boasts some good explosions and aerial scenes. **88m/C VHS, DVD.** Daniel Baldwin, Richard Tyson, Richard Portnow, Stacy Haiduk; ***D:*** Jim Wynorski; ***W:*** Lenny Juliano. **VIDEO**

Desert Trail 1/2 **1935** Wayne is a championship rodeo rider accused of bank robbery. **57m/B VHS, DVD.** John Wayne, Paul Fix, Mary Kornman; ***D:*** Robert North Bradbury; ***W:*** Lindsley Parsons; ***C:*** Archie Stout.

Desert Warrior **1988 (PG-13)** Earth becomes a waste site after a nuclear war. Ferrigno stars as a post-nuke hero in this low-budget action film. Very bad acting. **89m/C VHS.** Lou Ferrigno, Shari Shattuck, Kenneth Peer, Anthony East; ***D:*** Jim Goldman; ***W:*** Frederick Bailey.

Desert Winds **1995** Weird little fantastical romance finds Jackie (Graham), who lives near the New Mexican desert, regularly communing with nature on a rocky plateau. Lonely Jackie once heard the voice of Eugene (Nickles), who lives 500 miles away in Arizona, thanks to a rare phenomenon known as a wind tunnel, but it takes seven years before she hears his voice again. **97m/C VHS, DVD.** Heather Graham, Michael A. (M.A.) Nickles, Grace Zabriskie, Jack Kehler, Adam Ant; ***D:*** Michael A. (M.A.) Nickles; ***W:*** Michael A. (M.A.) Nickles; ***C:*** Denis Maloney; ***M:*** James McVay.

The Deserters 1/2 **1983** Sergeant Hawley, a Vietnam-era hawk, hunts deserters and draft-dodgers in Canada. There, he confronts issues of war and peace head-on. **110m/C VHS.** *CA* Alan Scarfe, Dermot Hennelly, Jon Bryden, Barbara March; ***D:*** Jack Darcus; ***W:*** Jack Darcus; ***C:*** Tony Westman; ***M:*** Michael Conway Baker.

The Designated Mourner 1/2 **1997 (R)** Adapted from the play by Wallace Shawn, this pointy-headed inaction movie laments the passing of the class of people who "appreciate the poetry of John Donne" and other forms of high art. It's probably the same class that would like this movie. Set in an unnamed politically repressive country that resembles a large table, Nichols plays the eponymous mourner Jack, a journalist who once ran with a literary crowd but betrayed their ideals for survival. Richardson plays his wife Judy, the daughter of final talking head Howard (de Keyser), who is a humanist poet who doesn't like people. If you need a lecture on culture written by a man who was in "Mom and Dad Save the World" and played the geeky social studies teacher in "Clueless," then this is your movie. To quote Shawn: "Inconceivable!" **94m/C VHS, DVD.** *GB* Mike Nichols, Miranda Richardson, David de Keyser; ***D:*** David Hare; ***W:*** Wallace Shawn; ***C:*** Oliver Stapleton; ***M:*** Richard Hartley.

Designing Woman **1957** Bacall and Peck star in this mismatched tale of romance. She's a chic high-fashion designer, he's a rumpled sports writer. The fun begins when they try to adjust to married life together. Neither likes the other's friends or lifestyle. Things get even crazier when Bacall has to work with her ex-lover Helmore on a fashion show and Peck's former love Gray shows up as well. And as if that weren't enough, Peck is being hunted by the mob because of a boxing story he's written. It's a fun, quick, witty tale that is all entertainment and no message. Bacall's performance is of note because Bogart was dying of cancer at the time. **118m/C VHS, DVD.** Gregory Peck, Lauren Bacall, Dolores Gray, Sam Levene, Tom Helmore, Mickey Shaughnessy, Jesse White, Chuck Connors, Edward Platt, Alvy Moore, Jack Cole; ***D:*** Vincente Minnelli; ***W:*** George Wells; ***C:*** John Alton; ***M:*** Andre Previn. Oscars '57: Story & Screenplay.

Desire **1936** Jewel thief Madeleine (Dietrich) manages to involve innocent tourist Tom (Cooper) into carrying her ill-gotten goods across the Spanish border. Then she entices him into joining her at the country estate of her partner-in-crime. By this time Tom is in love—and so is Madeleine but she doesn't think she's good enough for him. Lots of lying until the twosome can figure out what to do. Cooper manages to hold his own with the sophisticated Dietrich in their second film together (after "Morocco"). **96m/B VHS.** Marlene Dietrich, Gary Cooper, John Halliday, William Frawley, Ernest Cossart, Akim Tamiroff, Alan Mowbray; ***D:*** Frank Borzage; ***W:*** Edwin Justus Mayer, Waldemar Young; ***M:*** Frederick "Friedrich" Hollander.

Desire **1993 (R)** A free-spirited woman finds herself attracted to a local fisherman. Hardly her intellectual equal but then what she really wants is his body. **108m/C VHS, DVD.** Greta Scacchi, Vincent D'Onofrio; ***D:*** Andrew Birkin.

Desire **1995 (R)** Security consultant Lauren Allen (Hodge) is working for a perfume manufacturer whose fragrance, Desire, is the fave of a Beverly Hills serial killer who likes to douse his victims in the scent. The prime suspect is scent expert Gordon Lewis (Kemp) and naturally Lauren falls for him. Standard erotic thriller fare. **90m/C VHS.** Kate Hodge, Martin Kemp, Deborah Shelton, Robert Miranda; ***D:*** Rodney McDonald; ***W:*** Rodney McDonald.

Desire and Hell at Sunset Motel 1/2 **1992 (PG-13)** Low-budget thriller takes place at the Sunset Motel in 1950s Anaheim. Fenn is the bombshell wife of a toy salesman who's in town for a sales meeting, while she just wants to visit Disneyland. She's soon fooling around with another guy and her husband hires a psychotic criminal to spy on her as her new lover plots to kill hubby. Very confusing plot isn't worth figuring out. Film's only redeeming quality is the imaginative and creative work used in the visuals. Castle's directorial debut. **90m/C VHS, DVD.** Sherilyn Fenn, Whip Hubley, David Hewlett, David Johansen, Paul Bartel, Kenneth Tobey; ***D:*** Alien Castle; ***W:*** Alien Castle; ***C:*** Jamie Thompson.

Desire Under the Elms 1/2 **1958** Ives, the patriarch of an 1840s New England farming family, takes a young wife (Loren) who promptly has an affair with her stepson. Loren's American film debut. Based on the play by Eugene O'Neill. **114m/B VHS, DVD.** Sophia Loren, Anthony Perkins, Burl Ives, Frank Overton; ***D:*** Delbert Mann; ***C:*** Daniel F. Fapp; ***M:*** Elmer Bernstein.

Desiree 1/2 **1954** A romanticized historical epic about Napoleon and his 17-year-old mistress, Desiree. Based on the novel by Annemarie Selinko. Slightly better than average historical fiction piece. **110m/C** Charlotte Austin, Marlon Brando, Jean Simmons, Merle Oberon, Michael Rennie, Cameron Mitchell, Elizabeth Sellars, Cathleen Nesbitt; ***D:*** Henry Koster; ***W:*** Daniel Taradash; ***C:*** Milton Krasner; ***M:*** Alex North.

Desk Set *His Other Woman* **1957** One of the later and less dynamic Tracy/Hepburn comedies, about an efficiency expert who installs a giant computer in an effort to update a TV network's female-run reference department. Still, the duo sparkle as they bicker, battle, and give in to love. Based on William Marchant's play. **103m/C VHS, DVD.** Spencer Tracy, Katharine Hepburn, Joan Blondell, Gig Young, Dina Merrill, Neva Patterson, Harry Ellerbe, Nicholas Joy, Diane Jergens, Merry Anders; ***D:*** Walter Lang; ***W:*** Phoebe Ephron, Henry Ephron; ***C:*** Leon Shamroy; ***M:*** Cyril Mockridge.

Desolation Angels **1995** Nick Adams (Rodrick) returns to New York after a month spent unhappily visiting his mother and discovers his girlfriend Mary (Thomas) has been raped by his best friend Sid (Bassett). At least that's how Nick interprets the situation after an unwilling Mary admits they had sex. Nick goes after Sid, gets beaten up, hires a couple of thugs who botch a retaliation, and just gets increasingly enraged over his inability to settle the situation. The focus is on Nick and Rodrick is more than up to the director McCann's demands. **90m/C VHS, DVD.** Michael Rodrick, Peter Bassett, Jennifer Thomas; ***D:*** Tim McCann; ***W:*** Tim McCann; ***C:*** Matt Howe.

Despair *Eine Reise ins Licht* **1978** A chilling and comic study of a victimized chocolate factory owner's descent into madness, set against the backdrop of the Nazi rise to power in the 1930s. Adapted from the Nabokov novel by Tom Stoppard. **120m/C VHS.** *GE* Dirk Bogarde, Andrea Ferreol, Volker Spengler, Klaus Lowitsch; ***D:*** Rainer Werner Fassbinder; ***W:*** Tom Stoppard; ***C:*** Michael Ballhaus; ***M:*** Peer Raben.

Desperado *El Mariachi 2* **1995 (R)** Rodriguez's nameless guitar player-turned-gunman returns—this time in the persona of heartthrob Banderas. The director also has a studio budget to play with (a sizable increase over the $7000 for "El Mariachi"), so the action's on a bigger, more violent scale (you'll quickly lose count of flying bodies and bullets) as El Mariachi tracks infamous drug lord Bucho (de Almeida). Gringo Buscemi provides assistance, beautiful bookstore owner Carolina (Hayek) offers solace, and Tarantino meets his well-deserved cameo demise. You'll also find original Mariachi, Gallardo, in a cameo role as a musician/gunslinger amigo of the hero. Filmed in Mexico. **103m/C VHS, DVD.** Antonio Banderas, Salma Hayek, Joaquim de Almeida, Steve Buscemi, Richard "Cheech" Marin, Carlos Gomez; ***Cameos:*** Quentin Tarantino, Carlos Gallardo; ***D:*** Robert Rodriguez; ***W:*** Robert Rodriguez; ***C:*** Guillermo Navarro; ***M:*** Los Lobos.

The Desperadoes 1/2 **1943** Cheyenne Rogers (Ford) is a gunman trying to go straight. So he heads into the town of Red Valley, Utah, to see old pal-turned-sheriff Steve Upton (Scott). Unfortunately for Cheyenne, this is just after the town's bank has been robbed in a crooked scheme set up by a couple of sharpies (Hall, Buchanan) and he is framed for the crime. Now it's up to Cheyenne, Steve, and a couple of wild west gals (Trevor, Keyes) to prove his innocence. Set in 1863; adapted from a story by Max Brand. Columbia's first Technicolor film. **86m/C DVD.** Glenn Ford, Randolph Scott, Claire Trevor, Evelyn Keyes, Edgar Buchanan, Porter Hall, Guinn "Big Boy" Williams, Raymond Walburn; ***D:*** Charles Vidor; ***W:*** Robert Carson; ***C:*** George Meehan Jr.; ***M:*** John Leipold.

Desperados 1/2 **1969 (PG)** After the Civil War, a murderous renegade and two of his sons go on a looting rampage, eventually kidnapping the child of the third son who just wants to live in peace. Made in Spain. **90m/C VHS.** *SP* Jack Palance, Vince Edwards, Christian Roberts, George Maharis, Neville Brand, Sylvia Syms; ***D:*** Henry Levin; ***W:*** Walter Brough; ***C:*** Sam Leavitt.

The Desperados 1/2 *Apache Vengeance; Five Savage Men* **1970** When a young woman is raped by outlaws robbing her stagecoach, a bevy of western heroes band together to avenge her. **86m/C VHS, DVD.** Keenan Wynn, Henry Silva, Michele Carey, John Anderson, Joe Turkel; ***D:*** Ron Joy; ***W:*** Richard Bakalyan; ***M:*** Rupert Holmes.

Desperate 1/2 **1947** An honest truck driver witnesses a mob crime and must escape with his wife in this minor film noir. Eventually, the law is on his tail, too. **73m/B VHS.** Steve Brodie, Audrey Long, Raymond Burr, Jason Robards Sr., Douglas Fowley, William Challee, Ilka Gruning, Nan Leslie; ***D:*** Anthony Manh.

Desperate Cargo 1/2 **1941** Two showgirls stranded in a Latin American town manage to get aboard a clipper ship with hoodlums who are trying to steal the vessel's cargo. **69m/B VHS, DVD.** Ralph Byrd, Carol Hughes, Jack Mulhall; ***D:*** William Beaudine; ***W:*** Morgan Cox, John T. Coyle; ***C:*** Jack Greenhalgh.

Desperate Characters **1971 (R)** A slice-of-city-life story about a middle-class couple living in a once-fashionable section of Brooklyn, New York, who watch their neighborhood disintegrate around them. Their marriage on remote control, the two find their lives a series of small disappointments, routine work, uncertain friendships, and pervasive violence. Excellent performances, especially by MacLaine as the harried wife, but the film's depressing nature made it a complete boxoffice flop. **87m/C VHS.** Shirley MacLaine, Kenneth Mars, Gerald S. O'Loughlin, Sada Thompson, Michael Higgins, Rose Gregorio, Jack Somack, Chris Gampel, Mary Alan Hokanson, Patrick McVey, Carol Kane; ***D:*** Frank D. Gilroy; ***W:*** Frank D. Gilroy.

Desperate Crimes *Mafia Docks* **1993** Two rival mobs battle over the prostitution and drug trade. When an innocent woman is murdered her brother looks for revenge with the help of a beautiful prostitute. **92m/C VHS, DVD.** Traci Lords, Denise Crosby, Franco (Columbo) Columbu, Van Quattro, Rena Niehaus, Nicoletta Boris, Elizabeth Kaitan, Randi Ingerman; ***D:*** Andreas Marfori; ***W:*** Andreas Marfori; ***C:*** Marco Isoli.

Desperate Hours **1955** A tough, gritty thriller about three escaped convicts taking over a suburban home and holding the family hostage. Plenty of suspense and fine acting. Based on the novel and play by Joseph Hayes. **112m/B VHS, DVD.** Humphrey Bogart, Fredric March, Martha Scott, Arthur Kennedy, Gig Young, Dewey Martin, Mary Murphy, Robert Middleton, Richard Eyer, Ray Collins, Beverly Garland; ***D:*** William Wyler; ***C:*** Lee Garmes. Natl. Bd. of Review '55: Director (Wyler).

Desperate Hours **1990 (R)** An escaped prisoner holes up in a suburban couple's home, waiting for his lawyer/accomplice to take him to Mexico. Tensions heighten between the separated couple and the increasingly nerve-wracked criminals. Terrific, if not downright horrifying, performance by Rourke in an overall tepid remake of the 1955 thriller. **105m/C VHS, DVD.** Mickey Rourke, Anthony Hopkins, Mimi Rogers, Kelly Lynch, Lindsay Crouse, Elias Koteas, David Morse, Shawnee Smith, Danny Gerard, Matt McGrath; ***D:*** Michael Cimino; ***W:*** Mark Rosenthal, Larry Konner, Joseph Hayes; ***C:*** Doug Milsome; ***M:*** David Mansfield.

Desperate Journey 1/2 **1942** Flynn and Reagan are two of five Allied fighters shot down over Nazi occupied Poland. They go through various tight squeezes such as stealing Goering's car in Berlin, and eliminating a few Nazis at a chemical factory to get back to the safety of England. All the while they are hunted by Massey as Nazi Major Otto Baumester, who of course bumbles and fumbles the whole affair. Strictly propaganda intended to keep up morale on the homefront. Flynn was not pleased about having Reagan as his co-star, seeing as he was usually paired with female leads. **108m/B VHS.** Errol Flynn, Ronald Reagan, Raymond Massey, Nancy Coleman, Alan Hale, Arthur Kennedy, Helmut Dantine; ***D:*** Raoul Walsh; ***M:*** Max Steiner.

Desperate Lives **1982** High school siblings come into contact with drugs and join their guidance counselor in the war against dope. Average made for TV fare. **100m/C VHS.** Diana Scarwid, Doug McKeon, Helen Hunt, William Windom, Art Hindle, Tom Atkins, Sam Bottoms, Diane Ladd, Dr. Joyce Brothers; ***D:*** Robert Lewis; ***M:*** Bruce Broughton. **TV**

Desperate Living 1/2 **1977** Typical John Waters trash. A mental patient (Stole) is released and becomes paranoid that her family may be out to kill her. After aiding in the murder of her husband (the hefty maid, Hill, suffocates him by sitting on him), Stole and Hill escape to Mortville, a town populated by outcasts such as transsexuals, murderers, and the woefully disfigured. **90m/C VHS, DVD.** Mink Stole, Jean Hill, Edith Massey, Liz Renay, Mary Vivian Pearce, Cookie Mueller, Susan Lowe, Ed Peranio, Pat Moran, George Stover, Turkey Joe, Channing Wilroy; ***D:*** John Waters; ***W:*** John Waters; ***C:*** Thomas Loizeaux.

Desperate Measures 1/2 **1998 (R)** Police officer Frank Connor (Garcia) desperately searches for a bone marrow donor for his dying son. Turns out the perfect match is vicious murderer and prison inmate Pete McCabe (Keaton). McCabe seizes the opportunity to unleash an elaborate and violent prison escape in a San Francisco hospital. Keaton, as a poor man's Hannibal Lecter, offers this movie's only entertainment. If not for the dying child to propel its already ludicrious story along, it would be a great source for slapstick comedy. Film was held back for several months before its final release and you'll find out why the studio wanted to hide this one. **100m/C VHS, DVD.** Andy Garcia, Michael Keaton, Marcia Gay Harden, Brian Cox, Efrain Figueroa, Joseph Cross, Richard Riehle; *D:* Barbet Schroeder; *W:* Henry Bean, Neal Jimenez, David Klass; *C:* Luciano Tovoli; *M:* Trevor Jones.

The Desperate Mission **1960** Joaquin Murietta (Montelban) is a Mexican nobleman acting as a Robin Hood for those oppressed by corrupt authorities in gold-rushed 1840s California, along with his outlaw sidekick Three-Fingered Jack. Action scenes are well staged and direction is tight making for a greatly satisfying western. **96m/C VHS.** Ricardo Montalban, Slim Pickens, Roosevelt "Rosie" Grier, Earl Holliman; *D:* Earl Bellamy; *W:* Rick Collins, Jack Guss. **VIDEO**

Desperate Motives *Distant Cousins* **1992 (R)** Keith and his fiancee Helgenberger are a charming couple who arrive to stay with Keith's distant cousin (Katt) and his family. Only what the family doesn't realize is that the duo have escaped from an asylum for the criminally insane and want to take over their lives. **92m/C VHS.** Edward (Eddie) Bunker, David Keith, Marg Helgenberger, William Katt, Mel Harris, Mary Crosby, Brian Bonsall, Cyndi Pass; *D:* Andrew Lane; *W:* C. Courtney Joyner.

Desperate Moves **1986** An Oregon-transplanted geek in San Francisco sets out to make himself over in order to win his dream girl. Sometimes effective, often sappy treatment of his coming to terms with the big city. **90m/C VHS.** Isabel Sanford, Steve Tracy, Paul Benedict, Christopher Lee, Eddie Deezen; *D:* Ovidio G. Assonitis.

Desperate Prey 1/2 *Redheads* **1994 (R)** Lucy (Karvan) videotapes herself having sex with lawyer Brewster (Hembrow) and then accidentally films his murder. So she's stalked by the killer. **102m/C VHS.** *AU* Claudia Karvan, Catherine McClements, Mark Hembrow; *D:* Danny Vendramini; *W:* Danny Vendramini.

Desperate Remedies **1993 (R)** Enjoyment will rest on the viewer's appreciation of campy melodrama. In a Victorian-era New Zealand town, regal shop owner Dorothea Brook (Ward-Lealand) is trying to find a husband for her difficult younger sister Rose (Mills)—who happens to be pregnant and a drug addict. She spots handsome sailor Lawrence (Smith) and decides he'll do but Lawrence is instantly smitten with Dorothea (who's also having heart palpitations over the hunk). Unfortunately, her current lover is Anne (Chappell) and Dorothea has also decided on a marriage of convenience with ambitious politician William (Hurst). It's all very operatic. **92m/C VHS.** *NZ* Jennifer Ward-Lealand, Kevin Smith, Lisa Chappell, Michael Hurst, Kiri Mills, Clifford Curtis; *D:* Stewart Main, Peter Wells; *W:* Stewart Main, Peter Wells; *C:* Leon Narbey; *M:* Peter Scholes.

Desperate Target 1/2 **1980** Courageous people fight against all odds to survive. **90m/C VHS.** Chris Mitchum, Victoria Loveland; *D:* George Vieira; *C:* Jack Beckett.

The Desperate Trail 1/2 **1994 (R)** Prostitute, convicted of killing an abusive client, manages to escape from the marshal who's escorting her to her hanging. She teams up with a con man in a plot to rob a bank while the marshal enlists a posse to track her down. Strong performances augmented by blazing guns, hobbled by weak writing. **93m/C VHS, DVD.** Sam Elliott, Linda Fiorentino, Craig Sheffer, Frank Whaley; *D:* P.J. Pesce; *W:* P.J. Pesce, Tom Abrams; *C:* Michael Bonvillain; *M:* Stephen Endelman. **CABLE**

Desperate Women 1/2 **1978** Western about three unjustly accused female convicts rescued en route to prison by an ex-hired gun. **98m/C VHS.** Susan St. James, Dan Haggerty, Ronee Blakley, Ann Dusenberry, Susan Myers; *D:* Earl Bellamy. **TV**

Desperately Seeking Susan **1985 (PG-13)** Roberta (Arquette) is a bored New Jersey housewife who gets her kicks reading the personals. When she becomes obsessed with a relationship between two lovers who arrange their meetings through the columns, Roberta decides to find out for herself who they are. But after an accident, Robert loses her memory and thinks she is Susan, the free-spirited woman in the personals. Unfortunately, Susan (Madonna) is in a lot of trouble with all sorts of unsavory folk and our innocent housewife finds herself caught in the middle. Terrific characters, with special appeal generated by Arquette and Madonna. Quinn winningly plays Roberta's bewildered romantic interest, Dez. **104m/C VHS, DVD.** Rosanna Arquette, Madonna, Aidan Quinn, Mark Blum, Robert Joy, Laurie Metcalf, Steven Wright, John Turturro, Will Patton, Richard Hell, Annie Golden, Ann Magnuson, Richard Edson; *D:* Susan Seidelman; *W:* Leora Barish; *C:* Edward Lachman; *M:* Thomas Newman. British Acad. '85: Support. Actress (Arquette); Natl. Bd. of Review '85: Support. Actress (Arquette).

Despicable Me **2010** The one black house in a pretty suburban neighborhood has a hideout where evil Gru (voiced by Carrell) is planning to steal the moon. But the villain meets his match in orphans Margo, Edith, and Agnes who think Gru should become their new dad. **m/C DVD.** *US D:* Chris Renaud, Pierre Coffin; *W:* Ken Daurio, Cinco Paul; *V:* Steve Carell, Jason Segel, Miranda Cosgrove, Russell Brand, Elsie Fisher, Dana Gaier, Will Arnett, Danny McBride, Julie Andrews, Jemaine Clement, Kristen Wiig, Jack McBrayer, Mindy Kaling, Ken Jeong.

Destination Moon 1/2 **1950** Story of man's first lunar voyage contains Chesley Bonstell's astronomical artwork and a famous Woody Woodpecker cartoon. Includes previews of coming attractions from classic science fiction films. **91m/C VHS, DVD.** Warner Anderson, Tom Powers, Dick Wesson, Erin O'Brien-Moore; *D:* Irving Pichel; *W:* Alford "Rip" Van Ronkel, Robert Heinlein, James O'Hanlon; *C:* Lionel Lindon; *M:* Leith Stevens.

Destination Moonbase Alpha *Space: 2100* **1975** In the 21st century, an explosion has destroyed half the moon, causing it to break away from the Earth's orbit. The moon is cast far away, but the 311 people manning Alpha, a research station on the moon, must continue their search for other life forms in outer space. A thankless task. Pilot for the TV series "Space: 1999." **93m/C VHS.** *GB* Martin Landau, Barbara Bain, Barry Morse, Nick (Nicholas) Tate; *D:* Tom Clegg; *W:* Terence Feely; *M:* Derek Wadsworth. **TV**

Destination Saturn *Buck Rogers* **1939** Buck Rogers awakens from suspended animation in the 25th century. **90m/B VHS, DVD.** Buster Crabbe, Constance Moore; *D:* Ford Beebe.

Destination Tokyo **1943** A weathered WWII submarine actioner, dealing with the search-and-destroy mission of a U.S. sub sent into Tokyo harbor. Available in a colorized version. **135m/B VHS, DVD.** Cary Grant, John Garfield, Alan Hale, Dane Clark, John Ridgely, Warner Anderson, William Prince, Robert Hutton, Tom Tully, Peter Whitney, Faye Emerson, John Forsythe; *D:* Delmer Daves.

Destination Vegas **1995 (R)** Attorney Sommerfield is on the lam, driving across the Mojave trying to elude hitmen sent to prevent her testimony in a murder trial. She hooks up with drifter Duhamel, who just happens to be an ex-getaway driver, and it's put the pedal to the metal time. Low-budget familiar story with some saving humor. **78m/C VHS, DVD.** Jennifer Sommerfield, Claude Duhamel, Stephen Polk, Richard Lynch; *D:* Paul Wynne; *W:* Paul Wynne; *C:* William H. Molina; *M:* Peter Tomashek. **VIDEO**

Destiny *Der Mude Tod* **1921** Fritz Lang's silent fantasy is a version of the myth of Orpheus. Death takes a young man on the eve of his wedding, but agrees to return him if his fiancee can save three lives. In terms of style, it's really closer to Dreyer's "Vampyr" than to Lang's own "M." **99m/B VHS, DVD.** *GE* Lil Dagover, Rudolf Klein-Rogge, Bernhard Goetzke, Walther Jansson, Eduard von Winterstein, Paul Biensfieldt; *D:* Fritz Lang; *W:* Thea von Harbou; *C:* Fritz Arno Wagner, Erich Nitzschmann, Hermann Saalfrank.

Destiny *Al-Massir* **1997** Averroes (el-Cherif) is a 12th century Arab humanist philosopher living in Andalusia, Spain. When one of his disciples is burned at the stake for heresy, the man's son Youssef (Rahouma), following his father's wishes, travels to Andalusia to study with Averroes. Youssef finds that the ruling Caliph (Memida) supports Averroes but a fundamentalist Muslim cult hopes to overthrow the Caliph and destroy Averroes and his students. Arabic with subtitles. **135m/C VHS, DVD.** *EG* Nour (el-Sherif) el-Cherif, Fares Rahouma, Mahmoud Hemeida, Khaled el-Nabaoui, Laila Eloui; *D:* Youssef Chahine; *W:* Youssef Chahine, Khaled Youssef.

The Destiny of Marty Fine **1996** Lame low-budget drama about washed-up boxer Marty Fine (Gelfant), who witnesses the murder of mob boss Capelli (Ironside). He promises old-time gangster Daryl (Fell) he'll keep quiet but Daryl orders a hit anyway. So lowlife Marty tries to get out of L.A. **85m/B VHS.** Mark Ruffalo, Alan Gelfant, Norman Fell, James LeGros, Catherine Keener, Michael Ironside, Glenn Plummer, John Diehl, Sandra Seacat; *D:* Michael Hacker; *W:* Mark Ruffalo, Michael Hacker; *C:* Melinda Sue Gordon.

Destiny Turns on the Radio **1995 (R)** Mystic figure Johnny Destiny (Tarantino) dabbles in the lives of various stock characters in Las Vegas after emerging from a glowing swimming pool. Three years after this grand entrance, he enlists escaped con Julian and partner Thoreau (McDermott and Le Gros, respectively) to help him return to his place of origin. Julian has other plans, which involve getting his ex, Lucille (Travis), back from sleazy casino owner Tuerto (Belushi). Aggressively cheezy, dime novel dialogue and threadbare, convoluted plot wastes talents of interesting cast. Too much time and energy spent trying to be hip. Sadly, Tarantino's only participation was in front of the camera. **101m/C VHS.** Dylan McDermott, Nancy Travis, James LeGros, Quentin Tarantino, Allen (Goorwitz) Garfield, James Belushi, Tracey Walter, Bob(cat) Goldthwait, Richard Edson; *D:* Jack Baran; *W:* Robert Ramsey, Matthew Stone; *C:* James L. Carter; *M:* Steven Soles.

Destroy All Monsters 1/2 *Kaiju Soshingeki; All Monsters Attack; Operation Monsterland* **1968 (G)** When alien babes take control of Godzilla and his monstrous colleagues, it looks like all is lost for Earth. Adding insult to injury, Ghidra is sent in to take care of the loose ends. Can the planet possibly survive this madness? Classic Toho monster slugfest also features Mothra, Rodan, Son of Godzilla, Angila, Varan, Baragon, Spigas and others. **88m/C VHS, DVD.** *JP* Akira Kubo, Jun Tazaki, Yoshio Tsuchiya, Kyoko Ai, Yukiko Kobayashi, Kenji Sahara, Andrew Hughes, Yoshifumi Tajima, Nadao Kirino, Susumu Kurobe, Hisaya Ito; *D:* Inoshiro Honda; *W:* Inoshiro Honda, Takeshi Kimura; *C:* Taiichi Kankura; *M:* Akira Ifukube.

Destroy All Planets *Gamera Tai Viras; Gamera Tai Uchukaiju Bairasu; Gamera Vs. Viras; Gamera Vs. Outer Space Monster Viras* **1968** Aliens whose spaceships turn into giant flying squids are attacking Earth. It's up to Gammera, the flying, fire-breathing turtle to save the day. **75m/C VHS, DVD.** *JP* Peter Williams, Kojiro Hongo, Toru Takatsuka; *D:* Noriaki Yuasa.

Destroyer **1943** Trials and tribulations aboard a WWII destroyer result in tensions, but when the time comes for action, the men get the job done. **99m/B VHS.** Edward G. Robinson, Glenn Ford, Marguerite Chapman, Edgar Buchanan, Leo Gorcey, Regis Toomey, Edward Brophy, Larry Parks; *D:* William A. Seiter.

Destroyer **1988 (R)** Small-budget film crew goes to an empty prison to shoot, and are stalked by the ghost/zombie remains of a huge serial killer given the electric chair 18 months before. **94m/C VHS.** Anthony Perkins, Deborah Foreman, Lyle Alzado; *D:* Robert Kirk.

The Destructors *The Marseille Contract* **1974 (PG)** An American narcotics enforcement officer in Paris seeks the help of a hitman in order to catch a druglord. **89m/C VHS.** *GB* Anthony Quinn, Michael Caine, James Mason, Maureen Kerwin, Alexandra Stewart; *D:* Robert Parrish; *W:* Judd Bernard.

Destry Rides Again *Justice Rides Again* **1939** An uncontrollably lawless western town is whipped into shape by a peaceful, unarmed sheriff. A vintage Hollywood potpourri with Dietrich's finest post-Sternberg moment; standing on the bar singing "See What the Boys in the Back Room Will Have." The second of three versions of this Max Brand story. First was released in 1932; the third in 1954. **94m/B VHS, DVD.** James Stewart, Marlene Dietrich, Brian Donlevy, Charles Winninger, Mischa Auer, Irene Hervey, Una Merkel, Billy Gilbert, Jack Carson, Samuel S. Hinds, Allen Jenkins; *D:* George Marshall; *W:* Gertrude Purcell, Felix Jackson, Henry Myers; *C:* Hal Mohr; *M:* Frank Skinner. Natl. Film Reg. '96.

Details of a Duel: A Question of Honor 1/2 **1989** A butcher and a teacher collide in this comedy, and prodded by the church, militia and town officals, must duel before the entire town. In Spanish with English subtitles. **97m/C VHS.** *SP* Frank Ramirez, Florina Lemaitre, Vicky Hernandez, Humberto Dorado; *D:* Sergio Cabrera; *W:* Humberto Dorado; *C:* Jose Medeiros; *M:* Juan Marquez.

The Detective *Father Brown* **1954** Based on G.K. Chesterton's "Father Brown" detective stories, a slick, funny English mystery in which the famous priest tracks down a notorious, endlessly crafty antique thief. **91m/B VHS.** *GB* Alec Guinness, Peter Finch, Joan Greenwood, Cecil Parker, Bernard Lee; *D:* Robert Hamer; *W:* Maurice Rapf; *M:* Jerry Goldsmith.

The Detective **1968** A New York detective investigating the mutilation murder of a homosexual finds political and police department corruption. Fine, gritty performances prevail in this suspense thriller. Based on the novel by Roderick Thorpe. **114m/C VHS, DVD.** Frank Sinatra, Lee Remick, Ralph Meeker, Jacqueline Bisset, William Windom, Robert Duvall, Tony Musante, Jack Klugman, Al Freeman Jr., Horace McMahon, Lloyd Bochner, Pat Henry, Patrick McVey, "Sugar Ray" Robinson, Renee Taylor, Tom Atkins, George Plimpton; *D:* Gordon Douglas; *W:* Abby Mann; *C:* Joseph Biroc; *M:* Jerry Goldsmith.

Detective **1985** Style over substance as Godard has various characters/suspects investigating a murder committed in a Paris hotel two years previously. However, Godard seems more interested in the look than the plot. French with subtitles. **95m/C VHS.** *FR* Nathalie Baye, Claude Brasseur, Jean-Pierre Leaud, Johnny Hallyday, Laurent Terzieff, Alain Cuny; *D:* Jean-Luc Godard; *W:* Philippe Setbon, Alain Sarde; *C:* Bruno Nuytten.

Detective Sadie & Son *Sadie & Son* **1984** An elderly detective and her young son crack a case. **96m/C VHS.** Debbie Reynolds, Sam Wanamaker, Brian McNamara; *D:* John Llewellyn Moxey. **TV**

Detective School Dropouts *Dumb Dicks* **1985 (PG)** Since they couldn't pass detective school, are they smart enough to outwit a kidnapper? Find out and get a few laughs at the same time. **92m/C VHS.** Lorin Dreyfuss, David Landsberg, Christian de Sica, George Eastman; *D:* Filippo Ottoni.

Detective Story 1/2 **1951** Intense drama about a New York City police precinct with a wide array of characters led by a disillusioned and bitter detective (Douglas). Excellent casting is the strong point, as the film can be a bit dated. Based on Sydney Kingsley's Broadway play. **103m/B VHS, DVD.** Kirk Douglas, Eleanor Parker, Lee Grant, Horace McMahon, William Bendix, Craig Hill, Cathy O'Donnell, Bert Freed, George Macready, Joseph Wiseman, Gladys George, Frank Faylen, Warner Anderson, Gerald Mohr; *D:* William Wyler; *W:* Philip Yordan, Robert Wyler; *C:* Lee Garmes. Cannes '52: Actress (Grant).

Detention 1/2 **2003 (R)** Lungren is history teacher and ex-Special Forces soldier Decker, in charge of detention for a group of juvenile delinquents. The school is shut down by a group of drug dealers so they can use it to finish a heroin theft. Decker and the students must fight the bad guys in the usual hail of gunfire and explosions to regain control of the school. Cartoonish action flick isn't helped by the wooden presence of "The Dolphinator." **84m/C DVD.** *CA* Dolph Lundgren, Alex Karzis, Sidney J. Furie, John

Sheppard, Corey Sevier, Dov Tiefenbach, Chris Collins, Mpho Koaho, Larry Day, Danielle Hampton, Kata Dobo; *C:* Curtis Petersen; *M:* Amin Bhatia. **VIDEO**

Deterrence **2000 (R)** Stagy one-room thriller set during the presidential campaign of 2008. Veep Walter Emerson (Pollak) became prez when the incumbant died—now he's campaigning for re-election. He's at a Colorado primary when a blizzard forces Emerson and his aides (as well as a TV crew) to take shelter in a small town diner. The diner's cable TV hookup reports an international crisis—Iraq forces have invaded Kuwait and slaughtered American peacekeepers. So Emerson decides the thing to do is nuke Baghdad. Lots of pontificating. **101m/C VHS, DVD.** Kevin Pollak, Timothy Hutton, Sheryl Lee Ralph, Sean Astin, Clotilde Courau, Badja (Medu) Djola, Mark Thompson; *D:* Rod Lurie; *W:* Rod Lurie; *C:* Frank Perl; *M:* Lawrence Nash Groupe.

Detonator *Alistair MacLean's Death Train; Death Train* **1993 (R)** A renegade Russian general has stolen a nuclear bomb and is transporting it from Germany to Iraq via a hijacked train commandeered by his hired band of mercenaries. Stewart is the U.N. troubleshooter delegated to stop the plot, aided by a commando team featuring Brosnan and Paul. Based on the novel "Death Train" by Alistair MacLean. **98m/C VHS, DVD.** Pierce Brosnan, Patrick Stewart, Ted Levine, Alexandra Paul, Christopher Lee; *D:* David S. Jackson; *W:* David S. Jackson. **CABLE**

The Detonator 1/2 **2006 (R)** Yet another ho-hum actioner from Snipes. Homeland Security agent Sonni Griffith is involved in an arms deal that goes bad. After leaving too many dead bodies behind, Sonni is given a chance to redeem himself by escorting witness Nadia (Colloca) to New York. Except the arms dealer just happens to be after Nadia and some traitor in the CIA is providing him with intel. **96m/C DVD.** Wesley Snipes, Silvia Colloca, Michael Brandon, Matthew Leitch, William Hope; *D:* Po Chih Leong; *W:* Martin Wheeler; *C:* Richard Greatrex; *M:* Barry Taylor. **VIDEO**

Detonator 2: Night Watch 1/2 *Alistair MacLean's Night Watch; Night Watch* **1995 (R)** Brosnan and Paul return as operatives for the secret United Nations Anti-Crime Organization (UNACO). Mike Graham and Sabrina Carver are teamed by their boss Nick Caldwell (Devane) when it's discovered that Rembrandt's "Night Watch" has been replaced by a forgery. This takes our intrepid duo to Hong Kong, a shady computer expert/art collector (Shannon), and a suspicious satellite about to be launched by North Korea. Based on a story by Alistair MacLean. **99m/C VHS, DVD.** Pierce Brosnan, Alexandra Paul, William Devane, Michael J. Shannon, Lim Kay Siu, Irene Ng; *D:* David S. Jackson; *W:* David S. Jackson; *M:* John Scott. **CABLE**

Detour **1946** Considered to be the creme de la creme of "B" movies, a largely unacknowledged but cult-followed noir downer. Well-designed, stylish, and compelling, if a bit contrived and sometimes annoyingly shrill. Shot in only six days with six indoor sets. Down-on-his-luck pianist Neal hitches cross-country to rejoin his fiancee. His first wrong turn involves the accidental death of the man who picked him up, then he's en route to Destiny with a capital "D" when he picks up fatal femme Savage, as vicious a vixen as ever ruined a good man. Told in flashback, it's also been called the most despairing of all "B"-pictures. As noir as they get. **67m/B VHS, DVD.** Tom Neal, Ann Savage, Claudia Drake, Edmund MacDonald, Tim Ryan, Esther Howard, Don Brodie, Pat Gleason; *D:* Edgar G. Ulmer; *W:* Martin Goldsmith; *C:* Benjamin (Ben H.) Kline; *M:* Leo Erdody. Natl. Film Reg. '92.

Detour **1992 (R)** Remake of the 1945 noir classic even features Neal Jr. in the role that his dad made famous. He's the nightclub musician, hitching his way to Hollywood, who falls into big trouble thanks to fatale dame, Vera (Lavish). Not a patch on the original but not a complete waste of time either. **91m/B VHS.** Tom Neal Jr., Lea Lavish, Susanna Foster, Erin McGrane; *D:* Wade Williams; *W:* Wade Williams; *M:* Bill Crain. **VIDEO**

Detour **1999 (R)** Danny's (Fahey) in trouble with the mob when a $1 million robbery goes sour. So he high tails it to his rural hometown where one of his old friends (Madsen) is now the sheriff. But Danny still can't escape from his ex-partner (Russo) or the rest of the bad guys. Lots of action in a routine plot. **93m/C VHS.** Paul Sampson, Tim Thomerson, Evan Rachel Wood, Robert Miano, Stacie Randall, Darnell Williams, David Snedeker, Ellen Travolta, Jeff Fahey, Michael Madsen, James Russo, Gary Busey; *D:* Joey Travolta. **VIDEO**

Detour to Danger **WOOF!** **1945** Two young men set out on a fishing expedition and run into crooks and damsels in distress. Unintentionally hilarious "acting" by the no-name cast make this a grade-Z "B" movie. Of interest only because it was filmed in the three-color Kodachrome process used primarily in documentaries. **56m/C VHS.** Britt Wood, John Day, Nancy Brinckman; *D:* Richard Talmadge.

Detroit 9000 1/2 *Detroit Heat* **1973 (R)** A pair of Detroit policemen investigate a robbery that occurred at a black congressman's fundraising banquet. **106m/C VHS, DVD.** Alex Rocco, Scatman Crothers, Hari Rhodes, Lonette McKee, Herbert Jefferson Jr., Robert Phillips; *D:* Arthur Marks; *W:* Orville H. Hampton; *C:* Harry J. May; *M:* Luchi De Jesus.

Detroit Rock City **1999 (R)** It's 1978, and a group of dim Kiss fans will do anything to get into a sold-out Detroit concert. And non-Kiss fans should do anything to get out of watching this movie. Manages to be tasteless and humorless even when it's not obviously annoying. Co-producer Gene Simmons and the boys only perform the title song, so Kiss fans will be left searching their neighborhood for an Old Folks Kabuki Theater for a fix of the elderly in makeup. Director Rifkin re-created the 1978 Kiss Love Gun Show with the band performing in that haven of heavy metal: Hamilton, Ontario? **95m/C VHS, DVD.** Edward Furlong, Sam Huntington, Giuseppe Andrews, Lin Shaye, James DeBello, Natasha Lyonne, Gene Simmons, Paul Stanley, Ace Frehley, Peter Criss; *D:* Adam Rifkin; *W:* Carl DuPre; *C:* John R. Leonetti; *M:* J. Peter Robinson.

Deuce Bigalow: European Gigolo **WOOF!** **2005 (R)** Deuce returns to clear the name of his former pimp when he's accused of murder in Amsterdam. Crass, which is not unexpected, with some almost entertaining bits (but not nearly enough). **75m/C DVD, UMD.** *US* Rob Schneider, Eddie Griffin, Jeroen Krabbe, Til Schweiger, Hanna Verboom, Dana Min Goodman, Miranda Raison, Douglas Sills, Charles Keating, Carlos Ponce, Oded Fehr, Adam Sandler, Norm MacDonald, Fred Armisen; *D:* Mike Bigelow; *W:* Rob Schneider, David Garrett, Jason Ward; *C:* Marc Felperlaan; *M:* James L. Venable. Golden Raspberries '05: Worst Actor (Schneider).

Deuce Bigalow: Male Gigolo **1999 (R)** Schneider tries to enter the low-brow leading man territory now occupied by Adam Sandler (who exec produced) as Deuce Bigelow, a hapless tropical fish caretaker turned hapless gigolo. When Deuce is asked to nurse a stereotypically ethnic gigolo's fish to health, he proceeds to practically destroy his house and subsequently take over his "business" to pay for the repairs. With the help of pimp T.J. (Griffin), Deuce finds a clientele and the secret that the women want compassion, not sex. The gags (mostly of the tasteless, toilet humor variety) are very hit and miss, but they should play well to the intended audience of adolescent boys. **86m/C VHS, DVD.** Rob Schneider, William Forsythe, Eddie Griffin, Oded Fehr, Gail O'Grady, Richard Riehle, Jacqueline Obradors; *D:* Mike Mitchell; *W:* Rob Schneider, Harris Goldberg; *C:* Peter Lyons Collister; *M:* Teddy Castellucci.

Deuces Wild 1/2 **2002 (R)** Cliche piles upon cliche in this story of Brooklyn street gangs in the late '50s. The Deuces, led by Leon (Dorff) and his hot-headed younger brother Bobby (Renfro), and their rivals the Vipers, go to war over turf when Vipers leader Marco (Redus) is released from prison. Drug-dealing Marco was responsible for the heroin death of their older brother Sal, and the brothers want to keep their streets clean, which also puts them in conflict with local mobster Fritzy (Dillon) and his thugs. There's even a star-crossed romance since Bobby loves Vipers girl Annie (Balk). Director Kalvert did better with teens and drugs and violence in "The Basketball Diaries." **97m/C VHS, DVD.** *US* Stephen Dorff, Brad Renfro, Norman Reedus, Fairuza Balk, Max Perlich, Matt Dillon, Drea De Matteo, Frankie Muniz, Vincent Pastore, Balthazar Getty, James Franco, Louis Lombardi, Deborah Harry, Johnny Knoxville, Paul Sampson; *D:* Scott Kalvert; *W:* Paul Kimatian, Christopher Gambale; *C:* John A. Alonzo; *M:* Stewart Copeland.

Deutschland im Jahre Null 1/2 **1947** The acclaimed, unsettling vision of post-war Germany as seen through the eyes of a disturbed boy who eventually kills himself. Lyrical and grim, in German with subtitles. **75m/B VHS.** *GE* Franz Gruber; *D:* Roberto Rossellini.

Devastator *Kings Ransom; The Destroyers* **1985 (R)** A Vietnam vet exacts violent revenge on the murderer of an old army buddy. **79m/C VHS.** Richard (Rick) Hill, Katt Shea, Crofton Hardester; *D:* Cirio H. Santiago.

Devdas **1955** Third of at least six film versions of the novel by Saratchandra Chatterjee. Devdas (Dilip Kumar) and Parvati (Suchitra Sen) are childhood sweethearts, but his father disapproves and sends him to Calcutta. While he is away Parvati is arranged to marry a much older man. When Devdas learns of this upon returning he is crushed, and drowns his sorrows in alcohol, while the beautiful dancer who serves him tries to make him realize she is in love with him. **161m/C DVD.** *IN* Dilip Kumar, Vyjayanthimala, Motilal, Suchrita Sen, Nasir Hussain, Iftekhar, Shivraj, Mohan Choti; *D:* Bimal Roy; *W:* Rajinder Singh Bedi, Saratchandra Chatterjee, Nabendu Ghosh; *C:* Kamal Bose; *M:* Sachin Dev Burman.

Devdas **2002 (R)** Devdas (Sharukh Khan) is considered a slacker by his father, and sent to London to be educated (and to keep him away from his childhood sweetheart). Returning he asks to marry her, and his father rejects the idea, chiding him for trying to marry a woman of lower caste. Devdas retreats into a life of alcoholism and womanizing to forget the woman he loves, and to prevent himself from falling for another woman who has entered his life. **181m/C DVD.** *IN* Madhuri Dixit, Aishwarya Rai, Jackie Shroff, Kiron Kher, Sharulh Khan, Tiku Talsania, Dina Pathak, Smita Jaykar, Viyajendra Ghatge, Milind Gunaji, Ananya Khare, Manoj Joshi, Ava Mukherjee, Vijay Crishna, Muni Jha, Sunil Rege, Jaya Bhattacharya, Apara Mehta, Kapil Soni, Radhika Singh; *D:* Sanjay Leela Bhansali; *W:* Sanjay Leela Bhansali, Saratchandra Chatterjee, Prakash Kapadia; *C:* Vinod Pradhan; *M:* Ismail Darbar, Monty Sharma.

Devi 1/2 *The Goddess* **1960** A minor film in the Ray canon, it is, nonetheless, a strange and compelling tale of religious superstition. An Indian farmer becomes convinced that his beautiful daughter-in-law is the reincarnation of the goddess Kali. The girl is then pressured into accepting a worship that eventually drives her mad. In Bengali with English subtitles. **93m/B VHS.** *IN* Chhabi Biswas, Sharmila Tagore, Soumitra Chatterjee; *D:* Satyajit Ray; *W:* Satyajit Ray; *C:* Subrata Mitra; *M:* Ali Akbar Khan.

Devices and Desires *P.D. James: Devices & Desires* **1991** Typically complicated mystery adapted from the novel by P.D. James. Scotland Yard Commander Adam Dalgliesh (Marsden) is on holiday on the east coast of England where, of course, there's blackmail, murder, suicide, and trouble at a nearby nuclear power station for him to contend with. Made for TV; on six cassettes. **312m/C VHS.** *GB* Roy Marsden, Susannah York, Gemma Jones, James Faulkner, Tony Haygarth, Tom Georgeson, Tom Chadbon, Nicola Cowper, Suzan Crowley, Robert Hines, Harry Burton, Helena Michell; *D:* John Davies; *W:* Thomas Ellice. **TV**

The Devil and Daniel Johnston **2005 (PG-13)** Having lived in relative cult obscurity in the 1980s, singer/songwriter Daniel Johnston morphed into a quasi-celebrity in the early 1990s after Nirvana's Kurt Cobain wore a T-shirt promoting him. Director Feuerzeig's lively documentary follows Johnston from his teenage years—with material that Johnston captured himself on audio and videotape—to his rise to sort-of fame with some of his music being recorded by well-known acts such as Tom Waits and Pearl Jam. However, his life has been riddled with trouble caused by his manic depression. Tends to look mostly at the bright side of his talents and ignores those who contend that he is perhaps overrated. **110m/C DVD.** *US* *D:* Jeff Feuerzeig; *W:* Jeff Feuerzeig; *C:* Fortunato Procopio; *M:* Daniel Johnston.

The Devil & Daniel Webster 1/2 *All That Money Can Buy; Here Is a Man; A Certain Mr. Scratch* **1941** In 1840s New Hampshire, a young farmer, who sells his soul to the devil, is saved from a trip to Hell when Daniel Webster steps in to defend him. This classic fantasy is visually striking and contains wonderful performances. Adapted from the story by Stephen Vincent Benet who based it on Goethe's Faust. **106m/B VHS, DVD.** James Craig, Edward Arnold, Walter Huston, Simone Simon, Gene Lockhart, Jane Darwell, Anne Shirley, John Qualen, H.B. Warner; *D:* William Dieterle; *M:* Bernard Herrmann. Oscars '41: Orig. Dramatic Score.

Devil & Leroy Basset **1973 (PG)** Keema Gregwolf kills a deputy, breaks from jail with the Basset brothers, hijacks a church bus, kidnaps a family, and gets into other troublesome situations while on a posse-eluding cross-country adventure. **85m/C VHS.** Cody Bearpaw, John Goff, George "Buck" Flower; *D:* Robert E. Pearson; *M:* Les Baxter.

The Devil & Max Devlin 1/2 **1981 (PG)** Good cast wanders aimlessly in Disney family fantasy. The recently deceased Max Devlin strikes a bargain with the devil. He will be restored to life if he can convince three mortals to sell their souls. **95m/C VHS, DVD.** Elliott Gould, Bill Cosby, Susan Anspach, Adam Rich, Julie Budd, Sonny Shroyer, Helene Winston; *D:* Steven Hilliard Stern; *W:* Jimmy Sangster; *C:* Howard Schwartz; *M:* Marvin Hamlisch, Buddy (Norman Dale) Baker.

The Devil & Miss Jones 1/2 **1941** Engaging romantic comedy finds a big business boss posing as an ordinary salesclerk to weed out union organizers. He doesn't expect to encounter the wicked management or his beautiful co-worker, however. **90m/B VHS.** Jean Arthur, Robert Cummings, Charles Coburn, Edmund Gwenn, Spring Byington, William Demarest, S.Z. Sakall; *D:* Sam Wood; *C:* Harry Stradling Sr.

The Devil and the Deep 1/2 **1932** British submarine commander Sturm (Laughton), who's stationed on the North African coast, is insanely jealous of his bored wife Diana (Bankhead). When she's rescued from a mob by Lt. Sempter (Cooper), the two spend the night together and Sturm discovers her infidelity. Finally cracking, Sturm traps Diana aboard the sub with his crew before sinking the vessel but Diana isn't about to die. Laughton's Hollywood debut piles on the ham and cheese although his performance was praised at the time. **72m/B DVD.** Charles Laughton, Tallulah Bankhead, Gary Cooper, Cary Grant, Paul Porcasi, Henry Kolker, Juliette Compton, Arthur Hoyt; *D:* Marion Gering; *W:* Benn W. Levy; *C:* Charles B(ryant) Lang Jr.

The Devil at 4 O'Clock 1/2 **1961** An alcoholic missionary and three convicts work to save a colony of leper children from a South Seas volcano. Quality cast barely compensates for mediocre script. **126m/B VHS, DVD.** Spencer Tracy, Frank Sinatra, Kerwin Mathews, Jean-Pierre Aumont; *D:* Mervyn LeRoy; *C:* Joseph Biroc; *M:* George Duning.

The Devil Bat *Killer Bats* **1941** Madman Lugosi trains a swarm of monstrous blood-sucking bats to attack whenever they smell perfume. Followed by the sequel "Devil Bat's Daughter." DVD release is paired with the Lugosi vehicle "Scared to Death" (1946). **67m/B VHS, DVD.** Bela Lugosi, Dave O'Brien, Suzanne Kaaren, Yolande Donlan; *D:* Jean Yarbrough; *W:* John Thomas "Jack" Neville; *C:* Arthur Martinelli.

The Devil Bat's Daughter 1/2 **1946** A young woman, hoping to avoid becoming insane like her batty father, consults a psychiatrist when she starts to have violent nightmares. Unsuccessful sequel to "The Devil Bat." **66m/B VHS, DVD.** Rosemary La Planche, Michael Hale, John James, Molly Lamont; ***D:*** Frank Wisbar; ***W:*** Griffin Jay; ***C:*** James S. Brown Jr.

The Devil Came on Horseback 2007 Documentary showcasing the photographs and testimony of former U.S. Marine Captain Brian Steidle, who witnessed in person the genocide of Darfur. **85m/C DVD.**

Devil Diamond 🦴🦴 **1937** Mystery-suspense yarn about two amateur detectives who find themselves facing danger after tracking down a gang of evil jewel thieves. **61m/B VHS, DVD.** Kane Richmond, Frankie Darro, Joan Gale, Robert (Fisk) Fiske; ***D:*** Leslie Goodwins; ***W:*** Sherman Lowe; ***C:*** Jack Greenhalgh.

Devil Dog: The Hound of Hell 🦴 **1978** A family has trouble with man's best friend when they adopt a dog that is the son of the "Hound of Hell." **95m/C VHS, DVD.** Richard Crenna, Yvette Mimieux, Kim Richards, Victor Jory, Ike Eisenmann, Lou Frizzell, Ken Kercheval, R.G. Armstrong, Martine Beswick; ***D:*** Curtis Harrington; ***W:*** Elinor Karpf, Stephen Karpf; ***C:*** Gerald Perry Finnerman; ***M:*** Artie Kane. **TV**

Devil Dogs of the Air 🦴🦴 ½ **1935** Cagney and O'Brien team up in another air drama with Cagney once again the cocky pilot who, this time, joins the Marine Air Corp. O'Brien plays his flying idol (and later rival). Cagney finds all his wisecracking and luck are no match for knowledge and experience but he learns. Good stunt flying; shot on location at the San Diego naval air base. **85m/B VHS.** James Cagney, Pat O'Brien, Margaret Lindsay, Frank McHugh, Robert Barrat, Russell Hicks, Ward Bond; ***D:*** Lloyd Bacon.

Devil Doll 🦴🦴🦴 *The Witch of Timbuctoo* **1936** Paris banker Paul Lavond (Barrymore) is framed for robbery and murder by former associates and sent to Devil's Island prison where he hooks up with a scientist who's researching a method for reducing humans to mere inches. Levond engineers an escape from the island and returns to Paris were he sets about exacting his revenge on his betrayers. **80m/B VHS, DVD.** Lionel Barrymore, Maureen O'Sullivan, Frank Lawton, Rafaela (Rafael, Raphaella) Ottiano, Robert Greig, Lucy Beaumont; ***D:*** Tod Browning; ***W:*** Garrett Fort, Erich von Stroheim, Guy Endore, Abraham Merritt; ***C:*** Leonard Smith; ***M:*** Franz Waxman.

Devil Doll 🦴🦴 **1964** Ventriloquist's dummy, which contains the soul of a former performer, eyes a beautiful victim in the crowd. Newspaper guy senses trouble. Cut above the usual talking, stalking dummy story. **80m/B VHS, DVD.** *GB* Bryant Holiday, William Sylvester, Yvonne Romain, Sandra Dorne, Karel Stepanek, Francis De Wolff; ***D:*** Lindsay Shonteff; ***W:*** Lance Z. Hargreaves, George Barclay; ***C:*** Gerald Gibbs.

Devil Girl from Mars 🦴 ½ **1954** Sexy female from Mars and her very large robot arrive at a small Scottish inn to announce that a Martian feminist revolution has occurred. The distaff aliens then undertake a search of healthy Earth males for breeding purposes. Believe it or not, the humans don't want to go and therein lies the rub. A somewhat enjoyable space farce. **76m/B VHS, DVD.** *GB* Hugh McDermott, Hazel Court, Patricia Laffan, Peter Reynolds, Adrienne Corri, Joseph Tomelty, Sophie Stewart, John Laurie, Anthony Richmond; ***D:*** David MacDonald; ***W:*** John C. Mather, James Eastwood; ***C:*** Jack Cox; ***M:*** Edwin Astley.

Devil Horse 🦴🦴 **1932** A boy's devotion to a wild horse marked for destruction as a killer leads him into trouble. A serial in 12 chapters of 13 minutes each. **156m/B VHS.** Frankie Darro, Harry Carey Sr., Noah Beery Sr.; ***D:*** Otto Brower, Richard Talmadge.

Devil Hunter 🦴 ½ *Sexo canibal; The Gruesome Shock of the Devil; Mandingo Manhunter; The Man Hunter* **2008** A poor googly-eyed super cannibal with breathing problems has to deal with his home being invaded by brainless, tasty white women. Or a group of innocent girls on vacation is being stalked by a savage flesh eating monster. It's your call. Either way, the plot is secondary to Franco's fascination with certain female attributes. **89m/C DVD.** Al Cliver, Gisela Hahn, Werner Pochath, Antonio Mayans, Antonio de Cabo, Burt Altman, Melo Costa, Ursula Buchfellner; ***D:*** Jess (Jesus) Franco; ***W:*** Jess (Jesus) Franco, Julian Esteban; ***C:*** Juan Soler; ***M:*** Jess (Jesus) Franco. **VIDEO**

Devil in a Blue Dress 🦴🦴🦴 **1995 (R)** Down-on-his-luck Easy Rawlins (Washington) is an out of work aircraft worker in 1948 LA. He's hired to find mystery woman Daphne (Beals) by a shady businessman (Sizemore). What he finds are the usual noir staples: government corruption backed by thugs who want him to mind his own business. Easy and Daphne's torrid romance featured in the Walter Mosley novel is missing but the racism and violence are intact. Realism and accuracy in period detail enhance solid performance by Washington, though the deliberate, literary pace is at times lulling. Cheadle takes over whenever he shows up as Mouse, Rawlins' loyal friend and muscle. **102m/C VHS, DVD.** Nick(y) Corello, Denzel Washington, Jennifer Beals, Don Cheadle, Tom Sizemore, Maury Chaykin, Terry Kinney, Mel Winkler, Albert Hall, Renee Humphrey, Lisa Nicole Carson, John Roselius, Beau Starr; ***D:*** Carl Franklin; ***W:*** Carl Franklin; ***C:*** Tak Fujimoto; ***M:*** Elmer Bernstein. L.A. Film Critics '95: Support. Actor (Cheadle); Natl. Soc. Film Critics '95: Cinematog., Support. Actor (Cheadle).

The Devil in Silk 🦴🦴 ½ **1956** A composer marries a woman, not knowing that she is psychotically jealous. After she commits suicide, he must prove to the police that he did not kill her. Original dialogue in German. **102m/B VHS.** *GE* Lilli Palmer, Curt Jurgens, Winnie Markus; ***D:*** Rolf Hansen.

Devil in the Flesh 🦴🦴🦴 *Le Diable au Corps* **1946** Acclaimed drama about a French soldier's wife having a passionate affair with a high school student while her husband is away fighting in WWI. From the novel by Raymond Radiguet. Dubbed. Updated and remade in 1987. **112m/B VHS.** *FR* Gerard Philipe, Micheline Presle, Denise Grey; ***D:*** Claude Autant-Lara; ***W:*** Jean Aurenche, Pierre Bost; ***C:*** Michel Kelber; ***M:*** Rene Cloerec.

Devil in the Flesh 🦴🦴 *Il Diavolo in Corpo* **1987 (R)** A angst-ridden, semi-pretentious Italian drama about an obsessive older woman carrying on an affair with a schoolboy, despite her terrorist boyfriend and the objections of the lad's psychiatrist father, who had treated her. Famous for a graphic sex scene, available in the unrated version. Updated remake of the 1946 French film. Italian with subtitles. **110m/C VHS, DVD.** *IT* Riccardo De Torrebruna, Maruschka Detmers, Federico Pitzalis; ***D:*** Marco Bellocchio; ***W:*** Ennio de Concini, Enrico Palandri, Marco Bellocchio; ***C:*** Giuseppe Lanci; ***M:*** Carlo Crivelli.

Devil in the Flesh 🦴 ½ *Dearly Devoted* **1998 (R)** Troubled Debbie Strand (McGowan) has a crush on teacher Peter Rinaldi (McArthur) and no one is going to stop her getting what (or who) she wants. She tries blackmailing him when he doesn't respond and Peter learns Debbie has a very deadly past. **92m/C VHS, DVD.** Rose McGowan, Alex McArthur, Sherrie Rose, Phil Morris, Robert Silver; ***D:*** Steve Cohen. **VIDEO**

Devil in the Flesh 2 🦴🦴 ½ *Teacher's Pet* **2000 (R)** In this sequel to the '98 flick, disturbed Debbie (O'Keefe) escapes from the looney bin and causes the accidental death of the college coed who offers her a ride, so she assumes her identity. Passing herself off as wealthy Sydney Hollings, Debbie becomes infatuated with her writing prof Sam (Garcia), who's flattered by the attention. Except that anyone who gets in Debbie's way is permanently disposed of. Sly humor and O'Keefe is remarkably appealing considering she plays a psychopath. **90m/C VHS, DVD.** Jodi Lyn O'Keefe, Katherine Kendall, Jsu Garcia, Jeanette Brox, Bill Gratton, Todd McKee, Christiana Frank, Todd Robert Anderson; ***D:*** Marcus Spiegel; ***W:*** Richard Brandes; ***C:*** M. David Mullen. **VIDEO**

The Devil Is a Sissy 🦴🦴 ½ **1936** The 1930s three biggest juvenile stars are together in this melodrama. Upper-class English lad Claude (Bartholomew) is happy to live with his father for six months per his parents' divorce agreement. His wealthy mother doesn't feel the same since struggling dad lives in a New York slum area and Claude must attend public school. Claude has to prove himself to tough juvies Buck (Cooper) and Gig (Rooney) and everyone gets into lots of trouble before learning the lesson that crime doesn't pay. **91m/B DVD.** Freddie Bartholomew, Jackie Cooper, Mickey Rooney, Ian Hunter, Katherine Alexander, Peggy Conklin, Gene Lockhart, Jonathan Hale; ***D:*** Woodbridge S. Van Dyke; ***W:*** Richard Schayer, John Lee Mahin; ***C:*** Harold Rosson, George Schneiderman; ***M:*** Herbert Stothart.

The Devil Is a Woman 🦴🦴🦴 **1935** Dietrich vamps as money-hungry beauty Concha Perez, who soon has best friends and fellow military officers Pasqual (Atwill) and Antonio (Romero) dueling for her dubious affections. Turns out the man she desires may not be the man she truly needs. Flashbacks show how Concha seductively destroyed Pasquel some years earlier and how his jealousy lingered on. Based on the novel "The Woman and the Puppet" by Pierre Louys. After protests by the Spanish government over the depiction of the Spanish military, Paramount agreed to supress the film and few prints survived. **79m/B VHS.** Marlene Dietrich, Lionel Atwill, Cesar Romero, Edward Everett Horton, Alison Skipworth; ***D:*** Josef von Sternberg; ***W:*** John Dos Passos, S.K. Winston; ***C:*** Josef von Sternberg, Lucien Ballard.

Devil Monster 🦴 **1946** A world-weary traveler searches for a girl's fiance in the South Pacific, and is attacked by a large manta. **65m/B VHS.** Barry Norton, Blanche Mehaffey; ***D:*** S. Edwin Graham.

Devil of the Desert Against the Son of Hercules 🦴🦴 ½ **1962** The grandson of Zeus ventures into the wasteland to take on a feisty foe. **93m/C VHS, DVD.** *IT* Kirk Morris, Michele Girardon; ***D:*** Riccardo Freda.

Devil on Horseback 🦴🦴 **1954** A miner's son journeys to London to become a jockey in this comedy/drama. As he tries to bully his way into the racing circuit, he succeeds, but not in the way he anticipated. **88m/B VHS.** *GB* Googie Withers, John McCallum, Jeremy Spenser, Liam Redmond; ***D:*** Cyril Frankel; ***M:*** Malcolm Arnold.

The Devil on Wheels 🦴🦴 **1947** Inspired by his dad's reckless driving, a teenager becomes a hot rodder and causes a family tragedy. A rusty melodrama that can't be described as high-performance. **67m/B VHS, DVD.** James B. Cardwell, Noreen Nash, Darryl Hickman, Jan Ford, Damian O'Flynn, Lenita Love; ***D:*** Crane Wilbur; ***W:*** Crane Wilbur.

The Devil, Probably 🦴🦴 *Le Diable, Probablement* **1977** Ennui among Parisian youth, lost in their polluted, consumer society. Charles (Monnier) spins deeper into depression, despite the efforts of his friends, and finally makes a bargain with a junkie to shoot him in Pere Lachaise cemetery. French with subtitles. **95m/C VHS.** *FR* Antoine Monnier, Tina Irissari, Henri De Maublanc; ***D:*** Robert Bresson; ***W:*** Robert Bresson; ***C:*** Pasqualino De Santis; ***M:*** Philippe Sarde.

Devil Riders 🦴 ½ **1944** Unspectacular horse opera has a crooked lawyer trying to get his grubby hands on some choice land. Enter Crabbe to set things straight. **56m/B VHS.** Buster Crabbe, Al "Fuzzy" St. John, Patti McCarty, Charles "Blackie" King, John Merton, Kermit Maynard, Frank LaRue, Jack Ingram, George Chesebro, Edward Cassidy; ***D:*** Sam Newfield.

The Devil Rides Out 🦴🦴🦴 ½ *The Devil's Bride* **1968** Considered by many to be Hammer's finest achievement, though several other of the studio's films rate serious consideration. This one's a solid witchcraft tale written by Richard Matheson. In 1925, the Duc de Richleau (Lee), a "good" warlock, and the evil Mocata battle each other over De Richleau's friend Simon (Mower). Some of the effects are a little dated now, but director Terence Fisher builds suspense through a stately pace. Production values are highlighted by the usual excellent sets and a fleet of vintage cars. Lee's performance is one of his strongest in a conventionally heroic role. **95m/C DVD.** *GB* Christopher Lee, Charles Gray, Nike Arrighi, Leon Greene, Patrick Mower, Gwen Ffrangcon Davies, Sarah Lawson, Paul Eddington; ***D:*** Terence Fisher; ***W:*** Richard Matheson; ***C:*** Arthur Grant; ***M:*** James Bernard.

The Devil-Ship Pirates 🦴🦴 **1964** Hammer-produced swashbuckler stars Lee as Captain Robeles, a ruthless pirate fighting for Spain during the 1588 Armada. When his ship, the Diablo, is damaged, Robles docks it in a small English coastal village for repairs. The village is so isolated that most believe Robles when he says that Spain has defeated England and they are the new rulers. But not quite everyone is willing to accept the pirate's tale. **89m/C DVD.** *GB* Christopher Lee, John Cairney, Barry Warren, Andrew Keir, Duncan Lamont, Michael Ripper, Ernest Clark, Suzan Farmer, Philip Latham, Natasha Pyne; ***D:*** Don Sharp; ***W:*** Jimmy Sangster; ***C:*** Michael Reed; ***M:*** Gary Hughes.

The Devil Thumbs a Ride 🦴🦴🦴 **1947** A naive traveller picks up a hitchhiker, not knowing he's wanted for murder. Will history repeat itself in this interesting noir? **63m/B VHS.** Ted North, Lawrence Tierney, Nan Leslie; ***D:*** Felix Feist.

Devil Times Five 🦴 ½ *People Toys; The Horrible House on the Hill* **1974 (R)** To take revenge for being incarcerated in a mental hospital, five children methodically murder the adults who befriend them. **87m/C VHS, DVD.** Gene Evans, Sorrell Booke, Shelley Morrison; ***D:*** Sean McGregor.

The Devil Wears Prada 🦴🦴 ½ **2006 (PG-13)** This predictable plot (small town girl with big city dreams) gets an extra half-bone for Streep's sleek boss-from-hell. That would be Miranda Priestly, high priestess editor of the Manhattan fashion mag where wide-eyed Andy (Hathaway) is hired as a second assistant. A walking fashion faux pas, Andy slowly loses her ideals (and frumpy appearance) to the beguilement of power and designer trends. Can she be saved? Hathaway struggles to hold her own (she has the least showy role) against both Streep and the scene-stealing Tucci. Based on the chick lit book by Lauren Weisberger. **106m/C DVD, Blu-ray Disc.** *US* Anne Hathaway, Meryl Streep, Adrian Grenier, Simon Baker, Stanley Tucci, Emily Blunt, Tracie Thoms, David Marshall Grant, James Naughton, Daniel Sunjata, Rebecca Mader, Rich Sommer; ***D:*** David Frankel; ***W:*** Aline Brosh McKenna; ***C:*** Florian Ballhaus; ***M:*** Theodore Shapiro. Golden Globes '07: Actress—Mus./Comedy (Streep).

Devil Wears White 🦴 **1986 (R)** A student's vacation is disrupted when he becomes involved in a war with an insane arms dealer who wants to take over a Latin American Republic. **92m/C VHS, DVD.** Robert Livesy, Jane Higginson, Guy Ecker, Anthony Cordova; ***D:*** Steven A. Hull.

Devil Woman WOOF! 1976 (R) A Filipino Gorgon-woman seeks reptillian revenge on the farmers who killed her family. Bad news. **79m/C VHS.** *PH* Rosemarie Gil; ***D:*** Albert Yu, Felix Vilars.

Devilfish 🦴 *Shark: Red on the Ocean* **1984** A small seaside community is ravaged by berserk manta rays in this soggy saga. **92m/C VHS.** *IT* Michael Sopkiw, Valentine Monnier, Gianni "John" Garko, William Berger; ***D:*** Lamberto Bava; ***W:*** Gianfranco Clerici, Dardano Sacchetti; Herve Piccini; ***C:*** Giancarlo Ferrando; ***M:*** Guido de Angelis, Maurizio de Angelis.

The Devils 🦴🦴🦴 *The Devils of Loudun* **1971 (R)** In 1631 France, a priest is accused of commerce with the devil and sexual misconduct with nuns. Since he is also a political threat, the accusation is used to denounce and eventually execute him. Based on Aldous Huxley's "The Devils of Loudun," the movie features masturbating nuns and other excesses—shocking scenes typical of film director Russell. Supposedly this was Russell's attempt to wake the public to their desensitization of modern horrors of war. Controversial and flamboyant. **109m/C VHS.** *GB* Vanessa Redgrave, Oliver Reed, Dudley Sutton, Max Adrian, Gemma Jones, Murray Melvin, Michael Gothard, Georgina Hale, Christopher Logue, Andrew Faulds; ***D:*** Ken Russell; ***W:*** Ken Russell; ***C:*** David Watkin; ***M:*** Peter Maxwell Davies. Natl. Bd. of Review '71: Director (Russell).

The Devil's Advocate 1/2 **1997 (R)** Forget the actors, this film belongs to cinematographer Bartkowiak and production designer Bruno Rubeo, who offer a lush, rich look that's very enticing. And it's all about enticement—young Florida lawyer Kevin Lomax (Reeves) is seduced by the power and money of a position at an influential New York law firm run by the mysterious John Milton (Pacino). But soon Kevin's beautiful wife Mary Ann (Theron) is having a breakdown, his religious mother (Ivey) is prophesizing doom, and Kevin learns the boss is Satan—literally. Reeves is earnest, Pacino relishes his showy role, and the visual effects provide some much needed jolts. Based on the novel by Andrew Neiderman. **144m/C VHS, DVD.** Al Pacino, Keanu Reeves, Charlize Theron, Judith Ivey, Craig T. Nelson, Jeffrey Jones, Connie Nielsen, Ruben Santiago-Hudson, Debra Monk, Tamara Tunie, Vyto Ruginis, Laura Harrington, Pamela Gray, Heather Matarazzo, Delroy Lindo, Gloria Lynne Henry, Chris Bauer; ***D:*** Taylor Hackford; ***W:*** Tony Gilroy, Jonathan Lemkin; ***C:*** Andrzej Bartkowiak; ***M:*** James Newton Howard.

Devil's Angels **1967** A motorcycle gang clashes with a small-town sheriff. Cheap 'n' sleazy fare. **84m/C VHS.** John Cassavetes, Beverly Adams, Mimsy Farmer, Salli Sachse, Nai Bonet, Leo Gordon; ***D:*** Daniel Haller; ***W:*** Charles B. Griffith.

The Devil's Arithmetic 1/2 **1999** Modern teen Hannah Stern (Dunst) is indifferent to her Jewish faith and reluctant to attend her Aunt Eva's (Fletcher) Passover seder. After getting drunk, she passes out and is mysteriously transported to Poland in 1941, where she and her cousin Rivkah (Murphy) are imprisoned in a concentration camp and Hannah gets a first-hand look at faith and oppression. Pic doesn't play down the Nazi horrors and may not be suitable for the very young. Adapted from Jane Yolen's novel. **101m/C VHS, DVD.** Kirsten Dunst, Brittany Murphy, Louise Fletcher, Paul Freeman, Mimi Rogers; ***D:*** Donna Deitch; ***W:*** Robert J. Avrech; ***C:*** Jacek Laskus; ***M:*** Frederic Talgorn. **CABLE**

The Devil's Backbone *El Espinazo del Diablo* **2001 (R)** In the final days of the Spanish Civil War, staff and children at a remote orphanage run by loyalists Casares (Luppi) and Carmen (Paredes) prepare for an uncertain fate. Carlos (Tielve) is a new arrival who quickly learns that there are many secrets, including the (possible) ghost of schoolboy Santi. Sinister janitor Jacinto (Noriega) also thinks there's gold hidden somewhere and is determined to find it. Uneasy combination of history and the supernatural. Spanish with subtitles. **106m/C VHS, DVD.** *SP MX* Marisa Paredes, Federico Luppi, Eduardo Noriega, Fernando Tielve, Inigo Garces, Irene Visedo, Berta Ojea; ***D:*** Guillermo del Toro; ***W:*** Guillermo del Toro, Antonio Trashorras, David Munoz; ***C:*** Guillermo Navarro; ***M:*** Javier Navarrete.

The Devil's Brigade **1968** "Dirty Dozen" style film with Holden as the leader of special commando brigade consisting of the usual misfits and oddballs. The team is trained to take on the Nazis in Scandanavia but has their assignment cancelled. Instead, they take them on in the Italian Alps, making for some perilous adventures. Non-acting notables include former football great Hornung and former boxing champ Gene Fullmer. **130m/C VHS, DVD.** William Holden, Cliff Robertson, Vince Edwards, Andrew Prine, Claude Akins, Michael Rennie, Dana Andrews, Gretchen Wyler, Carroll O'Connor, Richard Jaeckel, Jack Watson, Paul Hornung, Jeremy Slate, Don Megowan, Patric Knowles, James Craig, Richard Dawson, Tom Stern, Luke Askew, Harry Carey Jr., Tom Troupe, Norman Alden, David Pritchard, Wilhelm von Homburg; ***D:*** Andrew V. McLaglen; ***W:*** William Roberts; ***C:*** William Clothier; ***M:*** Alex North.

The Devil's Brother *Fra Diavolo; Bogus Bandits; The Virtuous Tramps* **1933** In one of their lesser efforts, Laurel and Hardy star as bumbling bandits in this comic operetta based on the 1830 opera by Daniel F. Auber. **88m/B VHS, DVD.** Stan Laurel, Oliver Hardy, Dennis King, Thelma Todd, James Finlayson, Lucille Browne; ***D:*** Charles R. Rogers, Hal Roach.

Devil's Canyon **1953** An ex-lawman, serving time in an Arizona prison, is beset by a jailed killer seeking vengeance for his own incarceration. Filmed in 3-D. **92m/B VHS.** Dale Robertson, Virginia Mayo, Stephen McNally, Arthur Hunnicutt, Robert Keith, Jay C. Flippen, Whit Bissell; ***D:*** Alfred Werker.

The Devil's Cargo 1/2 **1948** When a man is accused of killing a racetrack operator, he calls in the Falcon to clear his name. The master detective finds this to be a most difficult task however, especially when the accused is found poisoned in his cell. One of the final three "Falcon" films, in which Calvert replaced Tom Conway. **61m/B VHS.** John Calvert, Rochelle Hudson, Roscoe Karns, Lyle Talbot, Tom Kennedy; ***D:*** John F. Link.

Devil's Crude **1971** Adventurous sailor and a young oil heir uncover a conspiracy within a giant corporation. **85m/C VHS.** *IT* Franco Nero, Francisco Rabal; ***D:*** Tommaso Dazzi.

The Devil's Daughter 1/2 *Pocomania* **1939** A sister's hatred and voodoo ceremonies play an important part in this all-black drama. **60m/B VHS, DVD.** Nina Mae McKinney, Jack Carter, Ida James, Hamtree Harrington; ***D:*** Arthur Leonard; ***C:*** Jay Rescher.

The Devil's Daughter **1991 (R)** Satan, in a desperate bid to take over the planet, orders his minions to flood the earth with horrific evil. Only one woman can prevent the HellMaster from succeeding, and she may be too late! **112m/C VHS.** *IT* Kelly Curtis, Herbert Lom, Maria Angela Giordano, Michel Hans Adatte, Carla Cassola, Angelika Maria Boeck, Tomas Arana; ***D:*** Michele (Michael) Soavi; ***W:*** Dario Argento; ***M:*** Pino Donaggio.

Devil's Den 1/2 **2006** Cheapie ghoul horror/comedy. Quinn and Nick are heading towards the U.S. border from Mexico with their drug stash when they happen upon the titular club. Being your normal horny dudes, they're happy to find a bevy of beautiful strippers, who are not what they seem. Now the doofs have to stay alive until dawn with the help of a gorgeous assassin and a demon-wasting samurai. **84m/C DVD.** Devon Sawa, Steven Schub, Kelly Hu, Ken Foree, Karen Maxwell, Ken Ohara, Dawn Olivieri; ***D:*** Jeff Burr; ***W:*** Mitch Gould; ***C:*** Viorel Sergovici Jr.; ***M:*** Jon Lee. **VIDEO**

The Devil's Disciple **1959** Entertaining adaptation of a minor George Bernard Shaw play set during the American Revolution. British Gen. Burgoyne (Olivier) and his troops are stuck in a northeastern village in 1777 awaiting orders and dealing with rebels. This includes troublemaking Richard Dudgeon (Douglas), whose father has been hanged by the Brits, and pastor Anthony Anderson (Lancaster), working in secret with the rebels. There's also a modest romantic triangle between the two men and Anderson's wife Judith (Scott). Film suffers from choppy direction, but the excellent cast more than makes up for it. **82m/B VHS.** *GB* Burt Lancaster, Kirk Douglas, Laurence Olivier, Janet Scott, Eva LeGallienne, Harry Andrews, Basil Sydney, George Rose; ***D:*** Guy Hamilton; ***W:*** John Dighton, Roland Kibbee; ***C:*** Jack Hildyard; ***M:*** Richard Rodney Bennett.

The Devil's Dominoes 1/2 **2007** A car crash kills the driver of one of the vehicles and leads to an attempted cover-up. The buddies who survived the accident find diamonds in the other car and learn the victim was the son of a Chicago mobster. Now the guys have the mob, local law enforcement, and each other to worry about. **93m/C DVD.** Vincent Pastore, Daniel Baldwin, Tom Bateman, Crag Degel, Christopher Mur; ***D:*** Scott Prestin; ***W:*** John Pizzo; ***C:*** Marc Menet. **VIDEO**

The Devil's Eye *Djavulens Oga* **1960** The devil dispatches Don Juan to tempt and seduce a young virgin bride-to-be, a reverend's daughter, no less. Based on the Danish radio play "Don Juan Returns." **90m/B VHS.** *SW* Stig Jarrel, Bibi Andersson, Jarl Kulle; ***D:*** Ingmar Bergman; ***W:*** Ingmar Bergman; ***C:*** Gunnar Fischer; ***M:*** Erik Nordgren.

Devil's Gift **WOOF!** **1984** A young boy's toy is possessed by a demon and havoc ensues. **112m/C VHS.** Bob Mendlesolin, Vicki Saputo, Steven Robertson; ***D:*** Kenneth Berton.

The Devil's Hand *Devil's Doll; The Naked Goddess; Live to Love* **1961** When Alda finds a doll that represents his ideal woman in a curio shop, the shop's owner (Hamilton, aka Commissioner Gordon), tells him the dream girl who modeled for the doll lives nearby. Trouble is, she's part of a voodoo cult, and guess who's head voodooman. Big trouble for Alda; big snooze for you. **71m/B VHS, DVD.** Linda Christian, Robert Alda, Neil Hamilton, Ariadne Welter; ***D:*** William Hole Jr.

Devil's Island *Djoflaeyjan* **1996** An abandoned military base is being used to house poor families outside Reykjavik in the '50s. The trash-filled landscape offers little to those who live there, including four generations of one eccentric no-hope family. The usual family dysfunction is all played for exaggerated caricature. Icelandic with subtitles. **103m/C VHS, DVD.** *IC* Gisli Halldorsson, Baltasar Kormakur, Sveinn Geirsson, Sigurveig Jonsdottir; ***D:*** Fridrik Thor Fridriksson; ***W:*** Einar Karason; ***C:*** Ari Kristinsson; ***M:*** Hilmar Orn Hilmarsson.

Devil's Kiss *The Wicked Caresses of Satan* **1975** Gothic horror including zombies, virgins, sorcery, and the inevitable living dead. **93m/C VHS.** *SP FR* Maria Silva, Olivier Mathot, Jose Nero, Dan (Daniel, Danny) Martin, Silvia Solar, Evelyn Scott; ***D:*** Jordi Gigo; ***W:*** Jordi Gigo; ***C:*** Julio Perez de Rozas; ***M:*** Alberto Argudo.

Devil's Knight **2003 (R)** Brothers Hector (Serna) and Ruben (Solano) Rivera are expert "low-rider" designers who end up murdered. Their sister Delia (Alvarez) leaves the Army to find their killers. With the help of a Vietman vet mechanic (Kove), she sets out to take her own brand of revenge, which consists of wearing bikinis and rubbing against pimped-out cars at custom shows. So-so actioner is fueled by the lovingly-shot Alvarez, and the even-more-lovingly-shot custom street machines. **97m/C VHS, DVD.** Elizabeth Alvarez, Jose Solano, Alexander Romanov, Martin Kove, Pepe Serna, Jaime Gomez, Garry Marshall; ***D:*** Quan Phillips; ***W:*** Quan Phillips; ***C:*** Robert Hayes. **VIDEO**

The Devil's Mercy 1/2 **2007** The Winters family—Beth (Valente), Matt (Cram), and young son Calvin (Everett)—have just moved into their renovated apartment in an old Connecticut house. Their downstairs neighbor Tyler Grant (Rea) is friendly and he has a niece, Kayla (Lochner), willing to hang out with Calvin. But the boy doesn't like his new abode, complaining to Beth that there are monsters in the house. And he's right. **90m/C DVD.** Stephen Rea, Hannah Lochner, Michael Cram, Deborah Valente, Dylan Everett; ***D:*** Melanie Orr; ***W:*** James A. McLean; ***M:*** Ryan Latham. **VIDEO**

The Devil's Mistress 1/2 **1968** A gang of criminals on a pillaging spree murder a man and rape his Indian wife, only to find out she's a she-demon who won't let bygones be bygones. Lame. **66m/C VHS.** Joan Stapleton, Robert Gregory, Forrest Westmoreland, Douglas Warren, Oren Williams, Arthur Resley; ***D:*** Orville Wanzer; ***W:*** Orville Wanzer.

The Devil's Nightmare 1/2 *Succubus; The Devil Walks at Midnight* **1971 (R)** A woman leads seven tourists (representing the seven deadly sins) on a tour of a medieval European castle. There they experience demonic tortures. Lots of creepy moments. Euro-horror/sex star Blanc is fantastic in this otherwise mediocre production. **88m/C VHS, DVD.** *BE IT* Erika Blanc, Jean Servais, Daniel Emilfork, Lucien Raimbourg, Jacques Monseau, Colette Emmanuelle, Ivana Novak, Shirley Corrigan, Frederique Hender; ***D:*** Jean Brismee; ***W:*** Patrice Rhomm, Vertunnio De Angelis, Charles Lecocq; ***C:*** Andre Goeffers; ***M:*** Alessandro Alessandroni.

Devils on the Doorstep *Guizi Laile* **2000** Chinese film needs some sharp editing before this black comedy about a tiny village's survival during WWII could be anything more than frustrating. Local peasant Ma Dasan is surprised when the Chinese Army dump two prisoners in their remote village—a Japanese POW and his Chinese interpreter. When no one comes for the prisoners after six months, the fearful villagers decide they should be executed and Ma is sent to hire an assassin. When this doesn't work out, the villagers try to return them to nearby Japanese troops. This idea isn't any better and by now the movie's exhausted a viewer's patience. Japanese and Mandarin with subtitles. **162m/B VHS, DVD.** *CH* Jiang Wen, Kagawa Teruyuki, Jiang Hongbo, Chen Qiang, Sawada Kenya, Yuan Ding; ***D:*** Jiang Wen; ***W:*** Jiang Wen; ***C:*** Gu Changwei. Cannes '00: Grand Jury Prize.

The Devil's Own **1996 (R)** Irish-American New York cop Tom O'Meara (Ford) and wife Sheila (Colin) take charming Irish emigre Rory Devaney (Pitt) into their home and make him part of the family. But Rory, AKA Frankie McGuire, turns out to be an IRA terrorist who has hustled out of trouble in Belfast and now has a bloody purpose for coming to America. When Tom discovers just what it is, he tries to stop Rory before he destroys any more lives—including his own. More a low-key character study than a slam-bang actioner, with Pitt cooly charismatic as the troubled gunman while Ford does his usual professional work as a good cop caught up in a bad situation. **110m/C VHS, DVD, Blu-ray Disc.** Harrison Ford, Brad Pitt, Margaret Colin, Ruben Blades, Treat Williams, George Hearn, Natascha (Natasha) McElhone, Mitchell Ryan, Simon Jones, Paul Ronan; ***D:*** Alan J. Pakula; ***W:*** Kevin Jarre, David Aaron Cohen, Vincent Patrick; ***C:*** Gordon Willis; ***M:*** James Horner.

The Devil's Partner 1/2 **1958** Yet another uninspired devil yarn in which an old-timer trades in his senior citizenship by dying and coming back in the form of his younger self. Young again, he takes a new wife and indulges in multiple ritual sacrifices. Noteworthy only by virtue of the cast's later TV notoriety—Buchanan and Foulger would later appear on "Petticoat Junction," Nelson played Dr. Rossi on "Peyton Place," and Crane beached a role on "Hawaiian Eye." **75m/B VHS, DVD.** Ed Nelson, Jean Allison, Edgar Buchanan, Richard Crane, Spencer Carlisle, Byron Foulger, Claire Carleton; ***D:*** Charles R. Rondeau.

Devil's Party **1938** A tenement boy's reunion party turns into a night of horror when one of the guests is killed. As a result, the childhood friends band together to uncover the murderer's identity. **65m/B VHS, DVD.** Victor McLaglen, Paul Kelly, William Gargan, Samuel S. Hinds, Scotty Beckett; ***D:*** Ray McCarey.

The Devil's Playground **1976** Sexual tension rises in a Catholic seminary, distracting the boys from their theological studies. The attentions of the priests only further their sexual confusion. **107m/C VHS, DVD.** *AU* Arthur Dignam, Nick (Nicholas) Tate, Simon Burke, Charles Frawley, Jonathan Hardy, Gerry Dugan, Thomas Keneally; ***D:*** Fred Schepisi; ***W:*** Fred Schepisi; ***C:*** Ian Baker; ***M:*** Bruce Smeaton. Australian Film Inst. '76: Actor (Tate), Actor (Burke), Cinematog., Director (Schepisi), Film, Screenplay.

Devil's Pond *Heaven's Pond* **2003 (R)** Spoiled rich girl Julianne (Reid) impulsively marries her boyfriend Mitch (Pardue) in order to get away from her controlling family. They honeymoon in an isolated cabin, with no communication to the outside world, and Julianne soon discovers that her new hubby has no intention of ever letting her go. This is one newlywed who wasn't expecting the "till death do us part" to come so soon. You'll have to like the pretty lead actors since it's their adventure. **92m/C VHS, DVD.** Tara Reid, Kip Pardue, Meredith Baxter, Dan Gunther; ***D:*** Joel Viertel; ***W:*** Alek Friedman, Mora Stephens; ***C:*** Matthew Jensen; ***M:*** Brad Caleb Kane. **VIDEO**

The Devil's Possessed 1/2 **1974** A Middle Ages despot tortures and maims the peasants in his region until they rise up and enact an unspeakable revenge. **90m/C VHS, DVD.** *AR SP* Paul Naschy; ***D:*** Leon Klimovsky.

The Devil's Prey **2001 (R)** Partyers attending a rave discover it's a front for satanic cult leader Minister Seth (Bergin) to obtain the young flesh he needs for his blood sacrifies. But Susan (Jones) is willing to fight for her life against the masked cult members. Fast-paced horror. **91m/C VHS, DVD.** Patrick Bergin, Ashley Jones, Charlie O'Connell, Bryan Kirkwood, Tim Thomerson; ***D:*** Bradford May. **VIDEO**

Devil's Rain 1/2 **1975 (PG)** The rituals and practices of devil worship, possession, and satanism are gruesomely related. Interesting cast. **85m/C VHS, DVD.** Ernest Borgnine, Ida Lupino, William Shatner, Eddie Albert, Keenan Wynn, Tom Skerritt, Joan Prather, Claudio Brook, John Travolta, Anton La Vey; ***D:*** Robert Fuest; ***W:*** James Ashton, Gabe Essoe, Gerald Hopman; ***C:*** Alex Phillips Jr.; ***M:*** Al De Lory.

The Devil's Rejects WOOF! 2005 (R) Tortuous recycling by director Zombie of his senseless "House of 1000 Corpses" tribute-driven horror movie, featuring the psychotic Firefly clan, which was enough of a cult hit for this pointless follow-up that also honors (or insults?) other serial killer and zombie flicks as well. Only Satan would order a third installment. **101m/C DVD, Blu-ray Disc, UMD.** *US GE* William Forsythe, Sid Haig, Sheri Moon Zombie, Bill Moseley, Tyler Mane, Leslie Easterbrook, Matthew McGrory, Ken Foree, Michael Berryman, Danny Trejo, Rosario Dawson, Deborah Van Valkenburgh, Geoffrey Lewis, Priscilla Barnes, Kate Norby, Dave Sheridan, Lew Temple, Elizabeth (E.G. Dailey) Daily, Diamond Dallas Page, Tom Towler, P.J. Soles, Chris Ellis, Mary Woronov, Daniel Roebuck, Duane Whitaker, Steve Railsback, Brian Posehn; ***D:*** Rob Zombie; ***W:*** Rob Zombie; ***C:*** Phil Parmet; ***M:*** Rob Zombie, Tyler Bates.

The Devil's Sleep 1951 When a crusading woman sets out to break up a teen narcotics ring, the threatened thugs attempt to draw her daughter into their sleazy affairs, thus assuring the mother's silence. **81m/B VHS, DVD.** Lita Grey Chaplin, Timothy Farrell, John Mitchum, William Thomason, Tracy Lynn; ***D:*** W. Merle Connell.

Devil's Son-in-Law WOOF! 1977 (R) A black stand-up comic makes a deal with a devil. **95m/C VHS, DVD.** Rudy Ray Moore; ***D:*** Cliff Roquemore.

The Devil's Tomb 2009 (R) Familiar but well-paced action-horror. War vet Mack (Gooding Jr.) leads his team of mercenaries into the desert on a rescue mission to free a scientist trapped in an underground lab. The squad soon learns that the lab was deliberately sealed to contain an ancient evil that shows them their dreams, desires, and nightmares and makes them all violent and stuff. **90m/C DVD.** Cuba Gooding Jr., Ron Perlman, Valerie Cruz, Taryn Manning, Henry Rollins, Jason London, Bill Moseley, Zack (Zach) Ward, Franky G., Stephanie Jacobsen, Ray Winstone; ***D:*** Jason Connery; ***W:*** Keith Kjornes; ***C:*** Tom Calloway; ***M:*** Bill Brown. **VIDEO**

The Devil's Undead ½ 1975 (PG) When a Scottish orphanage is besieged by a rash of cold-blooded murders, the detectives Lee and Cushing are summoned to investigate. Interesting spin on that old possessed by demons theme. **90m/C VHS.** *GB* Christopher Lee, Peter Cushing; ***D:*** Peter Sasdy.

Devil's Wanton ½ *Fangelse; Prison* **1949** A young girl tries to forget an unhappy relationship by beginning a new romance with an equally frustrated beau. Gloomy, but hopeful. **80m/B VHS, DVD.** *SW* Doris Svedlund, Eva Henning, Hasse (Hans) Ekman; ***D:*** Ingmar Bergman; ***W:*** Ingmar Bergman.

The Devil's Web ½ 1974 (PG) A demonic nurse infiltrates, manipulates, and corrupts three beautiful sisters. **73m/C VHS.** Diana Dors, Andrea Marcovicci, Ed Bishop, Cec Linder, Michael Culver; ***D:*** Shaun O'Riordan; ***W:*** Brian Clemens. **TV**

Devil's Wedding Night WOOF! *El Retorno de la Drequessa Dracula; The Return of the Duchess Dracula; Full Moon of the Virgins* **1973 (R)** An archaeologist and his twin brother fight over a ring that lures virgins into Count Dracula's Transylvanian castle. Vampire queen Bay seduces the dimwit twins and strips at every chance she gets. **85m/C VHS, DVD.** Mark Damon, Rosalba Neri, Frances Davis; ***D:*** Luigi (Paolo Solvay) Batzella.

Devlin 1992 (R) Devlin is a tough cop with an alcohol problem and a bad marriage. His father-in-law, Brennan, is a powerful local political boss. When Brennan's son is murdered, Devlin is the fall guy. Seeking to clear himself, he discovers a conspiracy going back 30 years. **110m/C VHS.** Bryan Brown, Lloyd Bridges, Roma Downey, Whip Hubley, Lawrence Dane, Lisa Eichhorn, Carol(e) Shelley, Jan Rubes, Frances Fisher, Gary Klar, Bruce MacVittie, Robert Cicchini, Gabrielle Rose; ***D:*** Rick Rosenthal; ***W:*** David Taylor; ***C:*** Neil Roach; ***M:*** John Altman. **CABLE**

Devon's Ghost: Legend of the Bloody Boy 2005 (R) Slasher flick. As a boy, Devon was nearly murdered by his parents. Now he's back (and not as a ghost) to continue his revenge against any young couple he sees. Which means all those horny teens had better watch out. **86m/C DVD.** Matt Moore, John Yong Bosch, Karan Ashely, Reza Bahador, Jonathan Cruz, Kristy Vaughan; ***D:*** John Yong Bosch, Koichi Sakamoto; ***W:*** Karan Ashely, Ron Day, Tim Grace; ***C:*** John Rhode, Sam Lazoya; ***M:*** Cody Westheimer. **VIDEO**

Devonsville Terror 1983 (R) Strange things begin to happen when a new school teacher arrives in Devonsville, a town that has a history of torture, murder, and witchcraft. The hysterical townspeople react by beginning a 20th-century witchhunt. **97m/C VHS, DVD.** Suzanna Love, Donald Pleasence, Deanna Haas, Mary Walden, Robert Walker Jr., Paul Willson; ***D:*** Ulli Lommel; ***W:*** Ulli Lommel; ***C:*** Ulli Lommel; ***M:*** Ray Colcord.

Devotion ½ 1931 A lovesick British miss disguises herself as a governess so she can be near the object of her affection, a London barrister. **80m/B VHS.** Ann Harding, Leslie Howard, Robert Williams, O.P. Heggie, Louise Closser Hale, Dudley Digges; ***D:*** Robert Milton.

Devotion 1995 (R) Lesbian comic Sheila (Derbyshire) is offered her own sitcom by now-married former lover Lynn (Girling), who admits there's still a spark. Should Sheila rekindle the flame or stay true to free-spirited lover Julie (Twa)? Cutesy at first but takes a welcome dramatic turn as the characters explore their true feelings. **124m/C VHS, DVD.** Jan Derbyshire, Cindy Girling, Kate Twa; ***D:*** Mindy Kaplan.

Devour 2005 (R) Jake (Ackles) and friends play a deadly Internet game called "The Pathway" that assigns its members bizarre tasks that initially seem harmless, but soon turn violent. Fascinating premise, but too many intertwined plots and themes involving uninteresting characters leave viewers confused and bored. **90m/C DVD.** Shannyn Sossamon, Dominique Swain, William Sadler, Martin Cummins, Jensen Ackles, Teach, Robert Stewart; ***D:*** David Winkler; ***W:*** Adam Gross, Seth Gross; ***C:*** Brian Pearson; ***M:*** Joseph LoDuca. **CABLE**

D.I. 1957 A tough drill sergeant is faced with an unbreakable rebellious recruit, threatening his record and his platoon's status. Webb's film features performances by actual soldiers. **106m/B VHS.** Jack Webb, Don Dubbins, Jackie Loughery, Lin McCarthy, Virginia Gregg; ***D:*** Jack Webb.

The Diabolical Dr. Z *Miss Muerte; Dans les Griffes du Maniaque* **1965** When dad dies of cardiac arrest after the medical council won't let him make the world a kinder gentler place with his personality-altering technique, his dutiful daughter—convinced the council brought on dad's demise—is out to change some personalities in a big way. **86m/B VHS, DVD.** *SP FR* Mabel Karr, Fernando Montes, Estella Blain, Antonio J. Escribano, Howard Vernon, Jess (Jesus) Franco, Jose Maria Prada, Guy Mairesse; ***D:*** Jess (Jesus) Franco; ***W:*** Jean-Claude Carriere, Jess (Jesus) Franco; ***C:*** Alejandro Ulloa; ***M:*** Jess (Jesus) Franco.

Diabolically Yours ½ *Diaboliquement Votre* **1967** A French thriller about an amnesiac who struggles to discover his lost identity. Tensions mount when his pretty spouse and friends begin to wonder if it's all a game. Dubbed. **94m/C VHS, DVD.** *FR* Alain Delon, Senta Berger; ***D:*** Julien Duvivier.

Diabolique ½ *Les Diabolique* **1955** Sadistic boarding school master Michel (Meurisse) has a wealthy, neurotic wife, Christina (Clouzet, the director's wife), and a cold-blooded mistress, Nicole (Signoret), who conspire to poison and then drown him in the school's swimming pool. But after the plot is carried out, Christina becomes convinced that Michel is still alive. Plot twists and double-crosses abound. Based on the novel "Celle Qui N'Etait Pas" by Pierre Boileau and Thomas Narcejac. French with subtitles. Remade for TV in 1974 as "Reflections of Murder." **107m/B VHS, DVD.** *FR* Simone Signoret, Vera Clouzot, Paul Meurisse, Charles Vanel, Michel Serrault, Georges Chamarat, Robert Dalban, Therese Dorny, Camille Guerini; ***D:*** Henri-Georges Clouzot; ***W:*** Henri-Georges Clouzot, Frederic Grendel, Jerome Geronimi, Rene Masson; ***C:*** Armand Thirard; ***M:*** Georges Van Parys. N.Y. Film Critics '55: Foreign Film.

Diabolique ½ 1996 (R) Remake of the 1955 French noir classic, updated for '90s sensibilities, finds timid teacher Mia (Adjani) married to overbearing school head Guy (Palminteri), who's having an affair with fellow teacher Nicole (Stone). The two women, who loathe Guy equally, plot to kill him. But when a P.I. (Bates) investigates, it seems possible that Guy isn't dead after all. If you're having trouble accessorizing with leopard skin, watch Stone. Otherwise, watch the far superior original. The usually publicity hungry Stone refused to have anything to do with this picture after its release due to a spat with director Chechik. **105m/C VHS, DVD.** Sharon Stone, Isabelle Adjani, Chazz Palminteri, Kathy Bates, Spalding Gray, Shirley Knight, Adam Hann-Byrd, Allen (Goorwitz) Garfield; ***D:*** Jeremiah S. Chechik; ***W:*** Don Roos; ***C:*** Peter James; ***M:*** Randy Edelman.

Dial Help ½ *Ragno Gelido; Minaccia d'Amore* **1988 (R)** A lame Italian-made suspenser about a model plagued by ghostly phone calls. **94m/C VHS.** *IT* Charlotte Lewis, Marcello Modugno, Mattia Sbragia, Victor Cavallo, William Berger, Carlo Monni, Carola Stagnaro; ***D:*** Ruggero Deodato; ***C:*** Renato Tafuri.

Dial "M" for Murder 1954 Unfaithful playboy Tony's (Milland) cash is all thanks to his marriage to heiress Margot (Kelly) and he fears losing her to writer Mark (Cummings). So Tony devises an elaborate plan to murder his wife for her money, but when she accidentally stabs the killer-to-be, with scissors no less, it's Tony who comes under the suspicious eye of Chief Inspector Hubbard (Williams). Filmed in 3-D. Based on the play by Frederick Knotts. Loosely remade in 1998 as "A Perfect Murder" starring Michael Douglas and Gwenyth Paltrow. **123m/C VHS, DVD.** Ray Milland, Grace Kelly, Robert Cummings, John Williams, Anthony Dawson; ***D:*** Alfred Hitchcock; ***W:*** Frederick Knott; ***C:*** Robert Burks; ***M:*** Dimitri Tiomkin.

Dial Red O 1955 War vet Ralph Wyatt (Larsen) escapes the psych ward after getting wind that his wife, Connie (Stanley), wants a divorce. Lieutenant Andy Flynn (Elliot) leads the manhunt; meanwhile Connie's hooked up with Norman Roper (Picerni), a guy from Ralph's former Marine unit—but when Roper refuses to drop his own wife for Connie, she's ticked, they fight, and tragedy ensues—leaving Wyatt under suspicion. **63m/B DVD.** Bill Elliott, Helene Stanley, Keith Larsen, Paul Picerni, Jack Kruschen, Elaine Riley, Robert Bice, Rick Vallin; ***D:*** Daniel Ullman; ***W:*** Daniel Ullman.

Diamond Dogs 2007 (R) Stupid title, cardboard plot, disposable characters, but with enough action to be mildly diverting. Mercenary Xander Ronson (Lundgren) is stuck in Mongolia trying to pay off his debts when art collector Chambers (Shriver) offers him a job obtaining an invaluable jeweled tapestry housed in a remote Buddhist temple. But a group of Russian treasure hunters are also after the prize. **94m/C DVD.** Dolph Lundgren, William Shiver, Yu Nan, Xue Zuren, Raicho Vasilev; ***D:*** Shimon Dotan; ***W:*** Leopold St-Pierre; ***C:*** Xiaobing Rao; ***M:*** Larry Cohen. **VIDEO**

Diamond Fleece ½ 1992 Rick (Cross) is a convicted diamond thief who's given a parole just so he can guard the world's largest uncut gemstone. But Inspector Outlaw (Dennehy) figures Rick will never be able to resist stealing the gem himself and the law can finally lock Rick away for good. Oh, and Holly, she thinks a maybe-ex-diamond thief will bring a little romance to her life. **93m/C VHS.** Ben Cross, Brian Dennehy, Kate Nelligan; ***D:*** Al Waxman; ***W:*** Michael Norell.

Diamond Girl ½ 1998 Claire (Collins) works for vineyard owner Denny (Otto) but he doesn't realize she's in love with him. His brother Regan (Cake) does and offers to make Denny jealous by pretending that Claire is his new girlfriend. Of course their romantic plan doesn't work as expected. From the Harlequin Romance Series; adapted from the Diana Palmer novel. **91m/C DVD.** *CA* Jonathan Cake, Kevin Otto, Dyan Cannon, Denise Virieux, Joely Collins, Royston Stoffels; ***D:*** Timothy Bond; ***W:*** Charles Lazar; ***C:*** Buster Reynolds; ***M:*** Tim McCauley. **TV**

Diamond Head ½ 1962 A Hawaiian landowner brings destruction and misery to his family via his stubbornness. Based on the Peter Gilman novel. **107m/C VHS, DVD.** Charlton Heston, Yvette Mimieux, George Chakiris, France Nuyen, James Darren; ***D:*** Guy Green; ***C:*** Sam Leavitt; ***M:*** John Williams.

Diamond Men 2001 Slice of life Americana that's a showcase for actor Forster. Eddie Miller (Forster), a guy in his fifties, is a longtime diamond salesman who travels to jewelry stores throughout Pennsylvania. After having a heart attack, his company wants Eddie to retire—after he trains brash Bobby Walker (Wahlberg) to take over his route. Bobby's an eager loudmouth who bullies while Eddie knows how to finesse his clientele. Still he wants to learn and to befriend Eddie but the story turns out to more than a reluctant old dog teaching a pup some tricks to get along. **100m/C VHS, DVD.** Robert Forster, Donnie Wahlberg, Bess Armstrong, Jasmine Guy, George Coe; ***D:*** Daniel M. Cohen; ***W:*** Daniel M. Cohen; ***C:*** John Huneck; ***M:*** Garrett Parks.

The Diamond of Jeru ½ 2001 Helen (Jefferson) and John (Carradine) travel to Borneo in search of adventure (and diamonds) in an effort to put some spice back into their marriage. Too bad Helen is very attracted to their guide, Mike (Zane). John gets jealous and decides he and the missus should head out on their own while Mike pursues them through the jungle in an effort to rescue them from certain doom. Based on the story "Off the Mangrove Coast" by Louis L'Amour. **89m/C VHS, DVD.** Billy Zane, Keith Carradine, Paris Jefferson, Jackson Raine, Khoa Do; ***D:*** Ian Barry, Dick Lowry; ***W:*** Beau L'Amour; ***C:*** Stephen Windon; ***M:*** Christopher Tyng. **VIDEO**

Diamond Run ½ 1990 (R) A streetwise American expatriate frantically searches for his girlfriend after unwittingly involving her in an assassination plot. **89m/C VHS.** William Bell Sullivan, Ava Lazar, Ayu Azhari, David Thornton, Peter Fox; ***D:*** Robert Chappell.

Diamond Run 2000 (R) Convoluted heist movie. J. Sloan (Lynch) leads a special forces unit that's gone over to the dark side. Sloan's planned a big diamond heist but loses the gems to thief Megan Marlow (Ljoka), who in turn is being sought by NYPD detective Jack Gates (Valentine). Gates gets to Megan first, only to have them both be stalked by Sloan's henchman, Walker (Gleek). And it seems Megan has another secret that could prove explosive. **98m/C VHS, DVD.** Richard Lynch, Linda Ljoka, Michael J. Valentine, Fred Gleek, Peter Harrington; ***D:*** David Giancola; ***W:*** Marty Poole, Derrick J. Costa; ***C:*** John McAleer. **VIDEO**

Diamond Trail ½ 1933 East Coast jewel thieves bring their operation to the West, trailed by a New York reporter. **58m/B VHS.** Rex Bell, Frances Rich, Bud Osborne, Lloyd Whitlock, Norman Feusier; ***D:*** Harry Fraser.

The Diamond Trap 1991 (PG) A Manhatten detective finds himself in the middle of a diamond heist and involved with a con artist. **93m/C VHS.** Howard Hesseman, Brooke Shields, Ed Marinaro, Twiggy; ***D:*** Don Taylor; ***W:*** David Peckinpah. **TV**

Diamondbacks ½ 1999 Militia group, led by O'Keefe, takes over a remote NASA station in order to reprogram a government weapons satellite for evil. And it's up to engineer Lottimer to stop them. Lots of action in a no-brainer adventure. **90m/C VHS, DVD.** Miles O'Keeffe, Chris Mitchum, Timothy Bottoms, Eb Lottimer; ***D:*** Bernard Salzman. **VIDEO**

Diamonds 1972 (PG) A tense film in which the Israel Diamond Exchange is looted by a motley array of criminal heisters.

Shaw plays a dual role as twin brothers. **108m/C VHS, DVD.** *IS* Robert Shaw, Richard Roundtree, Barbara Hershey, Shelley Winters; ***D:*** Menahem Golan.

Diamonds 1/2 **1999 (PG-13)** Douglas lends both dignity and humor to his first screen role since recovering from a stroke. Harry Agrensky (Douglas) is a one-time boxing champ (recovering from a stroke) who wants to live as independently as possible. He claims to have a fortune in diamonds, given to him by a mobster, hidden away in Reno and bullies his estranged son, Lance (Aykroyd), and his grandson Michael (Allred) to go on a road trip and retrieve them. There are various adventures and bonding moments and Douglas is re-united with Bacall (as a Nevada madam), with whom he worked in 1950's "Young Man with a Horn." **90m/C VHS, DVD.** Kirk Douglas, Dan Aykroyd, Corbin Allred, Lauren Bacall, Kurt Fuller, Jenny McCarthy, John Landis, Mariah O'Brien; ***D:*** John Mallory Asher; ***W:*** Allan Aaron Katz; ***C:*** Paul Elliott; ***M:*** Joel Goldsmith.

Diamonds Are Forever 1/2 **1971 (PG)** 007 once again battles his nemesis Blofeld, this time in Las Vegas. Bond must prevent the implementation of a plot to destroy Washington through the use of a space-orbiting laser. Fabulous stunts include Bond's wild drive through the streets of Vegas in a '71 Mach 1. Connery returned to play Bond in this film after being offered the then record-setting salary of $1 million. **120m/C VHS, DVD.** *GB* Sean Connery, Jill St. John, Charles Gray, Bruce Cabot, Jimmy Dean, Lana Wood, Bruce Glover, Putter Smith, Norman Burton, Joseph Furst, Bernard Lee, Desmond Llewelyn, Laurence Naismith, Leonard Barr, Lois Maxwell, Margaret Lacey, Joe Robinson, Donna Garrat, Trina Parks; ***D:*** Guy Hamilton; ***W:*** Tom Mankiewicz; ***C:*** Ted Moore; ***M:*** John Barry.

Diamond's Edge *Just Ask for Diamond* **1988 (PG)** An adolescent private eye and his juvenescent brother snoop into the affairs of the Fat Man, and find out that the opera ain't over until they find out what's in the Fat Man's mysterious box of bon-bons. A genre-parodying kid mystery, written by Horowitz, based on his novel, "The Falcon's Malteser." **83m/C VHS, DVD.** Susannah York, Peter Eyre, Patricia Hodge, Nickolas Grace; ***D:*** Stephen Bayly; ***W:*** Anthony Horowitz; ***M:*** Trevor Jones.

Diamonds of the Night *Demanty Noci* **1964** A breakthrough masterpiece of the Czech new wave, about two young men escaping from a transport train to Auschwitz and scrambling for survival in the countryside. Surreal, powerfully expressionistic film, one of the most important of its time. In Czech with English subtitles. Accompanied by Nemec's short "A Loaf of Bread." **71m/B VHS.** *CZ* Ladislav Jansky, Antonin Kumbera, Ilse Bischofova; ***D:*** Jan Nemec; ***W:*** Arnost Lustig, Jan Nemec.

Diana: Her True Story 1/2 **1993** Britain's royals are held up to scandalous review in this made for tv adaptaion of Andrew Morton's sympathetic bio of the Princess of Wales. Taking Diana from her lonely childhood to her "fairytale" nuptials and subsequent disillusionment with being a royal, including her bulimia and half-hearted suicide attempts. Charles is portrayed as an arrogant, emotional cold fish, only interested in farming and continuing his liaison with Camilla Parker-Bowles. Handsome production with appropriate inpersonations by the cast. **180m/C VHS, DVD.** Serena Scott Thomas, David Threlfall, Elizabeth Garvie, Jemma Redgrave, Tracy Hardwick, Anne Stallybrass, Jeffrey Harmer, Donald Douglas; ***D:*** Kevin Connor; ***W:*** Stephen Zito. **TV**

Diane **1955** Overstuffed medieval drama featuring Turner as Diane de Poitier, the mistress of a 16th century French King. Moore plays the king in his Hollywood debut. Gorgeous sets and costumes couldn't boost this film at the boxoffice, which had disappointing figures in spite of the expense bestowed upon it. Based on the novel "Diane de Poitier" by John Erskine. **110m/C VHS.** Lana Turner, Pedro Armendariz Sr., Roger Moore, Marisa Pavan, Cedric Hardwicke, Torin Thatcher, Taina Elg, John Lupton, Henry Daniell, Sean McClory, Michael Ansara; ***D:*** David Miller; ***W:*** Christopher Isherwood; ***M:*** Miklos Rozsa.

Diary 1/2 *Mon seung* **2006** Leung Win-na (Charlene Choi) is a pretty young woman who spends her days crafting her dolls, writing in her diary, and pining for her missing lover who seems to have abandoned her. Meeting a man who is almost his double, she convinces him to not only date her but move in, even after she says he reminds her of her past lover who died in a car accident. But later she tells him he died of cancer, and confusion begins to overcome Leung. **85m/C DVD.** *HK JP* Charlene (Cheuk-Yin) Choi, Isabella Leong, Shawn Yue; ***D:*** Oxide Pang Chun; ***W:*** Oxide Pang Chun, Thomas Pang; ***C:*** Anuchit Chotrattanasiri; ***M:*** Payont Permsith.

Diary of a Chambermaid **1946** A chambermaid wants to marry a rich man and finds herself the object of desire of a poor servant willing to commit murder for her. Excellent comic drama, but very stylized in direction and set design. Produced during Renoir's years in Hollywood. Adapted from a story by Octave Mirbeau, later turned into a play. Remade in 1964 by Luis Bumel. **86m/B VHS.** Paulette Goddard, Burgess Meredith, Hurd Hatfield, Francis Lederer, Judith Anderson, Florence Bates, Almira Sessions, Reginald Owen; ***D:*** Jean Renoir.

Diary of a Chambermaid 1/2 *Le Journal d'une Femme de Chambre; Il Diario di una Cameriera* **1964** Vintage Bunuelian social satire about a young girl taking a servant's job in a provincial French family, and easing into an atmosphere of sexual hypocrisy and decadence. In French with English subtitles. Remake of the 1946 Jean Renoir film. **97m/C VHS, DVD.** *FR* Jeanne Moreau, Michel Piccoli, Georges Geret, Francoise Lugagne, Daniel Ivernel; ***D:*** Luis Bunuel; ***W:*** Luis Bunuel, Jean-Claude Carriere; ***C:*** Roger Fellous.

Diary of a Country Priest 1/2 *Le Journal d'un Cure de Campagne* **1950** With "Balthazar" and "Mouchette," this is one of Bresson's greatest, subtlest films, treating the story of an alienated, unrewarded young priest with his characteristic austerity and Catholic humanism. In French and English subtitles. **120m/B VHS, DVD.** *FR* Nicole Maurey, Antonine Balpetre, Claude Layou, Jean Riveyre, Nicole Ladmiral; ***D:*** Robert Bresson; ***W:*** Robert Bresson; ***C:*** Leonce-Henri Burel; ***M:*** Jean Jacques Grunenwald.

Diary of a Hitman 1/2 **1991 (R)** A hitman is hired to knock off the wife and child of a commodities broker who claims his wife is a drug addict and the infant is a crack baby and not his. The hired killer wants out of the business, but needs to pull off one more job for a down payment on his apartment. Beset by doubts, he breaks conduct by conversing with the victim and discovers the broker lied. Based on the play "Insider's Price" by Pressman. **90m/C VHS.** Forest Whitaker, James Belushi, Sherilyn Fenn, Sharon Stone, Seymour Cassel, Lewis Smith, Lois Chiles, John Bedford-Lloyd; ***D:*** Roy London; ***W:*** Kenneth Pressman; ***M:*** Michel Colombier.

Diary of a Lost Girl 1/2 *Das tagebuch einer verlorenen* **1929** The second Louise Brooks/G.W. Pabst collaboration (after "Pandora's Box") in which a frail but mesmerizing German girl plummets into a life of hopeless degradation. Dark and gloomy, the film chronicles the difficulties she faces, from rape to an unwanted pregnancy and prostitution. Based on the popular book by Margarete Boehme. Silent. Made after flapper Brooks left Hollywood to pursue greater opportunities and more challenging roles under Pabst's guidance. **116m/B VHS, DVD.** *GE* Louise Brooks, Fritz Rasp, Josef Rovensky, Sybille Schmitz; ***D:*** G.W. Pabst; ***W:*** Rudolf Leonhard; ***C:*** Sepp Allgeier, Fritz Arno Wagner; ***M:*** Timothy Brock.

Diary of a Mad Black Woman **2005 (PG-13)** The critics spoke and the intended audience ignored every disparaging comment to make this soap opera a success. After an 18-year marriage, Helen (beautiful Elise) gets tossed out of her Atlanta mansion by nasty hubby Charles (Harris) for his long-time mistress, Brenda (Marcos). Weepy Helen flees to the home of her feisty grandmamma Madea (Perry in outrageous drag) and then learns to get her own back. She even finds a blue-collar prince in handsome, loving Orlando (Moore). Yep, it's a life-affirming, over-the-top fairytale with faith as the cornerstone. Perry plays two other roles as well as adapting the script from his play. **116m/C VHS, DVD.** *US* Kimberly Elise, Steve Harris, Shemar Moore, Tamara Taylor, Cicely Tyson, Lisa Marcos, Tiffany Evans, Tyler Perry; ***D:*** Darren Grant; ***W:*** Tyler Perry; ***C:*** David Claessen; ***M:*** Tyler Perry, Elvin D. Ross.

Diary of a Mad Housewife **1970 (R)** Despairing of her miserable family life, a housewife has an affair with a writer only to find him to be even more selfish and egotistical than her no-good husband. Snodgress plays her character perfectly, hearing the insensitive absurdity of her husband and her lover over and over again, enjoying her martyrdom even as it drives her crazy. **94m/C VHS.** Carrie Snodgress, Richard Benjamin, Frank Langella; ***D:*** Frank Perry. Golden Globes '71: Actress—Mus./Comedy (Snodgress); Natl. Bd. of Review '70: Support. Actor (Langella).

Diary of a Mad Old Man *Dagboek Van Een Oude Dwaas* **1988 (PG-13)** A wistful drama about an old man who's lost everything except his desire for his daughter-in-law, which sends him into fits of nostalgia. **93m/C VHS.** *BE FR NL* Derek de Lint, Ralph Michael, Beatie Edney; ***D:*** Lili Rademakers; ***W:*** Hugo Claus; ***C:*** Paul van den Bos; ***M:*** Egisto Macchi.

Diary of a Madman **1963** Price is once again possessed by an evil force in this gothic thriller. Fairly average Price vehicle, based on Guy de Maupassant's story. **96m/C VHS.** Vincent Price, Nancy Kovack, Chris Warfield, Ian Wolfe, Nelson Olmstead, Elaine Devry, Stephen Roberts; ***D:*** Reginald LeBorg; ***W:*** Robert E. Kent; ***C:*** Ellis W. Carter.

Diary of a Rebel *El Che Guevara* **1968** A fictional account of the rise of Cuban rebel leader Che Guevara. **89m/C VHS.** *IT* John Ireland, Francisco Rabal, Howard (Red) Ross, Andrea Checchi, Giacomo "Jack" Rossi-Stuart, Jose Torres, Susanna Martinkova; ***D:*** Paolo Heusch; ***W:*** Adriano Bolzoni; ***C:*** Luciano Trasatti; ***M:*** Nico Fidenco.

Diary of a Seducer *Le Journal du Seducteur; The Seducer's Diary* **1995** Claire's (Mastroianni) a bored 20-year-old Parisian whose ennui is lifted when she meets philosophy student Gregoire (Poupaud), who lends her a rare copy of Soren Kierkegaard's "Diary of a Seducer." The volume apparently has seductive powers and manages to affect everyone within Claire's orbit. French with subtitles. **98m/C VHS.** *FR* Danielle Dubroux, Chiara Mastroianni, Melvil Poupaud, Mathieu Amalric, Micheline Presle, Hubert Saint Macary, Jean-Pierre Leaud; ***D:*** Danielle Dubroux; ***W:*** Danielle Dubroux; ***C:*** Laurent Machuel; ***M:*** Jean-Marie Senia.

Diary of a Serial Killer **1997 (R)** Down-on-his-luck journalist Nelson Keece (Busey) witnesses a murder and then is invited by the killer, Stefan (Vosloo), to conduct an exclusive interview. Stefan keeps killing and Nelson keeps writing, but the cops begin to think that Keece is the killer. Then Stefan decides to target Keece's girlfriend Juliette (Campbell) as his next victim. **92m/C VHS, DVD.** Gary Busey, Arnold Vosloo, Michael Madsen, Julia Campbell; ***D:*** Alan Jacobs; ***W:*** Jennifer Badham-Stewart; ***C:*** Keith L. Smith; ***M:*** Stephen (Steve) Edwards. **VIDEO**

Diary of a Suicide 1/2 *Le Journal d'un Suicide* **1973** Dull drama with way too many flashbacks. A cruise ship tour guide becomes infatuated with the group's enigmatic interpreter who insists he woo her with stories. One of these is a complicated tale about a group of terrorists who blow up a politician, intending to also kill themselves. Only one of the terrorists survives and is sent to prison for life where she is guarded by a very strange jailer. French with subtitles. **82m/C DVD.** *FR* Delphine Seyrig, Marie-France Pisier, Sacha (Sascha) Pitoeff, Sami Frey; ***D:*** Stanislav Stanojevic; ***W:*** Stanislav Stanojevic; ***C:*** Jen-Jacques Flon.

Diary of a Teenage Hitchhiker **1982** Teen girl ignores family restrictions and police warnings about a homicidal rapist stalking the area and continues to thumb rides to her job at a beach resort. One night she's picked up for ride she'll never forget. **96m/C VHS.** Charlene Tilton, Dick Van Patten, Katherine Helmond, Dominique Dunne, Katy Kurtzman, Christopher Knight, James Carroll Jordan, Craig T. Nelson, Noelle North, Karlene Crockett, Don Mclean, Patricia Smith, Richard Sanders; ***D:*** Ted Post; ***M:*** Joe Renzetti.

Diary of a Wimpy Kid **2010 (PG)** Live-action translation of Jeff Kinney's charming illustrated novel chronicling the day-to-day misadventures of wisecracking student Greg Heffley (Gordon) and his best friend Rowley (Capron) as they navigate their first year of middle school. Neither have much interest in girls until the sharp-witted, beat-poet-reading Angie (Moretz) develops a liking for the boys. And things get a little strained when Greg thinks he might be too good to hang with Rowley. The young performers are by no means wimps, never dumbing down the source material so beloved by so many a tweener. But bringing those stick figures to life proved just as tough as Greg's life. **94m/C DVD.** Chloe Grace Moretz, Steve Zahn, Rachael Harris, Zachary Gordon, Devon Bostick; ***D:*** Thor Freudenthal; ***W:*** Jeff Filgo, Jackie Filgo, Jeff Judah, Gabe Sachs; ***C:*** Jack N. Green; ***M:*** Julia Michels.

Diary of a Young Comic **1979** New York comedian searches for the meaning of lunacy. He finds it after Improvisation in Los Angeles. **74m/C VHS.** Stacy Keach, Dom DeLuise, Richard Lewis, Bill Macy, George Jessel, Gary Muledeer, Nina Van Pallandt; ***D:*** Gary Weis.

The Diary of Anne Frank 1/2 **1959** In June 1945, a liberated Jewish refugee returns to the hidden third floor of an Amsterdam factory where he finds the diary kept by his youngest daughter, Anne. The document recounts their years in hiding from the Nazis. Based on the actual diary of 13-year-old Anne Frank, killed in a death camp during WWII. **150m/B VHS, DVD.** Millie Perkins, Joseph Schildkraut, Shelley Winters, Richard Beymer, Gusti Huber, Ed Wynn, Lou Jacobi, Diane Baker; ***D:*** George Stevens; ***C:*** William Mellor. Oscars '59: Art Dir./Set Dec., B&W, B&W Cinematog., Support. Actress (Winters).

The Diary of Anne Frank 1/2 **2008** Moggach's faithful script uses passages from Frank's diary to tell the story of a once-ordinary Jewish teenager (Kendricks in an engaging, nuanced performance) who is forced into tragic and extraordinary circumstances because of anti-Semitism and the Nazis. Originally shown as a five-part BBC miniseries; also available as a 100-minute feature film. **150m/C DVD.** *GB* Ellie Kendrick, Iain Glen, Tamsin Greig, Kate Ashfield, Geoff Breton, Lesley Sharp, Ron Cook, Roger Frost, Tim Dantay, Mariah Gale, Felicity Jones, Nicholas Farrell; ***D:*** Jon Jones; ***W:*** Deborah Moggach; ***C:*** Ian Moss; ***M:*** Charlie Mole. **TV**

The Diary of Ellen Rimbauer **2003 (R)** Prequel to Stephen King's "Rose Red," shows how the marriage of innocent Ellen (Brenner) to the unfaithful and twisted John Rimbauer (Brand) eventually found her possessed by the forces surrounding their haunted Seattle mansion. Diary passages highlight a series of deadly encounters on the estate. **88m/C VHS, DVD.** Lisa Brenner, Steven Brand, Kate Burton, Tsidii Leloka, Brad Greenquist, Tsai Chin; ***D:*** Craig R. Baxley; ***W:*** Ridley Pearson; ***C:*** Joao Fernandes; ***M:*** Gary Chang. **TV**

Diary of Forbidden Dreams *What?; Che?* **1973 (R)** A beautiful young girl finds herself drawn into bizarre incidents at an eccentric millionaire's mansion that cause her to go insane. Set on the Italian Riviera, it's the most offbeat rendition of "Alice in Wonderland" you're apt to find. Unfortunately, the convoluted plot lessens its appeal. Unedited version, under the original title "What!," released at 113 minutes, is also available. **94m/C VHS.** *IT* Marcello Mastroianni, Hugh Griffith, Sydne Rome, Roman Polanski; ***D:*** Roman Polanski; ***W:*** Roman Polanski, Gerard Brach.

Diary of the Dead **1976 (PG)** A newlywed kills his aggravating mother-in-law, only to have her repeatedly return from the grave. **93m/C** Hector Elizondo, Geraldine Fitzgerald, Salome Jens; ***D:*** Arvin Brown; ***W:*** I.C. Rapoport, Robert L. Fish; ***C:*** Robert M. "Bob" Baldwin Jr.; ***M:*** Jacques Urbont.

Diary of the Dead *George A. Romero's Diary of the Dead* **2007 (R)** Nearly 40 years after Romero's ultra-low-budget "Night of the Living Dead," he's taking another stab at the genre with his fifth zombie flick. This modern incarnation starts with some college kids shooting a horror movie in the woods when their filming is interrupted by radio reports of zombies afoot. Camera rolling, the plucky students and their professor abandon the shoot to head for safer ground, but director Jason instead gets footage of his pals succumbing to zombification. Not too much new here, but the familiarity, nostalgia and gooey gore will make some die-hards happy. Pay attention to the spoofs of the original. **95m/C DVD.** *US* Joshua Close, Joe Dinicol, Philip Riccio, Michelle Morgan, Shawn Roberts, Amy Lalonde, Scott Wentworth; ***D:*** George A. Romero; ***W:*** George A. Romero; ***C:*** Adam Swica; ***M:*** Norman Orenstein.

Dick **1999 (PG-13)** If you think Hollywood is done making fun of Nixon, then you don't know "Dick." Satire puts forth the theory that two dizzy teenage girls (Dunst and Williams) caused the downfall of Richard Nixon (Hedaya). They bump into all the major Watergate players, including Liddy (Shearer), Haldemann (Foley) and Dean (Breuer). The girls are blissfully blind to Tricky Dick's indiscretions, and one of them even develops a hilarious crush on him. When they overhear him abusing the presidential pup, however, they turn on him. Flouting the Constitution is one thing, but being mean to dogs is clearly icky behavior. They decide to become the famed Deep Throat for bickering reporters Woodward (Ferrell) and Bernstein (McCulloch). Rent this with "All the President's Men" and "Nixon," because this is the movie that Oliver Stone would've made if he had a sense of humor instead of flashbacks. **95m/C VHS, DVD.** Kirsten Dunst, Michelle Williams, Dan Hedaya, Will Ferrell, Dave Foley, Harry Shearer, Jim Breuer, Bruce McCulloch, Devon Gummersall, Ted McGinley, Ryan Reynolds, Saul Rubinek, Teri Garr, G.D. Spradlin, Ana Gasteyer; ***D:*** Andrew Fleming; ***W:*** Andrew Fleming, Sheryl Longin; ***C:*** Alexander Grusynski; ***M:*** John Debney.

Dick Barton, Special Agent **1948** Dick Barton is called in when a mad scientist threatens to attack London with germ-carrying bombs. The first film production for Hammer Studios, later to be known for its horror classics. **70m/B VHS.** *GB* Don Stannard, Geoffrey Ford, Jack Shaw; ***D:*** Alfred Goulding.

Dick Barton Strikes Back **1/2** **1948** "Mr. French" Cabot has a nuclear weapon and is willing to use it; that is, until Dick Barton arrives to put the Frenchman out of commission. Generally considered the best of the Dick Barton film series. **73m/B VHS.** *GB* Don Stannard, Sebastian Cabot, Jean Lodge; ***D:*** Godfrey Grayson.

Dick Tracy **1937** Serial, based on the comic-strip character, in 15 chapters. Tracy tries to find his kidnapped brother as he faces the fiend "Spider." The first chapter is 30 minutes and each additional chapter is 20 minutes. **290m/B VHS, DVD.** Ralph Byrd, Smiley Burnette, Irving Pichel, Jennifer Jones; ***D:*** John English, Alan James, Ray Taylor.

Dick Tracy **1/2** **1990 (PG)** Beatty wears the caps of producer, director, and star, performing admirably on all fronts. One minor complaint: his Tracy is somewhat flat in comparison to the outstanding performances and makeup of the unique villains, especially Pacino. Stylistically superior, shot in only seven colors, the timeless sets capture the essence rather than the reality of the city, successfully bringing the comic strip to life. Madonna is fine as the seductive Breathless Mahoney, belting out Stephen Sondheim like she was born to do it. People expecting the gothic technology of "Batman" may be disappointed, but moviegoers searching for a memory made real will be thrilled. ♫ Sooner or Later. **105m/C VHS, DVD.** Warren Beatty, Madonna, Charlie Korsmo, Glenne Headly, Al Pacino, Dustin Hoffman, James Caan, Mandy Patinkin, Paul Sorvino, Charles Durning, Dick Van Dyke, R.G. Armstrong, Catherine O'Hara, Estelle Parsons, Seymour Cassel, Michael J. Pollard, William Forsythe, Kathy Bates, James Tolkan; ***D:*** Warren Beatty; ***W:*** Jim Cash, Jack Epps Jr.; ***C:*** Vittorio Storaro; ***M:*** Danny Elfman, Stephen Sondheim. Oscars '90: Art Dir./Set Dec., Makeup, Song ("Sooner or Later").

Dick Tracy, Detective **1945** The first Dick Tracy feature film, in which Splitface is on the loose, a schoolteacher is murdered, the Mayor is threatened, and a nutty professor uses a crystal ball to give Tracy the clues needed to connect the crimes. **62m/B VHS, DVD.** Morgan Conway, Anne Jeffreys, Mike Mazurki, Jane Greer, Lyle Latell; ***D:*** William Berke; ***W:*** Eric Taylor; ***C:*** Frank Redman; ***M:*** Roy Webb.

Dick Tracy Meets Gruesome *Dick Tracy's Amazing Adventure; Dick Tracy Meets Karloff* **1947** Gruesome and his partner in crime, Melody, stage a bank robbery using the secret formula of Dr. A. Tomic. Tracy has to solve the case before word gets out and people rush to withdraw their savings, destroying civilization as we know it. **66m/B VHS, DVD.** Boris Karloff, Ralph Byrd, Lyle Latell, Anne Gwynne, Edward Ashley, June Clayworth, Tony Barrett, Skelton Knaggs; ***D:*** John Rawlins; ***W:*** Eric Taylor, Robertson White; ***C:*** Frank Redman; ***M:*** Paul Sawtell.

Dick Tracy Returns **1938** 15-chapter serial. Public Enemy Paw Stark and his gang set out on a wave of crime that brings them face to face with dapper Dick. **100m/B VHS.** Ralph Byrd, Charles Middleton; ***D:*** William Witney.

Dick Tracy: The Spider Strikes **1937** Dick Tracy, his bumbling sidekick, and his beautiful, brainy assistant go up against the master criminal, The Spider. **60m/B VHS, DVD.** Kay Hughes, Smiley Burnette, Lee Van Atta, Ralph Byrd, Francis X. Bushman; ***D:*** Alan James, Ray Taylor; ***W:*** Barry Shipman, Winston Miller; ***C:*** Edgar Lyons, William Nobles.

Dick Tracy vs. Crime Inc. **1941** Dick Tracy encounters many difficulties when he tries to track down a criminal who can make himself invisible. A serial in 15 chapters. **100m/B VHS.** Ralph Byrd, Ralph Morgan, Michael Owen; ***D:*** William Witney; ***W:*** John English.

Dick Tracy vs. Cueball **1946** Dick Tracy has his work cut out for him when the evil gangster Cueball appears on the scene. Based on Chester Gould's comic strip. **62m/B VHS, DVD.** Morgan Conway, Anne Jeffreys, Lyle Latell, Rita (Paula) Corday, Ian Keith, Dick Wessel, Skelton Knaggs; ***D:*** Gordon Douglas; ***W:*** Robert E. Kent, Dane Lussier; ***C:*** George E. Diskant; ***M:*** C. Bakaleinikoff, Phil Ohman.

Dick Tracy's Dilemma *Mark of the Claw* **1947** The renowned police detective Dick Tracy tries to solve a case involving the Claw. Based on the Chester Gould comic strip. **60m/B VHS, DVD.** Ralph Byrd, Lyle Latell, Kay Christopher, Jack Lambert, Ian Keith, Jimmy Conlin; ***D:*** John Rawlins; ***W:*** Robert Stephen Brode; ***C:*** Frank Redman; ***M:*** Paul Sawtell.

Dick Turpin **1/2** **1925** In this rare film, Mix plays the famed English highwayman who seeks adventure in historical Britain. **60m/B VHS.** Tom Mix, Alan Hale; ***D:*** John Blystone.

Dickie Roberts: Former Child Star **2003 (PG-13)** Spade plays the impish title character, a valet parking attendant who wishes to revive his former child-star sitcom fame. Without much help from his despondent agent (a dead-on Lovitz), Dickie scores a meeting with Rob Reiner (as himself!) who's casting the lead in his new movie. When Dickie loses the role due to a lack of real character, he hires a family to relive his lost youth and help him get a real life. Pic is at its crackling best when Spade is his usual, smarmy self, but suffers when trying for earnestness. Amusing cameos by the likes of Leif Garrett, Danny Bonaduce, and Corey Feldman, and the final credits include a fun and rousing anthem sung by a gaggle of former child stars. **99m/C VHS, DVD.** *US* David Spade, Mary McCormack, Craig Bierko, Jon Lovitz, Alyssa Milano, Doris Roberts, Jenna Boyd, Scott Tessa, Edie McClurg; ***Cameos:*** Rob Reiner, Leif Garrett, Brendan Fraser; ***D:*** Sam Weisman; ***W:*** David Spade, Fred Wolf; ***C:*** Thomas Ackerman; ***M:*** Christophe Beck, Waddy Wachtel.

Did You Hear About the Morgans? **2009 (PG-13)** Successful New York couple Meryl (Parker) and Paul (Grant) Morgan are in the midst of their unraveling marriage when they witness a murder and become the targets of a hitman. Placed into the Witness Protection Program, the Morgans trade upscale Manhattan for a tiny Wyoming town, and all-too-familiar, brutally unfunny "fish out of water" hijinks ensue. Grant and Parker display little of their individual charm in their phoned-in performances as the obnoxious Paul and grating Meryl. A cliche-ridden comedy filled with predictable jokes about how darn dumb city folk are when you take them to the heartland. The less you hear about the Morgans, the better. **103m/C DVD.** *US* Hugh Grant, Sarah Jessica Parker, Sam Elliott, Mary Steenburgen, Elisabeth (Elissabeth, Elizabeth, Liz) Moss, Michael Kelly, Seth Gilliam; ***D:*** Marc Lawrence; ***W:*** Marc Lawrence; ***C:*** Florian Ballhaus; ***M:*** Thomas S. Drescher.

Didn't You Hear? **1983 (PG)** An alienated college student discovers that dreams have a life of their own when he becomes immersed in his own fantasy world. **94m/C VHS.** Dennis Christopher, Gary Busey, Cheryl Waters, John Kauffman; ***D:*** Skip Sherwood.

Die Another Day **1/2** **2002 (PG-13)** The 20th film in the James Bond series carries a lot of "in" jokes referring to previous films, including the bikini and knife belt worn by NSA agent Jinx (shades of Ursula Andress in "Dr. No"). Of course, the beautiful Berry is well worth comtemplating, which is a good thing since this Bond is fairly tiresome with its convoluted plot and over-the-top action. It starts off well and Brosnan is comfortable in the role (even with the silly double entendres) but the main villain (Stephens) is another meglomaniac with designs on taking over the world (wrapped around some political cant) and the second half of the film is one chase scene after another. Yawn. **130m/C VHS, DVD, Blu-ray Disc.** *US* Pierce Brosnan, Halle Berry, Toby Stephens, Judi Dench, John Cleese, Rosamund Pike, Rick Yune, Michael Madsen, Will Yun Lee, Kenneth Tsang, Samantha Bond, Colin Salmon, Emilio Echeverria, Michael Gorevoy, Lawrence Makoare; ***D:*** Lee Tamahori; ***W:*** Neal Purvis, Robert Wade; ***C:*** David Tattersall; ***M:*** David Arnold. Golden Raspberries '02: Worst Support. Actress (Madonna).

Die! Die! My Darling! **1/2** *Fanatic* **1965** A young widow visits her mad ex-mother-in-law in a remote English village, and is imprisoned by the mourning woman as revenge for her son's death. Bankhead's last role. Based on Anne Blaisdell's novel. **97m/C VHS, DVD.** *GB* Tallulah Bankhead, Stefanie Powers, Peter Vaughan, Maurice Kaufmann, Donald Sutherland, Gwendolyn Watts, Yootha Joyce, Winifred Dennis; ***D:*** Silvio Narizzano; ***W:*** Richard Matheson; ***C:*** Arthur Ibbetson; ***M:*** Wilfred Josephs.

Die Grosse Freiheit Nr. 7 **1/2** *Great Freedom No. 7* **1945** A man tries to stop his niece's love affair with a sailor. Nazi propaganda minister Goebbels banned this film in Germany, since it showed German soldiers getting drunk and also had Hildebrand cast as a prostitute. After the war, however, it enjoyed great popularity throughout Germany. Albers sings the classic "Auf der Reeperbahn." In German with no English translation. **100m/C VHS.** *GE* Hans Albers, Hilde Hildebrand, Ilse Werner, Hans Sohnker, Helmut Kautner; ***D:*** Helmut Kautner; ***W:*** Helmut Kautner; ***C:*** Werner Krien; ***M:*** Werner Eisbrenner.

Die Hard **1988 (R)** It's Christmas Eve and NYC cop John McClane (Willis) has arrived in L.A. to spend the holiday with his estranged wife Holly (Bedelia) and their kids. Unfortunately, Holly is one of the hostages being held by a band of ruthless high-stakes terrorists in the Century City high-rise headquarters of a Japanese corporation. Soon it's the loner cop against the intruders, who are led by Eurotrash villain Hans Gruber (a marvelous performance by Rickman). A high-voltage action thriller that's just as unbelievable as it sounds, but you'll love it anyway. Based on the novel "Nothing Lasts Forever" by Roderick Thorp. **114m/C VHS, DVD, Blu-ray Disc, UMD.** Bruce Willis, Bonnie Bedelia, Alan Rickman, Alexander Godunov, Paul Gleason, William Atherton, Reginald VelJohnson, Hart Bochner, James Shigeta, Mary Ellen Trainor, De'voreaux White, Robert Davi, Ric(k) Ducommun, Clarence Gilyard Jr., Grand L. Bush, Al Leong, Wilhelm von Homburg; ***D:*** John McTiernan; ***W:*** Jeb Stuart, Steven E. de Souza; ***C:*** Jan De Bont; ***M:*** Michael Kamen.

Die Hard 2: Die Harder **1990 (R)** Fast, well-done sequel brings another impossible situation before the wise-cracking, tough-cookie cop. Our hero tangles with a group of terrorists at an airport under siege, while his wife remains in a plane circling above as its fuel dwindles. Obviously a repeat of the plot and action of the first "Die Hard," with references to the former in the script. While the bad guys lack the fiendishness of their predecessors, this installment features energetic and finely acted performances. Fairly gory, especially the icicle-in-the-eyeball scene. Adapted from the novel "58 Minutes" by Walter Wager and characters created by Roderick Thorp. **124m/C VHS, DVD, Blu-ray Disc, UMD.** Bruce Willis, William Atherton, Franco Nero, Bonnie Bedelia, John Amos, Reginald VelJohnson, Dennis Franz, Art Evans, Fred Dalton Thompson, William Sadler, Sheila McCarthy, Robert Patrick, John Leguizamo, Robert Costanzo, Tom Verica, Don Harvey, Tony Ganios, Vondie Curtis-Hall, Colm Meaney; ***D:*** Renny Harlin; ***W:*** Doug Richardson, Steven E. de Souza; ***C:*** Oliver Wood; ***M:*** Michael Kamen.

Die Hard: With a Vengeance **1/2** *Die Hard 3* **1995 (R)** Third time is not a charm in the "Die Hard" series. McClane (Willis) is back home in the Big Apple and having another bad day. More Eurotrash terrorists, led by the brilliant and vengeful Simon (Irons), are out to blow things up, snag some gold, and make life miserable for McClane and his reluctant partner, Zeus Carver (Jackson). The claustrophobic settings of the first two outings have been replaced by the exhausting expanse of New York City, to good effect, but frenetic action scenes and good chemistry between Willis and Jackson don't quite compensate for a lackluster script and more cartoony feel. Jackson brings a fresh perspective and vitality. **131m/C VHS, DVD, Blu-ray Disc.** Bruce Willis, Samuel L. Jackson, Jeremy Irons, Graham Greene, Colleen Camp, Larry Bryggman, Tony Peck, Nick Wyman, Sam (Leslie) Phillips; ***D:*** John McTiernan; ***W:*** Jonathan Hensleigh; ***C:*** Peter Menzies Jr.; ***M:*** Michael Kamen.

Die Laughing **WOOF!** **1980 (PG)** A cab driver unwittingly becomes involved in murder, intrigue, and the kidnapping of a monkey that has memorized a scientific formula that can destroy the world. Writer/actor/composer Benson might consider renaming it "Die from Embarassment." **108m/C VHS.** Robby Benson, Charles Durning, Bud Cort, Elsa Lanchester, Peter Coyote; ***D:*** Jeff Werner; ***W:*** Robby Benson, Scott Parker; ***M:*** Robby Benson.

Die Mommie Die! **1/2** **2003 (R)** Angela Arden (co-writer Busch, in drag) is a fading diva trapped in a loveless marriage. Her husband, Sol Hussman (Hall), a movie producer, refuses to give her a divorce. Like all good dysfunctional families, battle lines are drawn between dad, supported by daughter Edith (Lyonne) and Angela, supported by son Lance (Sands). Add in bisexual gigolo Tony Parker (Priestly) and fanatically religious maid Bootsie Carp (Conroy) plus some bawdy humor, and you've got the workings of a campy cult classic. Definitely one for John Waters fans. **90m/C VHS, DVD.** *US* Charles Busch, Natasha Lyonne, Jason Priestley, Frances Conroy, Philip Baker Hall, Stark Sands, Victor Raider-Wexler, Nora Dunn; ***D:*** Mark Rucker; ***W:*** Charles Busch; ***C:*** Kelly Evans; ***M:*** Dennis McCarthy.

Die, Monster, Die! *Monster of Terror* **1965** A reclusive scientist experiments with a radioactive meteorite and gains bizarre powers. Karloff is great in this adaptation of H.P. Lovecraft's "The Color Out of Space." **80m/C VHS, DVD.** *GB* Boris Karloff, Nick Adams, Suzan Farmer, Patrick Magee, Freda Jackson, Terence de Marney, Leslie Dwyer, Paul Farrell; ***D:*** Daniel Haller; ***W:*** Jerry Sohl; ***C:*** Paul Beeson; ***M:*** Don Banks.

Die Screaming, Marianne *Die, Beautiful Marianne* **1973** A girl is on the run from her father, a crooked judge, who wants to kill her before her 21st birthday, when she will inherit evidence that will put him away for life. **81m/C VHS, DVD.** *GB* Michael Rennie, Susan George, Karin Dor, Leo Genn; ***D:*** Pete

Walker; ***W:*** Murray Smith; ***C:*** Norman G. Langley; ***M:*** Cyril Ornadel.

Die Sister, Die! **1974** Thriller about a gothic mansion with an eerie secret in the basement features a battle between a senile, reclusive sister and her disturbed, tormenting brother. **88m/C VHS, DVD.** Jack Ging, Edith Atwater, Antoinette Bower, Kent Smith, Robert Emhardt; ***D:*** Randall Hood.

Die Watching **1/2 1993 (R)** Sleazy erotic thriller about a video director (Atkins) who not only likes to film some hot Hollywood babes but may also like to kill them as well. His latest discovery just could be the next victim. **92m/C VHS, DVD.** Christopher Atkins, Vali Ashton, Tim Thomerson, Carlos Palomino, Mike Jacobs Jr.; ***D:*** Charles Davis; ***W:*** Kenneth J. Hall; ***C:*** Howard Wexler; ***M:*** Scott Roewe.

Diecovery *Chum thaang rot fai phii* **2003** A man convinces a young woman to marry him and sign over her resort to him. When she finds out he intends to betray her, and go back to his ex-wife, she goes mad and falls off the hotel's railing while trying to attack said wife. She falls all of 10 feet. And is stone dead. They hide the body, and 25 years later her ghost suddenly seeks revenge. **92m/C DVD.** *TH* Chutima Avery, Suthiporn Meta, Natcha Songsuwan, Jaran Patchjaroen; ***D:*** Kulrachart Jittkajornvanit; ***C:*** Yuttadanai Mongkolphun, Sarawut Thongbhanyong.

Different for Girls **1996 (R)** Boyish motorcycle dispatch rider Paul Prentice (Graves) nearly gets run over by a London taxi whose passenger Kim Foyle (Mackintosh) seems strangely familiar. Then Paul discovers Kim used to be his boyhood school chum Karl. After a shaky start, the duo discover a genuine attraction but when they get into an argument that leads to a police call and Paul gets thrown in jail, Kim's first instincts are to retreat to her sister's (Reeves) family and back into her quiet life. Director Spence refrains from camping up the situation and some fine performances, especially from the engaging Graves, make this quirky film well worth a watch. **101m/C VHS, DVD.** *GB* Rupert Graves, Steven Mackintosh, Miriam Margolyes, Saskia Reeves, Neil Dudgeon, Charlotte Coleman; ***D:*** Richard Spence; ***W:*** Tony Merchant; ***C:*** Sean Van Hales; ***M:*** Stephen Warbeck. Montreal World Film Fest. '95: Film.

A Different Loyalty **2004 (R)** Gleaned from the true story of an American journalist, Sally (Stone), finds love with British government agent Leo (Everett) while in Beirut during the Cold War. They marry, but their happily ever after is interrupted when Leo goes missing. A desperate search takes her to the Soviet Union where his disturbing secret life endangers them both. **96m/C VHS, DVD.** Sharon Stone, Rupert Everett, Julian Wadham, Michael Cochrane, Anne Lambton, Jim Piddock, Richard McMillan, Mimi Kuzyk, Emily Van Camp, Tamara Hope, Damir Andrei, John Bourgeois, Sonja Smits, Edward Hibbert, Joss Ackland, Jack Galloway, Matthew Scurfield, Ron Lea, Mark Rendall; ***D:*** Marek Kanievska; ***C:*** Jean Lepine; ***M:*** Normand Corbeil. **VIDEO**

Different Story **1/2 1978 (PG)** Romance develops when a lesbian real estate agent offers a homosexual chauffeur a job with her firm. Resorts to stereotypes when the characters decide to marry. **107m/C VHS, DVD.** Perry King, Meg Foster, Valerie Curtin, Peter Donat, Richard Bull; ***D:*** Paul Aaron.

DIG! **2004 (R)** Seven year documentary chronicle of two indie-rock bands, charting rise of one and downfall of the other. The Dandy Warhols, led by Courtney Taylor, seem to be blessed by the angels as they meteorically rise in the world of alterna-pop. Anton Newcombe and band, Brian Jonestown Massacre, who are great mentors to Taylor's own band, seem to have no one but Newcombe to blame for their lack of success. Belligerent and out-of-control, Newcombe amazingly crafts brilliant album after album, but scares bandmates, record companies and friends away. Truly sad up-close look at the difficulties of remaining uncompromising in the ruthless music business. **110m/C DVD.** *US* ***D:*** Ondi Timoner; ***W:*** Ondi Timoner; ***C:*** Ondi Timoner, Vasco Lucas Nunes, David Timoner; ***M:*** David Brownlow.

Digby, the Biggest Dog in the World **1973 (G)** Poor comedy-fantasy about Digby, a sheepdog, who wanders around a scientific laboratory, drinks an experimental fluid, and grows and grows and grows. **88m/C VHS.** *GB* Jim Dale, Angela Douglas, Spike Milligan, Dinsdale Landen; ***D:*** Joseph McGrath; ***M:*** Edwin Astley.

Digger **1/2 1994 (PG)** Digger (Hann-Byrd) arrives at a Pacific Northwest island to stay with relatives, including his Grandma (Dukakis) who's being romanced by the fun-loving Arthur (Nielsen). He makes friends with another youth who turns out to have a terminal heart ailment. **92m/C VHS.** Adam Hann-Byrd, Olympia Dukakis, Leslie Nielsen, Joshua Jackson, Barbara Williams, Timothy Bottoms; ***D:*** Robert Turner; ***W:*** Rodney Gibbons; ***M:*** Todd Boekelheide.

Diggers **1/2 2006 (R)** Four 30-something buddies face life-changing decisions in this modest slice-of-life drama. In 1976, Long Islanders Hunt (Rudd), Jack (Eldard), Cons (Hamilton), and Lozo (Marino) continue their families' tradition as clam diggers, but their livelihood is threatened by a corporate fishery that's buying up prime water rights. Hunt's dad has just died so maybe he should finally move on but he's worried when lothario Jack starts sniffing around his divorced sister, Gina (Tierney). Meanwhile, Cons supplements his earnings dealing pot (although smoking most of it), and Lozo's large and increasing family strains his marriage and his temper. Charming and poignant despite its well-worn premise of breaking out of small-town working-class life. **90m/C DVD.** *US* Paul Rudd, Ron Eldard, Josh Hamilton, Ken Marino, Lauren Ambrose, Maura Tierney, Sarah Paulson; ***D:*** Katherine Dieckmann; ***C:*** Michael McDonough; ***M:*** David Mansfield.

Digging to China **1/2 1998 (PG)** Directorial debut of Hutton is the sentimental story of a sweet friendship between misfits—precocious 10-year-old Harriet (Wood) and mentally handicapped 30-year-old Ricky (Bacon). Harriet's alcoholic mom (Moriarty) runs a motel in rural New Hampshire (film is set in the mid-'60s) with Harriet's slutty older sister Gwen (Masterson). Ricky winds up at the motel with his dying mother Leah (Seldes), who was taking him to an institution when her car breaks down. Harriet thinks Ricky is a terrific playmate but after some shocking news, the young girl and her new friend decide to run away—causing a lot of trouble. **98m/C VHS, DVD.** Evan Rachel Wood, Kevin Bacon, Mary Stuart Masterson, Cathy Moriarty, Marian Seldes; ***D:*** Timothy Hutton; ***W:*** Karen Janszen; ***C:*** Jorgen Persson; ***M:*** Cynthia Millar.

Digging Up Business **WOOF! 1991 (PG)** Johnson tries to save the family funeral home business from financial ruin with some unique interment services. This film needs a decent burial. **89m/C VHS.** Lynn-Holly Johnson, Billy Barty, Ruth Buzzi, Murray Langston, Yvonne Craig, Gary Owens; ***D:*** Mark Byers.

Diggstown **1/2 1992 (R)** Lightweight, good-natured sports comedy about a boxing scam. Con man Gabriel Caine (Woods), fresh out of prison, heads for Diggstown and the unregulated boxing matches arranged by town boss, John Gillon (Dern). The bet is that Caine's one boxer can beat any 10 boxers, chosen by Gillon, in a 24-hour period. So Caine decides to hook up with an old friend, former prizefighter "Honey" Roy Palmer (Gosset Jr.), to run the scam of his life. Dern is sufficiently nasty and Woods his usual nervy self but it's Gossett Jr. who manages to hold everything together as the aging boxer. Based on the novel "The Diggstown Ringers" by Leonard Wise. **97m/C VHS, DVD.** James Woods, Louis Gossett Jr., Bruce Dern, Oliver Platt, Heather Graham, Randall "Tex" Cobb, Thomas Wilson Brown, Duane Davis, Willie Green, George D. Wallace, Wilhelm von Homburg; ***D:*** Michael Ritchie; ***W:*** Steven McKay; ***M:*** James Newton Howard.

Digital Man **1/2 1994 (R)** High-tech military super-soldier prototype has his programming sabotaged and a team of human and robotic commmandoes must prevent him from starting WWIII. **95m/C VHS.** Ken Olandt, Adam Baldwin, Ed Lauter, Matthias Hues, Kristen Dalton, Paul Gleason; ***D:*** Phillip J. Roth; ***W:*** Phillip J. Roth, Ronald Schmidt.

Dilemma **1/2 1997** On Death Row, Rudy Salazar (Trejo) volunteers to be a bone-marrow donor to a sick child. LAPD detective Quin (Howell) realizes that it's a set-up for an escape and he's right. Then the cops have to catch Salazar again, but they can't kill him without sacrificing the kid. **87m/C DVD.** C. Thomas Howell, Danny Trejo, Sofia Shinas; ***D:*** Eric Larsen; ***W:*** Ira Israel, Chuck Conaway; ***C:*** Mark Melville; ***M:*** Albritton McClain.

Dillinger **1945** John Dillinger's notorious career, from street punk to public enemy number one, receives a thrilling fast-paced treatment. Tierney turns in a fine performance in this interesting account of the criminal life. **70m/C VHS, DVD.** Lawrence Tierney, Edmund Lowe, Anne Jeffreys, Elisha Cook Jr.; ***D:*** Max Nosseck; ***W:*** Philip Yordan.

Dillinger **1/2 1973 (R)** The most colorful period of criminality in America is brought to life in this story of bank-robber John Dillinger, "Baby Face" Nelson, and the notorious "Lady in Red." **106m/C VHS, DVD.** Warren Oates, Michelle Phillips, Richard Dreyfuss, Cloris Leachman, Ben Johnson, Harry Dean Stanton; ***D:*** John Milius; ***W:*** John Milius; ***C:*** Jules Brenner; ***M:*** Barry DeVorzon.

Dillinger **1/2** *The Last Days of John Dillinger* **1991** Harmon stars as the Depression-era bank robber, who became public enemy number one, in this TV gangster story. Fenn's girlfriend Billy Frenchette, with Patton particularly beady-eyed as G-man Melvin Purvis. **95m/C VHS.** Mark Harmon, Sherilyn Fenn, Will Patton, Patricia Arquette, Vince Edwards, Bruce Abbott; ***D:*** Rupert Wainwright; ***C:*** Donald M. Morgan.

Dillinger and Capone **1/2 1995 (R)** Supposedly the FBI has killed the wrong Dillinger and the gangster (Sheen) decides to make a new life. But his old friend Al Capone (Abraham), newly released from prison, is holding Dillinger's wife (Hicks) and son hostage as insurance that first he'll retrieve $15 million from a mob-owned Chicago bank. **95m/C VHS, DVD.** Martin Sheen, F. Murray Abraham, Catherine Hicks, Stephen Davies, Don Stroud, Clint Howard, Joe Estevez; ***D:*** Jon Purdy; ***W:*** Michael B. Druxman; ***C:*** John Aronson; ***M:*** David Wurst, Eric Wurst.

Dillinger Is Dead **1/2** *Dillinger e Morto* **1969** Uneven combo of reality and fantasy is a trippy curiosity. Industrial designer Glauco unexpectedly finds a gun while cooking dinner and uses it to kill his wife then dreams about escaping to Tahiti. Or maybe he does. And maybe the.45 that Glauco finds belonged to American gangster John Dillinger but it doesn't seem to matter. Italian with subtitles. **90m/C DVD.** *IT* Michel Piccoli, Anita Pallenberg, Annie Girardot; ***D:*** Marco Ferreri; ***W:*** Marco Ferreri, Sergio Bazzini; ***C:*** Mario Vulpiani; ***M:*** Teo Usuelli.

Dim Sum: A Little Bit of Heart **1985 (PG)** The second independent film from the director of "Chan Is Missing." A Chinese-American mother and daughter living in San Francisco's Chinatown confront the conflict between traditional Eastern ways and modern American life. Gentle, fragile picture made with humor and care. In English and Chinese with subtitles. **88m/C VHS, DVD.** Laureen Chew, Kim Chew, Victor Wong, Ida F.O. Chong, Cora Miao, John Nishio, Joan Chen; ***D:*** Wayne Wang; ***W:*** Terrel Seltzer; ***M:*** Todd Boekelheide.

Dim Sum Funeral **1/2 2008 (R)** Uneasy and unsuccessful mix of sentimentality and comedy. Four estranged Chinese-American siblings are reunited in Seattle when their busybody mother dies since she wanted a traditional seven-day Chinese funeral. Secrets (none of them particularly shocking or surprising) are revealed. **95m/C DVD.** Julia Nickson-Soul, Russell Wong, Francoise Yip, Steph Song, Bai Ling, Talia Shire, Kelly Hu, Lisa Lu; ***D:*** Anna Chi; ***W:*** Donald Martin; ***C:*** Michael Balfry; ***M:*** Scott Starrett.

Diminished Capacity **2008** Recently fired Chicago political columnist Cooper (Broderick) is urged to return home to rural Illinois to convince his uncle Rollie (Alda) to check into a nursing home. Cooper and Rollie bond through a shared ailment: both suffer memory loss, Cooper from an old bar fight and Rollie from Alzheimer's. The gathered family soon discovers that one of Rollie's old baseball cards is worth a fortune and could bring him out of debt. So Cooper, an old flame (Madsen), and her son take a trip into the city in hopes of cashing it in at a sports card convention, where they haggle with dealers and fall into silly hijinks. Unfortunately, a tame script brings only light laughter and doesn't say much about anything. **92m/C DVD.** *US* Matthew Broderick, Alan Alda, Virginia Madsen, Louis CK, Jimmy Bennett, Dylan Baker, Bobby Cannavale, Jim True-Frost, Jeff(rey) Perry, Lois Smith; ***D:*** Terry Kinney; ***W:*** Sherwood Kinney; ***C:*** Vanja Cernjul; ***M:*** Robert Berger, Griffin Richardson.

Dimples **1/2 1936 (PG)** When Shirley's pickpocket grandfather is caught red-handed, she steps in, takes the blame, and somehow ends up in show business. Reissued version is rated. Also available colorized. ♫Hey, What Did the Bluebird Say?; He Was a Dandy; Picture Me Without You; Oh Mister Man Up in the Moon; Dixie-Anna; Get On Board; Swing Low Sweet Chariot. **78m/B VHS, DVD.** Shirley Temple, John Carradine, Frank Morgan, Helen Westley, Berton Churchill, Robert Kent, Delma Byron; ***D:*** William A. Seiter; ***W:*** Nat Perrin, Arthur Sheekman; ***C:*** Bert Glennon; ***M:*** Louis Silvers.

Diner **1/2 1982 (R)** A group of old high school friends meet at "their" Baltimore diner to find that more has changed than the menu. A bittersweet look at the experiences of a group of Baltimore twentysomethings, circa 1959, who find adulthood hard to face. Particularly notable was Levinson's casting of "unknowns" who have since become household names. Features many humorous moments and fine performances. **110m/C VHS, DVD.** Steve Guttenberg, Daniel Stern, Mickey Rourke, Kevin Bacon, Ellen Barkin, Timothy Daly, Paul Reiser, Michael Tucker, Jessica James, Kathryn Dowling, Colette Blonigan; ***D:*** Barry Levinson; ***W:*** Barry Levinson; ***C:*** Peter Sova; ***M:*** Bruce Brody, Ivan Kral. Natl. Soc. Film Critics '82: Support. Actor (Rourke).

Dingaka **1/2 1965** A controversial drama from the writer and director of "The Gods Must Be Crazy" about a South African tribesman who avenges his daughter's murder by tribal laws, and is then tried by white man's laws. A crusading white attorney struggles to acquit him. **96m/C VHS.** Stanley Baker, Juliet Prowse, Ken Gampu; ***D:*** Jamie Uys.

Dingo **1/2 1990** In Davis' only film appearance he's, what else, a famous jazz trumpeter. Paris-based Billy Cross (Davis) and his combo are on tour in 1969 and momentarily stuck at a remote Australian airstrip. They give an impromptu concert heard by John "Dingo" Anderson (Friels), who instantly decides that music is the life for him. Over the years Dingo keeps in touch with his idol as he works outback bars and secretly saves to go to Paris and check out the scene—even if it means sacrificing his wife and family. **108m/C VHS, DVD.** *FR AU* Colin Friels, Miles Davis, Helen Buday, Bernadette LaFont; ***D:*** Rolf de Heer; ***W:*** Marc Rosenberg; ***C:*** Denis Lenoir; ***M:*** Miles Davis, Michel Legrand.

The Dining Room **1/2 1986** Six performers play more than 50 roles in this adaptation of A.R. Gurney Jr.'s play set in a dining room, where people live out dramatic and comic moments in their lives. From the "American Playhouse" series. **90m/C VHS.** Remak Ramsay, Pippa Perthree, John Shea, Frances Sternhagen; ***D:*** Allan Goldstein.

Dinner and Driving **1/2 1997** Twentysomething writer Jason (a charming Slotnick) looks like a nebbish but must have something else going for him because he's caught between two babes. One is longtime girlfriend Laura (Devicq), who has pressured the reluctant Jason into a marriage proposal. The other is Grace (Bako), a hottie who was Jason's college sweetie and suddenly makes a reappearance in his life. Jason, who doesn't know if he can commit to one woman for life, seeks advice from his equally clueless friends and realizes that relationships aren't easy. **89m/C VHS, DVD.** Joey Slotnick, Paula DeVicq, Brigitte Bako, Sam Robards, Molly Shannon, Greg Grunberg; ***D:*** Lawrence Trilling; ***W:*** Lawrence Trilling, Steven Wolfson; ***C:*** Geary McLeod; ***M:*** Peter Himmelman.

Dinner at Eight **1933** Social-climbing Mrs. Jordan (Burke) and her husband Oliver (Lionel Barrymore) throw a dinner party for various members of the New York elite. During the course of the evening, all of the guests reveal too much. Special performances all around, especially John Barrymore in a parody of his drunken career, Dressler as a grande dame sliding down the social ladder, and Harlow as a gold-digging hussy. Superb comedic direction by Cukor. Adapted from the play by Edna Ferber and George Kaufman. **110m/C VHS, DVD.** John Barrymore, Lionel Barrymore, Wallace Beery, Madge Evans, Jean Harlow, Billie Burke, Marie Dressler, Phillips Holmes, Jean Hersholt, Lee Tracy, Edmund Lowe, Karen Morley, May Robson; ***D:*** George Cukor; ***W:*** Herman J. Mankiewicz, Frances Marion, Donald Ogden Stewart; ***C:*** William H. Daniels; ***M:*** William Axt.

Dinner at Eight **1989** A social-climbing romance novelist throws an elegant dinner party. TV remake of the 1933 film does not compare well. **100m/C VHS.** Lauren Bacall, Charles Durning, Ellen Greene, Harry Hamlin, John Mahoney, Marsha Mason, Tim Kazurinsky; ***D:*** Ron Lagomarsino. **TV**

Dinner at the Ritz ½ **1937** Daughter of a murdered Parisian banker vows to find his killer with help from her fiance. **78m/B VHS, DVD.** *GB* David Niven, Annabella, Paul Lukas, Patricia Medina; ***D:*** Harold Schuster.

Dinner for Schmucks **2010** Remake of the 1998 French film "The Dinner Game." Exec Tim (Rudd) attends his boss' monthly dinner where each invitee (if they want to get noticed by the head honcho) must bring the most pathetic person they can find. So Tim brings along IRS employee Barry (Carrell). **m/C DVD.** *US* Steve Carell, Paul Rudd, Lucy Punch, Bruce Greenwood, Zach Galifianakis, Ron Livingston, Jemaine Clement, Stephanie Szostak, Rick Overton; ***D:*** Jay Roach; ***W:*** Michael Handelman; ***C:*** Jim Denault.

The Dinner Game *Le Diner de Cons* **1998 (PG-13)** Smug publisher Pierre (Lhermitte) dines weekly with equally smug friends, their entertainment being to see who can bring the biggest fool as a dinner guest. This nasty joke gets the turnabout it deserves when Pierre intends to bring bumbling Francois (Villeret) to the party, only to have the man proceed to wreck Pierre's life before they even get there—all while Francois maintains his own sweet dignity. French with subtitles. **82m/C VHS, DVD.** *FR* Thierry Lhermitte, Jacques Villeret, Alexandra Vandernoot, Catherine Frot, Francis Huster, Daniel Prevost; ***D:*** Francis Veber; ***W:*** Francis Veber; ***C:*** Luciano Tovoli; ***M:*** Vladimir Cosma. Cesar '99: Actor (Villeret), Support. Actor (Prevost), Writing.

Dinner Rush **2000 (R)** Louis, owner of a trendy Manhattan restaurant and operator of a bookmaking enterprise, must deal with various problems and people from both of his occupations in one hectic night. His son, Udo has transformed the restaurant from a simple Italian place with his pursuit of nouvelle cuisine fame, two mob guys are trying to muscle him out of the bookie business (having already killed his partner), a snooty gallery owner is hassling his staff, his sous-chef is piling up gambling debts, and a powerful food critic just walked in the door. Although pic is overstuffed, Giraldi's deft direction, and excellent performances (especially Aiello's) make for a satisfying treat. Successful restauranteur Giraldi filmed in one of his own eateries. **98m/C VHS, DVD.** *US* Danny Aiello, Edoardo Ballerini, Vivian Wu, Mike McGlone, Kirk Acevedo, Sandra Bernhard, Summer Phoenix, Polly Draper, Mark Margolis, John Corbett, Alex Corrado; ***D:*** Bob Giraldi; ***W:*** Brian Kalata, Rick Shaughnessy; ***C:*** Tim Ives; ***M:*** Alexander Lasarenko.

Dinner with Friends ½ **2001** The main course is a look at the meaning of love, marriage, and friendship, with a heaping side of mid-life angst. Happily married couple Gabe (Quaid) and Karen (MacDowell) deal with the fallout of the breakup of their friends' marriage. Beth (Collette) shows up at their door after husband Tom (Kinnear) leaves her for another woman. When Gabe and Karen try to help (read: offer their advice), they're met with a less than enthusiastic response. **95m/C VHS, DVD.** Dennis Quaid, Andie MacDowell, Greg Kinnear, Toni Collette; ***D:*** Norman Jewison; ***W:*** Donald Margulies. **CABLE**

Dino ½ **1957** Social worker joins a young woman in helping a 17-year-old delinquent re-enter society. **96m/B VHS.** Sal Mineo, Brian Keith, Susan Kohner; ***D:*** Thomas Carr.

Dinosaur ½ **2000 (PG)** Young iguanodon Aladar is separated from his parents and raised by lemurs on an isolated island. Aladar must discover his heritage just as a meteor crash threatens to destroy his world. Raises the bar on animated adventures by having the impossibly realistic critters superimposed onto actual jungle footage. Pic represents the next step in animation evolution, but the amazing visuals are somewhat undercut by the script, which has a pieced-together feel at times. May be too scary for the wee ones since everything does look so lifelike. **82m/C VHS, DVD, Blu-ray Disc.** ***D:*** Ralph Zondag, Eric Leighton; ***W:*** John Harrison, Robert Nelson Jacobs; ***M:*** James Newton Howard; ***V:*** Julianna Margulies, Alfre Woodard, D.B. Sweeney, Ossie Davis, Della Reese, Max Casella, Samuel E. Wright, Joan Plowright, Hayden Panettiere, Peter Siragusa.

Dinosaur Island **1993 (R)** Five military men survive a plane crash and discover an island where scantily clad (leather bikinis being the fashion choice) lascivious ladies live. Will the awesome power of testosterone overcome the fierce dinosaurs which stand between the men and their objects of desire? **85m/C VHS.** Ross Hagen, Richard Gabai, Antonia Dorian, Peter Spellos, Tom Shell, Griffin (Griffen) Drew, Steve Barkett, Toni Naples, Michelle (McClellan) Bauer; ***D:*** Jim Wynorski, Fred Olen Ray; ***W:*** Bob Sheridan, Christopher Wooden; ***C:*** Gary Graver; ***M:*** Chuck Cirino.

Dinosaur Valley Girls ½ **1996** Hollywood action hero Tony Markham comes into posession of a magic stone that hurls him backwards through time into a prehistoric world. That just happens to be populated by fierce, beautiful babes in animal-print bikinis. A PG version is also available. **94m/C VHS, DVD.** Karen Black, William D. Russell, Ron Jeffries, Jeff Rector, Griffin (Griffen) Drew, Ed Fury; ***D:*** Don Glut; ***W:*** Don Glut.

Dinosaurus! **1960** Large sadistic dinosaurs appear in the modern world. They eat, burn, and pillage their way through this film. Also includes a romance between a Neanderthal and a modern-age woman. **85m/C VHS, DVD.** Ward Ramsey, Kristina Hanson, Paul Lukather, Fred Engelberg; ***D:*** Irvin S. Yeaworth Jr.; ***W:*** Dan E. Weisburd, Jean Yeaworth; ***C:*** Stanley Cortez; ***M:*** Ronald Stein.

Dinotopia ½ **2002** TV miniseries based on two books by author/illustrator James Gurney about a fantasy island paradise where humans and talking dinos coexist peacefully. Teenaged half-brothers Karl (Leitso) and David (Miller) survive a plane crash and wind up on Dinotopia where they are befriended by young princess Marion (Carr). But the island has problems—rogue carnivorous dinosaurs and sinister human Cyrus Crabb (Thewlis) as well as some magical sunstones that are losing their power. Fanciful storytelling with some fun special effects. **285m/C VHS, DVD.** Tyron Leitso, Wentworth Miller, Katie Carr, David Thewlis, Jim Carter, Alice Krige, Colin Salmon, Hannah Yelland, Stuart Wilson, Anna McGuire; ***D:*** Marco Brambilla; ***W:*** Simon Moore; ***C:*** Tony Pierce-Roberts; ***M:*** Trevor Jones; ***V:*** Lee Evans. **TV**

Diplomaniacs ½ **1933** Wheeler and Woolsey, official barbers on an Indian reservation, are sent to the Geneva peace conference to represent the interests of their tribe. Slim plot nevertheless provides quite a few laughs. Fun musical numbers. **62m/B VHS.** Bert Wheeler, Robert Woolsey, Marjorie White, Hugh Herbert; ***D:*** William A. Seiter; ***W:*** Joseph L. Mankiewicz, Henry Myers; ***M:*** Max Steiner.

Diplomatic Courier **1952** Cold-war espionage saga has secret agent Power attempting to re-steal sensitive documents from the hands of Soviet agents. Involved and exciting thriller. Michael Ansara, Charles Bronson and Lee Marvin made brief appearances. **97m/B VHS.** Tyrone Power, Patricia Neal, Stephen McNally, Hildegarde Knef, Karl Malden; ***D:*** Henry Hathaway; ***C:*** Lucien Ballard.

Diplomatic Immunity ½ **1991 (R)** Vicious killer gets off scot-free due to his diplomatic immunity. That is, until the victim's ex-soldier father follows this low-life to the jungles of Paraguay to exact revenge. A heap o' action. **95m/C VHS.** Bruce Boxleitner, Billy Drago, Meg Foster, Robert Forster; ***D:*** Peter Maris.

Diplomatic Siege *Enemy of My Enemy* **1999 (R)** The U.S. Embassy is taken over by Serbian terrorists who demand that foreign forces clear out of Bosnia or they'll kill their hostages. But General Buck Swain (Berenger) decides to get rid of the Serbs instead. And just to keep things interesting, CIA ops Steve Parker (Weller) and Erica Long (Hannah) are in the embassy basement trying to defuse a bomb. **94m/C VHS, DVD.** Tom Berenger, Daryl Hannah, Peter Weller; ***D:*** Gustavo Graef-Marino; ***W:*** Robert Boris, Kevin Bernhardt, Sam Bernard, Mark Amin; ***C:*** Steven Wacks; ***M:*** Terry Plumeri. **VIDEO**

Direct Contact ½ **2009 (R)** Typical action fare from Lundgren. Former Special Forces operative Mike Riggins is being held in a Russian prison. He's offered his freedom if he will find missing American Ana (May) but when he does so, he learns it's all a double-cross and now he needs to save Ana from the men who want her dead. **90m/C DVD.** Dolph Lundgren, Michael Pare, Bashar Rahal, James Chalke, Gina May; ***D:*** Dan Lerner; ***W:*** Les Weldon; ***C:*** Ross Clarkson; ***M:*** Stephen (Steve) Edwards. **VIDEO**

Direct Hit ½ **1993 (R)** A CIA assassin discovers retiring is not an option. John Hatch (Forsythe) decides he wants out, particularly when his next kill, Savannah (Champa), turns out to be an innocent pawn. So Hatch turns protector and decides to best the agency at its own deadly game. **91m/C VHS, DVD.** William Forsythe, Richard Norton, Jo Champa, John Aprea, Juliet Landau, George Segal; ***D:*** Joseph Merhi; ***W:*** Jacobsen Hart.

Dirkham Detective Agency ½ **1983** Three children team up to form the Dirkham Detective Agency and are hired by a veterinarian to recover two dognapped poodles. **60m/C VHS.** Sally Kellerman, Stan Shaw, John Quade, Gordon Jump, Randy Morton; ***D:*** Stuart Margolin; ***W:*** Chuck Menville, Brenda Wilson.

Dirt Bike Kid ½ **1986 (PG)** A precocious brat is stuck with a used motorbike that has a mind of its own. Shenanigans follow in utterly predictable fashion as he battles bankers and bikers with his bad bike. **91m/C VHS, DVD.** Peter Billingsley, Anne Bloom, Stuart Pankin, Patrick Collins, Sage Parker, Chad Sheets; ***D:*** Hoite C. Caston; ***W:*** Lewis Colick, David Brandes.

Dirt Boy ½ **2001** Ex-heroin addict Matty Matthews (Hedman) has decided to leave New York and take forensic courses in a creepy Cape Cod community where the local celeb is Attwater Bridges (Walsh), the writer of a non-fiction account of a serial killer called "Dirt Boy." But after talking to one near-victim, Matty has his own suspicions about what really happened. **90m/C VHS, DVD.** Jacob Lee Hedman, Arthur J. Walsh, Luca Bercovici, Michelle Guthrie; ***D:*** Gerald L. Frasco; ***W:*** Gerald L. Frasco; ***C:*** Jeffrey Greeley; ***M:*** Robert Robertson.

Dirt Gang **1971 (R)** A motorcycle gang terrorizes the members of a film crew on location in the desert. **89m/C VHS.** Paul Carr, Michael Pataki, Michael Forest; ***D:*** Jerry Jameson.

Dirty **2005 (R)** Paired on LAPD's anti-gang division with immoral cop Salim Adel (Gooding Jr. in an atypical bad-guy role), former street-thug-turned-good-guy Armando Sancho (Collins Jr.) agonizes over whether to turn Salim over to Internal Affairs for his fatal shooting of an innocent citizen until their commanding officers step in. More than subtle hint of the real-life 1990s Rampart scandal. **97m/C DVD.** *US* Cuba Gooding Jr., Clifton (Gonzalez) Collins Jr., Cole Hauser, Nelust Wyclef Jean, Wood Harris, Robert LaSardo, Lobo Sebastian, Khleo Thomas, Ramirez, Aimee Garcia; ***D:*** Chris Fisher; ***W:*** Chris Fisher, Gill Reavill, Eric Saks; ***C:*** Eliot Rockett, Dani Minnick; ***M:*** Peter Lopez.

Dirty Dancing **1987 (PG-13)** An innocent 17-year-old (Grey) is vacationing with her parents in the Catskills in 1963. Bored with the program at the hotel, she finds the real fun at the staff dances. Falling for the sexy dance instructor (Swayze), she discovers love, sex, and rock and roll dancing. An old story, with little to save it, but Grey and Swayze are appealing, the dance sequences fun, and the music great. Swayze, classically trained in ballet, also performs one of the sound-track songs. ♫ (I've Had) the Time of My Life; Be My Baby; Big Girls Don't Cry; Cry to Me; Do You Love Me?; Hey Baby; Hungry Eyes; In the Still of the Nite; Love is Strange. **97m/C VHS, DVD, Blu-ray Disc.** Patrick Swayze, Jennifer Grey, Cynthia Rhodes, Jerry Orbach, Jack Weston, Jane Brucker, Kelly Bishop, Lonny Price, Charles "Honi" Coles, Bruce 'Cousin Brucie' Morrow; ***D:*** Emile Ardolino; ***W:*** Eleanor Bergstein; ***C:*** Jeffrey Jur; ***M:*** John Morris. Oscars '87: Song ("(I've Had) the Time of My Life"); Golden Globes '88: Song ("(I've Had) the Time of My Life"); Ind. Spirit '88: First Feature.

Dirty Dancing: Havana Nights **2004 (PG-13)** Folks, it's not a sequel, it's not a prequel—it's a "re-imagining." This time around the dirty dancers are in Cuba (although filmed in Puerto Rico) and the year is 1958 on the eve of the Communist Revolution. Young Katey's (Garai) dad transplants the family and, bored, she meets Javier (Luna), the poor yet sexy busboy, and...well...really you know the rest. It's great eye candy and the couple is very appealing but they lack that certain something that Swayze (who makes a cameo) and Grey exuded. **86m/C VHS, DVD.** *US* Diego Luna, Romola Garai, Sela Ward, John Slattery, Jonathan Jackson, January Jones, Mika Boorem, Rene Lavan, Patrick Swayze, Mya; ***D:*** Guy Ferland; ***W:*** Boaz Yakin, Peter Sagal, Victoria Arch; ***C:*** Anthony B. Richmond; ***M:*** Hector Pereira.

Dirty Deeds **2002 (R)** In the late 1960s, Barry Ryan (Brown) is a Sydney crime boss who rules the slot machine trade. Having the local police chief (Neill) in his pocket is a help and Barry's Vietnam vet nephew Darcy (Worthington) is just joining the business, but Barry does have some personal trouble with his tough wife Sharon (Collette) and young mistress Margaret (Morassi). Then, a couple of Chicago wiseguys show up: down-to-earth Tony (Goodman) and his hot-headed colleague Sal (Williamson) have been instructed to muscle in on Barry's turf, but Barry is not about to let these interlopers interfere with his business. A bold combination of charm, comedy, and violence. **110m/C VHS, DVD.** *AU* Bryan Brown, Toni Collette, John Goodman, Sam Neill, Sam Worthington, Felix Williamson, Andrew S. Gilbert, Kestie Morassi; ***D:*** David Caesar; ***W:*** David Caesar; ***C:*** Geoffrey Hall; ***M:*** Paul Healy.

Dirty Dishes *La Jument Vapeur* **1978 (R)** A French film sardonically examining the fruitless life of the average housewife as she confronts a series of bizarre but pointless experiences during the day. Dubbed and subtitled versions available. The director is the American daughter-in-law of the late Luis Bunuel. **99m/C VHS.** *FR* Carole Laure, Pierre Santini; ***D:*** Joyce Bunuel; ***W:*** Joyce Bunuel, Suzanne Baron; ***C:*** Francois Protat; ***M:*** Jean-Marie Senia.

The Dirty Dozen **1967 (PG)** A tough Army major is assigned to train and command 12 hardened convicts offered absolution if they participate in a suicidal mission into Nazi Germany in 1944. Well-made movie is a standout in its genre. Rough and gruff Marvin is good as the group leader. Three made-for-TV sequels followed in the '80s. **149m/C VHS, DVD, Blu-ray Disc, HD DVD.** Lee Marvin, Ernest Borgnine, Charles Bronson, Jim Brown, George Kennedy, John Cassavetes, Clint Walker, Donald Sutherland, Telly Savalas, Robert Ryan, Ralph Meeker, Richard Jaeckel, Trini Lopez, Robert Webber, Stuart Cooper, Robert Phillips, Al Mancini; ***D:*** Robert Aldrich; ***W:*** Nunnally Johnson, Lukas Heller; ***C:*** Edward Scaife; ***M:*** Frank DeVol. Oscars '67: Sound FX Editing.

The Dirty Dozen: The Deadly Mission ½ **1987** A second made-for-TV sequel to the '67 movie finds Borgnine ordering another suicide mission. Savalas (killed in the original, he's playing a new character) must pick 12 convicted army prisoners for an assault on a Nazi-held French monastery. Their mission is to rescue six scientists who are working on a deadly new nerve gas. Followed by "The Dirty Dozen: The Fatal Mission." **96m/C VHS.** Ernest Borgnine, Telly Savalas, Vince Edwards, Gary (Rand) Graham, James Van Patten, Vincent Van Patten, Bo Svenson; ***D:*** Lee H. Katzin.

The Dirty Dozen: The Fatal Mission 1/2 **1988** This third TV sequel has Borgnine learning of a plan to bring a group of high-ranking Nazis to Instanbul via the Orient Express. Naturally, he assigns Savalas the task of getting his motley gang together to thwart the Nazi schemes. To add intrigue, a female has joined the ranks of the Dirty Dozen and a spy may also have infiltrated the group. **91m/C VHS.** Ernest Borgnine, Telly Savalas, Hunt Block, Jeff Conaway, Erik Estrada, Ray "Boom Boom" Mancini, Heather Thomas, Alex Cord; ***D:*** Lee H. Katzin.

The Dirty Dozen: The Next Mission 1/2 **1985** Disappointing TV sequel to the 1967 hit, with Marvin reprising his role as the leader of the motley pack. In this installment, the rag-tag toughs are sent on yet another suicide mission inside Nazi Germany, this time to thwart an assassination attempt of Hitler. Followed by two more sequels. **97m/C VHS.** Lee Marvin, Ernest Borgnine, Richard Jaeckel, Ken Wahl, Larry Wilcox, Sonny Landham, Ricco Ross; ***D:*** Andrew V. McLaglen. **TV**

Dirty Games 1/2 **1989** Nicola Kendra is part of a team sent to Africa to inspect a nuclear waste site. Once there, the scientists discover terrorists are plotting to blow up the nuclear complex unless Nicola and her new allies can prevent it. **97m/C VHS, DVD.** Jan-Michael Vincent, Valentina Vargas, Ronald France, Michael McGovern; ***D:*** Gray Hofmeyr.

Dirty Gertie from Harlem U.S.A. **1946** All-black cast performs a variation of W. Somerset Maugham's "Rain." Gertie goes to Trinidad to hide out from her jilted boyfriend. **60m/B VHS, DVD.** Francine Everett, Katherine Moore, Spencer Williams Jr., Alfred Hawkins; ***D:*** Spencer Williams Jr.

The Dirty Girls 1/2 **1964** Typical Metzger sexcapades featuring two stories about prostitute Garance, who works in Paris, and Monique, who plies her trade in Munich. **82m/B VHS, DVD.** Reine Rohan, Denise Roland, Marlene Sherter, Peter Parten, Lionel Bernier; ***D:*** Radley Metzger; ***W:*** Peter Fernandez.

Dirty Harry 1/2 **1971 (R)** Rock-hard cop Harry Callahan attempts to track down a psychopathic rooftop killer before a kidnapped girl dies. Harry abuses the murderer's civil rights, however, forcing the police to return the criminal to the streets, where he hijacks a school bus and Harry is called on once again. The only answer to stop this vicious killer seems to be death in cold blood, and Harry is just the man to do it. Taut, suspenseful direction by Siegel, who thoroughly understands Eastwood's on-screen character. Features Callahan's famous "Do you feel lucky?" line, the precursor to his "Go ahead, make my day." **103m/C VHS, DVD, Blu-ray Disc.** Clint Eastwood, Harry Guardino, John Larch, Andrew (Andy) Robinson, Reni Santoni, John Vernon, Albert "Poppy" Popwell, Craig G. Kelly, John Mitchum, Josef Sommer, Mae Mercer, Woodrow Parfrey, Angela Paton, Debralee Scott, Max Gail; ***D:*** Donald Siegel; ***W:*** Dean Riesner, Harry Julian Fink, Rita M. Fink; ***C:*** Bruce Surtees; ***M:*** Lalo Schifrin.

Dirty Heroes *Dalle Ardenne All'Inferno* **1971 (R)** A band of escaped WWII POWs battle the Nazis for a precious treasure in the war's final days. **117m/C VHS.** John Ireland, Curt Jurgens, Adolfo Celi, Daniela Bianchi, Michael Constantine; ***D:*** Alberto De Martino; ***M:*** Ennio Morricone.

Dirty Laundry WOOF! **1987 (PG-13)** Insipid wreck of a comedy about a klutz who accidentally gets his laundry mixed up with $1 million in drug money. Features Olympians Lewis and Louganis. Never released theatrically. **81m/C VHS.** Leigh McCloskey, Jeanne O'Brien, Frankie Valli, Sonny Bono, Carl Lewis, Greg Louganis, Nicholas Worth; ***D:*** William Webb. **VIDEO**

Dirty Laundry 1/2 **2007 (PG-13)** Preachy family comedy about acceptance with an either over-the-top or winning performance by Devine, depending on viewer perception. New York writer Sheldon (Dunbar) returns to his Georgia roots after a call from his mama (Devine). She introduces him to his 10-year-old son (a shocker for Sheldon), who's the product of a one-night stand, and does her best to not see that her boy is gay, even after his boyfriend (Costello) shows up. **100m/C DVD.** Rockmond Dunbar, Loretta Devine, Jenifer Lewis, Joey Costello, Aaron Grady Shaw, Terri J. Vaughn, Maurice Jamal; ***D:*** Maurice Jamal; ***W:*** Maurice Jamal; ***C:*** Rory King, Liz Rubin.

Dirty Little Secret 1/2 **1998 (R)** Sarah Weatley (Gold) hires some hoods to kidnap the adopted 10-year-old son of a wealthy, hot-tempered sheriff (Wagner). But there's more to this than meets the eye—both Sarah and the sheriff share a nasty secret and, after 10 years of keeping silent, what Sarah really wants is revenge. **92m/C VHS.** Tracey Gold, Jack Wagner, Mary Page Keller; ***D:*** Robert M. Fresco; ***W:*** Robert M. Fresco. **CABLE**

Dirty Love WOOF! **2005 (R)** Jenny McCarthy was funny once upon a time. Now, not so much. Rebecca (McCarthy) finds out her idiot boyfriend (Webster) is cheating on her, so she attempts to get back at him by sleeping with a constant stream of nerds, each more nerdy than the last. Her sidekicks Michelle (Electra) and Carrie (Heskin) are trashy, ineffectual, and stupid. In fact, everyone's stupid. An embarrassing film with little to recommend. **95m/C DVD.** *US* Jenny McCarthy, Carmen Electra, Eddie Kaye Thomas, Victor Webster, Kam Heskin, Lochlyn Munro, Kathy Griffin, Jessica Collins; ***D:*** John Mallory Asher; ***W:*** Jenny McCarthy; ***C:*** Eric Wycoff. Golden Raspberries '05: Worst Picture, Worst Actress (McCarthy), Worst Director (Asher), Worst Screenplay.

Dirty Mary Crazy Larry **1974 (PG)** A racecar driver, his mechanic, and a sexy girl hightail it from the law after pulling off a heist. Great action, great fun, and an infamous surprise ending. **93m/C VHS, DVD.** Peter Fonda, Susan George, Adam Roarke, Vic Morrow, Roddy McDowall, Craig G. Kelly; ***D:*** John Hough; ***W:*** Leigh Chapman.

Dirty Mind of Young Sally WOOF! **1972 (R)** Sally's erotic radio program broadcasts from a mobile studio, which must stay one step ahead of the police. **84m/C VHS, DVD.** George "Buck" Flower, Norman Fields, Sharon Kelly; ***D:*** Bethel Buckalew.

Dirty Pictures **2000 (R)** Dull telepic on controversial subject that features real-life interviews, which only serve to cut the story's momentum. Dennis Barrie (Woods) is the director of the Cincinnati Contemporary Arts Center who decides to book an exhibition of Robert Mapplethorpe photographs in 1990. He gets indicted on obscenity charges and decides on a court fight based on First Amendment rights though it costs him personally. **104m/C VHS, DVD.** James Woods, Diana Scarwid, Craig T. Nelson, Leon Pownall, David Huband, Judah Katz, R.D. Reid, Matt North; ***D:*** Frank Pierson; ***W:*** Ilene Chaiken; ***C:*** Hiro Narita; ***M:*** Mark Snow. **CABLE**

Dirty Pretty Things 1/2 **2003 (R)** Frears revisits the theme of the plight of illegal immigrants living in London with typically moving results. Okwe (Ejiofor), a doctor who was forced to flee his native Nigeria, is now scraping by as a hotel clerk and cabbie in London, where he befriends his Turkish co-worker Senay (Tautou), a chambermaid who later is forced into sweatshop labor and a compromising relationship with her new boss. Already living in fear of being caught by immigration agents, Okwe discovers an illegal organ-selling ring at the hotel. Engagingly illuminates the mysterious and tense underworld inhabited by illegals and those who seek to exploit them in this surprisingly effective thriller. Ejiofor delivers the goods in a darkly subtle turn while Tautou delightfully broadens her range. **107m/C VHS, DVD.** *GB* Chiwetel Ejiofor, Audrey Tautou, Sergi Lopez, Sophie Okonedo, Zlatko Buric, Benedict Wong; ***D:*** Stephen Frears; ***W:*** Steven Knight; ***C:*** Chris Menges; ***M:*** Nathan Larson.

Dirty Rotten Scoundrels **1988 (PG)** A remake of the 1964 "Bedtime Story," in which two confidence tricksters on the Riviera endeavor to rip off a suddenly rich American woman, and each other. Caine and Martin are terrific, Martin has some of his best physical comedy ever, and Headly is charming as the prey who's always one step ahead of them. Fine direction from Oz, the man who brought us the voice of Yoda in "The Empire Strikes Back." **112m/C VHS, DVD.** Steve Martin, Michael Caine, Glenne Headly, Anton Rodgers, Barbara Harris, Dana Ivey; ***D:*** Frank Oz; ***W:*** Stanley Shapiro, Paul Henning, Dale Launer; ***C:*** Michael Ballhaus; ***M:*** Miles Goodman.

A Dirty Shame **2004 (NC-17)** Outrageously tasteless fare has Waters back in familiar Baltimore territory with angry and repressed Sylvia Stickles (Ullman), who runs a convenience store with unfulfilled hubby Vaughn (Isaak). Their daughter Caprice (Blair) is locked in her room so she can't continue her career as a topless dancer. Sylvia suffers a concussion in a car crash and goes nympho—joining a cult of sex addicts led by local sexual healer Ray-Ray (Knoxville). Suddenly, their quiet blue-collar neighborhood is under siege from fetish freaks! It's all low-rent and tawdry exaggeration with a flimsy plot. It doesn't quite work, but then Waters has never let slick technique interfere with his fun. **89m/C DVD.** *US* Tracey Ullman, Johnny Knoxville, Selma Blair, Chris Isaak, Suzanne Shepherd, Mink Stole, Patty (Patricia Campbell) Hearst, Jackie Hoffman; ***Cameos:*** Ricki Lake, David Hasselhoff; ***D:*** John Waters; ***W:*** John Waters; ***C:*** Steve Gainer; ***M:*** George S. Clinton.

Dirty Tricks 1/2 **1981 (PG)** History professor Gould fights with bad guys for a letter written by George Washington. Thoroughly forgettable comedy lacking in laughs. **91m/C VHS.** *CA* Elliott Gould, Kate Jackson, Arthur Hill, Rich Little; ***D:*** Alvin Rakoff; ***W:*** William W. Norton Sr.; ***M:*** Hagood Hardy.

Dirty Work **1992 (R)** A drug-dealing bail bondsman (Ashton) steals counterfeit money from the mob and then sets up his partner (Dobson) as the fall guy. Can Dobson survive long enough to set things straight? **88m/C VHS.** John Ashton, Kevin Dobson, Roxann Biggs-Dawson, Donnelly Rhodes, Jim Byrnes, Mitchell Ryan; ***D:*** John McPherson; ***W:*** Aaron Julien.

Dirty Work 1/2 **1997 (PG-13)** You'll notice that star and ex-Saturday Night Live newsguy MacDonald isn't even trying to act, he's just doing his deadpan wise guy routine with a different name. His delivery and attitude, however, are about the only funny things in this tale of Mitch (MacDonald) and Sam (Lange), two losers who can't keep a job but have a talent for petty revenge. When Sam's father (Warden) has a heart attack, the boys decide to open a business specializing in dirty deeds done dirt cheap to pay for a heart transplant. Although the premise is good, the tricks are mostly of the junior high variety and don't seem quite dirty enough. Several unbilled cameos, including Adam Sandler, John Goodman and the late Chris Farley. **81m/C VHS, DVD.** Fred Wolf, Norm MacDonald, Artie Lange, Chevy Chase, Don Rickles, Jack Warden, Traylor Howard, Christopher McDonald, Chris Farley, Gary Coleman, Ken Norton, John Goodman, Adam Sandler; ***D:*** Bob Saget; ***W:*** Fred Wolf; ***C:*** Arthur Albert; ***M:*** Richard Gibbs.

Disappearance **1981 (R)** A hired assassin discovers an ironic link between his new target and his missing wife. **80m/C VHS.** *CA* Donald Sutherland, David Hemmings, John Hurt, Christopher Plummer, David Warner, Virginia McKenna; ***D:*** Stuart Cooper.

Disappearance 1/2 **2002 (PG-13)** The vacationing Henley family stumble across the ghost town of Weaver, New Mexico, decide to stop long enough to take some photos, and get stranded. Turns out that something is inhabiting the town and it probably isn't human. Ending's a let-down. **91m/C VHS, DVD.** Harry Hamlin, Susan Dey, Jeremy Lelliott; ***D:*** Walter Klenhard; ***W:*** Walter Klenhard; ***C:*** David Connell; ***M:*** Shirley Walker. **CABLE**

The Disappearance of Aimee **1976** Dramatic re-creation of events surrounding the 1926 disappearance of evangelist Aimee Semple McPherson. She claimed she was abducted, but her mother insisted she ran away to have an affair. Excellent TV movie with an exceptional cast. Originally was to star Ann-Margret. **110m/C VHS.** Faye Dunaway, Bette Davis, James Sloyan, James Woods, John Lehne, Lelia Goldoni, Barry Brown, Severn Darden; ***D:*** Anthony Harvey; ***W:*** John McGreevey; ***C:*** James A. Crabe. **TV**

The Disappearance of Christina 1/2 **1993 (PG-13)** Successful entrepreneur Joe Seldon (Stamos) is married to heiress Christina (Yarlett) and they seem to be the perfect couple. But when Christina mysteriously vanishes during a sailing trip, was it really an accident? Detective Nora Davis (Pounder) doesn't think so and naturally, Joe is suspect numero uno. **93m/C VHS.** John Stamos, Kim Delaney, Robert Carradine, Claire Yarlett, CCH Pounder; ***D:*** Karen Arthur; ***W:*** Camille Thomasson.

The Disappearance of Garcia Lorca 1/2 *Death in Granada; Lorca* **1996 (R)** In 1954, Spanish-born journalist Ricardo Fernandez (Morales) returns to Granada to look into the death of his idol, poet/playwright Gabriel Garcia Lorca (Garcia). Ricardo's family fled Spain for Puerto Rico in 1936, at the start of the Spanish Civil War, when anti-fascist Lorca was executed. Ricardo wants to find out just who Lorca's killers were but Franco's Spain is a country eager to bury its past. Based on two books by Ian Gibson. **114m/C VHS.** *SP* Esai Morales, Andy Garcia, Edward James Olmos, Jeroen Krabbe, Miguel Ferrer, Giancarlo Giannini, Marcela Wallerstein, Jose Coronado; ***D:*** Marcos Zurinaga; ***W:*** Marcos Zurinaga, Neil Cohen, Juan Antonio Ramos; ***C:*** Juan Ruiz-Anchia; ***M:*** Mark McKenzie.

The Disappearance of Kevin Johnson 1/2 **1995 (R)** Mockumentary about a British TV crew, doing a film about successful Brits in Hollywood, stumbling across the disappearance of wanna-be producer and wealthy Englishman, Kevin Johnson. So they begin asking questions of the agents, executives, stars, business associates, and women in Johnson's life. So just who is—or was—Kevin Johnson? **105m/C VHS.** Michael Brandon, Bridget Baiss, Keely Sims, Rick Peters, Kari Wuhrer, John Hillard, Heather Stephens, Richard Beymer, Richard Neil, Michael Laskin, Ian Ogilvy, Stoney Jackson; ***Cameos:*** Pierce Brosnan, James Coburn, Dudley Moore; ***D:*** Francis Megahy; ***W:*** Francis Megahy; ***C:*** John Newby; ***M:*** John Coda; ***Nar:*** Francis Megahy.

Disappearances **2006 (PG-13)** Quebec Bill (Kristofferson) and his teenaged son Wild Bill (McDermott) travel into the Canadian backwoods to run bootleg whiskey in 1932 so they can save the family's Vermont farm. Elements of magical realism throw off the simpler family adventure plot. Based on the novel by Howard Frank Mosher. **103m/C DVD.** Kris Kristofferson, Lothaire Bluteau, Luis Guzman, William Sanderson, Charlie McDermott, Gary Farmer, Genevieve Bujold; ***D:*** Jay Craven; ***W:*** Jay Craven; ***C:*** Wolfgang Held; ***M:*** Judy Hyman, Jeff Claus. **VIDEO**

The Disappeared **2008** Teenager Matthew suffers a breakdown and is institutionalized after his eight-year-old brother Tom goes missing while Matthew was partying. He blames himself and so does his violence-prone dad Jack (Wise), who's got his own secrets. When Matthew returns to their south London housing estate, he begins hearing Tom's voice asking for help and thinks he's going crazy again. But Matthew will do anything to find out what happened to his brother. **95m/C DVD.** *GB* Harry Treadway, Greg Wise, Tom Felton, Alex Jennings, Niki Amuka-Bird, Lewis Lemperuer Palmer, Ros Leeming, Finlay Robertson; ***D:*** Johnny Kevorkian; ***W:*** Johnny Kevorkian, Neil Murphy; ***C:*** Diego Rodriguez; ***M:*** Ilan Eshkeri.

Disappearing Acts 1/2 **2000 (R)** Zora Banks (Lathan) is a college-educated music teacher with dreams of becoming a singer. She meets high school dropout Franklin (Snipes), who's doing construction work and wants to become a contractor. Neither wants a relationship but opposites still attract and they get involved. But not without trouble. Based on the 1989 novel by Terry McMillan. **115m/C VHS, DVD.** Sanaa Lathan,

Wesley Snipes, Regina Hall, Clark Johnson, John Amos, CCH Pounder, Aunjanue Ellis, Lisa Arrindell Anderson, Kamaal Fareed, Michael Imperioli; *D:* Gina Prince-Bythewood; *W:* Lisa Jones; *C:* Tami Reiker. **CABLE**

Disaster at Silo 7 **1988** When the engine of a Titan missile goes on the fritz, the Air Force tries to prevent a nuclear disaster. Based on an actual Titan II missile incident near Little Rock, Arkansas. **92m/C VHS.** Peter Boyle, Patricia Charbonneau, Perry King, Michael O'Keefe, Joe Spano, Dennis Weaver; *D:* Larry Elikann; *W:* Douglas Lloyd McIntosh; *C:* Roy Wagner. **TV**

Disaster Movie WOOF! **2008 (PG-13)** Aptly titled flick with barely a premise, let alone a plot, to set it up. There's something about a guy trying to rescue his girlfriend from a library. Devolves into a vile stew of tired pop-culture references, scatological "humor," and an unrelenting stream of send-ups that are as unfunny as they are uninspired. Writers/directors Friedberg and Selzer insist on wringing out every drop of stupidity from their movie-spoof franchise. Thankfully they're running out of genres. **90m/C DVD, Blu-ray Disc.** *US* Matt Lanter, Tad Hilgenbrink, Carmen Electra, Vanessa Minnillo, Gary 'G-Thang' Johnson, Nicole Parker, Crista Flanagan, Kim Kardashian, Ike Barinholtz; *D:* Jason Friedberg, Aaron Seltzer; *W:* Jason Friedberg, Aaron Seltzer; *C:* Shawn Maurer; *M:* Christopher Lennertz.

The Disciple ½ **1915** Vintage silent western wherein Hart's unsmiling good-bad guy tries to clean up a lawless town and win back his wife, who has shamelessly fallen in with a corrupt saloon-keeper. **80m/B VHS.** William S. Hart, Dorothy Dalton, Robert McKim, Jean Hersholt; *D:* William S. Hart; *W:* Thomas Ince.

Disciple of Death **1972 (R)** Raven plays "The Stranger," a ghoul who sacrifices virgins to the Devil. **82m/C VHS, DVD.** *GB* Mike Raven, Ronald Lacey, Stephen Bradley, Virginia Wetherell; *D:* Tom Parkinson.

Disclosure **1994 (R)** Likable, responsible executive and family man (Douglas) finds himself sexually harassed by his ex-lover turned dragon-lady boss (Moore). But when he rejects her lusty come-on, she points the finger at him. One-dimensional characters and hollow material turn sexual harassment into a trivial issue. High-tech saga of corporate politics, while flashy, is nothing we haven't seen before. Douglas just can't pass up these "Regular Joe meets beautiful, horny babe, bad things happen" roles, can he? Based on the Michael Crichton novel. **129m/C VHS, DVD.** Michael Douglas, Demi Moore, Donald Sutherland, Caroline Goodall, Dylan Baker, Dennis Miller, Rosemary Forsyth, Roma Maffia; *D:* Barry Levinson; *W:* Paul Attanasio; *C:* Tony Pierce-Roberts; *M:* Ennio Morricone. Blockbuster '95: Drama Actress, T. (Moore); Blockbuster '96: Drama Actress, V. (Moore).

Disco Pigs ½ **2001** Pig (Murphy) and Runt (Cassidy) were born minutes apart in the same Dublin hospital and have grown up in adjoining houses. They share a telepathic bond as well as their own language and no one can separate them—until their first kiss when they turn 17. But Pig will stop at nothing to keep their bond. Adapted by Walsh from his play. **94m/C VHS, DVD.** *IR* Cillian Murphy, Elaine Cassidy, Geraldine O'Rawe, Eleanor Methven, Brian F. O'Byrne; *D:* Kristen Sheridan; *W:* Enda Walsh; *C:* Igor Jadue-Lillo; *M:* Gavin Friday, Maurice Seezer.

Disconnected ½ **1987** "Sorry, Wrong Number" is updated, with more than ample doses of sex and violence. **81m/C VHS.** Mark Walker, Frances Raines; *D:* Gorman Bechard; *W:* Gorman Bechard; *C:* Gorman Bechard.

Discontent ½ **1916** An early silent film by Lois Weber in which a cantankerous old vet goes to live with his wealthy nephew. The harmonious family life is disrupted by his meddling ways. **30m/B VHS.** Katherine Griffith, J. Edwin Brown, Charles Hammond, A(lva) D. Blake; *D:* Lois Weber; *W:* Lois Weber.

The Discovery Program ½ **1989** Four award-winning short films on one video: "Ray's Male Heterosexual Dance Hall," "Greasy Lake," "The Open Window," and "Hearts of Stone." The subjects range from humorous and offbeat to tragic and deadly serious. **106m/C VHS.** Tim Choate, Boyd Gaines, John Achorn, Eric Stoltz; *D:* Bryan Gordon, Steven E. Anderson, Damian Harris, Rupert Wainwright; *W:* Bryan Gordon.

The Discreet Charm of the Bourgeoisie *Le Charme Discret de la Bourgeoisie* **1972 (R)** Bunuel in top form, satirizing modern society. These six characters are forever sitting down to dinner, yet they never eat. Dreams and reality, actual or contrived, prevent their feast. **100m/C VHS, DVD.** *FR* Milena Vukotic, Fernando Rey, Delphine Seyrig, Jean-Pierre Cassel, Bulle Ogier, Michel Piccoli, Stephane Audran, Luis Bunuel; *D:* Luis Bunuel; *W:* Luis Bunuel, Jean-Claude Carriere; *C:* Edmond Richard. Oscars '72: Foreign Film; British Acad. '73: Actress (Seyrig), Screenplay; Natl. Soc. Film Critics '72: Director (Bunuel), Film.

Discretion Assured ½ **1993 (R)** Successful businessman Trevor McCabe (York) finds himself in a romantic quandry with three women, leading to his involvement in embezzlement and murder. **97m/C VHS, DVD.** Michael York, Jennifer O'Neill, Dee Wallace, Elizabeth (Ward) Gracen; *D:* Odorico Mendes.

The Disenchanted ½ *La Desenchantee* **1990** Seventeen-year-old Beth (Godreche) is having a rough time growing up. She's forced to look after her bedridden mother and younger brother and their survival depends on the generosity of her mother's ex-lover, who's now taking a more personal interest in the beautiful teenager. Meanwhile, Beth's arrogant boyfriend decides Beth should prove her love for him by sleeping with the ugliest man she can find. French with subtitles. **78m/C VHS, DVD.** *FR* Judith Godreche, Ivan Desny, Therese Liotard, Malcolm Conrath, Marcel Bozonnet; *D:* Benoit Jacquot; *W:* Benoit Jacquot; *C:* Caroline Champetier; *M:* Jorge Arriagada.

Disgrace **2008 (R)** Contemptuous, arrogant, predatory, and racist Cape Town university academic David Lurie (Malkovich) finally pays the price for his ill-advised affair with a student when he's dismissed from his position. David then decides to visit his daughter Lucy (Haines) at her Eastern Cape farm, eventually getting a job at the local animal shelter (where he euthanizes a number of stray dogs). David and Lucy are attacked by three black youths, leaving them with physical and emotional injuries, but Lucy refuses to involve the police in a personal post-apartheid attempt at reconciliation. Adaptation of the 1999 J.M. Coetzee novel; filmed on location in South Africa. **119m/C DVD.** *AU* John Malkovich, Eriq Ebouaney, Jessica Haines, Antoinette Engel; *D:* Steve Jacobs; *W:* Anna Maria Monticelli; *C:* Steve Arnold; *M:* Antony Partos, Greame Koehne.

The Dish **2000 (PG-13)** Tells the true story of a NASA official (Neill) and his group of local Aussie technicians as they manned the satellite dish responsible for bringing to TV sets around the world man's first footsteps on the moon in 1969. Originally only a backup plan, the Australian dish was called into action when the receiver in California became useless after a change in Apollo 11's flight path. Treats the central, spectacular event itself with dignity and appropriate awe, but also squeezes humor and emotion out of all that leads up to it. **104m/C VHS, DVD.** *AU* Sam Neill, Patrick Warburton, Tom Long, Kevin Harrington, Bille Brown, John McMartin, Tayler Kane, Eliza Szonert, Carl Snell; *D:* Rob Sitch; *W:* Rob Sitch, Santo Cilauro, Tom Gleisner, Jane Kennedy; *C:* Graeme Wood; *M:* Edmund Choi.

Dish Dogs ½ **1998 (R)** Morgan (Astin) and Jason (Lillard) are a couple of bachelor best friends who cruise SoCal in their old Chevy looking for the best surfing and work as dishwashers to make ends meets. But the slacker duo are beset by love (Ward, Elizabeth) and cracks surface in their buddyhood. **96m/C VHS, DVD.** Matthew Lillard, Sean Astin, Shannon Elizabeth, Maitland Ward, Brian Dennehy, Richard Moll; *D:* Bob (Robert) Kubilos; *W:* Ashley Scott Meyers, Nathan Ives; *C:* Mark Vicente; *M:* Herman Beeftink.

Dishdogz **2005 (PG-13)** Kevin (Allman) is tired of working hard to make a buck until he becomes part of the kitchen crew at an extreme sports summer camp. To win the affections of Cassidy (Duff), Kevin teams up with his fellow workers, who call themselves the Dishdogz, to take part in a camp competition to see who's the best skateboarder. Kevin also has to contend with his tough boss Tony (Perry), who just happens to know some old school tricks he might be willing to pass on. **90m/C DVD.** Marshall Allman, Luke Perry, Haylie Duff, Timothy Lee DePriest; *D:* Mikey Hilb; *W:* Steven Sessions; *C:* Christopher Gosch. **VIDEO**

Dishonorable Discharge *Ces Dames Preferent le Mambo; Women Prefer the Mambo* **1957** American sailor Burt Brickford (Constantine) gets mixed up with dames, drugs, crooks, and treasure hunters—all in a seedy European coastal town. Loosely based on Ernest Hemingway's "To Have and Have Not." Dubbed. **105m/B VHS.** *FR* Eddie Constantine, Jacques Castelot, Jean Murat, Pascale Roberts, Joelle Bernard, Robert Berri, Lisa Bourdin, Rene Harvard; *D:* Bernard Borderie; *W:* Bernard Borderie; *C:* Jacques Lemare; *M:* Charles Aznavour.

Dishonored ½ **1931** Dated spy drama has Dietrich playing secret agent X-27 in WWI and masquerading on the side as a peasant girl. Although not one of the more famous Dietrich-Sternberg productions, its camp plot and Dietrich's lavish performance make it worth watching. Based on the infamous spy Mata Hari, who was shot by the French in 1917 for espionage. **91m/B VHS.** Marlene Dietrich, Victor McLaglen, Lew Cody, Gustav von Seyffertitz, Warner Oland, Barry Norton, Davison Clark, Wilfrid Lucas; *D:* Josef von Sternberg; *W:* Josef von Sternberg, Daniel N. Rubin; *C:* Lee Garmes.

Dishonored Lady ½ **1947** After her ex-boyfriend is murdered, a female art director finds that she's the number one suspect. When put on trial for the dastardly deed, she takes the fifth in this mediocre melodrama. **85m/B VHS, DVD.** Hedy Lamarr, Dennis O'Keefe, William Lundigan, John Loder; *D:* Robert Stevenson.

Disney's Teacher's Pet *Teacher's Pet: The Movie* **2004 (PG)** Disney strikes again with this zany Pinocchio story about a blue dog who wants to become a real boy like his owner Leonard (Fleming). Wanna-be Spot (Lane) dresses as a boy (named Scott) and follows Leonard to school until he discovers his chance: a mad scientist named Ivan Krank (Grammar) who claims to be able to change animals into people. Unfortunately, no one considers Spot's "dog years," which cause him to end up not a boy but a middle-aged man. Creative script and visual style, excellent performances by Lane and Grammar, and loads of wit and charm make this an above-average cartoon that appeals to children and parents alike. Based on the ABC cartoon. **73m/C VHS, DVD.** *US* *D:* Timothy Bjorklund; *W:* Bill Steinkellner, Cheri(e) Steinkellner; *M:* Stephen James Taylor; *V:* Nathan Lane, Kelsey Grammer, David Ogden Stiers, Jerry Stiller, Shaun Fleming, Debra Jo Rupp, Paul (Pee-wee Herman) Reubens, Megan Mullally, Rob Paulsen, Wallace Shawn, Estelle Harris, Jay Thomas, Genie Francis, Anthony Geary, Pamela Segall, Lauren Tom, Ken Swofford, Mae Whitman, Rosalyn Landor.

Disney's The Kid **2000 (PG)** Cynical 40-year-old Willis comes face-to-face with his 8-year-old self (Breslin), who wants to know how he grew up to become such a jerk. It's Disney, so there are Important Lessons to be learned, and dramatic changes in behavior to be witnessed, but Breslin, Willis, and Tomlin as his assistant, make the schmaltz bearable with excellent performances. Wells' sophisticated, funny script helps smooth out Turtletaub's heavy-handed direction. **104m/C VHS, DVD.** Bruce Willis, Emily Mortimer, Jean Smart, Spencer Breslin, Chi McBride, Lily Tomlin, Dana Ivey, Daniel von Bargen, Nicholas Chinlund; *D:* Jon Turteltaub; *W:* Audrey Wells; *C:* Peter Menzies Jr.; *M:* Jerry Goldsmith.

Disorder ½ **2006 (R)** David Randall was accused of a double murder and sent to a mental hospital where he was diagnosed as a paranoid schizophrenic. Now released, David heads back to his hometown to prove his innocence but soon thinks that the same masked killer is now after his friend Melissa. His shrink and the sheriff think David has gone off his meds and may be dangerous. **103m/C DVD.** Darren Kendrick, Lauren Seikaly, Thomas Ruderstaller, Alan Samulski, Sean Eager; *D:* Jack Thomas Smith; *W:* Jack Thomas Smith; *C:* Jonathan Belinski; *M:* Joel Goodman. **VIDEO**

Disorderlies **1987 (PG)** Members of the popular rap group cavort as incompetent hospital orderlies assigned to care for a cranky millionaire. Fat jokes abound with performances by the Fat Boys. **86m/C VHS, DVD.** The Fat Boys, Ralph Bellamy; *D:* Michael A. Schultz; *M:* Anne Dudley.

Disorderly Orderly ½ **1964** When Jerry Lewis gets hired as a hospital orderly, nothing stands upright long with him around. Vintage slapstick Lewis running amuck in a nursing home. **90m/C VHS, DVD.** Jerry Lewis, Glenda Farrell, Everett Sloane, Kathleen Freeman, Susan Oliver; *D:* Frank Tashlin.

Disorganized Crime **1989 (R)** On the lam from the law, Bernsen attempts to organize a group of his ex-con buddies to pull off the perfect heist. Before the boys can organize, however, the cops are hot on Bernsen's trail, and he must vacate the meeting place. Good cast attempts to lift this movie beyond script. **101m/C VHS, DVD.** Lou Diamond Phillips, Fred Gwynne, Corbin Bernsen, Ruben Blades, Hoyt Axton, Ed O'Neill, Daniel Roebuck, William Russ; *D:* Jim Kouf; *W:* Jim Kouf; *C:* Ron Garcia; *M:* David Newman, Hoyt Axton.

Disraeli **1930** Arliss deservedly won the Best Actor Oscar for his title role as the famed British prime minister to Queen Victoria. This particular slice of the cunning statesman's life depicts his efforts to secure the Suez Canal for England against the Russians. Arliss' wife also played his screen spouse. One of Warner's earliest and best biographical pictures. Based on a play by Louis Napoleon Parker. **87m/B VHS.** George Arliss, Joan Bennett, Florence Arliss, Anthony Bushell, David Torrence, Doris Lloyd, Ivan Simpson, Gwendolyn Logan; *D:* Alfred E. Green; *C:* Lee Garmes. Oscars '30: Actor (Arliss).

Disraeli **1979** Flamboyant, irreverant, a dandy, and a womanizer, Benjamin Disraeli (McShane) was also England's first Jewish Prime Minister and one of its greatest. This British miniseries examines the controversial figure and the Victorian era his life and career spanned. **208m/C VHS.** *GB* Ian McShane, Mary Peach, Mark Dignam, Leigh Lawson, Rosemary Leach, Anton Rodgers, Margaret Whiting; *D:* Claude Whatham; *W:* David Butler.

Distant Drums **1951** A small band of adventurers tries to stop the Seminole War in the Florida Everglades. **101m/C VHS, DVD.** Gary Cooper, Mari Aldon, Robert Barrat, Richard Webb, Ray Teal, Arthur Hunnicutt; *D:* Raoul Walsh; *M:* Max Steiner.

Distant Justice ½ **1992 (R)** Tokyo police inspector Rio (Sugawara) is vacationing in Boston with his wife and daughter, where he can also visit old friend, Chief Bradfield (Kennedy). But Rio's wife is murdered and his daughter kidnapped by vicious drug dealer Roy Pennola (Carradine) and Bradfield assigns young officer Charlie Givens (Lutes) to see that Rio doesn't get himself killed as well. **91m/C VHS.** Bunta Sugawara, George Kennedy, David Carradine, Eric Lutes; *D:* Toru Murakawa.

Distant Thunder ½ *Ashani Sanket* **1973** A bitter, unrelenting portrait of a small Bengali neighborhood as the severe famines of 1942, brought about by the "distant thunder" of WWII, take their toll. A mature achievement from Ray; in Bengali with English subtitles. **92m/C VHS.** *IN* Soumitra Chatterjee, Sandhya Roy, Babita, Gobinda Chakravarty, Romesh Mukerji; *D:* Satyajit Ray; *W:* Satyajit Ray; *C:* Soumendu Roy; *M:* Satyajit Ray. Berlin Intl. Film Fest. '73: Golden Berlin Bear.

Distant Thunder **1988 (R)** A scarred Vietnam vet, who has become a recluse, and his estranged son reunite in the Washington State wilderness, causing him to reflect on his isolation. Strong premise and cast watered down by weak script. **114m/C VHS, DVD.** *CA* John Lithgow, Ralph Macchio, Kerrie Keane, Janet Margolin, Rick Rosenthal; ***D:*** Rick Rosenberg; ***C:*** Ralf Bode; ***M:*** Maurice Jarre.

A Distant Trumpet ½ **1964** Sixties teen crush Donahue is miscast in the last western directed by Raoul Walsh, who appears to have been just going through the motions. In 1883, West Point Army grad Matthew Hazard is sent to Arizona's desolate Fort Delivery, which is soon beset by attacking Apaches. The Red Rocks/Painted Desert locations are worth a look. **117m/C DVD.** Troy Donahue, Suzanne Pleshette, Diane McBain, James Gregory, William Reynolds, Claude Akins; ***D:*** Raoul Walsh; ***W:*** John Twist, Richard Fielder, Albert Beich; ***C:*** William Clothier; ***M:*** Max Steiner.

Distant Voices, Still Lives **1988** A profoundly executed, disturbing film chronicling a British middle-class family through the maturation of the three children, under the dark shadow of their abusive, malevolent father. An evocative, heartbreaking portrait of British life from WWII on, and of the rhythms of dysfunctional families. A film festival favorite. **87m/C VHS.** *GB* Freda Dowie, Pete Postlethwaite, Angela Walsh, Dean Williams, Lorraine Ashbourne; ***D:*** Terence Davies; ***W:*** Terence Davies; ***C:*** Patrick Duval. L.A. Film Critics '89: Foreign Film.

The Distinguished Gentleman **1992 (R)** A small-time con man (Murphy) manages to scam his way into a political career and winds up in Congress. The other characters serve mostly as foils for Murphy's comedic talent. Viewers will laugh despite the story's predictablity. **122m/C VHS, DVD.** Eddie Murphy, Lane Smith, Sheryl Lee Ralph, Joe Don Baker, Victoria Rowell, Grant Shaud, Kevin McCarthy, Charles S. Dutton, James Garner, Gary Frank; ***D:*** Jonathan Lynn; ***W:*** Marty Kaplan; ***C:*** Gabriel Beristain; ***M:*** Randy Edelman.

Distortions **1987 (PG)** Hussey is a widow whose evil aunt (Laurie) is holding her hostage. What the film lacks in suspense throughout most of the movie is made up for in the end. **90m/C VHS.** Piper Laurie, Steve Railsback, Olivia Hussey, Edward Albert, Rita Gam, Terence Knox; ***D:*** Armand Mastroianni.

District B13 *Banlieue 13* **2004 (R)** Fast-paced and suspenseful actioner set in 2010 outside Paris. Things are so bad that the authorities have walled off the drug-ridden district and left it to crime boss Taha. Local Leito takes a stand by flushing a shipment of Taha's dope and then runs for his life and into undercover cop Damien, who learns that a massive bomb is now in Taha's possession. French with subtitles. **85m/C DVD, Blu-ray Disc.** *FR* David Belle, Cyril Raffaelli, Larbi (Bibi) Naceri, Dany Verissimo; ***D:*** Pierre Morel; ***W:*** Luc Besson, Larbi (Bibi) Naceri; ***C:*** Manuel Teran.

District 9 **2009 (R)** Based on director Blomkamp's 2005 short film "Alive in Joburg" this is memorable, speculative sci fi that finds alien refugees unwillingly trapped above Johannesburg when their spacecraft breaks down. A fearful government confines the insectoid-looking creatures, derisively called 'prawns,' to an increasingly filthy shantytown. After 20 years, corporate bureaucrat Wilkus van der Merwe (Copley) is charged with moving the aliens to the even-more-remote District 10. Blithely going about his job, Wilkus finds his own life changing when he encounters alien goo that begins to alter him in ways that make him very valuable to the powers-that-be. **111m/C DVD.** *NZ* David James, Sharlto Copley, Mandla Gaduka, Vanessa Haywood; ***D:*** Neil Blomkamp; ***W:*** Neil Blomkamp, Terri Tatchell; ***C:*** Trent Opaloch; ***M:*** Clinton Shorter; ***V:*** Jason Cope.

District 13: Ultimatum *Banlieue 13: Ultimatum* **2009 (R)** This sequel to "District B13" has local criminal Leito (Belle) re-teaming with law enforcement buddy Damien (Raffaelli) to save the locked-down, crime-ridden sector of Paris known as District 13 once again. This time, corrupt cops led by Gassman (Duval) are trying to raze the lawless suburb and get rich off of the real estate rights. The plot is just a framework to hang the well-choreographed action sequences that utilize the acrobatic technique known as parkour, which star Belle helped originate. Fun for stunt fans, but not too deep. French with subtitles. **101m/C DVD.** *FR* Cyril Raffaelli, David Belle, Daniel Duval, Philippe Torreton, Elodie Yung; ***D:*** Patrick Alessandrin; ***W:*** Luc Besson; ***C:*** Jean-Francois Hensgens; ***M:*** Alexandre Mahout.

Disturbance ½ **1989** The two personas of a young schizophrenic get him entangled in a mysterious string of murders. **81m/C VHS.** Timothy Greeson, Lisa Geoffreion; ***D:*** Cliff Guest.

Disturbed **1990 (R)** Lusty mental hospital director McDowell meets sex starved and suicidal Gidley in this less-than-stellar erotic creeper. Redeemed only by McDowell's performance and more evidence that the droog's career hasn't been just peachy since "Clockwork Orange." **96m/C VHS.** Malcolm McDowell, Geoffrey Lewis, Priscilla Pointer, Pamela Gidley, Clint Howard; ***D:*** Charles Winkler; ***W:*** Emerson Bixby, Charles Winkler.

Disturbia ½ **2007 (PG-13)** Unacknowledged updated teen version of "Rear Window." Troubled Kale (LaBeouf) is placed on house arrest with an electronic ankle monitor after a school incident. His fed-up mom (Moss) cuts off his videogame/cable access, so Kale begins spying on the locals with his handy binoculars. At first he's mostly interested in hottie girl next door, Ashley (Roemer), but then Kale becomes suspicious of neighbor Mr. Turner (Morse) and whether he could actually be the serial killer from local news reports. Kale recruits Ashley and pal Ronnie (Yoo) to be his legs even though they question his accusations. Morse is effectively creepy in what amounts to the Raymond Burr role and LeBeouf makes the most of Kale's foolishness and smart-aleck wit. **105m/C DVD, Blu-ray Disc, HD DVD.** *US* Shia LaBeouf, David Morse, Carrie-Anne Moss, Jose Pablo Cantillo, Sarah Roemer, Aaron Yoo; ***D:*** D.J. Caruso; ***W:*** Christopher Landon, Carl Ellsworth; ***C:*** Rogier Stoffers; ***M:*** Geoff Zanelli.

Disturbing Behavior ½ **1998 (R)** Gavin (Stahl) welcomes new kid in town Steve (Marsden) by pointing out the social castes at Cradle Bay High School. The Uber-group is the goody-goody Blue Ribbons, an excessively straitlaced and perky group of athletes and cheerleaders. Along with fellow outcasts Rachel (Holmes) and U.V. (Donella), they joke about a possible conspiracy, but when Gavin shows up with a crewcut and an inordinate love of pep rallies and bake sales, his friends know something is up. They discover that parents have allowed the school shrink (Greenwood) to use drugs to tinker with the brains of the Blue Ribbons. They also discover that the Stepford Teens' vanilla lives are topped with sprinkles of homicidal fury. Director Nutter creates just the right creepy and paranoid mood in his feature debut. **84m/C VHS, DVD.** James Marsden, Nick Stahl, Katie Holmes, Bruce Greenwood, William Sadler, Chad E. Donella, Ethan (Randall) Embry, Steve Railsback; ***D:*** David Nutter; ***W:*** Scott Rosenberg; ***C:*** John Bartley; ***M:*** Mark Snow. MTV Movie Awards '99: Breakthrough Perf. (Holmes).

Diva ½ **1982 (R)** While at a concert given by his favorite star, a young French courier secretly tapes a soprano who has refused to record. The film follows the young man through Paris as he flees from two Japanese recording pirates, and a couple of crooked undercover police who are trying to cover-up for the chief who not only has a mistress, but runs a prostitution ring. Brilliant and dazzling photography compliment the eclectic soundtrack. **123m/C VHS, DVD.** *FR* Frederic Andrei, Roland Bertin, Richard Bohringer, Gerard Darmon, Jacques Fabbri, Wilhelmenia Wiggins Fernandez, Dominique Pinon; ***D:*** Jean-Jacques Beineix; ***W:*** Jean-Jacques Beineix; ***C:*** Philippe Rousselot; ***M:*** Vladimir Cosma. Cesar '82: Cinematog., Sound, Score; Natl. Soc. Film Critics '82: Cinematog.

The Dive **1989 (PG-13)** Two North Sea oil-rig workers are trapped far below the waves when the lifeline to their diving bell snaps in rough seas. **90m/C VHS.** Bjorn Sundquist, Frank Grimes, Einride Eidsvold, Michael Kitchen; ***D:*** Tristan De Vere Cole.

Dive Bomber **1941** Exciting aviation film that focuses on medical problems related to flying. Flynn stars as an aviator-doctor who conducts experiments to eliminate pilot-blackout. MacMurray, Toomey, and Heydt perform well as three flyboys stationed in Hawaii. Great flying sequences filmed at San Diego's naval base with extra scenes shot at Pensacola. Warner Bros. released this film just months before the Japanese attacked Pearl Harbor. Based on the story "Beyond the Blue Sky" by Frank Wead. **130m/B VHS, DVD.** Errol Flynn, Fred MacMurray, Ralph Bellamy, Alexis Smith, Regis Toomey, Robert Armstrong, Allen Jenkins, Craig Stevens, Herbert Anderson, Moroni Olsen, Dennie Moore, Louis Jean Heydt, Cliff Nazarro, Tod Andrews, Ann Doran, Charles Drake, Alan Hale Jr., William Forrest, Creighton Hale, Howard Hickman, Russell Hicks, George Meeker, Richard Travis, Addison Richards; ***D:*** Michael Curtiz; ***W:*** Frank Wead, Robert Buckner; ***C:*** Bert Glennon, Winton C. Hoch; ***M:*** Max Steiner.

Divided by Hate **1996 (PG-13)** In 1984, struggling farmer Louis Gibbs (Walsh), wife Carol (Roth), and their children fall under the spell of charismatic preacher Steve Riordan (Skerritt) whose anti-government sentiments lead to the forming of a local militia. Naturally, the FBI gets involved and there's a struggle between the feds and the militia, with the family caught in the middle. If it sounds familiar that's because it's based on the 1995 Branch Davidian incident. **92m/C VHS.** Dylan Walsh, Andrea Roth, Tom Skerritt; ***D:*** Tom Skerritt; ***W:*** Leonard Gross.

Divided Heaven *Der Geteilte Himmel* **1964** East German drama. In 1961, Rita returns to her childhood village to recover from a breakdown. She remembers her romance with chemist Manfred and how they dealt so differently with Communist worker ideology, which has the disillusioned Manfred leaving for West Berlin. He thinks Rita will follow but she remains behind even as the Berlin Wall goes up. German with subtitles; based on the novel by Wolf, who also wrote the screenplay. **109m/B DVD.** *GE* Renate Blume, Eberhard Esche, Hans Hardt-Hardtloff, Hilmar Thate; ***D:*** Konrad Wolf; ***W:*** Christa Wolf; ***C:*** Werner Bergmann; ***M:*** Hans-Dieter Hosalla.

Divided We Fall ½ *Musime si Pomahat* **2000 (PG-13)** In 1943, the inhabitants of an unnamed Czechoslovakian town are existing under the Nazi occupation. Josef (Polivka) recognizes his former employer David (Kassai), a Jew who has escaped the camps. Josef and his wife Marie (Siskova) agree to hide David in their home although they are under the scrutiny of Nazi collaborator Horst (Dusek), who keeps making passes at Marie. Although they are childless, Marie claims to be pregnant to get Horst to leave her alone. Which leads Josef to ask a delicate favor of David so they can make good on Marie's lie. Czech with subtitles. **123m/C VHS, DVD.** *CZ* Boleslav Polivka, Anna Siskova, Csongor Kassai, Jaroslav Dusek, Jiri Pecha, Simona Stasova, Marin Huba, Vladimir Marek, Jiri Kodet, Richard Tesarik; ***D:*** Jan Hrebejk; ***W:*** Petr Jarchovsky; ***C:*** Jan Malir; ***M:*** Ales Brezina.

Divided We Stand **2000 (R)** Naive college coed Lisa joins the Black Student Coalition and soon accuses fellow member Robey of rape. However, BSC member and law student Jarrod, who knows what really happened, is hesitant to get involved. **81m/C VHS, DVD.** Andrea Lisa, Crayton Robey, J.R. Jarrod; ***D:*** J.R. Jarrod; ***W:*** J.R. Jarrod; ***C:*** John Crawford; ***M:*** Charles D. Jackson, Sherwood Seward, Derek Seward.

Divine ½ **1990** Two Divine flicks from Waters. First, Divine plays a naughty girl who, not surprisingly, since this one is titled "The Diane Linkletter Story," ends up a successful suicide. "The Neon Woman" is a rare live performance, with Divine a woman who owns a strip joint and has a slew of problems you won't read about in Dear Abby. **110m/C VHS.** Divine; ***D:*** John Waters.

The Divine Enforcer ½ **1991** A monsignor in a crime-ridden L.A. neighborhood reaches his wit's end in trying to stave off perpetrators of injustice. Fortunately, help arrives in the form of a mysterious priest who is equally handy with his fists, nunchakus, and guns. From then on it's no more mister nice guy, and the criminals haven't a prayer. **90m/C VHS.** Jan-Michael Vincent, Erik Estrada, Jim Brown, Judy Landers, Don Stroud, Robert Z'Dar, Michael Foley, Carrie Chambers, Hiroko; ***D:*** Robert Rundle.

The Divine Lady ½ **1929** Lavish historical/romantic drama. Lower-class Emma Hart (Griffith) falls for the charms of aristocrat Charles Greville (Keith) but when he becomes embarrassed by her, Charles readily passes her off to his enamored uncle William Hamilton (Warner), the British ambassador to Naples. Hamilton marries Emma and she becomes instrumental in getting the ships of British fleet commander Nelson (Varconi), who is battling Napoleon, resupplied. Nelson and Emma fall in love, but their adulterous relationship causes a scandal when they return to England. The E. Barrington novel was remade as 1941's "That Hamilton Woman." **105m/B DVD.** Corinne Griffith, Victor Varconi, H.B. Warner, Ian Keith, Marie Dressler, Montagu Love, Dorothy (Dorothy G. Cummings) Cumming, Michael Vavitch, Helen Jerome Eddy; ***D:*** Frank Lloyd; ***W:*** Forrest Halsey; ***C:*** John Sietz.

Divine Nymph ½ **1971 (R)** Charts the erotic adventures of the beautiful and young Manuela, who is dangerously pursued by two cousins. **100m/C VHS.** *IT* Laura Antonelli, Marcello Mastroianni, Terence Stamp; ***D:*** Giuseppe Patroni-Griffi; ***M:*** Ennio Morricone.

Divine Secrets of the Ya-Ya Sisterhood **2002 (PG-13)** Southern dramedy with a group of girlfriends (Smith, Flanagan, Knight) who stage an intervention to help about-to-be-married, New York-based playwright Sidda Lee (Bullock) discover the truth about her eccentric, alcoholic Southern mama Vivi (Burstyn). Flashbacks ensue as we see the women as children in the 1930s when they formed their secret Ya-Ya society and then later to Vivi as a young women (played somewhat hysterically by Judd). The most fun bits, however, are those with the slightly cracked Southern belles now in their 70s. Female bonding, estrogen-fest gives short shrift to the men in these ladies' lives (shocking!). First time director Khouri lets these kooky dames (and the plot) run a little too wild. Based on the novels "Divine Secrets of the Ya-Ya Sisterhood" and "Little Altars Everywhere" by Rebecca Wells. **116m/C VHS, DVD.** *US* Ashley Judd, Sandra Bullock, Ellen Burstyn, Maggie Smith, James Garner, Fionnula Flanagan, Shirley Knight, Cherry Jones, Angus MacFadyen, Jacqueline McKenzie, Katy Selverstone, Kiersten Warren, Gina McKee, Matthew Settle, David Rasche, Frederick Koehler, Leslie Silva, Ron Dortoh, David Lee Smith; ***D:*** Callie Khouri; ***W:*** Callie Khouri, Mark Andrus; ***C:*** John Bailey; ***M:*** T-Bone Burnett.

The Diving Bell and the Butterfly ½ *Le Scaphandre et le Papillon* **2007 (PG-13)** The true story of French "Elle" magazine editor Jean-Dominique Bauby, who suffered a stroke that left him completely paralyzed but for his left eyelid. The film chronicles the process by which Bauby dictated his memoir by blinking that left eye as an assistant spoke the alphabet, signifying each individual letter with every blink. As if Bauby's story isn't tragic enough, he died just two days after his book was published in France. An emotionally wrenching, at times difficult to watch, poetic and richly-cinematic journey ripe with colorful and sensual images from Bauby's past life and his fully-functioning inner world as imagined by director Schnable. In French with subtitles and named after Bauby's biography. **112m/C DVD.** *FR* Mathieu Amalric, Emmanuelle Seigner, Marie Josee Croze, Patrick Chesnais, Max von Sydow, Anne Consigny, Isaach de Bankole, Niels Arestrup; ***D:*** Julian Schnabel; ***W:*** Ronald Harwood; ***C:*** Janusz Kaminski. British Acad. '07: Adapt. Screenplay; Golden Globes '08: Director (Schnabel), Foreign Film; Ind. Spirit '08: Cinematog., Director (Schnabel).

Diving In **1990 (PG-13)** Have you heard the one about the acrophobic diver? It seems a paralyzing fear of heights is the only thing between a young diver and Olympic gold. Much splashing about and heartstring-tugging. **92m/C VHS.** Burt Young, Matt Adler, Kristy Swanson, Matt Lattanzi, Richard Johnson, Carey Scott, Yolanda Jilot; ***D:*** Strathford Hamilton; ***C:*** Hanania Baer; ***M:*** Guy Moon, Paul Buckmaster.

Divorce American Style ½ **1967** Dated but still amusing look at love, marriage, and the big D. Richard (Van Dyke) and Barbara (Reynolds) Harmon find their longtime marriage in a tailspin as they spend all their time arguing. They split but find single life and the dating game have their own pitfalls. **103m/C VHS, DVD.** Dick Van Dyke, Debbie Reynolds, Jason Robards Jr., Jean Simmons, Van Johnson, Lee Grant, Joe Flynn, Shelley Berman, Martin Gabel, Tom Bosley, Dick Gautier, Eileen Brennan; ***D:*** Bud Yorkin; ***W:*** Norman Lear; ***C:*** Conrad L. Hall; ***M:*** Dave Grusin.

Divorce His, Divorce Hers
1972 The first half of this drama shows the crumbling of a marriage through the husband's eyes. The second half offers the wife's perspective. **144m/C VHS, DVD.** Richard Burton, Elizabeth Taylor; ***D:*** Waris Hussein. **TV**

Divorce—Italian Style 1/2 *Divorzio All'Italiana* **1962** A middle-aged baron bored with his wife begins directing his amorous attentions to a teenage cousin. Since divorce in Italy is impossible, the only way out of his marriage is murder—and the baron finds a little-known law that excuses a man from murdering his wife if she is having an affair (since he would merely be defending his honor). A hilarious comedy with a twist ending. Available in Italian with English subtitles or dubbed in English. **104m/B VHS, DVD.** *IT* Marcello Mastroianni, Daniela Rocca, Leopoldo Trieste, Stefania Sandrelli; ***D:*** Pietro Germi; ***W:*** Pietro Germi, Ennio de Concini, Alfredo Giannetti; ***C:*** Carlo Di Palma, Leonida Barboni; ***M:*** Carlo Rustichelli. Oscars '62: Story & Screenplay; British Acad. '63: Actor (Mastroianni); Golden Globes '63: Actor—Mus./Comedy (Mastroianni), Foreign Film.

The Divorce of Lady X 1/2 **1938** A spoiled British debutante, in the guise of "Lady X," makes a woman-hating divorce lawyer eat his words through romance and marriage. Based on the play by Gilbert Wakefield. **92m/C VHS.** *GB* Merle Oberon, Laurence Olivier, Ralph Richardson, Binnie Barnes; ***D:*** Tim Whelan; ***C:*** Harry Stradling Sr.; ***M:*** Miklos Rozsa.

The Divorcee 1/2 **1930** Early Leonard film (he'd later direct "The Great Ziegfield" and "Pride and Prejudice") casts Shearer as a woman out to beat her husband at philandering. Married to a journalist, she cavorts with her husband's best friend and a discarded old flame as only a pre-production code gal could. Shearer—who Lillian Hellman described as having "a face unclouded by thought"—grabbed an Oscar. Based on the novel "Ex-Wife" by Ursula Parrott. **83m/B VHS.** Norma Shearer, Chester Morris, Conrad Nagel, Robert Montgomery, Mary Doran, Tyler Brooke, George Irving, Helen Johnson; ***D:*** Robert Z. Leonard. Oscars '30: Actress (Shearer).

Dixiana 1/2 **1930** A Southern millionaire falls for a circus performer shortly before the start of the Civil War. Part color. ♫ Dixiana; Here's to the Old Days; A Tear, a Kiss, a Smile; My One Ambition is You; A Lady Loved a Soldier; Mr. & Mrs. Sippi; Guiding Star. **99m/B VHS, DVD.** Bebe Daniels, Bert Wheeler, Robert Woolsey, Dorothy Lamour, Bill Robinson; ***D:*** Luther Reed; ***M:*** Max Steiner.

Dixie: Changing Habits **1985** A New Orleans madam and a Mother Superior go head to head in this amusing TV movie. In the end all benefit as the nuns discover business sense and pay off a debt, while the former bordello owner cleans up her act. Above-average scripting and directing for the medium. **100m/C VHS.** Suzanne Pleshette, Cloris Leachman, Kenneth McMillan, John Considine, Geraldine Fitzgerald, Judith Ivey; ***D:*** George Englund. **TV**

Dixie Dynamite **1976 (PG)** The two daughters of a Georgia moonshiner set out to avenge the murder of their father. The music is performed by Duane Eddy and Dorsey Burnette. **88m/C VHS, DVD.** Warren Oates, Christopher George, Jane Anne Johnstone, Kathy McHaley, R.G. Armstrong, Wes Bishop; ***D:*** Lee Frost; ***W:*** Lee Frost, Wes Bishop.

Dixie Jamboree **1944** Low-budget musical has gangster on the lam using an unusual method to escape from St. Louis—the last Mississippi Showboat. ♫ Dixie Showboat; No, No, No; If It's a Dream; You Ain't Right with the Lord; Big Stuff. **69m/B VHS, DVD.** Guy Kibbee, Frances Langford, Louise Beavers, Charles Butterworth; ***D:*** Christy Cabanne.

Dixie Lanes **1988** A relentlessly nostalgic comedy set in a small town at the end of WWII. A woman, troubled by her nephew's restless antics, puts him to work. Unfortunately she adds to his plight, as her business involves the Black Market. **92m/C VHS, DVD.** Hoyt Axton, Karen Black, Art Hindle, John Vernon, Ruth Buzzi, Tina Louise, Pamela Springsteen, Nina Foch; ***D:*** Don Cato.

Django 1/2 **1968 (PG)** Django is a stranger who arrives in a Mexican-border town (dragging a coffin behind him) to settle a dispute between a small band of Americans and Mexicans. **90m/C VHS, DVD.** Franco Nero, Loredana Nusciak, Angel Alvarez, Jose Bodalo, Eduardo Fajardo, Simon Arriaga, Ivan Scratuglia; ***D:*** Sergio Corbucci; ***W:*** Sergio Corbucci, Bruno Corbucci, Jose Maesso, Piero Vivarelli, Franco (Fred Gardner) Rossetti; ***C:*** Enzo Barboni; ***M:*** Luis Bacalov.

Django Shoots First 1/2 *Django Spara per Primo* **1974** Spaghetti western with usual amount of action and plot twists. **96m/C VHS.** *IT* Glen Saxson, Evelyn Stewart, Alberto Lupo; ***D:*** Alberto De Martino; ***W:*** Alberto De Martino.

Django Strikes Again *Django 2: Il Grande Ritorno* **1987** Django (Nero) has abandoned his former life of violence in favor of the peaceful life of a monk. That is, until his daughter is kidnapped. Then he manages to find that old coffin and go after the dastardly dogs. **96m/C VHS, DVD.** *SP* Franco Nero, Donald Pleasence, Rodrigo Obregon, Christopher Connelly, William Berger; ***D:*** Nello Rossati; ***W:*** Nello Rossati; ***M:*** Gianfranco Plenizio.

DNA 1/2 **1997 (R)** Idealistic doctor Ash Mattley (Dacascos) mistakenly reveals his radical DNA theories to creepy scientist Wessinger (Prochnow), who uses the knowledge in mutant experiments. One mutant, an insect-like creature with super powers, lurks in the rain forest, waiting for prey, while Mattley sets out to destroy it. **94m/C VHS, DVD.** Mark Dacascos, Jurgen Prochnow, Robin McKee; ***D:*** William Mesa; ***W:*** Nick Davis; ***C:*** Gerry Lively; ***M:*** Christopher Stone.

Do I Love You? 1/2 **2002** Biking through the streets of London in search of answers to the mysteries of life and love is 30-something lesbian Marina (writer/director Gornick) who is sent adrift after a difficult split with girlfriend Romy (Cassidy). Overly chatty and rambling, much like her trek. **73m/C DVD.** Sarah Patterson, Lisa Gornick, Raquel Cassidy, Harri Alexander; ***D:*** Lisa Gornick; ***W:*** Lisa Gornick. **VIDEO**

Do Not Disturb 1/2 **1965** Filmed on the studio backlot, though the story is set in England and Paris, this so-so romantic comedy finds Janet Harper (Day) relocating to England with exec hubby Mike (Taylor). He promptly leaves her to settle in alone while dallying with his secretary, so Janet decides to invent her own admirer. But a real suitor, Paul (Fantoni), does show up and sweeps Janet off to Paris, thus making Mike insanely jealous. **102m/C DVD.** Doris Day, Rod Taylor, Sergio Fantoni, Hermione Baddeley, Reginald Gardiner; ***D:*** Ralph Levy; ***W:*** Richard L. Breen; ***C:*** Leon Shamroy; ***M:*** Lionel Newman.

Do or Die 1/2 **1991 (R)** Former "Playboy" centerfolds Speir and Vasquez team up as a couple of federal agent babes who take on international crime boss Morita. But the crimelord is ready for our scantily clad heroines with a sick game of revenge—and the stakes are their very lives! **97m/C VHS, DVD.** Erik Estrada, Dona Speir, Roberta Vasquez, Noriyuki "Pat" Morita, Bruce Penhall, Carolyn Liu, Stephanie Schick; ***D:*** Andy Sidaris; ***W:*** Andy Sidaris.

Do or Die 1/2 **2001** When her young son is diagnosed with leukemia, Dr. Samantha Sheppard (Ashfield) is forced to admit to her husband (Speer) that he is not the boy's biological father. That would be a convicted criminal (Long) who escapes from jail just as Samantha arrives in Australia to seek his help. Desperate, Samantha tries to track her ex-lover down before the cops can find him. Originally an Australian miniseries that has been edited to a fast-moving pace. **90m/C DVD.** *AU* Kate Ashfield, Tom Long, Hugo Speer, William McInnes, Martin Sacks; ***D:*** Rowan Woods; ***W:*** Christopher Lee; ***C:*** Martin McGrath; ***M:*** Edmund Butt. **TV**

Do or Die **2003** Die, please die. A rapid aging disease affects more than half the world's population and only one drug is available to slow the process. The drug is controlled by a single manufacturer and its head will stop at nothing to continue his company's monopoly. That includes threatening pregnant Ruth, who may have been given the key to a cure. A Sci-Fi Channel original. **89m/C DVD.** Shawn Doyle, Polly Shannon, Nigel Bennett, Alan Van Sprang, Guylaine St. Onge, Anthony Lemke; ***D:*** David S. Jackson; ***W:*** David S. Jackson; ***C:*** Rudolf Blahacek; ***M:*** Frederic Talgorn. **CABLE**

Do the Right Thing 1/2 **1989 (R)** An uncompromising, brutal comedy about the racial tensions surrounding a white-owned pizzeria in the Bed-Stuy section of Brooklyn on the hottest day of the summer, and the violence that eventually erupts. Ambivalent and, for the most part, hilarious; Lee's coming-of-age. **120m/C VHS, DVD.** Spike Lee, Danny Aiello, Richard Edson, Ruby Dee, Ossie Davis, Giancarlo Esposito, Bill Nunn, John Turturro, John Savage, Rosie Perez, Frankie Faison; ***D:*** Spike Lee; ***W:*** Spike Lee; ***C:*** Ernest R. Dickerson; ***M:*** Bill Lee. L.A. Film Critics '89: Director (Lee), Film, Support. Actor (Aiello), Natl. Film Reg. '99;; N.Y. Film Critics '89: Cinematog.

D.O.A. 1/2 **1949** A man is given a lethal, slow-acting poison. As his time runs out, he frantically seeks to learn who is responsible and why he was targeted for death. Dark film noir remade in 1969 as "Color Me Dead" and in 1988 with Dennis Quaid and Meg Ryan. Also available colorized. **83m/B VHS, DVD.** Edmond O'Brien, Pamela Britton, Luther Adler, Neville Brand, Beverly Garland, Lynne Baggett, William Ching, Henry Hart, Laurette Luez, Virginia Lee, Jess Kirkpatrick, Cay Forrester, Michael Ross; ***D:*** Rudolph Mate; ***W:*** Russell Rouse, Clarence Greene; ***C:*** Ernest Laszlo; ***M:*** Dimitri Tiomkin. Natl. Film Reg. '04.

D.O.A. 1/2 **1988 (R)** Well-done remake of the 1949 thriller with Quaid portraying a college professor who is poisoned and has only 24 hours to identify his killer. His search for the suspect is further complicated by the fact that he is being sought by the police on phony charges of murder. Directed by the same people who brought "Max Headroom" to TV screens. **98m/C VHS, DVD.** Dennis Quaid, Meg Ryan, Charlotte Rampling, Daniel Stern, Jane Kaczmarek, Christopher Neame, Jay Patterson; ***D:*** Rocky Morton, Annabel Jankel; ***W:*** Charles Edward Pogue; ***M:*** Chaz Jankel.

DOA: Dead or Alive **2006 (PG-13)** Female-centric martial arts actioner, based on a videogame, follows five woman fighters battling to the death on an island. Okay, not the most original concept in the world, but as a straightforward action-and-chicks, "turn-off-the-brain" time waster, you could do a lot worse. Hey, at least Uwe Boll didn't direct it. Corey Yuen, who knows a thing or two about staging martial arts action, did. And it does look like everyone's having a good time. **87m/C DVD.** *GB GE US* Devon Aoki, Sarah Carter, Natassia Malthe, Jaime Pressly, Eric Roberts, Steve Howey, Matthew Marsden, Collin Chou, Holly Valance, Kane (Takeshi) Kosugi, Kevin Nash, Brian White, Robin Shou, Derek Boyer, Silvio Simac; ***D:*** Corey Yuen; ***W:*** J.F. Lawton, Adam Gross, Seth Gross; ***C:*** Chi Ying Chan, Kwok-Man Keung.

The Doberman Gang **1972 (PG)** Clever thieves train a gang of Dobermans in the fine art of bank robbery. Sequelled by "The Daring Dobermans." **85m/C VHS.** Byron Mabe, Hal Reed, Julie Parrish, Simmy Bow, JoJo D'Amore; ***D:*** Byron Ross Chudnow; ***W:*** Frank Ray Perilli.

Doc Hollywood 1/2 **1991 (PG-13)** A hotshot young physician on his way to a lucrative California practice gets stranded in a small Southern town. Will the wacky woodsy inhabitants persuade the city doctor to stay? There aren't many surprises in this fish-out-of-water comedy, but the cast injects it with considerable charm. Adapted from Neil B. Shulman's book "What?...Dead Again?" **104m/C VHS, DVD.** Michael J. Fox, Julie Warner, Woody Harrelson, Barnard Hughes, David Ogden Stiers, Frances Sternhagen, Bridget Fonda, George Hamilton, Roberts Blossom, Helen Martin, Macon McCalman, Barry Sobel; ***D:*** Michael Caton-Jones; ***W:*** Daniel Pyne, Jeffrey Price, Peter S. Seaman; ***C:*** Michael Chapman; ***M:*** Carter Burwell.

Doc Savage 1/2 **1975 (PG)** Doc and "The Amazing Five" fight a murderous villain who plans to take over the world. Based on the novels of Kenneth Robeson. **100m/C VHS.** Ron Ely, Pamela Hensley, Paul Gleason, Paul Wexler, William Lucking; ***D:*** Michael Anderson Sr.; ***W:*** George Pal, Joe Morhaim; ***C:*** Fred W. Koenekamp.

Docks of New York **1928** Von Sternberg made his mark in Hollywood with this silent drama about two dockside losers finding love amid the squalor. A rarely seen, early masterpiece. **60m/B VHS.** George Bancroft, Betty Compson, Olga Baclanova; ***D:*** Josef von Sternberg; ***M:*** Gaylord Carter. Natl. Film Reg. '99.

The Doctor 1/2 **1991 (PG-13)** A hotshot doctor develops throat cancer and gets treated at his own hospital, an ordeal that teaches him a respect and compassion for patients that he formerly lacked. Potential melodrama is saved by fine acting and strong direction. Based on the autobiographical book "A Taste of My Own Medicine" by Dr. Edward Rosenbaum. **125m/C VHS, DVD.** William Hurt, Elizabeth Perkins, Christine Lahti, Mandy Patinkin, Wendy Crewson, Charlie Korsmo, Adam Arkin, Bill Macy; ***D:*** Randa Haines; ***W:*** Robert Caswell; ***C:*** John Seale; ***M:*** Michael Convertino.

Dr. Akagi *Kanzo Sensei* **1998** In 1945, the dedicated Dr. Akagi (Emoto) is more worried about a hepatitis epidemic in his seaside village that the Japanese wartime defeat. He becomes obsessed with finding a cure and assembles a ragtag group of compatriots to assist him, including a teenaged prostitute and an escaped Dutch prisoner of war. Based on the novel "Dr. Liver" by Ango Sakaguchi. Japanese with subtitles. **128m/C VHS, DVD.** *JP* Akira (Tsukamoto) Emoto, Jacques Gamblin, Kumiko Aso, Masanori Sera, Jyuro Kara, Keiko Matsuzaka; ***D:*** Shohei Imamura; ***W:*** Shohei Imamura, Daisuke Tengan; ***C:*** Shigeru Komatsubara; ***M:*** Yosuke Yamashita.

Dr. Alien **1988 (R)** Alien poses as beautiful scientist and turns a college freshman into a sex-addicted satyr. Likewise, the cast turns this flick into a dog. **90m/C VHS, DVD.** Billy Jacoby, Olivia Barash, Stuart Fratkin, Troy Donahue, Arlene Golonka, Judy Landers; ***D:*** David DeCoteau.

The Doctor and the Devils 1/2 **1985 (R)** Based on an old screenplay by Dylan Thomas, this is a semi-Gothic tale about two criminals who supply a physician with corpses to study, either digging them up or killing them fresh. **93m/C VHS, DVD.** *GB* Timothy Dalton, Julian Sands, Jonathan Pryce, Twiggy, Stephen Rea, Beryl Reid, Sian Phillips, Patrick Stewart, Phyllis Logan, T.P. McKenna; ***D:*** Freddie Francis; ***W:*** Ronald Harwood; ***M:*** John Morris.

Doctor at Large 1/2 **1957** A fledgling doctor seeks to become a surgeon at a hospital for the rich. Humorous antics follow. The third of the "Doctor" series. **98m/C VHS.** *GB* Dirk Bogarde, Muriel Pavlow, James Robertson Justice, Shirley Eaton, Donald Sinden, Anne Heywood; ***D:*** Ralph Thomas.

Doctor at Sea 1/2 **1956** To escape a troublesome romantic entanglement and the stresses of his career, a London physician signs on a cargo boat as a ship's doctor and becomes involved with French bombshell Bardot. The second of the "Doctor" series. **93m/C VHS.** *GB* James Robertson Justice, Dirk Bogarde, Brigitte Bardot; ***D:*** Ralph Thomas; ***W:*** Jack Davies.

Dr. Bell and Mr. Doyle: The Dark Beginnings of Sherlock Holmes 1/2 *Murder Rooms: The Dark Origins of Sherlock Holmes* **2000** In 1878, Arthur Conan Doyle (Laing) is a medical student at Edinburgh University. He is mentored by the gurff and brilliant, if unconventional, Dr. Joseph Bell (Richardson), who is a pioneer in the field of forensic science. Arthur is soon assisting Dr. Bell, who is helping the local police investigate the brutal murders of several young women. The case may also take a personal turn for Arthur when it appears his classmate and friend Elspeth (Wells) is a target. Well-done if sometimes gruesome; based in part on the letters and writings of Bell. **116m/C VHS, DVD.** *GB* Robin Laing, Ian Richardson, Charles Dance, Dolly Wells, Sean McGinley, Alec Newman; ***D:*** Paul Seed; ***W:*** David Pirie; ***C:*** John Kenway; ***M:*** Jim Parker. **TV**

Dr. Bethune *Bethune, The Making of a Hero* **1990** Canadian surgeon Norman Bethune was a larger-than-life hero with equally great flaws. A crusader for socialized medicine and an outspoken opponent of Fascism (as well as an alcoholic womanizer), he worked for the Loyalist forces in the Spanish Civil War and was instrumental in developing mobile medical units for treating battlefield wounded. He's also credited with bringing modern medical care to China, where he attended to Mao's revolutionary forces. Sutherland's strong performance shows the intensity and vision of a complicated man; he previously played the doctor in 1977's "Bethune." Awkward jumps in time and place rob the story of narrative drive. **115m/C VHS.** *CA FR* Donald Sutherland, Helen Mirren, Helen Shaver, Colm Feore, Anouk Aimee, Ronald Pickup, Harrison Liu; ***D:*** Phillip Borsos; ***W:*** Ted Allan; ***C:*** Raoul Coutard; ***M:*** Alan Reeves.

Dr. Black, Mr. Hyde *Dr. Black and Mr. White; The Watts Monster* **1976 (R)** Not-so-horrifying tale of a black Jekyll who metamorphoses into a white monster with the help of the special potion. Unintended laughs lessen suspense. **88m/C VHS.** Rosalind Cash, Stu Gilliam, Bernie Casey, Marie O'Henry; ***D:*** William Crain.

Doctor Blood's Coffin 1/2 **1962** The aptly named doctor performs hideous experiments on the unsuspecting denizens of a lonely village. Good cast in this effective chiller. **92m/C VHS, DVD.** *GB* Kieron Moore, Hazel Court, Ian Hunter; ***D:*** Sidney J. Furie.

Doctor Bull 1/2 **1933** Rogers is aw-shucks charming in the title role. George Bull is an opinionated small-town doctor who's subjected to much gossip, especially over his romance with widow Janet (Allen). When the town's water supply is contaminated and many fall ill, Bull diagnoses typhoid. Herbert Banning (Churchill), Janet's brother, tries to blame the good doctor since he's the town's health officer, but Janet defends him. **77m/B DVD.** Will Rogers, Marion (Marian) Nixon, Berton Churchill, Louise Dresser, Vera Allen, Howard Lally, Andy Devine; ***D:*** John Ford; ***W:*** Paul Green; ***C:*** George Schneiderman; ***M:*** Samuel Kaylin.

Doctor Butcher M.D. **WOOF!** *Queen of the Cannibals; Zombie Holocaust; The Island of the Last Zombies* **1980 (R)** Mad doctor's deranged dream of creating "perfect people" by taking parts of one person and interchanging them with another backfires as his monstrosities develop strange side effects. The M.D., by the way, stands for "Medical Deviate." Dubbed. **81m/C VHS, DVD.** *IT* Ian McCulloch, Alexandra Cole, Peter O'Neal, Donald O'Brien, Sherry Buchanan, Walter Patriarca; ***D:*** Frank Martin, Mariano Laurenti; ***W:*** Fabrizio de Angelis, Romano Scandariato; ***M:*** Nico Fidenco, Walter Sear.

Dr. Caligari **1989 (R)** The granddaughter of the original Dr. Caligari promotes "better living through chemistry" in her insane asylum while using her patients as guinea pigs in her bizarre sexual experiments. Nothing outstanding here in terms of story or performance, but "Dick Tracy" has nothing on the visually compelling set designs and make-up. **80m/C VHS.** Madeleine Reynal, Fox Harris, Laura Albert, Jennifer Balgobin, John Durbin, Gene Zerna, David Parry, Barry Phillips; ***D:*** Stephen Sayadian; ***W:*** Stephen Sayadian, Jerry Stahl; ***C:*** Stephen Sayadian.

Doctor Chance *Docteur Chance* **1997** Frustrated Angstel (Hestnes) decides it's time to make a big change in his life. He heads to a nightclub and buys the favors (with counterfeit cash) of dancer Ancetta (Elvire) but events get out of hand. Soon the duo are heading out of the city with a car trunk full of weapons and adventure on their minds. French with subtitles. **97m/C VHS, DVD.** *FR* Pedro Hestnes, Elvire, Marisa Paredes, Stephane Ferrara, Joe Strummer, Feodor Atkine; ***D:*** F.J. Ossang; ***W:*** F.J. Ossang; ***C:*** Remy Chevrin.

Dr. Christian Meets the Women 1/2 **1940** This entry in the "Dr. Christian" series of films has the small-town physician once again exposing a con man trying to filch the townspeople. **63m/B VHS, DVD.** Jean Hersholt, Edgar Kennedy, Rod La Rocque, Dorothy Lovett, Veda Ann Borg; ***D:*** William McGann.

Dr. Cyclops 1/2 **1940** The famous early Technicolor fantasia about a mad scientist miniaturizing a group of explorers who happen upon his jungle lab. Landmark F/X and a slow-moving story. **76m/C VHS.** Albert Dekker, Janice Logan, Victor Kilian, Thomas Coley, Charles Halton, Frank Yaconelli, Paul Fix, Frank Reicher; ***D:*** Ernest B. Schoedsack; ***W:*** Tom Kilpatrick; ***C:*** Winton C. Hoch, Henry Sharp; ***M:*** Gerard Carbonara, Albert Hay Malotte, Ernst Toch.

Dr. Death, Seeker of Souls **1973 (R)** Evil doctor discovers a process for transmigrating his soul into the bodies of people he murdered 1000 years ago. Now he seeks to revive his wife. Final role for 77-year-old "Stooge" Moe Howard. **93m/C VHS.** John Considine, Barry Coe, Cheryl Miller, Stewart Moss, Leon Askin, Jo Morrow, Florence Marly, Sivi Aberg, Athena Lorde, Moe Howard; ***D:*** Eddie Saeta.

Doctor Detroit **1983 (R)** Aykroyd is funny in thin film, portraying a meek college professor who gets involved with prostitutes and the mob, under the alias "Dr. Detroit." Aykroyd later married actress Donna Dixon, whom he worked with on this film. Features music by Devo, James Brown, and Pattie Brooks. **91m/C VHS, DVD.** Dan Aykroyd, Howard Hesseman, Donna Dixon, T.K. Carter, Lynn Whitfield, Lydia Lei, Fran Drescher, Kate Murtagh, George Furth, Andrew Duggan, James Brown, Glenne Headly; ***D:*** Michael Pressman; ***W:*** Carl Gottlieb, Robert Boris; ***M:*** Lalo Schifrin.

Doctor Dolittle **1967** An adventure about a 19th century English doctor who dreams of teaching animals to speak to him. Realistic premise suffers from poor script. Based on Hugh Lofting's acclaimed stories. ♫ Doctor Dolittle; My Friend the Doctor; Talk to the Animals; I've Never Seen Anything Like It; Beautiful Things; When I Look in Your Eyes; After Today; Fabulous Places; Where Are the Words?. **151m/C VHS, DVD.** Rex Harrison, Samantha Eggar, Anthony Newley, Richard Attenborough, Geoffrey Holder, Peter Bull; ***D:*** Richard Fleischer; ***W:*** Leslie Bricusse; ***C:*** Robert L. Surtees; ***M:*** Leslie Bricusse. Oscars '67: Song ("Talk to the Animals"), Visual FX; Golden Globes '68: Support. Actor (Attenborough).

Dr. Dolittle 1/2 **1998 (PG-13)** Loose non-musical adaption of the 1967 movie has Eddie Murphy playing straight man to a group of furry friends voiced by the likes of Chris Rock, Garry Shandling and Albert Brooks. He is reduced to reacting lamely, and is upstaged throughout by the wisecracking critters created by Jim Henson's Creature Shop. Fellow humans Dr. Weller (Platt) and Calloway (Boyle) are shallow villains created to prop up a shaky plot involving the corporate takeover of Dolittle's vet clinic. May contain a bit too much bathroom humor for some family tastes. No animals were harmed during the making of this movie, but there was probably cruel and unusual treatment of the interns involving pooper-scoopers. **85m/C VHS, DVD.** Eddie Murphy, Oliver Platt, Peter Boyle, Jeffrey Tambor, Ossie Davis, Richard Schiff, Kyla Pratt, Raven, Steven Gilborn; ***D:*** Betty Thomas; ***W:*** Nat Mauldin, Larry Levin; ***C:*** Russell Boyd; ***M:*** Richard Gibbs; ***V:*** Julie Kavner, Albert Brooks, Chris Rock, John Leguizamo, Garry Shandling, Norm MacDonald, Reni Santoni, Paul (Pee-wee Herman) Reubens, Gilbert Gottfried.

Dr. Dolittle 2 **2001 (PG)** The good doctor (Murphy) returns, along with his furry talking friends, who persuade him to save their forest from human developers. The vet must also find a mate for an endangered Pacific Western bear, but the only candidate is Archie (Zahn), a circus performer who has to be taught how to survive in the wilderness. Gastrointestinal and other bodily functions dominate the humor, and a subplot involving Dolittle's moody teenage daughter (Raven-Symone) nearly undoes the charm, but it's passable entertainment. Add half a bone if you're under 12 years old for this flatulence-obsessed outing. **87m/C VHS, DVD.** *US* Eddie Murphy, Jeffrey Jones, Kevin Pollak, Raven, Kyla Pratt, Kristen Wilson, Zane R. (Lil' Zane) Copeland Jr., Andy Richter; ***D:*** Steve Carr; ***W:*** Larry Levin; ***C:*** Daryn Okada; ***M:*** David Newman; ***V:*** Norm MacDonald, Lisa Kudrow, Steve Zahn, Mike Epps, Michael Rapaport, Jacob Vargas, Isaac Hayes, Andy Dick, Joey Lauren Adams, Richard Sarafian.

Dr. Dolittle 3 1/2 **2006 (PG)** Maya Dolittle (Pratt) can also talk to the animals, which doesn't make being a teenager any easier. When she gets into trouble, mom sends Maya to a Colorado dude ranch, where she tries to make some friends while yakking with the local barnyard critters. Since the ranch is in financial trouble, it's up to Maya and the animals to win big at the local rodeo and save the day. Harmless and silly cash-in on the Eddie Murphy features. **95m/C DVD.** *US* Kyla Pratt, Kristen Wilson, John Amos, Walker Howard, Luciana Carro, Tommy Snider, James Kirk; ***D:*** Rich Thorne; ***W:*** Nina Colman; ***C:*** Eric Goldstein; ***M:*** Christopher Lennertz. **VIDEO**

Dr. Dolittle 4: Tail to the Chief **2008 (PG)** Dog whisperer? In her latest adventure, Maya Dolittle (Pratt) is asked by the president to come to the White House and tame the rambunctious First Dog. **90m/C DVD.** Kyla Pratt, Peter Coyote, Malcolm Stewart, Christine Chatelain, Niall Matter; ***D:*** Craig Shapiro; ***W:*** Kathleen Laccinole, Matthew Lieberman; ***C:*** Ron Stannett; ***M:*** Don MacDonald. **VIDEO**

Dr. Dolittle: Million Dollar Mutts 1/2 **2009 (PG)** The fifth in the Dolittle series. Maya Dolittle (Pratt) heads off to San Francisco to study veterinary medicine but her rescue of a cat brings her to the attention of heiress/reality star Tiffany (Moss) and her neurotic pooch Princess. Maya heads to Hollywood to dog whisper to Princess and soon is offered a tacky show of her own by Tiffany's agent (Beverley). It sounds like a good opportunity but Maya soon learns some rude truths about showbiz. **87m/C DVD.** Kyla Pratt, Tegan Moss, Brandon Jay McLaren, Jason Bryden; ***D:*** Alex Zamm; ***W:*** Alex Zamm, Daniel Altiere, Steven Altiere; ***C:*** Albert J. Dunk; ***M:*** Chris Hajian; ***V:*** Norm McDonald. **VIDEO**

Dr. Ehrlich's Magic Bullet 1/2 **1940** Quite provocative for its time considering the subject matter is the cure for syphilis. Berlin research scientist Paul Ehrlich's (Robinson) experiments have him battling the medical establishment and underfunding as he develops the theory of poison immunity and a synthetic antimicrobial drug to cure diphtheria and syphilis. It takes him 606 tests before his 'magic bullet' works. A good Warner bio with a particularly compelling performance by Robinson. **103m/B DVD.** Edward G. Robinson, Ruth Gordon, Otto Kruger, Albert Bassermann, Donald Crisp, Maria Ouspenskaya, Montagu Love, Sig Rumann, Donald Meek; ***D:*** Donald Crisp, William Dieterle, John Huston; ***W:*** Ruth Gordon, Norman Burnside, Heinz Herald, John Huston; ***C:*** James Wong Howe; ***M:*** Max Steiner.

Doctor Faustus 1/2 **1968** A stilted, stagy, but well-meaning adaptation of the Christopher Marlowe classic about Faust, who sold his soul to the devil for youth and the love of Helen of Troy. **93m/C VHS, DVD.** Richard Burton, Andreas Teuber, Elizabeth Taylor, Ian Marter; ***D:*** Richard Burton, Nevill Coghill.

Dr. Frankenstein's Castle of Freaks **1974 (PG)** Dr. Frankenstein and his dwarf assistant reanimate a few Neanderthals that are terrorizing a nearby Rumanian village. **90m/C VHS, DVD.** *IT* Rossano Brazzi, Michael Dunn, Edmund Purdom, Christiane Royce, Simone Blondel; ***D:*** Robert (Dick Randall) Oliver; ***W:*** William Rose, Mark Smith, Robert Spano; ***C:*** Mario Mancini.

Dr. Giggles **1992 (R)** Drake plays the psycho-genius Dr. Giggles, an escaped mental patient who sets out to avenge the death of his psycho-genius father (dementia runs in the family). He returns to his family home to procure the necessary medical instruments, most notably a hypodermic needle, and starts killing people—on screen with the tools and in the audience with remarkably stupid one-liners. Opening scenes are especially mired in gore. **96m/C VHS, DVD.** Larry Drake, Holly Marie Combs, Glenn Quinn, Keith Diamond, Cliff DeYoung; ***D:*** Manny Coto; ***W:*** Manny Coto, Graeme Whifler; ***C:*** Rob Draper; ***M:*** Brian May.

Dr. Goldfoot and the Bikini Machine **1966** A mad scientist employs gorgeous female robots to seduce the wealthy and powerful, thereby allowing him to take over the world. Title song by the Supremes. **90m/C VHS, DVD.** Vincent Price, Frankie Avalon, Dwayne Hickman, Annette Funicello, Susan Hart, Kay Elkhardt, Fred Clark, Deanna Lund, Deborah Walley; ***D:*** Norman Taurog; ***M:*** Les Baxter.

Dr. Hackenstein 1/2 **1988 (R)** A doctor tries to revive his wife by "borrowing" parts from unexpected (and unsuspecting) guests. **88m/C VHS, DVD.** David Muir, Stacey Travis, Catherine Davis Cox, Dyanne DiRosario, Anne Ramsey, Logan Ramsey; ***D:*** Richard Clark.

Dr. Heckyl and Mr. Hype **1980 (R)** A naughty, comical version of the Jekyll and Hyde story. Exuberantly wicked performances from Reed and Coogan; stellar cast of "B" veterans. **100m/C VHS.** Oliver Reed, Sunny Johnson, Maia Danziger, Mel Welles, Virgil Frye, Kedrick Wolfe, Jackie Coogan, Corinne Calvet, Dick Miller, Lucretia Love; ***D:*** Charles B. Griffith; ***W:*** Charles B. Griffith; ***M:*** Richard Band.

Doctor in Clover 1/2 **1966** The series was running out of steam by this sixth effort that has the usual sight gags and innuendos. After Dr. Gaston Grimsdyke (Phillips) loses his job at a women's prison, he enrolls in a refresher course taught by his mentor Sir Lancelot Spratt (Robertson-Justice). Spratt is determined that Gaston will stop chasing nurses long enough to become a decent physician but that may be an impossible task. **97m/C DVD.** *GB* Leslie Phillips, James Robertson-Justice, Shirley Anne Field, John Fraser, Joan Sims, Fenella Fielding, Jeremy Lloyd; ***D:*** Ralph Thomas; ***W:*** Jack Davies; ***C:*** Ernest Steward; ***M:*** John Scott.

Doctor in Distress 1/2 **1963** Aging chief surgeon falls in love for the first time. His assistant tries to further the romance as well as his own love life. Comedic fourth in the six-film "Doctor" series. **102m/C VHS.** *GB* Dirk Bogarde, James Robertson Justice, Leo McKern, Samantha Eggar; ***D:*** Ralph Thomas.

Doctor in Love **1960** The fourth in the series, but the first without former lead Dirk Bogarde. This time the story focuses primarily on Dr. Richard Hare (Craig) and his romance with Dr. Nicola Barrington (Maskell). Meanwhile, his friend Dr. Tony Burke (Phillips) continues to sow his wild oats, which is how some strippers come to be involved. **93m/C DVD.** *GB* Michael Craig, Leslie Phillips, Virginia Maskell, Carole Lesley, Nicholas Phipps, Reginald Beckwith, Liz Fraser, Irene Handl, Moira Redmond, James Robertson-Justice, Joan Simms; ***D:*** Ralph Thomas; ***W:*** Nicholas Phipps; ***C:*** Ernest Steward; ***M:*** Bruce Montgomery.

Doctor in the House 1/2 **1953** Four medical student/roommates seek only to examine lovely women and make lots of cash. In the process, they are also tempted by the evils of drink, but rally to make their grades. A riotous British comedy with marvelous performances all around. Led to six sequels and a TV series. **92m/C VHS.** *GB* Dirk Bogarde, Muriel Pavlow, Kenneth More, Donald Sinden, Kay Kendall, James Robertson Justice, Donald Houston, Geoffrey Keen, George Coulouris, Shirley Eaton, Joan Hickson, Richard Wattis; ***D:*** Ralph Thomas. British Acad. '54: Actor (More).

Dr. Jekyll and Ms. Hyde 1/2 **1995 (PG-13)** Chemist Richard Jacks (Daly) stumbles across the secret formula of great-grandad Dr. Jekyll and, after trying to improve the potion, he finds himself transformed into wicked woman Helen Hyde (Young). Cheap cross-gender gags abound. **89m/C VHS, DVD.** Timothy Daly, Sean Young,

Lysette Anthony, Stephen Tobolowsky, Harvey Fierstein, Polly Bergen, Stephen Shellen; ***D:*** David F. Price; ***W:*** William Davies, William Osborne, Tim John, Oliver Butcher; ***C:*** Tom Priestley; ***M:*** Mark McKenzie.

Dr. Jekyll and Mr. Hyde **1920** The first American film version of Robert Louis Stevenson's horror tale about a doctor's experiments that lead to his developing good and evil sides to his personality. Silent. Kino Video's edition also contains the rarely seen 1911 version of the film, as well as scenes from a different 1920 version. **96m/B VHS, DVD.** John Barrymore, Martha Mansfield, Brandon Hurst, Charles Lane, J. Malcolm Dunn, Nita Naldi, Louis Wolheim; ***D:*** John S. Robertson; ***W:*** Clara Beranger; ***C:*** Karl Struss, Roy F. Overbaugh.

Dr. Jekyll and Mr. Hyde **1932** The hallucinatory, feverish classic version of the Robert Louis Stevenson story, in which the good doctor becomes addicted to the formula that turns him into a sadistic beast. Upright Dr. Jekyll (March) has a genteel fiance, Muriel (Hobart), while twisted alter-ego Hyde delights in torturing barmaid Ivy (Hopkins)—the bond between violence and sexuality in these scenes is highly charged. Possibly Mamoulian's and March's best work, and a masterpiece of subversive, pseudo-Freudian creepiness. Eighteen minutes from the original version, lost until recently, have been restored, including the infamous whipping scene. **96m/B VHS, DVD.** Fredric March, Miriam Hopkins, Halliwell Hobbes, Rose Hobart, Holmes Herbert, Edgar Norton; ***D:*** Rouben Mamoulian; ***W:*** Samuel Hoffenstein, Percy Heath; ***C:*** Karl Struss. Oscars '32: Actor (March); Venice Film Fest. '31: Actor (March).

Dr. Jekyll and Mr. Hyde **1941** Strangely cast adaptation of the Robert Louis Stevenson story about a doctor's experiment on himself to separate good and evil. **113m/B VHS, DVD.** Spencer Tracy, Ingrid Bergman, Lana Turner, Donald Crisp, Ian Hunter, Barton MacLane, Sara Allgood, Billy Bevan; ***D:*** Victor Fleming; ***W:*** John Lee Mahin; ***C:*** Joseph Ruttenberg; ***M:*** Franz Waxman.

Dr. Jekyll and Mr. Hyde *The Strange Case of Dr. Jekyll and Mr. Hyde* **1968** Yet another production of Robert Louis Stevenson's classic story of a split-personality. **90m/C VHS, DVD.** Jack Palance, Denholm Elliott, Tessie O'Shea, Oscar Homolka, Torin Thatcher; ***D:*** Charles Jarrott. **TV**

Dr. Jekyll and Mr. Hyde **1973** Dr. Jekyll discovers a potion that turns him into the sinister Mr. Hyde. Based on the classic story by Robert Louis Stevenson. **90m/C VHS.** Kirk Douglas, Michael Redgrave, Susan George, Donald Pleasence; ***D:*** David Winters.

Dr. Jekyll & Mr. Hyde **1999 (R)** Henry Jekyll (Baldwin) is a successful surgeon who is traveling to Hong Kong on his honeymoon. But shortly after his arrival, both he and his bride are killed in an explosion during a gang war. Henry is resurrected by Chinese healer Dr. Chau, although the potion he must take alters him physically and mentally. Henry only seeks revenge but he learns that his arrival was predestined and his fate is to become the legendary fighter known as the White Dragon. Obviously has little or nothing to do with the Robert Louis Stevenson story. **96m/C VHS, DVD.** *CA AU* Adam Baldwin, Steve Bastoni, Chang Tseng, Jason Chong, Richard Chong, Kira Clavel, Karen Cliche; ***D:*** Colin Budds; ***W:*** Peter M. Lenkov; ***C:*** Mark Wareham; ***M:*** Garry McDonald. **VIDEO**

Dr. Jekyll and Mr. Hyde **1/2 2008** Set in Boston, this erratic modern update of the Robert Louis Stevenson story finds respected doctor Henry Jekyll (Scott) conducting experiments on himself with a serum made from a rare flower he believes is able to separate the soul into dark and light. The dark part would be his serial-killing alter Edward Hyde. When an appalled Jekyll realizes what he's done, he turns himself into the cops and hires lawyer Claire Wheaton (Bridges) to represent him at his sensational trial. But her defense could prove misguided if not deadly. **80m/C DVD.** Dougray Scott, Krista Bridges, Tom Skerritt, Ellen David, Cas Anvar, Danette Mackay; ***D:*** Paolo Barzman; ***W:*** Paul B. Margolis; ***C:*** Pierre Jodoin. **TV**

Dr. Jekyll and Sister Hyde **1/2** **1971 (R)** A tongue-in-cheek variation on the split-personality theme, which has the good doctor transforming himself into a sultry, knife-wielding woman who kills prostitutes. **94m/C VHS, DVD.** *GB* Ralph Bates, Martine Beswick, Gerald Sim; ***D:*** Roy Ward Baker; ***W:*** Brian Clemens; ***C:*** Norman Warwick; ***M:*** Philip Martell, David Whitaker.

Dr. Jekyll and the Wolfman *Dr. Jekyll y el Hombre Lobo; Dr. Jekyll vs. the Werewolf* **1971 (R)** Naschy's sixth stint as El Hombre Lobo. This time he visits a mysterious doctor in search of a cure but ends up turning into Mr. Hyde, a man who likes to torture women. **85m/C VHS.** *SP* Paul Naschy, Shirley Corrigan, Jack Taylor, Barta Barry, Luis Induni, Mirta Miller; ***D:*** Leon Klimovsky; ***W:*** Paul Naschy; ***C:*** Francisco Fraile.

Dr. Jekyll's Dungeon of Death **1982 (R)** Dr. Jekyll and his lobotomized sister, Hilda, scour the streets of San Francisco looking for human blood to recreate his great-grandfather's secret serum. **90m/C VHS.** James Mathers, Dawn Carver Kelly, John Kearney, Jake Pearson; ***D:*** James Wood.

Dr. Kildare's Strange Case **1940** Dr. Kildare administers a daring treatment to a man suffering from a mental disorder of a dangerous nature. One in the film series. **76m/B VHS, DVD.** Lew Ayres, Lionel Barrymore, Laraine Day; ***D:*** Harold Bucquet.

Dr. Mabuse, The Gambler **1/2** *Doktor Mabuse der Spieler; Dr. Mabuse, Parts 1 & 2* **1922** The massive, two-part crime melodrama, introducing the raving mastermind/extortionist/villain to the world. The film follows Dr. Mabuse (Klein-Rogge) through his life of crime until he finally goes mad. Highly influential and inventive. Lang meant this to be a criticism of morally bankrupt post-WWI Germany. Lang also directed "The Crimes of Dr. Mabuse" (1932) and "The Thousand Eyes of Dr. Mabuse" (1960). **242m/B VHS, DVD.** *GE* Rudolf Klein-Rogge, Aud Egede Nissen, Alfred Abel, Gertrude Welcker, Lil Dagover, Paul Richter, Bernhard Goetzke; ***D:*** Fritz Lang; ***W:*** Fritz Lang, Thea von Harbou; ***C:*** Carl Hoffmann.

Dr. Mabuse vs. Scotland Yard **1/2 1964** A sequel to the Fritz Lang classics, this film features the arch-criminal attempting to take over the world with a mind-controlling camera. **90m/B VHS.** *GE* Sabine Bethmann, Peter Van Eyck; ***D:*** Paul May.

Doctor Mordrid: Master of the Unknown **1990 (R)** Two immensely powerful sorcerers from the 4th dimension cross over into present time with two very different missions—one wants to destroy the Earth, one wants to save it. **102m/C VHS.** Jeffrey Combs, Yvette Nipar, Jay Acovone, Brian Thompson; ***D:*** Albert Band, Charles Band; ***M:*** Richard Band.

Dr. No **1962 (PG)** The world is introduced to British secret agent 007, James Bond, when it is discovered that mad scientist Dr. No (Wiseman) is sabotaging rocket launchings from his hideout in Jamaica. The first 007 film is far less glitzy than any of its successors but boasts the sexiest "Bond girl" of them all in Andress as Honey Ryder who walks out of the surf in a white bikini, and promptly made stars of her and Connery. **111m/C VHS, DVD, Blu-ray Disc.** *GB* Sean Connery, Ursula Andress, Joseph Wiseman, Jack Lord, Zena Marshall, Eunice Gayson, Margaret LeWars, John Kitzmiller, Lois Maxwell, Bernard Lee, Anthony Dawson; ***D:*** Terence Young; ***W:*** Johanna Harwood, Richard Maibaum, Berkely Mather; ***C:*** Ted Moore; ***M:*** John Barry.

Doctor of Doom **WOOF!** *Wrestling Women vs. the Aztec Ape* **1962** An unclassifiable epic wherein female wrestlers battle a mad doctor and his Aztec robot gorilla. Dubbed badly, of course. Much anticipated follow-up to "Wrestling Women vs. the Aztec Mummy." **111m/C VHS, DVD.** *MX* Elizabeth Campbell, Lorena Lalazquez, Armando Silvestre, Roberto Canedo, Chucho Salinas, Sonia Infante; ***D:*** Rene Cardona Sr.; ***W:*** Alfredo Salazar; ***C:*** Enrique Wallace; ***M:*** Antonio Diaz Conde.

Dr. Orloff and the Invisible Man **1/2** *Orloff Against the Invisible Man* **1972** In this horror film, Dr. Orloff creates an invisible ape-monster that escapes and goes on a rampage. **91m/C VHS, DVD.** *FR SP* Howard Vernon, Brigitte Carva, Fernando (Fernand) Sancho; ***D:*** Pierre Chevalier; ***W:*** Pierre Chevalier.

Dr. Orloff's Monster **WOOF!** **1964** As if "The Awful Dr. Orloff" wasn't awful enough, the doctor is back, this time eliminating his enemies with his trusty killer robot. Awful awful. **88m/B VHS, DVD.** *SP* Jose Rubio, Agnes Spaak; ***D:*** Jess (Jesus) Franco; ***C:*** Alfonso Nieva.

Dr. Otto & the Riddle of the Gloom Beam **1/2 1986 (PG)** Ernest is in your face again. Fresh from the TV commercials featuring "Ernest" comes Varney playing a villain out to wreck the global economy. He also plays all the other characters, too. Way bizarre, "Know whut I mean?" **92m/C VHS, DVD.** Jim Varney; ***D:*** John R. Cherry III.

Dr. Petiot *Le Docteur Petiot* **1990** Based on the true life story of a French WWII doctor who promised to smuggle Jews to freedom but instead killed them for their money and possessions. He was executed in 1946—accused of 60 murders and convicted of 27. The gruesome details are left to the imagination rather than shown. In French with subtitles. **102m/C VHS.** *FR* Michel Serrault, Berangere Bonvoisin, Aurore Prieto, Nita Klein, Dominique Marcas, Andre Lacombe, Pierre Romans, Zbigniew Horoks, Claude Degliame, Martine Montgermont, Nini Crepon, Andre Julien, Andre Chaumeau, Axel Bogousslavsky, Maxime Collion, Nadege Boscher, Jean Dautremay, Michel Hart; ***D:*** Christian de Chalonge; ***W:*** Christian de Chalonge, Dominique Garnier; ***C:*** Patrick Blossier; ***M:*** Michel Portal.

Doctor Phibes Rises Again **1/2** **1972 (PG)** The despicable doctor contines his quest to revive his beloved wife. Fun, superior sequel to "The Abominable Dr. Phibes." **89m/C VHS, DVD.** *GB* Vincent Price, Robert Quarry, Peter Cushing, Beryl Reid, Hugh Griffith, Terry-Thomas, Valli Kemp, Peter Jeffrey, Fiona Lewis, Caroline Munro; ***D:*** Robert Fuest; ***W:*** Robert Fuest, Robert Blees; ***C:*** Alex Thomson; ***M:*** John Gale.

Dr. Renault's Secret **1/2 1942** Larry Forbes (Strudwick) arrives at the French village where his fiance Madeleine (Roberts) lives with her scientist father (Zucco) and the doctor's strange manservant Noel (Naish). Larry is suspicious of Noel, and with good reason, since Dr. Renault is your basic mad scientist and has been doing experiments that resulted in turning beast into man or, in this case, ape into Noel. **58m/B DVD.** George Zucco, Shepperd Strudwick, Lynne Roberts, J. Carrol Naish; ***D:*** Harry Lachman; ***W:*** Robert Metzler, William Bruckner; ***C:*** Virgil Miller; ***M:*** David Raskin.

Doctor Satan's Robot **1/2 1940** Indestructible robot is battled by insane Dr. Satan in reedited serial, "Mysterious Dr. Satan." **100m/B VHS.** Eduardo Ciannelli, Robert Wilcox, William "Billy" Newell, Ella Neal; ***D:*** William Witney, John English.

Dr. Seuss' Horton Hears a Who! *Horton Hears a Who!* **2008 (G)** Big-screen CG-animated adaptation of the Dr. Seuss classic. Toning down his shtick considerably, Jim Carrey voices Horton, an enlightened elephant who discovers an entire planet on a speck of dust. Within this planet is the harmonious city of Whoville, threatened to be crushed by imagination-hating tyranny. Its mayor (Carell), unaccustomed to dealing with crisis, turns to Horton to save it. A timeless, allegorical story that works for kids and adults alike. Its only fault is in trying to stretch a 10-minute bedtime story into an hour and a half, which leads to obvious interference with the original voice of Dr. Seuss. **88m/C DVD, Blu-ray Disc.** *US* ***D:*** Steve Martino, Jimmy Hayward; ***W:*** Cinco Paul; ***M:*** John Powell; ***V:*** Jim Carrey, Steve Carell, Carol Burnett, Will Arnett, Seth Rogen, Isla Fisher, Jonah Hill, Dan Fogler, Amy Poehler, Jaime Pressly, Josh Flitter, Jesse McCartney, Debi Derryberry, Laraine Newman, Joey King; ***Nar:*** Charles Osgood.

Dr. Seuss' How the Grinch Stole Christmas **1/2** *How the Grinch Stole Christmas; The Grinch* **2000 (PG)** If you've seen the cartoon, then you know it was padded. Just think of the stuff that Ron Howard added!/A new plot line here, an embellishment there, all Carreyed by a big star in green skin and hair./Crass Whos are shown doing frantic Yule shopping, and decoration-envy keeps each neighbor hopping./This anti-shop message is curiously told, considering the junk that this film clearly sold./Cindy Lou Who loses her Christmas-time zest, and starts to research the town's Yuletide pest./In a flashback it's shown why the Grinch is so mean, and a love interest is added from when he's a teen./He's elected Cheermeister of the holiday season; but again leaves bitter, and with good Grinchy reason./Mayor May Who, his rival for Martha May's hand, repeats an insult about too-active glands./The stage is now set for his Grinchy attacks, assisted by his trusty reindeer/dog Max./Though he gave back Christmas for all the Whos' sakes, the Grinch got away with huge boxoffice takes./Young tots may think that this Grinch is too scary, but big kids will like the antics of Carrey./Fair holiday flick, even though the plot thins. Narrated by Sir Anthony Hopkins. **102m/C VHS, DVD, HD DVD.** Jim Carrey, Jeffrey Tambor, Christine Baranski, Taylor Momsen, Molly Shannon, Josh Ryan Evans, Clint Howard, Bill Irwin, Sloane Momsen; ***D:*** Ron Howard; ***W:*** Jeffrey Price, Peter S. Seaman; ***C:*** Don Peterman; ***M:*** James Horner; ***Nar:*** Anthony Hopkins.

Dr. Seuss' The Cat in the Hat **1/2** *The Cat in the Hat* **2003 (PG)** Another megastar comedian goes deep under makeup cover to bring a beloved Dr. Seuss character to life. This time it's Myers, who dons the cat garb to bring some mischief to a bored brother and sister on a rainy afternoon. Conrad (Breslin) is an authority-defying slob, while Sally (Fanning) is an uptight over-achieving control freak. They rightfully distrust their neighbor Quinn (Baldwin) who has matrimonial designs on their mom (Preston), an overworked real estate agent. First-time helmer Welch reveals his art-director roots in the fully-realized Seussian sets, and in the failure to bring any joy or emotion to the proceedings. The screenwriters must also share the blame, as well, as they go to extremes to flesh out the book, only to drain the translation of charm. You'd be hard-pressed to recognize much that you or your kids love from the book. **82m/C VHS, DVD.** *US* Mike Myers, Dakota Fanning, Spencer Breslin, Kelly Preston, Alec Baldwin, Amy Hill, Sean P. Hayes; ***D:*** Bo Welch; ***W:*** Alec Berg, David Mandel, Jeff Schaffer; ***C:*** Emmanuel Lubezki; ***M:*** David Newman; ***V:*** Sean P. Hayes.

Dr. Strange **1/2 1978** TV pilot based upon the Marvel Comics character who, with the help of a sorcerer, practices witchcraft in order to fight evil. **94m/C VHS.** Peter Hooten, Clyde Kusatsu, Jessica Walter, Eddie Benton, John Mills; ***D:*** Philip DeGuere. **TV**

Dr. Strangelove, or: How I Learned to Stop Worrying and Love the Bomb **1964** Sellers plays a tour-de-force triple role in Kubrick's classic black anti-war comedy. When a crazed general (Hayden) initiates a nuclear attack on the Soviets, the U.S. President (Sellers) deals with the consequences, "aided" by a hawkish general (Scott) and a wheelchair-bound advisor with an obvious Nazi past. Famous for Pickens' wild ride on the bomb, Hayden's character's "purity of essence" philosophy, Scott's gumchewing militarist, a soft-drink vending machine dispute, and countless other scenes. Based on the novel "Red Alert" by Peter George. **93m/B VHS, DVD.** *GB* Peter Sellers, George C. Scott, Sterling Hayden, Keenan Wynn, Slim Pickens, James Earl Jones, Peter Bull, Tracy Reed, Shane Rimmer, Glenn Beck, Gordon Tanner, Frank Berry, Jack Creley; ***D:*** Stanley Kubrick; ***W:*** Stanley Kubrick, Terry Southern, Peter George; ***C:*** Gilbert Taylor; ***M:*** Laurie Johnson. AFI '98: Top 100; British Acad. '64: Film, Natl. Film Reg. '89;; N.Y. Film Critics '64: Director (Kubrick).

Dr. Syn **1937** The story of a seemingly respectable vicar of Dymchurch who is really a former pirate. The last film of George Arliss. **90m/B VHS, DVD.** *GB* George Arliss, Margaret Lockwood, John Loder; ***D:*** Roy William Neill.

Dr. Syn, Alias the Scarecrow **1/2 1964 (G)** A mild-mannered minister is, in reality, a smuggler and pirate avenging King George III's injustices upon the English people. Originally broadcast in three parts on the Disney TV show. **129m/C VHS, DVD.** Patrick McGoohan, George Cole, Tony Britton, Michael Hordern, Geoffrey Keen, Kay Cole; ***D:*** James Neilson. **TV**

Dr. T & the Women 2000 (R) Gere stars as Dr. Sullivan Travis, a charming and sensitive gynecologist to the affluent women of Dallas, Texas. Yet despite his respect for and adoration of the women in his life, Dr. T, as he is known, cannot truly fathom their complexity. And none are more baffling to him than those closest to him—his wife (Fawcett), who is slowly descending into mental illness, and his daughters (Hudson and Reid). Director Altman has set his sights on ordinary human weaknesses and shortcomings here, staying away from the social commentary and cynicism of some of his earlier films, and often hits his target with a sweet and humorous note. Gere's charm and mannerisms fit the doctor to a "T," while Dern, Hunt, and Long put in good performances as well. Screenwriter Ann Rapp also collaborated with Altman on his previous film, "Cookie's Fortune." **122m/C VHS, DVD.** Richard Gere, Farrah Fawcett, Kate Hudson, Helen Hunt, Lee Grant, Liv Tyler, Shelley Long, Laura Dern, Tara Reid, Andy Richter, Matt Malloy, Robert Hays, Janine Turner; ***D:*** Robert Altman; ***W:*** Anne Rapp; ***C:*** Jan Kiesser; ***M:*** Lyle Lovett.

Doctor Takes a Wife 1940 A fast, fun screwball comedy wherein two ill-matched career people are forced via a publicity mix-up to fake being married. **89m/B VHS.** Ray Milland, Loretta Young, Reginald Gardiner, Gail Patrick, Edmund Gwenn, George Metaxa, Charles Halton; ***D:*** Alexander Hall; ***W:*** George Seaton.

Dr. Tarr's Torture Dungeon WOOF! *Dr. Jekyll's Dungeon of Darkness; Mansion of Madness* **1975** (R) A mysterious man is sent to the forest to investigate the bizarre behavior of Dr. Tarr who runs a torture asylum. **90m/C VHS, DVD.** *MX* Claudio Brook, Ellen Sherman, Robert Dumont; ***D:*** Juan Lopez Moctezuma; ***W:*** Carlos Illescas.

Dr. Terror's House of Horrors ½ *The Blood Suckers* **1965** On a train, six traveling companions have their fortunes told by a mysterious doctor. Little do they realize that their final destination has changed. Creepy and suspenseful, especially the severed-hand chase sequence. Amazingly, Christopher Lee and Peter Cushing manage to appear in the movie but not the vampire story. **92m/C VHS.** *GB* Christopher Lee, Peter Cushing, Donald Sutherland, Roy Castle, Neil McCallum, Max Adrian, Ann Bell, Michael Gough, John Martin; ***D:*** Freddie Francis; ***W:*** Milton Subotsky; ***C:*** Alan Hume; ***M:*** Elisabeth Lutyens.

Doctor Who ½ **1996** The late British sci-fi series, which ended in 1989, has been resurrected in this TV movie. The TARDIS is forced down in 1999 San Francisco and renegade Time Lord The Master's sluglike remains escape from the Doctor (McCoy) and into a temporary host body (Roberts). Meanwhile, the Doctor's been hospitalized and a botched operation by Dr. Grace Holloway (Ashbrook) leaves him clinically dead—until he manages to regenerate once again (as McGann). With Grace's help, the Doctor tries to stop his enemy from destroying the world on New Year's Eve in a plot that will also give the Master the Doctor's body as his new home. Production design and special effects are lavish (particularly in relation to the cheesiness of the series). **95m/C VHS.** *GB CA* Paul McGann, Eric Roberts, Daphne Ashbrook, Yee Jee Tso, Sylvester McCoy; ***D:*** Geoffrey Sax; ***W:*** Matthew Jacobs; ***C:*** Glen MacPherson; ***M:*** John Debney. **TV**

Doctor X ½ **1932** An armless mad scientist uses a formula for "synthetic flesh" to grow temporary limbs and commit murder. A classic, rarely seen horror oldie, famous for its very early use of two-color Technicolor. **77m/C VHS, DVD.** Lionel Atwill, Fay Wray, Lee Tracy, Preston Foster, Arthur Edmund Carewe, Leila Bennett, Mae Busch; ***D:*** Michael Curtiz; ***W:*** Earl Baldwin, Robert Tasker; ***C:*** Ray Rennahan, Richard Towers.

Doctor Zhivago **1965** (PG-13) Sweeping adaptation of the Nobel Prize-winning Boris Pasternak novel. An innocent Russian poet-intellectual is caught in the furor and chaos of the Bolshevik Revolution. Essentially a poignant love story filmed as a historical epic. Panoramic film popularized the song "Lara's Theme." Overlong, with often disappointing performances, but gorgeous scenery. Lean was more successful in "Lawrence of Arabia," where there was less need for ensemble acting. **197m/C VHS, DVD.** Omar Sharif, Julie Christie, Geraldine Chaplin, Rod Steiger, Alec Guinness, Klaus Kinski, Ralph Richardson, Rita Tushingham, Siobhan McKenna, Tom Courtenay, Bernard Kay, Gerard Tichy, Noel Willman, Geoffrey Keen, Adrienne Corri, Jack MacGowran, Mark Eden, Erik Chitty, Peter Madden, Jose Maria Caffarell, Jeffrey Rockland, Wolf Frees, Lucy Westmore; ***D:*** David Lean; ***W:*** Robert Bolt; ***C:*** Frederick A. (Freddie) Young; ***M:*** Maurice Jarre. Oscars '65: Adapt. Screenplay, Art Dir./Set Dec., Color, Color Cinematog., Costume Des. (C), Orig. Score; AFI '98: Top 100; Golden Globes '66: Actor—Drama (Sharif), Director (Lean), Film—Drama, Screenplay, Score; Natl. Bd. of Review '65: Actress (Christie).

Doctor Zhivago ½ **2003** Miniseries version of the Pasternak novel focuses more on the story's romantic difficulties and slightly less on the politics of the Russian revolution. Noble doctor/poet Yury Zhivago (Matheson) marries his childhood sweetheart and cousin, Tonya (Lara), but falls madly in love with beautiful Lara (Knightley). As if this affair weren't dramatic enough, Lara is the obsession of the powerful Kormarovsky (Neill), who is determined to keep her as his possession and who is much more capable of bending with the changing political winds than the idealistic Yury. And if the ending seems different, you're right, it was changed for this re-telling. **214m/C VHS, DVD.** *GB* Hans Matheson, Keira Knightley, Sam Neill, Kris Marshall, Daniele Liotti, Celia Imrie, Bill Paterson, Alexandra Maria Lara, Maryam D'Abo; ***D:*** Giacomo Campiotti; ***W:*** Andrew Davies; ***C:*** Blasco Giurato; ***M:*** Ludovico Einaudi. **TV**

Doctors and Nurses **1982** A children's satire of soap operas wherein the adults play the children and vice-versa. **90m/C VHS.** Rebecca Rigg, Drew Forsythe, Graeme Blundell; ***D:*** Maurice Murphy.

Doctors' Wives ½ **1970** (R) An adaptation of the Frank Slaughter potboiler about a large city hospital's doctors, nurses, and their respective spouses, with plenty of affairs, medical traumas, and betrayals. **102m/C VHS.** Dyan Cannon, Richard Crenna, Gene Hackman, Carroll O'Connor, Rachel Roberts, Janice Rule, Diana Sands, Ralph Bellamy, John Colicos; ***D:*** George Schaefer; ***W:*** Daniel Taradash; ***C:*** Charles B(ryant) Lang Jr.; ***M:*** Elmer Bernstein.

Dodes 'ka-den ½ *Clickety Clack* **1970** In this departure from his samurai-genre films, Kurosawa depicts a throng of fringe-dwelling Tokyo slum inhabitants in a semi-surreal manner. Fascinating presentation and content. **140m/C VHS, DVD.** *JP* Yoshitaka Zushi, Junzaburo Ban, Kiyoko Tange; ***D:*** Akira Kurosawa; ***W:*** Shinobu Hashimoto, Hideo Oguni, Akira Kurosawa; ***C:*** Takao Saito, Yasumichi Fukuzawa; ***M:*** Toru Takemitsu.

Dodge City **1939** Flynn stars as Wade Hutton, a roving cattleman who becomes the sheriff of Dodge City. His job: to run a ruthless outlaw and his gang out of town. De Havilland serves as Flynn's love interest, as she did in many previous films. A broad and colorful shoot-em-up! **104m/C VHS, DVD.** Errol Flynn, Olivia de Havilland, Bruce Cabot, Ann Sheridan, Alan Hale, Frank McHugh, Victor Jory, Henry Travers, Charles Halton; ***D:*** Michael Curtiz; ***M:*** Max Steiner.

Dodgeball: A True Underdog Story **2004** (PG-13) Likable, easygoing schmoe (Vaughn) runs a gym for underachievers in direct competition with big box fitness fascist (Stiller) across the street. Stiller finds a way to expose Vaughn's financial failings to put him out of business. Vaughn enlists aid of his misfit patrons to win the pot of a professional dodgeball tournament—but they must beat Stiller's elite team first. Slobs vs. snobs comedy in the "Caddyshack/Meatballs" tradition, with plenty of crotch-crunching and boob humor. Don't miss Torn's crusty coach, who hurls wrenches as training. Nothing too original, but should please the frat crowd. Cameos by William Shatner, Lance Armstrong, David Hasselhoff, and Chuck Norris. **96m/C DVD, Blu-ray Disc, UMD.** *US* Ben Stiller, Vince Vaughn, Christine Taylor, Justin Long, Jason Bateman, Gary Cole, Missi Pyle, Stephen (Steve) Root, William Shatner, Rip Torn, Hank Azaria, Chris(topher) Williams, Alan Tudyk, David Hasselhoff; ***Cameos:*** Chuck Norris, Lance Armstrong; ***D:*** Rawson Marshall Thurber; ***W:*** Rawson Marshall Thurber; ***C:*** Jerzy Zielinski, Theodore Shapiro; ***M:*** Theodore Shapiro.

Dodson's Journey ½ **2001** Worried about the impact their impending divorce will have on 10-year-old Maggie (Morton), dad James (Elliott) decides to take his daughter on a bonding fly-fishing trip. Adapted from Dodson's book "Faithful Travelers." **120m/C VHS, DVD.** David James Elliott, Alicia Morton, Ellen Burstyn, Brenda James, Tantoo Cardinal, Nanci Chambers; ***D:*** Gregg Champion; ***W:*** John Pielmeier; ***C:*** Attila Szalay; ***M:*** Joseph Conlan. **TV**

Dodsworth ½ **1936** The lives of a self-made American tycoon and his wife are drastically changed when they take a tour of Europe. The success of their marriage seems questionable as they re-evaluate their lives. Huston excels as does the rest of the cast in this film, based upon the Sinclair Lewis novel. **101m/B VHS, DVD.** Walter Huston, David Niven, Paul Lukas, John Payne, Mary Astor, Ruth Chatterton, Maria Ouspenskaya, Charles Halton; ***D:*** William Wyler; ***W:*** Sidney Howard; ***C:*** Rudolph Mate; ***M:*** Alfred Newman. Natl. Film Reg. '90;; N.Y. Film Critics '36: Actor (Huston).

The Doe Boy **2001** A hemophiliac half-Cherokee youth tries to live up to his father's expectations, free himself from an over-protective mother, and forge an identify for himself. He also has to overcome the stigma of accidently killing a female deer instead of a buck during his first hunting trip (giving him his nickname and the movie its title). Redroad's directorial debut doesn't break much new ground, but deals with the themes in a satisfying way. Fine cast helps things along nicely. **83m/C VHS, DVD.** James Duval, Kevin Anderson, Andrew J. Ferchland, Jeri Arredondo, Jim Metzler, Gordon Tootoosis, Robert C. Anthony; ***D:*** Randy Redroad; ***W:*** Randy Redroad; ***C:*** Laszlo Kadar; ***M:*** Adam Dorn.

Does This Mean We're Married? **1990** (PG-13) A stand-up comedian is trying to find success in the comedy clubs of Paris but without her green card she may soon be deported. She finds a sleazy marriage broker who fixes her up with a womanizing songwriter who needs money. As usual, immigration officials suspect that the marriage is a fake and the mismatched couple must live together to prove them wrong. **93m/C VHS.** Patsy Kensit, Stephane Freiss; ***D:*** Carol Wiseman.

Dog Bite Dog **2006** Violent, if routine, Hong Kong action pic. A Cambodian hit man (Chen) is up against a cop (Lee) with anger issues. Chinese, Thai, and Cambodian with subtitles. **108m/C DVD.** *HK JP* Edison Chen, Sam Lee, Suet Lam, Weiying Pei, Siu-fai Cheung; ***D:*** Pou-soi Cheang; ***W:*** Matt Chow, Kam-yuen Szeto; ***C:*** Yuen Man Fung; ***M:*** Ben Cheung.

Dog Day ½ *Canicule* **1983** An American traitor, who is on the lam from the government, and his cronies, takes refuge on a small farm. A surprise awaits him when the farmers come up with an unusual plan to bargain for his life. **101m/C VHS, DVD.** *FR* Lee Marvin, Miou-Miou, Victor Lanoux; ***D:*** Yves Boisset.

Dog Day Afternoon ½ **1975** (R) Based on a true story, this taut, yet fantastic thriller centers on a bi-sexual and his slow-witted buddy who rob a bank to obtain money to fund a sex change operation for the ringleader's lover. Pacino is breathtaking in his role as the frustrated robber, caught in a trap of his own devising. Very controversial for its language and subject matter when released, it nevertheless became a huge success. Director Lumet keeps up the pace, fills the screen with pathos without gross sentiment. **124m/C VHS, DVD, Blu-ray Disc, HD DVD.** Dominic Chianese, Al Pacino, John Cazale, Charles Durning, James Broderick, Chris Sarandon, Carol Kane, Lance Henriksen, Dick Anthony Williams; ***D:*** Sidney Lumet; ***W:*** Frank Pierson; ***C:*** Victor Kemper. Oscars '75: Orig. Screenplay; British Acad. '75: Actor (Pacino); Natl. Bd. of Review '75: Support. Actor (Durning), Natl. Film Reg. '09;; Writers Guild '75: Orig. Screenplay.

Dog Eat Dog *Einer Frisst den Anderen; La Morte Vestita di Dollar* **1964** Centering on a heist scheme by Mitchell, this one has nothing to offer except Mansfield's attributes. **86m/B VHS, DVD.** Cameron Mitchell, Jayne Mansfield, Isa Miranda; ***D:*** Ray Nazarro.

Dog Gone ½ *Diamond Dog Caper* **2008** (PG) Fast-paced family comedy. Twelve-year-old Owen rescues a golden retriever from three bumbling thieves and, after reading about a diamond heist, realizes that the jewels are stashed with the dog (you really don't want to know where). Owen goes to the cops but they don't believe his story, so he and the dog he's named Diamond plan to bring the bad guys down themselves. **108m/C DVD.** Luke Benward, French Stewart, Kevin Farley, Garrett Morris, Kelly Perrine, Brittany Curran; ***D:*** Mark Stouffer; ***W:*** Mark Stouffer, Denis Johnson; ***C:*** Tom Camarda; ***M:*** Andrew Gross. **VIDEO**

Dog Gone Love ½ **2003** (R) While doing some research at the local vet office, struggling author Steven meets foxy assistant Rebecca who thinks he's gay. So he figures faking it would be fun until—oh my!—he falls for her. Plot is all bark and no bite. **89m/C VHS, DVD.** Lindsay Sloane, Richard Kind, Christopher Coppola, Brian Poth, Tom McGowan, Jordan Ladd, Chris Elwood, Marissa Hall, James Warwick, Alexander Chaplin, Marina Black, John Cantwell, Carmen Mormino, Alexandra Boyd, Jenni Pulos, Paul Korver, Steve Susskind, Mikyla, Brian O'Hare, Laura Pinner, Brian T. Lynch; ***D:*** Rob Lundsgaard; ***W:*** Rob Lundsgaard; ***C:*** Kristian Bernier; ***M:*** William V. Malpede. **VIDEO**

A Dog Named Christmas ½ **2009** Sentimental Christmas mush gets you all the time in this 237th presentation from the Hallmark Hall of Fame. Kansas farmer George McCray (Greenwood) has always been adamant that his family will not get a dog (flashbacks explain why). However, when his 20-year-old mentally-challenged son Todd (Fisher) hears about an adopt-a-dog program for the holidays sponsored by the local animal shelter, Todd and mom Mary Ann (Edmond) manage to persuade George to give in. Yellow Lab Christmas is, of course, an exceptionally appealing choice and you won't be surprised by how things turn out. Adapted from the novel by Greg Kincaid. **100m/C DVD.** Bruce Greenwood, Noel Fisher, Ken Pogue, Sonja Bennett, Linda Emond, Carrie Ruscheinsky; ***D:*** Peter Werner; ***W:*** Jenny Wingfield; ***C:*** Eric Van Haren Noman; ***M:*** Jeff Beal. **TV**

A Dog of Flanders ½ **1959** A young Dutch boy and his grandfather find a severely beaten dog and restore it to health. **96m/C VHS, DVD.** David Ladd, Donald Crisp, Theodore Bikel, Max Croiset, Monique Ahrens; ***D:*** James B. Clark.

A Dog of Flanders **1999** (PG) Fifth screen version of Marie Louise de la Ramee's 1872 children's story is put to sleep by slow pacing and murky settings. Orphan Nello (Kissner) and his grandfather Jehan (Warden) find an abused dog and nurse it back to health. The boy and his dog team up to support the household as Jehan's health begins to fade. Nello is noticed sketching in the town square by artist Michel (Voight), who then befriends and encourages the boy. As his artistic gifts flower, he attempts to win his childhood sweetheart Aloise (Monet) over the protests of her father. The rather depressing climax of the original story is replaced by a brighter ending in an attempt to make the movie more child-friendly, but the uneven acting and accents won't even fool the kiddies. **100m/C VHS, DVD.** Jack Warden, Jon Voight, Jeremy James Kissner, Jesse James, Cheryl Ladd, Bruce McGill, Steven Hartley, Dirk Lavrysen, Andrew Bicknell, Antje De Boeck; ***D:*** Kevin Brodie; ***W:*** Robert Singer, Kevin Brodie; ***C:*** Walther Vanden Ende; ***M:*** Richard Friedman.

Dog Park **1998** (R) Andy (Wilson) and Lorna (Henstridge) have only their doggy companions to keep them warm after their respective lovers take a hike. At least until they find each other while walking their pups. Not that the course of true love (or even dating) will run smoothly. Pleasant enough romantic comedy but Henstridge seems out of her element. **91m/C VHS, DVD.** *CA* Luke Wilson, Natasha Henstridge, Janeane Garofalo, Bruce McCulloch, Kathleen Robertson, Kristen Lehman, Mark McKinney, Gordon Currie, Amie Carey, Harland Williams; *D:* Bruce McCulloch; *W:* Bruce McCulloch; *C:* David Makin; *M:* Craig Northey. Genie '99: Support. Actor (McKinney).

Dog Pound Shuffle *Spot* **1975 (PG)** Two drifters form a new song-and-dance act in order to raise the funds necessary to win their dog's freedom from the pound. Charming Canadian production. **98m/C VHS.** *CA* Ron Moody, David Soul; *D:* Jeffrey Bloom; *W:* Jeffrey Bloom.

The Dog Problem 1/2 **2006 (R)** Solo (Ribisi) is at a personal and professional crossroads after squandering the rewards of his success on drugs, women, and therapy. At his last session with Dr. Noumand (Cheadle), the good psychiatrist suggests he get a pet to help overcome his loneliness. Upon doing so, his new pooch is soon chomped by a formidable hound in the care of a spunky stripper (Collins). This leads to a most unusual relationship plagued with canine complications. Holds your interest, develops nicely, with just the right touch of comedic urban disdain. **89m/C DVD.** Giovanni Ribisi, Don Cheadle, Lynn Collins, Kevin Corrigan, Mena Suvari, Scott Caan, Joanna Krupa; *D:* Scott Caan; *W:* Scott Caan; *C:* Phil Parmet; *M:* Mark Mothersbaugh.

Dog Soldiers **2001 (R)** Military werewolf flick finds a British army squad on manuevers in the Scottish highlands. When they find their Special Ops war-game foes half-eaten except for leader Ryan, they're set upon by the creatures. The survivors are rescued by a passing female zoologist and taken to a cabin to hold up for the night. Pic becomes an "Assault on Precinct 13"-type siege as the creatures try to get to the soldiers, some of whom have taken on distinctly canine tendences. Hit-and-miss black humor, paired with too-British banter and low-tech effects make this one a bit hard to swallow for most. **104m/C VHS, DVD.** *GB LU* Sean Pertwee, Kevin McKidd, Liam Cunningham, Thomas Lockyer, Emma Cleasby; *D:* Neil Marshall; *W:* Neil Marshall; *M:* Mark Thomas.

Dog Star Man **1964** The silent epic by the dean of experimental American film depicts man's spiritual and physical conflicts through Brakhage's characteristically freeform collage techniques. **78m/C VHS, DVD.** *D:* Stan Brakhage. Natl. Film Reg. '92.

The Dog Who Saved Christmas 1/2 **2009 (PG)** Former K-9 police dog Zeus is the newest member of the Bannister family. Left behind to guard the house when the Bannisters go away for the holiday, Zeus seizes his chance to act heroically when the usual comically-inept burglars try to rob the home. **90m/C DVD.** Dean Cain, Gary Valentine, Elisa Donovan, Mindy Sterling, Sierra McCormick, Charlie Stewart, Joey Diaz, Joe Torry; *D:* Michael Feifer; *W:* Michael Ciminiera, Richard Gnolfo; *C:* Hank Baumert Jr.; *M:* Andres Boulton; *V:* Mario Lopez. **VIDEO**

The Dog Who Stopped the War **1984 (G)** A Canadian children's film about a dog who puts a halt to an escalating snowball fight between rival gangs. **90m/C VHS, DVD.** *CA* Cedric Jourde, Marie-Pierre D'Amour, Julien Elie, Minh Vu Duc; *D:* Andre Melancon; *W:* Roger Cantin, Danyele Patenaude; *C:* Francois Protat; *M:* Germain Gauthier.

Dogfight **1991 (R)** It's 1963 and a baby-faced Marine and his buddies are spending their last night in San Francisco before leaving the U.S. for a tour of duty in Vietnam. They agree to throw a "dogfight," a competition to see who can bring the ugliest date to a party. Birdlace (Phoenix) chooses Taylor, a shy, average-looking waitress who dreams of becoming a folk singer and realizes too late that she doesn't deserve the treatment he's about to subject her to. This quiet film didn't see a wide release, but is worth renting due to an above average script which is held up by the splendid performances of Phoenix and Taylor. **94m/C VHS, DVD.** River Phoenix, Lili Taylor, Richard Panebianco, Anthony Clark, Mitchell Whitfield, Elizabeth (E.G. Dailey) Daily, Holly Near, Brendan Fraser, Margaret "Peg" Phillips; *D:* Nancy Savoca; *W:* Bob Comfort.

The Dogfighters **1995 (R)** Ex-Air Force pilot Rowdy Wells (Davi) is blackmailed into trying to destroy a plutonium plant in an eastern European country. That is, if Rowdy can survive an air battle with nemisis Lothar Krasna (Godunov). Small budget is reflected in the mediocre aerial sequences. **96m/C VHS.** Robert Davi, Alexander Godunov, Ben Gazzara, Lara Harris; *D:* Barry Zetlin; *W:* Sean Smith, Anthony Stark; *C:* Levie Isaacks; *M:* Jimmie Haskell.

Dogma 1/2 **1999 (R)** Smith packs a lot into his brave, controversial comedy on Catholicism and, as a Catholic himself, illustrates that he has some issues about his religion. He vents with a film that's both devilishly funny and agonizingly boring. A great cast does his dirty work, including Affleck and Damon as two cast out angels with a plan to re-enter heaven. Rock plays an angry apostle, Hayek is a muse turned stripper, and Rickman is the voice of God informing an abortion worker (Fiorentino) that she's to stop the angels. Rounding out the motley crew is Carlin as a cardinal. The first half is loaded with on-target jokes, but laughs are hard to find in the second hour, which falls victim to excessive religious yakety-schmakety. Smith's a talented screenwriter, unfortunately this time out, it's his directing that's really a sin. **125m/C VHS, DVD.** Ben Affleck, Matt Damon, Linda Fiorentino, Chris Rock, Salma Hayek, Jason Lee, George Carlin, Alan Rickman, Jason Mewes, Janeane Garofalo, Kevin Smith, Alanis Morissette, Bud Cort, Jeff Anderson, Guinevere Turner; *D:* Kevin Smith; *W:* Kevin Smith; *C:* Robert Yeoman; *M:* Howard Shore.

A Dog's Breakfast 1/2 **2007** Black comedy at its funniest. Patrick hates his younger sister Marilyn's fiance Ryan so much that he decides to murder him. Title is British slang for making a mess of things, although there is a dog (named Mars) and what he eats is important (and gross). **88m/C DVD.** David Hewlett, Paul McGillion, Rachel Luttrell, Christopher Judge, Kate Hewlett; *D:* David Hewlett; *W:* David Hewlett; *C:* James Alfred Menard; *M:* Tim Williams. **VIDEO**

Dogs in Space **1987** A low-budget Australian film about a clique of aimless Melbourne rock kids in 1978, caught somewhere between post-hippiedom and punk, free love and heroin addiction. Acclaimed. Includes music by Hutchence, Brian Eno, Iggy Pop, and others. **109m/C VHS.** *AU* Michael Hutchence, Saskia Post, Nique Needles, Tony Helou, Deanna Bond; *D:* Richard Lowenstein; *W:* Richard Lowenstein.

Dogs of Hell 1/2 **1983 (R)** The sheriff of an idyllic resort community must stop a pack of killer dogs from terrorizing the residents. **90m/C VHS.** Earl Owensby, Bill Gribble, Jerry Rushing; *D:* Worth Keeter.

The Dogs of War 1/2 **1981 (R)** A graphic depiction of a group of professional mercenaries, driven by nothing but their quest for wealth and power, hired to overthrow the dictator of a new West African nation. Has some weak moments which break up the continuity of the movie. Based on the novel by Frederick Forsyth. **102m/C VHS, DVD.** *GB* Christopher Walken, Tom Berenger, Colin Blakely, Paul Freeman, Hugh Millais, Victoria Tennant, JoBeth Williams; *D:* John Irvin; *W:* Gary De Vore; *C:* Jack Cardiff; *M:* Geoffrey Burgon.

Dogs: The Rise and Fall of an All-Girl Bookie Joint **1996** On the surface, this is a story about some twenty-something women who are bad at relationships and can't pay the rent. To solve one of their problems they turn their apartment into a bookie joint. However, underneath there is the story of the girl who has just lost her mother and needs money to pay for her funeral. The thread that weaves it all together is the drive to survive and rise above what life has given you, or sometimes what you give yourself. This is an indie, low-budget film and the acting and lighting reflect its limitations, but overall it is a good story with competent acting. **88m/C DVD.** Pam Columbus, Pam Gray, Eve Annenberg, Toby Huss, Leo Marks, Amedo D'Adamo; *D:* Eve Annenberg; *W:* Eve Annenberg; *C:* Wolfgang Held.

Dogtown **1997** Former beauty queen/cheerleader Dorothy Sternen feels trapped in her small town of Cuba, Missouri. Her longtime boyfriend Ezra Good is a bitter ex-athlete stuck in a dull job who sometimes gets violent. Then high school classmate Philip returns to town. Although he's a struggling actor, Philip is treated like a celebrity, and Dorothy starts giving him the eye. Tensions arise as they all realize how dissatisfied each of them are. **99m/C VHS, DVD.** Mary Stuart Masterson, Trevor St. John, Jon Favreau, Rory Cochrane, Karen Black, Natasha Gregson Wagner, Maureen McCormick, Harold Russell, John Livingston, Shawnee Smith; *D:* George Hickenlooper; *W:* George Hickenlooper; *C:* Kramer Morgenthau; *M:* Steve Stevens.

Dogville 1/2 **2003 (R)** Another "love it or hate it" offering from director von Trier brings us yet another troubled woman, Grace (Kidman), who is on the run from mobsters and picks Dogville (a made-up U.S. locale) to hide out, even offering up free labor to the townsfolk in return for their silence. But things go south for her as she is persecuted and eventually they do an about-face and consider ratting her out for a hefty reward-...though she's savvy enough to fight back. Set during the Depression and filmed on a minimalist set similar to the Thorton Wilder classic "Our Town," though the two stories are complete contradictions The Danish von Trier may be perceived as hateful toward the American way of life, whereas many will find his latest effort to be a memorably appalling, thought-provoking tale with Kidman flourishing in the challenging lead role. **178m/C DVD.** *DK NL SW FR NO FI GE IT* Nicole Kidman, Lauren Bacall, Paul Bettany, Philip Baker Hall, Blair Brown, James Caan, Patricia Clarkson, Jeremy Davies, Ben Gazzara, Siobhan Fallon Hogan, Zeljko Ivanek, Udo Kier, Harriet Andersson, Jean-Marc Barr, Thom Hoffman, Bill Raymond, Chloe Sevigny, Stellan Skarsgard; *D:* Lars von Trier; *W:* Lars von Trier; *C:* Anthony Dod Mantle; *Nar:* John Hurt.

Dogville Shorts 1/2 **1930** Two-disc compilation containing nine specialty shorts from 1930-31 of the "All-Barkie" Dogville Comedies. These featured various dog breeds spoofing human behavior (with human voiceovers) and the era's popular movie themes, including prison escapes, war heroics, jungle adventures, detective stories, romance, and musicals. **142m/B DVD.** *D:* Zion Myers, Jules White.

Dogwatch **1997 (R)** San Francisco police detective Charlie Falon (Elliott) tries to avenge his partner's murder but kills the wrong man. Then he learns dirty cops are behind the crime. Thriller takes the easy road by solving everything with violence. **100m/C VHS, DVD.** Sam Elliott, Esai Morales, Paul Sorvino, Dan Lauria, Richard Gilliland, Jessica Steen, Mimi (Meyer) Craven; *D:* John Langley; *W:* Martin Zurla; *C:* Robert Yeoman; *M:* Lennie Niehaus. **CABLE**

Doin' Time **1985 (R)** At the John Dillinger Memorial Penitentiary, the inmates take over the prison under the supervision of warden "Mongo." Silliness prevails. **80m/C VHS.** Jeff Altman, Dey Young, Richard Mulligan, John Vernon, Colleen Camp, Melanie Chartoff, Graham Jarvis, Pat McCormick, Eddie Velez, Jimmie Walker, Judy Landers, Nicholas Worth, Mike Mazurki, Muhammad Ali, Melinda Fee, Francesca "Kitten" Natividad, Ron Palillo; *D:* George Mendeluk; *W:* George Mendeluk, Dee Caruso, Ron Zwang, Franelle Silver; *M:* Charles Fox.

Doin' Time on Planet Earth 1/2 **1988 (PG-13)** A young boy feels out of place with his family and is convinced by two strange people (aliens themselves?) that he is really an extraterrestrial. Amusing, aimless fun directed by the son of Walter Matthau. **83m/C VHS.** Adam West, Candice Azzara, Hugh O'Brian, Matt Adler, Timothy Patrick Murphy, Roddy McDowall, Maureen Stapleton, Andrea Thompson; *D:* Charles Matthau.

Doing Time 1/2 *Kimusho No Naka* **2002** After spending several years in prison, Kazuichi Hanawa managed to turn his experiences into a successful comic, and then get it made into film. Every aspect of life in a Japanese prison is micromanaged and carefully controlled until the prisoners lose all sense of identity and individuality. Fans of prison films will want to see it for the stark and surprising differences in the American and Japanese prison systems, and fans of unconventional films may also wish to give it a go. **93m/C DVD.** *JP* Tsutomu Yamazaki; *D:* Yoichi Sai; *W:* Yoshihiro Nakamura, Yoichi Sai, Wui Sin Chong, Kazuichi Hanawa.

Doing Time for Patsy Cline 1/2 **1997** Yearning to make it big in faraway Nashville, Ralph (Day) forsakes his parents' down-under farm with guitar in hand. Hitchhiking with punk Boyd (Roxburgh) and pretty Patsy (Otto)—who claims country crooner Patsy Cline as her namesake—he finds out free rides don't usually end well (not in the movies anyhow) as the cops bust them on drug charges. Patsy flees, leaving the boys in the pen, though there's not much suspense to their fate as director Kennedy's story repeatedly jumps back and forth in time between locales. **95m/C DVD.** Richard Roxburgh, Miranda Otto, Matt(hew) Day, Tony Barry, Kiri Paramore, Laurence Coy; *D:* Chris Kennedy; *W:* Chris Kennedy; *C:* Andrew Lesnie; *M:* Peter Best.

Doing Time on Maple Drive 1/2 **1992** College boy Matt (McNamara) brings his fiancee Alison (Loughlin) home to meet his seemingly tranquil but secretly dysfunctional family. Dad (Sikking), a retired military man, and Mom (Besch) expect their children to be perfect but elder brother Tim (Carrey) is a not-so-secret alcoholic, neurotic daughter Karen's (Brook) marriage is in trouble, and Matt himself is hiding a big secret that threatens the harmonious family facade. Made for TV. **90m/C VHS, DVD.** William McNamara, James B. Sikking, Bibi Besch, Jim Carrey, Lori Loughlin, Jayne Brook, David Byron; *D:* Ken Olin; *W:* James Duff; *C:* Bing Sokolsky; *M:* Laura Karpman. **TV**

Doktor Faustus *Thomas Mann's Doktor Faustus* **1982** A composer sells his soul in return for a lifetime of creativity. Satan's condition is that Leverhuehn has no close human contacts but he violates the agreement with tragic consequences. Adapted from the Thomas Mann novel and updated to the 1930s and 40s as Germany descends into the coming war madness that mirrors Leverhuehn's own. German with subtitles. **137m/C DVD.** *GE* Jon Finch, Hanns Zischler, Andre Heller, Marie Breillat; *D:* Franz Seitz; *W:* Franz Seitz; *C:* Rudolf Blahacek; *M:* Rolf Wilhelm.

Dolemite 1/2 **1975 (R)** An ex-con attempts to settle the score with some of his former inmates. He forms a band of kung-fu savvy ladies. Strange combination of action and comedy. **88m/C VHS, DVD.** Rudy Ray Moore, Jerry Jones, D'Urville Martin, Lady Reeds; *D:* D'Urville Martin; *W:* Jerry Jones; *C:* Nicholas Josef von Sternberg; *M:* Arthur Wright.

Dolemite 2: Human Tornado 1/2 *The Human Tornado* **1976 (R)** Nobody ever said Moore was for everybody's taste. But, hey, when blaxploitation movies were the rage, Rudy the standup comic was out there rapping through a series of trashy movies that, when viewed today, have survived the test of time. This one's just as vile, violent, and sexist as the day it was released. When Rudy is surprised in bed with a white sheriff's wife, he flees and meets up with a madam and a house of kung-fu-skilled girls who are embroiled in a fight with a local mobster. **98m/C VHS, DVD.** Rudy Ray Moore, Lady Reeds, Ernie Hudson, Howard Jackson, Herb Graham, Jerry Jones, Jimmy Lynch; *D:* Cliff Roquemore; *W:* Jerry Jones; *C:* Fred Conde, Bob Wilson; *M:* Arthur Wright.

The Doll *La Poupee; He, She or It* **1962** A lonely night watchman happens upon two burglars and, in the chase, the thieves knock over a mannequin. The watchman reports the mannequin stolen, brings it home and begins to have conversations with it. Soon, the doll's needs cause him to steal jewelry and clothes, until his brutish neighbor discovers his secrets. In Swedish with English subtitles. **96m/B VHS.** *SW* Per Oscarsson, Gio Petre, Tor Isedal, Elsa Prawitz; *D:* Arne Mattson.

Doll Face 1/2 *Come Back to Me* **1946** Story of a stripper who wants to go legit and make it on Broadway. Film was adapted from the play "The Naked Genius" by tease queen Gypsy Rose Lee. ♫ Dig You Later; Here Comes Heaven Again; Chico-Chico; Somebody's Walkin' In My Dreams; Red Hot and Beautiful. **80m/B VHS, DVD.** Vivian Blaine, Dennis O'Keefe, Perry Como, Carmen Miranda, Reed Hadley; ***D:*** Lewis Seiler.

The Doll Squad *Hustler Squad* **1973 (PG)** Three voluptuous special agents fight an ex-CIA agent out to rule the world. **93m/C VHS, DVD.** Michael Ansara, Francine York, Anthony Eisley, John N. Carter, Rafael Campos, William Bagdad, Lisa Todd, Lillian Garrett, Herb Robbins, Tua Satana; ***D:*** Ted V. Mikels; ***W:*** Ted V. Mikels, Jack Pichesin, Pam Eddy; ***C:*** Anthony Salinas; ***M:*** Nicholas Carras.

Dollar **1938** The actress wife of an industrialist, convinced that he is having an affair, follows him to a ski lodge in attempt to catch him in the act. In Swedish with English subtitles. **74m/B VHS.** *SW* Georg Rydeberg, Ingrid Bergman, Kotti Chave, Tutta Rolf, Hakan Westergren, Elsa Burnett, Edvin Adolphson, Gosta Cederlund, Eric Rosen; ***D:*** Gustaf Molander.

Dollars *The Heist* **1971 (R)** A bank employee and his dizzy call-girl assistant plan to steal the German facility's assets while installing its new security system. Lighthearted fun. **119m/C VHS.** Warren Beatty, Goldie Hawn, Gert Frobe, Scott Brady, Robert Webber; ***D:*** Richard Brooks; ***W:*** Richard Brooks; ***M:*** Quincy Jones.

The Dollmaker 1/2 **1984** Excellent adaptation of Harriette Arnow's novel. A strong-willed Kentucky mother of five helps move her family to Detroit in the 1940s. Petrie's direction moves the story along and creates a lovely period vision. **140m/C VHS.** Jane Fonda, Levon Helm, Geraldine Page, Amanda Plummer, Susan Kingsley; ***D:*** Daniel Petrie. **TV**

Dollman 1/2 **1990 (R)** An ultra-tough cop from an Earth-like planet (even swear words are the same) crashes in the South Bronx—and on this world he's only 13 inches tall. The filmmakers squander a great premise and cast with bloody shootouts and a sequel-ready non-ending. **86m/C VHS, DVD.** Tim Thomerson, Jackie Earle Haley, Kamala Lopez, Humberto Ortiz, Nicholas Guest, Michael Halsey, Eugene Robert Glazer, Judd Omen, Frank Collison, Vincent Klyn; ***D:*** Albert Pyun.

Dollman vs Demonic Toys **1993 (R)** Let's combine elements from three separate films and make one disgusting sequel: "Dollman," the 13-inch cop from the planet Arturus; his new girlfriend, Dollchick, who was shrunk to a diminutive 10 inches in "Bad Channels"; and tough cop Judith Grey, who's once again battling those loathsome playthings from "Demonic Toys." If you feel the need for a plot—Dollchick is kidnapped by Baby Doll and needs to be rescued. **84m/C VHS.** Tim Thomerson, Tracy Scoggins, Melissa Behr, Phil Brock, Phil Fondacaro; ***D:*** Charles Band; ***W:*** Craig Hamann; ***M:*** Richard Band.

The Dolls WOOF! **1983** A tropically located photographer recruits an area beauty into the fashion world with his winning smile and macho charm, only to learn native traditions forbid her to follow him. **96m/C VHS.** Tetchie Agbayani, Max (Michael) Thayer, Carina Schally, Richard Seward; ***D:*** Hubert Frank.

Dolls 1/2 **1987 (R)** A group of people is stranded during a storm in an old, creepy mansion. As the night wears on, they are attacked by hundreds of antique dolls. Tongue-in-cheek. **77m/C VHS, DVD.** Ian Patrick Williams, Carolyn Purdy-Gordon, Carrie Lorraine, Stephen Lee, Guy Rolfe, Bunty Bailey, Cassie Stuart, Hilary Mason; ***D:*** Stuart Gordon; ***W:*** Ed Naha; ***M:*** Richard Band.

Dolls **2002** Lyrical Japanese film intertwines three character studies into a wistful movie about devotion and lost love. A man literally ties himself to the girl he loves after realizing his weakness drove her to attempt suicide. A gang lord remembers the promise given to a girlfriend 30 years earlier. Thirty years later he returns to the park where they met, finding her still waiting. The final chapter fumbles the connection a bit, focusing on a famous pop star becoming disfigured in an auto accident. She flees the public eye, only to let one devoted fan into her life. Lush photography and landscapes are pure dazzling eye candy, but the emotionally syrupy excess may turn off some audiences. **113m/C DVD.** Tatsuya Mihashi, Chieko Matsubara, Miho Kanno, Hidetoshi Nishijima, Kyoko Fukada, Sebastian Blenkov; ***D:*** Takeshi "Beat" Kitano; ***W:*** Takeshi "Beat" Kitano; ***C:*** Katsumi Yanagijima; ***M:*** Joe Hisaishi.

A Doll's House 1/2 **1959** An all-star cast is featured in this original TV production of Henrik Ibsen's classic play about an independent woman's quest for freedom in 19th-century Norway. **89m/B VHS.** Julie Harris, Christopher Plummer, Jason Robards Jr., Hume Cronyn, Eileen Heckart, Richard Thomas; ***D:*** George Schaefer. **TV**

A Doll's House 1/2 **1973 (G)** Fonda plays Nora, a subjugated 19th-century housewife who breaks free to establish herself as an individual. Based on Henrik Ibsen's classic play; some controversy regarding Fonda's interpretation of her role. **98m/C DVD.** Jane Fonda, Edward Fox, Trevor Howard, David Warner, Delphine Seyrig; ***D:*** Joseph Losey; ***W:*** Christopher Hampton; ***M:*** John Barry.

A Doll's House **1973 (G)** A Canadian production of the Henrik Ibsen play about a Norwegian woman's search for independence. **96m/C VHS, DVD.** *CA* Claire Bloom, Anthony Hopkins, Ralph Richardson, Denholm Elliott, Anna Massey, Edith Evans; ***D:*** Patrick Garland.

Dolly Dearest 1/2 **1992 (R)** Strange things start happening after an American family takes over a run-down Mexican doll factory. They create a new doll called "Dolly Dearest" with deadly results. In the same tradition as the "Chucky" series. **94m/C VHS, DVD.** Rip Torn, Sam Bottoms, Denise Crosby; ***D:*** Maria Lease.

The Dolly Sisters 1/2 **1946** Competent musical about sisters Jenny (Grable) and Rosie (Haver), who become turn-of-the-century vaudeville stars and also find romance. Good songs, extravagent costuming, fine support work, and the charms of the two leading actresses provide simple enjoyment. ♫ I Can't Begin to Tell You; I'm Always Chasing Rainbows; Powder, Lipstick and Rouge; Give Me the Moonlight; On the Mississippi; We Have Been Around; Carolina In the Morning; Arrah Go On, I'm Gonna Go Back to Oregon; The Darktown Strutter's Ball. **114m/C VHS, DVD.** Betty Grable, June Haver, John Payne, Frank Latimore, S.Z. Sakall, Reginald Gardiner, Gene Sheldon, Sig Rumann; ***D:*** Irving Cummings; ***W:*** Marian Spitzer, John Larkin; ***C:*** Ernest Palmer.

Dolores Claiborne **1994 (R)** Stephen King gets the Hollywood treatment again (the check cleared, King approved), with better results than previous outings (remember "Needful Things"?). Successful but neurotic New York journalist Selena (Leigh) confronts her troubled past when coarse, hard-talking mom Dolores (Bates) is accused of murdering her wealthy employer (Parfitt). Plummer is vengeful detective John Mackey who, like everyone else on the fictitious Maine island, believes Dolores murdered her husband 15 years before. Top-notch performances by Bates and Leigh highlight this sometimes manipulative tale. Straithairn is wonderfully despicable as the stereotypically abusive husband and father. **132m/C VHS, DVD.** Kathy Bates, Jennifer Jason Leigh, Christopher Plummer, Judy Parfitt, David Strathairn, John C. Reilly; ***D:*** Taylor Hackford; ***W:*** Tony Gilroy; ***C:*** Gabriel Beristain; ***M:*** Danny Elfman.

The Dolphin 1/2 **1987** A dolphin visits a Brazilian fishing village each full moon, turns himself into a man, and casts a spell of seduction over the women. Villagers are both enchanted and angered by the dolphin-man, since his presence creates desire in local women but scares fish from the waters. In Portuguese with English subtitles. **95m/C VHS.** *BR* Carlos Alberto Riccelli, Cassia Kiss, Ney Latorraca; ***D:*** Walter Lima Jr.; ***W:*** Walter Lima Jr.

Domestic Disturbance **2001 (PG-13)** Lame entry in the "evil stepparent" genre features Travolta as Frank, a hard-working boat builder who shares custody of his son Danny (O'Leary) with ex-wife Susan (Polo). Danny starts acting out by getting in trouble and lying after Susan gets involved with suave local businessman Rick (Vaughn). Although Danny is clued into Rick's dark side from the start, it takes the appearance of Ray (Buscemi), a sleazy hood from Rick's shady past, to awaken Frank's suspicion. When Danny hides in Rick's van and witnesses Ray's murder, nobody believes him except his dad. The stage is set for the "good dad" versus "bad dad" showdown, which is handled as clumsily and unbelievably as possible. Most of the performances seem listless, with the exception of Vaughn as the oily villain and O'Leary as the terrorized kid. **89m/C VHS, DVD.** *US* John Travolta, Vince Vaughn, Teri Polo, Matt O'Leary, Ruben Santiago-Hudson, Susan Floyd, Steve Buscemi, Angelica Torn; ***D:*** Harold Becker; ***W:*** Lewis Colick; ***C:*** Michael Seresin; ***M:*** Mark Mancina.

Dominick & Eugene **1988 (PG-13)** Dominick is a little slow, but he makes a fair living as a garbageman—good enough to put his brother through medical school. Both men struggle with the other's faults and weaknesses, as they learn the meaning of family and friendship. Well-acted, especially by Hulce, never melodramatic or weak. **96m/C VHS, DVD.** Ray Liotta, Tom Hulce, Jamie Lee Curtis, Todd Graff, Bill Cobbs, David Strathairn; ***D:*** Robert M. Young; ***W:*** Alvin Sargent, Corey Blechman; ***C:*** Curtis Clark; ***M:*** Trevor Jones.

Dominion 1/2 **1994 (R)** Six buddies take off for a weekend hunting trip that turns deadly when a murderous hunter believes they've trespassed on his territory and begins stalking them. **98m/C VHS.** Michael (Mike) Papajohn, Brad Johnson, Brion James, Tim Thomerson, Woody Brown, Glenn Morshower, Richard Riehle, Geoffrey Blake; ***D:*** Michael Kehoe; ***W:*** Woody Brown, Michael Kehoe.

Dominion: Prequel to the Exorcist 1/2 **2005 (R)** Paul Schrader's dark and intensely serious horror movie about demon-possession gone wrong. Released less because of the interest in another "Exorcist" spin-off, but more in hopes of cashing in on the curiosity to see such an unusual studio maneuver. This "prequel" disappointed the Morgan Creek execs, who then decided to re-shoot the entire movie with a new director and a few new actors. That movie became "Exorcist: The Beginning." With nothing to lose, the studio plunked in some CGI and released their original investment under this slightly different title. It's better than their reshoot, and makes for a fascinating experiment when paired up scene-for-scene with "The Beginning." **116m/C DVD.** *US* Stellan Skarsgard, Gabriel Mann, Clara Bellar, Andrew French, Israel Adurama, Eddie Osei, Antoine Kamerling, Julian Wadham, Ilario Bisi-Pedro; ***D:*** Paul Schrader; ***W:*** William Wisher, Caleb Carr; ***C:*** Vittorio Storaro; ***M:*** Trevor Rabin, Angelo Badalamenti, Dog Fashion Disco.

Dominique Is Dead **1979 (PG)** A woman is driven to suicide by her greedy husband; now someone is trying to drive him mad. A.K.A. "Dominique" and "Avenging Spirit." **95m/C VHS, DVD.** Cliff Robertson, Jean Simmons, Jenny Agutter, Simon Ward, Ron Moody; ***D:*** Michael Anderson Sr.

Domino **1988 (R)** A beautiful woman and a mysterious guy link up for sex, murder and double-crosses. Dubbed. Tries to be arty and avant-garde, but only succeeds in being a piece of soft-core fluff. **95m/C VHS, UMD.** *IT* Brigitte Nielsen, Tomas Arana, Daniela Alzone; ***D:*** Ivana Massetti.

Domino 1/2 **2005 (R)** Scott, who proved that he could hang with the Tarantino crowd in "True Romance," uses every trick in his cinematic arsenal to bring to life the "sort of" true story of model-turned-bounty-hunter Domino Harvey (Knightley). Domino joins the crew of a bail-bondsman, looking for passion and thrills, and finds herself in the center of screenwriter Richard Kelly's perfect storm of bombastic sex, gunplay, criminal conspiracies, and reality TV. The plot tends to drag and the supporting cast overwhelms Knightley a bit, but you've got to love a movie that brings together Christopher Walken, Mickey Rourke, and 90210's Ian Ziering, with every camera shot that Tarantino and Oliver Stone were too chicken to use themselves. **128m/C DVD, Blu-ray Disc.** *US* Keira Knightley, Mickey Rourke, Edgar Ramirez, Delroy Lindo, Mo'Nique, Lucy Liu, Christopher Walken, Mena Suvari, Macy Gray, Jacqueline Bisset, Dabney Coleman, Brian Austin Green, Ian Ziering, Stanley Kamel, Peter Jacobson, T.K. Carter, Kel O'Neill, Shondrella Avery, Lew Temple, Tom Waits, Rizwan Abbasi; ***D:*** Tony Scott; ***W:*** Richard Kelly, Steve Barancik; ***C:*** Dan Mindel; ***M:*** Harry Gregson-Williams.

The Domino Principle 1/2 *The Domino Killings* **1977 (R)** It's got nothing to do with pizza. Viet vet Hackman is a doltish convict sprung from the joint by a government organization to do some dirty work: working as a political assassin. Heavy-handed direction and lack of suspense make it less than it should be. **97m/C VHS, DVD.** Gene Hackman, Candice Bergen, Richard Widmark, Mickey Rooney, Edward Albert, Eli Wallach; ***D:*** Stanley Kramer; ***C:*** Fred W. Koenekamp; ***M:*** Billy Goldenberg.

Don Daredevil Rides Again **1951** A greedy political boss tries to take over homesteaders' claims for their mineral rights. One settler adopts the identity of an ancestor (Don Daredevil), and a black mask, and becomes a frontier avenger. A 12-episode serial. **180m/B VHS.** Ken Curtis, Aline Towne, Roy Barcroft; ***D:*** Fred Brannon.

The Don Is Dead 1/2 *Beautiful But Deadly* **1973 (R)** A violent Mafia saga wherein a love triangle interferes with Family business, resulting in gang wars. **96m/C VHS, DVD.** Anthony Quinn, Frederic Forrest, Robert Forster, Al Lettieri, Ina Balin, Angel Tompkins, Charles Cioffi; ***D:*** Richard Fleischer; ***W:*** Michael Butler; ***M:*** Jerry Goldsmith.

Don Juan 1/2 **1926** Barrymore stars as the swashbuckling Italian duke with Spanish blood who seduces a castleful of women in the 1500s before falling in love with innocent Astor. Many exciting action sequences, including classic sword fights in which Barrymore eschewed a stunt double. Great attention is also paid to the detail of the costumes and settings of the Spanish-Moor period. Noted for employing fledgling movie sound effects and as the first film with a synchronized musical score from the Vitaphone Company, which, ironically, were responsible for eclipsing the movie's reputation. Watch for Loy as an Asian vamp and Oland as a pre-Charlie Chan Cesare Borgia. **90m/B VHS.** John Barrymore, Mary Astor, Willard Louis, Estelle Taylor, Helene Costello, Myrna Loy, June Marlowe, Warner Oland, Montagu Love, Hedda Hopper, Gustav von Seyffertitz; ***D:*** Alan Crosland; ***W:*** Bess Meredyth; ***C:*** Byron Haskin; ***M:*** William Axt.

Don Juan DeMarco 1/2 **1994 (PG-13)** Burned-out clinical psychiatrist Dr. Jack Meckler (Brando) is romantically inspired by a cape-wearing, suicidal man-child from Queens (Depp), who thinks he's legendary lover Don Juan. Delusional Depp recounts, in a convincing Castilian accent, thousands of conquests as the sympathetic shrink decides it's time to bring some spice to his own ho-hum life and marriage (to Dunaway). Depp turns in a sincere, engaging performance that avoids the huge potential for melodrama and compensates for inconsistent pacing. Brando and Dunaway make a charmingly quirky couple. Watch for slain Tejano queen Selena in a musical interlude. **92m/C VHS, DVD.** Marlon Brando, Johnny Depp, Faye Dunaway, Geraldine Pailhas, Rachel Ticotin, Bob (Robert) Dishy, Talisa Soto; ***D:*** Jeremy Leven; ***W:*** Jeremy Leven; ***C:*** Ralf Bode; ***M:*** Michael Kamen.

Don Juan, My Love *Don Juan, Mi Querido Fantasma* **1990** Sexy comedy finds the ghost of Don Juan given a chance, after 450 years in Purgatory, to perform a good deed and free his soul. In Spanish with English subtitles. **96m/C VHS.** *SP* Juan Luis Galiardo, Rossy de Palma, Maria Barranco, Loles Leon; ***D:*** Antonio Mercero; ***M:*** Bernardo Bonezzi.

Don Juan (Or If Don Juan Were a Woman) *Don Juan 73; Ms. Don Juan; Si Don Juan Etait une Femme* **1973** Offers unintentional amusement with Bardot in the title role. Jeanne specializes in humiliation and seduction of, among others, her cousin the priest, a poltician, and a businessman. French with subtitles. **94m/C VHS, DVD.** *FR* Brigitte Bardot, Jane Birkin, Matthieu Carriere, Robert Hossein, Maurice Ronet, Michele Sand; ***D:*** Roger Vadim; ***W:*** Jean Cau; ***C:*** Henri Decae.

Don King: Only in America 1/2 **1997 (R)** Rhames reigns in this bio of flamboyant, notorious boxing promoter Don King. King starts off as a Cleveland numbers runner at ease with violence, which eventually sends him to a four-year prison term for manslaughter. Released in 1971, King uses his friendship with R&B singer Lloyd Price (Curtis-Hall) to meet Muhammed Ali (McCrary), leading to his set-up of the 1974 Ali-Foreman fight in Zaire. From there it's just more self-promotion. **112m/C VHS, DVD.** Gabriel Casseus, Ving Rhames, Vondie Curtis-Hall, Jeremy Piven, Darius McCrary, Keith David, Bernie Mac, Loretta Devine, Lou Rawls, Ron Leibman; ***D:*** John Herzfeld; ***W:*** Kario Salem; ***C:*** Bill Butler; ***M:*** Anthony Marinelli. **CABLE**

Don Q., Son of Zorro **1925** Zorro's son takes up his father's fight against evil and injustice. Silent sequel to the 1920 classic. **111m/B VHS, DVD.** Douglas Fairbanks Sr., Mary Astor, Donald Crisp; ***D:*** Donald Crisp; ***W:*** Jack Cunningham; ***C:*** Henry Sharp.

Don Quixote *Chaliapin: Adventures of Don Quixote* **1935** Miguel de Cervantes' tale of the romantic who would rather be a knight in shining armor than shining armor at night. Chaliapin stars as the knight-errant on his nightly errands, tilting at windmills and charging flocks of sheep. Certain scenes were adapted to fit the pre-WWII atmosphere, as it was filmed during the same time that the Nazis were burning books. **73m/B VHS, DVD.** Feodor Chaliapin Sr., George Robey, Sidney (Sydney) Fox, Miles Mander, Oscar Asche, Emily Fitzroy, Wally Patch; ***D:*** G.W. Pabst; ***W:*** Paul Morand, Alexandre Arnoux; ***M:*** Jacques Ibert.

Don Quixote 1/2 *Don Kikhot* **1957** The lauded, visually ravishing adaptation of the Cervantes classic, with a formal integrity inherited from Eisenstein and Dovshenko. In Russian with English subtitles. **110m/B VHS.** *SP RU* Nikolai Cherkassov, Yuri Tolubeyev; ***D:*** Grigori Kozintsev; ***W:*** Yevgeni Schwarz; ***C:*** Appolinari Dudko, Andrei Moskvin; ***M:*** Kara Karayev.

Don Quixote 1/2 *Orson Welles' Don Quixote* **1992** Welles started filming in 1955 but eventually abandoned the project; it was finished seven years after his death by one-time assistant Jess Franco. A patchwork mess of drawings and stills are used to fill-in the gaps of the Miguel de Cervantes novel with Quixote and his servant Sancho Panza setting off across a modern-day Spain. A rather useless addition to the Welles oeuvre; dubbed. **115m/B DVD.** *SP* Akim Tamiroff, Orson Welles, Francisco Reiguera; ***D:*** Orson Welles; ***W:*** Orson Welles; ***M:*** Daniel White.

Don Quixote **2000** Spanish nobleman Alonso Quijano of La Mancha (Lithgow) decides to dedicate himself to chivalry. With his sanity in question, he dubs himself a knight errant—becoming Don Quixote—picks up sidekick Sancho Panza (Hoskins), and finds his lady fair—washerwoman Dulcinea (Williams). Episodic retelling has a number of familiar touches (including windmill-tilting) but doesn't add up to much, although the Spanish scenery is a plus. Based on Miguel de Cervantes' 1605 novel. **150m/C VHS.** John Lithgow, Bob Hoskins, Vanessa L(ynne) Williams, Isabella Rossellini, James Purefoy, Lambert Wilson, Tony Haygarth, Peter Eyre; ***D:*** Peter Yates; ***W:*** John Mortimer; ***C:*** David Connell; ***M:*** Richard Hartley. **CABLE**

Don Segundo Sombra 1/2 **1969** An interesting film seen through the eyes of an old gaucho, who is the mentor of a young boy growing to manhood. Based on the novel by Ricardo Guiraldes. In Spanish with English subtitles. **110m/C VHS.** *SP* Juan Carballido, Juan Carlos Gene, Soledad Silveyra, Alejandra Boero; ***D:*** Manuel Antin.

Don Winslow of the Coast Guard **1943** Serial in 13 episodes features comic-strip character Winslow as he strives to keep the waters of America safe for democracy. **234m/B VHS.** Don Terry, Elyse Knox; ***D:*** Ford Beebe, Ray Taylor.

Don Winslow of the Navy **1943** Thirteen episodes centered around the evil Scorpion, who plots to attack the Pacific Coast, but is thwarted by comic-strip hero Winslow. **234m/B VHS, DVD.** Don Terry, Walter Sande, Anne Nagel; ***D:*** Ford Beebe, Ray Taylor.

Dona Flor and Her Two Husbands *Dona Flor e Seus Dois Maridos* **1978** Dona Flor (Braga) is widowed when her philandering husband Vadhino (Wilker) finally expires from drink, gambling, and ladies. She remarries, but her new husband Teodoro (Mendonca) is so boring and proper that she begins fantasizing spouse number one's return. But is he only in her imagination? Based on the novel by Jorge Amado. Portuguese with subtitles. Remade as "Kiss Me Goodbye." **106m/C VHS.** *BR* Sonia Braga, Jose Wilker, Mauro Mendonca; ***D:*** Bruno Barreto; ***W:*** Bruno Barreto; ***C:*** Maurilo Salles; ***M:*** Chico Buarque.

Dona Herlinda & Her Son *Dona Herlinda y Su Hijo* **1986** A Mexican sex comedy about a mother who manipulates her bisexual son's two lovers (one male, one female), until all four fit together into a seamless unit. In Spanish with English subtitles. Slow, but amusing. **90m/C VHS, DVD.** *MX* Guadalupe Del Toro, Arturo Meza, Marco Antonio Trevino, Leticia Lupersio; ***D:*** Jaime Humberto Hermosillo; ***W:*** Jaime Humberto Hermosillo; ***C:*** Miguel Ehrenberg.

Dondi **1961** American GIs are celebrating Christmas in WWII Italy when very young orphan Dondi (Kory) attaches himself to reluctant Dealey (Janssen). He then stows away on their troopship but gets lost in New York and has various adventures in Macy's department store. But Dondi wants to reunite with Dealey, longing for a real home and family. Ham-fisted direction by Zugsmith adds to the unbelievable treacle although the film is often fondly remembered by those who saw it as kids upon its release. Based on the Gus Edson and Irwin Hasen comic strip. **100m/B DVD.** David Janssen, Patti Page, Arnold Stang, Robert Strauss, Gale Gordon, Mickey Shaughnessy, Walter Winchell, David Kory; ***D:*** Albert Zugsmith; ***W:*** Albert Zugsmith, Gus Edson; ***C:*** Carl Guthrie; ***M:*** Tommy Morgan.

Donkey Punch **2008 (R)** Three English chicks on vacation in Spain allow themselves to be picked up by a quartet of Brit boys who are crewing on a yacht. During drug-fueled, videotaped sexcapades, one of the girls is accidentally killed by the title deviant act and the guys, fearing police involvement, decide to dump the body overboard. This leads to more violence and gore. **89m/C DVD.** *GB* Tom Burke, Julian Morris, Robert Boulter, Sian Brecklin, Nichola Burley, Jay Taylor, Jaime Winstone; ***D:*** Olly Blackburn; ***W:*** David Bloom, Olly Blackburn; ***C:*** Nanu Segal; ***M:*** Francoise-Eudes Chanfrault.

Donkey Skin *Peau d'Ane* **1970** A charming, all-star version of the medieval French fairy tale about a king searching for a suitable wife in a magical realm after his queen dies. In his quest for the most beautiful spouse, he learns that his daughter is that woman. She prefers Prince Charming, however. In French with English subtitles. **89m/C VHS, DVD.** *FR* Catherine Deneuve, Jean Marais, Delphine Seyrig, Jacques Perrin; ***D:*** Jacques Demy; ***C:*** Ghislan Cloquet; ***M:*** Michel Legrand.

Donner Pass: The Road to Survival **1984** Tame retelling of the western wagon-train pioneers who were forced to resort to cannibalism during a brutal snowstorm in the Rockies. The tragedy is lightly implied, keeping the film suitable for family viewing. **98m/C VHS.** Robert Fuller, Diane McBain, Andrew Prine, John Anderson, Michael Callan; ***D:*** James L. Conway.

Donnie Brasco **1996 (R)** Excellent look at the unglamourous working end of the mob and an undercover operation. In the late '70s, FBI agent Joe Pistone (Depp) infiltrates the New York Bonanno crime family, under the alias of Donnie Brasco, where he's mentored by aging low-level hood Lefty (Pacino). As Joe/Donnie gets deeper into the wiseguy life, Lefty takes a fatherly pride in his protege and the agent also becomes ensnared by his new identity—to the possible detriment of both feds and family. Terrific lead performances. Based on a true story and adapted from the book by Pistone and Richard Woodley. **126m/C VHS, DVD, Blu-ray Disc.** Johnny Depp, Al Pacino, Anne Heche, Michael Madsen, Bruno Kirby, James Russo, Zeljko Ivanek, Gerry Becker, Zach Grenier, Robert Miano; ***D:*** Mike Newell; ***W:*** Paul Attanasio; ***C:*** Peter Sova; ***M:*** Patrick Doyle. Natl. Bd. of Review '97: Support. Actress (Heche).

Donnie Darko **2001 (R)** Stylish, exciting debut by writer/director Kelly that, like "Mulholland Drive," leaves much unexplained as dark doings occur in an idyllic suburb, circa 1988. Aptly named Darko family is full of complex characters, including the gifted but schizophrenic Donnie, a teenager able to see the future with the aid of a life-size, doomsday-spewing rabbit named Frank. Donnie's psychiatrist (Ross) discovers he's sleepwalking on Frank's orders, which actually saves his life when a jet engine falls from a plane, landing squarely in the teen's bedroom. Even more mysteriously, no plane has reported a missing engine, which turns out to be just one of the many eerie events that may be real or imagined. McDonnell and Osborne are both fine as Donnie's upper-middle class Republican parents. Like "Harvey" on anti-psychotic meds, this challenging and complex film is worth the effort. **113m/C VHS, DVD, Blu-ray Disc, UMD.** *US* Jake Gyllenhaal, Jena Malone, Drew Barrymore, Mary McDonnell, James Duval, Maggie Gyllenhaal, Holmes Osborne, Katharine Ross, Patrick Swayze, Noah Wyle, Arthur Taxier, Stuart Stone; ***D:*** Richard Kelly; ***W:*** Richard Kelly; ***C:*** Steven Poster; ***M:*** Michael Andrews.

The Donor 1/2 **1994 (R)** Cartel stalks victims and kills them for a human organ black market. **94m/C VHS.** Jeff Wincott, Michelle Johnson, Gordon Thomson; ***D:*** Damian Lee; ***W:*** Neal Dobrofsky, Tippi Dobrofsky.

Donor Unknown **1995 (R)** Driven businessman Nicholas Stillman (Onorati) has always put work before his family—and both wife Alice (Krige) and teenaged daughter Danielle (Herbst) have suffered from his attitude. When Nick is hit by a massive heart attack and gets a transplant, he insists on knowing everything about the donor. What he uncovers is a black market in organ procurement and Nash Creed (Brown), who'll do anything to stop Nick from exposing his lucrative business. Based on the novel "Corazon" by William H. Mooney. **93m/C VHS.** Peter Onorati, Alice Krige, Clancy Brown, Becky Herbst, Sam Robards, Richard Portnow, T.J. Castranovo, Leo Garcia, John Dorman; ***D:*** John Harrison; ***W:*** John Harrison; ***C:*** Zoltan David; ***M:*** David Bergeaud.

Donovan's Brain **1953** Dedicated scientist Dr. Cory (Ayres) has succeeded in keeping a dismembered monkey's brain alive and gets his chance to experiment on a human when the victim of a plane crash is brought to his lab. Over the objections of his wife Janice (Davis) and assistant Frank (Evans), Cory keeps the brain alive in a tank. Too bad for him, since the organ belongs to a ruthless, vicious businessman (the titular Donovan) who begins to influence Cory in horrible ways. Based on the novel by Curt Siodmak, and also filmed as "The Lady and the Monster" (1944), "Vengeance" (1963), and "The Brain" (1965). **85m/B VHS, DVD.** Lew Ayres, Gene Evans, Nancy Davis, Steve Brodie; ***D:*** Felix Feist; ***W:*** Felix Feist, Hugh Brooke; ***C:*** Joseph Biroc; ***M:*** Eddie Dunstedter.

Donovan's Reef **1963** Two WWII buddies meet every year on a Pacific atoll to engage in a perpetual bar-brawl, until a stuck-up Bostonian maiden appears to find her dad, a man who has fathered a brood of lovable half-casts. A rollicking, good-natured film from Ford. **109m/C VHS, DVD.** John Wayne, Lee Marvin, Jack Warden, Elizabeth Allen, Dorothy Lamour, Mike Mazurki, Cesar Romero; ***D:*** John Ford; ***W:*** James Edward Grant, Frank Nugent; ***C:*** William Clothier; ***M:*** Cyril Mockridge.

Don's Party **1976** A rather dark comedy focusing on Australian Yuppie-types who decide to watch the election results on TV as a group. A lot more goes on at this party, however, than talk of the returns. Sexual themes surface. Cast members turn fine performances, aided by top-notch script and direction. **90m/C VHS, DVD.** *AU* Pat Bishop, Graham Kennedy, Candy (Candida) Raymond, Veronica Lang, John Hargreaves, Ray Barrett, Claire Binney, Graeme Blundell, Jeanie Drynan; ***D:*** Bruce Beresford; ***W:*** David Williamson; ***C:*** Donald McAlpine; ***M:*** Leos Janacek. Australian Film Inst. '77: Actress (Bishop).

Don't Answer the Phone *The Hollywood Strangler* **1980 (R)** Deeply troubled photographer stalks and attacks the patients of a beautiful psychologist talk-show hostess. **94m/C VHS, DVD.** James Westmoreland, Flo Gerrish, Ben Frank; ***D:*** Robert Hammer; ***W:*** Robert Hammer, Michael Castle; ***C:*** James L. Carter; ***M:*** Byron Allred.

Don't Be a Menace to South Central While Drinking Your Juice in the Hood **1995 (R)** Parody of "life in the hood" movies pokes fun at the attitudes and characters that are quickly becoming cliches in the genre. Shawn Wayans plays G-next-door Ashtray, sent by his mother to discover "what it is to be a man" from his father in South Central L.A. He hooks up with his homey Loc Dog (Marlon Wayans), a gun-crazed beer-swilling gangsta who packs a nuclear warhead. As the title implies, almost every major black film in recent memory is given the Wayans' drive-by treatment, with a majority of the plot lifted from "Boyz N the Hood." Fans of the TV series "In Living Color" will love this twisted look at ghetto life, but others may be offended. **88m/C VHS, DVD.** Shawn Wayans, Marlon Wayans, Tracey Cherelle Jones, Chris Spencer, Suli McCullough, Darrell Heath, Helen Martin, Isaiah Barnes, Lahmard Tate; ***Cameos:*** Keenen Ivory Wayans; ***D:*** Paris Barclay; ***W:*** Shawn Wayans, Marlon Wayans, Phil Beauman; ***C:*** Russ Brandt; ***M:*** John Barnes.

Don't Be Afraid of the Dark 1/2 **1973** A young couple move into their dream house only to find that demonic little critters are residing in their basement and they want more than shelter. Made for TV with creepy scenes and eerie makeup for the monsters. **74m/C VHS.** Kim Darby, Jim Hutton, Barbara Anderson, William Demarest, Pedro Armendariz Jr., Felix Silla, Patty Maloney, Tamara DeTreaux; ***D:*** John Newland; ***W:*** Giovanni Bergamini; ***C:*** Andrew Jackson; ***M:*** Billy Goldenberg. **TV**

Don't Bother to Knock 1/2 **1952** As a mentally unstable hotel babysitter, Monroe meets a pilot (Widmark) and has a brief rendezvous with him. When the little girl she is babysitting interrupts, Monroe is furious, and later tries to murder the girl. This is one of Monroe's best dramatic roles. Bancroft's film debut as the Widmark's girlfriend. **76m/B VHS, DVD.** Richard Widmark, Marilyn Monroe, Anne Bancroft, Elisha Cook Jr., Jim Backus, Lurene Tuttle, Jeanne Cagney, Donna Corcoran; ***D:*** Roy Ward Baker; ***W:*** Daniel Taradash; ***C:*** Lucien Ballard; ***M:*** Lionel Newman.

Don't Change My World 1/2 **1983 (G)** To preserve the natural beauty of the north woods, a wildlife photographer must fight a villainous land developer and a reckless poacher. Eco-correct. **89m/C VHS.** Roy Tatum, Ben Jones, Edie Kramer, George Macrenais, Paul Newmark, David Eidson; ***D:*** Robert Rector.

Don't Come Knocking **2005 (R)** Aging movie star Howard Spence (Shepard) is better known for his life of drugs, booze, and babes. Fed-up with his latest cowboy flick, he literally rides off the set, leaving chaos behind him. Spence heads to Nevada to visit his mother (Saint), whom he hasn't seen in 30 years. She blithely informs him that an ex-flame of his had once come calling with the news of her pregnancy, and Spence tracks down barkeep Doreen (Lange) and their bitter son, Earl (Mann). Seems Spence was more fertile than he knew when he's later accosted by Sky (Polley), who claims to be his daughter. Spence wants another chance but he's pretty much a jerk so it's hard to take any interest. The desert vistas (Utah, Montana) are beautiful, though. **110m/C DVD.** *US* Sam Shepard, Jessica Lange, Sarah Polley, Gabriel Mann, Tim Roth, Fairuza Balk, Eva Marie Saint, James Gammon, George Kennedy, Marley Shelton, Rodney A. Grant, Tim Matheson, Julia Sweeney, Kurt Fuller,

James Roday; *D:* Wim Wenders; *W:* Sam Shepard, Wim Wenders; *C:* Franz Lustig; *M:* T-Bone Burnett.

Don't Cry, It's Only Thunder 1/2 **1982 (PG)** A young army medic who works in a mortuary in Saigon becomes involved with a group of Vietnamese orphans and a dedicated army doctor. Based on a true story. **108m/C VHS.** Dennis Christopher, Susan St. James, Roger Aaron Brown, Li Lu, Thu Thuy, James Whitmore; *D:* Peter Werner; *M:* Maurice Jarre.

Don't Do It 1/2 **1994 (PG-13)** Three 20-something couples, attempting to find love, all wind up in the same cafe and try to tell the truth about how they feel and whom they desire. **90m/C VHS, DVD.** James Marshall, James LeGros, Sheryl Lee, Esai Morales, Alexis Arquette, Balthazar Getty, Sarah Trigger, Heather Graham; *D:* Eugene Hess; *W:* Eugene Hess; *C:* Ian Fox.

Don't Drink the Water 1/2 **1969 (G)** Based on Woody Allen's hit play, this film places an average Newark, New Jersey, family behind the Iron Curtain, where their vacation photo-taking gets them accused of spying. **100m/C VHS.** Jackie Gleason, Estelle Parsons, Joan Delaney, Ted Bessell, Michael Constantine; *D:* Howard Morris.

Don't Fence Me In **1945** Evans is a magazine photographer who heads west to do a story on a legendary character named Wildcat Kelly, who's supposedly dead. She meets rancher Rogers and sidekick Hayes and, of course, discovers that Rogers is the man she's looking for. **71m/B VHS.** Roy Rogers, Dale Evans, George "Gabby" Hayes, Robert "Bob" Livingston; *D:* John English; *W:* Dorrell McGowan, Stuart E. McGowan; *C:* William Bradford.

Don't Go in the House **1980 (R)** Long-dormant psychosis is brought to life by the death of a young man's mother. **90m/C VHS, DVD.** Dan Grimaldi, Robert Osth, Ruth Dardick; *D:* Joseph Ellison; *W:* Joseph Ellison, Ellen Hammill; *C:* Oliver Wood; *M:* Richard Einhorn.

Don't Go in the Woods WOOF! **1981 (R)** Routine exercise in "don't do that" terror genre (includes warnings about going into houses, answering phones, looking into basements, opening windows, etc.). This time, four young campers are stalked by a crazed killer armed with prerequisite ax. **88m/C VHS, DVD.** Angie Brown, James Hayden, Mary Gail Artz, Jack McClelland; *D:* James Bryan.

Don't Go Near the Water **1957** Somewhat amusing comedy about the happenings at a Naval installation on a South Pacific tropical paradise. Clark outshines the others in his role as a frustrated officer. Based on the novel by William Brinkley. **107m/C VHS.** Glenn Ford, Gia Scala, Earl Holliman, Anne Francis, Keenan Wynn, Fred Clark, Eva Gabor, Russ Tamblyn; *D:* Charles Walters; *W:* Dorothy Kingsley, George Wells.

Don't Go to Sleep **1982** After a fatal car crash, a young girl misses mom and dad so much she returns from the grave to take them where they can be one big happy family again. Better than most made-for-TV junk-food fright-fests, written by Keenan Wynn's son, Ned. **93m/C VHS.** Dennis Weaver, Valerie Harper, Robin Ignico, Kristin Cummings, Ruth Gordon, Robert Webber, Claudette Nevins; *D:* Richard Lang; *W:* Ned Wynn. **TV**

Don't Hang Up 1/2 *Separation* **1990** Handicapped New York actress Sarah (Arquette) wants to do a production of agoraphobic London writer Joe's (Suchet) play. So she calls him up to get his permission and the two begin a phone relationship that develops from business to romance. **84m/C VHS.** *GB* Rosanna Arquette, David Suchet; *D:* Barry Davis; *W:* Tom Kempinski. **TV**

Don't Let Me Die on a Sunday 1/2 *J'Aimerais pas Crever un Dimache* **1998** Bizarre, disturbing wallow in Parisian depravity begins in a morgue. That's where attendant Ben (Barr) meets Teresa (Bouchez). The details of that first encounter will not be recounted, but the two begin a downward spiral into joyless sex, angst, alienation, and despair. Not for the fainthearted. French with subtitles. **86m/C VHS, DVD.** *FR* Elodie Bouchez, Jean-Marc Barr, Martin Petitguyot, Patrick Catalifo, Gerard Loussine, Jeanne Casilas, Florence Darel; *D:* Didier Le Pecheur; *W:* Didier Le Pecheur; *C:* Denis Rouden; *M:* Philippe Cohen-Solal.

Don't Let Your Meat Loaf 1/2 **1995** Three struggling comedians take their act on the road, including subway stations and street corners, in order to get the money to open their own comedy club. **82m/C VHS.** Leander Sales, Dana S. Hubbard, Brad Albright; *D:* Leander Sales.

Don't Look Back **1996 (R)** Musician and heroin addict Jesse Parish (Stoltz) stumbles across a suitcase full of cash after witnessing a drug deal gone bad. He heads back to family and friends in Texas so he can kick his habit, but is marked for death by the dealers who want their money back. Strong script and performances. **91m/C VHS, DVD.** Eric Stoltz, John Corbett, Josh Hamilton, Annabeth Gish, Dwight Yoakam, Amanda Plummer; *D:* Geoff Murphy; *W:* Billy Bob Thornton, Tom Epperson. **CABLE**

Don't Look Back: The Story of Leroy "Satchel" Paige 1/2 **1981** Drama of the legendary baseball pitcher who helped break down racial barriers, based on his autobiography. Made-for-TV fare. Gossett hits a home run in the lead, but the overall effort is a ground-rule double. **98m/C VHS.** Louis Gossett Jr., Beverly Todd, Cleavon Little, Clifton Davis, John Beradino, Jim Davis, Ossie Davis, Hal Williams; *D:* George C. Scott, Richard A. Colla.

Don't Look Down 1/2 *Wes Craven Presents: Don't Look Down* **1998** TV reporte Carla (Ward) begins suffering from acrophobia after the falling death of her sister. She joins and extreme therapy group run by radical shrink Dr. Sadowski (Kinney) to overcome her fears. But it doesn't help when her fellow therapy mates beginning dying in fatal falls. **90m/C VHS, DVD.** Megan Ward, Billy Burke, Terry Kinney, Angela Moore, William McDonald, Kate Robbins, Tara Spencer-Nairn; *D:* Larry Shaw; *W:* Gregory Goodell; *C:* David Geddes; *M:* J. Peter Robinson. **TV**

Don't Look in the Attic WOOF! **1981** A couple finds a haunted house with cows in the attic. **90m/C VHS.** Beba Loncar, Jean-Pierre Aumont; *D:* Carl Ausino.

Don't Look in the Basement 1/2 **1973 (R)** Things get out of hand at an isolated asylum and a pretty young nurse is caught in the middle. Straight-jacketed by a low budget. **95m/C VHS, DVD.** Rosie Holotik, Anne MacAdams, William (Bill) McGhee, Rhea MacAdams, Gene Ross, Betty Chandler, Camilla Carr, Robert Dracup, Jessie Kirby, Hugh Feagin, Harryete Warren, Jessie Lee Fulton, Michael Harvey; *D:* S.F. Brownrigg; *W:* Tim Pope, Tom Pope; *M:* Robert Farrar.

Don't Look Now **1973 (R)** A psychological creepfest with a chilling climax, based on the novel by Daphne Du Maurier. John (Sutherland) and Laura (Christie) Baxter travel to a dank, off-season Venice in an attempt to put the drowning death of their young daughter behind them. But while working on a church restoration, John begins to have psychic visions which are encouraged by a pair of strange sisters (Matania, Mason). There's a steamy love scene between Sutherland and Christie that became the object of much gossip. **110m/C VHS, DVD.** *GB IT* Donald Sutherland, Julie Christie, Hilary Mason, Clelia Matania, Massimo Serato, Leopoldo Trieste, Adelina Porrio; *D:* Nicolas Roeg; *W:* Chris Bryant, Allan Scott; *C:* Anthony B. Richmond; *M:* Pino Donaggio.

Don't Lose Your Head *Carry On, Don't Lose Your Head* **1966** In the 13th series entry, two English fops, Sir Rodney Ffing (James) and Lord Darcy Pue (Dale), are horrified to hear about the French Revolution and decide to come to the rescue of their fellow aristocrats. So Sir Rodney disguises himself (badly) as the adventurous Black Fingernail (think a low-rent Scarlet Pimpernel) to tweak those Citizen Frenchies. **90m/C DVD.** *GB* Sidney James, Jim Dale, Kenneth Williams, Charles Hawtrey, Peter Butterworth, Dany Robin, Peter Gilmore, Joan Sims; *D:* Gerald Thomas; *W:* Talbot Rothwell; *C:* Alan Hume; *M:* Eric Rogers.

Don't Mess with My Sister! 1/2 **1985** A married, New York junkyard worker falls in love with a belly dancer he meets at a party. The affair leads to murder and subsequently, revenge. An interesting, offbeat film from the director of "I Spit on Your Grave." **90m/C VHS, DVD.** Joe Perce, Jeannine Lemay, Jack Gurci, Peter Sapienza, Laura Lanfranchi; *D:* Mier Zarchi.

Don't Open the Door! WOOF! **1974 (PG)** A young woman is terrorized by a killer located inside her house. **90m/C VHS, DVD.** Susan Bracken, Gene Ross, Jim Harrell; *D:* S.F. Brownrigg.

Don't Open Till Christmas WOOF! **1984** A weirdo murders various Santa Clauses in assorted gory ways. Best to take this one back to the department store. **86m/C VHS.** *GB* Edmund Purdom, Caroline Munro, Alan Lake, Belinda Mayne, Gerry Sundquist, Mark Jones; *D:* Edmund Purdom.

Don't Raise the Bridge, Lower the River **1968 (G)** After his wife leaves him, an American with crazy, get-rich-quick schemes turns his wife's ancestral English home into a Chinese discotheque. Domestic farce that comes and goes; if mad for Lewis, rent "The Nutty Professor." **99m/C VHS, DVD.** Jerry Lewis, Terry-Thomas, Jacqueline Pearce; *D:* Jerry Paris.

Don't Say a Word 1/2 **2001 (R)** Douglas plays the stable family man pushed to the brink once again in this chilly kidnaping thriller. Dr. Nathan Conrad (Douglas) is a psychiatrist whose idyllic life is shattered when his eight-year-old daughter Jessie (Bartusiak) is kidnaped by a gang of thieves. They threaten to kill his little girl unless he can retrieve a six-digit number locked in the brain of Nathan's new patient Elisabeth (Murphy), a raving lunatic who slashed an orderly to death. Meanwhile, the bad guys have rigged surveillance equipment in his apartment and are menacing his wife Aggie (Janssen), as cop Esposito stumbles across the plot, inadvertently threatening Nathan's efforts. All the plot threads are conveniently tied up in a standard final showdown scene. **112m/C VHS, DVD.** *US* Michael Douglas, Sean Bean, Brittany Murphy, Skye McCole Bartusiak, Famke Janssen, Guy Torry, Jennifer Esposito, Shawn Doyle, Victor Argo, Oliver Platt, Conrad Goode, Paul Schulze, Lance Reddick; *D:* Gary Fleder; *W:* Patrick Smith Kelly, Anthony Peckham; *C:* Amir M. Mokri; *M:* Mark Isham.

Don't Talk to Strangers 1/2 **1994 (R)** Formula thriller has Brosnan marrying divorcee Reed and becoming instant father to her nine-year-old son. But someone appears to be a whacko—is it the kid's real dad (Quinn) or is Brosnan just too good to be true? **94m/C VHS.** Pierce Brosnan, Shanna Reed, Terry O'Quinn; *D:* Robert Lewis; *W:* Neill D. Hicks, Jon George, Nevin Schreiner.

Don't Tell *La Bestia nel Cuore; The Beast in the Heart* **2005** An inexplicable Oscar nominee, this confusing melodrama concerns a brother and sister and family secrets coming to light. Voiceover actress Sabina (Mezzogiorno) lives in Rome with her actor boyfriend, Franco (Boni). After dubbing a rape scene, Sabina begins having nightmares about a scared child and decides to visit her brother, Daniele (Lo Cascio), who lives in Virginia. She pressures him to tell what he knows. Side stories involving Franco's work on a soap opera and a couple of Sabrina's friends finding (and losing) romance dissipate the tension. Attractive cast. Italian with subtitles. **120m/C DVD.** *IT* Giovanna Mezzogiorno, Stefania Rocca, Angela Finocchiaro, Alessio Boni, Luigi Lo Cascio, Valerio Binasco, Lewis Lemperuer Palmer, Jeke-Omer Boyayanlar, Lucy Akhurst, Guiseppe Battiston, Francesca Inaudi; *D:* Cristina Comencini; *W:* Francesca Marciano, Cristina Comencini, Giulia Calenda; *C:* Fabio Cianchetti; *M:* Franco Piersanti.

Don't Tell **2005** Lame family drama has three siblings (Eastwood, Root, Wlcek) reuniting in their dreary, small hometown after their hard-drinking farmer dad dies. This is a dysfunctional bunch with family secrets that don't inspire sympathy or involvement. **88m/C DVD.** *US* Alison Eastwood, Bonnie Root, James Wlcek; *D:* Isaac H. Eaton; *W:* Julie Anne Koehnen; *C:* Mike King; *M:* Larry Brown.

Don't Tell Her It's Me *The Boyfriend School* **1990 (PG-13)** Guttenberg is determined to win the heart of an attractive writer. With the assistance of his sister, he works to become a dream man. Clever premise, promising cast, lame comedy. From the novel by Sarah Bird. **101m/C VHS, DVD.** Steve Guttenberg, Jami Gertz, Shelley Long, Kyle MacLachlan, Madchen Amick; *D:* Malcolm Mowbray; *W:* Sarah Bird; *M:* Michael Gore.

Don't Tell Mom the Babysitter's Dead 1/2 **1991 (PG-13)** Their mother traveling abroad, the title situation leaves a houseful of teenagers with the whole summer to themselves. Eldest daughter Applegate cons her way into the high-powered business world while the metalhead son parties hardy. Many tepid comic situations, not adding up to very much. **105m/C VHS, DVD.** Christina Applegate, Keith Coogan, Joanna Cassidy, John Getz, Josh Charles, Concetta Tomei, Eda Reiss Merin; *D:* Stephen Herek; *W:* Neil Landau, Tara Ison; *C:* Tim Suhrstedt; *M:* David Newman.

Don't Torture a Duckling *Non Si Sevizia un Paperino* **1972** Newspaperman Andrea Martelli (Milian) investigates the deaths of several young boys in the Sicily village where his father was born. The suspicious villagers take their revenge on a couple of outcast locals but Martelli teams up with seductive Patrizia (Bouchet) to uncover the real killer. Creepy rather a gorefest, although Fulci recycled one of the more violent scenes for his later film, "The Psychic." **102m/C VHS, DVD.** *IT* Tomas Milian, Barbara Bouchet, Irene Papas, Florinda Bolkan, Marc Porel; *D:* Lucio Fulci; *W:* Lucio Fulci, Robert Gianviti; *C:* Sergio d'Offizi; *M:* Riz Ortolani.

Doogal *The Magic Roundabout* **2005 (G)** Animated kiddie adventure. Doogal the dog frees evil sorcerer Zeebad (Stewart) by mistake, and now the canine and his gang—a sassy cow (Goldberg), geeky snail (Macy), hippy bunny (Fallon), kind-hearted magician (McKellen), and a little girl (Minogue)—must keep the imp from making the world a big ball of ice. Compared with the inventive and beloved British TV show from the 1960s, the disappointment of this outing overpowers all the big-name celebrity voices involved. **80m/C DVD.** *D:* Frank Passingham, Dave Borthwick, Jean Duval; *W:* Paul Bassett Davies, Stephane Sanoussi, Raoff Sanoussi; *C:* Tad Safran; *M:* Mark Thomas; *V:* Tom Baker, Jim Broadbent, Joanna Lumley, Ian McKellen, Kylie Minogue, Bill Nighy, Ray Winstone, Lee Evans, Robbie Williams.

The Doolins of Oklahoma 1/2 *The Great Manhunt* **1949** Scott is the leader of the last of the southwestern outlaw gangs, pursued by lawmen and changing times with the onset of the modern age. Fast-paced and intelligent. **90m/B VHS.** Randolph Scott, George Macready, Louise Allbritton, John Ireland, Virginia Huston, Charles Kemper, Noah Beery Jr.; *D:* Gordon Douglas; *M:* George Duning.

Doom **2005 (R)** It's the live-action version of the videogame. If that's your thing, you'll enjoy the flick because everyone involved knows it's a game and they get to play Space Marines (led by the Rock and Urban) and use big guns to blow away flesh-eating mutants. Hey, what could be more fun? Anything else comes to mind. **104m/C DVD, Blu-ray Disc, UMD, HD DVD.** *US* Karl Urban, Rosamund Pike, DeObia Oparei, Ben Daniels, Raz Adoti, Richard Brake, Dexter Fletcher, Al Weaver, Brian Steele, Dwayne "The Rock" Johnson, Yao Chin; *D:* Andrzej Bartkowiak; *W:* David Callaham, Wesley Strick; *C:* Tony Pierce-Roberts; *M:* Clint Mansell.

Doom Asylum WOOF! **1988 (R)** Several sex kittens wander into a deserted sanatorium and meet up with the grisly beast wielding autopsy instruments. The people involved with this spoof should have been (more) committed. **77m/C VHS, DVD.** Patty Mullen, Ruth (Coreen) Collins, Kristin Davis, William Hay, Kenny L. Price, Harrison White, Dawn Alvan, Michael Rogen; *D:* Richard Friedman.

The Doom Generation **1995 (R)** Alienated trio on the road trip to hell (doubling as L.A.). Beautiful 17-year-old druggie Amy Blue (McGowan), her sweetly dim boyfriend Jordan White (Duval), and hot-tempered stud/drifter Xavier Red (Schaech) flee after Red kills a store clerk. They're basically from nowhere, going nowhere, and finding sex and (lots of gruesomely depicted) violence along the way. The subtitle, "A Heterosexual Movie by Gregg Araki," may be technically accurate but the homoerotic subtext is very clear. Terrific performances. Second film in Araki's teen trilogy, following "Totally F***ked Up," and preceding "Nowhere." An unrated version is also available. **84m/C VHS, DVD.** Parker Posey, Lauren Tewes, Christopher Knight, Margaret Cho, Skinny Puppy, Heidi Fleiss, Rose McGowan, James Duval, Johnathon Schaech; ***D:*** Gregg Araki; ***W:*** Gregg Araki; ***C:*** Jim Fealy; ***M:*** Don Gallo.

Doom Runners 🦴🦴 **1997** Ah, yes—another dark and dangerous postapocalyptic world. Evil ruler Dr. Kao (Curry) uses "mind-wiping" to erase the memories of his victims and maintains order with an army of "Doom Troopers." Teen Jada (Moreno) finds a map that will lead her to New Eden, the only free society left. And she's determined to make it, despite Kao's threats. **87m/C VHS.** Tim Curry, Lea Moreno, Bradley Michael Pierce, Nathan Jones; ***D:*** Brendan Maher; ***W:*** Barney Cohen, Ken Lipman; ***C:*** Steve Arnold; ***M:*** Braedy Neal. **CABLE**

Doomed at Sundown 🦴🦴 **1/2 1937** Decent Steele vehicle has the tough cowpoke as a sheriff's son known for playing practical jokes. When his father gets knifed, it's no laughing matter and he takes off after the killers. Based on a story by Fred Myton. **55m/B VHS, DVD.** Bob Steele, Laraine Day, Warner Richmond, Harold Daniels, David Sharpe; ***D:*** Sam Newfield; ***W:*** George Plympton.

Doomed Caravan 🦴🦴🦴 **1941** Hoppy and his pals lend a hand when some villains try to monopolize the wagon train business. Location shooting was done in the valleys of central California. **60m/B VHS, DVD.** William Boyd, Russell Hayden, Andy Clyde, Minna Gombell, Morris Ankrum, Georgia Hawkins, Trevor Bardette, Pat J. O'Brien; ***D:*** Lesley Selander.

Doomed Love 🦴🦴 **1/2 1983** Love is hell, especially when the object of your affection happens to be deceased. A professor of literature in the throes of unrequited love decides to reunite himself with his lost love. Won awards when released in Berlin. **75m/C VHS.** Allen Frame, Rosemary Moore, Jim Neu, Bill Rice; ***D:*** Andrew Horn; ***W:*** Andrew Horn; ***C:*** Carl Teitelaum; ***M:*** Evan Lurie.

Doomed to Die 🦴🦴 **1940** Cargo of stolen bonds leads to a tong war and the murder of a shipping millionaire. Part of Mr. Wong series. Worth a look if only for Karloff's performance. **67m/B VHS, DVD.** Boris Karloff, Marjorie Reynolds, Grant Withers; ***D:*** William Nigh.

Doomsday 🦴🦴 **1/2 1928** Vidor marries for wealth instead of love and, in classic fashion, finds that money doesn't buy happiness. **73m/B VHS.** Florence Vidor, Gary Cooper, Lawrence Grant; ***D:*** Rowland V. Lee.

Doomsday 🦴🦴 **2008 (R)** In 2035 the Reaper Virus has left Scotland a barren wasteland, quarantined from the rest of the world. But when satellite images reveal that life may still exist, a team of soldiers led by Eden Sinclair (Mitra) return in hopes of curing the survivors, instead discovering an underground civilization of psycho bikers and gutter punks. It's hard to tell if director Marshall has assembled a tribute, spoof, or rip-off of earlier doomsday flicks, because while this one doesn't make a lot of sense, it's still cheesy, over-the-top good fun. **109m/C DVD, Blu-ray Disc.** *US* Rhona Mitra, Malcolm McDowell, Bob Hoskins, Adrian Lester, Alexander Siddig, David O'Hara, MyAnna Buring, Craig Conway; ***D:*** Neil Marshall; ***W:*** Neil Marshall; ***C:*** Sam McCurdy; ***M:*** Tyler Bates.

The Doomsday Flight 🦴🦴 **1966** Uneven thriller in which O'Brien plants an altitude-triggered bomb on a jet in an effort to blackmail the airline. Search for the bomb provides some suspenseful and well-acted moments. **100m/C VHS.** Jack Lord, Edmond O'Brien, Van Johnson, John Saxon, Katherine Crawford, Michael Sarrazin, Ed Asner, Greg Morris, Richard Carlson, Don Stewart; ***D:*** William A. Graham; ***W:*** Rod Serling. **TV**

Doomsday Gun 🦴🦴 **1/2 1994** Fact-based thriller about arms manufacturer Gerald Bull (Langella), who dreams of building the world's biggest gun—a behemoth with a range of 1000 miles. Only problem is Bull's willingness to sell the weapon to the highest bidder, who happens to be Saddam Hussein. This doesn't sit well with Israeli Mossad agent Yossi (Arkin). **110m/C VHS, DVD.** Frank Langella, Alan Arkin, Kevin Spacey, Tony Goldwyn, James Fox, Michael Kitchen, Francesca Annis, Marianne (Cuau) Denicourt; ***D:*** Robert M. Young; ***W:*** Lionel Chetwynd, Walter Bernstein; ***C:*** Ian Wilson. **CABLE**

Doomsdayer 🦴 **1/2 1999 (R)** Okay, see how familiar this sounds. Jack Logan (Lara) works for a covert agency. His assignment is to prevent a new explosive from falling into terrorists' hands. This Doomsdayer device is currently held by a ruthless billionaire weapons dealer (Kier) and his equally nasty wife (Nielsen), who have their own island. Logan and his team run into trouble before they save the day. Now you won't have to actually watch the video. **93m/C VHS, DVD.** Joe Lara, Udo Kier, Brigitte Nielsen, Sandra Gomez, January Isaac, T.J. Storm, Paige Rowland, Ravil Isyanov; ***D:*** Michael J. Sarna; ***W:*** Bob Couttie; ***C:*** David Rakoczy. **VIDEO**

Doomsdayer 🦴🦴 **2001** An anti-terrorist organization is trying to track down a weapon called The Doomsdayer, capable of causing the meltdown of nuclear power plants, before it falls into the wrong hands. Mission specialist Jack Logan (Lara) finds the weapon's owner Max Gast (Kier) and discovers the device has been activated and there's seven days until mass destruction. **m/C VHS, DVD.** Joe Lara, Udo Kier, Brigitte Nielsen, January Isaac; ***D:*** Michael J. Sarna; ***W:*** Bob Couttie; ***C:*** David Rakoczy. **VIDEO**

Doomwatch 🦴🦴 **1/2 1972** A scientist discovers a chemical company is dumping poison into local waters, deforming the inhabitants of an isolated island when they eat the catch of the day. Unsurprising. **89m/C VHS, DVD.** *GB* Ian Bannen, Judy Geeson, John Paul, Simon Oates, George Sanders; ***D:*** Peter Sasdy; ***W:*** Clive Exton; ***C:*** Ken Talbot.

The Door in the Floor 🦴🦴🦴 **1/2 2004 (R)** This compelling feature gets an extra half-bone for Jeff Bridges' standout performance. He's dissolute but celebrated children's author/illustrator Ted Cole (the title refers to one of his books), who is spending the summer of 1958 in a Hamptons beach house with his inconsolable wife Marion (Basinger) and their precocious four-year-old daughter, Ruth (Fanning). Marion has not recovered from the car crash that killed the couple's two teenaged sons. Ted decides on a trial separation, which means he can continue an affair with wealthy Evelyn (Rogers), and he hires 16-year-old Eddie (Foster) to keep an eye on Marion. Eddie does more than that when he develops an obsession for the lonely woman who begins a sexual relationship with him. Adapted from the first section of John Irving's 1998 novel "A Widow of One Year." **111m/C DVD.** *US* Jeff Bridges, Kim Basinger, Jon Foster, Mimi Rogers, Elle Fanning, Bijou Philips, Louis Arcella; ***D:*** Tod Williams; ***W:*** Tod Williams; ***C:*** Terry Stacey; ***M:*** Marcelo Zarvos.

Door to Door 🦴🦴 **1984** Comedy about two door-to-door salesmen who race to stay one step ahead of the law and their own company. Fairly lightweight, but it has its moments. **93m/C VHS.** Ron Leibman, Jane Kaczmarek, Arliss Howard, Alan Austin; ***D:*** Patrick Bailey. **CABLE**

Door to Door Maniac 🦴 **1/2** ***Five Minutes to Live*** **1961** Criminals hold a bank president's wife hostage, unaware that the husband was looking to get rid of her in favor of another woman. Cash's screen debut. Aside from the strange cast ensemble, not particularly worth seeing. **80m/B VHS, DVD.** Johnny Cash, Ron Howard, Vic Tayback, Donald Woods, Cay Forrester, Pamela Mason; ***D:*** Bill Karn.

Door with the Seven Locks 🦴🦴 **1/2 1962** Bizarre Edgar Wallace story of man who leaves seven keys to a treasure vault in his will. Remake of "Chamber of Horrors." **96m/C VHS.** *GE* Eddi Arent, Heinz Drache, Klaus Kinski, Ady Berber; ***D:*** Alfred Vohrer.

The Doorbell Rang: A Nero Wolfe Mystery 🦴🦴 **1/2 2001** Detective Nero Wolfe (Chaykin) and his investigator Archie Goodwin (Hutton) get involved in the case of an eccentric woman who comes to Wolfe with a tale of FBI harassment that leads to murder. Based on the mystery by Rex Stout. **100m/C VHS, DVD.** Timothy Hutton, Maury Chaykin, Saul Rubinek, Debra Monk, Colin Fox; ***W:*** Timothy Hutton, Michael Jaffe. **CABLE**

The Doors 🦴🦴 **1/2 1991 (R)** Stone approached Jim Morrison with an early incarnation of this docudrama, but it's hard to believe even the Lizard King could play himself with any more convincing abandon than Kilmer, in a great performance. Trouble is, the story—one of drugs, abuse, and abject self-indulgence—grows tiresome, and the audience, with the exception of die-hard fans, may lose sight of any sympathy they might have had. Ryan is forgettable as Morrison's hippie-chick wife, MacLachlan sports a funny wig and dabbles on the keyboards as Ray Manszarek, and Quinlan is atypically cast as a sado-masochistic journalist paramour. Based on "Riders on the Storm" by John Densmore. **138m/C VHS, DVD, UMD.** Kelly Hu, Val Kilmer, Meg Ryan, Kevin Dillon, Kyle MacLachlan, Frank Whaley, Michael Madsen, Kathleen Quinlan, Crispin Glover, Josh Evans, John Densmore, William Jordan, Mimi Rogers, Paul Williams, Bill Graham, Billy Vera, William Kunstler, Wes Studi, Costas Mandylor, Billy Idol, Michael Wincott, Dennis Burkley; ***D:*** Oliver Stone; ***W:*** Oliver Stone, Ralph Thomas, Randy Johnson, J. Randall Johnson; ***C:*** Robert Richardson.

The Doorway 🦴 **1/2 2000 (R)** Four college students are fixing up a house that they discover is built over a doorway to hell—and they've just opened it up. So they ask the local expert on the paranormal (Scheider, whose role is very limited) for help. **91m/C VHS, DVD.** Roy Scheider, Lauren Woodland, Suzanne Bridgham, Teresa De Priest, Christian Harmony, Don Maloney; ***D:*** Michael B. Druxman; ***W:*** Michael B. Druxman; ***C:*** Yoram Astrakhan. **VIDEO**

Dopamine 🦴🦴 **1/2 2003 (R)** Rand (Livingston), a partner in a dot-com startup, develops an interactive, AI-type computer character. When they decide to test it in a classroom, Rand falls for the teacher, Sarah (Lloyd). Rand tries to sort out his feelings, and intellectual insticts, as he ponders whether love is emotional or chemical. Perhaps he's over-thinking a bit. **79m/C DVD.** *US* John Livingston, Sabrina Lloyd, Bruno Campos, Reuben Grundy, Kathleen Antonia, Nicole Wilder; ***D:*** Mark Decena; ***W:*** Mark Decena, Timothy Breitbach; ***C:*** Robert Humphreys; ***M:*** Eric Holland.

Dope Case Pending 🦴 **2000** Extremely low-budget urban action picture revolves around Devon King (Prime Time), who's got a bright future in athletics ahead of him until the cops are called to a party at his house and he's arrested for drug possession. It's a downward spiral from there on. Everything about the film is substandard. Semi-professional writing, acting, and directing. **91m/C DVD.** Prime Time, Thinline, Kid Frost, Coolio, Sean Levert, Tony Dorian; ***D:*** Patrick McKnight, Jeff Williams; ***W:*** Patrick McKnight; ***C:*** Steve Van Dyne; ***M:*** Prime Time.

Doppelganger: The Evil Within 🦴🦴 ***Doppleganger*** **1990 (R)** Holly Gooding (Barrymore) seems like such a nice girl—until the police suspect her of the brutal murder of her mother. Her new friend Patrick (Newbern) begins to see another side to the vulnerable Holly—a seductress capable of doing anything to get what she wants. **105m/C VHS, DVD.** Drew Barrymore, George Newbern, Dennis Christopher, Sally Kellerman, Leslie Hope; ***D:*** Avi Nesher; ***W:*** Avi Nesher.

Dorian Gray 🦴 **1/2** ***The Secret of Dorian Gray; Il Dio Chiamato a Dorian; Das Bildness des Dorian Gray; The Evils of Dorian Gray*** **1970 (R)** Modern-day version of the famous tale by Oscar Wilde about an ageless young man whose portrait reflects the ravages of time and a life of debauchery. More sex, less acting with Berger in lead. Not nearly as good as the original version, "The Picture of Dorian Gray." **92m/C VHS.** *GE IT* Richard Todd, Helmut Berger, Herbert Lom, Marie Liljedahl, Margaret Lee, Maria Rohm, Beryl Cunningham, Isa Miranda, Eleanora Rossi-Drago, Renato Romano; ***D:*** Massimo Dallamano; ***W:*** Massimo Dallamano, Marcello Costa; ***C:*** Otello Spila.

Dorm That Dripped Blood **WOOF!** **1982 (R)** Five college students volunteer to close the dorm during their Christmas vacation. A series of grisly and barbaric incidents eliminates the youngsters one by one. As the terror mounts, the remaining students slowly realize that they are up against a terrifyingly real psychopathic killer. Merry Christmas. **84m/C VHS, DVD.** Laura Lopinski, Stephen Sachs, Pamela Holland; ***D:*** Stephen Carpenter, Jeffrey Obrow; ***W:*** Stephen Carpenter.

Dororo 🦴🦴 **2007** Based on the classic manga by Osamu Tezuka (of "Astro Boy" fame), a madman exchanges the body parts of his infant son for power. Born little more than a stump with a head, his mother spirits the boy away and he is raised by a doctor who creates artificial limbs and body parts. Growing up he learns sword-fighting to kill the demons that possess his body parts, and reclaim his own. **139m/C DVD.** *JP* Kou Shibasaki, Satoshi Tsumabaki; ***D:*** Akihiko Shiota; ***W:*** Akihiko Shiota, Osamu Tezuka, Masa Nakamura.

Dostoevsky's Crime and Punishment 🦴🦴 ***Crime and Punishment*** **1999 (PG-13)** Muddled TV adaptation of the 1866 Dostoevsky novel is anchored by Dempsey's lead performance as impoverished student Rodya Raskolnikov. He murders the local pawnbroker in a "perfect crime" only to be consumed by guilt. Then he falls under the suspicious eyes of unrelenting inspector Porfiri (Kingsley), who waits for Rodya to make a mistake. **89m/C VHS.** Patrick Dempsey, Ben Kingsley, Julie Delpy, Eddie Marsan, Richard Bremmer, Lili Horvath, Carole Nimmons, Penny Downie, Michael Mehlmann, Sara Toth; ***D:*** Joseph Sargent; ***W:*** David Stevens; ***C:*** Elemer Ragalyi. **TV**

Dot the I 🦴🦴 **2003 (R)** Carmen (Verbeke) is about to marry boring stiff Barnaby (D'Arcy) when she meets sexy, dashing filmmaker Kit (Garcia Bernal) at her bachelorette party and begins an adulterous love affair with him. Surprisingly enough, bad things come of this love triangle, including Barnaby's angry jealousy and Kit's inability to separate his personal life from his work. Add in some additional plot twists that turn the last part of the movie from romantic drama into unpredictable noir, and what you get is a fluffy, hollow movie with little sense of direction. **92m/C DVD.** *US SP GB US* Gael Garcia Bernal, Natalia Verbeke, James D'Arcy, Thomas (Tom) Hardy, Charlie Cox; ***D:*** Matthew Parkhill; ***W:*** Matthew Parkhill; ***C:*** Alfonso Beato; ***M:*** Javier Navarrete.

Dot.Kill 🦴 **1/2 2005 (R)** Getting a cyber-thrill by broadcasting his victims' deaths via his website, a savage murderer is pursued by gruff, drug-addicted cop Charlie Daines (Assante) who gets put on the case and, as his bad luck would have it, ends up on the psycho's to-do list. Not much of a whodunit. **90m/C VHS, DVD.** Armand Assante, Sonny Marinelli, Raffaello Degruttola, Clare Holman, Frank Nasso; ***D:*** John Irvin; ***W:*** Andrew Charas, Robert Malkani; ***C:*** Damian Bromley. **VIDEO**

Double Agent 73 🦴 **1980 (R)** The title refers to star Chesty Morgan's amazing bust size. Here, she's a secret agent who has a camera/bomb implanted in her oh, never mind. The result is more curiosity than exploitation. Director Doris Wishman doesn't care about the plot and neither should you. **73m/C DVD.** Chesty Morgan, Frank Silvano, Saul Meth, Jill Harris, Louis Burdi, Peter Petrillo, Cooper Kent; ***D:*** Doris Wishman; ***W:*** Doris Wishman, Judy J. Kushner; ***C:*** Yuri Haviv.

Double Agents 🦴 ***La Nuit Des Espions; Night Encounter*** **1959** Two double agents are sent on a rendezvous to exchange vital government secrets. Dubbed in English. **81m/B VHS.** *FR* Marina Vlady, Michel Etcheverry, Roger Crouzet, Robert Hossein, Robert Le Beal, Clement Harari; ***D:*** Robert Hossein; ***W:*** Robert Hossein; ***C:*** Jacques Robin; ***M:*** Andre Gosselain.

Double Bang 🦴🦴 **2001 (R)** Honest cop Billy Benson decides to take the law into his own hands when his ex-partner is killed by a smalltime mobster. Standard actioner. **104m/C VHS, DVD.** William Baldwin, Adam Baldwin, Jon Seda, Elizabeth Mitchell, Richard Portnow, John Capodice, Sofia Milos; ***D:*** Heywood Gould; ***W:*** Heywood Gould; ***C:*** David Rush Morrison. **VIDEO**

Double Cross **1992 (R)** Tank Polling (Connery), a British journalist, uses the secrets of an ex-hooker (Donohoe) to get back at a corrupt politician who ruined Polling's life five years earlier. Lots of action and a few graphic murders in this thriller. **96m/C VHS.** Amanda Donohoe, Peter Wyngarde, Jason Connery; ***D:*** James A. Marcus.

Double Cross **1994 (R)** Man has what seems to be a chance erotic encounter with a beautiful blonde. But this wouldn't be a thriller if it ended there, so there's blackmail and murder to contend with as well. **95m/C VHS.** Patrick Bergin, Jennifer Tilly, Kelly Preston, Matt Craven, Kevin Tighe; ***D:*** Michael Keusch; ***C:*** Tobias Schliessler; ***M:*** Graeme Coleman.

Double Crossbones **1/2 1951** Rubbery comedian O'Connor becomes an unlikely scourge of the high seas. Meek Charleston shop assistant Dave is accused of piracy after stumbling onto the governor's (Emery) nefarious schemes. Stowing away on a brigantine, Dave goes through a series of adventures and winds up a notorious pirate captain who's determined to rescue beautiful Lady Sylvia (Carter), the governor's ward, from an arranged marriage. **75m/C DVD.** Donald O'Connor, Helena Carter, John Emery, Will Geer, Stanley Logan, Hayden Rorke, Kathryn Givney; ***D:*** Charles T. Barton; ***W:*** Oscar Brodney; ***C:*** Maury Gertsman; ***M:*** Frank Skinner.

Double-Crossed **1/2 1991** In 1984 Barry Seal agrees to inform on Colombia's Medellin Cartel and its links to the Sandanista government of Nicaragua in exchange for leniency on drug-smuggling charges. Little does he know that the personal consequences will turn deadly when his cover is blown and the government double-crosses him. Hopper's hyped-up performance as drug smuggler turned DEA informant Seal showcases this true-crime tale. **111m/C VHS.** Dennis Hopper, Robert Carradine, G.W. Bailey, Adrienne Barbeau; ***C:*** Donald M. Morgan; ***M:*** Richard Bellis.

Double Deal **1939** An honest man and a gangster are rivals in love. The gangster robs a jewelry store and tries to pin the crime on the good guy. This is a movie with a moral so don't expect him to get away with it. **60m/C VHS.** Monte Hawley, Jeni Le Gon, Edward Thompson, Florence O'Brien; ***D:*** Arthur Dreifuss.

Double Deal **1/2 1950** Murder, mayhem, and industrial espionage come into play as parties fight over an oil field. **65m/B VHS.** Marie Windsor, Richard Denning, Taylor Holmes; ***D:*** Abby Berlin.

Double Deal **1/2 1984** Unfaithful woman and her lover plot to steal priceless opal from hubby. Lifeless and silly. **90m/C VHS.** Louis Jourdan, Angela Punch McGregor; ***D:*** Brian Kavanagh.

Double Double Toil and Trouble **1/2 1994** The twins come to the financial rescue of their family when Dad's business gets into trouble and their home is threatened. But first they need to get a magic moonstone from their wicked Aunt Agatha (Leachman) and rescue kind Aunt Sophia, all before midnight on Halloween. Made for TV. **93m/C VHS, DVD.** Ashley (Fuller) Olsen, Mary-Kate Olsen, Cloris Leachman, Meshach Taylor; ***D:*** Jeff Franklin; ***W:*** Jeff Franklin. **TV**

Double Down **1/2** *Zigs* **2001 (R)** Five buddies, for whom gambling is a career, owe a lot of moolah to the local L.A. bookies. Naturally, they decide that one last bet will get them out of debt and on their way to their dream of owning a sports bar. Low-budget feature with lots of hanging around. **93m/C VHS, DVD.** Peter Dobson, Jason Priestley, Orien Richman, Kane Picoy, Richard Portnow, Luca Palanca, Alicia Coppola, Alexandra Powers, David Proval; ***D:*** Mars Callahan; ***W:*** Mars Callahan; ***C:*** Christopher Pearson. **VIDEO**

Double Dragon **1/2 1994 (PG-13)** Generally harmless brain candy, based on the videogame, finds orphaned brothers Jimmy (Dacascos) and Billy (Wolf) living in the rubble of post earthquake L.A., circa 2007. They have half of a mystical dragon amulet and obsessed mogul Koga Shuko (Patrick), who possesses the other half, after them. Seems he needs the entire amulet in order to control its vast power. Non-stop action should keep the kiddies amused. **96m/C VHS, DVD.** Scott Wolf, Mark Dacascos, Robert Patrick, Alyssa Milano, Kristina Malandro Wagner, Julia Nickson-Soul; ***D:*** Jim Yukich; ***W:*** Michael Davis, Peter Gould; ***C:*** Gary B. Kibbe; ***M:*** Jay Ferguson.

Double Dynamite **1/2** *It's Only Money* **1951** A bank teller is at a loss when his racetrack winnings are confused with the cash lifted from his bank during a robbery. Forgettable, forgotten shambles. Originally filmed in 1948. **80m/B VHS.** Frank Sinatra, Jane Russell, Groucho Marx, Don McGuire, Howard Freeman, Harry Hayden, Nestor Paiva, Lou Nova, Joe Devlin; ***D:*** Irving Cummings; ***W:*** Melville Shavelson.

Double Edge **1992 (PG-13)** The Palestinian-Israeli conflict is the focus of this drama about an ambitious reporter (Dunaway). On her first foreign assignment, New Yorker Faye Milano finds herself way out of her depth when she covers a colleague's beat in Jerusalem. Unable to remain a detached observer, Faye instead becomes an active participant, alternating between her affair with an Israeli reserves officer and her friendship with a family of Palestinian intifada leaders. Dunaway and Kollek are unfortunately stiff in their performances but the location (Israel and the West Bank) is interesting and the story surprisingly balanced. **85m/C VHS.** *IS* Faye Dunaway, Amos Kollek, Muhamad Bakri, Shmuel Shilo, Makram Khoury, Michael Schneider, Anat Atzmon, Ann Belkin; ***D:*** Amos Kollek; ***W:*** Amos Kollek.

Double Edge **1/2** *American Dragons* **1997 (R)** Obsessed NYC cop Tony Luca (Biehn) tries to bring down crimelord Rocco (Stark) but things go badly and instead he's taken off the case. His new assignment is investigating yakuza murders in Little Tokyo, which has also drawn the unwanted attention of South Korean detective Kim (Park), who recognizes the killer's MO. But when mobsters also start dying it turns out the bad guy is trying to get rid of the mob and the yakuza and take over. **95m/C VHS.** Michael Biehn, Joong-Hoon Park, Cary-Hiroyuki Tagawa, Don Stark, Byron Mann; ***D:*** Ralph Hemecker; ***W:*** Erik Saltzgaber; ***C:*** Ernest Holzman; ***M:*** Joel Goldsmith, K. Alexander (Alex) Wilkinson. **VIDEO**

Double Exposure **1982 (R)** A young photographer's violent nightmares become the next day's headlines. Unsurprising vision. **95m/C VHS.** Michael Callan, James Stacy, Joanna Pettet, Cleavon Little, Pamela Hensley, Seymour Cassel, David Young, Misty Rowe, Don Potter; ***D:*** William B. Hillman.

Double Exposure **1/2 1993 (R)** A possessive husband discovers his wife's infidelity and decides to get revenge, only his plan doesn't work out as he intends. **93m/C VHS.** Ron Perlman, Ian Buchanan, Jennifer Gatti, William R. Moses, James McEachin, Dedee Pfeiffer; ***D:*** Claudia Hoover; ***W:*** Christine Colfer, Bridget Hoffman, Claudia Hoover.

Double Exposure: The Story of Margaret Bourke-White **1/2** *Margaret Bourke-White* **1989** Beautifully shot but slow biography of a woman who became a well-known professional photographer for "Life" magazine during the 1930s and 1940s, as well as the first official female photojournalist of WWII. **105m/C VHS.** Farrah Fawcett, Frederic Forrest, Mitchell Ryan, David Huddleston, Jay Patterson, Ken Marshall; ***D:*** Lawrence Schiller; ***C:*** Robert Elswit. **CABLE**

Double Face **1/2 1970** A wealthy industrialist kills his lesbian wife with a car bomb, but she seems to haunt him through pornographic films. **84m/C VHS.** *IT GE* Christiane Kruger, Gunther Stoll, Sydney Chaplin, Klaus Kinski, Annabella Incontrera; ***D:*** Riccardo Freda; ***W:*** Riccardo Freda, Paul Hengge; ***C:*** Gabor Pogany; ***M:*** Nora Orlandi.

Double Happiness **1994 (PG-13)** Slice of life comedy-drama finds 20-something Chinese-Canadian Jade Li (Oh) struggling to balance her would-be acting career and new world romance with her family's traditional values. Jade wants to please her old world father (Chang) so she endures his arranged dates and puts on a pleasant demeanor for family friends. But Jade must decide who she wants to be when she gets involved with non-Asian college student Mark (Rennie). Fine performances and assured direction from Shum in her feature film debut. **87m/C VHS, DVD.** *CA* Sandra Oh, Stephen Chang, Alannah Ong, Frances You, Johnny Mah, Callum Keith Rennie; ***D:*** Mina Shum; ***W:*** Mina Shum; ***C:*** Peter Wunstorf. Genie '94: Actress (Oh), Film Editing.

Double Harness **1/2 1933** Naughty and unapologetic situations in a pre-Code romance. Joan (Harding) loves wealthy John Fletcher (Powell) but he prefers to play the field. So she arranges a compromising situation so he will be forced to marry her. John soon wants a divorce but Joan persuades him to wait and proves she's more than a gold-digger by helping him when his business runs into trouble. **70m/B DVD.** Ann Harding, William Powell, Henry Stephenson, Lillian Bond, George Meeker, Lucille Browne, Reginald Owen; ***D:*** John Cromwell; ***W:*** Jane Murdin; ***C:*** J. Roy Hunt.

The Double Hour*La Doppia Ora* **2009** Foreign-born Sonia (Rappoport) has just started working as a maid at a Turin hotel. Lonely, she tries speed-dating and hits it off with Guido (Timi) but then both are held at gunpoint during a robbery that may not be as straightforward as it seemed. Italian with subtitles. **95m/C DVD.** *IT* Antonia Truppo, Gaetano Bruno, Fausto Russo Alesi, Michele di Mauro, Lucia Poli, Kseniya Rappoport, Filippo Timi; ***D:*** Giuseppe Capondi; ***W:*** Alessandro Fabbri, Ludovica Rampoldi, Stefano Sardo; ***C:*** Tat Radcliffe; ***M:*** Pasquale Catalano.

Double Identity **1/2 1989 (PG-13)** Former college professor turned criminal Mancuso moves to a corn patch called New Hope in hopes of returning to the straight and narrow. He finds a good woman to stand by him, but, alas, crime, like smoking, is easier to start than to quit. Much intrigue and deceit. **95m/C VHS.** *CA FR* Nick Mancuso, Leah K. Pinsent, Patrick Bauchau, Anne LeTourneau, Jacques Godin; ***D:*** Yves Boisset.

Double Impact **1/2 1991 (R)** Van Damme plays twins re-united in Hong Kong to avenge their parents' murder by local bad guys, but this lunkhead kick-em-up doesn't even take advantage of that gimmick; the basic story would have been exactly the same with just one Jean-Claude. Lots of profane dialogue and some gratuitous nudity for the kiddies. **107m/C VHS, DVD.** Jean-Claude Van Damme, Cory (Corinna) Everson, Geoffrey Lewis; ***D:*** Sheldon Lettich; ***W:*** Jean-Claude Van Damme, Sheldon Lettich; ***C:*** Richard H. Kline; ***M:*** Arthur Kempel.

Double Indemnity **1944** The classic seedy story of insurance agent Walter Neff (MacMurray), who's seduced by deadly blonde Phyllis Dietrichson (Stanwyck) into killing her husband (Powers) so they can collect together from his company. But the husband's "accident" invites suspicions from claims adjustor Keyes (Robinson) and Walter and Phyllis begin to turn on each other. Terrific, influential film noir, the best of its kind. Based on the James M. Cain novel. **107m/B VHS, DVD.** Fred MacMurray, Barbara Stanwyck, Edward G. Robinson, Tom Powers, Porter Hall, Jean Heather, Byron Barr, Fortunio Bonanova; ***D:*** Billy Wilder; ***W:*** Raymond Chandler, Billy Wilder; ***C:*** John Seitz; ***M:*** Miklos Rozsa. AFI '98: Top 100, Natl. Film Reg. '92.

Double Jeopardy **1992 (R)** Boxleitner stars as a married man who risks his family and life when his sexy ex-lover returns to town. She easily involves him in deception—and murder. A cake-walk for Ward as the femme fatale. **101m/C VHS.** Bruce Boxleitner, Rachel Ward, Sela Ward, Sally Kirkland; ***D:*** Lawrence Schiller; ***M:*** Eduard Artemyev. **CABLE**

Double Jeopardy **1/2 1999 (R)** This film really doesn't make much sense. But it certainly struck a nerve, as well as box-office gold, as an entertaining thriller, probably because it doesn't give you much time to catch your breathe or think about plot holes. Libby (Judd) does time for murdering hubby Nick (Greenwood) after she's set up by the sleaze. Once she's released, she decides since she can't be tried for the same crime twice (this is actually faulty logic), she might as well get rid of the lowlife for real. Wisecracking parole officer Travis Lehman (Jones) winds up getting deeply involved ferreting out the truth of the messy situation. **105m/C VHS, DVD.** Ashley Judd, Tommy Lee Jones, Bruce Greenwood, Annabeth Gish, Roma Maffia, Jay Brazeau, Gillian Barber, Davenia McFadden, Spencer (Treat) Clark; ***D:*** Bruce Beresford; ***W:*** David Weisberg, Douglas S. Cook; ***C:*** Peter James; ***M:*** Normand Corbeil.

A Double Life **1947** Colman plays a Shakespearean actor in trouble when the characters he plays begin to seep into his personal life and take over. Things begin to look really bad when he is cast in the role of the cursed Othello. Colman won an Oscar for this difficult role, and the moody musical score garnered another for Rosza. **107m/B VHS, DVD.** Ronald Colman, Shelley Winters, Signe Hasso, Edmond O'Brien, Ray Collins, Millard Mitchell; ***D:*** George Cukor; ***W:*** Ruth Gordon, Garson Kanin; ***C:*** Milton Krasner; ***M:*** Miklos Rozsa. Oscars '47: Actor (Colman), Orig. Dramatic Score; Golden Globes '48: Actor—Drama (Colman).

The Double Life of Veronique *La Double Vie de Veronique* **1991 (R)** They say everyone has a twin, but this is ridiculous. Two women—Polish Veronika and French Veronique—are born on the same day in different countries, share a singing talent, a cardiac ailment, and, although the two never meet, a strange awareness of each other. Jacob is unforgettable as the two women, and director Krzysztof creates some spellbinding scenes but the viewer has to be willing to forgo plot for atmosphere. **96m/C VHS, DVD.** *FR PL* Irene Jacob, Philippe Volter, Sandrine Dumas, Aleksander Bardini, Louis Ducreux, Claude Duneton, Halina Gryglaszewska, Kalina Jedrusik; ***D:*** Krzysztof Kieslowski; ***W:*** Krzysztof Kieslowski, Krzysztof Piesiewicz; ***C:*** Slawomir Idziak; ***M:*** Zbigniew Preisner. Cannes '91: Actress (Jacob); Natl. Soc. Film Critics '91: Foreign Film.

The Double McGuffin **1979 (PG)** A plot of international intrigue is uncovered by teenagers—a la the Hardy Boys—when a prime minister and her security guard pay a visit to a small Virginia community. They're not believed, though. Action-packed from the makers of Benji. Dogs do not figure prominently here. **100m/C VHS, DVD.** Ernest Borgnine, George Kennedy, Elke Sommer, Ed "Too Tall" Jones, Lisa Whelchel, Vincent Spano; ***D:*** Joe Camp; ***M:*** Euel Box; ***V:*** Orson Welles.

The Double Negative **1/2** *Deadly Companion* **1980** A photojournalist pursues his wife's killer in a confusing story. Based on Ross MacDonald's "The Three Roads." **96m/C VHS.** *CA* Michael Sarrazin, Susan Clark, Anthony Perkins, Howard Duff, Kate Reid, Al Waxman, Elizabeth Shepherd, John Candy; ***D:*** George Bloomfield; ***W:*** Janis Allen.

The Double O Kid **1/2 1992 (PG-13)** Lance is a 17-year-old video game master who's interning at the Agency, a covert spy organization. Ordered to rush a package to Los Angeles, Lance discovers that a madman computer virus designer and his henchwoman desperately want what he's carrying. Aided by the prerequisite pretty girl, Lance must avoid all the hazards sent his way. **95m/C VHS.** Corey Haim, Wallace Shawn, Brigitte Nielsen, Nicole Eggert, John Rhys-Davies, Basil Hoffman, Karen Black; ***Cameos:*** Anne Francis; ***D:*** Duncan McLachlan; ***W:*** Andrea Buck, Duncan McLachlan.

Double Obsession **1/2 1993 (R)** College roommates Heather (Hemingway) and Claire (d'Abo) are inseparable friends—until Claire falls in love. Heather becomes possessive and, though the years pass, her obsession with Claire only grows. When Heather's affections turn deadly, can Claire stop her? **88m/C VHS.** Margaux Hemingway, Maryam D'Abo, Frederic Forrest, Scott Valentine; ***D:*** Eduardo Montes; ***W:*** Jeffrey Delman, R.J. Marx, Eduardo Montes.

Double or Nothing **1/2 1937** Lighthearted musical comedy. An eccentric millionaire believes people are basically honest. In his will, he instructs his lawyer to drop four money-filled wallets on the streets to see if they'll be returned. The honest folk get $5000 and a chance to inherit the rest of the Clark fortune if they double their money (legally) in a month, otherwise it goes to a group of greedy relatives. The four (Crosby, Raye, Devine, Frawley) decide to pool their efforts and Der Bingle takes a shot at opening a nightclub while withstanding a series of dirty tricks. **90m/B DVD.** Bing Crosby, Martha Raye, Andy Devine, William Frawley, Mary Carlisle, Samuel S. Hinds, Fay Holden, William Henry; ***D:*** Theodore Reed; ***W:*** Erwin Gelsey, John Moffitt, Charles Lederer, Duke Atteberry; ***C:*** Karl Struss; ***M:*** Boris Morros.

Double Parked 🦴🦴 1/2 **2000** Meter maid Rita (Thorne) is divorced from an alcoholic abuser and finally has a steady job. Which she needs to support her teenaged son Matt (Read) who suffers from cystic fibrosis and bad judgement since his best friend is a delinquent (Fleiss). Rita's been taken care of business while putting her personal needs on hold but that's about to change. Fine performances. **98m/C VHS, DVD.** Callie (Calliope) Thorne, Rufus Read, Noah Fleiss, William Sage, Anthony De Sando, Eileen Galindro, Michelle Hurd, P.J. Brown; ***D:*** Stephen Kinsella; ***W:*** Stephen Kinsella, Paul Solberg; ***C:*** Jim Denault; ***M:*** Craig Hazen, David Wolfert.

Double Platinum 🦴🦴 1/2 **1999 (PG)** Baby diva Brandy squares off against mega-diva Ross—the mommy who abandoned her for a fabulous career. Eighteen years later Brandy decides to pursue a singing career herself and meets Ross—not knowing about their relationship. But when she finds out, there are a lot of abandonment issues to deal with and this teen is determined to get even by besting mommy dearest at her own game. You go, girl! **91m/C VHS, DVD.** Diana Ross, Brandy Norwood, Harvey Fierstein, Roger Rees, Brian Stokes Mitchell, Christine Ebersole, Tony Payne; ***D:*** Robert Allan Ackerman; ***W:*** Nina Shengold, Katie Ford, Renee Longstreet. **TV**

Double Play 🦴🦴 1/2 *Prisoner of Zenda Inc* **1996 (PG)** Updated version of "The Prince and the Pauper" finds teenaged computer genius Rudy (Jackson) inheriting his dad's successful computer company. But his evil Uncle Mike (Shatner), who's not the boy's guardian, wants the company for himself and hires some thugs to kidnap the kid and force him to sign over control of the business. But Rudy just happens to have a double—a high school baseball star who's in town for the championship game—and confusion rules when he takes his place. Jackson's brother, Richard Lee Jackson, plays his cousin in the movie. **101m/C VHS, DVD.** Jonathan Jackson, William Shatner, Richard Lee Jackson, Jay Brazeau; ***D:*** Stefan Scaini; ***W:*** Richard Clark; ***C:*** Maris Jansons; ***M:*** John Welsman.

Double Revenge 🦴 1/2 **1989** Two men feel they have a score to settle after a bank heist gone sour leaves two people dead. **90m/C VHS.** Bobby DiCicco, Joe Dallesandro, Nancy Everhard, Leigh McCloskey, Richard Rust, Theresa Saldana; ***D:*** Armand Mastroianni.

Double Standard 🦴 1/2 **1988** You'll be less concerned with the plot—a community discovers that a prominent judge has maintained two marriages for nearly 20 years—than with the possibility that such dim-witted myopes might actually have existed in the real world. This made-for-TV slice of bigamy is for fans of the oops-I-forgot-I'm-married genre only. **95m/C VHS.** Robert Foxworth, Michele Greene, Pamela Bellwood, James Kee; ***D:*** Louis Rudolph.

Double Suicide 🦴🦴🦴 *Shinju Ten No Amijima* **1969** From a play by Monzarmon Chikamatsu, a tragic drama about a poor salesman in 18th century Japan who falls in love with a geisha and ruins his family and himself trying to requite the hopeless passion. Stylish with Iwashita turning in a wonderful dual performance. In Japanese with subtitles. **105m/B VHS, DVD.** *JP* Kichiemon Nakamura, Shima Iwashita, Yusuke Takita, Hosei Komatsu; ***D:*** Masahiro Shinoda; ***W:*** Masahiro Shinoda, Toru Takemitsu, Taeko Tomioka; ***C:*** Toichiro Narushima; ***M:*** Toru Takemitsu.

Double Take 🦴🦴 **1997 (R)** Writer Connor McEwen (Sheffer) witnesses a murder and identifies the suspect from a police lineup. But when he sees a dead ringer for the alleged murderer, he becomes convinced the police have arrested the wrong guy. **86m/C VHS.** Craig Sheffer, Costas Mandylor, Brigitte Bako, Torri Higginson, Maurice Godin; ***D:*** Mark L. Lester; ***W:*** Ed Rugoff, Ralph Rugoff; ***M:*** Paul Zaza.

Double Take 🦴 **2001 (PG-13)** Businessman Daryl Chase (Jones) is framed as a money-launderer for a drug cartel and assumes the identity of street hustler Freddy (Griffin) in order to clear his name. Fans of "Mad TV" and "Malcolm and Eddie" (Jones and Griffin's TV ventures, respectively) will probably be sorely disappointed with this action-comedy attempt. While the two stars trade zingers and dodge gunfire, you're left to wonder why you didn't rent "Midnight Run," or even "Beverly Hills Cop 3." **88m/C VHS, DVD.** *US* Orlando Jones, Eddie Griffin, Gary Grubbs, Daniel Roebuck, Sterling Macer, Garcelle Beauvais, Edward Herrmann, Benny Nieves, Shawn Elliott, Brent Briscoe, Carlos Carrasco; ***D:*** George Gallo; ***W:*** George Gallo; ***C:*** Theo van de Sande; ***M:*** Graeme Revell.

Double Tap 🦴🦴 **1998 (R)** Undercover FBI agent becomes personally interested in the vigilante she's pursuing—whose purpose is to bring down a drug cartel. Not much to recommend this one, except Stephen Rea's performance. **99m/C VHS.** Heather Locklear, Stephen Rea, Peter Greene, Mykelti Williamson, Kevin Gage, Robert LaSardo, Richard Edson, A. Martinez; ***D:*** Greg Yaitanes; ***C:*** John Peters; ***M:*** Moby.

Double Team 🦴🦴 **1997 (R)** Counter-terrorist expert Jack Quinn (Van Damme) teams with weapons specialist Yaz (Rodman, in his film debut) to take down international terrorist Stavros (Roarke). After Jack kills Stavros's son, he is sent to a high-security superspy retirement village. When his wife and newborn son are kidnapped, Jack escapes, with Yaz's help, to finish the job and try to save his family. Van Damme teams with his third famous Hong Kong action director, Tsui Hark (the other two are John Woo and Ringo Lam) to create yet another disappointment. He's slightly more charismatic than usual (not saying much), but Rodman easily steals the flick as he gets most of the good lines, and delivers them with relish. **93m/C VHS, DVD.** Jean-Claude Van Damme, Dennis Rodman, Mickey Rourke, Natasha Lindinger, Paul Freeman, Valeria Cavalli, Jay Benedict, Bruno Bilotta; ***D:*** Tsui Hark; ***W:*** Paul Mones, Don Jakoby; ***C:*** Peter Pau; ***M:*** Gary Chang. Golden Raspberries '97: Worst Support. Actor (Rodman), Worst New Star (Rodman).

Double Threat 🦴🦴 **1992 (R)** An aging sex star makes her return to the screen opposite a younger actor with whom she is having an affair. When the director wants to include nude sex scenes in the film she agrees to use a younger body-double. Then the actress discovers her lover is involved in off-screen action with the double as well. This does not please her and she decides to take a deadly revenge. An unrated version is also available. **94m/C VHS.** Sally Kirkland, Andrew Stevens, Lisa Shane, Richard Lynch, Anthony (Tony) Franciosa, Sherrie Rose, Chick Vennera; ***D:*** David A. Prior.

Double Trouble 🦴🦴 1/2 **1941** Langdon and Rogers are hired to work in a canning factory and accidentally package a valuable necklace in a can of beans. The rest is a mad chase to get the necklace back. Langdon was best known as a silent-screen comedian but he hadn't lost his farcical touch. **62m/B VHS.** Harry Langdon, Charles "Buddy" Rogers, Dave O'Brien, Wheeler Oakman, Catherine Lewis, Mira McKinney; ***D:*** William West; ***W:*** Jack Natteford; ***C:*** Arthur Martinelli; ***M:*** Ross DiMaggio.

Double Trouble 🦴🦴 **1967** When rock star Presley falls in love with an English heiress, he winds up involved in an attempted murder. The king belts out "Long Legged Girl" while evading cops, criminals, and crying women. A B-side. Based on a story by Marc Brandell. **92m/C VHS, DVD.** Elvis Presley, Annette Day, John Williams, Yvonne Romain, Michael Murphy, Chips Rafferty, Helene Winston; ***D:*** Norman Taurog; ***W:*** Jo Heims.

Double Trouble 🦴 **1991 (R)** Twin brothers—one a cop, one a jewel thief—team up to crack the case of an international jewel smuggling ring headed by a wealthy and politically well-connected businessman and his righthand man. **87m/C VHS.** David Paul, Peter Paul, James Doohan, Roddy McDowall, Steve Kanaly, A.J. (Anthony) Johnson, David Carradine; ***D:*** John Paragon.

Double Vision 🦴🦴 **1992 (PG-13)** Suspense thriller starring Cattrall as Caroline, a medical student who goes to London to check out the strange disappearance of her twin sister, Lisa. Assuming her identity, Caroline gets deeply involved in a kinky lifestyle that may result in murder. Based on a short story by Mary Higgins Clark. **92m/C VHS.** Kim Cattrall, Gale Hansen, Christopher Lee; ***D:*** Robert Knights.

Double Vision 🦴🦴 *Shuang Tong* **2002 (R)** FBI agent Kevin Richter (Morse) pairs up with troubled Taiwanese Foreign Affairs Officer and former detective Huang Huo-tu (Leung Ka Fai) to hunt for a serial killer who uses random methods that don't seem scientifically possible. But the victims do have one thing in common—a black fungus found in their brain that appears to cause deadly hallucinations. As Huang digs further he discovers the crimes mimic ritualized murders committed by an ancient mystic cult. English and Chinese with subtitles. **110m/C VHS, DVD.** *HK* Tony Leung Ka-Fai, David Morse, Rene Liu, Brett Climo, Leon Dai; ***D:*** Kuo-fu Chen; ***W:*** Kuo-fu Chen, Chao-Bin Ju; ***C:*** Arthur Wong Ngok Tai; ***M:*** Sin-yun Lee.

Double Wedding 🦴🦴🦴 **1937** Madcap comedy starring Powell as a wacky painter who doesn't believe in working and Loy as a workaholic dress designer. Loy has chosen a fiance for her younger sister, Irene, to marry, but Irene has plans of her own. When Irene and her beau meet bohemian Powell, the fun really begins. Script suffers slightly from too much slapstick and not enough wit, although the stars (in their seventh outing as a duo) play it well. Based on the play "Great Love" by Ferenc Molnar. **86m/B VHS, DVD.** William Powell, Myrna Loy, Florence Rice, John Beal, Jessie Ralph, Edgar Kennedy, Sidney Toler, Mary Gordon; ***D:*** Richard Thorpe; ***W:*** Jo Swerling.

Double Whammy 🦴🦴 **2001 (R)** DiCillo's attempt at Tarantino crimedy doesn't quite work out. Leary is Ray Pluto, a cop with a trick back with lousy timing and a past that haunts him. When his back gives out during a restaurant shooting, he's put on desk duty and sent to sexy chiropractor Hurley, who eventually heals his love life as well as his vertebrae. Weak subplots include his building super's attempted murder by his daughter, and a screenwriting duo who also, coincidentally, want to be the next Tarantino. Occasionally inspired, but DiCIllo can't make the comedy and romance fit with the sometimes brutal violence. **93m/C VHS, DVD.** Denis Leary, Elizabeth Hurley, Steve Buscemi, Luis Guzman, Victor Argo, Christopher Noth, Donald Adeosun Faison, Maurice Smith; ***D:*** Tom DiCillo; ***W:*** Tom DiCillo; ***C:*** Robert Yeoman; ***M:*** Jim Farmer.

Doubt 🦴🦴🦴 **2008 (PG-13)** Shanley adapts and directs his own Pulitzer Prize-winning play. Set in 1964 in a Bronx Catholic high school, young teacher Sister James (Adams) approaches stern principal Sister Aloysius (Streep) regarding possible improper behavior of a sexual nature by the seemingly benevolent Father Flynn towards the sole black student, 12-year-old Donald (Foster II). As a detractor of his liberal views, Sister Aloysius finally realizes an opportunity to target and entrap her supervisor, but even with her fervent determination the question of doubt constantly lurks in the shadows. Streep is forboding while Hoffman holds the secret close, though trumping them all is Davis in the role of the boy's mother with her meaty scene confronting Streep. **104m/C DVD.** *US* Meryl Streep, Philip Seymour Hoffman, Amy Adams, Viola Davis, Lloyd Clay Brown, Joseph Foster, Alice Drummond, Carrie Preston, John A. Costelloe, Audrie Neenan; ***D:*** John Patrick Shanley; ***W:*** John Patrick Shanley; ***C:*** Roger Deakins; ***M:*** Howard Shore. Screen Actors Guild '08: Actress (Streep).

Doubting Thomas 🦴🦴 1/2 **1935** Rogers' last film, which was in theatres when he was killed in a plane crash. Silly story of a husband and his doubts about his wife and her amateur-acting career. The show goes on in spite of his doubts, her forgotten lines, and wardrobe goofs. Remake of 1922's silent film "The Torch Bearers." **78m/B VHS.** Will Rogers, Billie Burke, Alison Skipworth, Sterling Holloway; ***D:*** David Butler.

Doughboys 🦴🦴 1/2 *Forward March* **1930** Keaton's second talkie is a so-so comedy about a rich man who mistakenly enlists in the Army during WWI. He manages to bumble his way through basic training and win the heart of a pretty girl. There are a few bright moments, particularly a musical number between Keaton and "Ukulele Ike" Edwards. **80m/B VHS.** Buster Keaton, Cliff Edwards, Edward Brophy, Sally Eilers, Victor Potel, Arnold Korff, Frank Mayo; ***D:*** Edward Sedgwick.

Doughboys 🦴🦴 **2008 (PG-13)** Italian-American brothers Frank (Iacono) and Lou (Lombardi) inherit the Bronx family bakery that's a neighborhood institution. Frank's the responsible one but Lou is the baking whiz. He also has a gambling addiction and owes a lot of money to a local mobster, which Frank, who has plans of his own, knows nothing about. **80m/C DVD.** Louis Lombardi, Andrew Keegan, James Madio, Vincent Pastore, Mike Starr, Gaetano Iacono; ***D:*** Louis Lombardi; ***W:*** Louis Lombardi, Evan Jacobs; ***C:*** Stephen Franciosa Jr.; ***M:*** Peter Cascone. **VIDEO**

Doughnuts & Society 🦴 1/2 **1936** Two elderly ladies who run a coffee shop suddenly strike it rich and find that life among the bluebloods is not all it's cracked up to be. No sprinkles. **70m/B VHS.** Louise Fazenda, Maude Eburne, Eddie Nugent, Ann Rutherford, Hedda Hopper, Franklin Pangborn; ***D:*** Lewis D. Collins; ***W:*** Karen De Wolf, Wallace MacDonald; ***C:*** William Nobles.

Doug's 1st Movie 🦴🦴🦴 **1999 (G)** Feature-length version of the children's animated series assumes sequels according to the title, but has problem stretching the storyline over an hour. However, kids who like the series will enjoy the adventures of 12-year-old Doug Funnie and his pal Skeeter as they try to hide the lake monster Herman Melville (so named because he tries to eat a copy of "Moby Dick") from the clutches of polluting bad guy Mr. Bluff. He also has to impress Patti before the big Valentine's Day Dance. Not overly preachy, but the animation will not impress children used to the glossy Disney style. **77m/C VHS.** ***D:*** Maurice Joyce; ***W:*** Ken Scarborough; ***M:*** Mark Watters; ***V:*** Guy Hadley, Eddie Korbich, Thomas McHugh, Fred Newman, Chris Phillips, Constance Shulman, Frank Welker, Alice Playten, Doris Belack, Doug Preis.

The Dove 🦴🦴 1/2 **1974 (PG-13)** The true story of a 16-year-old's adventures as he sails around the world in a 23-foot sloop. The trip took him five years and along the way he falls in love with a girl who follows him to exotic locales. Photography and scenery are magnificent. **105m/C VHS.** Joseph Bottoms, Deborah Raffin, Dabney Coleman, Peter Gwynne; ***D:*** Charles Jarrott; ***W:*** Peter S. Beagle; ***C:*** Sven Nykvist.

Down Among the Z Men 🦴🦴 **1952** Enlisted man helps a girl save an atomic formula from spies. Funny in spots but weighed down by musical numbers from a female entourage. From the pre-Monty Python comedy troupe "The Goons." **71m/B VHS, DVD.** *GB* Peter Sellers, Spike Milligan, Harry Secombe, Michael Bentine, Carole Carr; ***D:*** Maclean Rogers.

Down & Dirty 🦴🦴🦴 *Brutti, Sporchi, e Cattivi; Ugly, Dirty and Bad; Dirty, Mean and Nasty* **1976** A scathing Italian satire about a modern Roman family steeped in petty crime, incest, murder, adultery, drugs, and arson. In Italian with English subtitles. **115m/C VHS.** *IT* Nino Manfredi, Francesco Anniballi, Maria Bosco; ***D:*** Ettore Scola; ***W:*** Ruggero Maccari, Ettore Scola; ***C:*** Dario Di Palma; ***M:*** Armando Trovajoli. Cannes '76: Director (Scola).

Down and Out in Beverly Hills 🦴🦴 1/2 **1986 (R)** A modern retelling of Jean Renoir's classic "Boudu Saved from Drowning" with some nice star turns. Neurotic and wealthy Beverly Hills married Dave (Dreyfuss) and Barbara (Midler) find their lives turned upside down when they prevent suicidal bum Jerry Baskin (Nolte) from drowning in their pool. Jerry takes over the household—bedding Barbara, her daughter Jenny (Nelson), and their sultry maid Carmen (Pena)—offering encouragement to a frustrated Dave and his son Max (Richards)—and even solving family dog Matisse's identity crisis. Naturally, Jerry learns there's more to life than being a bum. **103m/C VHS, DVD.** Nick Nolte, Bette Midler, Richard Dreyfuss, Little Richard, Tracy Nelson, Elizabeth Pena, Evan Richards, Valerie Curtin, Barry Primus, Dorothy Tristan, Alexis Arquette; ***D:*** Paul Mazursky; ***W:*** Paul Mazursky, Leon Capetanos; ***C:*** Donald McAlpine; ***M:*** Andy Summers.

Down Argentine Way **1940** A lovely young woman falls in love with a suave Argentinian horse breeder. First-rate Fox musical made a star of Grable and was Miranda's first American film. ♫ South American Way; Down Argentina Way; Two Dreams Met; Mama Yo Quiero; Sing to Your Senorita. **90m/C VHS, DVD.** Don Ameche, Betty Grable, Carmen Miranda, Charlotte Greenwood, J. Carrol Naish, Henry Stephenson, Leonid Kinskey, Kay Aldridge, Chris-Pin (Ethier Crispin Martini) Martin, Charles (Judel, Judells) Judels; ***D:*** Irving Cummings; ***W:*** Rian James, Ralph Spence, Karl Tunberg; ***C:*** Leon Shamroy, Ray Rennahan; ***M:*** Mack Gordon.

Down by Law **1986 (R)** In Jarmusch's follow-up to his successful "Stranger than Paradise," he introduces us to three men: a pimp, an out-of-work disc jockey, and an Italian tourist. When the three break out of prison, they wander through the Louisiana swampland with some regrets about their new-found freedom. Slow-moving at times, beautifully shot throughout. Poignant and hilarious, the film is true to Jarmusch form: some will love the film's offbeat flair, and others will find it bothersome. **107m/B VHS, DVD.** John Lurie, Tom Waits, Roberto Benigni, Ellen Barkin, Billie Neal, Rockets Redglare, Vernel Bagneris, Nicoletta Braschi; ***D:*** Jim Jarmusch; ***W:*** Jim Jarmusch; ***C:*** Robby Muller; ***M:*** John Lurie, Tom Waits.

Down Came a Blackbird **1/2** **1994 (R)** Anna Lenka (Redgrave), a Holocaust survivor, runs a clinic for healing both the physical and psychological wounds of torture victims. Journalist Helen McNulty (Dern), herself a survivor, decides to write about the clinic but Anna believes Helen's covering up the pain she's never dealt with. Also at the clinic is Tomas Ramirez (Julia), a former college professor with a terrible secret, with whom Helen discovers a special rapport. Conventional script with some fine performances; Julia died shortly after principal photography was completed on the TV film, which is dedicated to his memory. **112m/C VHS.** Vanessa Redgrave, Laura Dern, Raul Julia, Jay O. Sanders, Cliff Gorman, Sarita Choudhury, L. Scott Caldwell, Jeffrey DeMunn; ***D:*** Jonathan Sanger; ***W:*** Kevin Droney; ***C:*** Kees Van Oostrum; ***M:*** Graeme Revell.

Down Dakota Way **1/2 1949** Strange coincidence between a recent murder and a fatal cow epidemic. Rogers helps some locals bring the link to light. **67m/C VHS, DVD.** Roy Rogers, Dale Evans, Pat Brady, Monte Montana, Elisabeth Risdon, Byron Barr, James B. Cardwell, Roy Barcroft, Emmett Vogan; ***D:*** William Witney.

Down in the Delta **1998 (PG-13)** Chicago matriarch Rosa Lynn (Alice) tries to prevent her jobless, single-mom daughter Loretta (Woodard) from succumbing to drugs, alcohol, and the other destructive forces that are a part of her rough neighborhood. She sends her Loretta and her two grandchildren (including an autistic boy) to her brother's home in the Mississippi delta, hoping that they'll reconnect to their roots. Though reluctant at first, Loretta finds herself slowly changing her ways as she works in Uncle Earl's restaurant; she is moved by his love of family, particularly his Alzheimer-ridden wife (Rolle). Poet-novelist Maya Angelou's first outing as a director skillfully demonstrates the importance of connecting to one's heritage. Woodard shines energetically as the strung-out mom and Freeman is nearly perfect as the elegant and tender Uncle Earl. **111m/C VHS, DVD.** Alfre Woodard, Al Freeman Jr., Mary Alice, Wesley Snipes, Esther Rolle, Loretta Devine, Anne-Marie Johnson, Mpho Koaho, Kulani Hassen, Richard Blackburn; ***D:*** Maya Angelou; ***W:*** Myron Goble; ***C:*** William Wages; ***M:*** Stanley Clarke. **CABLE**

Down in the Valley **2005 (R)** Wannabe cowboy hero Harlan (Edwards) befriends rebellious, aimless teen Tobe (Wood) and her shy younger brother Lonnie (Culkin). They're the children of tough San Fernando Valley sheriff Wade (Morse), who immediately distrusts this soft-spoken, tale-spinning stranger. And with good reason, since Harlan is delusional at best and dangerous at his worst. No matter the talent, flick stretches credibility—particularly in its last act. **114m/C DVD.** *US* Edward Norton, Evan Rachel Wood, David Morse, Rory Culkin, John Diehl, Kat Dennings, Hunter Parrish, Bruce Dern, Muse Watson, Geoffrey Lewis, Aviva, Aaron Fors, Heather Ashleigh; ***D:*** David Jacobson; ***W:*** David Jacobson; ***C:*** Enrique Chediak.

Down Mexico Way **1941** Two cowboys come to the aid of a Mexican town whose residents have been hoodwinked by a phony movie company. Very exciting chase on horseback, motorcycle, and in automobiles. **78m/B VHS, DVD.** Gene Autry, Smiley Burnette, Fay McKenzie, Duncan Renaldo; ***D:*** Joseph Santley.

Down, Out and Dangerous **1995 (R)** Expectant couple Brad (Davison) and Monica (Ettinger) Harrington find out that Tim (Thomas), the charming homeless man they've befriended, is really a psycho killer. **90m/C VHS.** Richard Thomas, Bruce Davison, Cynthia Ettinger, Steve Hytner, Christine Cavanaugh, George DiCenzo, Jason Bernard, Melinda Culea, Stuart Pankin; ***D:*** Noel Nosseck; ***W:*** Carey Hayes, Chad Hayes; ***C:*** Paul Maibaum; ***M:*** Mark Snow.

Down Periscope **1/2 1996 (PG-13)** Tom Dodge (Grammer) dreams of commanding a nuclear sub, but gets stuck with an out-of-mothballs, rusting WWII vintage tub with the usual goof-off crew. In order for Dodge to get his dream assignment, he and his losers must beat the nuclear subs of generic mean authority figure Admiral Graham (Dern), in a war game. Predictable comedy is kept afloat by amusing cast, especially Schneider as the weaselly Executive Officer Pascal. Many jokes revolve around Dodge's tattoo, which is on a body part that is normally private first-class. Denied cooperation from the U.S. Navy, the shipyard scenes were filmed on three barges tied together in the San Francisco Bay area, with empty discarded frigates and destroyers belonging to the U.S. Department of Transportation playing the fleet. **92m/C VHS, DVD.** Kelsey Grammer, Lauren Holly, Bruce Dern, Rob Schneider, Rip Torn, Harry Dean Stanton, William H. Macy, Ken H. Campbell, Toby Huss, Duane Martin, Jonathan Penner, Bradford Tatum, Harland Williams; ***D:*** David S. Ward; ***W:*** Hugh Wilson, Andrew Kurtzman, Eliot Wald; ***C:*** Victor Hammer; ***M:*** Randy Edelman.

Down Texas Way **1942** One of the "Rough Riders" series. When one of the boys is accused of murdering his best friend, his two companions search for the real killer. **57m/B VHS, DVD.** Buck Jones, Tim McCoy, Raymond Hatton; ***D:*** Howard Bretherton.

Down the Drain **1989 (R)** A broad-as-a-city-block farce about an unscrupulous criminal lawyer and his assortment of crazy clients. A fine first half but someone pulls the plug in the middle of the bath. **90m/C VHS.** Andrew Stevens, John Matuszak, Teri Copley, Joseph Campanella, Don Stroud, Stella Stevens, Jerry Mathers, Benny "The Jet" Urquidez; ***D:*** Robert C. Hughes.

Down the Wyoming Trail **1939** Western hero Ritter battles some rustlers who are terrorizing farmers during the winter, while still managing to find time to warble some tunes. **52m/B VHS.** Tex Ritter, Horace Murphy, Mary Brodel, Bobby Lawson, Charles "Blackie" King, Bob Terry; ***D:*** Al(bert) Herman; ***W:*** Peter Dixon, Roger Merton.

Down to Earth **1917** Ever-gallant lover Fairbanks overruns a mental hospital to save his sweetheart. Once inside, he's determined to show the patients that their illness is illusion, and reality's the cure. A quixotic gem from Fairbanks' pre-swashbuckling social comic days. Director Emerson's wife was the scenarist, and Victor Fleming, who went on to direct "The Wizard of Oz" and "Gone with the Wind" (to name a few), was the man behind the camera. **68m/B VHS.** Douglas Fairbanks Sr., Eileen (Elaine Persey) Percy, Gustav von Seyffertitz, Charles P. McHugh, Charles Gerrard, William H. Keith, Ruth Allen, Frederico Prosperi; ***D:*** John Emerson.

Down to Earth **1947** A lackluster musical and boxoffice flop with an impressive cast. Hayworth is the Greek goddess of dance sent to Earth on a mission to straighten out Broadway producer Parks and his play that ridicules the Greek gods. Anita Ellis dubs the singing of Hayworth. A parody of "Here Comes Mr. Jordan," remade in 1980 as "Xanadu." **101m/C VHS, DVD.** Rita Hayworth, Larry Parks, Marc Platt, Roland Culver, James Gleason, Edward Everett Horton, Adele Jergens, George Macready, William Frawley, James Burke, Fred F. Sears, Lynn Merrick, Myron Healey; ***D:*** Alexander Hall; ***W:*** Edwin Blum; ***M:*** George Duning.

Down to Earth **2001 (PG-13)** Rock is called to heaven before his time by angel Levy but the only body available to send him back in is that of a 60-ish white businessman. Rock's presence and comic sensibility saves what could've been a lame time-waster but he's the only reason to see it and if you don't like Rock, don't bother. Remake of "Heaven Can Wait," which was a remake of "Here Comes Mr. Jordan." **87m/C VHS, DVD.** *US* Chris Rock, Regina King, Chazz Palminteri, Eugene Levy, Frankie Faison, Mark Addy, Greg Germann, Jennifer Coolidge; ***D:*** Chris Weitz, Paul Weitz; ***W:*** Chris Rock, Lance Crouther, Ali LeRoi, Louis CK; ***C:*** Richard Crudo; ***M:*** Jamshield Sharifi.

Down to the Bone **1/2 2004** Sad tale of everyday addiction, portraying the issue with a bleakness that allows for authenticity that few films accomplish. Irene (Farmiga), a mother of two saddled with financial difficulties, begins using cocaine to get through her days working as a cashier in a suburban mega-store. But as time passes, her dependence, lies, and the personal tolls all mount. Eventually she seeks help at a rehab center and meets a nurse, Bob (Dillon), who is also a recovering user. The two become friends as they try to support each other's recovery. **105m/C DVD.** *US* Vera Farmiga, Hugh Dillon, Clint Jordan, Caridad "La Bruja" De La Luz, Jasper Moon Daniels, Taylor Foxhall; ***D:*** Debra Granik; ***W:*** Richard Lieske, Debra Granik; ***C:*** Michael McDonough; ***M:*** Jackie O Motherfucker. L.A. Film Critics '05: Actress (Farmiga).

Down to the Sea in Ships **1/2** *The Last Adventurers* **1922** Bow made her movie debut in this drama about the whalers of 19th-century Massachusetts. Highlighted by exciting action scenes of an actual whale hunt. Silent with music score and original tinted footage. **83m/B VHS, DVD.** Marguerite Courtot, Raymond (Ray) McKee, Clara Bow; ***D:*** Elmer Clifton; ***W:*** John L.E. Pell; ***C:*** Alexander Penrod.

Down to You **1/2 2000 (PG-13)** Light romantic comedy has appealing leads and a predictable plot (and references to about a gazillion similar movies). Aspiring chef Al (Prinze Jr.) and artist Imogen (Stiles) are immediately smitten when they meet at the campus dive. The relationship develops at headlong speed but then they both realize neither of them is ready for a lifelong commitment. So, do they just split or try being friends or slow things down or what? **92m/C VHS, DVD.** Freddie Prinze Jr., Julia Stiles, Selma Blair, Shawn Hatosy, Zak Orth, Rosario Dawson, Henry Winkler, Ashton Kutcher, Lucie Arnaz; ***D:*** Kris Isacsson; ***W:*** Kris Isacsson; ***C:*** Robert Yeoman; ***M:*** Edmund Choi.

Down Twisted **1989 (R)** A young woman gets involved with a thief on the run in Mexico in this "Romancing the Stone" derivative. The muddled plot deserves such a confusing title. **89m/C VHS.** Carey Lowell, Charles Rocket, Trudi Dochtermann, Thom Mathews, Linda Kerridge, Courteney Cox; ***D:*** Albert Pyun; ***W:*** Albert Pyun; ***C:*** Walt Lloyd; ***M:*** Eric Allaman.

Down Under **1986** Two gold-hungry beach boys go to Australia looking for riches, and document their adventures on film. Essentially a crudely shot, tongue-in-cheek travelogue narrated by Patrick Macnee. **90m/C VHS.** Don Atkinson, Donn Dunlop; ***W:*** Robert H. Jamieson; ***M:*** David Gibney; ***Nar:*** Patrick Macnee.

Down With Love **1/2 2003 (PG-13)** This uneven but amusing homage/satire to the Rock Hudson/Doris Day sex comedies of the early '60s gets the look and feel right, but loses something in the attitude by superimposing modern sensibilities and perspective over the whole thing. Proto-feminist author Barbara Novak (Zellweger) writes a book proclaiming that women should claim their equality in the workplace by acting like men when it comes to sex. This puts a crimp in the style of Babe magnet/cad Catcher Block (McGregor), a magazine writer who conspires to expose her as an old-fashioned girl at heart. McGregor and Zellweger do a good job channelling Hudson and Day, and the production design and costumes perfectly capture the movie version of 1962 Manhattan that never existed in real life. Pierce is perfect in the old Tony Randall role. **94m/C VHS, DVD.** *US* Renee Zellweger, Ewan McGregor, David Hyde Pierce, Sarah Paulson, Tony Randall, Jack Plotnick, Rachel Dratch, John Aylward, Jeri Ryan, Melissa George, Florence Stanley, Laura Kightlinger; ***D:*** Peyton Reed; ***W:*** Dennis Drake, Eve Ahlert; ***C:*** Jeff Cronenweth; ***M:*** Marc Shaiman.

Downdraft **1996 (R)** A special forces unit has six hours to penetrate a subterranean bunker, which protects a supercomputer that's about to launch a nuclear attack. Assaulted by a variety of sophisticated weapons, the unit must also outwit the computer's android defender. **101m/C VHS.** *HK* Jackie Chan, Paul Chang, Wai-Man Chan, Vincent Spano, Kate Vernon, Paul Koslo; ***D:*** Jackie Chan; ***W:*** Jackie Chan; ***C:*** Chung-Yuen Chan, Chin-Kui Chen.

Downfall **1/2** *Der Untergang* **2004 (R)** Controversial German film explores the last days of Hitler (Ganz) and his cronies in the bunker before the fall of Berlin in 1945. Overlong but engrossing look at the mundane, very human face of evil. Ganz is amazing in the role of a lifetime, virtually becoming the most hated man in history. All the smaller roles, Hitler's secretary Traudl Junge (Lara) for instance, are wonderfully fleshed out by an incredibly talented cast. **155m/C DVD.** *GE* Bruno Ganz, Agustin Lara, Corinna Harfouch, Ulrich Matthes, Heino Ferch, Christian Berkel, Matthias Habich, Thomas Kretschmann, Ulrich Noethen, Goetz Otto, Juliane Koehler, Donevan Gunia; ***D:*** Oliver Hirschbiegel; ***W:*** Bernd Eichinger; ***C:*** Rainer Klausmann; ***M:*** Stephan Zacharias.

Downhill Racer **1/2 1969 (PG)** An undisciplined American skier locks ski-tips with his coach and his new-found love while on his way to becoming an Olympic superstar. Character study on film. Beautiful ski and mountain photography keep it from sliding downhill. **102m/C VHS.** Robert Redford, Camilla Sparv, Gene Hackman, Dabney Coleman; ***D:*** Michael Ritchie.

Downhill Willie **1/2 1996 (PG)** Willie (Coogan) isn't the brightest guy around—except on skies. Now he wants to enter the Kamikaze Run, which takes place on an extreme race course, and win the half-million top prize as well as the prettiest snow bunny (Keanan) on the slopes. **90m/C VHS, DVD.** Keith Coogan, Staci Keanan, Lochlyn Munro, Estelle Harris, Fred Stoller, Lee Reherman; ***D:*** David Mitchell; ***W:*** Stephanie Cedar; ***C:*** David Pelletier; ***M:*** Norman Orenstein.

Downloading Nancy **1/2 2008** Deeply disturbing drama about a suicidal incest 'survivor' with a death wish. Nancy (Bello) was sexually abused as a child by her uncle and her rage and despair have remained despite therapy. Married to Albert (Sewell), an emotionally cold businessman, Nancy self-mutilates, eventually getting into the s/m scene via online chatrooms. It's here Nancy contacts Louis (Patric) who vows to honor her desire for death despite his attraction to her after they finally meet in person. Bello's performance is fearless but to no particular end since Nancy's only aim is to die, which isn't necessarily compelling to watch. **102m/C DVD.** *US* Maria Bello, Jason Patric, Rufus Sewell, Amy Brenneman, Michael Nyquist; ***D:*** Johan Renck; ***W:*** Pamela Cuming, Lee H. Ross; ***C:*** Christopher Doyle; ***M:*** Krister Linder.

Downtown **1/2 1989 (R)** Urban comedy about a naive white suburban cop who gets demoted to the roughest precinct in Philadelphia, and gains a streetwise black partner. Runs a routine beat. **96m/C VHS, DVD.** Anthony Edwards, Forest Whitaker, Joe

Pantoliano, Penelope Ann Miller; *D:* Richard Benjamin; *M:* Alan Silvestri.

D.P. **1985** A black orphan attaches to the only other black in post-WWII Germany. From a story by Kurt Vonnegut Jr. **60m/C VHS.** Stan Shaw, Rosemary Leach, Julius Gordon. **TV**

Drachenfutter *Dragon's Food; Dragon Chow* **1987** Powerful story dealing with a Pakistani immigrant's attempts to enter the Western world. Themes of alienation and helplessness are emphasized. Dialogues occur in 12 languages, predominantly German and Mandarin Chinese; subtitled in English. **75m/B VHS.** *GE SI* Bhasker, Ric Young, Buddy Uzzaman; *D:* Jan Schutte; *W:* Thomas Strittmatter; *M:* Claus Bantzer.

Dracula (Spanish Version) ½ **1931** Filmed at the same time as the Bela Lugosi version of "Dracula," using the same sets and the same scripts, only in Spanish. Thought to be more visually appealing and more terrifying than the English-language counterpart. The only thing it's missing is a presence like Lugosi. Based on the novel by Bram Stoker. **104m/B VHS, DVD.** Carlos Villarias, Lupita Tovar, Eduardo Arozamena, Pablo Alvarez Rubio, Barry Norton, Carmen Guerrero; *D:* George Melford; *W:* Garrett Fort.

Dracula **1931** Lugosi, in his most famous role, plays a vampire who terrorizes the countryside in his search for human blood. From Bram Stoker's novel. Although short of a masterpiece due to slow second half, deservedly rated a film classic. What would Halloween be like without this movie? Sequelled by "Dracula's Daughter." The 1999 re-release was re-scored by Philip Glass and performed by the Kronos Quartet. **75m/B VHS, DVD.** Bela Lugosi, David Manners, Dwight Frye, Helen Chandler, Edward Van Sloan, Frances Dade, Herbert Bunston; *D:* Tod Browning; *W:* Garrett Fort; *C:* Karl Freund. Natl. Film Reg. '00.

Dracula ½ *Bram Stoker's Dracula* **1973** Count on squinty-eyed Palance to shine as the Transylvanian vampire who must quench his thirst for human blood. Adaptation of the Bram Stoker novel that really flies. **105m/C VHS, DVD.** Jack Palance, Simon Ward, Fiona Lewis, Nigel Davenport, Pamela Brown, Penelope Horner, Murray Brown, Virginia Wetherell, Sarah Douglas, Barbara Lindley; *D:* Dan Curtis; *W:* Richard Matheson; *C:* Oswald Morris; *M:* Wojciech Kilar. **TV**

Dracula ½ **1979 (R)** Langella recreates his Broadway role as the count who needs human blood for nourishment. Notable for its portrayal of Dracula as a romantic and tragic figure in history. Overlooked since the vampire spoof "Love at First Bite" came out at the same time. **109m/C VHS, DVD.** Frank Langella, Laurence Olivier, Kate Nelligan, Donald Pleasence, Janine Duvitsky, Trevor Eve, Tony Haygarth; *D:* John Badham; *W:* W.D. Richter; *C:* Gilbert Taylor; *M:* John Williams.

Dracula **2006** Nonsensical adaptation of the Dracula story that uses little of Stoker's tale (and much ridiculous invention). Lord Holmwood (Stevens) discovers he has syphilis, which endangers his marriage to Lucy (Myles). Apparently inviting the fanged one (Warren)—who seems to now be a member of a sinister blood cult—to England will offer a potential cure. **90m/C DVD.** Marc Warren, Dan Stevens, Sophia Myles, David Suchet, Tom Burke, Stephanie Leonidas, Rafe Spall; *D:* Bill Eagles; *W:* Stewart Harcourt; *M:* Dominik Scherrer. **TV**

Dracula 2: Ascension ½ *Wes Craven Presents Dracula 2: Ascension* **2003 (R)** Wheelchair-bound medical scientist Lowell (Sheffer) and his students decide to use the blood from Dracula's burned corpse (from the first film, which is now in the local New Orleans morgue) to find a cure for Lowell's paralysis. But it's always a mistake to resurrect a vampire. Lame sequel to the "Dracula 2000" film has a cliffhanger ending to be resolved in "Dracula 3: Legacy." **85m/C VHS, DVD.** Jason Scott Lee, Jason London, Craig Sheffer, Diane Neal, Stephen Billington, Roy Scheider, Rutger Hauer; *D:* Patrick Lussier; *W:* Patrick Lussier, Joel Soisson; *C:* Doug Milsome; *M:* Kevin Kliesch. **VIDEO**

Dracula 3: Legacy **2005 (R)** Badass Father Uffizi (Lee) is back, accompanied by sidekick Luke (London), and they travel to Transylvania to hunt Dracula (Hauer) at his castle and get rid of him once and for all. Lots of action and a healthy helping of cheese. If you've seen the first two installments, you know what to expect. **90m/C DVD.** Jason Scott Lee, Jason London, Rutger Hauer, Roy Scheider, Diane Neal, Alexandra Wescourt; *D:* Patrick Lussier; *W:* Patrick Lussier, Joel Soisson; *C:* Doug Milsome; *M:* Kevin Kliesch, Cieri Torjussen. **VIDEO**

Dracula A.D. 1972 *Dracula Today* **1972** Lee returned to England for his sixth (and by most accounts, worst) go-round as Dracula for Hammer Films, where the creative juices seemed to be drying up. The decision was made to turn Dracula loose in the modern world. The movie actually opens in 1872 with a scene that is one of the highlights of the entire production—an action scene that features Dracula battling his nemesis Van Helsing (Cushing) atop a speeding stagecoach. When the coach is wrecked, Dracula is impaled on a wheel spoke and dies. From that point, the scene immediately jumps ahead one century. A Satanist named Johnny Alucard and a group of naive hippie teenagers revive the long-dead vampire in an abandoned church building in England. The teens and Dracula are opposed by Van Helsing's grandson (Cushing again) and his granddaughter Jessica (Beacham). Hammer's unwillingness to pay Lee to speak more than a few lines, together with a sterile plot that had Dracula essentially paralyzed by the modern world, forced the teenagers to carry the story. It appears that the idea for *Dracula A.D. 1972* came from the Count Yorga movies, which had some success in placing an Old World vampire in modern Los Angeles. However, the Yorga movies were only moderately successful and this Hammer copy did not even do that well. *Dracula A.D. 1972* was the sequel to *The Scars of Dracula* (1971) and was followed by *The Satanic Rites of Dracula* (1973). **95m/C VHS, DVD.** *GB* Christopher Lee, Peter Cushing, Christopher Neame, Stephanie Beacham, Michael Coles, Caroline Munro, Marsha A. Hunt, Philip Miller, Janet Key, William Ellis; *D:* Alan Gibson; *W:* Don Houghton; *C:* Dick Bush; *M:* Michael Vickers.

Dracula and Son ½ *Dracula Pere et Fils* **1976** Badly dubbed French satire finds the elegant Count (Lee) deciding that beautiful Hermaine (Marie-Helene Breillat) would be the perfect vampire mommy. Thus Dracula's son Ferdinand is born. Some 300 years later, Ferdinand (Menez) is proving to be a trial to his father, since he has yet to drink anyone's blood. Driven from their castle, the Count winds up in London and becomes a star in vampire films, while Ferdinand lives in Paris. When the two reunite, it's to feud over the beautiful Nicole (Catherine Breillat), who happens to be a dead ringer for Hermaine. Based on the novel "Paris Vampire" by Claude Klotz. **70m/C VHS.** *FR* Christopher Lee, Bernard Menez, Catherine Breillat, Marie Breillat; *D:* Edouard Molinaro; *W:* Edouard Molinaro.

Dracula Blows His Cool **1982 (R)** Three voluptuous models and their photographer restore an ancient castle and open a disco in it. The vampire lurking about the castle welcomes the party with his fangs. **91m/C VHS, DVD.** John Garco, Betty Verges; *D:* Carlo Ombra; *W:* Carlo Ombra.

Dracula: Dead and Loving It **WOOF!** **1995 (PG-13)** King of the spoofs Nielsen takes on the title role as the ever-loving, if clumsy, Count who still enjoys necking—particularly with luscious damsels in distress, Lucy (Anthony) and Mina (Yasbeck). And he's still got his bug-eating minion Renfield (MacNichol) and egomaniacal vampire-hunter Van Helsing (Brooks) around. As usual, Brooks throws everything possible on the screen, hoping some schtick will stick (not very much does). **90m/C VHS, DVD.** Leslie Nielsen, Mel Brooks, Peter MacNichol, Lysette Anthony, Amy Yasbeck, Steven Weber, Harvey Korman, Anne Bancroft, Darla Haun, Megan Cavanagh, Mark Blankfield, Clive Revill; *D:* Mel Brooks; *W:* Rudy DeLuca, Steve Haberman, Mel Brooks; *C:* Michael D. O'Shea; *M:* Hummie Mann.

Dracula Has Risen from the Grave ½ **1968 (G)** Lee's Dracula is foiled by the local priest before he can drain the blood from innocent villagers. Effectively gory. One of the Hammer series of Dracula films followed by "Taste the Blood of Dracula." **92m/C VHS, DVD.** *GB* Christopher Lee, Rupert Davies, Veronica Carlson, Barbara Ewing, Barry Andrews, Michael Ripper, Ewan Hooper, Marion Mathie; *D:* Freddie Francis; *W:* John (Anthony Hinds) Elder; *C:* Arthur Grant; *M:* James Bernard.

Dracula, Prince of Darkness *The Bloody Scream of Dracula; Disciple of Dracula; Revenge of Dracula* **1966** Sequel to 1958's "Horror of Dracula" finds the Count (Lee) extending his hospitality at Castle Dracula to four unwary tourists, one of whom is immediately killed for his blood. Then Dracula takes the dead man's wife (Shelley) and turns her into a vampire and the gruesome twosome go after the remaining couple. Standard Hammer horror. **90m/C VHS, DVD.** *GB* Christopher Lee, Barbara Shelley, Andrew Keir, Francis Matthews, Suzan Farmer, Charles "Bud" Tingwell, Thorley Walters, Philip Latham; *D:* Terence Fisher; *W:* John Sansom, John (Anthony Hinds) Elder; *C:* Michael Reed; *M:* James Bernard.

Dracula Rising ½ **1993 (R)** A modern-day art historian (Travis) turns out to have been a witch, burned at the stake, in a past life. She was also the blood-drinking Count's lost love. Now Dracula's a monk and when he sees this reincarnated beauty is he going to be able to keep his hands—er, fangs—off her? **85m/C VHS, DVD.** Christopher Atkins, Stacey Travis, Doug Wert, Zahari Vatahov; *D:* Fred Gallo.

Dracula Sucks **1979 (R)** A soft-core edit of a hardcore sex parody about Dracula snacking on the usual bevy of screaming quasi-virgins. **90m/C VHS.** James Gillis, Reggie Nalder, Annette Haven, Kay Parker, Serena, Seka, John Leslie; *D:* Philip Marshak.

Dracula: The Dark Prince ½ *Dark Prince: The True Story of Dracula* **2001 (R)** Costume bio on the life of Vlad the Impalder AKA Vlad Dracula (Martin). In the 15th century, Vlad and his brother are captured by the Turkish sultan who rules over their native Romania. During their captivity, the boys' father (the country's regent) is killed and when Vlad returns home years later he seeks to expel the Turks and rule himself. But his dreams of a unified country are undermined by tragedy and his own brutality. **89m/C VHS, DVD.** Rudolf Martin, Jane March, Peter Weller, Roger Daltrey, Michael Sutton, Christopher Brand; *D:* Joe Chappelle; *W:* Thomas Baum; *C:* Dermott Downs; *M:* Frankie Blue. **CABLE**

Dracula 2000 *Wes Craven Presents: Dracula 2000* **2000 (R)** Dracula finds his way to New Orleans to terrorize the modern world in this adaptation of the classic vampire tale that borrows freewheelingly from many supernatural legends. Butler plays Dracula well enough, but doesn't add anything memorable to a character that's been done, redone, and overdone so many times, while Plummer struggles to make the most of a bad situation. Horror fans will no doubt enjoy the gore, but the overall clumsiness is hard to take by anyone's standards. Presented by Wes Craven, but directed by Patrick Lussier, Craven's editor on many films, including the "Scream" trilogy. **98m/C VHS, DVD.** Jonny Lee Miller, Justine Waddell, Gerard Butler, Colleen (Ann) Fitzpatrick, Jennifer Esposito, Danny Masterson, Jeri Ryan, Lochlyn Munro, Sean Patrick Thomas, Omar Epps, Christopher Plummer; *D:* Patrick Lussier; *W:* Joel Soisson; *C:* Peter Pay; *M:* Marco Beltrami.

Dracula vs. Frankenstein *Assignment: Terror* **1969** An alien reanimates Earth's most infamous monsters in a bid to take over the planet. Rennie's last role. **91m/C VHS, DVD.** *IT GE SP* Michael Rennie, Paul Naschy, Karin Dor, Patty (Patti) Shepard, Craig Hill; *D:* Hugo Fregonese, Tulio Demicheli; *W:* Paul Naschy.

Dracula vs. Frankenstein **WOOF!** *Blood of Frankenstein; They're Coming to Get You; Dracula Contra Frankenstein; The Revenge of Dracula; Satan's Bloody Freaks* **1971 (PG)** The Count makes a deal with a shady doctor to keep him in blood. Vampire spoof that's very bad but fun. Last film for both Chaney and Naish. Features a cameo by genre maven Forrest J. Ackerman. **90m/C VHS, DVD.** *SP* J. Carrol Naish, Lon Chaney Jr., Regina Carrol, Russ Tamblyn, Jim Davis, Anthony Eisley, Zandor Vorkov, John Bloom, Angelo Rossitto, Forrest J Ackerman; *D:* Al Adamson; *W:* William Pugsley, Sam M. Sherman; *C:* Paul Glickman, Gary Graver; *M:* William Lava.

Dracula's Daughter **1936** Count Dracula's daughter, Countess Marya Zaleska, heads to London supposedly to find the cure to a mysterious illness. Instead she finds she has a taste for human blood, especially female blood. She also finds a man, falls in love, and tries to keep him by casting a spell on him. A good script and cast keep this sequel to Bela Lugosi's "Dracula" entertaining. **71m/B VHS, DVD.** Gloria Holden, Otto Kruger, Marguerite Churchill, Irving Pichel, Edward Van Sloan, Nan Grey, Hedda Hopper; *D:* Lambert Hillyer; *W:* Garrett Fort; *C:* George Robinson.

Dracula's Great Love **WOOF!** *Gran Amore del Conde Dracula; Count Dracula's Great Love; Dracula's Virgin Lovers; Vampire Playgirls* **1972 (R)** Four travellers end up in Dracula's castle for the night, where the horny Count takes a liking to one of the women. Left out in the sun too long. **96m/C VHS, DVD.** *SP* Paul Naschy, Charo Soriano, Haydee Politoff, Rossana Yanni, Ingrid Garbo, Mirta Miller; *D:* Javier Aguirre; *W:* Javier Aguirre, Paul Naschy.

Dracula's Last Rites **WOOF!** *Last Rites* **1979 (R)** Blood-curdling tale of a sheriff and a mortician in a small town who are up to no good. Technically inept: film equipment can be spotted throughout. Don't stick your neck out for this one. **86m/C VHS.** Patricia Lee Hammond, Gerald Fielding, Victor Jorge; *D:* Domonic Paris.

Dracula's Widow **1988 (R)** Countess Dracula, missing her hubby and desperately in need of a substitute, picks innocent Raymond as her victim. His girlfriend and a cynical cop fight to save his soul from the Countess' damnation. Directed by the nephew of Frances Ford Coppola. **85m/C VHS.** Sylvia Kristel, Josef Sommer, Lenny Von Dohlen, George Stover; *D:* Christopher Coppola.

Drag Me to Hell **2009 (PG-13)** Raimi returns to his lower-budget over-the-top horror roots. In order to impress her boss, L.A. loan officer Christine Brown (Lohman) refuses to allow Mrs. Ganush (Raver) a loan extension on her home. Big mistake since the elderly gypsy places a curse on Christine that involves an evil spirit that starts destroying her life and in three days—well, you can see what'll happen from the title. Lots of gross-out moments, delivered in Raimi's tongue-in-cheek schlock style with Lohman being a particularly good sport considering what her character goes through (mud, bugs, and projectile vomiting included). **99m/C DVD.** *US* Alison Lohman, Justin Long, Lorna Raver, David Paymer, Dileep Rao, Adriana Barraza, Chelcie Ross, Reggie Lee; *D:* Sam Raimi; *W:* Sam Raimi, Ivan Raimi; *C:* Peter Deming; *M:* Christopher Young.

Dragnet ½ **1954** Sgt. Joe Friday and Officer Frank Smith try to solve a mob slaying but have a rough time. Alexander plays the sidekick in "Dragnet" pre-Morgan days. Just the facts: feature version of the TV show that's suspenseful and well-acted. **88m/C VHS.** Jack Webb, Ben Alexander, Richard Boone, Ann (Robin) Robinson; *D:* Jack Webb.

Dragnet **1987 (PG-13)** Semi-parody of the vintage '60s TV cop show. Sgt. Joe Friday's straitlaced nephew (Aykroyd) and his sloppy partner Pep (Hanks) take on a crooked reverend (Plummer) and a pagan organization called, well, P.A.G.A.N. Neither Aykroyd nor Hanks can save this big-budget but lackluster spoof that's full of holes, although they both have their moments. **106m/C VHS, DVD.** Dan Aykroyd, Tom Hanks, Christopher Plummer, Harry (Henry) Morgan, Elizabeth Ashley, Dabney Coleman, Alexandra Paul, Kathleen Freeman, Jack O'Halloran; *D:* Tom Mankiewicz; *W:* Tom Mankiewicz, Alan Zweibel, Dan Aykroyd; *C:* Matthew F. Leonetti; *M:* Ira Newborn.

Dragon Fury ½ **1995** Evil dictator tries to conquer what remains of America in the year 2099—a world peopled by barbarians and victims of a deadly plague. Naturally, there's a martial arts hero around to stop him.

80m/C VHS. Robert Chapin, Richard Lynch, Chona Jason, Deborah Stamble; *D:* David Heavener.

Dragon Fury 2 ♂ 1/2 **1996** Futuristic action finds a heroic female struggling alone against a violent gang who want to rule the world (with the help of a computer chip). But a scientist unthaws an ancient warrior to help her out. Of course, things don't go exactly as expected. **90m/C VHS.** Mike Norris, Robert Chapin, Cathleen Ann Gardner, Cole Andersen, Walter O'Neill, Kayla Murphy; *D:* Bryan Michael Stoller; *W:* Parker Bostwick.

Dragon Lord ♂ **1982** Young kung-fu hero (Chan) defends his village against greedy outlaws. Comic interludes tend to slow the action. **90m/C VHS, DVD.** Jackie Chan.

The Dragon Painter ♂♂ **1919** Provincial painter Tatsu (Hayakawa) is obsessed with painting dragons, believing that his fantasy princess was captured by such a beast. Celebrated Tokyo artist Kano Indara (Peil) is looking for an apprentice and Tatsu accepts after meeting Kano's daughter Ume Ko (Aoki), whom he believes is his lost princess. They marry and Tatsu is so happy he gives up painting, so Ume Ko decides she must leave him for the sake of his art. **53m/B DVD.** Sessue Hayakawa, Edward Peil Sr., Toyo Fujita, Tsuru Aoki; *D:* William Worthington; *W:* Richard Schayer; *C:* Frank D. Williams.

Dragon Seed ♂♂ 1/2 **1944** The lives of the residents of a small Chinese village are turned upside down when the Japanese invade it. Based on the Pearl S. Buck novel. Lengthy and occasionally tedious, though generally well-made with heart-felt attempts to create Oriental characters, without having Asians in the cast. **145m/B VHS, DVD.** Katharine Hepburn, Walter Huston, Agnes Moorehead, Akim Tamiroff, Hurd Hatfield, J. Carrol Naish, Henry Travers, Turhan Bey, Aline MacMahon; *D:* Jack Conway.

Dragon Storm ♂ 1/2 **2004 (PG-13)** In this Sci-Fi Channel original production, medieval men must fight to free the planet from an other-worldly infestation of fearsome, foul, flying, fire-breathing alien dragons. And they didn't even call first! **92m/C VHS, DVD.** Tony Amendola, Angel Boris, Maxwell Caulfield, Jeff Rank, Iskra Angelova, Maxim Gentchev, Ivaylo Geraskov, John Hansson, Woon Young Park, Tyrone Pinkham, John Rhys-Davies, Richard Wharton; *D:* Stephen Furst; *W:* Patrick Phillips. **CABLE**

Dragon: The Bruce Lee Story ♂♂♂ **1993 (PG-13)** Entertaining, inspiring account of the life of Chinese-American martial-arts legend Bruce Lee. Jason Scott Lee (no relation) is great as the talented artist, exuding his joy of life and gentle spirit, before his mysterious brain disorder death at the age of 32. Ironically, this release coincided with son Brandon's accidental death on a movie set. The martial arts sequences in "Dragon" are extraordinary, but there's also romance as Lee meets and marries his wife (Holly, who acquits herself well). Based on the book "Bruce Lee: The Man Only I Knew" by his widow, Linda Lee Caldwell. **121m/C VHS, DVD.** Jason Scott Lee, Lauren Holly, Robert Wagner, Michael Learned, Nancy Kwan, Kay Tong Lim, Sterling Macer, Ric Young, Sven-Ole Thorsen; *D:* Rob Cohen; *W:* Edward Khmara, John Raffo, Rob Cohen; *C:* David Eggby; *M:* Randy Edelman.

Dragon Wars ♂ 1/2 *D-War; Dragon Wars: D-War* **2007 (PG-13)** Originally announced in 2002 but not released until five years later, this pic wracked up a massive budget that made it the most expensive Korean film ever made. Unfortunately it's far from the best. Apparently every 500 years a girl is born who can change an Imoogi (giant snake) into a celestial dragon. An evil Imoogi (Buraki) has attempted to kidnap her in the past, and attempts to do so again in the modern day. Thankfully she has some college kid to protect her from the evil 300-foot-long snake and his enormous army of monsters. Worth seeing for the monster attack scenes, but don't try following the plot. **90m/C DVD, Blu-ray Disc, UMD.** *KN* Jason Behr, Amanda Brooks, Robert Forster, Craig Robinson, Aimee Garcia, Chris Mulkey, John Ales, Elizabeth Pena, Billy Gardell, Cody Arens, Craig Anton, Hyun Jin Park, Hyojin Ban, Ji-hwan Min, Jongman Lee, Kyuho Moon, Cheyenne Alexis Dean, Roberta Farkas, Ethan Grant, Kerry Liu, Richard Steen; *D:* Hyung Rae Shim; *W:* Hyung Rae Shim; *C:* Hubert Taczanowski; *M:* Steve Jablonsky.

Dragonard ♂ 1/2 **1988 (R)** Slaves on a West Indies island rebel against their cruel masters. **93m/C VHS.** Eartha Kitt, Oliver Reed, Annabel Schofield, Patrick Warburton; *D:* Gerard Kikoine; *W:* R.J. Marx.

Dragonball: Evolution ♂ **2009 (PG)** Based on the popular Japanese manga created by Akira Toriyama, whose work spawned best selling graphic novels, video games, and a phenomenally successful television series. The live-action adventure centers on a team of warriors, each of whom possesses special abilities. Teenager Goku (Chatwin) must find Master Roshi (Chow) and gather all seven dragonballs before evil Lord Piccolo (Marsters) does so that he can prevent him from taking over the world. Unfortunately pic relies on martial arts action and uneven, unimpressive CGI. Only saved by a few entertaining fight scenes, which basically relegate it to a not-so-good video game. A complete waste of Hong Kong legend Chow Yun Fat's talent with horrible dialogue and enough cliches to choke a dragon. **84m/C DVD.** Justin Chatwin, James Marsters, Chow Yun-Fat, Emmy Rossum, Ernie Hudson, Randall Duk Kim, Texas Battle; *D:* James Wong; *W:* James Wong; *C:* Robert McLachlan; *M:* Brian Tyler.

Dragonfight ♂ 1/2 **1990 (R)** Corporations rule the world and vie for supremacy through gladiator combat in this action-adventure saga set in the near future. Fights are to the death and when the current champ refuses a new challenger the corporate honchos decide to provoke him into battle by having the challenger mow down innocent bystanders. Several execs also decide the slaughter has to stop but they may be the next targets. **84m/C VHS.** Robert Z'Dar, Michael Pare, Paul Coufos, Charles Napier, James Hong, Alexa Hamilton, Fawna MacLaren; *D:* Warren A. Stevens; *W:* Buddy Lewis; *C:* Curtis Petersen; *M:* Bob Mithoff.

Dragonfly ♂ 1/2 **2002 (PG-13)** I see dead performances. Cheesy, self-gratifying supernatural snorer has Costner as Chicago's dour ER doctor Joe Darrow, righteously widowed when his doctor wife bites the dust tending to the poor in Venezuela, while pregnant, no less. Unable to accept her death, Darrow is convinced she's trying to contact him from Beyond as he receives a series of cryptic messages, some from the children in his wife's pediatric oncology ward. Darrow's talking parrot provides some of the sillier scenes in this slow-paced, must-miss melodrama. Bates as the neighbor manages to liven up her scenes, anyway. Director Shadyac ("Patch Adams") certainly didn't want his lead here displaying any of his other doctor's kid-loving antics, and glum and glummer Costner is a dutiful downer as he pumps the kids in the ward for info about his dead wife. **103m/C VHS, DVD.** *US* Kevin Costner, Joe Morton, Susanna Thompson, Ron Rifkin, Linda Hunt, Kathy Bates, Jay Thomas, Matt Craven, Robert Bailey Jr., Lisa Banes, Jacob Smith; *D:* Tom Shadyac; *W:* David Seltzer, Brandon Camp, Mike Thompson; *C:* Dean Semler; *M:* John Debney.

Dragonfly Squadron ♂♂ **1954** Korean war drama about pilots and their romantic problems. Never gets off the ground. **82m/C VHS.** John Hodiak, Barbara Britton, Bruce Bennett, Jess Barker; *D:* Lesley Selander.

Dragonheart ♂♂ 1/2 **1996 (PG-13)** Okay, get past the fact that Connery's Scottish burr is coming out of the teeth-filled mouth of an 18 ft. tall, 43 ft. long dragon and you'll be well on your way to enjoying this 10th-century fantasy. Knightly Bowen (Quaid) is the one-time mentor of evil-hearted King Einon (Thewlis) and it's up to him, Draco the dragon, feisty Kara (Meyer), and some fearful peasants to band together and free themselves from the king's tyranny. There's some slow spots but Bowen and Draco make for an amusing pairing and the dragon does seem, well, real. Work on Draco took more than a year of Industrial Light & Magic's expertise. **103m/C VHS, DVD, HD DVD.** Dennis Quaid, David Thewlis, Pete Postlethwaite, Dina Meyer, Julie Christie, Jason Isaacs, Brian Thompson, Wolf Christian, Terry O'Neill; *D:* Rob Cohen; *W:* Charles Edward Pogue; *C:* David Eggby; *M:* Randy Edelman; *V:* Sean Connery, John Gielgud.

Dragonheart: A New Beginning ♂♂ **2000 (PG)** Geoff (Masteron) is a monastery stableboy who wants to become a knight. Then he discovers Friar Peter (Woodnutt) has secretly been raising a young dragon called Drake (voiced by Benson). When the evil Lord Osric (Van Gorkum) learns of the beast's existence, he wants to claim its powers for himself. But Geoff, who's aided by two mysterious warriors from the east, is determined to save both Drake and the kingdom. **85m/C VHS, DVD.** Christopher K. Masterson, Henry O, Harry Van Gorkum, John Woodnutt, Rona Figueroa, Ken Shorter; *D:* Doug Lefler; *W:* Shari Goodhartz; *C:* Buzz Feitshans IV; *V:* Robby Benson. **VIDEO**

Dragons Forever ♂ 1/2 *Dragon Forever* **1988** A big time lawyer is persuaded to work against a chemical plant who wants to take over a site used by local fisherman. Complications arise when he falls for the beautiful cousin of the fishery's owner. A comic king-fu battle between Chan, Hung, and Biao is the rousing finale. In Cantonese with English subtitles. **88m/C VHS, DVD.** *CH* Jackie Chan, Yuen Biao, Sammo Hung, Pauline Yeung, Yuen Wah; *D:* Sammo Hung, Corey Yuen; *W:* Roy Szeto, Gordon Chan.

Dragonslayer ♂♂♂ **1981 (PG)** A sorcerer's apprentice suddenly finds himself the only person who can save the kingdom from a horrible, fire-breathing dragon. Extreme violence but wonderful special effects, smart writing, and a funny performance by Richardson. **110m/C VHS, DVD.** Peter MacNichol, Caitlin Clarke, Ralph Richardson, John Hallam, Albert Salmi, Chloe Salaman; *D:* Matthew Robbins; *W:* Matthew Robbins, Hal Barwood; *M:* Alex North.

Dragonworld ♂♂ 1/2 **1994 (PG)** Five-year-old Johnny McGowan is sent to Scotland to live with his grandfather. A wish for a friend has Johnny mysteriously awakening a baby dragon he names Yowler. Years later, the financially strapped adult Johnny agrees to loan Yowler to an amusement park only to find out the park's owner never intends to give Yowler back. Both baby dragon and young Johnny are unbearably cute. **86m/C VHS.** Sam Mackenzie, Courtland Mead, Brittney Powell, John Calvin, Andrew Keir, Lila Kaye, John Woodvine; *D:* Ted Nicolaou; *W:* Ted Nicolaou, Suzanne Glazener Naha; *M:* Richard Band.

Dragonwyck ♂♂ **1946** In the 1840s, wealthy Nicholas Van Ryn (Price) is living on an estate called Dragonwyck in the Hudson Valley. He's unhappily married and blames wife Abigail (Revere) for not giving him a son and heir. When his beautiful distant cousin Miranda (Tierney) comes to be a companion to his daughters, it isn't long before Nicholas is a widower. Naive Miranda eventually becomes his bride but things don't work out very well for her either until local doctor Turner (Langan) becomes suspicious. Mankiewicz's directorial debut; adapted from the Anya Seton novel. **103m/B DVD.** Vincent Price, Gene Tierney, Walter Huston, Glenn Langan, Anne Revere, Spring Byington, Harry (Henry) Morgan; *D:* Joseph L. Mankiewicz; *W:* Joseph L. Mankiewicz; *C:* Arthur C. Miller; *M:* Alfred Newman.

Dragstrip Girl ♂♂ **1957** An 18-year-old girl comes of age while burning rubber at the dragstrip—the world of boys, hot rods, and horsepower. A definite "B" movie that may seem dated. **70m/B VHS.** Paul Blaisdell, Fay Spain, Steven Terrell, John Ashley, Frank Gorshin; *D:* Edward L. Cahn.

Dragstrip Girl ♂♂ 1/2 **1994** Remake of the 1857 "B" movie; a part of Showtime's Rebel Highway series. Latino Johnny (Dacasos) works as a valet during the day and goes drag racing at night. He's got big plans that may be derailed by rich white girl Laura (Wagner) who likes taking a walk on the wild side. **82m/C VHS, DVD.** Mark Dacascos, Natasha Gregson Wagner, Raymond Cruz, Traci Lords; *D:* Mary Lambert; *W:* Jerome Gary; *C:* Sandi Sissel. **CABLE**

The Drake Case ♂♂ **1929** A slight courtroom drama made during the waning days of the silent era. You'll probably recognize Brit Lloyd from her later career. **56m/B VHS.** Robert Frazer, Doris Lloyd, Gladys Brockwell; *D:* Edward Laemmle; *W:* Charles Logue; *C:* Jerome Ash.

The Draughtsman's Contract ♂♂♂ **1982 (R)** A beguiling mystery begins when a wealthy woman hires an artist to make drawings of her home. Their contract is quite unusual, as is their relationship. Everything is going along at an even pace until murder is suspected, and things spiral down to darker levels. A simple story turned into a bizarre puzzle. Intense enough for any thriller fan. **103m/C VHS, DVD.** *GB* Anthony (Corlan) Higgins, Janet Suzman, Anne Louise Lambert, Hugh Fraser; *D:* Peter Greenaway; *W:* Peter Greenaway; *C:* Sacha Vierny; *M:* Michael Nyman.

Draw! ♂♂ **1981** Two has-been outlaws warm up their pistols again in this old-fashioned Western. Star power and some smart moments make it worthwhile. Made for TV. **98m/C VHS.** Kirk Douglas, James Coburn, Alexandra Bastedo, Graham Jarvis; *D:* Steven Hilliard Stern.

Dream a Little Dream ♂♂ **1989 (PG-13)** Strange teen transformation drama about an old man and his wife trying mystically to regain their youth. When they collide bikes with the teenagers down the street, their minds are exchanged and the older couple with the now young minds are transported to a permanent dream-like state. Same old switcheroo made bearable by cast. **114m/C VHS, DVD.** Corey Feldman, Corey Haim, Meredith Salenger, Jason Robards Jr., Piper Laurie, Harry Dean Stanton, Victoria Jackson, Alex Rocco, William McNamara; *D:* Marc Rocco; *W:* Marc Rocco.

Dream a Little Dream 2 ♂ 1/2 **1994 (PG-13)** Friends Dinger Holefield (Haim) and Bobby Keller (Feldman) receive a mysterious package containing two pairs of sunglasses, which they discover have magic powers. The wearer of one pair is driven to do the bidding of the wearer of the second pair of specs—whether for good or evil. Naturally, there are evildoers who want the glasses as well. **91m/C VHS.** Corey Haim, Corey Feldman, Stacie Randall, Michael Nicolosi; *D:* James (Momel) Lemmo; *W:* David Weissman, Susan Forman.

The Dream Catcher ♂♂ 1/2 *The Dreamcatcher* **1999** With his girlfriend pregnant, Freddy (Compte) hits the road to look for his uncle, who might be able to give him some cash. With no car, he takes to hitchhiking and riding trains, and along the way befriends a klepto. When Freddy finds out his dad is out of prison. Quirky characters and a thoughtful script help this pleasing road flick along. **93m/C VHS, DVD.** Maurice Compte, Paddy Connor, Jeanne Heaton, Joseph Arthur, Larry John Meyers; *D:* Edward A. Radtke; *W:* Edward A. Radtke, M.S. Nieson; *C:* Terry Stacey; *M:* Georgiana Gomez.

Dream Chasers ♂ **1982 (PG)** A bankrupt old codger and an 11-year-old boy stricken with cancer run away together during the Great Depression. **97m/C VHS, DVD.** Wesley Bishop, Carolyn Carradine, Harold Gould, Justin Dana; *D:* Arthur Dubs, David E. Jackson; *W:* Wesley Bishop; *C:* Milas C. Hinshaw; *M:* William Loose.

Dream Date ♂♂ 1/2 **1993 (PG-13)** Lovely teenager is wooed by hip, playful suitor until trouble ensues when goofball sidekick enters the picture. Family entertainment. **96m/C VHS.** Tempestt Bledsoe, Clifton Davis, Kadeem Hardison, Anne-Marie Johnson, Pauly Shore, Richard Moll; *D:* Anson Williams.

Dream Demon ♂ **1988** The appearance of Wilhoite, a visiting American, disrupts the status quo at a spooky British manor where the charming Redgrave debates her impending marriage to wealthy rogue Greenstreet. Aside from a terrific opening dream sequence, most of the scary bits have been done before. **89m/C VHS.** *GB* Jemma Redgrave, Kathleen Wilhoite, Timothy Spall, Jimmy Nail, Mark Greenstreet; *D:* Harley Cokliss.

Dream for an Insomniac ♂ 1/2 **1996 (R)** Irritating characters put the kibbosh on this attempt at twentysomething romantic comedy. Whiny would-be actress Frankie (Skye) works at her Uncle Leo's (Cassel) cafe and hangs out with assorted, equally whiny friends. Frankie seems more interested in finding the "perfect" boyfriend than a career anyway and her interest is sparked by new guy David (a sweet Astin). Lots of overacting. Debut for writer/director DeBartolo. **108m/C VHS, DVD.** Ione Skye, MacKenzie Astin, Jennifer Aniston, Seymour Cassel, Michael Landes, Robert Kelker-Kelly; ***D:*** Tiffanie DeBartolo; ***W:*** Tiffanie DeBartolo; ***C:*** Guillermo Navarro; ***M:*** John Laraio.

A Dream for Christmas 1973 Earl Hamner Jr. (best known for writing the "The Waltons") wrote this moving story of a black minister whose church in Los Angeles is scheduled to be demolished. **100m/C VHS.** Hari Rhodes, Beah Richards, George Spell, Juanita Moore, Joel Fluellen, Robert DoQui, Clarence Muse; ***D:*** Ralph Senensky. **TV**

Dream House 1998 (R) This dream house of the future turns out to be a nightmare for its new owners. The supercomputer that runs everything has been misprogrammed and regards these humans as interlopers who must be killed. Tedious horror. **90m/C VHS.** *CA* Timothy Busfield, Jennifer Dale, Lisa Jakub; ***D:*** Graeme Campbell. **TV**

Dream Lover 1985 (R) Terrifying nightmares after an assault lead McNichol to dream therapy. Treatment causes her tortured unconscious desires to take over her waking behavior, and she becomes a violent schizophrenic. Slow, heavy, and not very thrilling. **105m/C VHS.** Kristy McNichol, Ben Masters, Paul Shenar, Justin Deas, Joseph Culp, Gayle Hunnicutt, John McMartin; ***D:*** Alan J. Pakula; ***W:*** Jon Boorstin; ***C:*** Sven Nykvist.

Dream Lover 1993 (R) Divorced architect Ray (Spader) meets and marries Lena (Amick), beautiful and seemingly perfect, who nonetheless warns him that she's just your average mixed-up gal. Suspense is supposed to come into play as Ray suspects Lena's been lying to him about her past. Visually appealing (considerably helped by the attractive leads) but good looks don't make up for the lack of substance and the minimal number of surprises expected in a thriller. Directorial debut of Kazan. Also available in an unrated version. **103m/C VHS, DVD.** James Spader, Madchen Amick, Frederic Lehne, Bess Armstrong, Larry Miller, Kathleen York, Blair Tefkin, Scott Coffey, William Shockley, Clyde Kusatsu; ***D:*** Nicholas Kazan; ***W:*** Nicholas Kazan; ***C:*** Jean-Yves Escoffier; ***M:*** Christopher Young.

Dream Lovers*Meng zhong ren* **1986** A supernatural love story which moves back and forth from contemporary Hong Kong to the mysterious Qin dynasty. When an orchestra conductor and the daughter of a noted architect meet at an exhibit featuring the famed terracotta army, an affair from the past is resurrected. In Cantonese with English subtitles. **95m/C VHS, DVD.** *CH* Chow Yun-Fat, Brigitte Lin, Cher Yeung; ***D:*** Tony Au; ***W:*** Yau Da Ah-Pin, Manfred Wong; ***C:*** Bill Wong.

Dream Machine 1/2 1991 (PG) A childish teen comedy, based on that old urban legend of the lucky kid given a free Porshe by the vengeful wife of a wealthy philanderer. The gimmick is that the husband's body is in the trunk; the murderer is in pursuit. The tape includes an anti-drug commerical—but nothing against reckless driving, which the picture glorifies. **88m/C VHS.** Corey Haim, Evan Richards, Jeremy Slate, Randall England, Tracy Fraim, Brittney Lewis, Susan Seaforth Hayes; ***D:*** Lyman Dayton.

Dream Man 1/2 1994 (R) Kris Anderson (Kensit) is a Seattle cop with the clairvoyant ability to see crimes as they're committed. But that doesn't stop her from getting involved with the handsome murder suspect (McCarthy) she's supposed to be investigating. **94m/C VHS.** Patsy Kensit, Andrew McCarthy, Bruce Greenwood; ***D:*** Rene Bonniere; ***W:*** Michael Alexander Miller; ***M:*** Graeme Coleman.

Dream No Evil 1/2 1970 A mentally disturbed woman is forced to commit bizarre murders to protect her warped fantasy world. **93m/C VHS, DVD.** Edmond O'Brien, Brooke Mills, Marc Lawrence, Arthur Franz; ***D:*** John Hayes; ***W:*** John Hayes; ***C:*** Paul Hipp; ***M:*** Jaime Mendoza-Nava.

A Dream of Kings 1969 (R) Quinn is exceptional in this Petrakis story of an immigrant working to get his dying son home to Greece. Last film appearance for Stevens before committing suicide at age 36. **107m/C VHS.** Anthony Quinn, Irene Papas, Inger Stevens, Sam Levene, Val Avery; ***D:*** Daniel Mann; ***M:*** Alex North.

A Dream of Passion 1/2 1978 (R) A woman imprisoned in Greece for murdering her children becomes the object of a publicity stunt for a production of "Medea," and she and the lead actress begin to exchange personalities. Artificial gobbledygook. **105m/C VHS.** *GR SI* Ellen Burstyn, Melina Mercouri, Andreas Voutsinas; ***D:*** Jules Dassin; ***W:*** Jules Dassin; ***C:*** Yorgos Arvanitis.

Dream Street 1921 A weak morality tale of London's lower classes. Two brothers, both in love with the same dancing girl, woo her in their own way, while a Chinese gambler plans to take her by force. Silent with music score. Based on Thomas Burke's "Limehouse Nights." **138m/B VHS.** Tyrone Power Sr., Carol Dempster, Ralph Graves, Charles Emmet Mack; ***D:*** D.W. Griffith.

The Dream Team 1/2 1989 (PG-13) On their way to a ball game, four patients from a mental hospital find themselves lost in New York City after their doctor is knocked out by murderers. Some fine moments from a cast of dependable comics. Watch for numerous nods to "One Flew Over the Cuckoo's Nest," another Lloyd feature. Keaton fans won't want to miss this one. **113m/C VHS, DVD.** Michael Keaton, Christopher Lloyd, Peter Boyle, Stephen Furst, Lorraine Bracco, Milo O'Shea, Dennis Boutsikaris, Philip Bosco, James Remar, Cynthia Belliveau; ***D:*** Howard Zieff; ***W:*** Jon Connolly, David Loucka; ***M:*** David McHugh.

D.R.E.A.M. Team 1999 (R) Garrison (Sheen) heads a secret United Nations agency that has uncovered terrorist activities in Puerto Rico involving a bomb laced with anthrax. He turns to CIA agent Zack (Kaake) to form a team of agents to stop the madness. Their cover just happens to be as models working on a fashion shoot, which means Zack gets to choose three babes to kick butt. **81m/C VHS, DVD.** Jeff Kaake, Angie Everhart, Traci Lords, Traci Bingham, Martin Sheen, Roger Moore, Ian McShane, James Remar; ***D:*** Dean Hamilton; ***W:*** Michael Snyder; ***M:*** Matthias Weber. **TV**

Dream to Believe 1985 Slice of the life of your typical high school coed—mom's dying, stepdad's from hell, sports injury hurts, and, oh yeah, championship gymnastic competitions loom. Designed to make you feel oh-so-good in that MTV kind of way. Reeves is most excellent as the girl's blushing beau. **96m/C VHS, DVD.** Rita Tushingham, Keanu Reeves, Olivia D'Abo, Jessica Steen; ***D:*** Paul Lynch.

Dream Trap 1/2 1990 A young man is obsessed with a girl in his dreams. When he meets a girl who really exists, fantasy louses up every opportunity for the real thing. **90m/C VHS.** Kristy Swanson, Sasha Jenson, Jeanie Moore; ***D:*** Tom Logan, Hugh Parks; ***W:*** Tom Logan.

Dream Wife 1953 A battle of the sexes comedy that doesn't seem quite so funny anymore. State department official Priscilla Effington (Kerr) is not willing to give up her career to marry Clemson Reade (Grant). A miffed Clem decides to make a formal marriage proposal to Princess Tarji (St. John), the daughter of the Khan (Franz) of oil-rich Bukistan where Clem previously worked. Effie is sent to Bukistan to solve an oil crisis and decides to inform Tarji about that whole female equality thing and suddenly Clem's perfect fiancee is thinking for herself. **99m/B DVD.** Cary Grant, Deborah Kerr, Walter Pidgeon, Betta St. John, Eduard Franz, Buddy Baer, Les Tremayne, Bruce Bennett, Richard Anderson; ***D:*** Sidney Sheldon; ***W:*** Sidney Sheldon, Herbert Baker, Alfred Lewis Levitt; ***C:*** Milton Krasner; ***M:*** Conrad Salinger.

Dream with the Fishes 1/2 1997 (R) Suicidal voyeur Terry (Arquette) is about to jump from a bridge when terminally ill thief Nick (Adams) strikes a strange deal with him. In exchange for funding a few of Nick's fantasies, he will kill Terry in a less messy way. After various strange escapades (including an unplanned robbery and nude bowling), the pair arrive in Nick's hometown, where he attempts to resolve old issues with an ex-girlfriend and his abusive father. As Nick's health fades, Terry reexamines his wish to die. As the story develops, the cliches of both the buddy and road movie genres fall away, letting you actually care about both of these guys. In an homage to the independent spirit of movies of the early 70s, the film stock copies their grainy look, gradually dissolving over the course of the movie to a clearer look. Debut for director Finn Taylor. **97m/C VHS, DVD.** David Arquette, Brad Hunt, Kathryn Erbe, Cathy Moriarty, Allyce Beasley, Patrick McGaw, J.E. Freeman; ***D:*** Finn Taylor; ***W:*** Finn Taylor; ***C:*** Barry Stone; ***M:*** Tito Larriva.

Dreamcatcher 1/2 2003 (R) Four childhood buddies with telepathic abilities bestowed on them by a mentally retarded boy they protected meet in the Maine woods for an annual hunting trip just in time for a body-snatching alien jamboree. Of course, the military is there, too, waiting for the chance to eliminate the aliens by toasting the town, literally. Convoluted story doesn't seem like an adaptation of King's novel, it's more like an adaptation of all of 'em, from "It" to "Stand By Me." With some "The Thing" and "Outbreak" thrown in for good measure. None of it works, unless you like bloody scenes of alien rectal excavation. **134m/C VHS, DVD.** *US* Morgan Freeman, Thomas Jane, Jason Lee, Damian Lewis, Timothy Olyphant, Tom Sizemore, Donnie Wahlberg, Michael O'Neill, Rosemary Dunsmore, Mike Holekamp, Reece Thompson, Giacomo Baessato, Joel Palmer, Andrew Robb; ***D:*** Lawrence Kasdan; ***W:*** Lawrence Kasdan, William Goldman; ***C:*** John Seale; ***M:*** James Newton Howard.

Dreamchild 1985 (PG) A poignant story of the autumn years of Alice Hargreaves, the model for Lewis Carroll's "Alice in Wonderland." Film follows her on a visit to New York in the 1930s, with fantasy sequences including Wonderland characters created by Jim Henson's Creature Shop invoking the obsessive Reverend Dodgson (a.k.a. Carroll). **94m/C VHS.** *GB* Coral Browne, Ian Holm, Peter Gallagher, Jane Asher, Nicola Cowper, Amelia Shankley, Caris Corfman, Shane Rimmer, James Wilby; ***D:*** Gavin Millar; ***W:*** Dennis Potter; ***C:*** Billy Williams; ***M:*** Max Harris, Stanley Myers.

Dreamer 1979 (PG) The excitement of bowling is exploited for all it's worth in this "strike or die" extravaganza. One of a kind. **86m/C VHS.** Tim Matheson, Susan Blakely, Jack Warden, Richard B. Shull; ***D:*** Noel Nosseck; ***W:*** Larry Bischof; ***M:*** Bill Conti.

Dreamer: Inspired by a True Story 1/2 2005 (PG) Family-friendly heart-warmer about a girl and her race horse. Ben Crane (Russell) has a failing Kentucky horse farm, so he's working as a trainer for stable owner Palmer (Morse). The stable's most promising filly Sonador ("Dreamer") breaks a leg during a race and is supposed to be put down, but Ben's plucky daughter Cale (Fanning) insists the horse is a keeper. So Ben quits his job, takes the filly as severance pay, and decides to not only nurse the horse back to health, but get her racing again. Well-matched cast with some especially good moments between Russell and Fanning. **98m/C DVD.** *US* Kurt Russell, Dakota Fanning, Kris Kristofferson, Elisabeth Shue, Luis Guzman, Freddy Rodriguez, David Morse, Oded Fehr, Ken Howard, Holmes Osborne; ***D:*** John Gatins; ***W:*** John Gatins; ***C:*** Fred Murphy; ***M:*** John Debney.

The Dreamers 2003 (NC-17) A carnal odyssey among a trio of cinephiles set against the political background of the 1968 Paris student riots. Matthew (Pitt), an impressionable American student, meets flirtatious Isabelle (Green) and her twin brother Theo (Garrel) at a protest march. He soon joins the siblings at their apartment even though he's uncomfortable at their closeness. Matthew's inhibitions dissolve as he begins a sexual relationship with Isabelle while there's increasing friction with the volatile Theo. Eventually, Matthew begins to question the insularity of the twins' privileged world. Bertolucci's a meticulous craftsman but here it's in the service of a sometimes overwrought romanticism. Screenwriter Adair adapted from his novel "The Holy Innocents." Some subtitled French. **115m/B VHS, DVD.** *US* Michael Pitt, Robin Renucci, Anna Chancellor, Mike Colter, Lucia Rijker, Florian Cadiou; ***D:*** Bernardo Bertolucci; ***W:*** Gilbert Adair; ***C:*** Fabio Cianchetti.

Dreamgirls 2006 (PG-13) The stage musical was coyly set in Chicago; Condon starts his movie off in 1962 Detroit, where three young black women—Effie (Hudson), Deena (Knowles), and Lorell (Rose)—are singing in a talent contest. Sharp wannabe manager Curtis Taylor Jr. (Foxx) takes them on as backup singers to soul shouter James Early (Murphy) and then sees the girl trio's potential to move into pop stardom, as long as the out-of-place Effie, who's a little too black, is replaced. Follows the up-and-down showbiz cliches with lots of intensity even if the music can't compare to the real Motown sound of the 60s and 70s. (Come on—as if the shades of Diana Ross and the Supremes aren't all over the plot.) Anyway, Hudson can belt out her big number, "And I Am Telling You I'm Not Going," with real heartache, and, man, Murphy just scorches the stage. **130m/C DVD, Blu-ray Disc, HD DVD.** *US* Jamie Foxx, Eddie Murphy, Beyonce Knowles, Anika Noni Rose, Jennifer Hudson, Danny Glover, Sharon Leal, Keith D. Robinson, Loretta Devine; ***D:*** Bill Condon; ***W:*** Bill Condon; ***C:*** Tobias Schliessler; ***M:*** Henry Krieger. Oscars '06: Sound, Support. Actress (Hudson); British Acad. '06: Support. Actress (Hudson); Golden Globes '07: Film—Mus./Comedy, Support. Actor (Murphy), Support. Actress (Hudson); Screen Actors Guild '06: Support. Actor (Murphy), Support. Actress (Hudson).

Dreaming About You 1/2 *Anoche Soñe Contigo* **1992** Teeangers Toto (Altomaro) and Quique (Mora) are spending their summer break biking around the neighborhood, dreaming about girls, and spying on Chabelita (Aguirre), Quique's family's pretty maid. But Toto will soon be doing more than dreaming when his attractive and experienced cousin Azucena (Perdigon) comes for a visit. Spanish with subtitles. **90m/C VHS, DVD.** *MX* Martin Altomaro, Moises Ivan Mora, Leticia Perdigon, Patricia Aguirre; ***D:*** Marisa Sistach; ***W:*** Jose Buil; ***C:*** Alex Phillips Jr.; ***M:*** Alberto Delgado.

Dreaming Lips 1/2 1937 An orchestra conductor's wife falls in love with her husband's violinist friend. Tragedy befalls the couple. Bergner outstanding in a familiar script. **70m/B VHS.** *GB* Raymond Massey, Elisabeth Bergner, Romney Brent, Joyce Bland, Charles Carson, Felix Aylmer; ***D:*** Lee Garmes, Paul Czinner; ***C:*** Lee Garmes.

Dreaming of Joseph Lees 1999 (R) Eva (Morton) has long had fantasies about her worldly older cousin Joseph Lees (Graves), but he's retreated from society after a terrible accident and lives in Italy. Meanwhile, lonely Eva is stuck in boring rural England in 1958. So she's willing to respond to the romantic gestures of working-class Harry Flyte (Ross) and, shockingly, decides to move in with him. Then Eva re-meets Joseph at a family wedding and, perversely, her desire for him only increases, which leads Harry to desperate measures. Strained symbolism pushes the plot but the accomplished performances take up the slack. **92m/C VHS.** *GB* Rupert Graves, Samantha Morton, Lee Ross, Miriam Margolyes, Frank Finlay, Nicholas Woodeson, Holly Aird; ***D:*** Eric Styles; ***W:*** Catherine Linstrum; ***C:*** Jimmy Dibling; ***M:*** Zbigniew Preisner.

Dreaming of Rita 1994 Bob (Oscarsson) named his daughter Rita after long-lost love Sabine's resemblance to Hollywood goddess, Rita Hayworth. Now an elderly widower, Bob suddenly decides to try and find Sabine, taking off across the Swedish countryside. The unhappily married Rita (Lagercrantz), leaving husband and children behind, goes after him—and meets sympathetic hitchhiker Erik (Ersgard), who's happy to offer a little romance. Swedish with subtitles. **108m/C VHS.** *SW* Per Oscarsson, Marika Lagercrantz, Patrick Ersgard, Philip Zanden; ***D:*** Jon Lindstrom; ***W:*** Jon Lindstrom, Rita Holst; ***C:*** Kjell Lagerros.

Dreaming Out Loud 1940 Screen debut of popular radio team Lum 'n Abner. The boys get involved in several capers to bring progress to their small Arkansas town. Rural wisecracks make for pleasant outing. First in film series for the duo. **65m/B VHS, DVD.** Frances Langford, Phil Harris, Clara Blandick, Robert Wilcox, Chester Lauck, Norris Goff, Frank Craven, Bobs Watson, Irving Bacon; ***D:*** Harold Young.

Dreamland 🦴🦴🦴 **2006 (PG-13)** Well-told (and cast) coming-of-age story. The title refers to the name of the New Mexico trailer park where 18-year-old Audrey (Bruckner) lives with her agoraphobic, hard-drinking, widowed dad Henry (Corbett). Because she's a natural caregiver, Audrey has put her college plans on hold and works at the local mini-mart while also looking out for her best friend Calista (Garner), whose beauty pageant dreams are hindered by her MS. When Mookie (Long) and his family move into the neighborhood, Audrey sets him and Calista up on a date even though she likes the guy herself—and discovers the feeling is mutual. **90m/C DVD.** Agnes Bruckner, Kelli Garner, Justin Long, John Corbett, Gina Gershon, Chris Mulkey, Brian Klugman; ***D:*** Jason Matzner; ***W:*** Tom Willett; ***C:*** Jonathan Sela; ***M:*** Anthony Marinelli.

The Dreamlife of Angels 🦴🦴🦴 *La Vie Revee des Anges* **1998** Deceptively simple debut from director Zouca follows the friendship of two opportunistic working class French women, Marie (Regnier) and Isa (Bouchez). Tensions between the two arise when Marie becomes involved with brutal nightclub owner Chriss (Cohn). Zouca had his female leads live together during filming to create the realistic bickering scenes. French with subtitles. **113m/C VHS, DVD.** *FR* Elodie Bouchez, Natacha Regnier, Gregoire Colin, Jo Prestia, Patrick Mercado; ***D:*** Erick Zonca; ***W:*** Erick Zonca, Roger Bohbot; ***C:*** Agnes Godard; ***M:*** Yann Tiersen. Cesar '99: Actress (Bouchez), Film.

Dreams 🦴🦴 *Kvinn odrom; Journey into Autumn* **1955** Unfocused film about the lives and loves of two successful women. Subtitled. **86m/B VHS.** *SW* Harriet Andersson, Gunnar Bjornstrand, Eva Dahlbeck, Ulf Palme; ***D:*** Ingmar Bergman; ***W:*** Ingmar Bergman; ***C:*** Hilding Bladh; ***M:*** Stuart Gorling.

Dreams Come True 🦴 **1984 (R)** Silly young comedy-romance about two young lovers who discover the trick of out-of-body travel, and have various forms of spiritual contact while their bodies are sleeping. **95m/C VHS.** Michael Sanville, Stephanie Shuford; ***D:*** Max Kalmanowicz.

Dreams Lost, Dreams Found 🦴 ½ **1987** A young widow journeys from the U.S. to Scotland in search of her heritage. The third "Harlequin Romance Movie." **102m/C VHS.** Kathleen Quinlan, Betsy Brantley, Charles Gray; ***D:*** Willi Patterson. **CABLE**

Dreams with Sharp Teeth 🦴🦴🦴 **2007** Documentarian Nelson had his hands full depicting such a larger-than-life character as writer Harlan Ellison. Ellison's immense body of work includes more than 2000 published stories as well as episodes for "The Outer Limits" and "Star Trek," but is nearly eclipsed by his own story. Described by friends as "a cranky old Jew" or "a skin graft on a leper" (in the case of good friend Robin Williams), Ellison no doubt has made a few enemies during his journey from runty Cleveland kid bullied by anti-semites to the self-made success, welcoming of any verbal joust, be it with a publishing executive or the driver in the next car. At its best, pic provides a view of the creative world of one of the most renowned popular writers of our time. **96m/C DVD.** *US* ***D:*** Erik Nelson; ***C:*** Wes Dorman; ***M:*** Richard Thompson.

Dreamscape 🦴🦴 ½ **1984 (PG-13)** When a doctor teaches a young psychic how to enter into other people's dreams in order to end their nightmares, somebody else wants to use this psychic for evil purposes. The special effects are far more convincing than the one man-saves-the-country-with-his-psychic-powers plot. **99m/C VHS, DVD, UMD.** Dennis Quaid, Max von Sydow, Christopher Plummer, Eddie Albert, Kate Capshaw, David Patrick Kelly, George Wendt, Jana Taylor; ***D:*** Joseph Ruben; ***W:*** Chuck Russell; ***C:*** Brian Tufano; ***M:*** Maurice Jarre.

Dresden 🦴🦴 ½ **2006** In 1945, German nurse Anna Mauth (Woll) discovers an injured British pilot, Robert Newman (Light), hiding in the hospital's cellar. She first helps him believing he's a German deserter, but even after discovering that Robert's an enemy combatant, Anna can't bring herself to betray him since they've fallen in love. But time is not on their side as the Allied bombing of the city of Dresden is about to begin. Made for German TV; English and German with subtitles. **180m/C DVD.** *GE* Heiner Lauterbach, Kai Wiesinger, Felicitas Woll, John Light, Benjamin Sadler, Katharina Meinecke, Marie Baumer; ***D:*** Roland Suso Richter; ***W:*** Stefan Kolditz; ***C:*** Holly Fink; ***M:*** Harald Kloser, Thomas Wanker. **TV**

The Dress 🦴🦴 **1996** The title character turns out to be a very malevolent object indeed, in this Dutch absurdist comedy. The bright blue dress with the striking leaf design first causes havoc for the fabric designer, who's nearly fired, while the garment manufacturers get into a fight over the pattern. The dress goes from wearer to wearer, causing havoc for them all, until it is finally destroyed. Dutch with subtitles. **103m/C VHS.** *NL* Henri Garcin, Ariane Schluter, Alex Van Warmerdam; ***D:*** Alex Van Warmerdam; ***W:*** Alex Van Warmerdam; ***C:*** Marc Felperlaan; ***M:*** Vincent van Warmerdam.

The Dress Code 🦴🦴 *Bruno* **1999 (PG-13)** Eight-year-old Bruno is the kind of meek kid who gets picked on by schoolyard bullies and is a disappointment to his dad. So his grandma comes up with a plan to toughen the kid up. **108m/C VHS, DVD.** Alex D. Linz, Gary Sinise, Jennifer Tilly, Kathy Bates, Joey Lauren Adams, Shirley MacLaine, Brett Butler, Gwen Verdon, Stacey Halprin, Kiami Davael; ***D:*** Shirley MacLaine; ***W:*** David Ciminello; ***C:*** Jan Kiesser; ***M:*** Chris Boardman.

Dress Gray 🦴🦴🦴 **1986** Fine, exciting adaptation of the Lucian K. Truscott IV novel about a coverup at an Eastern military academy. Baldwin is cadet Slaight, an upperclassman who finds more secrets than he can handle when a younger cadet (Cassidy), with whom he had an adversarial relationship, is murdered. He's torn between investigating the death or keeping quiet—for the sake of his career if not his life. **192m/C VHS.** Alec Baldwin, Hal Holbrook, Eddie Albert, Lloyd Bridges, Susan Hess, Timothy Van Patten, Patrick Cassidy, Alexis Smith, James B. Sikking, Lane Smith; ***D:*** Glenn Jordan; ***W:*** Gore Vidal; ***M:*** Billy Goldenberg. **TV**

Dress Parade 🦴 ½ **1927** A familiar plot even during the silent era. In order to win the heart of military commander's daughter Janet (Love), brash amateur boxer Vic (Boyd) enters West Point. He promptly alienates his classmates and the girl he loves because of his cocky behavior and must redeem himself in some heroic manner. **73m/B DVD.** William Boyd, Bessie Love, Clarence Gledart, Hugh Allan, Walter Yennyson, Maurice Ryan, Louis Natheaux; ***D:*** Donald Crisp; ***W:*** Douglas Z. Doty; ***C:*** J. Peverell Marley.

Dressed for Death 🦴 ½ *Straight on Till Morning; Til Dawn Do Us Part* **1974 (R)** A tale of true love gone bad as a woman is chased and murdered in her castle by the psychopath she loves. **121m/C VHS, DVD.** *GB* Rita Tushingham, Shane Briant, Tom Bell, Annie Ross, Katya Wyeth, James Bolam, Claire Kelly; ***D:*** Peter Collinson.

Dressed to Kill 🦴🦴 ½ **1946** Sherlock Holmes finds that a series of music boxes holds the key to plates stolen from the Bank of England. The plot's a bit thin, but Rathbone/Bruce, in their final Holmes adventure, are always a delight. **72m/B VHS, DVD.** Basil Rathbone, Nigel Bruce, Patricia Morison, Edmund Breon, Tom Dillon; ***D:*** Roy William Neill; ***W:*** Frank Gruber, Leonard Lee; ***C:*** Maury Gertsman; ***M:*** Hans J. Salter.

Dressed to Kill 🦴🦴 ½ **1980 (R)** Contemporary thriller merges bombastic DePalma with a tense Hitchcockian flare. Sexually unsatisfied Kate (Dickinson) is told to have an affair by her sympathetic shrink Dr. Elliott (Caine) and ends up in bed with a man who catches her eye in a museum. Then Kate's found brutally murdered by prostitute Liz (Allen). Kate's son Peter (Gordon) teams up with Liz to track and lure the killer into their trap. Suspenseful and fast paced. Dickinson's museum scene is wonderfully photographed and edited. DePalma was repeatedly criticized for using a stand-in during the Dickinson shower scene; he titled his next film "Body Double" as a rebuttal. **105m/C VHS, DVD.** Angie Dickinson, Michael Caine, Nancy Allen, Keith Gordon, Dennis Franz, David Margulies, Brandon Maggart; ***D:*** Brian De Palma; ***W:*** Brian De Palma; ***C:*** Ralf Bode; ***M:*** Pino Donaggio.

The Dresser 🦴🦴🦴 ½ **1983 (PG)** Film adaptation of Harwood's play (he also wrote the screen version) about an aging English actor/manager (Finney), his dresser (Courtenay), and their theatre company touring England during WWII. Marvelous showbiz tale is lovingly told, superbly acted. **119m/C VHS, DVD.** Albert Finney, Tom Courtenay, Edward Fox, Michael Gough, Zena Walker, Eileen Atkins, Cathryn Harrison; ***D:*** Peter Yates; ***W:*** Ronald Harwood; ***M:*** James Horner. Golden Globes '84: Actor—Drama (Courtenay).

Dressmaker 🦴🦴 ½ **1956** French comedian Fernandel stars as a man's tailor who designs dresses in secret so as not to compete with his dressmaker wife. Lightweight but entertaining. English subtitled. **95m/B VHS.** *FR* Fernandel, Francoise Fabian; ***D:*** Jean Boyer.

The Dressmaker 🦴🦴 ½ **1989** Two sisters in WWII Liverpool must deal with their young niece's romantic involvement with an American soldier. Plowright and Whitelaw turn in fine performances as the two siblings with very different outlooks on life. **90m/C VHS.** *GB* Pam(ela) Austin, Joan Plowright, Billie Whitelaw, Pete Postlethwaite, Jane Horrocks, Tim Ransom; ***D:*** Jim O'Brien; ***C:*** Michael Coulter; ***M:*** George Fenton.

Drift 🦴🦴 **2000** Angsty relationship drama concerns Ryan (Lee) who's working in an L.A. coffee shop as he tries to become a screenwriter. He's living with Joel (Dayne) but that situation becomes tenuous when Ryan meets young college student Leo (Roessler) and begins to wonder what would happen if he left Joel to pursue this new relationship. Three talky scenarios are offered. **86m/C DVD.** *CA* R. T. Lee, Greyson Dayne, Jonathon Roessler; ***D:*** Quentin Lee; ***W:*** Quentin Lee; ***C:*** Quentin Lee; ***M:*** Steven Panoto.

Drift Fence 🦴🦴 ½ *Texas Desperadoes* **1936** Good early oater about a Texas ranger who goes in search of the man responsible for the murder of his buddy. Routine story saved by high quality production. Based on the story "Nevada" by Zane Grey. **57m/B VHS, DVD.** Buster Crabbe, Katherine DeMille, Tom Keene, Benny Baker; ***D:*** Otho Lovering; ***W:*** Stuart Anthony, Robert Yost.

The Drifter 🦴🦴 **1932** A lumberjack makes sacrifices for the love between his brother and the lumbermill owner's daughter. **56m/B VHS.** William Farnum, Noah Beery Sr., Phyllis Barrington; ***D:*** William A. O'Connor; ***W:*** Oliver Drake; ***C:*** William Nobles.

The Drifter 🦴 ½ **1944** Billy Carson (Crabbe) discovers that his exact double, outlaw Drifter Davis, has been impersonating him in order to commit a series of bank robberies. The marshal jails Drifter (thinking he's Carson) so the real Carson pretends to be Drifter in order to get the goods on who's been helping Drifter. But Carson's pal Fuzzy breaks Drifter out of jail (thinking he's Billy) causing more complications. Confused yet? **62m/B DVD.** Al "Fuzzy" St. John, Buster Crabbe, Kermit Maynard, Carol Parker, Jack Ingram, Roy Brent, George Chesebro, Jimmy Aubrey, Slim Whitaker; ***D:*** Sam Newfield; ***W:*** Patricia Harper; ***C:*** Robert E. Cline.

The Drifter 🦴🦴 ½ **1988 (R)** It's psychos, psychos everywhere as a beautiful young woman learns to regret a one-night stand. A good, low-budget version of "Fatal Attraction." Director Brand plays the cop. **90m/C VHS, DVD.** Kim Delaney, Timothy Bottoms, Miles O'Keeffe, Al Shannon, Thomas Wagner, Larry Brand; ***D:*** Larry Brand; ***W:*** Larry Brand; ***C:*** David Sperling; ***M:*** Rick Conrad.

The Driftin' Kid 🦴 **1941** Poorly produced western has Keene posing as a rancher in order to nab a bunch of cattle rusters. So bad that even the sound of the punches are seconds off from the blows. **57m/B VHS.** Tom Keene, Betty Miles, Frank Yaconelli, Slim Andrews, Stanley Price, Glenn Strange; ***D:*** Robert Emmett Tansey; ***W:*** Robert Emmett Tansey, Frances Kavanaugh.

Driftin' River 🦴🦴 ½ **1946** A shipment of horses bound for the Army is hijacked and the soldiers sent to investigate the theft are murdered. Investigators Deans and Ates are sent to take care of the culprits. Routine oater. **57m/B VHS, DVD.** Eddie Dean, Roscoe Ates, Shirley Patterson, William "Bill" Fawcett, Dennis Moore, Bob Callahan, Lottie Harrison, Forrest Taylor; ***D:*** Robert Emmett Tansey; ***W:*** Frances Kavanaugh.

Drifting 🦴🦴 ½ *Nagooa* **1982** A controversial Israeli film about a homosexual filmmaker surviving in modern-day Jerusalem. First such movie to be made in Israel. In Hebrew with English titles. **103m/C VHS.** *IS* Jonathan Sagalle, Ami Traub, Ben Levine, Dita Arel; ***D:*** Amos Guttman.

Drifting Souls 🦴🦴 **1932** In order to save her father's life, a beautiful young woman marries for money instead of love. **65m/C VHS.** Lois Wilson, Theodore von Eltz, Shirley Grey, Raymond Hatton, Gene Gowing, Bryant Washburn; ***D:*** Louis King.

Drifting Weeds 🦴🦴🦴 ½ *Floating Weeds; The Duckweed Story; Ukigusa* **1959** A remake by Ozu of his 1934 silent film about a troupe of traveling actors whose leader visits his illegitimate son and his lover after years of separation. Classic Ozu. In Japanese with English subtitles. **128m/B VHS, DVD.** *JP* Ganjiro Nakamura, Machiko Kyo, Haruko Sugimura, Ayako Wakao; ***D:*** Yasujiro Ozu.

Drillbit Taylor 🦴🦴 **2008 (PG-13)** Three freshman dweebs find high-school life a nightmare, especially when two ruthless bullies are out for blood. Pooling together pocket change and savings, they hire Drillbit Taylor (Wilson), a panhander posing as a freelance body guard with plans to quietly steal from their nice suburban homes. Taylor's scheme is thwarted when he discovers a genuine sympathy for the boys, as well as a budding romance with a teacher (Mann). Wilson is typically sweet and likable, but he's lost in a bland script. **102m/C DVD, Blu-ray Disc.** *US* Owen Wilson, Leslie Mann, Troy Gentile, David Dorfman, Alex Frost, Josh Peck, Nate Hartley; ***D:*** Steven Brill; ***W:*** Seth Rogen, Kristofor Brown; ***C:*** Fred Murphy; ***M:*** Christophe Beck.

Driller Killer **WOOF!** **1979 (R)** Frustrated artist goes insane and begins to kill off Manhattan residents with a carpenter's drill. Likewise, the plot is full of holes. Director Ferrara starred in his own film under the name Jimmy Laine. **94m/C VHS, DVD.** Abel Ferrara, Carolyn Marz, Bob DeFrank, Peter Yellen, Baybi Day, Harry Schultz; ***D:*** Abel Ferrara; ***W:*** Nicholas St. John; ***C:*** Ken Kelsch; ***M:*** Joe Delia.

Drive 🦴🦴 **1996 (R)** A technologically enhanced man (Dacascos), running from biotech corporate hitmen, offers a down-on-his-luck stranger (Hardison) $5 million to drive him from San Francisco to L.A. And he won't take no for an answer. **99m/C VHS, DVD.** Mark Dacascos, Kadeem Hardison, Brittany Murphy, John Pyper-Ferguson, Tracey Walter, James Shigeta, Masaya Kato; ***D:*** Steve Wang.

Drive By 🦴🦴 ½ **2001 (R)** Ceasar (Acosta), the young brother of the leader of the neighborhood gang, hates the drugs and murder on the streets, but the pull of gang life is strong. He is tipped off about a set-up of his brother, and must choose between his future and his family. Not quite expertly filmed and acted, but the artistry is secondary to the message. The film's emotion and sincerity come through in the credible script (from obvious life experience). The non-professional actors and location shooting add to the realism. **98m/C DVD.** Mario Acosta, Felipe Camacho, Alberto Viruena, Raul Salinas, Vincente Zuniga C; ***D:*** Juan J. Frausto; ***W:*** Vincente Zuniga C, Juan J. Frausto; ***C:*** Gennadi Balitski; ***M:*** Christopher Morford. **VIDEO**

Drive-In **WOOF!** **1976 (PG)** A low-budget bomb showing a night in the life of teenage yahoos at a Texas drive-in. **96m/C VHS.** Lisa Lemole, Glenn Morshower, Gary Cavagnaro; ***D:*** Rod Amateau.

Drive-In Massacre **WOOF!** **1974 (R)** Two police detectives investigate a bizarre series of slasher murders at the local drive-in. Honk the horn at this one. **78m/C VHS, DVD.** Jake Barnes, Adam Lawrence, Austin Johnson, Douglas Gudbye, Valdesta; ***D:*** Stu Segall; ***W:*** George "Buck" Flower, John Goff.

Drive Me Crazy 🦴🦴 **1999 (PG-13)** Nicole (Hart) and Chase (Grenier) have grown up next door to each other and attend the same high school, but that's all they think they have in common. Pep rallying Nicole yearns to date BMOC Brad (Carpenter), but he's only interested in a rival cheerleader. Slacker-type Chase just wants to hang out at the coffeehouse with his animal activist girlfriend Dulcie (Larter), but he gets dumped hard. They conspire to win their dream dates to the prom by pretending to be a couple in order to provoke jealousy. As the two grow closer, they inevitably fall in love. Unfortunately, they don't do it in a very entertaining or amusing manner. Slow paced, unfunny and trite is no way to go through life, son. Based on the novel "How I Created My Perfect Prom Date" by Todd Strasser. **91m/C VHS, DVD.** Melissa Joan Hart, Adrian Grenier, Stephen Collins, Faye Grant, Susan May Pratt, Kris Park, Mark Webber, Ali Larter, Mark Metcalf, William Converse-Roberts, Gabriel Carpenter; ***D:*** John Schultz; ***W:*** Rob Thomas; ***C:*** Kees Van Oostrum; ***M:*** Greg Kendall.

Driven 🦴🦴 **2001 (PG-13)** Hotshot rookie racer Jimmy Bly (Pardue) is slipping in the rankings thanks to pressure from his promoter brother (Leonard) and his ongoing affair with Sophia (Warren), the girlfriend of top rival Beau (Schweiger). Owner Henry (Reynolds) brings in former hotshot Joe Tanto (Stallone) to straighten the kid out, but Joe has his own demons, including a horrific, nearlydeadly crash, an ex married to his arch-rival (De la Fuente), and a hovering female reporter (Edwards). There's a lot going on, what with all the CGI-created car crashes, the bed-hopping, and the tempers flaring, but it's all over the road, so as not to tax anyone's attention span. It doesn't get anywhere, but at least it gets there fast. **117m/C VHS, DVD.** *US* Sylvester Stallone, Burt Reynolds, Kip Pardue, Til Schweiger, Gina Gershon, Robert Sean Leonard, Stacy Edwards, Estella Warren, Christian de la Fuente, Brent Briscoe; ***D:*** Renny Harlin; ***W:*** Sylvester Stallone; ***C:*** Mauro Fiore; ***M:*** BT (Brian Transeau).

Driven to Kill 🦴🦴 **1990** No-name cast assemble in low-rent suspenser portraying the ugly side of love: bent on revenge, a man is out to obliterate the thugs who made his life a horrible experience highlighted by misery and boredom. **97m/C VHS.** Jake Jacobs, Chip Campbell, Michele McNeil; ***D:*** John Gazarian; ***W:*** Frank Norwood; ***C:*** Robert Hayes.

The Driver 🦴 ½ **1978 (PG)** A police detective will stop at nothing to catch "The Driver," a man who has the reputation of driving the fastest getaway car around. Chase scenes win out over plot. **131m/C VHS, DVD.** Ryan O'Neal, Bruce Dern, Isabelle Adjani, Ronee Blakley, Matt Clark; ***D:*** Walter Hill; ***W:*** Walter Hill.

Driver's Seat WOOF! *Psychotic; Identikit* **1973 (R)** Extremely bizarre film with a cult following that was adapted from the novel by Muriel Spark. Liz stars as a deranged woman trying to keep a rendezvous with her strange lover in Rome. In the meantime she wears tacky clothes and delivers stupid lines. **101m/C VHS, DVD.** *IT* Elizabeth Taylor, Ian Bannen, Mona Washbourne, Andy Warhol, Guido Mannari, Maxence Mailfort; ***D:*** Giuseppe Patroni-Griffi; ***W:*** Giuseppe Patroni-Griffi, Raffaele La Capria; ***M:*** Franco Mannino.

Driving Force 🦴 **1988 (R)** In an effort to capitalize on the popularity of the "Road Warrior" movies, features a lone trucker battling a gang of roadhogs in another post-holocaust desert. Ultimately, runs off the road. **90m/C VHS.** Sam Jones, Catherine Bach, Don Swayze; ***D:*** A.J. Prowse; ***W:*** Patrick Edgeworth.

Driving Lessons 🦴🦴 ½ **2006 (PG-13)** Red-headed Grint gets to step out from just being Harry Potter's sidekick in this cozy generational comedy. Ben is a shy teen who's usually dragged into helping steely mom Laura (Linney) with her Christian charity work, even agreeing to her suggestion of a summer job. He ends up with the alcoholic and somewhat delusional Evie (Walters), an over-the-hill actress who convinces Ben to drive her to Edinburgh, a trip that turns out to be quite eventful. It's a case of dueling divas for the carcass of one bewildered boy—predictable, but it's still a laugh. **98m/C DVD.** *GB* Julie Walters, Rupert Grint, Laura Linney, Nicholas Farrell, Jim Norton, Tamsin Egerton, Michaelle Duncan; ***D:*** Jeremy Brock; ***W:*** Jeremy Brock; ***C:*** David Katznelson; ***M:*** John Renbourn, Clive Carroll.

Driving Me Crazy 🦴 ½ **1991 (PG-13)** When an East German car inventor comes to America, it's laughs in the fast lane in this all-star comedy. **88m/C VHS.** Billy Dee Williams, Thomas Gottschalk, Dom DeLuise, Milton Berle, Steve Kanaly, Michelle Johnson, Richard Moll, Morton Downey Jr., George Kennedy; ***D:*** Jon Turteltaub.

Driving Miss Daisy 🦴🦴🦴 ½ **1989 (PG)** Tender and sincere portrayal of a 25-year friendship between an aging Jewish woman and the black chauffeur forced upon her by her son. Humorous and thought-provoking, skillfully acted and directed, it subtly explores the effects of prejudice in the South. The development of Aykroyd as a top-notch character actor is further evidenced here. Part of the fun is watching the changes in fashion and auto design. Adapted from the play by Alfred Uhry. **99m/C VHS, DVD.** Jessica Tandy, Morgan Freeman, Dan Aykroyd, Esther Rolle, Patti LuPone; ***D:*** Bruce Beresford; ***W:*** Alfred Uhry; ***C:*** Peter James; ***M:*** Hans Zimmer. Oscars '89: Actress (Tandy), Adapt. Screenplay, Makeup, Picture; British Acad. '90: Actress (Tandy); Golden Globes '90: Actor—Mus./Comedy (Freeman), Actress—Mus./Comedy (Tandy), Film—Mus./Comedy; Natl. Bd. of Review '89: Actor (Freeman); Writers Guild '89: Adapt. Screenplay.

The Drop 🦴 **2006 (R)** Naive college student Carter (Bondies) accepts suspiciously big bucks to drive a sports car from San Francisco to L.A. While waiting in a parking garage for the pickup, Carter gets curious about a briefcase in the trunk and makes the mistake of opening it. Supposed to be spooky; instead, the whole thing is silly and nonsensical. **?m/C DVD.** *US* John Savage, Sean Young, Michael P. Bondies; ***D:*** Kevin Lewis; ***W:*** Kevin Lewis; ***C:*** Chris Wilson. **VIDEO**

Drop Dead Fred WOOF! 1991 (PG-13) As a little girl, Lizzie Cronin had a manic, imaginary friend named Fred, who protected her from her domineering mother. When her husband dumps her 20 years later, Fred returns to "help" as only he can. Although the cast is fine, incompetent writing and direction make this a truly dismal affair. Plus, gutter humor and mean-spirited pranks throw the whole "heart-warming" premise out the window. Filmed in Minneapolis. **103m/C VHS, DVD.** Phoebe Cates, Rik Mayall, Tim Matheson, Marsha Mason, Carrie Fisher, Daniel Gerroll, Ron Eldard; ***D:*** Ate De Jong; ***W:*** Carlos Davis, Anthony Fingleton; ***M:*** Randy Edelman.

Drop Dead Gorgeous 🦴🦴 ½ *Dairy Queens* **1999 (PG-13)** Oh, the ambitions of stage moms and their daughters in this mockumentary of small-town Minnesota beauty pageants. Satire takes the lowest road whenever possible, because that's where the laughs happen to be. Naive Amber (Dunst) has a trailer-trash babe, Annette (Barkin), for a mom, while rival rich bitch, Becky (Richards), is stuck with the horror that is Gladys (Alley). And someone is taking the contest way too seriously, since other contestants are dropping like flies. Piles it on a little thick sometimes, but overall it works. Watch for Richards' cringe-inducing talent show dance number. **97m/C VHS, DVD.** Denise Richards, Kirsten Dunst, Kirstie Alley, Ellen Barkin, Allison Janney, Sam McMurray, Mindy Sterling, Amy Adams, Tara Redepenning, Sara Stewart, Shannon Nelson, Matt Malloy, Michael McShane, Brooke Bushman, Will Sasso, Brittany Murphy, Mo Gaffney, Nora Dunn, Amanda Detmer; ***Cameos:*** Adam West; ***D:*** Michael Patrick Jann; ***W:*** Lona Williams; ***C:*** Michael Spiller; ***M:*** Mark Mothersbaugh.

Drop Dead Sexy 🦴🦴 ½ **2005 (R)** The ick factor seems high but it's more comic/thriller than disturbing. Frank (Lee) and Eddie (Glover) are a couple of smalltime Texas losers: Frank works for a used car dealer, Eddie is a gravedigger, and both moonlight for thug Spider (Vince) to whom they owe money. After seeing the obit of Crystal (Keller), the beautiful blonde wife of the richest man (Berkeley) in town, Frank learns she's been buried with an expensive necklace. He convinces Eddie to dig up the body, only to find the necklace missing. They also can't immediately rebury the corpse. So Eddie takes the body home for safekeeping while Frank tries to come up with another plan. **83m/C DVD.** Jason Lee, Crispin Glover, Pruitt Taylor Vince, Xander Berkeley, Melissa Keller, Brad Dourif, Lin Shaye; ***D:*** Michael Philip; ***W:*** Michael Philip; ***C:*** Thomas Callaway; ***M:*** Deborah Lurie.

Drop-Out Mother 🦴🦴 **1988** A woman gives up her executive position to become a housewife and full-time mom; expected domestic turmoil follows. Standard TV fare and sort of a sequel to "Drop-Out Father," shown in 1982. **100m/C VHS.** Valerie Harper, Wayne Rogers, Carol Kane, Kim Hunter, Danny Gerard; ***D:*** Charles S. Dubin. **TV**

DROP Squad 🦴🦴 **1994 (R)** Not quite on target social satire revolving around buppie Burford Jackson Jr. (La Salle), a token minority ad exec who's job is to push questionable products, using gross stereotypes, to the black community. His family's appalled and Buford becomes a prime target of D.R.O.P. (Deprogramming and Restoration of Pride), a vigilante organization that kidnaps erring black brethren and leads them back to their cultural heritage. Frequently intense performances but the script raises some serious issues on which it doesn't deliver. Based on the short story "The Deprogrammer" by David Taylor. **88m/C VHS, DVD.** Eriq La Salle, Vondie Curtis-Hall, Ving Rhames, Kasi Lemmons, Vanessa Williams, Nicole Powell, Afemo Omilami, Spike Lee; ***D:*** David C(lark) Johnson; ***W:*** David C(lark) Johnson, Butch Robinson, David Taylor; ***C:*** Ken Kelsch; ***M:*** Michael Bearden.

Drop Zone 🦴🦴 ½ **1994 (R)** Routine action-thriller finds U.S. marshal Pete Nessip (Snipes) and his brother Terry (Warner) assigned to protect drug cartel snitch Earl Leedy (Jeter). The plane they're on is skyjacked by criminal Moncrief (Busey) who parachutes off with Leedy, Terry's killed, and while Pete's on suspension he decides to go undercover into the world of sky-driving with the aid of ex-con cutie Jessie (Butler). Plot holes are big enough to pilot a plane through but the stunts are good and Snipes is never less than professional. **101m/C VHS, DVD.** Wesley Snipes, Gary Busey, Yancy Butler, Michael Jeter, Corin "Corky" Nemec, Kyle Secor, Luca Bercovici, Malcolm Jamal Warner, Rex Linn, Grace Zabriskie, Sam Hennings, Claire Stansfield, Mickey Jones, Andy Romano; ***D:*** John Badham; ***W:*** John Bishop, Peter Barsocchini; ***C:*** Roy Wagner; ***M:*** Hans Zimmer.

The Dropkick 🦴🦴🦴 **1927** Erstwhile D.W. Griffith leading man Barthelmess stars in this pigskin whodunnit: a coach's suicide looks like murder, and the prime suspect is the team's most valuable player. Cast includes ten bona fide university football players and Hedda "nobody's interested in sweetness and light" Hopper, while The Duke makes cameo. Webb later went on to direct a musical with Eddie Cantor and Rudy Vallee ("Glorifying the American Girl"). Silent. Based on the story "Glitter" by Katherine Brush. **62m/B VHS.** Richard Barthelmess, Barbara Kent, Dorothy Revier, Eugene Strong, Alberta Vaughn, Brooks Benedict, Hedda Hopper; ***Cameos:*** John Wayne; ***D:*** Millard Webb; ***W:*** Winifred Dunn.

Drowning by Numbers 🦴🦴🦴 ½ **1987 (R)** Three generations of women, each named Cissie Colpitts, solve their marital problems by drowning their husbands and making deals with a bizarre coroner. Further strange visions from director Greenaway, complemented by stunning cinematography courtesy of Sacha Vierny. A treat for those who appreciate Greenaway's uniquely curious cinematic statements. **121m/C VHS.** *GB* Bernard Hill, Joan Plowright, Juliet Stevenson, Joely Richardson; ***D:*** Peter Greenaway; ***W:*** Peter Greenaway; ***C:*** Sacha Vierny; ***M:*** Michael Nyman.

Drowning Mona 🦴🦴 **2000 (PG-13)** Strident comedy about the low-IQ denizens of small town Verplanck, New York, where everybody still drives a Yugo (the town was a test market). Nasty Mona Dearly (Midler) drives her car into the Hudson River and drowns. It turns out to be murder and Chief Wyatt Rash (DeVito) must investigate. He's not lacking in suspects since Mona was the most hated woman in the community. Everyone in the cast looks like they're enjoying themselves which may be more than the viewer will say. **95m/C VHS, DVD.** Danny DeVito, Bette Midler, Jamie Lee Curtis, Casey Affleck, Neve Campbell, William Fichtner, Peter Dobson, Marcus Thomas, Kathleen Wilhoite, Tracey Walter, Paul Ben-Victor, Paul Schulze, Mark Pellegrino; ***D:*** Nick Gomez; ***W:*** Peter Steinfeld; ***C:*** Bruce Douglas Johnson; ***M:*** Michael Tavera.

Drowning on Dry Land 2000 (R) After being fired, Hershey decides to take a cross-country trip—by taxi—to find herself in the desert. Naturally, bonding goes on. **90m/C VHS, DVD.** Barbara Hershey, Naveen Andrews, Carol Lynley, John Doe, Stephen Polk; ***D:*** Carl Colpaert; ***W:*** Julie Jacobs, Sheila Nayar; ***C:*** Dean Lent; ***M:*** Richard Horowitz. **VIDEO**

The Drowning Pool 🦴🦴 **1975 (PG)** Newman returns as detective Lew Harper (after 1966's "Harper") to solve a blackmail case. Uneventful script and stodgy direction, but excellent character work from all the cast members keep this watchable. Title is taken from a trap set for Newman, from which he must escape using most of his female companion's clothing. Adapted from Ross MacDonald's novel about detective Lew Archer. **109m/C VHS, DVD.** Paul Newman, Joanne Woodward, Anthony (Tony) Franciosa, Murray Hamilton, Melanie Griffith, Richard Jaeckel; ***D:*** Stuart Rosenberg; ***W:*** Tracy Keenan Wynn, Walter Hill; ***C:*** Gordon Willis; ***M:*** Charles Fox.

Drug Wars: The Camarena Story 🦴🦴🦴 **1990 (PG-13)** Enrique "Kiki" Camerena (Bauer) is an undercover DEA agent working in Mexico in 1985 His discovery of a major drug operation leads to a top drug kingpin. When his cover is blown, Kiki is kidnapped, tortured, and murdered and the cover-up highlights corruption in the government itself. Based on the book "Desperados" by Elaine Shannon. **130m/C VHS, DVD.** Steven Bauer, Elizabeth Pena, Miguel Ferrer, Benicio Del Toro, Treat Williams, Craig T. Nelson, Guy Boyd, Tony Plana, Tomas Milian, Raymond J. Barry, Everett McGill, Eddie Velez, Rosalind Chao; ***D:*** Brian Gibson; ***W:*** Rose Schacht, Ann Powell, Christopher Canaan, Mel Frohman; ***C:*** Sandi Sissel; ***M:*** Charles Bernstein. **TV**

Drug Wars 2: The Cocaine Cartel 🦴🦴 **1992** Muddled drama featuring crazy unpredictable DEA agents executing the downfall of Colombia's Medellin drug kingpins. Average sequel to the award-winning miniseries "Drug Wars." **200m/C VHS.** Alex McArthur, Dennis Farina, Julie Carmen, John Glover, Karen Young, Michele Placido, Gustav Vintas, Geno Silva; ***D:*** Paul Krasny.

Drugstore Cowboy 🦴🦴🦴 ½ **1989 (R)** A gritty, uncompromising depiction of a pack of early 1970s drugstore-robbing junkies as they travel around looking to score. Brushes with the law and tragedy encourage them to examine other life-styles, but the trap seems impossible to leave. A perfectly crafted piece that reflects the "me generation" era, though it tends to glamorize addiction. Dillon's best work to date. Based on a novel by prison inmate James Fogle. **100m/C VHS, DVD.** Matt Dillon, Kelly Lynch, James Remar, James LeGros, Heather Graham, William S. Burroughs, Beah Richards, Grace Zabriskie, Max Perlich; ***D:*** Gus Van Sant; ***W:*** Gus Van Sant, Daniel Yost; ***C:*** Robert Yeoman; ***M:*** Elliot Goldenthal. Ind. Spirit '90: Actor (Dillon), Cinematog., Screenplay, Support. Actor (Perlich); L.A. Film Critics '89: Screenplay; N.Y. Film Critics '89: Screenplay; Natl. Soc. Film Critics '89: Director (Van Sant), Film, Screenplay.

Druids 🦴🦴 ½ *Vercingetorix* **2001 (R)** Gallic chieftain Vercingetorix (Lambert) must rally his people when they are threatened by Roman army commander Julius Caesar (Brandauer) in 60 B.C. The action is well-done even if the story drags occassionally. **115m/C VHS, DVD.** Christopher Lambert, Klaus Maria Brandauer, Max von Sydow, Ines Sastre, Stefan Ivanov, Barnard Pierre Donnadieu; ***D:*** Jacques Dorfmann; ***W:*** Jacques Dorfmann, Rospo Pallenberg, Norman Spinrad; ***M:*** Pierre Charvet. **VIDEO**

Drum WOOF! **1976 (R)** This steamy sequel to "Mandingo" deals with the sordid interracial sexual shenanigans at a Southern plantation. Bad taste at its best. **101m/C VHS.** Ken Norton, Warren Oates, Pam Grier, Yaphet Kotto, Fiona Lewis, Isela Vega, Cheryl "Rainbeaux" Smith; ***D:*** Steve Carver; ***C:*** Lucien Ballard.

Drum Beat 🦴🦴 **1954** An unarmed Indian fighter sets out to negotiate a peace treaty with a renegade Indian leader. Bronson is especially believable as chief. Based on historical incident. **111m/C VHS, DVD.** Alan Ladd, Charles Bronson, Marisa Pavan, Robert Keith, Rodolfo Acosta, Warner Anderson, Elisha Cook Jr., Anthony Caruso; ***D:*** Delmer Daves.

Drum Taps 🦴🦴 **1933** Maynard saves the day for a young girl who is being pushed off her land by a group of speculators. **55m/B VHS, DVD.** Ken Maynard, Dorothy Dix, Frank "Junior" Coghlan, Kermit Maynard; ***D:*** J(ohn) P(aterson) McGowan.

Drumline 🦴🦴🦴 **2002 (PG-13)** Devon Miles, (Cannon), a hip-hop drummer from Harlem, receives a full music scholarship to the fictitious Atlanta A&T University. Although his hotdogging antics brought him recognition at home, they aren't appreciated by bandleader Dr. Lee, who's philosophy is "one band, one sound." The university president is aching for more showmanship during halftime and supports Devon's hot-shot performing. This, along with Devon's wisecracking attitude, grates on section-leader and rival Sean, (Roberts). Stone does well dealing with ethnic issues without falling into character cliches and stereotypes, but with so many issues explored, some ideas go undeveloped. Good story is helped along by the flair and power of the marching band scenes. **118m/C VHS, DVD, Blu-ray Disc.** *US* Nick Cannon, Zoe Saldana, Orlando Jones, Leonard Roberts, GQ, Jason Weaver, Earl C. Poitier, Candace Carey, Afemo Omilami, Shay Rountree, Miguel A. Gaetan, J. Anthony Brown; ***D:*** Charles Stone III; ***W:*** Shawn Schepps, Tina Gordon Chism; ***C:*** Shane Hurlbut; ***M:*** John Powell.

Drums 🦴🦴 ½ *The Drum* **1938** A native prince helps to save the British army in India from being annihilated by a tyrant. Rich melodrama with interesting characterizations and locale. **96m/B VHS.** *GB* Sabu, Raymond Massey, Valerie Hobson, Roger Livesey, David Tree; ***D:*** Zoltan Korda.

Drums Along the Mohawk 🦴🦴🦴 ½ **1939** Grand, action-filled saga about pre-Revolutionary America, detailing the trials of a colonial newlywed couple as their village in Mohawk Valley is besieged by Indians. Based on the Walter Edmonds novel, and vintage Ford. **104m/C VHS, DVD.** Henry Fonda, Claudette Colbert, Edna May Oliver, Eddie Collins, John Carradine, Dorris Bowdon, Arthur Shields, Ward Bond, Jessie Ralph, Robert Lowery; ***D:*** John Ford; ***C:*** Ray Rennahan.

Drums in the Deep South 🦴🦴 **1951** A rivalry turns ugly as two former West Point roommates wind up on opposite sides when the Civil War breaks out. Historical drama hampered by familiar premise. **87m/C VHS, DVD.** James Craig, Guy Madison, Craig Stevens, Barbara Payton, Barton MacLane; ***D:*** William Cameron Menzies; ***W:*** Philip Yordan.

Drums of Africa 🦴 **1963** Low-budget travelogue uses stock African footage to tell a dull story about three do-gooders on safari in 1897 who get involved in doing away with the slave trade in East Africa. Avalon still finds time to sing. **91m/C DVD.** Frankie Avalon, Mariette Hartley, Lloyd Bochner, Torin Thatcher, Hari Rhodes; ***D:*** James B. Clark; ***W:*** Robin Estridge; ***C:*** Paul Vogel; ***M:*** Johnny Mandel.

Drums of Fu Manchu 🦴🦴🦴 **1940** Fu Manchu searches for the scepter of Genghis Khan, an artifact that would give him domination over the East. Brandon smoothly evil as the Devil Doctor. Originally a serial in 15 chapters. **150m/B VHS, DVD.** Henry (Kleinbach) Brandon, Robert Kellard, George Cleveland, Dwight Frye, Gloria Franklin, Tom Chatterton, Philip Ahn; ***D:*** William Witney, John English; ***W:*** Barney A. Sarecky, Frank (Franklyn) Adreon, Norman S. Hall, Morgan Cox; ***C:*** William Nobles; ***M:*** Cy Feuer.

Drums of Jeopardy 🦴 *Mark of Terror* **1931** A father wanders through czarist Russia and the U.S. to seek revenge on his daughter's killer. Cheap copy of "Dr. Fu Manchu." **65m/B VHS, DVD.** Warner Oland, June Collyer, Lloyd Hughes, George Fawcett, Mischa Auer; ***D:*** George B. Seitz.

Drums O'Voodoo WOOF! *She Devil* **1934** A voodoo princess fights to eliminate the town bad guy in this all-black feature that is greatly hampered by shoddy production values. **70m/B VHS.** Laura Bowman, J. Augustus Smith, Edna Barr; ***D:*** Arthur Hoerl.

Drunken Angel 🦴🦴🦴 *Yoidore tenshi* **1948** Alcoholic doctor gets mixed up with local gangster. Kurosawa's first major film aided by strong performances. With English subtitles. **108m/B VHS.** *JP* Toshiro Mifune, Takashi Shimura, Choko Iida; ***D:*** Akira Kurosawa; ***W:*** Keinosuke Uegusa; ***C:*** Takeo Ito; ***M:*** Fumio Hayasaka.

Drunken Monkey 🦴🦴 ½ *Chui Ma Lau* **2002 (R)** Wen Biao discovers his brother is conducting criminal acts through their security company and confronts him. Shortly after, Wen Biao goes missing and is assumed dead until he resurfaces again for a final martial arts showdown with his misguided sibling. Unfortunately typical in narrative and combat. Chinese with subtitles. **98m/C DVD.** *HK* Chia-Liang Liu, Wing-kin Lau, Jacky Wu, Shannon Yao, Chia Hui Liu; ***W:*** Pak Ling Li; ***C:*** Wong Bo Man; ***M:*** Tommy Wai.

Drunks 🦴🦴 **1996 (R)** Ensemble story set in a church basement in Manhattan where a diverse group of people go to their Alcoholics Anonymous meetings. Recovering alcoholic Jim (Lewis) has gone on a bender after his wife's death; Rachel's (Wiest) an overworked doctor with drug and alcohol dependencies; alcoholic Becky's (Dunaway) a divorcee with problem kids; Brenda's (Hamilton) an ex-heroin addict who's HIV positive; Joseph's (Rollins) still haunted by his son's death, which he caused while driving drunk. There's more and everyone gets their chance at the spotlight. Adapted from Lennon's play "Blackout." **88m/C VHS, DVD.** Richard Lewis, Faye Dunaway, Dianne Wiest, Lisa Gay Hamilton, Howard E. Rollins Jr., Parker Posey, Spalding Gray, Amanda Plummer, Calista Flockhart, George Martin, Anna Thomson; ***D:*** Peter Cohn; ***W:*** Gary Lennon; ***C:*** Peter Hawkins; ***M:*** Joe Delia.

Dry Cleaning 🦴🦴 *Nettoyage a Sec* **1997** Marrieds Nicole (Miou-Miou) and Jean-Marie (Berling) Kunstler are sharing a midlife crisis. The hard-working owners of a dry cleaning establishment are bored by their routine and decide to visit a racy nightclub where the featured performers are a brother/sister drag act. And before the Kunstlers know quite how it happened, they are both involved with handsome Loic (Merhar), whose sister has suddenly broken up their performing partnership. So Loic is now both working for and living with the Kunstlers and the erotic waters are getting very murky indeed. French with subtitles. **97m/C VHS.** *FR* Miou-Miou, Charles Berling, Stanislas Merhar, Mathilde Seigner; ***D:*** Anne Fontaine; ***W:*** Anne Fontaine, Gilles Taurand; ***C:*** Caroline Champetier.

A Dry White Season 🦴🦴🦴 **1989 (R)** A white Afrikaner living resignedly with apartheid confronts the system when his black gardener, an old friend, is persecuted and murdered. A well-meaning expose that, like many others, focuses on white people. **105m/C VHS, DVD.** Donald Sutherland, Marlon Brando, Susan Sarandon, Zakes Mokae, Janet Suzman, Jurgen Prochnow, Winston Ntshona, Susannah Harker, Thoko Ntshinga, Rowan Elmes; ***D:*** Euzhan Palcy; ***W:*** Colin Welland, Euzhan Palcy; ***M:*** Dave Grusin.

Drying Up the Streets 🦴 **1976** Tepid message tale of a police drug squad out to terminate the pattern that has young women turning to a life of prostitution and drugs. **90m/C VHS.** *CA* Len Cariou, Don Francks, Sarah Torgov, Calvin Butler; ***D:*** Robin Spry.

D3: The Mighty Ducks 🦴🦴 **1996 (PG)** Estevez proves that he'll quack for a dollar in the latest redux of the Disney franchise. This time the members of the rag-tag team are drafted by an exclusive prep school where, once again, they don't fit in. Go figure! Although billed as the star, Estevez only appears briefly at the beginning and end of the movie, leaving team captain Charlie (Jackson) as the focus of the story. Facing off against the new coach and the snooty elitist varsity team, the players learn lessons about maturity, responsibility and whacking people with sticks. In all probability, Disney will not be happy with just the hat trick, so don't be surprised if you see "D4: Mighty Old to Still Be Playing Kids" in a theatre near you soon. Cameo from professional Mighty Duck and fellow Disney employee Paul Kariya. **104m/C VHS, DVD.** Emilio Estevez, Jeffrey Nordling, Joshua Jackson, David Selby, Heidi Kling, Joss Ackland, Elden (Ratliff) Henson, Shaun Weiss, Matt Doherty, Michael Cudlitz, Vincent A. Larusso, Colombe Jacobsen, Aaron Lohr, Christopher Orr; ***D:*** Robert Lieberman; ***W:*** Steven Brill, Jim Burnstein; ***C:*** David Hennings; ***M:*** J.A.C. Redford.

D2: The Mighty Ducks 🦴🦴 *The Mighty Ducks 2* **1994 (PG)** When an injury forces Gordon (Estevez) out of the minor leagues, he is tapped by promotor Tibbles (Tucker) to coach Team U.S.A. in the Junior Goodwill Games. Upon arriving in LA, the coach's head is turned by the money to be made in endorsements, and he soon gets a lesson in character-building (hey, it's Disney). The duck redux premise is lame, but kids will want ice time to see more of the hockey action that made the first a hit. **107m/C VHS, DVD.** Emilio Estevez, Michael Tucker, Jan Rubes, Kathryn Erbe, Shaun Weiss, Kenan Thompson, Ty O'Neal; ***Cameos:*** Kristi Yamaguchi, Kareem Abdul-Jabbar, Wayne Gretzky; ***D:*** Sam Weisman; ***W:*** Steven Brill; ***M:*** J.A.C. Redford.

Du Barry Was a Lady 🦴🦴 ½ **1943** Skelton is a washroom attendant who daydreams that he is King Louis XV of France. Dorsey's band gets to dress in period wigs and costumes. ♫DuBarry Was a Lady; Do I Love You, Do I?; Friendship; Well, Did You Evah; Taliostro's Dance; Katie Went to Haiti; Madame, I Love Your Crepes Suzettes; Thinking of You; A Cigarette, Sweet Music and You. **112m/C VHS, DVD.** Lucille Ball, Gene Kelly, Red Skelton, Virginia O'Brien, Zero Mostel, Dick Haymes, Rags Ragland, Donald Meek, George Givot, Louise Beavers; ***D:*** Roy Del Ruth; ***W:*** Irving Brecher; ***C:*** Karl Freund.

Dual Alibi 🦴🦴 **1947** Identical twin trapeze artists murder a colleague for a winning lottery ticket. Lom plays the brothers in a dual role. **87m/B VHS.** *GB* Herbert Lom, Terence de Marney, Phyllis Dixey, Ronald Frankau, Abraham Sofaer, Harold Berens, Sebastian Cabot; ***D:*** Alfred Travers.

Duane Hopwood 🦴🦴🦴 **2005 (R)** Duane (Schwimmer), a casino pit boss, is a loving husband and father, with a steadfast unwillingness to deal with his alcoholism. It's a sad but familiar story in which Duane watches as his wife (Garofalo) and daughters drift away, he loses his job as a result of a costly mistake, and his life becomes increasingly defined by his drinking schedule, his drinking friends, and his drinking spots. While Duane's alcoholism is never fully resolved, his life is viewed from an entirely human, even sympathetic point of view. Cast somewhat against type, Schwimmer brings a visceral heartache to his portrayal. **83m/C DVD.** *US* David Schwimmer, Janeane Garofalo, Judah Friedlander, Susan Lynch, Dick Cavett, Steven R. Schirippa, John Krasinski, Lenny Venito; ***D:*** Matt Mulhern; ***W:*** Matt Mulhern; ***C:*** Mauricio Rubenstein; ***M:*** Michael Rohatyn.

Dubarry 🦴🦴 ½ **1930** Early sound version of the romantic experiences of Madame Dubarry, the alluring French heroine of David Belasco's "DuBarry." Talmadge's last film. **81m/B VHS.** Norma Talmadge, Conrad Nagel, William Farnum, Hobart Bosworth, Alison Skipworth; ***D:*** Sam Taylor.

Dubeat-E-O 🦴 ½ **1984** A filmmaker races against time to finish making a documentary about the Los Angeles underground hardcore punk scene, and becomes immersed in the subculture. Somewhat of a haphazard exercise in filmmaking that is best appreciated by rock fans. **84m/C VHS.** Ray Sharkey, Joan Jett, Derf Scratch, Len Lesser, Nora Gaye; ***D:*** Alan Sacks.

The Duchess 🦴🦴🦴 **2008 (PG-13)** Based on the tempestuous life and times of Georgiana, the Duchess of Devonshire, who was married off by her mother at age 16 to endure a scarring relationship with a husband who demanded obedience and used her for breeding much the way he did his beloved dogs. She grew to become one of Britain's most outspoken liberals and groundbreaking feminists, supporting the American and French revolutions and speaking publicly on politics. Impeccably detailed from the costumes to the sets to Knightly's powerhouse performance, crafted from cold, hard realism rather than some whimsical Jane Austin novel. Despite the historical accuracies, however, it sticks close to genre standards with scenes of endless debate broken up with the usual bed-hopping. **110m/C DVD.** Keira Knightley, Ralph Fiennes, Dominic Cooper, Hayley Atwell, Charlotte Rampling, Simon McBurney, Aidan McArdle, Georgia King; ***D:*** Saul Dibb; ***W:*** Saul Dibb, Jeffrey Hatcher, Anders Thomas Jensen; ***C:*** Gyula Pados; ***M:*** Rachel Portman. Oscars '08: Costume Des.; British Acad. '08: Costume Des.

The Duchess and the Dirtwater Fox 🦴 ½ **1976 (PG)** Period western strung together with many failed attempts at humor, all about a music-hall hooker who meets a bumbling card shark on the make. **105m/C VHS, DVD.** George Segal, Goldie Hawn, Conrad Janis, Thayer David; ***D:*** Melvin Frank; ***W:*** Barry Sandler; ***C:*** Joseph Biroc; ***M:*** Charles Fox.

The Duchess of Buffalo 🦴🦴 **1926** American dancer Marian (Talmadge) is performing in pre-Revolutionary Russia and falls in love with handsome Army officer Vladimir (Carminati). Unfortunately, Marian also draws the lecherous attentions of married Grand Duke Gregory (Martindel), which causes a scandal and a case of mistaken identity in this generally lighthearted farce. **75m/B DVD.** Constance Talmadge, Tullio Carminati, Edward Martindel, Madame Rose (Dion) Dione, Chester Conklin; ***D:*** Sidney Franklin; ***W:*** Hans Kraly; ***C:*** Oliver Marsh.

The Duchess of Duke Street 🦴🦴🦴 **1978** Cockney Rosa Lewis (Jones), a clockmaker's daughter born in 1869, goes into service with the ambition to become the best cook in London. She learns from a society household's French chef, where she was a kitchen maid, and eventually won success by an unexpected opportunity to cook for Edward, the Prince of Wales. A marriage-of-convenience and a mysterious legacy allows Rosa to buy the rundown Bentinck Hotel (actually the Cavendish) and cater fashionable dinners. By unceasing hard work, Rosa turns her establishment into an exclusive and discreet haunt for aristocrats, the wealthy, and various celebrities. British series on seven cassettes. **880m/C VHS.** *GB* Gemma Jones, Christopher Cazenove, John Welsh, George Pravda, June Brown, Victoria Plucknett, Richard Vernon, Doreen Mantle, Elizabeth Bennett, Donald Burton, John Cater, Holly DeJong, John Rapley; ***D:*** Cyril Coke, Gerry Mill, Simon Langton, Bill Bain, Raymond Menmuir; ***W:*** Julian Bond, Julia Jones, Rosemary Anne Sisson, Maggie Wadey, Jeremy Paul, Jack Rosenthal, Bill Craig, John Hawkesworth. **TV**

The Duchess of Idaho 🦴🦴 ½ **1950** Williams tries to help her roommate patch up a romance gone bad, but ends up falling in love herself. MGM guest stars liven up an otherwise routine production. ♫Baby Come Out of the Clouds; You Can't Do Wrong Doin' Right; Let's Choo Choo to Idaho; Of All Things; Or Was It Spring; Warm Hands, Cold Heart; Singlefoot Serenade; You Won't Forget Me. **98m/C VHS.** Esther Williams, Van Johnson, John Lund, Paula Raymond, Amanda Blake, Eleanor Powell, Lena Horne; ***D:*** Robert Z. Leonard.

The Duchess of Langeais 🦴🦴🦴 *Ne Touchez pas la Hache; Don't Touch the Axe* **2007** Set in 1820s Paris during the Restoration. The Duchess of Langeais, Antoinette (Balibar), is pursued by general Armand de Montriveau (Guillaume Depardieu—Gerard's son) who falls for her at first sight. She's a smart socialite, schooled in the ways of high living—he's a handsome Napoleonic war hero with stories of bravery. Although married, she's flattered by his attentions and engages him in a skillful game of cat and mouse. Montriveau eventually is angered by her game and attempts to exact his revenge, which finally piques Antoinette's interest—except now it may be too late. The politics of the period are palpable as the social constraints of the would-be lovers stand sentinel to their unrequited love. Gorgeous settings and painful formalities heighten the cruel irony of the ill-fated lovers, and it's oh-so-enticing to watch. **137m/C DVD.** *FR IT* Jeanne Balibar, Guillaume Depardieu, Bulle Ogier, Michel Piccoli, Barbet Schroeder; ***D:*** Jacques Rivette; ***W:*** Jacques Rivette, Pascal Bonitzer, Christian Laurent; ***C:*** William Lubtchansky; ***M:*** Pierre Allio.

Duck 🦴 1/2 **2005 (PG-13)** Ducks just don't have a lot of personality (unless they're the cartoon kind) so the story of a man and his feathered friend starts at a disadvantage. Aged Arthur (Hall) is homeless in L.A. without family or friends when an orphaned duck starts waddling after him. Arthur decides that he and Joe will head towards the ocean (shouldn't he just find a nice pond?) and as they meander along, they run into the usual assortment of oddballs. **98m/C DVD.** Philip Baker Hall, French Stewart, Bill Cobs, Bill Brochtrup; ***D:*** Nicole Bettauer; ***W:*** Nicole Bettauer; ***C:*** Ann Etheridge; ***M:*** Alan Ari Lazar.

Duck Season 🦴🦴🦴 *Temporada de patos* **2004 (R)** Left alone one afternoon in a Mexico City apartment, two young teenaged boys settle in with video games. A neighbor girl joins them, wanting to use their oven, followed by the pizza guy (who the boys refuse payment for supposedly being seconds late but who won't leave until he gets his money). This sets the stage for some genuinely warm exchanges among the quartet as they chatter about life and act goofy in the way only aimless youths can. Of course the marijuana-spiked brownies the girl cooks up adds to their careless mood. **90m/B DVD.** Enrique Arreola, Diego Catano, Daniel Miranda, Danny Perea; ***D:*** Fernando Eimbcke; ***W:*** Fernando Eimbcke, Paula Markovitch; ***C:*** Alexis Zabe; ***M:*** Alejandro Rosso.

Duck Soup 🦴🦴🦴🦴 **1933** The Marx Brothers satiric masterpiece (which failed at the box office). Groucho becomes the dictator of Freedonia, and hires Chico and Harpo as spies. Jam-packed with the classic anarchic and irreverent Marx shtick; watch for the mirror scene. Zeppo plays a love-sick tenor, in this, his last film with the brothers. **70m/B VHS, DVD.** Groucho Marx, Chico Marx, Harpo Marx, Zeppo Marx, Louis Calhern, Margaret Dumont, Edgar Kennedy, Raquel Torres, Leonid Kinskey, Charles Middleton; ***D:*** Leo McCarey; ***W:*** Harry Ruby, Nat Perrin, Bert Kalmar, Arthur Sheekman; ***C:*** Henry Sharp; ***M:*** Harry Ruby, Bert Kalmar. AFI '98: Top 100, Natl. Film Reg. '90.

DuckTales the Movie: Treasure of the Lost Lamp 🦴🦴 1/2 **1990 (G)** Uncle Scrooge and company embark on a lost-ark quest, ala Harrison Ford, for misplaced treasure (a lamp that can make the sky rain ice cream). Based on the daily Disney cartoon of the same name, it's more like an extended-version Saturday morning sugar smacks'n'milk 'toon. See it with someone young. **74m/C VHS.** ***D:*** Bob Hathcock; ***W:*** Alan Burnett; ***M:*** David Newman; ***V:*** Alan Young, Christopher Lloyd, Rip Taylor, June Foray, Chuck McCann, Richard Libertini, Russi Taylor, Joan Gerber, Terence McGovern.

The Dude Bandit 🦴🦴 **1933** An unscrupulous money-lender tries to gain control of a ranch but Gibson comes to the rescue. Gibson actually plays three roles: the rancher's best friend, an aw-shucks cowpoke disguise in order to find out what's going on, and the title character used to bedevil the crooks. **68m/B VHS.** Hoot Gibson, Gloria Shea, Hooper Atchley, Skeeter Bill Robbins, Horace Carpenter, Neal Hart, Lafe (Lafayette) McKee, Gordon DeMain; ***D:*** George Melford; ***W:*** Jack Natteford; ***C:*** Tom Galligan, Harry Neumann.

The Dude Goes West 🦴🦴 1/2 **1948** East Coast gunsmith Daniel (Albert) plans a move to Arsenic City, Arizona figuring he can make a fortune in the wild west. The only good thing to happen to the tenderfoot on the trail is meeting Liza (Storm), who's got a map to her murdered father's gold mine. Naturally, she needs a little help. **86m/B DVD.** Eddie Albert, Gale Storm, James Gleason, Binnie Barnes, Gilbert Roland, Barton MacLane; ***D:*** Kurt Neumann; ***W:*** Mary Loos, Richard Sale; ***C:*** Karl Struss; ***M:*** Dimitri Tiomkin.

Dude Ranger 🦴🦴 1/2 **1934** Well-acted Zane Grey story about an easterner who gets caught up in a range war and cattle rustling when he takes possession of some property out west. **58m/B VHS, DVD.** George O'Brien, Irene Hervey, Leroy Mason, Syd Saylor, Henry K. Hall; ***D:*** Edward F. (Eddie) Cline; ***C:*** Frank B. Good.

Dude, Where's My Car? 🦴🦴 **2000 (PG-13)** Slow-witted roommates Jesse and Chester wake one morning to a bizarre, seemingly unexplainable situation. To make matters worse, they appear to have trashed their girlfriends' home the night before and, of course, their car is missing. Dude. Too hung over to remember how this all came to be, the two boys set out to piece things together and, in the process, involve themselves with angry transsexuals, ostriches, and extraterrestrials. Follows the grand tradition of stoned and/or goofball duos like Cheech and Chong, Bill and Ted, and Wayne and Garth, but just can't reach their level. **83m/C VHS, DVD, UMD.** Ashton Kutcher, Seann William Scott, Jennifer Garner, Marla Sokoloff, Kristy Swanson, David Herman, Charlie O'Connell, Hal Sparks; ***D:*** Danny Leiner; ***W:*** Philip Stark; ***C:*** Robert M. Stevens; ***M:*** David Kitay.

Dudes 🦴 **1987 (R)** Three city kids head for the desert and run afoul of some rednecks. Tired grade-6 revenge story. **90m/C VHS.** Jon Cryer, Catherine Mary Stewart, Daniel Roebuck, Flea, Lee Ving, Calvin Bartlett, Pete Willcox, Glenn Withrow; ***D:*** Penelope Spheeris; ***M:*** Charles Bernstein.

Dudley Do-Right 🦴🦴 1/2 **1999 (PG)** Lightning didn't strike twice for Fraser, who successfully starred as Jay Ward's 60s cartoon character "George of the Jungle" and then decided to tackle Ward's brainless-but-noble Canadian Mountie, Dudley. The big goof is still protecting Semi-Happy Valley from the dastardly Snidely Whiplash (Molina), who manages to take over the town and rename it Whiplash City. Snidely is also twirling his mustache in the direction of Dudley's sweetie, fair maiden Nell Fenwick (Parker), which the right-minded Mountie won't allow. Unfortunately, the film only manages a few chuckles. **75m/C VHS, DVD.** Brendan Fraser, Sarah Jessica Parker, Alfred Molina, Robert Prosky, Eric Idle, Alex Rocco, Jack Kehler, Louis Mustillo, Regis Philbin, Kathie Lee Gifford; ***D:*** Hugh Wilson; ***W:*** Hugh Wilson; ***C:*** Donald E. Thorin; ***M:*** Steve Dorff; ***Nar:*** Corey Burton.

Due East 🦴🦴 1/2 **2002 (PG-13)** Sixteen-year-old Mary Faith (Bryant) is about to be named class valedictorian when she reveals she's pregnant. The small southern town of Due East is scandalized, especially when she refuses to name the father and intends to have the baby. But Mary Faith's predicament yields some unexpected blessings with new friendships and romance. Based on the young adult novels "Due East" and "How I Got Him Back" by Valerie Sayers. **104m/C VHS, DVD.** Clara Bryant, Robert Forster, Cybill Shepherd, Kate Capshaw, Erich Anderson, Katharine Isabelle, James Kirk; ***D:*** Helen Shaver; ***W:*** Tricia Brock. **CABLE**

Duel 🦴🦴🦴 **1971 (PG)** Spielberg's first notable film, a truly scary made-for-TV exercise in paranoia. A docile traveling salesman is repeatedly attacked and threatened by a huge, malevolent tractor-trailer on an open desert highway. Released theatrically in Europe. **90m/C VHS, DVD.** Dennis Weaver, Lucille Benson, Eddie Firestone, Cary Loftin, Jacqueline Scott, Lou Frizzell, Gene Dynarski; ***D:*** Steven Spielberg; ***W:*** Richard Matheson; ***C:*** Jack Marta; ***M:*** Billy Goldenberg. **TV**

Duel at Diablo 🦴🦴🦴 **1966** An exceptionally violent film that deals with racism in the Old West. Good casting; western fans will enjoy the action. **103m/C VHS, DVD.** James Garner, Sidney Poitier, Bibi Andersson, Dennis Weaver, Bill Travers; ***D:*** Ralph Nelson.

Duel at Silver Creek 🦴🦴 1/2 **1952** A group of claim jumpers murder anyone who gets in their way, including the family of the Silver Kid (Murphy), who's deputized by Sheriff Lightning (McNally) to help him get the varmints. **76m/B VHS, DVD.** Audie Murphy, Faith Domergue, Stephen McNally, Susan Cabot, Gerald Mohr, Eugene Iglesias, Kyle James, Lee Marvin; ***D:*** Donald Siegel; ***W:*** Gerald Drayson Adams; ***C:*** Irving Glassberg; ***M:*** Hans J. Salter.

Duel in the Sun 🦴🦴🦴 **1946** A lavish, lusty David O. Selznick production of a minor western novel about a vivacious half-breed Indian girl, living on a powerful dynastic ranch, who incites two brothers to conflict. Selznick's last effort at outdoing his epic success with "Gone With the Wind." **130m/C VHS, DVD.** Gregory Peck, Jennifer Jones, Joseph Cotten, Lionel Barrymore, Lillian Gish, Butterfly McQueen, Harry Carey Sr., Walter Huston, Charles Bickford, Herbert Marshall; ***D:*** King Vidor; ***W:*** Oliver H.P. Garrett, David O. Selznick; ***C:*** Ray Rennahan; ***M:*** Dimitri Tiomkin.

Duel of Champions 🦴 *Orazi e Curiazi* **1961** It's ancient Rome, and the prodigal gladiator has come home. Now the family must have a duel to decide who will rule. **90m/C VHS, DVD.** *IT SP* Alan Ladd, Francesca Bett; ***D:*** Ferdinando Baldi.

Duel of Fists 🦴 **1971** When the owner of a boxing institute dies, he instructs his son in his will to go searching for his long-lost brother in Thailand. All he can go on is an old photograph and the knowledge that his brother is a Thai boxer. **111m/C VHS.** *HK* David Chiang, Chen Hsing, Ti Lung, Tang Ti; ***D:*** Chen Chang; ***W:*** Kuang Ni.

Duel of Hearts 🦴🦴 **1992 (PG-13)** Beautiful Caroline falls in love with wealthy Lord Vane Brecon, who unfortunately is accused of murder. When Caroline tries to help him clear his name she discovers he's hiding a number of secrets. Based on the romance novel "Duel of Love" by Barbara Cartland. Nothing too inspiring here, although regency romance fans will appreciate the attention to detail. **95m/C VHS.** *GB* Alison Doody, Michael York, Geraldine Chaplin, Benedict Taylor, Billie Whitelaw, Virginia McKenna, Richard Johnson, Jeremy Kemp, Beryl Reid, Suzanna Hamilton, Jolyon Baker, Julie Kate; ***D:*** John Hough. **CABLE**

Duel to the Death 🦴🦴 **1982** A legendary battle is held every ten years between the best Japanese and Chinese martial arts experts to determine who's tops. During the Ming Dynasty, as the next duel approaches, the candidates are caught in a war between Shaolin monks and ninjas. Chinese with subtitles. **90m/C VHS, DVD.** *HK* Damian Lau, Borman Chu, Flora Cheung; ***D:*** Siu-Tung Ching.

The Duellists 🦴🦴🦴 **1977 (PG)** A beautifully photographed picture about the long-running feud between two French officers during the Napoleonic wars. Based on "The Duel" by Joseph Conrad. **101m/C VHS, DVD.** *GB* Keith Carradine, Harvey Keitel, Albert Finney, Edward Fox, Tom Conti, Christina Raines, Diana Quick, William Morgan Sheppard; ***D:*** Ridley Scott.

Duet for One 🦴🦴 **1986 (R)** A famous concert violinist learns she is suffering from multiple sclerosis and is slowly losing her ability to play. Convinced that her life is meaningless without music, she self-destructively drifts into bitter isolation. From the play by Tom Kempinski. **108m/C VHS.** Julie Andrews, Max von Sydow, Alan Bates, Liam Neeson; ***D:*** Andrei Konchalovsky.

Duets 🦴🦴 **2000 (R)** Bruce Paltrow misuses the talents of his fine ensemble cast (including daughter Gwyneth) in this off-key comedy-melodrama about karaoke culture. The three subplots each center on a pair of misfits en route to a karaoke contest in Omaha. Ricky (Lewis) is a karaoke hustler who meets his daughter Liv (Paltrow) for the first time after the death of her mother in Las Vegas. Suzi (Bello) is a steely waitress who bullies and beguiles mild cab driver Billy (Speedman) into taking her halfway across the country with the promise of sex. Todd's (Giamatti) a freaked-out businessman fleeing his family and Reggie's (Braugher) a deep-thinking escaped convict with a killer voice. Flashes of feeling and humor offset some of the hokiness of the characters, but not enough to save the movie. **112m/C VHS, DVD.** Gwyneth Paltrow, Maria Bello, Scott Speedman, Andre Braugher, Paul Giamatti, Huey Lewis, Marian Seldes, Kiersten Warren, Angie Phillips, Angie Dickinson; ***D:*** Bruce Paltrow; ***W:*** John Byrum; ***C:*** Paul Sarossy; ***M:*** David Newman.

The Duke 🦴🦴 1/2 **1999 (G)** Talk about the dog who has everything! Hubert is the faithful bloodhound companion to the Duke of Dingwall (Neville). When the Duke dies, Hubert inherits everything—even the title! Trusted butler Clive (Doohan) and his niece Charlotte (Draper) are there to make certain Hubert is safe from the plots of the late Duke's sniveling nephew, Cecil (Muirhead), who wants the estate for himself and even tries to arrange a doggie wedding to get the riches. **88m/C VHS, DVD.** *CA* James Doohan, John Neville, Courtnee Draper, Oliver Muirhead, Sophie Heyman, Judy Geeson; ***D:*** Philip Spink; ***W:*** Craig Detweiler, Anne Vince, Robert Vince; ***C:*** Mike Southon; ***M:*** Brahm Wenger. **VIDEO**

The Duke Is Tops 🦴🦴 1/2 **1938** In Horne's earliest existing film appearance, she's off to attempt the "big-time," while her boyfriend joins a traveling medicine show. ♫I Know You Remember. **80m/C VHS, DVD.** Ralph Cooper, Lena Horne, Lawrence Criner, Monte Hawley, Edward Thompson; ***D:*** William Nolte; ***W:*** Phil Dunham; ***C:*** Robert E. Cline, J. Henry Kruse; ***M:*** Harvey Brooks, Ben Ellison.

Duke of the Derby 🦴🦴 *Le Gentleman d'Epsom* **1962** A scheming racehorse handicapper bets over his head and ruins his higher-than-means lifestyle. In French with English subtitles. **83m/C VHS.** *FR* Madeleine Robinson, Frank Villard, Jean (Lefevre) Lefebvre, Jacques Marin, Jean Gabin; ***D:*** Gilles Grangier; ***W:*** Gilles Grangier; ***C:*** Louis Page; ***M:*** Michel Legrand.

The Duke of West Point 🦴🦴 **1938** Conceited but ultimately good-hearted Brit Earley (Hayward) immigrates to the States and enrolls at West Point. He immediately alienates everyone with his superior attitude but eventually shows his good side. Fontaine provides a fine performance; plus, she's about the only one who's young enough to make a convincing college student. Hokey and predictable, but pleasant enough if you're wondering why they don't make 'em like that anymore. **109m/B VHS.** Louis Hayward, Joan Fontaine, Richard Carlson, William "Billy" Bakewell, Donald (Don "Red") Barry, Charles D. Brown, Tom Brown, Alan Curtis, Emma Dunn, Edward Earle, Marjorie Gateson, Jonathan Hale, Kenneth Harlan, Mary MacLaren; ***D:*** Alfred E. Green; ***W:*** George Bruce; ***C:*** Robert Planck.

The Dukes of Hazzard 🦴🦴 1/2 **2005 (PG-13)** Yee-haw! The '70s TV show jumps (literally!) onto the big screen. Good ole Georgia boys, moonshinin' cousins Bo (Scott) and Luke (Knoxville) Duke try to keep their Hazzard County family farm from corrupt county commissioner Boss Hogg (Reynolds), with the help of Uncle Jessie (Nelson), Daisy (Simpson), and Cooter (Koechner). But then, you knew that, because that was the plot of every episode. This version is a little less lighthearted, but it is funny (thanks to script doctoring by the Broken Lizard troupe), and doesn't take itself as seriously as the show. What it does take seriously are the car chases and stunts, which show off the General Lee, the Dukes' beloved 1969 Dodge Charger, to great effect. If you were a fan then, especially of the General, you'll be pleased. If not, you're probably wondering why they bothered at all. **105m/C DVD, Blu-ray Disc, UMD, HD DVD.** *US* Johnny Knoxville, Seann William Scott, Burt Reynolds, Willie Nelson, M.C. Gainey, Michael Weston, Lynda Carter, David Koechner, Jessica Simpson, Jack Polick, Steve Lemme, Michael Roof, Nikki Griffin, Alice Greczyn, James Roday, Kevin Heffernan, Joe Don Baker, Jacqui Maxwell; ***D:*** Jay Chandrasekhar; ***W:*** Jay Chandrasekhar, Jonathan Davis; ***C:*** Lawrence Sher; ***M:*** Nathan Barr.

Duma 🦴🦴🦴 **2005 (PG)** Family friendly pic with a kid, a cat, and a beautiful setting. Xan (Michaletos) lives on a South African farm and adopts an orphaned cheetah cub he names Duma. When his father (Scott) dies, and Xan and his mom (Davis) must move to the city, Xan is determined to release Duma into the wild himself. Not a very bright idea, especially when he gets lost in the desert—only to be found by the shifty Ripkuna (Walker). Based on fact; adapted from the book "How It Was With Dooms" by Xan and Carol Hopcraft. And no, you can't have a pet cheetah, no matter how cute they are. **100m/C DVD.** *US* Eamonn Walker, Campbell Scott, Hope Davis, Alexander Michaletos; ***D:*** Carroll Ballard; ***W:*** Karen Janszen; ***C:*** Werner Maritz.

Dumb & Dumber 🦴🦴 1/2 **1994 (PG-13)** Moronic limo driver Lloyd Christmas (Carrey) and equally dense dog groomer

Harry Dunne (Daniels) travel (in the hilarious "sheep dog" van) from Rhode Island to Colorado—at one point going east!—to return a briefcase full of cash to a beautiful socialite (Holly). Engaging in all sorts of gross-out bathroom, bodily function, and slapstick humor, this one will definitely not appeal to the stuffy critic or arthouse snob. It will provide plenty of laughs, however embarrassingly rendered, for everyone else. Daniels proves a convincing dimwit sidekick, while Carrey mugs shamelessly. Occasional "Seinfeld" writer Farrelly makes his directorial debut. **110m/C VHS, DVD, Blu-ray Disc, UMD.** Jim Carrey, Jeff Daniels, Lauren Holly, Teri Garr, Karen Duffy, Mike Starr, Charles Rocket, Victoria Rowell, Felton Perry, Harland Williams, Rob Moran, Cam Neely, Lin Shaye, Fred Stoller; ***D:*** Peter Farrelly; ***W:*** Bennett Yellin, Bobby Farrelly, Peter Farrelly; ***C:*** Mark Irwin; ***M:*** Todd Rundgren. MTV Movie Awards '95: Comedic Perf. (Carrey), Kiss (Jim Carrey/Lauren Holly); Blockbuster '96: Comedy Actor, V. (Carrey).

Dumb and Dumberer: When Harry Met Lloyd **2003 (PG-13)** The title is probably the most inspired part of this flick. Harry (Richardson) and Lloyd (Olsen) meet in high school and are immediately recruited to attend a "special needs" class set up by the corrupt principal (Levy) to steal grant money. The school paper's star reporter (Nichols) investigates the scam, setting up possible romance. Richardson and Olsen do a commendable job impersonating Daniels and Carrey, but the charm of the original has been replaced by a double dose of poo and retard jokes, done with less subtlety and class (!) than the Farrelly outing. Stick with the original. **82m/C VHS, DVD.** *US* Derek Richardson, Eric Christian Olsen, Eugene Levy, Luis Guzman, Cheri Oteri, Rachel Nichols, Elden (Ratliff) Henson, William Lee Scott, Mimi Rogers, Shia LaBeouf, Lin Shaye, Teal Redmann, Josh Braaten, Michelle Krusiec, Julia Duffy; ***D:*** Troy Miller; ***W:*** Troy Miller, Robert Brener; ***C:*** Anthony B. Richmond; ***M:*** Eban Schletter.

Dumb Waiter **1987** A mini-play by Harold Pinter about two hitmen awaiting instructions for a job in an empty boardinghouse, and getting comically mixed messages. **60m/C VHS.** John Travolta, Tom Conti; ***D:*** Robert Altman; ***W:*** Harold Pinter; ***C:*** Pierre Mignot; ***M:*** Judith Gruber-Stitzer. **TV**

Dumbo **1941** Animated Disney classic about a baby elephant growing up in the circus who is ridiculed for his large ears, until he discovers he can fly. The little elephant who could fly then becomes a circus star. Expressively and imaginatively animated, highlighted by the hallucinatory dancing pink elephants sequence. Endearing songs by Frank Churchill, Oliver Wallace, and Ned Washington, including "Baby Mine," "Pink Elephants on Parade," and "I See an Elephant Fly." **63m/C VHS, DVD.** ***D:*** Ben Sharpsteen; ***W:*** Joe Grant, Dick Huemer; ***M:*** Frank Churchill, Oliver Wallace; ***V:*** Sterling Holloway, Edward Brophy, Verna Felton, Herman Bing, Cliff Edwards. Oscars '41: Scoring/Musical.

Dummy **2002 (R)** Sappy farce/ latent coming-of-ager about a man and his dummy. Shy outsider Steven (Brody), nearly 30 and still living at home with his parents, embarks on his dream career in ventriloquism. His wooden buddy, along with high-school friend Fanny (Jovovich), give Steven the confidence to woo his pretty unemployment counselor Lorena (Farmiga). Ranges from genuinely sweet to annoyingly cloying. Despite a decent turn from Oscar-winner Brody, who did all his own ventriloquism, lovable schmuck routine wears thin rather quickly. Supports are uniformly strong. **90m/C VHS, DVD.** *US* Adrien Brody, Milla Jovovich, Illeana Douglas, Vera Farmiga, Jessica Walter, Ron Leibman, Jared Harris; ***D:*** Greg Pritkin; ***W:*** Greg Pritkin; ***C:*** Horacio Marquinez; ***M:*** Paul Wallfisch.

The Dummy Talks **1943** When a ventriloquist is murdered, a midget goes undercover as a dummy to find the killer. Watch closely and you might see his lips move. **85m/B VHS.** *GB* Jack Warner, Claude Hulbert, Beryl Orde, Derna Derna-Hazell, Ivy Benson, Manning Whiley; ***D:*** Oswald Mitchell; ***W:*** Michael Barringer, Jack Clifford, Con West; ***C:*** James Wilson.

Dune **1984 (PG-13)** Lynch's sci-fi opus based on the Frank Herbert novel boasting great set design, muddled scripting, and a good cast. The story: controlling the spice drug of Arrakis permits control of the universe in the year 10991. Paul, the heir of the Atreides family, leads the Freemen in a revolt against the evil Harkhonens who have violently seized control of Arrakis, also known as Dune, the desert planet. That's as clear as it ever gets. **137m/C VHS, DVD, HD DVD.** Kyle MacLachlan, Francesca Annis, Jose Ferrer, Sting, Max von Sydow, Jurgen Prochnow, Linda Hunt, Freddie Jones, Dean Stockwell, Virginia Madsen, Brad Dourif, Kenneth McMillan, Silvana Mangano, Jack Nance, Sian Phillips, Paul Smith, Richard Jordan, Everett McGill, Sean Young, Patrick Stewart; ***D:*** David Lynch; ***W:*** David Lynch; ***C:*** Freddie Francis; ***M:*** Brian Eno.

Dune 1/2 *Frank Herbert's Dune* **2000** Frank Herbert's 1965 sci-fi classic was previously made into a disappointing 1984 film by David Lynch. This miniseries more successfully combines visuals with character, although the complicated plot is still somewhat overwhelming. Duke Leto (Hurt) of the House of Atreides has been appointed by the Emperor to harvest and export Spice—the most prized commodity on the desert planet of Arrakis (or Dune). But a rival faction, led by Baron Harkonnen (McNeice), causes trouble for Atreides and his heir, Paul (Newman), who must look to Dune's native inhabitants for support. **270m/C VHS, DVD, Blu-ray Disc.** Alec Newman, William Hurt, Saskia Reeves, Ian McNeice, P. H. Moriarty, Julie Cox, Matt Keeslar, Giancarlo Giannini, Barbara Kodetova, Robert Russell, Miljen Kreka Kljakovic; ***D:*** John Harrison; ***W:*** John Harrison; ***C:*** Vittorio Storaro, Harry B. Miller III; ***M:*** Graeme Revell. **CABLE**

Dune Warriors 1/2 **1991 (R)** Earth is a parched planet in the year 2040. Renegade bands cruise the desert, making short shrift of civilized people who band together in remote villages. When peaceful farmer Carradine's family falls prey to the pillagers, surely he and the most evil warlord of all must clash. Good action and stunts, if the dummy plot doesn't get you first. **77m/C VHS.** David Carradine, Richard (Rick) Hill, Luke Askew, Jillian McWhirter, Blake Boyd; ***D:*** Cirio H. Santiago.

The Dunera Boys **1985 (R)** Hoskins shines in this story about Viennese Jews who, at the onset of WWII, escape to England where they are suspected as German spies. Subsequently, the British shipped them all to an Australian prison camp, where they recreated in peace their Viennese lifestyle. **150m/C VHS.** *AU* Bob Hoskins, Joe Spano, Warren Mitchell, Joseph Furst, Moshe Kedem, Dita Cobb, John Meillon, Mary-Anne Fahey, Simon Chilvers, Steven Vidler; ***D:*** Sam Lewin.

Dungeon of Harrow **1964** Unbelievably cheap tale of shipwrecked comrades who encounter a maniacal family on an otherwise deserted island. Not your stranded-on-a-desert-island fantasy come true. Filmed in San Antonio; a harrowing bore. **74m/B VHS, DVD.** Russ Harvey, Helen Hogan, Bill McNulty, Pat Boyette; ***D:*** Pat Boyette.

Dungeonmaster 1/2 *Ragewar* **1983 (PG-13)** A warlord forces a computer wiz to participate in a bizarre "Dungeons and Dragons" styled game in order to save a girl held captive. Consists of seven segments, each by a different director. Save yourself the trouble. **80m/C VHS.** Jeffrey Byron, Richard Moll, Leslie Wing, Danny Dick; ***D:*** John Carl Buechler, Charles Band, Dave Allen, Stephen Ford, Peter Manoogian, Ted Nicolaou, Rosemarie Turko; ***W:*** Allen Actor; ***M:*** Richard Band.

Dungeons and Dragons 1/2 **2000 (PG-13)** Based (probably very loosely) on the role-playing game of the same name, "D & D" tells the story of the land of Izmer, whose reformer ruler, Empress Savina (Birch), wants to empower the lowly commoners and put them on equal footing with the ruling Mages. An elitist Mage, Profion (Irons, in an obvious pay-the-bills role) wants to overthrow her. Luckily, she's aided by young hero Ridley (Whalin) and his sidekick Snails (Wayans). It's hard to decide what's more ridiculous: plot, dialogue, settings, effects, costumes, or the idea that anyone would pay to see this mess. The mere title is enough to turn off anyone who never played the game as a kid, and the target audience will probably nit-pick it to death with "that's not like in the game"-type complaints. **107m/C VHS, DVD.** Justin Whalin, Marlon Wayans, Jeremy Irons, Thora Birch, Zoe McLellan, Kristen Wilson, Lee Arenberg, Bruce Payne, Richard O'Brien, Tom Baker, Robert Miano; ***D:*** Courtney Solomon; ***W:*** Topper Lilien, Carroll Cartwright; ***C:*** Doug Milsome; ***M:*** Justin Caine Burnett.

Dunston Checks In 1/2 **1995 (PG)** This just in: Hollywood thinks monkeys are funny. But, as far as "stupid people learn important life lessons from a monkey who wears clothes" movies go, this one's not bad. Robert Grant (Alexander) is the manager of a five-star hotel. His Leona Helmsley-esque boss (Dunaway) is convinced that aristocratic guest Lord Rutledge (Everett) is a travel guide critic who is there to bestow an elusive sixth star on the hotel. Actually he's a jewel thief, and Dunston the orangutan is his accomplice. When Dunston flees from his abusive owner, he's adopted by Grant's two children. Together, Dunston and the kids are left to straighten out the whole mess. **88m/C VHS, DVD.** Jason Alexander, Faye Dunaway, Eric Lloyd, Rupert Everett, Graham Sack, Paul (Pee-wee Herman) Reubens, Glenn Shadix, Nathan Davis, Jennifer Bassey; ***D:*** Ken Kwapis; ***W:*** Bruce Graham, John Hopkins; ***C:*** Peter Lyons Collister; ***M:*** Miles Goodman.

The Dunwich Horror **1970** Young warlock acquires a banned book of evil spells, starts trouble on the astral plane. Stockwell hammy. Loosely based on H. P. Lovecraft story. **90m/C VHS, DVD.** Sandra Dee, Dean Stockwell, Lloyd Bochner, Ed Begley Sr., Sam Jaffe, Joanna Moore, Talia Shire, Barboura Morris, Beach Dickerson, Michael Fox, Donna Baccala; ***D:*** Daniel Haller; ***W:*** Curtis Hanson, Henry Rosenbaum, Ronald Silkosky; ***C:*** Richard C. Glouner; ***M:*** Les Baxter.

Duplex **2003 (PG-13)** New York yuppies try to bump off a sweet old lady for her rent-controlled apartment in Brooklyn. Alex (Stiller) and Nancy (Barrymore), however, didn't start out as would-be assassins in the name of real estate. After moving into a picture-perfect duplex downstairs from Mrs. Connell, they discover that, although very old and in poor health, she still manages a host of irksome behaviors. With her health not declining nearly fast enough, the senior-crazed couple are driven to desperate measures. Stiller is top-notch and Barrymore a worthy co-star despite a far-fetched plot that revenge comedy specialist/director DeVito ultimately doesn't sell. **88m/C VHS, DVD.** *US* Drew Barrymore, Ben Stiller, Eileen Essell, Harvey Fierstein, Justin Theroux, Robert Wisdom, Amber Valletta, James Remar, Maya Rudolph, Swoosie Kurtz, Wallace Shawn, Michelle Krusiec; ***D:*** Danny DeVito; ***W:*** Larry Doyle; ***C:*** Anastas Michos; ***M:*** David Newman.

Duplicates **1992 (PG-13)** Harrison and Greist are a married couple whose young son has disappeared. When the boy is found he has no memory of his former life or parents. The couple discover he's the victim of secret experiments which transfer human memories into computer banks. Will they become the next targets? **92m/C VHS.** Gregory Harrison, Kim Greist, Cicely Tyson, Lane Smith, William Lucking, Kevin McCarthy; ***D:*** Sandor Stern.

Duplicity 1/2 **2009 (PG-13)** CIA officer Claire Stenwick (Roberts) and MI6 agent Ray Koval (Owen) have left the world of government intelligence to cash in on the highly profitable cold war raging between two rival multinational corporations. Their mission? Secure the formula for a product that will bring a fortune to the company that patents it first. Pic is a strange but surprisingly effective combination of romantic comedy and crime caper. From the two leads to the lavish hotel suites throughout Europe, everything looks exquisite. While it keeps the viewer guessing who is conning who, it begins to boarder on the absurd with one contrived, implausible double-cross after another. A worthy effort from writer/director Gilroy but not on the level of his excellent "Michael Clayton." **125m/C DVD.** *US* Julia Roberts, Clive Owen, Tom Wilkinson, Paul Giamatti, Carrie Preston, Thomas (Tom) McCarthy, Denis O'Hare, Kathleen Chalfant, Wayne Duvall, Rick Worthy, Oleg Stefan; ***D:*** Tony Golroy; ***W:*** Tony Golroy; ***C:*** Robert Elswit; ***M:*** James Newton Howard.

Dupont Lajoie *Rape of Innocence* **1974** At a tourist campground Lajoie (Carmet) accidentally kills his son's girlfriend when she resists his sexual advances. To save his life he accuses Arabs of committing the crime and begins a racist campaign of vengeance. French with subtitles. **103m/C VHS.** *FR* Jean Carmet; ***D:*** Yves Boisset.

Durango 1/2 **1999** Okay, the title sounds western and there is a cattle drive but this whimsical romance is set in the Irish countryside in 1939. Mark Doran (Keeslar) and his neighbors get together to drive their cattle to the railway (40 miles distant) when the local buyer tries to cheat them. He's also in love with a lassie (St. Alban) but is worried about her fearsome father (Bergin). Maybe, if Mark's plan succeeds, he'll have the confidence to get the girl as well. Based on the novel by John B. Keane. **98m/C VHS.** Matt Keeslar, Patrick Bergin, Brenda Fricker, Nancy St. Alban, George Hearn, Paul Ronan, Dermot Martin, Mark Lambert; ***D:*** Brent Shields; ***W:*** Walter Bernstein; ***C:*** Shelly Johnson; ***M:*** Mark McKenzie. **TV**

The Durango Kid 1/2 **1940** Bad guy Mace Ballard (MacDonald) blames the murder of a local rancher on the Durango Kid, which really irks Bill Lowry (Starrett) since he's actually the masked do-gooder. The Kid then steals money from Ballard to give to the homesteaders Ballard has burned out. Finally suspicious of Lowry, Ballard kidnaps his girlfriend Nancy (Walters) to lure him into a trap. Despite the Durango Kid retiring his mask at the end of the movie, Starrett resurrected the character for a series of westerns from 1945 to 1952. **61m/B DVD.** Charles Starrett, Luana Walters, Kenneth MacDonald, Forrest Taylor, Francis Walker, Melvin Lang; ***D:*** Lambert Hillyer; ***W:*** Paul Franklin; ***C:*** John Stumar.

Durango Valley Raiders 1/2 **1938** Sheriff is the leader of the outlaws, and a young cowboy finds out. **55m/B VHS.** Bob Steele; ***D:*** Sam Newfield.

Dust **1985** A white woman in South Africa murders her father when he shows affection for a young black servant. Controversial and intense. **87m/C VHS.** *FR BE* Jane Birkin, Trevor Howard, John Matshikiza, Nadine Uwampa, Lourdes Christina Sayo, Rene Diaz; ***D:*** Marion Hansel; ***W:*** Marion Hansel; ***M:*** Martin St. Pierre.

Dust 1/2 **2001 (R)** Skewered Euro-western set primarily in a war-torn Macedonia (where it was filmed) at the turn of the 20th century. It begins awkwardly in a present-day New York apartment where the aged Angela (Murphy) holds would-be burglar Edge (Lester) at gunpoint so he will listen to the story of her father and uncle. Gunfighter brothers Luke (Wenham) and Elijah (Fiennes) both fall for prostitute Lilith (Brochet), but it's Elijah who marries her. An embittered Luke eventually winds up in Macedonia, where revolutionary gangs battle the occupying Turks. Luke lends his gun, finds a girl (Kujaca), and then Elijah shows up. The old-west tale is visually stunning (and bloody) but the New York story is intrusive and sentimental. **124m/C VHS, DVD.** *GB GE IT MA* Joseph Fiennes, David Wenham, Adrian Lester, Rosemary Murphy, Anne Brochet, Nikolina Kujaca; ***D:*** Milcho Manchevski; ***W:*** Milcho Manchevski; ***C:*** Barry Ackroyd; ***M:*** Kiril Dzajkovski.

Dust Devil **1993 (R)** Three travelers find themselves in Namibia's vast desert: a policeman, a woman on the run, and her abusive husband. They all have the misfortune of meeting up with a supernatural being known as the "Dust Devil," who kills humans in order to steal their souls and increase his other worldly powers. **87m/C VHS, DVD.** *GB* Robert John Burke, Chelsea Field, Zakes Mokae, Rufus Swart, John Matshikiza, William Hootkins, Marianne Saegebrecht; ***D:*** Richard Stanley; ***W:*** Richard Stanley; ***C:*** Steven Chivers; ***M:*** Simon Boswell.

Dust to Glory **2005 (PG)** Son of "The Endless Summer" creator Bruce Brown, Dana Brown brings his father's sense of kineticism to the races in this high-octane documentary. The Baja 1000 is the world's more dangerous and notorious race, open to dirt bikes, souped-up VW bugs, 4x4s, and just about anything else. Its dusty trails and Mexican highways are captured in all their white-knuckled madness through the use of 50 different cameras, edited seamlessly. However, once a few of the race's more eccentric characters are introduced along the way, things slow down considerably. It takes a few jump starts to get going now and then, but overall it's a whopping 97-minute condensed version of this 16 hour trek. Racing legends Robby Gordon, Mario Andretti, and Jimmy Vasser join in the fun. **97m/C DVD.** *US* ***D:*** Dana Brown; ***W:*** Dana Brown; ***C:*** Kevin Ward; ***M:*** Nathan Furst.

Dusty **1985** Touching story of a wild dingo dog raised by an Australian rancher and trained to herd sheep. Filmed in the Australian bush and based on the children's book by Frank Dalby Davison. **89m/C VHS.** *AU* Bill Kerr, Noel Trevarthen, Carol Burns, Nicholas Holland, John Stanton; ***D:*** John Richardson.

Dusty and Sweets Mcgee **1971** Some weird leftover hippie tale about the dangers of drug addiction with a 'cast' of real-life, essentially nameless heroin addicts whose delusions about their lives are striking. It's not a documentary, although first-time film director Mutrux started off interviewing the addicts before filming. **87m/C DVD.** ***D:*** Floyd Mutrux; ***W:*** Floyd Mutrux; ***C:*** William A. Fraker; ***M:*** Ricky Nelson.

Dutch 1/2 **1991 (PG-13)** Working class boob attempts to pick up his girlfriend's son from boarding school. Their trip together gives them an unexpected chance to connect, if they don't kill each other first. Silly premise from the Hughes factory has little innovation and uses type-casting instead of acting. **107m/C VHS, DVD.** Ed O'Neill, Ethan (Randall) Embry, JoBeth Williams, Elizabeth (E.G. Dailey) Daily; ***D:*** Peter Faiman; ***W:*** John Hughes.

Dutch Girls **WOOF!** **1987** Muddled mayhem as a horny high school field hockey team travels through Holland, cavorts about, and discovers the meaning of life. **83m/C VHS, DVD.** *GB* Bill Paterson, Colin Firth, Timothy Spall; ***D:*** Giles Foster.

Dutch Treat **1986 (R)** Two nerds con a sultry, all-girl rock band into thinking they're powerful record company execs. Nobody's buying. **95m/C VHS.** Lorin Dreyfuss, David Landsberg; ***D:*** Boaz Davidson.

Dutchman **1967** Film presentation of Amiri Baraka's one act play depicting the claustrophobic reality of the black man's situation in America. Black man shares subway conversation with a white woman who questions his race and middle class aspirations. Enraged, one takes the other's life. **55m/C VHS, DVD.** *GB* Al Freeman Jr., Shirley Knight; ***D:*** Anthony Harvey; ***M:*** John Barry. Cannes '67: Film.

The Dybbuk 1/2 *Der Dibuk* **1937** A man's bride is possessed by a restless spirit. Set in the Polish-Jewish community before WWI and based on the play by Sholom Anski. Considered a classic for its portrayal of Jewish religious and cultural mores. In Yiddish with English subtitles. **123m/B VHS, DVD.** *PL* Abraham Morewski, Isaac Samberg, Moshe Lipman, Lili Liliana, Dina Halpern, Leon Liebgold; ***D:*** Michal Waszynski; ***W:*** S.A. Kacyzna, Marek Arenstein; ***C:*** Albert Wywerka; ***M:*** Krzysztof Komeda.

Dying Game **1994** Sorority girls are being stalked and murdered and the detective investigating the crimes falls for the sorority's president. Now, he has to find the killer before his girlfriend becomes the next victim. **85m/C VHS.** Michael Hughes, Mathea Webb, D.J. Boozer; ***D:*** Kris Hughes.

The Dying Gaul **2005 (R)** Elaine (Clarkson) is one twisted sister—although she has reason to act on her ugly impulses and feelings of betrayal. A former screenwriter, Elaine is the wife of powerful movie exec Jeffrey (Scott), who wants to buy the script of fledgling writer Robert (Sarsgaard). With one large caveat: Robert must change his tragic, autobiographical gay love story into a standard straight tearjerker. Robert caves and winds is seduced by the predatory Jeffrey as well. Elaine goes online under an assumed identity and learns about the affair. Elaine's revenge is outrageous and not too believable. The actors make it somewhat plausible. Lucas adapted his 1998 play for his directorial debut. **105m/C DVD.** *US* Patricia Clarkson, Campbell Scott, Peter Sarsgaard; ***D:*** Craig Lucas; ***W:*** Craig Lucas; ***C:*** Bobby Bukowski; ***M:*** Steven Reich.

Dying Room Only 1/2 **1973** Travelling through the desert, a woman's husband suddenly disappears after they stop at a secluded roadside diner. A real spooker. **74m/C VHS.** Cloris Leachman, Ross Martin, Ned Beatty, Louise Latham, Dana Elcar, Dabney Coleman; ***D:*** Philip Leacock; ***W:*** Richard Matheson; ***M:*** Charles Fox. **TV**

Dying to Get Rich *Susan's Plan* **1998 (R)** Slow pacing stunts the humor but doesn't manage to destroy it. Divorced Susan (Kinski) wants her lover, Sam (Zane), to knock off her ex-husband (Paul) so she can collect his life insurance policy. He hires the job out to a couple of losers (Schneider, Biehn), who fail. So the lovers hire a crazy biker (Aykroyd) to finish the job. **90m/C VHS, DVD.** Nastassja Kinski, Billy Zane, Dan Aykroyd, Rob Schneider, Lara Flynn Boyle, Adrian Paul, Michael Biehn, Carl Ballantine, Thomas Haden Church, Bill Duke, Sheree North; ***D:*** John Landis; ***W:*** John Landis; ***C:*** Ken Kelsch; ***M:*** Peter Bernstein.

Dying to Remember 1/2 **1993 (PG-13)** A fashion designer (Gilbert) regresses to a past life during hypnotherapy and discovers she was murdered in 1963. She flies to San Francisco to discover more about her past but finds that someome wants to keep things secret—and is willing to kill again. Tedious and predictable. **87m/C VHS.** Melissa Gilbert, Ted Shackleford, Scott Plank, Christopher Stone, Jay Robinson; ***D:*** Arthur Allan Seidelman; ***W:*** George Schenck, Frank Cardea, Brian Ross.

The Dying Truth *A Distant Scream* **1986** A wrongfully accused prisoner lies dying in his cell. Trouble is, he can't die in peace until he solves the murder they say he committed. Interesting mix of the supernatural and mystery, although perhaps not one of Carradine's more memorable roles. **80m/C VHS.** *GB* David Carradine, Stephanie Beacham, Stephen Greif, Stephan Chase, Larry Carby, Lesley Dunlop; ***D:*** John Hough; ***W:*** Martin Worth; ***C:*** Brian West; ***M:*** Paul Patterson.

Dying Young 1/2 **1991 (R)** Muted romance has a wealthy leukemia victim hire a spirited, unschooled beauty as his nurse. They fall in love, but the film is either too timid or too unimaginative to mine emotions denoted by the title. Nobody dies, in fact, a grim ending (faithful to the Marti Leimbach novel on which this was based) got scrapped after testing poorly with audiences. The actors try their best, photography is lovely, and Kenny G's mellow music fills the soundtrack, but this is basically overmelodramatic drivel. Scott is the late Dewhurst's son. **111m/C VHS, DVD.** Julia Roberts, Campbell Scott, Vincent D'Onofrio, Colleen Dewhurst, Ellen Burstyn, David Selby; ***D:*** Joel Schumacher; ***W:*** Richard Friedenberg; ***C:*** Juan Ruiz-Anchia.

Dynamite **1949** Romance explodes as two young demolitions experts vie for the same girl. Stand back. **68m/B VHS, DVD.** William Gargan, Virginia Welles, Richard Crane, Irving Bacon; ***D:*** William H. Pine.

Dynamite and Gold *Where the Hell's the Gold?* **1988 (PG)** Nelson and crew embark on a search for lost gold, battling hostile Indians, the Mexican army and assorted bandits along the way. A mediocre TV movie. **91m/C VHS.** Willie Nelson, Delta Burke, Jack Elam, Alfonso Arau, Gregory Sierra, Michael Wren, Gerald McRaney; ***D:*** Burt Kennedy; ***W:*** Burt Kennedy. **TV**

The Dynamite Brothers **1974 (R)** Two tough guys, one a Hong Kong immigrant with martial arts skills, the other a brother from the streets of the ghetto, team up to rid Los Angeles of a Chinese crimelord. **90m/C VHS, DVD.** James Hong, Aldo Ray, Alan Tang, Timothy Brown, Carolyn Ann Speed, Don Oliver; ***D:*** Al Adamson; ***M:*** Charles Earland.

Dynamite Canyon **1941** Average oater has villain Price committing murder in order to keep secret the location of a lode of copper. Standard western fare. **58m/B VHS, DVD.** Tom Keene, Evelyn Finley, Sugar Dawn, Stanley Price, Kenne Duncan; ***D:*** Robert Emmett Tansey; ***W:*** Robert Emmett Tansey, Frances Kavanaugh.

Dynamite Chicken **1970 (R)** Melange of skits, songs, and hippie satire is dated. Includes performances by Joan Baez, Lenny Bruce, B.B. King, and others. **75m/C VHS, DVD.** Joan Baez, Richard Pryor, Jimi Hendrix; ***D:*** Ernest Pintoff.

Dynamite Dan 1/2 **1924** A man knocks out the heavyweight boxing champion after he flirts with his girlfriend and decides to give up his day job to become a championship boxer. He is a success, and in the end he has to face the champion again. Will he win? **62m/B VHS, DVD.** Kenneth McDonald, Frank Rice, Boris Karloff, Eddie Harris, Diana Alden, Harry Woods, Jack (H.) Richardson; ***D:*** Bruce Mitchell.

Dynamite Pass **1950** Offbeat oater about disgruntled ranchers attempting to stop the construction of a new road. **61m/B VHS.** Tim Holt, Richard Martin, Regis Toomey, Lynne Roberts, Denver Pyle; ***D:*** Lew Landers.

Dynamite Ranch **1932** Ranchers fight tooth and nail to keep their rights and property in this Maynard oater. **60m/B VHS, DVD.** Ruth Hall, Alan Roscoe, Arthur Hoyt, Martha Mattox, Ken Maynard; ***D:*** Forrest Sheldon; ***W:*** Barry Barrington; ***C:*** Ted D. McCord.

Dynasty **1976** Pulitzer Prize-winning author James Michener creates the usual sweeping saga of a family torn by jealousy, deception, and rivalry in love and business as husband, wife, and brother-in-law seek their fortune in the Ohio frontier of the 1820s. **90m/C VHS, DVD.** Sarah Miles, Harris Yulin, Stacy Keach, Harrison Ford, Amy Irving, Granville Van Dusen, Charles Weldon, Gerrit Graham; ***D:*** Lee Philips; ***W:*** Sidney Carroll; ***C:*** William Cronjager; ***M:*** Gil Melle.

Dynasty **1977** A leader of the Ming Dynasty is killed by evil Imperial Court eunuch and his son the monk sets out to avenge him. In 3-D. Run-of-the-mill kung-fu stunts. **94m/C VHS, DVD.** Bobby Ming, Lin Tashing, Pai Ying, Tang Wei, Jin Gang; ***D:*** Zhang Meijun.

Dynasty of Fear 1/2 *Fear in the Night; Honeymoon of Fear* **1972 (PG)** Matters get rather sticky at a British boys' school when the headmaster's wife seduces her husband's assistant. Together they conspire to murder her husband and share his fortune. **93m/C VHS, DVD.** *GB* Peter Cushing, Joan Collins, Ralph Bates, Judy Geeson, James Cossins, John Bown, Brian Grellis, Gillian Lind; ***D:*** Jimmy Sangster; ***W:*** Jimmy Sangster, Michael Syson; ***C:*** Arthur Grant.

E. Nick: A Legend in His Own Mind **1984** Satire of videos and magazines designed for adults. **75m/C VHS.** Don Calfa, Cleavon Little, Andra Akers, Pat McCormick; ***D:*** Robert Hegyes.

Each Dawn I Die 1/2 **1939** Cagney stars as a reporter who is a fervent critic of the political system. Framed for murder and imprisoned, he is subsequently befriended by fellow inmate Raft, a gangster. Once hardened by prison life, Cagney shuns his friend and becomes wary of the system. Despite its farfetched second half and mediocre script, the film makes interesting viewing thanks to a stellar performance from Cagney. **92m/B VHS, DVD.** James Cagney, George Raft, George Bancroft, Jane Bryan, Maxie "Slapsie" Rosenbloom, Alan Baxter, Thurston Hall, Stanley Ridges, Victor Jory; ***D:*** William Keighley; ***W:*** Norman Reilly Raine; ***C:*** Arthur Edeson; ***M:*** Max Steiner.

The Eagle **1925** In this tale of a young Cossack "Robin Hood," Valentino assumes the persona of the Eagle to avenge his father's murder. The romantic rogue encounters trouble when he falls for the beautiful Banky much to the chagrin of the scorned Czarina Dresser. Fine performances from Valentino and Dresser. Silent, based on a Alexander Pushkin story. Released on video with a new score by Davis. **77m/B VHS, DVD.** Rudolph Valentino, Vilma Banky, Louise Dresser, George Nicholls Jr., James A. Marcus; ***D:*** Clarence Brown; ***C:*** George Barnes; ***M:*** Carl Davis.

The Eagle and the Hawk **1933** Americans Jerry Young (March), Henry Crocker (Grant), and Mike Richards (Oakie) volunteer for flying duty with the British Army in 1918. Jerry is a heroic pilot but becomes depressed by the horrors of war, while gung ho Henry, who's serving as his observer/gunner, also becomes his rival. On leave, Jerry briefly finds solace with a society babe (Lombard) only to discover on his return that Henry's cockiness has gotten their buddy Mike killed. He denounces the war but Henry manages to ensure Jerry's status as a hero despite his actions. **73m/B VHS.** Fredric March, Cary Grant, Jack Oakie, Carole Lombard, Guy Standing, Forrester Harvey, Kenneth Howell, Leyland Hodgson; ***D:*** Stuart Walker; ***W:*** Seton I. Miller, Bogart Rogers; ***C:*** Harry Fischbeck.

Eagle Eye **2008 (PG-13)** Slacker Jerry's (LaBeouf) twin brother has died under suspicious circumstances and single mom Rachel's (Monaghan) child is missing. The two strangers are thrown together when they get mysterious calls on their cell phones from an unknown woman who forces them into one death-defying situation after another, ultimately to frame them as terrorists planning a political assassination. FBI agent Morgan (Thornton) is on their trail but doesn't believe the pair are truly assassins. Too loud and too slick, it borrows unapologetically from better political thrillers while attempting to deliver serious messages about civil liberties, surveillance and technology in a post 9/11 America. **117m/C DVD, Blu-ray Disc.** *US* Shia LaBeouf, Michelle Monaghan, Billy Bob Thornton, Rosario Dawson, Michael Chiklis, Cameron Boyce, Bill Smitrovich, Anthony Mackie, Marc Singer, Nick Searcy, Lynn Cohen, Anthony Azizi; ***D:*** D.J. Caruso; ***W:*** Hillary Seitz, Dan McDermott, John Glenn, Travis Adam Wright; ***C:*** Dariusz Wolsi; ***M:*** Brian Tyler.

The Eagle Has Landed **1977 (PG)** Duvall, portraying a Nazi colonel in this WWII spy film, commissions Sutherland's Irish, English-hating character to aid him in his mission to kill Prime Minister Winston Churchill. Adapted from the bestselling novel by Jack Higgins. A restored version is available at 134 minutes. **123m/C VHS, DVD.** Michael Caine, Donald Sutherland, Robert Duvall, Larry Hagman, Jenny Agutter, Donald Pleasence, Treat Williams, Anthony Quayle; ***D:*** John Sturges; ***W:*** Tom Mankiewicz; ***C:*** Anthony B. Richmond; ***M:*** Lalo Schifrin.

The Eagle Has Two Heads *L'Aigle a Deux Tetes; The Eagle with Two Heads* **1948** Set during the 19th century, poet/anarchist Marais sets out to assassinate the queen, but when he sees the beautiful monarch, it's love at first sight. Adapted from Cocteau's hugely successful play. In French with English subtitles. **93m/B VHS.** *FR* Edwige Feuillere, Jean Marais; ***D:*** Jean Cocteau; ***W:*** Jean Cocteau.

Eagle vs. Shark 1/2 **2007 (R)** Lily (Horseley) and Jarrod (Clement) are small-town mall employees united by a decided lack of social skills who meet at a costume party dedicated to dressing as their favorite animals. Lily's sweet, Jarrod's completely unlikable, and something resembling clingy love ensues as the two bounce from awkward situation to awkward situation. Tries to be simultaneously edgy and charming but ultimately just makes jokes at the expense of its protagonists. **94m/C DVD.** *NZ* Brian Sergent, Craig Hall, Joel Tobeck, Jemaine Clement, Loren Horsley, Rachel House; ***D:*** Taika Waititi; ***W:*** Taika Waititi; ***C:*** Adam Clark; ***M:*** Phoenix Foundation.

Eagles Attack at Dawn 1/2 *The Big Escape; From Hell to Victory; Hostages in the Gulf* **1970 (PG)** After escaping from an Arab prison, an Israeli soldier vows to return with a small commando force to kill the sadistic warden. **96m/C VHS, DVD.** *IS* Rick Jason, Peter Brown, Joseph Shiloah, Yehuda Barkan, Yehoram Gaon; ***D:*** Menahem Golan; ***W:*** Menahem Golan; ***C:*** Ya'ackov Kallach; ***M:*** Dov Seltzer.

Eagles Over London 1/2 *La Battaglia d'Inghilterra* **1969** Italian-produced war action that's supposed to represent the Battle of Britain. German saboteurs kill a squad of British troops, steal their ID tags, and infiltrate England. Their intention is to blow up coastal radar installations so that the Luftwaffe can bomb London. Captain Paul Stevens discovers what's happening and tries to find the bad guys. **110m/C DVD.** *IT* Frederick Stafford, Francisco Rabal, Van Johnson, Luigi Pistilli, Ida Galli, Renzo Palmer; ***D:*** Enzo G. Castellari; ***W:*** Enzo G. Castellari, Tito Carpi, Vincenzo Flamini; ***C:*** Alejandro Ulloa; ***M:*** Francesco De Masi.

Eagle's Shadow 🦴 **1984** After a poor orphan boy rescues an aged beggar, the grateful old man tutors the lad in Snake-Fist techniques. **101m/C VHS, DVD.** Jackie Chan, Juan Jan Lee, Simon Yuen, Roy Horan; ***D:*** Yuen Woo Ping.

Eagle's Wing 🦴 1/2 **1979** John Briley, screenwriter of the award-winning epic "Gandhi," attempts to weave the threads of allegory smoothly in this white man vs. red man Western from England. The mediocre story finds Native American Waterston dueling white trapper Sheen in a quest to capture an elusive, exotic white stallion. **111m/C VHS.** *GB* Martin Sheen, Sam Waterston, Harvey Keitel, Stephane Audran, Caroline Langrishe; ***D:*** Anthony Harvey; ***W:*** John Briley; ***C:*** Billy Williams.

Early Days 🦴🦴 **1981** A cantankerous, salty, once-powerful politician awaits death. From the play by David Storey. **67m/C VHS.** *GB* Ralph Richardson, Edward Judd, Sheila Ballantyne, Mary Cruickshank; ***W:*** David Storey. **TV**

Early Frost 🦴 1/2 **1984** Near suspenseful whodunit centering around a simple divorce investigation that leads to the discovery of a corpse. **95m/C VHS, DVD.** Diana McLean, Jon Blake, Janet Kingsbury, David Franklin; ***D:*** Terry O'Connor.

An Early Frost 🦴🦴🦴 1/2 **1985** Highly praised, surprisingly intelligent drama following the anguish of a successful lawyer who tells his closed-minded family that he is gay and dying of AIDS. Sensitive performance by Quinn in one of the first TV films to focus on the devastating effects of HIV. Rowlands adeptly displays her acting talents as the despairing mother. **97m/C VHS, DVD.** Aidan Quinn, Gena Rowlands, Ben Gazzara, John Glover, D.W. Moffett, Sylvia Sidney; ***D:*** John Erman. **TV**

Early Summer 🦴🦴🦴 *Bakushu* **1951** A classic from renowned Japanese director Ozu, this film chronicles family tensions in post-WWII Japan caused by newly independent women rebelling against the social conventions they are expected to fulfill. Perhaps the best example of this director's work. Winner of Japan's Film of the Year Award. In Japanese with English subtitles. **150m/B VHS, DVD.** *JP* Ichiro Sugai, Chishu Ryu, Setsuko Hara, Chikage Awashima, Chieko Higashiyama, Haruko Sugimura, Kuniko Miyake, Kan Nihon-yanagi, Shuji Sano, Toyoko Takahashi, Seiji Miyaguchi; ***D:*** Yasujiro Ozu.

The Earrings of Madame De... 🦴🦴🦴🦴 *Diamond Earrings; Madame De* **1954** A simple story about a society woman who sells a pair of diamond earrings that her husband gave her, then lies about it. Transformed by Ophuls into his most opulent, overwrought masterpiece, the film displays a triumph of form over content. In French with English subtitles. **105m/C VHS.** *FR* Charles Boyer, Danielle Darrieux, Vittorio De Sica, Lea di Lea, Jean Debucourt; ***D:*** Max Ophuls; ***W:*** Max Ophuls, Marcel Archard, Annette Wademant; ***C:*** Christian Matras; ***M:*** Oscar Straus, Georges Van Parys.

Earth 🦴🦴🦴🦴 *Zemlya; Soul* **1930** Classic Russian silent film with English subtitles. Problems begin in a Ukrainian village when a collective farm landowner resists handing over his land. Outstanding camera work. Kino release runs 70 minutes. **101m/B VHS, DVD.** *RU* Semyon Svashenko, Nikolai Nademsky, Stephan Shkurat, Yelena Maximova, Yulia Solntseva; ***D:*** Alexander Dovzhenko; ***W:*** Alexander Dovzhenko; ***C:*** Daniil Demutsky.

Earth 🦴🦴 **1998** The second of Mehta's projected trilogy (after 1997's "Fire"), "Earth" follows the events surrounding the partitioning of India in 1947, forcing neighbors to take sides in a ferocious religious conflict. The story is seen through the eyes of eight-year-old Lenny (Sthna), the daughter of a wealthy Parsi family in Lahore who are trying to remain neutral. But Lenny is cared for by her lovely Hindu nanny, Shanta (Das), whose Muslim suitors are deeply affected by the violence. Based on the novel "Cracking India" by Bapsi Sidhwa. Hindi, Urdu, Parsi, and Punjabi with subtitles. **101m/C VHS, DVD.** *CA* Aamir Khan, Nandita Das, Rahul Khanna, Maia Sethna; ***D:*** Deepa Mehta; ***W:*** Deepa Mehta; ***C:*** Giles Nuttgens; ***M:*** A.R. Rahman.

Earth 🦴🦴 1/2 **2007 (G)** Feature-length version of the BBC/Discovery TV series "Planet Earth," which was originally released theatrically in Europe and Japan. The first theatrical release from DisneyNature, it follows the migration of a trio of animal families: polar bears, elephants, and humpback whales using cutting-edge photographic technology, which allowed filming from great distances so as not to disturb the subjects. Fothergill and Linfield worked for five years on the project, including 250 days of aerial photography, at some 200 locations in 64 countries. **90m/C DVD.** *GB GE* ***D:*** Alastair Fothergill, Mark Linfield; ***W:*** Alastair Fothergill, Mark Linfield, Leslie Megahey; ***M:*** George Fenton; ***Nar:*** James Earl Jones.

Earth & Water 🦴🦴 *Homa ke Nero* **1999** Twenty-year-old Nicholas and 18-year-old Constantina fall in love the first time they meet. But under pressure from her family, Constantina is forced to break things off—without telling Nicolas she is pregnant. Desperate, Nicholas sinks himself to the bottom of a river but resurfaces to a different world. A love story that crosses the border between dreams and reality. Greek with subtitles. **112m/C VHS, DVD.** *GR* Giorgios Karamichos, Photini Papododima, Lena Kitsopoulou, Vassias Eleftheriadis; ***D:*** Panos Karkanevatos; ***W:*** Panos Karkanevatos; ***C:*** Yannis Valeras; ***M:*** Yannis Aggelakas, Giorgos Christianakis, Asvlipios Zambetas.

Earth Entranced 🦴🦴 *Terra em Transe* **1966** A complex political lamentation from Rocha, the premiere director of Brazil's own new wave cinema. Here a writer switches his allegiance from one politician to another, only to find that he (and the masses) lose either way. In Portuguese with English subtitles. **105m/C VHS.** *BR* Jose Lewgoy, Paulo Gracindo, Jardel Filho, Glauce Rocha; ***D:*** Glauce Rocha; ***W:*** Glauce Rocha.

Earth Girls Are Easy 🦴🦴 1/2 **1989 (PG)** Valley girl Valerie is having a bad week: first she catches her fiancee with another woman, then she breaks a nail, then furry aliens land in her swimming pool. What more could go wrong? When the aliens are temporarily stranded, she decides to make amends by giving them a head-to-toe makeover. Devoid of their excessive hairiness, the handsome trio of fun-loving extraterrestrials set out to experience the Southern California lifestyle. Sometimes hilarious sci-fi/musical, featuring bouncy shtick and a gleeful dismantling of modern culture. **100m/C VHS, DVD.** *GB* Geena Davis, Jeff Goldblum, Charles Rocket, Julie Brown, Jim Carrey, Damon Wayans, Michael McKean, Angelyne, Larry Linville, Rick Overton, Diane Stilwell, Terrance McNally, Stacey Travis; ***D:*** Julien Temple; ***W:*** Charlie Coffey, Julie Brown, Terrance McNally; ***C:*** Oliver Stapleton; ***M:*** Nile Rodgers.

Earth II 🦴🦴 1/2 **1971** A space station set up for scientific research and as an example of worldwide peaceful cooperation is threatened when the Chinese launch a nuclear satellite. Astronauts David Seville (Lockwood) and Jim Capa (Hylands) debate the best course of action after failing to disarm the satellite as the Chinese decide to activate their weapon as payback for the station's interference. **94m/C DVD.** Gary Lockwood, Scott Hylands, Hari Rhodes, Anthony (Tony) Franciosa, Mariette Hartley, Edward Bell, Inga Swenson, Lew Ayres; ***D:*** Tom Gries; ***W:*** Allan Balter, William Read Woodfield; ***C:*** Michael Hugo; ***M:*** Lalo Schrifrin. **TV**

Earth vs. the Flying Saucers 🦴🦴 1/2 *Invasion of the Flying Saucers* **1956** Extraterrestrials land on Earth and issue an ultimatum to humans concerning their constant use of bombs and missiles. Peace is threatened when the military disregards the extraterrestrials' simple warning. Superb special effects by Ray Harryhausen. **83m/B VHS, DVD.** Hugh Marlowe, Joan Taylor, Donald Curtis, Morris Ankrum; ***D:*** Fred F. Sears; ***W:*** George Worthing Yates, Bernard Gordon; ***C:*** Fred H. Jackman Jr.; ***M:*** Mischa Bakaleinikoff.

Earth vs. the Spider 🦴 *The Spider* **1958** Man-eating giant mutant (teenage ninja?) tarantula makes life miserable for a small town in general and high school partyers in particular. Silly old drive-in fare is agony for many, camp treasure for a precious few. **72m/B VHS, DVD.** Edward Kemmer, June Kenney, Gene Persson, Gene Roth, Hal Torey, Mickey Finn; ***D:*** Bert I. Gordon; ***W:*** Laszlo Gorog, George Worthing Yates; ***C:*** Jack Marta.

Earth vs. the Spider 🦴🦴 **2001 (R)** Shares the title of the 1958 drive-in feature but not much else. Nerdy comic book fanatic Quentin (Gummersall) works as a security guard at a biotech research lab. After his partner is killed during a break-in, Quentin injects himself with a drug made from a mutated lab spider in the hopes of becoming an avenging superhero. Soon Quentin begins to mutate and no one is safe! **90m/C VHS, DVD.** Devon Gummersall, Dan Aykroyd, Amelia Heinle, Christopher Cousins, John Cho, Theresa Russell, Mario Roccuzzo; ***D:*** Scott Ziehl; ***W:*** Cary Solomon, Chuck Konzelman, Max Enscoe, Annie de Young; ***C:*** Thomas Callaway; ***M:*** Charles Bernstein. **CABLE**

Earthling 🦴🦴 1/2 **1980 (PG)** A terminally ill Holden helps a young Schroder survive in the Australian wilderness after the boy's parents are killed in a tragic accident. Lessons of life and the power of the human heart are passed on in this panoramic, yet mildly sentimental film. **102m/C VHS.** *AU* William Holden, Rick Schroder, Jack Thompson, Olivia Hamnett, Alwyn Kurts; ***D:*** Peter Collinson; ***W:*** Lanny Cotler.

Earthly Possessions 🦴🦴 1/2 **1999 (R)** Sarandon can't really pass for a drab housewife but she does her best in this adaptation of Anne Tyler's novel. Charlotte Emory (Sarandon) is the very sheltered wife of a smalltown minister (Sanders), who longs for a break from her tedious routine. She gets her chance when she's unexpectedly taken hostage by would-be bankrobber, Jake Simms Jr. (Dorff), who suffers from impulse control problems and continual bad luck. Both their fortunes change when Jake forces Charlotte on the road with him (he wants to see his pregnant girlfriend) and an increasingly close bond forms between the two strangers as they try to stay out of police custody. **120m/C VHS, DVD.** Susan Sarandon, Stephen Dorff, Jay O. Sanders, Elisabeth (Elissabeth, Elizabeth, Liz) Moss, Margo Martindale; ***D:*** James Lapine; ***W:*** Steven Rogers; ***C:*** David Franco; ***M:*** Stephen Endelman. **CABLE**

Earthquake 🦴🦴 **1974 (PG)** Less-than-mediocre drama centers on a major earthquake in Los Angeles and its effect on the lives of an engineer, his spoiled wife, his mistress, his father-in-law, and a suspended policeman. Filmed in much-hyped Sensurround—a technique intended to shake up the theatre a bit, but which will have no effect on your TV set. Good special effects, but not enough to compensate for lackluster script. **123m/C VHS, DVD.** Charlton Heston, Ava Gardner, George Kennedy, Lorne Greene, Genevieve Bujold, Richard Roundtree, Marjoe Gortner, Barry Sullivan, Victoria Principal, Lloyd Nolan, Walter Matthau, Scott Hylands; ***D:*** Mark Robson; ***W:*** Mario Puzo; ***C:*** Philip Lathrop; ***M:*** John Williams. Oscars '74: Sound, Visual FX.

Earthquake in Chile 🦴 1/2 *Erdbeben in Chili* **1974** Jeronimo is hired to tutor heiress Josefa and they fall in love. But their forbidden romance is discovered and she's shipped off to a convent; things get worse when it's discovered she's pregnant. Jeronimo tries to rescue her and gets thrown in jail but a fateful earthquake intervenes. German with subtitles; made for German television. **86m/C DVD.** *GE* Victor Alcazar, Fernando Villena, Julia Pena, Juan Amigo; ***D:*** Helma Sanders-Brahms; ***W:*** Helma Sanders-Brahms; ***C:*** Dietrich Lohmann. **TV**

Earthstorm 🦴 1/2 **2006** Cheesy low-budget B-pic from the Sci-Fi Channel. An asteroid hits the moon, resulting in changes to the ocean's tides that cause massive storms. With the moon now unstable and threatening to break apart, a crew of scientists, plus a demolitions expert, head into space to see if they can prevent further destruction. **89m/C DVD.** Stephen Baldwin, Dirk Benedict, John Ralston, Jason Blicker, Anna Silk, Amy Price-Francis, Matt Gordon, Conrad Coates; ***D:*** Terry Cunningham; ***W:*** Michael Kenyves; ***C:*** John Tarver. **CABLE**

Earthworm Tractors 🦴🦴 1/2 **1936** Ambitious tractor salesman Alexander Botts will do anything to make a sale. Brown excels as the fast-talking lead. Comedy is strengthened by its supporting cast. Based on characters first appearing in the "Saturday Evening Post." **63m/B VHS, DVD.** Joe E. Brown, June Travis, Guy Kibbee, Dick Foran, Carol Hughes, Gene Lockhart, Olin Howlin; ***D:*** Ray Enright.

The Easiest Way 🦴🦴 1/2 **1931** The way turns out to be not-so-easy for beautiful, poverty-stricken salesclerk Laura (Bennett) who gets a new job modeling for Willard Brockton's (Menjou) agency. Soon she's the suave Brockton's mistress and sending dough to her poor and disapproving family. Laura falls in love with Argentine tycoon Jack (Montgomery), who must suddenly return home to Buenos Aires. When he comes back, he's dismayed to find that Laura has continued her arrangement with Brockton. Includes two markedly different endings. **73m/B DVD.** Constance Bennett, Adolphe Menjou, Robert Montgomery, Anita Page, J. Farrell MacDonald, Clara Blandick, Marjorie Rambeau, Clark Gable; ***D:*** Jack Conway; ***W:*** Edith Ellis; ***C:*** John Mescall.

East and West 🦴🦴🦴 *Ost und West* **1924** Morris Brown, a worldly New York Jew, returns home to Galicia with his daughter Mollie for a traditional family wedding. She teaches the young villagers to dance and box but meets her romantic match in a young yeshiva scholar who forsakes tradition to win her heart. Picon shines as the exuberant flapper. With English and Yiddish intertitles. **85m/B VHS.** *AT* Molly Picon, Jacob Kalish, Sidney Goldin; ***D:*** Ivan Abramson, Sidney Goldin.

East Is East 🦴🦴🦴 **1999 (R)** Culture clash comedy is set in 1971 in the northern working-class community of Salford, England. Pakistani immigrant George Khan (Puri) is the would-be stern patriarch to a brood of six sons and one daughter. While he wants to raise his kids traditionally, they're rebelling. Especially in the marriage department: despite his own long marriage to the English Ella (Bassett), George tries to arrange marriages to fellow Pakistanis for his two eldest sons, with disastrous results. Story is swift-paced, definitely not p.c., and is told in amusingly broad strokes. Based on Khan-Din's play. **96m/C VHS, DVD.** *GB* Om Puri, Linda Bassett, Archie Panjabi, Chris Bisson, Jimi Mistry, Ian Aspinall, Jordan Routledge, Raji James; ***D:*** Damien O'Donnell; ***W:*** Ayub Khan-Din; ***C:*** Brian Tufano; ***M:*** Deborah Mollison. British Acad. '99: Film.

East L.A. Warriors 🦴 1/2 **1989** A mobster, Hilton-Jacobs, manipulates Los Angeles gangs in this non-stop action adventure. **90m/C VHS, DVD.** Tony Bravo, Lawrence-Hilton Jacobs, Kamar De Los Reyes, William (Bill) Smith; ***D:*** Addison Randall.

East of Borneo 🦴 1/2 **1931** Tropical adventure involving a "lost" physician whose worried wife sets out to find him in the jungle. She locates her love only to discover he has a prestigious new job tending to royalty and didn't want to be found. **76m/B VHS, DVD.** Charles Bickford, Rose Hobart, Georges Renavent; ***D:*** George Melford.

East of Eden 🦴🦴🦴🦴 **1954** Steinbeck's contemporary retelling of the biblical Cain and Abel story receives superior treatment from Kazan and his excellent cast. Dean, in his first starring role, gives a reading of a young man's search for love and acceptance that defines adolescent pain. Though filmed in the 1950s, this story still rivets today's viewers with its emotional message. **115m/C VHS, DVD.** James Dean, Julie Harris, Richard (Dick) Davalos, Raymond Massey, Jo Van Fleet, Burl Ives, Albert Dekker; ***D:*** Elia Kazan; ***W:*** Paul Osborn; ***M:*** Leonard Rosenman. Oscars '55: Support. Actress (Van Fleet); Golden Globes '56: Film—Drama.

East of Eden 🦴🦴 1/2 **1980** Remade into a TV mini series, this Steinbeck classic tells the tale of two brothers who vie for their father's affection and the woman who comes between them. Seymour is notable as the self-serving mother who abandons her babies to lead a disreputable life. Rife with biblical symbolism and allusions. **375m/C VHS.** Jane Seymour, Bruce Boxleitner, Warren Oates, Lloyd Bridges, Anne Baxter, Timothy Bottoms, Soon-Teck Oh, Karen Allen, Hart Bochner, Sam Bottoms, Howard Duff, Richard Masur, Wendell Burton, Nicholas Pryor, Grace Zabriskie, M. Emmet Walsh, Matthew "Stymie" Beard; ***D:*** Harvey Hart. **TV**

East of Elephant Rock 🦴 1/2 **1976** In 1948, a young first secretary of the British Embassy returns from leave in England to a tense atmosphere in a colony in southeast Asia. Beautiful scenery can't make up for weak plot. **93m/C VHS.** *GB* John Hurt, Jeremy Kemp, Judi Bowker, Christopher Cazenove; ***D:*** Don Boyd; ***W:*** Don Boyd.

East of Kilimanjaro 🦴🦴 *The Big Search* **1957** A freelance photographer and a doctor search frantically to find the carrier of a fatal disease near the slopes of the majestic Mt. Kilimanjaro. Routine killer virus flick filmed in Africa. **75m/C VHS.** Marshall Thompson, Gaby Andre, Fausto Tozzi; ***D:*** Arnold Belgard.

East Palace, West Palace 🦴🦴 *Behind the Forbidden City; Donggong, Xigong* **1996** Bold and controversial examination of a shadow world in Chinese society. A-Lan (Han) is a young homosexual, cruising the park outside the Forbidden Palace in Beijing. He's detained in a roundup by a cop, Xiao Shi (Jun), who takes him to the park's police station for interrogation. A-Lan is unashamed of his lifestyle and the cop presses him to tell his life story. It soon becomes clear that the Xiao Shi, though outwardedly homophobic, is actually sexually intrigued by A-Lan's presence as the duo mentally and verbally dance around the charged situation. Chinese with subtitles. **95m/C VHS, DVD.** *CH* Si Han, Hu Jun; ***D:*** Zhang Yuan; ***W:*** Zhang Yuan, Wang Xiaobo; ***C:*** Zheng Jian; ***M:*** Xiang Min.

East Side Kids 🦴🦴 **1940** Early East Side kids. A hoodlum wants to prevent his brother from beginning a similar life of crime. **60m/B VHS, DVD.** Leon Ames, Harris Berger, Dennis Moore, Joyce Bryant; ***D:*** Robert F. "Bob" Hill.

East Side of Heaven 🦴🦴 **1939** Denny (Crosby) is hired by drunken Cyrus Barrett Jr. (Kent) to deliver a singing telegram to his crusty father (Smith), who is threatening to take custody of his baby grandson. Mona (Hervey), Junior's wife, is an old friend of Denny's and leaves her son with him to sort out her troubled marriage. Denny's interference costs him his job and his chance to marry longtime girlfriend Mary (Blondell). Meanwhile, gossip columnist Claudius De Wolfe (Cowan) discovers that Denny is actually a long-lost relation of Barrett Sr. **88m/B DVD.** Joan Blondell, Mischa Auer, Irene Hervey, Bing Crosby, Sir C. Aubrey Smith, Robert Kent, Jerome Cowan; ***D:*** David Butler; ***W:*** William Conselman; ***C:*** George Robinson; ***M:*** Johnny Burke.

East Side Story 🦴 1/2 **2007** Handsome Diego's (Alvarado) life is in upheaval: he feels obligated to keep working in his grandma's (De Bari) Mexican restaurant rather than pursue his own dreams; his closeted boyfriend (Beron) just broke up with him; he's been outed by his desperate Aunt Blanca (Jimenez); and his East L.A. neighborhood is being gentrified. The last may not be so bad since Anglo Wesley (Callahan) moves in across the street—along with his jealous, patronizing boyfriend Jonathan (Schneider). Still, Diego may find more than one dream coming true. Some over-the-top performances mar what is frequently a sweet story. **88m/C DVD.** David Beron, Rene Alvarado, Steve Callahan, Cory Alan Schneider, Irene De Bari, Gladise Jimenez; ***D:*** Carlos Portugal; ***W:*** Carlos Portugal, Charo Toledo; ***C:*** Neil De la Pena; ***M:*** Steven Cahill.

East Side, West Side 🦴🦴 **1949** Stanwyck and Mason try hard to make this simple-minded soaper work, with mixed results. A wealthy couple experiences marital woes, aggravated by a ambitious young woman and a soft-hearted man suffering from unrequited love. Based on the popular novel by Marcia Davenport. **110m/B VHS.** Barbara Stanwyck, James Mason, Ava Gardner, Van Heflin, Gale Sondergaard, William Frawley, Nancy Davis; ***D:*** Mervyn LeRoy; ***C:*** Charles Rosher; ***M:*** Miklos Rozsa.

East-West 🦴🦴 *Est-Ouest* **1999 (PG-13)** In 1946, Stalin offered amnesty to any Russians who left the country after the 1917 revolution. But he executed or imprisoned many of the homesick expatriates and others found their gray motherland hard to bear (and impossible to leave). Russian doctor Alexei Golovin (Menshikov) bows to circumstances while his marriage to French wife Marie (Bonnaire) becomes increasingly strained. Marie befriends a champion swimmer, Sasha (Bodrov), with the hopes that they can both escape but things don't go as planned. Old-fashioned storytelling hampers the drama and the story (which leaps ahead months and years) becomes confused. French and Russian with subtitles. **125m/C VHS, DVD.** *FR* Sandrine Bonnaire, Oleg Menshikov, Sergei Bodrov Jr., Catherine Deneuve, Tatiana Dogileva; ***D:*** Regis Wargnier; ***W:*** Regis Wargnier, Sergei Bodrov, Rustam Ibragimbekov, Louis Gardel; ***C:*** Laurent Dailland; ***M:*** Patrick Doyle.

Easter Parade 🦴🦴🦴 1/2 **1948** Big musical star Don Hewes (Astaire) splits with his partner Nadine (Miller) claiming that he could mold any girl to replace her in the act. He tries and finally succeeds with clumsy chorus girl Hannah Brown (Garland) after much difficulty. Astaire and Garland in peak form, aided by a classic Irving Berlin score. ♫Happy Easter; Drum Crazy; It Only Happens When I Dance With You; Everybody's Doin' It; I Want to Go Back to Michigan; Beautiful Faces Need Beautiful Clothes; A Fella With an Umbrella; I Love a Piano; Snookey Ookums. **103m/C VHS, DVD.** Fred Astaire, Judy Garland, Peter Lawford, Ann Miller, Jules Munshin, Joi Lansing; ***D:*** Charles Walters; ***W:*** Sidney Sheldon, Frances Goodrich, Albert Hackett; ***C:*** Harry Stradling Sr.; ***M:*** Irving Berlin. Oscars '48: Scoring/Musical.

Eastern Condors 🦴🦴 **1987** At the end of the Vietnam War, a band of Chinese convicts are recruited by the U.S. Army (and promised their freedom) if they can destroy an ammunition dump before the Viet Cong can make use of it. Considered a Hong Kong version of "The Dirty Dozen," with the requisite level of high energy and blood. Dubbed or Chinese with English subtitles. **94m/C VHS, DVD.** *HK* Sammo Hung, Joyce Godenzi, Yuen Biao, Haing S. Ngor; ***D:*** Sammo Hung.

Eastern Promises 🦴🦴🦴 1/2 **2007 (R)** Midwife Anna (Watts) delivers a baby in a London hospital as the baby's mother, Tatiana, a teen prostitute from Russia, dies in Anna's arms. Haunted by the young girl's demise as well as her own demons, Anna's attempts to track down Tatiana's identity lead her to a Russian mafia gang led by Semyon (Mueller-Stahl). Seymon's son Kirill (Cassel) and bodyguard/driver Nikolai (a marvelous Mortenson) dole out a fierce brand of brutality, brought to full-tilt in a bloody bathhouse scene. Director Cronenberg's vision is unflinching, messy, and raw in all the right places in this complicated but resonating morality tale. **95m/C DVD, Blu-ray Disc, HD DVD.** *GB CA* Viggo Mortensen, Naomi Watts, Vincent Cassel, Armin Mueller-Stahl, Sinead Cusack, Jerzy Skolimowski, Donald (Don) Sumpter, Mina E. Mina; ***D:*** David Cronenberg; ***W:*** Steven Knight; ***C:*** Peter Suschitzky; ***M:*** Howard Shore.

Eastside 🦴🦴 **1999** After being released from prison, Antonio Lopez pays a visit to his successful lawyer brother and learns that he's a mouthpiece for the mob. So Antonio gets an in with East L.A. kingpin De La Rosa as a strongarm guy. Only when he's asked to intimidate the owner of an inner-city youth center, Antonio's latent conscience begins to bother him. Of course, if he betrays De La Rosa, he's dead. **94m/C VHS, DVD.** Mario Lopez, Efrain Figueroa, Mark Espinoza, Elizabeth Bogush, Gulshan Grover, Richard Lynch, Carlos Gallardo; ***D:*** Lorena David; ***W:*** Eric P. Sherman; ***C:*** Lisa Wiegand; ***M:*** Armando Avila. **VIDEO**

Easy Come, Easy Go 🦴🦴 **1967 (PG)** Elvis, as a Navy frogman, gets excited when he accidentally discovers what he believes is a vast sunken treasure. Music is his only solace when he finds his treasure to be worthless copper coins. ♫Easy Come, Easy Go; The Love Machine; Yoga Is As Yoga Goes; Sing, You Children; You Gotta Stop; I'll Take Love. **96m/C VHS, DVD.** Elvis Presley, Dodie Marshall, Pat Priest, Elsa Lanchester, Frank McHugh, Pat Harrington, Sonny Tufts; ***D:*** John Rich.

Easy Kill 🦴 1/2 **1989** A man takes the law into his own hands to exact revenge on drug lords. **100m/C VHS, DVD.** Jane Badler, Cameron Mitchell, Frank Stallone; ***D:*** Josh Spencer.

The Easy Life 🦴🦴🦴 **1963** Haunting film about a hedonistic man from a small Italian village who takes a mild-mannered student pleasure-seeking. The ride turns sour and the playboy is ultimately destroyed by his own brutality. **105m/B VHS.** *IT* Vittorio Gassman, Catherine Spaak, Jean-Louis Trintignant, Luciana Angiolillo; ***D:*** Dino Risi.

Easy Living 🦴🦴🦴 **1937** Exasperated Wall Street millionaire J.B. Ball (Arnold) throws his spoiled wife's (Nash) fur coat out their apartment window and it just happens to land on poor-but-hardworking secretary Mary Smith (Arthur). Ball insists Mary keep the coat and even buys her a matching hat. Soon, rumors are flying that Mary is the millionaire's tootsie. She meets cute with John (Milland), who turns out to be Ball's son and, after the usual misunderstandings, the twosome realize that they're meant for each other. **91m/B VHS.** Jean Arthur, Edward Arnold, Ray Milland, Franklin Pangborn, Mary Nash, William Demerest; ***D:*** Mitchell Leisen; ***W:*** Preston Sturges; ***C:*** Ted Tetzlaff; ***M:*** Boris Morros.

Easy Living 🦴🦴 1/2 **1949** Compromised melodrama about an over-the-hill football player who must cope with his failing marriage and looming retirement. Based on an Irwin Shaw story. **77m/B VHS.** Victor Mature, Lucille Ball, Jack Paar, Lizabeth Scott, Sonny Tufts, Lloyd Nolan, Paul Stewart; ***D:*** Jacques Tourneur.

Easy Money 🦴🦴 **1983 (R)** A basic slob has the chance to inherit $10 million if he can give up his loves: smoking, drinking, and gambling among others. Dangerfield is surprisingly restrained in this harmless, though not altogether unpleasing comedy. **95m/C VHS, DVD.** Rodney Dangerfield, Joe Pesci, Geraldine Fitzgerald, Jennifer Jason Leigh, Tom Ewell, Candice Azzara, Taylor Negron; ***D:*** James Signorelli; ***W:*** Rodney Dangerfield, Dennis Blair.

Easy Rider 🦴🦴🦴 1/2 **1969 (R)** Slim-budget, generation-defining movie. Two young men in late 1960s undertake a motorcycle trek throughout the Southwest in search of the real essence of America. Along the way they encounter hippies, rednecks, prostitutes, drugs, Nicholson, and tragedy. One of the highest-grossing pictures of the decade, undoubtedly an influence on two generations of "youth-oriented dramas," which all tried unsuccessfully to duplicate the original accomplishment. Psychedelic scenes and a great role for Nicholson are added bonuses. Look for the graveyard dancing scene in New Orleans. Features one of the best '60s rock scores around, including "Mean Streets" and "The Wanderers." **94m/C VHS, DVD.** Peter Fonda, Dennis Hopper, Jack Nicholson, Karen Black, Toni Basil, Robert Walker Jr., Luana Anders, Luke Askew, Warren Finnerty, Mac Mashorian, Antonio Mendoza, Sabrina Scharf, Phil Spector; ***D:*** Dennis Hopper; ***W:*** Terry Southern, Peter Fonda, Dennis Hopper; ***C:*** Laszlo Kovacs. AFI '98: Top 100, Natl. Film Reg. '98;; N.Y. Film Critics '69: Support. Actor (Nicholson); Natl. Soc. Film Critics '69: Support. Actor (Nicholson).

Easy Street 🦴🦴🦴 **1916** Chaplin portrays a derelict who, using some hilarious methods, reforms the residents of Easy Street. Chaplin's row with the town bully is particularly amusing. Silent with musical soundtrack added. **20m/B VHS, DVD.** Charlie Chaplin; ***D:*** Charlie Chaplin.

Easy to Love 🦴🦴 1/2 **1953** Williams is in love with her boss, but he pays her no attention until a handsome singer vies for her affections. Set at Florida's Cypress Gardens, this aquatic musical features spectacular water ballet productions choreographed by Busby Berkeley, and the title song penned by Cole Porter. ♫Easy to Love; Coquette; Beautiful Spring; That's What Rainy Day is For; Look Out! I'm Romantic; Didja Ever. **96m/C VHS.** Esther Williams, Van Johnson, Tony Martin, John Bromfield, King Donovan, Carroll Baker; ***D:*** Charles Walters; ***W:*** William Roberts.

Easy to Wed 🦴🦴 1/2 **1946** Mild MGM musical remake of 1936's "Libeled Lady." Wealthy J.B. Allenbury (Kellaway) is suing for big bucks after an unflattering write-up of his daughter Connie's (Williams) lifestyle (she's accused of being a playgirl who likes married men). So newspaper editor Warren Haggerty (Wynn) sends suave reporter Bill (Johnson) to pretend to be married and prove the accusations true while Haggerty's fiancee Gladys (Ball) gets caught in the middle of the farce. Williams is winning but Ball steals the picture. **109m/C DVD.** Esther Williams, Van Johnson, Keenan Wynn, Lucille Ball, Cecil Kellaway, Ben Blue, June Lockhart, Grant Mitchell, Paul Harvey, Jonathan Hale, James Flavin; ***D:*** Edward Buzzell; ***W:*** Dorothy Kingsley; ***C:*** Harry Strandling Jr.; ***M:*** Johnny Green.

Easy Virtue 🦴🦴 1/2 **1927** Hitchcock directs this adaptation of a Noel Coward play as a social melodrama. Larita is an unhappily married socialite with a lover. When her husband discovers her infideltiy they divorce and she is marked as a woman of loose morals. Her reputation is not enhanced by her marriage to a younger man whose family diapproves. **79m/B VHS, DVD.** *GB* Isabel Jeans, Ian Hunter, Franklin Dyall, Eric Bransby Williams, Robin Irvine, Violet Farebrother; ***D:*** Alfred Hitchcock.

Easy Virtue 🦴🦴 1/2 **2008 (PG-13)** In the mid-1920s, upper-class John Whittaker (Barnes) meets glamorous race car-driving Larita (Biel) in Monte Carlo and they impulsively marry. John then takes the all-too-modern American home to his all-too-hidebound aristocratic family, only to meet with swift disapproval by John's snappish, snobbish mother (Scott Thomas) who is determined to break up their union so her son can take a more suitable wife. John settles into the role of country squire (boring), although Larita realizes that the times have definitely changed. Director Elliot's production is lavish and Biel almost manages to hold her own (she looks lovely) against the pinched hauteur of Scott Thomas. Based on the 1924 play by Noel Coward. **96m/C DVD.** *GB US* Jessica Biel, Ben Barnes, Colin Firth, Kimberly Nixon, Kris Marshall, Pip Torrens, Charlotte Riley, Kristin Scott Thomas, Katharine Parkinson; ***D:*** Stephan Elliot; ***W:*** Stephan Elliot, Sheridan Jobbins; ***C:*** Martin Kenzie; ***M:*** Marius De Vries.

Easy Wheels 🦴🦴 1/2 **1989** Like most decent biker movies, "Wheels" is propelled by bad taste and a healthy dose of existentialist nihilism. But there's an unusual plot twist in this parody. A biker named She-Wolf and her gang kidnap female babies and let wolves rear the children. Their elaborate plan is to create a race of super women who will subdue the troublesome male population. But can this "noble" plan succeed? **94m/C VHS, DVD.** Paul LeMat, Eileen Davidson, Marjorie Bransfield, Jon Menick, Mark Holton, Karen Russell, Jami Richards, Roberta Vasquez, Barry Livingston, George Plimpton; ***D:*** David O'Malley; ***W:*** Ivan Raimi, Celia Abrams, David O'Malley; ***M:*** John Ross.

Eat a Bowl of Tea 🦴🦴🦴 **1989 (PG-13)** Endearing light drama-comedy concerning a multi-generational Chinese family. They must learn to deal with the problems of life in America and in particular, marriage, when Chinese women are finally allowed to immigrate with their husbands to the United States following WWII. Adaptation of Louis Chu's story, directed by the man who brought us "Dim Sum." A PBS "American Playhouse" presentation. **102m/C VHS, DVD.** Cora Miao, Russell Wong, Lau Siu Ming, Eric Tsiang Chi Wai, Victor Wong, Jessica Harper, Lee Sau Kee; ***D:*** Wayne Wang; ***W:*** Judith Rascoe; ***C:*** Amir M. Mokri; ***M:*** Mark Adler.

Eat and Run 🦴 **1986 (R)** A bloody comedy about a 400-pound alien with a taste for Italian (people, that is). **85m/C VHS.** Ron Silver, R.L. Ryan, Sharon Schlarth; ***D:*** Christopher Hart.

Eat Drink Man Woman 🦴🦴🦴 1/2 **1994 (R)** In Taipei, widowed master chef serves weekly feast of elaborate food and familial guilt to his three grown daughters, all of whom still live at home. They spend their time sorting out professional and romantic difficulties, searching for independence, and fulfilling traditional family obligations. Each character has a lot going on, but no one's story gets lost in the mix. Lee uses irony to great effect, introducing us to the culinary artist who has lost his sense of taste and has a daughter who works at a Wendy's. Food preparation scenes (more than 100 recipes are served up) illustrate a careful attention to detail (and are guaranteed to make you hungry). Lee's follow-up to "The Wedding Banquet" is a finely observed, comic tale of generational drift, the richness of tradition, and the power of love to redeem or improve. In Chinese with subtitles or dubbed. **123m/C VHS, DVD.** *TW* Sihung Lung, Kuei-Mei Yang, Yu-Wen Wang, Chien-Lien Wu, Sylvia Chang, Winston Chao, Ah-Leh Gua, Lester Chen; ***D:*** Ang Lee; ***W:*** Ang Lee, James Schamus, Hui-Ling Wang; ***C:*** Jong Lin; ***M:*** Mader. Natl. Bd. of Review '94: Foreign Film.

Eat My Dust 🦴🦴 **1976 (PG)** Teenage son of a California sheriff steals the best stock cars from a race track to take the town's heartthrob for a joy ride. Subsequently he leads the town on a wild car chase. Brainless but fast-paced. **89m/C VHS, DVD.** Ron Howard, Christopher Norris, Warren Kemmerling, Dave Madden, Robert Broyles, Jessica Potter, Don Brodie, Evelyn Russell, Clint Howard, Paul Bartel, Rance Howard, Corbin Bernsen; ***D:*** Charles B. Griffith; ***W:*** Charles B. Griffith; ***C:*** Eric Saarinen; ***M:*** David Grisman.

Eat, Pray, Love 2010 Based on Elizabeth Gilbert's 2006 memoir "Eat, Pray, Love: One Woman's Search for Everything Across Italy, India and Indonesia." Married Gilbert (Roberts) discovers her current life isn't what she wants, so after a protracted divorce she decides to travel extensively in a journey of self-discovery, including Italy for pleasure, India for meditation, and Indonesia for both the spiritual and an unexpected love affair. **m/C DVD.** *US* Julia Roberts, Javier Bardem, Richard Jenkins, Viola Davis, Billy Crudup, James Franco; ***D:*** Ryan Murphy; ***W:*** Ryan Murphy, Jennifer Salt; ***C:*** Robert Richardson; ***M:*** Dario Marianelli.

Eat the Peach 🦴🦴 **½ 1986** An idiosyncratic Irish comedy about two young unemployed rebels who attempt to break free from their tiny coast town by becoming motorcycle champs after seeing the Elvis Presley film "Roustabout." Together they create the "wall of death,"—a large wooden barrel in which they can perform various biker feats. **90m/C VHS.** *IR* Stephen Brennan, Eamon Morrissey, Catherine Byrne, Niall Toibin, Tony Doyle, Joe Lynch; ***D:*** Peter Ormrod; ***W:*** Peter Ormrod, John Kelleher; ***M:*** Donal Lunny.

Eat the Rich 🦴 **1987 (R)** A British farce about a group of terrorists who take over the popular London restaurant, Bastard's. Led by a former, disgruntled transvestite employee, they turn diners into menu offerings. Music by Motorhead. **89m/C VHS, DVD.** *GB* Nosher Powell, Lanah Pellay, Fiona Richmond, Ronald Allen, Sandra Dorne, Paul McCartney, Linda McCartney, Bill Wyman, Koo Stark, Miranda Richardson, Angie Bowie, Sandie Shaw; ***D:*** Peter Richardson; ***W:*** Peter Richardson; ***C:*** Witold Stok.

Eat Your Heart Out 🦴🦴 **½ 1996 (R)** Routine romantic comedy about talented but struggling young chef Daniel (Oliver) who gets his shot at success with his own TV cooking show. He doesn't realize his best gal pal (Seagall) loves him, while Daniel becomes intrigued by his sexy agent (San Giacomo). **96m/C VHS, DVD.** Christian Oliver, Laura San Giacomo, Pamela Segall, Linda Hunt; ***D:*** Felix Adlon; ***W:*** Felix Adlon; ***C:*** Judy Irola; ***M:*** Alex Wurman.

Eaten Alive 🦴🦴 *Death Trap; Starlight Slaughter; Legend of the Bayou; Horror Hotel Massacre* **1976 (R)** A Southerner takes an unsuspecting group of tourists into a crocodile death trap. Director Tobe Hooper's follow-up to "The Texas Chainsaw Massacre." Englund is more recognizable with razor fingernails as Freddy Krueger of the "Nightmare on Elm Street" films. **96m/C VHS, DVD.** Neville Brand, Mel Ferrer, Carolyn Jones, Marilyn Burns, Stuart Whitman, Robert Englund, William Finley, Roberta Collins, Kyle Richards, Janus Blythe; ***D:*** Tobe Hooper; ***W:*** Marti Rustam, Alvin L. Fast, Kim Henkel; ***C:*** Robert Caramico; ***M:*** Wayne Bell.

Eating 🦴🦴 **½ 1990 (R)** Set in Southern California, women gather to celebrate birthdays for three of their friends who are turning 30, 40 and 50. As the party commences, women from two generations discuss their attitudes towards food and men...and discover hilarious parallels. **110m/C VHS, DVD.** Nelly Alard, Frances Bergen, Mary Crosby, Lisa Richards, Gwen Welles, Daphna Kastner, Elizabeth Kemp, Marlena Giovi, Marina Gregory, Toni Basil; ***D:*** Henry Jaglom; ***W:*** Henry Jaglom; ***C:*** Hanania Baer.

Eating Out 2: Sloppy Seconds 🦴 **½ 2006** Goofy low-budget gay comedy. Kyle (Verraros) has been dumped by Marc (Chukerman) so he's on the prowl. He's drawn to hunky-but-dumb art class model Troy (Dapper), who says he's straight. Since Kyle and his gal pals Gwen (Brooke) and Tiffani (Kochan) have their doubts, Kyle claims he's a member of a "going straight" group and decides to take Troy to a meeting and see what happens. **85m/C DVD.** Mink Stole, Jim Verraros, Marco Dapper, Emily Brooke, Rebekah Kochan, Brett Chukerman; ***D:*** Phillip J. Bartell; ***W:*** Phillip J. Bartell, Q. Allan Brocka; ***C:*** Lisa Wiegand; ***M:*** Cary Berger, Boris Worister.

Eating Out 3: All You Can Eat WOOF! 2009 Pandering and inept gay sex comedy. Fag hag Tiffani befriends shy new boy Casey and tries to match him up with hunky Zack using a phony social networking profile. **80m/C DVD.** Daniel Skelton, Rebekah Kochan, Chris Salvatore, Leslie Jordan, Mink Stole, Michael Walker; ***D:*** Glenn Gaylord; ***W:*** Phillip J. Bartell; ***C:*** Tom Camarda. **VIDEO**

Eating Raoul 🦴🦴🦴 **½ 1982 (R)** The Blands are a happily married couple who share many interests: good food and wine, entrepreneurial dreams, and an aversion to sex. The problem is, they're flat broke. So, when the tasty swinger from upstairs makes a pass at Mary and Paul accidentally kills him, they discover he's got loads of money; Raoul takes a cut in the deal by disposing of—or rather recycling—the body. This may just be the way to finance that restaurant they've been wanting to open. Wonderful, offbeat, hilariously dark comedy. **83m/C VHS, DVD.** Mary Woronov, Paul Bartel, Robert Beltran, Buck Henry, Ed Begley Jr., Edie McClurg, John Paragon, Richard Blackburn, Hamilton Camp, Billy Curtis, Susan Saiger, Richard Paul, Don Steele, Mark Woods; ***D:*** Paul Bartel; ***W:*** Paul Bartel, Richard Blackburn; ***C:*** Gary Thieltges; ***M:*** Arlon Ober.

Eban and Charley 🦴 **½ 2001** Draggy romance about a couple of misfits—one of whom is underage. 29-year-old Eban (Fellows) returns to his parents' home in a coastal Oregon community after leaving his job as a soccer coach. He's hanging around town when he meets the 15-year-old Charley (Andrade), who's been sent to live with his resentful divorced father after Charley's mother dies. Eventually, the relationship becomes physical (there are no depictions of sex) and they're headed for trouble. **88m/C VHS, DVD.** Brent Fellows, Giovanni Andrade, Nolan V. Chard, Ron Upton, Pam Munter; ***D:*** James Bolton; ***W:*** James Bolton; ***C:*** Judy Irola; ***M:*** Stephin Merritt.

The Ebb-Tide 🦴🦴 **½ 1997** Capt. Chisholm (Coltrane) is bothered by a scandalous past, so he doesn't ask a lot of questions about transporting a secret cargo to Australia. A storm strands Chisholm and two sailors on an uncharted island that's inhabited by the malevolent Ellstrom (Terry) and has Chisholm in a battle of good versus evil. Based on a novel by Robert Louis Stevenson. **104m/C VHS.** Robbie Coltrane, Nigel Terry, Steven Mackintosh; ***D:*** Nicholas Renton; ***W:*** Simon Donald. **CABLE**

Ebbtide 🦴🦴 **½ 1994 (R)** Lawyer Jeff Warren (Hamlin) takes on the case of a mother who claims her son died from chemicals dumped by the Poseidon Pacific Co. Jeff got the case when the previous lawyer died mysteriously but this doesn't stop him checking out the chemical company or its beautiful president. **90m/C VHS.** John Waters, Harry Hamlin, Judy McIntosh, Susan Lyons, John Gregg, Frankie J. Holden; ***D:*** Craig Lahiff; ***W:*** Bob Ellis, Peter Goldsworthy.

Ebenezer 🦴🦴 **½ 1997 (PG)** Ebenezer (Palance) is a crumedgeonly crook in the wild west who doesn't believe in Christmas and even cheats at poker. He's told by the ghostly Jacob Marlowe (Halliday) to change his ways or else—and Ebenezer is visited by several spirits that show him the error of his ways. A western version of Charles Dickens' "A Christmas Carol" that's quite colorful. **94m/C VHS.** Jack Palance, Rick Schroder, Amy Locane, Albert Schultz, Richard Halliday, Richard Comar, Michelle Thrush, Susan Coyne, Joshua Silberg, Morris Chapdelaine; ***D:*** Ken Jubenvil; ***W:*** Donald Martin; ***C:*** Henry Lebo; ***M:*** Bruce Leitl. **CABLE**

Ebony Tower 🦴🦴 **½ 1986** Based on the John Fowles novel about a crusty old artist who lives in a French chateau with two young female companions. They are visited by a handsome young man, thereby initiating sexual tension and recognizably Fowlesian plot puzzles. Features some partial nudity. **80m/C** *GB* Laurence Olivier, Roger Rees, Greta Scacchi, Toyah Willcox; ***D:*** Robert Knights; ***M:*** Richard Rodney Bennett. **TV**

Echelon Conspiracy 🦴 **½** *The Gift* **2009 (PG-13)** Computer security analyst Max Peterson receives a series of text messages on his new cell phone promising gambling tips that make him rich. The situation turns out to be too good to be true since there's an international conspiracy involving government agencies collecting surveillance material that has Max running for his life. **105m/C DVD.** Shane West, Edward Burns, Ving Rhames, Martin Sheen, Sergey Gubanov; ***D:*** Greg Marcks; ***W:*** Kevin Elders, Michael Nitsberg; ***C:*** Lorenzo Senatore; ***M:*** Joseph Gutowski, Bobby Tahouri. **VIDEO**

Echo Murders 🦴 **½ 1945** A Sexton Blake mystery wherein he investigates a mine owner's mysterious death, opening up a veritable can of murdering, power-hungry worms. **75m/B VHS, DVD.** Julien Mitchell, Ferdinand "Ferdy" Mayne, Pamela Stirling, David Farrar, Dennis Price; ***D:*** John Harlow; ***W:*** John Harlow; ***C:*** James Wilson; ***M:*** Percival Mackey.

Echo of Murder 🦴🦴 *Who Killed Atlanta's Children?* **2000** Docudrama focuses on the 29 child murders in Atlanta, which took place in the late '70s and early '80s, from the point of view of investigative journalists Hines and Belushi. Their theory is that convicted killer Wayne Williams is the scapegoat for a police conspiracy and the killings were perpetrated by the Ku Klux Klan. But they seem to spend most of their time yelling at each other so the story's emotional impact is lost. **105m/C VHS, DVD.** James Belushi, Gregory Hines; ***D:*** Charles Robert Carner; ***W:*** Charles Robert Carner; ***C:*** Michael Goi; ***M:*** James Verboort. **CABLE**

The Echo of Thunder 🦴🦴 **½ 1998** It's a hard life in the Australian outback for Gladwyn (Davis) and Larry (Sheridan) Ritchie who, with their three children, raise specialty palm trees on their small farm. It's a struggle that's made more uncomfortable for Gladwyn when 15-year-old Lara (Hewett) arrives. Lara is Larry's daughter by his late first wife and Gladwyn doesn't think the city-bred girl will fit in, and she's also worried that Lara's presence will stir up old memories for her husband. Indeed, Lara's only friend seems to be the stray Dingo dog she adopts and names Thunderwith. Based on the novel "Thunderwith" by Libby Hathorn. **98m/C VHS.** Judy Davis, Jamey Sheridan, Bill Hunter, Lauren Hewett, Ernie Dingo, Michael Caton; ***D:*** Simon Wincer; ***W:*** H. Haden Yelin; ***M:*** Laurence Rosenthal. **TV**

Echo Park 🦴🦴 **½ 1986 (R)** An unsung sleeper comedy about three roommates living in Los Angeles' Echo Park: a body builder, a single-mother waitress, and an itinerant songwriter. Charts their struggles as they aim for careers in showbiz. Offbeat ensemble effort. **93m/C VHS, DVD.** *AU* Tom Hulce, Susan Dey, Michael Bowen, Richard "Cheech" Marin, Christopher Walker, Shirley Jo Finney, Cassandra Peterson, Yana Nirvana, Timothy Carey; ***D:*** Robert Dornhelm; ***W:*** Michael Ventura; ***C:*** Karl Kofler; ***M:*** David Rickets.

Echoes 🦴🦴 *Living Nightmare* **1983 (R)** A young painter's life slowly comes apart as he is tormented by nightmares that his stillborn twin brother is attempting to murder him. **90m/C VHS, DVD.** Gale Sondergaard, Mercedes McCambridge, Richard Alfieri, Ruth Roman, John Spencer, Nathalie Nell; ***D:*** Arthur Allan Seidelman; ***W:*** Richard Alfieri, Richard J. Anthony; ***C:*** Hanania Baer.

Echoes 🦴🦴 **½ 1988** Shopkeeper's daughter Clare O'Brien (Garahy) and doctor's son David Power (Hines) both want to escape from their 1950s Irish seaside town. They meet again at university in Dublin where their friendship turns to romance but their return home comes complete with family troubles and differing dreams. Based on the novel by Maeve Binchy. **208m/C VHS, DVD.** *GB* Siobhan Garahy, Robert Hines, Geraldine James, Stephen Holland, Alison Doody, Dermot Crowley; ***W:*** Donald Churchill, Barbara Rennie. **TV**

Echoes in the Darkness 🦴🦴 **½ 1987** Miniseries based on the true-life Joseph Wambaugh bestseller about the "Main Line" murder investigation in Pennsylvania in 1979. Police are baffled when a teacher is murdered and her children vanish. Suspicion falls on a charismatic coworker and the school's principal. **234m/C VHS.** Peter Coyote, Robert Loggia, Stockard Channing, Peter Boyle, Cindy Pickett, Gary Cole, Zeljko Ivanek, Alex Hyde-White, Treat Williams; ***D:*** Glenn Jordan. **TV**

Echoes of Paradise 🦴 **½** *Shadows of the Peacock* **1986 (R)** After a series of earth-shattering events, a depressed woman journeys to an island where she falls for a Balinese dancer. Soon she must choose between returning home or beginning life anew in paradise. **90m/C VHS.** *AU* Wendy Hughes, John Lone, Rod Mullinar, Peta Toppano, Steve Jacobs, Gillian Jones; ***D:*** Phillip Noyce; ***C:*** Peter James.

The Eclipse 🦴🦴🦴 **½** *L'eclisse* **1966** The last of Antonioni's trilogy (after "L'Avventura" and "La Notte"), wherein another fashionable and alienated Italian woman passes from one lover to another searching unsuccessfully for truth and love. Highly acclaimed. In Italian with subtitles. **123m/B VHS, DVD.** *IT* Monica Vitti, Alain Delon, Francisco Rabal, Louis Seigner; ***D:*** Michelangelo Antonioni; ***W:*** Tonino Guerra, Elio Bartolini, Ottiero Ottieri, Michelangelo Antonioni; ***C:*** Gianni Di Venanzo; ***M:*** Giovanni Fusco.

Eclipse 🦴 **½ 1994** Sexual roundelay set in Toronto shortly before a total solar eclipse, which is apparently affecting all the generally listless characters in such a way that they meet and mate in joyless abandon. First feature for Podeswa. **96m/C VHS.** *CA GE* Von Flores, John Gilbert, Pascale Montpetit, Manuel Aranguiz, Maria Del Mar, Matthew Ferguson, Earl Pastko, Greg Ellwand, Daniel MacIvor, Kirsten Johnson; ***D:*** Jeremy Podeswa; ***W:*** Jeremy Podeswa; ***C:*** Miroslaw Baszak; ***M:*** Ernie Tollar.

Ecstasy 🦴🦴 **½** *Extase; Ekstase; Symphony of Love* **1933** A romantic, erotic story about a young woman married to an older man, who takes a lover. Features Lamarr, then Hedy Kiesler, before her discovery in Hollywood. Film subsequently gained notoriety for Lamarr's nude scenes. In Czech with English subtitles. **90m/B VHS, DVD.** *CZ* Hedy Lamarr, Jaromir Rogoz, Aribert Mog; ***D:*** Gustav Machaty; ***W:*** Gustav Machaty.

Ecstasy WOOF! *Love Scenes* **1984 (R)** Soft core fluff about a film director's wife's erotic adventures. **82m/C VHS.** Tiffany Bolling, Franc Luz, Jack Carter, Britt Ekland, Julie Newmar; ***D:*** Bud Townsend; ***W:*** C. Penning Masters.

Ed WOOF! 1996 (PG) A must see for all fans of flatulent animatronic chimpanzees who play third base. Everyone else should stay away. LeBlanc (who should've been tipped off when they couldn't even get a real chimp to appear) plays Coop, a phenom pitcher stuck on a losing team in the minor leagues. After Ed the chimpanzee is bequeathed to the team by the late Mickey Mantle, (forgive them Mick, they know not what they do) he starts playing the hot corner like Brooks Robinson. Surprise! Ed becomes a national sensation, the team goes on a winning streak and sets up the showdown game climax. Most of the humor is derived from Ed tearing things up and passing gas, while LeBlanc yells in pop-eyed exasperation. Cameo from Tommy Lasorda playing a fat major league manager. **94m/C VHS, DVD.** Matt LeBlanc, Jayne Brook, Bill Cobbs, Jack Warden, Doren Fein, Patrick Kerr, Charlie Schlatter, Carl Anthony Payne II, Curt Kaplan,

Zack (Zach) Ward, Mike McGlone, James (Jim) Caviezel, Valente Rodriguez; ***D:*** Bill Couturie; ***W:*** David Mickey Evans; ***C:*** Alan Caso; ***M:*** Stephen Endelman.

Ed and His Dead Mother 1993 **(PG-13)** Ed's just an average guy who happens to really love his mother. So much so that when she dies Ed tries to bring her back from the dead—and succeeds. Only death has made a few changes in Mom's personality. Now she's a bug-eating, chainsaw-wielding fiend. Just what's a good son supposed to do? **93m/C VHS, DVD.** Ned Beatty, Steve Buscemi, John Glover, Miriam Margolyes, Sam Jenkins; ***D:*** Jonathan Wacks; ***W:*** Chuck Hughes.

Ed Gein 2001 Considering the subject matter, this is a mild account of murdering, grave-robbing, dismembering psycho/cannibal Ed Gein (Railsback) and the Wisconsin farm community who just can't believe what their neighbor has been up to. **88m/C VHS, DVD.** Steve Railsback, Carrie Snodgress, Pat Skipper, Sally Champlin; ***D:*** Chuck Parello; ***W:*** Stephen Johnston; ***C:*** Vanja Cernjul; ***M:*** Robert F. McNaughton.

Ed Wood 1/2 **1994 (R)** Leave it to Burton to bring to the screen the story of a director many consider to be the worst of all time (he's at least in the top three) and who now occupies a lofty position as a cult icon. In this hilarious and touching tribute to a Hollywood maverick with grade-Z vision, detailed homage is paid to Wood's single-mindedness and optimism in the face of repeated failure and lack of financing, even down to the black and white photography. Depp is convincing (and engaging) as Ed Wood, Jr., the cross-dressing, angora-sweater-wearing, low-budget auteur of such notoriously "bad" cult films as "Glen or Glenda" and "Plan 9 From Outer Space." Depp is supported by terrific portrayals of the motley Wood crew, led by Landau's morphine-addicted, down-on-his-luck Bela Lugosi. Burton focuses on Wood's relationship with Lugosi, whose career is over by the time Wood befriends him. Based on Rudolph Grey's book, "Nightmare of Ecstasy: The Life and Art of Edward D. Wood Jr." **127m/B VHS, DVD.** Max Casella, Johnny Depp, Sarah Jessica Parker, Martin Landau, Bill Murray, Jim Myers, Patricia Arquette, Jeffrey Jones, Lisa Marie, Vincent D'Onofrio, Ned Bellamy, Conrad Brooks, Rance Howard, Juliet Landau, G.D. Spradlin, Mike Starr, George "The Animal" Steele, Gregory Walcott; ***D:*** Tim Burton; ***W:*** Scott M. Alexander, Larry Karaszewski; ***C:*** Stefan Czapsky; ***M:*** Howard Shore. Oscars '94: Makeup, Support. Actor (Landau); Golden Globes '95: Support. Actor (Landau); L.A. Film Critics '94: Cinematog., Support. Actor (Landau), Score; N.Y. Film Critics '94: Cinematog., Support. Actor (Landau); Natl. Soc. Film Critics '94: Cinematog., Support. Actor (Landau); Screen Actors Guild '94: Support. Actor (Landau).

Eddie **1996 (PG-13)** Basketball nut Edwina (Goldberg) wins a chance to be honorary coach of her beloved Knicks in a free throw contest. When some of her courtside advice works, and the other fans seem to respond to her, the publicity-seeking maverick owner (Langella) gives her the job full-time. Predictable comedy with the usual "new team member leads underdogs to contention" characters won't suprise, or particularly thrill, anyone. Goldberg's lively performance somewhat redeems standard script but reduces everyone around her, including an All-Star roster of NBA players, to window dressing. Basically the hoops version of "Little Big League." **100m/C VHS, DVD.** Whoopi Goldberg, Frank Langella, Dennis Farina, Richard Jenkins, Lisa Ann Walter, John Benjamin Hickey, John Salley; ***D:*** Steve Rash; ***W:*** Jon Connolly, David Loucka, Eric Champnella, Keith Mitchell, Steve Zacharias, Jeff Buhai; ***C:*** Victor Kemper; ***M:*** Stanley Clarke.

Eddie and the Cruisers **1983 (PG)** In the early 1960s, rockers Eddie and the Cruisers score with one hit album. Amid their success, lead singer Pare dies mysteriously in a car accident. Years later, a reporter decides to write a feature on the defunct group, prompting a former band member to begin a search for missing tapes of the Cruisers' unreleased second album. Questions posed at the end of the movie are answered in the sequel. Enjoyable soundtrack by John Cafferty and the Beaver Brown Band. **90m/C VHS, DVD.** Tom Berenger, Michael Pare, Ellen Barkin, Joe Pantoliano, Matthew Laurance, Helen Schneider, David Wilson, Michael "Tunes" Antunes, Joe Cates, John Stockwell, Barry Sand, Vebe Borge, Howard Johnson, Robin Karfo, Rufus Harley, Bruce Brown, Louis D'Esposito, Michael Toland, Bob Garrett, Joanne Collins; ***D:*** Martin Davidson; ***W:*** Martin Davidson, Arlene Davidson; ***C:*** Fred Murphy; ***M:*** John Cafferty.

Eddie and the Cruisers 2: Eddie Lives! 1/2 **1989 (PG-13)** A sequel to the minor cult favorite, in which a rock star believed to be dead emerges under a new name in Montreal to lead a new band. The Beaver Brown Band again provides the music. **106m/C VHS.** *CA* Michael Pare, Marina Orsini, Matthew Laurance, Bernie Coulson, Anthony Sherwood; ***Cameos:*** Larry King, Bo Diddley, Martha Quinn, Merrill Shindler; ***D:*** Jean-Claude Lord; ***W:*** Charles Zev Cohen; ***C:*** Rene Verzier; ***M:*** Leon Aronson.

Eddie Macon's Run **1983 (PG)** Based on a true story; Eddie Macon has been unjustly jailed in Texas and plans an escape to run to Mexico. He is followed by a tough cop who is determined to catch the fugitive. Film debut of Goodman. **95m/C VHS.** Kirk Douglas, John Schneider, Lee Purcell, John Goodman, Leah Ayres; ***D:*** Jeff Kanew; ***M:*** Wendy Blackstone.

Eddie Presley 1/2 **1992** Eddie Presley is an Elvis impersonator at the lowest rung of the entertainment industry ladder. He's a true believer whose act is a heartfelt homage. He lives in his van and has a crappy security guard job, and has a tenuous hold on his dignity. When he gets a gig at a seedy hotel, he has a meltdown on stage and gives a performance the audience will never forget. Well-crafted, bittersweet showbiz drama is packed fine performances. Based on writer/star Whitaker's play. **106m/C DVD.** Duane Whitaker, Stacie Randall, Lawrence Tierney, Roscoe Lee Browne, Theodore (Ted) Raimi, Joe Estevez, Tom Everett, Clu Gulager, John Lazar, Francesca "Kitten" Natividad, Ian Ogilvy, Willard Pugh, Daniel Roebuck, Tim Thomerson, Patrick Thomas; ***Cameos:*** Quentin Tarantino, Bruce Campbell; ***D:*** Jeff Burr; ***W:*** Duane Whitaker; ***C:*** Thomas Callaway; ***M:*** Jim Manzie.

The Eddy Duchin Story **1956** Glossy tearjerker that profiles the tragic life of Eddy Duchin, the famous pianist/bandleader of the 30s and 40s. Features almost 30 songs, including classics by Cole Porter, George and Ira Gershwin, Hammerstein, Chopin, and several others. **123m/C VHS, DVD.** Tyrone Power, Kim Novak, Victoria Shaw, James Whitmore, Rex Thompson; ***D:*** George Sidney; ***W:*** Samuel A. Taylor; ***C:*** Harry Stradling Sr.; ***M:*** George Duning.

Eden **1993** Eden is a luxury resort designed to cater to personal fantasies and filled with numerous intrigues. Part-owner Eve Sinclair faces a number of professional and personal complications, including the tragic death of her husband, a brother-in-law who's interested in more than business, and an old friend with uncertain motives. Lots of sex in beautiful settings. **107m/C VHS, DVD.** Barbara Alyn Woods, Jack Armstrong, Steve Chase, Darcy Demoss, Jeff Griggs; ***D:*** Victor Lobl; ***W:*** Stephen Black, Henry Stern. **CABLE**

Eden **1998 (R)** Frustrated, Multiple Sclerosis-afflicted housewife Helen (Going) deals with the physical and emotional limitations of her life with dreams of astral projection. Husband Bill (Walsh) is a prep school teacher who doesn't want her to work even though she reaches one of his problem students (Flanery) more effectively than he can. First-time director Goldberg won a Sundance competition for his screenplay, but can't quite deliver on its promise. A tight budget and too many unanswered questions keep this one on the intriguing but ultimately disappointing level. **106m/C VHS, DVD.** Joanna Going, Dylan Walsh, Sean Patrick Flanery; ***D:*** Howard Goldberg; ***W:*** Howard Goldberg; ***C:*** Hubert Taczanowski; ***M:*** Brad Fiedel.

Eden 2 **1993 (R)** The continuing saga of the luxury resort Eden. Owner Eve is still having erotic dreams of late husband Grant while fending off the very real advances of his brother Josh and becoming attracted to Paul, her late husband's best friend. The guests are equally caught up in erotic dilemmas involving sexual blackmail. **102m/C VHS.** Barbara Alyn Woods, Jack Armstrong, Steve Chase, Darcy Demoss, Jeff Griggs; ***D:*** Kristine Peterson; ***W:*** Stephen Black, Henry Stern. **CABLE**

Eden 3 **1993 (R)** Yet another chapter in this sexy cable saga. Eve Sinclair risks losing her share of the tropical resort unless she remarries, which she doesn't want to do, although fitness trainer Randi would be delighted to pick up the option. Meanwhile, an heiress discovers her new bridegroom has murderous intentions. **?m/C VHS.** Barbara Alyn Woods, Jack Armstrong, Steve Chase, Darcy Demoss, Jeff Griggs, Dean Scofield; ***D:*** Victor Lobl. **CABLE**

Eden 4 **1993 (R)** Further adventures in the cable series. Eve, Eden's co-owner, must cope with both Josh's jealous rage and Randi's continuing scheming as she tries to keep her guests happy at the posh resort. One of the guests, a beautiful author, gets too caught up in her sexual fantasies and may find herself in danger. **?m/C VHS.** Barbara Alyn Woods, Jack Armstrong, Steve Chase, Darcy Demoss, Jeff Griggs, Dean Scofield; ***D:*** Kristine Peterson. **CABLE**

Eden Valley **1994** A low-key intensity marks this northeast England drama that's produced, written, and directed by an eight-member film cooperative, the Amber Production Team. Troubled Newcastle teenager Billy (Bell) is put on probation for drug and theft charges and in a last-ditch chance at turning his life around goes to live with his estranged father, Hoggy (Hogg). They haven't seen each other in 10 years and Hoggy lives on a farm in County Durham where he raises and trains horses for harness racing. Naturally, their relationship is strained and there aren't any easy solutions (kinda like in real life). **95m/C VHS.** *GB* Darren Bell, Brian Hogg, Mike Elliott, Jimmy Killeen; ***D:*** Amber Production Team; ***W:*** Amber Production Team; ***C:*** Amber Production Team; ***M:*** Amber Production Team.

The Edge 1/2 *Bookworm* **1997 (R)** Wealthy Charles Morse (Hopkins) isn't too pleased that fashion photog Bob Greene (Baldwin) takes such an interest in his lovely fashion model wife (Macpherson) and feels the two are out to kill him. Despite his conspiracy theory, Morse and Greene end up depending on each other for survival when their plane crashes in the Alaskan wilderness. To compound their problems, they must do battle with a stalking killer bear. Mamet screenplay dices things up a bit with cutting dialogue which leads to the mind games Mamet is so famous for. Hopkins and Baldwin give understated, intact performances, with an intensity shared only by Bart the Bear, in this small comtemporary parable on the meaning of life. The splendid Alaskan scenery is actually breathtaking aerial and ground footage in Canada. **120m/C VHS, DVD.** Anthony Hopkins, Alec Baldwin, Elle Macpherson, Harold Perrineau Jr., L.Q. Jones; ***D:*** Lee Tamahori; ***W:*** David Mamet; ***C:*** Donald McAlpine; ***M:*** Jerry Goldsmith.

Edge of Darkness 1/2 **1943** Compelling war-drama about the underground movement in Norway during Nazi takeover of WWII. Flynn plays a Norwegian fisherman who leads the local underground movement and Sheridan is his loyal fiancee. Although several problems occurred throughout filming, this picture earned high marks for its superb performances and excellent camera work. Based on the novel by William Woods. **120m/B VHS.** Errol Flynn, Ann Sheridan, Walter Huston, Nancy Coleman, Helmut Dantine, Judith Anderson, Ruth Gordon, John Beal; ***D:*** Lewis Milestone; ***W:*** Robert Rossen.

Edge of Darkness **1986** Miniseries mystery involves a police detective who investigates his daughter's murder and uncovers a web of espionage and intrigue. **307m/C VHS.** *GB* Bob Peck, Joe Don Baker, Jack Woodson, John Woodvine, Joanne Whalley; ***D:*** Martin Campbell; ***M:*** Eric Clapton, Michael Kamen. **TV**

Edge of Darkness **2010 (PG-13)** Widowed cop Thomas Craven's (Gibson) only child—activist daughter Emma—is gunned down in front of his home and it's assumed Thomas was actually the target. When he investigates, Thomas discovers more than he expected: a tangled web of corporate and political cover-ups and conspiracies. Based on the British miniseries, the movie is overpacked with more information than two hours can contain, and fails to put all the pieces of the puzzle together. Strong supporting roles, especially from Winstone, but Gibson crowds everyone else off the screen with a one-dimensional boiling rage as the movie devolves into a self-important "Death Wish." **126m/C DVD.** Mel Gibson, Ray Winstone, Danny Huston, Shawn Roberts, Denis O'Hare, Bojana Novakovic, Jay O. Sanders; ***D:*** Martin Campbell; ***W:*** William Monahan, Andrew Bovell; ***C:*** Phil Meheux; ***M:*** Howard Shore.

The Edge of Heaven *Auf der Anderen Seite; On the Other Side* **2007** Intertwining story focusing on six very different characters bouncing into each other across countries. Yeter, a devout Muslim and working prostitute, is taken in as a roommate by a lonely john named Ali, but soon is forced into sex slavery. Her daily torture eases after meeting Ali's son Nejat, a German-speaking professor. Unexpectedly, Yeter dies and Nejat takes it upon himself to travel to Turkey in search of Yeter's lost daughter. An excellent cast holds it all together, while director Akin smoothly transitions from story to story. **122m/C DVD.** *GE TU* Hanna Schygulla, Baki Davrak, Tuncel Kurtiz, Nursel Kose, Nurgul Yesilcay, Patrycia Ziolkowska; ***D:*** Fatih Akin; ***W:*** Fatih Akin; ***C:*** Rainer Klausmann; ***M:*** Shantel.

Edge of Honor 1/2 **1991 (R)** Young Eagle Scouts camping in the Pacific Northwest discover a woodland weapons cache and wage guerilla war against killer lumberjacks out to silence them. A boneheaded, politically correct action bloodbath; you don't have to like the logging industry to disapprove of the broad slurs against its men shown here. **92m/C VHS, DVD.** Corey Feldman, Meredith Salenger, Scott Reeves, Ken Jenkins, Christopher Neame, Don Swayze; ***D:*** Michael Spence; ***W:*** David O'Malley.

The Edge of Love 1/2 **2008** Despite the cast (and only Rhys is believable), Maybury's downbeat drama suffers from unlikeable characters and an overwrought plot. Welsh poet Dylan Thomas (Rhys), who's a drunken lout, is doing war work in London in 1940. He reconnects with ex-girlfriend Vera Phillips (Knightley) who then befriends Dylan's hard-drinking Irish wife Caitlin (Miller). Vera marries English soldier William Killick (Murphy) but sets up house with the Thomases when he's sent overseas. Much bad behavior, jealousy, and resentment ensues, leading to violence when a shell-shocked William returns. **110m/C DVD.** *GB* Matthew Rhys, Keira Knightley, Sienna Miller, Cillian Murphy; ***D:*** John Maybury; ***W:*** Sharman MacDonald; ***C:*** Jonathan Freeman; ***M:*** Angelo Badalamenti.

Edge of Madness 1/2 *A Wilderness Station* **2002 (R)** In 1850, naive Annie (Dhavernas) agrees to an arranged marriage with Manitoba homesteader Simon (Fehr). But although Annie befriends Simon's younger brother George (Sevier), her husband turns out to be angry and abusive. So she kills him after he attacks her. At least that's what she tells constable Mullen (Johansson) when the half-frozen and terrified Annie stumbles into town from her wilderness home. But when Mullen investigates, he finds only more questions. **99m/C VHS, DVD.** *CA* Caroline Dhavernas, Brendan Fehr, Paul Johansson, Corey Sevier, Tantoo Cardinal, Peter Wingfield, Currie Graham, Jonas Chernick; ***D:*** Anne Wheeler; ***W:*** Anne Wheeler, Charles Kristian Pitts.

Edge of Sanity 1/2 **1989 (R)** An overdone Jekyll-Hyde reprise, with cocaine serving as the villainous substance. Dr. Jekyll (Perkins) is working in his lab, testing cocaine for use as an anaesthetic, when a lab monkey knocks a liquid into the coke and the fumes cause the doc to turn into Jack Hyde, a prototype for Jack the Ripper. Perkins knows the schizoid territory and the production values are good but this is not for the easily queazy. Available in a 90 minute, unrated version. **85m/C VHS, DVD.** *GB* Anthony Perkins, Glynis Barber, David Lodge, Sarah Maur-Thorp, Ben Cole, Lisa Davis, Jill Melford; ***D:*** Gerard Kikoine; ***W:*** J.P. Felix, Ron Raley; ***C:*** Tony Spratling; ***M:*** Frederic Talgorn.

Edge of Seventeen ☙☙ 1/2 **1999** Perceptive gay coming of age tale set in 1984 Ohio. Naive 16-year-old Eric (Stafford) is eager to explore his burgeoning sexuality with the help of college man, Rod (Gabrych). Unfortunately for Eric, Rod's the love 'em and leave 'em type. Disillusioned, Eric tries to remake himself in Brit-pop, New Wave fashion (think Boy George and Duran Duran), while turning to best friend Maggie (Holmes), without realizing the depths of her feelings for him. Eric's coming out tellingly provides confusion not just for himself but for everyone around him. **100m/C VHS, DVD.** Chris Stafford, Tina Holmes, Andersen Gabrych, Stephanie McVay, Lea DeLaria, John Eby; ***D:*** David Moreton; ***W:*** Todd Stephens; ***C:*** Gina DeGirolamo; ***M:*** Tom Bailey.

Edge of the Axe **1989** A small town is held in the grip of terror by a demented slasher. **91m/C VHS.** Barton Faulks, Christina Marie Lane, Page Moseley, Fred Hollyday; ***D:*** Joseph (Jose Ramon Larraz) Braunstein.

Edge of the City ☙☙ 1/2 **1957** Axel North (Cassavetes) left his family, who blamed him for his brother's death, and now has gone AWOL from the Army. He gets a job working on the New York docks and becomes friendly with Tommy (Poitier), who stoically puts up with his racist boss Malik (Warden) until the man goads him into a fight. Tommy is killed and Alex stays quiet to the cops before confronting Malik on his own. Based on the play "A Man Is Ten Feet Tall" by Robert Alan Aurthur. Directorial debut of Ritt. **85m/B DVD.** John Cassavetes, Sidney Poitier, Jack Warden, Kathleen Maguire, Ruby Dee, Robert F. Simon, Ruth White; ***D:*** Martin Ritt; ***W:*** Robert Alan Aurthur; ***C:*** Joseph Brun; ***M:*** Leonard Rosenman.

Edge of the World ☙☙☙ **1937** Moody, stark British drama of a mini-society in its death throes, expertly photographed on a six-square-mile island in the Shetlands. A dwindling fishing community of fewer than 100 souls agonize over whether to migrate to the mainland; meanwhile the romance of a local girl with an off-islander takes a tragic course. Choral effects were provided by the Glasgow Orpheus Choir. **80m/B VHS, DVD.** *GB* Finlay Currie, Niall MacGinnis, Grant Sutherland, John Laurie, Michael Powell; ***D:*** Michael Powell; ***W:*** Michael Powell.

Edie & Pen ☙☙ 1/2 **1995 (PG-13)** Tilly seems to be making a career of playing the ditz who's smarter than she seems as she shows here as Edie, who meets Pen (Channing) in Reno where both are looking for quickie divorces. They hit a bar to celebrate and hook up with soft-hearted Harry (Glenn), who's been dumped by his wife. Some drunken life discussions follow and then Edie finds out that her fiance is Pen's cold-hearted, newly ex hubby (Wilson). Slight script, charming performances. **97m/C VHS, DVD.** Jennifer Tilly, Stockard Channing, Scott Glenn, Stuart Wilson; ***Cameos:*** Beverly D'Angelo, Louise Fletcher, Joanna Gleason, Michael McKean, Martin Mull, Michael O'Keefe, Chris Sarandon, Randy Travis, Jean Smart, Victoria Tennant; ***D:*** Matthew Irmas; ***W:*** Victoria Tennant; ***C:*** Alicia Weber; ***M:*** Shawn Colvin.

Edie in Ciao! Manhattan ☙☙ *Ciao! Manhattan* **1972 (R)** Real-life story of Edie Sedgwick, Warhol superstar and international fashion model, whose life in the fast lane led to ruin. **84m/C VHS, DVD.** Edie Sedgwick, Baby Jane Holzer, Roger Vadim, Paul America, Viva, Isabel Jewell, Pat Hartley; ***D:*** David Weisman, John Palmer; ***W:*** David Weisman, John Palmer; ***C:*** John Palmer, Kjell Rostand; ***M:*** Gino Piserchio.

Edison Force ☙ 1/2 *Edison* **2005 (R)** Pollack (Timberlake) is a junior reporter at a lowly community paper in suburban Edison when he stumbles across information on a police unit whose results at cleaning up crime (at any cost) have left them above the law they purportedly serve. When Pollack asks too many questions, bad things happen. Self-important and heavy-handed. **97m/C DVD.** Morgan Freeman, Kevin Spacey, Justin Timberlake, LL Cool J, Dylan McDermott, Cary Elwes, Piper Perabo, Roselyn Sanchez; ***D:*** David J. Burke; ***W:*** David J. Burke; ***C:*** Francis Kenny. **VIDEO**

Edison the Man ☙☙ 1/2 **1940** Story of Tommy Edison's early years of experimentation in the basement. The young genious eventually invents light bulbs, motion pictures, and a sound recording device. Well played by Tracy. **108m/C VHS.** Spencer Tracy, Rita Johnson, Lynne Overman, Charles Coburn, Gene Lockhart, Henry Travers, Felix Bressart; ***D:*** Clarence Brown.

Edith & Marcel ☙ 1/2 **1983** A fictionalization of the love affair between chanteuse Edith Piaf and boxer Marcel Cerdan (played by his son, Marcel Cerdan Jr.). French with English subtitles. **104m/C VHS.** *FR* Evelyne Bouix, Marcel Cerdan Jr., Charles Aznavour, Jacques Villeret; ***D:*** Claude Lelouch.

Edmond ☙☙ **2005 (R)** Dissatisfied with his middle-aged, middle-management life, Edmond (Macy) reacts to a psychic's dismal prophecy by leaving his wife and turning his regretful existence upside down with a homicidal night on the town. Following the dubious advice of a sleazeball barfly (Mantegna), Edmond, in a nutshell, gets kicked out of a strip club, kills a would-be mugger, beds then kills a waitress half his age (Stiles), and ends up the plaything of his burly, black cellmate (Woodbine). Sound unpleasant? It is. Macy's usual, utterly convincing portrayal earns pic a half bone. Based on a 1982 play by David Mamet, which ran off-Broadway. Rent it with "Bad Lieutenant" for a night that'll destroy your faith in humanity. **76m/C DVD.** *US* William H. Macy, Joe Mantegna, Jeffrey Combs, Denise Richards, Rebecca Pidgeon, Julia Stiles, Mena Suvari, Bai Ling, Dule Hill, Dylan Walsh, Russell Hornsby, Debi Mazar, Lionel Mark Smith, Bokeem Woodbine, Jack Wallace, George Wendt, Frances Bay; ***D:*** Stuart Gordon; ***W:*** David Mamet; ***C:*** Denis Maloney; ***M:*** Bobby Johnston.

Ed's Next Move ☙☙ 1/2 **1996 (R)** Genial indie NYC comedy with a Woody Allen feel is littered with whimsical one-liners. Title character Ed (Ross) moves from small-town Wisconsin to New York after a break-up with his girlfriend. Being that he's a rice geneticist, it's not a big leap to conclude that Ed's a bit uptight, so it's imperative that Ed's big city roommate, the suave Ray (Carroll), hip him up to better meet the ladies. Soon, Ed falls for boho Lee (Thorne) leader of a band called "Ed's Redeeming Qualities." Fun fantasy sequence involving Ed, his old girlfriend and two translators is a highlight. Low-budgeter, with a first time writer/director (Walsh), and it shows, but in a good-natured way. Though more could be asked visually, picture does boast good performers and well-drawn characters. **88m/C VHS.** Matt Ross, Callie (Calliope) Thorne, Kevin Carroll, Ramsey Faragallah, Nina Shevaleva, James (Jimmy) Cummings; ***D:*** John Walsh; ***W:*** John Walsh; ***C:*** Peter Nelson.

EDtv ☙☙ 1/2 **1999 (PG-13)** Ed (McConaughey) is a scruffy redneck video clerk who agrees to have his life broadcast 24/7 for a reality show produced by DeGeneres. Of course the show becomes a hit, and an entire nation watches breathlessly as Ed steals his brother's girlfriend Shari (Elfman), restocks shelves, and goes to the bathroom with the door open. His family life immediately turns melodramatic, with Ed learning "shocking secrets" about his mom (Kirkland), dad (Landau), and brother (Harrelson). Compared to the "The Truman Show," thanks to their back-to-back release in theatres, but director (and TV child star survivor) Ron Howard's version lacks the biting satire. **122m/C VHS, DVD.** Ellen DeGeneres, Sally Kirkland, Martin Landau, Elizabeth Hurley, Rob Reiner, Dennis Hopper, Adam Goldberg, Viveka Davis, Clint Howard, Larry "Flash" Jenkins, Donny Most, Rick Overton, RuPaul Charles, Gedde Watanabe, Harry Shearer, Jennifer Elise Cox, Matthew McConaughey, Jenna Elfman, Woody Harrelson; ***D:*** Ron Howard; ***W:*** Lowell Ganz, Babaloo Mandel; ***C:*** John Schwartzman; ***M:*** Randy Edelman.

Educating Rita ☙☙☙ 1/2 **1983 (PG)** Walters and Caine team beautifully in this adaptation of the successful Willy Russell play which finds Rita, an uneducated hairdresser, determined to improve her knowledge of literature. In so doing, she enlists the aid of tutor Frank: a disillusioned alcoholic, adeptly played by Caine. Together, the two find inspiration in one another's differences and experiences. Ultimately, the teacher receives a lesson in how to again appreciate his work and the classics as he observes his pupil's unique approach to her studies. Some deem this a "Pygmalion" for the '80s. **110m/C VHS, DVD.** *GB* Michael Caine, Julie Walters, Michael Williams, Maureen Lipman; ***D:*** Lewis Gilbert; ***W:*** Willy Russell. British Acad. '83: Actor (Caine), Actress (Walters), Film; Golden Globes '84: Actor—Mus./Comedy (Caine), Actress—Mus./Comedy (Walters).

An Education ☙☙☙ **2009 (PG-13)** Mulligan is bewitching as 16-year-old Jenny in a coming-into-womanhood story. Bored, bright and inexperienced, Jenny can't wait to throw off her sheltered suburban upbringing and the restraints of her strict girls' school in a drab 1961 London. Desperate to be thought a sophisticate, she's ripe for the plucking after she meets smooth-talking thirtysomething David (Sarsgaard), who starts taking her out on the town. But Jenny isn't quite the naif he thinks she is. Adapted from a memoir by journalist Lynn Barber. **100m/C DVD.** *GB* Carey Mulligan, Peter Sarsgaard, Dominic Cooper, Rosamund Pike, Alfred Molina, Olivia Williams, Emma Thompson, Cara Seymour, Matthew Beard, Sally Hawkins; ***D:*** Lone Scherfig; ***W:*** Nick Hornby; ***C:*** John de Borman; ***M:*** Paul Englishby. British Acad. '09: Actress (Mulligan); Ind. Spirit '10: Foreign Film.

The Education of Little Tree ☙☙☙ **1997 (PG)** Child's eye view of a large scale epic on par with modern classics like "The Secret Garden." In 1935, poor, orphaned, and part Native American Little Tree (Ashton) is sent to live with his grandfather (Cromwell) and Native American grandmother (Cardinal) in the Smokey Mountains of Tennessee. There he learns "The Way" of his Cherokee ancestors and how to make moonshine from his Scottish/Irish grandfather. A nosy, Bible-thumping Aunt tips off authorities and soon Little Tree is shipped off to an evil state institution to cure him of his inappropriate Indian ways. There, the old-fashioned discipline runs fierce and abusive. Adapted from a children's book by Forrest Carter. Cardinal and Cromwell carve out memorable performances alongside first-rate newcomer Joseph Ashton. **112m/C VHS, DVD.** James Cromwell, Tantoo Cardinal, Joseph Ashton, Graham Greene, Lisa Bronwyn Moore; ***D:*** Richard Friedenberg; ***W:*** Richard Friedenberg; ***C:*** Anastas Michos; ***M:*** Mark Isham.

The Education of Sonny Carson ☙☙ 1/2 **1974 (R)** Chilling look at the tribulations of a black youth living in a Brooklyn ghetto amid drugs, prostitution, crime, and other forms of vice. Based on Sonny Carson's autobiography. Still pertinent some 20 years after its theatrical release. **104m/C VHS, DVD.** Rony Clanton, Don Gordon, Paul Benjamin; ***D:*** Michael Campus.

The Edukators ☙☙ *Die Fetten Jahre sind vorbei* **2004 (R)** In Berlin, three twenty-something political idealists, dogmatic and naive, commit various property pranks on the bourgeoisie. Roomies Jan (Bruehl) and Peter (Erceg) and Peter's girlfriend Julie (Jentsche) (who likes Jan, too) happily vandalize until ineptly graduating to kidnapping when businessman Hardenberg (Klaussner) comes home early and interrupts them. Clueless, the trio decide to hide out with their captive (who turns out to be a former 60s radical) at a mountain cabin. Much generational talk and romantic tension ensues. German with subtitles. **126m/C DVD.** *GE AT* Daniel Bruhl, Julia Jentsch, Stipe Erceg, Burghart Klaussner; ***D:*** Hans Weingartner; ***W:*** Hans Weingartner, Katharina Held; ***C:*** Matthias Schellenberg, Daniela Knapp; ***M:*** Andreas Wodraschke.

Edvard Munch ☙☙ **1974** Biographical portrait of the Norwegian Expressionist painter and his tormented life in the stuffy society of 19th-century Oslo. Concentrates mainly on his early years, including the deaths of his mother and younger sister, his brother's suicide, Munch's affair with a married woman, and his struggle to maintain his sanity. Based on Munch's memoirs. In German and Norwegian with English subtitles. **167m/C VHS, DVD.** *NO* Geir Westby, Gro Fraas, Eli Ryg; ***D:*** Peter Watkins; ***W:*** Peter Watkins; ***C:*** Odd Geir Saether.

Edward and Mrs. Simpson ☙☙ **1980** Dramatic reconstruction of the years leading to the abdication of King Edward VIII, who forfeited the British throne in 1936 so that he could marry American divorcee Wallis Simpson. Originally aired on PBS. **270m/C VHS, DVD.** Edward Fox, Cynthia Harris; ***D:*** Waris Hussein. **TV**

Edward Scissorhands ☙☙☙ **1990 (PG-13)** Depp's a young man created by loony scientist Price, who dies before he can attach hands to his boy-creature. Then the boy is rescued from his lonely existence outside of suburbia by an ingratiating Avon lady. With scissors in place of hands, he has more trouble fitting into suburbia than would most new kids on the block, and he struggles with being different and lonely in a card-board-cutout world. Visually captivating fairy tale full of splash and color, however predictable the Hollywood-prefab denouement. **100m/C VHS, DVD, Blu-ray Disc.** Johnny Depp, Winona Ryder, Dianne Wiest, Vincent Price, Anthony Michael Hall, Alan Arkin, Kathy Baker, Conchata Ferrell, Caroline Aaron, Dick Anthony Williams, Robert Oliveri, John Davidson; ***D:*** Tim Burton; ***W:*** Tim Burton, Caroline Thompson; ***C:*** Stefan Czapsky; ***M:*** Danny Elfman.

Edward II ☙☙ 1/2 **1992 (R)** Jarman's controversial adaptation of Christopher Marlowe's play "The Troublesome Reign of Edward II" portrays the weak-willed monarch as neglecting his kingdom for love. Unfortunately, it's not for his queen but for his commoner male lover. His neglect of both queen and country lead to a swift and brutal downfall. Jarman's use of contemporary anachronisms, stream of conscienceness approach, and heavy symbolism may leave more than one viewer wondering what's going on. **91m/C VHS, DVD.** *GB* Steven Waddington, Kevin Collins, Andrew Tiernan, John Lynch, Dudley Sutton, Tilda Swinton, Jerome Flynn, Jody Graber, Nigel Terry, Annie Lennox; ***D:*** Derek Jarman; ***W:*** Derek Jarman; ***M:*** Simon Fisher Turner. Venice Film Fest. '92: Actress (Swinton).

Edward the King ☙☙ 1/2 **1975** British miniseries follows the long life of Prince Edward, who waited some 60 years for his overbearing mother, Queen Victoria, to die so he could ascend the throne. Bertie scandalized with his affairs and carousing but, nevertheless, proved his worth as king-in-waiting. On six cassettes. **708m/C VHS, DVD.** *GB* Timothy West, Annette Crosbie, John Gielgud, Francesca Annis, Robert Hardy; ***D:*** John Gorrie; ***C:*** Tony Imi. **TV**

Edwin ☙☙ 1/2 **1984** Sir Fennimore Truscott (Guinness) is a retired High Court Judge who suspects that his neighbor once had an affair with Truscott's wife. These long-fermenting fears assert themself as Truscott presents his case (to the audience) and even suspects the paternity of his son, Edwin. When Edwin comes for a visit, Truscott's obsessions are forced into the open. **78m/C VHS, DVD.** *GB* Alec Guinness, Paul Rogers, Renee Asherson; ***D:*** Rodney Bennett; ***W:*** John Mortimer. **TV**

Eegah! **WOOF!** **1962** Another Arch Hall-directed (under the Nicholas Merriwether pseud.) epic in which an anachronistic Neanderthal falls in love in '60s California. Reputed to be one of the worst films of all time. **93m/C VHS, DVD.** Marilyn Manning, Richard Kiel, Arch Hall Jr., William Waters, Carolyn Brandt, William Lloyd, Ray Dennis Steckler; ***D:*** Arch (Archie) Hall Sr.; ***W:*** Bob Wehling; ***C:*** Vilis Lapenieks; ***M:*** Arch Hall Jr.

The Eel ☙☙☙ *Unagi* **1996** Yamashita (Yakusho) has just been paroled after spending eight years in prison for killing his adulterous wife in a jealous rage. While there, he found and cared for an eel, which became his only confidante, and which accompanies him to his new life as a barber in a small town outside Tokyo. The newcomer is soon befriended by the locals but Yamashita's life changes most when he saves the suicidal Keiko (Shimizu) from drowning. She comes to work in his shop and would obviously like a more intimate relationship but some secrets in her past and some strange incidents in the town may jepordize Yamashita's hopes for a normal life. Based on the novel "Glimmering in the Dark" by Akira Yoshimura. Japanese with subtitles. **117m/C VHS, DVD.** *JP* Koji Yakusho, Misa Shimizu, Mitsuko Baisho, Shou Aikawa, Fujio Tsuneta, Akira (Tsukamoto) Emoto, Etsuko Ichihara, Tomorowo Taguchi, Ken Kobayashi, Sabu Kawahara; ***D:*** Shohei Imamura; ***W:*** Shohei Imamura, Motofumi Tomikawa, Daisuke Tengan; ***C:*** Shigeru Komatsubara; ***M:*** Shinichiro Ikebe. Cannes '97: Film.

The Effect of Gamma Rays on Man-in-the-Moon Marigolds ☙☙☙ **1973 (PG)** A wonderful drama based on the Pulitzer Prize winning play by Paul Zindel. The story centers around eccentric young Matilda and her depressed family. Matilda is preparing her experiment for the school science fair, determined to beat her competition. Her exhibit shows how radiation sometimes kills the helpless marigolds, but sometimes causes them to grow into even more beautiful mutations. This mirrors Matilda, who flowers even amidst the drunkenness of her mother and the dullness of her sister. **100m/C VHS.** Joanne Woodward, Nell Potts, Roberta Wallach, Judith Lowry, Richard Venture; ***D:*** Paul Newman; ***W:*** Paul Zindel. Cannes '73: Actress (Woodward).

Effi Briest ½ *Fontane Effi Briest* **1974** A 19th-century tragedy well-played by Schygulla and empowered with Fassbinder's directorial skills. Effi (Schygulla) is a 17 year-old beauty, unhappily married to a much older man. She drifts into a brief affair, which is not discovered for several years. When her husband does discover her past infidelity, the Prussian legal code permits him a chilling revenge. Based on a popular 19th-century novel by Theodor Fontane. In German with English subtitles. **135m/B VHS, DVD.** *GE* Hanna Schygulla, Wolfgang Schenck, Lilo Pempeit, Ulli Lommel; ***D:*** Rainer Werner Fassbinder; ***W:*** Rainer Werner Fassbinder; ***C:*** Jurgen Jurges, Dietrich Lohmann.

The Efficiency Expert ½ *Spotswood* **1992 (PG)** Lighthearted Australian comedy about a dingy moccasin factory where a rigid efficiency consultant is invited to save the eccentric family-run company from bankruptcy. Predictable ending contains a nevertheless timely message about the importance of the bottom line. **97m/C VHS, DVD.** *AU* Anthony Hopkins, Ben Mendelsohn, Alwyn Kurts, Bruno Lawrence, Angela Punch McGregor, Russell Crowe, Rebecca Rigg, Toni Collette; ***D:*** Mark Joffe; ***W:*** Andrew Knight, Max Dann; ***M:*** Ricky Fataar.

Egg ½ **1988** Striking film from Holland chronicles the life of a quiet, middle-aged baker who answers a personal ad from a schoolteacher. After much correspondence, the teacher visits the baker in his village, and the townspeople take great interest in what happens next. In Dutch with English subtitles. **58m/C VHS.** *NL* Johan Leysen, Marijke Vengelers; ***D:*** Danniel Danniel; ***W:*** Danniel Danniel.

Egg and I **1947** Based on the true-life adventures of best-selling humorist Betty MacDonald. A young urban bride agrees to help her new husband realize his life-long dream of owning a chicken farm. A dilapidated house, temperamental stove, and suicidal chickens test the bride's perseverance, as do the zany antics of her country-bumpkin neighbors, Ma and Pa Kettle, who make their screen debut. Plenty of old-fashioned laughs. **104m/B VHS, DVD.** Claudette Colbert, Fred MacMurray, Marjorie Main, Percy Kilbride, Louise Allbritton, Richard Long, Billy House, Donald MacBride; ***D:*** Chester Erskine; ***C:*** Milton Krasner.

The Egyptian ½ **1954** Based on the sword-and-sandal novel by Mika Waltari, this is a ponderous big-budget epic about a young Egyptian in Akhnaton's epoch who becomes physician to the Pharaoh. **140m/C VHS.** Angela (Clark) Clarke, Edmund Purdom, Victor Mature, Peter Ustinov, Bella Darvi, Gene Tierney, Henry Daniell, Jean Simmons, Michael Wilding, Judith Evelyn, John Carradine, Carl Benton Reid; ***D:*** Michael Curtiz; ***W:*** Philip Dunne, Casey Robinson; ***C:*** Leon Shamroy.

An Egyptian Story *Hadduta Misriya* **1982** An Egyptian film director (Dine) goes to London for open-heart surgery and as he hovers between life and death, he remembers his past. Scenes from Chahine's other films highlight the director's reminiscences. Part 2 of the Alexandria trilogy, preceded by "Alexandria...Why?" and followed by "Alexandria Again and Forever." Arabic with subtitles. **127m/C VHS, DVD.** *EG* Mohiel Dine, Nour (el-Sherif) el-Cherif, Oussama Nadir, Magda El Khatib; ***D:*** Youssef Chahine; ***W:*** Youssef Chahine; ***C:*** Mohsen Nasr; ***M:*** Gamal Salama.

The Eiger Sanction **1975 (R)** An art teacher returns to the CII (a fictionalized version of the CIA) as an exterminator hired to assassinate the killers of an American agent. In the process, he finds himself climbing the Eiger. Beautiful Swiss Alps scenery fails to totally compensate for several dreary lapses. Based on the novel by Trevanian. **125m/C VHS, DVD.** Clint Eastwood, George Kennedy, Vonetta McGee, Jack Cassidy, Thayer David; ***D:*** Clint Eastwood; ***W:*** Hal Dresner, Warren B. Murphy, Rod Whitaker; ***C:*** Frank Stanley; ***M:*** John Williams.

8-A *Ochoa* **1992** Reconstructs the 1989 trial and execution of Cuban general Arnaldo Ochoa Sanchez, a hero of the revolution who, along with other government officials, advocated the resignation of Fidel Castro as the solution to the country's economic and political crises. At the trial Ochoa and four other officials were convicted of illegal drug trafficking and shot by a firing squad. Spanish with subtitles. **84m/C VHS.** *CU* ***D:*** Orlando Jiminez-Leal; ***W:*** Orlando Jiminez-Leal; ***C:*** Emilio Guede Jr.

8 1/2 *Otto E Mezzo; Federico Fellini's 8 1/2* **1963** The acclaimed Fellini self-portrait of a revered Italian film director struggling with a fated film project wanders through his intermixed life, childhood memories, and hallucinatory fantasies. Subtitled in English. **135m/B VHS, DVD.** *IT* Marcello Mastroianni, Claudia Cardinale, Anouk Aimee, Sandra Milo, Barbara Steele, Rossella Falk, Eddra Gale, Mark Herron, Madeleine LeBeau, Caterina Boratto; ***D:*** Federico Fellini; ***W:*** Tullio Pinelli, Ennio Flaiano, Brunello Rondi, Federico Fellini; ***C:*** Gianni Di Venanzo; ***M:*** Nino Rota. Oscars '63: Costume Des. (B&W), Foreign Film; N.Y. Film Critics '63: Foreign Film.

8 1/2 Women ½ **1999 (R)** A typically baffling presentation from Greenaway concerns wealthy Swiss businessman Philip Emmeenthal (Standing), who is grief-stricken over the recent death of his wife. His son, Storey (Delamere), comes to Geneva to console his father. After seeing Fellini's "8 1/2" they suddenly decide to assemble their own harem of decidedly offbeat females and pursue sexual fantasies. Remarkably unappealing and dull. **122m/C VHS, DVD.** *GB* John Standing, Vivian Wu, Annie Shizuka Inoh, Matthew Delamere, Toni Collette, Amanda Plummer, Manna Fujiwara, Barbara Sarafian, Polly Walker, Karina Mano, Natacha Amal; ***D:*** Peter Greenaway; ***W:*** Peter Greenaway; ***C:*** Sacha Vierny.

Eight Below ½ **2006 (PG)** Disney goes to the dogs with appropriately tail-wagging results. Jerry (Walker), a guide at the U.S. National Science Research Base in Antarctica, is deeply devoted to his eight beautiful sled dogs. Ambitious scientist McClaren (Greenwood) gets them involved in a risky mission that results in evacuation for the humans—but not the dogs—due to early winter storms. While the dogs scavenge to survive, Jerry tries to organize a rescue trip to save his best friends. Shot in Canada, Norway, and Greenland. **120m/C DVD, Blu-ray Disc.** *US* Paul Walker, Bruce Greenwood, Jason Biggs, Gerard Plunkett, Connor Christopher Levins, August Schellenberg, Wendy Crewson, Moon Bloodgood, Belinda Metz; ***D:*** Frank Marshall; ***W:*** Dave DiGilio; ***C:*** Don Burgess; ***M:*** Mark Isham.

Eight Days a Week ½ **1997 (R)** Shy, nerdy high-schooler Peter (Schaefer) is obsessed with Erica (Russell), the popular babe who lives across the street. Peter decides a sit-in on her front lawn and constant protestations about his devotion is the way to get her attention. Title comes from the Beatles tune and is the cleverest thing in the movie. **92m/C VHS.** Joshua Schaefer, Keri Russell, R.D. Robb, Mark L. Taylor, Catherine Hicks; ***D:*** Michael Davis; ***W:*** Michael Davis; ***C:*** James Lawrence Spencer; ***M:*** Kevin Bassinson.

8 Heads in a Duffel Bag **1996 (R)** Mob bag man Tommy (Pesci, in a real stretch) loses his heads, the evidence of a successful hit, to med student Charlie Pritchett (Comeau), who's headed for a Mexican vacation with his fiance's (Swanson) uptight family. Desperate, Tommy "persuades" Charlie's roommates (Spade and Louiso) to help him find some replacement noggins. Excellent premise is almost done in by a timid script that relies a little too much on slapstick. Schulman's uneven directorial debut does little to mask the problem. Newcomer Comeau tries for a "Bachelor Party" era Tom Hanks thing, but doesn't quite get there. Pesci and Spade save flick from disaster, and get most of the good lines, pitted in a generational "battle of the smart-asses," but neither one strays from their previous screen personas. Louiso hilariously makes the most of his role as the naive roommate. **95m/C VHS, DVD.** Joe Pesci, David Spade, Andy Comeau, Kristy Swanson, George Hamilton, Dyan Cannon, Todd Louiso, Frank Roman, Anthony Mangano, Joe Basile, Ernestine Mercer, Howard George; ***D:*** Tom Schulman; ***W:*** Tom Schulman; ***C:*** Adam Holender; ***M:*** Andrew Gross.

800 Bullets ½ *800 Balas* **2002** Director Iglesia pays tribute to the films of Sergio Leone in this Spanish dramatic comedy. Fourteen-year-old Carlos (Castro) runs away from his uptight widowed mother, Laura (Maura), in search of his paternal grandfather. He finds his grandfather Julian (Gracia) living in Almeria, a region in Spain that doubled for the American West in countless spaghetti westerns. Julian, a former stuntman, is now an alcoholic employee of a theme park cobbled together from the abandoned sets of old cowboy movies. Julian and his fellow stuntmen welcome Carlos into their band of Lost Boys, that is, until Laura shows up, threatening to close the party down. Iglesia has great fun orchestrating complex comedic set pieces, but has trouble balancing the dramatic tone in the last act. **123m/C DVD.** Sancho Gracia, Carmen Maura, Eusebio Poncela, Terele Pavez, Angel de Andres Lopez, Luis Castro; ***D:*** Alex de la Iglesia; ***C:*** Flavio Martinez Labiano; ***M:*** Roque Banos.

800 Leagues Down the Amazon ½ **1993 (PG-13)** A 19th-century journey down the Amazon on a raft with a planter, his daughter, and various complications. Based on a novel by Jules Verne. **100m/C VHS, DVD.** Daphne Zuniga, Barry Bostwick, Adam Baldwin, Tom Verica, E.E. Bell; ***D:*** Luis Llosa; ***W:*** Laura Schiff, Jackson Barr; ***C:*** Pili Flores-Guerra; ***M:*** Jorge Tafur.

Eight Legged Freaks ½ **2002 (PG-13)** Attack of the B-Movie Redos! Boy (Arquette) meets girl (Wuhrer) and battle giant mutant spiders in this updated 1950s sci-fi horror/comedy. Prosperity, Arizona is the unlikely site of a toxic waste mishap near a spider farm, spawning SUV-sized creepy crawlies. Slow-witted but sweet local boy Arquette joins forces with foxy sheriff Wuhrer and a posse of locals to rid the town of the huge spideys. Scary, campy, self-parodying fun. Director Elkayem gives props to the '50s horror cult classic, "Them!" which plays in the background of one scene. **99m/C VHS, DVD.** *US* David Arquette, Kari Wuhrer, Scott Terra, Scarlett Johansson, Doug E. Doug, Riley Smith, Leon Rippy, Rick Overton, Eileen Ryan, Tom Noonan; ***D:*** Ellory Elkayem; ***W:*** Jesse Alexander, Ellory Elkayem; ***C:*** John Bartley; ***M:*** John Ottman.

Eight Men Out **1988 (PG)** Taken from Eliot Asinof's book, a moving, full-blooded account of the infamous 1919 "Black Sox" scandal, in which members of the Chicago White Sox teamed to throw the World Series for $80,000. A dirge of lost innocence, this is among Sayles' best films. Provides an interesting look at the "conspiracy" that ended "Shoeless" Joe Jackson's major-league career. The actual baseball scenes are first-rate, and Straithairn, Sweeney, and Cusack give exceptional performances. Sayles makes an appearance as Ring Lardner. Enjoyable viewing for even the non-sports fan. **121m/C VHS, DVD.** John Cusack, D.B. Sweeney, Perry Lang, Jace Alexander, Bill Irwin, Clifton James, Michael Rooker, Michael Lerner, Christopher Lloyd, Studs Terkel, David Strathairn, Charlie Sheen, Kevin Tighe, John Mahoney, John Sayles, Gordon Clapp, Richard Edson, James Read, Don Harvey, John Anderson, Maggie Renzi, Michael Mantell, Nancy Travis, Michael Laskin, Barbara Garrick, Wendy Makkena; ***D:*** John Sayles; ***W:*** John Sayles; ***C:*** Robert Richardson; ***M:*** Mason Daring.

8 Mile **2002 (R)** Although claiming to be fiction, director Hanson's thinly veiled bio of star Eminem's escape from the streets of Detroit will please more than the rapper's fans. Rabbit (Eminem) is a joyless autoworker living in the trailer park with his loose mother (Basinger) and little sister Lily (Greenfield). The only time that Rabbit has a chance to shine is at the rap battles organized by pal Future (Phifer), who sees talent in his friend. Also recognizing greatness (and a possible ticket out of the 'hood) is aspiring model Alex (Murphy), who quickly consummates a calculating relationship with Rabbit. The climactic rap battle allows Eminem to showcase the talent that made this "Rocky"-esque vehicle possible, although it wisely ends with Rabbit on the cusp of success and not at the pinnacle. Shot on location in Detroit. **118m/C VHS, DVD, UMD.** *US* Eminem, Kim Basinger, Brittany Murphy, Mekhi Phifer, Evan Jones, Eugene Byrd, Omar Benson Miller, De'Angelo Wilson, Taryn Manning, Michael Shannon, Anthony Mackie, Chloe Greenfield, Paul Bates, Craig Chandler; ***D:*** Curtis Hanson; ***W:*** Scott Silver; ***C:*** Rodrigo Prieto; ***M:*** Eminem. Oscars '02: Song ("Lose Yourself").

Eight Miles High ½ *Das Wilde Leben* **2007** Flashy, trashy autobiopic of frequently undressed German model/sixties icon Uschi Obermaier (Avelon), from her provincial childhood to her time at a radical Berlin commune and other adventures. Then there's her sexual exploits with Mick Jagger and Keith Richards (among other rockers) before Uschi runs off to explore the Third World with adventurer Deiter Bockhorn. Unless you're enamored of the era, you'll wonder what the fuss is about, though end credits showcase photos of the real Obermaier. English and German with subtitles. **114m/C DVD.** *GE* Natalia Avelon, David Scheller, Alexander Scheer, Friederike Kempter, Victor Noven; ***D:*** Achim Bornhak; ***W:*** Olaf Kraemer; ***C:*** Benjamin Dernbecker; ***M:*** Alexander Hacke.

Eight Miles High *Das Wilde Leben* **2008** Uschi Obermaier's name and face are not famous in America, but in Europe in the 1960s her image was synonymous with the counter cultural movement. This overly adoring biopic follows her from a boring middle class life and her time to a commune to her life as a supermodel and eventually a globe-trotting vagabond. There isn't much substance to the film, but as Uschi, Avelon manages to distract viewers with her body well enough that they probably won't notice. **114m/C DVD.** *GE* David Scheller, Alexander Scheer, Georg Friedrich, Natalia Avelon, Matthias Schweighofer, Friederike Kempter, Victor Noren, Milan Peschel; ***D:*** Achim Bornhak; ***W:*** Achim Bornhak, Dagmar Benke, Claus Peter Hant, Olaf Kraemer; ***C:*** Benjamin Dernbecker; ***M:*** Alexander Hacke. **VIDEO**

8mm ½ **1998 (R)** Surveillance expert Tom Welles (Cage) leads a normal family life until he's hired by widow Mrs. Christian (Carter). She wants him to find out the identity of a young girl apparently slashed to death in a porno film found in her late husband's safe. He descends into the underbelly of the pornography industry, guided by sleazeballs with names like Max California (Phoenix) and Dino Velvet (Stormare), and is both disgusted and fascinated by what he sees and learns. After he ferrets out the villain, he is forced into a showdown in order to save his family. Scripted by "Seven" writer Andrew Kevin Walker, but lacks some of the psychological punch of his previous effort. **123m/C VHS, DVD.** Nicolas Cage, Joaquin Rafael (Leaf) Phoenix, James Gandolfini, Peter Stormare, Anthony Heald, Catherine Keener, Chris Bauer, Myra Carter, Amy Morton; ***D:*** Joel Schumacher; ***W:*** Andrew Kevin Walker; ***C:*** Robert Elswit; ***M:*** Mychael Danna.

8 Million Ways to Die **1985 (R)** An ex-cop hires himself out to rescue a pimp-bound hooker, and gets knee-deep in a mess of million-dollar drug deals, murder, and prostitution. Slow-moving but satisfying. Based on the book by Lawrence Block. **115m/C VHS.** Jeff Bridges, Rosanna Arquette, Andy Garcia, Alexandra Paul; ***D:*** Hal Ashby; ***W:*** Oliver Stone; ***C:*** Stephen Burum; ***M:*** James Newton Howard.

Eight on the Lam **1967 (PG)** Unfunny comedy features widower Henry Dimsdale (Hope) taking off with his kids and family maid Golda (Diller) when he's accused of embezzling bank funds. Jasper Lynch (Winters) is on their trail until Henry can prove who the real culprit is. **103m/C VHS.** Bob Hope, Phyllis Diller, Jonathan Winters, Jill St. John, Shirley Eaton; ***D:*** George Marshall; ***W:*** Albert Lewin, Arthur Marx, Bob Fisher, Burt Styler; ***C:*** Alan Stensvold; ***M:*** George Romanis.

8 Seconds ½ *The Lane Frost Story* **1994 (PG-13)** Love, not sports, dominates the true-life story of rodeo star Lane Frost (Perry), a world champion bull rider killed in the ring at the age of 25 in 1990. A decent guy, he finds quick success on the rodeo circuit, marries (to Geary), and finds his career getting in the way of their happiness. Bull-riding sequences are genuinely stomach churning, the performances low-key. Title refers to the amount of time a rider must stay aboard his animal. **104m/C VHS, DVD.** Luke Perry, Cynthia Geary, Stephen Baldwin, James Rebhorn, Carrie Snodgress, Red Mitchell, Ronnie Claire Edwards; *D:* John G. Avildsen; *W:* Monte Merrick; *C:* Victor Hammer; *M:* Bill Conti.

Eight Witnesses **1954** Suspense thriller about a man being murdered in front of eight blind witnesses. **67m/B VHS, DVD.** *GB* Peggy Ann Garner, Dennis Price; *D:* Lawrence Huntington; *W:* Halsted Welles.

8 Women *8 femmes* **2002 (R)** Wacky musical murder mystery starring eight of France's top actresses. Grand dame Gaby (Deneuve) and her daughters, Suzon (Ledoyen) and Catherine (Sagnier), share a remote estate with her husband Marcel (Lamure), her mother Mamy (Darrieux), spinster sister Augustine (Huppert), loyal housemaid Mme. Chanel (Richard), and pouty chambermaid Louise (Beart). Louise discovers Marcel stabbed to death—the phone doesn't work, the car won't start, and there's a blizzard. To make matters more interesting, Marcel's estranged sister Pierrette (Ardant) literally comes in from the cold. Now, the eight women are trapped together. Is one of them a killer? Secrets and accusations spill out in song, like a Technicolor '50s musical melodrama. It may not make sense but with this cast, plot will be the last thing on your mind. Based on the play by Robert Thomas; French with subtitles. **103m/C VHS, DVD.** *FR* Catherine Deneuve, Isabelle Huppert, Emmanuelle Beart, Fanny Ardant, Virginie Ledoyen, Danielle Darrieux, Ludivine Sagnier, Firmine Richard, Dominique Lamure; *D:* Francois Ozon; *W:* Francois Ozon, Marina de Van; *C:* Jeanne Lapoirie; *M:* Krishna Levy.

Eighteen **2004** After leaving his dysfunctional family, Pip (Anthony) is living on the streets where his father (Houde) finds him when Pip turns 18. Dad hands his son a tape that his grandfather (McKellen) recorded about his own experiences at 18, which happened while he was a soldier during WWII. The flashbacks are the best part and, despite the "Pip" name, the story has nothing to do with Charles Dickens or "Great Expectations." **101m/C DVD.** *CA* Paul Anthony, Brendan Fletcher, Carly Pope, Serge Houde, Clarence Sponagle, Thea Gill; *D:* Richard Bell; *W:* Richard Bell; *C:* Kevin Van Niekerk; *M:* Bramwell Tovey.

18 Again! 1/2 **1988 (PG)** After a bump on the head, an 81-year-old man and his 18-year-old grandson mentally switch places, giving each a new look at his life. Lightweight romp with Burns in especially good form, but not good enough to justify redoing this tired theme. **100m/C VHS, DVD.** George Burns, Charlie Schlatter, Anita Morris, Jennifer Runyon, Tony Roberts, Red Buttons, Miriam Flynn, George DiCenzo, Pauly Shore, Anthony Starke; *D:* Paul Flaherty; *W:* Jonathan Prince, Josh Goldstein; *C:* Stephen M. Katz; *M:* Billy Goldenberg.

18 Fingers of Death 1/2 **2005 (PG-13)** Kung fu spoof about an actor, Buford Lee (Lew), who has starred in 803 low-budget action movies. When the producers cancel the film that he believes will make him a superstar, Lee really goes into fighting mode. **87m/C DVD.** James Lew, Noriyuki "Pat" Morita, Robin Shou, Lorenzo Lamas, Maurice Patton, Bokeem Woodbine, Don "The Dragon" Wilson, Lisa Arturo, Roark Critchlow; *D:* James Lew; *W:* James Lew; *C:* Jan Michalik; *M:* Eddie Griffin, Aaron Bolden. **VIDEO**

1860 **1933** During the Battle of Calatafimi in May of 1860, Sicilian peasants revolted against the King of Naples' army. The story focuses on four people caught up in the fighting: the spouse of a revolutionary, a foppish intellectual, a rebel priest, and the young shepherd who is sent with a message to Genoa asking for assistance. Blasetti made great use of location filming and natural light. In Italian with English subtitles. **72m/C VHS.** *IT* Giuseppe Gulino, Aida Bellia, Gianfranco Giachetti, Mario Ferrari; *D:* Alessandro Blasetti; *W:* Alessandro Biasetti, Emilio Cecchi; *C:* Anchise Brizzi; *M:* Nino Medin.

The Eighteenth Angel **1997 (R)** The unexpected death of his wife (Crewson) finds Hugh Stanton (McDonald) clinging to his 15-year-old daughter Lucy (Cook), who has fallen into a deep depression. Then a mysterious modeling agent "discovers" Lucy, claiming she has the face of an angel, and offers Lucy a trip to Italy. Unexplainable things happen during their stay and when Hugh investigates it seems that good and evil are in a battle for Lucy's soul. **90m/C VHS.** Christopher McDonald, Rachael Leigh Cook, Maximilian Schell, Stanley Tucci, Wendy Crewson, Ted Rusoff; *D:* William Bindley; *W:* David Seltzer; *C:* Thomas Ackerman.

The Eighth Day 1/2 *Le Huitieme Jour* **1995** Sugary story about workaholic businessman Harry (Auteuil), whose wife Julie (Miou-Miou) has just left him, taking their daughters. Driving home, Harry finds Georges (Duquenne) by the side of the road. Georges, who has Downs syndrome, has left the institution he's been living in and, though Harry tries to take him to the nearest police station, Georges refuses to leave him. Naturally, the emotionally deprived Harry begins to loosen up and, when Georges is finally returned to his group home, all his friends decide to help with Harry's attempts to win back his family. Thick with whimsy but the lead performances are excellent. French with subtitles. **108m/C VHS.** *FR BE* Daniel Auteuil, Pascal Duquenne, Miou-Miou, Henri Garcin, Fabienne Loriaux, Isabelle Sadoyan, Helene Roussel, Michele Maes; *D:* Jaco Van Dormael; *W:* Jaco Van Dormael; *C:* Walther Vanden Ende; *M:* Pierre Van Dormael. Cannes '96: Actor (Auteuil), Actor (Duquenne).

The Eighties 1/2 **1983** A comic, pseudo-documentary romp through the making of a musical. Not just another dime-a-dozen song-and-dance flick, but plays with the genre with humor and intelligence, treating us to an insider's view of a performance arranged at a shopping plaza, from the rigorous auditions to the tedium of the production of songs and routines. Treated in a lighthearted, sensitive, just on the verge of laughable manner, it concludes with 30 minutes of song and dance. In French with English subtitles. **86m/C VHS.** *FR* Aurore Clement, Lio, Magali Noel, Pascale Salkin; *D:* Chantal Akerman; *W:* Chantal Akerman, Jean Gruault.

80 Minutes **2008** Tedious wannabe thriller. Alex is waiting for girlfriend Mona to show up for his birthday but instead he gets bad guy Walter. Alex owes Walter $15,000, so Walter injects him with a poison and gives Alex 80 minutes to get the money and the antidote or die, sending Alex scrambling through the streets of Berlin to get the cash. **98m/C DVD.** *GE* Gabriel Mann, Natalia Avelon, Francis Fulton-Smith, Oliver Kieran-Jones, Joshua Dallas; *D:* Thomas Jahn; *W:* Thomas Jahn; *C:* Henning Jessel; *M:* Boris Salchow.

84 Charing Cross Road **1986 (PG)** A lonely woman in New York and a book-seller in London begin corresponding for business reasons. Over a 20-year period, their relationship grows into a friendship, and then a romance, though they communicate only by mail. Based on a true story and adapted from the book by Helene Hanff. **100m/C VHS, DVD.** Anne Bancroft, Anthony Hopkins, Judi Dench, Jean De Baer, Maurice Denham, Eleanor David, Mercedes Ruehl, Daniel Gerroll, Hugh Whitemore; *D:* David Hugh Jones; *W:* Hugh Whitemore; *C:* Brian West; *M:* George Fenton. British Acad. '87: Actress (Bancroft).

84 Charlie MoPic **1989 (R)** A widely acclaimed drama about the horrors of Vietnam seen through the eyes of a cameraman assigned to a special front-line unit. Filled with a cast of unknowns, this is an unsettling film that sheds new light on the subject of the Vietnam war. Powerful and energetic; music by Donovan. **89m/C VHS.** Richard Brooks, Christopher Burgard, Nicholas Cascone, Jonathan Emerson, Glenn Morshower, Jason Tomlins, Byron Thames; *D:* Patrick Sheane Duncan; *W:* Patrick Sheane Duncan; *C:* Alan Caso; *M:* Donovan.

88 Minutes 1/2 **2008 (R)** Predictable thriller sat on the shelves developing mold before Sony studios finally released it, and it's easy to see why. Jack Gramm (Pacino—either indifferent or ranting) is an allegedly hotshot forensic shrink whose testimony put away serial killer Jon Forster (McDonough). Forster is on death row when similar crimes are committed. Gramm gets the fisheye from FBI agent Parks (Forsythe) over the latest murder and then receives a call saying he's got 88 minutes to live. There's no sense of urgency and a viewer can easily discern who's sticking it to Jack, making suspense an afterthought. **108m/C DVD, Blu-ray Disc.** *US GE* Al Pacino, Alicia Witt, Leelee Sobieski, Amy Brenneman, Neal McDonough, William Forsythe, Deborah Kara Unger, Ben(jamin) McKenzie, Stephen Moyer; *D:* Jon Avnet; *W:* Gary Scott Thompson; *C:* Denis Lenoir; *M:* Ed Shearmur.

Eijanaika 1/2 *Why Not?* **1981** A gripping story of a poor Japanese man who returns to his country after a visit to America in the 1860s. Memorable performances make this an above-average film. In Japanese with English subtitles. **151m/C VHS.** *JP* Ken Ogata, Shigeru Izumiya; *D:* Shohei Imamura.

El *This Strange Passion* **1952** Bizarre black-comedy finds virginal middle-aged Francisco (De Cordova) marrying a beautiful young woman (Garces) and becoming jealously paranoid when he believes she's been unfaithful. He's eventually driven to insanity and attempted murder. Spanish with subtitles. **88m/B VHS.** *MX* Arturo de Cordova, Delia Garces, Luis Beristain, Aurora Walker; *D:* Luis Bunuel; *W:* Luis Bunuel, Luis Alcoriza; *C:* Gabriel Figueroa; *M:* Luis Hernandez Breton.

El Amor Brujo *Love, the Magician* **1986** An adaptation of the work of Miguel de Falla, in which flamenco dancers enact the story of a tragic romance. **100m/C VHS.** Antonio Gades, Cristina Hoyos, Laura Del Sol; *D:* Carlos Saura.

El Barbaro *Conquest* **1984** In the beginning of civilization, when evil powers rule, a barbarian has two ambitions in life: to seek revenge for his friend's death and to rescue the world from a sorcerer's power. **88m/C VHS.** *IT SP* Andrea Occhipinti, Gioia Scola, Violeta Cela, Sabrina Siani; *D:* Lucio Fulci; *W:* Gino Capone; *C:* Alejandro Ulloa; *M:* Claudio Simonetti.

El Bola *Pellet* **2000** A graphic portrayal of child abuse. 12-year-old Pablo (Ballesta) is nicknamed "Bola" or "Pellet" because he carries a small wooden ball as a good luck charm. Which he needs since his embittered father Mariano (Maron) regularly beats him. Pablo is quick to make friends with new kid in school, Alfredo (Galan), who eventually tells his own father, Jose (Gimenez), about the bruises he's seen on Pablo's body. Jose wants to get involved but it's not as simple as it seems. Spanish with subtitles. **88m/C DVD.** *SP* Juan Jose Ballesta, Pablo Galan, Alberto Gimenez, Manuel Maron, Nieve De Medina, Ana Wagener, Gloria Munoz; *D:* Achero Manas; *W:* Achero Manas; *C:* Juan Carlos Gomez; *M:* Eduardo Arbide.

El Bruto 1/2 *The Brute* **1952** A mid-Mexican-period Bunuel drama, about a brainless thug who is used as a bullying pawn in a struggle between a brutal landlord and discontented tenants. In Spanish with English titles. **83m/B VHS.** *MX* Pedro Armendariz Sr., Katy Jurado, Andres Soler, Rosita (Rosa) Arenas; *D:* Luis Bunuel.

El Camino 1/2 **2008** Minimalist road movie about self-discovery. When Matthew dies it bonds three strangers together on a road trip to scatter his ashes in Mexico. Elliot and Matthew were in foster care together; Lilly was his ex-girlfriend; and Gary, a current friend, felt Matthew was the anchor in his troubled life. The trip from North Carolina isn't very eventful, there are no big emotional revelations, and no romantic triangle develops. Cinematographer Neumann offers magnificent landscapes to make up for the lack of action. **86m/C DVD.** Leo Fitzpatrick, Christopher Denham, Elisabeth (Elissabeth, Elizabeth, Liz) Moss, Wes Studi, Amy Hargreaves, Richard Gallagher; *D:* Erik S. Weigel; *W:* Erik S. Weigel, Salvatore Interlandi; *C:* Till Neumann; *M:* Adam Balazs.

El Cantante **2006 (R)** Fiery passion is evident in this ode to a likely little-known artist who may be responsible for bringing salsa to the states. Puerto Rican-born Hector Lavoe—musician, singer, and addict—died of AIDS in 1993 at 46 after firing up the salsa scene in the U.S. The film showcases Lavoe and wife Puchi (Lopez) as they navigate the world of music, drugs, sex, and family. The music throbs but the story bobs, and we can't help but scratch our heads at the pair and their thorny relationship (he shares their bed with myriad others—of both sexes). It's the music that steals the show in this thumping, grinding tribute to a shooting star. **116m/C DVD.** *US* Marc Anthony, Jennifer Lopez, John Ortiz, Manny Perez, Vincent Laresca, Federico Castelluccio, Nelson Vasquez; *D:* Leon Ichaso; *W:* Leon Ichaso, David Darmstaedter, Todd Anthony Bello; *C:* Claudio Chea; *M:* Andres Levin.

El Carro 1/2 *The Car* **2004** Winning Colombian comedy about the Velez family and the arrival of its latest member, a cherry red Chevy. Narrated by the youngest daughter, Paola, recounting the drastic social and moral transformations brought on by this new car—a vehicle both for transportation and for plot development. Divided into quirky little episodes all revolving around the new wheels. Consistently funny. **93m/C DVD.** Cesar Badillo, Luly Bossa, Zaira Valenzuela, Diego Cadavid, Andrea Gomez; *D:* Luis Orjuela; *W:* Dago Garcia; *C:* J.C. Vasquez; *M:* Jymmi Pulido.

El Cid **1961** Charts the life of Rodrigo Diaz de Bivar, known as El Cid, who was the legendary 11th-century Christian hero who freed Spain from Moorish invaders. Noted for its insanely lavish budget, this epic tale is true to its setting and features elaborate battle scenes. **184m/C VHS, DVD.** Charlton Heston, Sophia Loren, Raf Vallone, Hurd Hatfield, Genevieve Page; *D:* Anthony Mann; *W:* Philip Yordan; *C:* Robert Krasker; *M:* Miklos Rozsa.

El Cochecito *The Wheelchair* **1960** Great Spanish actor Isbert stars as the head of a large family whose closest friends are all joined together in a kind of fraternity defined by the fact that they each use a wheelchair. He feels excluded because he does not have or need one, so he goes to great lengths to gain acceptance in this "brotherhood." In Spanish with English subtitles. **90m/B VHS.** *SP* Maria Luisa Ponte, Pedro Porcel, Antonio Gavilan, Jose Isbert; *D:* Marco Ferreri; *W:* Rafael Azcona, Marco Ferreri; *C:* Juan Julio Baena; *M:* Miguel Asins Arbo.

El Condor 1/2 **1970 (R)** Two drifters search for gold buried in a Mexican fort. **102m/C VHS.** *SP* Jim Brown, Lee Van Cleef, Patrick O'Neal, Marianna Hill, Iron Eyes Cody, Elisha Cook Jr.; *D:* John Guillermin; *W:* Larry Cohen, Steven W. Carabatsos; *M:* Maurice Jarre.

El Crimen Perfecto 1/2 *Ferpect Crime; Crimen Ferpecto; El Crimen Ferpecto* **2004** The "perfect crime"? Seemingly not, but this dark comedy delivers. Womanizing department store salesman Rafael (Toledo) finds himself in a predicament. A dressing room scuffle leaves his arch-nemesis and men's department manager (Varela) dead, and Rafael takes it upon himself to dispose of the body. But unattractive Lourdes (Cervera), a sales assistant in love with Rafael, saw it all and even helps him, only to later blackmail him into marriage. Now Rafael must find a way to loosen Lourdes' clutches. In Spanish with English subtitles. **105m/C DVD.** *SP IT* *D:* Alex de la Iglesia; *W:* Alex de la Iglesia, Jorge Guerricaechevarria; *C:* Jose L. Moreno; *M:* Roque Banos.

El Diablo 1/2 **1990 (PG-13)** A young man finds the West more wild than he expected. He finds "help" in the shape of Gossett as he tries to free a young girl who's being held by the notorious El Diablo. Better than average. **107m/C VHS, DVD.** Louis Gossett Jr., Anthony Edwards, John Glover, Robert Beltran, M.C. Gainey, Miguel (Michael) Sandoval, Sarah Trigger, Joe Pantoliano; *D:* Peter Markle; *W:* John Carpenter, Bill Phillips; *C:* Ron Garcia; *M:* William Olvis. **CABLE**

El Diablo Rides 1/2 **1939** A fierce feud between cattlemen and sheepmen develops, with touches of comedy in between. **57m/B VHS.** Bob Steele, Carleton Young, Kit Guard, Claire Rochelle, Ted Adams, Robert Walker; *D:* Ira Webb; *W:* Carl Krusada; *C:* Edward Kull.

El Diputado *The Deputy* **1978** A famous politician jeopardizes his career when he has an affair with a young man. In

Spanish with English subtitles. **111m/C VHS.** *SP* Jose Sacristan, Maria Luisa San Jose, Jose Alonso; *D:* Eloy De La Iglesia.

El Dorado **1967** A gunfighter rides into the frontier town of El Dorado to aid a reckless cattle baron in his war with farmers over land rights. Once in town, the hired gun meets up with an old friend—the sheriff—who also happens to be the town drunkard. Switching allegiances, the gunslinger helps the lawman sober up and defend the farmers. This Hawks western displays a number of similarities to the director's earlier "Rio Bravo" (1959), staring Wayne, Dean Martin, and Ricky Nelson—who charms viewers as the young sidekick "Colorado" much like Caan does as "Mississippi" in El Dorado. **126m/C VHS, DVD.** John Wayne, Robert Mitchum, James Caan, Charlene Holt, Ed Asner, Arthur Hunnicutt, Christopher George, R.G. Armstrong, Jim Davis, Paul Fix, Johnny Crawford, Michele Carey; *D:* Howard Hawks.

El Mariachi **1993 (R)** Extremely low-budget but clever mixture of humor and violence in a tale of mistaken identity set in a small Mexican border town. Unemployed singer/musician Gallardo wanders into a small town and is mistaken for a hitman who carries his weapons in a guitar case. Eventually, the real hitman also shows up. 24-year-old director Rodriguez makes his feature film debut with this $7000 feature, originally intended only for the Spanish-language market. Film festival awards and critical attention brought the work to wider release. Spanish with subtitles or dubbed. **81m/C VHS, DVD.** *MX* Carlos Gallardo, Consuelo Gomez, Peter Marquardt, Jaime de Hoyos, Reinol Martinez, Ramiro Gomez; *D:* Robert Rodriguez; *W:* Robert Rodriguez, Carlos Gallardo; *C:* Robert Rodriguez; *M:* Eric Guthrie. Ind. Spirit '94: First Feature; Sundance '93: Aud. Award.

El Matador **2003** Wanting to escape the doldrums of his pizza delivery job, young Mexican-American Johnny dreams of emulating his father by becoming a matador. But much absurdity ensues after a not-so-friendly loan shark captures the "family jewels"—bronzed bull testicles—and he must fight to regain the prized family heirloom. **74m/C VHS, DVD.** Robert Wolfskill, Martin Klebba, Gabriel Iglesias, Elilio Rivera; *D:* Joey Medina; *W:* Joey Medina; *C:* Tom Hobbs. **VIDEO**

El Muerto ½ **1975** In 19th-century Buenos Aires, a young man flees his home after killing an enemy. Arriving in Montevideo, he becomes a member of a smuggling ring. In Spanish with English subtitles. **103m/C VHS.** *SP* Thelma Biral, Juan Jose Camero, Francisco Rabal; *D:* Hector Olivera.

El Norte **1983 (R)** Gripping account of a Guatemalan brother and sister, persecuted in their homeland, who make an arduous journey north ("El Norte") to America. Their difficult saga continues as they struggle against overwhelming odds in an attempt to realize their dreams. Passionate, sobering, and powerful. In English and Spanish with English subtitles. Produced in association with the "American Playhouse" series for PBS. Produced by Anna Thomas who also co-wrote the story with Nava. **139m/C VHS, Blu-ray Disc.** *SP* David Villalpando, Zaide Silvia Gutierrez, Ernesto Cruz, Eracio Zepeda, Stella Quan, Alicia del Lugo, Lupe Ontiveros; *D:* Gregory Nava; *W:* Anna Thomas, Gregory Nava. Natl. Film Reg. '95.

El Paso ½ **1949** Frontier lawyer (and ex-soldier) Clayton Fletcher (Payne) reunites with former flame Susan Jeffers (Russell) but discovers her father, Judge Jeffers (Hull), has become a drunk and is under the thumb of crooked and land-grabbing town boss Donner (Hayden). In order to save the town, Fletcher has to take the law into his own hands. **91m/B DVD.** John Payne, Gail Russell, Sterling Hayden, George "Gabby" Hayes, Henry Hull, Dick Foran; *D:* Lewis R. Foster; *W:* Lewis R. Foster; *C:* Ellis W. Carter; *M:* Darrell Calker.

El Paso Stampede ½ **1953** Cowboy investigates raids on cattle herds used to feed Americans fighting in the Spanish-American War. **50m/B VHS.** Allan "Rocky" Lane, Eddy (Eddie, Ed) Waller, Phyllis Coates; *D:* Harry Keller.

El Super **1979** A Cuban refugee, still homesick after many years, struggles to make a life for himself in Manhattan as an apartment superintendent. In Spanish with English subtitles; an American production shot on location in New York City. **90m/C VHS.** *SP* Raymundo Hidalgo-Gato, Orlando Jiminez-Leal, Zully Montero, Raynaldo Medina, Juan Granda, Hilda Lee, Elizabeth Pena; *D:* Leon Ichaso; *W:* Leon Ichaso, Manuel Arce.

The Elder Son ½ **2006 (R)** L.A. car thief Bo (West) needs a place to hide out after a job goes wrong. So Bo manages to convince Russian immigrant musician Max (Serbedzija) that he's his long-lost son. Then the situation gets more complicated when Bo falls for his hottie "sister" Lolita (Sobieski). **84m/C DVD.** Shane West, Leelee Sobieski, Rade Serbedzija, Eric Balfour, Regina Hall, Ed Begley Jr.; *D:* Marius Balchunas; *W:* Marius Balchunas, Scott Sturgeon; *C:* Andrew Huebscher; *M:* Yagmur Kaplan. **VIDEO**

Ele, My Friend ½ **1993** The British Raj still rules India in the 1920s, when 10-year-old Charles comes across a herd of wild elephants living in the jungle. Charles befriends a baby elephant he names Ele but what can he do when hunters also discover the animals? Filmed on location in south India. **104m/C VHS, DVD.** Jacob Paul Guzman, Gazan Khan, R.S. Shivaji, Amjad Khan, Prabhu; *D:* Dharan Mandrayar; *W:* Dharan Mandrayar; *M:* Barry Phillips.

Eleanor & Franklin ½ **1976** An exceptional dramatization of the personal lives of President Franklin D. Roosevelt and his wife Eleanor. Based on Joseph Lash's book, this Emmy award-winning film features stunning performances by Alexander and Herrmann in the title roles. **208m/C VHS, DVD.** Jane Alexander, Edward Herrmann, Ed Flanders, Rosemary Murphy, MacKenzie Phillips, Pamela Franklin, Anna Lee, Linda Purl, Linda Kelsey, Lindsay Crouse; *D:* Daniel Petrie; *M:* John Barry. **TV**

Eleanor: First Lady of the World ½ **1982 (G)** Stapleton plays the former first lady after her husband's death as she goes on to work at the United Nations and emerges as even more of an influential public figure. **96m/C VHS.** Jean Stapleton, E.G. Marshall, Coral Browne, Joyce Van Patten, Gail Strickland, Kenneth Kimmins; *D:* John Erman; *M:* John Addison. **TV**

Election **1999 (R)** Payne uses a high school student council election to skewer the American political system in general and the election process in particular. Smart comedy has wildly ambitious Tracy (Witherspoon) running for council president unopposed until dedicated but flawed civics teacher Mr. McAllister (Broderick) decides she must be stopped. He recruits likeable but dim jock Paul (Klein) to run against her. Then Paul's lesbian (and anarchic) sister Tammy (Campbell) joins the race. As in Payne's previous effort, "Citizen Ruth," no side of the political spectrum is spared. Everyone's foibles and hypocrisy are shown, to great effect. Witherspoon gives an energized performance, while Broderick is excellent as the respected, conflicted mentor with a touch of Bueller in him. **105m/C VHS, DVD, Blu-ray Disc.** Matthew Broderick, Reese Witherspoon, Chris Klein, Jessica Campbell, Mark Harelik, Molly Hagan, Colleen Camp, Frankie Ingrassia, Matt Malloy, Holmes Osborne, Phil Reeves, Delaney Driscoll, Jeanine Jackson; *D:* Alexander Payne; *W:* Alexander Payne, Jim Taylor; *C:* James Glennon; *M:* Rolfe Kent. Ind. Spirit '00: Director (Payne), Film, Screenplay; N.Y. Film Critics '99: Screenplay; Natl. Soc. Film Critics '99: Actress (Witherspoon); Writers Guild '99: Adapt. Screenplay.

Elective Affinities ½ **1996** Adaptation of Goethe's 1809 novel, which the Taviani brothers transport to their native Tuscany. Aristocratic Charlotte (Huppert) and Edouard (Anglade) reunite after 20 years and decide to marry, retiring to a country villa. Their idyll is interrupted by the arrival of Edouard's best friend, Othon (Bentivoglio), and Charlotte's goddaughter Ottilie (Gillain). Soon, the married duo find themselves in love with their respective houseguests. But though the characters pursue their relationships, tragedy haunts them. French with subtitles. **98m/C VHS.** *FR IT* Isabelle Huppert, Jean-Hugues Anglade, Fabrizio Bentivoglio, Marie Gillain; *D:* Paolo Taviani, Vittorio Taviani; *W:* Paolo Taviani, Vittorio Taviani; *C:* Giuseppe Lanci; *M:* Carlo Crivelli.

Electra **1995** Sex-bomb Lorna (Tweed) does her oedipal best with stepson Billy (Tab), who was implanted with the secret of physical regeneration by his late scientist dad. Cybervillian Roach (Erik) wants the info, which can only be obtained through intimate contact, and Lorna's the right woman for the job. Funny how Billy's just so uncooperative. Very over-the-top. **85m/C VHS.** Shannon Tweed, Joe Tab, Sten Eirik; *D:* Julian Grant; *W:* Damian Lee; *C:* Gerald R. Goozie.

Electra Glide in Blue **1973 (R)** An Arizona motorcycle cop uses his head in a world that's coming apart at the seams. Good action scenes; lots of violence. **113m/C VHS, DVD.** Robert (Bobby) Blake, Billy Green Bush, Mitchell Ryan, Jeannine Riley, Elisha Cook Jr., Royal Dano; *D:* James W. Guercio; *W:* Robert Boris; *C:* Conrad L. Hall.

Electric Dragon 80,000V **2001** Filmed in black and white as is traditional for most Japanese cyberpunk films, Dragon Eye Morrison (Tadanobu Asano) is a man struck by lightning as a child and who is now a human battery obsessed with lizards and the electric guitar. A superhero known as the Thunderbolt Buddha (Masatoshi Nagase), was also struck by lightning as a child and covers his scarred face with a Buddha Mask while fighting crime. For some reason he gets ticked at Morrison for stealing his thunder and fries all of his pet lizards leading to an epic battle between the two of them. **55m/B DVD.** *JP* Tadanobu Asano, Masatoshi Nagase; *D:* Sogo Ishii; *W:* Sogo Ishii; *C:* Norimichi Kasamatsu; *M:* Hiroyuki Onogawa; *V:* Masakatsu Funaki.

Electric Dreams ½ **1984 (PG)** A young man buys a computer that yearns to do more than sit on a desk. First it takes over his apartment, then it sets its sights on the man's cello-playing neighbor—the same woman his owner is courting. To win her affections, the over-eager computer tries to dazzle her with a variety of musical compositions from his unique keyboard. Cort supplies the voice of Edgar the computer in this film that integrates a rock-music video format. **95m/C VHS.** Lenny Von Dohlen, Virginia Madsen, Maxwell Caulfield, Bud Cort, Koo Stark; *D:* Steven Barron.

The Electric Horseman ½ **1979 (PG)** Journalist Fonda sets out to discover the reason behind the kidnapping of a prized horse by an ex-rodeo star. The alcoholic cowboy has taken the horse to return it to its native environment, away from the clutches of corporate greed. As Fonda investigates the story she falls in love with rebel Redford. Excellent Las Vegas and remote western settings. **120m/C VHS, DVD.** Robert Redford, Jane Fonda, John Saxon, Willie Nelson, Valerie Perrine, Wilford Brimley, Nicolas Coster, James B. Sikking; *D:* Sydney Pollack; *W:* Robert Garland; *C:* Owen Roizman; *M:* Dave Grusin.

Electric Shadows **2004** Delivery man Mao Xiaobing (Xiz) is attacked by a strange young woman in the streets and lands in the hospital. After his release, he visits Ling Ling (Qi) at the police station and discovers they were childhood playmates who were both obsessed with the movies. She asks him to take care of her fish and Mao finds her apartment filled with movie memorabilia and a diary that details her fantasy life. Mandarin with subtitles. **95m/C DVD.** *CH* Xu Xia, Zhongyang Qi, Yihong Jiang; *D:* Xiao Jiang; *W:* Xiao Jiang, Qingsong Cheng; *C:* Hong Chen, Lun Yang; *M:* Lin Zhao.

The Electronic Monster *Escapement; The Electric Monster* **1957** Insurance claims investigator Cameron looks into the death of a Hollywood starlet and discovers an exclusive therapy center dedicated to hypnotism. At the facility, people vacation for weeks in morgue-like body drawers, while evil Dr. Illing uses an electronic device to control the sleeper's dreams and actions. Eerie. Intriguingly, it is one of the first films to explore the possibilities of brainwashing and mind control. **72m/B VHS.** *GB* Rod Cameron, Mary Murphy, Meredith Edwards, Peter Illing; *D:* Montgomery Tully.

The Elegant Criminal ½ **1992** Based on the true story of France's most infamous killer, Pierre Lacenaire. The film begins with Lacenaire in prison, writing his memoirs, receiving his admirers, and awaiting his execution (in 1836). A series of flashbacks detail his life and the supposed social clime which hindered his better instincts and turned him to the criminal life. However, Auteuil has such a wonderful time playing the charming bad guy that any blame to society fails to convince. In French with English subtitles. **120m/C VHS.** *FR* Daniel Auteuil, Jean Poiret, Jacques Weber, Marie-Armelle Deguy, Maiwenn Le Besco, Patrick Pineau; *D:* Francis Girod; *W:* Georges Conchon, Francis Girod.

Elegy ½ **2008 (R)** With a penchant for pursuing his much younger female graduate students, literature professor and serial seducer David Kepesh (Kingsley) is taken off-guard by his strong feelings for his latest, and particularly alluring conquest, Consuela (Cruz). Despite her hopes to the contrary, David is seemingly incapable of changing his bachelor ways, including his continued bedding of former student Carolyn (Clarkson). His life is further complicated by a strained relationship with his adult son. Hopper has an unusually understated role as David's ill-advised advice-giver. Based on the 2001 novel "The Dying Animal" by Philip Roth. **108m/C DVD.** *US* Ben Kingsley, Penelope Cruz, Dennis Hopper, Patricia Clarkson, Peter Sarsgaard, Deborah Harry, Sonja Bennett, Chelah Horsdal; *D:* Isabel Coixet; *W:* Nicholas Meyer; *C:* Jean-Claude Larrieu.

Elektra **2005 (PG-13)** When we last saw her in the movie "Daredevil," Elektra had died, but thanks to the magical healing power of her mentor Stick (Stamp) she's alive and kicking. Regrettably, she came back only to be in yet another wretched film. Elektra is an assassin-for-hire. Her next assignment is to kill 13-year-old Abby (Prout) and Abby's father (Visnjic) who are the target of a powerful faction called The Hand...which (dramatic music here) is a powerful secret society. Through heavy-handed flashbacks of her own childhood, Elektra instantly bonds with the girl and decides to protect them instead. **97m/C DVD.** *US* Jennifer Garner, Terence Stamp, Goran Visnjic, Cary-Hiroyuki Tagawa, Kirsten Prout, Will Yun Lee; *D:* Rob Bowman; *W:* Zak Penn, Stuart Zicherman, Raven Metzner; *C:* Bill Roe; *M:* Christophe Beck.

The Element of Crime ½ *Forbrydelsens Element* **1984** In a monochromatic, post-holocaust future, a detective tracks down a serial killer of young girls. Made in Denmark, this minor festival favorite features an impressive directional debut and awaits cult status. Filmed in Sepiatone. **104m/C VHS, DVD.** *DK* Michael Elphick, Esmond Knight, Jerold Wells, Me Me Lai, Astrid Henning-Jensen, Preben Leerdorff-Rye, Gotha Andersen; *D:* Lars von Trier; *W:* Lars von Trier, Niels Vorsel; *C:* Tom Elling; *M:* Bo Holten.

Element of Doubt ½ **1996** Beth Murray's (McKee) family have always been suspicious of her ambitious husband, Richard (Havers). Although Beth desperately wants children, Richard has persuaded her to wait until after he's closed some mysterious business deal. Suddenly, Richard promises Beth a home in the country and the family she desires. Then, Beth discovers her husband has been in close contact with his ex-wife. So, is Beth merely suffering from hysterics or is Richard actually contemplating murder? **90m/C VHS, DVD.** *GB* Nigel Havers, Gina McKee, Polly Adams, Judy Parfitt, Sarah Berger, Michael Jayston, Dennis (Denis) Lill, Robert Reynolds; *D:* Christopher Morahan; *C:* Brian Tufano; *M:* Stephen Warbeck. **TV**

The Elementary School *Obecna Skola* **1991** Screenwriter Sverak's memories of his childhood are the basis for this child's eye view of the mysteries surrounding the adult world. In 1945, 10-year-old Eda (Jakoubek) is living in a village outside Prague. His school class is so wild that the teacher quits and is replaced by the strict Igor Hnizdo (Triska), who turns out to have a weakness for young women. Czech with subtitles. **100m/C VHS.** *CZ* Jan Triska, Vaclav Jakoubek, Zdenek Sverak, Radoslav Budas, Libuse Safrankova, Rudolf Hrusinsky, Petr Cepek; *D:* Jan Sverak; *W:* Zdenek Sverak; *C:* F.A. Brabec.

Elena and Her Men *Paris Does Strange Things; Elena et les Hommes* **1956** The romantic entanglements and intrigues of a poor Polish princess are explored in this enjoyable French film. Beautiful cinematography by Claude Renoir. In French with subtitles. **98m/C VHS, DVD.** *FR* Ingrid Bergman, Jean Marais, Mel Ferrer, Jean Richard, Magali Noel, Pierre Bertin, Juliette Greco; ***D:*** Jean Renoir; ***C:*** Claude Renoir.

Eleni **1985 (PG)** The true story of "New York Times" reporter Nicholas Gage and his journey to Athens to discover the truth about his mother's execution by Communists during the Greek rebellion after WWII. Adapted by Steve Tesich from Gage's bestselling book. **117m/C VHS.** John Malkovich, Kate Nelligan, Linda Hunt, Oliver Cotton, Ronald Pickup, Dimitra Arliss, Rosalie Crutchley; ***D:*** Peter Yates; ***W:*** Steve Tesich; ***C:*** Billy Williams; ***M:*** Bruce Smeaton.

Elephant **2003 (R)** Made for HBO film depicting a day in the life at a typical American high school that ends in tragedy. Film lazily follows a number of the banal goings-on of various students before wandering to a shocking climax involving the violence of a Columbine-type massacre by two young social outcasts. The motivation of killers Alex and Eric (Frost and Deulen) isn't explored but merely offered up as fact, save a few shots of the boys watching a documentary about Hitler and sharing a brief kiss. Mainly utilizing non-actors and a largely improvised script, Van Sant genuinely imparts the reality of high school life in modern day America without trying to explain it but creates a sense of detachment from the characters and subject matter along the way. **81m/C VHS, DVD.** *US* Alex Frost, Eric Deulen, John Robinson, Elias McConnell, Nathan Tyson, Carrie Finklea, Kristen Hicks, Jordan Taylor, Nicole George, Brittany Mountain, Timothy Bottoms, Matt Malloy; ***D:*** Gus Van Sant; ***W:*** Gus Van Sant; ***C:*** Harris Savides. Cannes '03: Director (Van Sant), Film. **CABLE**

Elephant Boy **1937** An Indian boy helps government conservationists locate a herd of elephants in the jungle. Sabu's first film. Available in digitally remastered stereo. **80m/B VHS.** *GB* Sabu, Walter Hudd, W.E. Holloway; ***D:*** Robert Flaherty, Zoltan Korda. Venice Film Fest. '37: Director (Flaherty).

An Elephant Called Slowly 1/2 **1969 (G)** In a sequel of sorts to the 1966 hit "Born Free," McKenna and Travers star as an English couple who trek to Africa to meet game warden George Adamson (here playing himself). Once in Africa, they are introduced to a menagerie of animals, such as lions and hippos. Along the way, the meet Pole Pole (Swahili for "Slowly"), a baby elephant who adopts McKenna and Travers and attempts to travel with them. The first 20 minutes are rather slow, but the last 70 are very watchable with gorgeous cinematography and astounding nature shots. **91m/C VHS, DVD.** *GB* Virginia McKenna, Bill Travers, George Adamson, Joab Collins, Vinay Inambar, Ali Twaha; ***D:*** James Hill; ***W:*** Bill Travers, James Hill; ***C:*** Simon Trevor; ***M:*** Howard Blake, Bert Kaempfert.

The Elephant King 1/2 **2006 (R)** Jake Hunt (Robert) is staying put in Thailand after being accused of fraud. His introverted younger brother Oliver (Ellington) is sent by their parents to bring Jake back to the U.S. but Oliver succumbs to Jake's expat lifestyle of drinking and bar girls instead. A baby elephant figures into the plot too. **90m/C DVD.** Ellen Burstyn, Josef Sommer, Jonno Robert, Tate Ellington, Florence Faivre; ***D:*** Seth Grossman; ***C:*** Diego Quemada Diaz; ***M:*** Adam Balazs.

The Elephant Man **1980 (PG)** A biography of John Merrick, a severely deformed man who, with the help of a sympathetic doctor, moved from freak shows into posh London society. Lynch's first mainstream film, shot in black and white, it presents a startlingly vivid picture of the hypocrisies evident in the social mores of the Victorian era. Moving performance from Hurt in title role. **125m/B VHS, DVD.** Michael Elphick, Anthony Hopkins, John Hurt, Anne Bancroft, John Gielgud, Wendy Hiller, Freddie Jones, Kenny Baker; ***D:*** David Lynch; ***W:*** Eric Bergren, Christopher DeVore, David Lynch; ***C:*** Freddie Francis; ***M:*** John Morris, Samuel Barber. British Acad. '80: Actor (Hurt), Film; Cesar '82: Foreign Film.

Elephant Walk 1/2 **1954** Sri Lanka's balmy jungles provide the backdrop for a torrid love triangle in this post-prime Dieterle effort. Taylor, ignored by her wealthy drunkard hubby, finds solace in the arms of her spouse's sexy right-hand man. As if keeping the affair secret weren't a big enough task, she also braves a cholera epidemic and a pack of vengeful elephants who take an unscheduled tour of her humble home. Lethargic lead performances make this more of a sleep walk, but Sofaer and Biberman's supporting roles are worth the price of rental. Taylor replaced Vivian Leigh early in the filming after she fell ill, but footage of Leigh in faraway shots is included. **103m/C VHS, DVD.** Elizabeth Taylor, Dana Andrews, Peter Finch, Abraham Sofaer, Abner Biberman; ***D:*** William Dieterle; ***C:*** Loyal Griggs.

11:14 **2003 (R)** Rcounts the half hour of events prior to a tragedy at 11:14 pm from five character perspectives. First time effort by Marcks is laudable—smart writing, well shot, wonderfully cast. Characters could have been given more dimension, but the overall effect is acceptable. **85m/C DVD.** Henry Thomas, Blake Heron, Barbara Hershey, Clark Gregg, Hilary Swank, Shawn Hatosy, Colin Hanks, Ben Foster, Patrick Swayze, Rachael Leigh Cook, Stark Sands, Rick Gomez, Jason Segel; ***D:*** Greg Marcks; ***W:*** Greg Marcks; ***C:*** Shane Hurlbut; ***M:*** Clint Mansell. **VIDEO**

11 Harrowhouse *Anything for Love; Fast Fortune* **1974 (PG)** The Consolidated Selling System at 11 Harrowhouse, London, controls much of the world's diamond trade. Four adventurous thieves plot a daring heist relying on a very clever cockroach. A rather successful stab at spoofing detailed "heist" films. **95m/C VHS.** *GB* Charles Grodin, Candice Bergen, James Mason, Trevor Howard, John Gielgud; ***D:*** Aram Avakian; ***W:*** Jeffrey Bloom.

Eleven Men Out 1/2 *Strakarnir Okkar* **2005 (R)** Arrogant Ottar Thor is Iceland's top soccer player. Hoping for some extra publicity, he reveals in an interview that he's gay and the team's conservative owners ban him from playing. Ottar decides to join a friend's amateur team and soon other gay players are filling the ranks. Ottar's former team finds itself with a publicity backlash so the pros agree to a showcase match against the amateurs. Unpleasant characters and stereotypical situations don't provide much to attract a viewer. Icelandic with subtitles. **85m/C DVD.** *IC GB FI* Helgi Bjornsson, Sigurdur Skulason, Bjorn Hlynur Haraldsson, Lilja Nott Porarinsdottir, Porsteinn Bachmann, Arnmundur Ernst Bjornsson; ***D:*** Robert I. Douglas; ***W:*** Robert I. Douglas, Jon Alti Jonasson; ***C:*** G. Magni Agustsson; ***M:*** Bardi Johannsson.

The 11th Hour 1/2 **2007 (PG)** Global warming is certainly "the" hot topic, and this film doesn't present anything we haven't heard before, plus throws around enough stats and figures to make your head spin. Leonardo DiCaprio multitasks as narrator, actor, and co-writer; he even helped produce. It's grim, but provides some real solutions. Make no mistake—this is a documentary, not intended to entertain, but to inspire outrage and action. **95m/C DVD.** *US* ***D:*** Leila Conners Petersen, Nadia Conners; ***W:*** Leonardo DiCaprio, Leila Conners Petersen, Nadia Conners; ***C:*** Peter Youngblood Hills, Andrew Roland, Brian Knappenberger; ***M:*** Jean Pascal Beintus, Eric Avery; ***Nar:*** Leonardo DiCaprio.

Elf **2003 (PG)** As a baby, Buddy (Ferrell) had snuck into Santa's bag and found himself transported to the North Pole. The elves adopted the human and raised him as an elf. When he learns of his human origins (the enormous size difference didn't tip him off?), he goes to New York to search for his real father. Daddy turns out to be a Walter Hobbs (Caan), a highly insensitive children's book publisher who needs a good dose of Christmas cheer. While it's all straight-ahead Christmas movie formula, Ferrell's unabashed innocence and delight in everything helps pull it off. It also helps that he looks so darn funny in yellow tights. Director Favreau makes a cameo as a doctor. **95m/C VHS, DVD, UMD.** *US* Will Ferrell, James Caan, Bob Newhart, Ed Asner, Mary Steenburgen, Zooey Deschanel, Faizon Love, Daniel Tay, Peter Dinklage, Amy Sedaris, Michael Lerner, Andy Richter, Jon Favreau; ***D:*** Jon Favreau; ***W:*** David Barenbaum; ***C:*** Greg Gardiner; ***M:*** John Debney.

Eli Eli 1/2 **1940** An American Yiddish film about a family forced to live apart because of their farm's failure. Lighthearted and fun. In Yiddish with English titles. **85m/B VHS.** Esther Field, Lazar Fried, Muni Serebroff; ***D:*** Joseph Seiden; ***M:*** Sholom Secunda.

The Eliminators **1986 (PG)** A cyborgian creature endeavors to avenge himself on his evil scientist creator with help from a kung fu expert and a Mexican. The group uses time travel and other devices to achieve their mission. **95m/C VHS.** Roy Dotrice, Patrick Reynolds, Denise Crosby, Andrew Prine, Conan Lee; ***D:*** Peter Manoogian; ***W:*** Danny Bilson, Paul DeMeo; ***M:*** Richard Band.

Elisa **1994** Teenaged sexpot Marie (Paradis) has grown up in a reform school, thanks to her mother Elisa's suicide. Along with friends Solange (Courau) and Ahmed (Sall), Marie spends her time on the Paris streets shoplifting and flirting. Obsessed with finding her long-gone father, Marie discovers that Lebovitch (Depardieu), the writer of the popular song "Elisa," is daddy dearest. He's now a drunk, living on a fishing island, and Marie sets out to right the wrongs she believes drove her mother to suicide. Based on the song by Serge Gainsbourg. French with subtitles. **111m/C VHS.** *FR* Vanessa Paradis, Gerard Depardieu, Clotilde Courau, Sekkou Sall, Florence Thomassin; ***D:*** Jean Becker; ***W:*** Jean Becker, Fabrice Carazo; ***C:*** Etienne Becker; ***M:*** Zbigniew Preisner. Cesar '95: Support. Actress (Courau), Score.

Elisa, Vida Mia *Elisa, My Love; Elisa, My Life* **1977** A long-estranged father and daughter are reunited when he falls ill. She stays to help him write his biography and gradually begins to see things through his perspective. The shifting narrative can confuse but worth seeing are Rey and Chaplin's subtle performances. Spanish with subtitles. **125m/C VHS.** *SP* Fernando Rey, Geraldine Chaplin, Norman Brisky, Isabel Mestres, Joaquin Hinojosa; ***D:*** Carlos Saura; ***W:*** Carlos Saura. Cannes '77: Actor (Rey).

Elizabeth **1998 (R)** And you thought modern day politics were dirty! Indian director Kapur takes a look at the turbulent life of Queen Elizabeth I of England (a brilliant Blanchett) from her uncertain days as a beseiged Protestant Princess to her ascension to the throne and the machinations surrounding her early reign. Elizabeth indeed proves to be her father's daughter as she must keep her head (literally) while dealing with religion, war, assassination, and the vexing question of a political marriage. Rush is notable as spidery spymaster Walsingham and Eccleston's hissably evil as the arrogant Catholic Duke of Norfolk. Wonderful shadowy cinematography by Adefarasin adds to the atmosphere but it does help to know some history in order to keep the plots and plotters straight. **124m/C VHS, DVD, HD DVD.** *GB* Cate Blanchett, Geoffrey Rush, Joseph Fiennes, Christopher Eccleston, Richard Attenborough, Fanny Ardant, Vincent Cassel, Daniel Craig, Kathy Burke, James Frain, Edward Hardwicke, Eric Cantona, John Gielgud, Emily Mortimer; ***D:*** Shekhar Kapur; ***W:*** Michael Hirst; ***C:*** Remi Adefarasin; ***M:*** David Hirschfelder. Oscars '98: Makeup; British Acad. '98: Actress (Blanchett), Cinematog., Film, Score; Golden Globes '99: Actress—Drama (Blanchett); Natl. Bd. of Review '98: Director (Kapur); Broadcast Film Critics '98: Actress (Blanchett).

Elizabeth of Ladymead **1948** Four generations of a British family live through their experiences in the Crimean War, Boer War, WWI, and WWII. Neagle, playing the wives in all four generations, aptly explores the woman's side of war. Enjoyable performances from husband and wife team Neagle and Wilcox. **97m/C VHS.** Anna Neagle, Hugh Williams, Bernard Lee, Michael Lawrence, Nicholas Phipps, Isabel Jeans; ***D:*** Herbert Wilcox.

Elizabeth R **1972** Jackson is outstanding in the title role of this TV drama focusing on the life of Elizabeth I, from 17 to 70. Constantly besieged by court intrigue and political machinations, the Virgin Queen managed to restore England to glory and power amidst private and public turmoil. Six 90-minute cassettes. **540m/C VHS, DVD.** *GB* Glenda Jackson, Rosalie Crutchley, Robin Ellis, Robert Hardy, Peter Jeffrey, Stephen Murray, Vivian Pickles, Sarah Frampton, Ronald Hines; ***D:*** Claude Whatham, Herbert Wise, Roderick Graham, Richard Martin, Donald Whatham; ***W:*** Hugh Whitemore, John Hale, Julian Mitchell, John Prebble, Ian Rodger, Rosemary Anne Sisson.

Elizabeth I **2005** Mirren gives an outstanding performance as the imperious British monarch. In 1579, Elizabeth is being pressured to marry, but not her lover and confidante, the Earl of Leicester (Irons). Matters are complicated by the rebellion of her cousin, Mary Queen of Scots (Flynn), and war with Spain. On his deathbed, Leicester bequeaths his relationship to his handsome and arrogant stepson, the Earl of Essex (Dancy). Flattered and flustered, Elizabeth gradually realizes that the callow Essex is a threat to her throne. **220m/C DVD.** Helen Mirren, Jeremy Irons, Hugh Dancy, Ian McDiarmid, Patrick Malahide, Barbara Flynn, Toby Jones; ***D:*** Tom Hooper; ***W:*** Nigel Williams; ***C:*** Larry Smith; ***M:*** Robert (Rob) Lane. **CABLE**

Elizabeth: The Golden Age 1/2 **2007 (PG-13)** Kapur's 1998 film dealt with Elizabeth's early reign. She's now been in power 27 years and is still doing an intricate political dance to keep her head and her Protestant throne against the Catholic opposition, who want Mary, Queen of Scots (Morton) ruling in her place. Then there's pesky Philip II of Spain (Molla) and his armada threatening her shores. Blanchett returns in the titular role as does Rush as spymaster Walsingham. Owen's cast as a swashbuckling Sir Walter Raleigh (very Errol Flynn), whom Elizabeth uses as a distraction. Lavish pomp and circumstance, but a disappointingly routine costumer. **114m/C DVD.** *GB* Cate Blanchett, Geoffrey Rush, Clive Owen, Abbie Cornish, Rhys Ifans, Jordi Molla, Samantha Morton, Tom Hollander, David Threlfall, Eddie Redmayne, John Shrapnel, Antony Carrick; ***D:*** Shekhar Kapur; ***W:*** Michael Hirst, William Nicholason; ***C:*** Remi Adefarasin; ***M:*** Craig Armstrong. Oscars '07: Costume Des.

Elizabeth, the Queen *The Private Lives of Elizabeth and Essex* **1968** Historical drama re-creates the struggle for power by Robert Devereaux, Earl of Essex, whom the aging Queen Elizabeth I both loved and feared, and whose downfall she finally invoked. Part of "George Schaefer's Showcase Theatre." **76m/C VHS.** Judith Anderson, Charlton Heston; ***D:*** George Schaefer. **TV**

Elizabethtown **2005 (PG-13)** Over-stuffed romantic comedy from Crowe begins with the career meltdown of Drew Baylor (Bloom with a so-so American accent). Before Drew can wallow in suicidal depression, his manic mother Hollie (Sarandon) and sister Heather (Greer) inform Drew that dad died while visiting his hometown of Elizabethtown, Kentucky and Drew must deal with the funeral arrangements. This leads to his meeting cute but psychotically perky flight attendant Claire (Dunst), who decides she must console Drew at all costs. Drew discovers things about himself and his family that you may not care about at all, and takes a road trip—accompanied, as per usual in Crowe's movies, by copious amounts of music. **120m/C DVD.** *US* Orlando Bloom, Kirsten Dunst, Susan Sarandon, Judy Greer, Jessica Biel, Alec Baldwin, Paul Schneider, Loudon Wainwright III, Bruce McGill, Paula Deem, Gailard Sartain, Dan Biggers; ***D:*** Cameron Crowe; ***W:*** Cameron Crowe; ***C:*** John Toll; ***M:*** Nancy Wilson.

Eliza's Horoscope 1/2 **1970** A frail Canadian woman uses astrology in her search for love in Montreal, and experiences bizarre and surreal events. An acclaimed Canadian film. **120m/C VHS, DVD.** *CA* Tommy Lee Jones, Elizabeth Moorman; ***D:*** Gordon Sheppard.

Ella Cinders **1926** The American mania for breaking into the movies is satirized in this look at a girl who wins a trip to Hollywood in a small-town beauty contest. Silent with original organ score. **60m/B VHS.** Colleen Moore, Harry Langdon, Lloyd Hughes, Jed Prouty, Vera Lewis; ***D:*** Alfred E. Green.

Ella Enchanted **2004 (PG)** Enchanting modern Cinderella story is a fresh and funny mix of fantasy, romance, and pop culture. Hathaway appealingly plays the title's Ella of Frell, cursed by her fairy godmother Lucinda (Fox) with the spell of obedience, which forces the budding teen to obey every command she is given. She hooks up with the ogres, elves, and giants and begins a crusade for their equal rights. Her quest leads her to the total hottie Prince Charmont (Dancy) who is the intended victim of a coup planned by the throne-seeking Prince Edgar. Updated fairy tale sports top-notch special effects, a cool 70s soundtrack, and fun modern anachronisms. Based on the novel by Gail Carson Levine. **101m/C DVD.** Anne Hathaway, Hugh Dancy, Cary Elwes, Vivica A. Fox, Joanna Lumley, Minnie Driver, Patrick Bergin, Parminder K. Nagra, Jimi Mistry, Heidi Klum; ***D:*** Tommy O'Haver; ***W:*** Laurie Craig, Karen McCullah Lutz, Kirsten Smith, Jennifer Heath, Michele J. Wolff; ***C:*** John de Borman; ***M:*** Shaun Davey; ***V:*** Steve Coogan; ***Nar:*** Eric Idle.

Ellen Foster 1/2 **1997 (PG-13)** Coming-of-age TV drama concerns 10-year-old Ellen (Malone), who lives with her abusive, drunken dad (Levine) and her gentle mom (O'Connor). After mom dies, Ellen is shuffled between uncaring relatives, including a nasty grandma, Leonora (Harris), while trying to draw strength from the few friends and teachers who do care about her. Based on the book by Kaye Gibbons. **97m/C VHS.** Jena Malone, Julie Harris, Ted Levine, Glynnis O'Connor, Debra Monk, Barbara Garrick, Kate Burton, Zeljko Ivanek, Lynne Moody, Bill Nunn, Amanda Peet, Allison Jones, Timothy Olyphant; ***D:*** John Erman; ***W:*** Maria Nation, William Hanley; ***C:*** Brian West; ***M:*** John Morris. **TV**

Ellie 1/2 **1984 (R)** A murderous widow's stepdaughter tries to save her father from being added to the woman's extensive list of dearly departed husbands. **90m/C VHS.** Shelley Winters, Sheila Kennedy, Pat Paulsen, George Gobel, Edward Albert; ***D:*** Peter Wittman.

Ellie Parker **2005** Ellie (Watts) is the typical struggling actress in L.A., frantically driving from audition to audition, transforming her clothes and personality in an instant to please a series of dismissive casting directors. While Ellie wrestles with her integrity and the absurdity of Hollywood, her friends and manager (Chevy Chase, in an odd cameo role) try and fail to re-inspire her love of acting. Coffey uses 16-millimeter film to emphasize Ellie's disconsolate search for something authentic. A low-budget verite production, but Watts' performance is spot-on. **95m/C DVD.** *US* Naomi Watts, Rebecca Rigg, Chevy Chase, Mark Pelligrino, Blair Mastbaum, Scott Coffey; ***Cameos:*** Keanu Reeves; ***D:*** Scott Coffey; ***W:*** Scott Coffey; ***C:*** Blair Mastbaum, Scott Coffey; ***M:*** B.C. Smith.

Elling 1/2 **2001 (R)** Witty, gentle comedy has two Noregian misfits, recently released from a mental institution, living together in a government-subsidized Oslo flat in order to learn how to live in the outside world. Elling, who had to be dragged from his mother's home when she died, is extremely agoraphobic, fastidious, and socially inept. His roomie Kjell Bjarne is a hulking man with no sense of personal hygiene and an overdeveloped sexual imagination. Their friendship helps them to slowly and amusingly adapt to, and enter, the world. This allows Kjell to befriend, and become romantic with, their pregnant upstairs neighbor, while Elling writes poetry (and slips it into saurkraut packages at the market), finally attends a reading, and meets fellow poet Alfons. Sentimental without being cloying. **89m/C VHS, DVD.** *NO* Per Christian Ellefsen, Sven Nordin, Marit Pia Jacobsen, Jorgen Langhelle, Per Christensen; ***D:*** Petter Naess; ***W:*** Axel Hellstenius; ***C:*** Svein Krovel; ***M:*** Lars Lillo Stenberg.

Elmer 1/2 **1976 (G)** Follows the adventures of a temporarily blinded youth and a lovable hound dog who meet in the wilderness and together set off in search of civilization. **82m/C VHS.** Elmer Swanson, Phillip Swanson; ***D:*** Christopher Cain.

Elmer Gantry 1/2 **1960** The classic multi-Oscar-winning adaptation of the Sinclair Lewis novel written to expose and denounce the flamboyant, small-town evangelists spreading through America at the time. In the film, Lancaster is the amoral Southern preacher who exacts wealth and power from his congregation, and takes a nun as a mistress. Jones stars as his ex-girlfriend who resorts to a life of prostitution. **146m/C VHS, DVD.** Burt Lancaster, Shirley Jones, Jean Simmons, Dean Jagger, Arthur Kennedy, Patti Page, Edward Andrews, John McIntire, Hugh Marlowe, Rex Ingram, Wendell Holmes; ***D:*** Richard Brooks; ***W:*** Richard Brooks; ***C:*** John Alton; ***M:*** Andre Previn. Oscars '60: Actor (Lancaster), Adapt. Screenplay, Support. Actress (Jones); Golden Globes '61: Actor—Drama (Lancaster); Natl. Bd. of Review '60: Support. Actress (Jones); N.Y. Film Critics '60: Actor (Lancaster).

Elmore Leonard's Gold Coast 1/2 *Gold Coast* **1997 (R)** Miami mobster Frank DiCilia (Bradford) is dead and his widow Karen (Helgenberger) is not happy. Yes, she's inherited $15 mil but Frank's will also stipulates that she has to remain faithful to him forever. Too bad Karen and smalltime con man Maguire (Caruso) are instantly attracted to one another. And too bad Frank's also left behind loathsome hit man Roland (Kober) to enforce the edict (although if Karen wants him, Roland's willing to be flexible). Based on the novel by Elmore Leonard. **109m/C VHS.** David Caruso, Marg Helgenberger, Jeff Kober, Barry Primus, Richard Bradford, Wanda De Jesus; ***D:*** Peter Weller; ***W:*** Harley Peyton; ***C:*** Jacek Laskus; ***M:*** Peter Harris. **CABLE**

Eloise at the Plaza 1/2 **2003** Hyperactive adaptation of the first of Kay Thompsn's books about six-year-old enfant terrible Eloise (Vassilieva), who lives with her mother at the Plaza Hotel in New York. Mom is away in Paris, so it's up to Nanny (Andrews) to try to reign in her charge's exuberant behavior and frequently disastrous schemes. This time Eloise is determined to attend the prestigious Debutante's Ball that is being held at the Plaza, despite her age (and the lack of an invitation). **90m/C VHS, DVD.** Sofia Vassilieva, Julie Andrews, Jeffrey Tambor, Kenneth Welsh, Debra Monk, Jonas Chernick, Christine Baranski; ***D:*** Kevin Lima; ***W:*** Janet Brownell; ***C:*** James Chressanthis; ***M:*** Bruce Broughton. **TV**

Elsa, Elsa **1985** Satire of moviemaking life finds a scriptwriter-director distracted by the loss of his girlfriend and unable to concentrate on writing a memoir of his career as a child actor. He creates a subplot dealing with his romantic problems, and puts the film in jeopardy. Fine acting and witty dialogue. In French with English subtitles. **85m/C VHS.** *FR* Francois Cluzet, Lio, Tom Novembre, Catherine Frot; ***D:*** Didier Haudepin; ***W:*** Didier Haudepin; ***C:*** Gilberto Azevedo; ***M:*** Eric Lelann.

The Elusive Corporal 1/2 *Le Caporal Epingle* **1962** Set in a P.O.W. camp on the day France surrendered to Germany, this is the story of the French and Germans, complete with memories of a France that is no more. **108m/B VHS.** Jean-Pierre Cassel, Claude Brasseur, O.E. Hasse, Claude Rich; ***D:*** Jean Renoir.

The Elusive Pimpernel 1/2 *The Fighting Pimpernel* **1950** Niven sparkles in this otherwise undistinguished adaptation of Baroness Orczy's "The Scarlet Pimpernel." **109m/C VHS.** *GB* David Niven, Margaret Leighton, Jack Hawkins, Cyril Cusack, Robert Coote, Edmund Audran, Danielle Godet, Patrick Macnee; ***D:*** Michael Powell; ***W:*** Michael Powell, Emeric Pressburger.

Elves **1989 (PG-13)** A group of possessed, neo-Nazi elves perform serious human harm at Christmas time in this tongue-in-check thriller. **95m/C VHS.** Dan Haggerty, Deanna Lund, Julie Austin, Borah Silver; ***D:*** Jeffrey Mandel.

Elvira Madigan **1967 (PG)** Chronicles the true 19th-century Swedish romance between teenaged Elvira (Degermark), a beautiful circus tight-rope walker, and young Army officer Sixten Sparre (Berggren) who leaves his wife and children to be with her. Exceptional direction and photography and a notable use of classical music by Mozart and Vivaldi. Swedish with subtitles. **90m/C VHS, DVD.** *SW* Pia Degermark, Thommy Berggren, Lennart Malmer, Nina Widerberg, Cleo Jensen; ***D:*** Bo Widerberg; ***W:*** Johan Lindstroem Saxon, Bo Widerberg; ***C:*** Jorgen Persson; ***M:*** Ulf Bjorlin. Cannes '67: Actress (Degermark).

Elvira, Mistress of the Dark **1988 (PG-13)** A manic comedy based on Peterson's infamous B-movie horror-hostess character. The mega-busted terror-queen inherits a house in a conservative Massachusetts town and causes double-entendre chaos when she attempts to sell it. **96m/C VHS, DVD.** Cassandra Peterson, Jeff Conaway, Susan Kellerman, Edie McClurg, Daniel Greene, William Morgan Sheppard, Kurt Fuller, Pat Crawford Brown, William Duell, William Cort, John Paragon; ***D:*** James Signorelli; ***W:*** Sam Egan, Cassandra Peterson, John Paragon; ***C:*** Hanania Baer; ***M:*** James Campbell.

Elvira's Haunted Hills 1/2 **2002 (PG-13)** That bodacious vamp returns as Elvira (Peterson) and her French maid Zou Zou (Smith) are stranded in Carpathia in 1851. They manage to find shelter at the Transylavania castle of the twitchy Vladimir Hellsubus (O'Brien) where all sorts of high camp happenings occur. **89m/C VHS, DVD.** Cassandra Peterson, Richard O'Brien, Mary Jo Smith, Mary Scheer, Scott Atkinson; ***D:*** Sam Irvin; ***W:*** Cassandra Peterson, John Paragon; ***C:*** Viorel Segovia; ***M:*** Eric Allaman.

Elvis and Me 1/2 **1988** TV mini series based on Priscilla Beaulieu Presley's autobiography about her life with the Pelvis. Features many of Presley's biggest hits, sung by country star Ronnie McDowell. Film may aggravate Elvis fans, however, as the King is often depicted negatively from his ex-wife's point of view. **187m/C VHS.** Dale Midkiff, Susan Walters, Billy Green Bush, Linda Miller, Jon Cypher; ***D:*** Larry Peerce.

Elvis Has Left the Building 1/2 **2004 (PG-13)** Once upon a time Elvis gave Harmony Jones (Basinger) a ride in his pink Caddy, making her feel so indebted to the King that, years later, the cosmetics saleswoman thinks he's using her from beyond the grave when she begins unintentionally offing his impersonators. While on the lam from the law, Harmony teams up with Miles (Corbett), a down-and-out New York advertising executive who has his own issues with the King. Offbeat yet not amusing. **90m/C VHS, DVD.** Kim Basinger, John Corbett, Annie Potts, Sean Astin, Denise Richards, Mike Starr, Phill Lewis, Philip Charles MacKenzie, Billy Ray Cyrus, Richard Kind, David Leisure, Tom Hanks, Joel Zwick, Angie Dickinson, Noriyuki "Pat" Morita; ***D:*** Joel Zwick; ***W:*** Adam-Michael Garber, Mitchell Ganem; ***C:*** Paul Elliott; ***M:*** David Kitay. **VIDEO**

Elvis in Hollywood **1993** A tribute highlighting Presley's first four films, "Love Me Tender," "Loving You," "Jailhouse Rock," and "King Creole," completed prior to his reporting for active duty in the army. Features his 1956 screen test at Paramount Studios; photos from the movie sets; interviews with co-stars, directors, writers, business associates, songwriters, and friends; and home movies as well as out-take footage from "Jailhouse Rock." **65m/C VHS, DVD.** ***D:*** Frank Martin.

Elvis Meets Nixon 1/2 **1998 (PG-13)** Based on the bizarre (but true) visit of Elvis Presley (Peters) to the Nixon (Gunton) White House. **103m/C VHS.** Richard Beymer, Edwin Newman, Graham Nash, Wayne Newton, Bob Gunton, Rick Peters, Jackie Burroughs, Curtis Armstrong; ***D:*** Allan Arkush; ***W:*** Alan Rosen; ***C:*** Michael Storey; ***M:*** Larry Brown. **CABLE**

Elvis: The Movie 1/2 **1979** Biography of the legendary singer, from his high school days to his Las Vegas comeback. Russell gives a convincing performance and lip syncs effectively to the voice of the King (provided by country singer Ronnie McDowell). Also available in 150-minute version. **117m/C VHS.** Kurt Russell, Season Hubley, Shelley Winters, Ed Begley Jr., Dennis Christopher, Pat Hingle, Bing (Neil) Russell, Joe Mantegna; ***D:*** John Carpenter. **TV**

Emanon 1/2 **1986 (PG-13)** A coming-of-age tale about a young kid and the Christ-like vagabond, named Emanon (or "no name" if spelled in reverse), he befriends. **101m/C VHS.** Stuart Paul, Cheryl Lynn, Jeremy Miller; ***D:*** Stuart Paul.

The Embalmer *L'Imbalsamatore* **2003** Peppino (Mahieux) is a dwarfish middle-aged taxidermist (the Embalmer of the title) who attaches himself to handsome but dumb Valerio (Manzillo). Peppino hires Valerio, gives him a place to live, and uses hookers to put the two men in bed together at the same time. When Valerio meets Deborah, a beautiful drifter, on a business trip, the result is a tug-of-war for Valerio's attention. Mahieux is brilliant as the creepy Peppino, who supplements his income with shady underworld deals. Manzillo does an adequate job as the blank, naive Valerio, who can't decide between barracuda Deborah and a relationship he doesn't entirely understand with Peppino. Director Garrone fills every moment with lurking dread and foreboding, adding distinctive visual flourishes and gritty details. **104m/C DVD.** *IT* Ernesto Mahieux, Valerio Foglia Manzillo, Elisabetta Rocchetti, Pietro Biondi, David Ryall, Bernardino Terracciano, Marcella Granito; ***D:*** Matteo Garrone; ***W:*** Matteo Garrone, Ugo Chiti, Massimo Gaudioso; ***C:*** Marco Onorato; ***M:*** Banda Osiris.

Embassy *Target: Embassy* **1972** In this mediocre espionage thriller, von Sydow is a Soviet defector under asylum at the U.S. embassy in Beirut. Colonel Connors, a Russian spy, penetrates embassy security and wounds von Sydow. He is caught, escapes, is captured, escapes, and is caught again. Great cast, but script is often too wordy and contrived. **90m/C VHS, DVD.** *GB* Richard Roundtree, Chuck Connors, Max von Sydow, Ray Milland, Broderick Crawford, Marie-Jose Nat; ***D:*** Gordon Hessler.

Embassy **1985** An American family in Rome unknowingly possesses a secret computer chip, and thus is pursued by ruthless agents. **104m/C VHS.** Nick Mancuso, Blanche Baker, Eli Wallach, Sam Wanamaker, Richard Gilliland, Mimi Rogers, George Grizzard, Richard Masur, Kim Darby; ***D:*** Robert Lewis. **TV**

The Embezzled Heaven **1958** Teta works as a cook for an auspicious Austrian family and aspires to have a better place in heaven. In order to ensure this, she financially supports her nephew's seminary education. When she finally visits him she is rudely awakened to his scam, which sends her on a journey of repentance ending in Rome before the pope. In German with subtitles. **91m/B VHS.** *GE* Hans Holt, Viktor de Kowa, Anne Rosav, Vilma Degischer; ***D:*** Ernst Marischka; ***W:*** Ernst Marischka, Franz Werfel. **VIDEO**

Embrace of the Vampire **1995 (R)** Innocent young Charlotte (Milano) must make a choice between her college boyfriend Chris (Pruett) and a new nighttime lover (Kemp) with some decidedly different habits. Seems Charlotte looks exactly like a love lost hundreds of years ago and he's not going to take no for an answer. Also available in an unrated version. **92m/C VHS, DVD.** Alyssa Milano, Martin Kemp, Harrison Pruett, Charlotte Lewis, Jordan Ladd, Rachel True, Jennifer Tilly; ***D:*** Anne Goursaud; ***W:*** Halle Eaton, Nicole Coady, Rick Bitzelberger; ***C:*** Suki Medencevic; ***M:*** Joseph Williams. **VIDEO**

Embryo *Created to Kill* **1976 (PG)** An average sci-fi drama about a scientist who uses raw genetic material to artificially produce a beautiful woman, with ghastly results. **108m/C VHS, DVD.** Rock Hudson, Barbara Carrera, Diane Ladd, Roddy McDowall, Ann Schedeen, John Elerick, Dr. Joyce Brothers; ***D:*** Ralph Nelson; ***W:*** Anita Doohan, Jack W. Thomas; ***C:*** Fred W. Koenekamp; ***M:*** Gil Melle.

The Emerald Forest **1985 (R)** Bill (Boothe) moves his family to Brazil where he has a job as an engineer working on a dam project. His young son Tommy wanders into the rainforest and is taken in by a primitive tribe of Amazons. Bill searches 10 years for him, finally discovering a happily adjusted teenager named Tomme (Boorman, the director's son), who may not want to return to so-called civilization. An engrossing look at tribal life in the vanishing jungle. Beautifully photographed and based upon a true story. **113m/C VHS, DVD.** Powers Boothe, Meg Foster, Charley Boorman, Dira Paes, Rui Polonah; ***D:*** John Boorman; ***W:*** Rospo Pallenberg; ***C:*** Philippe Rousselot.

Emerald Jungle 1/2 *Eaten Alive by Cannibals; Eaten Alive; Mangiati Vivi dai Cannibali* **1980** While searching for her missing sister in the jungle, Agren encounters cannibal tribes and a colony of brainwashed cult followers. This Italian feature was cut for its U.S. release. **92m/C VHS, DVD.** *IT* Robert Kerman, Janet Agren, Mel Ferrer, Luciano Martino, Mino Loy, Ivan Rassimov, Paola Senatore, Me Me Lai, Meg Fleming, Franco Fantasia; ***D:***

Umberto Lenzi; *W:* Umberto Lenzi; *C:* Frederico Zanni.

Emerald of Artama 🦴 *The Girl of the Nile* **1967** Anyone viewing the most precious and sought after stone in the history of man does not live to tell about it. **93m/C VHS.** *SP* Francisco (Frank) Brana, Pilar Arenas, Rory Calhoun; *D:* Jose Maria Elorrieta; *W:* Jose Maria Elorrieta; *C:* Alfonso Nieva; *M:* Federico Contreras.

The Emigrants 🦴🦴🦴 *Utvandrarna* **1972 (PG)** Farmer von Sydow decides to gather his wife (Ullmann) and family together and leave 19th-century Sweden for the promise of a new life in America. Film is divided into their leaving, the voyage over, and the journey to a settlement in Minnesota. Pacing is somewhat slow; notable cinematography (by director Troell). Adapted from the novels by Vilhelm Moberg. Dubbed into English. Followed by "The New Land." Also edited with the sequel for TV as "The Emigrant Saga." **151m/C VHS.** *SW* Max von Sydow, Liv Ullmann, Allan Edwall, Eddie Axberg, Svenolof Bern, Aina Alfredsson, Monica Zetterlund, Pierre Lindstedt; *D:* Jan Troell; *W:* Jan Troell, Bengt Forslund; *C:* Jan Troell; *M:* Erik Nordgren. N.Y. Film Critics '72: Actress (Ullmann).

Emil and the Detectives 🦴🦴 ½ *Emil Und Die Detektive* **1964** A German ten-year-old is robbed of his grandmother's money by gangsters, and subsequently enlists the help of pre-adolescent detectives to retrieve it. Good Disney dramatization of the Erich Kastner children's novel. Remake of the 1931 German film starring Rolf Wenkhaus. **99m/C VHS.** Bryan Russell, Walter Slezak, Roger Mobley; *D:* Peter Tewkesbury; *W:* A.J. Carothers.

Emile 🦴🦴 ½ **2003 (R)** McKellen shines in this story of a man confronting the demons of his past. Emile, a respected British scientist and professor, travels to Canada to receive an honorary degree and visit his niece Nadia (Unger). Although Emile acts like the perfect uncle, in reality he deserted Nadia in an orphanage when her parents died and has never been a part of her life. Reconnecting with his past leads into a series of oddly-shot flashbacks to Emile's youth and his painful relationships with his brothers, and in the end Emile must come to terms with his own painful past as well as his selfish treatment of Nadia. Despite Bessai's efforts to break up the narrative, the story is routine and predictable, with McKellen's performance the most distinctive part of the film. **96m/C VHS, DVD.** *CA GB* Ian McKellen, Deborah Kara Unger, Tygh Runyan, Ian Tracey, Chris William Martin, Janet Wright; *D:* Carl Bessai; *W:* Carl Bessai; *C:* Carl Bessai; *M:* Vincent Mai.

Emily WOOF! **1977** Returning from her exclusive Swiss finishing school, licentious young Emily discovers mama is a prostitute and deals with the scalding news by delving into a series of erotic encounters at the hands of her willing "instructors." Stark's first venture into the realm of soft porn. **87m/C VHS.** Koo Stark; *D:* Henry Herbert; *C:* Jack Hildyard.

Emily Bronte's Wuthering Heights 🦴🦴 ½ *Wuthering Heights* **1992 (PG)** Miscast version of the tragic tale of doomed lovers Cathy (Binoche) and Heathcliff (Fiennes). While Fiennes may seem too refined for the role, he manages to be both brooding and brutal. However, the beautiful Binoche can't successfully supress her French accent enough to pass for a heedless Yorkshire lass. Good supporting cast, with O'Connor posing as writer/narrator Bronte. **107m/C VHS, DVD.** *GB* Ralph Fiennes, Juliette Binoche, Janet McTeer, Sophie Ward, Simon Shepherd, Jeremy Northam, Jason Riddington, Jonathan Firth, Paul Geoffrey, Sinead O'Connor; *D:* Peter Kosminsky; *W:* Anne Devlin; *C:* Mike Southon; *M:* Ryuichi Sakamoto.

Eminent Domain 🦴🦴 ½ **1991 (PG-13)** A communist party member wakes up to find himself stripped of power in a Kafkaesque purge, not knowing what he is accused of—or why. A potent premise, indifferently handled despite filming on location in Poland. Based on actual events that befell the family of scriptwriter Androej Krakowski. **102m/C VHS.** Donald Sutherland, Anne Archer, Paul Freeman, Bernard Hepton, Francoise Michaud, Jodhi May; *D:* John Irvin; *W:* Andrzej Krakowski, Richard Greggson; *M:* Zbigniew Preisner.

Emissary 🦴🦴 **1989 (R)** An American politician and his wife are blackmailed in Africa by the Russians into revealing state secrets that could spark WWIII. **98m/C VHS.** *SA* Robert Vaughn, Ted Leplat, Terry Norton, Andre Jacobs; *D:* Jan Scholtz.

Emma 🦴🦴 ½ **1932** Not the Jane Austen heroine. This Emma (Dressler) is hired as housekeeper/nanny to widow Frederick Smith's (Hersholt) children, spending 20 years looking after them until Smith proposes marriage while Emma takes a vacation in Niagara Falls. He dies shortly thereafter, leaving Emma his money, and three of the children she's looked after suddenly turn on her, accusing her of murdering their father for the inheritance. A trial ensues. **71m/B DVD.** Marie Dressler, Jean Hersholt, Richard Cromwell, Myrna Loy, Kathryn Crawford, George Meeker, Purnell Pratt, John Miljan; *D:* Clarence Brown; *W:* Zelda Sears, Leonard Praskins; *C:* Oliver Marsh.

Emma 🦴🦴 ½ **1972** BBC TV version of the Jane Austen saga with young Emma trying her matchmaking skills on all her friends and neighbors—with disastrous results. Mr. Knightly tries to provide both a voice of reason and romance, if only Emma could realize it. **257m/C VHS, DVD.** *GB* Doran Goodwin, Vivienne Moore, John Carson, Donald Eccles, Debbie Bowen; *D:* John Glenister.

Emma 🦴🦴🦴 **1996 (PG)** Jane Austen's 1816 novel about wealthy, 21-year-old Emma Woodhouse (Paltrow) who makes it her goal to "fix" the lives of all her friends, while ignoring her own problems (the modern adaptation was "Clueless"). Emma focuses much of her attention on Harriet Smith (Collete), a simple young woman who Emma believes is in need of the perfect mate. Meanwhile, Emma neglects to notice the attractive, and exasperated, Mr. Knightley (Northam). McGrath's screenplay makes Emma and Knightley more likable than in the book, but otherwise stays true. After the success of "Sense and Sensibility," Austen's name is making it in the movies in the footsteps of the likes of John Grisham. **120m/C VHS, DVD.** Gwyneth Paltrow, Jeremy Northam, Greta Scacchi, Toni Collette, Alan Cumming, Juliet Stevenson, Polly Walker, Ewan McGregor, James Cosmo, Sophie Thompson, Phyllida Law; *D:* Douglas McGrath; *W:* Douglas McGrath; *C:* Ian Wilson; *M:* Rachel Portman. Oscars '96: Orig. Score.

Emma 🦴🦴🦴 *Jane Austen's Emma* **1997** British TV adaptation of the Jane Austen novel featuring young, matchmaking Emma (Beckinsale) wrecking havoc amongst her friends and neighbors with her would-be romantic alliances. Screenplay is truer to the book, with slightly less likable personalities than the 1996 big-screen version. Excellent cast, and beautiful locations and costumes make this one worth seeing. A&E Network offered "Emma" after the overwhelming success of their miniseries "Pride and Prejudice," also adapted from Austen. **107m/C VHS, DVD.** *GB* Kate Beckinsale, Mark Strong, Samantha Bond, Prunella Scales, Bernard Hepton, Raymond Coulthard, Dominic Rowan, James Hazeldine, Samantha Morton, Lucy Robinson, Olivia Williams; *D:* Diarmuid Lawrence; *W:* Andrew Davis.

Emma 🦴🦴 ½ **2009** Cast wins out in this charmingly sunlit BBC adaptation of the Austen novel with Garai bright and well-meaning (if self-absorbed) in the title role. Wealthy Emma Woodhouse believes she has a future as a matchmaker but her efforts nearly cause a social disaster for new (and poor) friend Harriet Smith (Dylan) when Emma discourages a marriage proposal from someone she deems unsuitable. No wonder acerbic neighbor Mr. Knightley (Miller) finds Emma both exasperating and amusing. Of course neither can admit to a romantic attraction to each other. **240m/C DVD.** *GB* Romola Garai, Jonny Lee Miller, Louise Dylan, Rupert Evans, Laura Pyper, Blake Ritson, Jodhi May, Michael Gambon, Christina Cole, Robert Bathurst; *D:* Jim O'Hanlon; *W:* Sandy Welch; *C:* Adam Suschitzky; *M:* Samuel Sim. **TV**

Emmanuelle 🦴🦴 ½ **1974** Filmed in Bangkok, a young, beautiful woman is introduced by her husband to an uninhibited world of sensuality. Above-average soft-core skin film, made with sophistication and style. Kristel maintains a vulnerability and awareness, never becoming a mannequin. **92m/C VHS, DVD.** *FR* Sylvia Kristel, Alain Cuny, Marika Green, Daniel Sarky; *D:* Just Jaeckin; *W:* Jean-Louis Richard; *C:* Richard Suzuki; *M:* Pierre Bachelet.

Emmanuelle 4 🦴 **1984 (R)** Emmanuelle flees a bad relationship and undergoes plastic surgery to mask her identity. Ultimately, she becomes a beautiful young model in the form of a different actress, of course. **95m/C VHS, DVD.** *FR* Sylvia Kristel, Mia Nygren, Patrick Bauchau; *D:* Francis Giacobetti.

Emmanuelle 5 🦴 ½ **1987 (R)** This time around sexy Emmanuelle flees aboard a convenient yacht when she's chased by adoring fans at the Cannes Film Festival. But she winds up being forced to join an Arab sheik's harem of slaves. A good example of a series that should have quit while it was ahead. **78m/C VHS, DVD.** *FR* Monique Gabrielle, Charles Foster; *D:* Steve Barnett, Walerian Borowczyk; *M:* Pierre Bachelet.

Emmanuelle 6 🦴 **1988 (R)** The saga of the sexy beauty continues. This time Emmanuelle and a group of models head for the paradise of an Amazon jungle where they promptly become the prized captives of a drug lord. **80m/C VHS, DVD.** *FR* Natalie Uher, Jean-Rene Gossart, Thomas Obermuller, Gustavo Rodriguez; *D:* Jean Rollin, Bruno Zincone; *C:* Serge Godet; *M:* Olivier Day.

Emmanuelle & Joanna 🦴 **1978** A mistreated newlywed bride goes to her sister's whorehouse and stumbles across lots of soft-core antics. **90m/C VHS.** *FR* Sherry Buchanan, Danielle Dublino; *D:* Franco (Fred Gardner) Rossetti; *C:* Pier Luigi Santi; *M:* Enzo Petti.

Emmanuelle in the Country 🦴 *L'Infermiera di Campagna; Country Nurse* **1978** Emmanuelle becomes a nurse in an attempt to bring comfort and other pleasures to those in need. **90m/C VHS, DVD.** *IT* Laura Gemser, Gabriele Tinti, Aldo Sambrel; *D:* Mario Bianchi; *W:* Luigi Petrini; *C:* Umberto Galeassi; *M:* Ubaldo Continiello.

Emmanuelle on Taboo Island 🦴 ½ *La Spiaggia del Desiderio; A Beach Called Desire* **1976 (R)** Marooned young man discovers a beautiful woman on his island. This delights him. **95m/C VHS, DVD.** *IT* Laura Gemser, Paul(o) Giusti, Arthur Kennedy; *D:* Enzo D'Ambrosio; *W:* Enzo D'Ambrosio; *C:* Riccardo (Pallton) Pallottini; *M:* Marcello Giombini.

Emmanuelle, the Joys of a Woman 🦴 *Emmanuelle l'Antivierge; Emmanuelle's 7th Heaven; Emmanuelle 2* **1976** The amorous exploits of a sensuous, liberated couple take them and their erotic companions to exotic Hong Kong, Bangkok, and Bali. **92m/C VHS, DVD.** *FR* Sylvia Kristel, Umberto Orsini, Catherine Rivet, Frederic Lagache, Laura Gemser, Henri Czarniak, Tom Clark, Caroline Laurence; *D:* Francis Giacobetti; *W:* Francis Giacobetti, Jean-Marc Vasseur; *C:* Robert Fraisse; *M:* Pierre Bachelet, Francis Lai.

Emmanuelle, the Queen 🦴 *Black Emmanuelle; Mavri Emmanouella* **1979** Seeking revenge, Emmanuelle plots the murder of her sadistic husband. The lecherous assassin she hires tries to blackmail her, and she challenges him at his own game of deadly seduction. **90m/C VHS, DVD.** *GR* Laura Gemser, Gabriele Tinti, Livia Russo, Vagelis Vartan, Pantelis Agelopou; *D:* Ilias Milonakos; *W:* Ilias Milonakos; *C:* Vassilis Christomoglou; *M:* Giovanni Ullu.

Emmanuelle's Daughter 🦴 **1979** A Greek-made thriller in which a vapidly sensuous heroine cavorts amid episodes of murder, blackmail, and rape. **91m/C DVD.** *GR* Laura Gemser, Gabriele Tinti, Livia Russa, Vagelis Vartan, Nadia Neri; *D:* Ilias Mylonakos; *W:* Ilias Mylonakos; *C:* Vassilis Christomoglou; *M:* Giovanni Ullu.

Emma's Shadow 🦴🦴🦴 *Skyggen af Emma* **1988** In the 1930s, a young girl fakes her own kidnapping to get away from her inattentive family and comes to befriend an ex-convict sewer worker. In Danish with English subtitles. Winner of the Prix de la Jeunesse at Cannes, it was voted 1988's Best Danish Film. **93m/C VHS.** *DK* Borje Ahlstedt, Line Kruse; *D:* Soeren Kragh-Jacobsen; *W:* Soeren Kragh-Jacobsen; *C:* Dan Laustsen.

Emma's Wish 🦴🦴 **1998** Somewhat maudlin family drama, originally shown on CBS. Emma makes a wish on her 75th birthday to reunite with her estranged daughter Joy. The next morning Emma wakes up looking like she's 40 and sets out to see Joy, persisting until Joy agrees to hire her as a nanny. Emma finds out Joy's marriage is in trouble and tries to set things right. However, she has to complete her mission in a month before she turns geriatric again. **90m/C DVD.** Joanna Kerns, Harley Jane Kozak, William R. Moses, Della Reese, Seymour Cassel, Courtland Mead, Jeanne Allen; *D:* Mike Robe; *W:* Cynthia Whitcomb; *C:* Edward Pei; *M:* Laura Karpman. **TV**

The Emperor and the Assassin 🦴🦴 **1999 (R)** Sumptuous historical drama (and a complicated storyline) concerns a united China's first emperor. Set in 320 B.C., China is a collection of seven rival kingdoms with Ying Zheng, the King of Qin (Xuejian) obsessed with uniting the country and then dividing it into provinces for proper ruling (with himself as supreme head). Naturally, this means war. Also involved is his lover, Lady Zhao (Li), who plans a fake assassination attempt to aid Zheng. But the assassin she chooses, Jing Ke (Fengyi), is trying to reform and things don't go exactly according to plan. Remember—power corrupts. Mandarin with subtitles. **161m/C VHS, DVD.** *CH* Xuejian Li, Gong Li, Fengyi Zhang, Zhiwen Wang, Sun Zhou, Chen Kaige; *D:* Chen Kaige; *W:* Chen Kaige, Wang Peigong; *C:* Fei Zhao; *M:* Jiping Zhao.

Emperor Jones 🦴🦴 ½ **1933** Loosely based on Eugene O'Neill's play, film portrays the rise and fall of a railroad porter whose exploits take him from a life sentence on a chain gang to emperor of Haiti. Robeson re-creates his stage role in his first screen appearance. **72m/B VHS, DVD.** Paul Robeson, Dudley Digges, Frank Wilson, Fredi Washington, Ruby Elzy; *D:* Dudley Murphy. Natl. Film Reg. '99.

Emperor of the Bronx 🦴 **1989** A look at crime, sleaze, violence, and the actions of bad guys in the inner-city. **90m/C VHS, DVD.** Alex D'Andrea, Adrian Drake, Anthony Gioia, William (Bill) Smith; *D:* Joseph Merhi; *W:* Joseph Merhi, Sean Dash; *C:* Richard Pepin.

Emperor of the North Pole 🦴🦴🦴 *Emperor of the North* **1973 (PG)** Violent and well-done tale of hobos riding the rails during the Depression has Marvin as A#1, a legendary hobo who can get on any train, and his protege Cigaret (Carradine), trying to catch a ride on the train of sadistic conductor Shack (Borgnine), who's been known to kill to keep the hobos away. Tense and gritty, with the usual tight direction of Aldrich, beautiful cinematography, and a gripping screenplay. Borgnine is exceptional among a very strong cast. **118m/C VHS, DVD.** Lee Marvin, Ernest Borgnine, Keith Carradine, Charles Tyner, Malcolm Atterbury, Simon Oakland, Harry Caesar, Hal Baylor, Matt Clark, Elisha Cook Jr., Liam Dunn, Robert Foulk, Ray Guth, Sid Haig, Vic Tayback; *D:* Robert Aldrich; *W:* Christopher Knopf; *C:* Joseph Biroc; *M:* Frank DeVol.

Emperor Waltz 🦴🦴 ½ **1948** Typical Hollywood musical finds phonograph salesman Crosby travelling to Vienna, hoping to sell his goods to the Austrian royal family of Emperor Franz Joseph. He meets up with the Emperor's snobby niece (Fontaine) and attempts to charm her into an audience with her royal uncle. Naturally the two fall in love and everything ends in a happy fade-out. ♫ The Emperor's Waltz; Friendly Mountains; Get Yourself a Phonograph; The Kiss in Your Eyes; I Kiss Your Hand, Madame; The Whistler and His Dog. **106m/C VHS, DVD.** Bing Crosby, Joan Fontaine, Roland Culver, Richard Haydn, Lucile Watson, Sig Rumann, Harold Vermilyea; *D:* Billy Wilder; *W:* Billy Wilder, Charles Brackett; *C:* George Barnes; *M:* Victor Young.

The Emperor's Club 🦴🦴 *The Palace Thief* **2002 (PG-13)** "A man's character is his fate." This statement is eminently displayed through events both past and present of a prep school teacher (Kline) and one of his more challenging students (Hirsch). Ethics are questioned, schools of thought examined and hearts changed in this "Dead Poet Society" type drama. Hoffman's development of Ethan Canin's book "The Palace Thief" is unfortunately accomplished through manipulation and fake sincerity. **109m/C VHS, DVD.** *US* Kevin Kline, Emile Hirsch, Embeth Davidtz, Rob Morrow, Paul Franklin Dano, Edward Herrmann, Harris Yulin, Roger Rees, Jesse Eisenberg, Rishi Mehta, Joel Gretsch, Steven Culp, Patrick Dempsey, Rahul Khanna; ***D:*** Michael Hoffman; ***W:*** Neil Tolkin; ***C:*** Lajos Koltai; ***M:*** James Newton Howard.

The Emperor's New Clothes **1984** The story of an emperor and the unusual outfit he gets from his tailor. A "Faerie Tale Theatre" presentation. **60m/C VHS, DVD.** Art Carney, Alan Arkin, Dick Shawn; ***D:*** Peter Medak; ***Nar:*** Timothy Dalton. **CABLE**

The Emperor's New Clothes 1/2 **2001 (PG)** Historical comedy about Napoleon Bonaparte (Holm). Confined to the island of St. Helena by the British, the former emperor and his advisers plot to regain power in France by recruiting a look-alike named Eugene (Holm again) to trade places while the real Napoleon heads to Paris and restakes his claim to power. The first part of the plan works fine; the second part doesn't. Eugene likes playing the exiled ruler too much to reveal himself as an imposter and Napoleon turns out to enjoy his more simple life, especially with comely widow Pumpkin (Hjejle) proffering her charms. Loosely based on the French novel "The Death of Napoleon" by Simon Leys. **107m/C VHS, DVD.** *GB* Ian Holm, Iben Hjejle, Tim (McInnerny) McInnery, Tom Watson, Nigel Terry, Hugh Bonneville, Murray Melvin, Eddie Marsan, Clive Russell; ***D:*** Alan Taylor; ***W:*** Kevin Molony, Herbie Wave; ***C:*** Alessio Gelsini Torresi; ***M:*** Rachel Portman.

The Emperor's New Groove **2000 (G)** Animated fantasy about self-centered young emperor Kusco (Spade) who gets turned into a llama by sorceress Yzma (Kitt) and must team up with peasant Pacha (Goodman) to get his throne back. Refreshingly devoid of "important lessons" and sappy pop tunes, the only mission here is to provide laughs, and that it does. Like the great Warner Bros. cartoons of old, sarcastic and sophisticated humor abounds (Spade really helps out here), and the sidekicks get plenty of face (and hero) time, not to mention some of the best lines, including Warburton as Yzma's distracted and clumsy right-hand villain, Kronk. **79m/C VHS, DVD.** ***D:*** Mark Dindal; ***W:*** Dave Reynolds; ***M:*** John Debney; ***V:*** David Spade, John Goodman, Eartha Kitt, Patrick Warburton, Wendie Malick, Patti Deutsch, John Fiedler, Kellyann Kelso, Eli Russell Linnetz. Broadcast Film Critics '00: Song ("My Funny Friend and Me").

The Emperor's Shadow *Qin Song* **1996** Saga of two boyhood friends in China around 220 BC. Gao Jianli (You) is a famous musician and the childhood friend of powerful Emperor Ying Sheng (Wen). Jianli basically wants to be left alone to work on his music but the Emperor demands he stick around and compose a stirring imperial anthem. Add into the mix Yueyang (Qing), the Emperor's daughter who has the hots for the musician (and vice versa) although she's betrothed to another, and tragedy is bound to be the result. Mandarin with subtitles. **123m/C VHS, DVD.** *CH* Ge You, Jiang Wen, Xu Qing; ***D:*** Xiaowen Zhou; ***W:*** Wei Lu; ***C:*** Lu Gengxin; ***M:*** Jiping Zhao.

Empire 1/2 **2002 (R)** Leguizamo is Victor Rosa, a slick South Bronx drug entrepreneur hustling to keep his patch of heroin turf. Through narration, Victor walks us through his seedy world and his decision to leave it. His opportunity arises when he meets Wall Street couple Trish (Richards) and Jack (Sarsgaard). Jack cuts him in on an investment deal that helps launder his money, but Victor soon finds out that even a player can get played. Reyes's gangster flick aspires to the heights of "Scarface" and "The Godfather," but sinks in a quagmire of cliches and obvious plot devices. Excellent cast includes Rosellini as an over-the-top drug queenpin as well as rappers Fat Joe and Treach. **195m/C VHS, DVD.** John Leguizamo, Peter Sarsgaard, Denise Richards, Delilah Cotto, Vincent Laresca, Isabella Rossellini, Sonia Braga, Nestor Serrano, Fat Joe, Treach; ***D:*** Franc Reyes; ***W:*** Franc Reyes; ***C:*** Kramer Morgenthau; ***M:*** Ruben Blades.

Empire Falls 1/2 **2005** Passive Miles Roby (Harris), manager of the Empire Grill, has been unable to sever ties with either his economically depressed Maine mill town or his demanding family, including ne'er-do-well father Max (Newman), ex-wife Janice (Hunt), teen daughter Tick (Panabaker), and brother David (Quinn). Also in the picture is the town's manipulative matriarch (Woodward) and secrets involving Miles' dead mother (Wright Penn) and another man (Hoffman). HBO miniseries based on the Pulitzer Prize-winning book by Richard Russo is sometimes slow going but the cast is worth the effort. **240m/C DVD.** Ed Harris, Paul Newman, Joanne Woodward, Helen Hunt, Aidan Quinn, Robin Wright Penn, Philip Seymour Hoffman, Danielle Panabaker, Dennis Farina, William Fichtner, Estelle Parsons, Theresa Russell, Jeffrey DeMunn, Lou Taylor Pucci, Kate Burton, Josh(ua) Lucas; ***D:*** Fred Schepisi; ***W:*** Richard Russo; ***C:*** Ian Baker; ***M:*** Paul Grabowsky. **CABLE**

The Empire of Passion *In the Realm of Passion* **1976** A peasant woman and her low-life lover kill the woman's husband, but find the future they planned with each other is not to be. The husband's ghost returns to haunt them, and destroy the passionate bond which led to the murder. Oshima's follow-up to "In the Realm of the Senses." In Japanese with English subtitles. **110m/C VHS, DVD.** *JP* Nagisa Oshima, Kazuko Yoshiyuki, Tatsuya Fuji, Takahiro Tamura, Takuzo Kawatani; ***D:*** Nagisa Oshima. Cannes '78: Director (Oshima).

Empire of the Ants 1/2 **1977 (PG)** A group of enormous, nuclear, unfriendly ants stalk a real estate dealer and prospective buyers of undeveloped oceanfront property. Story originated by master science-fiction storyteller H. G. Wells. **90m/C VHS, DVD.** Joan Collins, Robert Lansing, John David Carson, Albert Salmi, Jacqueline Scott, Robert Pine; ***D:*** Bert I. Gordon; ***W:*** Bert I. Gordon; ***C:*** Reginald Morris.

Empire of the Sun **1987 (PG)** Spielberg's mature, extraordinarily vivid return to real storytelling, from the best-selling J.G. Ballard novel. Yearns to be a great film, but occasional flat spots keep it slightly out of contention. Young, wealthy British Jim (Bale) lives in Shanghai, but is thrust into a life of poverty and discomfort when China is invaded by Japan at the onset of WWII and he's separated from his family and interred in a prison camp. A mysterious, breathtaking work, in which Spielberg's heightened juvenile romanticism has a real, heartbreaking context. Two other 1987 releases explore the WWII memories of young boys: "Au Revoir Les Enfants" and "Hope and Glory." **153m/C VHS, DVD.** Christian Bale, John Malkovich, Miranda Richardson, Nigel Havers, Joe Pantoliano, Leslie Phillips, Rupert Frazer, Ben Stiller, Robert Stephens, Burt Kwouk, Masato Ibu, Emily Richard, David Neidorf, Ralph Seymour, Emma Piper, Peter Gale, Zhai Nai She, Guts Ishimatsu, J.G. Ballard; ***D:*** Steven Spielberg; ***W:*** Tom Stoppard, Menno Meyjes; ***C:*** Allen Daviau; ***M:*** John Williams. Natl. Bd. of Review '87: Director (Spielberg).

Empire of the Wolves 1/2 *L'Empire des Loups* **2005 (R)** Confusing police thriller. Anna Heymes (Jover) experiences terrifying dreams and memory loss. Later she learns that her face has been completely altered by plastic surgery. Meanwhile, young police detective Nerteaux (Quivrin) and his shady older partner Schiffer (Reno) are investigating the brutal murders of three women who were all illegal Turkish workers and they think the Turkish mafia has something to do with the crimes. Eventually, the link between Anna and the dead women will become apparent. French with subtitles. **128m/C DVD.** *FR* Arly Jover, Jean Reno, Jocelyn Quivrin, Vernon Dobtcheff, Laura Morante, Philippe Bas, David Kammenos; ***D:*** Chris Nahon; ***W:*** Chris Nahon, Jean-Christophe Grange; ***C:*** Michel Abramowicz.

Empire Records **1995 (PG-13)** Well, the soundtrack's good and that's about all this frantic movie has going for it (besides a photogenic cast). Joe's (LaPaglia) the manager of an independent record store about to be taken over by a faceless conglomerate unless he and his young-and-crisis-prone staff can come up with the cash to buy the place within 24 hours. **91m/C VHS, DVD.** Anthony LaPaglia, Rory Cochrane, Liv Tyler, Renee Zellweger, Johnny Whitworth, Robin Tunney, Ethan (Randall) Embry, Maxwell Caulfield, Debi Mazar; ***D:*** Allan Moyle; ***W:*** Carol Heikkinen; ***C:*** Walt Lloyd; ***M:*** Mitchell Leib.

Empire State **1987 (R)** When his friend disappears from a posh London nightclub, a young man searches for him and finds more action and intrigue than he can handle. Even so, this movie's still pretty bland. **102m/C VHS.** *GB* Cathryn Harrison, Martin Landau, Ray McAnally; ***D:*** Ron Peck.

The Empire Strikes Back *Star Wars: Episode 5—The Empire Strikes Back* **1980 (PG)** Second film in the epic "Star Wars" trilogy finds young Luke Skywalker and the Rebel Alliance plotting new strategies as they prepare to battle the evil Darth Vader and the forces of the Dark Side. Luke learns the ways of a Jedi knight from master Yoda, while Han and Leia find time for romance and a few adventures of their own. Introduces the charismatic Lando Calrissian and a mind-blowing secret from Vadar. Offers the same superb special effects and hearty plot as set by 1977's excellent "Star Wars." Followed by "Return of the Jedi" in 1983. **124m/C VHS, DVD.** Mark Hamill, Carrie Fisher, Harrison Ford, Billy Dee Williams, Alec Guinness, David Prowse, Kenny Baker, Frank Oz, Anthony Daniels, Peter Mayhew, Clive Revill, Julian Glover, John Ratzenberger, Jeremy Bulloch; ***D:*** Irvin Kershner; ***W:*** Leigh Brackett, Lawrence Kasdan; ***C:*** Peter Suschitzky; ***M:*** John Williams; ***V:*** James Earl Jones. Oscars '80: Sound, Visual FX.

Employee of the Month 1/2 **2006 (PG-13)** Amy (the ever-clueless Simpson) is the hot new employee at mega-store Super Club and rumor has it that she has a serious fetish for the employee of the month. This sparks a battle for the title between slacker Zack (weirdly appealing Cook) and 17-time consecutive winner Vince (Shepard). Dopey comedy is only rescued from complete mediocrity by some sharp jabs at consumerism. **103m/C DVD, Blu-ray Disc.** *US* Dane Cook, Jessica Simpson, Dax Shepard, Andy Dick, Tim Bagley, Danny Woodburn, Efren Ramirez, Harland Williams, Sean M. Whalen, Brian George; ***D:*** Greg Coolidge; ***W:*** Greg Coolidge, Dan Calame, Chris Conroy; ***C:*** Anthony B. Richmond; ***M:*** John Swihart.

Employees' Entrance **1933** William stars as a ruthless department store manager in this story about commerce and compromise during the Depression. Young gives an excellent performance as the wife of one of his employees. Outrageous, and racy, this pre-Code film was expertly directed by veteran craftsman Del Ruth. Based on a play by David Boehm. **74m/B VHS.** Warren William, Loretta Young, Wallace Ford, Alice White, Allen Jenkins; ***D:*** Roy Del Ruth; ***W:*** Robert Presnell Sr.; ***C:*** Barney McGill; ***M:*** Bernhard Kaun.

The Empty Acre **WOOF!** **2007** The idyllic world of Beth and Jacob Nance is shattered when their infant son is missing. Might it have something to do with the creepy acre of land on their property, where nothing grows and cattle die? And of course more people get abducted into the blackness that starts to rise from it. That's about as exciting and edge of your seat as it gets folks. Seriously suspense challenged. Not even eerie. **90m/C DVD.** Jennifer Plas, John Wilson, Robert Paisley, Ari Pavel, Sally Bremenkamp, Ric Averill; ***D:*** Patrick Rea; ***W:*** Patrick Rea; ***C:*** Jeremy Osbern; ***M:*** Don James.

The Empty Beach 1/2 **1985** A tough private detective investigates the disappearance of a wealthy business tycoon. **87m/C VHS.** *AU* Bryan Brown, Anna Maria Monticelli; ***D:*** Chris Thomson.

An Empty Bed **1990** Award-winning independent production depicting Bill Frayne, an older homosexual, and the challenges of his everyday life. Told mostly in flashbacks as Bill encounters people and places during the course of one day, this is a delicate drama with important statements about homosexuality, aging and honesty. **60m/C VHS, DVD.** John Wylie, Mark Clifford Smith, Conan McCarty, Dorothy Stinnette, Kevin Kelly, Thomas Hill, Harriet Bass; ***D:*** Mark Gasper; ***W:*** Mark Gasper.

Empty Canvas 1/2 *La Noia: L'Ennui Et Sa Diversion, L'Erotisme* **1964** A spiritually bankrupt artist becomes obsessively jealous of his mistress who refuses to marry him in the hope that someone better will come along. Based on the Alberto Moravia novel. **118m/B VHS.** *FR IT* Horst Buchholz, Catherine Spaak, Bette Davis; ***D:*** Damiano Damiani; ***M:*** Luis Bacalov.

The Empty Mirror **1999 (PG-13)** Boring fictionalized account of Hitler's (Rodway) final hours, hidden away in his bunker, as he realizes his Third Reich dreams have come to nothing. He does a lot of ranting but what is more interesting are the clips from Leni Riefenstahl's "Triumph of the Will" that are screened behind him. **108m/C VHS, DVD.** Norman Rodway, Joel Grey, Camilla Soeberg, Glenn Shadix, Peter Michael Goetz, Doug McKeon; ***D:*** Barry J. Hershey; ***W:*** Barry J. Hershey, R. Buckingham; ***C:*** Frederick Elmes; ***M:*** John (Gianni) Frizzell.

En la Cama *In Bed* **2005** Think of a naked version (with sex) of "Before Sunrise." Daniela (Lewin) and Bruno (Valenzuela) meet at a party in Santiago and wind up in a seedy motel room. There's some post-coital talk, some more sex, and then Bruno happens to mention he's taken a job in Belgium while Daniela retaliates that one-nighters mean nothing. The attractive duo reveal secrets because they never expect to meet again but the ending hints of further romantic possibilities. Spanish with subtitles. **85m/C DVD.** *CL GE* Blanca Lewin, Gonzalo Valenzuela; ***D:*** Matias Bize; ***W:*** Julio Rojas; ***C:*** Gabriel Diaz, Cristian Castro; ***M:*** Diego Fontecilla.

Enchanted **2007 (PG)** Princess Giselle (Adams) idly sings in wait for "true love's kiss" to rescue her. Vain Prince Edward (Marsden) hears her love song and falls fast, but meddling Queen Narissa (Sarandon) thinks they'll steal her queendom away so she banishes the princess to New York by tossing her down a wishing well (the film turns from animated to real once they hit the city). Divorce lawyer Robert (Dempsey) and his daughter rescue Giselle from the streets of Manhattan, where she promptly makes herself a new dress from his curtains and calls on her animal friends to clean the apartment. Edward has followed and is combing the streets gallantly searching for Giselle; meanwhile, Robert is falling for the princess. It would be a generally happy and fun little film if it ended about there, but no—the queen has more mayhem to unleash. Some painfully slow and cliche moments, but Adams, Marsden, and Dempsey keep up the charm. **107m/C DVD.** *US* Amy Adams, Patrick Dempsey, James Marsden, Timothy Spall, Idina Menzel, Susan Sarandon, Rachel Covey; ***D:*** Kevin Lima; ***W:*** Bill Kelly; ***C:*** Don Burgess; ***M:*** Alan Menken; ***Nar:*** Julie Andrews.

Enchanted April 1/2 **1992 (PG)** Lotte (Lawrence) and Rose (Richardson), tired of their overbearing husbands, rent a villa in Portofino, Italy, for a month with two other very different women—Lady Caroline (Walker), a beautiful but bored socialite, and crusty old Mrs. Fisher (Plowright), who has an impeccable literary pedigree. The effects of the charming villa, with plenty of wisteria and sunshine, do wonders for the women. A charming and romantic period piece. Based on the 1922 novel by Elizabeth von Arnim. **93m/C VHS.** *GB* Miranda Richardson, Joan Plowright, Josie Lawrence, Polly Walker, Alfred Molina, Jim Broadbent, Michael Kitchen, Adriana Fachetti; ***D:*** Mike Newell; ***W:*** Peter Barnes; ***C:*** Rex Maidment; ***M:*** Richard Rodney Bennett. Golden Globes '93: Actress—Mus./Comedy (Richardson), Support. Actress (Plowright).

The Enchanted Cottage 1/2 **1945** Represents Hollywood's "love conquers all" fantasy hokum, as a disfigured war vet and a homely girl retreat from the horrors of the world into a secluded cottage, where they both regain youth and beauty. A four-tissue heart-tugger. Adopted from the Arthur Pinero play. **91m/B VHS.** Dorothy McGuire, Robert Young, Herbert Marshall, Mildred Natwick, Spring Byington, Hillary Brooke, Richard Gaines, Robert Clarke; ***D:*** John Cromwell.

The Enchanted Forest 1/2 **1945** An elderly man teaches a boy about life and the beauty of nature when the boy gets lost in a forest. **78m/C VHS, DVD.** *AR* Harry Davenport, Edmund Lowe, Brenda Joyce; ***D:*** Lew Landers.

Enchanted Island 1/2 **1958** Sailor stops on an island to find provisions and ends up falling in love with a cannibal princess. Thinly based upon Herman Melville's "Typee." **94m/C VHS, DVD.** Jane Powell, Dana Andrews, Arthur Shields; ***D:*** Allan Dwan.

The Enchantress 1/2 *I Skiachtra* **1985** A daring boy experiences his first true loves and passions when he journeys through a mystical land in order to find a beautiful fairy. In Greek with subtitles. **93m/C VHS.** *GR* Alkis Kourkoulos, Sofia Aliberti, Lily Kokodi, Antogone Amanitou, Vicky Koulianou, Nicols Papaconstantinou, Stratos Pahis; ***D:*** Manoussos Manoussakis.

Encino Man *California Man* **1992 (PG)** Two, like, totally uncool Valley dudes dig up a 10,000-year-old caveman in the backyard. After giving him a makeover and teaching him the necessities like the four basic food groups (Milk Duds in the dairy group, Sweet Tarts in the fruit group), they use the gnarly caveman as their ticket to popularity and dates to the prom. Juvenile humor appealing to teens; strictly brain candy. **88m/C VHS, DVD.** Pauly Shore, Brendan Fraser, Sean Astin, Megan Ward, Robin Tunney, Ric(k) Ducommun, Mariette Hartley, Richard Masur, Michael DeLuise, Rose McGowan, Jack Noseworthy, Erik Avari; ***D:*** Les Mayfield; ***W:*** Shawn Schepps; ***C:*** Robert Brinkmann. Golden Raspberries '92: Worst New Star (Shore).

Encore **1952** The third W. Somerset Maugham omnibus (following "Quartet" and "Trio") which includes: "Winter Cruise," "The Ant and the Grasshopper," and "Gigolo and Gigolette." **85m/B VHS.** *GB* Nigel Patrick, Kay Walsh, Roland Culver, John Laurie, Glynis Johns, Ronald Squire, Noel Purcell, Peter Graves; ***D:*** Pat Jackson, Anthony Pelissier, Harold French; ***W:*** Eric Ambler.

Encounter at Raven's Gate 1/2 **1988 (R)** Punk rockers and extraterrestrials meet amid hard rock and gallons of gore. **85m/C VHS.** Eddie Cleary, Steven Vidler; ***D:*** Rolf de Heer.

Encounter with the Unknown 1/2 **1975** Relates three fully documented supernatural events including a death prophesy and a ghost. **90m/C VHS, DVD.** Rosie Holotik, Gene Ross; ***D:*** Harry Z. Thomason; ***Nar:*** Rod Serling.

Encounters at the End of the World **2007** McMurdo Station, headquarters of the National Science Foundation and the base for U.S. research at the South Pole, sits at the bottom of the Earth and is populated by about 1,000 scientists, loners, dreamers, and outcasts for a brief five-month period each year—the only time the Pole is remotely hospitable to research. Director Herzog doesn't lead, but lets McMurdo's unique residents tell their own stories about the stark and dramatic landscape that draws them to leave the rest of the world behind. Herzog gives us stunning images of the otherworldly, subzero terrain, including underwater cathedrals and glacial mountains. Although scientific evidence being gathered at McMurdo points to global warming, Herzog isn't filming to smack you over the head with it; rather, he's exploring the explorers. Absolutely unmissable. **99m/C DVD.** *US* ***D:*** Werner Herzog; ***W:*** Werner Herzog; ***C:*** Peter Zeitlinger; ***M:*** Henry Kaiser, David Lindley; ***Nar:*** Werner Herzog.

Encrypt **2003** By 2068, the Earth's atmosphere is ravaged and survivors fight for every scrap. Mercenary Garth (Show) is promised medicine and food if he and his men will recover what they are told is priceless art from an abandoned estate. Of course they've been lied to and they discover a very dangerous automated defense system is set to kill any intruder. But a hologram named Diana (Wu) may be the key to everyone's survival. A Sci-Fi Channel original. **90m/C DVD.** Grant Show, Vivian Wu, Steve Bacic, Hannah Lochner, Matthew G. Taylor; ***D:*** Oscar Luis Costo; ***W:*** Richard Taylor, Robinson Young; ***C:*** Michael Galbraith; ***M:*** Misha Segal. **CABLE**

The End **1978 (R)** Reynolds plays a young man who discovers he is terminally ill. He decides not to prolong his suffering and attempts various tried-and-true methods for committing suicide, receiving riotous but incompetent help from the crazed DeLuise. **100m/C VHS, DVD.** Burt Reynolds, Sally Field, Dom DeLuise, Carl Reiner, Joanne Woodward, Robby Benson, Kristy McNichol, Norman Fell, Pat O'Brien, Myrna Loy, David Steinberg; ***D:*** Burt Reynolds; ***W:*** Jerry Belson; ***C:*** Bobby Byrne; ***M:*** Paul Williams.

End Game 1/2 **2006 (R)** Secret Service agent Alex Thomas (Gooding Jr.) fails to prevent a presidential assassination. He's pulled out of his alcoholic funk by reporter Kate Crawford (Harmon) and the more the two dig, the more dangerous their situation becomes. Well-done conspiracy thriller. **93m/C DVD.** Cuba Gooding Jr., Angie Harmon, Peter Greene, James Woods, Anne Archer, Burt Reynolds, David Selby, Jack Scalia; ***D:*** Andy Cheng; ***W:*** Andy Cheng, J.C. Pollock; ***C:*** Chuck Cohen; ***M:*** Kenneth Burgomaster. **VIDEO**

End of August **1982 (PG)** A spinster of New Orleans Creole aristocracy, circa 1900, breaks out of her sheltered life and experiences new sexual and romantic awareness. Adapted from "The Awakening" by Kate Chopin. **104m/C VHS.** Sally Sharp, David Marshall Grant, Paul Roebling; ***D:*** Bob Graham; ***W:*** Anna Thomas, Gregory Nava; ***C:*** Robert Elswit.

End of Days **1999 (R)** Alcoholic ex-cop Jericho Cane (Schwarzenegger) becomes a reluctant savior, who must battle a literal Satan (Byrne) who has the opportunity to rule both Heaven and Hell if he can make young Christine (Tunney) his bride before the millennial midnight. There's lots of action, Arnold looks great (post heart surgery), and Byrne is a very sexy devil but there's also an excessive amount of gore and silly mumbo-jumbo to suffer through. **123m/C VHS, DVD, HD DVD.** Arnold Schwarzenegger, Gabriel Byrne, Robin Tunney, Kevin Pollak, CCH Pounder, Rod Steiger, Derrick O'Connor, Miriam Margolyes, Udo Kier; ***D:*** Peter Hyams; ***W:*** Andrew Marlowe; ***C:*** Peter Hyams; ***M:*** John Debney.

End of Desire **1962** Schell discovers that her husband, Marquand, has married her for her money and is having an affair with the maid in this melodrama based on De Maupassant's story, "Une Vie." A period piece that is a little on the slow side. In French with English subtitles. **86m/C VHS.** *FR* Maria Schell, Christian Marquand, Pascale Petit, Ivan Desny; ***D:*** Alexandre Astruc.

The End of Innocence **1990 (R)** In her attempts to please everyone in her life, a woman experiences a nervous breakdown. Released two years after Schaeffer's murder. **102m/C VHS, DVD.** Dyan Cannon, John Heard, George Coe, Lola Mason, Rebecca Schaeffer, Stephen Meadows, Billie Bird, Michael Madsen, Madge Sinclair, Renee Taylor, Viveka Davis; ***D:*** Dyan Cannon; ***W:*** Dyan Cannon; ***M:*** Michael Convertino.

The End of St. Petersburg 1/2 **1927** A Russian peasant becomes a scab during a workers' strike in 1914. He is then forced to enlist in the army prior to the 1917 October Revolution. Fascinating, although propagandistic film commissioned by the then-new Soviet government. Silent. **75m/B VHS, DVD.** Ivan Chuvelov; ***D:*** Vsevolod Pudovkin.

End of Summer 1/2 **1997 (R)** Bisset's performance is the highlight of this romantic drama. She's spinster Christine Van Buren who is spending the summer at a Saratoga Springs resort, circa 1890. She's stunned to encounter Theo (Weller), the man she loved and lost 20 years before. Christine and Theo are both willing to take a second chance but soon others are complicating the situation. **95m/C VHS.** Jacqueline Bisset, Peter Weller, Julian Sands, Amy Locane, Elizabeth Shepherd, Michael Hogan; ***D:*** Linda Yellen; ***W:*** Linda Yellen, Jonathan Platnick; ***C:*** David Bridges; ***M:*** Patrick Seymour. **CABLE**

End of the Affair **1955** In WWII London, Sarah (Kerr), the wife of a British civil servant (Cushing), falls in love with her neighbor Maurice (Johnson). The two make plans for their future together, but suddenly and mysteriously, Sarah brings the affair to an end. **105m/B DVD.** *GB* Deborah Kerr, Van Johnson, John Mills, Peter Cushing; ***D:*** Edward Dmytryk; ***W:*** Lenore Coffee; ***C:*** Wilkie Cooper; ***M:*** Benjamin Frankel.

The End of the Affair **1999 (R)** During the Blitz of WWII, married Londoner Sarah Miles (Moore) suddenly breaks off her affair with writer Maurice Bendrix (Fiennes). An unexpected meeting with her husband, Henry (Rea), leads Bendrix to believe Sarah is having a new affair and he hires a detective (Hart) to follow her. Instead, Bendrix discovers her reasons for breaking off with him and her spiritual reawakening. Compellingly adult drama about love, faith, and moral dilemmas that is based on the 1955 novel by Graham Greene. **101m/C VHS, DVD.** *GB* Ralph Fiennes, Julianne Moore, Stephen Rea, Ian Hart, Sam Bould, Jason Isaacs; ***D:*** Neil Jordan; ***W:*** Neil Jordan; ***C:*** Roger Pratt; ***M:*** Michael Nyman. British Acad. '99: Adapt. Screenplay.

End of the Century: The Story of the Ramones **2003** Documents the underground music scene in New York (and abroad) during the late 1970s and chronicles the music, addictions, lineup changes, and pressures of life on the road, as well as just about every petty squabble the Ramones ever had. **110m/C DVD.** ***D:*** Michael Gramaglia, Jim Fields; ***C:*** Jim Fields.

End of the Line 1/2 **1988 (PG)** Two old-time railroad workers steal a locomotive for a cross-country jaunt to protest the closing of the local railroad company. Produced by Steenburgen. **103m/C VHS, DVD.** Wilford Brimley, Levon Helm, Mary Steenburgen, Kevin Bacon, Holly Hunter, Barbara Barrie, Bob Balaban, Howard Morris, Bruce McGill, Clint Howard, Trey Wilson, Rita Jenrette; ***D:*** Jay Russell; ***W:*** John Wohlbruck; ***M:*** Andy Summers.

End of the Road 1/2 *Man of Mystery* **1944** Crime novelist Robert Kirby (Norris) is convinced the man imprisoned for the notorious "Flower Shop Murder" is the wrong guy. He sets out to befriend who he thinks is the real killer to get him to confess. **51m/B DVD.** Edward Norris, John Abbott, June Storey, Jonathan Hale, Pierre Watkin; ***D:*** George Blair; ***W:*** Denison Clift; ***C:*** William Bradford; ***M:*** Richard Sherwin.

End of the Road 1/2 **1970 (X)** Keach is a troubled college professor whose bizarre treatment by his psychologist (Jones) produces tragic results. He eventually enters into an affair with the wife of a co-worker. Fascinating, if uneven script adapted from John Barth's story. Rated X upon release for adult story and nudity. **110m/C VHS.** Stacy Keach, James Earl Jones, James Coco, Harris Yulin, Dorothy Tristan; ***D:*** Aram Avakian; ***W:*** Terry Southern; ***C:*** Gordon Willis.

End of the Spear **2006 (PG-13)** Based on the true events of a 1956 missionary trip during which five Americans were speared to death by the very Ecuadorian tribesmen they were seeking to convert. Unfortunately, studio production values coat the jungle and its visitors with a big bottle of syrup. To its credit, it at least tries to develop the tribesmen into something more than savages. Anyone looking for something more than an overt martyrs' tale will be disappointed. **112m/C DVD.** *US* Chad Allen, Chase Ellison, Louie Leonardo, Sara Kathryn Bakker, Cara Stoner, Jack Guzman, Christina Souza; ***D:*** Jim Hanon; ***W:*** Bart Gavigan, Jim Hanon, Bill Ewing; ***C:*** Robert A. Driskell Jr.; ***M:*** Ronald Owen.

End of the World WOOF! **1976 (PG)** A coffee machine explodes, sending a man through a window and into a neon sign, where he is electrocuted. A priest witnesses this and retreats to a convent where he meets his alien double and heads for more trouble with outer space invaders. Interesting premise. **88m/C VHS, DVD.** Christopher Lee, Sue Lyon, Lew Ayres, MacDonald Carey, Dean Jagger, Kirk Scott; ***D:*** John Hayes; ***M:*** Andrew Belling.

The End of Violence **1997 (R)** Slick, manipulative action-movie producer Mike Max (Pullman) evolves from his Hollywood roots to tranquility as a gardener after his own life is touched by the violence so pervasive in his pictures. There's a sinister government agent (Benzali) and a reclusive surveillance expert (Byrne) and Max gets kidnapped, only the kidnappers mysteriously wind up dead, and then he disappears. And, no, the plot doesn't really make much sense and all the characters are paranoid anyway. But it does give you something to try to figure out. Director Wenders drastically re-edited his movie after its lukewarm work-in-progress appearance at the 1997 Cannes Film Festival. **122m/C VHS, DVD.** *FR* Bill Pullman, Gabriel Byrne, Andie MacDowell, Daniel Benzali, Traci Lind, Rosalind Chao, Loren Dean, Nicole Ari Parker, Enrique Castillo, K. Todd Freeman, John Diehl, Pruitt Taylor Vince, Peter Horton, Udo Kier, Marshall Bell, Frederic Forrest, Henry Silva, Samuel Fuller; ***D:*** Wim Wenders; ***W:*** Nicholas Klein; ***C:*** Pascal Rabaud; ***M:*** Ry Cooder.

Endangered 1/2 **1994** Environmentalists battle bad guys for survival in the wilderness. **91m/C VHS.** Rick Aiello, Martin Kove, Sandra Hess, Tim Quill, Richard Hench, Dale Dye, Craig Alan, Kent MacLachlan, Renee Estevez; ***D:*** Nick Kellis; ***W:*** Nick Kellis.

Endangered Species 1/2 **1982 (R)** Offbeat thriller with sci-fi leanings about a retired New York cop on vacation in America's West who is drawn into a female sheriff's investigation of a mysterious series of cattle killings. Could it be UFOs? Based on a true story. **97m/C VHS.** Robert Urich, JoBeth Williams, Paul Dooley, Hoyt Axton, Peter Coyote, Harry Carey Jr., Dan Hedaya, John Considine; ***D:*** Alan Rudolph; ***W:*** Alan Rudolph, John Binder.

Endangered Species **2002 (R)** A spree of bizarre health spa murders and missing victims stumps police detective Sullivan (Roberts). Of course the culprit is an up-to-no-good alien who just wants human skin to make an out-of-this-world fashion statement. Luckily there's a rival alien who arrives to aide the confused copper. **90m/C VHS, DVD.** Eric Roberts, Arnold Vosloo, John Rhys-Davies, Tony LoBianco, Al Sapienza, James W. Quinn, Sarah Kaite Coughlan, Miranda Coughlan, Sophie Bielders, Alisa Hensley, Monika Verbutaite, Evgenija Zakarevieiute; ***D:*** Kevin S. Tenney; ***W:*** Kevin S. Tenney; ***C:*** Chris Manley; ***M:*** Harry Manfredini. **VIDEO**

Endgame **1985** Grotesquely deformed survivors of WWIII fight their way out of radioactive New York City to seek a better life. **98m/C VHS.** *IT* Al Cliver, Laura Gemser, Jack Davis, G.L. Eastman, Hal Yamanouchi; ***D:*** Joe D'Amato; ***W:*** G.L. Eastman, Joe D'Amato; ***C:*** Joe D'Amato; ***M:*** Carlo Maria Cordio.

Endgame **2001** Tom (Newman) is a troubled rent boy beholden to sadistic London gangster George Norris (McGann), who uses him in blackmail schemes. Norris is also involved in drug distribution with crooked cop Dunstan (Benfield). When Tom accidentally kills Norris during a fight, he goes to married neighbors Max (Johnson) and Nikki (Barry) for help in escaping Dunston's wrath. Only Nikki has a personal fascination for Tom that comes out when she agrees to hide him. Moody and sometimes brutal. **113m/C VHS, DVD.** *GB* Daniel Newman, Mark McGann, John Benfield, Toni Barry, Corey Johnson; ***D:*** Gary Wicks; ***W:*** Gary Wicks; ***C:*** David Bennett; ***M:*** Adrian Thomas.

Endgame 1/2 **2009** Sharply-told docudrama about the secret talks that bring about the end of apartheid in South Africa. In 1985, the segregationist government of President P.W. Botha is about to collapse and Nelson Mandela is in the final days of his prison term. But money is really the ruler as Michael Young (Miller), the chairman of the British mining company Consolidated Goldfields, initiates dialogues between white Afrikaner leaders and the African National Congress. Young arranges a series of discussions at an English estate (far from the violence) between ANC leader Thabo Mbeki (Ejifor) and Afrikaner professor Willie Esterhuyse (Hurt), who's being encouraged by Neil Barnard (Strong), the head of the National Intelligence Service. Meanwhile, Barnard himself is privately negotiating with Mandela (Peters). Based on the book "The Fall of Apartheid" by Robert Harvey. **109m/C DVD.** *GB* William Hurt, Chiwetel Ejiofor, Jonny Lee Miller, Mark Strong, Clarke Peters, John Kani, Derek Jacobi, Timothy West, Robert John Burke, Keith David; ***D:*** Billy Kent; ***W:*** Adam

Wierzbianski; ***C:*** Ramsay Nickell; ***M:*** Bruno Coon.

Endless Descent WOOF! *La Grieta* **1990 (R)** At least it seems endless. A group of scientist-types set out in search of a sunken sub, but somehow take a wrong turn into the rift, the deepest chasm at the bottom of the sea. There, they discover unimaginable horrors—that is, if you've never seen "Alien," or just about any other icky-monster flick. A Spanish film, shot in English, by director Simon, whose other works of art include "Pieces" and "Slugs." **79m/C VHS.** *SP* Jack Scalia, R. Lee Ermey, Ray Wise, Deborah Adair, Ely Pouget; ***D:*** J(uan) Piquer Simon; ***W:*** David Coleman.

The Endless Game **1989 (PG-13)** Cold War suspenser has British secret-agent-man Finney attempting to solve the murder of his erstwhile fellow agent/lover, much to the dismay of the government. Written by director Forbes, this cable would-be thriller is a decidedly mediocre waste of a talented cast. Also of note, it was actor-director Sir Anthony Quayle's final appearance. **123m/C VHS.** *GB* Albert Finney, George Segal, Derek de Lint, Monica Guerritore, Ian Holm, John Standing, Anthony Quayle, Kristin Scott Thomas; ***D:*** Bryan Forbes; ***W:*** Bryan Forbes; ***C:*** Brian Tufano; ***M:*** Ennio Morricone. **CABLE**

Endless Love **1981 (R)** Although only 17, David and Jade are in love. Her parents think they are too serious and demand that the two spend time apart. David attempts to win her parents' affection and approval, goes mad in the process, and commits a foolish act (he burns the house down) that threatens their love forever. Based on the novel by Scott Spencer. Of interest only to those with time on their hands or smitten by a love so bad that this movie will seem grand in comparison. Features Cruise's first film appearance. **115m/C VHS.** Brooke Shields, Martin Hewitt, Don Murray, Shirley Knight, Beatrice Straight, Richard Kiley, Tom Cruise, James Spader, Robert Moore, Jami Gertz; ***D:*** Franco Zeffirelli; ***W:*** Judith Rascoe; ***C:*** David Watkin.

Endless Night *Agatha Christie's Endless Night* **1971** An adaptation of an Agatha Christie tale. Focuses on a young chauffeur who wants to build a dream house, and his chance meeting with an American heiress. **95m/C VHS, DVD.** *GB* Hayley Mills, Hywel Bennett, Britt Ekland, George Sanders, Per Oscarsson, Peter Bowles; ***D:*** Sidney Gilliat; ***W:*** Sidney Gilliat; ***C:*** Harry Waxman; ***M:*** Bernard Herrmann.

The Endless Summer **1966** Classic surfing documentary about the freedom and sense of adventure that surfing symbolizes. Director Brown follows two young surfers around the world in search of the perfect wave. (They finally find it at a then-unknown break off Cape Saint Francis in South America.) Besides the excellent surfing photography, Big Kahuna Brown provides the amusing tongue-in-cheek narrative. Considered by many to be the best surf movie ever. **90m/C VHS, DVD, UMD.** Mike Hynson, Robert August; ***D:*** Bruce Brown; ***W:*** Bruce Brown; ***Nar:*** Bruce Brown. Natl. Film Reg. '02.

The Endless Summer 2 *Bruce Brown's The Endless Summer 2; Bruce Brown's The Endless Summer Revisited* **1994 (PG)** You don't have to personally hang ten to get stoked about this long-awaited sequel that once again follows two surfer dudes in their quest for the perfect wave. This time out pro surfers O'Connell and Weaver circle the globe seeking adventure and the world's best waves. Traces the evolution of surfing from the lazy, golden days of the '60s to the worldwide phenomenon it is today, complete with its own pro tour circuit. Breathtaking scenery and spectacular surfing sequences highlight this look at a unique subculture. Thirty years later and it's still a great ride, though the travelogue wears thin and the sub-culture's now fairly well exploited. **107m/C VHS, DVD.** Robert "Wingnut" Weaver, Pat O'Connell, Robert August; ***D:*** Bruce Brown; ***W:*** Bruce Brown, Dana Brown; ***Nar:*** Bruce Brown.

Endplay 1/2 **1975** An Australian-made crime/horror drama in which two brothers cover for each other in a series of murders involving blonde hitchhikers. Based on a novel by Russell Braddon. **110m/C VHS.** *AU* George Mallaby, John Waters, Ken Goodiet, Delvene Delaney, Charles "Bud" Tingwell, Robert Hewett, Kevin Miles; ***D:*** Tim Burstall.

Enduring Love **2004 (R)** Brit psychodrama, based on Ian McEwan's 1997 novel, is triggered by a bizarre accident. A runaway hot air balloon disturbs the country picnic of science prof Joe Rose (Craig) and his girlfriend Claire (Morton). Several men, including Joe, try to rescue the boy trapped inside the balloon's basket and one would-be rescuer is killed. Joe doesn't know how to react and his conflict is echoed by loner/misfit Jed (Ifans), also on the scene. In fact, Jed is convinced that he and Joe now share a profound connection. His increasingly chilling persistence leads to the breakdown of Joe and Claire's relationship and Joe's own fury. Film heads down a predictable path and the characters become cliches but Craig and Ifans manage to overcome those limitations. **98m/C DVD.** Daniel Craig, Rhys Ifans, Samantha Morton, Joe Dunton, Susan Lynch, Helen McCrory, Andrew Lincoln, Corin Redgrave; ***D:*** Roger Michell; ***W:*** Joe Penhall; ***C:*** Haris Zambarloukos; ***M:*** Jeremy Sams.

Enemies, a Love Story 1/2 **1989 (R)** A wonderfully resonant, subtle tragedy based on the novel by Isaac Bashevis Singer. A post-Holocaust Jew, living in Coney Island, can't choose between three women—his current wife (who hid him during the war), his tempestuous lover, and his reappearing pre-war wife he presumed dead. A hilarious, confident tale told with grace and patience. **119m/C VHS, DVD.** Ron Silver, Lena Olin, Anjelica Huston, Margaret Sophie Stein, Paul Mazursky, Alan King, Judith Malina, Rita Karin, Phil Leeds, Elya Baskin, Marie-Adele Lemieux; ***D:*** Paul Mazursky; ***W:*** Paul Mazursky; ***C:*** Fred Murphy; ***M:*** Maurice Jarre. N.Y. Film Critics '89: Director (Mazursky), Support. Actress (Olin); Natl. Soc. Film Critics '89: Support. Actress (Huston).

Enemies of Laughter 1/2 **2000** Aspiring playwright and TV sitcom writer Paul is dejected as his first big stage venture totally tanks—and he can't seem to find true love either despite a steady string of prospects. But as fate would have it his buddy makes a successful documentary about Paul's romantic woes that attracts the attention of a gorgeous producer who rattles him with her desire to revive his failed play. **91m/C VHS, DVD.** David Paymer, Judge Reinhold, Rosalind Chao, Bea Arthur, Peter Falk, Vanessa Angel, Kathy Griffin, Marilu Henner, Kristina Fulton, Daphne Zuniga, Shera Danese, Leila Kenzle, Glen Merzer; ***D:*** Joey Travolta; ***W:*** Glen Merzer; ***C:*** Kristian Bernier; ***M:*** Barry Coffing. **VIDEO**

The Enemy 1/2 **2001 (R)** Mike Ashton (Perry) lives in Canada with his retired chemist father (Buchholz) who has been keeping secrets from his son. But they don't stay hidden when the bad guys come looking for dad and his work on bio-weapons making. A kidnapping attempt and a murder bring in the authorities, including Penny (d'Abo) who has a past with Mike and isn't adverse to fanning some flames. Story gets too convoluted for its own good but the pace is fast. **98m/C VHS, DVD.** Luke Perry, Olivia D'Abo, Roger Moore, Horst Buchholz, Tom Conti, Hendrick Haese; ***D:*** Tom Kinninmont, Charlie Watson; ***W:*** John Penney; ***C:*** Mike Garfath; ***M:*** Gast Waltzing.

Enemy at the Gates **2000 (R)** World War II saga set during the siege of Stalingrad in 1942 as Russian sniper Zaitsev (Law) tracks his equal in German sniper Konig (Harris). Law is also involved in a romantic triangle with a female Russian soldier (Weisz) and smarmy commissar Danilov (Fiennes). Only the sniper story is based on actual events and real people, from William Craig's historical account. Otherwise, the story as put on screen leaves out a lot, namely any real exploration of either the German or the Russian social and political stances of the time. We're left with good-looking men shooting it out in front of dramatic scenery, and a World War II lacking historical commentary. **131m/C VHS, DVD.** *GE GB IR US* Jude Law, Ed Harris, Joseph Fiennes, Rachel Weisz, Bob Hoskins, Gabriel Marshall-Thomson, Eva Mattes, Ron Perlman, Matthias Habich; ***D:*** Jean-Jacques Annaud; ***W:*** Jean-Jacques Annaud, Alain Godard; ***C:*** Robert Fraisse; ***M:*** James Horner.

Enemy Below **1957** Suspenseful WWII sea epic, in which an American destroyer and a German U-Boat chase one another and square off in the South Atlantic. **98m/C VHS, DVD.** Robert Mitchum, Curt Jurgens, David Hedison, Theodore Bikel, Doug McClure, Russell Collins; ***D:*** Dick Powell.

Enemy Gold 1/2 **1993 (R)** A crime czar and a beautiful killer without a conscience go after federal agents who have stumbled across a cache of Confederate gold. Basically, a babes-with-guns blowout. **92m/C VHS, DVD.** Bruce Penhall, Rodrigo Obregon, Mark Barriere, Suzi Simpson, Tai Collins, Julie Strain; ***D:*** Drew Sidaris; ***W:*** Wess Rahn, Christian Sidaris.

Enemy Mine **1985 (PG-13)** A space fantasy in which two pilots from warring planets, one an Earthling, the other an asexual reptilian Drac, crash land on a barren planet and are forced to work together to survive. **108m/C VHS, DVD.** Dennis Quaid, Louis Gossett Jr., Brion James, Richard Marcus, Lance Kerwin, Carolyn McCormick; ***D:*** Wolfgang Petersen; ***W:*** Edward Khmara; ***C:*** Tony Imi; ***M:*** Maurice Jarre.

Enemy of the Law 1/2 **1945** Texas rangers battle evil in an old frontier town. **59m/B VHS, DVD.** Tex Ritter, Dave O'Brien; ***D:*** Harry Fraser.

An Enemy of the People **1977** Heavy-handed adaptation of the Henrik Ibsen play (which is no comedy to begin with). McQueen took a chance getting away from his action roles to portray a noble 19th-century doctor but it doesn't work. Thomas (McQueen) learns the local tannery is contaminating the water in the hot springs that brings tourists into the town. His brother, the mayor (Durning), warns him to keep quiet but Thomas can't and ends up the town pariah. **106m/C DVD.** Steve McQueen, Charles Durning, Bibi Andersson, Eric Christmas, Michael Cristofer, Richard Dysart; ***D:*** George Schaefer; ***W:*** Alexander Jacobs; ***C:*** Paul Lohmann; ***M:*** Leonard Rosenman.

Enemy of the State 1/2 **1998 (R)** Paranoia-thriller shows what the nerds would do if they really wanted revenge. After a friend slips him a videocassette without his knowledge, lawyer Robert Dean (Smith) is targeted by a surveillance-and-gizmo-happy government agency headed by the sinister Reynolds (Voight). They hound Dean relentlessly, cutting him off from everything he holds dear by ruining his career and marriage, forcing him underground. Just when he has no place left to turn, he is aided by Brill (Hackman), a remorseful ex-agent who helped create the cyber-surveillance monster. From this point, our two heroes bicker, buddy-film fashion, and things blow up until the inevitable shootout crescendo. Smith's good guy vibe sustains interest in tale of technology run amok. **132m/C VHS, DVD, Blu-ray Disc.** Will Smith, Gene Hackman, Jon Voight, Jason Lee, Regina King, Gabriel Byrne, Barry Pepper, Scott Caan, Loren Dean, Jake Busey, Lisa Bonet, Stuart Wilson, Tom Sizemore, James LeGros, Ian Hurt, Dan E. Butler, Jamie Kennedy, Rebeca Silva, Jason Robards Jr., Bobby Boriello, Anna Gunn, Seth Green, Philip Baker Hall, Lillo Brancato, John Capodice, Jack Black, Bodhi (Pine) Elfman; ***D:*** Tony Scott; ***W:*** David Marconi; ***C:*** Dan Mindel; ***M:*** Trevor Rabin, Harry Gregson-Williams.

Enemy of Women 1/2 *The Private Life of Paul Joseph Goebbels* **1944** Chronicles the life and loves of Nazi propagandist Dr. Joseph Goebbels. **90m/B VHS, DVD.** Claudia Drake, Paul Andor, Donald Woods, H.B. Warner, Sigrid Gurie, Ralph Morgan, Gloria Stuart, Charles Halton; ***D:*** Alfred Zeisler; ***W:*** Alfred Zeisler.

Enemy Territory **1987 (R)** A handful of citizens trapped in a New York City housing project after dark are stalked by a violent, murderous street gang. **89m/C VHS.** Ray Parker Jr., Jan-Michael Vincent, Gary Frank, Frances Foster; ***D:*** Peter Manoogian.

Enemy Unseen **1991 (R)** A bickering squad of merceneries slog through the African jungle to find a girl abducted by crocodile-worshipping natives. Dull Jungle-Jim-style adventure, notable for the hilariously phony crocs that occasionally clamp onto the characters. **90m/C VHS.** Vernon Wells, Stack Pierce, Ken Gampu, Michael McCabe, Angela O'Neill; ***D:*** Elmo De Witt.

The Enemy Within 1/2 **1994** Cable TV remake of the 1964 political thriller "Seven Days in May." Set in the late 1990s, President William Foster's (Waterston) approval rating is at an all-time low and his heavy defense cuts have certain government officials plotting a coup. Hero of the tale is Joint Chief of Staffs officer, Col. Mac Casey (Whitaker), whose military career is warring with his sense of ethics. The updating is fairly clunky; for true suspense stick with the original. **86m/C VHS, DVD.** Forest Whitaker, Sam Waterston, Josef Sommer, Jason Robards Jr., Dana Delany, George Dzundza; ***D:*** Jonathan Darby; ***W:*** Darryl Ponicsan, Ronald Bass; ***C:*** Kees Van Oostrum. **CABLE**

The Enforcer 1/2 *Murder, Inc* **1951** A district attorney goes after an organized gang of killers in this film noir treatment of the real-life "Murder, Inc." case. **87m/B VHS, DVD.** Humphrey Bogart, Zero Mostel, Ted de Corsia, Everett Sloane, Roy Roberts, Michael (Lawrence) Tolan, King Donovan, Bob Steele, Adelaide Klein, Don Beddoe, Tito Vuolo, John Kellogg; ***D:*** Bretaigne Windust, Raoul Walsh; ***W:*** Martin Rackin; ***C:*** Robert Burks.

The Enforcer 1/2 **1976 (R)** Dirty Harry takes on a female partner and a vicious terrorist group that is threatening the city of San Francisco. See how many "punks" feel lucky enough to test the hand of the tough cop. **96m/C VHS, DVD.** Clint Eastwood, Tyne Daly, Harry Guardino, Bradford Dillman, John Mitchum, Albert "Poppy" Popwell, Will MacMillan, John Crawford, Jocelyn Jones, DeVeren Bookwalter, Dick Durock, Joe Spano; ***D:*** James Fargo; ***W:*** Stirling Silliphant, Stuart Hagmann; ***C:*** Charles W. Short; ***M:*** Jerry Fielding.

Enforcer from Death Row **1978** An ex-con is recruited by a secret international peacekeeping organization to track down and eliminate a band of murderous spies. **87m/C VHS.** Cameron Mitchell, Leo Fong, Darnell Garcia, Booker T. Anderson, John Hammond, Mariwin Roberts; ***D:*** Efren C. Pinon; ***W:*** Leo Fong.

The English Patient **1996 (R)** Filled with flashbacks and moral ambiguities, this adult romance is a complicated WWII saga that finds fragile French-Canadian nurse Hana (Binoche) caring for Almasy (Fiennes), an enigmatic, dying burn patient, in an abandoned monastery in Tuscany. Hana's joined by thief-turned-spy Caravaggio (Dafoe), who has a private score to settle with Almasy, and two British bomb disposal experts, Kip (Andrews), a Sikh who falls in love with Hana, and Sgt. Hardy (Whately). Almasy spends his days recalling his illicit love affair with Katharine Clifton (Scott Thomas), the wife of fellow cartographer, Geoffrey (Firth), as they map the North African desert. Exquisitely photographed in a golden glow by Seale with wonderful performances by the entire cast. Based on the novel by Michael Ondaatje. **162m/C VHS, DVD.** Ralph Fiennes, Kristin Scott Thomas, Juliette Binoche, Willem Dafoe, Naveen Andrews, Colin Firth, Julian Wadham, Jurgen Prochnow, Kevin Whately, Clive Merrison, Nino Castelnuovo; ***D:*** Anthony Minghella; ***W:*** Anthony Minghella; ***C:*** John Seale; ***M:*** Gabriel Yared. Oscars '96: Art Dir./Set Dec., Cinematog., Costume Des., Director (Minghella), Film Editing, Picture, Sound, Support. Actress (Binoche), Orig. Dramatic Score; British Acad. '96: Adapt. Screenplay, Cinematog., Film, Support. Actress (Binoche), Score; Directors Guild '96: Director (Minghella); Golden Globes '97: Film—Drama, Score; L.A. Film Critics '96: Cinematog.; Natl. Bd. of Review '96: Support. Actress (Binoche), Support. Actress (Scott Thomas); Broadcast Film Critics '96: Director (Minghella), Screenplay.

An Englishman Abroad **1983** During a cultural exchange, British actress Coral Browne (playing herself in a pointed recreation) visits Moscow in 1961 and chances to meet notorious English spy/defector Guy Burgess (Bates). Behind their gossip and small talk is a tragicomic portrait of the exiled traitor/spy. Made for British TV; nuances may be lost on yank viewers. Winner of several British awards. **63m/C VHS.** *GB* Alan Bates, Coral Browne, Charles Gray; ***D:*** John Schlesinger; ***W:*** Alan Bennett; ***M:*** George Fenton. **TV**

An Englishman in New York 🦴🦴 1/2 **2009** Made-for-British TV with Hurt reprising his role as gay raconteur Quentin Crisp from 1975's "The Naked Civil Servant." Crisp moves to New York in 1981 at the age of 72, works on a one-man stage show, and writes for a gay magazine. However, after the aged contrarian quips that AIDS is a 'fad,' many in the gay community turn on him (especially after he refuses to apologize) despite his quiet support for various AIDS charities. Crisp still carried on and died in 1999 in England while preparing for a tour. **74m/C DVD.** *GB* John Hurt, Swoosie Kurtz, Denis O'Hare, Jonathan Tucker, Cynthia Nixon; ***D:*** Richard Laxton; ***W:*** Brian Fillis; ***C:*** Yaron Orbach; ***M:*** Paul Englishby. **TV**

The Englishman Who Went up a Hill But Came down a Mountain 🦴🦴🦴 **1995 (PG)** Charming if slight tale of town pride based on writer/director Monger's family stories. In 1917 two English cartographers—pompous George (McNeice) and naive Reginald (Grant)—travel into Wales to measure the height of Ffynnon Garw (a running gag has the surveyors struggling with the Welsh language). To the proud locals it is the first mountain in Wales, and without that designation they might as well redraw the maps and be part of England—God forbid. But in order to be designated a mountain Ffynnon Garw must be 1000 feet high, and she measures only 984. Grant stammers boyishly as the Englishman who is not only captivated by the village, but by spirited local lass Betty (Fitzgerald, with whom he starred in "Sirens"). Meaney slyly shines as innkeeper Morgan the Goat, leading the townful of color characters. Wales is shown to great advantage by cinematographer Layton. **96m/C VHS, DVD.** *GB* Hugh Grant, Tara Fitzgerald, Colm Meaney, Ian McNeice, Ian Hart, Kenneth Griffith; ***D:*** Christopher Monger; ***W:*** Christopher Monger; ***C:*** Vernon Layton; ***M:*** Stephen Endelman.

Enid Is Sleeping 🦴🦴 *Over Her Dead Body* **1990 (R)** Well-done comedy noir in the now-popular there's-a-corpse-in-the-closet subgenre. A woman in a mythical New Mexican town tries to hide the body of her sister Enid, who she's accidentally killed. Enid, it turns out, wasn't thrilled to discover her sister sleeping with her police-officer husband. Phillips and Perkins restored the film to its original state after it was ruthlessly gutted by the studio. **105m/C VHS, DVD.** Elizabeth Perkins, Judge Reinhold, Rhea Perlman; ***D:*** Maurice Phillips; ***W:*** Maurice Phillips; ***C:*** Alfonso Beato.

Enigma 🦴🦴 **1982 (PG)** Trapped behind the Iron Curtain, a double agent tries to find the key to five pending murders by locating a Russian coded microprocessor holding information that would unravel the assassination scheme. **101m/C VHS, DVD.** *FR GB* Martin Sheen, Brigitte Fossey, Sam Neill, Derek Jacobi, Frank Finlay, Michael (Michel) Lonsdale, Warren Clarke; ***D:*** Jeannot Szwarc; ***W:*** John Briley.

Enigma 🦴🦴 1/2 **2001 (R)** Tom Jericho (Scott) is a British codebreaker working at Bletchley Park during WWII. He has a breakdown after a romantic breakup with colleague Claire (Burrows), who's mysteriously disppeared. Could she have been working for the Germans? Tom is determined to find out, aided by Claire's roommate Hester (Winslet). Meanwhile, intelligence operative Wigram (Northam) is keeping an eye on them both, thinking they know more than they appear to. Excessive subplots make for some confusion but the story's still compelling. Based on a novel by Robert Harris. **117m/C VHS, DVD.** *GB* Dougray Scott, Kate Winslet, Saffron Burrows, Jeremy Northam, Nikolaj Waldau, Tom Hollander, Corin Redgrave, Robert Pugh, Matthew MacFadyen, Donald (Don) Sumpter; ***D:*** Michael Apted; ***W:*** Tom Stoppard; ***C:*** Seamus McGarvey; ***M:*** John Barry.

Enigma Secret 🦴🦴 **1979** Three Polish mathematicians use their noggins to break the Nazi secret code machine during WWII. Based on a true story; in Polish with English subtitles. **158m/C VHS, DVD.** *PL* Tadeusz Borowski, Piotr Fronczewski, Piotr Garlicki; ***D:*** Rom Wionczek; ***W:*** Rom Wionczek; ***C:*** Jacek Zygadio; ***M:*** Henryk Kuzniak, Jerzy Maksymiuk.

Enjo 🦴🦴 *Conflagration; The Flame of Torment* **1958** True story of a tormented young monk, studying at the Golden Pavilion in Kyoto, who becomes disillusioned by the pervasive corruption of the temple. In desperation, he sets fire to the national shrine in an attempt to preserve the monument from further contamination. Very disturbing yet beautiful to watch. Adapted from Mishima's novel "Temple of the Golden Pavilion." Japanese with subtitles. **98m/B VHS.** *JP* Raizo Ichikawa, Ganjiro Nakamura, Tatsuya Nakadai; ***D:*** Kon Ichikawa; ***W:*** Natto Wada, Keiji Hasebe, Toshiro Mayuzumi; ***C:*** Kazuo Miyagawa.

Enola Gay: The Men, the Mission, the Atomic Bomb 🦴🦴 **1980** Based on the bestselling book by Gordon Thomas and Max Gordon Witts, this drama tells the story of the airmen aboard the B-29 that dropped the first atomic bomb. Details the events during WWII leading up to the decision to bomb Hiroshima and the concerns of the crew assigned the task. **150m/C VHS.** Patrick Duffy, Billy Crystal, Kim Darby, Gary Frank, Gregory Harrison, Ed Nelson, Robert Walden, Stephen Macht, Robert Pine, James Shigeta, Henry Wilcoxon; ***D:*** David Lowell Rich; ***M:*** Maurice Jarre. **TV**

Enormous Changes 🦴🦴🦴 *Enormous Changes at the Last Minute* **1983** Three stories about New York City women and their personal relationships. Based on the stories of Grace Paley. **115m/C VHS.** Ellen Barkin, David Strathairn, Ron McLarty, Maria Tucci, Lynn Milgrim, Kevin Bacon; ***D:*** Mirra Bank; ***W:*** John Sayles.

Enough 🦴🦴 **2002 (PG-13)** Revenge fantasy that's been compared to both "Sleeping with the Enemy" (Julia Roberts) and "Double Jeopardy" (Ashley Judd). Working-class waitress Slim (Lopez) marries wealthy contractor Mitch (Campbell) and for a while everything appears perfect. But Mitch turns out to be an abusive, cheating, control freak who forces Slim to take their daughter and run. When Mitch finds and threatens her, Slim decides to literally toughen up and give Mitch a taste of his own medicine. Okay, it's nice to see Lopez kick butt but this movie has a very nasty taste and some lame advice for battered women (who probably won't discover that their biological fathers are filthy rich and can help them out financially). **115m/C VHS, DVD.** *US* Jennifer Lopez, Billy Campbell, Juliette Lewis, Dan Futterman, Noah Wyle, Tessa Allen, Fred Ward, Bill Cobbs, Christopher Maher, Janet Carroll; ***D:*** Michael Apted; ***W:*** Nicholas Kazan; ***C:*** Rogier Stoffers; ***M:*** David Arnold.

Enough! 🦴🦴 *Barakat!* **2006** The year is 1990 and emergency room doctor Amel (Brakni) is living through the Algerian civil war. When she returns home, she finds that her journalist husband has been abducted by fundamentalists and allegedly taken to one of the remote mountain villages. Determined to find him, Amel is accompanied by older nurse Khadidja (Bouamari), who's lived through years of her country's unrest and who offers advice on the perilous situation. Arabic and French with subtitles. **94m/C DVD.** *AL FR* Rachida Brakni, Fetouma Bouamari, Malika Belbey, Amine Kedam, Ahmed Berrhama; ***D:*** Djamila Sahraoui; ***W:*** Djamila Sahraoui, Cecile Vargaftig; ***C:*** Katell Dijan; ***M:*** Alla.

Enrapture 🦴 1/2 **1990 (R)** A chauffeur is the prime suspect when a promiscuous passenger is murdered in his limousine. The driver did it? **87m/C VHS.** Ona Simms, Harvey Siegel, Richard Parnes; ***D:*** Chuck Vincent.

Enron: The Smartest Guys in the Room 🦴🦴🦴 1/2 **2005** Based on the book by Fortune magazine reporters Bethany McLean and Peter Elkind. Director Gibney deftly compiles vast amounts of in-house video and audio footage along with after-the-fact interviews and Congressional hearings chronicling the devastating downfall in 2001 of corporate behemoth Enron. An engaging, thorough, and coherent profile of the hustle created by chief executives Kenneth Lay, Jeffrey Skilling, and Andy Fastow and the resulting economic destruction, from the loss of 20,000 jobs and $2 million in employee pensions to the $30 billion cost of California's energy crisis. Matter-of-fact narration by Peter Coyote contrasts well with sly use of several pop music songs. **110m/C DVD.** *US* ***D:*** Alex Gibney; ***W:*** Alex Gibney; ***C:*** Maryse Albert; ***M:*** Matt Hauser. Ind. Spirit '06: Feature Doc.; Writers Guild '05: Feature Doc.

Ensign Pulver 🦴🦴 **1964** A continuation of the further adventures of the crew of the U.S.S. Reluctant from "Mister Roberts," which was adapted from the Broadway play. **104m/C VHS.** Walter Matthau, Robert Walker Jr., Larry Hagman, Jack Nicholson, Millie Perkins, James Coco, James Farentino, Burl Ives, Gerald S. O'Loughlin, Al Freeman Jr.; ***D:*** Joshua Logan.

Entangled 🦴🦴 **1993 (R)** David Mirkin (Nelson) is a struggling writer living in Paris with his beautiful girlfriend Annabelle (Treil). As she becomes ever more successful as a fashion model, David becomes ever more jealous and mistrustful. So he hires a detective (Brosnan) to spy on her. And then there's the small matter of a murder. Adapted from the novel "Les Veufs" by Boileau Narcejac. **98m/C VHS.** Judd Nelson, Pierce Brosnan, Laurence Treil, Roy Dupuis; ***D:*** Max Fischer.

Enter Laughing 🦴🦴 **1967** Based on Reiner's semi-autobiographical novel and play, depicts the botched efforts of a Bronx-born schlump to become an actor. Worthwhile, but doesn't live up to the original. **112m/C VHS.** Reni Santoni, Jose Ferrer, Elaine May, Shelley Winters, Jack Gilford, Don Rickles, Michael J. Pollard, Janet Margolin, Rob Reiner; ***D:*** Carl Reiner; ***W:*** Carl Reiner; ***C:*** Joseph Biroc; ***M:*** Quincy Jones.

Enter the Dragon 🦴🦴🦴 *The Deadly Three* **1973 (R)** The American film that broke Bruce Lee worldwide combines Oriental conventions with 007 thrills. Spectacular fighting sequences including Karate, Judo, Tae Kwon Do, and Tai Chi Chuan are featured as Lee is recruited by the British to search for opium smugglers in Hong Kong. **98m/C VHS, DVD, UMD, HD DVD.** Bruce Lee, John Saxon, Jim Kelly, Ahna Capri, Shih Kien, Bob Wall, Angela (Mao Ying) Mao, Betty Chung, Jackie Chan, Tony Liu, Chuck Norris; ***D:*** Robert Clouse; ***W:*** Michael Allin; ***C:*** Gil Hubbs; ***M:*** Lalo Schifrin. Natl. Film Reg. '04.

Enter the Ninja 🦴 **1981 (R)** First and most serious of the Cannon canon of relatively well-done ninja epics (faint praise) that created original boxoffice stir for genre (mostly among adolescents needing outlet). Ninja Nero visits old friend in Philippines who's being terrorized by ruthless evil guy George. Nero dispatches numerous thugs before indulging in ninja slugfest with Kosugi. Just because they take it seriously doesn't mean you should. **99m/C VHS.** Franco Nero, Susan George, Sho Kosugi, Christopher George, Alex Courtney; ***D:*** Menahem Golan; ***W:*** Judd Bernard.

The Entertainer 🦴🦴🦴 1/2 **1960** Splendid drama of egotistical, third-rate vaudevillian Archie Rice (Olivier), who tries vainly to gain the fame his dying father Billy (Livesey) once possessed. His blatant disregard for his alcoholic wife Phoebe (De Banzie), his superficial sons (Bates and Finney), and his loyal daughter (Plowright) brings his world crashing down around him, as Archie discovers how self-destructive his life has been. Adapted from the play by John Osborne. Remade for TV in 1975 with Jack Lemmon. **104m/B VHS, DVD.** *GB* Laurence Olivier, Brenda de Banzie, Roger Livesey, Joan Plowright, Daniel Massey, Alan Bates, Shirley Anne Field, Albert Finney, Thora Hird; ***D:*** Tony Richardson; ***W:*** Nigel Kneale, John Osborne; ***C:*** Oswald Morris; ***M:*** John Addison.

Entertaining Angels: The Dorothy Day Story 🦴🦴 1/2 **1996 (PG-13)** Dorothy Day (Kelly) was a social activist who founded the left-wing publication The Catholic Worker and was dedicated to sheltering and feeding the poor, founding soup kitchens across America. A radical journalist and New York bohemian, Day converts to Catholicism in the '20s and is soon working with the city's poor and homeless. Episodic story works mainly on indignation and its heroine's compassion. **110m/C VHS.** Moira Kelly, Martin Sheen, Melinda Dillon, Lenny Von Dohlen, Heather Graham, Geoffrey Blake, Boyd Kestner, Allyce Beasley, Brian Keith; ***D:*** Michael Ray Rhodes; ***W:*** John Wells; ***C:*** Mike Fash; ***M:*** Bill Conti, Ashley Irwin.

Entertaining Mr. Sloane 🦴🦴 1/2 **1970** Playwright Joe Orton's masterpiece of black comedy concerning a handsome criminal who becomes the guest and love interest of a widow and her brother. **90m/C VHS.** *GB* Beryl Reid, Harry Andrews, Peter McEnery, Alan Webb; ***D:*** Douglas Hickox; ***W:*** Clive Exton, Joe Orton; ***C:*** Wolfgang Suschitzky.

The Entity 🦴🦴 **1983 (R)** Supposedly based on a true story about an unseen entity that repeatedly rapes a woman. Hershey's the victim whom nobody believes. She eventually ends up at a university for talks with parapsychologist Silver. Pseudo-science to the rescue as the over-sexed creature is frozen dead in its tracks. Exploitative violence, gore, and nudity aplenty, balanced to a degree by Hershey's strong performance. **115m/C VHS, DVD.** Barbara Hershey, Ron Silver, Alex Rocco; ***D:*** Sidney J. Furie; ***W:*** Frank De Felitta; ***C:*** Stephen Burum; ***M:*** Charles Bernstein.

Entrapment 🦴🦴 1/2 **1999 (PG-13)** Too tricky for its own good crime caper features insurance investigator Virginia Baker (Zeta-Jones) convincing her boss, Hector Cruz (Patton), that master thief Mac MacDougall (Connery) is behind the theft of a Rembrandt. Only when Gin catches up to Mac, she convinces him that she's also a thief and she has a very elaborate, very rich heist in mind, that needs his expertise. However, nobody involved in anything that goes on in this movie is exactly what they seem. Nice scenery (and not just that offered by the beautiful Zeta-Jones). **112m/C VHS, DVD, Blu-ray Disc.** Sean Connery, Catherine Zeta-Jones, Ving Rhames, Will Patton, Maury Chaykin; ***D:*** Jon Amiel; ***W:*** Ronald Bass, William Broyles Jr.; ***C:*** Phil Meheux; ***M:*** Christopher Young.

Entre-Nous 🦴🦴🦴 1/2 *Between Us; Coup de Foudre; At First Sight* **1983 (PG)** Two attractive, young French mothers find in each other the fulfillment their husbands cannot provide. One of the women was confined in a concentration camp during WWII; the other is a disaffected artist. In French with English subtitles. **112m/C VHS, DVD.** *FR* Jean-Pierre Bacri, Patrick Bauchau, Jacqueline Doyen, Isabelle Huppert, Miou-Miou, Guy Marchand; ***D:*** Diane Kurys; ***W:*** Alain Henry, Diane Kurys; ***C:*** Bernard Lutic; ***M:*** Luis Bacalov.

Entropy 🦴🦴 **1999** Dorff gives a gifted lead performance in this excessively stylistic romantic drama. It spans a year in the life of arrogant moviemaker Jake Walsh (Dorff), who describes how he meets French model Stella (Godreche) and experiences love at first sight. Although they live together, their careers frequently keep them apart and Jake's emotional immaturity eventually separates them. The cliched film-within-a-film narrative only manages to slow the main story down. **104m/C VHS.** Stephen Dorff, Judith Godreche, Kelly Macdonald, Lauren Holly, Jon Tenney, Frank Vincent, Paul Guilfoyle, Hector Elizondo; ***D:*** Phil Joanou; ***W:*** Phil Joanou; ***C:*** Carolyn Chen; ***M:*** George Fenton.

Entry Level 🦴🦴 **2007** Middle-aged chef Clay Maguire's (Sweeney) restaurant goes under and Clay decides to get out of the food business and look for a different line of work. Of course Clay has no other job skills (he can't even use a computer) so that really limits his choices, but he gets encouragement from some unlikely sources. **85m/C DVD.** D.B. Sweeney, Kurtwood Smith, Missi Pyle, Cedric Yarbrough, Taylor Negron, Steve Ryan, Lisa Ann Walter; ***D:*** Douglas Horn; ***W:*** Douglas Horn; ***C:*** Aasulv Austad; ***M:*** Brandon Roberts. **VIDEO**

Envy 🦴🦴 1/2 **2004 (PG-13)** Tim (Stiller) and Nick (Black) are buddies, neighbors, and coworkers at a sandpaper plant. Nick is a dreamer who's constantly coming up with wacky inventions that Tim reminds him are impossible or impractical. One of these ideas is Vapoorize, a spray that makes dog doo disappear. When Tim passes on a chance to get in on the deal and the spray becomes a monster success, his wife's (Weisz) scorn triggers a jealousy that sends him on a trail of petty revenge on Nick. Uneven comedy is elevated by the gleefully manic performance of Walken, as Tim's criminal inspiration, the J-Man. Black's clueless immersion in the overly opulent lifestyle is a kick, as well. **99m/C DVD.** *US* Ben Stiller, Jack Black, Rachel Weisz, Amy Poehler, Christopher Walken, Hector Elias, Edward "Blue" Deckert, Ariel Gade, Sam Lerner, Lily Jackson, Connor Matheus; ***D:*** Barry Levinson; ***W:*** Steve Adams; ***C:*** Tim Maurice-Jones; ***M:*** Mark Mothersbaugh.

Epic Movie WOOF! 2007 (PG-13) Another cobbled together, extremely unfunny spoof of popular movies. Four orphans (Mays, Penn, Chambers, Campbell) wind up in a chocolate factory where Glover is an even more sinister candy maker than Johnny Depp's Willy Wonka. Then they escape to a parody of "Narnia" (although Coolidge makes a fairly cool ice queen) and it just goes downhill from there. Someone somewhere must still finds this stuff funny. **85m/C DVD.** *US* Kal Penn, Adam Campbell, Jennifer Coolidge, Faune A. Chambers, Jayma Mays, Crispin Glover, Fred Willard, Hector Jimenez, Darrell Hammond, Carmen Electra, David Carradine; ***D:*** Jason Friedberg, Aaron Selzer; ***W:*** Jason Friedberg, Aaron Selzer; ***C:*** Shawn Maurer; ***M:*** Ed Shearmur.

Epoch ⚲⚲ ½ **2000 (PG-13)** Alien monolith suddenly appears and hovers over Bhutan, seemingly causing worldwide power disruptions and earthquakes. National security adviser Lysander (O'Neal) assigns special ops Kasia Czaban (Niznik) and weapons specialist Mason Rand (Keith) to figure out just what the object is—and wants—and, if necessary, to destroy it. **97m/C VHS, DVD.** David Keith, Stephanie Niznik, Ryan O'Neal, James Hong, Brian Thompson, Craig Wasson, Donna Magnani, Shannon Lee; ***D:*** Matt Cold; ***C:*** Ken Stipe. **CABLE**

Epoch: Evolution ⚲⚲ **2003 (R)** It's been 10 years since the alien monolith, Torus, wreaked havoc with the planet. In this passable sequel to 2000's Epoch, Rand (Keith) must now summon it as a drastic measure to prevent a catastrophic third world war. **90m/C VHS, DVD.** David Keith, Angel Boris, Billy Dee Williams, Brian Thompson; ***D:*** Ian Watson; ***M:*** Jason Christopherson. **CABLE**

Equal Impact ⚲ ½ **1996** Identical twin brothers Josh and Dave (Jay and Joe Gates) find themselves caught up in a deadly counterfeiting ring, headed by the sinister Donald Moss (Estevez). To escape, they enlist old friend Ray Tobin (Z'dar) and their own martial arts skills. **105m/C VHS.** Jay Gates, Joe Gates, Joe Estevez, Robert Z'Dar; ***D:*** Jon Steven Ward; ***W:*** Jon Steven Ward; ***C:*** Lon Magdich; ***M:*** Darin Isaacs.

Equalizer 2000 ⚲ **1986 (R)** A warrior in a post-holocaust future plots to overthrow a dictatorship by using a high-powered gun. **85m/C VHS.** Richard Norton, Corinne Wahl, William (Bill) Steis; ***D:*** Cirio H. Santiago.

Equilibrium WOOF! 2002 (R) It's the near future, in which society self-administers Prozium daily to thwart all emotions. The emotion cops, Grammaton Cleric, arrest sense offenders using the time-tested method of massive gun-kata battles. Agent John Preston's (Bale) position is compromised when he's attracted to Mary (Watson), a woman working with a resistance group. Poor attempt at sci-fi drama raises the question "Would the future suck less if we stopped making lousy movies about it in the present?" **106m/C VHS, DVD.** *US* Christian Bale, Emily Watson, Taye Diggs, Angus MacFadyen, Sean Bean, William Fichtner, Matthew Harbour; ***D:*** Kurt Wimmer; ***W:*** Kurt Wimmer; ***C:*** Dion Beebe; ***M:*** Klaus Badelt.

Equinox ⚲⚲⚲ *The Beast* **1971 (PG)** Young archaeologists uncover horror in a state forest. The ranger, questing for a book of spells that the scientists have found, threatens them with wonderful special effects, including winged beasts, huge apes, and Satan. Though originally an amateur film, it is deemed a minor classic in its genre. **80m/C VHS, DVD.** Edward Connell, Barbara Hewitt, Frank Bonner, Robin Christopher, Jack Woods, Fritz Leiber Jr., Patrick Burke, Jim Phillips; ***D:*** Dennis Muren, Jack Woods; ***W:*** Jack Woods; ***C:*** Mike Hoover; ***M:*** John Caper Jr.

Equinox ⚲⚲ **1993 (R)** Modine gets to try his hand (and does well) at a dual role, with his portrayal of identical twins, separated at birth and raised in completely different environs. Garage worker Henry lives in a tenement while slick brother Freddie is a gangster's chauffeur married to the materialistic Sharon (Singer). Fate brings the brothers together when a janitor discovers a letter that reveals their parentage and the fact that a fortune has been left to them. Set in the near future, in the surreal and decaying city of Empire, this is typical Rudolph with its moody stylized appearance and convoluted plot. **110m/C VHS.** Matthew Modine, Lara Flynn Boyle, Lori Singer, Marisa Tomei, Fred Ward, M. Emmet Walsh, Tyra Ferrell, Tate Donovan, Kevin J. O'Connor, Gailard Sartain; ***D:*** Alan Rudolph; ***W:*** Alan Rudolph; ***C:*** Elliot Davis.

Equinox Flower ⚲⚲ **1958** Ozu's first color film tells the sensitive story of two teenage girls who make a pact to protect each other from the traditional prearranged marriages their parents have set up. Lovely film that focuses on the generation gap between young and old in the Japanese family. In Japanese with English subtitles. **118m/C VHS.** *JP* Shin Saburi, Kinuyo Tanaka, Ineko Arima, Miyuki Kuwano, Chishu Ryu; ***D:*** Yasujiro Ozu.

Equus ⚲⚲ ½ **1977 (R)** A psychiatrist undertakes the most challenging case of his career when he tries to figure out why a stable-boy blinded horses. Based upon the successful play by Peter Shaffer, but not well transferred to film. **138m/C VHS, DVD.** Richard Burton, Peter Firth, Jenny Agutter, Joan Plowright, Colin Blakely, Harry Andrews; ***D:*** Sidney Lumet; ***W:*** Peter Shaffer; ***C:*** Oswald Morris; ***M:*** Richard Rodney Bennett. British Acad. '77: Support. Actress (Agutter); Golden Globes '78: Actor—Drama (Burton), Support. Actor (Firth).

Era Notte a Roma ⚲⚲⚲ *Escape by Night; Blackout in Rome* **1960** An American, Russian, and British soldier each escape from a concentration camp in the waning days of WWII and find refuge in the home of a young woman. **145m/C VHS.** *IT* Giovanna Ralli, Renato Salvatori, Leo Genn, Sergei Bondarchuk, Peter Baldwin; ***D:*** Roberto Rossellini; ***W:*** Roberto Rossellini; ***C:*** Carlo Carlini; ***M:*** Renzo Rossellini.

Eragon ⚲⚲ **2006 (PG)** The dragon, voiced with maternal concern by Weisz, is a lot more charismatic than its rider—the teenaged farm boy of the title (Speleers in his film debut). A sword-and-sorcery flick, based on the first novel in a trilogy by Christopher Paolini (who was a teen himself when he wrote it), has a bad king (Malkovich) and his evil wizard (Carlyle) oppressing the little people in a mythic land—until Eragon and his dragon Saphira, aided by mentor Brom (Irons), can rally the rebels (there's always rebels). The kids will probably enjoy the adventure—even though the film is left open-ended for a sequel—but it doesn't hold much crossover appeal for adults. **104m/C DVD, Blu-ray Disc.** *US* Jeremy Irons, Sienna Guillory, Robert Carlyle, John Malkovich, Ed Speleers, Djimon Hounsou, Garrett Hedlund, Joss Stone, Alun Armstrong, Gary Lewis, Christopher Egan, Richard Rifkin, Caroline Chikezie, Andrea Fazekas, Steve Speirs; ***D:*** Stefan Fangmeier; ***W:*** Peter Buchman; ***C:*** Hugh Johnson; ***M:*** Patrick Doyle; ***V:*** Rachel Weisz.

Eraser ⚲⚲ ½ **1996 (R)** Arnold returns to familiar big-budget action territory and looks right at home. He plays elite U.S. Marshal John Kruger, who protects federal witnesses by "erasing" their previous identities. When a beautiful witness uncovers a high-level conspiracy, the two go on the run to stay alive long enough to expose the truth. Fans of the big bang Schwarzenegger of yore will not be disappointed. Rumors of production delays and budget overruns, not to mention difficulties between director Russell and producer Kopelson, brought up the spectre of "Waterworld," but the final result is more reminiscent of the success of "True Lies." **115m/C VHS, DVD, Blu-ray Disc.** Arnold Schwarzenegger, Vanessa L(ynne) Williams, James Caan, James Coburn, Robert Pastorelli, Andy Romano, James Cromwell, Danny Nucci, Nicholas Chinlund, Mark Rolston, Gerry Becker, Joe (Johnny) Viterelli, Michael (Mike) Papajohn; ***D:*** Chuck Russell; ***W:*** Tony Puryear, Walon Green; ***C:*** Adam Greenberg; ***M:*** Alan Silvestri.

Eraserhead ⚲⚲⚲ **1978** The infamous cult classic about a numb-brained everyman wandering through what amounts to a sick, ironic parody of the modern urban landscape, innocently impregnating his girlfriend and fathering a pestilent embryonic mutant. Surreal and bizarre, the film has an inner, completely unpredictable logic all its own. Lynch's first feature-length film stars Nance, who later achieved fame in Lynch's "Twin Peaks" as Pete the Logger. **90m/B VHS, DVD.** Jack Nance, Charlotte Stewart, Allen Joseph, Jeanne Bates, Judith Anna Roberts, Laurel Near, V. Phipps-Willson, Jack Fisk, Jean Lange, Darwin Joston, Hal Landon Jr., Jennifer Lynch, Gill Dennis; ***D:*** David Lynch; ***W:*** David Lynch; ***C:*** Frederick Elmes, Herbert Cardwell; ***M:*** David Lynch, Fats Waller, Peter Ivers. Natl. Film Reg. '04.

Erendira ⚲⚲ ½ **1983** Based on Gabriel Garcia-Marquez's story about a teenage girl prostituting herself to support her witch-like grandmother after accidentally torching the elder's house. The film follows the two as they travel across the desert trying out new and inventive ways to survive. Unusual ending tops off a creative, if not eclectic, movie. In Spanish with English subtitles. **103m/C VHS.** *FR MX GE* Sergio Calderon, Blanca Guerra, Ernesto Cruz, Pierre Vaneck, Irene Papas, Claudia Ohana, Michael (Michel) Lonsdale, Rufus, Jorge Fegan; ***D:*** Ruy Guerra; ***W:*** Gabriel Garcia Marquez; ***C:*** Denys Clerval; ***M:*** Maurice Lecouer.

Eric ⚲⚲⚲ **1975** Tear-jerker about a young athlete who fights for his life after he's diagnosed with leukemia. Based on the true-life account written by Eric's mother, Doris Lund. **100m/C VHS.** Patricia Neal, John Savage, Claude Akins, Sian Barbara Allen, Mark Hamill, Nehemiah Persoff, Tom Clancy; ***D:*** James Goldstone; ***M:*** Dave Grusin. **TV**

Erik ⚲⚲ *One Man Out* **1990** An ex-government agent working in Central America finds his loyalties divided when he is approached by a female activist and his old CIA friends. They want him to help expose his current boss as a drug smuggler. **90m/C VHS.** Stephen McHattie, Deborah Van Valkenburgh; ***D:*** Michael Kennedy; ***W:*** Michael Kennedy; ***C:*** Ludek Bogner; ***M:*** Mychael Danna.

Erik, the Viking ⚲ **1965** The Norse Warrior discovers not only the New World but traitorous subordinates among his crew, calling for drastic measures. **95m/C VHS.** *IT SP* Giuliano Gemma, Gordon Mitchell; ***D:*** Mario Caiano; ***W:*** Mario Caiano; ***C:*** Enzo Barboni; ***M:*** Carlo Franci.

Erik the Viking ⚲ ½ **1989 (PG-13)** A mediocre Monty Pythonesque farce about a Viking who grows dissatisfied with his barbaric way of life and decides to set out to find the mythical Asgaard, where Norse gods dwell. Great cast of character actors is wasted. **104m/C VHS, DVD.** *GB* Tim Robbins, Terry Jones, Mickey Rooney, John Cleese, Imogen Stubbs, Anthony Sher, Gordon John Sinclair, Freddie Jones, Eartha Kitt, Gary Cady, Neil Innes, Jim Broadbent, Andrew MacLachlan, Charles McKeown; ***D:*** Terry Jones; ***W:*** Terry Jones; ***C:*** Ian Wilson; ***M:*** Neil Innes.

Erin Brockovich ⚲⚲⚲ **2000 (R)** Erin Brockovich (Roberts) is a divorced mom desperate for a job. She bullies her way into a file clerk position at the small law office of Ed Masry (Finney) where her salty language, take-no-prisoners attitude, and scanty attire unnerve her co-workers. But that's just the appeal that Erin needs when she uncovers and investigates some shady corporate dealings that eventually lead to a multimillion dollar settlement against a public utility over contaminated water. Standout role for Roberts who's ably backed-up by the rumpled Finney. Based on a true story and yes, the real Erin is a looker who dresses every bit as provocatively as her screen counterpart. **131m/C VHS, DVD, HD DVD.** Julia Roberts, Albert Finney, Aaron Eckhart, Marg Helgenberger, Cherry Jones, Veanne Cox, Conchata Ferrell, Tracey Walter, Peter Coyote; ***D:*** Steven Soderbergh; ***W:*** Susannah Grant; ***C:*** Edward Lachman; ***M:*** Thomas Newman. Oscars '00: Actress (Roberts); British Acad. '00: Actress (Roberts); Golden Globes '01: Actress—Drama (Roberts); L.A. Film Critics '00: Actress (Roberts), Director (Soderbergh); Natl. Bd. of Review '00: Actress (Roberts), Director (Soderbergh); N.Y. Film Critics '00: Director (Soderbergh); Natl. Soc. Film Critics '00: Director (Soderbergh); Screen Actors Guild '00: Actress (Roberts), Support. Actor (Finney); Broadcast Film Critics '00: Actress (Roberts), Director (Soderbergh).

Ermo ⚲⚲ **1994** Hard-working noodle-maker Ermo (Alia) supports her slothful husband, Chief (Zhijun), and their son in their northern China village. Her smitten truck-driver neighbor Blindman (Peiqi) has an equally unpleasant wife, Fat Woman (Haiyan), with whom Ermo has an ongoing rivalry. They own a color TV (the only one in the village) and Ermo becomes determined to get a bigger and better set by selling her noodles in a nearby town and compulsively saving her money. Of course, her entrepreneurship has some unexpected consequences. Mandarin Chinese with subtitles. **93m/C VHS.** *CH* Alia, Peiqi Liu, Ge Zhijun, Zhang Haiyan; ***D:*** Xiaowen Zhou; ***W:*** Lang Yun; ***C:*** Lu Gengxin; ***M:*** Xiaowen Zhou.

Ernest Goes to Africa ⚲ ½ **1997 (PG)** Ernest P. Worrel (Varney) finds himself in a heap 'o trouble when he's accused of buying some stolen diamonds and he and would-be girlfriend Renee are kidnapped and taken to Africa where a prince wants his property returned. Lots of sight gags and low humor. **90m/C VHS, DVD.** Jim Varney, Linda Kash, Jamie Bartlett; ***D:*** John R. Cherry III; ***W:*** John R. Cherry III; ***C:*** James Robb.

Ernest Goes to Camp ⚲ ½ **1987 (PG)** Screwball, slapstick summer camp farce starring the character Ernest P. Worrell as an inept camp counselor. When progress threatens the camp, Ernest leads the boys on a turtle-bombing, slop-shooting attack on the construction company. Followed by "Ernest Saves Christmas" and "Ernest Goes to Jail." **92m/C VHS, DVD.** Richard Speight Jr., Jim Varney, Victoria Racimo, John Vernon, Iron Eyes Cody, Lyle Alzado, Gailard Sartain, Daniel Butler, Hakeem Abdul-Samad; ***D:*** John R. Cherry III; ***W:*** John R. Cherry III.

Ernest Goes to Jail ⚲⚲ **1990 (PG)** The infamous loon Ernest P. Worrell winds up in the jury box and the courtroom will never be the same again. Jury duty suddenly becomes hard-time in the slammer for poor Ernest when he is mistaken for a big-wig organized crime boss. Sequel to "Ernest Goes to Camp" and "Ernest Saves Christmas." **81m/C VHS, DVD.** Jim Varney, Gailard Sartain, Randall "Tex" Cobb, Bill Byrge, Barry Scott, Charles Napier; ***D:*** John R. Cherry III; ***W:*** Charlie Cohen; ***M:*** Bruce Arntson.

Ernest Goes to School ⚲⚲ ½ **1994 (PG)** Ernest must finish high school if he wants to keep his job as school janitor. He's "aided" by two crazy science teachers who give him an experimental IQ booster. **89m/C VHS.** Jim Varney, Linda Kash, Bill Byrge; ***D:*** Coke Sams.

The Ernest Green Story ⚲⚲ ½ **1993** Drama based on the integration of Central High in Little Rock, Arkansas, by nine black students in 1957. Green was the only senior in the group and the movie follows a year of verbal and physical abuse, vandalism, and unfair academic treatment, as he struggles to withstand every difficulty in order to graduate. **92m/C VHS.** Sonny Shroyer, Morris Chestnut, CCH Pounder, Gary Grubbs, Tina Lifford, Avery Brooks, Ruby Dee, Ossie Davis; ***D:*** Eric Laneuville. **CABLE**

Ernest in the Army ⚲ ½ **1997 (PG)** Ernest is talked into joining the Army reserves and promptly causes all sorts of trouble when he's assigned to drive various military vehicles. **85m/C VHS, DVD.** Jim Varney, Hayley Tyson, David Muller, Ivan Lucas, Robert Foster; ***D:*** John R. Cherry III; ***W:*** Jeffrey Pillars; ***C:*** James Robb; ***M:*** Mark Adler.

Ernest Rides Again ⚲⚲ ½ **1993 (PG)** Ernest P. "Knowwhutlmean?" Worrell (Varney) is back, aiding a college professor friend who has a cockamamie theory that the British crown jewels were hidden in a Revolutionary War cannon. Naturally he's right and Ernest must battle British spies and a greedy antiquities collector to get the gems back. Goofy slapstick sticks to the formula of the other films. **93m/C VHS.** Jim Varney, Ron James, Duke Ernsberger, Jeffrey Pillars, Linda Kash, Tom Butler; ***D:*** John R. Cherry III; ***W:*** John R. Cherry III, William M. Akers; ***M:*** Bruce Arntson, Kirby Shelstad.

Ernest Saves Christmas ⚲ ½ **1988 (PG)** Ernest P. Worrell is back. When Santa decides that it's time to retire, Ernest must help him recruit a has-been children's show host who is a bit reluctant. For Ernest fans only, and only the most dedicated of those. Second in the series featuring the nimble-faced Varney, the first of which was "Ernest Goes to Camp," followed by "Ernest Goes to Jail." **91m/C VHS, DVD.** Jim Varney, Douglas Seale, Oliver Clark, Noelle Parker, Billie Bird; ***D:*** John R. Cherry III.

Ernest Scared Stupid 1/2 **1991 (PG)** Pea-brained Ernest P. Worrell returns yet again in this silly comedy. When he accidentally releases a demon from a sacred tomb a 200-year-old curse threatens to destroy his hometown, unless Ernest can come to the rescue. Would you want your town depending on Ernest's heroics? Who would have thought that the annoying Ernest P. Worrell could appear in one movie, let alone four? **93m/C VHS, DVD.** Jim Varney, Eartha Kitt, Austin Nagler, Jonas Moscartolo, Shay Astar; ***D:*** John R. Cherry III; ***W:*** John R. Cherry III; ***C:*** Hanania Baer; ***M:*** Bruce Arntson.

Ernesto 1/2 **1979** A lushly erotic Italian film depicting the troubled relationship between a young, devil-may-care gay youth and his older, coolly seducing lover. In Italian with subtitles. **98m/C VHS.** *IT* Martin Halm, Michele Placido; ***D:*** Salvatore Samperi.

Ernie Kovacs: Between the Laughter **1984** The television comic's life and career, ending with his tragic death in a car accident in 1962. Shows the brand of humor that made Kovacs famous as well as the devastation that he suffered after the tragic kidnapping of his children by his first wife during divorce proceedings. Kovac's second wife, Edie Adams, makes a brief appearance. **95m/C VHS.** Jeff Goldblum, Cloris Leachman, Melody Anderson, Madolyn Smith, John Glover; ***Cameos:*** Edie Adams; ***D:*** Lamont Johnson; ***M:*** Ralph Burns. **TV**

Eros 1/2 **2004 (R)** Three short films by renowned directors intended to convey their own interpretation of eroticism. Whether or not they're actually intended to be erotic is yet to be determined. Wong Kar-Wai's "The Hand" nails it. There's no nudity, no explicit sex, nothing to tell you what to feel. But it's poetic and stays with you. Steven Soderbergh's "Equilibrium" stars Robert Downey, Jr. as a patient explaining his sexually-obscure dream to psychiatrist Alan Arkin over and over and over. The doc doesn't listen much. Neither do we. Finally, director Michelangelo Antonioni closes the program with a real stinker. His Zabriskien roots place the characters in a land of causal nudity and dopey music. Trilogies need to get better with each installment, but this one rolls downhill the entire way. **104m/C DVD.** *US FR IT LU* Gong Li, Chang Chen, Tin Fung, Zhou Jianjun, Robert Downey Jr., Alan Arkin, Ele Keats, Christopher Buchholz, Regina Nemni, Luisa Ranieri; ***D:*** Wong Kar-Wai, Steven Soderbergh, Michelangelo Antonioni; ***W:*** Wong Kar-Wai, Steven Soderbergh, Michelangelo Antonioni; ***C:*** Tonino Guerra, Christopher Doyle, Marco Pontecorvo; ***M:*** Peer Raben, Enrica Antonioni, Vinicio Milani, Chico O'Farrill.

Erotic Escape *Les Bananes Mecaniques; Mechanical Bananas* **1972** Soft-core fun about party girls taking over a small French town. Originally in French, but dubbed in English. Check your brain at the door. **86m/C VHS.** *FR* Marie-Claire Davy, Pauline Larrieu, Anne Libert; ***D:*** Jean-Francois Davy; ***C:*** Roger Fellous; ***M:*** Raymond Ruer.

Erotic House of Wax 1/2 **1997** Young woman inherits her uncle's bizarre wax museum upon his death and discovers that the museum's inhabitants have this habit of coming to life and acting out their sexual fantasies. **90m/C VHS.** Jacqueline Lovell, Josie Hunter; ***D:*** Cybil (Sybil) Richards.

Erotic Images WOOF! 1985 (R) A beautiful psychology teacher publishes her doctoral thesis on sex and becomes a best-selling author, which threatens her marriage. **93m/C VHS.** Britt Ekland, Edd Byrnes, John McCann; ***D:*** Declan Langan.

Erotic Touch of Hot Skin **1965** Sex, murder, false identities, car crashes, and striptease in the Riviera. **78m/B VHS.** Fabienne Dali, Sophie Hardy, Jean Valmont, Francois Dryek; ***D:*** Max Pecas.

Erotique **1994** Sex quartet from female filmmakers. "Let's Talk About Sex" finds struggling Latina actress Rosie (Lopez-Dawson) supporting herself by working at a phone sex agency where a caller (Cranston) wants to know about her sexual fantasies. "Taboo Parlor" finds lesbian lovers Claire (Barnes) and Julia (Soeberg) picking up boy toy Victor (Carr) and planning some s/m games. "Wonton Soup" has Australian-born Chinese Adrian (Lounibos) reuniting with his lover Ann (Man) in Hong Kong and deciding to hold her interest by practicing some ancient Chinese sexual techniques. And in "Final Call," a school teacher (Ohana) tries a sexual adventure with a stranger. **120m/C VHS, DVD.** Kamala Lopez, Bryan Cranston, Priscilla Barnes, Camilla Soeberg, Michael Carr, Tim Lounibos, Hayley Man, Claudia Ohana; ***D:*** Lizzie Borden, Monika Treut, Clara Law, Ana Maria Magalhaes; ***W:*** Lizzie Borden, Monika Treut, Susie Bright, Eddie Ling-Ching Fong; ***C:*** Larry Banks, Elfi Mikesch, Arthur Wong Ngok Tai.

The Errand Boy 1/2 **1961** Jerry Lewis' patented babbling schnook hits Hollywood in search of a job. When he lands a position as an errand boy, Hollywood may never be the same again in this prototypical comedy; a must for Lewis fans only. **92m/B VHS, DVD.** Jerry Lewis, Brian Donlevy, Dick Wesson, Howard McNear, Felicia Atkins, Fritz Feld, Sig Rumann, Renee Taylor, Doodles Weaver, Mike Mazurki, Lorne Greene, Michael Landon, Dan Blocker, Pernell Roberts, Snub Pollard, Kathleen Freeman; ***D:*** Jerry Lewis; ***W:*** Jerry Lewis.

The Errors of Youth *Wild Oats* **1978** Dimitri (Zhdanko), a construction worker in Siberia, is disillusioned over a failed love affair and moves to Leningrad where he falls in with black marketeers and a marriage of convenience. Because of political problems, director Frumin left the film unfinished when he emigrated to the U.S. and it wasn't until 1989 that he returned to Leningrad to complete the project. Russian with subtitles. **87m/C VHS.** *RU* Stanislav Zhdanko, Marina Neyolova, Natalia Varley, Mikhail Vaskov; ***D:*** Boris Frumin.

Erskinville Kings 1/2 **1999** The plot borders on the cliched but White's debut feature has strong performances to carry it along. It's summer in a grimy Sydney suburb filled with run-down stores, bars, and neglected houses. Barky (screenwriter Chooney acting under the pseudonym Martin Denniss) is returning home after two years for his drunken, abusive father's funeral. He's hoping to have some kind of reconciliation with his brother Wace (Jackman) but Wace's bitterness may prevent that. **85m/C VHS.** *AU* Anik (Martin Denniss) Chooney, Hugh Jackman, Leah Vandenberg, Aaron Blabey, Andrew Wholley, Joel Edgerton; ***D:*** Alan White; ***W:*** Anik (Martin Denniss) Chooney; ***C:*** John Swaffield; ***M:*** Don Miller-Robinson.

Escanaba in da Moonlight **2001 (PG-13)** If you're not a "Yooper" or familiar with those denizens of Michigan's Upper Penisula, Daniels's film (based on his play) will probably be lost on you. This is the kind of local humor that rarely travels well. The story is basically a tall tale—middleaged Reuben Soady (Daniels) has reached his advanced years without ever having bagged a deer on his annual hunting trip with his dad (Presnell) and brother (Albright). He is a community laughingstock but that is about to change. **90m/C VHS, DVD.** *US* Jeff Daniels, Harve Presnell, Joey Albright, Wayne David Parker, Randall Goodwin, Kimberly Norris Guerrero; ***D:*** Jeff Daniels; ***W:*** Jeff Daniels; ***C:*** Richard Brawer.

Escapade **1955** Sons thinking their parents are en route to divorce court create a scheme to achieve peace worldwide. The pacifist father's reaction juxtaposes idealistic youth with the cynicism of adulthood. Adapted from a play by Roger MacDougall. **87m/B VHS.** *GB* John Mills, Yvonne Mitchell, Alastair Sim, Jeremy Spenser, Andrew Ray, Marie Lohr, Peter Asher; ***D:*** Philip Leacock; ***W:*** Donald Ogden Stewart.

Escapade in Florence **1962** As two students in Florence paint their way to immortality, an elaborate art-forging ring preys upon their talents. **81m/C VHS.** Tommy Kirk, Ivan Desny; ***D:*** Steve Previn.

Escapade in Japan **1957** A Japanese youth helps an American boy frantically search the city of Tokyo for his parents. Shot in Japan. **93m/C VHS.** Cameron Mitchell, Teresa Wright, Jon(athan) Provost, Roger Nakagawa, Philip Ober, Clint Eastwood; ***D:*** Arthur Lubin; ***M:*** Max Steiner.

Escape 1/2 **1990 (R)** A woman attempts to track down her brother's killer and finds an entire town mysteriously controlled by a sadistic and powerful man. Features General Hospital's bad-boy Shriner. **100m/C VHS.** Elizabeth Jeager, Kim Richards, Kin Shriner; ***D:*** Richard Styles.

Escape **1990 (PG)** A fun-loving, care-free Irish officer is sent to oversee the toughest POW prison in Scotland. There, he becomes consumed with keeping the facility secure despite the intricate escape plans laid out by a group of rioters. **90m/C VHS.** Brian Keith, Helmut Griem; ***D:*** Lamont Johnson.

The Escape 1/2 **1995** Prisoner Clayton (Dempsey) manages to escape incarceration and is then on the lam from sadistic prison guard, Hickman (Feore). Moody flashbacks show his crime, while in the present Clayton finds some sexual solace with the accommodating Sarah (Bako) as he tries to outwit his pursuers. **91m/C VHS.** Patrick Dempsey, Brigitte Bako, Colm Feore, Vincent Gale, Nathaniel DeVeaux, William Morgan Sheppard; ***D:*** Stuart Gillard; ***W:*** Scott Busby; ***C:*** Tobias Schliessler; ***M:*** Loek Dikker. **VIDEO**

The Escape Artist **1982 (PG)** Award-winning cinematographer Deschanel's first directorial effort is this quirky film about a teenage escape artist who sets out to uncover the identity of his father's killers. **96m/C VHS, DVD.** Griffin O'Neal, Raul Julia, Teri Garr, Joan Hackett, Desi Arnaz Sr., Gabriel Dell, Huntz Hall, Jackie Coogan, Elizabeth (E.G. Dailey) Daily; ***D:*** Caleb Deschanel; ***W:*** Melissa Mathison; ***C:*** Stephen Burum; ***M:*** Georges Delerue.

Escape Clause **1996 (R)** Insurance exec Richard Ramsay (McCarthy) gets a call from a hitman informing him that his wife Sarah (McNeil) has hired him to kill Richard. The hitman says if Richard will pay him, the contract's off. Instead Richard tries to figure out what's going on, with some help from police detective Ferrand (Sorvino), who discovers Richard has been treated for paranoid delusions. Fast-paced mystery with a few too many twists. **131m/C VHS.** Andrew McCarthy, Paul Sorvino, Kate McNeil, Peter Donaldson, Kenneth Welsh, Connie Britton, Stan(ford) Egi, John Evans; ***D:*** Brian Trenchard-Smith; ***W:*** Danilo Bach; ***M:*** Ken Thorne, Richard (Rick) Marvin. **VIDEO**

Escape from Alcatraz **1979 (PG)** A fascinating account of the one and only successful escape from the maximum security prison at Alcatraz in 1962. The three men were never heard from again. **112m/C VHS, DVD.** Clint Eastwood, Patrick McGoohan, Roberts Blossom, Fred Ward, Jack Thibeau, Paul Benjamin, Larry Hankin, Carl Lumbly, Danny Glover; ***D:*** Donald Siegel; ***W:*** Richard Tuggle; ***C:*** Bruce Surtees; ***M:*** Jerry Fielding.

Escape from Atlantis 1/2 **1997 (PG-13)** Workaholic attorney and single dad, Matt Spencer (Speakman), charters a sailboat and plans a cruise to the Bahamas so he and his three teenagers can have some quality time. The sailboat heads into the Bermuda Triangle and capsizes in a hurricane; when the Spencers come to, they're in the land of Atlantis, where fantasy is reality. **93m/C VHS.** Jeff Speakman, Brian Bloom, Tim Thomerson, Mercedes McNab, Michael Lee Goggin, Justin Burnette, Breck Wilson; ***D:*** Strathford Hamilton; ***W:*** Arne Olsen.

Escape from Cell Block 3 *Women Unchained* **1974** Five escaped female convicts take it on the lam for Mexico and freedom. **82m/C VHS.** Carolyn Judd, Teri Guzman, Bonita Kalem; ***D:*** Ken Osborne; ***W:*** Ken Osborne; ***C:*** Clancy B. Grass III; ***M:*** Hank Webster.

Escape from Death Row *Dio, Sei Proprio un Padreterno!* **1973 (R)** Convicted criminal mastermind, sentenced to die, devises a brilliant and daring plan of escape on the eve of his execution. **85m/C VHS, DVD.** *IT* Lee Van Cleef, Jean Rochefort, Tony LoBianco, Edwige Fenech, Fausto Tozzi, Mario Erpichini, Jess Hahn; ***D:*** Michele Lupo; ***W:*** Nicola Badalucco, Sergio Donati, Luciano Vincenzoni; ***C:*** Joe D'Amato, Aldo Tonti; ***M:*** Riz Ortolani.

Escape from DS-3 **1981** Bostwick and "Police Academy" alumnus Smith team up in a familiar story: framed for a serious crime, a man attempts to escape from a maximum security satellite prison. About as good as you'd expect. **88m/C VHS.** Jackson Bostwick, Bubba Smith; ***D:*** Bob Emenegger; ***W:*** Peter Dawson.

Escape from El Diablo **1983 (PG)** Two juvenile delinquents harass guards at a Mexican prison. Being from California, they use frisbees and skateboards to help their escape. **92m/C VHS.** *SP GB* Jimmy (James Vincent) McNichol, Timothy Van Patten, John Ethan Wayne; ***D:*** Gordon Hessler.

Escape from Fort Bravo 1/2 **1953** A Civil War era western set in an Arizona stockade. Holden is the hard-bitten Union cavalry officer who ruthlessly guards his Confederate prisoners, who are led by Forsythe. Parker is a southern spy whose job is to break the rebels out of jail by seducing Holden from his duty, which she does. When Holden discovers what's happened, he recaptures his prisoners only to be beset by hostile Mescalero Indians while trying to get everyone back to the fort. It's an old story but well-executed with lots of action. **98m/C VHS.** William Holden, Eleanor Parker, John Forsythe, William Demarest, William Campbell, Polly Bergen, Richard Anderson, Carl Benton Reid, John Lupton, Howard McNear, Alex Montoya, Forrest Lewis, Fred Graham, William "Billy" Newell; ***D:*** John Sturges; ***W:*** Frank Fenton; ***C:*** Robert L. Surtees.

Escape from Galaxy Three **1981 (G)** A pair of space travelers fight off a bevy of evil aliens. **90m/C VHS.** *IT* James Milton, Cheryl Buchanan; ***D:*** Bitto Albertini; ***W:*** John Thomas; ***C:*** Sandro Mancori; ***M:*** Don Powell.

Escape from Hell WOOF! *Hellfire on Ice, Part 2: Escape from Hell; Femmine Infernali* **1979** Two scantily clad women escape from a jungle prison and are pursued by their sadistic warden. **93m/C VHS, DVD.** *IT SP* Anthony Steffen, Ajita Wilson; ***D:*** Edward (Edoardo Mulargia) Muller.

Escape from L.A. 1/2 *John Carpenter's Escape from L.A* **1996 (R)** Well, Snake Plissken is back (Russell once again) and so's Carpenter, who did the original "Escape from New York" saga, and technology's advanced a lot in 15 years, so sit back and enjoy the action. In 2013, L.A.'s been turned into a gang-infested island, thanks to a 9.6 earthquake, where Snake is forced to find a doomsday weapon in just 10 hours. Seems he's been injected with a virus that will kill him unless he can complete his job and escape to get the antidote. Naturally, there's lots of bad guys who'll try to stop him. Russell not only reprises his old role but found Snake's original leathers, which still fit, and wore the outfit in some scenes of the sequel. **101m/C VHS, DVD.** Kurt Russell, Georges Corraface, Stacy Keach, Peter Fonda, Steve Buscemi, Pam Grier, Valeria Golino, Cliff Robertson, Michelle Forbes, Bruce Campbell, A.J. (Allison Joy) Langer; ***D:*** John Carpenter; ***W:*** Kurt Russell, John Carpenter, Debra Hill; ***C:*** Gary B. Kibbe; ***M:*** John Carpenter, Shirley Walker.

Escape from Mars **1999 (PG)** Astronauts make the first manned trip to Mars in the 21st century and must battle any number of internal and external problems to survive. **90m/C VHS.** *CA* Christine Elise, Peter Outerbridge, Allison Hossack, Michael Shanks; ***D:*** Neill Fearnley; ***W:*** Jim Henshaw; ***C:*** Peter Woeste; ***M:*** Peter Allen. **TV**

Escape from New York 1/2 **1981 (R)** The ultimate urban nightmare: a ruined, future Manhattan is an anarchic prison for America's worst felons. When convicts hold the President hostage, a disgraced war hero unwillingly attempts an impossible rescue mission. Cynical but largely unexceptional sci-fi action, putting a good cast through tight-lipped peril. **99m/C VHS, DVD, UMD.** Kurt Russell, Lee Van Cleef, Ernest Borgnine, Donald Pleasence, Isaac Hayes, Adrienne Barbeau, Harry Dean Stanton, Season Hubley, Tom Atkins, Charles Cyphers, George "Buck" Flower; *D:* John Carpenter; *W:* John Carpenter, Nick Castle; *C:* Dean Cundey; *M:* John Carpenter; *V:* Jamie Lee Curtis.

Escape from Planet Earth *The Doomsday Machine* **1967** A spaceship is damaged deep in space and only a few of the crew can make it back to Earth. But who will decide who lives or dies? (Unfortunately, the Earth has been totally destroyed so who cares anyway.) Lousy special effects. **91m/B VHS, DVD.** Grant Williams, Bobby Van, Ruta Lee, Henry Wilcoxon, Mala Powers, Casey Kasem, Mike Farrell, Harry Hope; *D:* Lee Sholem.

Escape from Safehaven WOOF! 1988 (R) Brutal slimeballs rule a mad, sadistic world in the post-apocalyptic future, and a family tries to escape them. In very poor taste. **87m/C VHS.** Rick Gianasi, Mollie O'Mara, John Wittenbauer, Roy MacArthur, William Beckwith; *D:* Brian Thomas Jones, James McCalmont.

Escape from Sobibor 1987 (PG-13) Nail-biting, true account of the largest successful escape from a Nazi prison camp, adapted from Richard Rashke's book. Made for TV. **120m/C VHS, DVD.** Alan Arkin, Joanna Pacula, Rutger Hauer, Hartmut Becker, Jack Shepherd; *D:* Jack Gold; *M:* Georges Delerue. **TV**

Escape from the Bronx 1985 (R) Invading death squads seek to level the Bronx. Local street gangs cry foul and ally to defeat the uncultured barbarians. Sequel to "1990: The Bronx Warriors." **82m/C VHS.** Mark Gregory, Henry Silva, Valeria (Valerie Dobson) D'Obici, Giancarlo Prete, Andrea Coppola; *D:* Enzo G. Castellari.

Escape from the KGB WOOF! 1987 A CIA agent escapes from a Soviet prison, taking plans for a new space installation with him. **99m/C VHS.** Thomas Hunter, Ivan Desny, Marie Versini, Walter Barns; *D:* Harald Phillipe.

Escape from the Planet of the Apes 1971 (G) Reprising their roles as intelligent, English-speaking apes, McDowall and Hunter flee their world before it's destroyed, and travel back in time to present-day America. In L.A. they become the subjects of a relentless search by the fearful population, much like humans Charlton Heston and James Franciscus were targeted for experimentation and destruction in simian society in the earlier "Planet of the Apes" and "Beneath the Planet of the Apes." Sequelled by "Conquest of..." and a TV series. **98m/C VHS, DVD.** Roddy McDowall, Kim Hunter, Sal Mineo, Ricardo Montalban, William Windom, Bradford Dillman, Natalie Trundy, Eric (Hans Gudegast) Braeden, Jason Evers, Harry Lauter, John Randolph, M. Emmet Walsh; *D:* Don Taylor; *W:* Paul Dehn; *C:* Joseph Biroc; *M:* Jerry Goldsmith.

Escape from Wildcat Canyon 1/2 1999 Grandfather Weaver and his young grandson must fight for survival after their small plane crashes in the mountains. **96m/C VHS, DVD.** Dennis Weaver, Michael Caloz, Peter Keleghan, Frank Schorpion, Vlasta Vrana; *D:* Marc Voizard. **CABLE**

Escape: Human Cargo *Human Cargo* **1998** Suspenseful and fact-based drama set in 1977. Texan John McDonald (Williams) thinks he's scored big when he gets a contract to build housing in Dhahran, Saudi Arabia. Despite government warnings, McDonald decides to travel there himself to oversee the deal. But his partners prove deceitful and when McDonald tries to enforce the contract, he's the one that winds up in prison. He's eventually released, but with his passport confiscated, the only way for McDonald to get out of the Middle East is to try smuggling himself home as cargo. Based on the book "Flight from Dhahran" by John McDonald and Clyde Burleson. **110m/C VHS, DVD.** Treat Williams, Stephen Lang, Sasson Gabai; *D:* Simon Wincer; *W:* William Mickelberry, Dan Vining; *C:* David Burr; *M:* Eric Colvin. **CABLE**

Escape Me Never 1/2 1947 Flynn plays a struggling composer in this sappy period piece about poverty-stricken artists in Italy at the turn of the century. Flynn falls for his brother's wealthy fiancee (Parker), although he is married to the faithful Lupino. Atypical role for Flynn and definitely not one of his best. Based on the novel "The Fool of the Family," by Margaret Kennedy and the play "Escape Me Never" by Kennedy. **101m/B VHS.** Errol Flynn, Ida Lupino, Eleanor Parker, Gig Young, Reginald Denny, Isobel Elsom; *D:* Peter Godfrey; *W:* Thomas Williamson.

Escape to Athena 1/2 1979 (PG) A motley group is stuck in a German P.O.W. camp on a Greek island during WWII. **102m/C VHS.** *GB* Roger Moore, Telly Savalas, David Niven, Claudia Cardinale, Richard Roundtree, Stefanie Powers, Sonny Bono, Elliott Gould, William Holden; *D:* George P. Cosmatos; *W:* Edward Anhalt; *M:* Lalo Schifrin.

Escape to Burma 1/2 1955 A man on the run for a murder he did not commit finds refuge and romance in an isolated jungle home. **86m/C VHS, DVD.** Barbara Stanwyck, Robert Ryan, Reginald Denny; *D:* Allan Dwan.

Escape to Love 1/2 1982 Beautiful student helps a famous dissident escape from Poland, only to lose him to another heroic venture. **105m/C** Clara Perryman, Louis Jourdan; *D:* Herbert Stein.

Escape to Paradise 1/2 1939 The last of Breen's films for RKO has him as a South American motorcycle-taxi driver acting as a guide for tourist Taylor. When Breen sets Taylor up with Shelton, trouble ensues. ♫ Tra-La-La; Rhythm of the Rio; Ay, Ay, Ay. **60m/B VHS.** Bobby Breen, Kent Taylor, Marla Shelton, Joyce Compton, Rosina Galli, Frank Yaconelli; *D:* Erle C. Kenton.

Escape to the Sun 1/2 *Habricha el Hashemesh* **1972 (PG)** Pair of Russian university students plan to flee their homeland so they can be allowed to live and love free from oppression. **94m/C VHS.** *IS* Laurence Harvey, Josephine Chaplin, John Ireland, Jack Hawkins, Lila Kedrova, Clive Revill; *D:* Menahem Golan.

Escape to Witch Mountain 1975 (G) Two young orphans with supernatural powers find themselves on the run from a greedy millionaire who wants to exploit their amazing gift. Adapted from a novel by Alexander Key. **97m/C VHS, DVD.** Kim Richards, Ike Eisenmann, Eddie Albert, Ray Milland, Donald Pleasence, Tony Giorgio, Walter Barnes, Denver Pyle, Reta Shaw; *D:* John Hough.

Escape 2000 WOOF! *Turkey Shoot* **1981 (R)** In a future society where individuality is considered a crime, those who refuse to conform are punished by being hunted down in a jungle. Gross, twisted takeoff of Richard Connell's "The Most Dangerous Game." **80m/C VHS, DVD.** *AU* Steve Railsback, Olivia Hussey, Michael Craig; *D:* Brian Trenchard-Smith; *W:* George Schenck; *M:* Brian May.

Escape under Pressure 1/2 2000 (R) Cheapie version of "Die Hard" holds interest thanks to lots of action. Engineer John Spencer (Lowe) and wife Chloe (Miller) are aboard a Greek ferry that get hijacked by lowlifes who are after a priceless ancient statue of Artemis. They manage to protect the statue but have to save themselves as well from the killers. **90m/C VHS, DVD.** Rob Lowe, Larisa Miller, Craig Wasson, Harry Van Gorkum, Stanley Kamel; *D:* Jean Pellerin; *W:* James Christopher; *C:* Richard Clabaugh. **CABLE**

Escape Velocity 1999 (R) Scientists Cal (Bergin), Billie (Crewson) and their daughter Ronnie (Beaudoin) are on a deep space project when they discover a seemingly abandoned space ship. They find one crewman, Nash (Outerbridge), in suspended animation and make the mistake of bringing him out of his deep sleep. Of course, he turns out to be a psychotic. **100m/C VHS, DVD.** Patrick Bergin, Wendy Crewson, Peter Outerbridge, Michelle Beaudoin; *D:* Lloyd A. Simandl; *M:* Peter Allen. **VIDEO**

Escapes 1986 In the tradition of "The Twilight Zone," Vincent Price introduces five short thrillers featuring time travel, aliens, and telepathy. Produced with computer assistance for sharper, more contrasted images. **72m/C VHS.** Vincent Price, Jerry Grisham, Lee Canfield, John Mitchum, Gil Reade; *D:* David Steensland.

Escapist WOOF! 1983 A professional escape artist becomes involved in a perverted corporate plot and must escape to save his life and livelihood. **87m/C VHS.** Bill Shirk, Peter Lupus; *D:* Eddie Beverly Jr.

The Escort 1997 (R) Debra Grey (Hall) runs a highly successful (and respectable) escort service and has just hired the charming Suzanne Lane (O'Brien). But behind Suzanne's charm lies the dreaded face of a psycho and she takes a very personal interest in Debra and her family. The unrated version is 90 minutes. **85m/C VHS.** Shauna O'Brien, Landon Hall; *D:* Gary Graver; *W:* Sean O'Bannon; *C:* Gary Graver. **VIDEO**

ESL: English as a Second Language 1/2 2005 (R) Bad title, good movie. Bolivar (Becker) is an illegal Mexican immigrant who comes to L.A. looking for work and winds up with a job as a stripper because the money is good and he has a pregnant wife back home. Bolivar's struggles are contrasted with those of privileged party girl Lola (Camastra), who has to do community service after a DUI conviction. She signs up to teach an ESL class where Bolivar is a student and, for all their differences in wealth and class, they have similar problems with identity, responsibility, and what makes the American Dream. English and Spanish with subtitles. **105m/C DVD.** Kuno Becker, Danielle Camastra, Maria Conchita Alonso, John Michael Higgins, Sal Lopez, Efrain Figueroa, Harold Gould, Treva Etienne; *D:* Youssef Delara; *W:* Youssef Delara; *C:* Ben Kufrin; *M:* Gary Chang.

Esmeralda Comes by Night 1/2 *De Noche Vienes, Esmeralda* **1998 (R)** Fluff Mexican comedy about a very nuturing nurse named Esmeralda (Rojo) who just loves men so much that she's married to five of them—at the same time. When she decides to take a sixth spouse, that's one man too many for one of her jealous hubbies and he formally accuses her of polyandry. She gets arrested and must explain herself to a grim inspector (Obregon), who will naturally fall under her considerable spell. Based on a story by Elena Poniatowska. Spanish with subtitles. **107m/C VHS.** *MX* Maria Rojo, Claudio Obregon, Roberto Cobo, Ernesto Laguardia, Humberto Pineda, Pedro Armendariz Jr., Alberto Estrella; *D:* Jaime Humberto Hermosillo; *W:* Jaime Humberto Hermosillo; *C:* Xavier Perez Grobet; *M:* Omar Guzman.

E.S.P. 1983 A young man is given the amazing power of extra-sensory perception. **96m/C VHS.** Jim Stafford, George Deaton; *D:* Julian Cole.

Espionage in Tangiers 1/2 *Marc Mato, Agent S.077* **1965** Bond rip-off with Davila as super-spy Mike Murphy, who's assigned to find a ray gun stolen from a lab. From there it's all gadgets, cars, villains, and babes (who get slapped around when they don't cooperate). Attractive settings in Nice and Tangiers; dubbed. Available as a Drive-In Double Feature with "Assassination in Rome." **92m/C DVD.** *IT SP* Luis Davila, Perla Cristal, Jose Greci, Ana Castor, Alfonso Rojas; *D:* Gregg Tallas; *W:* Gregg Tallas; *C:* Alvaro Mancori.

Essex Boys 1999 (R) British gangster movie inspired by the true-crime 1995 murders of three criminals. Ambitious young Billy (Creed-Miles) is hired to chauffeur violent Jason Locke (Bean), who's just out of prison. Jason partnered with John Dyke (Wilkinson) in the drug trade but times have changed and double-crosses are the new name of the game. Billy gets sucked in and betrayed, but beware, because the female (Kingston) does turn out to be deadlier than the male. **102m/C VHS, DVD.** *GB* Charlie Creed-Miles, Sean Bean, Tom Wilkinson, Alex Kingston, Larry Lamb, Terence Rigby, Billy Murray, Amelia Lowdell; *D:* Terry Winsor; *W:* Terry Winsor, Jeff Pope; *C:* John Daly; *M:* Colin Towns.

Estate of Insanity *The Black Torrent* **1964** An English lord and his second wife become involved in a web of death when a maniac stalks their ancient estate. **90m/C VHS, DVD.** *GB* John Turner, Heather Sears, Ann Lynn; *D:* Robert Hartford-Davis; *W:* Derek Ford, Donald Ford; *C:* Peter Newbrook; *M:* Robert Richards.

Esther 1/2 1998 Biblical story of a young Jewish girl named Esther who is sought as the bride of Ahasuerus, the King of Persia. She persuades him to stop the slaughter of her people. **91m/C VHS, DVD.** Louise Lombard, Thomas Kretschmann, F. Murray Abraham, Jurgen Prochnow, Ornella Muti; *D:* Raffaele Mertes. **CABLE**

Esther and the King 1/2 1960 Biblical costumer with Egan as Persian king and Collins as the Judean maiden he wants in place of the murdered queen. Long, rambling, and torturous. **109m/C VHS, DVD.** *IT* Joan Collins, Richard Egan, Denis O'Dea, Sergio Fantoni; *D:* Raoul Walsh; *W:* Raoul Walsh, Michael Elkins; *M:* Angelo Francesco Lavagnino.

Esther Kahn 2000 (PG) Esther (Phoenix) is growing up in the poor East End of London at the end of the 19th century—the daughter of a Jewish tailor. When Esther attends a Yiddish stage play, she decides that she must become an actress and approaches a local theatre for work. She is later taken under the wing of older actor Nathan (Holm), who advises her to take a lover for emotional experience. Esther gets involved with drama critic, Philip Haygard (Desplechin), is betrayed, but achieves a more-desired stage triumph. Adapted from a short story by Arthur Symons. **145m/C VHS, DVD.** *FR GB* Summer Phoenix, Ian Holm, Emmanuelle Devos, Fabrice Desplechin, Frances Barber, Laszlo Szabo; *D:* Arnaud Desplechin; *W:* Arnaud Desplechin, Emmanuel Bourdieu; *C:* Eric Gautier; *M:* Howard Shore.

E.T.: The Extra-Terrestrial 1982 (PG) Spielberg's famous fantasy, one of the most popular films in history, portrays a limpid-eyed alien stranded on earth and his special bonding relationship with a young boy. A modern fairy tale providing warmth, humor and sheer wonder. Held the first place spot as the highest grossing movie of all time for years until a new Spielberg hit replaced it—"Jurassic Park." Debra Winger contributed to the voice of E.T. **115m/C VHS, DVD.** Erika Eleniak, Henry Thomas, Dee Wallace, Drew Barrymore, Robert MacNaughton, Peter Coyote, C. Thomas Howell, Sean Frye, K.C. Martel; *D:* Steven Spielberg; *W:* Melissa Mathison; *C:* Allen Daviau; *M:* John Williams; *V:* Debra Winger. Oscars '82: Visual FX, Orig. Score; AFI '98: Top 100; Golden Globes '83: Film—Drama, Score; L.A. Film Critics '82: Director (Spielberg), Film, Natl. Film Reg. '94;; Natl. Soc. Film Critics '82: Director (Spielberg); Writers Guild '82: Orig. Screenplay.

The Eternal *The Eternal Kiss of the Mummy* **1999 (R)** Nora (Elliott) plays a young wife and mother who's tormented by blinding headaches and dizziness. Along with her husband and young son, she decides to return to her childhood home in Ireland to visit her ailing grandmother. But her symptoms worsen the closer she gets to her ancestral home, and Elliott discovers that her creepy uncle (Walken) has retrieved the body of a witch who died hundreds of years before. Only she's not quite dead. **95m/C VHS, DVD.** Alison Elliott, Jared Harris, Christopher Walken, Lois Smith, Karl Geary; *D:* Michael Almereyda; *W:* Michael Almereyda; *C:* Jim Denault; *M:* Simon Fisher Turner.

Eternal 2004 (R) Remarkably dull erotic vampire thriller (which only hints at kink). Detective Raymond Pope (Pla) is searching for his missing wife, which leads him to the Montreal estate of wealthy Elizabeth Kane (Neron) and her maid, Irina (Sanchez). Seems Elizabeth is actually 16th-century Countess Elizabeth Bathory, who kills and then bathes in the blood of young women to maintain her own beauty and immortality. Eventually, the obsessed Pope follows Elizabeth to a masked ball in Venice in order to stop the bloodletting. **107m/C DVD.** *CA* Conrad Pla, Caroline Neron, Victoria Sanchez, Liane Balaban, Sarah Manninen, Ilona Elkin, Nick Baillie; *D:* Wilhelm Liebenberg, Frederico Sanchez; *W:* Wilhelm Liebenberg, Frederico Sanchez; *C:* Jamie Thompson.

Eternal Evil 1987 (R) A bored TV director is taught how to have out-of-body experiences by his devil-worshipping girlfriend. He eventually realizes that when he leaves his body, it runs around killing people. **85m/C VHS, DVD.** Karen Black, Winston Rekert, Lois Maxwell; ***D:*** George Mihalka; ***W:*** Robert Geoffrion; ***C:*** Paul Van der Linden.

Eternal Return 1/2 *L'Eternel Retour; Love Eternal* **1943** A lush modern retelling of the Tristan/Isolde legend. Patrice (Marais) brings the beautiful Nathalie (Sologne) to his family's castle, as his uncle's (Murat) intended bride. But thanks to a love potion, it's Nathalie and Patrice who fall in love—with tragic results. In French with English subtitles. **111m/B VHS.** *FR* Jane (Jeanne) Marken, Alex(andre) Rignault, Roland Toutain, Yvonne de Bray, Jean Marais, Madeleine Sologne, Jean Murat; ***D:*** Jean Delannoy; ***W:*** Jean Cocteau; ***C:*** Roger Hubert; ***M:*** Georges Auric.

Eternal Sunshine of the Spotless Mind 1/2 **2004 (R)** Unhappy couple uses latest technology to try and vacuum their minds clean of each other and all associated memories in this black comedy. Carrey plays it mostly straight here as Joel, a lovesick sap who undergoes the memory-erasing procedure when he finds out his strident girlfriend Clementine (Winslet) had similar sci-fi style treatment to wipe him out of her trendy blue-streaked head. Carrey begins to have second thoughts, however, playing hide and seek with his memories of Clementine from the thoroughly unprofessional mind-erasing technicians (Ruffalo and Wood) who trash his apartment in the process. Clever story penned by Kaufman in his second venture with director Gondry. Leads earn their stellar salaries here, along with excellent supports, including Wood, Ruffalo, Wilkinson, and Dunst. **108m/C DVD, HD DVD.** *US* Jim Carrey, Kate Winslet, Elijah Wood, Mark Ruffalo, Thomas Jay Ryan, Jane Adams, David Cross, Kirsten Dunst, Tom Wilkinson, Ellen Pompeo, Paulie (Litowsky) Litt; ***D:*** Michel Gondry; ***W:*** Michel Gondry, Charlie Kaufman; ***C:*** Ellen Kuras; ***M:*** Jon Brion. Oscars '04: Orig. Screenplay; British Acad. '04: Film Editing, Orig. Screenplay; Writers Guild '04: Orig. Screenplay.

The Eternal Waltz *Ewiger Walzer* **1954** Overly sentimental chronicle of the life of composer Johann Strauss. Only director Verhoeven's touch holds the viewer's interest, though the production values are excellent. **97m/C VHS.** Bernhard Wicki, Hilde Krahl, Annemarie Duerringer, Friedl Loor, Eduard Strauss Jr., Gert Frobe, Arnulf Schroeder; ***D:*** Paul Verhoeven.

Eternally Yours 1/2 **1939** A witty magician's career threatens to break up his marriage. **95m/B VHS, DVD.** David Niven, Loretta Young, Hugh Herbert, Broderick Crawford, Sir C. Aubrey Smith, Billie Burke, Eve Arden, Zasu Pitts; ***D:*** Tay Garnett.

Eternity **1990 (R)** While trying to uncover corrupt corporate America, a TV reporter falls in love with a model who works for a media king and puts his credibility on the line. He believes he and the woman shared romance in a past life. **122m/C VHS.** Jon Voight, Armand Assante, Wilford Brimley, Eileen Davidson, Kaye Ballard, Lainie Kazan, Joey Villa, Steven Keats, Eugene Roche, Frankie Valli, John P. Ryan; ***D:*** Steven Paul.

Eternity and a Day *Mia Eoniotita Ke Mia Mera* **1997** Seriously ill writer Alexander (Ganz) is putting his affairs in order and revisiting his past, particularly moments with his beloved late wife, Anna (Renauld). But the present isn't finished with Alexander yet. He rescues a young boy (Skevis), an illegal immigrant from Albania, who says he was taken from his grandmother. Alexander decides to take the boy home and the two set out on the journey that will surely be Alexander's last. Greek with subtitles. **134m/C VHS, DVD.** *GR FR* Bruno Ganz, Isabelle Renauld, Achileas Skevis, Fabrizio Bentivoglio; ***D:*** Theo Angelopoulos; ***W:*** Theo Angelopoulos; ***C:*** Yorgos Arvanitis, Andreas Sinanos; ***M:*** Eleni Karaindrou. Cannes '98: Film.

Ethan 1/2 **1971** A missionary in the Philippines falls in love with a woman and exiles himself for his fall from grace. **91m/C VHS.** Robert Sampson, Rosa Rosal, Eddie Infante; ***D:*** Michael Du Pont.

Ethan Frome 1/2 **1992 (PG)** Neeson stars as the lonely, poverty-stricken 19th-century New England farmer who has long and faithfully cared for his bitter, invalid wife. When his wife's distant young cousin comes to take over as housekeeper they both succumb to their forbidden passion with tragic results. The performers carry the burden of the film's sluggish pacing, where the bleak setting of Massachusetts in winter tends to overwhelm the events. Based on the novel by Edith Wharton. **107m/C VHS, DVD.** Liam Neeson, Patricia Arquette, Joan Allen, Tate Donovan, Katharine Houghton, Stephen Mendillo; ***D:*** John Madden; ***W:*** Richard Nelson; ***C:*** Bobby Bukowski.

Eubie! **1982** The popular Broadway musical revue based on the life and songs of Eubie Blake is presented in a video transfer. Some of Eubie's best known songs, performed here by members of the original cast, include "I'm Just Wild About Harry," "Memories of You," "In Honeysuckle Time" and "The Charleston Rag." **100m/C VHS.** Gregory Hines, Maurice Hines, Leslie Dockery, Alaina Reed, Lynnie Godfrey, Mel Johnson Jr., Jeffrey V. Thompson; ***D:*** Julianne Boyd.

Eulogy 1/2 **2004 (R)** Unworkable ensemble black comedy that wastes its good cast. The dysfunctional Collins family is forced back together to bury their toxic family patriarch (Torn). Accommodating granddaughter Kate (Deschanel) is expected to deliver the eulogy but neither her brooding father (Azaria) nor his crude brother (Romano) or their neurotic sisters (Winger, Preston) have anything good to say. No wonder all the bickering is driving Grandma Charlotte (Laurie) to multiple suicide attempts. And yes, the contrivances extend to a not-unexpected surprise at the reading of the will. **91m/C VHS, DVD.** Hank Azaria, Jesse Bradford, Zooey Deschanel, Glenne Headly, Famke Janssen, Piper Laurie, Kelly Preston, Ray Romano, Rip Torn, Debra Winger, Curtis Garcia, Keith Garcia, Rene Auberjonois; ***D:*** Michael Clancy; ***W:*** Michael Clancy; ***C:*** Michael Chapman; ***M:*** Richard (Rick) Marvin.

Eureka! 1/2 **1981 (R)** A bizarre, wildly symbolic slab of Roegian artifice that deals with the dream-spliced life of a rich, bored gold tycoon who becomes tortured over his daughter's marriage and his own useless wealth. Eventually he is bothered by the Mafia and led to the courtroom by business competitors. From the book by Paul Mayersberg. **130m/C VHS, DVD.** *GB* Gene Hackman, Theresa Russell, Joe Pesci, Rutger Hauer, Mickey Rourke, Ed Lauter, Jane Lapotaire; ***D:*** Nicolas Roeg.

Eureka Stockade *Massacre Hill* **1949** Four early Australian gold prospectors join forces to fight their governor and the police for the rights to dig on the continent. **103m/B VHS.** *AU* Chips Rafferty, Peter Finch, Jane Barrett, Peter Illing; ***D:*** Harry Watt.

Europa, Europa 1/2 *Hitlerjunge Salomon* **1991 (R)** The incredible, harrowing and borderline-absurdist true story of Solomon Perel, a young Jew who escaped the Holocaust by passing for German at an elite, Nazi-run academy. Such a sharp evocation of the era that the modern German establishment wouldn't submit it for the Academy Awards. In German and Russian with English subtitles. **115m/C VHS, DVD.** *GE* Marco Hofschneider, Klaus Abramowsky, Michele Gleizer, Rene Hofschneider, Nathalie Schmidt, Delphine Forest, Julie Delpy; ***D:*** Agnieszka Holland; ***W:*** Agnieszka Holland; ***C:*** Jacek Petrycki, Jacek Zaleski; ***M:*** Zbigniew Preisner. Golden Globes '92: Foreign Film; Natl. Bd. of Review '91: Foreign Film; N.Y. Film Critics '91: Foreign Film.

Europa '51 1/2 *The Greatest Love* **1952** The despairing portrait of post-war malaise, as an American woman, whose son committed suicide, lives in Rome searching for some semblance of meaning, and ends up in an asylum. One of Bergman & Rossellini's least-loved films. In Italian with subtitles. **110m/B VHS.** Ingrid Bergman, Alexander Knox, Ettore Giannini, Giulietta Masina; ***D:*** Roberto Rossellini.

The Europeans **1979** Fine adaptation of Henry James's satiric novel. British brother and sister visit their staid American cousins in 19th-century New England in an effort to improve their prospects through fortuitous marriages. **90m/C VHS, DVD.** Lee Remick, Lisa Eichhorn, Robin Ellis, Wesley Addy, Tim Woodward; ***D:*** James Ivory; ***W:*** Ruth Prawer Jhabvala.

Eurotrip **2004 (R)** Straight-arrow Scotty, freshly dumped by his girlfriend, realizes his German pen-pal is not a man coming on to him over the internet but an insanely hot girl. What's a boy to do? Why, jet off to Europe with three friends to meet her, of course! Scott and Cooper (Pitts) get cheap tickets to England and plan to meet up with twins Jamie (Wester) and Jenny (Trachtenberg). At that point, the plot goes out the window as the movie descends into an endless string of insulting, laugh-free jokes about mimes, soccer hooligans, hookers, gay train passengers, and the Vatican. Recommended if you think bottom-of-the-barrel gags based on European stereotypes make a movie. Everyone else should avoid this Trip. **89m/C DVD.** *US* Scott Mechlowicz, Jacob Pitts, Michelle Trachtenberg, Travis Wester, Jessica Boehrs, Fred Armisen, Lucy Lawless, Vinnie Jones, Kristin Kreuk, Jeffrey Tambor, Matt Damon, Diedrich Bader, J.P. Manoux, Rade Serbedzija, Steve Hytner, Patrick Malahide, Joanna Lumley; ***D:*** Jeff Schaffer; ***W:*** Jeff Schaffer, Alec Berg, David Mandel; ***C:*** David Eggby; ***M:*** James L. Venable.

Eva 1/2 *Eva the Devil's Woman* **1962** Writer Tyvian (Baker) becomes obsessed with prostitute Eva (Moreau), spends all his money on her, leaves his fiancee Francesca (Lisi) for her, but all she does is taunt and abandon him. He marries Francesca but leaves his bride (who kills herself) for Eva, who discards him again, leaving Tyvian broke and betrayed. Based on the novel "Eve" by James Hadley Chase. **103m/B VHS, DVD.** *FR IT* Jeanne Moreau, Stanley Baker, Virna Lisi, James Villiers, Giorgio Albertazzi, Riccardo Garrone; ***D:*** Joseph Losey; ***W:*** Hugo Butler, Evan Jones; ***C:*** Gianni Di Venanzo; ***M:*** Michel Legrand.

Evan Almighty **2007 (PG)** Holy spinoff! Former TV anchor-turned-politician Evan (Carell) is about to give up his values and ruin the environment when God (Freeman, reprising his "Bruce Almighty" role) orders him to build an ark. Wife Joan (Graham) and his sons are doubtful, but eventually get on the boat. Smarmy blend of animal-based potty humor and tepid life-lessons about taking care of the environment and being nice fails to take advantage of Carell's talents. **95m/C DVD, Blu-ray Disc.** *US US* Steve Carell, Morgan Freeman, Lauren Graham, John Goodman, John Michael Higgins, Wanda Sykes, Jimmy Bennett, Johnny (John W.) Simmons, Jonah Hill, Ed Helms, Rachael Harris, Molly Shannon, Graham Phillips; ***D:*** Tom Shadyac; ***W:*** Steve Oedekerk, Josh Stolberg, Bob Florsheim; ***C:*** Ian Baker; ***M:*** John Debney.

Evangeline 1/2 **1929** Based on the Henry Wadsworth Longfellow poem about the struggles of Evangeline and the tragedy of lost love. Evangeline lives in an Acadian (with ties to France) village in Nova Scotia and is engaged to Gabriel. But when France and England declare war, the village sides with France and the men are forcibly deported to Louisiana. But Evangeline is determined to be reunited with her love. **90m/B VHS, DVD.** Dolores Del Rio, Roland (Walter Goss) Drew, Alec B. Francis, George F. Marion Sr., Donald Reed; ***D:*** Edwin Carewe; ***W:*** Finis Fox; ***C:*** Robert B. Kurrle; ***M:*** Hugo Riesenfeld, Philip Carli.

Eve of Destruction **WOOF! 1990 (R)** Hell knows no fury like a cutting-edge android-girl on the warpath. Modeled after her creator, Dr. Eve Simmons, Eve VII has android-babe good looks and a raging nuclear capability. Wouldn't you know, something goes haywire during her trial run, and debutante Eve turns into a PMS nightmare machine, blasting all the good Doctor's previous beaux. That's where military agent Hines comes in, though you wonder why. Dutch actress Soutendijk plays dual Eves in her first American film. **101m/C VHS, DVD.** Gregory Hines, Renee Soutendijk, Kurt Fuller, Ross Malinger, Eugene Robert Glazer, John M. Jackson, Loren Haynes, Michael Greene; ***D:*** Duncan Gibbins; ***W:*** Duncan Gibbins, Yale Udoff; ***C:*** Alan Hume.

Evel Knievel **1972 (PG)** The life of motorcycle stuntman Evel Knievel is depicted in this movie, as portrayed by George Hamilton. Stunts will be appreciated by Evel Knievel fans. **90m/C VHS, DVD.** George Hamilton, Bert Freed, Rod Cameron, Sue Lyon; ***D:*** Marvin J. Chomsky; ***W:*** John Milius; ***C:*** David M. Walsh; ***M:*** Patrick Williams.

Evelyn **2002 (PG)** Lovable but ale-soaked Desmond Doyle (Brosnan) is abandoned by his wife in 1953. At that time it was believed that a man couldn't care for his children alone, so the children are placed in a church orphanage. A barmaid (Margulies) takes pity on him and convinces him to sober up and seek legal counsel to regain custody. Beresford's straightforward classic style thankfully only alludes to the punishment the children faced rather than exploiting it, choosing instead to focus on the true story of the case against the Family Act of 1941. Faithful retelling brings pertinent items to light, with notable character development. It's refreshing to see Brosnan as an average bloke vs. his 007 persona, and Vavasseu, as the nine-year old Evelyn is one to watch. **94m/C VHS, DVD.** *IR GB* Pierce Brosnan, Aidan Quinn, Julianna Margulies, Sophie Vavasseur, Stephen Rea, Alan Bates, John Lynch, Andrea Irvine, Karen Ardiff, Niall Beagan, Hugh MacDonagh; ***D:*** Bruce Beresford; ***W:*** Paul Pender; ***C:*** Andre Fleuren; ***M:*** Stephen Endelman.

Evelyn Prentice 1/2 **1934** Powell and Loy again team up as a married couple (after their "The Thin Man" success) but this time things aren't so rosy. He is an attorney with a wandering eye who has an affair with Russell (in her film debut). Loy finds out and turns for sympathy to Stephens but then she decides to stay with her husband after all. Only she's written some steamy letters to Stephens and he tries blackmailing her—and winds up dead. Dramatic courtroom scene straightens things out. Adapted from the novel by W.E. Woodward. Film was remade as "Stronger Than Desire" in 1939. **78m/B VHS, DVD.** Myrna Loy, William Powell, Harvey Stephens, Isabel Jewell, Una Merkel, Rosalind Russell, Henry Wadsworth, Edward Brophy, Cora Sue Collins, Jessie Ralph, Sam Flint, Pat O'Malley; ***D:*** William K. Howard; ***W:*** Lenore Coffee.

Even Angels Fall **1990** One of heartthrob singer Humperdinck's scattered dramatic projects, a mystery thriller about a romance novelist moving into a New York brownstone whose previous inhabitant committed suicide—or was it murder? **?m/C VHS.** Morgan Fairchild, Engelbert Humperdinck; ***D:*** Thomas Calabrese. **TV**

Even Cowgirls Get the Blues 1/2 **1994 (R)** '70s counterculture loses its ill-defined charm in a meandering adaptation of cult author Tom Robbins' 1976 novel. An interesting failure, but likely to alienate both Van Sant and Robbins fans. Sissy Hackshaw (Thurman) possesses enormous thumbs which she hopes will make her the greatest hitchhiker in the world. But first they take her to a NYC modeling career for The Countess (Hurt in a high camp performance), who sends her to the Rubber Rose ranch, recently liberated by female cowhands, who are happy to welcome her. Theatrical release was delayed numerous times as Van Sant recut but it doesn't matter—the only successful feature is the soundtrack. **106m/C VHS, DVD.** Uma Thurman, John Hurt, Rain Phoenix, Lorraine Bracco, Noriyuki "Pat" Morita, Angie Dickinson, Keanu Reeves; ***Cameos:*** Sean Young, Crispin Glover, Roseanne, Ed Begley Jr.; ***D:*** Gus Van Sant; ***W:*** Gus Van Sant; ***C:*** Eric Alan Edwards, John Campbell; ***M:*** k.d. lang, Ben Mink.

Even Money 1/2 **2006 (R)** Dull ensemble drama despite some over-the-top performances. Basinger, DeVito, and Whitaker are gambling addicts who lie, cheat, and steal for another chance at that big score, despite having family and bookie problems. **108m/C DVD.** Danny DeVito, Kim Basinger, Forest Whitaker, Tim Roth, Kelsey Grammer, Jay Mohr, Ray Liotta, Nick Cannon, Carla Gugino, Grant Sullivan; ***D:*** Mark Rydell; ***W:*** Robert Tannen; ***C:*** Robbie Greenberg; ***M:*** Dave Grusin.

Evening 1/2 **2007 (PG-13)** Ann (Redgrave, chewing scenery) is on her deathbed, and she flashes back to a time when her younger self (Danes) experienced love and loss and possibly caused the death of a friend's brother. Meanwhile, her grown daughters (Collette and Richardson) struggle with their own issues while tending to their dying mother. Adapted by Minot from her novel, the film fails to escape its leaden dialogue, miscast actors, and unlikable, stereotypical characters. **117m/C DVD, Blu-ray Disc.** *US* Vanessa Redgrave, Natasha Richardson, Toni Collette, Meryl Streep, Claire Danes, Patrick Wilson, Hugh Dancy, Ebon Moss-Bachrach, Mamie Gummer, Eileen Atkins, Glenn Close, Barry Bostwick; ***D:*** Lajos Koltai; ***W:*** Susan Minot, Michael Cunningham; ***C:*** Gyula Pados; ***M:*** Jan A.P. Kaczmarek.

The Evening Star 🦴🦴 ½ **1996 (PG-13)** Sequel to 1983's "Terms of Endearment" starts in 1988 and finds the overbearing Aurora (MacLaine) now wreacking havoc on the lives of her three grown grandchildren (and vice versa). And Aurora's lovelife is as active as ever—old beau Hector Scott (Moffat) is hanging around, young psychiatrist Jerry Bruckner (Paxton) becomes her lover, and former astronaut flame Garrett Breedlove (Nicholson) also makes a brief appearance to cock an eyebrow at the shenanigans. Last screen role for Johnson as neighbor Arthur Cotten. Based on the novel by Larry McMurtry. Bring a hankie for the tears. **128m/C VHS, DVD.** Shirley MacLaine, Juliette Lewis, George Newbern, MacKenzie Astin, Bill Paxton, Miranda Richardson, Marion Ross, Ben Johnson, Donald Moffat, Scott Wolf, China Kantner, Jack Nicholson; ***D:*** Robert Harling; ***W:*** Robert Harling; ***C:*** Don Burgess; ***M:*** William Ross.

The Event 🦴 ½ **2003 (R)** Unbalanced effort begins with AIDS-stricken Matt dying at his so-called farewell party, arousing the suspicions of Assistant D.A. Nick (Posey). As Matt's suffering is recounted in flashbacks, Nick has a hard time pursuing the case after recently witnessing her father's painful death. **112m/C VHS, DVD.** *CA* Parker Posey, Don McKellar, Sarah Polley, Jane Leeves, Brent Carver, Olympia Dukakis, Joanna Adler, Rejean Cournoyer, Christina Zorich, Dick Latessa, Cynthia (Cyndy, Cindy) Preston, Gianna Marciante, Jaclyn Markowitz, Glen Michael Grant, Ruth Moore, Chaz Thorne; ***D:*** Thom Fitzgerald; ***W:*** Thom Fitzgerald, Steven Hillyer, Tim Marback; ***C:*** Thomas M. Harting; ***M:*** Christophe Beck. **VIDEO**

Event Horizon 🦴🦴 ½ **1997 (R)** Cross between "Alien" and "The Shining" has Fishburne heading an ensemble cast out to rescue a prototype spaceship that's been missing for seven years. Their own ship is sabatoged by their own demons and certain extraterrestial ones, too, that cause much mayhem on their once peaceful mission. **97m/C VHS, DVD.** Laurence Fishburne, Sam Neill, Kathleen Quinlan, Joely Richardson, Richard T. Jones, Jack Noseworthy, Sean Pertwee, Jason Isaacs; ***D:*** Paul W.S. Anderson; ***W:*** Philip Eisner; ***C:*** Adrian Biddle; ***M:*** Michael Kamen.

Ever After: A Cinderella Story 🦴🦴🦴 **1998 (PG-13)** The adorable Barrymore takes on Cinderella, renamed Danielle and very capable, in this not-quite-a-fairytale version set in 16th-century France. Huston's the peeved stepmom, Rodmilla, who reduces Danielle to the role of servant in her own home after her beloved father (Krabbe) dies. Danielle still falls for handsome Prince Henry (Scott), only she's not above trying to change the arrogant snob's opinions and tweak him about his privileged upbringing. Artist/genius Leonardo da Vinci (Godfrey) serves as the prince's confidante and there's still a lovely masked ball and a shoe to be lost (and found). **122m/C VHS, DVD.** Drew Barrymore, Anjelica Huston, Dougray Scott, Patrick Godfrey, Megan Dodds, Melanie Lynskey, Timothy West, Judy Parfitt, Jeroen Krabbe; ***Cameos:*** Jeanne Moreau; ***D:*** Andy Tennant; ***W:*** Andy Tennant, Susannah Grant, Rick Parks; ***C:*** Andrew Dunn; ***M:*** George Fenton.

Evergreen 🦴🦴 ½ **1934** The daughter of a retired British music hall star is mistaken for her mother and it is thought that she has discovered the secret of eternal youth. ♫Daddy Wouldn't Buy Me a Bow-Wow; When You've Got a Little Springtime in Your Heart; If I Give in to You; Tinkle, Tinkle, Tinkle; Dear, Dear; Dancing on the Ceiling; Just by Your Example; Over My Shoulder. **91m/B VHS.** *GB* Jessie Matthews, Sonnie Hale, Betty Balfour, Barry Mackay, Ivor McLaren, Hartley Power, Patrick Ludlow, Marjorie Gaffney; ***D:*** Victor Saville; ***W:*** Emlyn Williams; ***C:*** Glen MacWilliams; ***M:*** Richard Rodgers, Harry Woods, Lorenz Hart, Harry Woods.

Evergreen 🦴🦴 **2004 (PG-13)** Troubled mother Kate (Seymour) and daughter Henri (Land) move to a new community in hope of a fresh start. Henri resents her family's dire position and sets out to create a better niche with her newfound boyfriend's affluent but screwed up family. Dreary independent coming-of-age film is helped by good performances, especially from Land, but offers few surprises. **85m/C DVD.** *US* Cara Seymour, Mary Kay Place, Noah Fleiss, Gary Farmer, Bruce Davison, Addie Land; ***D:*** Enid Zentelis; ***W:*** Enid Zentelis; ***C:*** Matthew Clark; ***M:*** John Sirratt, Patrick Sansone.

Everlasting Moments 🦴🦴 ½ *Maria Larssons Eviga Ogonblick* **2008** Set in Sweden in 1907 and covering some 10 years, Troell's drama concerns downtrodden Maria Larsson's (Heiskanen) awakening to life's possibilities. Dockworker husband Sigfrid (Persbrandt) is an abusive womanizing drunk who doesn't support their large family. Needing money, Maria decides to pawn a camera but photographer Sebastian (Christensen) instead persuades Maria to take pictures herself. A natural talent, Maria begins making money and becomes more estranged from her husband as the years pass. Swedish with subtitles. **131m/C DVD.** *SW* Maria Heiskanen, Mikael Persbrandt, Jesper Christensen, Ghita Norby, Amanda Ooms, Callin Ohrvall, Emil Jensen, Claire Wikholm; ***D:*** Jan Troell; ***W:*** Jan Troell, Niklas Radstrom, Agneta Ulfster Troell; ***C:*** Jan Troell, Mischa Gavrjusjov; ***M:*** Matti Bye.

An Everlasting Piece 🦴🦴 ½ **2000 (R)** Director Levinson moves from working-class Baltimore to working-class Belfast in the 1980s in this goofball comedy. Best pals and fellow barbers Colm (McEvoy) and George (O'Byrne) don't let their different religions come between them. In fact, they decide it will be an advantage when they take on a new toupee business (called The Piece People)—Colm can sell to the Catholics and George will handle the Protestants. But it turns out they have a rival firm, Toupee or Not Toupee, and then Colm winds up with a substantial order from the IRA. He's willing to separate politics for business but is anyone else? **103m/C VHS, DVD.** *US* Barry McEvoy, Brian F. O'Byrne, Anna Friel, Billy Connolly, Pauline McLynn, Laurence Kinlan, Ruth McCabe; ***D:*** Barry Levinson; ***W:*** Barry McEvoy; ***C:*** Seamus Deasy; ***M:*** Hans Zimmer.

The Everlasting Secret Family 🦴🦴 **1988** Politics and family life make strange bedfellows. A top political figure joins a secret homosexual organization in his search for power. **93m/C VHS, DVD.** *AU* Arthur Dignam, Mark Lee, Dennis Miller, Heather Mitchell; ***D:*** Michael Thornhill.

Eversmile New Jersey 🦴 ½ **1989 (PG)** A dentist travels through Patagonia, offering dental care and advice to anyone in need, and a young woman, taken with the dental knight, dumps her boyfriend and stows away with him. When he discovers his admirer, he is less than ecstatic, but a chance tooth extraction on the road reveals the young woman's natural dental talents, and the two bond. From the director of "The Official Story." **88m/C VHS.** *AR* Daniel Day-Lewis, Mirjana Jokovic; ***D:*** Carlos Sorin; ***W:*** Jorge Goldenberg, Roberto Scheuer, Carlos Sorin.

Every Breath 🦴🦴 **1993 (R)** A kinky couple's games can be deadly and now they have someone new to play with. Jimmy couldn't resist the wife's seductive allure and if he wants to survive, he'll have to beat them at their own game. **88m/C VHS.** Judd Nelson, Joanna Pacula, Patrick Bauchau; ***D:*** Steve Bing; ***W:*** Judd Nelson, Andrew Fleming, Steve Bing; ***M:*** Nils Lofgren.

Every Day's a Holiday 🦴🦴 ½ **1938** In the 1890s, West stars as confidence woman Peaches O'Day, who sells the Brooklyn Bridge and is run out of New York City. But she comes back, in disguise as a French singer, to expose some crooked cops. The Hays office again came down heavily on Mae's suggestive behavior, which left her with little to rely on. West's last film for Paramount. **79m/B VHS.** Mae West, Edmund Lowe, Charles Butterworth, Charles Winninger, Walter Catlett, Lloyd Nolan, Herman Bing; ***D:*** Edward Sutherland; ***W:*** Mae West.

Every Girl Should Be Married 🦴🦴 ½ **1948** A shopgirl sets her sights on an eligible bachelor doctor. **84m/B VHS.** Cary Grant, Betsy Drake, Diana Lynn, Franchot Tone; ***D:*** Don Hartman.

Every Girl Should Have One 🦴 ½ **1978** A rambunctious comedy about a chase following a million-dollar diamond theft. **90m/C VHS.** Zsa Zsa Gabor, Robert Alda, Alice Faye, Sandra Vacey, John Lazar; ***D:*** Robert Hyatt; ***W:*** Robert Hyatt; ***C:*** Michael Jones; ***M:*** Johnny Pate.

Every Little Step 🦴🦴 ½ **2008 (PG-13)** Directors Stern and Del Deo track the audition process of Bob Avian's 2006 Broadway revival of creator-choreographer Michael Bennett's 1975's "A Chorus Line," which mirrors the musical's storyline. Included are reel-to-reel tapes of Bennett's 1974 workshop interviews, current interviews with some performers involved in the original production, casting calls, and selection of the final cast. **96m/C DVD.** *US* Donna McKechnie, Charlotte d'Amboise, Jacques D'Amboise, Marvin Hamlisch, Baayork Lee; ***D:*** James D. Stern, Adam Del Deo; ***M:*** Marvin Hamlisch, Jane Cornish.

Every Man for Himself 🦴🦴🦴🦴 *Slow Motion; Sauve qui peut; Sauve qui peut la vie* **1979** One of the funniest, most beautiful, and most deeply disturbing films of Godard's career. Set in the cold, symbolic neutrality of Switzerland, the three loosely intertwined plot threads tell of lovers who manipulate and control each other with varying degrees of passion and disgust, and for very different reasons. (A businessman's precisely choreographed "scene" with a prostitute is one of the more appalling and brilliant depictions of joyless, power-centered sexuality in cinema history.) Often hard to follow and maddeningly fragmented, it is also so rich that you may just have your priorities realigned. **87m/C DVD.** *FR* Roland Amstutz, Nathalie Baye, Jacques Dutronc, Isabelle Huppert, Anna Baldaccini, Monique Barscha, Michel Cassagna, Nicole Jacquet, Paule Muret, Fred Personne, Cecile Tanner; ***D:*** Jean-Luc Godard; ***W:*** Jean-Luc Godard, Jean-Claude Carriere, Anne-Marie Mieville; ***C:*** Renato Berta, William Lubtchansky, Barnard Menoud; ***M:*** Gabriel Yared.

Every Man for Himself & God Against All 🦴🦴🦴🦴 *The Mystery of Kaspar Hauser; Jeder fur Sich und Gott gegen Alle; The Enigma of Kaspar Hauser* **1975** Kaspar Hauser is a young man who mysteriously appears in the town square of Nuremberg, early in the 19th century. He cannot speak or stand upright and is found to have been kept in a dungeon for the first 18 years of his life. He becomes an attraction in society with his alternate vision of the world and attempts to reconcile with reality. A lovely, though demanding film which is based on a true story. In German with English subtitles. **110m/C VHS, DVD.** *GE* Bruno S, Brigitte Mira, Walter Ladengast, Hans Musaus, Willy Semmelrogge, Michael Kroecher, Henry van Lyck; ***D:*** Werner Herzog; ***W:*** Werner Herzog; ***C:*** Jorge Schmidt-Reitwein; ***M:*** Orlando Di Lasso.

Every Mother's Worst Fear 🦴🦴 **1998 (PG-13)** When her boyfriend dumps her, 16-year-old Martha Hoagland (Jordan Ladd) checks out the Internet chat rooms. She begins an online romance with Drew (Gale) but doesn't realize that hacker Mitch Carson (McGinley) is manipulating the entire situation. Soon Martha decides to slip away and meet Drew, and winds up Mitch's prisoner and the latest potential victim of his porn business. But it's mom Connie (Cheryl Ladd) to the rescue! **92m/C VHS.** Cheryl Ladd, Jordan Ladd, Ted McGinley, Vincent Gale, Robert Wisden, Tom Butler; ***D:*** Bill W.L. Norton; ***W:*** John Robert Bensink. **CABLE**

Every Other Weekend 🦴🦴🦴 *Un Week-end sur Deux* **1991** Camille Valmont (Baye) is an actress who has sacrified everything for her now-fading career. She's divorced loving husband Adrian (Manojlovic) and given him custody of their two young children—often ignoring her every other weekend visitation rights. In financial straits, Camille takes a job out of town and decides to take the kids with her, without telling Adrian. Self-centered and easily distracted, Camille tries to get close but manages to destroy what little rapport she has with her children. Camille isn't likable but Baye is such a gifted actress that you'll still feel pity. Director Garcia's debut; French with subtitles. **100m/C VHS.** *FR* Nathalie Baye, Miki (Predrag) Manojlovic, Joachim Serreau, Felicie Pasotti; ***D:*** Nicole Garcia; ***W:*** Nicole Garcia, Jacques Fieschi; ***C:*** William Lubtchansky; ***M:*** Oswald D'Andrea.

Every Second Counts 🦴🦴 ½ **2008** Entertaining Hallmark Channel family flick. Teen Brooke Preston (Apanowicz) is a champion in the rodeo sport of penning, trained by her dad Joe (Collins), a former champion himself. Brooke's dedication is partly to earn money because her family has hit hard times and the financial pressure may mean giving up her college dreams in favor of continuing on the rodeo circuit. **88m/C DVD.** Stephen Collins, Barbara Williams, Eric Keenleyside, Brett Dier, Magda Apanowicz; ***D:*** John Bradshaw; ***W:*** Kevin Commins, Robert Vaughn, Arthur Martin Jr., Barbara Kymlicka; ***C:*** Paul Mitchnick; ***M:*** Stacey Hersh. **CABLE**

Every Time We Say Goodbye 🦴🦴 ½ **1986 (PG-13)** In 1942, Jerusalem, an American flyboy falls in love with a young Sephardic Jewish girl, whose family resists the match. **97m/C VHS, DVD.** Tom Hanks, Christina Marsillach, Benedict Taylor, Anat Atzmon, Gila Almagor; ***D:*** Moshe Mizrahi; ***W:*** Moshe Mizrahi, Leah Appet; ***M:*** Philippe Sarde.

Every Which Way But Loose 🦴🦴 **1978 (R)** Fairly pointless Eastwood foray featuring Clint as a beer-guzzling, country-music loving truck driver earning a living as a barroom brawler. He and his orangutan travel to Colorado in pursuit of the woman he loves. Behind him are a motorcycle gang and an L.A. cop. All have been victims of his fists. Sequel is "Any Which Way You Can." **119m/C VHS, DVD, Blu-ray Disc.** Clint Eastwood, Sondra Locke, Geoffrey Lewis, Beverly D'Angelo, Ruth Gordon; ***D:*** James Fargo; ***W:*** Jeremy Joe Kronsberg; ***C:*** Rexford Metz; ***M:*** Steve Dorff.

Every Woman Knows a Secret 🦴🦴 **1999** Twenty-something Rob (Bettany) is blamed for the death of divorced, fortyish Jess's (Redmond) son in a drunk driving crash. Oddly drawn together by grief and guilt, the two begin an affair that reveals more secrets. **95m/C DVD.** *GB* Paul Bettany, Siobhan Redmond; ***D:*** Paul Seed; ***W:*** William Humble; ***C:*** Ian Punter; ***M:*** Nigel Hess. **TV**

Everybody Says I'm Fine! 🦴🦴 ½ **2006** A horrible accident during his childhood that left Xen (Engineer) an orphan also gave him the power as an adult to hear people's thoughts as he cuts hair for a living. While he uses his gift for the greater good by helping customers with problems in their lives, he's otherwise lonely and unhappy. He becomes intrigued by the beautiful Nikita (Purie) but is baffled when her thoughts are silent; his interest in her might be a dire mistake. **103m/C DVD.** *IN* Rehaan Engineer, Koel Purie, Rahul Bose, Pooja Bhatt, Anahita Oberoi; ***D:*** Rahul Bose; ***W:*** Rahul Bose. **VIDEO**

Everybody Sing 🦴🦴 **1938** A down-on-their-luck theatrical family, including Garland (who is kicked out of boarding school for singing Mendelssohn with a swing beat) decides to put on a show in hopes of making a comeback. Dumb plot and boring songs make this one for die-hard Garland fans only. ♫Swing, Mr. Mendelssohn, Swing; The One I Love; Down on Melody Farms; The Show Must Go On; I Wanna Swing; Never Was There Such a Perfect Day; Quainty Dainty Me; Why? Because; Snooks. **80m/B VHS.** Allan Jones, Fanny Brice, Judy Garland, Reginald Owen, Billie Burke, Reginald Gardiner, Lynne Carver, Monty Woolley; ***D:*** Edwin L. Marin; ***M:*** George Bassman.

Everybody Wants to Be Italian 🦴🦴 **2008 (R)** Jay Bianski (Jablonski), a fish market worker in Boston's North End, is having cold feet about asking his girlfriend Isabella (Petroro) to marry him. Fed up with Jay's indecisiveness, his co-workers invite Marisa (Vincent), a sexy veterinarian who shows up at the market looking for a cat, out to the local Italian-American club for drinks, hoping to spark something new for Jay. She's Hispanic, Jay think she's Italian. Jay's Polish, she thinks he's Italian. In a case of "mistaken ethnicity," the two anxiously prime themselves for the dos-and-don'ts when dating an Italian. Harmless and charmless, coming off like a cheap retread of "My Big Fat Greek Wedding." **105m/C DVD.** *US* Jay Jablonski, Cerina Vincent, Marisa Petroro, John Kapelos, John Enos, Richard Libertini, Dan Cortese, Penny Marshall; ***D:*** Jason Todd Ipson; ***W:*** Jason Todd Ipson; ***C:*** Michael Fimognari; ***M:*** Michael Cohen.

Everybody Wins **1990 (R)** A mystery-romance about a befuddled private eye trying to solve a murder and getting caught up with the bizarre prostitute who hired him. Arthur Miller based this screenplay on his stage drama "Some Kind of Love Story." Confused and, given its pedigree, disappointing mystery. **110m/C VHS, DVD.** Nick Nolte, Debra Winger, Will Patton, Jack Warden, Kathleen Wilhoite, Frank Converse, Frank Military, Judith Ivey; ***D:*** Karel Reisz; ***W:*** Arthur Miller; ***C:*** Ian Baker.

Everybody's All American **1988 (R)** Shallow, sentimental melodrama about a college football star and his cheerleader wife whose lives, subsequent to their youthful glories, is a string of disappointments and tragedies. Decently acted and based on Frank Deford's novel. **127m/C VHS, DVD.** Jessica Lange, Dennis Quaid, Timothy Hutton, John Goodman, Carl Lumbly, Ray Baker, Savannah Smith; ***D:*** Taylor Hackford; ***M:*** James Newton Howard.

Everybody's Dancin' 1/2 **1950** A ballroom proprietor's business is marred by random killings in her establishment as the bands play on. ♫Foolish Tears; Oblivious; Deep Freeze Dinah; I Shook; Rhumba Boogie. **66m/B VHS.** Spade Cooley, Dick Lane, Hal Derwin, Roddy McDowall; ***D:*** Will Jason.

Everybody's Famous! 1/2 *Iedereen Beroemd!* **2000 (R)** Factory worker Jean (De Pauw) is convinced that his teenaged daughter Marva (Van der Gucht) has the talent to become a famous singer, though she suffers from stage fright and seems hopeless. Devoted dad goes to the extreme of kidnapping Debbie (Reuten), a Belgian pop star burned out by her successful career. Jean's demand is that Debbie's lowlife manager (Loew) make Marva a star. Meanwhile, Debbie falls for her young co-kidnapper Willy (De Smedt). It's all played for laughs as it skewers the idea of media madness and fame at any price but there's a warped sweetness at the core as well. Dutch, Flemish, and French with subtitles. **99m/C VHS, DVD.** *BE* Josse De Pauw, Eva Van der Gucht, Werner De Smedt, Thekla Reuten, Victor Low, Gert Portael; ***D:*** Dominique Deruddere; ***W:*** Dominique Deruddere; ***C:*** Willy Stassen; ***M:*** Raymond van het Groenewoud.

Everybody's Fine 1/2 *Stanno Tutti Bene* **1990 (PG-13)** Mastroianni stars in this bittersweet story of a father on a mission to reunite his five grown children. His journey takes him all over Italy as he tries to bring them together in this touching film about enduring family love. In Italian with English subtitles. **115m/C VHS.** *IT* Marcello Mastroianni, Salvatore Cascio, Valeria Cavalli, Norma Martelli, Marino Cenna, Roberto Nobile, Michele Morgan, Fabio Iellini; ***D:*** Giuseppe Tornatore; ***W:*** Giuseppe Tornatore, Tonino Guerra; ***M:*** Ennio Morricone.

Everybody's Fine 1/2 **2009 (PG-13)** Nobody's even close to fine in this unappealing family dramedy. After none of his grown children show up at a planned family gathering, widower Frank (De Niro) decides to go on a road trip to catch up with them. What follows is a series of visits to children he realizes he barely knows as he discovers that none of them are leading the lives they've led him to believe. Unfortunately, that's all there is to offer, as De Niro deadpans his way through a mediocre story that no amount of charm from his co-leads Barrymore, Rockwell, or Beckinsale can save. A remake of Giuseppe Tornatore's 1990 film of the same name ("Stanno Tutti Bene," in Italian). **99m/C DVD.** *US* Robert DeNiro, Drew Barrymore, Kate Beckinsale, Sam Rockwell, Katherine Moenning, James Frain; ***D:*** Kirk Jones; ***W:*** Kirk Jones; ***C:*** Henry Braham; ***M:*** Dario Marianelli.

Everyman's Law 1/2 **1936** A cowboy who poses as a hired gunman is almost lynched by ranchers who think he is a murderer. **60m/B VHS.** Johnny Mack Brown, Beth Marion, Frank Campeau, Lloyd Ingraham, John (Jack) Beck, Charles "Slim" Whitaker; ***D:*** Albert Ray; ***W:*** Earle Snell; ***C:*** Jack Greenhalgh.

Everyone Says I Love You **1996 (R)** Woody sings! Granted, he doesn't sing very well, but who else could twist a story of love among the neurotic rich with lavish production numbers from the golden age of movie musicals? The excellent cast (who weren't told that they were in a musical until after they signed) prove that as singers, they're pretty good actors. The plot centers around the wandering love lives of Steffi (Hawn), her husband Bob (Alda), her ex-husband Joe (Allen) and their assorted children; especially the preppy Skylar (Barrymore) and her fiance Holden (Norton). Some of the musical productions are shaky (Allen's duet with Julia Roberts is straight out of Tin Ear Alley), but the feeling behind them is genuine; Besides, where else are you going to hear Groucho's "Hooray for Captain Spaulding" sung in French or a chorus of pregnant women sing "Makin' Whoopee"? **105m/C VHS, DVD.** Woody Allen, Alan Alda, Drew Barrymore, Goldie Hawn, Gaby Hoffman, Edward Norton, Natalie Portman, Julia Roberts, Tim Roth, Natasha Lyonne, Lukas Haas, David Ogden Stiers; ***D:*** Woody Allen; ***W:*** Woody Allen; ***C:*** Carlo Di Palma; ***M:*** Dick Hyman. L.A. Film Critics '96: Support. Actor (Norton); Natl. Bd. of Review '96: Support. Actor (Norton).

Everyone's Hero **2006 (G)** Reeve completed pre-production on this lackluster animated feature before his death, which is why he's sharing directorial credit (pic is also dedicated to both Christopher and Dana Reeve). During the 1932 World Series between the Yankees and the Chicago Cubs, Babe Ruth's lucky bat, Darlin' (Goldberg), is stolen. Pint-sized baseball fan Yankee Irving (Austin) hops the rails, accompanied by wisecracking baseball Screwie (Reiner), to find the bat, stolen by unhygienic Cubs pitcher Lefty (Macy), and get it to the Bambino in time to win the big game. Anachronistic adventure might distract the younger kiddies (the fart and booger jokes will probably help). **88m/C DVD.** *US* ***D:*** Christopher Reeve, Daniel St. Pierre, Colin Brady; ***W:*** Robert Kurtz, Jeff Hand; ***C:*** Andy Wang, Jan Carlee; ***M:*** John Debney; ***V:*** Jake T. Austin, Rob Reiner, Whoopi Goldberg, William H. Macy, Stanley Irving, Raven, Robert Wagner, Forest Whitaker, Brian Dennehy, Robin Williams, Joe Torre, Dana Reeve.

Everything for Sale *Wszysiko na Sprzedaz* **1968** An unacknowledged tribute to actor Zbigniew Cybulski, an actor who starred in several films for Wajda and who died in the same manner as the actor in this behind-the-scenes look at moviemaking. The lives of the director and actors are disrupted when their leading man, who lead a complicated offscreen life, is killed during filming. Polish with subtitles. **94m/C DVD.** *PL* Andrzej Lapicki, Daniel Olbrychski, Beata Tyszkiewicz, Elzbieta Czyzewska; ***D:*** Andrzej Wajda; ***W:*** Andrzej Wajda; ***C:*** Witold Sobocinski; ***M:*** Andrzej Korzynski.

Everything Happens at Night **1939** Rival reporters Milland and Cummings are torn between the woman they love and the story of a lifetime. One of Henie's best romantic skating vehicles due to the strong performances by the leading men. Henie does take to the ice for a couple of numbers, but this film was largely designed to expand her image as a serious actress. Although it failed to do that, it's good entertainment nonetheless. **76m/B VHS.** Sonja Henie, Ray Milland, Robert Cummings, Maurice (Moscovitch) Moscovitch, Leonid Kinskey, Alan Dinehart, Fritz Feld; ***D:*** Irving Cummings; ***W:*** Art Arthur, Robert Harari; ***C:*** Edward Cronjager; ***M:*** Cyril Mockridge.

Everything I Have is Yours **1952** The Gowers were better dancers than actors as they proved in their leading roles in this below-average MGM musical. The married Hubbards split up their Broadway act when Pamela retires to stay home and care for their baby. Chuck's wandering eye soon falls on new costar Sybil. **91m/C DVD.** Marge Champion, Gower Champion, Monica Lewis, Dennis O'Keefe, Dean Miller, Eduard Franz; ***D:*** Robert Z. Leonard; ***W:*** George Wells; ***C:*** William V. Skall.

Everything is Illuminated **2005 (PG-13)** Based on a novel by Jonathon Safran Foer, the film follows the journey of Jonathon (Wood), a fastidious New Yorker attempting to locate the Ukrainian woman he feels saved his grandfather from the Nazis. After traveling to the Ukraine, Jonathon employs Alex (Hutz), who narrates the film, and his grandfather (Leskin) as tour guides. The two specialize in taking "rich Jewish people" on trips to find ancestral homes and relatives. The beauty of the film is in finding its way from the humorous early scenes to the solemn conclusion. **104m/C DVD.** *US* Elijah Wood, Eugene Hutz, Boris Leskin, Laryssa Lauret; ***D:*** Liev Schreiber; ***W:*** Liev Schreiber; ***C:*** Matthew Libatique; ***M:*** Paul Cantloni.

Everything Put Together 1/2 **2000** Suburban housewife Angie (Mitchell) is pregnant as are her best friends Judith (Burns) and Barbie (Mullally). But Angie seems overly anxious and her worst fears are realized when her seemingly healthy son dies in the hospital from SIDS. Although husband Russ (Louis) tries to be as understanding and caring as possible, Anglie sinks into severe depression, especially when her friends, in their discomfort, begin to withdraw from her. **85m/C VHS, DVD.** Radha Mitchell, Megan Mullally, Justin Louis, Catherine Lloyd Burns, Alan Ruck, Matt Malloy, Michele Hicks; ***D:*** Marc Forster; ***W:*** Catherine Lloyd Burns, Adam Forgash; ***C:*** Roberto Schaefer; ***M:*** Thomas Koppel.

Everything Relative 1/2 **1996** Seven college buddies reunite and spend a weekend in the country together in this lesbian twist on "The Big Chill." A bris held by partners Katie and Sarah for their new baby brings the mostly single fortysomething women together, and bring out the unfulfilled desires and regrets of the six lesbians and one straight woman. Standouts include Weber as the stunt woman mourning the loss of a lover to a car accident 15 years prior, as well as the relationship between Josie (McLaughlin) and Maria (Negron), the woman who left her to get married and have children, and is now divorced and losing her children in the custody battle. Low budget ($100,000) indie debut of writer/director Pollack is right on the mark emotionally and manages to keep the characters and their stories engaging, but loses something with neatly pat solutions to the intricate problems facing these women. **110m/C VHS, DVD.** Stacey Nelkin, Ellen McLaughlin, Olivia Negron, Monica Bell, Andrea Weber, Gabriella Messina, Carol Schneider; ***D:*** Sharon Pollack; ***W:*** Sharon Pollack; ***C:*** Rachel Othmer; ***M:*** Frank London.

Everything That Rises 1/2 **1998** Quaid directs (his debut) and stars in this movie about tough rancher Jim Clay who struggles to hold onto the land that's been in his family for generations. An uncommunicative man, Jim is forced to re-examine his life when his young son Nathan (Merriman) is rendered a paraplegic after an auto accident caused by his dad. Winningham is devoted, stoic wife Kyle and Presnell is aging cowpoke/family friend Garth. **90m/C VHS.** Dennis Quaid, Mare Winningham, Harve Presnell, Ryan Merriman, Meat Loaf Aday, Bruce McGill; ***D:*** Dennis Quaid; ***W:*** Mark Spragg; ***C:*** Jack Conroy; ***M:*** David Robbins. **CABLE**

Everything You Always Wanted to Know about Sex (But Were Afraid to Ask) **1972 (R)** Satiric comical sketches about sex includes a timid sperm cell, an oversexed court jester, a sheep folly, and a giant disembodied breast. Quite entertaining in its own jolly way. Based on the book by Dr. David Reuben. **88m/C VHS, DVD.** Woody Allen, John Carradine, Lou Jacobi, Louise Lasser, Anthony Quayle, Geoffrey Holder, Lynn Redgrave, Tony Randall, Burt Reynolds, Gene Wilder, Robert Walden, Jay Robinson; ***D:*** Woody Allen; ***W:*** Woody Allen; ***C:*** David M. Walsh; ***M:*** Mundell Lowe.

Everything You Want **2005** Bookstore clerk/art student Abby seems to have a happy life, including a perfect boyfriend in Sy. Only problem is Sy isn't real, he's the imaginary friend Abby's had since childhood. Then Abby actually falls for the flesh-and-blood Quinn and has to make a decision. Seriously, a 20-something chick who still hangs out with her imaginary playmate sounds like a looney. **92m/C DVD.** Shiri Appleby, Nick Zano, Orlando Seale, Alexandra Holden, Will Friedle, Edie McClurg; ***D:*** Ryan Little; ***W:*** Steven A. Lee; ***C:*** Geno Salvatori; ***M:*** J Bateman. **CABLE**

Everything's Gone Green 1/2 **2006 (R)** Happy-go-lucky slacker Ryan (Costanzo) loses his job and girlfriend in one worst-day-of-his-life swoop. New employment at a lottery magazine draws him into a money laundering scheme that produces loot, ladies, and lots of opportunity for moral growth. Cleverly and hilariously weaves recurrent "green" references into each outlandish circumstance (dare you to tally them). Not a waste to watch but does lack that secret box-office hit ingredient. **95m/C DVD.** *CA* Paulo Costanzo, Steph Song, J.R. Bourne, Aidan Devine, Susan Hogan, Tom Butler, Gordon Michael Woolvett, Katharine Isabelle; ***D:*** Paul Fox; ***W:*** Douglas Coupland; ***C:*** David Frazee.

Eve's Bayou 1/2 **1997 (R)** Eve (newcomer Smollett) comes from the upper-middle class Batiste family that seems all too perfect on the outside, but secrets and lies slowly surface when she mistakenly catches her doctor father Louis (Jackson) doing more than a routine check-up with a female patient. With her innocence shattered by the discovery, Eve's torment soon affects her emotionally strained mother Roz (Whitfield) and adolescent tease older sister Cisely (Good). Set in Louisiana 1962, and told in flashback, film presents a mesmerizing and complex story with haunting visuals. Ghostly appearance from Carroll adds a touch of voodoo and heightens the melodramatic intensity. Jackson is solid as the charming, yet flawed womanizer and Whitfield his equal as the suspecting wife. Impressive, multi-layered directorial debut from Lemmons didn't draw much attention during theatrical run, but has gained a following since. **109m/C VHS, DVD.** Samuel L. Jackson, Lynn Whitfield, Debbi (Deborah) Morgan, Diahann Carroll, Jurnee Smollett, Meagan Good, Vondie Curtis-Hall, Lisa Nicole Carson, Jake Smollett, Ethel Ayler; ***D:*** Kasi Lemmons; ***W:*** Kasi Lemmons; ***C:*** Amy Vincent; ***M:*** Terence Blanchard; ***Nar:*** Tamara Tunie. Ind. Spirit '98: First Feature, Support. Actress (Morgan).

The Evictors **WOOF!** **1979 (PG)** Young couple moves into an abandoned, haunted farmhouse in a small Louisiana town. Unfortunately, they don't know anything about its horrible bloody history. And the real estate agent acts kinda funny. AIP Amityville scare-a-thon. **92m/C VHS.** Vic Morrow, Michael Parks, Jessica Harper, Sue Ane Langdon, Dennis Fimple; ***D:*** Charles B. Pierce; ***W:*** Charles B. Pierce.

Evidence of Blood 1/2 **1997 (PG-13)** Crime writer investigates a 40-year-old murder in a small town that would rather keep its secrets to itself. Based on the book by Thomas H. Cook. **109m/C VHS.** David Strathairn, Mary McDonnell; ***D:*** Andrew Mondshein; ***W:*** Dalene Young; ***C:*** Philip Linzey; ***M:*** Mason Daring.

The Evil **1978 (R)** A psychologist must destroy an evil force that is killing off the members of his research team residing at an old mansion. **80m/C VHS.** Richard Crenna, Joanna Pettet, Andrew Prine, Victor Buono, Cassie Yates, George O'Hanlon Jr., Lynne Moody, Mary Louise Weller, Milton Selzer; ***D:*** Gus Trikonis; ***W:*** Donald G. Thompson; ***C:*** Mario DiLeo.

Evil *Ondskan* **2003** Wanting her son to escape his stepdad's beatings, Erik's (Wilson) mom scrapes up the funds to send him to a supposedly classy boarding school. Unfortunately it's ruled by upperclassmen who like to keep the pecking order alive by tormenting younger students. But Erik's violent past—including his expulsion from his last school as a gang leader—makes him a poor target for their abuse, and despite his desire to please his mom he must fight to protect himself and the other victims. Based on Swede Jan Guillou's 1981 autobiographical novel "Ondskan." **113m/C DVD.** *SW* Marie Richardson, Andreas Wilson, Henrik Lundstrom, Gustaf Skarsgard, Linda Zilliacus, Johan Rabeus, Kjell Bergqvist, Magnus Roosman; ***D:*** Mikael Hafstrom; ***W:*** Mikael Hafstrom, Hans Gunnarsson; ***C:*** Peter Mokrosinski; ***M:*** Francis Shaw.

Evil Alien Conquerors **2002 (PG-13)** Extremely lame sci-fi comedy. Inept evil aliens My-ik and Du-ug, armed only with swords, are sent to Earth to behead the planet's entire population or suffer the wrath of giant Croker. With a two-day time limit they've got problems, especially since the dopey duo get distracted by alcohol, Earth women, and cows. **89m/C DVD.** Diedrich Bader, Chris Parnell, Tori Spelling, Elden (Ratliff) Henson, Beth Grant, Taylor Labine, Missy Yager; ***D:*** Chris Matheson; ***W:*** Chris Matheson; ***C:*** Russell Lyster; ***M:*** David E. Russo.

Evil Altar 🦴 **1989 (R)** A man controls a small town, but only so long as he offers sacrifices to the devil! **90m/C VHS.** William (Bill) Smith, Robert Z'Dar, Pepper Martin, Theresa Cooney, Ryan Rao; ***D:*** James R. Winburn.

The Evil Below 🦴 **1987** A couple hits the high seas in search of the lost treasure ship "El Diablo," resting on the ocean floor. In the process they trigger an evil curse and then must attempt to thwart it. **90m/C VHS, DVD.** *SA* June Chadwick, Wayne Crawford; ***D:*** Jean-Claude Dubois.

Evil Clutch 🦴 ½ **1989 (R)** A young couple vacationing in the Alps encounter several creepy locals when they find themselves in the midst of a haunted forest. The cinematography is extremely amateurish in this Italian gorefest and the English dubbing is atrocious. However, the special makeup effects are outstanding and the musical score adds a touch of class to this otherwise inept horror film. **88m/C VHS, DVD.** *IT* Coralina Cataldi-Tassoni, Diego Riba, Elena Cantarone, Luciano Crovato, Stefano Molinari; ***D:*** Andreas Marfori; ***W:*** Andreas Marfori; ***C:*** Marco Isoli.

Evil Dead 🦴🦴 ½ **1983 (NC-17)** Five college students, vacationing in the Tennessee mountains, take refuge in an abandoned cabin. They find a tape and a Book of the Dead, which unwittingly lets them resurrect demons, which transform the students into evil monsters until only Ash (Campbell) remains to fight the evil. Exuberantly gory low-budgeter followed by two sequels. **85m/C VHS, DVD, UMD.** Bruce Campbell, Ellen Sandweiss, Betsy Baker, Hal Delrich, Sarah York, Theodore (Ted) Raimi, Sam Raimi, Scott Spiegel; ***D:*** Sam Raimi; ***W:*** Sam Raimi; ***C:*** Tim Philo; ***M:*** Joseph LoDuca.

Evil Dead 2: Dead by Dawn 🦴🦴 ½ **1987 (R)** A gory, tongue-in-cheek sequel/remake of the original festival of gag and gore, in which an ancient book of magic invokes a crowd of flesh-snacking, joke-tossing ghouls. Followed by yet a third bloodfest. **84m/C VHS, DVD, Blu-ray Disc, UMD.** Bruce Campbell, Sarah Berry, Dan Hicks, Kassie Wesley, Theodore (Ted) Raimi, Denise Bixler, Richard Domeier, Scott Spiegel, Josh Becker, Lou Hancock; ***Cameos:*** Sam Raimi; ***D:*** Sam Raimi; ***W:*** Sam Raimi, Scott Spiegel; ***C:*** Peter Deming; ***M:*** Joseph LoDuca.

Evil Dead Trap 🦴🦴🦴 ½ **1988** Nami (Miyuki Ono), a Japanese late-night TV show host, is sent a tape that appears to show a brutal murder. Her cheap boss refuses to do anything, but she and her female crew decide to follow up on the tape and find the location where it was made. What follows in an abandoned factory owes much to Argento with even more visceral sex and violence. Director Ikeda's camera is almost never still. The script combines supernatural elements with a realistic setting and believable characters. **90m/C VHS, DVD.** *JP* Miyuki Ono, Fumi Katsuragi, Hitomi Kobayashi, Eriko Nakagawa; ***D:*** Toshiharu Ikeda; ***W:*** Takashi Ishii.

Evil Dead Trap 2: Hideki 🦴 ½ *Shiryo No Wana 2: Hideki* **1991** A shy theater film projectionist is haunted by a child (who may be from the first film), a quirky female reporter, and her equally quirky married boyfriend. They all have several things in common. They're all involved in a story about a recent series of serial killings, they all have serious emotional issues, and they're creepy. This sequel in name only is hard to watch, as the protagonists are clearly unsympathetic walking train wrecks. **102m/C DVD.** Shiro Sano, Shoko Nakajima, Jaimie Alexander; ***D:*** Izo Hashimoto.

Evil Ed 🦴 ½ **1996 (R)** Formerly mild-mannered film editor Ed (Ruebeck) becomes obsessed with the horror series he's working on, goes off the deep end, and begins a series of killings that mimic the ones from the films. Lots of splatter. **90m/C VHS, DVD.** *SW* Johan Ruebeck, Olof Rhodin, Pete Lofbergh; ***D:*** Anders Jacobsson; ***W:*** Anders Jacobsson; ***C:*** Anders Jacobsson; ***M:*** Goran Lundstrom.

Evil Eyes 🦴 ½ **2004 (R)** Hard-up screenwriter Jeff Stenn (Baldwin) is happy to accept a producer's (Kier) offer to pen a horror flick about a guy who went psycho and offed his family with an axe. But Jeff starts suffering from violent hallucinations and is soon living out his character's nightmare. Familiar plot moves briskly but if you really need see a crazy guy with an axe, watch "The Shining." **80m/C DVD.** Adam Baldwin, Udo Kier, Mark Sheppard, Jennifer Gates, Kristin Lorenz; ***D:*** Mark Atkins; ***W:*** Naomi L. Selfman; ***C:*** Mark Atkins. **VIDEO**

Evil Has a Face 🦴🦴 ½ **1996 (R)** Chicago police sketch artist Gwen McGarrell (Young) travels to rural Minnesota to help investigator Tom Sawyer (Moses) locate a child molester. But the face she draws turns out to be that of her abusive stepfather (Ross), who's been presumed dead. **92m/C VHS.** Sean Young, William R. Moses, Joe Guzaldo, Chelcie Ross, Brighton Hertford, Richard (Dick) Cusack; ***D:*** Robert M. Fresco; ***W:*** Robert M. Fresco; ***C:*** Stephen Lighthill; ***M:*** Joseph Vitarelli. **CABLE**

Evil Judgment 🦴 ½ **1985** A young girl investigates a series of murders and finds the culprit is a psychopathic judge. **93m/C VHS, DVD.** Pamela Collyer, Jack Langedijk, Nanette Workman; ***D:*** Claude Castravelli.

Evil Laugh WOOF! **1986 (R)** Medical students and their girlfriends party at an abandoned orphanage, until a serial killer decides to join them. **90m/C VHS, DVD.** Tony Griffin, Kim McKamy, Jody Gibson, Dominick Brascia; ***D:*** Dominick Brascia.

Evil Lives 🦴🦴 ½ *Soulmates* **1992** Now here's a horror premise you don't run into every day. Horror novelist Richard Wayborn (Rodgers) leaves a trail of dead women during his lecture tours. Seems he's really 700-years-old and his long-dead wife can temporarily resurrect herself using the nubile forms of other women. Now, Wayborn has chosen a new babe but so far she's managing to elude his deadly charms. **90m/C VHS, DVD.** Tristan Rogers, Arabella Holzbog, Tyrone Power Jr., Sonia Curtis, Griffin O'Neal, Melissa Moore, Wendy Barry, Paul Bartel, Dawn Wells; ***D:*** Thunder Levin.

The Evil Mind 🦴🦴 ½ *The Clairvoyant* **1934** A fraudulent mind reader predicts many disasters that start coming true. **80m/B VHS, DVD.** *GB* Claude Rains, Fay Wray, Jane Baxter, Felix Aylmer; ***D:*** Maurice Elvey; ***W:*** Charles Bennett.

Evil Obsession 🦴 **1996** Disturbed Homer (Feldman) obsessed with supermodel Margo (Stevens) and later becomes a suspect in the murders of 12 other models. **93m/C VHS.** Corey Feldman, Kimberly Stevens, Mark Derwin, Brion James, Stacie Randall; ***D:*** Richard W. Munchkin. **VIDEO**

The Evil of Frankenstein 🦴🦴 **1964** The third of the Hammer Frankenstein films, with the mad doctor once again finding his creature preserved in ice and thawing him out. Preceded by "The Revenge of Frankenstein" and followed by "Frankenstein Created Woman." **84m/C VHS, DVD.** *GB* Peter Cushing, Duncan Lamont, Peter Woodthorpe, Sandor Eles, Kiwi Kingston, Katy Wild; ***D:*** Freddie Francis; ***W:*** John (Anthony Hinds) Elder; ***C:*** John Wilcox; ***M:*** Don Banks.

Evil Roy Slade 🦴🦴🦴 **1971** Goofy family comedy (a failed TV pilot) that's a parody of every western cliche imaginable. Roy (Astin) is the meanest gunslinger in the west (he was raised by vultures) who's trying to turn over a new leaf after he falls for a pretty schoolteacher. He's aided by a shrink, who wants Roy to give up his weapons fetish, but singing glamour boy lawman Bing Bell (Shawn) has a score to settle with Roy. **97m/C VHS.** John Astin, Dick Shawn, Mickey Rooney, Pam(ela) Austin, Henry Gibson, Edie Adams, Milton Berle, Dom DeLuise, Noriyuki "Pat" Morita, Penny Marshall, John Ritter; ***Cameos:*** Jerry Paris; ***D:*** Jerry Paris; ***W:*** Garry Marshall, Jerry Belson; ***C:*** Sam Leavitt; ***Nar:*** Pat Buttram. **TV**

Evil Spawn 🦴 *Deadly Sting; Alive by Night; Alien Within* **1987** A fading movie queen takes an experimental drug to restore her youthful beauty, but it only turns her into a giant silverfish. Releases under several alternate titles, and with varying running times. **70m/C VHS, DVD.** Bobbie Bresee, John Carradine, Drew Godderis, John Terrance, Dawn Wildsmith, Jerry Fox, Pamela Gilbert, Forrest J Ackerman; ***D:*** Kenneth J. Hall; ***W:*** Kenneth J. Hall; ***C:*** Christopher Condon.

Evil Spirits 🦴 ½ **1991 (R)** Boardinghouse tenants are murdered while the crazy landlady cashes their social security checks. This seedy horror cheapie doesn't take itself seriously, and like-minded genre buffs may enjoy the cult-film cast. **95m/C VHS, DVD.** Karen Black, Arte Johnson, Virginia Mayo, Michael Berryman, Martine Beswick, Bert Remsen, Yvette Vickers, Robert Quarry, Mikel Angel, Debra Lamb; ***D:*** Gary Graver; ***W:*** Mikel Angel.

The Evil That Men Do 🦴🦴 **1984 (R)** A hitman comes out of retirement to break up a Central American government's political torture ring and, in the process, brings a friend's killer to justice. Based on the novel by R. Lance Hill. **90m/C VHS, DVD.** Charles Bronson, Theresa Saldana, Joseph Maher, Jose Ferrer, Rene Enriquez, John Glover, Raymond St. Jacques, Antoinette Bower, Enrique Lucero, Jorge Luke; ***D:*** J. Lee Thompson; ***W:*** John Crowther; ***C:*** Xavier Cruz; ***M:*** Ken Thorne.

Evil Toons 🦴 ½ **1990 (R)** A quartet of lovely coeds on a cleaning job venture into a deserted mansion. There they accidentally release a vulgar, lustful, animated demon who proceeds to cause their clothes to fall off. Can the girls escape the haunted mansion with their sanity, virtue and wardrobes intact? **86m/C VHS, DVD.** David Carradine, Dick Miller, Monique Gabrielle, Suzanne Ager, Stacy Nix, Madison Stone, Don Dowe, Arte Johnson, Michelle (McClellan) Bauer; ***D:*** Fred Olen Ray.

Evil Town 🦴 **1987 (R)** In this poorly made film, a wandering guy discovers a town overrun with zombies created by a mad doctor. **88m/C VHS.** Dean Jagger, James Keach, Robert Walker Jr., Doria Cook, Michele Marsh; ***D:*** Edward Collins.

Evil under the Sun 🦴🦴 **1982 (PG)** An opulent beach resort is the setting as Hercule Poirot attempts to unravel a murder mystery. Based on the Agatha Christie novel. **112m/C VHS, DVD.** *GB* Peter Ustinov, Jane Birkin, Maggie Smith, Colin Blakely, Roddy McDowall, Diana Rigg, Sylvia Miles, James Mason, Nicholas Clay; ***D:*** Guy Hamilton; ***W:*** Anthony Shaffer; ***C:*** Christopher Challis; ***M:*** Cole Porter.

The Evil Within WOOF! *Baby Blood* **1989 (R)** Parasitic beast, with an unquenchable thirst for blood, slithers from the center of the earth into the convenient womb of a young woman. She takes to murdering everyone within reach while preparing to give birth. As disgusting as it sounds. **88m/C VHS, DVD.** Emmanuelle Escourrou, Jean-Francois Guillotte; ***D:*** Alain Robak; ***W:*** Alain Robak, Serge Cukier.

Evils of the Night 🦴 **1985** Teenage campers are abducted by sex-crazed alien vampires. Bloody naked mayhem follows. **85m/C VHS, DVD.** John Carradine, Julie Newmar, Tina Louise, Neville Brand, Aldo Ray, Karrie Emerson, Bridget Holloman; ***D:*** Marti Rustam; ***W:*** Marti Rustam, Phillip D. Connors.

Evilspeak WOOF! **1982 (R)** Bumbling misfit enrolled at a military school is mistreated by the other cadets. With the help of his computer, he retaliates with satanic power. Bits, bytes, and gore. **89m/C VHS, DVD.** Clint Howard, Don Stark, Lou Gravance, Lauren Lester, R.G. Armstrong, Joe Cortese, Claude Earl Jones, Haywood Nelson, Lenny Montana; ***D:*** Eric Weston.

Evita 🦴🦴 ½ **1996 (PG)** Webber/Rice rock opera about the life and death of Eva Peron finally comes to the big screen with all its extravaganza intact. Madonna's in the title role (in fine voice, lavishly costumed but unflatteringly lit) about an ambitious poor girl willing to do anything to make her mark—in this version by sleeping her way up the ladder of power to Argentine strongman Juan Peron (Pryce as wax dummy). Evita becomes a would-be champion of the people, even as the government ruthlessly suppresses their freedoms. The surprisingly strong-voiced Banderas (perhaps his emphatic enunciation is to make his English as clear as possible) is everyman narrator Che (changed from the stage version's revolutionary Che Guevera). The highlight is still Madonna's balcony scene, singing "Don't Cry for Me, Argentina," but some of the other songs are drowned by loud orchestration. Director Parker has a cameo as a frustrated film director trying to work with Evita. ♫ A Cinema in Buenos Aires; Requiem for Evita; Oh, What a Circus; On This Night of a Thousand Stars; Eva and Magadi; Eva Beware of the City; Buenos Aires; Another Suitcase in Another Hall; Goodnight and Thank You. **133m/C VHS, DVD.** Madonna, Antonio Banderas, Jonathan Pryce, Jimmy Nail, Victoria Sus, Julian Littman, Olga Meediz, Laura Pallas, Julia Worsley; ***Cameos:*** Alan Parker; ***D:*** Alan Parker; ***W:*** Oliver Stone, Alan Parker; ***C:*** Darius Khondji; ***M:*** Andrew Lloyd Webber, Tim Rice. Oscars '96: Song ("You Must Love Me"); Golden Globes '97: Actress—Mus./Comedy (Madonna), Film—Mus./Comedy, Song ("You Must Love Me").

Evolution 🦴 ½ **2001 (PG-13)** A meteor containing microscopic organisms crashes in the New Mexico desert and they begin evolving at an enormous rate. A misfit team consisting of community college prof Duchovny, government scientist Moore, wannabe fireman Scott, and kooky geologist Jones try to prevent the spores (which evolve into a number of crazy critters) from taking over the planet. It's supposed to be sci-fi comedy, but the effectively scary monsters eliminate whatever comedic elements the writers and Reitman forgot to kill. **101m/C VHS, DVD.** *US* David Duchovny, Julianne Moore, Orlando Jones, Seann William Scott, Ted Levine, Ethan Suplee, Michael Ray Bower, Katharine Towne, Dan Aykroyd, Richard Moll, Gregory Itzin, Ty Burrell; ***D:*** Ivan Reitman; ***W:*** David Diamond, David Weissman, Don Jakoby; ***C:*** Michael Chapman; ***M:*** John Powell.

Evolver 🦴 ½ **1994 (R)** Teenager Kyle Baxter (Randall) wins a robot patterned after a video arcade game but the robot has a secret military weapon's program built into its brain, causing it to evolve into a killing machine. **90m/C VHS, DVD.** Ethan (Randall) Embry, John de Lancie, Cassidy Rae, Cindy Pickett, Paul Dooley; ***D:*** Mark Rosman; ***W:*** Mark Rosman; ***C:*** Jacques Haitkin; ***V:*** William H. Macy.

The Ewok Adventure 🦴🦴 ½ **1984 (G)** Those adorable, friendly and funny characters from "Return of the Jedi" make the jump from film to TV in a new adventure from George Lucas. In this installment, the Ewoks save a miraculous child from harm with the help of a young human. This fun-filled adventure has Lucas's thumbprint all over it and great special effects. Followed by "Ewoks: The Battle for Endor." **96m/C VHS, DVD.** Warwick Davis, Eric Walker, Aubree Miller, Fionnula Flanagan; ***D:*** John Korty; ***M:*** Elmer Bernstein, Peter Bernstein; ***Nar:*** Burl Ives. **TV**

The Ewoks: Battle for Endor 🦴🦴 ½ **1985** TV movie based on the furry creatures from "Return of the Jedi," detailing their battle against an evil queen to retain their forest home. Preceded by "The Ewok Adventure." **98m/C VHS, DVD.** Wilford Brimley, Warwick Davis, Aubree Miller, Sian Phillips, Paul Gleason, Eric Walker, Carel Struycken, Niki Botelho; ***D:*** Jim Wheat, Ken Wheat; ***M:*** Peter Bernstein. **TV**

The Ex 🦴🦴 ½ **1996 (R)** Architect David Kenyon (Mancuso) has a new life, with a sweet second wife (Amis) and a five-year-old son. Then the ex, Deirdre (Butler), comes sauntering back and it seems she and David had a very kinky relationship. Now Deirdre decides it's time to get revenge. Familiar plotline is given a high gloss and some chills. **87m/C VHS.** Yancy Butler, Nick Mancuso, Suzy Amis; ***D:*** Mark L. Lester; ***W:*** John Lutz, Larry Cohen; ***C:*** Richard Letterman; ***M:*** Paul Zaza.

The Ex 🦴🦴 *Fast Track* **2007 (PG-13)** Tom (Braff) loses his job after his wife (Peet) quits hers to raise their first child. To save the family, he moves them from New York to Ohio to accept an advertising job with his father-in-law. Then he discovers that his new boss is a wheelchair-bound paraplegic who had a one night stand with his wife in high school, and has been obsessing over her ever since. Plays like a mean sitcom, but without the laughs that would normally accompany black comedies. Although it might make you squirm like one. **90m/C DVD.** *US* Zach Braff, Amanda Peet, Jason Bateman, Charles Grodin, Mia Farrow, Donal Logue, Lucian Maisel, Amy Poehler, Fred Armisen, Bob Stephenson, Josh Charles, Paul Rudd, Amy Adams, Romany Malco; ***D:*** Jesse Peretz; ***W:*** Michael Handelman, Paul Guion; ***C:*** Tom Richmond; ***M:*** Ed Shearmur.

Ex-Cop **1993** Pete Danberg is a cop with a drinking problem. He's fired from the force but not before he puts away the "Las Vegas Slasher." Unfortunately for Pete the Slasher makes parole and is out for revenge—using Pete's kidnapped daughter as bait. **97m/C VHS.** Rick Savage, Sandy Hackett, Joan Chamberlain, Douglas Terry, Angi Davidson, Richard Cornell, Jim Williams; ***D:*** Patrick Kerby; ***W:*** Daniel S. Sample.

Ex-Lady **1933** Davis stars as a liberated woman who loves advertising writer Raymond, but doesn't want to marry him. However, she believes living together is the most suitable arrangement. The two open up an ad agency and complications ensue. Remake of "Illicit," which was filmed only two years earlier with Barbara Stanwyck in the lead role. **65m/B VHS.** Bette Davis, Gene Raymond, Frank McHugh, Claire Dodd, Monroe Owsley, Ferdinand Gottschalk; ***D:*** Robert Florey.

Ex-Mrs. Bradford **1936** Amateur sleuth Dr. Bradford teams up with his ex-wife to solve a series of murders at the race track. Sophisticated comedy-mystery; witty dialogue. **80m/B VHS.** William Powell, Jean Arthur, James Gleason, Eric Blore, Robert Armstrong; ***D:*** Stephen Roberts.

Excalibur ½ **1981 (R)** A sweeping, visionary retelling of the life of King Arthur, from his conception, to the sword in the stone, to the search for the Holy Grail and the final battle with Mordred. An imperfect, sensationalized version, but still the best yet filmed. **140m/C VHS, DVD, HD DVD.** Robert Addie, Keith Buckley, Niall O'Brien, Nigel Terry, Nicol Williamson, Nicholas Clay, Helen Mirren, Cherie Lunghi, Paul Geoffrey, Gabriel Byrne, Liam Neeson, Patrick Stewart, Charley Boorman, Corin Redgrave; ***D:*** John Boorman; ***W:*** Rospo Pallenberg, John Boorman; ***C:*** Alex Thomson; ***M:*** Trevor Jones.

Excellent Cadavers ½ **1999 (R)** Giovanni Falcone (Palminteri) was an incorruptible Italian prosecutor who took on the Mafia in Sicily in the 1980s. By the end of the decade, and with the help of informer Tommaso Buscetta (Abraham), Falcone had 300 convictions and sealed his own grim fate. Title refers to the corpses of public officials who challenged the mobsters. Based on the book by Alexander Stille. **86m/C VHS, DVD.** Chazz Palminteri, F. Murray Abraham, Anna Galiena, Bruno Bilotta; ***D:*** Ricky Tognazzi; ***W:*** Peter Pruce; ***M:*** Joseph Vitarelli. **CABLE**

Excess Baggage ½ **1996 (PG-13)** Attention-seeking rich girl Emily (Silverstone) fakes her own kidnapping to get back at dear old dad, involving car thief Vincent Roche (del Toro) in the crime. Things get out of control when her creepy "Uncle" Ray (Walken), who's an ex-CIA assassin, is hired by Emily's father to get her back. Silverstone's character is alternately whiny and pouting, you'll wonder why dad would want her back and why Vincent hangs on at all. First picture in Silverstone's pricey production deal with Columbia went through the rumor mill (for supposed clashes between Silverstone and director Brambilla) and was originally scheduled for release in the fall of '96. **101m/C VHS, DVD.** Alicia Silverstone, Benicio Del Toro, Christopher Walken, Harry Connick Jr., Jack Thompson, Nicholas Turturro, Michael Bowen, Leland Orser, Robert Wisden, Sally Kirkland; ***D:*** Marco Brambilla; ***W:*** Mikhaila Max Adams, Dick Clement, Ian La Frenais; ***C:*** Jean-Yves Escoffier; ***M:*** John Lurie.

Excessive Force ½ **1993 (R)** Routine actioner lives up to its title by offering lots of violence, but little else. Gang leader Young seeks revenge on the cops who he believes ruined a $3 million drug deal. Loner cop Griffith is the only one to survive the grudge killings and goes after Young himself. Talented cast underachieves. Limited theatrical release sent this one almost straight to video. **87m/C VHS, DVD.** Thomas Ian Griffith, Lance Henriksen, James Earl Jones, Charlotte Lewis, Tony Todd, Burt Young, W. Earl Brown; ***D:*** Jon Hess; ***W:*** Thomas Ian Griffith; ***C:*** Donald M. Morgan; ***M:*** Charles Bernstein.

Excessive Force 2: Force on Force ½ **1995 (R)** Special agent Harly Cordell (Randall) volunteers to hunt down an assassination squad that is turning L.A. into murder central. Seems her former lover Francis Lydell (Gauthier) is head killer and Harly's got a score to settle. Lots of action and nifty weapons. **88m/C VHS.** Stacie Randall, Dan Gauthier, Jay Patterson, John Mese; ***D:*** Jonathan Winfrey; ***W:*** Mark Sevi; ***C:*** Russ Brandt; ***M:*** Kevin Kiner.

The Execution ½ **1985** Five female friends who discover that the Nazi doctor who brutalized them in a concentration camp during WWII is now living a normal life in California. Together they plot his undoing. **92m/C VHS, DVD.** Loretta Swit, Valerie Harper, Sandy Dennis, Jessica Walter, Rip Torn, Barbara Barrie, Robert Hooks, Michael Lerner; ***D:*** Paul Wendkos; ***M:*** Georges Delerue.

Execution of Justice **1999 (R)** Emily Mann's play focused on the 1978 voluntary manslaughter verdict in the trial of city supervisor Dan White for the deaths of San Francisco Mayor George Moscone (Young) and openly gay elected official Harvey Milk (Coyote). You may remember the infamous "Twinkie Defense." This sporadically compelling cable docudrama delves into the mind of White (Daly) himself. **103m/C VHS.** Timothy Daly, Peter Coyote, Stephen Young, Amy Van Nostrand, Tyne Daly, Khalil Kain, Frank Pellegrino, Shannon Hile; ***D:*** Leon Ichaso; ***W:*** Michael Butler; ***C:*** Claudio Chea. **CABLE**

The Execution of Private Slovik ½ **1974** This quiet powerhouse of a TV movie recounts in straightforward terms the case of Eddie Slovik, a WWII misfit who became the only American soldier executed for desertion since the Civil War. The Levinson/Link screenplay (based on the book by William Bradford Huie) ends up deifying Slovik, which some might find hard to take. But there's no arguing the impact of the drama, or of Sheen's unaffected lead performance. **122m/C VHS.** Martin Sheen, Mariclare Costello, Ned Beatty, Gary Busey, Matt Clark, Ben Hammer, Warren Kemmerling; ***D:*** Lamont Johnson; ***W:*** Richard Levinson, William Link; ***C:*** Bill Butler. **TV**

Execution of Raymond Graham ½ **1985** The lawyers and family of Raymond Graham struggle to keep him from being executed for murder. Based on a true story. **104m/C VHS, DVD.** Morgan Freeman, Jeff Fahey, Kate Reid, Laurie Metcalf, Josef Sommer; ***D:*** Daniel Petrie. **TV**

The Executioner **1970 (PG)** A thriller wherein a British spy must prove that his former colleague is a double agent. Elements of backstabbing, betrayal, and espionage abound. **107m/C VHS.** *GB* Judy Geeson, Oscar Homolka, Charles Gray, Nigel Patrick, George Peppard, Joan Collins, Keith Michell; ***D:*** Sam Wanamaker.

The Executioner *Like Father, Like Son; Massacre Mafia Style* **1978 (R)** A very cheap, very "Godfather"-like story of a mafia family gone awry. **84m/C VHS.** Duke Mitchell, Vic Caesar, Dominic Micelli, John Strong, Jim Williams, Lorenzo Dodo; ***D:*** Duke Mitchell; ***W:*** Duke Mitchell.

Executioner of Venice **1963** Marauding pirates with time on hands swarm in from the Adriatic Sea and attempt to rob the Venetians blind. The Doge and his godson come to the rescue. **90m/C VHS.** Guy Madison, Lex Barker, Alessandra Panaro; ***D:*** Louis Capauno.

The Executioner, Part 2: Frozen Scream **1984 (R)** Brutal feud rocks the Mafia, and a crime kingpin's passionate son seeks revenge on his father's slayers. Not a sequel to any other films bearing similar titles. Strange thing is, no "Executioner, Part I" was ever made. Pretty laughable. **150m/C VHS.** Chris Mitchum, Aldo Ray, Antoine John Mottet, Renee Harmon; ***D:*** James Bryant.

The Executioners ½ **1993** When a nuclear explosion contaminates most of the city's drinking water, the remainder falls under the harsh control of the Black Knight. Now, it's up to the Heroic Trio to defeat their nemesis. Chinese with subtitles. **100m/C VHS, DVD.** *HK* Anita (Yim-Fong) Mui, Michelle Yeoh, Maggie Cheung; ***D:*** Ching Siu Tung; ***W:*** Susan Chan; ***C:*** Hang-Seng Poon; ***M:*** Cacine Wong.

The Executioner's Song ½ **1982** European version of the TV movie based on Norman Mailer's Pulitzer Prize-winner, recounting the life and death of convicted murderer Gary Gilmore. Features adult-minded footage not seen in the U.S. version. **157m/C VHS.** Tommy Lee Jones, Rosanna Arquette, Eli Wallach, Christine Lahti, Jenny Wright, Jordan Clark, Steven Keats; ***D:*** Lawrence Schiller.

Executive Action ½ **1973 (PG)** Political thriller providing a different look at the events leading to the assassination of JFK. In this speculation, a millionaire pays a professional spy to organize a secret conspiracy to kill President Kennedy. Ryan's final film. Adapted by Dalton Trumbo from Mark Lane's "Rush to Judgement." **91m/C VHS.** Burt Lancaster, Robert Ryan, Will Geer, Gilbert Green, John Anderson; ***D:*** David Miller; ***C:*** Robert Steadman; ***M:*** Randy Edelman.

Executive Decision **1996 (R)** Those wacky terrorists are at it again. You would think that after getting their butts kicked in almost every action picture since 1980 that they would learn. But here they are, hijacking a 747, cutting off communications, and affixing a nerve gas bomb to the plane. This time a group of high tech commandos, led by Russell and (briefly) Seagal, must sneak onto the plane and generally mess up the bad guys' plans. Brave stewardess Berry helps tango with the central casting mad dog terrorists. The title refers to the President's decision on whether or not to blow the plane up in order to avert disaster. Or maybe "Die Hard: Ad Nauseum" wasn't available. **132m/C VHS, DVD.** Mary Ellen Trainor, Kurt Russell, Halle Berry, Oliver Platt, John Leguizamo, Steven Seagal, Joe Morton, David Suchet, B.D. Wong, Len Cariou, Whip Hubley, J.T. Walsh; ***D:*** Stuart Baird; ***W:*** Jim Thomas, John Thomas; ***C:*** Alex Thomson; ***M:*** Jerry Goldsmith.

Executive Koala *Koara Kacho* **2006** In director Minoru Kawasaki's latest parody, a six-foot tall talking koala bear happens to be an executive at a pickle manufacturer and suffers blackouts. Unfortunately for him during one of these blackouts his ex suffers a bad case of death, and he looks to be the main suspect. Others soon follow, and it's a race for the poor Koala and his animal friends to prove his innocence. **86m/C DVD.** *JP* Lee Ho, Eiichi Kikuchi, Arthur Kuroda, Hironobu Nomura; ***D:*** Minoru Kawasaki; ***W:*** Minoru Kawasaki, Masakazu Migita; ***C:*** Yasatako Nagano.

Executive Power **1998 (R)** The President has a secret and his people will do anything to prevent a scandal. Secret Service agent Nick (Scheffer) realizes this when a staffer who knows turns up dead. Above average thriller. **115m/C VHS.** Craig Sheffer, Andrea Roth, Joanna Cassidy, John Heard, William Atherton, Denise Crosby, John Capodice; ***D:*** David Corley; ***W:*** David Corley. **VIDEO**

Executive Suite **1954** One of the first dog-eat-dog dramas about high finance and big business. The plot centers on the question of a replacement for the freshly buried owner of a gigantic furniture company. **104m/B VHS.** William Holden, June Allyson, Barbara Stanwyck, Fredric March, Walter Pidgeon, Louis Calhern, Shelley Winters, Paul Douglas, Nina Foch, Dean Jagger; ***D:*** Robert Wise; ***W:*** Ernest Lehman; ***C:*** George J. Folsey.

Executive Target **1997 (R)** Stunt-car driver Nick James (Madsen) is grabbed by a gang of mercenaries who want him as their getaway man when they attempt to kidnap the president (Scheider) and overthrow the U.S. government. He agrees because the gang have also taken his wife as a hostage. Lots of action sequences show where the money went. **96m/C VHS, DVD.** Michael Madsen, Keith David, Angie Everhart, Roy Scheider, Dayton Callie, Kathy Christopherson; ***D:*** Joseph Merhi; ***W:*** Dayton Callie; ***C:*** Ken Blakey. **VIDEO**

Exiled **2006 (R)** High-octane Hong Kong actioner. In 1998, Macau's gangsters are settling old scores and divvying up their loot before the Portuguese island is turned over to communist China. Wo (Nick Cheung) has just returned from exile but Boss Fay (Yam), whom he tried to kill, still wants revenge and sends Blaze (Wong Chau-Sang) and Fat (Lam) to do the deed. But when gangsters Tai (Ng) and Cat (Roy Cheung) show up, it's to prevent Wo's death. Turns out, all five men once belonged to the same gang and they agree to first hijack a gold shipment before finishing other business. Cantonese with subtitles or dubbed. **109m/C DVD.** *HK* Nick Cheung, Roy Cheung, Frances Ng, Suet Lam, Anthony Wong Chau-Sang, Katung Lam, Simon Yam, Josie Ho, Richie Jen; ***D:*** Johnny To; ***W:*** Kam-yeun Szeto, Tin-Shing Yip; ***C:*** Sui-keung Cheung; ***M:*** Guy Zerafa.

Exiled in America **1990** A Central American freedom fighter (Albert) flees his country for the United States, settling in a small town with his wife. She gets a waitressing job at a local diner, telling the owner her husband died in an accident, and the owner's son winds up falling in love with her. Things get complicated when the death squad, led by a corrupt CIA agent, follows Albert to his hiding place, and the local sheriff threatens to blow his cover. **84m/C VHS.** Maxwell Caulfield, Edward Albert, Viveca Lindfors, Kamala Lopez, Stella Stevens, Wings Hauser; ***D:*** Paul Leder; ***W:*** Paul Leder.

Exiled to Shanghai ½ **1937** A couple of newsreel men invent a television device that revolutionizes the business. **65m/B VHS.** Wallace Ford, June Travis, Dean Jagger, William "Billy" Bakewell, Arthur Lake, Jonathan Hale, William Harrigan, Sarah Padden; ***D:*** Nick Grinde.

The Exiles **1961** A slice-of-bygone-life drama, set in L.A., that briefly made the festival circuit and then disappeared until its 2008 restoration by the UCLA Film and Television Archive. Mackenzie, then a USC film student, turned his attention to the now-razed downtown neighborhood of Bunker Hill, an area peopled by immigrants and marginally employed Native Americans. He follows one fairly typical evening with several characters who spend their time worrying, drinking, and raising a little hell. **72m/B DVD.** *US* Yvonne Williams, Homer Nish, Tommy Reynolds; ***D:*** Kent Mackenzie; ***W:*** Kent Mackenzie; ***C:*** Erik Daarstad, Robert Kaufman, John Morrill; ***M:*** Anthony Hilder, Robert Hafner, Eddie Sunrise. Natl. Film Reg. '09.

eXistenZ ½ **1999 (R)** Typically scary and weird Cronenberg production finds security guard Law saving the life of computer-game designer Leigh. They both get sucked into one of her alternate-reality creations and are pursued by assassins. In this future world, game players are literally hooked up to their computer with an umbilical-like cord plugged directly into their spines—no doubt the fantasy of teenage boys everywhere. Surreal visuals and excellent performances won't help the viewer keep track of what's going on, but for Cronenberg linear plotting is rarely the point. **97m/C VHS, DVD.** *CA* Jennifer Jason Leigh, Jude Law, Ian Holm, Willem Dafoe, Sarah Polley, Christopher Eccleston, Don McKellar, Callum Keith Rennie; ***D:*** David Cronenberg; ***W:*** David Cronenberg; ***C:*** Peter Suschitzky; ***M:*** Howard Shore. Genie '99: Film Editing.

Exit ½ **1995 (R)** Gang of criminals, lead by pscho Charles (Bradley), take a strip club's dancers as hostages when their robbery attempt goes bad. Exotic dancer Diane (Whirry) manages to escape and hook up with ex-ATF agent Alex (Bucci) to stop the creeps. Lame action, silly dialogue, very attractive Whirry. **90m/C VHS.** Shannon Whirry, David Bradley, Larry Manetti, Joe Bucci; ***D:*** Ric Roman Waugh; ***W:*** Joe Augustyn, Brent Friedman, David Robinson; ***C:*** David B. Nowell; ***M:*** Kevin Kiner.

Exit in Red ½ **1997 (R)** Beverly Hills psychiatrist Ed Altman (Rourke) is hiding out after the suicide of one of his patients lead to professional misconduct charges. But he just can't leave the women alone and gets involved with unhappily married Ally (Schofield). When her husband turns up dead, Ed's charged with murder. It's a frame but just how's he going to prove it. **96m/C**

VHS. Mickey Rourke, Annabel Schofield, Anthony Michael Hall, Carre Otis; ***D:*** Yurek Bogayevicz; ***W:*** David Womack; ***C:*** Ericson Core; ***M:*** Michael Lorenc.

Exit Smiling 1/2 **1926** Wannabe actress Violet (Lillie in her film debut) joins a third-rate traveling troupe as their wardrobe mistress hoping for a chance to get onstage. During a railroad stop, Violet meets Jimmy Marsh (Pickford), a fugitive who's been falsely accused of embezzlement. Violet persuades him to disguise himself as their new male lead and, having fallen in unrequited love, works to clear his name. **77m/B DVD.** Beatrice Lillie, Jack Pickford, Doris Lloyd, Louise Lorraine, DeWitt Jennings, Harry C. (Henry) Myers, Franklin Pangborn, Tenen Holtz; ***D:*** Sam Taylor; ***W:*** Sam Taylor, Tim Whelan; ***C:*** Andre Barlatier.

Exit Speed 1/2 **2008 (R)** On Christmas Eve, ten strangers board a bus traveling across Texas. They accidentally collide with a meth-addict biker and his equally drug-crazed buds who force the bus off the road. The passengers take refuge in an abandoned junkyard where they improvise weapons to repel attacks by the murderous gang. **93m/C DVD.** Fred Ward, Desmond Harrington, Lea Thompson, Julie Mond, Gregory Jbara, David Rees Snell; ***W:*** Scott Ziehl, Michael Stokes; ***C:*** Thomas Callaway; ***M:*** Doug Besterman. **VIDEO**

Exit to Eden 1/2 **1994 (R)** Anne Rampling's (AKA Anne Rice) novel focused on fulfilling S&M sexual fantasies, but director Marshall goes for laughs with a buddy cops-out-of-water sitcom subplot, as undercover cops Aykroyd and O'Donnell track a suspected jewel thief to the fantasy resort of Eden, run by dominatrix Delany. (What was the pitch for this one? Think "Another Stakeout" meets "Tie Me Up, Tie Me Down." It'll be great. Really.) Neither plot works, resulting in a kinky movie with no kink, and a comedy with few laughs. O'Donnell holds up her end, providing what few yuks there are. Everyone else, especially Aykroyd and Delany, seem to be sleepwalking. Lucky for them. **113m/C VHS, DVD.** Dana Delany, Paul Mercurio, Dan Aykroyd, Rosie O'Donnell, Hector Elizondo, Stuart Wilson, Iman, Sandi Korn, Laura Elena Harring; ***D:*** Garry Marshall; ***W:*** Deborah Amelon, Bob Brunner; ***M:*** Patrick Doyle. Golden Raspberries '94: Worst Support. Actress (O'Donnell).

Exit Wounds **2001 (R)** Unpredictable, unorthodox Detroit police detective Orin Boyd (Seagal, of course) gets sent to the baddest part of town after successfully, but unconventionally, breaking up a plot to kill the Vice President. There, along with his rambunctious new partner (Washington), he uncovers corrupt cops and a drug-running scheme involving the notorious crime lord Walker (DMX). Lots of martial arts sequences and loads of gunfire from, presumably, really bad shots. Romance also blossoms between Mr. Loose Canon and a precinct commander played by Hennessy. Typical Seagal flick, sure to be enjoyed by fans. Others should be wary. **98m/C VHS, DVD.** *US* Steven Seagal, DMX, Isaiah Washington IV, Anthony Anderson, Michael Jai White, Bill Duke, Jill(ian) Hennessey, Tom Arnold, Bruce McGill, David Vadim, Eva Mendes; ***D:*** Andrzej Bartkowiak; ***W:*** Ed Horowitz, Richard D'Ovidio; ***C:*** Glen MacPherson; ***M:*** Jeff Rona, Damon Blackman.

Exodus **1960** Chronicles the post-WWII partition of Palestine into a homeland for Jews; the anguish of refugees from Nazi concentration camps held on ships in the Mediterranean; the struggle of the tiny nation with forces dividing it from within and destroying it from the outside; and the heroic men and women who saw a job to be done and did it. Based on the novel by Leon Uris; filmed in Cyprus and Israel. Preminger battled the Israeli government, the studio, and the novel's author to complete this epic. Cost more than $4 million, a phenomenal amount at the time. **208m/C VHS, DVD.** Paul Newman, Eva Marie Saint, Lee J. Cobb, Sal Mineo, Ralph Richardson, Hugh Griffith, Gregory Ratoff, Felix Aylmer, Peter Lawford, Jill Haworth, John Derek, David Opatoshu, Marius Goring, Alexandra Stewart, Michael Wager, Martin Benson, Paul Stevens, George Maharis; ***D:*** Otto Preminger; ***W:*** Dalton Trumbo; ***M:*** Ernest Gold. Oscars '60: Orig. Dramatic Score; Golden Globes '61: Support. Actor (Mineo).

Exorcism 1/2 *Exorcismo* **1974** A satanic cult in a small English village commits a series of gruesome crimes that have the authorities baffled. **90m/C VHS, DVD.** *SP* Paul Naschy, Maria Perschy, Maria Kosti, Grace Mills, Jorge Torras, Marta Avile; ***D:*** Juan Bosch; ***W:*** Juan Bosch, Paul Naschy; ***C:*** Francisco Sanchez.

The Exorcism of Emily Rose **2005 (PG-13)** Nineteen year old student Emily Rose (Carpenter) died during an exorcism performed by Father Richard Moore (Wilkinson), who is being tried for negligent homicide. Attorney Erin Bruner (Linney) hopes her defense of the priest will propel her career to the next level. This courtroom drama is interwoven with horror as the freakish circumstances of Emily's death are recounted from the stand. Somewhat predictable, but well worth the viewing for fans of the genre. **114m/C DVD, UMD.** *US* Laura Linney, Tom Wilkinson, Campbell Scott, Jennifer Carpenter, Colm Feore, Joshua Close, Kenneth Welsh, Duncan Fraser, J.R. Bourne, Mary Beth Hurt, Henry Czerny, Shohreh Aghdashloo; ***D:*** Scott Derrickson; ***W:*** Scott Derrickson, Paul Harris Boardman; ***C:*** Tom Stern; ***M:*** Christopher Young.

Exorcism's Daughter *House of Insane Women* **1974 (R)** While running an insane asylum, a man discovers that a woman has lost her mind because as a child, she witnessed her mother's death during an exorcism. Pretty grim but interesting for genre fans. A natural double feature with "House of Psychotic Women." **93m/C VHS.** *SP* Amelia Gade, Francisco Rabal, Espartaco (Spartaco) Santoni; ***D:*** Rafael Morena Alba.

The Exorcist 1/2 **1973 (R)** Truly terrifying story of a young girl who is possessed by a malevolent spirit. Brilliantly directed by Friedkin, with underlying themes of the workings and nature of fate. Impeccable casting and unforgettable, thought-provoking performances. A rare film that remains startling and engrossing with every viewing, it spawned countless imitations and changed the way horror films were made. Based on the bestseller by Blatty, who also wrote the screenplay. Not for the squeamish. When first released, the film created mass hysteria in theatres, with people fainting and paramedics on the scene. **120m/C VHS, DVD.** Ellen Burstyn, Linda Blair, Jason Miller, Max von Sydow, Jack MacGowran, Lee J. Cobb, Kitty Winn, Barton Heyman, Peter Masterson; ***D:*** William Friedkin; ***W:*** William Peter Blatty; ***C:*** Owen Roizman, Billy Williams; ***M:*** Jack Nitzsche; ***V:*** Mercedes McCambridge. Oscars '73: Adapt. Screenplay, Sound; Golden Globes '74: Director (Friedkin), Film—Drama, Screenplay, Support. Actress (Blair).

The Exorcist 2: The Heretic **1977 (R)** Unnecessary sequel to the 1973 hit "The Exorcist" which featured extensive recutting by Boorman. After four years, Blair is still under psychiatric care, suffering from the effects of being possessed by the devil. Meanwhile, a priest investigates the first exorcist's work as he tries to help the head-spinning lass. Decent special effects. **118m/C VHS, DVD.** Richard Burton, Linda Blair, Louise Fletcher, Kitty Winn, James Earl Jones, Ned Beatty, Max von Sydow, Paul Henreid; ***D:*** John Boorman; ***W:*** William Goodhart; ***C:*** William A. Fraker; ***M:*** Ennio Morricone.

Exorcist 3: Legion **1990 (R)** Apparently subscribing to the two wrongs make a right school of sequels, this time novelist Blatty is the director. The result is slightly better than the first sequel, but still a far cry from the original. Fifteen years later, Detective Kinderman (Scott) is faced with a series of really gross murders bearing the mark of a serial killer who was flambeed in the electric chair on the same night as the exorcism of the pea-soup expectorating devil of the original. With the aid of priests Flanders and Dourif, the detective stalks the transmigratory terror—without the help of Linda Blair, who was at the time spoofing "The Exorcist" in "Repossessed." **105m/C VHS, DVD.** George C. Scott, Ed Flanders, Jason Miller, Nicol Williamson, Scott Wilson, Brad Dourif, Nancy Fish, George DiCenzo, Viveca Lindfors, Patrick Ewing, Fabio; ***D:*** William Peter Blatty; ***W:*** William Peter Blatty; ***C:*** Gerry Fisher; ***M:*** Barry DeVorzon.

Exorcist Master *Kui moh do jeung; Qu mo dao zhang* **1993** A Catholic priest and a Taoist priest vie for the hearts and minds of the local village, with the Taoist often on the losing end as the locals have become enamored of Western civilization. The Catholic Church wishes to reopen a long sealed church in which one of their missionaries was slain years ago, and ends up releasing his corpse as a vampire who gains control of the local hopping vampires and goes on a rampage. Each priest finds out his powers are useless against the other civilization's undead, and they must team up to save everyone. **92m/C DVD.** *HK* Collin Chou, Ching-Ying Lam, Ma Wu, Wing-Cho Yip; ***D:*** Ma Wu.

Exorcist: The Beginning 1/2 **2004 (R)** Once upon a time, Paul Schrader was set to make a prequel to the 1973 horror classic "The Exorcist." He shot his film, which was rejected by the producer as insufficiently scary. So Renny Harlin was hired to basically re-shoot (and re-cast) the entire movie. This backstory has got to be more interesting than what finally showed up on screen. In 1949, Merrin (holdover Skarsgard) has temporarily rejected the priesthood and is working as an archeologist. He agrees to travel to Kenya and bring back an artifact unearthed at a mysteriously preserved Byzantine church. Scary, possibly supernatural, things begin to happen—a child even becomes possessed! Would that any of the cheap theatrics could, more than momentarily, hold a viewer's interest. Schrader's version is also expected to be released on DVD. **114m/C DVD.** Stellan Skarsgard, James D'Arcy, Izabela Scorupco, Remy Sweeney, Julian Wadham, Andrew French, Ben Cross, David Bradley; ***D:*** Renny Harlin; ***W:*** William Wisher, Caleb Carr, Alexi Hawley; ***C:*** Vittorio Storaro; ***M:*** Trevor Rabin.

Exotica **1994 (R)** Daunting look at eroticism, secrecy, and despair. Christina (Kirshner) is at the center of some complicated relationships. She dresses as a schoolgirl while working at the Exotica strip club in Toronto, where her former lover Eric (Koteas) is the creepily suggestive DJ. Christina's also the obsession of seemingly mild-mannered tax man Francis (Greenwood), who has turned her table dancing into a strange private ritual. Lest this seem to make sense be assured that director Egoyan has much, much more going on—not all of it clear and most of it disturbing. **104m/C VHS, DVD.** *CA* Mia Kirshner, Elias Koteas, Bruce Greenwood, Don McKellar, Victor Garber, Arsinee Khanjian, Sarah Polley, Calvin Green, David Hemblen; ***D:*** Atom Egoyan; ***W:*** Atom Egoyan; ***C:*** Paul Sarossy; ***M:*** Mychael Danna. Genie '94: Art Dir./Set Dec., Cinematog., Costume Des., Director (Egoyan), Film, Orig. Screenplay, Support. Actor (McKellar), Score; Toronto-City '94: Canadian Feature Film.

Expect No Mercy **1995 (R)** Government agent must rescue a fellow agent being held in a virtual reality center that trains assassins to commit murder. **91m/C VHS, DVD.** Wolf Larson, Laurie Holden, Real Andrews, Billy Blanks, Jalal Merhi; ***D:*** Zale Dalen; ***W:*** J. Stephen Maunder; ***C:*** Curtis Petersen; ***M:*** Varouje.

Expectations *Swedish Heroes; Svenska Hjaltar* **1997** Several interconnected tales follow a divorcing couple, a man trying to reconcile with his father, two young lovers, and an older man and woman poised on the edge of an affair. Swedish with subtitles. **95m/C VHS, DVD.** *SW* Niclas Olund, Kent-Arne Dahlgren, Stefan Sundstrom, Emma Warg, Anki Liden, Cajsa-Lisa Ejemyr, Janne Carlsson, Hans Klinga; ***D:*** Daniel Bergman; ***W:*** Reider Jonsson; ***C:*** Esa Vuorinen; ***M:*** Nicklas Frisk.

The Expendables 1/2 **1989 (R)** A rugged captain turns a platoon of criminals and misfits into a tough fighting unit for a particularly dangerous mission from which they might not return. See the "Dirty Dozen" instead. **89m/C VHS.** Anthony Finetti, Peter Nelson, Loren Haynes, Kevin Duffis; ***D:*** Cirio H. Santiago; ***W:*** Phillip Alderton.

The Expendables **2010** Triple-threat Stallone (cast, writer, and director) leads a group of mercenaries on a mission to overthrow a South American dictator. Naturally, the group is betrayed. **m/C DVD.** *US* Sylvester Stallone, Terry Crews, Randy Couture, Eric Roberts, Dolph Lundgren, Jet Li, Jason Statham, Mickey Rourke, Steve Austin, Bruce Willis, Arnold Schwarzenegger, Charisma Carpenter, Nick Searcy, Brittany Murphy, Danny Trejo, David Zayas, Gary Daniels; ***D:*** Sylvester Stallone; ***W:*** Sylvester Stallone, David Callaham; ***C:*** Jeffrey L. Kimball; ***M:*** Brian Tyler.

Experience Preferred... But Not Essential 1/2 **1983 (PG)** An English schoolgirl gets her first job at a resort where she learns about life. **77m/C VHS.** *GB* Elizabeth Edmonds, Sue Wallace, Geraldine Griffith, Karen Meagher, Ron Bain, Alun Lewis, Robert Blythe; ***D:*** Peter Duffell; ***W:*** June Roberts; ***C:*** Phil Meheux. **TV**

The Experiment **2001 (R)** A prestigious medical institute recruits 20 men to spend two weeks in a controlled prison environment for a psychology experiment. Eight are chosen as guards and the remaining 12 are prisoners. The guards, led by sadist Berus (von Dohnanyi), soon begin abusing their power and their prisoners while the prisoners, led by Tarek (Bleibtreu), challenge their authority and the scientists simply lose control of their experiment. Based on the novel "Black Box" by Giordano. German with subtitles. **119m/C VHS, DVD.** *GE* Moritz Bleibtreu, Christian Berkel, Justus von Dohnanyi, Oliver Stokowski, Wotan Wilke Mohring, Nicki von Tempelhoff, Timo Dierkes, Antoine Munot Jr., Edgar Selge, Andrea Sawatzki, Philip Hochmair; ***D:*** Oliver Hirschbiegel; ***W:*** Don Bohlinger, Mario Giordano, Christoph Darnstadt; ***C:*** Rainer Klausmann; ***M:*** Alexander von Bubenheim.

Experiment 1/2 **2005 (R)** Low-budget sci fi (filmed in Prague). Morgan (Hopkins) and Anna (French) both wake up in different parts of the same city with no idea who or where they are or what happened to them. But someone is watching them very closely and it turns out the unfortunate duo are the subjects of a mind control experiment. **95m/C DVD.** John Hopkins, David Grant, Georgina French, Nick Simons; ***D:*** Dan Turner; ***W:*** John Harrison, Dan Turner; ***C:*** Gareth Pritchard; ***M:*** John Rand. **VIDEO**

Experiment in Terror **1962** A psychopath kidnaps a girl in order to blackmail her sister, a bank teller, into embezzling $100,000. **123m/B VHS, DVD.** Lee Remick, Glenn Ford, Stefanie Powers, Ross Martin; ***D:*** Blake Edwards; ***M:*** Henry Mancini.

Experiment Perilous **1945** A psychologist and a recently widowed woman band together to find her husband's murderer. An atmospheric vintage mystery. **91m/B VHS.** Hedy Lamarr, Paul Lukas, George Brent, Albert Dekker; ***D:*** Jacques Tourneur.

The Expert **1995 (R)** Special operations expert John Lomax (Speakman) helps catch the creep who murdered his sister. But the killer gets a slap-on-the-wrist sentence, ticking Lomax off mightily. Now, the duo prepare for a deadly last confrontation. **92m/C VHS, UMD.** Jeff Speakman, James Brolin, Michael Shaner, Alex Datcher, Wolfgang Bodison, Elizabeth (Ward) Gracen, Red West, Jim Varney; ***D:*** Rick Avery; ***W:*** Max Allan Collins; ***C:*** Levie Isaacks; ***M:*** Ashley Irwin.

Expert Weapon 1/2 **1993** It's a low-budget, male version of "La Femme Nikita" with an imprisoned cop killer recruited as an assassin by a secret government org (are there any other kind in these flicks). He even falls in love and then wants out. Fat chance. **90m/C VHS, DVD.** Ian Jacklin, Sam Jones, Mel Novak, Judy Landers, Joe Estevez; ***D:*** Steve Austin.

The Experts **1989 (PG-13)** When the KGB needs real Americans for their spies to study, they kidnap two out-of-work New Yorkers who mistakenly believe that they have been hired to open a nightclub in Nebraska. Shot on location in Canada. Sometimes funny and directed by former Second City TV MacKenzie Brother, Dave Thomas. **94m/C VHS.** John Travolta, Arye Gross, Charles Martin Smith, Kelly Preston, James Keach, Deborah Foreman, Brian Doyle-Murray; ***D:*** Dave Thomas; ***W:*** Nick Thiel, Eric Alter; ***M:*** Marvin Hamlisch.

Explicit Ills **2008 (R)** Ensemble drama chronicles the lives of various residents of a tough North Philly neighborhood and their struggles with poverty, drugs, and health care. Webber's directorial debut. **87m/C DVD.** Paul Franklin Dano, Rosario Dawson, Naomie Harris, Lou Taylor Pucci, Tariq Trotter, Francisco Burgos, Frankie Shaw; ***D:*** Mark Webber; ***W:*** Mark Webber; ***C:*** Patrice Lucien Crochet; ***M:*** Khari Mateen.

Explorers 1/2 **1985 (PG)** Intelligent family fare involving three young boys who use a contraption from their makeshift laboratory to travel to outer space. From the director of "Gremlins," displaying Dante's characteristic surreal wit and sense of irony. **107m/C VHS, DVD.** Ethan Hawke, River Phoenix, Jason Presson, Amanda Peterson, Mary Kay Place, Dick Miller, Robert Picardo, Dana Ivey, Meshach Taylor, Brooke Bundy; ***D:*** Joe Dante; ***W:*** Eric Luke; ***M:*** Jerry Goldsmith.

Explosion 1/2 **1969 (R)** Distraught and disturbed young man evades the draft after losing a brother in Vietnam. Arriving in Canada, he meets another draft-dodger with whom he embarks on a murderous rampage. **96m/C VHS.** Don Stroud, Gordon Thomson, Michele Chicione, Richard Conte; ***D:*** Jules Bricken.

Expose WOOF! **1997** Congressman's daughter Tiffany gets mistaken for a call girl and propositioned by one of dad's colleagues. When the geezer pays her off to keep quiet, Tiff decides extortion is a viable career option. **78m/C VHS, DVD.** Tracy Tutor, Kevin E. West, Daneen Boone, Libby George; ***D:*** B.A. Rudnick.

Exposed **1983 (R)** High fashion model Kinski falls in with a terrorist gang through a connection with violinist Nureyev. Weak plotting undermines the end of this political thriller. However, Kinski is brilliant, stripping the barrier between performance and audience. **100m/C VHS.** Nastassja Kinski, Rudolf Nureyev, Harvey Keitel, Ian McShane, Bibi Andersson; ***D:*** James Toback; ***W:*** James Toback; ***C:*** Henri Decae; ***M:*** Georges Delerue.

Exposed 1/2 **2003 (R)** Bob Smith (Donovan) hosts a TV tabloid show that is digging for dirt on three popular female TV personalities who are all up for a big award: Martha Stewart-like Susan Andrews (Strong), Brit wit Jade Blake (Carides), and morning show host Laura Silvera (Cavazos). Lame satire. **95m/C DVD.** *US* Tate Donovan, Brenda Strong, Gia Carides, Lumi Cavazos, David Rasche, Missi Pyle, Tom Irwin, Coolio, Jane Lynch; ***D:*** Misti Barnes; ***W:*** Misti Barnes; ***M:*** Mark Lewis.

Exposure **1991 (R)** A rugged American photographer (Coyote) on assignment in Rio turns vigilante to locate the vicious killer of a young prostitute. Coyote and his girlfriend (Pays) get caught up in the deadly underworld of international arms trading and drug running as they search for the murderer. **99m/C VHS.** Peter Coyote, Amanda Pays, Tcheky Karyo; ***M:*** Todd Boekelheide.

The Express 1/2 **2008 (PG)** Raised in a poverty-stricken Pennsylvania coal-mining town, Ernie Davis (Brown) is determined to play football for Syracuse University coach Ben Schwartzwalder (Quaid), who is equally determined to win a national championship with the running back who will become the first African-American to win the Heisman Trophy. Set in the 1960s, pic does a decent if not original job of telling the predictable story of overcoming obstacles to achieve greatness, but liberal doses of cliche and melodrama detract from excellent performances. Davis died of leukemia at 23 before ever playing in the pros. **129m/C DVD.** *US* Rob Brown, Dennis Quaid, Clancy Brown, Charles S. Dutton, Darrin Dewitt Henson, Nelsan Ellis, Omar Benson Miller, Geoff Stults, Frank Grillo; ***D:*** Gary Fleder; ***W:*** Charles Leavitt; ***C:*** Kramer Morgenthau; ***M:*** Mark Isham.

Express to Terror 1/2 **1979** Passengers aboard an atomic-powered train en route to Los Angeles attempt to kill a sleazy theatrical agent. Pilot for the "Supertrain" series. **120m/C VHS.** Steve Lawrence, George Hamilton, Vic Morrow, Broderick Crawford, Robert Alda, Don Stroud, Fred Williamson, Stella Stevens, Don Meredith; ***D:*** Dan Curtis. **TV**

Expresso Bongo 1/2 **1959** Soho singer/bongo player (Richards) is "discovered" by seedy talent agent Johnny Jackson (Harvey) who manages the young man into a teen idol with a 50-50 contract. But women come between the duo and Johnny finds himself without a star. **111m/B VHS, DVD.** *GB* Laurence Harvey, Sylvia Syms, Yolande Donlan, Cliff Richard; ***D:*** Val Guest; ***W:*** Wolf Mankowitz; ***C:*** John Wilcox.

Exquisite Corpses 1/2 **1988** An Oklahoma hayseed charges to New York with a new, slick image. He meets the wife of a wealthy man, and together they organize a murderous operation. **95m/C VHS.** Zoe Tamerlis, Gary Knox, Daniel Chapman, Ruth (Coreen) Collins; ***D:*** Temistocles Lopez.

Extasis *Ecstasy* **1996** Petty thieves Rober (Bardem), Max (Guzman), and Ona (Berrocal) hatch a plan to rob celebrated theater director Daniel Peligro (Luppi). He's Max's biological father but has never met his son, and the trio decide there would be less emotional trouble if Rober poses as Max. Rober is surprised when Daniel actually welcomes him and he begins to enjoy his new lifestyle, but his partners are getting impatient. Spanish with subtitles. **92m/C DVD.** *SP* Javier Bardem, Federico Luppi, Daniel Guzman, Leire Berrocal, Silvia Munt; ***D:*** Mariano Barroso; ***W:*** Mariano Barroso, Joaquin Oristrell; ***C:*** Flavio Labiano; ***M:*** Bingen Mendizabal.

The Exterminating Angel 1/2 *El Angel exterminador* **1962** A fierce, funny surreal nightmare, wherein dinner guests find they cannot, for any definable reason, leave the dining room; full of dream imagery and characteristically scatological satire. One of Bunuel's best, in Spanish with English subtitles. **95m/B VHS.** *MX SP* Claudio Brook, Cesar del Campo, Lucy Gallardo, Enrique Garcia Alvarez, Tito Junco, Ofelia Montesco, Bertha Moss, Pancho Cordova, Silvia Pinal, Enrique Rambal, Jacqueline Andere, Jose Baviera, Augusto Benedico, Luis Beristain; ***D:*** Luis Bunuel; ***W:*** Luis Alcoriza, Luis Bunuel; ***C:*** Gabriel Figueroa; ***M:*** Raul Lavista.

Exterminator **1980 (R)** Vietnam veteran hunts down the gang that assaulted his friend and becomes the target of the police, the CIA and the underworld in this bloody banal tale of murder and intrigue. Followed by creatively titled "Exterminator II." **101m/C VHS, DVD, UMD.** Christopher George, Samantha Eggar, Robert Ginty, Steve James, Tony DiBenedetto, Dick Boccelli, Patrick Farrelly, Michele Harrell, Stan Getz, Roger Grimsby; ***D:*** James Glickenhaus; ***W:*** James Glickenhaus; ***C:*** Robert M. "Bob" Baldwin Jr.; ***M:*** Joe Renzetti.

Exterminator 2 **1984 (R)** The Exterminator battles the denizens of New York's underworld after his girlfriend is crippled, then murdered by the ruthless Mr. X. Violence galore. **88m/C VHS.** Robert Ginty, Mario Van Peebles, Deborah Geffner, Frankie Faison; ***D:*** Mark Buntzman; ***W:*** Mark Buntzman.

Exterminators in the Year 3000 WOOF! **1983 (R)** The Exterminator and his mercenary girlfriend battle with nuclear mutants over the last remaining tanks of purified water on Earth. Low-budget Road Warrior rip-off. **91m/C VHS.** *IT SP* Robert Jannucci, Alicia Moro, Alan Collins, Fred Harris; ***D:*** Jules Harrison.

The External *Michael Almereyda's The Mummy; Trance* **1999 (R)** Alcoholic Nora (Elliott) keeps experiencing strange trances that have nothing to do with her drinking. So, Nora, her husband (Harris) and their young son travel to Ireland to visit Nora's freaky uncle (Walken) in hopes of some kind of explanation. Yep, it all has something to do with a 2,000-year-old druid he's keeping in the basement of the family castle. No, it doesn't make much sense. **95m/C VHS, DVD.** Alison Elliott, Jared Harris, Christopher Walken, Karl Geary; ***D:*** Michael Almereyda.

Extra Girl **1923** A silent melodrama/farce about a farm girl, brilliantly played by Normand, who travels to Hollywood to be a star. Once in the glamour capital, she gets used and abused for her trouble. **87m/B VHS, DVD.** Mabel Normand, Ralph Graves, Vernon Dent; ***D:*** F. Richard Jones; ***W:*** Mack Sennett.

Extract **2009 (R)** Sketchy and fitfully amusing comedy finds mild-mannered Joel (Bateman), the owner of a flavor-extract factory, besieged at work and at home. An assembly-line accident lawsuit is trouble since Joel was about to sell the company while newly-hired hottie Cindy (Kunis) turns out to be a con woman whom Joel stills lusts after. Meanwhile, to appease his conscience, Joel tries to have himbo Brad (Mulligan) seduce Joel's frigid wife Suzie (Wiig). Doesn't really hold together but may follow Judge's other work-related flick "Office Space" into belated cultdom. **91m/C DVD.** *US* Jason Bateman, Mila Kunis, Kristen Wiig, Dustin Milligan, Ben Affleck, Clifton (Gonzalez) Collins Jr., J.K. Simmons, David Koechner, Gene Simmons; ***D:*** Mike Judge; ***W:*** Mike Judge; ***C:*** Tim Suhrstedt; ***M:*** George C. Clinton.

Extramarital **1998 (R)** Magazine editor Fahey assigns reporter Lords to investigate a woman whose affair with a mystery man turns deadly. **90m/C VHS, DVD.** Jeff Fahey, Traci Lords, Brian Bloom, Maria Isabel Diaz; ***D:*** Yael Russcol. **VIDEO**

Extramuros **1985** A nun (Maura), living in a convent during the Spanish Inquisition, tries to repress her lesbian desires while the convent vies for fame and money through faked visions. Spanish with subtitles. **120m/C VHS.** *SP* Carmen Maura; ***D:*** Miguel Picazo.

The Extraordinary Adventures of Mr. West in the Land of the Bolsheviks **1924** The first achievement from the Kuleshov workshop, a wacky satire on American insularity depicting a naive and prejudiced American visiting Russia and being taken advantage of. Silent. **55m/B VHS.** Vsevolod Pudovkin, Boris Barnet; ***D:*** Lev Kuleshov.

Extraordinary Measures 1/2 **2010 (PG)** John Crowley (Fraser) seems to have the perfect life with wife Aileen and their children until the two youngest are diagnosed with a fatal genetic disorder. John teams up with unconventional doctor Robert Stonehill (Ford) and they start a bio-tech company focused on developing a new drug to save his children. Only Ford distinguishes himself as the rest of the high profile cast struggles with the weak material they've been given in this predictable, run-of-the-mill tearjerker. The first production from CBS Films has the look and feel of a made-for-TV-movie. Based on a true story. **105m/C DVD.** Harrison Ford, Brendan Fraser, Keri Russell, Dee Wallace, Jared Harris, Patrick Bauchau, Courtney B. Vance, Alan Ruck, Sam Hall, Meredith Droeger, Diego Velazquez; ***D:*** Tom Vaughan; ***W:*** Robert Nelson Jacobs; ***C:*** Andrew Dunn; ***M:*** Alex Wurman, Andrea Guerra.

Extraordinary Rendition **2007** Low-budget and short run time work against this sketchy story that does have some powerful scenes. Zaafir Ahmadi (Berdouni), a British citizen of Moroccan descent, has made some inflammatory statements during his college lectures on terrorism and democracy. This gets him drugged and kidnapped off a London street, taken to an unnamed Mideastern country, and tortured by Maro (Serkis), who accuses Ahmadi of funding terrorists. Flashbacks and flash-forwards show his life before and after his release as the broken man tries to pick up the pieces of his life. **77m/C DVD.** *GB* Omar Berdouni, Andy Serkis, Ania Sowinski; ***D:*** Jim Threapleton; ***W:*** Jim Threapleton; ***C:*** Duncan Telford; ***M:*** James Edward Barker.

The Extreme Adventures of Super Dave 1/2 **1998 (PG)** Cable TV character Super Dave Osborne (Einstein) comes to the big screen as Super Dave comes out of retirement for one last megastunt. He and protege Van Wormer plot a death-defying leap to raise money for neighbor Carides who has an ill son (Lindner). **91m/C VHS, DVD.** Bob Einstein, Gia Carides, Carl Michael Lindner, Steve Van Wormer, Dan Hedaya; ***D:*** Peter Macdonald; ***W:*** Lorne Cameron, Don Lake; ***C:*** Bernd Heinl; ***M:*** Andrew Gross.

Extreme Dating **2004 (R)** Four young ad execs head to a ski resort to continue their concept of extreme dating, which has so far been a disaster. The latest scheme is equally stupid: Troy (Keegan) and his crush Amy (DiScala) will get kidnapped, Troy will save the day, and Amy will be forever grateful and in love. Only the ex-cons hired by their pals Daniel (Sawa) and Lindsay (Detmer) decide to change the plan. No hilarity ensues, just embarrassment. **96m/C DVD.** Devon Sawa, Amanda Detmer, Andrew Keegan, Jamie-Lynn Sigler, Ian Virgo, Meat Loaf Aday, Lee Tergesen, John DiMaggio; ***D:*** Lorena David; ***W:*** Jeff Schectman; ***C:*** Sonja Rom; ***M:*** Scott Gilman. **VIDEO**

Extreme Honor **2001 (R)** This is an action movie with little action until the finale and a too-familiar storyline. Brascoe (Anderson) is forced out of the Navy SEALS when he's framed by his partner (Gruner). Now he needs a lot of cash in order to pay for his son's cancer treatments. So Brascoe teams up with some crooks (Madsen, Bush) to rip off a billionaire (Ironside). **95m/C VHS, DVD.** Dan Anderson, Michael Ironside, Michael Madsen, Olivier Gruner, Grand L. Bush, Martin Kove, Antonio Fargas, Edward Albert, Charles Napier, Odile Corso; ***D:*** Steven Rush; ***W:*** Steven Rush; ***C:*** Ken Blakey; ***M:*** David Powell, Geoff Levin. **VIDEO**

Extreme Justice 1/2 **1993 (R)** A violent expose of the Special Investigations Section of the Los Angeles Police Department, an elite, undercover squad which specialized in catching violent repeat offenders. But their tactics left something to be desired. They were accused of stalking their prey until they committed a crime and then dealing with the criminal by shooting them in the act. Lots of gunplay. Originally a theatrical film that was pulled for release in the wake of the Rodney King verdict. **96m/C VHS, DVD.** Stephen (Steve) Root, Lou Diamond Phillips, Scott Glenn, Yaphet Kotto, Ed Lauter, Chelsea Field; ***D:*** Mark L. Lester; ***W:*** Robert Boris; ***C:*** Mark Irwin; ***M:*** David Michael Frank.

Extreme Limits **2001 (R)** CIA agent Williams heads to Alaska to find a plane that has crashed in the mountains. As well as helping the survivors, he must find a mystery bomb that's also being sought by terrorists. Typical action fare. Wynorski directed under the pseudonym Jay Andrews. **105m/C VHS, DVD.** Treat Williams, Hannes Jaenicke, John Beck, Susan Blakely, Gary Hudson, Julie St. Claire; ***D:*** Jim Wynorski; ***C:*** Andrea V. Rossotto. **VIDEO**

Extreme Measures 1/2 **1996 (R)** Dr. Grant, Action Guy! Cast against type, Grant takes on action-suspense in this urbane medical thriller, and it works. Plot is pretty standard for the genre—doctor Luthan (Grant) suspects foul play when homeless people are turning up with mysterious symptoms before expiring in his ward. Seeking to expose what he believes is a medical conspiracy, his "darn meddling" gets him in all kinds of trouble. Enter Dr. Lawrence Myrick (Hackman), a genius neurologist who reeks of suspicion. Luthan must get by him to uncover the dangerous human experimentation that's been going on. Producer and real-life love Hurley may have had something to do with the fact that Grant pulls off a mostly convincing turn, where his normally comic persona is used to humanize an otherwise cardboard hero. Adapted from a book by Michael Palmer. **118m/C VHS, DVD.** J.K. Simmons, Hugh Grant, Gene Hackman, Sarah Jessica Parker, David Cronenberg, Bill Nunn, Debra Monk, John Toles-Bey, Paul Guilfoyle, Andre De Shields, Shaun Austin-Olsen, Peter Appel; ***D:*** Michael Apted; ***W:*** Tony Gilroy; ***C:*** John Bailey; ***M:*** Danny Elfman.

Extreme Movie **2008 (R)** Raunchy sketch comedy about teen sex includes geek Mike after his dream girl; Fred wanting to hook up with a sex chatroom babe; Chuck's once-innocent girlfriend getting into kink; and a sex puppet called Blue Ballsy. **75m/C DVD.** Ryan Pinkston, Michael Cera, Frankie Muniz, Jamie Kennedy, Christina DeRosa, Cherilyn Wilson, Rob Pinkston; ***D:*** Adam Jay Epstein, Andrew Jacobson; ***W:*** Adam Jay Epstein, Andrew Jacobson; ***C:*** Eric Haase; ***M:*** Jim Latham. **VIDEO**

Extreme Ops 1/2 **2002 (PG-13)** Shameless attempt to cash in on the popularity of extreme sports does a faceplant in every area but stunt work. The plot revolves around the antics of a group of snowboarders and skiers as they film a commercial for director Ian (Sewell). In their exploration of a half-finished resort, boarders Silo (Absolom) and Kittie (Pallaske) accidentally film a supposedly dead Serbian war criminal (Lowitsch). The intrepid crew must then evade the villain's armed henchmen while still finding time to poke fun at frosty downhill skier Chloe (Wilson-Sampras). No reason to be stoked about this one. **93m/C VHS, DVD.** *GB GE* Devon Sawa, Bridgette Wilson-Sampras, Rupert Graves, Rufus Sewell, Heino Ferch, Liliana Komorowska, Klaus Lowitsch, Jean-Pierre Castaldi, Joe Absolom, Jana Pallaske, David Scheller; ***D:*** Christian Duguay; ***W:*** Michael Zaidan; ***C:*** Hannes Hubach; ***M:*** Normand Corbeil, Stanislas Syrewicz.

Extreme Prejudice 𝒥𝒥 **1987 (R)** A redneck Texas Ranger fights a powerful drug kingpin along the U.S.-Mexican border. Once best friends, they now fight for justice and the heart of the woman they both love. **104m/C VHS, DVD.** Nick Nolte, Powers Boothe, Maria Conchita Alonso, Michael Ironside, Rip Torn, Clancy Brown, Matt Mulhern, William Forsythe, Tommy (Tiny) Lister, Larry B. Scott; ***D:*** Walter Hill; ***W:*** Deric Washburn; ***M:*** Jerry Goldsmith.

Extreme Vengeance 𝒥𝒥 **1990** Police officer David puts mafia crime boss Mario Blanco away for ten years, then exposes police corruption and goes into hiding. When Blanco gets out, he seeks revenge on David's family, forcing David out of hiding to protect what is his. Available in Spanish subtitles. **97m/C VHS.** David A. Cox, Lisa Gay Hamilton, Michael De Costa, Tanya George; ***D:*** Raja Zahr; ***C:*** Edward Zare.

Extremedays 𝒥 ½ **2001 (PG)** Four buddies take an aimless road California trip after graduating from college, indulging in their love of extreme sports such as surfing, skateboarding, dirt bike racing, and snowboarding. But when one of the guys learns of his grandfather's death, they decide to make the trip into a pilgrimage to pay their respects. For the most part it's silly fluff. **93m/C VHS, DVD.** Dante Basco, Ryan Browning, A.J. Buckley, Derek Hamilton, Cassidy Rae; ***D:*** Eric Hannah. **VIDEO**

Extremely Dangerous 𝒥𝒥 ½ **1999** Convoluted thriller that originated as a four-part British miniseries. Neil Byrne (Bean) was a British intelligence agent working deep undercover after infiltrating a group of gangsters. But his life is blown apart when Neil is convicted of the brutal murders of his wife and daughter. Naturally, he's innocent and when he makes his escape from prison transport, he heads back to find the true killers and get his revenge while being pursued by mobsters, police, and the agency he worked for. Some of the violence is very nasty. **200m/C VHS, DVD.** *GB* Sean Bean, Juliet Aubrey, Ralph Brown, Anthony Booth, Ron Donachie, Sean Gallagher; ***D:*** Sallie Aprahamian; ***C:*** Peter Middleton; ***M:*** Rupert Gregson-Williams. **TV**

Extremities 𝒥𝒥 **1986 (R)** An adaptation of the topical William Mastrosimone play about an intended rape victim who turns on her attacker, captures him, and plots to kill him. Violent and exploitive. **83m/C VHS, DVD.** Farrah Fawcett, Diana Scarwid, James Russo, Alfre Woodard; ***D:*** Robert M. Young; ***W:*** William Mastrosimone; ***C:*** Curtis Clark; ***M:*** J.A.C. Redford.

Eye 𝒥𝒥 *Dead Innocent* **1996 (R)** When attorney Suzanne St. Laurent's (Bujold) daughter is kidnapped, only mom can outwit the video-obsessed culprit before her child is killed. **90m/C VHS, DVD.** *CA* Genevieve Bujold, Graham Greene, Jonathan Scarfe, Emily Hampshire, Nancy Beatty, Susan Glover; ***D:*** Sara Botsford; ***W:*** Mort Pattigo, Dolores Payne; ***C:*** Rodney Gibbons; ***M:*** David Findlay.

The Eye 𝒥𝒥 *Jian Gui* **2002 (R)** Stylish Asian ghost story follows the blind-since-childhood Mun (Lee), who receives a corneal transplant that restores her sight. Some adjustment is expected, but Mun sees shadowy figures lurking about that no one else sees, accident scenes miles from where they occurred, and, yes, dead people. Mun goes to a shrink, Dr. Wah (Chou), who doesn't think his patient is crazy. Instead, the doctor investigates the cornea donor—and is not reassured to discover the young woman committed suicide. Cantonese, Mandarin, and Thai with subtitles. **98m/C VHS, DVD.** *HK* Sin-Je (Angelica) Lee, Lawrence Chou, Chutcha Rujinanon, Candy Lo; ***D:*** Oxide Pang, Danny Pang; ***W:*** Oxide Pang, Danny Pang, Jojo Hui; ***C:*** Decha Seementa.

The Eye 𝒥 ½ **2008 (PG-13)** Sydney Wells (Alba) is a concert violinist who has been blind since a childhood firecracker accident. As an adult, she undergoes a corneal transplant and promptly begins seeing ghouls, fire, premonitions of death, and eventually the image of the cornea donor (Romero), who it seems is trying to communicate something important through her eyes. Naturally her doctor and everyone else around her assume she is merely struggling with her transition to the sighted world; boy, are they wrong. Another ho-hum Hollywood re-make of a popular Asian formula horror film, but Alba fans will appreciate the tight, lingering shots of her lovely face and her obligatory shower scene. **97m/C DVD, Blu-ray Disc.** *US* Jessica Alba, Alessandro Nivola, Parker Posey, Rade Serbedzija, Rachel Ticotin, Chloe Grace Moretz, Fernanda Romero, Obba Babatunde, Danny Mora; ***D:*** David Moreau, Xavier Palud; ***W:*** Sebastian Gutierrez; ***C:*** Jeffrey Jur; ***M:*** Marco Beltrami.

The Eye 2 𝒥𝒥 *Gin Gwai 2; Khon hen phi 2* **2004 (R)** Joey Cheng (Shu Qi) is feeling a little depressed and moody, and she should be. She's broken up with a married man, failed at committing suicide, and learned she's pregnant with his baby—and now she can see ghosts when near children or pregnant women. Some of them even defend her, and one even beats down a would-be rapist. Unfortunately her ghostly defender is also a rabid stalker, and Joey soon comes to believe it's only waiting around for her to give birth. **98m/C DVD.** *HK TH* Qi Shu, Eugenia Yuan, Jesdaporn Pholdee; ***D:*** Oxide Pang Chun, Danny Pang; ***W:*** Lawrence Cheng, Jojo Hui; ***C:*** Decha Srimantra; ***M:*** Payont Permsith.

The Eye 3 𝒥 ½ *Gin Gwai 3; The Eye 10; Gin Gwai 10* **2005** Four teens are on vacation in Thailand when a local friend introduces them to a book that highlights ten ways to see ghosts or contact the dead. They give it a try, but once they start seeing ghosts it seems they can't shut it off. And then they start disappearing. Each of the "3 Eye" films done by the Pang brothers is different; this one is a comedy as well as a horror flick, but the mix doesn't work very well. **86m/C DVD.** *HK TH* Isabella Leong, Ray Macdonald, Bo-lin Chen, Yu Gu, Kate Yeung; ***D:*** Oxide Pang Chun, Danny Pang; ***W:*** Oxide Pang Chun, Danny Pang, Mark Wu; ***C:*** Decha Srimantra; ***M:*** Payont Permsith.

The Eye Creatures 𝒥 **1965** Alien creatures in the form of eyeballs are fought off by a teenager and his girlfriend. A low-budget, gory, science fiction feature. **80m/B VHS, DVD.** John Ashley, Cynthia Hull, Warren Hammack, Chet Davis, Bill Peck; ***D:*** Larry Buchanan.

An Eye for an Eye 𝒥𝒥 **1981 (R)** A story of pursuit and revenge with Norris as an undercover cop pitted against San Francisco's underworld and high society. **106m/C VHS, DVD.** Chuck Norris, Christopher Lee, Richard Roundtree, Matt Clark, Mako, Maggie Cooper; ***D:*** Steve Carver; ***W:*** James Bruner; ***C:*** Roger Shearman; ***M:*** William Goldstein.

An Eye for an Eye 𝒥 **1995 (R)** A made-for-TV script that ended up on the feature film pile (and we do mean pile). Manipulative story has Karen McCann (Field) listening on the phone as her daughter is raped and killed by a scuzzball drifter (Sutherland). He's caught, but released on a technicality, driving Mom to join a vigilante group and plot revenge. Not a great career move for the director or surprisingly distinguished cast, who are given nothing but cardboard characters and push-button emotional cliches to work with. Shamelessly plays on middle class fears of crime and doubts about the judicial system. Based on the novel by Erika Holzer. **102m/C VHS, DVD.** Sally Field, Ed Harris, Kiefer Sutherland, Beverly D'Angelo, Joe Mantegna, Keith David; ***D:*** John Schlesinger; ***W:*** Amanda Silver, Rick Jaffa; ***C:*** Amir M. Mokri; ***M:*** James Newton Howard.

Eye of God 𝒥𝒥𝒥 **1997 (R)** Darkly dramatic story of lonely small-town waitress Ainsley (Plimpton), who marries newly released, born-again ex-con Jack (Anderson) with whom she has been corresponding. Movie kicks off when veteran sheriff (Holbrook) questions a shaken up youth, Tommy (Stahl), who is mysteriously covered in blood but rendered mute by his experience. First-time director Nelson's spare narrative seeks to explore deep issues like faith and violence in the Bible Belt locale. Performances are universally powerful, especially Plimpton's lovable dim-bulb and Anderson's maniacal Jack, giving credence to the clever but sometimes overly flashy cinematic style. **88m/C VHS, DVD.** Martha Plimpton, Kevin Anderson, Hal Holbrook, Nick Stahl, Richard Jenkins, Margo Martindale, Maggie Moore, Mary Kay Place; ***D:*** Tim Blake Nelson; ***W:*** Tim Blake Nelson; ***C:*** Russell Fine; ***M:*** David Van Tiegham.

Eye of the Beast 𝒥 **2007** Scientist Dan Leland (Van Der Beek) comes to the small Canadian fishing town of Fells Island, where several deaths have been reported off the coast. Locals blame a sea monster but fishery officer Katrina Tomas (Castillo) says it's a giant squid. Since the sea beastie is ruining the fishing industry, the locals organize to get the tentacled troublemaker. Because this creature feature is low-budget, you don't get much in the way of visuals (a tentacle here, a giant eye there) so the fright quotient is minimal. **90m/C DVD.** James Van Der Beek, Ryan Black, Alexandra Castillo, Brian Roach, Larissa Tobacco, Arne MacPherson; ***D:*** Gary Yates; ***W:*** Mark Mullin; ***C:*** Michael Marshall; ***M:*** Jonathan Goldsmith. **TV**

Eye of the Beholder 𝒥 **1999 (R)** Disengaged surveillence expert, known only as "The Eye" (McGregor), works for British intelligence out of their embassy in Washington. His latest assignment is to keep track of blackmailing Joanna (Judd), who turns out to be a psychotic serial killer of many identities. This must provide some strange turn-on, since instead of calling the cops, he proceeds to track her cross-country, protecting her from capture. Judd's an attractive femme fatale but the picture makes little sense and soon falls into the jaw-dropping, I-don't-believe-what-I'm-seeing category. Based on the novel by Marc Behm. **101m/C VHS, DVD.** Ewan McGregor, Ashley Judd, Patrick Bergin, k.d. lang, Jason Priestley, Genevieve Bujold; ***D:*** Stephan Elliott; ***W:*** Stephan Elliott; ***C:*** Guy Dufaux; ***M:*** Marius De Vries.

Eye of the Demon 𝒥 **1987** A couple moves to a small town in Massachusetts and discovers that the area had once been a haven for witchcraft. To their horror, they soon find that old habits die hard, and the spellcasting continues in a nearby graveyard. **92m/C VHS, DVD.** Tim Matheson, Pamela Sue Martin, Woody Harrelson, Barbara Billingsley, Susan Ruttan; ***D:*** Carl Schenkel. **CABLE**

Eye of the Dolphin 𝒥𝒥 ½ **2006 (PG)** Come on, who doesn't love a dolphin? After her mother's death, troubled teen Alyssa (Schroeder) is sent to live with her previously unknown father Hawk (Dunbar), who runs a dolphin research facility in the Bahamas. Alyssa discovers she has a natural ability to communicate with the dolphins and when the facility is threatened with closure, she and a wild dolphin pal come to the rescue. Good family fare. **100m/C DVD.** Carly Schroeder, Adrian Dunbar, Katharine Ross, Christine Adams, Jane Lynch, George Harris; ***D:*** Michael D. Sellers; ***W:*** Michael D. Sellers, Wendell Morris; ***C:*** Guy Livneh; ***M:*** Alan Derian. **VIDEO**

Eye of the Eagle 𝒥 ½ **1987 (R)** A special task force is given a dangerous assignment during the Vietnam war. **84m/C VHS, DVD.** Brett (Baxter) Clark, Ed Crick, Robert Patrick, William (Bill) Steis, Cec Verrell; ***D:*** Cirio H. Santiago.

Eye of the Eagle 2 𝒥 **1989 (R)** When his platoon is betrayed and killed in Vietnam, a surviving soldier joins with a beautiful girl and seeks revenge. **79m/C VHS, DVD.** Todd Field, Andy Wood, Ken Jacobson, Ronald Lawrence; ***D:*** Carl Franklin.

Eye of the Eagle 3 𝒥 ½ **1991 (R)** Filipino-made Vietnam-War shoot-em-up, rack-em-up, shoot-em-up again, with U.S. forces pinned down against seemingly overwhelming odds. Violent. **90m/C VHS, DVD.** Steve Kanaly, Ken Wright, Peter Nelson, Carl Franklin; ***D:*** Cirio H. Santiago; ***W:*** Carl Franklin.

Eye of the Killer 𝒥𝒥 ½ **1999 (R)** Mickey Hayden is a drunken detective who is forced to re-open the serial killer case that led to his present wretched state. But this time Mickey finds himself having psychic visions when he touches the victims' belongings that put him into the mind of the killer. Now he's tracking a serial killer that may tie into a ten-year-old case. **100m/C VHS, DVD.** Kiefer Sutherland, Henry Czerny, Polly Walker, Gary Hudson; ***D:*** Paul Marcus; ***W:*** Jeff Miller; ***C:*** Brian Pearson; ***M:*** Michael Hoenig.

Eye of the Needle 𝒥𝒥 ½ **1981 (R)** Based on Ken Follett's novel about a German spy posing as a shipwrecked sailor on a deserted English island during WWII. Lonely, sad, yet capable of terrible violence, he is stranded on an isolated island while en route to report to his Nazi commander. He becomes involved with an English woman living on the island, and begins to contemplate his role in the war. **112m/C VHS, DVD.** Donald Sutherland, Kate Nelligan, Ian Bannen, Christopher Cazenove, Philip Brown, Stephen MacKenna, Faith Brook, Colin Rix, Alex McCrindle, John Bennett, Sam Kydd, Rik Mayall, Bill Fraser; ***D:*** Richard Marquand; ***W:*** Stanley Mann; ***C:*** Alan Hume; ***M:*** Miklos Rozsa.

Eye of the Storm 𝒥𝒥 ½ **1991 (R)** At the highway gas station/motel/diner where they live, two young brothers witness their parent's murder. Their younger brother is blinded in the same incident. Ten years later both brothers are still there and the tragedy may have turned one of them psychotic. When the abusive Gladstone and his young and sexy wife are stranded at the gas station it brings out the worst in everyone, with a violent climax during an equally violent thunderstorm. **98m/C VHS, DVD.** Craig Sheffer, Bradley Gregg, Lara Flynn Boyle, Dennis Hopper, Leon Rippy, Wilhelm von Homburg; ***D:*** Yuri Zeltser.

Eye of the Storm 𝒥 ½ *The Farmhouse* **1998 (R)** What's the elegant Danner during in this horror mishmash? (Maybe it worked better as a stage play.) College student Jenny (Kendall) is in rural Kansas during research on a typical American family. That turns out not to be the Millers—the farming family Jenny is forced to shelter with because of a tornado. Seems mom Irma (Danner) went whacko and killed daughter Sally and the event was covered up by her husband and adult son. Now, Irma's delusions mistake Jenny for Sally and the local sheriff is also snooping into Sally's disappearance. Adapted by co-scripter Watson from his play "The Farmhouse." **100m/C VHS, DVD.** Katherine Kendall, Blythe Danner, Leo Burmester, Guy Ale, Kurt Deutsch, Keith Reddin; ***D:*** Marcus Spiegel; ***W:*** Marcus Spiegel, Randy Watson; ***C:*** Horacio Marquinez; ***M:*** Anton Sanko.

Eye of the Stranger 𝒥 ½ **1993 (R)** Suspenser about a nameless stranger who sets out to solve the mystery of a small western town and its corrupt mayor. **96m/C VHS, DVD.** David Heavener, Sally Kirkland, Martin Landau, Don Swayze, Stella Stevens, John Pleshette, Joe Estevez, Thomas F. Duffy; ***D:*** David Heavener; ***W:*** David Heavener; ***M:*** Robert Garrett.

Eye of the Tiger 𝒥𝒥 **1986 (R)** A righteous ex-con battles a crazed, crack-dealing motorcycle gang that terrorized and murdered his wife, and is moving on to infest his town. **90m/C VHS, DVD.** Gary Busey, Yaphet Kotto, Seymour Cassel, Bert Remsen, William (Bill) Smith, Judith Barsi; ***D:*** Richard Sarafian; ***W:*** Michael Thomas Montgomery; ***C:*** Peter Lyons Collister; ***M:*** Don Preston.

Eye of the Wolf 𝒥𝒥 ½ **1995 (PG-13)** Zoologist (Fahey) brings a wild wolf into civilization and then must fight to save the animal from execution. Kazan (a wolf-dog mix) is the true star—and rightly so. **96m/C VHS.** Jeff Fahey, Sophie Duez.

Eye on the Sparrow 𝒥𝒥 ½ **1991 (PG)** A couple (Winningham and Carradine) desperately want to raise a child of their own, but the system classifies them as unfit parents since they are both blind. Together they successfully fight the system in this inspiring movie that was based on a true story. **94m/C VHS.** Mare Winningham, Keith Carradine, Conchata Ferrell, Sandy McPeak, Karen Lee, Bianca Rose; ***D:*** John Korty. **TV**

Eye See You 𝒥𝒥 *D-Tox* **2001 (R)** Substandard cop vs. serial killer yarn has FBI man Jake Malloy (Stallone) tracking a serial killer who likes to remove his victims' eyes with a drill. When his girlfriend becomes the maniac's latest victim, Sly goes on the sauce and ends up in a Wyoming detox center for cops. Shortly after he arrives, the patients start dying in apparent suicides and Malloy suspects his old nemesis might be on the premises. The plot wavers between illogical and laughable, while everybody involved overacts in an apparent attempt to figure out what the heck's going on. **95m/C VHS, DVD.** Sylvester Stallone, Tom Berenger, Charles S. Dutton, Sean Patrick Flanery, Christopher Fulford, Dina Meyer, Robert Patrick, Robert Prosky, Courtney B. Vance, Polly Walker, Jeffrey Wright, Kris Kristofferson, Stephen Lang, Rance Howard; ***D:*** Jim Gillespie; ***W:*** Ron L. Brinkerhoff; ***C:*** Dean Semler; ***M:*** John Powell.

Eye Witness 🦴🦴 1/2 *Your Witness* **1949** An American attorney goes abroad to free a friend from the British legal system. A book of poems becomes the necessary device in deducing the whereabouts of the witness testifying to his friend's alibi. **104m/B VHS.** *GB* Robert Montgomery, Felix Aylmer, Leslie Banks, Michael Ripper, Patricia Wayne; ***D:*** Robert Montgomery; ***M:*** Malcolm Arnold.

Eye Witness 🦴🦴 *Sudden Terror* **1970 (PG)** The murder of an African dignitary is witnessed by a young boy who has trouble convincing his parents and the police about the incident. Suspenseful but less than original. Shot on location in Malta. **95m/C VHS, DVD.** *GB* Mark Lester, Lionel Jeffries, Susan George, Tony Bonner; ***D:*** John Hough; ***W:*** Bryan Forbes; ***C:*** David Holmes.

Eyeball WOOF! *Gatto Rossi In Un Labirinto Do Vetro* **1978 (R)** An intrepid policeman is stumped by a madman who is removing eyeballs from his victims. At least they won't have to watch this movie. **87m/C VHS.** *IT* John Richardson, Martine Brochard; ***D:*** Umberto Lenzi.

Eyes Behind the Stars 🦴 *Occhi Dalle Stelle* **1972** A news photographer accidentally gets a few pictures of invading aliens, but nobody takes him seriously, particularly the government. **95m/C VHS, DVD.** *IT* Martin Balsam, Robert Hoffman, Nathalie Delon, Sherry Buchanan; ***D:*** Mario Gariazzo.

Eyes of a Stranger WOOF! 1981 (R) Terrifying maniac stalks his female prey by watching their every move. Tewes is cast as a journalist, the stronger of the two sisters in this exploitative slasher. **85m/C VHS.** Lauren Tewes, John Disanti, Jennifer Jason Leigh; ***D:*** Ken Wiederhorn; ***W:*** Eric L. Bloom; ***M:*** Richard Einhorn.

Eyes of a Witness 🦴🦴 1/2 **1994** American businessman Roy Baxter (Travanti) travels to Kenya to rescue his daughter (Grey) from danger in the African bush. But Roy is falsely charged with murdering a government official and must take on the police to prove his innocence. **90m/C VHS.** Daniel J. Travanti, Jennifer Grey, Carl Lumbly; ***D:*** Peter R. Hunt; ***W:*** Charles Robert Carner, Walter Clayton III; ***C:*** James Devis; ***M:*** Charles Gross.

Eyes of an Angel 🦴🦴 1/2 **1991 (PG-13)** A widower (Travolta), who's heavily involved in gambling, is forced to go on the run with his young daughter (Raab) when a deal goes sour. She must abandon the family dog, who manages to follow them from Chicago to California anyway. Talk about loyalty! **91m/C VHS, DVD.** John Travolta, Ellie Raab, Jeffrey DeMunn; ***D:*** Robert Harmon.

Eyes of Fire 🦴🦴 **1984 (R)** In early rural America, a group of pioneers set up camp in the wilderness and are besieged during the night by Indian witchcraft. **86m/C VHS.** Dennis Lipscomb, Rebecca Stanley, Fran Ryan, Rob Paulsen, Guy Boyd, Karlene Crockett; ***D:*** Avery Crounse; ***W:*** Avery Crounse; ***M:*** Brad Fiedel.

Eyes of Julia Deep 🦴🦴 **1918** Rare silent film featuring the ill-fated Minter as Julia, a woman who prevents Terry (Forrest) from killing himself. Piano scored. **54m/B VHS.** Mary Miles Minter, Alan Forrest, Alice Wilson, George Periolat; ***D:*** Lloyd Ingraham.

Eyes of Laura Mars 🦴🦴 1/2 **1978 (R)** A photographer exhibits strange powers—she can foresee a murder before it happens through her snapshots. In time she realizes that the person responsible for a series of killings is tracking her. Title song performed by Barbra Streisand. **104m/C VHS, DVD.** Faye Dunaway, Tommy Lee Jones, Brad Dourif, Rene Auberjonois, Raul Julia, Darlanne Fluegel, Michael Tucker; ***D:*** Irvin Kershner; ***W:*** John Carpenter, David Zelag Goodman; ***C:*** Victor Kemper.

The Eyes of Tammy Faye 🦴🦴 1/2 **2000 (PG-13)** Documentary examines the eventful life of a not-particularly interesting woman, Tammy Faye Bakker Messner. She was most famous for being married to televangelist Jim Bakker when their PTL ministry went belly up. Since much of the story is told through static interviews and TV news footage, the image is nothing special. Neither is the sound, though the choice of RuPaul Charles as narrator is inspired. The film was a hit on the festival circuit, and is recommended to that audience. **79m/C DVD.** Tammy Faye Bakker, Jim Bakker; ***D:*** Fenton Bailey, Randy Barbato; ***Nar:*** RuPaul Charles.

Eyes of Texas 🦴 1/2 **1948** Bryant, a lawyer who uses a pack of killer dogs to get the land she wants, is pursued by a U.S Marshal played decently by Rogers. **54m/B VHS, DVD.** Roy Rogers, Lynne Roberts, Andy Devine, Nana Bryant, Roy Barcroft; ***D:*** William Witney.

The Eyes of the Amaryllis 🦴 1/2 **1982 (R)** A young girl becomes involved in a mysterious game when she arrives in Nantucket to care for her insane, invalid grandmother. Based on the story by Natalie Babbitt and filmed on location on Nantucket Island. **94m/C VHS.** Martha Byrne, Ruth Ford, Guy Boyd, Jonathan Bolt, Katharine Houghton; ***D:*** Frederick King Keller.

Eyes of the Beholder 🦴🦴 **1992 (R)** Janice is a psychopathic serial killer who suffered brain damage from a botched surgical attempt to reverse his insanity. Now he's escaped from the state mental institution, heading straight for the secluded home of the doctor who made him crazier than ever. During a raging storm, Janice stalks the doctor, his wife, and their two hapless dinner guests in a sadistic game of cat-and-mouse. **89m/C VHS.** Lenny Von Dohlen, Joanna Pacula, Matt McCoy, George Lazenby, Kylie Travis, Charles Napier; ***D:*** Lawrence L. Simeone; ***W:*** Lawrence L. Simeone; ***M:*** Greg Turner.

Eyes of the Panther 1990 One of Shelley Duvall's "Nightmare Classics" series, this adaptation of an Ambrose Bierce story concerns a pioneer girl haunted for years by the animal urges of a wild cat. **60m/C VHS.** Daphne Zuniga, C. Thomas Howell, John Stockwell; ***D:*** Noel Black.

The Eyes of Youth 🦴🦴 **1919** A young woman searches her soul for answers: to marry or not to marry is the question. A little foresight, in the form of a glimpse into the hypothetical future, helps her make the right choice. Very early Valentino fare in which the sheik plays a cad. **78m/B VHS.** Clara Kimball Young, Edmund Lowe, Rudolph Valentino; ***D:*** Albert Parker; ***W:*** Albert Parker; ***C:*** Arthur Edeson.

Eyes Right! 🦴🦴 **1926** Based on a story by Ernest Grayman, this portrayal of life in a military prep school has its main character experience struggle, recognition, love, jealousy, and triumph. Silent. **46m/B VHS.** Francis X. Bushman, Larry Kent, Frederick Vroom, Florence Fair, Dora Dean, Robert Hale; ***D:*** Louis Chaudet; ***W:*** Leslie Curtis; ***C:*** Allen Davey.

The Eyes, the Mouth 🦴🦴 **1983 (R)** A young man has an affair with his dead twin brother's fiancee. Happiness eludes them as they are haunted by the deceased's memory and the family's grief. In Italian with English subtitles. **100m/C VHS.** *FR IT* Lou Castel, Angela Molina; ***D:*** Marco Bellocchio; ***W:*** Marco Bellocchio.

Eyes Wide Shut 🦴🦴 **1999 (R)** Kubrick's psychosexual drama (two years in the making), and last film, turned out to be visually interesting (because everything was done on soundstages) but less than compelling. Society doc William Harford (Cruise) and wife Alice (Kidman) seem to have it all, until a stoned Alice confesses to having lustful thoughts for others besides her hubby. Bill can't admit to the same (he's kind of a chilly guy), but this revelation sends him reeling out into the Manhattan night looking for adventure. He ends his evening observing, but not joining in, an aristocratic, anonymous orgy before heading home, presumably a wiser man. Kidman's role basically fades out after her bravura confessional and Cruise seems more like an interested bystander than a man whose known world has crumbled. Based on Arthur Schnitzler's 1926 novel "Traumnovelle." **159m/C VHS, DVD, Blu-ray Disc, HD DVD.** Treva Etienne, Tom Cruise, Nicole Kidman, Sydney Pollack, Marie Richardson, Vinessa Shaw, Todd Field, Rade Serbedzija, Leelee Sobieski, Alan Cumming, Thomas Gibson, Sky Dumont, Fay Masterson; ***D:*** Stanley Kubrick; ***W:*** Stanley Kubrick; ***C:*** Larry Smith; ***M:*** Jocelyn Pook.

Eyewitness 🦴🦴 1/2 *The Janitor* **1981 (R)** When a murder occurs in the office building of a star-struck janitor, he fabricates a tale in order to initiate a relationship with the TV reporter covering the story. Unfortunately the killers think he's telling the truth, which plunges the janitor and reporter into a dangerous and complicated position, pursued by both police and foreign agents. Somewhat contrived, but Hurt and Weaver are always interesting. Woods turns in a wonderful performance as Hurt's somewhat-psychotic best friend. **102m/C VHS, DVD.** William Hurt, Sigourney Weaver, Christopher Plummer, James Woods, Kenneth McMillan, Pamela Reed, Irene Worth, Steven Hill, Morgan Freeman; ***D:*** Peter Yates; ***W:*** Steve Tesich.

Eyewitness to Murder 🦴 1/2 **1993** Stevens plays a cop who is assigned to protect beautiful artist Wolter. They both have their tragic flaws: he is a grieving widower, she has been blinded by an unknown attacker. Their flaws may draw them together. Somewhat more engaging than a TV police action drama. **75m/C VHS.** Andrew Stevens, Adrian Zmed, Sherilyn Wolter, Carl Strano, Robin Drue; ***D:*** Jag Mundhra.

F. Scott Fitzgerald in Hollywood 🦴🦴 **1976** Dramatization begins in the late 1930s when Fitzgerald was lured to Hollywood to work in the burgeoning film industry. It covers the period when, with his wife in a mental institution, he lived with Sheila Graham and struggled against alcoholism. Interesting story made dull and depressing by Miller's uninspired performance, but it's almost saved by Weld's portrayal of Zelda. **98m/C VHS.** Jason Miller, Tuesday Weld, Julia Foster, Dolores Sutton, Michael Lerner, James Woods, John Randolph; ***D:*** Anthony Page. **TV**

F/X 🦴🦴🦴 **1986 (R)** Rollie Tyler (Brown) is a New York-based special effects expert who is contracted by government agent Lipton (DeYoung) to fake an assassination in order to protect mob informer DeFranco (Orbach). After completing the assignment, Rollie learns that he's become involved in a real crime and is forced to reach into his bag of F/X tricks to survive, aided by tough cop Leo McCarthy (Dennehy), who's trying to figure out just what's going on. Twists and turns abound in this fast-paced story that was the sleeper hit of the year. Followed by a sequel. **109m/C VHS, DVD.** Bryan Brown, Cliff DeYoung, Diane Venora, Brian Dennehy, Jerry Orbach, Mason Adams, Joe Grifasi, Martha Gehman, Angela Bassett; ***D:*** Robert Mandel; ***W:*** Robert T. Megginson, Gregory Fleeman; ***C:*** Miroslav Ondricek; ***M:*** Bill Conti.

F/X 2: The Deadly Art of Illusion 🦴🦴 **1991 (PG-13)** Weak follow-up finds the special-effects specialist set to pull off just one more illusion for the police. Once again, corrupt cops use him as a chump for their scheme, an over-complicated business involving a stolen Vatican treasure. **107m/C VHS, DVD.** Bryan Brown, Brian Dennehy, Rachel Ticotin, Philip Bosco, Joanna Gleason; ***D:*** Richard Franklin; ***W:*** Bill Condon; ***C:*** Victor Kemper; ***M:*** Michael Boddicker, Lalo Schifrin.

Fabiola 🦴🦴🦴 **1948** The first of the big Italian spectacle movies, this one opened the door for a flood of low-budget imitators. Fabiola, the daughter of a Roman senator, becomes a Christian when her father's Christian servants are accused of murdering him. In the meantime, the Emperor Constantine speeds toward Rome to convert it to Christian status. You can bet plenty of Christians will lose their heads, be thrown to the lions and generally burn at the stake before he does. **96m/C VHS.** *IT* Michel Simon, Henri Vidal, Michele Morgan, Gino Cervi; ***D:*** Alessandro Blasetti.

The Fable of the Beautiful Pigeon Fancier 🦴🦴 1/2 *Fabula de la Bella Palomera* **1988** A powerful man who has always gotten what he wanted spies a beautiful young married woman and sets out to make her his own. Based on the Gabriel Gracia Marquez novel "Love in the Time of Cholera." In Spanish with English subtitles. **73m/C VHS.** *SP* Ney Latorraca, Claudia Ohana, Tonia Carrero, Dina Stat, Chico Diaz; ***D:*** Ruy Guerra; ***W:*** Ruy Guerra, Gabriel Garcia Marquez; ***C:*** Edgar Moura.

Fabled 🦴 1/2 **2002 (R)** Is it all in his head? And do you care? Paranoid Joseph Fable (Askew) believes his ex-girlfriend Liz (Winnick) is in cahoots with his shrink and that his co-workers have stolen his dog. His friend Alex (Nash) thinks Joe should stop mixing booze and his meds. **84m/C DVD.** *US* Desmond Askew, Katheryn Winnick, Michael Panes, J. Richey Nash; ***D:*** Ari Kirschenbaun; ***W:*** Ari Kirschenbaun; ***C:*** Yaron Orbach; ***M:*** Jack Lingo.

Fabulous Adventures of Baron Munchausen 🦴🦴 *Baron Munchausen; The Fabulous Baron Munchausen; The Original Fabulous Adventures of Baron Munchausen; Baron Prasil* **1961** The legendary Baron Munchausen, known for his tall tales, relates the story of his trek to the strange and beautiful land of Trukesban in a mixture of live action and animation. Wonderful special effects but a boring story line. In German with English subtitles. **84m/C VHS.** *GE* Milos Kopecky, Hana Brejchova, Rudolf Jelinek, Jan Werich; ***D:*** Karel Zeman; ***W:*** Karel Zeman; ***C:*** Jiri Tarantik; ***M:*** Zdenek Liska.

The Fabulous Baker Boys 🦴🦴🦴 **1989 (R)** Two brothers have been performing a tired act as nightclub pianists for 15 years. When they hire a sultry vocalist to revitalize the routine, she inadvertently triggers long-suppressed hostility between the "boys." The story may be a bit uneven, but fine performances by the three leading actors, the steamy atmosphere, and Pfeiffer's classic rendition of "Makin' Whoopee," are worth the price of the rental. **116m/C VHS, DVD.** Michelle Pfeiffer, Jeff Bridges, Beau Bridges, Ellie Raab, Jennifer Tilly; ***D:*** Steve Kloves; ***W:*** Steve Kloves; ***C:*** Michael Ballhaus; ***M:*** Dave Grusin. Golden Globes '90: Actress—Drama (Pfeiffer); L.A. Film Critics '89: Actress (Pfeiffer), Cinematog.; Natl. Bd. of Review '89: Actress (Pfeiffer); N.Y. Film Critics '89: Actress (Pfeiffer); Natl. Soc. Film Critics '89: Actress (Pfeiffer), Cinematog., Support. Actor (Bridges).

The Fabulous Dorseys 🦴🦴 **1947** The musical lives of big band leaders Tommy and Jimmy Dorsey are portrayed in this less than fabulous biography that's strong on song but weak on plot. Guest stars include Art Tatum, Charlie Barnet, Ziggy Elman, Bob Eberly and Helen O'Connell. Highlights are the tunes. ♫At Sundown; I'll Never Say Never Again; To Me; Green Eyes; Dorsey Concerto; Art's Blues; Everybody's Doin' It; The Object of My Affection; Runnin' Wild. **91m/B DVD.** Tommy Dorsey, Jimmy Dorsey, Janet Blair, Paul Whiteman, Sara Allgood, Arthur Shields; ***D:*** Alfred E. Green.

Fabulous Joe 🦴🦴 **1947** A talking dog named Joe gets involved in the life of a hen-pecked husband. **54m/C VHS.** Walter Abel, Donald Meek, Margot Grahame, Marie Wilson; ***D:*** Harve Foster.

Facade 🦴🦴 **1998 (R)** American real-estate whiz, Colin Wentworth, and Frenchman Frederic Colbert team up for a shady business deal to build a luxury hotel in Malibu. They use murder, so no one will stand in their way. Frederic even encourages Colin to kill his murdered partner's wife, Caroline. But strange things keep happening and what Colin believes to be true, turns out to be very far from reality. **93m/C VHS.** Eric Roberts, Angus MacFadyen, Camilla Overbye Roos, Joe (Johnny) Viterelli; ***D:*** Carl Colpaert; ***W:*** Carl Colpaert, Lance Smith. **VIDEO**

Face 🦴🦴 **1997 (R)** A violent Brit-take on "Reservoir Dogs" has a group of East End armed robbers realizing someone in their gang has betrayed them after a heist goes wrong. Chief among the crooks are Ray (Carlyle) and his partner Dave (Winstone), plus three rookies and the unexpected involvement of a crooked cop. Lots of energy but not much that's new. **107m/C VHS, DVD.** *GB* Robert Carlyle, Steven Waddington, Ray Winstone, Philip Davis, Damon Albarn, Peter Vaughan, Lena Headey, Andrew Tiernan; ***D:*** Antonia Bird; ***W:*** Ronan Bennett; ***C:*** Fred Tammes; ***M:*** Andy Roberts.

The Face at the Window 🦴🦴 **1939** Melodramatic crime story of a pair of ne'er-do-well brothers who terrorize Paris to conceal their bank robberies. **65m/B VHS, DVD.** Tod Slaughter, Marjorie Taylor, John Warwick, Robert Adair, Harry Terry; ***D:*** George King.

Face Down 🦴🦴 **1997 (R)** You've got your standard wisecracking New York excop-turned-PI Bob Signorelli (Mantegna), who has a one-nighter with your blonde bombshell type client Merre (Maroney), who has ties to a mystery man (Ant). There's a murder, there's Bob's ex-partner Lt. Cooper (Riegert), who's no friend, investigating the murder, and there's Bob trying to find the killer first. And you've certainly seen it all before. **107m/C VHS.** J.K. Simmons, Joe Mantegna, Peter Riegert, Kelli Maroney, Adam Ant; ***D:*** Thom Eberhardt; ***W:*** Thom Eberhardt; ***C:*** John Holosko; ***M:*** Gunther Schuller. **CABLE**

A Face in the Crowd 🦴🦴🦴 ½ **1957** Journalist (Neal) discovers a down-home philosopher (Griffith) and puts him on her TV show. His aw-shucks personality soon wins him a large following and increasing influence—even political clout. Off the air he reveals his true nature to be insulting, vengeful, and power-hungry—all of which Neal decides to expose. Marks Griffith's spectacular film debut as a thoroughly despicable character and debut of Remick as the pretty cheerleader in whom he takes an interest. Schulburg wrote the screenplay from his short story "The Arkansas Traveler." He and director Kazan collaborated equally well in "On the Waterfront." **126m/B VHS, DVD.** Andy Griffith, Patricia Neal, Lee Remick, Walter Matthau, Anthony (Tony) Franciosa; ***D:*** Elia Kazan; ***W:*** Budd Schulberg; ***C:*** Harry Stradling Sr. Natl. Film Reg. '08.

A Face in the Fog 🦴🦴 **1936** Two newspaper reporters set out to solve a number of murders that have plagued the cast of a play. Also interested is the playwright. Good low-budget thriller. **66m/B VHS, DVD.** June Collyer, Lloyd Hughes, Lawrence Gray, Al "Fuzzy" St. John, Jack Mulhall, Jack Cowell, John Elliott, Sam Flint, Forrest Taylor, Edward Cassidy; ***D:*** Robert F. "Bob" Hill.

A Face in the Rain 🦴🦴 **1963** American spy Rand (Calhoun) is hiding out in German-occupied Italy during WWII. It turns out Anna (Berti), the wife of his contact, is having an affair with the German officer (MacGinnis) who's hunting Rand. Mediocre. **82m/B VHS.** Rory Calhoun, Marina Berti, Niall MacGinnis, Massimo Giuliani; ***D:*** Irvin Kershner; ***W:*** Hugo Butler, Jean Rouveral; ***C:*** Haskell Wexler; ***M:*** Richard Markowitz.

Face of Another 🦴🦴 *Tanin no kao; I Have a Stranger's Face; Stranger's Face* **1966** A severely burned man gets a second chance when a plastic surgeon makes a mask to hide the disfigurement. Unfortunately this face leads him to alienation, rape, infidelity, and murder. In Japanese with English subtitles. **124m/B VHS, DVD.** *JP* Minoru Chiaki, Robert Dunham, Kyoko Kishida, Beverly (Bibari) Maeda, Eiji Okada, Koreya Senda, Tatsuya Nakadai, Machiko Kyo; ***D:*** Hiroshi Teshigahara; ***W:*** Kobe Abe; ***C:*** Hiroshi Segawa; ***M:*** Toru Takemitsu.

Face of the Screaming Werewolf 🦴 ½ *La Casa Del Terror; House of Terror* **1959** Originally a Mexican horror/comedy that was bought for U.S. distribution by Jerry Warren, who earned his spot in the horror hall of fame with "The Incredible Petrified World" and "Teenage Zombies." A scientist brings a mummy back to life, but when he removes the bandages (gasp), the subject turns out to be of the canine persuasion. Suffers from comic evisceration; not much to scream about. **60m/B VHS.** *MX* Lon Chaney Jr., Landa Varle, Raymond Gaylord; ***D:*** Gilberto Martinez Solares, Jerry Warren.

Face/Off 🦴🦴🦴 ½ **1997 (R)** Woo returns to his blood-soaked, violence-as-poetry-in-motion roots with the story of a fed who assumes the identity of the presumed-dead terrorist who killed his son. When the master criminal wakes up, he "steals" the cop's identity. Travolta's back for another wild ride, eating up the scenery when he takes on the bad-guy role. Cage, fresh from action hits in "The Rock" and "Con Air" gets to study the nature of good and evil (another Woo specialty) while he learns the nuances of the "leap across the room with two pistols blazing" move. Woo's Hong Kong efforts have always explored the blurry line between the good guys and the bad guys, and with Cage and Travolta, he has the perfect actors to display his findings. Woo cultists will welcome the return to the old style, while those only familiar with his stateside work will understand what all the fuss was about. **140m/C VHS, DVD, Blu-ray Disc, HD DVD.** John Travolta, Nicolas Cage, Joan Allen, Alessandro Nivola, Gina Gershon, Nick Cassavetes, Dominique Swain, Harve Presnell, Margaret Cho, CCH Pounder, Colm Feore, John Carroll Lynch, Matt Ross; ***D:*** John Woo; ***W:*** Mike Werb, Michael Colleary; ***C:*** Oliver Wood; ***M:*** John Powell. MTV Movie Awards '98: On-Screen Duo (John Travolta/Nicolas Cage), Action Seq.

Face the Evil 🦴 ½ **1997 (R)** TV star Sharon (Tweed) gets taken hostage in an art gallery where she's filming by a gang of thieves. But that's not the real problem—seems their leader, Dangler (Henriksen), wants to retrieve a shipment of nerve gas that's been hidden in some art work. **92m/C VHS, DVD.** Shannon Tweed, Lance Henriksen, Bruce Payne, Jayne Heitmeyer; ***D:*** Paul Lynch; ***W:*** Richard Beattie; ***C:*** Barry Gravelle; ***M:*** Paul Zaza. **VIDEO**

Face the Music 🦴 ½ **1992 (PG-13)** Ringwald and Dempsey were once stormily married and pursuing successful, collaborative careers as singer/songwriters for the movies. But they've abandoned the work, along with the marriage, until a movie producer makes them a very lucrative offer for a new song. Only Dempsey's new girlfriend has some voracious objections. **93m/C VHS.** Patrick Dempsey, Molly Ringwald, Lysette Anthony; ***D:*** Carol Wiseman; ***W:*** Randee Russell; ***C:*** Yves Dahan; ***M:*** Didier Vasseur.

Face the Music 🦴🦴 ½ **2000 (PG-13)** After being dumped by their record label, a band decides to have lead singer Dan (Christopher) fake his death for the publicity. But when a hot reporter (Lyons) arrives to cover the story, Dan finds it increasingly difficult to keep quiet. **85m/C DVD.** Tyler Christopher, Elena Lyons, Patrick Malone, Ted McGinley, Sharon Leal, Gloria Leroy, Jill Ritchie, Harry Van Gorkum; ***D:*** Jeffrey Howard; ***W:*** Beth Hollander-Harris; ***C:*** David Trulli; ***M:*** Philip W. Gough. **VIDEO**

Face to Face 🦴🦴 ½ **1952** Dramatic adaptation of two short stories, "The Secret Sharer," by Joseph Conrad, and Stephen Crane's "The Bride Comes to Yellow Sky." The Conrad story features Mason as a sea captain who discovers a fugitive stowaway aboard his ships. The Crane story features Preston as a sheriff threatened by an old-time gunfighter. **92m/B VHS.** Bretaigne Windust, James Mason, Michael Pate, Robert Preston, Marjorie Steele, Gene Lockhart, Minor Watson; ***D:*** John Brahm.

Face to Face 🦴🦴🦴 *Ansikte mot Ansikte* **1976** Bergman's harrowing tale of a mental breakdown. Ullmann has a bravura role as a psychiatrist deciding to vacation at her grandparent's house in the country. Once there she begins to experience depression and hallucinations tied to her past with both her mother and grandmother. Her deeply repressed feelings eventually lead to a suicide attempt, which brings some much needed help. Originally a four-hour series made for Swedish TV; subtitled. **136m/C VHS.** *SW* Liv Ullmann, Erland Josephson, Gunnar Bjornstrand, Aino Taube-Henrikson, Sven Lindberg, Kari Sylway, Sif Ruud; ***D:*** Ingmar Bergman; ***W:*** Ingmar Bergman; ***C:*** Sven Nykvist. Golden Globes '77: Foreign Film; L.A. Film Critics '76: Actress (Ullmann), Foreign Film; Natl. Bd. of Review '76: Actress (Ullmann); N.Y. Film Critics '76: Actress (Ullmann). **TV**

A Face to Kill For 🦴🦴 **1999 (PG-13)** Bernard has a horse farm, which her compulsive gambler husband Savant needs to sell to get some cash. So, he frames her for a crime and she's sent to prison. A fight with another inmate leads to facial disfigurement and when she does get out, Bernard decides plastic surgery will give her a whole new look. And with a new face, she plans to take some very sweet revenge. **91m/C VHS.** Crystal Bernard, Doug Savant, Barry Corbin, Billy Dean; ***D:*** Michael Toshiyuki Uno; ***W:*** Andrew Laskos, David Venable; ***C:*** Robert Steadman; ***M:*** Peter Himmelman. **CABLE**

Faceless 🦴🦴 *Les Predateurs de la Nuit* **1988** Franco gorefest has model Barbara disappear after going to a plastic surgery clinic run by the crazed Dr. Flamand. Her father sends a P.I. to find her, and he finds much more, as beautiful women are being killed for their skin and other needed accessories for the doctor's sister, who was disfigured in an acid-throwing incident. Bigger budget and better production values than Franco usually uses provides quality scares and squirms for fans of his work. Others may not be as enamored. **98m/C DVD.** *SP FR* Helmut Berger, Brigitte Lahaie, Chris Mitchum, Telly Savalas, Stephane Audran, Anton Diffring, Caroline Munro, Howard Vernon; ***D:*** Jess (Jesus) Franco; ***W:*** Fred (Rene Chateau) Castle, Pierre Ripert, Jean Mazarain, Michele Lebrun; ***C:*** Roger Fellous; ***M:*** Romano Musumarra.

Faces 🦴🦴🦴 ½ **1968 (R)** Cassavettes' first independent film to find mainstream success portrays the breakup of the 14-year marriage of middle-aged Richard (Marley) and Maria (Carlin) Forst. Both seek at least momentary comfort with others—Richard with prostitute Jeannie (Rowlands) and Maria with aging hippie Chet (Cassel). The director's usual improvisational and documentary style can either be viewed as compelling or tedious but the performances are first-rate. **129m/B VHS, DVD.** John Marley, Lynn Carlin, Gena Rowlands, Seymour Cassel, Val Avery, Dorothy Gulliver, Joanne Moore Jordan, Fred Draper, Darlene Conley; ***D:*** John Cassavetes; ***W:*** John Cassavetes; ***C:*** Al Ruban; ***M:*** Jack Ackerman. Natl. Soc. Film Critics '68: Screenplay, Support. Actor (Cassel).

Faces of Women 🦴🦴 **1985** Two stories about women in contemporary Africa. In the first, an unhappy young woman is married to a very jealous man. When her brother-in-law visits, she decides to give her husband something to worry about. The second story finds a businesswoman running into problems when she tries to open a restaurant—problems that her daughter helps to solve. French and indigenous languages with English subtitles. **103m/C VHS.** Eugenie Cisse Roland, Sidiki Bakaba, Albertine N'Guessan; ***D:*** Desire Ecare.

Facing the Enemy 🦴🦴 **2000 (R)** Harlan Moss (Caulfield) believes in revenge and he blames Detective Griff McCleary (Ashby) for the death of his wife (Preston). So his idea is to seduce McCleary's estranged wife (Paul)—and then kill her. The surprise ending isn't very and it's a familiar ride but if you're in the mood for a cop thriller, this one will pass the time. **98m/C VHS, DVD.** Linden Ashby, Maxwell Caulfield, Alexandra Paul, Cynthia (Cyndy, Cindy) Preston, Max Gail, Bruce Weitz, Melanie Wilson; ***D:*** Rob Malenfant; ***W:*** Martin Kitrosser; ***C:*** Steve Adcock; ***M:*** Richard Bowers. **VIDEO**

Facing Windows 🦴🦴 ½ *La Finestra di Fronte* **2003 (R)** Unhappy Giovanna (Mezzogiorno) is a working wife and mother with an oblivious husband, Filippo (Nigro), and a dull job in a chicken factory. Her only sliver of excitement is her handsome neighbor, Lorenzo (Bova), whom she ogles from her kitchen window (as he watches back). Things change when Filippo brings home a confused elderly gentleman who thinks his name is Davide (Girotti). Giovanna reluctantly allows the stranger to stay the night after spotting a concentration camp number tattooed on his arm. In a round about way, this leads to Giovanna getting involved with Lorenzo, learning about Davide's lost love, and even satisfying her secret dream of becoming a pastry chef. Poignant if undemanding slice of life drama. Girotti's last role; Italian with subtitles. **106m/C DVD.** *IT GB PT TU* Giovanna Mezzogiorno, Massimo Girotti, Raoul Bova, Filippo Nigro, Serra Yilmaz, Massimo Poggio, Ivan Bacchi; ***D:*** Ferzan Ozpetek; ***W:*** Ferzan Ozpetek, Gianni Romoli; ***C:*** Gianfilippo Corticelli; ***M:*** Andrea Guerra.

Factory Girl 🦴 ½ **2006 (R)** The brief life of Warhol wild child Edie Sedgwick (Miller) is retold in a conventional biopic. Blonde, beautiful, and from a wealthy-but-troubled family, Sedgwick trades in art school for the sixties New York scene and her chance as Warhol's (Pearce) latest muse. But Edie falls into a drug-fueled trap and bad romantic choices, including a seductive musician (Christensen). While Miller certainly looks the part, there's nothing substantial or particularly interesting about her performance or the flick. **90m/C DVD.** *US* Sienna Miller, Guy Pearce, Hayden Christensen, Jimmy Fallon, Mena Suvari, Shawn Hatosy, Illeana Douglas, James Naughton, Beth Grant, Jack Houston; ***D:*** George Hickenlooper; ***W:*** Captain Mauzner; ***C:*** Michael Grady; ***M:*** Ed Shearmur.

Factotum 🦴🦴🦴 **2006 (R)** Adaptation of Charles Bukowski's 1975 book of the same name is a bleak, darkly funny examination of ideals and ambivalence. Bukoswki's booze-soaked alter-ego Hank Chinaski (Dillon) lives by the slacker code with his series of changeable jobs and changeable women while he tends to his mediocre writing. Girlfriends Jan (Taylor) and Laura(Tomei) are excellent as Hank's enablers, but it's Dillon who brings style and swagger to a "man of many jobs" (a definition of the movie's title) who eschews soul-sucking opportunity and success in favor of being true to his distasteful, deep self. **94m/C DVD.** *US GE NO* Matt Dillon, Lili Taylor, Marisa Tomei, Fisher Stevens, Didier Flamand, Adrienne Shelly, Karen Young, Tom Lyons; ***D:*** Bent Hamer; ***W:*** Bent Hamer, Jim Stark; ***C:*** John Christian Rosenlund; ***M:*** Kristin Asbjornsen.

The Facts of Life 🦴🦴 ½ **1960 (PG-13)** Risque bedroom comedy finds Larry Gilbert (Hope) and Kitty Weaver (Ball) running off from boredom in suburbia and their respective spouses (Hussey and DeFore) to have a little interlude together. **103m/B VHS.** Bob Hope, Lucille Ball, Ruth Hussey, Don DeFore, Louis Nye, Philip Ober; ***D:*** Melvin Frank; ***W:*** Melvin Frank, Norman Panama; ***C:*** Charles B(ryant) Lang Jr.; ***M:*** Leigh Harline. Oscars '60: Costume Des. (B&W).

The Faculty 🦴🦴 ½ **1998 (R)** Nerd (Wood), beauty queen (Brewster), jock (Hatosy), new girl (Harris), rebel (Hartnett), and lovelorn girl (DuVall) come up against the greatest challenge of their lives. No, not the SATs. Parasitic aliens have nested in their high school and replaced the rumpled, frumpy staff with pleasure-seeking sexpots out for excitment. It's "The Breakfast Club" against "Them" in a battle royale! More style, less substance dictates the union between indie director Rodriguez and screenwriter Williamson. As expected, the dialogue is hip, the fashions are crisp, and kids are spunky, but pic never explains the aliens' visit. The multi-generational cast is enjoyable enough and the scares (however recycled they may be) are effective if you like icky scenes of alien projectiles sprouting from a human orifice or two. **102m/C VHS, DVD.** Jon Abrahams, Elijah Wood, Robert Patrick, Bebe Neuwirth, Salma Hayek, Jon Stewart, Piper Laurie, Famke Janssen, Christopher McDonald, Jordana Brewster, Clea DuVall, Laura Harris, Josh Hartnett, Usher Raymond; ***D:*** Robert Rodriguez; ***W:*** Kevin Williamson; ***C:*** Enrique Chediak; ***M:*** Marco Beltrami.

Fade to Black **WOOF!** **1980 (R)** Young man obsessed with movies loses his grip on reality and adopts the personalities of cinematic characters (Hopalong Cassidy and Dracula among them) to seek revenge on people who have wronged him. Thoroughly unpleasant, highlighted by clips from old flicks. **100m/C VHS, DVD.** Dennis Christopher, Tim Thomerson, Linda Kerridge, Mickey Rourke, Melinda Fee, Gwynne Gilford, Norman Burton, Morgan Paull, James Luisi, John Steadman, Marcie Barkin, Eve Brent; ***D:*** Vernon Zimmerman; ***W:*** Vernon Zimmerman; ***C:*** Alex Phillips Jr.; ***M:*** Craig Safan.

Fade to Black 🦴🦴 **1993 (R)** Busfield stars as a college professor with voyeuristic tendencies and a handy camcorder. After viewing his latest tape, he realizes he's filmed his neighbor's murder and that he can recognize the killer. Before he can warn the killer's girlfriend, she disappears and our nosy prof is framed for the death. **84m/C VHS.** Timothy Busfield, Heather Locklear, Michael Beck, Louis Giambalvo, Cloris Leachman, David Byron; ***D:*** John McPherson; ***W:*** Douglas Barr.

Fade to Black **2004 (R)** Jay-Z's brilliant goodbye letter to the public eye. What's touted as the final concert of his career is magnificently captured in an exploding Madison Square Gardens in November of 2003, along with studio time during the making of "The Black Album." Jay-Z waxes ill-osophic about the methods to his badness, gets a haircut, and scowls as his posse bumrush his ColecoVision, dropping furious rhymes everywhere he turns. The entire affair is a little too long, but the energy carries well. **109m/C DVD.** *US* ***D:*** Michael John Warren; ***C:*** Scott Lochmus, Theron Smith, Paul Bozymowski, Luke McCoubrey.

Fahrenheit 451 **1966** Chilling adaptation of the Ray Bradbury novel about a totalitarian futuristic society that has banned all reading material and the firemen whose job it is to keep the fires at 451 degrees: the temperature at which paper burns. Werner is Montag, a fireman who begins to question the rightness of his actions when he meets the book-loving teacher Clarisse (Christie)—who also plays the dual role of Werner's TV-absorbed wife, Linda. Truffaut's first color and English-language film. **112m/C VHS, DVD.** *FR GB* Oskar Werner, Julie Christie, Cyril Cusack, Anton Diffring, Alex Scott, Anna Palk, Ann Bell, Mark Lester, Tom Watson; ***D:*** Francois Truffaut; ***W:*** Francois Truffaut, Helen Scott, Jean-Louis Richard, David Rudkin; ***C:*** Nicolas Roeg; ***M:*** Bernard Herrmann.

Fahrenheit 9/11 **2004 (R)** Michael Moore's indictment of the Bush administration's handling of the Iraq War begins with the 2000 election and follows Bush up to and through the 9/11 attacks, pointing out lost opportunities to stop Bin Laden's plot. Continues through the War on Terrorism and the Iraq War. Party affiliation will determine viewer opinion, but Moore's poisoned pen letter of a documentary is effective and bracing. This is pure propaganda, but of the strongest kind. Moore uses every weapon in his arsenal to attack Bush and his cronies, with outtakes and bloopers by Ashcroft, Rumsfeld, and Bush especially juicy. Sobering, horrific footage of ongoing carnage in Iraq—the stuff they don't show on the nightly news—balances out some of the more outlandish buffoonery and lampooning. Viciously funny and gut-wrenchingly heartbreaking. **110m/C DVD.** *US* ***D:*** Michael Moore; ***W:*** Michael Moore; ***C:*** Mike Desjarlais; ***M:*** Bob Golden, Jeff Gibbs. Golden Raspberries '04: Worst Actor (Bush), Worst Support. Actor (Rumsfeld), Worst Support. Actress (Spears).

Fail-Safe **1/2 1964** A nail-biting nuclear age nightmare, in which American planes have been erroneously sent to bomb the USSR, with no way to recall them. An all-star cast impels this bitterly serious thriller, the straight-faced flipside of "Dr. Strangelove." **111m/B VHS, DVD.** Henry Fonda, Dan O'Herlihy, Walter Matthau, Larry Hagman, Fritz Weaver, Dom DeLuise; ***D:*** Sidney Lumet; ***W:*** Walter Bernstein; ***C:*** Gerald Hirschfeld.

Fail Safe **2000** Claustrophobic remake of the 1964 Cold War thriller shown originally as a live CBS TV broadcast. Thanks to a computer glitch, a nuclear strike is launched against the USSR and the president and the military must find a way to recall the bombers or deal with the consequences. **86m/B DVD.** George Clooney, Richard Dreyfuss, Noah Wyle, Brian Dennehy, Sam Elliott, Don Cheadle, Harvey Keitel, Hank Azaria, James Cronwell, John Diehl, Norman Lloyd; ***D:*** Stephen Frears; ***W:*** Walter Bernstein; ***C:*** John Alonzo. **TV**

Failure to Launch **2006 (PG-13)** Finally, a movie that lives up to its title. Tripp (McConaughey) is a 35-year-old slacker still living with his parents (Bradshaw and Bates). They want him out, so they hire a woman, Paula (Parker), who specializes at getting grown men to move out of their parents' homes. Along the way characters are bitten by a chipmunk, a lizard, a dolphin, even a mockingbird. Both Parker and McConaughey play their usual smiling, glowing selves. Since this is a romantic comedy, they eventually fall in love. Guess Paula's not used to these freeloaders being buff and charming. **97m/C DVD, Blu-ray Disc, HD DVD.** *US* Matthew McConaughey, Sarah Jessica Parker, Zooey Deschanel, Justin Bartha, Bradley Cooper, Terry Bradshaw, Kathy Bates, Katheryn Winnick, Tyrell Jackson Williams, Patton Oswalt, Stephen Tobolowsky, Peter Jacobson, Kate McGregor-Stewart; ***D:*** Tom Dey; ***W:*** Tom J. Astle, Matt Ember; ***M:*** Rolfe Kent.

Fair Game WOOF! **1982 (R)** Three young women decide to ditch their private school for a weekend of fun but find out the resort town they've chosen is run by sociopaths who get their kicks by stalking our chicks. **90m/C VHS.** *AU* Kim Trengove, Kerry Mack, Marie O'Loughlina, Karen West; ***D:*** Christopher Fitchett.

Fair Game WOOF! **1985** In the Australian outback, three loathesome excuses for human beings come across a beautiful woman alone on a remote farm. Naturally, they try to do despicable things but she fights back. **83m/C VHS, DVD.** *AU* Cassandra Delaney, Peter Ford, David Sandford, Gary Who; ***D:*** Mario Andreacchio; ***W:*** Rob George; ***C:*** Andrew Lesnie; ***M:*** Ashley Irwin.

Fair Game WOOF! *Mamba Snakes* **1989 (R)** A psychotic but imaginative ex-boyfriend locks his former girlfriend in her apartment with a lethal giant Mamba snake. Understandably uninterested in its serpentine attention, the young woman must trespass against the Hollywood code and keep her wits in the face of danger. Guaranteed not to charm you. **81m/C VHS, DVD.** *IT* Gregg Henry, Trudie Styler, Bill Moseley; ***D:*** Mario Orfini; ***W:*** Mario Orfini, Linda Ravera; ***C:*** Dante Spinotti; ***M:*** Giorgio Moroder.

Fair Game **1/2 1995 (R)** Miami police detective Max (Baldwin) defies orders so he can protect family attorney Kate (Crawford, in her big-screen debut) from high-tech assassins. Nice work if you can get it. Generic action plot provides Crawford and first-time director Sipes with relatively safe proving ground. Cindy wears the "Die Hard" dirty white tank top look fetchingly enough (and showers when the action slackens), while Baldwin is no slouch in the babe department (male division) either. Based on Paula Gosling's 1978 novel "Fair Game," which was previously filmed as 1986's "Cobra." **91m/C VHS, DVD.** William Baldwin, Cindy Crawford, Steven Berkoff, Miguel (Michael) Sandoval, Christopher McDonald, Johann Carlo, Salma Hayek, John Bedford Lloyd, Jenette Goldstein; ***D:*** Andrew Sipes; ***W:*** Charlie Fletcher; ***C:*** Richard Bowen; ***M:*** Mark Mancina.

Fairy Tales *Fairytales* **1976 (R)** A ribald musical fantasy follows the equally risque "Cinderella." In order to save the kingdom, the prince must produce an heir. The problem is that only the girl in the painting of "Princess Beauty" can "interest" the prince and she must be found. Good-natured smut. **83m/C VHS, DVD.** Don Sparks, Prof. Irwin Corey, Brenda Fogarty, Sy Richardson, Nai Bonet, Martha Reeves; ***D:*** Harry (Hurwitz) Tampa.

FairyTale: A True Story **1/2** *Illumination* **1997 (PG)** Discovery of hope and fantasy in bleak reality when two girls in 1917 war-torn England claim to have photographed fairies in their garden. Skeptical debunker Harry Houdini (Keitel) and spiritual believer Sir Arthur Conan Doyle (O'Toole) show up to investigate the photos of cousins Elsie (Hoath) and Frances (Earl). The issues of science and spiritualism are profusely debated between the two men, getting a little in the way of the girls and their story. Tries to appeal to both adults and children, which may leave both feeling a bit unsatisfied. Perky pixies flitting about throughout picture, courtesy of special f/x wizard Tim Webber, are bound to delight even hardened audience skeptics. Don't blink for Mel Gibson's cameo as Frances' father. This same true story, known as the Cottingley Fairies, is also part of the plotline in the surreal British film "Photographing Fairies." **99m/C VHS, DVD.** Harvey Keitel, Peter O'Toole, Florence Hoath, Elizabeth Earl, Paul McGann, Phoebe Nicholls, Bill Nighy, Bob Peck, Tim (McInnerny) McInnery; ***Cameos:*** Mel Gibson; ***D:*** Charles Sturridge; ***W:*** Ernie Contreras; ***C:*** Michael Coulter; ***M:*** Zbigniew Preisner.

Faith **1990 (R)** When young dancer Faith's parents are killed in an accident she winds up in a frightening foster home. Running away, she meets a gentlemanly mobster who helps her attain her dance dreams. Laughably implausible. **104m/C VHS.** Sylvia Seidel, Ami Dolenz, Richard Maldone; ***D:*** Ted Mather; ***W:*** Ted Mather; ***C:*** Dennis Peters; ***M:*** Guido de Angelis, Maurizio de Angelis.

Faith **1994** Nick Simon (Hannah) is a widowed tabloid journalist who falls in love with Holly (Harker), daughter of politician Peter Moreton (Gambon). Nick gets an unexpected scoop when Holly tells him about her father's affair and now must choose between using the information or protecting his girlfriend's dad even as Peter struggles to save his career. **206m/C DVD.** *GB* John Hannah, Michael Gambon, Susannah Harker, John Strickland; ***W:*** Simon Burke; ***C:*** Peter Fearon. **TV**

Faithful **1/2 1995 (R)** Black comedy about depressed, rich housewife Margaret (Cher) who is rudely interrupted by Tony the hitman (Palminteri) while trying to commit suicide on her 20th wedding anniversary. Unfaithful hubby Jack (O'Neal), who has put the contract out on Margaret, is conveniently away on business. As Margaret sits tied to a chair and Tony waits for a call to confirm the hit, the two connect and decide to turn the tables. Director Mazursky succeeds in bringing Palminteri's three-character play to the screen, even if it does suffer at times from too much stage talk and not enough action. First film for Cher since 1990's "Mermaids" and the first for O'Neal since 1989's "Chances Are." Big rift between Mazursky and the film's producers over final cut led him to threaten to pull his name from the credits. Mazursky cameos as the hitman's therapist. **91m/C VHS, DVD.** Cher, Ryan O'Neal, Chazz Palminteri; ***Cameos:*** Paul Mazursky; ***D:*** Paul Mazursky; ***W:*** Chazz Palminteri; ***C:*** Fred Murphy.

Faithless **1/2** *Trolosa* **2000 (R)** Ullman again directs a Bergman screenplay about raw emotions and the pain of broken relationships. Evidently semi-autobiographical (it's set on Bergman's island home of Faro), an aging filmmaker (Josephson) in a spare office contemplates his newest screenplay when he's visited by an actress. This visitation is wholly in his mind, however, as Marianne (Endre) aids "Bergman" in writing about a painful affair in his past. Married to Markus (Hanzon), Marianne falls into an affair with close family friend David, who turns out to be the filmmaker in his younger days. The affair wreaks havoc on all three, while Marianne and David's daughter becomes a pawn. While the older filmmaker is thoughtful and even wistful, Bergman shows his younger, more reckless self little sympathy, while Ullman captures the director's languorous style. In Swedish with subtitles. **142m/C VHS, DVD.** *SW* Lena Endre, Erland Josephson, Thomas Hanzon, Krister Henriksson, Philip Zanden, Marie Richardson, Michelle Gylemo, Juni Dahr, Therese Brunnander; ***D:*** Liv Ullmann; ***W:*** Ingmar Bergman; ***C:*** Jorgen Persson.

Fake Out *Nevada Heat* **1982** Nightclub singer is caught between the mob and the police who want her to testify against her gangland lover. Typical vanity outing for Zadora. **89m/C VHS, DVD.** Pia Zadora, Telly Savalas, Desi Arnaz Jr.; ***D:*** Matt Cimber.

Fakers **2004** A London con man (Rhys) orchestrates an art heist to pay back a $50,000 debt. With the help of an artist buddy (Chambers), who came to possess a lost sketch by an Italian master, they hope to produce five copies and sell them to various London galleries in one single morning, and then blow town before anyone is the wiser. Chirpy crime caper with a lackluster plot. **85m/C DVD.** *GB* Matthew Rhys, Kate Ashfield, Art Malik, Tony Haygarth, Tom Chambers; ***D:*** Richard Janes; ***W:*** Paul Gerstenberger; ***C:*** Balasz Bolygo; ***M:*** Kevin Sargent.

The Falcon and the Snowman **1985 (R)** True story of Daulton Lee and Christopher Boyce, two childhood friends who, almost accidentally, sell American intelligence secrets to the KGB in 1977. Hutton and Penn are excellent, creating a relationship we care about and strong characterizations. **110m/C VHS, DVD.** Sean Penn, Timothy Hutton, Lori Singer, Pat Hingle, Dorian Harewood, Richard Dysart, David Suchet, Jennifer Runyon, Priscilla Pointer, Nicholas Pryor, Joyce Van Patten, Mady Kaplan, Michael Ironside; ***D:*** John Schlesinger; ***W:*** Steven Zaillian; ***C:*** Allen Daviau; ***M:*** Lyle Mays, Pat Metheny.

The Falcon in Hollywood **1/2 1944** The falcon gets caught up with the murder of an actor who was part of a Tinseltown love triangle. The film takes place on RKO's back lot for a behind-the-scenes view of Hollywood. Part of the popular "Falcon" series from the 1940s. **67m/B VHS.** Tom Conway, Barbara Hale, Veda Ann Borg, Sheldon Leonard, Frank Jenks, Rita (Paula) Corday, John Abbott; ***D:*** Gordon Douglas.

The Falcon in Mexico **1/2 1944** When paintings from a supposedly dead artist turn up for sale in New York City, the Falcon and the artist's daughter wind up journeying to Mexico to solve the mystery. Part of "The Falcon" series. **70m/B VHS.** Tom Conway, Mona Maris, Nestor Paiva; ***D:*** William Berke.

The Falcon Takes Over **1/2 1942** Escaped con Moose Malloy (Bond) is trying to track down his missing ex-girlfriend Velma in New York. The Falcon (Sanders) becomes interested in the case and investigates alongside reporter Ann Riordan (Bari), uncovering a gambling operation. **65m/B VHS.** George Sanders, Lynn Bari, Ward Bond, James Gleason, Allen Jenkins, Helen Gilbert, Edward (Ed) Gargan, Anne Revere; ***D:*** Irving Reis; ***W:*** Lynn Root, Frank Felton; ***C:*** George Robinson.

The Falcon's Brother **1942** Enemy agents intent on killing a South American diplomat are foiled by the Falcon's brothers at a steep personal cost. The plot enabled Sanders' real-life brother Conway to take over the title role in "The Falcon" mystery series, a role which he played nine more times. **64m/B VHS.** Tom Conway, George Sanders, Keye Luke, Jane Randolph; ***D:*** Stanley Logan.

Fall **1997** Brainy supermodel falls for literary cabbie in this portrait of life in the Big Apple. Within minutes of a chance encounter in a cab, married fare Sarah Easton (DeCadenet) is whiling the hours that her gorgeous, rich, doting husband is away, listening to romantic hack Michael's poetry and writhing seductively while feasting on carry-out like it's "9 1/2 Weeks." Schaeffer places himself opposite yet another gorgeous model and egotistically pens his character as a super-sensitive writer (who does this guy think he is, Woody Allen?) faced with overwhelming acclaim after his first novel, who decides to chuck it all and drive a cab. Although nicely acted and not bad to look at, the main characters and both their dilemmas are just a little hard to relate to. **92m/C VHS, DVD.** Eric Schaeffer, Amanda DeCadenet, Francie Swift, Lisa Vidal, Rudolf Martin; ***D:*** Eric Schaeffer; ***W:*** Eric Schaeffer; ***C:*** Joe DeSalvo; ***M:*** Amanda Kravat.

The Fall **1998 (R)** Or should that be "The Patsy"? American novelist Sheffer, who's living in Budapest, gets chosen as the savior of femme de Fourgerolles, who is being stalked by Prochnow. Or so she says—and she wants Sheffer to kill her tormenter. **90m/C VHS, DVD.** Craig Sheffer, Jurgen Prochnow, Helene de Fougerolles; ***D:*** Andrew Piddington. **VIDEO**

The Fall **2006 (R)** The R-rating seems silly (although it's not for the kiddies) in this visually striking and dramatically absurd creation from Tarsem, which took four years to film. In an L.A. hospital, circa 1915, a five-year-old Romanian migrant worker named Alexandria (Untaru) is convalescing after a fall. Movie stuntman Roy (Pace) is in the same hospital also after an accident—but he is paralyzed. Bored, Alexandria is happy to have her new friend tell her stories that change with her imagination and limited grasp of English (Indians to her are the eastern kind with elephants and palaces). However, a despondent Roy (whose girlfriend has dumped him) has an ulterior motive for befriending Alexandria. Based on the 1981 Bulgarian movie "Yo Ho Ho." **117m/C DVD, Blu-ray Disc.** *US GB IN* Lee Pace, Justine Waddell, Leo Bill, Catinca Untaru, Marcus Wesley, Daniel Caltagirone; ***D:*** Tarsem; ***W:*** Dan Gilroy, Tarsem, Nico Soultanakis; ***C:*** Colin Watkinson; ***M:*** Krishna Levy.

Fall from Grace **1/2 1994** American and British intelligence officers take deadly risks in 1943 Europe in an effort to convince Hitler to end the war. **180m/C VHS.** *GB* James Fox, Michael York, Patsy Kensit, Gary Cole; ***D:*** Waris Hussein.

Fall from Innocence ½ **1988** A girl is driven to a life of prostitution and drugs by the sexual abuse inflicted upon her by her father. **81m/C VHS.** Isabelle Mejias, Thom Haverstock, Amanda Smith, Rob McEwan; ***D:*** Carey Connor.

Fall Guy **1947** Cocaine-addled Tom Cochrane (Penn) can't explain to the cops why he's covered in blood. He's accused of murder but escapes from jail and gets his girl, Lois (Loring), to help him figure out what's happened. Dead bodies and a set-up are involved. Adapted from the Cornell Woolrich story "Cocaine." **64m/B VHS.** Reginald LeBorg, Mack Stengler, Teala Loring, Robert Armstrong, Clifford Penn, Elisha Cook Jr., Douglas Fowley, Charles Arnt, Virginia Dale; ***W:*** Jerry Warner.

Fall Guy *Kamata Koshin-Kyoku* **1982** Ginshiro Kuraoka (Kazama) is a megalomaniac actor whose once-hot career is on the skids. He's planned a spectacular fight scene for his latest picture in order to one-up his acting rival, but it's so dangerous that no stuntman will take the job. Until desperate and loyal bit player Yasu (Hirata) comes along. Ginshiro has already foisted his pregnant mistress Konatsu (Matsuzaka) off on his lackey and to provide for his new bride (whom he has always loved), Yasu is ready to tackle the dangerous stunt. It's a comedy. Japanese with subtitles. **108m/C DVD.** *JP* Keiko Matsuzaka, Sonny Chiba, Morio Kazama, Mitsuru Hirata, Chika Takami, Keizo Kanie; ***D:*** Kinji Fukasaku; ***W:*** Kouhei Tsuka; ***C:*** Kiyoshi Kitasaka; ***M:*** Masato Kai.

The Fall of the House of Usher **1949** Lord Roderick Usher is haunted by his sister's ghost in this poor adaptation of the Poe classic. **70m/B VHS, DVD.** *GB* Kay Tendeter, Gwen Watford, Irving Steen, Lucy Pavey; ***D:*** Ivan Barnett.

The Fall of the House of Usher *House of Usher* **1960** The moody Roger Corman/Vincent Price interpretation, the first of their eight Poe adaptations, depicting the collapse of the famous estate due to madness and revenge. Terrific sets and solid direction as well as Price's inimitable presence. **85m/C VHS, DVD.** Vincent Price, Myrna Fahey, Mark Damon, Harry Ellerbe, Bill Borzage, Nadajan; ***D:*** Roger Corman; ***W:*** Richard Matheson; ***C:*** Floyd Crosby; ***M:*** Les Baxter. Natl. Film Reg. '05.

The Fall of the House of Usher ½ **1980 (PG)** Another version of Edgar Allan Poe's classic tale of a family doomed to destruction. Stray to the Roger Corman/Vincent Price version to see how it should have been done. **101m/C VHS, DVD.** Martin Landau, Robert Hays, Charlene Tilton, Ray Walston; ***D:*** James L. Conway.

The Fall of the Roman Empire **1964** An all-star, big budget extravaganza set in ancient Rome praised for its action sequences. The licentious son of Marcus Aurelius arranges for his father's murder and takes over as emperor while Barbarians gather at the gate. Great sets, fine acting, and thundering battle scenes. **187m/C VHS, DVD.** Sophia Loren, Alec Guinness, James Mason, Stephen Boyd, Christopher Plummer, John Ireland, Anthony Quayle, Eric Porter, Mel Ferrer, Omar Sharif; ***D:*** Anthony Mann; ***W:*** Philip Yordan; ***C:*** Robert Krasker. Golden Globes '65: Score.

Fall Time *Falltime* **1994 (R)** Crime drama set in small-town Minnesota, circa 1957. Three high schoolers set in motion a prank that turns bad when they pull up in front of the local bank. David (Arquette), Joe (Blechman), and Tim (London) intend to stage a mock robbery—but a real robbery is going down and the teens wind up the terrified hostages of creepy criminals Florence (Rourke) and Leon (Baldwin). Promising premise derailed by narrative inadequacies. **88m/C VHS, DVD.** Mickey Rourke, Stephen Baldwin, Jason London, David Arquette, Jonah Blechman, Sheryl Lee; ***D:*** Paul Warner; ***W:*** Steve Alden, Paul Skemp; ***C:*** Mark J. Gordon; ***M:*** Hummie Mann.

Fallen **1997 (R)** Take a police-story suspense thriller, add the occult and a big dose of the supernatural, stir in a heaping helping of philosophy, a dash of a wrong-man subplot, shake vigorously, and out pours the bitter "Fallen." After the execution of serial killer Edgar Reese (Koteas), crack cop Hobbes (Washington) is soon chasing down copycat killings springing up everywhere. The real culprit is not Reese, but a fallen angel who inhabits body after body, creating new killers with each new host. Washington manages to hold his own as the pic gets messy and overly complicated. Goodman's character provides needed earthbound common sense when the banter gets a bit too lofty, debating things like the meaning of life, existence of God, and other issues that don't belong here. Hoblit's second feature tries to take on way too much in it's already lengthy span. With a mish-mash of conflicting film styles and dicey dialogue, film manages to land on the careers of an otherwise talented cast and crew. **124m/C VHS, DVD.** Denzel Washington, Donald Sutherland, John Goodman, Elias Koteas, Embeth Davidtz, James Gandolfini, Robert Joy, Gabriel Casseus; ***D:*** Gregory Hoblit; ***W:*** Nicholas Kazan; ***C:*** Newton Thomas (Tom) Sigel; ***M:*** Tan Dun.

The Fallen **2005** Set in the beautiful Italian countryside during the latter stage of World War II, follows the daily struggles of German, Italian, and American soldiers in October 1944 as Italian rebels battle with Italian and German troops forcing common villagers to choose between fascism and communism. The Allies head north to attack Germany's "Gothic Line." Intimate look at the common soldier's life filmed on a modest budget (under $1 million) unusual to modern war films. **105m/C DVD.** *US* Fabio Sartor, Sergio Leone, John McVay, Thomas Pohn, Ruben Pla, Dirk Schmidt; ***D:*** Ari Taub; ***W:*** Caio Ribeiro, Nick Day; ***C:*** Claudia Amber, Ian Dudley; ***M:*** Sergei Dreznin.

Fallen Angel ½ **1981** Relationship between a child pornographer and a particular young girl he finds easily exploitable because of her unbalanced home situation. Fine cast, solid direction. **100m/C** Dana Hill, Richard Masur, Melinda Dillon, Ronny Cox; ***D:*** Robert Lewis; ***M:*** Richard Bellis. **TV**

Fallen Angel ½ *Revenge* **1999 (R)** Mystery woman seduces and murders her victims and a police detective tries to undercover the link between the crimes. **90m/C VHS, DVD.** Alexandra Paul, Vlasta Vrana, Anthony Michael Hall, Michelle Johnson; ***D:*** Marc S. Grenier; ***W:*** Neil Goldberg; ***C:*** Georges Archambault; ***M:*** Milan Kymlicka. **VIDEO**

Fallen Angel ½ **2003** Sentimental story about making peace with your past and your family. Successful L.A. lawyer Terry McQuinn (Sinise) returns to Maine when his father dies. A caretaker for wealthy summer home people, the senior McQuinn and Terry were long estranged. Katherine Wentworth (Richardson) also has parental issues—her father abandoned the family after a tragic car accident and her wealthy mother is a much-remarried cold fish. Terry remembers Katherine from a childhood tragedy and they are gradually drawn together for a second chance at love and family. Snyder adapted from his novel. **110m/C DVD.** Gary Sinise, Joely Richardson, Gordon Pinsent, Jordy Benattar; ***D:*** Michael Switzer; ***W:*** Don Snyder; ***C:*** William Wages; ***M:*** Ernest Troost. **TV**

Fallen Angels *Duoluo Tianshi* **1995** The visuals dazzle but the disjointed narrative proves a challenge in what Kar-Wai originally intended to be a third story for his film "Chungking Express." Contract killer Wong Chi-Ming (Lai) has been getting his assignments from a nameless female agent (Reis) who's fallen for him. Wong wants to retire, which upsets her. Then there's mute ex-con He Zhiwo (Kaneshiro) who gets involved with a strange young woman named Cherry (Young) who still loves her ex-boyfriend, and everybody crosses paths but there's really no connection and nothing makes much sense anyway. **97m/C VHS, DVD.** *HK* Leon Lai, Michelle Reis, Takeshi Kaneshiro, Charlie Young, Karen Mok; ***D:*** Wong Kar-Wai; ***W:*** Wong Kar-Wai; ***C:*** Christopher Doyle; ***M:*** Frankie Chan.

Fallen Angels 1 **1993** Trilogy of hard-boiled, film noirish tales set in Los Angeles. "The Frightening Frammis" concerns a grifter (Gallagher) who meets his match in a mystery woman (Rossellini) in this adaptation of a Jim Thompson story. Cruise's directorial debut. "Murder, Obliquely" finds a plain Jane (Dern) falling for a heel (Rickman) who may have murdered his previous girl in a Cornell Woolrich tale. "Since I Don't Have You" has Buzz Meeks (Busey) hired to find a dame sought by both Howard Hughes (Matheson) and gangster Mickey Cohen (Woods). From a story by James Elroy. **90m/C VHS.** Peter Gallagher, Isabella Rossellini, Nancy Travis, John C. Reilly, Bill Erwin, Laura Dern, Alan Rickman, Diane Lane, Robin Bartlett, Gary Busey, Tim Matheson, James Woods, Aimee Graham, Dick Miller, Ken Lerner; ***D:*** Tom Cruise, Alfonso Cuaron, Jonathan Kaplan; ***W:*** Jon Robin Baitz, Amanda Silver, Steven Katz; ***M:*** Elmer Bernstein. **CABLE**

Fallen Angels 2 **1993** Three more film noir stories set in L.A. "Dead End for Delia" finds a police detective (Oldman) arriving at a murder scene to find his estranged wife (Anwar) the victim. Based on a short story by William Campbell Gault. "I'll Be Waiting" has Kirby as a hapless hotel detective who falls for a beautiful guest (Helgenberger) and winds up a mob pawn. Adaptation of a Raymond Chandler tale. "The Quiet Room" has Bedelia and Mantegna as a pair of corrupt cops who find their shakedown schemes going very wrong. From a story by Jonathan Craig. **90m/C VHS.** Gary Oldman, Gabrielle Anwar, Meg Tilly, Patrick Massett, Vondie Curtis-Hall, Paul Guilfoyle, Dan Hedaya, John Putch, Wayne Knight, Bruno Kirby, Marg Helgenberger, Jon Polito, Peter Scolari, Dick Miller, Joe Mantegna, Bonnie Bedelia, Vinessa Shaw, J.E. Freeman, Peter Gallagher, Patrick Breen, Genia Michaela, Wayne Grace; ***Cameos:*** Tom Hanks; ***D:*** Phil Joanou, Tom Hanks, Steven Soderbergh; ***W:*** Scott Frank, C. Gaby Mitchell. **CABLE**

Fallen Champ: The Untold Story of Mike Tyson **1993** Director Kopple's provocative documentary on the boxing champ, from his roots in a Brooklyn ghetto to his conviction for rape in 1991. Tyson is shown as pathetic, vulnerable, and violent—psychologically unprepared for both acclaim and responsibility, as well as easily manipulated by promoters and opportunists. A mixture of ring footage and interviews with sportswriters, promoters, trainers, and others as well as media coverage of Tyson. **93m/C VHS.** ***D:*** Barbara Kopple. **TV**

The Fallen Idol *The Lost Illusion* **1949** A young boy wrongly believes that a servant he admires is guilty of murdering his wife. Unwittingly, the child influences the police investigation of the crime so that the servant becomes the prime suspect. Richardson as the accused and Henrey as the boy are notable. Screenplay adapted by Greene from his short story, "The Basement Room." **92m/B VHS, DVD.** *GB* Ralph Richardson, Bobby Henrey, Michele Morgan, Sonia Dresdel, Jack Hawkins, Bernard Lee, Denis O'Dea, Dora Bryan, Walter Fitzgerald, Karel Stepanek, Geoffrey Keen, James Hayter, Dandy Nichols, George Woodbridge, John Ruddock, Joan Young, Gerard Heinz; ***D:*** Carol Reed; ***W:*** Graham Greene, Lesley Storm, William Templeton; ***C:*** Georges Perinal. British Acad. '48: Film; Natl. Bd. of Review '49: Actor (Richardson); N.Y. Film Critics '49: Director (Reed).

The Fallen Sparrow **1943** Garfield is superb as a half-mad veteran of the Spanish Civil War. Captured and brutalized, he never revealed the whereabouts of a valuable possession. His return to the U.S. continues his torture as Nazi agent Slezak uses the woman Garfield loves to set a trap and finish the job. Solid performances and good plot are highlights. **94m/B VHS.** John Garfield, Maureen O'Hara, Walter Slezak, Patricia Morison, Martha O'Driscoll, Bruce Edwards, John Miljan, John Banner, Hugh Beaumont; ***D:*** Richard Wallace.

Falling *Fallen* **2006** Intimate character study of five women who reunite at the funeral of their former teacher. Together they crash a wedding, kick up their heels at a nightclub, and share secrets that liberate them. As things are brought to a close, one is left feeling empty and unfulfilled, much like the lives of our five friends. German with subtitles. **88m/C DVD.** *AT* Birgit Minichmayr, Ursula Strauss, Kathrin Resatarits, Nina Proll, Gabriela Hegedus; ***D:*** Barbara Albert; ***W:*** Barbara Albert; ***C:*** Bernhard Keller.

Falling Angels **2003** Domineering Jim Field has driven his wife Mary into alcoholism and depression, leaving their three teenaged daughters to make their own way in 1960s Saskatchewan. Eldest daughter Norma has no self-confidence and is burdened by the suspicious death of their infant brother; middle daughter Lou becomes rebellious; and youngest daughter Sandy gets involved with a married man with some kinky ideas. Adaptation of the Barbara Gowdy novel. **109m/C DVD.** *CA* Callum Keith Rennie, Miranda Richardson, Monte Gagne, Katharine Isabelle, Kristin Adams, Mark McKinney, Kett Turton; ***D:*** Scott Smith; ***W:*** Scott Smith, Esta Spalding; ***C:*** Gregory Middleton; ***M:*** Ken Whiteley.

Falling Down **1993 (R)** Douglas is "D-FENS" (taken from his license plate), a normally law-abiding white-collar geek who snaps while stuck in a traffic jam on a hot day in LA. Like Charles Bronson in "Death Wish," he decides to take matters into his own hands. Unlike Bronson, he is not avenging an attack by a specific criminal, but raging against whomever gets in his way. Duvall is a detective on his last day before retirement, Hershey has the thankless role of Douglas' ex. Essentially a revenge fantasy that was vilified by some for catering to the baser emotions. **112m/C VHS, DVD.** Michael Douglas, Robert Duvall, Barbara Hershey, Rachel Ticotin, Tuesday Weld, Frederic Forrest, Lois Smith, D.W. Moffett, Dedee Pfeiffer, Vondie Curtis-Hall, Michael Paul Chan, Raymond J. Barry, Jack Kehoe, John Diehl; ***D:*** Joel Schumacher; ***W:*** Ebbe Roe Smith; ***C:*** Andrzej Bartkowiak; ***M:*** James Newton Howard.

Falling Fire ½ *The Cusp* **1997 (R)** Good visual effects highlight this cable scifier that combines terrorists and asteroids. Daryl Boden (Pare) has the task of getting his spacecraft to steer an asteroid into earth orbit for the purpose of mining its resources. But an eco-terrorist group, led by Lopez (Vidosa), want to force the asteroid to crash into the planet, thus "cleansing" it of man. Oh, there's a terrorist aboard Boden's craft to help things along, while his ex-wife Marilyn (von Palleske) fights the eco-villians back on earth. **84m/C VHS, DVD.** *CA* Michael Pare, Heidi von Palleske, Christian Vidosa, Zehra Leverman; ***D:*** Daniel D'or; ***W:*** Daniel D'or; ***C:*** Jonathan Freeman; ***M:*** Donald Quan. **CABLE**

Falling for a Dancer ½ **1998** When young Elizabeth Sullivan (Dermot-Walsh) gets pregnant after a brief affair, there's not much she can do since she lives in Ireland during the 1930s. She's forced by her family into marriage with a drunken widower and resigns herself to loneliness until love is found again. Purcell adapted from her own novel. **200m/C VHS, DVD.** *GB* Elisabeth Dermot-Walsh, Dermot Crowley, Liam Cunningham, Rory Murray, Brian McGrath, Maureen O'Brien, Colin Farrell; ***D:*** Richard Standeven; ***W:*** Deirdre Purcell; ***C:*** Kevin Rowley; ***M:*** Stephen McKeon. **TV**

Falling from Grace ½ **1992 (PG-13)** Bud Parks (Mellencamp) is a successful country singer who, accompanied by his wife and daughter, returns to his small Indiana hometown to celebrate his grandfather's 80th birthday. He's tired of both his career and his marriage and finds himself taking up once again with an old girlfriend (Lenz), who is not only married to Bud's brother but is also having an affair with his father. Bud believes he's better off staying in his old hometown but the problems caused by his return may change his mind. Surprisingly sedate, although literate, family drama with good ensemble performances. Actor-director debut for Mellencamp. **100m/C VHS, DVD.** John Cougar Mellencamp, Mariel Hemingway, Kay Lenz, Claude Akins, Dub Taylor, Brent Huff, Deirdre O'Connell, Larry Crane; ***D:*** John Cougar Mellencamp; ***W:*** Larry McMurtry.

Falling in Love ½ **1984 (PG-13)** Two married New Yorkers unexpectedly fall in love after a coincidental meeting at the Rizzoli Book Store. Weak but gracefully performed reworking of "Brief Encounter," where no one seems to ever complete a sentence. An unfortunate re-teaming for Streep and De Niro after their wonderful work in "The Deer Hunter." **106m/C VHS, DVD.** Robert De Niro, Meryl Streep, Harvey Keitel, Dianne Wiest,

George Martin, Jane Kaczmarek, David Clennon; ***D:*** Ulu Grosbard; ***W:*** Michael Cristofer; ***C:*** Peter Suschitzky; ***M:*** Dave Grusin.

Falling in Love Again 🦴 1/2 *In Love* **1980 (PG)** Romantic comedy about middle-aged dreamer Gould and realistic wife York. They travel from Los Angeles to their hometown of New York for his high school reunion, where Gould is suddenly attacked by nostalgia vibes for his youth, seen in countless flashbacks, and prominently featuring Pfeiffer, notable in her film debut. Like watching a home movie about people you don't care about. **103m/C VHS, DVD.** Elliott Gould, Susannah York, Michelle Pfeiffer; ***D:*** Steven Paul; ***W:*** Ted Allan; ***C:*** Michael Mileham; ***M:*** Michel Legrand.

Fallout 🦴🦴 1/2 **2001** It is horribly ironic that filmmaker Palumbo chose to film the introduction to his independent feature on top of one of the World Trade Center towers. His film concerns the interplay among four high-rise office workers who flee a disaster of uncertain origin and find themselves trapped in a basement fallout shelter. His story really has nothing to do with the 9/11/01 atrocities. It's a well-made character study that attempts to work with some serious ideas within the limitations of a modest budget. It's mostly successful, too, and certainly doesn't need any extra baggage. Parallels to reality are difficult to ignore, however. **88m/C DVD.** Claire Beckman, Mark Deakins, Keith Randolph Smith, David Wasson; ***D:*** Robert Palumbo; ***W:*** Robert Palumbo, Mark Gallini; ***C:*** Wolfgang Held; ***M:*** Frank Ferrucci.

False Arrest 🦴🦴 1/2 **1992** A woman is falsely accused of killing her husband's business partner and winds up in prison where she continues to fight to prove her innocence. Mills does well in this less-than-glamorous role. Based on a true story. **102m/C VHS, DVD.** Donna Mills, Steven Bauer, James Handy, Lane Smith, Lewis Van Bergen, Dennis Christopher, Robert Wagner; ***D:*** Bill W.L. Norton. **TV**

False Colors 🦴 **1943** Hopalong Cassidy unmasks a crook posing as a ranch heir. This was the 49th Hopalong Cassidy feature. **54m/B VHS, DVD.** William Boyd, Robert Mitchum, Andy Clyde, Jimmy Rogers; ***D:*** George Archainbaud.

False Faces 🦴🦴 1/2 **1918** Secret agent known as The Lone Wolf is working in France for the Allies when he learns a German master spy is headed for the U.S. to cause trouble. So he heads for New York to stop him. Lots of thrills. **65m/B VHS.** Henry B. Walthall, Lon Chaney Sr., Mary Anderson, Milton Ross; ***D:*** Irvin Willat.

False Faces 🦴 1/2 **1932** A ruthless, money-hungry quack is hounded by the law and the victims of his unscrupulous plastic surgery. **80m/B VHS.** Lowell Sherman, Peggy Shannon, Lila Lee, Joyce Compton, Berton Churchill, David Landau, Eddie Anderson, Ken Maynard, Veda Ann Borg; ***D:*** Lowell Sherman.

False Identity 🦴 1/2 **1990 (PG-13)** A radio psychologist buys a Purple Heart medal at a garage sale and then tries to find out about the original recipient. But her questions are making a number of folks uneasy, including a potentially dangerous stranger. **97m/C VHS.** Genevieve Bujold, Stacy Keach, Veronica Cartwright, Tobin Bell, Mimi Maynard; ***D:*** James Keach; ***W:*** Sandra K. Bailey.

False Prophets 🦴 1/2 **2006 (R)** Waitress Maggie (Heuring) is pregnant and wants an abortion until a fundamentalist group talks her into adoption because they believe there's something miraculous about the baby. Except Maggie gets suspicious and runs away and winds up at a rural gas station with a spiritually-minded attendant named Manny (Lyons), who helps her give birth in a field. There's supposed to be some meaning to all this. **?m/C DVD.** Lori Heuring, Patrick Bergin, Clayne Crawford, Tucker Smallwood, Antonio David Lyons; ***C:*** David Gossard; ***M:*** Brian Arbuckle. **VIDEO**

False Witness 🦴🦴 1/2 **1989** A New Orleans district attorney and her lover, a private investigator, find themselves working the same rape-murder case. When their methods disagree both find themselves in danger. Adapted from a novel by Dorothy Uhnak. **96m/C VHS.** Phylicia Rashad, Philip Michael Thomas, Terri Austin, George Grizzard; ***D:*** Arthur Allan Seidelman; ***M:*** Charles Fox. **TV**

Fame 🦴🦴🦴 **1980 (R)** Follows eight talented teenagers from their freshmen year through graduation from New York's High School of Performing Arts. Insightful and absorbing, director Parker allows the kids to mature on screen, revealing the pressures of constantly trying to prove themselves. A faultless parallel is drawn between these "special" kids and the pressures felt by high schoolers everywhere. Great dance and music sequences. Basis for a TV series. ♫ Fame; Red Light; I Sing the Body Electric; Dogs in the Yard; Hot Lunch Jam; Out Here On My Own; Is It OK If I Call You Mine?. **133m/C VHS, DVD.** Irene Cara, Barry Miller, Paul McCrane, Anne Meara, Joanna Merlin, Richard Belzer, Maureen Teefy, Albert Hague; ***D:*** Alan Parker; ***M:*** Michael Gore. Oscars '80: Song ("Fame"), Orig. Score; Golden Globes '81: Song ("Fame").

Fame 🦴 1/2 **2009 (PG)** Unnecessary update of the 1980 musical (and subsequent TV series) about an ambitious group of students at New York's prestigious High School for the Performing Arts. The teens soon learn that getting into the program is only their first challenge. The actors are then required to play out a script riddled with stuffy cliches aimed at a hip teen audience that's way too smart for this type of outdated, soapy mush. The original R-rated account of the pain behind achieving dreams is now a watered-down, PG-rated knock-off of "High School Musical." **107m/C DVD.** *US* Paul Iacono, Kay Panabaker, Debbie Allen, Charles S. Dutton, Kristy Flores, Kelsey Grammer, Megan Mullally, Bebe Neuwirth, Tim Jo, Debbie Allen, Charles S. Dutton; ***D:*** Kevin Tancharoen; ***W:*** Allison Burnett, Christopher Gore; ***C:*** Scott Kevan; ***M:*** Mark Isham.

Fame Is the Spur 🦴🦴 1/2 **1947** A lengthy but interesting look at the way power corrupts, plus an insight into the Conservative versus Labor dynamics of British government. Redgrave is a poor, idealistic worker who decides to help his fellow workers by running for Parliament. There, he falls prey to the trappings of office with surprising consequences. Look hard for Tomlinson, who went on to star in "Mary Poppins" and "Bedknobs and Broomsticks" for Disney. **116m/B VHS.** *GB* Michael Redgrave, Rosamund John, Bernard Miles, Hugh Burden, Guy Verney, Carla Lehmann, Sir Seymour Hicks, David Tomlinson; ***D:*** Roy Boulting.

Familia 🦴🦴 **2005** Divorced Michele has a gambling problem and when she loses her job, she and rebellious teen daughter Marguerite impose on her childhood friend Janine for a place to stay. Uptight Janine lives a seemingly perfect life in suburban Montreal but the cracks are showing since her husband is a chronic adulterer and she is having trouble with her own two children. Janine's demure daughter Gabrielle easily bonds with Marguerite while Michele is soon betraying Janine's hospitality. English and French with subtitles. **102m/C DVD.** *CA* Sylvie Moreau, Macha Grenon, Juliette Gosselin, Mylene St-Sauveur, Paul Savoie, Vincent Graton; ***D:*** Louise Archambault; ***W:*** Louise Archambault; ***C:*** Andre Turpin; ***M:*** Ramachandra Bocar.

Familiar Strangers 🦴🦴 1/2 **2008 (PG-13)** Brian Worthington left home to get away from dad Frank, who can't understand any of his kids and prefers his pets. Brian finally returns for Thanksgiving and finds little has changed: mom Dottie is still trying to hold the family together; aimless 20-something Kenny still lives at home; and Erin has moved back in, with daughter Maddy, after a messy divorce. Brian does reconnect with family friend Allison but the shocker is when he gets pressured to dispose of the family member Frank loves the best—dog Argus. **86m/C DVD.** Shawn Hatosy, Tom Bower, Ann Dowd, DJ Qualls, Cameron Richardson, Georgia Mae Lively, Nikki Reed; ***D:*** Zackary Adler; ***W:*** John Bell; ***C:*** H. Michael Otano; ***M:*** Dawn Landes, Steve Salett.

The Family 🦴 1/2 *Violent City* **1970** As a New Orleans hit-man who resists joining the mob, Bronson initiates an all-out war on the syndicate and its boss, played by Savalas. A poorly dubbed Italian action film. **94m/C VHS, DVD.** *IT* Charles Bronson, Jill Ireland, Telly Savalas, George Savalas, Michel Constantin, Umberto Orsini; ***D:*** Sergio Sollima; ***W:*** Sergio Sollima; ***C:*** Aldo Tonti; ***M:*** Ennio Morricone.

The Family 🦴🦴🦴 *La Famiglia* **1987** An 80-year-old patriarch prepares for his birthday celebration reminiscing about his family's past triumphs, tragedies and enduring love. The charming flashbacks, convincingly played, all take place in the family's grand old Roman apartment. In Italian with English subtitles or dubbed. **128m/C VHS.** *IT* Vittorio Gassman, Fanny Ardant, Philippe Noiret, Stefania Sandrelli, Andrea Occhipinti, Jo Champa; ***D:*** Ettore Scola; ***W:*** Ettore Scola, Ruggero Maccari, Furio Scarpelli; ***M:*** Armando Trovajoli.

Family 🦴🦴🦴 **1994** Petty thief Charlo Spencer (McGinley) abuses wife Paula (Ryan) and their kids, with young son John Paul in danger of following in his dad's footsteps and teenage daughter Nicola just discovering her emerging sexuality. Narrative is divided into four chapters, each devoted to a different family member. Ordinary life with no melodrama but many priceless moments. Will seem familiar to followers of Roddy Doyle's Barrytown trilogy. **119m/C VHS.** *GB* Sean McGinley, Ger Ryan, Neili Conroy, Barry Ward; ***D:*** Michael Winterbottom; ***W:*** Roddy Doyle.

A Family Affair 🦴🦴 1/2 **2001** Rachel (Lesnick), a Jewish lesbian New Yorker, has been brutally dumped by her manipulative girlfriend Reggie (Greene). She flees to San Diego for the succor of her PFLAG mom (Golonka), who's more than happy to help her daughter find Ms. Right. And that seems to be blonde and perky WASP, Christine (Shaffer). Insecurity leads to romance leads to love—and the sudden re-appearance of Reggie. **107m/C VHS, DVD.** Helen Lesnick, Arlene Golonka, Erica Shaffer, Michele Greene, Suzanne Westenhoefer, Michael Moerman, Barbara Stuart; ***D:*** Helen Lesnick; ***W:*** Helen Lesnick; ***C:*** Jim Orr; ***M:*** Danny De La Isla, Kelly Neill, Robert Westlind.

Family Business 🦴🦴 1/2 **1989 (R)** A bright Ivy Leaguer, impressed by the exploits and vitality of his criminal grandfather, recruits him and his ex-con dad to pull off a high-tech robbery, which goes awry. Caper film, with its interest in family relationships and being true to one's nature. Casting Connery, Hoffman, and Broderick as the three leaves a big believability problem in the family department. **114m/C VHS, DVD.** Sean Connery, Dustin Hoffman, Matthew Broderick, Rosanna Desoto, Janet Carroll, Victoria Jackson, Bill McCutcheon, Deborah Rush, Marilyn Cooper, Salem Ludwig, Rex Everhart, James Tolkan, Tony DiBenedetto, Wendell Pierce, John Capodice, Luis Guzman; ***D:*** Sidney Lumet; ***W:*** Vincent Patrick; ***C:*** Andrzej Bartkowiak; ***M:*** Cy Coleman.

Family Enforcer 🦴 *Death Collector* **1976 (R)** A small-time hoodlum is bent on becoming the best enforcer in an underworld society. **82m/C VHS, DVD.** Joe Cortese, Lou Criscuola, Joe Pesci, Anne Johns, Keith Davis; ***D:*** Ralph De Vito; ***W:*** Ralph De Vito; ***C:*** Bob Bailin.

The Family Game 🦴🦴🦴 *Kazoku gaimu; Kazoku Game* **1983** An obsessive satire about a poor, belligerent college student hired by a wealthy contemporary Japanese family to tutor their spoiled teenage son. Provides an all-out cultural assault on the Japanese bourgeoisie. From an original story by Yohei Honma. In Japanese with English subtitles. **107m/C VHS, DVD.** *JP* Junichi Tsujita, Yusaku Matsuda, Juzo Itami, Saori Yuki, Ichirota Miyagawa; ***D:*** Yoshimitsu Morita; ***W:*** Yoshimitsu Morita; ***C:*** Yonezo Maeda.

The Family Holiday 🦴🦴 **2007** Con man Donald "Doc" Holiday (Coulier) must become the perfect family man (complete with kids and dog) before he can inherit his uncle's estate. He finds a couple of cute, mouthy orphans who have run away so they won't be separated in foster care and hires a nanny who doesn't realize it's all a scam. Except, of course, since it's also a holiday-set film, everything will turn out for the best. **94m/C DVD.** Dave Coulier, Christina Pickles, Craig Clyde, Alexa Fischer, Terisa Greenan; ***C:*** Paul Mayne; ***M:*** Justin Melland. **CABLE**

Family Jewels 🦴🦴 **1965** A spoiled child-heiress has to choose among her six uncles to decide which should be her new father. If you like Jerry Lewis, you can't miss this! In addition to playing all six uncles, Lewis plays the chauffeur, as well as serving as producer, director, and coauthor of the script. **100m/C VHS, DVD.** Jerry Lewis, Donna Butterworth, Sebastian Cabot, Robert Strauss; ***D:*** Jerry Lewis; ***W:*** Jerry Lewis.

Family Life 🦴🦴 1/2 *Wednesday's Child* **1971** A portrait of 19-year-old Janice Baldwin, who's forced to get an abortion by her parents and battles them constantly to establish her own identity. She is eventually sent to a mental institution for depression, where she is subjected to increasingly vigorous psychological interventions, including electro-shock. Documentary-style effort originally made for British TV. **108m/C VHS.** *GB* Sandy Ratcliff, Bill Dean, Grace Cave; ***D:*** Ken Loach. **TV**

Family Life 🦴🦴 *Zycie Rodzinne* **1971** Melancholy mood piece finds an engineer reluctantly returning to his family's delapidated country mansion after six years in Warsaw. He must confront his own life as well as his alcoholic father and slightly mad sister. Polish with subtitles. **93m/C VHS.** *PL* Daniel Olbrychski, Jan Nowicki, Jan Kreczmar, Maja Komorowska, Halina Mikolajska; ***D:*** Krzysztof Zanussi; ***W:*** Krzysztof Zanussi; ***M:*** Wojciech Kilar.

The Family Man 🦴🦴 **1979** A brief encounter-between a married Manhattanite (Asner) and a much younger single woman (Baxter Birney) is sensitively handled in this film which explores their passionate affair. **98m/C VHS.** Ed Asner, Meredith Baxter, Paul Clemens, Mary Joan Negro, Anne Jackson, Martin Short, Michael Ironside; ***D:*** Glenn Jordan; ***M:*** Billy Goldenberg. **TV**

Family Man 🦴🦴 **2000 (PG-13)** With the help of a guardian angel/taxi driver (Cheadle), money-loving investment banker Jack Campbell (Cage) gets to see how life could have been if he'd married college sweetie Leoni, had kids, and was living in New Jersey and working as a tire salesman. Lost in this new world of responsibility and funnel cakes, Jack can't help but pine for his old life. But, in the end, will he choose ambition and "freedom" over love? Darker and not as tidy as "It's a Wonderful Life," its obvious inspiration, "Family Man" seeks to teach Jack a lesson we see coming miles off. **125m/C VHS, DVD.** Nicolas Cage, Tea Leoni, Don Cheadle, Amber Valletta, Jeremy Piven, Saul Rubinek, Josef Sommer, Harve Presnell, Mary Beth Hurt, Kate Walsh; ***D:*** Brett Ratner; ***W:*** David Diamond, David Weissman; ***C:*** Dante Spinotti; ***M:*** Danny Elfman.

A Family Matter 🦴🦴 *Vendetta: Secrets of a Mafia Bride* **1991 (R)** A Mafia chieftain adopts a child whose father was killed by hit men. She grows into a beautiful woman bent on revenge. Melodramatic Italian-American co-production, made for TV. **100m/C VHS.** Eric Roberts, Carol Alt, Eli Wallach, Burt Young; ***D:*** Stuart Margoin; ***W:*** Stuart Margoin; ***C:*** Ennio Guarnieri; ***M:*** Bruce Ruddell. **TV**

Family of Cops 🦴🦴 1/2 **1995 (PG-13)** Trouble comes calling on Inspector Paul Fein's (Bronson) close-knit Milwaukee family when his party girl daughter Jackie (Featherstone) comes home to visit. She's soon accused of murdering a wealthy businessman she picked up in a drunken stupor and her cop family gets deeply involved in the investigation. Made for TV. **90m/C VHS, DVD.** Charles Bronson, Daniel Baldwin, Angela Featherstone, Sebastian Spence, Lesley-Anne Down, Barbara Williams, Simon MacCorkindale; ***D:*** Ted Kotcheff; ***W:*** Joel Blasberg. **TV**

Family of Cops 2: Breach of Faith 🦴🦴 1/2 *Breach of Faith: A Family of Cops 2* **1997 (PG-13)** The investigation of a priest's murder makes Inspector Paul Fein (Bronson) and his cop family the target of Russian mobsters. TV movie once again filmed in Toronto, which substitutes for Milwaukee. **90m/C VHS, DVD.** Charles Bronson, Joe Penny, Diane Ladd, Sebastian Spence, Angela Featherstone, Barbara Williams, Andrew Jackson, Matt Birman, Kim Weeks, David Hemblen, Mimi Kuzyk, Real Andrews; ***D:*** David Greene; ***W:*** Joel Blasberg; ***C:*** Ronald Orieux; ***M:*** Peter Manning Robinson. **TV**

Family of Cops 3 🦴🦴 1/2 **1998 (PG-13)** Police inspector Paul Fein (Bronson) decides to run for chief while detective son

Ben (Penny) investigates the murder of a banker. There's also a corruption problem and time for a little romance. **90m/C VHS, DVD.** Charles Bronson, Joe Penny, Kim Weeks, Sebastian Spence, Barbara Williams, Torri Higginson, Nikki de Boer; ***D:*** Sheldon Larry; ***W:*** Noah Jubelirer; ***C:*** Bert Dunk. **TV**

Family of Strangers 🦴 ½ **1993** Melodramatic made-for-TV fare. Before having brain surgery, Julie Lawson (Gilbert) needs her medical history and learns for the first time that she was adopted as a baby. This sends her on a quest to find her biological parents, but when Julie finds her birth mother Beth (Duke), she learns the disquieting reasons she was given up. **94m/C DVD.** Melissa Gilbert, Patty Duke, William Shatner, Gordon Clapp, Martha Gibson, Chuck Shamata, Eric McCormick; ***D:*** Sheldon Larry; ***W:*** Anna Sandor, William Gough; ***C:*** Ronald Orieux; ***M:*** Peter Manning Robinson. **TV**

Family Pictures 🦴🦴🦴 **1993** A photographer remembers growing up in the '50s with her autistic brother, the mother who lavished her attention on him almost to the exclusion of her five other children, and the father who blamed his wife for their son's deficiencies. Interesting portrait of an American family, which eventually cracks under pressure and splits up. Adapted from the novel by Sue Miller (no relation to screenwriter Jennifer). **240m/C VHS, DVD.** Anjelica Huston, Sam Neill, Kyra Sedgwick, Dermot Mulroney, Gemma Barry, Tara Strong, Torri Higginson, Jamie Harrold; ***D:*** Philip Saville; ***W:*** Jennifer Miller.

The Family Plan 🦴🦴 ½ **2005 (PG)** Charlie Mackenzie (Spelling) wants to keep her executive job, but new boss Ed Walcott (Germann) insists on family values and mistakenly believes Charlie is married. When she is forced to invite Ed and his wife (Vernon) to dinner, Charlie borrows a house and child (Breslin) from a friend and hires actor Buck (Bridges) to play her husband. Their ruse works for the evening, but Charlie is horrified to learn that the Walcotts are planning to rent the house next door. Should she keep lying or will the truth set Charlie free (or just make her unemployed)? **85m/C DVD.** Tori Spelling, Greg Germann, Jordan Bridges, Kate Vernon, Abigail Breslin, Jon Polito, Kail Rocha, Christopher Cass; ***D:*** David S. Cass Sr.; ***W:*** Richard Gitelson; ***C:*** James W. Wrenn; ***M:*** David Kitay. **CABLE**

Family Plot 🦴🦴 ½ **1976 (PG)** Alfred Hitchcock's last film focuses on the search for a missing heir which is undertaken by a phony psychic and her private-eye boyfriend, with all becoming involved in a diamond theft. Campy, lightweight mystery that stales with time and doesn't fit well into Hitchcock's genre. **120m/C VHS, DVD.** Karen Black, Bruce Dern, Barbara Harris, William Devane, Ed Lauter, Katherine Helmond, Cathleen Nesbitt, Warren Kemmerling, Edith Atwater, William Prince, Nicholas Colasanto, Alfred Hitchcock; ***D:*** Alfred Hitchcock; ***W:*** Ernest Lehman; ***C:*** Leonard J. South; ***M:*** John Williams.

Family Prayers 🦴🦴 ½ **1991 (PG)** Coming-of-age drama, set in 1969 Los Angeles, about 13-year-old Andrew and his family troubles. His father Martin (Mantegna) is a compulsive gambler which causes wife Rita (Archer) untold anxiety and constant friction between the two. Tension is heightened by Nan (LuPone), Rita's opinionated older sister who has bailed the family out of their money problems more than once. Meanwhile, Andrew tries to look out for his younger sister and prepare for his bar-mitzvah. A little too much of a nostalgic golden glow surrounds what is essentially a family tragedy. **109m/C VHS.** Tzvi Ratner-Stauber, Joe Mantegna, Anne Archer, Patti LuPone, Paul Reiser, Allen (Goorwitz) Garfield, Conchata Ferrell, David Margulies; ***D:*** Scott Rosenfelt; ***W:*** Steven Ginsburg.

Family Reunion 🦴 ½ **1979** The Andrews family is on vacation and visiting the ghost town of Sutterville. Grandpa Henry didn't want to stop and for good reason—it seems the town was once in the grip of a satanic cult. Forty years before, when Tom Andrews was a child, he was the designated satanic sacrifice and was rescued by Henry, who adopted him. Now Tom's real father has willed the family back to Sutterville to complete the ritual. **88m/C VHS, DVD.** Mel Novak, John Andes, A.J. Woods, Kaylin Cool, Pam Phillips, Mark McTague; ***D:*** Michael Hawes; ***W:*** Michael Hawes; ***C:*** Jack Anderson.

Family Reunion 🦴 ½ **1988** A young man brings a pretty hitchhiker to his family reunion where they mistake her for his fiancee (who recently dumped him). **97m/C VHS.** David Eisner, Rebecca Jenkins, Henry Beckman, Linda Sorensen; ***D:*** Dick Sarin.

Family Secrets 🦴🦴 ½ **1984** Drama about a daughter, mother, and grandmother overprotecting and manipulating each other during a weekend together. **96m/C** Maureen Stapleton, Stefanie Powers, Melissa Gilbert, James Spader; ***D:*** Jack Hofsiss. **TV**

Family Sins 🦴🦴 **1987** A domineering father dotes on his sports-oriented son while willfully neglecting the other. Eventually this leads to calamity. **93m/C VHS.** James Farentino, Jill Eikenberry, Andrew Bendarski, Mimi Kuzyk, Brent Spiner, Michael Durrell, Tom Bower; ***D:*** Jerrold Freedman. **TV**

The Family Stone 🦴🦴 **2005 (PG-13)** Parker plays against her "Sex in the City" role. She's still a New Yorker here, but an uptight one—who's dragged to boyfriend Everett's (Mulroney) family home for the holidays. Mix of characters (gay, deaf, African American, tomboy girl) hits all those let's-not-overlook-anyone buttons. Unfortunately, the likeable ones are rare. No one likes Meredith and they're not shy about it. Another attempt at screwball holiday comedy with a decent cast that delivers on low expectations. **102m/C DVD.** *US* Claire Danes, Diane Keaton, Rachel McAdams, Dermot Mulroney, Craig T. Nelson, Sarah Jessica Parker, Luke Wilson, Ty(rone) Giordano, Brian White, Elizabeth Reaser, Paul Schneider; ***D:*** Thomas Bezucha; ***W:*** Thomas Bezucha; ***C:*** Jonathan Brown; ***M:*** Michael Giacchino.

The Family That Preys 🦴 *Tyler Perry's The Family That Preys* **2008 (PG-13)** Lifelong pals and business partners Alice (Woodward) and Charlotte (Bates) clash when Alice's married son William (Hauser) sparks up an affair with Charlotte's daughter Andrea (Lathan), emptying the family closets of all its skeletons. Meanwhile, Andrea's dense husband Chris (Dunbar) continues to ask William for start-up money to open a construction business, while Andrea's sister Pam (Henson) and her husband Ben (Perry) can only stand back and watch the nutty circus go by. Despite criticism, Perry's cheap, melodramatic soap opera formula shows no sign of improving or appealing to any sense of artistry. Notable for the first Perry movie to treat a white character as more than a "white character." **m/C DVD.** *US* Alfre Woodard, Kathy Bates, Sanaa Lathan, Cole Hauser, Rockmond Dunbar, KaDee Strickland, Taraji P. Henson, Robin Givens, Tyler Perry, Sebastian Siegel; ***C:*** Toyomichi Kurita; ***M:*** Aaron Zigman.

A Family Thing 🦴🦴🦴 **1996 (PG-13)** Racial issues are addressed in this character-driven story of two brothers. Southerner Earl Pilcher (Duvall) learns his biological mother was black and that she died during his birth. In a letter written by the recently deceased woman who raised him, Earl discovers he also has a half brother, Ray (Jones), who is black and living in Chicago. He drives to Chicago, and seeks out Ray, who to Earl's surprise knows about him already, and is not exactly thrilled about the family ties, either. As the two brothers, expertly played by Duvall and Jones, slowly find common ground, Hall steals the show as the irascible Aunt T. **109m/C VHS, DVD.** Robert Duvall, James Earl Jones, Irma P. Hall, Michael Beach, Grace Zabriskie, Regina Taylor, Mary Jackson, Paula Marshall, Jim Harrell; ***D:*** Richard Pearce; ***W:*** Billy Bob Thornton, Tom Epperson; ***C:*** Fred Murphy.

Family Tree 🦴 ½ **2000 (G)** Slow-paced and preachy. A small town, suffering from high unemployment, is happy when a plastics company agrees to build a new factory. Only problem is that it means cutting down the town landmark—an ancient oak tree with generations of initials carved into its bark. However, young Mitch (Lawrence) decides to start a save-the-tree movement. **90m/C VHS.** Robert Forster, Cliff Robertson, Naomi Judd, Andy Laurence, Matthew Lawrence; ***D:*** Duane Clark; ***W:*** Paul Canterna; ***C:*** John Peters; ***M:*** Michael Curb, Randy Miller.

Family Upside Down 🦴🦴🦴 **1978** An aging couple fight their separation after the husband has a heart attack and is put into a nursing home. The fine cast received several Emmy nominations, with Astaire the winner. **100m/C VHS.** Helen Hayes, Fred Astaire, Efrem Zimbalist Jr., Patty Duke; ***D:*** David Lowell Rich; ***M:*** Henry Mancini. **TV**

Family Viewing 🦴🦴🦴 **1987** Surrealistic depiction of a family—obsessed with television and video—whose existence is a textbook model of home sweet dysfunctional home. An early, experimental film from Canada's Egoyan, it won considerable praise for its social commentary. **92m/C VHS, DVD.** *CA* David Hemblen, Adian Tierney, Gabrielle Rose, Arsinee Khanjian; ***D:*** Atom Egoyan; ***W:*** Atom Egoyan; ***C:*** Robert MacDonald, Peter Mettler; ***M:*** Mychael Danna. Toronto-City '87: Canadian Feature Film.

Famous Five Get into Trouble 🦴🦴 **1970** Four precocious youngsters and a dog get involved with a criminal plot and cutely wile their way out of it. Scandinavian; dubbed in English. **90m/C VHS.** *DK* Astrid Villaume, Ove Sprogoe, Lily Broberg; ***D:*** Katrine Hedman; ***C:*** Mikael Salomon; ***M:*** Betrand Bech.

The Fan 🦴🦴 **1981 (R)** A Broadway star is threatened and her immediate circle cut down when a lovestruck fan feels he has been rejected by his idol. The stellar cast makes this bloody and familiar tale seem better than it is. **95m/C VHS, DVD.** Lauren Bacall, Maureen Stapleton, James Garner, Hector Elizondo, Michael Biehn, Griffin Dunne; ***D:*** Edward Bianchi; ***W:*** Priscilla Chapman; ***C:*** Dick Bush; ***M:*** Pino Donaggio.

The Fan 🦴🦴 ½ **1996 (R)** Obsessed baseball fan Gil Renard (De Niro, who owns the copyright on playing deranged) stalks favorite player Bobby Rayburn (Snipes) who just signed a big contract with the hometown team. When Rayburn goes into a slump, Renard figures he can help his idol—by any means necessary. As an added bonus, Gil's a knife salesman. De Niro does the psycho thing with his usual aplomb, while Snipes successfully returns to the diamond. Scott keeps the familiar storyline from becoming tedious. Based on the book by Peter Abrahams. **117m/C VHS, DVD.** Jack Black, Chris Mulkey, Brandon Hammond, Charles Hallahan, Dan E. Butler, Michael Jace, Frank Medrano, M.C. Gainey, Eric Bruskotter, Kim Robillard, Robert De Niro, Wesley Snipes, Ellen Barkin, John Leguizamo, Benicio Del Toro, Patti D'Arbanville; ***D:*** Tony Scott; ***W:*** Phoef Sutton; ***C:*** Darius Wolski; ***M:*** Hans Zimmer.

Fanatic WOOF! *The Last Horror Film* **1982 (R)** Beautiful queen of horror films is followed to the Cannes Film Festival by her number one fan who, unbeknownst to her, is slowly murdering members of her entourage in a deluded and vain attempt to capture her attentions. Title refers to lack of plans for a sequel. **87m/C VHS, DVD.** Caroline Munro, Joe Spinell, Judd Hamilton, Devin Goldenberg, David Winters; ***D:*** David Winters; ***W:*** Tom Klassen, Judd Hamilton, David Winters; ***C:*** Thomas Denove; ***M:*** Jesse Frederick.

Fanboys 🦴🦴 ½ **2009 (PG-13)** Four Star Wars fanatics who've strayed since high school reunite over the news that their buddy Linus has cancer. Set in 1999, a few months before the release of "Star Wars: Episode 1 - The Phantom Menace," the posse decides that Linus needs to see this movie before things take a turn for the worse. They set out on a road trip to Skywalker Ranch with the intention of stealing an unreleased copy from George Lucas himself. Along the way they pick up hot comic book fanchick Zoe (Bell), run into William Shatner, and fall in love again with Carrie Fisher. Unfortunately, a great cast can't save an uninspired script that takes its dopey concept too seriously. Weinstein's insistence on removing the cancer subplot stalled post-production for almost two years. **90m/C DVD.** *US* Sam Huntington, Christopher Marquette, Dan Fogler, Jay Baruchel, Kristen Bell, Craig Robinson; ***D:*** Kyle Newman; ***W:*** Adam F. Goldberg, Ernest Cline; ***C:*** Lukas Ettlin; ***M:*** Mark Mothersbaugh.

Fanci's Persuasion 🦴 ½ **1995** San Francisco-set gay farce features lesbian Fanci (Patton) 24 hours away from marrying lover Loretta (Boa) and in panic mode. Her parents refuse to come to the ceremony and there are numerous and inexplicable complications to deal with. Deliberately over-the-top performances and contrived dialogue and situations can't really take the strain despite the pic's good looks. **78m/C VHS.** Jessica Patton, Boa, Justin Bond, Robert Coffman, Charles Herman-Wurmfeld; ***D:*** Charles Herman-Wurmfeld; ***W:*** Charles Herman-Wurmfeld; ***C:*** David Rush Morrison.

Fancy Pants 🦴🦴 ½ **1950** Remake of "Ruggles of Red Gap" features Hope, a British actor posing as a butler. Also featuring Ball, an amusing contrast. Fine performances all around. ♫Fancy Pants; Home Cookin'. **92m/C VHS, DVD.** Bob Hope, Lucille Ball, Bruce Cabot, Jack Kirkwood, Lea Penman, Eric Blore, John Alexander, Norma Varden; ***D:*** George Marshall; ***C:*** Charles B(ryant) Lang Jr.

Fandango 🦴🦴 ½ **1985 (PG)** Five college friends take a wild weekend drive across the Texas Badlands for one last fling before graduation and the prospect of military service. Expanded by Reynolds with assistance from Steven Spielberg, from his student film. Provides a look at college and life during the Vietnam crisis. **91m/C VHS, DVD.** Judd Nelson, Kevin Costner, Sam Robards, Chuck Bush, Brian Cesak, Elizabeth (E.G. Dailey) Daily, Suzy Amis, Glenne Headly, Pepe Serna, Marvin J. McIntyre; ***D:*** Kevin Reynolds; ***W:*** Kevin Reynolds; ***M:*** Alan Silvestri.

Fanfan la Tulipe 🦴🦴🦴 *Fanfan the Tulip; Fearless Little Soldier* **1951** Fanfan (Philipe) escapes an unwanted marriage by joining the army of Louis XV (Herrand), after being promised an illustrious career and a royal marriage. And after many heroics, it all comes true. Amusing satire of swashbucklers and historical romance movies. French with subtitles. **98m/B VHS, DVD.** *FR* Gerard Philipe, Gina Lollobrigida, Marcel Herrand, Sylvia Pelayo, Genevieve Page, Noel Roquevert; ***D:*** Christian-Jaque; ***W:*** Rene Wheeler, Jean Fallet, Christian-Jaque; ***C:*** Christian Matras; ***M:*** Georges Van Parys, Maurice Thiriet. Cannes '52: Director (Christian-Jaque).

Fangs 🦴 ½ **1975 (R)** Unfriendly reptile-stomping villagers take the life of Mr. Snakey's favorite serpent. He sends his slithering pets on a vengeful and poisonous spree. **90m/C VHS.** Les Tremayne, Janet Wood, Bebe Kelly, Marvin Kaplan, Alice Nunn; ***D:*** Vittorio Schiraldi.

Fangs of Fate 🦴 ½ **1925** A gang of bad guys battles the town's new marshal. **67m/B VHS.** Bill(y) (William Patten) Patton, Dorothy Donald; ***D:*** Horace Carpenter; ***W:*** Horace Carpenter; ***C:*** Paul H. Allen.

Fangs of the Living Dead 🦴 ½ *Malenka, the Vampire; La Nipote del Vampiro; The Niece of the Vampire; The Vampire's Niece* **1968** When a young woman inherits a castle, her uncle, who happens to be a vampire, tries to persuade her to remain among the undead. **80m/C VHS, DVD.** *SP IT* Anita Ekberg, Rossana Yanni, Diana Lorys, Fernando Bilbao, Paul Muller, Julian Ugarte, Andriana Ambesi; ***D:*** Armando de Ossorio; ***W:*** Armando de Ossorio.

Fangs of the Wild 🦴🦴 *Follow the Hunter* **1954** When a young boy witnesses a murder at his father's hunting lodge, no one but the killer believes him. When the killer decides to get rid of the boy, Buck the Wonder Dog gets involved. **72m/B VHS.** Charles Chaplin Jr., Onslow Stevens, Margia Dean, Freddy Ridgeway, Phil Tead, Robert Stevenson; ***D:*** William Claxton.

Fanny 🦴🦴🦴🦴 **1932** Second part of Marcel Pagnol's trilogy depicting the lives of the people of Provence, France. The poignant tale of Fanny, a young woman who marries an older man when Marius, her young lover, leaves her pregnant when he goes to sea. Remade several times but the original holds its own very well. "Marius" was first in the trilogy; "Cesar" was third. **128m/B VHS, DVD.** *FR* Raimu, Charpin, Orane Demazis, Pierre Fresnay, Alida Rouffe; ***D:*** Marc Allegret; ***W:*** Marcel Pagnol; ***M:*** Vincent Scotto.

Fanny 🦴🦴🦴 **1961** Young girl falls in love with an adventurous sailor, and finds herself pregnant after he returns to the sea. With the help of the sailor's parents, she finds, marries, and eventually grows to love a much older man, who in turn cares for her and adores her son as if he were his own. When the sailor returns, all involved must confront their pasts and define their futures. Beautifully made, with fine performances and a plot which defies age or nationality. Part of the "A Night at the Movies" series, this tape simulates a 1961 movie evening, with a Tweety Pie cartoon, a newsreel and coming attractions for "Splendor in the Grass" and "The Roman Spring of Mrs. Stone." **148m/C VHS.** *FR* Leslie Caron, Maurice Chevalier, Charles Boyer, Horst Buchholz, Lionel Jeffries; ***D:*** Joshua Logan; ***W:*** Julius J. Epstein; ***C:*** Jack Cardiff.

Fanny and Alexander *Fanny Och Alexander* **1983 (R)** The culmination of Bergman's career, this autobiographical film is set in a rural Swedish town in 1907. It tells the story of one year in the lives of the Ekdahl family, as seen by the young children, Fanny and Alexander. Magic and religion, love and death, reconciliation and estrangement are skillfully captured in this carefully detailed, lovingly photographed film. In Swedish with English subtitles or dubbed. **197m/C VHS, DVD.** *SW* Pernilla Allwin, Bertil Guve, Gunn Wallgren, Allan Edwall, Ewa Froling, Erland Josephson, Harriet Andersson, Jarl Kulle, Jan Malmsjo; ***D:*** Ingmar Bergman; ***W:*** Ingmar Bergman; ***C:*** Sven Nykvist; ***M:*** Daniel Bell. Oscars '83: Art Dir./Set Dec., Cinematog., Costume Des., Foreign Film; Cesar '84: Foreign Film; Golden Globes '84: Foreign Film; L.A. Film Critics '83: Cinematog., Foreign Film; N.Y. Film Critics '83: Director (Bergman), Foreign Film.

Fanny Hill **1983 (R)** A softcore adaptation of the racy Victorian classic. **80m/C VHS, DVD.** *GB* Alfred Marks, Lisa Raines, Shelley Winters, Wilfrid Hyde-White, Oliver Reed; ***D:*** Gerry O'Hara; ***W:*** Stephen Chesley; ***C:*** Tony Spratling; ***M:*** Paul Hoffert.

Fanny Hill 1/2 **2007** John Cleland's bawdy 18th-century novel is turned into an entertainingly smutty romp. Orphaned country girl Fanny Hill (Night) heads to London to make her fortune and winds up in the brothel of Mrs. Brown (Steadman). She falls in love and runs away with client Charles Standing (Robertson), but they are parted by his family and Fanny must use her considerable skills to make her own way while penning her scandalous memoirs. **117m/C DVD.** *GB* Alex Robertson, Alison Steadman, Hugo Speer, Philip Jackson, Samantha Bond, Rebecca Night, Emma Stansfield; ***D:*** James Hawes; ***W:*** Andrew Davies; ***C:*** James Aspinall; ***M:*** Rohan Stevenson. **TV**

Fanny Hill: Memoirs of a Woman of Pleasure **WOOF!** **1964** Sexual exploits of an innocent in bawdy 18th-century London, as directed by notorious "Super Vixen" Meyer (though by Meyer standards, proceedings are fairly innocuous, if inept). Based on the novel. **105m/B VHS.** *GE* Miriam Hopkins, Walter Giller, Alexander D'Arcy, Leticia Roman, Billy Frick, Heidi Hansen, Chris Howland, Ulli Lommel; ***D:*** Russ Meyer; ***W:*** Robert J. Hill; ***C:*** Heinz Hoelscher; ***M:*** Erwin Halletz.

Fantasia **1940** Disney's most personal animation feature first bombed at the boxoffice and irked purists who couldn't take the plotless, experimental mix of classical music and cartoons. It became a cult movie, embraced by more liberal generations of moviegoers. Reissue of the original version, painstakingly restored, ceased because of a planned remake. ♫Toccata & Fugue in D; The Nutcracker Suite; The Sorcerer's Apprentice; The Rite of Spring; Pastoral Symphony; Dance of the Hours; Night on Bald Mountain; Ave Maria; The Cossack Dance. **116m/C VHS, DVD.** ***D:*** Ben Sharpsteen, James Nelson Algar, Samuel Armstrong, Ford Beebe, Jim Handley, T. Hee, Wilfred Jackson, Hamilton Luske, Bill Roberts, Paul Satterfield; ***W:*** Lee Blair, Phil Dike, Otto Englander, Carl Fallberg, Campbell Grant, Albert Heath, Graham Heid, Arthur Heinemann, Bianca Majolie, William Martin, John McLeish, Sylvia Moberly-Holland, Perce Pearce, Bill Peet, Edward Penner, Joseph Sabo, Webb Smith, Leo Thiele, Norman Wright; ***M:*** Leopold Stokowski; ***V:*** Walt Disney; ***Nar:*** Deems Taylor. AFI '98: Top 100, Natl. Film Reg. '90.

Fantasia/2000 1/2 **2000 (G)** Lightweight continuation of Disney's 1940 film hangs on to Mickey Mouse's popular "The Sorcerer's Apprentice" and adds seven new animated sequences of varying charm with celebrity introductions. Probably the most fun sequence is that of the yo-yo-ing flamingo set to Saint-Saens' "Carnvial of the Animals." Music is conducted by James Levine and performed by the Chicago Symphony Orchestra. Originally released in the IMAX format. ♫Symphony No. 5 (Ludwig Van Beethoven); Pines of Rome (Ottorino Respighi); Rhapsody in Blue (George Gershwin); Piano Concerto No. 2, Allegro, Opus 102 (Dmitri Shostakovich); Carnvial of the Animals (Camille Saint-Saens); The Sorcerer's Apprentice (Paul Dukas); Pomp and Circumstance (Edward Elgar); Firebird Suite (Igor Stravinsky). **75m/C VHS, DVD.** ***D:*** Hendel Butoy, Eric Goldberg, James Nelson Algar, Gaetan Brizzi, Paul Brizzi, Pixote Hunt, Francis Glebas.

Fantasies **WOOF!** *And Once Upon a Love* **1973 (R)** Teenage lovers Derek and Hooten return to their Greek island home and decide to improve their village by turning it into a tourist haven. First collaboration of the Dereks is a loser, lacking plot, direction, and decent acting. Bo shows no talent but the obvious one and is actually credited as Kathleen Collins. **81m/C VHS, DVD.** Bo Derek, Peter Hooten, Anna Alexiades; ***D:*** John Derek.

The Fantasist **1989 (R)** Sex crime thriller features a deranged killer who makes obscene, yet seductive phone calls to young ladies before murdering them. **98m/C VHS.** Timothy Bottoms, Christopher Cazenove; ***D:*** Robin Hardy.

Fantastic Balloon Voyage *Viaje Fantastico en Globo* **1976 (G)** Three men embark on a journey across the equator in a balloon, experiencing myriad adventures along the way. Much hot air. **100m/C VHS.** *MX* Hugo Stiglitz, Jeff Cooper, Carlos East, Carmen Vicarte; ***D:*** Rene Cardona Jr.

Fantastic Four **2005 (PG-13)** Or, more like the "So-So Four." The Stan Lee/Jack Kirby Marvel Comic foursome, who made their print debut in 1961, finally get on the big screen, though beyond introducing them and showing off their newly-acquired superpowers from exposure to outer-space radiation, they don't have much to do. Lee cameos as mailman Willy Lumpkin. **105m/C DVD, Blu-ray Disc, UMD.** *US GE* Ioan Gruffudd, Jessica Alba, Michael Chiklis, Chris Evans, Julian McMahon, Kerry Washington, Stan Lee, Laurie Holden; ***D:*** Tim Story; ***W:*** Mark Frost, Michael France, Simon Kinberg; ***C:*** Oliver Wood; ***M:*** John Ottman.

Fantastic Four: Rise of the Silver Surfer 1/2 **2007 (PG)** They weren't fantastic the first time and this sequel is almost as dull. Mr. Fantastic (Gruffudd) keeps getting distracted while trying to marry invisible sweetie Sue (Alba). But he's got good reason, with intergalactic traveler Silver Surfer deciding to visit our little planet. Seems dead planets follow in the visitor's wake and the mild foursome doesn't want that happening to Earth. At least the 3-D animation for the Surfer deserves a look-see. **92m/C DVD, Blu-ray Disc.** *US* Ioan Gruffudd, Jessica Alba, Chris Evans, Michael Chiklis, Julian McMahon, Doug Jones, Andre Braugher, Kerry Washington, Gonzalo Menendez; ***D:*** Tim Story; ***W:*** Don Payne, Mark Frost; ***C:*** Larry Blanford; ***M:*** John Ottman; ***V:*** Laurence Fishburne.

Fantastic Mr. Fox **2009 (PG)** Animated adaptation of Roald Dahl's classic children's book by director Anderson, who puts his quirky dark humor to good use in telling the sardonic story of a clever fox forced to outwit the farmers after him and his family for stealing their chickens and cider. Great visual appeal with the use of stop-motion photography and miniature puppets instead of drawings. All-star cast delivers the goods with Anderson regulars, Murray and Schwartzman, plus Clooney, Streep, Blanchett, Gambon, Dafoe, and Wilson. And even though it has moments of trying a little too hard, all in all, as one of the characters might say, it's a "cussing" good time. **87m/C DVD.** ***D:*** Wes Anderson; ***W:*** Wes Anderson, Noah Baumbach; ***C:*** Tristan Oliver; ***M:*** Alexandre Desplat; ***V:*** George Clooney, Meryl Streep, Bill Murray, Willem Dafoe, Jason Schwartzman, Michael Gambon, Helen McCrory, Brian Cox, Adrien Brody, Owen Wilson, Wes Anderson, Karen Duffy.

The Fantastic Night *La Nuit Fantastique* **1942** Considering that this film was made in France during the Nazi occupation, it is a remarkably clear work. It's a fantasy about Denis (Gravey), who is visited by a beautiful woman (Presle) as he sleeps and then follows her through a series of adventures. According to the box copy, the star was working with the Resistance while he was making the film. French with subtitles. **90m/B VHS, DVD.** *FR* Fernand Gravey, Micheline Presle, Marcel Levesque, Christiane Nere; ***D:*** Marcel L'Herbier; ***W:*** Louis Chavance, Marcel L'Herbier; ***C:*** Pierre Montazel; ***M:*** Maurice Thiriet.

Fantastic Planet *La Planete Sauvage; Planet of Incredible Creatures; The Savage Planet* **1973 (PG)** A critically acclaimed French, animated, sci-fi epic based on the drawings of Roland Topor. A race of small humanoids are enslaved and exploited by a race of giants on a savage planet, until one of the small creatures manages to unite his people and fight for equality. **72m/C VHS, DVD.** *FR* ***D:*** Roland Topor, Rene Laloux; ***W:*** Roland Topor, Steve Hayes, Rene Laloux; ***C:*** Boris Baromykin, Lubomir Rejthar; ***M:*** Alain Goraguer; ***V:*** Barry Bostwick.

Fantastic Seven 1/2 **1979** The Fantastic Seven is a daredevil team sent to rescue a Hollywood sex symbol who has been kidnapped and held for ransom while shooting on location off the coast of Miami. **96m/C VHS.** Christopher Connelly, Christopher Lloyd, Soon-Teck Oh, Morgan Brittany, Bill Macy, Peter Haskell, Patrick Macnee, Elke Sommer; ***D:*** John Peyser; ***C:*** Frank Holgate; ***M:*** Bill Conti. **TV**

Fantastic Voyage *Microscopia; Strange Journey* **1966** An important scientist, rescued from behind the Iron Curtain, is so severely wounded by enemy agents that traditional surgery is impossible. After being shrunk to microscopic size, a medical team journeys inside his body where they find themselves threatened by the patient's natural defenses. Great action, award-winning special effects. **100m/C VHS, DVD.** Stephen Boyd, Edmond O'Brien, Raquel Welch, Arthur Kennedy, Donald Pleasence, Arthur O'Connell, William Redfield, James Brolin, Barry Coe, Brendan Fitzgerald, Shelby Grant, Ken Scott; ***D:*** Richard Fleischer; ***W:*** Harry Kleiner; ***C:*** Ernest Laszlo; ***M:*** Leonard Rosenman. Oscars '66: Art Dir./Set Dec., Color, Visual FX.

The Fantastic World of D.C. Collins **1984** Gary Coleman plays a daydreaming teenager who thinks he is being pursued by mysterious strangers seeking a videotape that was unknowingly slipped to him. **100m/C VHS.** Gary Coleman, Bernie Casey, Shelley Smith, Fred (John F.) Dryer, Marilyn McCoo, Philip Abbott, George Gobel, Michael Ansara; ***D:*** Leslie Martinson. **TV**

The Fantasticks 1/2 **1995 (PG)** The stage's longest-running musical gets the big-screen treatment with a story about two fathers (Grey and Hughes) who decide to matchmake for their children Matt (McIntyre) and Luisa (Kelly). They hire the members of a traveling carnival (called the Fantasticks) to kidnap Luisa, so that Matt can play the hero and rescue her. The plan seems to work but the course of true love never runs that smoothly. Adapted by Jones and Schmidt from their play. **86m/C VHS, DVD.** Jonathan Morris, Joel Grey, Barnard Hughes, Jean (Louisa) Kelly, Joe McIntyre; ***D:*** Michael Ritchie; ***W:*** Tom Jones, Harvey Schmidt; ***C:*** Fred Murphy; ***M:*** Harvey Schmidt.

Fantasy Island **1976** Three people fly ("De plane, boss!") to an island paradise and get to live out their fantasies for a price. Pilot for the TV series. **100m/C VHS.** Ricardo Montalban, Bill Bixby, Sandra Dee, Peter Lawford, Carol Lynley, Hugh O'Brian, Eleanor Parker, Dick Sargent, Victoria Principal; ***D:*** Richard Lang. **TV**

Fantasy Man 1/2 **1984** A restless middle-aged man tries to relieve his mid-life crisis with the help of three women. **100m/C VHS.** *AU* Harold Hopkins, Jeanie Drynan, Kerry Mack, Kate Fitzpatrick; ***D:*** John Meagher; ***W:*** John Meagher.

Fantasy Mission Force **1984** In this indescribably silly action comedy, Japanese troops capture an international group of generals (some in Civil War-era uniforms). An invasion of Canada is underway. Jackie is part of a group trying to rescue them: UN troops wear kilts; others wear armor. **90m/C VHS, DVD.** *HK* Jackie Chan, Brigitte Lin, Adam Cheng, Jimmy Wang Yu; ***D:*** Yen Ping Chu.

Far and Away 1/2 **1992 (PG-13)** Meandering old-fashioned epic about immigrants, romance, and settling the American West. In the 1890s, Joseph Donelly (Cruise) is forced to flee his Irish homeland after threatening the life of his landlord, and emigrates to America in the company of the landlord's daughter, feisty Shannon Christie (Kidman). Particularly brutal scenes of Cruise earning his living as a bare-knuckled boxer contrast with the expansiveness of the land rush ending. Slow, spotty, and a little too slick for its own good, though real-life couple Cruise and Kidman are an attractive pair. Filmed in 70-mm Panavision on location in Ireland and Montana. **140m/C VHS, DVD.** Tom Cruise, Nicole Kidman, Thomas Gibson, Robert Prosky, Barbara Babcock, Colm Meaney, Eileen Pollock, Michelle Johnson, Cyril Cusack, Clint Howard, Rance Howard; ***D:*** Ron Howard; ***W:*** Bob Dolman; ***C:*** Mikael Salomon; ***M:*** John Williams.

Far Away and Long Ago 1/2 **1974** Based on the autobiographical novel by Guillermo Hudson which details the memories which haunted his childhood—the Argentinian pampas, its gauchos, witchcraft, and women. In Spanish with English subtitles. **91m/C VHS.** *AR* Juan Jose Camero, Leonor Manso; ***D:*** Manuel Antin.

Far Country **1955** Cattlemen must battle the elements and frontier lawlessness in this classic. Stewart leads his herd to the Yukon in hopes of large profits, but ends up having to kidnap it back from the crooked sheriff and avenging the deaths of his friends. Entertaining and the Yukon setting takes it out of the usual Western arena. **97m/C VHS, DVD.** James Stewart, Ruth Roman, Walter Brennan, Harry (Henry) Morgan, Corinne Calvet, Jay C. Flippen, John McIntire; ***D:*** Anthony Mann; ***C:*** William H. Daniels; ***M:*** Henry Mancini.

Far Cry from Home **1981** A battered wife attempts to escape from her domineering husband before it's too late. **87m/C VHS.** *CA* Mary Ann McDonald, Richard Monette; ***D:*** Gordon Pinsent. **TV**

Far East 1/2 **1985** Two ex-lovers meet in Southeast Asia and join forces to find the woman's missing husband, a reporter. **105m/C VHS.** Bryan Brown, Helen Morse; ***D:*** John Duigan.

Far from Heaven 1/2 **2002 (PG-13)** Perfect '50s homemaker, mother, and wife Cathy (Moore) faces her husband Frank's (Quaid) emerging homosexual desires, which culminate in her witnessing him in an intimate kiss with another man at the office. When Cathy seeks comfort from her black gardener (Haysbert), scandal and hatred spread and wrenching truths are found. Melodramatic (in the Douglas Sirk tradition) tale of social/racial taboos and a woman's sacrifice is intriguing. Moore's performance is Oscar caliber (she got a nomination), Quaid's fearless, and Lachman's retro-chic visuals also exhibit stunning craftsmanship, while Bernstien's lush score sets the proper mood. **107m/C VHS, DVD.** *US* Julianne Moore, Dennis Quaid, Dennis Haysbert, Patricia Clarkson, James Rebhorn, Celia Weston, Viola Davis; ***D:*** Todd Haynes; ***W:*** Todd Haynes; ***C:*** Edward Lachman; ***M:*** Elmer Bernstein. Ind. Spirit '03: Actress (Moore), Cinematog., Director (Haynes), Film, Support. Actor (Quaid); L.A. Film Critics '02: Actress (Moore), Cinematog., Score; Natl. Bd. of Review '02: Actress (Moore); N.Y. Film Critics '02: Cinematog., Director (Haynes), Film, Support. Actor (Quaid), Support. Actress (Clarkson); Natl. Soc. Film Critics '02: Cinematog., Support. Actress (Clarkson).

Far from Home **1989 (R)** Drew Barrymore is the seductive teen being scoped by a psychotic killer while on vacation with her father. Lots of over-the-top performances by the familiar cast. **86m/C VHS, DVD.** Matt Frewer, Drew Barrymore, Richard Masur, Karen Austin, Susan Tyrrell, Anthony Rapp, Jennifer Tilly, Andras Jones, Dick Miller; ***D:*** Meiert Avis; ***C:*** Paul Elliott; ***M:*** Jonathan Elias.

Far from Home: The Adventures of Yellow Dog 🦴🦴 **1994 (PG)** Stalwart lad Angus (Bradford) and his faithful pooch Yellow (Dakotah) battle the elements, wild animals and fatigue as they try to get back home after being shipwrecked on a remote island in British Columbia. Good thing Dad (Davidson) gave them all those cool survival tips before they left, or else they never would've known that you can eat bugs. (Okay, the dog probably knew that already.) Mom (Rogers) does her bit by making sure the search mission stays focused. You usually can't go wrong with a kid and his dog lost in the wilderness, but this one is really short—on time and drama. Nice scenery, though. **81m/C VHS, DVD.** Jesse Bradford, Bruce Davison, Mimi Rogers, Tom Bower; ***D:*** Phillip Borsos; ***W:*** Phillip Borsos.

Far from the Madding Crowd 🦴🦴🦴 **1967 (PG)** A lavish, long adaptation of Thomas Hardy's 19th-century classic about the beautiful Bathsheba (Christie) and the three very different men who love her. Her first love is handsome and wayward soldier Sgt. Troy (Stamp), her second the local noble lord William Boldwood (Finch), and her third the ever-loving and long-patient farmer Gabriel Oaks (Bates). Christie is well cast as the much-desired beauty. Gorgeous cinematography by Nicolas Roeg. Remade for British TV in 1997. **165m/C VHS.** *GB* Julie Christie, Terence Stamp, Peter Finch, Alan Bates, Prunella Ransome; ***D:*** John Schlesinger; ***W:*** Frederic Raphael; ***C:*** Nicolas Roeg; ***M:*** Richard Rodney Bennett. Natl. Bd. of Review '67: Actor (Finch).

Far from the Madding Crowd 🦴🦴🦴 **1997** TV version of the Thomas Hardy novel (filmed for the big screen in 1967) that follows the adventures of young Bathsheba (Baeza), who's the object of desire for three very different men in 19th-century rural England. Independent-minded Bathsheba Everdene inherits a farm and insists on managing it herself. She's aided by steadfast head man Gabriel Oak (Parker), who loves her but doesn't feel he can offer her anything; wealthy older neighbor William Boldwood (Terry), whose love for Bathesheba becomes an obsession; and rakish Sgt. Frank Troy (Firth), who captivates Bathsheba but proves to be a scoundrel. **200m/C VHS, DVD.** *GB* Paloma Baeza, Nigel Terry, Nathaniel Parker, Jonathan Firth; ***D:*** Nicholas Renton; ***W:*** Philomena McDonagh. **TV**

Far Frontier 🦴🦴 **1948** Roy Rogers saves the day by thwarting a band of outlaws who are being smuggled across the border in soybean oil cans. Includes musical numbers and horse tricks. **60m/B VHS, DVD.** Roy Rogers, Andy Devine, Francis Ford, Gail Davis, Roy Barcroft, Clayton Moore, Robert Strange, Holly (Mike Ragan) Bane, Lane Bradford, Edmund Cobb; ***D:*** William Witney; ***W:*** Sloan Nibley; ***C:*** Jack Marta; ***M:*** R. Dale Butts.

Far Harbor 🦴🦴 **1996** An attractive cast of yuppie failures gather in a Long Island mansion to whine and snipe at each other over dinner. Among them is Frick (Atterton), a persona non grata English filmmaker, who becomes obsessed with a moored yacht that belongs to a Hollywood studio bigwig, and fragile hostess, Ellie (Connelly), who's written a screenplay based on her own traumas. **99m/C VHS.** Edward Atterton, Jennifer Connelly, Dan Futterman, Marcia Gay Harden, George Newbern, Jim True-Frost, Andrew Lauren, Tracee Ellis Ross; ***D:*** John Huddles; ***W:*** John Huddles; ***C:*** Tami Reiker.

The Far Horizons 🦴🦴 **1955** Meriwether Lewis (MacMurray) and William Clark (Heston) lead an expedition to survey the territory after the Louisiana Purchase. Along the way they gain the assistance of Sacajawea, played by blue-eyed Donna Reed. Vintage Hollywood at its "best" takes a historical premise and turns it into comical love-triangle that comes full circle—in the White House, no less. Check your knowledge of history at the door, but enjoy the beautiful scenery and some unintentional giggles. **107m/C DVD.** Fred MacMurray, Charlton Heston, Donna Reed, Barbara Hale, William Demarest, Eduardo Noriega, Herbert (Hayes) Heyes, Lester Matthews, Alan Reed, Larry Pennell; ***D:*** Rudolph Mate; ***W:*** Winston Miller, Edmund H. North; ***C:*** Daniel F. Fapp; ***M:*** Hans J. Salter.

Far North 🦴🦴 ½ **1988 (PG-13)** Quirky comedy about a woman who returns to her rural family homestead after her father is seriously injured by a horse, and tries to deal with her eccentric family's travails. Fine cast never reaches its potential. Shepard's directing debut. **96m/C VHS.** Jessica Lange, Charles Durning, Tess Harper, Donald Moffat, Ann Wedgeworth, Patricia Arquette, Nina Draxton; ***D:*** Sam Shepard; ***W:*** Sam Shepard; ***C:*** Robbie Greenberg.

Far North 🦴 ½ **2007 (R)** Nomadic Saiva (Yeoh) is constantly struggling to survive in the Arctic tundra. A shaman predicted she was cursed to bring harm to anyone she gets close to (flashbacks prove that point), so Saiva avoids people except for Anja (Krusiec), an orphan she's raised from infancy. One day Saiva finds a dying man (Bean) and impulsively decides to care for him, which invariably brings trouble. **89m/C DVD.** *GB* Michelle Yeoh, Michelle Krusiec, Sean Bean; ***D:*** Asif Kapadia; ***W:*** Asif Kapadia, Tim Miller; ***C:*** Roman Osin; ***M:*** Dario Marianelli.

A Far Off Place 🦴🦴 **1993 (PG-13)** Adolescent boy, adolescent girl, adolescent bushperson, and mature dog set out across the African desert to escape elephant poachers who want to kill them. The boy and girl find romance in the sand, bushperson finds water by listening, and dog gets very nice walk. Strong performances by the youthful leads lend charm to this Disney/Amblin flick, particularly Bok as the bushperson. Unusually violent film for studios involved (animals and people bite sand), though care is taken to edit actual blood shed on screen. Filmed in Zimbabwe and Namibia and based on the books "A Story Like the Wind" and "A Far Off Place" by Laurens van der Post. **107m/C VHS, DVD.** Reese Witherspoon, Ethan (Randall) Embry, Sarel Bok, Jack Thompson, Maximilian Schell, Robert John Burke, Patricia Kalember, Daniel Gerroll, Miles Anderson; ***D:*** Mikael Salomon; ***W:*** Robert Caswell, Jonathan Hensleigh, Sally Robinson; ***C:*** Juan Ruiz-Anchia; ***M:*** James Horner.

Far Out Man WOOF! *Soul Man 2* **1989 (R)** An unalterable middle-aged hippie is sent by his worried family and his psychiatrist on a cross-country journey to rediscover himself. The script makes no sense and has very few laughs. **81m/C VHS, DVD.** Thomas Chong, Rae Dawn Chong, C. Thomas Howell, Shelby Chong, Martin Mull, Paris Chong, Paul Bartel, Judd Nelson, Michael Winslow, Richard "Cheech" Marin; ***D:*** Thomas Chong; ***W:*** Thomas Chong.

The Far Pavilions 🦴🦴 ½ *Blade of Steel* **1984** A British officer falls in love with an Indian princess during the second Afghan War. Cross is appropriately noble and stiff-upper-lipped but Irving is miscast as his ethnic love. This lavish production was based on the romantic bestseller by M.M. Kaye. **108m/C VHS, DVD.** *GB* Ben Cross, Amy Irving, Omar Sharif, Benedict Taylor, Rossano Brazzi, Christopher Lee, John Gielgud, Rupert Everett; ***D:*** Peter Duffell; ***C:*** Jack Cardiff; ***M:*** Carl Davis. **CABLE**

The Far Side of Jericho 🦴 ½ **2006 (R)** In the 1880s, the widows of three executed outlaw brothers are forced to flee their homes and are pursued by a posse determined to find their husbands' buried ill-gotten gains. Routine oater. **99m/C DVD.** Patrick Bergin, James Gammon, Lawrence Pressman, C. Thomas Howell, Suzanne Andrews, Judith Burnett, Lissa Negrin, John Diehl, Jason Connery; ***D:*** Tim Hunter; ***W:*** Rob Sullivan, James Crumley; ***C:*** Patrick Cady; ***M:*** Mark Adler. **VIDEO**

Far Side of the Moon 🦴🦴 *La Face Cachee de la Lune* **2003** Lepage directed, wrote (an adaptation of his play), and stars as Quebec brothers Philippe and Andre. Philippe is a failed doctoral student obsessed with space, while gay younger brother Andre is a vacuous TV weatherman. They are brought into each other's orbit by the death of their mother, although Philippe has apparently never quite reached adulthood anyway. Alienation—rather than aliens—rule. French with subtitles. **105m/C DVD.** *CA* Robert Lepage, Anne-Marie Cadieux, Celine Bonnier, Marco Poulin; ***D:*** Robert Lepage; ***W:*** Robert Lepage; ***C:*** Ronald Plante; ***M:*** Benoit Jutras. **VIDEO**

Faraway, So Close! 🦴🦴 *In Weiter Ferne, So Nah!* **1993 (PG-13)** Wenders' erratic follow-up to his magnificent "Wings of Desire." Cassiel (Sander), the angel left behind when Damiel (Ganz) chose to become human, once again surveys Berlin, noticing the changes (not necessarily for the better). Angelic companion Raphaela (Kinski) watches events passively, including an old man's (Ruhamnn) reflections on life and the philosophical musings of Emit Flesti (Dafoe, Time Itself, get it?), even as Cassiel impulsively chooses humanity over his heavenly world. Falk makes a return appearance to little effect. Overlong and under-developed. **146m/C VHS, DVD.** *GE* Otto Sander, Peter Falk, Horst Buchholz, Nastassja Kinski, Heinz Ruhmann, Bruno Ganz, Solveig Dommartin, Ruediger Vogler, Willem Dafoe, Lou Reed; ***D:*** Wim Wenders; ***W:*** Ulrich Zieger, Richard Reitinger, Wim Wenders; ***C:*** Jurgen Jurges; ***M:*** David Darling, Laurent Petitgand. Cannes '93: Grand Jury Prize.

Farewell My Concubine 🦴🦴 *Bawang Bie Ji* **1993 (R)** Exotic film covers 50 years of sexual, social, and political Chinese history wrapped around the story of two male Peking Opera stars. Deposited as boys at the Opera's training school Douzi and Shitou become fast friends in their hermetically sealed world, but their friendship is tested during the chaos of Communism and the cultural revolution. Sumptuous and well-acted, but the sheer length and emotional detachment prove to be drawbacks. Adapted from a novel by Lee, who based the work on a 2000-year-old Chinese opera about an imperial concubine. Filmed on location in Beijing. In Mandarin Chinese with subtitles. **157m/C VHS, DVD.** *HK* Leslie Cheung, Fengyi Zhang, Gong Li, Lu Qi, Da(nniel) Ying, Ge You, Fei Yang, Ma Mingwei; ***D:*** Chen Kaige; ***W:*** Lilian Lee, Lu Wei; ***C:*** Gu Changwei; ***M:*** Jiping Zhao. British Acad. '93: Foreign Film; Cannes '93: Film; Golden Globes '94: Foreign Film; L.A. Film Critics '93: Foreign Film; Natl. Bd. of Review '93: Foreign Film; N.Y. Film Critics '93: Foreign Film, Support. Actress (Li).

Farewell, My Lovely 🦴🦴🦴 **1975 (R)** A remake of the 1944 Raymond Chandler mystery, "Murder, My Sweet," featuring private eye Phillip Marlowe hunting for an ex-convict's lost sweetheart in 1941 Los Angeles. Perhaps the most accurate of Chandler adaptations, but far from the best, this film offers a nicely detailed production. Mitchum is a bit too world-weary as the seen-it-all detective. **95m/C VHS, DVD.** *GB* Robert Mitchum, Charlotte Rampling, Sylvia Miles, John Ireland, Anthony Zerbe, Jack O'Halloran, Harry Dean Stanton, Sylvester Stallone, Cheryl "Rainbeaux" Smith; ***D:*** Dick Richards; ***W:*** David Zelag Goodman; ***C:*** John A. Alonzo; ***M:*** David Shire.

A Farewell to Arms 🦴🦴🦴 **1932** The original film version of Ernest Hemingway's novel about the tragic love affair between an American ambulance driver and an English nurse during the Italian campaign of WWI. The novelist disavowed the ambiguous ending, but the public loved the film. Fine performances and cinematography. **85m/B VHS, DVD.** Helen Hayes, Gary Cooper, Adolphe Menjou, Mary (Phillips) Philips, Jack La Rue, Blanche Frederici; ***D:*** Frank Borzage; ***W:*** Oliver H.P. Garrett, Benjamin Glazer; ***C:*** Charles B(ryant) Lang Jr. Oscars '33: Cinematog., Sound.

A Farewell to Arms 🦴 ½ **1957** Third version of the Hemingway novel, set during WWI, was designed as a vehicle for faded star Jones, wife of producer David O. Selznick. But she was too old for the part of the innocent young nurse who gets pregnant by ambulance driver Hudson (equally unconvincing). Selznick's interference with the script didn't help either (he actually wrote a letter of apology to Hemingway). The overblown production was a boxoffice bomb. **152m/C DVD.** Jennifer Jones, Rock Hudson, Alberto Sordi, Mercedes McCambridge, Oscar Homolka, Elaine Stritch, Kurt Kasznar, Vittorio De Sica; ***D:*** Charles Vidor; ***W:*** Ben Hecht; ***C:*** Piero Portalupi, Oswald Morris; ***M:*** Mario Nascimbene.

Farewell to the King 🦴🦴 ½ **1989 (PG-13)** During WWII, a ship-wrecked American deserter becomes the chief of a tribe of Borneo headhunters until his jungle kingdom is caught between the forces of the U.S. and Japanese. With the help of a British officer he helps them defend themselves when the Japanese invade. An old-fashioned war epic with a beautiful location and solid if uninspired-performances by the leads. Based on Pierre Schoendoerffer's novel "L'Adieu Au Roi." **114m/C VHS, DVD.** Nick Nolte, Nigel Havers, Marius Weyers, Frank McRae, Marilyn Tokuda, Elan Oberon, William Wise, James Fox, Aki Aleong; ***D:*** John Milius; ***W:*** John Milius; ***C:*** Dean Semler; ***M:*** Basil Poledouris.

Fargo 🦴🦴🦴 **1996 (R)** Another malicious, extra-dark comedy from the Coen brothers. Car salesman Jerry Lundegaard (Macy) hires a couple of losers to kidnap his wife so he can swindle the ransom money out of his father-in-law. Naturally, the scheme begins to unravel and the very pregnant police chief Marge Gunderson (McDormand) treks through the frozen tundra of Minnesota to put the pieces of the puzzle together. McDormand's performance as the chatty competent chief is first rate. Needling the flat-accented Midwesterners of their youth, the Coens have also returned to their filmmaking roots after the disappointing big-budget "Hudsucker Proxy." Because Minneapolis was having its warmest, driest winter in 100 years, the Coens were forced to shoot most of the exteriors in wintery North Dakota. **97m/C VHS, DVD.** William H. Macy, Frances McDormand, Steve Buscemi, Peter Stormare, Harve Presnell, Steve Reevis, John Carroll Lynch, Kristin Rudrud, Steve Park, Jose Feliciano; ***D:*** Joel Coen; ***W:*** Ethan Coen, Joel Coen; ***C:*** Roger Deakins; ***M:*** Carter Burwell. Oscars '96: Actress (McDormand), Orig. Screenplay; AFI '98: Top 100; Australian Film Inst. '96: Foreign Film; British Acad. '96: Director (Coen); Cannes '96: Director (Coen); Ind. Spirit '97: Actor (Macy), Actress (McDormand), Cinematog., Director (Coen), Film, Screenplay; Natl. Bd. of Review '96: Actress (McDormand), Director (Coen), Natl. Film Reg. '06;; N.Y. Film Critics '96: Film; Screen Actors Guild '96: Actress (McDormand); Writers Guild '96: Orig. Screenplay; Broadcast Film Critics '96: Actress (McDormand), Film.

Fargo Express 🦴 ½ **1932** When the kid brother of Maynard's true love is falsely accused of robbing a stagecoach, Maynard works to clear his name. Routine stuff. **60m/B VHS, DVD.** Ken Maynard, Helen Mack, Paul Fix; ***D:*** Alan James.

Farinelli 🦴🦴 *Farinelli the Castrato; Farinelli Il Castrato* **1994 (R)** A movie to make men cringe. Floridly depicts the complex professional and personal ties of 18th-century opera composer Riccardo Broschi (Lo Verso) and his younger brother Carlo (Dionisi), a celebrated castrato singer under the stage name "Farinelli." In part, because of an early church prohibition against women singing in public, boys were castrated before puberty to preserve their pure soprano voices while vocal power and agility grew as they became men. Castrati were the rock stars of their day and Farinelli lived a flamboyant life before retiring to the Spanish court of Philip V. The castrato voice heard in the movie is an electronic mixture of countertenor Derek Lee Ragin and soprano Ewa Mallas Godlewska. French and Italian with subtitles. **110m/C VHS, DVD.** *FR IT BE* Stefano Dionisi, Enrico Lo Verso, Jeroen Krabbe, Elsa Zylberstein, Caroline Cellier, Omero Antonutti, Jacques Boudet; ***D:*** Gerard Corbiau; ***W:*** Gerard Corbiau, Andree Corbiau, Marcel Beaulieu; ***C:*** Walther Vanden Ende; ***M:*** Christopher Rousset. Cesar '95: Art Dir./Set Dec., Sound; Golden Globes '95: Foreign Film.

Farmer & Chase 🦴🦴 **1996 (R)** It's always nice to see an old pro like Gazzara but it's a shame it couldn't have been in something less predictable. Farmer's (Gazzara) a hold-up man who's been working with partner Ollie (Jones) for 20 years. But when Ollie's killed, Farmer, who wants to pull one last job before retiring, makes the mistake of teaming up with his pacifist son Chase (Field). And then Chase involves his new gal pal Hillary (Boyle) in on the scheme. Dumb move, dumb movie. **97m/C VHS.** Ben Gazzara, Todd Field, Lara Flynn Boyle, Steven Anthony Jones, Ron Karell, David Booth; ***D:*** Michael Seitzman; ***W:*** Michael Seitzman; ***C:*** Michael Maley; ***M:*** Tony Saunders.

The Farmer Takes a Wife 🦴🦴 ½ **1935** Henry Fonda's first film, recreating his stage role, as a mid-19th century farmer at odds with the Erie canal builders and struggling to court the woman he loves. Remade as a musical in 1953. **91m/B VHS.** Janet Gaynor, Henry Fonda, Charles Bickford, Slim Summerville, Jane Withers; *D:* Victor Fleming.

The Farmer Takes a Wife
1953 Poor musical remake of the 1935 drama, about the trials of a struggling 1850s farmer and the Erie canal boat cook he loves. Contains no memorable music and Robertson can't compete with Henry Fonda's original role as the farmer. ♫ We're in Business; On the Erie Canal; We're Doing it for the Natives in Jamaica; When I Close My Door; Today I Love Everybody; Somethin' Real Special; With The Sun Warm Upon Me; Can You Spell Schenectady?. **81m/C VHS.** Betty Grable, Dale Robertson, Thelma Ritter, John Carroll, Eddie Foy Jr., Charlotte Austin, Merry Anders, Gwen Verdon, Kathleen Crowley, May Wynn; *D:* Henry Levin; *W:* Sally Benson, Walter Bullock, Joseph Fields; *C:* Arthur E. Arling; *M:* Cyril Mockridge, Harold Arlen.

The Farmer's Daughter **1947** Young portrays Katrin Holmstrom, a Swedish farm girl who becomes a maid to Congressman Cotten and winds up running for office herself (not neglecting to find romance as well). The outspoken and multi-talented character charmed audiences and was the basis of a TV series in the 1960s. **97m/B VHS.** Loretta Young, Joseph Cotten, Ethel Barrymore, Charles Bickford, Harry Davenport, Lex Barker, James Arness, Rose Hobart; *D:* H.C. Potter; *C:* Milton Krasner. Oscars '47: Actress (Young).

The Farmer's Other Daughter *Farm Girl* **1965** A rural comedy about Farmer Brown whose lovely daughter is eyed by all the farmhands. He also has to contend with dastardly Mr. Barksnapper who wants to take his farm away from him until one of his daughter's beaus comes to the rescue. **84m/C VHS.** Ernest Ashworth, Judy Pennebaker, Bill Michael; *D:* John Patrick Hayes.

The Farmer's Wife 1/2 **1928** Silent British comedy about a recently widowed farmer searching for a new wife. Meanwhile, his lovely housekeeper would be the perfect candidate. Based on Eden Philpott's play. **97m/B VHS, DVD.** *GB* Jameson Thomas, Lillian Hall-Davis, Gordon Harker; *D:* Alfred Hitchcock; *W:* Alfred Hitchcock; *C:* Jack Cox.

Farmhouse WOOF! 2008 (R) Icky torture porn that features a dead child and tries to tie up its plot holes with some supernatural hogwash. After Chad and Scarlet's baby dies, they decide to start over in a new city. They get into a car accident and are offered shelter at the farmhouse of crazy Samael and his wife Lilith (those names should be a warning). These are not folks you want to be under the same roof with. **95m/C DVD.** Jamie Anne Allman, William Lee Scott, Steven Weber, Kelly Hu; *W:* Daniel P. Coughlin, Jason Hice; *C:* Tim Hudson; *M:* Mark Petrie. **VIDEO**

Fascination WOOF! 2004 (R) Bisset's beauty at 60 is the only fascinating thing in this mess of a thriller. Dad (Naughton) dies in a mysterious swimming accident, son (Garcia) thinks foul play, Mom remarries quickly, son sleeps with new stepsister (Evans). The plot twists and surprise revelations stretch things beyond the point of believability, the dialogue is terrible, and the performances lack any spark. It all adds up to a shallow, painful movie that will either induce groans or laughs. **102m/C DVD.** Jacqueline Bisset, Adam Garcia, Alice Evans, James Naughton, Stuart Wilson; *D:* Klaus Menzel; *W:* Klaus Menzel; *C:* Reinhart Pesche, Reinhart Pesche; *M:* John Du Prez, John Du Prez.

Fashion Victims *Reine Geschmacksache* **2007** Disgruntled middle-aged Wolfgang Zenker is a travelling salesman of frumpy fashions for women. His position is threatened by younger rival Steven, who's peddling a trendier line of clothing to the same clients. Wolfgang has also over-extended himself financially, which he keeps secret from his frustrated wife Erika. When he loses his driver's license, Wolfgang forces his closeted teenaged son Karsten to chauffeur him around. Karsten makes cute with the outgoing, gay Steven and they begin a romance without realizing just who's who. The farce is somewhat spoiled by the fact that Wolfgang is completely unpleasant but the other characters are amusing. German with subtitles. **94m/C DVD.** *GE* Edgar Selge, Florian Bartholomai, Roman Knizka, Franziska Walser; *D:* Ingo Rasper; *W:* Ingo Rasper, Tom Steuber; *C:* Marc Achenbach; *M:* Martina Eisenreich.

Fashions of 1934 *Fashions* **1934** A typical, lightweight '30s musical with impressive choreography by Busby Berkeley. Powell plays a disreputable clothing designer who goes to Paris to steal the latest fashion designs and winds up costuming a musical and falls in love. ♫ Spin a Little Web of Dreams; Broken Melody. **78m/B VHS.** Bette Davis, William Powell, Frank McHugh, Hugh Herbert, Reginald Owen, Busby Berkeley; *D:* William Dieterle.

Fass Black **1977 (R)** Yet another man against the mob flick straight out of Bartlett's familiar plotlines. Amidst gratuitous music and violence, a disco owner locks horns with the syndicate after they try to take over his place. There's a good reason disco is dead. **105m/C VHS.** John Poole, Jeannie Bell, Cal Wilson, Harold Nicholas, Nicholas Lewis; *D:* D'Urville Martin.

Fast & Furious **2009 (PG-13)** The fourth installment in the series really is a prequel for *Tokyo Drift* and puts the original cast and characters back together in L.A. Dom (Diesel) and Brian (Walker) end their feud to combine forces against a common enemy and agree to help the feds bring down a heroin importer. Diesel will definitely draw his fans in, but in the end there's not much else but a bunch of sweet cars, flashy driving, fiery crashes, and all other manner of things blowing up real good. **107m/C DVD.** *US* Vin Diesel, Paul Walker, Michelle Rodriguez, Jordana Brewster, Laz Alonso; *D:* Justin Lin; *W:* Chris Morgan; *C:* Amir M. Mokri; *M:* Brian Tyler.

The Fast and the Furious
1954 On the lam after being falsely charged with murder, Ireland picks up a fast car and a loose woman (or is it a loose car and a fast woman?) and makes a run for the border by entering the Pebble Beach race. **73m/B VHS, DVD.** John Ireland, Dorothy Malone, Bruce Carlisle, Iris Adrian, Jean Howell; *D:* Edwards Sampson, John Ireland; *W:* Jerome Odlum, Jean Howell; *C:* Floyd Crosby; *M:* Alexander Gerens.

The Fast and the Furious 1/2 **2001 (PG-13)** Rookie L.A. cop Brian (Walker) goes undercover to infiltrate a street gang that adapts sports cars for illicit street racing and other, even less legal, uses. But first he has to earn the respect and trust of their leader, Dominic (Diesel), and the love of Dom's sister Mia (Brewster). Dominic is the head of a tight-knit "family" of quirky thieves hopped up on car exhaust and adrenaline, very much in the B-movie tradition of "Gone in 60 Seconds" (the original), "Eat My Dust," and "Grand Theft Auto." And hey, let's face it, kids. That's all this is, a summer B-movie where reality, plot, and dialogue have no place. Diesel does impress (again) in the patriarch-philosopher-thief role. **101m/C VHS, DVD, UMD, HD DVD.** *US* Vin Diesel, Paul Walker, Jordana Brewster, Michelle Rodriguez, Rick Yune, Ted Levine, Ja Rule, Thom Barry, Chad Lindberg, Johnny Strong, Matt Schulze, Vyto Ruginis; *D:* Rob Cohen; *W:* Gary Scott Thompson, Erik Bergquist, David Ayer; *C:* Ericson Core; *M:* BT (Brian Transeau).

The Fast and the Furious: Tokyo Drift 1/2 **2006 (PG-13)** In the third installment, the franchise heads to Japan (just like the Bad News Bears!) with new anti-hero Sean (Black), a bad-attitude teenager sent to live with his estranged military dad. Sean soon finds himself involved in the illegal neon world of drift racing and rebel/gangster types out to teach this gaijin some hard lessons. Pic delivers on its fast-cars-fast-races premise. **105m/C DVD, HD DVD.** *US* Lucas Black, Bow Wow, Sung Kang, Jason J. Tobin, Zachery Ty Bryan, Leonardo Nam, Brian Tee, Nathalie Kelley, Brian Goodman, Sonny Chiba, Nikki Griffin, Lynda Boyd, Keiko Kitagawa, Vincent Laresca, Vin Diesel; *D:* Justin Lin; *W:* Chris Morgan; *C:* Stephen Windon; *M:* Brian Tyler.

Fast Break 1/2 **1979 (PG)** New York deli clerk who is a compulsive basketball fan talks his way into a college coaching job. He takes a team of street players with him, with predictable results on and off the court. Kaplan's screen debut. **107m/C VHS.** Gabe Kaplan, Harold Sylvester, Randee Heller; *D:* Jack Smight; *M:* David Shire.

Fast Bullets 1/2 **1936** Texas Rangers fight a gang of smugglers and rescue a kidnap victim in this typical western. **52m/B VHS.** Tom Tyler, Rex Lease, Alan Bridge, William (Bill) Gould, Margaret Nearing, Robert Walker, Charles "Slim" Whitaker, George Chesebro, Jimmy Aubrey; *D:* Harry S. Webb; *W:* Carl Krusada; *C:* Pliny Goodfriend.

Fast, Cheap & Out of Control 1/2 **1997 (PG)** Director Morris' use of odd camera angles, unusual editing, and dark humor increases with each outing but always seems to enhance interest in the subject matter rather than detract from it. While his previous films have focused on just one subject, this one features four: a wild-animal trainer, a topiary gardener, a scientist who creates robotic insects, and a man who studies mole rats. Through inter-cutting and the overlapping of the subjects (at times audio from one is played over the visuals of another), Morris gives the impression that they are all linked together. Old movie footage is used to add an unreal quality, and the score by Caleb Sampson of the Alloy Orchestra hypnotically completes the surrealism. This is the story of four obsessed men, but none as obsessed as director Morris himself, with his need to show that truth is stranger than fiction. **82m/C VHS, DVD.** *D:* Errol Morris; *C:* Robert Richardson; *M:* Caleb Sampson. Natl. Bd. of Review '97: Feature Doc.; N.Y. Film Critics '97: Feature Doc.; Natl. Soc. Film Critics '97: Feature Doc.

Fast Company **1978** The life story of champion race car driver Lonnie Johnson including women, money, and the drag racing sponsors. **90m/C VHS, DVD.** William (Bill) Smith, John Saxon, Claudia Jennings, Nicholas (Nick) Campbell, Don Francks; *D:* David Cronenberg; *W:* David Cronenberg.

Fast Food **1989** A super-cheap, strangulated attempt at low comedy, wherein an entrepreneurial hamburger peddler invents a secret aphrodisiac sauce. Look for former porn-star Traci Lords. **90m/C VHS, DVD.** Clark Brandon, Tracy Griffith, Randal Patrick, Traci Lords, Kevin McCarthy, Michael J. Pollard, Jim Varney; *D:* Michael A. Simpson; *W:* Clark Brandon.

Fast Food Nation **2006 (R)** Director Richard Linklater's attempt to show the public that fast food is both figuratively and literally crappy suffers from some slow pacing and wandering plotlines, but its point is effectively super-sized. After Don (Kinnear), an executive at fictional restaurant chain Mickey's, discovers that some cows may have dropped a chalupa in the meat patties, he starts an investigation that crosses ethnic and class barriers. The story then weaves the lives of illegal immigrants (Moreno, Valderrama), cattle ranchers (Kristofferson, Willis) and suburbanites (Arquette, Hawke, Johnson) together to show why most burger shack value meals should be called the "number two." Linklater wrote the screenplay with Eric Schlosser, whose eponymous nonfiction book provided inspiration. Salad, anyone? **114m/C DVD.** *GB US* Patricia Arquette, Paul Franklin Dano, Luis Guzman, Ethan Hawke, Bobby Canavale, Greg Kinnear, Ashley Johnson, Kris Kristofferson, Avril Lavigne, Esai Morales, Catalina Sandino Moreno, Wilmer Valderrama, Bruce Willis; *D:* Richard Linklater; *W:* Richard Linklater, Eric Schlosser; *C:* Lee Daniel; *M:* Dean Martinez.

Fast Forward 1/2 **1984 (PG)** A group of eight teenagers from Ohio learn how to deal with success and failure when they enter a national dance contest in New York City. A break-dancing variation on the old show business chestnut. ♫ Fast Forward; How Do You Do; As Long As We Believe; Pretty Girl; Mystery; Curves; Showdown; Do You Want It Right Now?; Hardrock. **110m/C VHS.** John Scott Clough, Don Franklin, Tracy Silver, Cindy McGee; *D:* Sidney Poitier; *W:* Richard Wesley; *M:* Tom Bahler.

Fast Getaway **1991 (PG)** Chases scenes proliferate when a teen criminal mastermind plots bank heists for his outlaw father. Relatively painless adolescent action-comedy, cleverly acted, quickly forgotten. **91m/C VHS.** Corey Haim, Cynthia Rothrock, Leo Rossi, Ken Lerner, Marcia Strassman; *D:* Spiro Razatos.

Fast Getaway 2 1/2 **1994 (PG-13)** Ex-bank robber Nelson (Haim) has given up a life of crime to open a business with gal pal Patrice (Buxton) while waiting for his partner/dad Sam (Rossi) to get out of jail. Then Nelson gets set up by Lily (Rothrock) and finds himself trying to convince an FBI agent of his innocence. Innocuous. **90m/C VHS.** Corey Haim, Sarah Buxton, Leo Rossi, Cynthia Rothrock, Peter Paul Liapis; *D:* Oley Sassone; *W:* Mark Sevi; *M:* David Robbins.

Fast Girl 1/2 **2007 (PG)** After her dad is killed in a racing accident, Alex (Monroe) wants to prove she can win in the male-dominated sport. But her Uncle Bill (Brown), who runs the local speedway, refuses to allow her to compete, and then a romance with driver Darryl (Guarini) messes with Alex's concentration. **85m/C DVD.** Mircea Monroe, Justin Guarini, Dwier Brown, Caroline Rhea, James DuMont, Cameron Gordon; *D:* Daniel Zirilli; *W:* Luke Ricci, D. Glase Lomond; *C:* Jason Dittmer; *M:* Nicholas O'Toole. **VIDEO**

Fast Gun 1/2 **1993 (R)** Weapons-loving ex-CIA spook decides to take over a town—with your basic one lone hero to stop him. **90m/C VHS.** Richard (Rick) Hill, Kaz Garas, Robert Dryer, Brenda Bakke, Cirio H. Santiago; *D:* Cirio H. Santiago; *W:* Joe Mari Avellana, Frederick Bailey; *C:* Ricardo Remias; *M:* Jun Latonio.

Fast Kill **1973** A terrorist plot begins to fall apart when the conspirators fight among themselves. **94m/C VHS.** Tom Adams, Susie Hampton, Michael Culver, Peter Halliday; *D:* Lindsay Shonteff.

Fast Money 1/2 **1983** Three pals can't resist the temptation of big bucks from flying drugs in from Mexico, but they find danger along the way. **92m/C VHS.** Sammy Allred, Sonny Carl Davis; *D:* Doug Holloway.

Fast Money **1996 (R)** Car thief Francesca Marsh (Butler) and journalist Jack Martin (McCoy) go on the lam from the mob (and everyone else) with a briefcase containing $2.7 million. **93m/C VHS.** Yancy Butler, Matt McCoy, John Ashton, Trevor Goddard, Andy Romano, Carole Cook, Patrika Darbo; *D:* Alexander Wright; *W:* Alexander Wright; *C:* Thomas Jewett; *M:* Tony Riparetti.

The Fast Runner *Atanarjuat, the Fast Runner* **2001 (R)** The first Inuktikut language feature film is a remarkably compelling drama based on an ancient Inuit legend and set in the north Baffin region of the Candian Arctic. Atanarjuat (Ungalaaq) is in love with Atuat (Ivalu), who is already promised to the jealous Oki (Arnatsiaq) who decides to kill his rival. Atanarjuat manages to escape by running (naked) across the ice, outlasting his pursuers until he finds a safe refuge. Then he decides to go back to his community and settle the score. **172m/C VHS, DVD.** *CA* Pakkak Innuksuk, Natar Ungalaaq, Peter Henry Arnatsiaq, Sylvia Ivalu, Lucy Tulugarjuk; *D:* Zacharias Kunuk; *W:* Paul Apak Angilirq; *C:* Norman Cohn; *M:* Chris Crilly. Cannes '01: First Feature; Genie '01: Director (Kunuk), Film, Film Editing, Screenplay, Score.

Fast Sofa **2001 (R)** Lowlife, small-time L.A. drug dealer Rick (Busey) has a one-nighter with porn actress Ginger (Tilly) and decides to follow her to Palm Springs. Too bad her jealous (and violent) movie-producer husband (Roberts) is also about to show up. Based on the book by Bruce Craven. **95m/C VHS, DVD.** Jake Busey, Jennifer Tilly, Eric Roberts, Adam Goldberg, Crispin Glover, Natasha Lyonne, Bijou Phillips; *D:* Salome Breziner; *W:* Salome Breziner, Peter Chase, Bruce Craven; *C:* Dean Lent; *M:* William V. Malpede.

Fast Talking **1986** The story of a quick-talking, incorrigible, 15-year-old Australian boy's humorous though tragic criminal schemes. The young protagonist slides his way through a life marked by a degenerate home life, a brother who forces him to sell drugs, and a future that holds no promise. **93m/C VHS.** *AU* Steve Bisley, Tracy Mann, Peter Hehir, Dennis Moore, Rod Zuanic, Toni

Allaylis, Chris Truswell; *D:* Ken Cameron; *W:* Ken Cameron.

Fast Times at Ridgemont High 1982 (R) Teens at a Southern California high school revel in sex, drugs, and rock 'n' roll. A full complement of student types meet at the Mall—that great suburban microcosm percolating with angst-ridden teen trials—to contemplate losing their virginity, plot skipping homeroom, and move inexorably closer to the end of their adolescence. The talented young cast became household names: Sean Penn is most excellent as the California surfer dude who antagonizes teacher, Walston, aka "Aloha Mr. Hand." Based on the best-selling book by Cameron Crowe, it's one of the best of this genre. **91m/C VHS, DVD, HD DVD.** Sean Penn, Jennifer Jason Leigh, Judge Reinhold, Robert Romanus, Brian Backer, Phoebe Cates, Ray Walston, Scott Thomson, Vincent Schiavelli, Amanda Wyss, Forest Whitaker, Kelli Maroney, Eric Stoltz, Pamela Springsteen, James Russo, Martin Brest, Anthony Edwards, Nicolas Cage; *D:* Amy Heckerling; *W:* Cameron Crowe; *C:* Matthew F. Leonetti. Natl. Film Reg. '05.

Fast Walking 1982 (R) A prison guard is offered $50,000 to help a militant black leader escape from jail, the same man his cousin has contracted to kill. **116m/C VHS.** James Woods, Kay Lenz, M. Emmet Walsh, Robert Hooks, Tim McIntire, Timothy Carey, Susan Tyrrell; *D:* James B. Harris.

Faster, Pussycat! Kill! Kill! *The Leather Girls; Pussycat* **1965** It doesn't get any better than this! Three sexy go-go dancers get their after-work kicks by hot-rodding in the California desert. They soon find themselves enveloped in murder, kidnapping, lust and robbery after a particular race gets out of hand. Easily the most watchable, fun and funny production to spring from the mind of Russ Meyer. Those who haven't seen this cannot truly be called "cool." **83m/B VHS, DVD.** Tua Satana, Haji, Lori Williams, Susan Bernard, Stuart Lancaster, Paul Trinka, Dennis Busch, Ray Barlow, Mickey Foxx; *D:* Russ Meyer; *W:* Jack Moran, Russ Meyer; *C:* Walter Schenk; *M:* Paul Sawtell, Bert Shefter, The Bostweeds.

Fastest Guitar Alive 1/2 **1968** Debut of the legendary Orbison is strictly for inveterate fans only. Rebel operative/crooner during the Civil War, whose rhythm is good but timing is bad, steals a Union gold supply, but the war ends before he makes it back to the land of Dixie. Seems that makes him a common thief. **88m/C VHS.** Roy Orbison, Sammy Jackson, Margaret Pierce, Joan Freeman; *D:* Michael D. Moore; *M:* Fred Karger.

Fastest Gun Alive 1956 Suspenseful western with ex-gunfighter Ford challenged to a showdown by Crawford. **89m/C VHS.** Glenn Ford, Jeanne Crain, Broderick Crawford, Russ Tamblyn, Allyn Joslyn, Leif Erickson, John Dehner, Noah Beery Jr., J.M. Kerrigan, Rhys Williams; *D:* Russell Rouse; *W:* Russell Rouse, Frank D. Gilroy; *C:* George J. Folsey; *M:* Andre Previn.

Fat Albert 1/2 **2004 (PG)** Clunky live-action version of Bill Cosby's standup routines and the animated series "Fat Albert and the Cosby Kids." Depressed South Philly teen Doris (Pratt) is watching TV Land reruns of the show when a magic portal opens up allowing Fat Albert (an agreeable Thompson) and his gang to pop into her living room. F.A. feels obliged to offer advice to help Doris gain some self-esteem and even develops a crush on Doris' popular foster sister, Lauri (Ramirez). Meanwhile, the '70s-era tooners react to the real world of the 21st century in expected fish-out-of-water ways. Hey, hey, hey is more why, why, why? **93m/C VHS, DVD.** *US* Kenan Thompson, Kyla Pratt, Marques Houston, Dania Ramirez, Omari (Omarion) Grandberry, Shedrack Anderson III, Jermaine Williams, Keith D. Robinson, Alphonso McAuley, Aaron A. Frazier, J. Mack Slaughter Junior; ***Cameos:*** Bill Cosby; *D:* Joel Zwick; *W:* Bill Cosby, Charles Kipps; *C:* Paul Elliott; *M:* Richard Gibbs.

Fat City 1/2 **1972 (PG)** One of Huston's later triumphs, a seedy, street-level drama based on the Leonard Gardner novel about an aging alcoholic boxer trying to make a comeback and his young worshipful protege. Highly acclaimed. Tyrrell earned an Oscar nomination as the boxer's world-weary lover. **93m/C VHS, DVD.** Stacy Keach, Jeff Bridges, Susan Tyrrell, Candy Clark, Nicholas Colasanto; *D:* John Huston; *C:* Conrad L. Hall; *M:* Marvin Hamlisch.

Fat Guy Goes Nutzoid **WOOF!** *Zeisters* **1986** A crude farce about an obese mental patient who escapes from the mental hospital and joins two teenagers on a wild trip to New York City. **85m/C VHS.** Tibor Feldman, Peter Linari, John MacKay, Joan Allen; *D:* John Golden; *M:* Leo Kottke.

Fat Man and Little Boy 1/2 **1989 (PG-13)** A lavish, semi-fictional account of the creation of the first atomic bomb, and the tensions between J. Robert Oppenheimer and his military employer, Gen. Leslie Groves. Overlong but interesting. Cusack, whose character never existed, is especially worthwhile as an idealistic scientist. **127m/C VHS, DVD.** Paul Newman, Dwight Schultz, Bonnie Bedelia, John Cusack, Laura Dern, John C. McGinley, Natasha Richardson, Ron Frazier; *D:* Roland Joffe; *W:* Bruce Robinson, Tony Garnett, Roland Joffe; *M:* Ennio Morricone.

The Fat Spy **WOOF!** **1966** Campy beach movie parody has a gaggle of treasure hunting teens, a tycoon's daughter, her boyfriend, his twin brother, and the twin's girlfriend descending on an island off the Florida coast looking for the Fountain of Youth. Flick tries hard, with plenty of (awful) "rock" music by The Wild Ones, Jayne Mansfield, and Phyllis Diller among the participants wildly mugging for laughs. None of it works, as parody or straight comedy. Unless you're a fan of ulta-bad quickie exploitation, don't bother. **75m/C VHS, DVD.** Phyllis Diller, Jack E. Leonard, Brian Donlevy, Jayne Mansfield, Joseph Brun, Joel Hirschhorn, Al Kasha; *D:* Joseph Cates; *W:* Matthew Andrews; *C:* Joseph Brun; *M:* Al Kasha.

Fatal Attraction *Head On* **1980 (R)** Couple meet after an auto accident. They begin an affair which turns dark and bizarre. Fine cast doesn't get far with this peculiar premise, although every one tries hard. **90m/C VHS.** *CA* Sally Kellerman, Stephen Lack, John Huston, Lawrence Dane; *D:* Michael Grant.

Fatal Attraction **1987 (R)** When a very married New York lawyer is seduced by a beautiful blonde associate, the one-night stand leads to terror as she continues to pursue the relationship. She begins to threaten his family and home with possessive, violent acts. An expertly made, manipulative thriller; one of the most hotly discussed films of the 1980s. A successful change of role for Close as the sexy, scorned, and deadly other woman. Also available in a special "director's series" edition, featuring Lyne's original, controversial ending. **120m/C VHS, DVD.** Michael Douglas, Glenn Close, Anne Archer, Stuart Pankin, Ellen Hamilton-Latzen, Ellen Foley, Fred Gwynne, Meg Mundy, J.J. Johnston; *D:* Adrian Lyne; *W:* James Dearden; *C:* Howard Atherton; *M:* Maurice Jarre.

Fatal Beauty 1/2 **1987 (R)** A female undercover cop in Los Angeles tracks down a drug dealer selling cocaine (from which the title is taken). Elliott is the mob bodyguard who helps her out. Violent and sensational, the film tries to capitalize on the success of "Beverly Hills Cop" and fails miserably. Goldberg is wasted in this effort and the picture tiptoes around the interracial romance aspects that are implied. **104m/C VHS, DVD.** Whoopi Goldberg, Sam Elliott, Ruben Blades, Harris Yulin, Richard "Cheech" Marin, Brad Dourif; *D:* Tom Holland; *W:* Hilary Henkin, Dean Riesner; *C:* David M. Walsh; *M:* Harold Faltermeyer.

Fatal Bond 1/2 **1991 (R)** Blair plays a small-town hairdresser caught in an obsessive love affair with a drifter. When she suspects her boyfriend is committing a string of rape-murders, will she turn him in or protect him? Or is she next? **89m/C VHS.** Linda Blair, Jerome Ehlers, Stephen Leeder, Donal Gibson, Caz Lederman, Tao Gerbert, Penny Pederson, Joe Bugner; *D:* Vincent Monton; *W:* Phillip Avalon.

Fatal Charm **1992 (R)** There's a serial killer at work in a small town. So far six women have been raped and murdered. But cute-teen Valerie can't believe it when the townspeople accuse that sweet guy Adam, especially since he's the one boy Valerie is so very attracted to. **90m/C VHS, DVD.** Christopher Atkins, Amanda Peterson, Mary Frann, James Remar, Andrew (Andy) Robinson, Peggy Lipton; *D:* Alan Smithee; *W:* Nicholas Niciphor.

Fatal Chase *Nowhere to Hide* **1977** Van Cleef is a U.S. Marshal assigned to protect ex-hitman Musante from his vengeful former employers. And you thought you didn't get along with your boss. Typical made-for-TV fodder written by Anhalt, who usually manages to be a trifle more entertaining. **78m/C VHS.** Lee Van Cleef, Tony Musante, Charles Robinson, Lelia Goldoni, Noel Fournier, Russell Johnson, Edward Anhalt; *D:* Jack Starrett; *W:* Edward Anhalt.

Fatal Chase 1/2 **1992** Police investigation Marcus Lee and undercover cop Robin investigate drug dealer Dion. Robin and fellow officer Cynthia apprehend Dion in Hong Kong and bring him back to face charges in the Philippines. But Dion escapes and the duo are forced to deal with local officer Philip in order to get Dion back. Dubbed into English. **96m/C VHS.** *HK* Robin Shou, Yukari Oshima, Waise Lee; *D:* Ki Yee Chik.

Fatal Combat 1/2 *No Exit* **1996 (R)** Reclusive billionaire Houston Armstrong (Fitzpatrick) privately broadcasts a program called "No Exit" that features combat-to-the-death. (Live on TV!) But Armstrong tends to run out of combatants so when he hears about John Stoneman (Wincott), a master martial artist, he has his minions kidnap him along with Stoneman's pupil, Jason (Demambro). Now, it's fight or die. **93m/C VHS.** Jeff Wincott, Richard Fitzpatrick, Joe Demambro, Sven-Ole Thorsen; *D:* Damian Lee; *W:* Damian Lee, John Lawson; *C:* Gerald R. Goozie. **VIDEO**

Fatal Confinement 1/2 **1964** Wrenching drama finds Crawford, having lived 15 years in seclusion with her young daughter, forced to sell her land to a giant corporation bent on expansion. Interesting also for the similarities to Crawford's real-life "Mommie Dearest" lifestyle. **70m/C VHS.** *GB* Joan Crawford, Paul Burke, Charles Bickford; *D:* Robert Guest.

Fatal Contact: Bird Flu in America **2006** Oh no! Another really terrible disaster flick! Avian flu has mutated and is now transmittable from human to human, which causes widespread panic. Poor scientist Iris Varnack (Richardson) is trying to come up with a vaccine or something but gosh darn, it's just so hard with all those people running around screaming and dying! **83m/C DVD.** Joely Richardson, Scott Cohen, Stacy Keach, Justina Machado, Ann Cusack, David Ramsey; *D:* Richard Pearce; *W:* Ron McGee; *C:* Ivan Strasburg; *M:* Mark Adler. **TV**

Fatal Error 1/2 *Outsider in Amsterdam; The Outsider; Grijpstra and de Gier* **1983** Dutch police thriller about the investigation of a cop killing. Based on the mystery series by Janwillem van de Wetering. Dubbed. **85m/C VHS.** *NL* Rutger Hauer, Rijk de Gooyer, Willeke Van Ammelrooy, Donald M. Jones; *D:* Wim Verstappen; *M:* Ennio Morricone.

Fatal Error 1/2 **1999** Digicron, the world's largest media company, is about to connect all the televisions and computers worldwide. But Dr. Nick Baldwin (Sabato Jr.) and Army medical researcher Samantha Carter (Turner) discover that people are dying from an untraceable virus. So is the virus linked to Digicron. Well, what do you think? Adapted from the novel "Reaper" by Ben Mezrich. **91m/C VHS, DVD.** Antonio Sabato Jr., Janine Turner, Robert Wagner, Malcolm Stewart; *D:* Armand Mastroianni; *W:* Rockne S. O'Bannon; *C:* David Geddes; *M:* Ron Ramin. **CABLE**

Fatal Exposure **1990** The insatiably sanguinary Jack the Ripper lives on in the form of his great grandson, who avails himself of modern technology to capture those magic moments on videotape. Just goes to show home movies don't have to be bland. **96m/C VHS.** Blake Bahner, Ena Henderson, Julie Austin, Dan Schmale, Renee Cline, Gary Wise, Joy Ovington; *D:* Peter B. Good; *W:* Christopher Painter; *C:* Peter B. Good; *M:* Dean Richard Marino.

Fatal Exposure **1991 (PG-13)** A divorcee on vacation with her young sons accidentally picks up the wrong snapshots at the developers'. It turns out she has her hands on some incriminating photos, and the subject will resort to anything, even murder, to keep her quiet. **89m/C VHS.** Mare Winningham, Nick Mancuso, Christopher McDonald, Geoffrey Blake, Christopher Pettiet; *D:* Alan Metzger. **TV**

Fatal Fix 1/2 *Eroina* **1980** A French film expose of urban heroin addiction. Music by the Pretenders. **90m/C VHS.** *FR* Helmut Berger, Corinne Clery; *D:* Massimo Pirri.

Fatal Games 1/2 **1984** Young female athletes are mysteriously disappearing at the Falcon Academy of Athletics and a crazed killer is responsible. **88m/C VHS.** Sally Kirkland, Lynn Banashek, Sean Masterson, Teal Roberts; *D:* Michael Elliot; *W:* Michael Elliot; *C:* Alfred Taylor; *M:* Shuki Levy.

The Fatal Hour 1/2 **1940** Karloff is enlisted to aid police in solving the murder of a detective. As Karloff is rounding up suspects, three more murders take place. Feeble. **68m/B VHS, DVD.** Boris Karloff, Marjorie Reynolds, Grant Withers, Charles Trowbridge, John Hamilton, Frank Puglia, Jason Robards Sr.; *D:* William Nigh; *W:* Scott Darling, George Waggner; *C:* Harry Neumann.

The Fatal Image 1/2 **1990** A mother and daughter on vacation in Paris inadvertantly videotape an international mob hit, making them the target of ruthless assassins. Filmed on location in Paris. **96m/C VHS, DVD.** Michele Lee, Justine Bateman, Francois Dunoyer, Jean-Pierre Cassel, Sonia Petrovna; *D:* Thomas J. Wright; *C:* Jean-Yves Le Mener. **TV**

Fatal Images **1989** A camera mysteriously causes all the models who pose for it to die, prompting the photographer to investigate. **90m/C VHS.** Lane Coyle; *D:* Dennis Devine; *W:* Dennis Devine, Mike Bowler, Steve Jarvis.

Fatal Instinct 1/2 **1992 (R)** A tough-guy cop trying to solve a murder instead finds himself a victim of sexual obsession in this erotic thriller. Also available in an unrated version. Not to be confused with (but doesn't everything sound familiar) "Basic Instinct." **93m/C VHS.** Michael Madsen, Laura Johnson, Antony (Tony) Hamilton; *D:* John Dirlam.

Fatal Instinct **1993 (PG-13)** Spoof on erotic thrillers such as "Fatal Attraction" and "Basic Instinct." Suave Assante plays a guy with dual careers—he's both cop and attorney, defending the criminals he's arrested. Young plays a lovelorn psycho who's lost her panties. Plot is worth mentioning only in passing, since the point is to mercilessly skewer the entire film noir tradition. The gags occasionally hit deep-chuckle level, though for every good joke there's at least three that misfire. Clemons of "E Street Band" fame wanders around with sax for background music purposes, typical of the acute self-consciousness of the film. **90m/C VHS, DVD.** Armand Assante, Sean Young, Sherilyn Fenn, Kate Nelligan, Christopher McDonald, James Remar, Tony Randall; ***Cameos:*** Clarence Clemons, Doc Severinsen; *D:* Carl Reiner; *W:* David O'Malley; *M:* Richard Gibbs.

A Fatal Inversion 1/2 **1992** When 19-year-old Hodge inherits a remote English estate from his great-uncle, he invites best friend Northam to spend a carefree summer, after both have told their parents they're vacationing in Greece. The boys are soon joined by Todd, Ford, and Warnecke in an informal commune but several disasters cause them to break off all contact for 12 years—until the remains of two bodies are discovered on the grounds and a police investigation is started. Made for British TV; based on the psychological thriller by Ruth Rendell (writing as Barbara Vine). **150m/C VHS.** *GB* Douglas Hodge, Jeremy Northam, Saira Todd, Julia Ford, Gordon Warnecke, Nicholas Woodeson, Peter Attard, Rachel Joyce, Nicholas Le Prevost, Ben Chaplin; *D:* Tim Fywell; *W:* Sandy Welch; *C:* Barry McCann; *M:* David Ferguson. **TV**

Fatal Justice **1993** Mars is a topnotch assassin who's been in the business too long and knows too much so the agency he works for decides to kill him off. They send young and beautiful professional Diana to do the job but will she be able to when she discovers Mars is actually her father? **90m/C VHS, DVD.** Suzanne Ager, Richard Folmer, Tom Bertino, Joe Estevez; ***D:*** Gerald Cain; ***W:*** Bret McCormick; ***C:*** Gerald Cain; ***M:*** Jeff Walton.

Fatal Mission **1989 (R)** A Vietnam soldier captures a female Chinese guerilla and uses her as his hostage and guide through the jungle. **84m/C VHS, DVD.** Peter Fonda, Mako, Tia Carrere, Ted Markland, Jim Mitchum; ***D:*** George Rowe; ***C:*** Phil Parmet.

Fatal Passion *Dark Red* **1994** Two sisters escape from the city after an accidental murder but run straight into the middle of a sacrifical backwoods cult. **90m/C VHS, DVD.** Lisa Hayland, Joe Pilato; ***D:*** Hugh Parks; ***C:*** Greg Patterson.

Fatal Past **1994 (R)** Bodyguard gets up close and personal with his client—who happens to be a mobster's mistress. As if this weren't trouble enough their pasts provide doom and gloom as well. **85m/C VHS.** Costas Mandylor, Kasia (Katarzyna) Figura; ***D:*** Clive Fleury; ***W:*** Richard Ryan.

Fatal Pulse **WOOF! 1988** Sorority girls are being killed off in grisly ways. Basic slasher/gore. **90m/C VHS.** Michelle McCormick, Ken Roberts, Joe Estevez, Alex Courtney; ***D:*** Anthony J. Christopher; ***W:*** James Hundhausen; ***C:*** David Lewis; ***M:*** Martin Mayo.

Fatal Skies **1990** An evil schemer plots to dump toxic waste in a small town's water supply until a group of teens comes to the rescue. **88m/C VHS.** Tim Burke, J. Michael Esposito, Maureen Burns, Timothy Leary; ***D:*** Thomas Dugan; ***W:*** Thomas Dugan; ***C:*** Glenn Kershaw; ***M:*** Daniel May.

Fatal Vision 1/2 **1984** TV-murder-of-the-week version of Joe McGinniss's controversial book about the murder trial of Dr. Jeffrey MacDonald, the former Green Beret physician accused of murdering his whole family and blaming the killings on crazed hippies. McGinniss first believed MacDonald may have been innocent but his subsequent investigation, and his book, proved otherwise. Starring debut for Cole, who would go on to play a much better TV dad. MacDonald still protests his innocence. **192m/C VHS.** Gary Cole, Karl Malden, Eva Marie Saint, Andy Griffith, Barry Newman, Mitchell Ryan, Wendy Schaal, Barry Corbin, Gary Grubbs, Scott Paulin, Albert Salmi; ***D:*** David Greene; ***W:*** John Gay; ***C:*** Stevan Larner; ***M:*** Gil Melle. **TV**

Fatally Yours **1995** Real-estate agent Danny (Rossovich) decides to restore a long-vacant house where a mob massacre occurred in 1928. While in the house, he's "contacted" by the ghostly Sara (MacDonnell), whose husband and gangster father were among the dead. Sara tells him about a hidden treasure of jewels, which leads some present-day gangsters to take an interest in Danny's new property. **90m/C VHS.** Rick Rossovich, George Lazenby, Roddy McDowall, Sage Stallone, Sarah MacDonnell; ***D:*** Tim Everitt; ***C:*** Tim Everitt.

Fate 1/2 **1990 (PG-13)** Sweet comedy. A young man plans his love-affair carefully, but his biggest problem is meeting the girl of his dreams. Cheerful acting from Lynn and Paul. Stylish and charming. **115m/C VHS.** Cheryl Lynn, Stuart Paul, Kaye Ballard, Susannah York; ***D:*** Stuart Paul.

Fateless 1/2 *Sorstalansag* **2005** Gyuri is a 14-year-old Hungarian Jewish boy subjected to the horrors of three different concentration camps, surviving only to find isolation in the world around him. An emphasis on the dehumanization of the Jews as they were corralled into these camps gives a unique look and tone from that of other Holocaust pictures. Muddy and miserable perspective is nonetheless visually beautiful. Adapted from a novel by Nobel Prize-winning author Imre Kertesz. **114m/C DVD.** *HU GE GB* Marcell Nagy, Daniel Craig, Aron Dimeny, Andras M. Kecskes, Jozsef Gyabronka, Endre Harkanyi, Janos Ban, Judit Schell; ***D:*** Lajos Koltai; ***W:*** Imre Kertesz; ***C:*** Gyula Pados; ***M:*** Ennio Morricone.

Father *Apa* **1967** After WWII, a Hungarian youth makes up stories about his dead father's heroism that enhance his own position. Eventually he becomes obsessed with the facts surrounding his father's death at the hands of the enemy and, learning the truth, lays the past to rest. In Hungarian with English subtitles. **85m/B VHS, DVD.** *HU* Andras Balint, Miklos Gabor; ***D:*** Istvan Szabo; ***W:*** Istvan Szabo.

Father **1990 (PG-13)** A woman receives an anonymous telephone call telling her to watch a TV news program and learn the truth about her beloved father. What she sees is her father's face superimposed over that of a young Nazi soldier and an aging, unstable woman accusing her father of war crimes. The daughter fiercely believes her father to be a victim of mistaken identity but questions keep nagging at her. Very similiar in plot to "Music Box" and just as pedestrian in spite of some good performances. **106m/C VHS.** *AU* Max von Sydow, Carol Drinkwater, Julia Blake, Steve Jacobs; ***D:*** John Power. Australian Film Inst. '90: Actor (von Sydow), Actress (Blake).

Father and Scout 1/2 **1994 (PG)** Would-be Eagle Scout Michael (Bonsall) has a problem when he takes his city-bred, whiny, basically incompetent, dad Spenser (Saget) on a camping trip. Made for TV. **92m/C VHS, DVD.** Bob Saget, Brian Bonsall, Heidi Swedberg, Stuart Pankin, David Graf, Troy Evans; ***D:*** Richard Michaels; ***M:*** David Kitay. **TV**

Father and Son 1/2 *Otets I Syn* **2003** Intense look at a father-son relationship. The father (Shetini), a widower, and son (Neimyshev) have lived a largely hermetic life, creating a relationship that more closely resembles partners than of father and son (and not in the business sense either). As each face new choices, however, they are forced to realize that they may have to let go of their dependence on each other. Second chapter of Alexander Sokurov's trilogy on family relationships, the first being "Mother and Son". **83m/C DVD.** *GE* Andrei Shetinin, Alexei Neimyshev, Alexander Rasbash; ***D:*** Alexander Sokurov; ***W:*** Sergei Potepalov; ***C:*** Alexander Burov; ***M:*** Andrei Sigle.

The Father Clements Story 1/2 **1987** The true story of a black priest in Chicago who battled the Roman Catholic hierarchy in order to adopt a troubled teenager. **100m/C VHS.** Louis Gossett Jr., Malcolm Jamal Warner, Carroll O'Connor, Leon Robinson, Rosetta LeNoire, Ron McClarty; ***D:*** Edwin Sherin. **TV**

Father Figure 1/2 **1980** When a divorced man attends his ex-wife's funeral, he discovers that he must take care of his estranged sons. Well-done drama based on young adult writer Richard Peck's novel. **94m/C VHS.** Hal Linden, Timothy Hutton, Cassie Yates, Martha Scott, Jeremy Licht; ***D:*** Jerry London; ***M:*** Billy Goldenberg. **TV**

Father Goose 1/2 **1964** During WWII, a liquor-loving plane-spotter stationed on a remote Pacific isle finds himself stuck with a group of French refugee schoolgirls and their teacher. Some predictable gags, romance, and heroism fill out the running time pleasantly. Scriptwriters Stone and Tarloff, who were competitors, not collaborators on the project, shared an Oscar. **116m/C VHS, DVD.** Cary Grant, Leslie Caron, Trevor Howard; ***D:*** Ralph Nelson; ***W:*** Peter Stone, Frank Tarloff; ***C:*** Charles B(ryant) Lang Jr.; ***M:*** Cy Coleman. Oscars '64: Story & Screenplay.

Father Hood **1993 (PG-13)** Family drama has Swayze playing a small-time criminal whose daughter tracks him down after leaving the foster-care shelter where she and her brother are being abused. The family takes to the road, running from both the police and a journalist (Berry) who wants to expose the corrupt foster-care system. The children are obnoxious, Swayze is miscast, and the entire film is a misfire. **94m/C VHS, DVD.** Patrick Swayze, Halle Berry, Sabrina Lloyd, Brian Bonsall, Diane Ladd, Michael Ironside, Bob Gunton; ***D:*** Darrell Roodt; ***W:*** Scott Spencer.

Father of Lies 1/2 **2007** Bishop Calvin Jacobs (Powell) has a drinking problem and a church that's deep in debt and he's willing to go to some unscrupulous means to save his ministry. He learns that not trusting in the Lord is his biggest mistake. **102m/C DVD.** Clifton Powell, Vivica A. Fox, DMX, Clyde Jones, Veronica Berry, Lucius Basten; ***D:*** Phenomenon; ***W:*** Anthony Faia, Evan Scott.

Father of the Bride 1/2 **1950** A classic, quietly hilarious comedy about the tribulations of a father preparing for his only daughter's wedding. Tracy is suitably overwhelmed as loving father Stanley Banks and Taylor radiant as the bride, Kay. A warm vision of American family life, accompanied by the 1940 MGM short "Wedding Bills." Followed by "Father's Little Dividend" (1951) and later a TV series. Remade in 1991. **106m/C VHS, DVD.** Spencer Tracy, Elizabeth Taylor, Joan Bennett, Billie Burke, Leo G. Carroll, Russ Tamblyn, Don Taylor, Moroni Olsen; ***D:*** Vincente Minnelli; ***W:*** Frances Goodrich, Albert Hackett; ***C:*** John Alton.

Father of the Bride 1/2 **1991 (PG)** Remake of the 1950 comedy classic portrays one of the most overextravagant weddings in recent film history, but falls short of the original. Predictable plot and characters don't hide any surprises, but nothing detracts from the purpose of the film: to be a nice, charming movie. Martin is fine as the reluctant dad but Keaton is little more than window dressing as the bride's mom; Short is annoying as a pretentious wedding coordinator. Williams pulls off a nice film debut—and was almost immediately cast in a TV ad as a young-bride-to-be calling her dad long distance to tell him she's engaged. Adapted from a novel by Edward Streeter. **105m/C VHS, DVD.** Steve Martin, Diane Keaton, Kimberly Williams, Kieran Culkin, George Newbern, Martin Short, B.D. Wong, Peter Michael Goetz, Kate McGregor-Stewart, Martha Gehman, Eugene Levy; ***D:*** Charles Shyer; ***W:*** Charles Shyer, Nancy Meyers; ***C:*** John Lindley; ***M:*** Alan Silvestri.

Father of the Bride Part 2 1/2 **1995 (PG)** Sweetly sentimental update of the 1951 film "Father's Little Dividend" finds George Banks (Martin) once again thrown for a loop—first by his beloved daughter Annie's (Williams) pregnancy and then by wife Nina's (the radiant Keaton) announcement that they are about to become parents themselves. George doesn't deal very well with either situation but, aided by fey party planner Franck (Short), he manages to get through the predictable chaos. Martin's physical expressiveness and sly charm are a big plus. **106m/C VHS, DVD.** Steve Martin, Diane Keaton, Kimberly Williams, Martin Short, George Newbern, Kieran Culkin, Peter Michael Goetz, Kate McGregor-Stewart, Eugene Levy, B.D. Wong, Jane Adams; ***D:*** Charles Shyer; ***W:*** Nancy Meyers, Charles Shyer; ***C:*** William A. Fraker; ***M:*** Alan Silvestri.

Father of the Kamikaze *Aa Kessen Kokutai* **1974** A highly romanticized version of the events surrounding the life of Vice Admiral Takijiro Onishi (Kojiro Sasaki) in WWII. Onishi doesn't think Japan can defeat America because of its limited resources, but when the idea for the kamikaze attacks is thought up he repeats it to his superiors and they give it the green light. Despondent when the attacks fail to end the war Onishi commits seppuku, and the other officers attempt a mutiny when the Emperor surrenders to U.S. forces. **199m/C DVD, Blu-ray Disc.** *JP* Koji Tsuruta; ***D:*** Kosaku Yamashita; ***W:*** Kazuo Kasahara, Tatsuo Nogami.

Father Was a Fullback 1/2 **1949** College football coach (MacMurray) has a losing team, problems with the administration and alumni, and two daughters with growing pains at home. Wife O'Hara supplies the sympathetic shoulder. **99m/B VHS.** Fred MacMurray, Maureen O'Hara, Betty Lynn, Rudy Vallee, Thelma Ritter, Natalie Wood, Jim Backus; ***D:*** John M. Stahl; ***W:*** Mary Loos, Casey Robinson, Richard Sale; ***C:*** Lloyd Ahern; ***M:*** Cyril Mockridge.

Fatherland 1/2 **1994** It's 1964 and 20 years earlier Hitler has won WWII in this what-if TV movie. The Nazi leader is about to sign a historic alliance with the U.S. President in Berlin when a series of murders of high-ranking Third Reich officers begins. SS detective Xavier March (Hauer) investigates, along with visiting American journalist Charlie Maguire (Richardson), leading the two to the Gestapo coverup of the Holocaust. If the secret gets out it could ruin the summit, so guess who's in big danger? Intriguing premise but the thriller fails to sustain tension. Based on the novel by Robert Harris. Filmed in Prague, Czech Republic. **106m/C VHS.** Rutger Hauer, Miranda Richardson, Peter Vaughan, Jean Marsh, Michael Kitchen, John Woodvine, John Shrapnel, Clare Higgins; ***D:*** Christopher Menaul; ***W:*** Stanley Weiser, Ron Hutchinson; ***C:*** Peter Sova; ***M:*** Gary Chang. **CABLE**

Fathers and Sons 1/2 **1992 (R)** Max is a brooding, former bad-boy movie director living on the Jersey Shore. His wife's death causes him to rethink his life and deal with his drinking problem. He also tries to get to know his equally brooding teenage son, Ed. Turns out addiction may run in the family as Ed experiments with drugs. Ill-fitting subplot deals a serial killer stalking the community. Goldblum brings an uneasy gentleness to the father's role in an otherwise slow, talky, and obviously symbolic flick. **100m/C VHS.** Jeff Goldblum, Rory Cochrane, Mitchell Marchand, Famke Janssen, Natasha Gregson Wagner, Ellen Greene, Samuel L. Jackson, Joie Lee, Rosanna Arquette, Michael Disend; ***D:*** Paul Mones; ***W:*** Paul Mones; ***C:*** Ron Fortunato; ***M:*** Mason Daring.

A Father's Choice 1/2 *Cowboy Dad* **2000** After witnessing their mother's shooting death in L.A., young Chris and Kelly are sent to live in the country with their estranged rodeo-loving dad Mac. With the help of a counselor, the broken family begins to mend until their mother's sister Gayle becomes determined to gain custody of her nieces. Forget the murder subplot because the killer is never identified. **88m/C DVD.** Peter Strauss, Mary McDonnell, Yvonne Zima, Michelle Trachtenberg, Susan Hogan, Roger R. Cross, Eddie Velez; ***D:*** Christopher Cain; ***W:*** Richard Leder; ***C:*** William Wages; ***M:*** Steve Dorff. **TV**

Father's Day 1/2 **1996 (PG-13)** The comedy team of Williams and Crystal makes its feature film debut in this affable take on fatherhood. Freelance writer Putley (Williams) unites with attorney Lawrence (Crystal) to help their mutual ex-girlfriend Kinski search for her runaway son (she's led each man to believe he's the boy's father). Their quest leads to some inevitable sticky situations, but the erratic, adolescent Williams is wonderfully balanced by the calm, upstanding Crystal. Who needs a son when you have to deal with Williams? Together, they're fun to watch and almost make you forget the contrived plot. Almost. Remake of the 1984 French film "Les Comperes." **98m/C VHS, DVD.** Louis Lombardi, Robin Williams, Billy Crystal, Nastassja Kinski, Julia Louis-Dreyfus, Charlie Hofheimer, Bruce Greenwood, Jared Harris, Patti D'Arbanville, Charles Rocket, Dennis Burkley; ***D:*** Ivan Reitman; ***W:*** Lowell Ganz, Babaloo Mandel; ***C:*** Stephen Burum; ***M:*** James Newton Howard.

Father's Little Dividend **1951** Tracy expects a little peace and quiet now that he's successfully married off Taylor in this charming sequel to "Father of the Bride." However, he's quickly disillusioned by the news he'll soon be a grandfather—a prospect that causes nothing but dismay. Reunited the stars, director, writers, and producer from the successfull first film. **82m/B VHS, DVD.** Spencer Tracy, Joan Bennett, Elizabeth Taylor, Don Taylor, Billie Burke, Russ Tamblyn, Moroni Olsen; ***D:*** Vincente Minnelli; ***W:*** Frances Goodrich, Albert Hackett; ***C:*** John Alton; ***M:*** Albert Sendrey.

A Father's Revenge 1/2 **1988 (R)** Dennehy is the only reason to bother with this average hostage drama. He's the father of a stewardess who's one of a group being held by terrorists. They're scheduled to die in 72 hours unless Dennehy can find a way to rescue them. **93m/C VHS, DVD.** Brian Dennehy, Joanna Cassidy, Ron Silver; ***D:*** John Herzfeld; ***M:*** Klaus Doldinger. **TV**

Fathom 1/2 **1967** Welch and her bikini fill out the title role as Fathom Harvill, a parachutist who is hired to find a nuclear triggering device that has been lost in the Mediterranean. She eventually hooks up with spy guy Peter Merriweather (Franciosa) and gets involved in a case involving priceless jewelry stolen from China. Spy spoof is oh so '60s. Based on the novel by Larry Forrester. **104m/C VHS, DVD.** *GB* Raquel Welch, Anthony (Tony) Franciosa, Ronald Fraser, Clive

Revill, Richard Briers, Tom Adams; ***D:*** Leslie Martinson; ***W:*** Lorenzo Semple Jr.; ***C:*** Douglas Slocombe; ***M:*** John Dankworth.

Fatso 1/2 **1980 (PG)** After the shocking death of his obese cousin, an obsessive overeater struggles to overcome his neurosis with the aid of his sister and a self-help group called "Chubby Checkers." Bancroft's first work as both writer and director. **93m/C VHS, DVD.** Dom DeLuise, Anne Bancroft, Ron Carey, Candice Azzara; ***D:*** Anne Bancroft; ***W:*** Anne Bancroft.

Fatty Finn 1/2 **1984** A children's gag-fest about young kids and bullies during the Depression, based on Syd Nicholls' comic strip. **91m/C VHS.** *AU* Ben Oxenbould, Bart Newton; ***D:*** Maurice Murphy.

Fatwa **2006** Junior senator Maggie Davidson (Holly) lets her ambitions get the better of her when she takes a hard-line stance on Islamic terrorism. She attracts the notice of a D.C. sleeper cell that may decide to use a dirty bomb on the National Mall to make a point. **91m/C DVD.** *US* Lauren Holly, Rachel Miner, John Doman, Lacey Chabert, Angus MacFadyen, Mykelti Williamson, Ryan Sands; ***D:*** John Carter; ***W:*** Scott Schafer; ***C:*** Brian Gurley. **VIDEO**

Faust 1/2 *Faust-Eine deutsche Volkssage* **1926** The classic German silent based upon the legend of Faust, who sells his soul to the devil in exchange for youth. Based on Goethe's poem, and directed by Murnau as a classic example of Germanic expressionism. Remade as "All That Money Can Buy" in 1941. **117m/B VHS, DVD.** *GE* Emil Jannings, Warner Fuetterer, Gosta Ekman, Camilla Horn; ***D:*** F.W. Murnau; ***W:*** Hans Kyser; ***C:*** Carl Hoffmann; ***M:*** Timothy Brock, Werner R. Heymann.

Faust: Love of the Damned **2000 (R)** Very gory, visually impressive horror flick finds artist John Jaspers (Frost) selling his soul to Lucifer minion "M" (Divoff) in exchange for revenge on his wife's killers. Eventually, he gets sent to hell but returns as avenger Faust (in a red rubber suit). There's also a good guy detective (Combs) and a troubled shrink named Jade (Brook) involved in the action. Based on the comic book by Tim Vigil and David Quinn. An unrated version is also available. **96m/C VHS, DVD.** Mark Frost, Andrew Divoff, Jeffrey Combs, Isabel Brook; ***D:*** Brian Yuzna; ***W:*** David Quinn; ***C:*** Jacques Haitkin; ***M:*** Xavier Capellas.

The Favor 1/2 **1992 (R)** Light-hearted romance rife with comic confusion, vivid fantasies, secrets, and the all-important favor. Kathy (Kozak) seeks to relieve the boredom of her marriage through best friend Emily's (McGovern) tryst with Kathy's old beau, Tom. Or so she thinks, until Em spills all the juicy details. In a change of pace, the males take a back seat to the women. Good comic performances from Kozak and McGovern and witty dialogue help overcome the plot's sheer silliness. Damian Elwes (actor Cary's brother) provided Pitt's paintings. Theatrical release was delayed three years due to financial crisis at Orion Pictures. **97m/C VHS, DVD.** Harley Jane Kozak, Elizabeth McGovern, Bill Pullman, Brad Pitt, Ken Wahl, Larry Miller, Holland Taylor; ***D:*** Donald Petrie; ***W:*** Josann McGibbon, Sara Parriott; ***C:*** Tim Suhrstedt; ***M:*** Thomas Newman.

The Favor, the Watch, & the Very Big Fish **1992 (R)** Set in a fairytale version of Paris. Hoskins is a photographer of religious subjects searching for a man to pose as Jesus. He discovers his subject in the hirsute Goldblum, a mad bar pianist who actually thinks he's the savior. Richardson plays the object of Hoskin's shy affections, an actress who does dubbing work by providing the moaning and groaning for porno flicks. Messy attempt at screwball-comedy with some brief humorous moments. **89m/C VHS.** *GB FR* Jack Arnold, Bob Hoskins, Jeff Goldblum, Natasha Richardson, Michel Blanc, Jacques Villeret, Angela Pleasence, Jean-Pierre Cassel, Bruce Altman; ***D:*** Ben Lewin; ***W:*** Ben Lewin; ***C:*** Bernard Zitzermann; ***M:*** Vladimir Cosma.

The Favorite Son *Le Fils Prefere* **1994** Troubled family history is examined between three adult French brothers and their Italian immigrant father. A dutiful son, hotel manager Jean-Paul (Lanvin) regularly visits elderly father Raphael (Herlitzka). But Jean-Paul has problems. Desperate for cash to pay his loan shark, he approaches estranged younger brother Philippe (Barr), a wealthy lawyer, who is loath to help, while older schoolteacher brother Francis (Giraudeau) has little spare cash. Jean-Paul decides to take out a life insurance policy on dad—who promptly disappears—leaving the brothers to reluctantly come to terms in order to find him. French with subtitles. **100m/C VHS.** *FR* Gerard Lanvin, Jean-Marc Barr, Bernard Giraudeau, Roberto Herlitzka, Margherita Buy; ***D:*** Nicole Garcia; ***W:*** Nicole Garcia; ***C:*** Eric Gautier; ***M:*** Philippe Sarde. Cesar '95: Actor (Lanvin).

Fay Grim **2006 (R)** Hartley's sequel to 1998's "Henry Fool" follows the misbegotten adventures of Henry's estranged wife Fay (Posey). Henry's been on the lam for years, but CIA op Fulbright (Goldblum) suddenly turns up and informs Fay that A) Henry's dead; B) Henry was in the CIA; C) his notebook memoirs are actually coded secrets; and D) Fay needs to retrieve them from Paris. So Fay agrees, heads off to Europe, and discovers much chicanery, eventually winding up among terrorists in Istanbul. Posey's game but the elaborate, international thriller spoof of a plot is hard to swallow (or follow). **118m/C DVD.** *US GE* Parker Posey, Jeff Goldblum, James Urbaniak, Liam Aiken, Saffron Burrows, Elina Lowensohn, Leo Fitzpatrick, Chuck Montgomery, Thomas Jay Ryan; ***D:*** Hal Hartley; ***W:*** Hal Hartley; ***C:*** Sarah Crawley Cabiya.

FBI Girl **1952** An FBI clerk is used as bait to trap a murderer and break up a gang. Burr, pre-Perry Mason, plays a bad guy. **74m/B VHS, DVD.** Cesar Romero, George Brent, Audrey Totter, Raymond Burr, Tom Drake; ***D:*** William Berke.

The FBI Story **1959** Mr. Stewart goes to Washington in this anatomy of the Federal Bureau of Investigation. If you're a fan of the gangster genre (LeRoy earlier directed "Little Caesar"), and not especially persnickity about fidelity to the facts, this actioner offers a pseudo-factual (read fictional) glimpse—based on actual cases from the 1920s through the 1950s—into the life of a fictitious agent-family man. **149m/C VHS, DVD.** James Stewart, Vera Miles, Nick Adams, Murray Hamilton, Larry Pennell, Diane Jergens, Jean Willes, Joyce Taylor, Ann Doran, Parley Baer, Victor Millan; ***D:*** Mervyn LeRoy; ***W:*** Richard L. Breen, John Twist; ***C:*** Joseph Biroc; ***M:*** Max Steiner.

Fear **1946** An impoverished medical student murders the professor he believes is tormenting him and his life suddenly gets better. He falls in love and gets a scholarship but the police are closing in on his crime. Except...did any of it really happen? Or is he suffering from hallucinations. Low-budget psycho-drama with some good paranoid moments. **68m/B VHS.** Peter Cookson, Warren William, Anne Gwynne, James B. Cardwell, Nestor Paiva; ***D:*** Alfred Zeisler.

Fear *Honor Betrayed* **1988 (R)** A vacationing family is plagued by a murderous Vietnam vet and other psychotic cons. **96m/C VHS, DVD.** Edward (Eddie) Bunker, Frank Stallone, Cliff DeYoung, Kay Lenz, Robert Factor; ***D:*** Robert A. Ferretti.

Fear 1/2 **1990 (R)** A young psychic (Sheedy) delves into the minds of serial killers and writes novels about her experiences. But what happens when the next killer is also a psychic and decides to play mind-games with her? Above-average suspense sustains this cable thriller. **98m/C VHS, DVD.** Ally Sheedy, Lauren Hutton, Michael O'Keefe, Stan Shaw, Dina Merrill, John Agar, Marta DuBois; ***D:*** Rockne S. O'Bannon; ***M:*** Henry Mancini. **CABLE**

The Fear 1/2 **1994 (R)** Student psychologist (Bowz) takes a group to a remote cabin to explore their fears as part of his research project. Then, they begin to die horribly and gradually figure out that the cabin's wooden mascot, Morty (Weiss), is coming to life and doing them in. **98m/C VHS, DVD.** Eddie Bowz, Darin Heames, Anna Karin, Leland Hayward, Monique Mannen, Heather Medway, Antonio Todd, Erick Weiss, Vince Edwards, Ann Turkel, Wes Craven; ***D:*** Vincent Robert; ***W:*** Ron Ford; ***C:*** Bernd Heinl; ***M:*** Robert O. Ragland.

Fear 1/2 *No Fear* **1996 (R)** Wahlberg (the former Marky Mark) is a parents' worse nightmare: the violent, obsessed boyfriend of a 16-year-old girl (Witherspoon) as "Fatal Attraction" goes to the prom. Some cleverness, but ultimately follows a familiar, cliched path littered with one-dimensional characters and predictable plot twists. Gory, unconvincing climax kills any credibility that was left. The one standout is Petersen as the girl's protective father. **96m/C VHS, DVD.** Reese Witherspoon, Mark Wahlberg, William L. Petersen, Amy Brenneman, Alyssa Milano, Tracy Fraim, Christopher Gray, Todd Caldecott; ***D:*** James Foley; ***W:*** Christopher Crowe; ***C:*** Thomas Kloss; ***M:*** Carter Burwell. MTV Movie Awards '97: Song ("Machinehead").

Fear and Loathing in Las Vegas **1998 (R)** Hunter S. Thompson's 1971 cult memoir arrives on the big screen about 20 years too late to have any meaning or much entertainment value. Director Gilliam, never one to shy away from weirdness, overdoes everything in trying to capture the wretched excess of the book. Thompson's screen alter-ego Duke (Depp) packs his Caddy with illicit drugs and his equally wasted lawyer (Del Toro), and heads for his next writing assignment—to cover a drug enforcement conference in Vegas. Depp does a great job of impersonating the completely wasted and unlikable Thompson, while Del Toro passes out and pukes a lot in the sidekick role. It's most definitely a one-of-a-kind trip, but not one that most people will be willing to take. **119m/C VHS, DVD, HD DVD.** Johnny Depp, Benicio Del Toro, Christina Ricci, Gary Busey, Craig Bierko, Ellen Barkin, Cameron Diaz, Flea, Mark Harmon, Katherine Helmond, Michael Jeter, Penn Jillette, Lyle Lovett, Tobey Maguire, Harry Dean Stanton, Tim Thomerson; ***D:*** Terry Gilliam; ***W:*** Terry Gilliam, Alex Cox, Tony Grisoni, Tod Davies; ***C:*** Nicola Pecorini.

Fear, Anxiety and Depression 1/2 **1989 (R)** A neurotic aspiring playwright in New York has various problems with his love life. Sub-Woody Allen comedy attempt, with a few bright spots. The dregs of New York, with all the violence and degradation, are brought to the screen here. **84m/C VHS.** Todd Solondz, Stanley Tucci; ***D:*** Todd Solondz; ***W:*** Todd Solondz.

The Fear Chamber **WOOF!** *Torture Zone; Chamber of Fear; La Camara del Terror; Torture Chamber* **1968** Hardly a Karloff vehicle. Boris shot the footage for this and three other Mexican "horror" films in LA, an unfortunate swan song to his career, though he was fortunate to be quickly written out of this story. The near plot concerns a mutant rock that thrives on human fear. Doctor Karloff and his assistants make sure the rock is rolling in sacrificial victims (women, of course). A prodigious devaluation of the "B"-grade horror flick, it's so bad it's just bad. **88m/C VHS, DVD.** *MX* Boris Karloff, Yerye Beirut, Julissa, Carlos East, Sandra Chavez, Eva Muller, Pamela Rosas, Santanon, Isela Vega; ***D:*** Juan Ibanez, Jack Hill; ***W:*** Jack Hill, Luis Enrique Vergara; ***C:*** Austin McKinney, Raul Dominguez.

Fear City 1/2 **1985 (R)** Two partners who own a talent agency are after the psychopath who is killing off their prized strippers with the aid of a local cop. Sleazy look at Manhattan low life. **93m/C VHS, DVD.** Billy Dee Williams, Tom Berenger, Jack Scalia, Melanie Griffith, Rae Dawn Chong, Joe Santos, Maria Conchita Alonso, Rossano Brazzi; ***D:*** Abel Ferrara; ***W:*** Nicholas St. John; ***C:*** James (Momel) Lemmo; ***M:*** Dick Halligan.

The Fear: Halloween Night *Fear 2; Fear: Resurrection* **1999 (R)** Mike Hawthorne, the son of a psycho killer, has been plagued by blackouts. According to a friend, a Halloween eve ritual where a group of friends all face their worst fears could help Mike get rid of the fear of his father that continues to haunt him. Only when Mike awakens from another blackout, it's to discover a murdered friend. Palmer played another serial killer's mom (Jason) in "Friday the 13th." **87m/C VHS, DVD.** Gordon Currie, Stacy Grant, Brendan Beiser, Betsy Palmer, Emmanuelle Vaugier, Rachel Hayward, Larry Pennell, Phillip Rhys, Myc Agnew, Kelly Benson; ***D:*** Chris Angel; ***W:*** Kevin Richards. **VIDEO**

Fear in the City **1981** The Sicilian Mafia and a black crime gang battle for control of the streets. **90m/C VHS.** *IT* Michael Constantine, Fred Williamson, Gianni Manera; ***D:*** Gianni Manera.

Fear in the Night **1947** Suspenseful tale of a murder committed by a man under hypnosis. Fearing his nightmares are real Kelley talks his detective friend into investigating his "crime," which leads them to a mansion, a mirrored room, and a plot that takes some clever and unexpected twists. Remade in 1956 as "Nightmare." **72m/B VHS, DVD.** Paul Kelly, DeForest Kelley, Ann Doran, Kay Scott, Robert Emmett Keane; ***D:*** Maxwell Shane; ***W:*** Maxwell Shane; ***C:*** Jack Greenhalgh; ***M:*** Rudolph (Rudy) Schrager.

The Fear Inside 1/2 **1992 (R)** Lahti plays a woman suffering from agoraphobia who, because of her fear, has not left her home in more than a year. To help out, Lahti invites a seemingly charming college student to live with her. When the young woman's equally charming "brother" comes to visit, Lahti discovers the two aren't so charming after all. A standard woman-in-terror film with a better-than-average cast. **100m/C VHS.** Christine Lahti, Jennifer Rubin, Dylan McDermott, David Ackroyd, Thomas Ian Nicholas, Paul (Link) Linke, Leon Ichaso; ***D:*** Leon Ichaso; ***W:*** David Birke; ***C:*** Bojan Bazelli. **CABLE**

Fear No Evil **1980 (R)** A teenager who is the human embodiment of the demon Lucifer commits acts of demonic murder and destruction. His powers are challenged by an 18-year-old girl, who is the embodiment of the archangel Gabriel. First feature from La Loggia is better than it sounds. **90m/C VHS, DVD.** Stefan Arngrim, Kathleen Rowe McAllen, Elizabeth Hoffman; ***D:*** Frank Laloggia; ***W:*** Frank Laloggia.

Fear of a Black Hat **1994 (R)** Think "Spinal Tap" as gangsta rap and you've the plot of this good-natured imitator. The dim-witted Ice Cold (Cundieff), Tone-Def (Lawrence), and Tasty-Taste (Scott), the trio known as NWH (Niggaz With Hats), are touring in support of their album and trying to convince filmmaker Nina Blackburn (Lemmons) of their street cred. Like Tap's metal-heads, the more they explain themselves, the less sense they make. **87m/C VHS, DVD.** Larry B. Scott, Mark Christopher Lawrence, Kasi Lemmons, Rusty Cundieff, Lamont Johnson, Howie Gold, Faizon Love, Deezer D, Barry (Shabaka) Henley, Penny Johnson, Eric Laneuville; ***D:*** Rusty Cundieff; ***W:*** Rusty Cundieff; ***C:*** John L. (Ndiaga) Demps Jr.

Fear of Fear *Angst vor der Angst* **1975** Middleclass housewife Margot (Carstensen) begins experiencing intense fear after having her second child but her husband and family dismiss her concerns. So she turns to drugs and alcohol for relief, which only makes her situation worse. German with subtitles. **88m/C VHS, DVD.** *GE* Margit Carstensen, Brigitte Mira, Irm Hermann, Ulrich Faulhaber, Armin Meier, Adrian Hoven; ***D:*** Rainer Werner Fassbinder; ***W:*** Rainer Werner Fassbinder; ***C:*** Jurgen Jurges; ***M:*** Peer Raben.

Fear of the Dark **2002 (PG-13)** Brian doesn't sleep at night because he knows something in the dark is after him. His brother Dale thinks he's just trying to get attention, until the two are home alone when a storm knocks out the power. Creepy and atmospheric, but anyone over the age of 15 will be disappointed by the lack of gore or any over-the-top scares. **86m/C VHS, DVD.** *CA* Jesse James, Kevin Zegers, Linda Purl, Charles Powell, Rachel (Racheal) Skarsten; ***D:*** K.C. Bascombe; ***W:*** K.C. Bascombe, John Sullivan; ***C:*** Marc Charlebois; ***M:*** Sari Dijani. **VIDEO**

Fear Runs Silent **1999 (R)** High school class heads to the woods for an overnight campout. They get stranded. Can you guess what happens? Yes, someone or something tries to kill them! Busy production tries to make up for lack of storyline freshness. **90m/C VHS, DVD.** Stacy Keach, Billy Dee Williams, Dan Lauria, Bobby Jacoby, Suzanne Davis, Ethan Erickson, Elizabeth Low; ***D:*** Serge Rodnunsky; ***W:*** Serge Rodnunsky; ***C:*** Pierre Chemaly. **VIDEO**

Fear Strikes Out **1957** Perkins plays Jimmy Piersall, star outfielder for the Boston Red Sox, and Malden, his demanding father, in the true story of the baseball star's battle for sanity. One of Perkins' best screen performances. **100m/B VHS, DVD.** Anthony Perkins, Karl Malden, Norma Moore, Adam Williams, Perry Wilson; ***D:*** Robert Mulligan; ***W:*** Raphael David Blau; ***M:*** Elmer Bernstein.

Fear X **2003 (PG-13)** Grim, intense thriller stars Turturro as Harry, a security guard at a Wisconsin shopping mall obsessed with finding the truth about his wife's murder. His pursuit takes him across the Midwest into Montana and directly into the path of respected cop Peter (Remar) and his wife, Kate (Unger). Minimal in dialogue and feel, the movie depends on Turturro to hold it together and he does so impressively, portraying Harry as a man so disturbed by grief that the chase becomes more important than finding the truth. Swedish director Refn's American debut. **91m/C DVD.** John Turturro, Deborah Kara Unger, William Allen Young, James Remar, Stephen McIntyre, Eugene M. Davis, Mark Houghton, Jacqueline Ramel; ***D:*** Nicolas Winding Refn; ***W:*** Nicolas Winding Refn, Hubert Selby Jr.; ***C:*** Larry Smith; ***M:*** Brian Eno, J. Peter Schwalm.

Feardotcom *fear dot com* **2002 (R)** Cyber-thriller features a killer virus on the loose in Manhattan. All the victims shared one thing—48 hours before they logged onto the same web site, which features a live feed of sicko Alistair (Rea) torturing and murdering women. Detective Mike Reilly (Dorff) and Health Department investigator Terry Huston (McElhone) investigate. The visuals are actually interesting; too bad everything else about the movie is awful. **101m/C VHS, DVD.** *US GB GE LU* Stephen Dorff, Natascha (Natasha) McElhone, Stephen Rea, Jeffrey Combs, Udo Kier, Nigel Terry, Michael Sarrazin, Amelia Curtis; ***D:*** William Malone; ***W:*** Josephine Coyle; ***C:*** Christian Sebaldt; ***M:*** Nicholas Pike.

Fearless **1977** An Italian detective has found a Viennese banker's daughter, but continues to pursue the unanswered questions of the case, embroiling himself in a web of intrigue and plotting. **89m/C VHS, DVD.** *IT* Joan Collins, Maurizio Merli, Franz Antel; ***D:*** Stelvio Massi; ***W:*** Stelvio Massi; ***C:*** Riccardo (Pallton) Pallottini; ***M:*** Stelvio Cipriani.

Fearless **1993 (R)** Two plane crash survivors reach out to each other as they try and cope with everday life. Bridges is riveting as the transformed Max, and Perez compelling as the sorrowful Carla. Hulce provides dead-on amusement as a casualty lawyer who knows he's slime but can't help himself. Opening sequences of smoke in the corn fields are haunting as are flashbacks of the crash itself. Weir provides an engrossing look at facing death, both psychological and spiritual, but the ending is something of a letdown in its sappiness. Based on the novel by Yglesias. **122m/C VHS, DVD.** Jeff Bridges, Isabella Rossellini, Rosie Perez, Tom Hulce, John Turturro, Benicio Del Toro, Deirdre O'Connell, John de Lancie; ***D:*** Peter Weir; ***W:*** Rafael Yglesias; ***C:*** Allen Daviau; ***M:*** Maurice Jarre. L.A. Film Critics '93: Support. Actress (Perez).

Fearless Tiger **1/2** **1994 (R)** Martial arts action flick includes the usual combination of fierce swordplay, hand-to-hand showdowns, and the intrigue of exotic locations. **88m/C VHS.** *CA* Bolo Yeung, Monica Schnarre, Jamie Farr, Jalal Merhi; ***D:*** Ron Hulme; ***W:*** Ron Hulme; ***M:*** Varouje.

The Fearless Vampire Killers *Pardon Me, Your Teeth Are in My Neck; Dance of the Vampires* **1967** Underrated, off-off-beat, and deliberately campy spoof of vampire films in which Tate is kidnapped by some fangy villains. Vampire trackers MacGowran and Polanski pursue the villains to the haunted castle and attempt the rescue. Only vampire movie with a Jewish bloodsucker ("Boy, have you got the wrong vampire," he proclaims to a maiden thrusting a crucifix at him). Inside the castle, Polanski is chased by the count's gay vampire son. Highlight is the vampire ball with a wonderful mirror scene. Many other amusing moments. **98m/C VHS, DVD.** *GB* Jack MacGowran, Roman Polanski, Alfie Bass, Jessie Robins, Sharon Tate, Ferdinand "Ferdy" Mayne, Iain Quarrier, Terry Downes, Fiona Lewis, Ronald Lacey; ***D:*** Roman Polanski; ***W:*** Gerard Brach, Roman Polanski; ***C:*** Douglas Slocombe; ***M:*** Krzysztof Komeda.

Fearmaker **1/2** *House of Fear; Violent Rage; Rancho del Miedo* **1971 (PG)** After the mysterious death of her father, the heiress to his fortune is tangled in a web of treachery created by other potential inheritors. **90m/C VHS.** *MX* Katy Jurado, Paul Picerni, Sonia Amelio, Carlos East; ***D:*** Anthony Carras; ***W:*** Anthony Carras; ***C:*** Alex Phillips Jr.; ***M:*** Lex de Azevedo.

Feast **1/2** **2006 (R)** The third (and last) of Bravo's "Project Greenlight" series finds strangers hanging out in a dive desert bar when Hero (Dane) barges in with a shotgun and a thing's decapitated head. Hero quickly bites it but his wife, Heroine (Rawat), takes over and warns everyone that they are about to be attacked by carnivorous creatures and must work together to survive. Familiar horror story although fast-paced and mildly amusing. Also available unrated. **85m/C DVD, HD DVD.** *US* Navi Rawat, Balthazar Getty, Henry Rollins, Krista Allen, Clu Gulager, Judah Friedlander, Duane Whitaker, Eric Dane, Jenny Wade, Diane Goldner; ***D:*** John Gulager; ***W:*** Marcus Dunstan, Patrick Melton; ***C:*** Thomas Callaway; ***M:*** Stephen (Steve) Edwards.

Feast 2: Sloppy Seconds **1/2** **2008** The original was a plotless gorefest involving monsters assaulting a bar in the middle of nowhere in the dead of night. The sequel is a plotless gorefest involving monsters assaulting a small western town in the middle of nowhere in broad daylight. Despite the sequel's bold change of pace, it's really just more of the same. If only it revealed why biker chicks favor middle-of-nowhere western locales. **?m/C DVD.** Jenny Wade, Clu Gulager, Carl Anthony Payne II, Hanna Putnam, Diane Goldner, Chelsea Richards, Tom Gulager, Martin Klebba, Juan Garcia, Melissa Reed, Katie Supple Callais, Kent Jude Bernard; ***D:*** John Gulager; ***W:*** Patrick Melton, Marcus Dunstan; ***C:*** Kevin Atkinson; ***M:*** Stephen (Steve) Edwards. **VIDEO**

Feast for the Devil **1/2** *Feast of Satan* **1971** A woman searches for her missing sister in a mysterious coastal village, only to fall under the occult spell of a mad doctor. **90m/C VHS, DVD.** *SP* Krista Nell, Teresa Gimpera; ***D:*** Jose Maria Elorrieta; ***W:*** Jose Maria Elorrieta; ***C:*** Emmanuele Di Cola.

Feast of July **1995 (R)** Victorian-era drama, adapted from an H. E. Bates novel, has young Bella (Davidtz) pregnant and abandoned by super-cad Arch (Wise) whom she sets out to find. After a miscarriage, she is taken in by the Wainwright family where she becomes the object of the affections of the three grown sons. Predictably, she falls for and weds the troubled loafer, Con (Chaplin). Naturally (this being Victorian England) tragedy results. Well-crafted, a given considering the producers, but ultimately a familiar telling of an average story. Feature film debut for director Menaul, after an award-winning career in British TV. **116m/C VHS, DVD.** Embeth Davidtz, Ben Chaplin, Tom Bell, Gemma Jones, James Purefoy, Kenneth Anderson, Greg Wise; ***D:*** Christopher Menaul; ***W:*** Christopher Neame; ***C:*** Peter Sova; ***M:*** Zbigniew Preisner.

Feast of Love **1/2** **2007 (R)** University professor Harry (Freeman) dispenses wisdom at his friend Bradley's (Kinnear) coffee shop. And Bradley sure needs it: his wife Kathryn (Blair) has left him for another woman, and his new girlfriend Diana (Mitchell) is still sleeping with her married lover. Meanwhile, Harry also contemplates the love affair between Bradley's teenage employees Chloe (Davalos) and Oscar (Hemingway). As the narrator of these stories of love and loss, Harry doesn't seem to have any problems at all. Hmm. A strange movie that tries to be profound but is largely weightless. **102m/C DVD.** *US* Morgan Freeman, Greg Kinnear, Jane Alexander, Radha Mitchell, Billy Burke, Selma Blair, Alexa Davalos, Toby Hemingway, Fred Ward, Stana Katic; ***D:*** Robert Benton; ***W:*** Allison Burnett; ***C:*** Kramer Morgenthau; ***M:*** Stephen Trask.

Federal Agent **1936** Lots of cliches fill this crime film about a federal agent chasing foreign spys who are looking for a new explosive. **53m/B VHS.** William Boyd, Charles A. Browne, Irene Ware, George Cooper, Lentia Lace, Dan Alvarado; ***D:*** Sam Newfield.

Federal Agents vs. Underworld, Inc. *Golden Hands of Kurigal* **1949** Super G-Man Dave Worth goes up against Nila, a greedy villainess bent on finding the golden hands of Kurigal so she may rule the world. A 12-episode serial edited onto two cassettes. **167m/B VHS.** Kirk Alyn, Rosemary La Planche, Roy Barcroft, Carol Forman, James Dale, Bruce Edwards; ***D:*** Fred Brannon.

Federal Hill **1994 (R)** Familiar plot and characters are still well-handled by cast and first time writer/director Corrente. Federal Hill is a working-class, Little Italy section of Providence, Rhode Island. Five buddies, mostly losers, hang out together at a weekly card game. Nicky's (De Sando) a small-time dealer who meets his uptown Brown University sweetie, Wendy (Langdon), when he sells her cocaine. His friends try to warn him, especially short-fused burglar Ralphie (Turturro). And, of course, things go very wrong for practically everyone. The video is available colorized or in the director's version in B&W. **100m/B VHS, DVD.** Anthony De Sando, Nicholas Turturro, Libby Langdon, Michael Raynor, Jason Andrews, Frank Vincent, Robert Turano, Michael Corrente; ***D:*** Michael Corrente; ***W:*** Michael Corrente; ***C:*** Richard Crudo; ***M:*** Bob Held, David Bravo.

Federal Operator 99 **1/2** **1945** A fortune in stolen jewels, a chemical plant, and a priceless violin all figure in this 12 chapter serial. And it's up to Jerry Blake, Federal Operator 99, to save the day. Part of "The Cliffhanger Serials" series. **169m/B VHS.** Marten Lamont, Helen Talbot, George Lewis; ***D:*** Yakima Canutt, Spencer Gordon Bennett, Wallace Grissell; ***W:*** Albert DeMond, Jesse Duffy, Basil Dickey, Joseph Poland; ***C:*** Bud Thackery.

Federal Protection **1/2** **2002 (R)** Chicago mobster Frank Carbone (Assante) decides to go into the witness protection program after barely surviving a hit. But his suburban neighborhood heats up when next-door neighbor Leigh (Featherstone) finds out her husband is cheating on her with her own sister (Meyer) and she turns to Frank for comfort. Meanwhile, Frank is finding life a little too quiet and decides to stir things up by contacting his former partners. Slickly made genre piece if you don't mind watching a familiar story. **94m/C VHS, DVD.** Armand Assante, Angela Featherstone, Dina Meyer, David Lipper, Maxim Roy, Tony Calabretta; ***D:*** Anthony Hickox; ***W:*** Craig Smith.

Feds **1/2** **1988 (PG-13)** Two women enter the FBI Academy and take on the system's inherent sexism with feebly comic results. **82m/C VHS.** Rebecca De Mornay, Mary Gross, Ken Marshall, Fred Dalton Thompson, Larry Cedar, James Luisi, Raymond Singer; ***D:*** Dan Goldberg; ***W:*** Dan Goldberg, Len Blum; ***M:*** Randy Edelman.

Feed **WOOF!** **2005** Yuck. A police officer investigates a fetish website where a dominant feeder controls submissive gainers. Only he goes too far and they are force-fed to death. Will definitely put you off your dinner. **105m/C DVD.** *AU* Jack Thompson, Alex O'Loughlin, Patrick Thompson, Rose Ashton, Gabby Millgate; ***D:*** Brett Leonard; ***W:*** Kieran Galvin; ***C:*** Steve Aronold; ***M:*** Gregg Leonard. **VIDEO**

Feeders **WOOF!** **1996** Ya gotta love a low-budget film with the tagline "Earth was just an appetizer!" Okay, so maybe "love" isn't exactly what you'll be thinking. Anyway, Derek and Bennett are heading to the east coast for a vacation when they have a deadly UFO encounter with some flesh-eating aliens, who think earthlings are the perfect snack food. **80m/C VHS, DVD.** Jon McBride, John Polonia, Sebastian Barran, Melissa Torpy, Maria Russo, Todd Carpent, Gary LeBlanc; ***D:*** Jon McBride, John Polonia, Mark Alan Polonia; ***W:*** Jon McBride, Mark Alan Polonia; ***C:*** Arthur Daniels.

Feel My Pulse **1928** Silent comedy about a rich fanatic who leaves everything in his will to his young niece on the stipulation that she lead a germ-free life; when she reaches 21, she moves into the sanitarium she's inherited, not knowing it has become a base for prohibition-era rum runners. **86m/B VHS.** Bebe Daniels, Richard Arlen, William Powell; ***D:*** Gregory La Cava.

Feel the Motion **1986** A female auto-mechanic wants to make it big in the music biz. She sees her chance when she slips her demo tape onto a hit TV-music show. **98m/C VHS.** *GE* Sissy Kelling, Frank Meyer-Brockman, Ingold Locke, Falco, Meat Loaf Aday; ***D:*** Wolfgang Buld; ***W:*** Wolfgang Buld; ***C:*** Roland Willaert.

Feel the Noise **1/2** **2007 (PG-13)** Familiar scenario plays out to the sultry beat of reggaeton. When Harlem rapper Rob (Grandberry) tangles with a local gangster, his mom ships him off to Puerto Rico to live with his estranged dad (Esposito) and his family. Stepbrother Javi (Rasuk) introduces Rob to the local scene and music as well as sexy sweet dancer C.C. (Henao). She pushes Rob's musical ambitions, which eventually leads everyone back to New York. The soundtrack will probably do better than the movie. **86m/C DVD.** *US* Omari (Omarion) Grandberry, Victor Rasuk, James McCaffrey, Giancarlo Esposito, Zulay Henao, Kellita Smith, Melonie Diaz; ***D:*** Alejandro Chomski; ***W:*** Albert Leon; ***C:*** Zoran Popiv; ***M:*** Andres Levin.

Feelin' Screwy **1990** A couple of misfit dweebs attempt to rid their town of the local drug dealer in order to impress a couple of babes in this limp coming-of-ager. **90m/C VHS.** Quincy Reynolds, Larry Gamal, Darin McBride, Hassan Jamal, Marsha Carter, Brooks Morales, Anna Fuentes; ***D:*** Riffat A. Khan; ***W:*** Riffat A. Khan.

Feelin' Up **WOOF!** **1976 (R)** A young man sells all his possessions to come to New York in search of erotic adventures. **84m/C VHS.** Malcolm Groome, Kathleen Seward, Rhonda Hansome, Tony Collado, Charles Douglass; ***D:*** David Secter.

Feeling Minnesota **1996 (R)** A truly stupid movie about truly stupid, mostly nasty people. Petty criminal Jjaks (Reeves) shows up at sleazy older brother Sam's (D'Onofrio) wedding and promptly falls for beautiful-but-unhappy bride Freddie (Diaz), who's being forced into the marriage by local crime boss Red (Lindo). Manipulative Freddie easily convinces Jjaks to run away to Vegas with her but Sam isn't willing to let his bride go so easily. The only character who comes off with any dignity is the diner waitress played by Love. A very lame first effort from Baigelman. Title's from a Soundgarden song about "looking California and feeling Minnesota." **96m/C VHS, DVD.** Keanu Reeves, Cameron Diaz, Vincent D'Onofrio, Delroy Lindo, Dan Aykroyd, Courtney Love, Tuesday Weld, Levon Helm; ***D:*** Steven Baigelman; ***W:*** Steven Baigelman; ***C:*** Walt Lloyd.

Feet First **1/2** **1930** A shoe salesman puts on "upper crust" airs as he begins a shipboard romance with a girl who thinks he's wealthy. Lloyd's second sound film shows him grappling with technique and has scenes that recall highlights of his silent hits. **85m/B VHS, DVD.** Harold Lloyd, Barbara Kent, Robert McWade; ***D:*** Clyde Bruckman.

Felicia's Journey **1999 (PG-13)** Joseph Ambrose Hilditch (Hoskins) is a mild-mannered, fastidious, middle-aged Brit whose mother problems have turned him into a serial killer. He's a catering manager who watches tapes of his flamboyant late mother Gala's (Khanjian) cooking show, where young Hilditch was an embarassed foil. Into his structured world stumbles pregnant Irish teen, Felicia (Cassidy), who's trying to find the father of her baby. Hilditch begins to take a warped interest in Felicia, who may be naive but who isn't dumb. Cold and elegant adaptation of William Trevor's novel. **111m/C VHS, DVD.** *CA GB* Bob Hoskins, Elaine Cassidy, Arsinee Khanjian, Peter McDonald, Gerard McSorley, Brid Brennan, Claire Benedict; ***D:*** Atom Egoyan; ***W:*** Atom Egoyan; ***C:*** Paul Sarossy; ***M:*** Mychael Danna. Genie '99: Actor (Hoskins), Adapt. Screenplay, Cinematog., Score.

Felicidades *Merry Christmas* **2000** A not exactly joyous story set on Christmas Eve but probably much more realistic about the expectations that the holiday brings to people. A random group of men and women randomly cross paths during the evening—a doctor eager to seduce a beautiful woman, a father doing some last-minute shopping, a man in a wheelcar, a writer—all looking for some connection that they're not finding. Bittersweet rather than bitter but also frustrating because you learn so little about the characters. Spanish with subtitles. **100m/C VHS, DVD.** *AR* Gaston Pauls, Silke Klein, Luis Machin, Pablo Cedron, Carlos Bellaso, Marcello Mazzarello; ***D:*** Lucho Bender; ***W:*** Pablo Cedron, Lucho Bender, Emilio Bender; ***C:*** Daniel Sotelo; ***M:*** Andres Goldstein, Daniel Tarrals.

Felix the Cat: The Movie 🦴 1/2 **1991** Classic cartoon creation Felix returns in a trite feature. The feline and his bag of tricks enter a dimension filled with He-Man/Mutant Ninja Turtles leftovers; new-age princess, comic reptiles, robots and a Darth Vader clone who's defeated with ridiculous ease. Strictly for undemanding kids. **83m/C VHS.** ***D:*** Tibor Hernadi; ***V:*** Chris Phillips, Alice Playten, Maureen O'Connell.

Fellini: I'm a Born Liar 🦴🦴 *Fellini: Je suis un grand menteur; Federico Fellini: Sono un gran bugiardo; Fellini: Sono un gran bugiardo* **2003** Documentary includes an interview with the filmmaker Frederico Fellini, as well as with those who worked with him, most notably Donald Sutherland and Roberto Benigni. Director Pettigrew uses Fellini's interview as the foundation of the film, but focuses on Fellini the enigma rather than his work or his life. Clips from Fellini's films are used frequently but not labeled; nor are the numerous interviews with the people who have been part of the filmmaker's career. You get a sense of his style, but very little information about his life or his films. For dedicated Fellini fans only—everyone else should just start with his movies. **89m/C VHS, DVD.** *GE* Federico Fellini, Donald Sutherland, Terence Stamp, Giuseppe Rotunno, Roberto Benigni; ***D:*** Damian Pettigrew; ***W:*** Damian Pettigrew, Olivier Gal; ***C:*** Paco Wiser.

Fellini Satyricon 🦴🦴🦴 *Satyricon* **1969 (R)** Fellini's famous, garish, indulgent pastiche vision of ancient Rome, based on the novel "Satyricon" by Petronius, follows the adventures of two young men through the decadences of Nero's reign. Actually an exposition on the excesses of the 1960s, with the actors having little to do other than look good and react to any number of sexual situations. Crammed with excesses of every variety. In Italian with English subtitles. **129m/C VHS, DVD.** *IT FR* Martin Potter, Capucine, Hiram Keller, Salvo Randone, Max Born, Alain Cuny; ***D:*** Federico Fellini; ***W:*** Federico Fellini, Barnardino Zapponi; ***C:*** Giuseppe Rotunno; ***M:*** Nino Rota.

Fellini's Roma 🦴🦴 1/2 *Roma* **1972 (R)** Fellini reviews his youth in this stream-of-consciousness homage to Rome and Italy. Best left for fervent Fellini fans. **128m/C VHS, DVD.** *FR IT* Peter Gonzales, Britta Barnes, Pia de Doses, Fiona Florence, Marne Maitland, Renato Giovannoli; ***Cameos:*** Gore Vidal, Anna Magnani, Marcello Mastroianni; ***D:*** Federico Fellini; ***W:*** Federico Fellini; ***C:*** Giuseppe Rotunno; ***M:*** Nino Rota; ***V:*** Federico Fellini.

Fellow Traveler 🦴🦴🦴 **1989** Two old friends, an actor and a screenwriter, both successful, get blacklisted for reputed Communist leanings in 1950s Hollywood. Good performances and a literate script. **97m/C VHS.** Ron Silver, Hart Bochner, Daniel J. Travanti, Imogen Stubbs, Katherine Borowitz, Jonathan Hyde; ***D:*** Philip Saville; ***M:*** Colin Towns. **CABLE**

Felon 🦴🦴 **2008 (R)** Prison pic avoids preaching and exploitation. Wade Porter (Dorff) takes a swing at a burglar with a baseball bat, the intruder ends up dead, and Wade ends up in the joint for manslaughter. In the highly polarized prison atmosphere, Wade is forced to find allies, especially since the only way lead guard Jackson (Perrineau) keeps order is through violence. Wade's cellmate is lifer John Smith (Kilmer), who gives him a crash course in survival, and Wade's dehumanization begins. Filmed on location at a New Mexico correction facility. **104m/C DVD.** Stephen Dorff, Harold Perrineau Jr., Val Kilmer, Sam Shepard, Nicholas Chinlund, Johnny Lewis, Marisol Nichols, Anne Archer; ***D:*** Ric Roman Waugh; ***W:*** Ric Roman Waugh; ***C:*** Dana Gonzales; ***M:*** Gerhard Daum.

Felony 🦴 1/2 **1995 (R)** Police seek revenge when 12 cops are murdered. Turns out the culprit is a rogue CIA agent, whose spree was captured on video by a tabloid-show cameraman. **90m/C VHS, DVD.** Lance Henriksen, Leo Rossi, Joe Don Baker, Charles Napier, Ashley Laurence, Cory (Corinna) Everson; ***D:*** David A. Prior; ***W:*** David A. Prior; ***M:*** Jan A.P. Kaczmarek.

Female 🦴🦴 1/2 **1933** Feminist look at life in the '30s stars Chatterton as the wealthy president of an auto factory who wines and dines the office men and then gives them the strictly business line the next day. However, she finally meets her match when Brent walks through the door. (The two stars were a real-life married couple at the time.) Funny, role-reversal story directed by Curtiz of "Casablanca" fame. Based on a story by Donald Henderson Clark. **60m/B VHS.** Ruth Chatterton, George Brent, Philip Reed, Ruth Donnelly, Johnny Mack Brown, Lois Wilson, Gavin Gordon, Ferdinand Gottschalk; ***D:*** Michael Curtiz, William Dieterle; ***W:*** Gene Markey, Kathryn Scola.

The Female Bunch WOOF! **1969 (R)** The man-free world of an all-woman settlement is shattered by the arrival of a handsome stranger. Some of this garbage was filmed on location at the notorious Charles Manson ranch, and that's the least of its flaws. **86m/C VHS.** Jennifer Bishop, Russ Tamblyn, Lon Chaney Jr., Nesa Renet, Geoffrey Land, Regina Carrol; ***D:*** Al Adamson, John Cardos.

The Female Jungle 🦴 *The Hangover* **1956** Below-average whocares whodunnit directed by Roger Corman stock-company actor Ve Sota. Police sergeant Tierney is caught between a rock and a hard place. The prime suspect in a murder case, Tierney discovers a series of clues that implicate his friend Carradine. Interesting only for the screen debut of the nympho-typecast Miss Jayne—of whom Bette Davis said "Dramatic art in her opinion is knowing how to fill a sweater." **56m/B VHS.** Lawrence Tierney, John Carradine, Jayne Mansfield, Burt Kaiser, Kathleen Crowley, James Kodl, Duane Grey, Jack Hill, Bruno VeSota; ***D:*** Bruno VeSota; ***W:*** Burt Kaiser, Bruno VeSota; ***C:*** Elwood "Woody" Bredell; ***M:*** Nicholas Carras.

Female Perversions 🦴🦴 **1996 (R)** Psycho-sexual story of Los Angeles attorney Eve Stephens (Swinton), who, because of bizarre dreams and fantasies, leads a dual life. Successful Eve is being considered for appointment as a judge, but her enormous insecurity and neuroses only increase, landing her in kinky relationships with both sexes. During an unlikely reunion with her sister, Madelyn (Madigan), a kleptomaniac with a Ph.D., Eve is forced to spend time with Madelyn's motley roommates—her landlady and the landlady's odd daughter and sister. This semi-reunion brings about some self-realization on the part of both sisters about their dysfunctional behavior. Filled with detailed symbolism, powerful imagery, and dream sequences. Rife with Freudian psychology, movie is based on Louise J. Kaplan's feminist study on female behavior and sexuality, "Female Perversions: The Temptations of Emma Bovary." Extremely glossy visuals and rich production design brings life to this rather heavy story. **110m/C VHS, DVD.** Tilda Swinton, Amy Madigan, Karen Sillas, Laila Robins, Clancy Brown, Frances Fisher, Paulina Porizkova, Lisa Jane Persky, Dale Shuger; ***D:*** Susan Streitfeld; ***W:*** Susan Streitfeld, Julie Hebert; ***C:*** Teresa Medina; ***M:*** Debbie Wiseman.

Female Prisoner: Caged 🦴🦴 *Joshu Ori; Female Prisoner: Cage; Prison Heat* **1983** While not the best example of the Pinky or Pinku eiga genre (softcore nudie films, usually with action based storylines and revenge themes), pic is one of the more infamous and foregoes any kind of narrative for a series of ever more disturbing scenes. Part of the Nikkatsu studio's "Roman Porno" series (1971-1988), which took the genre a step further. **70m/C DVD.** *JP* Shigeru Muroi, Ryoko Watanabe; ***D:*** Masaru Konoma; ***W:*** Osamu Murakami; ***C:*** Shohei Ando.

Female Prisoner Sigma 🦴🦴 *Joshu Siguma* **2006** Ryou's (Shoko Hamada) sister commits suicide in prison, and Ryou requests she herself be sent to the same prison after failing to kill a man who has wronged her in some way. As usual the warden and guards are evil, and are turning the female prisoners into sex slaves. Unlike other women-in-prison films, this has a supernatural being stalking the premises as the inmates die one by one. **80m/C DVD.** *JP* Shoko Hamada, Koichi Kitamura; ***D:*** Sasuke Sasuga; ***W:*** Bakuto Ijuin; ***C:*** Sung-Bok Kim.

Female Trouble 🦴🦴 1/2 **1974 (R)** Divine leads a troublesome existence in this $25,000 picture. She turns to a life of crime and decadence, seeking to live out her philosophy: "Crime is beauty." Look closely at the Divine rape scene where she plays both rapist and victim. Climax of her deviant ways comes with her unusual night club act, for which the law shows no mercy. Trashy, campy; for die-hard Waters fans. **95m/C VHS, DVD.** Divine, David Lochary, Mary Vivian Pearce, Mink Stole, Edith Massey, Cookie Mueller, Susan Walsh, Michael Potter, Ed Peranio, Paul Swift, George Figgs, Susan Lowe, Channing Wilroy, Pat Moran, Elizabeth Coffey, George Stover; ***D:*** John Waters; ***W:*** John Waters; ***C:*** John Waters.

Female Vampire 🦴 *Erotikill; The Loves of Irina; Les Avaleuses; The Bare Breasted Contessa* **1973** Franco's dreamy, sanguine, produced-on-a-dime tale of a vampiress. She cruises the Riviera, seducing and nibbling on a variety of men and women. Not for most tastes. **95m/C VHS, DVD.** *FR SP GE* Lina Romay, Monica Swin, Jack Taylor, Alice Arno; ***D:*** Jess (Jesus) Franco; ***C:*** Jess (Jesus) Franco; ***M:*** Daniel White.

Femalien 🦴 **1996 (R)** Advanced alien beings, composed of pure light energy, travel to earth to assume corporal form so they can once again experience sexual pleasure. **90m/C VHS, DVD.** Vanessa Taylor, Jacqueline Lovell, Matt Schue; ***D:*** Cybil (Sybil) Richards, David DeCoteau; ***W:*** Cybil (Sybil) Richards, David DeCoteau. **VIDEO**

Femalien 2 🦴 1/2 **1998** Sofcore sequel offers more of the same, with slightly more wit and the semblance of story between the canoodling. Two more aliens come to Earth looking for their colleague Kara. Much sexy shenanigans and madcap things ensue, in typical exploitation fashion. **93m/C DVD.** Vanessa Taylor, Debra Summers, Bethany Lorraine, Josh Edwards, Summer Leeds, Damian Wells; ***D:*** Cybil (Sybil) Richards, David DeCoteau; ***W:*** Cybil (Sybil) Richards, David DeCoteau; ***C:*** Gary Graver; ***M:*** Wayne Scott Joness. **VIDEO**

The Feminine Touch 🦴🦴 1/2 *The November Conspiracy* **1995** Journalist Jennifer Barron (Turco) discovers a deadly conspiracy to take over U.S. politics by killing off presidential candidates. And the hitman who's doing the job thinks Jennifer's in possession of an informative computer disk so he goes after her. **99m/C VHS.** Paige Turco, Dirk Benedict, Conrad Janis, Bo Hopkins, George Segal, Elliott Gould, Lois Nettleton, Virginia Capers, Richard Kline, Warren Berlinger; ***D:*** Conrad Janis; ***W:*** Maria Grimm; ***C:*** Francis Mohajerin, Monty Rowan; ***M:*** Tony Humecke.

Femme Fatale 🦴🦴 1/2 *Fatal Woman* **1990 (R)** When a man's new bride disappears he teams up with an artist pal to track her down. Their search reveals her secret double life and takes them to L.A.'s avant-garde art scene—and deeper into deception and mystery. Billy Zane (Elijah) and Lisa Zane are brother and sister. **96m/C VHS.** Colin Firth, Lisa Zane, Billy Zane, Scott Wilson, Lisa Blount; ***D:*** Andre Guttfreund; ***W:*** John Brancato, Michael Ferris.

Femme Fatale 🦴🦴 1/2 **2002 (R)** DePalma's latest exercise in leering style over substance works because he does stunning, sparkling visuals so well, and because he uses Rebecca Romijn-Stamos to show them off. She's Laure, a sleek jewel thief who, when we first see her, is seducing the diamond-encrusted bra off a supermodel at Cannes. Convoluted heist-doublecross-mistaken-identity plot keeps the surprises coming often enough that you don't have much time to consider their plausibility as Laure goes from thief to grieving widow to ambassador's wife and back, while toying with paparazzo Banderas. **112m/C VHS, DVD.** *FR* Rebecca Romijn, Antonio Banderas, Peter Coyote, Gregg Henry, Eriq Ebouaney, Edouard Montoute, Rie Rasmussen, Thierry Fremont; ***D:*** Brian De Palma; ***W:*** Brian De Palma; ***C:*** Thierry Arbogast; ***M:*** Ryuichi Sakamoto.

Femme Fontaine: Killer Babe for the C.I.A. WOOF! **1995 (R)** Beautiful assassin Drew "Killer Babe" Fontaine (Hope) gets help from CIA-agent-turned-monk Master Sun (Hong) in order to avenge her father's death. Fishnet-clad women with big guns are always a Troma treat. **93m/C VHS.** Margot Hope, James Hong, Catherine Dao, David "Shark" Fralick, Kevin Fry, Harry Mok; ***D:*** Margot Hope; ***W:*** Margot Hope; ***C:*** Gary Graver; ***M:*** Gardner Cole.

Femmes de Paris 🦴🦴 *Women of Paris* **1953** A funny and risque French musical comedy about the comings and goings of the cast of a naughty nightclub shows. In French with English subtitles. **79m/C VHS.** *FR* Michel Simon, Brigitte Auber, Germain Kerjean, Georges Galley, Micheline Dax; ***D:*** Jean Boyer; ***W:*** Alex Joffe; ***C:*** Charles Suin; ***M:*** Paul Misraki.

The Fence 🦴🦴 1/2 **1994** Interesting presentation of standard bad boy grows up, attempts to go straight. Terry Griff (Wirth) has been bounced from juvenile detention to prison since he was 15. On the streets for the first time in 14 years, Terry wants to lead a clean life with potential girlfriend Jackie (Gimp). But when Terry gets on the wrong side of his dishonest parole officer, the harsh world of the streets pulls him back. Bleak urban drama with sincere performances. **90m/C VHS, DVD.** Billy Wirth, Erica Gimpel, Marc Alaimo, Paul Benjamin, Lorenzo Clemons; ***D:*** Peter Pistor; ***W:*** Peter Fedorenko; ***C:*** John Newby; ***M:*** Jeff Beal.

The Fencing Master 🦴🦴 1/2 **1992** The fencing master is the aristocratic Don Jaime de Astarloa (Antonutti) who secretly takes on female pupil, Adela de Otero (Serna), with whom he begins to fall in love. But when another pupil is murdered by de Astarloa's signature thrust to the throat, Don Jaime finds himself caught up in a bewildering world of political intrigue. Adapted from the novel by Antonio Perez Reverte. Spanish with subtitles. **88m/C VHS.** *SP* Assumpta Serna, Omero Antonutti, Joaquim de Almeida; ***D:*** Pedro Olea; ***W:*** Pedro Olea; ***C:*** Alfredo Mayo.

Fer-De-Lance 🦴 1/2 *Operation Serpent* **1974** A stricken submarine is trapped at the bottom of the sea, with a nest of deadly snakes crawling through the ship. **120m/C VHS, DVD.** David Janssen, Hope Lange, Ivan Dixon, Jason Evers; ***D:*** Russ Mayberry. **TV**

Fergie & Andrew: Behind Palace Doors 🦴🦴 **1993** More soap-opera from the British royals in this tale of feisty redhead, Sarah Ferguson, and the neglectful Prince Andrew. He's away a lot, she's bored by all the palace propriety and causes too many scandals, and their marriage falls apart. **92m/C VHS.** Pippa Hinchley, Sam Miller, Peter Cellier, Harold Innocent, Edita Brychta; ***D:*** Michael Switzer. **TV**

Fermat's Room 🦴🦴 *La Habitacion de Fermat* **2007** Locked-room thriller. Four mathematicians are invited by the mysterious Fermat to a secluded retreat to solve a series of logic puzzles. Which turn out to be how—and if—they'll survive as the walls of the room literally start closing in unless they get all the answers right. Spanish with subtitles. **92m/C DVD.** *SP* Alejo Sauras, Lluis Homar, Santi Millan, Elena Ballesteros, Federico Luppi; ***D:*** Luis Piedrahita, Rodrigo Sopena; ***W:*** Luis Piedrahita, Rodrigo Sopena; ***C:*** Miguel Amoedo; ***M:*** Federico Jusid.

Fernandel the Dressmaker 🦴🦴 1/2 **1957** Fernandel dreams of designing exquisite dresses, but when the opportunity arises, he finds his cheating partners get in the way. In French with English subtitles. **95m/B VHS.** *FR* Fernandel, Suzy Delair, Francoise Fabian, Georges Chamarat; ***D:*** Jean Boyer.

Ferngully: The Last Rain Forest 🦴🦴 1/2 **1992 (G)** Animated eco-musical follows the adventures of independent-minded flying sprite Crysta, who lives in a rain forest beset by pollution. She discovers the outside world and becomes smitten with the human Zak, who is helping to cut down the forest. Crysta decides to reduce him to her size and show him the error of his ways. She's aided by fellow sprite, Pips, and a crazy bat (Batty Koda with a voice provided by the lively Williams). So-so script with politically pristine environmental message may grow tiresome for both adults and children, though decent animation and brilliant coloring enlivens the tale. **80m/C VHS, DVD.** ***D:*** Bill Kroyer; ***W:*** Jim Cox; ***M:*** Alan Silvestri; ***V:*** Samantha Mathis, Christian Slater, Robin Williams, Tim Curry, Jonathan Ward, Grace Zabriskie, Richard "Cheech" Marin, Thomas Chong, Tone Loc, Jim Cox.

Ferocious Female Freedom Fighters 1988 A typical foreign-made action flick with female wrestlers is spoofed by the L.A. Connection comedy troupe which did the totally ridiculous dubbed dialog. **90m/C VHS, DVD.** Eva Arnaz, Barry Prima, Leyli Sagita, Wieke Widowati, Ruth Pelupessi, Aminah Cendrakasih; ***D:*** Yopi Burnama; ***W:*** Deddy Armand, Charles Kaufman, Joey Gaynor; ***C:*** Asmawi; ***M:*** Gatot Sudarto.

Ferris Bueller's Day Off 1986 **(PG-13)** It's almost graduation and if Ferris can get away with just one more sick day—it had better be a good one. He sweet talks his best friend into borrowing his dad's antique Ferrari and sneaks his girlfriend out of school to spend a day in Chicago. Their escapades lead to fun, adventure, and almost getting caught. Broderick is charismatic as the notorious Bueller with Grey amusing as his tattle-tale sister doing everything she can to see him get caught. Early Sheen appearance as a juvenile delinquent who pesters Grey. Led to TV series. One of Hughes' more solid efforts. **103m/C VHS, DVD.** Matthew Broderick, Mia Sara, Alan Ruck, Jeffrey Jones, Jennifer Grey, Cindy Pickett, Edie McClurg, Charlie Sheen, Del Close, Virginia Capers, Max Perlich, Louie Anderson, Richard Edson, Lyman Ward, Kristy Swanson, Larry "Flash" Jenkins, Ben Stein; ***D:*** John Hughes; ***W:*** John Hughes; ***C:*** Tak Fujimoto; ***M:*** Ira Newborn.

Ferry to Hong Kong ½ 1959 World-weary, heavy drinking traveler comes aboard the "Fat Annie," a ship skippered by the pompous Captain Hart. The two men clash, until an act of heroism brings them together. Embarrassingly hammy performance by Welles as the ferry skipper. **103m/C VHS.** Curt Jurgens, Orson Welles, Sylvia Syms; ***D:*** Lewis Gilbert.

Festival at Cannes ½ 2002 **(PG-13)** That would be the Cannes Film Festival where everyone is hustling in one way or another. American actress Alice (Scacchi) is looking for financing for her first directorial effort and offers the lead to aging actress Millie Marquand (Aimee). But Millie has been offered major moolah to play a mother role in a big studio pic by desperate producer Rick Yorkin (Silver). Then there's Millie's flagrantly unfaithful director/husband Viktor (Schell), wheeler-dealer Kaz (Norman), and Blue (Gabrielle), a starlet promoting an indie pic that's an unexpected hit, as well as numerous other associates, assistants, and hangers-on. **99m/C VHS, DVD.** *US* Greta Scacchi, Anouk Aimee, Ron Silver, Zack Norman, Jenny Gabrielle, Maximilian Schell, Kim Kolavich, Rachel Bailit, Alex Craig Mann, Peter Bogdanovich, Camilla Campanale; ***D:*** Henry Jaglom; ***W:*** Henry Jaglom; ***C:*** Hanania Baer; ***M:*** Gaili Schoen.

Festival Express 2003 **(R)** In 1970, rock promoters Ken Walker and Thor Eaton orchestrated a lollapalooza featuring Janis Joplin, the Grateful Dead, the Band, the Flying Burrito Bros., Delany & Bonnie, Ian & Sylvia, Buddy Guy and Sha Na Na. For five days the musicians traveled by private train across Canada, playing concerts, socializing, trading riffs, and partying. A film crew recorded the event, but in the chaos following the tour the footage was lost for decades, only to later be restored by the producer's son. The electrifying sequences of Janis Joplin capture her at the height of a self-consuming talent months prior to her death. A must-see for fans of the bands, the era, and its music. **90m/C DVD.** *CA* ***D:*** Bob Smeaton; ***C:*** Bob Fiore, Peter Biziou.

The Feud 1990 **(R)** Wacky comedy about the ultimate "family feud." The Bullards of Millville and the Bealers of Hornbeck engage in a battle of the witless, and no one in either town is safe. A silly, irreverent comedy of the slapstick variety. Based on a novel by Thomas Berger. **87m/C VHS.** Rene Auberjonois, Ron McLarty, Joe Grifasi, David Strathairn, Gale Mayron; ***D:*** Bill D'Elia; ***W:*** Bill D'Elia.

Feud Maker ½ 1938 Steele rides to the rescue in this range war between the bad guys and the cowmen. Hackett plays a schemer who falsely befriends both sides, plotting to buy up cheap land when the participants have killed each other off. Based on a story by Harry F. Olmsted. **55m/B VHS, DVD.** Bob Steele, Marion Weldon, Karl Hackett, Frank Ball, Budd Buster, Lew Meehan, Roger Williams; ***D:*** Sam Newfield; ***W:*** George Plympton.

Feud of the Trail 1937 A cowboy saves a range family's gold and falls in love with their daughter in the process. Tyler plays both the hero and the villain here. **56m/B VHS.** Tom Tyler, Harlin Wood, Guinn "Big Boy" Williams; ***D:*** Robert F. "Bob" Hill.

Feud of the West ½ 1935 Old West disagreements settled with guns in this outing for cowboy star Gibson, here portraying a rodeo performer. **60m/B VHS.** Hoot Gibson, Buzz Barton, Robert F. (Bob) Kortman, Edward Cassidy, Joan Barclay, Nelson McDowell, Reed Howes, Lew Meehan; ***D:*** Harry Fraser.

Fever 1981 Controversial Polish film based on Andrzej Strug's novel "The Story of One Bomb." Focusing on a period in Polish history marked by anarchy, violence, resistance, and revolution, it was banned before it won eventual acclaim at the Gdansk Film Festival. In Polish with English subtitles. **115m/C VHS.** *PL* Adam Ferency, Barbara Grabowska, Boguslaw Linda, Olgierd Kukaszewicz; ***D:*** Agnieszka Holland; ***W:*** Krzysztof Toeplitz; ***C:*** Jacek Petrycki; ***M:*** Jan Pawluskiewicz.

Fever 1988 **(R)** A once-honest cop trades his good life in for a shot at dealing drugs. Meanwhile, his wife's lover wants to murder him. **83m/C VHS.** Bill Hunter, Gary Sweet, Mary Regan, Jim Holt; ***D:*** Craig Lahiff.

Fever 1991 **(R)** An ex-con and a high-powered lawyer join forces to rescue the woman both of them love from a vicious killer. Available in Spanish. **99m/C VHS, DVD.** Armand Assante, Sam Neill, Marcia Gay Harden, Joe Spano, John Dennis Johnston, Mark Boone Jr., Jon(athan) Gries, Gordon Clapp, Gregg Henry, John Capodice, Rainbow Harvest, John David (J.D.) Cullum; ***D:*** Larry Elikann; ***W:*** Larry Brothers; ***C:*** Bojan Bazelli; ***M:*** Michel Colombier. **CABLE**

Fever 1999 **(R)** Twentysomething Nick Parker (Thomas) is a struggling artist living in a Brooklyn tenement and fighting a losing battle to keep both his physical health and his sanity. Neither are helped when his landlord's murder leads to a police investigation; a suspicious new tenant moves into the apartment above Nick's; and Nick realizes that he's been sleepwalking. Since the film is told from his fractured point-of-view, the viewer can never be sure just what's real. **90m/C VHS, DVD.** Henry Thomas, David O'Hara, Bill Duke, Teri Hatcher, Sandor Tecsy, Irma St. Paule, Marisol Padilla Sanchez; ***D:*** Alex Winter; ***W:*** Alex Winter; ***C:*** Joe DeSalvo; ***M:*** Joe Delia.

The Fever 2004 Works because of Redgrave's outstanding performance, although the idea teeters (if not topples) into pretension. A nameless privileged woman decides to shake up her life by traveling to a nameless country that's in the midst of a civil war. Falling ill, she has hallucinations, seeing images of violence and revolutionaries (including Jolie) who condemn her indifference and discuss oppression. Based on the play by Wallace Shawn. **83m/C DVD.** Vanessa Redgrave, Angelina Jolie, Geraldine James, Joely Richardson, Rade Serbedzija, Michael Moore; ***D:*** Carlo Gabriel Nero; ***W:*** Wallace Shawn; ***C:*** Mark Moriarty; ***M:*** Claudio Capponi. **CABLE**

Fever Mounts at El Pao ½ *Los Ambiciosos* 1959 A minor effort from director Bunuel about the regime of a dictator in an imaginary South American country. In Spanish with English subtitles. **97m/B VHS.** *MX* Gerard Philipe, Jean Servais; ***D:*** Luis Bunuel.

Fever Pitch WOOF! 1985 **(R)** Sordid story of a sports writer (O'Neal) who becomes addicted to gambling. Very poor script. **95m/C VHS.** Ryan O'Neal, Catherine Hicks, Giancarlo Giannini, Bridgette Andersen, Chad Everett, John Saxon, William (Bill) Smith, Patrick Cassidy, Chad McQueen; ***D:*** Richard Brooks; ***W:*** Richard Brooks; ***M:*** Thomas Dolby.

Fever Pitch ½ 1996 **(R)** Mildly amusing sports/romance based on Nick Hornby's 1992 sports memoir and set in late '80s London. English teacher/school coach Paul Ashworth (Firth) is an obsessed fan of the Arsenal football (soccer) club. Although completely oppposite in temperament, Paul begins a romance with fellow teacher, Sarah (Gemmell), who's only mildly interested in sports. When Sarah gets pregnant, they drift apart as Sarah begins more and more to resent Paul's perpetual adolescent behavior. Finally, it all comes down to Arsenal's championship match and how they both react. **103m/C VHS, DVD.** *GB* Colin Firth, Ruth Gemmell, Neil Pearson, Mark Strong, Holly Aird, Ken Stott, Stephen Rea, Lorraine Ashbourne; ***D:*** David Evans; ***W:*** Nick Hornby; ***C:*** Chris Seager; ***M:*** Neil MacColl, Boo Hewerdine.

Fever Pitch ½ 2005 **(PG-13)** Math teacher Ben meets unlucky-in-love career woman Lindsey. Looking for a change from the usual (successful) guys she dates, she agrees to go out with him, and a relationship ensues. Then the other spike drops. He's an obsessive Red Sox fan and must choose between his love for Lindsey and the Sox. Standard romantic comedy is raised a level by coinciding with the Red Sox' historic 2004 comeback against the Yankees and subsequent World Series victory. Adapted from Nick Hornby's novel about an obsessive soccer fan. A solid outing, but the brothers Farrelly show signs of losing a little zip off their fastball. **98m/C DVD.** *US* Jimmy Fallon, Drew Barrymore, KaDee Strickland, Ione Skye, Willie Garson, James B. Sikking, JoBeth Williams, Jack Kehler, Lenny Clarke, Siobhan Fallon Hogan, Marissa Jaret Winokur, Evan Helmuth, Scott Severance, Zen Gesner; ***D:*** Peter Farrelly, Bobby Farrelly; ***W:*** Lowell Ganz, Babaloo Mandel; ***C:*** Matthew F. Leonetti; ***M:*** Craig Armstrong.

A Few Days in September ½ *Quelques Jours en Septembre* 2006 Confusing spy thriller. CIA agent Elliott (Nolte) disappears ten days before 9/11 after contacting French agent Irene (Binoche). Elliott makes Irene responsible for his two children, half-siblings Orlando (Forestier) and David (Riley). But setting up a meeting proves difficult as they follow his trail from Paris to Venice, pursued by an over-the-top assassin (Turturro), in an effort to discover what Elliott's learned that's so dangerous. English, French, and Arabic with subtitles. **112m/C DVD.** *FR IT* Juliette Binoche, Nick Nolte, John Turturro, Sara Forestier, Tom Riley, Mathieu Demy, Said Amadia; ***D:*** Santiago Amigorena; ***W:*** Santiago Amigorena; ***C:*** Christophe Beaucarne; ***M:*** Laurent Martin.

A Few Good Men ½ 1992 **(R)** Strong performances by Cruise and Nicholson carry this story of a peacetime military coverup. Cruise is a smart aleck Navy lawyer sleepwalking through his comfortable career in DC. He's ready to write off two soldiers pinned for the murder of their cohort until he interviews their commanding officer, Nicholson. Cruise smells a rat, but Nicholson practically dares him to prove it. Moore is another military lawyer assigned to the case, though her function seems to be holding Kaffee's hand (there's no actual romance between the two). Incredible fireworks between Cruise and Nicholson in the courtroom. Based on the play by Sorkin, who also wrote the screenplay. **138m/C VHS, DVD, Blu-ray Disc.** Tom Cruise, Jack Nicholson, Demi Moore, Kevin Bacon, Kevin Pollak, Kiefer Sutherland, James Marshall, J.T. Walsh, Christopher Guest, J.A. Preston, Matt Craven, Wolfgang Bodison, Xander Berkeley, Cuba Gooding Jr., Noah Wyle; ***D:*** Rob Reiner; ***W:*** Aaron Sorkin; ***C:*** Robert Richardson; ***M:*** Marc Shaiman. MTV Movie Awards '93: Film; Natl. Bd. of Review '92: Support. Actor (Nicholson).

ffolkes *Assault Force; North Sea Hijack* 1980 **(PG)** Rufus Excalibur Ffolkes is an eccentric underwater expert who is called upon to stop a madman (Perkins, indulging himself) from blowing up an oil rig in the North Sea. Entertaining farce with Moore playing the opposite of his usual suave James Bond character. **99m/C VHS, DVD.** Roger Moore, James Mason, Anthony Perkins, David Hedison, Michael Parks; ***D:*** Andrew V. McLaglen.

The Fiance 1996 **(R)** Faith (Anthony) suspects husband Richard (Cassidy) of being unfaithful and confides her suspicions to the friendly Walter (Moses). Only the unbalanced guy then becomes unhealthily involved in Faith's life. **94m/C VHS, DVD.** William R. Moses, Lysette Anthony, Patrick Cassidy, Alina Thompson, Wanda Acuna, Gordon Thomson; ***D:*** Martin Kitrosser; ***W:*** Greg Walker, Frank Rehwaldt; ***C:*** M. David Mullen; ***M:*** Richard Bowers. **VIDEO**

Fiances *The Engagement; I Fidanzati; Ermanno Olmi's I Fadanzati* 1963 Young man from Milan takes a welding job in Sicily that will separate him from his fiancee for 18 months. He thinks the separation will be good for them but loneliness and the strange environment makes him long for her. Nonprofessional leads provide strength. Italian with subtitles. **84m/B VHS, DVD.** *IT* Carlo Carbrini, Anna Canzi; ***D:*** Ermanno Olmi; ***W:*** Ermanno Olmi; ***C:*** Lamberto Caimi; ***M:*** Gianni Ferrio.

Fiction Makers 1967 Roger Moore stars as Simon Templar, also known as "The Saint," a sophisticated detective who is hired to help Amos Klein. Klein turns out to be an alias for a beautiful novelist who is being threatened by the underworld crime ring. Based on the Leslie Chateris' character. **102m/C VHS.** *GB* Roger Moore, Sylvia Syms, Justine Lord, Kenneth J. Warren, Philip Locke, Tom Clegg; ***D:*** Roy Ward Baker; ***W:*** Harry Junkin, John Kruse; ***C:*** Michael Reed; ***M:*** Edwin Astley.

Fictitious Marriage 1988 Eldad Ilan, a high school teacher experiencing a mid-life crisis, travels to Israel to get away from his family in order to consider his life's direction. In Hebrew with English subtitles. **90m/C VHS, DVD.** Shlomo Bar-Aba, Irit Sheleg, Ofra Veingarten; ***D:*** Haim Bouzaglo.

Fiddler on the Roof ½ 1971 **(G)** Based on the long-running Broadway musical. The poignant story of Tevye, a poor Jewish milkman at the turn of the century in a small Ukrainian village, and his five dowry-less daughters, his lame horse, his wife, and his companionable relationship with God. Topol, an Israeli who played the role in London, is charming, if not quite as wonderful as Zero Mostel, the Broadway star. Finely detailed set decoration and choreography, strong performances from the entire cast create a sense of intimacy in spite of near epic proportions of the production. Play was based on the Yiddish stories of Tevye the Dairyman, written by Sholem Aleichem. ♫ Tradition; Matchmaker, Matchmaker; If I Were a Rich Man; Sabbath Prayer; To Life; Miracle of Miracles; Tevye's Dream; Sunrise, Sunset; Wedding Celebration. **184m/C VHS, DVD.** Chaim Topol, Norma Crane, Leonard Frey, Molly Picon, Paul Mann, Rosalind Harris, Michele Marsh, Neva Small, Paul Michael Glaser, Ray Lovelock; ***D:*** Norman Jewison; ***W:*** Joseph Stein; ***C:*** Oswald Morris; ***M:*** John Williams. Oscars '71: Cinematog., Sound, Orig. Song Score and/or Adapt.; Golden Globes '72: Actor—Mus./Comedy (Topol), Film—Mus./Comedy.

The Fiddlin' Buckaroo ½ 1933 Maynard plays a government agent who disguises himself as a musical ventriloquist to capture Kohler and his band of outlaws. Everybody sings a lot. **63m/B VHS.** Ken Maynard, Gloria Shea, Fred Kohler Sr., Frank Rice, Jack Mower, Charles "Slim" Whitaker, Robert F. (Bob) Kortman, Hank Bell, Jack Rockwell; ***D:*** Ken Maynard; ***W:*** Nate Gatzert.

Fidel 2002 Excellent bio of Fidel Castro's rise to power in Cuba loses a little steam in its later moments but keeps interest with a strong performance by Martin in the title role. The politics are also kept simple; Castro is an idealistic lawyer who fights for the underdog as a rebel leader after his country's military takeover by Batista (Plana). But once he himself takes power, Castro blurs the lines into a dictatorship of his own. Based on the books "Guerilla Prince" by Georgie Anne Geyer and "Fidel Castro" by Robert E. Quirk. **140m/C VHS, DVD.** Victor Huggo Martin, Gael Garcia Bernal, Patricia Velasquez, Maurice Compte, Tony Plana, Guillermo Diaz, Margarita d'Francisco, Enrique Arce; ***D:*** David Attwood; ***W:*** Stephen Tolkin; ***C:*** Checco Varese; ***M:*** John Altman. **CABLE**

Fido 2006 **(R)** Amusing—if mild—zom-com. In the near-future (although it looks like the 1950s), a radioactive cloud has turned the dead into zombies. But a shady corporation has domesticated some zombies (thanks to electronic collars), and turned them into household help. When Timmy's (Ray) family finally acquires one, the lonely kid names his loyal zombie Fido (Connolly) and makes him his best friend. Despite Fido's unwavering desire to eat the neighbors (hey, that old lady was mean!). **91m/C DVD.** *CA* Billy Connolly, Carrie-Anne Moss, Dylan Baker, Henry Czerny, Tim Blake Nelson, K'Sun Ray, Sonja Bennett; ***D:*** Andrew Currie; ***W:*** Andrew Currie, Robert Chomiak, Dennis Heaton; ***C:*** Jan Kiesser; ***M:*** Don MacDonald.

The Field 1/2 **1990 (PG-13)** After an absence from the big screen, intense and nearly over the top Harris won acclaim as an iron-willed peasant fighting to retain a patch of Irish land he's tended all his life, now offered for sale to a wealthy American. His uncompromising stand divides the community in this glowing adaptation of John B. Keane's classic play, an allegory of Ireland's internal conflicts. **113m/C VHS, DVD.** *GB* Richard Harris, Tom Berenger, John Hurt, Sean Bean, Brenda Fricker, Frances Tomelty, John Cowley, Sean McGinley, Jenny Conroy; ***D:*** Jim Sheridan; ***W:*** Jim Sheridan; ***C:*** Jack Conroy; ***M:*** Elmer Bernstein.

Field of Dreams 1/2 **1989 (PG)** Uplifting mythic fantasy based on W.P. Kinsella's novel "Shoeless Joe." Iowa corn farmer Ray Kinsella (Costner) heeds a mysterious voice that instructs "If you build it, he will come" and cuts a baseball diamond in his corn field. Soon the ball field is inhabited by the spirit of Joe Jackson (Liotta) and others who were disgraced in the notorious 1919 "Black Sox" baseball scandal. Jones is Terence Mann, a character based on reclusive author J.D. Salinger, is reluctantly pulled into the mystery. It's all about chasing a dream, maintaining innocence, finding redemption, reconciling the child with the adult, and celebrating the mythic lure of baseball. Costner and Madigan (as wife Anni) are strong, believable characters. **106m/C VHS, DVD, HD DVD.** Kevin Costner, Amy Madigan, James Earl Jones, Burt Lancaster, Ray Liotta, Timothy Busfield, Frank Whaley, Gaby Hoffman, Dwier Brown; ***D:*** Phil Alden Robinson; ***W:*** Phil Alden Robinson; ***C:*** John Lindley; ***M:*** James Horner.

Field of Fire **1992 (R)** One of America's top military experts has been taken hostage and it's up to a top general to rescue him. But the rescue doesn't come off as planned and all must fight their way through the Cambodian jungle to safety. **96m/C VHS.** David Carradine; ***D:*** Cirio H. Santiago; ***W:*** Thomas McKelvey Cleaver.

Field of Honor 1/2 **1986 (R)** A look at the harrowing experience of jungle combat through the eyes of a Dutch infantryman in Korea. **93m/C VHS.** Everett McGill, Ron Bradsteder, Hey Young Lee; ***D:*** Hans Scheepmaker.

Field of Honor 1/2 *Champ d'Honneur* **1987 (PG)** A quiet French anti-war drama set during the Franco-Prussian war in 1869 in which a peasant boy volunteers to fight in place of a rich man's son. He is befriended behind enemy lines by a young boy and both try to avoid capture. In French with English subtitles. **87m/C VHS.** *FR* Cris Campion, Eric Wapler, Pascale Rocard, Frederic Mayer; ***D:*** Jean-Pierre Denis. Cesar '88: Score.

The Fiend **1971 (R)** A religious cultist, already unbalanced, grabs a knife and starts hacking away Jack-the-Ripper style. **87m/C VHS, DVD.** *GB* Ann Todd, Patrick Magee, Tony Beckley, Madeline Hinde, Suzanna Leigh, Percy Herbert; ***D:*** Robert Hartford-Davis.

Fiend **WOOF! 1983** Glowing supernatural thing flits around graveyard before animating dead guy who needs to kill in order to go on living. Murderous dead guy becomes a small-town music teacher feeding parasitically on his students to satisfy his supernatural hunger. His neighbor suspects some discord. Low-budget time waster. **93m/C VHS, DVD.** Don Leifert, Richard Nelson, Elaine White, George Stover; ***D:*** Donald M. Dohler.

The Fiend Who Walked the West 1/2 **1958** Brutal western has incarcerated bankrobber Dan letting slip the location of his loot to fellow inmate Griffin, who unfortunately turns out to be psychotic and due for release. When Dan's family is endangered, lawmen release him for a show-down with Griffin. Tense remake of "Kiss of Death" provides effective atmosphere and graphic violence in an Old West setting. **101m/B VHS.** Hugh O'Brian, Robert Evans, Dolores Michaels, Linda Cristal, Stephen McNally, Ron Ely, Edward Andrews, Ken Scott, Emile Meyer, Gregory Morton; ***D:*** Gordon Douglas; ***W:*** Philip Yordan; ***C:*** Joe MacDonald; ***M:*** Les Baxter.

Fiend without a Face **1958** An isolated air base in Canada is the site for a scientist using atomic power in an experiment to make a person's thoughts materialize. Only his thoughts are evil and reveal themselves as flying brains with spinal cords that suck human brains right out of the skull. Tons of fun for '50s SF fans and anyone who appreciates the sheer silliness of it all. **77m/B VHS, DVD.** Marshall Thompson, Kim Parker, Terence (Terry) Kilburn, Michael Balfour, Gil Winfield, Shane Cordell, Kynaston Reeves; ***D:*** Arthur Crabtree; ***W:*** Herbert J. Leder; ***C:*** Lionel Banes; ***M:*** Buxton Orr.

The Fiendish Plot of Dr. Fu Manchu **WOOF! 1980 (PG)** A sad farewell from Sellers, who in his last film portrays Dr. Fu in his desperate quest for the necessary ingredients for his secret life-preserving formula. Sellers portrays both Dr. Fu and the Scotland Yard detective on his trail, but it's not enough to save this picture, flawed by poor script and lack of direction. **100m/C VHS.** *GB* Peter Sellers, David Tomlinson, Sid Caesar, Helen Mirren, Simon Williams, Steve Franken, Stratford Johns, John Le Mesurier, John Sharp, Clement Harari; ***D:*** Piers Haggard; ***W:*** Rudy Dochtermann, Jim Moloney; ***C:*** Jean Tournier; ***M:*** Marc Wilkinson.

Fierce Creatures **1996 (PG-13)** This not-really-a-sequel features the same cast as "A Fish Called Wanda" and was jokingly known as "Death Fish II" until a more appropriate title was thought of. A failing London zoo gets a new lease on life, and officious new manager Rollo Lee (Cleese) by stocking only man-eating predators. This plan has kindly, insect house manager Bugsy (Palin) tongue-tied at the thought of destroying the zoo's cuddly current occupants. Kline is again in fine form with his dastardly dual role of zoo's Aussie owner Rod McCain and his idiot son, Vince. Curtis displays her obvious talents as Willa Weston, Vince's more sympathetic partner. Despite inspired moments, flick's not as tightly told or as wickedly funny as "Fish," (an admittedly tough act to follow). A family-friendlier attitude has effectively declawed this "Creature." Many scenes were reshot after unfavorable advance screenings, necessitating a new director and the recall of the actors from far and wide. **93m/C VHS, DVD.** John Cleese, Jamie Lee Curtis, Kevin Kline, Michael Palin, Ronnie Corbett, Robert Lindsay, Carey Lowell, Bille Brown, Derek Griffiths, Cynthia Cleese; ***D:*** Robert M. Young, Fred Schepisi; ***W:*** John Cleese, Iain Johnstone; ***C:*** Adrian Biddle, Ian Baker; ***M:*** Jerry Goldsmith.

Fierce People **2005 (R)** In 1980, fifteen-year-old Finn (Yelchin) is supposed to summer in South America with his wayward anthropologist father. Instead, train-wreck addict/masseuse mom (Lane), who's trying her luck at sobriety, plucks him from their New York City existence to spend the season at the New Jersey country estate of super-loaded and super-eccentric Osborne (Sutherland), where the idle rich pursue their own brand of summer fun. Finn falls for the billionaire's granddaughter (Stewart), and a twisted coming-of-age story unfolds amid the darkness. Be warned: a brutal rape sequence is totally jarring, and the already thin plot never recovers. Teen drug use, bizarre twists, and outrageous characters send the entire mess over the top. **135m/C DVD.** *US* Diane Lane, Donald Sutherland, Anton Yelchin, Chris Evans, Kristen Stewart, Elizabeth Perkins, Christopher Shyer, Blu Mankuma; ***D:*** Griffin Dunne; ***W:*** Dirk Wittenborn; ***C:*** William Rexer; ***M:*** Nick Laird-Clowes.

Fiesta 1/2 **1995** Young, idealistic Spanish aristocrat Rafael (Colin) has been studying in France during the years since the Spanish Republic was declared. Now, it's 1936 and he has been summoned home to fight against the Communists under the command of Col. Masagual (Trintignant). Masagual assigns Rafael to the firing squad to toughen him up but Rafael eventually rediscovers his convictions and double-crosses his mentor. Based on an autobiographical novel by Jose Luis de Vilallonga. French with subtitles. **108m/C VHS.** *FR* Jean-Louis Trintignant, Gregoire Colin, Dayle Haddon, Marc Lavoine, Jean-Philippe Ecoffey, Laurent Terzieff; ***D:*** Pierre Boutron; ***W:*** Pierre Boutron; ***C:*** Javier Aguirresarobe; ***M:*** Wim Mertens.

15 Amore **1998** Dorothy's husband is off fighting in WWII while she struggles with the family farm and three young kids in rural Australia. But soon she gets the help of two Italian POWs, Alfredo and Joseph, who settle right in. Then, Dorothy takes in German Jewish refugees Frau Gutman and her daughter Rachel. While Dorothy and Alfredo have an unacknowledged love for each other, Joseph and Rachel engage in a secret romance. Secret until Rachel's disapproving mother finds out. A last-minute bombshell accusation needlessly skewers everything that's gone before. Title refers to a tennis score, one of the local pasttimes. **92m/C VHS, DVD.** *AU* Lisa Hensley, Steve Bastoni, Domenic Galati, Tara Jakszewicz, Gertraud Ingeborg; ***D:*** Maurice Murphy; ***W:*** Maurice Murphy; ***C:*** John Brock; ***M:*** Carlo Giacco.

15 Minutes 1/2 **2001 (R)** New York cop and publicity hound De Niro teams up with arson investigator Burns to hunt down a couple of violent criminals who are videotaping their crimes for celebrity purposes. Is writer/director Herzfeld exploring our culture's fascination with violence, nihilism, and fame, or just using images of those ideas to sell tickets? Most likely it's the latter, but either way, Warhol would probably approve. Grammer tries his hand at playing the sleazy, Jerry Springerish shock-TV host, and mostly pulls it off. **120m/C VHS, DVD.** *US* Robert De Niro, Edward Burns, Kelsey Grammer, Avery Brooks, Melina Kanakaredes, Vera Farmiga, Karel Roden, Oleg Taktarov, John DiResta, James Handy, Darius McCrary, Charlize Theron, Kim Cattrall, David Alan Grier; ***D:*** John Herzfeld; ***W:*** John Herzfeld; ***C:*** Jean-Yves Escoffier; ***M:*** Anthony Marinelli, J. Peter Robinson.

Fifth Avenue Girl 1/2 **1939** An unhappy millionaire brings home a poor young woman to pose as his mistress to make his family realize how they've neglected him. As this below-par social comedy drones toward its romantic conclusion, the rich folks see the error of their ways and love conquers all. **83m/B VHS.** Ginger Rogers, Walter Connolly, Tim Holt, James Ellison, Franklin Pangborn; ***D:*** Gregory La Cava.

Fifth Day of Peace **1972 (PG)** In the aftermath of the WWI armistice, two German soldiers are tried and executed for desertion by their commander, even though the Allies forbade German military trials. An interesting plot that is marred by too obvious plot twists. Based on a true story. **95m/C VHS, DVD.** *IT* Richard Johnson, Franco Nero, Larry Aubrey, Helmuth Schneider; ***D:*** Guiliano Montaldo.

The Fifth Element 1/2 **1997 (PG-13)** Besson's view of the future is colorful, loud and fashionable. Dressed in costumes by Jean Paul Gaultier, Willis (in a blonde dye job) is New York City cab driver turned unwilling hero Korban Dallas, who must save earth from destruction at the hands of evil arms dealer Zorg (Oldman). Bruce is up to the old heroics that made him a household name, and takes time to romance orange-haired nymph Jovovich, who holds the key to all the madness going on. Oldman is over-the-top as the icy villain with a distinct southern accent, which makes him more of a bad gag than a bad guy. Jumbled story fortunately takes a backseat to weird aliens and stunning visuals which makes this an eye-catching (albeit confusing) sci-fi trip. **125m/C VHS, DVD, Blu-ray Disc, UMD.** Bruce Willis, Gary Oldman, Ian Holm, Milla Jovovich, Luke Perry, Lee Evans, Chris Tucker, Brion James, Tommy (Tiny) Lister, John Neville, John Bluthal, Maiwenn Le Besco, Mathieu Kassovitz; ***D:*** Luc Besson; ***W:*** Luc Besson; ***C:*** Thierry Arbogast; ***M:*** Eric Serra. British Acad. '97: Visual FX; Cesar '98: Art Dir./Set Dec., Cinematog., Director (Besson).

The Fifth Floor **WOOF! 1980 (R)** College disco dancer overdoses on drugs and winds up in an insane asylum, complete with menacing attendant Hopkins and apathetic doctor Ferrer. Pathetic, exploitative trash. **90m/C VHS.** Bo Hopkins, Dianne Hull, Patti D'Arbanville, Mel Ferrer; ***D:*** Howard (Hikmet) Avedis; ***W:*** Howard (Hikmet) Avedis.

The Fifth Horseman Is Fear **1964** In Nazi-occupied Prague, Dr. Braun is forbidden from practicing medicine because he is a Jew. Instead, he catalogs confiscated property in a warehouse. But when a wounded resistance fighter is secretly brought to Braun for treatment, he journeys throughout the chaotic city trying to find morphine for his patient, whom he is hiding in his apartment building. But he fears his scared neighbors may become informers. Czech with subtitles. **100m/B DVD.** *CZ* Jiri Adamira, Miroslav Machacek, Josef Vinklar, Jiri Virtala; ***D:*** Zbynek Brynych; ***W:*** Zbynek Brynych; ***C:*** Jan Kalis.

The Fifth Monkey 1/2 **1990 (PG-13)** A man embarks on a journey to sell four monkeys in order to fill a dowry for his bride, but along the way he encounters all sorts of obstacles and adventures. Filmed on location in Brazil **93m/C VHS.** Ben Kingsley; ***D:*** Eric Rochant; ***W:*** Eric Rochant.

The Fifth Musketeer *Behind the Iron Mask* **1979 (PG)** A campy adaptation of Dumas's "The Man in the Iron Mask," wherein a monarch's evil twin impersonates him while imprisoning the true king. A good cast and rich production shot in Austria make for a fairly entertaining swashbuckler. **90m/C DVD.** *GB* Beau Bridges, Sylvia Kristel, Ursula Andress, Cornel Wilde, Ian McShane, Alan Hale Jr., Helmut Dantine, Olivia de Havilland, Jose Ferrer, Rex Harrison; ***D:*** Ken Annakin; ***W:*** David Ambrose; ***C:*** Jack Cardiff.

The Fifth Seal **1976** A group of friends are arrested when one makes a casual remark that offends a commandant. This leads to a series of tasks that test their commitment to their moral ideals. Set at the close of WWII in Hungary. In Hungarian with English subtitles. **116m/C VHS.** *HU* Lajos Oze, Laszlo Markus, Ferenc Bencze, Sandor Horvath; ***D:*** Zoltan Fabri; ***W:*** Zoltan Fabri; ***C:*** Gyorgy Illes; ***M:*** Gyorgy Vukan.

Fifty Dead Men Walking **2008** It's 1988 in Belfast with British soldiers in the streets and the IRA waging war. Petty hustler and criminal Martin McGartland (Sturgess) drifts into becoming an informant for intelligence agent Fergus (Kingsley). Then his friend Frankie (MacNeill) gets kneecapped and Martin wrangles his way into the IRA itself. Title refers to the 50 men Martin reputedly saved from IRA execution. Exceptional performances from Sturgess and Kingsley in a somewhat convoluted story. **118m/C DVD.** *GB CA* Jim Sturgess, Ben Kingsley, Kevin Zegers, Nathalie Press, Rose McGowan, Conor MacNeill; ***D:*** Keri Skogland; ***W:*** Keri Skogland; ***C:*** Jonathan Freeman; ***M:*** Ben Mink.

50 First Dates 1/2 **2004 (PG-13)** Barrymore is the sweet girl with no short-term memory and Sandler is the love-struck island veterinarian who tries to woo her...over and over again. Sweetly charming at times, as Sandler tones down his more outrageous behavior for a decent romantic comedy. Clark does a fine job as Barrymore's slightly over-protective but loving father. Astin goes 180 degrees from anything resembling a hobbit as the pumped-up brother. **96m/C DVD, Blu-ray Disc, UMD.** *US* Adam Sandler, Drew Barrymore, Rob Schneider, Sean Astin, Blake Clark, Dan Aykroyd, Amy Hill, Allen Covert, Maya Rudolph, Missi Pyle, Lusia Strus, Pomaika'i Brown; ***D:*** Peter Segal; ***W:*** George Wing; ***C:*** Jack N. Green; ***M:*** Teddy Castellucci.

$50,000 Reward 1/2 **1925** Maynard's first western finds him being victimized by an unscrupulous banker who wants Maynard's land deeds for property on which a new dam is being built. **49m/B VHS.** Ken Maynard, Esther Ralston, Edward Peil Sr., Bert Lindley, Lillian (Lillianne, Lyllian) Leighton, Frank Whitson; ***D:*** Clifford S. Elfelt; ***W:*** Frank Howard Clark; ***C:*** Bert Longenecker.

52 Pick-Up 1/2 **1986 (R)** After a fling, a wealthy industrialist is blackmailed by a trio of repulsive criminals and determines to save himself. First he becomes deeply caught in their web of murder. Based on an Elmore Leonard novel with lots of gruesome violence and good performances. **111m/C**

VHS. Roy Scheider, Ann-Margret, Vanity, John Glover, Doug McClure, Clarence Williams III, Kelly Preston, Robert Trebor, Lonny (Lonnie) Chapman; ***D:*** John Frankenheimer; ***W:*** John Steppling, Elmore Leonard; ***M:*** Gary Chang.

54 🦴 ½ **1998 (R)** The days of '70s disco, drugs, and hedonism rear their heads in this look back at New York's infamous Studio 54. Myers takes the drama route as druggie club co-owner Steve Rubell, while Phillippe starts off as innocent New Jersey boy Shane O'Shea, who gets a job as a bartender and is soon taking the low road to debauchery. Others hitting the dance floor include pouty soap star Julie (Campbell), coat-check girl/would-be disco diva Anita (Hayek), and her busboy hubby Greg (Meyer). But Shane is a dunce and his story a bore, while the effective Myers takes a decided backseat storywise. Film went through a lot of last-minute re-editing but it didn't seem to help. **92m/C VHS, DVD.** Mike Myers, Ryan Phillippe, Breckin Meyer, Salma Hayek, Neve Campbell, Sela Ward, Sherry Stringfield, Ellen A. Dow, Heather Matarazzo, Skipp (Robert L.) Sudduth, Cindy Crawford; ***Cameos:*** Lauren Hutton, Michael York; ***D:*** Mark Christopher; ***W:*** Mark Christopher; ***C:*** Alexander Grusynski.

55 Days at Peking 🦴🦴🦴 **1963** A costume epic depicting the Chinese Boxer Rebellion and the fate of military Britishers caught in the midst of the chaos. Standard fare superbly handled by director Ray and an all-star cast. **150m/C VHS, DVD.** Charlton Heston, Ava Gardner, David Niven, John Ireland, Flora Robson, Paul Lukas, Jacques Sernas; ***D:*** Nicholas Ray; ***W:*** Philip Yordan; ***C:*** Jack Hildyard.

The Fig Tree 1987 After her mother passes away, Miranda becomes tormented by the fear of death. Now her aunt must help her cope with this difficult part of life. Adapted from the short story by Katherine Anne Porter. Aired on PBS as part of the "Wonderworks" family movie series. **58m/C VHS.** Olivia Cole, William Converse-Roberts, Doris Roberts, Teresa Wright, Karron Graves; ***D:*** Calvin Skaggs.

Fight Club 🦴🦴🦴 ½ **1999 (R)** Young, male, repressed rage comes in the form of Norton's disillusioned yuppie, emotionally numbed by chronic insomnia, who meets the answer to all his pent-up frustrations in malcontent Pitt. Tyler's his name and anarchy's his game as the duo eventually establish fight clubs where the participants beat each other up and stage massive acts of terrorism to undermine the allure of consumerism. Bonham Carter plays a kinky, death-obsessed woman both men fancy. Fincher heads for the dark side again and puts a middle finger on the pulse of several hot topics without missing a beat or skirting the issues. Film's dark humor and stylistic vision of young male malaise is made even more biting by newcomer Uhl's faithful adaptation of Chuck Palahniuk's debut novel. Performances by all three leads are equal to the powerful subject matter. **139m/C VHS, DVD, UMD.** Brad Pitt, Edward Norton, Helena Bonham Carter, Meat Loaf Aday, Jared Leto, Eion Bailey; ***D:*** David Fincher; ***W:*** Jim Uhls; ***C:*** Jeff Cronenweth; ***M:*** Howard Shore.

Fight for Gold 🦴 **1986** In the frozen wastes of the North, a man becomes embroiled in a violent quest for gold. **107m/C VHS.** *GE* Doug McClure, Harald Leipnitz, Heinz Reinl, Roberto Bianco, Angelica Ott, Kristina Nel; ***D:*** Harald Reinl.

A Fight for Jenny 🦴🦴 **1990 (PG)** Miami Viceroy Thomas and Warren play an interracial couple who fight for custody of the wife's child from a previous marriage. Standard made-for-TV meaningful drama (bite-sized issues served with a modicum of melodrama). **95m/C VHS.** Philip Michael Thomas, Lesley Ann Warren, Jean Smart, Lynne Moody, William Atherton; ***D:*** Gilbert Moses.

Fight for the Title 🦴🦴 **1957** Benny Leonard's reign as the lightweight boxing champ has just begun when WWII is declared. Against his manager's wishes, Benny decides to enlist. **30m/C VHS, DVD.** Michael Landon, George Brenlin; ***D:*** Eric Kenton.

Fight for Us 🦴 ½ *L'Insoumis* **1989 (R)** A social activist, recently released from prison, takes on the death squads terrorizing the countryside in post-Marcos Philippines. In Spanish with English subtitles. **92m/C VHS.** Phillip Salvador, Dina Bonnevie, Gina Alajar, Benbol Roco; ***D:*** Lino Brocka; ***W:*** Jose F. Lacaba; ***C:*** Rody Lacap; ***M:*** Hugo Crotti.

Fight for Your Life 🦴 *Getting Even; Held Hostage; Staying Alive* **1977 (R)** Three escaped convicts—a white bigot, an Asian, and a Chicano—take a black minister's family hostage. After suffering all manner of vicious torture, the family exacts an equally brutal revenge. Shades of "The Desperate Hours" and "Extremities," but with much more graphic violence and a racial twist. **89m/C VHS, DVD.** *CA* William Sanderson, Robert Judd, Lela Small, Reggie Rock Bythewood; ***D:*** Robert A. Endelson; ***W:*** Straw Weisman; ***C:*** Lloyd Freidus; ***M:*** Jeff Slevin.

The Fighter 🦴🦴🦴 *The First Time* **1952** A Mexican patriot, involved in a struggle to overthrow a dictator, falls for a co-revolutionist. Flashbacks show the destruction of his family and village, and his pugilistic expertise, which he uses to fight for a huge purse to help the cause. Adapted from Jack London's "The Mexican." **78m/B VHS, DVD.** Richard Conte, Vanessa Brown, Lee J. Cobb, Frank Silvera, Roberta Haynes, Hugh Sanders, Claire Carleton, Martin Garralaga; ***D:*** Herbert Kline; ***W:*** Herbert Kline, Aben Kandel; ***C:*** Floyd Crosby, James Wong Howe; ***M:*** Vincente Gomez.

The Fighter 🦴 ½ **1995 (R)** French soldier Charlemont (Gruner) gets involved with desperate farmers opposing a greedy landlord (Ermey) and is forced to compete against former rival Ziegfield (Singer). Strange western/kickboxing hybrid that does have lots of action. **91m/C VHS.** Olivier Gruner, Marc Singer, R. Lee Ermey, Ian Ziering, James Brolin, Ashley Laurence; ***D:*** Isaac Florentine.

Fighter Attack 🦴🦴 **1953** Story of a WWII pilot, based in Corsica, who is shot down during a mission to destroy a Nazi supply station. He meets with a woman of the Italian underground, and succeeds in destroying his target with her help. **80m/C VHS.** Sterling Hayden, J. Carrol Naish, Joy Page; ***D:*** Lesley Selander.

Fightin' Ranch 🦴🦴 *Fighting Thru* **1930** A famous lawman saves his reputation, previously tainted. A Maynard classic. **60m/B VHS.** Jeanette Loff, Wallace MacDonald, Carmelita Geraghty, Ken Maynard; ***D:*** William Nigh; ***W:*** John Natteford; ***C:*** Ted D. McCord.

Fighting 🦴🦴 ½ **2009 (PG-13)** You can anticipate all the sports cliches within minutes, but for some reason it still has appeal. Alabama-born Shawn MacArthur (Tatum) hustles various jobs on the New York streets while going nowhere fast. Until he meets equally hustling fight coach Harvey Boarden (Howard), who introduces him to the world of underground bare-knuckles fighting. Shawn discovers he's a winner at something that may get him killed as the payday for the matches increases against better competitors. There's also some romance between Shawn and single mom/waitress Zulay (Henao) who falls for the lug despite her better judgment. **105m/C DVD.** *US* Channing Tatum, Terrence Howard, Luis Guzman, Brian White, Zulay Henao, Roger Guenveur Smith; ***D:*** Dito Montiel; ***W:*** Dito Montiel, Robert Munic; ***C:*** Stefan Czapsky; ***M:*** Dave Wittman, Jonathan Elias.

The Fighting American 🦴🦴 **1924** A frat boy proposes to a girl on a brotherly dare, and, unflattered by the fraternal proposal, the girl flees to the Far East to return to the bosom of her family. But it turns out the boy really does love the girl, by golly, and he's got just enough of that fighting American spirit to prove it. Predates Oland's Charlie Chan career by seven years. **65m/B VHS.** Pat O'Malley, Mary Astor, Raymond Hatton, Warner Oland; ***D:*** Tom Forman.

Fighting Back 🦴🦴 *Death Vengeance* **1982 (R)** Reactionary tale of an angry resident in a crime-ridden Philadelphia neighborhood who organizes a patrol of armed civilian vigilantes. The police attempt to head off a racial confrontation in this effective drama graced with some fine performances. **96m/C VHS.** Tom Skerritt, Patti LuPone, Michael Sarrazin, Yaphet Kotto; ***D:*** Lewis Teague; ***W:*** David Zelag Goodman; ***C:*** Franco Di Giacomo.

Fighting Black Kings 🦴 **1976 (PG)** Martial arts and karate masters appear in this tale of action. **90m/C VHS.** William Oliver, Charles Martin, Willie Williams, Mas Oyama; ***D:*** Shuji Goto; ***W:*** Shuji Goto; ***C:*** Kimiaki Kimura; ***M:*** Keisuke Hidaka.

Fighting Caballero 🦴 **1935** Lease and his pals effectively handle a gang of mine-harassing outlaws. **60m/B VHS.** Dorothy Gulliver, Earl Douglas, George Chesebro, Robert Walker, Wally Wales, Rex Lease; ***D:*** Elmer Clifton; ***W:*** Elmer Clifton; ***C:*** Bert Longenecker.

Fighting Caravans 🦴🦴 *Blazing Arrows* **1931** In this early big-budget western, based on a story by Zane Grey, a wagon train sets out west from Missouri. Cooper emerges as the hero after warding off an Indian attack that takes the lives of the original leaders. **80m/B VHS, DVD.** Gary Cooper, Ernest Torrence, Tully Marshall, Fred Kohler Sr., Lili Damita; ***D:*** Otto Brower, David Burton.

Fighting Champ 🦴 **1933** Cowpunching gives way to boxing as Steele steps into the ring and takes on all comers. Poor combination of riding and boxing makes for a disappointing Western. **57m/B VHS.** Bob Steele, Arletta Duncan, George "Gabby" Hayes, Charles "Blackie" King, Lafe (Lafayette) McKee, Kit Guard, George Chesebro; ***D:*** John P. McCarthy; ***W:*** Wellyn Totman.

Fighting Cowboy 🦴 **1933** Bill settles a tungsten mine dispute with a greedy miner and some outlaws. **50m/B VHS.** Buffalo Bill Jr., Allen Holbrook; ***D:*** Victor Adamson; ***C:*** Brydon Baker.

Fighting Devil Dogs 🦴🦴 **1943** Two Marine lieutenants are assigned the task of obtaining a deadly secret weapon controlled by crooks. A serial in 12 chapters. **195m/B VHS.** Lee Powell, Bruce Bennett; ***D:*** John English, William Witney.

The Fighting Eagle 🦴🦴 **1927** Etienne Girard (La Rocque), a young officer in Napoleon's army, saves a beautiful diplomatic courier (Haver) from the duplicitous Talleyrand (de Grasse) and uncovers a plot to overthrow the Emperor. Based on the comic "Brigadier Gerard" stories by Sir Arthur Conan Doyle. **71m/B DVD.** Rod La Rocque, Phyllis Haver, Sam De Grasse, Max Barwyn, Julia Faye, Clarence Burton, Sally Rand; ***D:*** Donald Crisp; ***W:*** Douglas Z. Doty; ***C:*** J. Peverell Marley.

Fighting Elegy 🦴🦴 *Kenka Ereji* **1966** A high school boy longs for an unattainable girl and channels all those teenaged hormones into brawling with street gangs. Then he has an encounter with an ultra-right wing militarist that changes his life and sets him on the path to fascism. Japanese with subtitles. **86m/B VHS.** *JP* Hideki Takahashi, Yusuke Kawazu, Jinko Asano, Mitsuo Kataoka; ***D:*** Seijun Suzuki.

Fighting Father Dunne 🦴🦴 **1948** Mega-hokey Hollywood steamroller about a tough priest caring for St. Louis newsboys in the early 1900s. Based on a true story. **92m/B VHS.** Pat O'Brien, Darryl Hickman, Charles Kemper, Una O'Connor, Arthur Shields, Harry Shannon, Joseph (Joe) Sawyer, Anna Q. Nilsson, Donn Gift, Myrna Dell; ***D:*** Ted Tetzlaff.

Fighting Fists of Shanghai Joe 🦴 **1965** Fearsome fighting man from the Far East engages a vile American land baron in a battle of honor. **94m/C VHS, DVD.** Klaus Kinski, Gordon Mitchell, Carla Romanelli, Claudio Undari, Chen Lee; ***D:*** Mario Caiano.

Fighting Fool 🦴 **1932** Average oater has McCoy as a sheriff constantly in pursuit of an outlaw named "The Shadow." Of course, romance blossoms between McCoy and Day, too. The real identity of "The Shadow" turns out to be quite a surprise for McCoy. **57m/B VHS.** Tim McCoy, Marceline Day, Robert Ellis, Arthur (L.) Rankin, Dorothy Granger; ***D:*** Lambert Hillyer.

Fighting Hero 🦴 ½ **1934** Tom Hall (Tyler) is an express company detective who poses as an outlaw to capture some bandits. Along the way he rescues Mexican miss Conchita (Borden) from a lynching when she's accused of a murder that was actually self-defense. But after Tom falls for the girl, he starts thinking she may be in cahoots with the thieves. **55m/B DVD.** Tom Tyler, Rene Borden, Edward Hearn, Dick Botiller, Murdock MacQuarrie, George Chesebro, Ralph Lewis, Tom London; ***D:*** George Chesebro, Harry S. Webb; ***W:*** Carl Krusada, Rose Gordon; ***C:*** J. Henry Kruse.

Fighting Jack 🦴🦴 **1926** After he saves a girl from a watery death, a man is accused of horse stealing and trespassing. **52m/B VHS.** Bill (William N.) Bailey, Hazel Deane, Frona Hale, John Byron, Sailor Sharkey, Herma Cordova; ***D:*** Louis Chaudet.

The Fighting Kentuckian 🦴🦴 ½ **1949** Homeward bound from the Battle of New Orleans in 1814, a Kentucky rifleman lingers in a French settlement in Alabama. His romance with the daughter of a French general is blocked by the father until the American saves the community from an assault by land grabbers. Hardy as a frontiersman is well worth the view. An action-packed, well-photographed hit. **100m/B DVD.** John Wayne, Oliver Hardy, Vera Hruba Ralston, Marie Windsor, Philip Dorn, John Howard, Hugo Haas, Grant Withers; ***D:*** George Waggner.

The Fighting Legion 🦴🦴 **1930** Maynard shows his foresight here, making this one of the first westerns to fully exploit sound by adding music and singing. Standard plot has Maynard going after the villain who murdered his brother. **69m/B VHS.** Ken Maynard, Dorothy Dwan, Ernie Adams, Stanley Blystone, Frank Rice; ***D:*** Harry Joe Brown.

Fighting Mad 🦴 ½ **1939** A singing Mountie tangles with border-crossing robbers and saves the reputation of a woman they exploit. One of the "Renfrew of the Mounties" series. **57m/B VHS.** James Newill, Milburn Stone, Sally Blane; ***D:*** Sam Newfield.

Fighting Mad 🦴🦴 ½ **1976 (R)** A peaceful land owner is driven to violence when he discovers that the business men who want his property are planning to murder two of his family members in order to get it. The local sheriff's apathy forces the man to take the law into his own hands. Unlike other Fonda films of the time which consist of chaotic violence and car crashes, this story is a well performed character study. **90m/C VHS, DVD.** Peter Fonda, Lynn Lowry, John Doucette, Phil Carey, Scott Glenn, Kathleen Miller; ***D:*** Jonathan Demme; ***W:*** Jonathan Demme.

Fighting Mad 🦴 ½ *Fierce* **1977 (R)** Soldiers leave their buddy for dead in wartime Vietnam. He is alive, but captured by Japanese soldiers who believe they are still fighting in WWII. **96m/C VHS, DVD.** James Iglehart, Jayne Kennedy, Leon Isaac Kennedy; ***D:*** Cirio H. Santiago.

Fighting Marines 🦴 ½ **1936** U.S. Marines are trying to establish an air base on Halfway Island in the Pacific, but are thwarted by the "Tiger Shark," a modern-day pirate. First appeared as a serial. **69m/B VHS, DVD.** Jason Robards Sr., Grant Withers, Ann Rutherford, Pat O'Malley; ***D:*** Joseph Kane, B. Reeves Eason; ***W:*** Barney A. Sarecky.

The Fighting Marshal 🦴🦴 **1932** After serving time for a crime he didn't commit, McCoy assumes the identity of a dead sheriff and tries to find the felons who done him wrong. **58m/B VHS.** Tim McCoy, Dorothy Gulliver, Mary Carr, Matthew Betz, Pat O'Malley; ***D:*** David Ross Lederman.

Fighting Parson 🦴 **1935** In order to infiltrate a lawless town Gibson, a gunsliging cowboy, dresses as a revivalist preacher. **65m/B VHS.** Hoot Gibson, Marceline Day, Robert Frazer, Stanley Blystone, Skeeter Bill Robbins, Charles "Blackie" King; ***D:*** Harry Fraser.

Fighting Pilot 1935 Talmadge is a real fighter in this classic talkie. His assignment is to rescue the plans for a secret aircraft from ill fate. **62m/B VHS, DVD.** Richard Talmadge, Victor Mace, Gertrude Messinger, Eddie Davis, Robert Frazer; ***D:*** Noel Mason Smith.

The Fighting Prince of Donegal 🦴🦴 ½ **1966** An Irish prince battles the invading British in 16th Century

Ireland. Escaping their clutches, he leads his clan in rescuing his mother and his beloved in this Disney swashbuckler. Based on the novel "Red Hugh, Prince of Donegal" by Robert T. Reilly. **110m/C VHS.** Peter McEnery, Susan Hampshire, Tom Adams, Gordon Jackson, Andrew Keir; ***D:*** Michael O'Herlihy; ***M:*** George Bruns.

The Fighting Rats of Tobruk 🦴🦴 *The Rats of Tobruk* **1944** Australian film about the Egyptian campaign against Rommel in World War II attempts to take a slightly documentary approach to the subject. It's notable mostly for providing an early role for Peter Finch. **71m/B VHS, DVD.** *AU* Grant Taylor, Peter Finch, Chips Rafferty, Pauline Garrick; ***D:*** Charles Chauvel; ***C:*** George Heath.

The Fighting Redhead 🦴🦴 **1950** Final entry in the "Red Ryder" series has Hart as a cattle rustling murderer and Bannon as the hero, Red Ryder. Based on the comic strip, "Red Ryder." **55m/C VHS, DVD.** Jim Bannon, Don Reynolds, Emmett Lynn, Marin Sais, Peggy Stewart, John Hart, Lane Bradford; ***D:*** Lewis D. Collins; ***W:*** Paul Franklin, Jerry Thomas.

Fighting Renegade 🦴 ½ **1939** The search for an Indian burial ground in Mexico prompts two murders and McCoy, disguised as a notorious bandit part of the time, is wrongly accused. Justice triumphs in the end. **60m/B VHS, DVD.** Joyce Bryant, Ben (Benny) Corbett, Ted Adams, Tim McCoy; ***D:*** Sam Newfield; ***W:*** William Lively; ***C:*** Arthur Reed.

The Fighting Rookie 🦴 ½ **1934** LaRue, better known for playing hoods, is a rookie cop set up and disgraced by the mob. But he fights back to regain his honor and bring the gang to justice. **65m/B VHS.** Ada Ince, DeWitt Jennings, Matthew Betz, Wally Wales, Arthur Belasco, Jack La Rue; ***D:*** Spencer Gordon Bennet; ***W:*** George Morgan; ***C:*** James S. Brown Jr.

Fighting Seabees 🦴🦴 ½ **1944** As a hot-tempered construction foreman who battles Navy regulations as well as the Japanese, Wayne emerges as a larger-than-life hero in this action-packed saga of the Pacific theater of WWII. Extremely popular patriotic drama depicts the founding of the Seabees, the naval construction corps, amidst the action and the would-be romance with a woman reporter. Also available colorized. **100m/B VHS, DVD.** John Wayne, Susan Hayward, Dennis O'Keefe, William Frawley, Grant Withers, Tom London, Wally Wales, Paul Fix, William Forrest, J.M. Kerrigan, Leonid Kinskey, Duncan Renaldo, Addison Richards, Ben Welden, Crane Whitley, Charles Trowbridge; ***D:*** Edward Ludwig; ***W:*** Borden Chase, Aeneas MacKenzie; ***C:*** William Bradford; ***M:*** Walter Scharf, Roy Webb.

Fighting Shadows 🦴 ½ **1935** McCoy plays a tough lawman who rids his town of an unscrupulous bandit gang guilty of harassing the locals. Highlighted by some excellent trick riding—for which Western star McCoy was known. **58m/B VHS.** Tim McCoy, Robert "Tex" Allen, Geneva Mitchell, Ward Bond, Si Jenks; ***D:*** David Selman; ***W:*** Ford Beebe.

The Fighting Sheriff 🦴 **1931** Routine oater mixes action and romance when a sheriff is thrown together with a society debutante. **65m/B VHS.** Buck Jones, Loretta Sayers, Robert Ellis, Harlan E. Knight, Paul Fix, Lilian Worth; ***D:*** Louis King; ***W:*** Stuart Anthony.

The Fighting 69th 🦴🦴🦴 **1940** Cornball but entertaining WWI drama with lots of action. Cagney is a Brooklyn street tough who joins the all-Irish 69th New York regiment but could care less about its famed military history. He promptly defies his superiors and barely scrapes through his training. Sent to France, the swaggering Cagney turns coward when confronted by the horrors of war but eventually redeems himself. O'Brien is the famed regimental chaplain Father Duffy, while Brent is commander "Wild Bill" Donovan, who would later found the OSS in WWII. Lots of heart-tugging emotion backed with a fine supporting cast. **90m/B VHS, DVD.** James Cagney, Pat O'Brien, George Brent, Jeffrey Lynn, Alan Hale, Frank McHugh, Dennis Morgan, William Lundigan, Dick Foran, Guinn "Big Boy" Williams, Henry O'Neill, John Litel, George Reeves, Frank "Junior" Coghlan, Sammy Cohen, Joseph Crehan, Eddie Dew, William Hopper, Frank Mayo, Herbert Anderson, Harvey Stephens, Charles Trowbridge, Roland Varno; ***D:*** William Keighley; ***W:*** Fred Niblo, Norman Reilly Raine, Dean Franklin; ***C:*** Gaetano Antonio "Tony" Gaudio; ***M:*** Adolph Deutsch.

The Fighting Stallion 🦴🦴🦴 **1926** Canutt stars as a drifter hired by a rancher who's determined to capture a beautiful wild stallion (played by Boy the Wonder Horse). Silent with original organ score. **76m/B VHS.** Yakima Canutt, Neva Gerber, Bud Osborne; ***D:*** Ben F. Wilson; ***W:*** George W. Pyper; ***C:*** Joseph Walker.

The Fighting Sullivans 🦴🦴🦴 ½ *The Sullivans* **1942** The true story of five brothers killed on the Battleship Juneau at Guadalcanal during WWII. The tale tells of the fury felt by the siblings after Pearl Harbor, their enlistment to fight for their country, and their tragic fate in the heat of battle. Truly a stirring tribute to all lives lost in combat. **110m/B VHS, DVD.** Anne Baxter, Thomas Mitchell, Selena Royle, Eddie Ryan, Trudy Marshall, James B. Cardwell, Roy Roberts, Ward Bond, Mary McCarty, Bobby Driscoll, Addison Richards, Selmer Jackson, Mae Marsh, Harry Strang, Barbara Brown, George Offerman Jr., John Campbell, John Alvin, Patrick Curtis, Nancy June Robinson, Marvin Davis; ***D:*** Lloyd Bacon; ***W:*** Edward Doherty, Mary C. McCall, Jules Schermer; ***C:*** Lucien N. Andriot; ***M:*** Cyril Mockridge, Alfred Newman.

The Fighting Temptations 🦴🦴 **2003 (PG-13)** New York adman Darrin marries a witch and hilarity ensues. Oh wait, that's something else. Okay, Darrin (Gooding, Jr.) is an adman in New York...for about 15 minutes. Before long he's unemployed and heading to his small Georgia hometown in order to collect an inheritance. Only there's a catch—he must return a gospel choir to its former greatness in order to collect. Wafer-thin plot is merely filler connecting the great gospel and R&B music that is the real star of this show. Beyonce Knowles is the love interest and mainstay of the choir, but she's only one of the prominent musical talents who help to raise this flick above the mundane. Shirley Caesar, Melba Moore, The O'Jays, Faith Evans, Eddie LeVert, and Montel Jordan are among the luminaries. **123m/C VHS, DVD.** *US* Cuba Gooding Jr., Beyonce Knowles, Mike Epps, LaTanya Richardson Jackson, Steve Harvey, Melba Moore; ***D:*** Jonathan Lynn; ***W:*** Elizabeth Hunter, Saladin Patterson; ***C:*** Alfonso Beato; ***M:*** Jimmy Jam, Terry Lewis, James "Big Jim" Wright.

Fighting Texans 🦴 **1933** An entire town invests in an oil well, on the advice of young salesman Bell, that the bankers are sure is a dud. Imagine their surprise when it turns out to be a gusler. **60m/B VHS.** Rex Bell, Luana Walters, Betty Mack, Gordon DeMain; ***D:*** Armand Schaefer.

Fighting Thru 🦴 *California in 1878* **1930** Maynard fights off the bad guys and wins the girl after some nifty riding in his first all-talkie western. **60m/B VHS.** Ken Maynard, Jeanette Loff; ***D:*** William Nigh.

The Fighting Trooper 🦴 ½ **1934** Based on the James Oliver Curwood story, "Footprints," this frontier tale presents a Mountie who goes undercover as a trapper in the Northwest. He is out to catch a murderer. **57m/B VHS.** Kermit Maynard, Barbara Worth, Leroy Mason, Charles Delaney, Robert Frazer, George Regas, Walter Miller, Joseph Girard; ***D:*** Ray Taylor; ***W:*** Forrest Sheldon; ***C:*** Edgar Lyons.

Fighting Valley 🦴🦴 **1943** Texas Rangers O'Brien, Newill, and Wilkerson ride off to break up an outlaw gang that is trying to monopolize the ore smelting business. O'Brien later went on to directing for TV and also wrote for Red Skelton. **60m/B VHS.** Dave O'Brien, James Newill, Guy Wilkerson, Patti McCarty, John Merton, Curley Dresden; ***D:*** Oliver Drake; ***W:*** Oliver Drake.

Fighting Vigilantes 🦴🦴 **1947** A villainous food distributor is terrorizing his rivals until LaRue whips him. Holt and her father put together a committee called "The Vigilantes" to help out. Holt is the daughter of movie good guy Jack Holt. **61m/B VHS.** Lash LaRue, Al "Fuzzy" St. John, Jennifer Holt, George Chesebro, Lee Morgan, Russell Arms, Steve Clark; ***D:*** Ray Taylor.

The Fighting Westerner 🦴 ½ *Rocky Mountain Mystery* **1935** Scott stars as a mining engineer who becomes entangled in mysterious murders. Mrs. Leslie Carter stars in a rare screen role. **54m/B VHS, DVD.** Randolph Scott, Charles "Chic" Sale, Ann Sheridan, Charles T. Barton.

Fighting with Anger 🦴 **2007** Hitwoman Ray (Fleming) is looking for answers to her past and doesn't realize that mentor Will (Nelson) is keeping things from her. These secrets prove problematic when her next assignment, which involves illegal antiques and the Korean government, goes bad and leaves Ray with a new enemy. Poorly acted with a laughably executed plot. **90m/C DVD.** Willie Nelson, Kelli Fleming, Jonathan Boatwright, Trant Batey; ***D:*** Sam Um; ***W:*** Sam Um, Lauran James; ***C:*** Phil Curry; ***M:*** Rick DeJonge. **VIDEO**

Fighting with Kit Carson 🦴🦴 **1933** Famous guide and Indian fighter lead bands of settlers westward. Action-packed. Twelve chapters. **230m/B VHS, DVD.** Johnny Mack Brown, Noah Beery Sr., Noah Beery Jr., Betsy King Ross; ***D:*** Armand Schaefer, Colbert Clark.

Film Geek 🦴🦴 ½ **2006** Pitiful Scotty (Malkasian) loses his video store job because of the pain and suffering he's caused coworkers and customers (and viewers) alike with his endless chit-chat about the cinema and his lame zero-visitor movie website. The forlorn film fanatic gets really bummed out until his life takes an undue fairytale-ending twist thanks in part to a cool movie-loving chick he's preoccupied with. **78m/C DVD.** *US* Melik Malkasian, Tyler Gannon, Matt Morris; ***D:*** James Westby; ***C:*** Jason Hughes; ***M:*** Jason Wells.

Filth 🦴🦴 ½ **2008** A gently satiric look at the real-life morality crusade of staid British teacher and housewife Mary Whitehouse (Walters). It might be the swinging '60s in London, but Mary and her genteel circle are appalled by the sex and vulgarities that are turning up on the telly. Mary's crusade eventually gains a momentum that even lecherous, haughty BBC head, Sir Hugh Greene (Bonneville), can't ignore forever. Unfortunately, the deeper Mary gets into her clean-up campaign, the more self-righteous she becomes. **90m/C DVD.** *GB* Julie Walters, Hugh Bonneville, Alun Armstrong, Ron Cook, Georgie Glen, Timothy Davies; ***D:*** Andy de Emmony; ***W:*** Amanda Coe; ***C:*** David Odd; ***M:*** Norwell & Green. **TV**

The Filth and the Fury 🦴🦴 ½ **1999 (R)** British punk anarchists The Sex Pistols get their documentary due. Combines new and old footage and interviews of the (surviving) band members (Sid Vicious died of a heroin overdose). Director Temple previously covered the group in 1980's "The Great Rock 'n' Roll Swindle," which was told from the viewpoint of their former manager, Malcolm McLaren. **105m/C VHS, DVD.** *GB* John (Johnny Rotten) Lydon, Paul Cook, Steve Jones, Malcolm McLaren, Sid Vicious, Glen Matlock, Nancy Spungen; ***D:*** Julien Temple; ***M:*** John (Johnny Rotten) Lydon.

Filth and Wisdom 🦴🦴 **2008** Pop queen, author, actress, and now director Madonna helms this uneven comedy focusing on three flatmates struggling to make a name for themselves in modern day London. Ukrainian-born singer-songwriter A.K. (Gogol Bordello frontman Eugene Hutz) pays the bills as a male dominatrix, dancer Holly (Weston) turns to stripping once ballet stops paying the bills, and pharmacist Juliette (McClure), trying to fund a nursing trip to Africa, has to put up with her married boss's leering stares. Unfairly ravaged by international critics once the Material Girl compared her aspirations to that of Godard and Fellini, but still aimless and amateurish. **80m/C DVD.** *GB* Eugene Hutz, Richard E. Grant, Stephen Graham, Holly Weston, Vicky McLure, Inder Manocha, Elliot Levey, Francesca Kingdon; ***D:*** Madonna; ***W:*** Madonna, Dan Cadan; ***C:*** Tim Maurice Jones.

Final 🦴🦴 ½ **2001 (R)** Bill (Leary) wakes up confused in a Connecticut psychiatric hospital after an apparent suicide attempt. He's assigned to Ann (Davis), a young staff therapist who tries to help Bill sort out his memories from his delusions, which include the fear that he's to be executed by lethal injection and must escape. The story takes on some strange twists, including patients' rights and conspiracy theories. **111m/C VHS, DVD.** Denis Leary, Hope Davis, J.C. MacKenzie, Jim Gaffigan; ***D:*** Campbell Scott; ***W:*** Bruce McIntosh; ***C:*** Dan Gillham; ***M:*** Guy Davis.

The Final Alliance 🦴 **1989 (R)** A tough loner takes on a vicious motorcycle gang that's terrorizing a small town, and realizes that they're also responsible for his family's death. **90m/C VHS.** David Hasselhoff, John Saxon, Bo Hopkins, Jeanie Moore; ***D:*** Mario DiLeo.

Final Analysis 🦴🦴 ½ **1992 (R)** Glossy thriller starring Gere as a San Francisco psychiatrist who falls for the glamorous sister of one of his patients. Basinger plays the femme fatale and Thurman is Gere's sexually neurotic patient. Although heavily influenced by "Vertigo," this film never comes close to attaining the depth of Hitchcock's cinematic masterpiece. Roberts gives the most gripping performance in this slick suspense movie as Basinger's sleazy gangster husband. **125m/C VHS, DVD.** Richard Gere, Kim Basinger, Uma Thurman, Eric Roberts, Paul Guilfoyle, Keith David, Robert Harper, Jolyon Baker, Harris Yulin, Agustin Rodriguez; ***D:*** Phil Joanou; ***W:*** Wesley Strick, Robert Berger; ***C:*** Jordan Cronenweth; ***M:*** George Fenton.

Final Appeal 🦴🦴 ½ **1993 (PG-13)** Christine Biondi (Williams) is an abused wife, living in terror of her drug-addicted doctor husband, Ed. When Christine walks in on Ed and his mistress, she's forced to kill him in self-defense. But Ed's mistress swears it was murder and Christine's on trial. Now her only chance is her hard-drinking lawyer brother Perry (Dennehy)—who doesn't believe her story. Fact-based made for TV fare. **94m/C VHS.** JoBeth Williams, Brian Dennehy, Lindsay Crouse, Tom Mason, Eddie Jones, Ashley Crow, Betsy Brantley, Michael Beach; ***M:*** Charles Bernstein. **TV**

Final Approach 🦴🦴 **1991 (R)** Test pilot Jason Halsey (Sikking) crashes in the desert and awakens in the office of psychiatrist Dio Gottlieb (Elizondo). Halsey can't remember anything about his past, or his own name for that matter, but through word association games and psychological tests, he begins to remember as Gottlieb tries to pry information from his brain. Showy computer effects are excellent, but they only serve to fill holes in a story that has an unsatisfying ending. Notable as first film mde with digital sound. Also available in a letterboxed version. **100m/C VHS.** James B. Sikking, Hector Elizondo, Madolyn Smith, Kevin McCarthy, Cameo Kneuer, Wayne Duvall; ***D:*** Eric Steven Stahl.

Final Approach 🦴🦴 *Junior Pilot* **2004** Hijackers take control of a plane full of elementary students and, to make things worse, the pilot collapses. Luckily 10-year-old Ricky (Garrett)—who has mastered computer flight simulation games—is put in charge of landing the plane. He and his friends must keep the terrorists at bay. Family-oriented though perhaps a little scary for the younger set. **92m/C DVD.** Jordan Garrett, Larry Miller, Eric Roberts, Mark Dacascos, Angela Watson, David Rasche, Tim Thomerson, Steve Hynter; ***D:*** James Becket; ***W:*** James Becket; ***C:*** Denis Maloney; ***M:*** Peter Tomashek. **VIDEO**

Final Approach 🦴🦴 **2008** FBI agent Jack Bender (Cain) is part of a raid on a white supremacist compound. Sometime later, he just happens to be aboard a flight that's hijacked by members of the group, lead by the ruthless Gilliad (Hall), who want their leader released from prison. Jack quietly enlists some of the other passengers to assist him in overpowering the bad guys but there's not much new about this hostage-crisis-in-the-sky saga. **130m/C DVD.** Dean Cain, Anthony Michael Hall, Ernie Hudson, Sunny Mabrey, Lea Thompson, Barry Livingston, Tracey Gold, Richard Roundtree, Scott Paulin, Christopher Cousins, William Forsythe; ***D:*** Armand Mastroianni; ***W:*** Adam Armus, Kay Foster; ***C:*** Dane Peterson; ***M:*** Kevin Kiner. **CABLE**

Final Assignment 🦴 *The Moscow Chronicle* **1980** A Canadian TV reporter agrees to smuggle a dissident Soviet scientist's ill granddaughter out of Russia for treatment along with a videotape documenting tragic experiments on children with steroids. She manages to evade the KGB while carrying on with a Russian press officer, and enlists the support of a Jewish fur trader. Location shooting in Canada instead of Russia is just one pitfall of this production. **101m/C VHS.** *CA* Genevieve Bujold, Michael York, Burgess Meredith, Colleen Dewhurst; ***D:*** Paul Almond.

Final Combination 1/2 **1993** Boxer Welton (Stretch) lures two girls to his hotel room where he rapes and beat them to death. Trying to catch the psycho is hard-bitten, hard-drinking L.A. cop Matt Dickson (Madsen), who figures out he's after a serial killer using the names of famous boxers as aliases. Also involved is supposed journalist Catherine Briggs (Bonet), who offers info to Dickson but has her own agenda. Ordinary thriller with sillier-than-usual dialogue. **92m/C VHS.** Michael Madsen, Lisa Bonet, Gary Stretch, Tim Russ, Damian Chapa, Carmen Argenziano, Susan Byun; ***D:*** Nigel Dick; ***W:*** Larry Golin; ***M:*** Rolfe Kent.

Final Comedown **1972 (R)** A black revolutionary attempts to get white radicals behind his war against racism. He fails and starts a racial bloodbath. **84m/C VHS, DVD.** Billy Dee Williams, D'Urville Martin, Celia Kaye, Raymond St. Jacques, Pamela Jones, R.G. Armstrong; ***D:*** Oscar Williams.

The Final Conflict 1/2 *Omen 3: The Final Conflict* **1981 (R)** Unwelcomed third installment in the "Omen" series, concerning Satan's son Damien. Now 32, and the head of an international conglomerate, he is poised for world domination but fears another savior is born. Several monks and many babies meet gruesome deaths before he gets his comeuppance. The last theatrical release; the next entry was made for TV. **108m/C VHS, DVD.** Sam Neill, Lisa Harrow, Barnaby Holm, Rossano Brazzi, Don Gordon, Mason Adams, Robert Arden, Marc Boyle, Tommy Duggan, Richard Oldfield, Arwen Holm; ***D:*** Graham Baker; ***W:*** Andrew Birkin; ***C:*** Phil Meheux, Robert Paynter; ***M:*** Jerry Goldsmith.

The Final Countdown **1980 (PG)** A U.S. nuclear-powered aircraft carrier, caught in a time warp, is transported back to 1941, just hours before the bombing of Pearl Harbor. The commanders face the ultimate decision—leave history intact or stop the incident and thus avoid WWII. Excellent photography and a surprise ending. **92m/C VHS, DVD, Blu-ray Disc.** Kirk Douglas, Martin Sheen, Katharine Ross, James Farentino, Charles Durning; ***D:*** Don Taylor; ***W:*** Thomas Hunter, David Ambrose.

Final Cut 1/2 **1988** While filming in a secluded swampland, a crew stumbles on a local sheriff's crooked scheme and one by one, the crew members disappear. **92m/C VHS, DVD.** Carla De Lane, T.J. Kennedy, Joe Rainer, Brett Rice, Jordan Williams; ***D:*** Larry G. Brown.

The Final Cut **1995** Follows "House of Cards" and "To Play the King" in portraying the political adventures of Francis Urquardt (Richardson), Prime Minister. At 65, Urquardt has two goals: he wants to beat Margaret Thatcher's 11-year reign and he wants to establish a secret retirement fund (the plot involves Cyprus and could—finally—leads to Urquardt's downfall). Author Michael Dobbs objected to the adaptation and insisted his name be removed from the script. On two cassettes. **200m/C VHS, DVD.** *GB* Ian Richardson, Diane Fletcher, Paul Freeman, Isla Blair, Nick Brimble, Erika Hoffman, Nickolas Grace, Julian Fellowes; ***D:*** Mike Vardy; ***W:*** Andrew Davies; ***C:*** Ian Punter; ***M:*** Jim Parker.

The Final Cut **1996 (R)** John Pierce (Elliott) is a retired bomb squad specialist who's unwillingly called back to active duty to stop a bomber who's targeting Seattle. Along with ambitious officer Kathleen Hardy (Ramsay), Pierce tries to discover the bomber's next move—only to have suspicion fall upon himself. **99m/C VHS.** Sam Elliott, Charles Martin Smith, Anne Elizabeth Ramsay, Matt Craven, Ray Baker, John Hannah, Amanda Plummer; ***D:*** Roger Christian; ***W:*** Raul Inglis; ***C:*** Mike Southon; ***M:*** Ross Vannelli.

Final Cut **1998 (R)** A self-indulgent, apparently largely improvised mess. Jude (Law) has died and after his friends pay their respects at his funeral, his wife Sadie (Frost) insists they view the home video he'd been working on for the past two years. It turns out Jude must have been quite the voyeur—hidden cameras recorded his pals at their worst behavior, all of which is now revealed to the uncomfortable ensemble. **93m/C VHS, DVD.** *GB* Jude Law, Sadie Frost, Ray Winstone, Ray Burdis, Dominic Anciano, Perry Benson, John Beckett; ***D:*** Ray Burdis, Dominic Anciano; ***W:*** Ray Burdis, Dominic Anciano; ***C:*** John Ward; ***M:*** John Beckett.

The Final Cut 1/2 **2004 (PG-13)** After "One Hour Photo" Williams plays another guy involved in images, this time in a subdued sci-fi thriller. In the near-future, newborns are implanted with a chip that records their entire life—good, bad, and in-between. Alan Hakman (Williams) is a cutter who splices the appropriate footage of the deceased together as a funeral memorial. Then Hakman is asked to create a memorial of the recently-deceased chipmaker, a guy with some shady dealings that put Hakman in danger. Caviezel plays an anti-chip activist who wants an expose and Sorvino is Williams' ex-girlfriend who didn't care for his video obsession. The premise has certainly been done before and in much more enthralling movies. **104m/C DVD.** *CA GE* Robin Williams, Mira Sorvino, James (Jim) Caviezel, Mimi Kuzyk, Brendan Fletcher, Vincent Gale, Thom Bishops, Casey Dubois, Liam Ranger; ***D:*** Omar Naim; ***W:*** Omar Naim; ***C:*** Tak Fujimoto; ***M:*** Brian Tyler.

The Final Days 1/2 **1989 (PG)** TV drama follows the presidency of Richard Nixon (Smith) from Watergate through his resignation. Based on the Pulitzer Prize-winning book by Bob Woodward and Carl Bernstein. **150m/C VHS.** Lane Smith, Richard Kiley, David Ogden Stiers, Ed Flanders, Theodore Bikel; ***D:*** Richard Pearce.

Final Destination **2000 (R)** Teenager Alex (Sawa) predicts that a plane filled with classmates will explode. It does but he and some others manage to make it off the plane beforehand. Things get interesting (and a little philosophical) when the survivors start dying. Seems Death feels cheated and is getting even. Typical body count slasher genre gets a twist from the machinations of fate...or whatever. Filmmakers paid tribute to some of their favorite horror stars and directors with the characters' surnames. **97m/C VHS, DVD.** Devon Sawa, Ali Larter, Kristen Cloke, Daniel Roebuck, Roger Guenveur Smith, Chad E. Donella, Seann William Scott, Tony Todd, Kerr Smith, Amanda Detmer; ***D:*** James Wong; ***W:*** Glen Morgan, James Wong, Jeffrey Reddick; ***C:*** Robert McLachlan; ***M:*** Shirley Walker.

The Final Destination *Final Destination 4; Final Destination: Death Trip 3D* **2009 (R)** It's probably not the end, although the cliched plot and characters couldn't be thinner and the actors couldn't be prettier or more wooden. While at the racetrack, Nick (Campo) has a horrible premonition of cars crashing, the stands collapsing, and his friends dying. He persuades them to leave just in time, which makes Death very unhappy, and soon the survivors are getting killed off in very gruesome ways, including decapitation, impalement, and mutilation. The killings get boring and the 3D effects generally just highlight blood and organs spewing at the audience. **75m/C DVD.** *US* Nick Zano, Krista Allen, Bobby Campo, Shantel VanSanten, Haley Webb, Mykelti Williamson, Justin Welborn; ***D:*** David R. Ellis; ***W:*** Eric Bress; ***C:*** Glen MacPherson; ***M:*** Brian Tyler.

Final Destination 2 **2003 (R)** Sequel has the same premise as the original. Kimberly (Cook) has a horrifying vision of a traffic accident as she heads onto the highway. She blocks the ramp with her SUV, thus saving the lives of the drivers behind her. However, Death doesn't like to be cheated and the drivers start to die in bizarre accidents. Less philosophical than the first one, it ups the ante on the gore factor. Death also has a tendency to lay elaborate, convoluted plans to bring the intended victims to their gruesome deaths (kinda like Bond villains). The accidents can be so improbable that it borders on being tiresome, but if you accept the premise on a certain level you can enjoy it as a guilty pleasure. Larter returns as the sole survivor from the first movie and Tony Todd has a cameo as a morgue attendent. **100m/C VHS, DVD.** *US* Ali Larter, A.J. Cook, Michael Landes, Terrence "T.C." Carson, Lynda Boyd, Jonathan Cherry, Keegan Connor Tracy, Sarah Carter, Tony Todd, Justina Machado, David Paetkau, James Kirk; ***D:*** David R. Ellis; ***W:*** J. Mackye Gruber, Eric Bress; ***C:*** Gary Capo; ***M:*** Shirley Walker.

Final Destination 3 **2006 (R)** Death stalks a whole new batch of interchangeable teenagers who survive a huge rollercoaster crash thanks to the premonition of Wendy (Winstead). You weren't really expecting anything different, were you? Demises come in really gross, over-the-top, more-gore-the-better ways as the Grim Reaper makes like a deranged Wile E. Coyote. **92m/C DVD.** *US* Mary Elizabeth Winstead, Ryan Merriman, Kris Lemche, Texas Battle, Jesse Moss, Crystal Lowe, Chelan Simmons, Alexz Johnson, Gina Holden, Sam Easton, Amanda Crew; ***D:*** James Wong; ***W:*** James Wong, Glen Morgan; ***C:*** Robert McLachlan; ***M:*** Shirley Walker.

Final Draft 1/2 **2007** Once-successful screenwriter Paul Twist (Van der Beek) has been on a downhill slide since his divorce and has a bad case of writer's block. Twist decides to isolate himself in his apartment to work on his new screenplay, which involves characters and situations from his past, including a childhood incident about a circus clown dying in a fire. Too bad Paul starts losing sight of the boundaries between fiction and reality. **92m/C DVD.** James Van Der Beek, Tara Spencer-Nairn, Darryn Luci, Jeff Roop; ***D:*** Jonathan Dueck; ***W:*** Darryn Luci; ***C:*** Mick Reynolds; ***M:*** Ryan Latham. **VIDEO**

Final Embrace 1/2 **1992 (R)** When Laurel's famous sister is murdered she decides to do a little investigating on her own. She's aided by a young cop who just happened to be obsessed with the murdered woman. **88m/C VHS.** Robert Rusler, Nancy Valen, Dick Van Patten, Linda Dona; ***D:*** Oley Sassone; ***W:*** R.J. Robertson, Jim Wynorski; ***M:*** Daniel Licht.

Final Encounter *For the Cause* **2000 (R)** Confusing sci-fier based on the Warhammer videogame. A 100-year-old war between two technologically advanced colonies may finally be decided by a weapon of mass destruction. Sutherland (Whalen) is told by Gen. Murran (Cain) to lead a unit into enemy territory and stop the devastation. They're aided by witches who can turn computer programs into physical monsters but they also have to deal with a traitor. **98m/C DVD.** Dean Cain, Justin Whalin, Thomas Ian Griffith, Jodi Bianca Wise, Michelle Krusiec; ***D:*** David Douglas, Tim Douglas; ***W:*** David Douglas, Christopher Salazar; ***C:*** Adolfo Bartoli; ***M:*** Kevin Memley. **VIDEO**

Final Engagement 1/2 **2007** Jacqueline is being used as a pawn by her Miami criminal dad Jimmy Bombay. In order to join with an international drug cartel, Jimmy's arranged a marriage between his daughter and the drug lord's son. Jacqueline turns to a priest for guidance, but he may not be exactly what he seems either. **96m/C DVD.** Peter Greene, Arlene Tur, Greg Schroeder, Mike Maria, John Trapani, Ted Bell; ***D:*** Ari Vovak; ***C:*** Ari Vovak; ***M:*** Mel Lewis. **VIDEO**

Final Equinox 1/2 **1995** Mysterious alien artifact, which has the power to spontaneously create new life, is stolen and both the government and the mob try to be the first to find—and control—it. Cop Kove opposes them both. **90m/C VHS.** Martin Kove, Joe Lara, David Warner, Gary Kasper; ***D:*** Serge Rodnunsky; ***W:*** Serge Rodnunsky.

Final Exam WOOF! **1981 (R)** Psychotic killer stalks college students during exam week. This one's too boring to be scary. You root for the psycho to off everyone just to have the movie over. **90m/C VHS.** Cecile Bagdadi, Joel Rice; ***D:*** Jimmy Huston.

Final Exam 1/2 **1998** Ghetto drama about racism. High school basketball star Javon Robinson (McCray) is counting on getting a scholarship to college to get away from the drugs and violence that surrounds him. But when he fails English, he takes his teacher hostage at gunpoint and blames his failure on racism. **93m/C VHS.** Alvin O. McCray, John Mollica, Mario Velasquez, Gregor Manns, Augustina Montesino; ***D:*** John Mollica; ***W:*** John Mollica; ***C:*** Mike Dolgetta. **VIDEO**

The Final Executioner *The Last Warrior* **1983** A valiant man finds a way to stop the slaughter of innocent people in a post-nuclear world. **95m/C VHS.** William Mang, Marina Costa, Harrison Muller, Woody Strode; ***D:*** Romolo Guerrieri.

Final Fantasy: The Spirits Within 1/2 **2001 (PG-13)** Photorealistic computer-generated animation may be the highlight of this fantasy adventure, which is based on the videogame series. In the year 2065, life on Earth is threatened by aliens who steal energy from all living things on the planet. A team of scientists, led by Aki Ross (Ming-Na) and Dr. Sid (Sutherland) are at odds with the military, in the form of General Hein (Woods) over how to deal with the creatures. Plot, dialogue, and characterization, the movie's obvious weaknesses, definitely take a back seat to the visuals. The human characters, while not completely lifelike, are the closest anyone's come so far. Where the techology shines is in the landscapes and non-human creatures, which are all striking. **104m/C VHS, DVD, Blu-ray Disc, UMD.** *US* ***D:*** Hironobu Sakaguchi; ***W:*** Al Reinert, Jeff Vintar; ***M:*** Elliot Goldenthal; ***V:*** Ming Na, Alec Baldwin, Steve Buscemi, Peri Gilpin, Ving Rhames, Donald Sutherland, James Woods, Keith David, Jean Simmons, Matt McKenzie.

The Final Goal 1/2 **1994 (R)** Evil businessman (and ex-soccer star) Paulo Ramirez (Estrada) meddles with his country's current soccer star, who's playing in the Global Cup of Soccer. He wants the player to throw the game and thinks death threats will accomplish his goal. **85m/C VHS, DVD.** Erik Estrada, Steven Nijjar, Dean Butler; ***D:*** Jon Cassar.

The Final Hit **2002 (R)** Washed-up Hollywood producer Sonny Wexler (Reynolds) prefers to reminisce about his past success than raise the money to option a hot script and get back in the game. Maybe he should stick with his memories, since Sonny hooks up with a shady businessman who expects a guaranteed return on his investment—or else. **90m/C VHS, DVD.** Burt Reynolds, Lauren Holly, Benjamin Bratt, Sean Astin; ***D:*** Burt Reynolds.

Final Impact 1/2 **1991 (R)** Nick Taylor seeks vengeance on reigning kickboxing champ Jake Gerard through his prodigy, Danny Davis. Will sweet revenge for the wicked beating, suffered at the hands of Gerard years earlier, be his? **99m/C VHS, DVD.** Lorenzo Lamas, Kathleen Kinmont, Mimi Lesseos, Kathrin Lautner, Jeff Langton, Mike Worth; ***D:*** Joseph Merhi, Stephen Smoke; ***M:*** John Gonzalez.

Final Judgment **1992 (R)** Daniel Tyrone (Dourif) is a former gang member, now a troubled priest, who's the prime suspect in the Los Angeles murder of a beautiful stripper. Determined to find the killer Father Tyrone heads into L.A.'s underground sex industry to search for clues, which brings him face to face with evil and his own desires. **90m/C VHS.** Brad Dourif, Isaac Hayes, Maria Ford, Karen Black, Orson Bean, David Ledingham; ***D:*** Louis Morneau; ***W:*** Kirk Honeycutt, Louis Morneau.

Final Justice **1984 (R)** A small-town Texan sheriff wages a war against crime and corruption that carries him to Italy and the haunts of Mafia hitmen. **90m/C VHS, DVD.** Joe Don Baker, Rossano Brazzi, Patrizia Pellegrino, Venantino Venantini; ***D:*** Greydon Clark; ***W:*** Greydon Clark; ***C:*** Nicholas Josef von Sternberg; ***M:*** David Bell.

Final Justice **1994 (R)** Icky revenge drama has bad guys Red (Huff) and Bobby (Marotta) hiding out in a woodsy cabin that's owned by lawyer Alan Massard (Brolin) and his wife Amy (Fitzgerald). Unfortunately for them, the Massards have chosen to invite some friends and hang out at the cabin for the weekend, where the bad guys do nasty things before Alan manages to kill Bobby and trap Red. Then there's a stupid debate on just what to do with Red and more violence. **92m/C VHS.** James Brolin, Annie Fitzgerald, Brent Huff, Rick Marotta, Beau Billingslea; ***D:*** Brent Huff; ***W:*** Brent Huff.

Final Justice 1/2 **1998** Teacher Gwen (O'Toole) is outraged when a sleazy attorney (McKean) gets her murdered gay brother's killer acquitted. So she kidnaps him for some rough justice of her own but then winds up on trial herself. **120m/C VHS, DVD.** Annette O'Toole, Michael McKean, CCH Pounder, Brian Wimmer; ***D:*** Tommy Lee Wallace; ***W:*** Babs Greyhosky; ***M:*** Brian Tyler. **CABLE**

Final Mission **1984** Vengeful one-man army follows the professional hit man who slaughtered his family from L.A. to Laos. His pursuit leads to a jungle showdown. Gee, sounds like "Rambo, First Blood," though obviously less grand and glorious. **97m/C VHS.** Richard Young, John Dresden, Kaz Garas, Christine Tudor; ***D:*** Cirio H. Santiago.

Final Mission **1993 (R)** Virtual reality becomes a weapon in a military conspiracy when pilots start dying. Air Force jets are supposed to be unstoppable thanks to the new technology and a general is only too willing to blame the deaths on pilot error but one fly boy is out to find the truth. **91m/C VHS.** Billy Wirth, Corbin Bernsen, Elizabeth (Ward) Gracen, Steve Railsback.

Final Move **2006 (R)** After using his psychic powers to help the LAPD solve a chess-related serial-killer case, former detective Dan Marlowe (Schulze) becomes obsessed by thoughts that he might have put an innocent man to death. A rash of similar slayings seems to confirm his worst fears, causing him to rejoin the force to crack the case. Produces a serious case of deja vu for the onslaught of rehashed plot twists. **90m/C DVD.** Matt Schulze, Lochlyn Munro, Amanda Detmer, Daniel Baldwin, David Carradine; ***D:*** Joey Travolta; ***W:*** Richard Preston Jr., David Shoshan. **VIDEO**

Final Notice **1989** A detective tracking a serial killer has as his only evidence a trail of shredded photos of nude women. Not released theatrically. **91m/C VHS.** Gil Gerard, Steve Landesberg, Jackie Burroughs, Melody Anderson, Louise Fletcher, David Ogden Stiers, Kevin Hicks; ***D:*** Steven Hilliard Stern; ***W:*** John Gay; ***M:*** Tom Scott.

The Final Option *Who Dares Wins* **1982 (R)** An agent of England's Special Air Services team goes undercover as one of a band of anti-nuclear terrorists that take over the U.S. Embassy in London. Violent, but unconvincing. **125m/C VHS.** *GB* Lewis Collins, Judy Davis, Richard Widmark, Robert Webber, Edward Woodward, Ingrid Pitt, Kenneth Griffith, Tony Doyle, John Duttine; ***D:*** Ian Sharp; ***W:*** Reginald Rose; ***C:*** Phil Meheux.

Final Payback WOOF! **1999** A cast of faded TV stars long since past their prime time (Richard Grieco of "21 Jump Street," Corbin Bernsen of "L.A. Law," Martin Kove of "Cagney and Lacey," Priscilla Barnes of "Three's Company") collect their paychecks for this ineptly directed thriller that leaves no direct-to-video cliche unturned. Grieco stars as an ex-cop who finds himself "pushed over the fence" after he is framed for the murder of the police chief's wife. Gee, you think the police chief himself (B-movie vet John Saxon) may be involved in the conspiracy? No nudity and only one car explosion. Why bother? **102m/C VHS, DVD, UMD.** Richard Grieco, Corbin Bernsen, Martin Kove, Priscilla Barnes, John Saxon; ***D:*** Art Camacho.

The Final Programme 1/2 *The Last Days of Man on Earth* **1973** In this futuristic story, a man must rescue his sister—and the world—from their brother, who holds a microfilmed plan for global domination. Meanwhile, he must shield himself from the advances of a bisexual computer programmer who wants to make him father to a new, all-purpose human being. Based on the Michael Moorcock "Jerry Cornelius" stories, the film has gained a cult following. **85m/C VHS, DVD.** *GB* Hugh Griffith, Harry Andrews, Jon Finch, Jenny Runacre, Sterling Hayden, Patrick Magee, Sarah Douglas; ***D:*** Robert Fuest; ***W:*** Robert Fuest; ***C:*** Norman Warwick; ***M:*** Gerry Mulligan, Paul Beaver, Bernard Krause.

Final Round 1/2 **1993 (R)** A kickboxer and his girlfriend are kidnaped by a millionaire who stages hunt the humans games for the pleasure of his gambling syndicate. Stiff but with a few good action sequences. **90m/C VHS.** Lorenzo Lamas, Anthony de Longis, Kathleen Kinmont, Clark Johnson, Isabelle Jamieson; ***D:*** George Erschbamer; ***W:*** Arne Olsen; ***M:*** Graeme Coleman.

Final Sanction 1/2 **1989** After a nuclear holocaust exhausts their military resources, the U.S. and the Soviets each send one-man armies to battle each other for final control of the world. **90m/C VHS.** Robert Z'Dar, Ted Prior; ***D:*** David A. Prior; ***W:*** David A. Prior.

The Final Season **2007 (PG)** A tiny city in Iowa revels in the success of the local high school baseball team, with its multiple state championships. But administrators are plotting to merge the school with a neighboring high school, putting both coaches and players in jeopardy. Brand new head coach Kent Stock (Astin) wants the team to end their legendary run on a high note. No surprises here—there's a romance, a troubled transfer student who straightens up, a legendary final game. Yet another based-on-a-true-story sports drama that makes up for its flaws with a whole lotta heart. **114m/C DVD.** *US* Sean Astin, Powers Boothe, Rachael Leigh Cook, James Gammon, Larry Miller, Marshall Bell, Tom Arnold, Michael Angarano, Angela Paton; ***D:*** David Mickey Evans; ***W:*** Art D'Alessandro, James Grayford; ***C:*** Daniel Styoloff; ***M:*** Nathan Wang.

Final Shot: The Hank Gathers Story 1/2 **1992** Inspirational story of Gathers, who rose from the ghetto to become one of America's top college basketball stars at Loyola Marymount, until tragedy strikes during a game. **92m/C VHS, DVD.** Victor Love, Duane Davis, Nell Carter, George Kennedy; ***D:*** Charles Braverman; ***W:*** Fred Johnson; ***C:*** Stephen Blake; ***M:*** Stanley Clarke.

The Final Terror *Campsite Massacre; Bump in the Night; The Forest Primeval* **1983 (R)** Group of young campers is stalked by a mad killer in a desolate, backwoods area. Better-than-average stalked-teens entry is notable for the presence of some soon-to-be stars. **90m/C VHS, DVD.** John Friedrich, Rachel Ward, Adrian Zmed, Daryl Hannah, Joe Pantoliano, Ernest Harden Jr., Mark Metcalf, Lewis Smith, Cindy Harrel, Akosua Busia; ***D:*** Andrew Davis.

Final Verdict 1/2 **1991** A trial lawyer defends a man he knows is guilty, throwing his life and his family into turmoil. **93m/C VHS.** Treat Williams, Glenn Ford, Amy Wright, Olivia Burnette; ***D:*** Jack Fisk; ***C:*** Paul Elliott. **CABLE**

Final Voyage **1999 (R)** Hijackers, led by Ice-T, take over the cruise ship Britannica and their robbery of the ship's vault leads to a threat to sink the boat as well. Bodyguard Walsh manages to escape and wages a one-man war against the bad guys throughout the ship. It's better than "Speed 2." Wynorski directed under the pseudonym Jay Andrews. **95m/C VHS, DVD.** Ice-T, Dylan Walsh, Erika Eleniak, Claudia Christian, Ric(k) Ducommun; ***D:*** Jim Wynorski; ***W:*** Jim Wynorski, J. Everitt Morley; ***C:*** Ken Blakey; ***M:*** David Wurst, Eric Wurst. **VIDEO**

Final Warning 1/2 *Chernobyl: The Final Warning* **1990** A dramatization of actual events surrounding the 1986 melt-down of the nuclear power plant at Chernobyl. **94m/C VHS.** Jon Voight, Jason Robards Jr., Sammi Davis; ***D:*** Anthony Page. **TV**

The Finances of the Grand Duke *Die Finanzen des Grossherzogs* **1924** Rare Murnau comedy. The Grand Duke of Abacco (Liedtke) is in desperate need of money to save his bankrupt duchy. He proposes to Olga (Christians), the Grand Duchess of Russia, but some revolutionaries wish to thwart his plans until the Duke's adventurous friend, Philip (Abel), intervenes. **77m/B DVD.** *GE* Harry Liedtke, Alfred Abel, Mady Christians, Walter Rilla, Adolphe Engers, Julius Falkenstein; ***D:*** F.W. Murnau; ***W:*** Thea von Harbou; ***C:*** Karl Freund, Franz Planer.

Find Me Guilty **2006 (R)** Amusingly cutting mockery of courtroom ritual from master Lumet that's based on a true story. From 1986-88, 20 members of the New Jersey-based Lucchese crime family were prosecuted by the feds; all had attorneys except for low-level goombah Giacomo "Jackie Dee" DiNorscio (Diesel), who represented himself. Jackie wisecracks throughout the trial, garnering unexpected sympathy while causing agita in both the presiding judge (Silver) and mob boss Nick Calabrese (Rocco). Performances are excellent; note Sciorra's cameo as Jackie's bitter ex-wife. **125m/C DVD.** *US* Vin Diesel, Peter Dinklage, Linus Roache, Ron Silver, Alex Rocco, Annabella Sciorra, Richard Portnow, Robert Stanton, Raul Esparza, Domenick Lombardozzi, Paul Borghese, Jerry Adler, Marcia Jean Kurtz; ***D:*** Sidney Lumet; ***W:*** Sidney Lumet, T.J. Mancini, Robert J. McCrea; ***C:*** Ron Fortunato; ***M:*** Richard Glasser.

Find the Lady 1/2 *Call the Cops; Kopek and Broom* **1976 (R)** Candy assumes a supporting role as a bumbling cop who is part of an incompetent police team trying to rescue a kidnapped socialite. **100m/C VHS.** *CA* John Candy, Peter Cook, Mickey Rooney, Lawrence Dane, Alexandra Bastedo, Robert McHeady, Dick Emery, Michael Kirby, Delroy Lindo; ***D:*** John Trent; ***W:*** David Main, Claude Harz; ***C:*** Harry Waxman.

Finder's Fee **2001 (R)** A basic psycho-thriller set primarily in a New York apartment. Tepper (Palladino) finds a wallet in the street and contacts the owner, Avery Phillips (Jones). Later, Tepper also discovers a lottery ticket worth $6 mil inside the wallet and spills the news to his poker buddy, Fishman (Lillard), who can't keep the news from the other guys—Quigley (Reynolds) and Bolan (Mihok). Then, Avery shows up and sits in on the game, suposedly unaware of his potential good fortune. Now, does Tepper keep the ticket? And will his buddies also keep quiet? **99m/C VHS, DVD.** Erik Palladino, James Earl Jones, Matthew Lillard, Ryan Reynolds, Dash Mihok, Carly Pope, Robert Forster, Frances Bay; ***D:*** Jeff Probst; ***W:*** Jeff Probst; ***C:*** Francis Kenny; ***M:*** B.C. Smith.

Finders Keepers **1984 (R)** A wild assortment of characters on board a train en route from California to Nebraska search for $5 million hidden in the baggage car. **96m/C VHS.** Michael O'Keefe, Beverly D'Angelo, Ed Lauter, Louis Gossett Jr., Pamela Stephenson, Jim Carrey, David Wayne, Brian Dennehy, John Schuck; ***D:*** Richard Lester; ***W:*** Ronny Graham.

Finding Amanda 1/2 **2008 (R)** TV writer Taylor (Broderick) is a not-so-recovering alcohol, drug, and gambling addict with a failing marriage and career. In an effort to redeem himself (so he says), he heads off to Vegas to find his 20-year-old niece Amanda (Snow), an overly-perky hooker, and get her to clean up her life. Veers from pathos to comedy (and back again) with about as much control as the characters have. **96m/C DVD.** Matthew Broderick, Brittany Snow, Maura Tierney, Peter Facinelli, Steve Coogan; ***D:*** Peter Tolan; ***W:*** Peter Tolan; ***C:*** Tom Houghton; ***M:*** Christopher Tyng.

Finding Buck McHenry 1/2 **2000** When 11-year-old Jason (Schiffman) gets cut from Little League, he decides to form his own team. He persuades school custodian Buck McHenry (Davis) to coach but the man's knowledge about the game leads Jason to suspect that Buck is a Negro League legend who's long dropped out of sight and he decides to uncover the truth. **88m/C VHS, DVD.** Ossie Davis, Ruby Dee, Ernie Banks, Michael Schiffman, Duane McLaughlin, Karl Pruner, Megan Bower, Catherine Blythe; ***D:*** Charles Burnett; ***W:*** Alfred Slote; ***C:*** John L. (Ndiaga) Demps Jr.; ***M:*** Stephen James Taylor. **CABLE**

Finding Forrester **2000 (PG-13)** Underprivileged kid (Brown) from the Bronx, who has smarts and basketball skills, wins a scholarship to an Upper East Side prep school where he's befriended by wealthy classmate Paquin and eccentric writer Connery. Predictable, cloying script almost undermines excellent performances by Connery and newcomer Brown. The only good thing about the screenplay is their dialogue together. **133m/C VHS, DVD.** Anna Paquin, Sean Connery, Rob Brown, F. Murray Abraham, Busta Rhymes, April Grace, Michael Nouri, Zane R. (Lil' Zane) Copeland Jr.; ***D:*** Gus Van Sant; ***W:*** Mike Rich; ***C:*** Harris Savides; ***M:*** Hal Willner.

Finding Graceland 1/2 **1998 (PG-13)** Down-on-his-luck Byron (Schaech) is driving his 1959 Cadillac convertible through New Mexico when he stops for a hitchhiker and Elvis impersonator (Keitel), who's on his way to Memphis. Except this Elvis believes he's the real thing and he's heading for his Graceland home. Odd things seem to happen to Byron as long as Elvis is around. Not the least being his finding Marilyn Monroe impersonator, Ashley (Fonda). **97m/C VHS, DVD.** Johnathon Schaech, Harvey Keitel, Bridget Fonda, Gretchen Mol; ***D:*** David Winkler; ***W:*** Jason Horwitch; ***C:*** Elliot Davis; ***M:*** Stephen Endelman.

Finding Home **2003 (PG-13)** Workaholic exec Amanda (Brenner) inherits her grandmother Esther's (Fletcher) B&B, located on a remote island off the Maine coast. When Amanda travels there to decide if she should sell the property, she begins having flashbacks of some terrible childhood event that she has repressed. But maybe things are better left forgotten. Conventional family melodrama in a picturesque setting. **124m/C DVD.** Lisa Brenner, Genevieve Bujold, Louise Fletcher, Johnny Messner, Justin Henry, Jason Miller, Misha Collins; ***D:*** Lawrence Foldes; ***W:*** Lawrence Foldes, Grafton S. Harper; ***C:*** Jeffrey Seckendorf; ***M:*** Joseph Conlan. **VIDEO**

Finding Nemo **2003 (G)** Despite the dead mom beginning, this is not from the Disney animation studio. It's Pixar (of "Toy Story" fame). Little clown fish Nemo (Gould) was born with an undersized fin and is the sole survivor of a barracuda attack. This makes nervous dad Marlin (Brooks) overprotective. When curious Nemo is scooped up by a scuba diver for life in a fish tank, it's dad to the rescue! He's aided by chipper blue tang Dory (DeGeneres), who unfortunately suffers from short-term memory loss, a sea turtle (director Stanton), and other denizens of both sea and air (including a helpful pelican), while Nemo is making new friends (and escape plans) with his tank mates. Since water is considered the hardest thing to animate, the undersea sequences are particularly breathtaking. There's the usual humor to keep adults interested as well as sweetness amidst the comedy. **101m/C VHS, DVD.** *US* ***D:*** Andrew Stanton; ***W:*** Andrew Stanton, Bob Peterson, Dave Reynolds; ***C:*** Sharon Calahan, Jeremy Lasky; ***M:*** Thomas Newman; ***V:*** Albert Brooks, Ellen DeGeneres, Willem Dafoe, Alexander Gould, Barry Humphries, Andrew Stanton, Brad Garrett, Allison Janney, Austin Pendleton, Stephen (Steve) Root, Vicki Lewis, Joe Ranft, Geoffrey Rush, Eric Bana, Bruce Spence, Elizabeth Perkins, Erik Per Sullivan, John Ratzenberger, Bill Hunter, LuLu Ebeling, Erica Beck, Bob Peterson. Oscars '03: Animated Film.

Finding Neverland **2004 (PG)** Genteel drama takes the usual biographical license and makes sometimes-obvious conclusions between the life and work of author J.M. Barrie (an equally genteel Depp). A celebrated writer in Edwardian London, Barrie is looking for inspiration when he meets recent widow Sylvia Llewelyn Davies (Winslet) and her four young sons: Peter (Highmore), Jack (Prospero), George (Roud), and Michael (Spill). The childless Barrie, detached from his own marriage, becomes increasingly involved with their lives, leading them in games and telling stories that revitalize his own creative juices, which result in the successful 1904 theatrical opening of his new work, "Peter Pan." Though Barrie maintains a courtly, platonic friendship with Sylvia, his actions alarm his wife, Mary (Mitchell), and Sylvia's formidable mother, Emma (Christie). A three-hanky affair, beautifully photographed by Schaefer, and adapted from the play "The Man Who Was Peter Pan" by Allan Knee. **108m/C DVD, Blu-ray Disc.** *US* Johnny Depp, Kate Winslet, Julie Christie, Radha Mitchell, Dustin Hoffman, Kelly Macdonald, Ian Hart, Eileen Essell, Freddie Highmore, Joe Prospero, Nick Roud, Luke Spill; ***D:*** Marc Forster; ***W:*** David Magee; ***C:*** Roberto Schaefer; ***M:*** Jan A.P. Kaczmarek. Oscars '04: Orig. Score.

Finding North **1997** Predictable dramedy about the friendship between a straight woman and gay man. Talkative, bored bank clerk Rhonda (Makkena) meets suicidal yuppie, Travis (Hickey), who's just lost his lover to AIDS, and decides to help him regain his emotional balance. Even if this means following him from New York to the small Texas town where Travis' late lover grew up. **95m/C VHS, DVD.** Wendy Makkena,

John Benjamin Hickey, Angela Pietropinto, Freddie Roman, Molly McClure; *D:* Tanya Wexler; *W:* Kim Powers; *C:* Michael Barrett; *V:* Jonathan Walker.

Finding Rin Tin Tin 🦴🦴 **2007 (PG)** How a star is discovered. Corporal Lee Duncan (Jensen) finds a German shepherd puppy in France and uses his expertise as a POW dog handler to train Rin Tin Tin to aid his WWI platoon. When the war is over, Lee decides to take his photogenic find to Hollywood and see if they can get in the movies, and the dog becomes a star. **90m/C DVD.** Ben Cross, William Hope, Todd Jensen, Tyler Jensen; *D:* Dan Lerner; *W:* David Rolland, Jim Tierney; *C:* Emil Topuzov; *M:* Stephen (Steve) Edwards.

Fine Dead Girls 🦴🦴 *Fine Mrtve Djevojke* **2002** Lesbian couple Iva and Marija try to keep their relationship a secret when they move to a new apartment in Zagreb. But what seems to be a safe haven turns out to be filled with creepy, sometimes violent neighbors and Olga, their nosy, bigoted landlady. Olga begins a witch-hunt against the new tenants that leads to rape, kidnapping, and murder, which writer/director Matanic uses as a microcosm for the upheavals of Croatian society at the time. Croatian with subtitles. **77m/C DVD.** *CR* Olga Pakalovic, Jadranka Djokic, Nina Violic, Kresimir Mikic, Inge Apelt, Ivica Vidovic; *D:* Dalibor Matanic; *W:* Dalibor Matanic; *C:* Branko Linta; *M:* Jura Ferina.

Fine Gold 🦴🦴 **1988** A false charge of embezzlement leaves a man without home and family, so he decides to turn the tables on those who betrayed him. **91m/C VHS.** Andrew Stevens, Ray Walston, Ted Wass, Stewart Granger, Lloyd Bochner, Jane Badler; *D:* Jose Antonio De La Loma.

A Fine Madness 🦴🦴🦴 **1966** A near-classic comedy about a lusty, rebellious poet thrashing against the pressures of the modern world, and fending off a bevy of lobotomy-happy psychiatrists. Shot on location in New York City, based on Elliot Baker's novel. **104m/C VHS, DVD.** Sean Connery, Joanne Woodward, Jean Seberg, Patrick O'Neal, Colleen Dewhurst, Clive Revill, John Fiedler, Werner Peters, Kay Medford, Jackie Coogan, Zohra Lampert, Sorrell Booke, Sue Ane Langdon, Bibi Osterwald, Gerald S. O'Loughlin, Richard S. Castellano; *D:* Irvin Kershner; *W:* Elliott Baker; *C:* Ted D. McCord; *M:* John Addison.

A Fine Mess 🦴 **1/2 1986 (PG)** Two buffoons cash in when one overhears a plan to dope a racehorse, but they are soon fleeing the plotters' slapstick pursuit. The plot is further complicated by the romantic interest of a gangster's wife. The TV popularity of the two stars did not translate to the big screen; perhaps it's Edwards's fault. **100m/C VHS, DVD.** Ted Danson, Howie Mandel, Richard Mulligan, Stuart Margolin, Maria Conchita Alonso, Paul Sorvino; *D:* Blake Edwards; *W:* Blake Edwards; *C:* Harry Stradling Jr.; *M:* Henry Mancini.

A Fine Romance 🦴🦴 **1992 (PG-13)** An improbable romance set in Paris features Andrews and Mastroianni as abandoned spouses falling in love. Andrews is the prim English Pamela who has been abandoned by her docter husband. Mastroianni is the irrepresible Cesareo, whose wife has just happened to run off with the aforementioned doctor. They meet to plan how to get their spouses back and wind up with opposites attracting. Not much story and the charm is spread thin. Based on the play "Tchin, Tchin" by Francois Billetdoux. **83m/C VHS, DVD.** Julie Andrews, Marcello Mastroianni, Ian Fitzgibbon, Jean-Pierre Castaldi, Jean-Jacques Dulon, Maria Machado, Jean-Michel Cannone, Catherine Jarrett, Gene Saks; *W:* Ronald Harwood; *M:* Pino Donaggio.

The Finest Hour 🦴 **1/2 1991 (R)** Two Navy buddies have a falling out when they both fall for the same woman. But they must put aside their differences when their next mission sends them to Iraq to deal with the deadly threat of biological warfare. **105m/C VHS.** Rob Lowe, Gale Hansen, Tracy Griffith, Eb Lottimer; *D:* Shimon Dotan; *W:* Shimon Dotan.

The Finger Man 🦴🦴 **1/2 1955** An ex-con cooperates with the feds rather than return to jail. The deal is that he gets the dirt on an underworld crime boss. Solid performances. **82m/B VHS.** Frank Lovejoy, Forrest Tucker, Peggy Castle, Timothy Carey, Glenn Gordon, John Cliff, William P. Leicester, John Close, Hugh Sanders, Joi Lansing, Charles Maxwell; *D:* Harold Schuster; *W:* Warren Douglas; *C:* William Sickner; *M:* Paul Dunlap.

Finger on the Trigger 🦴🦴 *El Dedo En El Gatillo* **1965** Veterans from both sides of the Civil War are after a hidden supply of gold, but find that they must band together to fend off an Indian attack. Routine. **89m/C VHS.** Rory Calhoun, James Philbrook, Todd Martin, Silvia Solar, Brad Talbot; *D:* Sidney W. Pink.

Fingerprints Don't Lie 🦴 **1951** A fingerprint expert pins the murder of the town mayor on an innocent guy, then suspects a frame-up. **56m/B VHS, DVD.** Richard Travis, Sheila Ryan, Tom Neal; *D:* Sam Newfield.

Fingers 🦴🦴🦴 **1978 (R)** Keitel is Johnny Fingers, a mobster's son, reluctantly working as a mob debt-collector, all the while dreaming of his ambitions to be a concert pianist. The divisions between his dreams and reality cause him to crack. Toback's first film generates psychological tension and excellent performances. **89m/C VHS, DVD.** Harvey Keitel, Tisa Farrow, Jim Brown, James Toback, Danny Aiello, Tanya Roberts, Marian Seldes, Michael V. Gazzo, Lenny Montana; *D:* James Toback; *W:* James Toback; *C:* Michael Chapman; *M:* George Barrie.

Finian's Rainbow 🦴🦴🦴 **1968 (G)** A leprechaun comes to America to steal back a pot of gold taken by an Irishman and his daughter in this fanciful musical comedy based on a 1947 Broadway hit. Both the sprite and the girl find romance; the sharecropping locals are saved by the cash; a bigot learns the error of his ways; and Finian (Astaire) dances off to new adventures. The fine production and talented cast are not used to their best advantage by the director who proved much better suited for "The Godfather." Entertaining, nonetheless. ♫ How Are Things in Glocca Morra?; Look To the Rainbow; That Old Devil Moon; If This Isn't Love; Something Sort of Grandish; The Be-Gat; This Time of Year; The Great Come and Get It Day; When I'm Not Near the Girl I Love. **141m/C VHS, DVD.** Fred Astaire, Petula Clark, Tommy Steele, Keenan Wynn, Al Freeman Jr., Don Francks, Susan Hancock, Dolph Sweet; *D:* Francis Ford Coppola.

Finish Line 🦴🦴 **1/2 1989** A high school track star turns to steroids to enhance his performance after being pushed by an overzealous father. The father-and-son Brolins play the pair. **100m/C VHS.** James Brolin, Josh Brolin, Mariska Hargitay, Kristoff St. John, John Finnegan, Billy Vera, Stephen Lang; *D:* John Nicolella. **CABLE**

Finish Line 🦴 **1/2 2008** Chachi's a bad guy—is nothing sacred? Mitch Camponella (Page) needs a new car to compete in the pro stock car racing circuit. So he agrees to become a bodyguard to Jessie (Cole), the flirty daughter of shady importer Frank Chase (Baio). Chase is smuggling bomb-making materials into the U.S. and naive Mitch is forced to work undercover for the FBI, which makes every situation more dangerous. **86m/C DVD.** Sam Page, Scott Baio, Dan Lauria, Ian Reed Kesler, John Enos, Taylor Cole, Timilee Romolini; *D:* Gerry Lively; *W:* Ron McGee; *C:* Maximo Munzi; *M:* Paul D'Amour. **TV**

Finishing School 🦴 **1/2 1933** Girls' school roommates Rogers and Dee experience heartaches and loves lost while enduring disinterested parents and snobbish peers. Boxoffice bomb when released, despite a strong cast. **73m/B VHS.** Ginger Rogers, Frances Dee, George Nicholls Jr., Beulah Bondi, Bruce Cabot, Billie Burke, John Halliday, Sara Haden, Jack Norton, Joan Barclay, Jane Darwell, John David Horsley; *D:* George Nicholls Jr.; *M:* Max Steiner.

The Finishing Touch 🦴🦴 **1992 (R)** Someone is stalking L.A.'s most gorgeous women and Detective Sam Stone (Nader) is assigned to the case. Stone discovers his prime suspect is a video artist with a taste for pornography. When Stone's investigation is cut short, his ex-wife, Detective Hannah Stone (Hack) is brought in to take over the case. Unfortunately, she finds herself falling for the suspect in this erotic thriller. **82m/C VHS.** Michael Nader, Shelley Hack, Arnold Vosloo, Art Evans, Clark Johnson, Theodore (Ted) Raimi; *D:* Fred Gallo.

Finnegan Begin Again 🦴🦴 **1984** A middle-aged schoolteacher and a grouchy, 65-year-old newspaper editor find romance despite their other obligations. Winning performances add charm to this cable TV movie. **112m/C VHS.** Mary Tyler Moore, Robert Preston, Sam Waterston, Sylvia Sidney, David Huddleston; *D:* Joan Micklin Silver. **CABLE**

Finnegan's Wake 🦴🦴 **1/2** *Passages from "Finnegans Wake"; Passages from James Joyce's "Finnegans Wake"* **1965** Portions of the filmed adaptation of James Joyce's novel are shown in this program along with an interview with producer/director Mary Ellen Bute. **92m/B VHS.** Peter Haskell, Martin J. Kelley, Jane Reilly, Page Johnson; *D:* Mary Ellen Bute; *W:* Mary Ellen Bute; *C:* Ted Nemeth; *M:* Elliot Kaplan.

Fiona 🦴 **1/2 1998** Fiona was abandoned as a baby, raised in an abusive foster home, and is now a crack-smoking hooker on the streets of New York. After casually killing three cops, she hides out in a crackhouse where she hooks up with Anita—who naturally turns out to be Fiona's long-lost mama. Film is a blend of fiction and documentary footage of real prostitutes and drug houses. **85m/C VHS, DVD.** Anna Thomson, Mike Hodge, Anna Grace, Felicia Maguire; *D:* Amos Kollek; *W:* Amos Kollek; *C:* Ed Talavera; *M:* Alison Gordy.

Fiorile 🦴🦴🦴 *Wild Flower* **1993 (PG-13)** Covers several generations of a Tuscan clan living under a family curse which dates back to Napoleon's invasion of Italy. At that time Jean, a handsome French lieutenant, falls in love with Tuscan peasant girl Elisabetta, nicknamed Fiorile. When Jean is executed for a theft committed by her brother, the pregnant Fiorile vows revenge. Throughout sucessive generations, haunted by the past, the family's personal bad luck persists. Several of the actors play their character's ancestors, lending continuity. Attractive cast does well with the Taviani brothers' visual style and romantic narrative. In Italian with English subtitles. **118m/C VHS.** *IT* Michael Vartan, Galatea Ranzi, Claudio Bigagli, Lino Capolicchio, Constanze Engelbrecht, Athina Cenci, Giovanni Guidelli, Chiara Caselli; *D:* Paolo Taviani, Vittorio Taviani; *W:* Paolo Taviani, Vittorio Taviani, Sandro Petraglia; *C:* Giuseppe Lanci; *M:* Nicola Piovani.

Fire 🦴 **1/2 1977** A fire started by an escaped convict rages through Oregon timberland in this suspenseful Irwin Allen disaster drama. **98m/C VHS.** Ernest Borgnine, Vera Miles, Patty Duke, Alex Cord, Donna Mills; *D:* Earl Bellamy. **TV**

Fire 🦴🦴 **1/2 1996** Follows the relationship of two sisters-in-law in New Delhi—both stuck in frustrating, loveless marriages—while examining the harsh patriarchal culture of India. Radha (Azmi) is married to Ashok (Kharbanda), a video store clerk who has taken a vow of celibacy under the teachings of a scruffy swami. Sita (Das) is married to Ashok's brother Jatin (Jaaferi), who is openly having an affair with a Chinese Canadian woman. As her frustration grows, the younger Sita acts on her attraction to her sister-in-law and the two begin a lesbian affair, which is taboo in the strict Hindu culture. Dialogue is in "Hinglish," or English with occasional Hindi phrases thrown in. The attitudes portrayed must exist, because the film was banned in India. **104m/C VHS, DVD.** *CA* Shabana Azmi, Nandita Das, Kulbashan Kharbanda, Jaaved Jaaferi, Ranjit (Chaudry) Chowdhry, Kushal Rekhi; *D:* Deepa Mehta; *W:* Deepa Mehta; *C:* Giles Nuttgens; *M:* A.R. Rahman.

Fire Alarm 🦴 **1932** A change of scene for Western star Brown as he portrays a fireman who, in-between his work, romances a career girl. **67m/B VHS, DVD.** Johnny Mack Brown, Noel Francis; *D:* Karl Brown; *W:* Karl Brown, I.E. Chadwick.

Fire and Ice 🦴🦴 **1/2 1983 (PG)** An animated adventure film that culminates in a tense battle between good and evil, surrounded by the mystical elements of the ancient past. Designed by Frank Frazetta. **81m/C VHS, DVD.** Randy Norton, Cynthia Leake; *D:* Ralph Bakshi; *W:* Ralph Bakshi, Willy Bogner, Gerry Conway; *V:* Susan Tyrrell, William Ostrander.

Fire and Ice 🦴 **1987 (PG)** A tale of love on the slopes. Two skiers realize that their feelings for each other are perhaps even stronger than their feelings about skiing. You won't care though, except for some fine ski footage. **83m/C VHS, DVD.** Suzy Chaffee, John Eaves; *D:* Willy Bogner; *W:* George Schlatter; *M:* Harold Faltermeyer; *Nar:* John Denver.

Fire and Rain 🦴🦴 **1989** Based on the real-life crash of a Delta Airlines plane in Dallas and the rescue efforts made following the disaster. Familiar cast-members turn in decent performance. **89m/C VHS.** Angie Dickinson, Charles Haid, Tom Bosley, David Hasselhoff, Robert Guillaume, Susan Ruttan, John Beck, Patti LaBelle, Dean Jones, Lawrence Pressman, Penny Fuller; *D:* Jerry Jameson; *W:* Gary Sherman. **TV**

Fire and Sword 🦴 **1982** A Cornish knight must choose between loyalty for king and country and the love of an Irish woman in this medieval drama. A not very inspired retelling of the Tristan and Isolde legend. **84m/C VHS.** *GB* Peter Firth, Leigh Lawson, Antonia Preser, Christopher Waitz; *D:* Veith von Furstenberg.

Fire Birds 🦴 *Wings of the Apache* **1990 (PG-13)** Army attack helicopters and the people who fly them are used in the war on drugs in South America. Failed to match the exciting flight sequences, the romantic interest, or the boxoffice of "Top Gun." **85m/C VHS, DVD.** Nicolas Cage, Tommy Lee Jones, Sean Young, Bryan Kestner, Dale Dye, Mary Ellen Trainor, J.A. Preston, Peter Onorati; *D:* David Green; *W:* Dale Dye, Nick Thiel, Paul F. Edwards; *M:* David Newman.

Fire Down Below 🦴 **1/2 1957** Hayworth is the been-around-the-block beauty who persuades Mitchum and Lemmon, two small-time smugglers, to take her to a safe haven, no questions asked. Both men fall for her obvious charms, causing them to have a falling out until a life or death situation puts their friendship to the test. An unoriginal melodrama indifferently acted by everyone but Lemmon. Good location work in Trinidad and Tobago. **116m/C VHS, DVD.** *GB* Robert Mitchum, Jack Lemmon, Rita Hayworth, Herbert Lom, Anthony Newley; *D:* Robert Parrish; *W:* Irwin Shaw; *C:* Desmond Dickinson; *M:* Arthur Benjamin, Douglas Gamley.

Fire Down Below 🦴 **1997 (R)** Seagal comes armed with his trademark ponytail, martial arts expertise, big leather jackets, and environment-friendly message to the Appalachians in this hoedown showdown. As undercover (yeah, he blends right in) EPA agent Jack Taggart, Seagal must stop evil industrialist Hanner (Kristofferson) from dumping toxic waste. Of course, the company town sends the usual band of thugs (thoughtfully attacking one at a time) to make him go away. He finds allies in the local outcasts (Helgenberger and Stanton) en route to the final confrontation. Not Seagal's worst, but that's not saying much. Even the usually impressive fight scenes become tedious after a while. At least he didn't try to direct this one. Originally conceived as a Bruce Willis project at Columbia. **105m/C VHS, DVD.** Steven Seagal, Marg Helgenberger, Kris Kristofferson, Harry Dean Stanton, Stephen Lang, Levon Helm, Brad Hunt, Richard Masur, Ed Bruce, Randy Travis, Mark Collie, Alex Harvey; *D:* Felix Alcala; *W:* Jeb Stuart; *C:* Tom Houghton; *M:* Nick Glennie-Smith.

Fire, Ice and Dynamite 🦴 **1/2 1991 (PG)** Moore is onscreen only briefly as an eccentric tycoon who fakes suicide to watch several teams of challengers scramble in a madcap winter-sports contest for his millions. A German-made avalanche of crazy stunts, bad jokes, and product plugs for countless European companies, commencing with a literal parade of guests, from astronaut Buzz Aldrin to soul man Isaac Hayes. Numbing; must be seen to be believed. **105m/C VHS.** Roger Moore, Shari Belafonte, Simon Shepherd, Uwe Ochsenknecht, Marjoe Gortner; *D:* Willy Bogner.

Fire in the Night 🦴 **1/2 1985** In a small Southern town, a beautiful and sure-footed woman battles the limitless resources of the town's predominant dynastic family. **89m/C VHS.** Patrick St. Esprit, Muni Zano, Graciela Casillas, John Martin; ***D:*** John Steven Soet; ***C:*** Gene Jackson.

Fire in the Sky **1993 (PG-13)** Mysterious disappearance of Sweeney sparks a criminal investigation, until he returns, claiming he was abducted by aliens. Though everybody doubts his story, viewers won't, since the alleged aliens have already made an appearance, shifting the focus to Sweeney as he tries to convince skeptics that his trauma is genuine. Perhaps this mirrors what director Lieberman went through while trying to convince backers the film should be made. He could have benefitted by understanding the difference between what he was telling viewers and what he was showing them. Captivating special effects are one of the few bright spots. Based on a story that might be true. **98m/C VHS, DVD.** D.B. Sweeney, Robert Patrick, Craig Sheffer, Peter Berg, James Garner, Henry Thomas; ***D:*** Robert Lieberman; ***W:*** Tracy Torme; ***M:*** Mark Isham.

The Fire in the Stone **1985** A young boy discovers an opal mine and dreams of using the treasure to reunite his family. However, when the jewels are stolen from him, he enlists his friends to help get them back. Based on the novel by Colin Thiele. **97m/C VHS.** *AU* Paul Smith, Linda Hartley, Theo Pertsindis; ***D:*** Gary Conway; ***W:*** Roger Dunn; ***C:*** Ross Berryman; ***M:*** Isabel Meier, Matthias Bonnefoy.

Fire Maidens from Outer Space **1956** Fire maidens prove to be true to the space opera code that dictates that all alien women be in desperate need of male company. Astronauts on an expedition to Jupiter's 13th moon discover the lost civilization of Atlantis, which, as luck would have it, is inhabited by women only. Possibly an idea before its time, it might've been better had it been made in the '60s, when space-exploitation came into its own. **80m/B VHS, DVD.** *GB* Anthony Dexter, Susan Shaw, Paul Carpenter, Harry Fowler, Jacqueline Curtiss, Sydney Tafler, Maya Koumani, Jan Holden, Kim Parker, Rodney Diak, Owen Berry; ***D:*** Cy Roth; ***W:*** Cy Roth; ***C:*** Ian Struthers.

Fire Monsters Against the Son of Hercules *Maciste Contro i Mostri* **1962** The son of the muscular one does battle with a hydra-headed monster in this average sword and sandal adventure. **82m/C VHS, DVD.** *IT* Reg Lewis, Margaret Lee; ***D:*** Guido Malatesta; ***W:*** Guido Malatesta, Arpad De Riso; ***C:*** Guiseppe La Torre; ***M:*** Guido Robuschi, Gian Stellari.

The Fire Next Time **1/2 1993** In the year 2017, the United States is being ravaged by an ecological holocaust caused by a deadly combination of pollution and global warming. Nelson, Bedelia, and their children are forced from their Louisiana home by a natural disaster and decide to head for better times in Canada. Their travels aren't easy. **195m/C VHS, DVD.** Craig T. Nelson, Bonnie Bedelia, Jurgen Prochnow, Richard Farnsworth, Justin Whalin, Charles Haid, Sal Lopez, Shawn Toovey, Ashley Jones; ***Cameos:*** Odetta; ***D:*** Tom McLoughlin; ***W:*** James Henerson. **TV**

Fire on the Amazon **1/2 1993 (R)** Really dumb "save-the-environment" movie with Bullock the rainforest activist and Sheffer the photojournalist. The duo hook up to investigate the assassination of an environmentalist. The big woo-hoo is Bullock's brief nude sex scene with Sheffer. **81m/C VHS, DVD.** Sandra Bullock, Craig Sheffer, Judith Chapman, Juan Fernandez; ***D:*** Luis Llosa; ***W:*** Catherine Cyran, Jane Gray; ***C:*** Pili Flores-Guerra; ***M:*** Roy J. Ravio.

Fire Over England **1937** Young naval officer volunteers to spy at the Spanish court to learn the plans for the invasion of his native England and to identify the traitors among the English nobility. He arouses the romantic interest of his queen, Elizabeth I, one of her ladies, and a Spanish noblewoman who helps with his missions, and later leads the fleet to victory over the huge Spanish Armada. The first on-screen pairing of Olivier and Leigh is just one of the many virtues of this entertaining drama. **81m/B VHS, DVD.** *GB* Flora Robson, Raymond Massey, Laurence Olivier, Vivien Leigh, Leslie Banks, James Mason; ***D:*** William K. Howard; ***W:*** Clemence Dane, Sergei Nolbandov; ***C:*** James Wong Howe; ***M:*** Richard Addinsell.

Fire Serpent **WOOF! 2007 (R)** Another laughably bad cheapie from the Sci-Fi Channel. Solar flares cast off living flames that occasionally make it to Earth, not only starting fires but possessing people. A firefighter (Brendon) is drawn into a government conspiracy involving flame hunter Dutch Fallon (Mantooth), an arson investigator (Holt), and a Fed (Beltran). **89m/C DVD.** Nicholas Brendon, Randolph Mantooth, Sandrine Holt, Robert Beltran; ***D:*** John Terlesky; ***W:*** Judith Reeves-Stevens, Garfield Reeves-Stevens; ***C:*** Patrick Mcgowan; ***M:*** Chuck Cirino. **CABLE**

Fire with Fire **1986 (PG-13)** A boy at a juvenile detention center and a Catholic school girl fall in love. However, they find themselves on the run from the law when he escapes to be with her. Sheffer and Madsen are appealing in this otherwise unspectacular film. **103m/C VHS.** Craig Sheffer, Virginia Madsen, Jon Polito, Kate Reid, Jean Smart, D.B. Sweeney; ***D:*** Duncan Gibbins; ***W:*** Bill Phillips, Paul Boorstin, Sharon Boorstin; ***M:*** Howard Shore.

The Fire Within *Le Feu Follet; Fuoco Fatuo* **1964** Ronet plays an alcoholic writer recently released from a sanitorium after a breakdown. Believing his life will only continue its downward spiral, he pays a final visit to friends and calmly plots his suicide. Malle clearly and pitilessly describes a man beyond despair. Based on a novel by Pierre Drieu La Rochelle, which itself fictionalized the suicide of writer Jacques Rigaut. In French with English subtitles. **104m/B VHS.** *FR* Bernard Noel, Jeanne Moreau, Alexandra Stewart, Henri Serre, Maurice Ronet, Lena Skerla, Yvonne Clech, Hubert Deschamps, Jean-Paul Moulinot; ***D:*** Louis Malle; ***W:*** Louis Malle; ***C:*** Ghislan Cloquet.

Fireback **1/2 1978** A Vietnam vet's wife is kidnapped by the mob, causing him to take up arms and spill blood yet again. **90m/C VHS, DVD.** Bruce Baron, Richard Harrison; ***D:*** Teddy Page; ***M:*** Patrick Wales.

Fireball 500 **1/2 1966** Your basic low-budget teen flick from AIP finds Frankie and Fabian as rival stock car drivers in South Carolina. Newcomer Frankie makes a play for Annette, who's already Fabian's girl. But then Frankie switches cars to romance wealthy raceway owner Parrish. Bootleggers try to trick Frankie into illegal doings during a cross-country race, but he wises up and helps the Feds close the moonshiners down. He also croons a few tunes and the action is a little more adventurous than in the "Beach Party" series. **92m/C DVD.** Frankie Avalon, Annette Funicello, Fabian, Julie Parrish, Chill Wills, Harvey Lembeck; ***D:*** William Asher; ***W:*** William Asher, Leo Townsend; ***C:*** Floyd Crosby; ***M:*** Les Baxter.

Fireball Forward **1/2 1972 (PG)** A battalion fighting in France during WWII is having a bad time until Gazzara takes over and turns them into a crack fighting team. Uses some battle footage from the movie "Patton." **100m/C VHS.** Ben Gazzara, Eddie Albert, Ricardo Montalban, Dana Elcar, L.Q. Jones, Anne Francis; ***D:*** Marvin J. Chomsky. **TV**

Fireballs **1/2 1990** Sexploitaton pic set at a firehouse, where a batch of female recruits turn up the heat for three stud hosebearers. The title should give you some idea of the intellectual level. **89m/C VHS.** Mike Shapiro, Goren Kalezik; ***D:*** Mike Shapiro.

Firebird 2015 A.D. **1981 (PG)** Dreary action adventure set in a 21st century society where automobile use is banned because of an extreme oil shortage. Private cars are hunted down for destruction by the Department of Vehicular Control. One over-zealous enforcer decides to make it a package deal and throws in the owners as well. Everyone connected with effort should have been cited for running stop sign. **97m/C VHS.** Darren McGavin, George Touliatos, Doug McClure; ***D:*** David Robertson.

Firecracker **1981** Female martial arts expert retaliates against the crooks who murdered her sister. **83m/C VHS.** Jillian Kesner, Darby Hinton; ***D:*** Cirio H. Santiago.

Firecreek **1/2 1968** Fonda and his thugs terrorize a small town protected by part-time sheriff Stewart. Beautiful photography and competent cast, but meandering and long. **104m/C VHS, DVD.** Henry Fonda, James Stewart, Inger Stevens, Gary Lockwood, Dean Jagger, Ed Begley Sr., Jay C. Flippen, Jack Elam, Barbara Luna; ***D:*** Vincent McEveety; ***C:*** William Clothier.

Fired Up! **1/2 2009 (PG-13)** Really? We're supposed to believe the two lead guys are high schoolers? 'Cause they look old enough to be teachers not students. So suspend all sense of reality and relax into a typically silly teen sex comedy. Football players Shawn (D'Agosto) and Nick (Olsen) decide they can bag more babes going to summer cheerleading camp than sweating over a pigskin. Considering the PG-13 rating, these two really get around with some minor complications, including a nasty rival cheer squad. **89m/C DVD.** *US* Nicholas D'Agosto, Eric Christian Olsen, Sarah Roemer, Molly Sims, Danneel Harris, AnnaLynne McCord, Philip Baker Hall, John Michael Higgins, Juliette Goglia, David Walton, Adhir Kalyan; ***D:*** Will Gluck; ***W:*** Freedom Jones; ***C:*** Thomas Ackerman; ***M:*** Richard Gibbs.

Firefall *Freefall* **1994** Wildlife photog Katy Mazur (Gidley) has a brief affair with sportsman Grant Orion (Roberts) while on assignment in Africa. When they meet again, Orion tells Katy he's actually an Interpol agent who's assigned to protect her—although she has no idea why. Katy's fiance (Fahey) thinks this is strange. **95m/C VHS, DVD.** Pamela Gidley, Eric Roberts, Jeff Fahey; ***D:*** John Irvin.

Firefight **1987** After a nuclear holocaust, convicted criminals endeavor to rule the wasteland. **100m/C VHS.** James Pfeiffer, Janice Carraher, Jack Tucker; ***D:*** Scott Pfeiffer.

Firefight **1/2 2003 (R)** Armored car driver Jonas (Bacic) is desperate to save his family's restaurant from bankruptcy so, aided by chopper pilot George (Mancuso), he robs his own vehicle and uses a forest fire as cover. But that's not Jonas's only problem—bad guy Wolf (Baldwin) learns about the crime and he's determined to get the cash for himself. **94m/C DVD.** Steve Bacic, Nick Mancuso, Stephen Baldwin, Sonya Salomaa; ***D:*** Paul Ziller; ***W:*** Paul Ziller, Elizabeth Sanchez; ***C:*** Kamal Derkaoui; ***M:*** Ken Williams. **VIDEO**

The Firefly **1/2 1937** Although slow-paced and long, this adaptation of the 1912 Rudolf Friml operetta was one of MacDonald's most popular films. Co-star Jones gets to sing the best song in the film, "Donkey Serenade," while MacDonald sings most of the others. ♫ Love Is Like a Firefly; English March; A Woman's Kiss; He Who Loves and Runs Away; When a Maid Comes Knocking at Your Heart; When the Wine Is Full of Fire; The Donkey Serenade; Giannina Mia; Sympathy. **140m/B VHS.** Jeanette MacDonald, Allan Jones, Warren William, Billy Gilbert, Henry Daniell, Douglass Dumbrille, George Zucco; ***D:*** Robert Z. Leonard.

Firefox **1/2 1982 (PG)** A retired pilot sneaks into the Soviet Union for the Pentagon to steal a top-secret, ultra-sophisticated warplane and fly it out of the country. Best for the low-altitude flight and aerial battle sequences, but too slow on character and much too slow getting started. **136m/C VHS, DVD.** Clint Eastwood, Freddie Jones, David Huffman, Warren Clarke, Ronald Lacey, Kenneth Colley, Nigel Hawthorne, Kai Wulff; ***D:*** Clint Eastwood; ***C:*** Bruce Surtees; ***M:*** Maurice Jarre.

Firehawk **1992 (R)** Several American soldiers survive the crash of their helicopter into the jungles of Vietnam. They think their only enemy is the Vietcong but when they discover the copter has been sabotaged the hunt is on for the traitor among them. **92m/C VHS.** Martin Kove, Matt Salinger, Vic Trevino; ***D:*** Cirio H. Santiago; ***W:*** Jeff Yonis.

Firehead **1/2 1990 (R)** A pyrokinetic Soviet defector begins using his powers to destroy American munitions in the name of peace. When a clandestine pro-war organization hears of this, they attempt to capture the man and use him for their own evil purposes. **88m/C VHS, DVD.** Christopher Plummer, Chris Lemmon, Martin Landau, Gretchen Becker, Brett Porter; ***D:*** Peter Yuval.

Firehouse **1972** Tempers ignite in a lily-white firehouse when a black rookie replaces an expired veteran. March—of "Paper Lion" renown—directed this made-for-TV emergency clone, which ran ever-so-briefly as an adventure series on TV in 1974 (with a largely different cast). **73m/C VHS, DVD.** Richard Roundtree, Vince Edwards, Andrew Duggan, Richard Jaeckel, Sheila Frazier, Val Avery, Paul LeMat, Michael Lerner; ***D:*** Alex March; ***M:*** Tom Scott. **TV**

Firehouse **1987 (R)** In the style of "Police Academy," three beautiful and sex-starved fire-fighting recruits klutz up an urban firehouse. A softcore frolic. **91m/C VHS, DVD.** Barrett Hopkins, Shannon Murphy, Violet Brown, John Anderson, Julia Roberts; ***D:*** J. Christian Ingvordsen; ***W:*** J. Christian Ingvordsen, Steven Kaman, Rick Marx; ***C:*** Steven Kaman; ***M:*** Michael Montes.

Firehouse Dog **2007 (PG)** Movie dog Rexxx, aka Dewey, is lost during an airplane stunt and winds up in the reluctant care of sullen 12-year-old Shane Fahey (Hutcherson). Shane and his dad, Connor (Greenwood), are going through a rough time as Connor has taken charge of an embattled inner-city fire station called Dogpatch. But the kid soon realizes that Dewey is no ordinary mutt and his furry pal becomes both a rescue dog and the perfect PR tool. There's lots of bonding and hey, it's a dog movie! What could be better? Okay there are a few things better than this particular dog movie. Like a trip to the vet. **111m/C DVD.** *US* Josh Hutcherson, Bruce Greenwood, Dash Mihok, Steven Culp, Bill Nunn, Bree Turner, Mayte Garcia; ***D:*** Todd Holland; ***W:*** Mike Werb, Michael Colleary, Claire-Dee Lim; ***C:*** Victor Hammer; ***M:*** Jeff Cardoni.

Firelight **1/2 1997 (R)** Governess Elisabeth (Marceau) needs to pay off her father's debts and makes a deal with married British aristocrat Charles Godwin (Dillane) to give him a child since his own wife is comatose from a riding accident. She gives her baby daughter up but, seven years later, is still so haunted by her memories that she decides to seek them out. So Elisabeth gets hired as her own spoiled daughter's governess. Charles is at least momentarily outraged but soon they can't keep their sexual desires quiescent any longer. Set in 1838. **104m/C VHS.** Sophie Marceau, Stephen (Dillon) Dillane, Joss Ackland, Kevin Anderson, Lia Williams, Dominique Belcourt; ***D:*** William Nicholson; ***W:*** William Nicholson; ***C:*** Nic Morris; ***M:*** Christopher Gunning.

The Fireman **1/2 1916** Chaplin portrays a fireman who becomes a hero. Silent with musical soundtrack added. **20m/B VHS, DVD.** Eric Campbell, Edna Purviance, Charlie Chaplin; ***D:*** Charlie Chaplin.

The Firemen's Ball *Hori, ma panenko* **1968** A critically acclaimed comedy about a small-town ball held for a retiring fire chief. Plans go amusingly awry as beauty contestants refuse to show themselves, raffle prizes and other items—including the gift for the guest of honor—are stolen, and the firemen are unable to prevent an old man's house from burning down. Forman's second film is sometimes interpreted as political allegory; Czech with subtitles. **73m/C VHS, DVD.** *CZ* Vaclav Stockel, Josef Svet; ***D:*** Milos Forman; ***W:*** Ivan Passer, Jaroslav Papousek, Vaclav Sasek, Milos Forman; ***C:*** Miroslav Ondricek; ***M:*** Karel Mares.

Firepower **1/2 1979 (R)** Loren blames her chemist husband's death on a rich industrialist and hires hitman Coburn to take care of the matter. Less than compelling. **104m/C VHS.** Dominic Chianese, Sophia Loren, James Coburn, O.J. Simpson, Christopher F. Bean; ***D:*** Michael Winner; ***W:*** Michael Winner; ***M:*** Gato Barbieri.

Firepower **1/2 1993 (R)** Two cops chase "The Swordsman" into a federally sanctioned area of legalized gambling, prostitution and crime (Las Vegas?), risking life and limb in the treacherous "Caged Ring of Death." **95m/C VHS, DVD.** Chad McQueen, Gary Daniels, Jim Hellwig, Joseph Ruskin, George Murdock; ***D:*** Richard Pepin; ***W:*** Michael January; ***C:*** Ken Blakey.

Fireproof 2008 (PG) Firefighter Caleb (Cameron) has let his obsession with work get in the way of his marriage to neglected spouse Catherine (Bethea) and they have separated. Caleb's dad (Malcom) urges him to attempt a reconciliation by trying a Christian-based 40-day marriage program but it won't be easy. Commendable and sincere effort that gets a little heavy-handed in its last act. **122m/C DVD.** *US* Kirk Cameron, Erin Bethea, Harris Malcom, Ken Bevel, Phyllis Malcom, James McLeod; ***D:*** Alex Kendrick; ***W:*** Alex Kendrick, Stephen Kendrick; ***C:*** Bob Scott; ***M:*** Mark Willard.

Fires on the Plain *Nobi* 1959 A grueling Japanese antiwar film about an unhinged private in the Philippines during WWII who roams the war-torn countryside encountering all manner of horror and devastation. In Japanese with English subtitles. **105m/B VHS, DVD.** *JP* Eiji Funakoshi, Osamu Takizawa, Mickey Custis, Asao Sano, Kyu Sazanka, Yoshihiro Hamaguchi, Hikaru Hoshi, Yasushi Sugita, Masaya Tsukida, Mantaro Ushio; ***D:*** Kon Ichikawa; ***W:*** Natto Wada; ***C:*** Setsuo Kobayashi; ***M:*** Yashushi Akutagawa.

Fires Within 1991 (R) A curiously flat romance with political overtones. After eight years as a political prisoner in Cuba, Nestor (Smits) is released and goes to Miami to be reunited with his wife and daughter. Once there he finds his wife has fallen in love with another man. Now Nestor must choose between his politics and the chance to win back his family. Secondary plotlines fizzle out and a talented cast is largely wasted. Scacchi is beautiful but hardly believable as the Cuban wife. **90m/C VHS, DVD.** Jimmy Smits, Greta Scacchi, Vincent D'Onofrio; ***D:*** Gillian Armstrong; ***W:*** Cynthia Cidre; ***C:*** David Gribble; ***M:*** Maurice Jarre.

Firestarter 1984 (R) A C.I.A.-like organization is after a little girl who has the ability to set anything on fire in this filmed adaptation of Stephen King's bestseller. Good special effects help a silly plot. **115m/C VHS, DVD.** David Keith, Drew Barrymore, Freddie Jones, Martin Sheen, George C. Scott, Heather Locklear, Louise Fletcher, Moses Gunn, Art Carney, Antonio Fargas, Drew Snyder; ***D:*** Mark L. Lester; ***W:*** Stanley Mann; ***C:*** Giuseppe Ruzzolini; ***M:*** Tangerine Dream.

Firestarter 2: Rekindled 2002 Original sequel to the 1984 film, based on the Stephen King novel. A now-adult Charlie (Moreau) is researching the project that sparked her fire-starting powers, without realizing that her former mentor (McDowell) wants to eliminate all survivors of the Lot 6 project. Meanwhile, insurance agent Vincent Sforza (Nucci) is looking for Charlie and a mysterious scientist (Hopper) is also involved. **168m/C VHS, DVD.** Marguerite Moreau, Malcolm McDowell, Danny Nucci, Dennis Hopper, Skye McCole Bartusiak, John Dennis Johnston, Darnell Williams, Deborah Van Valkenburgh; ***D:*** Robert Iscove; ***W:*** Philip Eisner; ***C:*** David Boyd. **CABLE**

Firestorm 1/2 1997 (R) Ex-NFL tough guy Long plays Jesse Graves, a parachuting firefighter with a really square head in his first starring role. Jesse, along with "smoke jumping" mentor Wynt (Glenn), must drop into a raging Wyoming forest fire in order to save a group of trapped firemen. Except they aren't really firemen, they're convicts in disguise who have escaped through a hole in the plot. Ringleader Shaye (Forsythe) had his lawyer set the fire so that he could use the volunteer murderer/fire fighter release program to escape and find the $37 million he has hidden. Happens all the time. The smoky chain gang also stumble across beautiful bird-watcher Jennifer (Amis) and take her hostage. Jesse must foil the bad guys, save the girl and douse the fire; all the while lugging around his humongous chin and speaking in monotone. Fire effects were enhanced by computer generated graphics. **89m/C VHS, DVD.** Howie Long, Scott Glenn, William Forsythe, Suzy Amis, Christianne Hirt, Garwin Sanford, Sebastian Spence, Michael Greyeyes, Benjamin Ratner, Barry Pepper, Vladimir Kulich, Tom McBeath; ***D:*** Dean Semler; ***W:*** Chris Soth; ***C:*** Stephen Windon; ***M:*** J. Peter Robinson.

Firestorm: 72 Hours in Oakland 1/2 1993 Residents of an Oakland community face the threat of a big brush fire. **94m/C VHS.** LeVar Burton, Jill Clayburgh, Michael Gross; ***D:*** Michael Tuchner.

Firetrap 1/2 2001 (R) Combo heist/disaster flick is routine material. Thief Jack (Cain) is hired to steal a computer chip from a L.A. high-rise corporate headquarters but is double-crossed by a crooked company insider (Tyson) who sets fire to the building, trapping Jack and the other occupants. **99m/C VHS, DVD.** Dean Cain, Richard Tyson, Lori Petty, Mel Harris, James Storm, Vanessa Angel, John O'Hurley, Elena Sahagun, Steven Williams; ***D:*** Harris Done; ***W:*** Richard Preston Jr., Diane Fine; ***C:*** Mark W. Gray; ***M:*** Sean Murray. **VIDEO**

Firewalker 1986 (PG) An "Indiana Jones" clone about three mercenaries endeavoring to capture a fortune in hidden gold. Paper-mache sets and a villain with an eye patch that consistently changes eyes are just some of the gaffes that make this one of the worst edited movies in history. **106m/C VHS, DVD.** Chuck Norris, Louis Gossett Jr., Melody Anderson; ***D:*** J. Lee Thompson; ***W:*** Norman Aladjem; ***M:*** Gary Chang.

Firewall 2006 (PG-13) The 60-something Ford does the heroic family man thing again. Here he plays Jack Stanfield, a security specialist at a Seattle bank, whose family is held hostage by psycho thief Bill Cox (Bettany) and his gang. Cox needs Jack to circumvent his own security system so that $100 million can be transferred to an offshore account. Jack, of course, decides to thwart their nefarious plan and save his family. Ford is his usual stalwart self, but the movie is a paint-by-numbers disappointment that brings nothing new to the well-worn genre **120m/C DVD, Blu-ray Disc, HD DVD.** *US* Harrison Ford, Paul Bettany, Virginia Madsen, Mary Lynn Rajskub, Robert Patrick, Robert Forster, Alan Arkin, Carly Schroeder, Jimmy Bennett, Vince Vieluf, Kett Turton, Vincent Gale, Nikolaj Coster-Waldau; ***D:*** Richard Loncraine; ***W:*** Joe Forte; ***C:*** Marco Pontecorvo; ***M:*** Alexandre Desplat.

Fireworks *Hana-Bi* 1997 Idiosyncratic mixture of drama, comedy, violence, and sentiment. Nishi (Kitano) is a tough detective whose wife, Miyuki (Kishimoto), is dying from leukemia. He's visiting her in the hospital when his partner Horibe (Osugi) is gunned down and paralyzed. Deciding to get justice on his own terms, Nishi quits the force and decides to settle his debts with the yakuza by robbing a bank (which also funds a last trip with his wife). Kitano (who uses his acting alias of Beat Takeshi) is the strong, silent, violent type and a very visual director. Those are Kitano's own paintings in the scenes where Horibe takes up art as his new hobby. Japanese with subtitles. **103m/C VHS, DVD.** *JP* Takeshi "Beat" Kitano, Kayoko Kishimoto, Ren Osugi, Susumu Terajima, Tetsu Watanabe; ***D:*** Takeshi "Beat" Kitano; ***W:*** Takeshi "Beat" Kitano; ***C:*** Hideo Yamamoto; ***M:*** Joe Hisaishi.

The Firing Line 1991 The Central American government hires a mercenary rebel-buster to squash insurgents. Everything's great until he finds out he agrees with the rebel cause, and he trains them to fight the government. Below average renegade-with-a-hidden-heart warpic. **93m/C VHS, DVD.** Reb Brown, Shannon Tweed, Michael Monty, Kathlena Marie, Melvin Davidson, Carl Terry, Andy Jacobson; ***D:*** John Gale; ***W:*** John Gale, Sonny Sanders; ***C:*** Carl Sommers; ***M:*** Martia Manuel.

The Firm 1993 (R) Top-flight cast promises a good time—the script based on the top-selling 1991 novel by John Grisham nearly guarantees it. Ambitious, idealistic Ivy League law school grad Cruise accepts a great offer from a small but wealthy Memphis law firm. As with anything that seems too good to be true, he discovers too late that nothing in life is free. Good performances by nearly everyone involved makes up for predictability. Sorvino has an uncredited cameo as a mob boss. Book fans beware: the script is fairly faithful until the end. The movie rights were snapped up before the book was published. Placed third in the 1993 race for top boxoffice gross. **154m/C VHS, DVD.** Tom Cruise, Jeanne Tripplehorn, Gene Hackman, Hal Holbrook, Terry Kinney, Wilford Brimley, Ed Harris, Holly Hunter, David Strathairn, Gary Busey, Steven Hill, Tobin Bell, Barbara Garrick, Jerry Hardin, Karina Lombard, John Beal, Paul Sorvino, Joe (Johnny) Viterelli; ***D:*** Sydney Pollack; ***W:*** Robert Towne, David Rayfiel; ***C:*** John Seale; ***M:*** Dave Grusin.

First a Girl 1/2 1935 Delivery girl Elizabeth (Matthews) is dropping off costumes at the local theatre, which is where she meets a female impersonator with throat trouble. He gets Elizabeth to take his place on stage and she becomes famous overnight. So she keeps up the charade until a princess (Lee) and her boyfriend (Jones) become suspicious and decide to uncover the truth. If the plot sounds familiar, it's because the film was remade as "Victor/Victoria" (1982). **93m/B VHS.** *GB* Jessie Matthews, Sonnie Hale, Anna Lee, Griffith Jones, Alfred Drayton, Martita Hunt; ***D:*** Victor Saville; ***W:*** Marjorie Gaffney; ***C:*** Glen MacWilliams.

First Affair 1983 A young girl undergoes the pressures of freshman life at college, including her first love affair, which is with the husband of a female professor. **95m/C VHS.** Loretta Swit, Melissa Sue Anderson, Joel Higgins; ***D:*** Gus Trikonis. **TV**

First & Ten: The Team Scores Again 1985 A sequel to the cable comedy "First and Ten" about a football team's relationship with their female owner. **101m/C VHS.** Delta Burke, Geoffrey Scott, Ruta Lee, Reid Shelton, Clayton Landey, Fran Tarkenton. **CABLE**

The First Auto 1927 In 1895, successful Hank Armstrong (Simpson) owns the town's livery stable and is also a prize-winning race horse owner. His son Bob (Mack) is enamored of the new horseless carriage, which appalls Hank. Over the years, the automobile takes over, Hank's business goes bust, and he is forced to sell his beloved horses. Becoming bitter, Hank sabotages an automobile, not realizing that Bob will be driving it in an exhibition race. Ironically, Mack was killed in a car accident during filming and he is notably absent in later scenes. **78m/B DVD.** Russell Simpson, Charles Emmet Mack, Frank Campeau, Patsy Ruth Miller, William Demarest, Douglas Gerrard; ***D:*** Roy Del Ruth; ***W:*** Darryl F. Zanuck; ***C:*** David Abel.

First Blood 1982 (R) Stallone is a former Green Beret survivor of Vietnam whose nightmares of wartime horrors are triggered by a wrongful arrest in a small town. He escapes into the mountains of the Northwest and leads his pursuers to all manner of bloody ends. Finally, the Army is summoned to crush him. Extremely violent and frequently confused, fueled on the revenge fantasy and not much concerned with the rules of plot realism. Screen debut of Caruso. Based on David Morrell's novel. A boxoffice hit that launched the "Rambo" series. Followed by "Rambo: First Blood, Part 2." **96m/C VHS, DVD, Blu-ray Disc, UMD.** Sylvester Stallone, Richard Crenna, Brian Dennehy, Jack Starrett, David Caruso; ***D:*** Ted Kotcheff; ***W:*** Sylvester Stallone; ***C:*** Andrew Laszlo; ***M:*** Jerry Goldsmith.

First Born 1/2 1984 (PG-13) In search of romance, divorced mother Garr finds an intriguing man, Weller. Trouble erupts when her son learns Weller is a cocaine dealer. Talented cast makes most of story. **100m/C VHS.** Teri Garr, Peter Weller, Christopher Collet, Corey Haim, Sarah Jessica Parker, Robert Downey Jr.; ***D:*** Michael Apted; ***C:*** Ralf Bode.

First Daughter 1/2 1999 Alex McGregor (Hemingway) is a Secret Service agent who saves President Johnathan Hayes's (Harrison) life and is rewarded for her efforts by being assigned to protect his bratty teen daughter, Jess (Keena), on a Colorado rafting trip. (Actually filmed in Australia.) The teen gets kidnapped by a paramilitary group and agent Alex, aided by river guide Grant Carlson (Savant), is determined to get her back. **94m/C VHS.** Mariel Hemingway, Doug Savant, Monica Keena, Gregory Harrison; ***D:*** Armand Mastroianni; ***W:*** Carey Hayes, Chad Hayes; ***C:*** Mark Wareham; ***M:*** Louis Febre. **CABLE**

First Daughter 1/2 2004 (PG) Ever hear of a flick called "Chasing Liberty" about a president's daughter who wants to escape from her duties and just have a little fun? Well, let's just play follow the government leader. Samantha Mackenzie (Holmes) chafes under the restrictions of being presidential dad's (Keaton) proper only offspring. So she heads to college in California where she tries to ditch her security detail to party with diva roommate Mia (Amerie), getting into some mild hijinks that cause mom Melanie (Colin) to lay down the law (it's an election year), even as Sam gets flirty with faculty adviser James (Blucas). Everyone seems to be sleepwalking (even director Whitaker) as if it's too much effort to pump some hot air into this snoozefest. **104m/C VHS, DVD.** *US* Katie Holmes, Marc Blucas, Margaret Colin, Michael Keaton, Amerie, Lela Rochon Fuqua; ***D:*** Forest Whitaker; ***W:*** Jessica Bendinger, Kate Kondell; ***C:*** Toyomichi Kurita; ***M:*** Michael Kamen, Blake Neely, Damon Elliot; ***Nar:*** Forest Whitaker.

The First Deadly Sin 1/2 1980 (R) Police lieutenant Sinatra tracks down a homicidal killer in spite of wife Dunaway's illness and his impending retirement. Read Lawrence Sanders' bestselling novel; it's a lot more exciting than this. **112m/C VHS, DVD.** Frank Sinatra, Faye Dunaway, David Dukes, Brenda Vaccaro, James Whitmore; ***D:*** Brian G. Hutton; ***W:*** Mann Rubin; ***C:*** Jack Priestley; ***M:*** Gordon Jenkins.

First Degree 1/2 1995 (R) N.Y.C. homicide detective Rick Mallory (Lowe) goes up against the mob while investigating the murder of a rich man and falling for the widow. **98m/C VHS, DVD.** *CA* Rob Lowe, Leslie Hope, Tom McCamus, Nadia Capone, Brett Halsey; ***D:*** Jeff Woolnough; ***W:*** Ron Base; ***C:*** Glen MacPherson. **CABLE**

First Degree *Charades; Felons* 1998 (R) Quinn (Wilder) and wife Lara (Kates) invite some friends and co-workers to their house for a barbecue. But there's more than hamburgers about to be grilled. Seems widow Jude (Black) is convinced that her husband Paul's killer is attending the festivities. And she soon has everyone turning on each other. **80m/C VHS, DVD.** Erika Eleniak, C. Thomas Howell, Jack Scalia, James Wilder, James Russo, Karen Black, Kimberley Kates, James Andronica; ***D:*** Stephen Eckelberry; ***W:*** S.P. Somtow; ***C:*** Susan Emerson. **VIDEO**

First Descent 2005 (PG-13) Documentary attempts to chronicle the history as well as the current state of free-ride snowboarding. Nick Perata, Shawn Farmer, Terji Haakonsen, Shaun White and Hannah Teter ride virgin powder throughout Alaska's spectacular Chugach Mountains. The narration darts around a bit but the obvious enthusiasm more than makes up. **110m/C DVD, UMD.** *US* ***D:*** Kevin Harrison; ***W:*** Kevin Harrison, Kemp Curley; ***C:*** Scott Duncan; ***M:*** Mark Mothersbaugh.

First Do No Harm 1/2 1997 (PG-13) Well-intentioned but routine TV movie depicts the crisis of the farming Reimuller family when the youngest child, four-year-old Robbie (Adkins), is diagnosed with epilepsy. Their health insurance won't cover Robbie's drug treatment and the bank is about to foreclose on the farm so dad Dave (Ward) takes up truck driving while mom Lori (Streep) tries to hold things together. Dismayed at Robbie's doctors, Lori also pursues an unorthodox treatment for Robbie that involves diet therapy rather than drugs. Director Abraham's own son has his epilepsy controlled by this alternative method. **94m/C VHS, DVD.** Meryl Streep, Fred Ward, Seth Adkins, Allison Janney, Michael Yarmush; ***D:*** Jim Abrahams; ***W:*** Ann Beckett; ***C:*** Pierre Letarte. **TV**

First Encounter 1/2 1997 Warning—when exploring space and encountering a mysteriously abandoned, apparently deserted ship—Leave It Alone! This crew decides to go sightseeing and it doesn't work out well. **88m/C VHS.** Redge Mahaffey, Roddy Piper, Trevor Goddard; ***D:*** Redge Mahaffey; ***W:*** Redge Mahaffey. **VIDEO**

First Family 1/2 1980 (R) Flat satire of life in the White House. The humor is weak and silly at best, despite the excellent comedy cast. Henry's first directorial effort. **100m/C VHS.** Bob Newhart, Madeline Kahn, Gilda Radner, Richard Benjamin; ***D:*** Buck Henry; ***W:*** Buck Henry; ***M:*** Ralph Burns.

First Kid 1996 (PG) Formulaic "Home Alone Guarding Tess" does have its moments, but if you're over 14, probably not enough of them. Latest in a bevy of films to be inaugurated into the white hot "White House" genre-of-the-moment. Innocuous family comedy casts Sinbad as Sam Simms, an offbeat Secret Service agent who is given the menial job of guarding Prez's bratty son Luke (Pierce). Simms sees that Luke is merely a misunderstood misfit like himself, and helps the lad have more fun than a Presidential son is allowed. Flick's clean, inoffensive humor makes it hard to dislike. Watch for cameo from Sonny Bono. **101m/C VHS, DVD.** Sinbad, Brock Pierce, James Naughton, Blake Boyd, Timothy Busfield, Art LaFleur, Robert Guillaume, Lisa Eichhorn, Zachery Ty Bryan, Bill Cobbs; ***D:*** David Mickey Evans; ***W:*** Tim Kelleher; ***C:*** Anthony B. Richmond; ***M:*** Richard Gibbs.

First Knight 1/2 **1995 (PG-13)** King Arthur/Camelot legend comes to life again, but isn't worth the time it takes to watch. Wandering swordsman Lancelot (Gere) saves beautiful Guinevere (Ormond), soon to be Arthur's (Connery) queen, from evil renegade knight Malagant. They yearn, they gaze, they kiss—you gag. Written like a Harlequin romance, the dialogue (especially when uttered by Gere) is unintentionally funny, and the plot will cause much eye-rolling. Connery's regal (he knows his costume epics) and Ormond's lovely, but Gere is badly miscast. He offers a contemporary take on the flawed hero complete with American accent, an amazing feat in the 13th century. Big-scale battles, betrayals, passion, even Disneyland-like Camelot sets—the pieces for a tremendous epic are all here, it just doesn't work. **134m/C VHS, DVD.** Sean Connery, Richard Gere, Julia Ormond, Ben Cross, John Gielgud, Liam Cunningham, Christopher Villiers, Valentine Pelka; ***D:*** Jerry Zucker; ***W:*** William Nicholson; ***C:*** Adam Greenberg; ***M:*** Jerry Goldsmith.

First, Last and Deposit 1/2 **2000** Christine and her daughter 13-year-old Tessa end up living in their car when Christine is unable to cover the rent on her cashier's salary after her boyfriend moves them to Santa Barbara, loses his job, and splits. Tessa tries to get along with her new classmates by lying about her home life as the bonds between mother and daughter begin to strain under the pressure of their situation. First-time director Hyoguchi's use of digital video helps convey the desparation and immediacy of the family's plight, as well as giving a sense of gritty realism. Mostly inexperienced cast does a fine job. **92m/C VHS, DVD.** Sara Wilcox, Jessica White, Don Margolin, Alanna Learned, Robin Alcorn, Katie Hatcher, Jason Hallows; ***D:*** Peter Hyoguchi; ***W:*** Peter Hyoguchi, Duffy Hecht.

First Legion 1/2 **1951** Boyer and Addy are seminarians struggling with their faith when they are confronted with a supposed miracle. Low-key examination of religion and conflict within a religious community. **77m/B VHS.** Charles Boyer, Barbara Rush, William Demarest, Leo G. Carroll; ***D:*** Douglas Sirk.

First Love 1/2 **1939** Best known for Durbin's first screen kiss, this lightweight romance finds orphaned Connie Harding moving to New York to live with her wealthy Uncle James Clinton (Pallette) and his family. Connie meets handsome rich boy Ted Drake (Stack's screen debut) but her snobby debutante cousin Barbara (Parrish) already has Ted in her sights. Barbara tries to prevent Connie from going to the Drakes fancy dance but, in Cinderella fashion, the Clinton family servants help her become the belle of the ball. Durbin also does some singing. ♫ One Fine Day; Amapola; Sympathy; A Change of Heart; Deserted; Spring In My Heart; Home Sweet Home. **85m/B VHS, DVD.** Deanna Durbin, Robert Stack, Eugene Pallette, Helen Parrish, Leatrice Joy, June Storey, Frank Jenks, Kathleen Howard, Charles Coleman, Mary Treen; ***D:*** Henry Koster; ***W:*** Bruce Manning, Lionel Houser; ***C:*** Joseph Valentine; ***M:*** Frank Skinner.

First Love 1/2 **1970 (R)** A 16-year-old lad falls in love with a slightly older woman only to have his feelings rejected and to discover that she's his father's mistress. Actor Schell's directorial debut. **90m/C VHS.** *GE SI* John Moulder-Brown, Dominique Sanda, Maximilian Schell, Valentina Cortese; ***D:*** Maximilian Schell; ***C:*** Sven Nykvist.

First Love 1/2 **1977 (R)** A story of an idealistic college student who takes love (and especially making love) more seriously than the rest of his peers, including his girlfriend. Based on Harold Brodkey's story "Sentimental Education." Darling's directorial debut. **92m/C VHS.** William Katt, Susan Dey, John Heard, Beverly D'Angelo, Robert Loggia; ***D:*** Joan Darling; ***M:*** John Barry.

First Love and Other Pains / One of Them 1/2 **1999** Two gay shorts explore first love. In "First Love" (50 minutes), Hong Kong college student Mark begins an English lit course with a stern British professor, Hugh Graham. Depressed by creative burnout, Hugh is flattered by Mark's attentions and they have a one-nighter—at least in Hugh's mind because Mark is looking for a longer-lasting romance. Cantonese and English with subtitles. In "One of Them" (47 minutes), two gay teens in the 60s strike up a friendship that makes their small, boring town almost bearable. **97m/C VHS, DVD.** Edward Strode, Alex Wong, Ciaran Pennington, Cameron J. Watt; ***D:*** Simon Chung, Stewart Main; ***W:*** Simon Chung, Peter Wells; ***C:*** Ping Hung Wong, Stewart Main.

First Love, Last Rites 1/2 **1998 (R)** Peretz moved his atmospheric debut feature (adapted from a short story by Ian McEwan) from the English coast to the bayous of Louisiana. There local gal Sissel (Gregson Wagner) is shacking up with fish-out-of-water Brooklyn boy Joey (Ribisi). They have a lot of sex. Sissel finally introduces Joey to her crazy father Henry (Burke) and the two men get involved in an eel-catching business. Then Sissel and Joey start spatting and soon they're not having sex anymore and their romance drifts away. The film does look really good. **93m/C VHS.** Natasha Gregson Wagner, Giovanni Ribisi, Robert John Burke, Eli Marienthal; ***D:*** Jesse Peretz; ***W:*** Jesse Peretz, David Ryan; ***C:*** Tom Richmond; ***M:*** Craig (Shudder to Think) Wedren.

First Man into Space *Satellite of Blood* **1959** An astronaut returns to Earth covered with strange space dust and with an organism feeding inside him (shades of "Alien"). The alien needs human blood to survive and starts killing in order to get it. **78m/B VHS, DVD.** Marshall Thompson, Marla Landi, Bill Edwards; ***D:*** Robert Day; ***W:*** John C. Cooper, Lance Z. Hargreaves; ***C:*** Geoffrey Faithfull; ***M:*** Buxton Orr.

First Men in the Moon **1964** A fun, special effects-laden adaptation of the H. G. Wells novel about an Edwardian civilian spacecraft visiting the moon and the creature found there. Visual effects by Ray Harryhausen. Finch makes a brief appearance. **103m/C VHS, DVD.** *GB* Martha Hyer, Edward Judd, Lionel Jeffries, Erik Chitty, Peter Finch; ***D:*** Nathan "Jerry" Juran; ***W:*** Nigel Kneale, Jan Read; ***C:*** Wilkie Cooper; ***M:*** Laurie Johnson.

First Monday in October 1/2 **1981 (R)** Clayburgh, as the first woman appointed to the Supreme Court, finds a friendly rival in colleague Matthau, a crusty but benign liberal judge. Though based on a Broadway hit, it ended up seeming to foreshadow the real-life appointment of Sandra Day O'Connor, which occurred at about the time the film was released. The title refers to the date the court begins its sessions. **99m/C VHS, DVD.** Walter Matthau, Jill Clayburgh, Barnard Hughes, James Stephens, Jan Sterling, James Stephens, Joshua Bryant, Noble Willingham; ***D:*** Ronald Neame; ***C:*** Fred W. Koenekamp; ***M:*** Ian Fraser.

First Name: Carmen *Prenom: Carmen* **1983** Carmen, although posing as an aspiring filmmaker, really is a bank robber and terrorist. She is also such a femme fatale that during a bank robbery one of the guards decides to run away with her. Godard cast himself as Carmen's uncle. Amusing late Godard. French with subtitles. **95m/C VHS, DVD.** *FR* Maruschka Detmers, Jacques Bonnaffe, Jean-Luc Godard, Myriem Roussel, Christophe Odent; ***D:*** Jean-Luc Godard; ***W:*** Anne-Marie Mieville; ***C:*** Raoul Coutard.

The First 9 1/2 Weeks WOOF! **1998 (R)** Prequel to "9 1/2 Weeks" finds investor Matt Wade trying to close the biggest deal of his career with eccentric New Orleans businessman Francois Dubois. But Dubois' wife starts raising Wade's temperature even more than steamy New Orleans. **99m/C VHS, DVD.** Paul Mercurio, Clara Bellar, Malcolm McDowell, Frederic Forrest, Dennis Burkley, James Black, Anna Jacyszyn, William Keane, Richard Durden; ***D:*** Alexander Wright; ***W:*** Alexander Wright; ***C:*** John Tarver; ***M:*** Norman Orenstein.

The First Nudie Musical **1975 (R)** A producer tries to save his studio by staging a 1930s style musical, but with a naked cast and risque lyrics. Has attained semi-cult/trash status. ♫ The First Nudie Musical; The Lights and the Smiles; Orgasm; Lesbian Butch Dyke; Dancing Dildos; Perversion; Honey, What Ya Doin' Tonight; Let 'Em Eat Cake; I Don't Have to Hide Anymore. **93m/C VHS, DVD.** Cindy Williams, Stephen Nathan, Diana Canova, Bruce Kimmel, Alan Abelew, Alexandra Morgan, Frank Doubleday, Kathleen Hietala, Leslie Ackerman, Ron Howard; ***D:*** Mark Haggard, Bruce Kimmel; ***W:*** Bruce Kimmel; ***C:*** Douglas Knapp; ***M:*** Bruce Kimmel.

The First Olympics: Athens 1896 1/2 **1984** Recounts the organization and drama surrounding the first modern-day Olympic games when the inexperienced American team shocked the games with their success. **260m/C VHS.** Louis Jourdan, Angela Lansbury, David Ogden Stiers, Virginia McKenna, Jason Connery, Alex Hyde-White, Honor Blackman, Bill Travers; ***D:*** Alvin Rakoff; ***M:*** Bruce Broughton. **TV**

The First Power 1/2 **1989** A detective and psychic join forces to track down a serial killer who, after being executed, uses his satanic powers to kill again. **90m/C VHS, DVD.** Lou Diamond Phillips, Tracy Griffith, Jeff Kober, Mykelti Williamson, Elizabeth Arlen; ***D:*** Robert Resnikoff; ***W:*** Robert Resnikoff; ***C:*** Theo van de Sande; ***M:*** Stewart Copeland.

The First Saturday in May 1/2 **2008 (PG-13)** That would be the Saturday that the Kentucky Derby is run. The Hennegan brothers are the sons of a thoroughbred trainer and their documentary follows six demographically disparate trainers as they try to qualify their horses for the big 2006 race. There's lots of off-track human and equine drama and that Derby was the one that featured the ill-fated Barbaro. **100m/C DVD.** *US* ***D:*** Brad Hennegan, John Hennegan; ***W:*** Brad Hennegan, John Hennegan; ***C:*** Brad Hennegan, John Hennegan; ***M:*** Mark Krewatch, Ryan Brothers.

First Snow **2007 (R)** Sleazy traveling salesman Jimmy (Pearce) impulsively gets his fortune told by Vacaro (Simmons), who suffers a seizure and abruptly ends their session. After his other predictions come true, Jimmy returns and insists that the psychic tell him the rest—which is of Jimmy's death by the first snowfall. Jimmy starts to unravel as his past mistakes catch up to him, but maybe his impending doom is a self-fulfilling prophecy. Pearce (angular and spooked) is made for paranoid types, although the flick ultimately underachieves. **102m/C DVD.** *US* Guy Pearce, Piper Perabo, William Fichtner, J.K. Simmons, Shea Whigham, Rick Gonzales; ***D:*** Mark Fergus; ***W:*** Mark Fergus, Hawk Ostby; ***C:*** Eric Alan Edwards; ***M:*** Cliff Martinez.

First Spaceship on Venus *Der Schweigende Stern; Milczaca Gwiazda* **1960** Eight scientists from various countries set out for Venus and find the remains of a civilization far in advance of Earth's that perished because of nuclear weapons. A sometimes compelling anti-nuclear sci-fi effort made with German and Polish backing. Originally released at 130 minutes. **78m/C VHS, DVD.** *GE PL* Yoko Tani, Oldrich Lukes, Ignacy Machowski, Julius Ongewe, Michal Postnikow, Kurt Rackelmann, Gunther Simon, Tang-Hua-Ta, Lucyna Winnicka; ***D:*** Kurt Maetzig; ***C:*** Joachim Hasler.

First Strike **1985** The United States and the USSR engage in nuclear submarine warfare when the Soviets hijack a U.S. sub and aims its weapons at Arab oil fields. **90m/C VHS.** Stuart Whitman, Persis Khambatta; ***D:*** Allan Kuskowski; ***W:*** Allan Kuskowski; ***C:*** Glenn Roland.

First Sunday **2008 (PG-13)** Durell (Ice Cube) and LeeJohn (Morgan) are buddies who both find themselves in need of some large money in a big hurry in order to escape tight spots. Naturally, they hatch a plan to rob the local Baltimore neighborhood church since, hey, who else has that kind of cash? Just one problem: someone has already unloaded the safe, and a handful of church officials are on hand to witness the whole caper. Undaunted, the two pals take the whole lot hostage, setting up a few lame attempts at humor as the characters find themselves stuck together. The overly sweet choirmaster (Williams) proves to be a high point in a mostly predictable and ridiculous movie. See this one if you have the entire N.W.A catalogue on your iPod. **98m/C DVD, Blu-ray Disc.** *US* Ice Cube, Katt Micah Williams, Tracy Morgan, Loretta Devine, Michael Beach, Chi McBride, Keith David, Regina Hall, Malinda Williams; ***D:*** David E. Talbert; ***W:*** David E. Talbert; ***C:*** Alan Caso; ***M:*** Stanley Clarke.

The First Texan 1/2 **1956** Mediocre bio of Sam Houston (McCrea) from young lawyer to the Battle of San Jacinto to gain Texas independence from Mexico to his presidency of the Republic of Texas. **82m/C DVD.** Joel McCrea, Felicia Farr, Jeff Morrow, James Griffin, David Silva, Carl Benton Reid, Wallace Ford, William Hopper, Dayton Lummis; ***D:*** Byron Haskin, Daniel Ullman; ***W:*** Daniel Ullman; ***C:*** Byron Haskin, Wilfrid M. Cline; ***M:*** Roy Webb.

The First Time 1/2 *You Don't Need Pajamas at Rosie's; The Beginners Three; The Beginners; They Don't Wear Pajamas at Rosie's; Doin' It* **1969 (R)** It's pre-Porky's zaniness as a vacationing youth understandably wants to spend his "first time" with Bisset. Other than her presence, this film has little to offer. **90m/C VHS.** Jacqueline Bisset, Wes Stern, Rick Kelman, Wink Roberts; ***D:*** James Neilson.

First Time 1/2 *Doin' It* **1982 (R)** A comedy about a college student who can't quite succeed with women, despite coaching from his roommate and counseling from a psychology professor whose assistance is part of a research project. **96m/C VHS.** Tim Choate, Krista Errickson, Marshall Efron, Wallace Shawn, Wendie Jo Sperber, Cathryn Damon; ***D:*** Charles Loventhal.

First Time Felon 1/2 **1997 (R)** Based on the true story of a young Chicago drug dealer Greg Yance (Epps), who's convicted as a first-time offender and sent to a prison boot camp to straighten up. But the real challenge is when he's released and returns to his old neighborhood, with its old temptations, and tries to find an honest job. **106m/C VHS, DVD.** Omar Epps, William Forsythe, Rachel Ticotin, Delroy Lindo; ***D:*** Charles S. Dutton; ***W:*** Daniel Therriault. **CABLE**

The First to Go **1997 (PG-13)** Impulsive Adam is the first of his crowd to get engaged. His friends don't approve of his decision and decide to take him on vacation to get him to change his mind. Only his fiancee decides to come along too and she has plans of her own. **91m/C VHS, DVD.** Zach Galligan, Laurel Holloman, Mark Harmon, Corin "Corky" Nemec, Steve Parlavecchio, Jennifer Jostyn, Lisanne Falk; ***D:*** John Jacobs.

First Turn On **1983 (R)** Not to be confused with "The Thomas Edison Story," this sex-comedy follows the adventures of several young campers who decide to die happy when an avalanche leaves them trapped in a cave. A longer unrated version is available. **88m/C VHS, DVD.** Georgia Harrell, Michael Sanville, Googy Gress, Jenny Johnson, Heide Basset, Vincent D'Onofrio, Sheila Kennedy; ***D:*** Michael Herz, Lloyd Kaufman; ***W:*** Michael Herz, Lloyd Kaufman, Stuart Strutin, Georgia Harrell; ***C:*** Lloyd Kaufman.

The First $20 Million is Always the Hardest **2002 (PG-13)** Dismal "comedy" about the late dot-com economy is itself late by at least a year. Not that timeliness would've helped this muddled, desparate-for-laughs mess. Marketing whiz Andy (Garcia) leaves his corporate gig to "do something important." He joins a hot tech firm run by digital guru Francis (Colantoni) who immediately resents him and assigns him to the hopeless project of trying to create a $99 PC. He assembles a quirky team of misfits for the project and geek jokes ensue. Only Dawson, as Andy's love interest, escapes with any dignity. Based on the Po

Bronson novel. **105m/C VHS, DVD.** Adam Garcia, Rosario Dawson, Jake Busey, Enrico Colantoni, Ethan Suplee, Gregory Jbara, Dan E. Butler, Linda Hart, Anjul Nigam; ***D:*** Mick Jackson; ***W:*** Jon Favreau, Gary Tieche; ***C:*** Ron Garcia; ***M:*** Marco Beltrami.

The First Wives Club 1/2 **1996 (PG)** As the first Mrs. Trump, who makes a most appropriate cameo, so wisely puts it, "Don't get mad, get everything." But to the three rich, middle-aged friends who are dumped by their husbands so the guys can marry younger "trophy" wives, there's just nothing like revenge. Comedy begins in 1969 with the young and idealistic Annie (Keaton), Brenda (Midler), Elise (Hawn) and Cynthia graduating college, then moves to the present with the wronged Cynthia (Channing) ledge-diving from her swanky Manhattan apartment because her husband left her. The remaining mistreated trio goes into action, using their exes' own money, businesses, power, and various mistresses against them. This film's appeal and success had Hollywood tongues wagging, predicting the dawn of new roles for older actresses. Based on the book by Olivia Goldsmith. **104m/C VHS, DVD.** Goldie Hawn, Diane Keaton, Bette Midler, Sarah Jessica Parker, Heather Locklear, Marcia Gay Harden, Elizabeth Berkley, Victor Garber, Dan Hedaya, Stephen Collins, Maggie Smith, Stockard Channing, Bronson Pinchot, Jennifer (Jennie) Dundas Lowe, Eileen Heckart, Philip Bosco, Rob Reiner, James Naughton, Dina Spybey, Timothy Olyphant, J.K. Simmons, Debra Monk, Edward Hibbert, Stephen Mendillo; ***D:*** Hugh Wilson; ***W:*** Robert Harling; ***C:*** Donald E. Thorin; ***M:*** Marc Shaiman.

First Yank into Tokyo *Mask of Fury* **1945** An American army pilot who grew up in Japan undergoes plastic surgery in order to infiltrate Japanese lines and get information from an American scientist. Some last minute editing to capitalize on current events made this the first American film to deal with the atomic bomb. **83m/B VHS.** Tom Neal, Richard Loo, Barbara Hale, Marc Cramer; ***D:*** Gordon Douglas.

A Fish Called Wanda **1988 (R)** Absurd, high-speed farce about four criminals trying to retrieve $20 million they've stolen from a safety deposit box—and each other. Meanwhile, barrister Archie Leech (Cleese) falls in love with the female thief, Wanda (Curtis). Some sick, but tastelessly funny, humor involves Palin's problem with stuttering and some very dead doggies. Written by Monty Python alum Cleese and director Crichton, who understand that silence is sometimes funnier than speech, and that timing is everything. Wickedly funny. **98m/C VHS, DVD.** John Cleese, Kevin Kline, Jamie Lee Curtis, Michael Palin, Tom Georgeson, Maria Aitken, Patricia Hayes, Geoffrey Palmer, Andrew MacLachlan; ***D:*** Charles Crichton; ***W:*** Charles Crichton, John Cleese; ***C:*** Alan Hume; ***M:*** John Du Prez. Oscars '88: Support. Actor (Kline); British Acad. '88: Actor (Cleese), Support. Actor (Palin).

Fish Hawk 1/2 **1979 (G)** When an alcoholic Indian, Fish Hawk, meets a young boy in the forest, they strike up a friendship and he attempts to clean up his act. Attempts to be heartwarming. **95m/C VHS, DVD.** *CA* Will Sampson, Charlie (Charles) Fields; ***D:*** Donald Shebib.

Fish in a Barrel **2001 (R)** Familiar heist gone wrong flick is supposed to be played for laughs but doesn't have any. Four petty thieves are suprised to find themselves with four million in uncut diamonds and then wind up with two more partners to split the loot—a hitwoman and a dirty cop. **85m/C VHS, DVD.** Jeremy Renner, Arly Jover, Kent Dalian, Stephen Ingle, Rene Rigal, David Kelsey; ***D:*** Kent Dalian; ***W:*** Kent Dalian; ***C:*** Lisa Wiegand; ***M:*** Matt Sorum, Lanny Cordola.

Fish Tank **2009** Raw and grim depiction of the life of a sexually awakening teen girl in lower-class London. Sullen 15-year-old Mia (Jarvis) has been kicked out of school and is trapped in a rough housing project with her boozy mum Joanne (Wareing) and her hostile sister Tyler (Griffiths). Alienated from her peers, Mia's only escape is breaking into an abandoned apartment where she practices hip-hop dance routines. Everything changes when Joanne brings home hunky boyfriend Connor (Fassbender), who may have designs on Mia as well. Jarvis, who carries the film with her performance, was a non-professional actress discovered by director Arnold while loudly fighting with her boyfriend in a train station. **123m/C DVD.** *GB* Michael Fassbender, Harry Treadway, Katie Jarvis, Kierston Wareing, Rebecca Griffiths, Sydney Mary Nash, Jason Maza; ***D:*** Andrea Arnold; ***W:*** Andrea Arnold; ***C:*** Robbie Ryan.

The Fish that Saved Pittsburgh **1979 (PG)** A floundering basketball team hires an astrologer to try and change their luck. She makes sure all the team members' signs are compatible with their star's Pisces sign (the fish). Produced a disco soundtrack with several Motown groups who also performed in the movie. **104m/C VHS.** Jonathan Winters, Stockard Channing, Flip Wilson, Julius Erving, Margaret Avery, Meadowlark Lemon, Nicholas Pryor, James Bond III, Kareem Abdul-Jabbar, Jack Kehoe, Debbie Allen; ***D:*** Gilbert Moses; ***M:*** Thom Bell.

Fish Without a Bicycle *Girls Will Be Girls* **2003 (R)** Too many dating cliches floating around in lead actress/writer Mattison's story of a woman who dumps her dutiful and handsome beau Danny (Rowe) to pursue her dreams of acting—and other men, including the self-absorbed director Michael (Callen). She also hooks up with her caring, studly co-star Ben (Green). Her lesbian best friend Vicki also has a thing for her. **95m/C DVD.** Brian Austin Green, Jenna Mattison, Brian Austin Green, Jennifer Blanc, Brad Rowe, Bryan Callen; ***D:*** Brian Austin Green; ***W:*** Jenna Mattison. **VIDEO**

The Fisher King **1991 (R)** In derelict-infested Manhattan a down-and-out radio deejay meets a crazed vagabond (Williams) obsessed with medieval history and in search of the Holy Grail. At first the whimsical mix of Arthurian myth and modern urban hell seems amazingly wrongheaded. In retrospect it still does. But while this picture runs it weaves a spell that pulls you in, especially in its quiet moments. Your reaction to the silly ending depends entirely on how well you're bamboozled by a script that equates madness with enlightment and the homeless with holy fools. Filmed on the streets of New York, with many street people playing themselves. **138m/C VHS, DVD.** Robin Williams, Jeff Bridges, Amanda Plummer, Mercedes Ruehl, Michael Jeter, Harry Shearer, John de Lancie, Kathy Najimy, David Hyde Pierce; ***D:*** Terry Gilliam; ***W:*** Richard LaGravenese; ***C:*** Roger Pratt; ***M:*** George Fenton. Oscars '91: Support. Actress (Ruehl); Golden Globes '92: Actor—Mus./Comedy (Williams), Support. Actress (Ruehl); L.A. Film Critics '91: Actress (Ruehl).

Fisherman's Wharf 1/2 **1939** Breen stars as an orphan adopted by a San Francisco fisherman who runs away when his aunt and bratty cousin come to live with them. **72m/B VHS, DVD.** Bobby Breen, Leo Carrillo, Henry Armetta, Lee Patrick, Rosina Galli, Leon Belasco; ***D:*** Bernard Vorhaus.

The Fishing Trip **1998** Jessie (Hood) and her younger sister Kristi (Erwin) are determined to track down the stepfather who molested them as children. They discover he's on a fishing trip at a remote British Columbia cabin and head after him, joined by Murdoch (Henry), their dope-smoking friend. The troubled trio are seeking resolution for their various problems and find it in an unexpected manner. **84m/C VHS.** *CA* Jhene Erwin, Melissa Hood, Anna Henry, Jim Kenney, Diana Tayback, T.J. Grist; ***D:*** Amnon Buchbinder; ***C:*** Derek Rogers. Genie '98: Song ("River Blue").

Fishtales 1/2 **2007 (PG)** Family fluff. Widowed history professor Thomas Bradley (Zane) is desperate to continue his studies on ancient Greek love spells. He's given one last chance to make an academic breakthrough before losing his research grant, so Thomas and his 12-year-old daughter Serena (Sawa) travel to the Greek island of Spetses. Serena tries playing matchmaker after meeting Neried (Brook), who turns out to be a mermaid. The Bradleys must then come to her rescue when she's menaced by a local fisherman (David) who wants Neried's jewel-encrusted tail. That's not the only problem: if the mermaid falls in love with a mortal, she gives up her immortality (and presumably the tail). **87m/C DVD.** Billy Zane, Kelly Brook, Amber Sawa, Alki David; ***D:*** Alki David; ***W:*** Melissa Painter, Alki David; ***C:*** Aggelos Viskadourakis. **VIDEO**

Fist *Black Fist; The Black Streetfighter; Homeboy* **1976 (R)** Street fighter battles his way through the urban jungle seeking personal freedom and revenge. **84m/C VHS, DVD.** Richard Lawson, Annazette Chase, Dabney Coleman, Philip Michael Thomas; ***D:*** Timothy Galfas, Richard Kaye; ***W:*** Tim Kelly; ***M:*** Ed Townsend.

F.I.S.T. 1/2 **1978 (R)** A young truck driver turns union organizer for idealistic reasons, but finds himself teaming with gangsters to boost his cause. His rise to the top of the union comes at the cost of his integrity, as Stallone does a character resembling Jimmy Hoffa. **145m/C VHS, DVD.** Sylvester Stallone, Rod Steiger, Peter Boyle, David Huffman, Melinda Dillon, Tony LoBianco, Kevin Conway, Peter Donat, Cassie Yates, Brian Dennehy; ***D:*** Norman Jewison; ***W:*** Sylvester Stallone; ***M:*** Bill Conti.

Fist Fighter 1/2 **1988 (R)** The ups and downs of a professional bare-knuckle fighter as he avenges a friend's murder. **99m/C VHS.** Jorge (George) Rivero, Edward Albert, Brenda Bakke, Mike Connors, Simon Andreu, Matthias Hues; ***D:*** Frank Zuniga; ***W:*** Max Bloom.

Fist of Fear, Touch of Death *Fist of Fear; The Dragon and the Cobra* **1980 (R)** Madison Square Garden is the scene for a high stakes martial arts face-off. Standard kung-fu film highlighted by short clips of the late Bruce Lee. **81m/C VHS, DVD.** Fred Williamson, Ron Van Clief, Adolph Caesar, Aaron Banks, Bill Louie; ***D:*** Matthew Mallinson; ***W:*** Ron Harvey; ***C:*** John Hazard; ***M:*** Keith Mansfield.

Fist of Glory 1/2 **1995 (R)** In the waning days of the Vietnam War, a commando searches for the comrade who saved his life. He discovers his pal is a drug-addicted POW who's forced to fight in order to survive. **93m/C VHS.** Dale "Apollo" Cook, Maurice Smith, Robert Marius, Eric Hahn; ***D:*** Joe Mari Avellana.

Fist of Honor **1992 (R)** A young boxer seeks to avenge his fiance's death, a beautiful girl squares off against a bad-cop, and two mobster leaders try to take control of the same city. When a member of one family breaks a truce and begins killing rival family members, the violence escalates and old scores will be settled. **90m/C VHS, DVD.** Sam Jones, Joey House, Harry Guardino, Nicholas Worth, Frank Sivero, Abe Vigoda, Bubba Smith; ***D:*** Richard Pepin; ***W:*** Charles Kanganis.

Fist of Legend **1994 (R)** Chen Zuen (Li) is a martial arts practitioner studying abroad during WWII, who returns to his homeland to avenge his teacher's death at the hands of the invading Japanese. Homage to Bruce Lee's 1972 "Fists of Fury" AKA "Chinese Connection." Cantonese with subtitles or dubbed. **92m/C VHS, DVD.** *HK* Jet Li, Yasuka Kurata; ***D:*** Woo-ping Yuen, Gordon Chan; ***M:*** Joseph Koo.

Fist of Steel 1/2 **1993** In this futuristic martial arts film, modern day gladiators fight to the death in tournaments run by a vicious syndicate. When top gladiator Amp makes an escape bid he's hunted by henchman Mainframe, who plans to meet Amp in a fixed fight in order to become the new champion. **97m/C VHS.** Dale "Apollo" Cook, Greg Douglass, Cynthia Khan, Don Nakaya Neilsen, Jim Gaines, Ned Hourani, Nick Nicholson, Kris Aguilar; ***D:*** Irvin Johnson; ***W:*** Anthony Jesu.

Fist of the North Star **1995 (R)** Legendary warrior Kenshiro (Daniels) returns from the grave to avenge the death of his father (McDowell) and restore his North Star clan. He must battle evil Lord Shin (Mandylor) and his henchmen in a post-apocalyptic future. Based on the Japanese comic book series, which is also available in anime form. **90m/C VHS, DVD.** Gary Daniels, Costas Mandylor, Christopher Penn, Julie Brown, Malcolm McDowell, Melvin Van Peebles, Isako Washio; ***D:*** Tony Randel; ***W:*** Tony Randel; ***C:*** Jacques Haitkin; ***M:*** Christopher Stone.

Fistful of Death *Ballad of Django; Stinky; Giu la Testa..Hombre* **1971** A truly awful and completly illogic Italian spaghetti western that somehow includes the characters of Butch Cassidy and the Sundance Kid (and Kinski—the John Carradine of European cinema—apparently out to make a buck). **84m/C VHS.** *IT* Klaus Kinski, Jack Betts, Gordon Mitchell, Giancarlo Prete; ***D:*** Demofilo Fidani; ***W:*** Demofilo Fidani; ***C:*** Joe D'Amato; ***M:*** Coriolano Gori.

A Fistful of Dollars **1964 (R)** The epitome of the "spaghetti western" pits Eastwood as "the man with no name" against two families who are feuding over land. A remake of Kurosawa's "Yojimbo," and followed by Leone's "For a Few Dollars More," and "The Good, The Bad, and The Ugly." **101m/C VHS, DVD.** *IT* Clint Eastwood, Gian Marie Volonte, Marianne Koch; ***D:*** Sergio Leone; ***W:*** Sergio Leone, Victor Andres Catena, Duccio Tessari, G. Schock; ***C:*** Massimo Dallamano, Federico G. Larraya; ***M:*** Ennio Morricone.

A Fistful of Dynamite *Duck, You Sucker; Giu la Testa* **1972 (PG)** A spaghetti western, with Leone's trademark humor and a striking score by Morricone. An Irish demolitions expert and a Mexican peasant team up to rob a bank during a revolution in Mexico. **138m/C VHS, DVD.** *IT* James Coburn, Rod Steiger, Romolo Valli; ***D:*** Sergio Leone; ***M:*** Ennio Morricone.

Fistful of Lead **1970** Hilton is Sartana, this film's version of Clint Eastwood's "Man with No Name" in a blatant rip-off of "Fistful of Dollars." Of the many copycats that came in the wake of Leone's classic, this is one of the better efforts, which considering the field is damning with faint praise. **92m/C VHS, DVD.** *IT* George Hilton, Charles Southwood, Pierro Lulli, Erika Blanc; ***D:*** Giuliano Carnimeo; ***W:*** Tito Carpi; ***C:*** Stelvio Massi; ***M:*** Francesco De Masi.

Fists of Blood 1/2 **1987** A martial arts expert seeks revenge on the drug baron who murdered his friend and kidnapped his girl. **90m/C VHS.** *AU* Eddie Stazak; ***D:*** Brian Trenchard-Smith.

Fists of Fury *The Big Boss; Tang Shan da Xiong* **1973 (R)** Bruce Lee stars in this violent but charming Kung Fu action adventure in which he must break a solemn vow to avoid fighting in order to avenge the murder of his teacher by drug smugglers. **102m/C VHS, DVD.** Bruce Lee, Maria Yi; ***D:*** Lo Wei; ***W:*** Lo Wei, Bruce Lee; ***C:*** Chen Ching Chu; ***M:*** Fu-ling Wang.

Fists of Iron 1/2 **1994 (R)** Tough guy, skilled in martial arts, seeks revenge on the fighter and promoter who caused the death of his best friend. **94m/C VHS.** Mike Worth, Matthias Hues, Sam Jones, Marshall Teague, Jenilee Harrison; ***D:*** Richard W. Munchkin; ***W:*** Sean Dash; ***C:*** Garett Griffin; ***M:*** Louis Febre.

Fit for a King **1937** A reporter becomes a princess' knight in shining armor when he foils an assassination plot in this screwball romance. **73m/B VHS, DVD.** Joe E. Brown, Leo Carrillo, Helen Mack, Paul Kelly, Harry Davenport; ***D:*** Edward Sedgwick; ***C:*** Paul Vogel.

Fit to Kill 1/2 **1993 (R)** Once again special agents Donna Hamilton and Nicole Justine (former Playboy centerfolds Speir and Vasquez) reteam for an adventure that matches them with an old enemy, double agents, diamonds, and revenge. Filmed on location in Hawaii. **94m/C VHS, DVD.** Dona Speir, Roberta Vasquez, R.J. (Geoffrey) Moore, Bruce Penhall, Julie Strain, Rodrigo Obregon, Cynthia Brimhall, Tony Peck; ***D:*** Andy Sidaris; ***W:*** Andy Sidaris.

Fitzcarraldo **1982 (PG)** Although he failed to build a railroad across South America, Fitzcarraldo is determined to build an opera house in the middle of the Amazon jungles and have Enrico Caruso sing there. Based on a true story of a charismatic Irishman's impossible quest at the turn of the century. Of note: No special effects were used in this movie—everything you see actually occurred during filming, including hauling a large boat over a mountain. **157m/C VHS, DVD.** *GE* Klaus Kinski, Claudia Cardinale, Jose Lewgoy, Miguel Angel Fuentes, Paul Hittscher; ***D:*** Werner Herzog; ***W:*** Werner Herzog; ***C:*** Thomas Mauch; ***M:*** Popul Vuh. Cannes '82: Director (Herzog).

Five 1951 A curiosity as an early (and low-budget) example of survivors after a nuclear holocaust plot. Pregnant Roseanne (Douglas), naturalist Michael (Phipps), black doorman Charles (Lampkin), elderly bank clerk Barnstaple (Lee), and cynical intellectual Eric (Anderson) find shelter together in a California house (designed by Frank Lloyd Wright) and have to decide what happens next. **93m/B DVD.** William Phipps, Susan Douglas, James Anderson, Charles Lampkin, Earl Lee; ***D:*** Arch Oboler; ***W:*** Arch Oboler; ***C:*** Louis Clyde Stoumen, Sid Lubow; ***M:*** Henry Russell.

5 Against the House 1955 College buddies, who are going to school on the G.I. Bill after serving in Korea, plan to rob a Reno casino just to prove they can and then give the money back. However, Brick (Keith) is mentally unstable after his war experiences and deeply in debt so he doesn't want to return the loot. Al (Madison) goes along out of loyalty but then his babe girlfriend Kay (Novak) gets pulled into the scheme. **84m/B DVD.** Guy Madison, Kim Novak, Brian Keith, Alvy Moore, Kerwin Mathews, William Conrad; ***D:*** Phil Karlson; ***W:*** Stirling Silliphant, William Bowers, John Barnwell; ***C:*** Lester White; ***M:*** George Duning.

Five Came Back 1939 When a plane with 12 passengers crashes in the South American jungle, only five can ride in the patched-up wreck. Since the remainder will be left to face head hunters, intense arguments ensue. Same director remade this as "Back from Eternity" in 1956. **93m/B VHS.** Lucille Ball, Chester Morris, John Carradine, Wendy Barrie, Kent Taylor, Joseph Calleia, Sir C. Aubrey Smith, Patric Knowles; ***D:*** John Farrow.

Five Card Stud 1/2 1968 (PG) Five members of a lynching party are being killed one by one, and a professional gambler, who tried to prevent the lynching, attempts to ensnare the killer with the aid of a preacher with a gun. The poor script was based on a novel by Ray Gaulden. **103m/C VHS, DVD.** Robert Mitchum, Dean Martin, Inger Stevens, Roddy McDowall, Yaphet Kotto, John Anderson, Katherine Justice; ***D:*** Henry Hathaway; ***W:*** Marguerite Roberts; ***C:*** Daniel F. Fapp; ***M:*** Maurice Jarre.

Five Cartridges *Funf Patronenhulsen* **1960** Five soldiers during the Spanish Civil War hide their dying commander's final message in five empty bullet casings to keep the message from falling into enemy hands. Now, they have to survive the fighting in order to deliver the message. German with subtitles. **85m/B VHS.** *GE* Erwin Geschonneck, Manfred Krug, Armin Mueller-Stahl, Ulrich Thein, Edwin Marran, Ernst-Georg Schwill; ***D:*** Frank Beyer; ***W:*** Walter Gorrish; ***C:*** Gunter Marczinkowski.

Five Corners 1988 (R) A quixotic, dramatic comedy about the inhabitants of the 5 Corners section of the Bronx in 1964, centering around a girl being wooed by a psychotic rapist, her crippled boyfriend, and the hero-turned-racial-pacifist who cannot rescue her out of principle. **92m/C VHS, DVD.** Jodie Foster, John Turturro, Todd Graff, Tim Robbins, Elizabeth Berridge, Rose Gregorio, Gregory Rozakis, Rodney Harvey, John Seitz; ***D:*** Tony Bill; ***W:*** John Patrick Shanley; ***C:*** Fred Murphy; ***M:*** James Newton Howard. Ind. Spirit '89: Actress (Foster).

5 Dark Souls 1/2 1996 Three high schoolers, anxious to be part of the "in" crowd, are sent by five members of the most popular clique on a sinister woodland adventure as stars in a snuff film. **90m/C VHS.** Tina Ona Paukstelis, Mick Wynhoff, Matthew Winkler, Christopher D. Harder, Karen Dilloo, Sy Stevens, William Krekling; ***D:*** Jason Paul Collum.

Five Days 1/2 2007 Leanne (Tremarco) and her two children disappear from their car while at a rest stop—all of which is captured by CCTV cameras. The children are later found but the police investigation becomes a major news story and the action unfolds on days 1, 3, 28, 33, and 79. As the story proceeds, it becomes clear that nothing (and no one) is quite as it seems, even when the missing persons case turns into a murder inquiry. **300m/C DVD.** *GB* David Oyelowo, Hugh Bonneville, Janet McTeer, Penelope Wilton, Patrick Malahide, Edward Woodward, Sarah Smart, Christine Tremarco, Philip Davis, Rory Kinnear, Niki Amuka-Bird; ***D:*** Simon Curtis, Otto Bathurst; ***W:*** Gwyneth Hughes; ***C:*** Florian Hoffmeister; ***M:*** Magnus Fiennes. **TV**

Five Days One Summer 1982 (PG) Set in 1932, the story of a haunting and obsessive love affair between a married Scottish doctor and a young woman who happens to be his niece. While on vacation in the Swiss Alps, the doctor must vie for her love with their handsome young mountain climbing guide. Based on a story by Kay Boyle. **108m/C VHS.** Sean Connery, Betsy Brantley, Lambert Wilson; ***D:*** Fred Zinnemann; ***W:*** Michael Austin; ***M:*** Elmer Bernstein.

$5 a Day 2008 Smoothly-done father-son road trip comedy. Aging Atlantic City con man Nat (Walken) is getting by on five bucks a day, lots of freebies, and his own agenda. That includes pressing estranged son Flynn (Nivola) into taking the wheel of a customized pink PT cruiser and heading out on a cross-country road trip. They make a stop in Amarillo, Texas so Nat can visit Flynn's former babysitter and successful swindler Dolores (Stone), who knows some family secrets that Flynn doesn't (yet). **90m/C DVD.** Christopher Walken, Alessandro Nivola, Sharon Stone, Peter Coyote, Amanda Peet; ***D:*** Nigel Cole; ***W:*** Neal Dobrofsky, Tippi Dobrofsky; ***C:*** Peter Donahue; ***M:*** Alex Wurman.

Five Dolls for an August Moon 1970 A group of investment speculators try to talk scientist Gerry Farrell (Berger) into selling them the rights to a new formula, while at a wild weekend retreat on an isolated island. As the competitors try to cheat one another with secret bids, Farrell seems disinterested, and tempers rise with the stakes. The wives and girlfriends along for the fun and games feel the tension as their men stray, or try to get them to use sex to close a deal. But once the murders begin, the possibility of anyone trusting anyone is left far behind. Allegedly a professional assignment given Bava with just two days' notice, the film is a fair murder mystery in which even this director's visual tricks can't sustain interest. The cast of connivers is interchangeable and hard to keep straight, and in some cases more easily identifiable by their now-hideous 1970 fashions than their faces. **78m/C DVD.** *IT* William Berger, Ira von Furstenberg, Edwige Fenech, Howard (Red) Ross, Helena Ronee, Teodoro Corra, Ely Galleani, Edith Meloni, Mauro Bosco, Maurice Poli; ***D:*** Mario Bava; ***W:*** Mario di Nardo; ***C:*** Antonio Rinaldi; ***M:*** Pierro Umiliani.

Five Easy Pieces 1970 (R) Nicholson's superb acting brings to life this character study of a talented musician who has given up a promising career and now works on the oil rigs. After a few years he returns home to attempt one last communication with his dying father and perhaps, reconcile himself with his fear of failure and desire for greatness. Black, Anspach, and Bush create especially memorable characters. Nicholson ordering toast via a chicken salad sandwich is a classic. **98m/C VHS, DVD.** Jack Nicholson, Karen Black, Susan Anspach, Lois Smith, Billy Green Bush, Fannie Flagg, Ralph Waite, Sally Struthers, Helena Kallianiotes, Richard Stahl, Lorna Thayer; ***D:*** Bob Rafelson; ***W:*** Adrien (Carole Eastman) Joyce, Bob Rafelson; ***C:*** Laszlo Kovacs. Golden Globes '71: Support. Actress (Black); Natl. Bd. of Review '70: Support. Actress (Black), Natl. Film Reg. '00;; N.Y. Film Critics '70: Director (Rafelson), Film, Support. Actress (Black); Natl. Soc. Film Critics '70: Support. Actress (Smith).

Five Element Ninjas *Rhen zhe wu di; Chinese Super Ninjas; Yan je mo dik; Super Ninjas* **1982** Two Kung-Fu schools are having a tournament to determine who is best, but when the Masters are to compete the Master of one school sends a Japanese Samurai to fight in his place. The Samurai is soundly defeated and before committing seppuku promises that the Ninjas of the 5 Elements will take revenge upon the school. Sure enough weird ninjas in theme costumes begin killing everyone in sight. Made as one of the last efforts director Chang Cheh did for the Shaw Brothers, it is entertaining for its sheer oddity. **104m/C DVD, Blu-ray Disc.** *HK* Meng Lo, Wai-Man Chan, Tien-chi Cheng, Tien Hsiang Lung, Chen Hei Psi, Wang Lieh, Ke Chu; ***D:*** Cheh Chang; ***W:*** Cheh Chang, Kuang Ni; ***C:*** Wen Yun Huang; ***M:*** Chin Yung Shing, Chun Hao So.

Five Fingers 1/2 *Operation Cicero* **1952** Under the alias "Cicero," Albanian valet Mason joins the espionage ring, selling highly confidential British war papers to the Germans during WWII. True story with odd real-life ending—unconvinced of document authenticity, the Nazis never acted on the information, even when they had the time and date of the European invasion! Fast-paced and absorbing. Adapted from the book "Operation Cicero" by L.C. Moyzisch. **108m/B VHS.** James Mason, Danielle Darrieux, Michael Rennie, Walter Hampden, Oscar Karlweis, Herbert Berghof, John Wengraf, Michael Pate, Ivan Triesault, Hannelore Axman, David Wolfe, Nestor Paiva, Richard Loo, Keith McConnell; ***D:*** Joseph L. Mankiewicz; ***W:*** Michael Wilson; ***M:*** Bernard Herrmann; ***Nar:*** John Sutton. Golden Globes '53: Screenplay.

Five Fingers 2006 (R) Idealistic Dutch pianist Martijn (Phillippe) travels to his girlfriend's home country of Morocco in order to start a food program for children. He and his guide Gavin (Meaney) are promptly kidnapped and wake up in a warehouse where Gavin is killed. Then Ahmat (Fishburne) begins to question Martijn, believing he's actually a CIA operative. When Ahmat doesn't think the pianist is telling the truth, he begins cutting off Martijn's fingers. Martijn starts changing his story, but is he lying or not? **89m/C DVD.** Laurence Fishburne, Ryan Phillippe, Gina Torres, Colm Meaney, Said Taghmaoui, Touriya Haoud; ***D:*** Laurence Malkin; ***W:*** Laurence Malkin, Chad Thumann; ***C:*** Alexander Grusynski; ***M:*** Vernon Reid, Noah Arguss.

Five for Hell 1967 The army picks five of its meanest men for a suicide mission during WWII. They must go behind German lines and find the plans for the enemy offensive. Parolini used the pseudonym Frank Kramer. **88m/C VHS, DVD.** *IT* Klaus Kinski, Gianni "John" Garko, Aldo Canti, Margaret Lee; ***D:*** Gianfranco Parolini.

Five Giants from Texas *I Cinque Della Vendetta* **1966** El cheapo spaghetti western features Madison, TV's former Wild Bill Hickock, as a rancher fighting off displaced Mexican peasants and outlaws. **103m/C VHS.** *IT* Guy Madison, Monica Randall; ***D:*** Aldo Florio.

Five Golden Dragons 1967 A typical action film about an American running afoul of ruthless gold trafficking in Hong Kong. Even this stellar cast can't help the script. **92m/C VHS.** *GB* Robert Cummings, Christopher Lee, Brian Donlevy, Klaus Kinski, George Raft, Dan Duryea, Margaret Lee; ***D:*** Jeremy Summers.

Five Graves to Cairo 1943 Tense WWII thriller finds British soldier John Bramble (Tone) stranded in a small desert town after the defeat of the British garrison by General Rommel's (Von Stroheim) Afrika Korps. Arab hotel owner Farid (Tamiroff) agrees to let Bramble assume the identity of a dead hotel waiter, much to the dismay of French maid Moush (Baxter), whose only interest is in getting her brother out of a German POW camp. The real waiter turns out to have been a secret Nazi spy, fortunately known to Rommel only by name, so Bramble attempts to learn where the German supply depots have been hidden (the "five graves" of the title)—that is, unless Moush decides to betray him to win her brother's release. Based on the play "Hotel Imperial" by Lajos Biro. **97m/B VHS.** Franchot Tone, Anne Baxter, Erich von Stroheim, Akim Tamiroff, Peter Van Eyck, Fortunio Bonanova, Miles Mander, Konstantin Shayne, Leslie Denison, Ian Keith, Frederick Giermann, Fred Nurney; ***D:*** Billy Wilder; ***W:*** Billy Wilder, Charles Brackett; ***C:*** John Seitz; ***M:*** Miklos Rozsa.

The Five Heartbeats 1991 (R) Well told story of five black singers in the 1960s, their successes and failures as a group and as individuals. Although every horror story of the music business is included, the story remains fresh and the acting excellent. Music is fine, but secondary to the people. Well written characters with few cliches. Skillfully directed by Townsend (of "Hollywood Shuffle") who did research by talking to the Dells. Less than memorable showing at the boxoffice but fun and entertaining. **122m/C VHS, DVD.** Robert Kevin Townsend, Tressa Thomas, Michael Wright, Harry J. Lennix, Diahann Carroll, Leon, Hawthorne James, Chuck Patterson, Roy Fegan, Tico Wells, John Canada Terrell, Harold Nicholas, Paul Benjamin, Norma Donaldson, Eugene Robert Glazer, Lamont Johnson; ***D:*** Robert Kevin Townsend; ***W:*** Keenen Ivory Wayans, Robert Kevin Townsend; ***C:*** Bill Dill; ***M:*** Stanley Clarke.

(500) Days of Summer 1/2 2009 (PG-13) Downbeat romantic comedy. Sweet-natured Tom (Gordon-Levitt) works for an L.A. greeting card company and is instantly smitten by new hire, the elusive Summer (Deschanel), although he's too shy to make the first move. He believes in true and lasting love, she does not and their romantic travails are indicated in a nonlinear 500 days. Told from the baffled male point-of-view, not just Tom's but his buddies Paul (Gubler) and McKenzie (Arend), so Summer is a generally enigmatic fantasy woman/object rather than a person who speaks for herself. **95m/C DVD.** *US* Joseph Gordon-Levitt, Zooey Deschanel, Geoffrey Arend, Chloe Grace Moretz, Matthew Grey Gubler, Clark Gregg, Rachel Boston; ***D:*** Marc Webb; ***W:*** Scott Neustadter, Michael H. Weber; ***C:*** Eric Steelberg; ***M:*** Mychael Danna, Rob Simonsen. Ind. Spirit '10: Screenplay.

Five Minutes of Heaven 1/2 2009 Director Hirschbiegel's tense thriller begins in 1975 during The Troubles in Northern Ireland as 17-year-old Alistair Little (Davison) tries to earn his stripes via an anti-Catholic assassination, initially unaware that the victim's 11-year-old brother Joe Griffen (O'Neill) witnesses the slaying. Based on fact, the story steps ahead three decades to the fabricated scenario of Griffen (Nesbitt) and Little's (Neeson) planned face-to-face meeting prompted by a TV reality program looking more for ratings than amends. After serving 12 years, Little now thrives in the field of conflict resolution, and hopes to reconcile, whereas behind Griffen's seemingly normal life masks a broken man seeking revenge, dubbed his "five minutes in heaven." Told in three parts, screenwriter Hibbert plays out this "what if" scenario with guidance from the real Alistair and Griffen. **89m/C DVD.** *GB IR* Liam Neeson, James Nesbitt, Mark David, Kevin O'Neill, Anamaria Marinca, Richard Dormer; ***D:*** Oliver Hirschbiegel; ***W:*** Guy Hibbert; ***C:*** Ruairi O'Brien; ***M:*** David Holmes, Leo Abrahams.

Five Minutes to Love *The Rotten Apple; It Only Take Five Minutes* **1963** McClanahan (one of TV's "Golden Girls") plays a young, sleazy hussy named "Poochie, the girl from the shack." This exploitation schlocker appears to be McClanahan's first film. **85m/B VHS, DVD.** Rue McClanahan, Paul Leder, King Moody; ***D:*** John Hayes.

The Five of Me 1/2 1981 A man with five personalities finds that livin' ain't easy and seeks professional help. Based on the autobiography of Henry Hawksworth. **100m/C VHS.** David Birney, Dee Wallace, Mitchell Ryan, John McLiam, James Whitmore Jr., Ben Piazza; ***D:*** Paul Wendkos. **TV**

The Five Pennies 1/2 1959 Sentimental biography starring Kaye as famed jazzman Red Nichols features performances by legendary musicians Bob Crosby, Bobby Troup, Ray Anthony and Louis Armstrong. This movie marked Weld's film debut. ♫ Good Night Sleep Tight; The Five Pennies; Battle Hymn of the Republic; When the Saints Go Marching In; The Music Goes 'Round and Around; Jingle Bells; Carnival of Venice; Paradise. **117m/C VHS, DVD.** Danny Kaye, Louis Armstrong, Barbara Bel Geddes, Tuesday Weld, Harry Guardino; ***D:*** Melville Shavelson; ***W:*** Melville Shavelson, Jack Rose; ***C:*** Daniel F. Fapp.

The Five Senses 1999 Follows the trials of five urbanites, each of whom is linked to a missing child, as well as being linked to one of the five senses. Massage therapist Ruth (Rose) is losing her sense of touch; cake baker Rona (Parker) has an impaired sense of taste; housecleaner Robert (MacIvor) believes his acute sense of smell will lead to love; optholmologist Richard (Volter) is losing his hearing; and teenager Rachel (Litz) is drawn into spying games (sight) with a voyeur. Suprisingly accessible given the complex construct, each story is not only well-acted but frequently warm and witty. **105m/C VHS, DVD.** *CA*

Mary-Louise Parker, Philippe Volter, Gabrielle Rose, Daniel MacIvor, Molly Parker, Pascale Bussieres, Marco Leonardi, Brendan Fletcher, Nadia Litz; *D:* Jeremy Podeswa; *W:* Jeremy Podeswa; *C:* Gregory Middleton; *M:* Alex Pauk, Alexina Louie. Genie '99: Director (Podeswa); Toronto-City '99: Canadian Feature Film.

The 5000 Fingers of Dr. T **1953 (G)** In Dr. Seuss' only non-animated movie, a boy tries to evade piano lessons and runs right into the castle of the evil Dr. Terwilliger, where hundreds of boys are held captive for piano lessons. Worse yet, they're forced to wear silly beanies with "happy fingers" waving on top. Luckily, the trusted family plumber is on hand to save the day through means of an atomic bomb. Wonderful satire, horrible music, mesmerizing Seussian sets. The skating brothers (who are joined at their beards) are a treat. **88m/C VHS, DVD.** Peter Lind Hayes, Mary Healy, Tommy Rettig, Hans Conried, Noel Cravat; *D:* Roy Rowland; *W:* Theodore "Dr. Seuss" Geisel, Allan Scott; *C:* Franz Planer; *M:* Frederick "Friedrich" Hollander, Hans J. Salter.

5x2 1/2 *Cinq fois deux; Five Times Two* **2004 (R)** The unhappy marriage of Marion (Bruni-Tedeschi) and Gilles (Freiss) is chronicled backwards in five scenes (with two characters, hence the title), beginning with their divorce and ending with their first meeting and includes a dinner party, childbirth, and their wedding night. The couple is basically a disaster from the beginning of their relationship and you won't be terribly sympathetic (or surprised) about what happens. French with subtitles. **90m/C DVD.** *FR* Valeria Bruni-Tedeschi, Stephane Freiss, Geraldine Pailhas, Francoise Fabian, Michael (Michel) Lonsdale, Antoine Chappey; *D:* Francois Ozon; *W:* Francois Ozon, Emmanuele Bernheim; *C:* Yorick Le Saux; *M:* Philippe Rombi.

The $5.20 an Hour Dream **1980** Lavin is a divorced mother and factory worker burdened with debt and determined to get and keep a job on the higher-paying, traditionally all-male assembly line. Lesser feminist drama on the heels of "Norma Rae." **96m/C VHS.** Linda Lavin, Richard Jaeckel, Nicholas Pryor, Pamela McMyler, Mayf Nutter, Taurean Blacque, Robert Davi, Dennis Fimple, Dana Hill, Ernie Hudson; *D:* Russ Mayberry. **TV**

Five Weeks in a Balloon **1962 (PG)** This adaptation of the Jules Verne novel follows the often-comic exploits of a 19th-century British expedition that encounters many adventures on a balloon trek across Africa. Pleasant fluff with a good cast. **101m/C VHS, DVD.** Fabian, Peter Lorre, Red Buttons, Cedric Hardwicke, Barbara Eden; *D:* Irwin Allen; *W:* Charles Bennett, Irwin Allen; *C:* Winton C. Hoch.

The Fix *The Agitators* **1984** A group of cocaine smugglers get their just desserts as the federal government catches them in a sting operation. **95m/C VHS.** Vince Edwards, Richard Jaeckel, Julie Hill, Charles Dierkop, Byron Cherry, Robert Tessier; *D:* Will Zens.

Fixed Bayonets! 1/2 **1951** Fuller's second Korean War epic is just as gritty as his first ("Steel Helment"), and it stood in direct contrast to the sappy and/or nostalgic WWII pictures of the time. A unit covering the retreat of a division from an icy mountainous terrain sees its commanding officers killed off until Corporal Menno (Baseheart) remains to lead the men. Menno, hesitant to kill, learns whether he can do what needs to be done for the survival of his men. One of Fuller's best films, and that's saying a lot. **92m/B DVD.** Richard Basehart, Gene Evans, Michael O'Shea, Richard Hylton, Craig Hill, Skip Homeier, Richard Monahan, James Dean, John Doucette; *D:* Samuel Fuller; *W:* Samuel Fuller; *C:* Lucien Ballard; *M:* Roy Webb.

The Fixer **1968 (PG-13)** Based on the true story of a Jewish handyman (Bates) in 1911 Tsarist Russia who's accused of murdering a gentile boy. Wrongly imprisoned he's tortured to confess to the crime, which he refuses to do. Bogarde is the lawyer who tries to help him. Strong direction and acting in an unrelenting drama. Adapted from Bernard Malamud's Pulitzer Prize-winning novel. **132m/C VHS.** Alan Bates, Dirk Bogarde, Georgia Brown, Hugh Griffith, Elizabeth Hartman, Ian Holm, David Opatoshu, David Warner, Carol White, Murray Melvin, Peter Jeffrey, William Hutt; *D:* John Frankenheimer; *W:* Dalton Trumbo; *M:* Maurice Jarre.

The Fixer 1/2 **1997** Jack Killoran (Voight) is a corrupt Chicago lawyer who can get anything done for a price. But after he's temporarily paralyzed in an accident, Jack has a crisis of conscience and decides he'd like to go legit. However, his bosses decide he knows too much to let him go. **105m/C VHS.** Jon Voight, Brenda Bakke, J.J. Johnston, Miguel (Michael) Sandoval, Karl Pruner, Brent Jennings, Jack Wallace; *D:* Charles Robert Carner; *W:* Charles Robert Carner; *C:* Michael Goi; *M:* Lennie Niehaus. **CABLE**

Flags of Our Fathers 1/2 **2006 (R)** Director Eastwood tells the dark and ultimately sad story behind Joe Rosenthal's iconic 1945 photograph, the flag-raising by six soldiers at Iwo Jima, in his most ambitious outing to date. The government decides to whisk the three survivors home and use them on a nationwide war bonds drive, although only marine Rene Gagnon (Bradford) takes to the hoopla. Navy corpsman "Doc" Bradley (Phillippe) is haunted by the deaths and those left behind while alcoholic Pima Indian Ira Hayes (Beach) would rather fight than be subjected to the casual prejudice he constantly experiences. Successfully avoids the cliches and Hollywood conventions injected into most war stories, leaving room for surprise and genuine emotion. "Letters from Iwo Jima," also released in 2006, is Eastwood's companion film, told from the Japanese point of view. **131m/C DVD, Blu-ray Disc, HD DVD.** *US* Ryan Phillippe, Jesse Bradford, Adam Beach, Barry Pepper, John Benjamin Hickey, John Slattery, Jamie Bell, Paul Walker, Robert Patrick, Neal McDonough, Thomas (Tom) McCarthy, Melanie Lynskey, Joseph Cross, Judith Ivey, Chris Bauer, Harve Presnell, George Grizzard, Len Cariou; *D:* Clint Eastwood; *W:* William Broyles Jr., Paul Haggis; *C:* Tom Stern; *M:* Clint Eastwood.

Flakes 1/2 **2007** Slacker comedy set in New Orleans. Hippie geezer Willie (Lloyd) owns the titular restaurant that serves only breakfast cereal. It's managed by would-be rocker Neal (Stanford), whose arty girlfriend Pussy Katz (Deschanel) is frustrated by his lack of ambition. So she's delighted when yuppie Stuart (O'Donnell) opens a slick competitor across the street. An outraged Neal engages in a series of dirty tricks to deal with the upstart but Pussy goes to work for Stuart, hoping that if Neal is left jobless he'll finally take his music career seriously. Very fitfully amusing, though Deschanel is an oddball charmer. **81m/C DVD.** Aaron Stanford, Zooey Deschanel, Christopher Lloyd, Keir O'Donnell, Frank Wood, Ryan Donowho; *D:* Michael Lehmann; *W:* Karey Kirkpatrick, Chris Poche; *C:* Nancy Schreiber; *M:* Jason Derlatka, Jon Ehrlich.

Flambards 1/2 **1978** In the early 1900s, teenaged orphan Christine is sent to live with her tyrannical Uncle Russell and his two sons on their crumbling English estate, Flambards. Bitter rivalries and jealousies abound between arrogant, tradition-bound Mark and younger brother William, who's obsessed with the new-fangled airplane. Quarrels intensify as both young men fall in love with Christine and WWI begins, leading to sacrifice and tragedy. Based on the trilogy by K.M. Peyton. **676m/C VHS, DVD.** *GB* Christine McKenna, Stephen Grives, Alan Parnaby, Edward Judd, Sebastian Abineri, Peter Settelen, Carol Leader, Frank Mills; *D:* Lawrence Gordon-Clark, Peter Duffell. **TV**

The Flame & the Arrow **1950** Dardo the Arrow, a Robin Hood-like outlaw in medieval Italy, leads his band of mountain fighters against a mercenary warlord who has seduced his wife and kidnapped his son. Spectacular acrobatics, with Lancaster performing his own stunts, add interest to the usual swashbuckling. **88m/C VHS.** Burt Lancaster, Virginia Mayo, Aline MacMahon, Nick Cravat, Robert Douglas, Frank Allenby; *D:* Jacques Tourneur; *M:* Max Steiner.

The Flame Is Love 1/2 **1979** Adaptation of one of Barbara Cartland's romantic novels. A turn-of-the-century American heiress falls tragically in love with a Parisian journalist despite her engagement to an Englishman. **98m/C VHS.** Linda Purl, Timothy Dalton, Shane Briant; *D:* Michael O'Herlihy. **TV**

Flame of Araby 1/2 **1951** When Princess Tanya's (O'Hara) father is murdered, she's threatened with an unwanted marriage and loss of the throne. But if she can win a horse race, Tanya has a chance for freedom. Now, if she can only convince handsome Bedouin chief Tamerlane (Chandler), who has the fastest black stallion in the desert, to come to her aid. **78m/C VHS.** Maureen O'Hara, Jeff Chandler, Lon Chaney Jr., Buddy Baer, Maxwell Reed, Susan Cabot, Royal Dano, Richard Egan; *D:* Charles Lamont; *W:* Gerald Drayson Adams; *C:* Russell Metty.

The Flame of New Orleans **1941** Dietrich is naturally the flame in question as Claire, Countess of New Orleans. She becomes engaged to Girard (Young) but then is attracted to sailor Robert (Cabot) and strings both men along while she tries to decide what to do. Claire's temporary solution is a harebrained plan involving her posing as a lookalike cousin, just come to town. French director Clair's first U.S. film was critically panned upon its release. **79m/B VHS.** Marlene Dietrich, Bruce Cabot, Roland Young, Mischa Auer, Andy Devine, Frank Jenks, Franklin Pangborn, Laura Hope Crews; *D:* Rene Clair; *W:* Norman Krasna; *C:* Rudolph Mate; *M:* Frank Skinner.

Flame of the Barbary Coast 1/2 **1945** A rancher from Montana vies with a gambling czar for a beautiful dance hall queen and control of the Barbary Coast district of San Francisco. The great earthquake of 1906 provides the plot with a climax. Also available colorized. **91m/B DVD.** John Wayne, Ann Dvorak, Joseph Schildkraut, William Frawley; *D:* Joseph Kane.

Flame of the Islands **1955** De Carlo plays a smoldering, passionate chanteuse who struggles with love and gangsters for possession of a Bahamian casino in this tropical heat wave. **92m/C VHS.** Yvonne De Carlo, Howard Duff, Zachary Scott, James Arness, Kurt Kasznar, Barbara O'Neil; *D:* Edward Ludwig.

Flame Over India *Northwest Frontier* **1960** When Moslems lay siege to a British fortress in India, Governess Wyatt (Bacall) and Captain Scott (More) save the Maharaja's son and escape by commandeering a train. Along the way they find treason, adventure and love. **130m/C VHS.** *GB* Kenneth More, Lauren Bacall, Herbert Lom, Wilfrid Hyde-White, I.S. Johar, Ursula Jeans, Ian Hunter, Eugene Deckers, Jack (Gwyllam) Gwillim, Govind Raja Ross, Frank Olegario; *D:* J. Lee Thompson; *C:* Geoffrey Unsworth.

Flame to the Phoenix 1/2 **1985** A WWII drama about the Polish cavalry forces' decimation to German Panzer tanks. **80m/C VHS.** *GB* Paul Geoffrey, Ann(e) Firbank, Frederick Treves; *D:* William Brayne.

The Flame Trees of Thika **1981** In 1913, a British family travels to East Africa to start a coffee plantation. Seen through the eyes of the young daughter, her childhood consists of the local Masai and Kikuyu tribes, the eccentric and sometimes unhappy English neighbors, and the wild animals that roam the plains. Based on the memoirs of writer Elspeth Huxley. Four cassettes; shown on PBS "Masterpiece Theatre." **366m/C VHS, DVD.** *GB* Hayley Mills, Holly Aird, David Robb, Ben Cross; *D:* Roy Ward Baker; *W:* John Hawkesworth; *C:* Ian Wilson; *M:* Alan Blaikley.

Flaming Bullets **1945** Last of the Texas Rangers series has solid action scenes, but little else. Ritter leads the Texas Rangers in breaking up a gang with a devious scheme: breaking men out of jail, then killing them for the cash reward. **55m/B VHS.** Tex Ritter, Dave O'Brien, Guy Wilkerson, Charles "Blackie" King, Patricia Knox, I. Stanford Jolley; *D:* Harry Fraser; *W:* Harry Fraser; *C:* Robert E. Cline.

Flaming Frontiers **1938** A frontier scout matches wits against gold mine thieves. In 15 episodes. **300m/B VHS, DVD.** Johnny Mack Brown, Eleanor Hanson, Ralph Bowman; *D:* Ray Taylor.

Flaming Lead 1/2 **1939** A hard-drinkin' ranch owner hires a nightclub cowboy to help him get an Army horse contract. **57m/B VHS, DVD.** Ken Maynard, Eleanor Stewart, Walter Long, Tom London; *D:* Sam Newfield.

Flaming Signal 1/2 **1933** Featuring Flash the Wonder Labrador, this action-packed film deals with a pilot who crash-lands near a Pacific island, just as the natives, provoked by an exploitative German trader, are rising up against the whites. Both Flash and his master manage to rescue the missionary's pretty daughter. **64m/B VHS.** Noah Beery Sr., Marceline Day, Carmelita Geraghty, Mischa Auer, Henry B. Walthall, John David Horsley; *D:* Charles E. Roberts, George Jeske; *W:* Charles E. Roberts; *C:* Irvin Akers; *M:* Lee Zahler.

Flaming Star **1960** In 1870s Texas, a family with a white father and an Indian mother is caught in the midst of an Indian uprising. The mixed-blood youth, excellently played by Presley, must choose a side with tragic results for all. A stirring, well-written drama of frontier prejudice and one of Presley's best films. **101m/C VHS, DVD.** Elvis Presley, Dolores Del Rio, Barbara Eden, Steve Forrest, John McIntire, Richard Jaeckel, L.Q. Jones, Douglas Dick, Rodolfo Acosta, Ford Rainey, Karl Swenson; *D:* Donald Siegel; *W:* Nunnally Johnson, Clair Huffaker; *C:* Charles G. Clarke; *M:* Cyril Mockridge.

The Flaming Teen-Age **1956** Schlocky pseudo-documentary demonstrating the evils of drugs and alcohol. Exploitative, and the teenagers look really old. Cheaply made, and it shows. **67m/B VHS, DVD.** Noel Reyburn, Ethel Barrett, Jerry Frank, Shirley Holmes; *D:* Irvin S. Yeaworth Jr., Charles Edwards.

The Flaming Urge **1953** A small town is plagued by mysterious fires. Could a pyromaniac be on the loose? **67m/B VHS, DVD.** Harold Lloyd Jr., Cathy Downs; *D:* Harold Ericson; *W:* Harold Ericson; *C:* Clark Ramsey; *M:* Raoul Krayshaar.

The Flamingo Kid **1984 (PG-13)** Brooklyn teen Jeffrey Willis (Dillon) gets a summer job at a fancy beach club on Long Island. His plumber father, Arthur (Elizondo), remembers how to dream but is also aware of how rough the world is on dreamers. Suddenly making lots of money at a mostly easy job, the kid's attracted to the high style of local sports car dealer Phil Brody (Crenna), and finds his father's solid life a bore. By the end of the summer, he's learned the true value of both men, and the kind of man he wants to be. Excellent performances all around, nice ensemble acting among the young men who play Dillon's buddies. Great sound track. Film debut of Jones, who seems a little old for her part as a California college sophomore. **100m/C VHS, DVD.** Matt Dillon, Hector Elizondo, Molly McCarthy, Martha Gehman, Richard Crenna, Jessica Walter, Carole (Raphaelle) Davis, Janet Jones, Fisher Stevens, Bronson Pinchot; *D:* Garry Marshall; *W:* Garry Marshall, Neil Marshall; *C:* James A. Contner; *M:* Curt Sobel.

The Flamingo Rising 1/2 **2001** Impetuous Herbert T. Lee (Benben) decides to build the world's largest drive-in movie theatre in his '60s Florida community. Unfortunately, the spot he picks is right across the street from the funeral parlor run by Turner Knight (Hurt), who doesn't see it as an appropriate venue. Caught in the middle are Lee's two adopted children and his wife, Edna (McGovern), who tries to make both men see reason. Based on the novel by Larry Baker. **98m/C VHS.** Brian Benben, William Hurt, Elizabeth McGovern, Angela Bettis, Erin Broderick, Joe Torry, Chris Larkin, Olivia Oguma; *D:* Martha Coolidge; *W:* Richard Russo; *C:* Johnny E. Jensen; *M:* David Newman. **TV**

Flamingo Road **1949** A scandalously entertaining melodrama in which Crawford portrays a carnival dancer who intrigues Scott and Brian in a small Southern town where the carnival stops. Crawford shines in a role that demands her to be both tough and sensitive in a corrupt world full of political backstabbing and sleazy characters. Remade as a TV movie and television soap-opera series in 1980. **94m/B VHS.** Joan Crawford, Zachary Scott, David Brian, Sydney Greenstreet, Gertrude Michael, Gladys George, Virginia Huston, Fred Clark, Alice White; *D:* Michael Curtiz; *W:* Edmund H. North, Robert Wilder; *M:* Max Steiner.

Flanders **2006** Dumont's work (with nonprofessionals) is an acquired, frequently polarizing taste, and in this case, numbingly boring. Andre (Boidin) is a brute of a farmer who boffs local trollop Barbe (Leroux). He gets drafted and goes off to fight some nameless war in the desert. One of his fellow soldiers is Blondel (Cretel), who also knew Barbe in the biblical sense. She's back home having an abortion and going temporarily nuts while the soldiers pay the price for brutal acts against the local militia. French with subtitles. **91m/C DVD.** *FR* Samuel Boidin, Adelaide Leroux, Henri Cretel; ***D:*** Bruno Dumont; ***W:*** Bruno Dumont; ***C:*** Yves Cape.

Flannel Pajamas **2006 (R)** Raw but talky look at the nearly-three year relationship between two New Yorkers from their first date to their final breakup. Jewish Stuart (Kirk) and Catholic Nicole (Nicholson) date, marry, and try to settle into domestic life while family dilemmas (Nicole's mother is an anti-Semite, among other problems) and personal and professional disappointments take their toll. Equal opportunity nudity by both leads. **124m/C DVD.** Julianne Nicholson, Justin Kirk, Rebecca Schull, Jamie Harrold, Tom Bower, Stephanie March, Chelsea Altman; ***D:*** Jeff Lipsky; ***W:*** Jeff Lipsky; ***C:*** Martina Radwan; ***M:*** Paul Hsu.

The Flash **1990** When police scientist Barry Allen is accidentally doused by chemicals and then struck by lightening the combination makes him into a new superhero. His super quickness help his quest in fighting crime in Central City where he's aided by fellow scientist Tina McGee (the only other person to know his secret). In this adventure, the Flash seeks out the violent and mesmerizing leader of a biker gang who caused the death of Barry's brother. Based on the DC comic book character, this is the pilot episode for the short-lived TV series. The look is dark and stylized and not played for camp. **94m/C VHS.** John Wesley Shipp, Amanda Pays, Michael Nader; ***M:*** Danny Elfman. **TV**

Flash **1998** Fourteen-year-old Connor's (Black) best friend is a horse named Flash. When his family hits hard times, Connor's dad (Kerwin) joins the merchant marines, his grandmother (Burstyn) goes to work in a factory, and Connor is forced to sell Flash. The teen takes a job in the new owner's stables and when he sees how badly the animal is treated, Connor steals Flash and sets off to meet his father's ship in New York. **90m/C VHS, DVD.** Lucas Black, Ellen Burstyn, Brian Kerwin, Shawn Toovey, Tom Nowicki, Dan Biggers; ***D:*** Simon Wincer. **TV**

Flash & Firecat **1975 (PG)** A beautiful blonde and a crazy thief steal and race their way across the country in a dune buggy with the police hot on their trail. **90m/C VHS.** Roger Davis, Tricia Sembera, Dub Taylor, Richard Kiel; ***D:*** Ferd Sebastian.

Flash Gordon **1980 (PG)** Camp version of the adventures of Flash Gordon in outer space. This time, Flash and Dale Arden are forced by Dr. Zarkov to accompany him on a mission to far-off Mongo, where Ming the Merciless is threatening the destruction of Earth. Music by Queen. **111m/C VHS, DVD.** Sam Jones, Melody Anderson, Chaim Topol, Max von Sydow, Ornella Muti, Timothy Dalton, Brian Blessed; ***D:*** Mike Hodges; ***W:*** Lorenzo Semple Jr.; ***C:*** Gilbert Taylor; ***M:*** Howard Blake.

Flash Gordon Conquers the Universe *Purple Death from Outer Space* **1940** Ravaging plague strikes the earth and Flash Gordon undertakes to stop it. A serial in 12 chapters. **240m/B VHS, DVD.** Buster Crabbe, Carol Hughes, Charles Middleton, Frank Shannon, Anne Gwynne, John Hamilton, Herbert Rawlinson, Tom Chatterton; ***D:*** Ford Beebe, Ray Taylor; ***W:*** George Plympton, Basil Dickey, Barry Shipman; ***C:*** Jerome Ash, William Sickner.

Flash Gordon: Mars Attacks the World *The Deadly Rays from Mars; Flash Gordon's Trip to Mars* **1939** The earth is plagued by the evil Ming, but Flash Gordon steps in. From the serial. **97m/B VHS, DVD.** Buster Crabbe, Jean Rogers, Charles Middleton; ***D:*** Robert F. "Bob" Hill, Ford Beebe.

Flash Gordon: Rocketship ½ *Spaceship to the Unknown; Perils from Planet Mongo; Space Soldiers; Atomic Rocketship* **1940** Re-edited from the original Flash Gordon serial in which Flash and company must prevent the planet Mongo from colliding with Earth. Good character acting and good clean fun. **82m/B VHS, DVD.** Buster Crabbe, Jean Rogers, Frank Shannon, Charles Middleton, Priscilla Lawson, Jack Lipson; ***D:*** Frederick Stephani.

Flash of Genius ½ **2008 (PG-13)** In 1967 Detroit, engineering professor Robert Kearns patented an idea for intermittent windshield wipers—ones that aren't just set at on or off. He pitched the idea, without giving away the mechanics, to Ford, who stole the idea and didn't pay up. Two decades later, Kearns sued and won, with automakers coming to a settlement without admitting to any wrongdoing. Kearns, played affectionately by Kinnear, struggles to perfect his invention, testing the patience of his business partner (Mulroney) and his lawyer (Alda), while trying to squeeze in time for his loved ones. In the end, the audience is left to decide whether all those maddening years that resulted in ruined friendships and family strife were worth the payoff. **120m/C DVD.** *US* Greg Kinnear, Lauren Graham, Dermot Mulroney, Daniel Roebuck, Jake Abel, Tim Kelleher, Alan Alda, Bill Smitrovich; ***D:*** Marc Abraham; ***W:*** Philip Railsback; ***C:*** Dante Spinotti; ***M:*** Aaron Zigman.

A Flash of Green **1985** A crooked politician is helping a construction firm exploit valuable waterfront property. He enlists the influence of a hesitant local journalist, who then falls for the woman leading the homeowner's conservation drive against the development plan. Made for American Playhouse and produced by costar Jordon. Based on the work of John D. MacDonald. **122m/C VHS.** Ed Harris, Blair Brown, Richard Jordan, George Coe; ***D:*** Victor Nunez; ***W:*** Victor Nunez; ***M:*** Charles Engstrom.

Flash Point ½ *Dou fo sin; Flashpoint; City with No Mercy; Dao huo xian; Po jun* **2007** Detective Sergeant Ma Jun (Donnie Yen) is a cop who always gets his man, no matter how much collateral damage is done in the process. His lifelong nemeses are three Vietnamese brothers who are rising stars in organized crime, and he assigns a cop named Wilson (Louis Koo) to infiltrate their gang. Although Wilson violently disagrees with Jun, he does as ordered, and gets caught. **87m/C DVD, Blu-ray Disc.** *CH HK* Donnie Yen, Louis Koo, Collin Chou, Bingbing Fan, Kent Cheng, Ben Lam, Ray Lui, Yu Xing, Qing Xu, Lan Law, Irene Wang, Austin Wai, Wai Ai, Chi Wai Wong, Aaron Leung; ***D:*** Wilson (Wai-Shun) Yip; ***W:*** Kam-yeun Szeto, Lik-Kei Tang; ***C:*** Man Po Cheung; ***M:*** Kwong Wing Chan.

Flashback **1989 (R)** FBI agent Sutherland's assignment sounds easy: escort aging 1960s radical Hopper to prison. But Hopper is cunning and decides not to go without a fight. He uses his brain to outwit the young Sutherland and to turn him against himself. Good moments between the two leads and with Kane, as a woman who never left the '60s behind. **108m/C VHS.** Dennis Hopper, Kiefer Sutherland, Carol Kane, Cliff DeYoung, Paul Dooley, Michael McKean, Richard Masur; ***D:*** Franco Amurri; ***M:*** Barry Goldberg.

Flashbacks of a Fool ½ **2008 (R)** Washed-up British movie star Joe Scot (Craig) is living in L.A. and spending more time with drugs and sex than his career. News of the sudden death of his best childhood mate leads Joe to a drunken night, a suicide attempt, and an extended flashback to his teenaged years in 1970s Britain and an ultimately tragic affair with a married woman. Not terribly compelling or coherent despite the cast. **113m/C DVD.** *GB* Daniel Craig, Harry Eden, Jodhi May, Felicity Jones, Max Deacon, Claire Forlani, Olivia Williams, Eve, Helen McCrory, Mark Strong, Keeley Hawes, James D'Arcy; ***D:*** Baillie Walsh; ***W:*** Baillie Walsh; ***C:*** John Mathieson.

Flashdance **1983 (R)** 18-year-old Alex (Beals) wants to dance. She works all day as a welder, has a hot affair going with her boss Nick (Nouri), dances at a local bar at night, and hopes someday to get enough courage to audition for a spot at the School of Ballet. Glossy music video redeemed somewhat by exciting choreography with Marine Jahan doing the dancing for Beals. Oscar-winning title song sung by Irene Cara. Inspired the torn-sweatshirt trend in fashion of the period. ♫ Flashdance...What a Feeling; I Love Rock 'n Roll; Manhunt; Gloria; Lady, Lady, Lady; Seduce Me Tonight. **95m/C VHS, DVD.** Jennifer Beals, Michael Nouri, Belinda Bauer, Lilia Skala, Cynthia Rhodes, Sunny Johnson, Lee Ving, Kyle T. Heffner, Ron Karabatsos, Robert Wuhl, Elizabeth Sagal; ***D:*** Adrian Lyne; ***W:*** Joe Eszterhas; ***C:*** Don Peterman; ***M:*** Giorgio Moroder. Oscars '83: Song ("Flashdance...What a Feeling"); Golden Globes '84: Song ("Flashdance...What a Feeling"), Score.

Flashfire ½ **1994 (R)** The torching of an apartment building and the murder of a cop seem unrelated until troubled detective Jack Flinder (Zane) becomes involved. Soon, he and murder witness Lisa (Minter) are on the run from the arsonists and crooked police. **88m/C VHS, DVD.** Billy Zane, Kristin Minter, Louis Gossett Jr.; ***D:*** Elliot Silverstein; ***W:*** John Warren, Dan York; ***C:*** Albert J. Dunk; ***M:*** Sylvester Levay.

Flashpoint **1984 (R)** A pair of Texas border patrolmen discover an abandoned jeep that contains a fortune in cash, apparently from the 1960s. As they try to figure out how it got there, they become prey to those who want to keep the secret. With this cast, flick ought to be better. **95m/C VHS, DVD.** Terry Alexander, Treat Williams, Kris Kristofferson, Tess Harper, Rip Torn, Miguel Ferrer, Roberts Blossom; ***D:*** William (Bill) Tannen; ***W:*** Michael Butler.

Flashpoint Africa ½ **1984** When a news team follows a terrorist group's activities it winds up in a power struggle with terrifying consequences. **99m/C VHS.** Trevor Howard, Gayle Hunnicutt, James Faulkner, Ken Gampu; ***D:*** Francis Megahy.

Flat Top ½ **1952** The training of Navy fighter pilots aboard "flat top" aircraft carriers during WWII provides the drama here. A strict commander is appreciated only after the war when the pilots realize his role in their survival. The film makes good use of actual combat footage; fast-paced and effective. **85m/C VHS, DVD.** Sterling Hayden, Richard Carlson, Keith Larsen, John Bromfield; ***D:*** Lesley Selander.

Flatbed Annie and Sweetiepie: Lady Truckers ½ *Flatbed Annie* **1979** A couple of good ol' gals hit the road and encounter a variety of bad guys out to steal their truck. **100m/C VHS.** Annie Potts, Kim Darby, Harry Dean Stanton, Arthur Godfrey, Rory Calhoun, Billy Carter, Avery Schreiber; ***D:*** Robert Greenwald. **TV**

Flatfoot *The Knock-Out Cop* **1978 (PG)** Tough police officer will let nothing stop him from finding and arresting drug smugglers. Good for laughs as well as lots of action. **113m/C VHS, DVD.** *IT GE* Bodo, Werner Pochath, Bud Spencer, Enzo Cannavale, Dagmar Lassander, Joe Stewardson; ***D:*** Steno.

Flatliners **1990 (R)** A group of medical students begin after-hours experimentation with death and out-of-body experiences. Some standard horror film images but Roberts and Sutherland create an energy that makes it worth watching. **111m/C VHS, DVD, Blu-ray Disc.** Kiefer Sutherland, Julia Roberts, William Baldwin, Oliver Platt, Kevin Bacon, Kimberly Scott, Joshua Rudoy, Aeryk Egan; ***D:*** Joel Schumacher; ***W:*** Peter Filardi; ***C:*** Jan De Bont; ***M:*** James Newton Howard.

Flawless **1999 (R)** Former New York City cop and resident tough guy Walt Koontz (De Niro) lives across the hall from nosily outrageous drag queen Rusty (Hoffman). The odd couple have a mutual animosity that's put to the test when Walt suffers a stroke and it's recommended that he take singing lessons to help him recover his ability to speak. So he makes an offer to Rusty who needs the cash. Soon they're not only tolerating each other but bonding as well. There are distracting subplots about hidden drug money and a drag queen beauty contest that take the focus off of what could have worked as a two-character study about an unlikely friendship. **111m/C VHS, DVD.** Robert De Niro, Philip Seymour Hoffman, Barry Miller, Chris Bauer, Skipp (Robert L.) Sudduth, Wanda De Jesus, Daphne Rubin-Vega, Rory Cochrane; ***D:*** Joel Schumacher; ***W:*** Joel Schumacher; ***C:*** Declan Quinn; ***M:*** Bruce Roberts.

Flawless **2007 (PG-13)** A soon-to-retire janitor (Caine) of the London Diamond Corporation convinces the company's only female executive (Moore) to help him make off with the merchandise—a scheme she easily agrees to after years of sexist, lying bosses stepping on her head to climb higher on the ladder. Set in 1960's London, told in flashback by an elderly, heavily made-up Moore. Slow pace and cheesy ending keep the drama and suspense in mediocrity. **108m/C DVD.** *LU GB US* Demi Moore, Michael Caine, Joss Ackland, Lambert Wilson; ***D:*** Michael Radford; ***W:*** Edward A. Anderson; ***C:*** Richard Greatrex; ***M:*** Stephen Warbeck.

Fled **1996 (R)** Charles Piper (Fishburne) and Luke Dodge (Baldwin) are combative prison escapees who need to find a stash of cash and a computer disk that could save them from both the Cuban mob and the cops. Bombshell Cora (Hayek) decides to help the duo and tries to get steamy with Piper. Lots of chases, lots of violence, not much sense. The climatic battle (the film was shot around Atlanta) takes place in a sightseeing gondola at Georgia's Stone Mountain. **98m/C VHS, DVD.** Laurence Fishburne, Stephen Baldwin, Salma Hayek, Will Patton, Robert John Burke; ***D:*** Kevin Hooks; ***W:*** Preston A. Whitmore II; ***C:*** Matthew F. Leonetti; ***M:*** Graeme Revell.

Fleeing by Night ½ *Ye Ben* **2000** Old-fashioned romantic melodrama set in 1930s China. A small town businessman owns a theater and invites a Beijing opera company to perform there. His naive daughter Wei Ing-er (Liu) is smitten by moody performer Lin Chung (Yin) as is (unexpectedly) her American-schooled fiance Hsu Shao-dung (Huang). But the twosome have a rival for Lin Chung's affections—the wealthy and jealous Huang Zilei (Tai), whose sexual interest is blatant. The dialogue is frequently florid (as probably befits the setting) and it's operatic soap all the way. Mandarin with subtitles. **123m/C DVD.** *TW* Rene Liu, Lei Huang, Chao-te Yin, Li-jen Tai, Ah-Leh Gua; ***D:*** Li-Kong Hsu, Chi Yin; ***W:*** Hui-Ling Wang, Mingxia Wang; ***C:*** Cheng-hui Tsai; ***M:*** Chris Babida.

Flesh *Andy Warhol's Flesh* **1968** An Andy Warhol-produced seedy urban farce about a bisexual street hustler who meets a variety of drug-addicted, deformed, and sexually deviant people. Dallesandro fans will enjoy his extensive exposure (literally). **90m/C VHS, DVD.** Joe Dallesandro, Geraldine Smith, Patti D'Arbanville, Candy Darling, Jackie Curtis, Geri Miller, Barry Brown; ***D:*** Paul Morrissey; ***W:*** Paul Morrissey; ***C:*** Paul Morrissey.

Flesh and Blood **1922** An unjustly convicted lawyer is released from prison to find out his wife has died. He vows revenge on those who falsely imprisoned him and assumes the disguise of a crippled beggar to begin his plot. Silent with musical score. **75m/B VHS, DVD.** Lon Chaney Sr.; ***D:*** Irving Cummings.

Flesh and Blood ½ *The Rose and the Sword* **1985 (R)** A rowdy group of 16th Century hellions makes off with a princess who is already spoken for and pillage and plunder their way to revenge. Hauer leads the motley group through sword fights, raids, and the like. Dutch director Verhoeven's first English language film. Not for children; with rape scenes, nudity, and graphic sex. **126m/C VHS, DVD.** Rutger Hauer, Jennifer Jason Leigh, Tom Burlinson, Susan Tyrrell, Jack Thompson, Ronald Lacey, Brion James, Bruno Kirby; ***D:*** Paul Verhoeven; ***W:*** Paul Verhoeven, Gerard Soeteman; ***C:*** Jan De Bont; ***M:*** Basil Poledouris.

Flesh and Blood Show *Asylum of the Insane* **1973 (R)** Rehearsal turns into an execution ritual for a group of actors at a mysterious seaside theatre. Truth in titling: features blood, gore, and some sex. Shot in part in 3-D. **93m/C VHS, DVD.** *GB* Robin Askwith, Candace Glendenning, Tristan Rogers, Ray Brooks, Jenny Hanley, Luan Peters, Patrick Barr, Judy Matheson, Penny Meredith; ***D:*** Pete Walker; ***W:*** Alfred Shaughnessy; ***C:*** Peter Jessop.

Flesh and Bone **1993 (R)** Quaid is exact as a vending machine distributor with a desolate rural Texas circuit, haunted by the memory of a decades-old murder committed by his father (Caan) during a botched farmhouse robbery. Alcoholic Ryan (Quaid's real-life wife) emerges from a bad marriage and helps Quaid rebuild his life, never suspecting that they may have met before. Challenging but successful role for Ryan, better known for her girlish, romantic-comedy appeal. Paltrow's unforgettable as a heartless casket robber and Caan's partner/girlfriend. Director Kloves extracts moments of earthy beauty from the bleak, humble West Texas setting. **127m/C VHS, DVD.** Dennis Quaid, Meg Ryan, James Caan, Gwyneth Paltrow, Scott Wilson, Christopher Rydell; ***D:*** Steve Kloves; ***W:*** Steve Kloves; ***M:*** Thomas Newman.

The Flesh and the Devil 🦴🦴🦴 1/2 **1927** Classic Garbo at her seductive best as a woman who causes a feud between two friends. Gilbert is an Austrian officer, falls for the married Garbo and winds up killing her husband in a duel. Banished to the African Corps he asks his best friend (Hanson) to look after his lady love. But Hanson takes his job too seriously, falling for the lady himself. Great silent movie with surprise ending to match. The first Gilbert and Garbo pairing. **112m/B VHS, DVD.** John Gilbert, Greta Garbo, Lars Hanson, Barbara Kent, George Fawcett, Eugenie Besserer; ***D:*** Clarence Brown; ***C:*** William H. Daniels. Natl. Film Reg. '06.

The Flesh and the Fiends 🦴🦴 1/2 *Mania; Fiendish Ghouls; Psycho Killers* **1960** Fine adaptation of the Burke and Hare grave robbing legend. Cushing is the doctor who needs corpses and Pleasence and Rose provide them by any means. Highly atmospheric representation of dismal, 19th century Edinburgh. Very graphic for its time. **87m/B VHS, DVD.** *GB* Peter Cushing, June Laverick, Donald Pleasence, George Rose, Dermot Walsh, Renee Houston, Billie Whitelaw, John Cairney, Michael Balfour; ***D:*** John Gilling; ***W:*** John Gilling, Leon Griffiths; ***C:*** Monty Berman; ***M:*** Stanley Black.

Flesh and the Spur 🦴 1/2 **1957** A cowboy tracks the killer of his brother. Future Mannix Mike Connors (nicknamed 'Touch' at the time) joins the search. Unedifying western with oddball touches, notably a theme song by Chipmunks creator Ross Bagdasarian. **78m/C VHS.** John Agar, Marla English, Mike Connors, Raymond Hatton, Maria Monay, Joyce Meadows, Kenne Duncan; ***D:*** Edward L. Cahn.

The Flesh Eaters 🦴 1/2 **1964** A claustrophobic low-budget thriller about a film queen and her secretary who crash-land on an island inhabited by your basic mad scientist. His latest experiment is with tiny flesh-eating sea creatures. Shock ending. **87m/C VHS, DVD.** Martin Kosleck, Rita Morley, Byron Sanders, Barbara Wilkin, Ray Tudor; ***D:*** Jack Curtis; ***W:*** Arnold Drake; ***C:*** Carson Davidson.

Flesh Eating Mothers 🦴 **1989** Housewives are transformed into cannibals after a mystery virus hits their town. Their kids must stop the moms from eating any more people. **90m/C VHS, DVD.** Robert Lee Oliver, Donatella Hecht, Valorie Hubbard, Neal Rosen, Terry Hayes; ***D:*** James Aviles Martin.

Flesh Feast WOOF! **1969 (R)** Classically horrendous anti-Nazi bosh, in which a mad female plastic surgeon (Lake) rejuvenates Hitler and then tortures him to death with maggots to avenge her mother's suffering. Lake's last film, and the sorriest sign-off any actress ever had. **72m/C VHS, DVD.** Veronica Lake, Phil Philbin, Heather Hughes, Martha Mischon, Yanka (Doris Keating) Mann, Dianne Wilhite, Chris Martell; ***D:*** Brad F. Ginter.

Flesh Gordon 🦴 **1972** Soft-core spoof of the "Flash Gordon" series. Flesh takes it upon himself to save Earth from the evil Wang's sex ray; Wang, of course, being the leader of the planet Porno. Lackluster special effects and below par story dull an already ridiculous movie. Look for cameo by real-life porn starlet Candy Samples. The restored (90-minute) version also includes the theatrical trailer; a 72-minute R-rated version is also available. **90m/C VHS, DVD.** Jason Williams, Suzanne Fields, Joseph Hudgins, John Hoyt, Howard Zieff, Michael Benveniste; ***Cameos:*** Candy Samples; ***D:*** Howard Ziehm, Michael Benveniste; ***W:*** Michael Benveniste; ***C:*** Howard Ziehm; ***M:*** Ralph Ferraro; ***V:*** Craig T. Nelson.

Flesh Gordon 2: Flesh Gordon Meets the Cosmic Cheerleaders 🦴 **1990** Emperor Wang (Hunt) threatens the Universe with his powerful Impotence ray. Flesh (Murdocco), along with Dale (Kelly) and Dr. Flexi Jerkoff (Travis), do battle with a belt of farting assteroids and other weirdos. Director Ziehm delivers this one on a shoestring of under $1 million, even improving technically on the original. The sex scenes are, however, more watered down in an apparent attempt to gain a wider audience. Scatological jokes are the basis for much of the humor. **98m/C VHS, DVD.** *CA* Vince Murdocco, Tony Travis, William Dennis Hunt, Robyn Kelly, Morgan Fox, Melissa Mounds; ***D:*** Howard Ziehm; ***W:*** Howard Ziehm; ***C:*** Danny Nowak.

Fleshburn 🦴🦴 **1984 (R)** An Indian Vietnam War veteran escapes from a mental institution to get revenge on the four psychiatrists who committed him. **91m/C VHS, DVD.** Steve Kanaly, Karen Carlson, Sonny Landham, Macon McCalman; ***D:*** George Gage; ***W:*** George Gage, Beth Gage, Brian Garfield; ***M:*** Arthur Kempel.

Fleshpot on 42nd Street 🦴 **1971** Stark, realistic look at the streetwalking profession. Dusty leaves her blue collar boyfriend to move in with a transvestite and then she meets a dashing young Staten Island native (like the director). Their romance blooms until he is run over by a car, sending Dusty into a tailspin which lands her back on 42nd Street. Along the way, various rustic hookers and venerable old floozies liven up director Mulligan's version of New York. Less emphasis on the sleaze than the grittiness. **78m/C VHS.** Diana Lewis, Lynn Flanagan, Bob Walters; ***D:*** Andy Milligan.

Fleshtone 🦴🦴 **1994 (R)** Artist Matthew Greco's (Kemp) work is not for the faint-hearted since he paints grisly suicides and murders. No wonder he's lonely—so lonely that he answers a phone-sex ad and is hooked up with Edna (Cutter), who becomes an obsession. Matthew even depicts her murder in one of his paintings and then she's found dead—only it turns out not to be Edna, who doesn't exist. Just what has Matthew gotten himself into? Provocative but ending is a letdown. An unrated version is also available. **89m/C VHS.** Martin Kemp, Lise Cutter, Tim Thomerson; ***D:*** Harry Hurwitz; ***W:*** Harry Hurwitz.

Fletch 🦴🦴 **1985 (PG)** Somewhat charming comedy. When newspaper journalist Fletch goes undercover to get the scoop on the local drug scene, a wealthy young businessman enlists his help in dying. Something's rotten in Denmark when the man's doctor knows nothing of the illness and Fletch comes closer to the drug scene than he realizes. Throughout the entire film, Chevy Chase assumes a multitude of flippant comic characters to discover the truth. Based on Gregory McDonald's novel. **98m/C VHS, DVD.** Chevy Chase, Tim Matheson, Joe Don Baker, Dana Wheeler-Nicholson, M. Emmet Walsh, Kenneth Mars, Geena Davis, Richard Libertini, George Wendt, Kareem Abdul-Jabbar, Alison La Placa, George Wyner, Tony Longo, James Avery, William Sanderson, Beau Starr, Ralph Seymour, Larry "Flash" Jenkins; ***D:*** Michael Ritchie; ***W:*** Andrew Bergman; ***C:*** Fred Schuler; ***M:*** Harold Faltermeyer.

Fletch Lives 🦴🦴 **1989 (PG)** In this sequel to "Fletch," Chase is back again as the super-reporter. When Fletch learns of his inheritance of a Southern estate he is eager to claim it. During his down-home trip he becomes involved in a murder and must use his disguise skills to solve it before he becomes the next victim. Based on the novels of Gregory MacDonald. **95m/C VHS, DVD.** Chevy Chase, Hal Holbrook, Julianne Phillips, Richard Libertini, R. Lee Ermey, Cleavon Little, Randall "Tex" Cobb, Richard Belzer, Geoffrey Lewis, Patricia Kalember, Phil Hartman, George Wyner; ***D:*** Michael Ritchie; ***W:*** Leon Capetanos; ***M:*** Harold Faltermeyer.

Flexing with Monty 🦴 **2010** So what happens to your film when your lead actor suddenly dies (as Goddard did in 2003)? Well, Albo (who also had financial problems) apparently carried on in some fashion to finally get a release. Bigoted, narcissist bodybuilder Monty (Goddard) lives to indulge his gym rat obsession and to torment his emotionally fragile younger brother Bertin (Davis). Their delicately-balanced lives are upended by the arrival of Catholic nun Lilith (Kirkland), who's fundraising for a very strange charity. **90m/C DVD.** Trevor Goddard, Rudi Davis, Sally Kirkland; ***D:*** John Albo; ***W:*** John Albo; ***C:*** Thomas Denove; ***M:*** Miriam Cutler. **VIDEO**

Flicka 🦴🦴 1/2 **2006 (PG)** A girl and her horse. Katy McLaughlin (Lohman) is happy to return to her family's struggling Wyoming ranch after having blown her year at boarding school. She would much rather help her traditionalist father, Rob (McGraw), breed quarter horses, although dad is leaning on her older brother Howard (Kwanten). Mom Nell (Bello) plays peacemaker. The situation worsens when Katy corrals and decides to tame the wild black stallion of the title. But when dad sells Flicka to the rodeo, Katy is determined to get the horse back. C-W singing star McGraw is a natural while the twentysomething Lohman can still easily pass for a big-hearted, hard-headed teen. **94m/C DVD.** *US* Alison Lohman, Tim McGraw, Maria Bello, Ryan Kwanten, Dallas Roberts, Nick Searcy, Jeffrey Nordling, Danny Pino; ***D:*** Michael Mayer; ***W:*** Mark Rosenthal, Larry Konner; ***C:*** J.(James) Michael Muro; ***M:*** Aaron Zigman.

Flickering Lights 🦴 1/2 *Blikende Lygter* **2001** Trokild (Pilmark) is deeply in debt to gangster Eskimo (Andersson). He and pals Peter (Thomsen), Arne (Mikkelsen), and Stefan (Kaas) are surprised to discover the briefcase they've been forced to steal contains a lot of money. They decide to keep the cash and are heading for Spain when their getaway truck breaks down in the woods. The foursome finds refuge in an abandoned inn and Torkild, who's tired of the criminal life, decides to use the money to buy the inn and open it back up so they can all start new lives. Of course, Eskimo may have other ideas when he finds them. An uncertain mixture of dark humor and sentimentality. Danish with subtitles. **109m/C VHS, DVD.** *DK* Soren Pilmark, Ulrich Thomsen, Mads Mikkelsen, Nikolaj Lie Kaas, Peter Andersson, Sofie Grabol, Iben Hjejle, Frits Helmuth; ***D:*** Anders Thomas Jensen; ***W:*** Anders Thomas Jensen; ***C:*** Eric Kress; ***M:*** Bent Fabricius-Bjerre, Jeppe Kaas.

Flickers 🦴🦴 1/2 **1980** Uncouth, ambitious Cockney Arnie Cole (Hoskins), wants to go from bioscope exhibitor to owner of his own silent-film production company. But he needs money—and upper middle-class Maud (de la Tour) needs a husband since she's pregnant and being a single mum won't do. The oddball duo make a business arrangement that turns into something more, all the while surrounded by the eccentrics and egotists who are involved with Arnie's new venture. Hoskins and de la Tour are an amusing visual mismatch (she's a stork and he's a fireplug) and a delight as sparring partners. 6 episodes. **307m/C DVD.** *GB* Bob Hoskins, Frances de la Tour, Peggy Wood, Dickie Arnold, Valerie Holliman, Fraser Cains, Granville Saxon, Jim Hooper, Joanna Foster; ***D:*** Cyril Coke; ***W:*** Roy Clarke. **TV**

Flicks *Hollyweird; Loose Joints* **1985 (R)** A compilation of skits parodying the tradition of Saturday afternoon matinees, including coming attractions and a cartoon. Never released theatrically. **79m/C VHS.** Martin Mull, Joan Hackett, Pamela Sue Martin, Betty Kennedy, Richard Belzer; ***D:*** Peter Winograd.

The Flight 🦴🦴 **1989** A non-narrative view of glider planes as they soar over the countryside and rivers of the Laurentians and Canadian Rockies. Useful in language arts classes. **96m/C VHS.** Eli Danker, Sandy McPeak, Lindsay Wagner; ***D:*** Paul Wendkos.

Flight from Glory 🦴🦴 1/2 **1937** A group of pilots fly supplies over the Andes from their isolated base camp to even more isolated mines. Morris is their leader who watches as, one by one, the men are killed on their dangerous flights. To make a bad situtation worse, Heflin arrives as a new recruit—along with his pretty wife. **66m/B VHS, DVD.** Chester Morris, Onslow Stevens, Whitney Bourne, Van Heflin; ***D:*** Lew Landers.

Flight from Singapore 🦴 1/2 **1962** Transporting desperately needed blood to Malaysia, a flight crew is forced to crash land in the jungle. Nicely done if trite. **74m/B VHS.** *GB* Patrick Allen, Patrick Holt, William Abney, Harry Fowler; ***D:*** Dudley Birch; ***W:*** Dudley Birch.

Flight from Vienna 🦴🦴 **1956** A high-ranking Hungarian security officer, disenchanted with communism, stages a daring escape from his country. In Vienna, he asks the British for political asylum, but is sent back to Hungary to help a scientist escape in order to prove his loyalty. Cold war drama hangs together on strength of Bikel's performance. **54m/B VHS.** Theodore Bikel, John Bentley, Donald Gray, Adrienne Scott, Carina Helm; ***D:*** Denis Kavanagh; ***W:*** Denis Kavanagh; ***C:*** Hal Morey.

Flight of Black Angel 🦴🦴 1/2 **1991 (R)** Wacked-out F-16 pilot fancies himself an angel of death, and, after annihilating a number of trainees, sets out to make Las Vegas a nuked-out ghost town. Squadron commander Strauss, however, is not pleased with his pilot's initiative. Made-for-cable script runs out of gas and heads into a nosedive. **102m/C VHS, DVD.** Peter Strauss, William O'Leary, James O'Sullivan, Michael Keys Hall; ***D:*** Jonathan Mostow; ***W:*** John Brancato. **CABLE**

Flight of Dragons 🦴🦴 1/2 **1982** Animated tale takes place between the Age of Magic and the Age of Science, in a century when dragons ruled the skies. **98m/C VHS.** ***D:*** Arthur Rankin Jr., Jules Bass; ***V:*** John Ritter, Victor Buono, James Earl Jones, Donald E. Messick, Larry Storch.

A Flight of Rainbirds 🦴🦴 **1981** In a dual role, Krabbe plays a biologist who dreams he must lose his virginity within a week or die and his alter ego who joins him in the search for the perfect woman. In Dutch with English subtitles. **94m/C VHS.** *NL* Jeroen Krabbe, Willeke Van Ammelrooy, Marijke Merckens; ***D:*** Ate De Jong; ***W:*** Ate De Jong; ***C:*** Paul van den Bos; ***M:*** Laurens van Rooyen.

Flight of the Eagle 🦴🦴 1/2 **1982** Based on the actual ill-fated expedition of Salomon Andree who, with two friends, attempted to fly from Sweden to the North Pole in a hydrogen balloon in 1897. The last half of the film drags somewhat as the three struggle to survive in the frozen north after their balloon crashes. Beautifully photographed adventure. In Swedish with English subtitles. **115m/C VHS.** *SW* Max von Sydow, Goran Stangertz, Clement Harari, Sverre Anker; ***D:*** Jan Troell.

Flight of the Grey Wolf 🦴 1/2 **1976** A tame, innocent wolf is mistaken for a killer and must run for his life with the help of his boy-owner. **82m/C VHS.** Bill Williams, Barbara Hale, Jeff East; ***D:*** Frank Zuniga; ***W:*** Calvin Clements Jr.

Flight of the Innocent 🦴🦴 1/2 **1993 (R)** The innocent 10-year-old Vito comes from a family who make their living as kidnappers. He is the only witness (and the only survivor) when his family is massacred by a rival gang. Vito flees the carnage and sets off to find his cousin who lives in Rome. But his journey truly ends when he is taken in by a wealthy industrialist family whose own son has been kidnapped. Directorial debut of Carlei who tends to rely on striking visuals rather than his characters. In Italian with English subtitles. **105m/C VHS, DVD.** *IT* Manuel Colao, Francesca Neri, Jacques Perrin, Frederico Pacifici, Sal Borgese; ***D:*** Carlo Carlei; ***W:*** Carlo Carlei, Gualtiero Rosella.

Flight of the Intruder 🦴 1/2 **1990 (PG-13)** Vietnam naval pilots aboard an aircraft carrier don't like the way the war is being handled, so they go rogue and decide to go on a mission to bomb an enemy air base in Hanoi. Loads of male bonding. **115m/C VHS, DVD.** Danny Glover, Willem Dafoe, Brad Johnson, Rosanna Arquette, Tom Sizemore, Ving Rhames, David Schwimmer; ***D:*** John Milius; ***W:*** Robert Dillon; ***C:*** Fred W. Koenekamp; ***M:*** Basil Poledouris.

Flight of the Living Dead: Outbreak on a Plane 🦴🦴 *Plane Dead* **2007** Campy, fast-paced gore. A scientist brings a corpse infected with a genetically engineered virus aboard a flight from L.A. to Paris. The zombie escapes from the cargo hold and infects the passengers, who really have nowhere to run. **93m/C DVD.** Kevin J. O'Connor, Derek Webster, Raymond J. Barry, Dale Midkiff, David Chisum, Kristen Kerr, Erik Avari, Richard Tyson; *D:* Scott Thomas; *W:* Scott Thomas, Mark Onspaugh; *C:* Mark Eberle; *M:* Nathan Wang. **VIDEO**

Flight of the Navigator 1/2 **1986 (PG)** A boy boards an alien spacecraft and embarks on a series of time-travel adventures with a crew of wisecracking extraterrestrial creatures. When he returns home eight years later, a NASA investigation ensues. Paul Reubens, better known as Pee-wee Herman, provides the voice of the robot. **90m/C VHS, DVD.** Joey Cramer, Veronica Cartwright, Cliff DeYoung, Sarah Jessica Parker, Matt Adler, Howard Hesseman; *D:* Randal Kleiser; *W:* Michael Burton, Matt MacManus; *M:* Alan Silvestri; *V:* Paul (Pee-wee Herman) Reubens.

The Flight of the Phoenix **1965** A group of men stranded in the Arabian desert after a plane crash attempt to rebuild their plane in order to escape before succumbing to the elements. Big budget, all-star survival drama based on the novel by Elleston Trevor. **147m/C VHS, DVD.** James Stewart, Richard Attenborough, Peter Finch, Hardy Kruger, Dan Duryea, George Kennedy, Ernest Borgnine, Ian Bannen; *D:* Robert Aldrich; *C:* Joseph Biroc.

Flight of the Phoenix 1/2 **2004 (PG-13)** Old-fashioned remake of Robert Aldrich's 1965 film makes use of both Lukas Heller's original screenplay and the Elleston Trevor novel. Frank Towns (Quaid) is the tough, cynical pilot of a rusty C-119 cargo plane who has just picked up a disparate group of oil rig workers, including lone woman Kelly (Otto), from the Mongolian desert. They crash during a sandstorm and their survival comes to depend on arrogant oddball Elliott (Ribisi). Claiming to be an aircraft designer, Elliott announces he can make a new plane from the crash pieces, if the reluctant Towns will cede him authority. Tensions grow, supplies dwindle, and desert nomads wait like vultures to prey on the weakening survivors. Remake has CGI advantages but less-compelling characters. **112m/C VHS, DVD, Blu-ray Disc.** *US* Dennis Quaid, Miranda Otto, Giovanni Ribisi, Tyrese Gibson, Hugh Laurie, Tony Curran, Kirk "Sticky Fingaz" Jones, Jacob Vargas, Scott Michael Campbell, Kevork Malikyan; *D:* John Moore; *W:* Scott Frank, Edward Burns; *C:* Brendan Galvin; *M:* Marco Beltrami.

Flight of the Red Balloon *Le Voyage du Ballon Rouge* **2008** Hou's homage to Albert Lamorisse's 1956 film "The Red Balloon" does have a red balloon, a little boy, and Paris, but Simon (Iteanu) doesn't wander the streets accompanied by the balloon so much as he wanders with his new nanny Song (Fang), a Taiwanese film student who serves as Hou's calm observer. Simon's single mom is frazzled bleach-blonde Suzanne (Binoche), who doesn't seem to be coping with her son, her career, or her emotions very well. Not much actually happens so the film can be something of a slog but it looks beautiful. French with subtitles. **113m/C DVD.** *FR TW* Juliette Binoche, Hippolyte Girardot, Simon Iteanu, Song Fang, Louise Margolin, Anna Sigalevitch; *D:* Hou Hsiao-Hsien; *W:* Hou Hsiao-Hsien, Francois Margolin; *C:* Mark Lee Ping-Bin; *M:* Constance Lee.

Flight to Fury 1/2 **1966** A cheap independent adventure film, featuring the novice Hellman-Nicholson team, about a few assorted mercenaries searching for a horde of diamonds when their plane crashes in the wilderness of the Philippines. Based on a story by director/producer Hellman. **73m/B VHS.** Jack Nicholson, Dewey Martin, Fay Spain, Vic Diaz, Jacqueline Hellman; *D:* Monte Hellman; *W:* Jack Nicholson.

Flight to Mars **1952** An expedition crash lands on the red planet and discovers an advanced underground society that wants to invade earth using the U.S. spacecraft. Includes previews of coming attractions from classic science fiction films. First movie of this genre to be shot in color. **72m/C VHS, DVD.** Cameron Mitchell, Marguerite Chapman, Arthur Franz, Virginia Huston; *D:* Lesley Selander; *W:* Arthur Strawn; *C:* Harry Neumann; *M:* Marlin Skiles.

Flight to Nowhere **WOOF!** **1946** An FBI agent tracks down a stolen map of atomic bomb source material with the help of a charter pilot and a dizzy blonde. Muddled plot and no discernable acting. **74m/B VHS, DVD.** Alan Curtis, Evelyn Ankers, Jack Holt; *D:* William Rowland.

Flightplan 1/2 **2005 (PG-13)** Kyle Pratt (Foster) and her daughter Julia (Lawston) are on the flight from Berlin to New York to bury Kyle's husband who, she's told, died after falling (or jumping?) from their apartment roof. She happens to be a propulsion engineer who knows planes inside and out. Kyle wakes from a nap to find Julia simply gone. Worse, the crew and even the passengers don't recall Julia being there, as flight and boarding lists seem to confirm that she wasn't. Tense, psychological and... implausible, but Foster makes it work. Not for the claustrophobic—most of the film's 90 minutes is spent inside the plane. **93m/C DVD, Blu-ray Disc.** *US* Jodie Foster, Peter Sarsgaard, Erika Christensen, Sean Bean, Kate Beahan, Greta Scacchi, Judith Scott, Michael Irby, Brent Sexton, Marlene Lawston, Haley Ramm, Stephanie Faracy; *D:* Robert Schwentke; *W:* Billy Ray, Peter A. Dowling; *M:* James Horner.

Flim-Flam Man *One Born Every Minute* **1967** A con man teams up with an army deserter to teach him the fine art of flim-flamming as they travel through small southern towns. Love may lead the young man back to the straight and narrow, but not his reprobate mentor. Scott is wonderful; and the slapstick episodes move at a good pace. **104m/C VHS.** George C. Scott, Michael Sarrazin, Slim Pickens, Sue Lyon, Jack Albertson, Harry (Henry) Morgan; *D:* Irvin Kershner; *C:* Charles B(ryant) Lang Jr.; *M:* Jerry Goldsmith.

Flinch **1994 (R)** Two models, who work as live mannequins, witness a murder and wonder if they'll be the next victims. **90m/C VHS.** Judd Nelson, Nick Mancuso, Gina Gershon; *D:* George Erschbamer.

Fling *Lie to Me* **2008 (R)** Samantha and Mason seem like the perfect couple and talk a good game about having an open relationship. Then they attend the wedding of Sam's sister and Sam sees her ex James, who's still smitten. Meanwhile, Mason does some serious canoodling with his best pal Luke's teenaged sister Olivia. When they reveal their peccadilloes to each other, the reactions are unexpected. **98m/C DVD.** Courtney Ford, Steve Sandvoss, Brandon Routh, Nick Wechsler, Shoshana Bush, Ellen Hollman; *D:* John Stewart Muller; *W:* John Stewart Muller, Laura Boersma; *C:* Frederick Schroeder; *M:* Nick Urata.

The Flintstones 1/2 **1994 (PG)** Preceded by massive hype, popular '60s cartoon comes to life thanks to a huge budget and creative sets and props. Seems that Fred's (Goodman) being set up by evil corporate types Cliff Vandercave (MacLachlan) and Miss Rosetta Stone (Berry) to take the fall for their embezzling scheme. Soon he gives up dining at RocDonald's for Cavern on the Green and cans best buddy Barney (Moranis). Forget the lame plot (32 writers took a shot at it) and sit back and enjoy the spectacle. Goodman's an amazingly true-to-type Fred, O'Donnell has Betty's giggle down pat, and Perkins looks a lot like Wilma. Wilma's original voice, VanderPyl, has a cameo as Mrs. Feldspar; listen for Korman's voice as the Dictabird. Add half a bone if you're under 12. **92m/C VHS, DVD.** John Goodman, Rick Moranis, Elizabeth Perkins, Rosie O'Donnell, Elizabeth Taylor, Kyle MacLachlan, Halle Berry, Jonathan Winters, Richard Moll, Irwin Keyes, Dann Florek; ***Cameos:*** Laraine Newman, Jean Vander Pyl, Jay Leno; *D:* Brian Levant; *W:* Tom S. Parker, Jim Jennewein, Steven E. de Souza; *C:* Dean Cundey; *M:* David Newman; *V:* Harvey Korman. Golden Raspberries '94: Worst Support. Actress (O'Donnell), Worst Screenplay.

The Flintstones in Viva Rock Vegas **2000 (PG)** In a prequel to the 1994 film, a young Fred (Addy) and his best pal Barney (Baldwin) take their girlfriends Wilma (Johnson) and Betty (Krakowski) on a would-be romantic weekend to Rock Vegas. There's a whole lot going on, as runaway society girl Wilma is being wooed by playboy Chip Rockefeller (Gibson), Chip's trying to bankrupt and frame Fred, and the Great Gazoo (Cumming) is on hand to observe earthly mating habits. Everything is appropriately cartoonish, including the story and the acting. Unfortunately, the only ones who'll be entertained are the ones who are too young to remember the original series (or the original movie for that matter). **90m/C VHS, DVD.** Mark Addy, Kristen Johnston, Stephen Baldwin, Jane Krakowski, Thomas Gibson, Joan Collins, Alan Cumming, Harvey Korman, Alex Meneses; *D:* Brian Levant; *W:* Harry Elfont, Deborah Kaplan, Jim Cash, Jack Epps Jr.; *C:* Jamie Anderson; *M:* David Newman.

Flipper **1963** A fisherman's son befriends an injured dolphin, is persuaded to return him to the wild, and earns the animal's gratitude. Prime kids' fare, as its sequels and TV series attest. **87m/C VHS, DVD.** Chuck Connors, Luke Halpin, Kathleen Maguire, Connie Scott; *D:* James B. Clark.

Flipper **1996 (PG)** They still call him Flipper! Flipper, who in some scenes is played by a robot dolphin, reappears in a feature film for the first time since 1966. Sullen 14-year-old city boy Sandy Ricks (Wood) must spend the summer with crusty bachelor uncle Porter (Hogan), who would rather fish than look after his troublesome nephew. The duo witness the heartless killing of Flipper's family and are adopted by him. In addition to causing their seafood bill to skyrocket, the dolphin helps them uncover an illegal toxic waste dumper, who happens to be the same guy who made Flipper's mama sleep with the fishes. Updated along with the story is the soundtrack, which features a version of the famous theme song by Mathew Sweet. **97m/C VHS, DVD.** Elijah Wood, Paul Hogan, Chelsea Field, Isaac Hayes, Jonathan Banks, Luke Halpin; *D:* Alan Shapiro; *W:* Alan Shapiro; *C:* Bill Butler; *M:* Joel McNeely.

Flipper's New Adventure *Flipper and the Pirates* **1964** Believing they are to be separated, Flipper and Sandy travel to a remote island. Little do they know, a British family is being held for ransom on the island they have chosen. It's up to the duo to save the day. An enjoyable, nicely done family adventure. **103m/C VHS, DVD.** Luke Halpin, Pamela Franklin, Tom Helmore, Francesca Annis, Brian Kelly, Joe Higgins, Ricou Browning; *D:* Leon Benson.

Flipper's Odyssey **1966** Flipper has disappeared and his adopted family goes looking for him, but when one of the boys gets trapped in a cave, Flipper is his only hope. **77m/C VHS.** Luke Halpin, Brian Kelly, Tommy Norden; *D:* Paul Landres.

Flipping **1996 (R)** Quartet of none-too-bright wiseguy wanna-bes serve as debt collectors for gangster Leo Richards (David). Turns out gay undercover cop Billy (Proval) has infiltrated the gang—only to fall for ambitious hoodlum Michael (Amos)—and violent double-crosses abound. Debut for writer/director Mitchell. **102m/C VHS.** David Amos, David Proval, Gene Mitchell, Keith David, Shant Benjamin, Barry Primus, Mike Starr, Tony Burton, Paul Klar; *D:* Gene Mitchell; *W:* Gene Mitchell; *C:* Phil Parmet.

Flirt 1/2 **1995 (R)** Three variations on the same theme: love, jealousy, and the problems of committing are what comprise this interesting portrait of modern romance in three countries. One character in each of the three stories is faced with an ultimatum to commit and is given a 90-minute deadline. Each are already involved in various other romantic entanglements. The best scenes show the confused flirts receiving very amusing advice from strangers. First episode is the best, as the pace subsequently slows. **84m/C VHS.** *GE JP* William Sage, Parker Posey, Martin Donovan, Dwight Ewell, Dominik Bender, Geno Lechner, Miho Nikaido, Toshizo Fujisawa; *D:* Hal Hartley; *W:* Hal Hartley; *C:* Michael Spiller; *M:* Hal Hartley.

Flirtation Walk 1/2 **1934** West point musical that has cadet Powell falling in love with the general's daughter (Keeler), who is already engaged to lieutenant Eldredge. Some fairly good numbers, including "Mr. and Mrs. Is The Name," and "Flirtation Walk." In an attempt to change her image, Keeler hardly dances at all, which is too bad for the viewer. Based on a story by Lou Edelman and Delmer Daves. **98m/B VHS.** Dick Powell, Ruby Keeler, Pat O'Brien, Ross Alexander; *D:* Frank Borzage; *W:* Delmer Daves.

Flirting **1989 (R)** Set in an Australian boarding school in 1965, a charming story following the misadventures of the adolescent Danny Embling, who has the misfortune to be both bright and sensitive, putting him seriously at odds with his masculine peers. He finds love with an outcast at the neighboring girls boarding school, the daughter of a diplomat from Uganda. Kidman has a supporting role as a snobbish older boarding school girl, not quite as bad as she seems. Tender and amusing. The second of director Duigan's coming-of-age trilogy, preceded by "The Year My Voice Broke" (the third film isn't yet completed). **100m/C VHS, DVD.** *AU* Noah Taylor, Thandie Newton, Nicole Kidman, Bartholomew Rose, Felix Nobis, Josh Picker, Kiri Paramore, Marc Gray, Joshua Marshall, David Wieland, Craig Black, Leslie Hill; *D:* John Duigan; *W:* John Duigan. Australian Film Inst. '90: Film.

Flirting with Disaster **1995 (R)** Mel Coplin (Stiller) is your average neurotic New York entomologist searching for his birth parents so he can finally name his four-month-old child and make love to his wife. Tagging along on his bumpy ride are his wife Nancy (Arquette), a beautiful quirky adoption agency shrink (Leoni), and a pair of bisexual FBI agents. The excellent cast also features Moore as Mel's bra-baring adoptive mother, Segal as his weirdly paranoid adoptive father, and Alda and Tomlin as hilarious send-ups of ex-hippie mentality. As events spin madly out of control, every type of relationship is satirized, and every character is left in their underwear. This is director Russell's first big-budget movie, and is as close to a vintage screwball comedy as you'll see in the '90s. **92m/C VHS, DVD.** Ben Stiller, Patricia Arquette, Tea Leoni, Alan Alda, Mary Tyler Moore, George Segal, Lily Tomlin, Josh Brolin, Richard Jenkins, Celia Weston, Glenn Fitzgerald, Beth Ostrosky, Cynthia Lamontagne, David Patrick Kelly, John Ford Noonan, Charles Oberly; *D:* David O. Russell; *W:* David O. Russell; *C:* Eric Alan Edwards; *M:* Stephen Endelman.

Flirting with Fate **1916** Early Fairbanks-cum-acrobat vehicle. Having hired a hitman to rub himself out, a young man decides he doesn't want to die, after all. Seems there's a girl involved.. **51m/B VHS.** Douglas Fairbanks Sr., Jewel Carmen, Howard Gaye, William E. Lawrence, George Beranger, Dorothy Hadel, Lillian Langdon; *D:* Christy Cabanne.

Flirting with Forty 1/2 **2009** Sunny romantic fantasy from Lifetime is an adaptation of the Jane Porter novel. Recently divorced mom and successful businesswoman Jackie (Locklear) is feeling blue about turning forty. Her pal Kristine (Williams) talks her into a restorative Hawaiian vacation where Jackie promptly has a romance with her twenty-something surf instructor, free-spirit Kyle (Buckley). But when it turns out to be more than a fling, her kids, ex, and jealous friends make a big deal out of the situation. **87m/C DVD.** Heather Locklear, Vanessa Williams, Cameron Bancroft, Robert Buckley, Sam Duke, Anne Hawthorne; *D:* Mikael Salomon; *W:* Julia Dahl; *C:* Jon Joffin; *M:* Jeff Beal. **CABLE**

Floating **1997** Van (Reedus) is a moody 20-year-old ex-high school swimming champ who's basically treading water. He looks after his drunken paraplegic father (Lyman) in their run-down cottage and drifts into home burglaries with two equally loser friends. It's Van's idea to stash their ill-gotten gains in the basement of his former family home—of course the empty dwelling immediately gets a new owner—and Van winds up befriending the family's son, Doug (Lowe), who's not only a swimming champ but has Dad problems as well. This male bonding leads to some (predictable) attitude changes but the sincerity of the cast goes a long way in overcoming the cliches. **91m/C VHS, DVD.** Norman Reedus, Chad Lowe, Will Lyman, Jonathan Quint, Josh Marchette, Sybil Temchen; *D:* William Roth; *W:* William Roth; *C:* Wolfgang Held; *M:* David Mansfield.

Floating Life **1995** The Chans have decided to emigrate from Hong Kong before the mainland China takeover and join daughter Bing (Yip) and her family in Sydney. High-strung Bing's determined to assimilate as much as possible into Australian society and bullies her newly arrived family, who are naturally disoriented. The arrival of laggard son Gar Ming (Wong) and easy-going daughter Yen (Shun-Wah), who's been living in Germany, only provide further complications for a family completely adrift in their new world. Cantonese, German, and English dialogue. **95m/C VHS.** *AU* Annie Yip, Annete Shun-Wah, Anthony Wong, Edwin Pang, Cecilia Fong Sing Lee, Toby Wong, Toby Chan, Bruce Poon; *D:* Clara Law; *W:* Clara Law, Eddie Ling-Ching Fong; *C:* Dion Beebe; *M:* Davood A. Tabrizi.

The Flock 🦴🦴 **2007 (R)** Burned-out federal agent Erroll Babbage (Gere) is training his replacement, Allison Laurie (Danes), while investigating a missing girl he thinks is the victim of a paroled sex offender. First English-language pic for Hong Kong director Lau, best-known for "Infernal Affairs," but the reshoots were done by Niels Mueller. Having another director take over is not considered a good sign. Sleazy and confusing, but features some good work by Gere and Danes. **91m/C DVD.** *US* Richard Gere, Claire Danes, KaDee Strickland, Matt Schulze, Russell Sams, Avril Lavigne, Ray Wise, French Stewart, Kristina Sisco; *D:* Andrew Lau; *W:* Hans Bauer, Craig Mitchell; *C:* Enrique Chediak; *M:* Guy Farley.

Flood! 🦴🦴 **1976** Irwin Allen's first made-for-TV disaster film. A dam bursts and devastates a small town, so a helicopter pilot must save the day. Good cast is swept along in a current of disaster-genre cliches. **98m/C VHS.** Robert Culp, Martin Milner, Barbara Hershey, Richard Basehart, Carol Lynley, Roddy McDowall, Cameron Mitchell, Teresa Wright, Francine York; *D:* Earl Bellamy. **TV**

Flood 🦴 ½ **2007** Typical disaster flick. A storm of hurricane proportions devastates Scotland and moves along the coast on its way to London. Authorities are convinced the city is safely protected by the Thames Barrier but discredited scientist Leonard Morrison (Courtenay) thinks otherwise and turns to his estranged son Rob (Carlyle), an engineer, for help. In turn, Rob gets his ex-wife Sam (Gilsig), the operations director for the barrier project, to listen but it still isn't enough to prevent water, water everywhere. **188m/C DVD.** *GB CA* Robert Carlyle, Jessalyn Gilsig, Tom Courtenay, Joanne Whalley, David Suchet, Nigel Planer, Martin Ball; *D:* Tony Mitchell; *W:* Justin Bodle, Matthew Cope; *C:* Pierre Jodoin; *M:* Debbie Wiseman. **TV**

Flood: A River's Rampage 🦴🦴 ½ **1997 (PG-13)** Community struggles to rebuild after a devastating flood. **92m/C VHS, DVD.** Richard Thomas, Kate Vernon, Jan Rubes; *D:* Bruce Pittman. **TV**

Flooding 🦴🦴 ½ **1997** Clever homage to Alfred Hitchcock on a budget. Joyce Calloway (Gibson) has become agoraphobic after the unsolved murder of her husband and has spent the past six months in her house. She is working with a new doctor (who comes to the house, of course) to get over her fear of the outside world, and she better hurry, because her parents are selling the house in an effort to get her to go outside. After a fling, a man comes to her back door, falls inside, and dies after uttering a name she doesn't recognize. The tension mounts as it becomes clear that her subconscious mind is holding out on her and that someone wants her dead or at least out of the way. The why of the story is the weak link in the film; it is the journey to the answer that is absorbing. This is not a perfect film, but it is worth watching for fans of suspense. **86m/C DVD.** Brenna Gibson, Lauren Bailey, Kary Cawley; *D:* Todd Portugal; *W:* Todd Portugal.

The Floorwalker 🦴🦴🦴 **1917** Chaplin becomes involved with a dishonest floorwalker in a department store. Silent. **20m/B VHS, DVD.** Charlie Chaplin; *D:* Charlie Chaplin.

Flor Silvestre 🦴 *Wild Flower* **1958** The son of a rich rancher romances a young woman against the background of the Mexican Revolution. **90m/B VHS.** *MX* Dolores Del Rio, Pedro Armendariz Sr.; *D:* Emilio Fernandez.

Florence Nightingale 🦴🦴 ½ **1985** Respectable bio of Florence Nightingale (Smith), a privileged Victorian who rejects marriage for the chance to become a nurse. Appalled by reports of Army hospital care for British soldiers during the Crimean War, Florence and 40 volunteer nurses travel to Turkey in 1854 only to face hostility and rejection by the military and medical establishments. Florence forges ahead—making nursing a respectable profession and improving patient care despite her own doubts. The beautiful Smith may seem an odd casting choice and her English accent wobbles but she's as determined as her character to succeed. **140m/C DVD.** Jaclyn Smith, Timothy Dalton, Jeremy Brett, Claire Bloom, Peter McEnery, Brian Cox, Jeremy Child, Stephan Chase; *D:* Daryl Duke; *W:* Ivan Moffett; *C:* Jack Hildyard; *M:* Stanley Myers. **TV**

Florence Nightingale 🦴 ½ **2008** BBC co-production, along with Faith & Values Media, that focuses on Florence Nightingale's (Fraser) spiritual calling, leading her to reject her privileged life to become a nurse. Despite medical and military objections, Florence improves conditions for soldiers during the Crimean War and then continues pushing for reforms using her wealth and political connections. There are a number of music-hall interludes that are supposed to help tell the story but they're odd interruptions. **130m/C DVD.** *GB* Laura Fraser, Michael Pennington, Barbara Marten, Sean McKenzie, Wendy Patterson; *D:* Norman Shore; *C:* Mike J. Fox; *M:* Jeremy Soule. **TV**

The Florentine 🦴🦴 **1998 (R)** A decaying steel town is home to a bar called The Florentine, its owner Whitey (Madsen), and the usual drinking denizens. But with profits sinking, Whitey may lose his livelihood. And then there's his sister Molly's (Madsen) problems. Her wedding to Frankie (Perry) is in jeopardy because of a con man (Belushi) and her ex-fiance, Teddy (Sizemore), who's back in town. **104m/C VHS, DVD.** Michael Madsen, Virginia Madsen, Luke Perry, Tom Sizemore, James Belushi, Mary Stuart Masterson, Christopher Penn; *D:* Nick Stagliano. **VIDEO**

The Florida Connection 🦴 **1974** An action thriller set in the Florida Swamps with a collection of villains and a vague plot about smuggling. **90m/C VHS.** Dan Pastorini, June Wilkinson, Bill (Billy) Thurman; *D:* Robert Emery; *W:* Robert Emery.

Florida Straits 🦴🦴 **1987 (PG-13)** A recently released Cuban prisoner hires a few losers and their boat to return to the island, supposedly to find the girl he loves. The real quest is for gold buried during the Bay-of-Pigs invasion in this none-too-original cable movie that at least offers a good cast. **98m/C VHS.** Raul Julia, Fred Ward, Daniel H. Jenkins, Antonio Fargas; *D:* Mike Hodges; *W:* Stephen Metcalfe; *M:* Michel Colombier. **CABLE**

Floundering 🦴 ½ **1994 (R)** Misguided satire uses the 1992 L.A. riots as a backdrop to tell the saga of unemployed James Boyz (LeGros), whose life is a walking disaster. He owes the IRS, his unemployment compensation has run out, his brother (Hawke) has fled from a drug rehab clinic, and he finds his girlfriend (Zane) in bed with another man. John drags himself among the city's downtrodden as he fantasizes about life. Drag pretty much sums up the film despite good performances by LeGros and Hawke. **97m/C VHS, DVD.** James LeGros, Ethan Hawke, Steve Buscemi, John Cusack, Lisa Zane, Sy Richardson, Jeremy Piven, Billy Bob Thornton; *D:* Peter McCarthy; *W:* Peter McCarthy; *C:* Denis Maloney; *M:* Pray for Rain.

Flourish 🦴🦴 **2006 (PG-13)** Desperate for cash, Gaby (Morrison) agrees to babysit precocious 16-year-old Lucy (Meester), who soon disappears from the house. Now Gaby spends an increasingly wild night, running into lots of very strange people, trying to find Lucy before her parents get home. **95m/C DVD.** Jenny (Jennifer) Morrison, Leighton Meester, Jesse Spencer, Connie Ray, Daniel Roebuck, Olivia Burnette; *D:* Kevin Palys; *W:* Kevin Palys; *C:* Maximilian Gutierrez; *M:* Luigi Pittorino, Melinda Doring.

Flower & Snake 🦴🦴 *Hana to hebi* **2004** Originally a series of fetish novels by Dan Oniroku, there have been as many as 10 different versions of this film made, this one by Takashi Ishii (best known in Japan for his horror and erotica films). An internationally famous tango dancer is sold by her estranged husband to a local Yakuza to whom he owes a great deal of money. Despite excellent cinematography and themes of sexual and social liberation, most viewers will only remember the many bondage scenes. **115m/C DVD.** *JP* Aya Sugimoto, Renji Ishibashi, Kenichi Endo, Misaki Mori, Yoshiyuki Yamaguchi, Shun Nakayama, Shigeo Kobayashi, Naoki Matsuda, Tomoo Yageta, Miyako Kawahara, Mr. Buddhaman, Tomezo Tsunokake, Diasuke Iijima, Go Arisue, Susumu Terajima, Hironobu Nomura; *D:* Takashi Ishii; *W:* Takashi Ishii, Oniroku Dan; *C:* Takashi Komatsu, Kazuto Sato, Hiro'o Yanagida; *M:* Goro Yasukawa.

Flower & Snake 2 🦴🦴 *Hana to hebi 2: Pari/Shizuko* **2005** Still together with her husband after the events of the first film, Shizuko (Aya Sugimoto) finds that her increasingly aging husband can't always perform, but likes watching her in erotic situations. He hires a painter to bring their fantasies to life and she becomes the object of desire to a parade of rich lechers. Still as pretty as the first film, still has a bit of a message, all of which will still be lost in all the nakedness. **113m/C DVD.** *JP* Aya Sugimoto, Kenichi Endo, Fujiko, Mieko Arai, Toru Shinagawa, Joe Shishido; *D:* Takashi Ishii; *W:* Takashi Ishii, Oniroku Dan; *C:* Takashi Komatsu, Hiro'o Yanagida; *M:* Goro Yasukawa.

Flower & Snake '74 🦴 ½ *Hana to hebi; Flowers and Snakes* **1974** With actual porn putting a dent in their money in the mid-80s, Pink Film producers Nikkatsu began a series of nostalgic remakes of S&M films with this one based on the novels by Dan Oniroku. A young boy kills an American soldier for consorting with his mother, and grows up impotent unless he can tie up and whip his girlfriends. When the president of the company he works for asks the man to abduct his wife and educate her sexually, she doesn't exactly receive the education he is thinking of. **90m/C DVD.** *JP* Naomi Tani, Nagatoshi Sakamoto; *D:* Masaura Konuma; *W:* Oniroku Dan, Yozo Tanaka; *C:* Shohei Ando; *M:* Richiro Manabe.

Flower Drum Song 🦴🦴 **1961** The Rodgers and Hammerstein musical played better on Broadway than in this overblown adaptation of life in San Francisco's Chinatown. Umeki plays the young girl who arrives from Hong Kong for an arranged marriage. Her intended (Soo) is a fast-living nightclub owner already enjoying the love of singer Kwan. Meanwhile Umeki falls for the handsome Shigeta. Naturally, everything comes together in a happy ending. ♫ I Enjoy Being A Girl; Don't Marry Me; Grant Avenue; You Are Beautiful; A Hundred Million Miracles; Fan Tan Fanny; Chop Suey; The Other Generation; I Am Going to Like It Here. **133m/C VHS, DVD.** Nancy Kwan, Jack Soo, James Shigeta, Miyoshi Umeki, Juanita Hall; *D:* Henry Koster; *C:* Russell Metty; *M:* Richard Rodgers. Natl. Film Reg. '08.

The Flower of My Secret 🦴🦴🦴 *La Flor de My Secreto* **1995 (R)** Emotional yet restrained story about middle-aged Leo (Paredes), whose longtime marriage is fast ending (and it's not her idea). Leo writes hugely popular romance novels under a pseudonym but her current work is so bleak it's unpublishable. So, Leo gets a job at a newspaper where editor Angel (Echanove) immediately falls for her, and indeed, lives up to his name as her guardian. Willfully myopic about her own life, Leo undergoes further trials until she slowly realizes the mess she's in and becomes willing to change. Surprisingly subdued given Almodovar's usual flamboyance but it's a welcome change of pace. Spanish with subtitles. **107m/C VHS, DVD.** *SP FR* Marisa Paredes, Juan Echanove, Imanol Arias, Carmen Elias, Rossy de Palma, Chus (Maria Jesus) Lampreave, Joaquin Cortes, Manuela Vargas; *D:* Pedro Almodovar; *W:* Pedro Almodovar; *C:* Alfonso Beato; *M:* Alberto Iglesias.

Flowers for Algernon 🦴 ½ **2000** Previously filmed as the 1968 feature "Charly," this TV adaptation of Daniel Keyes' novel unfortunately descends into mawkish sentimentality. Mentally handicapped bakery worker Charlie Gordon (Modine) is chosen to be part of an experimental surgery to enhance intelligence. The method was previously tested on a mouse called Algernon with apparent success. It works on Charlie as well (to an overwhelming extent) but he's able to figure out that the effect is only temporary when Algernon has problems and learns he'll soon regress to his former mental state. **120m/C DVD.** Matthew Modine, Kelli Williams, Ron Rifkin, Bonnie Bedelia, Richard Chevolleau; *D:* Jeff Bleckner; *W:* John Pielmeier; *C:* Mike Fash; *M:* Mark Adler. **TV**

Flowers in the Attic 🦴 ½ **1987 (PG-13)** Based on the V.C. Andrews bestseller, a would-be thriller about four young siblings locked for years in their family's old mansion by their grandmother with their mother's selfish acquiescence. A chicken-hearted, clumsy flop that skimps on the novel's trashier themes. **93m/C VHS, DVD.** Victoria Tennant, Kristy Swanson, Louise Fletcher, Jeb Stuart Adams; *D:* Jeffrey Bloom; *W:* Jeffrey Bloom; *C:* Gil Hubbs; *M:* Christopher Young.

Flowers of Reverie 🦴🦴 **1984** A former soldier is imprisoned for his work in the resistance during the Hungarian Revolution (1848-9), leading to tragedy. In Hungarian with English subtitles. **106m/C VHS.** *HU* Gyorgy Cserhalmi, Grazyna Szapolowska, Jiri Adamira, Boguslaw Linda; *D:* Laszlo Lugossy; *W:* Laszlo Lugossy; *C:* Elemer Ragalyi; *M:* Gyorgy Selmeczi.

The Flowers of St. Francis 🦴🦴🦴 *Francesco, giullare di Dio; Francis, God's Jester* **1950** Rossellini's presentation of St. Francis and his friars' attainment of spiritual harmony. In Italian with English subtitles. This is the British release version, 10-15 minutes longer than the U.S. version. **75m/B VHS, DVD.** *IT* Aldo Fabrizi, Brother Nazario Gerardi, Arabella Lemaitre; *D:* Roberto Rossellini; *W:* Father Antonio Lisandrini, Father Felix Morion, Federico Fellini, Roberto Rossellini; *C:* Otello Martelli; *M:* Enrico Buondonno, Renzo Rossellini.

Flowers of Shanghai 🦴🦴 *Haishang Hua* **1998** Slow costume drama/soap opera set in the brothels of late 19th-century Shanghai. In this self-contained world, the elegant "flower girls" depend on their ability to hold onto wealthy clients and Crimson (Hada) seems to be losing her charms. Her longtime patron, Wang (Leung Chui Wai), is also seeing Jasmin (Wei). Meanwhile, among the other ladies, Emerald (Reis) is working to buy her freedom and Jade (Hsuan) is refusing other clients because she believes Zhu (Chang) will marry her. Based on the novel "Biographies of Flowers of Shanghai" by Han Ziyun. Mandarin with subtitles. **125m/C VHS, DVD.** *JP TW* Tony Leung Chiu-Wai, Michiko Hada, Hsiao-hui Wei, Jack Kao, Michelle Reis, Annie Shizuka Inoh, Fang Hsuan, Simon Chang; *D:* Hou Hsiao-Hsien; *W:* Tien-wen Chu; *C:* Mark Lee Ping-Bin; *M:* Yoshihiro Yanno.

Flu Birds **WOOF!** *Flu Bird Horror* **2008 (R)** Even the box art is misleading in this Sci-Fi Channel dreck. A group of juvenile delinquents are at some kind of wilderness boot camp (or something) and become prey to giant mutant birds infected by a killer virus. A local doc and a park ranger try to help. **95m/C DVD.** Clare Carey, Lance Guest, Sarah Butler, Brent Lydic, Bill Posley; *D:* Leigh Scott; *W:* Brian J. Smith, Tony Daniel; *C:* Gabriel Kosuth; *M:* Alan Howarth. **CABLE**

Flubber 🦴🦴 **1997 (PG)** Bland remake of Disney's "The Absent-Minded Professor" with Williams as the befuddled, yet brilliant Prof. Brainard. Putting his wedding on the back Bunsen burner, much to the dismay of his fiancee Sara Jean (Harden), Brainard invents a bouncy, flying green slime named "flubber." As the substance becomes the cure-all for romantic turmoil and fledging school basketball teams, it also attracts the attention of a corrupt businessman and his moronic henchmen. Due to the dull subplots, kids and adults will be disappointed that the main attraction (the cute green goo) doesn't have much screen time. Williams, oddly enough, seems comfortable playing second banana to a substance that could describe his comedic skills. **93m/C VHS, DVD.** Robin Williams, Marcia Gay Harden, Christopher McDonald, Raymond J. Barry, Clancy Brown, Ted Levine, Wil Wheaton, Edie McClurg; *D:* Les Mayfield; *W:* John Hughes; *C:* Dean Cundey; *M:* Danny Elfman.

The Fluffer 🦴🦴 **2001** Naive aspiring filmmaker Sean (Cunio) has his romantic illusions destroyed and is rather rudely forced to grow up. Gay Sean gets a job with a Hollywood porn production company and falls for one of the company's stars—the immature and self-destructive gay-for-pay

Mikey (Gurney) whose nom-de-porn is Johnny Rebel. Mikey's on a downward slide despite Sean's admiration and the love of his stripper girlfriend Julie (Day) and if the two aren't careful, Mikey will take them with him. Title refers to one of the personal services Sean is expected to offer Mikey. **94m/C VHS, DVD.** Michael Cunio, Scott Gurney, Rozanne Day, Richard Riehle, Taylor Negron, Tim Bagley, Adina Porter, Deborah Harry; ***D:*** Richard Glatzer, Wash West; ***W:*** Wash West; ***C:*** Mark Putnam.

Fluke **1995 (PG)** "Ghost" meets "Oh, Heavenly Dog" as Tom (Modine) dies in a suspicious car accident and is reincarnated as a dog who remembers his past life. He returns to his former family (Travis and Pomeranc) to protect them from his former business partner (Stoltz), battling such puppy perils as cosmetic testing labs and dogcatchers along the way. While there's plenty of squishy sentimentality to go around, some of the scenes involving animal abuse may be a little much for the target audience of pre-teen kids. Jackson and Stoltz trade "Pulp Fiction" for pup fiction, but this dog won't hunt. Based on the novel by James Herbert. **96m/C VHS, DVD.** Matthew Modine, Nancy Travis, Eric Stoltz, Max Pomeranc, Ron Perlman, Jon Polito, Bill Cobbs, Frederico Pacifici, Collin Wilcox-Paxton; ***D:*** Carlo Carlei; ***W:*** James Carrington, Carlo Carlei; ***C:*** Raffaele Mertes; ***M:*** Carlo Siliotto; ***V:*** Samuel L. Jackson.

Flush **1981** Unorthodox comedy involving funny noises. **90m/C VHS.** William Calloway, William Bronder, Jeannie Linero; ***D:*** Andrew J. Kuehn.

Flushed Away **2006 (PG)** The Aardman studio ventures from its usual clay figure stop-motion look into computer animation but the inventiveness remains. Roddy (Jackman) is a posh London pet mouse who is unceremoniously flushed down the loo by baddie sewer rat Sid (Richie). Roddy discovers a raucous underground community that is threatened by evil gangster The Toad (McKellen) and his French cousin Le Frog (Reno). Fortunately, the pampered Roddy is taken in by tough working-class rat Rita (Winslet) as they try to save the day. The harmonizing singing slugs are an added highlight. **84m/C DVD.** *US GB* ***D:*** David Bowers, Sam Fell; ***W:*** Dick Clement, Ian La Frenais, Chris Lloyd, Joe Keenan, William Davies; ***M:*** Harry Gregson-Williams; ***V:*** Hugh Jackman, Kate Winslet, Ian McKellen, Jean Reno, Bill Nighy, Andy Serkis, Kathy Burke, David Suchet, Shane Richie, Miriam Margolyes, Rachel Rawlinson.

The Fly **1958** The historic, chillingly original '50s sci-fi tale about a hapless scientist experimenting with teleportation who accidentally gets anatomically confused with a housefly. Campy required viewing; two sequels followed, and a 1986 remake which itself has spawned one sequel. **94m/C VHS, DVD.** David Hedison, Patricia Owens, Vincent Price, Herbert Marshall, Kathleen Freeman, Betty Lou Gerson, Charles Herbert; ***D:*** Kurt Neumann; ***W:*** James Clavell; ***C:*** Karl Struss; ***M:*** Paul Sawtell.

The Fly **1986 (R)** A sensitive, humanistic remake of the 1958 horror film about a scientist whose flesh is genetically intermixed with a housefly via his experimental transportation device. A thoughtful, shocking horror film, with fine performances from Goldblum and Davis and a brutally emotional conclusion. Followed by "The Fly II" in 1989. **96m/C VHS, DVD.** Jeff Goldblum, Geena Davis, John Getz, Joy Boushel, Cosette Lee; ***D:*** David Cronenberg; ***W:*** David Cronenberg, Charles Edward Pogue; ***C:*** Mark Irwin; ***M:*** Howard Shore. Oscars '86: Makeup.

The Fly 2 **1/2 1989 (R)** Inferior sequel to Cronenberg's opus, in which the offspring of Seth Brundle achieves full genius maturity in three years, falls in love, and discovers the evil truth behind his father's teleportation device and the corporate auspices that backed it. **105m/C VHS, DVD.** Eric Stoltz, Daphne Zuniga, Lee Richardson, John Getz, Harley Cross; ***D:*** Chris Walas; ***W:*** Ken Wheat, Frank Darabont, Mick Garris, Jim Wheat; ***C:*** Robin Vidgeon; ***M:*** Christopher Young.

Fly Away Home *Father Goose; Flying Wild* **1996 (PG)** Does for geese what "Babe" did for pigs. Young Amy (Paquin) withdraws when she loses her mother in a car crash and is forced to live with her estranged father, Thomas (Daniels), a scruffy sculptor/inventor, in rural Ontario. Still dealing with her own mother's death, Amy suddenly becomes a mother herself to a tiny gaggle of goslings when she happens upon a nest of uprooted eggs. Extraordinary technical achievements make up for some unnecessary melodrama in the second half as the geese head South, led by Amy, in a glider built by her father. Touching but unsentimental, mostly well scripted and acted, and extraordinarily shot. Based on the true story of inventor Bill Lishman, who led domesticated geese on a winter migration from Toronto, Canada to North Carolina, leading the formation in his motor-powered glider. **107m/C VHS, DVD.** Jeff Daniels, Anna Paquin, Dana Delany, Terry Kinney, Jeremy Ratchford; ***D:*** Carroll Ballard; ***W:*** Robert Rodat, Vince McKewin; ***C:*** Caleb Deschanel; ***M:*** Mark Isham.

Fly Boy **1/2 1999 (PG)** Gramps (Karen) is a still-adventurous WWII vet whose remote-controlled model airplanes are the terror of the neighborhood and the delight of his 10-year-old grandson, Ray (Hughes). In fact, Ray would like to help Gramps fulfill his big dream—to fly a real plane one last time. **86m/C VHS.** Miko Hughes, James Karen, Kathleen Lloyd, Gregory Itzin; ***D:*** Richard Stanley. **VIDEO**

Fly by Night **1993 (PG-13)** Mismatched New York rappers Rich and I join forces to make it big as hard-core gangstas. When they're propelled to the top of the charts, forces both personal and professional work to tear them apart. **93m/C DVD.** Jeffrey D. Sams, Ron Brice, Daryl (Chill) Mitchell, Todd Graff, Leo Burmester, Soulfood Jed, Larry (Lawrence) Gilliard Jr., Omar Carter, Maura Tierney, Yul Vazquez, M.C. Lyte, Christopher-Michael Gerrard, Ebony Jo-Ann; ***D:*** Steve Gomer; ***W:*** Todd Graff; ***C:*** Larry Banks; ***M:*** Kris Parker, Sidney Mills, Dwayne Sumal. Sundance '93: Filmmakers Trophy.

Fly Me to the Moon **1/2 2008 (G)** A literal "fly on the wall" perspective of 1969's historic Apollo 11 launch to the moon, as experienced by three young stowaway houseflies aboard the shuttle. Its crude computer animation is saved only by its innovative 3-D tricks, carefully planned out by director Stassen, fresh off his duties on "Wild Safari 3-D." Nevertheless, preschool jokes, not-so-clever "2001" references, and an awkward script that mixes kiddy fun with sterile technical information about the mission ultimately bring about its failure to launch. **84m/C DVD.** *US* Philip Daniel Bolden, Christopher Lloyd; ***D:*** Ben Stassen; ***W:*** Domonic Paris; ***M:*** Ramin Djawadi; ***V:*** Trevor Gagnon, Kelly Ripa, David Gore, Nicolette Sheridan, Tim Curry, Buzz Aldrin, Lorraine Nicholson.

Fly with the Hawk **1985** A troubled teenager gets lost in the wilderness for a year, and learns some important things from nature to take back to civilization. **90m/C VHS.** Peter Ferri, Peter Snook, Shelley Lynne Speigel; ***D:*** Robert Tanos.

Flyboys **1/2 2006 (PG-13)** Old-fashioned war flick based on the exploits of the Lafayette Escadrille—young Americans who volunteered for the French military during WWI, before the U.S. entered the war. Formulaic script has the new recruits, who had a life expectancy as biplane pilots of six weeks, training under the paternal eye of Capt. Thenault (Reno). Besides the heroics, there's a corny romance between laconic Texan Rawlings (Franco) and local beauty Lucienne (Decker). Extensive CGI is combined with actual footage for the dynamic air sequences. **139m/C DVD, Blu-ray Disc.** James Franco, Martin Henderson, Jean Reno, Philip Winchester, David Ellison, Jennifer Decker, Tyler Labine, Abdul Salis, Christien Anholt; ***D:*** Tony Bill; ***W:*** Blake T. Evans, David S. Ward, Phil Sears; ***C:*** Henry Braham; ***M:*** Trevor Rabin.

Flying Blind **1/2 1941** Foreign agents are thwarted in their attempt to steal a vital air defense secret. Unconvincing espionage plot cobbled into a story about a Los Angeles-Las Vegas puddle jumper. **69m/B VHS, DVD.** Richard Arlen, Jean Parker, Marie Wilson, Nils Asther, Roger Pryor, Eddie Quillan, Grady Sutton, Dick Purcell; ***D:*** Frank McDonald; ***W:*** Richard Murphy, Maxwell Shane; ***C:*** Fred H. Jackman Jr.; ***M:*** Dimitri Tiomkin.

Flying By **1/2 2009 (PG-13)** Real estate developer George Barron (Cyrus) goes to his 25-year high school reunion, sans wife Pamela (Locklear), and discovers his old band has reunited. After sitting in, he agrees to rehearse with the guys and gets the old music bug back, especially when they have a successful gig at the local bar. Pamela gets worried when George's midlife crisis starts interfering with their marriage and his work, especially when he contemplates touring with the band. **90m/C DVD.** Billy Ray Cyrus, Heather Locklear, Patricia Neal, Olesya Rulin; ***D:*** Jim Amatulli; ***W:*** Jim Amatulli; ***C:*** Chris Chomyn; ***M:*** Geoff Levin. **VIDEO**

The Flying Deuces *Flying Aces* **1939** Ollie's broken heart lands Laurel and Hardy in the Foreign Legion. The comic pair escape a firing squad only to suffer more indignities. A musical interlude with a Laurel soft shoe while Hardy sings "Shine On, Harvest Moon" is one of the film's highlights. **65m/B VHS, DVD.** Stan Laurel, Oliver Hardy, Jean Parker, Reginald Gardiner, James Finlayson; ***D:*** Edward Sutherland; ***W:*** Ralph Spence, Charles R. Rogers, Harry Langdon, Alfred Schiller; ***C:*** Elmer Dyer, Art Lloyd; ***M:*** Leo Shuken, John Leopold.

Flying Down to Rio **1/2 1933** The first Astaire-Rogers musical, although they are relegated to supporting status behind Del Rio and Raymond. Still, it was enough to make them stars and a team that epitomizes the height of American musical films. The slim story revolves around singer Del Rio's two suitors and receives a splendid, art deco production. Showgirls dancing on plane wings in flight provide another memorable moment. ♫ Music Makes Me; The Carioca; Orchids in the Moonlight; Flying Down to Rio. **89m/B VHS, DVD.** Fred Astaire, Ginger Rogers, Dolores Del Rio, Eric Blore, Gene Raymond, Franklin Pangborn; ***D:*** Thornton Freeland; ***M:*** Vincent Youmans, Max Steiner.

The Flying Fool **1929** Ace pilot Bill returns from the war to find his younger brother has fallen for a singer. When Bill meets the lady, he also notices her charms and the two brothers have a duel in the skies to see who'll get the girl. **75m/B VHS.** William Boyd, Marie Prevost, Russell Gleason; ***D:*** Tay Garnett; ***W:*** James Gleason.

Flying from the Hawk **1/2 1986** A 12-year-old boy sees something he shouldn't and soon finds that his friends and relatives are mysteriously vanishing. **110m/C VHS.** John Ireland, Diane McBain; ***D:*** Cecil Barker; ***W:*** Jesse Goldstein, Dave O'Brien; ***C:*** Manuel Berenguer; ***M:*** Adolfo Waitzman.

Flying High **1931** MGM musical comedy, based on the 1930 Broadway production, with choreography by Busby Berkeley. Lahr reprises his stage role (in his first film lead) as Rusty, a goofy inventor/pilot, who inadvertently breaks the record for high-altitude flying in an experimental aerocopter. Greenwood steals the film as gawky spinster Pansy who is determined to get the flummoxed Rusty to marry her, even coming to his airborne rescue. Note the Prohibition booze scene when Rusty undergoes a physical exam. **79m/B DVD.** Bert Lahr, Charlotte Greenwood, Pat O'Brien, Kathryn Crawford, Charles Winninger, Hedda Hopper, Guy Kibbee; ***D:*** Charles Riesner; ***W:*** Charles Riesner, Robert Hopkins, A.P. Younger; ***C:*** Merritt B. Gerstad.

The Flying Irishman **1/2 1939** Film version of aviator "Wrong Way" Corrigan's life story and his 1938 flight from New York to California—that landed him near Dublin, Ireland instead. Only screen appearance of Corrigan, whose trip was suspected to be a publicity stunt since he was eager to emulate the exploits of friend Charles Lindbergh. **71m/B VHS.** Paul Kelly, Robert Armstrong, Gene Reynolds, Eddie Quillan, Donald MacBride, J.M. Kerrigan, Douglas Corrigan; ***D:*** Leigh Jason; ***W:*** Dalton Trumbo, Ernest Pagano; ***C:*** J. Roy Hunt.

Flying Leathernecks **1951** Tough squadron leader Wayne fights with his fellow officer Ryan in Guadalcanal when their leadership styles clash. But when the real fighting begins all is forgotten as Wayne leads his men into victorious battle, winning the admiration and devotion of his fliers. Memorable WWII film deals with war in human terms. **102m/C VHS, DVD.** John Wayne, Robert Ryan, Janis Carter, Don Taylor, James Bell, James Dobson, Jay C. Flippen, Gordon Gebert, William Harrigan, Brett King, Adam Williams, Carleton Young, Dick Wessel, Gail Davis, Harlan Warde, Michael (Steve Flagg) St. Angel, Maurice Jara, John Mallory, Britt Nelson, Lynn Stalmaster; ***D:*** Nicholas Ray; ***W:*** Kenneth Gamet, James Edward Grant; ***C:*** William E. Snyder; ***M:*** Roy Webb.

The Flying Saucer **1/2 1950** U.S. and Russian scientists clash over their search for a huge flying saucer that is hidden under a glacier. The first movie to deal with flying saucers. The cassette includes animated opening and closing sequences plus previews of coming attractions. **71m/B VHS, DVD.** Mikel Conrad, Pat Garrison, Hanz von Teuffen; ***D:*** Mikel Conrad; ***W:*** Howard Irving Young, Mikel Conrad; ***C:*** Philip Tannura; ***M:*** Darrell Calker.

The Flying Scotsman **1/2 1929** A fired railroad worker tries to wreck an express train on the engineer's last journey. The daughter of the intended victim saves the day. Silent, with sound added. **60m/B VHS, DVD.** Ray Milland, Pauline Johnson, Moore Marriott; ***D:*** Castleton Knight.

The Flying Scotsman **1/2 2006 (PG-13)** Based on the story of Graeme Obree, a Scottish amateur cyclist who broke several world speed records using a bike of his own design made from, among other things, parts from a washing machine, "Scotsman" highlights his nightmarish problems of self doubt and depression. Despite the litany of cliches, it's well enough done, and there are good moments, though some will find it a definite downer. **96m/C DVD.** *GB* Johnny Miller, Sean Brown, Julie Austin, Billy Boyd, Laura Fraser, Brian Cox, Ron Donachie, Morven Christie, Steven Berkoff, Philip Wright, Adrian Smith, Joseph Carney, Niall Macgregor, Christopher Anderson, Moray Hunter, Niall Greig Fulton, Daniel Andre Pageon, Gudrun Mangel, Muzaffer Cakar; ***D:*** Douglas Mackinnon; ***W:*** John Brown, Declan Hughes, Simon Rose; ***C:*** Gavin Finney; ***M:*** Martin Phipps.

Flying Tigers **1/2 1942** Salutes the All-American Volunteer Group which flew for China under General Claire Chennault against the Japanese before the U.S. entered WWII. A squadron leader and a brash new recruit both vie for the affections of a pretty nurse in-between their flying missions. Romance and a few comic touches take a back seat to graphic scenes of aerial battles and dramatization of heroic sacrifice in this rousing war film. **101m/B VHS, DVD.** John Wayne, Paul Kelly, John Carroll, Anna Lee, Mae Clarke, Gordon Jones; ***D:*** David Miller.

Flying Wild **1/2 1941** A gang of saboteurs is out to steal top-secret airplane blueprints. Who else but the Bowery Boys could conceivably stop them? **62m/B VHS, DVD.** Leo Gorcey, Bobby Jordan, Donald Haines, Joan Barclay, David Gorcey, Bobby Stone, Sammy (Earnest) Morrison; ***D:*** William West; ***W:*** Al Martin; ***C:*** Fred H. Jackman Jr.; ***M:*** Johnny Lange, Lew Porter.

Flynn **1/2** *My Forgotten Man* **1996** Details the adventurous early years of Tasmania-born Errol Flynn (Pearce) before he became the swashbuckling hero of Hollywood films. His sexual exploits get him kicked out of school and he makes his way as gigolo, thief, liar, and alleged spy. **96m/C VHS, DVD.** *AU* Guy Pearce, Claudia Karvan, Steven Berkoff; ***D:*** Frank Howson; ***W:*** Frank Howson; ***C:*** John Wheeler; ***M:*** Anthony Marinelli.

Flypaper **1997 (R)** Parking-lot big-shot Marvin (Loggia) and his business associate Jack (Brolly) help out junkie Natalie (Frost), who is being pressured by low-rent hood Bobby Ray (Sheffer). There's actually three separate but connected stories revolving around a big score and the various lowlifes who want to get their hands on it one California afternoon. **111m/C VHS, DVD.** Robert Loggia, Sadie Frost, Craig Sheffer, Shane Brolly, Lucy Liu, James Wilder, Illeana Douglas, Talisa Soto, John C. McGinley; ***D:*** Klaus Hoch; ***W:*** Klaus Hoch; ***C:*** Jurgen Baum; ***M:*** Peter Manning Robinson.

FM *Citizen's Band* **1978 (PG-13)** The disc jockeys at an L.A. radio station rebel in the name of rock'n'roll. Despite the promising cast and setting (Mull makes his movie debut as a memorable space case), this is just disjointed and surprisingly unhip; one producer took his name off it due to creative difficulties. The decent soundtrack includes concert footage of Jimmy Buffet and Linda Ronstadt. ♫ FM; Do It Again; FM Reprise; Livingston Saturday Night; The Key To My Kingdom; Green Grass and High Tides; Life In The Fast Lane; Bad Man; Poor, Poor, Pitiful Me. **104m/C VHS, DVD.** Eileen Brennan, Alex Karras, Cleavon Little, Martin Mull, Cassie Yates, Linda Ronstadt, Jimmy Buffett; ***D:*** John A. Alonzo; ***W:*** Ezra Sacks; ***C:*** David Myers.

Focus 🦴🦴 1/2 **2001 (PG-13)** Based on a 1945 novel by playwright Arthur Miller, this exploration of anti-Semitism and bigotry features Macy as Larry Newman, a nebbish personnel worker who lives with his invalid mother. After 20 years on the job, he is demoted after he gets glasses because they make him look "too Jewish" to his bosses. After quitting his job in protest, he is interviewed for a new job by Gertrude (Dern), a woman that he had turned away from his firm because she may or may not have been a Jew. A whirlwind romance ensues, and the two are soon married as their neighborhood is becoming a battleground of ethnic tension. Strong-arm tactics are used on local newsstand owner Finkelstein (Paymer), and he warns the Newmans about collective hate. Macy gives a great performance, but the material is a bit blunt and preachy. **106m/C VHS, DVD.** William H. Macy, Laura Dern, David Paymer, Meat Loaf Aday, Michael Copeman, Kenneth Welsh, Kay Hawtrey, Joseph Ziegler, Arlene Meadows; ***D:*** Neil Slavin; ***W:*** Kendrew Lascelles; ***C:*** Juan Ruiz-Anchia; ***M:*** Mark Adler.

The Fog 🦴🦴 **1978 (R)** John Carpenter's blustery follow-up to his success with "Halloween." An evil fog containing murderous, vengeful ghosts envelops a sleepy seaside town and subjects the residents to terror and mayhem. **91m/C VHS, DVD.** Hal Holbrook, Adrienne Barbeau, Jamie Lee Curtis, Janet Leigh, John Houseman, Tom Atkins; ***D:*** John Carpenter; ***W:*** John Carpenter, Debra Hill; ***C:*** Dean Cundey; ***M:*** John Carpenter.

The Fog 🦴 1/2 **2005 (PG-13)** Remake of the 1980s film of the same name, this foggy feature is updated by utterly ludicrous special effects. It does, however, stay true to the original film's roots, where a misty fog overtakes the sleepy (and fictional) town of Antonio Bay, bringing in the ghosts of some seafarers murdered 100 years ago. Of course, the ghosts are ticked off and they exact revenge on the poor townsfolk. The original was at least scarier, and even better-acted, which isn't saying a whole lot. **100m/C VHS, DVD, UMD.** *US* Tom Welling, Maggie Grace, Selma Blair, DeRay Davis, Kenneth Welsh, Sara Botsford, Rade Serbedzija, Adrian Hough; ***D:*** Rupert Wainwright; ***W:*** Cooper Layne; ***C:*** Nathan Hope; ***M:*** Graeme Revell.

Fog Island 🦴 1/2 **1945** Murder and terror lurk after a greedy inventor, who was framed for fraud by his business partner, is released from prison. He plots revenge by inviting his foes to his island home. **72m/B VHS, DVD.** George Zucco, Lionel Atwill, Terry Morse, Jerome Cowan, Veda Ann Borg; ***D:*** Terry Morse; ***W:*** Pierre Gendron; ***C:*** Ira Morgan.

The Fog of War: Eleven Lessons from the Life of Robert S. McNamara 🦴🦴🦴 1/2 **2003 (PG-13)** Oscar winner for Best Documentary not only gave prolific documentarian Morris his first Academy Award, but also presents a startlingly honest and three-dimensional portrayal of one of the major architects of twentieth-century American history, Robert McNamara. A former president of the Ford Automotive Company and the Secretary of Defense for both Kennedy and Johnson, McNamara speaks frankly about his role in the Bay of Pigs and the Vietnam War, alternating between offering fascinating insights and arguing with his off-screen interviewer. He'll make you love him one moment and cringe the next. A must-see for history buffs. **106m/C DVD.** *US* ***D:*** Errol Morris; ***C:*** Peter Donahue, Robert Chappell; ***M:*** Philip Glass. Oscars '03: Feature Doc.; Ind. Spirit '04: Feature Doc.; L.A. Film Critics '03: Feature Doc.; Natl. Bd. of Review '03: Feature Doc.

Folks! 🦴 **1992 (PG-13)** Selleck is a Chicago stockbroker whose wife and kids have left him, the FBI is after him, and, worst of all, his parents have moved in with him. His parents don't want to be a burden, so Selleck decides that the best way to solve his financial woes is to help his parents commit suicide so he can collect on their insurance policies. Tasteless comedy that makes fun of aging and Alzheimer's Disease. Selleck is too sweet and cuddly for his role, but Ameche is good as the senile father, and Ebersole is great as Selleck's unpleasant sister. **109m/C VHS, DVD.** Tom Selleck, Don Ameche, Anne Jackson, Christine Ebersole, Wendy Crewson, Robert Pastorelli, Michael Murphy, Kevin Timothy Chevalia, Margaret Murphy; ***D:*** Ted Kotcheff; ***M:*** Michel Colombier.

Follies Girl 🦴🦴 **1943** There's folly in expecting that this wartime tuner would hold up today. An army private romances a dress designer and a musical show somehow results. ♫ Keep the Flag A-Flying; No Man In The House; Someone to Love; I Told A Lie; Shall We Gather at the Rhythm?; Fascination; I Knew Your Father's Son; Thoity Poiple Boids. **74m/B VHS.** Wendy Barrie, Doris Nolan, Gordon Oliver, Anne Barrett, Arthur Pierson; ***D:*** William Rowland.

Follies in Concert **1985** A filmed record of the famed Stephen Sondheim musical play, performed at Lincoln Center in New York with an all-star cast. Songs include "I'm Still Here," "Losing My Mind," "Broadway Baby" and "The Ladies Who Lunch." **90m/C VHS, DVD.** Carol Burnett, Lee Remick, Betty Comden, Andre Gregory, Adolph Green, Mandy Patinkin, Phyllis Newman, Elaine Stritch, Jim Walton, Licia Albanese.

Follow Me 🦴🦴 **1969 (G)** Round-the-world odyssey of three moon doggies searching for adventure—and the perfect wave. Spectacular surfing scenes are complemented by songs performed by Dino, Desi, and Billy. **90m/C VHS.** Claude Codgen, Mary Lou McGinnis, Bob Purvey; ***D:*** Gene McCabe.

Follow Me, Boys! 🦴🦴🦴 **1966** A Disney film about a simple man who decides to put down roots and enjoy the quiet life, after one year too many on the road with a ramshackle jazz band. That life is soon interrupted when he volunteers to lead a high-spirited boy scout troop. **120m/C VHS, DVD.** Fred MacMurray, Vera Miles, Lillian Gish, Charlie Ruggles, Elliott Reid, Kurt Russell, Luana Patten, Ken Murray; ***D:*** Norman Tokar; ***W:*** Louis Pelletier; ***M:*** George Bruns.

Follow Me Quietly 🦴🦴🦴 **1949** Serial strangler who only kills in the rain is stalked by Lundigan. Very good little thriller which packs a punch in less than an hour. **59m/B VHS.** William Lundigan, Dorothy Patrick, Jeff Corey, Nestor Paiva, Charles D. Brown, Paul Guilfoyle; ***D:*** Richard Fleischer.

Follow That Camel 🦴 1/2 *Carry On Follow That Camel* **1967** Foreign Legion sergeant who invents acts of heroism finally gets a chance to really help out a friend in need. Part of the "Carry On" series. **95m/C VHS.** *GB* Phil Silvers, Kenneth Williams, Anita Harris, Jim Dale; ***D:*** Gerald Thomas.

Follow That Car 🦴 **1980 (PG)** Three southern kids become FBI agents and begin a thigh-slappin', rip-snortin' down-home escapade. **96m/C VHS.** Dirk Benedict, Tanya Tucker, Teri Nunn; ***D:*** Daniel Haller.

Follow That Dream 🦴🦴 **1961 (G)** Elvis plays a musical hillbilly whose family is trying to homestead on government land along the sunny Florida coast. Based on Richard C. Powell's novel "Pioneer Go Home." The songs—the only reason to see this movie—include "Angel," "What a Wonderful Life," and the title track. **111m/C VHS, DVD.** Elvis Presley, Arthur O'Connell, Anne Helm, Simon Oakland, Jack Kruschen, Joanna Moore, Howard McNear; ***D:*** Gordon Douglas; ***W:*** Charles Lederer; ***C:*** Leo Tover; ***M:*** Hans J. Salter.

Follow That Rainbow 🦴 **1979** Believing that her long-lost father is a popular touring singer, a young lass pursues him from Switzerland to South Africa. **90m/C VHS.** *SA* Joe Stewardson, Memory Jane, Joan Bickhill; ***D:*** Louis Burke.

Follow the Boys 🦴🦴🦴 **1944** Vaudeville performer Tony West (Raft) heads out to California to try his luck and gets a double break when he's noticed by leading lady Gloria Vance (Zorina). Not only does he become a star but he marries Gloria as well. When WWII breaks out Tony's turned down for military service, so he organizes camp shows for the soldiers. They're a big success but misunderstandings have put his marriage in jeopardy. Plot's merely an excuse to have haute Hollywood (including Marlene Dietrich, Orson Welles, Jeanette MacDonald, and W.C. Fields) sing, dance, and tell jokes. ♫ Beyond the Blue Horizon; I'll See You In My Dreams; The Bigger the Army and the Navy; Some of These Days; I'll Get By; I'll Walk Alone; Mad About Him Blues; The House I Live In. **111m/B VHS.** George Raft, Vera Zorina, Grace McDonald, Charles Butterworth, Martha O'Driscoll, Charley Grapewin, Elizabeth Patterson; ***D:*** Edward Sutherland; ***W:*** Lou Breslow, Gertrude Purcell.

Follow the Fleet 🦴🦴🦴 **1936** A song-and-dance man joins the Navy and meets two sisters in need of help in this Rogers/Astaire bon-bon featuring a classic Berlin score. Look for Betty Grable, Lucille Ball, and Tony Martin in minor roles. Hilliard went on to be best known as the wife of Ozzie Nelson in TV's "The Adventures of Ozzie and Harriet." ♫ Let's Face the Music and Dance; We Saw the Sea; I'm Putting All My Eggs In One Basket; Get Thee Behind Me, Satan; But Where Are You?; I'd Rather Lead a Band; Let Yourself Go. **110m/B VHS, DVD.** Fred Astaire, Ginger Rogers, Randolph Scott, Harriet Hilliard Nelson, Betty Grable, Lucille Ball; ***D:*** Mark Sandrich; ***M:*** Irving Berlin, Max Steiner.

Follow the Leader 🦴🦴 *East of the Bowery* **1944** On leave from the Army, Hall and Gorcey discover that one of the gang has been jailed on a trumped-up charge and set about finding the real culprit. ♫ Now and Then; All I Want to Do Play the Drums. **65m/B VHS.** Leo Gorcey, Huntz Hall, Gabriel Dell, Jack La Rue, Joan Marsh, William Benedict, Mary Gordon, Sammy (Earnest) Morrison; ***D:*** William Beaudine; ***M:*** Gene Austin.

Follow the River 🦴🦴 1/2 **1995 (PG)** It's 1775 and Mary Ingles (Lee) is living with her husband and family on a frontier farm in the Blue Ridge Mountains. The community is raided by the Shawnee, lead by Wildcat (Schweig), who take Mary and several other settlers miles away to their home camp. Once there, Mary befriends another captive, the older Gretl (Burstyn), proves her courage to the smitten Wildcat, and plots to escape and find her way home. Based on the 1981 novel by James Alexander Thom; filmed in North Carolina. **93m/C VHS, DVD.** Sheryl Lee, Eric Schweig, Ellen Burstyn, Tim Guinee, Renee O'Connor; ***D:*** Martin Davidson.

Follow the Stars Home 🦴🦴 1/2 **2001** Dianne (Williams) falls for charming fisherman Mark McCune (Close), they get married, and she's soon pregnant. But when Dianne learns that their baby daughter will be born will severe disabilities, Mark can't cope and leaves her. Flash forward six years, with Dianne making a life for herself and Julia—aided by her mother (Brown) and Mark's steadfast pediatrician brother, David (Scott), who obviously loves her. Then an accident brings Mark back into their lives, but will Dianne make a different choice this time? Based on the novel by Luanne Rice. A Hallmark Hall of Fame production that's a predictable tearjerker. **97m/C VHS, DVD.** Kimberly Williams, Campbell Scott, Eric Close, Blair Brown, Alexa Vega, Roxanne Hart; ***D:*** Dick Lowry; ***W:*** Sally Robinson. **TV**

Follow the Sun 🦴🦴 1/2 **1951** Ford excels as Ben Hogan, who was seriously injured in a car accident and fought his way back to become a golf legend. Details Hogan's painful recovery and the support he received from his wife Valerie (Baxter). Real life pros (and legends in their own right) Sam Snead, Jimmy Demaret, and Cary Middlecoff have cameos. **93m/B VHS.** Glenn Ford, Anne Baxter, Dennis O'Keefe, June Havoc, Larry Keating, Roland Winters, Nana Bryant, Myrtle Anderson; ***Cameos:*** Sam Snead; ***D:*** Sidney Lanfield; ***W:*** Frederick Hazlitt Brennan; ***C:*** Leo Tover; ***M:*** Cyril Mockridge.

Following 🦴🦴 **1999 (R)** Nolan's feature debut is an odd little neo-noir about a young man named Bill (Theobald) who likes to follow strangers. He picks the wrong guy in burglar Cobb (Haw) who has his own voyeuristic tastes. Cobb turns the tables on Bill and decides to become his mentor in crime. And sticking with the noir tradition, there's a mysterious blonde femme (Russell) whose relationship to the men is gradually revealed. As in his 2001 film "Memento," Nolan plays twister with the chronology, which means more than one viewing may be necessary to figure things out. **71m/B VHS, DVD.** Jeremy Theobald, Alex Haw, Lucy Russell, John Nolan; ***D:*** Christopher Nolan; ***W:*** Christopher Nolan; ***C:*** Christopher Nolan; ***M:*** David Julyan.

A Fond Kiss 🦴🦴 **2004 (R)** A modern-day Scottish "Romeo & Juliet," with star-crossed mediocrity between a Pakistani DJ and a Catholic music teacher. The culture-clash throws both families into panic (you know the story). Another notch in a series of socially-adept films from director Ken Loach and writer Paul Laverty. This time around they bring a little less humor and a little more drama, albeit stilted, which, along with weak performances and nearly unintelligible accents may turn off a majority of Western audiences. **104m/C VHS, DVD.** Eva Birthistle, Atta Yaqub, Ahmad Riaz, Shabana Bakhsh, Shamshad Akhtar, Ghizala Avan, Pasha Bocarie, Gerard Kelly; ***D:*** Ken Loach; ***C:*** Barry Ackroyd; ***M:*** George Fenton.

Food, Inc. 🦴 1/2 **2008 (PG)** Despite the rating, this muckraking expose on the food industry isn't something for younger children to see and will probably be of limited interest to most adults. It covers familiar territory—basically stating that almost everything we buy and eat is bad for us because the food industry is a big agri-business with big government subsidies and is more interested in volume and profit than in consumer health. Nor does it reasonably address the fact that most consumers are unable to find or afford so-called organic food easily or cheaply and it makes fast food a convenient villain (which we have seen before). **94m/C DVD.** *US* ***D:*** Robert Kenner; ***C:*** Richard Pearce; ***M:*** Mark Adler.

Food of Love 🦴🦴 **2002** Melodramatic gay romance set in the world of classical music. 18-year-old piano student Paul Porterfield (Bishop) is hired as a page turner for a concert given by his idol, middle-aged pianist Richard Kennington (Rhys). While traveling in Barcelona with his clinging mother Pamela (Stevenson), Paul re-meets Richard and they have a fling, which means more to Paul than to Richard whose longtime lover is his manager Joseph (Corduner). At school in New York, Paul happens to meet Joseph (lots of coincidences here) and Pamela finally realizes her son is gay. Based on the novel "The Page Turner" by David Leavitt. Spanish director Pons's English-language debut feels abrupt and Paul is an unsympathetic character. **112m/C VHS, DVD.** *SP GE* Kevin Bishop, Paul Rhys, Juliet Stevenson, Allan Corduner, Geraldine McEwan; ***D:*** Ventura Pons; ***W:*** Ventura Pons; ***C:*** Mario Montero; ***M:*** Carles Cases.

Food of the Gods WOOF! **1976 (PG)** On a secluded island giant rats, chickens, and other creatures crave human flesh, blood, bones, etc. This cheap, updated version of the H. G. Wells novel suffers from lousy performances and a lack of imagination. **88m/C VHS.** Marjoe Gortner, Pamela Franklin, Ralph Meeker, Ida Lupino, Jon Cypher; ***D:*** Bert I. Gordon.

Food of the Gods: Part 2 WOOF! *Gnaw: Food of the Gods 2* **1988 (R)** The killer beasts and animals of the first film (and of H.G. Wells' classic novel) strike again; gigantic rats maim young girls. Easily as bad as the original. **93m/C VHS, DVD.** Paul Coufos, Lisa Schrage; ***D:*** Damian Lee; ***W:*** E. Kim Brewster.

A Fool and His Money 🦴🦴 1/2 **1988 (R)** Adman Morris Codman (Penner) decides to market a shady new religion based on greed but, naturally, finds the true road. Bullock is skeptical girlfriend Debby. **84m/C VHS.** Jonathan Penner, Sandra Bullock, Gerald Orange, George Plimpton; ***D:*** Daniel Adams; ***W:*** Daniel Adams.

Fool for Love 🦴🦴 **1986 (R)** Explores the mysterious relationship between a modern-day drifter and his long-time lover, who may or may not be his half-sister, as they confront each other in a seedy New Mexico motel. Adapted by Shepard from his play. **108m/C VHS, DVD.** Sam Shepard, Kim Basinger, Randy Quaid, Harry Dean Stanton; *D:* Robert Altman; *W:* Sam Shepard; *M:* George Burt.

The Fool Killer 1/2 *Violent Journey* **1965** In the post-Civil War south, a 12 year-old boy learns that a terrifying legend about an axe-murderer may be all too real. Offbeat film with striking visuals and photography. Debut film for Albert and another choice psycho role for Perkins. **100m/B VHS.** Anthony Perkins, Edward Albert, Dana Elcar, Henry Hull, Salome Jens, Arnold Moss; *D:* Servando Gonzalez.

A Fool There Was 1/2 **1914** The rocket that blasted Theda Bara to stardom and launched the vamp film genre. One of the few extant Bara films, it tells the now familiar story of a good man whom crumbles from the heights of moral rectitude thanks to the inescapable influence of an unredeemable vamp. Bette Davis described Bara as "divinely, hysterically, insanely malevolent." Much heavy emoting; subtitled (notoriously) "Kiss Me, My Fool!" Based on Rudyard Kipling's "The Vampire." **70m/B VHS, DVD.** Mabel Frenyear, Victor Benoit, Theda Bara, Edward Jose, Runa Hodges, Clifford Bruce; *D:* Frank Powell; *W:* Roy L. McCardell; *C:* George Schneiderman.

Foolin' Around 1/2 **1980 (PG)** An innocent Oklahoma farm boy arrives at college and falls in love with a beautiful heiress. He will stop at nothing to win her over, including crashing her lavish wedding ceremony. **101m/C VHS.** Michael Talbott, William H. Macy, Gary Busey, Annette O'Toole, Eddie Albert, Tony Randall, Cloris Leachman; *D:* Richard T. Heffron; *W:* Michael Kane; *C:* Philip Lathrop; *M:* Charles Bernstein.

Foolish WOOF! **1999 (R)** Foolish? You bet it is. Eddie Griffin stars as the title character, a struggling comic who rips off old Eddie Murphy routines to a hip-hop beat. He butts heads with his brother Fifty Dollah, played by rapper/sports agent/bad actor Master P, who also wrote and executive produced this clunker. The boom mike falls into the picture so often that you expect Master P to grab it and bust a rhyme at any given moment. Strictly for sucka MCs. **96m/C VHS, DVD.** Eddie Griffin, Master P, Frank Sivero, Amy Petersen, Jonathan Banks, Andrew (Dice Clay) Silverstein, Marla Gibbs, Daphne Lynn Duplaix, Sven-Ole Thorsen, Bill Nunn, Bill Duke; *D:* Dave Meyers; *W:* Master P; *C:* Steve Gainer; *M:* Wendy Melvoin, Lisa Coleman.

Foolish Wives 1/2 **1922** A remake of Von Stroheim's classic depicting the confused milieu of post-war Europe as reflected through the actions of a bogus count and his seductive, corrupt ways. Comes as close as possible to the original film. **107m/B VHS, DVD.** Erich von Stroheim, Mae Busch, Maud(e) (Ford) George, Cesare Gravina, Harrison Ford; *D:* Erich von Stroheim; *W:* Erich von Stroheim; *C:* William H. Daniels; *M:* Sigmund Romberg. Natl. Film Reg. '08.

Fools **1970 (PG)** Two lonely people—he an aging horror film actor and she a young woman estranged from her husband—start a warm romance when they meet in San Francisco. The husband reacts violently. Good cast seems lost. **93m/C VHS.** Jason Robards Jr., Katharine Ross, Scott Hylands; *D:* Tom Gries.

Fool's Gold 1/2 **2008 (PG-13) 112m/C DVD, Blu-ray Disc.** *US* Matthew McConaughey, Kate Hudson, Donald Sutherland, Alexis Dziena, Ewen Bremner, Ray Winstone, Kevin Hart, Malcolm Jamal Warner, Brian Hooks, David Roberts; *D:* Andy Tennant; *W:* Andy Tennant, John Claflin, Daniel Zelman; *C:* Don Burgess; *M:* George Fenton.

Fool's Gold: The Story of the Brink's-Mat Robbery 1/2 **1992** True story focuses on a robbery that nets the thieves a windfall—and the problems that follow. In November of 1983, Mickey McAvoy (Bean) has set up a heist to rob the high-security warehouse of Brink's-Mat at Heathrow airport. The thieves are after gold bullion but what they find in the vaults are 6,800 gold bars, worth roughly eight times more than their intended haul. The police are quickly on to various members of the gang, but just what happened to all that loot? (Most of the bars have never been recovered; the police believe some were smelted down, but many may be buried. McAvoy was sentenced in 1984 to 25 years in prison.) **93m/C VHS, DVD.** *GB* Sean Bean, Larry Lamb, Trevor Byfield, George Jackos, Brian Croucher, David Cardy, Jeremy Child, Rob Spendlove; *D:* Terry Winsor; *W:* Terry Winsor, Jeff Pope; *C:* Dick Pope; *M:* William Woolf. **TV**

Fools of Fortune 1/2 **1990 (PG-13)** Adaptation of William Trevor's novel depicting Willie Clinton's childhood and adult experiences of family dramatics played against the backdrop of post-WWI Ireland. During the Irish war for independence, a family is attacked by British soldiers, creating emotional havoc for the survivors. Though well-acted and poignant, it's a rather disjointed and straying shamrock opera. **104m/C VHS.** *GB* Mary Elizabeth Mastrantonio, Iain Glen, Julie Christie, Michael Kitchen, Sean McClory, Frankie McCafferty, Mick (Michael) Lally; *D:* Pat O'Connor; *W:* Michael Hirst; *M:* Hans Zimmer.

Fools Rush In **1997 (PG-13)** Uptight eastern yuppie Alex Whitman (Perry) meets cute in Vegas with beautiful Latina casino worker Isabel Fuentes (Hayek) and the duo spend the night together. Three months later, Isabel shows up at Alex's New York door to announce her pregnancy and say she's keeping the baby. Movie cliches collide with movie stereotypes when they decide to marry but find the relationship suffers over their vast ethnic and cultural differences. At least the leads are attractive. Perry's real-life dad plays his character's father. **110m/C VHS, DVD.** Matthew Perry, Salma Hayek, Jon Tenney, Carlos Gomez, Tomas Milian, John Bennett Perry, Jill Clayburgh, Stanley DeSantis, Anne Betancourt; *D:* Andy Tennant; *W:* Katherine Reback; *C:* Robbie Greenberg; *M:* Alan Silvestri.

The Foot Fist Way **2008 (R)** Cringe-worthy, slapdash, and super-cheap comedy about self-deluded Fred Simmons (McBride) who teaches tae kwon do (the title is an English translation) at a strip mall dojo where he belittles and sexually harasses his inexplicably devoted students. A bonehead, Fred's wannabe macho behavior is undermined when his bimbo wife Suzie (Bostic) cheats and then leaves him, causing Fred to fall apart. Besides his domestic woes, Fred is obsessed with meeting his idol, Chuck 'The Truck' Wallace (Best), which naturally turns into a disaster. Under the radar for most audiences, it's a big hit among comedians. **85m/C DVD.** *US* Danny McBride, Mary Jane Bostic, Ben Best, Spencer Moreno, Carlos Lopez IV, Jody Hill; *D:* Jody Hill; *W:* Danny McBride, Ben Best, Jody Hill; *C:* Brian Mandle; *M:* Pyramid.

Footlight Glamour **1943** Dagwood is actually hired to run a new tool manufacturing plant but Blondie causes trouble when she casts the boss' daughter in a local play against the man's wishes. **68m/B VHS.** Penny Singleton, Arthur Lake, Larry Simms, Jonathan Hale, Thurston Hall, Ann Savage, Marjorie Ann Mutchie, Irving Bacon, Danny Mummert; *D:* Frank Strayer; *W:* Karen De Wolf, Connie Lee; *C:* Philip Tannura.

Footlight Parade **1933** Broadway producer Cagney is out of work. Sound films have scared off his backers until his idea for staging live musical numbers before the cinema features lures them back. Lots of authentic backstage action precedes three spectacular Busby Berkeley-choreographed numbers that climax the film, including the giant water ballet featuring more than 100 performers. ♫ Ah, the Moon is Here; Sittin' on a Backyard Fence; Honeymoon Hotel; By A Waterfall; Shanghai Lil. **104m/B DVD.** James Cagney, Joan Blondell, Dick Powell, Ruby Keeler, Guy Kibbee, Ruth Donnelly; *D:* Lloyd Bacon; *C:* George Barnes. Natl. Film Reg. '92.

Footlight Serenade 1/2 **1942** A boxer falls for a beautiful dancer with whom he's costarring in a Broadway play. Unfortunately, she's secretly married to another of the actors and her husband is becoming jealous of the boxer's intentions. Light, fun musical. One of a series of Grable movies made to boost morale during WWII. ♫ Are You Kidding?; I'm Still Crazy About You; I Hear the Birdies Sing; Living High; I'll Be Marching to a Love Song; Land On Your Feet; I'm Stepping Out With a Memory Tonight. **80m/B VHS.** Betty Grable, Victor Mature, John Payne, Jane Wyman, Phil Silvers, James Gleason, Mantan Moreland; *D:* Gregory Ratoff; *C:* Lee Garmes.

Footloose 1/2 **1984 (PG)** When a city boy moves to a small Midwestern town, he discovers some disappointing news: rock music and dancing have been forbidden by the local government. Determined to bring some '80s-style life into the town, he sets about changing the rules and eventually enlists the help of the daughter of the man responsible for the law. Rousing music, talented young cast, and plenty of trouble make this an entertaining musical-drama. ♫ Footloose; Let's Hear it for the Boy; The Girl Gets Around; Dancing in the Sheets; Somebody's Eyes; Almost Paradise; I'm Free; Never; Holding Out for a Hero. **107m/C VHS, DVD.** Kevin Bacon, Lori Singer, Christopher Penn, John Lithgow, Dianne Wiest, John Laughlin, Sarah Jessica Parker; *D:* Herbert Ross; *M:* Miles Goodman.

Footsteps *Expose* **1998 (R)** Reporter Jason Davis (Chapa) gets a tip that makes him an eyewitness to a judge's murder. Separated from wife Nancy (Alonso), Jason gets involved with photographer Amber (Lombard), who is also connected to D.A. Steve Carlen (Schanley). When Jason turns up evidence that links Amber and Carlen to the murdered judge and he begins to receive threatening messages, Jason can trust only himself to catch the killer. **93m/C VHS, DVD.** Damian Chapa, Karina Lombard, Tom Schanley, Maria Conchita Alonso, Steven Schub, Sandra Bernhard, Tippi Hedren; *D:* Daphna Edwards; *W:* Daphna Edwards; *C:* David J. Miller; *M:* Alex Wurman. **VIDEO**

Footsteps **2003** Suspense novelist Daisy Lowendahl (Bergen) is still recovering from a nervous breakdown when she decides to face her fear of being alone by spending time at her isolated Long Island beach house. But she's soon disturbed by over-zealous fan Spencer (Hall) and detective Eddie Bruno (Brown) who says Daisy's husband (Murphy) wants him to keep an eye on her. But Daisy just can't shake this feeling that something's wrong. **95m/C DVD.** Candice Bergen, Bug Hall, Bryan Brown, Michael Murphy; *D:* John Badham; *W:* Shelley Evans; *C:* Ron Stannett; *M:* Christopher Franke. **TV**

Footsteps in the Dark 1/2 **1941** Fairly amusing comedy-mystery with investment counselor Flynn doubling as detective. Based on the play "Blondie White" by Ladislaus Fodor, Bernard Merivale, and Jeffrey Dell. **96m/B VHS.** Errol Flynn, Brenda Marshall, Ralph Bellamy, Alan Hale, Lee Patrick, Allen Jenkins, Lucile Watson, William Frawley, Roscoe Karns, Grant Mitchell, Maris Wrixon, Noel Madison, Jack La Rue, Turhan Bey; *D:* Lloyd Bacon, Hugh MacMullen; *W:* Lester Cole, John Wexley.

For a Few Dollars More 1/2 **1965 (PG)** The Man With No Name returns as a bounty hunter who teams up with a gunslinger/rival to track down the sadistic leader of a gang of bandits. Violent. Sequel to "A Fistful of Dollars" (1964) and followed by "The Good, The Bad, and The Ugly." **127m/C VHS, VHS, DVD, Blu-ray Disc.** *IT* Clint Eastwood, Lee Van Cleef, Klaus Kinski, Gian Marie Volonte; *D:* Sergio Leone; *W:* Sergio Leone, Luciano Vincenzoni; *C:* Massimo Dallamano; *M:* Ennio Morricone.

For a Lost Soldier *Voor een Verloren Soldaat* **1993** Middle-aged Dutch choreographer Jeroen (Krabbe), working on a piece about the Allied liberation, recalls his relationship with a Canadian soldier more than 40 years before. During WWII, the 13-year-old Jeroen (Smit) is sent from Amsterdam to live in the country with a foster family. With the first twinges of puberty and sexuality he longs for a special friend, whom he finds in Walt (Kelley), a young gay Canadian soldier who is part of the Allied liberation forces. Very provocative subject, delicately handled, without any implication of child abuse. In English and Dutch with subtitles. **92m/C VHS, DVD.** *NL* Marten Smit, Andrew Kelley, Jeroen Krabbe, Feark Smink, Elsje de Wijn, Derk-Jan Kroon; *D:* Roeland Kerbosch; *W:* Roeland Kerbosch; *C:* Nils Post; *M:* Joop Stokkermans.

For Better and for Worse 1/2 **1992 (PG)** A nice young couple is planning to have your average nice wedding when one of their friends gets hold of an invitation and decides to jokingly invite the Pope to attend. But the joke is on them when the Pope accepts. Talk about upstaging the bride! **94m/C VHS.** Patrick Dempsey, Kelly Lynch; *D:* Paolo Barzman; *W:* Tony Gilroy; *C:* Yves Dahan; *M:* John Goldstein.

For Better or Worse **1995 (PG-13)** Pathetic loser Michael Makeshift (Alexander, also making his directorial debut) falls in love with his new sister-in-law Valerie (Davidovich) even as he gets entangled in his brother Reggie's (Woods) business scams. **95m/C VHS.** Jason Alexander, Lolita (David) Davidovich, James Woods, Joe Mantegna, Jay Mohr, Bea Arthur, Robert Costanzo, John Amos, Eda Reiss Merin; ***Cameos:*** Rob Reiner, Rip Torn; *D:* Jason Alexander; *W:* Jeff Nathanson; *C:* Wayne Keenan; *M:* Miles Goodman. **CABLE**

For Ever Mozart **1996** Godard's film puzzle makes references to literature, music, and cinema itself without making any particular sense. Veteran film director Vicky Vitalis (Messica) agrees to help his daughter Camille (Assas) stage a comedic play by Alfred de Musset in Sarajevo, in order to cheer up its war-tired residents. This doesn't go well, but the director has already abandoned the project to return to his latest film idea, which also turns out to be a disaster. French with subtitles. **85m/C VHS.** *FR SI* Vicky Messica, Madeleine Assas, Frederic Pierrot, Ghalia Lacroix; *D:* Jean-Luc Godard; *W:* Jean-Luc Godard; *C:* Christophe Pollock.

For Heaven's Sake **1926** Lloyd's first film for Paramount has him making an accidental donation to a skid row mission, then marrying the preacher's daughter and converting all the neighborhood tough guys. **60m/B VHS, DVD.** Harold Lloyd, Jobyna Ralston, Noah Young, James Mason, Paul Weigel; *D:* Sam Taylor.

For Heaven's Sake 1/2 *Heaven Only Knows* **1979** A bumbling basketball team is lent some heavenly assistance in the form of a meddling angel. But can he hit the jumper? **90m/C VHS.** Ray Bolger, Kent McCord; *D:* Jerry Thorpe; *W:* William Blinn. **TV**

For Hire 1/2 **1998** Suffering from cancer and with a pregnant wife, Chicago cabbie Mitch Lawrence (Lowe) is desperate for money. So, he agrees to kill an associate of famous writer Louis Webber (Mantegna) for $50,000. When the job is done, Mitch learns just why he was chosen to do the deed. **96m/C VHS, DVD.** Rob Lowe, Joe Mantegna, Dominic Philie, Bronwen Black; *D:* Jean Pellerin; *M:* Alan Reeves.

For Keeps 1/2 **1988 (PG-13)** Two high school sweethearts on the verge of graduating get married after the girl becomes pregnant, and suffer all the trials of teenage parenthood. Tends toward the unrealistic and trite. **98m/C VHS, DVD.** Molly Ringwald, Randall Batinkoff, Kenneth Mars; *D:* John G. Avildsen; *W:* Tim Kazurinsky, Denise DeClue; *M:* Bill Conti.

For Ladies Only **1981** A struggling actor takes a job as a male stripper to pay the rent. Among the leering ladies is Davis, daughter of former President Reagan. **100m/C VHS.** Gregory Harrison, Patricia (Patti) Davis, Dinah Manoff, Louise Lasser, Lee Grant, Marc Singer, Viveca Lindfors, Steven Keats; *D:* Mel Damski. **TV**

For Love Alone **1986** A young Australian college co-ed in the 1930s falls in love with a handsome, controversial teacher and follows him to London, only to discover he's not her Mr. Right after all. **102m/C VHS.** *AU* Helen Buday, Sam Neill, Hugo Weaving; *D:* Stephen Wallace.

For Love of Ivy **1968 (PG)** Poitier is a trucking executive who has a gambling operation on the side. Ivy is the Black maid of a rich white family who is about to leave her job to look for romance. The two are brought together but the road to true love doesn't run smooth. Based on a story by Poitier. **102m/C VHS, DVD.** Sidney Poitier, Abbey Lincoln, Beau Bridges, Carroll O'Connor, Nan Martin; *D:* Daniel

Mann; *M:* Quincy Jones.

For Love of the Game 1/2 **1999 (PG-13)** The baseball glove has long been gold for Costner. In his third baseball outing, he moderately scores as veteran Detroit Tigers pitcher Billy Chapel, facing a crossroad in his professional and personal life. In 1-2-3 manner, he learns that the team he's played on for 20 years has been sold, the new owners want to trade him, and his longtime girlfriend, Jane (Preston), is dumping him prior to an important game with the Yankees. Magically, he's this close to pitching a perfect game, as the last five years of his life flash before him. Sudsy, predictable romance overshadows the game action, but harder-edged Raimi, with his own love for the game, injects some striking visual flair. Based on the novel by Michael Shaara. **137m/C VHS, DVD, HD DVD.** Michael (Mike) Papajohn, Kevin Costner, Kelly Preston, John C. Reilly, Jena Malone, Brian Cox, J.K. Simmons, Bill E. Rogers, Vin Scully, Carmine D. Giovinazzo, Hugh Ross, Steve Lyons; *D:* Sam Raimi; *W:* Dana Stevens; *C:* John Bailey; *M:* Basil Poledouris.

For Love or Country: The Arturo Sandoval Story 1/2 **2000 (PG-13)** Biopic of Cuban trumpeter Arturo Sandoval (Garcia) who stays in Cuba for the sake of wife Marianela (Maestro) and their children, all the while chafing under his artistic restrictions. Finally, his wife agrees to defect and during a tour in Athens, Sandoval asks for political asylum. Both Garcia and Maestro have a believable chemistry but also look for Dutton's portrayal of Dizzy Gillespie, who hired Sandoval for his U.N. Orchestra, allowing the musician to travel abroad. **120m/C VHS, DVD.** Andy Garcia, Mia Maestro, Charles S. Dutton, David Paymer, Gloria Estefan, Tomas Milian, Freddy Rodriguez, Jose Zuniga, Steven Bauer, Fionnula Flanagan, Michael O'Hagan; *D:* Joseph Sargent; *W:* Timothy J. Sexton; *C:* Donald M. Morgan; *M:* Arturo Sandoval. **CABLE**

For Love or Money **1963** A super-rich hotel owner wants her lawyer to find her three beautiful daughters. However, she doesn't trust him enough not to meddle in the search. Lavish production and a good cast can't overcome the mediocrity of the script and direction. **108m/C VHS.** Kirk Douglas, Mitzi Gaynor, Thelma Ritter, William Bendix, Julie Newmar, Gig Young, Leslie Parrish, William Windom, Dick Sargent; *D:* Michael Gordon.

For Love or Money 1/2 **1984** Game-show contestants find money and romance. **91m/C VHS.** Jamie Farr, Suzanne Pleshette, Gil Gerard, Ray Walston, Lawrence Pressman, Mary Kay Place; *D:* Terry Hughes; *M:* Billy Goldenberg. **TV**

For Love or Money **1988 (PG-13)** A real estate man with Career on the mind has to choose between the woman in his life and the condo development that stands firmly between them and happily-ever-afterdom. **89m/C VHS.** Timothy Daly, Haviland (Haylie) Morris, Kevin McCarthy, David Doyle, Shelley Fabares; *D:* Todd Hallowell; *W:* Bart Davis; *C:* Igor Sunara; *M:* Jim Lang.

For Love or Money 1/2 **1993 (PG)** Struggling hotel concierge with a heart of gold finds himself doing little "favors" for a slimy entrepreneur who holds the key to his dreams—the cash to open an elegant hotel of his own. Romantic comedy is reminiscent of the classic screwball comedies of the '30s and '40s, but lacks the trademark tight writing and impeccable timing. Fox is appealing and likable as the wheeling and dealing concierge, a role undermined by a mediocre script offering too few laughs. **89m/C VHS, DVD.** Michael J. Fox, Gabrielle Anwar, Isaac Mizrahi, Anthony (Corlan) Higgins, Michael Tucker, Bobby Short, Dan Hedaya, Bob Balaban, Udo Kier, Patrick Breen, Paula Laurence; *D:* Barry Sonnenfeld; *W:* Mark Rosenthal, Larry Konner; *M:* Bruce Broughton.

For Me and My Gal 1/2 **1942** In his film debut, Kelly plays an opportunistic song-and-dance man who lures a young vaudevillian (Garland) away from her current partners. WWI interrupts both their career and romance, but you can count on them being reunited. Loaded with vintage tunes. ♫ For Me and My Gal; They Go Wild, Simply Wild Over Me; The Doll Shop; Oh, Johnny, Oh; Oh, You Beautiful Doll; When You Wore A Tulip; Don't Leave Me Daddy; Do I Love You; By The Beautiful Sea. **104m/B VHS, DVD.** Gene Kelly, Judy Garland, George Murphy, Martha Eggerth, Ben Blue, Richard Quine, Keenan Wynn, Stephen McNally; *D:* Busby Berkeley; *M:* George Bassman.

For One More Day 1/2 *Oprah Winfrey Presents: Mitch Albom's For One More Day* **2007** As the sap rises. Chick Benetto (Imperioli) is a washed-up baseball player turned alcoholic who's made such a mess of his life that he's suicidal. Suddenly, Chick's dead mom Posey (Burstyn) shows up and leads Chick on a trip down memory lane to show him that he can still turn his life around. A weepie family drama adapted from Albom's novel. **92m/C DVD.** Michael Imperioli, Ellen Burstyn, Samantha Mathis, Alice Drummond, Vadim Imperioli, Scott Cohen, Emily Wickersham; *D:* Lloyd Kramer; *W:* Mitch Albom; *C:* Tami Reiker; *M:* Lennie Niehaus. **TV**

For Pete's Sake *July Pork Bellies* **1974 (PG)** Topsy-turvy comedy about a woman whose efforts to get together enough money to put her husband through school involve her with loan sharks, a madame, and even cattle rustling in NYC. Not one of Streisand's best. **90m/C VHS, DVD.** Barbra Streisand, Michael Sarrazin, Estelle Parsons, William Redfield, Molly Picon; *D:* Peter Yates; *W:* Stanley Shapiro, Maurice Richlin; *C:* Laszlo Kovacs; *M:* Artie Butler.

For Real 1/2 **2002 (PG-13)** Mac (Reid) is a wealthy, workaholic middle-aged black record promotor, living in the suburbs of Richmond, Virigina, and looked after by his housekeeper Hardy (Lepart). When Hardy's inner-city, 18-year-old niece CeCe (Curry) gets into serious trouble, Hardy and Mac ask for leniency from the judge and Mac is expected to keep CeCe on the straight and narrow. But there's a generation clash since CeCe thinks Mac is a sellout and Mac thinks CeCe is a punk with a fatalistic attitude. But CeCe's opportunities may be threatened by her own insecurities and her narrow notions of what being "real" mean, while Mac has to learn to loosen up. **95m/C VHS, DVD.** Tim Reid, Tamara Curry, Kweli Leapart, Eugene Long, Susan Fales-Hill; *D:* Tim Reid; *W:* Tim Reid, Shirley Pierce. **VIDEO**

For Richer, for Poorer 1/2 *Father, Son and the Mistress* **1992 (PG)** A very rich, successful businessman notices his son is happy just to sit back and let dad earn all the dough while he waits for his share. In order to teach his son a lesson, Dad decides to give all his money away. But the plan backfires when both realize that earning a second fortune may not be as easy as they assumed. Below average cable fare. **90m/C VHS, DVD.** Jack Lemmon, Talia Shire, Joanna Gleason, Jonathan Silverman, Madeline Kahn, George Wyner; *D:* Jay Sandrich; *W:* Stan Daniels. **CABLE**

For Richer or Poorer **1997 (PG-13)** Definitely poorer. Don't pity the Amish because they can't defend themselves against movies like this—envy them because they don't have to see it. Shallow New York real-estate hustler Brad (Allen) is supposed to be divorcing socialite wife Caroline (Alley). Their inept accountant (Knight), however, has cooked the books, causing them to head for the Pennsylvania hills. They hide out with a community of Amish people, rediscovering their love along with a bunch of manure jokes. Proves once again the inherent unfunniness of butter churns and barn raisings. **122m/C VHS, DVD.** Tim Allen, Kirstie Alley, Wayne Knight, Larry Miller, Jay O. Sanders, Michael Lerner, Miguel A. Nunez Jr., Megan Cavanagh, John Pyper-Ferguson, June Claman, Katie Moore; *D:* Bryan Spicer; *W:* Jana Howington, Steve Lukanic; *C:* Buzz Feitshans IV; *M:* Randy Edelman.

For Roseanna 1/2 *Roseanna's Grave* **1996 (PG-13)** Romantic comedy (despite the subject matter) about Marcello (Reno), the owner of a trattoria in an Italian village and his ailing wife Cecilia (Ruehl), whose dream is to be buried next to their daughter in one of the three remaining plots in their ancient local cemetery. Marcello goes to great lengths to ensure the health of the town's more at-risk citizens to save his wife's spot. Pleasant enough comedy boasts a fine job by an excellent cast, and the Italian scenery is beautiful. Overlooked at the time of its theatrical release, but worth a look for the sentimentally inclined. **99m/C VHS, DVD.** Jean Reno, Mercedes Ruehl, Polly Walker, Mark Frankel, Trevor Peacock, Fay Ripley, Giuseppe Cederna, Luigi Diberti, Renato Scarpa, George Rossi, Roberto Della Casa, Romano Ghini; *D:* Paul Weiland; *W:* Saul Turteltaub; *C:* Henry Braham; *M:* Trevor Jones.

For Sale *A Vendre* **1998** After France (Kiberlain) leaves her groom-to-be at the altar, he hires private detective Luigi (Castellito) to track her down and bring her back. Luigi discovers France has left a string of lovers in her wake and that she has been charging them for her favors. The more he learns, the more obsessed he becomes with a woman he has yet to meet in the flesh. French with subtitles. **116m/C VHS, DVD.** *FR* Sandrine Kiberlain, Sergio Castellitto, Jean-Francois Stevenin, Chiara Mastroianni, Aurore Clement, Samuel Le Bihan; *D:* Laetitia Masson; *W:* Laetitia Masson; *C:* Antoine Hebale; *M:* Siegfried.

For Sale by Owner 1/2 **2009 (PG-13)** Preservation architect Will Custis (Cooper) undertakes the restoration of a colonial-era house near Chesapeake Bay and may finally discover the fate of British colonists who vanished from a nearby settlement. Of course finding this out may be a big mistake. **94m/C DVD.** Scott Cooper, Rachel Nichols, Skeet Ulrich, Kris Kristofferson, Tom Skerritt, Joanna Cassidy, Frankie Faison; *D:* Robert Wilson; *W:* Scott Cooper; *C:* Bill Roe; *M:* Joseph Conlan. **VIDEO**

For the Boys **1991 (R)** Midler stars as Dixie Leonard, a gutsy singer-comedian who hooks up with Eddie Sparks (Caan) to become one of America's favorite USO singing, dancing, and comedy teams. The movie spans 50 years and three wars—including Korea and Vietnam—and raises such issues as the blacklist and the role of politics in showbiz. Glitzy Hollywood entertainment falters despite Midler's strong performance. ♫ Billy-A-Dick; Come Rain or Come Shine; In My Life; Stuff Like That There. **120m/C VHS, DVD.** Bette Midler, James Caan, George Segal, Patrick O'Neal, Christopher Rydell, Arye Gross, Norman Fell, Rosemary Murphy, Dori Brenner, Bud Yorkin, Jack Sheldon, Melissa Manchester, Brandon Call, Arliss Howard; *D:* Mark Rydell; *W:* Marshall Brickman, Neal Jimenez, Lindy Laub; *C:* Stephen Goldblatt; *M:* Dave Grusin. Golden Globes '92: Actress—Mus./Comedy (Midler).

For the First Time 1/2 **1959** In his last film, Lanza plays an opera singer who tours European cities to raise money for his deaf girlfriend's medical treatment. ♫ Oh Mon Amour; Bavarian Drinking Song; Ave Maria; Vesti La Giubba; La Donna e Mobile; Niun Mi Tema; Grand March; O Solo Mio; Ich Liebe Dich. **97m/C VHS.** Mario Lanza, Zsa Zsa Gabor, Johanna von Koczian, Kurt Kasznar, Hans Sohnker, Peter Capell, Renzo Cesana, Sandro Giglio; *D:* Rudolph Mate; *W:* Andrew Solt.

For the Love of Angela 1/2 **1982** Pretty and young shop clerk involves herself with both the shopkeeper and his son. **90m/C** Sarah Rush, David Winn, Margaret Fairchild, Barbara Malloy, Peter Paul Liapis, Louis Jourdan; *D:* Rudy Veyar; *W:* Paul C. Elliot.

For the Love of Benji **1977 (G)** In this second "Benji" film, the adorable little dog accompanies his human family on a Greek vacation. He is kidnapped to be used as a messenger for a secret code, but escapes, to have a series of comic adventures in this entertaining family fare. **85m/C VHS, DVD.** Benji, Patsy Garrett, Cynthia Smith, Allen Finzat, Ed Nelson; *D:* Joe Camp; *W:* Joe Camp; *C:* Don Reddy; *M:* Euel Box.

For the Love of It 1/2 **1980** TV stars galore try to hold together this farce about car chases in California, stolen secret documents, and (of course) true love. Outstandingly mediocre. **100m/C VHS.** Deborah Raffin, Jeff Conaway, Tom Bosley, Norman Fell, Don Rickles, Henry Gibson, Noriyuki "Pat" Morita, William (Bill) Christopher, Lawrence-Hilton Jacobs, Adrian Zmed, Barbi Benton, Adam West; *D:* Hal Kanter. **TV**

For the Love of Mary 1/2 **1948** Durbin retired after this fluff romantic comedy (with some musical numbers) in which she played White House switchboard operator Mary Peppertree. Mary has three potential suitors and juggling her romances causes job-related problems. Includes a second ending and song, which runs an additional eight minutes. ♫ Moonlight Bay; Let Me Call You Sweetheart; I'll Take You Home Again, Kathleen; On the Wings of a Song; Largo al Factotum. **91m/B VHS.** Deanna Durbin, Edmond O'Brien, Don Taylor, Jeffrey Lynn, Harry Davenport, Ray Collins, Hugo Haas; *D:* Fred de Cordova; *W:* Oscar Brodney; *C:* William H. Daniels.

For the Moment 1/2 **1994 (PG-13)** Aussie aviator Lachlan (Crowe) has joined the British Commonwealth Training Plan in 1942, a crash course for fighter pilots that drew men from several countries to bases across Canada. Stationed with best buddy Johnny (Outerbridge) in Manitoba, Lachlan falls for the married Lill (Hirt), sister of Johnny's honey Kate (McMillan), whose husband is away fighting. The emotional stakes are high for all concerned since they know the fliers will soon be sent off to combat. Old-fashioned (and sometimes slow-moving) romance with excellent performances and some gorgeous scenery. **120m/C VHS, DVD.** *CA* Russell Crowe, Christianne Hirt, Peter Outerbridge, Sara McMillan, Wanda Cannon, Scott Kraft; *D:* Aaron Kim Johnston; *W:* Aaron Kim Johnston; *C:* Ian Elkin; *M:* Victor Davies.

For Us, the Living **1988** The life and assassination of civil rights activist Medgar Evers are dramatically presented in this production of "American Playhouse" for PBS. Provides insight into Evers' character, not just a recording of the events surrounding his life. Adapted from the biography written by Evers' widow. **84m/C VHS.** Howard E. Rollins Jr., Rocky Aoki, Paul Winfield, Irene Cara, Margaret Avery, Roscoe Lee Browne, Laurence Fishburne, Janet MacLachlan, Dick Anthony Williams; *D:* Michael A. Schultz.

For Which He Stands **1998** Johnny Rochetti (Forsythe) is a popular Vegas club owner with a loving wife (Alonso) and child. Then his life comes undone one night when he protects a young woman and kills her attacker in the process. Although vindicated by the cops, Johnny finds his troubles are just beginning when he learns the dead man was the brother of a Columbian druglord (Davi). Johnny's wife and child are taken hostage in order to force a deadly showdown between the two men. **94m/C VHS.** William Forsythe, Robert Davi, Maria Conchita Alonso, Ernie Hudson, John Ashton, Robert Costanzo, Ed Lauter, Jose Zuniga, Robert Miranda, Anthony John (Tony) Denison, Ed McMahon; *D:* Nelson McCormick; *W:* Gianni Russo, Nelson McCormick; *C:* Larry Blanford. **VIDEO**

For Whom the Bell Tolls 1/2 **1943** Hemingway novel, gorgeously translated to the big screen, features a star-crossed romantic tale of derring-do. American schoolteacher Robert Jordan (Cooper) decides to join the Spanish Civil War and fight the fascists. He's ordered to rendezvous with peasant guerillas, to aid in blowing up a bridge, and in the rebel camp Jordan meets the beautiful Maria (Bergman). Lots of heroics (and some romance under the stars). Both leads were personally selected by the author. Originally released at 170 minutes. **130m/C VHS, DVD.** Gary Cooper, Ingrid Bergman, Akim Tamiroff, Katina Paxinou, Arturo de Cordova, Vladimir Sokoloff, Mikhail Rasumny, Fortunio Bonanova, Victor Varconi, Joseph Calleia, Alexander Granach, Yakima Canutt, George Coulouris, Yvonne De Carlo, Martin Garralaga, Soledad Jiminez, Duncan Renaldo, Tito Renaldo, Pedro de Cordoba, Frank Puglia, John (Jack) Mylong, Eric Feldary, Lilo Yarson, Leo Bugakov, Antonio Molina; *D:* Sam Wood; *W:* Dudley Nichols; *C:* Ray Rennahan; *M:* Victor Young. Oscars '43: Support. Actress (Paxinou).

For Your Consideration 1/2 **2006 (PG-13)** Writing team Guest and Levy drop their patented "mockumentary" format, but not their sly satire in this send-up of Hollywood's awards season. Marilyn Hack (O'Hara) is a fading actress stuck in a bad low-budget movie until an Internet rumor deems her performance Oscar-worthy. As the buzz grows, she and her co-stars (Shearer, Posey) begin campaigning for nominations and the studio head (Gervais) becomes interested. Levy and Guest get the most out of their ensemble cast (including themselves), especially O'Hara. Fred Willard and

Jane Lynch are a highlight as clueless entertainment show hosts. **86m/C DVD.** *US* Catherine O'Hara, Harry Shearer, Parker Posey, John Michael Higgins, Christopher Moynihan, Jennifer Coolidge, Fred Willard, Jane Lynch, Ricky Gervais, Bob Balaban, Michael McKean, Ed Begley Jr., Jim Piddock, Rachael Harris, Eugene Levy, Carrie Aizley, Christopher Guest; ***D:*** Christopher Guest; ***W:*** Eugene Levy, Christopher Guest; ***C:*** Roberto Schaefer; ***M:*** C.J. Vanston.

For Your Eyes Only **1981 (PG)** In this James Bond adventure, 007 must keep the Soviets from getting hold of a valuable instrument aboard a sunken British spy ship. Sheds the gadgetry of its more recent predecessors in the series in favor of some spectacular stunt work and the usual beautiful girl and exotic locale. Glen's first outing as director, though he handled second units on previous Bond films. Sheena Easton sang the hit title tune. **136m/C VHS, DVD.** *GB* Roger Moore, Carole Bouquet, Chaim Topol, Lynn-Holly Johnson, Julian Glover, Cassandra Harris, Jill Bennett, Michael Gothard, John Wyman, Jack Hedley, Lois Maxwell, Desmond Llewelyn, Geoffrey Keen, Walter Gotell, Charles Dance; ***D:*** John Glen; ***W:*** Michael G. Wilson; ***C:*** Alan Hume; ***M:*** Bill Conti.

For Your Love Only **1979** A beautiful young student falls in love with her teacher and is blackmailed, leading her to murder her tormentor. Soap opera made for German TV. Dubbed in English. **90m/C VHS.** *GE* Nastassja Kinski, Christian Quadflieg, Judy Winter, Klaus Schwarzkopf; ***D:*** Wolfgang Petersen. **TV**

Forbidden 1/2 **1985** In Nazi Germany, a German countess has an affair with a Jewish intellectual, and she winds up hiding him from the S.S. Based on the novel "The Last Jews of Berlin" by Leonard Gross. Slow made-for-cable movie. **116m/C VHS.** Jacqueline Bisset, Jurgen Prochnow, Irene Worth, Peter Vaughan, Amanda Cannings, Avis Bunnage; ***D:*** Anthony Page; ***W:*** Leonard Gross. **CABLE**

Forbidden Choices *The Beans of Egypt, Maine* **1994 (R)** Problems and attractions of the white trash Bean family as observed by enthralled neighbor girl Earlene (Plimpton). Hot-tempered Reuben Bean (Hauer) has just landed a long prison term, leaving his brood of nine in the care of lover Roberta (Lynch), who's also involved with Bean nephew Beal (McGaw). Downtrodden Earlene is only too eager to give in to handsome Beal's charms, leading to more heartbreak. Based on Carolyn Chute's novel "The Beans of Egypt, Maine." Directorial debut of Warren. **109m/C VHS.** Martha Plimpton, Kelly Lynch, Rutger Hauer, Patrick McGaw, Richard Sanders; ***D:*** Jennifer Warren; ***W:*** Bill Phillips; ***C:*** Stevan Larner; ***M:*** Peter Manning Rob.

The Forbidden Christ *Il Cristo Proibito* **1950** Bruno (Vallone) returns from the war to his Tuscan village after years as a POW, only to learn his younger brother, a Resistance fighter, was killed by the Nazis after being betrayed by someone in the town. Bruno wants revenge but when no one will help him find the truth, his rage leads him to kill the wrong man. The only film made by writer Malaparte, which was inspired by actual events, was a boxoffice disaster and caused him to abandon future film plans. Italian with subtitles. **98m/B VHS.** *IT* Raf Vallone, Gino Cervi, Alain Cuny, Elena Varzi; ***D:*** Curzio Malaparte; ***W:*** Curzio Malaparte; ***C:*** Gabor Pogany; ***M:*** Curzio Malaparte.

The Forbidden City **1918** San San is a young Chinese maiden who has the misfortune to fall in love with a Western diplomat. After he is sent away on business San San keeps secret the fact she has born her lover a child but her actions are unforgiven by her father, a deposed mandarin. **72m/B VHS.** Norma Talmadge, Thomas Meighan; ***D:*** Sidney Franklin.

The Forbidden Dance WOOF! **1990 (PG-13)** The first of several quickies released in 1990 applying hackneyed plots to the short-lived Lambada dance craze. The nonsensible plot has a Brazilian princess coming to the U.S. in order to stop further destruction of the rain forest. Instead, she winds up falling for a guy, teaching him to Lambada, and going on TV for a dance contest. Features an appearance by Kid Creole and the Coconuts. **90m/C VHS, DVD.** Laura Elena Harring, Jeff James, Sid Haig, Richard Lynch; ***D:*** Greydon Clark.

Forbidden Fruit *Le Fruit Defendu* **1952** Widowed country doctor (Fernandel), who lives with his domineering mother (Sylvie), marries an equally demanding woman (Nollier) and then finds himself involved with a compliant young prostitute (Arnoul). Comic Fernandel does very well with his change of pace role as a man whose illusions of middle-class respectibility are destroyed. Based on "Letter a Mon Juge" by Georges Simenon. French with subtitles. **103m/B VHS.** *FR* Fernandel, Francoise Arnoul, Claude Nollier, Sylvie, Jacques Castelot; ***D:*** Henri Verneuil; ***W:*** Jacques Companeez, Jean Manse, Henri Verneuil; ***C:*** Henri Alekan; ***M:*** Paul Durand.

Forbidden Games *Les Jeux Interdits* **1952** Famous anti-war drama about two French children play-acting the dramas of war amid the carnage of WWII. Young refugee Fossey sees her parents and dog killed. She meets a slightly older boy whose family takes the girl in. The children decide to bury the animals they have seen killed in the same way that people are buried—even stealing crosses from the cemetery to use over the animal graves. Eventually they are discovered and Fossey is again separated from her newfound home. Acclaimed; available in both dubbed and English-subtitled versions. **90m/B VHS, DVD.** *FR* Brigitte Fossey, Georges Poujouly, Amedee, Louis Herbert, Suzanne Courtal, Jacques Marin, Laurence Badie, Andre Wasley, Louis Sainteve; ***D:*** Rene Clement; ***W:*** Rene Clement, Jean Aurenche, Pierre Bost, Francois Boyer; ***C:*** Robert Juillard; ***M:*** Narciso Yepes. Oscars '52: Foreign Film; British Acad. '53: Film; N.Y. Film Critics '52: Foreign Film; Venice Film Fest. '52: Film.

Forbidden Games **1995 (R)** When a modeling agency head is murdered, the investigator finds there are more than enough suspects to go around. **89m/C VHS, DVD.** Jeff Griggs, Gail Harris, Amy Weber, Lesli Kay, Jefferson Wagner; ***D:*** Edward Holzman; ***W:*** Edward Holzman; ***C:*** Harris Done; ***M:*** K. Alexander (Alex) Wilkinson.

Forbidden Homework *La Tarea Prohibida* **1992** A young man (Pastor) needs to complete an assignment for his film class and persuades middle-aged Maria (Rojo), a friend of the family, to help him rehearse a scene. What she doesn't know is that he's recording their rehearsal—which happens to be a simulated sexual encounter that turns all too real. Spanish with subtitles. **80m/C VHS, DVD.** *MX* Maria Rojo, Julian Pastor, Esteban Soberanes; ***D:*** Jaime Humberto Hermosillo; ***W:*** Jaime Humberto Hermosillo; ***C:*** Alex Phillips Jr.; ***M:*** Omar Guzman.

The Forbidden Kingdom 1/2 **2008 (PG-13)** Introduce the kiddies to kung fu action-lite in this mild adventure (that could easily be a PG). Boston teen Jason (Angarano) is magically transported back to ancient China thanks to a golden staff that must be returned to its imprisoned owner, the Monkey King (Li). He's helped by drunken fighter Lu Yan (Chan), orphaned babe Golden Sparrow (Yifei), and a guy known as the Silent Monk (Li again). They're opposed by the Jade Warload (Chou), white-haired witch Ni Chang (Bing Bing Li), and various evil minions. Plays it safe but it's also (surprisingly) the first pairing between martial art stars Chan and Li, so that's a treat. **105m/C DVD, Blu-ray Disc.** *US* Michael Angarano, Jackie Chan, Jet Li, Collin Chou, Bingbing Li, Liu Yifei, Morgan Benoit; ***D:*** Rob Minkoff; ***W:*** John Fusco; ***C:*** Peter Pau; ***M:*** David Buckley.

Forbidden Love **1982** A man in his early 20s falls in love with a woman twice his age, much to the chagrin of her daughters. **96m/C VHS.** Andrew Stevens, Yvette Mimieux, Dana Elcar, Lisa Lucas, Jerry Houser, Randi Brooks, Lynn Carlin, Hildy Brooks, John Considine; ***D:*** Steven Hilliard Stern; ***M:*** Hagood Hardy. **TV**

Forbidden Passion: The Oscar Wilde Movie 1/2 *Oscar* **1985** A British-made look at Wilde's later years, emphasizing his homosexuality and the Victorian repression that accompanied it. **120m/C VHS.** *GB* Michael Gambon, Robin Lermitte; ***D:*** Henry Herbert; ***W:*** John Hawkesworth; ***C:*** Garth Tucker; ***M:*** Carl Davis.

Forbidden Planet 1/2 **1956** In A.D. 2200, a space cruiser visits the planet Altair-4 to uncover the fate of a previous mission of space colonists. They are greeted by Robby the Robot and discover the only survivors of the Earth colony which has been preyed upon by a terrible space monster. A classic science-fiction version of the Shakespearean classic "The Tempest." **98m/C VHS, DVD, HD DVD.** Walter Pidgeon, Anne Francis, Leslie Nielsen, Warren Stevens, Jack Kelly, Richard Anderson, Earl Holliman, George D. Wallace, Robert Dix, Frankie Darro; ***D:*** Fred M. Wilcox; ***W:*** Cyril Hume; ***C:*** George J. Folsey; ***M:*** Bebe Barron, Louis Barron; ***V:*** Marvin Miller; ***Nar:*** Les Tremayne.

The Forbidden Quest **1993** In 1941, a journalist (Ward) tracks down the only survivor of the Hollandia's 1905 expedition to Antarctica, ship's carpenter Sullivan (O'Conor), to find out about the tragic journey. Director Delpeut mixes archival footage of actual turn-of-the-century voyages to reveal the Hollandia's murderous secrets. **75m/C VHS, DVD.** *NL* Joseph O'Conor, Roy Ward; ***D:*** Peter Delpeut; ***W:*** Peter Delpeut.

Forbidden Sins **1999 (R)** Defense attorney Maureen Doherty (Tweed) is hired to defend an arrogant multi-millionaire accused of murdering a stripper during kinky sex games. Maureen's search for the truth soon takes her into forbidden territory, in opposition to her ex-husband, the detective assigned to the case. **87m/C VHS, DVD.** Shannon Tweed, Corbin Timbrook; ***D:*** Robert Angelo; ***W:*** Daryl Haney, Hel Styverson; ***C:*** Michael Goi; ***M:*** Herman Beeftink. **VIDEO**

Forbidden Sun **1989 (R)** An Olympic gymnastics coach and her dozen beautiful students go to Crete to train. When one of them is brutally raped, vengeance is meted out by the girls. **88m/C VHS, DVD.** Lauren Hutton, Cliff DeYoung, Renee Estevez; ***D:*** Zelda Barron.

Forbidden Trails 1/2 **1941** Rough Riders adventure has Silver the horse saving his owner from the vengeance of two outlaws. Two more heroes go under cover to bring the bad guys to justice. **60m/B VHS, DVD.** Buck Jones, Tim McCoy, Raymond Hatton; ***D:*** Robert North Bradbury.

Forbidden Valley 1/2 **1938** Ring Hazzard (Beery) has been raised in a remote New Mexico canyon by his father (Hinds), who years earlier fled a bogus murder charge. Ring meets rancher's daughter, Wilda Lanning (Robinson), when he has to save her from stampeding horses, but his father is killed by a wild bronco so he and Wilda begin to drive a herd of mustangs into town to sell them and begin a life together. Their plan is interrupted by rattle snake bites and a rival, Matt Rogan (Kohler), who attempts to steal Ring's herd. **68m/B DVD.** Noah Beery Jr., Frances Robinson, Fred Kohler Sr., Alonzo Price, Samuel S. Hinds; ***D:*** Wyndham Gittens; ***W:*** Stuart Hardy; ***C:*** Elwood "Woody" Bredell.

Forbidden World WOOF! *Mutant* **1982 (R)** Lives of a genetic research team become threatened by the very life form they helped to create: a man-eating organism capable of changing its genetic structure as it grows and matures. Corman-produced quickie follow-up to "Galaxy of Terror" is a graphically violent rip-off of "Alien." **82m/C VHS.** Jesse Vint, Dawn Dunlap, June Chadwick, Linden Chiles, Scott Paulin, Michael Bowen; ***D:*** Allan Holzman; ***W:*** Jim Wynorski, R.J. Robertson, Tim Curnen; ***C:*** Tim Suhrstedt; ***M:*** Susan Justin.

Forbidden Zone 1/2 **1980 (R)** A sixth dimension kingdom is ruled by the midget, King Fausto, and inhabited by dancing frogs, bikini-clad tootsies, robot boxers, and degraded beings of all kinds. Original music by Oingo Boingo, and directed by founding member Elfman. **75m/B VHS, DVD.** Herve Villechaize, Susan Tyrrell, Viva, Marie-Pascale Elfman, Joe Spinell, Richard Elfman, Danny Elfman; ***D:*** Richard Elfman; ***W:*** Matthew Bright, Richard Elfman; ***C:*** Gregory Sandor; ***M:*** Danny Elfman.

Forbidden Zone: Alien Abduction **1996 (R)** Three babes sharing a sauna also share sexual confidences and discover they've each had an encounter with the same unusual man. Then one of the girls figures out they've had an alien encounter of the very close kind. **90m/C VHS, DVD.** Darcy Demoss, Pia Reyes, Dumitri Bogmaz, Carmen Lacatus, Alina Chivulescu, Florin Chiriac, Meredyth Holmes; ***D:*** Lucian S. Diamonde; ***W:*** Vernon Lumley; ***C:*** Adolfo Bartoli; ***M:*** Reg Powell.

The Force **1994 (R)** Rookie LAPD cop Cal Warner (Gedrick) crosses paths with maverick homicide detective Des Flynn (Hudson), who's on the trail of a brutal killer. But when Flynn dies mysteriously, it's Cal who's haunted by bizarre dreams—and finding the truth could be equally deadly. **94m/C VHS.** Jason Gedrick, Gary Hudson, Cyndi Pass, Kim Delaney; ***D:*** Mark Rosman; ***W:*** Randall Frakes, Mitch Marcus; ***C:*** Jacques Haitkin; ***M:*** Louis Febre.

Force Five **1975** A group of excons form an anti-crime undercover force turning their skills toward justice. Nothing new in this TV pilot. **78m/C VHS.** Gerald Gordon, Nicholas Pryor, James Hampton, David Spielberg, Leif Erickson, Bradford Dillman, Victor Argo; ***D:*** Walter Grauman. **TV**

Force: Five **1981 (R)** Mercenary gathers a group of like-minded action groupies together to rescue the daughter of a powerful man from a religious cult. All action and no brains. **95m/C VHS.** Joe Lewis, Pam Huntington, Master Bong Soo Han; ***D:*** Robert Clouse; ***W:*** Robert Clouse; ***M:*** William Goldstein.

Force of Evil **1949** A cynical attorney who works for a mob boss and for Wall Street tries to save his brother from the gangster's takeover of the numbers operation. The honorable, though criminal, brother refuses the help of the amoral lawyer, and he is finally forced to confront his conscience. Garfield's sizzling performance and the atmospheric photography have made this a film noir classic. **82m/B VHS, DVD.** John Garfield, Thomas Gomez, Marie Windsor, Sheldon Leonard, Roy Roberts; ***D:*** Abraham Polonsky; ***W:*** Abraham Polonsky; ***C:*** George Barnes. Natl. Film Reg. '94.

Force of Evil **1977** A paroled murderer returns to his hometown to brutalize the family that refused to fabricate an alibi for him. **100m/C VHS.** Lloyd Bridges, Eve Plumb, William Watson, Pat(ricia) Crowley; ***D:*** Richard Lang. **TV**

Force of Impulse **1960** J.D. schlocker featuring an impressive cast involved with everything from hot rods to robbery to parental problems. **84m/B VHS.** J. Carrol Naish, Robert Alda, Tony Anthony, Christina Crawford, Jody McCrea, Lionel Hampton; ***D:*** Saul Swimmer; ***W:*** Richard Bernstein, Francis Swann; ***C:*** Clifford Poland; ***M:*** Joseph Liebman.

Force of One **1979 (PG)** A team of undercover narcotics agents is being eliminated mysteriously, and karate expert Norris saves the day in this sequel to "Good Guys Wear Black." **91m/C VHS, DVD, UMD.** Chuck Norris, Bill Wallace, Jennifer O'Neill, Clu Gulager; ***D:*** Paul Aaron.

Force of the Ninja **1988 (R)** When Kazuko Tokugawa (Ball), the daughter of a member of Japan's imperial family, is kidnapped and two of her friends are killed, Kenji (Ivan) is forced to take action. A U.S. agent studying the art of the ninja, he learns that the kidnapping is part of an international arms deal lead by a mercenary named Ryan (Williams). Now Kenji must return home and save the situation using his new warrior skills. **100m/C VHS.** Douglas Ivan, Patricia Ball, Brook Lynne, Lee Thomas; ***D:*** Emmett Alston; ***M:*** Dan Slider.

Force on Thunder Mountain **1977** A father and son go camping and encounter ancient Indian lore and flying saucers. **93m/C VHS, DVD.** Christopher Cain, Todd Dutson.

Force 10 from Navarone **1978 (PG)** So-so sequel to Alistair MacLean's "The Guns of Navarone," follows a group of saboteurs whose aim is to blow up a bridge vital to the Nazi's in Yugoslavia. Keep an eye out for Ford, Nero, and Bach. Lots of double-crosses and action sequences, but doesn't quite hang together. **118m/C VHS, DVD.** Robert Shaw, Harrison Ford, Barbara Bach, Edward Fox, Carl Weathers, Richard Kiel, Franco Nero; *D:* Guy Hamilton; *W:* Robin Chapman; *C:* Christopher Challis; *M:* Ronald Goodwin.

Forced Entry 🦴 *The Last Victim* **1975 (R)** Psychopathic killer-rapist hesitates over one of his victims, and she murders him instead. **92m/C VHS.** Tanya Roberts, Ron Max, Nancy Allen; *D:* Jim Sotos.

Forced March 🦴🦴 ½ **1990** On location in Hungary, an actor portrays a poet who fought in WWII and became a victim of the Holocaust. However, the deeper he gets into his role, the thinner the line between illusion and reality becomes. Flat drama. **104m/C VHS.** Chris Sarandon, Renee Soutendijk, Josef Sommer, John Seitz; *D:* Rick King.

Forced to Kill 🦴 ½ **1993 (R)** A repo man is on his way to deliver a Jaguar when he's captured by a bizarre family and forced to fight in an illegal bare-fist tournament run by the local lunatic sheriff. Professional stuntman Eubanks has his work cut out for him in this actioner. **91m/C VHS, DVD.** Corey Michael Eubanks, Michael Ironside, Rance Howard, Don Swayze, Clint Howard, Brian Avery, Kari Whitman, Mickey Jones, Carl Ciarfalio, Cynthia J. Blessington, Alan Gelfant; *D:* Russell Solberg; *W:* Corey Michael Eubanks; *M:* Martin D. Bolin.

Forced Vengeance 🦴🦴 **1982 (R)** Vietnam vet pits himself against the underworld in Hong Kong. With Norris in the lead, you can take it for granted there will be plenty of martial arts action. **103m/C VHS, DVD.** Chuck Norris, Mary Louise Weller; *D:* James Fargo; *M:* William Goldstein.

Forces of Nature 🦴🦴 **1999 (PG-13)** Lightweight romantic screwball comedy has straight-laced nice guy Ben (Affleck) trying to get to Savannah in time for his wedding with Tierney. When his plane skids off the runway, he's paired up with free spirit Sarah (Bullock) on an obstacle-filled trip down south. Some fine moments and unusually well done characterization are undone by inconsistency and a lack of chemistry. Enjoyment of the conclusion depends on your opinion of romantic comedy conventions. **104m/C VHS, DVD.** Jack Kehler, Sandra Bullock, Ben Affleck, Maura Tierney, Steve Zahn, Blythe Danner, Ronny Cox, Michael Fairman, Janet Carroll, Richard Schiff, Meredith Scott Lynn, George D. Wallace, John Doe, Steve Hytner, David Strickland; *D:* Bronwen Hughes; *W:* Marc Lawrence; *C:* Elliot Davis; *M:* John Powell.

Ford: The Man & the Machine 🦴 ½ **1987** Episodic biography of ruthless auto magnate Henry Ford I from the building of his empire to his personal tragedies. The cast lacks spark and Robertson (Ford) is positively gloomy. The only one appearing to have any fun is Thomas (Ford's mistress). Based on the biography by Robert Lacey. **200m/C VHS, DVD.** Cliff Robertson, Hope Lange, Heather Thomas, Michael Ironside, Chris Wiggins, R.H. Thomson; *D:* Allan Eastman; *C:* Thomas Burstyn.

A Foreign Affair 🦴🦴🦴 **1948** Amusing comedy finds straitlaced congresswoman Phoebe Frost (Arthur) heading a committee that travels to Berlin to check on the morale (and morals) of American troops stationed there. Phoebe is suspicious of sultry singer Erika Von Schluetow (Dietrich), whose under the protection of a mysterious American officer. After Phoebe falls for Captain John Pringle (Lund), guess who turns out to be the heel in question? Of course, he's got a perfectly reasonable explanation. **115m/B VHS.** Marlene Dietrich, Jean Arthur, John Lund, Millard Mitchell, Stanley Prager, Peter Von Zerneck, Freddie (Fred) Steele; *D:* Billy Wilder; *W:* Billy Wilder, Charles Brackett, Richard L. Breen; *C:* Charles B(ryant) Lang Jr.; *M:* Frederick "Friedrich" Hollander.

Foreign Affairs 🦴🦴🦴 **1993** Vinnie Miller (Woodward) is a prim New England college teacher off to London on a research sabbatical. On the flight Vinnie's seatmate is boisterous good-ole-boy Chuck Mumpson (Dennehy), with whom she appears to have nothing in common. Naturally the two middle-aged romantics find a funny, though bittersweet, love together. A rather distracting subplot find's Vinnie's young colleague Fred (Stolz) involved in an affair with an older, eccentric British actress (Beacham). Based on the novel by Alison Lurie. **100m/C VHS.** Joanne Woodward, Brian Dennehy, Eric Stoltz, Stephanie Beacham, Ian Richardson, Robert Hands; *D:* Jim O'Brien; *W:* Chris Bryant; *C:* Michael Coulter. **CABLE**

Foreign Body 🦴🦴 ½ **1986 (PG-13)** An Indian (played by "Passage to India" star, Banerjee) visiting London pretends to be a doctor and finds women flocking to him. Excellent overlooked British comedy. Based on the novel by Roderick Mann. **108m/C VHS.** *GB* Victor Banerjee, Warren Mitchell, Trevor Howard, Geraldine McEwan, Amanda Donohoe, Denis Quilley, Eve Ferret, Anna Massey; *D:* Ronald Neame; *W:* Celine La Freniere; *M:* Ken Howard.

Foreign Correspondent 🦴🦴🦴🦴 **1940** A classic Hitchcock tale of espionage and derring-do. A reporter is sent to Europe during WWII to cover a pacifist conference in London, where he becomes romantically involved with the daughter of the group's founder and befriends an elderly diplomat. When the diplomat is kidnapped, the reporter uncovers a Nazi spy-ring headed by his future father-in-law. **120m/B VHS, DVD.** Joel McCrea, Laraine Day, Herbert Marshall, George Sanders, Robert Benchley, Albert Bassermann, Edmund Gwenn, Eduardo Ciannelli, Harry Davenport, Martin Kosleck, Charles Halton; *D:* Alfred Hitchcock; *W:* Robert Benchley, Charles Bennett, Joan Harrison, James Hilton; *M:* Alfred Newman.

Foreign Exchange 🦴 ½ **2008 (R)** Teen sex comedy about four high schoolers determined to take the easiest classes possible in their senior year so they can devote their time to hosting the school's sexy exchange students. As usual, their plans get derailed and humiliations follow. **85m/C DVD.** Ryan Pinkston, Vanessa Lengies, Jennifer Coolidge, Curtis Armstrong, Clint Howard, Miles Thompson, Tania Raymonde, Ashley Edner, Randy Wayne, Daniel Booko; *D:* Danny Roth; *W:* Danny Roth. **VIDEO**

A Foreign Field 🦴🦴 ½ **1993** Comedy/drama focuses on several WW2 veterans returning to the Normandy beaches in honor of the 50th anniversary of the invasion. Blustery British Cyril (McKern) and equally demanding Yank Waldo (Randolph) also must deal with their 50-year rivalry over their wartime love, the cheerfully vulgar Angelique (Moreau). Veteran performers get the chance to show their stuff but film descends into pathos. **90m/C VHS, DVD.** *GB* Leo McKern, John Randolph, Jeanne Moreau, Lauren Bacall, Alec Guinness, Edward Herrmann, Geraldine Chaplin; *D:* Charles Sturridge; *W:* Roy Clarke; *M:* Geoffrey Burgon.

Foreign Land 🦴🦴 *Terra Estrangeira* **1995** Twenty-one-year-old Paco is an impoverished student living in Sao Paulo who naively agrees to take a suitcase to Lisbon for shady businessman Igor (Melo) and give it to his compatriot, Miguel (Borges). But Paco discovers Miguel has been murdered—leading him to the dead man's girlfriend, unhappy Brazilian exile, Alex (Torres). The two bond while seeking to avoid the newly arrived Igor and Miguel's other treacherous associates. Portuguese with subtitles. **100m/B VHS, DVD.** *BR PT* Alexandre Borges, Tcheky Karyo, Fernanda Torres, Laura Cardoso, Joao Lagarto, Luis Mello, Fernando Pinto; *D:* Walter Salles; *W:* Walter Salles, Marcos Bernstein, Daniela Thomas; *C:* Walter Carvalho; *M:* Jose Miguel Wisnik.

Foreign Student 🦴🦴 ½ **1994 (R)** In 1956 Philippe (Hofschneider) is a French exchange student at a tradition-bound Virginia college. At a professor's home he meets part-time housekeeper April (Givens), who wants to practice her schoolbook French (among other things). They begin a romance but, since April is black, there's trouble. Hofschneider is charming though Givens appears too glamorous and self-aware. Dutton and Battle are notable in their small roles as blues musicians Howlin' Wolf and Sonny Boy Williamson. Directorial debut for Sereny. Based on the novel "The Foreign Student" by Philippe Labro. **96m/C VHS.** Marco Hofschneider, Robin Givens, Jack Coleman, Edward Herrmann, Rick Johnson, Charlotte Ross, Charles S. Dutton, Hinton Battle; *D:* Eva Sereny; *W:* Menno Meyjes; *C:* Franco Di Giacomo; *M:* Jean-Claude Petit.

The Foreigner 🦴 **1978** Secret agent who comes to New York City to meet his contact becomes entrapped in a series of mysterious events revolving around the underground club scene. **90m/B VHS, DVD.** Eric Mitchell, Patti Astor, Deborah Harry; *D:* Amos Poe; *W:* Amos Poe.

The Foreigner 🦴 **2003 (R)** Ludicrous would-be actioner stars immovable hulk Seagal as a former spy turned mercenary. His latest job is to carry the black box recorder from a downed plane from France to Germany but the sinister Van Arken (Van Gorkum) has other ideas. **96m/C VHS, DVD.** Steven Seagal, Harry Van Gorkum, Sherman Augustus, Anna-Louise Plowman; *D:* Michael Oblowitz; *W:* Darren O. Campbell; *C:* Michael Slovis; *M:* David Wurst, Eric Wurst. **VIDEO**

The Foreman Went to France 🦴 ½ *Somewhere in France* **1942** Industrial engineer travels to France during WWII to help prevent secret machinery from falling into the hands of the Nazis and their allies. **88m/B VHS.** *GB* Clifford Evans, Constance Cummings, Robert Morley, Gordon Jackson, Ernest Milton, Charles Victor, Mervyn Johns, Bill Blewitt, Paul Bonifas, Ronald Adam; *D:* Charles Frend; *W:* Leslie Arliss, John Dighton, Angus MacPhail; *C:* Wilkie Cooper; *M:* William Walton.

Foreplay **WOOF!** *The President's Women* **1975** Inane trilogy of comedy segments involving characters with White House connections. Stories are introduced by former President Mostel discussing his downfall in a TV interview. Lame rather than risque, wasting talents of all involved. Each segment was scripted and directed by a different team. **100m/C VHS, DVD.** Pat Paulsen, Jerry Orbach, Estelle Parsons, Zero Mostel; *D:* Bruce Malmuth, John G. Avildsen; *C:* Ralf Bode.

Forest of Little Bear 🦴🦴 **1987** A man returns to his impoverished family in 1928 and decides to seek the reward put on the head of a one-eared man-eating bear. He kills the bear but faces a dilemma when he sees the bear left a helpless cub behind. In Japanese with English subtitles. **124m/C VHS.** *JP* Takahiro Tamura, Junko Sakurado, Hiroshi Miyata; *D:* Toshio Goto; *W:* Ryunosuke Ono; *C:* Takaya Yamazaki; *M:* Masaru Sato.

Forest Warrior 🦴🦴 **1995 (PG)** Children fight to save the local forests of Tanglewood Mountain from greedy developer Kiser with the help of ghostly mountain man John McKenna (Norris), who was murdered in the same woods a century before. Mild adventure with good ecology theme. **98m/C VHS.** Chuck Norris, Terry Kiser, Max Gail, Roscoe Lee Browne, William Sanderson; *D:* Aaron Norris; *W:* Ron Swanson; *C:* Joao Fernandes.

Forever 🦴🦴 ½ **1978** A teenage girl experiences true love for the first time and struggles with its meaning. Adaptation of Judy Blume's novel. **100m/C VHS.** Stephanie Zimbalist, Dean Butler, John Friedrich, Beth Raines, Diana Scarwid; *D:* John Korty. **TV**

Forever: A Ghost of a Love Story 🦴🦴 ½ **1992 (R)** Coogan is a hot-shot music video director who moves into a haunted house and soon meets the resident ghost, who just happens to be a beautiful woman. He falls for the ghostly presence but his all-too-real female agent is also making her moves. **93m/C VHS.** Keith Coogan, Sean Young, Diane Ladd, Sally Kirkland, Terence Knox, Nicholas Guest, Renee Taylor, Steve Railsback; *D:* Thomas Palmer Jr.; *W:* Thomas Palmer Jr.

Forever Amber 🦴🦴 ½ **1947** Seventeenth century rags to riches story features Darnell as the poverty stricken girl who uses sex to gain wealth and status. She makes it to the bed of King Charles II, only to lose the one man she ever really loved (Wilde). The censorship of the 1940s hindered the film's erotic potential. Adapted from the best-selling novel by Kathleen Winsor. **140m/C VHS.** Linda Darnell, Cornel Wilde, Richard Greene, George Sanders, Richard Haydn, Jessica Tandy, Anne Revere, John Russell, Leo G. Carroll, Robert Coote, Margaret Wycherly, Alma Kruger, Edmund Breon, Alan Napier, Bill Ward, Richard Bailey, Skelton Knaggs, Norma Varden, Edith Evanson, Ellen Corby; *D:* Otto Preminger; *W:* Philip Dunne, Ring Lardner Jr.; *C:* Leon Shamroy; *M:* David Raksin.

Forever and a Day 🦴🦴🦴🦴 **1943** Tremendous salute to British history centers around a London manor originally built by an English admiral during the Napoleonic era and the exploits of succeeding generations. The house even manages to survive the blitz of WWII showing English courage during wartime. Once-in-a-lifetime casting and directing. **104m/B VHS, DVD.** Brian Aherne, Robert Cummings, Ida Lupino, Charles Laughton, Herbert Marshall, Ray Milland, Anna Neagle, Merle Oberon, Claude Rains, Victor McLaglen, Buster Keaton, Jessie Matthews, Roland Young, Sir C. Aubrey Smith, Edward Everett Horton, Elsa Lanchester, Edmund Gwenn; *D:* Rene Clair, Edmund Goulding, Cedric Hardwicke, Frank Lloyd, Victor Saville, Robert Stevenson, Herbert Wilcox, Kent Smith; *W:* Christopher Isherwood, Gene Lockhart, Donald Ogden Stewart, Charles Bennett, Michael Hogan, Peter Godfrey; *C:* Robert De Grasse, Lee Garmes, Russell Metty, Nicholas Musuraca; *M:* Anthony Collins.

Forever Darling 🦴🦴 **1956** Mixed effort from the reliable comedy duo sees Desi playing a dedicated chemist who neglects his wife while pursuing the next great pesticide. Lucy calls on her guardian angel (Mason) to help her rekindle her marriage. He advises her to go with Desi when he tests his new bug killer, and a series of hilarious, woodsy calamities occur. Lucy and Desi are always fun to watch, but '60s TV sitcom fans will enjoy the fact that Mrs. Howell (Schaefer) and Jane Hathaway (Kulp) appear in the same picture. **91m/C VHS, DVD.** Lucille Ball, Desi Arnaz Sr., James Mason, Louis Calhern, John Emery, John Hoyt, Natalie Schafer, Nancy Kulp; *D:* Alexander Hall.

Forever Emmanuelle 🦴 *Laure* **1975 (R)** Sensual young woman finds love and the ultimate erotic experience in the wilds of the South Pacific in this sequel to the porn-with-production-values "Emmanuelle." **89m/C VHS.** *IT FR* Annie Belle, Emmanuelle Arsan, Al Cliver; *D:* Emmanuelle Arsan, Ovidio G. Assonitis; *W:* Emmanuelle Arsan; *C:* Roberto D'Ettorre Piazzoli; *M:* Franco Micalizzi.

Forever Evil 🦴 **1987** The vacationing denizens of a secluded cabin are almost killed off by the cult followers of a mythic god. **107m/C VHS, DVD.** Red Mitchell, Tracey Huffman, Charles Trotter, Howard Jacobsen, Kent Johnson; *D:* Roger Evans; *W:* Freeman Williams; *C:* Horacio Fernandez; *M:* Marianne Pendino.

Forever Female 🦴🦴🦴 **1953** Bright comedy about show business, egos, and love. Holden is a young playwright whose first play is accepted by stage producer Douglas on the condition that the lead role, featuring a 19-year-old heroine, be rewritten for his ex-wife Rogers. She's an aging leading lady smitten by Holden's charms—as is the ingenue Crowley, who would be perfect for the role as written. Complications and manipulations abound as the play makes its way to production. Adaptation of the Sir James Barrie play "Rosalind." **93m/B VHS.** Ginger Rogers, William Holden, Paul Douglas, Pat(ricia) Crowley, James Gleason, Jesse White, George Reeves, Marjorie Rambeau, King Donovan, Vic Perrin, Marion Ross; *D:* Irving Rapper; *W:* Julius J. Epstein, Philip G. Epstein.

Forever Love 🦴🦴 ½ **1998** Lizzie Brooks (McEntire) is a wife and mother who has just awakened from a 20-year coma. Her daughter Emma (Stephens) is a grownup, her husband Peter (Matheson) is a stranger, and she discovers her best friend Gail (Armstrong) has taken her place in both her home and Peter's heart. Now Lizzie seeks to find her own place in a totally new world. Based on a true story. **120m/C VHS.** Reba McEntire, Tim Matheson, Bess Armstrong, Heather Stephens, Richard Biggs, Scott Foley; *D:* Michael Switzer; *W:* Joyce Heft Brotman. **TV**

Forever, Lulu 🦴 *Crazy Streets* **1987 (R)** A down-on-her-luck novelist winds up involved with the mob and a gangster's girlfriend. Completely laughless comedy with amateurish direction. **86m/C VHS, DVD.** Hanna Schygulla, Deborah Harry, Alec Baldwin, Annie Golden, Paul Gleason, Dr. Ruth Westheimer; *D:* Amos Kollek.

Forever Mary ♂♂♂ *Mery per Sempre* **1989** A teacher tries to better the lives of the boys sentenced to a reformatory in Palermo, Sicily, when a teenage transvestite prostitute (the title character) is admitted to the school. In Italian with English subtitles. **100m/C VHS.** *IT* Michele Placido, Alessandro DiSanzo, Francesco Benigno; ***D:*** Marco Risi; ***W:*** Sandro Petraglia.

Forever Mine ♂♂ **1999 (R)** In 1973, cabana boy Alan (Fiennes) meets Ella (Mol), the seductive young wife of politico Mark (Liotta) at the Miami Beach resort where he works. It's lust at first sight but ends badly when Mark discovers the affair. But in 1987, Alan re-enters both their lives with a new identity, a new occupation, and a desire for revenge. Noir wannabe whose story doesn't always hold together (but is at least titillating for the sex scenes). **117m/C VHS, DVD.** Joseph Fiennes, Ray Liotta, Gretchen Mol, Vincent Laresca; ***D:*** Paul Schrader; ***W:*** Paul Schrader; ***C:*** John Bailey; ***M:*** Angelo Badalamenti.

Forever Strong ♂ **2008 (PG-13)** High-strung rugby star Rick Penning (Faris) gets nailed with a DUI, and the way out of trouble puts him on a rival team, where he clashes with the hard-nosed coach. Then a shot at the national championship puts Rick's loyalty and character to the test. Tired bad-boy jock redemption story does itself in with sap and schmaltz. Based on an all-too-familiar but true story of sports glory that finds freshness only because it doesn't involve football, baseball, basketball, or hockey. **112m/C DVD.** *US* Sean Faris, Gary Cole, Julie Warner, Neal McDonough, Penn Badgley, Sean Astin, Arielle Kebbel, Nathan West, Larry Bagby; ***D:*** Ryan Little; ***W:*** David Pliler; ***C:*** T.C. Christensen; ***M:*** J Bateman.

Forever Together ♂♂ 1/2 *Can't Be Heaven* **2000 (PG)** The perils of young, first love are sweetly explored as fatherless seventh-grader Danny (Burke) thinks he's falling in love with best friend, Julie (Tractenberg). His widowed mom (Ticotin) is having her own romantic troubles, so Danny turns for advice to a friendly jazz musician (Macchio). **88m/C VHS, DVD.** Michelle Trachtenberg, Rachel Ticotin, Ralph Macchio, Bryan Burke, Matt McCoy, Diane Ladd, Garry Marshall; ***D:*** Richard Friedman. **VIDEO**

Forever Young ♂♂ **1985** A young boy immerses himself in Catholicism. Admiring a priest, he is unaware that the priest's friend is involved with his mother. Tangled, but delicate handling of the coming-of-age story. **85m/C VHS.** *GB* James Aubrey, Nicholas Gecks, Alec McCowen; ***D:*** David Drury; ***W:*** Ray Connolly. **TV**

Forever Young ♂♂ 1/2 **1992 (PG)** When test pilot Gibson's girlfriend is hit by a car and goes into a coma, he volunteers to be cryogenically frozen for one year. Oops!—he's left frozen for 50 years, until he is accidentally thawed out by a couple of kids. Predictable, designed to be a tear jerker, though it serves mostly as a star vehicle for Gibson who bumbles with '90s technology, finds his true love, and escapes from government heavies, adorable as ever. Through all the schmaltz, the relationship Gibson develops with the young Wood turns out to be the most authentic and endearing love in the film. **102m/C VHS, DVD.** Mel Gibson, Jamie Lee Curtis, Elijah Wood, Isabel Glasser, George Wendt, Joe Morton, Nicolas Surovy, David Marshall Grant, Art LaFleur, John David (J.D.) Cullum; ***D:*** Steve Miner; ***W:*** J.J. (Jeffrey) Abrams; ***C:*** Russell Boyd; ***M:*** Jerry Goldsmith.

Forfeit ♂ 1/2 **2007 (R)** A teenaged Frank skedaddled out of L.A. after killing his abusive father, leaving girlfriend Karen behind. Years later, Frank returns, gets a job at an armored car company, and wants to reconnect with Karen. Only problem is Frank is a whacko who believes a TV evangelist is giving him signs about what to do. In this case, it's plan a heist, fake his death, and put the blame on poor, bewildered Karen. **84m/C DVD.** Billy Burke, Sherry Stringfield, Gregory Itzin, Wayne Knight, Kirk Baltz; ***D:*** Andrew Shea; ***W:*** John Rafter Lee; ***C:*** Roberto Blasini; ***M:*** Andrew Gross. **VIDEO**

Forger of London ♂♂ **1961** Edgar Wallace tale in which Scotland Yard investigates a counterfeit ring connected to a prime suspect, an amnesiac playboy. **91m/C VHS.** *GE* Eddi Arent, Karin Dor, Viktor de Kowa, Hellmut Lange, Robert Graf; ***D:*** Harald Reinl.

Forget About It ♂♂ **2006 (PG-13)** In a trailer park outside Phoenix, retired war vets Sam (Reynolds), Carl (Loggia), and Eddie (Durning) genially vie for the attention of sexy neighbor Christine (Welch) while enjoying their golden years. Then wiseguy Angelo Nitti (Paloma) is relocated as part of the Witness Protection Program without admitting that he's stolen four million bucks from his cohorts. When the trio find the cash and begin to live it up, they also find themselves pursued by the mob and the feds. **85m/C DVD.** Burt Reynolds, Raquel Welch, Robert Loggia, Charles Durning, Richard Grieco, Tim Thomerson, Phyllis Diller, Joanna Pacula, Michael Paloma; ***D:*** B.J. Davis; ***W:*** Julia Davis; ***C:*** Mark Trengove.

Forget Mozart ♂♂ *Zabudnite na Mozarta* **1985** On the day of Mozart's death, the head of the secret police gathers a group together for questioning. They include the composer's wife, his lyricist, the head of a Masonic lodge, and Salieri, Mozart's rival. Each has a different story to tell to the investigator about the composer's life and death. The film makes use of a number of sets and costumes from "Amadeus" and was also filmed on location in Prague. In German with English subtitles. **93m/C VHS.** *GE* Armin Mueller-Stahl, Catarina Raacke; ***D:*** Salvo Luther.

Forget Paris ♂♂ 1/2 **1995 (PG-13)** Pro basketball referee Mickey (Crystal) and airline executive Ellen (Winger) meet in Paris, fall in love and get married. But once the honeymoon is over, the marital bliss unravels due to conflicting work schedules and the lack of romantic scenery. This look at yuppie love and courtship finds Crystal in pre-"City Slickers 2" form, launching three-point oneliners and "When Harry Met Sally" sentiment. Bland direction and an obligation to be cute intensify the "been-there-seen-that" feeling. Winger's presence may hint of miscasting, but she has one of the films funniest scenes involving a stray pet and a pigeon. **101m/C VHS, DVD.** Billy Crystal, Debra Winger, Joe Mantegna, Cynthia Stevenson, Richard Masur, Julie Kavner, William Hickey, Cathy Moriarty, John Spencer; ***D:*** Billy Crystal; ***W:*** Lowell Ganz, Babaloo Mandel, Billy Crystal; ***C:*** Don Burgess; ***M:*** Marc Shaiman.

Forgetting Sarah Marshall ♂♂ **2008 (R)** Apatow produced this raunchy arrested male development comedy that stars (and was written by) second-banana Segel. Slacker couch potato Peter is an underachieving L.A. composer of TV music who's devastated when he's dumped by ambitious starlet hottie girlfriend Sarah (Bell). The woebegone Peter eventually decides to vacation at a Hawaiian resort but—ta-da!—finds Sarah and her new beau, self-absorbed Brit rocker Aldous Snow (Brand), are also guests. Despite frequent humiliations, Peter sticks it out, supported by brunette beauty Rachael (Kunis) and various odd hotel encounters. Segel is game since he gets naked (twice) and does a lot of crying and moping, but you're more likely to say "get over it already" than be amused. **112m/C DVD, Blu-ray Disc.** *US* Jason Segel, Kristen Bell, Mila Kunis, Bill Hader, Russell Brand, Jonah Hill, Paul Rudd, William Baldwin, Jason Bateman, Maria Thayer, Steve Landesberg, Jack McBrayer, Liz Cackowski, Gedde Watanabe; ***D:*** Nicholas Stoller; ***W:*** Jason Segel; ***C:*** Russ T. Alsobrook; ***M:*** Lyle Workman.

Forgive and Forget ♂♂ **1999** Macho London construction worker David (Shepherd) can't admit to himself or anyone else that he's gay, including his best mate since childhood, Theo (Simon). But when Theo decides to move in with his girlfriend Hannah (Fraser), David schemes to break them up. He also decides to publicly declare his love by appearing with Theo on a TV talk show, with unforgettable consequences. **96m/C VHS, DVD.** *GB* Steve John Shepherd, John Simm, Laura Fraser, Maurice Roeves, Ger Ryan, Meera Syal; ***D:*** Aisling Walsh; ***W:*** Mark Burt; ***C:*** Kevin Rowley; ***M:*** Hal Lindes.

The Forgotten ♂♂ **1989** After 17 years as POWs, six Green Berets are freed, only to face a treacherous government conspiracy aimed at eliminating them. **96m/C VHS.** Keith Carradine, Steve Railsback, Stacy Keach, Pepe Serna, Don Opper, Richard Lawson; ***D:*** James Keach; ***W:*** Keith Carradine, Steve Railsback, James Keach. **TV**

The Forgotten ♂♂ **2004 (PG-13)** Convoluted conspiracy-minded sci-fi thriller. Telly (Moore) is still acutely grieving over her young son's death in a plane crash 14 months before. Despite the help of hubby Jim (Edwards) and shrink Jack Munce (Sinise), Telly can't let go of the pain until the mementos of her son's life disappears. Now Jim claims they never had a child. Ash (West), the father of a daughter killed on the same flight, can't remember his child and thinks Telly is nuts. But Telly knows she's not—someone is erasing the evidence of their kids' existence and she's going to find out who and why (even if it means getting chased by those nasty men in black). **89m/C VHS, DVD.** *US* Julianne Moore, Dominic West, Gary Sinise, Alfre Woodard, Robert Wisdom, Jessica Hecht, Anthony Edwards, Linus Roache; ***D:*** Joseph Ruben; ***W:*** Gerald Di Pego; ***C:*** Anastas Michos; ***M:*** James Horner, Paul Kelly.

Forgotten City ♂♂ *The Vivero Letter* **1998 (R)** James Wheeler is out to uncover a city from the Mayan civilization but he faces a rival expedition, an unhappy native tribe, and mysterious disappearances and deaths that point to someone—or something—wanting the city and its treasures to remain undisturbed. Based on the novel "The Vivero Letter" by Desmond Bagley. Filmed on location in Costa Rica. **96m/C VHS, DVD.** Robert Patrick, Fred Ward, Chiara Caselli; ***D:*** H. Gordon Boos; ***W:*** Denne Bart Petitclerc, Arthur Sellers; ***C:*** Fabrizio Lucci. **VIDEO**

The Forgotten One ♂ 1/2 **1989 (R)** An uninspired author and a female reporter become mixed up in a century-old murder and the restless ghost it spawned. **89m/C VHS.** Kristy McNichol, Terry O'Quinn, Blair Parker, Elisabeth Brooks; ***D:*** Phillip Badger; ***W:*** Phillip Badger; ***C:*** James Mathers.

Forgotten Prisoners ♂♂ *Forgotten Prisoners: The Amnesty Files* **1990 (R)** Celluloid proof that conviction and true grit do not always entertainment make. Greenwald—whose credits range from "Xanadu" to "The Burning Bed"—directed this righteous but stationary drama about an Amnesty International official (Silver) who's assigned to look into the incarceration and egregious mistreatment of Turkish citizens. **92m/C VHS.** Ron Silver, Roger Daltrey, Hector Elizondo; ***D:*** Robert Greenwald; ***M:*** Brad Fiedel. **CABLE**

Forgotten Silver ♂♂♂ **1996** Jackson's mockumentary finds the director and co-director Botes "discovering" the lost films of Colin McKenzie, a pioneering New Zeland filmmaker of the early 1900s. These include McKenzie's epic film "Salome" which the duo decide to restore. The entire escapade is a fiction, including the silent film footage that's shown. The tape also includes the short film "Signing Off" about the final show for a radio DJ and the special request he has trouble fulfilling. **70m/C VHS, DVD.** *NZ* Costa Botes, Sam Neill, Leonard Maltin, Harvey Weinstein, John O'Shea, Hannah McKenzie, Lindsay Shelton, Johnny Morris, Marguerite Hurst; ***D:*** Peter Jackson, Costa Botes, Robert Sarkies; ***W:*** Peter Jackson, Costa Botes; ***C:*** Alun Bollinger; ***Nar:*** Jeffrey Thomas.

A Forgotten Tune for the Flute ♂♂♂ **1988** A delightful, Glasnost-era romantic comedy. A bureaucrat caught up in a dull, stuffy existence has a heart attack and winds up falling in love with his nurse. He then must decide between his comfortable, cared-for life or the love which beckons him. In Russian with English subtitles. **131m/C VHS.** *RU* Leonid Filatov, Tatiana Dogileva, Irina Kupchenko; ***D:*** Edgar Ryazanov.

Forgotten Warrior ♂ 1/2 **1986 (R)** Vengeance is the name of the game as a Vietnam vet tracks down the fellow officer who tried to kill him and shot his commander. **76m/C VHS.** Quincy Frazer, Sam T. Lapuzz, Ron Marchini, Joe Meyer; ***D:*** Nick Cacas, Charlie Ordonez.

Forlorn River ♂ 1/2 **1937** Nevada and Weary, two law-abiding men, seek to return their hometown to peace by eliminating a gang of outlaws. Based on a novel by Zane Grey. **62m/B VHS.** Buster Crabbe, June Martel, John D. Patterson, Harvey Stephens, Chester Conklin, Lew Kelly, Syd Saylor; ***D:*** Charles T. Barton.

The Formula ♂ 1/2 **1980 (R)** Convoluted story about a secret formula for synthetic fuel that meanders it's way from the end of WWII to the present. A U.S. soldier waylays, and then joins forces with, a German general entrusted with the formula. Years later, after the American is murdered, his friend, a hard-nosed L.A. cop, starts investigating, meeting up with spies and a reclusive oil billionaire. Scott and Brando have one good confrontation scene but the rest of the movie is just hot air. From the novel by Steve Shagan. **117m/C VHS.** Marlon Brando, George C. Scott, Marthe Keller, G.D. Spradlin, Beatrice Straight, John Gielgud, Richard Lynch; ***D:*** John G. Avildsen; ***M:*** Bill Conti.

Formula 51 ♂ *The 51st State* **2001 (R)** Good cast is wasted in this ridiculous plot revolving around drugs and crime lords. Elmo (Jackson) is a pharmacology grad student who loses his ability to work in the field due to a marijuana bust. He ends up toiling for drug kingpin Lizard (Meat Loaf) and invents a drug that is allegedly more powerful than crack, heroin or ecstasy. After he arranges an unpleasant surprise for Lizard, he flees to Liverpool in an attempt to sell his formula to English criminal Durant (Tomlinson). Aside from the asinine and convoluted storyline, Jackson is inexplicably forced to parade around in a kilt for most of the film. Just say no. **92m/C VHS, DVD.** *GB CA* Samuel L. Jackson, Robert Carlyle, Emily Mortimer, Meat Loaf Aday, Sean Pertwee, Ricky Tomlinson, Rhys Ifans; ***D:*** Ronny Yu, David Wu; ***W:*** Stel Pavlou; ***C:*** Hang-Seng Poon.

Formula for a Murder ♂ **1985** A very rich but paralyzed woman marries a scheming con artist who plots to kill her and inherit everything. **89m/C VHS.** *IT* Christina Nagy, David Warbeck, Rossano Brazzi; ***D:*** Alberto De Martino; ***W:*** Alberto De Martino; ***C:*** Gianlorenzo Battaglia; ***M:*** Francesco De Masi.

Formula 17 ♂♂ *Shi qi sui de tian kong* **2004** Classic romantic comedy—that is if you live in director DJ Chen's world set in an apparent hetero-free Taipei. This is a boy meets boy tale about young, attractive, sexually innocent country boy Tien's (Tang) move to the big city in search of love. Soon after arriving he runs into an old friend from home, Yu (Chin), who is a gay club bartender. Naturally he's swept into a hilarious circle of new friends including flamer CC (JI) and fitness trainer Alan (Yang). Tien meets a hot one-night-stand artist named Bai (Duncan) who deflowers Tien but can't deliver the relationship Tien expects. High energy sinopop soundtrack and attractive cast carries this light-hearted film. **93m/C DVD.** Tony Yang, Duncan, King Chin, Dada JI, Jimmy Yang, Jason Chang; ***D:*** D.J. Chen; ***W:*** Rady Fu; ***C:*** Chen Huei-Sheng; ***M:*** George Chen, Hung Tze-Li.

Forrest Gump ♂♂♂ 1/2 **1994 (PG-13)** Grandly ambitious and slightly flawed, amounting to a wonderful bit of movie magic. As the intelligence-impaired Gump with a heart of gold and more than enough character and dignity, Hanks supplies another career highlight. Field contributes a nice turn as his dedicated mama (they were last together in "Punchline"), while Sinise is particularly effective as a handicapped Vietnam veteran with a bad attitude. Incredible special effects put Gump in the middle of historic events over a four decade period, but the real story is the life-affirming, non-judgmental power of Gump to transform the lives of those around him. From the novel by Winston Groom. **142m/C VHS, DVD.** Tom Hanks, Robin Wright Penn, Sally Field, Gary Sinise, Mykelti Williamson, Haley Joel Osment, Michael Conner Humphreys, Hanna Hall, Sonny Shroyer, Siobhan Fallon Hogan, Peter Dobson, Michael Jace, Geoffrey Blake, Mary Ellen Trainor, David Brisbin; ***D:*** Robert Zemeckis; ***W:*** Eric Roth; ***C:*** Don Burgess; ***M:*** Alan Silvestri. Oscars '94: Actor (Hanks), Adapt. Screenplay, Director (Zemeckis), Film Editing, Picture, Visual FX; AFI '98: Top 100; Directors Guild '94: Director (Zemeckis); Golden Globes '95: Actor—Drama (Hanks), Director (Zemeckis), Film—Drama; Natl. Bd. of Review '94: Actor (Hanks), Film, Support. Actor (Sinise); Screen Actors Guild '94: Actor (Hanks); Writers Guild '94: Adapt. Screenplay; Blockbuster '95: Movie, T., Drama Actor, T. (Hanks); Blockbuster '96: Drama Actor, V. (Hanks).

The Forsaken 2001 (R) Vampire films need a little smarts to go with their gore but this film has only the latter. It was apparently gutted by the studio prior to release so maybe there was a story at some point. Sean (Smith) is driving from L.A. to Miami when he picks up hitchhiker Nick (Fehr) and the disoriented Megan (Miko). Both turn out to be infected by a blood disease thanks to a vampire's bite. They have to kill the sire if they don't want to become bloodsuckers themselves and then Megan bites Sean, so now it's personal. The vamp in question is suave Kit (Schaech), who has the usual band of trashy minions. The whole movie is trashy but not in a fun way. **90m/C VHS, DVD.** *US* Kerr Smith, Izabella Miko, Johnathon Schaech, Brendan Fehr, Simon Rex, Carrie Snodgress, Phina Oruche; ***D:*** J.S. Cardone; ***W:*** J.S. Cardone; ***C:*** Steven Bernstein; ***M:*** Johnny Lee Schell, Timothy S. (Tim) Jones.

Forsaking All Others 1/2 **1935** Screwball comedy featuring several MGM superstars. Friends since childhood, Gable has been in love with Crawford for 20 years, but she never realizes it and plans to marry Montgomery. Crawford is very funny in this delightful story of a wacky romantic triangle. **84m/B VHS.** Joan Crawford, Clark Gable, Robert Montgomery, Charles Butterworth, Billie Burke, Rosalind Russell, Frances Drake; ***D:*** Woodbridge S. Van Dyke; ***W:*** Joseph L. Mankiewicz; ***C:*** George J. Folsey.

Fort Apache 1/2 **1948** The first of director Ford's celebrated cavalry trilogy, in which fanatical Lt. Col. Owen Thursday (a decidely unsympathetic Fonda) leads his reluctant men to an eventual slaughter when he battles Apache chief Cochise (Inclan), recalling George Custer at Little Big Horn. Wayne is his seasoned second-in-command Kirby Yorke, who's unable to prevent what occurs. In residence: Ford hallmarks of spectacular landscapes and stirring action, as well as many vignettes of life at a remote outpost. Don't forget to catch "She Wore a Yellow Ribbon" and "Rio Grande," the next films in the series. **125m/B VHS, DVD.** Henry Fonda, John Wayne, Shirley Temple, John Agar, Pedro Armendariz Sr., Victor McLaglen, Ward Bond, Anna Lee, Guy Kibbee, Miguel Incian, Mae Marsh; ***D:*** John Ford; ***W:*** Frank Nugent; ***C:*** Archie Stout; ***M:*** Richard Hageman.

Fort Apache, the Bronx **1981 (R)** A police drama set in the beleaguered South Bronx of NYC, based on the real-life experiences of two former New York cops who served there. Newman is a decent cop who goes against every kind of criminal and crazy and against his superiors in trying to bring law and justice to a downtrodden community. **123m/C VHS, DVD.** Paul Newman, Ed Asner, Ken Wahl, Danny Aiello, Rachel Ticotin, Pam Grier, Kathleen Beller; ***D:*** Daniel Petrie; ***W:*** Heywood Gould; ***C:*** John Alcott; ***M:*** Jonathan Tunick.

Fort Saganne **1984** Charles Saganne (Depardieu), a soldier from a peasant background, is posted to the French Sahara, where he becomes a natural leader. He gains fame and fortune, marries, and then WWI begins. Good, if cliched, adventure saga. Based on the novel by Louis Gardel. French with subtitles. **180m/C VHS.** *FR* Gerard Depardieu, Catherine Deneuve, Philippe Noiret, Sophie Marceau, Michel Duchaussoy; ***D:*** Alain Corneau; ***W:*** Alain Corneau, Louis Gardel; ***M:*** Philippe Sarde.

Fort Yuma Gold 1/2 *For a Few Extra Dollars; Per Pochi Dollari Ancora; Die Now, Pay Later* **1966** Former Confederate Gary Diamond has become a scout at the end of the war. He's leading some Union soldiers to Fort Yuma to help prevent Confederate fanatic Sanders from attacking. But unbeknownst to Diamond what Sanders is really after is the gold that's hidden in the fort. Dubbed spaghetti western. **105m/C DVD.** *IT* Giuliano Gemma, Dan Vadis, Jacques Sernas, Nello Pazzafini, Sophie Daumier, Jose Calvo, Angel Del Pozo; ***D:*** Giorgio Ferroni; ***W:*** Massimilano Capriccioli; ***C:*** Rafael Pacheco; ***M:*** Gianni Ferrio.

Fortress **1985 (R)** A teacher and her class are kidnapped from their one-room schoolhouse in the Australian outback. They must use their ingenuity and wits to save their lives in this violent suspense drama. **90m/C VHS, DVD.** *AU* Rachel Ward, Sean Garlick, Rebecca Rigg; ***D:*** Arch Nicholson; ***M:*** Danny Beckerman. **CABLE**

Fortress **1993 (R)** How come the future is never a place you'd want to be? Thanks to overpopulation a woman is only allowed one pregnancy. When John and Karen Brennick are caught trying to have a second child they are shipped to the Fortress, an underground prison in the middle of the desert. Discipline is enforced with numerous sadistic toys, including the intestinator, so-called because it's implanted in the stomach of each prisoner and infractions result in excruciating laser-activated pain. Lambert does well with his action hero but it's character actor Smith as the warden, a techno-human with some sick fantasies, who has the real fun in this horrific depiction of the future. **91m/C VHS, DVD.** Christopher Lambert, Kurtwood Smith, Loryn Locklin, Lincoln Kilpatrick; ***D:*** Stuart Gordon; ***W:*** Steve Feinberg, Troy Neighbors, Terry Curtis Fox; ***C:*** David Eggby.

Fortress 2: Re-Entry **1999 (R)** John Brennick (Lambert) and his wife and son have escaped from a maximum security prison known as The Fortress. But Brennick is re-captured and his new prison is in orbit, 26,000 miles from Earth. Brennick wants to escape but there's mucho surveillance to overcome (including a camera placed inside his body) and the problem of returning to Earth. **92m/C VHS, DVD.** Christopher Lambert, Pam Grier, Patrick Malahide, Nick Brimble; ***D:*** Geoff Murphy; ***W:*** Steve Feinberg, Troy Neighbors. **VIDEO**

Fortress of Amerikka 1/2 **1989** In the not-too-distant future, mercenaries get their hands on a secret weapon that could allow them to take over the USA. **97m/C VHS, DVD.** Gene Le Brock, Kellee Bradley; ***D:*** Eric Louzil; ***W:*** Eric Louzil; ***C:*** Ron Chapman; ***M:*** Dave Ouimet.

Fortune and Men's Eyes **1971 (R)** Exploitative and depressing film about life in a Canadian prison. A naive young man is sent to prison for marijuana possession and has to make a difficult choice—be regularly sodomized by a man who will protect him or be raped by everyone else. Based on the play by John Herbert. **102m/C VHS.** Wendell Burton, Michael Greer, Zooey Hall, Danny Freedman; ***D:*** Harvey Hart; ***W:*** John Herbert.

The Fortune Cookie *Meet Whiplash Willie* **1966** After receiving a minor injury during a football game, a TV cameraman is convinced by his seedy lawyer brother-in-law to exaggerate his injury and start an expensive lawsuit. A classic, biting comedy by Wilder. First of several Lemmon-Matthau comedies. **125m/B VHS, DVD.** Jack Lemmon, Walter Matthau, Ron Rich, Cliff Osmond, Judi West, Lurene Tuttle; ***D:*** Billy Wilder; ***W:*** Billy Wilder, I.A.L. Diamond; ***C:*** Joseph LaShelle; ***M:*** Andre Previn. Oscars '66: Support. Actor (Matthau).

Fortune Dane 1/2 **1986 (PG)** Police detective Fortune Dane goes undercover to clear his name after he is framed for murder. **83m/C VHS.** Carl Weathers, Adolph Caesar; ***D:*** Nicholas Sgarro; ***W:*** Charles Correll.

Fortunes **2005 (R)** Three thirty-something buddies are having early midlife crises in this surprisingly appealing comedy-drama. After a bar night, two of the guys impulsively stop at a fortune teller. Married Phil (Hale) is told his young son is in danger and he becomes neurotically overprotective, while Lewis (Urbaniak) becomes a weird recluse after suddenly quitting his stressful job. This leaves cocky James (McGlone) to help out his boys while dealing with a career setback when he fails to get an expected promotion. **91m/C DVD.** James Urbaniak, Mike McGlone, Tony Hale, Diana Henry; ***D:*** Parker Cross; ***W:*** Matt Salzberg; ***M:*** Tobin Sprout.

Fortune's Fool **1921** A beef king and profiteer marries a younger woman and soon discovers the problems that ambition can cause. Silent. **60m/B VHS.** *GE* Emil Jannings, Daguey Servaes, Reinhold Schunzel; ***D:*** Reinhold Schunzel.

Fortunes of War **1987** British professor Guy Pringle arrives with his bride, Harriet, to take up a teaching post in the Balkans in 1939. The idealistic Guy soon becomes enmeshed in anti-fascist politics and involved with the local members of the British embassy. When threatened by war they travel to Athens and then Cairo, where Guy's increasing involvement in the political situation, and his neglect of Harriet, causes a crisis in their marriage. Slow-moving drama with some self-centered characters is redeemed by the acting skills of those involved. Based on the autobiographial novels of Olivia Manning. Originally shown on "Masterpiece Theater" on PBS. **160m/C VHS, DVD.** *GB* Kenneth Branagh, Emma Thompson, Rupert Graves, Ronald Pickup, Robert Stephens, Charles Kay, James Villiers, Harry Burton, Ciaran Madden, Diana Hardcastle, Greg Hicks, Alan Bennett, Jeremy Brundell, Jeremy Sinden; ***D:*** James Cellan Jones; ***W:*** Alan Plater.

Fortunes of War **1994 (R)** Peter Kernan (Salinger) is a burned-out relief worker in Thailand. Desperate for money, he agrees to smuggle a rare medicine across the Cambodian border to a rural war lord. Travelling with refugee Khoy Thoun (Ngor) and French Red Cross worker, Johanna (Jenkins), Peter begins to realize his need to do the right thing, even if the cost is high. Filmed on location in Manila. **107m/C VHS, DVD.** Matt Salinger, Michael Ironside, Haing S. Ngor, Sam Jenkins, Martin Sheen, Michael Nouri; ***D:*** Thierry Notz; ***W:*** Mark Lee.

Forty Carats 1/2 **1973 (PG)** Ullmann plays the just-turned 40 divorcee who has a brief fling with the half-her-age Albert while on vacation in Greece. She figures she'll never see him again but, back in New York, he turns up on the arm of her beautiful daughter (Raffin). Except he's still interested in mom. The rest of the movie is spent trying to convince Ullmann that love can conquer all. Ullmann's very attractive but not well-suited for the part; Raffins's screen debut. Based on the Broadway hit. **110m/C VHS.** Liv Ullmann, Edward Albert, Gene Kelly, Binnie Barnes, Deborah Raffin, Nancy Walker; ***D:*** Milton Katselas; ***W:*** Jay Presson Allen; ***C:*** Charles B(ryant) Lang Jr.

40 Days and 40 Nights 1/2 **2002 (R)** Abstinence comedy has womanizer Matt (Hartnett) suffering from a brutal romantic break-up, so for Lent he vows to go cold turkey in the sack. His always-supportive friends and co-workers rush to place odds on when Matt's self-control will eventually crumble, even posting his progress on the Internet. With babes aplenty seemingly everywhere, Matt's vow is really tested when, of course, he meets the girl of his dreams (Sossamon). Director Lehmann deftly directs the crew of likeable characters, keeping things light and moving along. Memorable funny scenes includes a dinner with Matt's dad describing sex with a hip replacement, and any with Bagel Guy (Maronna). **94m/C VHS, DVD.** *US* Josh Hartnett, Shannyn Sossamon, Maggie Gyllenhaal, Vinessa Shaw, Paulo Costanzo, Glenn Fitzgerald, Emmanuelle Vaugier, Michael Maronna, Mary Gross, Stanley Anderson, Adam Trese, Barry Newman, Griffin Dunne, Monet Mazur, Dylan Neal, Chris Gauthier; ***D:*** Michael Lehmann; ***W:*** Rob Perez; ***C:*** Elliot Davis; ***M:*** Rolfe Kent.

Forty Days of Musa Dagh **1985** Based on the true story of Armenia's fight for freedom against Turkey in the 1914 uprising and the dreadful cost. From the novel by Franz Werfel. **120m/C VHS.** Kabir Bedi, Maurice Sherbanee, Ronnie Carol, Victoria Woodbeck, Michael Constantine, David Opatoshu; ***D:*** Sarky Mouradian; ***W:*** Alex Hakobian; ***C:*** Gregory Sandor; ***M:*** Jaime Mendoza-Nava.

48 Angels 1/2 **2006 (PG-13)** Nine-year-old Seamus (newcomer Flynn) is terminally ill. Inspired by the story of Saint Columcille, he sets off in a rowboat to find God and ask for a miracle. When Seamus meets wounded Darry (Brolly) and teenaged runaway James (Travers), the unlikely trio decides to stay together and help each other. Touching but not maudlin story; beautiful Irish scenery. **90m/C DVD.** *IR* Shane Brolly, John Travers, Darragh Kelly, Ciaran Flynn; ***D:*** Marion Comer; ***W:*** Marion Comer; ***M:*** Patrick Duffner.

44 Minutes: The North Hollywood Shootout 1/2 **2003 (R)** In 1997, two heavily-armed, media-junkie bank robbers (Bryniarski, Taktarov) hold the ill-prepared LAPD at bay for 44 minutes when their heist goes wrong. Told from the point-of-view of various officers, detectives, and SWAT team members called to the scene. **120m/C VHS, DVD.** Michael Madsen, Ron Livingston, Mario Van Peebles, Andrew Bryniarski, Oleg Taktarov, Ray Baker, Douglas Spain, Alex Meneses, Dale Dye, J.E. Freeman; ***D:*** Yves Simoneau; ***W:*** Tim Metcalfe; ***C:*** David Franco; ***M:*** George S. Clinton. **CABLE**

Forty Guns 1/2 **1957** Typically over-the-top Fuller production filled with melodrama, violence, and lots of sexual innuendo. The Bonnel brothers—Griff (Sullivan), Wes (Barry), and Chico (Dix)—are lawmen out to arrest Brockie (Ericson), the nasty younger brother of tough, whip-cracking Jessica Drummond (Stanwyck). Jessica basically owns and runs everything and everyone around her with the help of her hired guns. Griff falls for this western wildcat, making his job more difficult. A climatic shootout helps the movie live up to its title. **79m/B DVD.** Barbara Stanwyck, Barry Sullivan, Gene Barry, Robert Dix, John Ericson, Dean Jagger, Eve Brent; ***D:*** Samuel Fuller; ***W:*** Samuel Fuller; ***C:*** Joseph Biroc; ***M:*** Harry Sukman.

The Forty-Niners **1932** A forgettable oater about the hysteria surrounding the finding of gold in California. **59m/B VHS.** Tom Tyler, Betty Mack, Alan Bridge, Fern Emmett, Gordon Wood, Frank Ball; ***D:*** John P. McCarthy.

The Forty-Ninth Parallel *The Invaders* **1941** Six Nazi servicemen, seeking to reach neutral American land, are trapped and their U-boat sunk by Royal Canadian Air Force bombers, forcing them into Canada on foot, where they run into an array of stalwart patriots. Dated wartime propaganda made prior to the U.S. entering the war; riddled with entertaining star turns. **90m/B VHS, DVD.** *GB* Laurence Olivier, Leslie Howard, Eric Portman, Raymond Massey, Glynis Johns, Finlay Currie, Anton Walbrook; ***D:*** Michael Powell; ***W:*** Emeric Pressburger, Rodney Ackland. Oscars '42: Story.

40 Pounds of Trouble 1/2 **1962** Lake Tahoe casino/hotel manager Steve McCluskey (Curtis) likes to avoid complications in his life. But first he's charmed by his boss' niece Chris (Pleshette), the hotel's new headliner, and then he becomes a surrogate father to five-year-old Penny (Wilcox), abandoned by her debt-ridden dad. So what does Steve decide to do? Why take them to Disneyland, of course! Director Jewison's feature film debut. **106m/C VHS.** Tony Curtis, Suzanne Pleshette, Claire Wilcox, Phil Silvers, Larry Storch, Howard Morris, Stubby Kaye, Edward Andrews, Mary Murphy, Kevin McCarthy, Sharon Farrell; ***D:*** Norman Jewison; ***W:*** Marion Hargrove; ***M:*** Mort Lindsey.

Forty Shades of Blue 1/2 **2005** Character study set in Memphis in which music industry legend Alan James (Torn), his much younger Russian live-in, Laura (Korzun), and adult son from a previous marriage, Michael (Burrows) are brought together when Alan is given a prestigious music industry award. The film unwinds painfully slowly as each character's flawed motivations and dark compromises are examined. Use of local music is a high point in this Sundance award winner. **107m/C DVD.** *US* Rip Torn, Dina Korzun, Darren E. Burrows, Paprika Steen, Red West, Jenny O'Hara; ***D:*** Ira Sachs; ***W:*** Ira Sachs; ***M:*** Michael Rohatyn, Dickon Hinchliffe.

Forty Thousand Horsemen 1/2 **1941** The story of the ANZACS of Australia, created to fight Germany in the Middle East during WWII. This Australian war drama is full of cavalry charges, brave young lads, and "Waltzing Matilda." **86m/B VHS.** *AU* Chips Rafferty, Grant Taylor, Betty Bryant, Pat Twohill; ***D:*** Charles Chauvel; ***W:*** Elsa Chauvel; ***C:*** George Heath; ***M:*** Lindley Evans.

The 40 Year Old Virgin **2005 (R)** Forty year old Andy (Carell) is a virgin, obsessed with pre-teen pursuits like video games, action heroes and collectibles. His work buddies find out his terrible secret and take on the task of initiating Andy into the world of adulthood and sex. Yes, it's raunchy and sophomoric, but the underlying sweetness and the well-done slapstick humor are worth it. Along with "Wedding Crashers," helped bring back the successful R-rated comedy. **116m/C DVD, Blu-ray Disc, HD DVD.** *US* Steve Carell, Catherine Keener, Paul Rudd, Romany Malco, Elizabeth Banks, Leslie Mann, Jane Lynch, Seth Rogen, Kat Dennings, David Koechner, Loudon Wainwright III; ***D:*** Judd Apatow; ***W:*** Steve Carell, Judd Apatow; ***C:*** Jack N. Green; ***M:*** Lyle Workman. L.A. Film Critics '05: Actress (Keener).

42nd Street 1933 A Broadway musical producer faces numerous problems in his efforts to reach a successful opening night. Choreography by Busby Berkeley. A colorized version of the film is also available. ♫You're Getting to Be a Habit with Me; Shuffle off to Buffalo; Young and Healthy; 42nd Street; It Must Be June. **89m/B VHS, DVD.** Warner Baxter, Ruby Keeler, Bebe Daniels, George Brent, Dick Powell, Guy Kibbee, Ginger Rogers, Una Merkel, Busby Berkeley, Ned Sparks, George E. Stone; ***D:*** Lloyd Bacon; ***W:*** Rian James, James Seymour; ***C:*** Sol Polito; ***M:*** Harry Warren, Al Dubin. Natl. Film Reg. '98.

.45 2006 (R) New York bad girl Kat (Jovovich) hates being controlled by her violent, gun-selling boyfriend Big Al (Macfayden). She starts making her own deals and is willing to go to any lengths to break free, with the help of the hopelessly-devoted Riley (Dorff) and her lesbian friend Vic (Strange). Good tough role for Jovovich in a woman's revenge flick. **97m/C DVD.** Milla Jovovich, Stephen Dorff, Angus MacFadyen, Aisha Tyler, Sarah Strange, Vincent Laresca; ***D:*** Gary Lennon; ***W:*** Gary Lennon; ***C:*** Teodoro Maniaci; ***M:*** John Robert Wood. **VIDEO**

47 Ronin, Part 1 *The Loyal 47 Ronin; 47 Samurai* **1942** Turn of the 18th-century epic chronicling the samurai legend. The warriors of Lord Asano set out to avenge their leader, tricked into committing a forced seppuku, or hara-kiri. The photography is generously laden with views of 18th century gardens as well as panoramic vistas. This is the largest and most popular film of the Kabuki version of the story by Seika Mayama. In Japanese with English subtitles. **111m/C VHS, DVD.** *JP* Yoshisaburo Arashi, Utaemon Ichikawa, Chojuro Kawarazaki, Kunitaro Kawarazaki, Mantoyo Mimasu, Micko Takamine; ***D:*** Kenji Mizoguchi; ***W:*** Yoshikata Yoda, Kenchiro Hara; ***C:*** Kohei Sugiyama; ***M:*** Shiro Fukai.

47 Ronin, Part 2 1942 Second half of the film in which the famous Japanese folklore tale of Lord Asano and his warriors is told. The film follows Asano's samurai as they commit themselves to avenging their leader in 1703. In Japanese with English subtitles. **108m/C VHS, DVD.** *JP* Yoshisaburo Arashi, Utaemon Ichikawa, Chojuro Kawarazaki, Kunitaro Kawarazaki, Mantoyo Mimasu; ***D:*** Kenji Mizoguchi; ***W:*** Kenchiro Hara, Yoshikata Yoda; ***C:*** Kohei Sugiyama; ***M:*** Shiro Fukai.

48 Hrs. 1982 (R) An experienced San Francisco cop (Nolte) springs a convict (Murphy) from jail for 48 hours to find a vicious murdering escaped con. Murphy's film debut is great and Nolte is perfect as his gruff foil. **97m/C VHS, DVD.** Ned Dowd, Nick Nolte, Eddie Murphy, James Remar, Annette O'Toole, David Patrick Kelly, Sonny Landham, Brion James, Denise Crosby; ***D:*** Walter Hill; ***W:*** Walter Hill, Larry Gross, Steven E. de Souza, Roger Spottiswoode; ***M:*** James Horner.

48 Hours to Live *Man in the Middle* **1960** A reporter travels to a nuclear scientist's secluded island only to find the scientist held hostage by nuclear weapon-seeking terrorists. **86m/B VHS.** *SW* Anthony Steel, Ingemar Johannson, Marlies Behrens; ***D:*** Peter Bourne; ***W:*** Peter Bourne; ***C:*** Bengt Lindstrom; ***M:*** Harry Arnold.

The Foul King 1/2 *Banchikwang* **2000** Dae-Ho (Song Kang-ho) is bullied by his boss and father, so to deal with his frustration he decides to train as a professional wrestler known as the villainous Foul King. After accidentally winning his first match, he is challenged to a tag-team match by the sport's reigning champion, who needs an easy win to bolster his own career. Purists should note the only available version in the U.S. is dubbed in Chinese, and subtitled in English. Foreign editions are required to view it in its original language. **112m/C DVD.** *KN* Kang-ho Song, Jin-Young Yang, Su-ro Kim; ***D:*** Ji-woon Kim; ***W:*** Ji-woon Kim.

Foul Play 1976 Bearing no similarity to the Goldie Hawn vehicle of the same name, this Polish crimer is based on a true story, and stars two of Poland's Olympic boxers. A young man, accused of theft, is coerced by the Warsaw police to go undercover in return for having the charges against him dropped. With English subtitles. **98m/C VHS.** *PL* Marek Piwowski, Jan Szczepanski, Jerzy Kulej; ***D:*** Marek Piwowski; ***W:*** Marek Piwowski; ***C:*** Witold Stok; ***M:*** Piotr Figiel.

Foul Play 1978 (PG) Hawn is a librarian who picks up a hitchhiker which leads to nothing but trouble. She becomes involved with San Francisco detective Chase in an effort to expose a plot to kill the Pope during his visit to the city. Also involved is Moore as an English orchestra conductor with some kinky sexual leanings. Chase is charming (no mugging here) and Hawn both bubbly and brave. A big winner at the boxoffice; features Barry Manilow's hit tune "Ready to Take a Chance Again." **116m/C VHS, DVD.** Goldie Hawn, Chevy Chase, Dudley Moore, Burgess Meredith, Billy Barty, Rachel Roberts, Eugene Roche, Brian Dennehy, Chuck McCann, Bruce Solomon, Marc Lawrence, Don Calfa, Marilyn Sokol, Frances Bay; ***D:*** Colin Higgins; ***W:*** Colin Higgins; ***C:*** David M. Walsh; ***M:*** Charles Fox.

Found Alive 1934 After a painful divorce, a woman kidnaps her son and steals away into the Mexican jungle, with only the help of her faithful butler. **65m/B VHS.** Barbara Bedford, Maurice Murphy, Robert Frazer, Edwin Cross; ***D:*** Charles (Hutchison) Hutchinson.

The Fountain 2006 (PG-13) Given the pic's long and troubled production history, maybe Aronofsky getting anything onscreen is a miracle. Of course this fantastical odyssey may be considered as a new "2001" and best seen by an audience in the same trippy condition. Anyway, Jackman and Weisz tackle three time periods and three characters but not in a linear fashion. In the 16th-century, Spanish conquistador Tomas is dispatched by Queen Isabel to find the Tree of Life worshipped by the Mayans. In the present, Tommy is a medical researcher who is trying to cure his dying wife, Izzi, who's writing a novel called "The Fountain." And in the 26th century, Tom is floating in a space bubble towards a nebula and Izzi shows up in his dreams. Or something. Feel free to interpret as you wish or just call it hooey and forget it. **95m/C DVD, Blu-ray Disc, HD DVD.** *US* Hugh Jackman, Rachel Weisz, Ellen Burstyn, Clifford Curtis, Mark Margolis; ***D:*** Darren Aronofsky; ***W:*** Darren Aronofsky; ***C:*** Matthew Libatique; ***M:*** Clint Mansell.

The Fountainhead 1949 Cooper is an idealistic, uncompromising architect who refuses to change his designs. When he finds out his plans for a public housing project have been radically altered he blows up the building and winds up in court defending his actions. Neal is the sub-plot love interest. Based on the novel by Ayn Rand. **113m/C VHS, DVD.** Gary Cooper, Patricia Neal, Raymond Massey, Ray Collins, Henry Hull, Robert Douglas, Kent Smith, Moroni Olsen, Ann Doran; ***D:*** King Vidor; ***C:*** Robert Burks; ***M:*** Max Steiner.

Four Adventures of Reinette and Mirabelle 1989 Small but touching Rohmer tale of the friendship between two women—one a naive country girl (Miquel, as Reinette), the other a sophisticated Parisian (Forde, as Mirabelle)—who share an apartment and a number of experiences, but who have a very different manner of inhabiting those experiences. A thoroughly French human comedy, one of Rohmer's better studies. In French with English subtitles. **95m/C VHS.** *FR* Joelle Miquel, Jessica Forde, Philippe Laudenbach, Marie Riviere, Beatrice Romand, Yasmine Haury; ***D:*** Eric Rohmer; ***W:*** Eric Rohmer.

Four and a Half Women 1/2 *Chocolate for Breakfast* **2005** Cute comedy about four roommates dealing with the day-to-day shuffle of being young, female, and running wild around the Big Apple. Things get complicated when one of the girls becomes pregnant after a one-night-stand and decides to keep the baby. **125m/C VHS.** Isabel Gillies, Marin Hinkle, Callie (Calliope) Thorne, Michael Showalter, Josh Hamilton; ***D:*** Emily Baer; ***W:*** Emily Baer; ***C:*** Joaquin Boca-Asay; ***M:*** Jason Frederick.

Four Bags Full 1/2 1956 A bitter comedy about two smugglers during WWII who try to get a slaughtered pig to the black market under the Nazis' noses. In French with English subtitles. **82m/C VHS.** *FR* Jean Gabin, Louis de Funes, Andre Bourvil, Jeanette Batti; ***D:*** Claude Autant-Lara.

Four Brothers 1/2 2005 (R) Urban remake of "The Sons of Katie Elder." Ma Mercer (Flanagan) is gunned down in a Detroit market hold-up, which brings her four adopted sons, two white and two black, to reunite and avenge her not-so-accidental death, leading to an elaborate conspiracy implicating the upper echelons of Motor City politics. For all its action scenes, violence and verbal ugliness, the final result is disappointing. **109m/C DVD, Blu-ray Disc, UMD, HD DVD.** *US* Mark Wahlberg, Andre Benjamin, Tyrese Gibson, Garrett Hedlund, Josh Charles, Chiwetel Ejiofor, Fionnula Flanagan, Terrence Howard, Sofia Vergara, Taraji P. Henson, Barry (Shabaka) Henley, Kenneth Welsh; ***D:*** John Singleton; ***W:*** David Elliot, Paul Lovett; ***C:*** Peter Menzies Jr.

Four Christmases 2008 (PG-13) When Kate (Witherspoon) and Brad's (Vaughn) holiday vacation plans are ruined by weather, they no longer have an excuse not to visit each of their divorced parents on Christmas. Brad can't wait for the day of parents, steps, sibs, and other relations to be over with, while Kate discovers she enjoys all the familial hoopla. Flick is awkward and uneven as first half leans on slapstick humor for a few cheap laughs while second half devolves into contrived schmaltz. And there's no zip between the mismatched leads, as her honed, straight cuteness doesn't mesh with his loose, off-the-cuff goofiness. Might be the worst film starring five Oscar-winners ever. **88m/C DVD.** *US* Reese Witherspoon, Vince Vaughn, Robert Duvall, Kristin Chenoweth, Jon Favreau, Dwight Yoakam, Tim McGraw, Sissy Spacek, Jon Voight, Mary Steenburgen, Katy Mixon, Colleen Camp; ***D:*** Seth Gordon; ***W:*** Jon Lucas, Scott Moore, Matt R. Allen, Caleb Wilson; ***C:*** Jeffrey L. Kimball; ***M:*** Alex Wurman.

Four Daughters 1938 Classic, three-hankie outing in which four talented daughters of music professor Rains fall in love and marry. Garfield shines, in a role tailor-made for him, as the world-weary suitor driven to extremes in the name of love. Great performances from all. Based on the novel "Sister Act" by Fannie Hurst. **90m/B VHS.** Claude Rains, John Garfield, May Robson, Priscilla Lane, Lola Lane, Rosemary Lane, Gale Page, Dick Foran, Jeffrey Lynn, Frank McHugh; ***D:*** Michael Curtiz; ***W:*** Lenore Coffee, Julius J. Epstein; ***C:*** Ernest Haller; ***M:*** Max Steiner.

Four Days 1/2 1999 (R) Fourteen-year-old Simon (Zegers) is devoted to his small-time crook dad Milt (Forsythe) who's just double-crossed his partner, Fury (Meany), in a bank robbery after arranging for Simon to get the money and meet him in a pre-selected location. But unbeknownst to Simon, Milt has been killed and Fury is on his trail—at least Simon has gotten a lift from over-sexed Crystal (Davidovitch), so things may not be so bad. Based on the novel by John Buell. **88m/C VHS.** *CA* Kevin Zegers, Lolita (David) Davidovich, Colm Meaney, William Forsythe, Anne-Marie Cadieux, Patrick Goyette; ***D:*** Curtis Wehrfritz; ***W:*** Pickney Benedict; ***C:*** Miroslaw Baszak; ***M:*** Tom Third.

Four Days in July 1985 Two couples from Belfast, one Catholic and one Protestant, find they have something in common when they meet in the maternity ward as both couples become first-time parents. Script and dialog were mainly improvised, which provides both dull stretches and the film's charm. **99m/C VHS, DVD.** *GB* Des McAleer, Brid Brennan, Charles Lawson, Paula Hamilton, Shane Connaughton, Eileen Pollock, Stephen Rea; ***D:*** Mike Leigh. **TV**

Four Days in September 1997 (R) Based on the true story of Charles Burke Elbrick (Arkin), the American ambassador to Brazil who, in 1969, was kidnapped by four idealistic students, part of a Marxist revolutionary group protesting their government's military dictatorship. Their leader, Fernando Gabeira (Cardoso), wants the release of political prisoners and gives the government four days to meet his terms. Adapted from the book "What's Up, Comrade?" by Gabeira. **105m/C VHS, DVD.** *BR* Alan Arkin, Pedro Cardoso, Marco Ricca, Fernanda Torres; ***D:*** Bruno Barreto; ***W:*** Leopoldo Serran; ***C:*** Felix Monti; ***M:*** Stewart Copeland.

Four Deuces 1/2 1975 Gang war is underway between the Chico Hamilton mob and Vic Morano and the Four Deuces during the Depression. Comedy and action combine with elements of strong language, strong sex, and strong violence. **87m/C VHS, DVD.** Jack Palance, Carol Lynley, Warren Berlinger, Adam Roarke; ***D:*** William H. Bushnell Jr.

Four Dogs Playing Poker 1/2 2000 (R) Four friends plan an art heist and then lose the prize, which gets them into trouble with the gangster who's expecting the goods. So they come up with another scheme that involves collecting on one of the group's life insurance policies (to pay off the gangster)—which means one of them will have to die. Sketchy thriller. **98m/C VHS, DVD.** Olivia Williams, Balthazar Getty, Stacy Edwards, Daniel London, Tim Curry, Forest Whitaker, George Lazenby, John Taylor; ***D:*** Paul Rachman; ***W:*** Thomas Durham, William Quist; ***C:*** Claudio Rocha; ***M:*** Brian Tyler, Scott Hackwith.

Four Dollars of Revenge 1/2 *Cuatro Dolares de Venganza; Four Dollars for Vengeance* **1966** Typical spaghetti western. Wounded after an ambush, Lt. Roy Dexter (Woods) is charged with the theft of the gold shipment he was supposed to deliver. Then he's given a long sentence at hard labor and all he wants is revenge. Spanish with subtitles or dubbed. **88m/C DVD.** *IT SP* Robert Woods, Dana Ghia, Angelo Infanti, Antonio Casas, Jose Martin, Gerard Tichy; ***W:*** Jaime Jesus Balcazar, Bruno Corbucci, Aldo Grimaldi, Giovanni Grimaldi; ***C:*** Victor Monreal; ***M:*** Angelo Francesco Lavagnino.

Four Eyes and Six Guns 1/2 1993 In 1882 a New York optometrist, who's a fan of the popular dime-store western novels, moves to Tombstone, Arizona, in search of adventure. He's just in time, too, because Sheriff Wyatt Earp is trying to rid the town of those pesky Doom Brothers but is having a problem with his eyesight (causing his gunshots to go astray). Now if the greenhorn can just get Earp to wear his new glasses. Silly but harmless fluff. **92m/C VHS.** Judge Reinhold, Patricia Clarkson, Dan Hedaya, M. Emmet Walsh, Austin Pendleton, Fred Ward; ***D:*** Piers Haggard; ***W:*** Leon Prochnik. **CABLE**

Four Faces West 1/2 *They Passed This Way* **1948** McCrea is an honest rancher who nevertheless robs the local bank in order to save his father's ranch from foreclosure. His humanity in helping a diphtheria-ridden family leads to his capture, but the sheriff promises a light sentence, since he is not a typical bad guy. Fine performances strengthen this low-key western. **90m/B VHS, DVD.** Joel McCrea, Frances Dee, Charles Bickford; ***D:*** Alfred E. Green.

Four Fast Guns 1959 Gunfighter Tom Sabin (Craig) travels to Purgatory in the guise of helping the townspeople wrest control away from wheelchair-bound town boss Hoag (Richards). Hoag doesn't want any interference so he hires three outlaws, believing one of them will be able to kill Sabin. The showdown winds up involving Sabin and his outlaw brother Johnny Naco (Halsey). **72m/B DVD.** James Craig, Paul Richards, Brett Halsey, Martha Vickers, Edgar Buchanan, Richard Martin, John Swift, Blu Wright; ***D:*** William Hole Jr.; ***W:*** James Edmiston, Dallas Gaultois; ***C:*** John M. Nickolaus Jr.

The Four Feathers 1939 A grand adventure from a story by A.E.W. Mason. After resigning from the British Army a young man is branded a coward and given four white feathers as symbols by three of his friends and his lady love. Determined to prove them wrong he joins the Sudan campaign of 1898 and rescues each of the men from certain death. They then take back their feathers as does his girl upon learning of his true courage. Excellent performances by Smith and Richardson. **99m/C VHS, DVD.** *GB* Alexander Knox, John Clements, Ralph Richardson, Sir C. Aubrey Smith, June Duprez, Donald Gray, Jack Allen, Allan Jeayes, Frederick

Culley, Hal Walters, Henry Oscar, John Laurie, Clive Baxter, Robert Rendel, Derek Elphinstone, Norman Pierce, Amid Taftazani, Archibald Batty, Hay Petrie; *D:* Zoltan Korda; *W:* R.C. Sherriff, Lajos Biro, Arthur Wimperis; *C:* Osmond H. Borradaile, Georges Perinal, Jack Cardiff; *M:* Miklos Rozsa.

The Four Feathers **1978** Determined to return the symbols of cowardice, four feathers, to his friends and fiance, a man courageously saves his friends' lives during the British Sudan campaign and regains the love of his lady, in this fifth remake of the story. **95m/C VHS, DVD.** Beau Bridges, Jane Seymour, Simon Ward, Harry Andrews, Richard Johnson, Robert Powell; *D:* Don Sharp. **TV**

The Four Feathers **2002 (PG-13)** Featherweight remake has Ledger as Harry, a British officer in the late 1800's in love and engaged to marry hottie Ethne (Hudson, sporting an unfortunate English accent). Best friend and fellow officer Jack (Bentley) also fancies English muffin Ethne, unbeknownst to Harry. When Harry resigns from service with battle in the Sudan looming, he's labeled a coward and given four white feathers as a sign of his cowardice. Ditched and dissed, a suitably shamed Harry, determined to prove his courage, disguises himself as an African native (Riiight) and heads to the Sudan. Seem dated and implausible, but action scenes are well done. Based on A.E.W. Mason's 1902 novel. **130m/C VHS, DVD.** *US* Heath Ledger, Wes Bentley, Kate Hudson, Djimon Hounsou, Michael Sheen, Kris Marshall, Rupert Penry-Jones, Tim Pigott-Smith, Alex Jennings; *D:* Shekhar Kapur; *W:* Michael Schiffer, Hossein Amini; *C:* Robert Richardson; *M:* James Horner.

Four Flies on Grey Velvet *Quattro Moschi di Velluto Grigio* **1972** Convoluted pulp thriller from Argento. Roberto Tobias (Brandon) accidentally kills a stalker, an act witnessed by a mask-wearing figure. He's then plagued by nightmares of decapitation and starts getting blackmail threats as his relationship with high-strung wife Nina (Farmer) is increasingly strained. The body count rises but the answers lie closer to home than Roberto thinks. **102m/C DVD.** *IT* Michael Brandon, Mimsy Farmer, Jean-Pierre Marielle, Francine Racette, Bud Spencer, Marissa Fabbri, Oreste Lionello; *D:* Dario Argento; *W:* Dario Argento; *C:* Franco Di Giacomo; *M:* Ennio Morricone.

Four for Texas **1963** Perhaps Aldrich's later success with "The Dirty Dozen" can be attributed, in part, to this exercise in how not to make a comic western; poorly made, over long, and far too dependant on the feminine charisma of Ekberg and Andress. Slow-moving Sinatra-Martin vehicle tells the tale of con men in the Old West who battle bandits and bad bankers for a stash of loot. **124m/C VHS, DVD.** Frank Sinatra, Dean Martin, Anita Ekberg, Ursula Andress, Charles Bronson, Victor Buono, Jack Elam, Arthur Godfrey, Moe Howard, Larry Fine, Joe DeRita; *D:* Robert Aldrich; *W:* Robert Aldrich, Teddi Sherman, W.R. Burnett; *C:* Ernest Laszlo; *M:* Nelson Riddle.

Four Friends *Georgia's Friends* **1981 (R)** The magical good and bad dream of the 1960s is remembered in this story of four friends. A young woman and the three men in love with her first come together in high school and then separate, learning from college, war and drug abuse, and each other in this ambitious movie from Steve Tesich, the writer of "Breaking Away." Good performances by all. **114m/C VHS, DVD.** James Leo Herlihy, Craig Wasson, Jodi Thelen, Michael Huddleston, Jim Metzler, Reed Birney; *D:* Arthur Penn; *W:* Steve Tesich; *C:* Ghislan Cloquet.

The Four Horsemen of the Apocalypse 1/2 **1921** Silent classic and star maker for Valentino concerning an Argentine family torn apart by the outbreak of WWI. Valentino is a painter who moves from his native Argentina to France and is persuaded to enlist by a recruiter who invokes the image of the Biblical riders. His excellence as a soldier, however, proves to be his undoing. The 1962 remake can't hold a candle to original, adapted from a novel by Vicente Blasco-Ibanez. **110m/B VHS.** Rudolph Valentino, Alice Terry, Pomeroy Cannon, Josef Swickard, Alan Hale, Mabel van Buren, Nigel de Brulier, Bowditch Turner, Wallace Beery, Bridgetta Clark, Virginia Warwick, Stuart Holmes, John St. Polis, Mark Fenton, Derek Ghent; *D:* Rex Ingram; *W:* June Mathis; *C:* John Seitz; *M:* Louis F. Gottschalk. Natl. Film Reg. '95.

The Four Horsemen of the Apocalypse 1/2 **1962** The members of a German family find themselves fighting on opposite sides during WWII. This remake of the vintage Valentino silent failed at the boxoffice, with complaints about its length, disjointed script, and uninspired performances. The title refers to the horrors of conquest, pestilence, war, and death. Adapted from the book by Vincente Blasco-Ibanez. **153m/C VHS, DVD.** Glenn Ford, Charles Boyer, Lee J. Cobb, Paul Henreid, Yvette Mimieux; *D:* Vincente Minnelli; *W:* John Gay; *C:* Milton Krasner; *M:* Andre Previn.

The 400 Blows *Les Quartre Cents Coups* **1959** The classic, groundbreaking semi-autobiography that initiated Truffaut's career and catapulted him to international acclaim, about the trials and rebellions of 12-year-old French schoolboy, Antoine Doinel (Leaud). One of the greatest and most influential of films, and the first of Truffaut's career-long Doinel series. French with subtitles. **97m/B VHS, DVD.** *FR* Francois Truffaut, Jean-Pierre Leaud, Claire Maurier, Albert Remy, Guy Decomble, Georges Flament, Patrick Auffay, Jeanne Moreau, Jean-Claude Brialy, Jacques Demy, Robert Beauvais; *D:* Francois Truffaut; *W:* Francois Truffaut, Marcel Moussey; *C:* Henri Decae; *M:* Jean Constantin. Cannes '59: Director (Truffaut); N.Y. Film Critics '59: Foreign Film.

Four in a Jeep 1/2 **1951** In Vienna in 1945, soldiers from different countries are serving as an international military police force. They clash as a result of political demands and their love for the same woman. Shot on location in Austria. **83m/B VHS.** Ralph Meeker, Viveca Lindfors, Joseph Yadin, Michael Medwin; *D:* Leopold Lindtberg.

Four Jacks and a Jill **1941** Four musicians are left in the lurch when their band singer leaves them for her gangster boyfriend and they must frantically search for a replacement. Not completely uninteresting, but rather bland and old now. Earlier versions of the story were released as "Street Girl" and "That Girl from Paris." ♫I'm in Good Shape For the Shape I'm In; You Go Your Way and I'll Go Crazy; I Haven't A Thing to Wear; Wherever You Are; Boogie Woogie Conga. **68m/B VHS.** Anne Shirley, Ray Bolger, Desi Arnaz Sr., Jack Durant, June Havoc, Eddie Foy Jr., Fritz Feld; *D:* Jack B. Hively.

Four Jills in a Jeep 1/2 **1944** Francis, Landis, Raye, and Mayfair all play themselves in this Fox musical comedy that has Francis organizing a USO tour (as they'd actually done in 1943) for the boys overseas. Landis married an airman she met (and wrote about it) so their romance is chronicled as well. Many other Fox players offer support, including Alice Faye, Betty Grable, Carmen Miranda, George Jessel, and Jimmy Dorsey and his band. **89m/B DVD.** Kay Francis, Carole Landis, Martha Raye, John Harvey, Phil Silvers, Dick Haymes, Mitzi Mayfair; *D:* William A. Seiter; *W:* Helen Logan, Snag Werris, Robert Ellis; *C:* J. Peverell Marley.

Four Last Songs 1/2 **2006** Lounge pianist Larry (Tucci) is trying for musical acclaim by holding a tribute concert to a late classical composer, who was a native of his Mediterranean resort town. However, life keeps getting in his way. There's his long-lost daughter, neurotic lovers and friends, and eccentric neighbors ruining his big chance. Lots of over-acting. **110m/C DVD.** *GB SP* Stanley Tucci, Rhys Ifans, Hugh Bonneville, Jena Malone, Jessica Stevenson, Marisa Paredes, Emmanuelle Seigner, Karl Johnson, Virgile Bramly; *D:* Francesca Joseph; *W:* Francesca Joseph; *C:* Javier Salmones; *M:* Dan (Daniel) Jones.

Four Men and a Prayer **1938** The four Leigh brothers (Greene, Sanders, Niven, Henry) seek the truth behind their colonel father's (Smith) dismissal from military service in India and his alleged suicide, which they believe was murder. Stiff upper lips prevail as the siblings travel from India to Argentina to Egypt and back home to England to restore the family honor. **85m/B DVD.** Richard Greene, George Sanders, David Niven, William Henry, Sir C. Aubrey Smith, Loretta Young, Alan Hale Jr., John Carradine, Reginald Denny, J. Edward Bromberg, Berton Churchill, Barry Fitzgerald; *D:* John Ford; *W:* Sonya Levien, Richard Sherman, Walter Ferris; *C:* Ernest Palmer.

The Four Minute Mile **1988** Four athletes become determined to break the record of running the mile in under four minutes. **186m/C VHS.** *GB* Richard Huw, Nique Needles, John Philbin, Lewis Fitz-Gerald, Michael York; *D:* Jim Goddard; *W:* David Williamson; *C:* Ian Warburton.

4 Months, 3 Weeks and 2 Days 1/2 *4 Luni, 3 Saptamani si 2 Zile* **2007** Stunning, intense thriller about two college roommates who seek an illegal abortion for one of them in the hellish totalitarian state of 1987 Romania. To do so they must enter the Romanian underworld and find someone to do the procedure while dealing with low-lifes who threaten them with violence, blackmail, and humiliation every step of the way. A tightly crafted noir that uses the challenging issue of abortion as a backdrop rather than a centerpiece, instead focusing on the struggles of the two women in the face of a dangerous world they aren't meant to see. **113m/C DVD.** *RO* Laura Vasiliu, Anamaria Marinca, Alex Potocean, Vlad Ivanov; *D:* Cristian Mungiu; *W:* Cristian Mungiu; *C:* Oleg Mutu.

The Four Musketeers *The Revenge of Milady* **1975 (PG)** A fun-loving continuation of "The Three Musketeers," reportedly filmed simultaneously. Lavish swashbuckler jaunts between France, England, and Italy, in following the adventures of D'Artagnan and his cohorts. Pictures give an amusing depiction of Lester-interpreted 17th-century Europe, with fine performances especially by Dunaway as an evil countess seeking revenge on our heroes and Welch as the scatterbrained object of York's affections. Followed, in 1989, by "The Return of the Musketeers." **108m/C VHS, DVD.** Michael York, Oliver Reed, Richard Chamberlain, Frank Finlay, Raquel Welch, Christopher Lee, Faye Dunaway, Jean-Pierre Cassel, Geraldine Chaplin, Simon Ward, Charlton Heston, Roy Kinnear, Nicole Calfan; *D:* Richard Lester; *W:* George MacDonald Fraser; *C:* David Watkin; *M:* Lalo Schifrin.

The 4 Musketeers 1/2 *D'Artagnan et les Trois Mousquietaires; D'Artagnan and the Three Musketeers* **2005 (R)** Yet another (remarkably dull and silly) version of the Dumas swashbuckler, only this time the evil Milady de Winter (Beart) has made a pact with the devil for some supernatural powers. The musketeers still use their swords a lot and battle the corrupt Cardinal Richelieu (Karyo) as well. Made for French TV; dubbed into English. **190m/C DVD.** *FR* Emmanuelle Beart, Tcheky Karyo, Vincent Elbaz, Gregori Derangere, Heino Ferch, Stefania Rocca, Tristan Ulloa, Gregory Gadebois, Diana Amft; *D:* Pierre Aknine; *W:* Pierre Aknine; *C:* Allen Smith; *M:* Matt Dunkley. **TV**

Four Robbers **1987** The ruthless Ma initiates his series of crimes throughout the Far East, somehow staying ahead of the cops. When the final showdown occurs, it's an all out kung fu massacre. **90m/C VHS.** *HK* Lau Chun, Shek Hon, Kong Seng, Lee Wing Shan; *D:* Gam Loi Sung; *W:* Gam Loi Sung.

Four Rode Out **1969** A Mexican outlaw is pursued by his girlfriend, one-time partner, and the law. Brutal, inferior western. **99m/C VHS, DVD.** Pernell Roberts, Sue Lyon, Leslie Nielsen, Julian Mateos; *D:* John Peyser.

Four Rooms **1995 (R)** Four stories by four hot indie filmers set in the same L.A. hotel on New Year's Eve are tied together by bellboy Roth, stumbling around in a Jerry/Carrey-like stupor. Leading off is Anders's roomful of witches trying to resurrect spirit of '50s stripper DeCadenet. After this disappointing start is Rockwell's bland look at infidelity, with wife Beals tied and gagged by her husband (Proval) over an alleged fling with Roth. Bandaras heads the best seg as a mobster who leaves his demonic children in Roth's hands. Tarantino is the anchor man with his take on Hitchcock, dealing with a macabre bet involving the removal of body parts. Altogether disjointed and uninspired. **98m/C VHS, DVD.** Tim Roth, Antonio Banderas, Jennifer Beals, Paul Calderon, Sammi Davis, Valeria Golino, Madonna, Ione Skye, Marisa Tomei, Tamlyn Tomita, Bruce Willis, David Proval, Lili Taylor, Alicia Witt, Amanda DeCadenet, Danny Verduzco, Lana McKissack, Quentin Tarantino; ***Cameos:*** Salma Hayek; *D:* Quentin Tarantino, Alexandre Rockwell, Robert Rodriguez, Allison Anders; *W:* Quentin Tarantino, Alexandre Rockwell, Robert Rodriguez, Allison Anders; *C:* Phil Parmet, Guillermo Navarro, Andrzej Sekula, Rodrigo Garcia; *M:* Combustible Edison, Esquivel. Golden Raspberries '95: Worst Support. Actress (Madonna).

The Four Seasons 1/2 **1981 (PG)** Three upper-middle-class New York couples share their vacations together, as well as their friendship, their frustrations and their jealousies. Alda's first outing as a film director is pleasant and easy on the eyes. **108m/C VHS, DVD.** Alan Alda, Carol Burnett, Sandy Dennis, Len Cariou, Jack Weston, Rita Moreno, Bess Armstrong; *D:* Alan Alda; *W:* Alan Alda.

Four Sheets to the Wind **2007 (R)** Seminole-Cree Cufe Smallhill discovers that his ill father has committed suicide. When his older sister Miri comes home for the funeral, she persuades Cufe that he needs a break from their small hometown and should come and stay with her in Tulsa. Miri is a party-hard gal and Cufe finds more sympathy from her neighbor Francie and a chance to decide what's next in his life. **81m/C DVD.** Cody Lightning, Jeri Arredondo, Christian Kane, Tamara Podemski, Laura Bailey; *D:* Sterlin Harjo; *W:* Sterlin Harjo; *C:* Frederick Schroeder; *M:* Jeff Johnson.

Four Sided Triangle **1953** Two mad scientists find their friendship threatened when they discover that they are both in love with the same woman. So they do what anyone would do in this situation—they invent a machine and duplicate her. **81m/B VHS, DVD.** *GB* James Hayter, Barbara Payton, Stephen Murray, John Van Eyssen, Percy Marmont; *D:* Terence Fisher; *W:* Terence Fisher, Paul Tabori; *C:* Reg Wyer; *M:* Malcolm Arnold.

Four Sons **1928** Mother Bernle lives with her four sons in Burgendorf, Bavaria. Joseph has a job offer in America and his mother gives him money to help him immigrate. The other three boys enlist in WWI and when America enters the war, Joseph enlists on the other side. After the war is over, and after much hardship and sorrow, Mother Bernle goes through Ellis Island herself. **100m/B DVD.** Margaret Mann, James Hall, George Meeker, June Collyer, Charles Morton, Ralph Bushman, Earle Foxe, Albert Gran; *D:* John Ford; *W:* Philip Klein; *C:* George Schneiderman.

Four Times That Night *Quante Volte...Quella Notte* **1969 (R)** Though he's known for his work in horror, Mario Bava also made one sex comedy and it's not a bad little movie, though its appeal is mostly nostalgia. Technically, it's a "Rashomon" story with the events of one night told from different points of view. What happens when Gianni (Halsey) takes the lovely Tina (Giordano) to his bachelor pad? Is it date rape or does she seduce him? The film is still grand stuff for '60s fans. The shagadelic apartment must be seen to be believed. **83m/C DVD.** *IT* Brett Halsey, Daniela Giordano, Pascale Petit, Brigitte Skay; *D:* Mario Bava; *M:* Lallo Gori.

Four Ways Out 1/2 **1957** Four average guys are fed up by their lot in life and stage a boxoffice robbery of their local soccer stadium. They don't get to enjoy their ill-gotten gains. In Italian with subtitles or dubbed. **77m/B VHS.** *IT* Gina Lollobrigida, Renato Baldini, Paul Muller; *D:* Pietro Germi.

Four Weddings and a Funeral **1994 (R)** Refreshing, intelligent adult comedy brimming with stiff upper-lip wit and sophistication. Thirtyish Brit bachelor Charles (Grant) spends his time attending the weddings of his friends, but manages to avoid taking the plunge himself. Then he falls for American Carrie (MacDowell), who's about to wed another. Great beginning offers loads of laughs as the first two weddings unfold, then becomes decidedly bittersweet. While Grant makes this a star turn as the romantic bumbler, MacDowell charms without seeming particularly needed.

Supporting characters are superb, especially Coleman as the "flirty" Scarlett and Atkinson as a new minister. Surprising boxoffice hit found a broad audience. **118m/C VHS, DVD.** *GB* Hugh Grant, Andie MacDowell, Simon Callow, Kristin Scott Thomas, James Fleet, John Hannah, Charlotte Coleman, David Bower, Corin Redgrave, Rowan Atkinson, Rosalie Crutchley, Jeremy Kemp, Sophie Thompson, Kenneth Griffith, David Haig; ***D:*** Mike Newell; ***W:*** Richard Curtis; ***C:*** Michael Coulter; ***M:*** Richard Rodney Bennett. Australian Film Inst. '94: Foreign Film; British Acad. '94: Actor (Grant), Director (Newell), Film, Support. Actress (Scott Thomas); Golden Globes '95: Actor—Mus./Comedy (Grant); Writers Guild '94: Orig. Screenplay.

The 4D Man 🦴🦴 1/2 **1959** A physicist makes two fateful discoveries while working on a special project that gets out of control, leaving him able to pass through matter and see around corners. He also finds that his touch brings instant death. Cheap but effective sci-fier. Young Duke has a small part. **85m/C VHS, DVD.** Robert Lansing, Lee Meriwether, James Congdon, Guy Raymond, Robert Strauss, Patty Duke; ***D:*** Irvin S. Yeaworth Jr.; ***W:*** Theodore Simonson, Cy Chermack; ***C:*** Theodore J. Pahle; ***M:*** Ralph Carmichael.

Four's a Crowd 🦴🦴 1/2 **1938** Rather complicated screwball comedy with some unexpected romantic complications. With her newspaper about to fold, reporter Jean Christy (Russell) persuades publisher Patterson Buckley (Knowles) to rehire former editor Robert Lansford (Flynn), who's now doing public relations. Ambitious Lansford wants to get tightwad millionaire John Dillingwell (Connolly) as a client and change his image using the media so he agrees, especially after meeting Dillingwell's daughter Lorri (de Havilland). Jean says Lorri is her romantic rival for Patterson, but later Lansford decides he's in love with Lorri and Dillingwell doesn't approve in either case. **91m/B DVD.** Errol Flynn, Olivia de Havilland, Rosalind Russell, Patric Knowles, Walter Connolly, Hugh Herbert, Melville Cooper, Franklin Pangborn, Margaret Hamilton; ***D:*** Michael Curtiz; ***W:*** Sid Herzig, Casey Robinson; ***C:*** Ernest Haller; ***M:*** Heinz Roemheld, Ray Heindorf.

The Foursome 🦴 1/2 **2006 (PG-13)** Four buddies reunite at their twentieth college reunion, discussing work, money, wives, and sex. Still competitive, the guys indulge in a golf game that results in some personal and awkward revelations. Harmless enough but leans toward boring and dumb. **80m/C DVD.** Kevin Dillon, Siri Baruc, Chris Gauthier, Paul Jarrett, John Shaw; ***D:*** William Dear; ***W:*** Jackson Davies; ***M:*** Chris Ainscough. **VIDEO**

1408 🦴🦴 1/2 **2007 (PG-13)** Professional skeptic Mike Enslin (Cusack) specializes in debunking haunted houses and other paranormal spots in his bestselling books. His next target is room 1408 at Manhattan's Dolphin Hotel, despite the warnings of manager Gerald Olin (Jackson) that it's just plain evil. The room preys on an occupant's deepest, darkest fears and since Mike is grieving the death of his young daughter Katie (Anthony), should he be surprised when she shows up? Creepiness builds effectively. Adapted from a Stephen King short story. **94m/C DVD, Blu-ray Disc.** *US* John Cusack, Samuel L. Jackson, Mary McCormack, Jasmine Jessica Anthony; ***D:*** Mikael Hafstrom; ***W:*** Matt Greenberg, Scott M. Alexander, Larry Karaszewski; ***C:*** Benoit Delhomme; ***M:*** Gabriel Yared.

1492: Conquest of Paradise 🦴🦴 1/2 **1992 (PG-13)** Large-scale Hollywood production striving for political correctness is a drawn-out account of Columbus's (Depardieu) discovery and subsequent exploitation of the "New World." Skillful directing by Ridley Scott and impressive scenery add interest, yet don't make up for a script which chronicles events but tends towards trite dialogue and characterization. Available in both pan-and-scan and letterbox formats. **142m/C VHS, DVD.** Gerard Depardieu, Sigourney Weaver, Armand Assante, Frank Langella, Loren Dean, Angela Molina, Fernando Rey, Michael Wincott, Steven Waddington, Tcheky Karyo, Kario Salem; ***D:*** Ridley Scott; ***W:*** Roselyne Bosch; ***M:*** Vangelis.

The Fourth Angel 🦴🦴 **2001 (R)** London-based journalist Jack Elgin (Irons) is on holiday with his family when their plane is hijacked by terrorists. Jack's wife and two daughters are among the dead. He's naturally outraged after learning the hijackers have been released and decides to hunt the criminals himself, which draws the attention of CIA agents Bernard (Whitaker) and Davidson (Priestley). A not unfamiliar revenge thriller. Based on the novel "Angel" by Robin Hunter. **95m/C VHS, DVD.** Jeremy Irons, Forest Whitaker, Jason Priestley, Charlotte Rampling, Lois Maxwell, Timothy West, Ian McNeice; ***D:*** John Irvin; ***W:*** Allan Scott; ***C:*** Mike Molloy; ***M:*** Paul Zaza.

The 4th Dimension 🦴 1/2 **2006** Child genius turned OCD loner, Jack Emitni's (Morabito) fascinated with Einstein's unsolved Unified Field Theory. Yeah, we don't know what that is either, which is probably a good thing since it seems to drive Jack nuts. He also regards sleeping as the fourth dimension, allowing him to travel between his memories or something like that. The directors don't have anything so mundane as a linear, clear plot. Mostly filmed in B&W with some scenes in color. **82m/B DVD.** Louis Morabito, Karen Peakes, Miles Williams, Kate LaRoss, Suzanne Inman; ***D:*** Tom Mattera, Dave Mazzoni; ***W:*** Tom Mattera, Dave Mazzoni; ***C:*** Daniel Watchulonis; ***M:*** John Avarese.

The 4th Floor 🦴🦴 **1999 (R)** Lewis, who's engaged to older and successful TV weatherman Hurt, inherits a rent-controlled apartment and is then terrorized by her neighbor, who may be working for someone else. Twist ending leaves viewer with more questions than answers. **90m/C VHS, DVD.** Juliette Lewis, William Hurt, Austin Pendleton, Shelley Duvall, Artie Lange, Tobin Bell; ***D:*** Josh Klausner; ***W:*** Josh Klausner; ***C:*** Michael Slovis; ***M:*** Brian Tyler.

The Fourth Kind 🦴 **2009 (PG-13)** Dopey alien abduction pic with fake documentary footage that's allegedly based on actual psychological case studies. Nome, Alaska shrink Dr. Tyler (Jovovich) uses hypnosis on her patients who have a tendency to levitate or go insane. And the good doc isn't too reliable either since her husband was murdered and she hears weird voices and has hallucinations of white owls (as do her patients). Not campy enough to fall into the 'so-bad-it's-good' category, it's just boring. **98m/C DVD.** *US* Milla Jovovich, Corey Johnson, Enzo Cilenti, Alisha Seaton, Elias Koteas, Will Patton, Hakeem Kae-Kazim, Mia McKenna-Bruce; ***D:*** Olatunde Osunsanmi; ***W:*** Olatunde Osunsanmi; ***C:*** Lorenzo Senatore; ***M:*** Atli Orvarsson.

The 4th Man 🦴🦴🦴 1/2 *Die Vierde Man* **1979** Steeped in saturated colors and jet black comedy, with an atmospheric score, Verhoeven's nouveau noir mystery enjoyed considerable art-house success but was not released in the US until 1984. The story is decidedly non-linear, the look stylish and symbolic. Krabbe is an alcoholic bisexual Catholic writer who inadvertently becomes the hypotenuse of a love triangle involving Herman, a young man he encounters at a railway station, and his lover Christine, who owns the Sphinx beauty parlor and whose three husbands died, shall we say, mysteriously. In Dutch with English subtitles. **102m/C VHS, DVD.** *NL* Jeroen Krabbe, Renee Soutendijk, Thom Hoffman, Jon (John) DeVries, Geert De Jong; ***D:*** Paul Verhoeven; ***W:*** Gerard Soeteman; ***C:*** Jan De Bont; ***M:*** Loek Dikker. L.A. Film Critics '84: Foreign Film.

The Fourth Protocol 🦴🦴🦴 **1987 (R)** Well-made thriller based on the Frederick Forsyth bestseller about a British secret agent trying to stop a young KGB agent from destroying NATO and putting the world in nuclear jeopardy. Brosnan, as the totally dedicated Russkie, gives his best performance to date while Caine, as usual, is totally believable as he goes about the business of tracking down the bad guys. **119m/C VHS.** *GB* Michael Caine, Pierce Brosnan, Ned Beatty, Joanna Cassidy, Julian Glover, Ray McAnally, Michael Gough, Ian Richardson, Betsy Brantley, Matt Frewer, Peter Cartwright, David Conville; ***D:*** John MacKenzie; ***W:*** Frederick Forsyth, Richard Burridge, George Axelrod; ***C:*** Phil Meheux; ***M:*** Lalo Schifrin, Francis Shaw.

The Fourth Sex 🦴 1/2 *Le Quatrieme Sexe* **1961** Wealthy American, Sand, spends her time in Paris painting her girlfriends in the nude and throwing very wild parties. When she meets newcomer Caroline, she immediately sets out to add her to her harem. **82m/B VHS.** *FR* Nicole Burgot, Brigette Juslin, Richard Winckler; ***D:*** Michel Wichard.

Fourth Story 🦴🦴🦴 **1990 (PG-13)** A misfit detective is hired by a beautiful woman to find her missing husband. The investigation reveals some unseemly facts about the gentleman. Characterizations and plot twists keep this mystery interesting. **91m/C VHS.** Mark Harmon, Mimi Rogers, Cliff DeYoung, Paul Gleason, M. Emmet Walsh; ***D:*** Ivan Passer; ***W:*** Andrew Guerdat. **CABLE**

The 4th Tenor 🦴🦴 1/2 **2002 (PG-13)** Well, Rodney doesn't get much respect in this movie either—at least not at first. Italian restauranteur Lupo (Dangerfield) has fallen for one of his operatic singing waitresses (Gurwitch) but she doesn't return his interest. So he decides he has to learn to sing himself to impress her and flies to Italy for professional coaching, only to be taken in by a couple of con men. **97m/C VHS, DVD.** Rodney Dangerfield, Robert Davi, Annabelle Gurwitch, Anita De Simone, Charles Fleischer, Richard Libertini, Vincent Schiavelli; ***D:*** Harry Basil; ***W:*** Rodney Dangerfield, Harry Basil; ***C:*** Ken Blakey; ***M:*** Christopher Lennertz. **VIDEO**

The Fourth War 🦴🦴 **1990 (R)** Scheider and Prochnow are American and Russian colonels, respectively, assigned to guard the West German-Czechoslovakian border against each other. With the end of the cold war looming, these two frustrated warriors begin to taunt each other with sallies into the other's territory, threatening to touch off a major superpower conflict. **109m/C VHS.** Roy Scheider, Jurgen Prochnow, Tim Reid, Lara Harris, Harry Dean Stanton, Dale Dye; ***D:*** John Frankenheimer; ***M:*** Bill Conti.

Fourth Wise Man 🦴🦴 **1985** A Biblical Easter story about a rich physician searching for Christ in Persia. **72m/C VHS, DVD.** Martin Sheen, Lance Kerwin, Alan Arkin, Harold Gould, Eileen Brennan, Ralph Bellamy, Adam Arkin, Richard Libertini; ***D:*** Michael Ray Rhodes; ***W:*** Tom Fontana; ***C:*** Jon Kranhouse; ***M:*** Bruce Langhorne.

Fourth Wish 🦴🦴 **1975** When a single father learns that his son is dying, he vows to make his son's last months as fulfilling as possible. Bring lots of hankies. **107m/C VHS.** John Meillon, Robert Bettles, Robyn Nevin; ***D:*** Don Chaffey; ***C:*** Geoff Burton. Australian Film Inst. '75: Actor (Meillon).

Fowl Play **WOOF!** *Supercock; Superchicken; A Fistful of Feathers* **1975 (PG)** An unlikely threesome encounter various hardships and mishaps on their way to the first cock-fighting Olympics. Let's hope it's the last cock-fighting Olympics. **90m/C VHS.** Nancy Kwan, Ross Hagen; ***D:*** Gus Trikonis; ***W:*** Ross Hagen, Gus Trikonis; ***C:*** Fred C. Soriano Jr.; ***M:*** Tito Sotto.

Fox and His Friends 🦴🦴🦴 1/2 *Faustrecht der Freiheit; Fist Right of Freedom* **1975** Fassbinder's breakthrough tragi-drama, about a lowly gay carnival barker who wins the lottery, thus attracting a devious, exploiting lover, who takes him for everything he has. In German with English subtitles. **123m/C VHS, DVD.** *GE* Rainer Werner Fassbinder, Peter Chatel, Karl-Heinz Boehm, Adrian Hoven, Harry Baer, Ulla Jacobsson, Kurt Raab; ***D:*** Rainer Werner Fassbinder; ***C:*** Michael Ballhaus.

The Fox and the Hound 🦴🦴🦴 **1981 (G)** Sweet story of the friendship shared by a fox and hound. Young and naive, the animals become friends and swear their allegiance to one another when they are separated for a season. Upon return, the hound has become his master's best hunting dog and warns his friend the fox to stay clear of their hunting grounds, for the master is determined to catch the docile fox. Saddened, the fox retreats but soon finds himself boldly standing his ground against a bear that attacks the hound, and the hound inevitably protects the fox from the mean-spirited hunter. Very good animation, but not in the same class as other Disney favorites like "Beauty and the Beast." **83m/C VHS, DVD.** ***D:*** Art Stevens, Ted Berman, Richard Rich; ***W:*** Art Stevens, Peter Young, Steve Hulett, Earl Kress, Vance Gerry, Laury Clemmons, Dave Michener, Burny Mattinson; ***M:*** Buddy (Norman Dale) Baker; ***V:*** Mickey Rooney, Kurt Russell, Pearl Bailey, Jack Albertson, Sandy Duncan, Jeannette Nolan, Pat Buttram, John Fiedler, John McIntire, Richard Bakalyan, Paul Winchell, Keith Coogan, Corey Feldman.

The Fox and the Hound 2 🦴🦴 **2006 (G)** Fox Tod and hound dog Copper are still buddies but their friendship is tested when Copper's head is turned by a group of hound dog howlers. **69m/C DVD.** ***D:*** Jim Kammerud; ***W:*** Rich Burns, Roger S.H. Schulman; ***M:*** Joel McNeely; ***V:*** Reba McEntire, Jeff Foxworthy, Patrick Swayze, Rob Paulsen. **VIDEO**

Foxes 🦴🦴 **1980 (R)** Four young California girls grow up with little supervision from parents still trying to grow up themselves. They rely on each other in a world where they have to make adult choices, yet are not considered grown-up. They look for no more than a good time and no tragic mistakes. **106m/C VHS, DVD.** Jodie Foster, Cherie Currie, Marilyn Kagan, Scott Baio, Sally Kellerman, Randy Quaid, Laura Dern; ***D:*** Adrian Lyne; ***W:*** Gerald Ayres.

Foxfire 🦴🦴🦴 **1987 (PG)** In the role that won her Tony and Emmy awards, Tandy stars as Annie Nations, a woman who has lived her entire life in the Blue Ridge Mountains. Widowed, all she has left are the memories of her beloved husband, with whom she regularly communes. Her son tries to convince her to move, and it becomes a clash of the wills as Annie tries to decide to stay in her past or change her future. **118m/C VHS, DVD.** Jessica Tandy, Hume Cronyn, John Denver, Gary Grubbs, Harriet Hall; ***D:*** Jud Taylor; ***C:*** Thomas Burstyn. **TV**

Foxfire 🦴🦴 **1996 (R)** Not much more than "The Craft" without the hocus-pocus. Lusty Legs Sadovsky (Jolie) is a liberated drifter who empowers a quartet of abused teens to take action against their molester, who happens to be their biology teacher. Based on the book by Joyce Carol Oates originally written in the 1950s, modern adaptation suffers from time warp, most notably when the girls expose their teacher's behavior to their principal and he promptly suspends them without further ado. After some bonding and tattooing in an abandoned house, flick descends into the more masculine and mundane territory of car chases, kidnapping and gunplay. Filmmakers rather timidly back off of leather-clad Legs' obvious lesbianism and her relationship with the adoring Maddy (Burress). Decent acting by most would've benefitted from a more cohesive screenplay. **102m/C VHS, DVD.** Angelina Jolie, John Diehl, Jenny Lewis, Cathy Moriarty, Richard Beymer, Hedy Burress, Jenny Shimizu, Sarah Rosenberg, Peter Facinelli; ***D:*** Annette Haywood-Carter; ***W:*** Elizabeth White; ***C:*** Newton Thomas (Tom) Sigel; ***M:*** Michel Colombier.

Foxfire Light 🦴 **1982 (PG)** A young woman vacationing in the Ozarks is drawn into a romance with a cowboy. But her mother's social ambitions and her own indecesion may tear them apart. **102m/C VHS.** Tippi Hedren, Lara Parker, Leslie Nielsen, Barry Van Dyke; ***D:*** Allen Baron; ***C:*** Thomas Ackerman.

Foxstyle 🦴 1/2 **1973** A wealthy nightclub owner struggles with his country roots and his city sophistication. **84m/C VHS.** Juanita Moore, Richard Lawson, John Taylor, Jovita Bush; ***D:*** Clyde Houston.

Foxtrap 🦴 **1985** An L.A. courier is hired to find a runaway girl and, upon finding her in Europe, discovers he's been led into a trap. A low budget Italian co-production. **89m/C VHS.** *IT* Fred Williamson, Christopher Connelly, Arlene Golonka; ***D:*** Fred Williamson.

Foxtrot 🦴🦴 *The Other Side of Paradise* **1976 (R)** A wealthy count isolates himself, his wife, and their two servants, on an island but cannot escape his past or the horrors of WWII. Even the good cast can't save the pretentious script and inadequate production. **91m/C VHS.** *SI MX* Peter O'Toole, Charlotte Rampling, Max von Sydow, Jorge Luke; ***D:*** Arturo Ripstein.

Foxy Brown 🦴 **1974 (R)** A bitter woman poses as a prostitute to avenge the mob-backed deaths of her drug dealer brother and undercover cop boyfriend. Extremely violent black exploitation flick. **92m/C VHS, DVD.** Pam Grier, Terry Carter, Antonio Fargas, Kathryn Loder, Peter Brown, Sid Haig, Juanita Brown, Tony Giorgio; ***D:*** Jack Hill; ***W:*** Jack Hill; ***C:*** Brick Marquard; ***M:*** Willie Hutch.

F.P. 1 🦴🦴 **1933** An artifical island (Floating Platform 1) in the Atlantic is threatened by treason. This slow-moving 1930s technothriller is the English-language version of the German "F.P. 1 Antwortet Nicht" ("F.P. 1 Doesn't Answer"). Both were directed at the same time by Hartl, using different casts. **74m/B VHS.** *GE* Leslie Fenton, Conrad Veidt, Jill Esmond; ***D:*** Karl Hartl.

F.P. 1 Doesn't Answer 🦴🦴 *F.P. 1 Antwortet Nicht* **1933** A mid-Atlantic refueling station (Floating Platform 1) is threatened by treason and a pilot sets out to put things right. Features pre-Hollywood vintage Lorre; Albers was Germany's number one boxoffice draw at the time. In German. **74m/B VHS.** *GE* Hans Albers, Sybille Schmitz, Paul Hartmann, Peter Lorre, Hermann Speelmanns; ***D:*** Karl Hartl.

Fracture 🦴🦴 ½ **2007 (R)** Old Turk vs. young Turk as Hopkins and Gosling play mind games. Arrogant Ted Crawford (Hopkins) shoots his adulterous trophy wife Jennifer (Davitz). Prosecutor Willy Beachum (Gosling) is leaving for a cushy private job when he gets the case, which proceeds to fall apart. Since Ted is taunting him, Willy can't let things go, no matter what it costs. Hopkins plays his part with sadistic relish (yes, Hannibal Lecter will come to mind), while Gosling handles an emotional roller-coaster from cockiness to vulnerability to determination. **112m/C DVD.** *US* Anthony Hopkins, Ryan Gosling, David Strathairn, Rosamund Pike, Embeth Davidtz, Billy Burke, Clifford Curtis, Fiona Shaw, Bob Gunton, Xander Berkeley, Josh Stamberg, Zoe Kazan; ***D:*** Gregory Hoblit; ***W:*** Daniel Pyne, Glen Gers; ***C:*** Kramer Morgenthau; ***M:*** Mychael Danna, Jeff Danna.

Fragments 🦴 ½ *Winged Creatures* **2008 (R)** Another ensemble drama that follows characters dealing with the aftermath of a tragedy. A gunman randomly opens fire in an L.A. diner, killing several people. The survivors cope (or don't) in various fashion: a waitress begins neglecting her young son; a teen turns to religion after her father is killed; a doctor who felt powerless begins poisoning his wife so he can save her; and a driving instructor, who was shot, decides to try his newfound luck at the casinos. **96m/C DVD.** Dakota Fanning, Kate Beckinsale, Embeth Davidtz, Soren Fulton, Tim Guinee, Forest Whitaker, Jeanne Tripplehorn, Robin Weigert, Guy Pearce, Jackie Earle Haley, Jennifer Hudson, Beth Grant, Josh Hutcherson, Hayley McFarland, Kevin Cooney, Walton Goggins, Troy Garity, Brooke Mackenzie; ***D:*** Rowan Woods; ***C:*** Eric Alan Edwards; ***M:*** Marcelo Zarvos.

Frailty 🦴🦴🦴 **2002 (R)** Impressive directorial debut by Paxton has him as Dad, a seemingly normal West Texas widower. One day, however, he tells his boys that their family has been chosen by God to destroy demons who are disguised as normal people. This sounds okay by impressionable nine year old Adam (Sumpter), but older Fenton (O'Leary) seems skeptical. Told mostly in flashback, from the point of view of now-grown, haunted Fenton (McConaughey), the story keeps the gore mostly offscreen, while focusing on such lofty ideas as the wages of religious fanaticism, the trust between parents and their kids, and toll of insanity. Screenwriting debut for Hanley. Paxton acquits himself well on both sides of the camera, but it's O'Leary who shines. McConaughey turns in his best performance to date. **100m/C VHS, DVD.** *US* Bill Paxton, Matthew McConaughey, Powers Boothe, Luke Askew, Matt O'Leary, Jeremy Sumpter, Derk Cheetwood, Missy (Melissa) Crider, Alan Davidson, Cynthia Ettinger, Vincent Chase, Levi Kreis; ***D:*** Bill Paxton; ***W:*** Brent Hanley; ***C:*** Bill Butler; ***M:*** Brian Tyler.

Frame by Frame 🦴🦴 ½ **1995 (R)** Cop partners Ekberg (Helgenberger) and Stash (Biehn), who share a passion on and off the job, become implicated in the mob-style murder of Stash's wife. **97m/C VHS.** Michael Biehn, Marg Helgenberger, Ron White, Dan Lett, Von Flores; ***D:*** Douglas Barr; ***W:*** Douglas Barr; ***C:*** Rodney Charters; ***M:*** Mark Snow. **CABLE**

Frame Up 🦴🦴 **1991 (R)** A small town sheriff is trying to investigate a murder tied to a fraternity's initiation. However, he runs into opposition from the most powerful man in town. **90m/C VHS.** Wings Hauser, Bobby DiCicco, Frances Fisher, Dick Sargent, Robert Picardo; ***D:*** Paul Leder.

Framed 🦴🦴 **1975 (R)** A nightclub owner is framed for murder, which understandably irks him. He's determined to get paroled and then seek revenge on the crooked cops responsible for his incarceration. This action melodrama features the writer, director and star of "Walking Tall." **106m/C VHS.** Joe Don Baker, Gabriel Dell, Brock Peters, Conny Van Dyke, John Marley; ***D:*** Phil Karlson; ***W:*** Mort Briskin.

Framed 🦴🦴 **1990** An art forger gets tripped up by a beautiful con artist. However, when they meet again he is willingly drawn into her latest swindle. **87m/C VHS.** Jeff Goldblum, Kristin Scott Thomas, Todd Graff; ***D:*** Dean Parisot.

Framed 🦴🦴🦴 **1993** British miniseries about a mediocre cop and a master criminal. Sgt. Larry Jackson (Morrissey) is on vacation in Spain when he spots the supposedly dead master thief/murderer Eddie Myers (Dalton). Once back in London, Larry's assigned the dubious task of guarding Eddie and finding out the names of his associates. Only the sophisticated Eddie starts to dangle temptation in front of the younger man until Larry begins to waver in his duty. Intricate plotting, with Dalton particular fine as the suave, immoral crook. LaPlante also wrote the very successful "Prime Suspect" police dramas for TV. **115m/C VHS, DVD.** *GB* Timothy Dalton, David Morrissey, Timothy West, Annabelle Apsion, Penelope Cruz, Rowena King, Francis Johnson, Glyn Grimstead, Wayne Foskett, Trevor Cooper; ***D:*** Geoffrey Sax; ***W:*** Lynda La Plante; ***M:*** Nick Bicat. **TV**

Framed for Murder 🦴 ½ **2007** Predictable woman-in-jeopardy movie from Lifetime. June (Donovan) argues with her philandering husband, hits him with a heavy object, and splits. The cops find him dead and June goes to the slammer for eight years. When released, June is still declaring her innocence, but proving who really dunnit could be perilous for her health. **94m/C DVD.** Elisa Donovan, Susan Walters, Perry King, Kevin Jubinville, Claire Brosseau, Jonathan Higgins, Sophie Gendron; ***D:*** Douglas Jackson; ***W:*** Christine Conradt, Richard Dana Smith; ***C:*** Bert Tougas; ***M:*** Steve Gurevitch. **CABLE**

Fran 🦴🦴 **1985** A young woman is torn between her desperate need for a male companion and the care of her children. Well made, albeit depressing, Australian production. **92m/C VHS.** *AU* Noni Hazlehurst, Annie Byron, Alan Fletcher; ***D:*** Glenda Hambly. Australian Film Inst. '85: Actress (Hazlehurst).

Frances 🦴🦴🦴 **1982** The tragic story of Frances Farmer, the beautiful and talented screen actress of the '30s and early '40s, who was driven to a mental breakdown by bad luck, drug and alcohol abuse, a neurotic, domineering mother, despicable mental health care, and her own stubbornness. After being in and out of mental hospitals, she is finally reduced to a shadow by a lobotomy. Not nearly as bleak as it sounds, this film works because Lange understands this character from the inside out, and never lets her become melodramatic or weak. **134m/C VHS, DVD.** Jessica Lange, Kim Stanley, Sam Shepard, Jeffrey DeMunn, Gerald S. O'Loughlin, Chris Pennock, John Randolph, Lane Smith; ***D:*** Graeme Clifford; ***W:*** Christopher DeVore, Nicholas Kazan, Eric Bergren; ***C:*** Laszlo Kovacs; ***M:*** John Barry.

Francesco 🦴🦴 **1993 (PG-13)** Set in 13th-century Italy and depicting the life of St. Francis of Assisi. Follows the pleasure-loving son of a wealthy merchant through his religious awakening, and the founding of the Franciscan order of monks. Rourke, in a definite change-of-pace role, is actually believable, while Bonham Carter offers fine support as a devoted disciple. **119m/C VHS, DVD.** Mickey Rourke, Helena Bonham Carter, Paolo Bonacelli, Andrea Ferreol, Hanns Zischler, Peter Berling; ***D:*** Liliana Cavani; ***W:*** Liliana Cavani; ***C:*** Giuseppe Lanci, Ennio Guarnieri; ***M:*** Vangelis.

The Franchise Affair 🦴🦴 **1952** A teenage girl in need of an alibi accuses two reclusive women of kidnapping and abusing her. It's up to a lawyer to sort out the truth. Based on the novel by Josephine Tey. **149m/C VHS.** *GB* Michael Denison, Dulcie Gray, Anthony Nicholls, Marjorie Fielding, Athene Seyler, Ann Stephens, Patrick Troughton; ***D:*** Lawrence Huntington.

The Franchise Affair 🦴🦴 ½ **1988** A scandal is about to overtake the sleepy village of Milford in 1947. An elderly lady and her daughter, the owners of a forbidding country house, are accused of kidnapping and beating a teenaged girl until she agreed to work as their servant. A British TV production based on the novel by Josephine Tey and previously filmed for the big screen in 1952. **155m/C VHS.** *GB* Patrick Malahide, Rosalie Crutchley, Joanna McCallum, Alex Jennings; ***D:*** Leonard Lewis; ***W:*** James Andrew Hall; ***M:*** Paul Hart. **TV**

Francis Covers the Big Town 🦴🦴 ½ **1953** The fourth in the series finds Peter Stirling (O'Connor) trying to become an ace reporter with a New York newspaper. Thanks to Francis he gets some big scoops but then runs afoul of the mob and is accused of murder. And it's up to his smarter pal to come to the rescue. **86m/B VHS, DVD.** Donald O'Connor, Yvette Dugay, Gene Lockhart, Nancy Guild, Larry Gates, Gale Gordon; ***D:*** Arthur Lubin; ***W:*** Oscar Brodney; ***C:*** Carl Guthrie; ***M:*** Joseph Gershenson; ***V:*** Chill Wills.

Francis Gary Powers: The True Story of the U-2 Spy 🦴🦴 ½ **1976** Dramatization of the true experiences of Gary Powers, a CIA spy pilot whose plane was shot down over the Soviet Union in 1960. His capture, trial, and conviction are all portrayed in detail, taken from Power's own reminiscences. **120m/C VHS.** Lee Majors, Noah Beery Jr., Nehemiah Persoff, Lew Ayres, Brooke Bundy; ***D:*** Delbert Mann. **TV**

Francis Goes to the Races 🦴🦴 ½ **1951** The second in the talking-mule series finds O'Connor and Francis taking up residence on Kellaway's failing horse ranch. When mobsters seize control of the property to pay off a debt, Francis decides to check with the horses at the Santa Anita race track and find a sure winner to bet on. **88m/B VHS, DVD.** Donald O'Connor, Piper Laurie, Cecil Kellaway, Jesse White, Barry Kelley, Hayden Rorke, Vaughn Taylor, Larry Keating; ***D:*** Arthur Lubin; ***W:*** Oscar Brodney; ***M:*** Frank Skinner; ***V:*** Chill Wills.

Francis Goes to West Point 🦴🦴 ½ **1952** Peter (O'Connor) and Francis get into West Point where the unfortunate freshman winds up last in his class. But thanks to Francis, Peter makes it past school hazing, grades, and other campus hijicks. Look for Leonard Nimoy in the bit role of a football player. Third in the series. **81m/B VHS, DVD.** Donald O'Connor, Lori Nelson, William Reynolds, Gregg (Hunter) Palmer, Alice Kelley, Les Tremayne, David Janssen, Paul Burke; ***D:*** Arthur Lubin; ***W:*** Oscar Brodney; ***C:*** Carl Guthrie; ***M:*** Joseph Gershenson; ***V:*** Chill Wills.

Francis in the Haunted House 🦴 ½ **1956** The sixth and last entry in the series finds star Donald O'Connor, director Arthur Lubin, and even Chill Wills (the voice of Francis) all abandoning the sinking series. So, its left to Rooney (as hapless David Prescott) to get himself into trouble (trapped in a haunted house with thieves) and for Francis to get him out. Ho-hum. **80m/B VHS.** Mickey Rooney, Virginia Welles, James Flavin, Paul Cavanagh, David Janssen, Richard Deacon; ***D:*** Charles Lamont; ***W:*** Herbert Margolis, William Raynor; ***C:*** George Robinson; ***M:*** Joseph Gershenson; ***V:*** Paul Frees.

Francis in the Navy 🦴🦴 **1955** The precocious talking mule, Francis, is drafted, and his buddy, played by O'Connor, comes to the rescue. The loquacious beast proves he has the superior grey matter however, and ends up doing all the thinking. Look for Clint Eastwood in his second minor role. **80m/B VHS, DVD.** Donald O'Connor, Martha Hyer, Jim Backus, Paul Burke, David Janssen, Clint Eastwood, Martin Milner; ***D:*** Arthur Lubin.

Francis Joins the WACs 🦴🦴 ½ **1954** The fifth entry in the series finds O'Connor working as a bank clerk when he is mistakenly drafted back into the military—and sent to a WAC base. Francis tries to keep him out of trouble with the ladies. Wills, the voice of Francis, also turns up as a general. **94m/B VHS.** Donald O'Connor, Julie Adams, Chill Wills, Mamie Van Doren, Lynn Bari, Zasu Pitts, Joan Shawlee, Mara Corday, Allison Hayes; ***D:*** Arthur Lubin; ***V:*** Chill Wills.

Francis the Talking Mule 🦴🦴🦴 *Francis* **1949** The first of the silly but funny series about, what else, a talking mule. Peter Stirling (O'Connor) is the dim-bulb G.I. who hooks up with Francis while fighting in Burma. Francis helps Peter become a war hero but of course everyone thinks he's crazy when Peter insists the mule can talk. The joke is that Francis is smarter than any of the humans. O'Connor starred in six of the films, with Mickey Rooney taking over the final adventure. Director Lubin went on to create the TV series "Mr. Ed," about a talking horse. Watch for Tony Curtis in a small role. **91m/B VHS, DVD.** Donald O'Connor, Patricia Medina, Zasu Pitts, Ray Collins, John McIntire, Eduard Franz, Howland Chamberlain, Frank Faylen, Tony Curtis; ***D:*** Arthur Lubin; ***M:*** Frank Skinner; ***V:*** Chill Wills.

Frank 🦴🦴 **2007 (PG)** When Jennifer York (Watros) inherits her family's vacation home on the beach, she and her uptight hubby Colin (Gries) take protesting teen daughter Anna (Robertson) and young son Patrick (Dierks) there for the summer. The kids find a large, slobbery, injured stray dog and plead until reluctant Colin agrees to let them care for Frank with the proviso that he's put up for adoption before they go home. Right, like that's really going to happen. **90m/C DVD.** Jon(athan) Gries, Cynthia Watros, Brittany Robertson, Ashton Dierks, Brian Burnett; ***D:*** Douglas Cheney; ***W:*** Robin Bradford; ***C:*** Paul Mayne; ***M:*** Massimiliano Frani. **VIDEO**

Frank and Jesse 🦴🦴 ½ **1994 (R)** Another revisionist western finds outlaw Jesse James (Lowe) brooding about his violent existence while brother Frank (Paxton) keeps the gang together and they all try to avoid capture by a vengeful Alan Pinkerton (Atherton) and his detective agency. **106m/C VHS, DVD.** Rob Lowe, Bill Paxton, Randy Travis, William Atherton, Alexis Arquette; ***D:*** Robert Boris; ***W:*** Robert Boris; ***C:*** Walt Lloyd; ***M:*** Mark McKenzie.

Frank McKlusky, C.I. 🦴🦴 **2002 (PG-13)** Frank McKlusky (Sheridan) is a klutzy but dedicated insurance claims investigator with an over-protective mama (Parton) who worries that her sonny boy will end up in a coma like his daredevil dad (Quaid). But Frank learns it can't always be safety first when he and his gay partner Jimmy (Farley) investigate a couple of slimy lawyers (Pollak, Morgan). **83m/C VHS, DVD.** Dave Sheridan, Dolly Parton, Randy Quaid, Kevin Farley, Kevin Pollak, Tracy Morgan, Orson Bean, Joanie Laurer, Andy Richter; ***D:*** Arlene Sanford; ***W:*** Mark Perez; ***C:*** Tim Suhrstedt; ***M:*** Randy Edelman. **VIDEO**

Frankenfish 🦴🦴 **2004 (R)** Hungry, jumbo-sized mutant fish feast on any humans they can get their fins on in the Louisiana Bayou whether they're on land or water. **84m/C VHS, DVD.** Tory Kittles, K.D. Aubert, China Chow, Tomas Arana, Richard Edson, Muse Watson, Raoul Trujillo, Matthew Rauch, Donna Biscoe, Mark Boone Jr., Reggie Lee, Noelle Evans, Eugene Collier, Sean Patterson; ***D:*** Mark Dippe; ***W:*** Simon Barrett, Scott Clevenger; ***C:*** Eliot Rockett; ***M:*** Ryan Beveridge. **VIDEO**

Frankenhooker 🦴 ½ **1990 (R)** Jeffrey Franken is a nice guy; he didn't mean to mow his fiancee down on the front lawn. But sometimes bad things just happen to good people. Luckily Jeff thought to save her head and decides to pair it up with the body of some sexy streetwalkers. Voila! You have Frankenhooker: the girlfriend with (someone else's) heart of gold. The posters say it best, "A Terrifying Tale of Sluts and Bolts." **90m/C VHS, DVD.** James Lorinz, Patty Mullen, Charlotte J. Helmkamp, Louise Lasser, Shirley Stoler, Joseph Gonzalez, Beverly Bonner, John Zacherle; ***D:*** Frank Henenlotter; ***W:*** Frank Henenlotter, Robert Martin; ***C:*** Robert M. "Bob" Baldwin Jr.; ***M:*** Joe Renzetti.

Frankenstein **1931** The definitive expressionistic Gothic horror classic that set the mold. Adapted from the Mary Shelley novel about Dr. Henry Frankenstein (Clive), the scientist who creates a terrifying, yet strangely sympathetic monster aided by his hunchbacked assistant, Fritz (Frye). Great performance by Karloff as the creation, which made him a monster star (in part, thanks to Jack Pierce's makeup). Several powerful scenes, excised from the original version, have been restored, including that of young Maria (Marilyn Harris), who is spotted by the monster innocently picking flowers by a pond. The first in the Universal series. **71m/B VHS, DVD.** Boris Karloff, Colin Clive, Mae Clarke, John Boles, Dwight Frye, Edward Van Sloan, Frederick Kerr, Lionel Belmore, Arletta Duncan; ***D:*** James Whale; ***W:*** Garrett Fort, John Lloyd Balderston, Robert Florey, Francis Edwards Faragoh; ***C:*** Arthur Edeson; ***M:*** David Broekman. AFI '98: Top 100, Natl. Film Reg. '91.

Frankenstein **½ 1973** A brilliant scientist plays God, unleashing a living monster from the remains of the dead. A TV movie version of the legendary horror story. Good atmosphere provided by producer Dan "Dark Shadows" Curtis. **130m/C VHS, DVD.** Robert Foxworth, Bo Svenson, Willie Aames, Susan Strasberg; ***D:*** Glenn Jordan.

Frankenstein **½ 1982** A remake of the horror classic, closely following the original story, wherein the creature speaks (and waxes philosophical), the doctor sees him as his dark subconscious, and the two die in an arctic confrontation. **81m/C VHS.** Robert Powell, Carrie Fisher, David Warner, John Gielgud; ***D:*** James Ormerod.

Frankenstein **½ 1993** Yet another remake of Mary Shelley's 1818 novel. Bergin stars as Dr. Victor Frankenstein, fanatically believing in the power of science to solve all mankind's ills. This leads him to prove his theories on the "secret of life" with his creation of the monster (Quaid), which Frankenstein finds he cannot ultimately control. Slow-moving story but while the monster isn't really terrifying, he's vengeful and intelligent enough to be a good enemy. **117m/C VHS.** Patrick Bergin, Randy Quaid, John Mills, Lambert Wilson, Fiona Gillies, Jacinta Mulcahy, Timothy Stark; ***D:*** David Wickes; ***W:*** David Wickes. **CABLE**

Frankenstein 1970 **½ 1958** Victor (Karloff), the horribly scarred grandson of the late Baron von Frankenstein, wants to continue granddad's experiments but lacks the cash to do so. He agrees to rent his castle to a TV crew, giving him the money to buy an atomic reactor (it was the 1950s after all) to bring his monster to life. The title is apparently meaningless and Karloff enjoys hamming up the horror but it's a minor pleasure at best. **83m/C DVD.** Boris Karloff, Tommy Duggan, Jana Lund, Donald (Don "Red") Barry, Charlotte Austin, Irwin Berke; ***D:*** Howard W. Koch; ***W:*** Richard H. Landau, George Worthing Yates; ***C:*** Carl Guthrie.

Frankenstein and Me **½ 1996 (PG)** Monster-mad 12-year-old Earl Williams (Boulanger) lives in a small Mojave desert town and dreams about bringing Frankenstein's creature back to life. On Halloween, Earl and his friends visit a traveling carnival that claims to have the "authentic" monster, which happens to fall off the truck when the show leaves. Earl finds the dummy and makes numerous attempts to bring the creature back to life. Lots of fantasy sequences and the picture's fun without being too scary. **91m/C VHS.** *CA* Jamieson Boulanger, Ricky Mabse, Louise Fletcher, Burt Reynolds, Myriam Cyr; ***D:*** Robert Tinnell; ***W:*** David Sherman, Richard Goudreau; ***C:*** Roxanne Di Santo; ***M:*** Normand Corbeil.

Frankenstein and the Monster from Hell **1974 (R)** A young doctor is discovered conducting experiments with human bodies and thrown into a mental asylum run by none other than Dr. Frankenstein himself. They continue their gruesome work together, creating a monster who develops a taste for human flesh. This really lame film was the last of the Hammer Frankenstein series. **93m/C VHS, DVD.** *GB* Peter Cushing, Shane Briant, Madeleine Smith, David Prowse, John Stratton, Bernard Lee, Patrick Troughton, Sydney Bromley; ***D:*** Terence Fisher; ***W:*** John (Anthony Hinds) Elder; ***C:*** Brian Probyn; ***M:*** James Bernard.

Frankenstein Conquers the World **½** *Furankenshutain tai chitai kaiju Baragon; Frankenstein Meets the Giant Devil Fish; Frankenstein vs. Baragon; Frankenstein vs. the Subterranean Monster; Furankensuten to Baragon; Frankenstein vs. the Giant Devil Fish* **1964** During WWII the heart of Frankenstein's monster is taken from Europe by the Nazis and sent to Japan, where it is irradiated by the blast at Hiroshima. Years later a disfigured young boy is caught eating local animals, and at a local hospital it's discovered that he is becoming immune to radiation. He begins growing, and as the doctors and scientists study him, they come to believe he has eaten Frankenstein's heart. He escapes and is blamed for massive destruction, which is actually caused by the newly awakened gigantic reptile monster Baragon. Hounded by the military, the new Frankenstein's monster and Baragon eventually clash. It spawned a sequel, "War of the Gargantuas," but all references to this film were removed from the American version for some reason. **94m/C DVD.** *JP* Tadao Takashima, Nick Adams, Kumi Mizuno, Yoshio Tsuchiya, Keiko Sawai, Haruo Nakajima, Koji Furuhata, Peter Mann, Kenichiro Kawaji; ***D:*** Ishio Honda; ***W:*** Takeshi Kimura, Jerry Sohl, Reuben Bercovitch; ***C:*** Hajime Koizumi; ***M:*** Akira Ifukube.

Frankenstein Created Woman *Frankenstein Made Woman* **1966** In Hammer's fourth take on the Frankenstein story, traditional lab scenes are replaced with less expensive "soul" translocations, though the filmmakers retain an ongoing fascination with decapitations. Oddly, the story has a warmth that's often lacking in the genre, and it's aimed at a younger audience, reflecting the changes that were going on when it was made. **86m/C DVD.** Peter Cushing, Susan Denberg, Thorley Walters, Robert Morris, Duncan Lamont, Peter Blythe, Alan MacNaughton, Peter Madden, Barry Warren, Derek Fowlds; ***D:*** Terence Fisher; ***W:*** John (Anthony Hinds) Elder; ***C:*** Arthur Grant.

Frankenstein '80 **WOOF!** *Mosaic* **1979** Guy named Frankenstein pieces together a monster who goes on a killing spree. Bottom of the barrel Italian production with funky music and lots of gore. **88m/C VHS, DVD.** *IT GE* John Richardson, Gordon Mitchell, Leila Parker, Dada Galloti, Marisa Travers, Xiro Papas, Renato Romano; ***D:*** Mario Mancini; ***W:*** Mario Mancini, Ferdinando De Leone; ***C:*** Emilio Varriano.

Frankenstein General Hospital **WOOF! 1988** A completely laughless horror spoof wherein the 12th grandson of the infamous scientist duplicates his experiments in the basement of a modern hospital. A must see for Frankenstein fans; considered by some the worst Frankenstein movie ever made. **90m/C VHS.** Mark Blankfield, Kathy Shower, Leslie Jordan, Irwin Keyes, Jonathan Farwell, Hamilton Mitchell, Lou (Cutel) Cutell, Bobby "Boris" Pickett; ***D:*** Deborah Roberts; ***W:*** Robert Deel, Michael F. Kelly; ***C:*** Tom Fraser.

Frankenstein Island **WOOF! 1981 (PG)** Four balloonists get pulled down in a storm and end up on a mysterious island. They are greeted by one Sheila Frankenstein and encounter monsters, amazons, and other obstacles. Completely inept; Carradine "appears" in a visionary sequence wearing his pajamas. **97m/C VHS, DVD.** Cameron Mitchell, Andrew Duggan, John Carradine; ***D:*** Jerry Warren.

Frankenstein Meets the Space Monster **WOOF!** *Mars Invades Puerto Rico; Frankenstein Meets the Spacemen; Duel of the Space Monsters* **1965** A classic grade-Z epic about a space robot gone berserk among Puerto Rican disco dancers. **80m/B VHS, DVD.** James Karen, Nancy Marshall, Marilyn Hanold, David Kerman, Robert Reilly, Lou (Cutel) Cutell; ***D:*** Robert Gaffney; ***W:*** George Garret; ***C:*** Saul Midwall.

Frankenstein Meets the Wolfman **1942** The two famous Universal monsters meet and battle it out in this typical grade-B entry, the fifth from the series. The Werewolf wants Dr. Frankenstein to cure him, but only his monster (played by Lugosi) remains. **73m/C VHS, DVD.** Lon Chaney Jr., Bela Lugosi, Patric Knowles, Lionel Atwill, Maria Ouspenskaya, Ilona Massey, Dwight Frye; ***D:*** Roy William Neill; ***W:*** Curt Siodmak; ***C:*** George Robinson.

Frankenstein Must Be Destroyed **½ 1969** Evil Dr. Frankenstein (Cushing) gets interested in brain transplants but discovers the expert, Dr. Pravda, he hoped to work with has gone mad and is in an asylum. He forces a young medical couple to help him free Pravda but the man is accidentally killed. Nevertheless, Frankenstein transplants Pravda's brain into the body of an asylum inmate that Frankenstein has murdered. These things never work out as intended. Followed by "The Horror of Frankenstein." **97m/C VHS, DVD.** *GB* Peter Cushing, Veronica Carlson, Freddie Jones, Maxine Audley, Simon Ward, Thorley Walters, George Pravda, Colette O'Neil; ***D:*** Terence Fisher; ***W:*** Bert Batt; ***C:*** Arthur Grant.

Frankenstein Reborn **½ 1998 (PG)** Thirteen-year-old Anna Frankenstein is impressed with her eccentric scientist uncle, Victor, but things get a little spooky when she meets his latest creation. Yes, Uncle Vic is still working on creating a man from stitched together parts of dead bodies and this time his creature has a human soul. DeCoteau used the pseudonym Julian Breen. **70m/C VHS, DVD.** Jaason Simmons, Ben Gould, Haven Burton, Ethan Wilde; ***D:*** David DeCoteau. **VIDEO**

Frankenstein Sings... The Movie **½ 1995 (PG)** Musical horror spoof finds young couple seeking shelter in a creepy mansion that happens to belong to Dr. Frankenstein. Also visiting (it just happens to be Halloween) are Mr. and Mrs. Dracula, the Wolfman and his mother, and the mummified remains of Elvis and his agent. Some amusing one-liners and mediocre music; adapted from a stage musical. **83m/C VHS.** Candace Cameron, Ian Bohen, Jimmie Walker, Anthony Crivello; ***D:*** Joel Cohen, Alec Sokolow.

Frankenstein Unbound *Roger Corman's Frankenstein Unbound* **1990 (R)** Corman returns after nearly 20 years with a better than ever B movie. Hurt plays Dr. Joseph Buchanan, a nuclear physicist time traveler who accidentally goes back to 1816 and runs into Lord Byron (Patric), Percy (Hutchence) and Mary (Fonda) Shelley and their neighbor Baron Frankenstein (Julia) and his monster (Brimble). But Frankenstein is not done experimenting just yet. Great acting, fun special effects, intelligent and subtle message, with a little sex to keep things going. **86m/C VHS, DVD.** John Hurt, Raul Julia, Bridget Fonda, Jason Patric, Michael Hutchence, Catherine Rabett, Nick Brimble, Catherine Corman, Mickey Knox; ***D:*** Roger Corman; ***W:*** F.X. Feeney, Roger Corman; ***C:*** Michael Scott, Armando Nannuzzi; ***M:*** Carl Davis; ***V:*** Terri Treas.

Frankenstein's Daughter *She Monster of the Night* **1958** Demented descendant of Dr. Frankenstein sets a den of gruesome monsters loose, including the corpse of a teenaged girl he revitalizes, as he continues the mad experiments of his forefathers. **85m/B VHS, DVD.** John Ashley, Sandra Knight, Donald Murphy, Felix Locher, Sally Todd, Harry Wilson; ***D:*** Richard Cunha; ***C:*** Meredith Nicholson; ***M:*** Nicholas Carras.

Frankenstein's Great Aunt Tillie **WOOF! 1983** An excrutiatingly bad send up of the Frankenstein saga with the good doctor about to be evicted from his estate because of back taxes. Gabor appears for a few seconds in a flashback. **99m/C VHS, DVD.** Donald Pleasence, Yvonne Furneaux, Aldo Ray, June Wilkinson, Zsa Zsa Gabor; ***D:*** Myron G. Gold; ***W:*** Myron G. Gold.

Frankenweenie **½ 1984 (PG)** "Frankenweenie" is the tale of a lovable spunky dog named Sparky and his owner, Victor Frankenstein. When Sparky is hit by a car, Victor brings him back to life through the use of electric shock. This affectionate parody of "Frankenstein" launched renowned director Burton's career. **27m/B VHS, DVD.** Shelley Duvall, Daniel Stern, Barret Oliver, Paul Bartel, Joseph Maher, Jason Hervey; ***D:*** Tim Burton; ***W:*** Tim Burton; ***C:*** Thomas Ackerman; ***M:*** Michael Convertino, David Newman.

Frankie and Johnny **1936** Based on the song of the same name, famed torch singer Morgan portrays a singer in a bordello who shoots her unfaithful lover. Release was delayed two years by the Hays Office's intervention in how a house of prostitution could be portrayed on screen. Too bad they reached an agreement. Not even Morgan's rendition of the title song redeems this. **68m/B VHS.** Helen Morgan, Chester Morris; ***D:*** Chester Erskine.

Frankie and Johnny **½ 1965** Elvis is a riverboat gambler/singer with lousy luck until Kovack changes the odds. This upsets his girlfriend Douglas who shoots him (but not fatally). Elvis wears period costumes, but this is otherwise similar to his contemporary films. ♫When the Saints Go Marching In; Look Out Broadway; Shout It Out; Frankie and Johnny; Chesay; Come Along; Petunia; The Gardner's Daughter; Beginner's Luck. **88m/C VHS, DVD.** Elvis Presley, Donna Douglas, Harry (Henry) Morgan, Audrey Christie, Anthony Eisley, Sue Ane Langdon, Robert Strauss, Nancy Kovack; ***D:*** Fred de Cordova; ***W:*** Alex Gottlieb; ***C:*** Jacques "Jack" Marquette; ***M:*** Fred Karger.

Frankie and Johnny **1991 (R)** Ex-con gets a job as a short-order cook and falls for a world-weary waitress. She doesn't believe in romance, but finally gives into his pleas for a chance and finds out he may not be such a bad guy after all. Nothing can make Pfeiffer dowdy enough for this role, but she and Pacino are charming together. In a change of pace role, Nelligan has fun as a fellow waitress who loves men. Based on the play "Frankie and Johnny in the Clair de Lune" by McNally who also wrote the screenplay. **117m/C VHS, DVD.** Al Pacino, Michelle Pfeiffer, Hector Elizondo, Nathan Lane, Kate Nelligan, Jane Morris, Greg Lewis, Al Fann, K. Callan, Phil Leeds, Tracy Reiner, Dey Young; ***D:*** Garry Marshall; ***W:*** Terrance McNally; ***C:*** Dante Spinotti; ***M:*** Marvin Hamlisch. British Acad. '91: Support. Actress (Nelligan); Natl. Bd. of Review '91: Support. Actress (Nelligan).

Frankie Starlight **½ 1995 (R)** Bernadette (Parillaud) leaves France after WWII, smuggled aboard an American troop ship. By the time the ship reaches Ireland, she's pregnant and gives birth to her dwarf son, Frankie, in Dublin. She's taken in by the family of customs officer Jack Kelly (Byrne), who instills in the boy a lifelong love of the stars. The adult Frankie (Walker) becomes a celebrity when he writes a novel combining his obsession with the cosmos and his mother's erotic history. Raymo adapts from his 1993 novel "The Dork of Cork." Great performances by both Pentony and Walker as the child and adult Frankies. **100m/C VHS.** *IR* Corban Walker, Alan Pentony, Gabriel Byrne, Anne Parillaud, Matt Dillon, Georgina Cates, Dearbhla Molloy, Niall Toibin, Rudi Davies; ***D:*** Michael Lindsay-Hogg; ***W:*** Chet Raymo, Ronan O'Leary; ***C:*** Paul Laufer; ***M:*** Elmer Bernstein.

Frantic *Elevator to the Gallows; Ascenseur pour L'Echafaud* **1958** From Louis Malle comes one of the first French New Wave film noir dramas. A man kills his boss with the connivance of the employer's wife, his lover, and makes it look like suicide. Meanwhile, teenagers have used his car and gun in the murder of a tourist couple and he is indicted for that crime. Their perfectly planned murder begins to unravel into a panic-stricken nightmare. A suspenseful and captivating drama. Director Malle's first feature film. Musical score by jazz legend Miles Davis. **92m/B VHS, DVD.** *FR* Maurice Ronet, Jeanne Moreau, Georges Poujouly; ***D:*** Louis Malle; ***C:*** Henri Decae; ***M:*** Miles Davis.

Frantic **1988 (R)** While in Paris, an American surgeon's wife is kidnapped when she inadvertantly picks up the wrong suitcase. Her kidnappers want their hidden tresure returned, which forces the husband into the criminal underground and into unexpected heroism when he seeks to rescue her. Contrived ending weakens on the whole, but Polanski is still master of the dark film thriller. **120m/C VHS, DVD.** Harrison Ford, Betty Buckley, John Mahoney, Emmanuelle Seigner, Jimmie Ray Weeks, Yorgo Voyagis, David Huddleston, Gerard Klein; ***D:*** Roman Polanski; ***W:*** Roman Polanski, Gerard Brach; ***C:*** Witold Sobocinski; ***M:*** Ennio Morricone.

Franz 1972 A French mercenary and an insecure woman struggle with a doomed love affair. In French with English subtitles. **90m/C VHS.** *FR* Daniele Evenou, Barbara, Louis Navarre, Jacques Brel; ***D:*** Jacques Brel; ***W:*** Paul Andreota, Jacques Brel; ***C:*** Alain Levent; ***M:*** Jacques Brel.

Frasier the Sensuous Lion *Frasier the Lovable Lion* **1973 (PG)** A zoology professor is able to converse with Frasier, a lion known for his sexual stamina and whose potency is coveted by a billionaire (shadow of monkey glands rejuvenation therapy). A fairly typical, if slightly risque, talking critter film. **97m/C VHS.** Michael Callan, Katherine Justice, Frank De Kova, Malachi Throne, Victor Jory, Peter Lorre Jr., Marc Lawrence; ***D:*** Pat Shields.

The Fraternity *The Circle* **2001 (R)** Despite the title, these aren't frat boys but a group of elite boarding school students who call themselves "The Circle" and run Runice Academy until headmaster Williams discovers their involvement in a cheating scandal and one of them is expelled. When the alleged informant winds up dead, another (Dunne) in the group decides he has to come clean about the group's other activities. **100m/C VHS, DVD.** Treat Williams, Robin Dunne, Gordon Currie; ***D:*** Sidney J. Furie. **VIDEO**

Fraternity Vacation **1985 (R)** Two college fraternity men show a nerd the greatest time of his life while he's on vacation in Palm Springs. **95m/C VHS, DVD.** Stephen Geoffreys, Sheree J. Wilson, Cameron Dye, Leigh McCloskey, Tim Robbins, Matt McCoy, Amanda Bearse, John Vernon, Nita Talbot, Barbara Crampton, Kathleen Kinmont, Max Wright, Julie Payne, Franklin Ajaye, Charles Rocket, Britt Ekland; ***D:*** James Frawley; ***W:*** Lindsay Harrison; ***C:*** Paul Ryan; ***M:*** Brad Fiedel.

Frauds 1/2 **1993 (R)** Collins is an immoral insurance investigator who takes his victims for everything he can. Then he meets a couple who are out to beat him at his own game. **94m/C VHS.** Phil Collins, Hugo Weaving, Josephine Byrnes; ***D:*** Stephan Elliott; ***W:*** Stephan Elliott; ***C:*** Geoff Burton; ***M:*** Guy Gross.

Frayed **2007 (R)** Really? It took five writers to come up with this slasher dreck? Small-town sheriff Pat Baker's worst nightmare comes true when his deranged son Kurt escapes from a psych hospital where he was incarcerated for the murder of his mother when he was only eight. Kurt (wearing a clown mask) runs into the woods and the sheriff is horrified when he figures out that daughter Sara is camping in the same area with some friends. As Kurt becomes even more unhinged, he goes on a killing spree. **111m/C DVD.** Tony Doupe, Kellee Bradley, Alena Dashiell, Aaron Blakely, Don Brady, Tasha Smith-Floe; ***D:*** Norb Caoili, Rob Portman; ***W:*** Norb Caoili, Rob Portman, Kurt Svennungsen, Dana Svennungsen, Dino Moore; ***C:*** Karel Bauer; ***M:*** Norb Caoili. **VIDEO**

Freaked *Hideous Mutant Freekz* **1993 (PG-13)** Bizarre little black comedy throws everything at the screen, hoping some of the gross-out humor will prove amusing (and some does). Greedy TV star Ricky Coogin (Winter) agrees to be the spokesman for E.E.S. Corporation, which markets a toxic green slime fertilizer to the third world. He's sent to South America to promote the product and is captured by the mad scientist proprietor (Quaid) of a mysterious sideshow, who douses him with the fertilizer. Before you know it he's an oozing half-man, half-beast, perfect to join other freaks as the latest attraction. Lots of yucky makeup. Reeves has an uncredited cameo as the Dog Boy. **80m/C VHS, DVD.** Alex Winter, Randy Quaid, Megan Ward, Michael Stoyanov, Brooke Shields, William Sadler, Derek McGrath, Alex Zuckerman, Karyn Malchus, Mr. T, Morgan Fairchild; ***Cameos:*** Keanu Reeves, Tom Stern, Tim Burns; ***D:*** Alex Winter, Tom Stern; ***W:*** Alex Winter, Tom Stern, Tim Burns; ***C:*** Jamie Thompson, Jene Omens; ***M:*** Kevin Kiner; ***V:*** Bob(cat) Goldthwait.

The Freakmaker *Mutations; The Mutation* **1973 (R)** Mad professor attempts to breed plants with humans in his lab and has the usual bizarre results. Experiments that fail go to Dunn, a dwarf who runs a freak show. Shamelessly includes real freaks as if plot was not strange enough. **90m/C VHS, DVD.** *GB* Donald Pleasence, Tom Baker, Brad Harris, Julie Ege, Michael Dunn, Jill Haworth, Olga Anthony, Lisa Collings, Scott Antony; ***D:*** Jack Cardiff; ***W:*** Edward Andrew (Santos Alcocer) Mann, Robert D. Weinbach; ***C:*** Paul Beeson; ***M:*** Basil Kirchin.

Freaks 1/2 *Nature's Mistakes; Forbidden Love; The Monster Show* **1932** The infamous, controversial, cult-horror classic about a band of circus freaks that exact revenge upon a beautiful aerialist and her strongman lover after enduring humiliation and exploitation. Based on Ted Robbins story "Spurs." It was meant to out-horror "Frankenstein" but was so successful that it was repeatedly banned. Browning's film may be a shocker but it is never intended to be exploitative since the "Freaks" are the only compassionate, loyal, and loving people around. **66m/B VHS, DVD.** Wallace Ford, Olga Baclanova, Leila Hyams, Roscoe Ates, Harry Earles, Henry Victor, Daisy Earles, Madame Rose (Dion) Dione, Daisy Hilton, Violet Hilton; ***D:*** Tod Browning; ***W:*** Al Boasberg, Willis Goldbeck, Leon Gordon, Edgar Allen Woolf; ***C:*** Merritt B. Gerstad. Natl. Film Reg. '94.

Freakshow **1995 (R)** Two teens wander into the sideshow at a local carnival and meet the Freakmaster (Hansen), whose grisly exhibits have equally grisly stories to tell. Campy horror with routine special effects. **102m/C VHS, DVD.** Gunnar Hansen, Veronica Carlson, Brian D. Kelly, Shannon Michelle Parsons; ***D:*** William Cooke, Paul Talbot.

Freaky Friday 1/2 **1976 (G)** A housewife and her teenage daughter inadvertently switch bodies and each then tries to carry on the other's normal routine. Mary Rodgers' popular book is brought to the screen with great charm in this above average Disney film. **95m/C VHS, DVD.** Barbara Harris, Jodie Foster, Patsy Kelly, John Astin, Dick Van Patten, Ruth Buzzi, Kaye Ballard, Charlene Tilton, James Van Patten; ***D:*** Gary Nelson; ***W:*** Mary Rodgers.

Freaky Friday **2003 (PG)** Worthy remake of the 1976 Disney original breathes some life into the body-switch genre. Curtis plays Tess, a widowed psychiatrist and mom to rebellious 15-year-old Anna (Lohan). Anna's upset that her mom is about to remarry. Following a fight over said wedding at a Chinese restaurant, mom and daughter are hexed by a cursed fortune cookie and wake up the next day in each other's bodies. After the initial shock wears off, the talented leads seem right at home in the other's role, resulting in more laughs than you'd expect from a Disney remake. Curtis is especially fun to watch, successfully tapping into her inner teen and kicking out the jams in Anna's garage band. Light comedy deftly blends with morality in fun family comedy. **93m/C VHS, DVD.** *US* Jamie Lee Curtis, Lindsay Lohan, Mark Harmon, Harold Gould, Chad Michael Murray, Ryan Malgarini, Stephen Tobolowsky, Christina Vidal, Rosalind Chao, Willie Garson, Dina Spybey; ***D:*** Mark S. Waters; ***W:*** Leslie Dixon, Heather Hach; ***C:*** Oliver Wood; ***M:*** Rolfe Kent.

Fred Claus **2007 (PG)** Vaughn attempts to bring his familiar shtick to pre-teens and fails miserably in this story about Santa's repo man brother, who's looking to make a quick buck in order to start a restaurant. Santa (Giamatti) offers Fred (Vaughn) money if he comes back to the North Pole to help with the Christmas rush, and something that fails to resemble hilarity ensues. The laughs are few, and the considerable talents of Vaughn, Giamatti, and fellow cast members Spacey, Weisz, and Bates are frittered, as the pic seems to rely exclusively on Vaughn's trademark big mouth and cliched family-movie sap. **115m/C DVD.** *US* Vince Vaughn, Paul Giamatti, Miranda Richardson, Rachel Weisz, John Michael Higgins, Kathy Bates, Trevor Peacock, Chris Bridges, Elizabeth Banks, Jeremy Swift, Elizabeth Berrington, Kevin Spacey; ***D:*** David Dobkin; ***W:*** Dan Fogelman; ***C:*** Remi Adefarasin; ***M:*** Christophe Beck.

Freddie the Frog 1/2 *Freddie as F.R.O.7* **1992 (G)** Prince Frederick's life is shattered when his father is killed by his evil Aunt Messina, who wants to rule the kingdom. She even changes Frederick into a frog—but he manages to escape her with the help of friendly sea monster Nessie. But Freddie discovers that he has also been given super-frog powers, just in time to save Britain's landmarks, which are disappearing thanks to Aunt Messina's spells. **72m/C VHS.** *GB* ***D:*** Jon Acevski; ***W:*** Jon Acevski, David Ashton; ***V:*** Ben Kingsley, Nigel Hawthorne, Jenny Agutter, John Sessions, Brian Blessed, Billie Whitelaw, Jonathan Pryce, Phyllis Logan, Michael Hordern; ***Nar:*** James Earl Jones.

Freddy Got Fingered **WOOF!** **2001 (R)** Green, making his feature directorial debut, is our hero, Gord, a dedicated slacker who refuses to get a job and move out of his father's (Torn) house. Green the director loves Green the "actor," almost as much as he loves human and animal bodily fluids—all of them. What he does to horses and elephants will poison forever your fond memories of trips to the zoo. He also enjoys oral sex, performed by a wheelchair-bound girlfriend, of course. Then, just to appeal to the family-values crowd, he falsely accuses his overbearing father of sexually abusing his younger brother. Taken in small doses, Green's act can induce "I can't believe I'm laughing at this"-type chuckles, but an hour and a half could cause permanent brain damage. Look what its apparently done to him! To say "Freddy" wallows in the gutter is to besmirch the gutter's good name. **88m/C VHS, DVD.** *US* Tom Green, Rip Torn, Harland Williams, Eddie Kaye Thomas, Julie Hagerty, Anthony Michael Hall, Marisa Coughlan; ***D:*** Tom Green; ***W:*** Tom Green, Derek Harvie; ***C:*** Mark Irwin; ***M:*** Mike Simpson. Golden Raspberries '01: Worst Picture, Worst Actor (Green), Worst Director (Green), Worst Screenplay.

Freddy vs. Jason 1/2 **2003 (R)** Highly anticipated cinematic showdown between Freddy Krueger and Jason Vorhees begins with the clever premise that Freddy is dying of neglect. The children of Elm Street have forgotten about him, so Freddy is ceasing to exist. Freddy gets it into his head to inject a little horror into the real world and summons Jason from whatever hell he's been languishing in and sets him loose. The only problem is that Jason is taking center stage, which displeases Freddy. Ronny Yu's frenetic direction sets a suitable pace, but after the setup, it all settles into standard "slasher film" mode until the climactic battle. Forgettable cast of victims adequately plays off of Robert Englund's scene-devouring Freddy. **97m/C VHS, DVD, UMD.** *US* Robert Englund, Ken Kirzinger, Monica Keena, Jason Ritter, Kelly Rowland, Katharine Isabelle, Brendan Fletcher, Tom Butler, Lochlyn Munro, James Callahan; ***D:*** Ronny Yu; ***W:*** Damian Shannon, Mark Swift; ***C:*** Fred Murphy; ***M:*** Graeme Revell.

Freddy's Dead: The Final Nightmare *A Nightmare on Elm Street 6: Freddy's Dead* **1991 (R)** Freddy's daughter journeys to Springwood, Ohio, to put a stop to her father's evil ways. Will she be able to destroy this maniac, or is a new reign of terror just beginning? The sixth film in the "Nightmare" series; followed by "Wes Craven's New Nightmare." **96m/C VHS, DVD.** Robert Englund, Lisa Zane, Shon Greenblatt, Lezlie (Dean) Deane, Ricky Dean Logan, Breckin Majer, Yaphet Kotto, Elinor Donahue, Roseanne, Johnny Depp, Alice Cooper, Tom Arnold; ***D:*** Rachel Talalay; ***W:*** Michael De Luca; ***C:*** Declan Quinn.

Frederick Forsyth's Icon 1/2 **2005 (PG-13)** Based on bestseller Frederick Forsyth's book Icon. Jason Monk (Swayze), an ex-CIA agent, comes out of retirement to save an entire country from the brink of ruin. Russian presidential candidate Igor Komarov (Bergin) promises his people a new Russia, but his plan is based on a secret "Black Manifesto" that lays a foundation for dictatorship and military rule, among other evils. Monk's also charged with seeking out Anatoli Grishin (Cross), an evil KGB officer whom Monk has a personal vendetta against. Forsyth fans may be disappointed by the many deviations from the book; breathtaking Russian scenery and some thrilling suspense may make up for it. **180m/C DVD.** Patrick Swayze, Patrick Bergin, Michael York, Ben Cross, Annika Peterson, Jeff Fahey, Joss Ackland; ***D:*** Charles Martin Smith; ***W:*** Adam Armus, Nora Kay Foster; ***C:*** David Cannell; ***M:*** Daniel Licht. **CABLE**

Free Amerika Broadcasting **1989** A drama about an alternate reality in which Richard Nixon was assassinated, leaving Spiro Agnew president. As a result, the country turns to violent revolution. **80m/C VHS.** Brian Kincaid; ***D:*** Dean Wilson.

Free and Easy 1/2 *Easy Go* **1930** Keaton plays the incompetent manager of a beauty contest winner (Page) from Gopher City, Kansas. Page and her overbearing mother, accompanied by Keaton, go to Hollywood to make the girl a star. They gatecrash the MGM studio where all cause havoc and it turns out Keaton is the one who lands in front of the cameras (Page has to settle for romancing Montgomery). Provides a behind-the-scenes look at the MGM studio, with a number of MGM stars making cameo appearances. **92m/B VHS, DVD.** Buster Keaton, Anita Page, Robert Montgomery, Trixie Friganza, Fred Niblo; ***Cameos:*** Cecil B. DeMille, Jackie Coogan, Lionel Barrymore, William Haines; ***D:*** Edward Sedgwick.

Free Enterprise 1/2 **1998 (R)** Funny and inventive semi-autobiographical tale of a couple of aspiring filmmakers facing 30 without a clue about becoming adults. Schlock screenwriter Robert (Weigel) and best bud, film editor Mark (McCormack), filter their existence through sci fi and '70s TV shows. The two are completely geeked by a chance meeting with their "Star Trek" idol William Shatner (who slyly pokes fun at his own persona), who offers them enouragement. The duo actually make some attempts at that grown-up thing by the clever finale. **114m/C VHS, DVD.** Eric McCormack, Rafer Weigel, William Shatner, Audie England, Patrick Van Horn, Jonathan Slavin, Phil LaMarr, Deborah Van Valkenburgh; ***D:*** Robert Meyer Burnett; ***W:*** Robert Meyer Burnett, Mark Altman; ***C:*** Charles L. Barbee; ***M:*** Scott Spock.

Free Grass *Scream Free!* **1969** A gang of thoughtless hippie drug smugglers and abusers escape from the police, drink acid-spiked wine, shoot each other, and have love-ins. **82m/C VHS.** Russ Tamblyn, Richard Beymer, Casey Kasem, Lana Wood, Warren Finnerty, Elizabeth Thompson, Lindsay Crosby, Jody McCrea; ***D:*** Bill Brame, John Lawrence; ***W:*** James Gordon White, Gerald Wilson; ***C:*** Austin McKinney.

Free Money **1999 (R)** Kinda dumb buddy comedy finds Bud (Sheen) and Larry (Church) stuck in North Dakota and forced to marry the twin daughters of local prison warden The Swede (Brando, overacting as usual). The two losers decide the best way to get away from their father-in-law's watchful eye is to rob a train loaded with cash. **94m/C VHS, DVD.** Charlie Sheen, Marlon Brando, Donald Sutherland, Thomas Haden Church, Mira Sorvino, David Arquette; ***D:*** Yves Simoneau; ***W:*** Tony Peck, Joseph Brutsman; ***C:*** David Franco.

Free of Eden 1/2 **1998** Successful New York businessman Poitier reluctantly agrees to mentor a troubled inner-city teenaged girl (played by Poitier's daughter). **97m/C VHS, DVD.** Sidney Poitier, Sydney Tamiia Poitier, Phylicia Rashad, Robert Hooks; ***D:*** Leon Ichaso; ***W:*** Delle Chatman, Yule Caise; ***C:*** Claudio Chea; ***M:*** Terence Blanchard. **CABLE**

Free Ride **1986 (R)** A kooky kid steals a sportscar to impress a girl, and gets involved with local hoods. They chase each other around. **92m/C VHS.** Gary Hershberger, Reed Rudy, Dawn Schneider, Peter DeLuise, Brian MacGregor; ***W:*** Robert Bell, Ron Zwang.

A Free Soul 1/2 **1931** Tippling litigator Barrymore helps low-life mobster Gable beat a murder rap, only to discover the hood has stolen his daughter's heart. Bargaining with his ditzy daughter, he vows to eschew the bottle if she'll stay away from good-for-nothing Gable. Directed by Brown, best known for his work with Garbo, and based on the memoirs of Adela Rogers St. John. The final courtroom scene—a cloak-and-gavel classic—cinched Barrymore's Oscar. Remade with Liz Taylor as "The Girl Who Had Everything" (although, ironically, the earlier version is the racier of the two). **94m/B VHS.** Norma Shearer, Leslie Howard, Lionel Barrymore, Clark Gable, James Gleason, Lucy Beaumont; ***D:*** Clarence Brown; ***C:*** William H. Daniels. Oscars '31: Actor (Barrymore).

Free Style 1/2 **2009 (PG)** Generic inspirational family/sports film that will probably appeal most to Bleu's fans. Hard-working Cale Bryant (Bleu) is forced to put his college plans on hold to help support his family—struggling single mom Jeanette (Parker) and cutie younger sis Bailey (Pettis). He's also determined to beat the odds and win a spot on the Grand National motocross racing team without sacrificing his family and friends while also making goo-goo eyes at bright hottie Alex (Echeverria). Both Bleu and Echeverria are appealing and can use the film as an eventual stepping stone to more complicated fare. **97m/C DVD.** *US CA* Sandra Echeverria, Corbin Bleu, Penelope Ann Miller, Madison Pettis, David Reivers, Tegan Moss, Jesse Moss, Jeff Nicholson; ***D:*** William Dear; ***W:*** Joshua Leibner, Jeff Nicholson; ***M:*** Stephen Endelman.

Free to Love **1925** Screen idol Bow plays a young woman, fresh out of prison, who is taken in by a kindly, affluent patron. But, as the silent drama axiom would have it, there's no escaping the past, and she's forced to defend her former life when her guardian is murdered. **61m/B VHS.** Clara Bow, Donald Keith, Raymond (Ray) McKee; ***D:*** Frank O'Connor.

Free, White, and 21 **1962** A black motel owner is accused of raping a white civil rights worker. Produced in a "pseudo-documentary" form which sometimes drags. **104m/B VHS.** Frederick O'Neal, Annalena Lund, George Edgely, John Hicks, Hugh Crenshaw, George Russell; ***D:*** Larry Buchanan.

Free Willy 1/2 **1993 (PG)** Sentimental story about a 12-year-old runaway (Richter) who befriends a whale. Should appeal to children for its heartwarming story and delightful sea acrobatics. An electronically operated stand-in whale was used for far-off shots; a domesticated performing whale named Keiko for the close-ups. Director Wincer was known to grumble about the temperamental Keiko during shooting. Suggested viewing for students of animal behavior. Proof that family films can make money, "Free Willy" placed tenth for total boxoffice receipts in 1993. **112m/C VHS, DVD.** Jason James Richter, Lori Petty, Jayne Atkinson, August Schellenberg, Michael Madsen; ***D:*** Simon Wincer; ***W:*** Keith A. Walker, Corey Blechman; ***C:*** Robbie Greenberg; ***M:*** Basil Poledouris. MTV Movie Awards '94: Song ("Will You Be There").

Free Willy 2: The Adventure Home 1/2 **1995 (PG)** While camping in the Pacific Northwest, Jesse is reunited with his orca-pal Willy, who has found a new home along with his whale siblings. But an offshore oil spill separates Willy from his family and threatens their lives, so his human friends must once again come to the rescue. All the principal characters are back, except for Willy (real name Keiko), who is recuperating from a skin virus in Mexico. Animatronics and Gump-like digital effects were used to replicate the real Willy. **98m/C VHS, DVD.** Jason James Richter, Michael Madsen, Jayne Atkinson, August Schellenberg, Jon Tenney, Elizabeth Pena; ***D:*** Dwight Little; ***W:*** Corey Blechman, John Mattson; ***C:*** Laszlo Kovacs; ***M:*** Basil Poledouris.

Free Willy 3: The Rescue 1/2 **1997 (PG)** Isn't this poor whale ever going to be left in peace? This time around an illegal whaling operation threatens Willie and his orca pod. But 17-year-old Jesse (Richter), who has a summer job as a whale tracker on a research vessel, is determined to rescue his friend, aided by 10-year-old Max (Berry), who's horrified to discover his commercial fisherman father (Kilpatrick) is one of the whalers. **86m/C VHS, DVD.** Jason James Richter, Vincent Berry, August Schellenberg, Annie Corley, Patrick Kilpatrick; ***D:*** Sam Pillsbury; ***W:*** John Mattson; ***C:*** Tobias Schliessler; ***M:*** Cliff Eidelman.

Free Zone 1/2 **2005** Three women with ethnic ties to the Middle East converge in Jordan and become traveling companions for dissimilar reasons. An American with Israeli roots, Rebecca (Portman) kicks things off with a 10-minute crying jag in a cab by the Wailing Wall, though her sorrow appears connected not to religion but to her break-up with her fiance after he makes an appalling admission to her. The cab driver is Hanna (a spirited Laslo), an Israeli woman who has endured the regional turmoil but needs to collect cash that an associate of her husband owes to her. Woman number three, Leila (Abbass), is a Palestinian who works at Hanna's husband's office, who informs Hanna that the associate has vanished, causing the women to embark on a road trip to the Free Zone to look for him—and the cash. While an interesting trip, the political lessons stall out along the way. **94m/C DVD.** *BE FR IS SP* Natalie Portman, Uri Klauzner, Carmen Maura, Hiam Abbass, Hanna Laslo, Makram Khoury, Aki Avni; ***D:*** Amos Gitai; ***W:*** Amos Gitai, Marie-Jose Sanselme; ***C:*** Laurent Brunet.

The Freebie **2010** Darren (Shepard) and Annie (Aselton) have been married for seven years and still appear annoyingly happy. Only they can't remember the last time they had sex so they decide each of them can take a night off to go out and fool around with a stranger. Set in L.A.'s Silverlake neighborhood. **m/C DVD.** *US* Dax Shepard, Ken Kennedy, Sean Nelson, Bellamy Young, Kate Aselton, Leonora Gershman, Marguerite Phillips,; ***D:*** Kate Aselton; ***W:*** Kate Aselton; ***C:*** Benjamin Kasulke; ***M:*** Julian Wass.

Freebie & the Bean 1/2 **1974 (R)** Two San Francisco cops nearly ruin the city in their pursuit of a numbers-running mobster. Top-flight car chases and low-level, bigoted humor combine. Watch for Valerie Harper's appearance as Arkin's wife. Followed by a flash-in-the-pan TV series. **113m/C VHS.** Alan Arkin, James Caan, Loretta Swit, Valerie Harper, Jack Kruschen, Mike Kellin; ***D:*** Richard Rush.

Freedom 1/2 **1982** A young man finds the price of freedom to be very high when he tries to escape from Australian society in a silver Porsche. **102m/C VHS.** *AU* Jon Blake, Candy (Candida) Raymond, Jad Capelja, Reg Lye, John Clayton, Charles "Bud" Tingwell, Chris Haywood; ***D:*** Scott Hicks; ***W:*** John Emery; ***C:*** Ron Johanson; ***M:*** Don Walker.

Freedom Is Paradise **1989** With his mother dead and his father missing, 13-year-old Sasha is growing up in a bleak reform school. Every time he runs away he is caught and severely beaten upon his return. When Sasha learns of his father's whereabouts he sets out on a 1,000 mile journey to the gulag-style prison where is father is being held. Bodrov's directorial debut. In Russian with English subtitles. **75m/C VHS.** *RU* Alexander Burejev, Vladimir Kosyrev, Svetlana Gajtan, Vitautas Tomkus; ***D:*** Sergei Bodrov; ***W:*** Sergei Bodrov; ***C:*** Yuri Skhirtladze. Montreal World Film Fest. '89: Film.

Freedom Road **1979** Drama about a Reconstruction Era ex-slave, portrayed by heavyweight champion Ali, who is elected to the U.S. Senate and subsequently killed while trying to obtain total freedom for his race. Based on a novel by Howard Fast. **186m/C VHS.** Ron O'Neal, Edward Herrmann, John McLiam, Ernest Dixon, Alfre Woodard, Kris Kristofferson, Muhammad Ali; ***D:*** Jan Kadar. **TV**

Freedom Song **2000** In Mississippi in 1961, Will Walker (Glover) is a black man both angry and afraid. Civil rights, freedom rights and increasing racial violence make for tense times for the Walker family as teenaged Owen (Shannon) is drawn to organizer Daniel Wall (Curtis-Hall). Complex, conflicted people and situations make for a fine drama. **150m/C VHS, DVD.** Danny Glover, Vondie Curtis-Hall, Vicellous Shannon, Loretta Devine, Glynn Turman, Stan Shaw, Michael Jai White, Rae'ven (Alyia Larrymore) Kelly, John Beasley, Jason Weaver, Marcello Thedford, David Strathairn; ***D:*** Phil Alden Robinson; ***W:*** Phil Alden Robinson, Stanley Weiser; ***M:*** James Horner. **CABLE**

Freedom Strike 1/2 **1998 (R)** Navy pilots Stone and MacDonald are sent on a covert mission to sabotage an Iraqui nuclear reactor before terrorists can use it. **93m/C VHS, DVD.** Michael Dudikoff, Tone Loc, Felicity Waterman; ***D:*** Jerry P. Jacobs. **VIDEO**

Freedom Writers 1/2 **2007 (PG-13)** Oh so earnest (yet affecting) dedicated teacher true story set in 1994. White-bread newbie Erin Gruwell (Swank) is unprepared for teaching freshman English to an ethnically diverse, underprivileged class at a Long Beach high school. In order to get their attention, Erin, inspired by "The Diary of Anne Frank," gives her students journals to write about their own lives in their own raw vernacular. A collection of entries is eventually published as "The Freedom Writers Diary," which continues to cause classroom/parental clashes for its eye-opening depictions of teen experience. Swank, complete with gleaming smile and pearls, is filled with can-do spirit while Dempsey is wasted as her neglected hubby. **123m/C DVD, Blu-ray Disc, HD DVD.** *US* Hilary Swank, Patrick Dempsey, Scott Glenn, Imelda Staunton, John Benjamin Hickey, Pat Carroll, April Lee Hernandez, Deance Wyatt, Mario, Vanetta Smith; ***D:*** Richard LaGravenese; ***W:*** Richard LaGravenese; ***C:*** Jim Denault; ***M:*** Mark Isham.

Freedomland 1/2 **2006 (R)** White girl (Moore) from "the right side of the tracks" walks into a medical center in the projects with the story of a carjacking/kidnapping of her son. Black detective Lorenzo (Jackson) must find out the truth and prevent a riot as the cops, one of whom (Eldard) is her brother, lock down the neighborhood. Tension is effectively built as Lorenzo works the case while trying to balance his allegiances to his instincts, his neighborhood, and his job. Jackson's presence is vital to keeping the movie from spinning out of control into preachy "good-for-you" territory. Still gets a bit heavy, and more than a little depressing. **113m/C DVD.** *US* Samuel L. Jackson, Julianne Moore, Edie Falco, Ron Eldard, William Forsythe, Aunjanue Ellis, Anthony Mackie, LaTanya Richardson Jackson, Clarke Peters; ***D:*** Joe Roth; ***W:*** Richard Price; ***C:*** Anastas Michos; ***M:*** James Newton Howard.

Freejack 1/2 **1992 (R)** Futuristic thriller set in the year 2009, where pollution, the hole in the ozone layer, and the financial gap between the social classes have grown to such horrific proportions that the rich must pillage the past to find young bodies to replace their own. Estevez is a young race car driver whose sudden death makes him an ideal candidate for this bizarre type of surgery. Once transported to the future, he becomes a "Freejack" who must run for his life. Good cast including Jagger and Hopkins brings this one up slightly. Adapted from the novel "Immortality Inc." by Robert Sheckley. **110m/C VHS, DVD.** Emilio Estevez, Mick Jagger, Rene Russo, Anthony Hopkins, Jonathan Banks, David Johansen, Amanda Plummer, Grand L. Bush, Frankie Faison, Esai Morales, John Shea; ***D:*** Geoff Murphy; ***W:*** Dan Gilroy, Ronald Shusett, Steven Pressfield; ***C:*** Amir M. Mokri; ***M:*** Michael Boddicker, Trevor Jones.

Freelance *Con Man* **1971** Robin Mitchell is a small-time con man on the fringes of London's underworld. He witnesses a brutal mob hit, which means they want him dead, and his girlfriend has decided it's just too dangerous being a part of his life. But Mitchell is convinced his luck will change for the better as he puts together a million-dollar long-shot that could secure him for life—if he survives. **91m/C VHS.** Ian McShane, Gayle Hunnicutt, Keith Barron, Alan Lake, Luan Peters; ***D:*** Francis Megahy.

Freeway 1/2 **1988 (R)** A nurse attempts to find the obsessive killer who shot her husband. The murderer phones a radio psychiatrist from his car, using Biblical quotes, while cruising for new victims. Okay thriller, based on the L.A. freeway shootings. **91m/C VHS, DVD.** Darlanne Fluegel, James Russo, Billy Drago, Richard Belzer, Michael Callan, Steve Franken, Kenneth Tobey, Clint Howard; ***D:*** Francis Delia; ***W:*** Larry Ketron, Darrell Fetty, Francis Delia; ***M:*** Joe Delia.

Freeway 1/2 **1995 (R)** Grubby modern retelling of "Little Red Riding Hood" finds surly 16-year-old Vanessa (Witherspoon) escaping from her parole officer to avoid foster care when the cops arrest her mom and stepdad. She takes the family car and heads off to grandma's but car trouble on the freeway leads to a ride from the big bad wolf—Bob Wolverton (Sutherland)—a serial killer preying on young women. Lots of lurid unpleasantness. **102m/C VHS, DVD.** Reese Witherspoon, Kiefer Sutherland, Brooke Shields, Wolfgang Bodison, Dan Hedaya, Amanda Plummer, Bokeem Woodbine, Brittany Murphy, Michael T. Weiss, Guillermo Diaz, Susan Barnes, Alanna Ubach, Conchata Ferrell, Tara Subkoff, Sydney Lassick; ***D:*** Matthew Bright; ***W:*** Matthew Bright; ***C:*** John Thomas; ***M:*** Danny Elfman.

Freeway 2: Confessions of a Trickbaby **1999 (R)** The 1995 film was a violent modern update of "Little Red Riding Hood" and the sequel is a twisted fairytale "Hansel and Gretel." Crystal (Lyonne) escapes from juvenile prison with cell buddy Cyclona (Celedonio) and heads to Tijuana where she hopes psychic Sister Gomez (Gallo) can cure her of her compulsion to murder. The body count rises a lot on their journey. As grubby and unappealing as its predecessor. **90m/C VHS, DVD.** Natasha Lyonne, Maria Celedonio, Vincent Gallo, David Alan Grier, Michael T. Weiss, John Landis, Max Perlich; ***D:*** Matthew Bright; ***W:*** Matthew Bright; ***C:*** Joel Ransom; ***M:*** Kennard Ramsey. **VIDEO**

The Freeway Maniac **1988 (R)** A low budget thriller about an escaped convict who ends up on a movie set where he continues his former career: murder. Music by former "Doors" guitarist Robby Krieger. **94m/C VHS.** Loren Winters, James Courtney, Shepard Sanders, Donald Hotton; ***D:*** Paul Winters; ***M:*** Robby Krieger.

Freeze-Die-Come to Life 1/2 *Zamri Oumi Voskresni* **1990** First feature film from Kanevski, who spent eight years in a labor camp before glasnost. The story of two children who overcome the crushing poverty and bleakness of life in a remote mining community with friendship and humor. Beautifully filmed images, fine acting, touching but never overly sentimental story. The title comes from a children's game of tag. In Russian with English subtitles. **105m/B VHS.** *RU* Pavel Nazarov, Dinara Drukarova; ***D:*** Vitaly Kanevski; ***W:*** Vitaly Kanevski; ***C:*** Vladimir Brylyakov; ***M:*** Sergei Banevich.

Freeze Frame 1/2 **1992** Doherty is a high school TV reporter who's determined to capture a biotech conspiracy on video in this funny, fast-paced action flick. Nothing objectionable here. **78m/C VHS.** Shannen Doherty, Charles Haid, Robyn Douglass, Seth Michaels; ***D:*** William Bindley; ***W:*** William Bindley.

Freeze Frame **2004 (R)** Sean Vail (Evans) was accused of multiple murders but released on a technicality. Ten years later, Sean's paranoia is in full bloom and he obsessively videotapes every moment of his life so he will have an alibi if it's ever needed, which happens when a new victim is discovered. But Sean can't account for his whereabouts because the tapes of those specific hours are mysteriously missing. Brit Evans is best known for his comedy so this psychothriller is a real departure. Strong visually, the flick falls apart at the end. **90m/C DVD.** *IR GB* Lee Evans, Sean McGinley, Rachael Stirling, Ian McNeice, Colin Salmon, Rachel O'Riordan; ***D:*** John Simpson; ***W:*** John Simpson; ***C:*** Mark Garret; ***M:*** Debbie Wiseman.

Freezer Burn: The Invasion of Laxdale **2008 (R)** Laxdale is a Canadian farming community where crop circles have been popping up in the cornfields and the temperature is unnaturally high. An odd oil company exec (Glover) is trying to buy the local grain silo but bitter former hockey player Bill Swanson (Green) refuses to sell. Then Bill stumbles across a dead alien wearing an oil company uniform and tries to warn the townspeople about what's really going on. **90m/C DVD.** *CA* Tom Green, Crispin Glover, Sarain Boylan, Scott Hylands, Paul J. Spence, David Brown; ***D:*** Grant Harvey; ***W:*** Grant Harvey; ***C:*** John Spooner; ***M:*** Michael Shields.

French Can-Can *Only the French Can!* **1955** Dramatically sparse but visually stunning depiction of the can-can's revival in Parisian nightclubs. Gabin plays the theatre impressario who discovers laundress Arnoul and decides to turn her into the dancing star of his new revue at the Moulin Rouge. In French with English subtitles. **93m/C VHS, DVD.** *FR* Jean Gabin, Francoise Arnoul, Maria Felix, Jean-Roger Caussimon, Edith Piaf, Patachou; ***D:*** Jean Renoir.

The French Connection 1/2 **1971 (R)** Popeye Doyle (Hackman) and his partner Buddy Russo (Scheider) are a couple of hard-nosed NYC narcotics detectives who stumble onto what turns out to be one of the biggest narcotics rings of all time, involving French mastermind Alain Charnier (Rey). Cat-and-mouse thriller will keep you on the edge of your seat; contains one of the most exciting chase scenes ever filmed. Hackman's portrayal of Doyle is exact and the teamwork with Scheider special. Based on a true story from the book by Robin Moore. Followed in 1975 by "French Connection 2." **102m/C VHS, DVD, Blu-ray Disc.** Gene Hackman, Roy Scheider, Fernando Rey, Tony LoBianco, Eddie Egan, Sonny Grosso, Marcel Bozzuffi; ***D:*** William Friedkin; ***W:*** Ernest Tidyman; ***C:*** Owen Roizman; ***M:*** Don Ellis. Oscars '71: Actor (Hackman), Adapt. Screenplay, Director (Friedkin), Film Editing, Picture; AFI '98: Top 100; British Acad. '72: Actor (Hackman); Directors Guild '71: Director (Friedkin); Golden Globes '72: Actor—Drama (Hackman), Director (Friedkin), Film—Drama; Natl. Bd. of Review '71: Actor (Hackman), Natl. Film Reg. '05;; N.Y. Film Critics '71: Actor (Hackman); Writers Guild '71: Adapt. Screenplay.

French Connection 2 **1975 (R)** New York policeman "Popeye" Doyle goes to Marseilles to crack a heroin ring headed by his arch nemesis, Frog One, whom he failed to stop in the United States. Dour, supergritty sequel to the 1971 blockbuster, and featuring one of Hackman's most uncompromising performances. **118m/C VHS, DVD, Blu-ray Disc.** Gene Hackman, Fernando Rey, Bernard Fresson; ***D:*** John Frankenheimer; ***W:*** Robert Dillon; ***C:*** Claude Renoir; ***M:*** Don Ellis.

The French Detective **1975** Two detectives, one an old-time tough guy and the other a young cynic, are after a ruthless politician and his pet hood. Grim but entertaining. **90m/C VHS.** *FR* Lino Ventura, Patrick Dewaere, Victor Lanoux; ***D:*** Pierre Granier-Deferre.

French Exit **1997 (R)** Another "meet cute" Hollywood romantic comedy. Neophyte screenwriters David Lake (Silverman) and Zina Hart (Amick) have a fender bender in an L.A. intersection. Flirtatious sparks fly amid their bickering but later they discover they're vying for the same big break script job. So will professional rivalry destroy the romantic fire? What do you think. **88m/C VHS.** Kurt Fuller, Beth Broderick, Jonathan Silverman, Madchen Amick, Molly Hagan; ***D:*** Daphna Kastner; ***W:*** Daphna Kastner, Michael Alan Lerner; ***C:*** Geza Sinkovics; ***M:*** Alex Wurman.

French Fried Vacation *Les Bronzes* **1979** Zany antics erupt when a group of unattached and consenting adults vacation in Africa. French with English subtitles. **90m/C VHS, DVD.** *FR* Josiane Balasko, Michel Blanc, Mariann (Marie-Anne) Chazel, Thierry Lhermitte, Gerard Jugnot, Dominique Lavanant, Christian Clavier; ***D:*** Patrice Leconte.

French Intrigue *Cannabis* **1970 (R)** International agents track drug lords from the U.S. to France in a so-so spy thriller. **90m/C VHS.** Serge Gainsbourg, Paul Nicholas, Gabriele Ferzetti, Jane Birkin, Curt Jurgens; ***D:*** Pierre Koralnik; ***W:*** Franz-Andre Burguet; ***C:*** Willy Kurant; ***M:*** Serge Gainsbourg.

French Kiss **1/2 1995 (PG-13)** Ultra cute Kate (Ryan) has a fear of flying but she's more afraid of losing her fiance (Hutton) to a newly met French babe. She jets off to Paris and on the way meets a dashing, but disheveled, French rogue (Kline). What happens next is predictable, but amusing just the same. Plot drags a bit in the middle, but the scenery and banter between Ryan and Kline are a pleasant enough diversion. Kline is at his charming best, while Ryan is typically perky. Watch for Spielvogel's stereotypically rude French hotel concierge. He's a hoot. **111m/C VHS, DVD.** Meg Ryan, Kevin Kline, Timothy Hutton, Jean Reno, Francois Cluzet, Renee Humphrey, Michael Riley, Susan Anbeh, Laurent Spielvogel; ***D:*** Lawrence Kasdan; ***W:*** Adam Brooks; ***C:*** Owen Roizman; ***M:*** James Newton Howard.

The French Lesson **1/2** *The Frog Prince* **1986 (PG)** A romantic British farce from a screenplay by cartoonist Simmonds, dealing with an English girl who goes to school in Paris and finds love. **90m/C VHS.** *GB* Alexandre Sterling, Jane Snowdon; ***D:*** Brian Gilbert; ***W:*** Posy S. Simmonds.

The French Lieutenant's Woman **1/2 1981 (R)** Romantic love and tragedy in the form of two parallel stories, that of an 19th-century woman who keeps her mysterious past from the scientist who loves her, and the lead actor and actress in the film of the same story managing an illicit affair on the set. Extraordinary performances and beautifully shot. Based on the John Fowles novel. **124m/C VHS, DVD.** Meryl Streep, Jeremy Irons, Leo McKern, Lynsey Baxter; ***D:*** Karel Reisz; ***W:*** Harold Pinter; ***C:*** Freddie Francis; ***M:*** Carl Davis. British Acad. '81: Actress (Streep); Golden Globes '82: Actress—Drama (Streep); L.A. Film Critics '81: Actress (Streep).

The French Line **1954** A millionairess beauty travels incognito while trying to sort out which men are after her money, and which ones aren't. The 3-D presentation of Russell's physique in skimpy costumes earned this the condemnation of the Catholic Legion of Decency, which pumped the box-office even higher. Lacks the charm of "Gentlemen Prefer Blonds," which it imitates. ♫Comment Allez-Vous; Well, I'll Be Switched; Any Gal From Texas; What Is This That I Feel?; With A Kiss; By Madame Fuelle; Wait Till You See Paris; Poor Andre; The French Line. **102m/C VHS.** Jane Russell, Gilbert Roland, Craig Stevens, Kim Novak, Arthur Hunnicutt, Scott Elliott, Joi Lansing; ***D:*** Lloyd Bacon.

French Postcards **1979 (PG)** Three American students study all aspects of French culture when they spend their junior year of college at the Institute of French Studies in Paris. By the same writers who penned "American Graffiti" a few years earlier. **95m/C VHS.** Miles Chapin, Blanche Baker, Valerie Quennessen, Debra Winger, Mandy Patinkin, Marie-France Pisier; ***D:*** Willard Huyck; ***W:*** Gloria Katz, Willard Huyck.

French Quarter **1/2 1978 (R)** A dual story about a young girl in the modern-day French Quarter of New Orleans who is also the reincarnation of a turn-of-the-century prostitute. Everyone gets to play two roles but this film is more curiosity than anything else. **101m/C VHS, DVD.** Bruce Davison, Virginia Mayo, Lindsay Bloom, Alisha Fontaine, Lance LeGault, Anne Michelle; ***D:*** Dennis Kane.

French Quarter Undercover **1985 (R)** Two undercover cops in New Orleans thwart a terrorist plot aimed at the World's Fair. **84m/C VHS.** Michael Parks, Bill Holiday; ***D:*** Joe Catalanotto.

French Silk **1/2 1994 (PG-13)** Homicide detective (Horsley) falls for a lingerie designer (Lucci) who's a murder suspect. Filmed on location in New Orleans. Made for TV production with additional footage. "R" rating is for nudity (not Lucci's). Based on the novel by Sandra Brown. **90m/C VHS, DVD.** Susan Lucci, Lee Horsley, Shari Belafonte, R. Lee Ermey, Sarah Marshall, Bobby Hosea, Jim Metzler, Joe Warfield, Paul Rosenberg; ***D:*** Noel Nosseck. **TV**

The French Touch **1/2 1954** Fernandel stars in this French farce about a shepherd who decides to open his own clip joint as a hairdresser and finds himself a hit among the Parisiennes. Fair to middling comedy. **84m/B VHS.** *FR* Fernandel, Renee Devillers, Georges Chamarat; ***D:*** Jean Boyer.

French Twist **1/2** *Bushwhacked; Gazon Maudit* **1995 (R)** Romantic comedy about housewife Loli (Abril), tiredly coping with her realtor/husband Laurent (Chabat) and their two sons. Then Loli meets appealing stranger Marijo (Balasko), a very matter-of-fact lesbian, and when she discovers her hubby is a chronic philanderer, Loli gets revenge by inviting Marijo to move in with them. Laurent realizes he loves his wife but she's having too much fun and there's finally an interesting showdown between Laurent and Marijo over Loli. The French title, which translates literally to "Cursed Lawn," is an old slang term for lesbian. French with subtitles. **100m/C VHS, DVD.** *FR* Victoria Abril, Alain Chabat, Josiane Balasko, Ticky Holgado; ***D:*** Josiane Balasko; ***W:*** Josiane Balasko, Telsche Boorman; ***C:*** Gerard de Battista; ***M:*** Manuel Malou. Cesar '96: Writing.

The French Way **1/2 1940** One of the legendary Baker's few films, in which she portrays a Parisian nightclub owner playing matchmaker for a young couple. In French with English subtitles. **72m/B VHS.** *FR* Josephine Baker, Micheline Presle, Georges Marchal; ***D:*** Jacques de Baroncelli.

The French Woman **1979 (R)** Soft-core story of blackmail, murder, and sex involving French cabinet ministers mixing passion and politics. From the director of "Emmanuelle." **97m/C VHS, DVD.** Francoise Fabian, Klaus Kinski; ***D:*** Just Jaeckin; ***M:*** Serge Gainsbourg.

Frenchman's Creek **1/2 1944** Adventure set in the 17th century features English noblewoman Lady Dona (Fontaine) fleeing her spineless husband Harry St. Columb (Forbes) and his lecherous friend, Lord Rockingham (Rathbone). She finds a Frenchman's ship anchored in a creek off her country estate and becomes dazzled by its dashing pirate captain (de Cordova). Unfortunately, the pirate is also a spy (since the Frenchies and the Brits are fighting as usual) and Rockingham discovers their secrets. When the Frenchman is captured, Lady Dona risks all to rescue him. Based on the novel by Daphne du Maurier and remade for British TV in 1998. **112m/C VHS.** Joan Fontaine, Arturo de Cordova, Basil Rathbone, Ralph Forbes, Nigel Bruce, Cecil Kellaway, Moyna MacGill; ***D:*** Mitchell Leisen; ***W:*** Talbot Jennings; ***C:*** George Barnes; ***M:*** Victor Young. **TV**

Frenchman's Creek **1/2 1998** Lady Dona St. Columb (Fitzgerald) is bored both with London society and her husband, Sir Harry (Fleet), so she and her children head for her family's estate on the Cornish coast. There, Dona discovers dashing French privateer, Jean Aubrey (Delon), is using a nearby cove to anchor his ship while he spies on the English. Dona and the pirate get very, very close and she decides to help him outwit the authorities. But soon Dona must choose between passion and duty. **120m/C VHS.** *GB* Tara Fitzgerald, Anthony Delon, Tim Dutton, James Fleet, Danny (Daniel) Webb, Jeremy Child; ***D:*** Ferdinand Fairfax; ***W:*** Patrick Harbinson; ***C:*** Chris Seager. **TV**

Frenchman's Farm **1/2 1987 (R)** A young woman witnesses a killing at a deserted farmhouse. When she tells the police, they tell her that the murder happened 40 years before. Average thriller that probably won't keep you on the edge of your seat. **90m/C VHS, DVD.** *AU* Tracey Tanish, David Reyne, John Meillon, Norman Kaye, Tui Bow; ***D:*** Ron Way.

Frenzy **1/2** *Latin Quarter* **1946** A sculptor, pushed over the brink of sanity when he discovers that his wife is having an affair, turns to his art for solace...and seals his wife's corpse in a statue. Creepy. **75m/B VHS, DVD.** *GB* Derrick DeMarney, Frederick Valk, Joan Greenwood, Joan Seton, Valentine Dyall, Martin Miller; ***D:*** Vernon Sewell; ***W:*** Vernon Sewell.

Frenzy **1972 (R)** The only film in which Hitchcock was allowed to totally vent the violence and perverse sexuality of his distinctive vision, in a story about a strangler stalking London women in the late '60s. Finch plays the convicted killer-only he's innocent and must escape prison to find the real killer. McGowen is wonderful as the put-upon police inspector. A bit dated, but still ferociously hostile and cunningly executed. **116m/C VHS, DVD.** *GB* Jon Finch, Barry Foster, Barbara Leigh-Hunt, Anna Massey, Alec McCowen, Vivien Merchant, Billie Whitelaw, Jean Marsh, Bernard Cribbins, Michael Bates, Rita Webb, Jimmy Gardner, Clive Swift, Madge Ryan, George Tovey, Noel Johnson; ***D:*** Alfred Hitchcock; ***W:*** Anthony Shaffer; ***C:*** Gilbert Taylor; ***M:*** Ronald Goodwin.

Frequency **1/2 2000 (PG-13)** In 1999, New York cop John (Caviezel) finds he can communicate with his dead father (Quaid) in 1969 through dad's old ham radio. Since his father was a fireman who died in a warehouse fire almost exactly 30 years ago, John decides to tell him how not to get killed. This leads to changes in the present (messing with the past always does), including the murder of John's mother by a serial killer. Father and son must solve and prevent the killings in the past and the present using their respective skills and, amazingly, John's knowledge of the 1969 World Series. It's all very convoluted and ridiculous (especially the ending), but the underlying sentiment, and the fine work of Caviezel and Quaid make it easy to suspend disbelief and go along for the ride. **117m/C VHS, DVD.** Dennis Quaid, James (Jim) Caviezel, Elizabeth Mitchell, Andre Braugher, Shawn Doyle, Noah Emmerich, Jordan Bridges, Melissa Errico, Daniel Henson; ***D:*** Gregory Hoblit; ***W:*** Toby Emmerich; ***C:*** Alar Kivilo; ***M:*** Michael Kamen.

Fresh **1/2 1994 (R)** Intelligent 12-year-old boy runs heroin in the morning and sells crack after school in a tough Brooklyn neighborhood. Enterprising young man draws life lessons from chess-hustler father Jackson and heroin-dealing mentor Esposito, so he looks for a way out of the dead-end business. First time director Yakin plays it straight, foregoing the usual Hollywood-style rap and automatic weapons approach to convey the message that circumstances can kill innocence just as effectively as a bullet. Startling but subdued atmosphere allows the plot and characters to become more complicated than first suspected. Excellent performance by newcomer Nelson as the kid. **114m/C VHS, DVD.** *FR* Samuel L. Jackson, Giancarlo Esposito, Sean Nelson, N'Bushe Wright, Ron Brice, Jean LaMarre, Luis Lantigua, Yul Vazquez, Cheryl Freeman; ***D:*** Boaz Yakin; ***W:*** Boaz Yakin; ***C:*** Adam Holender. Ind. Spirit '95: Debut Perf. (Nelson); Sundance '94: Special Jury Prize, Filmmakers Trophy.

Fresh Cut Grass **1/2 2004** Debut for writer/director Coppola is an overly earnest story about college grad and wannabe writer Zac (Wilke). After his father's death, Zac's biding his time cutting lawns while deciding what to do next. He finds romance with the exotically named Eastern Star (Hansz), who helps him on the path to adulthood. **101m/C DVD.** Katy Hansz, James McCaffrey, Bobby Cannavale, Dylan Bruno, David Wilke, Alicia Coppola; ***D:*** Matthew Coppola; ***W:*** Matthew Coppola; ***C:*** Tom Agnello.

Fresh Horses **1988 (PG-13)** A wrong-side-of-the-tracks Depression-era romance. McCarthy is the engaged college boy who falls for backwoods girl Ringwald, who turns out to have a destructive secret. **92m/C VHS, DVD.** Molly Ringwald, Andrew McCarthy, Patti D'Arbanville, Ben Stiller, Viggo Mortensen; ***D:*** David Anspaugh; ***M:*** David Foster.

Fresh Kill **1987** A young guy from Chicago goes to Hollywood, and gets mixed up in drugs and murder. **90m/C VHS.** Flint Keller, Patricia Parks; ***D:*** Joseph Merhi. **VIDEO**

The Freshman **1925** Country boy Lloyd goes to college and, after many comic tribulations, saves the day with the winning touchdown at the big game and wins the girl of his dreams. This was one of the comedian's most popular films. **75m/B VHS, DVD.** Harold Lloyd, Jobyna Ralston, Brooks Benedict, James Anderson, Hazel Keener; ***D:*** Fred Newmeyer, Sam Taylor; ***W:*** Sam Taylor. Natl. Film Reg. '90.

The Freshman **1/2 1990 (PG)** Brando, in an incredible parody of his Don Corleone character, makes this work. Broderick is a college student in need of fast cash, and innocent enough to believe that any work is honest. A good supporting cast and a twisty plot keep things interesting. Sometimes heavy handed with its sight gags, but Broderick and Brando push the movie to hilarious conclusion. Don't miss Bert Parks's musical extravaganza. **102m/C VHS, DVD.** Marlon Brando, Matthew Broderick, Penelope Ann Miller, Maximilian Schell, Bruno Kirby, Frank Whaley, Jon Polito, Paul Benedict, Richard Gant, B.D. Wong, Bert Parks; ***D:*** Andrew Bergman; ***W:*** Andrew Bergman; ***C:*** William A. Fraker; ***M:*** David Newman.

Freshman Orientation **1/2** *Home of Phobia* **2004 (R)** Would-be campus comedy that also seems to be trying (and failing) to teach a lesson on personal responsibility and identity. College freshman Clay (Huntington) is sure he's going to bag a lot of girls but he's a social zero on campus. Freshman Amanda (Doubleday) is a sorority pledge whose initiation includes picking up a certain type of campus outcast and taking him to a sorority party where humiliation is on the agenda. Amanda's supposed to bring a gay guy and mistakenly picks Clay, who goes along for the chance to be with a pretty girl. He gets lessons in gay behavior from outgoing bartender Rodney (Goodman) but eventually the ruse is exposed. Debut film for Shiraki. **91m/C DVD.** Sam Huntington, Kaitlin Doubleday, John Goodman, Heather Matarazzo, Marla

Sokoloff, Mike Erwin, Judy Tylor, Bryce Johnson; ***D:*** Ryan Shivaki; ***W:*** Ryan Shivaki; ***C:*** Amelia Vincent; ***M:*** Tomandandy.

Freud Leaving Home **1991** Freud (Roor) is the nickname of 25-year-old Angelique, who lives with her Jewish family in Stockholm. Problems erupt when her sister and brother return home for their mother's 60th birthday and all learn of her fatal illness. The siblings are forced to confront themselves and their relationships with each other and their mother. Swedish with subtitles. **100m/C VHS.** *SW* Gunilla Roor, Ghita Norby, Philip Zanden, Jessica Zanden; ***D:*** Suzanne (Susanne) Bier.

Frida **1/2 1984** The life of controversial Mexican painter Frido Kahlo is told via deathbed flashbacks using the artist's paintings to set the scenes. In Spanish with English subtitles. **108m/C VHS, DVD.** *SP* Ofelia Medina, Juan Jose Gurrola, Max Kerlow; ***D:*** Paul Leduc.

Frida **1/2 2002 (R)** Biography of nonconformist Mexican artist Frida Kahlo (Hayek) from her teen years to her death at the age of 44. The story relies heavily on her stormy marriage and continued relationship with famed muralist Diego Rivera (Molina). Director Julie Taymor also surrealistically brings to life several of Kahlo's paintings, although her glamorization of the famously uni-browed and mustachioed painter drew fire from ardent fans. Based on the book by Hayden Herrera. **120m/C VHS, DVD.** *US* Salma Hayek, Alfred Molina, Ashley Judd, Geoffrey Rush, Antonio Banderas, Roger Rees, Edward Norton, Valeria Golino, Mia Maestro, Saffron Burrows, Patricia Reyes Spindola, Margarita Sanz, Diego Luna; ***D:*** Julie Taymor; ***W:*** Gregory Nava, Anna Thomas, Clancy Sigeland, Diane Lake; ***C:*** Rodrigo Prieto; ***M:*** Elliot Goldenthal. Oscars '02: Makeup, Score; British Acad. '02: Makeup; Golden Globes '03: Score.

Friday **1/2 1995 (R)** It's "Boyz N' the Hood" meets "Good Times." Ice Cube wrote and stars as Craig in this humorous look into life in the 'hood. Craig's just lost his job and spends his time sitting on the porch with his pot smoking sidekick Smokey (Tucker), with the two getting mixed up in a variety of crazy antics involving their kooky neighbors. The laughs come at the expense of overworn cliches and sterotypical characters, but there's originality in the movie's energy and boldness (i.e. the local dope dealer is also the neighborhood ice cream man). To some, this "Friday" could be something to look forward to. **91m/C VHS, DVD, UMD.** Ice Cube, Chris Tucker, Bernie Mac, John Witherspoon, Regina King, Nia Long, Tommy (Tiny) Lister, Anna Maria Horsford, LaWanda Page; ***D:*** F. Gary Gray; ***W:*** DJ Pooh, Ice Cube; ***C:*** Gerry Lively; ***M:*** Frank Fitzpatrick.

Friday After Next **1/2 2002 (R)** Third installment of the series shows Christmas in the 'hood, as heroes Craig (Ice Cube) and Day-Day (Epps) are forced to take jobs as mall security guards after a ghetto Santa (Smiley) steals their presents and rent money. The usual brand of lowbrow humor is shoveled out in heaping piles and most of the regulars return, including John Witherspoon as Craig's chronically flatulent father. **85m/C VHS, DVD.** *US* Ice Cube, Mike Epps, John Witherspoon, Don "DC" Curry, Anna Maria Horsford, Clifton Powell, Terry Crews, BeBe Drake, Sommore, Starletta DuPois, K.D. Aubert, Katt Micah Williams, Rickey Smiley, Joel McKinnon Miller, Reggie Gaskins; ***D:*** Marcus Raboy; ***W:*** Ice Cube; ***C:*** Glen MacPherson; ***M:*** John Murphy.

Friday Foster **1/2 1975 (R)** A beautiful, young photographer investigates an assassination attempt and uncovers a conspiracy against black politicians. Based on the Chicago Tribune comic strip. **90m/C VHS, DVD.** Pam Grier, Yaphet Kotto, Thalmus Rasulala, Carl Weathers, Godfrey Cambridge; ***D:*** Arthur Marks; ***W:*** Orville H. Hampton; ***C:*** Harry J. May; ***M:*** Luchi De Jesus.

Friday Night *Vendredi Soir* **2002** Laure (Lemercier) is packing up her Paris apartment one wintery evening prior to moving in with her lover. She's a little uncertain about the upcoming changes as she heads out to dinner with friends. There's a public transport strike and a massive traffic jam, so Laure takes to watching the stranded commuters, one of whom is burly and calm Jean (Lindon). It's bitterly cold and Laure decides to offer Jean a ride. Laure also decides to cancel her plans and make new ones (the one-night stand kind) with Jean. Based on the novel by Emmanuele Bernheim. French with subtitles. **90m/C DVD.** *FR* Valerie Lemercier, Vincent Lindon; ***D:*** Claire Denis; ***W:*** Claire Denis, Emmanuele Bernheim; ***C:*** Agnes Godard; ***M:*** Dickon Hinchliffe.

Friday Night Lights **2004 (PG-13)** Excellent tale about West Texas and its love for high school football. Based on the 1990 nonfiction account written by H.G. Bissinger of the 1988 season of the Odessa-Permian Panthers team, the film showcases the be-all, end-all small town fervor for the game and the all-consuming impact that has on its teenaged players. Among those are arrogant star running back James "Boobie" Miles (Luke), shy and insecure quarterback Mike Winchell (Black), and troubled tailback Don Billingsley (Hedlund), who's abused by his alcoholic dad (country singer McGraw, making a notable debut). Thornton gives a fine performance as Coach Gaines, a reserved man who knows his job is on the line if the team doesn't make the state championship. **117m/C VHS, DVD, Blu-ray Disc, UMD, HD DVD.** *US* Billy Bob Thornton, Derek Luke, Jay Hernandez, Lucas Black, Garrett Hedlund, Connie Britton, Lee Jackson, Lee Thompson Young, Tim McGraw, Grover Coulson; ***D:*** Peter Berg; ***W:*** Peter Berg, David Aaron Cohen; ***C:*** Tobias Schliessler; ***M:*** Brian Reitzell, David Torn.

Friday the 13th **2009 (R)** The guys who brought you the remake of "Texas Chainsaw Massacre" no doubt want to reignite another franchise with this slasher re-do about a group of teens who encounter hockey-masked Jason Voorhees (Mears) at the boarded-up Camp Crystal Lake. Sadly, Jason barely had time to decompose after the last of the tired franchise's bombs before being dug up and trotted out to slaughter his way to the bank. The gritty, low-rent camp that was key to the first few has been replaced with high-tech, high-gloss production and a menace that takes itself too seriously. Even the standard gratuitous sex, violence and gore is overdone—a hack job for sure. **99m/C DVD.** *US* Jared Padalecki, Danielle Panabaker, Amanda Righetti, Travis Van Winkle, Derek Mears, Aaron Yoo, Willa Ford, Nana Visitor; ***D:*** Marcus Nispel; ***W:*** Mark Swift, Damian Shannon; ***C:*** Daniel Pearl; ***M:*** Steve Jablonsky.

Friday the 13th **1980 (R)** Notable as among the first in a very long series of slasher flicks, with effects by Tom Savini. A New Jersey camp reopens after it's been closed for 20 years after a history of "accidental" deaths. And the horror begins again. Six would-be counselors arrive to get the place ready. Each is progressively murdered: knifed, speared, and axed. Followed by numerous, equally gory sequels. **95m/C VHS, DVD.** Betsy Palmer, Adrienne King, Harry Crosby, Laurie Bartram, Mark Nelson, Kevin Bacon, Jeannine Taylor, Robbi Morgan, Peter Brouwer, Walt Gorney; ***D:*** Sean S. Cunningham; ***W:*** Victor Miller; ***C:*** Barry Abrams; ***M:*** Harry Manfredini.

Friday the 13th, Part 2 WOOF! 1981 (R) New group of teen camp counselors are gruesomely executed by the still undead Jason. Equally as graphic as the first installment; followed by several more gorefests. **87m/C VHS, DVD.** Amy Steel, John Furey, Adrienne King, Betsy Palmer, Kirsten Baker, Stu Charno, Warrington Gillette, Walt Gorney, Marta Kober, Bill Randolph, Jack Marks; ***D:*** Steve Miner; ***W:*** Ron Kurz; ***C:*** Peter Stein; ***M:*** Harry Manfredini.

Friday the 13th, Part 3 WOOF! 1982 (R) Yet another group of naive counselors at Camp Crystal Lake fall victim to the maniacal Jason. The 3-D effects actually helped lessen the gory effects, but this is still awful. Followed by more disgusting sequels. **96m/C VHS, DVD.** Dana Kimmell, Paul Kratka, Richard Brooker, Catherine Parks, Jeffrey Rogers, Tracie Savage, Larry Zerner; ***D:*** Steve Miner; ***W:*** Martin Kitrosser, Carol Watson; ***C:*** Gerald Feil.

Friday the 13th, Part 4: The Final Chapter WOOF! 1984 (R) Jason escapes from the morgue to once again slaughter and annihilate teenagers at a lakeside cottage. Preceded by three earlier "Friday the 13th" films, equally as graphic. The title's also a lie since there's several more sequels to look forward to. **90m/C VHS, DVD.** Erich Anderson, Judie Aronson, Kimberly Beck, Peter Barton, Tom Everett, Corey Feldman, Crispin Glover, Richard Brooker; ***D:*** Joseph Zito; ***W:*** Barney Cohen; ***C:*** Joao Fernandes.

Friday the 13th, Part 5: A New Beginning WOOF! 1985 (R) The hapless and anonymous residents of a secluded halfway house are the designated victims here. The sequels, and the sameness, never stop. See Part 6... **92m/C VHS, DVD.** John Shepherd, Melanie Kinnaman, Shavar Ross, Richard Young, Juliette Cummins, Corey Feldman, Carol Lacatell, Vernon Washington; ***D:*** Danny Steinmann; ***W:*** Danny Steinmann, David M. Cohen, Martin Kitrosser; ***C:*** Stephen Posey.

Friday the 13th, Part 6: Jason Lives WOOF! 1986 (R) One of the few youths not butchered by Jason digs him up and discovers he's not (and never will be) dead. Carnage ensues..and the sequels continue. **87m/C VHS, DVD.** Thom Mathews, Jennifer Cooke, David Kagen, Kerry Noonan, Renee Jones, Tom Fridley, C.J. Graham, Darcy Demoss; ***D:*** Tom McLoughlin; ***W:*** Tom McLoughlin; ***C:*** Jon Kranhouse; ***M:*** Harry Manfredini.

Friday the 13th, Part 7: The New Blood WOOF! 1988 (R) A young camper with telekinetic powers accidentally unchains Jason from his underwater lair with the now-familiar results. There's still another bloody sequel to go. **90m/C VHS, DVD.** Lar Park-Lincoln, Kevin Blair Spirtas, Susan Blu, Terry Kiser, Kane Hodder, Elizabeth Kaitan, John Otrin, Heidi Kozak; ***D:*** John Carl Buechler; ***W:*** Daryl Haney; ***C:*** Paul Elliott.

Friday the 13th, Part 8: Jason Takes Manhattan **1989 (R)** Yet another sequel, with the hockey-masked walking slaughterhouse transported to New York. Most of the previous action in the movie takes place on a cruise ship. This one is less gruesome than others in the series. Followed by "Jason Goes to Hell: The Final Friday." **96m/C VHS, DVD.** Kelly Hu, Jensen (Jennifer) Daggett, Scott Reeves, Peter Mark Richman, Barbara Bingham, Kane Hodder, Martin Cummins, Sharlene Martin, Vincent Craig Dupree; ***D:*** Rob Hedden; ***W:*** Rob Hedden; ***C:*** Bryan England.

Fridays of Eternity **1981** A romantic comedy about loyalty, fidelity, love, and lovers all with a tinge of the supernatural. In Spanish with English subtitles. **89m/C VHS.** *AR* Thelma Biral, Hector Alterio; ***D:*** Hector Olivera.

Fried Green Tomatoes **1991 (PG-13)** Two stories about four women, love, friendship, Southern charm, and eccentricity are untidily held together by wonderful performances. Unhappy, middle-aged Evelyn (Bates), meets the talkative 83-year-old Ninny Threadgoode (Tandy). Ninny reminisces about her Depression-era life in the town of Whistle Stop, Alabama and the two women, Idgie (Masterson) and Ruth (Parker), who ran the local cafe. Back-and-forth narrative as it tracks multiple storylines is occasionally confusing, though strong character development holds interest. Surprising box office hit adapted by Fannie Flagg from her novel "Fried Green Tomatoes at the Whistle Stop Cafe." **130m/C VHS, DVD.** Kathy Bates, Jessica Tandy, Mary Stuart Masterson, Mary-Louise Parker, Cicely Tyson, Chris O'Donnell, Stan Shaw, Gailard Sartain, Timothy Scott, Gary Basaraba, Lois Smith, Grace Zabriskie; ***D:*** Jon Avnet; ***W:*** Fannie Flagg, Carol Sobieski; ***C:*** Geoffrey Simpson; ***M:*** Thomas Newman.

Frieda **1/2 1947** An RAF officer brings his German wife home after the war and she is naturally distrusted by his family and neighbors. An interesting look at post-war bigotry. **97m/B VHS.** *GB* David Farrar, Glynis Johns, Mai Zetterling, Flora Robson, Albert Lieven; ***D:*** Basil Dearden.

Friend of the Family **1/2** *Elke* **1995** While backpacking across the U.S., Elke (O'Brien) is invited to stay in Malibu with the Stillman family—husband Jeff, wife Linda, and their 20-something children, Josh and Montana. Naturally, the sexy Elke becomes very involved with the family. **98m/C VHS, DVD.** Shauna O'Brien, C.T. Miller, Griffin (Griffen) Drew, Lisa Boyle; ***D:*** Edward Holzman; ***W:*** Edward Holzman, April Moskowitz; ***C:*** Kim Haun; ***M:*** Richard Bronskill.

Friend of the Family 2 **1996 (R)** Disturbed young woman decides to get revenge on the man who used and abandoned her by becoming his family's nanny. Also available in an unrated version. Ray used the pseudonym Nicholas Medina. **90m/C VHS, DVD.** Shauna O'Brien, Paul Michael Robinson, Jenna Bodnar, Jeff Rector; ***D:*** Fred Olen Ray; ***W:*** Henry Krinkle; ***C:*** Gary Graver.

Friendly Fire **1979** Based on a true story of an American family in 1970 whose soldier son is killed by "friendly fire" in Vietnam, and their efforts to uncover the circumstances of the tragedy. Touching and powerful, with an excellent dramatic performance by Burnett. **146m/C VHS.** Carol Burnett, Ned Beatty, Sam Waterston, Timothy Hutton; ***D:*** David Greene. **TV**

Friendly Persuasion *Except for Me and Thee* **1956** Earnest, solidly acted tale about a peaceful Quaker family struggling to remain true to its ideals in spite of the Civil War which touches their farm life in southern Indiana. Cooper and McGuire are excellent as the parents with Perkins fine as the son worried he's using his religion to hide his cowardice. Based on a novel by Jessamyn West. **140m/C VHS, DVD.** Gary Cooper, Dorothy McGuire, Anthony Perkins, Marjorie Main, Charles Halton; ***D:*** William Wyler; ***W:*** Michael Wilson; ***C:*** Ellsworth Fredericks; ***M:*** Dimitri Tiomkin. Cannes '57: Film.

Friends **1971 (R)** Ho-hum drama about an orphaned French girl and an unloved English boy who meet, become friends, and decide to run away together, setting up house in a deserted beach cottage. They even have a baby before they're discovered. Provides no insight into the teenagers dilemmas. Followed by "Paul and Michelle." **101m/C VHS.** *GB* Sean Bury, Anicee Alvina, Pascale Roberts, Sady Rebbot, Ronald Lewis; ***D:*** Lewis Gilbert; ***M:*** Elton John.

Friends **1995** Story of three South African women sharing an apartment in Johannesburg. Fox is a white political activist, Burgers, an Afrikaner archaeologist, and Kente, a black teacher. When Fox plants a bomb that takes two innocent lives, their loyalties are tested. Debut for director Proctor. **109m/C VHS.** Kerry Fox, Michele Burgers, Dambisa Kente; ***D:*** Elaine Proctor; ***W:*** Elaine Proctor.

Friends & Crocodiles **2005** Flashy real estate mogul Paul Reynolds (Lewis) is living a hedonistic lifestyle in 1980s London. He hires practical Lizzie Thomas (May) as his secretary but she's disturbed by his reckless, sometimes criminal, behavior and soon quits. Over a 20-year period, Paul's fortunes unravel while life is kinder to Lizzie, and the two maintain a sometimes strained friendship. **105m/C DVD.** *GB* Damian Lewis, Jodhi May, Robert Lindsay, Patrick Malahide, Eddie Marsan, Allan Corduner, Chris Larkin; ***D:*** Stephen Poliakoff; ***W:*** Stephen Poliakoff; ***C:*** Barry Ackroyd; ***M:*** Adrian Johnston. **TV**

Friends and Family **1/2 2001** Very broad comedy tries to shoehorn in a few too many subplots but it's slickly-done and harmless. Danny (Gartin) and Stephen (Lauren) are enforcers for New York mobster Victor Patrizzi (Lo Bianco), who has no problem with the fact that they are gay. Nor do Stephen's parents, who decide to make a surprise visit to the city to celebrate Mr. Torcelli's (Pellegrino) birthday. But what Stephen's parents don't know is what the two actually do for a living—the guys have been passing themselves off as caterers. With Patrizzi's assistance, they arrange a celebration that unexpectedly turns into an inept hostage situation. **87m/C VHS, DVD.** Greg Lauren, Christopher Gartin, Tony LoBianco, Rebecca Creskoff, Brian Lane Green, Meshach Taylor, Edward Hibbert, Beth Fowler, Frank Pellegrino, Tovah Feldshuh, Anna Maria Alberghetti, Frank Minucci, Patrick Collins; ***D:*** Kristen Coury; ***W:*** Joseph Triebwasser; ***C:*** John Leuba; ***M:*** Kurt Hoffman.

Friends & Lovers **1/2 1999** Nonsensical and mediocre would-be romantic comedy about wealthy widower, Richard (Rasche), who invites his estranged son, Ian

(Newbern), and his son's L.A. friends to spend Christmas with him at his Park City chalet. Everyone has some kind of sexual agenda except for Richard, who just wants to come to terms with Ian. **104m/C VHS, DVD.** David Rasche, George Newbern, Stephen Baldwin, Danny Nucci, Robert Downey Jr., Leon, Alison Eastwood, Suzanne Cryer, Neill Barry, Claudia Schiffer; ***D:*** George Haas; ***W:*** George Haas; ***C:*** Carlos Montaner; ***M:*** Emilio Kauderer.

Friends Forever 1986 Conformity, sexuality, and friendship are explored in this coming-of-age drama. Kristian is a shy, conformist 16-year-old, starting off at a new school. He finds himself drawn to two different young men who equally dominate his class. Henrik's androgynous sexual charm is equaled by his independence while the moody Patrick is the leader of a band of troublemakers. Kristian gains in self-confidence by their friendship but is tested when he learns Patrick is gay. **95m/C VHS.** *DK* Stefan Christian Henszelman, Claus Bender Mortensen, Thomas Elholm, Christine Skou; ***D:*** Stefan Christian Henszelman; ***C:*** Marcel Berga; ***M:*** Kim Sagild.

Friends, Lovers & Lunatics 1/2 *Crazy Horse; She Drives Me Crazy* **1989** A weekend turns into a romantic nightmare/laugh-fest when a man visits his ex-girlfriend and her new "friend," and winds up in a new romance himself. **87m/C VHS.** *CA* Daniel Stern, Deborah Foreman, Sheila McCarthy, Page Fletcher, Elias Koteas; ***D:*** Stephen Withrow.

Friends with Money 1/2 **2006 (R)** L.A.-set story about the friendship between three wealthy, married, middle-aged women and their slightly younger, unmarried, and decidedly not-rich pal. That's Olivia (Aniston), who has quit her teaching job in a fit of ennui to become a maid. Her friend Franny (Cusack) is a generous stay-at-home mom with a great marriage to Matt (Germann), while Jane (McDormand) is a continuously furious fashion designer whose metrosexual Brit hubby Aaron (McBurney) is suspected of being gay. Screenwriting partners Christine (Keener) and David (Isaacs) discover they don't even like each other as their marriage fractures. The women talk and support one another (and the actresses are great fleshing out some thin characters) but not much happens. **88m/C DVD.** *US* Jennifer Aniston, Joan Cusack, Catherine Keener, Frances McDormand, Jason Isaacs, Scott Caan, Simon McBurney, Greg Germann, Ty Burrell, Bob Stephenson; ***D:*** Nicole Holofcener; ***W:*** Nicole Holofcener; ***C:*** Terry Stacey; ***M:*** Craig Richey, Rickie Lee Jones. Ind. Spirit '07: Support. Actress (McDormand).

A Friendship in Vienna 1/2 **1988** The friendship of two young teenage girls, one Jewish, and the other the daughter of a Nazi collaborator, is tested as WWII looms over Europe and the Nazis begin their persecution of Austrian Jews. Adapted from the book "Devil in Vienna" by Doris Orgel. **100m/C VHS.** Jenny Lewis, Ed Asner, Jane Alexander, Stephen Macht, Rosemary Forsyth, Ferdinand "Ferdy" Mayne, Kamie Harper; ***D:*** Arthur Allan Seidelman; ***W:*** Richard Alfieri; ***Nar:*** Jean Simmons. **CABLE**

Fright *Spell of the Hypnotist* **1956** A woman—convinced that she died in 1889 as part of a suicide pact with Prince Rudolph of Austria—seeks help from a psychiatrist who promptly falls in love with her (didn't Freud say it was supposed to be the other way around?). **68m/B VHS, DVD.** Nancy Malone, Eric Fleming, Frank Marth, Humphrey Davis, Ned Glass, Norman Burton; ***D:*** W. Lee Wilder.

Fright *Night Legs* **1971** A baby-sitter is menaced by a mental hospital escapee. He turns out to be the father of the boy she is watching. Tense but violent thriller. **87m/C VHS, DVD.** *GB* Susan George, Honor Blackman, Ian Bannen, John Gregson, George Cole, Dennis Waterman, Tara Collinson, Maurice Kaufmann, Michael Brennan, Roger Lloyd-Pack; ***D:*** Peter Collinson; ***W:*** Tudor Gates; ***C:*** Ian Wilson; ***M:*** Harry Robinson.

Fright House **1989 (R)** Two stories of terror. "Fright House" features witches preparing an old mansion for a visit from the Devil. "Abandon" explains the prolonged youth of a teacher to her young student. **110m/C VHS.** Al Lewis, Duane Jones; ***D:*** Len Anthony.

Fright Night 1/2 **1985 (R)** It's Dracula-versus-the-teens time when Charley suspects that his new neighbor descends from Count Vlad's line. He calls in the host of "Fright Night," the local, late-night, horror-flick series, to help de-ghoul the neighborhood. But they have a problem when the vampire discovers their plans (and nobody believes them anyway). Sarandon is properly seductive as the bloodsucker. **106m/C VHS, DVD.** William Ragsdale, Chris Sarandon, Amanda Bearse, Roddy McDowall, Stephen Geoffreys, Jonathan Stark, Dorothy Fielding, Art Evans; ***D:*** Tom Holland; ***W:*** Tom Holland; ***C:*** Jan Kiesser; ***M:*** Brad Fiedel.

Fright Night 2 **1988 (R)** The sequel to the 1985 release "Fright Night," in which the harassed guy from the original film learns slowly that the vampire's sister and her entourage have come to roost around his college. Not quite as good as the original but the special effects are worth a look. **108m/C VHS, DVD.** Roddy McDowall, William Ragsdale, Traci Lind, Julie Carmen, Jon(athan) Gries, Russ Clark, Brian Thompson; ***D:*** Tommy Lee Wallace; ***W:*** Tommy Lee Wallace, Tim Metcalfe, Miguel Tejada-Flores; ***C:*** Mark Irwin; ***M:*** Brad Fiedel.

The Frightened City 1/2 **1961** Waldo Zhernikov (Lom) decides to unite all six of London's crime syndicates into one conglomerate that would control the city. But when he gets power-mad, rival gangster Harry Foulcher (Marks) breaks away and forms his own organization. Naturally, there's a war between the factions. Paddy Damion (Connery in an early role), one of Waldo's gunsels, is sent to get rid of Foulcher. **91m/B VHS, DVD.** *GB* Herbert Lom, John Gregson, Sean Connery, Alfred Marks, Yvonne Romain, Kenneth Griffith, Olive McFarland, Frederick Piper, John Stone, David Davies, Tom Bowman, Robert Cawdron, Norrie Paramor; ***D:*** John Lemont; ***W:*** Leigh Vance; ***C:*** Desmond Dickinson; ***M:*** Norrie Paramor.

The Frightened Man **1952** Julius Roselli (Walsh) is kicked out of Oxford after a drunken brawl, which disappoints his junk dealer father (Victor). Soon Julius gets involved with a gang of jewel thieves who use his father as their fence. Neither father nor son knows of the other's involvement, which figures in when the old man tips off the police about an upcoming robbery after being cut out of the deal. **69m/B DVD.** *GB* Dermot Walsh, Charles Victor, Barbara Murray, John Blythe, Michael Ward, Thora Hird, John Horsley; ***D:*** John Gilling; ***W:*** John Gilling; ***C:*** Monty Berman; ***M:*** John Lanchbery.

The Frightened Woman **1971** Wealthy Sayer (Leroy) likes to get his sexual kicks by playing master and slave in his villa outside Rome. When his usual hired call girl isn't available, he decides to lure a lovely journalist (Lassander) into his domination games. Dubbed into English. **90m/C VHS, DVD.** *IT* Phillippe LeRoy, Dagmar Lassander; ***D:*** Piero Schivazappa; ***W:*** Piero Schivazappa; ***M:*** Stelvio Cipriani.

The Frighteners 1/2 **1996 (R)** Con man Frank Bannister (Fox) has a unique scam—he works with a group of ghosts who haunt a home until Frank comes along to drive them out, for the right price. But the small town of Fairwater is plagued by a serial killer's evil spirit and Frank and his spiritual cronies face the challenge of getting rid of the ghost before the police decide to get rid of Frank. Interesting horror-comedy takes a lot of twists and turns to get where its going, but the payoff in gore and humor is worth it for fans of the genre. New Zealand helmer Jackson makes his American directorial debut. **106m/C VHS, DVD, HD DVD.** Michael J. Fox, Trini Alvarado, Peter Dobson, Dee Wallace, John Astin, Jeffrey Combs, Troy Evans, Chi McBride, Jake Busey, R. Lee Ermey, Jim Fyfe; ***D:*** Peter Jackson; ***W:*** Peter Jackson, Fran Walsh; ***C:*** Alun Bollinger, John Blick; ***M:*** Danny Elfman.

Frightmare 1/2 *Frightmare 2* **1974 (R)** A seemingly quiet British couple do indulge in one strange habit—they're cannibals. Released on video as "Frightmare 2" to avoid confusion with the 1981 film. **86m/C VHS, DVD.** *GB* Deborah Fairfax, Kim Butcher, Rupert Davies, Sheila Keith; ***D:*** Pete Walker; ***W:*** David McGillivray; ***C:*** Peter Jessop; ***M:*** Stanley Myers.

Frightmare **1981 (R)** Great horror star dies, but he refuses to give up his need for adoration and revenge. **84m/C VHS, DVD.** Ferdinand "Ferdy" Mayne, Luca Bercovici, Nita Talbot, Peter Kastner; ***D:*** Norman Thaddeus Vane.

The Fringe Dwellers 1/2 **1986 (PG)** An Aborigine family leave their shantytown and move to the white, middle-class suburbs of Australia, encountering prejudice and other difficulties. Well acted and interesting but the ending's a letdown. **98m/C VHS.** *AU* Kristina Nehm, Justine Saunders, Bob Maza, Kylie Belling, Denis Walker, Ernie Dingo; ***D:*** Bruce Beresford; ***W:*** Bruce Beresford, Rhoisin Beresford; ***M:*** George Dreyfus.

Frisco Jenny **1932** Pregnant Jenny (Chatterton) loses both her father and lover during the 1906 San Francisco earthquake. Without a home, she eventually gives up her illegitimate son to a wealthy couple and becomes a successful bordello madam on the Barbary Coast. Son Dan (Cook) grows up to be a crusading district attorney, but a criminal cohort (Calhern) of Jenny's wants him dead. Her actions save Dan but lead to her own downfall. **70m/B DVD.** Ruth Chatterton, Donald Cook, Louis Calhern, James Murray, Hallam Cooley, Harold Huber, Helen Jerome Eddy, Berton Churchill; ***D:*** William A. Wellman; ***W:*** Wilson Mizner, Robert Lord; ***C:*** Sid Hickox.

The Frisco Kid *No Knife* **1979 (R)** An innocent orthodox rabbi (Wilder) from Poland is sent to the wilds of San Francisco during the 1850s gold rush to lead a new congregation. He lands in Philadelphia, joins a wagon train and is promptly robbed and abandoned. He eventually meets up with a not-too-bright robber (Ford) who finds himself unexpectly befriending the man and undergoing numerous tribulations in order to get them both safely to their destination. This isn't a laugh riot and some scenes fall distinctly flat but Wilder is sweetness personified and lends the movie its charm. **119m/C VHS, DVD.** Gene Wilder, Harrison Ford, Ramon Bieri, Val Bisoglio, George DiCenzo, Penny Peyser, William (Bill) Smith; ***D:*** Robert Aldrich; ***W:*** Michael Elias; ***C:*** Robert B. Hauser.

Frisk **1995** Disturbing depictions of sex/murder fantasies come courtesy of letters written by Dennis (Gunther), a part of the L.A. S&M scene, to his former boyfriend, Julian (Laplante). Just exactly how far Dennis has gone with some of his like-minded sexual partners is the question. Has he become the killer he claims to be? Adapted from Dennis Cooper's 1991 novel. **87m/C VHS, DVD.** Michael Gunther, Jaie Laplante, Craig Chester, Parker Posey, James Lyons, Alexis Arquette, Raoul O'Connell, Michael Stock; ***D:*** Todd Verow; ***W:*** Todd Verow, Jim Dwyer, George LaVoo; ***C:*** Greg Watkins.

Fritz the Cat **1972** Ralph Bakshi's animated tale for adults about a cat's adventures as he gets into group sex, college radicalism, and other hazards of life in the '60s. Loosely based on the underground comics character by Robert Crumb. Originally X-rated. **77m/C VHS, DVD.** ***D:*** Ralph Bakshi; ***W:*** Ralph Bakshi; ***C:*** Ted C. Bemiller, Gene Borghi; ***M:*** Ed Bogas, Ray Shanklin; ***V:*** Skip Hinnant, Rosetta LeNoire, John McCurry.

Frog and Wombat 1/2 **1998** Alli, whose codename is "Frog," tries to convince her best friend Jane, code named "Wombat," that their new school principal (Cox) is up to no good, especially when she discovers the man's niece is missing. So the intrepid duo prepare to investigate. **90m/C VHS.** Katie Stuart, Ronny Cox, Lindsay Wagner, Ross Malinger, Emily Lipoma; ***D:*** Laurie Agard; ***W:*** Laurie Agard; ***C:*** Ray Preziosi; ***M:*** Greg Edmonson.

Frogs 1/2 **1972 (PG)** An environmental photographer working on a small island in Florida interrupts the birthday celebration of a patriarch. He and the folks at the party soon realize that various amphibians animals in the surrounding area are going berserk and attacking humans. One of the first environmentally motivated animal-vengeance films, and one of the best to come out of the '70s. **91m/C VHS, DVD.** Ray Milland, Sam Elliott, Joan Van Ark, Adam Roarke, Judy Pace, Lynn Borden, Mae Mercer, David Gilliam, George Skaff, Holly Irving; ***D:*** George McCowan; ***W:*** Robert Blees, Robert Hutchison; ***C:*** Mario Tosi; ***M:*** Les Baxter.

Frogs for Snakes **1998 (R)** Self-conscious black comedy about New York loan shark Al Santana (Coltrane) who also spends his time as a wanna-be East Village theatrical impressario. And how everybody who works for Al as a collector is even more desperate to be an actor, including his struggling ex-wife Eva (Hershey). And how all the characters suddenly break into monologues from their favorite movies. And how none of this makes much sense and the actors have really done better work elsewhere. **98m/C VHS.** Barbara Hershey, Robbie Coltrane, Harry Hamlin, Ian Hart, John Leguizamo, Lisa Marie, Debi Mazar, David Deblinger, Ron Perlman, Clarence Williams III, Justin Theroux, Nicholas Chinlund, Mike Starr, Taylor Mead; ***D:*** Amos Poe; ***W:*** Amos Poe; ***C:*** Enrique Chediak.

Frolics on Ice *Everything's on Ice* **1939** Pleasant musical-comedy about a family man saving to buy the barber shop at which he works. Irene Dare is featured in several ice skating production numbers. **65m/B VHS.** Roscoe Karns, Lynne Roberts, Irene Dare, Edgar Kennedy, Eric Linden, George Meeker, Bobby Watson, Mary Currier; ***D:*** Erle C. Kenton; ***W:*** Sherman Lowe, Adrian Landis; ***C:*** Russell Metty.

From a Far Country: Pope John Paul II **1981** TV biography of Polish Pope John Paul II begins in 1926 as Karol Wojtila celebrates Christmas with his father and continues through the important highlights of his life. **120m/C VHS, DVD.** *PL GB* Sam Neill, Christopher Cazenove, Warren Clarke, Kathleen Byron, Maurice Denham, Lisa Harrow; ***D:*** Krzysztof Zanussi; ***W:*** Krzysztof Zanussi; ***C:*** Slawomir Idziak; ***M:*** Wojciech Kilar; ***Nar:*** Michael Jayston. **TV**

From Beyond **1986 (R)** A gruesome, tongue-in-cheek adaptation of the ghoulish H.P. Lovecraft story. Scientists discover another dimension through experiments with the pineal gland. From the makers of "Re-Animator," and just as funny. **90m/C VHS.** Jeffrey Combs, Barbara Crampton, Ted (Theodore) Sorel, Ken Foree, Carolyn Purdy-Gordon, Bunny Summers, Bruce McGuire; ***D:*** Stuart Gordon; ***W:*** Dennis Paoli, Brian Yuzna; ***C:*** Mac Ahlberg; ***M:*** Richard Band.

From Beyond the Grave *Creatures* **1973 (PG)** This horror compendium revolves around a mysterious antique shop whose customers experience various supernatural phenomena, especially when they try to cheat the shop's equally mysterious owner. **98m/C VHS, DVD.** *GB* Peter Cushing, David Warner, Ian Bannen, Donald Pleasence, Margaret Leighton, Lesley-Anne Down, Diana Dors, Ian Ogilvy; ***D:*** Kevin Connor.

From Dusk Till Dawn 1/2 **1995 (R)** Escaped cons Seth and Richie Gecko (Clooney and Tarantino) pick up an ex-preacher (Keitel) and his two kids (Lewis and Liu) as hostages en route to their Mexican rendezvous spot, a raunchy biker joint run (unbenownst to them) by vampires. Feels like two movies in one, as Rodriguez's and Tarantino's styles don't necessarily mesh as much as they coexist. The first half features Tarantino's gift for snappy dialogue and somewhat sympathetic scumbags while the barroom finale shows off Rodriguez's mastery of the go-for-broke action set piece. Clooney proves the jump from TV to movies can be made successfully. Penned by Tarantino in 1990 during his video store days, he used the fee to get "Reservoir Dogs" off the ground. **108m/C VHS, DVD, UMD.** George Clooney, Quentin Tarantino, Harvey Keitel, Juliette Lewis, Ernest Liu, Fred Williamson, Richard "Cheech" Marin, Salma Hayek, Michael Parks, Tom Savini, Kelly Preston, John Saxon, Danny Trejo, Tia Texada; ***D:*** Robert Rodriguez; ***W:*** Quentin Tarantino; ***C:*** Guillermo Navarro; ***M:*** Graeme Revell. MTV Movie Awards '96: Breakthrough Perf. (Clooney).

From Dusk Till Dawn 2: Texas Blood Money *Texas Blood Money* **1998 (R)** Buck (Patrick) and his partner-in-crime Luther (Whitaker) decide to get a few bad men together and knock over a bank in Mexico. However, the group unwittingly come into contact with the vampire denizens of the Titty Twister bar and soon join the ranks of the undead. Except for Buck, who's somehow managed to avoid having the bite put on him—for now. Direct-to-video sequel is set two weeks after the first film's carnage. **88m/C VHS, DVD.** Robert Patrick,

Bo Hopkins, Muse Watson, Duane Whitaker, Raymond Cruz, Tiffani(-Amber) Thiessen, Brett Harrelson, Danny Trejo, Bruce Campbell; **D:** Scott Spiegel; **W:** Duane Whitaker, Scott Spiegel; **C:** Philip Lee; **M:** Joseph Williams. **VIDEO**

From Dusk Till Dawn 3: The Hangman's Daughter 1999 **(R)** This is actually a prequel to the "From Dusk Till Dawn" mayhem. In 1914, a group of refugees wind up in an isolated Mexican saloon, "La Tetilla del Diablo," that's the home of Santanico Pandemonium, the Queen of the Vampires (Braga). Oh, and the hangman's daughter is lovely Esmeralda (Celi), who doesn't know that Santanico is her mom. **94m/C VHS, DVD.** Michael Parks, Sonia Braga, Marco Leonardi, Rebecca Gayheart, Temuera Morrison, Lenny Y. Loftin, Danny Trejo, Ara Celi; **D:** P.J. Pesce. **VIDEO**

From Hell 2001 **(R)** The Hughes brothers take on the legend of Jack the Ripper in this grisly period thriller. Inspector Abberline (Depp) is the fictional opium-addled detective charged with finding the notorious killer of London's ladies of the night in 1888. With the help of his police sidekick Godley (Coltrane) and the cockney hooker-with-a-heart-of-gold Mary (Graham), Abberline pries into the medical community, the royal family and other less respectable areas in his search for the Ripper. Beautiful visuals and taut suspense raise this effort a notch above other adaptions of the material. Based on a graphic novel (a.k.a. fancy-schmancy comic book) by Alan Moore and Eddie Campbell. **121m/C VHS, DVD, Blu-ray Disc.** *US* Johnny Depp, Heather Graham, Ian Holm, Robbie Coltrane, Ian Richardson, Jason Flemyng, Katrin Cartlidge, Terence Harvey, Susan Lynch, Lesley Sharp, Annabelle Apsion; **D:** Albert Hughes, Allen Hughes; **W:** Terry Hayes, Rafael Yglesias; **C:** Peter Deming; **M:** Trevor Jones.

From Hell It Came WOOF! **1957** And to hell it should return for complete mind-numbing stupidity. Scientists studying residue left from an atomic bomb blast on a South Sea island are befriended by chief's son Kimo who gets killed by witch doctor Tano for breaking tribal law. Kimo curses said doctor and comes back as a tree stump spirit/monster (because a tree grew on the grave) and lumbers around getting revenge. **71m/B DVD.** Gregg (Hunter) Palmer.

From Hell to Borneo 1/2 **1964 (PG)** A mercenary must defend his secluded island from pirates and gangsters. **90m/C VHS.** George Montgomery, Torin Thatcher, Julie Gregg, Lisa Moreno; **D:** George Montgomery.

From Hell to Victory **1979 (PG)** Group of friends of different nationalities vow to meet each year in Paris on the same date but WWII interrupts their lives and friendships. Director Lenzi used the alias Hank Milestone. Good battle scenes but nothing special. **100m/C VHS, DVD.** *SP FR* George Peppard, George Hamilton, Horst Buchholz, Jean-Pierre Cassel, Capucine, Sam Wanamaker, Anny (Annie Legras) Duperey, Ray Lovelock; **D:** Umberto Lenzi.

From Here to Eternity **1953** Complex, hard-hitting look at the on and off-duty life of soldiers at the Army base in Honolulu in the days before the Pearl Harbor attack. There's sensitive Pvt. Prewitt (Clift), his always in trouble best friend Maggio (Sinatra), and their good-guy top sergeant (Lancaster) who just happens to be having a torrid affair with the commander's wife (Kerr). Prewitt, meanwhile, is introduced to a club "hostess" (Reed) who is a lot more vulnerable than she's willing to admit. A movie filled with great performances. Still has the best waves-on-the-beach love scene in filmdom. Based on the novel by James Jones, which was toned down by the censors. **118m/B VHS, DVD.** Burt Lancaster, Montgomery Clift, Frank Sinatra, Deborah Kerr, Donna Reed, Ernest Borgnine, Philip Ober, Jack Warden, Mickey Shaughnessy, George Reeves, Claude Akins, Harry Bellaver, John Dennis, Tim Ryan, John Bryant, John Cason, Doug(las) Henderson, Robert Karnes, Robert J. Wilke, Carleton Young, Merle Travis, Arthur Keegan, Barbara Morrison, Tyler McVey; **D:** Fred Zinnemann; **W:** Daniel Taradash; **C:** Burnett Guffey; **M:** George Duning. Oscars '53: B&W Cinematog., Director (Zinnemann), Film Editing, Picture, Screenplay, Sound, Support. Actor (Sinatra), Support. Actress (Reed); AFI '98: Top 100; Directors Guild '53: Director (Zinnemann); Golden Globes '54: Support. Actor (Sinatra), Natl. Film Reg. '02;; N.Y. Film Critics '53: Actor (Lancaster), Director (Zinnemann), Film.

From Here to Eternity 1/2 **1979 (PG-13)** From here to eternity...and back on the silver screen. Remake of the 1953 classic is based on James Jones's novel about life on a Hawaiian military base just before WWII. Decent actioner, but no Oscar-winner this time around. **110m/C VHS.** Natalie Wood, Kim Basinger, William Devane, Steve Railsback, Peter Boyle, Will Sampson, Andy Griffith, Roy Thinnes, Barbara Hershey; **D:** Buzz Kulik; **W:** Harold Gast. **TV**

From Here to Maternity 1/2 **1985** A soap opera-based spoof about modern maternity. Three women want to be pregnant but their significant others aren't interested in paternity. **40m/C VHS.** Carrie Fisher, Arleen (Arlene) Sorkin, Lauren Hutton, Griffin Dunne, Paul Reiser; **D:** Tom Schiller. **TV**

From Hollywood to Deadwood **1989 (R)** A beautiful starlet is kidnapped and the private eye searching for her discovers blackmail and danger. **90m/C VHS.** Scott Paulin, Jim Haynie, Barbara Schock; **D:** Rex Pickett; **W:** Rex Pickett; **C:** Peter Deming.

From Justin to Kelly WOOF! **2003 (PG)** Justin Guarini and Kelly Clarkson hurry to cash in on their "American Idol" success with another remake of "Where the Boys Are." Justin and Kelly chase romance between ludicrous dance numbers. In the pantheon of bad pop star flicks, this ranks well south of Elvis's worst fare, and even manages to sneak under the Unholy Trinity of Vanilla Ice-Mariah-Britny. **90m/C VHS, DVD.** Justin Guarini, Kelly Clarkson, Katherine Bailess, Anika Noni Rose, Greg Siff, Brian Dietzen; **D:** Robert Iscove; **W:** Kim Fuller; **C:** Francis Kenny; **M:** Michael Wandmacher.

From Noon Till Three 1/2 **1976 (PG)** A change of pace role for Bronson as a two-bit gunfighter in a spoof of western legends. Bronson has a brief romance with Ireland who, believing him dead, fictionalizes their relationship in a series of books and builds the mediocre Dorsey into a western hero. When he turns up alive no one, including Ireland, believes that he is the real Dorsey and he's gradually driven crazy. Good script, weak direction but Bronson is likeable. **99m/C VHS.** Charles Bronson, Jill Ireland, Douglas Fowley, Stan Haze, Damon Douglas; **D:** Frank D. Gilroy; **W:** Frank D. Gilroy; **C:** Lucien Ballard; **M:** Elmer Bernstein.

From Other Worlds 1/2 **2004** Dull sci-fi comedy. Depressed Brooklyn housewife Joanne believes she has been abducted by aliens and decides to meet with a group of fellow abductees, who include Abraham. They bond and begin to look for clues, meeting an alien who gives them advice on saving Earth from destruction. **88m/C DVD.** Cara Buono, Isaach de Bankole, David Lansbury, Joel de la Fuente, Robert Peters, Melissa Leo; **D:** Barry Strugatz; **W:** Barry Strugatz; **C:** Morris Flam; **M:** Pierre Foldes.

From Paris With Love **2010 (R)** James (Rhys Meyers) is a desk jockey at the American embassy in Paris who longs to be a CIA field agent. He gets his chance when he is called to spring loose-cannon operative Charlie (Travolta) from French customs agents. The two then team up to foil plots by Chinese drug smugglers and Pakistani bombers. The confused plot is merely an excuse for Travolta to chew up the scenery and spray bullets and catchphrases at various stuntmen. The action is chaotic and the humor isn't very funny in this lame attempt at a buddy flick/thriller. Acceptable for those who just want to see gunplay and explosions, but those who prefer a sensible plot may want to send this one packing. **92m/C DVD.** John Travolta, Jonathan Rhys Meyers, Richard Durden, Amber Rose Revah, Kasia Smutniak, Yin Bing; **D:** Pierre Morel; **W:** Adi Hasak; **C:** Michel Abramowicz; **M:** David Buckley.

From Russia with Love 1/2 **1963 (PG)** Bond is back and on the loose in exotic Istanbul looking for a super-secret coding machine. He's involved with a beautiful Russian spy and has the SPECTRE organization after him, including villainess Rosa Klebb (she of the killer shoe). Lots of exciting escapes but not an overreliance on the gadgetry of the later films. The second Bond feature, thought by many to be the best. **125m/C VHS, DVD, Blu-ray Disc.** *GB* Sean Connery, Daniela Bianchi, Pedro Armendariz Sr., Lotte Lenya, Robert Shaw, Eunice Gayson, Walter Gotell, Lois Maxwell, Bernard Lee, Desmond Llewelyn, Nadja Regin, Alizia Gur, Martine Beswick, Leila; **D:** Terence Young; **W:** Johanna Harwood, Richard Maibaum; **C:** Ted Moore; **M:** John Barry.

From the Dead of Night **1989** A spooky chiller about a near-death experience. Fashion designer Wagner narrowly escapes death but gets close enough to the other side that six of the dead feel cheated that she didn't join them. They decide to rectify the mistake and Wagner is pursued by the shadowy figures. Based on the novel "Walkers" by Gary Bradner. **192m/C VHS, DVD.** Lindsay Wagner, Bruce Boxleitner, Diahann Carroll, Robert Prosky, Robin Thomas, Merritt Butrick, Joanne Linville; **D:** Paul Wendkos. **TV**

From the Earth to the Moon **1958** A mad scientist invents a new energy source and builds a rocket which takes him, his daughter, and two other men for some adventures on the moon. Based on the novel by Jules Verne. **100m/C VHS.** George Sanders, Joseph Cotten, Debra Paget, Don Dubbins; **D:** Byron Haskin; **W:** Robert Blees.

From the Earth to the Moon **1998** Executive producer Tom Hanks shows off his fascination with the space program in this 12-part series covering the Apollo space program through the 1960s and '70s. Covers behind-the-scenes at NASA, the heroics of the astronauts and their missions, and the families that are left behind to wait and worry. On six cassettes. **720m/C VHS, DVD.** David Andrews, Bryan Cranston, Timothy Daly, Al Franken, Tony Goldwyn, Chris Isaak, Cary Elwes, Brett Cullen, Robert John Burke, Peter Scolari, Nick Searcy, Lane Smith, Dan Lauria, Mark Rolston, Mason Adams, Ronny Cox, Dakin Matthews, Kevin Pollak, Ben Marley, Joe Spano, Daniel Hugh-Kelly, Stephen (Steve) Root, Dann Florek, John Slattery, Ted Levine, Ann Cusack, Jo Anderson, James Rebhorn, Mark Harmon, Rita Wilson, Tom Amandes, John Aylward, Dylan Baker, Adam Baldwin, Reed Birney, Betsy Brantley, Bart Braverman, David Brisbin, Jimmy Buffett, Dan E. Butler, David Clennon, Gary Cole, Matt Craven, Wendy Crewson, Blythe Danner, Dave Foley, Jack Gilpin, John Michael Higgins, Peter Horton, Clint Howard, Zeljko Ivanek, Tcheky Karyo, John Carroll Lynch, Ann Magnuson, Joshua Malina, Andrew Masset, DeLane Matthews, Paul McCrane, Doug McKeon, Jay Mohr, Kieran Mulroney, Holmes Osborne, Conor O'Farrell, Elizabeth Perkins, Ethan Phillips, Andrew Rubin, Alan Ruck, Diana Scarwid, Grant Shaud, Cynthia Stevenson, Tom Verica, Gareth Williams, JoBeth Williams, Max Wright, Steve Zahn; **D:** Tom Hanks, David Frankel, Lili Fini Zanuck, Graham Yost, Frank Marshall, Jon Turteltaub, Gary Fleder, David Carson, Sally Field, Jonathan Mostow; **W:** Tom Hanks, Graham Yost, Stephen Katz, Remi Aubuchon, Al Reinert, Andy Wolk, Jeffrey Alladin Fiskin, Karen Janszen, Jonathan Marc Feldman; **C:** Gale Tattersall; **M:** Michael Kamen, Mark Mancina. **CABLE**

From the Edge of the City **1998** Sasha (Papadopoulos) is a teenaged emigre from Russia, who's working the Athens streets as a hustler. His older (and ruthless) mentor Giorgos (Papoulidis) is a pimp and offers Sasha the chance to move up by temporarily turning over the management of one of his girls—fellow emigre, Natasha (Tzimou). But Sasha, who isn't nearly as hardened as some of his friends, struggles not to become emotionally involved with the girl, to disastrous effect. Greek with subtitles. **94m/C VHS, DVD.** *GR* Stathis Papadopoulos, Dimitris Papoulidis, Theadora Tzimou, Costas Cotsianidis; **D:** Constantine Giannaris; **W:** Constantine Giannaris; **C:** George Argiroiliopoulos; **M:** Akis Daoutis.

From the Hip **1986 (PG)** A young lawyer (Nelson) gets the chance of a lifetime when his office assigns a murder case to him. The only problem is that he suspects his client is very guilty indeed and must discover the truth without breaking his code of ethics. Nelson's courtroom theatrics are a bit out of hand, as he flares his nostrils at every opportunity. The movie is encumbered by a weak script and plot as well as a mid-story switch from comedy to drama. **111m/C VHS, DVD.** Judd Nelson, Elizabeth Perkins, John Hurt, Ray Walston; **D:** Bob (Benjamin) Clark; **W:** Bob (Benjamin) Clark, David Kelly; **C:** Dante Spinotti; **M:** Paul Zaza.

From the Journals of Jean Seberg **1995** An imaginary look at the life of the ill-fated actress, who began her career as a 17-year-old, miscast in Otto Preminger's "Saint Joan," achieved fame in Godard's "Breathless," and became a suicide at age 40 in 1979. Seberg (Hurt) dispassionately narrates her life story as she views film clips, from small-town Iowa teenager to would-be star, through abusive relationships, drugs and drinking, political activisim, and FBI harassment. **97m/C VHS, DVD.** Mary Beth Hurt; **D:** Mark Rappaport; **W:** Mark Rappaport; **C:** Mark Daniels.

From the Life of the Marionettes **1980 (R)** A repressed man in a crumbling marriage rapes and kills a young prostitute. Another look at the powers behind individual motivations from Bergman, who uses black and white and color to relate details of the incident. **104m/C VHS, DVD.** *SW* Robert Atzorn, Christine Buchegger, Martin Benrath, Rita Russek, Lola Muethel, Walter Schmidinger, Heinz Bennent; **D:** Ingmar Bergman; **W:** Ingmar Bergman; **C:** Sven Nykvist.

From the Manger to the Cross **1915** This version of the Passion play was the first film to be done on location in Palestine. Re-enacts the Nativity, the flight into Egypt, and the crucifixion. Color-tinted. **71m/B VHS, DVD.** R. Henderson-Bland, Alice Hollister, Gene Gauthier; **D:** Sidney Olcott; **W:** Gene Gauthier, Sidney Olcott. Natl. Film Reg. '98.

From the Mixed-Up Files of Mrs. Basil E. Frankweiler 1/2 **1995 (PG)** Runaway siblings (Barnwell and Lee) secretly hide out in a New York art museum. They get caught up in trying to determine the authenticity of a sculpture (could it be the work of Michelangelo?) and turn to the statue's last owner, elusive art patron Mrs. Basil E. Frankweiler (Bacall). Based on the Newbery Award-winning novel by E.L. Konigsburg. Made for TV. **92m/C VHS, DVD.** Lauren Bacall, Jean Marie Barnwell, Jesse Lee; **D:** Marcus Cole. **TV**

From the Terrace 1/2 **1960** Newman is a wealthy Pennsylvania boy who goes to New York and marries into even more money and social position when he weds Woodward. He gets a job with her family's investment company and neglects his wife for business. She turns to another man and when he goes home for a visit he also finds a new romance which leads to some emotional soul searching. The explicitness of O'Hara's very long novel was diluted by the censors and Newman's performance is a stilted disappointment. Loy, as Newman's alcoholic mother, earned the best reviews. **144m/C VHS, DVD.** Paul Newman, Joanne Woodward, Myrna Loy, Ina Balin, Felix Aylmer, Leon Ames, George Grizzard, Patrick O'Neal, Barbara Eden, Mae Marsh; **D:** Mark Robson; **W:** Ernest Lehman; **C:** Leo Tover; **M:** Elmer Bernstein.

The Front **1976 (PG)** Woody is the bookmaker who becomes a "front" for blacklisted writers during the communist witch hunts of the 1950s in this satire comedy. The scriptwriter and several of the performers suffered blacklisting themselves during the Cold War. Based more or less on a true story. **95m/C VHS, DVD.** Woody Allen, Zero Mostel, Herschel Bernardi, Michael Murphy, Danny Aiello, Andrea Marcovicci; **D:** Martin Ritt; **W:** Walter Bernstein; **C:** Michael Chapman; **M:** Dave Grusin.

The Front Line **2006** Joe (Ebouaney), a political refugee from the Congo, is working as a bank security guard in Dublin. Psycho Eddie (Frain) and his gang kidnap Joe's family, using them as leverage to make Joe their inside man for their heist. Only Joe isn't the innocent he seems and when things go wrong, he utilizes an underground network of fellow African immigrants to track the gang down, including crime boss Erasmus

(Kae-Kazim), another Congolese native. **90m/C DVD.** *GB IR* Eriq Ebouaney, James Frain, Gerard McSorley, Ian McElhinney, Hakeem Kae-Kazim, Fatou N'Diaye, Bryan Eli Sebunya; ***D:*** David Gleeson; ***W:*** David Gleeson; ***C:*** Volker Tittel; ***M:*** Patrick Cassidy.

Front of the Class 🦴🦴 1/2 **2008** Inspirational Hallmark Hall of Fame drama based on a true story. Brad Cohen's outbursts are regarded by his stern father (Williams) and his teachers as simple misbehavior, although his mother (Heaton) believes otherwise. Eventually Brad is diagnosed with Tourette's, a little understood neurological disorder. Based on his own experiences, Brad wants to become a teacher but must struggle with acceptance in both his professional and personal lives. **95m/C DVD.** Patricia Heaton, Treat Williams, Sarah Drew, Kathleen York, Joseph Chrest, Dominic Scott Kay, Jimmy Wolk; ***D:*** Peter Werner; ***W:*** Thomas (Tom) Rickman; ***C:*** Paul Elliott; ***M:*** Ernest Troost. **TV**

The Front Page 🦴🦴🦴 1/2 **1931** The original screen version of the Hecht-MacArthur play about the shenanigans of a battling newspaper reporter and his editor in Chicago. O'Brien's film debut here is one of several hilarious performances in this breathless pursuit of an exclusive with an escaped death row inmate. **101m/B VHS, DVD.** Adolphe Menjou, Pat O'Brien, Edward Everett Horton, Mae Clarke, Walter Catlett; ***D:*** Lewis Milestone; ***C:*** Hal Mohr.

The Front Page 🦴🦴 1/2 **1974 (PG)** A remake of the Hecht-MacArthur play about the managing editor of a 1920s Chicago newspaper who finds out his ace reporter wants to quit the business and get married. But first an escaped convicted killer offers the reporter an exclusive interview. **105m/C VHS, DVD.** Jack Lemmon, Walter Matthau, Carol Burnett, Austin Pendleton, Vincent Gardenia, Charles Durning, Susan Sarandon; ***D:*** Billy Wilder; ***W:*** I.A.L. Diamond, Billy Wilder; ***C:*** Jordan Cronenweth; ***M:*** Billy May.

Frontier Days 🦴 1/2 **1934** Cody goes undercover to capture the leader of a gang of stagecoach robbers. He also manages to capture a killer along the way. **60m/B VHS.** Bill Cody, Ada Ince, Wheeler Oakman; ***D:*** Sam Newfield.

Frontier Fugitives 🦴 1/2 **1945** When a trapper is murdered—allegedly by Indians—the Texas Rangers ride in to investigate. **58m/B VHS.** Tex Ritter, Dave O'Brien, Guy Wilkerson, Lorraine Miller, I. Stanford Jolley, Jack Ingram; ***D:*** Harry Fraser.

Frontier Horizon 🦴🦴 **1939** Wayne and the Three Mesquiteers help out ranchers whose land is being bought up by crooked speculators. **55m/B VHS, DVD.** John Wayne, Jennifer Jones, Ray Corrigan, Raymond Hatton; ***D:*** George Sherman.

Frontier Justice 🦴🦴 **1935** Gibson is the foolish son of a cattle owner who has been forced into an insane asylum because of a battle over water rights. Naturally, he must take on responsibility and rescue his father. **56m/B VHS, DVD.** Hoot Gibson, Richard Cramer; ***D:*** Robert McGowan.

Frontier Law 🦴 1/2 **1943** Hayden and the boys ride into town to clean out the bad guys and clear a friend wrongly accused of murder. **55m/B VHS.** Russell Hayden, Jennifer Holt, Dennis Moore, Fuzzy Knight, Jack Ingram, Hal Taliaferro; ***D:*** Elmer Clifton; ***W:*** Elmer Clifton.

Frontier of Dawn 🦴 1/2 *La Frontiere de L'aube* **2008** An unhappy love triangle with some silly supernatural elements. Photographer Francois (Garrel, son of the director) is hired to shoot actress Carole (Smet) who, despite her recent marriage, is all too eager to begin an affair. Shallow Francois is willing to oblige though Carole is soon shown to be sexy-but-crazy. French with subtitles. **106m/B DVD.** *FR* Louis Garrel, Laura Smet, Clementine Poidatz, Emmanuel Broche, Olivier Massart, Eric Rulliat; ***D:*** Philippe Garrel; ***W:*** Philippe Garrel, Arlette Langmann, Marc Cholodenko; ***C:*** William Luctchansky; ***M:*** Jean-Claude Vannier.

Frontier Outlaws 🦴🦴 **1944** A gang of villains is selling stolen cattle, and Crabbe poses as an interested buyer to catch them in the act. Laughs are provided by Lynn as a judge, and "Fuzzy" St. John as Crabbe's sidekick. **58m/B VHS, DVD.** Buster Crabbe, Al "Fuzzy" St. John, Frances Gladwin, Marin Sais, Charles "Blackie" King, Jack Ingram, Kermit Maynard, Edward Cassidy, Emmett Lynn, Budd Buster; ***D:*** Sam Newfield.

Frontier Pony Express 🦴🦴 **1939** Roy and Trigger do their best to help the Pony Express riders who are being attacked by marauding gangs in California during the time of the Civil War. Plenty of action here. **54m/B VHS.** Roy Rogers; ***D:*** Joseph Kane.

Frontier Scout 🦴🦴 **1938** Action-packed western has Wild Bill Hickock, portrayed by former opera singer Houston, forcing Lee's surrender in the Civil War before pursuing cattle rustlers out West. **60m/B VHS, DVD.** George Houston, Mantan Moreland; ***D:*** Sam Newfield.

Frontier Uprising 🦴 1/2 **1961** Stunning cinematography makes up for weak narrative in this otherwise routine oater. Davis stars as a frontier scout battling hordes of Mexicans and Indians while trying to gain control of California for the U.S. Based on the short story "Kit Carson" by George Bruce. **68m/B VHS.** Jim Davis, Nancy Hadley, Ken Mayer, Nestor Paiva, Don O'Kelly; ***D:*** Edward L. Cahn; ***W:*** Owen Harris.

Frontier Vengeance 🦴 1/2 **1940** Barry is falsely accused of murder and works to clear his name while at the same time romancing a stagecoach driver who's trying to win a race with a rival stagecoach line. **54m/B VHS.** Donald (Don "Red") Barry, Betty Moran, George Offerman Jr., Ivan Miller, Yakima Canutt, Griff Barnett; ***D:*** Nate Watt; ***W:*** Barry Shipman, Bennett Cohen; ***C:*** Reggie Lanning; ***M:*** Cindy Walker.

The Frontiersmen 🦴🦴 **1938** Things plod along at the little red schoolhouse until Hoppy and the guys have to take off after some rustlers. Features the members of the St. Brendan Boys Choir as the schoolboys. Unusual for its lack of gunplay until near the end. **71m/B VHS.** William Boyd, George "Gabby" Hayes, Russell Hayden, Evelyn Venable, Clara Kimball Young, Charles Hughes, Dick(ie) Jones, Roy Barcroft, Emily Fitzroy; ***D:*** Lesley Selander.

Frost/Nixon 🦴🦴🦴 1/2 **2008 (R)** Engrossing dramatization of the 1977 interviews between British journalist David Frost (Sheen) and former president Richard Nixon (Langella), about three years after Nixon's resignation due to the Watergate scandal. Follows Frost as he struggles to earn credibility within journalistic circles and has to front $600,000 of his own funds to entice Nixon. Figuring he can easily handle Frost, a beleaguered Nixon hopes to redeem himself to the nation, but his underestimation leads to a surprising admission. Adapted by Peter Morgan from his highly acclaimed 2006 play of the same name; the lead actors reprise their stage roles and a stellar Langella lives up to the Tony he received. Director Howard filmed at actual locations such as Nixon's San Clemente, California, home as well as Frost's hotel suite. **122m/C DVD.** *US* Michael Sheen, Frank Langella, Sam Rockwell, Kevin Bacon, Rebecca Hall, Matthew Macfayden, Oliver Platt, Toby Jones, Pat McCormick, Jenn Gotzon; ***D:*** Ron Howard; ***W:*** Peter Morgan; ***C:*** Salvatore Totino; ***M:*** Hans Zimmer.

Frostbiter: Wrath of the Wendigo 🦴 **1994 (R)** Disappointing Troma entry takes itself a bit too seriously. It wants to be an "Evil Dead on Ice" (we even see a movie poster for same in the flick); the plot involves hunters trapped in the frozen woods of Northern Michigan by the evil spirit "Wendigo." It's short on original horror and the laff-factor is not up to usual Troma standards (although the killer chili was a nice touch). The only saving grace is the quirky soundtrack, including said chili's theme song by Randall and Allan Lynch, "March of the Undead" by the 3-D Invisibles, and "I'm a Hellbilly" by Elvis Hitler. Based on the comic book character of the same name. **90m/C VHS, DVD.** Ron Asheton, Lori Baker, Patrick Butler, Devlin Burton; ***D:*** Tom Chaney; ***W:*** Tom Chaney; ***C:*** Tom Chaney.

Frozen 🦴🦴 **1998** Flashback look at the suicide of struggling Beijing performance artist Qi Lei (Hongshen), who dies by freezing himself to death in an "ice burial" as part of his art. Focuses on the aftermath of Tienanmen Square and its disaffected younger generation. Mandarin with subtitles. Working without authorization, the director hid behind a pseudonym that translates as "No Name." The film was smuggled out of China and completed in Amsterdam. **90m/C VHS.** *CH* Hongshen Jia, Ma Xiaoqing, Bai Yu, Li Geng, Wei Ye; ***D:*** Xiaoshuai Wang; ***W:*** Xiaoshuai Wang, Pang Ming; ***C:*** Yang Shu; ***M:*** Roeland Dol.

Frozen 🦴 1/2 **2010 (R)** Dim college-aged snowboarders Joe (Ashmore), Dan (Zegers) and Parker (Bell) become trapped on a ski lift as a blizzard approaches. Since they're apparently the only people their age without cell phones, the trio must overcome the perils of frostbite, ravenous wildlife, poor decision-making and even worse dialogue. At turns tedious and gory. All this movie proves is that while you can suspend three people in the air indefinitely, you can't suspend the audience's disbelief that long. In a touch of irony, Ashmore played the character of Iceman in the "X-Men" series. **94m/C DVD.** *US* Kevin Zegers, Shawn Ashmore, Emma Bell, Rileah Vanderbilt, Adam Johnson, Ed Ackerman, Chris York; ***D:*** Adam Green; ***W:*** Adam Green; ***C:*** Will Barratt; ***M:*** Andy Garfield.

Frozen Alive 🦴 **1964** A scientist experiments with suspended animation but, wouldn't you know, someone murders his wife while he's on ice. Apparently being frozen stiff does not an alibi make, and he becomes the prime suspect. Much unanimated suspense. **80m/B VHS, DVD.** *GB GE* Mark Stevens, Marianne Koch, Delphi Lawrence, Joachim Hansen, Walter Rilla, Wolfgang Lukschy; ***D:*** Bernard Knowles.

Frozen Assets 🦴 **1992 (PG-13)** Pathetic attempt at comedy from Long and Bernsen. He's an ambitious executive who finds the "bank" of his corporation's latest acquisition deals in sperm and not cash. Still, he expects this acquisition to be a success and comes up with a number of tacky ways, much to the horror of the facility's administrator, to make that profit margin grow. **93m/C VHS.** Corbin Bernsen, Shelley Long, Larry Miller, Dody Goodman, Gerrit Graham, Paul Sand, Teri Copley, Matt Clark, John Bloom; ***D:*** George Miller; ***W:*** Don Klein, Tom Kartozian.

Frozen in Fear 🦴🦴 *The Flying Dutchman* **2000** Variation on the 1933 film "The Mystery of the Wax Museum" and the Vincent Price 1953 remake "House of Wax." Admiring art dealer Oxenberg tracks reclusive painter Roberts down to his remote cabin in Montana. Turns out the artist uses real female bodies for his work—killing young women, arranging them in provocative poses, and then encasing them in ice. Will Oxenberg become part of his next tableau? **91m/C VHS, DVD.** Eric Roberts, Catherine Oxenberg, Rod Steiger, Scott Plank, Barry Sigismondi, Joan Benedict, Douglas Sebern; ***D:*** Robin P. Murray. **VIDEO**

Frozen River 🦴🦴🦴🦴 **2008 (R)** Unsentimental and honest independent film set in a shabby trailer park on the U.S.-Quebec border, following the desperate attempts of two single mothers to break free of their economic struggles. Ray Eddy (Leo), mother of two and part-time employee at the local dollar store, is left scrambling to pay the bills after her husband disappears on a gambling spree. Lila Littlejohn (Upham), now living alone after her mother-in-law snatched up her one-year-old, discovers the keys to Ray's husband's abandoned car and drives off. Ray follows Lila and soon the two women hatch a scheme to smuggle illegal aliens across the border. First-time director Courtney Hunt never drags the material into cheap thriller mode, instead trusting Leo and Upham to carry the story through their incredible chemistry. Winner of the Grand Jury Prize at Sundance 2008. **97m/C DVD.** *US* Melissa Leo, Charlie McDermott, Michael O'Keefe, Mark Boone Jr., Misty Upham, James Reilly, Jay Klaitz, John Canoe; ***D:*** Courtney Hunt; ***W:*** Courtney Hunt; ***C:*** Reed Dawson Morano; ***M:*** Peter Golub, Shahzad Ali Ismaily. Ind. Spirit '09: Actress (Leo).

Fudoh: The New Generation 🦴🦴 1/2 *Gokudo sengokushi: Fudo* **1996** Riki Fudoh (Tanihara) is a high school kid whose father is a Yakuza. Dear old dad murders Riki's brother to save himself when he angers his bosses, and Riki decides the old man and his cronies have to go. Aiding him in his quest are his crack team of assassins composed of a giant teenage boy, two 10 year old kids, a few teenage schoolgirl strippers, and the occasional hermaphrodite. This ultra-violent film led to infamous Japanese director Takashi Miike receiving international attention. **100m/C DVD.** *JP* Shosuke Tanihara, Kenji Takano, Marie Jino, Tamaki Kenmochi, Toru Menigishi, Miho Nomoto, Riki Takeuchi, Takeshi Caesar; ***D:*** Takashi Miike; ***W:*** Hitoshi Tanimura, Toshiyuki Morioka; ***C:*** Hideo Yamamoto; ***M:*** Chu Ishikawa.

Fuel 🦴🦴🦴 **2008** Eleven years in the making, director and narrator Tickell spiritedly expounds upon the merits of biofuels over the oil industry, as supported by such celebrities as Sheryl Crow, Woody Harrelson, and Willie Nelson, as well as more credible folks actually working in the field with footage taken from his "Veggie Van" travels—a van using vegetable oil as fuel. Despite his predisposition against big oil after growing up in an industrial-polluted section of Louisiana, Tickell uses his background to share what he's learned for a fair debate, though no opposing viewpoint is put forth. Tweaked after his 2008 festival showing, the alternative fuel focus was switched from ethanol due to concerns about its use and environmental hazards. But the bigger question of the effects of energy dependence on mankind and the planet still loom. **112m/C DVD.** Joshua Tickell; ***D:*** Joshua Tickell; ***W:*** Johnny O'Hara; ***C:*** Jim Mulryan; ***M:*** Ryan Demaree, Edgar Rothermich.

The Fugitive 🦴🦴🦴🦴 **1948** Fonda is a priest devoted to God and the peasants under his care when he finds himself on the run after religion is outlawed in this nameless South-of-the-border dictatorship. Despite the danger of capture, he continues to minister to his flock. His eventual martyrdom unites the villagers in prayer. Considered Fonda's best performance; Ford's favorite film. Shot on location in Mexico. Excellent supporting performances. Based on the Graham Greene novel "The Power and the Glory" although considerably cleaned up for the big screen—Greene's priest had lost virtually all of his faith and moral code. Here the priest is a genuine Ford hero. A gem. **99m/B VHS.** Henry Fonda, Dolores Del Rio, Pedro Armendariz Sr., J. Carrol Naish, Leo Carrillo, Ward Bond, Robert Armstrong, John Qualen; ***D:*** John Ford; ***W:*** Dudley Nichols.

The Fugitive 🦴🦴🦴 1/2 **1993 (PG-13)** Exciting big-screen version of the '60s TV series with the same basic storyline: Dr. Richard Kimble's (Ford) wife (Ward) is murdered and he's convicted, so he escapes and goes on the lam to find the real killer, the mysterious one-armed man. Dogged marshal Sam Gerard (Jones) is determined to retrieve his man. Lots of mystery and action, particularly a spectacular train/bus crash sequence, keeps the tension high. Due to illness, Richard Jordan was replaced by Krabbe after production had begun. Alec Baldwin was originally slated to star as Kimble, but backed out and Ford was cast. Sound familiar? Ford also replaced Baldwin as Jack Ryan in "Patriot Games." **127m/C VHS, DVD, Blu-ray Disc, HD DVD.** Harrison Ford, Tommy Lee Jones, Jeroen Krabbe, Julianne Moore, Sela Ward, Joe Pantoliano, Andreas Katsulas, Daniel Roebuck; ***D:*** Andrew Davis; ***W:*** David N. Twohy, Jeb Stuart; ***C:*** Michael Chapman; ***M:*** James Newton Howard. Oscars '93: Support. Actor (Jones); Golden Globes '94: Support. Actor (Jones); L.A. Film Critics '93: Support. Actor (Jones); MTV Movie Awards '94: On-Screen Duo (Harrison Ford/Tommy Lee Jones), Action Seq.; Blockbuster '95: Action Actor, V. (Ford).

Fugitive Among Us 🦴🦴 **1992** Dedicated cop is determined to return an escaped rapist to a life behind bars and he's aided by a victim who would really rather forget the whole thing. Made for TV. **97m/C VHS, DVD.** Peter Strauss, Eric Roberts, Elizabeth Pena, Lauren Holly. **TV**

Fugitive Champion 🦴🦴 **1999** Gangsters bust motor-cross champion Jake McKnight (Mayer) out of a chain-gang so that he can search for his kidnapped daughter, a participant in an internet sex site. The silly plot is a framework upon which to hang some inventive lively chase scenes. Standard action for a video premiere with a generic title. **94m/C DVD.** Chip (Christopher) Mayer, Charlene Blaine, Thomas Burr, Carlos Cervantes; *D:* Max Kleven; *W:* Steven Baio, Jack Burkhead Jr.; *C:* Jason C. Poteet; *M:* Ennio di Berardo. **VIDEO**

The Fugitive Kind ✂✂ 1/2 **1960** A young drifter walks into a sleepy Mississippi town and attracts the attention of three of its women with tragic results. Based upon the Tennessee Williams' play "Orpheus Descending." good performances but the writing never hangs well-enough together for coherence. **122m/B VHS, DVD.** Marlon Brando, Anna Magnani, Joanne Woodward, Victor Jory, R.G. Armstrong, Maureen Stapleton; *D:* Sidney Lumet; *C:* Boris Kaufman.

Fugitive Mind ✂ 1/2 **1999 (PG-13)** Robert Dean (Dudikoff) is suffering from severe memory loss. As he begins to piece together his past, Dean discovers his mind has been programmed to carry out bizarre crimes. So now what does he do? **94m/C VHS, DVD.** Michael Dudikoff, Heather Langenkamp, Michele Greene, David Hedison, Ian Ogilvy; *D:* Fred Olen Ray; *W:* Sean McGinley, Tripp Reed; *C:* Theo Angell; *M:* David Wurst, Eric Wurst. **VIDEO**

Fugitive Rage ✂✂ **1996 (R)** Tara McCormick (Schumacher) winds up behind bars when she shoots the mobster who was acquitted for murdering her sister. She teams up with her cellmate Josie (O'Brien) to fight back against the mob who's put a bounty on her head and a covert government agency also out to use her. Prerequisite prison shower sequences, tough babes, and lots of action. **90m/C VHS.** Wendy Schumacher, Shauna O'Brien, Jay Richardson; *D:* Fred Olen Ray.

Fugitive Road ✂✂ **1934** The great von Stroheim stars as a crusty but soft-hearted border guard who arbitrarily detains people at the crossing. **69m/B VHS.** Erich von Stroheim, Wera Engels, Leslie Fenton, Harry Holman; *D:* Frank Strayer.

The Fugitive: Taking of Luke McVane ✂✂ **1915** An early silent western in which Hart upholds the cowboy code of honor. **28m/B VHS.** William S. Hart, Enid Markey, Cliff(ord) Smith; *D:* William S. Hart, Cliff(ord) Smith.

Fugitive Valley ✂ 1/2 **1941** Muddled plot has villains-turned-heroes on the trail of some outlaws and stolen money. Terhune shows off some of his vaudeville skills, and King sings some songs. **61m/B VHS, DVD.** Ray Corrigan, John "Dusty" King, Max Terhune, Julie Duncan, Glenn Strange, Robert F. (Bob) Kortman, Tom London, Reed Howes; *D:* S. Roy Luby.

Fugitive X ✂ 1/2 **1996** Advertising exec gets to be the prey for a group of thrill-seeking hunters. He's got a handgun, a small head start, and the slime taking bets on how long he'll last. You've seen this before. **97m/C VHS.** David Heavener, Richard Norton, Lynn-Holly Johnson, William Windom, Chris Mitchum, Robert Z'Dar; *D:* David Heavener; *W:* David Heavener.

Fulfillment ✂✂ 1/2 *The Fulfillment of Mary Gray* **1989 (PG-13)** Ladd stars as Mary Gray, a turn-of-the-century woman comfortably married to good but unexciting farmer, Jonathan (Levine). He's unable to give his wife the child they both desperately want and when his younger brother, Aaron (Smith), visits, the hope is Aaron can be persuaded to help out. The naturally volatile situation is heightened by the fact Mary is very drawn to the handsome Aaron anyway, and the feeling is mutual. Based on the novel "The Fulfillment" by LaVyrle Spencer. **96m/C VHS.** Cheryl Ladd, Ted Levine, Lewis Smith; *D:* Piers Haggard. **TV**

Full Body Massage ✂✂ **1995 (R)** Wealthy art gallery owner Nina (Rogers) spends much of her time alone at her California dream home—except for a weekly appointment with young masseur Douglas (Burgard). But one week, the older Fitch (Brown) comes instead and begins discussing life and personal spirituality while he massages away the self-indulgent cares of the world-weary Nina. Good work by the leads in a chatty cable movie. **93m/C VHS.** Mimi Rogers, Bryan Brown, Christopher Burgard, Elizabeth Barondes; *D:* Nicolas Roeg; *W:* Dan Gurskis; *C:* Anthony B. Richmond; *M:* Harry Gregson-Williams. **CABLE**

Full Circle ✂✂ *The Haunting of Julia* **1977 (R)** Peter Straub wrote this eerie tale about a grief-stricken young woman whose child has recently died. To overcome her loss, she moves into a new house—which is haunted by the ghost of a long-dead child. **96m/C VHS.** *CA GB* Mia Farrow, Keir Dullea, Tom Conti, Jill Bennett, Robin Gammell; *D:* Richard Loncraine; *M:* Colin Towns.

Full Contact ✂✂ *Xia dao Gao Fei* **1992** Nightclub bouncer Jeff helps his friend Sam escape from a loan shark. But Sam has doublecrossed him and now thinks that Jeff is dead in an arranged explosion. But Jeff's survived and plans to seek a suitable revenge. Cantonese with subtitles. **99m/C VHS, DVD.** *HK* Chow Yun-Fat, Anthony Wong, Simon Yam, Bonnie Fu, Franklin Chin, Ann Bridgewater, Chan Chi Leung; *D:* Ringo Lam; *W:* Yin Nam; *M:* Teddy Robin Kwan.

Full Contact ✂✂ **1993 (R)** Farmhand Luke Powers heads for the decadence of Los Angeles to find his older brother. When three thugs make the mistake of trying to rob him, Luke shows off his martial arts skills. When Luke finds out his brother has been murdered by gamblers involved in an illegal back alley kickboxing circuit, he vows to get revenge. **97m/C VHS, DVD.** Jerry Trimble, Howard Jackson, Alvin Prouder, Gerry Blanck, Denise Buick; *D:* Rick Jacobson; *W:* Beverly Gray.

Full Count ✂✂ *Lenexa, 1 Mile* **2006 (R)** Sports figure in, but this is more a story about friendship despite the curves in the plot. Five high school buddies are spending their last summer in their Kansas hometown before separating to go to college. They play a money game of basketball against the local cops and celebrate their win by getting drunk and driving. When disgruntled cop Russ pulls the boys over, he gets even by taking the money back and threatening them with arrest. They retaliate and things go downhill until there's another showdown between the boys (who have joined a softball league) and Russ' team. (And no, there's no showing of the "big game".) **90m/C DVD.** Austin Nichols, Paul Wesley, Jason Ritter, Chris Klein, Josh Stewart, Timothy Ryan Hensel, Michael Rooker, William Baldwin, Michael Beach; *D:* Jason Wiles; *W:* Jason Wiles, Shem Bitterman; *C:* David Boyd; *M:* Gary Clark Jr.

Full Disclosure ✂✂ 1/2 **2000 (R)** Veteran journalist McWhirter (Ward) gets an incredible opportunity when a group of radicals he sent to prison ask him to protect a Palestinian operative (Ticotin) involved in the murder of a pro-Israeli media mogul. But neither an FBI agent (Plummer) nor an assassin (Miller) want McWhirter in the way and he'll have to decide just how badly he wants this story. **137m/C VHS, DVD.** Fred Ward, Christopher Plummer, Penelope Ann Miller, Rachel Ticotin, Virginia Madsen, Kim Coates, Nicholas (Nick) Campbell, Dan Lauria, Roberta Maxwell; *D:* John Bradshaw; *W:* Tony Johnston; *C:* Barry Stone; *M:* Claude Desjardins, Eric N. Robertson. **VIDEO**

Full Eclipse ✂✂ **1993 (R)** Max Dire (Van Peebles) is seduced by the fetching Casey (Kensit) into joining a fierce elite group of underground cops whose mission is to wipe out crime. However, Max soon learns that the secret of their power is a serum which turns them into werewolves. Max is now faced with a decision: join forces with them, or expose them. Either way, blood will flow. Interesting special effects. Unrated version also available. **97m/C VHS, DVD.** Mario Van Peebles, Patsy Kensit, Bruce Payne, Anthony John (Tony) Denison; *D:* Anthony Hickox; *W:* Richard Christian Matheson; *C:* Sandi Sissel.

Full Exposure: The Sex Tape Scandals ✂ 1/2 **1989 (R)** Sleazy drama about a murdered call girl who was blackmailing her clients with sex videos. A cop and his inexperienced female partner are assigned to catch the killer. **95m/C VHS, DVD.** Jennifer O'Neill, Lisa Hartman Black, Vanessa L(ynne) Williams, Anthony John (Tony) Denison, Peter Jurasik; *D:* Noel Nosseck; *W:* Stephen Zito; *M:* Dana Kaproff. **TV**

Full Fathom Five ✂ 1/2 **1990 (PG)** Central American militants, angered by America's invasion of Panama, hijack a submarine and threaten a nuclear assault on Houston. Boring and dumb. **81m/C VHS.** Michael Moriarty, Maria Rangel, Michael Cavanaugh, John Lafayette, Todd Field, Daniel Faraldo; *D:* Carl Franklin; *W:* Bart Davis.

Full Frontal ✂ 1/2 **2002 (R)** Despite its suggestive title, Soderbergh's film is arty, meandering, and uninvolving. Shot mostly on digital video in 18 days, the director's unofficial sequel to "sex, lies and videotape" tracks the loosely related lives and loves of various Los Angeles movie business types working on a film called "Rendezvous" over a 24-hour period. Katt, hilarious as a self-involved stage actor playing Hitler; Keener, as the somewhat demented Lee; and masseuse McCormack are the real standouts. However, improv-feel performances are good all around, with canny insider humor. The film's ambiguous presentation, including voice-overs, plays within movies, and movies-within-movies-within movies (whew!), undermine its intention to reveal the whole Hollywood circus that is really best kept under wraps. **101m/C VHS, DVD.** *US* David Duchovny, Nicky Katt, Catherine Keener, Mary McCormack, David Hyde Pierce, Julia Roberts, Blair Underwood, Enrico Colantoni, Dina Spybey; *D:* Steven Soderbergh; *W:* Coleman Hough; *C:* Steven Soderbergh.

Full Hearts & Empty Pockets ✂ 1/2 **1963** Follows the happy-go-lucky adventures of a young, handsome, impoverished gentleman on the loose in Rome. Dubbed in English. **88m/B VHS.** *IT GE* Linda Christian, Gino Cervi, Senta Berger; *D:* Camillo Mastrocinque.

Full Metal Jacket ✂✂✂ 1/2 **1987 (R)** A three-act Vietnam War epic, about a single Everyman impetuously passing through basic training then working in the field as a Marine Corps photojournalist and fighting at the onset of the Tet offensive. First half of the film is the most realistic bootcamp sequence ever done. Unfocused but powerful. Based on the novel by Hasford, who also co-scripted. **116m/C VHS, DVD, Blu-ray Disc, HD DVD.** Matthew Modine, R. Lee Ermey, Vincent D'Onofrio, Adam Baldwin, Dorian Harewood, Arliss Howard, Kevyn Major Howard, Ed O'Ross, John Terry, Jon Stafford, Marcus D'Amico, Kieron Jecchinis, Bruce Boa, Kirk Taylor, Tim Colceri, Ian Tyler, Gary Landon Mills, Sal Lopez, Ngoc Le, Peter Edmund, Tan Hung Francione, Leanne Hong, Costas Dino Chimona; *D:* Stanley Kubrick; *W:* Stanley Kubrick, Michael Herr, Gustav Hasford; *C:* Doug Milsome; *M:* Abigail Mead.

Full Metal Ninja ✂ **1989** When his family is kidnapped, a trained martial artist trails their abductors and swears revenge. **90m/C VHS.** Patrick Allen, Pierre Kirby, Sean Odell, Jean Paul, Renato Sala; *D:* Godfrey Ho.

The Full Monty ✂✂✂ **1996 (R)** A group of laid off Yorkshire mill workers come up with a unique way to earn some money in this amusing Britcom. When exuberant Gaz (Carlyle) notices the local women lining up to see the Chippendale dancers, he persuades his mates to launch a striptease act themselves. But these guys are hardly cover boy material—they're variously overweight, middle-aged, depressed, and shy. Nevertheless, they turn out to be an unexpected success despite numerous mishaps and misunderstandings. Title refers to the fact that they strip down to their birthday suits. The film audience merely gets the moon view. **90m/C VHS, DVD.** *GB* Robert Carlyle, Tom Wilkinson, Mark Addy, Steve Huison, William Snape, Paul Barber, Hugo Speer, Lesley Sharp, Emily Woof, Deirdre Costello; *D:* Peter Cattaneo; *W:* Simon Beaufoy; *C:* John de Borman; *M:* Anne Dudley. Oscars '97: Orig. Mus./Comedy Score; British Acad. '97: Actor (Carlyle), Film, Support. Actor (Wilkinson); Screen Actors Guild '97: Cast.

Full Moon in Blue Water ✂✂ 1/2 **1988 (R)** His wife's been dead a year, he owes back taxes on his bar, his father has Alzheimer's, and his only form of entertainment is watching old home movies of his wife. Floyd has problems. Enter Louise, a lonely spinster who feels that it is her personal duty to change his life. If she doesn't do it, the bizarre things that happen after her arrival will. **96m/C VHS, DVD.** Gene Hackman, Teri Garr, Burgess Meredith, Elias Koteas, Kevin Cooney, David Doty; *D:* Peter Masterson; *W:* Bill Bozzone; *C:* Fred Murphy; *M:* Phil Marshall.

Full Moon in Paris ✂✂ 1/2 *Les Nuits de la Pleine* **1984 (R)** A young woman in Paris moves out on her architect lover in order to experience freedom. Through a couple of random relationships, she soon finds that what she hoped for is not what she really wanted. The fourth of Rohmer's Comedies and Proverbs series. French with subtitles. **101m/C VHS, DVD.** *FR* Pascale Ogier, Tcheky Karyo, Fabrice Luchini; *D:* Eric Rohmer; *W:* Eric Rohmer; *C:* Renato Berta. Venice Film Fest. '84: Actress (Ogier).

Full of It ✂ 1/2 **2007 (PG-13)** Mildly amusing teen comedy. Sam (Pinkston) is the small, geeky kid who tries to fit it at his new high school by telling a few white lies. Only by the next morning they've magically come true. But it's a definite case of "be careful what you wish for," including Sam almost losing out on the right girl (Mara) because of his typical teen boy cheerleader (Walsh) fantasy. **91m/C DVD.** *US* Kate Mara, Craig Kilborn, John Carroll Lynch, Cynthia Stevenson, Amanda Walsh, Derek McGrath, Teri Polo, Joshua Close, Ryan Pinkston; *Cameos:* Carmen Electra; *D:* Christian Charles; *W:* Jon Lucas, Scott Moore; *C:* Kramer Morgenthau; *M:* John Swihart.

Full of Life ✂✂ 1/2 **1956** Holliday stars in this domestic comedy about a non-religious young woman who had married, in a civil ceremony, into a strict, Italian-Catholic family. Although Emily is now eight months pregnant the family still wants her and husband Nick (Conte) to have a church wedding. Holliday is a winning personality and the humor is lightly handled. Fante adapts from his own novel. **91m/B VHS.** Judy Holliday, Richard Conte, Salvatore Baccaloni, Esther Minciotti; *D:* Richard Quine; *W:* John Fante.

Full Ride ✂✂ **2002 (PG-13)** Typical teen romance with a sports background. High school senior Matt (Smith) is picked to play in the all-state football game but his bad attitude keeps getting him in trouble. It's clear that he doesn't care about the game until Matt meets Amy (Monroe), one of the town's hosts, who tells him he'll be missing out on the chance of a full college scholarship if he doesn't become a team player. **95m/C DVD.** Riley Smith, Meredith Monroe, Bob Cady, Jonathan Wayne Wilson, Mario Foxbaker; *D:* Mark Hoeger; *W:* George Mills, Don Winslow; *C:* Andy Anderson; *M:* Peter Buffett. **TV**

Full Speed ✂✂ *A Toute Vitesse* **1996** Quentin (Cervo) has published a semi-autobiographical novel about disenfranchised youth that's based on his friends from a Lyon housing project, including drug-dealing DJ, Jimmy (Rideau). Although he has a girlfriend, Julie (Bouchez), Quentin flirts with Algerian-born Samir (Bardadi) in order to learn about Samir's murdered boyfriend, so he can use the story in his writing. Julie, meanwhile, becomes involved with the charismatic Jimmy when Quentin decides to go to Paris. There are several melodramatic twists in Morel's feature debut about live-for-today youth and racial tensions. French with subtitles. **84m/C VHS.** *FR* Pascal Cervo, Stephane Rideau, Elodie Bouchez, Meziane Bardadi; *D:* Gael Morel; *W:* Gael Morel, Catherine Corsini; *C:* Jeanne Lapoirie.

Full Tilt Boogie ✂✂ 1/2 **1997 (R)** Director Sarah Kelly's documentary films the making of hipster crime-vampire flick "From Dusk Till Dawn" by Quentin Tarantino and Robert Rodriguez. Watching this clash of show biz egos is actually more fun than watching the movie they made. Probes the inner workings of big shots Tarantino, Clooney, Keitel, and the interns that hate to go to Taco Bell for them. Keitel, in his best "I can't believe you talked me into making this movie" tone, has a brief monologue about...well, he probably had a point when he started talking. Also shows the problems that went on during the production, including the destruction of a set by fire and the process of saving it. Included on the "From Dusk Till Dawn" special edition DVD. **110m/C VHS, DVD.** *D:* Sarah Kelly; *C:* Chris Gallo; *M:* Cary Berger, Dominic Kelly.

Full Time Killer ✂✂ 1/2 *Fulltime Killer; Chunchik satsau; Chuen jik sat sau* **2001 (R)** O (Sorimachi) is the number one assassin in

Hong Kong. Despondent over the murder of his housekeeper with whom he was in love, he has shut himself off from the outside world and become obsessed with her replacement. Tok (Lau) is a loud up-and-coming assassin eager to be number one, who seduces O's housekeeper to lure him out of hiding into a confrontation. **98m/C DVD.** *HK* Andy Lau, Simon Yam, Kelly Lin, Suet Lam, Takashi Sorimachi, Cherrie Ying, Teddy Lin; ***D:*** Johnny To; ***W:*** Kai-Fai Wai, Ho-Cheung Pang, Joey O'Bryan; ***C:*** Siu Keung Cheng; ***M:*** Guy Zerafa, Alex Khaskin.

The Fuller Brush Girl ✂✂ 1/2 **1950** Lots of slapstick with Ball as a door-to-door saleswoman unexpectedly involved in a murder. She and dim-bulb boyfriend Albert are chased by cops, murderers, and smugglers in this frantic farce. Sequel to Red Skelton's (who has a cameo) 1948 film "The Fuller Brush Man." **84m/B VHS.** Lucille Ball, Eddie Albert, Carl Benton Reid, Gale Robbins, Jeff Donnell, John Litel, Fred Graham, Lee Patrick; ***Cameos:*** Red Skelton; ***D:*** Lloyd Bacon; ***W:*** Frank Tashlin.

The Fuller Brush Man ✂✂ 1/2 *That Man Mr. Jones* **1948** A newly hired Fuller Brush man becomes involved in murder and romance as he tries to win the heart of his girlfriend. A slapstick delight for Skelton fans. **93m/B VHS.** Red Skelton, Janet Blair, Don McGuire, Adele Jergens; ***D:*** Frank Tashlin.

Fun ✂✂ **1994** Another in the thrill kill genre. 14-year-old Bonnie (Witt) and 15-year-old Hillary (Humphrey) are best friends (and possibly lovers) who have stabbed to death an old woman—seemingly for kicks and to cement their loyalty to each other. (Can you say Leopold and Loeb?) Convicted and in a reformatory, they're documenting their actions, separately (in black & white sequences), to counselor Jane (Hope) and tabloid journalist John (Moses). Bleak dysfunction adapted by Bosley from his play. **95m/C VHS, DVD.** Alicia Witt, Renee Humphrey, Leslie Hope, William R. Moses, Ania Suli; ***D:*** Rafal Zielinski; ***W:*** James Bosley; ***C:*** Jens Sturup; ***M:*** Marc Tschantz.

Fun & Fancy Free ✂✂✂ **1947 (G)** Part-animated, part-live-action Disney feature is split into two segments: "Bongo" with Dinah Shore narrating the story of a happy-go-lucky circus bear looking for love; and "Mickey and the Beanstalk"—a "new" version of an old fairy tale. Disney's last performance as the voice of Mickey and the only film to star Mickey, Donald Duck, Jiminy Cricket and Goofy. **73m/C VHS, DVD.** ***D:*** Jack Kinney, Hamilton Luske, William M. Morgan; ***C:*** Charles P. Boyle; ***M:*** Paul J. Smith, Oliver Wallace, Eliot Daniel; ***V:*** Walt Disney, Cliff Edwards, Billy Gilbert, Clarence Nash, Anita Gordon; ***Nar:*** Edgar Bergen, Dinah Shore.

Fun Down There WOOF! **1988** This smalltown boy-comes-to-the-big city is so bad, it's—bad. A naive—and unsympathetic—gay man from upstate New York moves to Greenwich Village and has fun down there (and they don't mean Australia). **110m/C VHS, DVD.** Michael Waite, Nickolas Nagurney, Gretschen Somerville, Martin Goldin, Kevin Och; ***D:*** Roger Stigliano; ***W:*** Michael Waite, Roger Stigliano.

Fun in Acapulco ✂✂ **1963 (PG)** Former trapeze artist Elvis romances two beauties and acts as a part-time lifeguard and night club entertainer. He must conquer his fear of heights for a climactic dive from the Acapulco cliffs. Features ten musical numbers. ♫ Fun in Acapulco; Vino, Dinero y Amor; Mexico; The Bullfighter Was A Lady; El Toro; Marguerita; (There's) No Room To Rhumba (In A Sports Car); I Think I'm Going To Like It Here; You Can't Say No In Acapulco. **97m/C VHS, DVD.** Elvis Presley, Ursula Andress, Elsa Cardenas, Paul Lukas, Alejandro Rey, Larry Domasin, Howard McNear; ***D:*** Richard Thorpe; ***C:*** Daniel F. Fapp.

Fun with Dick and Jane ✂✂ **1977 (PG)** An upper-middle class couple turn to armed robbery to support themselves when the husband is fired from his job. Though it has good performances, the film never develops its intended bite. **104m/C VHS, DVD.** George Segal, Jane Fonda, Ed McMahon; ***D:*** Ted Kotcheff; ***W:*** Jerry Belson, David Giler, Mordecai Richler; ***C:*** Fred W. Koenekamp; ***M:*** Ernest Gold.

Fun With Dick and Jane ✂✂ **2005 (PG-13)** Recycled version of the 1977 film with Jane Fonda and George Segal. Dick (Carrey) has a great life with gorgeous wife Jane (Leoni), a super house and an important executive position. Then Dick's company goes bust in a big way, and his efforts to find a comparable job (or any job) go bust as well. So what do they do? Why, of course, they turn to a life of crime. None-too-subtle political message (an Enron-esque company blowup) is rendered ineffective by too much gas and not enough go. If Jim Carrey's trademark slapstick doesn't drive you nuts, you'll get a few laughs out of it. **90m/C DVD, UMD, HD DVD.** *US* Jim Carrey, Tea Leoni, Alec Baldwin, Richard Jenkins, Angie Harmon, John Michael Higgins, Richard Burgi, Carlos Jacott, Aaron Michael Drozin, Gloria Garayua; ***D:*** Dean Parisot; ***W:*** Judd Apatow, Nicholas Stoller; ***C:*** Jerzy Zielinski; ***M:*** Theodore Shapiro, Randall Poster.

The Funeral ✂✂✂ 1/2 *Funeral Rites; Ososhiki* **1984** A sharp satire of the clash of modern Japanese culture with the old. The hypocrisies, rivalries and corruption in an average family are displayed at the funeral of its patriarch who also happened to own a house of ill repute. Itami's breakthrough film; Japanese with subtitles. **112m/C VHS, DVD.** *JP* Tsutomu Yamazaki, Nobuko Miyamoto, Kin Sugai, Ichiro Zaitsu, Nekohachi Edoya, Hideji Otaki; ***D:*** Juzo Itami; ***W:*** Juzo Itami; ***C:*** Yonezo Maeda; ***M:*** Joji Yuasa.

The Funeral ✂✂✂ **1996 (R)** Ferrara fuels fantastic performances from his famous thesps in this fatalistic tale of a family of gangsters in 1930s New York. Flashbacks from the opening funeral scene show a complex and troubled family of Italian brothers (Walken, Penn, and Gallo), from their formative years through their quest for justice after youngest brother Johnny is murdered. Not just another mob movie; characters are multi-dimensional with interesting quirks and Penn, especially, sprints into his role. More subtle than "Bad Lieutenant" and less pretentious than "The Addiction," this Ferrara flick is the one to see. **96m/C VHS, DVD.** Christopher Walken, Benicio Del Toro, Vincent Gallo, Christopher Penn, Isabella Rossellini, Annabella Sciorra, John Ventimiglia, Paul Hipp, Gretchen Mol; ***D:*** Abel Ferrara; ***W:*** Nicholas St. John; ***C:*** Ken Kelsch; ***M:*** Joe Delia.

Funeral for an Assassin ✂ 1/2 **1977 (PG)** A professional assassin seeks revenge for his imprisonment by the government of South Africa, a former client. Planning to kill all of the country's leading politicians, he masquerades as a black man, a cover which is designed to fool the apartheid establishment. **92m/C VHS, DVD.** Vic Morrow, Peter Van Dissel; ***D:*** Ivan Hall.

Funeral Home ✂ 1/2 *2 Cries in the Night* **1982** Terrified teen spends her summer vacation at her grandmother's tourist home, a former funeral parlor. Rip-off of "Psycho." **90m/C VHS, DVD.** *CA* Lesleh Donaldson, Kay Hawtrey; ***D:*** William Fruet.

Funeral in Berlin ✂✂✂ **1966 (R)** Second of the Caine/Harry Palmer espionage films (following up "Ipcress File"), in which the deadpan antihero British secret serviceman arranges the questionable defection of a Russian colonel (Homolka). Good look at the spy biz and postwar Berlin. Based on the novel by Len Deighton. "Billion Dollar Brain" continues the series. **102m/C VHS, DVD.** Michael Caine, Eva Renzi, Oscar Homolka, Paul (Christian) Hubschmid, Guy Doleman, Hugh Burden; ***D:*** Guy Hamilton; ***W:*** Evan Jones; ***C:*** Otto Heller; ***M:*** Konrad Elfers.

The Funhouse ✂ 1/2 **1981 (R)** Four teenagers spend the night at a carnival funhouse, witness a murder, and become next on the list of victims. From the director of cult favorite "The Texas Chainsaw Massacre," but nothing that hasn't been seen before. **96m/C VHS, DVD.** Elizabeth Berridge, Shawn Carson, Cooper Huckabee, Largo Woodruff, Sylvia Miles, Miles Chapin, Kevin Conway, William Finley, Wayne Doba; ***D:*** Tobe Hooper; ***W:*** Larry Block; ***C:*** Andrew Laszlo; ***M:*** John Beal.

Funky Forest: The First Contact ✂✂ 1/2 *Naisu no mori: The First Contact* **2006** A collection of semi-related comedy, sci-fi, and avant-garde skits involving three brothers and some extremely odd people. And aliens. And hot women. And freaky televisions made from butts. **150m/C DVD.** *JP* Tadanobu Asano, Ryo Kase, Rinko Kikuchi, Kenji Mizuhashi, Maya Banno, Yoshiyuki Morishita, Kazue Fukishii, Chizuru Ikewaki, Shihori Kanjiya; ***D:*** Katushito Ishii, Hajime Ishimine, Shunichiro Miki; ***W:*** Katushito Ishii, Hajime Ishimine, Shunichiro Miki.

Funland ✂ **1989 (PG-13)** In the world's weirdest amusement park a clown goes nuts over the new corporate owners' plans for the place and decides to seek revenge. **86m/C VHS, DVD.** David Lander, William Windom, Bruce Mahler, Michael McManus; ***D:*** Michael A. Simpson.

Funny About Love ✂ 1/2 **1990 (PG-13)** Fairly absurd tale with dashes of inappropriate black humor about a fellow with a ticking biological clock. Nimoy sheds his Spock ears to direct a star-studded cast in this lame tale of middle-aged cartoonist Wilder who strays from wife Lahti after having problems on the conception end into the welcoming arms of fertile college co-ed Masterson in his quest to contribute to the population count. **107m/C VHS, DVD.** Gene Wilder, Christine Lahti, Mary Stuart Masterson, Robert Prosky, Stephen Tobolowsky, Anne Jackson, Susan Ruttan, David Margulies; ***D:*** Leonard Nimoy; ***W:*** Norman Steinberg, David Frankel.

Funny Bones ✂✂✂ **1994 (R)** Struggling comedian Tommy Fawkes (Platt) bombs in Vegas big-time while his Mr. Showbiz father George (Lewis) easily overshadows him at every turn. So Tommy decides to head back to his childhood home in Blackpool, England and figure out his life. What he discovers are the Parkers, a family of British vaudevillians, and the fact that his father stole their routines and, briefly, Mrs. Parker (Caron), resulting in half-brother Jack (Evans) who has all the natural talent Tommy can only dream about. Serious, funny, and hostile with notable performances from Platt and Evans. **128m/C VHS, DVD.** Oliver Platt, Lee Evans, Leslie Caron, Jerry Lewis, Oliver Reed, Ian McNeice, Ruta Lee, Richard Griffith, George Carl, Freddie Davies; ***D:*** Peter Chelsom; ***W:*** Peter Chelsom, Peter Flannery; ***C:*** Eduardo Berra; ***M:*** John Altman.

Funny, Dirty Little War ✂✂ 1/2 *No Hambra mas Penas ni Olvido; Funny Little Dirty War* **1983** An Argentinian farce about the petty rivalries in a small village erupting into a violent, mini-civil war. Based on the novel by Osvaldo Soriano. In Spanish with English subtitles. **80m/C VHS, DVD.** *AR* Federico Luppi, Julio de Grazia, Miguel Angel Sola; ***D:*** Hector Olivera; ***W:*** Hector Olivera, Roberto Cassa; ***C:*** Leonardo Solis; ***M:*** Oscar Cardozo Ocampo.

Funny Face ✂✂✂ **1957** Musical satire on beatniks and the fashion scene also features the May-December romance between Astaire and the ever-lovely Hepburn. He is a high-fashion photographer (based on Richard Avedon); she is a Greenwich Village bookseller fond of shapeless, drab clothing. He decides to take her to Paris and show her what modeling's all about. The elegant musical score features classic Gershwin. ♫ Let's Kiss and Make Up; He Loves and She Loves; Funny Face; How Long Has This Been Going On?; Clap Yo' Hands; S'Wonderful; Bonjour Paris; On How To Be Lovely; Marche Funebre. **103m/C VHS, DVD.** Fred Astaire, Audrey Hepburn, Kay Thompson, Suzy Parker; ***D:*** Stanley Donen; ***M:*** Ira Gershwin.

The Funny Farm ✂ 1/2 **1982** Comedy about a group of ambitious young comics striving to make it in the crazy world of comedy at Los Angeles' famous comedy club, The Funny Farm. **90m/C VHS.** *CA* Tracy Bregman, Miles Chapin, Eileen Brennan, Peter Aykroyd; ***D:*** Ron Clark; ***W:*** Ron Clark.

Funny Farm ✂✂ **1988 (PG)** Chevy Chase as a New York sportswriter finds that life in the country is not quite what he envisioned. The comedy is uneven throughout, with the best scenes coming at the end. **101m/C VHS, DVD.** Chevy Chase, Madolyn Smith, Joseph Maher, Jack Gilpin, Brad Sullivan, MacIntyre Dixon; ***D:*** George Roy Hill; ***W:*** Jeffrey Boam; ***C:*** Miroslav Ondricek; ***M:*** Elmer Bernstein.

Funny Games ✂✂ **1997** Georg (Muhe), his wife, Anna (Lothar), and young son, Georgie (Clapczynski) are vacationing at their lakeside cottage when their peace is invaded by psycho Paul (Frisch) and his sniveling partner Frank (Giering). The family is tied up and forced to play humiliating games with a couple of amoral killers. Most of the physical violence occurs off-screen but the psychological torture is relentless. German with subtitles. **103m/C VHS, DVD.** *AT* Susanne Lothar, Ulrich Muhe, Frank Giering, Arno Frisch, Stefan Clapczynski; ***D:*** Michael Haneke; ***W:*** Michael Haneke; ***C:*** Jurgen Jurges.

Funny Games ✂✂✂ **2007 (R)** Haneke's shot-by-shot remake of his 1997 German art house thriller about two preppy 20-somethings, Paul and Peter (Pitt and Corbet), who descend upon a family, first as annoying guests, then as vicious sadists out for blood. Haneke had always said this movie would work better in America as social commentary, and he's probably right. Roth and Watts turn in harrowing performances as the tortured husband and wife, with Watts also credited as producer. Deliberately shocking and manipulative, which may validate its premise, but still, a nasty little flick. **112m/C DVD.** *IT GE FR GB US* Naomi Watts, Tim Roth, Michael Pitt, Brady Corbet, Devon Gearhart; ***D:*** Michael Haneke; ***W:*** Michael Haneke; ***C:*** Darius Khondji.

Funny Girl ✂✂✂ **1968 (G)** Follows the early career of comedian Fanny Brice, her rise to stardom with the Ziegfeld Follies, and her stormy romance with gambler Nick Arnstein in a fun and funny look at back stage music hall life in the early 1900s. Streisand's film debut followed her auspicious performance of the role on Broadway. Score was augmented by several tunes sung by Brice during her performances. Excellent performances from everyone, captured beautifully by Wyler in his musical film debut. Followed by "Funny Lady." ♫ My Man; Second Hand Rose; I'd Rather Be Blue Over You; People; Don't Rain On My Parade; I'm The Greatest Star; Sadie, Sadie; His Love Makes Me Beautiful; You Are Woman, I Am Man. **151m/C VHS, DVD.** Barbra Streisand, Omar Sharif, Walter Pidgeon, Kay Medford, Anne Francis; ***D:*** William Wyler; ***W:*** Isobel Lennart; ***C:*** Harry Stradling Sr.; ***M:*** Jule Styne, Walter Scharf. Oscars '68: Actress (Streisand); Golden Globes '69: Actress—Mus./Comedy (Streisand).

Funny Lady ✂✂ 1/2 **1975 (PG)** A continuation of "Funny Girl," recounting Fanny Brice's tumultuous marriage to showman Billy Rose in the 1930s and her lingering affection for first husband Nick Arnstein. One of the rare sequels which are just as good, or at least almost, as the original. ♫ How Lucky Can You Get?; Great Day; More Than You Know; Blind Date; So Long, Honey Lamb; Isn't This Better; Let's Hear It For Me; I Like Him/I Like Her; It's Only a Paper Moon. **137m/C VHS, DVD.** Barbra Streisand, Omar Sharif, James Caan, Roddy McDowall, Ben Vereen, Carole Wells, Larry Gates, Heidi O'Rourke; ***D:*** Herbert Ross; ***W:*** Jay Presson Allen, Arnold Schulman; ***C:*** James Wong Howe.

Funny Money ✂ **1982** Pointed, satirical look at the British habit of financing life with the almighty credit card. Sometimes uneven comedy. **92m/C VHS.** *GB* Gregg Henry, Elizabeth (E.G. Dailey) Daily, Gareth Hunt, Derren Nesbitt, Annie Ross; ***D:*** James Kenelm Clarke.

Funny People ✂✂ **2009 (R)** Apatow might think longer is better, but brevity is the soul of comedy. Endless raunchy dialogue spouted by boy-men just can't sustain the pic's length. Superstar comedian George Simmons (Sandler) learns he has a rare and probably fatal illness. George, of course, lives only for performing and has no friends because offstage he's such a jerk. Aspiring comedian Ira (Rogen) can write material but he's a lousy performer so George makes him his personal assistant. George decides to seriously go after his onetime love (Mann) who's married with children. (Let's see—agonizing over Eric Bana or Adam Sandler? Only in Apatow-land.) Momentum mostly gets lost in the third act when it goes all serious. **146m/C DVD.** *US* Adam Sandler, Seth Rogen, Leslie Mann, Eric Bana, Jonah Hill, Jason Schwartzman, Aubrey Plaza, Iris Apatow, Maude Apatow, RZA; ***D:*** Judd Apatow; ***W:*** Judd Apatow; ***C:*** Janusz Kaminski; ***M:*** Michael Andrews.

A Funny Thing Happened on the Way to the Forum ✂✂✂ **1966** A bawdy Broadway farce set in ancient Rome where a conniving, slave plots his way to freedom by aiding in the romantic escapades of his master's inept son. Terrific performances by Mostel and Gilford. Keaton's second-to-last film role. The Oscar-winning score includes such highlights as "Comedy Tonight," "Lovely," and "Everybody Ought to Have a Maid." **100m/C VHS, DVD.** Zero Mostel, Phil Silvers, Jack Gilford, Buster Keaton, Michael Hordern, Michael Crawford, Annette Andre; ***D:*** Richard Lester; ***W:*** Melvin Frank, Michael Pertwee; ***C:*** Nicolas Roeg; ***M:*** Ken Thorne. Oscars '66: Adapt. Score.

Funny Valentine **2005 (R)** Josh (Hall) is having trouble with New York's singles scene so his buddies Tim (Lord Jamar) and Sean (Martin) offer dating advice, including placing a personal ad and vetting the responses. Embittered single mom Doreen (Marron) is not one of their choices but Josh decides to follow his heart. A romantic comedy that's weak on both the romance and the comedy. There is a lot of unwarranted seminudity that is more appropriate to softcore porn. **90m/C DVD.** Anthony Michael Hall, Marlo Marron, Ivan Martin, Larry Storch, Lord Jamar; ***D:*** Jeff Oppenheim; ***W:*** Jeff Oppenheim; ***C:*** Stephen Treadway; ***M:*** Greg Arnold. **VIDEO**

Funnyman **1994 (R)** Cartoon splatter courtesy of a demon dressed in classic British jester regalia. Rock 'n' roll mogul Young obtains Lee's creepy ancestral home in a card game but when he visits with his family, everyone but Young is killed by the Funnyman, who uses his victims own weaknesses to dispatch them. A second set of likely candidates arrive when Young's brother Devitt shows up with a motley collection of hangers-on, including psychic Black, who's the only one to realize something's seriously off. **89m/C VHS, DVD.** *GB* Tim James, Benny Young, Matthew Devitt, Pauline Black, Ingrid Lacey; ***Cameos:*** Christopher Lee; ***D:*** Simon Sprackling; ***W:*** Simon Sprackling.

Fur: An Imaginary Portrait of Diane Arbus **2006 (R)** Imaginary indeed as tall, pale Kidman looks nothing like the small, dark Arbus, not to mention that Downey's character Lionel Sweeney suffers from an extreme form of hirsuteness that covers him in hair so he's reduced to acting with eyes and voice. So here's this married 1950s New York housewife who helps out husband Allan (Burrell) with his commercial photography career suddenly transforming herself into a snapper of those marginalized by society. Apparently Diane is tired of being the good girl and wants to take a walk on the wild side and fulfill her own artistic desires. It's a well-intentioned but somehow unsatisfactory effort. **120m/C DVD.** *US* Nicole Kidman, Robert Downey Jr., Ty Burrell, Harris Yulin, Jane Alexander; ***D:*** Steven Shainberg; ***W:*** Erin Cressida Wilson; ***C:*** Bill Pope; ***M:*** Carter Burwell.

The Furies **1/2 1950** Huston's last film is a brooding western from director Mann with Stanwyck as the ultimate daddy's girl who wants revenge when she feels betrayed. In 1870s New Mexico, ruthless widowed rancher T.C. Jeffords (Huston) has secured a large bank loan in exchange for driving off some squatters, including a Mexican family whom daughter Vance (Stanwyck) regards as friends. Vance is furious when daddy marries scheming socialite Florence (Anderson), so she attacks her unwelcome stepmommy. There's also problems involving Vance's dowry (and who's getting the money) and Rip (Corey), a gambler-turned-banker with his own agenda when he teams up with Vance to ruin her father. **109m/B DVD.** Walter Huston, Barbara Stanwyck, Wendell Corey, Judith Anderson, Gilbert Roland, Thomas Gomez, Beulah Bondi, Albert Dekker, Wallace Ford, John Bromfield; ***D:*** Anthony Mann; ***W:*** Charles Schnee; ***C:*** Victor Milner; ***M:*** Franz Waxman.

Furry Vengeance **2010** A real estate developer moves his family to rural Oregon for his work on a new housing project. But construction threatens the local forest population and the animals come out with fur and feathers flying, seeking to sabotage construction and save their homes. **m/C DVD.** Brendan Fraser, Brooke Shields, Matt Prokop, Ken Jeong, Samantha Bee, Dick Van Dyke; ***D:*** Roger Kumble; ***W:*** Michael Carnes, Josh Gilbert; ***C:*** Peter Lyons Collister; ***M:*** Paul Kate.

The Further Adventures of Tennessee Buck **1988 (R)** Mercenary adventurer travels through tropical jungles acting as a guide to a dizzy couple. Along the way, they encounter cannibals, headhunters, and other bizarre jungle things in this lame take on "Indiana Jones." Shot on location in Sri Lanka. **90m/C VHS, DVD.** David Keith, Kathy Shower, Brant Van Hoffman; ***D:*** David Keith; ***M:*** John Debney.

Further Adventures of the Wilderness Family, Part 2 **1/2** *Wilderness Family, Part 2* **1977 (G)** Depicts the Robinson family who left civilization for the freedom of the Colorado wild. Predictable retread, but more good family adventure drama from the makers of "Adventures of the Wilderness Family." **104m/C VHS.** Heather Rattray, Ham Larsen, George "Buck" Flower, Robert F. Logan, Susan Damante-Shaw; ***D:*** Frank Zuniga.

Fury **1/2 1936** Tracy gives an excellent performance as an innocent young man framed for kidnapping and then nearly murdered by a lynch mob. His plans for revenge are thwarted by his girlfriend, who fears that he will turn into the murderer he has been accused of being. Powerful anti-violence message is well-made, with strong ensemble acting. Lang's favorite of his American-made films. **96m/B VHS, DVD.** Spencer Tracy, Sylvia Sidney, Walter Abel, Bruce Cabot, Edward Ellis, Walter Brennan, Frank Albertson; ***D:*** Fritz Lang; ***C:*** Joseph Ruttenberg. Natl. Film Reg. '95.

Fury **1978** A man and woman meet in the Amazonian jungle and the sparks begin to fly. **75m/C VHS.** *IT SP* Pilar Velasquez, Francisco Algora, Stuart Whitman, Laura Gemser; ***D:*** Jose Maria Froque; ***W:*** Jose Maria Froque; ***C:*** Alejandro Ulloa; ***M:*** Carlo Savina.

The Fury **1978 (R)** The head of a government institute for psychic research finds that his own son is snatched by supposed terrorists who wish to use his lethal powers. The father tries to use another a young woman with psychic power to locate him, with bloody results. A real chiller. **117m/C VHS, DVD.** Kirk Douglas, John Cassavetes, Carrie Snodgress, Andrew Stevens, Amy Irving, Charles Durning, Carol Rossen, Rutanya Alda, William Finley, Jane Lambert, Joyce Easton, Daryl Hannah, Dennis Franz, James Belushi; ***D:*** Brian De Palma; ***W:*** John Farris; ***C:*** Richard H. Kline; ***M:*** John Williams.

The Fury of Hercules **1/2** *La Furia Di Ercole; Fury of Samson* **1961** It's up to the mighty son of Zeus to free an enslaved group of people from an oppressive, evil ruler. Surely all who stand in his way will be destroyed. Another Italian muscleman film. **95m/C VHS.** *IT* Brad Harris, Luisella Boni, Mara Berni, Carlo Tamberlani, Serge Gainsbourg, Elke Arendt, Alan Steel; ***D:*** Gianfranco Parolini.

The Fury of the Wolfman *La Furia del Hombre Lobo* **1970** A murdering werewolf is captured by a female scientist who tries to cure his lycanthropy with drugs and brain implants. Pretty slow going, but hang in there for the wolfman versus werewoman climax. **80m/C VHS, DVD.** *SP* Paul Naschy, Perla Cristal, Michael Rivers, Mark Stevens, Veronica Lujan; ***D:*** Jose Maria Zabalza; ***W:*** Paul Naschy.

Fury on Wheels *Jump* **1971 (PG)** Tale of men who race cars and wreak havoc and vice versa. **89m/C VHS.** Tom Ligon, Logan Ramsey, Collin Wilcox-Paxton, Sudie Bond, Conrad Bain, Sally Kirkland, Jack Nance, Judd Hirsch; ***D:*** Joseph Manduke; ***W:*** Richard Wheelwright; ***C:*** Gregory Sandor.

Fury to Freedom: The Life Story of Raul Ries **1985** A young man raised in the volatile world of abusive and alcoholic parents grows into an abusive and violent adult. One night, however, he meets something he can't beat up, and it changes his life. **78m/C VHS, DVD.** Gil Gerard, John Quade, Tom Silardi; ***D:*** Eric Jacobson; ***W:*** Eric Jacobson; ***C:*** Don Burgess.

The Fury Within **1998 (PG-13)** Mike (Mandylor) and Jo (Sheedy) Hanlon are an estranged couple who, along with their two young children, are terrorized by the supernatural. Turns out the poltergeist is a manifestation of Jo's anger about her upcoming divorce. Gives new meaning to the saying about scorned women. **91m/C VHS.** Ally Sheedy, Costas Mandylor, Vincent Berry; ***D:*** Noel Nosseck. **CABLE**

Fuse **2003** Two years after the civil war, the Bosnian town of Tesanj expects a visit from President Bill Clinton. The entire community is determined to present a wholesome image (turning the brothel into a cultural center) but a black marketeer, a crazy ex-police chief, and a continuing Serbian rivalry could derail the process. Bosnian and Serbian with subtitles. **105m/C DVD.** *BS* Bogdan Diklic, Enis Beslagic, Sasa Petrovic, Izudin Bajrovic; ***D:*** Pjer Zalica; ***W:*** Pjer Zalica; ***C:*** Mirsad Herovic; ***M:*** Sasa Losic.

Future Cop *Trancers* **1976** A hard-nosed, old-fashioned cop is forced to team with the ultimate partner—a robot. Silly made-for-TV movie, but likable leads. **78m/C VHS.** Ernest Borgnine, Michael J. Shannon, John Amos, John Larch, Herbert Nelson, Ronnie Clair Edwards; ***D:*** Jud Taylor; ***W:*** Danny Bilson, Paul DeMeo.

Future Fear **1/2 1997 (R)** Genetic scientist Dr. John Denniel (Wincott) has to find a solution for a flesh-eating virus that threatens mankind. Along with wife Anna (Ford), John tries cominbing human DNA with that of other species. But it turns out the virus was engineered by maniacal General Wallace (Keach) as a form of human cleansing—and he's not happy when he hears about a potential cure. **82m/C VHS, DVD.** Shawn Thompson, Jeff Wincott, Maria Ford, Stacy Keach; ***D:*** Lewis Baumander; ***W:*** Lewis Baumander; ***C:*** Graeme Mears; ***M:*** Donald Quan. **VIDEO**

Future Force **1989 (R)** In the crime-filled future cops can't maintain order. They rely on a group of civilian mercenaries to clean up the streets. **90m/C VHS, DVD.** David Carradine, Robert Tessier, Anna Rapagna, William Zipp; ***D:*** David A. Prior; ***W:*** David A. Prior; ***C:*** Andy Parke; ***M:*** Mark Mancina.

Future Hunters **1988** In the holocaust-blitzed future, a young couple searches for a religious artifact that may decide the future of the planet. **96m/C VHS.** Robert Patrick, Linda Carol, Ed Crick, Bob Schott; ***D:*** Cirio H. Santiago.

Future Kill **1985 (R)** Anti-nuclear activists battle fraternity brothers in this grim futuristic world. Shaky political alliances form between revenge-seeking factions on both sides. **83m/C VHS, DVD.** Edwin Neal, Marilyn Burns, Doug Davis; ***D:*** Ronald W. Moore; ***W:*** Ronald W. Moore.

The Future of Emily *Flugel und Fesseln* **1985** Film actress Isabelle (Fossey) has essentially given over the raising of her young daughter Emily (Raymond) to her parents, who live quietly in Normandy. After finishing a film shoot in Berlin, Isabelle comes for a visit but her smitten co-star Friedrich (Treusch) unexpectedly follows, leading to a clash between Isabelle and her mother Paula (Knef) about responsibility and Emily's future. German and French with subtitles. **106m/C DVD.** *GE* Brigitte Fossey, Hildegarde Knef, Ivan Desny, Herman Treusch, Camille Raymond; ***D:*** Helmer Sanders-Brahms; ***W:*** Helmer Sanders-Brahms; ***C:*** Sacha Vierny; ***M:*** Jurgen Knieper.

Future Shock **1993 (PG-13)** Dr. Russell Langdon is a psychiatrist who has been experimenting with virtual reality technology. Unbeknownst to three of his patients he decides to use them as guinea pigs in his work. But confronting their deepest fears only leads to new terrors. Also available in an unrated version. **93m/C VHS, DVD.** Bill Paxton, Vivian Schilling, Brion James, Martin Kove; ***D:*** Eric Parkinson, Matt Reeves, Oley Sassone; ***W:*** Vivian Schilling.

Future Zone **1990 (R)** In an attempt to save his father from being murdered, a young man travels backwards in time. **88m/C VHS.** David Carradine, Charles Napier, Ted Prior; ***D:*** David A. Prior.

Futurekick **1/2 1991 (R)** In the not so distant future, a kickboxer with an attitude and cyborg capabilities must use every ounce of strength in a battle against evil. **80m/C VHS, DVD.** Don "The Dragon" Wilson, Meg Foster, Christopher Penn, Eb Lottimer, Linda Dona, Maria Ford; ***D:*** Damian Klaus; ***W:*** Damian Klaus, Catherine Cyran; ***C:*** Ken Arlidge; ***M:*** Stan Ridgway.

Futuresport **1/2 1998 (R)** In 2025, Tre Ramsey (Cain) is the arrogant star of a popular violent sport that's a combo of skateboarding and basketball. Only the key game turns out to have more on the line than endorsements when terrorists take over the arena. Tre's mentor, and Futuresport creator Orbike Fixx (Snipes), suggests it's just a gigantic turf war and that matters can be settled by an arena match to the death. Caught in the middle is newscaster Alejandra (Williams), the woman Tre once loved and left behind. **89m/C VHS, DVD.** Dean Cain, Vanessa L(ynne) Williams, Wesley Snipes, Bill Smitrovich, Francoise Yip; ***D:*** Ernest R. Dickerson; ***W:*** Robert Hewitt Wolfe. **TV**

Futureworld **1976 (PG)** In the sequel to "Westworld," two reporters junket to the new "Futureworld" theme park, where they first support a scheme to clone and control world leaders. Includes footage shot at NASA locations. **107m/C VHS, DVD.** Peter Fonda, Blythe Danner, Arthur Hill, Yul Brynner, Stuart Margolin; ***D:*** Richard T. Heffron; ***W:*** George Schenck.

Futz **1/2 1969** Story from off-Broadway is of a man who loves his pig and the world that can't understand the attraction. Better in original stage production. **90m/C VHS.** John Pakos, Victor Lipari, Sally Kirkland; ***D:*** Tom O'Horgan.

Fuzz **1/2 1972 (PG)** Reynolds in the Boston cop on the track of a bomber killing policemen, punks setting winos on fire, and some amorous fellow officers. Combines fast action and some sharp-edged humor. **92m/C VHS, DVD.** Burt Reynolds, Tom Skerritt, Yul Brynner, Raquel Welch, Jack Weston, Charles Martin Smith, Albert "Poppy" Popwell; ***D:*** Richard A. Colla; ***M:*** Dave Grusin.

Fyre **1/2 1978 (R)** Young beautiful girl moves from the Midwest to Los Angeles and becomes a prostitute. **90m/C VHS.** Allen (Goorwitz) Garfield, Lynn Theel, Tom Baker, Cal Haynes, Donna Wilkes, Bruce Kirby; ***D:*** Richard Grand.

G **1/2 2002 (R)** Black urban adaptation of "The Great Gatsby." Successful hip-hop mogul Summer G (Jones) uses his bling to buy a mansion in the Hamptons and throw lots of parties. G is still upset that lover Sky (Maxwell) ran off long ago to marry old-money rich Chip Hightower (Underwood). Chip's cheating on his wife so G figures it's time to get Sky back. Journalist Tre (Royo) documents the happenings. Contrived mish-mash was filmed in 2001. **96m/C DVD.** *US* Richard T. Jones, Chenoa Maxwell, Blair Underwood, Andrew Lauren, Laz Alonso, Andre Royo; ***D:*** Christopher Scott Cherot; ***W:*** Andrew Lauren, Charles E. Drew Jr.; ***C:*** Horacio Marquinez; ***M:*** Bill Conti.

G-Force **1/2 2009 (PG)** Silly 3-D comic adventure, basically for the preteen set, about a covert government program that trains rodents to work as operatives. Guinea pigs—squad leader Darwin (Rockwell), weapons expert Blaster (Morgan), and martial arts pro Juarez (Cruz)—are joined by computer specialist mole Speckles (Cage) to prevent greedy billionaire Saber (Nighy) from using household appliances (that he can turn into robots) from taking over the world. References to more adult Jerry Bruckheimer-produced movies will go over the heads of the kiddie set although parents might appreciate the nod in their direction. **86m/C DVD.** *US* Steve Buscemi, Bill Nighy, Will Arnett, Zach Galifianakis, Kelli Garner, Tyler Patrick Jones, Piper Mackenzie Harris; ***D:*** Hoyt Yeatman; ***W:*** Cormac Wibberley, Marianne S. Wibberley, Tim Firth; ***C:*** Bojan Bazelli; ***M:*** Trevor Rabin; ***V:*** Sam Rockwell, Tracy Morgan, Penelope Cruz, Nicolas Cage, Jon Favreau.

"G" Men **1/2 1935** Powerful story based loosely on actual events that occurred during FBI operations in the early 1930s, with Cagney on the right side of the law, though still given to unreasonable fits of anger. Raised and educated by a well-known crime kingpin, a young man becomes an attorney. When his friend the FBI agent is killed in the line of duty, he joins the FBI to seek vengeance on the mob. But his mob history haunts him, forcing him to constantly prove to his superiors that he is not under its influence. Tense and thrilling classic. **86m/B VHS, DVD.** James Cagney, Barton MacLane, Ann Dvorak, Margaret Lindsay, Robert Armstrong, Lloyd Nolan, William Harrigan, Regis Toomey; *D:* William Keighley; *W:* Seton I. Miller; *C:* Sol Polito.

G-Men Never Forget *Code 645* **1948** Moore, former stunt-man and future Lone Ranger, stars in this 12-part serial about FBI agents battling the bad guys. Lots of action. On two cassettes. **167m/B VHS.** Clayton Moore, Roy Barcroft, Ramsay Ames, Drew Allen, Tommy Steele, Eddie Acuff; *D:* Fred Brannon, Yakima Canutt.

G-Men vs. the Black Dragon 1943 Reedited serial of "Black Dragon of Manzanar" stars Cameron as Fed who battles Asian Axis agents during WWII. Action-packed. **244m/B VHS.** Rod Cameron, Roland Got, Constance Worth, Nino Pipitone, Noel Cravat; *D:* William Witney.

G2: Mortal Conquest ☠☠ **1999 (R)** In the year 2003, Steven Colin (Bernhardt) unknowingly possesses the secret of an ancient martial arts power he learned in a former incarnation. Now the foes from the ancient battle have returned and Colin must remember his past if he's to save his present. **93m/C VHS, DVD.** Daniel Bernhardt, James Hong; *D:* Nick Rotundo; *W:* Nick Rotundo; *M:* Gary Koftinoff. **VIDEO**

G. Whilliker! ☠☠ **1993** Brothers have decided a guy named Gus Whilliker is the perfect match for their older sister/guardian. Too bad she's already dating someone. **93m/C VHS.** Dan Brook, Robin Brooks, Matthew Tompkins, Jay Michael Ferguson, William Ryan Tilk, Chris Lloyd, Jody Miller; *D:* David McClendon; *W:* Brenda Brown-Canary, Michael Helderman; *M:* Drew F. Barlow.

Gabbeh ☠☠☠½ **1996** Gabbeh is not only the name of the film's heroine (Djobat), it is also the name of the finely embroidered woolen rugs that the nomadic Ghashgai tribe is known for. Gabbeh has a simple desire—she wishes to marry a mysterious horseman but her father keeps placing obstacles in her path. She tells her story to an old married couple, who are washing their own gabbeh in a stream. The film is visually lush but a challenge for Western sensibilities with its slow pace and allegorical content. Farsi with subtitles. **75m/C VHS, DVD.** *IA* Shaghayeh Djodat, Hossein Moharami, Rogheih Moharami, Abbas Sayah; *D:* Mohsen Makhmalbaf; *W:* Mohsen Makhmalbaf; *C:* Mahmoud Kalari; *M:* Hossein Alizadeh.

Gabriel & Me ☠½ **2001** Rather unlikeable characters (and strong accents) put a crimp in this family fantasy/drama. Jimmy Spud is 11 and lives with his working-class family in Newcastle. Jimmy wants to become an angel and prays about his job aspirations while in church, resulting in a visit from the archangel Gabriel. Jimmy's dad thinks he's daft but he's got bigger problems—lung cancer—so Jimmy decides Gabriel can help him perform a miracle to save his dad. Adapted from a radio play. **84m/C DVD.** *GB* Billy Connolly, Iain Glen, Rosie Rowell, David Bradley, Jordan Routledge, Sean Landless, Ian Cullen; *D:* Udayan Prasad; *W:* Lee Hall; *C:* Alan Almond; *M:* Stephen Warbeck.

Gabriel Over the White House ☠☠☠ **1933** Part political satire, part fantasy, and completely fascinating. Huston is venal politician Judson Hammond, completely in thrall to his crooked cohorts, who manages to get elected President. While recuperating from an auto accident Hammond thinks he sees a vision of the Archangel Gabriel, who essentially tells him to change his crooked ways. From bought man Hammond changes to righteous do-gooder, much to the dismay of his criminal companions, who'll stop at nothing to get rid of the man they think has simply gone insane. Huston gives a powerful performance in this decidedly oddball film. **86m/B VHS.** Walter Huston, Karen Morley, Arthur Byron, Franchot Tone, Dickie Moore, C. Henry Gordon, David Landau, Samuel S. Hinds, Jean Parker; *D:* Gregory La Cava; *W:* Carey Wilson.

Gabriela ☠☠ **1984 (R)** A sultry romance develops between a Brazilian tavern keeper and the new cook he's just hired. Derived from Jorge Amado's novel. In Portuguese with English subtitles. **102m/C VHS.** *BR* Sonia Braga, Marcello Mastroianni, Nelson Xavier, Antonio Cantafora; *D:* Bruno Barreto; *W:* Bruno Barreto; *C:* Carlo Di Palma; *M:* Antonio Carlos.

Gabriela ☠☠ ½ **2001 (R)** Student Gabriela (Lopez) takes a job at a mental health clinic where she meets social worker Mike (Gomez). She's pretty, he's handsome, there's a strong mutual attraction but Gabriela is engaged to Pat (Galligan) even though she doesn't really love him and only agreed to please her strict mother (Fernandez). So will this twosome manage to overcome their romantic obstacles and be together? Expect the expected. **93m/C VHS, DVD.** Seidy Lopez, Jaime Gomez, Zach Galligan, Troy Winbush, Evelina Fernandez, Lupe Ontiveros, Stacy Haiduk; *D:* Vincent Jay Miller; *W:* Vincent Jay Miller; *C:* Adrian Rudomin; *M:* Craig Stuart Garfinkle.

Gabrielle ☠☠ ½ **2005** French superstars give this highly stylized French period piece some bite despite one set and a whole lot of arguing, crying, and talking. Wealthy publisher Jean (Gregory) is living the high life, complete with a statue-filled mansion, an army of servants and a beautiful but dissatisfied wife, Gabrielle, (Huppert) with whom he barely has a relationship. Gabrielle upsets their high-end facade when she leaves her husband a Dear John letter, only to inexplicably return just as he begins to digest its contents. The bulk of the film is spent watching, sometimes painfully, as the two dissect their phony marriage and sacrifices in the name of appearances. Based on the short story, "The Return," by Joseph Conrad. **90m/C DVD.** *FR GE IT* Isabelle Huppert, Pascal Greggory, Chantal Neuwirth, Claudia Coli, Thierry Hancisse, Thierry Fortineau, Louise Vincent, Clement Hervieu-Leger; *D:* Patrice Chereau; *W:* Patrice Chereau, Anne-Louise Trividic; *C:* Eric Gautier; *M:* Fabio Vacchi.

Gaby: A True Story ☠☠☠ **1987 (R)** The story of a woman with congenital cerebral palsy who triumphs over her condition with the help of family and loved ones, and ends up a college graduate and acclaimed author. Based on a true story. **115m/C VHS.** Rachel Levin, Liv Ullmann, Norma Aleandro, Robert Loggia, Lawrence Monoson, Robert Beltran, Tony Goldwyn; *D:* Luis Mandoki; *W:* Martin Salinas, Michael James Love; *C:* Lajos Koltai; *M:* Maurice Jarre.

Gal Young 'Un ☠☠☠ **1979** Set during the Prohibition era, a rich, middle-aged woman living on her property in the Florida backwoods finds herself courted by a much younger man. She discovers she is being used to help him set up a moonshining business. Unsentimental story of a strong woman. Based on a Marjorie Kinnan Rawlings story. **105m/C VHS.** Dana Preu, David Peck, J. Smith, Timothy McCormack, Gene Densmore, Jenny Stringfellow; *D:* Victor Nunez; *W:* Victor Nunez; *C:* Victor Nunez. Sundance '81: Grand Jury Prize.

Galactic Gigolo WOOF! **1987 (R)** An alien broccoli (yes, the vegetable) descends to earth on vacation, and discovers he's irresistible to Connecticut women. Must be something in the water. Amateurish effort intended as science-fiction satire, but there's more sleaze than humor. **80m/C DVD.** Carmine Capobianco, Debi Thibeault, Ruth (Coreen) Collins, Angela Nicholas, Frank Stewart; *D:* Gorman Bechard.

Galaxies Are Colliding ☠☠ ½ *Planet of Love* **1992 (R)** Adam (Brown) is so afraid of tying the knot that he abandons his bride at the altar and takes off on a journey of enlightenment, accompanied by best friend Peter (Grammer). They naturally meet any number of eccentrics along the way. **97m/C VHS.** Dwier Brown, Kelsey Grammer, Susan Walters, Karen Medak; *D:* John Ryman; *W:* John Ryman; *C:* Philip Lee; *M:* Stephen Barber.

Galaxina ☠½ **1980 (R)** In the 31st century, a beautiful robot woman capable of human feelings is created. Stumbling parody of superspace fantasies features murdered Playmate Stratten in one of very few film appearances. **95m/C VHS, DVD, HD DVD.** Dorothy Stratten, Avery Schreiber, Stephen Macht, James D. Hinton, Ronald J. Knight, Lionel Mark Smith, Tad Horino, Herb Kaplowitz, Nancy McCauley; *D:* William Sachs; *W:* William Sachs; *C:* Dean Cundey.

Galaxis ☠ ½ **1995 (R)** The physically impressive Nielsen stars as space- and time-traveling freedom fighter Landera, who beams down to Earth to battle your basic evil, intergalatic villain Kyla (Moll) who has the power source that could save her civilization. **91m/C VHS.** Brigitte Nielsen, Richard Moll, Craig Fairbrass; *D:* William Mesa.

Galaxy Invader ☠ **1985 (PG)** Chaos erupts when an alien explorer crash lands his spacecraft in a backwoods area of the United States. **79m/C VHS, DVD.** Richard Ruxton, Faye Tilles, Don Leifert; *D:* Donald M. Dohler; *W:* Donald M. Dohler.

Galaxy of Terror ☠ ½ *Mindwarp: An Infinity of Terror; Planet of Horrors* **1981 (R)** Astronauts sent to rescue a stranded spaceship get killed by vicious aliens. Big first: Moran (Joanie on "Happy Days") explodes. Inferior Corman-produced "Alien" imitation still manages to shock and displays generous gore. Followed by "Forbidden World." **85m/C VHS, DVD.** Erin Moran, Edward Albert, Ray Walston, Grace Zabriskie, Zalman King, Taaffe O'Connell, Robert Englund, Bernard Behrens, Jack Blessing, Sid Haig; *D:* Bruce (B.D.) Clark; *W:* Bruce (B.D.) Clark, Mark Siegler; *C:* Jacques Haitkin; *M:* Barry Schrader.

Galaxy Quest ☠☠ ½ **1999 (PG)** An ingratiating goof on "Star Trek" and other cheesy TV shows that draw rabid fans and typecast actors. At a sci-fi convention, the actors from the campy '70s TV space series "Galaxy Quest" are mistaken for real space traveling heroes by naive aliens who need them to aid in an intergalactic war and whisk the troupe off to a galaxy far, far away (or thereabouts). Naturally, the "crew" is ill-prepared for their latest mission. Playful acting includes Allen's vain leader Peter Nesmith, blond bosomy babe Gwen DeMarco (Weaver), and cynical Brit, Alexander Dane (Rickman). **104m/C VHS, DVD.** Tim Allen, Sigourney Weaver, Alan Rickman, Tony Shalhoub, Sam Rockwell, Daryl (Chill) Mitchell, Robin Sachs, Enrico Colantoni, Missi Pyle; *D:* Dean Parisot; *W:* David Howard, Robert Gordon; *C:* Jerzy Zielinski; *M:* David Newman.

Gale Force ☠☠ ½ **2001 (R)** The reality TV show "Treasure Hunt" involves eight contestants, one of whom is L.A. detective Sam Garrett (Williams), competing to find 10 million buried on the remote island on which they are marooned. But Sam is suspicious of executive producer Stuart McMahon (DeYoung), who'll do anything for ratings, and show host Jack MacRae (Nozick), who has a plot to get the money for himself. Oh, and then Mother Nature decides to make things even more interesting. Lots of action, including a good storm sequence. Wynorski directs under his Jay Andrews pseudonym. **96m/C VHS, DVD.** Treat Williams, Michael Dudikoff, Tim Thomerson, Curtis Armstrong, Cliff DeYoung, Bruce Nozick; *D:* Jim Wynorski. **VIDEO**

Galgameth ☠☠ ½ *The Adventures of Galgameth* **1996 (PG)** Old-fashioned tale of a boy-hero and a friendly monster. 14-year-old Prince Davin (Oatway) accidentally injures his father during a joust and blames himself when the king suddenly dies. But his majesty's actually been poisoned by knight El El (Macht), who declares himself regent and terrorizes the kingdom. Davin's only hope to restore peace is a magical statue called Galgameth that the prince is able to bring to life. Romanian location provides proper storybook castles and medieval villages. **99m/C VHS.** Devin Oatway, Stephen Macht, Sean McNamara, Johna Stewart, Tom Dugan; *D:* Sean McNamara; *W:* James Angeli; *C:* Christian Sebaldt; *M:* Richard (Rick) Marvin.

Gallagher's Travels ☠ **1987** A screwball male/female reporting team chase an animal smuggling ring through the wilds of Australia. **94m/C VHS.** *AU* Ivar Kants, Joanne Samuel, Stuart Campbell, Jennifer Hagan; *D:* Michael Caulfield.

The Gallant Fool ☠ ½ **1933** A man is wrongly accused of murder and tries to clear his name while eluding the law. **57m/B VHS, DVD.** Bob Steele, Arletta Duncan, George "Gabby" Hayes, John Elliott; *D:* Robert North Bradbury; *W:* Robert North Bradbury.

The Gallant Hours ☠☠☠ **1960** Biography of Admiral "Bull" Halsey (Cagney) covers five weeks, October 18 through December 1, 1942, in the WWII battle of Guadalcanal in the South Pacific. Director Montgomery forgoes battle scenes to focus on the human elements in a war and what makes a great leader. Fine performance by Cagney. **115m/B VHS.** James Cagney, Dennis Weaver, Ward (Edward) Costello, Richard Jaeckel, Les Tremayne, Robert Burton, Raymond Bailey, Karl Swenson, Harry Landers, James T. Goto, Walter Sande, Vaughn Taylor, Leon Lontoc, Carleton Young, James Yagi, Carl Benton Reid, Selmer Jackson, Nelson Leigh, John McKee, Tyler McVey, William Schallert, John Zaremba, Richard Carlyle, Herbert Lylton, Sydney Smith, Art Gilmore; *D:* Robert Montgomery; *W:* Frank D. Gilroy, Beirne Lay Jr.; *C:* Joe MacDonald; *M:* Roger Wagner.

Gallery of Horrors ☠ *Dr. Terror's Gallery of Horrors* **1967** Really low-budget AIP horror anthology with lots of stock footage to fill in the scenery. Carradine serves as narrator and also appears in "The Witch's Clock" about a cursed antique clock. A doctor (Chaney) brings an executed killer back from the dead in "A Spark of Life." A corpse comes back to life in "Monster Raid." And Dracula appears in "Count Alucard" and "King of the Vampires." **83m/C DVD.** John Carradine, Lon Chaney Jr., Mitch Evans, Roger Gentry, Vic McGee, Karen Joy, Ron Doyle; *D:* David L. Hewitt; *W:* David Prentiss, Gary Heacock; *C:* Austin McKinney.

Gallipoli ☠☠☠☠ **1981 (PG)** History blends with the destiny of two friends as they become part of the legendary WWI confrontation between Australia and the German-allied Turks. A superbly filmed, gripping commentary on the wastes of war. Haunting score; excellent performances by Lee and a then-unknown Gibson. Remake of a lesser 1931 effort "Battle of Gallipoli." **111m/C VHS, DVD.** *AU* Mel Gibson, Mark Lee, Bill Kerr, David Argue, Tim McKenzie, Robert Grubb, Graham Dow, Stan Green, Heath Harris, Harold Hopkins, Charles Yunupingu, Ronny Graham, Gerda Nicolson; *D:* Peter Weir; *W:* Peter Weir, David Williamson; *C:* Russell Boyd; *M:* Brian May. Australian Film Inst. '81: Actor (Gibson), Film.

Galloping Dynamite ☠ ½ **1937** Early western based on a James Oliver Curwood story. A ranger avenges the death of his brother killed for gold. **58m/B VHS, DVD.** Kermit Maynard; *D:* Harry Fraser.

The Galloping Ghost ☠☠ ½ **1931** A 12-chapter serial starring football great "Red" Grange about big games, gambling, and underworld gangs. Grange is ousted from football when he's accused of throwing a game and he sets out to prove his innocence. **226m/B VHS, DVD.** Harold "Red" Grange, Dorothy Gulliver, Walter Miller, Tom Dugan; *D:* B. Reeves Eason.

Galloping Romeo ☠ ½ **1933** Steele stars as a heartthrob on horseback in this romantic Western. Steele had a hard time pulling off the light comedy he was asked to do, so clips from his previous films were used to pad the movie. **59m/B VHS, DVD.** Bob Steele, Doris Hill, George "Gabby" Hayes, Frank Ball, Ernie Adams; *D:* Robert North Bradbury; *W:* Harry Fraser.

Gallowglass ☠☠☠ **1995** A "gallowglass" is an ancient Gaelic term for a servant willing to sacrifice his life for his master. In this moody TV mystery that is dim Joe (Sheen), whose life was saved by manipulative, handsome Sandor (Rhys), who now demands his absolute loyalty. Sandor needs his help in kidnapping Nina (Whitely), an unhappy ex-model who was the victim of a kidnapping years before in Italy and now lives with her husband in wealthy seclusion in the country. There, Nina is under the protection of bodyguard/chauffeur Paul (McArdle), and their mutual attraction leads to unexpected complications. Based on the thriller by Ruth Rendell (writing as Barbara Vine). **150m/C VHS.** *GB* Paul Rhys, Michael Sheen, Arkie Whiteley, John McArdle, Claire Hackett, Gary Waldhorn; *D:* Tim Fywell; *C:* Rex Maidment. **TV**

Galyon ☠ **1977 (PG)** Soldier of fortune is recruited by an oil tycoon to find his daughter and son-in-law who have been kidnapped by terrorists in South America. **92m/C VHS.** Stan Brock, Lloyd Nolan, Ina Balin, Ron Hayes; ***D:*** Ivan Tors.

Gambit 1/2 **1966** Caine's first Hollywood film casts him as a burglar who develops a "Topkapi"-style scheme to steal a valuable statue with MacLaine as the lure and Lom as the equally devious owner. Once Caine's careful plan is put into operation, however, everything begins to unravel. **109m/C VHS.** Shirley MacLaine, Michael Caine, Herbert Lom, Roger C. Carmel; ***D:*** Ronald Neame; ***W:*** Alvin Sargent, Jack Davies; ***M:*** Maurice Jarre.

The Gamble **1988 (R)** A young man (Modine) seeks to rescue his father from gambling debts by wagering himself against a lustful countess (Dunaway). When he loses the bet, however, he flees and joins up with a runaway (Beals) with the countess and her henchmen in close pursuit. **108m/C VHS, DVD.** Matthew Modine, Jennifer Beals, Faye Dunaway; ***D:*** Carlo Vanzina.

Gamble on Love **1986** Woman returns to her father's Las Vegas casino and falls for the man who manages the gaming room. **90m/C** Beverly Garland; ***D:*** Jim Balden.

The Gambler **1974 (R)** College professor Axel Freed has a gambling problem so vast that it nearly gets him killed by his bookies. He goes to Las Vegas to recoup his losses and wins big, only to blow the money on stupid sports bets that get him deeper into trouble. Excellent character study of a compulsive loser on a downward spiral. **111m/C VHS, DVD.** James Caan, Lauren Hutton, Paul Sorvino, Burt Young, James Woods, Jacqueline Brookes, M. Emmet Walsh; ***D:*** Karel Reisz; ***W:*** James Toback; ***C:*** Victor Kemper; ***M:*** Jerry Fielding.

The Gambler **1997** In St. Petersburg in 1866, Russian writer Dostoyevsky (Gambon) is a middle-aged compulsive gambler who is currently indebted to his publisher Stellovsky (Jansen) and must now write a new novel in 27 days to pay him off. He hires poverty-stricken Anna (May) to be his secretary and the dictated novel turns out to be the story of a gambling couple who are trying to get out of hock at a German resort. The real and fictional intertwine as Anna becomes more and more protective of Dostoyevsky and is determined to help him succeed. **97m/C VHS, DVD.** *GB NL HU* Michael Gambon, Jodhi May, Polly Walker, Dominic West, Luise Rainer, John Wood, Johan Leysen, Thom Jansen, Angeline Ball; ***D:*** Karoly Makk; ***W:*** Charles Cohen, Nick Dear, Katharine Odgen; ***C:*** Jules Van Den Steenhoven; ***M:*** Brian Lock.

The Gambler & the Lady 1/2 **1952** A successful London-based gambler and casino owner endeavors to climb the social ladder by having an affair with a member of the British aristocracy. He not only has to contend with his jilted nightclub singer girlfriend but also with the gangsters who would like to take over his clubs. Dull direction and a mediocre script. **72m/B VHS, DVD.** *GB* Dane Clark, Naomi Chance, Kathleen Byron, Meredith Edwards, Eric Pohlmann, George Pastell; ***D:*** Patrick Jenkins, Sam Newfield; ***W:*** Sam Newfield; ***C:*** Walter J. (Jimmy W.) Harvey; ***M:*** Ivor Slaney.

The Gambler Returns: The Luck of the Draw 1/2 **1993** You'll see lots of familiar western TV stars as Rogers returns yet again as debonair gambler Brady Hawkes. This time he's on a cross country trip to San Francisco and the biggest card game around—only some varmints are out to stop him playing that first hand. **180m/C VHS, DVD.** Kenny Rogers, Reba McEntire, Rick Rossovich, Chuck Connors, Patrick Macnee, Linda Evans, James Drury, Mickey Rooney, Jere Burns, Clint Walker, Claude Akins, Gene Barry, Doug McClure, Hugh O'Brian, Brian Keith, Park Overall, Jack Kelly, David Carradine, Johnny Crawford, Marianne Rogers; ***D:*** Dick Lowry. **TV**

The Gambler, the Girl and the Gunslinger 1/2 **2009** In this Hallmark Channel western Cain steals every scene as smooth-talking 1860s gambler Shea McCall. He wins half-ownership of a ranch, much to the dismay of the other half-owner, semi-retired gunslinger B.J. Stoker (Tupper). McCall then causes a romantic kerfuffle when he flirts with Stoker's widowed neighbor Liz (Hossack). However, trouble with some would-be land grabbers turns them into reluctant allies. **90m/C DVD.** Dean Cain, James Tupper, Allison Hossack, Michael Eklund, Keith Mackechnie; ***D:*** Anne Wheeler; ***W:*** Larry Cohen, Bob Barbash; ***C:*** Paul Mitchnick. **CABLE**

Gambler's Choice **1944** A police lieutenant and his boyhood friend find themselves on opposite sides of the law in this crime drama. Even though both men are romantically involved with the same woman, their friendship remains intact. **66m/B VHS, DVD.** Chester Morris, Nancy Kelly, Russell Hayden, Sheldon Leonard, Lee Patrick, Lloyd Corrigan, Tom Dugan, Lyle Talbot, Charles Arnt; ***D:*** Frank McDonald; ***W:*** Maxwell Shane, Irving Reis, James Edward Grant, Howard Emmett Rogers; ***C:*** Fred H. Jackman Jr.

The Gambling Samurai *Kunisada Chuji* **1960** A samurai returns to his village to find it besieged by a ruthless government. Instead of attacking, he bides his time and works to undermine the government—finally achieving his revenge. In Japanese with English subtitles. **101m/C VHS.** *JP* Toshiro Mifune, Michiyo Aratama; ***D:*** Senkichi Taniguchi.

Gambling Ship 1/2 **1933** Tired of life as a gambling boss, Ace Corbin (Grant) decides to retire and assumes a new identity as a businessman on a cross-country train trip. He meets Eleanor (Hume), who's pretending to be a socialite but is really the mistress of Joe (Vinton), who owns a failing gambling ship. Ace winds up buying the venture to settle a score with rival Pete (LaRue) but Pete doesn't take kindly to his new competition. **72m/B VHS.** Cary Grant, Benita Hume, Glenda Farrell, Roscoe Karns, Arthur Vinton, Jack LaRue; ***D:*** Louis Gasnier, Max Marcin; ***W:*** Max Marcin; ***C:*** Charles B(ryant) Lang Jr.; ***M:*** Werner R. Heymann, Oscar Levant.

The Gambling Terror **1937** A cowboy goes after a mobster selling protection to hapless ranchers. **53m/B VHS.** Johnny Mack Brown, Charles "Blackie" King; ***D:*** Sam Newfield.

The Game **1989** Three friends arrange a puzzle-murder-mystery for a selected group of guilty people, with $1 million as the prize—and death for the losers. **91m/C VHS.** Tom Blair, Debbie Martin; ***D:*** Curtis Brown; ***W:*** Curtis Brown.

The Game **1997 (R)** Investment banker Nicholas Van Orton (Douglas) is an uptight corporate control freak. He receives a dangerous birthday present from his black-sheep younger brother Conrad (Penn). It's a subscription to Consumer Recreation Services, a real life-and-death version of a role-playing game that is designed to tap the hidden emotional and physical resources of the client. His life is overrun with an escalating series of traps and terrors, with the game reaching into every facet of his life. Excellent portrayal by Douglas as a man stuck in a Hitchcockian nightmare. **128m/C VHS, DVD, HD DVD.** Michael Douglas, Sean Penn, Deborah Kara Unger, Armin Mueller-Stahl, James Rebhorn, Peter Donat, Carroll Baker, Anna (Katerina) Katarina; ***D:*** David Fincher; ***W:*** John Brancato, Michael Ferris; ***C:*** Harris Savides; ***M:*** Howard Shore.

Game for Vultures 1/2 **1986 (R)** Racial unrest in Rhodesia is the backdrop for this tale of a black revolutionary who fights racist sanctions. The noble topic suffers from stereotypes and oversimplification. **113m/C VHS.** *GB* Richard Harris, Richard Roundtree, Joan Collins, Ray Milland; ***D:*** James Fargo.

The Game Is Over 1/2 *La Curee* **1966 (R)** A wealthy neglected wife falls in love with her grown stepson, causing her to divorce her husband and shatter her life. A good performance by Fonda, then Vadim's wife. Modern version of Zola's "La Curee." **96m/C VHS, DVD.** *FR* Jane Fonda, Peter McEnery, Michel Piccoli, Tina Aumont; ***D:*** Roger Vadim; ***W:*** Roger Vadim; ***C:*** Claude Renoir; ***M:*** Jean Bouchety.

Game of Death *Goodbye Bruce Lee: His Last Game of Death; Bruce Lee's Game of Death* **1979 (R)** Bruce Lee's final kung fu thriller about a young martial arts movie star who gets involved with the syndicate. Lee died halfway through the filming of this movie and it was finished with out-takes and a double. **100m/C VHS, DVD.** Bruce Lee, Dean Jagger, Kareem Abdul-Jabbar, Colleen Camp, Chuck Norris; ***D:*** Robert Clouse; ***M:*** John Barry.

The Game of Love *Tonight's the Night* **1987 (PG)** Olin presides over Henry's bar, the lost and found of lonely hearts and lust, where people go to quench that deep thirst for love. **94m/C VHS.** Ed Marinaro, Belinda Bauer, Ken Olin, Robert Rusler, Tracy Nelson, Max Gail, Janet Margolin, Brynn Thayer; ***D:*** Bobby Roth; ***W:*** Sue Grafton, Steve Humphrey; ***C:*** Steven Fierberg; ***M:*** Tangerine Dream. **TV**

Game of Seduction *Une Femme Fidele* **1976** A murdering, womanizing playboy pursues a married woman and gets caught up in a treacherous cat-and-mouse game. Dubbed. **81m/C VHS.** *FR* Sylvia Kristel, Jon Finch, Nathalie Delon; ***D:*** Roger Vadim; ***W:*** Daniel Boulanger, Roger Vadim; ***C:*** Claude Renoir; ***M:*** Pierre Porte.

Game of Survival **1989** A young rebel warrior from another planet is sent to earth to battle six of the galaxy's most brutal warriors. **85m/C VHS.** Nikki Hill, Cindy Coatman, Roosevelt Miller Jr.; ***D:*** Armand Gazarian.

The Game of Their Lives **2005 (PG)** Bland account of the United States' long-shot 1950 soccer team—a hodgepodge of players haphazardly rounded up—that jolted a heavily superior English team in the first round of the World Cup in Brazil. Weak script that, while it scores on facts, gives the cast of mostly cookie-cut pretty boys very little to get fired up about. **101m/C DVD.** *US* Gerard Butler, Wes Bentley, Jay Rodan, Gavin Rossdale, Costas Mandylor, Louis Mandylor, Zachery Ty Bryan, Patrick Stewart, Jimmy Jean-Louis, Terry Kinney, John Rhys-Davies, Marilyn Dodds Frank, Richard Jenik, Bill Smitrovich; ***D:*** David Anspaugh; ***W:*** Angelo Pizzo; ***C:*** Johnny E. Jensen; ***M:*** William Ross.

The Game Plan 1/2 **2007 (PG)** The Rock is the only one who scores in this Disney retread. Swaggering star quarterback Joe Kingman (Johnson) suddenly finds his bachelor lifestyle cramped by the sudden arrival of Peyton (Pettis), the eight-year-old daughter he never knew he had. In a premise that only Disney could serve up, Peyton is from a previous marriage, although the idea that somehow Joe had no idea that his ex-wife had a child is not the most ridiculous aspect of the movie. This sets up an endless series of gags based on Joe not knowing how to interact with a little girl or, really, anyone outside of his agent (Sedgwick). Johnson's charm is undeniable, and Pettis is button-cute, but the rest is lukewarm family fare. **110m/C DVD, Blu-ray Disc.** *US* Dwayne "The Rock" Johnson, Kyra Sedgwick, Roselyn Sanchez, Morris Chestnut, Madison Pettis, Brian White, Paige Turco, Gordon Clapp, Hayes Macarthur, Jamal Duff, Jackie Flynn; ***D:*** Andy Fickman; ***W:*** Nichole Millard, Kathryn Price; ***C:*** Greg Gardiner; ***M:*** Nathan Wang.

Game 6 1/2 **2005 (R)** It's October 25, 1986, and Nicky (Keaton) has quite the dilemma—should he attend his play's opening night or watch his beloved Bosox battle the New York Mets in the soon-o-be-legendary game six of the World Series? With his crumbling marriage (having a mistress doesn't help), distant daughter, stalled career, and a cutthroat theater critic set to make or break his new work, he feels just as wrapped in failure as his once-cursed baseball team. Keaton clearly fields his distressed-man act but the story flubs the grounder. **87m/C DVD.** *US* Michael Keaton, Robert Downey Jr., Griffin Dunne, Catherine O'Hara, Bebe Neuwirth, Shalom Harlow, Roger Rees, Ari Graynor, Nadia Dajani, Harris Yulin, Tom Aldredge, Lillias White, Amir Ali Said; ***D:*** Michael Hoffman; ***W:*** Don DeLillo; ***C:*** David M. Dunlap; ***M:*** Yo La Tengo.

Gamebox 1.0 **2004 (PG-13)** Video game tester Charlie gets hooked on a new virtual-reality system that's plugged directly into a user's brain. The object is to rescue the Princess, who looks suspiciously like Charlie's dead girlfriend. The game infests Charlie's brain so the only way for him to survive is to win. The CGI's not bad considering the low budget, but the story's formulaic. **83m/C DVD.** Danielle Fishel, Patrick Kilpatrick, Patrick Cavanaugh, Nate Richert; ***D:*** David Hillenbrand, Scott Hillenbrand; ***W:*** Patrick Casey, Worm Miller; ***C:*** Philip D. Schwartz. **VIDEO**

Gamer *Game* **2009 (R)** Performing in the online game "Slayers" is death row inmate Kable (the ever-so-macho Butler)—a controlled avatar of 17-year-old virtual game master Simon (Lerman)—who gets closer to winning his freedom with each violent and victorious battle he endures. Meanwhile, his desperate wife is an avatar forced to act out the deviant sexual desires in another game, all created by Ken Castle (Hall) who has grown filthy rich in the process. But a hacker resistance group threatens the whole operation. Lost amidst the not-unexpected hyper action of writers/directors Neveldine and Taylor is the message that technology isn't always such a good thing. **95m/C DVD.** *US* Gerard Butler, Michael C. Hall, Milo Ventimiglia, Alison Lohman, Amber Valletta, Logan Lerman, Kyra Sedgwick, John Leguizamo, Terry Crews, Zoe Bell; ***D:*** Mark Neveldine, Brian Taylor; ***W:*** Mark Neveldine, Brian Taylor; ***C:*** Ekkehart Pollack; ***M:*** Robert Williamson, Geoff Zanelli.

Gamera the Brave 1/2 *Gamera: Chiisaki yusha-tachi; Gamera: Little Braves* **2006** The original Gamera films were targeted at youngsters, while the redone series from the 1990s were more for adults. This sequel to the newer trilogy returns to its kid-oriented roots while retaining the higher production values. A young boy raises a newly hatched turtle, which turns out to be a baby Gamera. Thank goodness, because a man-eating monster has just appeared and there's a need for another giant critter to fight him, as the world's military is apparently capable of nuking countries, but can't put down one really big salamander. **96m/C DVD.** *JP* Kanji Tsuda, Susumu Terajima, Kaho; ***D:*** Ryuta Tazaki; ***W:*** Yukari Tatsui.

Gamera, the Invincible 1/2 *Gamera; Gammera; Daikaiju Gamera* **1966** This Japanese monster flick features the ultimate nuclear super-turtle who flies around destroying cities and causing panic. First in the series of notoriously bad films, this one is cool in black and white and has some impressive special effects. Dubbed in English. **86m/B VHS, DVD.** *JP* Eiji Funakoshi, Harumi Kiritachi, Junichiro Yamashiko, Yoshiro Uchida, Brian Donlevy, Albert Dekker, Diane Findlay, John Baragrey, Dick O'Neill; ***D:*** Noriaki Yuasa; ***W:*** Fumi Takahashi; ***C:*** Nobuo Munekawa.

Gamera vs. Barugon 1/2 *Gamera Tai Barugon; Gambara vs. Barugon; The War of the Monsters* **1966** The monstrous turtle returns to Earth from his outer space prison, now equipped with his famous leg-jets. He soon wishes he had stayed airborne, however, when he is forced to do battle with 130-foot lizard Barugon and his rainbow-melting ray. Tokyo and Osaka get melted in the process. **101m/C VHS, DVD.** *JP* Kojiro Hongo, Kyoko Enami; ***D:*** Shigeo Tanaka.

Gamera vs. Gaos 1/2 *The Return of the Giant Monsters; Gamera vs. Gyaos; Boyichi and the Supermonster; Gamera Tai Gaos* **1967** Now fully the good guy, Gamera slugs it out with a bat-like critter named Gaos. Suspense rules the day when Gaos tries to put out the super turtle's jets with his built-in fire extinguisher but luckily for Earth, Gamera has a few tricks of his own up his shell. **87m/C VHS, DVD.** *JP* Kojiro Hongo, Kichijiro Ueda, Naoyuki Abe; ***D:*** Noriaki Yuasa.

Gamera vs. Guiron *Attack of the Monsters; Gamera Tai Guiron* **1969** Gamera risks it all to take on an evil, spear-headed monster on a distant planet. Highlight is the sexy, leotard clad aliens who want to eat the little Earth kids' brains. **88m/C VHS, DVD.** *JP* Nobuhiro Kashima, Christopher Murphy, Miyuki Akiyama, Yuko Hamada, Eiji Funakoshi; ***D:*** Noriaki Yuasa.

Gamera vs. Zigra *Gamera Tai Shinkai Kaiju Jigara; Gamera vs. the Deep Sea Monster Zigra* **1971** Gamera the flying turtle chose an ecological theme for this, his final movie. It seems that the alien Zigrans have come to Earth to wrest the planet from the hands of the pollutive humans who have nearly destroyed it. The aliens kill the staunch turtle, but the love and prayers of children revive him that he may defend Earth once more. **91m/C VHS.** *JP* Reiko Kasahara, Mikiko Tsubouchi, Koji Fujiyama, Arlene Zoellner, Gloria Zoellner; *D:* Noriaki Yuasa.

Gamers 🦴 1/2 **2006** If you're big into role-playing games you might find this mockumentary amusing, otherwise it's sorta weirdly disturbing. Five socially inept geeks—still living with their parents and working minimal effort jobs—are about to break the all-time record for the most hours spent playing "Demons, Nymphs, and Dragons." They have been playing for 23 years but the nearer they get to their goal, the more tensions arise within the group. **87m/C DVD.** Scott Rinker, Dave Hanson, John Heard, Beverly D'Angelo, Kevin Kirkpatrick, Joe Nieves, Kevin Sherwood; *D:* Christopher Folino; *W:* Christopher Folino; *C:* Roberto Blasini; *M:* Tom Hite. **VIDEO**

Games 🦴🦴 1/2 **1967** Bored married Manhattanites Paul (Caan) and Jennifer (Ross), who are looking for some kinky entertainment, get involved with amateur medium Lisa (Signoret). Suddenly what's "real," isn't and there's more than one double-cross to cope with. Lots of atmosphere but not enough suspense. **100m/C VHS.** Simone Signoret, James Caan, Katharine Ross, Don Stroud, Kent Smith, Estelle Winwood, Marjorie Bennett, Ian Wolfe; *Cameos:* Florence Marly, Luana Anders; *D:* Curtis Harrington; *W:* Gene R. Kearney; *C:* William A. Fraker; *M:* Samuel Matlovsky.

Games Girls Play 🦴 1/2 *The Bunny Caper; Sex Play* **1975** The daughter of an American diplomat organizes a contest at a British boarding school to see which of her classmates can seduce important dignitaries. **90m/C VHS.** Christina Hart, Jane Anthony, Jill Damas, Drina Pavlovic; *D:* Jack Arnold.

Games of Love and Chance 🦴🦴 *L'esquive* **2003** Centered around North African immigrant Krimo (Elkharraz), a closed-up teenager living in a Paris suburb whose emotional walls force girlfriend Magali (Ganito) to dump him. He quickly finds a new love interest in the extroverted Lydia (Forestier) and pushes his way into a school play to be near her. The camera provides a close view of the many effusive confrontations between the teenaged cast, all of whom are played by acting neophyte residents of the working class suburb where the film is set. Many of the themes explored are universal to the teen movie genre. This film, Kechiche's second effort, has been an award-winning hit in France. **119m/C DVD.** *FR* Osman Elkharraz, Sara Forestier, Sabrina Ouazani, Nanou Benhamou, Aurelie Ganito, Rachid Hami; *D:* Abdellatif Kechiche; *W:* Abdellatif Kechiche; *C:* Lubomir Bakchev.

The Gamma People WOOF! **1956** A journalist discovers a Balkan doctor shooting children with gamma rays, creating an army of brainless zombies. Cult-renowned grade-Z tripe. **83m/B VHS.** *GB* Walter Rilla, Paul Douglas, Eva Bartok; *D:* John Gilling; *C:* Ted Moore.

Gandhi 🦴🦴🦴 1/2 **1982 (PG)** The biography of Mahatma Gandhi, from the prejudice he encounters as a young attorney in South Africa, to his role as spiritual leader to the people of India and his use of passive resistance against the country's British rulers, and his eventual assassination. Kingsley is a marvel in his Academy Award-winning role and the picture is a generally riveting epic worthy of its eight Oscars. **188m/C VHS, DVD.** *GB* Ben Kingsley, Candice Bergen, Edward Fox, John Gielgud, John Mills, Saeed Jaffrey, Trevor Howard, Ian Charleson, Roshan Seth, Athol Fugard, Martin Sheen, Daniel Day-Lewis, Rohini Hattangady, Ian Bannen, Geraldine James, Nigel Hawthorne, Om Puri, John Ratzenberger; *D:* Richard Attenborough; *W:* John Briley; *C:* Billy Williams; *M:* George Fenton. Oscars '82: Actor (Kingsley), Art Dir./Set Dec., Cinematog., Costume Des., Director (Attenborough), Film Editing, Orig. Screenplay, Picture, Sound; British Acad. '82: Actor (Kingsley), Director (Attenborough), Film, Support. Actress (Hattangady); Directors Guild '82: Director (Attenborough); Golden Globes '83: Actor—Drama (Kingsley), Director (Attenborough), Foreign Film, Screenplay; L.A. Film Critics '82: Actor (Kingsley); Natl. Bd. of Review '82: Actor (Kingsley); N.Y. Film Critics '82: Actor (Kingsley), Film.

Gang Boys 🦴 1/2 **1997** When a young man is brutally beaten by an L.A. street gang, mom Blair does not take things lying down. She contacts her estranged, ex-cop husband Hauser and he organizes a group of local victims to fight back. This time it's the gang members who should watch out. **87m/C VHS, DVD.** Wings Hauser, Linda Blair, Cole Hauser, Daryl Roach, Carmen Zapata, Ernest Harden Jr., Talbert Morton, Dave Buzzotta; *D:* Wings Hauser; *W:* Maria Dylan, Wings Hauser; *C:* Francis Grumman; *M:* Geoff Levin, Chris Many. **VIDEO**

Gang Bullets 🦴 **1938** Mobster tries to continue his dirty systems in a new town, but finds the legal force incorruptible. **62m/B VHS, DVD.** Anne Nagel, Robert Kent, Charles Trowbridge, Morgan Wallace, J. Farrell MacDonald, Arthur Loft, John Merton; *D:* Lambert Hillyer.

Gang Busters 🦴🦴 **1942** Men battle crime in the city in this serial in 13 episodes based on the popular radio series of the same name. **253m/B VHS, DVD.** Kent Taylor, Irene Hervey, Robert Armstrong, Ralph Morgan, Richard Davies, Ralf Harolde; *D:* Ray Taylor, Noel Mason Smith; *W:* Morgan Cox, Phillips Lord, Victor McLeod, George Plympton; *C:* John Boyle, William Sickner.

Gang Busters 🦴 1/2 **1955** Prisoners plan a breakout. Slow and uninteresting adaptation of the successful radio series. Filmed in Oregon. **78m/B VHS, DVD.** Myron Healey, Sam Edwards, Frank Gerstle; *D:* Bill Karn.

Gang in Blue 🦴🦴 1/2 **1996 (R)** Black officer Michael Rhoades (Van Peebles) is secretly investigating a white supremacist group of cops, called the Phantoms, within the LAPD. Marine Corp vet and police rookie Keith DeBruler (Brolin) becomes Rhoades's new partner and his racial comments make him a likely initiate for the Phantoms. So can he be trusted to be Rhoades's inside man and help Michael expose the corruption within the ranks? **99m/C VHS, DVD.** Mario Van Peebles, Josh Brolin, Melvin Van Peebles, J.T. Walsh, Cynda Williams, Stephen Lang, Sean McCann; *D:* Mario Van Peebles, Melvin Van Peebles; *W:* David Fuller, Rick Natkin; *C:* Rhett Morita; *M:* Larry Brown. **CABLE**

Gang Justice 🦴 **1994** Low-budget melodrama finds sensitive Asian student Paul (Kim) battling racists at school and his crippled alcoholic father at home. Some martial arts fight scenes but this is amateur time. **92m/C VHS, DVD.** Joon Kim, Jonathan Gorman, Erik Estrada, Angel Dashek; *D:* Richard W. Park.

Gang of Roses 🦴🦴 **2003 (R)** In the old west, Rachel, Chasity, Kim, Ming Li, and Maria formed the Rose Gang. Successful bank robbers, they retired after five years but regroup when Rachel's sister is killed. **88m/C VHS, DVD.** Monica Calhoun, Stacey Dash, LisaRaye, Marie Matiko, Kimberly (Lil' Kim) Jones, Bobby Brown, Louis Mandylor; *C:* Ben Kufrin; *M:* Michael Cohen. **VIDEO**

Gang Related 🦴 1/2 **1996 (R)** Rodriguez (Shakur) and Divinci (Belushi) are a couple of scuzzball homicide cops who set up drug deals with impounded dope, then kill the customers. They keep the dope and the money, and call the murders "gang-related." Their plan unravels when they whack an undercover DEA agent posing as a dealer. They try to play a game of "pin the crime on the wino" with a derelict (Quaid) who the duo thinks is easy prey. As their scheming spins out of control, Rodriguez tries to hold things together, while Divinci rips them apart. Shakur rises above the average material as the most likable of the entirely distasteful cast of characters. **109m/C VHS, DVD.** James Belushi, Tupac Shakur, Dennis Quaid, Lela Rochon, James Earl Jones, David Paymer, Wendy Crewson, Gary Cole, Terrence "T.C." Carson, Brad Greenquist, James Handy, Victor Love, Robert LaSardo, Gregory Scott Cummins; *D:* Jim Kouf; *W:* Jim Kouf; *C:* Brian Reynolds; *M:* Mickey Hart.

Gang War 🦴 **1940** Low-budget gangster film with an all-black cast about two gangs fighting for control of the city's jukebox business. **60m/B VHS, DVD.** Ralph Cooper, Gladys Snyder, Reggie Fenderson, Lawrence Criner, Monte Hawley, Jesse C. Brooks, Maceo B. Sheffield; *D:* Leo Popkin.

Gang Wars 🦴 *Devil's Express* **1975 (R)** There's a riot going on as Puerto Rican, Black, and Chinese gangs fight it out for control of the city. **82m/C VHS.** Warhawk Tanzania, Larry Fleishman, Sam DeFazio, Wilfred Roldan, Elsie Roman, Sarah Nyrick; *D:* Barry Rosen.

Gangland 🦴 **2000 (R)** In 2010 there's been a small nuclear disaster and a flesh-eating virus, and the survivors are essentially on their own. Jared (Mitchell) and Derek (Mandylor) are imprisoned by the local gang but they escape and hook up with fugitive Alexis (Kinmont). The trio decides payback is in order, especially when they discover that gang leader Lucifer (Klyn) is keeping the antidote to the virus all to himself. Don't get excited seeing Ice-T and Coolio on the box art because they play cops who get offed in the first scene. Talk about bait-and-switch. **93m/C DVD.** Sasha Mitchell, Costas Mandylor, Kathleen Kinmont, Vincent Klyn, Tim Thomerson, Jennifer Gareis, Ice-T, Coolio; *Cameos:* Kristanna Loken; *D:* Art Comacho; *W:* David DeFalco; *C:* Andrea V. Rossotto; *M:* Thomas Morse. **VIDEO**

The Gang's All Here 🦴 1/2 **1940** Darro joins a trucking firm whose rigs are being run off the road and hijacked by a competitor. Features "Charlie Chan" regulars Luke and Moreland. **63m/B VHS, DVD.** Frankie Darro, Marcia Mae Jones, Jackie Moran, Mantan Moreland, Keye Luke; *D:* Jean Yarbrough.

The Gang's All Here 🦴🦴 *The Girls He Left Behind* **1943** Produced smack in the middle of World War II, the film has (what else?) a war backdrop, but set to the tunes of Benny Goodman and his crew. On leave from his army post, playboy Andy Mason (Willock) falls for showgirl Edie Allen (Miranda), sweeping her off her feet for an evening of romance that leaves her swooning, only to leave for duty the next morning. He returns, but with a secret. **103m/C VHS.** Carmen Miranda, Phil Baker, Benny Goodman, Eugene Pallette, Charlotte Greenwood, Edward Everett Horton, James Ellison, Alice Faye, Dave Willock q, Tony De Marco; *D:* Busby Berkeley; *W:* Nancy Wintner, George Root Jr.

Gangs, Inc. 🦴🦴 *Crimes, Inc.; Paper Bullets* **1941** A woman is sent to prison for a hit-and-run accident, actually the fault of a wealthy playboy. When she learns his identity she vows revenge and turns to crime to achieve her evil ends. Okay thriller suffers from plot problems. Ladd has a minor role filmed before he became a star. **72m/B VHS, DVD.** Joan Woodbury, Jack LaRue, Linda Ware, John Archer, Vince Barnett, Alan Ladd, Gavin Gordon, Selmer Jackson, George Pembroke; *D:* Phil Rosen; *W:* Martin Mooney; *C:* Arthur Martinelli.

Gangs of New York 🦴🦴🦴 **2002 (R)** Scorsese's flawed but rich and powerful epic recounts the mid-19th Century struggles in New York's Five Points section between the Irish immigrant gang the Dead Rabbits and the second-generation nativist gangs led by the brutal but mesmerizing Bill the Butcher (Day-Lewis). Young Amsterdam Vallon (DeCaprio) witnesses the death of his father (Neeson), the leader of the Rabbits, in a bloody street melee and is sent away. When he returns, unrecognized, he insinuates himself into Bill's inner circle, waiting for his chance at vengeance and catching the eye of pickpocket Jenny (Diaz). This plot is set against the backdrop of the political corruption of "Boss" Tweed's New York empire and the draft riots that were tearing the city apart at the time. Scorsese's vision is realized through meticulous attention to period detail, a standout performance by Day-Lewis, and the willingness to show hero and villain alike as well-rounded characters. Uneven pacing and underuse (probably out of necessity) of excellent supporting cast are the only complaints. Loosely based on the 1928 book by Herbert Asbury. **168m/C VHS, DVD, Blu-ray Disc.** *US* Leonardo DiCaprio, Daniel Day-Lewis, Cameron Diaz, Liam Neeson, Jim Broadbent, John C. Reilly, Henry Thomas, Brendan Gleeson, Gary Lewis, Stephen Graham, Eddie Marsan, Alec McCowen, David Hemmings, Larry (Lawrence) Gilliard Jr., Cara Seymour, Roger Ashton-Griffiths, Cian McCormack; *Cameos:* Martin Scorsese; *D:* Martin Scorsese; *W:* Jay Cocks, Steven Zaillian, Kenneth Lonergan; *C:* Michael Ballhaus; *M:* Howard Shore. British Acad. '02: Actor (Day-Lewis); Golden Globes '03: Director (Scorsese), Song ("The Hands That Built America"); L.A. Film Critics '02: Actor (Day-Lewis); N.Y. Film Critics '02: Actor (Day-Lewis); Screen Actors Guild '02: Actor (Day-Lewis).

Gangs of Sonora 🦴 1/2 **1941** Crooked commissioner Sam Tredwell is determined to remain in charge with the help of his lackey lawyer David Connors. When newspaper editor Beecham argues for making Wyoming a state, he's murdered. Connors' mother, Kansas Kate, is disgusted and takes over running the newspaper, with the help of the Mesquiteers. The 38th film in the series. **56m/B DVD.** Robert "Bob" Livingston, Bob Steele, Rufe Davis, Robert Frazer, Helen MacKellar, Malcolm "Bud" McTaggart, William Farnum, June Johnson; *D:* John English; *W:* Doris Schroeder, Albert DeMond; *C:* Bud Thackery.

The Gangster 🦴🦴 1/2 **1947** Sullivan plays a small-time slum-bred hood who climbs to the top of the underworld, only to lose his gang because he allows his fears to get the better of him. (There's nothing to fear except when someone knows you're afeared.) Noir crimer with an interesting psychological perspective, though a bit sluggish at times. **84m/B VHS.** Barry Sullivan, Joan Lorring, Akim Tamiroff, Harry (Henry) Morgan, John Ireland, Fifi d'Orsay, Shelley Winters; *D:* Gordon Wiles.

Gangster No. 1 🦴🦴 1/2 **2000 (R)** An aging London crime boss—who's only known as Gangster 55 (McDowall)—learns that his mentor Freddie Mays (Thewlis) is just out of prison after a 30-year stretch for murder. Flashback to 1968, when a young, ruthless Gangster (a ferocious Bettany) earns his place by taking on Freddie's rivals. Then Gangster becomes jealous of Freddie's girlfriend, Karen (Burrows), and learns of a plot to rub out Freddie. He plans on setting up his boss and becoming head man but never expects to have to confront his past someday. Based on the play by Louis Mellis and David Scinto. **103m/C VHS, DVD.** *GB GE* Malcolm McDowell, Paul Bettany, David Thewlis, Saffron Burrows, Kenneth Cranham, Jamie Foreman, Eddie Marsan, Andrew Lincoln; *D:* Paul McGuigan; *W:* Johnny Ferguson; *C:* Peter Sova; *M:* John Dankworth.

Gangster Wars 🦴🦴 **1981** A specially edited-for-video version of the TV miniseries "The Gangster Chronicles." Based on fact, it deals with the growth of organized crime in America from the early days of this century, through the eyes of three ghetto kids who grow up to become powerful mobsters. **121m/C VHS.** Michael Nouri, Joe Penny, Brian Benben, Kathleen Lloyd, Madeleine Stowe, Robert Davi; *D:* Richard Sarafian. **TV**

Gangster World 🦴🦴 **1998 (R)** In the 21st century, Gangster World is an adult theme part that caters to fulfilling a human's most decadent fantasies—aided by cyborgs in a 1930s setting. But with a name like that, it's easy to believe that a battle for control turns the park into the most dangerous place in the universe. Lots of action and decent enough special effects. **91m/C VHS, DVD.** Xavier DeClie, David Leisure, Gabriel Dell Jr., Stacey Williams, Bridget Flannery; *D:* David Bishop. **VIDEO**

Gangsters 🦴 **1979** City is ruled by the mob and nothing can stop their bloody grip except "The Special Squad." **90m/C VHS.** *IT* Michael V. Gazzo, Tony Page, Vicki Sue Robinson, Nai Bonet; *D:* Mac Ahlberg.

Gangster's Den 🦴 **1945** A gang of renegades scare a woman out of buying a gold-laden piece of land and Billy the Kid comes to her rescue. **56m/B VHS, DVD.** Buster Crabbe, Kermit Maynard, Al "Fuzzy" St. John, Charles "Blackie" King; *D:* Sam Newfield.

Gangster's Law WOOF! **1986** A look at a seedy gangster's downfall. Filmed on location in Italy. Dubbed. **89m/C VHS.** Klaus Kinski, Maurice Poli, Susy Andersen, Max Delys; *D:* Siro Marcellini.

Gangsters of the Frontier 🦴 **1944** The people of Red Rock are forced to work in the town mines by two prison escapees until Ritter and his friends ride to the rescue. Part of the "Texas Ranger" series. **56m/B VHS.** Tex Ritter, Dave O'Brien; *D:* Elmer Clifton; *W:* Elmer Clifton.

Gangway 1/2 **1937** Pat Wayne (Matthews), a London newspaper reporter, is mistaken for a jewel thief and kidnapped by gangsters aboard a New York-bound ocean liner. In the meantime, the real thief is aboard posing as a Hollywood actress (Blakeney), and it's up to Scotland Yard inspector Bob Deering (Mackay) to solve the crime. Matthews was considered by many to be the English equivalent of America's Eleanor Powell. Based on an original story by Dwight Taylor. **90m/B VHS.** *GB* Jessie Matthews, Barry Mackay, Olive Blakeney, Liane Ordeyne, Patrick Ludlow, Nat Pendleton, Noel Madison, Alastair Sim, Doris Rogers, Laurence Anderson, Bennie Dorn; ***D:*** Sonnie Hale; ***W:*** Sonnie Hale, Lesser Samuels.

Ganja and Hess 1/2 *Blood Couple; Black Vampire; Double Possession; Black Out: The Moment of Terror; Black Evil* **1973 (R)** Jones plays a professor of African studies who is turned into a vampire by another vampire. He then marries the villain's ex-wife, played by Clark, a veteran of Russ Meyer films. Not much of a story but the acting is actually quite good and there are some creepy moments thanks mainly to an interesting score. **110m/C VHS, DVD.** Duane Jones, Marlene Clark, Bill Gunn, Sam Waymon, Leonard Jackson, Candece Tarpley, Mabel King; ***D:*** Bill Gunn; ***W:*** Bill Gunn; ***C:*** James E. Hinton; ***M:*** Sam Waymon.

Ganjasaurus Rex **1987 (R)** Monster spoof about a giant green dinosaur emerging from the pot-laden hills of California. Maybe it's all in your head, man. **100m/C VHS.** Paul Bassis, Dave Fresh, Rosie Jones; ***D:*** Ursi Reynolds.

Ganked **2005 (PG-13)** Ricky (Mitchell) is an undiscovered songwriter living in his parents' basement hoping to hit the big-time any day now. When he wins a contest and is offered a position in a record company he thinks he's made it. Instead, he's stuck working in their mailroom, while the company's sexy singer Kennedy Ross (Bombay) steals his song and his glory. And he won't rest until he's got his revenge. **108m/C DVD.** Kel Mitchell, Katt Micah Williams, Antwon Tanner, Bombay; ***D:*** Kenn Michael; ***W:*** Kel Mitchell; ***C:*** Kenn Michael; ***M:*** Kel Mitchell, Kenn Michael. **VIDEO**

Gappa the Trifibian Monster 1/2 *Daikyoju Gappa; Monster from a Prehistoric Planet* **1967 (PG)** Researchers visiting a tropical island find a giant egg and take it back to Tokyo with them, dismaying the egg's giant monster parents. Dubbed. **90m/C VHS, DVD.** *JP* Tamio Kawaji, Yoko Yamamoto, Tatsuya Fuji, Koji Wada, Yuji Okada; ***D:*** Haruyasu Hoguchi; ***W:*** Ryuzo Nakanishi; ***C:*** Muneo Ueda.

Garage Days 1/2 **2003 (R)** Sydney, Australia garage band tries to hit it big in this goofy comedy directed by Proyas. Freddy (Gurry) just wants to make it big as the singer of a rock and roll band, but he has to cope with the quirks and problems of his bandmates: girlfriend/bassist Tanya (Miranda), guitarist with an identity crisis Joe (Stiller), and dedicated drug user/drummer Lucy (Sadrinna) who spends more time creating pharmaceutical cocktails than practicing the drums. Further complicating the mix is the attraction between Freddy and Joe's girlfriend, Kate (Stange) and the band's misguided attempt to blackmail a big-time manager (Csokas) to come see them play. Proyas fills the movie with inventive visuals and keeps the comedy level high, but with characters that alternate between appealing and one-dimensional, and a familiar plot, some may find too little substance to go with the style. **105m/C DVD.** *AU* Maya Stange, Russell Dykstra, Andy Anderson, Marton Csokas, Kick (Christopher) Gurry, Pia Miranda, Brett Stiller, Chris Sadrinna, Tiriel Mora; ***D:*** Alex Proyas; ***W:*** Alex Proyas, Dave Warner; ***C:*** Simon Duggan; ***M:*** Antony Partos, David McCormack.

The Garbage Pail Kids Movie WOOF! **1987 (PG)** The disgusting youngsters, stars of bubblegum cards, make their first and last film appearance in this live action dud. The garbage is where it should be thrown. **100m/C VHS, DVD.** Anthony Newley, MacKenzie Astin, Katie Barberi; ***D:*** Rod Amateau; ***W:*** Rod Amateau.

The Garbage-Picking, Field Goal-Kicking Philadelphia Phenomenon 1/2 **1998** Sports recruiters discover the natural kicking talents of sanitation engineer Barney Gorman (Danza) and turn his life upside down by giving him the chance to be the new placekicker for the Philadelphia Eagles. TV movie. **85m/C VHS.** Tony Danza, Jessica Tuck, Art LaFleur, Al Ruscio, Ray Wise, Chris Berman; ***D:*** Tom Kelleher. **TV**

Garbo Talks **1984 (PG-13)** A dying eccentric's last request is to meet the reclusive screen legend Greta Garbo. Bancroft amusingly plays the dying woman whose son goes to extreme lengths in order to fulfill his mother's last wish. **104m/C VHS, DVD.** Anne Bancroft, Ron Silver, Carrie Fisher, Catherine Hicks, Steven Hill, Howard da Silva, Dorothy Loudon, Harvey Fierstein, Hermione Gingold; ***D:*** Sidney Lumet; ***C:*** Andrzej Bartkowiak; ***M:*** Cy Coleman.

The Garden **1990** Eternally provocative director Jarman does another take on sex and religion. He examines the role of the Church in the persecution of homosexuality by recreating the story of the Passion and replacing the figure of Christ in some sequences with two male lovers, who are arrested, humiliated, and tortured. **90m/C VHS.** *GB* Tilda Swinton, Johnny Mills, Philip MacDonald, Roger Cook, Kevin Collins, Pete Lee-Wilson, Spencer Lee, Jody Graber; ***D:*** Derek Jarman; ***W:*** Derek Jarman; ***M:*** Simon Fisher Turner.

The Garden of Allah **1936** Dietrich finds hyper-romantic encounters in the Algerian desert with Boyer, but his terrible secret may doom them both. This early Technicolor production, though flawed, is an absolute must for Dietrich fans. Yuma, Arizona substituted for the exotic locale. **85m/C VHS, DVD.** Alan Marshal, Marlene Dietrich, Charles Boyer, Basil Rathbone, Sir C. Aubrey Smith, Tilly Losch, Joseph Schildkraut, Henry (Kleinbach) Brandon, John Carradine; ***D:*** Richard Boleslawski; ***W:*** W.P. Lipscomb, Lynn Riggs; ***C:*** William Howard Greene; ***M:*** Max Steiner.

The Garden of Delights **1970** A wicked black comedy about a millionaire, paralyzed and suffering from amnesia after a car accident. His horrendously greedy family tries to get him to remember and reveal his Swiss bank account number. Acclaimed; in Spanish with English subtitles. **95m/C VHS.** *SP* Jose Luis Lopez Vasquez, Lina Canelajas, Luchy Soto, Francisco Pierra, Charo Soriano; ***D:*** Carlos Saura.

The Garden of Eden **1928** Milestone—whose "Two Arabian Nights" had won an Academy Award the previous year, and who went on to direct "All Quiet on the Western Front" and "Of Mice and Men"—directed this sophisticated ersatz Lubitsch sex comedy. Griffith, the so-called "Orchid Lady," is a young girl who dreams of divadom but falls deep into the underbelly of the seedy side of Budapest. With the aid of a fallen baroness, however, she finds her way to Monte Carlo and has her turn in the limelight. A handsome production designed by William Cameron Menzies, art director for "Gone With the Wind." **115m/B VHS, DVD.** Corinne Griffith, Louise Dresser, Charles Ray, Lowell Sherman; ***D:*** Lewis Milestone; ***W:*** Hans Kraly; ***C:*** John Arnold.

Garden of Evil 1/2 **1954** On their way to the gold fields, Hooker (Cooper), Fiske (Widmark), and Daly (Mitchell) are stranded in a Mexican village. Leah (Hayward) offers the three strangers big bucks if they'll rescue her husband (Marlowe), who was injured in a gold mining accident. The mine is located in a remote mountain region and the group find themselves besieged by Apaches. Equal excitement went on behind the camera as a temperamental Hayward walked off the set whenever she didn't like Hathaway's brusque directing. **100m/C DVD.** Gary Cooper, Susan Hayward, Richard Widmark, Cameron Mitchell, Hugh Marlowe, Victor Manuel Mendoza, Rita Moreno; ***D:*** Henry Hathaway; ***W:*** Frank Fenton; ***C:*** Milton Krasner; ***M:*** Bernard Herrmann.

The Garden of Redemption 1/2 **1997 (PG-13)** Italian priest Don Paolo (LaPaglia) has his faith tested when his Tuscan village is occupied in 1944 by German troops and he has to decide whether to overcome his fears and join with the partisan resistance movement. That village beauty Adriana (Davidtz) is eager to help him with the decision only complicates matters more. **99m/C VHS.** Anthony LaPaglia, Embeth Davidtz, Dan Hedaya, Peter Firth, David Neal, Jorge Sanz, James Acheson; ***D:*** Thomas Michael Donnelly; ***W:*** Thomas Michael Donnelly; ***C:*** Jacek Laskus; ***M:*** John Altman. **CABLE**

The Garden of the Finzi-Continis *Il Giardino Del Finzi-Contini* **1971 (R)** Acclaimed film by De Sica about an aristocratic Jewish family living in Italy under increasing Fascist oppression on the eve of WWII. The garden wall symbolizes the distance between the Finzi-Continis and the Nazi reality about to engulf them. Flawless acting and well-defined direction. Based on the novel by Giorgio Bassani, who collaborated on the script but later repudiated the film. Music by De Sica's son, Manuel. In Italian with English subtitles or dubbed. **94m/C VHS, DVD.** *IT* Dominique Sanda, Helmut Berger, Lino Capolicchio, Fabio Testi, Romolo Valli; ***D:*** Vittorio De Sica; ***W:*** Cesare Zavattini; ***C:*** Ennio Guarnieri; ***M:*** Bill Conti, Manuel De Sica. Oscars '71: Foreign Film; Berlin Intl. Film Fest. '71: Golden Berlin Bear.

Garden Party 1/2 **2008** It's a too-familiar story about chasing fame (and finding humiliation) in Hollywood. Realtor Sally (Shaw) has a successful pot operation sideline that becomes the focal point for the other lost souls, including a runaway teen, a porn photographer, a would-be dancer, and a struggling musician, as they drift along and momentarily cross paths. **88m/C DVD.** Vanessa Shaw, Patrick Fischler, Christopher Allport, Ross Patterson, Willa Holland, Alex Cendese, Erik Scott Smith, Richard Gunn, Jeff Newman, Fiona Duff; ***D:*** Jason Freeland; ***W:*** Jason Freeland; ***C:*** Robert Benavides; ***M:*** John Swihart.

Garden State **2004 (R)** Zach Braff stars in his directorial debut (which he also wrote) as Andrew Largeman, Large to his friends, a struggling actor whose biggest role so far has been a retarded quarterback in a cable movie. Things aren't going well. He works at a Vietnamese restaurant, is in a perpetually medicated state, and his father just called to tell him his mother died. Large flies home to New Jersey for the first time in nine years for the funeral, leaving his medication behind. Reunited with his high school friends, who form a motley crew ranging from a gravedigger to a millionaire who invented silent Velcro, Large begins to experience life again. His awakening is further helped by the arrival of Sam (Portman), a cute, quirky free spirit. While there are some minor flaws, the stellar cast and some genuinely amusing moments are well worth a look. **109m/C DVD.** *US* Zach Braff, Ian Holm, Ron Leibman, Method Man, Natalie Portman, Ann Dowd, Denis O'Hare, Peter Sarsgaard, Michael Weston, Jean Smart, Jim Parsons, Jackie Hoffman, Amy Ferguson, Ato Essandoh; ***D:*** Zach Braff; ***W:*** Zach Braff; ***C:*** Lawrence Sher; ***M:*** Chad Fisher. Ind. Spirit '05: First Feature.

Gardens of Stone **1987 (R)** A zealous young cadet during the Vietnam War is assigned to the Old Guard patrol at Arlington Cemetery, and clashes with the patrol's older officers and various pacifist civilians. Falls short of the mark, although Jones turns in an excellent performance. **112m/C VHS, DVD.** James Caan, James Earl Jones, D.B. Sweeney, Anjelica Huston, Dean Stockwell, Lonette McKee, Mary Stuart Masterson, Bill Graham, Sam Bottoms, Casey Siemaszko, Laurence Fishburne, Dick Anthony Williams, Elias Koteas, Peter Masterson, Carlin Glynn, Eric Holland; ***D:*** Francis Ford Coppola; ***W:*** Ronald Bass; ***C:*** Jordan Cronenweth; ***M:*** Carmine Coppola.

Gardens of the Night **2008 (R)** The first half of the film is the most harrowing and then it sorta peters out. Deviant child pornographer Alex (Arnold) and his sidekick Frank (Zegers) kidnap 8-year-old Leslie (Simpkins) and dump her in their lair alongside young Donnie (Smith). They eventually convince both children that their parents don't want them and the youngsters bond over their ordeal. Years later, they are homeless teens hustling the streets of San Diego until Leslie (Jacobs) enters a teen rescue program that could reunite her with her family. **110m/C DVD.** Tom Arnold, Ryan Simpkins, Kevin Zegers, Gillian Jacobs, Jermaine Scooter Smith, Evan Ross, Jeremy Sisto, Harold Perrineau Jr., John Malkovich, Raynold Gideon, Cornelia Guest, Kyle Gallner; ***D:*** Damian Harris; ***W:*** Damian Harris; ***C:*** Paul Huidobro; ***M:*** Craig Richey.

Garfield: A Tail of Two Kitties 1/2 **2006 (PG)** Jon (Meyer), his fat (CGI-rendered) kitty (voiced again by Murray), and dumb dog Odie follow vet Liz (Hewitt) to London where Garfield eventually switches places with a spoiled look-alike named Prince (Curry) who just inherited a country estate. Except Lord Dargis (Connolly), next in line to inherit, wants to do the feline in. It's like a furry version of "The Prince and the Pauper." **80m/C DVD.** *US* Jennifer Love Hewitt, Breckin Meyer, Billy Connolly, Lucy Davis, Ian Abercrombie, Roger Rees, Lucy Davis; ***D:*** Tim Hill; ***W:*** Joel Cohen, Alec Sokolow; ***C:*** Peter Lyons Collister; ***M:*** Christophe Beck; ***V:*** Bill Murray, Tim Curry, Bob Hoskins, Jane Leeves, Jane Horrocks, Sharon Osbourne, Richard E. Grant, Vinnie Jones, Rhys Ifans, Roscoe Lee Browne.

Garfield: The Movie 1/2 **2004 (PG)** The best thing that this escapee from the comic pages has going for it is that fat, nap-taking, lasagna-loving orange cat Garfield (a CGI-creation) is perfectly voiced by the sardonic Murray. The lazy feline dominates nice guy owner Jon (Meyer) and is appalled when life in paradise is threatened by the arrival of excitable mongrel Odie, who arrives via Garfield's sexy vet, Dr. Liz (Hewitt). Naturally, Garfield does his best to get rid of his doggy nuisance until Odie winds up in the clutches of nasty TV show host Happy Chapman (Tobolowsky), who's a decidedly unhappy guy. So it's Garfield to the rescue! Despite the daily comic strip, Garfield's long past his cultural prime, so it's a mystery how he made it to the big screen, especially in this unfunny, slapstick exercise in tedium. **80m/C DVD.** *US* Breckin Meyer, Jennifer Love Hewitt, Stephen Tobolowsky, Mark Christopher-Lawrence, Evan Arnolds Christopher; ***D:*** Peter Hewitt; ***W:*** Joel Cohen, Alec Sokolow; ***C:*** Dean Cundey; ***M:*** Christophe Beck; ***V:*** Bill Murray, Debra Messing, Brad Garrett, Alan Cumming, David Eigenberg, Nick Cannon, Jimmy Kimmel.

Gargantua 1/2 **1998** Marine biologist Jack Ellway (Baldwin) and his son are studying the effects of seismic activity on marine life on a Polynesian island, that's also been the scene of a number of mysterious drownings. Then Jack discovers a nearby underwater trench houses a family of giant reptiles. When a two-foot long baby lizard comes ashore, it's clear mom and dad must be close behind. Kinda the small screen version of "Godzilla," and you know how successful that was. **91m/C VHS.** Adam Baldwin, Julie Carmen, Bobby Hosea, Emile Hirsch; ***D:*** Bradford May; ***W:*** Ronald Parker; ***C:*** John Stokes. **TV**

Gargoyles, The Movie: The Heroes Awaken 1/2 **1994 (G)** Mythical crimefighting creatures, trapped in stone by day thanks to a sorcerer's spell but released to live at night, are displaced in time from their medieval Scottish home, winding up in modern-day New York City. But they discover they still have old enemies to fight. First aired as a five-episode part of the animated TV series. **80m/C VHS, DVD.** ***D:*** Saburo Hashimoto; ***W:*** Eric Luke, Michael Reaves; ***M:*** Carl Johnson; ***V:*** Ed Asner, Keith David, Jonathan Frakes, Marina Sirtis, Bill Fagerbakke, Salli Richardson, Frank Welker, Thom Adcox, Jeff Glenn Bennett.

The Garment Jungle 1/2 **1957** Rather luridly told pro-union film. Korean war vet Alan Mitchell (Mathews) discovers his father Walter (Cobb), who owns a dress company, has been paying protection money to union-busting mobster Ravidge (Boone). Having joined the firm, Alan likes what union boss Tulio Renata (Loggia) has to say and tries to convince his pops, which results in two murders. So Alan looks for dirt on Ravidge to take to the D.A. after getting some personal revenge first. Director Robert Aldrich was replaced by Sherman near the end of the shoot and went uncredited. **88m/B DVD.** Kerwin Mathews, Lee J. Cobb, Richard Boone, Robert Loggia, Gia Scala, Valerie French, Joseph Wiseman; ***D:*** Vincent Sherman; ***W:*** Harry Kleiner; ***C:*** Joseph Biroc; ***M:*** Leith Stevens.

Garringo **1969** Lawmen attempt to bring to justice a man who is intent on killing the soldiers responsible for his father's death. **95m/C VHS.** *IT SP* Anthony Steffen, Peter Lee Lawrence, Jose Bodalo; ***D:*** Rafael Romero Marchent.

Garuda 1/2 *Paksa wayu* **2004** Marketed as the first Thai giant monster film, Garuda is about an evil being imprisoned long ago in Thailand freed by an excavation for a train tunnel. They unleash a 20-foot-tall birdlike monster named after the somewhat more benevolent Garuda from Hindu religion. A military unit specializing in monsters is called in to stop it, and they do their best while promoting racism against their one biracial member (a poor subplot). **112m/C DVD.** *TH* Sornram Theppitak, Sara Legge, Dan Fraser, Chalad Na Songkhla, Yani Tramod; ***D:*** Monthon Arayangkoon; ***W:*** Monthon Arayangkoon; ***C:*** Jiradeht Samnansanor.

Gas WOOF! 1981 (R) This dog has tycoon Hayden buying up all the gas stations in town to create a crisis that will make him richer. Everyone in the cast wastes their time, especially Sutherland as a hip DJ reporting on the gas shortage. **94m/C VHS.** *CA* Donald Sutherland, Susan Anspach, Sterling Hayden, Peter Aykroyd, Howie Mandel, Helen Shaver; ***D:*** Les Rose; ***W:*** Dick Wolf.

Gas Food Lodging **1992 (R)** Saga casts Adams as Nora, a weary waitress in Laramie, New Mexico, trying her best to raise two teenaged daughters on her own. The daughters, Skye and Balk, are disillusioned about love and family. Balk's special friend is Darius, an eccentric window dresser, played by Leitch, Skye's brother. Nothing works out quite as intended but multi-dimensional characters, poignant situtations, and enormous emotional appeal highlight the directorial debut of Anders. Based on the Richard Peck novel "Don't Look and It Won't Hurt." **100m/C VHS, DVD.** Brooke Adams, Ione Skye, Fairuza Balk, James Brolin, Robert Knepper, Donovan Leitch, David Lansbury, Jacob Vargas, Chris Mulkey, Tiffany Anders; ***D:*** Allison Anders; ***W:*** Allison Anders; ***C:*** Dean Lent; ***M:*** J. Mascis, Barry Adamson. Ind. Spirit '93: Actress (Balk).

Gas Pump Girls 1/2 **1979 (R)** Comedy about five lovely ladies who manage a gas station and use their feminine wiles to win the battle against a shady oil sheik. **102m/C VHS.** Kirsten Baker, Dennis Bowen, Huntz Hall, Steve Bond, Leslie King, Linda Lawrence; ***D:*** Joel Bender.

Gas-s-s-s! 1/2 *Gas-s-s-s... or, It May Become Necessary to Destroy the World in Order to Save It* **1970 (PG)** A gas main leak in an Alaskan defense plant kills everyone beyond 30-something and the post-apocalyptic pre-boomer survivors are left to muddle their way through the brume. Trouble is, AIP edited the heck out of the movie, much to Corman's chagrin, and the result is a truncated comedy; Corman was so displeased, in fact, he left to create New World studios. **79m/C VHS, DVD.** Robert Corff, Elaine Giftos, Pat Patterson, George Armitage, Alex Wilson, Ben Vereen, Cindy Williams, Bud Cort, Talia Shire; ***D:*** Roger Corman; ***W:*** George Armitage; ***C:*** Ron Dexter; ***M:*** Barry Melton.

Gaslight 1/2 *Angel Street* **1940** A forgotten British classic that fell victim to the American production of the same title and theme that was filmed only four years later. Set in late Victorian London, Wynyard is the rich innocent married to the calculating Walbrook, who slowly tries driving his bride insane in order to discover some hidden family jewels. She comes under the protection of a Scotland Yard detective (Pettingell) who suspects Walbrook has already murdered once. An outstandingly eerie psychological thriller. Based on the play "Angel Street" by Patrick Hamilton. **88m/C VHS, DVD.** *GB* Anton Walbrook, Diana Wynyard, Frank Pettingell, Cathleen Cordell, Robert Newton, Jimmy Hanley, Minnie Rayner, Mary Hinton, Marie Wright, Jack Barty, Moyna MacGill, Darmora Ballet; ***D:*** Thorold Dickinson; ***W:*** A.R. Rawlinson, Bridget Boland; ***C:*** Bernard Knowles; ***M:*** Richard Addinsell.

Gaslight 1/2 *The Murder in Thorton Square* **1944** Lavish remake of the 1940 film, based on the Patrick Hamilton play "Angel Street." A man tries to drive his beautiful wife insane while searching for priceless jewels. Her only clue to his evil acts is the frequent dimming of their gaslights. A suspenseful Victorian era mystery. Lansbury's film debut, as the tarty maid. **114m/B VHS, DVD.** Charles Boyer, Ingrid Bergman, Joseph Cotten, Angela Lansbury, Terry Moore, May Whitty, Barbara Everest, Emil Rameau, Edmund Breon, Halliwell Hobbes, Tom Stevenson; ***D:*** George Cukor; ***W:*** John Van Druten, Walter Reisch, John Lloyd Balderston; ***C:*** Joseph Ruttenberg; ***M:*** Bronislau Kaper. Oscars '44: Actress (Bergman); Golden Globes '45: Actress—Drama (Bergman).

Gasoline Alley 1/2 **1951** The first in the film series based on the Frank O. King comic strip. Corky and Hope get married and open a diner, then have to deal with financial problems. Family and friends come to their rescue. Followed by "Corky of Gasoline Alley." **76m/B DVD.** Scotty Beckett, Susan Morrow, James Lydon, Don Beddoe, Dick Wessel, Gus Schilling, Pat Brady; ***D:*** Edward L. Bernds; ***C:*** Lester White.

The Gate **1987 (PG-13)** Kids generally like to explore and Dorff and Tripp are no exception. When a large hole is exposed in their backyard, it would be a childhood sin not to see what's in it, right? What they don't know is that this hole is actually a gateway to and from Hell. The terror they unleash includes more than just run-of-the-mill demons. Good special effects. Followed by "Gate 2." **85m/C VHS, DVD.** Christa Denton, Stephen Dorff, Louis Tripp, Kelly Rowan, Jennifer Irwin; ***D:*** Tibor Takacs; ***W:*** Michael Nankin; ***C:*** Thomas Vamos.

Gate 2 1/2 **1992 (R)** Tripp returns in his role as Terry, a young student of demonology in this lame sequel to "The Gate." Terry and a few of his teen buddies call up a group of demons that have been confined behind a gate for billions of years. The demons are used to grant modest wishes, but the wishes end up having very evil effects. Incredibly weak plot saved only by the special monster effects, which include live action and puppetry. **90m/C VHS, DVD.** Louis Tripp, Simon Reynolds, Pamela Segall, James Villemaire, Neil Munro, James Kidnie, Andrea Ladanyi; ***D:*** Tibor Takacs; ***W:*** Michael Nankin; ***C:*** Bryan England; ***M:*** George Blondheim.

Gate of Flesh *Nikutai No Mon* **1964** In postwar Japan, four prostitutes survive the American Occupation by sticking to their own code of conduct, including a restriction on anyone giving away their services for free. However, conduct becomes a flexible point when the women harbor a wounded black marketeer whom each comes to desire. Based on a novel by Taijiro Tamura. Japanese with subtitles. **90m/C VHS.** *JP* Joe Shishido, Yumiko Nogawa, Kayo Matsuo, Satoko Kasai, Misako Tominaga, Tomiko Ishi; ***D:*** Seijun Suzuki.

Gate of Hell 1/2 *Jigokumen* **1954** Set in 12th-century Japan. A warlord desires a beautiful married woman and seeks to kill her husband to have her. However, he accidentally kills her instead. Filled with shame and remorse, the warlord abandons his life to seek solace as a monk. Heavily awarded and critically acclaimed; the first Japanese film to use color photography. In Japanese with English subtitles. **89m/C VHS.** *JP* Kazuo Hasegawa, Machiko Kyo, Isao Yamagata, Koreya Senda; ***D:*** Teinosuke Kinugasa; ***W:*** Teinosuke Kinugasa; ***C:*** Kohei Sugiyama; ***M:*** Yashushi Akutagawa. Oscars '54: Costume Des. (C), Foreign Film; Cannes '54: Film.

Gates of Hell WOOF! *Paura Nella Citta Dei Morti Viventi; City of the Living Dead; The Fear; Twilight of the Dead; Fear in the City of the Living Dead* **1980** The Seven Gates of Hell have been opened and in three days the dead will rise and walk the earth. A reporter (George) and a psychic (MacColl) fight to close the portals before Salem, Massachusetts is overrun by the risen dead. A gorefest that tried to disguise itself under many other titles. **93m/C VHS, DVD.** *IT* Christopher George, Janet Agren, Katherine (Katriona) MacColl, Robert Sampson, Carlo De Mejo, Antonella Interlenghi, Lucio Fulci, Michele (Michael) Soavi; ***D:*** Lucio Fulci; ***W:*** Dardano Sacchetti, Lucio Fulci; ***C:*** Sergio Salvati; ***M:*** Fabio Frizzi.

Gates of Hell 2: Dead Awakening **1996** Occultists performing an initiation rite reopen the portal to hell and a creature from its depths reawakens to cause the usual unholy terror. **87m/C VHS, DVD.** Tom Campitelli, Tamara Hext, Randy Strickland; ***D:*** G.D. Marcum.

The Gathering 1/2 **1977** A dying man seeks out the wife and family he has alienated for a final Christmas gathering. James Poe authored this well-acted holiday tearjerker that won the 1977-78 Emmy for outstanding TV drama special. **94m/C VHS.** Ed Asner, Maureen Stapleton, Lawrence Pressman, Stephanie Zimbalist, Bruce Davison, Gregory Harrison, Veronica Hamel, Gail Strickland; ***D:*** Randal Kleiser; ***M:*** John Barry. **TV**

The Gathering **2002 (R)** Backpacker Cassie (Ricci) is headed for the English village of Ashby Wake when she's hit by a car. The driver, Marion Kirkman (Fox), takes Cassie to her house to recover since she's lost her memory. Marion's husband Simon (Dillane) is researching a recently uncovered first-century church with some unusual iconography that's drawing a number of strangers to the site. Cassie begins to have premonitions about the Kirkmans and the church and her possible ties to the mystery. **92m/C DVD.** *US GB* Christina Ricci, Ioan Gruffudd, Kerry Fox, Stephen (Dillon) Dillane, Simon Russell Beale, Robert Hardy, Peter McNamara; ***D:*** Brian Gilbert; ***W:*** Anthony Horowitz; ***C:*** Martin Fuhrer; ***M:*** Anne Dudley.

A Gathering of Eagles 1/2 **1963** Hudson portrays a hard-nosed Air Force colonel during peacetime whose British wife must adjust to being a military spouse. **115m/C VHS.** Rock Hudson, Rod Taylor, Mary Peach, Barry Sullivan, Kevin McCarthy, Henry Silva, Leif Erickson; ***D:*** Delbert Mann; ***M:*** Jerry Goldsmith.

The Gathering: Part 2 **1979** Sequel in which a widow has a Christmas reunion with her family, but conflict arises when she introduces a new man in her life. Not as effective as the original, also made for TV. **98m/C VHS.** Maureen Stapleton, Efrem Zimbalist Jr., Jameson Parker, Bruce Davison, Lawrence Pressman, Gail Strickland, Veronica Hamel; ***D:*** Charles S. Dubin. **TV**

The Gathering Storm **1974** Based on the first book of memoirs from Sir Winston Churchill, this drama examines the pre-WWII years. **72m/C** Richard Burton, Virginia McKenna, Ian Bannen; ***D:*** Herbert Wise.

The Gathering Storm **2002** Finney stars as a typically pugnacious Winston Churchill, who in the mid-1930s is in the political wilderness as he tries to warn an indifferent England about German re-armament and Hitler's rise to power. But he also has problems at home, since he beloved wife Clemmie (Redgrave) has gone off on an extended trip abroad to ease some marital strain and Winston is feeling lonely, jealous, and vulnerable. **96m/C VHS, DVD.** Albert Finney, Vanessa Redgrave, Jim Broadbent, Linus Roache, Lena Headey, Tom Wilkinson, Derek Jacobi, Ronnie Barker, Celia Imrie, Hugh Bonneville; ***D:*** Richard Loncraine; ***W:*** Hugh Whitemore; ***C:*** Peter Hannan; ***M:*** Trevor Jones. **CABLE**

The Gatling Gun 1/2 *King Gun* **1972 (PG)** Poor tale of the Cavalry, Apache Indians, and renegades all after the title weapon. **93m/C VHS, DVD.** Guy Stockwell, Woody Strode, Patrick Wayne, Robert Fuller, Barbara Luna, John Carradine, Pat Buttram, Phil Harris; ***D:*** Robert Gordon.

Gator **1976 (PG)** Sequel to "White Lightning" (1973) follows the adventures of Gator (Reynolds), who is recruited to gather evidence to convict a corrupt political boss who also happens to be his friend. Reynolds in his good ole' boy role with lots of chase scenes. Talk show host Michael Douglas made his film debut in the role of the governor. First film Reynolds directed. **116m/C VHS, DVD.** Sonny Shroyer, Mike Douglas, Burt Reynolds, Jerry Reed, Lauren Hutton, Jack Weston, Alice Ghostley, Dub Taylor; ***D:*** Burt Reynolds; ***W:*** William W. Norton Sr.; ***M:*** Charles Bernstein.

Gator Bait 1/2 **1973 (R)** The Louisiana swamp is home to the beautiful Desiree, and woe be unto any man who threatens her family. Aims to please fans of the raunchy and violent. Followed by an equally vile sequel. **91m/C VHS.** Claudia Jennings, Clyde Ventura, Bill (Billy) Thurman, Janit Baldwin; ***D:*** Ferd Sebastian, Beverly Sebastian; ***W:*** Ferd Sebastian, Beverly Sebastian.

Gator Bait 2: Cajun Justice **1988 (R)** A city girl comes to the Louisiana swamp and turns violent in an effort to exact revenge on the men who have been tormenting her. **94m/C VHS.** Jan MacKenzie, Tray Loren, Paul Muzzcat, Brad Kepnick, Jerry Armstrong, Ben Sebastian; ***D:*** Ferd Sebastian, Beverly Sebastian; ***W:*** Ferd Sebastian, Beverly Sebastian.

Gator King 1/2 **1970 (R)** Villainous Santos (Fargas) imports Chinese crocodiles to serve them up as dinner at his restaurant and for other nefarious purposes. Spunky journalist Maureen (Foley) and her ex-beau Ranger Ronny (Richardson) decide to investigate. It's a standard-issue micro-budget action flick with nothing really to recommend it, even to fans of the genre. **86m/C DVD.** Antonio Fargas, Jay Richardson, Shannon K. Foley, Michael Berryman, Joe Estevez; ***D:*** Grant Austin Waldman; ***W:*** John L. Denk; ***C:*** Richard Lacy; ***M:*** Joe Pegram.

Gattaca **1997 (PG-13)** It's a future world where genetic tinkering allows parents to tweak their children's DNA before birth and a caste system of "perfect" humans exists. Vincent (Hawke) dreams of employment with the aerospace corporation Gattaca, so he assumes the identity of the genetically superior Jerome (Law). Soon Vincent is falling for icy co-worker Thurman and getting involved in a murder investigation, which could uncover his true identity. Thinking man's sci-fi (read: no spaceships or explosions) along the lines of George Lucas' "THX-1138." **112m/C VHS, DVD, Blu-ray Disc.** Ethan Hawke, Uma Thurman, Jude Law, Gore Vidal, Alan Arkin, Loren Dean, Jayne Brook, Elias Koteas, Tony Shalhoub, Ernest Borgnine; ***D:*** Andrew Niccol; ***W:*** Andrew Niccol; ***C:*** Slawomir Idziak; ***M:*** Michael Nyman.

The Gaucho **1927** Fairbanks stars as the title character, an immoral swashbuckler who lusts after a virginal religious (Greear) before undergoing a change of heart (but not before dancing a red-hot tango with the less-than-virginal Velez). **96m/B VHS, DVD.** Douglas Fairbanks Sr., Lupe Velez, Geraine Greear, Gustav von Seyffertitz; ***D:*** F. Richard Jones; ***W:*** Lotta Woods; ***C:*** Gaetano Antonio "Tony" Gaudio.

Gaucho Serenade 1/2 **1940** Former rodeo stars Gene (Autry) and Frog (Burnette) set out to help the son of their ex-partner, who's the kidnapping target of gangsters. Lots of singing, not much action. ♫ Gaucho Serenade; A Song at Sunset; The Singing Hills; Give Out with a Song; Wooing of Kitty MacFuty. **66m/B VHS.** Gene Autry, Smiley Burnette, Duncan Renaldo, June Storey, Mary Lee; ***D:*** Frank McDonald; ***W:*** Bradford Ropes; ***C:*** Reggie Lanning.

Gauchos of El Dorado 1/2 **1941** Gaucho leaves Bart Braden's gang with some of the stolen money from a bank robbery and a bullet wound. The Mesquiteers find him dying and agree to take the money to his mother so she can pay off her mortgage without knowing it's ill-gotten goods. The 40th film in the series. **56m/B DVD.** Bob Steele, Tom Tyler, Rufe Davis, Lois Collier, Duncan Renaldo, Rosina Galli, Norman Willis; ***D:*** Willie Fung; ***W:*** Albert DeMond; ***C:*** Reggie Lanning.

Gaudi Afternoon **2001** Cassandra (Davis) is a translator, working in Barcelona, who gets caught up in the volatile relationship between transsexual Frankie (Harden) and her estranged female lover Ben (Taylor), who is now involved with hippie April (Lewis). It seems that Frankie and Ben also share a daughter and a custody fight is brewing that Cassandra doesn't want to get caught up in. On the other hand, all the melodrama is making her life quite interesting. Based on a novel by Barbara Wilson. **88m/C VHS, DVD.** *SP* Judy Davis, Marcia Gay Harden, Lili Taylor, Juliette Lewis, Maria Barranco, Christopher Bowen, Courtney Jines; ***D:*** Susan Seidelman; ***W:*** James Mhyre; ***C:*** Josep Civit; ***M:*** Bernardo Bonezzi.

The Gauntlet **1977 (R)** Clint is a broken-down cop ordered to Las Vegas to bring back a key witness for an important trial—but the witness turns out to be a beautiful prostitute being hunted by killers. Violence-packed action with some decent setpieces. **111m/C VHS, DVD.** Clint Eastwood, Sondra Locke, Pat Hingle, Bill McKinney; ***D:*** Clint Eastwood; ***W:*** Michael Butler; ***C:*** Rexford Metz; ***M:*** Jerry Fielding.

The Gay Bed and Breakfast of Terror 🦴 **2007** Camp horror cheapie populated with obnoxious characters whose murders you'll be openly rooting for. Squabbling couples arrive at the remote, ramshackle desert Sahara Salvation Inn, run by a religious nutjob, for an annual gay bash and soon are shrieking and dying. **110m/C DVD.** Shannon Lee, Mari Marks, Michael Soldier, Georgia Jean, Robert Borzych, Hilary Schwartz, Vinny Markus, Derek Long, Denise Heller, Lisa Block-Wieser, Allie Rivenbark, Noah Naylor; ***D:*** Jaymes Thompson; ***W:*** Jaymes Thompson; ***C:*** Joel Deutsch; ***M:*** Swerve South.

The Gay Buckaroo 🦴 ½ **1932** Don't anybody get the wrong idea. Successful horse rancher Clint Hale is in love with Mildred, the daughter of gold miner "Sporty" Bill Field, who has become a gentleman cattle rancher. Silly Mildred is taken with gambler Dave Dumont, so Clint tries to become a flashier guy (hence the title), with little success. Clint beats Dumont in a crooked card game, so then Dumont tries to frame Clint for murder. **66m/B DVD.** Hoot Gibson, Edward Peil Sr., Merna Kennedy, Roy D'Arcy, Lafe (Lafayette) McKee, Charles King; ***D:*** Phil Rosen; ***W:*** Philip Graham White.

The Gay Deceivers 🦴🦴 **1969 (R)** Unmistakably grounded in the '60s, the performances of this comedy are still fresh, but the script is a little stale. Danny (Coughlin) and Elliot (Casey) are two straight guys who avoid the draft by posing as a loving couple. When an army Colonel appears to be investigating the duo, they move into a gay apartment complex to carry on their scam. Naturally, hilarity ensues. The jokes are stereotype-based and show no true skill from the writer or director. Unfortunately, the film is credited with ruining the careers of its leads. **97m/C DVD.** Kevin Coughlin, Lawrence Casey, Brooke Bundy; ***D:*** Bruce Kessler; ***W:*** Gil Lasky, Jerome Wish; ***C:*** Richard C. Glouner; ***M:*** Stu Phillips.

The Gay Desperado 🦴🦴 ½ **1936** Mexican bandit Pablo (Carrillo), who styles himself after American screen gangsters, kidnaps singing caballero Chivo (Martini) and heiress Jane (Lupino). The reason everybody is so gay is that they're always singing in this goofy musical comedy. **85m/B VHS, DVD.** Leo Carrillo, Ida Lupino, Harold Huber, Nino Martini, Stanley Fields, Mischa Auer; ***D:*** Rouben Mamoulian; ***W:*** Wallace Smith; ***C:*** Lucien N. Andriot; ***M:*** Alfred Newman.

The Gay Divorcee 🦴🦴🦴 *The Gay Divorce* **1934** Astaire pursues Rogers to an English seaside resort, where she mistakes him for the hired correspondent in her divorce case. Based on the musical play "The Gay Divorce" by Dwight Taylor and Cole Porter. The title was slightly changed for the movie because of protests from the Hays Office. ♫ Don't Let It Bother You; A Needle in a Haystack; Let's K-nock K-nees; Night and Day; The Continental. **107m/B VHS, DVD.** Fred Astaire, Ginger Rogers, Edward Everett Horton, Eric Blore, Alice Brady, Erik Rhodes, Betty Grable; ***D:*** Mark Sandrich; ***M:*** Max Steiner. Oscars '34: Song ("The Continental").

The Gay Dog 🦴 ½ **1954** Working-class Northerner Jim Gay (Pickles) has all his friends betting on his greyhound Raving Beauty to win a big race. But after seeing the competition, Jim bets his money on a rival dog! **83m/B DVD.** *GB* Wilfred Pickles, Petula Clark, John Blythe, Margaret Barton, William Russell, Megs Jenkins; ***D:*** Maurice Elvey; ***W:*** Peter Rogers; ***C:*** James Wilson.

Gay in Amsterdam 🦴 ½ **2004** Long-time lovers Max (Metser) and Pascal (van de Sande) are involved in the trendy Amsterdam gay scene while maintaining a stable relationship that gets tested by a hot new arrival from the States. Max enters into an affair with Ken (van Bohemen) and Pascal realizes it's last-chance time to reclaim his partner. Dutch with subtitles. **90m/C DVD.** *NL* Hugo Metser, Joris van de Sande, Caspar van Bohemen, Nienke Brinkhuis; ***D:*** Tom Six; ***W:*** Tom Six; ***C:*** Goof de Koning.

The Gay Lady 🦴🦴 ½ *Trottie True* **1949** Light romantic comedy set in the 1890s about an actress who climbs to stardom in London theatre and winds up marrying into the aristocracy. Look for Christopher Lee and Roger Moore in early bit parts. **95m/C VHS.** *GB* Jean Kent, James Donald, Hugh Sinclair, Lana Morris, Bill Owen, Michael Medwin, Andrew Crawford; ***D:*** Brian Desmond Hurst.

Gay Purr-ee 🦴🦴 **1962** Delightful tale of feline romance in the City of Lights. For all ages. **85m/C VHS, DVD.** ***D:*** Abe Levitow; ***W:*** Chuck Jones; ***M:*** Harold Arlen; ***V:*** Judy Garland, Robert Goulet, Red Buttons, Hermione Gingold, Mel Blanc.

The Gay Ranchero 🦴🦴 **1942** Rogers, without Dale Evans, in an average tale of old west meets new crooks. Rogers is the sheriff who foils gangsters trying to take over an airport. The action doesn't stop him from singing a duet with leading lady Frazee on "Wait'll I Get My Sunshine in the Moonlight." **55m/B VHS, DVD.** Roy Rogers, Andy Devine, Tito Guizar, Jane Frazee, Estelita Rodriguez; ***D:*** William Witney.

The Gazebo 🦴🦴🦴 **1959** Wacky comedy about a TV writer who is being blackmailed by someone who has nude photos of his Broadway star wife. He decides murder is the only solution to this problem. Reynolds sings "Something Called Love." Based on a play by Alec Coppel from a story by Myra and Alec Coppel. **102m/B VHS.** Glenn Ford, Debbie Reynolds, Carl Reiner, John McGiver, Doro Merande, Bert Freed, Martin Landau; ***D:*** George Marshall; ***W:*** George Wells.

Geek Maggot Bingo 🦴 *The Freak from Suckweasel Mountain* **1983** It's too bad director Zedd waited until mid-"Bingo" to post a sign warning "Leave Now, It Isn't Going Get Any Better!" Conceived by the New York underground's don of the "Cinema of Transgression" to be an off-the-rack cult classic, this horror spoof is too long on in-jokes and short on substance to earn its number in the cult hall of fame. It does, however, boast Death as Scumbalina the vampire queen and Hell as a punk cowboy crooner (before alternative country hit the airwaves). TV horrormeister Zacherle narrates. **70m/C VHS, DVD.** Robert Andrews, Richard Hell, Donna Death, Brenda Bergman, Tyler Smith, Bruno Zeus, John Zacherle; ***D:*** Nick Zedd; ***W:*** Nick Zedd; ***C:*** Nick Zedd.

Geek Mythology 🦴 **2008** Bumbling geek Tim has no luck with women unlike his best friend Steve who has a beautiful girlfriend, Renee. Then Tim finds a magical statue that makes him a chick magnet but Renee is one of the chicks that comes under the statue's spell, which causes problems for Tim. **81m/C DVD.** Gregg Martin, Joy Boden, Cullen Cowan, Dave Gist, Michelle Davis, Sandra Rapale; ***D:*** Phil Hwang; ***W:*** Phil Hwang; ***C:*** Marco Escobar; ***M:*** Phil Hwang. **VIDEO**

Geheimakte WB1 🦴🦴 *Secret Paper WB1* **1942** Historical drama centering on the invention of the U-boat by Sergeant Wilhelm Bauer during Denmark's WWII blockade of the ports of Schleswig-Holstein. In German with no subtitles. **91m/B VHS.** *GE* Alexander Golling; ***D:*** Herbert Selpin.

A Geisha 🦴🦴🦴 *Gion Bayashi; Gion Festival Music* **1953** Miyoharu (Kogure) is a passive elderly geisha who agrees to train the naive young Eiko (Wakao) in her new role. But Eiko discovers her romantic notions of the geisha life are far from it's modern reality. Poignant look at the changing status of the geisha in Japan after WWII and the country's social upheavals. In Japanese with English subtitles. **86m/B VHS.** *JP* Michiyo Kogure, Ayako Wakao, Seizaburo Kawazu, Chieko Naniwa, Eitaro Shindo; ***D:*** Kenji Mizoguchi; ***W:*** Yoshikata Yoda; ***M:*** Ichiro Saito.

The Geisha Boy 🦴🦴 **1958** Jerry is a floundering magician who joins the USO and tours the Far East. His slapstick confrontations with the troupe leader and an officer who dreams of attending his own funeral provide hearty laughs, plus Lewis finds romance with a Japanese widow after her son claims him as a father. Pleshette's film debut, with an appearance by the Los Angeles Dodgers. **98m/C VHS.** Jerry Lewis, Marie McDonald, Sessue Hayakawa, Barton MacLane, Suzanne Pleshette, Nobu McCarthy; ***D:*** Frank Tashlin.

Geisha Girl 🦴 ½ **1952** Forgotten sci-fi film about a mad scientist and his Japanese cohorts who develop small explosive pills that are more powerful than nuclear bombs. Their plans of world conquest are thwarted when the pills inadvertently fall into the hands of two American G.I.s. **67m/B VHS.** Martha Hyer, William Andrews, Archer MacDonald, Kekao Yokoo, Teddy Nakamura; ***D:*** George Breakston, C. Ray Stahl; ***W:*** C. Ray Stahl.

Gemini Affair 🦴 **1974** Two women go to Hollywood to become rich and famous but end up being very disappointed. **88m/C VHS.** Marta Kristen, Kathy Kersh, Anne Seymour; ***D:*** Matt Cimber.

Gen-X Cops 🦴🦴 *Tejing Xinrenlei* **1999 (R)** Hong Kong police break a ring of smugglers, who are selling a massive shipment of explosives. But the cops then lose the goods to major criminal, Akatura (Nakamura). So a rebellious trio of young cops go undercover and discover the bad guy has very sinister plans. Cantonese with subtitles. **113m/C VHS, DVD.** *HK* Nicholas Tse, Stephen Fung, Sam Lee, Grace Kip, Toru Nakamura, Jackie Chan; ***D:*** Benny Chan; ***W:*** Benny Chan; ***C:*** Arthur Wong Ngok Tai.

The Gendarme of Saint-Tropez 🦴🦴 ½ **1964** Officer Ludovic Cruchot's plans for career advancement are on shaky ground after he is transferred to St. Tropez where his daughter has a little too much fun at the beach. Also available dubbed. **80m/C VHS.** *FR* Louis de Funes, Michel Galabru, Genevieve Grad, Jean (Lefevre) Lefebvre, Christian Marin; ***D:*** Jean Girault; ***W:*** Richard Balducci, Jean Girault; ***C:*** Marc Fossard; ***M:*** Raymond Lefevre.

The Gene Generation 🦴🦴 **2007 (R)** Cyberpunk action. In the futuristic city of Olympia, scientists discover a human gene therapy that can stop any disease but the downside is genetic mutations. DNA hackers steal the technology for evil purposes and assassin Michelle (Ling) is hired to stop them. When Michelle's naive brother Jackie (Shen) gets pulled in, she goes hunting in a dangerous cyber-underworld. Adapted from director Teo's graphic novel. **96m/C DVD.** Bai Ling, Parry Shen, Alec Newman, Faye Dunaway, Robert David Hall, Michael Shamus Wiles; ***D:*** Pearry Reginald Teo; ***W:*** Keith Collea; ***C:*** Anthony G. Nakonechnyi; ***M:*** Scott Glasgow, Ronan Harris. **VIDEO**

The Gene Krupa Story 🦴🦴 ½ **1959** The story of the famous jazz drummer and his career plunge after a drug conviction. Krupa recorded the soundtrack, mimed by Mineo, who was too young for a convincing portrayal. Gavin McLeod (of "Love Boat" fame) has a small part as Mineo's dad. **101m/B VHS, DVD.** Sal Mineo, James Darren, Susan Kohner, Susan Oliver, Anita O'Day, Red Nichols; ***D:*** Don Weis.

Genealogies of a Crime 🦴🦴 *Genealogies d'un Crime* **1997** Complex puzzle with the ever-beautiful Deneuve in dual roles. In one role, she's Solange, a criminal lawyer who agrees to defend a young man, Rene (Poupaud), who's accused of murdering his psychologist aunt Jeanne (Deneuve again, in flashback). Jeanne, who raised Rene, long suspected him of homicidal tendencies, became his shrink, and even expected to be killed by him. Solange believes Jeanne's ministrations programmed Rene to kill. As Solange investigates Rene's background, she becomes too involved with the unstable young man—leading her down the path to madness as well. French with subtitles. **114m/C VHS, DVD.** *FR* Catherine Deneuve, Melvil Poupaud, Michel Piccoli, Andrzej Seweryn, Bernadette LaFont, Hubert Saint Macary; ***D:*** Raul Ruiz; ***W:*** Raul Ruiz, Pascal Bonitzer; ***C:*** Stefan Ivanov; ***M:*** Jorge Arriagada.

The General 🦴🦴🦴🦴 **1926** Keaton's masterpiece and arguably the most formally perfect and funniest of silent comedies. Concerns a plucky Confederate soldier who single-handedly retrieves a pivotal train from Northern territory. Full of eloquent man-vs-machinery images and outrageous sight gags. Remade as "The Great Locomotive Chase" in 1956 with Fess Parker. **78m/B VHS, DVD.** Buster Keaton, Marion Mack, Glen Cavender, Jim Farley, Joe Keaton, Frederick Vroom, Charles Smith, Frank Barnes, Mike Donlin; ***D:*** Clyde Bruckman, Buster Keaton; ***W:*** Clyde Bruckman, Al Boasberg, Charles Henry Smith, Buster Keaton; ***C:*** Bert Haines, Devereaux Jennings. Natl. Film Reg. '89.

The General 🦴🦴🦴 **1998 (R)** Biopic of maverick Dublin crime lord Martin Cahill (Gleeson), nicknamed "The General" for his planning abilities. Film is one long flashback as it begins in 1994 with Cahill's assassination. Cahill supports his family through various burglaries, making a mockery of the local cops, including Ned Kenny (Voight). But Cahill's rise from petty criminal to local mobster is noted by the IRA and when he refuses to cut them in on his profits, things turn very dicey for the cocky, ruthless Cahill. **123m/B VHS, DVD.** *IR GB* Brendan Gleeson, Adrian Dunbar, Sean McGinley, Jon Voight, Maria Doyle Kennedy, Angeline Ball, Ciaran Fitzgerald, Eamon Owens; ***D:*** John Boorman; ***W:*** John Boorman; ***C:*** Seamus Deasy; ***M:*** Richie Buckley. Cannes '98: Director (Boorman).

The General Died at Dawn 🦴🦴🦴 **1936** A clever, atmospheric suspense film about an American mercenary in Shanghai falling in love with a beautiful spy as he battles a fierce Chinese warlord who wants to take over the country. Playwright-to-be Odets' first screenplay; he, O'Hara and '30s gossip hound Skolsky have cameos as reporters. **93m/B VHS, DVD.** Gary Cooper, Madeleine Carroll, Akim Tamiroff, Dudley Digges, Porter Hall, William Frawley, Philip Ahn; ***Cameos:*** John O'Hara, Clifford Odets, Sidney Skolsky; ***D:*** Lewis Milestone; ***W:*** Clifford Odets; ***C:*** Victor Milner.

The General Line 🦴🦴🦴🦴 *The Old and the New* **1929** Eisenstein's classic pro-Soviet semi-documentary about a poor farm woman who persuades her village to form a cooperative. Transgresses its party-line instructional purpose by vivid filmmaking. The director's last silent film. **90m/B VHS.** *RU* Marfa Lapkina; ***D:*** Sergei Eisenstein.

General Spanky 🦴🦴 **1936** The only feature "Our Gang" comedy goofed by transplanting them to a Civil War milieu popular at the time. Confederate kids Spanky and Alfalfa play soldier, ultimately outsmarting Union troops. The rascals are still funny sometimes, but Buckwheat's role as an eager slave is disturbing today. **73m/B VHS.** George "Spanky" McFarland, Phillips Holmes, Ralph Morgan, Irving Pichel, Rosina Lawrence, Billie "Buckwheat" Thomas, Carl "Alfalfa" Switzer, Louise Beavers; ***D:*** Fred Newmeyer.

Generale Della Rovere 🦴🦴🦴 ½ *Il Generale Della-Rovere* **1960** A WWII black marketeer is forced by the Nazis to go undercover in a local prison. To find out who the resistance leaders are, he poses as a general. But when prisoners begin to look to him for guidance, he finds the line between his assumed role and real identity diminished, leading to a tragic conclusion. Acclaimed film featuring a bravura lead performance by veteran director De Sica. In Italian with English subtitles. **139m/B VHS.** *IT* Vittorio De Sica, Otto Messmer, Sandra Milo; ***D:*** Roberto Rossellini; ***W:*** Roberto Rossellini, Sergio Amidei, Diego Fabbri, Indro Montanelli; ***C:*** Carlo Carlini; ***M:*** Renzo Rossellini.

The General's Daughter 🦴🦴 **1999 (R)** Disturbing and convoluted military thriller based on the 1992 bestseller by Nelson DeMille. Paul Brenner (Tavolta) is an Army criminal investigator whose latest case is the rape and murder of Capt. Elisabeth Campbell (Stefanson), whose father (Cromwell) is a legendary general. Elisabeth specialized in psychological warfare but she had more than a few mental problems of her own. Naturally, for the good of the service, everyone but Brenner would like a quick and tidy solution to the sleazy goings-on. Goes a little too over the top (including some performances) and you may come out wondering just who done what. **116m/C VHS, DVD.** John Travolta, Madeleine Stowe, James Cromwell, Timothy Hutton, James Woods, Leslie Stefanson, Clarence Williams III, Daniel von Bargen, Boyd Kestner, Mark Boone Jr., John Beasley, Peter Weireter, John Benjamin Hickey, Rick Dial, Brad Beyer; ***D:***

Simon West; *W:* William Goldman, Christopher Bertolini; *C:* Peter Menzies Jr.; *M:* Carter Burwell.

A Generation 🦴🦴🦴 *Pokolenie* **1954** During WWII, a young man escapes from the Warsaw Ghetto and finds his way to the Polish Resistance. He falls in love with the leader of the local group and finds the courage to fight for his freedom. Strong directorial debut from Wajda. Part 1 of his "War Trilogy," followed by "Kanal" and "Ashes and Diamonds." Scripted by Czeszko from his novel "Pokolenie." Polish with subtitles. **90m/B VHS, DVD.** *PL* Tadeusz Lomnicki, Urszula Modrzynska, Zbigniew Cybulski, Roman Polanski; *D:* Andrzej Wajda; *W:* Bohdan Czeszko; *C:* Jerzy Lipman; *M:* Andrzej Markowski.

Generation 🦴🦴 *A Time For Caring* **1969** A very pregnant bride informs everyone she'll give birth at home without doctors, and creates a panic. Based on the Broadway play by William Goodhart. **109m/C VHS.** David Janssen, Kim Darby, Carl Reiner, Peter Duel, Andrew Prine, James Coco, Sam Waterston; *D:* George Schaefer; *W:* William Goodhart; *C:* Lionel Lindon; *M:* Dave Grusin.

Generation Kill 🦴🦴🦴 **2008** Based on the book by "Rolling Stone" reporter Evan Wright that gives his first-person account of being embedded with the First Recon unit of Marines during the first 40 days of the Iraq invasion. The scene is chaotic, tense, and claustrophobic as the foul-mouthed grunts deal with bureaucratic screw-ups and contradictory orders from officers they frequently disdain as incompetent. **362m/C DVD.** Lee Tergesen, Alexander Skarsgard, James Ransone, Jon Huertas, Stark Sands, Billy Lush, Pawel Szajda, Jonah Lotan, Wilson Bethel; *D:* Susanna White, Simon Cellan Jones; *W:* David Simon, Ed Burns; *C:* Ivan Strasburg. **CABLE**

Genesis II 🦴🦴 **1973** Failed TV pilot by Roddenberry finds scientist Dylan Hunt (Cord) taking part in a NASA suspended animation experiment that goes wrong. He is revived 150 years later to a post-WWIII Earth. A confused Hunt is cared for sexy Lyra-a (Hartley), a member of a mutant race called the Tyranians. It seems the Tyranians are battling the Pax movement for control of what's left of the planet and Hunt gets caught in the middle. **74m/C DVD.** Alex Cord, Mariette Hartley, Ted Cassidy, Harvey Jason, Tito Vandia, Percy Rodrigues, Lynn(e) Marta; *D:* John Llewellyn Moxey; *W:* Gene Roddenberry; *C:* Gerald Perry Finnerman; *M:* Harry Sukman. **TV**

Genevieve 🦴🦴🦴 **1953** A 1904 Darracq roadster is the title star of this picture which spoofs "classic car" owners and their annual rally from London to Brighton. Two married couples challenge each other to a friendly race which becomes increasingly intense as they near the finish line. **86m/C VHS, DVD.** *GB* John Gregson, Dinah Sheridan, Kenneth More, Kay Kendall, Geoffrey Keen, Reginald Beckwith, Arthur Wontner, Joyce Grenfell, Leslie Mitchell, Michael Medwin, Michael Balfour, Edie Martin, Harold Siddons; *D:* Henry Cornelius; *W:* William Rose; *C:* Christopher Challis; *M:* Larry Adler. British Acad. '53: Film; Golden Globes '55: Foreign Film.

Genghis Cohn 🦴🦴 1/2 **1993** Black comedy follows the misadventures of a former Nazi concentration camp commander (Lindsay) who has settled in a small Bavarian town and taken on the position of police chief. But his quiet life is rocked by a series of murders, an affair with a kinky Baroness (Rigg), and by the ghost of Jewish comedian Genghis Cohn (Sher), a victim of the camps whose haunting presence exacts a particularly appropriate revenge. Adapted from Romain Gary's novel "The Dance of Genghis Cohn." Made for British TV. **100m/C VHS.** *GB* Robert Lindsay, Diana Rigg, Anthony Sher; *D:* Elijah Moshinsky; *W:* Stanley Price. **TV**

Genie of Darkness 🦴 **1962** The ashes of Nostradamus himself are retrieved in a bid to destroy his vampiric descendent. Edited from a Mexican serial; if you were able to sit through this one, look for "Curse of Nostradamus" and "The Monster Demolisher." **77m/B VHS.** *MX* German Robles; *D:* Frederick Curiel.

Gentle Giant 🦴🦴 **1967** An orphaned bear is taken in by a boy and his family and grows to be a 750 pound giant who must be returned to the wild. "Gentle Ben" TV series was derived from this feature. **93m/C VHS.** Dennis Weaver, Vera Miles, Ralph Meeker, Clint Howard, Huntz Hall; *D:* James Neilson.

Gentle Savage 🦴🦴 1/2 *Camper John* **1973 (R)** When an Indian is wrongly accused of raping and beating a white woman, the white community seeks revenge. The vengeful mob, led by the victim's step-father, is unaware that it's really their ringleader who is responsible for the crime. When the accused's brother is slain, the Indian community retaliates. Violent but well-crafted. **85m/C VHS.** William (Bill) Smith, Gene Evans, Barbara Luna, Joe Flynn; *D:* Sean McGregor.

A Gentle Woman 🦴🦴 *A Gentle Creature; Une Femme Douce* **1969** Adaptation of Dostoevsky's short story about a young married woman who kills herself. Sanda marries pawnbroker Frangin, is miserable in her marriage, toys with killing her husband, and commits suicide instead, leaving the bewildered Frangin to try to figure out why. Several theories are offered but nothing is ever made clear. Debut of Sanda; Bressons' first film in color. French with subtitles. **89m/C VHS.** *FR* Dominique Sanda, Guy Frangin, Jane Lobre; *D:* Robert Bresson; *W:* Robert Bresson; *C:* Ghislan Cloquet; *M:* Jean Wiener.

A Gentleman After Dark 🦴🦴 **1942** Poor script but a good lead performance by Donlevy. Harry Melton escapes from prison in order to protect his daughter (who was raised by others) from his blackmailing wife, Flo (Hopkins). This monster mom is threatening to spoil the girl's upcoming marriage by revealing her sordid antecedents. A remake of 1936's "Forgotten Faces." **78m/B VHS.** Brian Donlevy, Miriam Hopkins, Preston Foster, Harold Huber, Philip Reed, Gloria Holden, Douglass Dumbrille, Sharon Douglas; *D:* Edwin L. Martin; *W:* George Bruce, Patterson McNutt; *C:* Milton Krasner; *M:* Dimitri Tiomkin.

Gentleman Bandit 🦴🦴 **1981** So-so drama about Father Bernard Pagano, a Boston priest mistakenly arrested as a stickup artist. Based on a true story. **96m/C VHS.** Ralph Waite, Julie Bovasso, Jerry Zaks, Joe Grifasi, Estelle Parsons, Tom Aldredge; *D:* Jonathan Kaplan. **TV**

The Gentleman from California 🦴 *The Californian* **1937** The dashing son of a Mexican landowner returns home and finds his people's land stolen from them by greedy tax collectors. **56m/B VHS, DVD.** Ricardo Cortez, Marjorie Weaver, Katherine DeMille; *D:* Gus Meins.

Gentleman from Dixie 🦴🦴 **1941** After LaRue is released from prison, he looks to change his life by joining his brother on a farm and seeking revenge on the man who put him in the pokey. **61m/B VHS.** Jack La Rue, Marian Marsh, Clarence Muse, Mary Ruth, Robert Kellard, John Holland, Herbert Rawlinson; *D:* Al(bert) Herman.

Gentleman from Texas 🦴 **1946** Ropin', ridin', and romance figure in this less than dramatic oater. **55m/B VHS.** Johnny Mack Brown, Raymond Hatton, Claudia Drake, Reno Blair, Christine McIntyre; *D:* Lambert Hillyer.

Gentleman Jim 🦴🦴🦴 1/2 **1942** A colorful version of the life of old-time heavyweight boxing great Jim Corbett, transformed from a typical Warner Bros. bio-pic by director Walsh into a fun-loving, anything-for-laughs donnybrook. Climaxes with Corbett's fight for the championship against the great John L. Sullivan. One of Flynn's most riotous performances. **104m/B VHS, DVD.** Errol Flynn, Alan Hale, Alexis Smith, Jack Carson, Ward Bond, Arthur Shields, William Frawley; *D:* Raoul Walsh.

The Gentleman Killer 🦴 **1969** A man-with-no-name clears a ravaged border town of murdering bandits. **95m/C VHS.** *IT SP* Anthony Steffen, Silvia Solar; *D:* Giorgio Stegani; *W:* Jaime Jesus Balcazar; *C:* Francis Marin; *M:* Bruno Nicolai.

Gentleman's Agreement 🦴🦴🦴 **1947** Magazine writer Phil Green (Peck) looks for a new angle when he agrees to write a series of articles on anti-Semitism for publisher John Minify (Dekker). Phil pretends to be Jewish, and his new identity pervades his life in unexpected ways, almost destroys his relationships. Garfield has a small but powerful role as Phil's Jewish friend Dave, who has long had to deal with both overt and covert prejudice. This movie was Hollywood's first major attack on anti-Semitism. Controversial in its day, yet still timely. **118m/B VHS, DVD.** Gregory Peck, Dorothy McGuire, John Garfield, Celeste Holm, Anne Revere, June Havoc, Albert Dekker, Jane Wyatt, Dean Stockwell, Nicholas Joy; *D:* Elia Kazan; *W:* Moss Hart; *C:* Arthur C. Miller; *M:* Alfred Newman. Oscars '47: Director (Kazan), Picture, Support. Actress (Holm); Golden Globes '48: Director (Kazan), Film—Drama, Support. Actress (Holm); N.Y. Film Critics '47: Director (Kazan), Film.

A Gentleman's Game 🦴🦴 1/2 **2001 (R)** Twelve-year-old Timmy (Gamble) is a gifted young golfer who is pushed by his father to improve his game. He becomes a caddy at the local country club and manages to get tips from reluctant club pro Foster Pearce (Sinise) but learns about more than just golf. Based on the novel by Coyne, who co-scritped. **91m/C VHS, DVD.** Mason Gamble, Gary Sinise, Philip Baker Hall, Dylan Baker, Henry Simmons, Ellen Muth, Brian Doyle-Murray; *D:* J. Mills Goodloe; *W:* J. Mills Goodloe, Tom Coyne; *C:* Conrad W. Hall; *M:* Jeff Beal.

Gentlemen Broncos 🦴 1/2 **2009 (PG-13)** When misfit teenager Benjamin Purvis (Angarano) attends a fantasy writers convention, he discovers that one of his stories has been ripped off and rewritten by blocked fantasy novelist Ronald Chevalier (Clement) and is even being made into a movie by a local filmmaker. This sets off a series of slow, stuffy events as Benjamin fights for his craft. Writer-director Hess attempts to relive the offbeat charm of his debut, "Napoleon Dynamite," but it's stilted and forced with the opening credits being by far the best part. **90m/C DVD.** *US* Michael Angarano, Jemaine Clement, Sam Rockwell, Mike White, Jennifer Coolidge, Hector Jimenez, Josh Pais, Halley Feiffer; *D:* Jared Hess; *W:* Mike White, Jared Hess, Jerusha Hess; *C:* Munn Powell; *M:* David Wingo.

Gentlemen Prefer Blondes 🦴🦴🦴 **1953** Amusing satire involving two show-business girls from Little Rock trying to make it big in Paris. Seeking rich husbands or diamonds, their capers land them in police court. Monroe plays Lorelei Lee, Russell is her sidekick. Despite an occasionally slow plot, the music, comedy, and performances are great fun. Film version of a Broadway adaption of a story by Anita Loos. Followed by (but without Monroe) "Gentlemen Marry Brunettes." ♫ A (Two) Little Girl(s) From Little Rock; Bye, Bye Baby; Ain't There Anyone Here For Love?; When Love Goes Wrong; Diamonds Are A Girl's Best Friend. **91m/C VHS, DVD.** Marilyn Monroe, Jane Russell, Charles Coburn, Elliott Reid, Tommy Noonan, George Winslow; *D:* Howard Hawks; *W:* Charles Lederer; *C:* Harry Wild; *M:* Leo Robin, Jule Styne, Lionel Newman.

Gentlemen's Relish 🦴🦴 1/2 **2001** Artist Kingdom Swann (Connolly) is dismayed to learn Edwardian London finds his paintings old-fashioned, so loyal servant Violet (Lancashire) buys him a camera so he can experiment. With the help of unscrupulous assistant Marsh (Henshall), Swann becomes a successful society photographer, progressing into "artistic" nudes. However, Marsh is selling the increasingly naughty pics to a specialist clientele without the naive Swann's knowledge. **89m/C DVD.** *GB* Billy Connolly, Sarah Lancashire, Douglas Henshall, Katie Blake; *D:* Douglas Mackinnon; *W:* David Nobbs; *C:* Gavin Finney; *M:* Julian Nott. **TV**

Genuine Risk 🦴 1/2 **1989 (R)** Gorgeous young woman turns off her crime boss boyfriend bigtime when she seduces his bodyguard. Genuine tripe. **89m/C VHS.** Terence Stamp, Michelle Johnson, Peter Berg, Michael (M.K.) Harris; *D:* Kurt Voss; *W:* Kurt Voss.

Geordie 🦴🦴 1/2 *Wee Geordie* **1955** A wee, if charming, comedy. As a youngster growing up in the Scottish Highlands, Geordie is puny and bullied. He takes up a body-building course and a few years later is muscled enough to be the hammer-throwing champion at the Highland Games. This makes Geordie a member of the Olympic team traveling to Melbourne, Australia, where he meets Danish shot-putter Helga, who's instantly smitten. When Geordie breaks the world record, Helga's enthusiastic reaction is misinterpreted, leaving Geordie with a lot of explaining to do back home to his heartbroken girlfriend Jean. **96m/C DVD.** *GB* Bill Travers, Alastair Sim, Paul Young, Francis De Wolff, Norah Gorsen, Doris Goddard, Molly Urquhart; *D:* Frank Launder; *W:* Frank Launder, Sidney Gilliat; *C:* Wilkie Cooper; *M:* William Alwyn.

George! 🦴 1/2 **1970 (G)** A carefree bachelor takes his girlfriend and his 250-pound St. Bernard on a trip to the Swiss Alps where he proves that a dog is not always man's best friend. **87m/C VHS, DVD.** Marshall Thompson, Jack Mullaney, Inge Schoner; *D:* Wallace C. Bennett; *W:* Wallace C. Bennett.

George A. Romero's Land of the Dead 🦴🦴🦴 *Land of the Dead* **2005 (R)** Romero brings the walkers back for a fourth time, but with a tasty new twist—they aren't as dumb as they used to be. And worse yet, they've stumbled upon some ammo. But the upper-crust think they're now safe in their walled-in super tower until a renegade supplies runner, who's living among the poverty-plagued street people and angry because the elite won't invite him in, threatens their comfy confines. Compelling statement about societal classes embedded within usual gore. **93m/C DVD, Blu-ray Disc, UMD, HD DVD.** *FR CA US* Simon Baker, John Leguizamo, Asia Argento, Robert Joy, Dennis Hopper, Eugene Clark, Boyd Banks, Joanne Boland, Krista Bridges, Jennifer Baxter, Pedro Miguel Arce, Boyd Banks, Phil Fondacaro, Simon Pegg; *D:* George A. Romero; *W:* George A. Romero; *C:* Miroslaw Baszak; *M:* Reinhold Heil, Johnny Klimek.

George and the Dragon 🦴🦴 1/2 **2004 (PG)** The CGI may not be the best in this low-budget fantasy but it's still good family fare. Heroic medieval knight George (Purefoy) returns to England after the First Crusade intending to settle down. King Edgar (Callow) offers George some land in exchange for finding his daughter, Princess Luma (Perabo), who has run away from her betrothal to bad Sir Garth (Swayze). But the Princess is having her own adventure; after finding a cave-dwelling dragon down by the lake, she unexpectedly becomes the protector of the dragon's egg. **93m/C DVD.** James Purefoy, Piper Perabo, Patrick Swayze, Simon Callow, Jean-Pierre Castaldi, Rollo Weeks, Paul Freeman, Michael Clarke, Bill Treacher; *D:* Tom Reeve; *W:* Tom Reeve, Michael Burks; *C:* Joost van Starrenburg; *M:* Gast Waltzing.

George Balanchine's The Nutcracker 🦴🦴 1/2 *The Nutcracker* **1993 (G)** Pas de deux redeux. Tchaikovsky's classic ballet about the magic of Christmas and a little girl (Cohen) who dreams on Christmas Eve that she is in an enchanted kingdom. Culkin lamely grins through his wooden performance as the Nutcracker Prince, but the talent of the Sugarplum Fairy (Kistler) and the other dancers is such that conventional camera techniques sometimes fail to keep up with their exacting moves. Adapted from the 1816 book by E.T.A. Hoffmann. **93m/C VHS, DVD.** Macaulay Culkin, Jessica Lynn Cohen, Bart Robinson Cook, Darci Kistler, Damian Woetzel, Kyra Nichols, Wendy Whelan, Gen Horiuchi, Margaret Tracey; *D:* Emile Ardolino; *W:* Susan Cooper; *C:* Ralf Bode; *Nar:* Kevin Kline.

George of the Jungle 🦴🦴🦴 **1997 (PG)** The '60s cartoon hero goes big screen and live-action with Fraser starring as the clumsy (but very hunky) jungle hero. While on safari, socialite Ursula (Mann) falls in love with George and takes him back to San Francisco, leaving behind obnoxious fiancee Lyle (Church). But when poachers capture George's "brother" Ape (voiced by Cleese), he returns to save the day (aided by various jungle companions). Fraser is an appealing lead, and the script is sweetly funny while retaining creator Ward's smart, subversive edge. The stunts are more impressive than you'd usually expect from a cartoon adaptation. **91m/C VHS, DVD.** Brendan Fraser, Leslie Mann, Thomas Haden Church, Holland Taylor, Richard Roundtree, Greg Cruttwell, Abraham Benrubi, John Bennett Perry, Kelly Miller; *D:* Sam Weisman; *W:* Dana Olsen, Audrey Wells; *C:* Thomas Ackerman; *M:* Marc Shaiman; *V:* John Cleese; *Nar:* Keith Scott.

The George Raft Story 🦴🦴 1/2 **1961** Often in financial difficulty, actor Raft sold his life story, which became a fairly typical Hollywood bio. Raft (Danton) starts off as a dancer in a Hell's Kitchen joint but gets on the wrong side of mobster Frank Donatella (de Santis). So he departs for Hollywood and gets his (typecasting) break in "Scarface." Unable to resist the company of wiseguys, Raft's career eventually fades and he then gets involved in a Havana casino operation that ends with the Castro revolution. The film ends when Raft gets a role (parodying his tough guy image) in "Some Like It Hot." **103m/B DVD.** Ray Danton, Jayne Mansfield, Julie London, Barrie Chase, Frank Gorshin, Barbara Nichols, Brad Dexter, Neville Brand, Joe De Santis, Herschel Bernardi, Margo Moore; ***D:*** Joseph M. Newman; ***W:*** Daniel Mainwaring, Crane Wilbur; ***C:*** Carl Guthrie; ***M:*** Jeff Alexander.

George Wallace 🦴🦴 1/2 **1997** Follows 20 years (1955-1975) in the life of politician George Wallace (Sinise) from his career as a state circuit judge, his four terms as Alabama's hard-line segregationist governor, to the first years after he was paralyzed by a would-be assassin while campaigning for the presidency. Some elements are disturbingly dramatized, including Archie (Williams), the fictional black manservant who serves as Wallace's conscience. Based on the book "Wallace" by co-scripter Frady. **178m/C VHS.** Gary Sinise, Mare Winningham, Clarence Williams III, Joe Don Baker, Angelina Jolie, Mark Valley, Cliff DeYoung, Skipp (Robert L.) Sudduth, Mark Rolston, William Sanderson, Terry Kinney; ***D:*** John Frankenheimer; ***W:*** Marshall Frady, Paul Monash; ***C:*** Alan Caso; ***M:*** Gary Chang. **CABLE**

George Washington 🦴🦴 1/2 **1984** Bostwick stars as the father of our country in this made TV adaptation of James Thomas Flexner's biography. The destitute young Washington develops a close friendship with the wealthy Will Fairfax (Dukes), who provides him with the support to pursue his dreams, even though Washington has secretly fallen in love with Sally (Smith), Will's flirtatious wife. George himself has married the widowed Martha (Duke) and begins his military career, leading the American colonies against the Brits in the Revolutionary War. **398m/C VHS.** Barry Bostwick, David Dukes, Jaclyn Smith, Patty Duke, Hal Holbrook, Lloyd Bridges, Jose Ferrer, Trevor Howard, Richard Kiley, James Mason, Clive Revill, Robert Stack; ***W:*** Richard Fielder. **TV**

George Washington Slept Here 🦴🦴🦴 **1942** Hilarious side-splitter about a couple who moves from their Manhattan apartment to an old, broken-down country home in Connecticut. It's one catastrophe after another as the couple tries to renovate their home and deal with a greedy neighbor. Based on the play by George S. Kaufman and Moss Hart. **93m/B VHS.** Jack Benny, Ann Sheridan, Charles Coburn, Percy Kilbride, Hattie McDaniel, William Tracy; ***D:*** William Keighley.

George Washington: The Forging of a Nation 🦴🦴 1/2 **1986** Sequel to the "George Washington" miniseries finds Bostwick and Duke reprising their roles as George and Martha. Unfortunately, the later part of Washington's life isn't nearly as exciting. **208m/C VHS.** Barry Bostwick, Patty Duke, Penny Fuller, Jeffrey Jones, Richard Bekins; ***D:*** William A. Graham; ***M:*** Bruce Broughton. **TV**

George White's Scandals 🦴🦴 **1945** RKO musical based on White's Broadway revues has a flimsy plot to tie the many production numbers together. Performer Joan (Davis) announces she's engaged to Jack (Haley) much to the disapproval of his sister Clarabelle (Hamilton). Stage manager Tom (Terry) hires new dancer Jill (Holliday) and they fall in love. But there's obstacles to their romance too since she's hiding her identity as an English socialite so she won't embarrass her parents. **95m/B DVD.** Joan Davis, Jack Haley, Phillip Terry, Martha Holliday, Margaret Hamilton, Jane Greer, Glenn Tryon; ***D:*** Felix Feist; ***W:*** Hugh Wedlock Jr., Howard Snyder, Howard J. Green, Peter Levy; ***C:*** Robert De Grasse.

George's Island 🦴🦴🦴 **1991 (PG)** When young George is placed with the worst foster parents in the world, his eccentric grandfather helps him escape. They wind up on Oak's Island, where, legend has it, Captain Kidd's ghost and buried treasure reside. They soon find out the legends are true! **89m/C VHS.** Ian Bannen, Sheila McCarthy, Maury Chaykin, Nathaniel Moreau, Vicki Ridler, Brian Downey, Gary Reineke; ***D:*** Paul Donovan; ***W:*** J. William Ritchie; ***M:*** Marty Simon.

Georgia 🦴🦴 **1987** Tough lawyer Nina Bailey (Davis) explores her past when she begins a search for information on her biological mother, Georgia White, a photographer who drowned herself years before. Only Nina has no idea about the Pandora's box of secrets she's about to unleash. Frequent flashbacks to Georgia's mysterious life and death (Davis well plays both roles). **90m/C VHS.** *AU* Judy Davis, Julia Blake, John Bach; ***D:*** Ben Lewin.

Georgia 🦴🦴🦴 **1995 (R)** Character study about sibling rivalry, self-destruction, and the Seattle music scene. Struggling rock singer Sadie (Leigh), who relies on booze, drugs, and men to help her make it through the night, returns to Seattle to crash with big-sister Georgia (Winningham). Settled, with loving husband and kids, the much more talented Georgia is also a popular folk icon and has the type of personal/career success angry and ambitious Sadie can only dream about. Fine performances—particularly from the chameleonlike Leigh; both leads do their own singing. Screenwriter Turner is Leigh's mother. **117m/C VHS, DVD.** Mina (Badiyi) Badie, Jennifer Jason Leigh, Mare Winningham, Ted Levine, Max Perlich, John Doe, John C. Reilly, Jimmy Witherspoon; ***D:*** Ulu Grosbard; ***W:*** Barbara Turner; ***C:*** Jan Kiesser. Ind. Spirit '96: Support. Actress (Winningham); Montreal World Film Fest. '95: Actress (Leigh), Film; N.Y. Film Critics '95: Actress (Leigh).

Georgia, Georgia 🦴 1/2 **1972 (R)** Sands is a black entertainer on tour in Sweden who falls for a white photographer. Her traveling companion, who hates whites, takes drastic action to separate the lovers. Poor acting, script, and direction. Based on a book by Maya Angelou. **91m/C VHS.** Diana Sands, Dirk Benedict, Minnie Gentry; ***D:*** Stig Bjorkman; ***W:*** Maya Angelou.

Georgia Rule 🦴 1/2 **2007 (R)** Generally misbegotten female family saga from director Marshall takes a decided turn into the unpleasant. Rebellious troubled teen Rachel (Lohan) finally screws up so badly that her alcoholic mom Lily (Huffman) sends her off for a summer of tough love at her own estranged mother Georgia's (Fonda) small-town home in Idaho Mormon territory. Rachel proceeds to be both outrageous and obnoxious, casually revealing that she's been molested by stepdad Arnold (Elwes), although she's such a liar no one knows what to believe. Then Lily shows up, also seeking a safe haven and adding to the family tension. Yes, this is the film where Lohan's own outrageous and obnoxious behavior drew public reprimands from the producer and others. **113m/C DVD.** *US* Jane Fonda, Lindsay Lohan, Felicity Huffman, Dermot Mulroney, Cary Elwes, Garrett Hedlund, Laurie Metcalf, Hector Elizondo; ***D:*** Garry Marshall; ***W:*** Mark Andrus; ***C:*** Karl Walter Lindenlaub; ***M:*** John Debney.

Georgy Girl 🦴🦴🦴 **1966** Redgrave finely plays the overweight ugly-duckling Georgy who shares a flat with the beautiful and promiscuous Meredith (Rampling). Georgy is, however, desired by the wealthy and aging Mason and soon by Meredith's lover (Bates) who recognizes her good heart. When Meredith becomes pregnant, Georgy persuades her to let her raise the baby, leaving Georgy with the dilemma of marrying the irresponsible Bates (the baby's father) or the settled Mason. The film and title song (sung by the Seekers) were both huge hits. Based on the novel by Margaret Foster who also co-wrote the screenplay. **100m/B VHS, DVD.** *GB* Lynn Redgrave, James Mason, Charlotte Rampling, Alan Bates, Bill Owen, Claire Kelly, Rachel Kempson, Denise Coffey, Dorothy Alison, Peggy Thorpe-Bates, Dandy Nichols; ***D:*** Silvio Narizzano; ***W:*** Margaret Forster, Peter Nichols; ***C:*** Ken Higgins. Golden Globes '67: Actress—Mus./Comedy (Redgrave); N.Y. Film Critics '66: Actress (Redgrave).

Gepetto 🦴🦴 **2000** Kinda goopy Pinocchio update that focuses on toymaker dad, Geppetto (Carey). His longing for a kid of his own is granted by the Blue Fairy (Louis-Dreyfus), who makes puppet Pinocchio (Adkins) come alive. But Geppetto's parenting skills leave something to be desired and soon his new son disappears with travelling showman, Stromboli (Spiner), and gets into all kinds of trouble. Some catchy tunes. **90m/C VHS, DVD.** Drew Carey, Seth Adkins, Julia Louis-Dreyfus, Brent Spiner, Rene Auberjonois, Usher Raymond, Ana Gasteyer, Wayne Brady; ***D:*** Tom (Thomas R.) Moore; ***W:*** David Stern; ***C:*** Stephen M. Katz; ***M:*** Stephen Schwartz. **TV**

Germany in Autumn 🦴🦴 *Deutschland im Herbst* **1978** Twelve West German filmmakers offer political statements and artistic commentary on the political situation in their country after the kidnapping and murder of industrialist Hans Martin Schleyer. In German with English subtitles. **124m/C VHS.** *GE* ***D:*** Volker Schlondorff, Rainer Werner Fassbinder, Alf Brustellin, Alexander Kluge, Maximiliane Mainka, Edgar Reitz, Katja Rupe, Hans Peter Cloos, Bernhard Sinkel, Beate Mainka-Jellinghaus, Peter Schubert, Heinrich Boll; ***W:*** Heinrich Boll.

Germany, Pale Mother 🦴🦴 *Deutschland, Bleiche Mutter* **1980** In 1939, young, pregnant German hausfrau Lene (Mattes) sends her husband, Hans (Jacobi), to the front lines. Lene and her daughter struggle for survival through the war years until she has a bittersweet reunion with the embittered Hans. Director Sanders-Brahms based her story on her own mother's wartime experiences but the film suffers from the relentless parade of atrocities. German with subtitles. **123m/C VHS.** *GE* Eva Mattes, Ernst Jacobi; ***D:*** Helmer Sanders-Brahms; ***W:*** Helmer Sanders-Brahms; ***C:*** Jurgen Jurges; ***M:*** Jurgen Knieper.

Germicide 🦴 **1974** Scientist tries to warn the world of the threat posed by a horrifying bacterial weapon. Terrorists and his mistress hatch plots against him. **90m/C** Rod Taylor, Bibi Andersson, Matthieu Carriere, Christian Barbier; ***D:*** Sergio Gobbi; ***C:*** Jean Badal.

Germinal 🦴🦴🦴 **1993 (R)** Recounts the struggle of working-class coal miners in France, led by Depardieu and wife Miou-Miou, to stave off poverty. While greedy investors debate how far they should lower miners' wages, the Maheu family, spurred on by newly arrived Marxist and off-camera French pop star Renaud, lead a strike. Minor themes revolving around management's adulterous adventures provide some momentary relief to relieve short attention spans. Seems so self-consciously an epic drama, however, that the overall effect is ponderous. Adaptation of the 19th century novel by Zola. In French with English subtitles. **158m/C VHS.** *FR* Gerard Depardieu, Miou-Miou, Bernard Fresson, Jean Carmet, Laurent Terzieff, Anny (Annie Legras) Duperey, Renaud, Jacques Dacqmine, Judith Henry; ***D:*** Claude Berri; ***W:*** Claude Berri, Arlette Langmann; ***C:*** Yves Angelo; ***M:*** Jean-Louis Roques. Cesar '94: Cinematog., Costume Des.

Geronimo 🦴🦴 1/2 **1962** In typical Hollywood casting Connors stars as the Indian leader on the warpath against the cavalry over broken treaties. Lots of action and the Indians are actually the good guys. **101m/C VHS.** Chuck Connors, Ross Martin, Pat Conway, Kamala Devi, Adam West, Lawrence (Larry) Dobkin, Denver Pyle, Enid Jaynes, Armando Silvestre, John Anderson; ***D:*** Arnold Laven.

Geronimo 🦴🦴🦴 **1993** Not to be confused with the big screen version, this made-for-cable drama uses three actors to portray the legendary Apache warrior (1829-1909) at various stages of his life. The intrepid teenager who leads attacks on Mexican troops, the adult fighting the duplicitous bluecoats, and the aged man witnessing the destruction of his way of life. The true story is told from the point of view of Native American culture and historical records. Somewhat overly earnest. **120m/C VHS.** Joseph Runningfox, Jimmy Herman, Ryan Black, Nick Ramus, Michelle St. John, Michael Greyeyes, Tailinh Forest Flower, Kimberly Norris, August Schellenberg, Geno Silva, Harrison Lowe; ***D:*** Roger Young; ***W:*** J.T. Allen; ***M:*** Patrick Williams. **CABLE**

Geronimo: An American Legend 🦴🦴 1/2 **1993 (PG-13)** Well-intentioned bio-actioner about the legendary Apache leader who fought the U.S. Army over forcing Native Americans onto reservations. The division of young Army officer Gatewood (Patric) is to round up the renegades led by Geronimo (Studi), whom Gatewood naturally comes to admire. Hackman and Duvall (as a General and a scout respectively) steal any scene they're in although the leads manage to hold their own. An unknown Damon plays the narrator, Lt. Britton Davis. Too noble for its own good and somewhat plodding. Great location filming around Moab, Utah. **115m/C VHS, DVD.** Wes Studi, Jason Patric, Robert Duvall, Gene Hackman, Matt Damon, Rodney A. Grant, Kevin Tighe, Carlos Palomino, Stephen McHattie; ***D:*** Walter Hill; ***W:*** John Milius, Larry Gross; ***C:*** Lloyd Ahern II; ***M:*** Ry Cooder.

Geronimo's Revenge 🦴 1/2 **1960** When Geronimo starts a battle with the settlers, a rancher he has befriended finds himself caught in the middle. The fourth soggy Disney TV oater from the "Tales of Texas John Slaughter" series. **77m/C VHS.** Tom Tryon, Darryl Hickman; ***D:*** Harry Keller.

Gerry 🦴🦴 **2002 (R)** Even for Van Sant, this is a bizarro film with a number of obscure (and-not-so-obscure) influences. Two young men, both named Gerry (Damon, Affleck), are driving along a desert highway when they decide to get out of the car and hike along a wilderness trail. They get lost and start wandering around. They have no food or water and, after a couple of days, start to hallucinate, eventually the Affleck Gerry can't go on (but the film does). Something to make you go hmmmmmm. Or maybe, what were they thinking?! **103m/C DVD.** *US* Matt Damon, Casey Affleck; ***D:*** Gus Van Sant; ***W:*** Matt Damon, Casey Affleck, Gus Van Sant; ***C:*** Harris Savides; ***M:*** Arvo Part.

Gertrud 🦴🦴🦴 1/2 **1964** The simple story of an independent Danish woman rejecting her husband and lovers in favor of isolation. Cold, dry, minimalistic techniques make up Dreyer's final film. In Danish with subtitles. **116m/B VHS, DVD.** *DK* Nina Pens Rode, Bendt Rothe, Ebbe Rode, Baard Owe; ***D:*** Carl Theodor Dreyer; ***W:*** Carl Theodor Dreyer; ***C:*** Arne Abrahamsen, Henning Bendtsen; ***M:*** Jorgen Jersild.

Gervaise 🦴🦴🦴 **1956** The best of several films of Emile Zola's "L'Assommoir." A 19th-century middle-class family is destroyed by the father's plunge into alcoholism despite a mother's attempts to save them. Well acted but overwhelmingly depressing. In French with English subtitles. **89m/B VHS.** *FR* Maria Schell, Francois Perier, Suzy Delair, Armand Mestral; ***D:*** Rene Clement; ***M:*** Georges Auric. British Acad. '56: Actor (Perier), Film; N.Y. Film Critics '57: Foreign Film; Venice Film Fest. '56: Actress (Schell).

Get a Clue! 🦴🦴 *The Westing Game* **1998 (PG)** Teenaged Turtle discovers the body of a millionaire recluse and then learns that whoever can find the murderer will be awarded $20 million. Adapted from the book "The Westing Game." **95m/C VHS, DVD.** Ashley Peldon, Diane Ladd, Sally Kirkland, Cliff DeYoung, Ray Walston, Lewis Arquette, Billy Morrissette, Ernest Liu, Shane West, Sandy Faison; ***D:*** Terence H. Winkless; ***W:*** Dylan Kelsey Hadley; ***C:*** Kurt Brabbee; ***M:*** Parmer Fuller. **VIDEO**

Get a Clue 🦴🦴 1/2 **2002 (G)** Pampered rich girl and school gossip columnist (Lohan) becomes an amateur detective when one of her teachers goes missing. Lohan fans will love this good-natured Disney Channel teen mystery, others probably not so much. **107m/C DVD.** Lindsay Lohan, Bug Hall, Ian Gomez, Brenda Song, Amanda Plummer, Charles Shaughnessy, Dan Lett, Kimberly Roberts; ***D:*** Maggie Greenwald; ***W:*** Alana Sanko; ***C:*** Rhett Morita; ***M:*** David Mansfield. **CABLE**

Get Carter 🦴🦴🦴 **1971 (R)** Tough and stylish crime drama that has gained in stature since its release. Small-timer London hood Jack Carter (Caine) arrives in Newcastle determined to find out who killed his brother. After meeting local crime boss Cyril Kinnear (Osborne), Carter is told to go back home and leave things alone. But he doesn't and things (and the film) don't turn out exactly as expected. Caine shows just how ruthless he can make a character. Film debut for director Hodges. Based on the novel "Jack's Return Home" by Ted Lewis. Remade in 1972 as "Hit Man" and in 2000. **112m/C VHS, DVD.** *GB* Michael Caine, Ian Hendry, John Osborne, Geraldine Moffatt, Glynn Edwards, Dorothy White, Petra Markham, Bryan Mosley, Britt Ekland, Tony Beckley, George Sewell, Alun Armstrong, Bernard Hepton, Terence Rigby; ***D:*** Mike Hodges; ***W:*** Mike Hodges; ***C:*** Wolfgang Suschitzky; ***M:*** Roy Budd.

Get Carter **2000 (R)** Stallone is Las Vegas tough guy Jack Carter, who goes home to Seattle for his brother's funeral and decides that his death wasn't natural. Hoping to redeem himself in the eyes of sister-in-law Gloria (Richardson) and niece Doreen (Cook), Carter searches the seedy underbelly for the killers. Or he may be searching for some decent lighting, since most of the scenes are dark even for a seedy underbelly. His injury-inducing tour of the underworld leads him to a sleazy pornographer (Roarke) and whiny billionaire (Cumming), setting the stage for a climactic showdown involving Doreen. Remake fails because Stallone's catalog of cinematic carnage waters down the feeling of nihilistic violence of the original 1971 Brit thriller. Michael Caine (who had the original title role) makes an appearance as a wily bar owner. **104m/C VHS, DVD.** Sylvester Stallone, Michael Caine, Rachael Leigh Cook, Alan Cumming, Miranda Richardson, Mickey Rourke, John C. McGinley, Rhona Mitra, Johnny Strong, John Cassini, Garwin Sanford, Gretchen Mol; ***D:*** Stephen Kay; ***W:*** David McKenna; ***C:*** Mauro Fiore; ***M:*** Tyler Bates.

Get Christie Love! **1974** Vintage blaxploitation from the genre's halcyon days, when going undercover meant a carte blanche for skimpy outfits. Based on Dorothy Uhnak's detective novel, the eponymous policewoman goes undercover to bring a thriving drug empire to it knees. The outcome: a TV series. Graves previously appeared on TV as one of the "Laugh-In" party girls. **95m/C VHS, DVD.** Teresa Graves, Harry Guardino, Louise Sorel, Paul Stevens, Andy Romano, Debbie Dozier; ***D:*** William A. Graham. **TV**

Get Crazy 1/2 *Flip Out* **1983** The owner of the Saturn Theatre is attempting to stage the biggest rock-and-roll concert of all time on New Year's Eve 1983, and everything is going wrong in this hilarious, off-beat film. **90m/C VHS, DVD.** Malcolm McDowell, Allen (Goorwitz) Garfield, Daniel Stern, Gail Edwards, Ed Begley Jr., Lou Reed, Bill Henderson, Fabian, Bobby Sherman, Miles Chapin, Howard Kaylan, Franklin Ajaye, Mary Woronov, Paul Bartel, Jackie Joseph, Dick Miller, Lee Ving, Clint Howard; ***D:*** Allan Arkush; ***W:*** Henry Rosenbaum, Danny Opatoshu, David Taylor; ***C:*** Thomas Del Ruth; ***M:*** Michael Boddicker.

Get Him to the Greek **2010 (R)** "The Greek" is L.A.'s Greek Theatre and record company intern Aaron Green (Hill), who exaggerated his abilities to get the job, is sent to escort uncooperative British bad boy rocker Aldous Snow (Brand) from London to L.A. for the start of his worldwide tour. Snow has some other ideas. Judd Apatow produces so you may know what to expect as far as boy-men behaving stupidly. **m/C DVD.** *US* Jonah Hill, Russell Brand, Rose Byrne, Elisabeth (Elissabeth, Elizabeth, Liz) Moss, Sean (Puffy, Puff Daddy, P. Diddy) Combs; ***D:*** Nicholas Stoller; ***W:*** Nicholas Stoller.

Get Low **2009** Depression-era story about taciturn eccentric Felix Bush (Duvall), who has been a backwoods-Tennessee hermit for decades. Then he decides to plan his own memorial service, but wants to be there to hear what folks say about him. Funeral parlor director Frank Quinn (Murray) agrees to Felix's idea and decides to ensure a large turnabout by holding a raffle with Felix's property as the prize. **102m/C DVD.** *US* Bill Murray, Sissy Spacek, Bill Cobbs, Robert Duvall, Lucas Black, Gerald McRaney, Scott Cooper, Lori Beth Edgeman; ***D:*** Aaron Schneider; ***W:*** Chris Provenzano, C. Gaby Mitchell; ***C:*** Aaron Schneider, David Boyd; ***M:*** Jan A.P. Kaczmarek.

Get On the Bus **1996 (R)** Lee looks at the personal side of the Million Man March through a fictional group of men who board a bus in south central L.A. and head for Washington, D.C. Practically ignoring the event itself, Lee and writer Bythewood focus on the the men who participated, their reasons, and their interaction with each other. Standouts in the melting pot of characters include Dutton as the attentive bus driver, a brash young actor (Braugher), a likable old man (Davis), an absentee father (Byrd) and his potentially delinquent son (Bonds), and a cop (Smith). Despite low budget (2.4 mil) and tight shooting schedule (21 days), Lee manages to drive the story home with fine dialogue and characterization that (for the most part) avoids stereotypes. **122m/C VHS, DVD.** Andre Braugher, Ossie Davis, Charles S. Dutton, De'Aundre Bonds, Gabriel Casseus, Albert Hall, Hill Harper, Harry J. Lennix, Bernie Mac, Wendell Pierce, Roger Guenveur Smith, Isaiah Washington IV, Steve White, Thomas Jefferson Byrd, Richard Belzer, Randy Quaid; ***D:*** Spike Lee; ***W:*** Reggie Rock Bythewood; ***C:*** Elliot Davis; ***M:*** Terence Blanchard.

Get Out Your Handkerchiefs 1/2 *Preparez Vous Mouchoirs* **1978 (R)** Unconventional comedy about a husband desperately attempting to make his sexually frustrated wife happy. Determined to go to any lengths, he asks a Mozart-loving teacher to become her lover. She is now, however, bored by both men. Only when she meets a 13-year-old genius at the summer camp where the three adults are counselors does she come out of her funk and find her sexual happiness. Laure is a beautiful character, but Depardieu and Dewaere are wonderful as the bewildered would-be lovers. Academy Award winner for Best Foreign Film. In French with English subtitles. **109m/C VHS, DVD.** *FR* Gerard Depardieu, Patrick Dewaere, Carole Laure; ***D:*** Bertrand Blier; ***W:*** Bertrand Blier; ***C:*** Jean Penzer; ***M:*** Georges Delerue. Oscars '78: Foreign Film; Cesar '79: Score; Natl. Soc. Film Critics '78: Film.

Get Over It! 1/2 **2001 (PG-13)** Professes to be thematically related to "A Midsummer Night's Dream," but don't let this get your hopes up. Thankfully, there's little chance of that happening, as the practice of basing teen comedies on Shakespeare plays reached the saturation point not too long ago and audiences realized that a film claiming to have been inspired by the Bard rarely met such high expectations. So it goes with this below-average kiddie comedy, which follows the sad breakup of Berke Landers (Foster), the nice but slightly dull boy, and Alison (Sagemiller), his popular former girlfriend, who soon takes up with Striker (West), the hot new boy in school. Berke's obsession with his old flame seems unrelenting until Kelly (Dunst) enters the scene. **90m/C VHS, DVD.** *US* Kirsten Dunst, Ben Foster, Colin Hanks, Melissa Sagemiller, Sisqo, Shane West, Martin Short, Swoosie Kurtz, Ed Begley Jr., Zoe Saldana, Mila Kunis, Carmen Electra; ***Cameos:*** Coolio, Colleen (Ann) Fitzpatrick; ***D:*** Tommy O'Haver; ***W:*** R. Lee Fleming Jr.; ***C:*** Maryse Alberti; ***M:*** Steve Bartek.

Get Real 1/2 **1999 (R)** Gay coming of age tale about Brit suburban teen, Steven (Silverstone), deciding to come out of the closet. Steven's only confidante is fellow outsider Linda (Brittain). Then he has an unexpected encounter with popular jock John (Gorton), who's confused about his sexuality and terrified that anyone will suspect he's gay, even to the point of helping his jock buddies gay-bash Steven. Eventually, Steven decides secrecy is not worth the pain. Good performances in a somewhat self-conscious drama. Adapted from Wilde's play "What's Wrong with Angry?" **111m/C VHS, DVD.** *GB* Ben Silverstone, Brad Gorton, Charlotte Brittain, Stacy A. Hart, Kate McEnery, Jacquetta May, David Lumsden, Louise J. Taylor, Tim Harris; ***D:*** Simon Shore; ***W:*** Patrick Wilde; ***C:*** Alan Almond; ***M:*** John Lunn.

Get Rich or Die Tryin' 1/2 **2005 (R)** Gangsta melodrama loosely based on the experiences of star/rapper 50 Cent and something of a departure for Irish director Sheridan. Thug Marcus wants easy money by selling drugs; instead he gets into some nasty turf wars and winds up in prison. He reconnects with homeboy Bama (Howard) who offers to be his manager if Marcus wants to pursue that rap career. He also gets a good woman, Charlene (Bryant), who loves and believes in him. None of this is particularly interesting, maybe because familiarity breeds, if not contempt, then indifference. **134m/C DVD.** *US* Curtis "50 Cent" Jackson, Terrence Howard, Joy Bryant, Bill Duke, Adewale Akinnuoye-Agbaje, Omar Benson Miller, Viola Davis, Tory Kittles, Marc John Jefferies, Brian O'Hara, Sullivan Walker, Russell Hornsby, Ashley Walters, Serena Reeder, Mpho Koaho; ***D:*** Jim Sheridan; ***W:*** Terence Winter; ***C:*** Declan Quinn; ***M:*** Quincy Jones, Gavin Friday, Maurice Seezer.

Get Rita *Gun Moll; Poopsie; Oopsie Poopsie; La Puppa del Gangster* **1975** Italian prostitute sets up her gangster boyfriend for a murder she committed and she winds up as mob boss. **90m/C VHS.** Sophia Loren, Marcello Mastroianni; ***D:*** Tom Rowe.

Get Shorty **1995 (R)** Low-level Miami loan shark and film buff Chili Palmer (Travolta) heads to Hollywood via Las Vegas, looking for a deadbeat drycleaner (Paymer) and a grade-Z movie producer (Hackman) who owes Vegas $150,000. Aided by B-movie scream-queen Russo, Palmer is pitted against a variety of shady Hollywood-types, including an egomaniacal star (DeVito) while trying to get into showbiz himself. Snappy scripting and performances finally do screen justice to an Elmore Leonard novel. DeVito, with the smaller title role, was originally cast as Chili Palmer, a role Travolta twice turned down until the ubiquitous Quentin Tarantino advised him to take it. **105m/C VHS, DVD.** John Travolta, Gene Hackman, Danny DeVito, Rene Russo, Dennis Farina, Delroy Lindo, David Paymer, James Gandolfini, Bobby Slayton; ***Cameos:*** Bette Midler, Harvey Keitel, Penny Marshall; ***D:*** Barry Sonnenfeld; ***W:*** Scott Frank; ***C:*** Don Peterman; ***M:*** John Lurie. Golden Globes '96: Actor—Mus./Comedy (Travolta).

Get Smart 1/2 **2008 (PG-13)** Excellent casting brings the dusty 1960s TV comedy series back to life. Maxwell Smart (played brilliantly by Carell), the bumbling secret agent, is promoted within the CONTROL organization (like the CIA, but not as cool) and sent to Russia to take out super-villain Siegfried (Stamp). Balancing Smart's buffoonery is his new partner, the beautiful Agent 99 (Hathaway), who continually saves him from his own blunders. Not a cheap knock-off, but a slick spy spoof that could easily pass for a James Bond installment (if weren't so funny, that is). **110m/C DVD.** *US* Steve Carell, Anne Hathaway, Dwayne "The Rock" Johnson, Alan Arkin, Terence Stamp, Terry Crews, David Koechner, Ken Davitian, Bill Murray, Masi Oka, Bernie Kopell, Nate Torrence, Patrick Warburton, James Caan; ***D:*** Peter Segal; ***W:*** Tom J. Astle, Matt Ember; ***C:*** Dean Semler; ***M:*** Trevor Rabin.

Get Smart, Again! 1/2 **1989** Would you believe Maxwell Smart is back again as CONTROL's most incompetent agent? How about Agent 99 as his sidekick? Hymie the robot and those no-good-niks at KAOS? Well, it's all true. This second reunion movie (following "The Nude Bomb") from the '60s TV show highlights all the wacky gadgetry, including the shoe phone, but fails to find the show's original outlandishness. **93m/C VHS, DVD.** Don Adams, Barbara Feldon, Dick Gautier, Bernie Kopell, Kenneth Mars, Harold Gould, Roger Price, Fritz Feld, Robert Karvelas, King Moody; ***D:*** Gary Nelson. **TV**

Get That Girl **1932** Minor western action pic marred by former silent-screen player Talmadge's heavy German accent which soon lead to him giving up acting for a directing career. **54m/B VHS.** Richard Talmadge, Shirley Grey, Carl Stockdale; ***D:*** George Crone.

Get That Man **1935** When a cabby is mistaken for the murdered heir to a vast fortune, his life suddenly becomes complex. **57m/B VHS.** Wallace Ford, Leon Ames, Lillian Miles, E. Alyn (Fred) Warren; ***D:*** Spencer Gordon Bennet.

Get to Know Your Rabbit **1972** Absurdist indie satire from De Palma. Fed-up businessman Donald Beeman (Smothers) shucks his career to enroll in Mr. Delasandro's (Welles) magic school. Donald finds minor success as a tap-dancing magician (complete with rabbit) while his ex-boss Mr. Trumbull (Astin) goes off the rails. Trumbull becomes Donald's manager, eventually exploiting him by opening a fantasy camp for execs needing a corporate break, using the beleaguered Donald as a role model. **91m/C DVD.** Tom Smothers, John Astin, Orson Welles, Suzanne Zenor, Allen (Goorwitz) Garfield, Katharine Ross, Samantha Jones; ***D:*** Brian De Palma; ***W:*** Jordan Crittenden; ***C:*** John A. Alonzo; ***M:*** Jack Elliott, Allyn Ferguson.

Get Well Soon 1/2 **2001 (R)** Disjointed romantic comedy finds midnight TV talk show host Bobby Bishop (Gallo) suffering a nervous breakdown that results in a number of scandals. Bobby takes off to see ex-girlfriend Lily (Cox) in New York but she's not happy to see him when he arrives and neither is her new boyfriend (Donovan). **95m/C VHS, DVD.** Vincent Gallo, Courteney Cox, Jeffrey Tambor, Tate Donovan, Elina Lowensohn, Anne Meara; ***D:*** Justin McCarthy; ***W:*** Justin McCarthy; ***M:*** Vincent Gallo, Ric Markmann.

The Getaway **1972 (PG)** McQueen plays a thief released on a parole arranged by his wife (McGraw) only to find out a corrupt politician wants him to rob a bank. After the successful holdup, McQueen finds out his cohorts are in the politician's pocket and trying to doublecross him. McQueen and McGraw are forced into a feverish chase across Texas to the Mexican border, pursued by the politician's henchmen and the state police. Completely amoral depiction of crime and violence with McQueen taciturn as always and McGraw again showing a complete lack of acting skills. Based on a novel by Jim Thompson. McQueen and McGraw had a romance during filming and later married. Remade in 1993. **123m/C VHS, DVD, Blu-ray Disc, HD DVD.** Steve McQueen, Ali MacGraw, Ben Johnson, Sally Struthers, Al Lettieri, Slim Pickens, Jack Dodson, Dub Taylor, Bo Hopkins; ***D:*** Sam Peckinpah; ***W:*** Walter Hill; ***C:*** Lucien Ballard; ***M:*** Quincy Jones.

The Getaway 1/2 **1993 (R)** It was a bad movie in 1972 and the remake hasn't improved the situation. Doc and Carol are husband and wife crooks (played by marrieds Basinger and Baldwin). Doc gets double-crossed and winds up in a Mexican jail; Carol gets a well-connected crook (Woods) to spring her hubby—by sleeping with him and promising Doc will pull off another heist. The robbery's botched, there are double-crosses galore, and the couple go on the run. The stars are pretty but everything's predictable. An unrated version is also available. **110m/C VHS, DVD, HD DVD.** Alec Baldwin, Kim Basinger, James Woods, Michael Madsen, Jennifer Tilly, David Morse; ***D:*** Roger Donaldson; ***W:*** Walter Hill, Amy Holden Jones; ***C:*** Peter Menzies Jr.; ***M:*** Mark Isham.

Getting Away With Murder **WOOF!** **1996 (R)** An utterly distasteful bomb that proves the Holocaust just isn't as funny as it used to be. College professor Aykroyd takes matters into his own hands when he learns that his kindly neighbor (Lemmon) is a Nazi war criminal. After finding out he may have been a wee bit hasty, he marries the coot's daughter as penance. Writer-director Miller tries to squeeze gags out of such topics as Nazi death camps and Holocaust denial. Definitely career lows for everyone involved. (What were they thinking?) One of the last films released (with no advance warning and no advance screenings) by Savoy pictures. **92m/C VHS, DVD.** Dan Aykroyd, Lily Tomlin, Jack Lemmon, Bonnie Hunt, Brian Kerwin; ***D:*** Harvey Miller; ***W:*** Harvey Miller; ***C:*** Frank Tidy; ***M:*** John Debney.

Getting Even 1/2 *Hostage: Dallas* **1986 (R)** A maniac threatens to poison the entire population of Texas with a deadly gas unless he gets $50 million. An adventurous businessman sets out to stop him. **90m/C VHS.** Edward Albert, Joe Don Baker, Audrey Landers; ***D:*** Dwight Little; ***C:*** Peter Lyons Collister.

Getting Even **1992 (R)** Dundee and Evans served together in Vietnam. Fifteen years later they're reunited by the FBI to track a former Marine, who once betrayed Evans to the enemy. Seems he's now a drug trafficker and arms dealer who also gets his sadistic pleasures by killing women. The two ex-Marines find they have one last battle to fight. **93m/C VHS.** Richard Roundtree, Michael J. Aronin; ***D:*** Leandro Lucchetti.

Getting Even with Dad 1/2 **1994 (PG)** Crook Danson can't find the money he stole in his last heist. Why? because his precocious son has hidden it with the intention of blackmailing dear old dad into going straight and acting like a real father. Title is unintentionally funny in light of Mac's domineering dad Kit, who makes everybody in Hollywood want to go hide when he appears. Fairly bland family film squanders charm of Danson and Culkin, running formulaic plot into ground. Headly is likewise wasted as district attorney who prosecutes and then falls for Pops. **108m/C VHS, DVD.** Macaulay Culkin, Ted Danson, Glenne Headly, Hector Elizondo, Saul Rubinek, Gailard Sartain, Kathleen Wilhoite, Sam McMurray, Dann Florek; ***D:*** Howard Deutch; ***W:*** Tom S. Parker, Jim Jennewein; ***C:*** Tim Suhrstedt; ***M:*** Miles Goodman.

Getting Gertie's Garter **1927** Engaged lawyer Ken Walrick (Ray) is embarrassed by his one-time gift to showgirl Gertie (Prevost)—an engraved jeweled garter he feels he must retrieve before his jealous fiancee Barbara (Ridgeway) finds out about his former dalliance. **70m/B DVD.** Marie Prevost, Charles Ray, Fritzi Ridgeway, Franklin Pangborn, Sally Rand, Harry C. (Henry) Myers; ***D:*** E. Mason Hopper; ***W:*** F. McGrew Willis; ***C:*** Harold Rosson.

Getting Gertie's Garter 1/2 **1945** Light romantic farce that hinges on the fact the befuddled lead doesn't dare mention a lady's undergarment in public. (Yes, life was once like that.) Ken (O'Keefe) has just obtained a swell promotion and is happily married to Patty (Ryan). But in his reckless youth, he gave former flame Gertie (McDonald) a bejeweled garter as a token of his affections. Now, Gertie is about to get married to Ken's friend Ted (Sullivan) and that darn garter is wantd by the District Attorney as evidence in a robbery. Ken needs to quietly retrieve the garter before Patty, Ted, the D.A., and Ken's stuffy board of directors gets wind of the scandalous trinket. Lots of standard farce moments such as hiding in closets and shimmying down drainpipes. **72m/B VHS, DVD.** Dennis O'Keefe, Marie McDonald, Barry Sullivan, Binnie Barnes, Sheila Ryan, J. Carrol Naish, Jerome Cowan; ***D:*** Allan Dwan; ***W:*** Allan Dwan, Karen DeWolf; ***C:*** Charles Lawton Jr.

Getting Gotti 1/2 **1994 (R)** Story of the seven-year investigation and six-month trial by U.S. Attorney's Office prosecutor Diane Giacalone (Bracco) against reputed mobster "Teflon Don" John Gotti. (She lost.) **93m/C VHS, DVD.** Lorraine Bracco, Anthony John (Tony) Denison, Kathleen Lasky, August Schellenberg, Kenneth Welsh, Ellen Burstyn, Lawrence Bayne; ***D:*** Roger Young; ***W:*** James Henerson; ***M:*** Patrick Williams. **TV**

Getting In 1/2 *Student Body* **1994 (R)** Pressured by the family tradition of attending Johns Hopkins Medical School, Gabriel Higgs (Mailer) decides to bribe the rivals ahead of him on the waiting list. But one of them (McCarthy) decides the easiest thing to do is murder the other candidates and frame Gabe. **94m/C VHS.** Steven Mailer, Kristy Swanson, Andrew McCarthy, Dave Chappelle; ***D:*** Doug Liman; ***W:*** P.J. Posner, Joel Posner, Jonathan Lewin.

Getting It **2006** Teen sex comedy hero Silver is unlucky in love until by some twist of fate a rumor spreads about town that he has a two-foot (fill in the blank). Suddenly the ladies are lined up around the block to boyfriend young Silver. But alas, true love rules as he decides to woo back his dream girl. **97m/C DVD.** Patrick Censoplano, Cheryl Dent, Sajen Corona, Sandra Staggs, Salvatore Crivelo; ***D:*** Nick Gaitatjis; ***W:*** Nick Gaitatjis; ***C:*** Jonathan Hale; ***M:*** Holly Amber Church. **VIDEO**

Getting It On **1983 (R)** High school student uses his new-found video equipment for voyeuristic activity. **100m/C VHS, DVD.** Martin Yost, Heather Kennedy, Jeff Edmond, Kathy Rockmeier, Mark Alan Ferri; ***D:*** William Olsen.

Getting It Right 1/2 **1989 (R)** A sweet-natured British comedy about an inexperienced, shy adult male who is quite suddenly pursued by a middle-aged socialite, a pregnant, unstable rich girl, and a modest single mother. Novel and screenplay by Elizabeth Jane Howard. **101m/C VHS.** *GB* Jesse Birdsall, Helena Bonham Carter, Lynn Redgrave, Peter Cook, John Gielgud, Jane Horrocks, Richard Huw, Shirley Anne Field, Pat Haywood, Judy Parfitt, Bryan Pringle; ***D:*** Randal Kleiser; ***W:*** Elizabeth Jane Howard; ***M:*** Colin Towns, Steve Tyrell.

The Getting of Wisdom 1/2 **1977** A 13-year-old girl from the Australian outback tries to establish her identity, and her individuality, within the restricting confines of a Victorian girl's boarding school. Based on the novel by Henry Handel Richardson. **100m/C VHS.** *AU* Susannah Fowle, Hilary Ryan, Alix Longman, Sheila Helpmann, Patricia Kennedy, Barry Humphries, John Waters; ***D:*** Bruce Beresford.

Getting Out 1/2 **1994** Arlie (DeMornay) is an ex-con on her way home to Georgia and what she hopes will be a reunion with the son she bore in jail. She thinks he's in a foster home but instead her mother (Burstyn) had the child adopted and if she interferes, Arlie's parole will be revoked. Arlie's trying desperately to rehabilitate herself but the system and old contacts are close to dragging her back down. TV movie adapted from Marsha Norman's 1977 play. **92m/C VHS, DVD.** Rebecca De Mornay, Ellen Burstyn, Robert Knepper, Richard Jenkins, Carol Mitchell-Leon, Tandy Cronyn, Norman Skaggs; ***D:*** John Korty; ***W:*** Eugene Corr, Ruth Shapiro; ***M:*** Mason Daring.

Getting Over **1981** A black promoter is hired as a figurehead by a bigoted record company president and proceeds to try to run the company his own way. He develops an all-girl group called "The Love Machine" and gets involved in a singer's kidnapping and a record company run by gangsters. Filled with cliches and stereotypes. **108m/C VHS.** John Daniels, Gwen Brisco, Mary Hopkins, John Goff, Andrew "Buzz" Cooper; ***D:*** Bernie Rollins; ***W:*** Bernie Rollins.

Getting Physical 1/2 **1984** After being mugged, a secretary decides to get in shape and enters the world of female body building. Crammed with workout scenes and disco music. **95m/C VHS.** Alexandra Paul, Sandahl Bergman, David Naughton; ***D:*** Steven Hilliard Stern; ***M:*** William Goldstein. **TV**

Getting Played 1/2 **2005 (PG-13)** Three attractive women bet that any man can be seduced, but their mark knows their game and decides to play it his way. Slight story, predictable ending, attractive cast. **85m/C DVD.** Vivica A. Fox, Carmen Electra, Stacey Dash, Bill Bellamy, Joe Torry, Dorian Gregory, Kathy Najimy; ***D:*** David Silberg; ***W:*** David Silberg; ***C:*** Francis Kenny; ***M:*** David Lawrence. **VIDEO**

Getting Straight **1970 (R)** A returning Vietnam soldier (Gould) goes back to his alma mater to secure a teaching degree and gets involved in the lives of his fellow students and the turbulence of the end of the '60s, including campus riots. A now-dated "youth" picture somewhat watchable for Gould's performance. **124m/C VHS.** Elliott Gould, Candice Bergen, Jeff Corey, Cecil Kellaway, Jeannie Berlin, Harrison Ford, John Rubinstein, Robert F. Lyons, Max Julien; ***D:*** Richard Rush.

Getting Up and Going Home 1/2 **1992** Jack (Skerritt) is a married man with a midlife crisis. So what does he do? Get involved with not one, but two, other women. Is he asking for trouble or what? Adapted from the book by Robert Anderson. **93m/C VHS.** Tom Skerritt, Blythe Danner, Roma Downey, Julianne Phillips, Bruce Kirby, Gary Frank, Dorian Harewood, Paul Sand; ***D:*** Steven Schachter; ***W:*** Peter Nelson.

Getting Wasted 1/2 **1980 (PG)** Set in 1969 at a military academy for troublesome young men, chaos ensues when the cadets meet hippies. **98m/C VHS, DVD.** Brian Kerwin, Stephen Furst, Cooper Huckabee, David Caruso, Stefan Arngrim; ***D:*** Paul Fritzler; ***C:*** Daniel Pearl.

Gettysburg 1/2 **1993 (PG)** Civil War buff Ted Turner (who has a cameo as a Confederate soldier) originally intended Michael Shaara's Pulitzer Prize-winning novel "The Killer Angels" to be adapted as a three-part miniseries for his "TNT" network, but the lure of the big screen prevailed, marking the first time the battle has been committed to film and the first time a film crew has been allowed to film battle scenes on the Gettysburg National Military Park battlefield. The greatest battle of the war and the bloodiest in U.S. history is realistically staged by more than 5,000 Civil War re-enactors. The all-male cast concentrates on presenting the human cost of the war, with Daniels particularly noteworthy as the scholarly Colonel Chamberlain, determined to hold Little Round Top for the Union. Last film role for Jordan, to whom the movie is co-dedicated. The full scale recreation of Pickett's Charge is believed to be the largest period scale motion-picture sequence filmed in North America since D.W. Griffith's "Birth of a Nation." **254m/C VHS, DVD.** Jeff Daniels, Martin Sheen, Tom Berenger, Sam Elliott, Richard Jordan, Stephen Lang, Kevin Conway, C. Thomas Howell, Maxwell Caulfield, Andrew Prine, James Lancaster, Royce D. Applegate, Brian Mallon, Cooper Huckabee, Bo Brinkman, Kieran Mulroney, Patrick Gorman, William Morgan Sheppard, James Patrick Stuart, Tim Ruddy, Joseph Fuqua, Ivan Kane, Warren Burton, MacIntyre Dixon, George Lazenby, Alex Harvey, John Diehl, John Rothman, Richard Anderson, Billy Campbell, David Carpenter, Donal Logue, Dwier Brown, Mark Moses, Ken Burns, Ted Turner; ***D:*** Ronald F. Maxwell; ***W:*** Ronald F. Maxwell; ***C:*** Kees Van Oostrum; ***M:*** Randy Edelman.

The Ghastly Ones **WOOF!** **1968** Three couples must stay in a haunted mansion to inherit an estate, but they're soon being violently killed off. No budget and no talent. Remade as "Legacy of Blood." **81m/C VHS, DVD.** Don Williams, Maggie Rogers, Hal Belsoe, Veronica Redburn, Hal Sherwood; ***D:*** Andy Milligan; ***W:*** Andy Milligan, Hal Sherwood; ***C:*** Andy Milligan.

Ghetto Blaster **1989 (R)** A Vietnam vet takes on out-of-control street gangs to make his neighborhood safe. **86m/C VHS.** R.G. Armstrong, Richard Hatch, Richard Jaeckel, Harry Caesar, Rose Marie, Kamar De Los Reyes; ***D:*** Alan L. Stewart.

Ghetto Dawg 1/2 **2002 (R)** Standard urban actioner finds Tariq (J-King) wanting to escape his job working for mobster Gresh (Winslow) after falling for Robin (Coe). But Gresh wants Tariq to help him in his illegal pit bull fights and threatens to hurt Tariq's loved ones if he won't cooperate. **89m/C VHS, DVD.** Drena De Niro, J-King, Portia Coe, Gianna Palminteri, Lawrence Winslow, P.J. Marshall; ***D:*** Brian Averill; ***W:*** Allen Cognata; ***C:*** Shawn Kim; ***M:*** Wendell Hanes. **VIDEO**

Ghetto Dawg 2: Out of the Pits 1/2 **2005 (R)** Aimless teen Donte (Outlaw) has revenge on his mind when his brother is murdered. He joins his brother's violent crew but discovers he's not the killer type. Hooker girlfriend Brynn (Faith) comes up with a scheme to rip off crime boss Big Daddy (Torres) but there's one last thing Donte needs to do before blowing town with his squeeze and it involves dog-fighting competitions. A basic rehash of the first flick. **88m/C VHS, DVD.** Daniel Outlaw, Janisha Faith, Lou Torres, Paris Campbell, J-Hood, Randi Pannell; ***D:*** Jeff Crook, Josh Crook; ***W:*** Christine Conradt; ***C:*** Till Newman; ***M:*** Capone. **VIDEO**

Ghetto Revenge *The Bus Is Coming* **1971** An embittered Vietnam vet gets caught between white supremacists and black radical activists in this coming home story. He returns and tries to build a life but succumbs to the desire for vengeance and things are never the same. **109m/C VHS.** Mike Sims, Stephanie Faulkner, Burl Bullock, Tony Sweeting; ***D:*** Wendell Franklin; ***W:*** Horace Jackson, Robert H. Raff, Mike Rhodes; ***C:*** Mike Rhodes; ***M:*** Tom McIntosh.

Ghidrah the Three Headed Monster 1/2 *Ghidorah Sandai Kaiju Chikyu Saidai No Kessan; Ghidora, the Three-Headed Monster; Ghidrah; The Greatest Battle on Earth; The Biggest Fight on Earth; Monster of Monsters* **1965** When a three-headed monster from outer-space threatens the world, humans, having nowhere else to turn, appeal to the friendly Mothra, Rodan, and Godzilla. Rock'em, sock 'em giant thrashing about as Tokyo once again gets trampled. Dependable afternoon monster fare complete with usual dubious dubbing. **85m/C VHS.** *JP* Akiko Wakabayashi, Yosuke Natsuki, Yuriko Hoshi, Hiroshi Koizumi, Takashi Shimura, Emi Ito, Yumi Ito, Kenji Sahara, Hisaya Ito; ***D:*** Inoshiro Honda; ***W:*** Shinichi Sekizawa; ***C:*** Hajime Koizumi; ***M:*** Akira Ifukube.

The Ghost 1/2 *Lo Spettro; Lo Spettro de Dr. Hitchcock; The Spectre* **1963** A woman is driven mad by her supposedly dead husband and their evil housekeeper. Sequel to "The Horrible Dr. Hichcock." **96m/C VHS, DVD.** *IT* Barbara Steele, Peter Baldwin, Leonard Eliott, Harriet White, Harriet Medin, Umberto Raho; ***D:*** Riccardo Freda; ***W:*** Riccardo Freda, Oreste Biancoli; ***C:*** Raffaele Masciocchi; ***M:*** Franco Mannino, Roman Vlad.

Ghost **1990 (PG-13)** Zucker, known for overboard comedies like "Airplane!" and "Ruthless People," changed tack and directed this undemanding romantic thriller, which was the surprising top grosser of 1990. Murdered investment consultant Sam Wheast (Swayze) attempts (from somewhere near the hereafter) to protect his lover, Molly (Moore), from imminent danger when he learns he was the victim of a hit gone afoul. Goldberg is medium Oda Mae Brown, who suddenly discovers that the powers she's been faking are real. A winning blend of action, special effects (from Industrial Light and Magic) and romance. **127m/C VHS, DVD.** Stephen (Steve) Root, Patrick Swayze, Demi Moore, Whoopi Goldberg, Tony Goldwyn, Rick Aviles, Vincent Schiavelli, Gail Boggs, Armelia McQueen, Phil Leeds; ***D:*** Jerry Zucker; ***W:*** Bruce Joel Rubin; ***C:*** Adam Greenberg; ***M:*** Maurice Jarre. Oscars '90: Orig. Screenplay, Support. Actress (Goldberg); British Acad. '90: Support. Actress (Goldberg); Golden Globes '91: Support. Actress (Goldberg).

The Ghost 1/2 *Ryeong; Dead Friend* **2004** Ji-won (Kim Ha-neul) has some sort of accident that wipes out her memory. And it must've been a pretty bad event because all her friends are shunning her when she comes back to school. While she tries to figure out what the deal is, they all start drowning. That'll show 'em! Of course the rest of her acquaintances blame her for the troubles, and the more she remembers the more she comes to realize they may be right. **94m/C DVD.** *KN* Yi Shin, Ha-Neul Kim, Sang-mi Nam, Bin, Hie-ju Jeon, Yun-ji Lee; ***D:*** Tae-kyeong Kim; ***W:*** Tae-kyeong Kim.

The Ghost and Mrs. Muir **1947** A charming, beautifully orchestrated fantasy about a feisty widow who, with her young daughter, buys a seaside house and refuses to be intimidated by the crabby ghost of its former sea captain owner. When the widow falls into debt, the captain dictates his sea adventures, which she adapts into a successful novel. The ghost also falls in love with the beautiful lady. Tierney is exquisite and Harrison is sharp-tongued and manly. Based on R. A. Dick's novel. **104m/B VHS, DVD.** Gene Tierney, Rex Harrison, George Sanders, Edna Best, Anna Lee, Vanessa Brown, Robert Coote, Natalie Wood, Isobel Elsom; ***D:*** Joseph L. Mankiewicz; ***W:*** Philip Dunne; ***C:*** Charles B(ryant) Lang Jr.; ***M:*** Bernard Herrmann.

The Ghost and Mr. Chicken 1/2 **1966** Fraidy cat Luther Heggs (Knotts) works for a small town newspaper and longs to be a hot-shot reporter. One night he thinks he sees a woman's corpse at the vacant Simmons mansion but of course there's no body when the cops come. The house is considered haunted and there is a 20-year-old murder scandal, so Luther is very reluctantly persuaded to spend the night and solve the sinister goings-on. **90m/C VHS, DVD.** Don Knotts, Joan Staley, Dick Sargent, Liam Redmond, Skip Homeier, Reta Shaw, Lurene Tuttle, Philip Ober; ***D:*** Alan Rafkin; ***W:*** James Fritzell; ***C:*** William Margulies; ***M:*** Vic Mizzy.

The Ghost and the Darkness 1/2 **1996 (R)** Based on the true story of two man-eating lions who killed 130 people and nearly derailed the building of the East African railroad in 1896. Engineer John Patterson (Kilmer) is sent to build a bridge over the Tsavo river, but as African liaison Samuel (Kani) informs him, Tsavo prophetically means place of slaughter. The workers become convinced the lions, nicknamed "The Ghost" and "The Darkness" are actually demons and, try as he might, Patterson has little luck killing the beasts. Then, legendary big game hunter Remington (Douglas) is called in—but the lions still seem to have the advantage. Lots of crunching bones, slurping blood, and quick cut editing is used to depict the lions' attacks. **110m/C VHS, DVD.** Val Kilmer, Michael Douglas, John Kani, Bernard Hill, Om Puri, Brian McCardie, Tom Wilkinson, Emily Mortimer, Henry Cele; ***D:*** Stephen Hopkins; ***W:*** William Goldman; ***C:*** Vilmos Zsigmond; ***M:*** Jerry Goldsmith. Oscars '96: Sound FX Editing.

The Ghost and the Guest 1/2 **1943** Newlyweds spend their honeymoon in a house in the country only to find that gangsters are using the place as a hideout. Chases involving secret passages ensue. **59m/B VHS, DVD.** James Dunn, Florence Rice, Mabel Todd, Robert Bice, Anthony Warde, Anthony Caruso, Edward Foster; ***D:*** William Nigh; ***W:*** Morey Amsterdam; ***C:*** James N. Toney, Robert E. Cline.

The Ghost Breakers **1940** As a follow-up to the Hope/Goddard 1939 comedy thriller "The Cat and the Canary," this spooky comedy was even better. Lots of laughs and real chills as Hope and Goddard investigate a haunted mansion that she's inherited in Cuba. Effective horror scenes are expertly handled by director Marshall. Remade in 1953 as "Scared Stiff" with Dean Martin and Jerry Lewis. Based on the play by Paul Dickey and Charles Goddard. **83m/B VHS, DVD.** Bob Hope, Paulette Goddard, Richard Carlson, Paul Lukas, Willie Best, Pedro de Cordoba, Noble Johnson, Anthony Quinn; ***D:*** George Marshall; ***W:*** Walter DeLeon; ***C:*** Charles B(ryant) Lang Jr.

The Ghost Brigade 1/2 *The Killing Box; Grey Knight* **1993 (R)** Civil War ghost story finds a Union general (Sheen) trying to discover who's slaughtering both Confederate and Union soldiers on the battlefield. So he sends Captain Harling (Pasdar) to investigate, with the help of rebel prisoner Strayn (Bernsen) and a slave (Williams). What they find is an evil brigade of soldiers—who already happen to be dead—and are eager for new recruits. **80m/C VHS, DVD.** Corbin Bernsen, Martin Sheen, Adrian Pasdar, Ray Wise, Cynda Williams, Roger Wilson, Billy Bob Thornton, Alexis Arquette, David Arquette, Roger Wilson, Dean Cameron, A.J. (Allison Joy) Langer, Matt LeBlanc; ***D:*** George Hickenlooper; ***W:*** Matt Greenberg; ***C:*** Kent Wakeford.

The Ghost Camera 1/2 **1933** Slight story of a man falsely accused of murder. A photograph taken at the murder scene can prove his innocence if only the missing camera can be discovered. **68m/B VHS.** *GB* Henry Kendall, Ida Lupino, John Mills; ***D:*** Bernard Vorhaus.

Ghost Chase 1/2 **1988 (PG-13)** A young filmmaker desperate for funds inherits his dead relative's clock, from which issues the ghost of the deceased's butler. The ghostly retainer aids in a search for the departed's secret fortune. Neither scary nor funny. **89m/C VHS, DVD.** Jason Lively, Jill Whitlow, Tim McDaniel, Paul Gleason, Chuck "Porky" Mitchell; ***D:*** Roland Emmerich; ***W:*** Roland Emmerich, Oliver Eberle; ***C:*** Karl Walter Lindenlaub.

Ghost Chasers 1/2 **1951** The Bowery Boys become mixed up in supernatural hijinks when a seance leads to the appearance of a ghost that only Sach can see. **70m/B VHS.** Leo Gorcey, Huntz Hall, William Benedict, David Gorcey, Buddy Gorman, Bernard Gorcey, Jan Kayne, Philip Van Zandt, Lloyd Corrigan; ***D:*** William Beaudine.

Ghost City **1932** Our hero must deal with a masked gang that is "haunting" a town. **60m/B VHS.** Bill Cody, Helen Foster, Ann Rutherford, John Shelton, Reginald Owen; ***D:*** Harry Fraser.

Ghost Crazy *Crazy Knights* **1944** Three wild comedians and a gorilla create mayhem in a haunted house. **63m/B VHS.** Shemp Howard, Billy Gilbert, Maxie "Slapsie" Rosenbloom, Tim Ryan; ***D:*** William Beaudine; ***W:*** Tim Ryan; ***C:*** Marcel Le Picard.

Ghost Dad **1990 (PG)** A widowed workaholic dad is prematurely killed and returns from the dead to help his children prepare for the future. Cosby walks through doors, walls, and other solid objects for the sake of comedy—only none of it is funny. **84m/C VHS, DVD.** Bill Cosby, Denise Nicholas, Ian Bannen, Christine Ebersole, Dana Ashbrook, Arnold Stang; ***D:*** Sidney Poitier; ***W:*** S.S. Wilson, Brent Maddock; ***M:*** Henry Mancini.

Ghost Dance **1983** Sacred Indian burial ground is violated, with grim results. **93m/C VHS, DVD.** Sherman Hemsley, Henry Ball, Julie Amato; ***D:*** Peter Bufa.

Ghost Dog: The Way of the Samurai 1/2 **1999 (R)** Jarmusch takes a Far Eastern approach to the Mob-hit man genre with "Dog," whose title character, a contract killer played excellently by Whitaker, pledges himself to small-time hood Louie in the tradition of the Samurai after Louie saves his life. When one of his hits goes wrong, Ghost Dog is targeted for elimination, which leads to many dead bodies. Like most Jarmusch offerings, this one's quirky, disjointed, and not for everyone, but Whitaker's performance, and the offbeat humor make up for a lot. **116m/C VHS, DVD.** Forest Whitaker, Cliff Gorman, Henry Silva, John Tormey, Isaach de Bankole, Tricia Vessey, Victor Argo, Gene Ruffini, Richard Portnow, Camille Winbush; ***D:*** Jim Jarmusch; ***W:*** Jim Jarmusch; ***C:*** Robby Muller.

Ghost Fever WOOF! **1987 (PG)** Two bumbling cops try to evict the inhabitants of a haunted house and get nowhere. A bad rip-off of "Ghostbusters." Alan Smithee is a pseudonym used when a director does not want his or her name on a film—no wonder. **86m/C VHS.** Sherman Hemsley, Luis Avalos; ***D:*** Alan Smithee; ***W:*** Oscar Brodney.

The Ghost Goes West **1936** A brash American family buys a Scottish castle and transports the pieces to the United States along with the Scottish family ghost (Donat). Also along is the ghost's modern-day descendant (also played by Donat) who is the new castle caretaker and in love with the new owner's daughter. It turns out to be up to the ghost to get the two lovers together and find his own eternal rest. A rather lovable fantasy. Rene Clair's first English film. Available in digitally remastered stereo with original movie trailer. **90m/B VHS.** *GB* Robert Donat, Jean Parker, Eugene Pallette, Elsa Lanchester, Ralph Bunker, Patricia Hilliard, Everley Gregg, Morton Selten, Chili Bouchier, Mark Daly, Herbert Lomas, Elliot Mason, Jack Lambert, Hay Petrie; ***D:*** Rene Clair; ***W:*** Robert Sherwood, Geoffrey Kerr; ***C:*** Harold Rosson.

Ghost in the Invisible Bikini 1/2 **1966** Yes, it is very silly and you can understand why the seventh film in AIP's "Beach Party" series was also the last, but it's still a guilty pleasure. Greedy millionaire Hiram Stokley (Karloff) has died but because of his misdeeds he can't get into heaven. Then ghostly Cecily (Hart), whom Hiram once knew, shows up to say if he can perform a good deed within 24 hours he'll get through the pearly gates. Hiram realizes that his sinister lawyer Ripper (Rathbone) is going to kill off the benefactors of his will, so thwarting him will be his good deed. Ripper's invited the heirs (who include Kirk, Walley, and Kelly) to Hiram's creepy mansion to carry out his evil plan. **82m/C DVD.** Boris Karloff, Susan Hart, Basil Rathbone, Tommy Kirk, Deborah Walley, Patsy Kelly, Aron Kincaid, Quinn O'Hara, Jesse White, Harvey Lembeck, Bobbi Shaw, Nancy Sinatra, Benny Dubin; ***D:*** Don Weis; ***W:*** Louis M. Heyward; ***C:*** Stanley Cortez; ***M:*** Les Baxter.

Ghost in the Machine 1/2 **1993 (R)** Serial killer dies while undergoing an X-ray scan and somehow, because of a lightning storm and a power outage, his soul manages to infiltrate the hospital's computer and go on to terrorize more victims via their home computers and appliances. (You expect this to make sense?) Outlandish, predictable flick hovers between high-tech horror and satiric comedy and wastes some pretty decent talent. Horror buffs may get a kick out of it but be forewarned: You may never view your microwave, dishwasher, or electrical outlets in quite the same way again. **104m/C VHS, DVD.** Karen Allen, Chris Mulkey, Ted Marcoux, Jessica Walter, Ric(k) Ducommun, Wil Horneff, Nancy Fish, Brandon Adams; ***D:*** Rachel Talalay; ***W:*** William Davies, William Osborne; ***M:*** Graeme Revell.

Ghost in the Noonday Sun WOOF! **1974** Crew of a treasure-seeking pirate ship sets sail for high sea silliness in this slapstick adventure film. Not a theatrical release for one obvious reason—it's terrible. **90m/C VHS.** *GB* Peter Sellers, Spike Milligan, Anthony (Tony) Franciosa, Clive Revill, Rosemary Leach, Peter Boyle; ***D:*** Peter Medak.

Ghost in the Shell *Koukaku Kidoutai* **1995** Major Motoko Kusanagi of the Security Police Section 9 is on the trail of a super hacker known as the Puppet Master. His techniques are so advanced that almost nothing is known about him. The time is 2029 and many people are cybernetically enhanced which allows the Puppet Master to make almost anyone his pawn. The more the Major works on the case, the more conflicted she becomes, for all that remains of her original body is a small slice of brain. In a world where the only humanity some people have are their ghosts (or souls), where they may or may not be within the shells (or bodies) they were born with, what happens when a ghost exists where it should not? Along with the philosophical questions about the nature of humanity that are heavily interlaced within the plot, this anime features a slick science fiction story and top-quality animation. Based on the story by Masamune Shirow. A special edition is available which includes the 30-minutes documentary "The Making of Ghost in the Shell." **82m/C VHS, DVD, UMD.** *JP* ***D:*** Mamoru Oshii; ***W:*** Kazunori Ito.

Ghost Keeper **1980** Three girls are trapped in a mansion with an old hag and various supernatural apparitions. **87m/C VHS.** Riva Spier, Murray Ord, Georgie Collins; ***D:*** Vernon Sewell.

Ghost of a Chance *Eonios Ftitis* **2001** Vera is a dealer at a casino where med student Takis tries to make some cash. After becoming lovers, they rig a roulette game, take the money, and leave it with Vera's mother while they hide out at a friend's house. But their romantic dreams soon succumb to reality and when Vera returns home for her father's funeral, she's confronted by the casino boss who threatens her unless he gets his money back. Greek with subtitles. **100m/C VHS, DVD.** *GR* Maria Solomou, Emilios Chilakis, Mae Savastopoulou, Spyros Stavrinidis; ***D:*** Vangelis Seitanidis; ***W:*** Vangelis Seitanidis; ***C:*** Alekos Yannaros; ***M:*** Fotini Baxevani, Dimitris Tsakas.

The Ghost of Dragstrip Hollow **1959** Low-budget AIP teen fodder has the members of the hotrod, drag-racing Zenith Club losing their hangout. Anastasia Abernathy (Neumann), a friend of member Lois' (Fair) family, offers the teens her old mansion if they can get rid of the resident ghost. They decide to hold a come as your favorite monster Halloween bash to celebrate and discover there's a party-crasher! **65m/B DVD.** Jody Fair, Russ Bender, Dorothy Neumann, Elaine DuPont, Henry McCann, Martin Braddock, Leon Tyler, Kirby Smith; ***D:*** William Hole Jr.; ***W:*** Lou Rusoff; ***C:*** Gilbert Warrenton; ***M:*** Ronald Stein.

The Ghost of Frankenstein 1/2 **1942** Fourth Frankenstein film in the Universal Studios series with Chaney filling in for Karloff as the monster. Not as good as its predecessors, but the cast is enjoyable, especially Lugosi as the monster's deformed sidekick, Ygor. Based on a story by Eric Taylor. **68m/B VHS, DVD.** Cedric Hardwicke, Lon Chaney Jr., Lionel Atwill, Ralph Bellamy, Bela Lugosi, Evelyn Ankers, Dwight Frye; ***D:*** Erle C. Kenton; ***W:*** Scott Darling; ***C:*** Milton Krasner; ***M:*** Charles Previn.

The Ghost of Rashmon Hall *Night Comes Too Soon* **1947** Doctor tries to rid his home of the ghosts of a sailor, his wife and her lover. **52m/B VHS, DVD.** *GB* Valentine Dyall, Anne Howard, Alex Flavorsham, Howard Douglas, Beatrice Marsden, Arthur Brander, Antony Baird, Monti DeLyle, Nina Erber, John Desmond; ***D:*** Denis Kavanagh; ***W:*** Pat Dixon; ***C:*** Ray Densham.

The Ghost of Spoon River *The Mystery of Spoon River* **2000 (R)** Chicago lawyer Emma Masters (Sinclair) heads home to defend her brother-in-law Jesse (McNamara) who's been accused of killing the local game warden. A killing that seems racially motivated and seems to tie into the town's dark past and a 1941 lynching. And despite the title, this standard thriller has really nothing to do with Edgar Lee Masters' "Spoon River Anthology." **90m/C VHS, DVD.** Lauren Sinclair, Brian McNamara, Richard Portnow, Michael Monks; ***D:*** Scott A. Meehan. **VIDEO**

Ghost of the Needle **2003 (R)** Jacob (Avenet-Bradley) is a serial killer who likes to drug, photograph, and vacuum seal his female victims—watching as they suffocate. Except his latest victim, Aimee (Christian), is apparently getting her revenge from beyond the grave. **86m/C DVD.** Brian Avenet-Bradley, Frank Warlick, Greg Thompson, Leigh Hill; ***D:*** Brian Avenet-Bradley; ***W:*** Brian Avenet-Bradley; ***C:*** Laurence Avenet-Bradley; ***M:*** Mark Lee Fletcher.

The Ghost of Yotsuya 1/2 **1958** Based on the Japanese legend of a man who must betray his wife to get the power he seeks. When he does, however, what follows is a horrifying revenge. In Japanese with English subtitles. **76m/C VHS.** *JP* Shigeru Amachi, Noriko Kitazawa; ***D:*** Nobuo Nakagawa; ***W:*** Yoshihiro Ishikawa; ***C:*** Tadashi Nishimoto; ***M:*** Michiaki Watanabe.

Ghost on the Loose **1943** The Bowery Boys take on Nazi spies. **65m/C VHS, DVD.** Leo Gorcey, Huntz Hall, Bela Lugosi; ***D:*** William Beaudine.

Ghost Patrol 1/2 **1936** A cowboy duo kidnaps the inventor of a ray gun in order to hijack mail planes, but they're stopped by G-Man McCoy and friends. An odd hybrid of science fiction and western, to say the least. **57m/B VHS, DVD.** Tim McCoy, Walter Miller, Wheeler Oakman; ***D:*** Sam Newfield.

Ghost Rider **1935** A lawman is aided in his outlaw-nabbing efforts by the ghost of a gunfighter. **56m/B VHS.** Rex Lease, Bobby Nelson, Franklyn Farnum, Lloyd Ingraham, Eddie (Ed, Eddy, Edwin) Parker, Lafe (Lafayette) McKee; ***D:*** Jack Levine.

Ghost Rider **1943** Former football baller Brown rides the range once again, this time with an element of the supernatural nipping at his heels. **58m/B VHS.** Johnny Mack Brown, Raymond Hatton, Tim Seidel, Beverly Boyd, Milburn (Milt) Morante; ***D:*** Wallace Fox.

Ghost Rider 1/2 **2007 (PG-13)** Critic-proof nonsense based on the Marvel comic character with the flaming skull head and motorcycle. Stunt rider Johnny Blaze (Cage) makes a deal with the devil (Fonda) who, naturally, doesn't follow through as intended. So Johnny is left as hell's bounty hunter, up against devil spawn Blackheart (Bentley). Beautiful Mendes is wasted in the girl role while Cage and Bentley overact, Fonda and Elliott stay cool, and viewers wait for some superhero fire to ignite. **108m/C DVD, Blu-ray Disc, UMD.** *US* Nicolas Cage, Eva Mendes, Wes Bentley, Sam Elliott, Donal Logue, Peter Fonda, Brett Cullen, Matt Long, Raquel Alessi; ***D:*** Mark Steven Johnson; ***W:*** Mark Steven Johnson; ***C:*** Russell Boyd; ***M:*** Christopher Young.

The Ghost Ship 1/2 **1943** A young sailor signs on as third mate on a ship, only to find out theat the captain is a sadistic martinet who doesn't mind endangering his crew to prove his authority. Better than it should have been B-picture was supposedly commissioned because the studio had an expensive leftover ship set and wanted an excuse to use it again. **69m/B DVD.** Richard Dix, Russell Wade, Edith Barrett, Lawrence Tierney, Steve Forrest, Ben Bard, Edmund Glover; ***D:*** Mark Robson; ***W:*** Donald Henderson Clarke; ***C:*** Nicholas Musuraca; ***M:*** Roy Webb.

Ghost Ship 1/2 **1953** Young couple is tortured by ghostly apparitions when they move into an old yacht with a dubious past. Grade-B haunting featuring the murdered wife of the ship's former owner as the poltergeist. **69m/B VHS, DVD.** *GB* Dermot Walsh, Hazel Court, Hugh Burden, John Robinson; ***D:*** Vernon Sewell.

Ghost Ship **2002 (R)** Promising premise sinks into formulaic horror-on-the-high-seas after a gruesome and startling beginning. A boat salvage crew led by Murphy (Byrne) is working in a remote area of the Bering Sea when they're led to the remains of a passenger liner that's been missing for more than 40 years. First mate Epps (Margulies) is the first crewmember to figure out that things are not as they should be, but the rest are caught in a web of greed that may have been the undoing of the ship's original passengers. **88m/C VHS, DVD.** *US* Julianna Margulies, Ron Eldard, Desmond Harrington, Isaiah Washington IV, Gabriel Byrne, Alex Dimitriades, Karl Urban, Emily Browning, Francesca Rettondini; *D:* Steve Beck; *W:* John Pogue, Mark Hanlon; *C:* Gale Tattersall; *M:* John (Gianni) Frizzell.

Ghost Son ½ **2006** Mark (Hannah) and his American wife Stacey (Harring) live on a ranch in South Africa. When he dies in a car crash, the suicidal Stacey begins to see (and feel) his ghost. After delivering a son, Stacey is certain that her baby is possessed by Mark's spirit and is out to kill her. **97m/C DVD.** Laura Elena Harring, John Hannah, Pete Postlethwaite, Coralina Cataldi-Tassoni, Mosa Kaiser, Mary Twala; *D:* Lamberto Bava; *W:* Lamberto Bava, Silvia Ranfagni; *C:* Tani Canivari; *M:* Paolo Vivaldi.

Ghost Story **1981 (R)** Four elderly men, members of an informal social club called the Chowder Society, share a terrible secret buried deep in their pasts—a secret that comes back to haunt them to death. Has moments where it's chilling, but unfortunately they're few. Based on the best-selling novel by Peter Straub. **110m/C VHS, DVD.** Fred Astaire, Melvyn Douglas, Douglas Fairbanks Jr., John Houseman, Craig Wasson, Alice Krige, Patricia Neal; *D:* John Irvin; *W:* Lawrence D. Cohen; *C:* Jack Cardiff; *M:* Philippe Sarde.

Ghost Town **1937** Good guy Carey saves a mine from claim jumpers, but not before he is mistakenly incarcerated as his friend's murderer, and then proved innocent. **65m/B VHS.** Harry Carey Sr.; *D:* Harry Fraser.

Ghost Town ½ **1988 (R)** Fine sleeper about a modern sheriff who follows a gal through a supernatural sandstorm and discovers a literal ghost town of bad guys. **85m/C VHS.** Franc Luz, Catherine Hickland, Jimmie F. Skaggs, Penelope Windust, Bruce Glover, Blake Conway, Laura Schaefer; *D:* Richard Governor; *W:* Duke Sandefur; *M:* Harvey R. Cohen.

Ghost Town **2008 (PG-13)** Dentist Bertram Pincus (Gervais), an unmarried, friendless, and overall grumpy guy, is granted the ability to hang out with ghosts after momentarily dying during a colonoscopy. A gift or a curse, he's not sure, but either way he finds it incredibly annoying. Enter Frank Herlihy (Kinnear), a man cheating on his girlfriend with his yoga instructor, who is hit by a bus. Frank desperately pleads with his new supernatural middleman to find his girlfriend Gwen (Leoni) and let her know that he's sorry. Of course, as despicable as Bertram may be, he and Gwen fall in love, to the endless frustration of helpless Frank. A light comedy, carried and saved by its performances, especially the brilliant and effortless Gervais. **102m/C DVD, Blu-ray Disc.** *US* Ricky Gervais, Greg Kinnear, Tea Leoni, Dana Ivey, Billy Campbell, Kristen Wiig, Alan Ruck; *D:* David Koepp; *W:* David Koepp, John Kamps; *C:* Fred Murphy; *M:* Geoff Zanelli.

Ghost Town Gold **1936** The Three Mesquiteers series continues as the trio outwits bank robbers who have hidden their loot in a ghost town. **53m/B VHS, DVD.** Robert "Bob" Livingston, Ray Corrigan, Max Terhune; *D:* Joseph Kane.

Ghost Town Law ½ **1942** The Rough Riders step in to save the day when a group of outlaws defend their hideout by murdering anyone who approaches. **62m/B VHS, DVD.** Buck Jones, Tim McCoy, Raymond Hatton; *D:* Howard Bretherton.

Ghost Town Renegades **1947** A pair of government agents prevent a crook from gaining control of a mining town. **57m/B VHS.** Lash LaRue, Al "Fuzzy" St. John, Jennifer Holt; *D:* Ray Taylor.

Ghost Town Riders ½ **1938** An outlaw gang is holed up in an abandoned town, threatening to steal Shannon's gold mine, until Baker comes to the rescue. **55m/B VHS.** Bob Baker, Fay McKenzie, George Cleveland, Glenn Strange, Forrest Taylor, Hank Worden, Murdock MacQuarrie; *D:* George Waggner.

The Ghost Train ½ **1941** Badly dated mystery/thriller. Grating musical hall comedian Tommy Gander (Askey) causes a group of passengers to miss their connecting train and they are all forced to wait overnight in an eerie Cornish station. The stationmaster (Lomas) tells them that the station is haunted by a ghost train (the result of a deadly rail disaster) and that very night is the anniversary of the original tragedy. But what happens next turns out to be far less supernatural (note the film was made during wartime). **82m/B DVD.** *GB* Arthur Askey, Richard Murdock, Kathleen Harrison, Peter Murray-Hill, Herbert Lomas, Morland Graham, Carole Lynne, Betty Jardine, Stuart Latham; *D:* Walter Forde; *W:* Val Guest, J.O.C. Orton, Marriott Edgar; *C:* Jack Cox.

Ghost Valley ½ **1932** When Keene and Kennedy inherit land rich in unmined ore, the administrator (Harris) attempts to scare them off. To foil his plan, Keene conceals his identity and takes a job as the administrator's assistant. Based on a story by Adele Buffington. **54m/B VHS.** Tom Keene, Merna Kennedy, Mitchell Harris, Billy Franey, Harry Bowen, Kate Campbell, Ted Adams, Buck Moulton, Harry Semels, Al Taylor, Charles "Slim" Whitaker; *D:* Fred Allen.

The Ghost Walks **1934** A playwright has his new masterpiece acted out in front of an unsuspecting producer, who thinks that a real murder has taken place. But when the cast really does start disappearing, who's to blame? **69m/B VHS, DVD.** John Miljan, June Collyer, Richard Carle, Spencer Charters, Johnny Arthur, Henry Kolker; *D:* Frank Strayer.

Ghost World ½ **2001 (R)** Zwigoff makes his feature debut with this dark comedy that contains echoes of his documentary "Crumb." Enid (Birch) and Rebecca (Johansson) are not your typical acid-tongued teenage outsiders. Instead of struggling to fit in, they wear their contempt for the empty mall culture that surrounds them like a badge of honor. On a whim, the girls answer a personal ad from Seymour, a middle-aged schmoe who collects old records. Seymour, whose personal quirks are similar to those of former Zwigoff documentary subject R. Crumb, is also baffled by modern culture and Enid is eventually drawn to him. She decides to help him in his attempt to find a woman, developing a special yet strange bond with him. Swinging from bleak to hilarious, the plot refuses to follow your standard romantic formula. That would be, like, so mainstream. Based on the underground comics of Daniel Clowes. **111m/C VHS, DVD.** *US* Thora Birch, Scarlett Johansson, Steve Buscemi, Brad Renfro, Illeana Douglas, Bob Balaban, Teri Garr, Stacey Travis, Dave Sheridan, Brian George; *D:* Terry Zwigoff; *W:* Daniel Clowes, Terry Zwigoff; *C:* Alfonso Beato; *M:* David Kitay. Ind. Spirit '02: Support. Actor (Buscemi); N.Y. Film Critics '01: Support. Actor (Buscemi); Natl. Soc. Film Critics '01: Support. Actor (Buscemi).

Ghost Writer **1989 (PG)** A writer discovers the ghost of a movie star haunting her beach house, and together they solve the dead vamp's murder. **94m/C VHS.** Audrey Landers, Judy Landers, Jeff Conaway, David Doyle, Anthony (Tony) Franciosa, Joey Travolta, John Matuszak, David Paul, Peter Paul; *D:* Kenneth J. Hall.

The Ghost Writer **2010 (PG-13)** A successful British ghostwriter (McGregor), known only as The Ghost, is hired to complete the memoirs of former British prime minister Adam Lang (Brosnan). He travels to the Long Island mansion where Lang and his family are staying just when Lang is accused of turning suspected terrorists over to the CIA for torture during his tenure. The place is soon swarming with reporters and protesters and The Ghost's work may just uncover secrets no one wants revealed. Robert Harris co-scripted from his novel. **128m/C DVD.** Ewan McGregor, Pierce Brosnan, Kim Cattrall, Olivia Williams, Tom Wilkinson, Timothy Hutton, James Belushi, Eli Wallach, Tim Preece, Jon Bernthal; *D:* Roman Polanski; *W:* Roman Polanski, Robert Harris; *C:* Pawel Edelman; *M:* Alexandre Desplat.

Ghostboat ½ **2006** The British sub Scorpion goes missing (presumably sunk) in WWII and lone survivor Jack Hardy has amnesia. The sub suddenly reappears 40 years later, minus all signs of its crew. The government wants Jack (Jason), now a marine biologist, to join the crew they're sending to retrace the sub's course and figure out what happened. Of course, this is a mistake. An anti-climatic ending spoils the chills. **145m/C DVD.** *GB* David Jason, Ian Puleston-Davies, Tony Haygarth, Julian Wadham, Crispin Bonham Carter, James Laurenson, Jonathan Cullen; *D:* Stuart Orme; *W:* Guy Burt; *C:* Tony Coldwell; *M:* Colin Towns. **TV**

Ghostbusters **1984 (PG)** After losing their scholastic funding, a group of "para-normal" investigators decide to go into business for themselves, aiding New York citizens in the removal of ghosts, goblins and other annoying spirits. Comedy-thriller about Manhattan being overrun by ghosts contains great special effects, zany characters, and some of the best laughs of the decade. Oscar nominated title song written and sung by Ray Parker Jr. Followed by a sequel. **103m/C VHS, DVD, UMD.** Bill Murray, Dan Aykroyd, Harold Ramis, Rick Moranis, Sigourney Weaver, Annie Potts, Ernie Hudson, William Atherton, David Margulies, Steven Tash, Reginald VelJohnson, Timothy Carhart; *D:* Ivan Reitman; *W:* Dan Aykroyd, Harold Ramis; *C:* Laszlo Kovacs; *M:* Elmer Bernstein.

Ghostbusters 2 ½ **1989 (PG)** After being sued by the city for the damages they did in the original "Ghostbusters," the boys in khaki are doing kiddie shows at birthday parties. When a river of slime that is actually the physical version of evil is discovered running beneath the city, the Ghostbusters are back in action. They must do battle with a wicked spirit in a painting or the entire world will fall pray to its ravaging whims. Murray is the highlight of this serviceable sequel, although MacNicol gives him a good run as the painting's henchman. **102m/C VHS, DVD.** Bill Murray, Dan Aykroyd, Sigourney Weaver, Harold Ramis, Rick Moranis, Ernie Hudson, Peter MacNichol, David Margulies, Wilhelm von Homburg, Harris Yulin, Annie Potts, Ben Stein, Richard "Cheech" Marin, Brian Doyle-Murray, Janet Margolin, Mary Ellen Trainor; *D:* Ivan Reitman; *W:* Dan Aykroyd, Harold Ramis; *C:* Michael Chapman; *M:* Randy Edelman.

Ghosted ½ *Ai Mei* **2009** German artist Sophie (Busch) is in Taipei with an art exhibit dedicated to her late lover Ai-ling (Ke). She's approached for an interview by pushy reporter Mei-li (Hu), who seems to also want a more personal relationship to commence. Flashbacks to Sophie's previous life and Ai-ling's search for her father are more confusing than enlightening. English, Mandarin and German with subtitles. **92m/C DVD.** *GE TW* Jack Kao, Inga Busch, Huan-ru Ke, Ting-Ting Hu, Jana Schulz, Marek Hartoff; *D:* Monika Treut; *W:* Monika Treut, Astrid Stroher; *C:* Bernd Meiners; *M:* Uwe Haas.

Ghosthouse **1988** It looks like an average suburban house, but it's haunted by the ghost of a little girl—and when she comes, evil is sure to follow. **91m/C VHS.** Lara Wendel, Gregg Scott; *D:* Humphrey Humbert.

Ghostriders **1987** One hundred years after their hanging, a band of ghostly outlaws take revenge on the townfolk's descendents. **85m/C VHS.** Bill Shaw, Jim Peters, Ricky Long, Cari Powell, Mike Ammons, Arland Bishop; *D:* Alan L. Stewart.

Ghosts Can Do It ½ *Those Dear Departed* **1987** The Hound doesn't like jumping to conclusions, but is it possible this obscurity was titled to be reminiscent of the more publicized Bo Derek vehicle "Ghosts Can't Do It" comedy about a man who returns to his sexy wife despite her efforts at killing him. **88m/C VHS.** *AU* Garry McDonald, Pamela Stephenson; *D:* Ted Robinson; *W:* Steve J. Spears; *C:* David Burr; *M:* Phillip Scott.

Ghosts Can't Do It **1990 (R)** Another wet-shirted, Bo-dacious softcore epic, involving a young woman who would like to have the spirit of her virile, but unfortunately dead, husband return to inhabit a living body. **91m/C VHS.** Bo Derek, Anthony Quinn, Don Murray, Leo Damian; *D:* John Derek. Golden Raspberries '90: Worst Picture, Worst Actress (Derek), Worst Director (Derek).

Ghosts Never Sleep **2005 (R)** A screenwriter sells a script that exposes a family secret his wife doesn't know about and his mother wants to keep hidden at all costs. Dunaway keeps her drama queen mannerisms to a minimum. **?m/C DVD.** Faye Dunaway, Tony Goldwyn, Sean Young, Shea Alexander; *D:* Steve Freeedman; *W:* Steve Freeedman, Christopher Joyce; *C:* Jan Michalik; *M:* Craig Stuart Garfinkle. **VIDEO**

Ghosts of Berkeley Square ½ **1947** The ghosts of two retired soldiers of the early 18th century are doomed to haunt their former home, and only a visit from a reigning monarch can free them. **85m/B VHS.** Wilfrid Hyde-White, Robert Morley, Felix Aylmer; *D:* Vernon Sewell.

Ghosts of Girlfriends Past ½ **2009 (PG-13)** Here's a plot that sounds suspiciously like something you'd expect at Christmas (Scrooge, anyone?). Celebrity photog Connor Mead (McConaughey) is a romantic jerk and his attitude threatens to ruin his brother Paul's (Meyer) wedding. Until the ghosts of jilted girlfriends make an appearance to see if Connor can change his caddish ways. Douglas is comically creepy as Connor's ghostly uncle—a womanizer who taught Connor how to be a heartless sleaze. But plucky Garner is wasted as Jenny, the woman Connor should never have let get away, mainly because she's obviously too smart to ever fall for Connor's smarm. **115m/C DVD.** *US* Matthew McConaughey, Michael Douglas, Breckin Meyer, Jennifer Garner, Lacey Chabert, Robert Forster, Anne Archer, Emma Stone, Daniel Sunjata, Devin Brochu; *D:* Mark S. Waters; *W:* Jon Lucas, Scott Moore; *C:* Daryn Okada; *M:* Rolfe Kent.

The Ghosts of Hanley House ½ **1968** No-budget spooker with no-brain plot. Several unlucky guests spend an evening in a creepy mansion...sound familiar? Shot in Texas. **80m/C VHS, DVD.** Barbara Chase, Wilkie De Martel, Elsie Baker, Cliff Scott; *D:* Louise Sherrill; *W:* Louise Sherrill; *M:* David C. Parsons.

Ghosts of Mississippi *Ghosts from the Past* **1996 (PG-13)** Director Reiner attempts to tell the story of civil rights leader Medgar Evers, murdered in 1963, and the three trials of Byron De la Beckwith (Woods), who was finally convicted (after two hung juries) in 1994. Unfortunately, he filters the story through the eyes of white assistant D.A. Bobby De Laughter (Baldwin) while ignoring Evers' accomplishments almost completely. Woods chews up the scenery as the wily old racist, bringing perhaps a little too much glee into a portrait of true evil. Goldberg sleepwalks through her role as Evers' widow, Myrlie; Evers' sons, Darrell and Van, play themselves; daughter Reena plays a juror while her character is played by Yolanda King, the daughter of slain civil rights leader Martin Luther King, Jr. Filmed on location in Jackson, Mississippi. **123m/C VHS, DVD.** Alec Baldwin, Whoopi Goldberg, James Woods, Craig T. Nelson, Wayne Rogers, William H. Macy, Michael O'Keefe, Yolanda King, Susanna Thompson, Lucas Black, James Pickens Jr., Virginia Madsen, Bill Cobbs, Alexa Vega, Jerry Levine, Bill Smitrovich, Terry O'Quinn, Rex Linn, Richard Riehle, Bonnie Bartlett, Diane Ladd, Andy Romano, Rance Howard, Margo Martindale; *D:* Rob Reiner; *W:* Lewis Colick; *C:* John Seale; *M:* Marc Shaiman.

Ghosts That Still Walk **1977** Spooky phenomena occur. The demons possessing a young lad's soul may be responsible. **92m/C VHS.** Ann Nelson, Matt Boston, Jerry Jenson, Caroline Howe, Rita Crafts; *D:* James T. Flocker.

Ghostwarrior *Swordkill* **1986 (R)** A 16th-century samurai warrior's ice-packed body is revived and runs amuck in the streets of modern-day Los Angeles. **86m/C VHS.** Hiroshi Fujioka, Janet (Johnson) Julian, Andy Wood, John Calvin; *D:* Larry Carroll; *W:* Tim Curnen; *C:* Mac Ahlberg.

GhostWatcher ½ **2002 (R)** A horrid ordeal makes Laura too scared to leave the house but then some evil spirits had to go and ruin that too. Things only get worse when the ghost hunter she hires turns out to be a fraud. **94m/C VHS, DVD.** Jillian Byrnes, Marianne Hayden, Jennifer Servary, Kevin Floyd, Kevin Quinn, Ray Schueler; *D:* David Cross; *W:* David Cross; *C:* Dan Poole; *M:* David Cross, Jerry Gaskill, Doug Pinnick, Ty Tabor. **VIDEO**

Ghostwriter **1984** Based on Philip Roth's best-selling novel, the story is of a writer coming to terms with his past. Roth co-wrote the screenplay. First seen on PBS. **90m/C VHS.** Sam Wanamaker, Claire Bloom, Rose Arrick, MacIntyre Dixon, Cecile Mann, Joseph Wiseman, Mark Linn-Baker, Paulette Smit; ***D:*** Tristam Powell; ***W:*** Phillip J. Roth.

The Ghoul 🦴🦴 ½ **1934** An eccentric English Egyptologist desires a sacred jewel to be buried with him and vows to come back from the grave if the gem is stolen. When that happens, he makes good on his ghostly promise. A minor horror piece with Karloff only appearing at the beginning and end of the film. This leaves the middle very dull. **73m/B VHS, DVD.** *GB* Boris Karloff, Cedric Hardwicke, Ernest Thesiger, Dorothy Hyson, Ralph Richardson, Anthony Bushell, Kathleen Harrison, Harold Huth, D. A. Clarke-Smith, Jack Raine; ***D:*** T. Hayes Hunter; ***W:*** Roland Pertwee, John Hastings Turner, Rupert Downing; ***C:*** Gunther Krampf.

The Ghoul 🦴🦴 **1975 (R)** A defrocked clergyman has a cannibal son to contend with—especially after the drivers in a local auto race begin to disappear. Hurt is the lunatic family gardener. **88m/C VHS, DVD.** *GB* Peter Cushing, John Hurt, Alexandra Bastedo, Don Henderson, Stewart Bevan; ***D:*** Freddie Francis.

Ghoul School 🦴 **1990 (R)** A spoof of horror films and college flicks, with lots of scantily clad women and bloody creatures in dark hallways. **90m/C VHS, DVD.** Joe Franklin, Nancy Siriani, William Friedman; ***D:*** Timothy O'Rawe; ***W:*** Timothy O'Rawe; ***C:*** Michael Raso; ***M:*** Rodney Shields.

Ghoulies 🦴 **1984 (PG-13)** A young man gets more than he bargained for when he conjures up a batch of evil creatures when dabbling in the occult. Ridiculous but successful. Followed by three sequels. **81m/C VHS, DVD.** Lisa Pelikan, Jack Nance, Scott Thomson, Tamara DeTreaux, Mariska Hargitay, Bobbie Bresee; ***D:*** Luca Bercovici; ***W:*** Luca Bercovici; ***C:*** Mac Ahlberg; ***M:*** Richard Band.

Ghoulies 2 🦴 **1987 (R)** Inept sequel to "Ghoulies" (1985), wherein the little demons haunt a failing carnival horror house, whose revenues begin to soar. Followed by a second sequel. **89m/C VHS, DVD.** Damon Martin, Royal Dano, Phil Fondacaro, J. Downing, Kerry Remsen; ***D:*** Albert Band.

Ghoulies 3: Ghoulies Go to College WOOF! **1991 (R)** Third in the series has the best special effects and the worst storyline. Not satisfied with ripping off "Gremlins," this one imposes Three Stooges personae upon a trio of demons at large on a beer- and babe-soaked campus. **94m/C VHS.** Kevin McCarthy, Griffin O'Neal, Evan Mackenzie; ***D:*** John Carl Buechler.

Ghoulies 4 🦴 ½ **1993 (R)** Dopey series continues with the satanic creatures roaming the streets of Los Angeles, searching for a way to return to their netherworld home. They get their chance when they meet a Satan-worshipping dominatrix out on a killing spree. **84m/C VHS.** Bobby DiCicco, Barbara Alyn Woods, Peter Paul Liapis; ***D:*** Jim Wynorski; ***W:*** Mark Sevi.

Ghouls 🦴 **2007** Typically low-budget trash from the Sci-Fi Channel. Jennifer (Renton) accompanies her parents to her grandmother's funeral in a small town in Romania. She meets Thomas (DeBello), a spirit-hunting Druid, who tells Jen that there's ghouls haunting the local forest, preying on the townspeople, and her family has a connection to the creatures. Turns out her dad (Atherton) intends to sacrifice Jennifer, making her the new ghoul queen. **88m/C DVD.** James DeBello, William Atherton, Erin Gray, Ion Haiduc, Kristen Renton, Dan Badarau, Lucia Maier, Constantin Florescu; ***D:*** Gary Jones; ***W:*** Brian D. Young; ***C:*** Toni Cartu; ***M:*** Alan Howarth. **VIDEO**

G.I. Blues 🦴🦴 **1960 (PG)** Three G.I.'s form a musical combo while stationed in Germany. Prowse is the nightclub singer Presley falls for. Presley's first film after his military service. ♫ Shopping Around; Tonight Is So Right For Love; What's She Really Like?; Frankfurt Special; Didya Ever; Big Boots; Pocketful of Rainbows; Doin' the Best I Can; Blue Suede Shoes. **104m/C VHS, DVD.** Elvis Presley, Juliet Prowse, Robert Ivers, Leticia Roman, Ludwig Stossel, James Douglas, Jeremy Slate; ***D:*** Norman Taurog; ***C:*** Loyal Griggs.

G.I. Executioner 🦴 *Wit's End; Dragon Lady* **1971 (R)** An adventure set in Singapore featuring a Vietnam veteran turned executioner. **86m/C VHS, DVD.** Tom Kenna, Victoria Racimo, Angelique Pettyjohn, Janet Wood, Walter Hill; ***D:*** Joel M. Reed.

G.I. Jane 🦴 **1951** A TV producer faints when he gets his draft notice and dreams his company is stranded at a desert post with a company of WACs. **62m/B VHS.** Jean Porter, Tom Neal, Iris Adrian, Jimmy Lloyd, Mara Lynn, Michael Whalen; ***D:*** Reginald LeBorg; ***W:*** Henry Blankfort.

G.I. Jane 🦴🦴 ½ *In Pursuit of Honor; Navy Cross* **1997 (R)** Moore is buffed, bold and bald in this modern day fable of the first female to become a Navy SEAL. As Jordan O'Neil, Moore endures grueling training exercises and sexist remarks from male colleagues that are tortuous for her, but enjoyable for those who sat through Moore's three previous films. Impressive supporting cast, including Mortensen as the vicious and misogynist master chief and Bancroft as a fiesty senator with a secret political agenda, pick things up when the story flags in the middle. The beginning holds the most interest, but the movie's length encourages improbable plot points. Scott shows he still knows how to make a movie look great, even if the writing doesn't quite measure up. **124m/C VHS, DVD, Blu-ray Disc.** Demi Moore, Viggo Mortensen, Anne Bancroft, Jason Beghe, Scott Wilson, Morris Chestnut, Lucinda Jenney, James (Jim) Caviezel; ***D:*** Ridley Scott; ***W:*** David N. Twohy, Danielle Alexandra; ***C:*** Hugh Johnson; ***M:*** Trevor Jones. Golden Raspberries '97: Worst Actress (Moore).

G.I. Joe: The Rise of Cobra 🦴🦴 **2009 (PG-13)** When a flick is based on a toy—even if it's a classic one—the expectations are already low, as seen here: a basic plot, a bunch of interchangeable military-type characters, and a lot of CGI action. Cobra is an evil organization bent on world domination and there's an arms dealer and a super weapon and a bad ninja and a good ninja and the various members of the G.I. Joe squad running around Paris, but the blinding and deafening explosions and dazzling gizmos will distract from all that anyway. **117m/C DVD.** *US* Brendan Fraser, Channing Tatum, Joseph Gordon-Levitt, Sienna Miller, Dennis Quaid, Rachel Nichols, Ray Park, Marlon Wayans, Christopher Eccleston, Arnold Vosloo, Jonathan Pryce, Said Taghmaoui, Adewale Akinnuoye-Agbaje, Byung-hun Lee, Brandon Soo Hoo; ***D:*** Stephen Sommers; ***W:*** Stuart Beattie, Skip Woods; ***C:*** Mitchell Amundsen; ***M:*** Alan Silvestri. Golden Raspberries '09: Worst Support. Actress (Miller).

G.I. War Brides 🦴🦴 **1946** Linda Powell (Lee) stows away aboard a ship heading for the States to find her soldier beau. She assumes the identity of English war bride Joyce Giles, who has decided she wants to stay in England. When Linda arrives, she discovers her G.I. no longer loves her and reporter Steve (Ellison) discovers Linda's deception but falls for the pretty English rose anyway. **69m/B VHS.** Anna Lee, James Ellison, Harry Davenport, William Henry, Robert Armstrong, Joseph (Joe) Sawyer, Stephanie Bachelor, Doris Lloyd, Mary McLeod, Carol Savage; ***D:*** George Blair; ***W:*** John K. Butler; ***C:*** Alfred S. Keller; ***M:*** Ernest Gold, Joseph Dubin.

Gia 🦴🦴 **1998 (R)** Based on the life of self-destructive supermodel/drug addict Gia Carangi (Jolie), who died from AIDS at the age of 26. Gia grew up in an abusive Philadelphia family and hid her insecurities under a tough and wanton persona. Taken under the wing of New York modeling exec Wilhelmina Cooper (Dunaway), Gia's exoticness gets her noticed but the hedonistic lifestyle of the late '70s quickly leads to her downfall. Jolie goes all out for the title role. **120m/C VHS, DVD.** Angelina Jolie, Mercedes Ruehl, Kylie Travis, Faye Dunaway, Elizabeth Mitchell, Louis Giambalvo, John Considine, Scott Cohen; ***D:*** Michael Cristofer; ***W:*** Michael Cristofer, Jay McInerney; ***C:*** Rodrigo Garcia; ***M:*** Terence Blanchard. **CABLE**

Giant 🦴🦴🦴 ½ **1956** Based on the Edna Ferber novel, this epic saga covers two generations of a wealthy Texas cattle baron (Hudson) who marries a strong-willed Virginia woman (Taylor) and takes her to live on his vast ranch. It explores the problems they have adjusting to life together, as well as the politics and prejudice of the time. Dean plays the resentful ranch hand (who secretly loves Taylor) who winds up striking oil and beginning a fortune to rival that of his former boss. Dean's last movie—he died in a car crash shortly before filming was completed. **201m/C VHS, DVD.** Elizabeth Taylor, Rock Hudson, James Dean, Carroll Baker, Chill Wills, Dennis Hopper, Rod Taylor, Earl Holliman, Jane Withers, Sal Mineo, Mercedes McCambridge; ***D:*** George Stevens; ***W:*** Ivan Moffat, Fred Guiol; ***C:*** William Mellor. Oscars '56: Director (Stevens); AFI '98: Top 100; Directors Guild '56: Director (Stevens), Natl. Film Reg. '05.

The Giant Claw 🦴 ½ **1957** Giant, winged (and stringed) bird attacks from outer space and scientists Morrow, Corday and Ankrum attempt to pluck it. Good bad movie; Corday was Playboy's Miss October, 1958. **76m/B VHS.** Jeff Morrow, Mara Corday, Morris Ankrum, Louis D. Merrill, Edgar Barrier, Robert Shayne, Morgan Jones, Clark Howat; ***D:*** Fred F. Sears.

Giant from the Unknown WOOF! **1958** Giant conquistador is revived after being struck by lightning and goes on a murderous rampage. Unbelievably bad. **80m/B VHS, DVD.** Edward Kemmer, Buddy Baer, Bob Steele, Sally Fraser, Morris Ankrum; ***D:*** Richard Cunha; ***W:*** Ralph Brooke, Frank Hart Taussig; ***C:*** Richard Cunha; ***M:*** Albert Glasser.

The Giant Gila Monster 🦴 ½ **1959** A giant lizard has the nerve to disrupt a local record hop, foolishly bringing upon it the wrath of the local teens. Rear-projection monster isn't particularly effective, but the film provides many unintentional laughs. **74m/B VHS, DVD.** Don Sullivan, Lisa Simone, Shug Fisher, Jerry Cortwright, Beverly Thurman, Don Flourney, Pat Simmons; ***D:*** Ray Kellogg; ***W:*** Jay Simms; ***C:*** Wilfrid M. Cline; ***M:*** Jack Marshall.

The Giant of Marathon 🦴🦴 **1960** Reeves shrugs off the role of Hercules to play Philippides, a marathoner (who uses a horse) trying to save Greece from invading Persian hordes. Lots of muscle on display, but not much talent. **90m/C VHS.** *IT* Steve Reeves, Mylene Demongeot, Daniela Rocca, Ivo Garrani, Alberto Lupo, Sergio Fantoni; ***D:*** Jacques Tourneur; ***C:*** Mario Bava.

The Giant of Metropolis 🦴🦴 *Il Gigante Di Metropolis* **1961** Muscle-bound hero goes shirtless to take on the evil, sadistic ruler of Atlantis (still above water) in 10,000 B.C. Ordinary Italian adventure, but includes interesting sets and bizarre torture scenes. **92m/C VHS, DVD.** *IT* Gordon Mitchell, Roldano Lupi, Bella Cortez, Liana Orfei; ***D:*** Umberto Scarpelli.

The Giant Spider Invasion 🦴 **1975 (PG)** A meteorite carrying spider eggs crashes to Earth and soon the alien arachnids are growing to humongous proportions. Notoriously bad special effects, but the veteran "B" cast has a good time. **76m/C VHS, DVD.** Steve Brodie, Barbara Hale, Leslie Parrish, Robert Easton, Alan Hale Jr., Dianne Lee Hart, Bill Williams, Christiane Schmidtmer, Kevin Brodie; ***D:*** Bill Rebane; ***W:*** Bill Rebane, Richard L. Huff, Robert Easton; ***C:*** Jack Willoughby.

Giant Steps 🦴🦴 **1992** Williams plays Slate Hopson, a moody jazz legend idolized by a talented young trumpet player. When the two meet Hopson clues the boy into some of life's lessons and rediscovers his own joy at making music. **94m/C VHS.** Billy Dee Williams, Michael Mahonen; ***D:*** Richard Rose; ***W:*** Paul Quarrington, Greg Dummett; ***C:*** Paul Sarossy; ***M:*** Eric Leeds, Eric Leeds.

Giants of Rome WOOF! **1963** Rome is in peril at the hands of a mysterious secret weapon that turns out to be a giant catapult. Ludicrous all around. **87m/C VHS, DVD.** *IT* Richard Harrison, Ettore Manni; ***D:*** Antonio Margheriti; ***W:*** Ernesto Gastaldi, Luciano Martino; ***C:*** Fausto Zuccoli; ***M:*** Carlo Rustichelli.

The Giants of Thessaly 🦴🦴 **1960** Jason and Orpheus search for the Golden Fleece, encountering and defeating monsters, wizards, and a scheming witch. **86m/C VHS, DVD.** *IT* Roland Carey, Ziva Rodann, Massimo Girotti, Alberto (Albert Farley) Farnese; ***D:*** Riccardo Freda.

Gideon 🦴 ½ **1999** Clunky schmaltz about the slightly retarded Gideon (Lambert), who moves into a rest home and changes the lives of its depressed residents for the better. **100m/C VHS.** Christopher Lambert, Shelley Winters, Carroll O'Connor, Charlton Heston, Shirley Jones, Mike Connors, Harvey Korman, Barbara Bain, Taylor Nichols, Crystal Bernard, Mykelti Williamson, Christopher McDonald; ***D:*** Claudia Hoover; ***W:*** Brad Mirman; ***C:*** Joao Fernandes; ***M:*** Anthony Marinelli.

Gideon's Daughter 🦴🦴 **2005** Public relations whiz Gideon Warner (Nighy) is a professional star and a personal disaster. As he struggles to maintain some kind of relationship with estranged daughter Natasha (Blunt), Gideon finds unexpected romance with Stella (Richardson), who's grieving over the death of her young son. **144m/C DVD.** *GB* Bill Nighy, Miranda Richardson, Emily Blunt, Robert Lindsay; ***D:*** Stephen Poliakoff; ***W:*** Stephen Poliakoff; ***C:*** Barry Ackroyd; ***M:*** Adrian Johnston. **TV**

Gideon's Trumpet 🦴🦴 ½ **1980** True story of Clarence Earl Gideon, a Florida convict whose case was decided by the Supreme Court and set the precedent that everyone is entitled to defense by a lawyer, whether or not they can pay for it. Based on the book by Anthony Lewis. **104m/C VHS.** Henry Fonda, Jose Ferrer, John Houseman, Dean Jagger, Sam Jaffe, Fay Wray; ***D:*** Robert E. Collins. **TV**

Gidget 🦴🦴 **1959** A plucky, boy-crazy teenage girl (whose nickname means girl midget) discovers romance and wisdom on the beaches of Malibu when she becomes involved with a group of college-aged surfers. First in a series of Gidget/surfer films. Based on a novel by Frederick Kohner about his daughter. **95m/C VHS.** Sandra Dee, James Darren, Cliff Robertson, Mary Laroche, Arthur O'Connell, Joby Baker; ***D:*** Paul Wendkos; ***W:*** Gabrielle Upton; ***C:*** Burnett Guffey.

Gidget Goes Hawaiian 🦴🦴 **1961** Gidget is off to Hawaii with her parents and is enjoying the beach (and the boys) when she is surprised by a visit from boyfriend "Moondoggie." Sequel to "Gidget" and followed by "Gidget Goes to Rome." **102m/C VHS, DVD.** Deborah Walley, James Darren, Carl Reiner, Peggy Cass, Michael Callan, Eddie Foy Jr.; ***D:*** Paul Wendkos.

Gidget Goes to Rome 🦴 ½ **1963** Darren returns in his third outing as boyfriend "Moondoggie" to yet another actress playing "Gidget" as the two vacation in Rome and find themselves tempted by other romances. Second sequel to "Gidget." **104m/C VHS, DVD.** Cindy Carol, James Darren, Jeff Donnell, Cesare Danova, Peter Brooks, Jessie Royce Landis; ***D:*** Paul Wendkos; ***M:*** John Williams.

The Gift 🦴🦴 ½ **1982 (R)** Story of a 55-year-old man who chooses early retirement in the hopes of changing his dull and boring life. Unbeknownst to him, his co-workers arrange the ultimate retirement gift—a woman. Silly French sexual farce. Dubbed. **105m/C VHS.** *FR* Pierre Mondy, Claudia Cardinale, Clio Goldsmith, Jacques Francois, Cecile Magnet, Remy Laurent; ***D:*** Michael (Michel) Lang.

The Gift 🦴🦴 **2000 (R)** Widowed mom Blanchett uses her psychic gifts to help find the murderer of rich girl Holmes in their Georgia town. Among those involved are battered wife Swank, abuser Reeves, Holmes's fiance Kinnear and mentally slow tow-truck driver Ribisi. By-the-numbers thriller loses steam after a promising start, but is saved by the performances of a fine cast. The characters are stock Southern Gothic types, but they're given dimension by the portrayals. Raimi shows (early on) that he still knows how to startle an audience and create a creepy atmosphere. **112m/C VHS, DVD.** Cate Blanchett, Katie Holmes, Hilary Swank, Keanu Reeves, Greg Kinnear, Giovanni Ribisi, Michael Jeter, Gary Cole, Kim Dickens, Rosemary Harris, J.K. Simmons, Chelcie Ross, John Beasley; ***D:*** Sam Raimi; ***W:*** Billy Bob Thornton, Tom Epperson; ***C:*** Jamie Anderson; ***M:*** Christopher Young.

The Gift Horse 🦴🦴 *Glory at Sea* **1952** A WWII British naval officer dispatches his duties with an iron hand in an attempt to overturn the legacy of a court-martial eight years earlier. Angry rumblings from his crew threaten to upset the ship's stability. Against this foreboding backdrop, the Nazis give battle. Not historically accurate, but exciting. Based on a story by Ivan Goff and Ben Roberts. **99m/B VHS.** *GB* Trevor Howard, Richard Attenborough, Sonny Tufts, Bernard Lee; ***D:*** Compton Bennett; ***W:*** William Fairchild; ***C:*** Harry Waxman; ***M:*** Clifton Parker.

The Gift of Love 1/2 **1990** Saccharine TV adaption of O. Henry's Christmas romance "The Gift of the Magi." **96m/C VHS, DVD.** James Woods, Marie Osmond, Timothy Bottoms, June Lockhart, David Wayne; ***D:*** Don Chaffey. **TV**

Gifted Hands: The Ben Carson Story 1/2 **2009** Inspirational, though conventionally told, biopic. Ben Carson (Gooding Jr.) is the head of pediatric neurosurgery at Johns Hopkins Children's Center. As he works to separate twins who are conjoined at the head, flashbacks depict how Carson, though initially a poor student, is pushed to succeed by his illiterate single mother Sonya (Elise) and overcome the racism and setbacks he encounters. **90m/C DVD.** Cuba Gooding Jr., Kimberly Elise, Aunjanue Ellis, Gus Hoffman, Jaishon Fisher; ***D:*** Thomas Carter; ***W:*** John Pielmeier; ***C:*** John Aronson; ***M:*** Martin Davich. **CABLE**

The Gig 1/2 **1985** In this small, independently made film, a band of middle-aged amateur jazz musicians give up their stable occupations for a once-in-a-lifetime shot at a two-week gig in the Catskills. Film succeeds on the strength of it's well fleshed-out characters. **95m/C VHS.** Wayne Rogers, Cleavon Little, Warren Vache, Joe Silver, Daniel Nalbach, Andrew Duncan, Jay Thomas, Jerry Matz; ***D:*** Frank D. Gilroy; ***W:*** Frank D. Gilroy.

Gigantic **2008 (R)** Mattress salesman Brian (Dano) wants to better himself, adopt a Chinese baby, and leave the shadow of his brothers, not necessarily in that order. Into his store and life comes Happy (Deschanel) who falls asleep on one of his products and then wreaks havoc when a relationship blooms. Overly quirky, albeit intermittently engaging, this one seems to be trying just a little too hard to be offbeat. The uniformly excellent cast helps leaven the whimsy a bit. **98m/C DVD.** *US* Paul Franklin Dano, Zooey Deschanel, Ed Asner, Jane Alexander, John Goodman, Zach Galifianakis, Marthe Keller, Sean Dugan; ***D:*** Matt Aselton; ***W:*** Matt Aselton, Adam Nagata; ***C:*** Peter Donahue; ***M:*** Roddy Bottum.

Gigi **1958** Based on Colette's story of a young Parisian girl (Caron) trained to become a courtesan to the wealthy Gaston (Jourdan). But he finds out he prefers her to be his wife rather than his mistress. Chevalier is Gaston's roguish uncle, who casts an always admiring eye on the ladies. Gingold is Gigi's grandmother and former Chevalier flame, and Gabor amuses as Gaston's current, and vapid, mistress. One of the first MGM movies to be shot on location, this extravaganza features some of the best tributes to the French lifestyle ever filmed. Score includes memorable classics. ♫Gigi; Ah Yes, I Remember It Well; Thank Heaven For Little Girls; The Night They Invented Champagne; She's Not Thinking of Me; It's a Bore; Gossip; I'm Glad I'm Not Young Anymore; The Parisians. **119m/C VHS, DVD.** Leslie Caron, Louis Jourdan, Maurice Chevalier, Hermione Gingold, Eva Gabor, Isabel Jeans, Jacques Bergerac; ***D:*** Vincente Minnelli; ***W:*** Alan Jay Lerner; ***C:*** Joseph Ruttenberg; ***M:*** Frederick Loewe. Oscars '58: Adapt. Screenplay, Art Dir./Set Dec., Color Cinematog., Costume Des., Director (Minnelli), Film Editing, Picture, Song ("Gigi"), Scoring/Musical; Directors Guild '58: Director (Minnelli); Golden Globes '59: Director (Minnelli), Film—Mus./Comedy, Support. Actress (Gingold), Natl. Film Reg. '91.

Gigli **2003 (R)** The one where Ben met Jen. The title is pronounced "Geely" and is the last name of smalltime mobster hitman Larry (Affleck). His latest job is to kidnap and babysit a prosecutor's mentally impaired brother (Bartha in his film debut) as leverage in mob boss Starkman's (an overacting Pacino) trial, but he begins to feel sorry for his hostage. So his worried boss Louis (Venito) decides to send Ricki (Lopez), another contract killer, to keep an eye on them. Oh, and Ricki's a lesbian, which doesn't preclude Larry hitting on her. Not quite as bad as most of Madonna's oeuvre but the film's vulgar come-on of "gobble, gobble" succintly describes the movie—it's a turkey. **124m/C VHS, DVD.** *US* Ben Affleck, Jennifer Lopez, Justin Bartha, Christopher Walken, Al Pacino, Lainie Kazan, Missy (Melissa) Crider, Lenny Venito; ***D:*** Martin Brest; ***W:*** Martin Brest; ***C:*** Robert Elswit; ***M:*** John Powell. Golden Raspberries '03: Worst Picture, Worst Actor (Affleck), Worst Actress (Lopez), Worst Director (Brest), Worst Screenplay.

Gilda 1/2 **1946** An evil South American gambling casino owner hires young American Ford as his trusted aide, unaware that Ford and his sultry wife Hayworth have engaged in a steamy affair. Hayworth does a striptease to "Put the Blame on Mame" in this prominently sexual film. This is the film that made Hayworth into a Hollywood sex goddess. **110m/B VHS, DVD.** Rita Hayworth, Glenn Ford, George Macready, Joseph Calleia, Steven Geray; ***D:*** Charles Vidor; ***W:*** Jo Eisinger, Marion Parsonnet; ***C:*** Rudolph Mate.

The Gilded Cage **1954** Two brothers are falsely accused of art theft and must find the real crooks in order to clear their names. **77m/B VHS.** *GB* Alex Nicol, Veronica Hurst, Clifford Evans, Ursula Howells, Elwyn Brook-Jones, John Stuart; ***D:*** John Gilling.

Gildersleeve on Broadway 1/2 **1943** Longtime bachelor Throckmorton Gildersleeve (Peary) has finally proposed to girlfriend Matilda (Doran) when he decides to make a trip to New York. He has two purposes: to track down niece Margie's (Landry) wandering beau Jimmy (Road) and to help out town druggist Mr. Peavey (LeGrand), which leads him into the company of lonely widow (and pharmaceutical company owner) Laura (Burke). Soon there are three women, including blonde babe Francine (Carleton), after our man. Third of four films based on the radio serial "The Great Gildersleeve." **65m/B VHS.** Harold (Hal) Peary, Billie Burke, Claire Carleton, Ann Doran, Hobart Cavanaugh, Margaret Landry, Richard LeGrand, Freddie Mercer, Michael Road; ***D:*** Gordon Douglas; ***W:*** Robert E. Kent; ***C:*** Jack MacKenzie.

Gimme an F **WOOF!** *T & A Academy 2* **1985 (R)** The handsome cheerleading instructor at Camp Beaver View ruffles a few pom-poms when he discovers that the camp's owner is about to enter into a shady deal with some foreigners. The film certainly deserves an "F" for foolishness if nothing else. **100m/C VHS.** Stephen Shellen, Mark Keyloun, John Karlen, Jennifer Cooke; ***D:*** Paul Justman.

Gimme Shelter 1/2 **1970** The '60s ended as violence occurred at a December 1969 free Rolling Stones concert attended by 300,000 people in Altamont, California. This "Woodstock West" became a bitter remembrance in rock history, as Hell's Angels (hired for security) do some ultimate damage to the spectators. A provocative look at an out-of-control situation. **91m/C VHS, DVD.** Mick Jagger, Keith Richards, Charlie Watts, Bill Wyman, Mick Taylor, Marty Balin, Grace Slick, Paul Kantner, Jerry Garcia, David Crosby, Stephen Stills, Graham Nash, Tina Turner, Ike Turner, Melvin Belli, Bill Graham; ***D:*** David Maysles, Albert Maysles, Charlotte Zwerin; ***C:*** Haskell Wexler; ***M:*** Rolling Stones.

Gin Game **1984** Taped London performance of the Broadway play about an aging couple who find romance in an old age home. Two-character performance won awards; touching and insightful. **82m/C VHS, DVD.** Jessica Tandy, Hume Cronyn; ***D:*** Mike Nichols.

Ginger **1972** Fabulous super-sleuth Ginger faces the sordid world of prostitution, blackmail and drugs. Prequel to "The Abductors" and followed eventually by "Girls Are for Loving." **90m/C VHS, DVD.** Cheri Caffaro, William Grannel, Calvin Culver, Cindy Barnett, Lise Mauer, Michele Norris, Linda Susoeff; ***D:*** Don Schain; ***W:*** Don Schain; ***C:*** R. Kent Evans; ***M:*** Robert G. Orpin.

Ginger Ale Afternoon **1989** A smutty comedy revolving around a triangle formed by a married couple and their sexy next-door neighbor. The film tries for fizz but only comes up flat. **88m/C VHS.** Dana Anderson, John M. Jackson, Yeardley Smith; ***D:*** Rafal Zielinski; ***W:*** Gina Wendkos; ***M:*** Willie Dixon.

Ginger and Cinnamon *Dillo con Parole Mie* **2003** Fun in the summer sun in this equally light romance set on a picturesque Greek island. Thirty-year-old Stefania (Montorsi) has broken up with longtime beau Andrea (Morelli) and ends up vacationing with 14-year-old neice, Meggy (Merlino), on Ios. Meggy's decided her vacation is the perfect opportunity to lose her viriginity and she's found the perfect guy—who turns out to be Andrea. Italian with subtitles. **105m/C DVD.** *IT* Stefania Montorsi, Giampaolo Morelli, Martina Merlino, Alberto Cucca; ***D:*** Daniele Luchetti; ***W:*** Stefania Montorsi, Daniele Luchetti, Ivan Cotroneo; ***C:*** Paolo Carnera.

Ginger & Fred **1986 (PG-13)** An acclaimed story of Fellini-esque poignancy about an aging dance team. Years before they had gained success by reverently impersonating the famous dancing duo of Astaire and Rogers. Now, after 30 years, they reunite under the gaudy lights of a high-tech TV special. Wonderful performances by the aging Mastroianni and the still sweet Masina. Italian with English subtitles. **126m/C VHS, DVD.** *IT* Marcello Mastroianni, Giulietta Masina, Franco Fabrizi, Frederick Von Ledenberg, Martin Blau, Toto Mignone; ***D:*** Federico Fellini; ***W:*** Federico Fellini, Tonino Guerra, Tullio Pinelli; ***C:*** Tonino Delli Colli; ***M:*** Nicola Piovani.

Ginger in the Morning **1973** A salesman is enamored of a young hitchhiker whom he picks up on the road. This is the same year Spacek played the innocent-gone-twisted in "Badlands." **90m/C VHS, DVD.** Sissy Spacek, Slim Pickens, Monte Markham, Susan Oliver, Mark Miller; ***D:*** Gordon Wiles.

Ginger Snaps **2001 (R)** Modern teen horror goes for quite a ride. Teenaged sisters Ginger (Isabelle) and Brigitte (Perkins) are proud misfits in their quiet Canadian community. Then they're attacked by a werewolf in the woods and Ginger starts behaving very strangely (even for her). Brigitte turns to local pot dealer Sam (Lemche) for help while Ginger just gets more and more aggressive. **107m/C VHS, DVD.** *CA* John Bourgeois, Peter Keleghan, Emily Perkins, Katharine Isabelle, Kris Lemche, Mimi Rogers, Jesse Moss, Danielle Hampton; ***D:*** John Fawcett; ***W:*** Karen Walton; ***C:*** Thom Best; ***M:*** Michael Shields.

Ginger Snaps Back: The Beginning *Ginger Snaps 3* **2004 (R)** The trilogy snaps back from the depths of hell in this prequel that finds sisters Ginger and Brigitte time-warped to 19th century Canada and seeking shelter from the woods at an all-male trading fort that—unbeknownst to them—has been trying to fend off those pesky werewolves. **94m/C VHS, DVD.** *CA* Katharine Isabelle, Emily Perkins, Nathaniel Arcand, J.R. Bourne, Hugh Dillon, Adrien Dorval, Brendan Fletcher, David La Haye, Tom McCamus, Matthew (Matt) Walker; ***D:*** Grant Harvey; ***W:*** Stephen Massicotte, Christina Ray; ***C:*** Michael Marshall. **VIDEO**

Ginger Snaps: Unleashed *Ginger Snaps 2: The Sequel* **2004 (R)** In this why-did-they-bother sequel, it's Brigitte's turn to be afflicted with a case of the lycanthropy, but she keeps it at bay with wolfsbane. The whole thing goes haywire when she's taken to a rehab clinic after being mauled by another werewolf and can't take her meds. **93m/C VHS, DVD.** *CA* Emily Perkins, Katharine Isabelle, Janet Kidder, Tatiana Maslany, Eric Johnson, Pascale Hutton, Jack Mackinnon; ***D:*** Brett Sullivan; ***W:*** Megan Martin; ***C:*** Gavin Smith; ***M:*** Kurt Swinghammer. **VIDEO**

The Gingerbread Man 1/2 **1997 (R)** Lawyer Rick Macgruder (Branagh) falls for a scheming femme (Davidtz) who hires him to have her deranged, stalker father (Duvall) committed. Set in the new hot spot of filmdom, steamy Savannah, it becomes clear that nothing is clear and plot takes on noirish twists and turns of intrigue and suspense before the cigarette smoke clears. Shakespeare savant Branagh proves he can also master a Southern accent. Hannah, as Rick's mousy partner, surprises with an unusually good performance. Grisham's first original screenplay. Studio Polygram disliked Altman's original cut, replaced his editor, and recut the movie to its own specifications, angering Altman who threatened to remove his name from the film. Though not an Altman masterpiece, sly thriller doesn't fail to entice. **114m/C VHS, DVD.** Sonny Shroyer, Kenneth Branagh, Embeth Davidtz, Robert Duvall, Tom Berenger, Daryl Hannah, Robert Downey Jr., Famke Janssen, Mae Whitman, Jesse James; ***D:*** Robert Altman; ***W:*** John Grisham, Al Hayes; ***C:*** Gu Changwei; ***M:*** Mark Isham.

Ginostra 1/2 **2002 (R)** Dull crime drama. FBI agent Matt Benson takes his wife and young daughter along when he's sent to Sicily to interview 11-year-old Ettore, the only survivor of a car bombing that killed his family. Ettore's mobster dad was going against omerta to testify against a fellow wiseguy with ties to New York organized crime. The title is the name of the local volcano, which erupts. **135m/C DVD.** *FR* Harvey Keitel, Andie MacDowell, Harry Dean Stanton, Stefano Dionisi, Mattia de Martino; ***D:*** Manuel Pradal; ***W:*** Manuel Pradal; ***C:*** Maurizio Calvesi; ***M:*** Carlo Crivelli.

The Girl **1968** The first of Meszaros' trilogy, dealing with a young girl who leaves an orphanage to be reunited with her mother, a traditional country peasant. In Hungarian with English subtitles. Meszaros' first film. Followed by "Riddance" (1973) and "Adoption" (1975). **86m/B VHS.** *HU* Adam Szirtes, Kati Kovacs, Teri Horvath; ***D:*** Marta Meszaros; ***W:*** Marta Meszaros; ***C:*** Tamas Somlo; ***M:*** Levente Szorenyi.

The Girl 1/2 **1986 (R)** Nero is a wealthy attorney who agrees to pay Powney 300 crowns to have his way with her. Although somewhat ambivalent because of her scandalous age, he takes her anyway. Soon he informs his wife he needs to go on a long business trip, which fits in with her own adulterous plans. A snooping reporter (Brennan) out for some dirt upsets the apple cart, eventually leading to murder. **104m/C VHS.** Franco Nero, Christopher Lee, Bernice Stegers, Clare Powney, Frank Brennan; ***D:*** Arne Mattson.

Girl 1/2 **1998 (R)** Suburban 18-year-old Andrea Marr (Swain) is bored by her usual life and her virginity. She decides to try on the local club scene and spots musician Todd Sparrow (Flanery), becoming his groupie, and also taking up with cool chick singer Cybil (Reid) and her friends who are in a band. This try at self-discovery ultimately proves less-than-satisfying for Andrea. Lots of cliched issues are dealt with in the most cursory fashion. Based on the novel by Blake Nelson. **99m/C VHS, DVD.** Dominique Swain, Sean Patrick Flanery, Tara Reid, Summer Phoenix, Selma Blair, Channon Roe, Portia de Rossi, Christopher K. Masterson, Rosemary Forsyth, James Karen; ***D:*** Jonathan Kahn; ***W:*** David E. Tolchinsky; ***C:*** Tami Reiker; ***M:*** Michael Tavera.

The Girl 1/2 **2001** Stylish lesbian love story has a Paris artist meeting sultry nightclub singer and initiating a one-night stand which becomes a torrid affair. This upsets the club owner, who considers the singer his property. First time director (and co-writer) Zeig has confidence and an eye for subtle nuance, but occasionally wanders into pretentiousness (an occupational hazard for a first-time director). **84m/C VHS, DVD.** Claire Keim, Agathe de la Boulaye, Sandra N'Kake, Cyril Lecomte; ***D:*** Sande Zeig; ***W:*** Monique Wittig.

A Girl, 3 Guys and a Gun **2001 (R)** Best buds Neil (Leffler), Frank (Florence), and Joey (Luper) want to blow out of their smalltown by getting involved in a botched robbery that leads to an unexpected kidnapping. An indie that starts off as larky and then turns serious (and somewhat confusing). **88m/C VHS, DVD.** Christian Leffler, Josh Holland, Tracy Zahoryin, Michael Trucco, Tava Smiley, Kenny Luper, Brent Florence; ***D:*** Brent Florence; ***W:*** Brent Florence; ***C:*** Matt Davis.

A Girl, a Guy and a Gob *The Navy Steps Out* **1941** A shy rich boy falls in love with a girl who has her sights on another. Silly but enjoyable cast. **91m/B VHS.** Lucille Ball, Edmond O'Brien, George Murphy, Franklin Pangborn, Henry Travers, Lloyd Corrigan; ***D:*** Richard Wallace.

The Girl by the Lake *La Ragazza del Lago* **2007** Beautiful local girl Anna is found dead by the side of a lake near a small town in the Italian Dolomites and police inspector Sanzio (Servillo) is called in from the provincial capital. There's several possible suspects but Sanzio's investigation just brings up more questions in this troubling, compelling thriller. Italian with subtitles. **95m/C DVD.** *IT* Toni Servillo, Fabrizio Gifuni, Valeria Golino, Nello Mascia, Marco Baliani, Fausto Maria Sciarappa, Franco Ravera, Guilia Michelini, Alessia Piovan; ***D:*** Andrea Molaioli; ***W:*** Sandro Petraglia; ***C:*** Ramiro Civita; ***M:*** Teho Teardo.

The Girl Can't Help It 🦴🦴 1/2 **1956** Satiric rock and roll musical comedy about a retired mobster who hires a hungry talent agent to promote his girlfriend, a wanna-be no-talent singer. Mansfield's first starring role. Classic performances by some of the early greats including Eddie Cochran, Gene Vincent, the Platters, Little Richard, and Fats Domino. **99m/B VHS, DVD.** Jayne Mansfield, Tom Ewell, Edmond O'Brien, Julie London, Ray Anthony, Henry Jones, John Emery, Juanita Moore, Barry J. Gordon, Fats Domino, Abbey Lincoln, Eddie Fontaine, Little Richard, Eddie Cochran, Gene Vincent; ***D:*** Frank Tashlin; ***W:*** Frank Tashlin, Herbert Baker; ***C:*** Leon Shamroy; ***M:*** Lionel Newman.

Girl Crazy 🦴🦴🦴 *When the Girls Meet the Boys* **1943** A wealthy young playboy is sent to an all-boy school in Arizona to get his mind off girls. Once there, he still manages to fall for a local girl who can't stand the sight of him. The eighth film pairing for Rooney and Garland. ♫Sam and Delilah; Embraceable You; I Got Rhythm; Fascinating Rhythm; Treat Me Rough; Bronco Busters; Bidin' My Time; But Not For Me; Do. **99m/B VHS.** Mickey Rooney, Judy Garland, Nancy Walker, June Allyson; ***D:*** Norman Taurog; ***C:*** William H. Daniels; ***M:*** Ira Gershwin.

A Girl Cut in Two 🦴🦴 1/2 *La Fille Coupee en Deux* **2007** Innocent young TV weather girl Gabrielle (Sagnier) finds herself prey for two oversexed men in another of director Claude Chabrol's black comedies that highlights self-destructive and sexually perverse behavior. Sparks fly when the older, successful writer Charles (Berleand) is interviewed at the TV station and charms Gabrielle into becoming his Parisian plaything. The fact that he's married only seems to add fuel to the fantasy, infuriating Gabrielle's younger suitor Paul (Magimel), a spoiled playboy and heir to the family fortune. Those familiar with director Chabrol's prolific career as a sexual satirist will find more of the same, as well as his usual commentary on class struggle. **115m/C DVD.** *FR GE* Ludivine Sagnier, Benoit Magimel, Francois Berleand, Mathilda May, Marie Bunel, Valeria Cavalli, Caroline Sihol; ***D:*** Claude Chabrol; ***W:*** Claude Chabrol, Cecile Maistre; ***C:*** Eduardo Serra; ***M:*** Matthieu Chabrol.

Girl from Calgary 🦴 **1932** A female rodeo champ ropes her boyfriends much like she ropes her cows, but not without a knock-down, drag-out fight between the two which forces our cowgirl to make the choice she seems to know is fated. Stock rodeo footage is intercut with the heroine riding an obviously mechanical bucking bronc. **66m/B VHS, DVD.** Fifi d'Orsay, Paul Kelly; ***D:*** Philip H. (Phil, P.H.) Whitman.

Girl from Chicago 🦴🦴 **1932** In this crime melodrama a secret service agent falls in love while on assignment in Mississippi. When he's back in New York he finds a good friend of his girl's in serious trouble with the numbers racket. **69m/C VHS, DVD.** Starr Calloway, Grace Smith, Eugene Brooks, Frank Wilson; ***D:*** Oscar Micheaux.

Girl from Hunan 🦴🦴🦴 **1986** Turn-of-the-century China, a 12-year-old girl is married to a two-year-old boy in a typical arranged marriage. She grows into womanhood treating her toddler husband with sibling affection, but conducts a secret love affair with a farmer. Intolerant village laws against adultry place her life in jeopardy. In Mandarin with English subtitles. **99m/C VHS.** Na Renhua, Deng Xiaotuang, Yu Zhang; ***D:*** Xie Fei.

The Girl from Missouri 🦴🦴🦴 *One Hundred Percent Pure* **1934** Cute comedy in which Harlow tries to snag a millionaire without sacrificing her virtues. Lots of laughs and hilarious action, especially the scene where Harlow arrives at the yacht in Florida. Kelly is great as Harlow's wise-cracking girlfriend. Witty dialogue by Emerson and Loos, who also wrote "Gentleman Prefer Blondes." **75m/B VHS.** Jean Harlow, Lionel Barrymore, Franchot Tone, Lewis Stone, Patsy Kelly, Alan Mowbray, Clara Blandick, Russell Hopton, John David Horsley; ***D:*** Jack Conway; ***W:*** Anita Loos, John Emerson.

The Girl From Monaco 🦴🦴 *La Fille de Monaco* **2008 (R)** An uneasy mix of sex farce with thrillerish tendencies. Controlled, 50-something Paris lawyer Bertrand Beauvois (Luchini) arrives in Monaco to defend 70-something widow Edith Lasalle Audran, who is accused of murdering her young Russian gigolo. Because said gigolo was reputed to have mob ties, Edith's son Louis (Cohen) hires street-smart Christophe Abadi (Zem) to bodyguard the irritated Bertrand. But it's really not about the murder and subsequent trial, it's about the sexually voracious, beautiful bimbo weather girl Audrey (Bourgoin in her film debut), who makes a successful play for Betrand who knows amour fou when it strikes him but can't resist despite Christophe's warnings (he's been one of Audrey's numerous lovers). French with subtitles. **95m/C DVD.** *FR* Fabrice Luchini, Roschdy Zem, Louise Bourgoin, Stephane Audran, Gilles Cohen, Jeanne Balibar; ***D:*** Anne Fontaine; ***W:*** Anne Fontaine, Benoit Graffin, Jacques Fieschi; ***C:*** Patrick Blossier; ***M:*** Philippe Rombi.

The Girl from Paris 🦴🦴🦴 *Une Hirondelle a Fait le Printemps* **2002** A Parisian internet worker leaves the city and buys a mountaintop farm from a cranky farmer. Sandrine (Seigner) gives up her high-stress city life and buys a goat farm from Adrien (Serrault), who's ready to be done with farming but resentfully agrees to stick around for 18 months to help out. Sandrine initially does big business through internet advertising, drawing visitors who buy the farm's products and sleep in the barn, but soon must confront the harsh, relentless realities of managing a farm by herself. As she does, her adversarial relationship with Adrien evolves into a friendship. Moves a bit slowly, but farm-raised Carion directs it with sincerity and precision, and creates an honest story of country life and the relationships it builds. **103m/C DVD.** *FR* Michel Serrault, Mathilde Seigner, Jean-Paul Roussillon, Frederic Pierrot, Marc Berman, Francoise Bette; ***D:*** Christian Carion; ***W:*** Christian Carion, Eric Assous; ***C:*** Antoine Heberle; ***M:*** Philippe Rombi.

The Girl from Petrovka 🦴 1/2 **1974 (PG)** A high-spirited Russian ballerina falls in love with an American newspaper correspondent. Their romance is complicated by the suspicious KGB. Bittersweet with a bleak ending. **103m/C VHS.** Goldie Hawn, Hal Holbrook, Anthony Hopkins; ***D:*** Robert Ellis Miller; ***W:*** Chris Bryant, Allan Scott; ***M:*** Henry Mancini.

The Girl from Tobacco Row 🦴 **1966** A Southern slut involved with a cache of stolen cash fools with both a convict and the sheriff. **90m/C VHS.** Tex Ritter, Rachel Romen, Earl Richards, Tim Ormond, Rita Faye, Ralph Emery; ***D:*** Ron Ormond.

The Girl Getters 🦴🦴 *The System* **1966** Tinker (Reed) and his rowdy London pals take a vacation at a seaside resort, where they proceed to pick fights, chase girls, and cause general (minor) mayhem. Tinker's busy chasing Nicola (Merrow) but surprises himself when he actually starts to fall for her. **79m/B VHS.** *GB* Oliver Reed, Jane Merrow, David Hemmings, John Alderton, Harry Andrews; ***D:*** Michael Winner; ***W:*** Peter Draper; ***C:*** Nicolas Roeg.

Girl Happy 🦴🦴 **1965** The King's fans will find him in Fort Lauderdale, Florida this time as the leader of a rock 'n' roll group. His mission: to chaperone the daughter of a Chicago mobster who naturally falls for him. Why not? ♫Girl Happy; Cross My Heart and Hope to Die; Do Not Disturb; Spring Fever; Wolf Call; Do the Clam; Fort Lauderdale Chamber of Commerce; Puppet On a String; I've Got to Find About My Baby. **96m/C VHS, DVD.** Elvis Presley, Harold J. Stone, Shelley Fabares, Gary Crosby, Nita Talbot, Mary Ann Mobley, Jackie Coogan; ***D:*** Boris Sagal; ***W:*** Harvey Bullock.

Girl Hunters 🦴🦴 1/2 **1963** That intrepid private eye, Mike Hammer (played by his creator, Spillane), is caught up with communist spies, wicked women, and a missing secretary. Hammer is his usual judge-and-jury character but the action is fast-paced. **103m/B VHS, DVD.** Mickey Spillane, Lloyd Nolan, Shirley Eaton, Hy Gardner, Scott Peters, Charles Farrell; ***D:*** Roy Rowland; ***W:*** Roy Rowland, Robert Fellows; ***C:*** Ken Talbot; ***M:*** Philip Green.

A Girl in a Million 🦴🦴 **1946** Williams dumps his verbose wife and seeks peace and quiet in a men-only War Department office. All is well until the arrival of a colonel and his daughter, mute from trauma. Finding her silence appealing, he marries her, but another trauma restores her speech. Sexist comedy may have played better in its day. **90m/B VHS.** *GB* Hugh Williams, Joan Greenwood, Naunton Wayne, Wylie Watson, Garry Marsh; ***D:*** Francis Searle.

The Girl in a Swing 🦴 1/2 **1989 (R)** An Englishman impulsively marries a beautiful German girl and both are subsequently haunted by phantoms from her past—are they caused by her psychic powers? Cliche-ridden silliness. Based on the Richard Adams novel. **119m/C VHS.** Meg Tilly, Rupert Frazer, Elspet Gray, Lynsey Baxter, Nicholas Le Prevost, Jon Kroll; ***D:*** Gordon Hessler.

Girl in Black 🦴🦴 *To Koritsi Me Ta Mavra* **1956** The shy daughter of a once wealthy household gets the chance to escape her genteel poverty when she falls in love with the young man boarding with her family. He is attracted to her but a shocking tragedy changes everything. In Greek with English subtitles. **100m/B VHS, DVD.** *GR* Ellie Lambetti, Eleni Zafirou, Georges Foundas, Dimitri Horne, Stefanos Stratigos; ***D:*** Michael Cacoyannis; ***W:*** Michael Cacoyannis; ***C:*** Walter Lassally; ***M:*** Manos Hadjidakis.

Girl in Black Stockings 🦴🦴 **1957** Beautiful women are mysteriously murdered at a remote, Utah hotel. Interesting, little known thriller similar to Hitchcock's "Psycho," but pre-dating it by three years. **75m/B VHS.** Lex Barker, Anne Bancroft, Mamie Van Doren, Ron Randell, Marie Windsor, John Dehner, John Holland, Diana Van Der Vlis; ***D:*** Howard W. Koch; ***M:*** Les Baxter.

The Girl in Blue 🦴🦴 **1974 (R)** A lawyer, ill at ease with his current romance, suddenly decides to search for a beautiful woman he saw once, and instantly fell in love with, years before. **103m/C VHS, DVD.** *CA* Maud Adams, David Selby, Gay Rowan, William Osler, Diane Dewey, Michael Kirby; ***D:*** George Kaczender.

A Girl in Every Port 🦴🦴 1/2 **1928** Sailors Spike (McLaglen) and Salami (Armstrong) travel the world in search of adventure and dames. Spike thinks he's found true love with French gold-digger Marie (flapper Brooks) but Salami convinces him otherwise. **62m/B VHS.** Victor McLaglen, Robert Armstrong, Louise Brooks, Natalie Joyce; ***D:*** Howard Hawks; ***W:*** Seton I. Miller; ***C:*** L.W. O'Connell, Rudolph Bergquist.

A Girl in Every Port 🦴🦴 1/2 **1952** Navy buddies acquire an ailing racehorse and try to conceal it aboard ship along with a healthy horse they plan to switch it with in an upcoming race. Groucho flies without his brothers in this zany film. **86m/B VHS.** Groucho Marx, William Bendix, Marie Wilson, Don DeFore, Gene Lockhart; ***D:*** Chester Erskine.

Girl in Gold Boots 🦴 **1969** Aspiring starlet meets up with a draft evader and a biker on her way to Hollywood where she gets a job as a go-go dancer in a sleazy club. But things don't go smoothly when a murder and a drug theft are revealed. ♫Do You Want to Laugh or Cry?; For You; Hello, Michelle; One Good Time, One Good Place; Lonesome Man; You Gotta Come Down; Everything I Touch Turns to Gold; Cowboy Santa; Wheels of Love. **91m/C VHS, DVD.** Jody Daniels, Leslie McRae, Tom Pace, Mark Herron; ***D:*** Ted V. Mikels; ***W:*** Art Names, Leighton J. Peatman, John T. Wilson; ***C:*** Robert Maxwell; ***M:*** Nicholas Carras.

Girl in His Pocket 🦴🦴 *Amour de Poche; Nude in His Pocket* **1957** Mad scientist creates a potion that turns things into three-inch statues. He uses it mostly to have trystes with his lab assistant so his fiancee won't find out. Based on "The Diminishing Draft" by Waldemar Kaempfert. **82m/C VHS.** *FR* Jean Marais, Genevieve Page, Agnes Laurent; ***D:*** Pierre Kast; ***C:*** Ghislan Cloquet.

The Girl in Lover's Lane 🦴🦴 **1960** A drifter falls in love with a small town girl but becomes a murder suspect when she turns up dead. Interesting mainly for Elam's uncharacteristic portrayal of a village idiot. **78m/B VHS, DVD.** Brett Halsey, Joyce Meadows, Lowell Brown, Jack Elam; ***D:*** Charles R. Rondeau.

The Girl in Room 2A WOOF! **1976 (R)** A young woman is trapped in a mansion with the elderly owner and her demented son. Routine horrorfest. **90m/C VHS.** Raf Vallone, Daniela Giordano; ***D:*** William Rose.

Girl in the Cadillac 🦴🦴 1/2 **1994 (R)** Modern-day B-movie wanna-be loosely adapted from the James M. Cain novella "The Enchanted Isle." 17-year-old freespirited Amanda (Eleniak) wants to get out of stifling small town Texas. She buys a bus ticket to find her long-gone daddy and winds up with not-too-smart cowpoke Rick (McNamara) instead. A bank robbery gone bad finds the twosome on the loose with $75 thou, a cherry red El Dorado convertible, and Rick's partners after them. Appealing lead performers can't overcome the cliches. **89m/C VHS.** Erika Eleniak, William McNamara, Michael Lerner, Bud Cort, Valerie Perrine, Ed Lauter, William Shockley; ***D:*** Lucas Platt; ***W:*** John Warren; ***C:*** Nancy Schreiber; ***M:*** Anton Sanko.

The Girl in the Cafe 🦴🦴 1/2 **2005** When a tender but offbeat romance develops between Lawrence (Nighy), a mellow-and-lonely middle-aged British public official, and Gina (MacDonald), a younger New Ager, he decides to take her along on his trip to the G8 Summit in Iceland but is taken aback when she abruptly shocks the crowd with a rant about the starvation of African children. **95m/C DVD.** Bill Nighy, Kelly Macdonald, Ken Stott, Penny Downie, Meneka Das; ***D:*** David Yates; ***W:*** Richard Curtis. **CABLE**

The Girl in the News 🦴🦴 1/2 *The Girl in the Case* **1941** Wealthy wheelchair-bound Edward Bentley (Goldie) is poisoned by his butler Tracy (Williams), who is having an affair with Mrs. Bentley (Scott). He frames Bentley's nurse Anne Graham (Lockwood), who was acquitted of murdering another of her elderly patients. Her lawyer, Stephen Garrington (Barnes), takes the new case but wonders about Anne's innocence until the big courtroom denouement. **78m/B DVD.** *GB* Margaret Lockwood, Barry Barnes, Emlyn Williams, Margaretta Scott, Roger Livesey, Basil Radford, Irene Handl, Felix Aylmer, Wyndham Goldie; ***D:*** Carol Reed; ***W:*** Sidney Gilliat; ***C:*** Otto Kanturek; ***M:*** Louis Levy.

The Girl in the Picture 🦴🦴 1/2 **1986 (PG-13)** Sinclair stars in this light comedy as an unlucky photo clerk who discovers only too late that his ex-girlfriend may be the woman of his dreams. Typical understated but entertaining effort. **89m/C VHS.** *GB* John Gordon-Sinclair, Irina Brook, David McKay, Catherine Guthrie, Paul Young, Gregor Fisher; ***D:*** Cary Parker.

The Girl in the Red Velvet Swing 🦴🦴 **1955** Rather genteel reworking of a 1906 New York society scandal. Evelyn Nesbit (Collins) is a hotsy showgirl who's being courted by famous married architect Stanford White (Milland). However, Evelyn marries wealthy-but-unstable society boy Harry Thaw (Granger). Harry is pathologically jealous of Evelyn's relationship with White and shoots him dead in public. Then he uses an insanity plea (and family money) to avoid the death penalty in the ensuing trial. Collins is catnip but her character is depicted as boringly naive. **109m/C DVD.** Joan Collins, Ray Milland, Farley Granger, Luther Adler, Glenda Farrell, Cornelia Otis Skinner, Frances Fuller, Philip Reed, Gale Robbins, John Hoyt, Harvey Stephens, Emile Meyer, Richard Travis, Jack Raine, Ainslie Pryor, Kay Hammond, Kay Hammond, Edith Evanson; ***D:*** Richard Fleischer; ***W:*** Walter Reisch, Charles Brackett; ***C:*** Milton Krasner; ***M:*** Leigh Harline, Edward B. Powell.

Girl, Interrupted 🦴🦴 1/2 **1999 (R)** Ryder stars as neurotic 18-year-old Susanna who, after making a half-hearted suicide attempt, is diagnosed with borderline personality disorder. So, in 1967, she's sent to Claymoore, a psychiatric hospital outside Boston, where she'll spend the next two years. There, Susanna meets some young woman who are truly disturbed, including compelling sociopath, Lisa (Jolie). Yes, the story's predictable but it's also touching—just don't expect the fireworks of "One Flew Over a Cuckoo's Nest." Based on the 1993 memoir by Susanna Kaysen. **127m/C VHS, DVD.** Winona Ryder, Angelina Jolie, Vanessa Redgrave, Whoopi Goldberg, Clea DuVall, Brittany Murphy, Elisabeth (Elissabeth, Elizabeth, Liz) Moss, Jared Leto, Jeffrey Tambor, Mary Kay Place; ***D:*** James Mangold; ***W:*** James Mangold, Anna Hamilton Phelan, Lisa Loomer; ***C:*** Jack N. Green; ***M:*** Mychael Danna. Oscars '99: Support. Actress (Jolie); Golden Globes '00: Support. Actress (Jolie); Screen Actors Guild '99: Support. Actress (Jolie); Broadcast Film Critics '99: Support. Actress (Jolie).

The Girl Most Likely 1/2 **1957** Light musical comedy about a romance-minded girl who dreams of marrying a wealthy, handsome man. She runs into a problem when she finds three prospects. Remake of 1941's "Tom, Dick and Harry" with Ginger Rogers. Choreography by great Gower Champion. ♫The Girl Most Likely; All the Colors of the Rainbow; I Don't Know What I Want; Balboa; We Gotta Keep Up With the Joneses; Crazy Horse. **98m/C VHS.** Jane Powell, Cliff Robertson, Tommy Noonan, Kaye Ballard, Una Merkel; ***D:*** Mitchell Leisen; ***W:*** Paul Jarrico.

The Girl Next Door 1/2 **1953** Widowed comic strip writer Bill Carter (Dailey) is a single dad to 10-year-old son Joe (Gray). Then pretty nightclub star Jeannie (Haver) moves in next-door and their romance causes friction. Haver's last film before she decided to enter a convent for several months. **92m/C DVD.** Dan Dailey, June Haver, Billy Gray, Dennis Day, Cara Williams, Natalie Schafer; ***D:*** Richard Sale; ***W:*** Isobel Lennart; ***C:*** Leon Shamroy; ***M:*** Cyril Mockridge.

The Girl Next Door **1998 (R)** Married doctor Czerny agrees to keep an eye on his neighbor's 18-year-old hot-babe daughter (Shannon) while her parents are out of town. Only he takes the good neighbor relationship too far. When the teen winds up dead, the local Sheriff (Busey) is out to discover just what happened. **100m/C VHS, DVD.** *CA* Henry Czerny, Gary Busey, Polly Shannon, Robin Gammell, Alberta Watson, Simon MacCorkindale; ***D:*** Eric Till.

The Girl Next Door **2004 (R)** Porn goddess Danielle (Cuthbert) moves to suburbia to taunt and tease nerdy teen next door, Matt (Hirsch). The two meet cute and a "Risky Business" redo ensues: Matt hooks up with Danielle, to the delight of his two geeky friends (Marquette and Dano), who inform Matt of the illicit past Danielle is trying to leave behind. That past includes former producer Olyphant, who shows up to woo Danielle back to "the life" while schooling the studious Matt in the ways of the world. He must then juggle a trip to a Vegas porn convention and work on a speech on morality to win a scholarship to Georgetown. Though Cuthbert and Hirsch are attractive and have decent chemistry, it's Olyphant that scores with an above average comedic performance in this otherwise uninspired genre fare. **108m/C DVD.** *US* Elisha Cuthbert, Emile Hirsch, Timothy Olyphant, James Remar, Christopher Marquette, Paul Franklin Dano, Timothy Bottoms, Donna Bullock, Amanda Swisten, Jacob Young, Brian Kolodziej; ***D:*** Luke Greenfield; ***W:*** David T. Wagner, Brent Goldberg, Stuart Blumberg; ***C:*** Jamie Anderson; ***M:*** Paul Haslinger.

Girl of the Golden West **1938** A musical version of the David Belasco chestnut about a Canadian frontier girl loving a rogue. One of Eddy and MacDonald's lesser efforts but features Ebsen's song and dance talents. ♫Camptown Races; Shadows on the Moon; Soldiers of Fortune; Soldiers of Fortune Reprise; Shadows on the Moon Reprise; The Wind in the Trees; Liebestraum; Ave Maria; Senorita. **120m/B VHS.** Jeanette MacDonald, Nelson Eddy, Walter Pidgeon, Leo Carrillo, Buddy Ebsen, Leonard Penn, Priscilla Lawson, Bob Murphy, Olin Howlin, Cliff Edwards, Billy Bevan; ***D:*** Robert Z. Leonard.

A Girl of the Limberlost **1990** A young Indiana farmgirl fights to bring her estranged parents back together, in spite of a meddling aunt and the unexplained phenomena that haunt her. Fine acting and beautiful scenery. Originally broadcast as part of PBS's "Wonderworks" family movie series, it's best appreciated by young teens. Adapted from Gene Stratton Porter's much-filmed novel. **120m/C VHS, DVD.** Annette O'Toole, Joanna Cassidy, Heather Fairfield; ***D:*** Burt Brinckerhoff; ***W:*** Pamela Douglas; ***C:*** Gordon C. Lonsdale; ***M:*** Misha Segal. **TV**

The Girl of Your Dreams 1/2 *La nina de tus ojos* **1999 (R)** Macarena Granada (Cruz) headlines a troop of Spanish actors who travel from their war-torn country to Berlin in 1938 to turn an Andalusian musical into a movie. Things get grimly messy when she seeks to rescue a prisoner from a nearby concentration camp. In Spanish, with subtitles. **121m/C VHS, DVD.** Penelope Cruz, Antonio Resines, Jorge Sanz, Rosa Maria Sarda, Santiago Segura, Loles Leon, Jesus Bonilla, Neus Asensi, Miroslav Taborsky, Karel Dobry, Johannes Silberschneider, Goetz Otto, Hanna Schygulla, Maria Barranco, Juan Luis Galiardo, Heinz Rilling, Jan Preucil, Borivoj Navratil, Martin Faltyn, Otto Sevcik; ***D:*** Fernando Trueba; ***W:*** Rafael Azcona, Miguel Angel Egea, Carlos Lopez, David Trueba; ***C:*** Javier Aguirresarobe; ***M:*** Antoine Duhamel. **VIDEO**

Girl on a Chain Gang WOOF! **1965** A girl on the run gets caught by police and does her time on a chain gang—an otherwise all-male chain gang. Predictable. **96m/B VHS.** William Watson, Julie Ange, R.K. Charles; ***D:*** Jerry Gross; ***W:*** Jerry Gross.

The Girl on a Motorcycle *Naked under Leather; La Motocyclette* **1968 (R)** Singer Faithfull is a bored housewife who dons black leather and hops on her motorcycle to meet up with her lover (Delon), all the while remembering their other erotic encounters. **92m/C VHS, DVD.** *GB* Alain Delon, Marianne Faithfull, Roger Mutton; ***D:*** Jack Cardiff; ***W:*** Gillian Freeman, Ronald Duncan; ***C:*** Jack Cardiff; ***M:*** Les Reed.

A Girl on Her Own **1976** A young actress embarking on her first big role in Paris must also deal with family and political considerations in this drama set during the political upheaval of 1935. **112m/C VHS.** *FR* Sophie Chemineau, Bruno La Brasca; ***D:*** Philippe Nahon.

The Girl on the Bridge *Le Fille sure le Pont* **1998 (R)** An unconventional romance that finds middle-aged professional knife-thrower Gabor (Auteuil) calmly engaging in conversation with suicidal Adele (Paradis), the titular character. After a young lifetime of perpetual bad luck, what could be better for Adele than to risk everything every night by becoming Gabor's new partner. The duo seem to have a telepathic communication that makes them a great success but luck has a way of changing. Great chemistry between the world-weary Auteuil and the gamine Paradis that is all the more apparent because their characters maintain a hands-off relationship. French with subtitles. **92m/B VHS, DVD.** *FR* Daniel Auteuil, Vanessa Paradis, Demetre Georgalas, Isabelle Petit-Jacques; ***D:*** Patrice Leconte; ***W:*** Serge Frydman; ***C:*** Jean-Marie Dreujou. Cesar '00: Actor (Auteuil).

The Girl on the Train *La Fille du RER* **2009** Based on a 2004 media-sensational true story. Aimless early 20-something Jeanne (Dequenne) lives with her respectable widowed mother Louise (Deneuve) in the insular Parisian suburbs. After a bad breakup with her thuggish boyfriend Franck (Duvauchelle), Jeanne suddenly pretends that she was violently attacked on a train by Arab and black youths who thought she was Jewish. The assault makes international news but Jeanne is soon forced to admit that she lied. What you never find out from the enigmatic Jeanne is why she did it. In contrast, writer/director Techine also introduces the liberal Jewish Bleistein family whose lawyer patriarch Samuel (Blanc), an old acquaintance of Louise, comes to Jeanne's aid. French and Hebrew with subtitles. **105m/C DVD.** *FR* Emilie Dequenne, Catherine Deneuve, Michel Blanc, Ronit Elkabetz, Mathieu Demy, Nicolas Duvauchelle; ***D:*** Andre Techine; ***W:*** Andre Techine, Odile Barski, Jean-Marie Besset; ***C:*** Julien Hirsch; ***M:*** Philippe Sarde.

Girl Play **2004** When two lesbians meet while doing a play they begin to fall for one another despite the fact Robin (Greenspan) has a long-term partner and Lacie (Harmon) loathes commitment. Drawn from the real-life story of the lead actresses who adapted the script from their play "Real Girls." **74m/C VHS, DVD.** Mink Stole, Dom DeLuise, Robin Greenspan, Lacie Harmon, Katherine Randolph; ***D:*** Lee Friedlander; ***W:*** Lee Friedlander, Robin Greenspan, Lacie Harmon. **VIDEO**

Girl Rush **1944** Two bad vaudeville comics are stuck in California during the gold rush and are promised sacks of gold if they can persuade some women to come to a rowdy mining town. ♫Annabella's Bustle; Rainbow Valley; If Mother Could Only See Us Now; Walking Arm in Arm With Jim. **65m/B VHS.** Wally Brown, Alan Carney, Frances Langford, Barbara Jo Allen, Robert Mitchum, Paul Hurst, Patti Brill, Sarah Padden, Cy Kendall; ***D:*** Gordon Douglas.

The Girl Said No 1/2 *With Words and Music* **1937** A sleazy bookie poses as a theatrical producer in order to get even with a dance hall floozy who once stiffed him. **72m/B VHS.** Robert Armstrong, Irene Hervey, William Haines; ***D:*** Andrew L. Stone; ***W:*** Andrew L. Stone.

Girl Shy **1924** Harold is a shy tailor's apprentice who is trying to get a collection of his romantic fantasies published. Finale features Lloyd chasing wildly after girl of his dreams. **65m/B VHS, DVD.** Harold Lloyd, Jobyna Ralston, Richard Daniels; ***D:*** Fred Newmeyer; ***W:*** Sam Taylor.

Girl 6 1/2 **1996 (R)** Aspiring actress (Randle) takes job as a phone sex operator in order to make ends meet. After finally finding stardom in the world of titillating telecommunications, she starts to take her work home. Bound to be compared, unfairly and probably unfavorably, to Lee's debut "She's Gotta Have It." Terrific performance by Randle is hampered by the lack of a strong story and too many unresolved subplots. Features the obligatory Lee cameo, while Tarantino shows up as a young hotshot director. Prince provides old and new tunes (as well as his previous moniker, apparently) to the proceedings. **107m/C VHS, DVD.** Theresa Randle, Isaiah Washington IV, Ron Silver, John Turturro, Naomi Campbell, Halle Berry, Madonna, Quentin Tarantino, Debi Mazar, Peter Berg, Richard Belzer, Spike Lee, Jenifer Lewis, Michael Imperioli, Kristen Wilson, Dina Pearlman, Maggie Rush, Desi Moreno, Susan Batson; ***D:*** Spike Lee; ***W:*** Suzan-Lori Parks; ***C:*** Malik Hassan Sayeed; ***M:*** Prince.

The Girl, the Body and the Pill **1967** Sexploitation pic from director Lewis has a high school instructor getting fired for her sex education lectures—so she continues them in the privacy of her own home. Meanwhile, her students take up playing musical beds and learn about "the pill." **80m/C VHS.** Pamela Rhae, Bill Rogers, Nancy Lee Noble, George Brown, Roy Collodi, Todd Harris, James Nelson, Ray Sager, Valedia Hill; ***D:*** Herschell Gordon Lewis; ***W:*** Allison Louise Downe; ***C:*** Roy Collodi; ***M:*** Larry Wellington.

A Girl Thing **2001** In four individual stories, shrink Dr. Noonan (Channing) listens to her female patients' dreams and woes. Macpherson is a successful lawyer who finds herself attracted to Capshaw in a complicated affair. Headly and her sisters DeMornay and Janney bicker over their mother's final request—they must spend a week together in her house in order to collect their inheritance. Whitfield suspects her husband Bakula is having an affair and hires Hamilton to check things out. Manheim stars as a deeply disturbed patient who forces the doctor to re-evaluate her own life and profession. **237m/C VHS, DVD.** Stockard Channing, Elle Macpherson, Kate Capshaw, Glenne Headly, Rebecca De Mornay, Allison Janney, Lynn Whitfield, Linda Hamilton, Camryn Manheim, Scott Bakula, Bruce Greenwood, Brent Spiner, Mia Farrow; ***D:*** Lee Rose. **CABLE**

A Girl to Kill For 1/2 **1990 (R)** A temptress lures a randy college guy into a plot of murder and betrayal. **85m/C VHS.** Sasha Jenson, Karen Austin, Alex Cord, Rod McCary, Karen Medak; ***D:*** Richard Oliver.

Girl Under the Sheet **1961** A con-man/archaeologist moves into an ancient castle and begins romancing a beautiful resident ghost. **89m/C VHS.** *IT* Chelo Alonso, Walter Chiari; ***D:*** Marino Girolami; ***W:*** Marino Girolami; ***C:*** Augusto Tiezzi; ***M:*** Carlo Savina.

The Girl Who Had Everything 1/2 **1953** Good melodrama with top cast, intelligent script and smooth direction. Taylor plays the spoiled daughter of a criminal lawyer (Powell) who falls for her father's client (Lamas), a suave, underground syndicate boss. Remake of the 1931 film "A Free Soul," which starred Norma Shearer, Clark Gable, and Lionel Barrymore. Based on the novel of the same name by Adela Rogers St. John. **69m/B VHS.** Elizabeth Taylor, Fernando Lamas, William Powell, Gig Young, James Whitmore, Robert Burton; ***D:*** Richard Thorpe; ***M:*** Andre Previn.

The Girl Who Knew Too Much 1/2 *La Ragazza Che Sapeva Troppo; The Evil Eye* **1963** Ten years ago in Italy a string of "alphabet murders" began on "A" and ended on "C." Now a pretty young American named Nora Davis (Roman) is visiting a family friend in Italy. When the friend dies and Nora goes for help—in the middle of the night, in the rain, wearing only a raincoat, alone, through an empty plaza—she witnesses a murder that happened ten years ago or does she? She shouldn't worry, though, because handsome young Dr. Marcello Bassi (Saxon speaking fluent Italian) wants to help her. Typically fun and frightening Bava fare with the script, cinematography and direction working much more smoothly than usual. **86m/B DVD.** *IT* Leticia Roman, John Saxon, Valentina Cortese, Robert Buchanan; ***D:*** Mario Bava; ***W:*** Mario Bava, Ennio de Concini, Mino Guerrini; ***C:*** Mario Bava.

The Girl Who Spelled Freedom **1986** A young Cambodian girl, speaking little English, strives to adjust to life in Chattanooga, Tennessee. She faces her challenges by becoming a champion at the national spelling bee. Based on a true story. **90m/C VHS.** Wayne Rogers, Mary Kay Place, Jade Chinn, Kieu Chinh, Kathleen Sisk; ***D:*** Simon Wincer. **TV**

Girl with a Pearl Earring 1/2 **2003 (PG-13)** Based on the novel by Tracy Chevalier about the fictional relationship between the famous Dutch painter Vermeer and the servant girl who posed for his most famous work. Griet (Johansson, bearing an uncanny similarity to the actual painting) is sent to work for Vermeer after her father can no longer support the family. Vermeer (Firth) is intrigued by her intuitive sensibilities to art and soon has her helping in the studio and then posing for him. Johansson gives an exceptionally flawless performance in an intelligent and visually stunning film. **95m/C VHS, DVD.** *GB LU* Colin Firth, Scarlett Johansson, Tom Wilkinson, Judy Parfitt, Essie Davis, Cillian Murphy, Alakina Mann, Joanna Scanlan; ***D:*** Peter Webber; ***W:*** Olivia Hetreed; ***C:*** Eduardo Serra; ***M:*** Alexandre Desplat. L.A. Film Critics '03: Cinematog.

The Girl with a Suitcase *La Ragazza con la Valgia* **1960** Young nightclub singer Aida (Cardinale) falls for rich cad Marcello (Pani) and leaves her job to follow him to his family home in Parma. He was just stringing her along and instructs his 16-year-old brother Lorenzo (Perrin) to get rid of Aida. But instead Lorenzo decides to become her protector and the unlikely duo fall in love. Italian with subtitles; the original release was 135 minutes. **111m/B VHS, DVD.** *IT* Claudia Cardinale, Jacques Perrin, Corrado Pani, Luciana Angiolillo, Romolo Valli, Gian Marie Volonte; ***D:*** Valerio Zurlini; ***W:*** Valerio Zurlini; ***C:*** Tino Santoni; ***M:*** Mario Nascimbene.

Girl with Green Eyes 1/2 **1964** Kate Brady (Tushingham) is a young Catholic farm girl who comes to Dublin for work and falls in love with much older divorced writer Eugene Gaillard (Finch). She moves in with him despite her moral misgivings but both discover their differences are too great to sustain their relationship. O'Brien adapted the screenplay from her novel "The Lonely Girl." **91m/B VHS, DVD.** *GB* Peter Finch, Rita Tushingham, Lynn Redgrave, Marie Kean, Julian Glover, T.P. McKenna, Yolande Finch, Arthur O'Sullivan; ***D:*** Desmond Davis; ***W:*** Edna O'Brien;

C: Manny Wynn; M: John Addison.

The Girl With the Dragon Tattoo 🦴🦴🦴 *Man Som Hatar Kvinnor* **2009** This thriller based on the novel by Stieg Larsson was already an international critical and box-office success before landing on American shores. The eponymous tattooed girl is Lisbeth (Rapace), a goth private eye/hacker who helps reporter Mikael (Nyqvist) investigate the 40-year-old disappearance of a girl from a rich and powerful family. The girl's uncle Henrik (Taube) suspects that the person responsible is a member of his loathsome family. Rapace excels as the angry and rebellious Lisbeth, who has some secrets of her own. Some scenes may be too graphic for squeamish viewers, but they reinforce the original Swedish title: "Men Who Hate Women." In Swedish with subtitles. **152m/C DVD.** *SW DK GE* Michael Nyqvist, Noomi Rapace, Sven-Bertil Taube, Ingvar Hirdwall, Marika Lagercrantz, Ewa Froling, Peter Haber; *D:* Niels Arden Oplev; *W:* Rasmus Heisterberg, Nicolaj Arcel; *C:* Jens Fischer, Eric Kress; *M:* Jacob Groth.

The Girl with the Hat Box 🦴🦴 **1927** Early Russian production about a poor working girl who's paid with a lottery ticket rather than rubles (an ironic pre-communist theme?). When she strikes it rich in the lottery, her boss gives chase and silent antics ensue. Silent with orchestral score. **67m/B VHS, DVD.** *RU* Anna Sten, Vladimar Fogel, Serafina Birman, Ivan Koval-Samborsky; *D:* Boris Barnet.

The Girl with the Hungry Eyes 🦴🦴 **1994 (R)** In 1937, top fashion model and hotel owner Louise (Fulton) kills herself over a cheating fiancee. Except Louise doesn't die, instead she becomes a vampire and, in the present-day, decides to return to her now-derelict haunts. Louise is determined to restore her hotel to its former glory and get her revenge on men in general. Filmed in Miami's South Beach. Adapted from a short story by Fritz Leiber. **84m/C VHS, DVD.** Christina (Kristina) Fulton, Isaac Turner, Leon Herbert, Bret Carr, Susan Rhodes; *D:* Jon Jacobs; *W:* Jon Jacobs; *M:* Paul Inder.

Girlfight 🦴🦴🦴 **1999 (R)** Scrappy feminist coming-of-age drama is the feature debut from director Karyn Kusama. Diana (Rodriguez) is a high-school senior with a bad temper and a penchant for trouble. Her single dad, Sandro (Calderon), encourages her brother Tiny (Santiago) to work with a boxing trainer but refuses to allow his daughter to participate. Diana decides to train anyway, and her determination finds her becoming the gym's first female champ. She falls in love with fellow promising amateur Adrian (Douglas), setting the stage for an unlikely mixed gender bout between the two. The movie strains reality when it has Diana fight Adrian, but the feeling throughout is heartfelt without being overly sentimental. And at least she doesn't howl "Yo Adrian" afterwards. **90m/C VHS, DVD.** Jamie Tirelli, Michelle Rodriguez, Santiago Douglas, Ray Santiago, Elisa Bacanegra, Paul Calderon, John Sayles; *D:* Karyn Kusama; *W:* Karyn Kusama; *C:* Patrick Cady; *M:* Theodore Shapiro. Ind. Spirit '01: Debut Perf. (Rodriguez); Sundance '00: Director (Kusama), Grand Jury Prize.

The Girlfriend Experience 🦴🦴 **2009 (R)** Soderbergh's digitally-shot, brief film indulgence into five days (set before the 2008 election) in the life of high-end Manhattan call girl Chelsea (Grey), who thinks her life is all under control. Chelsea offers her clients more than just the sexual experience, she gives them the illusion of being a 'girlfriend:' going out to dinner, inquiring after their families, listening to their chatter, and asking for financial advice (then the sex). But despite her website and apparent sophistication, there's a good deal of self-delusion as well. Grey, better-known as a porn actress, has a blank beauty that serves her well. **78m/C DVD.** *US* Sasha Grey, Chris Santos, Peter Zizzo, Glenn Kenny; *D:* Steven Soderbergh; *W:* Brian Koppelman, David Levien; *C:* Steven Soderbergh; *M:* Ross Godfrey.

Girlfriend from Hell 🦴 **1989 (R)** The Devil inhabits the body of a teenage wallflower and turns her into an uncontrollable vamp. **95m/C VHS.** Liane (Alexandra) Curtis, Dana Ashbrook, Lezlie (Dean) Deane, James Daughton, Anthony Barrie, James Karen; *D:* Daniel M. Peterson; *W:* Daniel M. Peterson.

Girlfriends 🦴🦴🦴 **1978 (PG)** Bittersweet story of a young Jewish photographer learning to make it on her own. Directorial debut of Weill reflects her background in documentaries as the true-to-life episodes unfold. **87m/C VHS.** Melanie Mayron, Anita Skinner, Eli Wallach, Christopher Guest, Amy Wright, Viveca Lindfors, Bob Balaban, Kathryn Walker, Kristopher Tabori, Mike Kellin, Kenneth McMillan; *D:* Claudia Weill; *W:* Vicki Polon; *C:* Fred Murphy. Sundance '78: Grand Jury Prize.

Girls Are for Loving 🦴 **1973** Undercover agent Ginger faces real adventure when she battles it out with her counterpart, a seductive enemy agent. Her third adventure following "Ginger" (1970) and "The Abductors" (1971). **90m/C VHS, DVD.** Cheri Caffaro, Timothy Brown, William Grannel, Scott Ellsworth, Robert C. Jefferson, Jocelyn Peters, Yuki Shimoda, Fred Vincent; *D:* Don Schain; *W:* Don Schain; *M:* Robert G. Orpin.

Girls Can't Swim 🦴🦴 ½ *Les Filles Ne Savent Pas Nager* **1999** Fifteen-year-old Gwen (Le Bresco) and her best friend Lise (Alyx) always spend their summers together on the Brittany coast where Gwen lives and Lise's family rents a cottage. But when there's a family tragedy, Lise must stay home until the gloomy atmosphere has her traveling to Gwen's on her own. Gwen's parents (who have their own problems) let Lise stay but things between the friends have changed. Gwen has been flaunting her sexuality with the local boys and comes to resent Lise, who feels abandoned. Gwen's thoughtless sexual impulses finally cause the divisions between the girls to spin out of control. French with subtitles. **98m/C VHS, DVD.** *FR* Islid Le Besco, Karen Alyx, Pascal Elso, Pascale Bussieres, Julien Cottereau, Marie Riviere; *D:* Anne-Sophie Birot; *W:* Anne-Sophie Birot, Christophe Honore; *C:* Nathalie Durand; *M:* Ernest Chausson.

Girl's Dormitory 🦴🦴 ½ **1936** French actress Simon made her American debut in this sharp romance. Dr. Stephen Dominik (Marshall), the middle-aged headmaster of a strict Swiss girls' finishing school, is secretly loved by teenaged student Marie (Simon) and attractive professor Anna (Chatterton). Marie is in despair after being threatened with expulsion for writing Stephen a steamy love letter. She's comforted by the headmaster, who now believes that he does have feelings for the chit. Power had a one-scene role as a dashing young count romancing Marie and he made such an impression on the audience that the Fox studio started giving him bigger and better roles. **65m/B DVD.** Herbert Marshall, Ruth Chatterton, Simone Simon, Constance Collier, J. Edward Bromberg, Tyrone Power, Dixie Dunbar; *D:* Irving Cummings; *W:* Gene Markey; *C:* Merritt B. Gerstad; *M:* Arthur Lange, Charles Maxwell.

A Girl's Folly 🦴🦴 ½ **1917** A country girl falls in love with the leading man of a film shooting on location. She wants to become a rich actress, but fails miserably. The actor offers her all the luxuries she wants if she'll become his mistress. When she finally agrees, her mother shows up. What will our country maid do now? **66m/B VHS.** Robert Warwick, Doris Kenyon, June Elvidge, Johnny Hines; *D:* Maurice Tourneur.

Girls! Girls! Girls! 🦴🦴 **1962 (PG)** Poor tuna boat fisherman Elvis moonlights as a nightclub singer to get his father's boat out of hock. He falls for a rich girl pretending to be poor; and after some romantic trials, there's the usual happy ending. ♫ The Nearness of You; Never Let Me Go; Girls, Girls, Girls; Return to Sender; We're Coming in Loaded; A Boy Like Me, A Girl Like You; Song of the Shrimp; Earth Boy; The Walls Have Ears. **106m/C VHS, DVD.** Elvis Presley, Stella Stevens, Laurel Goodwin, Jeremy Slate, Benson Fong, Robert Strauss, Ginny Tiu, Guy Lee, Beulah Quo, Frank Puglia, Nestor Paiva, Alexander Tiu, Elizabeth Tiu, Lili Valenty; *D:* Norman Taurog; *W:* Edward Anhalt; *C:* Loyal Griggs; *M:* Joseph J. Lilley.

Girls in Chains 🦴 ½ **1943** Girls in a reformatory, a teacher, a corrupt school official, and the detective trying to nail him. There's also a murder with the killer revealed at the beginning of the film. **72m/B VHS.** Arline Judge, Roger Clark, Robin Raymond, Barbara Pepper, Dorothy Burgess, Clancy Cooper, Sid Melton, Betty Blythe, Peggy Stewart, Francis Ford; *D:* Edgar G. Ulmer; *W:* Albert Beich; *C:* Ira Morgan; *M:* Leo Erdody.

Girls in Prison 🦴 ½ **1956** Anne Carson is sent to prison for a bank robbery she didn't commit, and although the prison chaplain believes her story, the other prisoners think she knows where the money is hidden. They plan a prison break, forcing Carson to go with them and get the money, but they soon run across the real robber, also searching for the loot. A below-average "B" prison movie, lacking the camp aspects of so many of these films. **87m/B VHS.** Richard Denning, Joan Taylor, Adele Jergens, Helen Gilbert, Lance Fuller, Jane Darwell, Raymond Hatton; *D:* Edward L. Cahn.

Girls in Prison 🦴🦴 **1994 (R)** Not exactly a remake of the same-titled 1956 film (although it's still set in the '50s) but it's a familiar "babes behind bars" saga. Aspiring country singer Aggie (Crider) is wrongfully convicted of murdering a record company exec and winds up in the big house. Then she learns an inmate has been contracted to kill her. Can she find the hit girl before it's too late (and find out who's framing her)? **82m/C VHS.** Missy (Melissa) Crider, Ione Skye, Anne Heche, William Boyett, Tom Towler, Miguel (Michael) Sandoval, Jon Polito, Richmond Arquette; *D:* John McNaughton; *W:* Christa Lang, Samuel Fuller; *C:* Jean De Segonzac; *M:* Hummie Mann. **CABLE**

Girls Just Want to Have Fun 🦴 ½ **1985 (PG)** An army brat and her friends pull out all the stops and defy their parents for a chance to dance on a national TV program. **90m/C VHS, DVD.** Sarah Jessica Parker, Helen Hunt, Ed Lauter, Holly Gagnier, Morgan Woodward, Lee Montgomery, Shannen Doherty, Biff Yeager; *D:* Alan Metter; *W:* Janice Hirsch, Amy Spies; *C:* Thomas Ackerman; *M:* Thomas Newman.

Girls Next Door 🦴 **1979 (R)** A bevy of boisterous beauties cavort and cause havoc in buffoon-cluttered suburbia. **85m/C VHS.** Kirsten Baker, Perry Lang, Leslie Cederquist, Richard Singer; *D:* James Hong.

Girls' Night 🦴🦴 ½ **1997** The acting's fine but the story's weak in this old-fashioned weepie. Brit wives Dawn (Blethyn) and Jackie (Walters) are best friends and in-laws, who even work at the same factory. Both women are also suffering from the marriage blues and find solace at the local bingo parlor. When Dawn wins very big, she splits the money with Jackie and then discovers that she has cancer. The duo decide this is the time for their dream Las Vegas vacation, where they even meet a Prince Charming—in the form of cowpoke Cody (Kristofferson). **106m/C VHS.** *GB* Brenda Blethyn, Julie Walters, Kris Kristofferson, George Costigan, James Gaddas, Philip Jackson; *D:* Nick Hurran; *W:* Kay Mellor; *C:* David Odd; *M:* Ed Shearmur.

Girls Night Out 🦴 *The Scaremaker* **1983 (R)** Ex-cop must stop a killer who is murdering participants in a sorority house scavenger hunt and leaving cryptic clues on the local radio station. **96m/C VHS, DVD.** Hal Holbrook, Rutanya Alda, Julia Montgomery, James Carroll; *D:* Robert Deubel.

The Girls of Huntington House 🦴🦴 **1973** A teacher in a school for unwed mothers finds herself becoming increasingly absorbed in her students' lives. **73m/C VHS.** Shirley Jones, Mercedes McCambridge, Sissy Spacek, William Windom, Pamela Sue Martin, Darrell Larson; *D:* Alf Kjellin. **TV**

Girls of the White Orchid 🦴 *Death Ride to Osaka* **1985** A naive American girl thinks she's getting a job singing in a Japanese nightclub, but it turns out to be a front for a prostitution ring run by the Japanese Yakuza. Based on real stories, though the producers concentrate on the seamy side. **96m/C VHS, DVD.** Thomas Jefferson Byrd, Carolyn Seymour, Mako, Ann Jillian, Jennifer Jason Leigh; *D:* Jonathan Kaplan; *C:* John Lindley; *M:* Brad Fiedel. **TV**

Girls on the Road 🦴 ½ **1973 (PG)** Two girls are just out for fun cruising the California coast, but that handsome hitchhiker turns out to be a deadly mistake. **91m/C VHS.** *CA* Kathleen (Kathy) Cody, Michael Ontkean, Dianne Hull, Ralph Waite, Rigg Kennedy; *D:* Thomas J. Schmidt.

Girls Riot 🦴 **1988** Young, female juvenile delinquents have had enough! They decide to give their warden-like headmistress a taste of her own violence. **100m/C VHS.** Jocelyne Boisseau, Cornelia Calwer, Angelica Domrose, Ute Freight; *D:* Manfred Purzer.

Girls School Screamers 🦴 **1986 (R)** Six young women and a nun are assigned to spend the weekend checking the contents for sale in a scary mansion bequeathed to their school. Unfortunately, the psychotic killer inhabiting the place doesn't think that's a good idea. **85m/C VHS, DVD.** Mollie O'Mara, Sharon Christopher, Vera Gallagher; *D:* John P. Finegan; *W:* John P. Finegan; *C:* Albert R. Jordan; *M:* John Hodian.

Girls' Town 🦴 *The Innocent and the Damned* **1959** Typical bad girls and drag racing '50s flick has Van Doren sent to a correctional institute, run by nuns. This tough girl sees the error of her wicked ways and turns into a goody-two-shoes. **90m/B VHS.** Mamie Van Doren, Mel Torme, Paul Anka, Ray Anthony, Margaret (Maggie) Hayes, Cathy Crosby, Elinor Donahue, Gigi Perreau, Jim Mitchum, Gloria Talbott, Harold Lloyd Jr., Charles Chaplin Jr., Peggy Moffitt; *D:* Charles F. Haas; *W:* Robert Smith, Robert D. (Robert Hardy) Andrews; *C:* John L. "Jack" Russell; *M:* Van Alexander, Paul Anka.

Girls Town 🦴🦴 **1995 (R)** Tough look at the lives of three working-class high school seniors who are shattered by the suicide of Nikki (Ellis), the fourth member of their group, who killed herself from guilt over an undisclosed rape. Single mom Patti (Taylor), ambitious Emma (Grace), and strong-willed Angela (Harris) argue, commiserate, battle their foes (Patti's abusive boyfriend, Nikki's rapist), and lean on each other as they struggle to figure out themselves and their ambiguous futures. Lots of time's spent in the girls' bathroom at school (how realistic can you get?) **90m/C VHS.** Lili Taylor, Anna Grace, Bruklin Harris, Aunjanue Ellis, Guillermo Diaz, John Ventimiglia; *D:* Jim McKay; *W:* Denise Casano, Jim McKay, Lili Taylor, Anna Grace, Bruklin Harris, Aunjanue Ellis; *C:* Russell Fine. Sundance '96: Filmmakers Trophy.

Girly 🦴 *Mumsy, Nanny, Sonny, and Girly* **1970 (R)** An English gothic about an excessively weird family that lives in a crumbling mansion and indulges in murder, mental aberration, and sexual compulsion. **101m/C VHS.** *GB* Michael Bryant, Ursula Howells, Pat Heywood, Howard Trevor, Vanessa Howard, Michael Ripper; *D:* Freddie Francis.

Git! 🦴 ½ **1965** A young runaway and his faithful dog are taken in by a wealthy dog-breeder and trained by him into a crack hunting team. **90m/C VHS.** Jack Chaplain, Richard Webb, Heather North; *D:* Ellis Kadison.

Git Along Little Dogies 🦴 ½ **1937** It's cattle ranchers versus oil men with Autry caught in the middle of the petro/cow war. But Gene still finds a little time to romance the town banker's pretty daughter. **60m/B VHS.** Gene Autry, Judith Allen, Smiley Burnette, William Farnum; *D:* Joseph Kane.

Giuliani Time 🦴🦴 **2005** A mostly-warts documentary on Rudy Giuliani, from his early career at the Department of Justice to his controversial two terms as the mayor of New York City and his response to the disaster of 9/11, ending with his speech at the 2004 Republican National Convention. Filmmaker Keating is not a fan. **119m/C DVD.** *US* *D:* Kevin Keating; *C:* Kevin Keating; *M:* David Carbonara.

Give a Girl a Break 🦴🦴 ½ **1953** Three talented but unknown babes vie for the lead in a stage production headed for Broadway after the incumbent prima donna quits. After befriending one of the various men associated with the production, each starlet thinks she's a shoe-in for the part. Entertaining but undistinguished musical with appealing dance routines of Fosse and the Champions. Ira Gershwin, collaborating for the first and only time with Burton Lane, wrote the lyrics to two of the songs. ♫ Give the Girl a

Break; In Our United State; It Happens Every Time; Nothing is Impossible; Applause, Applause; Challenge Dance. **84m/C VHS.** Marge Champion, Gower Champion, Debbie Reynolds, Helen Wood, Bob Fosse, Kurt Kasznar, Richard Anderson, William Ching, Larry Keating, Donna (Dona Martel) Martell; ***D:*** Stanley Donen; ***M:*** Andre Previn.

Give 'Em Hell, Harry! 1975 James Whitmore's one-man show as Harry S. Truman filmed in performance on stage; Whitmore was nominated for a Tony. **103m/C VHS.** James Whitmore; ***D:*** Steve Binder.

Give Me a Sailor ½ 1938 Hope and Whiting play brothers, and fellow Naval officers, who meet sisters Grable and Raye on shore leave. Naturally, there's comic romantic complications until a double wedding ends the farce. Not much of a musical score from Ralph Rainger and Leo Robin but the movie's fun. Based on a play by Anne Nichols. ♫ What Goes Here in My Heart?; A Little Kiss at Twilight; Give Me a Sailor; The US and You; It Don't Make Sense. **71m/B VHS, DVD.** Bob Hope, Martha Raye, Betty Grable, Jack Whiting, Clarence (C. William) Kolb, Nana Bryant, Emerson Treacy; ***D:*** Elliott Nugent; ***W:*** Frank Butler, Doris Anderson.

Give Me Your Hand 2009 Identical teenaged twin brothers alternate between fighting, rivalry, and protectiveness on a road trip across France as they head to Spain for their mother's funeral while indulging in various sexual escapades. The Carrils are so inexpressive and the plot so simplistic that all a viewer will want is for the trip to end as quickly as possible. French with subtitles. **77m/C DVD.** *FR* Alexandre Carril, Victor Carril, Samir Harrag, Anais Demoustier; ***D:*** Pascal-Alex Vincent; ***W:*** Pascal-Alex Vincent, Martin Drouot, Olivier Nicklaus; ***C:*** Alexis Kavyrchine; ***M:*** Bernd Jestram, Ronald Lippock.

Give My Regards to Broad Street 1984 **(PG)** McCartney film made for McCartney fans. Film features many fine versions of the ex-Beatle's songs that accompany his otherwise lackluster portrayal of a rock star in search of his stolen master recordings. ♫ Eleanor Rigby; Ballroom Dancing; Good Day, Sunshine; Silly Love Songs; No Values; No More Lonely Nights; Yesterday; Not Such a Bad Boy; The Long and Winding Road. **109m/C VHS, DVD.** *GB* Paul McCartney, Bryan Brown, Ringo Starr, Barbara Bach, Tracey Ullman, Ralph Richardson, Linda McCartney; ***D:*** Peter Webb.

Giving It Up ½ *Casanova Falling* **1999 (R)** Bland and predictable romantic comedy. Successful New York ad exec Ralph (Feuerstein) is a sexaholic. This pleases his boss Jonathan (Coleman) since it seems to enhance Ralph's work but makes him a pariah to his female co-workers. He meets his match in sophisticated Elizabeth (Redford) and decides to change his horn dog ways for true love. Only Ralph slips when he gets a chance with supermodel Amber (Larter). It ain't pretty when Liz finds out. **90m/C VHS, DVD.** Mark Feuerstein, Dabney Coleman, Ali Larter, Amy Redford, Callie (Calliope) Thorne, James Toback; ***D:*** Christopher Kublan; ***W:*** Christopher Kublan; ***C:*** Leland Krane.

The Gladiator ½ 1938 Brown stars as a mild-mannered collegiate who accidently ingests a serum which turns him into a real he-man. Things take a turn for the funniest when the effects wear off, just as he is to wrestle Man Mountain Dean. Chock-full of Brown's trademark physical humor. **70m/B VHS.** Joe E. Brown, Man Mountain Dean, June Travis, Dickie Moore, Lucien Littlefield, Robert Kent, Ethel Wales; ***D:*** Edward Sedgwick.

The Gladiator ½ 1986 An angry Los Angeles citizen turns vigilante against drunk drivers after his brother is one of their victims. **94m/C VHS, DVD.** Ken Wahl, Nancy Allen, Robert Culp, Stan Shaw, Rosemary Forsyth; ***D:*** Abel Ferrara. **TV**

Gladiator ½ **1992 (R)** When suburban Golden Gloves boxing champion Tommy Riley (Marshall) is forced to move to the inner city because of his father's gambling debts, he becomes involved with an evil boxing promotor who thrives on pitting different ethnic races against each other in illegal boxing matches. Eventually Riley is forced to fight his black friend Lincoln (Gooding), even though Lincoln has been warned that another blow to the head could mean his life. Although this film tries to serve some moral purpose, it falls flat on the mat. **98m/C VHS, DVD.** Cuba Gooding Jr., James Marshall, Robert Loggia, Ossie Davis, Brian Dennehy, Cara Buono, John Heard, Jon Seda, Lance Slaughter; ***D:*** Rowdy Herrington; ***W:*** Lyle Kessler, Robert Mark Kamen; ***C:*** Tak Fujimoto; ***M:*** Brad Fiedel.

Gladiator **2000 (R)** Emperor Marcus Aurelius (Harris) decides to name victorious general Maximus (Crowe) his heir over the ruler's own son, the decadent Commodus (Phoenix). But Commodus manages to take over the Empire anyway. Maximus is betrayed, his family killed, and he is sold as a slave, eventually learning the ways of a gladiator. Then he returns to Rome to fight before the new Emperor and get his revenge. Last role for Reed (playing owner/trainer Proximo), who died during production. Unlike the cheesy Italian muscle epics of the early '60s this is swords, sandals, and killer beasts for a new generation, with a compelling hero in Crowe. **154m/C VHS, DVD.** Russell Crowe, Joaquin Rafael (Leaf) Phoenix, Connie Nielsen, Djimon Hounsou, Ralph (Ralf) Moeller, Derek Jacobi, Oliver Reed, Richard Harris, David Schofield, John Shrapnel, Tomas Arana, Spencer (Treat) Clark, Tommy Flanagan, David Hemmings, Sven-Ole Thorsen; ***D:*** Ridley Scott; ***W:*** David Franzoni, John Logan, William Nicholson; ***C:*** John Mathieson; ***M:*** Hans Zimmer. Oscars '00: Actor (Crowe), Costume Des., Film, Sound, Visual FX; British Acad. '00: Cinematog., Film; Golden Globes '01: Film—Drama, Score; Natl. Bd. of Review '00: Support. Actor (Phoenix); Broadcast Film Critics '00: Actor (Crowe), Cinematog., Film, Support. Actor (Phoenix).

Gladiator Cop: The Swordsman 2 ½ **1995 (R)** A legendary sword, believed to have magic powers, is stolen and an ex-detective winds up fighting modern-day gladiators and a man who believes himself to be a reincarnation of Alexander the Great. **92m/C VHS, DVD.** James Hong, Frank Anderson, Christopher Lee Clements, Heather Gillan, Lorenzo Lamas; ***D:*** Nick Rotundo; ***W:*** Nick Rotundo; ***C:*** Edgar Egger; ***M:*** Guy Zerafa.

Gladiator of Rome *Il Gladiatore Di Roma* **1963** A gladiator flexes his pecs to save a young girl from death at the hands of evil rulers. **105m/C VHS, DVD.** *IT* Gordon Scott, Wandisa Guida, Roberto Risso, Ombretta Colli, Alberto (Albert Farley) Farnese; ***D:*** Mario Costa.

The Gladiators *The Peace Game; Gladiatorerna* **1970** Televised gladiatorial bouts are designed to subdue man's violent tendencies in a futuristic society until a computer makes a fatal error. **90m/C VHS, DVD.** Arthur Pentelow, Frederick Danner; ***D:*** Peter Watkins.

Gladiators 7 ½ **1962** Sparta must be freed from the tyrannical rule of the Romans. In lieu of samurai or cowboys, who better than the Gladiators 7 to do the deed? Plenty of sword-to-sword action and scantily clad Italian babes. **92m/C VHS, DVD.** *SP IT* Richard Harrison, Loredana Nusciak, Livio Lorenzon, Gerard Tichy, Edoardo Toniolo, Joseph Marco, Barta Barry; ***D:*** Pedro Lazaga.

Glam 1997 **(R)** Eccentric writer Sonny Daye (McNamara) arrives in L.A. and is promptly exploited. His cousin Franky (Frank) takes Sonny's journal to a pair of schlocky producers who are impressed by the writing. So vain and ruthless Sid Dalgren (Danza) decides to control Sonny even while his tootsie, Vanessa (Wagner), begins to fall for the oddball's sweetness. Very talky. Director Evan's mom, Ali McGraw, has a cameo. **93m/C VHS, DVD.** William McNamara, Frank Whaley, Natasha Gregson Wagner, Tony Danza, Valerie Kaprisky, Caroline Lagerfelt, Lou (Cutel) Cutell, Robert DoQui, Jon Cryer, Donal Logue; ***Cameos:*** Ali MacGraw; ***D:*** Josh Evans; ***W:*** Josh Evans; ***M:*** Josh Evans.

Glass ½ **1990** A normally complacent man is driven to the brink of savagery when a killer begins stalking his employees. **92m/C VHS.** Alan Lovell, Lisa Peers, Adam Stone, Natalie McCurry; ***D:*** Chris Kennedy; ***W:*** Chris Kennedy; ***C:*** Peter De Vries; ***M:*** Mario Gregorie.

The Glass Bottom Boat ½ **1966** A bubbly but transparent Doris Day comedy, in which she falls in love with her boss at an aerospace lab. Their scheme to spend time together gets her mistaken for a spy. Made about the time they stopped making them like this anymore, it's innocuous slapstick romance with a remarkable 1960s cast, including a Robert Vaughn cameo as the Man From U.N.C.L.E. Doris sings "Que Sera, Sera" and a few other numbers. **110m/C VHS, DVD.** Doris Day, Rod Taylor, Arthur Godfrey, Paul Lynde, Eric Fleming, Alice Pearce, Ellen Corby, John McGiver, Dom DeLuise, Dick Martin, Edward Andrews; ***Cameos:*** Robert Vaughn; ***D:*** Frank Tashlin; ***W:*** Everett Freeman; ***C:*** Leon Shamroy.

The Glass Cage 1996 **(R)** Ex-CIA agent Paul Yeager (Tyson) takes a bartending job in New Orleans' French Quarter in order to get back his exotic dancer girlfriend Jacqueline (Lewis) but the bar's jealous owner and dirty cop Montrachet (Roberts) have other plans in mind for the duo. **96m/C VHS.** Richard Tyson, Charlotte Lewis, Eric Roberts, Stephen Nichols, Joseph Campanella, Richard Moll, Maria Ford, Lisa Marie Scott; ***D:*** Michael Schroeder; ***W:*** David Keith Miller; ***C:*** John Aronson.

The Glass House *Truman Capote's The Glass House* **1972** Alda stars as a middle-aged college professor, convicted on a manslaugter charge, who is sent to a maximum security prison and must learn to deal with life inside. Filmed at Utah State Prison, real-life prisoners as supporting cast add to the drama. Still has the power to chill, with Morrow particularly effective as one of the inmate leaders. Adapted from a Truman Capote story. **92m/C VHS, DVD.** Alan Alda, Vic Morrow, Clu Gulager, Billy Dee Williams, Dean Jagger, Kristopher Tabori; ***D:*** Tom Gries; ***M:*** Billy Goldenberg. **TV**

The Glass House ½ **2001 (PG-13)** With a brittle plot you can see right through, this flick is aptly named. After their parents are killed in a car accident, 16-year-old Ruby (Sobieski) and her little brother Rhett (Morgan) are sent to live with their former neighbors Erin and Terry Glass (Lane and Skarsgaard). The Glasses live in a swanky glass mansion with all the charm of a Windex bottle. Although they lavish the kids with clothes and gadgets, Ruby begins to suspect what we already know: evil stepparents! Ruby then tries to tell all the adults in her life that the Glasses have ugly streaks, but no one believes her or even suggests a rinsing agent. Obvious plot devices and cliched techniques (including the ever-popular "tinkling danger piano music") shatter what could have been a great thriller given the cast and concept. **111m/C VHS, DVD.** *US* Leelee Sobieski, Stellan Skarsgard, Diane Lane, Trevor Morgan, Bruce Dern, Kathy Baker, Christopher Noth, Rita Wilson, Michael O'Keefe, Vyto Ruginis; ***D:*** Daniel Sackheim; ***W:*** Wesley Strick; ***C:*** Alar Kivilo; ***M:*** Christopher Young.

Glass House: The Good Mother **2006 (R)** Orphaned Abby (Hinson) and her younger brother Ethan (Coleman) are adopted by a seemingly perfect couple, Eve (Harmon) and Raymond (Gretsch) Goode. Soon uptight Eve is doting exclusively on Ethan, who suddenly gets sick, and Abby is suspicious. She learns the Goodes have previously fostered several young boys who have all disappeared. She also figures out that Raymond has been covering for his wife. But Abby is determined her brother will not become their next victim. **93m/C DVD.** Angie Harmon, Joel Gretsch, Jason London, Jordan Hinson, Bobby Coleman; ***D:*** Steve Antin; ***W:*** Brett Merryman; ***C:*** Bobby Bukowski; ***M:*** Steve Gutheinz. **VIDEO**

The Glass Jungle **1988** Will a cab driver save Los Angeles? When armed terrorists and the FBI battle it out in the sunny California city an innocent cabby seems to hold the solution to survival. **94m/C VHS.** Lee Canalito, Joe Filbeck, Diana Frank, Mark High, Frank Scala; ***D:*** Joseph Merhi.

The Glass Key 1942 Previously filmed in 1935, this version of Dashiell Hammet's novel is a vintage mystery concerning nominally corrupt politician Madvig (Donlevy) being framed for murder, and his assistant Ed Beaumont (Ladd) sleuthing out the real culprit. One of Ladd's first starring vehicles; Lake is the mystery woman who loves him, and Bendix a particularly vicious thug. **85m/B VHS.** Alan Ladd, Veronica Lake, Brian Donlevy, William Bendix, Bonita Granville, Richard Denning, Joseph Calleia, Moroni Olsen, Dane Clark; ***D:*** Stuart Heisler; ***W:*** Jonathan Latimer; ***C:*** Theodor Sparkuhl; ***M:*** Victor Young.

The Glass Menagerie 1987 **(PG)** An aging Southern belle deals with her crippled daughter Laura, whose one great love is her collection of glass animals. The third film adaptation of the Tennessee Williams classic, which preserves the performances of the Broadway revival cast, is a solid-but-not-stellar adaptation of the play. All-star acting ensemble. **134m/C VHS, DVD.** Joanne Woodward, Karen Allen, John Malkovich, James Naughton; ***D:*** Paul Newman; ***W:*** Tennessee Williams; ***C:*** Michael Ballhaus; ***M:*** Henry Mancini.

The Glass Shield ½ **1995 (PG-13)** Timely look at racism and corruption in the Los Angeles sheriff's department as seen through the eyes of African American rookie J.J. Johnson (Boatman). His dream of being a police officer turns to disillusionment when he slowly realizes his own department is framing a black man (Ice Cube) for a murder he did not commit. First half grabs your attention, but the momentum is lost in murky plot twists and a rushed ending. Made on a shoestring, but has an interesting cast, including the reliably slimy Ironside as (what else) one of the bad cops and an almost unrecognizable Petty, who becomes Johnson's only ally on the force. **109m/C VHS, DVD.** Michael Boatman, Lori Petty, Michael Ironside, M. Emmet Walsh, Ice Cube, Richard Anderson, Elliott Gould; ***D:*** Charles Burnett; ***W:*** Charles Burnett; ***C:*** Elliot Davis; ***M:*** Stephen James Taylor.

The Glass Slipper 1955 In this version of the "Cinderella" saga, Caron plays an unglamourous girl gradually transformed into the expected beauty. Winwood is the fairy godmother who inspires the girl to find happiness, rather then simply providing it for her magically. The film is highlighted by the stunning dance numbers, choreographed by Roland Petit and featuring the Paris ballet. **93m/C VHS.** Leslie Caron, Michael Wilding, Keenan Wynn, Estelle Winwood, Elsa Lanchester, Barry Jones, Amanda Blake, Lurene Tuttle; ***D:*** Charles Walters; ***Nar:*** Walter Pidgeon.

Glass Tomb *The Glass Cage* **1955** At a circus, a man performs the world's longest fast inside a glass cage, and becomes the raison d'etre for murder. **59m/B VHS, DVD.** John Ireland, Honor Blackman, Eric Pohlmann, Tonia Bern, Sidney James; ***D:*** Montgomery Tully.

The Glass Trap ½ **2004 (PG-13)** It's never pretty when an experiment goes afoul, resulting in freakishly large, angry, and human-hungry ants. Naturally, this can't be good for the scientists responsible for the demons when they get stuck in a really big skyscraper with them. **90m/C VHS, DVD.** C. Thomas Howell, Stella Stevens, Siri Baruc, Brent Huff, Chick Vennera; ***D:*** Fred Olen Ray; ***W:*** Lisa Morton, Brett Thompson. **VIDEO**

Gleaming the Cube ½ **1989 (PG-13)** A skateboarding teen investigates his brother's murder. Film impresses with its stunt footage only. For those with adolescent interests. **102m/C VHS, DVD.** Christian Slater, Steven Bauer, Min Luong, Art Chudabala, Le Tuan; ***D:*** Graeme Clifford; ***W:*** Michael Tolkin; ***M:*** Jay Ferguson.

The Gleiwitz Case *Der Fall Gleiwitz; The Affair Gleiwitz* **1961** A reconstruction of an actual event. On August 31, 1939, six Germans living in Poland are selected for a secret mission: to take over a radio transmitter near Gleiwitz on the German-Polish border. Under the command of an SS officer, the attack will appear to come from Polish insurgents and thus justify the Nazi invasion of Poland. German with subtitles. **70m/B DVD.** *GE* Hilmar Thate, Hannjo Hasse, Herwart Grosse, Georg Leopold; ***D:*** Gerhard Klein; ***W:*** Wolfgang Kohlaas, Gunther Ruckev; ***C:*** Jan Curik; ***M:*** Kurt Scheaen.

Glen and Randa ½ **1971 (R)** Two young people experience the world after it has been destroyed by nuclear war. Early McBride, before the hired-gun success of "The Big Easy." **94m/C VHS.** Steven Curry, Shelley Plimpton; ***D:*** Jim McBride; ***W:*** Rudy Wurlitzer, Jim McBride.

Glen or Glenda? WOOF! *He or She; I Changed My Sex; I Led Two Lives; The Transvestite; Glen or Glenda: The Confessions of Ed Wood* **1953** An appalling, quasi-docudrama about transvestism, interspersed with meaningless stock footage, inept dream sequences and Lugosi sitting in a chair spouting incoherent prattle at the camera. Directorial debut of Wood, who, using a pseudonym, played the lead; one of the phenomenally bad films of this century. An integral part of the famous anti-auteur's canon. **67m/B VHS, DVD.** Edward D. Wood Jr., Bela Lugosi, Lyle Talbot, Timothy Farrell, Dolores Fuller, Charles Crafts, Tommy Haynes, Captain DeZita, Evelyn Wood, Shirley Speril, Conrad Brooks, Henry Bederski, William C. Thompson, Mr. Walter, Harry Thomas, George Weiss; ***D:*** Edward D. Wood Jr.; ***W:*** Edward D. Wood Jr.; ***C:*** William C. Thompson.

Glengarry Glen Ross **1992 (R)** Seven-character study chronicling 48 hours in the lives of some sleazy real estate men in danger of getting the ax from their hard-driving bosses. A standout cast includes Pacino as the glad-handing sales leader, Lemmon as the hustler fallen on dim prospects, and Baldwin, briefly venomous, as the company hatchet-man. Brutal and hard-edged with very strong language. Mamet scripted from his Tony-award winning Broadway play. **100m/C VHS, DVD.** Al Pacino, Jack Lemmon, Ed Harris, Alec Baldwin, Alan Arkin, Kevin Spacey, Jonathan Pryce, Bruce Altman, Jude Ciccolella; ***D:*** James Foley; ***W:*** David Mamet; ***C:*** Juan Ruiz-Anchia; ***M:*** James Newton Howard. Natl. Bd. of Review '92: Actor (Lemmon); Venice Film Fest. '93: Actor (Lemmon).

The Glenn Miller Story **1954 (G)** The music of the Big Band Era lives again in this warm biography of the legendary Glenn Miller, following his life from the late '20s to his untimely death in a WWII plane crash. Stewart's likably convincing and even fakes the trombone playing well. ♫Moonlight Serenade; In the Mood; Tuxedo Junction; Little Brown Jug; Adios; String of Pearls; Pennsylvania 6-5000; Stairway to the Stars; American Patrol. **113m/C VHS, DVD.** James Stewart, June Allyson, Harry (Henry) Morgan, Gene Krupa, Louis Armstrong, Ben Pollack; ***D:*** Anthony Mann; ***W:*** Oscar Brodney, Valentine Davies; ***C:*** William H. Daniels; ***M:*** Henry Mancini. Oscars '54: Sound.

The Glimmer Man 1/2 **1996 (R)** When a vicious LA serial killer starts dispatching whole families, NY detective Jack Cole (Seagal) is teamed with local homicide detective Jim Campbell (Wayans). Since, however, this is a Seagal movie, things have to be a little different. Cole, for example, is an ex-CIA operative who has been convinced by a Buddhist monk to stop killing people and start wearing goofy Nehru jackets and prayer beads. Campbell is a couch potato who cries over old movies (or perhaps he was watching the dailies from this one). After Cole's ex-wife is killed, he's implicated; and then somehow the Russian Mafia and the CIA are brought into the mix. Cole uses his unique brand of non-violence to slash, chop and impale his way to justice. Predictable when it's not being unbelievable, this could have been called "Hard to Watch." **92m/C VHS, DVD.** Steven Seagal, Keenen Ivory Wayans, Michelle Johnson, Brian Cox, Bob Gunton, Stephen Tobolowsky, Johnny Strong, Ryan Cutrona, Peter Jason, Nikki Cox, Richard Gant, Alexa Vega; ***D:*** John Gray; ***W:*** Kevin Brodbin; ***C:*** Rick Bota; ***M:*** Trevor Rabin.

A Glimpse of Hell 1/2 **2001 (PG-13)** Excellent depiction of the 1989 explosion aboard the USS Iowa, and the subsequent investigations by the Navy, Congress. Lt. Dan Meyer (Leonard) is put in charge of a gun turret but soon finds equipment problems, unauthorized munitions experiments, and lax training of the gunnery crew. When one of the turrets is rocked by an explosion and 47 men are killed, the Navy, and the ship's commander, Capt. Moosally (Caan), ignore the mounting physical evidence of accidental explosion to focus on a sabotage scenario involving one of the crew, Clay Hartwig (Eaves), supposedly distraught over the end of a homosexual affair with a fellow crewmember. As the investigations progress, Moosally comes to defend his men, and both he and Meyer must struggle with the question of truth vs. career. **85m/C VHS, DVD.** Robert Sean Leonard, James Caan, Daniel Roebuck, Jamie Harrold, Cherie Devanney, Dashiell Eaves; ***D:*** Mikael Salomon; ***W:*** Charles C. Thompson II, David Freed. **TV**

Glitch! 1/2 **1988 (R)** A throng of beautiful Hollywood hopefuls draw two youngsters unconnected with the film into posing as the film's director and producer in the hopes of conducting personal interviews on the casting couch. **88m/C VHS, DVD.** Julia Nickson-Soul, Will Egan, Steve Donmyer, Dan Speaker, Dallas Cole, Ji-Tu Cumbuka, Dick Gautier, Ted Lange, Teri Weigel, Fernando Carzon, John Kreng, Lindsay Carr; ***D:*** Nico Mastorakis; ***W:*** Nico Mastorakis; ***C:*** Peter C. Jensen; ***M:*** Tom Marolda. **VIDEO**

Glitter WOOF! 2001 (PG-13) Following in the footsteps of "Cool as Ice" and "Spice World," this may be the third in the pop star "why was this allowed to happen?" trilogy. Mariah Carey, showing her acting range of two emotions ("Yay!" and "Huh?"), stars as Billie Frank, a backup singer who climbs to stardom with the help from her svengali boyfriend Dice (Beesley). Together they struggle through the hard times and the wooden dialogue. Will success and the crappy plot stolen from "A Star is Born" tear them apart? You'll be wishing that wild dogs will tear them apart before the end of this mess. So bad it's nearly unintentionally funny. The key word is nearly. **104m/C VHS, DVD.** *US* Mariah Carey, Max Beesley, Tia Texada, Da Brat, Valarie Pettiford, Ann Magnuson, Terrence Howard, Dorian Harewood, Grant Nickalls, Eric Benet, Padma Lakshmi, Isabel Gomes; ***D:*** Vondie Curtis-Hall; ***W:*** Kate Lanier; ***C:*** Geoffrey Simpson; ***M:*** Terence Blanchard. Golden Raspberries '01: Worst Actress (Carey).

The Glitter Dome 1/2 **1984** Two policemen discover the sleazier side of Hollywood when they investigate the murder of a pornographer. Based upon the novel by Joseph Wambaugh. **90m/C VHS.** Stuart Margolin, John Marley, James Garner, John Lithgow, Margot Kidder, Colleen Dewhurst; ***D:*** Stuart Margolin. **TV**

Glitz 1/2 **1988** A Miami cop and an Atlantic City lounge singer team up to investigate a call-girl's death and wind up too close to a drug ring. Based on the novel by Elmore Leonard. **96m/C VHS.** Jimmy Smits, John Diehl, Markie Post, Ken Foree, Madison Mason, Robin Strasser; ***D:*** Sandor Stern. **TV**

A Global Affair 1/2 **1963** Hope is a department head in the United Nations who finds an abandoned baby in the building. The inept bachelor is wooed by a number of international beauties seeking to adopt the child for their various countries but he becomes increasingly attached to the little tyke. **84m/B VHS.** Bob Hope, Lilo (Liselotte) Pulver, Michele Mercier, Yvonne De Carlo, Miiko Taka, Robert Sterling, Nehemiah Persoff, John McGiver, Mickey Shaughnessy; ***D:*** Jack Arnold; ***W:*** Charles Lederer, Arthur Marx, Bob Fisher; ***C:*** Joseph Ruttenberg.

Gloomy Sunday *Ein Lied von Liebe und Tod* **2002** Story of a complex love triangle and Nazi oppression in 1930's Budapest, told in extended flashback. Jewish restaurant owner Laszlo (Krol), his waitress/lover Ilona (Marozsan) and pianist Andras (Dionisi) are all involved with one another when German salesman Hans (Ben Becker) falls for Ilona and eventually befriends the trio. Inspired by Ilona, Andras composes a hit song (the titular "Gloomy Sunday") that causes a rash of suicides. Three years later, Hans returns to Budapest as an SS colonel and is immediately torn between his dedication to the ideals of the Third Reich and his three friends. The characters are complex and well-written, and the tension is thick as they all struggle with the ethical implications of their actions as war encroaches on Budapest. Somewhat marred by stilted, melodramatic moments, but the excellent story and fine acting more than makes up for it. **114m/C DVD.** *GE HU* Joachim Krol, Stefano Dionisi, Ben Becker, Erika Marozsan, Sebastian Koch, Laszlo I. Kish, Rolf Becker; ***D:*** Rolf Schuebel; ***W:*** Rolf Schuebel, Ruth Thoma; ***C:*** Edward Klosinski; ***M:*** Detlef Petersen, Rezso Seress.

Gloria 1/2 **1980 (PG)** She used to be a Mafia moll, now she's outrunning the Mob after taking in the son of a slain neighbor. He's got a book that they want, and they're willing to kill to get it. Trademark Cassavetes effort in which he has actors plumb their souls to discomfiting levels. **123m/C VHS, DVD.** Gena Rowlands, John Adams, Buck Henry, Julie Carmen; ***D:*** John Cassavetes; ***M:*** Bill Conti. Venice Film Fest. '80: Film; Golden Raspberries '80: Worst Support. Actor (Adams).

Gloria **1998 (R)** Remake of the 1980 Cassavetes film, with Stone as title character, a gang moll who reluctantly becomes the guardian of a boy whose parents were killed by her low-life boyfriend Kevin (Northam). Entertainment value is derived from listening to Stone mangle her Noo Yawk accent. Stick with the original. **108m/C VHS, DVD.** Sharon Stone, Jeremy Northam, Cathy Moriarty, George C. Scott, Mike Starr, Don Billett, Tony DiBenedetto, Bonnie Bedelia, Jean-Luke Figueroa, Barry McEvoy, Jerry Dean, Teddy Atlas; ***D:*** Sidney Lumet; ***W:*** Steve Antin; ***C:*** David Watkin; ***M:*** Howard Shore.

Glorifying the American Girl **1930** Eaton's a chorus girl performing in the Ziegfeld Follies, which lends itself to numerous production numbers. The only film Ziegfeld ever produced. ♫What I Wouldn't Do For That Man; Blue Skies; I'm Just a Vagabond Lover; Baby Face; At Sundown; Beautiful Changes; Sam the Old Accordian Man; There Must Be Someone Waiting For Me. **96m/B VHS, DVD.** Mary Eaton, Dan Healey, Eddie Cantor, Rudy Vallee; ***D:*** Millard Webb.

Glory **1956** O'Brien is a racehorse owner who tussles with her grandmother over how to keep the family farm open on a shoestring budget. Brennan enters the picture as the financial guru who lands them back on track, with enough left over to enter their prize filly in the Kentucky Derby. Lupton plays O'Brien's love interest. No surprises here. **100m/C VHS.** Margaret O'Brien, Walter Brennan, Charlotte Greenwood; ***D:*** David Butler.

Glory 1/2 **1989 (R)** A rich, historical spectacle chronicling the 54th Massachusetts, the first black volunteer infantry unit in the Civil War. The film manages to artfully focus on both the 54th and their white commander, Robert Gould Shaw. Based on Shaw's letters, the film uses thousands of accurately costumed "living historians" (re-enactors) as extras in this panoramic production. A haunting, bittersweet musical score pervades what finally becomes an anti-war statement. Stunning performances throughout, with exceptional work from Freeman and Washington. **122m/C VHS, DVD.** Matthew Broderick, Morgan Freeman, Denzel Washington, Cary Elwes, Jihmi Kennedy, Andre Braugher, John Finn, Donovan Leitch, John David (J.D.) Cullum, Bob Gunton, Jane Alexander, Raymond St. Jacques, Cliff DeYoung, Alan North, Jay O. Sanders, Richard Riehle, Ethan Phillips, Ron-Reaco Lee, Peter Michael Goetz; ***D:*** Edward Zwick; ***W:*** Kevin Jarre, Marshall Herskovitz; ***C:*** Freddie Francis; ***M:*** James Horner. Oscars '89: Cinematog., Sound, Support. Actor (Washington); Golden Globes '90: Support. Actor (Washington).

Glory & Honor 1/2 **1998** Covers explorer Robert Peary's (Czerny) treks to the North Pole (he was finally successful in 1909). Peary was accompanied by his black valet Matthew Henson (Lindo), who proved to be resourceful and a source of calm to the driven explorer, and was eventually credited as a co-discoverer. Filmed on location near the Arctic Circle. **94m/C VHS.** Henry Czerny, Delroy Lindo; ***D:*** Kevin Hooks; ***W:*** Susan Rhinehart. **CABLE**

The Glory Boys 1/2 **1984** A secret agent is hired to protect an Israeli scientist who is marked for assassination by the PLO and IRA. **78m/C VHS, DVD.** Rod Steiger, Anthony Perkins, Gary Brown, Aaron Harris; ***D:*** Michael Ferguson.

Glory Daze **1996 (R)** Gen-X comedy about graduation week for five Santa Cruz college friends/housemates. There's Jack (Affleck), Mickey (DeRamus), Rob (Rockwell), Josh (Hong), and Dennis (Stewart) who basically party and kvetch about their uncertain futures, with various girlfriends, professors, and parents around to nag the boys. Not much you haven't seen before, although a number of the cast have gone on to bigger and better things. **100m/C VHS, DVD.** Ben Affleck, Sam Rockwell, French Stewart, Vinnie DeRamus, Vien Hong, Alyssa Milano, Megan Ward, John Rhys-Davies, Elizabeth Ruscio, Spalding Gray, Mary Woronov; ***Cameos:*** Matthew McConaughey, Brendan Fraser, Matt Damon, Meredith Salenger; ***D:*** Rich Wilkes; ***W:*** Rich Wilkes; ***C:*** Christopher Taylor.

Glory Enough for All: The Discovery of Insulin 1/2 **1992** The drama behind the discovery of insulin in the 1920s focuses on the research of four men, sometimes not-so-friendly rivals, searching for a treatment for diabetes mellitus. Dr. Frederick Banting and science student Charles Best are granted permission by James Macleod, a Professor of Physiology at the University of Toronto, to conduct experiments on the pancreas. Macleod then assigns biochemist James Collip to assist them on developing a viable serum, an extract named insulin. Banting and Macleod were awarded the Nobel prize in 1923 for their discovery (though Banting felt Macleod was undeserving). Adapted from "The Discovery of Insulin" by Michael Bliss. **196m/C VHS.** *CA* R.H. Thomson, Robert Wisden, John Woodvine, Michael Zelniker, Martha Henry, Heather Hess; ***D:*** Eric Till; ***W:*** Grahame Woods. **TV**

Glory! Glory! **1990 (R)** Slashing satire about TV evangelism. Thomas as the meek son of founder of Church of the Champions of Christ brings in lewd female rock singer to save the money-machine ministry from financial ruin. Rock music, sex, and MTV-like camera work make it worth seeing. Whitmore is a treat. **152m/C VHS.** Ellen Greene, Richard Thomas, Barry Morse, James Whitmore, Winston Rekert; ***D:*** Lindsay Anderson; ***W:*** Stan Daniels.

Glory Road 1/2 **2006 (PG)** Yet another inspirational, fact-based sports drama. In 1966, the Miners, an under-funded basketball team at small Texas Western, became legends by defeating the sport's Goliaths—the all-white University of Kentucky Wildcats—in the NCAA championship. Their coach, Don Haskins (Lucas), made history when he recruited seven black players and had five of them in his starting lineup. Naturally, there are problems leading up to their triumph, which are dealt with efficiently by first-time director Gartner. End credits showcase Haskins and several of the actual players reflecting on the game. **106m/C DVD, Blu-ray Disc.** *US* Josh(ua) Lucas, Derek Luke, Austin Nichols, Jon Voight, Evan Jones, Alphonso McAuley, Sam Jones III, Emily Deschanel, Al Shearer, Schin A.S. Kerr, Mehcad Brooks, Damaine Radcliff; ***D:*** James Gartner; ***W:*** Chris Cleveland, Bettina Gilois; ***C:*** John Toon, Jeffrey L. Kimball; ***M:*** Trevor Rabin.

The Glory Stompers WOOF! 1967 Hopper prepares for his Easy Rider role as the leader of a motorcycle gang who battles with a rival leader over a woman. Very bad, atrocious dialogue, and a "love-in" scene that will be best appreciated by insomniacs. **85m/C VHS.** Dennis Hopper, Jody McCrea, Chris Noel, Jock Mahoney, Lindsay Crosby, Robert Tessier, Casey Kasem; ***D:*** Anthony M. Lanza.

The Glory Trail 1/2 *Glorious Sacrifice* **1936** A group of railroad workers and soldiers are constantly harassed by Indian attacks. **63m/B VHS.** Tom Keene, Joan Barclay, James Bush, Frank Melton, Walter Long; ***D:*** Lynn Shores.

Glory Years **1987** Three old friends find themselves in charge of the scholarship fund at their 20th high school reunion. Unfortunately, they decide to increase the fund by gambling in Las Vegas and lose it all on a fixed fight! **150m/C VHS, DVD.** George Dzundza, Archie Hahn, Tim Thomerson, Tawny Kitaen, Donna Pescow, Donna Denton; ***D:*** Arthur Allan Seidelman.

The Glove 1/2 *The Glove: Lethal Terminator; Blood Mad* **1978 (R)** Ex-cop turned bounty hunter has his toughest assignment ever. It's his job to bring in a six-and-a-half foot, 250-pound ex-con who's been wreaking havoc with an unusual glove—it's made of leather and steel. **93m/C VHS, DVD.** John Saxon, Roosevelt "Rosie" Grier, Joanna Cassidy, Joan Blondell, Jack Carter, Aldo Ray; ***D:*** Ross Hagen.

The Gnome-Mobile **1967** A lumber baron and his two grandchildren attempt to reunite a pair of forest gnomes with a lost gnome colony. Brennan has a dual role as both a human and a gnome grandfather. Wynn's last film. Based on a children's novel by Upton Sinclair. **84m/C VHS, DVD.** Walter Brennan, Richard Deacon, Ed Wynn, Karen Dotrice, Matthew Garber; ***D:*** Robert Stevenson; ***C:*** Edward Colman; ***M:*** Buddy (Norman Dale) Baker.

Go **1999 (R)** Episodic tale of Christmas Eve in L.A. and Vegas follows grocery clerk Ronna (Polley) as she takes over a shift for Vegas-bound co-worker Simon (Askew) and also agrees to sub as a go-between for a drug deal between two actors (Mohr and Wolf) and Simon's dealer Todd (Olyphant). Three-part narrative also shows Simon's wild ride in Vegas with his buddies and the actors' involvement with a weird cop (Fichtner). Everybody seems to be doing everything at a break-neck pace, and the fact that all the activity is dangerous or illegal makes it that much more fun. Liman does a fine job of sorting out characters and plotlines, and the performances tag this as a star maker for a few of the cast members, most notably Polley and Diggs. **103m/C VHS, DVD.** Sarah Polley, Katie Holmes, Scott Wolf, Jay Mohr, Desmond Askew, Taye Diggs, William Fichtner, Breckin Meyer, Jane Krakowski, Timothy Olyphant, J.E. Freeman, James Duval, Nathan Bexton, Jay Paulson, Jimmy Shubert; ***D:*** Doug Liman; ***W:*** John August; ***C:*** Doug Liman.

The Go-Between 1/2 **1971 (PG)** Wonderful tale of hidden love. Young boy Guard acts as a messenger between the aristocratic Christie and her former lover Bates. But tragedy befalls them all when the lovers are discovered. The story is told as the elderly messenger (now played by Redgrave) recalls his younger days as the go-between and builds to a climax when he is once again asked to be a messenger for the lady he loved long ago. Based on a story by L.P. Hartley. **116m/C VHS.** *GB* Julie Christie, Alan Bates, Dominic Guard, Margaret Leighton, Michael Redgrave, Michael Gough, Edward Fox; ***D:*** Joseph Losey; ***W:*** Harold Pinter; ***C:*** Gerry Fisher; ***M:*** Michel Legrand. British Acad. '71: Screenplay, Support. Actor (Fox), Support. Actress (Leighton); Cannes '71: Film.

Go Down Death 1/2 **1941** In this early all-black film, a minister is caught in a moral dilemma literally between Heaven and Hell. Scenes of the afterlife are taken from early silent films. **63m/B VHS, DVD.** Myra D. Hemmings, Samuel H. James, Eddy L. Houston, Spencer Williams Jr., Amos Droughan; ***D:*** Spencer Williams Jr.

Go Fish **1994 (R)** Low-budget girl-meets-girl romantic comedy finds Kia (McMillan) playing matchmaker for her roommate, energetic Max (Turner), by setting her up with shy Ely (Brodie). The opposites do, eventually, attract, with their friends eager for every detail. Good-natured and candid, with a welcome lack of melodrama. **87m/B VHS, DVD.** Guinevere Turner, V.S. Brodie, T. Wendy McMillan, Anastasia Sharp, Migdalia Melendez; ***D:*** Rose Troche; ***W:*** Guinevere Turner, Rose Troche; ***C:*** Ann T. Rossetti; ***M:*** Brendan Dolan, Jennifer Sharpe.

Go for Broke! 1/2 **1951** Inexperienced officer Johnson heads a special WWII attack force which is made up of Japanese Americans. Sent to fight in Europe, they prove their bravery and loyalty to all. Good, offbeat story. **92m/B VHS, DVD.** Van Johnson, Gianna Maria Canale, Warner Anderson, Lane Nakano, George Miki; ***D:*** Robert Pirosh; ***W:*** Robert Pirosh; ***C:*** Paul Vogel; ***M:*** Alberto Colombo.

Go for It **1983 (PG)** Oddball super-cops go after a mad scientist—who has created a deadly "K"-bomb—and they encounter killer whales, karate busboys and malevolent Shirley Temple clones along the way. **109m/C VHS.** *IT* Bud Spencer, Terence Hill, David Huddleston; ***D:*** E.B. (Enzo Barboni) Clucher.

Go for the Gold **1984** A young marathon runner risks his girlfriend's love when he decides to pursue fame and fortune. **98m/C VHS.** James Ryan, Cameron Mitchell, Sandra Horne; ***D:*** Jackie Cooper; ***M:*** David McHugh.

Go for Zucker *Alles Auf Zucker!* **2005** Two estranged Jewish brothers, one living in eastern Germany, the other in the west, must clean up their act in order to receive the inheritance their recently-deceased mother left behind. As stated in the will, they must reconcile their differences and, more importantly, adhere to strict Jewish Orthodox conventions. Contrived storyline and loads of Jewish stereotypes drag this one into sitcom territory. A hit in Germany, but something is lost in translation for sure. **90m/C DVD.** Henry Hubchen, Hannelore Elsner, Udo Samel, Sebastian Blomberg, Rolf Hoppe, Golda Tencer, Steffen Groth, Anja Franke, Elena Uhlig; ***D:*** Dani Levy; ***W:*** Dani Levy, Holgar Franke; ***C:*** Carl F. Koschnick; ***M:*** Niki Reiser.

Go Further 1/2 **2003** Documentary follows Woody Harrelson and his "Merry Hempsters" as they travel up and down the Pacific coast by bike, preaching the virtues of a Green lifestyle. Pushing its message to the converted, film is cloying and about as subtle as a jackhammer. Harrelson does, however, come across as surprisingly intelligent and well-informed. Who could have guessed? **80m/C DVD.** *CA* Woody Harrelson; ***D:*** Ron Mann; ***C:*** Robert Fresco; ***M:*** Guido Luciani.

Go-Get-'Em-Haines **1935** Newsman Boyd follows a fleeing bankrupt utilities tycoon onto an ocean liner for an interview only to end up trying to solve the tycoon's murder. **61m/C VHS, DVD.** William Boyd, Sheila Terry, Eleanor Hunt, Leroy Mason, Lloyd Ingraham, Jimmy Aubrey, Clarence Geldart, Louis Natheaux, Lee Shumway; ***D:*** Sam Newfield.

The Go-Getter **1954** Wild slapstick fun in the world of business. **78m/C VHS.** Hank McCune, Beverly Garland, Thurston Hall, Ray Collins, Andrew Tombes; ***D:*** Leslie Goodwins, Leigh Jason; ***W:*** Earl Baldwin, Charles Maxwell; ***C:*** Charles Straumer.

The Go-Getter **2007 (R)** Quirky indie with a certain charm. Aimless 19-year-old Mercer White (Pucci) needs to inform his long-gone half-brother Arlen (Garcia) that their mother has died. So he steals a station wagon and heads off on a road adventure. A cell phone left behind rings and it's car owner Kate (Deschanel), who for some reason that will eventually be revealed, allows Mercer to continue his journey as long as he fills her in on his progress. Which is problematic since Arlen's a louse who has left trouble wherever he's been. Eventually, Mercer hooks up with Kate in the flesh and there's a confrontation with Arlen down Mexico way. **93m/C DVD.** Lou Taylor Pucci, Zooey Deschanel, Jena Malone, Jsu Garcia, William Lee Scott, Julio Oscar Mechoso, Nick Offerman; ***Cameos:*** Bill Duke; ***D:*** Martin Hynes; ***W:*** Martin Hynes; ***C:*** Byron Shah; ***M:*** M. Ward.

Go Into Your Dance **1935** Irresponsible Broadway star Al Howard (Jolson) is blackballed by producers so his agent sister Molly (Farrell) teams him with her dancer friend Dorothy (Keller) for a Chicago nightclub gig. When they're a success, Al wants to open his own club in New York and borrows money from gangster Duke (Maclane). Then he ignores sweet Dorothy for sultry chanteuse Luana (Morgan), who's already involved with Duke. Jolson and Keeler were married at the time they filmed this. **89m/B DVD.** Al Jolson, Ruby Keeler, Barton MacLane, Glenda Farrell, Helen Morgan, Patsy Kelly; ***D:*** Archie Mayo; ***W:*** Earl Baldwin; ***C:*** Gaetano Antonio "Tony" Gaudio.

Go, Johnny Go! **1959** Rock promoter Alan Freed molds a young orphan into rock sensation "Johnny Melody." Musical performances include Ritchie Valens (his only film appearance), Eddie Cochran, Jackie Wilson. **75m/B VHS.** Alan Freed, Sandy Stewart, Chuck Berry, Jimmy Clanton, Eddie Cochran, Jackie Wilson, Ritchie Valens; ***D:*** Paul Landres.

Go Kill and Come Back **1968 (PG)** A bounty hunter tracks down a notoriously dangerous train robber. **95m/C VHS, DVD.** Gilbert Roland, George Helton, Edd Byrnes; ***D:*** Enzo G. Castellari.

The Go-Masters *Mikan No Taikyoku* **1982** Historic co-production between Japan and China, centering on the ancient strategy board game "Go." A young competitor becomes obsessed with winning at any price. Episodic tale of the relationships between a Japanese and Chinese family spans 30 years and was critically acclaimed in both China and Japan. In Japanese and Chinese with English subtitles. **134m/C VHS.** *JP CH* Huang Zong-Ying, Du Peng, Yu Shao-Kang, Lui Xin, Yoshiko Mita, Keiko Matsuzaka, Mayumi Ogawa, Rentaro Mikuni, Daolin Sun, Shen Guan-Chu, Misako Honno; ***D:*** Junya Sato, Duan Jishun. Montreal World Film Fest. '83: Film.

Go Now 1/2 **1996** Regular guy Nick (Carlyle), a soccer-playing construction worker meets and falls in love with hotel management trainee Karen (Aubrey). All is going well until Nick starts experiencing physical problems—dropping things, double vision, numbness. As his condition worsens, it's confirmed that he's been stricken with Multiple Sclerosis. Nick goes through the usual stages of dealing with the disease, but Winterbottom's film doesn't go through the usual disease-of-the-week motions. Straightforward look at the effects of a debilitating disease doesn't create martyrs or heroes, opting instead for realistic characters and honest emotions and situations. First-rate performance by Carlyle. **87m/C VHS.** *GB* Robert Carlyle, Juliet Aubrey, James Nesbitt, Sophie Okonedo, Berwick Kaler, Tom Watson; ***D:*** Michael Winterbottom; ***W:*** Jimmy McGovern, Paul Powell; ***C:*** Daf Hobson; ***M:*** Alastair Gavin.

Go Tell It on the Mountain 1/2 **1984** Young black boy tries to gain the approval of his stern stepfather in this fine adaptation of James Baldwin's semiautobiographical novel. Set in the 1930s; originally a PBS "American Playhouse" presentation. **100m/C VHS, DVD.** Paul Winfield, Olivia Cole, Ruby Dee, Alfre Woodard, James Bond III, Rosalind Cash, Linda Hopkins; ***D:*** Stan Lathan.

Go Tell the Spartans **1978 (R)** In Vietnam, 1964, a hard-boiled major is ordered to establish a garrison at Muc Wa with a platoon of burned out Americans and Vietnamese mercenaries. Blundering but politically interesting war epic pre-dating the flood of 1980s American-Vietnam apologetics. Based on Daniel Ford's novel. **114m/C VHS, DVD.** Burt Lancaster, Craig Wasson, David Clennon, Marc Singer, Jonathan Goldsmith, Joe Unger, Dennis Howard, Evan C. Kim, John Megna, Hilly Hicks, Dolph Sweet, Clyde Kusatsu, James Hong; ***D:*** Ted Post; ***W:*** Wendell Mayes; ***C:*** Harry Stradling Jr.; ***M:*** Dick Halligan.

Go West 1/2 *Marx Brothers Go West* **1940** The brothers Marx help in the making and un-making of the Old West. Weak, late Marx Bros., but always good for a few yucks. **80m/B VHS, DVD.** Groucho Marx, Chico Marx, Harpo Marx, John Carroll, Diana Lewis, Walter Woolf King, George Lessey, Robert Barrat, June MacCloy; ***D:*** Edward Buzzell; ***W:*** Irving Brecher; ***C:*** Leonard Smith; ***M:*** George Bassman, Roger Edens.

Go West **2005** Ambitious but not always successful stew of ethnic hatred, war, romance, and identity. Kenan (Drmac) is Muslim; his lover Milan (Filpovic) is a Bosnian Serb and when the ethnic conflicts break out in Sarajevo in 1992, the two decide to flee to the Netherlands. Only their train is stopped by Bosnian soldiers, so Milan disguises Kenan as a woman and says she's his wife. Forced to find refuge with Milan's father Ljubo (Serbedzija) in his Bosnian hometown, the two attempt to continue their deception. Then Milan gets drafted and barkeep Ranka (Burina) discovers Kenan's secret. Bosnian with subtitles. **97m/C DVD.** *BS* Rade Serbedzija, Mirjana Karanovic, Tarik Filpovic, Mavio Drmac, Haris Burina; ***Cameos:*** Jeanne Moreau; ***D:*** Ahmed Imamovic; ***W:*** Ahmed Imamovic, Enver Puska; ***C:*** Mustafa Mustafic; ***M:*** Enes Zlatar.

Go West, Young Man 1/2 **1936** West is a movie star whose latest film is premiering in a small town, where she's naturally a sensation. Scott is the muscular farm boy who catches her eye and she decides to hang around in order to catch the rest of him as well. The censors again cut West's most overt sexual and satiric barbs. **80m/B VHS, DVD.** Mae West, Randolph Scott, Warren William, Alice Brady, Elizabeth Patterson, Lyle Talbot, Isabel Jewell; ***D:*** Henry Hathaway; ***W:*** Mae West; ***C:*** Karl Struss.

Goal 2: Living the Dream **2007 (PG-13)** Now that Santiago (Becker) has gained experience with the Newcastle United football (soccer) team, he gets transferred to superstar club Real Madrid. There he's reunited with his old friend Gavin (Nivola), who's thinking about retirement (and some guy named Beckham, who's got a cameo). But with success comes the expansion of Santiago's ego, which alienates fiancee Roz (Friel), among others. **115m/C DVD.** *GB* Kuno Becker, Alessandro Nivola, Anna Friel, Rutger Hauer, Leonor Varela, Stephen (Dillon) Dillane, Elizabeth Pena, Miriam Colon, Sean Pertwee, Frances Barber; ***Cameos:*** David Beckham; ***D:*** Jaume Collet-Serra; ***W:*** Mike Jefferies; ***C:*** Flavio Labiano; ***M:*** Stephen Warbeck.

Goal! The Dream Begins 1/2 **2006 (PG)** Illegal Mexican immigrant Santiago Munez (Becker) dreams of making it big playing soccer. L.A. talent scout Foy (Dillane), who's got U.K. contacts, offers a tryout with Newcastle United. First, the poor Santiago has to get across the pond (grandma helps) but his adjustment is difficult until his partying superstar teammate Gavin (Nivola) gives him a boost. Hits all the inspirational sports cliches (it's a Disney release) but it's good-hearted and good-looking (and that's not just the players). First of a planned trilogy. **118m/C DVD.** *US* Kuno Becker, Alessandro Nivola, Marcel Iures, Stephen (Dillon) Dillane, Anna Friel, Kieran O'Brien, Sean Pertwee, Gary Lewis, Cassandra Bell, Tony Plana, Miriam Colon, Jorge Cervera, Lee Ross, Ashley Walters, Frances Barber, Kevin Knapman; ***Cameos:*** Kieron Dyer, David Beckham; ***D:*** Danny Cannon; ***W:*** Dick Clement, Ian La Frenais, Adrian Butchart; ***C:*** Michael Barrett; ***M:*** Graeme Revell, Graeme Revell.

The Goalie's Anxiety at the Penalty Kick 1/2 *Die Angst Tormannes beim Elfmeter* **1971** A chilling landmark film that established Wenders as one of the chief film voices to emerge from post-war Germany. The story deals with a soccer player who wanders around Vienna after being suspended, commits a random murder, and slowly passes over the brink of sanity and morality. A suspenseful, existential adaptation of the Peter Handke novel. In German with English subtitles. **101m/C VHS.** *GE* Arthur Brauss, Erika Pluhar, Kai (Kay) Fischer; ***D:*** Wim Wenders; ***W:*** Peter Handke, Wim Wenders; ***C:*** Robby Muller; ***M:*** Jurgen Knieper.

Goblin WOOF! **1993** Newlywed couple regret the purchase of their new home when the devilish creature once brought to life by the previous homeowner, a witchcraft performing farmer, is raised from the depths of hell to rip to pieces anyone in its view. Any movie whose promo says "You won't believe your eyes...until he rips them from their sockets" is sure to be a crowd pleaser. Enjoy. **75m/C VHS.** Bobby Westrick, Jenny Admire; ***D:*** Todd Sheets.

God Bless the Child **1988** A young single mother loses her home and she and her seven-year-old daughter are forced to live on the streets. Harrowing TV drama providing no easy answers to the plight of the homeless. **93m/C VHS, DVD.** Mare Winningham, Dorian Harewood, Grace Johnston, Charlaine Woodard, Obba Babatunde, L. Scott Caldwell; ***D:*** Larry Elikann; ***W:*** Dennis Nemec; ***M:*** David Shire. **TV**

God Grew Tired of Us **2006 (PG)** Continuation of 2003's "The Lost Boys of Sudan," which revisits three young Sudanese men—John Bul Dau, Panther Bior, and Daniel Abul Pach—and their adjusting to life in the U.S. as refugees. **89m/C DVD.** *US* John Bul Dau, Panther Bior, Daniel Abul Pach; ***D:*** Christopher Quinn; ***C:*** Paul Daley; ***M:*** Mark Nelson, Mark McAdam, Jamie Staff.

God is My Co-Pilot **1945** Based on the book by Col. Robert Lee Scott (played by Morgan), an ace fighter pilot with Maj. Gen. Chennault's (Massey) famed Fighting Tigers squadron. After multiple engagements against the Japanese in the air over China, Scott is battling illness and nerves in 1942 when he's grounded just before a major air assault. Fairly standard hero story, told in flashbacks, although there's an emphasis on Scott's faith sustaining him, as you might guess from the title. **88m/B VHS.** Dennis Morgan, Raymond Massey, Dane Clark, Alan Hale, Andrea King, John Ridgely, Stanley Ridges, Craig Stevens, Richard Loo, Warren Douglas; ***D:*** Robert Florey; ***W:*** Abem Finkel, Peter Milne; ***C:*** Sid Hickox; ***M:*** Franz Waxman.

God, Man and Devil 1/2 **1949** A wager between God and Satan begins this allegory of money versus the spirit. A poor

Torah scribe, Hershele Dubrovner, has a life that glorifies God until Satan, disguised as a business partner, turns him greedy and dishonest. Dubrovner's success destroys both his religion and his community leaving only betrayal and abandonment. In Yiddish with English subtitles. **100m/B VHS.** Mikhal Mikhalesko, Gustav Berger; ***D:*** Joseph Seiden.

God on Trial ♂♂ **2008** Grim but thoughtful argument about religion (supposedly based on a true incident). Several Jewish prisoners at Auschwitz decide to hold a tribunal to prove that God broke his covenant with Israel by allowing the Holocaust to happen. A trio of judges presides over the trial but the real intent is the discussion about survival and maintaining sanity. **86m/C DVD.** *GB* Anthony Sher, Rupert Graves, Dominic Cooper, Stellan Skarsgard, Stephen (Dillon) Dillane, Jack Shepherd, Blake Ritson, Eddie Marsan; ***D:*** Andy de Emmony; ***W:*** Frank Cottrell Boyce; ***C:*** Wojciech Szepel. **TV**

God Said "Ha!" ♂♂♂ **1999 (PG-13)** Julia Sweeney recounts a very trying year in her life in this adaptation of her one-woman Broadway show. She tells of her brother's fight with lymphoma, which caused him (as well as her parents) to move in with her, as well as her own battle with cervical cancer. Sweeney's wry observations and loving rememberances prevent melodrama from seeping in. As with most monologues-turned-movies, this one works much better in the small-screen setting. **87m/C VHS.** Julia Sweeney; ***D:*** Julia Sweeney; ***W:*** Julia Sweeney; ***C:*** John Hora; ***M:*** Anthony Marinelli.

God Told Me To ♂♂ 1/2 *Demon* **1976 (R)** A religious New York cop is embroiled in occult mysteries while investigating a series of grisly murders. He investigates a religious cult that turns out to be composed of half-human, half-alien beings. A cult-fave Larry Cohen epic. **89m/C VHS, DVD.** Tony LoBianco, Deborah Raffin, Sylvia Sidney, Sandy Dennis, Richard Lynch, Sam Levene, Andy Kaufman, Robert Drivas, Mike Kellin; ***D:*** Larry Cohen; ***W:*** Larry Cohen; ***C:*** Paul Glickman; ***M:*** Frank Cordell.

The Goddess ♂♂♂ **1958** Sordid story of a girl who rises to fame as a celluloid star by making her body available to anyone who can help her career. When the spotlight dims, she keeps going with drugs and alcohol to a bitter end. **105m/B VHS.** Kim Stanley, Lloyd Bridges, Patty Duke; ***D:*** John Cromwell; ***W:*** Paddy Chayefsky.

The Godfather ♂♂♂♂ **1972 (R)** Coppola's award-winning adaptation of Mario Puzo's novel about a fictional Mafia family in the late 1940s. Revenge, envy, and parent-child conflict mix with the rituals of Italian mob life in America. Minutely detailed, with excellent performances by Pacino, Brando, and Caan as the violence-prone Sonny. Film debut of Coppola's daughter Sofia, the infant in the baptism scene, who returns in "Godfather III." The horrific horse scene is an instant chiller. Indisputably an instant piece of American culture. Followed by two sequels. **171m/C VHS, DVD.** Marlon Brando, Al Pacino, Robert Duvall, James Caan, Diane Keaton, John Cazale, Talia Shire, Richard Conte, Richard S. Castellano, Abe Vigoda, Alex Rocco, Sterling Hayden, John Marley, Al Lettieri, Sofia Coppola, Al Martino, Morgana King, Joe Spinell, Gianni Russo, Lenny Montana, Richard Bright, Tony Giorgio, Victor Rendina, Simonetta Stefanelli, Angelo Infanti; ***D:*** Francis Ford Coppola; ***W:*** Mario Puzo, Francis Ford Coppola; ***C:*** Gordon Willis; ***M:*** Nino Rota. Oscars '72: Actor (Brando), Adapt. Screenplay, Picture; AFI '98: Top 100; Directors Guild '72: Director (Coppola); Golden Globes '73: Actor—Drama (Brando), Director (Coppola), Film—Drama, Screenplay, Score; Natl. Bd. of Review '72: Support. Actor (Pacino), Natl. Film Reg. '90;; N.Y. Film Critics '72: Support. Actor (Duvall); Natl. Soc. Film Critics '72: Actor (Pacino); Writers Guild '72: Adapt. Screenplay.

The Godfather 1902-1959: The Complete Epic ♂♂♂♂ **1981** Coppola's epic work concerning the lives of a New York crime family. Comprises the first two "Godfather" films, reedited into a chronological framework of the Corleone family history, with much previously discarded footage restored. **386m/C VHS.** Marlon Brando, Al Pacino, Robert Duvall, James Caan, Richard S. Castellano, Diane Keaton, Robert De Niro, John Cazale, Lee Strasberg, Talia Shire, Michael V. Gazzo, Troy Donahue, Joe Spinell, Abe Vigoda, Alex Rocco, Sterling Hayden, John Marley, Richard Conte, G.D. Spradlin, Bruno Kirby, Harry Dean Stanton, Roger Corman, Al Lettieri; ***D:*** Francis Ford Coppola; ***W:*** Mario Puzo, Francis Ford Coppola.

The Godfather, Part 2 ♂♂♂♂ **1974 (R)** A continuation and retracing of the first film, interpolating the maintenance of the Corleone family by the aging Michael, and its founding by the young Vito (De Niro, in a terrific performance) 60 years before in NYC's Little Italy. Often considered the second half of one film, the two films stand as one of American film's greatest efforts, and as a 1970s high-water mark. Combined into one work for TV presentation. Followed by a sequel. **200m/C VHS, DVD.** Al Pacino, Robert De Niro, Diane Keaton, Robert Duvall, James Caan, Danny Aiello, John Cazale, Lee Strasberg, Talia Shire, Michael V. Gazzo, Troy Donahue, Joe Spinell, Abe Vigoda, Marianna Hill, Fay Spain, G.D. Spradlin, Bruno Kirby, Harry Dean Stanton, Roger Corman, Kathleen Beller, John Aprea, Morgana King, Dominic Chianese, Frank Sivero, Gianni Russo, Peter Donat; ***D:*** Francis Ford Coppola; ***W:*** Francis Ford Coppola, Mario Puzo; ***C:*** Gordon Willis; ***M:*** Nino Rota, Carmine Coppola. Oscars '74: Adapt. Screenplay, Art Dir./Set Dec., Director (Coppola), Picture, Support. Actor (De Niro), Orig. Dramatic Score; AFI '98: Top 100; Directors Guild '74: Director (Coppola), Natl. Film Reg. '93;; Natl. Soc. Film Critics '74: Director (Coppola); Writers Guild '74: Adapt. Screenplay.

The Godfather, Part 3 ♂♂♂ **1990 (R)** Don Corleone (Pacino), now aging and guilt-ridden, determines to buy his salvation by investing in the Catholic Church, which he finds to be a more corrupt brotherhood than his own. Meanwhile, back on the homefront, his young daughter discovers her sexuality as she falls in love with her first cousin. Weakest entry of the trilogy is still a stunning and inevitable conclusion to the story; Pacino adds exquisite finishing touches to his time-worn character. Beautifully photographed in Italy by Gordon Willis. Video release contains the final director's cut featuring nine minutes of footage not included in the theatrical release. **170m/C VHS, DVD.** Al Pacino, Diane Keaton, Andy Garcia, Joe Mantegna, George Hamilton, Talia Shire, Sofia Coppola, Eli Wallach, Don Novello, Bridget Fonda, John Savage, Al Martino, Raf Vallone, Franc D'Ambrosio, Donal Donnelly, Richard Bright, Helmut Berger; ***D:*** Francis Ford Coppola; ***W:*** Mario Puzo, Francis Ford Coppola; ***C:*** Gordon Willis; ***M:*** Carmine Coppola. Golden Raspberries '90: Worst Support. Actress (Coppola), Worst New Star (Coppola).

Godmoney ♂♂ 1/2 **1997 (R)** Nathan (Rodney) is a New York street kid who tries to clean up his life of drugs and crime by moving to the Los Angeles suburbs where he is recruited by Matthew (Field), a dealer who tries to get him back into his old ways. Director Doane's debut made an impression on the festival circuit, and it deserves its reputation. Despite a background in music videos, he is able to tell a coherent story about interesting characters without letting style overpower substance. **99m/C VHS, DVD.** Rick Rodney, Bobby Field, Christi Allen; ***D:*** Darren Doane; ***W:*** Darren Doane, Sean Atkins, Sean Nelson; ***M:*** Nicholas Rivera.

Gods and Generals ♂♂ **2003 (PG-13)** Maxwell's ambitious second film in his "Civil War trilogy" is exquisite in its attention to period detail, and grand in its depiction of the battles it covers, but suffers when it gets to the stories of the men it portrays. A prequel to 1993's "Gettysburg," this one covers the years 1861-63, beginning with Gen. Lee (Duvall) declining command of the Union Army, through the battles of First Manassas, Fredericksburg, and Chancelorsville, and finishing with Stonewall Jackson's death and the events leading up to Gettysburg. The main problem is that the dialogue (housed in many self-important and overlong speeches) is stilted, lifeless, and humorless, which handcuffs a very talented cast. Historic personages are raised to icon status, showing none of the real-life flaws that would've made them interesting. Based on the novel by Jeffrey M. Shaara. **220m/C VHS, DVD, Blu-ray Disc, HD DVD.** *US* Jeff Daniels, Stephen Lang, Robert Duvall, Kevin Conway, C. Thomas Howell, Patrick Gorman, Brian Mallon, Matt Letscher, William Sanderson, Mira Sorvino, Frankie Faison, Jeremy London, Kail Rocha, Bruce Boxleitner, Billy Campbell, Bo Brinkman, Mia Dillon, Stephen Spacek, Royce D. Applegate, William Morgan Sheppard; ***Cameos:*** Ted Turner; ***D:*** Ronald F. Maxwell; ***W:*** Ronald F. Maxwell; ***C:*** Kees Van Oostrum; ***M:*** John (Gianni) Frizzell, Randy Edelman.

Gods and Monsters ♂♂♂ 1/2 **1998** Although British director James Whale (McKellen) had a varied (if short) Hollywood career in the '30s and '40s, his name rested on his Universal horror films: "The Invisible Man," "Frankenstein," and "The Bride of Frankenstein." Now long-retired and suffering from ill-health, the openly gay Whale lives quietly in L.A. with his protective housekeeper, Hanna (Redgrave). Whale does enjoy the company of his new gardener—hunky, hetero ex-Marine Clayton Boone (Fraser)—but a stroke has left the director with a confusing sense of reality—returning him to his soldiering days in WWI and "Frankenstein" re-creations. Brilliant performance from McKellen, with solid support from Fraser and Redgrave. Based on the novel "Father of Frankenstein" by Christopher Bram. **105m/C VHS, DVD.** Ian McKellen, Brendan Fraser, Lynn Redgrave, Lolita (David) Davidovich, David Dukes, Kevin J. O'Connor, Brandon Kleyla, Jack Plotnick, Rosalind Ayres, Arthur Dignam, Jack Betts, Martin Ferrero, David Millbern; ***D:*** Bill Condon; ***W:*** Bill Condon; ***C:*** Stephen M. Katz; ***M:*** Carter Burwell. Oscars '98: Adapt. Screenplay; Golden Globes '99: Support. Actress (Redgrave); Ind. Spirit '99: Actor (McKellen), Film, Support. Actress (Redgrave); L.A. Film Critics '98: Actor (McKellen); Natl. Bd. of Review '98: Actor (McKellen), Film; Broadcast Film Critics '98: Actor (McKellen).

God's Bloody Acre WOOF! **1975 (R)** Three backwoods mountain-dwelling brothers kill construction workers in order to defend their land, and then begin preying on vacationers. **90m/C VHS.** Scott Lawrence, Jennifer Gregory, Sam Moree, Shiang Hwa Chyang; ***D:*** Harry Kerwin.

God's Comedy ♂♂ *A Comedia de Deus* **1995** Joao de Deus (Monteiro) is a lecherous ice-cream maker who indulges himself with the ice cream counter girls and some nighttime fantasies. But when he asks the daughter of the local butcher to indulge him as well, her father decides that Joao needs to be taught a lesson. Portuguese with subtitles. **163m/C VHS, DVD.** *PT* Joao Cesar Monteiro, Claudia Teixeira, Manuela de Freitas, Raquel Ascensao, Saraiva Serrano; ***D:*** Joao Cesar Monteiro; ***W:*** Joao Cesar Monteiro; ***C:*** Mario Barroso.

God's Country ♂♂ **1946** A loner kills a man in self-defense and escapes the pursuing law by disappearing into California Redwood country with his dog. **62m/C VHS.** Robert Lowery, Helen Gilbert, William Farnum, Buster Keaton; ***D:*** Robert Emmett Tansey.

God's Country and the Man ♂♂ **1937** Typical western adventurer about a cowboy out to nab a gunman who's been threatening the life of a dance hall girl. Plenty of two-fisted action when law-abiding Keene shows up. **56m/B VHS, DVD.** Tom Keene, Betty Compson, Charlotte Henry, Charles "Blackie" King, Billy Bletcher, Eddie (Ed, Eddy, Edwin) Parker; ***D:*** Robert North Bradbury; ***W:*** Robert Emmett.

God's Gun ♂ *A Bullet from God* **1975 (R)** Preacher who was once a gunfighter seeks revenge on the men who tried to kill him. Parolini used the pseudonym Frank Kramer. **93m/C VHS, DVD.** Richard Boone, Lee Van Cleef, Jack Palance, Sybil Danning; ***D:*** Gianfranco Parolini.

God's Little Acre ♂♂♂ **1958** Delves into the unexpectedly passionate lives of Georgia farmers. One man, convinced there's buried teasure on his land, nearly brings himself and his family to ruin trying to find it. Based on the novel by Erskine Caldwell. **110m/B VHS, DVD.** Robert Ryan, Tina Louise, Michael Landon, Buddy Hackett, Vic Morrow, Jack Lord, Aldo Ray, Fay Spain; ***D:*** Anthony Mann; ***W:*** Philip Yordan; ***C:*** Hans J. Haller; ***M:*** Elmer Bernstein.

God's Lonely Man ♂♂ **1996** Ernest Rackman (Wyle) is one of life's losers. He gets fired from his videostore job and suffers bouts of violence and suicidal impulses. Then he poses as a police officer in order to "rescue" teenaged prostitute Christiane (McComb) so they can begin a new life together but this also doesn't go as planned. **98m/C VHS, DVD.** Michael Wyle, Heather McComb, Justine Bateman, Paul Dooley, Roxana Zal, Wallace (Wally) Langham, Kieran Mulroney; ***D:*** Frank Von Zerneck; ***W:*** Frank Von Zerneck; ***C:*** Dennis Smith; ***M:*** James Fearnley.

The Gods Must Be Crazy ♂♂♂ 1/2 **1984 (PG)** An innocent and charming film. A peaceful Bushman travels into the civilized world to return a Coke bottle "to the gods." Along the way he meets a transplanted schoolteacher, an oafishly clumsy microbiologist and a gang of fanatical terrorists. A very popular film, disarmingly crammed with slapstick and broad humor of every sort. Followed by a weak sequel. **109m/C VHS, DVD.** *SA* N!xau, Marius Weyers, Sandra Prinsloo, Louw Verwey, Jamie Uys, Michael Thys, Nic de Jager; ***D:*** Jamie Uys; ***W:*** Jamie Uys; ***C:*** Robert M. Lewis, Buster Reynolds; ***M:*** John Boshoff, Johnny Bishop.

The Gods Must Be Crazy 2 ♂♂ 1/2 **1989 (PG)** A slapdash sequel to the original 1981 African chortler, featuring more ridiculous shenanigans in the bush. This time the bushman's children find themselves in civilization and N!xau must use his unique ingenuity to secure their safe return. **90m/C VHS, DVD.** N!xau, Lena Farugia, Hans Strydom, Eiros Nadies, Eric Bowen; ***D:*** Jamie Uys; ***M:*** Charles Fox.

Gods of the Plague ♂♂♂ *Gotter der Pest* **1969** Fassbinder goes noir—or grey with lots of sharp lighting—in this gangster-auteur tale of robbery gone awry. The requisite trappings of the crime genre (guys and dolls and cops and robbers) provide a vague backdrop (and a vague plot) for a moody story full of teutonic angst and alienation, and that certain Fassbinder feeling (which, need we say, isn't to everyone's taste). An early effort by the director, who remade the story later the same year as "The American Soldier" (Fassbinder acts in both). In German with (difficult-to-read) English subtitles. **92m/C VHS, DVD.** *GE* Hanna Schygulla, Harry Bear; ***D:*** Rainer Werner Fassbinder.

Gods of Wu Tang WOOF! *Godz of Wu Tang; Duel of the Masters; Fei cheung goh hiu; Fei xiang guo he* **1983** Two egotistical Kung Fu fighters have spent their entire lives fighting one another, but now team together once they realize that if they don't train disciples nobody will carry on their art (or their feud). Asked to investigate a haunted house they discover a couple of con artists. And then a hopping vampire comes along just to spoil their success. **95m/C DVD.** *HK* Emily Chu, Norman Chu, Hark-On Fung, Wilson Tong, Brandy Yuen; ***D:*** Wilson Tong.

God's Sandbox ♂ 1/2 *Tahara* **2002** This one takes a strange turn from family drama and romance into politics and religion and never finds its proper path again. Israeli author Liz tries to reconnect with rebellious daughter Rachel, who is working at a Sinai Desert resort. Liz is mistrustful of Rachel's friendship with co-worker Mustapha because he is a Bedouin, but he is eager to regale her with a local legend. Seems in the 1960s another wild child Israeli, Leila, fell in love with a local sheik's son, but her acceptance into his tribe revolves around her agreeing to the rite of female circumcision. And yes, the two stories tie together. Arabic and Hebrew with subtitles. **86m/C DVD.** *IS* Razia Israeli, Orli Perel, Sami Samir, Meital Dohan, Juliano Merr; ***D:*** Doran Eran; ***W:*** Yoav Halevy, Hanita Halevy; ***C:*** Claudio Steinberg; ***M:*** Arik Rudich.

The Godsend ♂ **1979 (R)** "Omen" rip-off about a little girl who is thrust upon a couple. After adopting her, they lose their natural family to her evil ways. **93m/C VHS.** *CA* Cyd Hayman, Malcolm Stoddard, Angela Pleasence, Patrick Barr; ***D:*** Gabrielle Beaumont.

Godsend ♂♂ **2004 (PG-13)** Playing like a dozen similar demon-child redos, pic tries for originality by combining modern technology with typical genre supernatural creepiness. Cute 8-year-old Adam Duncan is killed in a freak auto accident. Grieving parents Paul (Kinnear) and Jessie (Romijn-Stamos) have no sooner buried their adored son when they are approached by Dr. Wells (De Niro) who offers to harvest their dead son's cells for cloning and subsequent rebirth via Jessie. Naturally, the couple agree. When the Adam clone reaches his eighth birthday, however, things start to go eerily awry. Kinnear and Romijn-Stamos are convincing while De Niro has more problems with his cliched character. **102m/C VHS, DVD.** *US* Greg Kinnear, Rebecca Romijn, Cameron Bright, Robert De Niro, Merwin Mondesir, Deborah Odell, Jack Simons, Elle Downs, Zoie Palmer; ***D:*** Nick Hamm; ***W:*** Mark Bomback; ***C:*** Kramer Morgenthau; ***M:*** Brian Tyler.

The Godson **1998 (PG-13)** When Guiseppe "the Guppy" Calzone becomes the head of his crime family, he realizes his son and heir will need some tutoring to become the next big boss. So he sends the kid to Mafia U. to pick up some tricks of the trade. But the head of a rival family sees this as the perfect opportunity to get rid of the Calzone clan. Really, really dumb, despite the comic cast. **100m/C VHS, DVD.** Rodney Dangerfield, Dom DeLuise, Kevin McDonald, Fabiana Udenio, Lou Ferrigno, Barbara Crampton; ***D:*** Bob Hoge; ***W:*** Bob Hoge; ***C:*** Tom Lappin; ***M:*** Boris Elkis. **VIDEO**

Godspell **½ 1973 (G)** Musical retelling of the story of Jesus, set in New York City. Adapted from an enjoyable Broadway play but the film version comes off as silly. Good dancing and interesting score. ♫ Day by Day; By My Side; Alas For You; On the Willows; O, Bless the Lord My Soul; Prepare Ye the Way of the Lord; Turn Back O Man; Beautiful City; Save the People. **103m/C VHS, DVD.** Victor Garber, David Haskell, Jerry Sroka, Lynne Thigpen, Gilmer McCormick; ***D:*** David Greene; ***M:*** Stephen Schwartz.

Godzilla **½ 1998 (PG-13)** Over-the-top remake of the 1954 cult classic has nuclear testing in France creating a giant mutant lizard to destroy all boats, piers, people, and buildings that happen to get in its way. Gone are the days of a man in a rubber suit menacing Tokyo, replaced by state-of-the-art special effects. Third rate storyline has wimpy biologist Niko Tatopoulos (Broderick) hired to track down and connect with the beast, only to realize that Godzilla has chosen the Big Apple as the birthing place for its huge brood. When various supporting characters (including Reno as a French secret agent out to destroy Godzilla) cross paths with the creature, what results looks amazingly similar to one hugely successful dinosaur movie and its sequel. Ending leaves door wide open for an inevitable sequel of its own. **138m/C VHS, DVD, UMD.** Matthew Broderick, Jean Reno, Maria Pitillo, Hank Azaria, Kevin Dunn, Michael Lerner, Harry Shearer, Arabella Field, Vicki Lewis, Doug Savant, Malcolm Danare; ***D:*** Roland Emmerich; ***W:*** Roland Emmerich, Dean Devlin; ***C:*** Ueli Steiger; ***M:*** David Arnold. Golden Raspberries '98: Worst Remake/Sequel, Worst Support. Actress (Pitillo).

Godzilla, King of the Monsters ½ *Gojira* **1956** An underwater prehistoric reptile emerges from the depths to terrorize Tokyo after he has been awakened by atomic testing. Burr's scenes are intercut in the American version, where he serves as a narrator telling the monster's tale in flashbacks. Ridiculously primitive special effects even in its own day. One of the first post-WWII Japanese films to break through commercially in the U.S. **80m/B VHS, DVD.** *JP* Raymond Burr, Takashi Shimura, Akira Takarada, Akihiko Hirata, Momoko Kochi, Sachio Sakai, Fuyuki Murakami, Ren Yamamoto; ***D:*** Inoshiro Honda, Terry Morse; ***W:*** Inoshiro Honda, Takeo Murata; ***C:*** Masao Tamai, Guy Roe; ***M:*** Akira Ifukube.

Godzilla 1985 ½ **1985 (PG)** Godzilla is awakened from underwater slumber by trolling nuclear submarines belonging to the superpowers near Japan. The giant monster's newly acquired appetite for nuclear energy inadvertently precipitates an international incident. Burr is called in (as the only living American witness to Godzilla's destructive 1955 outburst) to help mediate the conflict. Film released to coincide with the 30th anniversary of the original. **91m/C VHS.** *JP* Keiju Kobayashi, Ken Tanaka, Raymond Burr, Yasuka Sawaguchi, Shin Takumaa; ***D:*** Kohji Hashimoto, Robert J. Kizer; ***W:*** Shuichi Nagahara, Lisa Tomei; ***C:*** Kazutami Hara; ***M:*** Reijiro Koroku.

Godzilla on Monster Island *Godzilla vs. Gigan* **1972** Even Godzilla himself cannot hope to take on both Ghidra and Gigan alone and hope to succeed. Therefore he summons his pal Angillus for help. Together, they offer Earth its only hope of survival. Though the terror may repel you, the movie is a must for Godzilla fans; it's his first speaking part. **89m/C VHS, DVD.** *JP* Hiroshi Ichikawa, Tomoko Umeda, Yuriko Hishimi, Minoru Takashima, Zan Fujita; ***D:*** Jun Fukuda.

Godzilla Raids Again *Gigantis, the Fire Monster; Godzilla's Counter Attack* **1955** Warner Bros. had a problem securing rights to Godzilla's name. Yearning for a change of pace, the King of Monsters opts to destroy Osaka instead of Tokyo, but the spiny Angorous is out to dethrone our hero. Citizens flee in terror when the battle royale begins. The first Godzilla sequel. **78m/B VHS, DVD.** *JP* Hugo Grimaldi, Makayama, Minoru Chiaki; ***D:*** Motoyoshi Oda; ***W:*** Shigeaki Hidaka; ***C:*** Seichi Endo; ***M:*** Masaru Sato.

Godzilla 2000 **1999 (PG)** Any other bigger-than-life movie-house hero starring in a series of films that span almost 50 years would have to answer some serious questions about plot repetition—but not Godzilla. The familiarity is what you pay to see. If Godzilla didn't clumsily destroy Tokyo office buildings and knock commuter trains off their elevated tracks, you'd be asking for a refund, pronto. So, with the latest Japanese flick to make it to our shores—featuring the REAL Godzilla, not that sophisticated American excuse for a Godzilla from a couple of years back—all is well. Funny dubbing, rubber suits, miniature sets—perfect comfort food on a rainy afternoon. As far as the plot goes...in short, spacecraft attacks Tokyo—the radioactive dinosaur comes to the rescue. **97m/C VHS, DVD.** *JP* Takehiro Murata, Shiro Sano, Hiroshi Abe, Naomi Nishida, Mayu Suzuki; ***D:*** Takao Okawara; ***W:*** Hiroshi Kashiwabara, Waturu Mimura; ***C:*** Katsuhiro Kato; ***M:*** Takayuki Hattori.

Godzilla vs. Biollante *Gojira tai Biorante* **1989 (PG)** Five years after Japan was destroyed, scientists are studying Godzilla's cells. Desparate spies, who apparently can't find their own Godzilla cells on all the ruined buildings, relaease Godzilla from his volcanic prison. When one scientist's attempt to create a super-plant goes awry and creates the behemoth Biollante, the monsters go at it in a giant territorial rumble. Japan (or a really small model thereof) is once again underfoot. Sequel to "Godzilla 1985." **104m/C VHS.** *JP* Koji Takahashi, Yoshiko Tanaka, Megumi Odaka, Kunihiko Mitamura, Masahiro Takashima, Kenpachiro Satsuma; ***D:*** Kazuki Omori; ***W:*** Kazuki Omori; ***C:*** Yudai Kato.

Godzilla vs. King Ghidora ½ **1991** Tokyo begins to panic when aliens from the 23rd century make an appearance. But these aliens supposedly come in peace—warning that Godzilla will soon reawaken and destroy Japan unless he can be destroyed first. But it turns out these beings aren't so benign and soon Godzilla is confronted by his arch-enemy—flying, three-headed King Ghidora. **89m/C VHS, DVD.** *JP* Richard Berger, Kiwako Harada, Kent Gilbert, Shoji Kobayashi; ***D:*** Kazuki Omori; ***W:*** Kazuki Omori; ***C:*** Yoshinori Sekiguchi; ***M:*** Akira Ifukube.

Godzilla vs. Mechagodzilla II ½ **1993** Mechagodzilla II, a mammoth robot fueled by a nuclear reactor and sheathed in a synthetic diamond shield, is supposed to protect Japan from Godzilla. The mechanical monster has its work cut out for it now that Godzilla and Rodan have both arrived to claim the recently hatched baby Godzilla from a team of scientists. **108m/C VHS, DVD.** *JP* Masahiro Takashima, Leo Mangetti; ***D:*** Takao Okawara.

Godzilla vs. Megalon ½ *Gojira tai Megaro* **1976 (G)** Godzilla's creators show their gratitude to misguided but faithful American audiences by transforming the giant monster into a good guy. This time, the world is threatened by Megalon, the giant cockroach, and Gigan, a flying metal creature, simultaneously. Fortunately, the slippery hero's robot pal Jet Jaguar is on hand to slug it out side by side with Tokyo's ultimate defender. **80m/C VHS, DVD.** *JP* Katsuhiko Sasakai, Hiroyuki Kawase, Yutaka Hayashi, Robert Dunham, Kotaro Tomita; ***D:*** Jun Fukuda; ***W:*** Jun Fukuda, Shinichi Sekizawa; ***C:*** Yuzuru Aizawa; ***M:*** Richiro Manabe.

Godzilla vs. Monster Zero *Monster Zero; Battle of the Astros; Invasion of the Astro-Monsters; Invasion of the Astros; Invasion of Planet X; Kaiju Daisenso; The Great Monster War; War of the Monsters* **1968 (G)** Novel Godzilla adventure with the big guy and Rodan in outer space. Suspicious denizens of Planet X require the help of Godzilla and Rodan to rid themselves of the menacing Ghidra, whom they refer to as Monster Zero. Will they, in return, help Earth as promised, or is this just one big, fat double cross? **93m/C VHS, DVD.** *JP* Akira Takarada, Nick Adams, Kumi Mizuno, Jun Tazaki, Akira Kubo, Keiko Sawai, Yoshio Tsuchiya, Noriko Sengoku, Fuyuki Murakami; ***D:*** Inoshiro Honda; ***W:*** Shinichi Sekizawa; ***C:*** Hajime Koizumi; ***M:*** Akira Ifukube.

Godzilla vs. Mothra *Godzilla vs. the Thing; Godzilla vs. the Giant Moth; Godzilla Fights the Giant Moth; Mothra vs. Godzilla; Mosura tai Gojira* **1964** Mighty Mothra is called in to save the populace from Godzilla, who is on a rampage; and he's aided by two junior Mothras who hatch in the nick of time. The hesitant moth avoids the fire-breathing behemoth until succumbing to the pleadings of the Peanut Sisters to save humanity. Hilarious special effects inspire more laughter from derision than anything else. **88m/C VHS, DVD.** *JP* Akira Takarada, Yuriko Hoshi, Hiroshi Koizumi, Emi Ito, Yumi Ito, Yoshifumi Tajima, Kenji Sahara, Yu Fujiki; ***D:*** Inoshiro Honda; ***W:*** Shinichi Sekizawa; ***C:*** Hajime Koizumi; ***M:*** Akira Ifukube.

Godzilla vs. the Cosmic Monster *Godzilla Versus the Bionic Monster; Godzilla vs. Mechagodzilla; Gojira Tai Meka-Gojira* **1974 (G)** Godzilla's worst nightmares become a reality as he is forced to take on the one foe he cannot defeat—a metal clone of himself! To make matters worse, Earth is in dire peril at the hands of cosmic apes. We all need friends, and Godzilla is never more happy to see his buddy King Seeser, who gladly lends a claw. **80m/C VHS, DVD.** *JP* Masaki Daimon, Kazuya Aoyama, Reiko Tajima, Barbara Lynn, Akihiko Hirata; ***D:*** Jun Fukuda.

Godzilla vs. the Sea Monster **WOOF!** *Nankai No Kai Ketto; Ebirah, Terror of the Deep; Big Duel in the North* **1966** Godzilla makes friends with former rival Mothra (a giant moth) and together they bash on Ebirah, an enormous lobster backed by an evil cadre of (human) totalitarians. The unrepentant crusteacean turns the tables on our heroes, however, by growing a new tentacle everytime one is ripped off. Meanwhile, a frenzied batch of helpless humans are trapped on an island about to explode, if they aren't drowned first in a shower of reptilian backwash. **80m/C VHS, DVD.** *JP* Kumi Mizuno, Chotaro Togin, Hideo Sunazuka, Akira Tekarada; ***D:*** Jun Fukuda; ***W:*** Shinichi Sekizawa, Kazuo Yamada; ***C:*** Masaru Sato.

Godzilla vs. the Smog Monster *Gojira Tai Hedora; Godzilla vs. Hedora* **1972 (G)** Godzilla battles a creature borne of pollution, a 400-pound sludge blob named Hedora. Early 1970s period piece conveys interesting attitude towards pollution; it's treated as a sinister force that people are powerless to stop. Japanese teenagers marshal their dancing talents to combat the threat amid the hypnotic swirl of disco lighting. Great opening song: "Save the Earth." Dubbed in English. **87m/C VHS, DVD.** *JP* Akira Yamauchi, Hiroyuki Kawase, Toshio Shibaki; ***D:*** Yoshimitu Banno.

Godzilla's Revenge *Oru Kaiju Daishingeki* **1969** A young boy who is having problems dreams of going to Monster Island to learn from Minya, Godzilla's son. Using the lessons in real life, the boy captures some bandits and outwits a bully. Uses footage from "Godzilla vs. the Sea Monster" and "Son of Godzilla" for battle scenes. One of the silliest Godzilla movies around. **70m/C VHS, DVD.** *JP* Kenji Sahara, Tomonori Yazaki, Machiko Naka, Sachio Sakai, Chotaro Togin, Yoshifumi Tajima, Eisei Amamoto, Ikio Sawamura; ***D:*** Inoshiro Honda; ***W:*** Shinichi Sekizawa; ***C:*** Sokei Tomioka; ***M:*** Kunio Miyauchi.

The Goebbels Experiment **2005** Documentary on Joseph Goebbels, Hitler's minister of propaganda, taken from diaries covering 1924 to 1945. Archival footage illustrates the readings. Kenneth Branagh narrates the English version; Udo Samel the German one. **107m/C DVD.** ***D:*** Lutz Hachmeister; ***W:*** Lutz Hachmeister, Michael Kloft; ***C:*** Hajo Schomerus; ***M:*** Hubert Bittman.

Goin' Coconuts **1978 (PG)** Donny and Marie are miscast as Donny and Marie in this smarmy story of crooks and jewels. Seems someone covets the chanteuse's necklace, and only gratuitous crooning can spare the twosome from certain swindling. Big bore on the big island. **93m/C VHS.** Donny Osmond, Marie Osmond, Herb Edelman, Kenneth Mars, Ted Cassidy, Marc Lawrence, Harold Sakata; ***D:*** Howard Morris.

Goin' South **1978 (PG)** An outlaw is saved from being hanged by a young woman who agrees to marry him in exchange for his help working a secret gold mine. They try to get the loot before his old gang gets wind of it. A tongue-in-cheek western that served as Nicholson's second directorial effort. Movie debuts of Steenburgen and Belushi. **109m/C VHS, DVD.** Jack Nicholson, Mary Steenburgen, John Belushi, Christopher Lloyd, Veronica Cartwright, Richard Bradford, Danny DeVito, Luana Anders, Ed Begley Jr., Anne Ramsey; ***D:*** Jack Nicholson; ***W:*** Charles Shyer; ***C:*** Nestor Almendros; ***M:*** Perry Botkin.

Goin' to Town **½ 1935** Complicated yarn with West as a woman who inherits an oil field and becomes the wealthiest woman in the state. She falls for British engineer Cavanagh and decides to become a "lady" in order to get his attention. There's a subplot about Buenos Aires and a crooked horse race, an in-name-only marriage to a high society type, and a murder before Mae finally gets her man. **71m/B VHS, DVD.** Mae West, Paul Cavanagh, Gilbert Emery, Ivan Lebedeff, Marjorie Gateson, Tito Coral, Monroe Owsley; ***D:*** Alexander Hall; ***W:*** Mae West; ***C:*** Karl Struss.

Goin' to Town **1944** Radio team Lum and Abner in one of their last films, as two conmen who scheme to make money from a phony oil well. **77m/B VHS.** Chester Lauck, Norris Goff, Barbara Hale, Grady Sutton, Florence Lake; ***D:*** Leslie Goodwins; ***W:*** Charles E. Roberts, Charles Marion; ***C:*** Robert Pittack; ***M:*** Lud Gluskin.

Going All the Way **½ 1997 (R)** Korean War vets Sonny Burns (Davies) and Gunner Casselman (Affleck) find themselves becoming best buds after returning to their Indianapolis hometown in 1954. Gunner's the self-confident stud, who vaguely wants to be an artist, while aspiring photographer Sonny's an anxious geek. The boys have mom troubles (Sonny's is a bible-thumper while Gunner's is a seductive flirt) and chase girls with varying success but the true bonding is strictly male. Davies is appropriately twitchy while Affleck gets to effectively use his natural charisma. Wakefield adapted from his 1970 novel. **110m/C VHS, DVD.** Jeremy Davies, Ben Affleck, Jill Clayburgh, Lesley Ann Warren, Rose McGowan, Rachel Weisz, Amy Locane; ***D:*** Mark Pellington; ***W:*** Dan Wakefield; ***C:*** Bobby Bukowski.

Going Ape! **1981 (PG)** Danza inherits a bunch of orangutans. If the apes are treated well, a legacy of $5 million will follow. This is all you need to know. **87m/C VHS.** Tony Danza, Jessica Walter, Danny DeVito, Art Metrano, Rick Hurst; ***D:*** Jeremy Joe Kronsberg; ***M:*** Elmer Bernstein.

Going Back **½ 1983** Four friends reunite after college to relive a memorable summer they spent together after graduating from high school. **85m/C VHS.** Bruce Campbell, Christopher Howe, Perry Mallette, Susan W. Yamasaki; ***D:*** Ron Teachworth.

Going Bananas **1988 (PG)** Wacky adventure about a chimp who is being chased by a sinister circus owner. The monkey runs through Africa dragging along a boy, his caretaker, and a guide. The cast says it all. **95m/C VHS.** Dom DeLuise, Jimmie Walker, David Mendenhall, Herbert Lom; ***D:*** Boaz Davidson.

Going Berserk 🦴🦴 1/2 **1983 (R)** The members of SCTV's television comedy troupe are featured in this comedy which lampoons everything from religious cults to kung fu movies. Has moments of inspired lunacy, interspersed with more pedestrian fare. Includes wicked send-up of "Father Knows Best," with former cast member Donahue. **85m/C VHS.** *CA* John Candy, Joe Flaherty, Eugene Levy, Paul Dooley, Pat Hingle, Richard Libertini, Ernie Hudson, Alley Mills, Dixie Carter, Murphy Dunne, Elinor Donahue; ***D:*** David Steinberg.

Going for the Gold: The Bill Johnson Story 🦴🦴 **1985** Biographical tale of the American downhill skier who went from hard-luck punk to Olympic champion in the 1984 games at Sarajevo, Yugoslavia. **100m/C VHS.** Anthony Edwards, Dennis Weaver, Sarah Jessica Parker, Deborah Van Valkenburgh, Wayne Northrop; ***D:*** Don Taylor.

Going Greek 🦴 1/2 **2001 (R)** College freshman/football star Jake (Bruno) is in school on a scholarship and must keep up his grades. That's not going to be easy when his geeky cousin Gil (James) wants to join a fraternity and won't be accepted unless Jake agrees to pledge as well. Jake finds himself loosening up with all the raucous antics of his frat brothers, but his grades begin to suffer as does his relationship with girlfriend Paige (Harris), who despises all fraternities. Gross-out gags and gratuitous nudity abound as you might expect. **90m/C VHS, DVD.** Dylan Bruno, Laura Harris, Simon Rex, Dublin James, Corey Pearson, Oliver Hudson, Steve Monroe; ***D:*** Justin Zackham; ***W:*** Justin Zackham; ***C:*** Kirk Douglas; ***M:*** Nathan Barr. **VIDEO**

Going Hollywood 🦴🦴🦴 **1933** Amusing musical/romantic fluff about a French teacher (Davies) who falls in love with a radio crooner (Crosby in his first MGM film). He's got the movie bug and heads for Hollywood, where he becomes an overnight sensation with a sultry costar (D'Orsay). Davies follows and proceeds to get Crosby out of D'Orsay's clutches and winds up replacing her rival in the film, promptly becoming a star herself. The underrated Davies was a fine light comedienne and supplied glamour to the production as well. Kelly, in her film debut, supplied the slapstick. The last Hearst-Cosmopolitan production made with MGM. ♫ Temptation; We'll Make Hay While the Sun Shines; Going Hollywood; Our Big Love Scene; After Sundown; Cinderella's Fella; Beautiful Girl; Just an Echo in the Valley. **78m/B VHS.** Marion Davies, Bing Crosby, Fifi d'Orsay, Stuart Erwin, Patsy Kelly, Ned Sparks; ***D:*** Raoul Walsh; ***W:*** Donald Ogden Stewart; ***C:*** George J. Folsey.

Going Home 🦴🦴 1/2 **1986** During WWI, Canadian soldiers held in British camps awaiting transport back home stage a riot over the endless delays and intolerable conditions. A fact-based story of the events leading up to this tragedy. **100m/C VHS.** Nicholas (Nick) Campbell, Paul Maxwell, Eugene Lipinski; ***D:*** Terence Ryan; ***C:*** Paul Reed.

Going in Style 🦴🦴🦴 1/2 **1979 (PG)** Three elderly gentlemen, tired of doing nothing, decide to liven up their lives by pulling a daylight bank stick-up. They don't care about the consequences because anything is better than sitting on a park bench all day long. The real fun begins when they get away with the robbery. Great cast makes this a winner. **91m/C VHS, DVD.** George Burns, Art Carney, Lee Strasberg; ***D:*** Martin Brest; ***W:*** Martin Brest.

Going My Way 🦴🦴🦴 1/2 **1944** A musical-comedy about a progressive young priest assigned to a downtrodden parish who works to get the parish out of debt, but clashes with his elderly curate, who's set in his ways. Followed by "The Bells of St. Mary's." Fitzgerald's Oscar-winning Supporting Actor performance was also nominated in the Best Actor category. ♫ The Day After Forever; Swinging on a Star; Too-ra-loo-ra-loo-ra; Going My Way; Silent Night; Habanera; Ave Maria. **126m/B VHS, DVD.** Bing Crosby, Barry Fitzgerald, Rise Stevens, Frank McHugh, Gene Lockhart, Porter Hall; ***D:*** Leo McCarey; ***W:*** Frank Butler, Frank Cavett, Leo McCarey; ***C:*** Lionel Lindon. Oscars '44: Actor (Crosby), Director (McCarey), Picture, Screenplay, Song ("Swinging on a Star"), Story, Support. Actor (Fitzgerald); Golden Globes '45: Director (McCarey), Film—Drama, Support. Actor (Fitzgerald), Natl. Film Reg. '04;; N.Y. Film Critics '44: Actor (Fitzgerald), Director (McCarey), Film.

Going Overboard 🦴 *Babes Ahoy* **1989 (R)** Cruise ship waiter dreams of becoming a comedian and gets his big break when the ship's comic disappears. **99m/C VHS, DVD.** Adam Sandler, Burt Young, Billy Zane, Peter Berg; ***D:*** Valerie Breiman.

Going Places 🦴🦴🦴 *Les Valseuses; Making It* **1974 (R)** A cynical, brutal satire about two young thugs traversing the French countryside raping, looting and cavorting as they please. Moreau has a brief role as an ex-con trying to go straight. An amoral, controversial comedy that established both its director and two stars. In French with English subtitles or dubbed. **122m/C VHS, DVD.** *FR* Gerard Depardieu, Patrick Dewaere, Miou-Miou, Isabelle Huppert, Jeanne Moreau, Brigitte Fossey; ***D:*** Bertrand Blier; ***W:*** Bertrand Blier; ***C:*** Bruno Nuytten; ***M:*** Stephane Grappelli.

Going Postal 🦴🦴 *Postal Worker* **1998** Psychologist Dr. Nicolas Brink (Portnow) is hired to create an early warning system to prevent the ticking timebombs of the postal world from going off. But he may be too late as paranoid postal worker Oren Starks (Garrett) becomes obsessed with fellow worker Tammy (Cavanagh), who has already survived one postal shootout. Oren gets fired for harrassment and then Tammy's boyfriend Harry (Futzgerald) gets fired as well for nearly killing another employee in a machinery mishap. So just which of these two will go postal first? A very dark and violent satire. **98m/C VHS, DVD.** Brad Garrett, Grace Cavanaugh, Rob Roy Fitzgerald, Richard Portnow, William Long Jr.; ***D:*** Jeffrey F. Jackson; ***W:*** Jeffrey F. Jackson; ***C:*** Mark Parry; ***M:*** Tim Bryson, Tracy Adams.

Going Shopping 🦴🦴 **2005 (PG-13)** Jaglom indulges his penchant for talky, femme-centered comedies by focusing on Holly (Foyt), the deeply in debt (a man done her wrong) owner of a trendy boutique. She searches for an infusion of cash while hoping a big Mother's Day sale will draw in customers and help salvage her enterprise. Interspersed with Holly's travails is a chorus of women who offer their thoughts on what shopping means to them. **106m/C DVD.** *US* Victoria Foyt, Rob Morrow, Lee Grant, Mae Whitman, Bruce Davison, Cynthia Sikes, Martha Gehman, Pamela Bellwood, Juliet Landau; ***D:*** Henry Jaglom; ***W:*** Victoria Foyt, Henry Jaglom; ***C:*** Hanania Baer; ***M:*** Harriet Schock.

Going the Distance **2010** Aspiring journalist Erin (Barrymore) moves to San Francisco while her boyfriend Garrett (Long), a music scout, remains in Manhattan. They try the bicoastal relationship thing but miscommunication and bad advice as well as their own ambitions could derail their love. **m/C DVD.** *US* Drew Barrymore, Justin Long, Charlie Day, Jason Sudeikis, Ron Livingston, Kelli Garner, Christina Applegate, Jim Gaffigan; ***D:*** Nanette Burstein; ***W:*** Geoff LaTulippe; ***C:*** Eric Steelberg.

Going Under **1991 (PG)** Subsurface military satire about the U.S.S. Sub Standard, the worst nuclear vessel in the Navy. It's so poorly constructed that the brass would rather sink than inspect it—if only they could. Interesting cast sinks with script headed for dry dock. **81m/C VHS.** Bill Pullman, Wendy Schaal, Ned Beatty, Robert Vaughn, Bud Cort, Michael Winslow; ***D:*** Mark W. Travis; ***W:*** Randolph Davis, Darryl Zarubica; ***C:*** Victor Hammer; ***M:*** David Michael Frank.

Going Undercover 🦴 **1988 (PG-13)** A bumbling private investigator is hired to protect a rich, beautiful, and spoiled young woman on her European vacation. Poor excuse for a comedy. **90m/C VHS, DVD.** Lea Thompson, Jean Simmons, Chris Lemmon; ***D:*** James Kenelm Clarke.

Going Upriver: The Long War of John Kerry 🦴🦴 1/2 **2004** Director Butler has known former senator and 2004 presidential candidate John Kerry for some 40 years and has been photographing him since 1969. This matter-of-fact documentary looks at Kerry's military service (with some archival footage shot in Vietnam) and his later role in helping establish the group Vietnam Veterans Against the War. Based on the nonfiction book "Tour of Duty" by Douglas Brinkley. **89m/C DVD.** *US* ***D:*** George Butler; ***W:*** Joseph Dorman; ***C:*** Sandi Sissel; ***M:*** Philip Glass.

The Gold & Glory 🦴 *Coolangatta Gold* **1988 (PG-13)** Two brothers, one a musician, the other an athlete, vie for the affections of the same girl by competing in a footrace for a golden purse. **102m/C VHS.** *AU* Colin Friels, Josephine Smulders, Grant Kenny; ***D:*** Igor Auzins; ***W:*** Peter Schreck; ***C:*** Keith Wagstaff; ***M:*** Bill Conti.

Gold Diggers in Paris 🦴🦴 **1938** A low budget (by musical standards) didn't deter choreographer Busby Berkeley from putting on a girlie show in back-lot Paris. Terry (Vallee) and Duke (Jenkins) own the failing Club Ballee and are quick to accept the mistaken invitation to take their dancers to the Paris International Dance Exposition. A shipboard romance ensues between singer Terry and ballet dancer Kay (Lane) but the troupe is eventually exposed as imposters before a decision is made to let them perform anyway. **100m/B DVD.** Rudy Vallee, Hugh Herbert, Rosemary Lane, Allen Jenkins, Gloria Dickson, Mabel Todd, Melville Cooper, Fritz Feld, Curt Bois, Edward Brophy; ***D:*** Ray Enright; ***W:*** Warren Duff, Earl Baldwin; ***C:*** George Barnes, Sol Polito; ***M:*** Harry Warren.

Gold Diggers of 1933 🦴🦴🦴 1/2 **1933** In this famous period musical, showgirls help a songwriter save his Busby Berkeley-choreographed show. Followed by two sequels. ♫ We're in the Money; Shadow Waltz; I've Got to Sing a Torch Song; Pettin' in the Park; Remember My Forgotten Man. **96m/B VHS, DVD.** Joan Blondell, Ruby Keeler, Aline MacMahon, Dick Powell, Guy Kibbee, Warren William, Ned Sparks, Ginger Rogers; ***D:*** Mervyn LeRoy. Natl. Film Reg. '03.

Gold Diggers of 1935 🦴🦴🦴 **1935** The second Gold Diggers film, having something to do with a New England resort, romance, and a charity show put on at the hotel. Plenty of Berkeleian large-scale drama, especially the bizarre, mock-tragic "Lullaby on Broadway" number, which details the last days of a Broadway baby. ♫ I'm Going Shopping With You; The Words Are in My Heart; Lullaby of Broadway. **95m/B VHS, DVD.** Dick Powell, Adolphe Menjou, Gloria Stuart, Alice Brady, Frank McHugh, Glenda Farrell, Grant Mitchell, Hugh Herbert, Wini Shaw; ***D:*** Busby Berkeley; ***C:*** George Barnes. Oscars '35: Song ("Lullaby of Broadway").

Gold Diggers of 1937 🦴🦴 **1936** Choreographer Busby Berkeley got an Oscar nomination for his dance direction in this glossy film with so-so musical numbers. Insurance agent Peek (Powell) is pressured into selling a million dollar policy to Broadway producer J.J. Hobart (Moore). When J.J. realizes his crooked partners (Perkins, Brown) lost the dough to put on their latest musical, he has a breakdown and Peek and his showgirl squeeze Norma (Blondell) come to the rescue. **101m/B DVD.** Dick Powell, Joan Blondell, Victor Moore, Osgood Perkins, Charles D. Brown, Glenda Farrell, Lee Dixon; ***D:*** Lloyd Bacon; ***W:*** Warren Duff; ***C:*** Arthur Edeson; ***M:*** Harold Arlen.

Gold Diggers: The Secret of Bear Mountain 🦴🦴 1/2 **1995 (PG)** Thirteen-year-old Beth (Ricci) moves to the small town of Wheaton, Washington, and forms an unlikely friendship with rebellious tomboy Jody (Chlumsky). Together, the girls set out on a treasure hunt that takes them into a dangerous trek through sea-coast mountain terrain. The grownups are dumb (and the story's fairly boring) but the two heroines have real appeal. **94m/C VHS.** Christina Ricci, Anna Chlumsky, Polly Draper, Brian Kerwin, Diana Scarwid, David Keith; ***D:*** Kevin James Dobson; ***W:*** Barry Glasser; ***C:*** Ross Berryman; ***M:*** Joel McNeely.

The Gold of Naples 🦴🦴🦴 *L'Oro Di Napoli* **1954** A four-part omnibus film about life in Naples, filled with romance and family tragedies, by turns poignant, funny and pensive. Originally six tales; two were trimmed for U.S. release. In Italian with subtitles. **107m/B VHS.** *IT* Vittorio De Sica, Eduardo de Filippo, Paolo Stoppa, Sophia Loren, Silvana Mangano; ***D:*** Vittorio De Sica.

Gold of the Amazon Women 🦴 *Amazon Women* **1979** When two explorers set out to find gold, they stumble onto a society of man-hungry women who follow them into the urban jungle of Manhattan. There is also a European "R" rated version. **94m/C VHS, DVD.** Bo Svenson, Anita Ekberg, Bond Gideon, Donald Pleasence; ***D:*** Mark L. Lester; ***W:*** Stanley Ralph Ross; ***C:*** David Quaid; ***M:*** Gil Melle. **TV**

Gold of the Seven Saints 🦴 1/2 **1961** Cheaply-made western adventure story has partners Jim (Walker) and Shaun (Moore) striking gold and then trying to transport it through desert and mountain territory with every crook around chasing after them for their treasure. **88m/B DVD.** Clint Walker, Roger Moore, Gene Evans, Chill Wills, Leticia Roman, Robert Middleton; ***D:*** Gordon Douglas; ***W:*** Leonard Freeman, Leigh Brackett; ***C:*** Joseph Biroc; ***M:*** Howard Jackson.

Gold Raiders 🦴 **1951** Larry, Moe, and Shemp team up with an insurance agent to take on the bad guys in the wild west. The Stooges are long past their prime. **56m/B VHS, DVD.** George O'Brien, Moe Howard, Moe Howard, Shemp Howard, Larry Fine, Sheila Ryan, Clem Bevans, Lyle Talbot; ***D:*** Edward L. Bernds.

Gold Raiders 🦴 1/2 **1983** Team of secret agents are sent to the Jungles of Laos to find a plane carrying $200 million worth of gold, and nothing will get in their way. **106m/C VHS.** *GB* Robert Ginty, Sarah Langenfeld, William Steven, Dusty Rhodes; ***D:*** P. (Philip) Chalong.

The Gold Rush 🦴🦴🦴🦴 **1925** Chaplin's most critically acclaimed film. The best definition of his simple approach to film form; adept maneuvering of visual pathos. The "Little Tramp" searches for gold and romance in the Klondike in the mid-1800s. Includes the dance of the rolls, pantomime sequence of eating the shoe, and Chaplin's lovely music. **85m/B VHS, DVD.** Charlie Chaplin, Mack Swain, Tom Murray, Georgia Hale; ***D:*** Charlie Chaplin; ***W:*** Charlie Chaplin; ***C:*** Roland H. Totheroh, Jack Wilson; ***M:*** Charlie Chaplin. AFI '98: Top 100, Natl. Film Reg. '92.

The Golden Bowl 🦴🦴🦴 **1972** Wealthy widower Adam Verver (Morris) and his naive daughter, Maggie (Townsend), are utterly devoted to each other. A situtation that doesn't change with Maggie's marriage to an impoverished Italian prince (Massey). Then Maggie decides her lonely father should also remarry and who could be better than Maggie's old chum, the beautiful Charlotte (Hunnicutt). But what the Ververs don't realize is how well the Prince and Charlotte already know each other. However, a gilded crystal cup—The Golden Bowl—will bring unwelcome knowledge. Based on the novel by Henry James. **270m/C VHS.** *GB* Barry Morse, Jill Townsend, Daniel Massey, Gayle Hunnicutt, Cyril Cusack, Kathleen Byron; ***D:*** James Cellan Jones; ***W:*** Jack Pulman. **TV**

The Golden Bowl 🦴🦴 1/2 **2000 (R)** Beautiful but bloodless Merchant/Ivory adaptation of Henry James' complex 1904 novel set in turn-of-the-century London. Wealthy American aesthete Adam Verver (Nolte) dotes on his only daughter, Maggie (Beckinsale), and even buys her a husband—an impoverished Italian aristocrat, Prince Amerigo (a miscast Northam), whom she loves. But, unknown to both Ververs, the prince and Maggie's best friend, the equally poor Charlotte (Thurman), had a long ago affair that gets rekindled, even though Charlotte has become the wife of Adam. A studied menage a quartre where just what anyone knows (or suspects) is never made clear. **130m/C VHS, DVD.** *GB US FR* Nick Nolte, Uma Thurman, Kate Beckinsale, Jeremy Northam, Anjelica Huston, James Fox, Madeleine Potter, Peter Eyre; ***D:*** James Ivory; ***W:*** Ruth Prawer Jhabvala; ***C:*** Tony Pierce-Roberts; ***M:*** Richard Robbins.

Golden Boy 🦴🦴🦴 **1939** Holden plays a young and gifted violinist who earns money for his musical education by working as a part-time prizefighter. Fight promoter Menjou has Stanwyck cozy up to the impressionable young man to convince him to make the fight game his prime concern. She's successful but it leads to tragedy. Holden's screen debut, with Cobb as his immigrant father and Stanwyck successfully slinky as the corrupting love interest. Classic pugilistic drama with well-staged fight scenes. Based on Clifford Odets' play with toned down finale. **99m/B VHS.** William Holden, Adolphe Menjou, Barbara Stanwyck, Lee J. Cobb, Joseph Calleia, Sam Levene, Don Beddoe, Charles Halton; ***D:*** Rouben Mamoulian; ***W:*** Daniel Taradash, Victor Heerman, Sarah Y. Mason.

The Golden Boys 🦴 1/2 **2008 (PG)** Surprisingly boring flick billed as a romantic comedy that's not very romantic. It's set in 1905 on Cape Cod where three grisly retired sea captains decide one of them should marry so they can be looked after properly. Widow Martha Snow answers their newspaper ad but Perez and Jeremiah try to back out of the arrangement, leaving Zebulon to woo the take-charge female. **97m/C DVD.** David Carradine, Bruce Dern, Rip Torn, Mariel Hemingway, Charles Durning, John Savage, Angelica Torn, Julie Harris; ***D:*** Daniel Adams; ***W:*** Daniel Adams; ***C:*** Philip D. Schwartz; ***M:*** Jonathan Edwards.

The Golden Child 🦴🦴 **1986 (PG-13)** When a Tibetan child with magic powers is kidnapped and transported to Los Angeles, Chandler, a professional "finder of lost children" must come to the rescue. The search takes him through Chinatown in a hunt that cliches every Oriental swashbuckler ever made. Good fun. **94m/C VHS, DVD.** Eddie Murphy, Charlotte Lewis, Charles Dance, Victor Wong, Randall "Tex" Cobb, James Hong; ***D:*** Michael Ritchie; ***W:*** Dennis Feldman; ***C:*** Donald E. Thorin; ***M:*** Michel Colombier.

The Golden Coach 🦴🦴🦴 *Le Carrosse D'Or* **1952** Based on a play by Prosper Merimee, the tale of an 18th-century actress in Spanish South America who takes on all comers, including the local viceroy who creates a scandal by presenting her with his official coach. Rare cinematography by Claude Renoir. **101m/C VHS, DVD.** *FR* Anna Magnani, Odoardo Spadaro, Nada Fiorelli, Dante Rino, Duncan Lamont; ***D:*** Jean Renoir; ***W:*** Ginette Doynel, Jack Kirkland, Giulio Macchi, Jean Renoir; ***C:*** Claude Renoir, Ronald Hill; ***M:*** Antonio Vivaldi.

The Golden Compass 🦴🦴 **2007 (PG-13)** 12-year-old Lyra (Richards) lives in a world similar to Victorian England and ruled by the church-like Magisterium, who seem dead set on controlling the minds of everyone in the world and eliminating free will. When best friend Roger (Walker) disappears, Lyra, alongside a strange assortment of allies including a talking, armored bear (McKellan) and a pilot with a Texas accent (Elliot), travels north to rescue him, despite the Magisterium and their ice-queen agent Ms. Coulter's(Kidman) best efforts to stop her. The all-star cast is exceptional, but the story may confound without the book as a roadmap. The film stirred a mild controversy because of the anti-religion themes of the book upon which it was based (the first installment of Philip Pullman's popular British fantasy trilogy), even though writer/director Weitz mostly cut those parts from the movie. **118m/C DVD, Blu-ray Disc.** *US* Nicole Kidman, Daniel Craig, Eva Green, Christopher Lee, Dakota Blue Richards, Sam Elliott, Ben Walker, Tom Courtenay, Derek Jacobi, Kathy Bates; ***D:*** Chris Weitz; ***W:*** Chris Weitz; ***C:*** Henry Braham; ***M:*** Alexandre Desplat; ***V:*** Kristin Scott Thomas, Freddie Highmore, Ian McKellen, Ian McShane. Oscars '07: Visual FX; British Acad. '07: Visual FX.

Golden Dawn 🦴 **1930** A legendarily bad production with a very strange plot that's based on the 1927 Broadway operetta (yes, there's singing in the movie too). Dawn (Siegel) is a white woman, apparently adopted and raised by a native tribe in WWI-era Dutch East Africa. She's first shown in a German POW camp but is released when trouble arises with her tribe since Dawn has been chosen as the sacrificial bride to the tribe's god. However, Dawn is in love with rubber planter Tom Allen (King), who must rescue her. It was originally filmed in two-strip Technicolor although those prints have been lost. **81m/B DVD.** Vivienne Siegel, Walter Woolf King, Noah Beery Sr., Lupino Lane, Alice Gentle, Edward Martindel; ***D:*** Ray Enright; ***W:*** Walter Anthony; ***C:*** Devereaux Jennings.

Golden Demon 🦴🦴 1/2 *Konjiki Yasha* **1953** An acclaimed Japanese epic, from the novel by Koyo Ozaki, about the destructive powers of wealth on the lives of two star-crossed lovers in medieval Japan. In Japanese with English subtitles. **95m/C VHS.** *JP* Jun Negami, Fujiko Yamamoto; ***D:*** Koji Shima.

Golden Earrings 🦴🦴 1/2 **1947** Enjoyable, yet incredulous story about British agent Milland joining up with gypsy Dietrich for espionage work. Absurd film was so bad it became a camp classic overnight. Although Dietrich and Milland couldn't stand each other and battled constantly during production, the movie did quite well at the boxoffice. Based on a novel by Yolanda Foldes. **95m/B VHS, DVD.** Ray Milland, Marlene Dietrich, Bruce Lester, Dennis Hoey, Quentin Reynolds, Reinhold Schunzel, Ivan Triesault; ***D:*** Mitchell Leisen; ***W:*** Abraham Polonsky, Frank Butler, Helen Deutsch; ***C:*** Daniel F. Fapp.

Golden Gate 🦴🦴 **1993 (R)** Young Fed Dillon is thrown into the hysteria of the communist witch hunt in 1952 San Francisco. He snares Song, a Chinese labor activist, on some very dubious charges. Ten years later he finds himself getting involved with Song's daughter Marilyn (Chen), who knows nothing about her lover's involvement with her family. Then she finds out. Ever-changing moods, sometimes film noir, sometimes a love story, sometimes a nostalgic look back, are confusing. Promising storyline meanders and fades as Director Madden tries to do too much in a short time. Beware of broad stereotypes in every character. **95m/C VHS.** Matt Dillon, Joan Chen, Bruno Kirby, Teri Polo, Tzi Ma, Stan(ford) Egi, Peter Murnik, Jack Shearer, George Giudall; ***D:*** John Madden; ***W:*** David Henry Hwang; ***C:*** Bobby Bukowski; ***M:*** Elliot Goldenthal.

Golden Gloves 🦴 1/2 **1940** Early example of the boxing noir genre looks inside the seedy world of racketeer Naish (Taggerty), who operates small clubs featuring badly mismatched fights to give the customers the brutal knockouts they're hungry for. When a young fighter is killed in a match, Richard Denning (Crane), a regular in Naish's clubs joins newspaperman Robert Paige (Matson) in an effort to clean up the amateur matches. Naish doesn't take the threat to his racket lying down and sends out his goons with the classic cloak and dagger. **66m/B DVD.** Richard Denning, J. Carrol Naish, Robert Paige, William Frawley; ***D:*** Edward Dmytryk, Felix Feist; ***W:*** Lewis R. Foster, Maxwell Shane, Joe Ansen; ***C:*** Henry Sharp, John L. "Jack" Russell; ***M:*** Arthur Lange.

Golden Lady 🦴 1/2 **1979** Beautiful woman leads her female gang in a deadly game of international intrigue. **90m/C VHS.** Christina World, Suzanne Danielle, June Chadwick; ***D:*** Joseph (Jose Ramon) Larraz.

Golden Rendezvous 🦴🦴 *Nuclear Terror* **1977** A tale of treachery aboard a "gambler's paradise" luxury liner which is hijacked and held for ransom. Based on Alistair MacLean's novel. **103m/C VHS.** Richard Harris, David Janssen, John Carradine, Burgess Meredith, Ann Turkel, John Vernon; ***D:*** Ashley Lazarus.

The Golden Salamander 🦴🦴 **1951** Howard shines in otherwise lackluster adventure about archaeologist searching for ancient ruins in Tunisia who must deal with gun runners and their evil leader, while torridly romancing a beautiful Tunisian girl. Filmed on location in Tunis. Based on the novel by Victor Canning. **96m/B VHS.** *GB* Trevor Howard, Anouk Aimee, Herbert Lom, Miles Malleson, Walter Rilla, Jacques Sernas, Wilfrid Hyde-White, Peter Copley, Eugene Deckers, Henry Edwards, Marcel Poncin, Percy Walsh, Sybilla Binder, Kathleen Boutall, Valentine Dyall; ***D:*** Ronald Neame; ***C:*** Oswald Morris.

The Golden Seal 🦴🦴 1/2 **1983 (PG)** Tale of a small boy's innocence put in direct conflict, because of his love of a rare wild golden seal and her pup, with the failed dreams, pride and ordinary greed of adults. **94m/C VHS, DVD.** Steve Railsback, Michael Beck, Penelope Milford, Torquil Campbell; ***D:*** Frank Zuniga; ***M:*** John Barry.

The Golden Spiders: A Nero Wolfe Mystery 🦴🦴 1/2 **2000** It's actually not much of a mystery but writer Rex Stout's eccentric Wolfe (Chaykin) and his idiosyncratic cast of helpers as well as the setting (Manhattan in the late '40s) make for some amusing moments. Gourmand and orchid grower Wolfe never leaves his brownstone, preferring right-hand man Archie Goodwin (Hutton) take care of the leg work. The golden spiders of the title are a pair of flashy earrings worn by a damsel in distress that leads to several hit-and-run deaths, blackmail, and fraud. **100m/C VHS, DVD.** Maury Chaykin, Timothy Hutton, Bill Smitrovich, Saul Rubinek, Mimi Kuzyk, Beau Starr, Robert Clark, Larissa Lapchinski, Gary Reineke, Nicky Guadagni, Robert Bockstael, Trent McMullen; ***D:*** Bill Duke; ***W:*** Paul Monash; ***C:*** Mike Fash; ***M:*** Michael Small. **CABLE**

The Golden Stallion 🦴 1/2 **1949** Trigger falls in love with a stunning mare. He sees her villainous owners abusing her and kills them. Roy takes the blame for his equine pal, but true love triumphs to save the day. **67m/B VHS.** Roy Rogers, Dale Evans, Estelita Rodriguez, Pat Brady, Douglas Evans, Frank Fenton; ***D:*** William Witney.

Golden Swallow 🦴🦴🦴 *Jin yan zi; The Girl with the Thunderbolt Kick; The Shaolin Swallow* **1968** Not to be confused with a Chinese ghost film from the 1980s with a similar name, this is technically a sequel to the film "Come Drink With Me." The Golden Swallow (Cheng Pei-pei) must investigate several murders that have her trademark calling card left at the scene, thus implicating her. She discovers a young man seeking revenge for the murder of his loved ones and eventually agrees to help him bring them to justice. Far more violent than the previous film, it also includes an unfortunate romantic triangle, as our young would-be hero and another kung fu fighter vie for Golden Swallow's affections. **104m/C DVD.** *HK* Pei Pei Cheng, Yu Wang, Lie Lo, Hsin Yen Chao; ***D:*** Cheh Chang; ***W:*** Cheh Chang, Yun Chih Tu; ***C:*** Hsueh Li Pao; ***M:*** Fu-ling Wang.

Golden Voyage of Sinbad 🦴🦴 1/2 **1973 (G)** In the mysterious ancient land of Lemuria, Sinbad and his crew encounter magical and mystical creatures. A statue of Nirvana comes to life and engages in a sword fight with Sinbad. He later meets up with a one-eyed centaur and a griffin. Ray Harryhausen can once again claim credit for the unusual and wonderful mythical creatures springing to life. **105m/C VHS, DVD.** John Phillip Law, Caroline Munro, Tom Baker, Douglas Wilmer, Martin Shaw, John David Garfield, Gregoire Aslan; ***D:*** Gordon Hessler; ***W:*** Brian Clemens; ***C:*** Ted Moore; ***M:*** Miklos Rozsa.

Goldeneye 🦴🦴🦴 **1995 (PG-13)** Bond is back, in the long-awaited (eight years) debut of Brosnan as legendary Brit agent 007. Since we're through the Cold War, Bond has to make do with the villainy of the Russian Mafia, who are planning to sabotage global financial markets utilizing the "Goldeneye" satellite weapon. There's a spectacularly impossible stunt to start things out in familiar territory and lots more noisy (if prolonged) action pieces. Brosnan (who looks great in a tux) is slyly self-aware that his character is more myth than man and Janssen does a suitably over-the-top job as bad Bond girl Xenia Onatopp. Tina Turner sings the dreary title track. **130m/C VHS, DVD.** Pierce Brosnan, Famke Janssen, Sean Bean, Izabela Scorupco, Joe Don Baker, Robbie Coltrane, Judi Dench, Tcheky Karyo, Gottfried John, Alan Cumming, Desmond Llewelyn, Michael Kitchen, Serena Gordon, Samantha Bond, Minnie Driver; ***D:*** Martin Campbell; ***W:*** Jeffrey Caine, Michael France; ***C:*** Phil Meheux; ***M:*** Eric Serra. Blockbuster '96: Action Actor, T. (Brosnan).

Goldeneye: The Secret Life of Ian Fleming 🦴🦴 1/2 *Spymaster* **1989** James Bond's creator lead quite an interesting life himself. The debonair author joins His Majesty's Secret Service and gets involved in numerous romantic exploits. Not to be confused with the British TV movie "Spymaker," which also covered Fleming's early career. **103m/C VHS.** *GB* Charles Dance, Phyllis Logan, Julian Fellowes, Patrick Ryecart, Ed Devereaux; ***D:*** Don Boyd; ***W:*** Reg Gadney; ***C:*** Mike Southon; ***M:*** Michael Berkeley. **TV**

Goldengirl 🦴🦴 **1979 (PG)** A neo-Nazi doctor tries to make a superwoman of his daughter who has been specially fed, exercised, and emotionally conditioned since childhood to run in the Olympics. Anton's starring debut. **107m/C VHS.** Susan Anton, James Coburn, Curt Jurgens, Robert Culp, Leslie Caron, Harry Guardino, Jessica Walter; ***D:*** Joseph Sargent; ***M:*** Bill Conti.

Goldenrod 🦴 1/2 **1977** A successful rodeo champion is forced to reevaluate his life when he sustains a crippling accident in the ring. **100m/C VHS.** *CA* Tony LoBianco, Gloria Carlin, Donald Pleasence, Donnelly Rhodes; ***D:*** Harvey Hart. **TV**

Goldfinger 🦴🦴🦴 **1964 (PG)** Ian Fleming's James Bond, Agent 007, attempts to prevent international gold smuggler Goldfinger and his pilot Pussy Galore from robbing Fort Knox. Features villainous assistant Oddjob and his deadly bowler hat. The third in the series is perhaps the most popular. Shirley Bassey sings the theme song. **117m/C VHS, DVD.** *GB* Sean Connery, Honor Blackman, Gert Frobe, Shirley Eaton, Tania Mallet, Harold Sakata, Cec Linder, Bernard Lee, Lois Maxwell, Desmond Llewelyn, Nadja Regin; ***D:*** Guy Hamilton; ***W:*** Paul Dehn, Richard Maibaum; ***C:*** Ted Moore; ***M:*** John Barry. Oscars '64: Sound FX Editing.

Goldilocks & the Three Bears 🦴🦴 1/2 **1983** Entry from "Faerie Tale Theatre" tells the story of Goldilocks, who wanders through the woods and finds the home of three bears—only in this version Goldilocks is a nasty child, and it's the bears who'll get your sympathy. **60m/C VHS, DVD.** Tatum O'Neal, Alex Karras, Brandis Kemp, Donovan Scott, Hoyt Axton, John Lithgow, Carole King; ***D:*** Gilbert Cates.

Goldrush: A Real Life Alaskan Adventure 🦴🦴 1/2 **1998** Well-bred Frances (Milano) decides to leave New York society life behind and join an expedition to Alaska (as a would-be gold miner) during the 1899 gold rush. **89m/C VHS.** Alyssa Milano, Bruce Campbell, Stan Cahill, Tom Scholte, William Morgan Sheppard; ***D:*** John Power; ***W:*** Jacqueline Feather, David Seidler. **TV**

Goldstein 🦴🦴 1/2 **1964** After strolling out of Lake Michigan, a mysterious old man roams around Chicago and causes a profound reaction in the people he meets. One man, a sculptor, becomes so affected that he scours the city for him while trying to make up with his pregnant ex-girlfriend, who decides to have an abortion that becomes an oddly comical experience. Unique debut film of notable director Kaufman was filmed in various locations throughout Chicago in the 1960s. **79m/B DVD.** Lou Gilbert, Tomas Erhart, Severn Darden, Ellen Madison, Benito Carruthers; ***D:*** Philip Kaufman, Benjamin Manaster; ***W:*** Philip Kaufman, Benjamin Manaster; ***C:*** Jean-Phillippe Carson; ***M:*** Meyer Kupferman.

The Goldwyn Follies 🦴🦴 **1938** Lavish disjointed musical comedy about Hollywood. A movie producer chooses a naive girl to give him advice on his movies. George Gershwin died during the filming. ♫ Romeo and Juliet; Water Nymph; Here, Pussy, Pussy; Serenade To a Fish; Love Walked In; Love is Here to Stay; Spring Again; I Was Doing Alright; La Serenata. **115m/C VHS, DVD.** Adolphe Menjou, Vera Zorina, Al Ritz, Harry Ritz, Jimmy Ritz, Helen Jepson, Phil Baker, Bobby Clark, Ella Logan, Andrea Leeds, Edgar Bergen; ***D:*** George Marshall; ***C:*** Gregg Toland; ***M:*** George Gershwin, Ira Gershwin.

The Golem 🦴🦴🦴 1/2 *Der Golem, wie er in die Welt kam* **1920** A huge clay figure is given life by a rabbi in hopes of saving the Jews in the ghetto of medieval Prague. Rarely seen Wegener expressionist mythopus that heavily influenced the "Frankenstein" films of the sound era. **80m/B VHS, DVD.** *GE* Paul Wegener, Albert Steinruck, Ernst Deutsch, Lyda Salmonava, Otto Gebuehr, Max Kronert, Loni Nest, Greta Schroder, Hans Sturm; ***D:*** Carl Boese, Paul Wegener; ***W:*** Henrik Galeen, Paul Wegener; ***C:*** Karl Freund; ***M:*** Hans Landberger.

Goliath Against the Giants 🦴 1/2 *Goliath Contro I Giganti; Goliat Contra Los Gigantes; Goliath and the Giants* **1963** Goliath takes on Bokan, who has stolen his throne. Goliath must fight Amazons, storms, and sea monsters to save the lovely Elea. Goliath conquers all. **95m/C VHS.** *IT SP* Brad Harris, Gloria Milland, Fernando Rey, Barbara

Carroll; ***D:*** Guido Malatesta.

Goliath and the Barbarians 🦴🦴 *Il Terror Dei Barbaberi* **1960** Goliath and his men go after the barbarians who are terrorizing and ravaging the Northern Italian countryside during the fall of the Roman Empire. A basic Reeves muscleman epic. **86m/C VHS.** *IT* Steve Reeves, Bruce Cabot; ***D:*** Carlo Campogalliani; ***M:*** Les Baxter.

Goliath and the Dragon WOOF! *La Vendetta di Ercole* **1961** Even Goliath must have doubts as he is challenged by the evil and powerful King Eurystheus. A must for fans of ridiculous movies with ridiculous monsters. **90m/C VHS, DVD.** *IT FR* Bruce Cabot, Mark Forest, Broderick Crawford, Gaby Andre, Leonora Ruffo; ***D:*** Vittorio Cottafavi; ***W:*** Marco Piccolo, Archibald Zounds Jr.; ***C:*** Mario Montuori; ***M:*** Les Baxter.

Goliath and the Sins of Babylon 🦴🦴 *Maciste, L'Eroe Piu Grande Del Mondo* **1964** Well-sculpted Forest plays yet another mesomorph to the rescue in this poorly dubbed spaghetti legend. Goliath must spare 24 virgins whom the evil Crisa would submit as human sacrifice. Forest—who played the mythic Maciste in a number of films—was randomly assigned the identity of Goliath, Hercules, or Samson for U.S. viewing; go figure. **80m/C VHS.** *IT* Mark Forest, Eleanora Bianchi, Jose Greco, Giuliano Gemma, Paul Muller; ***D:*** Michele Lupo.

Goliath Awaits 🦴🦴 **1981** Harmon plays an oceanographer who discovers a ship that was sunk by German U-boats during WWI. Nothing much new there, except that the survivors still reside on board the vessel, some 40 years after the oceanliner was torpedoed. And get this: they're living a quasi-Utopian existence. Kind of hard to swallow. Made for TV, it originally aired in two parts. **110m/C VHS.** Mark Harmon, Robert Forster, Christopher Lee, Eddie Albert, John Carradine, Alex Cord, Emma Samms, Jean Marsh; ***D:*** Kevin Connor; ***M:*** George Duning. **TV**

Gomorrah 🦴🦴🦴 **2008** This is nothing like "The Godfather." Instead it's a dramatization of Saviano's expose of Neapolitan crime as controlled by the so-called Camorra families. Director Garrone avoids glamorizing the violence as he uses five interconnecting stories to demonstrate their insidious control in all areas of daily life. Then things actually get worse as rival factions start a turf war. It's complicated keeping track of the different characters and power struggles but it's slice-of-life realism at its best. Italian with subtitles. **137m/C DVD.** *IT* Salvatore Abruzzese, Gianfelice Imparato, Maria Nazionale, Toni Servillo, Carmine Paternoster, Salvatore Cantalupo, Gigio Morra, Marco Macor, Ciro Petrone, Ciro Petrone; ***D:*** Matteo Garrone; ***W:*** Matteo Garrone, Ugo Chiti, Massimo Gaudioso, Roberto Saviano, Maurizio Braucci; ***C:*** Marco Onorato; ***M:*** Neil Davidge, Robert Del Naja, Euan Dickinson.

Gone Are the Days 🦴🦴 ½ *The Man From C.O.T.T.O.N., Purlie Victorious* **1963** Shaky adaptation of the play, "Purlie Victorious." A black preacher wants to cause the ruin of a white plantation owner. Alda's screen debut. **97m/B VHS, DVD.** Ossie Davis, Ruby Dee, Sorrell Booke, Godfrey Cambridge, Alan Alda, Beah Richards; ***D:*** Nicholas Webster; ***W:*** Ossie Davis; ***C:*** Boris Kaufman.

Gone Are the Days 🦴🦴 **1984** Government agent (Korman) is assigned to protect a family who witnessed an underworld shooting, but the family would like to get away from both the mob and the police. Disney comedy is well-acted but done in by cliches. **90m/C VHS, DVD.** Harvey Korman, Susan Anspach, Robert Hogan; ***D:*** Gabrielle Beaumont. **CABLE**

Gone Baby Gone 🦴🦴🦴 **2007 (R)** In working-class Dorchester (Boston), four-year-old Amanda McCready has been abducted. Cops Jack Doyle (Freeman) and Remy Bressant (Harris) are on the scene, but it's not enough for Amanda's Aunt Beatrice (Madigan). She hires private detectives Patrick Kenzie (the younger Affleck) and Angie Gennaro (Monaghan), locals with better access to neighborhood folks who may not talk to police. Mom Helene (Ryan) is tough to sympathize with—a drinker and druggie who lives in near squalor and who seems apathetic at best about her daughter's disappearance. Stellar performances, nuance, plot twists, and a distinctly un-Hollywood gritty Boston backdrop create a crime thriller that offers an uncomfortable edge of moral dilemma. The brothers Affleck and the rest of the crew put out a commendable effort, with Ben a pleasant surprise behind the camera and Casey an equally pleasant surprise in front of it. **115m/C DVD, Blu-ray Disc.** *US* Casey Affleck, Michelle Monaghan, Morgan Freeman, Ed Harris, John Ashton, Amy Ryan, Amy Madigan, Titus Welliver, Michael K. Williams, Edi Gathegi, Jill Quigg; ***D:*** Ben Affleck; ***W:*** Ben Affleck, Aaron Stockard; ***C:*** John Toll; ***M:*** Harry Gregson-Williams.

Gone Dark 🦴🦴 *The Limit* **2003 (R)** Out to score a big drug bust, undercover agent Monica (Forlani) is in too deep as she has affairs with the kingpin and his right-hand man, Denny, all while becoming addicted to heroin. When Denny ends up dead, Monica fears that an elderly neighbor, May (Bacall), might know too much and in her frenzied state she holds her captive but May's not about to succumb. Forlani and Bacall do their best to redeem director Webb's freshman effort as it labors through jerky scene cuts. **83m/C VHS, DVD.** Claire Forlani, Lauren Bacall, Henry Czerny, Pete Postlethwaite; ***D:*** Lewin Webb; ***W:*** Matt Holland; ***C:*** Curtis Petersen; ***M:*** Norman Orenstein. **VIDEO**

Gone Fishin' WOOF! 1997 (PG) Long delayed comedy (thanks to some on-set disasters and well founded doubts about quality) finds best friends and bassmasters of disaster Gus (Glover) and Joe (Pesci) thinking they're going on a peaceful fishing trip. Instead they meet two women (Arquette and Whitfield) who are on the trail of a dangerous British con artist (Brimble). Pesci and Glover have reeled in one stinky old shoe of a movie here. Granted, it's not entirely their fault, but they should've known better. There are no surprises (or laughs) as every joke and set piece is tipped way ahead of time, just so you won't miss it. Less fun than a fish hook in the eye. **94m/C VHS, DVD.** Danny Glover, Joe Pesci, Rosanna Arquette, Lynn Whitfield, Willie Nelson, Nick Brimble, Gary Grubbs, Carol Kane, Edythe Davis; ***D:*** Christopher Cain; ***W:*** J.J. (Jeffrey) Abrams, Jill Mazurzsky Cody; ***C:*** Dean Semler; ***M:*** Randy Edelman.

Gone in 60 Seconds 🦴 ½ **1974** Car thief working for an insurance adjustment firm gets double-crossed by his boss and chased by the police. Forty minutes are consumed by a chase scene which destroyed more than 90 vehicles. **105m/C VHS, DVD.** H.B. Halicki, Marion Busia, George Cole, James McIntyre, Jerry Daugirda; ***D:*** H.B. Halicki; ***W:*** H.B. Halicki; ***C:*** Jack Vacek; ***M:*** Philip Kachaturian.

Gone in 60 Seconds 🦴🦴 **2000 (PG-13)** Cage is an ex-car thief who must steal 50 cars in one night in order to save his ne'er-do-well brother (Ribisi) while gung-ho cop Castleback (Lindo) stays on his tail. "Rounding-up-the-old-crew" montage ensues, followed by much highway mayhem and the odd humorous one-liner. As with most Bruckheimer-produced epics, flash and stunts run roughshod over plot and character, but the target audience won't care because the cars just look so damn cool. Jolie is woefully underutilized in the girlfriend/partner-in-crime role. Remake of the 1974 film notable for its 40-minute chase scene. **117m/C VHS, DVD, Blu-ray Disc, UMD.** Nicolas Cage, Angelina Jolie, Giovanni Ribisi, Robert Duvall, Scott Caan, Vinnie Jones, Will Patton, Delroy Lindo, Chi McBride, Christopher Eccleston, Timothy Olyphant, William Lee Scott, Frances Fisher, Grace Zabriskie, James Duval, TJ Cross, Arye Gross, Bodhi (Pine) Elfman, Master P; ***D:*** Dominic Sena; ***W:*** Scott Rosenberg; ***C:*** Paul Cameron; ***M:*** Trevor Rabin.

Gone to Ground 🦴 **1976** Mad killer terrorizes a group of vacationers who are trapped in an isolated beach house. **74m/C VHS.** *AU* Charles "Bud" Tingwell, Elaine Lee, Eric Oldfield, Marion Johns, Robyn Gibbes, Judy Lynne, Dennis Grosvenor, Alan Penney, Marcus Hale; ***D:*** Kevin James Dobson; ***W:*** Bruce A. Wishart; ***C:*** Russell Boyd. **TV**

Gone with the West 🦴 ½ **1972** Little Moon and Jud McGraw seek revenge upon the man who stole their cattle. **92m/C VHS, DVD.** James Caan, Stefanie Powers, Sammy Davis Jr., Aldo Ray, Michael Conrad, Michael Walker Jr.; ***D:*** Bernard Giraudeau.

Gone with the Wind 🦴🦴🦴🦴 **1939** Epic Civil War drama focuses on the life of petulant southern belle Scarlett O'Hara. Starting with her idyllic lifestyle on a sprawling plantation, the film traces her survival through the tragic history of the South during the Civil War and Reconstruction, and her tangled love affairs with Ashley Wilkes and Rhett Butler. Classic Hollywood doesn't get any better than this; one great scene after another, equally effective in intimate drama and sweeping spectacle. The train depot scene, one of the more technically adroit shots in movie history, involved hundreds of extras and dummies, and much of the MGM lot was razed to simulate the burning of Atlanta. Based on Margaret Mitchell's novel, screenwriter Howard was assisted by producer Selznick and novelist F. Scott Fitzgerald. For its 50th anniversary, a 231-minute restored version was released that included the trailer for "The Making of a Legend: GWTW." **231m/C VHS, DVD.** Clark Gable, Vivien Leigh, Olivia de Havilland, Leslie Howard, Thomas Mitchell, Hattie McDaniel, Butterfly McQueen, Evelyn Keyes, Harry Davenport, Jane Darwell, Ona Munson, Barbara O'Neil, William "Billy" Bakewell, Rand Brooks, Ward Bond, Laura Hope Crews, Yakima Canutt, George Reeves, Marjorie Reynolds, Ann Rutherford, Victor Jory, Carroll Nye, Paul Hurst, Isabel Jewell, Cliff Edwards, Eddie Anderson, Oscar Polk, Eric Linden, Violet Kemble-Cooper, Fred Crane, Howard Hickman, Leona Roberts, Cammie King, Mary Anderson, Frank Faylen; ***D:*** Victor Fleming; ***W:*** Sidney Howard; ***C:*** Ray Rennahan; ***M:*** Max Steiner. Oscars '39: Actress (Leigh), Color Cinematog., Director (Fleming), Film Editing, Picture, Screenplay, Support. Actress (McDaniel); AFI '98: Top 100, Natl. Film Reg. '89;; N.Y. Film Critics '39: Actress (Leigh).,

Gonin 2 🦴 ½ *Five Women* **1996** A sequel in name only. A factory owner in debt to the Yazuka is beaten, and his wife commits suicide after being raped by the gangsters because her husband can't pay his debts. He sets out on a killing spree after making himself a sword, and he wanders into a jewelry store to get his dead wife a diamond ring, only to find that five women who have just fought off several Yakuza thieves are robbing the store themselves. They escape with the ring he wanted, and he follows to get the ring back. **107m/C DVD.** *JP* Ken Ogata, Yui Natsukawa, Shinobu Ootake, Kimiko Yo, Mai Kitajima, Yumi Nishiyama, Yumi Takigawa; ***D:*** Takashi Ishii; ***W:*** Takashi Ishii; ***C:*** Yasushi Sasakibara; ***M:*** Goro Yasukawa.

Gonza the Spearman 🦴🦴 ½ **1986** A gifted samurai lancer is accused of having an affair with the wife of the lord of his province. The lancer must leave to save the woman's honor, because to stay would mean death to them both. In Japanese with English subtitles. **126m/C VHS.** *JP* Hiromi Goh, Shima Iwashita; ***D:*** Masahiro Shinoda.

Gonzo: The Life and Work of Dr. Hunter S. Thompson 🦴🦴🦴 **2008 (R)** Chronicles his life and career through interviews of the many famous people who knew (or at least encountered) Thompson, the "Rolling Stone" columnist known as the father of gonzo journalism (wherein the reporter involves himself in the events he's reporting on to the extent the story revolves around himself), as well as his massive use of psychedelic drugs and his stubborn hatred of authority. Wildly popular in the 1960s and 1970s, his career declined in his later years, and in 2005 he was found dead from a self-inflicted gunshot wound. **120m/C DVD.** ***D:*** Alex Gibney; ***W:*** Alex Gibney; ***C:*** Maryse Alberti; ***M:*** David Schwartz. **VIDEO**

Good 🦴 ½ **2008** Passive to the point of inertia, even Mortensen can't do much with his character—German university professor John Halder who's willfully blind to Nazi atrocities in order to protect himself. A proponent of euthanasia, Halder's position is but one neat propaganda step to justify the 'final solution' as far as Hitler's chancellery is concerned. Stuck in a marriage to an unstable wife (Hille), Halder is only too willing to let himself be guided by others, including his Aryan mistress Anne (Whittaker). Isaacs gives the most energized performance as fellow teacher Maurice, a Jew whose friendship is betrayed by Halder. Adapted from the play by C.P. Taylor. **96m/C DVD.** *GB* Viggo Mortensen, Jason Isaacs, Jodie Whittaker, Anastasia Hille, Steven Mackintosh, Mark Strong, Gemma Jones; ***D:*** Vicente Amorim; ***W:*** John Wrathall; ***C:*** Andrew Dunn; ***M:*** Simon Lacey.

Good Advice 🦴🦴 ½ **2001 (R)** Stockboker Ryan Turner (Sheen) loses all his money on a bad stock tip and decides to ghostwrite his ex-girlfriend's (Richards) lame newspaper advice column. Suddenly the column is hot and the newspaper's publisher (Harmon) is showing interest in more than newsprint. **93m/C VHS, DVD.** Charlie Sheen, Denise Richards, Angie Harmon, Jon Lovitz, Rosanna Arquette, Estelle Harris, Barry Newman; ***D:*** Steve Rash; ***W:*** Robert Horn, Daniel Margosis; ***C:*** Daryn Okada; ***M:*** Teddy Castellucci.

A Good Baby 🦴🦴 ½ **1999** In a sparsely populated North Carolina community, loner Raymond Toker (Thomas) dicovers an abandoned newborn in the woods. He rescues the infant and attempts to find the baby's parents but no one will claim her. Toker gets more and more attached to the baby when slick traveling salesman Truman Lester (Strthairn) suddenly appears in town and the child's origins are finally revealed. Hasty ending mars an otherwise notably affecting debut for director Dieckmann. **98m/C VHS, DVD.** Henry Thomas, David Strathairn, Cara Seymour, Danny Nelson; ***D:*** Katherine Dieckmann; ***W:*** Katherine Dieckmann, Leon Rooke; ***C:*** Jim Denault; ***M:*** David Mansfield.

Good Boy! 🦴🦴 **2003 (PG)** "E.T." meets "Benji" in this amiable talking dog pic with very young kiddie appeal. Twelve-year-old Owen (Aiken) is a lonely little boy who begs his parents for a pup of his own when a doggie-piloted spacecraft conveniently crashes into his neighborhood carrying the adorable Hubble, who comes from (where else?) the Dog Star. Owen adopts Hubble but quickly realizes this is no ordinary pooch. Soon Owen is speaking dog while Hubble tries to train Earthling dogs to begin taking charge or face the threat of a en-masse canine "recall" to the home planet. While visual mechanics of the animal's speech are crude, vital performances of both humans and hounds alike elevate this recycled story. **89m/C VHS, DVD.** *US* Liam Aiken, Molly Shannon, Kevin Nealon, Brittany Moldowan, Hunter Elliot; ***D:*** John Hoffman; ***W:*** John Hoffman; ***C:*** James Glennon; ***M:*** Mark Mothersbaugh; ***V:*** Matthew Broderick, Delta Burke, Donald Adeosun Faison, Vanessa Redgrave, Richard "Cheech" Marin, Brittany Murphy, Carl Reiner.

Good Burger 🦴🦴 ½ **1997 (PG)** Teen actors Kel and Kenan from Nickelodeon fame make their feature film debut in this innocent, silly romp as employees trying to prevent the takeover of their fast food restaurant by the mega burger conglomerate across the street. Similar to comedy teams of the past, Kel is the dim-witted Ed and Kenan is the schemer Dexter, always looking for a quick way out of hard labor. The pre-adolescent humor of the film is as goofy as it is charming and the energetic duo of K&K serves up an entertaining meal for the kiddies. Shaquille O'Neal makes a cameo as does funk meister George Clinton. And yes, that is Abe Vigoda by that fry machine! **95m/C VHS, DVD.** Kenan Thompson, Kel Mitchell, Sinbad, Abe Vigoda, Dan Schneider, Shar Jackson, Jan Schweiterman, Ron Lester; ***Cameos:*** Shaquille O'Neal, George Clinton; ***D:*** Brian Robbins; ***W:*** Kevin Kopelow, Heath Seifert, Dan Schneider; ***C:*** Mac Ahlberg; ***M:*** Stewart Copeland.

Good-bye, Emmanuelle 🦴 ½ **1977 (R)** Follows the further adventures of Emmanuelle in her quest for sexual freedom and the excitement of forbidden pleasures. The second sequel to "Emmanuelle." **92m/C VHS, DVD.** Sylvia Kristel, Umberto Orsini, Jean-Pierre Bouvier, Charlotta Alexandra; ***D:*** Francois Leterrier; ***W:*** Emmanuelle Arsan, Francois Leterrier; ***C:*** Jean Badal; ***M:*** Serge Gainsbourg.

Good Bye, Lenin! 🦴🦴🦴 **2003 (R)** Communism has come to an end as the Berlin Wall falls in 1989 which may be too much of a shock for Alex's (Bruhl) mom Christiane (Sass)—a staunch Socialist—who has a heart attack right before the event and slips into an eight-month coma. In an effort to protect her from the changes capitalism has brought, he comically yet believably revives the vestiges of the fallen regime and even goes so far as to stage a newscast as part of the clever ruse. Although the practicality of the scenario is stretched, Bruhl impressively delivers in this offbeat farce. In German, with English subtitles. Winner of the 2003 European Film Awards for best picture. **121m/C DVD.** Chulpan Khamatova, Alexander Beyer, Daniel Bruhl, Katrin Sass, Maria Simon, Florian Lukas; ***D:*** Wolfgang Becker; ***W:*** Wolfgang Becker, Bernd Lichtenberg; ***C:*** Martin Kukula; ***M:*** Yann Tiersen.

Good Day for a Hanging 1/2 **1958** Marshal Ben Cutler (MacMurray) finds unexpectedly opposition from the townspeople when he captures killer Eddie Campbell (Vaughn). The charismatic outlaw gains their sympathy and Cutler is going to have trouble when Campbell is sentenced to hang. **85m/C VHS, DVD.** Fred MacMurray, Robert Vaughn, Joan Blackman, Margaret (Maggie) Hayes, James Drury, Wendell Holmes, Emile Meyer, Bing (Neil) Russell; ***D:*** Nathan "Jerry" Juran; ***W:*** Daniel Ullman, Maurice Zimm; ***C:*** Henry Freulich.

A Good Day to Die 1/2 *Children of the Dust* **1995 (R)** Western made-for-TV saga, set during the 1880s land rush of the Oklahoma Territory, and adapted from the novel by Clancy Carlile. Half-black, half-Cherokee gunslinger Gypsy Smith (Poitier) reluctantly agrees to lead a wagontrain of freed slaves west to found their own community. Naturally, there's trouble with the Klan and Gypsy isn't the only one involved—young Cherokee brave White Wolf (Wirth), who has been raised among whites, has a forbidden romance with his foster sister, Rachel (Going), leading to lots of heartbreak. Fawcett has a brief role as the young Rachel's high-strung mother. Filmed in Alberta, Canada. **120m/C VHS, DVD.** Sidney Poitier, Michael Moriarty, Joanna Going, Billy Wirth, Regina Taylor, Hart Bochner, Shirley Knight, Robert Guillaume, Farrah Fawcett; ***D:*** David Greene; ***W:*** Joyce Eliason; ***C:*** Ronald Orieux; ***M:*** Mark Snow.

The Good Earth 1/2 **1937** Pearl S. Buck's classic re-creation of the story of a simple Chinese farm couple beset by greed and poverty. Outstanding special effects. MGM's last film produced by master Irving Thalberg and dedicated to his memory. Rainer won the second of her back-to-back Best Actress Oscars for her portrayal of the self-sacrificing O-Lan. **138m/B VHS, DVD.** Paul Muni, Luise Rainer, Charley Grapewin, Keye Luke, Walter Connolly; ***D:*** Sidney Franklin; ***C:*** Karl Freund. Oscars '37: Actress (Rainer), Cinematog.

Good Evening, Mr. Wallenberg 1/2 **1993** Raoul Wallenberg was an upper-class Swede who imported luxury goods from Hungary. He was also responsible for saving thousands of Hungarian Jews from extermination by the Nazis. Using phony documents he first has small groups of Jews smuggled to safety but when he learns that the 65,000 Jews of the Budapest ghetto are to be killed he uses a bluff to prevent the deaths. Later taken prisoner by the Soviet Army, Wallenberg's fate has never been determined. Characters are dwarfed by the immensity of the events and Wallenberg remains an enigma. In Swedish, German, and Hungarian with English subtitles. **115m/C VHS, DVD.** *SW* Stellan Skarsgard, Erland Josephson, Katharina Thalbach; ***D:*** Kjell Grede; ***W:*** Kjell Grede.

The Good Fairy **1935** Charming romantic comedy based on the play by Ferenc Molnar and given the stardust touch of screenwriter Sturges. Luisa (a charming Sullavan) has just left a Budapest orphanage for a job where she attracts the amorous advances of millionaire Konrad (a scene-stealing Morgan). She pretends to be married and picks the first name out of the phone book as her "husband," that of struggling Max Sporum (Marshall), who goes along with the deception because he's instantly smitten with Luisa. She decides she can play "good fairy" to Max by using Konrad's bankroll but it's not that simple. Remade as 1947's "I'll Be Yours" with Deanna Durbin in the lead. **98m/B VHS, DVD.** Margaret Sullavan, Herbert Marshall, Frank Morgan, Reginald Owen, Alan Hale, Beulah Bondi, Cesar Romero; ***D:*** William Wyler; ***W:*** Preston Sturges; ***C:*** Norbert Brodine.

The Good Father **1987 (R)** An acclaimed British TV movie about a bitter divorced man trying to come to terms with his son, his ex-wife, and his own fury by supporting the courtroom divorce battle of a friend. **90m/C VHS, DVD.** *GB* Anthony Hopkins, Jim Broadbent, Harriet Walter, Frances Viner, Joanne Whalley, Simon Callow, Michael Byrne; ***D:*** Mike Newell; ***W:*** Christopher Hampton; ***C:*** Michael Coulter; ***M:*** Richard Hartley.

Good Fences 1/2 **2003 (R)** In the mid-1970s, upwardly mobile black lawyer Tom Spader (Glover) moves with his wife Mabel (Goldberg) and their kids into a posh Greenwich, Connecticut, suburb and embraces all sorts of WASP-y behavior—much to Mabel's disgust. Self-indulgent and simplistic satire. Based on the novel by Ericka Ellis. **119m/C VHS, DVD.** Danny Glover, Whoopi Goldberg, Mo'Nique; ***D:*** Ernest R. Dickerson; ***W:*** Trey Ellis; ***C:*** Jonathan Freeman; ***M:*** George Duke. **CABLE**

The Good Fight 1/2 **1992** Grace Cragin (Lahti) is a lawyer at a small firm who's asked by her son's best friend to represent him in a tough case against a powerful corporation. The young man is dying of mouth cancer and he wants to sue the tobacco company that makes the chewing tobacco he blames for his illness. Grace is wary of the high-powered litigation necessary but with the increasingly personal aid of her prominent lawyer ex-husband (O'Quinn), she is ready to battle the odds. Another fine performance by Lahti in this cable drama. **91m/C VHS.** Christine Lahti, Terry O'Quinn, Kenneth Welsh, Lawrence Dane, Adam Trese, Tony Rosato, Andrea Roth, Jonathan Crombie; ***D:*** John David Coles; ***W:*** Beth Gutcheon; ***M:*** W.G. Snuffy Walden. **CABLE**

The Good German 1/2 **2006 (R)** A throwback to 1940s noir, director Soderbergh makes it the real deal by only using technology of the era, with mixed results. The black-and-white drama begins during WWII as war correspondent Jake (Clooney) has an affair with the married Lena (an intense Blanchett). After the war ends he returns on assignment with hopes of finding her but is disheartened to see that she's taken up hooking with Tully (Maguire), a boyish pimp who fronts as a motor-pool soldier and becomes Jake's driver. The desolate Lena is desperate to leave Germany and her misery behind but can't because the U.S. and Russian governments are searching for her possibly dead husband—a Nazi scientist—who's disappeared. Visually nifty tribute to classic Hollywood might have pulled it off if the story were better. Based on Joseph Kanon's 2001 novel of the same name. **107m/B DVD.** *US* George Clooney, Cate Blanchett, Tobey Maguire, Beau Bridges, Tony Curran, Leland Orser, Jack Thompson, Robin Weigert, Christian Oliver, Ravil Isyanov, Don Pugsley; ***D:*** Steven Soderbergh; ***W:*** Paul Attanasio; ***C:*** Steven Soderbergh; ***M:*** Thomas Newman.

The Good Girl **2002 (R)** Justine (Aniston) spends her days in the retail hell of Retail Rodeo, a West Texas discount mart, and her nights with her pothead housepainter hubby (Reilly), while longing for something better in director Arteta's excellent and biting indie dramedy. She finds just that in college dropout and new employee, the self-named Holden (as in Caufield) played by Gyllenhaal. Justine and the brooding, malcontent (read: would-be writer) embark on an affair with interesting results. Small-screen star Aniston gives an excellent, convincing performance. Deschanel is a standout as Cheryl, who makes creative use of the store's PA system for the benefit of the unaware, zombie-like customers. Nelson is the narrow-minded boss who provides a good portion of the comedy. Successful re-teaming of Arteta and actor/writer White. **93m/C VHS, DVD.** *US* Jennifer Aniston, Jake Gyllenhaal, John C. Reilly, Tim Blake Nelson, Zooey Deschanel, Mike White, Deborah Rush, John Carroll Lynch, John Doe, Roxanne Hart; ***D:*** Miguel Arteta; ***W:*** Mike White; ***C:*** Enrique Chediak. Ind. Spirit '03: Screenplay.

Good Girls Don't 1/2 **1995** Jeannie (Estevez) and Bettina (Parton) are framed for murder and take it on the lam in a red convertible with a half million in cash. It's a comedy. **85m/C VHS.** Renee Estevez, Julia Parton, Mary Woronov, Christopher Knight; ***D:*** Rick Sloane; ***W:*** Rick Sloane.

The Good Guy **2010 (R)** The twist in DePietro's romantic comedy directorial debut is that Beth's (Bledel) boyfriend Tommy (Porter) is a shallow, loathsome cad who loses the girl to much more worthy sweetheart of a guy Daniel (Greenberg). Wall Street broker/shark Tommy needs to fill a job vacancy quickly and offers a promotion to office computer whiz Daniel. He also introduces shy Daniel to Beth, which is the beginning of the end of Tommy and Beth's oppressive relationship. **90m/C DVD.** *US* Alexis Bledel, Scott Porter, Anna Chlumsky, Aaron Yoo, Bryan Greenberg, Andrew McCarthy, Andrew Stewart-Jones; ***D:*** Julio DePietro; ***W:*** Julio DePietro; ***C:*** Seamus Tierney; ***M:*** Tomandandy.

The Good Guys and the Bad Guys 1/2 **1969 (PG)** When Kennedy is abandoned by his gang of outlaws for being too old to keep up, he finds himself being hunted by lifelong marshall nemesis Mitchum. **91m/C VHS, DVD.** Robert Mitchum, George Kennedy, David Carradine, Tina Louise, Douglas Fowley, Lois Nettleton, Martin Balsam, John Carradine; ***D:*** Burt Kennedy; ***W:*** Ronald M. Cohen; ***C:*** Harry Stradling Jr.

Good Guys Wear Black **1978 (PG)** A mild-mannered professor keeps his former life as leader of a Vietnam commando unit under wraps until he discovers that he's number one on the CIA hit list. Sequel is "A Force of One." **96m/C VHS, DVD.** Chuck Norris, Anne Archer, James Franciscus; ***D:*** Ted Post; ***W:*** Mark Medoff; ***M:*** Craig Safan.

Good Hair 1/2 **2009 (PG-13)** Documentary was sparked when one of comedian Chris Rock's young daughters asked why she didn't have 'good' hair. Rock then offers diverse interviews from the black community about hair and societal expectations, the lucrative hair care industry (relaxers and weaves included), and visiting the Bronner Bros. International Hair Show, the annual Atlanta-based convention for hair stylists. **95m/C DVD.** Chris Rock; ***D:*** Jeff Stilson; ***W:*** Chris Rock, Jeff Stilson, Lance Crouther, Chuck Sklar; ***C:*** Cliff Charles; ***M:*** Marcus Miller.

The Good Humor Man **2005 (R)** Coming of age story set in 1976. Underachieving high school buddies Jay (Stevens) and Mt. Rushmore (Garcia) kill time smoking weed and playing pranks. They and their buddies crash a party where Jay meets Wendy (Robinson) and there's a brawl with some jocks that results in a stabbing. When the boy later dies, suspicions point to Mt. Rushmore as the culprit and Jay tries to stay loyal through a bad situation. **112m/C DVD.** Jorge Garcia, Cameron Richardson, Jason Segel, Kelsey Grammer, Nathan Stevens, James Ransone, Elise Robertson; ***D:*** Tenney Fairchild; ***W:*** Tenney Fairchild; ***C:*** Scott Henriksen; ***M:*** Robin Trower.

The Good Life 1/2 **2007 (R)** A misfit in his football-mad Nebraska town, Jason Prayer (Webber) works minimum-wage jobs to support his mom and finds pleasure in helping out his aging friend Gus (Stanton) run his neighborhood cinema and watching old movies. And who walks into the joint? Why Frances (Deschanel), the perfect film noir babe who wouldn't know the truth if it slapped her across the kisser. Jason is instantly smitten and Frances is kind enough to encourage him to get out of town and start a new life, but can Jason really do it? **89m/C DVD.** Mark Webber, Zooey Deschanel, Harry Dean Stanton, Bill Paxton, Chris Klein, Patrick Fugit, Drea De Matteo, Bruce McGill, Donal Logue; ***D:*** Steve Berra; ***W:*** Steve Berra; ***C:*** Patrice Lucien Cochet; ***M:*** Don Davis, Joel Peterson.

Good Luck 1/2 **1996 (R)** Inspirational buddy movie that manages to avoid the worst of sentimental excess. Tony Olezniak (D'Onofrio) is a football player left blind because of a game injury. He's on a downward spiral and winds up in jail, which is where paraplegic Bernard Lemley (Hines), once Tony's tutor, finds him. Bernard wants to enter a rigorous whitewater raft race held on Oregon's Rogue River and he needs Tony's strength to help him do it. The emotional payoff comes as the two bicker and bond. Lots of charm. **95m/C VHS, DVD.** Vincent D'Onofrio, Gregory Hines, Max Gail, James Earl Jones, Sarah Trigger, Joe Theismann; ***D:*** Richard LaBrie; ***W:*** Bob Comfort; ***C:*** Maximo Munzi; ***M:*** Tim Truman.

Good Luck Chuck **WOOF! 2007 (R)** Charlie Logan (Cook) is a successful dentist whose office is conveniently adjacent to that of his long-time buddy, boob-obsessed plastic surgeon Stu (Fogler). Charlie's requisite fatal flaw is that he carries a curse placed on him during his preteen years by a rebuffed goth girl. As a result every woman he dates dumps him and immediately meets the man of her dreams. So legendary is the curse that heaps of women pursue him to ensure Mr. Right's arrival. When he meets klutzy but sweet beauty Cam (Alba), he faces a double dilemma: what to do with the Mr. Right-seeking bimbos, and how to hang on to Cam in light of the curse. Charlie and Cam are cute, but the gags are crude and the sex scenes are gross. **96m/C DVD, Blu-ray Disc.** *US* Dane Cook, Jessica Alba, Dan Fogler, Ellia English, Chelan Simmons, Lonny Ross; ***D:*** Mark Helfrich; ***W:*** Josh Stolberg; ***C:*** Anthony B. Richmond; ***M:*** Aaron Zigman.

A Good Man in Africa **1994 (R)** Bumbling low-level British diplomat gets caught up in the high-level political turmoil of a newly independent African state. Confusing plot has borderline incompetent blackmailed by corrupt politician into bribing respected doctor for local land rights. Wow, corrupt officials, ineffectual bureaucrats—go figure! Does to the British diplomatic corps what "A Fish Called Wanda" did to England's legal community, without the humor. Performances by Connery, Gossett and Lithgow almost make up for shortcomings in key areas such as writing and direction. Adapted from the novel by William Boyd. **95m/C VHS.** Colin Friels, Sean Connery, Louis Gossett Jr., John Lithgow, Joanne Whalley, Diana Rigg; ***D:*** Bruce Beresford; ***W:*** William Boyd; ***C:*** Andrzej Bartkowiak.

Good Morning *Ohayo* **1959** One of Ozu's first color efforts, "Good Morning" is a light social comedy revolving around two young Japanese boys who try to talk their parents into buying them one of those new-fangled television sets. Not likely, since the Dad feels that the boob tube will dull the senses of the Japanese youth...talk about your ESP. The kids feel that there's too much small talk going on. Ozu keeps the camera at kids' eye-level, emphasizing the sympathetic perspective of the children and giving a unique look to the film. Bold colors populate the screen and Ozu keeps the story whimsical while commenting on Japanese society (very much like Juzo Itami would years later). The characters are well-fleshed out and likable. **94m/C DVD.** *JP* Masahiko Shimazu, Koji Shigaragi, Chishu Ryu, Kuniko Miyake; ***D:*** Yasujiro Ozu; ***W:*** Yasujiro Ozu, Kogo Noda; ***C:*** Yuuharu Atsuta; ***M:*** Toshiro Mayuzumi.

Good Morning, Babylon *Good Morning Babilonia* **1987 (PG-13)** The Taviani brothers' first American film. Two young Italian brothers skilled in cathedral restoration come to America and find success building the sets to D.W. Griffith's "Intolerance." Eventually, their fortune is shattered by the onslaught of WWI. **113m/C VHS.** Vincent Spano, Joaquim de Almeida, Greta Scacchi, Charles Dance, Desiree Becker, Omero Antonutti, David Brandon; ***D:*** Paolo Taviani, Vittorio Taviani; ***W:*** Paolo Taviani, Vittorio Taviani, Tonino Guerra; ***M:*** Nicola Piovani.

Good Morning, Vietnam **1987 (R)** Based on the story of Saigon DJ Adrian Cronauer, although Williams' portrayal is reportedly a bit more extroverted than the personality of Cronauer. Williams spins great comic moments that may have been scripted but likely were not as a man with no history and for whom everything is manic radio material. The character ad-libs, swoops, and swerves, finally accepting adult responsibility. Engaging all the way with an outstanding period soundtrack. **121m/C VHS, DVD.** Robin Williams, Forest Whitaker, Bruno Kirby, Richard Edson, Robert Wuhl, J.T. Walsh, Noble Willingham, Floyd Vivino, Tung Thanh Tran, Chintara Sukapatana, Richard Portnow, Juney Smith, Cu Ba Nguyen, Dan Stanton, Don Stanton; ***D:*** Barry Levinson; ***W:*** Mitch Markowitz; ***C:*** Peter Sova; ***M:*** Alex North. Golden Globes '88: Actor—Mus./Comedy (Williams).

The Good Mother 1/2 **1988 (R)** A divorced mother works at creating a fulfilling life for herself and her daughter, with an honest education for her daughter about every subject, including sex. But her ex-husband, unsure of how far this education is being taken, fights her for custody of their eight-year-old daughter after allegations of sexual misconduct against the mother's new lover. Based on Sue Miller's bestselling novel. Well acted, weakly edited and scripted. **104m/C VHS, DVD.** Diane Keaton, Liam Neeson, Jason Robards Jr., Ralph Bellamy, James Naughton, Teresa Wright, Asia Vieira, Joe Morton, Katey Sagal, Tracy Griffith, Charles Kimbrough, Matt Damon; ***D:*** Leonard Nimoy; ***W:*** Michael Bortman; ***C:*** David Watkin; ***M:*** Elmer Bernstein.

Good Neighbor Sam **1964** A married advertising executive (Lemmon) agrees to pose as a friend's husband in order for her to collect a multimillion-dollar inheritance. Complications ensue when his biggest client mistakes the friend for his actual wife and decides they're the perfect couple to promote his wholesome product—milk. **130m/C VHS.** Louis Nye, Edward Andrews, Robert Q. Lewis, Anne Seymour, Charles Lane, Peter Hobbs, Tristram Coffin, Neil Hamilton, William Forrest, Bernie Kopell, Jack Lemmon, Romy Schneider, Dorothy Provine, Mike Connors, Edward G. Robinson, Joyce Jameson, David Swift; ***D:*** David Swift; ***W:*** James Fritzell, Everett Greenbaum, David Swift; ***C:*** Burnett Guffey; ***M:*** Frank DeVol.

Good News 1/2 **1947** A vintage Comden-Green musical about the love problems of a college football star, who will flunk out if he doesn't pass his French exams. Revamping of the 1927 Broadway smash features the unlikely sight of Lawford in a song-and-dance role. ♫ Varsity Drag; He's a Lady's Man; Good News; Tait Song; Students Are We; Just Imagine; If You're Not Kissing Me; Football; I Feel Pessimistic. **92m/C VHS, DVD.** June Allyson, Peter Lawford, Joan McCracken, Mel Torme; ***D:*** Charles Walters; ***W:*** Betty Comden; ***C:*** Charles E. Schoenbaum; ***M:*** Hugh Martin, Ralph Blane, Roger Edens.

The Good Night 1/2 **2007 (R)** Has-been pop star Gary (Freeman) composes commercial jingles and lives in Manhattan with his nagging girlfriend Dora (Paltrow). But Gary transcends his humdrum existence in his own mind with Anna (Cruz), literally the girl of his dreams—and she's more than happy to cater to his every whim. After a frustrated Dora skips town, Gary hires dream expert Mel (DeVito) to find Anna. Mel delivers model Melodia, who hardly lives up to her dreamy counterpart. Director Jake Paltrow's (yes, Gwyneth's brother) feature debut has some clever moments and film-student charm, but never quite manages to keep the rest of us awake. **93m/C DVD.** *US* Martin Freeman, Penelope Cruz, Gwyneth Paltrow, Simon Pegg, Danny DeVito; ***D:*** Jake Paltrow; ***W:*** Jake Paltrow; ***C:*** Giles Nuttgens; ***M:*** Alec Puro.

Good Night, and Good Luck 1/2 **2005 (PG)** Nearly flawless portrayals and script combine with smoky black and white shooting to transport you back to the McCarthy era, where television newsman Edward R. Murrow (Strathairn) faces off with Senator Joseph McCarthy and the House Un-American Activities Committee. Murrow is pressured to back down, but he and CBS staff are intent on exposing McCarthy's fear-based witch-hunt for communist activity. McCarthy plays his own role by way of archival footage; performances by Jeff Daniels and Robert Downey Jr. don't disappoint. A labor of love for George Clooney, he co-wrote and directed, and plays Fred Friendly, Murrow's producer at CBS. Though spare, the dialogue and acting create a scene and mood that, whether you remember the era or not, makes it completely real and utterly believable. **93m/B DVD, Blu-ray Disc, UMD, HD DVD.** *US GB FR JP* David Strathairn, Patricia Clarkson, George Clooney, Jeff Daniels, Robert Downey Jr., Frank Langella, Ray Wise, Robert John Burke, Reed Edward Diamond, Tate Donovan, Grant Heslov, Thomas (Tom) McCarthy, Matt Ross, Alex Borstein, Peter Jacobson, Robert Knepper, Dianne Reeves, Rose Abdoo, John David (J.D.) Cullum, Glenn Morshower; ***D:*** George Clooney; ***W:*** George Clooney, Grant Heslov; ***C:*** Robert Elswit. Ind. Spirit '06: Cinematog.; L.A. Film Critics '05: Cinematog.; Natl. Bd. of Review '05: Film.

The Good Old Boys 1/2 **1995** Debuting as both director and co-writer, Jones also stars as aging cowpoke Hewey Calloway. The n'er-do-well Hewey makes a surprise visit to the hardscrabble 1906 Texas farm of brother Walter (Kinney), whose wife Eve (McDormand) is none too happy to see the wanderer. But Walter needs help, the local banker (Brimley) is about to foreclose, and Hewey is also taken with spirited schoolmarm Spring Renfro (Spacek, who also starred with Jones in "Coal-Miner's Daughter"). And even Hewey realizes that the 20th century is going to change his way of life forever. Easy-going drama with a fine cast. **118m/C VHS.** Tommy Lee Jones, Sissy Spacek, Terry Kinney, Frances McDormand, Wilford Brimley, Sam Shepard, Walter Olkewicz, Matt Damon, Bruce McGill, Park Overall, Richard Jones; ***D:*** Tommy Lee Jones; ***W:*** J.T. Allen, Tommy Lee Jones; ***C:*** Alan Caso; ***M:*** John McEuen.

Good People, Bad Things 1/2 **2008** Architect Danny (Redman) finds his wife Angie (Regis) in bed with another man and goes out and gets drunk. While driving under the influence, he hits and kills a pedestrian and leaves the scene, which was witnessed by Bryan (Lennarson). Soon Bryan is blackmailing Danny to help him in a series of cons and robberies until finally Danny has had enough. **90m/C DVD.** *CA* Dean Redman, Nels Lennarson, Nadine Wright, Marsha Regis; ***D:*** Patrick Phillips; ***W:*** Patrick Phillips, Myra Mero; ***C:*** David Puff; ***M:*** Neale Ramakrishnan. **VIDEO**

Good Sam **1948** An incurable "Good Samaritan" finds himself in one jam after another as he tries too hard to help people. Lots of missed opportunities for laughs with McCrarey's mediocre direction. **116m/B VHS.** Gary Cooper, Ann Sheridan, Ray Collins, Edmund Lowe, Joan Lorring, Ruth Roman; ***D:*** Leo McCarey.

The Good Shepherd **2006 (R)** The birth of the CIA was apparently accomplished by a bunch of gray-faced, unassuming men from the same social milieu, who wore dull suits and neglected their private lives for the good of their country. Edward Wilson (Damon) knocks up and then marries senator's daughter Clover (Jolie), but that is about the most human behavior he'll show in decades as he moves from WWII through the Cold War with paranoia as his distinguishing characteristic. De Niro's second directorial effort is a long slog through the spy biz where everyone lies and betrays. If you want to see a spymaster at work, watch Alec Guinness in any of his incarnations as George Smiley; at least he's more human than robotic. **160m/C DVD, HD DVD.** *US* Matt Damon, Angelina Jolie, Alec Baldwin, Tammy Blanchard, Billy Crudup, Michael Gambon, William Hurt, Timothy Hutton, Keir Dullea, John Turturro, Joe Pesci, Gabriel Macht, Eddie Redmayne, Lee Pace, John Sessions, Robert De Niro, Martina Gedeck, Mark Ivanir; ***D:*** Robert De Niro; ***W:*** Eric Roth; ***C:*** Robert Richardson; ***M:*** Marcelo Zarvos, Bruce Fowler.

The Good Son **1993 (R)** In a grand departure from cute, Culkin tackles evil as a 13-year-old obsessed with death and other unseemly hobbies. During a stay with his uncle, Mark (Wood) watches as his cousin (Culkin) gets creepier and creepier, and tries to alert the family. But will they listen? Nooo—they choose to ignore the little warning signs like the doll hanging by a noose in Culkin's room. And then there's the untimely death of a sibling. Hmmm. Culkin isn't as bad as expected, but doesn't quite get all the way down to bone-chilling terror either. Original star Jesse Bradford was dropped when Papa Culkin threatened to pull Mac off "Home Alone 2" if he wasn't cast in the lead. **87m/C VHS, DVD.** Macaulay Culkin, Elijah Wood, Wendy Crewson, David Morse, Daniel Hugh-Kelly, Quinn Culkin; ***D:*** Joseph Ruben; ***W:*** Ian McEwan; ***C:*** John Lindley; ***M:*** Elmer Bernstein.

The Good Student 1/2 **2008 (R)** The sudden disappearance of a popular teenaged girl spells trouble for the unpopular high school teacher who was too interested in her. But is the obvious suspect too obvious? **77m/C DVD.** Hayden Panettiere, Timothy Daly, William Sadler, Sarah Steele; ***D:*** David Ostry; ***W:*** Adam Targum. **VIDEO**

The Good, the Bad, and Huckleberry Hound **1988** Journeying out West to begin a ranch, Huckleberry Hound winds up becoming a sheriff in the small town of Two-Bit. Huckleberry stands up against a group of bully brothers who have been terrorizing the town. **94m/C VHS.** ***D:*** Ray Patterson; ***V:*** Daws Butler.

The Good, the Bad and the Ugly 1/2 **1967** Leone's grandiloquent, shambling tribute to the American Western. Set during the Civil War, it follows the seemingly endless adventures of three dirtbags in search of a cache of Confederate gold buried in a nameless grave. Violent, exaggerated, beautifully crafted, it is the final and finest installment of the "Dollars" trilogy: a spaghetti Western chef d'oeuvre. **161m/C VHS, DVD.** *IT* Clint Eastwood, Eli Wallach, Lee Van Cleef, Chelo Alonso, Luigi Pistilli, Rada Rassimov, Livio Lorenzon, Mario Brega; ***D:*** Sergio Leone; ***W:*** Sergio Leone, Sergio Donati, Furio Scarpelli, Luciano Vincenzoni, Agenore Incrocci; ***C:*** Tonino Delli Colli; ***M:*** Ennio Morricone.

The Good Thief **2003 (R)** Jordan's stylish remake of Jean-Pierre Melville's "Bob le Flambeur" serves as a showcase for Nolte's magnificent performance. Nolte is Bob, an American inveterate gambler, heroin addict, and master thief whom everyone likes, including the French cop (Karyo) who wants to save him from himself. When Bob loses the last of his money at the track, he's talked into masterminding an art heist at a casino with the usual band of multinational partners. Along the way, he rescues a young waitress from a pimp, taking her under his wing. Jordan provides plenty of atmosphere and noir-heist dialogue, although the plot gets a little tricky and may induce some head-scratching at the end. **109m/C VHS, DVD.** *FR GB IR* Nick Nolte, Tcheky Karyo, Said Taghmaoui, Gerard Darmon, Nutsa Kukhianidze, Emir Kusturica, Marc Lavoine, Mark Polish, Michael Polish, Ouassini Embarek, Sarah Bridges; ***Cameos:*** Ralph Fiennes; ***D:*** Neil Jordan; ***W:*** Neil Jordan; ***C:*** Chris Menges; ***M:*** Elliot Goldenthal.

Good Times 1/2 **1967** Pop silliness as Sonny and Cher (playing themselves) are offered a movie deal by an eccentric tycoon (Sanders). Sonny thinks the script is terrible and dreams up various parts that he and Cher could play. Friedkin's directorial debut. **91m/C VHS, DVD.** Cher, Sonny Bono, George Sanders, Norman Alden, Edy Williams, China Lee, Larry Duran, Kelly Thordsen; ***D:*** William Friedkin; ***W:*** Tony Barrett; ***C:*** Robert Wyckoff; ***M:*** Sonny Bono.

The Good Wife 1/2 *The Umbrella Woman* **1986 (R)** A bored and sexually frustrated wife scandalizes her small Australian town by taking up with the new hotel barman. There's no denying Ward's sexuality, but overall the movie is too predictable. **97m/C VHS, DVD.** *AU* Rachel Ward, Bryan Brown, Sam Neill, Steven Vidler, Bruce Barry, Jennifer Claire; ***D:*** Ken Cameron; ***W:*** Peter Kenna; ***C:*** James Bartle; ***M:*** Cameron Allan.

Good Will Hunting 1/2 **1997 (R)** Good, if predictable, first effort from screenwriting actors Damon and Affleck. Troubled, young Will Hunting (Damon) is a janitor at MIT who also happens to be an unsung mathematical genius. This gift is discovered by big-shot Professor Lambeau (Skarsgard), who must vouch for Will with the parole board by giving him weekly math sessions and taking him to a therapist to work on his anger. Naturally, only the equally troubled shrink Sean Maguire (Williams) is willing to help Hunting get beyond his blue-collar roots. But Will resists the help—not sure that he wants to leave his neighborhood and best friends behind. The Damon/Williams scenes are affecting but the southie Boston accents offer an unexpected challenge. **126m/C VHS, DVD.** Matt Damon, Robin Williams, Ben Affleck, Stellan Skarsgard, Minnie Driver, Casey Affleck, Cole Hauser; ***D:*** Gus Van Sant; ***W:*** Matt Damon, Ben Affleck; ***C:*** Jean-Yves Escoffier; ***M:*** Danny Elfman. Oscars '97: Orig. Screenplay, Support. Actor (Williams); Golden Globes '98: Screenplay; Screen Actors Guild '97: Support. Actor (Williams); Broadcast Film Critics '97: Breakthrough Perf. (Damon), Orig. Screenplay.

The Good Witch 1/2 **2008** Cassandra Nightingale (Bell) moves into a small town's haunted mansion, intending to open a shop selling crystals, charms, and other odd paraphernalia. At least odd to the conservative members of the community who are sure Cassie is a witch and want to run her out of town. Of course, since she has a romance going with town sheriff Jake (Potter), he might object to that notion. A Hallmark Channel original movie. **89m/C DVD.** Catherine Bell, Chris Potter, Catherine Disher, Peter MacNeill, Allan Royal; ***D:*** Craig Pryce; ***W:*** Rod C. Spence. **CABLE**

A Good Woman 1/2 **2004 (PG)** Lackluster reworking of Oscar Wilde's 1892 drawing room comedy "Lady Windermere's Fan" that is now set on Italy's Amalfi coast in 1930. Penniless adventuress Mrs. Erlynne (Hunt) sets her apparently greedy eyes on wealthy American newlywed Robert Windermere (Umbers), who's honeymooning with wife Meg (Johansson). Meanwhile, devilish Lord Darlington (Campbell Moore) has designs on the naive bride. But appearances generally deceive. Hunt and Johansson are miscast and can't comfortably manage Wilde's arch bon mots, though the British actors do much better. Pic at least looks very good. **99m/C DVD.** *US GB IT SP* Helen Hunt, Scarlett Johansson, Mark Umbers, Stephan Campbell Moore, Tom Wilkinson, Milena Vukotic, Roger Hammond, John Standing, Diana Hardcastle; ***D:*** Mike Barker; ***W:*** Howard Himelstein; ***C:*** Ben Seresin; ***M:*** Richard G. Mitchell.

A Good Year **2006 (PG-13)** Certainly everyone involved had a wonderful time swilling wine and eating foie gras in Provence, but Crowe should be forbidden from taking any role that calls for him to play a Hugh Grant-ish floppy-haired Brit. Max is a London bonds trader who lives life on the fast track. When he unexpectedly inherits his Uncle Max's (Finney) vineyard, he travels down to the property with the intention of selling it quickly. That is until all that wine, not to mention French babe Fanny (Cotillard), start Max thinking he's missing out on life's true pleasures. The setting is really, really pretty. **118m/C DVD.** *US* Russell Crowe, Albert Finney, Marion Cotillard, Abbie Cornish, Tom Hollander, Freddie Highmore, Kenneth Cranham, Archie Panjabi, Didier Bourdon, Isabelle Candelier; ***D:*** Ridley Scott; ***W:*** Marc Klein; ***C:*** Philippe Le Sourd; ***M:*** Marc Streitenfeld.

Goodbye Again 1/2 *Aimez-Vous Brahms* **1961** A romantic drama based on the novel by Francoise Sagan. Bergman is a middle-aged interior decorator whose lover, Montand, has a roaming eye. She finds herself drawn to the son (Perkins) of a client and begins an affair—flattered by the young man's attentions. Montand is outraged and vows to change his ways and marry Bergman if she will give up the young man. A bit soapy, but a must for Bergman fans. **120m/B VHS.** Jessie Royce Landis, Ingrid Bergman, Anthony Perkins, Yves Montand, Diahann Carroll; ***D:*** Anatole Litvak; ***W:*** Samuel A. Taylor. Cannes '61: Actor (Perkins).

The Goodbye Bird 1/2 **1993 (G)** Frank is accused by his school principal of stealing her prized talking parrot. With the aid of a kindly veterinarian Frank tries to discover who the thief really is. **91m/C VHS.** Cindy Pickett, Concetta Tomei, Wayne Rogers, Christopher Pettiet; ***D:*** William Clark.

Goodbye Charlie **1964** Very much a product of its time with its swingin'-'60s playboy aura. Hollywood writer Charlie Sorel is murdered by film producer Leopold Sartori (Matthau) when he catches Charlie with his wife. But the playboy is reincarnated as a woman (Reynolds)—much to the confusion of the male Charlie's best friend, George (Curtis). And the female Charlie decides to see how the other half lives, loves, and gets revenge. Based on the play by George Axelrod. **117m/C VHS.** Debbie Reynolds, Tony Curtis, Pat Boone, Walter Matthau, Joanna Barnes, Ellen Burstyn, Laura Devon, Martin Gabel, Roger C. Carmel; ***D:*** Vincente Minnelli; ***W:*** Harry Kurnitz; ***C:*** Milton Krasner; ***M:*** Andre Previn.

Goodbye Columbus **1969 (PG)** Philip Roth's novel about a young Jewish librarian who has an affair with the spoiled daughter of a nouveau riche family is brought to late-'60s life, and vindicated by superb performances all around. Benjamin and McGraw's first starring roles. **105m/C VHS, DVD.** Richard Benjamin, Ali MacGraw, Jack Klugman, Nan Martin, Jaclyn Smith; ***D:*** Larry Peerce; ***M:*** Charles Fox. Writers Guild '68: Adapt. Screenplay.

Goodbye Cruel World 1/2 **1982 (R)** Black comedy about a suicidal TV anchorman who decides to spend his last day filming the relatives who drove him to the brink. **90m/C VHS.** Dick Shawn, Cynthia Sikes, Chuck "Porky" Mitchell; ***D:*** David Irving.

Goodbye, Dragon Inn *Bu san* **2003** Long on atmosphere and short on plot, this slow-moving drama is centered around a decaying movie palace in Taiwan that appears to have become a gay cruising spot. A Japanese tourist wanders in to get in out of the rain (or maybe for other reasons), the crippled ticket girl decides to finally act on her crush on the film projectionist, and two elderly patrons weep as they watch the feature, King Hu's 1966 epic, "Dragon Inn." Melancholy rules. Chinese with subtitles. **81m/C VHS, DVD.** Kang-sheng Lee, Tien Miao, Kiyonobu Mitzmura, Shian-chyi Chen, Shih Chun; ***D:*** Ming-liang Tsai; ***W:*** Ming-liang Tsai; ***C:*** Liao Pen-yung.

The Goodbye Girl **1977 (PG)** Neil Simon's story of a former actress, her precocious nine-year-old daughter and the aspiring actor who moves in with them. The daughter serves as catalyst for the other two to fall in love. While Mason's character is fairly unsympathetic, Dreyfuss is great and Simon's dialogue witty. **110m/C VHS, DVD.** Richard Dreyfuss, Marsha Mason, Quinn Cummings, Barbara Rhoades, Marilyn Sokol; ***D:*** Herbert Ross; ***W:*** Neil Simon; ***M:*** Dave Grusin. Oscars '77: Actor (Dreyfuss); British Acad. '78: Actor (Dreyfuss); Golden Globes '78: Actor—Mus./Comedy (Dreyfuss), Actress—Mus./Comedy (Mason), Film—Mus./Comedy, Screenplay; L.A. Film Critics '77: Actor (Dreyfuss).

Goodbye Love 1/2 **1934** Dull comedy about a group of ex-husbands who refuse to pay alimony and end up in jail. **65m/B VHS, DVD.** Charlie Ruggles, Verree Teasdale, Sidney Blackmer, Mayo Methot, Phyllis Barry, Ray Walker, John Kelly, Hale Grace, Luis Alberni; ***D:*** Herbert Ross.

Goodbye, Lover **1999 (R)** Sandra (Arquette) and Ben (Johnson) are hot 'n' heavy lovers. Jake (Mulrony) is husband to one and brother to the other. Peggy (Parker) has eyes for Ben and works with Jake. Since this is a contemporary noir comedy, there's plot twists, betrayal, blackmail, murder, a fortune in insurance money, and two cops (DeGeneres and McKinnon) trying to piece it all together. Overshoots comedy and ultimately lands in silly territory, but looks good doing it. Johnson comes out the best, kicking pic up a notch whenever he's on screen. DeGeneres (as the jaded cop) and McKinnon (the wide-eyed newbie) plod through the odd-couple schtick. **104m/C VHS, DVD.** Don Johnson, Patricia Arquette, Dermot Mulroney, Ellen DeGeneres, Mary-Louise Parker, Ray McKinnon, Alex Rocco, Andre Gregory, John Neville, Nina Siemaszko, David Brisbin, Lisa Eichhorn, George Furth, Barry Newman, Max Perlich, Frances Bay; ***D:*** Roland Joffe; ***W:*** Joel Cohen, Alec Sokolow, Ron Peer; ***C:*** Dante Spinotti; ***M:*** John Ottman.

Goodbye, Miss 4th of July 1/2 **1988** Inspired by the true story of the teenage daughter of Greek immigrants living in pre-WWI West Virginia, the prejudice they encounter, the relationship that begins between the family and an aging African-American ex-boxer, and the girl's efforts in the influenza epidemic. Based on the 1985 book by her brother. **89m/C VHS.** Richard Speight Jr., Roxana Zal, Louis Gossett Jr., Chris Sarandon, Chantal Contouri, Chynna Phillips, Mitchell Anderson, Conchata Ferrell, Ed Lauter; ***D:*** George Miller.

Goodbye, Mr. Chips 1/2 **1939** An MGM classic, the sentimental rendering of the James Hilton novel about shy Latin professor Charles Chipping (Donat), who teaches in an English public school, marrying the vivacious Katherine (Garson) only to tragically lose her. He spends the rest of his life devoting himself to his students and becoming a school legend. Multi award-winning soaper featuring Garson's first screen appearance, which was Oscar nominated. Remade in 1969 as a fairly awful musical starring Peter O'Toole. **115m/B VHS, DVD.** Robert Donat, Greer Garson, Paul Henreid, John Mills, Terence (Terry) Kilburn; ***D:*** Sam Wood; ***W:*** R.C. Sherriff, Sidney Franklin, Claudine West, Eric Maschwitz; ***C:*** Frederick A. (Freddie) Young. Oscars '39: Actor (Donat).

Goodbye, Mr. Chips **1969** Ross debuted as director with this big-budget (but inferior musical re-make) of the classic James Hilton novel about a gentle teacher at an English all-boys private school and the woman who helps him demonstrate his compassion and overcome his shyness. O'Toole, although excellent, is categorically a non-singer, while Clark, a popular singer at the time ("Downtown"), musters very little talent in front of the camera. The plot is altered unnecessarily and updated to the WWII era for little reason; the music is thoroughly forgettable. ♫Fill The World With Love; Where Did My Childhood Go; London is London; And the Sky Smiled; When I Am Older; Walk Through the World; What Shall I Do with Today?; What a Lot of Flowers; Schooldays. **151m/C VHS, DVD.** Peter O'Toole, Petula Clark, Michael Redgrave, George Baker, Sian Phillips, Michael Bryant, Jack Hedley, Elspeth March, Herbert Ross; ***D:*** Herbert Ross; ***C:*** Oswald Morris; ***M:*** Leslie Bricusse, John Williams. Golden Globes '70: Actor—Mus./Comedy (O'Toole); Natl. Bd. of Review '69: Actor (O'Toole); Natl. Soc. Film Critics '69: Support. Actress (Phillips).

Goodbye, Mr. Chips 1/2 **2002** Teachers don't get more dedicated than Arthur Chipping (Clunes), the Latin master at the cloistered Brookfield boys' boarding school. Shy, gruff, and somewhat eccentric, Chips' life is transformed when he meets unconventional Kathie (Hamilton) and they marry. Her devotion transforms his nature until tragedy strikes. Covers some 50 years from the late 1870s to the 1920s. Based on the novel by James Hilton. **120m/C VHS, DVD.** *GB* Martin Clunes, Victoria Hamilton, John Wood, Conleth Hill, Patrick Malahide, Christopher Fulford, David Horovitch; ***D:*** Stuart Orme; ***W:*** Brian Finch, Frank Delaney; ***C:*** Martin Fuhrer; ***M:*** Colin Towns. **TV**

Goodbye My Fancy **1951** Congresswoman Agatha Reed (Crawford) accepts an honorary degree from her alma mater despite the fact she was expelled after an escapade with young professor James Merrill (Young), who's now president of the school. She's hoping to re-kindle their old romance but journalist Matt Cole (Lovejoy), another former flame, wants Agatha to marry him. There's also a subplot about Agatha working to bring the school's old-fashioned curriculum into the modern age. Crawford has more chemistry with Young than Lovejoy (whom she overwhelms). Second banana Arden does the wisecracking aide role to perfection. Adapted from the Fay Kanin play; title is taken from a Walt Whitman poem. **107m/B DVD.** Joan Crawford, Robert Young, Frank Lovejoy, Eve Arden, Janice Rule, Lurene Tuttle, Howard St. John, Ellen Corby, Morgan Farley; ***D:*** Vincent Sherman; ***W:*** Ivan Goff, Ben Roberts; ***C:*** Ted D. McCord; ***M:*** Ray Heindorf.

Goodbye, My Lady **1956** Based on the novel by James Street, this is a tear-jerking film about a young Mississippi farmboy who finds and cares for a special dog that he comes to love but eventually must give up. **95m/B VHS.** Brandon de Wilde, Walter Brennan, Sidney Poitier, Phil Harris, Louise Beavers; ***D:*** William A. Wellman.

Goodbye, New York **1985 (R)** A New York yuppie on a vacation finds herself penniless and stranded in Israel. She makes the best of the situation by joining a kibbutz and falling for a part-time soldier. Well, of course. **90m/C VHS.** *IS* Julie Hagerty, Amos Kollek, Shmuel Shilo; ***D:*** Amos Kollek; ***M:*** Michael Abene.

Goodbye, Norma Jean **1975 (R)** Detailed and sleazy re-creation of Marilyn Monroe's early years in Hollywood. Followed by "Goodnight, Sweet Marilyn." **95m/C VHS, DVD.** Misty Rowe, Terrence Locke, Patch MacKenzie; ***D:*** Larry Buchanan; ***M:*** Joe Beck.

The Goodbye People 1/2 **1983** Balsam is an elderly man who decides to reopen his Coney Island hot dog stand that folded 22 years earlier. Hirsch and Reed help him realize his impossible dream in this sweetly sentimental film. **104m/C VHS.** Judd Hirsch, Martin Balsam, Pamela Reed, Ron Silver; ***D:*** Herb Gardner; ***W:*** Herb Gardner.

Goodbye Pork Pie 1/2 **1981 (R)** With the police on their trail, two young men speed on a 1000-mile journey in a small, brand-new, yellow stolen car. Remember: journey of thousand miles always begin in stolen car. **105m/C VHS, DVD.** *NZ* Tony Barry, Kelly Johnson; ***D:*** Geoff Murphy; ***C:*** Alun Bollinger.

Goodbye Solo **2008 (R)** Taciturn codger William makes a deal with Senegalese immigrant cabbie Solo, hiring Solo to take him on a one-way ride to Winston-Salem's nearby Blowing Rock National Park in two weeks time. Realizing the old man plans to commit suicide, the effusive Solo tries to change William's mind by forcibly befriending him—having William meet his family, taking him on jaunts around the city, and trying to get William to talk about his unhappy past while Solo reveals his own hopes for the future. **91m/C DVD.** Souleymane Sy Savane, Red West, Diana Franco-Galindo, Carmen Leyva; ***D:*** Ramin Bahrani; ***W:*** Ramin Bahrani, Bahareh Azimi; ***C:*** Michael Simmonds.

Goodbye South, Goodbye *Nanguo Zaijian, Nanguo* **1996** Restless camera follows equally restless losers through Taiwan's sprawling suburbs. Kao (Kao) and his sidekick Flathead (Giong) are minor gangsters running gambling dens and various scams. A kickback scheme involving corrupt bureaucrats and cops goes awry, Flathead gets beaten, and retaliation is in order. Thin characters tend not to hold a viewer's interest. Taiwanese with subtitles. **116m/C VHS, DVD.** *JP TW* Jack Kao, Lim Giong, Kuei-ying Hsu, Annie Shizuka Inoh; ***D:*** Hou Hsiao-Hsien; ***W:*** Tien-wen Chu; ***C:*** Mark Lee Ping-Bin, Hwai-en Chen; ***M:*** Lim Giong.

Goodfellas **1990 (R)** Quintessential picture about "wiseguys," at turns both violent and funny. A young man grows up in the mob, works hard to advance himself through the ranks, and enjoys the life of the rich and violent, oblivious to the horror of which he is a part. Cocaine addiction and many wiseguy missteps ultimately unravel his climb to the top. Excellent performances (particularly Liotta and Pesci, with De Niro pitching in around the corners), with visionary cinematography and careful pacing. Watch for Scorsese's mom as Pesci's mom. Based on the life of Henry Hill, ex-mobster now in the Witness Protection Program. Adapted from the book by Nicholas Pileggi. **146m/C VHS, DVD, Blu-ray Disc, HD DVD.** Robert De Niro, Ray Liotta, Joe Pesci, Paul Sorvino, Lorraine Bracco, Frank Sivero, Mike Starr, Frank Vincent, Samuel L. Jackson, Henny Youngman, Tony Darrow, Chuck Low, Frank DiLeo, Christopher Serrone, Jerry Vale, Illeana Douglas, Debi Mazar, Michael Imperioli, Peter Onorati, Beau Starr, Angela Pietropinto, Joseph (Joe) D'Onofrio, Catherine Scorsese, G. Anthony "Tony" Sirico, Vincent Pastore; ***D:*** Martin Scorsese; ***W:*** Nicholas Pileggi, Martin Scorsese; ***C:*** Michael Ballhaus. Oscars '90: Support. Actor (Pesci); AFI '98: Top 100; British Acad. '90: Adapt. Screenplay, Director (Scorsese), Film; L.A. Film Critics '90: Cinematog., Director (Scorsese), Film, Support. Actor (Pesci), Support. Actress (Bracco); Natl. Bd. of Review '90: Support. Actor (Pesci), Natl. Film Reg. '00;; N.Y. Film Critics '90: Actor (De Niro), Director (Scorsese), Film; Natl. Soc. Film Critics '90: Director (Scorsese), Film.

Goodnight, Michelangelo 1/2 **1989 (R)** Funny, engaging and somewhat confusing story of the life of an Italian immigrant family as seen through the eyes of its youngest member, eight-year-old Michelangelo. Winner of the 1990 Best Comedy Award at the Greater Fort Lauderdale Film Festival. **91m/C VHS.** *IT* Lina Sastri, Kim Cattrall, Giancarlo Giannini, Daniel Desanto; ***D:*** Carlo Liconti; ***W:*** Carlo Liconti.

Goodnight, Mr. Tom 1/2 **1999** Tom Oakley (Thaw) is an elderly widower, living reclusively in rural England at the onset of WWII. When abused, nine-year-old Londoner Willie Beech (Robinson) is evacuated to the countryside with a number of other children, he winds up in Tom's care. Naturally, the curmudgeonly old man and the wary young boy develop a strong friendship, which is threatened when Willie's mother unexpectedly turns up. Based on the novel by Michelle Magorian. **90m/C VHS, DVD.** *GB* John Thaw, Nick Robinson; ***D:*** Jack Gold; ***W:*** Brian Finch.

Goodnight, Sweet Marilyn **1989 (R)** Supposed "never-before-told" story of Marilyn Monroe's tragic death. According to this, her death was the result of pre-arranged "mercy-killing." Follow-up to director Buchanan's "Goodbye, Norma Jean" (1977) with Lane as the 1960s Marilyn intercut with scenes of Rowe from the first film as young Marilyn. You'd be better off leaving "Sweet Marilyn" to rest in peace. **100m/C VHS.** Paula Lane, Jeremy Slate, Misty Rowe; ***D:*** Larry Buchanan.

The Goods: Live Hard, Sell Hard 1/2 *The Goods: The Don Ready Story* **2009 (R)** Vulgar clunker of a comedy. Hustling Don Ready (Piven) and his freelance team are shady used car liquidators hired to save the Temecula franchise of Ben Selleck (Brolin). Ben's import-selling rival Stu Harding (Thicke) is ready to take over Ben's failing business unless Ready can move all the merchandise off the lot over the 4th of July weekend (between drinking, strip clubs, and various sexual situations). **89m/C DVD.** *US* Jeremy Piven, Ving Rhames, Tony Hale, David Koechner, Kathryn Hahn, Jordana Spiro, Ken Jeong, Ed Helms, James Brolin, Alan Thicke, Rob Riggle, Charles Napier; ***D:*** Neal Brennan; ***W:*** Andy Stock, Rick Stempson; ***C:*** Daryn Okada; ***M:*** Lyle Workman.

Goof Balls **WOOF!** **1987 (R)** The tourist denizens of a island golf resort putt and cavort about, and golf isn't all that's on their minds. **87m/C VHS.** Ben Gordon, Laura Robinson; ***D:*** Brad Turner; ***W:*** Skip West; ***C:*** Barney Stewart; ***M:*** Robert Rettberg.

A Goofy Movie 1/2 **1994 (G)** The dog finally gets his day. After 63 years of supporting roles, Disney's Goofy stars in his own movie along with his teenage son Max. When it comes to Goofy's attention that his rock music obsessed son is goofing off in school, Goofy decides to spend some quality time with Max via a road trip through the country. Their journey is plagued with mishaps, but through the obstacles, father and son bridge their generational gap and bond in the true Disney sense. A modest animated treat with six new songs that may induce some finger snapping and toe tapping. **78m/C VHS, DVD.** ***D:*** Kevin Lima; ***W:*** Jymn Magon, Brian Pimental, Chris Matheson; ***V:*** Bill Farmer, Jason Marsden, Jim (Jonah) Cummings, Kellie Martin, Rob Paulsen, Wallace Shawn, Florence Stanley, Jo Anne Worley.

Goon Movie *Stand Easy; Down Among the Z Men* **1952** The cast of "The Goon Show," Britain's popular radio comedy series, perform some of their best routines in this, their only film appearance. **75m/B VHS.** Peter Sellers, Spike Milligan, Harry Secombe, Carole Carr, Michael Bentine; ***D:*** Maclean Rogers; ***W:*** Charles Francis, Jimmy Grafton; ***C:*** Geoffrey Faithfull; ***M:*** Jack Jordan.

The Goonies 1/2 **1985 (PG)** Two brothers who are about to lose their house conveniently find a treasure map. They pick up a couple of friends and head for the "X." If they can recover the treasure without getting caught by the bad guys, then all will be saved. Steven Spielberg produced this high-energy action fantasy for kids of all ages. **114m/C VHS, DVD, UMD.** Sean Astin, Josh Brolin, Jeff B. Cohen, Corey Feldman, Martha Plimpton, John Matuszak, Robert Davi, Anne Ramsey, Mary Ellen Trainor, Jonathan Ke Quan, Kerri Green, Joe Pantoliano; ***D:*** Richard Donner; ***W:*** Chris Columbus, Steven Spielberg; ***C:*** Nick McLean; ***M:*** Dave Grusin.

Gor 1/2 **1988 (PG)** Sword and sorcery: a magic ring sends a meek college professor to "Gor," a faraway world in which survival goes to the fittest and the most brutal. Followed by "Outlaw of Gor." **95m/C VHS.** Urbano Barberini, Rebecca Ferratti, Jack Palance, Paul Smith, Oliver Reed; ***D:*** Fritz Kiersch; ***W:*** R.J. Marx.

Gorath *Yosei Gorasu* **1962** The world's top scientists are racing to stop a giant meteor from destroying the Earth. **77m/C VHS.** *JP* Ryo Ikebe, Yumi Shirakawa, Takashi Shimura, Akira Kubo; ***D:*** Inoshiro Honda; ***W:*** Takeshi Kimura; ***C:*** Hajime Koizumi; ***M:*** Ken Ishii.

Gordon's War **1973 (R)** When a Vietnam vet returns to his Harlem home, he finds his wife overdosing on the drugs that have infiltrated his neighborhood. He leads a vigilante group in an attempt to clean up the area, which makes for a lot of action; however, there's also an excessive amount of violence. **89m/C VHS.** Paul Winfield, Carl Lee, David Downing, Tony King, Grace Jones; ***D:*** Ossie Davis; ***M:*** Angelo Badalamenti.

Gordy 1/2 **1995 (G)** Perky talking porker Gordy manages to escape his fate as future bacon and find a couple of equally perky kids—motherless country-song-singing Jinnie Sue (Young) and lonely rich boy Hanky (Roescher), whom the pig manages to save from drowning. Plot scarcely matters and all the 25 piggies who performed as Gordy generally manage to outshine the humans, though country singer Stone (in his film debut) displays an easy charm. **90m/C VHS, DVD.** Doug Stone, Michael Roescher, Kristy Young, James Donadio, Deborah Hobart, Tom Lester, Ted Manson; ***D:*** Mark Lewis; ***W:*** Leslie Stevens; ***C:*** Richard Michalak; ***M:*** Tom Bahler; ***V:*** Justin Garms.

The Gore-Gore Girls *Blood Orgy* **1972** Splatter horror director Lewis' final film follows a detective's search for a madman who's been mutilating and killing beautiful young bar dancers. **84m/C VHS, DVD.** Frank Kress, Amy Farrel, Hedda Lubin, Henny Youngman, Russ Badger, Nora Alexis, Phil Laurensen, Frank Rice, Jackie Kroeger, Corlee Bew, Emily Mason, Lena Bousman, Ray Sager; ***D:*** Herschell Gordon Lewis; ***W:*** Alan J. Dachman; ***C:*** Alex Ameri.

Gore-Met Zombie Chef from Hell **WOOF! 1987** A demon/vampire opens up a seafood restaurant and slaughters his customers. Deliberately campy and extremely graphic. **90m/C VHS.** Theo Depuay, Kelley Kunicki, C.W. Casey, Alan Marx, Michael O'Neill; ***D:*** Don Swan; ***W:*** Don Swan, Jeff Baughn, William Highsmith; ***C:*** Don Swan; ***M:*** Don Swan, Steve Cunningham, Dan Smith.

Gore Vidal's Billy the Kid 1/2 **1989** An unusual treatment of the William Bonney legend in which the Kid is merely a misunderstood teenager caught up in the midst of the brutal range wars. **100m/C VHS.** Val Kilmer, Duncan Regehr, Wilford Brimley, Julie Carmen, Michael Parks, Rene Auberjonois, Albert Salmi; ***D:*** William A. Graham. **CABLE**

Gore Vidal's Lincoln 1/2 *Lincoln* **1988** Waterston is a low-key but sympathetic Lincoln, with Moore as his high-strung wife Mary, in this made for TV adaptation of the Vidal best-seller. Follows the couple from their first day in Washington, through the Civil War, family tragedies, up to the day of the President's burial. **190m/C VHS, DVD.** Sam Waterston, Mary Tyler Moore, John Houseman, Richard Mulligan, John McMartin, Ruby Dee, Cleavon Little, Jeffrey DeMunn, James Gammon, Deborah Adair, Robin Gammell; ***D:*** Lamont Johnson; ***W:*** Ernest Kinoy; ***M:*** Ernest Gold. **TV**

Gorgeous 1/2 *Glass Bottle; Bor Lei Jun* **1999 (PG-13)** Ah Bu (Shu), a young woman from a small Taiwan fishing village, finds a glass bottle with a romantic message inside. An adventurous spirit, she travels to Hong Kong to find the author of the note. Albert (Leung Chui Wai), the missive's writer, turns out to be a gay make-up artist but Ah Bu also meets millionaire businessman, C.N. Chan (Chan), who manages to fall for Ah Bu while battling corporate rival, Yi Lung (Jen). There may be romance amongst the action but Jackie is more than up to the challenge. Cantonese with subtitles. **99m/C VHS, DVD.** *HK* Jackie Chan, Tony Leung Chiu-Wai, Qi Shu, Hsein-Chi Jen; ***D:*** Vincent Kok; ***W:*** Vincent Kok; ***C:*** Man Po Cheung; ***M:*** Dang-Yi Wong.

The Gorgeous Hussy **1936** Crawford stars in this fictionalized biography of Peggy Eaton, Andrew Jackson's notorious belle, who disgraces herself and those around her. A star-studded cast complete with beautiful costumes isn't enough to save this overly long and dull picture. **102m/B VHS.** Joan Crawford, Robert Taylor, Lionel Barrymore, Melvyn Douglas, James Stewart, Franchot Tone, Louis Calhern; ***D:*** Clarence Brown; ***C:*** George J. Folsey.

Gorgo 1/2 **1961** An undersea explosion off the coast of Ireland brings to the surface a prehistoric sea monster, which is captured and brought to a London circus. Its irate mother appears looking for her baby, creating havoc in her wake. **76m/C VHS, DVD.** *GB* Bill Travers, William Sylvester, Vincent Winter, Bruce Seton, Christopher Rhodes; ***D:*** Eugene Lourie; ***W:*** Robert L. Richards, Daniel James; ***C:*** Frederick A. (Freddie) Young; ***M:*** Angelo Francesco Lavagnino.

The Gorgon **1964** In pre-WWI Germany, the lovely assistant to a mad brain surgeon moonlights as a snake-haired gorgon, turning men to stone. A professor arrives in the village to investigate, only to become another victim. **83m/C VHS.** *GB* Peter Cushing, Christopher Lee, Richard Pasco, Barbara Shelley, Michael Goodliffe, Patrick Troughton, Jack Watson, Jeremy Longhurst, Toni Gilpin, Prudence Hyman; ***D:*** Terence Fisher; ***W:*** John Gilling; ***C:*** Michael Reed; ***M:*** James Bernard.

The Gorilla **1939** Bumbling Ritzes are hired to protect a country gentleman receiving threats from a killer. Lugosi portrays the menacing butler. Derived from the play by Ralph Spence. **67m/B VHS, DVD.** Al Ritz, Harry Ritz, Jimmy Ritz, Anita Louise, Patsy Kelly, Lionel Atwill, Bela Lugosi; ***D:*** Allan Dwan.

Gorilla **1956** A rampaging gorilla is sought by the local game warden and a journalist researching the natives. Filmed on location in the Belgian Congo. **79m/B VHS.** *SW* Gio Petre, Georges Galley; ***D:*** Sven Nykvist, Lar Henrik Ottoson.

Gorillas in the Mist **1988 (PG-13)** The life of Dian Fossey, animal rights activist and world-renowned expert on the African gorilla, from her pioneering contact with mountain gorillas to her murder at the hands of poachers. Weaver is totally appropriate as the increasingly obsessed Fossey, but the character moves away from us, just as we need to see and understand more about her. Excellent special effects. **117m/C VHS, DVD.** Sigourney Weaver, Bryan Brown, Julie Harris, Iain Cuthbertson, John Omirah Miluwi, Constantin Alexandrov, Waigwa Wachira; ***D:*** Michael Apted; ***W:*** Anna Hamilton Phelan; ***C:*** John Seale; ***M:*** Maurice Jarre. Golden Globes '88: Actress—Drama (Weaver); Golden Globes '89: Score.

Gorky Park **1983 (R)** Adaptation of Martin Cruz Smith's bestseller. Three strange, faceless corpses are found in Moscow's Gorky Park. There are no clues for the Russian police captain investigating the incident. He makes the solution to this crime his personal crusade, and finds himself caught in a web of political intrigue. Excellent police procedure yarn. **127m/C VHS, DVD.** William Hurt, Lee Marvin, Brian Dennehy, Joanna Pacula; ***D:*** Michael Apted; ***W:*** Dennis Potter; ***C:*** Ralf Bode; ***M:*** James Horner.

Gorp **WOOF! 1980 (R)** Sex, fun, and lewd, sophomoric humor reign at a summer camp. For the bored and witless or those who aspire. **90m/C VHS.** Dennis Quaid, Rosanna Arquette, Michael Lembeck, Philip Casnoff, Fran Drescher; ***D:*** Joseph Ruben.

Gosford Park **2001 (R)** Altman's ensemble take on a British country house murder mystery set in 1932 that showcases both the upstairs and downstairs inhabitants. Actually, the murder is given short shrift in this look at the manners and mores of the snobs and their servants. Sir William McCordle (Gambon), a self-made man, is giving a weekend shooting party whose guests seem mainly to be the grasping relatives of his cold, aristocratic wife, Lady Sylvia (Scott Thomas). He's the murder victim but nobody really seems to care much (he's not a very nice guy). There's even a couple of American interlopers—movie producer Morris Weissman (Balaban) and his "valet" Henry (Phillippe). Keeping who's who straight is confusing and the pacing is sedate but the cinematography is gorgeous and the cast are all-pro. **137m/C VHS, DVD.** *GB* Michael Gambon, Kristin Scott Thomas, Maggie Smith, Helen Mirren, Eileen Atkins, Alan Bates, Bob Balaban, Ryan Phillippe, Kelly Macdonald, Clive Owen, Jeremy Northam, Emily Watson, Richard E. Grant, Charles Dance, Geraldine Somerville, Tom Hollander, James Wilby, Sophie Thompson, Stephen Fry, Ron Webster, Camilla Rutherford, Claudie Blakley, Natasha Wrightman, Jeremy Swift, Teresa Churcher; ***D:*** Robert Altman; ***W:*** Julian Fellowes; ***C:*** Andrew Dunn; ***M:*** Patrick Doyle. Oscars '01: Orig. Screenplay; British Acad. '01: Costume Des., Film; Golden Globes '02: Director (Altman); N.Y. Film Critics '01: Director (Altman), Screenplay, Support. Actress (Mirren); Natl. Soc. Film Critics '01: Director (Altman), Screenplay, Support. Actress (Mirren); Screen Actors Guild '01: Support. Actress (Mirren), Cast; Writers Guild '01: Orig. Screenplay; Broadcast Film Critics '01: Cast.

Gospa 1/2 **1994 (PG)** Based on the true story of Father Jozo Zovko (Sheen), who was put on trial for treason by the communist government in Yugoslavia in 1981 when he protected six Croatian children who repeatedly claimed that they saw visions of the Virgin Mary. Somewhat ponderous but well-meaning story that also suffers from a plethora of accents. "Gospa" means "Our Lady" in Croatian. **121m/C VHS.** Paul Guilfoyle, Martin Sheen, Michael York, Morgan Fairchild, Frank Finlay; ***D:*** Jakov Sedlar; ***W:*** Ivan Aralica, Paul Gronseth; ***C:*** Vjekoslav Vrdoljak; ***M:*** Nona Hendryx.

The Gospel **2005 (PG)** Young pals David and Frank both aspire to be ministers, but a family clash leads David on another path. Fifteen years later, David (Kodjoe) is now a hot pop star who returns to his minister father (Powell) and his father's church, which are both ailing. Not without bumps, romance, and clashes of will, David has to lead the church back to fiscal freedom. Gospel heavy hitters clinch the tunes, and American Idol finalist Tamyra Gray shows up, as well. Simple but effective (even non-preachy) plot and loads of solid gospel music will make fans very happy. **103m/C DVD, UMD.** *US* Boris Kodjoe, Idris Elba, Clifton Powell, Aloma Wright, Omar Gooding, Keisha Knight Pulliam, Nona Gaye, Michael J. Pagan, Donnie McClurkni, Tamyra Gray; ***D:*** Rob Hardy; ***W:*** Rob Hardy; ***C:*** Matthew MacCarthy; ***M:*** Stanley A. Smith.

The Gospel According to St. Matthew *Il Vangelo Secondo Matteo; L'Evangile Selon Saint-Matthieu* **1964** Perhaps Pasolini's greatest film, retelling the story of Christ in gritty, neo-realistic tones and portraying the man less as a divine presence than as a political revolutionary. The yardstick by which all Jesus-films are to be measured. In Italian with English subtitles or dubbed. **142m/B VHS, DVD.** *IT* Enrique Irazoqui, Susanna Pasolini, Margherita Caruso, Marcello Morante, Mario Socrate; ***D:*** Pier Paolo Pasolini; ***W:*** Pier Paolo Pasolini; ***C:*** Tonino Delli Colli; ***M:*** Luis Bacalov.

The Gospel According to Vic *Heavenly Pursuits* **1987 (PG-13)** A Scottish comedy about a skeptical teacher at a remedial school, who, having survived miraculously from a fall, is taken for proof of the sainthood of the school's patron namesake. **92m/C VHS.** *GB* Tom Conti, Helen Mirren; ***D:*** Charles Gormley; ***C:*** Michael Coulter.

Gospel Hill **2008** The residents of the black neighborhood of Gospel Hill are being forced out of their homes to make way for a golf development. John Malcolm (Glover) feels echoes of 30 years ago when his civil rights activist brother was murdered and racist sheriff Jack Herrod (Bower) let the investigation lapse. Now John's wife Sarah (Basset) decides to start a public protest and she rattles more than one skeleton. **98m/C DVD.** Danny Glover, Tom Bower, Angela Bassett, Adam Baldwin, Taylor Kitsch, Julia Stiles, Samuel L. Jackson, Giancarlo Esposito; ***D:*** Giancarlo Esposito; ***W:*** Terrell Tannen, Jeff Stacy, Jeffrey Pratt Gordon; ***C:*** David Tumblety; ***M:*** Scott Bomar.

The Gospel of John 1/2 **2003 (PG-13)** Plodding along in this verbatim telling of the Gospel of John, Saville methodically shows Jesus as he performs miracles and guides his disciples, culminating in the Crucifixion and Resurrection. Plummer strains to add vitality via his narration. **180m/C VHS, DVD.** Henry Ian Cusick, Stuart Bunce, Daniel Kash, Alan Van Sprang, Lynsey Baxter, Steven Russell, Diana Berriman, Scott Handy, Cedric Smith; ***D:*** Philip Saville; ***W:*** John Goldsmith; ***C:*** Miroslaw Baszak; ***M:*** Jeff Danna; ***Nar:*** Christopher Plummer.

Gossip **1999 (R)** Intriguing premise goes over-the-top. Bored rich boy Derrick (Marsden) share his pad with fellow college students Cathy (Headey) and Travis (Reedus). They all take a class where the prof (Bogosian) rants about the blurring of gossip and news. Then Derrick sees campus ice queen Naomi (Hudson) passed out a party with her jock boyfriend Beau (Jackson). So Derrick persuades his pals that they should all spread a rumor that Naomi did the wild thing with Beau and see how the slander takes on a life of its own. Only what no one anticipates is that Naomi comes to believe she's been raped and Beau gets arrested. **91m/C VHS, DVD.** James Marsden, Lena Headey, Norman Reedus, Kate Hudson, Joshua Jackson, Marisa Coughlan, Edward James Olmos, Sharon Lawrence, Eric Bogosian; ***D:*** Davis Guggenheim; ***W:*** Gregory Poirier, Theresa Rebeck; ***C:*** Andrzej Bartkowiak; ***M:*** Graeme Revell.

Gotcha! 1/2 **1985 (PG-13)** The mock assassination game "Gotcha!" abounds on the college campus and sophomore Edwards is one of the best. What he doesn't know is that his "assassination" skills are about to take on new meaning when he meets up with a female Czech graduate student who is really an international spy. **97m/C VHS, DVD.** Anthony Edwards, Linda Fiorentino, Alex Rocco, Jsu Garcia, Marla Adams, Klaus Lowitsch, Christopher Rydell; ***D:*** Jeff Kanew; ***W:*** Dan Gordon; ***M:*** Bill Conti.

Gotham **1988** A wealthy financier hires private-eye Jones to track down beautiful wife Madsen. It seems that she keeps dunning her husband for money. Sounds easy enough to Jones until he learns that she has been dead for some time. Mystery ventures into the afterlife and back as it twists its way to its surprise ending. Intriguing throwback to '40s detective flicks. **100m/C VHS, DVD.** Tommy Lee Jones, Virginia Madsen, Colin Bruce, Kevin Jarre, Denise Stephenson, Frederic Forrest; ***D:*** Lloyd Fonvielle; ***C:*** Michael Chapman; ***M:*** George S. Clinton. **TV**

Gothic **1987 (R)** Mary Shelley (Richardson), Lord Byron (Byrne), Percy Bysshe Shelley (Sands), Claire Clairmont (Cyr), and Dr. John Polidori (Spall) spend the night of June 16, 1816 in a Swiss villa telling each other ghost stories and experimenting with laudanum and sexual partner combinations. The dreams and realizations of the night will color their lives ever after. Interesting premise, well-carried out, although burdened by director Russell's typical excesses. **87m/C VHS, DVD.** Julian Sands, Gabriel Byrne, Timothy Spall, Natasha Richardson, Myriam Cyr; ***D:*** Ken Russell; ***W:*** Stephen Volk; ***C:*** Mike Southon; ***M:*** Thomas Dolby.

Gothika 1/2 **2003 (R)** Prison psychiatrist Dr. Miranda Grey (Berry) veers off the road after seeing an apparition and wakes up three days later in her own mental ward accused of killing her husband (Dutton). Flimsy plot is further hampered by the film's indecision as to whether to be a ghost story or woman-wrongfully-accused yarn. The most perplexing part is trying to figure out why such good actors agreed to be in it. **95m/C VHS, DVD, Blu-ray Disc, HD DVD.** *US* Halle Berry, Robert Downey Jr., Charles S. Dutton, Penelope Cruz, John Carroll Lynch, Bernard Hill, Dorian Harewood, Bronwen Mantel, Kathleen Mackey; ***D:*** Mathieu Kassovitz; ***W:*** Sebastian Gutierrez; ***C:*** Matthew Libatique; ***M:*** John Ottman.

Gotti 1/2 **1996 (R)** Follows the career of the New York mobster known as the "Teflon Don." Gotti's (Assante) mentor is Neil Dellacroce (Quinn), underboss to the aging head of the Gambino crime family. When Gambino (Lawrence) dies, Gotti is incensed that Paul Castellano (Sarafian) is named as family successor and eventually has him killed. He then grabs power (and lots of tabloid headlines), manages to beat his first federal racketeering rap, but is brought down with the aid of his own underboss, Sammy the Bull (Forsythe), whom the feds get into court. **118m/C VHS, DVD.** Armand Assante, William Forsythe, Anthony Quinn, Richard Sarafian, Vincent Pastore, Robert Miranda, Frank Vincent, Marc Lawrence, Al Waxman, Alberta Watson, Silvio Oliviero, Nigel Bennett, Dominic Chianese, G. Anthony "Tony" Sirico, Scott Cohen, Raymond Serra; ***D:*** Robert Harmon; ***W:*** Steve Shagan; ***C:*** Alar Kivilo; ***M:*** Mark Isham. **CABLE**

The Governess 1/2 **1998 (R)** Rosina da Silva (Driver) is a young Jewish woman living in 1840s London. After her doting father dies, she changes her name to Mary Blackchurch in order to pass herself off as a Gentile and secure a position as a governess. Rosina then gets a job with the Cavendish family in remote Scotland, with her charges being randy teenager Henry (Rhys Meyers) and spoiled brat Clementina (Hoath). Her free-spirit entrances stodgy father Charles (Wilkinson), whom she aids in his obsession with the new art of photography. Where there's a dark room and chemistry, more than photos are bound to develop; and soon Mr. Cavendish comes up with a fixation of his own. Starts as a depiction of a woman adapting to different surroundings, but ends up like a history of the first girlie photos. In the end, her Jewishness isn't that big of a deal, leaving that portion of the story a dead end. **114m/C VHS, DVD.** Minnie Driver, Tom Wilkinson, Harriet Walter, Florence Hoath, Jonathan Rhys Meyers, Arlene Cockburn, Emma Bird, Adam Levy, Bruce Meyers; ***D:*** Sandra Goldbacher; ***W:*** Sandra Goldbacher; ***C:*** Ashley Rowe; ***M:*** Ed Shearmur.

Government Agents vs. Phantom Legion 🦴🦴 **1951** Agent Hal Duncan must stop an evil group who is stealing uranium shipments from under the government's nose. Edited from 12 episodes of the original serial on two cassettes. **167m/B VHS.** Walter Reed, Mary Ellen Kay, Dick Curtis, John Pickard; ***D:*** Fred Brannon; ***W:*** Ronald Davidson; ***C:*** John L. "Jack" Russell; ***M:*** Stanley Wilson.

Goya in Bordeaux 🦴🦴 **1999 (R)** On the eve of his death at age 82 in 1828, Spanish artist Fracisco De Goya Lucientes (Rabal), living in political exile in France, remembers the wild creative days of his youth, particularly his passionate affair with the Duchess of Alba (Verdu), his struggles as a court painter to King Charles of Spain, and the deafness that afflicted him from the age of 46. This is a lavish production, filled with sumptuous sets and costumes. It's also a fairly standard bio-pic that settles back on cliches in the second half. **105m/C VHS, DVD.** *SP IT* Francisco Rabal, Jose Coronado, Maribel Verdu, Daphne Fernandez, Eulalia Ramon; ***D:*** Carlos Saura; ***W:*** Carlos Saura; ***C:*** Vittorio Storaro; ***M:*** Roque Banos.

Goya's Ghosts 🦴🦴 **2006 (R)** Fictionalized account of the life of Spanish painter Francisco Goya (Skarsgard), who lived and worked during the Inquisition. Straddling the eras of courtiers and modernists, Goya navigates the brutality and religious politics of his time. One of Goya's subjects, Ines Bibatua (Portman), is jailed under suspicion that she is Jewish. He must also take commissions from church officials, giving him a glimpse of the unholy and inhumane treatment handed out by the inquisitor and his minions. A well-crafted costume drama; lovely but light on script. **114m/C DVD.** *SP US* Javier Bardem, Natalie Portman, Stellan Skarsgard, Randy Quaid, Jose Luis Gomez, Michael (Michel) Lonsdale, Blanca Portillo; ***D:*** Milos Forman; ***W:*** Milos Forman, Jean-Claude Carriere; ***C:*** Javier Aguirresarobe; ***M:*** Varham Bauer.

Goyokin 🦴🦴🦴 *Official Gold; Steel Edge of Revenge* **1969** The Shogunate has passed an unfair tax, and a clan on the brink of financial ruin spreads rumors about the local peasants in preparation for stealing the Shogun's gold. Unfortunately the plan requires that they silence any witnesses. One of the clans samurai (Tatsuya Nakadai) decides to leave and turn Ronin rather than participate. Years later, he realizes that events are about to repeat themselves, and haunted by his guilt he attempts to prevent the massacre. **124m/C DVD.** *JP* Tatsuya Nakadai, Kinnosuke Nakamura, Tetsuro Tamba, Yoko Tsukasa, Isao Natsuyagi, Koichi Sato, Hisashi Igawa, Susumu Kurobe, Kunie Tanaka, Ruriko Asaoka, Ben Hiura, Shinnosuke Ogata, Shingo Osawa, Tsuyoshi Haraguchi, Kenjiro Hoshino, Hajime Araki, Hiroyoshi Yamaguchi, Tsuyoshi Date, Kujiro Tanaka; ***D:*** Hideo Gosha; ***W:*** Hideo Gosha, Kei Tasaka; ***C:*** Kozo Okazaki; ***M:*** Masaru Sato.

Gozu 🦴 1/2 *Gokudo kyofu dai-gekijo* **2003** Japanese freakmeister Miike revisits his yakuza world in this surreal adventure. Yakuza soldier Ozaki's (Aikawa) paranoia is causing trouble for his boss (Ishibashi) who decides he should be discreetly disposed of by newbie Minami (Sone). So Minami drives them into the country and then botches the job. He tries to find Ozaki's missing body and finds instead, well, a lot of really weird stuff. Title refers to a demon with a cow's head and a human body that Minami has nightmares about. You will too. Japanese with subtitles. **129m/C DVD.** Hideki Sone, Ryo Ishibashi, Sho Aikawa, Kimika Yoshino, Shohei Hino, Keiko Tomita, Harumi Sone; ***D:*** Takashi Miike; ***C:*** Kazunari Tanaka; ***M:*** Koji Endo.

Grace 🦴 1/2 **2009 (R)** Killer baby, obsessed mom, overdone horror. Madeline (Ladd) insists on carrying her dead baby to term and is rewarded with the birth of a living daughter who has an appetite for human blood (that also gives a new take on breastfeeding). Baby Grace also happens to attract flies—probably because she smells like dead flesh. Whatever happens, you don't want to threaten this new little family. **85m/C DVD.** Jordan Ladd, Samantha Ferris, Gabrielle Rose, Malcolm Stewart, Serge House, Stephen Park; ***D:*** Paul Soles; ***W:*** Paul Soles; ***C:*** Zoran Popovic; ***M:*** Austin Wintory.

Grace & Glorie 🦴🦴 1/2 **1998** Somewhat sappy and predictable story adapted from the play by Tom Ziegler. Aging Grace (Rowlands) is fiercely independent and resents having to have help in her country home as she recovers from a broken hip. But help she gets—in the form of ex-New Yorker turned hospice volunteer Glorie (Lane). Naturally, the younger woman has some hurts of her own to deal with and Grace decides to help her. **98m/C VHS.** Gena Rowlands, Diane Lane, Neal McDonough, Chris Beetem; ***D:*** Arthur Allan Seidelman; ***W:*** Grace McKeaney; ***C:*** Mike Fash; ***M:*** J.A.C. Redford. **TV**

Grace Is Gone 🦴🦴🦴 **2007 (PG-13)** Stanley (Cusack) must tell his daughters—12-year-old Heidi (O'Keefe) and 8-year-old Dawn (Bednarczyk)—that their soldier mother Grace has been killed in Iraq, but he is too overcome with grief and his own insecurities. Instead, to buy himself time, he takes the girls on a road trip from Minnesota to Florida. Along the way, Stanley must confront his own demons as his daughters get more and more suspicious of that their impromptu vacation. Cusack (who also co-produced) goes against type, playing Stanley as an essential good but weak man. Movie avoids ideology to explore the powerful emotional effect of war on a family. Score was written by Clint Eastwood after he saw the movie at Sundance. **92m/C DVD.** *US* John Cusack, Alessandro Nivola, Dana Gilhooley, Shelan O'Keefe, Grace Bednarczyk; ***D:*** James C. Strouse; ***W:*** James C. Strouse; ***C:*** Jean-Louis Bompoint; ***M:*** Clint Eastwood.

The Grace Kelly Story 🦴🦴 1/2 **1983** Ladd stars as the beautiful Philadelphia society girl who became an Oscar-winning actress and a seemingly fairy tale princess when she leaves Hollywood behind to marry Prince Rainier of Monaco. Standard TV bio but Ladd does look the part. **104m/C VHS.** Cheryl Ladd, Diane Ladd, Lloyd Bridges, Ian McShane, Alejandro Rey, William Schallert, Marta DuBois, Salome Jens, Edith Fellows; ***D:*** Anthony Page; ***W:*** Cynthia Mandelberg.

Grace of My Heart 🦴🦴 1/2 **1996 (R)** Edna Buxton (Douglas), from a rich Philadelphia family, wins a song contest and winds up in New York at Manhattan's Brill Building, pop music's '60s song factory, where she's transformed into Denise Waverly and told to write the music—not sing it. She pens a lot of hits, winds up in hippie Malibu, and finally gets the courage to record her own concept album (think Carole King's "Tapestry"). Along the way there's a succession of wrong men and heartbreak before her independent triumph. Douglas does a fine job (her singing's dubbed by Kristen Vigard) but last minute melodrama turns this into typical showbiz kitsch. **116m/C VHS, DVD.** Illeana Douglas, John Turturro, Matt Dillon, Eric Stoltz, Bruce Davison, Patsy Kensit, Bridget Fonda, Jennifer Leigh Warren, Chris Isaak; ***D:*** Allison Anders; ***W:*** Allison Anders; ***C:*** Jean-Yves Escoffier; ***M:*** Larry Klein; ***V:*** Peter Fonda.

Grace Quigley 🦴 1/2 *The Ultimate Solution of Grace Quigley* **1984 (PG)** An elderly woman, tired of life, hires a hitman to kill her. Instead they go into business together, bumping off other elderly folk who decide they'd rather be dead. Notoriously inept black comedy noted for being the career embarrassment for both of its stars. **87m/C VHS.** Katharine Hepburn, Nick Nolte, Walter Abel, Chip Zien, Elizabeth Wilson, Kit Le Fever, William Duell, Jill Eikenberry; ***D:*** Anthony Harvey; ***M:*** John Addison.

Gracie 🦴🦴 1/2 **2007 (PG-13)** Formulaic sports drama that's still ingratiating. In 1978, the soccer-mad Bowen family suffers a tragedy when varsity star Johnny (Soffer) dies in a car crash. His rebellious 15-year-old sister Gracie (a winning Schroeder) is determined to replace him on the team. Everyone's discouraging, citing the "girls aren't tough enough to play with the boys" and "sexuality of female athletes is well suspect" arguments. But Gracie is stubborn as well as talented. Loosely based on a real-life tragedy in the Shue family. **92m/C DVD.** *US* Carly Schroeder, Elisabeth Shue, Dermot Mulroney, Andrew Shue, Julia Garro, John Doman, Jesse Lee Stoffer, Joshua Caras, Christopher Shand; ***D:*** Davis Guggenheim; ***W:*** Karen Janszen; ***C:*** Chris Manley; ***M:*** Mark Isham.

The Gracie Allen Murder Case 🦴 1/2 **1939** Gracie tries to outsleuth the sleuth and ends up being no help at all to Philo Vance's murder case. Needless to say this is more comedy than mystery. **78m/B VHS, DVD.** Gracie Allen, Warren William, Ellen Drew, Kent Taylor, Jed Prouty, Jerome Cowan; ***D:*** Alfred E. Green; ***W:*** Nat Perrin. **VIDEO**

Gracie's Choice 🦴🦴 1/2 **2004** Drug-addicted Rowena (Heche) makes a lot of bad choices for herself and her kids. Broke and in trouble, the family eventually winds up with frail Grandma Lou (Ladd) for a temporary stay. But eldest child, 17-year-old Gracie (Bell), has had enough and decides to petition to become her siblings' legal guardian while she finishes high school and works to support them. Lifetime original TV movie is based on a true story. **90m/C DVD.** Kristen Bell, Anne Heche, Diane Ladd, Roberta Maxwell, Shedrack Anderson III; ***D:*** Peter Werner; ***W:*** Joyce Eliason; ***C:*** Neil Roach; ***M:*** Richard (Rick) Marvin. **CABLE**

Grad Night 🦴 **1981 (R)** The anticipation for graduation in a small town high school brings surprises no one could have predicted, unless they've seen all the other typical adolescent films. **85m/C VHS.** Joey Johnson, Suzanna Fagan, Barry Stolze, Sam Whipple, Caroline Bates; ***D:*** John Tenorio; ***C:*** Arledge Armenaki.

Gradiva 🦴🦴 **2006 (R)** Last film for Robbe-Grillet focuses on British art historian John Locke (Wilby) who's doing research on French painter Eugene Delacroix in Morocco. Locke wants to track down a set of previously unknown prints and becomes obsessed with the same sort of erotic fetishes that occupied Delacroix. Locke's memory starts playing tricks after he encounters a mystery blonde (Dombasle) and he becomes implicated in a murder, which may have actually happened 100 years before. Title refers to a ghost or figure of death. French with subtitles. **119m/C DVD.** *FR* James Wilby, Arielle Dombasle, Dany Verissimo; ***D:*** Alain Robbe-Grillet, Michael Scott; ***W:*** Alain Robbe-Grillet, Bruce Graham; ***C:*** Dominique Colin; ***M:*** Philip Griffin.

The Graduate 🦴🦴🦴🦴 **1967 (PG)** Famous, influential slice of comic Americana stars Hoffman as Benjamin Braddock, a shy, aimless college graduate who, without any idea of responsibility or ambition, wanders from a sexual liaison with a married woman (the infamous Mrs. Robinson) to pursuit of her engaged daughter. His pursuit of Elaine right to her wedding has become a film classic. Extremely popular and almost solely responsible for establishing both Hoffman and director Nichols. The career advice given to Benjamin, "plastics," became a catchword for the era. Watch for Dreyfuss in the Berkeley rooming house, Farrell in the hotel lobby, and screenwriter Henry as the desk clerk. Based on the novel by Charles Webb. **106m/C VHS, DVD.** Dustin Hoffman, Anne Bancroft, Katharine Ross, Murray Hamilton, Brian Avery, Marion Lorne, Alice Ghostley, William Daniels, Elizabeth Wilson, Norman Fell, Buck Henry, Richard Dreyfuss, Mike Farrell; ***D:*** Mike Nichols; ***W:*** Buck Henry, Calder Willingham; ***C:*** Robert L. Surtees; ***M:*** Paul Simon, Art Garfunkel, Dave Grusin. Oscars '67: Director (Nichols); AFI '98: Top 100; British Acad. '68: Director (Nichols), Film, Screenplay; Directors Guild '67: Director (Nichols); Golden Globes '68: Actress—Mus./Comedy (Bancroft), Director (Nichols), Film—Mus./Comedy, Natl. Film Reg. '96;; N.Y. Film Critics '67: Director (Nichols).

Graduation 🦴🦴 **2007** High school senior Carl (Marquette) needs a lot of dough to pay for his mother's cancer treatment, which her insurance won't cover. Polly (Lucio) is angry that her banker dad (Arkin) is having an affair so she suggests a heist of old cash that's about to be destroyed. Along with friends Tom (Lowell) and Chauncey (Smith), they plan the robbery for graduation day. Naturally the heist goes wrong, the cops surround the bank, and the story flashes back two weeks to how the whole mess got started. **82m/C DVD.** Christopher Marquette, Shannon Lucio, Riley Smith, Adam Arkin, Chris Lowell, Glynnis O'Connor; ***D:*** Michael Mayer; ***W:*** Michael Mayer, D. Cory Turner; ***C:*** Matthew Uhry; ***M:*** Brian Ralston. **VIDEO**

Graduation Day 🦴 **1981 (R)** Another teen slasher about the systematic murder of members of a high school track team. Notable mainly for brief appearance by Vanna White. **85m/C VHS, DVD.** Christopher George, Patch MacKenzie, E. Danny Murphy, Vanna White; ***D:*** Herb Freed.

The Graffiti Artist 🦴🦴 1/2 **2004** Street artist Nick is used to a lonely existence until he befriends fellow artisan Jesse. Romance seems to be in the air for the men when Jesse makes a quick exit, leaving a crushed Nick to scour the city for him. **79m/C VHS, DVD.** Ruben Bansie-Snellman, Pepper Fajans; ***D:*** James Bolton; ***W:*** James Bolton; ***C:*** Sarah Levy; ***M:*** Kid Loco. **VIDEO**

Graffiti Bridge 🦴 1/2 **1990 (PG-13)** Prince preaches love instead of sex and the result is boring. The Lavender One is a Minneapolis nightclub owner who battles with Day over the love of a beautiful woman. Chauvinistic attitudes toward women abound, but the females in the film don't seem to mind. Which must mean they were "acting." Visually interesting, although not as experimental as "Purple Rain." Music made Top Ten. **90m/C VHS, DVD.** Prince, Morris Day, Jerome Benton, Jill Jones, Mavis Staples, George Clinton, Ingrid Chavez; ***D:*** Prince; ***W:*** Prince; ***C:*** Bill Butler.

Grain of Sand 🦴🦴🦴 **1984** Based on a true story, an understated French drama about a troubled woman searching her past, and her home town in Corsica, for the man of her dreams. Directorial debut of Meffre. In French with English subtitles. **90m/C VHS.** *FR* Delphine Seyrig, Genevieve Fontanel, Coralie Seyrig, Michel Aumont; ***D:*** Pomme Meffre.

Grambling's White Tiger 🦴🦴 1/2 **1981** The true story of Jim Gregory, the first white man to play on Grambling College's all-black football team. Jenner's a little too old, but Belafonte, in his TV acting debut, is fine as legendary coach Eddie Robinson. Based on book by Bruce Behrenberg. **98m/C VHS, DVD.** Bruce Jenner, Harry Belafonte, LeVar Burton, Ray Vitte, Byron Stewart; ***D:*** Georg Stanford Brown; ***M:*** John D'Andrea. **TV**

Gran Torino 🦴🦴🦴 **2008 (R)** After his wife dies, Korean War vet and retired autoworker Walt Kowalski (Eastwood) spurns his sons and their comfy suburban existence and digs his heals in at his working-class Detroit neighborhood, where he is in the minority among the Hmong immigrants. Sitting on his porch with a permanent scowl and weaponry at hand, Walt catches Thao (Vang) of the Hmong family next door trying to steal his cherished 1972 Grand Torino—a car he built while working the line—after pressure from gang members. Thao's teenaged sister Sue (Ahney Her) offers Thao's services to make amends even though both are uncomfortable about it. But Walt is drawn to his neighbors—and particularly the breezy Sue, who's not thrown by Walt's racist mentality and language—so much so that he becomes their defender despite his prejudices. Solid effort gives Eastwood another chance to show his directorial chops and, in perhaps his last appearance, gives him another memorable character to explore. **116m/C DVD.** *US* Clint Eastwood, Brian Haley, Brian Howe, Dreama Walker, Geraldine Hughes, John Carroll Lynch, Christopher Carley, Bee Vang, Ahney Her; ***D:*** Clint Eastwood; ***W:*** Nick Schenk; ***C:*** Tom

Stern; ***M:*** Kyle Eastwood, Michael Stevens.

Grand Avenue 1/2 **1996** TV drama follows the lives of three Native American families living in a working-class section of northern California's Santa Rosa. Widowed Mollie (Tousey) and her three kids have just moved to Grand Avenue, discovering that her one-time boyfriend, teacher-activist Steven (Martinez), lives nearby with his wife and son. Meanwhile, Mollie's cousin Anna (Gago) has her own troubles caring for a cancer-stricken daughter. Sprawling storylines, lots of crises. Based on a book of short stories by Sarris, who also wrote the script. **?m/C VHS.** Sheila Tousey, A. Martinez, Jenny Gago, Irene Bedard, Tantoo Cardinal, Alexis Cruz, Deeny Dakota, Diane DeBassige, Cody Lightning, Simi Mehta, August Schellenberg, Eloy Casados; ***D:*** Daniel Sackheim; ***W:*** Greg Sarris; ***C:*** James L. Carter; ***M:*** Peter Melnick.

Grand Canyon **1991 (R)** Diverse group of characters is thrown together through chance encounters while coping with urban chaos in L.A. The main focus is the growing friendship between an immigration lawyer (Kline) and a tow-truck driver (Glover) who meet when Kline's car breaks down in a crime-ridden neighborhood. First-rate performances by the cast make up for numerous moral messages thrown at viewers with the subtlety of a brick. Sometimes funny, sometimes preachy became more relevant in light of the violence that exploded in L.A. during the summer of '92. **134m/C VHS, DVD.** Randle Mell, Sarah Trigger, K. Todd Freeman, Jack Kehler, Marley Shelton, Danny Glover, Kevin Kline, Steve Martin, Mary McDonnell, Mary-Louise Parker, Alfre Woodard, Jeremy Sisto, Tina Lifford, Patrick Malone, Mary Ellen Trainor; ***D:*** Lawrence Kasdan; ***W:*** Lawrence Kasdan, Meg Kasdan; ***C:*** Owen Roizman; ***M:*** James Newton Howard.

Grand Canyon Trail 1/2 **1948** Our hero is the owner of a played-out silver mine who is the target of an unscrupulous engineer who thinks there's silver to be found if you know where to look. The first appearance of the Riders of the Purple Sage, who replaced the Sons of the Pioneers. **68m/B VHS, DVD.** Roy Rogers, Andy Devine, Charles Coleman, Jane Frazee, Robert "Bob" Livingston; ***D:*** William Witney.

Grand Central Murder 1/2 **1942** Cocky private eye Rocky Custer (Heflin) becomes a suspect after actress Mida King (Dane) is murdered in a private train car in Grand Central Station. He must now race to solve the case before he's booked for the deed. Heflin shines in this mystery though unfolding the intricate plot comes at the cost of some character development. Director Simon captures the atmosphere of the famous train station well considering that it was not filmed on location. **72m/B DVD.** Van Heflin, Patricia Dane, Cecilia Parker, Virginia Grey, Samuel S. Hinds; ***D:*** S. Sylvan Simon; ***W:*** Sue MacVeigh, Peter Ruric; ***C:*** George J. Folsey; ***M:*** David Snell.

The Grand Duchess and the Waiter **1926** Menjou is a French millionaire who disguises himself as a waiter in order to enter the service of a grand duchess with whom he has fallen in love. **70m/B VHS.** Adolphe Menjou, Florence Vidor, Lawrence Grant; ***D:*** Malcolm St. Clair.

The Grand Duel **1973** More spaghetti thrills as Lee plays a mysterious gunman who also acts as protector of a young ruffian falsely accused of murder. **98m/C VHS, DVD.** *IT* Lee Van Cleef, Peter O'Brien, Jess Hahn, Horst Frank; ***D:*** Giancarlo Santi; ***W:*** Ernesto Gastaldi; ***C:*** Mario Vulpiani; ***M:*** Luis Bacalov.

Grand Hotel 1/2 **1932** A star-filled cast is brought together by unusual circumstances at Berlin's Grand Hotel and their lives become hopelessly intertwined over a 24 hour period. Adapted (and given the red-carpet treatment) from a Vicki Baum novel; notable mostly for Garbo's world-weary ballerina. Time has taken its toll on the concept and treatment, but still an interesting star vehicle. **112m/B VHS, DVD.** Greta Garbo, John Barrymore, Joan Crawford, Lewis Stone, Wallace Beery, Jean Hersholt, Lionel Barrymore; ***D:*** Edmund Goulding; ***C:*** William H. Daniels. Oscars '32: Picture, Natl. Film Reg. '07.

Grand Illusion *La Grande Illusion* **1937** Unshakably classic anti-war film by Renoir, in which French prisoners of war attempt to escape from their German captors during WWI. An indictment of the way Old World, aristocratic nobility was brought to modern bloodshed in the Great War. Renoir's optimism remains relentless, but was easier to believe in before WWII. In French, with English subtitles. **111m/B VHS, DVD.** *FR* Jean Gabin, Erich von Stroheim, Pierre Fresnay, Marcel Dalio, Julien Carette, Gaston Modot, Jean Daste, Dita Parlo, Georges Peclet, Werner Florian, Sylvain Itkine, Jacques Becker; ***D:*** Jean Renoir; ***W:*** Jean Renoir, Charles Spaak; ***C:*** Christian Matras; ***M:*** Joseph Kosma. N.Y. Film Critics '38: Foreign Film.

Grand Isle 1/2 **1992** At the turn of the century Grand Isle is the place Louisiana gentry leisurely spend their summers. This is where Edna Pontellier (McGillis), the wife of a rich stockbroker, meets sensitive Creole artist Robert LeBrun (Pasdar). Robert gives Edna all the attention sorely lacking in her marriage and they fall in love. However, Edna's attempts to liberate herself from the strictures of society lead her to tragedy. Based on "The Awakening" by Kate Chopin. **94m/C VHS.** Kelly McGillis, Adrian Pasdar, Julian Sands, Jon (John) DeVries, Glenne Headly, Anthony De Sando, Ellen Burstyn; ***D:*** Mary Lambert; ***W:*** Hesper Anderson; ***C:*** Toyomichi Kurita. **CABLE**

Grand Larceny **1992** The daughter of a millionaire/thief has to prove that she can take over the family "business." Lots of action and stunts. **95m/C VHS, DVD.** Marilu Henner, Omar Sharif, Ian McShane, Louis Jourdan; ***D:*** Jeannot Szwarc.

Grand National Night 1/2 *Wicked Wife* **1953** Gerald Coates should be basking in the fact that his horse is entered in the Grand National but his drunken wife Babs makes that impossible. When Gerald accidentally kills her, he panics and stuffs her body into the trunk of a stranger's car at the racetrack. Now he has to convince the coppers that he doesn't know anything. **75m/B DVD.** *GB* Nigel Patrick, Moira Lister, Michael Hordern, Beatrice Campbell, Betty Ann Davies, Noel Purcell; ***D:*** Bob McNaught; ***W:*** Bob McNaught, Val Valentine; ***C:*** Jack Asher; ***M:*** Johnny Greenwood.

Grand Prix **1966** A big-budget look at the world of Grand Prix auto racing, as four top competitors circle the world's most famous racing circuits. Strictly for those who like cars racing round and round; nothing much happens off the track. **161m/C VHS, DVD, HD DVD.** James Garner, Eva Marie Saint, Yves Montand, Toshiro Mifune, Brian Bedford; ***D:*** John Frankenheimer; ***C:*** Lionel Lindon; ***M:*** Maurice Jarre. Oscars '66: Film Editing, Sound, Sound FX Editing.

The Grand Role *Le Grande Role* **2004** A Hollywood director comes to Paris to film a Yiddish version of Shakespeare's "Merchant of Venice," setting the thespian world all atwitter. After being cast as Shylock, Maurice rushes home to tell his ailing wife of his big break. When the part ends up going to a more famous American actor, Maurice plays the role of his life in order to prolong his wife's happiness as her condition grows worse. In French with unfortunately inadequate subtitles. **90m/C DVD.** Stephane Freiss, Peter Coyote, Lionel Abelanski, Francois Berleand, Berenice Bejo; ***D:*** Steve Suissa; ***W:*** Daniel Cohen. **VIDEO**

Grand Theft Auto **1977 (PG)** In Howard's initial directorial effort, a young couple elopes to Las Vegas in a Rolls Royce owned by the bride's father. The father, totally against the marriage and angered by the stolen Rolls, offers a reward for their safe return and a cross-country race ensues. **84m/C VHS, DVD.** Ron Howard, Nancy Morgan, Marion Ross, Barry Cahill, Clint Howard, Elizabeth Rogers, Paul Bartel, Rance Howard; ***D:*** Ron Howard; ***W:*** Ron Howard, Rance Howard; ***C:*** Gary Graver; ***M:*** Peter Ivers.

Grand Theft Parsons **2003 (PG-13)** Phil Kaufman (Knoxville), manager of legendary country-rock singer Gram Parsons (Macht), has promised to cremate him at Joshua Tree National Monument. But the two are not together when the singer dies and Kaufman must beat out Parson's father (Forster) and greedy girlfriend (Applegate) to get the body first. He enlists the aid of a vivid hippy (Shannon), and the two abscond with the corpse in a brightly painted hearse. Supposedly based upon Kaufman's real-life story, film plays too hard for obvious laughs. Knoxville, Forster, and Shannon give confident performances, but Applegate is a shrill cartoon. Parsons himself seems to get lost somewhere along the way. Sadly, this isn't much of a memorial to the late great artist. **83m/C DVD.** *US GB* Johnny Knoxville, Gabriel Macht, Marley Shelton, Christina Applegate, Robert Forster, Michael Shannon; ***D:*** David Caffrey; ***W:*** Jeremy Drysdale; ***C:*** Bob Hayes; ***M:*** Richard G. Mitchell.

Grand Tour: Disaster in Time **1992 (PG-13)** Greenglen is a quiet, small Midwestern town, until it is visited by a sinister group of time-traveling aliens. Daniels plays a widowed innkeeper who must save the town from destruction and save his daughter from being kidnapped by the fiends. **98m/C VHS, DVD.** Jeff Daniels, Ariana Richards, Emilia Crow, Jim Haynie, Nicholas Guest, Marilyn Lightstone, George Murdock; ***D:*** David N. Twohy; ***W:*** David N. Twohy. **CABLE**

The Grandfather *El Abuelo* **1998 (PG)** Frail and nearly blind, old Count Albrit (Fernan-Gomez) returns to Spain from Peru, having lost the family's money. While he was away, the Count's only son died and from his belongings, the old man learned that his daughter-in-law was unfaithful and one of his lovely granddaughters is not his flesh-and-blood. He becomes determined to discover who is true heir, while his equally determined daughter-in-law wants to protect her children and what remains of their inheritance. Based on the novel by Benito Perez-Galdos. Spanish with subtitles. **145m/C VHS, DVD.** *SP* Fernando Fernan-Gomez, Cayetana Guillen Cuervo, Rafael Alonso, Augustin Gonzalez; ***D:*** Jose Luis Garci; ***W:*** Jose Luis Garci, Horacio Valcarcel; ***C:*** R(aul) P. Cubero; ***M:*** Manuel Balboa.

Grandma's Boy 1/2 **2006 (R)** Oh, Mrs. Partridge, how could you?! Slacker pothead Alex (Covert) is a 35-year-old videogame tester who moves in with his dotty grandma, Lilly (Roberts), and her two roommates—space case Bea (Knight) and easy-of-virtue Grace (Jones). Supposedly Alex is grown-up enough to actually have a girlfriend, co-worker Samantha (Cardellini), but this doesn't seem credible. Of course, neither does the flick but what do you expect since it comes from Adam Sandler's production company. Rob Schneider and David Spade cameo. **96m/C DVD.** *US* Allen Covert, Doris Roberts, Shirley Jones, Shirley Knight, Linda Cardellini, Joel David Moore, Kevin Nealon, Rob Schneider, David Spade, Peter Dante, Nick Swardson, Jonah Hill, Jonathan Loughran; ***D:*** Nicholaus Goossen; ***W:*** Allen Covert, Nick Swardson, Barry Wernick; ***C:*** Mark Irwin; ***M:*** Waddy Wachtel.

Grandma's House *Grandmother's House* **1988 (R)** A brother and sister discover that the house in which they live with their grandmother is chock-full of secrets and strange happenings, including madness, incest, and murder. **90m/C VHS, DVD.** Eric Foster, Kim Valentine, Brinke Stevens, Ida Lee, Len Lesser; ***D:*** Peter Rader; ***W:*** Peter C. Jensen; ***C:*** Peter C. Jensen.

A Grandpa for Christmas 1/2 **2007** In this Hallmark Channel holiday film, 90-year-old Borgnine is an old-time song-and-dance man who's surprised when his young granddaughter Becca (Goglia) shows up on his doorstep. His long-estranged daughter Marie (Nelson) is in a coma after an accident and Becca needs looking after. Grandpa Bert isn't sure what to do until Becca gets involved in the school holiday show and all those showbiz instincts take over. **85m/C DVD.** Ernest Borgnine, Katherine Helmond, Jamie Farr, Richard Libertini, Juliette Goglia, Tracy Nelson; ***D:*** Harvey Frost; ***W:*** David Alexander; ***C:*** Brian Shanley; ***M:*** David Lawrence. **CABLE**

Grandview U.S.A. 1/2 **1984 (R)** A low-key look at low-rent middle America, centering on a foxy local speedway owner and the derby-obsessed boys she attracts. Pre-"Dirty Dancing" choreography from Patrick Swayze and wife Lisa Niemi. **97m/C VHS.** Jamie Lee Curtis, Patrick Swayze, C. Thomas Howell, M. Emmet Walsh, Troy Donahue, William Windom, Jennifer Jason Leigh, Ramon Bieri, John Cusack, Joan Cusack, Jason Court; ***D:*** Randal Kleiser; ***M:*** Thomas Newman.

The Granny 1/2 **1994 (R)** Evil Granny Gargoli (Stevens) is so mean that just before she dies she swallows an ancient potion, enabling her to haunt her survivors. When Kelly (Whirry), the only one to really care for Granny, is cheated out of her inheritance, the rest of the family is in for some nasty shocks from the zombiefied oldster. Can't decide whether to be camp or horrific. **85m/C VHS.** Shannon Whirry, Stella Stevens; ***D:*** Luca Bercovici; ***W:*** Luca Bercovici.

The Grapes of Wrath 1/2 **1940** John Steinbeck's classic American novel about the Great Depression. We follow the impoverished Joad family as they migrate from the dust bowl of Oklahoma to find work in the orchards of California and as they struggle to maintain at least a little of their dignity and pride. A sentimental but dignified, uncharacteristic Hollywood epic. **129m/B VHS, DVD.** Henry Fonda, Jane Darwell, John Carradine, Charley Grapewin, Zeffie Tilbury, Doris Bowdon, Russell Simpson, John Qualen, Eddie Quillan, O.Z. Whitehead, Grant Mitchell; ***D:*** John Ford; ***W:*** Nunnally Johnson; ***C:*** Gregg Toland. Oscars '40: Director (Ford), Support. Actress (Darwell); AFI '98: Top 100, Natl. Film Reg. '89;; N.Y. Film Critics '40: Director (Ford), Film.

The Grass Harp 1/2 **1995 (PG)** Rather dull retelling (with an excellent cast) of the Truman Capote novella covering the eccentricities of small town Southern life in the '30s and '40s. Teenaged Collin Fenwick (Furlong) is sent to live with his maiden aunts, artistic, impractical Dolly (Laurie) and shrewd, hard businesswoman Verena (Spacek). Charlie Cool's (Matthau) the retired judge who's sweet on Dolly, Morris Ritz (Lemmon) is a shady Chicago entrepreneur with plans for Verena's money, and there are various opinionated townspeople with stories to tell as well. Screen nostalgia directed by Matthau's son Charles. **107m/C VHS, DVD.** Sissy Spacek, Piper Laurie, Edward Furlong, Walter Matthau, Nell Carter, Jack Lemmon, Mary Steenburgen, Roddy McDowall, Joe Don Baker, Charles Durning, Sean Patrick Flanery, Mia Kirshner; ***D:*** Charles Matthau; ***W:*** Stirling Silliphant; ***C:*** John A. Alonzo; ***M:*** Patrick Williams.

The Grass Is Always Greener Over the Septic Tank **1978** Based on Erma Bombeck's best-seller. A city family's flight to the supposed peace of the suburbs turns out to be a comic compilation of complications. **98m/C VHS.** Carol Burnett, Charles Grodin, Linda Gray, Alex Rocco, Robert Sampson, Vicki Belmonte, Craig Richard Nelson, Anrae Walterhouse, Eric Stoltz; ***D:*** Robert Day. **TV**

The Grass Is Greener 1/2 **1961** An American millionaire invades part of an impoverished Earl's mansion and falls in love with the lady of the house. The Earl, who wants to keep his wife, enlists the aid of an old girlfriend in a feeble attempt to make her jealous. The two couples pair off properly in the end. **105m/C VHS, DVD.** Cary Grant, Deborah Kerr, Jean Simmons, Robert Mitchum; ***D:*** Stanley Donen; ***W:*** Hugh Williams; ***C:*** Christopher Challis; ***M:*** Noel Coward.

The Grasshopper **1969** The beautiful Bisset stars as a teenager who hops from man to man with unhappy results. Christine abandons her dull L.A. boyfriend when she meets comic Danny (Monica) who takes her to Vegas where she becomes a showgirl. Christine also meets former football star Tommy (Brown), now a hotel greeter, and they marry but Christine attracts the wrong kind of attention from mobster Dekker (Bieri) and things end badly. Which is how they continue. **95m/C DVD.** Jacqueline Bisset, Jim Brown, Joseph Cotten, Corbett Monica, Ramon Bieri, Christopher Stone, Ed Flanders; ***D:*** Jerry Paris; ***W:*** Jerry Belson, Garry Marshall; ***C:*** Sam Leavitt; ***M:*** Billy Goldenberg.

The Grave 1/2 **1995 (R)** Rednecks King (Scheffer) and Tyn (Charles) escape from a North Carolina prison farm after learning about a possible fortune buried in a grave. Unfortunately, they can't keep their mouths shut and soon every other lowlife around them is hunting as well. **90m/C VHS.**

Craig Sheffer, Josh Charles, Gabrielle Anwar, Donal Logue, John Diehl, Anthony Michael Hall, Eric Roberts; ***D:*** Jonas Pate; ***W:*** Jonas Pate, Josh Pate; ***C:*** Frank Prinzi.

Grave Indiscretions ♪♪ *The Grotesque; Gentlemen Don't Eat Poets* **1996 (R)** Eccentric aristocrat, and amateur paleontologist, Sir Hugo Coal (Bates) is much more interested in the dinosaur skeleton he's attempting to assemble than in his crumbling estate or unsatisfied wife Harriet (Russell). Although he does take a dislike to the married servants his wife hires—sly butler Fledge (Sting) and his dipso cook/wife Doris (Styler). And then there's daughter Cleo (Headey) who's about to marry useles poet Sidney (Mackintosh) until he suddenly disappears. Which raises all sorts of questions, including just what the pigs have been eating recently. Based on McGrath's 1989 novel, "The Grotesque." **97m/C VHS.** *GB* Sting, Alan Bates, Theresa Russell, Trudie Styler, Lena Headey, Steven Mackintosh, Anna Massey, Jim Carter, James Fleet, Maria Aitken; ***D:*** John-Paul Davidson; ***W:*** Patrick McGrath; ***C:*** Andrew Dunn; ***M:*** Anne Dudley.

Grave of the Fireflies ♪♪♪ *Hotaru no Haka* **1988** In post-war Japan, in the city of Kobe's train station, a young boy lies dying. A janitor finds a metal canister lying next to the boy and when he opens it ashes fall out. As fireflies gather around, ghostly figures of the boy and his little sister appear, as the story flashes back to the orphaned, homeless Seita and his sister. The two youngsters struggle in the Japanese countryside but find they cannot escape the hardships of war and have no chance for survival. Stunning animated testimony to the human spirit. Based on the novel by Akiyuki Nosaka. In Japanese with English subtitles. **88m/C VHS, DVD.** *JP* ***D:*** Isao Takahata; ***W:*** Isao Takahata.

Grave of the Vampire ♪ *Seed of Terror* **1972 (R)** A vampire rapes and impregnates a modern-day girl. Twenty years later, their son, who grows up to be a bitter bloodsucker, sets out to find his father and kill him. **95m/C VHS, DVD.** William (Bill) Smith, Michael Pataki, Lyn Peters, Diane Holden, Jay Adler, Kitty Vallacher, Jay Scott, Lieux Dressler; ***D:*** John Hayes.

Grave Secrets ♪ ½ **1989 (R)** A professor of psychic phenomena teams up with a medium to find out who—or what—is controlling the life of a young woman. **90m/C VHS.** Paul LeMat, Renee Soutendijk, David Warner, Olivia Barash, Lee Ving; ***D:*** Donald P. Borchers.

Grave Secrets: The Legacy of Hilltop Drive ♪♪ **1992** The Williams family finds out their dream house is built on the site of an old graveyard. The spirits are not only restless, they're deadly. Based on a true story. **94m/C VHS, DVD.** Jonelle Allen, Patty Duke, David Selby, David Soul, Blake Clark; ***D:*** John D. Patterson.

Gravesend ♪♪ ½ **1997 (R)** Big cajones, puny budget: mini-Scorsese Stabile delivers the goods. Tracks a night in the life of four delinquent Brooklyn buddies who find themselves with a dead body on their hands. To avoid police involvement, the boys recruit local drug dealer JoJo (Aquilino) to aid in the body's disposal. JoJo demands $500 and a finger from the victim in return. Rest of pic deals with the fellows' quest for the cash and incorporates a deluge of dark humor which, outside of the pat, in your face dialogue and action, is the picture's real draw. Nineteen at the time of shooting, film school dropout's $5,000 auspicious first picture grabbed the attention of such heavyweights as Spielberg (Stabile now has a two picture deal with his Dreamworks SKG) and Oliver Stone. **85m/C VHS, DVD.** Tony Tucci, Michael Parducci, Tom Malloy, Thomas Brandise, Macky Aquilino; ***D:*** Salvatore Stabile; ***W:*** Salvatore Stabile; ***C:*** Joseph Dell'Olio; ***M:*** Bill Laswell.

The Graveyard ♪♪ *Persecution; Terror of Sheba; Sheba* **1974** A mommy spends many years torturing her little boy, David. In one blood-filled day, the fellow seeks his revenge. **90m/C VHS.** Lana Turner, Trevor Howard, Ralph Bates, Olga Georges-Picot, Suzan Farmer; ***D:*** Don Chaffey.

Graveyard of Honor ♪♪ ½ *Shin Jingi No Hakaba* **2002** Miike's remake of the 1975 classic follows Rikuo Ishimatsu, a lowly disherwasher, to the height of gang power, after he unknowingly saves the life of a gang leader. Well-executed script delves more deeply into the relationship Rikuo has with his heroin-addicted girlfriend and brings a comedic flair to gangster leader Ishimatsu's character. Japanese with subtitles. **131m/C DVD.** *JP* Goro Kishitani, Shingo Yamashiro, Narumi Arimori, Ryosuke Miki; ***D:*** Takashi Miike; ***W:*** Shigenori Takechi; ***C:*** Hideo Yamamoto; ***M:*** Koji Endo.

Graveyard of Horror ♪ **1971** His wife and baby dead, a man seeking revenge discovers a horrible secret: his brother, a doctor, is stealing the heads from corpses. Dubbed. **105m/C VHS, DVD.** *SP* Bill Curran, Francisco (Frank) Brana, Beatriz Lacy; ***D:*** Miguel Madrid.

Graveyard Shift ♪ ½ **1987 (R)** A New York cabby on the night shift is actually a powerful vampire who uses his fares to build an army of vampires. Not to be confused with the 1990 Stephen King scripted film. Followed by "Understudy: Graveyard Shift II." **89m/C VHS, DVD.** *IT* Silvio Oliviero, Helen Papas, Cliff Stoker; ***D:*** Gerard Ciccoritti.

Graveyard Shift ♪ *Stephen King's Graveyard Shift* **1990 (R)** Just because Stephen King wrote the original story doesn't mean its celluloid incarnation is guaranteed to stand your hair on end; unless that's your response to abject boredom. When a man takes over the night shift at a recently reopened textile mill, he starts to find remnants..and they aren't fabric. Seems there's a graveyard in the neighborhood. **89m/C VHS, DVD.** David Andrews, Kelly Wolf, Stephen Macht, Brad Dourif, Andrew Divoff; ***D:*** Ralph S. Singleton; ***W:*** Stephen King, John Esposito; ***C:*** Peter Stein; ***M:*** Brian Banks.

Gray Lady Down ♪♪ **1977 (PG)** A nuclear submarine sinks off the coast of Cape Cod and with their oxygen running out, a risky escape in an experimental diving craft seems to be their only hope. Dull, all-star suspenser. **111m/C VHS, DVD.** Charlton Heston, David Carradine, Stacy Keach, Ned Beatty, Ronny Cox, Christopher Reeve, Michael O'Keefe, Rosemary Forsyth; ***D:*** David Greene.

Gray Matters ♪♪ **2006 (PG-13)** Artificial screwball comedy finds loft-sharing siblings Gray (Graham) and Sam (Cavanagh) deciding they're too co-dependent and each needs to find a romantic partner—except they don't realize they'll want the same woman. Sam and beautiful Charlie (Moynahan) meet and are soon planning to elope to Vegas, with Gray as a witness. The gals share a drunken night out and an impulsive kiss (which Charlie doesn't remember) and suddenly the thirty-something Gray realizes she really, really likes girls. Fanciful if awkward debut from writer/director Kramer. **96m/C DVD.** *US* Heather Graham, Tom Cavanagh, Bridget Moynahan, Alan Cumming, Molly Shannon, Sissy Spacek, Rachel Shelley; ***Cameos:*** Gloria Gaynor; ***D:*** Sue Kramer; ***W:*** Sue Kramer; ***C:*** John Bartley; ***M:*** Andrew Hollender.

Grayeagle ♪♪ **1977 (PG)** When a frontier trapper's daughter is kidnapped by Cheyenne Indians, he launches a search for her recovery. More style than pace in this Western, but worth a look for fans of Johnson. **104m/C VHS.** Ben Johnson, Iron Eyes Cody, Lana Wood, Alex Cord, Jack Elam, Paul Fix, Cindy Butler, Charles B. Pierce; ***D:*** Charles B. Pierce; ***W:*** Charles B. Pierce.

Gray's Anatomy ♪♪ ½ **1996** Yet another monologue from Gray, this time about his medical crisis involving a rare eye disease. **80m/C VHS, DVD.** Spalding Gray; ***D:*** Steven Soderbergh.

Grbavica: The Land of My Dreams ♪♪ **2006** In postwar Sarajevo, single mother Esma is forced to work as a waitress in a gangster-run club in order to supplement the government aid she needs to raise defiant adolescent daughter Sara. They argue over many things, including the truth about Sara's father, whom she believes died fighting for Bosnia. Title refers to the rundown district, formerly the site of a prison camp, where they live. Bosnian with subtitles. **90m/C DVD.** *AT BS GE* Mirjana Karanovic, Bogdan Diklic, Luna Mijovic, Leon Lucev, Kenan Catic; ***D:*** Jasmila Zbanic; ***W:*** Jasmila Zbanic; ***C:*** Christine A. Maier; ***M:*** Enes Zlatar.

Grease ♪♪♪ **1978 (PG)** Film version of the hit Broadway musical about summer love. Set in the 1950s, this spirited musical follows a group of high-schoolers throughout their senior year. The story offers a responsible moral: act like a tart and you'll get your guy; but, hey, it's all in fun anyway. Followed by a weak sequel. ♫Grease; Summer Nights; Hopelessly Devoted to You; You're the One That I Want; Sandy; Beauty School Dropout; Look at Me, I'm Sandra Dee; Greased Lightnin'; It's Raining on Prom Night. **110m/C VHS, DVD.** John Travolta, Olivia Newton-John, Jeff Conaway, Stockard Channing, Didi Conn, Eve Arden, Frankie Avalon, Sid Caesar, Dinah Manoff, Joan Blondell, Alice Ghostley, Dody Goodman, Kelly Ward, Michael Tucci, Barry Pearl, Edd Byrnes, Susan Buckner, Lorenzo Lamas, Fannie Flagg, Eddie Deezen, Michael Biehn; ***D:*** Randal Kleiser; ***W:*** Allan Carr; ***C:*** Bill Butler; ***M:*** John Farrar, Barry Gibb.

Grease 2 ♪♪ **1982 (PG)** Continuing saga of the T-Birds, the Pink Ladies, and young love at Rydell High. Newton-John and Travolta have graduated, leaving Pfeiffer to lead on love-struck book-neb Caulfield. Some okay tunes, though lame story lacks good-humor flair of the original. **115m/C VHS, DVD.** Maxwell Caulfield, Michelle Pfeiffer, Adrian Zmed, Lorna Luft, Didi Conn, Eve Arden, Sid Caesar, Tab Hunter, Christopher McDonald; ***D:*** Patricia Birch; ***M:*** Artie Butler.

Greased Lightning ♪♪ ½ **1977 (PG)** The story of the first black auto racing champion, Wendell Scott, who had to overcome racial prejudice to achieve his success. Slightly better-than-average Pryor comedy vehicle. **95m/C VHS, DVD.** Richard Pryor, Pam Grier, Beau Bridges, Cleavon Little, Vincent Gardenia; ***D:*** Michael A. Schultz; ***W:*** Leon Capetanos, Melvin Van Peebles; ***M:*** Fred Karlin.

Greaser's Palace ♪♪ ½ *Zoot Suit Jesus* **1972** Seaweedhead Greaser, owner of the town's saloon, faces his arch-nemesis in this wide-ranging satiric Christ allegory from the director of "Putney Swope." **91m/C VHS, DVD.** Albert Henderson, Allan Arbus, Michael Sullivan, Luana Anders, James Antonio, Ronald Nealy, Larry Moyer, John Paul Hudson, Herve Villechaize; ***D:*** Robert Downey; ***W:*** Robert Downey; ***C:*** Peter Powell; ***M:*** Jack Nitzsche.

The Great Adventure ♪♪♪ ½ *Det Stora Aventyret* **1953** Two farm boys capture and attempt to train a wild otter. Unfortunately, the otter longs to once again join his kind despite the boys' efforts. Arne Sucksdorff won an Oscar for his arresting view of animal life. **73m/B VHS.** *SW* Anders Norberg, Kjell Sucksdorff, Arne Sucksdorff; ***D:*** Arne Sucksdorff; ***W:*** Arne Sucksdorff.

Great Adventure ♪♪ **1975 (PG)** In the severe environment of the gold rush days on the rugged Yukon territory, a touching tale unfolds of a young orphan boy and his eternal bond of friendship with a great northern dog. Based on a Jack London story. Baldanello used the pseudonym Paul Elliotts and Fred Romer is actually Fernando Romero. **90m/C VHS, DVD.** *IT SP* Jack Palance, Joan Collins, Fred Romer, Elisabetta Virgili, Remo de Angelis, Manuel de Blas; ***D:*** Gianfranco Baldanello.

The Great Alligator ♪ *Il Fiume del Grande Caimano; Alligators* **1981** As if you couldn't guess, this one's about a huge alligator who does what other huge alligators do...terrorizes the people at a resort. **89m/C VHS, DVD.** Barbara Bach, Mel Ferrer, Richard Johnson, Claudio Cassinelli, Romano Puppo; ***D:*** Sergio Martino; ***W:*** Sergio Martino, Ernesto Gastaldi, Luigi Montefiore, Maria Chiaretta; ***C:*** Giancarlo Ferrando.

The Great American Broadcast ♪♪♪ **1941** Two WWI vets want more than anything to strike it rich. After many failed endeavors, the two try that new-fangled thing called radio. The station takes off, as does the plot. The girlfriend of one vet falls for his partner and numerous other misunderstandings and complications ensue. Charming and crazy musical with an energetic cast. ♫I've Got a Bone To Pick With You; It's All In a Lifetime; I Take to You; Long Ago Last Night; Where You Are; The Great American Broadcast; Albany Bound; Give My Regards to Broadway; If I Didn't Care. **92m/B VHS.** Alice Faye, John Payne, Jack Oakie, Cesar Romero, James Newill, Mary Beth Hughes; ***D:*** Archie Mayo; ***C:*** Leon Shamroy.

The Great American Sex Scandal ♪♪ ½ *Jury Duty* **1994 (PG-13)** Sanford Lagelfust (Pinchot) is an meek accountant on trial for embezzlement, but when the prosecution's main witness turns out to be his sexy girlfriend Hope (Scoggins) the case turns into a courtroom sex scandal. Silly Canadian TV production. **94m/C VHS, DVD.** *CA* Bronson Pinchot, Tracy Scoggins, Heather Locklear, Stephen Baldwin, Lynn Redgrave, Alan Thicke, Madchen Amick, Barbara Bosson, Ilene Graff, Mark Blankfield, Danny Pintauro, Reginald VelJohnson, Jacklyn Zeman; ***D:*** Michael A. Schultz.

Great American Traffic Jam ♪ ½ *Gridlock* **1980 (PG)** Farce about the humorous variety of characters interacting on the interstate during a massive California traffic jam. **97m/C VHS.** Ed McMahon, Vic Tayback, Howard Hesseman, Abe Vigoda, Noah Beery Jr., Desi Arnaz Jr., John Beck, Shelley Fabares, James Gregory; ***D:*** James Frawley. **TV**

The Great Armored Car Swindle ♪♪ **1964** An anonymous English businessman becomes involved in international intrigue when he becomes a pawn in a plan to transfer money to a Middle Eastern government under communist rule. But thanks to his wife things don't go off as planned. **58m/B VHS.** Peter Reynolds, Dermot Walsh, Joanna Dunham, Lisa Gastoni, Brian Cobby; ***D:*** Lance Comfort.

Great Balls of Fire ♪♪ ½ **1989 (PG-13)** A florid, comic-book film of the glory days of Jerry Lee Lewis, from his first band to stardom. Most of the drama is derived from his marriage to his 13-year-old cousin. Somewhat overacted but full of energy. The soundtrack features many of the "Killer's" greatest hits re-recorded by Jerry Lee Lewis for the film. **108m/C VHS, DVD.** Dennis Quaid, Winona Ryder, Alec Baldwin, Trey Wilson, John Doe, Lisa Blount, Steve Allen, Stephen Tobolowsky, Lisa Jane Persky, Michael St. Gerard, Peter Cook; ***D:*** Jim McBride; ***W:*** Jack Baran, Jim McBride; ***C:*** Alfonso Beato; ***M:*** Jack Baran, Jim McBride.

Great Bank Hoax ♪♪ ½ *The Great Georgia Bank Hoax; Shenanigans* **1978 (PG)** Three bank managers decide to rob their own bank to cover up the fact that all the assets have been embezzled. **89m/C VHS.** Richard Basehart, Ned Beatty, Burgess Meredith, Michael Murphy, Paul Sand, Arthur Godfrey; ***D:*** Joseph Jacoby; ***C:*** Walter Lassally.

Great Bikini Off-Road Adventure ♪ ½ **1994 (R)** Duke Abbey is about to lose his jeep tour company because business is so slow that he can't pay the rent. Then Duke's niece Lori decides to get her bikini-clad friends to hire on as drivers, showing lots of sights on their desert tours. **90m/C VHS.** Avalon Anders, Lauren Hays, Floyd Irons, Laura Hudspeth, Dan Frank; ***D:*** Gary Orona.

The Great Buck Howard **2009 (PG)** Bored law school dropout Troy (Hanks the younger) takes a job as personal assistant to small-time illusionist Buck Howard (Malkiovich), much to the chagrin of his father (Hanks the elder). Troy and Buck bond on the road and soon an entry-level publicist (Blunt) joins them, set to help launch Howard's comeback with an "amazing stunt," but the results aren't what anyone expected. **87m/C DVD.** Colin Hanks, Tom Hanks, John Malkovich, Emily Blunt, Griffin Dunne, Tom Arnold, Patrick Fischler, Wallace (Wally) Langham, Stacey Travis, Steve Zahn, Ricky Jay, Donny Most, Jacquie Barnbrook, Matt Hoey; ***Cameos:*** Conan O'Brien, George Takei; ***D:*** Sean McGinly; ***W:*** Sean McGinly; ***C:*** Tak Fujimoto; ***M:*** Blake Neely.

The Great Caruso ♪♪ ½ **1951** The story of opera legend Enrico Caruso's rise to fame, from his childhood in Naples, Italy, to his collapse on the stage of the Metropolitan Opera House. Lanza is superb as the singer, and there are 27 musical numbers to satisfy the opera lover. ♫The Loveliest Night of the Year; Over the Waves; Vesti la Giubba; M'Appari; Celeste Aida; Numi, Pieta; La Fatal Pietra; Sextet from Lucia di Lammermoor; La

Donne a Mobile. **113m/C VHS, DVD.** Angela (Clark) Clarke, Jarmila Novotna, Richard Hageman, Carl Benton Reid, Eduard Franz, Ludwig Donath, Alan Napier, Shepard Menken, Nestor Paiva, Ian Wolfe, Mario Lanza, Ann Blyth, Dorothy Kirsten; ***D:*** Richard Thorpe; ***C:*** Joseph Ruttenberg; ***M:*** Johnny Green. Oscars '51: Sound.

The Great Challenge *Les Fils du Vent; Sons of the Wind* **2004 (PG-13)** Extreme athletes travel to Bangkok to set up a gym and explore the city. But they encounter a Thai gang who are allied with Japanese yakuza to take control of the city. For fans of the martial arts genre; French with subtitles. **93m/C DVD.** *FR* Williams Belle, Chau Belle Dinh, Malik Diouf, Yann Hnautra; ***D:*** Julien Seri; ***W:*** Julien Seri; ***C:*** Michel Taburiaux; ***M:*** Christian Henson.

The Great Commandment **1941** Young man throws himself into a revolution against the overbearing Roman Empire in A.D. 30. His brother joins him but is killed. The man, who has become influenced by the teachings of Christ, decides to give up his revolution and go off with his brother's widow. (He always loved her anyway.) **78m/B VHS, DVD.** John Beal, Maurice (Moscovitch) Moscovich, Albert Dekker, Marjorie Cooley, Warren McCollum; ***D:*** Irving Pichel.

Great Dan Patch **1/2 1949** The story of the great Dan Patch, the horse that went on to become the highest-earning harness racer in history. **92m/B VHS, DVD.** Dennis O'Keefe, Gail Russell, Ruth Warrick, Charlotte Greenwood, Henry Hull, John Hoyt, Arthur Hunnicutt, Clarence Muse; ***D:*** Joseph M. Newman; ***W:*** John Taintor Foote; ***C:*** Gilbert Warrenton; ***M:*** Rudolph (Rudy) Schrager.

Great Day **1/2 1946** A soap opera set around the wartime visit of first lady Eleanor Roosevelt to a small British town. It focuses mainly on the wife and daughter of a bitter, alcoholic WWI vet. **62m/B VHS.** Eric Portman, Flora Robson, Sheila Sim, Isabel Jeans, Walter Fitzgerald, Philip Friend, Marjorie Rhodes, Maire O'Neill, Beatrice Varley; ***D:*** Lance Comfort.

Great Day in the Morning **1/2 1956** A rebel sympathizer and a Northern spy are both after Colorado gold to help finance the Civil War. But our Southern gentlemen soon find themselves equally interested in the local ladies. **92m/C VHS.** Robert Stack, Ruth Roman, Raymond Burr, Virginia Mayo, Alex Nicol, Regis Toomey; ***D:*** Jacques Tourneur.

The Great Debaters **2007 (PG-13)** Inspirational story focusing on the debate team from all black Wiley College in East Texas who took on—and beat—all comers, including vaunted white rivals, during the 1930s. Debate coach (and labor/civil rights organizer) Melvin B. Tolson (director Washington) winnows down his prospects to four: earnest Hamilton Burgess (Williams), debonair Henry Lowe (Parker), aspiring lawyer and rare female debater Samantha Booke (Smollett), and studious, teenaged prodigy James Farmer Jr. (Denzel Whitaker), who's trying to please his theology professor father (Forest Whitaker, no relation). Naturally in the Jim Crow south they run into lots of problems before the big confrontation with the oh-so-superior Harvard team. The pros graciously step back to allow their younger colleagues room to shine. **127m/C DVD.** *US* Denzel Washington, Forest Whitaker, Nathaniel Parker, Jurnee Smollett, Denzel Whitaker, Jermaine Williams, Gina Ravera, John Heard, Kimberly Elise; ***D:*** Denzel Washington; ***W:*** Robert Eisele; ***C:*** Philippe Rousselot; ***M:*** James Newton Howard, Peter Golub.

The Great Dictator **1940** Chaplin's first all-dialogue film, a searing satire on Nazism in which he has dual roles as a Jewish barber with amnesia who is mistaken for a Hitlerian dictator, Adenoid Hynkel. A classic scene involves Hynkel playing with a gigantic balloon of the world. Hitler banned the film's release to the German public due to its highly offensive portrait of him. The film also marked Chaplin's last wearing of the Little Tramp's (and Hitler's equally little) mustache. **126m/B VHS, DVD.** Charlie Chaplin, Paulette Goddard, Jack Oakie, Billy Gilbert, Reginald Gardiner, Henry Daniell, Maurice (Moscovitch) Moscovich, Emma Dunn, Bernard Gorcey, Paul Weigel, Chester Conklin, Grace Hayle, Carter DeHaven; ***D:*** Charlie Chaplin; ***W:*** Charlie Chaplin; ***C:*** Roland H. Totheroh, Karl Struss; ***M:*** Meredith Willson. Natl. Film Reg. '97;, N.Y. Film Critics '40: Actor (Chaplin).

The Great Elephant Escape **1/2 1995** Vacationing American teen Gordon-Levitt teams up with Kenyan M'Cormac, who works at an animal orphanage, to save a baby elephant from an unscrupulous businessman and his poacher friends. Made for TV. **90m/C VHS.** Joseph Gordon-Levitt, Frederick M'Cormac, Stephanie Zimbalist, Leo Burmester, Julian Sands; ***D:*** George Miller; ***W:*** John Sweet, Christopher Canaan. **TV**

The Great Escape **1/2 1963** During WWII, troublesome allied POWs are thrown by the Nazis into an escape-proof camp, where they join forces in a single mass break for freedom. One of the great war movies, with a superb ensemble cast and lots of excitement. The story was true, based on the novel by Paul Brickhill. McQueen performed most of the stunts himself, against the wishes of director Sturges. Followed by a made for TV movie 25 years later. **170m/C VHS, DVD.** Tom Adams, Steve McQueen, James Garner, Richard Attenborough, Charles Bronson, James Coburn, Donald Pleasence, David McCallum, James Donald, Gordon Jackson, Hannes Messemer, John Leyton, Nigel Stock, Jud Taylor, Hans Reiser, Robert Freitag, Karl Otto Alberty, Angus Lennie, Robert Graf, Harry Riebauer; ***D:*** John Sturges; ***W:*** James Clavell, W.R. Burnett; ***C:*** Daniel F. Fapp; ***M:*** Elmer Bernstein.

The Great Escape 2: The Untold Story **1988** Bland actioner can't decide whether it's a remake of the original or a sequel; it pretends to be a sequel yet spends a lot of time retelling—poorly—the first great escape. Once it gets around to the sequel part, it dispenses with protocol: Pleasence, an escapee in the original, is a Nazi bad guy in this go-round. Poor casting, especially Reeves, unconvincing as a German-speaking British officer who rallies the surviving escapees in revenge against their WWII captors. TV movie was originally shown in two parts, but mercifully shortened for video. **93m/C VHS.** Christopher Reeve, Judd Hirsch, Ian McShane, Donald Pleasence, Anthony John (Tony) Denison, Michael Nader, Charles Haid; ***D:*** Jud Taylor, Paul Wendkos. **TV**

Great Expectations **1/2 1934** Weak Hollywood adaptation of the Dickens novel, easily dwarfed by the brilliant 1946 version. Holmes is Pip, the orphan who rises in the world thanks to a mysterious benefactor (Hull), with Wyatt as Pip's disdainful love, Estrella. **102m/B VHS.** Phillips Holmes, Henry Hull, Jane Wyatt, Florence Reed, Francis L. Sullivan, Alan Hale, Anne Howard; ***D:*** Stuart Walker; ***W:*** Gladys Unger; ***C:*** George Robinson.

Great Expectations **1946** Lean's magisterial adaptation of the Dickens tome, in which a young English orphan is graced by a mysterious benefactor and becomes a well-heeled gentleman. Hailed and revered over the years; possibly the best Dickens on film. Well-acted by all, but especially notable is Hunt's slightly mad and pathetic Miss Havisham. Remake of the 1934 film. **118m/B VHS, DVD.** *GB* John Mills, Valerie Hobson, Anthony Wager, Alec Guinness, Finlay Currie, Jean Simmons, Bernard Miles, Francis L. Sullivan, Martita Hunt, Freda Jackson, Torin Thatcher, Hay Petrie, Eileen Erskine, George "Gabby" Hayes, Everley Gregg, O.B. Clarence; ***D:*** David Lean; ***W:*** David Lean, Ronald Neame; ***C:*** Guy Green; ***M:*** Walter Goeher. Oscars '47: Art Dir./Set Dec., B&W, B&W Cinematog.

Great Expectations **1981** Miniseries adaptation of the Dickens epic about Pip and his mysterious benefactor in Victorian London. **300m/C VHS, DVD.** *GB* Gerry Sundquist, Stratford Johns, Joan Hickson; ***D:*** Julian Amyes; ***W:*** James Andrew Hall. **TV**

Great Expectations **1989** Dickens classic retold on three cassettes. A mysterious benefactor turns a poor orphan boy into a gentleman of means. **325m/C VHS.** *GB* Jean Simmons, Anthony Hopkins, John Rhys-Davies; ***D:*** Kevin Connor. **TV**

Great Expectations **1997 (R)** Expecting "Great Expectations?" The title and basic storyline are about all the filmmakers took for their contemporary updating of Dickens' story. The artistic, orphaned Finn (Hawke) is living a meager existence with his trashy sister and his "uncle" Joe in a Florida fishing town. His destiny is intertwined with an escaped convict (De Niro) he aids, the rich and loony Ms. Dinsmoor (Bancroft) and Dinsmoor's beautiful niece Estella (Paltrow). After being spurned by Estella as a teen, Finn quits painting and drawing entirely. Years later a mysterious art dealer offers him a one-man show in New York if he will move there and start creating again. Estella inevitably reappears in his life, providing more than a little inspiration. More style than substance. Although the visuals are stunning, the director should have learned that beauty on the surface isn't all it's cracked up to be from, say...hmm... "Great Expectations" by Charles Dickens maybe? **112m/C VHS, DVD.** Ethan Hawke, Robert De Niro, Gwyneth Paltrow, Hank Azaria, Anne Bancroft, Chris Cooper, Josh Mostel, Kim Dickens, Nell Campbell, Stephen Spinella; ***D:*** Alfonso Cuaron; ***W:*** Mitch Glazer; ***C:*** Emmanuel Lubezki; ***M:*** Patrick Doyle.

Great Expectations **1/2 1999** British TV version of the Dickens story about the expectations of Pip (Gruffudd). As a boy, he helps escaped convict Magwitch (Hill), a kindness that will change the course of Pip's life, though he doesn't realize it. Also a continuing part of his life is haughty beauty, Estella (Waddell), who has been raised by the eccentric Miss Havisham (Rampling) to wreak havoc on the male gender. A respectable retelling and rather dull. **180m/C VHS, DVD.** Ioan Gruffudd, Justine Waddell, Charlotte Rampling, Bernard Hill, Clive Russell, Laila Morse, Nicholas Woodeson, Lesley Sharp, Emma Cunniffe, Daniel Evans; ***D:*** Julian Jarrold; ***W:*** Tony Marchant. **TV**

Great Expectations: The Untold Story **1/2 1987** Magwitch is an escaped convict, hiding out in the Victorian English countryside, who is aided by the young orphan, Pip. Captured and sent to the penal colonies in Australia, Magwitch serves his time and then discovers a fortune in gold, which he decides to use to make Pip into a gentleman. But Magwitch's enemies would like to get Pip's inheritance for themselves. Based on the Dickens classic, this three-tape miniseries is also available in a 102-minute feature length version. **287m/C VHS.** John Stanton, Sigrid Thornton, Robert Coleby, Todd Boyce, Anne Louise Lambert, Ron Haddrick, Noel Ferrier; ***D:*** Tim Burstall. **TV**

Great Flamarion **1/2 1945** A woman-hating trick-shot artist is nevertheless duped into murdering the husband of his femme fatale assistant after he comes to believe she loves him. He's wrong. **78m/B VHS.** Dan Duryea, Erich von Stroheim, Mary Beth Hughes; ***D:*** Anthony Mann.

The Great Gabbo **1929** A ventriloquist can express himself only through his dummy, losing his own identity and going mad at the end. Von Stroheim's first talkie. May quite possibly be the first mentally-twisted-ventriloquist story ever put on film. Von Stroheim hated the movie, believing it to be analogous to his own life. When he tried to buy the rights to the film, presumably to destroy the prints, he found that the property had been already purchased by real-life ventriloquist, Edgar Bergen. Based on a story by Ben Hecht. ♫The New Step; I'm Laughing Ickey; I'm in Love With You; The Ga-Ga Bird; The Web of Love; Every Now and Then. **82m/B VHS, DVD.** Erich von Stroheim, Betty Compson, Donald "Don" Douglas, Marjorie "Babe" Kane; ***D:*** James Cruze; ***W:*** Ben Hecht, F. Hugh Herbert; ***C:*** Ira Morgan; ***M:*** Howard Jackson, Charley Chase.

The Great Garrick **1/2 1937** Renowned 18th-century actor David Garrick (Aherne) leaves London's Drury Lane for Paris' Comedie Francaise but not before insulting French acting abilities. Wanting to teach the English upstart a lesson, the French troupe concocts an elaborate hoax by taking over the inn where Garrick is staying, but he's on to the prank. Except for the fact that beautiful runaway Germaine (de Havilland) isn't part of the scheme. He insults her but manages to make amends when they meet again. Whale was best-known for directing horror films but he did fine with this period farce (although the script is rickety). **89m/B DVD.** Brian Aherne, Olivia de Havilland, Edward Everett Horton, Melville Cooper, Luis Alberni, Lionel Atwill, Etienne Girardot, Marie Wilson, Lana Turner; ***D:*** James Whale; ***W:*** Ernest Vadja; ***C:*** Ernest Haller; ***M:*** Adolph Deutsch.

The Great Gatsby **1/2 1949** Follows the silent 1926 version of F. Scott Fitzgerald's Jazz Era novel. Mysterious Jay Gatsby (Ladd) is a wealthy gangster and bootlegger who tries to buy his way into fast-living New York society. He befriends well-bred but penniless Nick Carraway (Carey), who serves as Gatsby's one true friend and eyewitness to the unfolding events. Gatsby rekindles his love for decorative Daisy (Field), who married into money and society and merely toys with leaving it all behind for Gatsby. Finally, the shallowness and selfishness all about prove to be Gatsby's undoing. **92m/B VHS.** Alan Ladd, Betty Field, MacDonald Carey, Ruth Hussey, Barry Sullivan, Howard da Silva, Shelley Winters, Henry Hull, Ed Begley Sr., Elisha Cook Jr.; ***D:*** Elliott Nugent; ***W:*** Cyril Hume, Richard Maibaum; ***C:*** John Seitz; ***M:*** Robert Emmett Dolan.

The Great Gatsby **1/2 1974 (PG)** Adaptation of F. Scott Fitzgerald's novel of the idle rich in the 1920s. A mysterious millionaire crashes Long Island society, and finds his heart captured by an impetuous and emotionally impoverished girl. Skillful acting and directing captures the look and feel of this era, but the movie doesn't have the power of the book. **144m/C VHS, DVD.** Robert Redford, Mia Farrow, Bruce Dern, Karen Black, Patsy Kensit, Sam Waterston, Howard da Silva, Edward Herrmann; ***D:*** Jack Clayton; ***W:*** Francis Ford Coppola; ***M:*** Nelson Riddle. Oscars '74: Costume Des., Orig. Song Score and/or Adapt.; Golden Globes '75: Support. Actress (Black).

The Great Gatsby **1/2 2001** Wealthy Jay Gatsby (Stephens) was a poor boy with a questionable past who fell in love with rich girl Daisy (Sorvino), who married another (Donovan). Now Jay, who wants to make it in Jazz Age Newport society, renews his involvement with superficial Daisy, which leads to tragedy. All the drama is observed by Daisy's cousin Nick (Rudd). Adapted from the 1925 F. Scott Fitzgerald novel. **100m/C VHS, DVD.** Toby Stephens, Mira Sorvino, Martin Donovan, Paul Rudd, Francie Swift, Matt Malloy; ***D:*** Robert Markowitz; ***W:*** John McLaughlin; ***C:*** Guy Dufaux; ***M:*** Carl Davis. **CABLE**

The Great Gildersleeve **1943** Throckmorton P. Gildersleeve adds another problem to his list; the sister of a local judge wants to marry him. His niece and nephew won't allow it and his attempts to juggle everyone's desires make for fine fun. Peary was also the voice for the popular radio series of the same name. **62m/B VHS.** Harold (Hal) Peary, Jane Darwell, Nancy Gates, Charles Arnt, Thurston Hall; ***D:*** Gordon Douglas.

Great Gold Swindle **1984** A dramatization of the 1982 swindling of the Perth Mint in Australia of over $650,000 worth of gold. **101m/C VHS.** John Hargreaves, Robert C. Hughes, Tony Rickards, Barbara Llewellyn; ***D:*** John Power; ***W:*** David White; ***C:*** David Sanderson; ***M:*** John Stuart.

The Great Gundown **1/2 1975** A violent tale set in the Old West. The peace of frontier New Mexico erupts when a half-breed Indian leads a brutal assault on an outlaw stronghold. **98m/C VHS.** Robert Padilla, Richard Rust, Milila St. Duval; ***D:*** Paul Hunt.

Great Guns **1941** Stan and Ollie enlist in the army to protect a spoiled millionaire's son but wind up being targets at target practice instead. Not one of their better efforts. **74m/B VHS, DVD.** Stan Laurel, Oliver Hardy, Sheila Ryan, Dick Nelson; ***D:*** Montague (Monty) Banks.

Great Guy **1/2** *Pluck of the Irish* **1936** One of Cagney's lesser roles as an ex-boxer turned food inspector who wipes out graft in his town. **50m/B VHS, DVD.** James Cagney, Mae Clarke, Edward Brophy; ***D:*** John Blystone.

The Great Impostor **1/2 1961** The true story of Ferdinand Waldo Demara Jr. who, during the 1950s, hoodwinked people by impersonating a surgeon, a college professor, a monk, a prison warden, and a schoolteacher, with the FBI always one step behind him. **112m/C VHS.** Tony Curtis, Edmond O'Brien, Arthur O'Connell, Gary Merrill, Raymond Massey, Karl Malden, Mike Kellin, Frank Gorshin; ***D:*** Robert Mulligan; ***C:*** Robert Burks; ***M:*** Henry Mancini.

Great Jesse James Raid 🦴 1/2 **1949** Jesse James comes out of retirement to carry out a mine theft. Routine. **73m/C VHS, DVD.** Willard Parker, Barbara Payton, Tom Neal, Wallace Ford; ***D:*** Reginald LeBorg.

Great K & A Train Robbery 🦴🦴 1/2 **1926** A railroad detective is hired to find and stop the bandits who have been preying on the K & A Railroad. Silent. **55m/B VHS.** Tom Mix, Dorothy Dwan, William Walling, Harry Grippe, Carl Miller; ***D:*** Lewis Seiler.

The Great Land of Small 🦴🦴 **1986 (G)** Two children enter a fantasy world and try to save it from Evil. For kids. **94m/C VHS.** Karen Elkin, Michael Blouin, Michael Anderson Jr., Ken Roberts; ***D:*** Vojtech Jasny.

The Great Lie 🦴🦴🦴 **1941** A great soaper with Davis and Astor as rivals for the affections of Brent, an irresponsible flyer. Astor is the concert pianist who marries Brent and then finds out she's pregnant after he's presumed dead in a crash. The wealthy Davis offers to raise the baby so Astor can continue her career. But when Brent does return, who will it be to? Sparkling, catty fun. Astor's very short, mannish haircut became a popular trend. **107m/B VHS.** Bette Davis, Mary Astor, George Brent, Lucile Watson, Hattie McDaniel, Grant Mitchell, Jerome Cowan; ***D:*** Edmund Goulding; ***C:*** Gaetano Antonio "Tony" Gaudio; ***M:*** Max Steiner. Oscars '41: Support. Actress (Astor).

The Great Locomotive Chase 🦴🦴 1/2 *Andrews' Raiders* **1956** During the Civil War, Parker and his fellow Union soldiers head into Confederate territory to disrupt railroad supply lines. They take over a locomotive, but are pursued by Confederate Hunter, the conductor of another train; and soon a pursuit is underway. Based on the true story of Andrews' Raiders. **85m/C VHS, DVD.** Fess Parker, Jeffrey Hunter, Kenneth Tobey; ***D:*** Francis D. Lyon; ***W:*** Lawrence Edward Watkin; ***C:*** Charles P. Boyle; ***M:*** Paul J. Smith.

The Great Los Angeles Earthquake 🦴 1/2 *The Big One: The Great Los Angeles Earthquake* **1991** Made-for-TV disaster movie is the same old story; multiple soap-opera plotlines are spun around terrifying special effects, as L.A. is devastated by three major earth tremors and attendant disasters. Condensed from a two-part miniseries. **106m/C VHS, DVD.** Ed Begley Jr., Joanna Kerns; ***D:*** Larry Elikann.

The Great Lover 🦴🦴 1/2 **1949** Aboard an ocean liner, a bumbler chaperoning school kids gets involved with a gambler, a duchess and a murder. Vintage Bob Hope. **80m/B VHS, DVD.** Bob Hope, Rhonda Fleming, Roland Young, Roland Culver, George Reeves, Jim Backus, Jack Benny; ***D:*** Alexander Hall; ***W:*** Edmund Beloin, Melville Shavelson, Jack Rose; ***C:*** Charles B(ryant) Lang Jr.

The Great Madcap 🦴🦴 **1949** A wealthy man believes in lavishly indulging himself which drives his excessively conservative family crazy. Bunuel satirizes behavioral extremes, Christianity, advertising, sex, and a number of other popular absurdities. In Spanish with English subtitles. **90m/B VHS.** *MX* Fernando Soler, Rosario Granados, Ruben Rojo; ***D:*** Luis Bunuel.

The Great Man Votes 🦴🦴🦴 **1938** Alcoholic college professor Barrymore falls into a deep depression after his wife's death. His children then plan to create a situation wherein his vote will decide the fate of the new town mayor, thus instilling in him a newly found sense of importance for himself and his children. Satiric and funny. **72m/B VHS.** John Barrymore, Peter Holden, Virginia Weidler, Katherine Alexander, Donald MacBride, Elisabeth Risdon, Granville Bates, Luis Alberni, J.M. Kerrigan, William Demarest, Roy Gordon; ***D:*** Garson Kanin; ***C:*** Russell Metty.

The Great Man's Lady 🦴🦴 1/2 **1942** Stanwyck stars in a "stand by your man" story in which she supported and was responsible for the good deeds of a now past town hero. Told in flashback sequence, Stanwyck's character, 109-year-old Hanna Sampler, reveals to a young biographer the trials and tribulations of her life with Ethan Hoyt, founder of Hoyt City, who is being honored with the dedication of a statue in the opening of the film. The picture reveals their secrets and the truth about the woman behind the man. Based on the story "The Human Side" by Vina Delmar. **91m/B VHS.** Barbara Stanwyck, Joel McCrea, Brian Donlevy; ***D:*** William A. Wellman; ***W:*** Seena Owen, W.L. Rivers, Adela Rogers St. John; ***C:*** William Mellor; ***M:*** Victor Young.

The Great McGinty 🦴🦴🦴 1/2 *Down Went McGinty* **1940** Sturges' directorial debut, about the rise and fall of a small-time, bribe-happy politician is an acerbic, ultra-cynical indictment of modern politics that stands, like much of his other work, as bracingly courageous as anything that's ever snuck past the Hollywood censors. Political party boss Tamiroff chews the scenery with gusto while Donlevy, in his first starring role, is more than his equal as the not-so-dumb political hack. **82m/B VHS.** Brian Donlevy, Muriel Angelus, Akim Tamiroff, Louis Jean Heydt, Arthur Hoyt, William Demarest; ***D:*** Preston Sturges; ***W:*** Preston Sturges; ***C:*** William Mellor. Oscars '40: Orig. Screenplay.

Great McGonagall 🦴 1/2 **1975** Tale of an unemployed Scot trying to become Britain's poet laureate. Sellers adds a semi-bright spot with his portrayal of Queen Victoria! **95m/C VHS.** *GB* Peter Sellers, Spike Milligan, Julia Foster; ***D:*** Joseph McGrath.

The Great Mike 🦴🦴 1/2 **1944** Unlikely but moving story of a young boy who convinces track management that his work horse has a chance against the touted thoroughbred. Sentimental, with little innovation, but generally well-acted. **72m/B VHS, DVD.** Stuart Erwin, Robert "Buzzy" Henry, Pierre Watkin, Gwen Kenyon, Carl "Alfalfa" Switzer, Edythe Elliott, Marion Martin; ***D:*** Wallace Fox.

Great Missouri Raid 🦴🦴 **1951** Follows the famous adventures of the James/Younger gang and their eventual demise. **81m/C VHS.** Wendell Corey, MacDonald Carey, Ellen Drew, Ward Bond; ***D:*** Gordon Douglas; ***C:*** Ray Rennahan.

The Great Moment 🦴🦴 **1944** Story of the Boston dentist who discovered ether's use as an anesthetic in 1845. Confusing at times, changing from comedy to drama and containing flashbacks that add little to the story. Surprisingly bland result from ordinarily solid cast and director. **87m/B VHS.** Joel McCrea, Betty Field, Harry Carey Sr., William Demarest, Franklin Pangborn, Porter Hall; ***D:*** Preston Sturges; ***C:*** Victor Milner.

The Great Mouse Detective 🦴🦴🦴 *The Adventures of the Great Mouse Detective* **1986 (G)** Animated version of the book "Basil of Baker Street" by Eve Titus. Fun adventure concerning the Sherlock-of-the-mouse-world, Basil, who must prevent his arch nemesis, Professor Ratigan, from overthrowing Queen Mousetoria. Not as good as some of the other Disney animated features, but kids will enjoy it nonetheless. **74m/C VHS, DVD.** ***D:*** John Musker, Ron Clements, Dave Michener, Burny Mattinson; ***W:*** Ron Clements, Dave Michener; ***M:*** Henry Mancini; ***V:*** Vincent Price, Barrie Ingham, Val Bettin, Susanne Pollatschek, Candy Candido, Eve Brenner, Alan Young, Melissa Manchester.

The Great Muppet Caper 🦴🦴🦴 **1981 (G)** A group of hapless reporters (Kermit, Fozzie Bear, and Gonzo) travel to London to follow up on a major jewel robbery. **95m/C VHS, DVD.** Charles Grodin, Diana Rigg, John Cleese, Robert Morley, Peter Ustinov, Peter Falk, Jack Warden; ***D:*** Jim Henson; ***W:*** Jack Rose; ***C:*** Oswald Morris; ***V:*** Frank Oz.

The Great New Wonderful 🦴 1/2 **2006 (R)** Five stories about neurotic New Yorkers that are linked by occurring in September 2002, a year after the terrorist attacks (which are never directly mentioned). So you're just left to guess how the characters were actually affected, making for some dull storytelling. **88m/C DVD.** *US* Maggie Gyllenhaal, Thomas (Tom) McCarthy, Judy Greer, Naseeruddin Shah, Tony Shalhoub, Jim Gaffigan, Olympia Dukakis, Dick Latessa, Sharat Saxena, Edie Falco, Stephen Colbert, Jeremy Shamos, Will Arnett, Rosemarie DeWitt, Seth Gilliam, Jim Parsons, Bill Donner, Ed Setrakian, Ari Graynor, Martha Millan, Priscilla Shanks, Sam Catlin; ***D:*** Danny Leiner; ***W:*** Sam Catlin; ***C:*** Harlan Bosmajian; ***M:*** John Swihart.

The Great Northfield Minnesota Raid 🦴🦴 1/2 **1972 (PG)** The Younger/James gang decides to rob the biggest bank west of the Mississippi, but everything goes wrong. Uneven, offbeat western, but Duvall's portrayal of the psychotic Jesse James and Robertson's cunning Cole Younger are notable. **91m/C VHS.** Cliff Robertson, Robert Duvall, Elisha Cook Jr., Luke Askew, R.G. Armstrong, Donald Moffat, Matt Clark; ***D:*** Philip Kaufman; ***W:*** Philip Kaufman; ***C:*** Bruce Surtees; ***M:*** Dave Grusin.

The Great Outdoors 🦴🦴 **1988 (PG)** Good cast is mostly wasted in another John Hughes's tale of vacation gone bad. A family's peaceful summer by the lake is disturbed by their uninvited, trouble-making relatives. Aykroyd and Candy are two funny guys done in by a lame script that awkwardly examines friendship and coming of age and throws in a giant bear when things get unbearably slow. May be fun for small fry. **91m/C VHS, DVD.** Dan Aykroyd, John Candy, Stephanie Faracy, Annette Bening, Chris Young, Lucy Deakins, John Bloom; ***D:*** Howard Deutch; ***W:*** John Hughes; ***C:*** Ric Waite; ***M:*** Thomas Newman.

The Great Plane Robbery 🦴 1/2 **1940** Gang leader Joe Colson (Madison) has insured his life for big bucks, which has the insurance company worried. So they hire PI Mike Henderson (Holt) to make sure Colson stays alive until his policy runs out. Not an easy task when the plane they're flying in is hijacked by racketeer Frankie Toller (Fields) who wants Colson to reveal where he's hiding his dough. **61m/B VHS.** Jack Holt, Stanley Fields, Noel Madison, Milburn Stone, Paul Fix, Vickie Lester; ***D:*** Lewis D. Collins; ***W:*** Albert DeMond; ***C:*** James S. Brown Jr.; ***M:*** Lee Zahler.

The Great Race 🦴🦴 1/2 **1965** A dastardly villain, a noble hero, and a spirited suffragette are among the competitors in an uproarious New York-to-Paris auto race circa 1908, complete with pie fights, saloon brawls, and a confrontation with a feisty polar bear. Overly long and only sporadically funny. **160m/C VHS, DVD.** Jack Lemmon, Tony Curtis, Natalie Wood, Peter Falk, Keenan Wynn, George Macready; ***D:*** Blake Edwards; ***M:*** Henry Mancini. Oscars '65: Sound FX Editing.

The Great Raid 🦴🦴 **2005 (R)** Workmanlike retelling of the 1944 rescue of more than 500 American POWs from a Japanese prison camp located in a remote area of the Philippines. You've got the outside planners, Army Rangers Mucci (Bratt) and Prince (Franco) and their Filipino allies, led by Pajota (Montano); the insiders, led by malaria sufferer Gibson (Fiennes); and nurse Margaret (Nielsen), who's also a resistance leader. Film has a looooong build-up before the raid comes off, which dissipates the tension. Completed in 2002, flick sat on the Miramax shelves until its brief 2005 big screen release. **132m/C DVD, Blu-ray Disc.** *US* Benjamin Bratt, James Franco, Connie Nielsen, Joseph Fiennes, Marton Csokas, Robert Mammone, Natalie Mendoza, Motoki Kobayashi, Cesar Montano, Maximillian Martini, James Carpinello, Craig McLachlan, Dale Dye, Paolo Montalban, Gotaro Tsunashima; ***D:*** John Dahl; ***W:*** Carlo Bernard, Doug Miro; ***C:*** Peter Menzies Jr.; ***M:*** Trevor Rabin.

Great Ride 🦴 **1978** State police are after two dirt bikers who are riding through areas where bike riding is illegal. **90m/C VHS.** Perry Lang, Michael MacRae, Michael Sullivan; ***D:*** Don Hulette.

The Great Riviera Bank Robbery 🦴🦴 1/2 **1979** A genius executes a bank robbery on the French Riviera netting $15 million. Based on a true story, the film chronicles the unfolding of the heist. **98m/C VHS.** Ian McShane, Warren Clarke, Stephen Greif, Christopher Malcolm; ***D:*** Francis Megahy.

The Great Rupert 🦴🦴🦴 *A Christmas Wish* **1950** Durante and family are befriended by a helpful squirrel (a puppet) in obtaining a huge fortune. Good fun; Durante shines. **86m/B VHS, DVD.** Jimmy Durante, Terry Moore, Tom Drake, Frank Orth, Sara Haden, Queenie Smith; ***D:*** Irving Pichel; ***W:*** Laszlo Vadnay; ***C:*** Lionel Lindon.

The Great St. Louis Bank Robbery 🦴🦴 1/2 **1959** Three career criminals (Denton, Clarke, Dukas) and young turk McQueen are brought together for a bank heist. They don't trust each other, which proves fatal when the heist goes bad. Based on a true story and filmed in semi-documentary style. Nineteen-year-old McQueen's follow-up to "The Blob." **86m/B VHS, DVD.** Graham Denton, David Clarke, James Dukas, Steve McQueen, Molly McCarthy; ***D:*** Charles Guggenheim; ***W:*** Richard T. Heffron; ***C:*** Victor Duncan; ***M:*** Bernardo Segall.

The Great St. Trinian's Train Robbery 🦴🦴 **1966** Train robbers hide their considerable loot in an empty country mansion only to discover, upon returning years later, it has been converted into a girls' boarding school. When they try to recover the money, the thieves run up against a band of pestiferous adolescent girls, with hilarious results. Based on the cartoon by Ronald Searle. Sequel to "The Pure Hell of St. Trinian's." **90m/C VHS.** *GB* Dora Bryan, Frankie Howerd, Reg Varney, Desmond Walter-Ellis; ***D:*** Sidney Gilliat, Frank Launder; ***M:*** Malcolm Arnold.

The Great Santini 🦴🦴🦴 *Ace* **1980 (PG)** Lt. Col. Bull Meechum, the "Great Santini," a Marine pilot stationed stateside, fights a war involving his frustrated career goals, repressed emotions, and family. His family becomes his company of marines, as he abuses them in the name of discipline, because he doesn't allow himself any other way to show his affection. With a standout performance by Duvall, the film successfully blends warm humor and tenderness with the harsh cruelties inherent with dysfunctional families and racism. Based on Pat Conroy's autobiographical novel, the movie was virtually undistributed when first released, but re-released due to critical acclaim. **118m/C VHS, DVD.** Robert Duvall, Blythe Danner, Michael O'Keefe, Julie Ann Haddock, Lisa Jane Persky, David Keith; ***D:*** Lewis John Carlino; ***W:*** Lewis John Carlino; ***C:*** Ralph Woolsey; ***M:*** Elmer Bernstein. Montreal World Film Fest. '80: Actor (Duvall).

Great Scout & Cathouse Thursday 🦴 1/2 *Wildcat* **1976 (PG)** Marvin and Reed vow to take revenge on their third partner, Culp, who made off with all their profits from a gold mine. The title refers to Marvin's May-December romance with prostitute Lenz. Already forgotten, unfunny, all-star comedy with cutesy title. **96m/C VHS.** Lee Marvin, Oliver Reed, Robert Culp, Elizabeth Ashley, Kay Lenz; ***D:*** Don Taylor.

The Great Skycopter Rescue 🦴 **1982** Ruthless businessmen hire a motorcycle gang to terrorize and scare away the inhabitants of an oil-rich town. A local teenage flying enthusiast organizes his friends into an attack force to fight back. **96m/C VHS.** William Marshall, Aldo Ray, Russell Johnson, Terry Michos, Terry Taylor; ***D:*** Lawrence Foldes.

Great Smokey Roadblock 🦴🦴 *Last of the Cowboys* **1976 (PG)** While in the hospital, a 60-year-old truck driver's rig is repossessed by the finance company. Deciding that it's time to make one last perfect cross country run, he escapes from the hospital, steals his truck, picks up six prostitutes, heads off into the night with the police on his tail, and becomes a folk hero. **84m/C VHS, DVD.** Henry Fonda, Eileen Brennan, Susan Sarandon, John Byner, Austin Pendleton, Robert Englund, Dub Taylor, Melanie Mayron, Leigh French, Gary Sandy, Valerie Curtin, Bibi Osterwald, Lyman Ward, Sander Vanocuer; ***D:*** John Leone; ***W:*** John Leone; ***C:*** Edward R. Brown; ***M:*** Craig Safan.

The Great Texas Dynamite Chase 🦴 1/2 *Dynamite Women* **1976 (R)** Two sexy young women drive across Texas with a carload of dynamite. They leave a trail of empty banks with the cops constantly on their trail. **90m/C VHS, DVD.** Claudia Jennings, Jocelyn Jones, Johnny Crawford,

Chris Pennock, Tara Strohmeier, Miles Watkins, Bart Braverman; ***D:*** Michael Pressman; ***C:*** Jamie Anderson; ***M:*** Craig Safan.

The Great Train Robbery *The First Great Train Robbery* **1979 (PG)** A dapper thief arranges to heist the Folkstone bullion express in 1855, the first moving train robbery. Well-designed, fast-moving costume piece based on Crichton's best-selling novel. **111m/C VHS, DVD.** *GB* Sean Connery, Donald Sutherland, Lesley-Anne Down, Alan Webb; ***D:*** Michael Crichton; ***W:*** Michael Crichton; ***C:*** Geoffrey Unsworth; ***M:*** Jerry Goldsmith.

Great Treasure Hunt **1972** Four Western rogues help a blind man steal a wealthy crook's gold. **90m/C VHS.** Mark Damon, Stelvio Rosi, Luis Marin; ***D:*** Tonino Ricci.

The Great Waldo Pepper **1975 (PG)** Low key and (for Hill) less commercial film about a WWI pilot-turned-barnstormer who gets hired as a stuntman for the movies. Features spectacular vintage aircraft flying sequences. **107m/C VHS, DVD.** Robert Redford, Susan Sarandon, Margot Kidder, Bo Svenson, Scott Newman, Geoffrey Lewis, Edward Herrmann; ***D:*** George Roy Hill; ***W:*** William Goldman; ***C:*** Robert L. Surtees; ***M:*** Henry Mancini.

A Great Wall *The Great Wall is a Great Wall* **1986 (PG)** A Chinese-American family travels to mainland China to discover the country of their ancestry and to visit relatives. They experience radical culture shock. Wang's first independent feature. In English and Chinese with subtitles. **103m/C VHS, DVD.** Peter Wang, Sharon Iwai, Kelvin Han Yee, Lin Qinqin, Hy Xiaoguang; ***D:*** Peter Wang; ***W:*** Peter Wang, Shirley Sun; ***M:*** David Liang, Ge Ganru.

The Great Wallendas **1978** The true story of the tragedies and triumphs of the Wallendas, a seven-person acrobatic family, who were noted for creating a pyramid on the high wire without nets below them. **96m/C VHS.** Lloyd Bridges, Britt Ekland, Cathy Rigby; ***D:*** Larry Elikann. **TV**

The Great Waltz **1938** The first of two musical biographies on the life of Johann Strauss sees the musician quit his banking job to pursue his dream of becoming a successful composer. A fine, overlooked production rich with wonderful music and romantic comedy. ♫ Tales of Vienna Woods; There'll Come A Time; One Day When We Were Young; Voices of Spring; Du und Du; The Bat; I'm In Love With Vienna; Revolutionary March. **102m/B VHS, DVD.** Luise Rainer, Fernand Gravey, Milza Korjus, Hugh Herbert, Lionel Atwill, Curt Bois, Leonid Kinskey, Al Shean, Minna Gombell, George Houston, Bert Roach, Herman Bing, Alma Kruger, Sig Rumann; ***D:*** Julien Duvivier; ***C:*** Joseph Ruttenberg. Oscars '38: Cinematog.

The Great War *La Grande Guerre* **1959** Two Italian soldiers find themselves in the midst of WWI, much against their will. They try a number of schemes to get out of fighting and working, but their circumstance dictates otherwise. Slightly muddled, but generally good acting. **118m/B VHS.** *FR IT* Vittorio Gassman, Alberto Sordi, Silvana Mangano, Folco Lulli; ***D:*** Mario Monicelli; ***M:*** Nino Rota.

The Great Water *Golemata voda; Velka voda* **2004** Aging Macedonian politician Lem Nikodinoski (Jovanovski) is rushed to the hospital after suffering a heart attack and has the time to reflect on his childhood, which was spent in a Stalinist camp intended to indoctrinate the young into proper communists. There, an orphaned 12-year-old Lem (Kekenovski) is taken under the wing of charismatic teen Isak (Stankovska, an actress cast as a boy), which ultimately leads to a wrenching betrayal. Based on the novel by Zivko Cingo; in English and Macedonian with subtitles. **90m/C DVD.** Nikolina Kujaca, Meto Jovanovski, Saso Kekenovski, Maja Stankovska, Mitko Apostolovski, Verica Nedeska, Risto Gogovski; ***D:*** Ivo Trajkov; ***W:*** Ivo Trajkov, Vladimir Blazevski; ***C:*** Suki Medencevic; ***M:*** Kiril Dzajkovski.

The Great White Hope ½ **1970 (PG-13)** A semi-fictionalized biography of boxer Jack Johnson, played by Jones, who became the first black heavyweight world champion in 1910. Alexander makes her film debut as the boxer's white lover, as both battle the racism of the times. Two Oscar-nominated performances in what is essentially an "opened-out" version of the Broadway play. **103m/C VHS, DVD.** James Earl Jones, Jane Alexander, Lou Gilbert, Joel Fluellen, Chester Morris, Robert Webber, Hal Holbrook, R.G. Armstrong, Moses Gunn, Scatman Crothers; ***D:*** Martin Ritt; ***C:*** Burnett Guffey.

The Great White Hype ½ **1996 (R)** Screenwriter Shelton, who penned "Bull Durham" and "White Men Can't Jump," returns to the sports arena with this satire of the sleazy world of boxing. Jackson's the Don King-esque promoter and manager of heavyweight champ Wayans. Noticing that pay-per-view revenues are slipping, he searches for a white boxer to generate interest and dollars and finds boxer-turned-musician Berg, who beat the champ in their Golden Glove days, and the publicity machine is cranked up for a veritable Lollapalooka. Jackson's performance as the flamboyant Rev. Fred Sultan fuels the entire movie. Concentrating on the shady wheeling and dealing, the boxing action is kept to a minimum. **95m/C VHS, DVD.** Samuel L. Jackson, Damon Wayans, Peter Berg, Jeff Goldblum, Jon Lovitz, Corbin Bernsen, Richard "Cheech" Marin, John Rhys-Davies, Salli Richardson, Rocky Carroll, Jamie Foxx, Michael Jace; ***D:*** Reginald (Reggie) Hudlin; ***W:*** Ron Shelton, Tony Hendra; ***C:*** Ron Garcia; ***M:*** Marcus Miller.

Great World of Sound **2007 (R)** Martin (Healy) sees an ad to become a record producer and joins the shady company of the title. He's partnered with exuberant (and once homeless) Clarence (Holliday) to hit those southern highways and byways and audition and "sign" musical talent. It's a scam, but both men need the job too badly to let their consciences guide them. **108m/C DVD.** Pat Healy, Kene Holliday, Rebecca Mader, Jonathan Baker, Robert Longstreet, Adam Stone, Tricia Paoluccio; ***D:*** Craig Zobel; ***W:*** Craig Zobel, George Smith; ***M:*** David Wingo.

The Great Yokai War ½ *The Great Goblin War; Yokai Daisenso; Spook Warfare; Hobgoblins & the Great War* **2005 (PG-13)** A young boy moves to a small town after his parents divorce, and he ends up involved in a spiritual war between the Yokai (odd monsters or spirits from Japanese folklore with magical powers) and a foreign spirit of toxic waste that moves into their territory. Shockingly this is a children's film directed by Takashi Miike, known for far less tame fare ("Audition," "Visitor Q," "Ichi the Killer," etc). Special effects abound, and while there are many cultural nuances that Western audiences will be oblivious to, fantasy film fans will still be able to appreciate the bevy of unique monsters. **124m/C DVD.** *JP* Ryunosuke Kamiki, Chiaki Kuriyama, Bunta Sugawara, Kaho Minami, Hiroyuki Miyasako, Etsushi Toyokawa, Naoto Takenaka, Kenichi Endo, Sadao Abe, Renji Ishibashi, Toshie Negishi, Tokitoshi Shiota, Riko Narumi, Kiyoshiro Yamawano, Mai Takahashi, Masaomi Kando, Takashi Okamura, Asumi Miwa, Hiroshi Aramata, Natshuhiko Kyogoku, Shigeru Mizuki, Toshiya Nagasawa, Minori Fujikura, Mame Yamada, Hiromasa Taguchi, Rei Yoshii, Kanji Tsuda; ***D:*** Takashi Miike; ***W:*** Takashi Miike, Hiroshi Aramata, Mistuhiko Sawamura, Takehiko Itakura; ***C:*** Hideo Yamamoto; ***M:*** Koji Endo.

The Great Ziegfeld ½ **1936** Big bio-pic of the famous showman; acclaimed in its time as the best musical biography ever done, still considered the textbook for how to make a musical. Look for cameo roles by many famous stars, as well as a walk-on role by future First Lady Pat Nixon. The movie would have stood up as a first-rate biography of Ziegfeld, even without the drop-dead wonderful songs. ♫ Won't You Come Play With Me?; It's Delightful to be Married; If You Knew Susie; Shine On Harvest Moon; A Pretty Girl is Like a Melody; You Gotta Pull Strings; She's a Follies Girl; You; You Never Looked So Beautiful. **179m/B VHS, DVD.** William Powell, Luise Rainer, Myrna Loy, Frank Morgan, Reginald Owen, Nat Pendleton, Ray Bolger, Virginia Bruce, Harriet Hocter, Ernest Cossart, Robert Greig, Gilda Gray, Leon Errol, Dennis Morgan, Mickey Daniels, William Demarest; ***Cameos:*** Fanny Brice; ***D:*** Robert Z. Leonard; ***W:*** William Anthony McGuire. Oscars '36: Actress (Rainer), Picture; N.Y. Film Critics '36: Actress (Rainer), Actress (Rainer).

The Greatest ½ **1977 (PG)** Autobiography of Cassius Clay, the fighter who could float like a butterfly and sting like a bee. Ali plays himself, and George Benson's hit "The Greatest Love of All" is introduced. **100m/C VHS, DVD.** Muhammad Ali, Robert Duvall, Ernest Borgnine, James Earl Jones, John Marley, Roger E. Mosley, Dina Merrill, Paul Winfield; ***D:*** Tom Gries; ***W:*** Ring Lardner Jr.; ***C:*** Harry Stradling Jr.; ***M:*** Michael Masser.

The Greatest Game Ever Played ½ **2005 (PG)** Classic kid-from-the-wrong-side-of-the-tracks story tells how 20-year-old amateur golfer Francis Ouimet (LaBeouf) beat his boyhood idol and defending champ Harry Vardon (Dillane) to win the 1913 U.S. Open. Ouimet's working-class background precludes him from playing at the country club course where he caddies, but he learns to play on his own. Class barriers abound, and there's lots and lots of golfing. The draw of the underdog, the fact that it's a true story, and some fine performances, ultimately carries the day. **115m/C DVD.** *US* Shia LaBeouf, Stephen (Dillon) Dillane, Elias Koteas, Marnie McPhail, Stephen Marcus, Peter Firth, Michael Weaver, Josh Flitter, Peyton List, James Paxton, Matthew Knight, Len Cariou, Luke Askew; ***D:*** Bill Paxton; ***W:*** Mark Frost; ***C:*** Shane Hurlbut; ***M:*** Brian Tyler.

The Greatest Question ½ **1919** Gish is a girl menaced by a married couple whom she saw commit a murder years before. A rush job by Griffith to fulfill his studio obligations but Gish's performance is fine. **80m/B VHS.** Lillian Gish, Robert "Bobbie" Harron, Ralph Graves, Eugenie Besserer, George Fawcett, George Nicholls Jr., Josephine Crowell, Carl Stockdale; ***D:*** D.W. Griffith.

The Greatest Show on Earth **1952** DeMille is in all his epic glory here in a tale of a traveling circus wrought with glamour, romance, mysterious clowns, a tough ringmaster, and a train wreck. **149m/C VHS, DVD.** Betty Hutton, Cornel Wilde, James Stewart, Charlton Heston, Dorothy Lamour, Lawrence Tierney, Gloria Grahame; ***D:*** Cecil B. DeMille. Oscars '52: Picture, Story; Golden Globes '53: Director (DeMille), Film—Drama.

The Greatest Story Ever Told **1965** Christ's journey from Galilee to Golgotha is portrayed here in true international-all-star-epic treatment by director Stevens. A lackluster version of Christ's life, remarkable only for Heston's out-of-control John the Baptist. **196m/C VHS, DVD.** Max von Sydow, Charlton Heston, Sidney Poitier, Claude Rains, Jose Ferrer, Telly Savalas, Angela Lansbury, Dorothy McGuire, John Wayne, Donald Pleasence, Carroll Baker, Van Heflin, Robert Loggia, Shelley Winters, Ed Wynn, Roddy McDowall, Pat Boone; ***D:*** George Stevens; ***W:*** George Stevens, James Lee Barrett; ***C:*** William Mellor, Loyal Griggs; ***M:*** Alfred Newman.

Greed **1924** A wife's obsession with money drives her husband to murder. Although the original version's length (eight hours) was trimmed to 140 minutes, it remains one of the greatest and most highly acclaimed silent films ever made. Effective use of Death Valley locations. Adapted from the Frank Norris novel, "McTeague." **140m/B VHS.** Dale Fuller, Gibson Gowland, Zasu Pitts, Jean Hersholt, Chester Conklin; ***D:*** Erich von Stroheim. Natl. Film Reg. '91.

The Greed of William Hart *Horror Maniacs* **1948** Reworking of the Burke and Hare legend has grave robbers providing Edinburgh medical students with the requisite cadavers. **78m/B VHS, DVD.** *GB* Tod Slaughter, Henry Oscar, Jenny Lynn, Winifred Melville; ***D:*** Oswald Mitchell.

Greedy ½ **1994 (PG-13)** Money-grubbing family suck up to elderly millionaire uncle (Douglas) when they fear he'll leave his money to the sexy, young former pizza delivery girl (d'Abo) he's hired as his nurse. Fox is the long-lost nephew who comes to the rescue. Wicked comedy from veterans Ganz and Mandel should zing, but instead falls flat thanks to a descent into the maudlin. Fox bares his backside and Douglas has fun as the mean old miser, but check out Hartman, a riot as a snarky relative. **109m/C VHS, DVD.** Mary Ellen Trainor, Kirk Douglas, Michael J. Fox, Olivia D'Abo, Phil Hartman, Nancy Travis, Ed Begley Jr., Bob Balaban, Colleen Camp, Jere Burns, Khandi Alexander, Jonathan Lynn; ***D:*** Jonathan Lynn; ***W:*** Lowell Ganz, Babaloo Mandel; ***C:*** Gabriel Beristain; ***M:*** Randy Edelman.

Greedy Terror *The Great Ride* **1978** A cross-country motorcycle trip becomes a real nightmare when two young men realize they're being stalked by a maniac with a thirst for blood. **90m/C VHS.** Michael MacRae, Perry Lang; ***D:*** Don Hulette; ***W:*** Walter Dallenbach; ***M:*** Don Hulette.

Greek Street *Latin Love* **1930** The owner of small cafe in London discovers a poor girl singing in the street for food. He takes her in and spotlights her songs in his cafe. **51m/B VHS.** *GB* Sari Maritza, Arthur Ahmbling, Martin Lewis; ***D:*** Sinclair Hill.

The Greek Tycoon ½ **1978 (R)** Old familiar story about widow of an American president who marries a billionaire shipping magnate and finds that money cannot buy happiness. A transparent depiction of the Onassis/Kennedy marriage, done to a turn. **106m/C VHS.** Anthony Quinn, Jacqueline Bisset, James Franciscus, Raf Vallone, Edward Albert; ***D:*** J. Lee Thompson.

Green Archer **1940** Fifteen episodes of the famed serial, featuring a spooked castle complete with secret passages and tunnels, trapdoors, and the mysterious masked figure, the Green Archer. **283m/B VHS, DVD.** Victor Jory, Iris Meredith, James Craven, Robert (Fisk) Fiske; ***D:*** James W. Horne.

The Green Berets WOOF! **1968 (G)** Cliched wartime heroics co-directed by Wayne and based on Robin Moore's novel. The Duke stars as a Special Forces colonel, leading his troops against the Viet Cong. Painfully insipid pro-war propaganda, notable as the only American film to come out in support of U.S. involvement in Vietnam. Truly embarrassing but did spawn the hit single "Ballad of the Green Beret" by Barry Sadler. **135m/C VHS, DVD.** John Wayne, David Janssen, Jim Hutton, Aldo Ray, George Takei, Raymond St. Jacques, Bruce Cabot, Jack Soo, Patrick Wayne, Luke Askew, Irene Tsu, Edward Faulkner, Jason Evers, Mike Henry, Chuck Roberson, Eddy Donno; ***D:*** John Wayne; ***W:*** James Lee Barrett; ***C:*** Winton C. Hoch; ***M:*** Miklos Rozsa.

The Green Butchers ½ *De Gronne Slagtere* **2003 (R)** Beware the sausage you're eating-particularly if it came from a certain Danish butcher shop. Friends and coworkers Svend (Mikkelsen) and Bjarne (Kaas) decide to open their own shop but business isn't going so well until Svend discovers the body of an electrician who accidentally froze to death in their store's meat locker. For some reason, Svend decides to add some human flesh to his sausage recipe and soon can't sell enough of the resulting delicacy. In order to keep up with demand, Svend turns to murder. It's a comedy. Danish with subtitles. **100m/C DVD.** Mads Mikkelsen, Line Kruse, Nicolas Bro, Nikolaj Lie Kaas; ***D:*** Anders Thomas Jensen; ***W:*** Anders Thomas Jensen; ***C:*** Sebastian Blenkov; ***M:*** Jeppe Kaas.

Green Card ½ **1990 (PG-13)** Some marry for love, some for money, others for an apartment in the Big Apple. Refined, single MacDowell covets a rent-controlled apartment in Manhattan, but the lease stipulates that the apartment be let to a married couple. Enter brusque and burly Depardieu, who covets the elusive green card. The counterpoint between MacDowell, as a stuffy horticulturist, and Depardieu, as a French composer works well, and the two adroitly play a couple whose relationship covers the romantic continuum. Director Weir wrote the screenplay with Depardieu in mind. Depardieu's English-language debut. **108m/C VHS, DVD.** Gerard Depardieu, Andie MacDowell, Bebe Neuwirth, Gregg Edelman, Robert Prosky, Jessie Keosian, Ann Wedgeworth, Ethan Phillips, Mary Louise Wilson, Lois Smith, Simon Jones; ***D:*** Peter Weir; ***W:*** Peter Weir; ***M:*** Hans Zimmer. Golden Globes '91: Actor—Mus./Comedy (Depardieu), Film—Mus./Comedy.

The Green Cockatoo *Four Dark Hours; Race Gang* **1937** Eileen (Ray) has just arrived in London and is still at the train station when Dave (Newton) stumbles into her. He's been stabbed by some crooks and dies and Eileen becomes a suspect. She flees the police to deliver a message to Dave's brother, nightclub entertainer Jim (Mills), and he wants revenge. Based on the book by Graham Greene. **65m/B DVD.** *GB* John Mills, Rene Ray, Robert Newton, Charles Oliver, Bruce Seton, Frank Atkinson, Allan Jeayes, Julien Vedey; ***D:*** William Cameron Menzies; ***W:*** Arthur Wimperis, Edward Berkman; ***C:*** Mutz Greenbaum; ***M:*** Miklos Rozsa.

Green Dolphin Street 1/2 **1947** Flimsy romantic epic set in 19th century New Zealand. A young girl marries the beau she and her sister are battling over in this Oscar-winning special effects show which features one big earthquake. Based on the Elizabeth Goudge novel, this was one of MGM's biggest hits in 1947. **161m/B VHS.** Lana Turner, Van Heflin, Donna Reed, Edmund Gwenn; ***D:*** Victor Saville; ***C:*** George J. Folsey.

Green Dragon 1/2 **2001 (PG-13)** Tai (Duong) is a former Army translator now appointed camp manager at a Vietnamese refugee camp in 1975. He brings a nephew, Minh, and a niece, Anh, as well as a boatload of guilt over leaving their mother behind. He forms a bond with his boss, Jim (Swayze) who seems gruff but has his own issues. The camp cook (Whitaker) helps Minh open up by teaching him to paint and working with him on a mural depicting an idealized American melting pot, with the titular Green Dragon at its center. Various subplots and periods of heavy-handed sentimantality threaten to overwhelm fine character study, but overall this is an engaging look at a period of American history previously ignored. **113m/C VHS, DVD.** Don Duong, Patrick Swayze, Forest Whitaker, Hiep Thi Le, Kieu Chinh, Billinger C. Tran, Trung Hieu Nguyen, Long Nguyen, Jennifer Tran; ***D:*** Timothy Linh Bui; ***W:*** Tony Bui, Timothy Linh Bui; ***C:*** Kramer Morgenthau; ***M:*** Mychael Danna, Jeff Danna.

Green Eyes 1/2 **1934** A costume party in a country mansion sets the scene for a routine murder mystery when the guests find their host stabbed to death in a closet. Based on the novel "The Murder of Stephen Kester" by H. Ashbrook. **68m/B VHS, DVD.** Shirley Grey, Charles Starrett, Claude Gillingwater, John Wray, Dorothy Revier; ***D:*** Richard Thorpe; ***W:*** Melville Shyer.

Green Eyes 1/2 **1976** Winfield, an ex-GI, returns to postwar Vietnam to search for his illegitimate son who he believes will have green eyes. A highly acclaimed drama featuring moving performances from Winfield and Jonathan Lippe. **100m/C VHS.** Paul Winfield, Rita Tushingham, Jonathon Lippe, Victoria Racimo, Royce Wallace, Claudia Bryar; ***D:*** John Erman. **TV**

Green Fields 1/2 *Grine Felder; Gruner Felder* **1937** A quiet romance based on Peretz Hirschbein's legendary tale of a young scholar of the Talmud who leaves the shelter of the synagogue in order to learn about people in the real world. The search takes him to the countryside where he finds himself in the middle of a battle between two families who both want him as a tutor and a suitor for their daughters. In Yiddish with English subtitles. **95m/B VHS, DVD.** Michael Goldstein, Herschel Bernardi, Helen Beverly; ***D:*** Jacob Ben-Ami.

Green Fire 1/2 **1955** The screen sizzles when emerald miner Granger meets plantation-owner Kelly in the exotic jungles of South America. Usual plot complications muddle the story, but who cares when the stars are this attractive? **100m/C VHS.** Stewart Granger, Grace Kelly, Paul Douglas, John Ericson, Murvyn Vye, Jose Torvay, Robert Tafur, Nacho Galindo; ***D:*** Andrew Marton; ***W:*** Ivan Goff, Ben Roberts; ***M:*** Miklos Rozsa.

Green for Danger **1947** A detective stages a chilling mock operation to find a mad killer stalking the corridors of a British hospital during WWII. Sim's first great claim to fame (pre-"A Christmas Carol"). **91m/B VHS, DVD.** *GB* Trevor Howard, Alastair Sim, Leo Genn; ***D:*** Sidney Gilliat.

The Green Glove 1/2 **1952** A jewel thief steals a beautiful relic from a tiny church. WWII makes it impossible for him to fence it and the church finds a relentless ally to track the thief. Excellent action sequences lift this standard plot slightly above the ordinary. **88m/B VHS, DVD.** Glenn Ford, Geraldine Brooks, Cedric Hardwicke, George Macready, Gaby Andre, Roger Treville, Juliette Greco, Jean Bretonniere; ***D:*** Rudolph Mate; ***W:*** Charles Bennett.

Green Grow the Rushes *Brandy Ashore* **1951** The English government tries to put a stop to brandy smuggling on the coast, but the townspeople drink up the evidence. A young Burton highlights this watered-down comedy. Based on a novel by co-scripter Harold Clewes. **77m/B VHS, DVD.** *GB* Roger Livesey, Honor Blackman, Richard Burton, Frederick Leister; ***D:*** Derek Twist.

Green Horizon 1/2 *Afurika Monogatari; A Tale of Africa* **1980** A bucolic old codger faces a dilemma when he must choose between his granddaughter's future and his disaster-prone natural environment. **80m/C VHS.** James Stewart, Philip Sayer, Elenora Vallone; ***D:*** Simon Trevor, Susumu Hani; ***W:*** Shintaro Tsuji; ***C:*** Tsuguzo Matsumae.

The Green Hornet **1939** The feature version of the original serial, in which the Green Hornet and Kato have a series of crime-fighting adventures. **100m/B VHS, DVD.** Gordon Jones, Keye Luke, Anne Nagel, Wade Boteler, Walter McGrail, Douglas Evans, Cy Kendall; ***D:*** Ford Beebe, Ray Taylor; ***W:*** George Plympton, Basil Dickey; ***C:*** Jerome Ash, William Sickner.

The Green House *The Greenhouse; Le Jardin des Plantes* **1996** Fernand Bonard (Rich) is the aged caretaker of the Paris zoo's botanical gardens during the waning days of WWII. His son Armand (Labarthe) is a collaborator who arrives at his father's home with eight-year-old daughter, Philippine (Stevenin), to celebrate her birthday. When Armand is suddenly killed by the Gestapo, Fernand begins an elaborate deception for his granddaughter, portraying her father as a hero of the French Resistance but his illusions take an unexpected turn. French with subtitles. **93m/C VHS.** *FR* Claude Rich, Salome Stevenin, Samuel Labarthe, Catherine Jacob, Rose Thiery; ***D:*** Philippe de Broca; ***W:*** Philippe de Broca, Alexandre Jardin; ***C:*** Janos Kende; ***M:*** Charles Court.

Green Ice 1/2 **1981** An American electronics expert gets involved with a brutal South American government dealing with emeralds and plans a heist with his girlfriend and other cohorts. A little bit of romance, a little bit of action, a lot of nothing much. **109m/C VHS.** *GB* Ryan O'Neal, Anne Archer, Omar Sharif, John Larroquette; ***D:*** Ernest Day; ***W:*** Edward Anhalt, Robert De Laurentis.

Green Inferno *Tarzan and the Jungle Mystery* **1972** A wealthy eccentric who lives deep in the South American jungle incites the natives to rebel. Mercenary agents are then hired to kill him. **90m/C VHS.** *SP* Richard Yesteran, Didi Sherman, Caesar Burner; ***D:*** Miguel Iglesias.

The Green Man **1991** Maurice Allington (Finney), the alcoholic and randy owner of the Green Man Inn in rural England, jokes about the spirits that supposedly haunt the inn. It's not too funny, however, when he discovers the spirits are real and he has to figure out who the spirit of a 17th-century murderer is inhabiting before he kills again. A classy ghost story based on the novel by Kingsley Amis. **150m/C VHS.** *GB* Albert Finney, Sarah Berger, Linda Marlowe, Michael Hordern, Nickolas Grace, Michael Culver; ***D:*** Elijah Moshinsky; ***W:*** Malcolm Bradbury.

Green Mansions **1959** Screen adaptation of W. H. Hudson's novel suffers due to miscasting of Hepburn as Rima the Bird Girl, who is not permitted to leave her sanctuary. Perkins is good as the male lead who fled to the jungle in search of wealth and instead finds a powerful love. Hepburn was married to director Ferrer at the time. **104m/C VHS.** Audrey Hepburn, Anthony Perkins, Lee J. Cobb, Sessue Hayakawa, Henry Silva, Nehemiah Persoff, Michael Pate; ***D:*** Mel Ferrer; ***W:*** Dorothy Kingsley; ***C:*** Joseph Ruttenberg.

The Green Mile 1/2 **1999 (R)** Lightning didn't exactly strike twice when Darabont directed this follow-up to "The Shawshank Redemption," another period prison drama by Stephen King. Paul Edgecomb (Hanks) is the decent head guard at Louisiana's Cold Mountain Penitentiary in 1935. He works E block, which is death row (title refers to the color of the floor). Among his prisoners is hulking black man John Coffey (Duncan), whose intimidating size belies a sweet nature. And something else—it seems Coffey has the power to heal. Overlong and watching the executions takes a strong stomach; characters are more symbols than human beings. **187m/C VHS, DVD, Blu-ray Disc.** Tom Hanks, Michael Clarke Duncan, David Morse, Bonnie Hunt, Michael Jeter, Sam Rockwell, James Cromwell, Patricia Clarkson, Graham Greene, Barry Pepper, Doug Hutchison, Jeffrey DeMunn, Harry Dean Stanton, Dabbs Greer, Eve Brent, William Sadler, Gary Sinise; ***D:*** Frank Darabont; ***W:*** Frank Darabont; ***C:*** David Tattersall; ***M:*** Thomas Newman. Broadcast Film Critics '99: Adapt. Screenplay, Support. Actor (Duncan).

Green Pastures **1936** An adaptation of Marc Connelly's 1930 Pulitzer Prize-winning play, which attempts to retell Biblical stories in black English vernacular of the '30s. Southern theatre owners boycotted the controversial film which had an all-Black cast. **93m/C VHS, DVD.** Rex Ingram, Oscar Polk, Eddie Anderson, George Reed, Abraham Graves, Myrtle Anderson, Frank Wilson; ***D:*** William Keighley, Marc Connelly; ***C:*** Hal Mohr.

Green Plaid Shirt **1996** In 1978, Phillip and Guy are exploring first love while their friends, Devon, Jerry, and Todd are exploring life. Ten years later, Phillip is the only one to survive the AIDS impact on the gay community as he tries to make sense of what happened and what comes next. **90m/C VHS, DVD.** Gregory Phelan, Kevin Blair Spirtas, Russell Scott Lewis, Richard Israel, Jonathan Klein; ***D:*** Richard Natale; ***W:*** Richard Natale; ***C:*** Amit Bhattacharya; ***M:*** Norman Noll.

The Green Promise *Raging Waters* **1949** A well-meaning but domineering farmer and his four motherless children face disaster as a result of the father's obstinacy. But when he is laid up, the eldest daughter takes over, tries modern methods and equipment, and makes the farm a success. **90m/B VHS, DVD.** Ted Donaldson, Connie Marshall, Robert Ellis, Irving Bacon, Milburn Stone, Walter Brennan, Marguerite Chapman, Robert Paige, Natalie Wood; ***D:*** William D. Russell; ***W:*** Monte (Monty) Collins Jr.; ***C:*** John L. "Jack" Russell; ***M:*** Rudolph (Rudy) Schrager.

The Green Room *La Chambre Verte* **1978 (PG)** Truffaut's haunting tale of a man who, valuing death over life, erects a shrine to all the dead he has known. Offered a chance at love, he cannot overcome his obsessions to take the risk. Based on the Henry James story "Altar of the Dead." In French with subtitles. **95m/C VHS.** *FR* Antoine Vitez, Jane Lobre, Marcel Berbert, Francois Truffaut, Nathalie Baye, Jean Daste; ***D:*** Francois Truffaut; ***W:*** Jean Gruault; ***C:*** Nestor Almendros; ***M:*** Maurice Jaubert.

The Green Slime **WOOF!** *Gamma Sango Uchu Daisakusen; Battle Beyond the Stars; Death and the Green Slime* **1968 (G)** Danger and romance highlight the journey of a space ship assigned to intercept an oncoming asteroid. Little do the astronauts realize, but they have brought aboard the ship the malevolent alien creatures known as green slime (and we ain't talking jello here). Cheap, U.S./Japanese co-production will leave you feeling lousy in the morning. The title song is legendary among genre aficionados. **90m/C VHS.** *JP* Robert Horton, Richard Jaeckel, Luciana Paluzzi, Bud Widom, Ted Gunther, Robert Dunham; ***D:*** Kinji Fukasaku; ***W:*** Ivan Reiner, Charles Sinclair, Bill Finger; ***C:*** Yoshikazu Yamasawa; ***M:*** Charles Fox, Toshiaki Tsushima.

Green Snake **1993** Combo of mysticism and action based on a Chinese fable. Green Snake (Cheung) and Son Ching (Wong) are actual reptiles who have been practicing taking human form. When self-righteous Buddhist monk Fa-Hai discovers them, he thinks it's a sin to tamper with the natural order. The snakes don't appreciate his lack of compassion and plot destruction. Cantonese with subtitles. **102m/C VHS, DVD.** *HK* Maggie Cheung, Joey Wong; ***D:*** Tsui Hark.

Green Street Hooligans 1/2 **2005 (R)** Matt Buckner (Wood) is expelled from Harvard weeks before graduating when he's forced to take the fall for his wealthy roommate after cocaine is found in their room. He accepts $10,000 in hush money and takes off for London to visit his sister Shannon (Forlani) and brother-in-law Steve (Warren). Steve's younger brother Pete (Hunnam) takes Matt to a West Ham football match, where he's introduced to the violent world of the Green Street Elite, the gang of rabid fans committed to supporting the West Ham football club through bloody street warfare with supporters of opposing teams. Yank's eye view of the gritty nature of soccer hooliganism will leave you both fascinated and repelled. **106m/C DVD.** *GB US* Elijah Wood, Charlie Hunnam, Claire Forlani, Marc Warren, Leo Gregory, Henry Goodman, Geoff Bell, Ross McCall, Rafe Spall, Kieran Bew, Francis Pope, Christopher Hehir, Terence Jay; ***D:*** Lexi Alexander; ***W:*** Lexi Alexander, Dougie Brimson, Josh Shelov; ***C:*** Alexander Buono; ***M:*** Christopher Franke.

Green Street Hooligans 2 **2009** After a particularly brutal brawl, members of the Green Street Elite and their Millwall rivals end up in the same prison where the violence escalates. Almost every prison cliche you can imagine is on display to no great effect and the pic has little in common with its 2005 predecessor except for its violence. **94m/C DVD.** *GB* Ross McCall, Nicky Holender, Luke Massy, Graham McTavish, Marina Sirtis, Treva Etienne, Terence Jay; ***D:*** Jesse Johnson; ***W:*** T. Jay O'Brien; ***C:*** Jonathan Hall.

The Green Wall **1970** A city-dwelling young man attempts to homestead with his family in the Amazon. A lovely and tragic film with stunning photography of the Peruvian forests. First Peruvian feature to be shown in the U.S. In Spanish with English subtitles. **110m/C VHS.** *SP* Julio Aleman, Sandra Riva; ***D:*** Armando Robles Godoy; ***W:*** Armando Robles Godoy.

Green Zone **2010 (R)** Reuniting the director and star of two of the "Bourne" series of action flicks, this thriller takes a more serious and realistic look at military secrecy. During the U.S.-led occupation of Baghdad, Roy Miller (Damon) is sent to find weapons of mass destruction allegedly stockpiled in the Iraqi desert. The only thing Miller discovers, however, is faulty intelligence and a region becoming increasingly unstable. Encounters with a slick State Department boss (Kinnear) and a jaded CIA agent (Gleeson) show him the dangers of less obvious minefields as well. Director Greengrass uses his patented "shaky-cam" technique once again, but the action sequences are never over-the-top and lend a real sense of the danger the troops face. **114m/C DVD.** Matt Damon, Greg Kinnear, Amy Ryan, Jason Isaacs, Brendan Gleeson; ***D:*** Paul Greengrass; ***W:*** Brian Helgeland; ***C:*** Barry Ackroyd; ***M:*** John Powell.

Greenberg 1/2 **2010 (R)** Cranky, unmotivated ex-rocker-turned-carpenter Roger Greenberg (Stiller), newly released from a mental hospital, uproots from New York to housesit for his brother in Los Angeles. While there, his abrasive personality begins to win over his brother's personal assistant, Florence (Gerwig), who's been assigned to look out for him. Dry, subtle but uneven, coming-of-middle-age comedy that often fumbles, accurately expressing the pain and humor of its characters' lives. **107m/C DVD.** *US* Ben Stiller, Greta Gerwig, Rhys Ifans, Brie Larson, Juno Temple, Mark Duplass, Jennifer Jason Leigh, Dave Franco, Chris Messina; ***D:*** Noah Baumbach; ***W:*** Noah Baumbach; ***C:*** Harris Savides.

Greenfingers 1/2 **2000 (R)** One of those strange-but-true stories that barely stays ahead of being twee, thanks to its cast. Surly prisoner Colin Briggs (Owen) has just been transferred to Edgefield, an "open" prison that aims at building job skills. When Colin accidentally turns out to be a prime gardener (with greenfingers in British parlance), warden Hodge (Clarke) assigns him to garden detail along with his twinkly, dying, elderly cellmate Fergus (Kelly). Then the prison garden comes to the attention of TV star gardener Georgina Woodhouse (Mirren) and she sponsors their efforts in a very prestigious flower show. Remember the Brits take their gardening very seriously indeed. **90m/C VHS, DVD.** *GB US* Clive Owen, Helen Mirren, David Kelly, Warren Clarke, Danny Dyer,

Paterson Joseph, Natasha Little, Adam Fogerty; ***D:*** Joel Hershman; ***W:*** Joel Hershman; ***C:*** John Daly; ***M:*** Guy Dagul.

Greenmail 🦴 **2001 (R)** A Seattle serial bomber is targeting corporations that harm the environment. Naturally, the bomb squad must stop him. Even things getting blowed up good can't save this one. **92m/C VHS, DVD.** Stephen Baldwin, Tom Skerritt, Kelly Rowan, D.B. Sweeney; ***D:*** Jonathan Heap; ***W:*** Raul Inglis, James Makichuk; ***C:*** Michael G. Wojciechowski. **VIDEO**

Greenwich Village 🦴🦴 **1944** Would-be classical composer Kenneth Harvey (Ameche) finds his work being adapted for a musical revue by speakeasy owner Danny O'Mara (Bendix). But Harvey isn't too upset when he discovers singer Bonnie Watson (Blaine in her screen debut) is working on the show. Miranda is the club's fortune-telling comic foil. **82m/C DVD.** Don Ameche, William Bendix, Vivian Blaine, Carmen Miranda, Felix Bressart; ***D:*** Walter Lang; ***W:*** Earl Baldwin, Ernest Pagano, Michael Fessier, Walter Bullock; ***C:*** Leon Shamroy, Harry Jackson; ***M:*** Emil Newman, Chuck Henderson.

Greetings 🦴🦴🦴 **1968 (R)** De Niro stars in this wild and crazy comedy about a man who tries to help his friend flunk his draft physical. One of DePalma's first films, and a pleasantly anarchic view of the late '60s, wrought with a light, intelligent tone. Followed by the sequel "Hi, Mom." **88m/C VHS, DVD.** Robert De Niro, Jonathan Warden, Gerrit Graham, Allen (Goorwitz) Garfield, Megan McCormick, Bettina Kugel, Jack Cowley, Richard Hamilton; ***D:*** Brian De Palma; ***W:*** Brian De Palma, Charles Hirsch; ***C:*** Robert Fiore.

Gregory's Girl 🦴🦴🦴 **1/2 1980** Sweet, disarming comedy established Forsyth. An awkward young Scottish schoolboy falls in love with the female goalie of his soccer team. He turns to his 10-year-old sister for advice, but she's more interested in ice cream than love. His best friend is no help, either, since he has yet to fall in love. Perfect mirror of teenagers and their instantaneous, raw, and all-consuming loves. Very sweet scene with Gregory and his girl lying on their backs in an open space illustrates the simultaneous simplicity and complexity of young love. **91m/C VHS, DVD.** *GB* Gordon John Sinclair, Dee Hepburn, Jake D'Arcy, Chic Murray, Alex Norton, John Bett, Clare Grogan; ***D:*** Bill Forsyth; ***W:*** Bill Forsyth; ***C:*** Michael Coulter. British Acad. '81: Screenplay.

Gremlins 🦴🦴🦴 **1984 (PG)** Comedy horror with deft satiric edge. Produced by Spielberg. Fumbling gadget salesman Rand Peltzer is looking for something really special to get his son Billy. He finds it in a small store in Chinatown. The wise shopkeeper is reluctant to sell him the adorable "mogwai" but relents after fully warning him "Don't expose him to bright light, don't ever get him wet, and don't ever, ever feed him after midnight." Naturally, this all happens and the result is a gang of nasty gremlins who decide to tear up the town on Christmas Eve. Followed by "Gremlins 2: The New Batch" which is less black comedy, more parody, and perhaps more inventive. **106m/C VHS, DVD.** Zach Galligan, Phoebe Cates, Hoyt Axton, Polly Holliday, Frances Lee McCain, Keye Luke, Dick Miller, Corey Feldman, Judge Reinhold, Glynn Turman, Scott Brady, Jackie Joseph; ***D:*** Joe Dante; ***W:*** Chris Columbus; ***C:*** John Hora; ***M:*** Jerry Goldsmith; ***V:*** Howie Mandel.

Gremlins 2: The New Batch 🦴🦴🦴 **1/2 1990 (PG-13)** The sequel to "Gremlins" is superior to the original, which was quite good. Set in a futuristic skyscraper in the Big Apple, director Dante presents a less violent but far more campy vision, paying myriad surreal tributes to scores of movies, including "The Wizard of Oz" and musical extravaganzas of the past. Also incorporates a Donald Trump parody, takes on TV news, and body slams modern urban living. Great fun. **107m/C VHS, DVD.** Zach Galligan, Phoebe Cates, John Glover, Christopher Lee, Robert Prosky, Robert Picardo, Haviland (Haylie) Morris, Dick Miller, Jackie Joseph, Keye Luke, Belinda Balaski, Paul Bartel, Kenneth Tobey, John Astin, Henry Gibson, Leonard Maltin, Hulk Hogan, Charles S. Haas; ***Cameos:*** Jerry Goldsmith; ***D:*** Joe Dante; ***W:*** Charles S. Haas; ***C:*** John Hora; ***M:*** Jerry Goldsmith; ***V:*** Howie Mandel, Tony Randall.

Grendel, Grendel, Grendel 🦴🦴 **1982** An utterly urbane dragon wants to be friends, but for some reason people are just terrified of Grendel. It's true, he bites a head off once in a while, but nobody's perfect! An ingenious, animated retelling of Beowulf. **90m/C VHS.** *AU* ***D:*** Alexander Stitt; ***M:*** Bruce Smeaton; ***V:*** Peter Ustinov, Arthur Dignam, Julie McKenna, Keith Michell.

Greta 🦴🦴🦴 **1986** During WWII, a young Polish boy escapes from a detention camp. Now on the run, several bizarre twists of fate place him in the care of Greta, a young girl whose father is an officer in the S.S. In Polish with English subtitles. **60m/C VHS.** *PL* Janusz Grabowski, Agnieszka Kruszewska, Eva Borowik, Tomasz Grochoczki, Andrzej Precig; ***D:*** Krzysztof Gruber.

The Grey Fox 🦴🦴🦴 **1/2 1983 (PG)** Based on the true story of Canada's most colorful and celebrated outlaw. Gentlemanly old stagecoach robber Bill Miner (Farnsworth) tries to pick up his life after 30 years in prison. Unable to resist another heist, he tries train robbery, and winds up hiding out in British Columbia where he meets photographer Kate Flynn (Burroughs), come to document the changing West. Farnsworth is perfect as the man who suddenly finds himself in the 20th century trying to work at the only craft he knows. Borso's first feature film after his work as a documentary filmmaker. **92m/C VHS.** *CA* Richard Farnsworth, Jackie Burroughs, Wayne Robson, Timothy Webber, Ken Pogue; ***D:*** Phillip Borsos; ***W:*** John Hunter; ***C:*** Frank Tidy; ***M:*** Michael Conway Baker. Genie '83: Director (Borsos), Film, Support. Actress (Burroughs).

Grey Gardens 🦴🦴🦴 **2009** Stellar performances from both Barrymore and Lange in a cable flick that was inspired by the 1973 documentary by the Maysles brothers, with director Michael Sucsy devotedly recreating a number of scenes. In the 1930s, vivacious 'Big Edie' Beale (Lange) is a party-thrower par excellence while her teenaged daughter 'Little Edie' (Barrymore) wants to be a starlet. As the years roll by, resources dwindle, eccentricities (and co-dependence) grow, and their East Hampton mansion becomes unlivable. In the early 1970s, things get so bad that the authorities raid the place and Jacqueline Kennedy Onassis (Tripplehorn), a relative, makes an ultimately unsuccessful attempt to help the recluses. **104m/C DVD.** Drew Barrymore, Jessica Lange, Jeanne Tripplehorn, Ken Howard, Daniel Baldwin, Malcolm Gets, Arye Gross, Justin Louis; ***D:*** Michael Sucsy; ***W:*** Patricia Rozema, Michael Sucsy; ***C:*** Mike Eley; ***M:*** Rachel Portman. **CABLE**

Grey Owl 🦴🦴 **1/2 1999 (PG-13)** Interesting old-fashioned biopic suffers from miscasting (and it's not Brosnan, although he takes a little getting used to). Based on the true story of Archie Grey Owl (Brosnan), an Ojibway trapper in 1930s Canada who changes his occupation and becomes an ardent early environmentalist and celebrity lecturer and writer. Only after his death does the truth come out—Archie was in fact Englishman Archibald Belaney. Film bogs down in its romantic aspects with Galipeau, as Grey Owl's young Mohawk girlfriend, sadly out of her depths. **117m/C VHS, DVD.** *GB CA* Pierce Brosnan, Annie Galipeau, Vlasta Vrana, Nathaniel Arcand, David Fox, Charles Powell, Renee Asherson, Stephenie Cole, Graham Greene; ***D:*** Richard Attenborough; ***W:*** William Nicholson; ***C:*** Roger Pratt; ***M:*** George Fenton. Genie '99: Costume Des.

The Grey Zone 🦴🦴 **2001 (R)** Nelson adapted his own play, which centers on the Sonderkommandos, Jewish prisoners who worked in the crematoriums (in this case at Auschwitz), disposed of remains, and were given special privileges by the Nazis. In October of 1944, the prisoners plan an uprising and blew up two of the gas chambers. The film can't transcend its theatrical origins and is both surreal and excruciating (since Nelson doesn't spare depicting the atrocities) to watch. **108m/C VHS, DVD.** *US* David Arquette, Daniel Benzali, Steve Buscemi, David Chandler, Allan Corduner, Harvey Keitel, Natasha Lyonne, Mira Sorvino; ***D:*** Tim Blake Nelson; ***W:*** Tim Blake Nelson; ***C:*** Russell Fine; ***M:*** Jeff Danna.

Greyfriars Bobby 🦴🦴 **1/2 1961** A true story of a Skye terrier named Bobby who, after his master dies, refuses to leave the grave. Even after being coaxed by the local children into town, he still returns to the cemetery each evening. Word of his loyalty spreads, and Bobby becomes the pet of 19th century Edinburgh. Nicely told, with fine location photography and good acting. Great for children and animal lovers. **91m/C VHS, DVD.** Donald Crisp, Laurence Naismith, Kay Walsh; ***D:*** Don Chaffey.

Greystoke: The Legend of Tarzan, Lord of the Apes 🦴🦴 **1984 (PG)** The seventh Earl of Greystoke becomes a shipwrecked orphan and is raised by apes. Ruling the ape-clan in the vine-swinging persona of Tarzan, he is discovered by an anthropologist and returned to his ancestral home in Scotland, where he is immediately recognized by his grandfather. The contrast between the behavior of man and ape is interesting, and Tarzan's introduction to society is fun, but there's no melodrama or cliff-hanging action, as we've come to expect of the Tarzan genre. Due to her heavy southern accent, Andie MacDowell (as Jane) had her voice dubbed by Glenn Close. **130m/C VHS, DVD.** Christopher Lambert, Ralph Richardson, Ian Holm, James Fox, Andie MacDowell, Ian Charleson, Cheryl Campbell, Nigel Davenport; ***D:*** Hugh Hudson; ***W:*** Michael Austin. N.Y. Film Critics '84: Support. Actor (Richardson).

Gridiron Gang 🦴🦴 **2006 (PG-13)** Based on the true story of correctional officer Sean Porter (The Rock), who recruits a bunch of gangbangers stuck in a juvie camp for his football team. Naturally, the teens find hope through the help of the game and their tough coach. Heavily motivational sports cliche; the documentary footage shown at the end, of the real team and the real coach, may be the best part of the movie. **125m/C DVD, Blu-ray Disc.** *US* Dwayne "The Rock" Johnson, Xzibit, Leon Rippy, Kevin Dunn, Willie Weathers; ***D:*** Phil Joanou; ***W:*** Jeff Maguire; ***C:*** Jeff Cutler; ***M:*** Trevor Rabin.

Gridlock'd 🦴🦴🦴 **1996 (R)** Junkies and sometime-musicians Spoon (Shakur) and Stretch (Roth) decide to kick the habit after their singer Cookie (Newton) overdoses and slips into a coma. The hapless pair are thrown into the switches of social services programs and government offices where they shuffle endlessly but nothing happens. Think "Waiting for Godot" meets "Waiting for the Man." Meanwhile, their dealer is murdered and they're the prime suspects, pursued by the cops and the actual killers, who believe that they've stolen said dealer's stash. Shakur shows flashes of the brilliance that might have been as the more sensitive and sane of the pair, while Roth complements him perfectly as his bug-crazy short-sighted partner. Fellow actor Curtis-Hall's directorial debut. **91m/C VHS, DVD.** Tim Roth, Tupac Shakur, Thandie Newton, Charles Fleischer, Howard Hesseman, James Pickens Jr., John Sayles, Tom Towler, Eric Payne; ***Cameos:*** Vondie Curtis-Hall; ***D:*** Vondie Curtis-Hall; ***W:*** Vondie Curtis-Hall; ***C:*** Bill Pope; ***M:*** Stewart Copeland.

Grief 🦴🦴 **1994** Mark (Chester) is a writer on the syndicated daytime TV show "The Love Judge." Still numb from his lover's death from AIDS the previous year, Mark begins to take an interest in fellow writer Bill (Arquette), while writer Paula (Gutteridge) desires to become the show's new producer and secretary Leslie (Douglas) wants to take her place as the new writer. Present producer Jo (Beat) tries to keep her office family in line while sorting out her personal life. Writer-director Glatzer knows his territory since he spent five years writing for "Divorce Court." **86m/C VHS, DVD.** Craig Chester, Alexis Arquette, Lucy Gutteridge, Illeana Douglas, Jackie Beat, Carlton Wilborn, Paul Bartel, Mary Woronov; ***D:*** Richard Glatzer; ***W:*** Richard Glatzer; ***C:*** David Dechant.

Grievous Bodily Harm 🦴🦴 **1989 (R)** Morris Martin's wife Claudine is missing. When he finds a videotape of Claudine in very compromising positions, he becomes murderously determined to find out where she has gone. **136m/C VHS.** John Waters, Colin Friels, Bruno Lawrence; ***D:*** Mark Joffe.

Griffin & Phoenix 🦴 **1/2 2006 (PG-13)** Despite the effective leads, this is a sentimental tearjerker of the worst sort (and a remake of the 1976 TV movie). Divorced workaholic Henry Griffin (Mulroney) learns that his inoperable cancer leaves him less than two years to live. While auditing a college course on death and dying, Henry meets Sarah Phoenix (Peet) and they decide to take a chance on romance. But it comes as no shocker that Sarah is hiding her own terminal secret. **102m/C DVD.** Dermot Mulroney, Amanda Peet, Sarah Paulson, Blair Brown, Alison Elliott, Lois Smith; ***D:*** Ed Stone; ***W:*** John Hill; ***C:*** David M. Dunlap; ***M:*** Roger Neill.

Griffin and Phoenix: A Love Story 🦴🦴 **1/2 1976** A sentimental film about the mortality of two vital people. Falk deserts his family when he learns he has terminal cancer. Clayburgh, also terminally ill, meets him for a short but meaningful affair. Good performances help overcome the tear-jerker aspects of the story. **110m/C VHS.** Peter Falk, Jill Clayburgh, Dorothy Tristan, John Lehne; ***D:*** Daryl Duke. **TV**

The Grifters 🦴🦴🦴 **1/2 1990 (R)** Evocative rendering of a terrifying sub-culture. Huston, Cusak, and Bening are con artists, struggling to stay on top in a world where violence, money, and lust are the prizes. Bening and Huston fight for Cusak's soul, while he's determined to decide for himself. Seamless performances and dazzling atmosphere, along with superb pacing, make for a provocative film. Based on a novel by Jim Thompson. **114m/C VHS, DVD.** Anjelica Huston, John Cusack, Annette Bening, Pat Hingle, J.T. Walsh, Charles Napier, Henry Jones, Gailard Sartain, Jeremy Piven; ***D:*** Stephen Frears; ***W:*** Donald E. Westlake; ***C:*** Oliver Stapleton; ***M:*** Elmer Bernstein. Ind. Spirit '91: Actress (Huston), Film; L.A. Film Critics '90: Actress (Huston); Natl. Soc. Film Critics '90: Actress (Huston), Support. Actress (Bening).

Grilled 🦴 **1/2** *Men Don't Quit* **2006 (R)** Struggling meat salesmen Maurice (Romano) and Dave (James) have their bacon on the line if they don't make a big sale. There's also a mobster, his girl, and a couple of hitmen that also involve the guys. The duo did much better on the small screen, having misplaced their comedy chops while making this yawner. **77m/C DVD.** *US* Ray Romano, Kevin James, Juliette Lewis, Sofia Vergara, Michael Rapaport, Barry Newman, Burt Reynolds, Kim Coates, Eric Allen Kramer, Jack Kehler, Jon Polito, Lisa Jane Persky, Mary Lynn Rajskub, Caroline Aaron, Richard Libertini, Lisa Edelstein; ***D:*** Jason Ensler; ***W:*** William Tepper; ***C:*** Lawrence Sher; ***M:*** Adam Cohen. **VIDEO**

Grim 🦴 **1995 (R)** Lives up to its title as an extremely icky and evil subterranean creature is awakened from a long sleep by miners. Apparently not long enough, since he proceeds to rip apart anyone he comes in contact with. **86m/C VHS, DVD.** Emmanuel Xuereb, Tres Handley, Peter Tregloan; ***D:*** Paul Matthews; ***W:*** Paul Matthews; ***C:*** Alan M. Trow; ***M:*** Dennis Michael Tenney.

Grim Prairie Tales 🦴🦴 **1989 (R)** A city slicker and a crazed mountain man meet by a campfire in the high plains one night and pass the time sharing four tales of Western horror. Dourif and Jones are fun, the stories scary, making for an interesting twist on both the horror and the Western genres. **90m/C VHS.** Brad Dourif, James Earl Jones, Marc McClure, William Atherton, Scott Paulin, Lisa Eichhorn; ***D:*** Wayne Coe; ***W:*** Wayne Coe; ***C:*** Janusz Kaminski.

The Grim Reaper 🦴🦴🦴 *La Commare Secca* **1962** 22-year-old Bertolucci directed his first feature with this grim and brutal treatment of the investigation of the murder of a prostitute, told via flashbacks and from the disparate perspectives of three people who knew the woman. A commercial bust, the critics were no kinder than the public at the time; not until two years later, with "Before the Revolution," did Bertolucci earn his directorial spurs. The script was written by Pasolini, with whom the erstwhile poet had collaborated on "Accattone" the previous year (as assistant). In Italian with English subtitles. **100m/B VHS, DVD.** *IT* Francesco Rulu, Giancarlo de Rosa; ***D:*** Bernardo Bertolucci; ***W:*** Pier Paolo Pasolini.

Grim Reaper 🦴 **1/2 1981 (R)** Mia Farrow's sister is one of a group of American students vacationing on a Greek island. Farrow learns of the twisted cannibalistic murderer who methodically tries to avenge the tragic deaths of his family. **81m/C VHS, DVD.** *IT* Tisa Farrow, George Eastman; ***D:*** Joe D'Amato.

Grind 🦴🦴 **1996** Dysfunctional blue-collar family saga set in New Jersey. Eddie Dolan (Crudup), just out of the joint, moves in with brother Terry (Schulze) and sister-in-law Janey (Shelly). He gets a dull factory job and fixes up old cars to go drag-racing on the weekend—as well as helping out Terry, who has a sideline working with a car theft ring. Since gorgeous Eddie works nights, he and sulky stay-at-home-with-the-baby Janey get to be real close daytime buddies. Naturally their affair causes trouble for all. A paint-by-numbers plot with some decent acting. **96m/C VHS, DVD.** Billy Crudup, Adrienne Shelly, Paul Schulze, Frank Vincent, Saul Stein, Amanda Peet, Steven Beach, Tim Devlin; ***D:*** Chris Kentis; ***W:*** Chris Kentis, Laura Lau; ***C:*** Stephen Kazmierski; ***M:*** Brian Kelly.

Grind 🦴🦴 **2003 (PG-13)** Lightweight tale of teens and their quest for fame and the booty that comes with it rides the rails of the newly-hip extreme sports genre. The straight-outta-Central Casting group of grinders consists of good-looking Eric (Vogel); ladies man Sweet Lou (Kern); goofy, sex-crazed Matt (Vieluf); and the nerdy Dustin (Brody). They follow their skateboarding hero Jimmy Wilson (London) on tour and hope to grab the pro's attention with their skateboarding antics in order to win a coveted sponsorship and ensuing fame and fortune. Pic finds moderate success when sticking to the 'board action (even if it's obviously stand-in work) while gross-out and slacker humor too often misses the mark. **100m/C VHS, DVD.** *US* Vince Vieluf, Mike Vogel, Adam Brody, Joey Kern, Jenny (Jennifer) Morrison, Jason London, Randy Quaid, Christopher McDonald, Summer Altice; ***D:*** Casey La Scala; ***W:*** Ralph Sall; ***C:*** Richard Crudo; ***M:*** Ralph Sall.

Grindin' 🦴🦴 **2007** Actor T.O. is constantly distracted from his work by all the pleasures Hollywood has to offer. With his career in shreds, T.O. has to find the motivation to get back on track, even if it's because he doesn't want to lose another part to rival Morris. **90m/C DVD.** Omar Benson Miller, French Stewart, Regina King, Lawrence Adisa, Sam Sarpong, Richard Whitten; ***D:*** Marcello Thedford; ***W:*** Lawrence Adisa; ***C:*** John Savedra; ***M:*** Damone Arnold. **VIDEO**

Grindstone Road 🦴 ½ **2007** Hannah Sloan (Balk) was in a car accident that has left son Daniel in an extended coma. Hoping for a fresh start, Hannah and husband Graham (Bryk) move into an old farmhouse, but Hannah is soon insisting strange things are happening. Graham thinks all the anti-depressants his wife is popping are the problem but it's never that simple. **88m/C DVD.** Fairuza Balk, Greg Bryk, Joan Gregson, Walter Learning; ***D:*** Melanie Orr; ***W:*** Paul Germann; ***C:*** Simon Shohet; ***M:*** Eric Cadesky, Nick Dyer. **VIDEO**

Grisbi 🦴🦴 *Touchez pas au Grisbi; Honour Among Thieves; Touchez Pas Au Grisbi* **1953** King of the French underworld, Gabin finds there's no honor among thieves when a gold heist goes wrong and the loot comes up missing. Moreau is the quintessential moll. French with subtitles. **94m/B VHS, DVD.** *FR* Jean Gabin, Jeanne Moreau, Lino Ventura, Daniel Cauchy, Gaby Basset; ***D:*** Jacques Becker; ***W:*** Jacques Becker, Maurice Griffe; ***M:*** Jean Wiener. Venice Film Fest. '54: Actor (Gabin).

The Grissom Gang 🦴🦴🦴 **1971 (R)** Remake of the 1948 British film "No Orchids for Miss Blandish." Darby is a wealthy heiress kidnapped by a family of grotesques, led by a sadistic mother. The ransom gets lost in a series of bizarre events, and the heiress appears to be falling for one of her moronic captors. Director Robert Aldrich skillfully blends extreme violence with dark humor. Superb camera work, editing, and 1920s period sets. **127m/C VHS, DVD.** Kim Darby, Scott Wilson, Tony Musante, Ralph Waite, Connie Stevens, Robert Lansing, Wesley Addy; ***D:*** Robert Aldrich; ***W:*** Leon Griffiths; ***C:*** Joseph Biroc; ***M:*** Gerald Fried.

Grizzly 🦴 *Killer Grizzly* **1976 (PG)** Giant, killer grizzly terrorizes a state park in this blatant "Jaws" rip-off. From the same folks who produced "Abby," a blatant "Exorcist" rip-off. Filmed in Georgia. **92m/C VHS, DVD.** Christopher George, Richard Jaeckel, Andrew Prine, Victoria (Vicki) Johnson, Charles Kissinger; ***D:*** William Girdler; ***W:*** Harvey Flaxman, David Sheldon; ***M:*** Robert O. Ragland.

Grizzly Adams: The Legend Continues 🦴 ½ **1990** A small town is saved from three desperados by Grizzly and his huge grizzly bear pet, Martha. **90m/C VHS.** Gene Edwards, Link Wyler, Red West, Tony Caruso, Acquanetta, L.Q. Jones; ***D:*** Ken Kennedy.

Grizzly Falls 🦴🦴 ½ **1999 (PG)** Old-fashioned family fare, set in 1913, finds 13-year-old Harry (Clark) setting out on a wilderness adventure in the Canadian Rockies with his dad, Tyrone (Brown). Tyrone is out to capture a grizzly and bring it back (alive) for study. But when Tyrone finds a female grizzly and captures the bear's two cubs, Mom Grizzly gets back at him by making off with Harry. The boy and the bear bond but this interspecies relationship can't last and eventually boy and cubs end up with the right species of parent. **94m/C VHS, DVD.** *CA GB* Daniel Clark, Bryan Brown, Tom Jackson, Oliver Tobias, Richard Harris; ***D:*** Stewart Raffill; ***W:*** Richard Beattie; ***C:*** Thom Best; ***M:*** Paul Zaza, David Reilly.

Grizzly Man 🦴🦴🦴 ½ **2005 (R)** Timothy Treadwell spent 13 summers, beginning in 1990, in the Alaskan wilderness living among grizzly bears until 2003, when he and his girlfriend were killed in a bear attack. Director Herzog is an ideal choice to tell the story of one self-absorbed man's obsession (tinged with madness) as the animals' self-appointed guardian and protector. Herzog includes amateur naturalist Treadwell's video footage as well as interviews and his own narration. **103m/C DVD.** *US* ***D:*** Werner Herzog; ***C:*** Peter Zeitlinger; ***M:*** Richard Thompson. Directors Guild '05: Feature Doc. (Herzog); L.A. Film Critics '05: Feature Doc.; N.Y. Film Critics '05: Feature Doc.; Natl. Soc. Film Critics '05: Feature Doc.

Grizzly Mountain 🦴🦴 ½ **1997 (G)** Dylan (Dylan Haggerty) and his sister Nicole (Lund) are camping in Oregon with their parents when they decide to explore a cave. After some mysterious rumbling and shaking, the siblings emerge in the 1870s. They meet mountain man Jeremiah (Haggerty), who promises to help them return home, but he's got problems of his own—bad guy Burt (Stephens) wants to dynamite the mountain so the railroad can come through. Pic wanders back and forth between the two time periods and the kids learn a lesson in ecology (and are reunited with their parents). Easy-going; some beautiful scenery. **96m/C VHS, DVD.** Dan Haggerty, Dylan Haggerty, Nicole Lund, Perry Stephens, Kim Morgan Greene, Martin Kove, Robert Budaska, E.E. Bell, Marguerite Hickey, Don Borza; ***D:*** Jeremy Haft; ***W:*** Peter White, Jeremy Haft; ***C:*** Andy Parke; ***M:*** Jon McCallum.

Grizzly Rage 🦴 **2007** Mama's got every right to be mad when four dumb teenagers run over and kill her baby. Ritch, Wes, Sean, and Lauren take a trip to celebrate high school graduation and wander off the main roads. After hitting the bear cub, they plow their jeep into a tree, which means they're stranded in the woods when Mother Grizzly shows up. **86m/C DVD.** Tyler Hoechlin, Kate Todd, Graham Kosakoski, Brody Harms; ***D:*** David DeCoteau; ***W:*** Arne Olsen; ***C:*** Barry Gravelle; ***M:*** Joe Silva. **TV**

Grocer's Son 🦴🦴 *Le Fils de L'Epicier* **2007** Sullen 30-year-old Antoine returns to his rural hometown in Provence when his father becomes ill and his older brother Francois insists it's time Antoine help out. While their mother minds their small grocery, Antoine must operate the van selling goods to the area's residents. His brusqueness frequently upsets the elderly customers until his friend Claire visits and joins Antoine on his rounds. Soon Antoine is not only warming up to her but to his rural surroundings. French with subtitles. **96m/C DVD.** *FR* Nicolas Cazale, Clotilde Hesme, Daniel Duval, Paul Crauchet, Jeanne Goupil, Stephen Guerin-Tillie, Liliane Rovere; ***D:*** Eric Guirado; ***W:*** Florence Vignon, Eric Guirado; ***C:*** Laurent Brunet; ***M:*** Christophe Boutin.

Groom Lake 🦴 ½ **2002** Minor sci-fi effort from Shatner with a not too interesting plot. Kate is dying so she and boyfriend Andy decide to visit Groom Lake (near Area 51) to see if the alien sightings are true and if outer space visitors can somehow help her. The government is keeping a UFO under wraps but it's actually part of a project that's just been cancelled, much to the anger of project leader Gossner (Shatner). **92m/C DVD.** William Shatner, Amy Acker, Dan Gauthier, Tom Towler, Dick Van Patten, John Prosky, Dan Martin; ***D:*** William Shatner; ***W:*** William Shatner; ***C:*** Mac Ahlberg; ***M:*** Richard John Baker.

The Groomsmen 🦴🦴 **2006 (R)** Writer, director, actor Ed Burns mines familiar territory with yet another story of Irish-American males struggling with growing up. This time Burns casts himself as a reluctant father-to-be who gets together with his longtime pals to discuss, continuously, their individual plights and struggles, none of which are very interesting or extraordinary, before resigning himself to a life of monogamy and responsibility. Nearly everything is a retread of past Burns' flicks except for the excellent ensemble cast, which includes Jay Mohr as still juvenile cousin Mike and John Leguizamo as T.C., the prodigal friend who returns with a long-held secret. Burns' first version of this story, "The Brothers McMullen" (1995), is still his best. **99m/C DVD.** *US* Edward Burns, Donal Logue, Jay Mohr, John Leguizamo, Matthew Lillard, Shari Albert, Spencer Fox, John A. Russo, Heather Burns, Jessica Capshaw, Brittany Murphy, Arthur J. Nascarelli, Marion McCorry, Joe Pistone, John F. O'Donohue, Jamie Tirelli, Kevin Kash, Catharine Bolz, Amy Leonard; ***D:*** Edward Burns; ***W:*** Edward Burns; ***C:*** William Rexer; ***M:*** Robert Gray, P.T. Walkley.

Groove 🦴🦴🦴 ½ **2000 (R)** Editor Greg Harrison's directorial debut is an economically paced examination of the "rave" scene. It features a terrific ensemble cast, but at heart, the film is an old-fashioned boy-meets-girl romance. The setting is an abandoned building on a San Francisco pier. That's where the squarish David (Linklater) is attending his first rave. Leyla (Glaudini) has perhaps been to too many. Over the course of the night they and the other rave kids go through a series of changes fueled by drugs, emotion, and sexual indecision. In another time, the same story with more limited sexual roles and consciousness-altering substances could have been told about a homecoming dance or spring break. The changes and discoveries the characters make have not changed. Even though the film was made on a restricted budget—actually shot in Super 16mm.—it looks very good. **86m/C VHS, DVD.** Steve Van Wormer, Lola Glaudini, Hamish Linklater, Denny Kirkwood, Rachel True, MacKenzie Firgens, Nick Offerman, Ari Gold; ***D:*** Greg Harrison; ***W:*** Greg Harrison; ***C:*** Matthew Irving.

The Groove Tube 🦴🦴 ½ **1972 (R)** A TV series called "The Groove Tube" is the context for these skits that spoof everything on TV from commercials to newscasts. Chevy Chase's movie debut. **75m/C VHS, DVD.** Lane Sarasohn, Chevy Chase, Richard Belzer, Marcy Mendham, Bill Kemmill, Ken Shapiro, Alex Stephens, Berkeley Harris, Buzzy Linhart, Richmond Baier; ***D:*** Ken Shapiro; ***W:*** Lane Sarasohn, Ken Shapiro; ***C:*** Bob Bailin.

Gross Anatomy 🦴🦴 ½ **1989 (PG-13)** Lightweight comedy/drama centers on the trials and tribulations of medical students. Modine is the very bright, but somewhat lazy, future doctor determined not to buy into the bitter competition among his fellow students. His lack of desire inflames Lahti, a professor dying of a fatal disease who nevertheless believes in modern medicine. She pushes and inspires him to focus on his potential, and his desire to help people. Worth watching, in spite of cheap laughs. Interesting cast of up-and-comers. **107m/C VHS, DVD.** Matthew Modine, Daphne Zuniga, Christine Lahti, John Scott Clough, Alice Carter, Robert Desiderio, Zakes Mokae, Todd Field; ***D:*** Thom Eberhardt; ***W:*** Ron Nyswaner; ***M:*** David Newman.

Gross Misconduct 🦴🦴 **1993 (R)** Charismatic university professor Justin Thorne (Smits) makes the nearly fatal mistake of getting involved with his student, Jennifer (Watts). Seems she's one of those obsessive types and when Thorne wants to break off the affair for the sake of his marriage, Jennifer goes over the edge. Thorne's charged with rape and unless Jennifer changes her story his life is over. Based on a true story that happened in the '50s but this version is set in the '90s. **97m/C VHS.** *AU* Jimmy Smits, Naomi Watts, Sarah Chadwick, Adrian Wright, Alan Fletcher; ***D:*** George Miller; ***W:*** Lance Peters, Gerard Maguire; ***C:*** David Connell.

Grosse Fatigue 🦴🦴🦴 *Dead Tired* **1994 (R)** Diminutive comic everyman Blanc successfully takes up the challenge of a dual role of mistaken identity (as well as directing and writing chores). He first plays himself, bewildered by accusations of lechery and other escapades, who learns he has a psychopath double who's stolen his celebrity. So it's up to Michel and pal Carole (the gorgeous Bouquet) to track down the mischief-maker before Blanc's reputation is in complete tatters. French with subtitles. **85m/C VHS, DVD.** *FR* Michel Blanc, Carole Bouquet, Philippe Noiret, Josiane Balasko; ***Cameos:*** Charlotte Gainsbourg, Mathilda May, Thierry Lhermitte, Roman Polanski; ***D:*** Michel Blanc; ***W:*** Michel Blanc; ***C:*** Eduardo Serra; ***M:*** Rene Marc Bini.

Grosse Pointe Blank 🦴🦴🦴 **1997 (R)** Stressed-out Martin Q. Blank (Cusack) debates with his nervous shrink (Arkin) about whether to attend his 10-year high school reunion. He doesn't want to deal with the Debi (Driver), the girl he ditched on prom night, the incessant small talk, or the prospect of telling his classmates that he's a professional hit man. Then there's the matter of rival pro Grocer (Aykroyd), who wants to start an assassins union. Dark comedy with excellent writing, a charmingly off-center lead by Cusack, who attended his own reunion as research, and a surprising amount of action. Pasadena fills in for most of Grosse Pointe, but the Detroit shots are real. **107m/C VHS, DVD.** John Cusack, Minnie Driver, Dan Aykroyd, Alan Arkin, Joan Cusack, Jeremy Piven, Mitchell Ryan, Hank Azaria, Michael Cudlitz, Benny "The Jet" Urquidez, Barbara Harris, Ann Cusack, K. Todd Freeman; ***D:*** George Armitage; ***W:*** Tom Jankiewicz, D.V. DeVincentis, Steve Pink, John Cusack; ***C:*** Jamie Anderson; ***M:*** Joe Strummer.

Grotesque **WOOF!** **1987 (R)** After slaughtering a young woman's family as they vacationed in a remote mountain cabin, a gang of bloodthirsty punks are attacked by the family secret, the deformed son. The title says it all. **79m/C VHS.** Linda Blair, Tab Hunter, Guy Stockwell, Donna Wilkes, Nels Van Patten, Brad Wilson, Sharon Hughes, Robert Z'Dar, Billy Frank, Michelle Bensoussan, Mikel Angel; ***D:*** Joe Tornatore; ***W:*** Mikel Angel.

Ground Control 🦴🦴 **1998 (PG-13)** Jack Harris (Sutherland) is a former air traffic controller, who retired after a fatal plane crash. Years later, a old friend asks Jack to help out during a busy night at the Phoenix airport and Jack finds himself being forced to aid a plane with no radar, contact or control. **98m/C VHS, DVD.** Kiefer Sutherland, Robert Sean Leonard, Kelly McGillis, Henry Winkler, Michael Gross, Margaret Cho, Charles Fleischer, Farrah Forke, Bruce McGill, Kristy Swanson; ***D:*** Richard Howard.

The Ground Truth 🦴🦴 ½ **2006 (R)** Compelling but unabashedly biased, go-for-the-jugular documentary about the effect of the Iraq War on the soldiers who've fought it. Filmmaker Foulkrod interviews scores of vets about the violence of the war (especially against Iraqi civilians) and the struggle to reintegrate into American society in the face of an uncaring government bureaucracy. The movie raises important points about the effect of war on those who wage it but doesn't maintain focus, leaving some of its most effective arguments unresolved. The combination of bias and disturbing violence makes this one most effective for those who already agree with its premise, but doesn't reach out to those who think otherwise. **72m/C DVD.** *US* ***D:*** Patricia Foulkrod; ***C:*** Reuben Aaronson; ***M:*** Dave Hodge.

Ground Zero 🦴 ½ **1988 (R)** Ground Zero is the term used to describe the site of a nuclear explosion. San Francisco is threatened with just such a new name in this story of nuclear blackmail. Someone plants an atomic bomb on the Golden Gate Bridge. It must be defused and the culprit caught. **90m/C VHS.** Ron Casteel, Melvin Belli, Yvonne D'Angiers; ***D:*** James T. Flocker.

Ground Zero 🦴🦴🦴 **1988 (R)** Political thriller, set in the Australian outback in the '50s, in which a man searches for the reasons for his father's murder in the films of the British nuclear tests. **109m/C VHS.** *AU* Colin Friels, Jack Thompson, Donald Pleasence, Natalie Bate, Simon Chilvers, Neil Fitzpatrick, Bob Maza, Peter Cummins; ***D:*** Bruce Myles, Michael Pattinson.

Groundhog Day **1993 (PG)** Phil (Murray), an obnoxious weatherman, is in Punxatawney, PA to cover the annual emergence of the famous rodent from its hole. After he's caught in a blizzard that he didn't predict, he finds himself trapped in a time warp, doomed to relive the same day over and over again until he gets it right. Lighthearted romantic comedy takes a funny premise and manages to carry it through to the end. Murray has fun with the role, although he did get bitten by the groundhog during the scene when they're driving. Elliott is perfectly cast as a smart-mouthed cameraman. **103m/C VHS, DVD, Blu-ray Disc.** Bill Murray, Andie MacDowell, Chris Elliott, Stephen Tobolowsky, Brian Doyle-Murray, Marita Geraghty, Angela Paton; ***D:*** Harold Ramis; ***W:*** Harold Ramis, Daniel F. Rubin; ***C:*** John Bailey; ***M:*** George Fenton. British Acad. '93: Orig. Screenplay, Natl. Film Reg. '06.

The Groundstar Conspiracy **1972 (PG)** Spy thriller brings to life L.P. Davies' novel, "The Alien." After an explosion kills all but one space project scientist, Peppard is sent to investigate suspicions of a cover-up. Meanwhile, the surviving scientist (Sarrazin) suffers from disfigurement and amnesia. He pursues his identity while Peppard accuses him of being a spy. Splendid direction by Lamont Johnson. Sarrazin's best role. **96m/C VHS, DVD.** *CA* George Peppard, Michael Sarrazin, Christine Belford, Cliff (Potter) Potts, James Olson, Tim O'Connor, James McEachin, Alan Oppenheimer; ***D:*** Lamont Johnson; ***W:*** Matthew Howard; ***C:*** Michael Reed; ***M:*** Paul Hoffert.

The Group **1/2 1966** Based upon the novel by Mary McCarthy, the well-acted story deals with a group of graduates from a Vassar-like college as they try to adapt to life during the Great Depression. Has some provocative subject matter, including lesbianism, adultery, and mental breakdowns. Soapy, but a good cast with film debuts of Bergen, Hackett, Pettet, Widdoes, and Holbrook. **150m/C VHS.** Candice Bergen, Joanna Pettet, Shirley Knight, Joan Hackett, Elizabeth Hartman, Jessica Walter, Larry Hagman, James Broderick, Kathleen Widdoes, Hal Holbrook, Mary-Robin Redd, Richard Mulligan, Carrie Nye; ***D:*** Sidney Lumet; ***C:*** Boris Kaufman.

Group Marriage **1/2 1972 (R)** Six young professionals fall into a marriage of communal convenience and rapidly discover the many advantages and drawbacks of their thoroughly modern arrangement. **90m/C VHS.** Victoria Vetri, Aimee (Amy) Eccles, Zack Taylor, Jeff Pomerantz, Claudia Jennings, Jayne Kennedy, Milt Kamen; ***D:*** Stephanie Rothman.

Grown Ups **1980** A newly married couple move into their first home only to discover that the wife's ditzy sister expects to live with them and that their next door neighbor was their former high school teacher. **95m/C VHS, DVD.** *GB* Philip Davis, Lesley Manville, Sam Kelly, Lindsay Duncan, Brenda Blethyn, Janine Duvitsky; ***D:*** Mike Leigh; ***W:*** Mike Leigh. **TV**

Grown Ups **1986** A journalist watches his family slowly disintegrating around him in this adaptation of Jules Feiffer's play. **106m/C VHS.** Jean Stapleton, Martin Balsam, Charles Grodin, Marilu Henner, Kerry Segal; ***D:*** John Madden.

Grown Ups **2010** Five buddies, who were all players on a championship basketball team, decide to reunite after 30 years in honor of the passing of their coach. They return to the lake cottage where they first celebrated their victory—only this time they're accompanied by wives and kids over a July 4th weekend **m/C DVD.** *US* Adam Sandler, Kevin James, Chris Rock, Rob Schneider, David Spade, Salma Hayek, Maria Bello, Maya Rudolph, Tim Meadows, Jamie Chung, Norm MacDonald, Joyce Van Patten, Colin Quinn, Tim Herlihy; ***D:*** Dennis Dugan; ***W:*** Adam Sandler, Fred Wolf; ***C:*** Theo van de Sande; ***M:*** Rupert Gregson-Williams.

The Grudge **1/2 2004 (PG-13)** Shimizu remade his own 2003 horror flick "Ju-On" and there are still more groans (of disbelief) than shrieks. Studying social work as an exchange student in Tokyo, Karen (Gellar) discovers elderly Emma (Zabriskie) home alone, her family (Mapother, DuVall) missing. She sees a ghostly boy (Ozeki, who was in two of the Japanese films) and his demonic mother (Fuji, who's been in all five). Karen's scruffy boyfriend (Behr) is lured in, as is her boss (Raimi) and a local detective (Ishibashi). Pullman also appears briefly as an American professor who was an early victim of the house of horrors. Gellar's an old hand at battling things that go bump in the night but this experience isn't worth her expertise. **96m/C DVD, UMD.** *US US* Sarah Michelle Gellar, Jason Behr, William Mapother, Clea DuVall, KaDee Strickland, Grace Zabriskie, Bill Pullman, Rosa Blasi, Theodore (Ted) Raimi, Ryo Ishibashi, Yuya Ozeki, Takako Fuji, Yoko Maki; ***D:*** Takashi Shimizu; ***W:*** Takashi Shimizu; ***C:*** Hideo Yamamoto.

The Grudge 2 **1/2 2006 (PG-13)** Same shriek, different day. Hospitalized in Japan after her last ordeal, Karen (Gellar in a cameo) kills herself in front of her horrified sister Aubrey (Tamblyn). Naturally, Aubrey now wants to discover what lead her sis to suicide, which involves those weird mother-child demons and a haunted house best left alone. It's creepy, but lacks new ideas since writer-director Shimizu sticks to his formula, which has served him through four "Ju-On" flicks and two American remakes. **95m/C DVD.** *US* Amber Tamblyn, Arielle Kebbel, Sarah Michelle Gellar, Jennifer Beals, Christopher Cousins, Edison Chen, Takako Fuji, Kim Miyori, Oga Tanaka, Teresa Palmer, Misako Uno; ***D:*** Takashi Shimizu; ***W:*** Stephen Susco; ***C:*** Katsumi Yanagijima; ***M:*** Christopher Young.

The Grudge 3 **1/2 2009 (R)** Picks up where '2' left off as survivor Jake (Knight) is in a psych hospital babbling about his ordeal to Dr. Sullivan (Smith). When Jake is killed, Sullivan goes to his Chicago apartment to investigate and finds landlord Max (Mckinney) having trouble with a couple of Japanese ghosts who have gotten very, very violent. **90m/C DVD.** Shawnee Smith, Matthew Knight, Marina Sirtis, Aiko Horiuchi, Shimba Tsuchiya, Gil McKinney, Johanna Braddy, Jadie Hobson, Emi Ikehata; ***D:*** Toby Wilkins; ***W:*** Brad Keene; ***C:*** Anton Bakarski; ***M:*** Sean McMahon. **VIDEO**

Gruesome Twosome **1967** Another guts/cannibalism/mutilation fun-fest by Lewis, about someone who's marketing the hair of some very recently deceased college coeds. **75m/C VHS, DVD.** Elizabeth Davis, Gretchen Wells, Chris Martell, Rodney Bedell, Ronnie Cass, Karl Stoeber, Dianne Wilhite, Andrea Barr, Dianne Raymond, Sherry Robinson, Barrie Walton, Michael Lewis, Ray Sager; ***D:*** Herschell Gordon Lewis; ***W:*** Allison Louise Downe; ***C:*** Roy Collodi; ***M:*** Larry Wellington.

Grumpier Old Men **1995 (PG-13)** Max (Matthau) and John (Lemmon) are back at each other's throats, but with John happily married to Ariel (Ann-Margaret), he's not much of an adversary. Enter Maria (Loren), who wants to turn the boys' favorite bait shop into an Italian restaurant. In a twist that should surprise no one, Max soon falls for the beautiful Maria, and she with him. Jokes are similar but more adolescent than in the first, and subplots involving John and Max's kids' wedding and Grandpa's (Meredith) romantic interests are forced. Suffers the standard sequel fate of not measuring up to the original. **101m/C VHS, DVD.** Jack Lemmon, Walter Matthau, Ann-Margaret, Sophia Loren, Kevin Pollak, Burgess Meredith, Daryl Hannah, Ann Guilbert; ***D:*** Howard Deutch; ***W:*** Mark Steven Johnson; ***C:*** Tak Fujimoto; ***M:*** Alan Silvestri.

Grumpy Old Men **1993 (PG-13)** Lemmon and Matthau team for their seventh movie, in parts that seem written just for them. Boyhood friends and retired neighbors, they have been feuding for so long that neither of them can remember why. Doesn't matter much, when it provides a reason for them to spout off at each other every morning and play nasty practical jokes every night. This, and ice-fishing, is life as they know it, until feisty younger woman Ann-Margret moves into the neighborhood and lights some long-dormant fires. 83-year-old Meredith is a special treat playing Lemmon's 90-something father. Filmed in Wabasha, Minnesota, and grumpy, in the most pleasant way. **104m/C VHS, DVD.** Jack Lemmon, Walter Matthau, Ann-Margret, Burgess Meredith, Daryl Hannah, Kevin Pollak, Ossie Davis, Buck Henry, Christopher McDonald; ***D:*** Donald Petrie; ***W:*** Mark Steven Johnson; ***C:*** Johnny E. Jensen; ***M:*** Alan Silvestri.

Grunt! The Wrestling Movie
WOOF! **1985 (R)** A spoof of documentaries about the behind-the-scenes world of wrestling. For fans only. **91m/C VHS.** Wally Greene, Steven Cepello, Dick Murdoch, John Tolos; ***D:*** Allan Holzman.

Gryphon **1988** Ricky's new teacher can do all sorts of magical things. Hidden among her tricks are lessons about creativity, beauty, and imagination. Adapted from the short story by Charles Baxter. Aired on PBS as part of the "Wonderworks" family movie series. **58m/C VHS.** Amanda Plummer, Sully Diaz, Alexis Cruz; ***D:*** Mark Cullingham.

Guadalcanal Diary **1/2 1943** A vintage wartime flag-waver, with a typical crew of Marines battling the "Yellow Menace" over an important base on the famous Pacific atoll. Based on Richard Tregaskis' first-hand account. **93m/B VHS, DVD.** Preston Foster, Lloyd Nolan, William Bendix, Richard Conte, Anthony Quinn, Richard Jaeckel, Roy Roberts, Minor Watson, Miles Mander, Ralph Byrd, Lionel Stander, Reed Hadley, John Archer, Eddie Acuff, Selmer Jackson, Paul Fung; ***D:*** Lewis Seiler; ***W:*** Lamar Trotti, Jerome Cady; ***C:*** Charles G. Clarke; ***M:*** David Buttolph.

Guantanamera **1995** A famous singer returns to her hometown of Guantanamo for the first time in 50 years, is reunited with her first sweetheart, and promptly dies. Her niece Georgina (Ibarra) comes to take her remains back to Havana, along with her husband Adolfo (Cruz), an oafish Communist Party worker who has devised a bizarre relay system to transport corpses in order to save gasoline. Also in the caravan is Mariano (Perugorria), a former student of Georgina's who had a crush on her. Mariano attempts to seduce Georgina, while Adolfo attempts to get a clue. Celebrates the lives of everyday Cubans and skewers bumbling government bureaucrats. The final collaboration between directors Gutierrez Alea, who died in 1996, and Tabio. Spanish with subtitles. **104m/C VHS, DVD.** *CU* Carlos Cruz, Mirta Ibarra, Jorge Perugorria, Raul Eguren, Pedro Fernandez; ***D:*** Tomas Gutierrez Alea, Juan Carlos Tabio; ***W:*** Tomas Gutierrez Alea, Juan Carlos Tabio, Eliseo Alberto Diego; ***C:*** Hans Burman; ***M:*** Jose Nieto.

Guantanamero *Arritmia* **2007 (R)** Ali awakens on a deserted beach without any idea how he got there. He's found by Good Samaritan Ivan, who takes Ali home so his dancer sister Manuela can look after him. Ali finds out he's in Cuba and then starts having flashbacks to being interrogated in prison. Well, the title kinda provided some clues, didn't it? **86m/C DVD.** *GB SP* Rupert Evans, Natalia Verbeke, Derek Jacobi, Ismael de Diego; ***D:*** Vicente Penarrocha; ***W:*** Phillip W. Palmer, Vicente Penarrocha; ***C:*** Kiko de la Rica; ***M:*** Richard File.

The Guardian **1/2 1984 (R)** Residents of a chic New York apartment building hire a security expert/ex-military man to aid them in combatting their crime problem. But one of the liberal tenants thinks their guard's methods may come at too high a cost. **102m/C VHS.** Martin Sheen, Louis Gossett Jr., Arthur Hill; ***D:*** David Greene; ***M:*** Jonathan Goldsmith. **CABLE**

The Guardian **1990 (R)** A young couple unwittingly hires a human sacrificing druid witch as a babysitter for their child. Based on the book "The Nanny" by Dan Greenburg. **92m/C VHS, DVD.** Jenny Seagrove, Dwier Brown, Carey Lowell, Brad Hall, Miguel Ferrer, Natalija Nogulich, Pamela Brull, Gary Swanson; ***D:*** William Friedkin; ***W:*** William Friedkin, Stephen Volk, Dan Greenberg; ***C:*** John A. Alonzo; ***M:*** Jack Hues.

The Guardian **1/2 2000 (R)** Uninspired actioner finds Marine John Kross (Van Peebles) witnessing some freaky stuff during Desert Storm. He winds up in the hospital with a strange map carved on his chest. Flash-forward 12 years and Kross is an L.A. cop chasing down some new street drug that's made from a mystery powder from Iraq. And then there's something about a demon, a young prophet who needs protection, and his guardian who is Kross of course. Who cares. **89m/C VHS, DVD.** Mario Van Peebles, James Remar, Ice-T, Daniel Hugh Kelly, Stacy Oversier; ***D:*** John Terlesky; ***W:*** John Terlesky, Jeff Yagher, Gary J. Tunnicliffe; ***C:*** Maximo Munzi. **VIDEO**

Guardian **1/2 2001 (R)** So soldier Van Peebles witnesses the escape of a demon while stationed in the middle east (although he doesn't know what he's really seen) and 12 years later must battle said demon to save the world. There are other plot threads but they don't make much sense either. **89m/C VHS, DVD.** James Remar, Ice-T, Mario Van Peebles; ***D:*** John Terlesky, Gary J. Tunnicliffe; ***W:*** Jeff Yagher. **VIDEO**

The Guardian **1/2 2006 (PG-13)** Costner has settled comfortably into mentor mode in this familiar action story. Legendary Coast Guard rescue swimmer Ben Randall's wife has left him, his crew died during their last mission, and he's become an unwilling and unorthodox instructor to the Guard's latest recruits. Naturally, his biggest challenge is a cocky, younger version of himself—Jake Fischer (Kutcher). But Ben is just the guy to whip Jake into shape as they bond over past mistakes and insecurities. Kutcher's a surprisingly good match for Costner as the troubled newbie. **139m/C DVD.** *US* Kevin Costner, Ashton Kutcher, Melissa Sagemiller, Clancy Brown, Bonnie Bramlett, Sela Ward, Neal McDonough, John Heard, Brian Geraghty, Dule Hill, Shelby Fenner, Alex Daniels; ***D:*** Andrew Davis; ***W:*** Ron L. Brinkerhoff; ***C:*** Stephen St. John; ***M:*** Trevor Rabin.

Guardian Angel **1/2** *Beyond Justice* **1994 (R)** Detective Christy McKay (Rothrock) quits the force after her partner/lover is killed by icy seductress Nina (Denier), who manages to escape from jail. When McKay is hired to protect playboy Lawton Hobbs (McVicar), she finds that the threat comes from a psycho ex-girlfriend. Guess who. **97m/C VHS, DVD.** Cynthia Rothrock, Lydie Denier, Daniel McVicar, Kenneth McLeod, Marshall Teague, John O'Leary, Dale Jacoby; ***D:*** Richard W. Munchkin.

Guardian of the Abyss **1982** A young couple who buy an antique mirror get more than they bargained for when they discover that it is the threshold to Hell and the devil wants to come through. **60m/C VHS, DVD.** Ray Lonnen, Rosalyn Landor, Paul Darrow, Barbara Ewing; ***D:*** Don Sharp.

Guarding Eddy **1/2 2004 (PG)** Autistic 18-year-old Eddy Patterson (Presley) runs away from home to fulfill his dream of playing basketball with the Los Angeles Clippers. He winds up in a homeless shelter and meets injured NBA hopeful Mike Jeffreys (Ellsworth), who's doing community service. Naturally, the two bond in this sappy inspirational flick. **96m/C DVD.** Brian Presley, Kiko Ellsworth, Lee Garlington, Anna Maria Hosford; ***D:*** Scott McKinsey; ***W:*** Paul Davidson; ***C:*** Christopher Norr; ***M:*** Scott Kay. **VIDEO**

Guarding Tess **1994 (PG-13)** Long-suffering Secret Service agent Cage is nearing the end of his three-year assignment to crotchety widowed First Lady MacLaine when the Prez extends his tour of duty. Feels like a TV movie, not surprising since writers Torokvei and Wilson have several sitcoms to their credit, including "WKRP in Cinncinnati." Nice chemistry between Cage and MacLaine results in a few funny moments, but there are too many formulaic plot twists. End result: a pleasant, if somewhat slow buddy comedy. **98m/C VHS, DVD.** Shirley MacLaine, Nicolas Cage, Austin Pendleton, Edward Albert, Richard Griffiths, Dale Dye; ***D:*** Hugh Wilson; ***W:*** Hugh Wilson, Peter Torokvei; ***C:*** Brian Reynolds; ***M:*** Michael Convertino.

The Guardsman **1931** Broadway's illustrious couple Lunt and Fontanne shine in this adaptation of the clever marital comedy by French playwright Molnar in which they also starred. This sophisticated comedy was their only starring film, although they were offered large sums of money to appear in other movies—they just couldn't tear themselves away from the stage. Remade as "The Chocolate Soldier" and "Lily in Love." **89m/B VHS.** Alfred Lunt, Lynn Fontanne, Roland Young, Zasu Pitts, Maude Eburne, Herman Bing, Ann Dvorak; ***D:*** Sidney Franklin.

Guerilla Brigade 🦴🦴 1/2 *Riders* **1939** A rarely seen Ukrainian epic about Russian/ Ukrainian solidarity during the Civil War. In Russian with English subtitles. **90m/B VHS.** *RU* Stephan Shkurat, Lev Sverdlin, Pyotr Masokha, Vladimir Osvetsimsky; ***D:*** Igor Savchenko; ***W:*** Vsevolod Pavlovsky; ***C:*** Vladimir Okulich; ***M:*** Sergei Pototsky.

Guess What We Learned in School Today? WOOF! 1970 (R) Parents in a conservative suburban community protest sex education in the schools. Intended as a satire, but it only reinforces stereotypes. **85m/C VHS.** Richard Carballo, Devin Goldenberg; ***D:*** John G. Avildsen.

Guess Who 🦴🦴 **2005 (PG-13)** Guess who thought it was a good idea to remake the classic 1967 Spencer Tracy/Sidney Poitier drama as a tepid comedy starring two sitcom actors? Columbia Pictures, apparently, but they're definitely in the minority. On the eve of his anniversary, successful black businessman Percy Jones (Mac) is introduced to his daughter's new boyfriend, goofy white dude Simon (Kutcher). Unnerved by the interracial relationship, Percy struggles to cope, while Simon tries his best to fit in and win Percy over. Mac works overtime to rise above the material, but the repetitive "white guy" jokes and inappropriate slapstick diminish the film's message of racial tolerance, making it come across instead as a low-rent "Meet the Parents" rip-off. **105m/C DVD, UMD.** *US* Bernie Mac, Ashton Kutcher, Zoe Saldana, Judith Scott, Hal Williams, RonReaco Lee, Kellee Stewart, Robert Curtis Brown, Nicole Sullivan, Jessica Cauffiel, Kimberly Scott, Denise Dowse, Niecy Nash, Sherri Shepherd, David Krumholtz, Mike Epps; ***D:*** Kevin Rodney Sullivan; ***W:*** Peter Tolan, Jay Scherick, David Ronn; ***C:*** Karl Walter Lindenlaub; ***M:*** John Murphy.

Guess Who's Coming to Dinner 🦴🦴🦴 **1967** Controversial in its time. A young white woman brings her black fiance home to meet her parents. The situation truly tests their open-mindedness and understanding. Hepburn and Tracy (in his last film appearance) are wonderful and serve as the anchors in what would otherwise have been a rather sugary film. Houghton, who portrays the independent daughter, is the real-life niece of Hepburn. **108m/C VHS, DVD.** Katharine Hepburn, Spencer Tracy, Sidney Poitier, Katharine Houghton, Cecil Kellaway, Beah Richards, Roy Glenn, Isabel Sanford; ***D:*** Stanley Kramer; ***W:*** William Rose; ***C:*** Sam Leavitt; ***M:*** Frank DeVol. Oscars '67: Actress (Hepburn), Story & Screenplay; AFI '98: Top 100; British Acad. '68: Actor (Tracy), Actress (Hepburn).

Guest in the House 🦴🦴 1/2 **1944** A seemingly friendly young female patient is invited to stay in the family home of her doctor. She skillfully attempts to dissect the family's harmony in the process. **121m/B VHS, DVD.** Anne Baxter, Ralph Bellamy, Ruth Warrick, Marie McDonald, Margaret Hamilton, Aline MacMahon, Scott McKay, Jerome Cowan, Percy Kilbride, Connie Laird; ***D:*** John Brahm; ***W:*** Ketti Frings; ***C:*** Lee Garmes; ***M:*** Werner Janssen.

Guest Wife 🦴🦴 1/2 **1945** Determined to impress his sentimental boss, a quick-thinking bachelor talks his best friend's wife into posing as his own wife, but the hoax gets a bit out of hand and nearly ruins the real couple's marriage. **90m/B VHS.** Claudette Colbert, Don Ameche, Dick Foran, Charles Dingle, Wilma Francis; ***D:*** Sam Wood; ***C:*** Joseph Valentine.

A Guide for the Married Man 🦴🦴🦴 **1967** One suburban husband instructs another in adultery, with a cast of dozens enacting various slapstick cameos. Based on Frank Tarloff's novel of the same name. Followed by "A Guide for the Married Woman." **91m/C VHS, DVD.** Walter Matthau, Robert Morse, Inger Stevens, Sue Ane Langdon, Claire Kelly, Elaine Devry; ***Cameos:*** Lucille Ball, Sid Caesar, Jack Benny, Wally Cox, Jayne Mansfield, Louis Nye, Carl Reiner, Phil Silvers, Terry-Thomas, Sam Jaffe, Jeffrey Hunter, Polly Bergen; ***D:*** Gene Kelly; ***W:*** Frank Tarloff; ***M:*** John Williams.

A Guide for the Married Woman 🦴 1/2 **1978** A bored housewife tries to take the romantic advice of a girlfriend to add a little spice to her life. A poor TV follow-up to "A Guide for the Married Man." **96m/C VHS, DVD.** Cybill Shepherd, Barbara Feldon, Eve Arden, Chuck Woolery, Peter Marshall, Charles Frank; ***D:*** Hy Averback. **TV**

A Guide to Recognizing Your Saints 🦴🦴 1/2 **2006 (R)** More than anything Dito Montiel (LeBeouf) wants to get out of his 1986 Queens' Astoria neighborhood and away from his irascible father Monty (Palminteri). But for now, Dito hangs out with his pals, especially tough thug Antonio (Tatum) and Irish newcomer Mike (Compston), as well as girlfriend Laurie (Diaz). But the streets are changing—and not for the better. Years later, Dito (now played by Downey Jr.) returns home because his dad is dying. However, not everyone he knew is there to say hello. Based on debut writer/ director Montiel's coming-of-age memoir. **98m/C DVD.** *US* Shia LaBeouf, Robert Downey Jr., Chazz Palminteri, Dianne Wiest, Channing Tatum, Melonie Diaz, Martin Compston, Eric Roberts, Rosario Dawson; ***D:*** Dito Montiel; ***W:*** Dito Montiel; ***C:*** Eric Gautier; ***M:*** Jonathan Elias.

The Guilty 🦴🦴 **1999 (R)** Lawyer Callum Crane (Pullman) has a drunken sexual tryst with his new secretary, Sophie (Anwar), and suddenly his life is spiraling out-of-control. Sophie tries to blackmail him when Crane is appointed a federal judge and he decides to hire Nathan (Sawa), a young man who's just been released from prison, to bump her off. But Nathan's not exactly who he seems and, of course, nothing goes exactly as planned. It's a complex thriller with a good ensemble cast. **112m/C VHS, DVD.** Bill Pullman, Gabrielle Anwar, Devon Sawa, Angela Featherstone, Joanne Whalley, Jaimz Woolvett, Ken Tremblett, Camilla Overbye Roos; ***D:*** Anthony Waller; ***W:*** William Davies; ***C:*** Tobias Schliessler; ***M:*** Debbie Wiseman.

Guilty as Charged 🦴 1/2 **1992 (R)** A butcher rigs his own private electric chair and captures and executes paroled killers in his personal quest for justice. But when a politician frames an innocent man for murder how far will this vigilante go? **95m/C VHS, DVD.** Rod Steiger, Lauren Hutton, Heather Graham, Isaac Hayes; ***D:*** Sam Irvin; ***M:*** Steve Bartek.

Guilty as Sin 🦴🦴 **1993 (R)** Johnson is a ruthless Casanova accused of murdering his very wealthy wife and decides lawyer DeMornay is just the woman to defend him. Question is, who'll defend DeMornay from him? Johnson has fun as the menacing smoothie but DeMornay's supposedly hotshot criminal attorney is just plain dumb. It sounds like "Jagged Edge" but there's no sexual involvement between client and lawyer and no thrill in this thriller. **120m/C VHS, DVD.** Don Johnson, Rebecca De Mornay, Jack Warden, Stephen Lang, Dana Ivey, Ron White, Sean McCann, Luis Guzman; ***D:*** Sidney Lumet; ***W:*** Larry Cohen; ***C:*** Andrzej Bartkowiak.

Guilty by Association 🦴🦴 **2003** Very graphic look at street life and its consequences set in Washington, DC. A young man tries to support his girlfriend and their daughter without turning to drug dealing and other criminal activities but the local gang members show him the supposed lure of easy money and what it can buy. Although Freeman's name and face on prominently featured on the box art, his part as a good cop is small. **80m/C VHS, DVD.** Daemon Moore, Jeff Edward, Morgan Freeman; ***D:*** Po Johns; ***W:*** Howard Gibson; ***C:*** Sean Morrison; ***M:*** Nicholas Rivera. **VIDEO**

Guilty by Suspicion 🦴🦴 1/2 **1991 (PG-13)** Examination of the 1950s McCarthy investigations by the House Un-American Activities Committee comes off like a bland history lesson. De Niro plays a director who attended a Communist party meeting in the '30s but who otherwise doesn't have any red connections. He takes the moral high ground and refuses to incriminate his buddy (Wendt) to get off the hook and finds himself blacklisted. Characterized by average performances (excepting Wettig who goes overboard) and a lightweight script. "The Front" (1976) does a better job on this topic. Directorial debut for producer Winkler. **105m/C VHS, DVD.** Robert De Niro, Annette Bening, George Wendt, Patricia Wettig, Sam Wanamaker, Chris Cooper, Ben Piazza, Martin Scorsese, Barry Primus, Gailard Sartain, Stuart Margolin, Barry Tubb, Roxann Biggs-Dawson, Robin Gammell, Brad Sullivan, Luke Edwards, Adam Baldwin, Stephen (Steve) Root, Tom Sizemore, Ileana Douglas, Jon Tenney; ***D:*** Irwin Winkler; ***W:*** Irwin Winkler; ***C:*** Michael Ballhaus; ***M:*** James Newton Howard.

Guilty Conscience 🦴🦴🦴 **1985** Anthony Hopkins plays a successful attorney who plots his wife's murder, but is it fantasy or reality? Excellent cast and intricate plot combine for a satisfying mystery. **90m/C DVD.** Anthony Hopkins, Blythe Danner, Swoosie Kurtz; ***D:*** David Greene; ***W:*** Richard Levinson, William Link; ***C:*** Stevan Larner; ***M:*** Billy Goldenberg. **TV**

Guilty of Innocence 🦴🦴 **1987 (PG)** A young African-American man finds he's guilty until proven innocent when he runs into the law in Texas. A bold lawyer joins his fight for justice. Based on a true story. **95m/C VHS.** Dorian Harewood, Dabney Coleman, Hoyt Axton, Paul Winfield, Dennis Lipscomb, Debbi (Deborah) Morgan, Marshall Colt, Victor Love; ***D:*** Richard T. Heffron. **TV**

Guilty of Treason 🦴🦴 1/2 **1950** A documentary on the life and times of Joszef Cardinal Mindszenty of Hungary, who was imprisoned by the communists as an enemy of the state for speaking out against the totalitarian regime. At the trial, it was revealed that the Cardinal's confession was obtained only by the use of drugs, hypnosis, and torture. A realistic look at the dark side of Communism. **86m/B VHS, DVD.** Charles Bickford, Paul Kelly, Bonita Granville, Richard Derr, Berry Kroeger, Elisabeth Risdon, Roland Winters, John Banner; ***D:*** Felix Feist.

The Guinea Pig 🦴🦴 1/2 *The Outsider* **1948** Jack Read (Attenborough), the son of a tobacconist, is sent to a posh public school as an experiment but finds problems between his simple upbringing and the reactions of the teachers and other students. **97m/B VHS.** *GB* Richard Attenborough, Joan Hickson, Bernard Miles, Sheila Sim, Robert Flemyng, Timothy Bateson; ***D:*** Roy Boulting; ***W:*** Bernard Miles, Roy Boulting.

Guinevere 🦴🦴🦴 **1999 (R)** Harper (Polley) is an uncertain, inexperienced 20-year-old in San Francisco who ditches family responsibilites at her sister's wedding reception in order to talk to fortysomething photographer Connie Fitzpatrick (Rea). Worldly wise and a natural charmer, Connie soon has Harper as his latest "Guinevere," the innocent young women he beds and nurtures until they outgrow the need for his guidance. Harper certainly doesn't seem to have much personality on her own but Connie also needs something of a lifeline as his drinking increases while his job prospects decline. Polished production with compelling performances by both Polley and Rea. **104m/C VHS, DVD.** Stephen Rea, Sarah Polley, Jean Smart, Gina Gershon, Paul Dooley, Francis Guinan, Jasmine Guy, Sandra Oh, Emily Procter, Gedde Watanabe; ***D:*** Audrey Wells; ***W:*** Audrey Wells; ***C:*** Charles Minsky; ***M:*** Christophe Beck. Sundance '99: Screenplay.

The Guitar 🦴 1/2 **2008 (R)** Fatal beauty. On the same day that Melody (Burrows) gets fired and dumped by her boyfriend, she also learns that she has inoperable throat cancer. With a definite time limit, Melody decides to max out her credit cards and enjoy herself; among her purchases is a coveted red guitar. Also apparently without friends or family, Melody then indulges herself sexually with a couple of delivery people but otherwise not much happens. **95m/C DVD.** Saffron Burrows, Paz de la Huerta, Isaach de Bankole; ***D:*** Amy Redford; ***W:*** Amos Poe; ***C:*** Bobby Bukowski; ***M:*** David Mansfield.

Guitarman 🦴 **1995** Modern version of "The Pied Piper of Hamlin" finds a mysterious musician saving a farming community's crops from a plague of locusts. But when the mayor reneges on paying the piper (so to speak), he takes the town's children instead. **92m/C VHS.** Nicholas (Nick) Campbell, Donnelly Rhodes, Andrea Martin, Shawn Ashmore, Jack Semple; ***D:*** Will Dixon.

Gulag 🦴🦴 1/2 **1985** An American sportscaster is wrongly sentenced to ten years of hard labor in a Soviet prison, and plans his escape from the cruel guards. Good suspense. **130m/C VHS.** *GB* David Keith, Malcolm McDowell, David Suchet, Warren Clarke, John McEnery; ***D:*** Roger Young; ***M:*** Elmer Bernstein. **TV**

Gulliver's Travels 🦴🦴 1/2 **1939** The Fleischer Studio's animated version of Jonathan Swift's classic about the adventures of Gulliver, an English sailor who is washed ashore in the land of Lilliput, where everyone is about two inches tall. **74m/C VHS, DVD, Blu-ray Disc.** ***D:*** Dave Fleischer; ***W:*** Dan Gordon, Tedd Pierce, Edmond Seward, Izzy Sparber; ***C:*** Charles Schettler; ***V:*** Lanny Ross, Jessica Dragonette.

Gulliver's Travels 🦴🦴 **1977 (G)** In this partially animated adventure the entire land of Lilliput has been constructed in miniature. Cartoon and real life mix in a 3-dimensional story of Dr. Lemuel Gulliver and his discovery of the small people in the East Indies. From the classic by Jonathan Swift. **80m/C VHS, DVD.** *GB* Richard Harris, Catherine Schell; ***D:*** Peter Hunt.

Gulliver's Travels 🦴🦴 1/2 **1995 (PG)** Faithful TV version of Jonathan Swift's 1726 satiric novel. Lemuel Gulliver (Danson) is confined to Bedlam, an English insane asylum, after having been lost at sea for eight years. While in the asylum he relates his very odd adventures—in the tiny land of Lilliput, among the giants of Brobdingnag, with the silly and impractical intellectuals of Laputa, and finally amidst the brutish human Yahoos, who are ruled by rational talking horses, the Houyhnhnms. Meanwhile, Gulliver's wife Mary (Steenburgen) and son Tom (Sturridge) struggle to prove his sanity and win his release. On two cassettes. **187m/C VHS, DVD.** Ted Danson, Mary Steenburgen, Edward Fox, Thomas Sturridge, Edward Woodward, Nicholas Lyndhurst, Peter O'Toole, Phoebe Nicholls, Ned Beatty, Kate Maberly, Alfre Woodard, Geraldine Chaplin, John Gielgud, Kristin Scott Thomas, Omar Sharif, John Standing, Warwick Davis, Robert Hardy, Shashi Kapoor, Karyn Parsons, Edward Petherbridge; ***D:*** Charles Sturridge; ***W:*** Simon Moore; ***C:*** Howard Atherton; ***M:*** Trevor Jones. **TV**

Gumball Rally 🦴🦴 **1976 (PG)** An unusual assortment of people converge upon New York for a cross country car race to Long Beach, California where breaking the rules is part of the game. **107m/C VHS, DVD.** Michael Sarrazin, Gary Busey, Raul Julia, Nicholas Pryor, Tim McIntire, Susan Flannery; ***D:*** Charles "Chuck" Bail; ***W:*** Leon Capetanos.

Gumby: The Movie 🦴🦴 1/2 **1995 (G)** Gumby and his musical group, the Clayboys, seek to save their neighbors' farms from foreclosure by putting on a benefit concert. And yes, pal Pokey is along to help out. But 90 minutes of our gentle clay hero stretches the patience of even the most enthusiastic fan. **90m/C VHS.** ***D:*** Art Clokey; ***W:*** Art Clokey.

Gummo WOOF! 1997 (R) "Kids" scripter and first time helmer Korine shamelessly parades out the freaks and calls it entertainment. More like a series of grisly images than a cohesive narrative when nihilism pervades a group of disaffected Xenia, Ohio teens who explore every brand of atrocity for kicks. Disturbing, not only in the graphic violence of the bored juvies but also in the frightening lack of a point to this uneven and self-indulgent shock-fest. Touted as modern movie's golden-boy, 23 year-old Korine doesn't let any dark humor slip in to detract from the purely revolting scenarios. The images that do summon up some truth about growing up in a dead-end town are far overshadowed by the collection of images as a whole. Renowned French cinematographer Escoffier lends style to this lost cause. **88m/C VHS, DVD.** Chloe Sevigny, Jacob Reynolds, Jacob Sewell, Nick Sutton, Carisa Bara, Darby Dougherty, Max Perlich, Linda Manz; ***D:*** Harmony Korine; ***W:*** Harmony Korine; ***C:*** Jean-Yves Escoffier.

Gumshoe 🦴🦴 1/2 **1972 (G)** An homage to American hard-boiled detectives. Finney plays a small-time worker in a Liverpool nightclub who decides to become a detective like his movie heroes. He bumbles through a number of interconnecting cases, but finds his way in the end. Good satire of film noir detectives. **85m/C VHS.** *GB* Albert Finney, Billie Whitelaw, Frank Finlay, Janice Rule, Carolyn Seymour; ***D:*** Stephen Frears; ***W:*** Neville Smith; ***C:*** Chris Menges; ***M:*** Andrew Lloyd Webber.

The Gumshoe Kid *The Detective Kid* **1989 (R)** A college-bound kid enters the family detective business to prevent his mother from being evicted. He gets in over his head though, trying to track the fiancee of a wealthy mobster. **98m/C VHS.** Jay Underwood, Tracy Scoggins, Vince Edwards, Arlene Golonka, Pamela Springsteen; ***D:*** Joseph Manduke.

A Gun, a Car, a Blonde **1997** Paraplegic Richard Spraggins (Metzler) escapes from his pain-filled life by imagining himself to be living in a '50s film noir world, where he takes on the persona of tough private eye Rick Stone. Naturally, as in all good noir worlds, he must save a femme fatale blonde (Thompson) from a killer. **101m/C VHS, DVD.** Jim Metzler, Billy Bob Thornton, Andrea Thompson, John Ritter, Kay Lenz, Victor Love, Paula Marshall; ***D:*** Stefani Ames; ***W:*** Stefani Ames, Tom Epperson; ***C:*** Carlos Gaviria; ***M:*** Harry Manfredini.

Gun Cargo **1949** Muddled story about a conniving shipowner who fires his crew for demanding shore leave. He replaces them with assorted low-lifes, resulting in the usual hijinks. A terrible performance by an otherwise great cast. **49m/C VHS.** Rex Lease, Smith Ballew, William Farnum, Gibson Gowland; ***D:*** Jack Irwin; ***W:*** Jack Irwin; ***C:*** Edward A. Kull.

Gun Code **1/2 1940** The white-hatted cowboy-hero puts a stop to small-town racketeering. **52m/B VHS.** Tim McCoy, Ina Guest; ***D:*** Sam Newfield.

Gun Crazy *Deadly Is the Female* **1949** Annie Laurie Starr—Annie Oakley in a Wild West show—meets gun-lovin' Bart Tare, who says a gun makes him feel good inside, "like I'm somebody." Sparks fly, and the two get married and live happily ever after—until the money runs out and fatal femme Laurie's craving for excitement and violence starts to flare up. The two become lovebirds-on-the-lam. Now a cult fave, it's based on a MacKinlay Kantor story. Ex-stuntman Russell Harlan's photography is daring; the realism of the impressive robbery scenes is owed in part to the technical consultation of former train robber Al Jennings. And watch for a young Tamblyn as the 14-year-old Bart. **87m/B VHS, DVD.** Peggy Cummins, John Dall, Berry Kroeger, Morris Carnovsky, Anabel Shaw, Nedrick Young, Trevor Bardette, Russ Tamblyn, Harry Lewis, Mickey Little, Paul Frison, Dave Bair, Stanley Prager, Virginia Farmer, Anne O'Neal, Frances Irwin, Don Beddoe, Robert Osterloh, Shimen Ruskin, Harry Hayden; ***D:*** Joseph H. Lewis; ***W:*** Dalton Trumbo; ***C:*** Russell Harlan; ***M:*** Victor Young. Natl. Film Reg. '98.

Gun Crazy **1/2** *A Talent for Loving* **1969** A gambler becomes enmeshed in an arranged marriage with a cursed Mexican family. Lightweight comedy, good cast. **110m/C VHS.** Richard Widmark, Chaim Topol, Cesar Romero, Genevieve Page, Judd Hamilton, Caroline Munro; ***D:*** Richard Quine.

Gun Fury **1/2 1953** A panoramic western about a Civil War veteran pursuing the bandits who kidnapped his beautiful bride-to-be. First screened as a 3-D movie. **83m/C VHS, DVD.** Rock Hudson, Donna Reed, Phil Carey, Lee Marvin; ***D:*** Raoul Walsh.

Gun Girls **1956** Campy exploitation flick about a gun-toting gang of girls who rob anything or anyone. The guy who fences their goods ends up getting one of them pregnant. **67m/C VHS.** Timothy Farrell, Jean Ferguson, Jacquelyn Park, Eve Brent; ***D:*** Robert Deltano.

Gun Glory **1/2 1957** Granger plays Tom Early, a gunslinger who returns home after three years to find the town would rather not have him. He regains the town's respect when he stops a murderer from invading the town with his cattle herd. Based on the novel "Man of the West" by Philip Yordan. **88m/C VHS.** Stewart Granger, Rhonda Fleming, Chill Wills, Steve Rowland, James Gregory, Jacques Aubuchon, Arch Johnson, William "Bill" Fawcett, Lane Bradford, Michael Dugan, Bud Osborne, May McAvoy, Charles Herbert, Carl Pitti; ***D:*** Roy Rowland; ***W:*** William Ludwig; ***M:*** Jeff Alexander.

Gun Grit **1/2 1936** An FBI agent is sent west to break up a protection racket. **51m/B VHS.** Jack Perrin, Ethel Beck, David Sharpe, Roger Williams, Budd Buster; ***D:*** William Berke.

The Gun in Betty Lou's Handbag **1992 (PG-13)** Shy, small town librarian with a dull marriage is looking for excitement when she stumbles across a gun used in a murder. She decides excitement will follow her (false) confession to the crime leaving her husband thunderstruck, the police confused, and the gossip line humming. She also intrigues the real bad guy, who comes looking for her. Lame silliness is redeemed somewhat by Miller, but there's some surprisingly nasty violence given the comedy label. **99m/C VHS, DVD.** Penelope Ann Miller, Eric Thal, Alfre Woodard, Cathy Moriarty, William Forsythe, Julianne Moore, Xander Berkeley, Michael O'Neill, Christopher John Fields; ***D:*** Allan Moyle; ***W:*** Grace Cary Bickley; ***M:*** Richard Gibbs.

A Gun in the House **1981** While being attacked in her own home, a woman shoots one of her assailants. The police find no conclusive evidence of attack and arrest the woman for murder. Exploitive drama on gun control. **100m/C VHS.** Sally Struthers, David Ackroyd, Joel Bailey, Jeffrey Tambor; ***D:*** Ivan Nagy. **TV**

Gun Law **1/2 1933** The hero tackles the Sonora Kid, an outlaw terrorizing Arizona folk. One of the few sound westerns with Hoxie, a silent-era star who hung up his spurs when his voice proved non-photogenic. **59m/B VHS.** Jack Hoxie, Paul Fix, Mary Carr, Edmund Cobb, Robert Burns; ***D:*** Lewis D. Collins.

Gun Lords of Stirrup Basin **1937** A cattleman and the daughter of a homesteader are in love in the Old West, but a seedy lawyer wants to douse their flame. Bullets and fists fly as a result. **55m/B VHS.** Bob Steele, Louise Stanley, Karl Hackett, Ernie Adams, Frank LaRue, Frank Ball, Steve Clark; ***D:*** Sam Newfield.

Gun Packer **1938** When an outlaw gang robs stagecoaches of their gold and uses the booty to salt barren mine shafts so the unsuspecting can be swindled out of their money on worthless gold mine certificates, hard-riding Randall is called in to save the day. **51m/B VHS.** Addison "Jack" Randall, Louise Stanley, Charles "Blackie" King, Glenn Strange; ***D:*** Wallace Fox; ***W:*** Robert Emmett.

Gun Play *Lucky Boots* **1936** Brother and sister venture west to run their father's ranch. Mexican bandits believe the ranch's property houses a revolutionary fortune, and set about recovering it. The brother defends his father's ranch along with a sidekick, who sweeps the sister off her feet. **59m/B VHS.** Guinn "Big Boy" Williams, Frank Yaconelli, Marion Shilling, Wally Wales, Charles French; ***D:*** Al(bert) Herman.

The Gun Ranger **1/2 1934** Our hero plays a Texas Ranger who becomes fed up with soft judges and shady prosecutors and decides to take the law into his own hands. **56m/B VHS, DVD.** Bob Steele, Eleanor Stewart, John Merton, Ernie Adams, Budd Buster; ***D:*** Robert North Bradbury.

Gun Riders **1/2** *Five Bloody Graves; Five Bloody Days to Tombstone; Lonely Man* **1969** Gunman must seek out and stop a murderer of innocent people. **98m/C VHS, DVD.** Scott Brady, Jim Davis, John Carradine; ***D:*** Al Adamson.

Gun Shy **2000 (R)** Psychiatry and organized crime collide again, but this time it's the cops in therapy. Well, one of 'em at least. Charlie (Neeson) is a burned-out DEA agent forced back undercover as a go-between for an Italian gangster (Platt) who knows he's a cliche and a Colombian drug cartel leader (Zuniga) who believes investing in bean futures is some sort of ethnic no-no. Charlie's work problems lead him to a men's therapy group and a nurse (Bullock) dubbed the "Enema Queen." Yep, it's mostly that kind of humor. The crime figures are thin, and Blakenly needs to work on his comic and scene timing, but Neeson fares pretty well. The group sessions are highlights, but the payoff isn't as big as one would hope. **102m/C VHS, DVD.** Liam Neeson, Oliver Platt, Sandra Bullock, Jose Zuniga, Richard Schiff, Andrew Lauer, Mitch Pileggi, Paul Ben-Victor, Mary McCormack, Frank Vincent, Michael Mantell, Louis Giambalvo, Gregg Daniel, Michael Delorenzo; ***D:*** Eric Blakeney; ***W:*** Eric Blakeney; ***C:*** Tom Richmond; ***M:*** Rolfe Kent.

Gun Smoke **1931** A gang of big city thugs high-tails it west when they're about to get busted for murder and robbery. They land in a small western town in Idaho, where their fancy suits and brim hats get them quickly mistaken for a different type of gang—one with big bucks who will invest in the city. It doesn't take the city boys long to figure out that they can take this rinky-dink town, and soon reinforcements are arriving by train to help them. But one smart cowboy had them pegged for trouble from the get-go. **71m/B VHS.** Richard Arlen, Mary Brian, William Boyd, Eugene Pallette, Charles Winninger, Louise Fazenda, Brooks Benedict; ***D:*** Edward Sloman; ***W:*** Grover Jones.

Gunblast **1974** A convict is released from San Quentin and wastes no time in getting involved with mob-powered drug smuggling. **70m/C VHS.** Lloyd Allan, Christine Cardan, James Cunningham; ***D:*** Nick Millard; ***W:*** Nick Millard.

Guncrazy **1992 (R)** Girl from the wrong side of the tracks, abused her entire life, finds her freedom in a gun. She winds up killing the man who raped her, takes up with an equally lost ex-con, and the two armed misfits go on the run from the law. Barrymore's convincing and the movie is another well-made variation on the lovers-on-the-run theme. Film was inspired by, but is not a remake of, the 1949 movie "Gun Crazy." **97m/C VHS, DVD.** Drew Barrymore, James LeGros, Billy Drago, Rodney Harvey, Ione Skye, Joe Dallesandro, Michael Ironside; ***D:*** Tamra Davis; ***W:*** Matthew Bright; ***C:*** Lisa Rinzler.

A Gunfight **1971 (PG)** When Cash is stranded in a small Western town, he meets up with fellow old-time gunfighter Douglas. The two strike up a friendship, but discover the town folk expect a gun battle. Needing money, the two arrange a gunfight for paid admission—winner take all. Cash makes his screen debut. **90m/C** Kirk Douglas, Johnny Cash, Jane Alexander, Karen Black, Dana Elcar, Keith Carradine, Raf Vallone; ***D:*** Lamont Johnson; ***W:*** Harold Jack Bloom.

Gunfight at Comanche Creek **1/2 1964** In 1875, Bob Gifford (Murphy) is working as an undercover operative for the National Detective Agency. He's tracking a gang that springs other criminals from jail, uses them as fronts in robberies, and then kills the convicts for the increased reward money. Bob infiltrates the gang and gets into a lot of trouble. **90m/C DVD.** Audie Murphy, Ben Cooper, Colleen Miller, DeForest Kelley, Jan Merlin, John Hubbard, Adam Williams; ***D:*** Frank McDonald, Edward L. Bernds; ***C:*** Joseph Biroc; ***M:*** Marlin Skiles.

The Gunfight at Dodge City **1959** Bat Masterson (McCrea) is pressured to become the sheriff of Dodge City and immediately has problems with the crooked local politicians and then more trouble when his old gang shows up in town. Typical oater that McCrea originally intended to be his final picture before his retirement from the screen. **80m/C DVD.** Joel McCrea, Julie Adams, John McIntire, Nancy Gates, Richard Anderson, Don Haggerty, James Westerfield; ***D:*** Joseph M. Newman; ***W:*** Martin Goldsmith, Daniel Ullman; ***C:*** Carl Guthrie; ***M:*** Hans J. Salter.

Gunfight at Red Sands *Gringo; Duello Nel Texas* **1963** Landmark western in the history of Italian cinema. Long before Leone's Eastwood trilogy, this film introduced the theme of an avenging stranger to the genre. Harrison stars as the dark, brooding hero who is out for revenge after learning that his family has been attacked by a gang of bandits. **97m/C VHS, DVD.** *SP IT* Richard Harrison, Giacomo "Jack" Rossi-Stuart, Sara Lezana, Dan (Daniel, Danny) Martin; ***D:*** Ricardo Blasco; ***W:*** Albert Band, Ricardo Blasco; ***C:*** Massimo Dallamano; ***M:*** Ennio Morricone.

Gunfight at the O.K. Corral **1957** The story of Wyatt Earp and Doc Holliday joining forces in Dodge City to rid the town of the criminal Clanton gang. Filmed in typical Hollywood style, but redeemed by its great stars. **122m/C VHS, DVD.** Burt Lancaster, Kirk Douglas, Rhonda Fleming, Jo Van Fleet, John Ireland, Kenneth Tobey, Lee Van Cleef, Frank Faylen, DeForest Kelley, Earl Holliman, Dennis Hopper, Martin Milner, Jack Elam, Olive Carey, Joan Camden; ***D:*** John Sturges; ***W:*** Leon Uris; ***C:*** Charles B(ryant) Lang Jr.; ***M:*** Dimitri Tiomkin.

The Gunfighter **1/2 1950** A mature, serious, Hollywood-western character study about an aging gunfighter searching for peace and quiet but unable to avoid his reputation and the duel-challenges it invites. One of King's best films. **85m/B VHS.** Angela (Clark) Clarke, Gregory Peck, Helen Westcott, Millard Mitchell, Jean Parker, Karl Malden, Skip Homeier, Mae Marsh; ***D:*** Henry King; ***C:*** Arthur C. Miller.

Gunfighter **1998 (PG-13)** Gunfighter Sheen is out to avenge the murder of some townsfolk. Then an outlaw kidnaps his girlfriend and things get even more personal. **94m/C VHS, DVD.** Robert Carradine, Martin Sheen, Clu Gulager; ***D:*** Christopher Coppola.

The Gunfighters **1/2 1987** Lackluster pilot of a proposed Canadian series pits three individualistic relatives against a powerful empire-builder. **100m/C VHS, DVD.** *CA* Art Hindle, Reiner Schone, Anthony Addabbo, George Kennedy, Michael Kane, Lori Hallier; ***D:*** Clay Borris. **TV**

Gunfighter's Moon **1/2 1996 (PG-13)** Legendary gunslinger Frank Morgan (Henriksen) is called on by former lover, Linda (Lenz), to help her sheriff husband prevent a jailbreak. Frank's tired of his constant challengers but can't seem to make another life for himself. **95m/C VHS, DVD.** Lance Henriksen, Kay Lenz, David McIlwraith, Ivan Sergei, Nikki Deloach; ***D:*** Larry Ferguson; ***W:*** Larry Ferguson; ***C:*** James L. Carter; ***M:*** Lee Holdridge.

Gunfire **1/2 1950** A Frank James look-alike cavorts, robs and loots the countryside until the real James decides to set things straight. **59m/B VHS, DVD.** Donald (Don "Red") Barry, Robert Lowery, Pamela Blake, Wally Vernon, Jan Sterling; ***D:*** William Berke.

Gunfire *China 9, Liberty 37* **1978** A gunfighter is rescued from the hangman's noose by railroad tycoons who want him to kill a farmer. He doesn't kill the man, but runs off with his wife instead, and the incensed railway honchos send assassins after the double-crossing gunman. Peckinpah's part is pretty puny in this leisurely horse opera. **94m/C VHS, DVD.** *IT* Fabio Testi, Warren Oates, Jenny Agutter, Sam Peckinpah; ***D:*** Monte Hellman; ***M:*** Pino Donaggio.

Gung Ho! **1943** Carlson's Raiders are a specially trained group of Marine jungle fighters determined to retake the Pacific island of Makin during WWII. **88m/B VHS, DVD.** Robert Mitchum, Randolph Scott, Noah Beery Jr., Alan Curtis, Grace McDonald; ***D:*** Ray Enright; ***C:*** Milton Krasner.

Gung Ho **1/2 1985 (PG-13)** A Japanese firm takes over a small-town U.S. auto factory and causes major cultural collisions. Keaton plays the go-between for employees and management while trying to keep both groups from killing each other. From the director of "Splash" and "Night Shift." Made into a short-lived TV series. **111m/C VHS, DVD.** Michael Keaton, Gedde Watanabe, George Wendt, Mimi Rogers, John Turturro, Clint Howard, Michelle Johnson, So Yamamura, Sab Shimono; ***D:*** Ron Howard; ***W:*** Babaloo Mandel, Lowell Ganz; ***M:*** Thomas Newman.

Gunga Din **1939** The prototypical "buddy" film. Three veteran British sergeants in India try to suppress a native uprising, but it's their water boy, the intrepid Gunga Din, who saves the day. Friendship, loyalty, and some of the best action scenes ever filmed. Based loosely on Rudyard Kipling's famous poem, the story is credited to Ben Hecht, Charles MacArthur, and William Faulkner (who is uncredited). Also available colorized. **117m/B VHS, DVD.** Cary Grant, Victor McLaglen, Douglas Fairbanks Jr., Sam Jaffe, Eduardo Ciannelli, Montagu Love, Joan Fontaine, Abner Biberman, Robert Coote, Lumsden Hare, Cecil Kellaway, Roland Varno, George Regas, Reginald (Reggie, Reggy) Sheffield, Clive Morgan; ***D:*** George Stevens; ***W:*** Fred Guiol, Joel Sayre, Ben Hecht, William Faulkner;

C: Joseph August; *M:* Alfred Newman. Natl. Film Reg. '99.

The Gunman 1/2 *A Promise Kept* **2003 (R)** Already tormented by the murder of his wife, police detective Ben Simms (Flanery) is plunged further into turmoil when given the duty of catching a vigilante who enjoys offing the bad guys...and he discovers that her killer is up next. **91m/C VHS, DVD.** Sean Patrick Flanery, Joey Lauren Adams, Mimi Rogers, Brian McNamara, Tom Wright, Jeff Speakman, Emma Nicolas, Steve Krieger, Alaina Kalanj, Daniel Millican; *D:* Daniel Millican; *W:* Daniel Millican. **VIDEO**

Gunman from Bodie 1/2 *Gun Man from Bodie* **1941** Second of the Rough Rider series. Jones, McCoy, and Hatton rescue a baby orphaned by rustlers and then go after the bad guys. **62m/B VHS, DVD.** Tim McCoy, Buck Jones, Raymond Hatton; *D:* Spencer Gordon Bennet.

Gunman's Walk 1/2 **1958** Rancher Lee Hackett (Heflin) gained his power through his gunslinging skill but wants his two sons to be respectable citizens. However, hot-tempered eldest son Ed (Hunter) wants to best the old man's reputation while younger son Davy (Darren) has his own problems when he falls for Sioux half-breed Clee (Grant), whose brother was murdered by Ed. As Ed gets more ruthless, his father must decide how far he's willing to go to protect him. **95m/C VHS.** Van Heflin, Tab Hunter, James Darren, Kathryn Grant, Mickey Shaughnessy, Robert F. Simon, Edward Platt, Bert Convy; *D:* Phil Karlson; *W:* Frank Nugent; *C:* Charles Lawton Jr.

Gunmen **1993 (R)** A reluctant buddy team face down some bad guys. DEA agent Cole (Van Peebles) teams up with smuggler Dani (Lambert) to find stolen drug money also wanted by wheelchair-bound villain Loomis (Stewart) and his violence-loving henchman (Leary). Adds comedy to the mix as well as shameless action rip-offs from spaghetti westerns. **90m/C VHS, DVD.** Christopher Lambert, Mario Van Peebles, Denis Leary, Patrick Stewart, Kadeem Hardison, Sally Kirkland; *Cameos:* Big Daddy Kane, Ed Lover, Eric B. Rakim, Dr. Dre; *D:* Deran Sarafian; *W:* Stephen Sommers; *M:* John Debney.

Gunner Palace **2004 (PG-13)** Frenetic documentary follows the 2/3 Field Artillery Division (known as "The Gunners") of the U.S. Army's First Armored Division as they serve their tour of duty in Iraq. The Gunners have set up camp in a once-opulent Iraqi palace, formerly occupied by one of Saddam Hussein's sons. Tucker and Epperlein ignore the politics behind the war, but rather emphasize the chaotic existence of the soldiers on the frontlines. We watch their daily routines, see them laugh and interact, and listen to them express their feelings about putting their lives on the line. The ugly, grainy camerawork might turn some off, but overall, it presents a compelling snapshot of life during wartime. **85m/C DVD.** *US D:* Michael Tucker, Petra Epperlein; *C:* Michael Tucker.

Gunners & Guns **1934** Vintage western starring King. **51m/B VHS.** Black King, Edmund Cobb, Edna Asetin, Eddie Davis; *D:* Robert Hoyt.

Gunplay 1/2 **1951** Two cowboys befriend a boy whose father has been killed and search for the murderer. **61m/B VHS.** Tim Holt, Joan Dixon, Richard Martin, Robert Bice, Harper Carter, Mauritz Hugo; *D:* Lesley Selander; *W:* Ed Earl Repp; *C:* J. Roy Hunt; *M:* Paul Sawtell.

Gunpowder **1987** Two Interpol agents endeavor to stop a crime lord from causing the collapse of the world economy. **85m/C VHS.** David Gilliam, Martin Potter, Gordon Jackson, Anthony Schaeffer; *D:* Norman J. Warren; *W:* Roy MacLean; *C:* Alistair Cameron; *M:* Jeffrey Wood.

The Gunrunner 1/2 **1984 (R)** Costner plays a Canadian mobster, involved in liquor smuggling, who aids a Chinese rebellion in this 1920s drama. Interesting concept. Received more attention after Costner gained notoriety in later films. **92m/C VHS.** *CA* Kevin Costner, Sara Botsford, Paul Soles; *D:* Nardo Castillo.

Guns **1990 (R)** An international gunrunner puts the moves on buxom women between hair-raising adventures. **95m/C VHS, DVD.** Erik Estrada, Dona Speir; *D:* Andy Sidaris; *W:* Andy Sidaris.

Guns **2008 (R)** Canadian miniseries. British expat Paul Duguid (Feore) is a legitimate arms dealer who also sells illegal weapons to street thugs. His son Bobby (Smith) comes under police surveillance, is implicated in the murder of a U.S. senator's father, and has his girlfriend Frances (Cuthbert) willing to smuggle guns across the border if it'll help him out. **180m/C DVD.** *CA* Colm Feore, Gregory Edward Smith, Elisha Cuthbert, Shawn Doyle, Lyriq Bent, Alan Van Sprang, Al Sapienza; *D:* David Sutherland; *C:* Arthur E. Cooper. **TV**

The Guns and the Fury 1/2 **1983** Two American oil riggers in the Middle East, circa 1908, are forced to fight off an attack by a vicious Arab sheik and his tribe. **90m/C VHS.** Peter Graves, Cameron Mitchell, Michael Ansara, Albert Salmi; *D:* Tony Zarindast.

Guns at Batasi 1/2 **1964** Attenborough plays a tough British Sergeant Major stationed in Africa during the anti-colonial 1960s. Ultimately the regiment is threatened by rebel Africans. Fine performances make this rather predictable film watchable. **103m/B VHS, DVD.** *GB* Richard Attenborough, Jack Hawkins, Mia Farrow, Flora Robson, John Leyton; *D:* John Guillermin; *M:* John Addison.

Guns Don't Argue **1957** Entertaining schlocker about the rise and fall of famous criminal Dillinger. Non-stop action also features Bonnie and Clyde, Pretty Boy Floyd and Baby Face Nelson. **92m/C VHS, DVD.** Myron Healey, Jim Davis, Lyle Talbot, Paul Dubov, Sam Edwards, Richard Crane; *D:* Richard C. Kahn, Bill Karn; *W:* Phillips Lord; *C:* William Clothier; *M:* Paul Dunlap.

Guns for Dollars *They Call Me Hallelujah* **1973** Mex-Western has four men, including a secret agent and a cossack, tangled up in the Mexican Revolution as they search for a fortune in smuggled jewels. **94m/C VHS.** *MX* George Hilton, Charles Southwood, Agata Flory, Roberto Camardiel, Paolo Gozlino, Rick Boyd; *D:* Giuliano Carnimeo.

Guns in the Dark **1937** A cowboy vows never to use a gun again when he believes that he accidentally shot his best friend. **60m/C VHS, DVD.** Johnny Mack Brown, Claire Rochelle; *D:* Sam Newfield.

Guns of Diablo **1964** Wagon train master Bronson has to fight a gang that controls the supply depot, all the while showing his young helper (beardless boy Russell) the fascinating tricks of the trade. **91m/C VHS, DVD.** Charles Bronson, Kurt Russell, Susan Oliver; *D:* Boris Sagal.

Guns of Fury 1/2 *The Daring Caballero* **1949** Cisco and Pancho solve the troubles of a small boy in this standard oater. **60m/B VHS.** Duncan Renaldo, Leo Carrillo, Charles Halton, Nassim Abdi, Pedro de Cordoba, Stephan Chase, Edmund Cobb, Mickey Little; *D:* Wallace Fox; *W:* Betty Burbridge; *C:* Lester White; *M:* Albert Glasser.

Guns of Justice *Colorado Ranger* **1950** Undercover Colorado rangers stop a swindler from forcing homesteaders off their land. **60m/B VHS.** James Ellison, Russell Hayden, Tom Tyler, Raymond Hatton; *D:* Thomas Carr.

The Guns of Navarone 1/2 **1961** During WWII, British Intelligence in the Middle East sends six men to the Aegean island of Navarone to destroy guns manned by the Germans. Consistently interesting war epic based on the Alistair MacLean novel, with a vivid cast. **159m/C VHS, DVD, Blu-ray Disc.** Gregory Peck, David Niven, Anthony Quinn, Richard Harris, Stanley Baker, Anthony Quayle, James Darren, Irene Papas, Gia Scala, James Robertson Justice, Bryan Forbes, Allan Cuthbertson, Michael Trubshawe, Percy Herbert, Walter Gotell, Tutte Lemkow; *D:* J. Lee Thompson; *W:* Carl Foreman; *C:* Oswald Morris; *M:* Dimitri Tiomkin. Golden Globes '62: Film—Drama, Score.

Guns of the Law 1/2 **1944** The Texas Rangers try to stop a shifty lawyer who attempts to swindle a family out of a potential fortune in property. **56m/B VHS, DVD.** Dave O'Brien, James Newill, Guy Wilkerson, Jack Ingram, Robert F. (Bob) Kortman, Bob (Robert) Barron; *D:* Elmer Clifton; *W:* Elmer Clifton.

Guns of the Magnificent Seven 1/2 **1969 (G)** The third remake of "The Seven Samurai." Action-packed western in which the seven free political prisoners and train them to kill. The war party then heads out to rescue a Mexican revolutionary being held in an impregnable fortress. **106m/C VHS, DVD.** George Kennedy, Monte Markham, James Whitmore, Reni Santoni, Bernie Casey, Joe Don Baker, Scott Thomas, Michael Ansara, Fernando Rey; *D:* Paul Wendkos; *M:* Elmer Bernstein.

Gunshy **1998 (R)** Familiar crime genre has some fine performances and an intelligent script. Journalist Jake Bridges (Petersen) heads to Atlantic City after catching his wife cheating on him. His drunken ranting gets him trouble, but Jake is rescued by likeable smalltime mob guy Frankie (Wincott) and his hot girlfriend, Melissa (Lane). Jake hangs around watching Frankie work and making passes at Melissa but it just might be that Jake has his own hidden agenda, as well. **101m/C VHS, DVD.** William L. Petersen, Michael Wincott, Diane Lane, Kevin Gage, Michael Byrne, Meat Loaf Aday, Eric Schaeffer, Musetta Vander, John Fleck, Badja (Medu) Djola, R. Lee Ermey, Natalie Canerday; *D:* Jeff Celentano; *W:* Larry Gross; *C:* John Aronson; *M:* Hal Lindes.

The Gunslinger 1/2 **1956** A woman marshall struggles to keep law and order in a town overrun by outlaws. Unique western with a surprise ending. **83m/C VHS, DVD.** John Ireland, Beverly Garland, Allison Hayes, Jonathan Haze, Dick Miller, Bruno VeSota, William Schallert; *D:* Roger Corman; *W:* Charles B. Griffith, Mark Hanna; *C:* Frederick E. West; *M:* Ronald Stein.

Gunslinger 1/2 *Have a Nice Funeral; Stranger's Gold; Buon Funerale, Amigos!* **1970** Armed to the teeth with weaponry, Sartana shows a mining town's heavies how to sling a gun or two. **90m/C VHS, DVD.** *IT SP* Gianni "John" Garko, Antonio Vilar, Daniela Giordano, Ivano Staccioli; *D:* Giuliano Carnimeo; *W:* Robert Gianviti, Giovanni Simonelli; *C:* Stelvio Massi; *M:* Bruno Nicolai.

Gunslinger's Revenge *Il Mio West* **1998 (PG-13)** After 20 years Doc Lowen's (Pieraccioni) gun-toting, outlaw father Johnny (Keitel) resurfaces much to Doc's dismay as he's devoted his life to a peace-loving existence with his wife and young son. While they try to resolve their issues Johnny must also contend with the return of his former nemesis Jack Sikora (Bowie) who's bent on revenge. Pace is slow on the draw (even for a Western) and a dubbed-over Keitel shoots a blank though Bowie followers will want to lasso this one. In Italian with English subtitles. **87m/C DVD.** Harvey Keitel, David Bowie, Sandrine Holt, Vincenzo Pardini, Leonardo Pieraccioni; *D:* Giovanni Veronesi; *W:* Giovanni Veronesi, Vincenzo Pardini. **VIDEO**

Gunsmoke 1/2 **1953** Reb Kittredge (Murphy) is a gun-for-hire who's offered a job by greedy rancher Matt Telford (Randolph). Instead, Kittredge decides to go with Telford's enemy, Dan Saxon (Kelly), so Telford hires another gunslinger (Drake) to get rid of them both. Cabot provides the usual romantic lure as Saxon's daughter. Based on the novel "Roughshod" by Norman A. Fox. **78m/C VHS.** Audie Murphy, Susan Cabot, Paul Kelly, Donald Randolph, Charles Drake, Mary Castle, Jack Kelly, Jesse White, William Reynolds; *D:* Nathan "Jerry" Juran; *W:* D.D. Beauchamp; *C:* Charles P. Boyle.

Gunsmoke: Return to Dodge 1/2 **1987** The first of the TV movies that reunited most of the cast of the classic TV western. Matt Dillon returns to Dodge and Miss Kitty after 12 years only to be trailed by a ruthless adversary. **100m/C VHS, DVD.** James Arness, Amanda Blake, Buck Taylor, Fran Ryan, Earl Holliman, Steve Forrest; *D:* Vincent McEveety. **TV**

Gunsmoke Trail 1/2 **1938** Cowpoke Randall saves an heiress from losing her estate to a phony uncle in low-budget western. Also features the prolific "Fuzzy" St. John in his cowboy's sidekick stage (interestingly, St. John, a nephew of Fatty Arbuckle, later co-starred in the "Lone Rider" series with Randall's brother, Robert Livingston). **59m/C VHS, DVD.** Louise Stanley, Henry Roquemore, Ted Adams, John Merton, Addison "Jack" Randall, Al "Fuzzy" St. John; *D:* Sam Newfield; *W:* Fred Myton; *C:* Jack Greenhalgh.

The Guru 1/2 **2002 (R)** Naive dance instructor Ramu Gupta (Mistry) leaves India to pursuit stardom in New York. After being fired from his job as a waiter, he auditions for a movie company, but it turns out to be for a porn film. Unable to perform despite coaching from Sharrona (Graham), a porn starlet, Ramu is fired from this job as well. As luck (and script) would have it, he's re-hired by his former boss to replace the drunken swami that was scheduled to appear at a party for socialite Lexi (Tomei). Regurgitating his porn co-star's advice, Ramu becomes a hit as a sex guru. Soon Ramu is the toast of the town as the mystical sex therapist (think Deepak Chopra as Dr Ruth). The movie has some genuinely funny moments, but suffers for trying to be both a light-hearted romantic comedy and a social satire. **91m/C VHS, DVD.** *GB FR US* Jimi Mistry, Heather Graham, Marisa Tomei, Michael McKean, Christine Baranski, Rob Morrow, Malachy McCourt, Dash Mihok; *D:* Daisy von Scherler Mayer; *W:* Tracey Jackson; *C:* John de Borman; *M:* David Carbonara.

Gus 1/2 **1976 (G)** A Disney film about the California Atoms, a football team that has the worst record in the league until they begin winning games with the help of their field goal kicking mule of a mascot, Gus. The competition then plots a donkey-napping. Enjoyable comedy for the whole family. **96m/C VHS, DVD.** Ed Asner, Tim Conway, Dick Van Patten, Ronnie Schell, Bob Crane, Tom Bosley; *D:* Vincent McEveety; *W:* Arthur Alsberg; *M:* Robert F. Brunner.

The Guy from Harlem **1977** He's mad, he's from Harlem, and he's not going to take it any more. **86m/C VHS.** Loye Hawkins, Cathy Davis, Patricia Fulton, Wanda Starr; *D:* Rene Martinez Jr.

A Guy Named Joe 1/2 **1944** A sentimental, patriotic Hollywood fantasy about the angel of a dead WWII pilot guiding another young pilot through battle and also helping him to romance his girl, who's still too devoted to his memory. Remade in 1989 as "Always." **121m/B VHS.** Spencer Tracy, Irene Dunne, Van Johnson, Ward Bond, James Gleason, Lionel Barrymore, Esther Williams; *D:* Victor Fleming; *W:* Dalton Trumbo; *C:* Karl Freund.

A Guy Thing **2003 (PG-13)** Paul (Lee), wakes up after his bachelor party to find free spirit Becky (Stiles) besides him in bed. Of course his fiancee walks in just as Paul is able to shoo Becky out, thus avoiding a rather embarrassing situation. Or not. Becky turns out to be his fiancee's cousin and keeps popping up into Paul's life, as does her insanely possessive, cop ex-boyfriend. Lee and Stiles are likable enough, unfortunately the material is too bland to make anything out their chemistry. **101m/C VHS, DVD.** *US* Jason Lee, Julia Stiles, Selma Blair, Shawn Hatosy, James Brolin, Diana Scarwid, Lochlyn Munro, Julie Hagerty, Jackie Burroughs, David Koechner, Thomas Lennon; *D:* Chris Koch; *W:* Matt Tarses, Bill Wrubel, Greg Glienna, Pete Schwaba; *C:* Robbie Greenberg; *M:* Mark Mothersbaugh.

The Guyana Tragedy: The Story of Jim Jones **1980** Dramatization traces the story of the Reverend Jim Jones and the People's Temple from its beginnings in 1953 to the November 1978 mass suicide of more than 900 people. Boothe is appropriately hypnotic as the Reverend. **240m/C VHS.** Powers Boothe, Ned Beatty, Randy Quaid, Brad Dourif, Brenda Vaccaro, LeVar Burton, Colleen Dewhurst, James Earl Jones; *D:* William A. Graham; *C:* Gil Hubbs; *M:* Elmer Bernstein. **TV**

The Guys 1/2 **2002 (PG)** Cinematic adaptation of Anne Nelson's timely play about September 11. A fateful introduction brings a journalist (Weaver) to collaborate with an emotionally wrought, inarticulate New York City Fire Department captain (LaPaglia) on poignant, heartfelt eulogies for his fallen brothers. Both leads do a fine job bringing their characters from stage to screen. Some archival footage feels awkwardly placed but on the whole film presents a dignified and humanistic perspective on an event whose world impact is still unfolding. Shot on location in New York, with very little budget in just two weeks, then reshot in another two weeks after discovering some lighting equipment had failed. Simpson and Weaver's daughter makes a cameo appearance along with Nelson's two sons. **98m/C VHS, DVD.** *US* Sigourney Weaver, Anthony LaPaglia; ***D:*** Jim Simpson; ***W:*** Ann Nelson, Jim Simpson; ***C:*** Maryse Alberti; ***M:*** Ron Carter.

Guys and Balls 𝒮𝒮 *Manner wie wir* **2004 (R)** Small-town baker's son Ecki (Bruckner) is the goalie on the local soccer team. After losing an important game, Ecki is discovered in a drunken embrace with another man and his teammates throw him off the squad. Vowing to get even, Ecki decides to put together an all-gay team and challenge his hometown's homophobes to a grudge match. So he heads to the city to recruit players and, naturally, finds mostly stereotypical oddballs. Lots of good-natured crass humor and rowdiness. German with subtitles. **106m/C DVD.** *GE* Christian Berkel, Maximilian Bruckner, Rolf Zacher, Lisa Maria Potthoff, David Rott, Mariele Millowitsch; ***D:*** Sherry Hormann; ***W:*** Benedikt Gollhardt; ***C:*** Hanno Lentz; ***M:*** Martin Todsharow.

Guys and Dolls 𝒮𝒮𝒮 **1955** New York gambler Sky Masterson takes a bet that he can romance a Salvation Army lady. Based on the stories of Damon Runyon with Blaine, Kaye, Pully, and Silver recreating their roles from the Broadway hit. Brando's not-always-convincing musical debut. ♫ More I Cannot Wish You; My Time of Day; Guys and Dolls; Fugue for Tinhorns; Follow the Fold; Sue Me; Take Back Your Mink; If I Were a Bell; Luck Be a Lady. **150m/C VHS, DVD.** Marlon Brando, Jean Simmons, Frank Sinatra, Vivian Blaine, Stubby Kaye, Sheldon Leonard, Veda Ann Borg, Regis Toomey; ***D:*** Joseph L. Mankiewicz; ***W:*** Joseph L. Mankiewicz; ***C:*** Harry Stradling Sr.; ***M:*** Frank Loesser. Golden Globes '56: Actress—Mus./Comedy (Simmons), Film—Mus./Comedy.

The Guyver 𝒮 ½ **1991** A young college student is transformed into a super-human fighting machine thanks to his discovery of an alien device, "The Guyver." A CIA agent (Hamill) must keep the secret device from falling into the hands of human mutants, the Zoanoids. Based on a Japanese comic book. **92m/C VHS, DVD.** Mark Hamill, Vivian Wu, David Gale, Jeffrey Combs, Michael Berryman; ***D:*** Steve Wang.

Guyver 2: Dark Hero 𝒮 ½ **1994 (R)** The Guvyer discovers an alien ship filled with weapons capable of destroying the planet. Naturally, he must battle the evil mutant Zoanoids in order to save the world. Adapted from a Japanese comic book. **127m/C VHS, DVD.** David Hayter, Kathy Christopherson, Christopher Michael; ***D:*** Steve Wang; ***W:*** Nathan Long.

Gym Teacher: The Movie 𝒮𝒮 ½ **2008** This Nickelodeon family comedy stars Meloni as short shorts-wearing Dave Stewie, a former gymnast who suffered an unfortunate accident at the Olympics and never quite recovered his equilibrium. Now a suburban junior high gym teacher, Stewie is determined to win the national gym-teacher-of-the-year award and he won't be thwarted by the athletic nightmare that is uncoordinated eighth-grader Roland Waffles (Kress). **94m/C DVD.** Christopher Meloni, Nathan Kress, Amy Sedaris, David Alan Grier, Chelah Horsdal; ***D:*** Paul Dinello; ***W:*** Steven Altiere, Daniel Altiere; ***C:*** Attila Szalay; ***M:*** Daniel Licht. **CABLE**

Gymkata 𝒮 **1985 (R)** A gymnast (Olympian Thomas) must use his martial arts skills to conquer and secure a military state in a hostile European country. **89m/C VHS, DVD.** Kurt Thomas, Tetchie Agbayani, Richard Norton, Conan Lee; ***D:*** Robert Clouse; ***W:*** Charles Robert Carner.

The Gymnast 𝒮𝒮 ½ **2006** A devastating injury ended the Olympic gymnastic hopes of Jane Hawkins. Years later, the unhappily married, middle-aged Jane gets a chance at performing in Las Vegas in a cirque-style aerial act with the beautiful younger Serena. As they practice for the show, Jane is surprised to feel so close to her new partner. Great shots of the aerial fabric act and a romantic story. **98m/C DVD.** Allison Mackie, Dreya Webber, Addie Yungmee, David De Simone, Mam Smith; ***D:*** Ned Farr; ***W:*** Ned Farr; ***C:*** Marco Fargnoli; ***M:*** Craig Richey.

Gypsy 𝒮𝒮𝒮 **1962** The life story of America's most famous striptease queen, Gypsy Rose Lee (Wood). Russell gives a memorable performance as the infamous Mama Rose, Gypsy's stage mother. Based on both Gypsy Rose Lee's memoirs and the hit 1959 Broadway play by Arthur Laurents. ♫ Small World; All I Need is the Girl; You'll Never Get Away From Me; Let Me Entertain You; Some People; Everything's Coming Up Roses; You Gotta Have a Gimmick; Baby Jane and the Newsboys; Mr. Goldstone, I Love You. **144m/C VHS, DVD.** Rosalind Russell, Natalie Wood, Karl Malden, Ann Jillian, Parley Baer, Paul Wallace, Betty Bruce; ***D:*** Mervyn LeRoy; ***W:*** Arthur Laurents, Leonard Spigelgass; ***C:*** Harry Stradling Sr.; ***M:*** Jule Styne, Stephen Sondheim. Golden Globes '63: Actress—Mus./Comedy (Russell).

Gypsy 𝒮𝒮 **1975** A modern day gypsy-blooded Robin Hood cavorts between heists and romantic trysts. Dubbed. **90m/C VHS.** Alain Delon, Annie Girardot, Paul Meurisse; ***D:*** Jose Giovanni.

Gypsy 𝒮𝒮 ½ **1993** If you like Bette brassy and larger than life, as only she can be, than this is the production for you. This TV re-creation of the 1959 Broadway musical stars Midler as notorious stage mother Mama Rose, who tries to realize all her frustrated ambitions by pushing her two young daughters, June and Louise, into vaudeville show biz. Her wish eventually comes true, in an unexpected fashion, when an adult Louise (Gibb) transforms herself into stripper Gypsy Rose Lee. ♫ Everything's Coming Up Roses; You've Gotta Have a Gimmick; All I Need Is the Girl; Rose's Turn; Some People; Mr. Goldstone, I Love You; You'll Never Get Away From Me; Together, Wherever We Go. **150m/C VHS, DVD.** Bette Midler, Peter Riegert, Cynthia Gibb, Ed Asner, Christine Ebersole, Michael Jeter, Andrea Martin, Jennifer Beck, Linda Hart, Rachel Sweet; ***D:*** Emile Ardolino; ***W:*** Arthur Laurents; ***C:*** Ralf Bode; ***M:*** Jule Styne, Stephen Sondheim. **TV**

Gypsy Angels 𝒮 **1994 (R)** A daredevil stunt pilot has a terrifying accident and develops amnesia. With the help of a stripper (who is in love with him), he tries to rebuild his life, this time with her in it. White's no actress and unless you like stunt flying (and there's a lot of it), fly by this one. (You'll note the director won't admit to this, since Smithee is a pseudonym.) **92m/C VHS.** Vanna White, Richard Roundtree, Gene Bicknell; ***D:*** Alan Smithee.

Gypsy Blood 𝒮𝒮 **1918** One of the first screen versions of "Carmen," closer to Prosper Merrimee's story than to the opera, depicting the fated love between a dancing girl and a matador. Lubitsch's first notable film. Silent. **104m/B VHS, DVD.** Pola Negri; ***D:*** Ernst Lubitsch.

Gypsy Colt 𝒮𝒮 ½ **1954 (G)** Gypsy is the horse beloved by the young Corcoran. But a drought forces her family to sell the animal to a racing stable 500 miles from their home. Gypsy is having none of this, escapes the stables, and returns home to be with Corcoran. Both horse and child actress are naturally appealing. **72m/C VHS.** Donna Corcoran, Ward Bond, Frances Dee, Lee Van Cleef, Larry Keating; ***D:*** Andrew Marton.

Gypsy 83 𝒮𝒮 **2001** Rue is goth girl Gypsy Vale, a Stevie Nicks wanna-be named after her idol's famous song, who unhappily resides in decidedly un-hip Sandusky, Ohio with her hippie dad and abandoned by her still-aspiring rock star mother. Desperate to flee the quiet Midwestern berg where she and her only friend Clive (Turton) serve merely as social outcasts, the two black-clad souls head to a New York nightclub to participate in the "Night of 1000 Stevies" Nicks tribute bash. The two encounter some predictable problems along the way, including being hassled about the way they look by various small-minded locals but also meet some reassuring kindred spirits, including wash-up lounge singer Black and Amish boy Scoville. Typical rebel without a cause premise made slightly better by a decent Rue and Turton. **94m/C VHS, DVD.** *US* Sara Rue, Karen Black, John Doe, Paulo Costanzo, Kett Turton, Anson Scoville; ***D:*** Todd Stephens; ***W:*** Todd Stephens; ***C:*** Gina DeGirolamo; ***M:*** Marty Beller.

The Gypsy Moths 𝒮𝒮 **1969** It's not actually about a bug infestation. Instead, it's a Frankenheimer melodrama about three barnstorming skydivers arriving in a small Kansas town to give an exhibition. They're staying with the aunt (Kerr) and uncle (Windom) of young Malcolm (Wilson) and Aunt Elizabeth is immediately drawn to fatalistic, taciturn leader Mike Rettig (Lancaster). After their one-night stand, Rettig is scheduled to perform an extremely risky jump, but tragedy strikes. Because Malcolm and Joe (Hackman) need money to bury Mike, Malcolm decides to perform the same stunt to draw a big crowd. **106m/C VHS, DVD.** Burt Lancaster, Deborah Kerr, Gene Hackman, Scott Wilson, William Windom, Bonnie Bedelia, Sheree North, Ford Rainey; ***D:*** John Frankenheimer; ***W:*** William Hanley; ***C:*** Philip Lathrop; ***M:*** Elmer Bernstein.

The Gypsy Warriors 𝒮 ½ **1978** Two Army captains during WWII infiltrate Nazi-occupied France in order to prevent the distribution of a deadly toxin and are aided by a band of Gypsies. **77m/C VHS.** Tom Selleck, James Whitmore Jr., Joseph Ruskin, Lina Raymond; ***D:*** Lou Antonio. **TV**

H 𝒮𝒮 **1990** Two junkies try to kick their heroin addiction and face the difficult withdrawal period. Includes glimpses into their past that shed light on the reasons they turned to drugs. Contains explicit footage. **93m/C VHS.** *CA* Martin Neufeld, Pascale Montpetit; ***D:*** Darrell Wasyk. Genie '91: Actress (Montpetit); Toronto-City '90: Canadian Feature Film.

H-Bomb WOOF! **1971** Mitchum stars as a CIA agent who is sent to Bangkok to retrieve two stolen nuclear warheads from a terrorist. It just so happens that his ex-girlfriend's father is the terrorist he must contend with in this stupid movie. **98m/C VHS.** Olivia Hussey, Chris Mitchum, Krung Savilai; ***D:*** P. (Philip) Chalong.

H-Man WOOF! *Bijo to Ekitainigen* **1959** A Japanese sci-fi woofer about a radioactive mass of slime festering under Tokyo. Extremely lame special effects get quite a few unintentional laughs. Dubbed. **79m/C VHS.** *JP* Koreya Senda, Kenji Sahara, Yumi Shirakawa, Akihiko Hirata; ***D:*** Inoshiro Honda.

Habit 𝒮𝒮 **1997** A very low-budget New York vampire tale that tweaks tradition. Wastrel Sam (Fessenden) is at loose ends when he meets intriguing Anna (Snaider). This first encounter is a bust (Sam's very drunk) but a later meeting leads to an intense sexual encounter—and Sam waking up alone in Battery Park with a prominently cut lip and some hazy memories. All their encounters are similarly intense (and in public places) but Anna refuses to reveal anything about herself. Sam is soon a confused physical wreck but when Anna's around, he just doesn't care. **112m/C VHS, DVD.** Larry Fessenden, Meredith Snaider, Aaron Beall, Heather Woodbury, Patricia Coleman; ***D:*** Larry Fessenden; ***W:*** Larry Fessenden; ***C:*** Frank DeMarco; ***M:*** Geoffrey Kidde.

Habitat 𝒮𝒮 ½ **1997 (R)** Nature goes wild when high school student Andreas (Getty) moves with his scientist parents, Hank (Karyo) and Clarissa (Krige), to the small Southwestern burg of Pleasanton. Hank's experiment with accelerated evolution takes some unexpected blips, with Hank turning into particles of matter, their house transformed into a vegetation-covered fortress, and Clarissa becoming a very earthy earth mother. Some eerie special effects. **103m/C VHS, DVD.** Alice Krige, Balthazar Getty, Tcheky Karyo, Kenneth Welsh, Lara Harris; ***D:*** Renee Daalder; ***W:*** Renee Daalder; ***C:*** Jean Lepine; ***M:*** Ralph Grierson. **CABLE**

The Habitation of Dragons 𝒮 ½ **1991** Family fueds and melodrama in 1930s West Texas. Wandering lawyer George Tolliver (Davis) argues with successful businessman brother Leonard (Forrest) while matriarch Leonora (Stapleton) presides and family skeletons rattle. Confusing hodgepodge. **94m/C VHS.** Jean Stapleton, Frederic Forrest, Brad Davis, Pat Hingle, Hallie Foote, Maureen O'Sullivan; ***D:*** Michael Lindsay-Hogg; ***W:*** Horton Foote; ***M:*** David Shire. **TV**

Hachiko: A Dog's Tale 𝒮𝒮 ½ *Hachi: A Dog's Tale* **2009 (G)** Family-friendly, sentimental tearjerker (a remake of a 1987 Japanese film) based on real events that occurred in Japan in the 1920s although the plot is much like 1961's "Greyfriars Bobby." The story has been moved to small town New England in the 1990s with a framing story set in 2007. Parker Wilson (Gere) finds a lost Akita puppy at the train station and winds up raising the rambunctious dog with the help of his wife Cate (Allen). Every morning and evening, Hachiko escorts Wilson to and from the station. One day Wilson doesn't get off the train although Hachiko continues to keep his vigil for years and becomes a local celebrity. **93m/C DVD.** Richard Gere, Joan Allen, Cary-Hiroyuki Tagawa, Jason Alexander, Erik Avari, Kevin Decoste; ***D:*** Lasse Hallstrom; ***W:*** Stephen P. Lindsay; ***C:*** Ron Fortunato; ***M:*** Jan A.P. Kaczmarek.

Hack! 𝒮𝒮 **2007 (R)** Horror fans Vincent King (Kanan) and his wife Mary (Landau) want to create the ultimate slasher flick—with the unwitting participation of a group of college students. Emily (McKellar) and her pals are on a biology field trip at a remote island where they find the woods to be a lot worse than just a bad case of poison ivy. Low-budget but with a number of clever horror movie references. **100m/C DVD.** Sean Kanan, Juliet Landau, Danica McKellar, Lochlyn Munro, Jay Kenneth Johnson, Tony Burton, Adrienne Frantz, Burt Young, William Forsythe, Kane Hodder; ***D:*** Matt Flynn; ***W:*** Matt Flynn; ***C:*** Roger Chingirian; ***M:*** Scott Glasgow. **VIDEO**

Hack O'Lantern 𝒮 *Halloween Night* **1987** Granddad worships Satan, and gets his grandson involved; the result is much bloodshed, violence, and evil. **90m/C VHS.** Hy Pyke, Gregory Scott Cummins, Katrina Garner, Carla Baron; ***D:*** Jag Mundhra; ***W:*** Carla Robinson; ***C:*** Stephen Blake; ***M:*** Greg Haggard.

Hackers 𝒮𝒮 **1995 (PG-13)** Group of teenaged computer cyber-geeks surf the 'net and become the prime suspects in an industrial conspiracy when hacker Dade (Miller) breaks into the computer at Ellingson Oil Company. It's really an inside job but just try getting anyone (read "adult") to believe him. So the techno whiz kids band together, with cops and security all wanting to shut them down. Jolie (hacker Acid Burn) is the daughter of actor Jon Voight. **105m/C VHS, DVD.** Felicity Huffman, Jonny Lee Miller, Angelina Jolie, Fisher Stevens, Lorraine Bracco, Jesse Bradford, Wendell Pierce, Alberta Watson, Laurence Mason, Renoly Santiago, Matthew Lillard, Penn Jillette; ***D:*** Iain Softley; ***W:*** Rafael Moreu; ***C:*** Andrzej Sekula; ***M:*** Simon Boswell.

The Hades Factor 𝒮𝒮 ½ *Covert One: The Hades Factor; Robert Ludlum's Covert One: The Hades Factor* **2006** Covert One, a top secret intelligence agency, must stop an air-borne virus that terrorists are planning to release throughout the U.S. Lots of running, chasing, double-crosses, snarling, and blood (it's not for the squeamish). Loosely based on the novel by Robert Ludlum and Gayle Lynds. **184m/C DVD.** *US* Stephen Dorff, Mira Sorvino, Blair Underwood, Colm Meaney, Danny Huston, Sophia Myles, Josh Hopkins, Jeffrey DeMunn, Kenneth Welsh, Anjelica Huston; ***D:*** Mick Jackson; ***W:*** Elwood Reid; ***C:*** Ivan Strasburg; ***M:*** J. Peter Robinson. **TV**

Hadley's Rebellion 𝒮 ½ **1984 (PG)** A Georgia farm boy adjusts to relocation at an elitist California boarding school by flaunting his wrestling abilities. **96m/C VHS.** Griffin O'Neal, Charles Durning, William Devane, Adam Baldwin, Dennis Hage, Lisa Lucas; ***D:*** Fred Walton; ***W:*** Fred Walton.

Haiku Tunnel 𝒮𝒮 **2000 (R)** Josh (Kornbluth) takes a temp job with high-powered attorney Bob Shelby (Keith) and then accepts an offer for a permanent position. This soon begins to freak commitment-phobic Josh out, resulting in his inablility to complete the simple task of mailing out 17 important letters. As his anxiety grows, Josh has even more trouble dealing with his chipper coworkers and his impatient boss. **88m/C VHS, DVD.** Josh Kornbluth, Warren Keith, Helen Shumaker, June Lomena, Amy Resnick; ***D:*** Josh

Kornbluth, Jacob Kornbluth; ***W:*** Josh Kornbluth, Jacob Kornbluth, John Bellucci; ***C:*** Don Matthew Smith.

Hail *Hail to the Chief; Washington, B.C* **1973 (PG)** A biting satire of what-might-have-been if certain key cabinet members had their way. **85m/C VHS.** Richard B. Shull, Dick O'Neill, Phil Foster, Joseph Sirola, Dan Resin, Willard Waterman, Gary Sandy; ***D:*** Fred Levinson.

Hail Caesar 1/2 **1994 (PG)** His job at an eraser factory is the only thing standing between Julius Caesar MacGruder (Hall) and fame and fortune as a rock 'n' roll singer. **93m/C VHS, DVD.** Anthony Michael Hall, Robert Downey Jr., Frank Gorshin, Samuel L. Jackson, Judd Nelson, Nicholas Pryor, Leslie Danon, Bobbie Phillips; ***D:*** Anthony Michael Hall; ***W:*** Robert Mittenthal; ***M:*** Roger Tallman.

Hail, Hero! 1/2 **1969 (PG)** A dated Vietnam War era drama about a confused hippie rebelling against his parents and the draft. First film for both Douglas and Strauss. Adapted from the novel by John Weston. Includes music by Gordon Lightfoot. **97m/C VHS.** Michael Douglas, Arthur Kennedy, Teresa Wright, John Larch, Charles Drake, Deborah Winters, Peter Strauss; ***D:*** David Miller; ***C:*** Robert B. Hauser.

Hail Mafia *Je Vous Salue, Mafia* **1965** American gangster Rudy (Constantine) has fled to France because his cohorts believe he's going to testify against them. So hitmen Phil (Klugmen) and Schaft (Silva) have been contracted to kill Rudy. They travel from Paris to Marseille in search of their quarry and for Schaft the job is strictly business, but for Phil it's more personal. Dubbed. **88m/C DVD.** *FR IT* Eddie Constantine, Jack Klugman, Henry Silva, Micheline Presle, Elsa Martinelli; ***D:*** Raoul Levy; ***W:*** Raoul Levy; ***C:*** Raoul Coutard; ***M:*** Hubert Rostaing.

Hail Mary 1/2 *Je Vous Salue Marie* **1985 (R)** A modern-day virgin named Mary inexplicably becomes pregnant in this controversial film that discards notions of divinity in favor of the celebration of a lively, intellectual humanism. Godard rejects orthodox narrative structure and bourgeois prejudices. Very controversial, but not up to his breathless beginning work. In French with English subtitles. **107m/C VHS.** *FR SI GB* Myriem Roussel, Thierry Rode, Philippe Lacoste, Manon Anderson, Juliette Binoche, Johan Leysen; ***D:*** Jean-Luc Godard; ***W:*** Jean-Luc Godard.

Hail the Conquering Hero 1/2 **1944** A slight young man is rejected by the Army. Upon returning home, he is surprised to find out they think he's a hero. Biting satire with Demarest's performance stealing the show. **101m/B VHS, DVD.** Eddie Bracken, Ella Raines, William Demarest, Franklin Pangborn, Raymond Walburn, Freddie (Fred) Steele; ***D:*** Preston Sturges.

Hair 1/2 **1979 (PG)** Film version of the explosive 1960s Broadway musical about the carefree life of the flower children and the shadow of the Vietnam War that hangs over them. Great music, as well as wonderful choreography by Twyla Tharp help portray the surprisingly sensitive evocation of the period so long after the fact. Forman has an uncanny knack for understanding the textures of American life. Watch for a thinner Nell Carter. **122m/C VHS, DVD.** Treat Williams, John Savage, Beverly D'Angelo, Annie Golden, Nicholas Ray, Nell Carter; ***D:*** Milos Forman; ***W:*** Michael Weller; ***C:*** Miroslav Ondricek; ***M:*** Galt MacDermot.

Hair Show 1/2 **2004 (PG-13)** Flick could have used a can of hair spray to give its limp premise some hold. Outgoing (i.e. loud) Peaches (Mo'Nique) works at a low-rent Baltimore hair salon while her successful sister Angie (Smith) has gone up-scale out in L.A. Owing a wad of cash to the IRS, Peaches heads for the west coast to visit her estranged sis and discovers that an annual competitive hairstyling pageant offers enough money to pay off her debt should she win. Angie thinks the event is beneath her but may just be jealous that rival salon owner Marcella (Torres) has won several years in a row. Peaches has no problem jumping into the action. It's all one giant cliche. **105m/C VHS, DVD.** Mo'Nique, Kellita Smith, Gina Torres, David Ramsey, Keiko Agena, Cee Cee Michaela, Joe Torry, Andre B. Blake, Taraji P. Henson; ***D:*** Leslie Small; ***C:*** Keith Smith; ***M:*** Kennard Ramsay.

The Hairdresser's Husband *Le Mari de la coiffeuse* **1992 (R)** Antoine (Rochefort) has had an odd obsession since boyhood—hairdressers—and in middle age he finds love with Mathilde (Galiena), a hairdresser he meets and proposes to as she cuts his hair. She accepts, and the two live their quiet lives in her barber shop as she cuts hair and he watches, occasionally breaking out in Arabian dances. A dark and odd yet refreshing film with fine performances by Rochefort and Galiena in this story about fetishism, obsession, and hair. In French with English subtitles. **84m/C VHS.** *FR* Jean Rochefort, Anna Galiena, Roland Bertin, Maurice Chevit, Philippe Clevenot, Jacques Mathou, Claude Aufaure; ***D:*** Patrice Leconte; ***W:*** Claude Klotz, Patrice Leconte; ***C:*** Eduardo Serra; ***M:*** Michael Nyman.

Hairspray **1988 (PG)** Waters' first truly mainstream film, if that's even possible, and his funniest. Details the struggle among teenagers in 1962 Baltimore for the top spot in a local TV dance show. Deals with racism and stereotypes, as well as typical "teen" problems (hair-do's and don'ts). Filled with refreshingly tasteful, subtle social satire (although not without typical Waters touches that will please die-hard fans). Lake is lovable and appealing as Divine's daughter; Divine, in his last film, is likeable as an iron-toting mom. Look for Waters in a cameo and Divine as a man. Great '60s music, which Waters refers to as "the only known remedy to today's Hit Parade of Hell." **94m/C VHS, DVD.** Ricki Lake, Divine, Jerry Stiller, Colleen (Ann) Fitzpatrick, Sonny Bono, Deborah Harry, Ruth Brown, Leslie Ann Powers, Michael St. Gerard, Shawn Thompson, Clayton Prince, Pia Zadora, Ric Ocasek, Mink Stole, Mary Vivian Pearce, Alan J. Wendl, Susan Lowe, George Stover, Toussaint McCall; ***Cameos:*** John Waters; ***D:*** John Waters; ***W:*** John Waters; ***C:*** David Insley; ***M:*** Kenny Vance.

Hairspray **2007 (PG)** Remake of the 1988 John Waters surprise hit that later became a Broadway musical. In spite of the rehash, this new iteration finds its freshness by upping the bounce and fun. The story remains intact, with less-than-popular teenager Tracy Turnblad (newcomer Blonsky, a treat) shaking up her 1960s-era town with her efforts to integrate the local television dance show. Supported by her mother Edna (Travolta in plus-size drag), she turns dance into social activism and has a blast doing it. **115m/C DVD, Blu-ray Disc.** *US* John Travolta, Christopher Walken, Michelle Pfeiffer, Queen Latifah, Nicole Blonsky, Amanda Bynes, James Marsden, Zac Efron, Brittany Snow, Allison Janney, Elijah Kelley, Jerry Stiller, Paul Dooley, Taylor Parks; ***D:*** Adam Shankman; ***W:*** Leslie Dixon, Thomas Meehan, Mark O'Donnell; ***C:*** Bojan Bazelli; ***M:*** Marc Shaiman.

The Hairy Ape **1944** Screen adaptation of the Eugene O'Neill play. A beast-like coal stoker becomes obsessed with a cool and distant passenger aboard an ocean liner. **90m/B VHS.** William Bendix, Susan Hayward, John Loder, Dorothy Comingore, Roman Bohnen, Alan Napier; ***D:*** Alfred Santell.

Half a Lifetime **1986** The stakes are too high for four friends playing a game of poker. **85m/C VHS.** *CA* Keith Carradine, Gary Busey, Nick Mancuso, Saul Rubinek; ***D:*** Daniel Petrie; ***W:*** Stephen Metcalfe.

Half a Loaf of Kung Fu *Dian Zhi Gong Fu Gan Chian Chan* **1978** The worthy bodyguards of Sern Chuan are called upon to deliver a valuable jade statue. Thwarted again and again by ruthless robbers, they falter. Only Chan carries on, meeting the enemy alone. Fast action, good story. **98m/C VHS, DVD.** *HK* Jackie Chan, James Tien; ***D:*** Chi-Hwa Chen; ***W:*** Ming Chi Tang; ***C:*** Chin-Kui Chen; ***M:*** Frankie Chen.

Half a Sixpence **1967** Former musician Sidney, who earlier directed "Showboat" and "Kiss Me Kate," shows a bit less verve in this production. Based on H.G. Wells' 1905 novel, "Kipps," it sports much of the original cast from its Broadway incarnation. Edwardian orphan Steele, a cloth-dealer-in-training, comes into a large sum of money and proceeds to lose it with great dispatch. Somewhere along the way he loses his girlfriend, too, but she takes him back because musicals end happily. ♫Half a Sixpence; Flash, Bang, Wallop!; All In The Cause Of Economy; I'm Not Talking To You; Money To Burn; The Race Is On; I Don't Believe A Word Of It; A Proper Gentleman; She's Too Far Above Me. **148m/B VHS, DVD.** Tommy Steele, Julia Foster, Penelope Horner, Cyril Ritchard, Grover Dale; ***D:*** George Sidney; ***W:*** Beverley Cross; ***C:*** Geoffrey Unsworth.

Half a Soldier *Half a Sinner* **1940** A spoiled girl gets a big surprise when she steals a car and discovers the body of a gangster in the trunk. **59m/B VHS.** Constance Collier, Tom Dugan, Heather Angel, John "Dusty" King; ***D:*** Al Christie; ***W:*** Fred Jackson Jr.; ***C:*** Charles Van Enger.

Half-Baked **1997 (R)** Four seedy roommates whose problems stem from their love of marijuana float through life with loser jobs that give them just enough money to buy their next bag. When Kenny (H.Williams) is arrested for killing a diabetic police horse during a munchies run, the three remaining friends must put their resinated brains together and come up with a way to bail him out. Thurgood (Chapelle), a custodian for a pharmaceutical company, decides to steal some high-grade grass from the lab; and along with Brian (Breuer, doing a very convincing stoned) and Scarface (Diaz), he begins dealing. This puts them afoul of the law as well as local drug lord Samson Simpson (C. Williams). Just say no. Trust me, dude, this stuff is bogus and it won't get you off. **83m/C VHS, DVD, HD DVD.** Tracy Morgan, Harland Williams, Dave Chappelle, Jim Breuer, Guillermo Diaz, Rachel True, Clarence Williams III, Thomas Chong, Jon Stewart, Stephen Baldwin, Willie Nelson, Janeane Garofalo, Steven Wright, Laura Silverman, Snoop Dogg; ***D:*** Tamra Davis; ***W:*** Neal Brennan, Dave Chappelle; ***C:*** Steven Bernstein; ***M:*** Alf Clausen.

The Half-Breed **1951** Routine oater with settlers and Apaches fighting, and the obligatory half-breed stuck in the middle. **81m/B VHS.** Robert Young, Jack Buetel, Janis Carter, Barton MacLane, Reed Hadley, Porter Hall, Connie Gilchrist; ***D:*** Stuart Gilmore.

Half Broken Things **2007** And completely broken people. Professional house-sitter Jean (Wilton) is due to retire after her last job at Walden Manor. When two strangers show up at the door—pregnant Steph (Matthews), who's run away from her abusive boyfriend, and Michael (Mays), who's helping her—lonely Jean takes them in. The troubled trio is soon lost amid delusions of family life and home until reality begins to intrude. **93m/C DVD.** *GB* Penelope Wilton, Sinead Matthews, Daniel Mays, Nicholas Le Prevost, Sian Thomas, Lara Cazalet, Crispin Redman; ***D:*** Tim Fywell; ***W:*** Alan Whiting; ***C:*** David Odd; ***M:*** Colin Towns. **TV**

Half-Caste **2004 (R)** See Bobby go to South Africa with his buddies to capture on film the fabled "Half-Caste"—half man, half leopard—that finds humans to be tasty treats. See Bobby's friends go bye-bye in not-at-all-surprising hideousness leaving him to persuade the coppers that he isn't the evil-doer. Look elsewhere for scary horror movie. **86m/C VHS, DVD.** Sebastian Apodaca, Kim Te Roller, Robert Pike Daniel, Rob Zazzali, Kathy Wagner, Greg Good, Kelly Cohen; ***D:*** Sebastian Apodaca; ***W:*** Sebastian Apodaca; ***C:*** Cooper Donaldson; ***M:*** Charlie Brissette, Manu Hanu, Hanu-Manu. **VIDEO**

Half Human 1/2 **1958** Dull Japanese monster movie about an ape-human who terrorizes Northern Japan. When released in the U.S., Carradine and Morris were added. Without subtitles, just Carradine's narration. Director Honda made better movies before and after, with Godzilla and Rodan. **78m/B VHS.** *JP* John Carradine, Akira Takarada, Morris Ankrum; ***D:*** Inoshiro Honda.

Half Light **2005 (R)** Rachel's (Moore) life as a well-known writer is sent spiraling when her five-year-old son accidentally drowns and she finds herself unable to write. Attempting to revive her career and escape her sorrow, she treks to a remote Scottish village where she seeks comfort from a local lighthouse operator. On cue, the tranquil setting is disrupted by not only visions of her dead child but by a shocking murder in town. Moore somewhat makes up for what's lacking in this not-quite-so-spooky tale. **102m/C DVD.** Demi Moore, Henry Ian Cusick, Nicholas Gleaves, Beans El-Balawi, Kate Isitt; ***D:*** Craig Rosenberg; ***W:*** Craig Rosenberg. **VIDEO**

Half Moon Street *Escort Girl* **1986 (R)** A brilliant woman scientist supplements her paltry fellowship salary by becoming a hired escort and prostitute, which leads her into various incidents of international intrigue. Adapted from a story by Paul Theroux, "Dr. Slaughter." **90m/C VHS, DVD.** Sigourney Weaver, Michael Caine, Keith Buckley, Ian Maclnnes; ***D:*** Bob Swaim.

The Half Naked Truth 1/2 **1932** Carnival barker Jimmy Bates (Tracy) has big plans, which are realized when he transforms sideshow hoochie dancer Teresita (Velez) into Princess Exotica and makes her a Broadway star. But when she begins dating the show's producer (Morgan), Jimmy gets jealous and tries to sabotage the dame's career (all in the name of love of course). **77m/B VHS.** Lee Tracy, Shirley Chambers, Lupe Velez, Eugene Pallette, Frank Morgan, Franklin Pangborn; ***D:*** Gregory La Cava; ***W:*** Gregory La Cava; ***C:*** Bert Glennon; ***M:*** Max Steiner.

Half Nelson **2006 (R)** Get high, Mr. Chips. Crackhead Brooklyn schoolteacher Dan Dunne (Gosling) manages to do the inspiring inner-city educator thing until 12-year-old Drey (Epps in a stellar debut performance), no stranger to addicts, discovers him passed out in a bathroom stall after a basketball game, pipe in hand. This leads to a tentative, complicated relationship between the two, with Dan's ironic efforts to save Drey from a drug dealer's plans to bring her into his fold somehow offering the pair the possibility of salvation. Gosling is raw and sympathetic portraying Dan's contradictions, and the film smartly avoids the usual feel-good trappings. **106m/C DVD.** *US* Ryan Gosling, Anthony Mackie, Tina Holmes, Deborah Rush, Shareeka Epps, Monique Gabriela Curnen, Jay O. Sanders, Karen Chilton; ***D:*** Ryan Fleck; ***W:*** Ryan Fleck, Anna Boden; ***C:*** Andrij Parekh. Ind. Spirit '07: Actor (Gosling), Actress (Epps).

Half of Heaven *La Mitad del Cielo* **1986** A critically popular film about a young Spanish woman who begins to share certain telepathic powers with her wizened grandmother. In Spanish with English subtitles. **95m/C VHS.** *SP* Angela Molina, Margarita Lozano; ***D:*** Manuel Gutierrez Aragon.

Half Past Dead **2002 (PG-13)** Steven Seagal hauls his bloated carcass through the motions in this action dud that's far past half dead. He plays Sascha, an undercover government agent working in a new-fangled Alcatraz prison. During the planned execution of thief/murderer Lester (Weitz), a corrupt government official (Chestnut) and his kick-boxing henchwoman (Peeples) take a Supreme Court justice (Thorson) hostage in an effort to find out where Lester hid his loot. Seagal allies with Nick (Ja Rule), his former FBI sting target, in order to save the day. Peeples delivers the film's only standout fight scene, although the backstage duel between Seagal and the buffet table must have been quite a sight. TV producer/novelist Stephen J. Cannell appears as a prison bureau chief. **97m/C VHS, DVD.** Steven Seagal, Morris Chestnut, Ja Rule, Nia Peeples, Michael "Bear" Taliferro, Claudia Christian, Linda Thorson, Bruce Weitz, Kurupt, Mo'Nique, Matt Battaglia, Richard Bremmer, Stephen J. Cannell, Don Michael Paul, Tony Plana; ***D:*** Don Michael Paul; ***W:*** Don Michael Paul; ***C:*** Michael Slovis; ***M:*** Tyler Bates.

Half-Shot at Sunrise **1930** Madcap vaudeville comedians play AWOL soldiers loose in 1918 Paris. Continuous one-liners, sight gags, and slapstick nonsense. First film appearance of comedy team Wheeler and Woolsey. **78m/B VHS, DVD.** Bert Wheeler, Robert Woolsey, Dorothy Lee, Robert Rutherford, Edna May Oliver; ***D:*** Paul Sloane; ***M:*** Max Steiner.

Half Slave, Half Free 1/2 *Solomon Northrup's Odyssey* **1985** The true story of a free black man in the 1840s who is kidnapped and forced into slavery for 12 years. Part of the "American Playhouse" series on PBS. Followed by "Charlotte Forten's Mission: Experiment in Freedom." **113m/C VHS, DVD.** Avery Brooks, Mason Adams, Petronia Paley, John Saxon, Joe Seneca, Michael (Lawrence) Tolan, Lee Bryant, Rhetta Greene, Janet League; ***D:*** Gordon Parks. **TV**

The Halfback of Notre Dame 1/2 **1996 (G)** Star football player (and coach's son) Craig Modeau (Hogan) is a lumbering misfit, ripe for high school teasing, anywhere but on the gridiron. But French exchange student Esmeralda (Vaugier) thinks he's sweet—much to the dismay of current boyfriend, obnoxious quarterback Archie (Cutler). Then Craig decides to quit the team right before the big game when dad says no fraternizing and it's up to his French flame to get the jock to change his mind. Made for TV reworking of Victor Hugo's "The Hunchback of Notre Dame." **97m/C VHS.** Gabriel Hogan, Emmanuelle Vaugier, Scott Hylands, Sandra Nelson, Allen (Culter) Cutler; ***D:*** Rene Bonniere; ***W:*** Richard Clark, Mark Trafficante; ***C:*** Maris Jansons; ***M:*** George Blondheim. **TV**

Halfmoon *Paul Bowles: Halbmond* **1995** Trilogy of stories by Paul Bowles. "Merkala Beach" looks at the friendship of two young Moroccan men who are both seduced by the same mysterious woman. "Call at Corazon" finds the honeymoon journey of a mismatched British couple turning into a nightmare as they sail up the Amazon on a crowded cargo boat. "Allal" is a Moroccan boy who's an outcast in his village because of his illegitimacy. He befriends an old snake dealer and steals one of his cobras in order to charm the reptile. Then Allal winds up in a magical transformation with the creature. English and Arabic with subtitles. **90m/C VHS, DVD.** *GE GE* Samir Guesmi, Khalid Ksouri, Sondos Belhassan, Veronica Quilligan, Sam Cox, Said Zakir, Mohammed Belfquih; ***D:*** Irene von Alberti, Frieder Schlaich; ***W:*** Irene von Alberti, Frieder Schlaich; ***C:*** Volker Tittel; ***M:*** Roman Bunka; ***Nar:*** Paul Bowles.

Hallelujah! 1/2 **1929** Haynes plays an innocent young man who turns to religion and becomes a charasmatic preacher after a family tragedy. He retains all his human weaknesses, however, including falling for the lovely but deceitful McKinney. Great music included traditional spirituals and songs by Berlin, such as "At the End of the Road" and "Swanee Shuffle." Shot on location in Tennessee. The first all-black feature film and the first talkie for director Vidor was given the go-ahead by MGM production chief Irving Thalberg, though he knew the film would be both controversial and get minimal release in the deep South. **90m/B VHS, DVD.** Daniel L. Haynes, Nina Mae McKinney, William Fontaine, Harry Gray, Fannie Belle DeKnight, Everett McGarrity; ***D:*** King Vidor; ***M:*** Irving Berlin. Natl. Film Reg. '08.

Hallelujah, I'm a Bum 1/2 *Hallelujah, I'm a Tramp; The Heart of New York; Happy Go Lucky; Lazy Bones* **1933** A happy-go-lucky hobo reforms and begins a new life for the sake of a woman. Bizarre Depression-era musical with a Rodgers and Hart score and continuously rhyming dialogue. The British version, due to the slang meaning of "bum," was retitled, substituting "tramp." ♫ You Are Too Beautiful; I'll Do It Again; I've Got To Get Back To New York; What Do You Want With Money?; Hallelujah, I'm A Bum; My Pal Bumper; Dear June; Bumper Found a Grand. **83m/B VHS, DVD.** Al Jolson, Madge Evans, Frank Morgan, Chester Conklin, Edgar Connor; ***D:*** Lewis Milestone; ***W:*** Ben Hecht, S.N. Behrman; ***M:*** Richard Rodgers, Lorenz Hart.

The Hallelujah Trail **1965** Denver mining town in the late 1800s is about to batten down the hatches for a long winter, and there's not a drop of whiskey to be had. The U.S. Cavalry sends a shipment to the miners, but temperance leader Cora Templeton Massingale (Remick) and her bevy of ladies against liquor stand between the shipment and the would-be whistle whetters. Limp Western satire directed by Preston Sturges' brother, who fared much better when he kept a straight face (he also directed "The Great Escape"). Based on Bill Gulick's novel, "The Hallelujah Train." **166m/C VHS, DVD.** Burt Lancaster, Lee Remick, Jim Hutton, Pamela Tiffin, Donald Pleasence, Brian Keith, Martin Landau; ***D:*** John Sturges; ***W:*** John Gay; ***C:*** Robert L. Surtees; ***M:*** Elmer Bernstein; ***Nar:*** John Dehner.

Hallowed **WOOF! 2005 (R)** Lame slasher flick. At 10, Gabriel witness his father murder his mother. Now, 20 years later, he believes it's his sacred duty to kill the vulnerable just like his religious daddy did. Naturally, Gabriel is a whack job. **80m/C DVD.** Corey Foxx, Richard Lava, Rosslyn Roberson, Andrew Martin; ***D:*** Rocky Costanzo; ***W:*** Rocky Costanzo; ***C:*** Joseph Brown; ***M:*** Peter Gorritz. **VIDEO**

Halloween 1/2 **1978 (R)** John Carpenter's horror classic has been acclaimed "the most successful independent motion picture of all time." A deranged youth returns to his hometown with murderous intent after 15 years in an asylum. Very, very scary—you feel this movie more than see it. **90m/C VHS, DVD, Blu-ray Disc, UMD.** Jamie Lee Curtis, Donald Pleasence, Nancy Loomis, P.J. Soles, Charles Cyphers, Kyle Richards, Brian Andrews, John Michael Graham, Nancy Stephens, Arthur Malet, Mickey Yablans, Brent Le Page, Adam Hollander, Robert Phalen, Sandy Johnson, David Kyle, Nick Castle; ***D:*** John Carpenter; ***W:*** John Carpenter, Debra Hill; ***C:*** Dean Cundey; ***M:*** John Carpenter. Natl. Film Reg. '06.

Halloween **2007 (R)** Director Rob Zombie trades suspense and chills for action and shock in this remake of the classic 1970s horror movie and loses what made the original so scary in the first place. The tale is essentially the same, but this time crazed serial killer Michael Myers (Mane) gets an extended backstory, complete with a good-hearted stripper mom (Moon-Zombie) and evil step-dad (Forsythe). Once we get to the actual story, in which Myers stalks and murders his long-lost sister's (Taylor-Compton) friends, it's been shortened so much that there's barely any time to build any tension, instead just going for your standard action-crazed stabfest. Diehard fans will deem it far better than most of the films in this series, but it doesn't hold a candle to the original. **110m/C DVD.** *US* Malcolm McDowell, Tyler Mane, Scout Taylor-Compton, Brad Dourif, Danny Trejo, William Forsythe, Danielle Harris, Hanna Hall, Sheri Moon Zombie, Dee Wallace; ***D:*** Rob Zombie; ***W:*** Rob Zombie; ***C:*** Phil Parmet; ***M:*** Tyler Bates.

Halloween 2: The Nightmare Isn't Over! 1/2 **1981 (R)** Trying to pick up where "Halloween" left off, the sequel begins with the escape of vicious killer Michael, who continues to murder and terrorize the community of Haddonfield, Illinois. Lacking the innovative intentions of its predecessor, it relies on old-fashioned buckets of blood. No chills, just trauma. Co-scripted by Carpenter, director of the original. **92m/C VHS, DVD.** Jamie Lee Curtis, Donald Pleasence, Jeffrey Kramer, Charles Cyphers, Lance Guest; ***D:*** Rick Rosenthal; ***W:*** John Carpenter, Debra Hill; ***C:*** Dean Cundey; ***M:*** John Carpenter.

Halloween 3: Season of the Witch **1982 (R)** Modern druid plans to kill 50 million children with his specially made Halloween masks. Produced by John Carpenter, this second sequel to the 1978 horror classic is not based on the events or characters of its predecessors or successors. Followed by Halloweens 4, 5, and 6. **98m/C VHS, DVD.** Tom Atkins, Stacey Nelkin, Dan O'Herlihy, Ralph Strait, Michael Currie; ***D:*** Tommy Lee Wallace; ***W:*** Tommy Lee Wallace; ***C:*** Dean Cundey; ***M:*** John Carpenter.

Halloween 4: The Return of Michael Myers **1988 (R)** The third sequel, wherein the lunatic that won't die returns home to kill his niece. **89m/C VHS, DVD.** Donald Pleasence, Ellie Cornell, Danielle Harris, Michael Pataki, George P. Wilbur, Beau Starr, Kathleen Kinmont, Sasha Jenson, Gene Ross; ***D:*** Dwight Little; ***W:*** Alan B. McElroy; ***C:*** Peter Lyons Collister; ***M:*** Alan Howarth, John Carpenter.

Halloween 5: The Revenge of Michael Myers 1/2 **1989 (R)** Fifth in the series, this Halloween is an improvement over 2, 3, and 4, thanks to a few well directed scare scenes. Unfortunately, the plot remains the same: a psycho behemoth chases down and kills more teens. An open ending promises yet another installment. **96m/C VHS, DVD.** Donald Pleasence, Ellie Cornell, Danielle Harris, Don Shanks, Betty Carvalho, Beau Starr, Wendy Kaplan, Jeffrey Landman; ***D:*** Dominique Othenin-Girard; ***W:*** Dominique Othenin-Girard, Shem Bitterman, Michael Jacobs; ***C:*** Rob Draper; ***M:*** John Carpenter, Alan Howarth.

Halloween 6: The Curse of Michael Myers *Halloween: The Origin of Michael Myers* **1995 (R)** First the return. Then his revenge. And now, his curse, aimed square at the viewer. Lame series entry connects Michael Meyers to an ancient Celtic ritual that drives him to murder whole families in his old stompin' grounds of Haddonfield. Before he finishes his reign of terror, Meyers has to contend with Dr. Loomis (Pleasence), the man who knows his true evil. Though still a profit-making monster (the entire franchise had a combined budget of $20 million and grossed over $200 million), Michael should probably join Freddy and Jason at the old slashers' retirement home. Film marks the final screen appearance of Pleasence, who died shortly after its completion. **88m/C VHS, DVD.** Donald Pleasence, Mitchell Ryan, Marianne Hagan, Leo Geter, George P. Wilbur, Kim Darby, Bradford English, Devin Gardner, Paul Rudd; ***D:*** Joe Chappelle; ***W:*** Daniel Farrands; ***C:*** Billy Dickson; ***M:*** Alan Howarth.

Halloween: H20 *Halloween: H20 (Twenty Years Later); Halloween 7* **1998 (R)** Jamie Lee Curtis treads familiar water in this return to the wellspring of the slasher genre. She reprises her role as Laurie Strode, sister of relentless psycho-killer Michael Myers. After faking her own death and changing her name, she becomes the headmistress of a private school in California. Now an overprotective single mom, she battles with the spirit of her brother, as well as the spirit of vodka. Her rebellious son John (Harnett) blows off a field trip for a romantic weekend with girlfriend Molly (Williams). They are accompanied by fellow lust-ridden Michael fodder Charlie (Hann-Byrd) and Sarah (O'Keefe) on the dimly lit campus. Either Laurie extracts her final revenge or you can anticipate "Halloween 8: The Social Security Checks of Michael Myers." Also features Curtis' mother Janet Leigh in a family reunion of screaming divas. **86m/C VHS, DVD.** Jamie Lee Curtis, Adam Arkin, Josh Hartnett, Michelle Williams, Adam Hann-Byrd, Jodi Lyn O'Keefe, Janet Leigh, LL Cool J, Joseph Gordon-Levitt, Nancy Stephens, Branden Williams, Chris Durand; ***D:*** Steve Miner; ***W:*** Matt Greenberg, Robert Zappia; ***C:*** Daryn Okada; ***M:*** John Ottman, John Carpenter.

Halloween II 1/2 *H2 : Halloween 2* **2009 (R)** Zombie's sequel to his "Halloween" re-do, which is a kinda remake of John Carpenter's 1981 sequel, follows the aftermath of Michael Myers's rampage through the eyes of survivor Laurie Strode. It's so gross and filled with caricatures that maybe the franchise can finally be laid to rest. Michael (Mane) returns to Haddonfield to continue his slaughter and a nightmare-plagued Laurie (Taylor-Compton) realizes she's Myers's baby sis, thanks to a bestselling book by publicity hound shrink Dr. Loomis (McDowell). Naturally this does nothing for her grip on her sanity. **101m/C DVD.** *US* Scout Taylor-Compton, Tyler Mane, Malcolm McDowell, Sheri Moon Zombie, Brad Dourif, Danielle Harris, Howard Hesseman, Margot Kidder, Brea Grant, Mary Birdsong; ***D:*** Rob Zombie; ***W:*** Rob Zombie; ***C:*** Brandon Trost; ***M:*** Tyler Bates.

Halloween Night **1990 (R)** Ancient evil rises up to destroy the perfect small town. **90m/C VHS.** Hy Pyke, Katrina Garner; ***D:*** Emilio P. Miraglio.

Halloween: Resurrection 1/2 **2002 (R)** The producers would like you to ignore the fact that psycho Michael Myers has been killed about 957 times in this franchise, and that the entire genre has been parodied into the ground. You should ignore this movie instead. Internet entrepreneur Rhymes arranges for a group of stupid kids to stay in Michael Myers' house as a publicity stunt for a live webcast. Naturally, Mike doesn't like the interlopers and proceeds to permanently cut their internet connections. Nothing new is added to the series, and drug-use and sexual hi-jinks are still the best way for the young uns to get an interesting new piercing. Jamie Lee Curtis and Rosenthal, who directed "Halloween 2," also return. **86m/C VHS, DVD.** *US* Busta Rhymes, Sean Patrick Thomas, Jamie Lee Curtis, Bianca Kajlich, Tyra Banks, Thomas Ian Nicholas, Ryan Merriman, Luke Kirby, Brad Loree, Daisy McCrackin, Katee Sackhoff; ***Cameos:*** Rick Rosenthal; ***D:*** Rick Rosenthal; ***W:*** Larry Brand, Sean Hood; ***C:*** David Geddes; ***M:*** Danny Lux.

Halloween with the Addams Family **WOOF! 1979** A really pathetic production spawned during the "reunion" craze of the late '70s, sparked only by the lively performance of Coogan's Uncle Fester and the always lovable Lurch. **87m/C VHS.** John Astin, Carolyn Jones, Jackie Coogan, Ted Cassidy; ***D:*** George Tibbles, David Steinmetz; ***C:*** Jacques "Jack" Marquette; ***M:*** Vic Mizzy. **TV**

Halloweentown 1/2 **1998** Gwen Piper has relinquished her witchy powers to live life as a mortal. Her children don't know about her colorful past until Grandma Aggie comes to visit, wanting to start 13-year-old Marnie on her training despite her mother Gwen's objections. When Aggie returns to Halloweentown, a haven for creatures who go bump in the night, Marnie and her siblings follow and learn an evil force is threatening the peaceful residents. **84m/C DVD.** Debbie Reynolds, Kimberly J. Brown, Judith Hoag, Joey Zimmerman, Robin Thomas, Phillip Van Dyke, Emily Roeske; ***D:*** Duwayne Dunham; ***W:*** Jon Cooksey, Ali Matheson; ***C:*** Michael Slovis; ***M:*** Mark Mothersbaugh. **CABLE**

Halloweentown 2: Kalabar's Revenge 1/2 **2001** Marnie has been training to be a witch and Grandma Aggie has come to live with the family to help out. Marnie is smitten by new boy in town Kal, but when he visits he steals Aggie's spell book. Aggie and Marnie return to Halloweentown and discover it's losing its magic while monsters are popping up in the mortal world. **81m/C DVD.** Kimberly J. Brown, Debbie Reynolds, Daniel Kountz, Judith Hoag, Joey Zimmerman, Emily Roeske, Phillip Van Dyke, Robin Thomas, Blu Mankuma; ***D:*** Mary Lambert; ***W:*** Jon Cooksey, Ali Matheson; ***C:*** Tony Westman; ***M:*** Mark Mothersbaugh. **CABLE**

Halloweentown High *Halloweentown 3* **2004** Marnie asks the Halloweentown Council if some students can become part of the exchange program at her high school. Meanwhile, grandma Aggie is their eccentric new science teacher. They all participate in running the school's holiday haunted house but the magic students are threatened by a group of ancient foes for having ventured into the mortal world. **82m/C DVD.** Kimberly J. Brown, Debbie Reynolds, Judith Hoag, Joey Zimmerman, Clifton Davis, Lucas Grabeel, Olesya Rulin, Finn Wittrock, Eliana Reyes, Todd Michael Schwartzman; ***D:*** Mark Dippe; ***W:*** Daniel Berendsen; ***C:*** Robert E. Seaman; ***M:*** Kenneth Burgomaster. **CABLE**

The Halls of Montezuma 1/2 **1950** Large, bombastic WWII combat epic. Depicts the Marines fighting the Japanese in the Pacific. **113m/C VHS, DVD.** Richard Widmark, Jack Palance, Reginald Gardiner, Robert Wagner, Karl Malden, Richard Boone, Richard Hylton, Skip Homeier, Jack Webb, Neville Brand, Martin Milner, Bert Freed; ***D:*** Lewis Milestone; ***W:*** Michael Blankfort; ***C:*** Winton C. Hoch, Harry Jackson; ***M:*** Sol Kaplan.

Hallucination **WOOF!** *Hallucination Generation* **1967** Early flower-power exploiter about expatriate acid heads who murder an antique dealer under the influence of LSD and then attempt to hide at a monastery. Depicts LSD as the catalyst in bringing out the group's criminal behavior. In sepia while everyone's cool, breaking into color during the head trips. **90m/C VHS.** George Montgomery, Danny Stone; ***D:*** Edward Andrew (Santos Alcocer) Mann; ***W:*** Edward Andrew (Santos Alcocer) Mann.

Hallucinations of a Deranged Mind *Delirios de Um Anormal* **1978** A compilation of all the magic moments ever censored by the Brazilian military dictatorship. Includes scenes banned from over 10 different Mojica Marins films, including his "Coffin Joe" character. In Portugese with English subtitles. **86m/C VHS.** *BR* Jose Mojica Marins; ***D:*** Jose Mojica Marins; ***W:*** Jose Mojica Marins.

Hambone & Hillie **1984 (PG)** An elderly woman makes a 3000-mile trek across the United States to search for the dog she lost in an airport. **97m/C VHS.** Lillian Gish, Timothy Bottoms, Candy Clark, O.J. Simpson, Robert Walker Jr., Jack Carter, Alan Hale Jr., Anne Lockhart; *D:* Roy Watts; *W:* Sandra K. Bailey.

The Hamburg Cell 🦴🦴 ½ **2004** Based on the events leading up to 9/11 from the hijackers' perspective. Ziad Jarrah (who will take over United Flight 93) is studying in Hamburg and begins going to the local mosque to learn how to become a better Muslim. A desire to belong somewhere soon leads to Jarrah being recruited by Al Qaeda. Alongside jihadists Mohammad Atta and Ramzi bin al Shibh, Jarrah's plans being to take shape; the story ends with the hijackers boarding their various flights. **101m/C DVD.** *GB* Karem Saleh, Kamel, Agni Tsangaridou, Kammy Darweish, Omar Berdouni, Adnan Maral; *D:* Antonia Bird; *W:* Ronan Bennett, Alice Berman; *C:* Florian Hoffmeister; *M:* Adrian Corker, Paul Conboy. **TV**

Hamburger Hill 🦴🦴 ½ **1987 (R)** Popular war epic depicting the famous battle between Americans and Viet Cong over a useless hill in Vietnam. Made in the heyday of 1980s Vietnam backlash, and possibly the most realistic and bloodiest of the lot. **104m/C VHS, DVD.** Michael Dolan, Daniel O'Shea, Dylan McDermott, Tommy Swerdlow, Courtney B. Vance, Anthony Barille, Michael Boatman, Don Cheadle, Tim Quill, Don James, Michael A. (M.A.) Nickles, Harry O'Reilly, Steven Weber, Tegan West, Kieu Chinh, Doug Goodman, J.C. Palmore; *D:* John Irvin; *W:* James (Jim) Carabatsos; *C:* Peter Macdonald; *M:* Philip Glass.

Hamburger... The Motion Picture 🦴 **1986 (R)** The life and times of students at Busterburger U., the only college devoted to hamburger franchise management. **90m/C VHS.** Leigh McCloskey, Dick Butkus, Randi Brooks, Sandy Hackett; *D:* Mike Marvin; *M:* Elmer Bernstein.

Hamlet 🦴🦴🦴🦴 **1948** Splendid adaptation of Shakespeare's dramatic play. Hamlet vows vengeance on the murderer of his father in this tight version of the four hour stage play. Some scenes were cut out, including all of Rosencrantz and Guildenstern. Beautifully photographed in Denmark. An Olivier triumph. Remade several times. **153m/B VHS, DVD.** *GB* Laurence Olivier, Basil Sydney, Felix Aylmer, Jean Simmons, Stanley Holloway, Peter Cushing, Christopher Lee, Eileen Herlie, John Laurie, Esmond Knight, Anthony Quayle; *D:* Laurence Olivier; *W:* Alan Dent; *C:* Desmond Dickinson; *M:* William Walton; *V:* John Gielgud. Oscars '48: Actor (Olivier), Art Dir./Set Dec., B&W, Costume Des. (B&W), Picture; British Acad. '48: Film; Golden Globes '49: Actor—Drama (Olivier); N.Y. Film Critics '48: Actor (Olivier).

Hamlet 🦴🦴 ½ **1969 (G)** Williamson brings to the screen his stage performance as the classic Shakespeare character. Something is lost in the process, although there are some redeeming moments including those with Faithfull as Ophelia. **114m/C VHS.** *GB* Nicol Williamson, Anthony Hopkins, Marianne Faithfull, Gordon Jackson, Judy Parfitt, Mark Dingham, Anjelica Huston; *D:* Tony Richardson.

Hamlet 🦴🦴🦴 ½ **1990 (PG)** Zeffirelli—in his fourth attempt at Shakespeare—creates a surprisingly energetic and accessible interpretation of the Bard's moody play. Gibson brings charm, humor and a carefully calculated sense of violence, not to mention a good deal of solid flesh, to the eponymous role, and handles the language skillfully (although if you seek a poetic Dane, stick with Olivier). Exceptional work from Scofield and Bates; Close seems a tad hysterical (not to mention too young to play Gibson's mother), but brings insight and nuance to her role. Purists beware: this isn't a completely faithful adaptation. Beautifully costumed; shot on location in Northern Scotland. **135m/C VHS, DVD.** Mel Gibson, Glenn Close, Alan Bates, Paul Scofield, Ian Holm, Helena Bonham Carter, Nathaniel Parker, Pete Postlethwaite; *D:* Franco Zeffirelli; *W:* Franco Zeffirelli, Christopher DeVore; *C:* David Watkin.

Hamlet 🦴🦴🦴🦴 **1996 (PG-13)** Branagh tackles Shakespeare once again with the uncut, four-hour long story of the melancholy Dane (played by you-know-who). Branagh's decision to use the complete text, and move the action ahead 600 years to the 19th century adds an interesting external political dimension to the palace intrigue and gives this sixth screen adaptation the stature of Olivier's 1948 masterpiece. Jacobi and Christie stand out among a very large and brilliant cast. Lemmon and Crystal, however, should stick to American comedy. A two and a half hour version was also prepared for those with shorter attention spans, but the uncut version is well worth the time invested. **242m/C VHS.** *GB* Kenneth Branagh, Kate Winslet, Julie Christie, Derek Jacobi, Richard Briers, Brian Blessed, Michael Maloney, Timothy Spall, Reece Dinsdale, Jack Lemmon, Nicholas Farrell, Charlton Heston, Rosemary Harris, Gerard Depardieu, Robin Williams, Billy Crystal, Simon Russell Beale, Michael Bryant, John Gielgud, Richard Attenborough, Rufus Sewell, Judi Dench, Ian McElhinney, John Mills; *D:* Kenneth Branagh; *W:* Kenneth Branagh; *C:* Alex Thomson; *M:* Patrick Doyle.

Hamlet 🦴🦴🦴 **2000 (R)** It's mopey Hawke's turn as the title character but in this update he's hardly a Danish prince. Instead he's an experimental filmmaker in New York whose murderous uncle Claudius (MacLachlan) runs the family conglomerate, Denmark, Inc. Thanks to Almereyda's respect for Shakespeare's language, as well as his excellent adaptation to present-day corporate America, this interpretation loses none of the play's power, and adds some insights that prove its timelessness. **111m/C VHS, DVD.** Ethan Hawke, Kyle MacLachlan, Sam Shepard, Diane Venora, Bill Murray, Julia Stiles, Liev Schreiber, Karl Geary, Paula Malcomson, Steve Zahn, Dechen Thurman, Jeffrey Wright, Paul Bartel, Rome Neal, Casey Affleck; *D:* Michael Almereyda; *W:* Michael Almereyda; *C:* John de Borman; *M:* Carter Burwell.

Hamlet 🦴🦴 ½ **2001** Every actor wants to play Shakespeare's melancholy Dane and in this cable adaptation, it's Scott (co-directing as well) who takes on the title role. This version is set at the turn of the 20th century. Good cast and some clever supernatural visuals for enchancement. **179m/C VHS, DVD.** Campbell Scott, Jamey Sheridan, Blair Brown, Roscoe Lee Browne, Lisa Gay Hamilton, John Benjamin Hickey, Roger Guenveur Smith, Sam Robards, Michael Imperioli, Byron Jennings; *D:* Campbell Scott, Eric Simonson; *C:* Dan Gillham. **CABLE**

Hamlet 2 🦴🦴🦴 **2008 (R)** Irreverent satire of Inspiration-teacher flicks, Middle American values, and religious views with nutty high school drama teacher Dana Marschz (Coogan), conceiving a sequel to Hamlet for his students to produce. Dana is never deterred, even at the fact that the major characters all died at the end of Shakespeare's play, even tossing in Jesus, Einstein, and Hillary Clinton for good measure. Wackiness aside, it hits on all the elements critical to amateur theatre: teacher's pets getting the leads, lousy costumes, and a dissapproving school board. Along with Coogan's neurotic brilliance, a talented supporting cast, including Elizabeth Shue as herself, makes director-writer Andrew Fleming's hilarious script come to ridiculously fun life. **92m/C DVD.** *US* Steve Coogan, Catherine Keener, Marshall Bell, Amy Poehler, Skylar Astin, Phoebe Strole, Joseph Julian Soria, David Arquette, Elisabeth Shue, Melonie Diaz, Marco Rodriguez; *D:* Andrew Fleming; *W:* Andrew Fleming, Pam Brady; *C:* Alexander Grusynski; *M:* Ralph Sall.

The Hammer 🦴🦴 ½ **2007 (R)** After getting dumped by his girlfriend on his 40th birthday, carpenter/boxing instructor Jerry Ferro (Carolla), aka "The Hammer" quits his lousy day job for a return to the ring with Olympic hopes. He soon sparks up a romance with one of his students (Juergensen) and catches the eye of big-time boxing coach Eddie Bell (Quinn), who takes him under his wing. Not so much a spoof of triumphant sports movies, but a realistic underdog comedy that works as a goofy "Rocky" tribute. Nearly semi-autobiographical, written by Carolla, an actual former Golden Glover (and carpenter), who plays his usual self-deprecating, snarky self with surprising success. **93m/C DVD.** *US* Adam Carolla, Heather Juergensen, Jonathan Hernandez, Oswaldo Castillo, Tom Quinn, Raimu; *D:* Charles Herman-Wurmfeld; *W:* Kevin Hench; *C:* Marco Fagnoli; *M:* John Swihart, Matt Mariano.

Hammers over the Anvil 🦴🦴 ½ **1991** Young Alan Marshall (Outhred) has a case of hero worship for local horse trainer East Driscoll (Crowe). But East has also caught the eye of the upper-class (and married) English beauty, Grace McAlister (Rampling), with whom he is having an affair, and which Alan witnesses. But East wants Grace more than just part-time and is determined to force her to run away with him—with disastrous consequences. **98m/C VHS, DVD.** *AU* Charlotte Rampling, Russell Crowe, Alexander Outhred, John Rafter Lee, Kirsty McGregor, Jake Frost; *D:* Ann Turner; *W:* Ann Turner, Peter Hepworth; *C:* James Bartle.

Hammersmith Is Out 🦴 ½ **1972 (R)** A violent lunatic cons an orderly into letting him escape. Chases, romance and craziness follow. **108m/C VHS.** Richard Burton, Elizabeth Taylor, Peter Ustinov, Beau Bridges, John Schuck; *D:* Peter Ustinov.

Hammett 🦴🦴 **1982 (PG)** After many directors and script rewrites, Wenders was assigned to this arch neo-noir what-if scenario. Depicts Dashiell Hammett solving a complex crime himself, an experience he uses in his novels. Interesting, but ultimately botched studio exercise, like many from executive producer Francis Coppola, who is said to have reshot much of the film. **98m/C VHS, DVD.** Frederic Forrest, Peter Boyle, Sylvia Sidney, Elisha Cook Jr., Marilu Henner; *D:* Wim Wenders; *C:* Joseph Biroc; *M:* John Barry.

Hamsin 🦴🦴🦴 **1983** A Jewish landowner and an Arab worker encounter difficulties in their relationship when the government announces plans to confiscate Arab land. In Hebrew with English subtitles. **90m/C VHS.** Shlomo Tarshish, Yasin Shawap, Hemda Levy, Ruth Geler; *D:* Daniel Wachsmann.

Hamsun 🦴🦴 **1996** Highly regarded Norwegian Nobel Prize-winning writer Knut Hamsun (von Sydow) stunned his countrymen when he sided with the Nazis in WWII and urged them to stop resisting the invaders of their homeland. An ardent nationalist, the elderly Hamsun apparently heard only what he wanted to about Hitler's policies and regarded Britain as the greater threat to Europe. After the war Hamsun and his equally outspoken pro-German wife, Marie (Norby), are deemed traitors and are put on trial. Based on a book by Thorkild Hansen. Swedish, Danish, and Norwegian with subtitles. **154m/C VHS, DVD.** *NO DK SW* Max von Sydow, Ghita Norby, Sverre Anker Ousdal, Ernst Jacobi, Anette Hoff, Erik Hivju; *D:* Jan Troell; *W:* Per Olof Enquist; *C:* Jan Troell; *M:* Arvo Part.

Hana & Alice 🦴🦴🦴 *Hana to Arisu* **2004** Hana (Anne Suzuki) and Arisu (Yu Aoi) are best friends. When Arisu gets a boyfriend, she hooks Hana up with one of his friends so she won't feel like a third wheel. But then she breaks up with her boyfriend because she's fallen for Hana's beau. When he gets amnesia from walking into a wall, she convinces him she is his girlfriend. Originated from a series of candy commercials. **135m/C DVD.** *JP* Anne Suzuki, Yu Aoi, Tomohiro Kaku; *D:* Shunji Iwai; *W:* Shunji Iwai; *C:* Noboru Shinoda; *M:* Shunji Iwai.

Hancock 🦴🦴 **2008 (PG-13)** John Hancock (Smith) is a crusty drunk who has superhero powers, although he doesn't know why or how. He might save the day, but he creates havoc and financial ruin in the process. After Hancock saves his life, PR guy Ray Embrey (Bateman) steps in to spiff up Hancock's image. Hancock has a history with Ray's wife Mary (Theron), only he doesn't remember and she's not talking (yet). But Mary's secret comes out, and Hancock is thrown for a loop. Some fun amid a flimsy plot, which won't matter for Smith fans anyway. **92m/C DVD.** *US* Will Smith, Jason Bateman, Charlize Theron, Eddie Marsan, Johnny Galecki, Thomas Lennon, Jae Head; *D:* Peter Berg; *W:* Vince Gilligan, Vy Vincent Ngo; *C:* Tobias Schliessler; *M:* John Powell.

The Hand 🦴 ½ **1960** During WWII, three British POWs are tortured by the Japanese. Refusing to give information, two of them have their right hands cut off. The third opts to talk, thereby keeping his hand. After the war, a series of murders occur in London where the victims have their hands amputated. Could there be a connection? **61m/B VHS, DVD.** *GB* Derek Bond, Ronald Lee Hunt, Reed de Rouen, Ray Cooney, Brian Coleman; *D:* Henry Cass.

The Hand 🦴🦴🦴 **1981 (R)** A gifted cartoonist's hand is severed in a car accident. Soon, the hand is on the loose with a mind of its own, seeking out victims with an obsessive vengeance. Stone's sophomore directorial outing is a unique, surreal psycho-horror pastiche consistently underrated by most critics. **105m/C VHS.** *GB* Michael Caine, Andrea Marcovicci, Annie McEnroe, Bruce McGill, Viveca Lindfors; *Cameos:* Oliver Stone; *D:* Oliver Stone; *W:* Oliver Stone; *C:* King Baggot; *M:* James Horner.

Hand Gun 🦴🦴 ½ **1993 (R)** Jack McCallister (Cassel) is wounded in a shoot-out with police but still manages to get away with half-a-million from a robbery. When word gets out, everybody begins looking for Jack, including his two sons—gun happy George (Williams) and small time con artist Michael (Schulze). **90m/C VHS, DVD.** Seymour Cassel, Treat Williams, Paul Schulze, Michael Rapaport; *D:* Whitney Ransick; *W:* Whitney Ransick; *C:* Michael Spiller; *M:* Douglas J. Cuomo.

The Hand that Rocks the Cradle 🦴🦴 ½ **1992 (R)** DeMornay is Peyton Flanders, the nanny from hell, in an otherwise predictable thriller. Sciorra's role is a thankless one as pregnant and unbelievably naive Claire Bartel, who unwittingly starts a horrific chain of events when she levels charges of molestation against her obstetrician. Transparent plot preys on the worst fears of viewers, and doesn't offer anything innovative or new. See this one for DeMornay's Jekyll and Hyde performance. **110m/C VHS, DVD.** Annabella Sciorra, Rebecca De Mornay, Matt McCoy, Ernie Hudson, Julianne Moore, Madeline Zima, John de Lancie, Mitchell Laurance; *D:* Curtis Hanson; *W:* Amanda Silver; *C:* Robert Elswit; *M:* Graeme Revell. MTV Movie Awards '92: Villain (De Mornay).

A Handful of Dust 🦴🦴 **1988 (PG)** A dry, stately adaptation of the bitter Evelyn Waugh novel about a stuffy young aristocrat's wife's careless infidelity and how it sends her innocent husband to a tragic downfall. A well-meaning version that captures Waugh's cynical satire almost in spite of itself. Set in post-WWI England. **114m/C VHS, DVD.** *GB* James Wilby, Kristin Scott Thomas, Rupert Graves, Alec Guinness, Anjelica Huston, Judi Dench, Cathryn Harrison, Pip Torrens, John Junkin; *D:* Charles Sturridge; *W:* Charles Sturridge, Tim Sullivan, Derek Granger; *C:* Peter Hannan; *M:* George Fenton. British Acad. '88: Support. Actress (Dench).

The Handmaid's Tale 🦴🦴 ½ **1990 (R)** A cool, shallow but nonetheless chilling nightmare based on Margaret Atwood's bestselling novel, about a woman caught in the machinations of a near-future society so sterile it enslaves the few fertile women and forces them into being child-bearing "handmaids." **109m/C VHS, DVD.** Natasha Richardson, Robert Duvall, Faye Dunaway, Aidan Quinn, Elizabeth McGovern, Victoria Tennant, Blanche Baker, Traci Lind; *D:* Volker Schlondorff; *W:* Harold Pinter; *C:* Igor Luther; *M:* Ryuichi Sakamoto.

Hands Across the Border 🦴 ½ **1943** A musical western in which Roy helps a woman find the men who killed her father. **72m/B VHS, DVD.** Roy Rogers, Ruth Terry, Guinn "Big Boy" Williams, Onslow Stevens, Mary Treen, Joseph Crehan; *D:* Joseph Kane.

Hands Across the Table 🦴🦴🦴 **1935** Regi Allen (Lombard) is a fortune-hunting manicurist in a swanky hotel barber shop. Has-been millionaire playboy Theodore Drew III (MacMurray) falls for her but he's about to marry money (Allwyn) and Regi's got a wheelchair-bound rich man (Bellamy) just waiting for her to say "I do." Snappy dialogue and light-hearted performances. Based on the story "Bracelets" by Vina Delmar. **80m/B VHS, DVD.** Carole Lombard, Fred MacMurray, Ralph Bellamy, Astrid Allwyn, Ruth Donnelly, Marie Prevost, William Demarest, Edward (Ed) Gargan; *D:* Mitchell Leisen; *W:* Norman Krasna, Vincent Lawrence, Herbert Fields; *C:* Ted Tetzlaff.

Hands of a Murderer 🦴🦴 ½ *Sherlock Holmes and the Prince of Crime* **1990** Sherlock Holmes (Woodward) and the faithful Dr. Watson (Hillerman) are in pursuit of the great detective's most evil nemisis—the nefarious Moriarty (Andrews). This time, the fiend has escaped the gallows and stolen government secrets from the safe of Holmes' brother Mycroft. TV movie. **100m/C VHS, DVD.** Edward Woodward, John Hillerman, Anthony Andrews, Kim Thomson, Peter Jeffrey, Warren Clarke; ***D:*** Stuart Orme; ***W:*** Charles Edward Pogue.

Hands of a Stranger **1962** Another undistinguished entry in the long line of remakes of "The Hands of Orlac." A pianist who loses his hands in an accident is given the hands of a murderer, and his new hands want to do more than tickle the ivories. Kellerman has a very small role as does former "Sheena" McCalla. **95m/B VHS, DVD.** Paul Lukather, Joan Harvey, James Stapleton, Sally Kellerman, Irish McCalla; ***D:*** Newton Arnold; ***C:*** Henry Cronjager Jr.

Hands of a Stranger 1/2 **1987** Policeman's wife is raped during an adulterous tryst. As the painful truth dawns on the cop, he himself dallies with a compassionate lady D.A. while hunting the attacker. About as sordid as a network TV-movie gets without toppling into sleaze; strong acting and a sober script pull it through. But the plot, from Robert Daly's novel, doesn't justify miniseries treatment; the two-cassette package is excessively long. **179m/C VHS.** Armand Assante, Beverly D'Angelo, Blair Brown, Michael Lerner, Philip Casnoff, Arliss Howard; ***D:*** Larry Elikann; ***W:*** Arthur Kopit. **TV**

The Hands of Orlac *Orlacs Hande* **1925** Classic silent film about a pianist whose hands are mutilated in an accident. His hands are replaced by those of a murderer, and his urge to kill becomes overwhelming. Contains restored footage. **92m/B VHS.** *AT* Conrad Veidt, Fritz Kortner, Carmen Cartellieri, Paul Askonas, Alexandra Sorina, Fritz Strassny; ***D:*** Robert Wiene; ***W:*** Ludwig Nerz; ***C:*** Gunther Krampf, Hans Androschin.

The Hands of Orlac *Hands of the Strangler; Hands of a Strangler* **1960** Third remake of Maurice Renard's classic tale. When a concert pianist's hands are mutilated in an accident, he receives a graft of a murderer's hands. Obsession sweeps the musician, as he believes his new hands are incapable of music, only violence. Bland adaptation of the original story. **95m/B VHS, DVD.** *GB FR* Mel Ferrer, Christopher Lee, Felix Aylmer, Basil Sydney, Donald Wolfit, Donald Pleasence, Dany Carrel, Lucile Saint-Simon, Peter Reynolds, Campbell Singer, David Peel; ***D:*** Edmond T. Greville; ***W:*** Edmond T. Greville, John Baines, Donald Taylor; ***C:*** Desmond Dickinson; ***M:*** Claude Bolling.

Hands of Steel WOOF! **1986 (R)** A ruthless cyborg carries out a mission to find and kill an important scientist. Terrible acting, and lousy writing: an all-around woofer! **94m/C VHS, DVD.** Daniel Greene, John Saxon, Janet Agren, Claudio Cassinelli, George Eastman; ***D:*** Sergio Martino.

Hands of the Ripper 1/2 **1971 (R)** Jack the Ripper's daughter returns to London where she works as a medium by day and stalks the streets at night. Classy Hammer horror variation on the perennial theme. **85m/C VHS.** *GB* Eric Porter, Angharad Rees, Jane Merrow, Keith Bell, Derek Godfrey, Dora Bryan, Marjorie Rhodes, Norman Bird; ***D:*** Peter Sasdy; ***W:*** L.W. Davidson; ***C:*** Ken Talbot; ***M:*** Christopher Gunning.

Hands Up 1/2 **1926** Jaunty Confederate spy (played by much-overlooked American comedian Griffith) attempts, amidst much comic nonsense, to thwart Yankee gold mining during the Civil War. Silent. **50m/B VHS.** Raymond Griffith, Mack Swain, Marion (Marian) Nixon, Montagu Love; ***D:*** Clarence Badger. Natl. Film Reg. '05.

Hands Up *Rece do Gory* **1981** Famed Polish film finished in 1967 but not released until 1981 for political reasons (prologue shot in '81 included). Doctors at a medical school reunion reflect upon the effect of Stalinist rule on their education and lives. In Polish with English subtitles. **78m/C VHS.** *PL* Tadeusz Lomnicki, Bogumil Kobiela, Alan Bates, Joanna Szczerbic, Jerzy Skolimowski; ***D:*** Jerzy Skolimowski; ***W:*** Jerzy Skolimowski; ***C:*** Witold Sobocinski, Andrzej Kostenko; ***M:*** Jozef Skrzek.

Hang 'Em High 1/2 **1967 (PG-13)** A cowboy is saved from a lynching and vows to hunt down the gang that nearly killed him in this American-made spaghetti western. Eastwood's first major vehicle made outside of Europe. **114m/C VHS, DVD.** *IT* Clint Eastwood, Inger Stevens, Ed Begley Sr., Pat Hingle, James MacArthur; ***D:*** Ted Post; ***W:*** Leonard Freeman, Mel Goldberg; ***C:*** Richard H. Kline, Leonard J. South; ***M:*** Dominic Frontiere.

Hangar 18 1/2 *Invasion Force* **1980 (PG)** Silly sci-fi drama about two astronauts who collide with a UFO during a shuttle flight. Later they learn that the government is hiding it in a hangar and they try to prove its existence. Shown on TV as "Invasion Force" with an entirely new ending. **97m/C VHS, DVD.** Darren McGavin, Robert Vaughn, Gary Collins, James Hampton, Philip Abbott, Pamela Bellwood, Tom Hallick, Cliff Osmond, Joseph Campanella; ***D:*** James L. Conway; ***W:*** David O'Malley.

The Hanged Man 1/2 **1974** Gunman James Devlin (Forrest) is wrongly convicted of murder but survives the hanging a changed (and free) man. He decides to help those in trouble, beginning with young widow Carrie (Acker), whose property is coveted by a mining tycoon (Mitchell). Made as a TV pilot. **73m/C DVD.** Steve Forrest, Sharon Acker, Cameron Mitchell, Rafael Campos, William (Bill) Bryant, Dean Jagger, Barbara Luna, John Mitchum, Will Geer; ***D:*** Michael Caffey; ***W:*** Ken Trevey; ***C:*** Keith C. Smith; ***M:*** Richard Markowitz. **TV**

Hangfire **1991 (R)** When a New Mexican prison is evacuated thanks to a nasty chemical explosion, several prisoners decide it's time for a furlough, and they elect the local sheriff's wife as a traveling companion. Another mediocre actioner from director Maris, it gets an extra bone for stunts kids shouldn't try at home. **91m/C VHS.** Brad Davis, Yaphet Kotto, Lee DeBroux, Jan-Michael Vincent, George Kennedy, Kim Delaney, James Tolkan, Lou Ferrigno, Lyle Alzado, Collin Bernsen; ***D:*** Peter Maris; ***W:*** Brian D. Jeffries; ***C:*** Mark Morris.

Hangin' with the Homeboys **1991 (R)** One night in the lives of four young men. Although the Bronx doesn't offer much for any of them, they have little interest in escaping its confines, and they are more than willing to complain. Characters are insightfully written and well portrayed, with strongest work from Serrano as a Puerto Rican who is trying to pass himself off as Italian. Lack of plot may frustrate some viewers. **89m/C VHS, DVD.** Mario Joyner, Doug E. Doug, John Leguizamo, Nestor Serrano, Kimberly Russell, Mary B. Ward, Christine Claravall, Rosemark Jackson, Reggie Montgomery; ***D:*** Joseph B. Vasquez; ***W:*** Joseph B. Vasquez; ***C:*** Anghel Decca. Sundance '91: Screenplay.

The Hanging Garden **1997 (R)** Bizarre family drama mixes the matter-of-fact and the surreal. Gay 25-year-old Sweet William (Leavins) returns to his rural Nova Scotia home and family after a 10-year absence for the marriage of his sister, Rosemary (Fox). The reunion brings up lots of painful memories and flashes back to the 15-year-old Sweet William (Veinotte), when he was emotionally and physically abused by his psycho father Whiskey Mac (MacNeill). After more crises, the teen hangs himself from a backyard tree. Oh yes, everyone in the present can still see the teen's ghost hanging there, including the adult William. You figure it out. **91m/C VHS, DVD.** *CA* Chris Leavins, Peter MacNeill, Kerry Fox, Seana McKenna, Troy Veinotte, Sarah Polley, Christine Dunsworth, Joel S. Keller, Joan Orenstein; ***D:*** Thom Fitzgerald; ***W:*** Thom Fitzgerald; ***C:*** Daniel Jobin. Genie '97: Screenplay, Support. Actor (MacNeill), Support. Actress (McKenna); Toronto-City '97: Canadian Feature Film.

Hanging on a Star **1978 (PG)** A small rock band encounters many comic adventures as it climbs its way up the charts. Raffin stars as the band's persistent and competent road agent. **92m/C VHS.** Deborah Raffin, Lane Caudell, Wolfman Jack, Jason Parker, Danil Torppe; ***D:*** Mike MacFarland.

The Hanging Tree **1959** Cooper plays a frontier doctor who rescues a thief (Piazza) from a lynch mob and nurses a temporarily blind girl (Schell). Malden is the bad guy who tries to attack Schell and Cooper shoots him. The townspeople take Cooper out to "The Hanging Tree" but this time it's Schell and Piazza who come to his rescue. Slow-paced western with good performances. Scott's screen debut. **108m/B VHS.** Gary Cooper, Maria Schell, Ben Piazza, Karl Malden, George C. Scott, Karl Swenson, Virginia Gregg, King Donovan; ***D:*** Delmer Daves; ***W:*** Wendell Mayes, Halsted Welles; ***M:*** Max Steiner.

Hanging Up 1/2 **1999 (PG-13)** Strident, schmaltzy comedy about family. Married working mom and middle sister Eve (Ryan) seems to be the one that has to deal with family dilemmas, in this case her cantankerous dying father Lou (Matthau). Older sis Georgia (Keaton) is a workaholic Manhattan magazine exec while ditzy younger sis Maddy (Kudrow) is an actress working on a soap. They check in by phone but duck out on their share of the responsibilities although sibling rivalry rears its head. Based on the novel by Delia Ephron. **93m/C VHS, DVD.** Meg Ryan, Diane Keaton, Lisa Kudrow, Walter Matthau, Adam Arkin, Cloris Leachman, Jesse James, Duke Moosekian, Ann Bortolotti; ***D:*** Diane Keaton; ***W:*** Delia Ephron, Nora Ephron; ***C:*** Howard Atherton; ***M:*** David Hirschfelder.

The Hanging Woman 1/2 *Return of the Zombies; Beyond the Living Dead; La Orgia de los Muertos; Dracula, the Terror of the Living Dead; Orgy of the Dead; House of Terror* **1972** A man is summoned to the reading of a relative's will, and discovers the corpse of a young woman hanging in a cemetery. As he investigates the mystery, he uncovers a local doctor's plans to zombify the entire world. Not bad at all and quite creepy once the zombies are out in force. Euro-horror star Naschy plays the necrophiliac grave digger, Igor. **91m/C VHS, DVD.** *SP IT* Stelvio Rosi, Vickie Nesbitt, Marcella Wright, Catherine Gilbert, Gerard Tichy, Paul Naschy, Dianik Zurakowska, Maria Pia Conte, Carlos Quiney; ***D:*** Jose Luis Merino; ***W:*** Jose Luis Merino.

Hangman **2000 (R)** A serial killer plays a lethal game of hangman, sending a videotape of each murder to detective Nick Roos (Phillips). Roos joins psychiatrist Grace Mitchell (Amick) to catch the killer but she may be the killer's next intended victim. **96m/C VHS, DVD.** Lou Diamond Phillips, Madchen Amick, Dan Lauria, Mark Wilson, Vincent Corazza; ***D:*** Ken Girotti; ***W:*** Vladimir Nemirovsky; ***C:*** Gerald Packer; ***M:*** Steven Stern. **VIDEO**

Hangman's Curse *The Veritas Project: Hangman's Curse* **2003 (PG-13)** It's the jocks vs. the Goths in a high school where the jocks are suddenly stricken with a deadly disease. No one's sure whether the deaths are caused by the ghost of a bullied student, drugs, or witchcraft, so an undercover family of occult investigators is brought in to solve the mystery. Convoluted plot with a predictable ending doesn't work as horror, because it's not all that scary, and the mystery elements don't hold up. Christians looking for a "family values thriller" might like it, though. **106m/C VHS, DVD.** David Keith, Mel Harris, Edwin Hodge, William R. Moses, Leighton Meester, Douglas Smith, Bobby Brewer, Daniel Farber, Andrea Morris, Frank Peretti, George Humphreys; ***W:*** Kathy Mackel, Stan Foster.

Hangman's House **1928** Dying "hanging" judge James O'Brien (Bosworth) tries to ensure his daughter Connaught's (Collyer) future by marrying her to wealthy James D'Arcy (Foxe), even though she despises him. Meanwhile, exiled patriot Hogan (McLaglen) returns to Ireland to kill the man responsible for his sister's suicide (guess who). **72m/B DVD.** Victor McLaglen, June Collyer, Earle Foxe, Hobart Bosworth, Larry Kent; ***D:*** John Ford; ***W:*** Malcolm Stuart Boylan; ***C:*** George Schneiderman.

Hangman's Knot 1/2 **1952** Members of the Confederate Cavalry rob a Union train, not knowing that the war is over. Now facing criminal charges, they are forced to take refuge in a stagecoach stop. Well-done horse opera with a wry sense of humor. **80m/C VHS, DVD.** Randolph Scott, Donna Reed, Claude Jarman Jr., Frank Faylen, Glenn Langan, Richard Denning, Lee Marvin, Jeannette Nolan; ***D:*** Roy Huggins.

Hangmen WOOF! **1987 (R)** Ex-CIA agents battle it out on the East side of New York. If you're into very violent, very badly acted films, then this one's for you. **88m/C VHS, DVD.** Jake LaMotta, Rick Washburne, Dog Thomas, Sandra Bullock; ***D:*** J. Christian Ingvordsen; ***W:*** J. Christian Ingvordsen, Steven Kaman; ***C:*** Steven Kaman; ***M:*** Michael Montes.

Hangmen Also Die 1/2 **1942** Lang's anti-Nazi propaganda film was inspirated by the actual May, 1942 assassination of Reinhard Heydrich. Franz Svoboda (Donlevy) is the member of the Czech resistance who assassinates Heydrich. The Nazis seek revenge and begin rounding up and executing Czech citizens, aided by the traitorous Emil (Lockhart). Franz wants to give himself up to prevent further slaughter but is persuaded to turn the tables on Emil and make him appear to be the assassin. Bertolt Brecht had a hand in the original screenplay but did not receive screen credit and later said most of his work was cut out. **134m/B VHS, DVD.** Brian Donlevy, Gene Lockhart, Walter Brennan, Anna Lee, Dennis O'Keefe, Alexander Granach, Jonathan Hale, Margaret Wycherly, Hans von Twardowski; ***D:*** Fritz Lang; ***W:*** John Wexley; ***C:*** James Wong Howe; ***M:*** Hanns Eisler.

The Hangover **2009 (R)** The stuff of urban legend is touted in this immature-men-behaving-badly, morning-after look at a Vegas bachelor party none of the participants can remember. Despite the chicken, tiger, baby, stolen police car, missing tooth—and missing groom-to-be. Bland Doug (Bartha) is accompanied to Sin City by cynical married Phil (Cooper), milquetoast dentist Stu (Helms) and his fiancee's brother Alan (Galifianakis), none-too-bright and somewhat creepily overeager to belong. After many booze-fueled hours of debauchery, the groomsmen struggle to retrace their steps in an effort to find Doug, meeting (or re-meeting) sweet stripper/hooker Jade (Graham) as well as tiger-owning Mike Tyson and a trash-talking gangster (Jeong). Rowdy, raunchy, and more clever than it needs to be. **100m/C DVD.** *US* Bradley Cooper, Ed Helms, Zach Galifianakis, Justin Bartha, Heather Graham, Ken Jeong, Jeffrey Tambor, Rachael Harris, Mike Epps, Mike Tyson, Sasha Barrese; ***D:*** Todd Phillips; ***W:*** Jon Lucas, Scott Moore; ***C:*** Lawrence Sher; ***M:*** Christophe Beck. Golden Globes '10: Film—Drama.

Hangover Square 1/2 **1945** Foggy, gaslit London, 1903. High-strung composer George (Cregar) has periodic blackouts and thinks he's a murderer although the police clear him. Then he gets involved with lush music hall singer Netta (Darnell), who strings him along. When George discovers her betrayal, his blackouts get worse and he really does become a killer. And what happens to the two-timing Netta is still genuinely shocking. Cregar's last film—he died of a heart attack before its release. **77m/B DVD.** Laird Cregar, Linda Darnell, George Sanders, Glenn Langan, Alan Napier; ***D:*** John Brahm; ***W:*** Barre Lyndon; ***C:*** Joseph LaShelle; ***M:*** Bernard Herrmann.

Hank Aaron: Chasing the Dream **1995** Docudrama combines archival footage, interviews, and reenactments to tell the story of the life and career of Henry Aaron. Follows Aaron's development as a Hall of Fame outfielder for the Milwaukee and Atlanta Braves and as a leader in the civil rights movement. Emphasis on personal and societal issues, as well as on-the-field accomplishments, raises this one above most sports biography documentaries. **120m/C VHS.** ***D:*** Mike Tollin; ***W:*** Mike Tollin; ***C:*** Chuck Cohen, Derek Britt; ***M:*** Ed Smart; ***Nar:*** Dorian Harewood.

Hank and Mike **2008 (R)** You will never think about the Easter Bunny the same way again. Hank and Mike are pink, furry blue-collar Easter Bunnies who work for Easter Enterprises. (Not guys dressed up in costumes but the actual 'delivers baskets on Easter Sunday' bunnies.) When they mistakenly miss a house one Easter they get downsized by their cost-cutting corporation. The duo fail at an assortment of odd jobs, get into debt, wind up homeless, and find even their longtime friendship unraveling. **86m/C DVD.** *CA* Thomas Michael, Paolo Mancini, Joe Mantegna, Chris Klein, Maggie Castle, Tony Nappo, Jane McLean; ***D:*** Matthew Klinck; ***W:*** Thomas Michael, Paolo Mancini; ***C:*** Glen Keenan; ***M:*** Phil Electric.

Hanky Panky 𝒥 1/2 **1982 (PG)** Insipid comic thriller in which Wilder and Radner become involved in a search for top-secret plans. **107m/C VHS, DVD.** Gene Wilder, Gilda Radner, Richard Widmark, Kathleen Quinlan; ***D:*** Sidney Poitier.

Hanna K. 𝒥𝒥 **1983 (R)** Story of divided passions set in the tumultuous state of Israel. American lawyer Clayburgh tries to settle her personal and political affairs with various Middle Eastern men. Mediocre and disappointing. Release generated controversy over pro-Palestine stance. **111m/C VHS.** *FR* Jill Clayburgh, Gabriel Byrne, Jean Yanne, Muhamad Bakri, David Clennon, Oded Kotler; ***D:*** Constantin Costa-Gavras.

Hannah and Her Sisters 𝒥𝒥𝒥 1/2 **1986 (PG)** Allen's grand epic about a New York showbiz family, its three adult sisters and their various complex romantic entanglements. Excellent performances by the entire cast, especially Caine and Hershey. Classic Allen themes of life, love, death, and desire are explored in an assured and sensitive manner. Witty, ironic, and heartwarming. **103m/C VHS, DVD.** Mia Farrow, Barbara Hershey, Dianne Wiest, Michael Caine, Woody Allen, Maureen O'Sullivan, Lloyd Nolan, Sam Waterston, Carrie Fisher, Max von Sydow, Julie Kavner, Daniel Stern, Tony Roberts, John Turturro, Lewis Black; ***D:*** Woody Allen; ***W:*** Woody Allen; ***C:*** Carlo Di Palma. Oscars '86: Orig. Screenplay, Support. Actor (Caine), Support. Actress (Wiest); British Acad. '86: Director (Allen), Orig. Screenplay; Golden Globes '87: Film—Mus./Comedy; L.A. Film Critics '86: Film, Screenplay, Support. Actress (Wiest); Natl. Bd. of Review '86: Director (Allen), Support. Actress (Wiest); N.Y. Film Critics '86: Director (Allen), Film, Support. Actress (Wiest); Natl. Soc. Film Critics '86: Support. Actress (Wiest); Writers Guild '86: Orig. Screenplay.

Hannah Montana: The Movie 𝒥𝒥 **2009 (G)** Hannah's star continues to climb, while Miley is in danger of being lost in the shuffle. To help bring her back to Earth, Miley's dad (Billy Ray Cyrus) takes her to their hometown of Crowley Corners, Tennessee, where there's plenty of love and laughter in the air. Appealing to preteen girls who won't notice the cliches; however, their poor parents will pray for a quick end to this exercise in unabated commercialism. The goal of this big screen version of the Disney Channel series is clearly to further the franchise, with nothing original—ultimately making this an extended music video with a little "story" thrown in. Along with the usual cast, also features country singers Rascal Flatts and Taylor Swift. **102m/C DVD.** *US* Miley Cyrus, Emily Osment, Billy Ray Cyrus, Heather Locklear, Jason Earles, Dolly Parton, Moises Arias, Lucas Till, Vicki Lawrence; ***D:*** Peter Chelsom; ***W:*** Daniel Berendsen; ***C:*** David Hennings; ***M:*** Alan Silvestri. Golden Raspberries '09: Worst Support. Actor (Cyrus).

Hannah Takes the Stairs 𝒥 **2007** Part of the "mumblecore" film movement with ultra-low-budgets and improvised plot, dialogue, and camerawork, and centered around aimless twenty-somethings. Self-absorbed Hannah (Gerwig) breaks up with Mike (Duplass), hooks up with her neglectful boss Paul (Bujalski), and then turns to writer/coworker Matt (Osborne). If you're part of the demographic you might find it distracting; if not, it's tedious and banal. **83m/C DVD.** Kent Osborne, Greta Gerwig, Mark Duplass, Andrew Bujalski; ***D:*** Joe Swanberg; ***W:*** Kent Osborne, Greta Gerwig, Joe Swanberg; ***C:*** Joe Swanberg; ***M:*** Kevin Bewersdorf.

Hanna's War 𝒥𝒥 1/2 **1988 (PG-13)** A moving film about Hanna Senesh, a young Hungarian Jew living in Palestine, who volunteered for a suicide mission behind Nazi lines during WWII. After her capture by the Germans, she was killed, and is now considered by many to have been a martyr. Detmers is very believable as Hanna and Burstyn puts in a good performance as her mother. **148m/C VHS.** Ellen Burstyn, Maruschka Detmers, Anthony Andrews, Donald Pleasence, David Warner, Denholm Elliott, Vincenzo Ricotta, Ingrid Pitt; ***D:*** Menahem Golan; ***W:*** Menahem Golan; ***M:*** Dov Seltzer.

Hannibal 𝒥𝒥 **2001 (R)** The long-awaited sequel to the much loved "Silence of the Lambs," and the lesser-known but equally praised "Manhunter," is more gruesome than scary, but it still managed to bring loads of people to the theatre, most likely to enjoy a heapin' helping of Hopkins's Hannibal. This time the infamous Dr. Lecter and FBI agent Clarice Starling (now played by Moore) are brought together by one of Hannibal's vengeful victims, the severely disfigured Verger (played by Oldman, under layers of prosthetics), and his trained wild pigs. Based on the novel by Thomas Harris. **131m/C VHS, DVD.** *US* Anthony Hopkins, Julianne Moore, Gary Oldman, Ray Liotta, Frankie Faison, Giancarlo Giannini, Francesca Neri, Zeljko Ivanek, Hazelle Goodman, David Andrews, Francis Guinan, Enrico Lo Verso; ***D:*** Ridley Scott; ***W:*** David Mamet, Steven Zaillian; ***C:*** John Mathieson; ***M:*** Hans Zimmer.

Hannibal Rising 𝒥 1/2 **2007 (R)** How Hannibal became a cannibal. Harris adapts his own novel but the fiendish spark is gone. A teenaged Hannibal (Ulliel) and his family fall prey to vicious roving thugs in 1944 (his plump little sister suffers an especially nasty fate). He's then taken in by his widowed Japanese aunt, Lady Murasaki (Li), who introduces him to the ways of the samurai and a handy stash of swords. Hannibal then tracks his quarry and dispatches them in gory ways while practicing his supercilious sneer. A distinct comedown for a franchise character. **117m/C DVD.** *US GB FR* Gaspard Ulliel, Gong Li, Rhys Ifans, Kevin McKidd, Dominic West, Aaron Thomas, Helena-Lia Tachovska; ***D:*** Peter Webber; ***W:*** Thomas Harris; ***C:*** Benjamin Davis; ***M:*** Ilan Eshkeri, Shigeru Umebay Ashi.

Hannie Caulder 𝒥𝒥 **1972 (R)** A woman hires a bounty hunter to avenge her husband's murder and her own rape at the hands of three bandits. Excellent casting but uneven direction. Boyd is uncredited as the preacher. **87m/C VHS.** Raquel Welch, Robert Culp, Ernest Borgnine, Strother Martin, Jack Elam, Christopher Lee, Diana Dors, Stephen Boyd; ***D:*** Burt Kennedy; ***W:*** Burt Kennedy.

Hanoi Hilton 𝒥 1/2 **1987 (R)** A brutal drama about the sufferings of American POWs in Vietnamese prison camps. Nonstop torture, filth, and degradation. **126m/C VHS.** Michael Moriarty, Paul LeMat, Jeffrey Jones, Lawrence Pressman, Stephen Davies, David Soul, Rick Fitts, Aki Aleong, Gloria Carlin; ***D:*** Lionel Chetwynd; ***W:*** Lionel Chetwynd.

Hanover Street 𝒥𝒥 **1979 (PG)** An American bomber pilot and a married British nurse fall in love in war-torn Europe. Eventually the pilot must work with the husband of the woman he loves on a secret mission. A sappy, romantic tearjerker. **109m/C VHS, DVD.** Harrison Ford, Lesley-Anne Down, Christopher Plummer, Alec McCowen; ***D:*** Peter Hyams; ***W:*** Peter Hyams; ***C:*** David Watkin; ***M:*** John Barry.

Hans Brinker 𝒥𝒥 1/2 **1969** Young Hans Brinker and his sister participate in an ice skating race, hoping to win a pair of silver skates. A musical version of the classic tale. **103m/C VHS, DVD.** Robin Askwith, Eleanor Parker, Richard Basehart, Cyril Ritchard, John Gregson; ***D:*** Robert Scheerer.

Hans Christian Andersen 𝒥𝒥 **1952** Sentimental musical story of Hans Christian Andersen, a young cobbler who has a great gift for storytelling. Digitally remastered editions available with stereo sound and original trailer. ♫ The King's New Clothes; I'm Hans Christian Andersen; Wonderful Copenhagen; Thumbelina; The Ugly Duckling; Anywhere I Wander; The Inch Worm; No Two People. **112m/C VHS, DVD.** Danny Kaye, Farley Granger, Zizi Jeanmaire, Joey Walsh; ***D:*** Charles Vidor; ***W:*** Moss Hart; ***C:*** Harry Stradling Sr.; ***M:*** Frank Loesser.

Hansel and Gretel 𝒥𝒥 1/2 **1982** From Shelly Duvall's "Faerie Tale Theatre" comes the story of two young children who get more than they bargained for when they eat a gingerbread house. **51m/C VHS, DVD.** Rick Schroder, Joan Collins, Paul Dooley, Bridgette Andersen; ***D:*** James Frawley. **CABLE**

Hanussen 𝒥𝒥𝒥 1/2 **1988 (R)** The third of Szabo and Brandauer's price-of-power trilogy (after "Mephisto" and "Colonel Redl"), in which a talented German magician and clairvoyant (based on a true life figure) collaborates with the Nazis during their rise to power in the 1930s, although he can foresee the outcome of their reign. In German with English subtitles. **110m/C VHS.** *GE HU* Klaus Maria Brandauer, Erland Josephson, Walter Schmidinger; ***D:*** Istvan Szabo; ***W:*** Peter Dobai, Istvan Szabo; ***C:*** Lajos Koltai; ***M:*** Gyorgy Vukan.

The Happening 𝒥 1/2 **2008 (R)** Shyamalan's self-proclaimed attempt at the best B-movie of all-time is another miss. One day in Central Park people begin doing inexplicably freaky things—wandering backwards, mumbling, and killing themselves. This phenomenon spreads across the Northeast and into Philadelphia, where high school teacher Elliot Moore (Wahlberg) and his wife Alma (Deschanel) pick up the kids and try to flee before they're next. It looks great, and it's jam-packed with suspense, but the payoff pales compared to any good episode of "The Twilight Zone." **91m/C DVD.** *US* Mark Wahlberg, Zooey Deschanel, John Leguizamo, Spencer Breslin, Betty Buckley, Joel de la Fuente, Frank Collison, Ashlyn Sanchez, Robert Bailey Jr.; ***D:*** M. Night Shyamalan; ***W:*** M. Night Shyamalan; ***C:*** Tak Fujimoto; ***M:*** James Newton Howard.

Happenstance 𝒥𝒥 1/2 *The Beating of the Butterfly's Wings; Le Battement d'Ailes du Papillon* **2000 (R)** Is it fate? destiny? chance? that brings people together? Clerk Irene (Tautou) chats with a woman on the subway who tells her that she will meet her true love that day. He turns out to be Faudel (Younes) but of course the made-for-each-other duo's actually getting together is a maze of complications. Amusing romantic comedy; French with subtitles. **97m/C VHS, DVD.** *FR* Audrey Tautou, Faudel, Eric Savin, Eric Feldman, Nathalie Besancon, Lysaine Meis, Lily Boulogne, Francoise Bertin, Frederique Bouraly, Irene Ismailoff; ***D:*** Laurent Firode; ***W:*** Laurent Firode; ***C:*** Jean-Rene Duveau; ***M:*** Peter Chase.

The Happiest Days of Your Life 𝒥𝒥𝒥 **1950** During the London Blitz, a girls' academy is evacuated to the country and mistakeningly billeted with a boys' school. The headmaster and headmistress clash and the bewildered students all try to get along. Good cast, lots of laughs. Adapted from a play by John Dighton. **81m/B VHS.** *GB* Alastair Sim, Margaret Rutherford, Joyce Grenfell, Edward Rigby, Guy Middleton, John Bentley, Bernadette O'Farrell, Richard Wattis, Muriel Aked, Patricia Owens, John Turnbull, Arthur Howard; ***D:*** Frank Launder; ***W:*** Frank Launder, John Dighton; ***M:*** Mischa Spoliansky.

The Happiest Millionaire 𝒥𝒥 **1967** A Disney film about a newly immigrated lad who finds a job as butler in the home of an eccentric millionaire. Based on the book "My Philadelphia Father," by Kyle Crichton. ♫ What's Wrong With That?; Watch Your Footwork; Valentine Candy; Strengthen the Dwelling; I'll Always Be Irish; Bye-Yum Pum Pum; I Believe in This Country; Detroit; There Are Those. **118m/C VHS, DVD.** Fred MacMurray, Tommy Steele, Greer Garson, Geraldine Page, Lesley Ann Warren, John Davidson; ***D:*** Norman Tokar; ***W:*** A.J. Carothers; ***C:*** Edward Colman; ***M:*** Richard M. Sherman, Robert B. Sherman.

Happily Ever After 𝒥𝒥 **1982** Las Vegas star-maker recruits and manipulates two green performers. Show business life in Vegas is given a truthful treatment in this drama. **95m/C VHS.** Suzanne Somers, John Rubinstein, Eric (Hans Gudegast) Braeden; ***D:*** Robert Scheerer. **TV**

Happily Ever After 𝒥𝒥 *Alem Da Paixao* **1986** A Brazilian housewife meets a bisexual transvestite and has a passionate affair, bringing her into the depths of the criminal underworld. In Portuguese with English subtitles. Contains nudity. **106m/C VHS.** *BR* Regina Duarte, Paul Castelli; ***D:*** Bruno Barreto; ***C:*** Alfonso Beato.

Happily Ever After 𝒥 1/2 **1993 (G)** Sequel to "Snow White" begins where the original ends, but isn't connected to the Walt Disney classic. Snow White and her Prince prepare for their wedding when the Wicked Queen is found dead by her brother, who vows revenge. So it's up to Snow and the Dwarfelles (Disney said no to using the Dwarfs), female cousins of the original Dwarfs, to rescue him. Interesting choices from the casting department: Diller is Mother Nature and Asner provides the voice of a rapping owl. Poorly animated drivel designed to ride in on Disney's coattails. While the kids might enjoy it, save your money for the original, finally slated for a video release. **74m/C VHS, DVD.** ***D:*** John Howley; ***W:*** Martha Moran, Robby London; ***V:*** Dom DeLuise, Phyllis Diller, Zsa Zsa Gabor, Ed Asner, Sally Kellerman, Irene Cara, Carol Channing, Tracey Ullman.

Happily Ever After 𝒥𝒥 *Ils se Marient et Eurent Beaucoup D'Enfants; ...And They Lived Happily Ever After* **2004** The wandering eye of the married man. Vincent (writer/director Attal) is happily married to Gabrielle (Gainsbourg) but, when egged on by his horndog bachelor pal Fred (Cohen), has sex with a hot masseuse (David). When Gabrielle finds out, she's hurt but gives a Gallic shrug and decides it's nothing she can't handle, especially since infantile Vincent knows he's being stupid. And Gabrielle knows she can find someone else, too. Depp has a cameo as a tempting stranger. French with subtitles. **100m/C DVD.** Yvan Attal, Charlotte Gainsbourg, Alain Chabat, Emmanuelle Seigner, Alain Cohen, Johnny Depp, Anouk Aimee, Claude Berri; ***D:*** Yvan Attal; ***W:*** Yvan Attal; ***C:*** Remy Chevrin.

Happily N'Ever After 𝒥𝒥 **2007 (PG)** Animated spoof of fairytales where the bad guys take over. A wizard (Carlin) goes on vacation and his two idiot assistants (Shawn, Dick) lose control of Fairy Tale Land to wicked stepmother Frieda (Weaver). Now, everyone from Cinderella to Rapunzel has their stories rewritten, and not for the better. Good voice work makes up for lackluster animation. **87m/C DVD, Blu-ray Disc.** *US GE* Lisa Kaplan; ***D:*** Paul J. Bolger; ***W:*** Rob Moreland; ***C:*** David Dulac; ***M:*** Paul Buckley; ***V:*** Sarah Michelle Gellar, Freddie Prinze Jr., Sigourney Weaver, Andy Dick, Wallace Shawn, Patrick Warburton, George Carlin, Michael McShane, Kath Soucie.

Happiness 𝒥𝒥 **1932** Another zany comedy from the land of the hammer and sickle. Banned in Russia for 40 years, it was deemed to be risque and a bit too biting with the social satire. Silent with orchestral score. **69m/B VHS, DVD.** *RU* Nikolai Cherkassov, Mikhail Gipsi, Yelena Yegorova; ***D:*** Alexander Medvedkin, Alexander Medvedkin; ***W:*** Alexander Medvedkin; ***C:*** Gleb Troyanski.

Happiness 𝒥𝒥𝒥 **1998** Very disturbing film made for the "love it or hate it" category. There are three middleclass New Jersey sisters—perky housewife Trish (Stevenson), underachieving Joy (Adams) and glamourous writer Helen (Boyle). Trish is married to shrink Bill (Baker) and they have an 11-year-old son, Billy (Read), who's getting curious about sex. His dad is the wrong person to ask since he's a pedophile who abuses his son's friends. Then there's Allen (Hoffman), one of Bill's patients. He makes obscene phone calls to Helen, who turns out to be turned on by the dirty talk. Suburban hell, indeed. Some riveting performances, especially Baker and Hoffman. **139m/C VHS, DVD.** Dylan Baker, Cynthia Stevenson, Lara Flynn Boyle, Jane Adams, Philip Seymour Hoffman, Ben Gazzara, Louise Lasser, Rufus Read, Jared Harris, Jon Lovitz, Camryn Manheim, Elizabeth Ashley, Marla Maples; ***D:*** Todd Solondz; ***W:*** Todd Solondz; ***C:*** Maryse Alberti; ***M:*** Robbie Kondor.

Happiness Ahead 𝒥𝒥 **1934** Bored society heiress Joan Bradford (Hutchinson in her screen debut) likes it when she gets a kiss from window washer Bob Lane (Powell) on New Year's Eve, so she pretends to be working-class so they can date. Bob needs money to start his own business and Joan arranges for her father to secretly back Bob's plans but there's trouble when Bob learns who Joan really is. **86m/B DVD.** Dick Powell, Josephine Hutchinson, John Halliday, Ruth Donnelly, Allen Jenkins, Dorothy Dare, Frank McHugh, Marjorie Gateson; ***D:*** Mervyn LeRoy; ***W:*** Harry Sauber; ***C:*** Gaetano Antonio "Tony" Gaudio.

The Happiness of the Katakuris 𝒥𝒥 *Katakuri-ke no kofuku* **2001 (R)** Theoretically this is a remake of the Korean film "Choyonghan kajok," and tells the story of a family opening an Inn that seems cursed with bad luck and death. But this remake is done by notorious Japanese director Takashi Miike. It slips effortlessly from genre to genre without warning, from romantic drama, to supernatural horror, to black comedy, to musical, seemingly at random. Some of it is live action, some is claymation. Not as gory or disturbing as some of his other films, but the surreal style in which it is done is an acquired taste. It has many film and pop culture references in the musical numbers, many of which will be lost as the audience stares in numbed disbelief. **113m/C DVD.** *JP* Kenji Sawada, Keiko Matsuzaka, Shinji Takeda, Naomi Nishida, Tetsuro Tamba, Naoto Takenaka, Kenichi Endo, Yoshiyuki Morishita, Kiyoshiro Imawano, Tamaki Miyazaki, Takashi Matsuzaki, Yoshiki Arizono, Chihiro Asakawa, Yumeki Kanazawa, Tokitoshi Shiota, Masahiro Asakawa, Moeko Ezawa, Akiko Hatakeyama, Maro, Aya Meguro, Yuka Nakatani, Miho Sawada; ***D:*** Takashi Miike; ***W:*** Ai Kennedy, Kikumi Yamagishi; ***C:*** Hideo Yamamoto; ***M:*** Koji Endo, Koji Makaino.

Happy Accidents 𝄞𝄞 1/2 **2000 (R)** Quirky sci-fi/romance offers a breath of fresh air by going against the grain of both genres. Ruby (Tomei) is a neurotic loser in romance who always tries to "fix" the men she dates. She meets Sam (D'Onofrio), who appears to be the well-adjusted guy she doesn't have to change. They fall for each other, and then Sam drops the other shoe. He claims to be a time-traveler from the year 2470, and he's come back to save her life by breaking the "causal chain of events" that will result in a fatal accident. Ruby then has to decide whether to believe him or write him off as another lunatic. D'Onofrio amusingly goes from seemingly normal to spouting surreal "history" without blinking. Light on the special effects (especially for sci-fi), but they're effective when they are used. Pic went through a time warp of its own, as it was shot in 1999, debuted at Sundance in 2000 and released in theatres in 2001. **110m/C VHS, DVD.** *US* Marisa Tomei, Vincent D'Onofrio, Tovah Feldshuh, Nadia Dajani, Holland Taylor, Richard Portnow, Sean Gullette, Cara Buono, Liana Pai, Tamara Jenkins, Jose Zuniga; ***Cameos:*** Anthony Michael Hall; ***D:*** Brad Anderson; ***W:*** Brad Anderson; ***C:*** Terry Stacey; ***M:*** Evan Lurie.

Happy Birthday, Gemini 𝄞 1/2 **1980 (R)** A coming-of-age comedy about a young man on his 21st birthday worrying about his sexual identity. Based on the play "Gemini" by Albert Innaurato. The closeness of the characters on stage did not translate to the screen. **107m/C VHS.** Robert Viharo, Madeline Kahn, Rita Moreno, Alan Rosenberg, Sarah Holcomb, David Marshall Grant, David McIlwraith; ***D:*** Richard Benner; ***W:*** Richard Benner.

Happy Birthday to Me 𝄞 1/2 **1981 (R)** Several elite seniors at an exclusive private school are mysteriously killed by a deranged killer who has a fetish for cutlery. **108m/C VHS, DVD.** *CA* Melissa Sue Anderson, Glenn Ford, Tracy Bregman, Jack Blum, Matt Craven, Lawrence Dane, Lenore Zann, Sharon Acker, Frances Hyland, Earl Pennington, David Eisner, Richard Rebrere, Lesleh Donaldson; ***D:*** J. Lee Thompson; ***W:*** Timothy Bond, Peter Jobin, John C.W. Saxton, John Beaird; ***C:*** Miklos Lente; ***M:*** Bo Harwood, Lance Rubin.

Happy Campers 𝄞𝄞 **2001 (R)** Director of Camp Bleeding Dove (Stormare) is sidelined by an injury, so his teen counselors take charge and seek to spice up their boring daily routines. Routine summer camp flick with a better-than-average cast. **94m/C VHS, DVD.** Brad Renfro, Dominique Swain, Emily Bergl, Jaime (James) King, Jordan Bridges, Peter Stormare, Justin Long, Keram Malicki-Sanchez; ***D:*** Daniel Waters; ***W:*** Daniel Waters; ***C:*** Elliot Davis; ***M:*** Rolfe Kent. **VIDEO**

The Happy Ending 𝄞𝄞 1/2 **1969 (PG)** Woman struggles with a modern definition of herself and her marriage, causing pain and confusion for her family. Simmons is solid as the wife and mother seeking herself. Michel LeGrand's theme song "What Are You Doing With the Rest of Your Life?" was a big hit. **112m/C VHS.** Jean Simmons, John Forsythe, Lloyd Bridges, Shirley Jones, Teresa Wright, Dick Shawn, Nanette Fabray, Bobby Darin, Tina Louise; ***D:*** Richard Brooks; ***W:*** Richard Brooks; ***C:*** Conrad L. Hall.

Happy Endings 𝄞𝄞 1/2 **2005 (R)** Director Roos somewhat successfully juggles several storylines about life, love, gay love, blackmail, deceit, and making babies that focus on two women whose paths eventually cross. There's Mamie (Kudrow) whose teenage fling with her unrelated stepbrother Charley (Coogan) resulted in a forsaken child and a cheerless, regret-filled life; meanwhile, vagabond Jude (a dynamic Gyllenhaal) manages to weasel her way into her gay friend Otis' home and his widowed father's heart. **128m/C DVD.** *US* Tom Arnold, Jesse Bradford, Bobby Cannavale, Sarah Clarke, Steve Coogan, Laura Dern, Maggie Gyllenhaal, Lisa Kudrow, Jason Ritter, David Sutcliffe, Hallee Hirsh, Eric Jungmann, Johnny Galecki; ***D:*** Don Roos; ***W:*** Don Roos; ***C:*** Clark Mathis.

The Happy Face Murders 𝄞𝄞 1/2 **1999 (R)** A puzzling murder and witnesses who keep changing their stories are the problem in this mystery, inspired by true events, that doesn't quite live up to its potential. Dowdy grandmother Lorraine Petrovich (Ann-Margaret) accuses abusive younger boyfriend Rusty (Campbell) of murder. Cynical detective Jen Powell (Helgenberger) and her naive assistant, Dylan (Thomas), must try and find the truth as everyone else keeps lying. The murder is brutal and each retelling only dramatizes the gore. **99m/C VHS.** Ann-Margret, Marg Helgenberger, Henry Thomas, Nicholas (Nick) Campbell, Rick Peters, David McIlwraith, Bruce Gray, Emily Hampshire; ***D:*** Brian Trenchard-Smith; ***W:*** John Pielmeier; ***C:*** Albert J. Dunk; ***M:*** Elmer Bernstein. **CABLE**

Happy Feet 𝄞𝄞𝄞 **2006 (PG)** Beautifully computer animated tale of Mumbles (Wood), a penguin who can't sing after being dropped as an egg by his father (Jackman). Instead, he hoofs like Savion Glover, whose moves were motion-captured for Mumbles' dance sequences. Exiled from his group and his love Gloria (Murphy), Mumbles has adventures with predators, other penguins and a certain two-legged animal that is apparently ruining the planet. Some situations may scare smaller children and the ecological message is a little ominous, so assure them that it will all work out fine and you'll remember to cut up those plastic six-pack thingies before you throw them out. **87m/C DVD, Blu-ray Disc, HD DVD.** *US* ***D:*** George Miller; ***W:*** George Miller, John Collee, Judy Morris, Warren Coleman; ***M:*** John Powell; ***V:*** Elijah Wood, Robin Williams, Brittany Murphy, Hugh Jackman, Nicole Kidman, Hugo Weaving, Anthony LaPaglia, Magda Szubanski, Elizabeth (E.G. Dailey) Daily, Steve Irwin, Miriam Margolyes. Oscars '06: Animated Film; British Acad. '06: Animated Film; Golden Globes '07: Song ("The Song of the Heart").

Happy Gilmore 𝄞𝄞 **1996 (PG-13)** Skating-impaired hockey player Gilmore (Sandler) translates his slap shot into a 400-yard tee shot and joins the pro golf tour. His unique style brings a new, less refined breed of fan to the game and upsets the reigning tour hotshot (McDonald). Sandler improves on "Billy Madison," which isn't saying much. There's still plenty of ammo for his many detractors, but the laughs are more frequent and consistent. Replacing bathroom humor with abusive behavior, the mis-named Happy swears at or beats up about 90% of the supporting cast, including Bob Barker in a charity pro-am. **92m/C VHS, DVD, UMD, HD DVD.** Adam Sandler, Christopher McDonald, Carl Weathers, Julie Bowen, Frances Bay, Ben Stiller, Richard Kiel, Joe Flaherty, Kevin Nealon, Allen Covert, Robert Smigel, Bob Barker, Dennis Dugan; ***D:*** Dennis Dugan; ***W:*** Adam Sandler, Tim Herlihy; ***C:*** Arthur Albert; ***M:*** Mark Mothersbaugh. MTV Movie Awards '96: Fight (Adam Sandler/Bob Barker).

Happy Go Lovely 𝄞𝄞 **1951** Chorus girl Janet (Vera-Ellen) is part of an American troupe that's in Scotland hoping to open a show. Producer Frost (Romero) needs financial backing and, after seeing Janet exit a limo, thinks she's found a rich beau and offers her the show's lead in hopes of getting her boyfriend's money. When the limo's owner, stodgy millionaire B.G. Bruno (Niven), does show up, Janet mistakes him for a reporter and falls in love with the guy. Tired plot, but good performances in this lightweight musical. ♫ One-Two-Three; Would You, Could You; London Town. **95m/C VHS, DVD.** *GB* Sandra Dorne, Vera-Ellen, David Niven, Cesar Romero, Bobby Howes; ***D:*** H. Bruce Humberstone; ***W:*** Val Guest; ***C:*** Erwin Hillier; ***M:*** Mischa Spoliansky.

Happy-Go-Lucky 𝄞𝄞𝄞 **2008 (R)** The title perfectly describes the lead, ever-optimistic London schoolteacher Poppy, who finds a silver lining no matter the situation. Her attitude leads her to romance, but she's tested by an obsessive, abusive driving instructor. Sounds simple, but it's actually a sophisticated character study with insidious charm. Director Leigh's famously morose mood couldn't be more different in this feel-good comedy about feeling good (without aid of chemicals). Poppy's cheerful disposition and perpetually rosy outlook are strangely contagious and not grating, thanks largely to Hawkins' memorable turn. **118m/C DVD.** *GB* Sally Hawkins, Eddie Marsan, Sylvestria Le Touzel, Alexis Zegerman, Samuel Roukin, Sinead Matthews, Kate O'Flynn, Sarah Niles, Karina Fernandez; ***D:*** Mike Leigh; ***W:*** Mike Leigh; ***C:*** Dick Pope; ***M:*** Gary Yershon. Golden Globes '09: Actress—Mus./Comedy (Hawkins).

Happy Hell Night 𝄞𝄞 **1992 (R)** A fraternity prank helps a crazed priest escape from a mental institution and again take up his hobby fom 25 years ago—killing local fraternity members. Oh, the irony is delicious! Unfortunately, the direction and script are not, and they bury some genuinely scary moments. Look for a pre-stardom Rockwell and pre-"CSI" Fox, along with McGavin making a mortgage payment or two. **84m/C DVD.** Nick Gregory, Darren McGavin, Sam Rockwell, Jorja Fox, Ted Clark, Frank John Hughes, Irfan Mensur, Gala Videnovic, Laura Carney, Charles Cragin; ***D:*** Brian Owens; ***W:*** Brian Owens; ***C:*** Sol Negrin.

The Happy Hooker 𝄞𝄞 1/2 **1975 (R)** Xaviera Hollander's cheeky (and bestselling) memoir of her transition from office girl to "working girl" has been brought to the screen with a sprightly (though sanitary) air of naughtiness, with Redgrave enjoyable in title role. Followed by "The Happy Hooker Goes to Washington" and "The Happy Hooker Goes Hollywood." **96m/C VHS.** Lynn Redgrave, Jean-Pierre Aumont, Nicholas Pryor; ***D:*** Nicholas Sgarro.

The Happy Hooker Goes Hollywood 𝄞 **1980 (R)** Third film inspired by the title of Xaviera Hollander's memoirs, in which the fun-loving Xaviera comes to Hollywood with the intention of making a movie based on her book, but soon meets up with a series of scheming, would-be producers. **86m/C VHS.** Martine Beswick, Chris Lemmon, Adam West, Phil Silvers; ***D:*** Alan Roberts.

The Happy Hooker Goes to Washington 𝄞 1/2 **1977 (R)** Further adventures of the world's most famous madam. Heatherton (not Redgrave) is Xaviera Hollander this time, testifying before the U.S. Senate in defense of sex. Fairly stupid attempt to milk boxoffice of original. Second in the holy trilogy of Happy Hooker pictures, which also include "The Happy Hooker" and "The Happy Hooker Goes Hollywood." **89m/C VHS.** Joey Heatherton, George Hamilton, Ray Walston, Jack Carter; ***D:*** William A. Levey.

Happy Hour 𝄞 1/2 **1987 (R)** A young brewing scientist discovers a secret formula for beer, and everyone tries to take it from him. Little turns in a good performance as a superspy. **88m/C VHS.** Richard Gilliland, Jamie Farr, Tawny Kitaen, Ty Henderson, Rich Little; ***D:*** John DeBello; ***W:*** John DeBello.

Happy Hour 𝄞 1/2 **2003** Tulley (LaPaglia) is a self-loathing drunk. A failed writer who works as a copywriter at a New York ad agency, Tulley lives in the shadow of his famous author father (Vaughn). Tulley and best bud/coworker Levine (Stoltz) spend time at their favorite watering hole where Tulley meets Natalie (Feeney) who becomes his instant girlfriend. Then Tulley gets diagnosed with advanced cirrhosis and has to decide what to do with his so-far wasted life. Not as maudlin as it could have been but if its familiarity doesn't breed contempt, it does breed boredom despite the talent involved. **93m/C DVD.** *US* Anthony LaPaglia, Eric Stoltz, Caroleen Feeney, Robert Vaughn, Sandrine Holt, Tom Sadoski; ***D:*** Mike Bencivenga; ***W:*** Mike Bencivenga, Richard Levine; ***C:*** Giselle Chamma; ***M:*** Jeff Taylor.

Happy Landing 𝄞𝄞 1/2 **1938** Predictable, yet entertaining Henie vehicle about a plane that makes a forced landing in Norway near Henie's home. Romance follows with bandleader Romero and manager Ameche. ♫ Hot and Happy; Yonny and his Oompah; You Are The Music to the Words in my Heart; A Gypsy Told Me; You Appeal to Me. **102m/B VHS.** Sonja Henie, Don Ameche, Jean Hersholt, Ethel Merman, Cesar Romero, Billy Gilbert, Wally Vernon, El Brendel; ***D:*** Roy Del Ruth; ***W:*** Milton Sperling, Boris Ingster.

Happy New Year 𝄞𝄞𝄞 *The Happy New Year Caper; La Bonne Annee* **1973** Charming romantic comedy in which two thieves plan a robbery but get sidetracked by the distracting woman who works next door to the jewelry store that's their target. Available in both subtitled and dubbed versions. Remade in 1987. **114m/C VHS, DVD.** *FR IT* Francoise Fabian, Lino Ventura, Andre Falcon, Charles Gerard; ***D:*** Claude Lelouch; ***W:*** Claude Lelouch, Pierre Uytterhoeven.

A Happy New Year! 𝄞𝄞 **1979** Two men and a woman, all engineers in a chemical plant, try to fight off a hangover as they deal with the comings and goings of friends throughout the day and night. In Hungarian with English subtitles. **84m/C VHS.** *HU* Istvan Bujtor, Erika Bodnar, Cecilia Esztergalyos, Andras Balint; ***D:*** Reszo Szoreny; ***W:*** Peter Modos, Reszo Szoreny.

Happy New Year 𝄞𝄞 1/2 **1987 (PG)** Two sophisticated thieves plan and execute an elaborate jewel heist that goes completely awry. Remake of the 1974 French film of the same name. **86m/C VHS.** Peter Falk, Wendy Hughes, Tom Courtenay, Charles Durning, Joan Copeland; ***D:*** John G. Avildsen; ***W:*** Warren Lane; ***M:*** Bill Conti.

Happy Since I Met You 𝄞𝄞𝄞 **1989** Comedy-drama about a scatterbrained drama teacher and a struggling young actor who become romantically involved. **55m/C VHS.** *GB* Julie Walters, Duncan Preston; ***Cameos:*** Tracey Ullman, Jim Bowen; ***D:*** Baz Taylor; ***W:*** Victoria Wood.

Happy Tears 𝄞 1/2 **2009 (R)** Disjointed and awkwardly handled questionable comedy about a dysfunctional family. No-nonsense Laura (Moore) and ditzy younger sister Jayne (Posey) must very reluctantly return to their Pittsburgh hometown to figure out how to handle their dementia-afflicted dad Joe (Torn) and his entrenched floozy, druggie girlfriend Shelly (Barkin). Naturally, there's a lot of past resentment to wade through and many uncomfortable moments ensue. **95m/C DVD.** *US* Parker Posey, Demi Moore, Rip Torn, Ellen Barkin, Christian Camargo, Billy Magnussen, Sebastien Roche, Patti D'Arbanville, Victor Slezak; ***D:*** Mitchell Lichtenstein; ***W:*** Mitchell Lichtenstein; ***C:*** Jamie Anderson; ***M:*** Robert Miller.

Happy, Texas 𝄞𝄞𝄞 **1999 (PG-13)** Producer/director Mark Illsley's quirky little debut hearkens back to such classic Hollywood comedies as "Some Like It Hot." Escaped prisoners Harry Sawyer (Northam) and Wayne Wayne Wayne Jr. (Zahn) steal a camper and assume the identity of its owners in order to evade the law. The trouble is that the owners are a pair of gay men who organize kiddie beauty pageants. When they arrive in the town of Happy, Texas, the populace thinks that they're there to stage the Little Miss Fresh Squeezed contest and greet them with open arms. Wayne is forced to summon up fashion and choreography skills not commonplace in your average hardened criminal, while Harry hobnobs with the local gentry while plotting to knock over the town bank. Romantic complications involving a schoolmarm (Douglas), lady banker (Walker) and a sexually confused sheriff (Macy) arise, setting the stage for a happy (but unnecessarily tidy) ending. **104m/C VHS, DVD.** Steve Zahn, Jeremy Northam, Ally Walker, Illeana Douglas, William H. Macy, M.C. Gainey, Ron Perlman, Michael Hitchcock, Paul Dooley; ***D:*** Mark Illsley; ***W:*** Phil Reeves, Ed Stone, Mark Illsley; ***C:*** Bruce Douglas Johnson; ***M:*** Peter Harris. Ind. Spirit '00: Support. Actor (Zahn).

Happy Times 𝄞𝄞 1/2 *Xingfu Shiguang* **2000 (PG)** Underneath this light comedy hides an intimate tale of an aging loser and his unexpected relationship with a young, blind teenager. When Zhao (Bensham) tries to woo plus-sized divorcee (Lihua) by pretending to be a rich hotel owner, she demands that he give her blind stepdaughter Wu Ying (Jie) a job, unaware that Zhao's only experience in hotel management was renting out a dilapidated bus to couples by the hour. With the help of friends, Zhao sets up an elaborate ruse: outfitting an abandoned factory as the "hotel" where Wu, a masseuse, employs her craft on Zhao's friends posing as clients who pay her in phony money. Zhao finds redemption of a sort in the sullen but honest Wu, who in turn blossoms in her new job. Acclaimed Chinese director Yimou elicits excellent performances in his scaled-down allegory. In Mandarin with subtitles. **106m/C VHS, DVD.** *CH* Benshan Zhao, Jie Dong, Xuejian Li, Lifan Dong, Qibin Leng, Biao Fu, Ben Nu; ***D:*** Yimou Zhang; ***W:*** Giu Zi; ***C:*** Hou Yong; ***M:*** San Bao.

Happy Together 1989 (PG-13) An eager freshman accidentally gets a beautiful, impulsive girl as his roommate. Together they meet the challenges of secondary education. **102m/C VHS, DVD.** Helen Slater, Patrick Dempsey, Dan Schneider, Marius Weyers, Barbara Babcock, Brad Pitt; ***D:*** Mel Damski; ***M:*** Robert Folk.

Happy Together *Cheun Gwong Tsa Sit* **1996** Lovers Lai Yiu-Fai (Leung) and Ho Po-Wing (Cheung) travel to Argentina from Hong Kong looking for adventure but soon go their separate ways. Lai is working as a doorman at a tango bar when a badly beaten Ho unexpectedly re-enters his life. Lai looks after the self-destructive Ho but his restlessness causes him to desert Lai once again, even as Lai befriends young Taiwanese Chang (Chen). After Chang returns to Taipei, Lai begins to suffer from depression and serious homesickness, as well as still worrying about Ho. Edgy visuals and playful performances bely a serious nature. Chinese and Spanish with subtitles. **92m/C VHS, DVD.** *HK* Leslie Cheung, Tony Leung Chiu-Wai, Chang Chen; ***D:*** Wong Kar-Wai; ***W:*** Wong Kar-Wai; ***C:*** Christopher Doyle; ***M:*** Danny Chung. Cannes '97: Director (Kar-Wai).

The Happy Years 1/2 **1950** Based on "The Lawrenceville Stories" by Owen Johnson. Concerned dad Samuel Stover (Ames) sends his troublemaking teenaged son Dink (Stockwell) to a turn-of-the-century prep school in the hopes of turning him into a responsible young man. Bullied by some older students (who all have odd nicknames), Dink has to earn their respect in class and on the football field. **110m/C DVD.** Dean Stockwell, Darryl Hickman, Scotty Beckett, Leon Ames, Margalo Gillmore, Leo G. Carroll, Peter Thompson, David Blair, Claudia Barrett; ***D:*** William A. Wellman; ***W:*** Harry Ruskin; ***C:*** Paul Vogel; ***M:*** Leigh Harline.

Harakiri 1/2 *Seppuku* **1962** An old samurai (Nakadai) wishes to commit ritual suicide on the grounds of a feudal lord, where he learns that his son-in-law, also a samurai, was forced to commit seppuku with a bamboo blade while seeking work. He tells the younger warrior's story to the assembled warlords, who abandoned the samurai when they were no longer needed. Beautifully told and shot film is a scathing indictment of the treatment of men of honor after the battles that defined them have been fought. A classic of the genre, focusing on the aftermath rather than the glory. **135m/B VHS, DVD.** *JP* Hisashi Igawa, Yoshio Inaba, Akira Ishihama, Shima Iwashita, Rentaro Mikuni, Masao Mishima, Tatsuya Nakadai, Tetsuro Tamba, Shichisaburo Amatsu, Yoshio Aoki, Jo Azumi, Akiji Kobayashi, Ichiro Nakaya, Kei Sato, Ryo Takeuchi; ***D:*** Masaki Kobayashi; ***W:*** Shinobu Hashimoto, Yasuhiko Takiguchi; ***C:*** Yoshio Miyajima; ***M:*** Toru Takemitsu.

Hard As Nails 1/2 **2001 (R)** Over-achieving video premiere is a genre piece that leaves no cliche unturned, but it also has moments of real style. Gangster Alex (Scotti) and stripper Kat (Yates) are caught between Russian and Japanese gangs in Los Angeles. A cop (Craig) and a hooker (Farentino) are involved, too. Doublecrosses abound. Some of the stunt work is wonderfully acrobatic. Director Katkin makes the most of a pocket-change budget. **88m/C DVD.** Allen Scotti, Kim Yates, Andrew Craig, Matt Westmore, Lorissa McComas, Stella Farentino; ***D:*** Brian Katkin; ***W:*** Brian Katkin; ***C:*** Marco Cappetta; ***M:*** Chris Farrell. **VIDEO**

Hard-Boiled 1/2 *Lashou Shentan* **1992** Police Inspector Yuen (Woo regular Yun-Fat) is investigating, with his usual excessive force, the Triads organized crime syndicate and a group of gun smugglers who killed his partner. He joins forces with Tony, an undercover cop who's working as a gangster hitman. There's lots of gunplay and betrayals among all the participants. Usual Woo way with violence and action sequences although the plot is more contrived. In Mandarin and Chinese with English subtitles. **126m/C VHS, DVD.** *HK* Chow Yun-Fat, Tony Leung Chiu-Wai, Philip Chan, Anthony Wong, Teresa Mo, Bowie Lam, Hoi-Shan Kwan, Philip Kwok, John Woo; ***D:*** John Woo; ***W:*** Barry Wong, John Woo; ***C:*** Wing-Heng Wang; ***M:*** Michael Gibbs.

Hard-Boiled Mahoney 1/2 **1947** Slip, Sach, and the rest of the Bowery Boys try to solve a mystery involving mysterious women and missing men. The last film in the series for Bobby Jordan, whose career was ended when he was injured in an accident involving a falling elevator. **64m/B VHS.** Leo Gorcey, Huntz Hall, Bobby Jordan, William Benedict, David Gorcey, Gabriel Dell, Teala Loring, Dan Seymour, Bernard Gorcey, Patti Brill, Betty Compson; ***D:*** William Beaudine.

Hard Bounty 1/2 **1994 (R)** After five years of chasing desperadoes, bounty hunter Martin B. Kanning hangs up his guns to open a saloon—complete with frontier prostitutes. When one of his ladies is murdered, the other gals decide to chase after the killer. Naturally, Kanning can't let them go alone. **90m/C VHS, DVD.** Matt McCoy, Kelly Le Brock, Rochelle Swanson, Felicity Waterman, Kimberly Kelley; ***D:*** Jim Wynorski; ***W:*** Karen Kelly; ***C:*** Zoran Hochstatter; ***M:*** Taj.

Hard Candy **2006 (R)** Page is scary-good as 14-year-old Hayley, a seeming Lolita out to tempt 32-year-old photographer Jeff (Wilson). They first flirt in an online chat room and then face-to-face in a coffee shop. Jeff invites pixie-ish Hayley back to his home for drinks, only whatever you think may happen, doesn't. Hayley drugs Jeff, ties him to a chair, and accuses him of being a child pornographer, pedophile, and possible murderer before threatening him with castration for his "crimes." Is she right or just a very dangerous hysteric? First feature for commercial/video director Slade. **103m/C DVD.** *US* Ellen Page, Patrick Wilson, Sandra Oh, Odessa Rae, Gilbert John; ***D:*** David Slade; ***W:*** Brian Nelson; ***C:*** Jo Willems; ***M:*** Molly Nyman, Harry Esscott.

Hard Cash 1/2 *Run for the Money* **2001 (R)** Thief Tom Taylor (Slater) wants to go legit after being released from prison but instead hooks up with a new crew for a job. When they discover the money is marked, Taylor finds himself embroiled with corrupt FBI agent Mark Cornell (Kilmer). Despite the billing, Kilmer has limited screen time and this caper film is a predictable yawner. **98m/C VHS, DVD.** Christian Slater, Bokeem Woodbine, Val Kilmer, Daryl Hannah, Verne Troyer, Balthazar Getty, Vincent Laresca, Peter Woodward, William Forsythe, Sara Downing; ***D:*** Pedrag (Peter) Antonijevic; ***W:*** Willie Dreyfus; ***C:*** Phil Parmet; ***M:*** Stephen (Steve) Edwards.

Hard Choices **1984** A 15-year-old Tennessee boy is unjustly charged as an accessory to murder, until a female social worker decides to help him. From then on, nothing is predictable. Excellent work by Klenck, McCleery, and Seitz. Don't miss Sayles as an unusual drug dealer. Intelligent, surprising, and powerful. Based on a true story, this is a low profile film that deserves to be discovered. **90m/C VHS.** Margaret Klenck, Gary McCleery, John Seitz, John Sayles, Liane (Alexandra) Curtis, J.T. Walsh, Spalding Gray; ***D:*** Rick King; ***W:*** Rick King.

Hard Core Logo **1996 (R)** Mockumentary about a group of Canadian veteran punk rock musicians who, at thirtysomething, have reunited for one last benefit concert. The semi-legendary Vancouver band are so pleased by how well the concert goes that they decide to head back on the road (in a decrepit van) for one last shot at glory, trailed by a documentary film crew (led by director McDonald). The documentary inserts reveal the band's ups and downs and the ego trips that ultimately drove them apart. Adapted from a novel by Michael Turner. McDonald describes "Hard Core Logo" as the last of his rock 'n' roll road trilogy, following "Roadkill" and "Highway 61." **96m/C VHS, DVD.** *CA* Hugh Dillon, Callum Keith Rennie, John Pyper-Ferguson, Bernie Coulson; ***D:*** Bruce McDonald; ***W:*** Noel S. Baker; ***C:*** Danny Nowak; ***M:*** Shaun Tozer. Genie '96: Song ("Swamp Baby, Who the Hell Do You Think You Are?").

Hard Country 1/2 **1981 (PG)** Caught between her best friend's success as a country singer and the old values of a woman's place, a small town girl questions her love and her life style. A warm and intelligent rural drama. Basinger's debut. **104m/C VHS.** Jan-Michael Vincent, Kim Basinger, Michael Parks, Gailard Sartain, Tanya Tucker, Ted Neeley, Daryl Hannah, Richard Moll; ***D:*** David Greene; ***W:*** Michael Kane; ***M:*** Michael Martin Murphey.

A Hard Day's Night 1/2 **1964** The Beatles' first film is a joyous romp through an average "day in the life" of the Fab Four, shot in a pseudo-documentary style with great flair by Lester and noted as the first music video. ♫ A Hard Day's Night; Tell Me Why; I Should Have Known Better; She Loves You; I'm Happy Just to Dance with You; If I Fell; And I Love Her; This Boy; Can't Buy Me Love. **90m/B VHS, DVD.** *GB* John Lennon, Paul McCartney, George Harrison, Ringo Starr, Wilfrid Brambell, Norman Rossington, John Junkin, Victor Spinetti, Anna Quayle, Deryck Guyler, Richard Vernon, Lionel Blair, Eddie Malin, Robin Ray, Alison Seebohm, David Saxon, Patti Boyd; ***D:*** Richard Lester; ***W:*** Alun Owen; ***C:*** Gilbert Taylor; ***M:*** George Martin, John Lennon, Paul McCartney.

Hard Drive 1/2 **1994** A high tech, interactive network offers shared fantasies to Will and Delilah. Then they become obsessed with making their dreams a reality. **92m/C VHS, DVD.** Matt McCoy, Christina (Kristina) Fulton, Edward Albert, Leo Damian, Stella Stevens; ***D:*** James Merendino; ***W:*** James Merendino; ***C:*** Sead Muhtarevic; ***M:*** Nels Cline.

Hard Drivin' **1960** Rowdy action featuring Southern stock car drivers with well shot race scenes from the Southern 500. **92m/C VHS.** Rory Calhoun, John Gentry, Alan Hale Jr.; ***D:*** Paul Helmick.

Hard Eight *Sydney* **1996 (R)** Performances are the highlight of this low-key story set in Reno, Nevada. Sydney (Hall) is a professional gambler who decides to take under his wing the destitute John (Reilly) and teach him the trade. John falls for waitress/hooker Clementine (Paltrow) but there has to be some snake in this gambler's would-be paradise and it shows up in the malevolent form of the scary Jimmy (Jackson), who the dim John befriends despite Sydney's warnings. Debut for writer/director Anderson. **101m/C VHS, DVD.** Philip Baker Hall, John C. Reilly, Gwyneth Paltrow, Samuel L. Jackson, F. William Parker, Philip Seymour Hoffman, Nathanael Cooper, Wynn White, Robert Ridgely, Michael J. Rowe, Kathleen Campbell, Melora Walters; ***D:*** Paul Thomas Anderson; ***W:*** Paul Thomas Anderson; ***C:*** Robert Elswit; ***M:*** Michael Penn, Jon Brion.

Hard Evidence 1/2 **1994 (R)** Trent Turner (Harrison) winds up with major regrets when he joins his mistress (Timmins) on a business trip. Seems her "business" involves drug smuggling and he's forced to shoot a DEA agent to protect them. Some protection—now Turner and his wife (Severance) are caught up in murder, drugs, and blackmail. **100m/C VHS.** Gregory Harrison, Joan Severance, Cali Timmins, Andrew Airlie, Nathaniel DeVeaux; ***D:*** Michael Kennedy; ***W:*** William Martell; ***C:*** Bruce Worrall; ***M:*** Barron Abramovitch.

Hard, Fast and Beautiful **1951** The title sounds like film noir but it's actually a sports drama with Trevor as grasping mom Milly Farley who sees her teen tennis prodigy daughter Florence (Forrest) as her meal ticket to money and fame. Florence is successful (but unhappy) on the amateur circuit while Milly accepts payola and pushes her daughter on a European tour. It's when mom tries to breakup Florence's romance with Gordon (Clarke) that Florence finally rebels. **71m/B DVD.** Claire Trevor, Sally Forrest, Robert Clarke, Kenneth Patterson, Carleton Young, Joseph Kearns; ***D:*** Ida Lupino; ***W:*** Martha Wilkerson; ***C:*** Archie Stout; ***M:*** Roy Webb.

Hard Frame 1/2 *Hunters Are For Killing* **1970** An ex-con returns home hoping all will turn to sweetness and light when he attempts to make nice-nice with his stepdad, who wouldn't stick by him during his trial. Reynolds' debut into TV moviedom; could be the hirsute actor was thinking of this one when he said his movies were the kind they show in prisons and airplanes because nobody can leave. **100m/C VHS.** Burt Reynolds, Melvyn Douglas, Suzanne Pleshette, Larry Storch, Martin Balsam, Peter Brown, Jill Banner, Donald (Don "Red") Barry, Angus Duncan, Ivor Francis, A. Martinez; ***D:*** Bernard Girard; ***W:*** Charles Kuenstle; ***C:*** Gerald Perry Finnerman; ***M:*** Jerry Fielding.

Hard Hombre **1931** Gibson rides and shoots across the screen in one of his best western adventures. **60m/B VHS, DVD.** Hoot Gibson, Lena Basquette, Skeeter Bill Robbins, Jack Byron, Glenn Strange; ***D:*** Otto Brower.

Hard Hunted 1/2 **1992 (R)** Three macho undercover agents try to avoid death at the hands of high-tech guerillas trying to steal nuclear weapons. No-brain actioner, heavy on the display of feminine charms. **97m/C VHS, DVD.** Dona Speir, Roberta Vasquez, Cynthia Brimhall, Bruce Penhall, R.J. (Geoffrey) Moore, Tony Peck, Rodrigo Obregon, Al Leong, Michael J. Shane; ***D:*** Andy Sidaris; ***W:*** Andy Sidaris.

Hard Justice **1995 (R)** Bureau of Alcohol, Tobacco & Firearms agent Nick Adams (Bradley) goes undercover in prison to find his partner's killer and discovers that Warden Pike (Napier) is running an illegal gun operation. Now, who's he gonna trust? Lots of action thrills in a routine story. **95m/C VHS.** David Bradley, Charles Napier, Yuji Okumoto, Vernon Wells; ***D:*** Greg Yaitanes; ***W:*** Nicholas Amendolare, Chris Bold; ***C:*** Moshe Levin; ***M:*** Don Peake.

Hard Knocks **1979** A young man on the run is tormented by an aging actress and her husband. His attempt to leave a past of violence and pain creates even more havoc. **90m/C VHS.** Michael Christian, John Crawford, Donna Wilkes, Keenan Wynn.

Hard Knocks 1/2 **1980** An ex-con goes from one tragic situation to another, and is eventually stalked by shotgun-wielding rednecks in this grim, powerful drama. Excellent performance by Mann holds this picture together. **85m/C** *AU* Tracy Mann, John Arnold, Bill Hunter, Max Cullen, Tony Barry; ***D:*** Don McLennan; ***W:*** Don McLennan. Australian Film Inst. '80: Actress (Mann).

Hard Knox **1983** A hard-nosed Marine pilot is dumped from the service and takes up command at a military school filled with undisciplined punks. A made-for-television movie. **96m/C VHS, DVD.** Robert Conrad, Frank Howard, Alan Ruck, Red West, Bill Erwin, Dean Hill, Joan Sweeney; ***D:*** Peter Werner.

Hard Labour **1973** Middle-aged housekeeper is humiliated at home by her children and tyrannical daughter-in-law. **70m/C VHS, DVD.** *GB* Alison Steadman, Ben Kingsley, Clifford Kershaw; ***D:*** Mike Leigh. **TV**

Hard Lessons 1/2 *The George McKenna Story* **1986** Washington stars as the newly appointed principal of George Washington High in Los Angeles. The school is located in South Central, a gang and drug-infested war zone where the students are armed for their own protection. The situation appears hopeless but McKenna refuses to give up. Based on a true story. **95m/C VHS, DVD.** Denzel Washington, Lynn Whitfield, Akosua Busia, Richard Masur; ***D:*** Eric Laneuville; ***W:*** Charles Eric Johnson; ***C:*** Isidore Mankofsky; ***M:*** Herbie Hancock. **TV**

Hard Luck **2001** Trevor "Lucky" O'Donnell's life certainly doesn't live up to his nickname. He's doing time in a mental ward when his childhood sweetheart Sheryl visits to let him know that his buddy, her brother Eric, is dying of cancer. So Lucky escapes and heads to his hometown of Gold Beach, Oregon, determined that the threesome will take one last trip together to their favorite childhood haunt. Too bad they're being pursued by Sheryl's cop husband Matt and her and Eric's dad, who just happens to be the Chief of Police. **85m/C VHS, DVD.** Kirk Harris, Renee Humphrey, Matthew Faber, Ron Gilbert, Gareth Williams, Karen Black, Joanne Baron, Darrell Bryan, Tony Longo, Luca Bercovici, Jon

Jacobs; *D:* Jack Rubio; *W:* Kirk Harris.

Hard Part Begins 1973 A naive country singer gets sucked into the pratfalls of show business. **87m/C VHS.** *CA* Donnelly Rhodes, Nancy Belle Fuller, Paul Bradley; *D:* Paul Lynch; *W:* John Hunter; *C:* Robert Saad; *M:* Ian Guenther.

Hard Pill 2005 Tim (Slavin) is young, lonely, and gay—uncomfortable with the club scene and the personals. So when he learns about a new pill that claims to turn homosexuals straight, he decides to be a test case and finds himself dealing with the consequences. Debut feature for Baumgartner. **94m/C DVD.** *US* Jonathan Slavin, Jennifer Elise Cox, Scotch Ellis Loring, Susan Slome, Mike Begovich, Jason Bushman, John Baumgartner; *D:* John Baumgartner; *W:* John Baumgartner; *M:* Mike Petrone.

Hard Promises 1992 (PG) Absence doesn't necessarily make the heart fonder, as Joey finds out when he's accidentally invited to his wife's wedding. He's been away from home for so long he doesn't even realize he's been divorced and hightails it home to win his sweetheart back. Average performances and script round out this innocuous domestic comedy-drama. **95m/C VHS, DVD.** Sissy Spacek, William L. Petersen, Brian Kerwin, Mare Winningham, Peter MacNichol, Ann Wedgeworth, Amy Wright, Lois Smith, Rip Torn; *D:* Martin Davidson; *M:* George S. Clinton. **CABLE**

Hard Rain *Flood* 1997 (R) Armored car guards Tom (Slater) and his uncle Charlie (Asner) are transporting $3 million to high ground during a flood in a small Indiana town. When their truck gets stuck in the mud, a band of jet-skiin' motor boatin' thieves arrive and try to steal the money. Tom hides the dough and alerts the local sheriff (Quaid) who, being your normal American elected official, decides he wants to steal it, too. Tom forms an uneasy alliance with head bad guy Jim (Freeman) to thwart the lawman and his toadies. While all this is happening, Tom manages to find love interest Karen (Driver), who's there to protect her church restoration work and wear wet blouses. And now the weather report: floods are the least cinematic disasters. Everything just gets soggy and waterlogged (especially the action sequences). Director Salomon created the huge flooded town set inside a tank in Palmdale, California. **96m/C VHS, DVD.** Morgan Freeman, Christian Slater, Randy Quaid, Minnie Driver, Ed Asner, Richard Dysart, Betty White, Mark Rolston, Peter Murnik, Dann Florek, Wayne Duvall, Michael Goorjian; *D:* Mikael Salomon; *W:* Graham Yost; *C:* Peter Menzies Jr.; *M:* Christopher Young.

The Hard Ride 1/2 1971 (PG) Above average biker movie about a Vietnam vet who brings the body of a black buddy back home, then tries to persuade the dead man's white girlfriend and the leader of his motorcycle gang to attend the funeral. **93m/C VHS.** Robert Fuller, Sherry Bain, Tony Russell, Marshall Reed, Biff (Elliott) Elliot, William Bonner, R.L. Armstrong; *D:* Burt Topper; *W:* Burt Topper.

Hard Rock Zombies 1/2 1985 (R) Four heavy metal band members die horribly on the road and are brought back from the dead as zombies. This horror/heavy metal spoof is somewhat amusing in a goofy way. **90m/C VHS, DVD.** E.J. Curcio, Sam Mann; *D:* Krishna Shah; *W:* David Ball.

Hard Target 1/2 1993 (R) Van Damme continues his action-hero ways as Chance Boudreaux, a Cajun (which explains the accent) merchant seaman, who comes to the rescue of Natasha (Butler), albeit with lots of violence. Brimley provides the humor as Chance's bayou uncle. It's another variation of "The Most Dangerous Game" story but it moves. American directorial debut of over-the-top Hong Kong action director Woo who had to tone down his usual stylistic effects and repeatedly cut some of the more violent scenes to earn an "R" rating. **97m/C VHS, DVD.** Jean-Claude Van Damme, Lance Henriksen, Yancy Butler, Arnold Vosloo, Wilford Brimley, Kasi Lemmons, Eliott Keener, Theodore (Ted) Raimi, Chuck Pfarrer; *D:* John Woo; *W:* Chuck Pfarrer; *C:* Russell Carpenter; *M:* Graeme Revell.

Hard Ticket to Hawaii 1987 (R) A shot-on-video spy thriller about an agent trying to rescue a comrade in Hawaii from a smuggling syndicate. Supporting cast includes many Playboy Playmates. **96m/C VHS, DVD.** Ron Moss, Dona Speir, Hope Marie Carlton, Cynthia Brimhall, Harold Diamond, Rodrigo Obregon, Rustam Branaman, Kwan Hi Lim; *D:* Andy Sidaris; *W:* Andy Sidaris; *C:* Howard Wexler; *M:* Gary Stockdale.

Hard Times 1975 (PG) A Depression-era drifter becomes a bare knuckle street fighter, and a gambler decides to promote him for big stakes. One of grade-B meister Hill's first genre films. A quiet, evocative drama. **92m/C VHS, DVD.** Charles Bronson, James Coburn, Jill Ireland, Strother Martin; *D:* Walter Hill; *W:* Walter Hill, Bryan Gindoff, Bruce Henstell; *C:* Philip Lathrop; *M:* Barry DeVorzon.

Hard to Die *Tower of Terror* 1990 Director Wynorski's comic homage to Carol Frank's "Sorority House Massacre." Five beauties (former Playboy Playmates Harris, Taylor, Dare, Moore, and Carney) find employment moving boxes in a deserted lingerie factory. The film takes off from there as they uncover a mysterious spirit called the Sorority House Killer in an ancient "Soul Box." Desperate to extinguish the evil threat, they focus their efforts in an armed struggle involving high-powered weaponry against the building maintenance man, whom they fear is possessed by the spirit. Accompanied by a lovely, touching group shower scene. **77m/C VHS.** Robin Harris, Melissa Moore, Debra (Deborah Dutch) Dare, Lindsay Taylor, Bridget Carney, Forrest J Ackerman, Orville Ketchum; *D:* Jim Wynorski.

Hard to Forget 1/2 1998 Private eyes Max Warner (Dutton) and Doug Hart (Campbell) are hired by grieving mother Helen Applewhite (Maxwell). Her daughter Nicky (Shannon) was supposedly killed in a boat explosion but a body was never found and someone claims to have spotted Nicky in Johannesburg. So Max heads to South Africa and takes a safari with lookalike guide Sandra. Max falls in love while trying to discover the truth. From the Harlequin Romance Series; adapted from the Evelyn Crowe novel. **95m/C DVD.** *CA* Tim Dutton, Polly Shannon, Nicholas (Nick) Campbell, Lois Maxwell, Chad Everett, Michael McManus; *D:* Vic Sarin; *W:* Gerald Wexler; *C:* Buster Reynolds; *M:* John McCarthy. **TV**

Hard to Get 1/2 1938 **82m/B DVD.** Dick Powell, Olivia de Havilland, Charles Winninger, Bonita Granville, Allen Jenkins, Thurston Hall, Isabel Jeans, Penny Singleton; *D:* Ray Enright; *W:* Maurice Leo, Jerry Wald, Richard Macaulay; *C:* Charles Rosher.

Hard to Hold 1/2 *Paid to Dance* 1937 Undercover agents William Dennis (Terry) and Joan Barclay (Wells) are trying to solve the mystery of some missing dancers. The "taxi-dancers," as they're known around town, worked at dance halls run by sleazeball Jack Miranda (Loft) and his henchman Nifty (Fix), who don't take kindly to the two government agents snooping around. **55m/B DVD.** Don Terry, Julie Bishop, Rita Hayworth, Arthur Loft, Paul Fix; *D:* Charles C. Coleman; *W:* Robert E. Kent, Leslie T. White; *C:* George Meehan Jr.; *M:* Morris Stoloff.

Hard to Hold 1/2 1984 (PG) Rockin' Rick's lukewarm film debut where he falls in love with a children's counselor after an automobile accident. Springfield sings "Love Somebody" with music by Peter Gabriel. **93m/C VHS, DVD.** Rick Springfield, Janet Eilber, Patti Hansen, Albert Salmi, Monique Gabrielle; *D:* Larry Peerce.

Hard to Kill 1989 (R) Policeman Seagal is shot and left for dead in his bedroom, but survives against the odds, though his wife does not. After seven years, he is well enough to consider evening the score with his assailants. He hides while training in martial arts for the final battle. Strong outing from Seagal, with good supporting cast. **96m/C VHS, DVD.** Steven Seagal, Kelly Le Brock, William Sadler, Frederick Coffin, Bonnie Burroughs, Zachary Rosencrantz, Dean Norris; *D:* Bruce Malmuth; *W:* Steven McKay; *C:* Matthew F. Leonetti; *M:* Charles Fox.

Hard Traveling 1985 (PG) An unemployed Depression-era farmworker is accused of murder. He must fight a hostile court system to maintain his dignity and salvage the love and respect of his wife. Based on a novel by Alvah Bessie. **99m/C VHS.** J.E. Freeman, Ellen Geer, Barry Corbin, James Gammon, Jim Haynie; *D:* Dan Bessie; *W:* Dan Bessie; *C:* David Myers.

The Hard Truth 1/2 1994 (R) By-the-book actioner finds cop Jonah (Rooker) suspended for having an itchy trigger finger. His gal Lisa (Anthony) knows her sleazy boss has lots of mob money handy and proposes they grab it. But then Lisa gets a look at Chandler (Roberts), the electronic whiz blackmailed to assist in the heist, and the triangle leads to trouble. **100m/C VHS.** Michael Rooker, Eric Roberts, Lysette Anthony, Ray Baker, Don Yesso; *D:* Kristine Peterson; *W:* Jonathan Tydor; *C:* Ross Berryman.

Hard Vice 1/2 1994 (R) Vice cops Joe Owens (Jones) and Andrea Thompson (Tweed) have their work cut out for them on their Las Vegas beat. When the bodies start piling up, the prime suspects turn out to be a group of high-priced hookers. **86m/C VHS, DVD.** Shannon Tweed, Sam Jones, James Gammon, Rebecca Ferratti; *D:* Joey Travolta; *W:* Joey Travolta; *C:* F. Smith Martin; *M:* Jeff Lass.

Hard Way 1980 A world-weary assassin is pressured by his boss to perform one last assignment. A surprise awaits him if he accepts. **88m/C VHS.** Patrick McGoohan, Lee Van Cleef, Donal McCann, Edna O'Brien, Lewis Black; *D:* Mihael Dryhurst.

The Hard Way 1991 (R) Hollywood superstar Fox is assigned to hardened NYC cop Woods to learn the ropes as he trains for a role. Nothing special in the way of script or direction, but Woods and Fox bring such intensity and good humor to their roles that the package works. Fox pokes fun at the LA lifestyle as the annoying, self-absorbed actor, and Marshall has an entertaining appearance as his agent. Woods is on familiar over-the-edge turf as the brittle but dedicated detective. Silly finale almost destroys the film, but other small vignettes are terrific. **91m/C VHS, DVD.** James Woods, Michael J. Fox, Annabella Sciorra, Stephen Lang, Penny Marshall, LL Cool J, John Capodice, Christina Ricci, Karen (Lynn) Gorney, Luis Guzman; *D:* John Badham; *W:* Daniel Pyne, Lem Dobbs; *C:* Robert Primes; *M:* Arthur B. Rubinstein.

The Hard Word 1/2 2002 (R) Pearce is Dale, the eldest of three criminal brothers who are enticed into one last job upon their release from prison. Since they've been pulling jobs all along, thanks to a "work-release" program cooked up by their slimy lawyer, Frank Malone (Taylor), and some crooked cops, it doesn't seem like a bad idea. Problems arise when Dale finds out that Frank is setting them up, and having an affair with his femme-fatale wife Carole (Griffiths). Aussie caper flick sizzles on the strength of lived-in performances by Pearce and Griffiths, as well as a grungy feel that makes the whole thing resonate with suspicion. **102m/C VHS, DVD.** *AU GB* Guy Pearce, Rachel Griffiths, Robert Taylor, Joel Edgerton, Damien Richardson, Rhonda Findleton, Kate Atikinson, Vince Colosimo, Paul Sonkkila, Kim Gyngell, Dorian Nkono; *D:* Scott Roberts; *W:* Scott Roberts; *C:* Brian J. Breheny; *M:* David Thrussell.

Hardball 2001 (PG-13) Loosely based on Daniel Coyle's book "Hardball: A Season in the Projects," the plot plays like a watered down "Bad News Bears" with a dark edge. Conor O'Neill (Reeves) is a gambler who owes money all over Chicago. He asks broker pal Jimmy (McGlone) for financial help, but it comes at a cost. Jimmy has him take over a baseball team from the Cabrini-Green projects as part of his company's community outreach program. Conor and the foul-mouthed little tykes inevitably get off on the wrong foot, setting up the eventual "rag-tag bunch of misfits turn into champions" scenario. Grimmer overtones show up, however, with the realities of the projects and a tragedy that deeply affects Conor and the team. The kids' teacher Elizabeth (Lane) is the guiding influence/unfulfilled love interest. The kids, especially Griffith and Warren, steal pic from the grown-ups with their performances. **106m/C VHS, DVD.** *US* Keanu Reeves, Diane Lane, John Hawkes, Bryan C. Hearne, Julian Griffith, A. Delon Ellis Jr., DeWayne Warren, Michael B. Jordan, D.B. Sweeney, Mike McGlone, Graham Beckel, Mark Margolis; *D:* Brian Robbins; *W:* John Gatins; *C:* Tom Richmond; *M:* Mark Isham.

Hardbodies 1984 (R) Three middle-aged men hit the beaches of Southern California in search of luscious young girls. They find them. Mid-life crisis done stupidly. Followed by a sequel. **88m/C VHS.** Grant Cramer, Teal Roberts, Gary Wood, Michael Rapport, Sorrels Pickard, Roberta Collins, Cindy Silver, Courtney Gains, Kristi Somers, Crystal Shaw, Kathleen Kinmont, Joyce Jameson; *D:* Mark Griffiths; *W:* Eric Alter.

Hardbodies 2 WOOF! 1986 (R) A sequel to the original comedy hit, dealing with film crew in Greece that is distracted by hordes of nude natives. Sophomoric humor dependent on nudity and profanity for laughs. **89m/C VHS.** Brad Zutaut, Brenda Bakke, Fabiana Udenio, James Karen; *D:* Mark Griffiths; *W:* Eric Alter; *M:* Eddie Arkin.

Hardcase and Fist 1989 (R) A framed cop leaves prison with his mind on revenge. The godfather who used him is just his first target. **92m/C VHS, DVD.** Maureen Lavette, Ted Prior, Tony Zarindast, Christine Lunde, Carter Wang; *D:* Tony Zarindast; *W:* Tony Zarindast, Bud Fleischer; *C:* Robert Hayes; *M:* Matthew Tucciarone, Tom Tucciarone. **VIDEO**

Hardcore 1/2 *The Hardcore Life* 1979 (R) A Midwestern businessman who is raising a strict Christian family learns of his daughter's disappearance while she is on a church trip. After hiring a streetwise investigator, he learns that his daughter has become an actress in pornographic films out in California. Strong performance by Scott and glimpse into the hardcore pornography industry prove to be convincing points of this film, though it exploits what it condemns. **106m/C VHS, DVD.** George C. Scott, Season Hubley, Peter Boyle, Dick Sargent; *D:* Paul Schrader; *W:* Paul Schrader; *C:* Michael Chapman; *M:* Jack Nitzsche.

Hardcore 1/2 2004 Two teenage prostitutes partner up for a string of power plays that eventually lead to murder. In Greek with subtitles **96m/C DVD.** Dimitris Liolios, Andreas Marianos, Konstadinos Markoulakis, Ioannis Papazisis; *D:* Dennis Iliadis; *W:* Dennis Iliadis. **VIDEO**

The Harder They Come 1/2 1972 (R) A poor Jamaican youth becomes a success with a hit reggae record after he has turned to a life of crime out of desperation. Songs, which are blended nicely into the framework of the film, include "You Can Get It If You Really Want it" and "Sitting In Limbo." **93m/C VHS, DVD.** *JM* Jimmy Cliff, Janet Barkley, Carl Bradshaw, Bobby Charlton, Ras Daniel Hartman, Basil Keane, Winston Stona; *D:* Perry Henzell; *W:* Perry Henzell, Trevor D. Rhone; *C:* Peter Jessop, David McDonald; *M:* Desmond Dekker, Jimmy Cliff.

The Harder They Fall 1956 A cold-eyed appraisal of the scum-infested boxing world. An unemployed reporter (Bogart in his last role) promotes a fighter for the syndicate, while doing an expose on the fight racket. Bogart became increasingly debilitated during filming and died soon afterward. Based on Budd Schulberg's novel. **109m/B VHS, DVD.** Humphrey Bogart, Rod Steiger, Jan Sterling, Mike Lane, Max Baer Sr., Albert "Poppy" Popwell; *D:* Mark Robson; *W:* Philip Yordan; *C:* Burnett Guffey.

Hardhat & Legs 1980 Comic complications arise when a New York construction worker falls in love with the woman who's teaching the modern sexuality course in which he's enrolled. **96m/C VHS.** Sharon Gless, Kevin Dobson, Raymond Serra, Elva Josephson, Bobby Short, Jacqueline Brookes, W.T. Martin; *D:* Lee Philips; *W:* Ruth Gordon; *M:* Brad Fiedel. **TV**

Hardly Working 1981 (PG) A circus clown finds it difficult to adjust to real life as he fumbles about from one job to another. Lewis's last attempt at resuscitating his directorial career. His fans will love it, but others need not bother. **90m/C VHS.** Jerry Lewis, Susan Oliver, Roger C. Carmel, Gary Lewis, Deanna Lund; *D:* Jerry Lewis; *W:* Jerry Lewis.

Hardware 1/2 1990 (R) Rag-tag ripoff in which McDermott is a post-apocalyptic garbage picker who gives girlfriend Travis some robot remains he collected (ours is not to ask why), oblivious to the fact that the tidy android was a government-spawned population controller programmed to destroy warm bodies. Seems old habits die hard, and that spells danger, danger, Will Robinson. Much violence excised to avoid x-rating. **94m/C VHS, DVD.** Dylan McDermott, Stacey Travis, John Lynch, Iggy Pop; ***D:*** Richard Stanley; ***M:*** Simon Boswell.

Hardwired ☝ 1/2 **2009 (R)** Derivative and dull sci-fi. Luke Gibson's (Gooding Jr.) family was killed in a car crash and he nearly died as well. Awakening in a hospital with amnesia, Luke learns a microchip has been implanted in his brain by a mysterious corporation headed by Virgil (Kilmer) that is monitoring him as a human guinea pig and that has the prerequisite sinister plans for their techno breakthrough. **94m/C DVD.** Cuba Gooding Jr., Val Kilmer, Tatiana Maslany, Juan Riedinger, Michael Ironside, Alastair Gamble; ***D:*** Ernie Barbarash; ***W:*** Michael Hurst; ***C:*** Stephen Jackson; ***M:*** Shaun Tozer. **VIDEO**

Harem ☝ **1985** A beautiful stockbroker gets kidnapped by a wealthy OPEC oil minister and becomes part of his harem. Kingsley stars as the lonely sheik who longs for the love of a modern woman. **107m/C VHS.** *FR* Ben Kingsley, Nastassja Kinski; ***D:*** Arthur Joffe.

Harem ☝☝ **1986** In the early 1900s, a dastardly Turkish sultan kidnaps an American beauty to add to his harem—mightily displeasing his jealous first wife. Lots of overwrought romance and drama until she is finally rescued. **200m/C VHS.** Omar Sharif, Nancy Travis, Ava Gardner, Julian Sands, Art Malik, Sarah Miles, Yaphet Kotto, Cherie Lunghi; ***D:*** William (Billy) Hale. **TV**

Harem ☝☝ *Harem Suare* **1999 (R)** Exotic but not particularly erotic saga of young beauty Safiye (Gillain) who is sold as a concubine to the Sultan of the Ottoman Empire. She becomes his favorite and official wife but this does not prevent her from turning to palace eunuch Nadir (Descas) for affection. Nor does it protect Safiye or the rest of the harem's women when the empire falls, the Sultan flees to Europe, and the women are abandoned to fend for themselves. Turkish, French, and Italian with subtitles. **107m/C VHS, DVD.** *IT* Marie Gillain, Alex Descas, Valeria Golino, Lucia Bose; ***D:*** Ferzan Ozpetek; ***W:*** Ferzan Ozpetek, Gianni Romoli; ***C:*** Pasquale Mari; ***M:*** Aldo De Scalzi.

Harlan County, U.S.A. ☝☝☝☝ **1976 (PG)** The emotions of 180 coal mining families are seen up close in this classic documentary about their struggle to win a United Mine Workers contract in Kentucky. Award-winning documentary. **103m/C VHS, DVD.** ***D:*** Barbara Kopple; ***C:*** Phil Parmet. Oscars '76: Feature Doc., Natl. Film Reg. '90.

Harlan County War ☝☝ 1/2 **2000** Ruby Kincaid (Hunter) is the wife of striking Kentucky coal miner Silas (Levine). After a court order severely restricts the union members' protests, Ruby leads the wives into action, even allowing her arrest to be used as propaganda by union rep Warren Jakopovich (Skarsgard) to her husband's dismay. Good lead performances, although the dramatic power of the story is subdued. Inspired by Barbara Kopple's 1976 documentary, "Harlan County, U.S.A." **104m/C VHS, DVD.** Holly Hunter, Stellan Skarsgard, Ted Levine, Wayne Robson; ***D:*** Tony Bill; ***W:*** Peter Silverman; ***C:*** Flavio Martinez Labiano; ***M:*** Van Dyke Parks. **CABLE**

Harlem Nights ☝☝ **1989 (R)** Two Harlem nightclub owners in the 1930s battle comically against efforts by the Mob and crooked cops to take over their territory. High-grossing, although somewhat disappointing effort from Murphy, who directed, wrote, produced, and starred in this film. **118m/C VHS, DVD.** Eddie Murphy, Richard Pryor, Redd Foxx, Danny Aiello, Jasmine Guy, Michael Lerner, Arsenio Hall, Della Reese, Eugene Robert Glazer; ***D:*** Eddie Murphy; ***W:*** Eddie Murphy; ***C:*** Woody Omens; ***M:*** Herbie Hancock. Golden Raspberries '89: Worst Screenplay.

Harlem on the Prairie ☝ *Bad Man of Harlem* **1938** This first-ever western with an all-black cast has Jeffries helping a young lady find hidden gold and foiling a villain. Even though the technical standards and acting are below par, this is worth watching for the singing and a comedy routine done by a well-known contemporary black team. ♫Harlem On The Prairie; Romance In The Rain. **54m/B VHS.** Herbert Jeffries, Mantan Moreland, F.E. (Flourney) Miller, Connie Harris, Maceo B. Sheffield, William Spencer Jr.; ***D:*** Sam Newfield.

Harlem Rides the Range ☝ 1/2 **1939** Jeffries must outsmart villainous Brooks, who means to swindle a radium mine away from its rightful owner. Early oater of interest only because of its atypical all-black cast and crew. **58m/B VHS, DVD.** Herbert Jeffries, Lucius Brooks, Artie Young, F.E. (Flourney) Miller, Spencer Williams Jr., Clarence Brooks, Tom Southern, Wade Dumas, Leonard Christmas; ***D:*** Richard C. Kahn; ***W:*** F.E. (Flourney) Miller, Spencer Williams Jr.

Harley ☝☝ **1990 (PG)** Diamond is Harley, an L.A. thug-on-a-hog, who's on his way to an extended stay at one of the state's luxury institutions when he's sent to a Texas rehabilitation community. There, he bonds with an ex-biker, and may just find his way back down the straight and narrow. And the local longhorn rednecks applaud his efforts-...not. **80m/C VHS.** Lou Diamond Phillips, Eli Cummins, DeWitt Jan, Valentine Kim; ***D:*** Fred Holmes; ***W:*** Frank Kuntz, Sandy Kuntz.

Harley Davidson and the Marlboro Man ☝ **1991 (R)** An awful rehash of "Butch Cassidy and the Sundance Kid" with blatant vulgarity and pointless sci-fi touches. The title duo are near-future outlaws who rob a bank to save their favorite bar, then find they've stolen mob money. Some action, but it's mostly talk: lewd, meant-to-be-whimsical soul-probing chats between H.D. and M.M. that would bore even the biker crowd—and did. **98m/C VHS, DVD.** Kelly Hu, Mickey Rourke, Don Johnson, Chelsea Field, Tom Sizemore, Vanessa L(ynne) Williams, Robert Ginty, Daniel Baldwin; ***D:*** Simon Wincer; ***W:*** Don Michael Paul; ***C:*** David Eggby; ***M:*** Basil Poledouris.

A Harlot's Progress ☝☝ **2006** In London, painter William Hogarth (Jones) meets young whore Mary Collins (Tapper) in a Covent Garden brothel, and the social critic and satirist decides to use her as his muse. In 1731, Hogarth begins a series of six paintings (those of the title) that will bring him fame and fortune, featuring Mary's miserable fate from innocent country girl to city prostitute to early death. (The paintings were later destroyed in a fire but Hogarth's engravings remain.) **100m/C DVD.** *GB* Toby Jones, Zoe Tapper, John Castle, Geraldine James, Nicholas (Nick) Rowe, Sophie Thompson; ***D:*** Justin Hardy; ***W:*** Clive Bradley; ***C:*** Douglas Hartington; ***M:*** Richard Blair-Oliphant. **TV**

Harlow ☝☝ 1/2 **1965** The more lavish of the two Harlow biographies made in 1965, both with the same title. A sensationalized "scandal sheet" version of Jean Harlow's rise to fame that bears little resemblance to the facts of her life. **125m/C VHS.** Carroll Baker, Martin Balsam, Red Buttons, Mike Connors, Angela Lansbury, Peter Lawford, Raf Vallone, Leslie Nielsen; ***D:*** Gordon Douglas; ***W:*** John Michael Hayes; ***C:*** Joseph Ruttenberg.

Harmon of Michigan ☝☝ 1/2 **1941** College football hero Harmon starred in this loosely adapted story of his life in and out of the pros and his career at Michigan. **65m/B VHS.** Tom Harmon, Anita Louise, Forest Evashevski, Oscar O'Shea, Warren Ashe, Stanley Crown, Ken Christy, Tim Ryan, Lloyd Bridges, William Hall, Chester Conklin, Larry Parks; ***D:*** Charles T. Barton; ***W:*** Howard J. Green.

The Harmonists ☝☝ **1999 (R)** Actor/singer Harry Frommermann (Noethen) is frustrated by his lack of success and decides to put together his own a cappella group—a musical sextet known as "The Comedian Harmonists," who find great success in Germany. Unfortunately, as the '20s give way to the '30s and the rise of Nazism, the group begins to run into trouble since three of its members are Jewish. Eventually, the political pressures force the group to disband and send its Jewish members into exile. German with subtitles. **114m/C VHS.** *GE* Ulrich Noethen, Ben Becker, Heino Ferch, Heinrich Schafmeister, Max Tidof, Kai Wiesinger, Meret Becker, Katja Riemann, Dana Vavrova; ***D:*** Joseph Vilsmaier; ***W:*** Klaus Richter; ***C:*** Joseph Vilsmaier; ***M:*** Harald Kloser.

Harmony Lane ☝☝ **1935** Highly romanticised rendition of the life of American composer, Stephen Collins Foster (1826-1864). Montgomery, as Foster, manages to lend a hint of credibility to the syrupy, melodramatic script. Very little attention is given to historical fact and almost every scene is orchestrated to showcase the composer's songs. The music steals the show. ♫Beautiful Dreamer; Old Folks at Home; Swanee River; Oh! Susanna; De Camptown Races. **84m/B VHS.** Douglass Montgomery, Evelyn Venable, Adrienne Ames, Joseph Cawthorn, William Frawley, Florence Roberts, Smiley Burnette, Hattie McDaniel; ***D:*** Joseph Santley.

Harm's Way ☝ **2007** Darlene and her daughter Victoria come to Bea's isolated farmhouse, which is supposed to be a refuge for abused women. But Bea is soon co-opting Victoria, turning her against her mother. When Darlene learns that other women have disappeared and confronts Bea, she finds the woman has murder on her mind. **83m/C DVD.** Kathleen Quinlan, Hannah Lochner, Ingrid Kavelaars, David Sparrow, Claudia Witt; ***D:*** Melanie Orr; ***W:*** William Brent Bell; ***C:*** Marcus Elliott; ***M:*** Eric Cadesky. **VIDEO**

Harnessing Peacocks ☝☝ 1/2 **1992** Hebe (Scott Thomas) has a one-night stand with a mystery man during carnival time in Venice, gets pregnant, and winds up living a very independent life with her son in a British seaside community. She supports herself as both a chef and as an expensive mistress, with a very select group of admirers, but always dreams of reuniting with her son's father. Based on the novel by Mary Wesley. **108m/C VHS.** *GB* Serena Scott Thomas, Peter Davison, Renee Asherson. **TV**

Harold ☝ 1/2 **2008 (PG-13)** Single joke comedy and not a funny joke at that. Thirteen-year-old Harold (Breslin) suffers from premature male-pattern baldness and acts likes somebody's elderly grandpa for no discernable reason. After moving to a new town with his family, Harold comes in for a lot of ridicule at his new school while getting advice from self-confident janitor Cromer (Gooding Jr.) **90m/C DVD.** Spencer Breslin, Cuba Gooding Jr., Ally Sheedy, Nicole Blonsky, Fred Willard, Chris Parnell, Rachel Dratch, Colin Quinn, Suzanne Shepherd, Stella Maeve; ***D:*** T. Sean Shannon; ***W:*** T. Sean Shannon, Greg Fields; ***C:*** Christopher Levasseur; ***M:*** Brady Harris. **VIDEO**

Harold & Kumar Escape from Guantanamo Bay ☝☝ **2008 (R)** Scatological, un-PC stoner comedy finds amiable dopers Harold (Cho) and Kumar (Penn) in federal trouble when Kumar can't resist lighting up his homemade bong in the airplane lavatory on their Amsterdam-bound flight. The bong is mistaken for a bomb and overzealous, idiotic Homeland Security dude Fox (Corddry) is sure the boys are terrorists (can you say ethnic profiling?). So they wind up at Gitmo, where predictable humiliations follow, before escaping and going on a road trip to Texas (an amiable fake Dubya makes an appearance), where they hope Harold's well-connected pal Colton (Winter) can keep them from wearing orange jumpsuits for the rest of their days. If you liked their first buddy adventure (NPH!), this is way more of the same. **102m/C DVD.** *US* John Cho, Kal Penn, Rob Corddry, Jack Conley, Roger Bart, Paula Garces, Neil Patrick Harris, Missi Pyle, Danneel Harris, Eric Winter, James Adomian, Beverly D'Angelo, David Krumholtz, Eddie Kaye Thomas, Ed Helms, Clyde Kusatsu, Christopher Meloni, Paula Garces; ***D:*** Jon Hurwitz, Hayden Schlossberg; ***W:*** Jon Hurwitz, Hayden Schlossberg; ***C:*** Daryn Okada; ***M:*** George S. Clinton.

Harold and Kumar Go to White Castle ☝☝ 1/2 **2004 (R)** Uptight junior banker Harold (Cho) and his laid-back med student pal Kumar (Penn) take the edge of encroaching adulthood by getting high. A lot. One such session produces cravings for White Castle hamburgers and sets the pair on a convoluted quest, despite Harold's need to finish an important work project. The journey is complicated by broken down vehicles, side trips for weed, creepy tow-truck drivers, skateboard punks, over-enthusiastic cops, and a hilariously Ecstacy-fueled Neil Patrick Harris. The pair's odd-couple chemistry helps smooth over the more ridiculous plot twists, and the target audience, properly medicated, should enjoy themselves long after the final credits have rolled. **96m/C DVD, UMD.** John Cho, Kal Penn, Paula Garces, David Krumholtz, Eddie Kaye Thomas, Fred Willard, Ethan (Randall) Embry, Neil Patrick Harris, Christopher Meloni, Ryan Reynolds, Anthony Anderson, Kate Kelton, Brooke D'Orsay; ***D:*** Danny Leiner; ***W:*** Jon Hurwitz, Hayden Schlossberg; ***C:*** Bruce Douglas Johnson; ***M:*** David Kitay.

Harold and Maude ☝☝☝☝ **1971 (PG)** Cult classic pairs Cort as a deadpan disillusioned 20-year-old obsessed with suicide (his staged attempts are a highlight) and a loveable Gordon as a fun-loving 80-year-old eccentric. They meet at a funeral (a mutual hobby), and develop a taboo romantic relationship, in which they explore the tired theme of the meaning of life with a fresh perspective. The script was originally the 20-minute long graduate thesis of UCLA student Higgins, who showed it to his landlady, wife of film producer Lewis. Features music by the pre-Islamic Cat Stevens. **92m/C VHS, DVD.** Ruth Gordon, Bud Cort, Cyril Cusack, Vivian Pickles, Charles Tyner, Ellen Geer, Eric Christmas, G(eorge) Wood, Gordon Devol; ***D:*** Hal Ashby; ***W:*** Colin Higgins; ***C:*** John A. Alonzo; ***M:*** Cat Stevens. Natl. Film Reg. '97.

Harold Robbins' Body Parts ☝☝ *Body Parts; Vital Parts* **1999 (R)** An unsurprising formula revenge flick. Ty Kinnick (Grieco) is double-crossed by his best friend (Stewart) and wife (Massey) during a drug deal. Five years later, he's back and finds that the intrigues are still being played out. **87m/C DVD.** Richard Grieco, Will Foster Stewart, Athena Massey; ***D:*** Craig Corman; ***W:*** Craig Corman.

Harper ☝☝☝ *The Moving Target* **1966** A tight, fast-moving genre piece about cynical LA private eye Lew Harper (Newman) who is hired by Mrs. Sampson (Bacall) to investigate the disappearance of her wealthy husband. Along the way he gets involved with an aging actress (Winter), a junkie singer (Harris), a religious nut (Martin), and a smuggling operation. From the Ross McDonald novel "The Moving Target." Later sequelled in "The Drowning Pool." **121m/C VHS, DVD.** Paul Newman, Shelley Winters, Lauren Bacall, Julie Harris, Robert Wagner, Janet Leigh, Arthur Hill, Pamela Tiffin; ***D:*** Jack Smight; ***W:*** William Goldman; ***C:*** Conrad L. Hall; ***M:*** Johnny Mandel.

Harper Valley P.T.A. ☝☝ **1978 (PG)** Eden raises hell in Harper Valley after the PTA questions her parental capabilities. Brain candy was adapted from a hit song; TV series followed. **93m/C VHS, DVD.** Barbara Eden, Nanette Fabray, Louis Nye, Pat Paulsen, Ronny Cox, Ron Masak, Audrey Christie, John Fiedler, Bob Hastings; ***D:*** Richard Bennett; ***W:*** Barry Schneider.

Harrad Experiment ☝ 1/2 **1973 (R)** Adaptation of Robert Rimmer's love-power bestseller in which an experiment-minded college establishes a campus policy of sexual freedom. Famous for the Hedren/Johnson relationship, shortly before Johnson married Hedren's real-life daughter Melanie Griffith. Followed by "The Harrad Summer." **98m/C VHS, DVD.** James Whitmore, Tippi Hedren, Don Johnson, Bruno Kirby, Laurie Walters, Victoria Thompson, Elliot Street, Sharon Taggart, Robert Middleton, Billy (Billie) Sands, Melanie Griffith; ***D:*** Ted Post; ***W:*** Ted Cassedy, Michael Werner; ***C:*** Richard H. Kline; ***M:*** Artie Butler.

Harrad Summer ☝☝ **1974 (R)** Sequel to "The Harrad Experiment." College coeds take their sex-education to the bedroom where they can apply their knowledge by more intensive means. **103m/C VHS.** Angela (Clark) Clarke, Richard Doran, Victoria Thompson, Laurie Walters, Robert Reiser, Bill Dana, Marty Allen; ***D:*** Steven Hilliard Stern.

Harriet Craig ☝☝☝ **1950** Tailor-made Crawford role finds her as seemingly perfect wife Harriet Craig. In reality, she's a domineering shrew, who's also a bully and a clean freak. Harriet squelches husband Walter's (Corey) promotion because it means he'll be travelling abroad, ruins his relationship with best friend Billy (Joslyn), and manages to sabotage her young cousin Clare's (Stevens) romance before anybody stands up to her. Third film adaptation of George Kelly's 1925 play "Craig's Wife." **94m/B VHS.** Joan Crawford, Wendell Corey, Allyn Joslyn, William Bishop, K.T. Stevens, Lucile Watson, Raymond Greenleaf, Ellen Corby; *D:* Vincent Sherman; *W:* James Gunn; *C:* Joseph Walker; *M:* George Duning.

Harriet the Spy 1/2 **1996 (PG)** Sixth-grade, 11-year-old tomboy Harriet M. Welsch (Trachtenberg) spies on everyone around her and, encouraged by her nanny Ole Golly (O'Donnell), writes down everything going on in her secret notebook, because she's determined to become a great writer. Unfortunately, Harriet's imagination sometimes gets the best of her and when her notebook is found, her friends and family are not too happy about its contents. Based on the award-winning novel by Louise Fitzhugh. Lovers of the book may not be enthusiastic about some of the changes but generally it's enjoyable fare. **102m/C VHS, DVD.** Michelle Trachtenberg, Rosie O'Donnell, Vanessa Lee Chester, Gregory Edward Smith, Robert Joy, Eartha Kitt, J. Smith-Cameron; *D:* Bronwen Hughes; *W:* Douglas Petrie, Theresa Rebeck; *C:* Francis Kenny; *M:* Jamshield Sharifi.

Harrison's Flowers **2002 (R)** Sometimes goopy, sometimes harrowing story of a naive woman searching for her missing husband. Newsweek photojournalist Harrison Lloyd (Strathairn) promises wife Sarah (MacDowell) that his '91 assignment to Yugoslavia (at the beginning of the Balkan conflict) will be his last. Maybe in more ways than one, since he's reported missing, which Sarah doesn't believe. So she's takes off for Croatia and promptly gets a hard lesson in the confusion of war. Fellow correspondents Kyle (Brody), Stevenson (Gleeson), and Yeager (Koteas) agree to help Sarah even though they think she's nuts. Watch the guys, particularly Brody, since all MacDowell has to do is alternate between noble, frightened, and stubborn. **122m/C VHS, DVD.** *FR* Andie MacDowell, David Strathairn, Elias Koteas, Adrien Brody, Brendan Gleeson, Alun Armstrong, Caroline Goodall, Diane Baker, Gerard Butler, Marie Trintignant; *D:* Elie Chouraqui; *W:* Elie Chouraqui, Didier Le Pecheur, Isabel Ellsen; *C:* Nicola Pecorini; *M:* Cliff Eidelman.

Harry and Max **2004** Harry (Johnson) is a teenage pretty boy in a pop band, his brother Max (Williams) is a slightly younger pretty boy model. They're jealous of one another, and steal one another's sex partners, one being a quite older adult yoga teacher (Gilroy). While there is never any real sex or nudity on screen, one has to wonder what kind of audience this movie meant to please. Truly awful, in spite of cast's dire attempts to inject some believability into the absurd story. **74m/C DVD.** *US* Bryce Johnson, Cole Williams, Rain Phoenix, Tom Gilroy, Michelle Phillips, Katherine Ellis, Justin Zachery, Roni Deitz; *D:* Christopher Munch; *W:* Christopher Munch; *C:* Rob Sweeney; *M:* Michael Tubbs.

Harry & Son **1984 (PG)** A widowed construction worker faces the problems of raising his son. Newman is miscast as the old man and we've all seen Benson play the young role too many times. **117m/C VHS.** Paul Newman, Robby Benson, Ellen Barkin, Wilford Brimley, Judith Ivey, Ossie Davis, Morgan Freeman, Joanne Woodward; *D:* Paul Newman; *M:* Henry Mancini.

Harry and the Hendersons 1/2 **1987 (PG)** Ordinary American family vacationing in the Northwest has a collision with Bigfoot. Thinking that the big guy is dead, they throw him on top of the car and head home. Lo and behold, he revives and starts wrecking the furniture and in the process, endears himself to the at-first frightened family. Nice little tale efficiently told, with Lithgow fine as the frustrated dad trying to hold his Bigfoot-invaded home together. Basis for the TV series. **111m/C VHS, DVD.** John Lithgow, Melinda Dillon, Don Ameche, David Suchet, Margaret Langrick, Joshua Rudoy, Kevin Peter Hall, Lainie Kazan, M. Emmet Walsh, John Bloom; *D:* William Dear; *W:* William Dear, William E. Martin, Ezra D. Rappaport; *C:* Allen Daviau; *M:* Bruce Broughton. Oscars '87: Makeup.

Harry and Tonto **1974** A gentle comedy about an energetic septuagenarian who takes a cross-country trip with his cat, Tonto. Never in a hurry, still capable of feeling surprise and joy, he makes new friends and visits old lovers. Carney deserved his Oscar. Mazursky has seldom been better. **115m/C VHS, DVD.** Art Carney, Ellen Burstyn, Larry Hagman, Geraldine Fitzgerald, Chief Dan George, Arthur Hunnicutt, Josh Mostel, Cliff DeYoung, Philip Bruns, Rene Enriquez, Herbert Berghof, Michael (Mick) McCleery, Melanie Mayron, Michael C. Butler; ***Cameos:*** Paul Mazursky; *D:* Paul Mazursky; *W:* Paul Mazursky; *C:* Michael C. Butler; *M:* Bill Conti. Oscars '74: Actor (Carney); Golden Globes '75: Actor—Mus./Comedy (Carney).

Harry & Walter Go to New York **1976 (PG)** At the turn of the century, two vaudeville performers are hired by a crooked British entrepreneur for a wild crime scheme. The cast and crew try their hardest, but it's not enough to save this boring comedy. The vaudeville team of Caan and Gould perhaps served as a model for Beatty and Hoffman in "Ishtar." **111m/C VHS, DVD.** James Caan, Elliott Gould, Michael Caine, Diane Keaton, Burt Young, Jack Gilford, Charles Durning, Lesley Ann Warren, Carol Kane; *D:* Mark Rydell; *W:* John Byrum; *M:* David Shire.

Harry Black and the Tiger *Harry Black* **1958** Jungle adventure involving a one-legged hunter and a man-eating tiger. The hunter initally teams up with the old war buddy who cost him his leg. The motivation grows with each failure to catch the beast and to make matters worse, the friend's wife and son are lost somewhere in the perilous jungle. Filmed in India. **107m/C VHS.** *GB* Stewart Granger, Barbara Rush, Anthony Steel; *D:* Hugo Fregonese.

Harry Potter and the Chamber of Secrets 1/2 **2002 (PG)** Action-packed sequel tops its predecessor with less exposition and more adventure as Harry (Radcliffe) and his friends at Hogwarts try to discover the force that's terrorizing the school. In his second year at school, the young (but obviously growing) wizard re-teams with fellow school chums Ron (Grint) and Hermione (Watson) to brave new dangers posed by the Chamber of Secrets, which may lie somewhere in the halls of the school, unbeknownst to professors Rickman, Smith, and even headmaster Harris. Everything about this outing is bigger and better, including a delightfully expanded, labyrinthine Hogwarts. Sometimes over-the-top thrills may be a lot for younger viewers. Book two in Rowling's series. **161m/C VHS, DVD, Blu-ray Disc, HD DVD.** *US* Daniel Radcliffe, Rupert Grint, Emma Watson, Kenneth Branagh, Robbie Coltrane, Richard Harris, Maggie Smith, John Cleese, Jason Isaacs, Tom Felton, Alan Rickman, Warwick Davis, Richard Griffiths, Fiona Shaw, Julie Walters, Shirley Henderson, Mark Williams, Julian Glover, Miriam Margolyes, Christian Coulson, Gemma Jones, David Bradley, Bonnie Wright; *D:* Chris Columbus; *W:* Steve Kloves; *C:* Roger Pratt; *M:* John Williams; *V:* Toby Jones.

Harry Potter and the Goblet of Fire 1/2 **2005 (PG-13)** If you aren't already swept up in the book-turned-film craze created by Rowling, this film might just do it. Harry (Radcliffe) and his trusty pals Ron (Grint) and Hermione (Watson), now teens in their fourth year at Hogwarts, battle the forces of evil that swirl around Harry's mysterious past. Lord Voldemort makes a showing, and new character Mad Eye Moody (Gleeson) joins forces with the good guys to help Harry compete in the frightening and dangerous Tri-Wizard Tournament. Special effects are even better than the previous three films—old fans won't be disappointed; new fans will want to play catch-up. **157m/C DVD, Blu-ray Disc, UMD, HD DVD.** *US* Daniel Radcliffe, Rupert Grint, Emma Watson, Robbie Coltrane, Ralph Fiennes, Michael Gambon, Brendan Gleeson, Jason Isaacs, Gary Oldman, Miranda Richardson, Alan Rickman, Maggie Smith, Timothy Spall, Frances de la Tour, Pedja Bjelac, David Bradley, Warwick Davis, Tom Felton, Robert Hardy, Shirley Henderson, Roger Lloyd-Pack, Mark Williams, Stanislav Ianevski, Robert Pattinson, Clarence Poesy, David Tennant, James Phelps, Oliver Phelps, Bonnie Wright, Katie Leung, Matthew Lewis, Afshan Azad, Shefali Chowhury; *D:* Mike Newell; *W:* Steve Kloves; *C:* Roger Pratt; *M:* Patrick Doyle.

Harry Potter and the Half-Blood Prince 1/2 **2009 (PG)** The sixth Potter adventure lays the groundwork for the final two films (since Rowling's seventh book is being broken down into two parts) with Harry (Radcliffe) accompanying mentor Dumbledore (Gambon) to recruit retired potions professor Horace Slughorn (Broadbent) back to Hogwarts because Dumbledore wants to know how former star pupil Tom Riddle became Voldemort. Meanwhile, reptilian Severus Snape (Rickman) becomes allied with Voldemort recruit Draco Malfoy (Felton). Teen hormones also rage when Harry finds himself interested in his best friend Ron's sister, Ginny (Wright), while Hermione (Watson) pines for an oblivious Ron (Grint), who's dating Lavender Brown (Cave). As usual, Radcliffe gets stuck with the part of the rather dull straight man with a very colorful (and large) crowd surrounding him. **153m/C DVD.** *US* Daniel Radcliffe, Emma Watson, Rupert Grint, Michael Gambon, Alan Rickman, Jim Broadbent, Helena Bonham Carter, Robbie Coltrane, Maggie Smith, David Thewlis, Tom Felton, Bonnie Wright, Julie Walters, Mark Williams, Helen McCrory, Fiona Shaw, Jessie Cave, Richard Griffiths, Timothy Spall, David Bradley, Warwick Davis; *D:* David Yates; *W:* Steve Kloves; *C:* Bruno Delbonnel; *M:* Nicholas Hooper.

Harry Potter and the Order of the Phoenix **2007 (PG-13)** Warner Brothers turned to Yates, their least recognizable director yet, for this fifth chapter of the Potter series and, regrettably, he doesn't bring much to the table. Angsty Potter (Radcliffe) returns to Hogwarts to discover that most of the wizarding world doesn't believe him about the Dark Lord's return, so he begins training his school chums in wizard-on-wizard combat under the nose of Ministry stooge Dolores Umbridge (Staunton). It's all quite dark and moody, but the story is nearly incomprehensible, and Yates bungles most of the sequences that made the book so much fun to read. **139m/C DVD, Blu-ray Disc, HD DVD.** *US* Daniel Radcliffe, Emma Watson, Rupert Grint, Michael Gambon, Alan Rickman, Gary Oldman, Imelda Staunton, Jason Isaacs, Ralph Fiennes, Helena Bonham Carter, David Thewlis, Robbie Coltrane, Fiona Shaw, Maggie Smith, Emma Thompson, Brendan Gleeson, Tom Felton, Katie Leung, Richard Griffiths, Julie Walters, Evanna Lynch, Mark Williams, Bonnie Wright, Warwick Davis, Robert Hardy, David Bradley; *D:* David Yates; *W:* Michael Goldberg; *C:* Slawomir Idziak; *M:* Nicholas Hooper.

Harry Potter and the Prisoner of Azkaban 1/2 **2004 (PG)** Harry's back at Hogwarts, but he's still dealing with evil entities trying to kill him. Sirius Black (Oldman), a rogue wizard and convicted murderer has escaped from Azkaban Prison. Harry also has to deal with the onset of puberty and the trials of being a teenager. Michael Gambon takes over the role of Dumbledore from the late Richard Harris. Cuaron is more faithful to the spirit of the books, driven more by emotion and feeling, and less by the marketing department. Cuaron was author J.K. Rowling's choice to direct the franchise from the start. **141m/C DVD, Blu-ray Disc, HD DVD.** Daniel Radcliffe, Emma Watson, Rupert Grint, Michael Gambon, Gary Oldman, Robbie Coltrane, Alan Rickman, Maggie Smith, Julie Walters, David Thewlis, Tom Felton, Emma Thompson, Julie Christie, Timothy Spall; *D:* Alfonso Cuaron; *W:* Steve Kloves; *C:* Michael Seresin; *M:* John Williams.

Harry Potter and the Sorcerer's Stone *Harry Potter and the Philosopher's Stone* **2001 (PG)** Much-anticipated screen adaptation of J.K. Rowling's first book about a Dickensian orphan who discovers his wizardly legacy, didn't disappoint its legions of built-in fans. Director Columbus remains painstakingly faithful to the book, although film plays, understandably, like a highlights version and sometimes lacks any personality of its own. This may have been intentional (directors Steven Spielberg and Terry Gilliam were perhaps passed over because their personal stamp would override the material), and it doesn't detract from the outstanding production and captivating storytelling. Stellar all-Brit cast is fun to watch, and the special effects are what you'd expect given a $125-million budget and use of no less than nine effects houses. Even those not familiar with the book will enjoy the film's many charms. Good mix of entertainment for kids and adults, although a bit long for the very young. **152m/C VHS, DVD, Blu-ray Disc, UMD, HD DVD.** *US* Daniel Radcliffe, Rupert Grint, Emma Watson, Robbie Coltrane, Richard Harris, Maggie Smith, Zoe Wanamaker, Alan Rickman, Ian Hart, John Hurt, Tom Felton, Harry Melling, Richard Griffiths, Fiona Shaw, John Cleese, Warwick Davis, Julie Walters, Sean Biggerstaff, David Bradley, Matthew Lewis; *D:* Chris Columbus; *W:* Steve Kloves; *C:* John Seale; *M:* John Williams.

Harry Tracy 1/2 *Harry Tracy—Desperado* **1983 (PG)** Whimsical tale of the legendary outlaw whose escapades made him both a wanted criminal and an exalted folk hero. **111m/C VHS, DVD.** *CA* Bruce Dern, Gordon Lightfoot, Helen Shaver, Michael C. Gwynne; *D:* William A. Graham; *C:* Allen Daviau.

Harry's War **1984 (PG)** A middle-class, middle-aged American declares military war on the IRS in this overdone comedy. **98m/C VHS.** Edward Herrmann, Geraldine Page, Karen Grassle, David Ogden Stiers; *D:* Keith Merrill.

Harsh Times **2005 (R)** Bale's truly scary as Jim Davis, a haunted Gulf War vet who drinks and drugs too much, which only exacerbates his natural volatility. Jim also manages to drag best bud, weak-willed Mike (Rodriguez), into his twilight life, which takes a crazy turn when, after being turned down by the LAPD, Jim is offered a job with Homeland Security. But it's in Colombia, which means choosing between work and love with his Mexican honey (Trull). Since writer/director Ayer also wrote "Training Day," you know this isn't going to end well. **119m/C DVD, HD DVD.** *US* Christian Bale, Freddy Rodriguez, Eva Longoria, Terry Crews, Tammy Trull, J.K. Simmons, Noel Guglielmi; *D:* David Ayer; *W:* David Ayer; *C:* Steve Mason; *M:* Graeme Revell.

Hart's War 1/2 **2002 (R)** Willis is leathery Col. McNamara, ranking U.S. POW officer in a German stalag who clashes with newly imprisoned Lt. Thomas Hart (Farrell), Yale law student and son of a U.S. Senator. Hart is recruited to lead a court martial proceeding against African-American prisoner Scott (Howard), accused of killing racist fellow prisoner Bedford (Hauser). McNamara seems to have ulterior motives for this court martial, however, and seems to be undermining Hart at every turn. Howard shines as the accused who doesn't even begin to expect a fair trial, and Iures is brilliant as the urbane, Yankee culture loving German Col. Visser, who also happens to be a Yale alum. Beautiful cinematography helps offset occasional heavy-handed direction and, at times, overwrought plot. **128m/C VHS, DVD, Blu-ray Disc.** *US* Bruce Willis, Colin Farrell, Terrence Howard, Cole Hauser, Marcel Iures, Linus Roache, Rory Cochrane, Michael Weston, Vicellous Shannon, Scott Michael Campbell, Adrian Grenier, Jonathan Brandis, Joe Spano, Sam Worthington; *D:* Gregory Hoblit; *W:* Billy Ray, Terry George; *C:* Alar Kivilo; *M:* Rachel Portman.

Harum Scarum *Harem Holiday* **1965** Elvis tune-fest time! When a movie star (Presley) travels through the Middle East, he becomes involved in an attempted assassination of the king and falls in love with his daughter. He also sings at the drop of a veil: "Shake That Tambourine," "Harem Holiday," and seven others. **95m/C VHS, DVD.** Elvis Presley, Mary Ann Mobley, Fran Jeffries, Michael Ansara, Billy Barty, Theo Marcuse, Jay Novello; *D:* Gene Nelson; *W:* Gerald Drayson Adams; *C:* Fred H. Jackman Jr.; *M:* Fred Karger.

Harvard Man 1/2 **2001 (R)** Dropping a metric ton of acid while getting chased by the Mafia and the FBI: it's all just a day in the life of Harvard student Alan Jensen (Grenier). Meanwhile, the busy scholar/basketball player is also juggling two girlfriends: a mobster's daughter/cheerleader (Gellar), and older philosophy professor (Adams), as well as the throwing of a basketball game. Stoltz and Gayheart play the mobster's bookies with a twist. Inspired by his own '60s acid trip, director Toback's modern coming-of-age comedy is long on mayhem-inspired action and dialogue but short on characters to care about and isn't as fun as it sounds. The all-too-real depiction of a bad trip alone, however, is worth a look. **100m/C VHS, DVD.** *US* Adrian Grenier, Sarah Michelle Gellar, Joey Lauren Adams, Eric Stoltz, Rebecca Gayheart, Gianni Russo, Ray Allen, Michael Aparo, Al Franken; *D:* James Toback; *W:* James Toback; *C:* David Ferrara; *M:* Ryan Shore.

Harvest *Regain* **1937** A classically Pagnolian rural pageant-of-life melodrama, wherein a pair of loners link up together in an abandoned French town and completely revitalize it and the land around it. From the novel by Jean Giono. In French with English subtitles. **128m/B VHS.** *FR* Fernandel, Gabriel Gabrio, Orane Demazis, Edouard Delmont, Henri Poupon; ***D:*** Marcel Pagnol; ***W:*** Marcel Pagnol; ***C:*** Willy; ***M:*** Arthur Honegger. N.Y. Film Critics '39: Foreign Film.

The Harvest ✂✂ 1/2 **1992 (R)** Sultry temptress Leilani sends Miguel's internal thermometer into convulsions with her preference for ice during lovemaking. However, their tryst turns sour (for him) when she takes Miguel to the beach where mystery thugs beat him unconscious and swipe his kidney. Bizarre story sure to ignite a small cult following. **97m/C VHS, DVD.** Miguel Ferrer, Leilani Sarelle Ferrer, Harvey Fierstein, Anthony John (Tony) Denison, Tim Thomerson, Matt Clark, Henry Silva; ***D:*** David Marconi; ***W:*** David Marconi; ***M:*** Dave Allen, Rick Boston.

Harvest ✂✂ *Cash Crop* **1998** Andy (Horneff) is shocked to discover that his seemingly straight-arrow parents (DeMunn and Emery) have held on to the family farm by growing and selling pot. And they're not the only ones, although the local sheriff (Slattery) has been neighborly looking the other way. But trouble arrives with a feisty DEA agent (McCormack). Not very memorable. **96m/C VHS, DVD.** Wil Horneff, Jeffrey DeMunn, John Slattery, Lisa Emery, Mary McCormack, James Van Der Beek, Evan Handler, Frederick Weller; ***D:*** Stuart Burkin; ***W:*** Stuart Burkin, James Biederman, David A. Korn; ***C:*** Oliver Bokelberg.

Harvest Melody ✂✂ **1943** Singing star Gilda Parker travels to farm country for a mere publicity stunt but decides to stay. Corny in more ways than one. ♫You Could Have Knocked Me Over With A Feather; Put It In Reverse; Let's Drive Out To The Drive-In; Tenderly. **70m/B VHS.** Rosemary Lane, Johnny Downs, Sheldon Leonard, Charlotte Wynters, Luis Alberni, Claire Rochelle, Syd Saylor; ***D:*** Sam Newfield.

Harvest of Fire ✂✂ 1/2 **1995 (PG)** A close-knit Amish farming community in Iowa has been the target of a series of barn burnings, which come under the investigation of FBI agent Sally Russell (Davidovich). But the community doesn't want an outsider around and Sally needs some help, which she finds with Amish widow Annie Beiler (Duke). And gradually the disparate duo find some common ground. A Hallmark Hall of Frame presentation. **90m/C VHS.** Patty Duke, Lolita (David) Davidovich, J.A. Preston, Jean (Louisa) Kelly, Tom Aldredge, James Read, Craig Wasson; ***D:*** Arthur Allan Seidelman; ***W:*** Richard Alfieri; ***C:*** Neil Roach; ***M:*** Lee Holdridge. **TV**

Harvey ✂✂✂ 1/2 **1950** Straightforward version of the Mary Chase play about a friendly drunk with an imaginary six-foot rabbit friend named Harvey, and a sister who tries to have him committed. A fondly remembered, charming comedy. Hull is a standout, well deserving her Oscar. **104m/B VHS, DVD.** James Stewart, Josephine Hull, Victoria Horne, Peggy Dow, Cecil Kellaway, Charles Drake, Jesse White, Wallace Ford, Nana Bryant; ***D:*** Henry Koster; ***W:*** Oscar Brodney; ***C:*** William H. Daniels; ***M:*** Frank Skinner. Oscars '50: Support. Actress (Hull); Golden Globes '51: Support. Actress (Hull).

The Harvey Girls ✂✂✂ **1946** Lightweight musical about a restaurant chain that sends its waitresses to work in the Old West. ♫In the Valley Where the Evening Sun Goes Down; Wait and See; On the Atchison, Topeka and Santa Fe; It's a Great Big World; The Wild Wild West. **102m/C VHS, DVD.** Judy Garland, Ray Bolger, John Hodiak, Preston Foster, Angela Lansbury, Virginia O'Brien, Marjorie Main, Chill Wills, Kenny L. Baker, Selena Royle, Cyd Charisse; ***D:*** George Sidney; ***C:*** George J. Folsey; ***M:*** Harry Warren, Johnny Mercer. Oscars '46: Song ("On the Atchison, Topeka and Santa Fe").

The Hasty Heart ✂✂ **1986** A rowdy, terminally ill Scotsman brings problems and friendships to a makeshift war-time hospital built in the jungles of Burma. Remake of 1949 flick with Richard Todd and Ronald Reagan in leading roles. **100m/C VHS.** Gregory Harrison, Cheryl Ladd, Perry King; ***D:*** Martin Speer.

Hat Box Mystery ✂✂ **1947** A detective's secretary is tricked into shooting a woman and private eye Neal is determined to save her from prison. Although not outstanding, it's worth seeing as perhaps the shortest detective film (a mere 44 min.) to ever make it as a feature. **44m/B VHS, DVD.** Tom Neal, Pamela Blake, Allen Jenkins; ***D:*** Lambert Hillyer.

Hatari! ✂✂✂ **1962** An adventure-loving team of professional big game hunters ventures to East Africa to round up animals for zoos around the world. Led by Wayne, they get into a couple of scuffs along the way, including one with lady photographer Martinelli who is doing a story on the expedition. Extraordinary footage of Africa and the animals brought to life by a fantastic musical score. **158m/C VHS, DVD.** John Wayne, Elsa Martinelli, Red Buttons, Hardy Kruger, Gerard Blain, Bruce Cabot; ***D:*** Howard Hawks; ***W:*** Leigh Brackett; ***C:*** Russell Harlan; ***M:*** Henry Mancini.

Hatchet for the Honeymoon ✂ *Blood Brides; Una Hacha para la Luna de Miel; Il Rosso Segmo della Follia; An Axe for the Honeymoon; The Red Sign of Madness* **1970** A rather disturbed young man goes around hacking young brides to death as he tries to find out who murdered his wife. Typical sick Bava horror flick; confusing plot, but strong on vivid imagery. **90m/C VHS, DVD.** *SP IT* Stephen Forsyth, Dagmar Lassander, Laura Betti, Gerard Tichy, Femi Benussi, Alan Collins, Jesus Puente; ***D:*** Mario Bava; ***W:*** Mario Bava, Santiago Moncada, Mario Musy; ***C:*** Mario Bava; ***M:*** Santa Maria Romitelli.

Hate ✂✂✂✂ *La Haine; Hatred* **1995** Twenty-hours in the lives of young, disenfranchised Said (Taghmaoui), Vinz (Cassel), and Hubert (Kounde), who are living in a housing project outside Paris. A riot breaks out, thanks to police brutality of an Arab resident, and Vinz finds a gun the cops lost. A Paris sojourn leads to a police interrogation of Hubert and Said, a fight with some skinheads, a return to their home turf, and an unexpected conclusion. Intelligent look at the idiocy engendered by societal oppression and a buildup of hatred. French with subtitles. **95m/B VHS, DVD.** *FR* Vincent Cassel, Hubert Kounde, Said Taghmaoui, Francois Levantal; ***D:*** Mathieu Kassovitz; ***W:*** Mathieu Kassovitz; ***C:*** Pierre Aim, Georges Diane. Cannes '95: Director (Kassovitz); Cesar '96: Film, Film Editing.

Hate Crime ✂ 1/2 **2005** Overwrought melodrama. Robbie (Peterson) and Trey (Smith) are a contented gay couple whose new neighbor, Chris (Donella), is the homophobic son of a fundamentalist pastor (Davison). Naturally, the neighbors soon clash. When Trey is beaten to death at a local park, Robbie is sure who's guilty, but the cops aren't. **103m/C DVD.** *US* Bruce Davison, Chad E. Donella, Cindy Pickett, Brian J. Smith, Seth Peterson, Susan Blakely, Giancarlo Esposito, Farah White; ***D:*** Tommy Stovall; ***W:*** Tommy Stovall; ***C:*** Ian W. Ellis; ***M:*** Ebony Tay.

The Hatfields & the McCoys ✂✂ **1975** A re-telling of the most famous feud in American history—the legendary mountain war between the Hatfields and the McCoys. **90m/C VHS.** Jack Palance, Steve Forrest, Richard Hatch, Karen Lamm; ***D:*** Clyde Ware. **TV**

Hats Off ✂ **1937** Clarke and Payne star as opposing press agents in this tedious musical. The only bright spot is the finale, which features white-robed girls on a cloud-covered carousel. ♫Where Have You Been All My Life?; Little Old Rhythm; Twinkle, Twinkle, Little Star; Let's Have Another; Zilch's Hats; Hats Off. **65m/B VHS.** Mae Clarke, John Payne, Helen Lynd, Luis Alberni, Richard "Skeets" Gallagher, Franklin Pangborn; ***D:*** Boris L. Petroff.

The Haunted ✂ **1979** The ancient curse of an Indian woman haunts a present day family by possessing the body of a beautiful girl. Through the girl, a horrible vengeance is carried out. **81m/C VHS.** Aldo Ray, Virginia Mayo, Anne Michelle, Jim Negele; ***D:*** Michael de Gaetano.

Haunted ✂✂ 1/2 **1995 (R)** At their Sussex home, David Ash watches helplessly as his younger sister Juliet drowns. Flash-forward to 1925 and the grownup David (Quinn) returns to teach a university course debunking the supernatural. Still, he's drawn to a supposedly haunted mansion, inhabited by artist Robert Mariell (Andrews), his sister Christina (Beckinsale), brother Simon (Lowe), and their elderly nanny (Massey). David starts experiencing visions of his dead sister, while mysterious fires and other unexplained manifestations occur—all of which seem tied to the unholy Mariell trio. Based on a novel by James Herbert. **108m/C VHS, DVD.** *GB* Aidan Quinn, Kate Beckinsale, Anthony Andrews, Alex Lowe, Anna Massey, Geraldine Somerville, Victoria Shalet; ***Cameos:*** John Gielgud; ***D:*** Lewis Gilbert; ***W:*** Lewis Gilbert, Bob Kellett, Tim Prager; ***C:*** Tony Pierce-Roberts; ***M:*** Debbie Wiseman.

Haunted ✂✂ 1/2 **1998** The first production of the play "Turpitude" resulted in a number of mysterious accidents and the opening night death of the star, Kay Taggert. Fifteen years later, producer Sol Brosky wants to take another shot mounting a new production at the original theatre. Problems arise almost immediately and people claim the ghost of Kay Taggart is haunting the play. Parapsychologist Charles Mooreland is called in to discover whether it's a spirit or a corporeal form wreaking havoc. **91m/C VHS.** Peter Tomarken, Suzan Spann, Yvette McClendon; ***D:*** Dennis Devine; ***W:*** Steve Jarvis.

The Haunted Airman ✂ 1/2 **2006 (R)** Clumsy and slow-moving BBC psychodrama loosely based on Dennis Wheatley's novel "The Haunting of Toby Jugg." Wounded and confined to a wheelchair, WWII flight lieutenant Toby Jugg (Pattinson) retreats to a convalescent home in Wales to recuperate. Suffering from terrible hallucinations, Toby comes to believe that his doctor (Sands) is actually trying to drive him crazy. **70m/C DVD.** *GB* Robert Pattinson, Julian Sands, Rachael Stirling, Melissa Lloyd, Scott Handy; ***D:*** Chris Durlacher; ***W:*** Chris Durlacher; ***C:*** Jeff Baynes; ***M:*** Daniel Pemberton. **TV**

The Haunted Castle ✂✂✂ *Schloss Vogelod* **1921** One of Murnau's first films, and a vintage, if crusty, example of German expressionism. A nobleman entertains guests at his country mansion when strange things start to occur. Silent, with English titles. **56m/B VHS.** Arnold Korff, Lulu Keyser-Korff; ***D:*** F.W. Murnau.

Haunted Gold ✂✂ **1932** A young Wayne, in his first Western for Warners, battles gold-hungry desperadoes and a mysterious cloaked phantom. Remake of "The Phantom City." **57m/B VHS, DVD.** John Wayne, Sheila Terry, Harry Woods; ***D:*** Mack V. Wright; ***W:*** Adele Buffington.

Haunted Harbor ✂✂ 1/2 *Pirate's Harbor* **1944** A high-seas financier has been murderd by a crooked crony and Captain Jim Marsden's alibi is all wet. He's got to find the gold, the girl, and avoid the goons. Part of "The Cliffhanger Serials" series. **243m/B VHS.** Kane Richmond, Kay Aldridge, Roy Barcroft.

Haunted Highway ✂ *Death Ride* **2005** Photographer Greg (Gamble) has an affair with his model, Yumi (Yoshikawa), which his wife, Amanda (Putney), finds out about. Greg accidentally kills Amanda during an argument and puts her body in his car trunk for disposal in a remote location. Then Amanda starts to haunt him. Dumb rather than scary. **83m/C DVD.** *US* Rand Gamble, Hinano Yoshikawa, Laura Putney; ***D:*** Junichi Suzuki; ***W:*** Junichi Suzuki; ***C:*** Takuro Ishizaka. **VIDEO**

Haunted Honeymoon ✂ **1986 (PG)** Arthritic comedy about a haunted house and a couple trapped there. Sad times for the Mel Brooks alumni participating in this lame horror spoof. **82m/C VHS, DVD.** Gene Wilder, Gilda Radner, Dom DeLuise, Jonathan Pryce, Paul Smith, Peter Vaughan, Bryan Pringle, Roger Ashton-Griffiths, Jim Carter, Eve Ferret; ***D:*** Gene Wilder; ***W:*** Terence Marsh, Gene Wilder; ***C:*** Fred Schuler.

The Haunted Mansion ✂ 1/2 **2003 (PG)** Inspired by the popular Disney ride of the same name. Jim Evers (Murphy) is a workaholic real estate agent who takes his family along to see a mansion whose owner wants to sell. They soon find out that the mansion is inhabited with ghosts, lots of them. Coincidentally enough, it turns out that Evers's wife Sara (Thomason) bears a striking resemblance to the owner's long dead lover, who had committed suicide. So why wouldn't they want to live there? While the production design of the mansion is quite impressive, it still doesn't make up for the lack of an original story or dialogue. Murphy's comedic talent is largely wasted. Skip the movie, go for the ride. **99m/C VHS, DVD, Blu-ray Disc.** *US* Eddie Murphy, Marsha Thomason, Terence Stamp, Wallace Shawn, Jennifer Tilly, Nathaniel Parker, Marc John Jeffries, Aree Davis, Dina Spybey; ***D:*** Rob Minkoff; ***W:*** David Barenbaum; ***C:*** Remi Adefarasin; ***M:*** Mark Mancina.

The Haunted Palace ✂✂ 1/2 **1963** Price plays both a 17th-century warlock burned at the stake and a descendant who returns to the family dungeon and gets possessed by the mutant-breeding forebearer. The movie has its own identity crisis, with title and ambience from Poe but story from H.P. Lovecraft's "The Case of Charles Dexter Ward." Respectable but rootless chills. **87m/C VHS, DVD.** Vincent Price, Debra Paget, Lon Chaney Jr., Frank Maxwell, Leo Gordon, Elisha Cook Jr., John Dierkes, Barboura Morris, Bruno VeSota; ***D:*** Roger Corman; ***W:*** Charles Beaumont, Floyd Crosby; ***M:*** Ronald Stein.

Haunted Ranch ✂ 1/2 **1943** Reno Red has been murdered and a shipment of gold bullion is missing. A gang on the lookout for the gold tries to convince people that Red's ranch is haunted by his ghost. **56m/B VHS, DVD.** John "Dusty" King, David Sharpe, Max Terhune, Rex Lease, Julie Duncan; ***D:*** Robert Emmett Tansey.

The Haunted Sea ✂✂ **1997 (R)** The crew of the Patna discovered an abandoned ship that's filled with Aztec treasure. But when the Patna's crew members begin disappearing, those remaining must discover what's guarding the treasure. **74m/C VHS.** James Brolin, Joanna Pacula, Krista Allen, Don Stroud; ***D:*** Dan Golden; ***C:*** John Aronson; ***M:*** David Wurst, Eric Wurst.

The Haunted Strangler ✂✂ 1/2 *The Grip of the Strangler* **1958** Boris Karloff is a writer investigating a 20-year-old murder who begins copying some of the killer's acts. **78m/B VHS, DVD.** *GB* Boris Karloff, Anthony Dawson, Elizabeth Allan, Timothy Turner, Diane Aubrey, Dorothy Gordon, Jean Kent, Vera Day; ***D:*** Robert Day; ***W:*** John C. Cooper, Jan Read; ***C:*** Lionel Banes; ***M:*** Buxton Orr.

Haunted Summer ✂✂ **1988 (R)** Soft-focus, sex-and-drugs period piece of the bacchanalian summer of 1816 spent by free spirits Lord Byron, Percy Shelley, Mary Shelley, and John Polidori and others that led Mary Shelley to write "Frankenstein." Based on the novel of the same name by Anne Edwards. **106m/C VHS.** Alice Krige, Eric Stoltz, Philip Anglim, Laura Dern, Alex Winter; ***D:*** Ivan Passer; ***W:*** Lewis John Carlino.

Haunted Symphony ✂✂ *Blood Song; Last Resurrection; Hellfire* **1994 (R)** In the 18th century, a deranged composer (Wert) is discovered creating a symphony for the devil and killed by a mob. Years later, his niece Gabrielle (Burns) discovers the unfinished symphony hidden in an old piano and hires choir master Marius (Cross) to complete the score. But when he tries, demonic things begin to occur. **85m/C VHS.** Jennifer Burns, Ben Cross, Doug Wert, Beverly Garland; ***D:*** David Tausik; ***W:*** Beverly Gray, David Hartwell.

Haunted: The Ferryman ✂✂ **1974** Adapted by Julian Bond from a Kingsley Amis story, the film deals with a novelist who is mysteriously confronted with various events and macabre set-pieces from his own novel, including a dead ferryman rising from the grave. **50m/C VHS.** *GB* Jeremy Brett, Natasha Parry, Lesley Dunlop; ***D:*** John Irvin.

HauntedWeen ✂ 1/2 **1991** All trick, no treat, as a guy nailed by a frat house prank 20 years ago comes-back-for-revenge. **88m/C VHS.** Brien Blakely, Blake Pickett, Brad Hanks, Bart White, Leslee Lacey, Ethan Adler; ***D:*** Doug Robertson.

The Haunting ✂✂✂ 1/2 **1963** A subtle, bloodless horror film about a weekend spent in a monstrously haunted mansion by a parapsychologist (Johnson), the mansion's skeptic heir (Tamblyn), and two mediums (Harris and Bloom). A chilling adaptation of Shirley

Jackson's "The Haunting of Hill House," in which the psychology of the heroine is forever in question. There's a silly 1999 remake that's all special effects and no scares. **113m/B VHS, DVD.** *GB* Julie Harris, Claire Bloom, Russ Tamblyn, Richard Johnson, Fay Compton, Rosalie Crutchley, Lois Maxwell, Valentine Dyall, Diane Clare; ***D:*** Robert Wise; ***W:*** Nelson Gidding; ***C:*** Davis Boulton; ***M:*** Humphrey Searle.

The Haunting ½ *The Haunting of Hill House* **1999 (PG-13)** Tiny Lili Taylor gets to play avenging angel with an assortment of ghosties and ghoulies in this silly would-be frightener based on the novel by Shirley Jackson and originally filmed in 1963. Dr. Marrow (Neeson) enlists three subjects to stay at Hill House for a study in insomnia that's (unknown to them) actually a study in fear response. There's brash Theo (Zeta-Jones), dopey Luke (Wilson), and fragile Nell (Taylor), who turns out to have unexpected ties to the haunted mansion. Big-budget doesn't make for big frights, just big, mocking laughter from the audience—certainly not what director De Bont must have intended. Dern appears briefly as the scruffy caretaker, with Seldes his Mrs. Danvers-like wife. **114m/C VHS, DVD.** Lili Taylor, Liam Neeson, Catherine Zeta-Jones, Owen Wilson, Bruce Dern, Marian Seldes, Virginia Madsen, Todd Field, Alix Koromzay; ***D:*** Jan De Bont; ***W:*** David Self; ***C:*** Caleb Deschanel; ***M:*** Jerry Goldsmith.

Haunting Fear **1991** Poe's "The Premature Burial" inspired this pale cheapie about a wife with a fear of early interment. After lengthy nightmares and graphic sex, her greedy husband uses her phobia in a murder plot. **88m/C VHS, DVD.** Jan-Michael Vincent, Karen Black, Brinke Stevens, Michael Berryman; ***D:*** Fred Olen Ray; ***W:*** Sherman Scott.

The Haunting in Connecticut **2009 (PG-13)** Strange things are afoot in a spooky old house a family moves into while their son is being treated for cancer at a nearby clinic. The house has a past as a funeral home, and thanks to a clairvoyant previous occupant, a supposed way station for demons and other unsavory supernatural types. Little more than the typical haunted house-ghost story, despite being supposedly based on actual events (wasn't the same said about "The Blair Witch Project?"). More creepy than scary, pic is completely unoriginal and its scare tactics rely heavily on standard horror cliches as well as computer-generated special effects. A waste of Madsen's talent, as she sleepwalks through the overwrought script. **102m/C DVD.** Virginia Madsen, Kyle Gallner, Elias Koteas, Amanda Crew, Martin Donovan, Ty Wood, Adam Simon, Tim Metcalfe, Sophi Knight, Erik J. Berg, John Bluethner; ***D:*** Peter Cornwell; ***C:*** Adam Swica; ***M:*** Robert Kral.

Haunting of Harrington House **1982** Tame teenage haunted house film. **50m/C VHS.** Dominique Dunne, Roscoe Lee Browne, Edie Adams, Phil Leeds; ***D:*** Murray Golden. **TV**

The Haunting of Hell House *Henry James' The Ghostly Rental; The Ghostly Rental* **1999 (R)** Remember when Hammer Studios made all those horror movies based on Edgar Allan Poe stories and they were a lot of campy fun (if not truly creepy)? Well, that's what this Victorian Gothic wants to (or should) be and isn't. Tormented James (Bowen) took his girlfriend to an abortionist and she died. James seeks advice from the mysterious Professor Ambrose (York), whose family past is also filled with tragedy. **90m/C VHS, DVD.** Andrew Bowen, Michael York, Claudia Christian, Aideen O'Donnell; ***D:*** Mitch Marcus; ***W:*** Mitch Marcus, L.L. Shapira; ***C:*** Russ Brandt; ***M:*** Ivan Koutikov.

The Haunting of Marsten Manor ½ **2007 (PG)** Low-budget horror with a faith-based message. Jill (who's blind) travels with friends to the creepy mansion she inherited from a missing aunt. Dark secrets are revealed by a ghostly soldier though her friends think Jill is imagining things. **81m/C DVD.** C. Thomas Howell, Brianne Davis, Ezra Buzzington, Ken Luckey, Janice Knickrehm, Julie Sapp; ***D:*** David Sapp; ***W:*** Julie Sapp, David Sapp; ***C:*** David Sapp; ***M:*** Julie Sapp. **VIDEO**

The Haunting of Molly Hartley **2008 (PG-13)** Misfit Molly Hartley (Bennett) has trouble adapting to her new life at a private school. As if the constant nosebleeds, headaches, and mysterious voices aren't bad enough, she's haunted by the fact that her mother's in a mental institution. As her eighteen birthday approaches, Molly begins to realize the horrible truth behind her ailments. A weak teen horror flick, knocked out quickly and cheaply in time for Halloween. The entire cast, along with first-time director Liddell (a longtime TV producer), should stick to the small screen. **86m/C DVD.** *US* Haley Bennett, Chace Crawford, Shannon Marie Woodward, Nina Siemaszko, Jessica Lowndes, Marin Hinkle, Jake Weber, AnnaLynne McCord, Shanna Collins, Ron Canada, Kevin Cooney; ***D:*** Mickey Liddell; ***W:*** John Travis, Rebecca Sonnenshine; ***C:*** Sharon Meir; ***M:*** James T. Sale.

The Haunting of Morella **1991 (R)** Poe-inspired cheapjack exploitation about a an executed witch living again in the nubile body of her teen daughter. Ritual murders result, in between lesbian baths and nude swims. Producer Roger Corman did the same story with more class and less skin in his earlier anthology "Tales of Terror." **82m/C VHS, DVD.** David McCallum, Nicole Eggert, Maria Ford, Lana Clarkson; ***D:*** Jim Wynorski; ***W:*** Jim Wynorski, R.J. Robertson.

Haunting of Sarah Hardy **1989** Ward, as a recently wed heiress, returns to the scene of her unhappy childhood home. In a standard plot, Ward is torn between an apparent haunting and the question of her own sanity. TV film is redeemed by the creditable acting. **92m/C VHS.** Sela Ward, Michael Woods, Roscoe Born, Polly Bergen, Morgan Fairchild; ***D:*** Jerry London; ***C:*** Bojan Bazelli. **TV**

The Haunting of Seacliff Inn ½ **1994 (PG-13)** Susan and Mark Enright struggle to start a bed-and-breakfast in their newly acquired Mendocino Victorian manse. But psychic Susie senses something—seems the former owner died violently, and, a hundred years ago, an owner was accused of murdering his wife in the house. Not-too-frightening ghost story but good cast work. **94m/C VHS.** Ally Sheedy, William R. Moses, Louise Fletcher, Lucinda Weist, Maxine Stuart, Tom McCleister, James Horan; ***D:*** Walter Klenhard; ***W:*** Walter Klenhard, Tom Walla. **CABLE**

The Haunting Passion ½ **1983** Newlywed Seymour moves into a haunted house only to be seduced by the ghost of the former occupant's dead lover. Effective and erotic presentation. **100m/C VHS, DVD.** Jane Seymour, Gerald McRaney, Millie Perkins, Ruth Nelson, Paul Rossilli, Ivan Bonar; ***D:*** John Korty. **TV**

Haunts ½ *The Veil* **1977 (PG)** Tormented woman has difficulty distinguishing between fantasy and reality after a series of brutal slayings lead police to the stunning conclusion that dead people have been committing the crimes. **97m/C VHS.** Cameron Mitchell, Aldo Ray, May Britt, William Gray Espy, Susan Nohr; ***D:*** Herb Freed; ***M:*** Pino Donaggio.

Haunts of the Very Rich ½ **1972** A loose remake of "Outward Bound" in which a group of spoiled people on a vacation find themselves spiritually dead. Made for TV. **72m/C VHS.** Lloyd Bridges, Anne Francis, Donna Mills, Tony Bill, Robert Reed, Moses Gunn, Cloris Leachman, Ed Asner; ***D:*** Paul Wendkos. **TV**

Hav Plenty **1997 (R)** Moving in the circles of young black professionals, Lee Plenty (Cherot) is an unemployed would-be writer who doesn't seem to care too much about getting a job. The materialistic and ambitious Havilland (Maxwell),a friend of his from college, invites him to a New Year's Eve party when she finds that her fiance Michael (Harper) is playing around on her. The sedate holiday weekend turns into a frenzy of surprises, as Lee is chased by Hav's hairdo-happy friend Caroline (Jones) and newlywed sister Leigh (Lee). Screwball romantic comedy comes off as a hybrid of Spike Lee and Woody Allen, with writer/director/editor Cherot's own personal touches thrown in. Performances are excellent, especially Cherot himself, who only starred when the actor hired to play his part bowed out as filming started. **87m/C VHS, DVD.** Christopher Scott Cherot, Chenoa Maxwell, Hill Harper, Tammi Katherine Jones, Robine Lee, Betty Vaughn, Reginald James, Kenneth "Babyface" Edmonds; ***D:*** Christopher Scott Cherot; ***W:*** Christopher Scott Cherot; ***C:*** Kerwin Devonish; ***M:*** Wendy Melvoin, Lisa Coleman.

Havana ½ **1990 (R)** During the waning days of the Batista regime, a gambler travels to Havana in search of big winnings. Instead, he meets the beautiful wife of a communist revolutionary. Unable to resist their mutual physical attraction, the lovers become drawn into a destiny which is far greater than themselves. Reminiscent of "Casablanca." **145m/C VHS, DVD.** Robert Redford, Lena Olin, Alan Arkin, Raul Julia, Tomas Milian, Tony Plana, Betsy Brantley, Lise Cutter, Richard Farnsworth, Mark Rydell, Daniel Davis; ***D:*** Sydney Pollack; ***W:*** Judith Rascoe, David Rayfiel; ***C:*** Owen Roizman; ***M:*** Dave Grusin.

Havana Widows **1933** Gold-digging chorus girls Mae (Blondell) and Sadie (Farrell) squeeze some money out of Herman Brody (Jenkins) and take off for Havana on a mission to bilk money from the millionaires there. They pose as wealthy widows and have their sights set on Deacon Jones (Kibbee), when their whole plot goes to pot as Brody suddenly shows up. Plus, Mae finds herself attracted to Deacon's son Bob-only he's broke. **62m/B VHS.** Joan Blondell, Glenda Farrell, Guy Kibbee, Allen Jenkins, Lyle Talbot, Frank McHugh; ***D:*** Ray Enright; ***W:*** Earl Baldwin.

Have No Fear: The Life of Pope John Paul II **2005** Cut-and-dried made-for-TV bio is told in flashback after the Pontiff (Kretschmann) begins to review his life after a pilgrimage to Jerusalem in 2000. He reflects on growing up as Karol Wojtyla in Nazi-occupied Poland and his journey from entering the clergy, up the priestly ladder to his elevation to Pope John Paul II. **87m/C DVD.** Thomas Kretschmann, Bruno Ganz, John Albasiny, Charles Kay, Joaquim DeAlmeida, Sabrino Javor; ***D:*** Jeff Bleckner; ***W:*** Michael Hirst, Judd Parkin; ***C:*** Roberto Benvenuti; ***M:*** Carlo Siliotto. **TV**

Have Rocket Will Travel ½ **1959** Three janitors (guess who) help a scientist who is about to lose her job if she can't send a rocket to Venus. They accidently initiate the launch while still on board and introduce their brand of slapstick to a whole new planet. First of the late '50s-early '60s feature films to capitalize on the renewed popularity of the Three Stooges. **76m/B VHS.** Moe Howard, Larry Fine, Joe DeRita, Anna-Lisa, Jerome Cowan, Bob Colbert; ***D:*** David Lowell Rich; ***W:*** Raphael Hayes.

Have Sword, Will Travel ½ *Bao Biao; Bo biu; The Bodyguard* **1969** The leader of a caravan guarding service has fallen so ill he cannot protect the yearly caravan of silver sent to the capitol, and so entrusts the job to two young fighters in his service. They are joined by a down-on-his-luck warrior and the three quickly form a romantic triangle (one of them is a woman). Eventually bandits get the silver, and the chase is on. **103m/C DVD.** *HK* Ching Lee, Lung Ti, David Chiang, Miao Ching, Feng Ku, Chung Wang; ***D:*** Cheh Chang; ***W:*** Kuang Ni; ***C:*** Kung Mo To; ***M:*** Fu-ling Wang.

Haven ½ **2004 (R)** Overly-complicated story begins with corrupt businessman Carl Ridley (Paxton) taking his daughter Pippa (Bruckner) and getting out of Miami with a suitcase full of cash just ahead of the feds. Ridley goes to the Caymans, hoping to arrange something with his double-dealing attorney Allan (Dillane). Meanwhile, dock worker Shy (Bloom) makes the mistake of romancing wealthy Andrea (Saldana), greatly upsetting her violent brother Hammer (Mackie). A local crime boss (Adoti) is clued into Ridley's money, Pippa hooks up with the wrong crowd, and things just get more confusing. **98m/C DVD.** *US GB GE SP* Orlando Bloom, Agnes Bruckner, Bill Paxton, Zoe Saldana, Anthony Mackie, Bobby Cannavale, Stephen (Dillon) Dillane, Victor Rasuk, Raz Adoti, Robert Wisdom; ***D:*** Frank E. Flowers; ***W:*** Frank E. Flowers; ***C:*** Michael Bernard; ***M:*** Hector Pereira.

Having a Wonderful Time **1938** City girl secretary Teddy (Rogers) heads to the country for some R&R, staying at a holiday camp for singles. She meets Chick (Fairbanks Jr.), who's working as a waiter to put himself through law school, and they insult each other before finding romance. Kober had to tone down the 'Jewish' elements of his play (which was originally set at a Catskills resort) to make it palatable for Hollywood. **71m/B DVD.** Ginger Rogers, Douglas Fairbanks Jr., Peggy Conklin, Lucille Ball, Eve Arden, Lee Bowman, Red Skelton, Donald Meek, Jack Carson; ***D:*** Alfred Santell; ***W:*** Arthur Kober; ***C:*** Robert De Grasse.

Having It All **1982** A wry comedy about a love triangle. Dyan Cannon stars as a successful business woman with a husband on each coast, who finds dividing her time is more than she bargained for. **100m/C VHS.** Dyan Cannon, Barry Newman, Hart Bochner, Melanie Chartoff, Sylvia Sidney; ***D:*** Edward Zwick; ***M:*** Miles Goodman. **TV**

Having Our Say: The Delany Sisters' First 100 Years ½ **1999** Based on the book and the Broadway play that looks at life through the aging eyes of the black Delany sisters: 103-year-old Sadie (Carroll) and 101-year-old Bessie (Dee). They share their experiences with New York Times reporter Amy Hill Hearth (Madigan), who has come to interview them in 1991. Their father was born a slave but all 12 of the Delany children graduated from college, with Bessie becoming a teacher and Sadie a dentist in Harlem. (The real Bessie died in 1995 and Sadie in 1999.) **90m/C VHS.** Diahann Carroll, Ruby Dee, Mykelti Williamson, Lonette McKee, Lisa Arrindell Anderson, Audra McDonald, Richard Roundtree, Della Reese; ***D:*** Lynne Littman; ***W:*** Emily Mann; ***C:*** Frank Byers. **TV**

Having Wonderful Crime ½ **1945** Madcap comedy-thriller about a newly married couple who combine sleuthing with a honeymoon. With their criminal lawyer friend along, the trio winds up searching for a magician who has vanished. Fast-paced action and quick dialogue. **70m/B VHS.** Pat O'Brien, George Murphy, Carole Landis, Lenore Aubert, George Zucco, Gloria Holden, Richard Martin, Blanche Ring, Charles D. Brown; ***D:*** Edward Sutherland; ***W:*** Howard J. Green; ***C:*** Frank Redman; ***M:*** Leigh Harline.

Having Wonderful Time ½ **1938** A young girl tries to find culture and romance on her summer vacation at a resort in the Catskills. Film debut of comic Red Skelton, who wasn't always as old as the hills. Based on a Broadway hit by Arthur Kober. **71m/B VHS, DVD.** Ginger Rogers, Lucille Ball, Eve Arden, Red Skelton, Douglas Fairbanks Jr.; ***D:*** Alfred Santell.

Havoc 2: Normal Adolescent Behavior *Normal Adolescent Behavior* **2007 (R)** It's kinda scary to think that this is a realistic portrait of modern teen life. Six teens, who have known each other since kindergarten, have decided to have sexual relationships only with each other at their Saturday night parties. But Wendy (Tamblyn) falls for her new neighbor Sean (Holmes) and wants to change the rules, leaving clique leader Billie (Garner) very unhappy. **93m/C DVD.** Amber Tamblyn, Ashton Holmes, Kelli Garner, Raviv (Ricky) Ullman, Stephen Colletti, Hilarie Burton, Daryl Sabara, Kelly Lynch, Julia Garro, Edward Tournier; ***D:*** Beth Schacter; ***W:*** Beth Schacter; ***C:*** Harlan Bosmajian; ***M:*** Craig DeLeon.

Hawaii **1966** James Michener's novel about a New England farm boy who decides in 1820 that the Lord has commanded him to the island of Hawaii for the purpose of "Christianizing" the natives. Filmed on location. Also available in a 181 minute version with restored footage. Available in director's cut version with an additional 20 minutes. **161m/C VHS, DVD.** Max von Sydow, Julie Andrews, Richard Harris, Carroll O'Connor, Bette Midler, Gene Hackman, Jocelyn Lagarde; ***D:*** George Roy Hill; ***W:*** Daniel Taradash, Dalton Trumbo; ***M:*** Elmer Bernstein. Golden Globes '67: Support. Actress (Lagarde), Score.

Hawaii Calls **1938** Two young stowaways on a cruise ship are allowed to stay on after one of them (Breen) struts his stuff as a singer. The two then turn sleuth to catch a gang of spies. More ham than a can of Spam, but still enjoyable. ♫That's The Hawaiian In Me; Hawaii Calls; Down Where The Trade Winds Blow; Macushia; Aloha Oe.

72m/B VHS. Bobby Breen, Ned Sparks, Irvin S. Cobb, Warren Hull, Gloria Holden, Pua Lani, Raymond Paige, Philip Ahn, Ward Bond; *D:* Edward F. (Eddie) Cline.

Hawaiian Buckaroo 1938 A couple of cowboys fight to save their pineapple plantation from a sneaky foreman. **62m/B VHS.** Smith Ballew, Evalyn Knapp, Benny Burt, Harry Woods, Pat J. O'Brien; *D:* Ray Taylor.

The Hawk 1/2 **1993 (R)** Okay thriller about suburban housewife Annie (Mirren) who suspects that her husband Stephen (Costigan) is a serial killer known as the Hawk. Since Annie has a history of depression and her husband is a known louse, her suspicions are dismissed as delusional. Some surprise twists help the weak story along. Contains some graphic views of corpses. Based on the novel by Ransley. **84m/C VHS, DVD.** *GB* Helen Mirren, George Costigan, Owen Teale, Rosemary Leach; *D:* David Hayman; *W:* Peter Ransley; *M:* Nick Bicat.

Hawk and Castile *The Hawk of Castile* **1967** Bandits murder, pillage, and terrorize the nobility in Medieval Europe until the Hawk comes onto the scene. **95m/C VHS.** *SP* Alvaro de Luna, Julio Perez Tabernero, Nuria Torray, German Cobos, Felix Defauce, Mari Real; *D:* Jose Maria Elorrieta; *W:* Jose Maria Elorrieta; *C:* Alfonso Nieva; *M:* Fernando Garcia Morcillo.

The Hawk Is Dying 1/2 **2006** And so's the flick. Gloomy George Gattling (Giamatti) is stuck in a boring life, helping his sister (Schwimmer) with her autistic son, Fred (Pitt). When tragedy strikes, George becomes obsessed with catching and taming a wild red-tail hawk, seeking to control something in his life, no matter the cost or consequences. Williams shows up occasionally as a stoner co-ed willing to boff George. Based on the novel by Harry Crews. **106m/C DVD.** Paul Giamatti, Michelle Williams, Michael Pitt, Robert Wisdom, Rusty Schwimmer, Ann Wedgeworth; *D:* Julian Goldberger; *W:* Julian Goldberger; *C:* Bobby Bukowski; *M:* Julian Goldberger.

The Hawk of Powder River 1948 Cheapie western has Dean getting involved with a beautiful outlaw gang leader with a murderous streak. A large part of this film was lifted from earlier Dean oaters, as are all the tunes. **54m/B VHS, DVD.** Eddie Dean, Roscoe Ates, Jennifer Holt, June Carlson, Terry Frost, Lane Bradford; *D:* Ray Taylor.

Hawk of the Wilderness *Lost Island of Kioga* **1938** A man, shipwrecked as an infant and reared on a remote island by native Indians, battles modern day pirates after an explorer finds a cache of treasure. Serial in 12 episodes. **213m/B VHS.** Bruce Bennett, Mala, William Boyle; *D:* William Witney.

Hawk the Slayer 1/2 **1981** A comic book fantasy. A good warrior struggles against his villainous brother to possess a magical sword that bestows upon its holder great powers of destruction. Violent battle scenes; Palance makes a great villain. **93m/C VHS, DVD.** Jack Palance, John Terry, Harry Andrews, Roy Kinnear, Ferdinand "Ferdy" Mayne, William Morgan Sheppard; *D:* Terry Marcel.

Hawken's Breed **1987 (R)** Drifter meets American Indian beauty and hears her tale of woe; the two fall for each other and set out together to avenge the murder of the woman's husband and son. Nothing much to crow about. **93m/C VHS.** Peter Fonda, Serene Hedin, Jack Elam; *D:* Charles B. Pierce.

Hawkeye 1/2 **1988** After his best friend is murdered by gangsters in a seedy drug deal, Hawkeye, a rough and tumble Texas cop, and his slick new partner hit the streets of Las Vegas with a vengeance. **90m/C VHS.** Troy Donahue, Chuck Jeffreys, George Chung, Stan Wertlieb; *D:* Leo Fong.

Hawks 1/2 **1989 (R)** Somewhere on the road to black-comedy this film gets waylaid by triviality. Two terminally ill men break out of the hospital, determined to make their way to Amsterdam for some last-minute fun. Mediocre at best. **105m/C VHS.** *GB* Anthony Edwards, Timothy Dalton, Janet McTeer, Jill Bennett, Sheila Hancock, Connie Booth, Camille Coduri; *D:* Robert Ellis Miller; *W:* Roy Clarke; *C:* Doug Milsome.

The Hawks & the Sparrows *Uccellacci e Uccellini* **1967** Shortly after "Mr. Ed" came Pasolini's garrulous crow, which follows a father and son's travels through Italy spouting pithy bits of politics. A comic Pasolinian allegory-fest full of then-topical political allusions, the story comes off a bit wooden. Worth watching to see Toto, the Italian comic, in his element. **91m/B VHS, DVD.** *IT* Toto, Ninetto Davoli, Femi Benussi; *D:* Pier Paolo Pasolini; *W:* Pier Paolo Pasolini; *M:* Ennio Morricone.

Hawk's Vengeance **1996 (R)** While investigating his police detective stepbrother's murder British Royal Marine Lt. Eric "Hawk" Kelly (Daniels) discovers a bizarre connection between a skinhead gang called the Death Skulls, a martial arts master crime boss (Magda), and the black market organ trade. Hard to believe this was based on a real life incident. **96m/C VHS, DVD.** Jayne Heitmeyer, Vlasta Vrana, Gary Daniels, Cass Magda; *D:* Marc Voizard; *W:* Jim Cirile; *C:* John Berrie; *M:* Eleanor Academia.

Hawmps! WOOF! **1976 (G)** Idiotic comedy about a Civil War lieutenant who trains his men to use camels. When the soldiers and animals begin to grow fond of each other, Congress orders the camels to be set free. Hard to believe this was based on a real life incident. **98m/C VHS.** James Hampton, Christopher Connelly, Slim Pickens, Denver Pyle; *D:* Joe Camp; *W:* William Bickley; *M:* Euel Box.

Hawthorne of the USA 1/2 **1919** Reid stars as Anthony Hamilton Hawthorne, American extraordinaire. After gambling a fortune away in Monte Carlo, Hawthorne heads to mainland Europe for rest and revelry. Instead, he finds the love of a princess and a Communist coup in the making. Silent with orchestral score. **55m/B VHS.** Wallace Reid, Harrison Ford, Lila Lee, Tully Marshall; *D:* James Cruze.

Haxan: Witchcraft through the Ages *Haxan; Witchcraft through the Ages* **1922** The demonic Swedish masterpiece in which witches and victims suffer against various historical backgrounds. Nightmarish and profane, especially the appearance of the Devil as played under much make-up by Christiansen himself. Silent. **74m/B VHS, DVD.** *SW* Maren Pedersen, Clara Pontoppidan, Oscar Stribolt, Benjamin Christiansen, Tora Teje, Elith Pio, Karen Winther, Emmy Schonfeld, John Andersen, Astrid Holm, Gerda Madsen; *D:* Benjamin Christiansen; *W:* Benjamin Christiansen; *C:* Johan Ankerstjerne; *Nar:* William S. Burroughs.

Haywire 1/2 **1980** Based on Brooke Hayward's Hollywood memoir about her dysfunctional family—actress mother Margaret Sullavan (Remick) and producer/agent father Leland Hayward (Robards). Despite her professional success, Sullavan desperately wanted to achieve the perfect family life while Hayward was wayward and the two would divorce with their three children caught up in their parents' career and marital troubles. Told in flashback, after Sullavan commits suicide in 1960. **184m/C DVD.** Lee Remick, Jason Robards Jr., Deborah Raffin, Dianne Hull, Hart Bochner, Linda Gray; *D:* Michael Tuchner; *W:* Ivan Davis; *C:* Howard Schwartz; *M:* Billy Goldenberg. **TV**

Hazel's People 1/2 *Happy as the Grass Was Green* **1973 (G)** Bitter and hostile college student attends his friend's funeral in Mennonite country. He discovers not only a way of life he never knew existed, but a personal faith in a living Christ. From the Merle Good novel, "Happy as the Grass Was Green." **105m/C VHS.** Geraldine Page, Pat Hingle, Graham Beckel, Rachel Thomas; *D:* Charles Davis; *W:* Charles Davis; *C:* Stan Martin; *M:* Gordon Zahler.

The Hazing 1/2 *Dead Scared* **2004** A demon is set loose at a campus mansion where college frat students spend a grisly initiation evening possessed by the wicked dude. **87m/C VHS, DVD.** Brad Dourif, Tiffany Shepis, Parry Shen, David Tom, Robert Donovan, Philip Andrew, Jeremy Maxwell, Nectar Rose, Charmaine DeGrate, Brooke Burke, Jeff LeBeau; *Cameos:* Robert Donovan; *D:* Rolfe Kanefsky; *W:* Rolfe Kanefsky; *M:* Chris Farrell. **VIDEO**

He Died With a Felafel in His Hand **2001** Ya gotta love the title—if nothing else about this adaptation of John Birmingham's seriocomic 1994 novel. Three distinct Australian cities play their part: subtropical Brisbane inspires indolence and wacky sunstruck behavior; cool Melbourne fosters navel-gazing and an overly-ernest dedication to causes; and seaside Sydney is dedicated to hedonism. Wannabe Brisbane writer Danny (Taylor) is looking for some kind of purpose in life and turns to friend Sam (Hamilton) for advice. The duo wind up in Melbourne after Sam's breakup with gal pal Anya (Bohringer) and finally make their way to Sydney where their chaotic lives don't become any more stable. Oh, and the title refers to one of the duo's many strange roommates. **107m/C DVD.** *AU IT* Noah Taylor, Emily Hamilton, Romane Bohringer, Sophie Lee, Francis McMahon, Brett Stewart; *D:* Richard Lowenstein; *W:* Richard Lowenstein; *C:* Andrew de Groot.

He Found a Star 1/2 **1941** Struggling talent agent Lucky (Oliver) and his loyal secretary Ruth (Churchill) specialize in giving a break to unknowns. Lucky finally gets lucky when he changes the act of singer Frank Forrester (Atkins), which leads slinky nightclub singer Suzanne (Dall) to ask him to help her. Suzanne's a bad bet (she's troubled), so it's Ruth to the rescue when she fills in for the unreliable dame. **89m/B DVD.** *GB* Sarah Churchill, Joan Greenwood, Gabrielle Brune, Vic Oliver, Evelyn Dall, Robert Atkins; *D:* Jack Paddy Carstairs; *W:* Bridget Boland, Austin Melford; *C:* Ernest Palmer.

He Got Game 1/2 **1998 (R)** Lee hops all over the place with this basketball drama that reveals more of his love for the game than cohesive filmmaking. Actually two movies in one: High school basketball great Jesus Shuttlesworth (newcomer and Milwaukee Bucks player Allen) must decide between college or a lucrative NBA contract. Then up pops his incarcerated pops, Jake, (a haggard Washington) to pressure him to chose his warden's alma mater, which turns the film into a shallow look at a strained father-son relationship. Washington is dynamic as the embittered father and Allen is evenly effective. Yet, the reunion is never fully developed and sometimes abandoned, while Lee scores visually by beautifully photographing the glorious hoop moves. Extraneous, stereotypical characters and rauchy sex sequences drag the film further from its dramatic resonance. **134m/C VHS, DVD.** Denzel Washington, Ray Allen, Milla Jovovich, Rosario Dawson, Hill Harper, Zelda Harris, Jim Brown, Ned Beatty, Lonette McKee, John Turturro, Michele Shay, Bill Nunn, Thomas Jefferson Byrd; *D:* Spike Lee; *W:* Spike Lee; *C:* Malik Hassan Sayeed.

He Is My Brother 1/2 **1975 (G)** Two boys survive a shipwreck, landing on an island that houses a leper colony. **90m/C VHS.** Keenan Wynn, Bobby Sherman, Robbie (Reist) Rist; *D:* Edward Dmytryk.

He Kills Night After Night After Night 1/2 *Night After Night After Night* **1969** British police are baffled as they seek the man who has been killing women in the style of Jack the Ripper. And he keeps doing it. **88m/C VHS.** *GB* Donald (Don) Sumpter, Terry Scully, Jack May, Linda Marlowe, Justine Lord, Gilbert Wynne; *D:* Lindsay Shonteff; *W:* Dail Ambler.

He Knows You're Alone **1980 (R)** Lame horror flick that focuses on a psychotic killer terrorizing a bride-to-be and her bridal party in his search for a suitable bride of his own. **94m/C VHS, DVD.** Don Scardino, Caitlin (Kathleen Heaney) O'Heaney, Tom Rolfing, Paul Gleason, Elizabeth Kemp, Tom Hanks, Patsy Pease, Lewis Arlt, James Rebhorn, Joseph Leon, James Carroll; *D:* Armand Mastroianni; *W:* Scott Parker; *C:* Gerald Feil; *M:* Alexander Peskanov, Mark Peskanov.

He Lives: The Search for the Evil One **1967** A man who was imprisoned by Nazis as a child attempts to keep Hitler, now living in Buenos Aires, from starting a 4th Reich. **90m/C VHS.** Henry (Kleinbach) Brandon, Lisa Pera, Pitt Herbert, Lee Patterson; *D:* Joseph Kane; *C:* Gary Galbraith; *M:* John Caper Jr.

He Loves Me ... He Loves Me Not *A la Folie...Pas de Tout* **2002** Art student Angelique (Tautou) is obsessively enthralled with her married lover, cardiologist Loic (Le Bihan), and refuses to believe that he won't leave his pregnant wife Rachel (Carre). When Loic stands Angelique up before they are about to take a holiday, she begins to unravel and attempts suicide. Then the film takes us back to the beginning and shows Loic's very different point-of-view: Angelique is delusional and stalking Loic who barely knows the girl. And her madness just excels from there. French with subtitles. **92m/C VHS, DVD.** *FR* Audrey Tautou, Samuel Le Bihan, Isabelle Carre, Sophie Guillemin, Clement Sibony; *D:* Laetitia Colombani; *W:* Laetitia Colombani, Caroline Thival; *C:* Pierre Aim; *M:* Jerome Coullet.

He Said, She Said 1/2 **1991 (R)** Romance is the topic, but this isn't a typical dating film, instead a couple's relationship unfolds from differing points of view: first, the guy's (by Kwapis) and then the girl's (by Silver). Bacon and Perkins, Baltimore journalists and professional rivals, tell how their romance wound up on the rocks, and why (or so they say). The end result is overlong and lacks the zing of other war between the sexes movies, but real-life couple Silver and Kwapis do humorously highlight the fact that men and women often view the same incidents very differently. Bacon overacts, Perkins overreacts, and Stone shines as Bacon's ex-girl. **115m/C VHS, DVD.** Elizabeth Perkins, Kevin Bacon, Sharon Stone, Nathan Lane, Anthony LaPaglia, Stanley Anderson, Charlaine Woodard, Danton Stone, Phil Leeds, Rita Karin; *D:* Marisa Silver, Ken Kwapis; *W:* Brian Hohlfield; *C:* Stephen Burum; *M:* Miles Goodman.

He Sees You When You're Sleeping 1/2 **2002 (PG)** Recently deceased stockbroker Sterling's superficial life doesn't pass muster with the powers-that-be at the pearly gates. But his guardian angel sets him up with one last selfless earthly task to make amends—save a single mom and her seven-year-old daughter from the evil clutches of the local mob. A Christmas-themed Mary Higgins Clark adaptation. **100m/C VHS, DVD.** Cameron Bancroft, Erika Eleniak, Greg Evigan, Udo Kier, Sean Campbell, Pam Hyatt, David Palffy, Eli Gabay, Nickol Tschenscher, Landy Cannon, Roger Haskett, Rheta Hutton, Jason Low, Craig March, Claire Riley; *D:* David Winning; *W:* Carl Binder; *C:* David Pelletier; *M:* Michael Richard Plowman. **TV**

He Walked by Night 1/2 **1948** Los Angeles homicide investigators track down cop killer Ray Morgan (Basehart) in this excellent drama. The final confrontation takes place in the L.A. County Flood Control System, consisting of some 700 miles of underground tunnels. Based on a true story from the files of the Los Angeles police, this first rate production reportedly inspired Webb to create "Dragnet." **80m/B VHS, DVD.** Richard Basehart, Scott Brady, Roy Roberts, Jack Webb, Whit Bissell; *D:* Alfred Werker, Anthony Mann; *W:* John C. Higgins; *C:* John Alton; *M:* Leonid Raab.

He Was a Quiet Man 1/2 **2007** Milquetoast Bob Maconel (Slater) is a paranoid and angry office drone who likes to keep a loaded gun in his desk. He accidentally becomes a hero when a co-worker does go postal and Bob kills him. This earns him a promotion. But he's dismayed to find out that his secret crush, Vanessa (Cuthbert), was paralyzed by a bullet and wants Bob to help her die. He can't, so they start a romance instead, or do they? Ending leaves a lot to puzzle out. **95m/C DVD.** Christian Slater, Elisha Cuthbert, William H. Macy, Sascha Knopf, John Gulager, Jamison Jones; *D:* Frank A. Capello; *W:* Frank A. Capello; *C:* Brandon Trost; *M:* Jeff Beal.

He Who Gets Slapped **1924** Chaney portrays a brilliant scientist whose personal and professional humiliations cause him to join a travelling French circus as a masochistic clown (hence the title). There he falls in love with a beautiful circus performer and plans a spectacular revenge. Brilliant use of lighting and Expressionist devices by director Sjostrom (who used the Americanized version of his name-Seastrom-in the credits). Adapted from the Russian play "He, The One Who Gets Slapped" by Leonid Andreyev. **85m/B VHS.** Lon Chaney Sr., Norma Shearer, John Gilbert, Tully Marshall, Ford Sterling, Marc McDermott; ***D:*** Victor Sjostrom; ***W:*** Carey Wilson, Victor Sjostrom.

He Who Walks Alone 🦴🦴 ½ **1978** Documents the life of Thomas E. Gilmore, who became the South's first elected black sheriff in the 1960s. **74m/C VHS.** Louis Gossett Jr., Clu Gulager, Mary Alice, James McEachin, Barton Heyman, Barry Brown, Lonny (Lonnie) Chapman; ***D:*** Jerrold Freedman. **TV**

The Head 🦴🦴 **1959** A scientist comes up with a serum that can keep the severed head of a dog alive. Before too long, he tries the stuff out on a woman, transferring the head from her own hunchbacked body to that of a beautiful stripper. Weird German epic sports poor special effects and unintentional laughs, but is interesting nonetheless. **92m/B VHS, DVD.** *GE* Horst Frank, Michel Simon, Paul Dahlke, Karin Kernke, Helmut Schmidt; ***D:*** Victor Trivas; ***W:*** Victor Trivas.

Head 🦴🦴🦴 **1968 (G)** Infamously plotless musical comedy starring the TV fab four of the '60s, the Monkees, in their only film appearance. A number of guest stars appear and a collection of old movie clips are also included. ♫ Circle Sky; Can You Dig It; Long Title: Do I Have to Do This All Over Again; Daddy's Song; As We Go Along; The Porpoise Song. **86m/C VHS, DVD.** Peter Tork, Mickey Dolenz, Davy Jones, Michael Nesmith, Frank Zappa, Annette Funicello, Teri Garr, Timothy Carey, Logan Ramsey, Victor Mature, Jack Nicholson, Bob Rafelson, Dennis Hopper; ***D:*** Bob Rafelson; ***W:*** Jack Nicholson, Bob Rafelson; ***C:*** Michael Hugo; ***M:*** Ken Thorne.

Head Above Water 🦴🦴 **1996 (PG-13)** Remake of same-titled 1993 Norwegian black comedy is now set on an island off the Maine coast where marrieds Nathalie (Diaz) and George (Keitel) are vacationing at her family's cottage. George goes off on an overnight fishing trip, but Nathalie isn't alone for long—former boyfriend Kent (Zane) shows up, the duo get drunk catching up on old times, and Nathalie wakes up the next morning with Kent's corpse. The unstable Nathalie hides the body, which is quickly found by George, who discards the corpse in a more permanent manner involving cement. Then Natalie suddenly decides George must have murdered Kent and is now after her. Plot doesn't hang together well and Keitel is frequently too low-key but Diaz is watchable. **92m/C VHS, DVD.** Cameron Diaz, Harvey Keitel, Craig Sheffer, Billy Zane; ***D:*** Jim Wilson; ***W:*** Theresa Marie; ***C:*** Richard Bowen; ***M:*** Christopher Young.

Head in the Clouds 🦴🦴 **2004 (R)** Beautiful Theron turns heads as hedonistic socialite Gilda, who briefly storms into the life of shy Irishman Guy (Townsend) in 1933. His torch remains ablaze as she later summons him to Paris, where Gilda is dabbling as a photographer and with a Spanish refugee named Mia (Cruz). Their triangular idyll is troubled by the political idealism displayed by both Mia and Guy, who are committed to the anti-fascist cause in the Spanish Civil War. Gilda feels betrayed when they leave her behind. When Guy finally sees her again in 1944, he's a British spy smuggled into Paris and Gilda is romancing Nazi officer Bietrich (Kretschmann). But is she really the unfeeling collaborator she seems? A plush potboiler with a pretty cast. **124m/C DVD.** *GB CA* Charlize Theron, Penelope Cruz, Stuart Townsend, Thomas Kretschmann, Steven Berkoff, Karine Vanasse, Gabriel Hogan, David LaHaye, Peter Cockett, John Jorgenson, John Robinson, Lisa Bronwyn Moore; ***D:*** John Duigan; ***W:*** John Duigan; ***C:*** Paul Sarossy; ***M:*** Terry Frewer.

Head of State 🦴🦴 **2003 (PG-13)** Just because Rock played a director in "Jay and Silent Bob Strike Back" doesn't mean he can do it in real life, at least not yet. Rock plays Mays Gilliam, a D.C. alderman drafted to run for President after the unnamed party's candidates die in a plane crash. The party leadership doesn't want him to win, just provide diversity cred for the next election. With his brother Mitch (Mac) as running mate, Mays fights his handlers to create his own identity. Unfortunately, in the hands of writer and director Rock, candidate Rock isn't given much consistent identity to work with. Maybe with a proven director, and more than token effort at plot and characterization, this one might've been better. **95m/C VHS, DVD.** *US* Chris Rock, Bernie Mac, Dylan Baker, Nick Searcy, Lynn Whitfield, Robin Givens, Tamala Jones, Stephanie March, James Rebhorn, Keith David, Tracy Morgan, Robert Stanton, Jude Ciccolella, Nate Dogg; ***D:*** Chris Rock; ***W:*** Chris Rock, Ali LeRoi; ***C:*** Donald E. Thorin; ***M:*** Marcus Miller, David "DJ Quik" Blake.

Head of the Family 🦴🦴 ½ **1971 (PG)** After a woman sacrifices her political ideals and career goals for her role as a family matriarch, she eventually falls apart. **105m/C VHS.** *IT FR* Nino Manfredi, Leslie Caron, Ugo Tognazzi, Claudine Auger; ***D:*** Nanni Loy; ***W:*** Nanni Loy.

Head of the Family 🦴 ½ **1996 (R)** Lance (Bailey) moves to Nob Hollow and discovers the Stackpool family's dreadful secrets—they're telepathic quadruplets under the control of brother Myron (Perra), who just happens to be a giant head that gets around in a wheelchair. Lance decides to use the whacko family to get rid of babe girlfriend Loretta's (Lovell) inconvenient husband. **82m/C VHS, DVD.** Blake Bailey, Jacqueline Lovell, Bob Schott, J.W. Perra; ***D:*** Robert Talbot; ***W:*** Benjamin Carr; ***C:*** Adolfo Bartoli; ***M:*** Richard Band.

Head Office 🦴🦴 **1986 (PG-13)** A light comedy revolving around the competition between corporate management and the lower echelon for the available position of chairman. **90m/C VHS, DVD.** Danny DeVito, Eddie Albert, Judge Reinhold, Rick Moranis, Jane Seymour; ***D:*** Ken Finkleman; ***M:*** James Newton Howard.

Head On 🦴🦴🦴 **1998** Nineteen-year-old Ari (Dimitriades) is forced to confront his Greek heritage and its idea of manhood with the homosexuality he keeps secret from his traditional family. Much of his day is spent killing time with his friends until he can meet Sean (Garner), the young man Ari is attracted to, at a bar that night. Bored and restless, Ari is out to have a good time with as little pain to himself as possible. Adapted from the book "Loaded" by Christos Tsiolkas. **104m/C VHS, DVD.** *AU* Alex Dimitriades, Paul Capsis, Julian Garner, Damien Fotiou, Elena Mandalis, Andrea Mandalis, Tony Nikolakopoulos, Eugenia Fragos, Maria Mercedes; ***D:*** Ana Kokkinos; ***W:*** Ana Kokkinos, Mira Robertson, Andrew Bovell; ***C:*** Jaems Grant; ***M:*** Ollie Olsen.

Head On 🦴🦴 *Gegen die Wand* **2004** Cahit (Unel) is a Turkish immigrant in Hamburg whose drunken, self-destructive behavior lands him in a psych ward. He meets fellow immigrant Sibel (Kekilli), a wrist-slasher who needs to escape her conservative Muslim family either by death or a marriage of convenience. Cahit figures he has nothing to lose and agrees when Sibel says she will keep him in alcohol. But their arrangement eventually spirals into mad love and violent consequences. Turkish and German with subtitles. **118m/C DVD.** Birol Unel, Sibel Kekilli, Catrin Striebeck, Guven Kirac, Meltem Cumbul, Cem Akin, Aysel Iscan, Demir Gokgol, Stefan Gebelhoff, Hermann Lause, Adam Bousdoukos, Ralph Misske, Mehmet Kurtulus; ***D:*** Fatih Akin; ***W:*** Fatih Akin; ***C:*** Rainer Klausmann.

Head Over Heels 🦴🦴🦴 **1967** A model married to an older man has an affair with a younger one and cannot decide between them. In French with subtitles. **89m/C VHS.** *FR* Brigitte Bardot, Laurent Terzieff, Michael Sarne; ***D:*** Serge Bourguignon.

Head Over Heels 🦴 ½ **2001 (PG-13)** New York art restorer Amanda (Potter) has sworn off men after a bad breakup, but finds herself back in the game when she meets her dashing and mysterious neighbor, Jim (Prinze). Having conveniently taken up residence in an apartment that offers a perfect view of the one occupied by Jim, her attraction grows as she and her supermodel roommates follow the young man's every move. Works well during its romantic comedy stretches, but loses points for its reliance on an ill-conceived plot point revolving around a possible murder, and for lowering itself to much crude, scatological humor. **86m/C VHS, DVD.** *US* Monica Potter, Freddie Prinze Jr., Shalom Harlow, Ivana Milicevic, China Chow, Jay Brazeau, Sarah O'Hare, Tomiko Fraser, Stanley DeSantis; ***D:*** Mark S. Waters; ***W:*** Ron Burch, David Kidd; ***C:*** Mark Plummer; ***M:*** Randy Edelman, Steve Porcaro.

Head Winds 🦴🦴 **1925** Silent romance in which Mr. Right spares helpless girl against her will from marrying Mr. Wrong. **52m/B VHS.** House Peters Sr., Patsy Ruth Miller; ***D:*** Herbert Blache; ***W:*** Edward T. Lowe; ***C:*** John Stumar.

Headhunter 🦴 ½ **1989** Voodoo-esque killers are leaving headless bodies all around Miami. Plenty of prosthetic make-up. **92m/C VHS.** Kay Lenz, Wayne Crawford, John Fatooh, Steve Kanaly, June Chadwick, Sam Williams; ***D:*** Francis Schaeffer.

Headhunter 🦴🦴 **2005** Ben Caruso (Parrillo) wants a new job and is advised to see Sarah (Clainos), a professional headhunter. Sarah gets Ben a higher-paying desk job but it's on the graveyard shift, and weird things immediately start happening. When Ben does some investigating, he learns Sarah was a murder victim who was decapitated and has been using her "clients" to find her missing head. And if they can't, they may have to look for their own. Offers some surprises for the indie horror genre. **90m/C DVD.** Ben Parrillo, Kristi Clainos, Mark Aiken; ***D:*** Paul Tarantino; ***W:*** Paul Tarantino; ***C:*** Seth Kotok; ***M:*** Vincent Gillioz. **VIDEO**

Headin' for the Rio Grande 🦴 **1936** A cowboy and his sheriff brother drive off cattle-rustlers in this Western saga. Ritter's film debut. Songs include "Campfire Love Song," "Jailhouse Lament," and "Night Herding Song." **60m/B VHS, DVD.** Tex Ritter, Eleanor Stewart, Syd Saylor, Warner Richmond, Charles "Blackie" King; ***D:*** Robert North Bradbury.

Headin' Home 🦴🦴 ½ **1920** A very early version of the Babe Ruth story—starring none other than the Babe himself. A fair print, this film is orchestra scored. **56m/B VHS, DVD.** Babe Ruth, Margaret Seddon, Ruth Taylor, William Sheer; ***D:*** Lawrence Windom; ***W:*** Arthur Baer.

Heading for Heaven 🦴🦴 **1947** A mistaken medical report leaves a frazzled realtor believing he has only three months to live, and when he disappears the family suspects the worst. A minor comedy based on a play by Charles Webb. **65m/B VHS, DVD.** Stuart Erwin, Glenda Farrell, Russ Vincent, Irene Ryan, Milburn Stone, George O'Hanlon; ***D:*** Lewis D. Collins.

Heading South 🦴🦴🦴 *Vers le Sud* **2005** French pic set in the late '70s tells the story of three women "of a certain age," as the euphemism goes, who travel to an accommodating beachside resort in Haiti to satisfy their still-burning sexual needs. Each woman has her own backstory and reason for seeking out the pleasures of a more-than-willing local teenager, and each take a turn explaining this frankly and directly to the camera. The wretched conditions and dangers of life for the locals are shown in frightening, sharp contrast to the self-indulgence of the foreigners. Veteran French director Laurent Cantet elicits excellent performances from cast, most notably Charlotte Rampling as queen bee Ellen. Based on short stories by Haitian writer Dany Laferriere. **105m/C DVD.** *CA FR* Charlotte Rampling, Karen Young, Louise Portal, Menothy Cesar, Lys Ambroise, Jackenson Pierre Olmo Diaz, Wilfried Paul; ***D:*** Laurent Cantet; ***W:*** Laurent Cantet, Robin Campillo; ***C:*** Pierre Milon.

Headless Body in Topless Bar 🦴🦴 ½ **1996** Based on a famous New York Post headline and the crime that inspired it, this black comedy contains more than its lurid title lets on. Except for street footage at the opening and closing, the entire movie is set in a seedy strip club. After shooting the bartender in a robbery attempt, a crazed ex-con holds the patrons and employees hostage. He forces them to play a mind game called "Nazi truth," revealing the distasteful truth about the captives. Director Bruce and screenwriter Koper first worked together filming re-creations for "America's Most Wanted." The cast worked for "hostage scale," meaning if those playing captives stole the gun from the robber (a plot point), they got his pay for the day. If not, then he got their wages. **105m/C VHS, DVD.** Raymond J. Barry, Jennifer MacDonald, David Selby, Taylor Nichols, Paul Williams, Biff Yeager, Rustam Branaman, April Grace; ***D:*** James Bruce; ***W:*** Peter Koper; ***C:*** Kevin Morrisey; ***M:*** Charles P. Barnett.

Headless Eyes 🦴 ½ **1983** Gory entry into the psycho-artist category. An artist is miffed when mistaken by a woman as a burglar he loses an eye. Not one to forgive and forget, he becomes quite the eyeball fetishist, culling donations from unsuspecting women. An eye for an eye ad finitum. **78m/C VHS.** Bo Brundin, Gordon Raman, Mary Jane Early; ***D:*** Kent Bateman; ***W:*** Kent Bateman.

The Headless Woman 🦴 ½ *La Mujer Sin Cabeza* **2008** Middle-aged Veronica (Onetto) is driving on a remote road when she is distracted by her ringing cell phone and hits something. She drives off but is burdened by guilt (there were children playing by the road) and finally confesses to her husband about what may have happened. Spanish with subtitles. **89m/C DVD.** *AR* Maria Onetto, Cesar Bordon, Daniel Genoud, Claudia Cantero, Ines Efron; ***D:*** Lucrecia Martel; ***W:*** Lucrecia Martel; ***C:*** Barbara Alvarez.

Headline Woman 🦴🦴 **1935** An ongoing feud between a police commissioner and a newspaper's city editor causes a reporter to make a deal with a policeman in exchange for news. A good cast makes this otherwise tired story tolerable. **75m/B VHS, DVD.** Heather Angel, Roger Pryor, Jack La Rue, Ford Sterling, Conway Tearle; ***D:*** William Nigh.

Heads 🦴🦴 ½ **1993 (R)** Unassuming copyreader Guy Franklin (Cryer) gets promoted to reporter and his first assignment is a doozy. He's to cover a series of decapitation murders in a small town. Can he do the job without become the next victim—or being accused of the crimes? Filmed in Manitoba, Canada. **102m/C VHS.** *CA* Jon Cryer, Jennifer Tilly, Ed Asner, Roddy McDowall; ***D:*** Paul Shapiro; ***W:*** Adam Brooks; ***M:*** Jonathan Goldsmith. **CABLE**

Headspace 🦴 ½ **2002 (R)** Something triggers Alex's (Denham) brain into hyperdrive and gives him immense mental abilities, including super-fast speed reading and chess-playing invincibility. But the drawbacks are wicked, as his repressed childhood memory of dad blowing away mom returns, along with hellish visions of ghastly monsters. To make things worse, the people around him are winding up dead, causing him the all-too-obvious concern that he's in some way responsible. **90m/C DVD.** *US* Sean Young, Larry Fessenden, William Atherton, Dee Wallace, Christopher Denham, Erick Kastel, Olivia Hussey, Mark Margolis, Udo Kier; ***D:*** Andrew van den Houten; ***W:*** Steve Klausner, William M. Miller; ***C:*** William M. Miller; ***M:*** Ryan Shore.

Healer 🦴 ½ *Little Pal* **1936** A doctor forgets his pledge to help the lame and becomes a fashionable physician. A young crippled lad helps him eventually remember his original purpose was to serve others. **80m/B VHS, DVD.** Mickey Rooney, Ralph Bellamy, Karen Morley, Judith Allen, Robert McWade; ***D:*** Reginald Barker.

The Healer 🦴🦴 *Julie Walking Home* **2002** When her cancer-stricken son is unable to accept traditional treatment, Julie frantically seeks out a mystic healer in Poland to cure him. In the midst of a divorce from her cheating husband she unexpectedly finds romance there as well. **113m/C VHS, DVD.** Miranda Otto, William Fichtner, Lothaire Bluteau, Jerzy Nowak, Ryan Smith, Bianca Crudo, Boguslawa Schubert; ***D:*** Agnieszka Holland; ***W:*** Agnieszka Holland, Arlene Sarner; ***C:*** Jacek Petrycki; ***M:*** Antoni Lazarkiewicz. **TV**

Hear My Song 🦴🦴🦴 ½ **1991 (R)** Mickey O'Neill (Dunbar) is an unscrupulous club promoter, who books singers with names like Franc Cinatra, while trying to revive his failing nightclub in this charming, hilarious comedy. He hires the mysterious Mr. X, who claims he is really the legendary exiled singer Josef Locke, only to find out he is an imposter. To redeem himself with his fiancee and her mother, he goes to Ireland to find the real Locke (Beatty) and bring him to Liverpool to sing. Dunbar is appealing in his role, and Beatty is magnificent as the legendary Locke—so much so that he was nominated for a Golden Globe for Best Supporting Actor. **104m/C VHS.** *GB* Ned Beatty, Adrian Dunbar, Shirley Anne Field, Tara Fitzgerald, William Hootkins, David McCallum, Gladys Sheehan; ***D:*** Peter Chelsom; ***W:*** Peter Chelsom; ***C:*** Sue Gibson; ***M:*** John Altman.

Hear No Evil 1/2 **1993 (R)** Below average thriller with a deaf victim (Matlin) involved in a game of cat-and-mouse with a corrupt cop (Sheen) who's looking for a valuable coin. Weak script plays up the woman in jeopardy theme but lacks the crucial element of suspense. A waste of an otherwise talented cast. **98m/C VHS, DVD.** Marlee Matlin, D.B. Sweeney, Martin Sheen, John C. McGinley, Christina Carlisi, Greg Elam, Charley Lang; ***D:*** Robert Greenwald; ***W:*** Randall Badat, Kathleen Rowell; ***M:*** Graeme Revell.

Hearing Voices 1/2 **1990** Joyless Erica is a commercial model who suffers from a form of scoliosis. If she capitalized on her infirmity by advertising medical aids, she could make a lot of money but she firmly refuses her lover's pleas to do this. When her doctor suggests reconstructive surgery, she storms out of his office but not before attracting the attention of Lee, his gay lover. Erica and Lee begin a complex emotional relationship, upsetting to everyone around them. Uninvolving characters, inert direction, and amateurish acting work against Greytak's feature film debut. **87m/C VHS.** Erika Nagy, Stephen Gatta, Tim Ahearn, Michael Davenport; ***D:*** Sharon Greytak; ***W:*** Sharon Greytak.

The Hearse WOOF! 1980 (PG) Incredibly boring horror film in which a young school teacher moves into a mansion left to her by her late aunt and finds her life threatened by a sinister black hearse. **100m/C VHS, DVD.** Trish Van Devere, Joseph Cotten, Donald Hotton, David Gautreaux; ***D:*** George Bowers; ***W:*** William Bleich; ***C:*** Mori Kawa.

The Hearst and Davies Affair 1/2 **1985** Married, middle-aged newspaper tycoon William Randolph Hearst falls for teenage Ziegfeld girl Marion Davies and tries to turn her into a Hollywood star. Davies was generally thought to be talented as a comedienne but Hearst insisted on choosing ill-suited dramatic roles for the blonde and her career was problematic. Their lavish lifestyle was enhanced when Hearst built San Simeon for Davies and their scandalous affair lasted 35 years. **97m/C VHS.** Robert Mitchum, Virginia Madsen, Fritz Weaver; ***D:*** David Lowell Rich. **TV**

Heart 1/2 **1987 (R)** A down-and-out small-time boxer is given a chance to make a comeback, and makes the Rocky-like most of it. **93m/C VHS, DVD.** Brad Davis, Jesse Doran, Sam Gray, Steve Buscemi, Frances Fisher; ***D:*** James (Momel) Lemmo.

Heart 1/2 **1999 (R)** Gruesome wannabe thriller (told in flashback) finds Gary Ellis (Eccleston) suffering a jealousy-induced heart attack after discovering wife Tess's (Hardie) philandering with Alex (Ifans). Gary gets a heart transplant—the donor being a young man killed in a motorcycle accident—and contacts the man's mother, Maria Ann (Reeves) after he gets out of the hospital. Too bad she's crazy. **85m/C VHS, DVD.** *GB* Christopher Eccleston, Saskia Reeves, Kate Hardie, Rhys Ifans, Bill Paterson, Anna Chancellor, Matthew Rhys; ***D:*** Charles McDougall; ***W:*** Jimmy McGovern; ***C:*** Julian Court; ***M:*** Stephen Warbeck.

Heart and Souls 1/2 **1993 (PG-13)** Reincarnation comedy casts Downey Jr. as a mortal whose body is inhabited by four lost souls who died on the night he was born. Now an adult, he must finish what they could not, no matter how outrageous it may be. Talented cast wears plot that's old hat. Downey Jr. must be looking to do a trilogy of tired reincarnated soul roles—this is his second, "Chances Are" was his first. **104m/C VHS, DVD.** Robert Downey Jr., Charles Grodin, Tom Sizemore, Alfre Woodard, Kyra Sedgwick, Elisabeth Shue, David Paymer; ***D:*** Ron Underwood; ***W:*** Erik Hansen, Brent Maddock, S.S. Wilson, Gregory Hansen; ***C:*** Michael Watkins; ***M:*** Marc Shaiman.

Heart Beat 1/2 **1980 (R)** The fictionalized story of Jack Kerouac (author of "On the Road"), his friend and inspiration Neal Cassady, and the woman they shared, Carolyn Cassady. Based on Carolyn Cassady's memoirs. Strong performances, with Nolte as Cassady and Spacek as his wife, overcome the sometimes shaky narrative. **105m/C VHS.** Nick Nolte, John Heard, Sissy Spacek, Ann Dusenberry, Ray Sharkey, Tony Bill, Steve Allen, John Larroquette; ***D:*** John Byrum; ***W:*** John Byrum; ***M:*** Jack Nitzsche.

Heart Condition 1/2 **1990 (R)** A deceased black lawyer's heart is donated to a bigoted Los Angeles cop who was stalking the lawyer when he was alive. Soon afterwards the lawyer's ghost returns to haunt the police officer, hoping the officer will help to avenge his murder. Both Hoskins and Washington display fine performances given the unlikely script. **95m/C VHS, DVD.** Bob Hoskins, Denzel Washington, Chloe Webb, Ray Baker, Ja'net DuBois, Alan Rachins, Roger E. Mosley, Jeffrey Meek; ***D:*** James D. Parriott; ***C:*** Arthur Albert.

The Heart Is a Lonely Hunter **1968 (G)** Set in the South, Carson McCuller's tale of angst and ignorance, loneliness and beauty comes to the screen with the film debuts of Keach and Locke. Arkin gives an instinctive, gentle performance as the deaf mute. **124m/C VHS, DVD.** Alan Arkin, Cicely Tyson, Sondra Locke, Stacy Keach, Chuck McCann, Laurinda Barrett; ***D:*** Robert Ellis Miller; ***C:*** James Wong Howe; ***M:*** Dave Grusin. N.Y. Film Critics '68: Actor (Arkin).

The Heart Is Deceitful Above All Things **2004 (R)** Sarah (writer/director Argento) is the worst kind of trailer trash—an alcoholic druggie who doesn't say no to any scum's sexual advances—yet social services returns her 7-year-old boy Jeremiah to her, taking him from stable foster parents. After corrupting him with her lifestyle, she dumps him on her very religious parents for three years, but just as the damage is undone, skanky Sarah returns and takes him on the road for more misery. Based on a supposed autobiographical novel by J.T. LeRoy that was later outed as a ruse created by writer Laura Albert. **98m/C DVD.** *US* Asia Argento, Jimmy Bennett, Cole Sprouse, Dylan Sprouse, Peter Fonda, Ben Foster, Ornella Muti, Kip Pardue, Michael Pitt; ***D:*** Asia Argento; ***W:*** Asia Argento, Alessandro Magania; ***C:*** Eric Alan Edwards; ***M:*** Marco Castoldi, Sonic Youth.

Heart Like a Wheel 1/2 **1983 (PG)** The story of Shirley Muldowney, who rose from the daughter of a country-western singer to the leading lady in drag racing. The film follows her battles of sexism and choosing whether to have a career or a family. Bedelia's perfomance is outstanding. Fine showings from Bridges and Axton in supporting roles. **113m/C VHS, DVD.** Bonnie Bedelia, Beau Bridges, Bill McKinney, Leo Rossi, Hoyt Axton, Dick Miller, Anthony Edwards; ***D:*** Jonathan Kaplan; ***W:*** Ken Friedman.

Heart of a Champion: The Ray Mancini Story **1985** Made-for-TV movie based on the life of Ray "Boom Boom" Mancini, former lightweight boxing champion. Inspired by the career his father never had due to WWII, Mancini fought his way to the top. Sylvester Stallone staged the fight sequences. **94m/C VHS.** Robert (Bobby) Blake, Doug McKeon, Mariclare Costello; ***D:*** Richard Michaels.

Heart of a Nation *Untel Pere et Fils; Immortal France* **1943** Saga of the Montmarte family and their life during three wars, beginning with the Franco-Prussian War and ending with the Nazi occupation in France. Although ordered to be destroyed by the Nazis, this film was saved, along with many others, by the French "Cinema Resistance." In French with English subtitles. **111m/B VHS, DVD.** *FR* Louis Jouvet, Raimu, Suzy Prim, Michele Morgan, Renee Devillers, Harry Krimer; ***D:*** Julien Duvivier; ***Nar:*** Charles Boyer.

Heart of America WOOF! 2003 (R) You might know Boll from his embarrassingly bad video game movies, but this school-shooting melodrama is easily the director's worst film yet. Your mind will boggle at how shamelessly Boll milks the Columbine tragedy in his desperate attempt to reinvent himself as a serious filmmaker. Set on the last day of high school, the film leaves no Afterschool Special cliche unturned as it follows various students and teachers hours before two brooding loners decide to take out their angst Charlton Heston-style. It's heady material, but Boll is no Michael Moore. Instead, he prefers to shoot inappropriate softcore T&A in a scene where a bully molests a mentally-handicapped girl known as "Slow White." Yeah, classy stuff all around. **87m/C DVD.** *CA GE* Jurgen Prochnow, Michael Pare, Patrick Muldoon, Kett Turton, Elisabeth (Elissabeth, Elizabeth, Liz) Moss, Maria Conchita Alonso, Clint Howard, Brendan Fletcher, Lochlyn Munro, Maeve Quinlan, Michaela Mann, Will Sanderson; ***D:*** Uwe Boll; ***W:*** Uwe Boll, Robert Dean Klein; ***C:*** Mathias Neumann; ***M:*** Reinhard Besser.

Heart of Darkness **1993** Joseph Conrad's 1902 menacing novella set in the Belgian Congo is told through flashbacks by Marlow (Roth), whose employers, a Belgian trading company, hire him to find Kurtz (Malkovich), head of a remote trading station, who is rumored to be hoarding a huge cache of ivory. Marlow's journey up the river is beset by obstacles and Kurtz is rumored to be either insane or a prophet in his jungle kingdom. Filmed in Belize. Francis Ford Coppola's updated adaptation became "Apocalyse Now." **120m/C VHS.** Tim Roth, John Malkovich, James Fox, Isaach de Bankole, Patrick Ryecart, Geoffrey Hutchings, Peter Vaughan, Phoebe Nicholls, Allan Corduner, Alan Scarfe, Iman, Timothy Bateson; ***D:*** Nicolas Roeg; ***W:*** Benedict Fitzgerald; ***M:*** Stanley Myers. **TV**

The Heart of Dixie **1989 (PG)** Three college co-eds at a southern university in the 1950s see their lives and values change with the influence of the civil rights movement. College newspaper reporter Sheedy takes up the cause of a black man victimized by racial violence. Lightweight social-conscience fare. **96m/C VHS, DVD.** Virginia Madsen, Ally Sheedy, Phoebe Cates, Treat Williams, Kyle Secor, Francesca Roberts, Barbara Babcock, Don Michael Paul, Kurtwood Smith, Richard Bradford; ***D:*** Martin Davidson; ***W:*** Tom McCown; ***C:*** Robert Elswit; ***M:*** Kenny Vance.

Heart of Dragon **1985** Police officer Chan takes care of his mentally challenged brother Hung, who gets mistaken for a robbery suspect. So Chan has to track down the real crooks. Features a 20-minute fight finale. Chinese with subtitles or dubbed. **85m/C VHS, DVD.** *HK* Jackie Chan, Sammo Hung, Emily Chu; ***D:*** Sammo Hung; ***W:*** Barry Wong; ***C:*** Arthur Wong Ngok Tai; ***M:*** Man Yee Lam.

Heart of Glass *Herz aus Glas* **1974** A pre-industrial Bavarian village becomes deeply troubled when their glass-blower dies without imparting the secret of making his unique Ruby glass. The townspeople go to extremes, from madness to murder to magic, to discover the ingredients. From German director Herzog (who hypnotized his cast daily), this somewhat apocalyptic tale is based on legend. The colors are incredible in their intensity. In German with English subtitles. **93m/C VHS, DVD.** *GE* Josef Bierbichler, Stefan Guttler, Clemens Scheitz, Volker Prechtel, Sonia Skiba; ***D:*** Werner Herzog; ***W:*** Werner Herzog, Herbert Achternbusch; ***C:*** Jorge Schmidt-Reitwein; ***M:*** Popul Vuh.

Heart of Humanity 1918 An intense drama of love, patriotism, and sacrifice just before the war in a small Canadian village. A traveler who is really a Prussian army lieutenant finds his way to the house of a young man who is about to wed. He ends up falling in love with his fiancee and war is declared just before the wedding. A silent film with music score. **133m/B VHS.** Dorothy Phillips, Erich von Stroheim; ***D:*** Allen Holubar.

Heart of Light *Lysets Hjerte* **1997** Marginalized Inuit family, living in Danish-occupied Greenland, suffer from being cut off from their native culture. Teenager Nisi has a breakdown, goes on a killing spree, and then turns the gun on himself. His drunken father, Rasmus, decides to leave the community on an old dogsled and encounters a hermit who leads him on a mystical journey into the past. Filmed on location in Greenland. Inuit and Danish with subtitles. **92m/C VHS, DVD.** *DK* Rasmus Lyberth, Anda Kristensen, Vivi Nielsen, Niels Platow; ***D:*** Jacob Gronlykke; ***W:*** Jacob Gronlykke; ***C:*** Dan Laustsen; ***M:*** Joachim Holbek.

The Heart of Me 1/2 **2002 (R)** Rather staid adaptation of Rosamond Lehmann's 1953 novel "The Echoing Grove," which follows the romantic trials of bohemian Dinah (Bonham Carter) and her adulterous affair with her chilly older sister Madeleine's (Williams) husband, Rickie (Bettany). Soapy melodrama covers approximately the mid-thirties to the post-war period. **96m/C VHS, DVD.** *GB* Helena Bonham Carter, Olivia Williams, Paul Bettany, Eleanor Bron; ***D:*** Thaddeus O'Sullivan; ***W:*** Lucinda Coxon; ***C:*** Gyula Pados; ***M:*** Nicholas Hooper.

Heart of Midnight 1/2 **1989 (R)** An emotionally unstable young woman inherits a seedy massage parlor. She works hard to turn it, and herself, into something better. Nice performance by Leigh. **93m/C VHS.** Jennifer Jason Leigh, Brenda Vaccaro, Frank Stallone, Peter Coyote, Gale Mayron, Sam Schacht, Denise Dumont; ***D:*** Matthew Chapman; ***W:*** Matthew Chapman; ***M:*** Yanni.

Heart of Stone **2001 (R)** Sexy L.A. mom Mary (Everhart) is suffering from a stale marriage and empty nest syndrome when her daughter goes off to college. So she's easy prey for the seductive Steve (Wilder), who becomes violently obsessed with Mary. And then there's a little problem of a killer targeting college coeds—could Mary's daughter become the next victim? And is Mary's unhinged lover the killer? **90m/C VHS, DVD.** Angie Everhart, James Wilder, Peter J. Lucas, Gregor Toerzs; ***D:*** Dale Trevillion, Marty Pistone. **VIDEO**

Heart of Texas Ryan 1/2 **1917** Flamboyant cowboy star fights with kidnappers and wins in this silent film. **50m/B VHS.** Tom Mix, George Fawcett, Bessie Eyton, Frank Campeau, Charles Gerrard; ***D:*** E.A. Martin; ***W:*** Gilson Willets.

Heart of the Beholder **2005 (R)** Writer/director Tipton's own experiences are the basis for this well-done and infuriating drama. In 1980, Mike Howard (Letscher) convinces his pregnant wife Diane (Brown) to open the first video rental store in their St. Louis hometown. By 1988, it's become a successful chain but Mike's targeted by fundamentalist preacher Brewer (Prosky) and his Citizens for Decency after he refuses to remove so-called "objectionable" material. The CFD increase their harassment, even threatening the Howards' young daughter. Then DA Eric Manion (Dye), who's being blackmailed by the group for his sexual indiscretions, takes Mike to court on trumped-up obscenity charges. His business and family are destroyed by the publicity but Mike eventually gets an unexpected revenge. **106m/C DVD.** Sarah Brown, John Dye, Arden Myrin, Greg Germann, Michael Dorn, Tony Todd, Matt Letcher, John Prosky; ***D:*** Ken Tipton; ***W:*** Ken Tipton; ***C:*** George Mooradian; ***M:*** Peter Rafelson.

The Heart of the Game 1/2 **2005 (PG-13)** Filmed over seven years, director Serrill follows Bill Resler's unorthodox approach to coaching the Roughriders, the girls' varsity basketball team at Seattle's middle-class Roosevelt High School. He turns the losing team into winners over the seasons, especially after recruiting gifted and volatile Darnellia Russell, an African-American from the inner-city, to join the predominantly white team. **97m/C DVD.** *US* ***D:*** Ward Serrill; ***W:*** Ward Serrill; ***C:*** Ward Serrill.

Heart of the Golden West **1942** Roy protects ranchers of Cherokee City from unjust shipping charges. **65m/B VHS.** Roy Rogers, Smiley Burnette, George "Gabby" Hayes, Bob Nolan, Ruth Terry; ***D:*** Joseph Kane.

Heart of the Rio Grande 1/2 **1942** Spoiled young rich girl tries to trick her father into coming to her "rescue" at a western dude ranch. **70m/B VHS, DVD.** Gene Autry, Smiley Burnette, Fay McKenzie, Edith Fellows, Joseph Stauch Jr.; ***D:*** William M. Morgan.

Heart of the Rockies 1/2 **1937** The Three Mesquiteers stop a mountain family's rustling and illegal game trappers. **54m/B VHS, DVD.** Robert "Bob" Livingston, Ray Corrigan, Max Terhune, Lynne Roberts, Yakima Canutt, J(ohn) P(aterson) McGowan; ***D:*** Joseph Kane.

Heart of the Rockies 🦴 1/2 **1951** Roy, along with his trusty horse and dog, takes care of a highway construction project. **67m/B VHS, DVD.** Roy Rogers, Penny Edwards, Gordon Jones, Ralph Morgan, Fred Graham, Mira McKinney; ***D:*** William Witney.

Heart of the Stag 🦴🦴 1/2 **1984 (R)** On an isolated sheep ranch in the New Zealand outback, a father and daughter suffer the repercussions of an incestuous relationship when she becomes enamored with a hired hand. **94m/C VHS, DVD.** *NZ* Bruno Lawrence, Mary Regan, Terence Cooper; ***D:*** Michael Firth.

Heartaches 🦴🦴 **1947** A reporter tries to track down a murderer who has killed twice. **71m/B VHS.** Ann Staunton, Chill Wills, Sheila Ryan, Edward Norris, James Seay, Frank Orth, Lash LaRue; ***D:*** Basil Wrangell; ***W:*** George Bricker, Monte (Monty) Collins Jr.; ***C:*** Jack Greenhalgh; ***M:*** Emil Cadkin.

Heartaches 🦴🦴🦴 **1982** A young pregnant woman (Potts) meets up with a crazy girlfriend (Kidder) in this touching film about love and friendship. Although a study in contrasts, the two end up sharing an apartment together in Toronto. Fine performances from Potts and Kidder give life to this romantic comedy. **90m/C VHS.** *CA* Margot Kidder, Annie Potts, Robert Carradine, Winston Rekert; ***D:*** Donald Shebib. Genie '82: Actress (Kidder).

Heartbeat 🦴🦴 1/2 **1946** If you thought pointless Hollywood remakes of French films were a new phenomenon (see "Pure Luck," for example), then note this lighthearted remake of a 1940 Gallic farce. Rogers becomes the best student in a Parisian school for pickpockets, but when she tries out her skills on a dashing diplomat they fall in love instead. **100m/B VHS, DVD.** Ginger Rogers, Jean-Pierre Aumont, Adolphe Menjou, Basil Rathbone, Melville Cooper, Mona Maris, Henry Stephenson, Eduardo Ciannelli; ***D:*** Sam Wood; ***C:*** Joseph Valentine.

Heartbeat Detector 🦴🦴 *La Question Humaine; The Human Question* **2007** Leisurely-paced French political thriller that raises intriguing questions about past and present actions. Cool and collected Simon (Amalric) is the in-house psychologist and human resources head at the Paris office of a German petrochemical firm. He's asked to quietly assess director Mathias Just (Lonsdale), who's been acting erratically. But, thanks to anonymous letters and company archives, Simon's investigation gets very complicated and involves the firm's past connection to the Third Reich. French with subtitles. **143m/C DVD.** *FR* Mathieu Amalric, Michael (Michel) Lonsdale, Jean-Pierre Kalfon, Lou Castel, Delphine Chuillot, Edith Scob, Valerie Dreville; ***D:*** Nicolas Klotz; ***W:*** Elisabeth Perceval; ***C:*** Josee Deshaies; ***M:*** Syd Matters.

Heartbeeps 🦴 1/2 **1981 (PG)** Mildly amusing romantic comedy about a couple of robot household servants (Kaufman and Peters) who fall in love, escape from domestic service, and begin a family of their own (they assemble a child robot from spare parts). **88m/C VHS, DVD.** Andy Kaufman, Bernadette Peters, Randy Quaid, Kenneth McMillan, Melanie Mayron, Christopher Guest, Richard B. Shull, Dick Miller, Kathleen Freeman, Mary Woronov, Paul Bartel; ***D:*** Allan Arkush; ***W:*** John Hill; ***C:*** Charles Rosher Jr.; ***M:*** John Williams.

Heartbreak Hotel 🦴🦴 1/2 **1988 (PG-13)** Johnny Wolfe kidnaps Elvis Presley from his show in Cleveland and drives him home to his mother, a die-hard Elvis fan. Completely unbelievable, utterly ridiculous, and still a lot of fun. **101m/C VHS, DVD.** David Keith, Tuesday Weld, Charlie Schlatter, Angela Goethals, Jacque Lynn Colton, Chris Mulkey, Karen Landry, Tudor Sherrard, Paul Harkins; ***D:*** Chris Columbus; ***W:*** Chris Columbus; ***M:*** Georges Delerue.

Heartbreak House 🦴🦴 1/2 **1986** A production of George Bernard Shaw's classic play about a captain and his daughter who invite an odd assortment of people into their home for a few days. In the course of their visit, each person shares his ambitions, hopes, and fears. From the "American Playhouse" TV series. **118m/C VHS.** Rex Harrison, Rosemary Harris, Amy Irving; ***D:*** Anthony Page. **TV**

The Heartbreak Kid 🦴🦴🦴 **1972 (PG)** Director May's comic examination of love and hypocrisy. Grodin embroils himself in a triangle with his new bride and a woman he can't have, an absolutely gorgeous and totally unloving woman he shouldn't want. Walks the fence between tragedy and comedy, with an exceptional performance from Berlin. Based on Bruce Jay Friedman's story. **106m/C VHS, DVD.** Charles Grodin, Cybill Shepherd, Eddie Albert, Jeannie Berlin, Audra Lindley, Art Metrano; ***D:*** Elaine May; ***W:*** Neil Simon; ***C:*** Owen Roizman; ***M:*** Garry Sherman, Cy Coleman, Sheldon Harnick. N.Y. Film Critics '72: Support. Actress (Berlin); Natl. Soc. Film Critics '72: Support. Actor (Albert), Support. Actress (Berlin).

The Heartbreak Kid 🦴 1/2 **2007 (R)** In the hands of the increasingly uninspired Farrelly brothers, this lame remake of the 70s film about an unlikable putz who marries too quickly and finds the real girl of his dreams on his honeymoon turns into yet another showcase of gross-out jokes and Stiller-style neuroses. He plays unsympathetic Eddie, who's desperately trying to get out of his marriage to sexpot Lila (Akerman) so he can woo nice girl Miranda (Monaghan). Portrays none of the original's wit or bite, and Stiller blows what little chance the movie has with a by-the-numbers, unappealing performance. **115m/C DVD, HD DVD.** *US* Ben Stiller, Michelle Monaghan, Malin Akerman, Jerry Stiller, Rob Corddry, Danny McBride, Scott Wilson, Carlos Mencia; ***D:*** Bobby Farrelly, Peter Farrelly; ***W:*** Bobby Farrelly, Peter Farrelly, Scot Armstrong, Leslie Dixon, Kevin Barnett; ***C:*** Matthew F. Leonetti; ***M:*** Bill Ryan, Brendan Ryan.

Heartbreak Ridge 🦴🦴🦴 **1986 (R)** An aging Marine recon sergeant is put in command of a young platoon to whip them into shape to prepare for combat in the invasion of Grenada. Eastwood whips this old story into shape too, with a fine performance of a man who's given everything to the Marines. The invasion of Grenada, though, is not epic material. (Also available in English with Spanish subtitles.) **130m/C VHS, DVD.** Clint Eastwood, Marsha Mason, Everett McGill, Arlen Dean Snyder, Bo Svenson, Moses Gunn, Eileen Heckart, Boyd Gaines, Mario Van Peebles, Vincent Irizarry, Ramon Franco, Tom Villard, Pete Koch, Richard Venture, J.C. Quinn, Peter Jason, Thom Sharp; ***D:*** Clint Eastwood; ***W:*** James (Jim) Carabatsos; ***C:*** Jack N. Green; ***M:*** Lennie Niehaus.

Heartbreaker 🦴 1/2 **1983 (R)** Eastern Los Angeles explodes with vicious turf wars when Beto and Hector battle for the affection of Kim, the neighborhood's newest heartbreaker. **90m/C VHS, DVD.** Fernando Allende, Dawn Dunlap, Michael D. Roberts, Robert Dryer, Apollonia; ***D:*** Frank Zuniga.

Heartbreakers 🦴🦴🦴 **1984 (R)** Two male best friends find themselves in the throes of drastic changes in their careers and romantic encounters. On target acting makes this old story new, with a fine performance by Wayne, in her last film before her death. **98m/C VHS.** Peter Coyote, Nick Mancuso, Carole Laure, Max Gail, James Laurenson, Carol Wayne, Jamie Rose, Kathryn Harrold; ***D:*** Bobby Roth; ***W:*** Bobby Roth; ***C:*** Michael Ballhaus; ***M:*** Tangerine Dream.

Heartbreakers 🦴🦴 1/2 **2001 (PG-13)** Max and Page, played by Weaver and Hewitt, are a mother-daughter con-artist team who delight in seducing men right out of their bank accounts and billfolds. Tobacco billionaire William B. Tensy is Max's latest target, but proves to be a tougher case than she realized. Meanwhile, daughter Page has her sights set on Jack, the handsome Palm Beach bar owner, but can't decide if it's just another con, or true love. Hackman excels as the obnoxious Tensy. Director Mirkin's first feature since "Romy and Michelle's High School Reunion." **123m/C VHS, DVD.** *US* Sigourney Weaver, Jennifer Love Hewitt, Gene Hackman, Ray Liotta, Jason Lee, Anne Bancroft, Jeffrey Jones, Nora Dunn, Julio Oscar Mechoso, Ricky Jay, Stacey Travis; ***D:*** David Mirkin; ***W:*** Paul Guay, Robert Dunn, Stephen Mazur; ***C:*** Dean Semler; ***M:*** John Debney.

Heartburn 🦴🦴🦴 **1986 (R)** Based on Nora Ephron's own semi-autobiographical novel about her marital travails with writer Carl Bernstein, this is a tepid, bitter modern romance between writers already shell-shocked from previous marriages. **109m/C VHS, DVD.** Meryl Streep, Jack Nicholson, Steven Hill, Richard Masur, Stockard Channing, Jeff Daniels, Milos Forman, Catherine O'Hara, Maureen Stapleton, Karen Akers, Joanna Gleason, Mercedes Ruehl, Caroline Aaron, Yakov Smirnoff, Anna Maria Horsford, Wilfrid Hyde-White; ***D:*** Mike Nichols; ***W:*** Nora Ephron; ***C:*** Nestor Almendros; ***M:*** Carly Simon.

Heartland 🦴🦴🦴 1/2 **1981 (PG)** Set in 1910, this film chronicles the story of one woman's life on the Wyoming frontier, when she contracts to become a housekeeper for a rancher. Elinore (Ferrell) and her young daughter arrive at the home of Clyde Stewart (Torn) and face any number of hazards, which test her courage and spirit. Stunningly realistic and without cliche. Based on the diaries of Elinore Randall Stewart. **95m/C VHS, DVD.** Conchata Ferrell, Rip Torn, Barry Primus, Lilia Skala, Megan Folson; ***D:*** Richard Pearce; ***W:*** Beth Ferris; ***C:*** Fred Murphy. Sundance '81: Grand Jury Prize.

Hearts & Armour 🦴🦴 **1983** A holy war between Christians and Moors erupts when a Moorish princess is kidnapped. Based on Ludovico Ariosto's "Orlando Furioso." **101m/C VHS.** *IT* Tanya Roberts, Leigh McCloskey, Ron Moss, Rick Edwards, Giovanni Visentin; ***D:*** Giacomo Battiato.

Heart's Desire 🦴 1/2 **1937** Opera great Tauber stars in this musical of an unknown Viennese singer who falls in love with an English girl. **79m/B VHS.** *GB* Richard Tauber, Lenora Corbett, Kathleen Kelly, Paul Graetz; ***D:*** Paul Stein.

Heart's Haven 🦴🦴 1/2 **1922** An insensitive wife (Adams), who doesn't appreciate how wonderful her husband is, winds up running away with another man. **61m/B VHS.** Claire Adams, Robert McKim, Carl Gantvoort, Jean Hersholt; ***D:*** Benjamin B. Hampton.

Hearts in Atlantis 🦴🦴 1/2 **2001 (PG-13)** Coming-of-age tale tinged with creeps benefits from the odd combination of a story by Stephen King and direction from Scott Hicks, who also directed "Shine" and "Snow Falling on Cedars." Bobby (Yelchin) is an 11-year-old boy living in lower middle class Connecticut circa 1960 with his widowed mother Liz (Davis). When enigmatic Ted (Hopkins) rents a room in their attic, he offers the boy a job reading him the daily newspaper. He also has Bobby keep an eye out for the "low men" (CIA agents? Mafia?) he believes are pursuing him. Ted offers the male role model and adult attention Bobby craves and the two quickly become close. Ted, it seems, has some kind of psychic ability, which he also sees in Bobby. Although lushly filmed, the plot seems a bit stagnant and listless for a story about young people. **101m/C VHS, DVD.** *US* Anthony Hopkins, Anton Yelchin, Hope Davis, Mika Boorem, David Morse, Alan Tudyk, Tom Bower, Celia Weston, Adam LeFevre, Timothy Reifsnyder, Deirdre O'Connell, Will Rothhaar; ***D:*** Scott Hicks; ***W:*** William Goldman; ***C:*** Piotr Sobocinski; ***M:*** Mychael Danna.

Hearts of Darkness: A Filmmaker's Apocalypse 🦴🦴🦴🦴 **1991 (R)** This riveting, critically acclaimed documentary about the making of Francis Ford Coppola's masterpiece "Apocalypse Now" is based largely on original footage shot and directed by his wife Eleanor. Also included are recent interviews with cast and crew members including Coppola, Martin Sheen, Robert Duvall, Frederic Forrest and Dennis Hopper. **96m/C VHS.** Sam Bottoms, Eleanor Coppola, Francis Ford Coppola, Robert Duvall, Laurence Fishburne, Frederic Forrest, Albert Hall, Dennis Hopper, George Lucas, John Milius, Martin Sheen; ***D:*** Fax Bahr, George Hickenlooper; ***W:*** Fax Bahr, George Hickenlooper; ***M:*** Todd Boekelheide. Natl. Bd. of Review '91: Feature Doc.

Hearts of Fire 🦴 **1987** A trio of successful rock 'n' roll stars work out their confused romantic entanglements. Barely released at all, and not even in the U.S. Sad outing for the cast, especially legendary Dylan. **90m/C VHS.** Bob Dylan, Fiona, Rupert Everett, Julian Glover; ***D:*** Richard Marquand; ***W:*** Joe Eszterhas; ***M:*** John Barry.

Hearts of Humanity 🦴🦴 **1932** Mawkish melodrama concerning a Jewish antique dealer and his relationship with the son of an Irish cop. An early "Chico and the Man" variant. **56m/B VHS.** Jean Hersholt, Jackie Searl, J. Farrell MacDonald, Claudia Dell, Charles Delaney, Lucille LaVerne, George Humbert; ***D:*** Christy Cabanne.

Hearts of the West 🦴🦴🦴 1/2 *Hollywood Cowboy* **1975 (PG)** A fantasy-filled farm boy travels to Hollywood in the 1930s and seeks a writing career. Instead, he finds himself an ill-suited western movie star in this small offbeat comedy-drama that's sure to charm. **103m/C VHS.** Jeff Bridges, Andy Griffith, Donald Pleasence, Alan Arkin, Blythe Danner; ***D:*** Howard Zieff; ***W:*** Rob Thompson. N.Y. Film Critics '75: Support. Actor (Arkin).

Hearts of the World 🦴🦴🦴 **1918** A vintage Griffith epic about a young boy who goes off to WWI and the tribulations endured by both him and his family on the homefront. Overly sentimental but powerfully made melodrama, from Griffith's waning years. Silent with music score. **152m/B VHS.** Lillian Gish, Robert "Bobbie" Harron, Dorothy Gish, Erich von Stroheim, Ben Alexander, Josephine Crowell, Noel Coward, Mary Gish; ***D:*** D.W. Griffith.

Hearts of War 🦴 1/2 *The Poet* **2007 (R)** In 1939, reluctant (and poetical) German soldier Oscar Koenig (Scarfe) is sent to Poland where he rescues beautiful Rachel (Dobrev) during a snowstorm. She turns out to be a Rabbi's daughter and engaged to someone else. They fall in love anyway but Oscar realizes that he must let her go and tells Rachel to flee towards the Russian front to escape the Nazis atrocities. A pregnant Rachel marries Bernard (Bennett), who accepts Oscar's son as his own, and they eventually all meet again at a German camp where more sacrifices must be made. **96m/C DVD.** *CA* Jonathan Scarfe, Nina Dobrev, Zachary Bennett, Roy Scheider, Kim Coates, Daryl Hannah, Colm Feore; ***D:*** Damian Lee; ***W:*** Jack Crystal; ***C:*** David Pelletier; ***M:*** Zion Lee.

Heartstopper 🦴 **1992** Benjamin Latham, an innocent physician in Pittsburgh, was accused of being a vampire in colonial times and hung. 200 years later, he emerges from the grave, unscathed. While trying to figure out what has happened, he falls in love with a photojournalist, who helps him find his own descendent, Matthew Latham. Unfortunately, his deep freeze has left him with the compulsion to kill, but only evil members of society. **96m/B VHS.** Moon Zappa, Tom Savini, Kevin Kindlin; ***D:*** John A. Russo; ***W:*** John A. Russo; ***C:*** John Rice.

Heartstrings 🦴🦴 *The Perfect Man* **1993** Melissa wants everything in her life to be perfect, including having the perfect man, which she thinks is New York gallery owner Peter. But will Melissa's heart compromise her ambitions? **94m/C VHS.** *CA* Garwin Sanford, Brian Jensen, Michelle Little, Phyllis Diller; ***D:*** Wendy Hill-Tout; ***W:*** Wendy Hill-Tout; ***C:*** Peter Wunstorf; ***M:*** George Blondheim.

Heartwood 🦴🦴 **1998 (PG-13)** Frank (Mills) is an outcast living in the woods of a failing lumber town. He falls for Sylvia (Swank), the daughter of the engineer hired by mill owner Logan Reese (Robards) to save the mill and the town as well. But when Frank discovers gold, he's the one who comes up with a plan. **92m/C VHS, DVD.** Eddie Mills, Hilary Swank, Jason Robards Jr., Randall Batinkoff, Stanley DeSantis; ***D:*** Lanny Cotler.

Heat 🦴🦴🦴 *Andy Warhol's Heat* **1972** Another Andy Warhol-produced journey into drug-addled urban seediness. Features a former child actor/junkie and a has-been movie star barely surviving in a run-down motel. This is one of Warhol's better film productions; even non-fans may enjoy it. **102m/C VHS, DVD.** Joe Dallesandro, Sylvia Miles, Pat Ast, Andrea Feldman, Ray Vestal; ***D:*** Paul Morrissey; ***W:*** Paul Morrissey; ***C:*** Paul Morrissey; ***M:*** John Cale.

Heat 🦴 1/2 **1987 (R)** A Las Vegas bodyguard avenges the beating of an old flame by a mobster's son, and incites mob retaliation. Based on the William Goldman novel. **103m/C VHS, DVD.** Burt Reynolds, Karen Young, Peter MacNichol, Howard Hesseman; ***D:*** R.M. Richards; ***W:*** William Goldman; ***M:*** Michael Gibbs.

Heat 1/2 **1995 (R)** Pacino and De Niro in the same scene. Together. Finally. Obsessive master thief McCauley (De Niro) leads a crack crew on various military-style heists across L.A. while equally obsessive detective Hanna (Pacino) tracks him. Each man recognizes and respects the other's ability and dedication, even as they express the willingness to kill each other, if necessary. Excellent script with all the fireworks you'd expect, as well as a surprising look into emotional and personal sacrifice. Beautiful cinematography shows industrial landscape to great effect. Writer-director Mann held onto the screenplay for 12 years. **171m/C VHS, DVD, UMD.** Robert De Niro, Al Pacino, Val Kilmer, Jon Voight, Diane Venora, Ashley Judd, Wes Studi, Tom Sizemore, Mykelti Williamson, Amy Brenneman, Ted Levine, Dennis Haysbert, William Fichtner, Natalie Portman, Hank Azaria, Henry Rollins, Kevin Gage, Tone Loc, Bud Cort, Jeremy Piven, Tom Noonan, Xander Berkeley; ***D:*** Michael Mann; ***W:*** Michael Mann; ***C:*** Dante Spinotti; ***M:*** Elliot Goldenthal.

Heat and Dust **1982 (R)** A young bride joins her husband at his post in India and is inexorably drawn to the country and its prince of state. Years later her great niece journeys to modern day India in search of the truth about her scandalous and mysterious relative. More than the story of two romances, this is the tale of women rebelling against an unseen caste system which keeps them second-class citizens. Ruth Jhabvala wrote the novel and screenplay. **130m/C VHS, DVD.** *GB* Julie Christie, Greta Scacchi, Shashi Kapoor, Christopher Cazenove, Nickolas Grace, Julian Glover, Susan Fleetwood, Patrick Godfrey, Jennifer Kendal, Madhur Jaffrey, Barry Foster, Amanda Walker, Sudha Chopra, Sajid Khan, Zakir Hussain, Ratna Pathak, Charles McCaughan, Parveen Paul; ***D:*** James Ivory; ***W:*** Ruth Prawer Jhabvala, Saeed Jaffrey, Harish Khare; ***C:*** Walter Lassally; ***M:*** Richard Robbins. British Acad. '83: Adapt. Screenplay.

Heat and Sunlight 1/2 **1987** A photographer becomes obsessively jealous of his lover as their relationship comes to an end. Director Nilsson again used a unique improvisational, video-to-film technique, as he did with his previous film, "Signal 7." **98m/B VHS, DVD.** Rob Nilsson, Consuelo Faust, Bill Bailey, Don Bajema, Ernie Fosselius; ***D:*** Rob Nilsson; ***W:*** Rob Nilsson; ***C:*** Tomas Tucker; ***M:*** Mark Adler. Sundance '88: Grand Jury Prize.

Heat of Desire *Plein Sud* **1984 (R)** A philosophy professor abandons everything (including his wife) for a woman he barely knows and is conned by her "relatives." With English subtitles. **90m/C VHS.** *FR* Clio Goldsmith, Patrick Dewaere, Jeanne Moreau, Guy Marchand; ***D:*** Luc Beraud.

The Heat of the Day 1/2 **1991** A British officer is accused of treason. As he attempts to find those who framed him, he meets a lovely woman all too willing to help. But whose side is she really on? Set in WWII. Tense and well-acted; made for TV. **120m/C VHS.** Michael York, Patricia Hodge, Peggy Ashcroft, Anna Carteret, Michael Gambon; ***W:*** Harold Pinter. **TV**

Heat of the Flame **1976** A vicious woodsman captures and rapes a beautiful girl. Psychological games, eroticism and exploitive nudity ensue. **88m/C VHS.** *SP* Tony Ferrandis, Ellie MacLure, Raymond Young, Anthony (Jose, J. Antonio, J.A.) Mayans; ***D:*** Rafael Romero Marchent.

Heat of the Sun **1999** Former Scotland Yard detective Albert Tyburn (Eve) has been sent to work in Nairobi, Kenya in the hedonistic expatriate community of the 1930s, known as "Happy Valley." But despite his disdain for the community's racial and social lines, Tyburn is soon involved in murder and mayhem. In "Private Lives," Tyburn investigates the death of Lady Ellesmere and discovers drug-running, adultery, and murder. "Hide in Plain Sight" finds Tyburn investigating the death of a native girl and the disappearance of other girls from the local Christian mission. "The Sport of Kings" finds Tyburn involved in the murder of a young boy against the backdrop of Nairobi's premier social event, Race Week. **360m/C VHS, DVD.** *GB* Trevor Eve, Michael Byrne, Susannah Harker, Tim Woodward, Daniel Betts, James Callis, Freddie Annobil-Dodoo, Kate McKenzie, Hugh Bonneville, Cathryn Harrison, Julian Rhind-Tutt, Diana Quick, Deborah Findlay, Joss Ackland, Richard McCabe, Sonya Walger; ***D:*** Adrian Shergold, Diarmuid Lawrence, Paul Seed; ***W:*** Russell Lewis, Tim Prager. **TV**

Heat Street **1987** Two thugs exact revenge on street gangs for the murders of loved ones. Made for video. **90m/C VHS.** Quincy Adams, Deborah Gibson, Wendy MacDonald, Del Zamora; ***D:*** Joseph Merhi. **VIDEO**

Heat Wave 1/2 *The House Across the Lake* **1954** A writer gets involved with a "femme fatale" who kills her wealthy husband for the love of a young pianist. **60m/B VHS, DVD.** *GB* Alex Nicol, Hillary Brooke, Sidney James, Susan Stephen, Paul Carpenter; ***D:*** Ken Hughes; ***W:*** Ken Hughes; ***C:*** Walter J. (Jimmy W.) Harvey; ***M:*** Ivor Slaney.

Heat Wave **1990 (R)** The Watts ghetto uprising of 1965 is a proving ground for a young black journalist. Excellent cast and fine script portrays the anger and frustration of blacks in Los Angeles and the U.S. in the 1960s and the fear of change felt by blacks and whites when civil rights reform began. Strong drama with minimal emotionalism. **92m/C VHS, DVD.** Blair Underwood, Cicely Tyson, James Earl Jones, Sally Kirkland, Margaret Avery, David Strathairn, Robert Hooks, Adam Arkin, Paris Vaughan, Charlie Korsmo; ***D:*** Kevin Hooks; ***W:*** Kevin Hooks, Michael Lazarou; ***C:*** Mark Irwin; ***M:*** Thomas Newman. **CABLE**

Heated Vengeance **1987 (R)** A Vietnam vet returns to the jungle to find the woman he left behind, and runs into some old enemies. **91m/C VHS.** Richard Hatch, Michael J. Pollard, Dennis Patrick, Mills Watson, Cameron Dye; ***D:*** Edward Murphy.

Heater **1999** Two homeless men come into possession of an electric space heater that, despite the December cold, is useless to them since they don't have any place to plug it in. So they decide to travel from their inner city haunt to a suburban shopping mall—by foot—in hopes they can return the heater for a cash refund. **87m/C VHS, DVD.** *CA* Gary Farmer, Stephen Ouimette; ***D:*** Terrance Odette; ***W:*** Terrance Odette; ***C:*** Arthur E. Cooper; ***M:*** Neil Clark.

Heathers 1/2 **1989 (R)** Clique of stuck-up girls named Heather rule the high school social scene until the newest member (not a Heather) decides that enough is enough. She and her outlaw boyfriend embark (accidentally on her part, intentionally on his) on a murder spree disguised as a rash of teen suicides. Dense, take-no-prisoners black comedy with buckets of potent slang, satire and unforgiving hostility. Humor this dark is rare; sharply observed and acted, though the end is out of place. Slater does his best Nicholson impression. **102m/C VHS, DVD, Blu-ray Disc.** Winona Ryder, Christian Slater, Kim Walker, Shannen Doherty, Lisanne Falk, Penelope Milford, Glenn Shadix, Lance Fenton, Patrick Laborteaux, Jeremy Applegate, Renee Estevez; ***D:*** Michael Lehmann; ***W:*** Daniel Waters; ***C:*** Francis Kenny; ***M:*** David Newman. Ind. Spirit '90: First Feature.

The Heat's On *Tropicana* **1943** Gaxton is a broadway producer with a failing musical and an unhappy star in West. He cranks up the publicity machine and gets the show declared immoral by the Legion of Purity which results in its closing (not what he expected). Gaxton then runs a scam to become the producer of West's new show, which just happens to be financed by some Legion members. Very uneven plot and performances with thrown-in musical numbers. West wrote her own dialogue but unlike her early films she had little control over the production and it showed. West didn't make another movie for 27 years (the appalling "Myra Breckenridge"). ♫ Just a Stranger in Town; Hello, Mi Amigo; The White Keys and the Black Keys; There Goes That Guitar; Antonio; The Caissons Go Rolling Along; There Goes My Heart. **79m/B VHS.** Mae West, William Gaxton, Victor Moore, Almira Sessions, Lester Allen, Mary Roche, Alan Dinehart, Lloyd Bridges; ***D:*** Gregory Ratoff; ***W:*** Fitzroy Davis, George S. George, Fred Schiller.

Heatseeker **1995 (R)** Corporations use mechanical fighters to participate in brutal kickboxing contests in 2019 New America. Human Chance (Cooke) must battle cyborg opponent Xao if he wants to save his kidnapped trainer. Lots of action and even some intentional humor. **91m/C VHS.** Keith Cooke, Gary Daniels, Norbert Weisser, Thom Mathews; ***D:*** Albert Pyun.

Heatwave **1983 (R)** Local residents oppose a multi-million dollar residential complex in Australia. Davis portrays a liberal activist, who wages war with the developers, and, in return, becomes involved with a possible murder case. **92m/C VHS.** *AU* Judy Davis, Richard Moir, Chris Haywood, Bill Hunter, John Gregg, Anna Maria Monticelli; ***D:*** Phillip Noyce.

Heaven **1987 (PG-13)** An exploration of "heaven" including the idea, the place, and people's views about it. Questions such as "How do you get there?" and "What goes on up there?" are discussed. Offbeat interviews mixed with a collage of celestial images. **80m/C VHS, DVD.** ***D:*** Diane Keaton; ***M:*** Howard Shore.

Heaven **1999 (R)** Robert Marling (Donovan) is an architect with a broken marriage and a compulsion to gamble (and lose) at a sleazy strip joint owned by the odious and brutual Stanner (Schiff). One of the performers is a psychic transvestite named Heaven (Edwards), who predicts that Robert will win big in the lottery. This info gets back to evil shrink Melrose (Malahide), who has both Robert and Heaven as patients, and who just happens to be having an affair with Robert's bitter wife, Jennifer (Going). And the coincidental silliness doesn't stop there. Based on a novel by Chad Taylor. **103m/C VHS, DVD.** *NZ* Martin Donovan, Joanna Going, Patrick Malahide, Danny Edwards, Richard Schiff; ***D:*** Scott Reynolds; ***W:*** Scott Reynolds; ***C:*** Simon Raby; ***M:*** Victoria Kelly.

Heaven 1/2 **2001 (R)** Themes of despair and redemption fuel this story of Philippa (Blanchett), a woman who has accidentally killed four innocent people while trying to assassinate drug lord Vendice. As she's questioned by the authorities (who are in cahoots with Vendice), young police translator Filippo (Ribisi) falls in love with her. The two escape thanks to police incompetence and go after Vendice. Directed by Tom Tykwer from a script written by late film legend Krzysztof Kieslowski ("The Decalogue" series and "Three Colors" trilogy) **96m/C VHS, DVD.** *US GE* Cate Blanchett, Giovanni Ribisi, Stefania Rocca, Remo Girone, Mattia Sbragia, Alberto Di Stasio, Stefano Santospago, Alessandro Sperduti; ***D:*** Tom Tykwer; ***W:*** Krzysztof Kieslowski, Krzysztof Piesiewicz; ***C:*** Frank Griebe.

Heaven & Earth **1990 (PG-13)** A samurai epic covering the battle for the future of Japan between two feuding warlords. The overwhelming battle scenes were actually filmed on location in Canada. In Japanese with English subtitles. **104m/C VHS.** *JP* Masahiko Tsugawa, Takaaki Enoki, Atsuko Asano, Tsunehiko Watase, Naomi Zaizen, Binpachi Ito; ***D:*** Haruki Kadokawa; ***W:*** Haruki Kadokawa; ***M:*** Daisuke Hinata; ***Nar:*** Stuart Whitman.

Heaven and Earth **1993 (R)** Conclusion of Stone's Vietnam trilogy (after "Platoon" and "Born on the Fourth of July") focuses on Vietnamese woman (film debut of Le) and her life under the French and American occupations. Jones is the American soldier who marries her and eventually brings her to the U.S. Not one for subtleties, Stone chases melodramatic excess with finesse of lumberjack, sawing away at guilt and remorse from a "woman's point of view." Cranky Tommy Lee shows up too late to save flick and is saddled with a perplexing I.D. to boot. Flawed, ambitious, and interesting if a student of Stone. Based on the two autobiographies of Le Ly Haslip, "When Heaven and Earth Changed Places" and "Child of War, Woman of Peace." Filmed on location in Thailand. **142m/C VHS, DVD.** Hiep Thi Le, Tommy Lee Jones, Joan Chen, Haing S. Ngor, Debbie Reynolds, Conchata Ferrell, Dustin Nguyen, Liem Whatley, Dale Dye; ***D:*** Oliver Stone; ***W:*** Oliver Stone; ***C:*** Robert Richardson; ***M:*** Kitaro. Golden Globes '94: Score.

Heaven & Hell *Di san lei da dou; Di yu; Heaven and Hell Gate; Sha chu di yu mun; Shaolin Hellgate* **1978** Xin Ling (Yi-min Ling) is sent by the Queen of Heaven to capture an earthly couple. When he allows them to live out of mercy, the Queen kills him, and he reincarnates as a taxi driver only to die saving another couple. Sentenced to Hell, he decides to gather a few lost souls who were meant to go to heaven and fight his way out. Truly one of the most bizarre of Shaw Brothers kung-fu films, it is famous for re-uniting the cast of the "5 Deadly Venoms." **88m/C DVD.** *HK* David Chiang, Ging Man Fung, Sheng Fu, Philip Kwok, Lin Lin Li, Chen Chi Lin, Yi-min Li, Meng Lo, Chien Sun, Yan Tsan Tang, Jenny Tseng, Dick Wei; ***D:*** Cheh Chang; ***W:*** Cheh Chang, Lang Chou, Kuang Ni; ***C:*** Fen Chen, Ying-Chaun Kuan, Mu-To Kung; ***M:*** Yung-Yu Chen, Chia Chang Liu.

Heaven Before I Die **1996 (PG)** Sheltered Jacob (Velasquez) travels from the Middle East to Toronto and is taken under the questionable wing of a small-time thief (Giannini) and a beautiful waitress (Pacula). But when Jacob finds a measure of success as a Charlie Chaplin impersonator, his innocence gets a dose of culture shock. **98m/C VHS, DVD.** *CA* Andy Velasquez, Giancarlo Giannini, Catherine Oxenberg; ***Cameos:*** Joanna Pacula, Omar Sharif, Burt Young, Joseph Bologna; ***D:*** Izidore K. Musallam.

Heaven Can Wait **1943** Social satire in which a rogue tries to convince the Devil to admit him into Hell by relating the story of his philandering life and discovers that he was a more valuable human being than he thought. A witty Lubitsch treat based on the play "Birthdays." **112m/C VHS, DVD.** Don Ameche, Gene Tierney, Laird Cregar, Charles Coburn, Marjorie Main, Eugene Pallette, Allyn Joslyn, Spring Byington, Signe Hasso, Louis Calhern, Dickie Moore, Florence Bates, Scotty Beckett, Charles Halton; ***D:*** Ernst Lubitsch.

Heaven Can Wait **1978 (PG)** A remake of 1941's "Here Comes Mr. Jordan." L.A. Rams quarterback Joe Pendleton (Beatty) is summoned to heaven before his time. When archangel Mr. Jordan (Mason) realizes the mistake, Joe is returned to Earth but it's in the body of a wealthy industrialist who's about to be murdered by his unfaithful wife Julia (Cannon) and his nervous secretary, Tony (Grodin). But Joe is about to let a little thing like murder prevent him from playing in the Super Bowl—new body or not. Christie's the new love interest; Warden's the gruff coach. Not to be confused with the 1943 film of the same name. **101m/C VHS, DVD.** Warren Beatty, Julie Christie, Charles Grodin, Dyan Cannon, James Mason, Jack Warden, Buck Henry; ***D:*** Warren Beatty, Buck Henry; ***W:*** Elaine May, Warren Beatty; ***C:*** William A. Fraker; ***M:*** Dave Grusin. Oscars '78: Art Dir./Set Dec.; Golden Globes '79: Actor—Mus./Comedy (Beatty), Film—Mus./Comedy, Support. Actress (Cannon); Writers Guild '78: Adapt. Screenplay.

Heaven Help Us 1/2 *Catholic Boys* **1985 (R)** Three mischievous boys find themselves continually in trouble with the priests running their Brooklyn Catholic high school during the mid-1960s. Realistic and humorous look at adolescent life. **102m/C VHS, DVD.** Andrew McCarthy, Mary Stuart Masterson, Kevin Dillon, Malcolm Danare, Jennifer (Jennie) Dundas Lowe, Kate Reid, Wallace Shawn, Jay Patterson, John Heard, Donald Sutherland, Yeardley Smith, Sherry Steiner, Calvert Deforest, Philip Bosco, Patrick Dempsey, Christopher Durang; ***D:*** Michael Dinner; ***W:*** Charles Purpura; ***M:*** James Horner.

Heaven Is a Playground 1/2 **1991 (R)** On Chicago's South Side an inner city basketball coach and an idealistic young lawyer are determined to change the fate of a group of high school boys. The men use the incentive of athletic scholarships to keep their team in school and away from drugs and gangs. **104m/C VHS, DVD.** D.B. Sweeney, Michael Warren, Richard Jordan, Victor Love; ***D:*** Randall Fried; ***W:*** Randall Fried; ***C:*** Tom Richmond; ***M:*** Patrick O'Hearn.

Heaven Knows, Mr. Allison **1957** Terrific two-character WWII drama finds tough (but tender-hearted) Marine sergeant Allison (Mitchum) stranded with Irish nun, Sister Angela (Kerr), on a Pacific island overrun by Japanese troops. The duo hide out during the day and forage for food by night, gradually revealing their pasts to each other. He falls hard while she resists his advances and they struggle to stay alive until U.S. forces invade the island. Lots of action and good performances. Based on the novel by Charles Shaw. **106m/C VHS, DVD.** Robert Mitchum, Deborah Kerr; ***D:*** John Huston; ***W:*** John Huston, John Lee Mahin; ***C:*** Oswald Morris; ***M:*** Georges Auric.

Heaven on Earth ✂✂ 1/2 **1989** The story of two orphaned British children who, along with thousands of orphans shipped from England to Canada between 1867 and 1914, try to make new lives in the Canadian wilderness. **101m/C VHS.** *CA* R.H. Thomson, Sian Leisa Davies, Torquil Campbell, Fiona Reid; ***D:*** Allen Kroeker; ***W:*** Margaret Atwood.

Heaven or Vegas ✂✂ **1998 (R)** Rachel (Bleeth) is a part-time Vegas prostitute who falls for gigolo Navy (Grieco), who offers her a new life with him in Montana. But first Rachel wants to visit the home she ran away from years before. Too bad Rachel's sister Lilli starts making eyes at her man and when Navy appears interested, Rachel runs away again. Can Navy find her and convince Rachel he loves only her? It's a modern-day fairytale so what do you think? **110m/C VHS.** Yasmine Bleeth, Richard Grieco; ***D:*** Gregory C. Haynes; ***W:*** Gregory C. Haynes. **VIDEO**

Heaven Tonight ✂✂ 1/2 **1993 (R)** Ex-rock star dad copes with midlife crisis by trying for his big comeback, this time with his son. **97m/C VHS.** *AU* John Waters, Rebecca Gilling, Guy Pearce, Kim Gyngell; ***D:*** Pino Amenta; ***C:*** David Connell.

Heavenly Bodies WOOF! **1984 (R)** A young woman who dreams of owning a health club will stop at nothing to accomplish her goals. When a rival tries to put her out of business, a "dance-down" takes place in this lame low-budget aerobics musical. **99m/C VHS.** *CA* Cynthia Dale, Richard Rebrere, Laura Henry, Stuart Stone, Walter George Alton, Cec Linder; ***D:*** Lawrence Dane; ***W:*** Lawrence Dane, Ron Base; ***C:*** Thomas Burstyn.

The Heavenly Body ✂✂ **1944** Stylish light comedy. Astronomer William Whitley (Powell) is so obsessed with his work that he ignores the heavenly body of wife Vicky (Lamarr) at home. Feeling unloved, Vicky turns to local astrologer Margaret Sibyll (Bainter) for advice and she predicts Vicky will fall for the new man who enters her life. Then air raid warden Lloyd Hunter (Craig) shows up at her door. When they continue to cross paths, both Lloyd and Vicky start taking their meetings more seriously and hubby William finally starts getting jealous. **95m/B DVD.** William Powell, Hedy Lamarr, James Craig, Fay Bainter, Henry O'Neill, Spring Byington; ***D:*** Alexander Hall; ***W:*** Harry Kurnitz, Walter Reisch, Michael Arlen; ***C:*** Robert Planck; ***M:*** Bronislau Kaper.

Heavenly Creatures ✂✂✂ 1/2 **1994 (R)** Haunting and surreal drama chronicles the true-life case of two young schoolgirls, Pauline and Juliet, who were charged with clubbing to death Pauline's mother in Christchurch, New Zealand, in 1954. Opens two years before the murder, and follows the friendship as the two teens become obsessed with each other, retreating into a rich fantasy life. They create an elaborate, medieval kingdom where they escape to their dream lovers and romantic alter egos. Elaborate morphing and animation effects vividly express the shared inner fantasy world, while innovative camera work creates the sensations of hysteria and excitement that the girls experience as their infatuation becomes uncontrollable. Leads Lynsky and Winslet are convincing as the awkward, quiet Pauline and the pretty, intelligent, upper class Juliet. Bizarre crime story is stylish and eerily compelling, and made more so by real life events: after the film was released, mystery writer Anne Perry was revealed as Juliet Hulme. **110m/C VHS, DVD.** *NZ* Melanie Lynskey, Kate Winslet, Sarah Pierse, Diana Kent, Clive Merrison, Simon O'Connor; ***D:*** Peter Jackson; ***W:*** Peter Jackson, Fran Walsh; ***C:*** Alun Bollinger; ***M:*** Peter Dasent.

The Heavenly Kid ✂✂ **1985 (PG-13)** Leather-jacketed "cool" guy who died in a '60s hot rod crash finally receives an offer to exit limbo and enter heaven. The deal requires that he educate his dull earthly son on more hip and worldly ways. A big problem is that the soundtrack and wardrobe are 1955, whereas the cocky cool greaser supposedly died 17 years ago in 1968. Mildly entertaining. **92m/C VHS, DVD.** Lewis Smith, Jane Kaczmarek, Jason Gedrick, Richard Mulligan; ***D:*** Cary Medoway; ***W:*** Cary Medoway, Martin Copeland.

Heaven's a Drag ✂✂ 1/2 *To Die For* **1994** Low-budget British cross between a tearjerker and a supernatural comedy. HIV-positive London drag performer Mark (Williams) lives with Simon (Arklie), a TV repairman who keeps his sexuality a secret from his co-workers and his emotional distance from his stricken lover. When Mark dies, Simon is quick to get on with his life—too quick for Mark, who's ghostly presence puts a damper on Simon's dating possibilities and brings up some old resentments. **96m/C VHS, DVD.** *GB* Thomas Arklie, Ian Patrick Williams, Dilly Keane, Tony Slattery, Jean Boht, John Altman; ***D:*** Peter MacKenzie Litten; ***W:*** Johnny Byrne; ***C:*** John Ward; ***Nar:*** Ian McKellen.

Heavens Above ✂✂✂ **1963** A sharp, biting satire on cleric life in England. Sellers stars as the quiet, down-to-earth reverend who is appointed to a new post in space. **113m/B VHS, DVD.** *GB* Peter Sellers, Cecil Parker, Isabel Jeans, Eric Sykes, Ian Carmichael; ***D:*** John Boulting, Roy Boulting; ***M:*** Richard Rodney Bennett.

Heaven's Burning ✂✂ **1997 (R)** Fast-paced road movie with some unexpected twists. Midori (Kudoh) is a young Japanese woman who is honeymooning in Sydney with new hubby Yukio (Isomura). But Midori fakes her own kidnapping to wait for her lover to arrive (who doesn't show). Yukio and the cops quickly discover her plotting but, in the meantime, Midori's been caught up in the midst of a bank robbery. When the robbery goes wrong, she becomes the quasi-hostage of driver Colin (Crowe), who takes off across Australia, pursued by the cops, his ex-partners, and the humiliated husband who wants revenge. Midori and Colin bond and things get increasingly stranger. **96m/C VHS, DVD.** *AU* Youki Kudoh, Russell Crowe, Kenji Isomura, Ray Barrett, Robert Mammone, Petru Gheorghiu, Matthew Dyktynski, Anthony Phelan, Colin Hay, Susan Prior, Norman Kaye; ***D:*** Craig Lahiff; ***W:*** Louis Nowra; ***C:*** Brian J. Breheny; ***M:*** Michael Atkinson.

Heavens Fall ✂✂ 1/2 **2006 (PG-13)** Nine young blacks are pulled off an Alabama freight train in 1931, accused of raping two white women. Quickly convicted, they were all sentenced to the electric chair. Their case is appealed to the U.S. Supreme Court and, in 1933, New York attorney Sam Leibowitz (Hutton) travels to the deeply segregated South to work on their defense. Straightforward retelling of the case of the Scottsboro Boys and a landmark judicial decision. **105m/C DVD.** Timothy Hutton, David Strathairn, Bill Sage, Leelee Sobieski, Anthony Mackie, Azura Skye, Bill Smitrovich, James Tolkan, Maury Chaykin; ***D:*** Terry Green; ***W:*** Terry Green; ***C:*** Paul Sanchez; ***M:*** David Reynolds.

Heaven's Fire ✂✂ **1999** Dean (Roberts) finds himself trying to prevent former co-worker Quentin (Prochnow) from stealing U.S. currency engraving plates from the treasury building. Dean foils the getaway but the crooks (and a group of tourists) are trapped in the building by a couple of explosions. So Dean then tries to protect the innocent while keeping Quentin at bay. **91m/C VHS, DVD.** Eric Roberts, Jurgen Prochnow, Cali Timmins; ***D:*** David Warry-Smith; ***W:*** Rob Kerchner, Charles Philip Moore; ***C:*** Gordon Verheul; ***M:*** Deddy Tzur. **CABLE**

Heaven's Gate ✂✂ **1981 (R)** The uncut version of Cimino's notorious folly. A fascinating, plotless, and exaggerated account of the Johnson County cattle war of the 1880s. Ravishingly photographed, the film's production almost single-handedly put United Artists out of business. **220m/C VHS, DVD.** Kris Kristofferson, Christopher Walken, Isabelle Huppert, John Hurt, Richard Masur, Mickey Rourke, Brad Dourif, Joseph Cotten, Jeff Bridges, Sam Waterston, Terry O'Quinn, Geoffrey Lewis; ***D:*** Michael Cimino; ***W:*** Michael Cimino; ***C:*** Vilmos Zsigmond. Golden Raspberries '81: Worst Director (Cimino).

Heaven's Prisoners ✂✂ 1/2 **1995 (R)** Dave Robicheaux (Baldwin) is an ex-New Orleans homicide detective and recovering alcoholic, living a quiet life on a bayou with patient wife Annie (Lynch). They witness a plane crash and Dave rescues the only survivor, a young Salvadoran girl, whom they adopt. But the crash wasn't an accident and Dave's snooping around involves him with drug runners and local crime bosses, including old high school buddy, Bubba Rocque (Roberts), and his sirenish wife, Claudette (Hatcher). Convoluted plot with some moody touches but Baldwin scores as the flawed hero. Based on the mystery series by James Lee Burke. **135m/C VHS, DVD.** Paul Guilfoyle, Alec Baldwin, Kelly Lynch, Mary Stuart Masterson, Eric Roberts, Teri Hatcher, Vondie Curtis-Hall, Badja (Medu) Djola, Joe (Johnny) Viterelli, Hawthorne James; ***D:*** Phil Joanou; ***W:*** Scott Frank, Harley Peyton; ***C:*** Harris Savides; ***M:*** George Fenton.

Heavy ✂✂✂ **1994 (R)** Sensitive character study supported by an excellent ensemble, led by Vince as Victor, an obese, painfully withdrawn, 30-ish cook. He lives with his domineering mother (a subdued Winters) and helps her run their roadside diner, along with veteran waitress Delores (Harry). Then beautiful teenager Callie (Tyler) is hired and Victor develops a suitably massive crush. Tyler is all pout and promise as Callie, making it clear why a guy like Victor could fall hard for her. Harry brings a rich cynical and sexual edge to Delores. Director Mangold's feature debut is both eloquent and economical, though at times paced to a near standstill. **104m/C VHS, DVD.** Pruitt Taylor Vince, Shelley Winters, Liv Tyler, Deborah Harry, Evan Dando, Joe Grifasi; ***D:*** James Mangold; ***W:*** James Mangold; ***C:*** Michael Barrow; ***M:*** Thurston Moore. Sundance '95: Special Jury Prize.

Heavy Metal ✂✂✂ **1981 (R)** Yes, the animated cult flick is now legally available on video, its copyright disputes finally resolved. A collection of science-fiction and fantasy stories, inspired by the same-titled magazine and offered in a variety of graphic styles, that all encompass the theme of good versus evil. And don't always bet on the good. Features a soundtrack compiled from the work of many top metal artists of the time as well as Bernstein's score with the London Philharmonic Orchestra. A three-minute transitional segment, called "Neverwhere Land," that was cut from the original version has been restored as an epilogue. **90m/C VHS, DVD, UMD.** *CA* ***D:*** Gerald Potterton; ***W:*** Dan Goldberg, Len Blum; ***C:*** Brian Tufano; ***M:*** Elmer Bernstein; ***V:*** John Candy, Joe Flaherty, Don Francks, Eugene Levy, Rodger Bumpass, Jackie Burroughs, Harold Ramis, Richard Romanus, Doug Kenney.

Heavy Metal 2000 ✂ 1/2 **2000 (R)** The original 1981 film was cutting edge but this video game-ish sequel is average at best. Warrior babe Julie is tracking a group of space pirates, led by villain Lord Tyler, who destroyed her home and forced her sister into slavery. Julie assumes a new name, F.A.K.K. (Federation Assigned Ketogenic Killzone), and the usual avenger mission. **88m/C VHS, DVD.** ***D:*** Michael Coldewey, Michel Lemire; ***W:*** Robert Payne Cabeen; ***C:*** Bruno Philip; ***M:*** Frederic Talgorn; ***V:*** Julie Strain, Michael Ironside, Billy Idol, Sonja Ball.

Heavy Petting ✂✂ 1/2 **1989** A hilarious compilation of "love scene" footage from feature films of the silent era to the '60s, newsreels, news reports, educational films, old TV shows, and home movies. **75m/C VHS, DVD.** David Byrne, Josh Mostel, Sandra Bernhard, Allen Ginsberg, Ann Magnuson, Spalding Gray, Laurie Anderson, John Oates, Abbie Hoffman, Jacki Ochs; ***D:*** Obie Benz; ***C:*** Sandi Sissel.

Heavy Petting ✂✂ 1/2 **2007** Charlie (Hines) falls for Daphne (Akerman), which means he has to get along with her new dog, Babydoll. But Charlie hates dogs and Babydoll feels the same way about Charlie. The more time Charlie spends with Babydoll and her owner, the more he realizes that he really likes the dog better than the girl, so he needs to keep Daphne happy. **98m/C DVD.** Brendan P. Hines, Malin Akerman, Kevin Sussman; ***D:*** Marcel Sarmiento; ***W:*** Marcel Sarmiento; ***C:*** Tim Ives; ***M:*** Julian Nott.

Heavy Traffic ✂✂✂ **1973** Ralph Bakshi's animated fantasy portrait of the hard-edged underside of city life. A young cartoonist draws the people, places, and paranoia of his environment. **77m/C VHS, DVD.** Joseph Kaufmann, Beverly Hope Atkinson, Michael Brandon, Frank De Kova, Terri Haven, Mary Dean Lauria, Lillian Adams, Jamie Farr, Robert Easton; ***D:*** Ralph Bakshi; ***W:*** Ralph Bakshi; ***C:*** Ted C. Bemiller, Gregg Heschong; ***M:*** Ed Bogas.

Heavyweights ✂ **1994 (PG)** A product of Disney's sometimes assembly line approach to family entertainment (think "Mighty Ducks"). Nothing new saga of overweight youngsters sent to a fat camp run by tyrannical fitness guru Tony Perkis (Stiller). His methods cause the kids to band together and overthrow him and his "evil" tactics. Oh, by the way, there's a baseball competition with the more athletic camp kids on the other side of the lake. Guess who wins. Stiller as the fame obsessed fitness fanatic, sporting a David Copperfield make-over, is the only highlight in this exercise of excess fluff. Directorial debut of Brill. **98m/C VHS, DVD.** Jeffrey Tambor, Ben Stiller, Jerry Stiller, Anne Meara, Shaun Weiss, Kenan Thompson; ***D:*** Steven Brill; ***W:*** Judd Apatow, Steven Brill; ***C:*** Victor Hammer; ***M:*** J.A.C. Redford.

Heckler ✂✂ **2008** After getting drubbed by the critics for "Son of the Mask," Kennedy and Addis decided to make this documentary of ticked off celebrities who are tired of being bullied by hecklers and critics. While it starts off pretty good, the buildup of bile starts to grate towards the end. **78m/C DVD.** Jamie Kennedy; ***D:*** Michael Addis. **VIDEO**

Heck's Way Home ✂✂ 1/2 **1995** Heck is the Neufeld family dog and best friend of 11-year-old Luke (Krowchuk). The family is moving from Winnipeg to Australia and have a three-day layover in Vancouver. Heck is supposed to come along but instead, unbeknownst to the family, he gets captured by the local dogcatcher (Arkin) and the family are forced to leave without him. Naturally, Heck escapes and starts off on a 2000-mile journey to find his family before they fly away forever. **92m/C VHS, DVD.** Chad Krowchuk, Alan Arkin, Michael Riley, Shannon Lawson; ***D:*** Michael Scott; ***C:*** Maris Jansons. **CABLE**

Hedd Wyn ✂✂ **1992** True story of talented young poet Ellis Evans (Garmon), writing under the pseudonym Hedd Wyn, who dreams of winning a coveted literary prize. His hopes are put on hold when he's forced to fight in WWI, although he submits his antiwar poem "The Hero" to the competition. Welsh with subtitles. **123m/C VHS.** *GB* Huw Garmon, Catrin Fychan, Ceri Cunnington, Llio Silyn; ***D:*** Paul Turner; ***W:*** Alan Llwyd; ***C:*** Ray Orton; ***M:*** John E.R. Hardy.

Hedda ✂✂ 1/2 **1975** A dramatization of the Henrik Ibsen play, "Hedda Gabler," about a middle-class pregnant woman. The story finds her frustrated with her life and manipulating those around her with tragic results. **102m/C VHS.** *GB* Glenda Jackson, Peter Eyre, Timothy West, Jennie Linden, Patrick Stewart; ***D:*** Trevor Nunn.

Hedwig and the Angry Inch ✂✂✂ **2000 (R)** Creator-star Mitchell adapted and directed his Off Broadway stage rock musical along with composer-lyricist Trask (who's also in the film) and opened up his gender-bending '70s kitsch fantasy. Hedwig was once Hansel, an East Berlin boy, whose sex-change operation was botched and who was abandoned in a Kansas trailer park by her G.I. husband. Betrayed in love by teen-aged boy toy Tommy (Pitt), who also steals Hedwig's songs, Hedwig and her band embark on a low-rent tour while Hedwig sings her life story to the disinterested and stalks a much-more successful Tommy. **95m/C VHS, DVD.** *US* John Cameron Mitchell, Michael Pitt, Andrea Martin, Miriam Shor, Alberta Watson, Maurice Dean Wint, Rob Campbell, Stephen Trask, Theodore Liscinski, Michael Aranov; ***D:*** John Cameron Mitchell; ***W:*** John Cameron Mitchell; ***C:*** Frank DeMarco; ***M:*** Stephen Trask.

Heidi ✂✂ 1/2 **1937** Johanna Spyri's classic tale puts Shirley Temple in the hands of a mean governess and the loving arms of her Swiss grandfather. Also available colorized. Remade in 1967. **88m/B VHS, DVD.** Shirley Temple, Jean Hersholt, Helen Westley, Arthur Treacher, Sidney Blackmer, Marcia Mae Jones, Mary Nash; ***D:*** Allan Dwan; ***W:*** Walter Ferris; ***C:*** Arthur C. Miller; ***M:*** Julien Josephson.

Heidi ✂✂ 1/2 **1952** The Swiss do their own version of the children's classic by Johanna Spyri. A precocious little girl enjoys life in the Swiss Alps with her grandfather, until her stern aunt takes her away to live in the village in the valley. **98m/B VHS.** *SI* Elsbeth Sigmund, Heinrich Gretler, Thomas Klameth, Elsie Attenoff; ***D:*** Luigi Comencini.

Heidi **1965** The classic story from Johanna Spyri's novel is filmed beautifully in the Swiss Alps in Eastmancolor. Heidi is kidnapped by her mean aunt and forced to work as a slave for a rich family. Her kindly old grandfather comes to her rescue. Family entertainment for all, dubbed in English. **95m/C VHS.** *AT GE* Eva Maria Singhammer, Gustav Knuth, Lotte Ledl; ***D:*** Werner Jacobs.

Heidi **1967** The second American adaptation of the classic Johanna Spyri novel tells the story of an orphaned girl who goes to the Swiss Alps to live with her grandfather. **100m/C VHS, DVD.** Maximilian Schell, Jennifer Edwards, Michael Redgrave, Jean Simmons; ***D:*** Delbert Mann; ***W:*** Earl Hamner; ***M:*** John Williams. **TV**

Heidi **1993 (G)** Yet another version of the children's classic, from German writer Johanna Spyri's 1881 novel. Thornton is charming as the orphan shuttled from relative to relative until she happily ends up with her crotchety grandfather (Robards) in his mountain cabin. Then her cousin comes along and whisks her off to the city to be a companion to the invalid Klara (Randall). Seymour is the snobbish, scowling governess. This "Heidi" is spunky enough to keep the sugar level tolerable. Filmed on location in Austria. **167m/C VHS, DVD.** Noley Thornton, Jason Robards Jr., Jane Seymour, Lexi (Faith) Randall, Sian Phillips, Patricia Neal, Benjamin Brazier, Michael Simkins, Andrew Bicknell, Jane Hazlegrove; ***D:*** Michael Rhodes; ***W:*** Jeanne Rosenberg; ***M:*** Lee Holdridge. **TV**

The Heidi Chronicles **1/2 1995** Some 25 years of boomer angst and friendship are covered in this cable adaptation of Wasserstein's 1988 Pulitzer Prize-winning play. Heidi Holland (Curtis) goes from prep school to Vassar to an art history career while searching for self-fulfillment, feminist ideals, and some romance along the way. The romance is on-and-off, thanks to caddish journalist Scoop (Friedman), but Heidi can always depend on soul mate, gay pediatrician Peter (Hulce), and Susan (Cattrall), her follow-the-fads confidante. Heidi's sometimes too morose for her own good but you won't mind spending a couple of hours in her company. **94m/C VHS.** Jamie Lee Curtis, Tom Hulce, Kim Cattrall, Peter Friedman, Eve Gordon, Shari Belafonte, Sharon Lawrence, Julie White, Debra Eisenstadt, Roma Maffia; ***D:*** Paul Bogart; ***W:*** Wendy Wasserstein; ***C:*** Isidore Mankofsky; ***M:*** David Shire.

Height of the Sky **1/2 1999** In rural Arkansas, 1935, the poor Jones family farms a small plot of land, which they rent from the rich Caldwells. When Gabriel Jones (Moninger) succumbs to tuberculosis, family patriarch Wendel Jones (Stewart) decides to hide Gabriel in an old cabin thereby leaving the strong-willed Leora (Weedon) in charge of the family. Jennifer must convince Mr. Caldwell (Palazzo) that all is well on their farm while she covers for her father's absence. Written and directed by Lyn Clinton, cousin of President Bill Clinton. **116m/C DVD.** Grant Moninger, Evan Palazzo, Jackie Stewart, Jennifer Weedon; ***D:*** Lyn Clinton; ***W:*** Lyn Clinton; ***C:*** John R. Zilles; ***M:*** Boris Zelkin.

Heights **1/2 2004 (R)** Mildly entertaining debut from Terrio follows the lives of several New Yorkers over 24 hours. Diana (Close) is an award-winning diva who gives acting classes at Juillard. Struggling Alec (Bradford) auditions for Diana and she decides to use him to console herself about her husband's latest romance by inviting Alec to her big birthday bash. Meanwhile, her photographer daughter Isabel (Banks) is worried about her upcoming wedding to handsome lawyer Jonathan (Marsden), who is dodging journalist Peter (Light) for suspicious reasons. Based on co-writer Fox's play. **93m/C DVD.** *US* Glenn Close, Elizabeth Banks, James Marsden, Jesse Bradford, Thomas Lennon, Matthew Davis, Isabella Rossellini, John Light, George Segal, Eric Bogosian, Michael Murphy; ***D:*** Chris Terrio; ***W:*** Amy Fox; ***C:*** Jim Denault; ***M:*** Martin Erskine, Ben Butler.

Heimat 1 **1/2** *Heimat-Eine deutsche Chronik* **1984** Sixteen-hour series follows the lives, loves, and tragedies of the German Simon family from the end of WWI to 1982. Based on Reitz's own family and his childhood. Shot over two years, the series has 28 lead performances and more than 140 speaking roles. German with subtitles. **924m/C VHS.** *GE* Marita Breuer; ***D:*** Edgar Reitz; ***W:*** Edgar Reitz, Peter F. Steinbach; ***C:*** Gernot Roll; ***M:*** Nikos Mamangakis.

Heimat 2 **1/2 1992** The continuation of the saga is composed of 25 half-hour segments and follows Hermann Simon's life in Munich from 1960 to 1970. A modernist musician and composer, Hermann falls in with a group of students, artists, and rebels. German with subtitles. **750m/C VHS.** *GE* Daniel E. Smith, Henry Arnold, Salome Kammer, Hannelore Hoger, Anke Sevenich, Noemi Steuer; ***D:*** Edgar Reitz; ***W:*** Edgar Reitz; ***C:*** Gernot Roll, Gerard Vandenburg, Christian Reitz; ***M:*** Nikos Mamangakis.

The Heiress **1/2 1949** Based on the Henry James novel "Washington Square." Catherine (de Havilland) is the plain, awkward daughter of wealthy widowed doctor Austin Sloper (Richardson), who is a belittling tyrant to his only child. Catherine has no suitors until handsome, fortune-seeking Morris Townsend (Clift) approaches her. Naturally, Dr. Sloper dismisses his interest and warns that his daughter will only end up with a broken heart. No happy endings here but the performances are superb. Remade as "Washington Square" in 1997. **115m/B VHS, DVD.** Olivia de Havilland, Montgomery Clift, Ralph Richardson, Miriam Hopkins, Vanessa Brown, Mona Freeman, Ray Collins, Selena Royle; ***D:*** William Wyler; ***W:*** Ruth Goetz, Augustus Goetz; ***C:*** Leo Tover; ***M:*** Aaron Copland. Oscars '49: Actress (de Havilland), Art Dir./Set Dec., B&W, Costume Des. (B&W), Orig. Dramatic Score; Golden Globes '50: Actress—Drama (de Havilland); Natl. Bd. of Review '49: Actor (Richardson), Natl. Film Reg. '96;; N.Y. Film Critics '49: Actress (de Havilland).

The Heirloom **1/2** *Zhaibian; House Transformations* **2005** A wealthy family commits mass suicide and 20 years later the mystery remains. James (Chang) inherits the abandoned Taipei mansion and decides to move in with girlfriend Yo (Kwan). Nasty things begin to happen. James' character fades into the background while Yo fights off the creepies. Chinese with subtitles. **97m/C DVD.** *TW* Jason Chang, Terri Kwan, Yu-Chen Chang, Tender Huang; ***D:*** Leste Chen; ***W:*** Dorian Li; ***C:*** Pung-Leung Kwan; ***M:*** Jeffrey Cheng.

The Heist **1989** An ex-con, upon regaining his freedom, sets out to rip off the crook who framed him. Entertaining enough story with a first-rate cast. **97m/C VHS, DVD.** Pierce Brosnan, Tom Skerritt, Wendy Hughes, Noble Willingham, Tom Atkins, Robert Prosky; ***D:*** Stuart Orme; ***C:*** Jiri (George) Tirl; ***M:*** Arthur B. Rubinstein. **CABLE**

The Heist *Hostile Force* **1996** Con artist plots the hijacking of a transport company's fleet and starts out by taking the firm's employees hostage. But one of the workers is an ex-cop who failed once to stop a robbery and is not about to fail again. **99m/C VHS, DVD.** *GE* Hannes Jaenicke, Cali Timmins, Andrew McCarthy, Cynthia Geary, Wolf Larson; ***D:*** Michael Kennedy; ***W:*** Michael January; ***C:*** Bruce Worrall. **TV**

Heist **2001 (R)** Hackman is Joe, a master thief who's planning to retire after his latest job, but fence Bergman (DeVito) has other ideas, holding Joe's payoff until he agrees to a big-time gold heist. And just to make things interesting, Bergman sends his nephew Silk (Rockwell) along. This complicates things even more, especially with Joe's wife, Fran (Pidgeon). In classic Mamet fashion, doublecrosses, plot twists, misdirection, great dialogue and perfect casting convene to create an excellent caper film. Lindo and Jay add plenty of spark as Joe's loyal crew members. **107m/C VHS, DVD.** *US* Gene Hackman, Danny DeVito, Delroy Lindo, Sam Rockwell, Rebecca Pidgeon, Ricky Jay, Patti LuPone, Jim Frangione; ***D:*** David Mamet; ***W:*** David Mamet; ***C:*** Robert Elswit; ***M:*** Theodore Shapiro.

Helas pour Moi *Oh Woe is Me* **1994** Perplexing, contemplative film on faith and love—and maybe a miracle. Told in flashback, publisher Alexander Klimt (Verley) travels to a Swiss lakeside town where it's rumored that the beautiful Rachel Donnadieu (Masliah) has been "visited" by God, who wishes to experience the pleasures of love, in the form of her own husband, simple fisherman Simon (Depardieu). Story is derived from the Greek myth concerning Zeus, who seduced Alcmene in the shape of her husband Amphitryon. French with subtitles. **84m/C VHS.** *FR SI* Gerard Depardieu, Laurence Masliah, Bernard Verley; ***D:*** Jean-Luc Godard; ***W:*** Jean-Luc Godard; ***C:*** Caroline Champetier.

Held for Murder *Her Mad Night* **1932** When a vacationing daughter is accused of murder, her mom lovingly takes the blame. Will the daughter come back to clear her mom, or will she let her fry in the electric chair? **67m/B VHS, DVD.** Irene Rich, Conway Tearle, Mary Carlisle, Kenneth Thomson, William B. Davidson; ***D:*** E. Mason Hopper.

Held for Ransom **1/2 1938** Confusing and weak crime drama. Femme fed Betty Mason (Mehaffey) is sent to help out on a kidnapping case where the ransom money has disappeared. She also has to juggle the affections of her partner Morrison (Mulhall) and those of Larry (Withers), the victim's son. **59m/B DVD.** Blanche Mehaffey, Grant Withers, Jack Mulhall, Bruce Warren, Kenneth Harlan, Edward Foster, Richard Lancaster; ***D:*** Clarence Bricker; ***W:*** Barry Barrington; ***C:*** Roland Price, Arthur Reed.

Held Hostage **1991** The true story of Jerry Levin, a reporter kidnapped by terrorists while on assignment in Beirut, and his wife, Sis, who struggled with the State Department for his release. **95m/C VHS.** Marlo Thomas, David Dukes, G.W. Bailey, Edward Winter, Robert Harper, William Schallert; ***D:*** Roger Young. **TV**

Held Up **1/2** *Inconvenienced* **2000 (PG-13)** Engaged couple Foxx and Long are having a hard time staying together when after they have a fight and Foxx becomes a hostage during a botched convenience store robbery in a sleepy southwestern town. Broad comedy works in all the black-guy-meets-white-yokels gags, but they've all been done before by funnier writers. Foxx has some appeal, but not enough to overcome this mess. It could've been worse: Rob Schneider bailed after four days of filming. **88m/C VHS, DVD.** Jamie Foxx, Nia Long, Jake Busey, John Cullum, Barry Corbin, Eduardo Yanez, Mike Wiles, Sarah Paulson, Julie Hagerty; ***D:*** Steve Rash; ***W:*** Jeff Eastin; ***C:*** David Makin; ***M:*** Robert Folk.

The Helen Morgan Story **1957** Musical bio of tragic Jazz Age torch singer Helen Morgan (Blyth) from her carnival days to Broadway stardom. She's constantly loving and getting left by bootlegger Larry Maddox (Newman), a charismatic louse. Then Helen gets involved with married lawyer Russell Wade (Carlson). Booze eventually is the downfall to her career. Most of the plot is fictional anyway with a prerequisite upbeat ending tacked on. Gogi Grant dubbed Blyth's singing. **118m/B DVD.** Ann Blyth, Paul Newman, Richard Carlson, Gene Evans, Alan King, Walter Woolf King, Cara Williams; ***D:*** Michael Curtiz; ***W:*** Oscar Saul, Stephen Longstreet, Nelson Gidding, Dean Riesner; ***C:*** Ted D. McCord; ***M:*** Larry Prinz.

Helen of Troy **1/2 1956** Mythological fantasy finds Helen (Podesta), the beautiful daughter of Zeus, falling in love with Trojan prince Paris (Sernas)—an event that leads to the siege of Troy. Ignores script for lavish effects. Video includes behind-the-scenes footage. **135m/C VHS, DVD.** Rossana Podesta, Jacques Sernas, Cedric Hardwicke, Stanley Baker, Niall MacGinnis, Nora Swinburne, Robert Douglas, Torin Thatcher, Harry Andrews, Janette Scott, Ronald Lewis, Brigitte Bardot; ***D:*** Robert Wise; ***W:*** John Twist, N. Richard Nash; ***C:*** Harry Stradling Sr.; ***M:*** Max Steiner.

Helen of Troy **1/2 2003** Since Helen was the face that launched a thousand ships for the Trojan War, she needs to be a looker and, in the person of Guillory, she is. Which is good, since the cable miniseries is fairly ordinary. Helen is married to weak-willed Menelaus (Callis), the King of Sparta but falls crazy in love with Paris (Marsden), a Prince of Troy. The lovers hightail it to Troy, where King Priam (Rhys-Davies) offers protection. Menelaus's brother Agamemnon (a snakey Sewell) leads the Spartans on a 10-year battle to get Helen back. Remember the Trojan Horse is a big deal. **177m/C VHS, DVD.** Sienna Guillory, Matthew Marsden, Rufus Sewell, Stellan Skarsgard, John Rhys-Davies, Maryam D'Abo, Emilia Fox, James Callis, James Lapine, Nigel Whitmey; ***D:*** John Kent Harrison; ***W:*** Ronni Kern; ***C:*** Edward Pei; ***M:*** Joel Goldsmith. **CABLE**

Hell Comes to Frogtown **1988 (R)** In a post-nuclear holocaust land run by giant frogs, a renegade who is one of the few non-sterile men left on earth must rescue some fertile women and impregnate them. Sci-fi spoof is extremely low-budget, but fun. Stars "Rowdy" Roddy Piper of wrestling fame. **88m/C VHS, DVD.** Roddy Piper, Sandahl Bergman, Rory Calhoun, Donald G. Jackson, Cec Verrell; ***D:*** Robert J. Kizer, Donald G. Jackson; ***W:*** Randall Frakes; ***C:*** Donald G. Jackson.

Hell Commandos **1/2 1969** Soldiers in WWII struggle to prevent the Nazis from releasing a deadly bacteria that will kill millions. Dubbed. **92m/C VHS, DVD.** *IT* Guy Madison, Stelvio Rosi; ***D:*** Jose Luis Merino.

Hell Fire Austin **1/2 1932** Maynard finds himself mixed up with outlaws in the Old West. **60m/B VHS.** Ken Maynard, Nat Pendleton, Jack Perrin; ***D:*** Forrest Sheldon.

Hell Harbor **1930** Caribbean love, murder and greed combine to make this early talkie. Exterior shots were filmed on the west coast of Florida and the beauty of the Tampa area in the 1930s is definitely something to see. **65m/B VHS.** Lupe Velez, Gibson Gowland, Jean Hersholt, John Holland; ***D:*** Henry King.

Hell High **1986 (R)** Four high schoolers plan a night of torture and humiliation for an annoying teacher, only to find she has some deadly secrets of her own. Dumber than it sounds. **84m/C VHS, DVD.** Christopher Stryker, Christopher Cousins, Millie Prezioso, Jason Brill; ***D:*** Douglas Grossman.

Hell Hounds of Alaska **1973 (G)** The Yukon, Yugoslav-style. European co-production goes back to the Gold Rush days for an adventure about a frontiersman tracking down a stolen shipment of the precious ore while trying to save the life of an injured boy. **90m/C VHS.** Doug McClure, Harald Leipnitz, Angelica Ott; ***D:*** Harald Reinl.

Hell Hunters **1987** Nazi-hunters foil the plot of an old German doctor to poison the population of L.A. Meanwhile, a daughter avenges the death of her mother by blowing up the doctor's jungle compound. **98m/C VHS.** Stewart Granger, Maud Adams, George Lazenby, Candice Daly, Romulo Arantes, William Berger; ***D:*** Ernst R. von Theumer; ***W:*** James Dalesandro, Louis LaRusso II; ***C:*** Mario DiLeo, Barry Samson; ***M:*** Larry Fallon.

Hell in the Pacific **1969 (PG)** A marvelously photographed (by Conrad Hall) psycho/macho allegory, about an American and a Japanese soldier stranded together on a tiny island and the mini-war they fight all by themselves. Overly obvious anti-war statement done with style. **101m/C VHS, DVD.** Lee Marvin, Toshiro Mifune; ***D:*** John Boorman; ***W:*** Eric Bercovici, Alexander Jacobs; ***C:*** Conrad L. Hall; ***M:*** Lalo Schifrin.

Hell Is for Heroes **1/2 1962** McQueen stars as the bitter leader of a small infantry squad outmanned by the Germans in this tight WWII drama. A strong cast and riveting climax make this a must for action fans. **90m/B VHS, DVD.** Steve McQueen, Bobby Darin, Fess Parker, Harry Guardino, James Coburn, Mike Kellin, Nick Adams, Bob Newhart, L.Q. Jones, Don Haggerty, Joseph Hoover, Michele Montau, Bill Mullikin; ***D:*** Donald Siegel; ***W:*** Robert Pirosh, Richard Carr; ***C:*** Harold Lipstein; ***M:*** Leonard Rosenman.

Hell Night **WOOF!** **1981 (R)** Several young people must spend the night in a mysterious mansion as part of their initiation into Alpha Sigma Rho fraternity in this extremely dull low-budget horror flick. **100m/C VHS, DVD.** Linda Blair, Vincent Van Patten, Kevin Brophy, Peter Barton, Jenny Neumann; ***D:*** Tom De Simone; ***W:*** Randy Feldman; ***C:*** Mac

Ahlberg; *M:* Danny Wyman.

Hell of the Living Dead WOOF! *Apocalipsis Canibal; Night of the Zombies; Zombie Creeping Flesh* **1983** Staff of a scientific research center are killed and then resurrected as cannibals who prey on the living. The living will suffer again if trapped into watching. Mattel is pseudonym for director Vincent Dawn. Cheap, dubbed, and possessing minimal coherence. **103m/C VHS, DVD.** *IT SP* Margit Evelyn Newton, Frank Garfield, Selan Karay; *D:* Bruno Mattei; *W:* J.M. Cunilles, Claudio Fragasso; *C:* John Cabrera.

Hell on Frisco Bay ♪♪ 1/2 **1955** An ex-waterfront cop, falsely imprisoned for manslaughter, sets out to clear his name. His quest finds him taking on the Mob, in this '30s-style gangster film. Good performances all around, especially Robinson, who steals every scene he's in. **93m/C VHS.** Alan Ladd, Edward G. Robinson, Joanne Dru, Fay Wray, William Demarest, Jayne Mansfield; *D:* Frank Tuttle; *M:* Max Steiner.

Hell on the Battleground ♪ 1/2 **1988 (R)** Group of inexperienced recruits are led into combat by two battle-hardened veterans. Their only hope for survival is a counterattack by U.S. tanks. **91m/C VHS.** William (Bill) Smith, Ted Prior, Fritz Matthews; *D:* David A. Prior; *W:* David A. Prior.

Hell on Wheels ♪♪ **1967** Two successful brothers in the racing industry are torn apart by the same girl. Brotherly love diminishes into a hatred so deep that murder becomes the sole purpose of both. **96m/C VHS, DVD.** Marty Robbins, Jennifer Ashley, John Ashley, Gigi Perreau, Robert Dornan, Connie Smith, Frank Gerstle; *D:* Will Zens.

Hell Raiders ♪ 1/2 **1968** A force invades a supposedly defenseless Pacific island, and finds itself fiercely attacked. **90m/C VHS.** John Agar, Richard Webb, Joan Huntington; *D:* Larry Buchanan.

Hell Ride ♪ **2008 (R)** Exploitation biker flick past its sell-by date. Bishop, a veteran of the 60s/70s genre, writes, directs, and stars as Pistolero, president of the Victors. He's still looking for revenge against the rival gang who killed his honey over stolen drug money and soon the glowering, riding, sexual exploitation of women, and killing is on! Oh yeah, apparently the similar "Grindhouse" wasn't enough for Quentin Tarantino, who is one of the executive producers. **84m/C DVD.** Larry Bishop, Michael Madsen, Eric Balfour, Vinnie Jones, David Carradine, Dennis Hopper, Leonor Varela; *D:* Larry Bishop; *W:* Larry Bishop; *C:* Scott Kevan; *M:* Daniele Luppi.

Hell River ♪♪ **1975 (PG)** In 1941 Yugoslavia, Yugoslav partisans and Nazis battle it out at a place called Hell River. **100m/C VHS.** Rod Taylor, Adam West; *D:* Stole Jankovic.

Hell-Ship Morgan ♪♪ 1/2 **1936** Bancroft is a womanizing tuna boat captain who falls for and marries Sothern. When they set up married life on the boat, she starts eyeing first mate Jory. And Bancroft finds out. **65m/B VHS.** George Bancroft, Ann Sothern, Victor Jory, George Regas, Howard Hickman, Ralph Byrd; *D:* David Ross Lederman.

Hell Ship Mutiny ♪ 1/2 **1957** Man comes to the aid of a lovely island princess, whose people have been forced to hand over their pearls to a pair of ruthless smugglers. Excellent cast in an unfortunately tepid production. **66m/B VHS, DVD.** Jon Hall, John Carradine, Peter Lorre, Roberta Haynes, Mike Mazurki, Stanley Adams; *D:* Lee Sholem, Elmo Williams.

Hell Squad ♪ 1/2 **1958** Lost in North Africa during WWII, five American GIs wander through the desert. They find numerous pitfalls and unexpected help. Overall, dismal and disappointing. **64m/B VHS.** Wally Campo, Brandon Carroll; *D:* Burt Topper.

Hell Squad ♪ **1985 (R)** Unable to release his son from the Middle Eastern terrorists who kidnapped him, a U.S. ambassador turns to the services of nine Las Vegas showgirls. These gals moonlight as vicious commandos in this low-budget action film with skin. **88m/C VHS.** Bainbridge Scott, Glen Hartford, Tina Lederman; *D:* Kenneth Hartford; *W:* Kenneth Hartford; *M:* Charles P. Barnett.

Hell to Eternity ♪♪ 1/2 **1960** The true story of how WWII hero Guy Gabaldon persuaded 2,000 Japanese soldiers to surrender. Features several spectacular scenes. **132m/B VHS, DVD.** Jeffrey Hunter, Sessue Hayakawa, David Janssen, Vic Damone, Patricia Owens; *D:* Phil Karlson.

Hell Up in Harlem WOOF! **1973 (R)** A black crime lord recuperates from an assassination attempt and tries to regain his power. Poor sequel to the decent film "Black Caesar." **98m/C VHS, DVD.** Fred Williamson, Julius W. Harris, Margaret Avery, Gerald Gordon, Gloria Hendry, D'Urville Martin, Mindi Miller, Tony King, Bobby Ramsen, James Dixon; *D:* Larry Cohen; *W:* Larry Cohen; *C:* Fenton Hamilton; *M:* Fonce Mizell, Freddie Perren.

Hellbenders ♪ 1/2 *Il Crudeli; Los Despiadados* **1967 (PG)** A confederate veteran robs a Union train and must fight through acres of Civil War adversity. Dubbed. Poorly directed and acted. **92m/C VHS, DVD.** *IT SP* Joseph Cotten, Norma Bengell, Julian Mateos; *D:* Sergio Corbucci; *M:* Ennio Morricone.

Hellbent ♪ 1/2 **1988** A crazed musician and a revenge-obsessed housewife embark on an unusual adventure that challenges their very sanity. **90m/C VHS.** Phil Ward, Lynn Levand, Cheryl Slean, David Marciano; *D:* Richard Casey; *W:* Richard Casey.

Hellbent ♪ 1/2 **2004** Amusingly schlocky gay slasher pic, set on Halloween. Buff bad guy, wearing a devil-horn mask, stalks hunks in West Hollywood, decapitating his victims. Gay rookie cop Eddie (Fergus) is assigned to catch the killer. Debut effort for writer/director Etheredge-Ouzts ratchets up the tension at the end. **85m/C DVD.** *US* Bryan Kirkwood, Hank Harris, Kris Andersson, Shaun Benjamin, Miguel Caballero, Samuel Phillips, Dylan Fergus, Wren Brown, Andrew Levitas, Matt Phillips; *D:* Paul Etheredge-Ouzts; *W:* Paul Etheredge-Ouzts; *C:* Mark Mervis; *M:* Mike Shapiro.

Hellblock 13 ♪♪ 1/2 **1997** Anthology of three low-budget short horror tales is told with grainy, raw-edged energy and a distinct regional flavor. Tara (Rochon) writes stories while she's on Death Row and shows them to her stolid guard (Hansen, "Leatherface" from "Texas Chainsaw Massacre"). Rochon brings a welcome note of humor to what might have been your basic madwoman stereotype. The individual films get better and funnier as they go along. **91m/C VHS, DVD.** Debbie Rochon, Gunnar Hansen, J.J. North, Jennifer Peluso, David G. Holland; *D:* Paul Talbot; *W:* Paul Talbot, Jeff Miller, Michael R. Smith.

Hellbound ♪♪ 1/2 **1994 (R)** Prosatanos (Neame), a powerful 12th-century wizard, is imprisoned and the source of his power (a scepter) is supposedly destroyed. Fast-forward several hundred years when Prosatanos manages to free himself and seek out the pieces of his scepter. Which happens to lead him to Chicago and a couple of unsuspecting cops (Norris, Levels). **95m/C VHS, DVD.** Chuck Norris, Christopher Neame, Calvin Levels, Sheree J. Wilson; *D:* Aaron Norris.

Hellbound: Hellraiser 2 ♪♪ *Hellraiser 2* **1988 (R)** In this, the first sequel to Clive Barker's inter-dimensional nightmare, the traumatized daughter from the first film is pulled into the Cenobites' universe. Gore and weird imagery abound. An uncut, unrated version is also available. **96m/C VHS, DVD.** *GB* Ashley Laurence, Clare Higgins, Kenneth Cranham, Imogen Boorman, William Hope, Oliver Smith, Sean Chapman, Doug Bradley; *D:* Tony Randel; *W:* Peter Atkins; *C:* Robin Vidgeon; *M:* Christopher Young.

Hellboy ♪♪ 1/2 **2004 (PG-13)** Faithful adaptation of the cult Dark Horse comic is a success, thanks mostly to del Toro's smart direction and Perlman's amusing yet complex portrayal of the titular demon/hero. During WWII, the Nazis and Rasputin team up to try to bring about the reign of the seven gods of chaos. What they bring to earth is actually a baby demon who is found and adopted by Dr. Bruttenholm of the FBI's Bureau of Paranormal Research and Defense. Sixty years later, Hellboy is an adult working with the doc, breaking in a new handler, and pining over former bureau denizen Liz (Blair). Rasputin and his Nazi friends plan on using Hellboy to bring about the Apocalypse. Perlman gives Hellboy depth (even under all the prosthetics), but he has lots of help from a strong supporting cast. **125m/C DVD, Blu-ray Disc, UMD.** *US* Ron Perlman, John Hurt, Selma Blair, Rupert Evans, Karel Roden, Jeffrey Tambor, Biddy Hodson, Doug Jones, Ladislav Beran, Kevin Trainor, Corey Johnson, Stephen H. Fisher; *D:* Guillermo del Toro; *W:* Guillermo del Toro, Peter Briggs; *C:* Guillermo Navarro; *M:* Marco Beltrami; *V:* David Hyde Pierce.

Hellboy II: The Golden Army ♪♪♪ **2008 (PG-13)** Director Del Toro creates a stunning backdrop for big red monster Hellboy (Pearlman) to return. In flashback, young Hellboy hears a story of a king who assembles but disbands a golden army of elves to destroy the human world. But the elves are on a comeback, as if Hellboy didn't already have his hands full working through commitment issues with pyrokinetic girlfriend Liz (Blair) and drowning his sorrows with his scaly fish-man pal. With battles and action almost constant, lush visuals, and uber-quirky Barry Manilow-loving characters, it's near perfect for genre fans. **110m/C DVD.** *US* Ron Perlman, Selma Blair, Doug Jones, Luke Goss, Roy Dotrice, John Hurt, Jeffrey Tambor, Brian Steele, Anna Walton; *D:* Guillermo del Toro; *W:* Guillermo del Toro, Mike Mignola; *C:* Guillermo Navarro; *M:* Danny Elfman; *V:* Thomas Kretschmann, Seth MacFarlane.

Hellcats WOOF! **1968 (R)** A mob of sleazy, leather-clad female bikers terrorize small Midwestern towns in this violent girl-gang thriller. Even biker movie fans might find this one unworthy. **90m/C VHS.** Ross Hagen, Dee Duffy, Sharyn Kinzie, Del (Sonny) West, Bob Slatzer; *D:* Bob Slatzer.

Hellcats of the Navy ♪ 1/2 **1957** Soggy true saga of the WWII mission to sever the vital link between mainland Asia and Japan. The only film that Ronald and Nancy Davis Reagan starred in together and the beginning of their grand romance. **82m/B VHS, DVD.** Ronald Reagan, Nancy Davis, Arthur Franz, Robert Arthur; *D:* Nathan "Jerry" Juran; *W:* Bernard Gordon, David Lang.

Helldorado ♪♪ *Heldorado* **1946** A lively western starring the singing cowboy, Roy Rogers. **54m/B VHS, DVD.** Roy Rogers, George "Gabby" Hayes, Dale Evans, Paul Harvey; *D:* William Witney.

Heller in Pink Tights ♪♪ **1960** Offbeast western, based on a novel by Louis L'Amour, that follows the adventures of a seedy vaudeville troupe in the 1880s. Manager Tom Healy (Quinn) stays barely ahead of his creditors, with Angela (Loren) as his leading asset (and Loren's assets are the film's highlight). She dallys with gunslinger Clint Mabry (Forest), who pursues her out of town and there's an Indian attack and more gunslinging until the troupe manages to find a safe haven. The story was hardly sophisticated director Cukor's specialty, which may account for the unbelievable characters and confused plot. **100m/C VHS, DVD.** Sophia Loren, Anthony Quinn, Margaret O'Brien, Steve Forrest, Edmund Lowe, Ramon Novarro, Eileen Heckart; *D:* George Cukor; *W:* Walter Bernstein; *C:* Harold Lipstein; *M:* Daniele Amfitheatrof.

Hellfighters ♪♪ **1968 (G)** Texas oil well fire fighters experience trouble between themselves and the women they love. **121m/C VHS, DVD.** John Wayne, Katharine Ross, Jim Hutton, Vera Miles, Bruce Cabot, Jay C. Flippen; *D:* Andrew V. McLaglen; *W:* Clair Huffaker; *C:* William Clothier; *M:* Leonard Rosenman.

Hellfire ♪♪ **1948** A gambler promises to build a church and follow the precepts of the Bible after a minister sacrifices his life for him. **90m/B VHS.** William (Wild Bill) Elliott, Marie Windsor, Forrest Tucker, Jim Davis; *D:* R.G. Springsteen.

The Hellfire Club ♪♪ **1961** In 18th century Britain, a young man reaches adulthood and attempts to claim the estate of his father. No ordinary dad, his led the infamous Hellfire Club, an organization specializing in debauchery and depravity. His cousin challenges his claim and kidnaps his fiancee. Historical hokum, complete with swordplay. **88m/C VHS.** *GB* Keith Michell, Kai (Kay) Fischer, Adrienne Corri, Peter Arne, David Lodge, Bill Owen, Peter Cushing, Francis Matthews, Desmond Walter-Ellis; *D:* Robert S. Baker, Monty Berman; *W:* Jimmy Sangster.

Hellgate ♪♪ **1952** Medical man Gil Hanley (Hayden) gets caught between renegade Confederate soldiers and the Army in 1867 Kansas. A former Reb himself, Hanley gets railroaded into the military prison at Hellgate, New Mexico. Prison warden Voorhees (Bond) is determined to make everyone suffer but he doesn't expect an epidemic to sweep through, which means Hanley's doctoring skills are needed. **87m/C DVD.** Sterling Hayden, Ward Bond, James Arness, Peter Coe, John Pickard, Joan Leslie, James Anderson; *D:* Charles Marquis Warren; *W:* Charles Marquis Warren, John C. Champion; *C:* Ernest Miller; *M:* Paul Dunlap.

Hellgate WOOF! **1989 (R)** A woman hitchhiking turns out to be one of the living dead. Her benefactor lives to regret picking her up. **96m/C VHS, DVD.** Abigail Wolcott, Ron Palillo, Carel Trichardt, Petrea Curran, Evan J. Klisser, Joanne Ward; *D:* William A. Levey; *W:* Michael O'Rourke; *C:* Peter Palmer.

Hellhole ♪ **1985 (R)** A young woman who witnesses her mother's murder is sent to a sanitarium where the doctors are perfecting chemical lobotomies. Extremely weak script and poor acting make this a suspenseless thriller. **93m/C VHS.** Judy Landers, Ray Sharkey, Mary Woronov, Marjoe Gortner, Edy Williams, Terry Moore, Dyanne Thorne, Lynn Borden; *D:* Pierre De Moro; *W:* Vincent Mongol; *C:* Stephen Posey; *M:* Jeff Sturges.

Hellmaster ♪ **1992** Your basic sicko mad scientist experiments on some unsuspecting college students by injecting them with an addictive drug. The drug also causes some horrifying mutations and makes its victims superhuman (but also super-ugly). Lots of gore. Creative special effects and make-up will appeal to fans of horror. **92m/C VHS, DVD.** John Saxon, David Emge, Amy Raasch; *D:* Douglas Schulze; *W:* Douglas Schulze.

Hello Again ♪♪ **1987 (PG)** The wife of a successful plastic surgeon chokes to death on a piece of chicken. A year later she returns to life, with comical consequences, but soon discovers that life won't be the same. **96m/C VHS, DVD.** Shelley Long, Corbin Bernsen, Judith Ivey, Gabriel Byrne, Sela Ward, Austin Pendleton, Carrie Nye, Robert Lewis, Madeleine Potter; *D:* Frank Perry; *M:* William Goldstein.

Hello, Dolly! ♪♪ **1969 (G)** Widow Dolly Levi, while matchmaking for her friends, finds a match for herself. Based on the hugely successful Broadway musical adapted from Thornton Wilder's play "Matchmaker." Lightweight story needs better actors with stronger characterizations. Original Broadway score helps. ♫ Hello Dolly; Just Leave Everything to Me; Love is Only Love; Dancing; Walter's Gavotte; It Only Takes a Moment; Ribbons Down My Back; Elegance; It Takes a Woman. **146m/C VHS, DVD.** Barbra Streisand, Walter Matthau, Michael Crawford, Louis Armstrong, E.J. Peaker, Marianne McAndrew, Tommy Tune; *D:* Gene Kelly; *W:* Ernest Lehman; *C:* Harry Stradling Sr.; *M:* Jerry Herman. Oscars '69: Art Dir./Set Dec., Sound, Scoring/Musical.

Hello Down There ♪♪ 1/2 **1969 (G)** Harmless—if dated—family comedy. Inventor Fred Miller (Randall) persuades his reluctant family to participate in a month-long experiment that has them living in a prototype underwater home. Wife Vivian (Leigh) is afraid of the water and his teenaged children are distressed because their pop band has a chance at a record deal. Meanwhile, the living room pool attracts sharks and an overly-friendly seal. Shot in Florida. **97m/C DVD.** Tony Randall, Janet Leigh, Jim Backus, Ken Berry, Charlotte Rae, Richard Dreyfuss, Roddy MacDowall; *D:* Jack Arnold; *W:* Frank Telford, John McGreevey; *C:* Clifford Poland; *M:* Jeff Barry.

Hello, Frisco, Hello ♪♪ 1/2 **1943** San Francisco's wild Barbary Coast is the setting for this romantic musical. Smoothie Payne opens up a saloon that features Faye, who's in love with him, as the star singing attraction. Unfortunately, Payne is involved with a society snob and Faye heads off to European success. When she returns, it's to a sadder and wiser man. Hello, Frisco, Hello; You'll Never Know; San Francisco; Ragtime Cowboy Joe; Sweet Cider Time; Has Anybody Here Seen Kelly; King Chanticleer; When You Wore a Tulip; Strike Up the Band, Here Comes a Sailor. **98m/C VHS.** Alice Faye, John Payne, Jack Oakie, Lynn Bari, Laird Cregar, June Havoc, Ward Bond, Aubrey Mather, John Archer; ***D:*** H. Bruce Humberstone; ***W:*** Robert Ellis, Helen Logan. Oscars '43: Song ("You'll Never Know").

Hello Goodbye **2008** Despite the cast, this culture clash comedy doesn't work thanks to annoying characters and situations. Gisele (Ardant) converted to Judaism to marry Alain (Depardieu) although the long-time married couple was never religious. What they are is bored and a trip to Israel impulsively convinces them to start over again in Tel Aviv. But doctor Alain's promised job falls through, their apartment isn't habitable, and most of their luggage is lost in transit. A zealous Gisele gets involved with questionable rabbi Yoshi (Ashkenazi) as Alain decides to explore his religious roots as well. English, French, and Hebrew with subtitles. **98m/C DVD.** *FR IS* Fanny Ardant, Gerard Depardieu, Lior Loui Ashkenazi, Jean Benguigui, Gilles Gaston-Dreyfus, Manu Payet; ***D:*** Graham Guit; ***W:*** Graham Guit, Michael Lelouche; ***C:*** Gerard Stein.

Hello, Hemingway **1990** Living in 1950s Havana, Larita hopes to be able to study in the United States and is inspired by Ernest Hemingway's "The Old Man and the Sea." She even tries to meet the writer but he's away hunting in Africa. However, the poverty of Larita's life may thwart her ambitions, and meanwhile the political situation in Cuba is becoming ever-more turbulent. Spanish with subtitles. **84m/C DVD.** *CU* Laura De la Uz, Raul Paz, Herminia Sanchez, Caridad Hernande, Enrique Molina; ***D:*** Fernando Perez; ***W:*** Maydo Royero; ***C:*** Julio Valdes; ***M:*** Edesio Alejandro.

Hello Mary Lou: Prom Night 2 1/2 *The Haunting of Hamilton High; Prom Night 2* **1987 (R)** A sequel to the successful slasher flick, wherein a dead-for-30-years prom queen relegates the current queen to purgatory and comes back to life in order to avenge herself. Wild special effects. **97m/C VHS.** *CA* Michael Ironside, Wendy Lyon, Justin Louis, Lisa Schrage, Richard Monette; ***D:*** Bruce Pittman; ***W:*** Ron Oliver; ***C:*** John Herzog.

Hello Trouble 1/2 **1932** A Texas Ranger accidentally kills his friend, who was a former Ranger turned bandit, causing him to hang up his guns. **63m/C VHS.** Buck Jones, Lena Basquette, Wallace MacDonald, "Spec" (Walter) O'Donnell, Ward Bond, Frank Rice, Ruth Warren; ***D:*** Lambert Hillyer.

Hellraiser 1/2 **1987 (R)** A graphic, horror fantasy about a woman who is manipulated by the monstrous spirit of her husband's dead brother. In order for the man who was also her lover to be brought back to life, she must lure and kill human prey for his sustenance. Grisly and inventive scenes keep the action fast-paced; not for the faint-hearted. **94m/C DVD, UMD.** *GB* Andrew (Andy) Robinson, Clare Higgins, Ashley Laurence, Sean Chapman, Oliver Smith, Robert Hines, Doug Bradley, Nicholas Vince, Dave Atkins; ***D:*** Clive Barker; ***W:*** Clive Barker; ***C:*** Robin Vidgeon; ***M:*** Christopher Young.

Hellraiser *Clive Barker Presents: Hellraiser* **2009** Based on Barker's "The Hellbound Heart" and a remake of the 1987 film, although how can anyone but Doug Bradley play Pinhead? Anyway, the plot revolves around a man who finds the doorway to hell and the bargain his loved ones must make to get him back. **m/C DVD.** *US* ***D:*** Julien Maury, Alexandre Bustillo; ***W:*** Marcus Dunstan, Patrick Melton.

Hellraiser 3: Hell on Earth **1992 (R)** Pinhead is back in this film based on characters created by horrormeister Clive Barker. A strange black box holds the key to sending Pinhead back to Hell and is sought by the heroine, a TV newswoman (Farrell). But Pinhead's human henchman, a nasty nightclub owner, isn't going to make things easy. Imaginative special effects and Bradley's commanding presence as Pinhead aid this shocker, which becomes unfortunately mired in excessive gore. An unrated version at 97 minutes is also available. **91m/C VHS, DVD.** Doug Bradley, Terry Farrell, Kevin Bernhardt, Paula Marshall, Ken Carpenter, Peter Boynton, Ashley Laurence; ***D:*** Anthony Hickox; ***W:*** Peter Atkins; ***C:*** Gerry Lively.

Hellraiser 4: Bloodline **1995 (R)** You can't keep a bad Pinhead in Hell, as this unfortunate sequel demonstrates. Bradley reprises his role as the big bad S&M pincushion in the latest and supposedly last installment of Clive Barker's blood drenched series. Tracing the origin of the infernal Rubik's Cube that releases Pinhead, the plot jumps between 18th century France, present day New York, and a 22nd century space station. Along the way, the Pointy One gets to flay, skewer, and impale to his evil heart's content. Special f/x guru Kevin Yeagher was so embarrassed by this outing that he took his director's credit off of the picture. Bad acting, bad plot, bad complexion. **81m/C VHS, DVD.** Bruce Ramsay, Valentina Vargas, Doug Bradley, Kim Myers, Christina Harnos, Charlotte Chatton, Paul Perri, Mickey Cotrell; ***D:*** Alan Smithee, Kevin Yagher; ***W:*** Peter Atkins; ***M:*** Daniel Licht.

Hellraiser 5: Inferno **2000 (R)** Los Angeles detective Joseph (Sheffer) wakes up one day literally in hell. In order to escape he must find the puzzle box, which is in Pinhead's possession. This one is not only boring, it's confusing, and Pinhead has little more than a cameo appearance. **99m/C VHS, DVD.** Craig Sheffer, Doug Bradley, Nicholas Turturro, James Remar, Lindsay Taylor; ***D:*** Scott Derrickson; ***W:*** Scott Derrickson, Paul Harris Boardman. **VIDEO**

Hellraiser: Deader *Hellraiser 7: Deader* **2005 (R)** Wanting to break the big story about a freaky Bucharest cult that supposedly rouses the deceased, a female reporter unearths the terrifying truth behind who they want to bring back to life. **88m/C VHS, DVD.** Doug Bradley, Kari Wuhrer, Paul Rhys, Marc Warren, Georgina Rylance; ***D:*** Rick Bota; ***W:*** Neal Marshall Stevens, Tim(othy) Day; ***M:*** Henning Lohner. **VIDEO**

Hellraiser: Hellseeker **2002 (R)** The fifth sequel in the 15-year-old series looks great, thanks to debuting director Bota, who's a veteran cinematographer. But the story doesn't have enough Pinhead to please fans. Kristy (Laurence) has escaped from the Cenobites and is driving with her husband Trevor (Winters) when her body vanishes after a traffic accident. The same accident has caused Trevor to suffer from hallucinations that turn out to be real and make him a multiple murder suspect. **89m/C VHS, DVD.** Ashley Laurence, Dean Winters, Doug Bradley; ***D:*** Rick Bota; ***W:*** Carl DuPre, Tim(othy) Day; ***C:*** John Drake; ***M:*** Stephen (Steve) Edwards. **VIDEO**

Hellraiser: Hellworld **2005 (R)** Pinhead (Bradley) and the Cenobites torment some computer hackers through the use of the hellworld.com site (possibly by manning the tech support phones). Ridiculously resilient franchise plods along, helped by the presence of Henriksen, on haitus from whatever Alien sequel they're probably working on. **2005m/C DVD.** Doug Bradley, Lance Henriksen, Henry Cavill, Katheryn Winnick; ***D:*** Rick Bota; ***W:*** Joel Soisson, Carl DuPre; ***C:*** Gabriel Kosuth; ***M:*** Lars Anderson. **VIDEO**

Hellriders **WOOF!** **1984 (R)** A motorcycle gang rides into a small town and subjects its residents to a reign of terror. **90m/C VHS.** Adam West, Tina Louise, Ross Alexander, Renee Harmon; ***D:*** James Bryan; ***W:*** Renee Harmon, James Bryan.

Hell's Angels **1930** Classic WWI aviation movie is sappy and a bit lumbering, but still an extravagant spectacle with awesome air scenes. Studio owner Hughes fired directors Howard Hawks and Luther Reed, spent an unprecedented $3.8 million, and was ultimately credited as director (although Whale also spent some time in the director's chair). Three years in the making, the venture cost three pilots their lives and lost a bundle. Harlow replaced Swedish Greta Nissen when sound was added and was catapulted into blond bombshelldom as a two-timing dame. And the tinted and two-color scenes—restored in 1989—came well before Ted Turner ever wielded a crayola. **135m/B VHS, DVD.** Jean Harlow, Ben Lyon, James Hall, John Darrow, Lucien Prival, Frank Clarke, Roy "Baldy" Wilson, Douglas Gilmore, Jane Winton, Evelyn Hall; ***D:*** Howard Hughes; ***W:*** Harry Behn, Howard Estabrook, Joseph Moncure March; ***C:*** Elmer Dyer, Harry Perry, E. Burton Steene, Dewey Wrigley, Gaetano Antonio "Tony" Gaudio; ***M:*** Hugo Riesenfeld.

Hell's Angels Forever **1983 (R)** A revealing ride into the world of honor, violence, and undying passion for motorcycles on the road. Documentary was filmed with cooperation of the Angels. Features appearances by Willie Nelson, Jerry Garcia, Bo Diddley, Kevin Keating and Johnny Paycheck. **93m/C VHS.** Willie Nelson, Jerry Garcia, Johnny Paycheck, Bo Diddley; ***D:*** Richard Chase, Leon Gast, Kevin Keating.

Hell's Angels on Wheels 1/2 **1967** Low-budget, two-wheeled Nicholson vehicle that casts him as a gas station attendant who joins up with the Angels for a cross country trip. Laszlo Kovacs is responsible for the photography. One of the better 1960s biker films. **95m/C VHS, DVD.** Jack Nicholson, Adam Roarke, Sabrina Scharf, Jana Taylor, John Garwood, Sonny Barger, Bruno VeSota; ***D:*** Richard Rush; ***W:*** Robert W(right) Campbell; ***C:*** Laszlo Kovacs; ***M:*** Stu Phillips.

Hell's Angels '69 **1969 (PG)** Figuring on robbing Caesar's Palace for the thrill, two wealthy brothers plot a deadly game by infiltrating the ranks of the Hell's Angels. Upon figuring out that they've been duped, the Angels seek revenge. Average biker epic filmed in Nevada features Hell's Angels Oakland chapter. **97m/C VHS, DVD.** Tom Stern, Jeremy Slate, Conny Van Dyke, G.D. Spradlin, Sonny Barger, Steve Sandor; ***D:*** Lee Madden; ***W:*** Tom Stern, Jeremy Slate, Don Tait; ***C:*** Paul Lohmann.

Hell's Belles 1/2 *Girl in the Leather Suit* **1969** Biker has his ride stolen by a rival, who leaves a chick as payment. The two team up to get revenge, chasing the gang across the Arizona desert and picking them off one by one. **95m/C VHS, DVD.** Jeremy Slate, Adam Roarke, Jocelyn Lane, Angelique Pettyjohn, Michael Walker, William Lucking; ***D:*** Maury Dexter; ***W:*** James Gordon White, Robert McMullen; ***M:*** Les Baxter.

Hell's Belles **WOOF!** **1995 (R)** The Devil's bored so he leaves hell for some mortal fun but in order to stay he and his henchmen must sacrifice five ladies. **90m/C VHS.** Terence Cooper, Nadine Kalmes, K.C. Kelly, Eric Liddy, Martin Howeller, Robert Mansbridge, Jeffrey Richardson; ***D:*** Ed Hansen; ***W:*** Ed Hansen, George "Buck" Flower, Simon Hartwell; ***C:*** Rick Lamb.

Hell's Bloody Devils 1/2 *Operation M; Smashing the Crime Syndicate; Swastika Savages; The Fakers* **1970 (PG)** Mark Adams (Gabriel) is an FBI agent assigned to infiltrate a counterfeiting ring composed of bikers, right wing American Neo-Nazis, the Mafia, and an actual Nazi war criminal named Count von Delberg (Taylor). Originally produced under the titles "The Fakers" and "Operation M," the biker subplot was added (along with its more exploitative title name) when distributors balked at releasing the film. It has also been released since then without the biker footage under the name "Smashing the Crime Syndicate." **92m/C DVD.** John Gabriel, Anne Randall, Broderick Crawford, Scott Brady, Kent Taylor, Robert Dix, Keith Andes, Jack Starrett, Erin O'Donnell, Vicki Volante, Emily Banks; ***D:*** Al Admason; ***W:*** Jerry Evans; ***C:*** Gary Graver, Laszlo Kovacs, Frank Ruttencutter; ***M:*** Nelson Riddle, Don Ginnis.

Hell's Brigade: The Final Assault **WOOF!** **1980 (PG)** Low-budget, poorly acted film in which a small band of American commandos is ordered on the most dangerous and important mission of WWII. **99m/C VHS.** Jack Palance, John Douglas, Carlos Estrada; ***D:*** Henry Mankiewirk.

Hell's Gate 1/2 *Bad Karma* **2001 (R)** Dangerous and crazy Agnes Thatcher (Kensit) believes her shrink, Dr. Trey Cambell (Muldoon), is the reincarnation of Jack the Ripper and that she was his mistress. She escapes from the looney bin and decides to eliminate Trey's family so that they can be reunited. Standard psycho-horror fare with some nudity for titillation (no pun intended). **92m/C VHS, DVD.** Patsy Kensit, Patrick Muldoon, Amy Locane, Damian Chapa; ***D:*** John Hough; ***C:*** Jacques Haitkin; ***M:*** Harry Manfredini. **VIDEO**

Hell's Headquarters **1932** A startling tale of murder and greed involving a hunt for a fortune in African ivory. **59m/B VHS, DVD.** Jack Mulhall, Barbara Weeks, Frank Mayo; ***D:*** Andrew L. Stone.

Hell's Hinges **1916** The next to last Hart western, typifying his good/bad cowboy character. This time he's a gunslinger who falls for the new preacher's sister, while the minister himself is led astray by a saloon gal. Perhaps Hart's best film. **65m/B VHS, DVD.** William S. Hart, Clara Williams, Jack Standing, Robert McKim; ***D:*** William S. Hart. Natl. Film Reg. '94.

Hell's House **1932** After his mother dies, young lad Durkin goes to the city to live with relatives, gets mixed up with moll Davis and her bootlegger boyfriend O'Brien, and is sent to a brutal reform school. Interesting primarily for early appearances by Davis and O'Brien (before he was typecast as the indefatigable good-guy). **80m/B VHS, DVD.** Junior Durkin, Pat O'Brien, Bette Davis, Frank "Junior" Coghlan, Charley Grapewin, Emma Dunn; ***D:*** Howard Higgin.

Hell's Kitchen NYC 1/2 **1997 (R)** Ex-con Johnny Miles (Phifer) returns home to New York's notorious Hell's Kitchen after serving five years for a crime he did not commit. More or less a redemption drama, the film benefits from a good cast, especially Jolie as a revenge-driven street urchin and Arquette as her drugged-out mom. Despite the trappings of his "convict-into-street angel" role, Phifer exudes a quiet strength that never seems out of place, even when the action gets hysterical. Director Cinciripini scores points in creating scenes of drug addiction that invoke a kind of horrific absurdity, guiding seemingly over-the-top moments with a sure hand and a rock-solid purpose. It's in the more preachy aspects of his script where he loses control, the rising saccharine quotient potentially diluting the potency of his worthwhile message. **101m/C DVD.** Rosanna Arquette, William Forsythe, Michael Spiller, Angelina Jolie, Mekhi Phifer, Johnny Whitworth, Michael Nicolosi, Ryan Slater, Sharif Rashed; ***D:*** Tony Cinciripini; ***W:*** Tony Cinciripini; ***C:*** Derek Wiesehahn; ***M:*** Tony Cinciripini, Nat Robinson.

The Hellstrom Chronicle **1971 (G)** A powerful quasi-documentary about insects, their formidable capacity for survival, and the conjectured battle man will have with them in the future. **90m/C VHS.** Lawrence Pressman; ***D:*** Walon Green; ***W:*** David Seltzer. Oscars '71: Feature Doc.

Helltown 1/2 *Born to the West* **1938** A western programmer based on Zane Grey's novel in which Wayne tracks down a cattle rustler. **60m/B VHS, DVD.** John Wayne, Marsha Hunt, Johnny Mack Brown, Monte Blue, Syd Saylor, John D. Patterson; ***D:*** Charles T. Barton; ***W:*** Stuart Anthony, Robert Yost; ***C:*** Devereaux Jennings.

Help! *Eight Arms to Hold You* **1965 (G)** Ringo's ruby ring is the object of a search by Arab cult members Clang (McKern) and Ahme (Bron) who chase the Fab Four all over the globe in order to acquire the bauble. A crazy scientist (Spinelli) and his assistant (Kinnear) also want the ring and join in the pursuit. Help!; You're Gonna Lose That Girl; You've Got to Hide Your Love Away; The Night Before; Another Girl; Ticket to Ride; I Need You. **90m/C VHS, DVD.** *GB* John Lennon, Paul McCartney, Ringo Starr, George Harrison, Leo McKern, Eleanor Bron, Victor Spinetti, Roy Kinnear, John Bluthal, Patrick Cargill, Alfie Bass, Warren Mitchell, Peter Copley, Bruce Lacey; ***D:*** Richard Lester; ***W:*** Charles Wood, Marc Behm; ***C:*** David Watkin; ***M:*** George Martin, Ken Thorne, John Lennon, Paul McCartney, Ringo Starr, George Harrison.

Help Wanted Female **1968** Jo Jo, a prostitute with kung fu skills who likes to rob traveling salesmen, is in a quandary over her lesbian roommate's acid dropping friends, including Mr. Gregory, who has a penchant for murder. After recounting a previous trip in which he murdered an acquaintance, he succeeds in alienating his current companions, who must fight for their life to escape him. **71m/B VHS, DVD.** Anthony (Tony) Vorno, Inga Olsen; ***D:*** Harold Perkins.

Help Wanted: Male 🦴 1/2 **1982** When a magazine publisher discovers that her fiance cannot have children, she looks for someone else who can do the job right. **97m/C VHS.** Suzanne Pleshette, Gil Gerard, Bert Convy, Dana Elcar, Harold Gould, Caren Kaye; ***D:*** William Wiard. **TV**

Helter Skelter 🦴🦴 1/2 **1976** The harrowing story of the murder of actress Sharon Tate and four others at the hands of Charles Manson and his psychotic "family." Based on the book by prosecutor Vincent Bugliosi, adapted by J.P. Miller. Features an outstanding performance by Railsback as Manson. **194m/C VHS, DVD.** Steve Railsback, Nancy Wolfe, George DiCenzo, Marilyn Burns, Christina Hart, Alan Oppenheimer, Cathy Paine; ***D:*** Tom Gries; ***W:*** J(ames) P(inckney) Miller; ***M:*** Billy Goldenberg. **TV**

Helter Skelter Murders WOOF! 1971 (R) An independently made version of the Charles Manson story, with sequences filmed at Spawn Ranch. Includes Manson's own recording of his songs "Mechanical Man" and "Garbage Dump" on the soundtrack. **83m/B VHS, DVD.** Brian Klinknett, Debbie Duff, Phyllis Estes; ***D:*** Frank Howard; ***W:*** J.J. Wilkie, Duke Howze; ***C:*** Frank Howard.

The Henderson Monster 🦴🦴 1/2 **1980** Experiments of a genetic scientist are questioned by a community and its mayor. A potentially controversial drama turns into typical romantic fluff. **105m/C VHS, DVD.** Jason Miller, Christine Lahti, Stephen Collins, David Spielberg, Nehemiah Persoff, Larry Gates; ***D:*** Waris Hussein. **TV**

Hendrix 🦴🦴 1/2 **2000 (R)** Biopic of legendary rock guitarist Jimi Hendrix (Harris) from his first teenaged band to his drug overdose death in 1970. There are some fine re-creations of such notable Hendrix performances at the 1967 Monterey Pop Festival and Woodstock in 1969. **103m/C VHS, DVD.** Wood Harris, Vivica A. Fox, Billy Zane, Christian Potenza, Dorian Harewood, Kris Holden-Ried, Christopher Ralph, Michie Mee; ***D:*** Leon Ichaso; ***W:*** Art Washington, Hal Roberts, Butch Stein; ***C:*** Claudio Chea; ***M:*** Daniel Licht. **CABLE**

Hennessy 🦴🦴 1/2 **1975 (PG)** An IRA man plots revenge on the Royal family and Parliament after his family is violently killed. Tense political drama, but slightly far-fetched. **103m/C VHS.** *GB* Rod Steiger, Lee Remick, Richard Johnson, Trevor Howard, Peter Egan, Eric Porter; ***D:*** Don Sharp; ***W:*** John Gay.

Henri Langlois: The Phantom of the Cinematheque 🦴🦴🦴 *Le Fantome D'henri Langlois* **2004** Documentary follows the career of the eccentric, longtime curator and film preservationist of the Cinematheque Francaise, founded by Langlois and Georges Franju in 1936. A fanatical collector, Langlois began by preserving silent films and hiding banned works from the Nazis during their occupation of Paris. Later, Langlois offered screenings of his collection, which heavily influenced such budding directors as Godard and Truffaut. Langlois also had a fractious relationship with the French government, who provided a subsidy and tried to exert control over the organization. A somewhat lengthy labor of love from director Richard; French with subtitles. **128m/B DVD.** ***D:*** Jacques Richard; ***C:*** Jerome Blumberg; ***M:*** Nicolas Baby, Liam Farell.

Henry IV 🦴🦴 1/2 **1985** The adaptation of the Luigi Pirandello farce about a modern-day recluse who shields himself from the horrors of the real world by pretending to be mad and acting out the fantasy of being the medieval German emperor Henry IV. In Italian with English subtitles. **94m/C VHS, DVD.** *IT* Marcello Mastroianni, Claudia Cardinale, Leopoldo Trieste, Paolo Bonacelli, Luciano Bartoli, Latou Chardons; ***D:*** Marco Bellocchio; ***W:*** Marco Bellocchio, Tonino Guerra, Astor Piazzolla.

Henry V 🦴🦴🦴🦴 **1944** Classic, epic adaptation of the Shakespeare play, and Olivier's first and most successful directorial effort, dealing with the medieval British monarch that defeated the French at Agincourt. Distinguished by Olivier's brilliant formal experiment of beginning the drama as a 16th Century performance of the play in the Globe Theatre, and having the stage eventually transform into realistic historical settings of storybook color. Filmed at the height of WWII suffering in Britain (and meant as a parallel to the British fighting the Nazis), the film was not released in the U.S. until 1946. **136m/C VHS, DVD.** *GB* Laurence Olivier, Robert Newton, Leslie Banks, Esmond Knight, Renee Asherson, Leo Genn, George Robey, Ernest Thesiger, Felix Aylmer, Ralph Truman, Harcourt Williams, Max Adrian, Valentine Dyall, Russell Thorndike, Roy Emerton, Robert Helpmann, Freda Jackson, Griffith Jones, John Laurie, Niall MacGinnis, Michael Shepley; ***D:*** Laurence Olivier; ***W:*** Alan Dent, Dallas Bower, Laurence Olivier; ***C:*** Robert Krasker; ***M:*** William Walton. Natl. Bd. of Review '46: Actor (Olivier); N.Y. Film Critics '46: Actor (Olivier).

Henry V 🦴🦴🦴🦴 **1989** Stirring, expansive retelling of Shakespeare's drama about the warrior-king of England. Branagh stars as Henry, leading his troops and uniting his kingdom against France. Very impressive production rivals Olivier's 1945 rendering but differs by stressing the high cost of war—showing the ego-mania, doubts, and subterfuge that underlie conflicts. Marvelous film-directorial debut for Branagh (who also adapted the screenplay). Wonderful supporting cast includes some of Britain's finest actors. **138m/C VHS, DVD.** *GB* Kenneth Branagh, Derek Jacobi, Brian Blessed, Alec McCowen, Ian Holm, Richard Briers, Robert Stephens, Robbie Coltrane, Christian Bale, Judi Dench, Paul Scofield, Michael Maloney, Emma Thompson, Patrick Doyle, Richard Clifford, Richard Easton, Paul Gregory, Harold Innocent, Charles Kay, Geraldine McEwan, Christopher Ravenscroft, John Sessions, Simon Shepherd, Jay Villiers, Danny (Daniel) Webb; ***D:*** Kenneth Branagh; ***W:*** Kenneth Branagh; ***C:*** Kenneth Macmillan; ***M:*** Patrick Doyle. Oscars '89: Costume Des.; British Acad. '89: Director (Branagh); Natl. Bd. of Review '89: Director (Branagh).

Henry & June 🦴🦴🦴 1/2 **1990 (NC-17)** Based on the diaries of writer Anais Nin which chronicled her triangular relationship with author Henry Miller and his wife June, a relationship that provided the erotic backdrop to Miller's "Tropic of Capricorn." Set in Paris in the early '30s, the setting moves between the impecunious expatriate's cheap room on the Left bank—filled with artists, circus performers, prostitutes, and gypsies—to the conservative, well-appointed home of Nin and her husband. Captures the heady atmosphere of Miller's gay Paris; no one plays an American better than Ward (who replaced Alec Baldwin). Notable for having prompted the creation of an NC-17 rating because of its adult theme. **136m/C VHS, DVD.** Fred Ward, Uma Thurman, Maria De Medeiros, Richard E. Grant, Kevin Spacey; ***D:*** Philip Kaufman; ***W:*** Philip Kaufman; ***C:*** Philippe Rousselot; ***M:*** Mark Adler.

Henry & Verlin 🦴🦴 **1994** Verlin (Macintosh) is a nine-year-old who doesn't talk. He lives in rural Ontario (during the Depression) with his overprotective mother Minnie (Beatty) and indifferent father Ferris (Joy), as well as Ferris' childlike brother Henry (Farmer) who befriends Verlin. The misfit duo develop a strong bond that includes disabled retired prostitute Mabel (Kidder)—much to the resentment of some of the less-enlightened townsfolk. There's some melodramatic events but the performances skirt maudlin excess. **87m/C VHS, DVD.** *CA* Gary Farmer, Keegan Macintosh, Nancy Beatty, Robert Joy, Margot Kidder, Eric Peterson; ***Cameos:*** David Cronenberg; ***D:*** Gary Ledbetter; ***W:*** Gary Ledbetter.

Henry Fool 🦴🦴🦴 **1998 (R)** Simon Grim (Urbaniak) is a socially inept garbage man treated with contempt by his depressed mother (Porter) and caustic sister (Posey). Henry Fool (Ryan), an alcoholic homeless man, claims to be a great writer and sees a bit of poet in Simon as well. After he moves Henry into the family's basement, Simon takes his first steps as a poet and Henry takes liberties with both of the women. Simon turns out to be a natural artist, and writes a poem that profoundly moves and/or shocks the public and creates a controversy on the Internet. As Simon is courted by publishers, he champions Henry's unread work as well. Their respective fortunes rise and fall as Henry's work is unveiled and the price of fame affects their lives. Director Hartley pulls very different elements such as the artistry of Samuel Beckett and the myth of Faust together to create a bizarre urban fable. **138m/C VHS, DVD.** Thomas Jay Ryan, James Urbaniak, Parker Posey, Maria Porter, Kevin Corrigan, James Saito; ***D:*** Hal Hartley; ***W:*** Hal Hartley; ***C:*** Michael Spiller; ***M:*** Hal Hartley.

Henry Hill 🦴🦴 **2000** Misfit Henry (Harrold) was a childhood musical prodigy who left his rural Maine home for New York City. But his extreme stage fright means his dreams of becoming a concert violinist are remote and a failed suicide attempt finds Henry returning to his loony family who run a gas station/diner. To Henry's rescue (maybe) is Cynthia (Kelly), a troubled loner in a red car who takes an interest in Henry and decides to hang around until she can persuade him to go back to New York with her and try again. **85m/C VHS, DVD.** Jamie Harrold, Moira Kelly, Susan Blommaert, John Griesemer, Eden Riegel; ***D:*** David G. Kantar; ***W:*** David G. Kantar; ***C:*** Luke Eder; ***M:*** Dave Eggar.

Henry Poole Is Here 🦴🦴🦴 **2008 (PG)** Low-key comedy based on the Catholic idea of miracles and public fascination with divine imagery. Fed up with life-as-he-knows-it, Henry (Wilson) abruptly leaves his fiancee and family business, retreating to a small house in an LA suburb in search of complete isolation. However, nosy neighbors won't leave him alone, and one in particular, Esperanza (Barrazza), discovers a water stain on his house in the shape of Jesus that quickly becomes a pilgrimage destination for those looking to relieve their ailments and burdens. Soon the skeptical Henry discovers the healing power in hope. A perfectly-balanced comedy that refreshingly believes in itself, opting out of snarky punchlines and cynical jabs at religion without getting preachy or sappy. For believers and skeptical audiences alike. **100m/C DVD, Blu-ray Disc.** *US* Luke Wilson, Radha Mitchell, George Lopez, Cheryl Hines, Adriana Barraza, Richard Benjamin, Beth Grant, Morgan Lily, Rachel Seiferth; ***D:*** Mark Pellington; ***W:*** Albert Torres; ***C:*** Eric Schmidt; ***M:*** John (Gianni) Frizzell.

Henry: Portrait of a Serial Killer 🦴🦴🦴🦴 **1990 (R)** Based on the horrific life and times of serial killer Henry Lee Lucas, this film has received wide praise for its straight-forward and uncompromising look into the minds of madmen. The film follows ex-cons Henry (Rooker) and his roommate Otis (Towles) as they set out on mindless murder sprees (one of which they videotape). Extremely disturbing and graphic film. Unwary viewers should be aware of the grisly scenes and use their own discretion when viewing this otherwise genuinely moving film. **90m/C VHS, DVD.** Michael Rooker, Tom Towler, Tracy Arnold, David Katz; ***D:*** John McNaughton; ***W:*** John McNaughton, Richard Fire; ***C:*** Charlie Lieberman; ***M:*** Robert F. McNaughton.

Henry: Portrait of a Serial Killer 2: Mask of Sanity 🦴 *Henry 2: Portrait of a Serial Killer* **1996 (R)** Michael Rooker gave a chilling performance as serial killer Henry in part 1 but Giuntoli is merely dull. A sullen drifter, Henry manages to get a job and fellow worker Kai (Komenich) invites him to crash at his place. Turns out Kai is a part-time arsonist for hire and Henry helps him out—also introducing Kai to the pleasures of casual murder. The gore is actually limited to a few bloody scenes (usually more is heard than shown) but the whole project is boring. **84m/C VHS, DVD.** Neil Giuntoli, Rich Komenich, Kate Walsh, Carri Levinson, Penelope Milford; ***D:*** Chuck Parello; ***W:*** Chuck Parello; ***C:*** Michael Kohnhurst; ***M:*** Robert F. McNaughton.

Her Alibi 🦴🦴 **1988 (PG)** When successful murder-mystery novelist Phil Blackwood runs out of ideas for good books, he seeks inspiration in the criminal courtroom. There he discovers a beautiful Romanian immigrant named Nina who is accused of murder. He goes to see her in jail and offers to provide her with an alibi. Narrated by Blackwood in the tone of one of his thriller novels. Uneven comedy, with appealing cast and arbitrary plot. **95m/C VHS, DVD.** Tom Selleck, Paulina Porizkova, William Daniels, James Farentino, Hurd Hatfield, Patrick Wayne, Tess Harper, Joan Copeland; ***D:*** Bruce Beresford; ***W:*** Charlie Peters; ***C:*** Freddie Francis; ***M:*** Georges Delerue.

Her and She and Him 🦴🦴 *Claude et Greta* **1969** Young Swedish beauty Greta arrives in Paris with only her guitar. Penniless, she takes up with another woman but soon feels she's only a sexual prisoner. So Greta seduces a young painter who is having an obsessive affair with a gay artist. Dubbed into English. **90m/C VHS.** *FR* Astrid Frank, Yves Vincent; ***D:*** Max Pecas; ***C:*** Robert Lefebvre.

Her Best Move 🦴🦴 1/2 **2007 (G)** Sara (Pipes) is a 15-year-old soccer phenom being pushed by her domineering coach dad (Patterson) to make the U.S. national team. She would really like the chance to just be a typical teen and maybe get a date and a kiss from cute Josh (Bell). Sara tries to juggle soccer, school, dance lessons, a part-time job, a best friend, her parents, and a potential boyfriend until something has to give. Cute, chipper story with a well-filmed big soccer game finale. **100m/C DVD.** Scott Patterson, Lisa Darr, Drew Tyler Bell, Daryl Sabara, Lalaine; ***D:*** Norm Hunter; ***W:*** Norm Hunter, Tony Vidal; ***C:*** Paul Ryan; ***M:*** Didier Rachou. **VIDEO**

Her First Romance 🦴🦴 1/2 *The Right Man* **1940** Mixed-up romance with Fellows and Wells as sisters, Linden their cousin, and Ladd her fiance. The sisters fall for Evans and use Ladd in their schemes, causing him to believe Evans is actually after Linden. Eventually, everyone pairs up properly. **77m/B VHS.** Edith Fellows, Julie Bishop, Alan Ladd, Judith Linden, Wilbur Evans, Roger Daniel; ***D:*** Edward Dmytryk; ***W:*** Adele Comandini.

Her Husband's Affairs 🦴 **1947** Tone is an advertising wonder and Ball is his loving wife who always gets credit for his work. Tone does the advertising for an inventor who is searching for the perfect embalming fluid in this rather lifeless comedy. **83m/B VHS.** Lucille Ball, Franchot Tone, Edward Everett Horton, Gene Lockhart, Larry Parks; ***D:*** S. Sylvan Simon; ***M:*** George Duning.

Her Life as a Man 🦴 1/2 **1983** A female reporter is refused a job as a sportswriter because of her gender. She makes herself up as a man, gets the job, and creates havoc when she has to deal with lustful women on the job. **93m/C VHS.** Robyn Douglass, Joan Collins, Robert Culp, Marc Singer, Laraine Newman; ***D:*** Robert Ellis Miller. **TV**

Her Majesty 🦴🦴 **2001** Young New Zealander Elizabeth Wakefield (Andrews) can't believe it when, in 1953, she learns that her hero, Queen Elizabeth II, will be visiting her hometown during a commonwealth tour. Elizabeth is friends with Hira Mata (Haughton), an aged Maori whose shack is considered an eyesore by town busybody Virginia Hobson (Holloway). When Virginia wants to clean up the community by displacing the old woman, things take a turn for the worst thanks to Elizabeth's spiteful brother (Elliott). **105m/C DVD.** *NZ* Vicky Haughton, Sally Andrews, Craig Elliott, Liddy Holloway, Annabel Leach; ***D:*** Mark J. Gordon; ***W:*** Mark J. Gordon; ***C:*** Stephen M. Katz; ***M:*** William Ross.

Her Name Is Cat 🦴🦴 1/2 **1999 (R)** Yet another Hong Kong hitwoman (Almen Wong) agrees to yet another "last job" before retiring...fans know the drill. Explosions and slo-mo shoot outs are plentiful, though the fight choreography isn't going to make anyone forget John Woo or Ringo Lam. **94m/C DVD.** *HK* Michael Wong, Almen Wong, Kent Masters King; ***D:*** Clarence (Fok) Ford; ***W:*** Wong Jing. **VIDEO**

Her Silent Sacrifice 🦴 1/2 **1918** A silent melodrama about a French girl torn between material wealth and true love. **42m/B VHS.** R. Payton Gibb, Edmund Pardo, Blanche Craig, Benjamin Struckman, Alice Brady, Henry Clive; ***D:*** Edward Jose; ***W:*** Eve Unsell.

Herbie: Fully Loaded 🦴🦴 **2005 (G)** On her way out of town, college graduate Maggie Peyton (Lohan) spends 75 bucks to free a '63 VW Beetle from the junkyard scrap pile and has boy pal Kevin (Long) restore it. Lo and behold, it's Herbie and he helps Maggie prove her driving skills to her NASCAR champ daddy (Keaton)—who's spent his energies on his not-as-talented son—as they race against pompous archenemy Trip Murphy (Dillon). The sassy Lohan, in her third Disney venture, picks up the speed for an uninspired-and-somewhat-CGI Herbie. Fifth feature in a series that, 15 years before, seemed out of gas. **101m/C DVD, UMD.** *US* Lindsay Lohan, Matt Dillon, Justin Long, Breckin Meyer, Michael Keaton, Jill Ritchie, Cheryl Hines, Thomas Lennon, Jimmi Simpson, Jeremy Roberts; ***D:*** Angela Robinson; ***W:*** Robert Ben Garant, Alfred Gough, Miles Millar, Thomas Lennon; ***C:*** Greg Gardiner; ***M:*** Mark Mothersbaugh.

Herbie Goes Bananas 1/2 **1980 (G)** While Herbie the VW is racing in Rio de Janeiro, he is bothered by the syndicate, a pickpocket, and a raging bull. The fourth and final entry in the Disney "Love Bug" movies, but Herbie later made his way to a TV series. **93m/C VHS, DVD.** Cloris Leachman, Charles Martin Smith, Harvey Korman, John Vernon, Alex Rocco, Richard Jaeckel, Fritz Feld; ***D:*** Vincent McEveety.

Herbie Goes to Monte Carlo **1977 (G)** While participating in a Paris-to-Monte-Carlo race, Herbie the VW takes a detour and falls in love with a Lancia. Third in the Disney "Love Bug" series. **104m/C VHS, DVD.** Dean Jones, Don Knotts, Julie Sommars, Roy Kinnear; ***D:*** Vincent McEveety; ***W:*** Arthur Alsberg.

Herbie Rides Again 1/2 **1974 (G)** In this "Love Bug" sequel, Herbie comes to the aid of an elderly woman who is trying to stop a ruthless tycoon from raising a skyscraper on her property. Humorous Disney fare. Two other sequels followed. **88m/C VHS, DVD.** Helen Hayes, Ken Berry, Stefanie Powers, John McIntire, Keenan Wynn; ***D:*** Robert Stevenson; ***M:*** George Bruns.

Hercules 1/2 *La Tatiche de Ercole* **1958** The one that started it all. Reeves is perfect as the mythical hero Hercules who encounters many dangerous situations while trying to win over his true love. Dubbed in English. **107m/C VHS, DVD.** *IT* Steve Reeves, Sylva Koscina, Fabrizio Mioni, Gianna Maria Canale, Arturo Dominici; ***D:*** Pietro Francisci; ***C:*** Mario Bava.

Hercules **1983 (PG)** Lackluster remake of 1957 original finds legendary muscle guy Hercules in the person of Ferrigno's Hulkster fighting against the evil King Minos for his own survival and the love of Cassiopeia, a rival king's daughter. **100m/C VHS, DVD.** *IT* Lou Ferrigno, Sybil Danning, William Berger, Brad Harris, Ingrid Anderson, Mindi Miller; ***D:*** Lewis (Luigi Cozzi) Coates; ***W:*** Lewis (Luigi Cozzi) Coates; ***M:*** Pino Donaggio. Golden Raspberries '83: Worst Support. Actress (Danning), Worst New Star (Ferrigno).

Hercules 1/2 **1997 (G)** After a couple of animated downers, Disney's latest adventure goes for a happy heroic tone by taking on Greek myths. Baby Herc is the son of Zeus, who rules on Mt. Olympus. Hades, Lord of the Underworld, plans a takeover and learns that only Hercules' strength will stand in his way. Hades manages to kidnap the tyke and turn him mortal but when the teenaged Herc learns his true origins, he also discovers that if he proves himself to be a hero he can regain his immortality and return to Mt. Olympus. He's aided by his flying horse Pegasus, satyr-like trainer Phil, and smart gal Meg, while Hades has his less-than-bright minions Pain and Panic. Lots of fun and lots of merchandising (even the movie makes fun of the inevitable tie-ins). ♫ The Gospel Truth; Go the Distance; One Last Hope; I Won't Say; Zero to Hero. **92m/C VHS, DVD.** ***D:*** John Musker, Ron Clements; ***W:*** John Musker, Ron Clements, Bob Shaw, Donald McEnery, Irene Mecchi; ***M:*** Alan Menken, David Zippel; ***V:*** Tate Donovan, James Woods, Danny DeVito, Matt Frewer, Bob(cat) Goldthwait, Susan Egan, Rip Torn, Samantha Eggar, Paul Shaffer, Barbara Barrie, Hal Holbrook, Amanda Plummer, Carol(e) Shelley; ***Nar:*** Charlton Heston.

Hercules 2 *The Adventures of Hercules* **1985 (PG)** The muscle-bound demigod returns to do battle with more evil foes amidst the same stunningly cheap special effects. **90m/C VHS, DVD.** *IT* Lou Ferrigno, Claudio Cassinelli, Milly Carlucci, Sonia Viviani, William Berger, Carlotta Green; ***D:*** Lewis (Luigi Cozzi) Coates; ***M:*** Pino Donaggio.

Hercules against the Moon Men *Maciste la Regina di Samar* **1964** It's no holds barred for the mighty son of Zeus when evil moon men start killing off humans in a desperate bid to revive their dead queen. **88m/C VHS, DVD.** *IT FR* Alan Steel, Jany Clair, Anna Maria Polani, Nando Tamberlani, Delia D'Alberti, Jean-Pierre Honore; ***D:*** Giacomo Gentilomo; ***W:*** Arpad De Riso, Nino Scolaro; ***C:*** Oberdan Troiani; ***M:*** Carlo Franci.

Hercules and the Captive Women *Hercules and the Haunted Women; Hercules and the Conquest of Atlantis; Ercole Alla Conquista di Atlantide* **1963** Hercules' son is kidnapped by the Queen of Atlantis, and the bare-chested warrior goes on an all-out rampage to save the boy. Directed by sometimes-lauded Cottafavi. **93m/C VHS, DVD.** *IT* Reg Park, Fay Spain, Ettore Manni; ***D:*** Vittorio Cottafavi.

Hercules and the Princess of Troy 1/2 **1965** Hercules is up to his pecs in trouble as he battles a hungry sea monster in order to save a beautiful maiden. Originally a pilot for a prospective TV series, and shot in English, not Italian, with Hercules played by erstwhile Tarzan Scott. Highlights are special effects and color cinematography. **50m/C VHS, DVD.** *IT* Gordon Scott, Diana Hyland, Paul Stevens, Everett Sloane; ***D:*** Albert Band; ***W:*** Larry Forrester; ***C:*** Enzo Barboni; ***M:*** Fred Steiner. **TV**

Hercules in New York 1/2 *Hercules: The Movie; Hercules Goes Bananas* **1970 (G)** Motion picture debut of Schwarzenegger (his voice is dubbed) as a Herculean mass of muscle sent by dad Zeus to Manhattan, where he behaves likes a geek out of water and eventually becomes a professional wrestling superstar. 250 pounds of stupid, lighthearted fun. **93m/C VHS, DVD.** Arnold Schwarzenegger, Arnold Stang, Deborah Loomis, James Karen, Ernest Graves, Taina Elg; ***D:*** Arthur Allan Seidelman; ***W:*** Aubrey Wisberg; ***C:*** Leo Lebowitz; ***M:*** John Balamos.

Hercules in the Haunted World 1/2 *Ercole al Centro Della Terra* **1964** Long before the days of 24-hour pharmacies, Hercules—played yet again by Reeves-clone Park—must journey to the depths of Hell in order to find a plant that will cure a poisoned princess. Better than most muscle operas, thanks to Bava. **91m/C VHS, DVD.** *IT* Reg Park, Leonora Ruffo, Christopher Lee, George Ardisson; ***D:*** Mario Bava.

Hercules, Prisoner of Evil **1964** Spaghetti myth-opera in which Hercules battles a witch who is turning men into werewolves. Made for Italian TV by director Dawson (the nom-de-cinema of Antonio Margheriti). **90m/C VHS.** *IT* Reg Park; ***D:*** Anthony M. Dawson. **TV**

Hercules the Legendary Journeys, Vol. 1: And the Amazon Women 1/2 **1994** Half-man, half-god Hercules (Sorbo) and his friend Ioleus (Hurst) are summoned to a village to kill the beasts stealing livestock. Turns out those responsible are the village's women, who are mad at their husbands and have formed a band of Amazons, lead by Hippolyta (Downey), who happens to be working for Hercules' immortal enemy, the goddess Hera. Now it's up to Herc to convince Hippolyta that men and women can work together and outsmart Hera at the same time. **91m/C VHS, DVD.** Kevin Sorbo, Michael Hurst, Roma Downey, Anthony Quinn, Lucy Lawless; ***D:*** Bill W.L. Norton; ***M:*** Joseph LoDuca. **TV**

Hercules the Legendary Journeys, Vol. 2: The Lost Kingdom 1/2 **1994** Hera has hidden the kingdom of Troy and only a magic compass can point Hercules (Sorbo) in the right direction. He rescues a sacrificial virigin (O'Connor) and the duo manage to find the compass and get into Troy where she learns her father was once its king. Turns out dad sent his daughter away so he wouldn't have to sacrifice her to Hera and lost his kingdom instead. Now she wants her kingdom back and Hera still wants her sacrifice—especially if it's Hercules. **91m/C VHS, DVD.** Kevin Sorbo, Michael Hurst, Anthony Quinn, Renee O'Connor, Robert Trebor; ***D:*** Harley Cokliss; ***M:*** Joseph LoDuca. **TV**

Hercules the Legendary Journeys, Vol. 3: The Circle of Fire 1/2 **1994** Hera's stolen fire from mankind, which is slowly freezing to death, keeping one eternal torch for herself. A villager named Deianeira (Kitaen) enlists Hercules (Sorbo) to search for Prometheus (Ferguson), the god of fire, but Hera's stolen his flame as well. When Herc finds the torch it's encircled in a ring of fire, which Hera knows can destroy Hercules' immortality. **92m/C VHS.** Kevin Sorbo, Michael Hurst, Anthony Quinn, Tawny Kitaen, Mark Ferguson; ***D:*** Doug Lefler; ***M:*** Joseph LoDuca. **TV**

Hercules the Legendary Journeys, Vol. 4: In the Underworld 1/2 **1994** Having married Deianeira (Kitaen), Herc's a pretty happy guy until a mysterious maiden, Iole, comes to him for help. Seems a deadly crack has opened up in the earth and is swallowing villagers. But Iole has actually been sent by Hera to destroy Hercules and when Deianeira discovers her treachery she goes to warn her husband. Only Hera manages to trick her into walking off a clift and falling to her death. Hercules must go into the underworld to save the world from Hera but when he learns Deianeira's fate, he accepts an impossible challenge from Hades (Ferguson) to bring his wife back to life. **91m/C VHS.** Kevin Sorbo, Michael Hurst, Anthony Quinn, Tawny Kitaen, Mark Ferguson; ***D:*** Bill W.L. Norton; ***M:*** Joseph LoDuca. **TV**

Hercules Unchained *Ercole e la Regina de Lidia* **1959** Sequel to "Hercules" finds superhero Reeves must use all his strength to save the city of Thebes and the woman he loves from the giant Antaeus. **101m/C VHS, DVD.** *IT* Steve Reeves, Sylva Koscina, Silvia Lopel, Primo Carnera; ***D:*** Pietro Francisci.

Hercules vs. the Sons of the Sun 1/2 *Hercules Against the Sons of the Sun; Ercole Contro I Figli del Sole* **1964** Herc (Forest) battles the evil King of the Incas by building unstoppable fighting machines. Typical of the genre. **91m/C VHS, DVD.** *IT SP* Mark Forest, Giuliano Gemma, Riccardo Valle, Andrea Scotti, Anna Maria Pace, Angela Rhu, Giulio Donnini; ***D:*** Osvaldo Civirani; ***W:*** Osvaldo Civirani; ***C:*** Osvaldo Civirani, Julio Ortas; ***M:*** Coriolano Gori.

Here and Elsewhere 1/2 *Ici et Ailleurs* **1976** Godard, Gorin, and Mieville contrast the story of a French family with a look at the Palestine revolution as seen through the media of television, books, and pictures. The film was originally titled "Until Victory" and commissioned by the Palestinians to examine life in the Palestinian camps. After the defeat of the Palestinian army in the Six Day War, Godard and his cohorts transformed the film with their French family ("Here") and their impressions of Palestine ("Elsewhere"). French with subtitles. **60m/C VHS.** *FR* Anne-Marie Mieville; ***D:*** Jean-Pierre Gorin, Jean-Luc Godard; ***W:*** Jean-Pierre Gorin, Jean-Luc Godard.

Here Come the Co-Eds 1/2 **1945** Bud & Lou are the caretakers of an all-girl college which is about to go bankrupt unless the boys can find a way to pay off the mortgage. And come to the rescue they do, including Bud getting into the wrestling ring with the "Masked Marvel" (Chaney Jr. as the villain). There's also a classic silent scene with Lou served a bowl of oyster stew containing a live oyster, which promptly grabs his tie, bites his fingers, and squirts in his face. **90m/B VHS, DVD.** Bud Abbott, Lou Costello, Lon Chaney Jr., Peggy Ryan, Martha O'Driscoll, June Vincent, Donald Cook, Charles Dingle; ***D:*** Jean Yarbrough; ***W:*** Arthur T. Horman, John Grant.

Here Come the Girls 1/2 **1953** An unfunny musical-comedy about a chorus boy (Hope) fired for incompetence and then rehired to set a trap when the new singer (Martin) is stalked by a killer. Weak script, weak songs. ♫ Girls Are Here To Stay; Never So Beautiful; You Got Class; Desire; When You Love Someone; Ali Baba Be My Baby; Heavenly Days; See the Circus; Peace. **100m/C VHS.** Bob Hope, Tony Martin, Arlene Dahl, Rosemary Clooney, Millard Mitchell, William Demarest, Fred Clark, Robert Strauss; ***D:*** Claude Binyon; ***W:*** Hal Kanter.

Here Come the Littles: The Movie 1/2 **1985** A 12-year-old boy finds many new adventures when he meets The Littles—tiny folks who reside within the walls of people's houses. Adapted from the books and TV series. **76m/C VHS.** ***D:*** Bernard Deyries.

Here Come the Marines *Tell It To the Marines* **1952** The Bowery Boys accidentally join the marines and wind up breaking up a gambling ring. **66m/B VHS.** Leo Gorcey, Huntz Hall, Tim Ryan; ***D:*** William Beaudine.

Here Come the Nelsons 1/2 **1952** In between the radio show, "The Adventures of Ozzie and Harriet," and the TV series came this feature film. Ad man Ozzie is trying to develop a campaign for a women's wear company while the town's centennial celebration is causing problems on the homefront. Seems Harriet's houseguest for the festivities is Rock Hudson! **76m/B VHS.** Ozzie Nelson, Harriet Hilliard Nelson, David Nelson, Ricky Nelson, Rock Hudson, Barbara Lawrence, Sheldon Leonard, Jim Backus; ***D:*** Fred de Cordova; ***W:*** Don Nelson, Ozzie Nelson.

Here Come the Waves **1945** Easy-going wartime musical finds Der Bingle as a singing idol drafted into the Navy, assigned to direct WAVE shows. The crooner meets identical twins (both played by Hutton) and falls hard. Only problem is he can't tell the gals apart—and one twin can't stand him. Amusing romantic complications mix well with some spoofing of a star's life. ♫ Ac-cent-tchu-ate the Positive; I Promise You; Let's Take the Long Way Home; That Old Black Magic; There's a Fellow Waiting in Poughkeepsie; Here Come the Waves; My Mama Thinks I'm a Star; Join the Navy. **99m/B VHS, DVD.** Bing Crosby, Betty Hutton, Sonny Tufts, Ann Doran, Noel Neill, Mae Clarke, Gwen Crawford, Catherine Craig; ***D:*** Mark Sandrich; ***W:*** Zion Myers.

Here Comes Cookie 1/2 **1935** Amusing farce finds Gracie (Allen) the daughter of wealthy Harrison Allen (Barbier), who's afraid of the fortune hunters eyeing other daughter Phyllis (Furness). So he temporarily turns over the family fortune to Gracie, who promptly turns their Park Avenue mansion into a home for down-on-their-luck vaudevillians. Lots of specialty acts and Burns is around as straight man. **65m/B VHS, DVD.** Gracie Allen, George Burns, George Barbier, Betty Furness; ***D:*** Norman Z. McLeod; ***W:*** Don Hartman, Sam Mintz; ***C:*** Gilbert Warrenton.

Here Comes Kelly 1/2 **1943** Controlling his temper and hanging on to his job is more than our hero can handle. **63m/C VHS.** Eddie Quillan, Joan Woodbury, Maxie "Slapsie" Rosenbloom; ***D:*** William Beaudine.

Here Comes Mr. Jordan **1941** Montgomery is the young prizefighter killed in a plane crash because of a mix-up in heaven. He returns to life in the body of a soon-to-be murdered millionaire. Rains is the indulgent and advising guardian angel. A lovely fantasy/romance remade in 1978 as "Heaven Can Wait." **94m/B VHS, DVD.** Robert Montgomery, Claude Rains, James Gleason, Evelyn Keyes, Edward Everett Horton, Rita Johnson, John Emery; ***D:*** Alexander Hall; ***W:*** Sidney Buchman, Seton I. Miller; ***M:*** Frederick "Friedrich" Hollander. Oscars '41: Screenplay, Story.

Here Comes Santa Claus 1/2 **1984** A young boy and girl travel to the North Pole to deliver a very special wish to Santa Claus. **78m/C VHS.** Karen Cheryl, Armand Meffre; ***D:*** Christian Gion.

Here Comes the Groom **1951** Late, stale Capra-corn, involving a rogue journalist who tries to keep his girlfriend from marrying a millionaire by becoming a charity worker. Includes a number of cameos. ♫ In the Cool, Cool, Cool of the Evening; Bonne Nuit, Good Night; Misto Cristofo Columbo; Your Own Little House. **114m/B VHS, DVD.** Bing Crosby, Jane Wyman, Franchot Tone, Alexis Smith, James Barton, Connie Gilchrist, Robert Keith, Anna Maria Alberghetti, Charles Halton; ***Cameos:*** Dorothy Lamour, Phil Harris, Louis Armstrong; ***D:*** Frank Capra. Oscars '51: Song ("In the Cool, Cool, Cool of the Evening").

Here is My Heart 1/2 **1934** It's a classic plot: someone pretends to be someone they're not, all for love. In this musical comedy a famous (and wealthy) singer pretends to be a waiter, all to position himself nearer to the woman of his dreams. Only she's a European princess. Will she even notice him? **77m/B VHS.** Bing Crosby, Kitty Carlisle Hart, Roland Young, Alison Skipworth, Reginald Owen, William Frawley; ***D:*** Frank Tuttle; ***W:*** Alfred Savoir; ***M:*** Leo Robin, Ralph Rainger.

Here on Earth 🦴🦴 **2000 (PG-13)** Predictable teary teen romantic drama with a very pretty cast doing what they can with one-note roles. Smalltown beauty Samantha (Sobieski) waits tables at the family diner and hangs out with long-time boyfriend Jasper (Hartnett), who's rivals with snotty prep, Kelley (Klein). Their rivalry causes a disaster for Sam and her family that the boys must rectifiy, even as Kelley and Sam turn to each other. Oh yeah, and then Sam's recurring knee problems turn out to be cancer and everyone has to pull together. **96m/C VHS, DVD.** Chris Klein, Leelee Sobieski, Josh Hartnett, Michael Rooker, Annie Corley, Bruce Greenwood, Annette O'Toole, Stuart Wilson, Tac Fitzgerald; ***D:*** Mark Piznarski; ***W:*** Michael Seitzman; ***C:*** Michael D. O'Shea; ***M:*** Andrea Morricone.

Here We Go Again! 🦴🦴 **1942** Fibber McGee and Molly are planning a cross-country trip for their 20th anniversary celebration, but complications abound. Based on the popular NBC radio series. **76m/B VHS, DVD.** Marian Jordan, Jim Jordan, Harold (Hal) Peary, Gale Gordon, Edgar Bergen, Ray Noble; ***D:*** Allan Dwan.

Here's Flash Casey 🦴 1/2 **1938** Shutterbug Flash Casey finds the newspaper game hard going since he's just a minor assistant. Then he takes some society shots as a favor to his columnist girlfriend Kay, which include a prominent citizen with a young woman. The shots are altered by a would-be blackmailer but Flash gets the blame and has to sort out the mess to save his reputation. **57m/B DVD.** Eric Linden, Patricia "Boots" Mallory, Holmes Herbert, Harry Harvey, Cully Richards, Victor Adams; ***D:*** Lynn Shores; ***W:*** John Krafft; ***C:*** Marcel Le Picard.

Heritage of the Desert 🦴 1/2 **1933** One of the earlier westerns made by the rugged Scott. **62m/B VHS, DVD.** Randolph Scott, Sally Blane, Guinn "Big Boy" Williams; ***D:*** Henry Hathaway.

The Hero 🦴 1/2 *Bloomfield* **1971 (PG)** A popular soccer player agrees to throw a game for big cash, and then worries about losing the respect of a young boy who idolizes him. Nothing new in this overly sentimental sports drama. **97m/C VHS.** Richard Harris, Romy Schneider, Kim Burfield, Maurice Kaufmann; ***D:*** Richard Harris.

Hero 🦴🦴🦴 **1992 (PG-13)** Interesting twist on Cinderella fable and modern media satire has TV reporter Davis looking for the man who saved her life, expecting a genuine hero, and accepting without question the one who fits her vision. Critically considered disappointing, but wait—Garcia and Hoffman make a great team, and Davis is fetching as the vulnerable media person. Strong language and dark edges may keep away some of the kids, but otherwise this is a fine fable. **116m/C VHS, DVD.** Geena Davis, Dustin Hoffman, Andy Garcia, Joan Cusack, Kevin J. O'Connor, Chevy Chase, Maury Chaykin, Stephen Tobolowsky, Christian Clemenson, Tom Arnold, Warren Berlinger, Susie Cusack, James Madio, Richard Riehle, Don Yesso, Darrell Larson; ***D:*** Stephen Frears; ***W:*** David Peoples; ***C:*** Oliver Stapleton; ***M:*** George Fenton.

Hero 🦴🦴🦴 *Ying Xiong* **2003 (PG-13)** Visually stunning movie combines martial arts, tragedy, historical drama, and philosophy into one complex, satisfying epic. Set in 3rd century B.C. China, the story revolves around swordsman Nameless (Li), who hunts down three assassins for the ruthless King (Chen), who used brutal methods to bring the various states of China under his leadership. Told mostly in flashback, Nameless unveils his encounters with the warriors (Leung, Cheung, and Yen) to the King, but all is not as it seems, and in the end Nameless faces a choice of what his place in the King's newly unified China should be. Features meticulous, creative cinematography (each segment has its own color theme) and beautiful martial arts sequences, but is hindered by inconsistent performances. The most expensive Chinese production ever made at $30 million, it has been criticized for appearing to endorse the government's stance on a unified China. **98m/C DVD, Blu-ray Disc, UMD.** *HK CH* Jet Li, Maggie Cheung, Donnie Yen, Zhang Ziyi, Tony Leung Chiu-Wai, Daoming Chen; ***D:*** Yimou Zhang; ***W:*** Yimou Zhang, Feng Li, Bin Wang; ***C:*** Christopher Doyle; ***M:*** Tan Dun.

A Hero Ain't Nothin' but a Sandwich 🦴🦴 1/2 **1978 (PG)** A young urban black teenager gets involved in drugs and is eventually saved from ruin. Slow-moving, over-directed and talky. However, Scott turns in a fine performance. Based on Alice Childress' novel. **107m/C VHS, DVD.** Cicely Tyson, Paul Winfield, Larry B. Scott, Helen Martin, Glynn Turman, David Groh; ***D:*** Ralph Nelson.

Hero and the Terror 🦴 1/2 **1988 (R)** Perennial karate guy Norris plays a sensitive policeman who conquers his fear of a not-so-sensitive maniac who's trying to kill him. Plenty of action and a cheesy subplot to boot. **96m/C VHS, DVD.** Chuck Norris, Brynn Thayer, Steve James, Jack O'Halloran, Ron O'Neal, Billy Drago; ***D:*** William (Bill) Tannen; ***W:*** Michael Blodgett; ***C:*** Eric Van Haren Noman; ***M:*** David Michael Frank.

Hero at Large 🦴🦴 1/2 **1980 (PG)** An unemployed actor foils a robbery while dressed in a promotional "Captain Avenger" suit, and instant celebrity follows. Lightweight, yet enjoyable. **98m/C VHS, DVD.** John Ritter, Anne Archer, Bert Convy, Kevin McCarthy, Kevin Bacon; ***D:*** Martin Davidson; ***W:*** A.J. Carothers.

Hero Bunker 🦴🦴 **1971** Hero bunk about a platoon of heroic Greek soldiers who attempt, at the expense of their personal longevity, to defend an important bunker from enemy invasion. **93m/C VHS.** Giannis Voglis, Maria Xenia; ***D:*** George Andrews.

Hero of Rome **1963** Rome has many who could be called "hero," but one stands biceps and pecs above the rest. **90m/C VHS, DVD.** *IT* Massimo Serato, Gabriele Antonini, Gordon Scott, Gabriella Pallotta; ***D:*** Giorgio Ferroni; ***W:*** Alberta Montanti, Antonino Visont; ***C:*** Augusto Tiezzi; ***M:*** Angelo Francesco Lavagnino.

Hero of the Year 🦴🦴 **1985** The characters from Falk's "Top Dog" return in this story of a Polish TV personality who loses his job and is forced to face unemployment and job-seeking. **115m/C VHS.** *PL* Jerzy Stuhr, Mieczyslaw Franaszek, Piotr Machalica, Marian Opania; ***D:*** Feliks Falk; ***W:*** Feliks Falk; ***C:*** Witold Adamek; ***M:*** Jan Pawluskiewicz.

Hero Wanted 🦴🦴 **2008 (R)** Garbage collector Liam Case (Gooding) becomes a local hero when he rescues a young girl from a burning car, but that one moment doesn't bring the changes to his life Liam anticipates. He happens to be at the bank, flirting with a pretty teller, when a heist is attempted. Liam and the teller are among the shooting victims and Liam vows revenge. But the detective (Liotta) on the case gets suspicious about Liam's true role in the bank job. Lots of flashbacks and a few plot twists. **95m/C DVD.** Cuba Gooding Jr., Ray Liotta, Christa Campbell, Jean Smart, Norman Reedus, Tommy Flanagan, Kim Coates, Ben Cross; ***D:*** Chad Law; ***W:*** Evan Law, Evan Law; ***C:*** Larry Blanford; ***M:*** Kenneth Burgomaster. **VIDEO**

Herod the Great 🦴 **1960** Biblical epic of the downfall of Herod, the ruler of ancient Judea. Scantily clad women abound. Dubbed. **93m/C VHS.** *IT* Edmund Purdom, Sandra Milo, Alberto Lupo; ***D:*** Arnaldo Genoino.

Heroes 🦴🦴 **1977 (PG)** An institutionalized Vietnam vet (Winkler) escapes, hoping to establish a worm farm which will support all his crazy buddies. On the way to the home of a friend he hopes will help him, he encounters Field. Funny situations don't always mix with serious underlying themes of mental illness and post-war adjustment. **97m/C VHS.** Henry Winkler, Sally Field, Harrison Ford; ***D:*** Jeremy Paul Kagan; ***W:*** James (Jim) Carabatsos; ***M:*** Jack Nitzsche.

Heroes Die Young 🦴 1/2 **1960** A cheap independent feature depicting an American command mission with orders to sabotage German oil fields during WWII. **76m/B VHS.** Krika Peters, Scott Borland, Robert Getz, James Strother; ***D:*** Gerald Shepard; ***W:*** Gerald Shepard; ***C:*** Glen R. Smith; ***M:*** Al Pellegrini.

Heroes for Sale 🦴🦴🦴 **1933** Fascinating melodrama about a WWI veteran who returns home and manages to survive one disaster after another. Barthelmess is great in his performance as an American Everyman who must deal with everything from morphine addiction to finding work during the Depression. Fast-paced, patriotic film is helped by ambitious script and the expert direction of Wellman. **72m/B VHS.** Richard Barthelmess, Loretta Young, Aline MacMahon, Robert Barrat, Grant Mitchell, Douglass Dumbrille, Charley Grapewin, Ward Bond; ***D:*** William A. Wellman; ***W:*** Robert Lord, Wilson Mizner.

Heroes in Blue 🦴🦴 **1939** Two brothers join the police force, but one goes astray and hooks up with gangsters. Plenty of action distracts from the cliched story. **60m/B VHS.** Dick Purcell, Charles Quigley, Bernadene Hayes, Edward (Ed Kean, Keene) Keane; ***D:*** William Watson.

Heroes in Hell 🦴 1/2 *Eroi All'Inferno* **1973** Escaped WWII POW joins the Allied underground in an espionage conspiracy against the Third Reich by kidnapping a German general. **90m/C VHS.** *IT* Klaus Kinski, Ettore Manni; ***D:*** Joe D'Amato; ***W:*** Joe D'Amato; ***C:*** Joe D'Amato.

The Heroes of Desert Storm 🦴🦴 **1991** The human spirit of the people who fought in the high-tech Persian Gulf War is captured in this film that also features real war footage from ABC News. **93m/C VHS.** Daniel Baldwin, Angela Bassett, Marshall Bell, Michael Alan Brooks, William Bumiller, Michael Champion, Maria Isabel Diaz; ***D:*** Don Ohlmeyer; ***W:*** Lionel Chetwynd.

The Heroes of Telemark 🦴🦴 1/2 **1965** In 1942, Norway is under Nazi occupation and Nazi scientists are dangerously close to producing an essential element for making an atomic bomb in a secret factory. Underground leader Knut Straud (Harris) enlists the help of Norwegian scientist Rolf Pedersen (Douglas) and a group of saboteurs to destroy the factory. But their raid only provides a short delay and our heroes must now prevent shipment of the component from ever reaching Germany. Filmed on location in Norway, with former members of the underground serving as technical advisors for director Mann. **130m/C VHS, DVD.** *GB* Richard Harris, Kirk Douglas, Michael Redgrave, Ulla Jacobsson, David Weston, Sebastian Breaks, Alan Howard, Roy Dotrice, Patrick Jordan, Anton Diffring, Eric Porter, Ralph Michael; ***D:*** Anthony Mann; ***W:*** Ben Barzman; ***C:*** Robert Krasker; ***M:*** Malcolm Arnold.

Heroes of the Alamo 🦴 1/2 **1937** Remember the Alamo...but forget this movie. Dull, threadbare dramatization of the battle that was scorned even back in '37. **75m/B VHS, DVD.** Rex Lease, Lane Chandler, Roger Williams, Earle Hodgins, Julian Rivero; ***D:*** Harry Fraser.

Heroes of the Heart 🦴🦴 1/2 **1994** Residents ofa West Viriginia trailer park are devastated when their homes are destroyed in a flood. But then Basquette claims she was visited by God, who's directed her to bring the poor community together so that each can be granted their most secret wish. Nicely eccentric characters, serious theme with some whimsical touches, and a country-music soundtrack. **102m/C VHS, DVD.** Lena Basquette, Larry Groce, Dusty Rhodes, Webb Wilder, John McIntire, Jennifer Gurney, Johnny Paycheck; ***D:*** Daniel Boyd; ***W:*** Daniel Boyd; ***C:*** Larry Kopelman; ***M:*** Michael Lipton.

Heroes of the Hills 🦴 1/2 **1938** The Three Mesquiteers back up a plan that would allow trusted prisoners to work for neighboring ranchers. Part of "The Three Mesquiteers" series. **54m/B VHS.** Robert "Bob" Livingston, Ray Corrigan, Max Terhune, Priscilla Lawson, Leroy Mason, James Eagles, Roy Barcroft, Carleton Young; ***D:*** George Sherman; ***W:*** Betty Burbridge; ***C:*** Reggie Lanning; ***M:*** Cy Feuer.

Heroes of the Saddle 🦴 1/2 **1940** When a friend of the Mesquiteers dies in an accident, the boys are forced to place his young daughter Peggy into an orphanage until they can raise the dough to adopt her. But when they visit Peggy, they find some suspicious goings-on and Stony fears that the kids are being used as sweatshop labor. The 27th film in the series. **59m/B DVD.** Robert Livingstone, Raymond Hatton, Duncan Renaldo, Loretta Weaver, Patsy Lee Parsons, Byron Foulger, William Royle, Kermit Maynard; ***D:*** William Whitney; ***W:*** Jack Natteford; ***C:*** William Nobles.

Heroes Shed No Tears 🦴🦴 *Ying Xiong Wei Lei; The Sunset Warrior* **1986** Chinese mercenaries are hired by the Thai government to capture a drug lord from the Golden Triangle. Cantonese with subtitles. **93m/C VHS, DVD.** *HK* Eddy Ko, Ching-Ying Lam, Chen Yue Sang, Kuo Sheng; ***D:*** John Woo; ***W:*** John Woo.

Heroes Stand Alone 🦴 **1989 (R)** When a U.S. spy plane is downed in Central America, a special force is sent in to rescue the crew. Another "Rambo" rip-off. **84m/C VHS.** Bradford Dillman, Chad Everett, Wayne Grace, Rick Dean; ***D:*** Mark Griffiths; ***W:*** Thomas McKelvey Cleaver.

Heroes Three 🦴🦴 **1984** When his crewmate is murdered while on leave in in the Far East, a Navy officer enlists the aid of a Chinese detective to track down the killer. **90m/C VHS.** Rowena Cortes, Mike Kelly, Laurens C. Postma, Lawrence Tan; ***D:*** S.H. Lau.

The Heroic Trio 🦴🦴 1/2 *Dong Fang San Xia* **1993** Three superheroines battle the Lord of the Underground to prevent him from stealing any more human babies. Lots of martial arts and supernatural action. Chinese with subtitles or dubbed. **87m/C VHS, DVD.** *HK* Damian Lau, Michelle Yeoh, Maggie Cheung, Anita (Yim-Fong) Mui, Anthony Wong; ***D:*** Ching Siu Tung, Johnny To; ***W:*** Sandy Shaw; ***C:*** Hang-Seng Poon, Tom Lau; ***M:*** William Hu.

He's Just Not That Into You 🦴🦴 **2009 (PG-13)** Comic take on the relationship book by Greg Behrendt and Liz Tuccillo, set in Baltimore, following five women through their struggles with modern-day relationships. Beth (Aniston) has been living with the perfect man for years who won't commit to marriage. Gigi (Goodwin) waits by the phone all day, hoping the dream guy who asked for her number will call. Janine (Connelly) is upset that her new husband Ben isn't excited by home decor. Mary (Barrymore) is surrounded by great guys, problem is, they're all gay. Then there's Anna (Johansson), who's being pursued by Mr. Right, but she's already committed to a married man who won't commit back. Cute and harmless, but doesn't think too highly of these five women with its paper-thin material. **129m/C DVD.** *US* Drew Barrymore, Jennifer Aniston, Kevin Connolly, Jennifer Connelly, Bradley Cooper, Ginnifer Goodwin, Justin Long, Scarlett Johansson, Ben Affleck, Wilson Cruz, Kris Kristofferson, Cory Hardrict, Leonardo Nam; ***D:*** Ken Kwapis; ***W:*** Abby Kohn, Marc Silverstein; ***C:*** John Bailey; ***M:*** Cliff Eidelman.

He's My Girl 🦴 1/2 **1987 (PG-13)** When a rock singer wins a trip for two to Hollywood, he convinces his agent to dress up as a woman so they can use the free tickets. **104m/C VHS.** David Hallyday, T.K. Carter, Misha McK, Jennifer Tilly; ***D:*** Gabrielle Beaumont; ***W:*** Terence H. Winkless, Taylor Ames, Charles F. Bohl; ***C:*** Peter Lyons Collister.

Hesher **2010** Paul Forney (Wilson) is mourning the car accident death of his wife two months earlier while his young son T.J. (Brochu) is obsessed with getting the auto back from the salvage yard and grandma Madeleine (Laurie) tries to look after them. Their home is suddenly invaded by antisocial, violent, foul-mouthed, tattooed Hesher (Gordon-Levitt) who makes himself completely at home. **105m/C DVD.** *US* Joseph Gordon-Levitt, Devin Brochu, Rainn Wilson, Piper Laurie, Natalie Portman, John Carroll Lynch; ***D:*** Spencer Susser; ***W:*** Spencer Susser, David Michod; ***C:*** Morgan Susser.

Hester Street 🦴🦴🦴 1/2 **1975** Set at the turn of the century, the film tells the story of a young Jewish immigrant who ventures to New York City to be with her husband. As she re-acquaints herself with her husband, she finds that he has abandoned his Old World ideals. The film speaks not only to preserving the heritage of the Jews, but to cherishing all heritages and cultures. Highly regarded upon release, unfortunately forgotten today. **92m/B VHS, DVD.** Carol Kane, Doris Roberts, Steven Keats, Mel Howard, Dorrie Kavanaugh, Stephen Strimpell; *D:* Joan Micklin Silver; *W:* Joan Micklin Silver; *C:* Kenneth Van Sickle; *M:* William Bolcom.

Hexed 🦴 1/2 **1993 (R)** Walter Mitty lives in the person of bellboy Matthew Welsh, who enjoys masquerading as a debonair bon vivant. He finagles his way into the life of Hexina, a beautiful psychotic model who has checked into the hotel where Matthew works in order to murder her blackmailer. She tries to kill Matthew, apparently getting in a little practice, but he'll still follow her anywhere. Inane, charmless comedy that intends to satirize "Fatal Attraction" and similar films. **93m/C VHS, DVD.** Arye Gross, Claudia Christian, Adrienne Shelly, R. Lee Ermey, Norman Fell, Michael E. Knight; *D:* Alan Spencer; *W:* Alan Spencer.

Hey Arnold! The Movie 🦴🦴 **2002 (PG)** Kidpic based on the Nickelodeon series has the cranial oddity cast getting civic-minded about saving their endangered 'hood from an evil corporate developer. Eerily upbeat Arnold battles strangely Ronald Reagan-sounding Scheck who wants to raze their inner-city neighborhood. Together with his more realistic, flat-topped friend Gerald, Arnold employs a variety of ways to save his diverse urban home, from organizing a block party (good) to breaking and entering (hmm...this is for kids?). Castellaneta is the voice of Grandpa, who has explosive plans of his own to save the street. Big names (well, their voices) cameo. Some of the charm of the series remains but lacks feature-length punch. Animation suffers from the big screen treatment, as well. **76m/C VHS, DVD.** *US D:* Tuck Tucker; *W:* Craig Bartlett, Steve Viksten; *M:* Jim Lang; *V:* Spencer Klein, Francesca Marie Smith, Jamil Walker Smith, Dan Castellaneta, Tress MacNeille, Paul Sorvino, Jennifer Jason Leigh, Christopher Lloyd, Vincent Schiavelli, Maurice LaMarche.

Hey, Babu Riba 🦴🦴 1/2 **1988 (R)** A popular Yugoslavian fit of nostalgia about four men convening at the funeral of a young girl they all loved years before, and their happy, Americana-bathed memories therein. In Serbo-Croatian with English subtitles. **109m/C VHS, DVD.** *YU* Gala Videnovic, Nebojsa Bakocevic, Dragan Bjelogric, Marko Todorovic, Goran Radakovic, Relja Basic, Milos Zutic; *D:* Jovan Acin; *W:* Jovan Acin.

Hey Good Lookin' 🦴🦴 1/2 **1982** Ralph Bakshi's irreverent look at growing up in the 1950s bears the trademark qualities that distinguish his other adult animated features, "Fritz the Cat" and "Heavy Traffic." **87m/C VHS.** *D:* Ralph Bakshi; *W:* Ralph Bakshi.

Hey, Happy! 🦴🦴 **2001** Camp comedy set in a post-apocalyptic Winnipeg where survivors of some type of environmental plague seem blase about a coming flood of biblical proportions. So enterprising DJ Sabu (Yuen) decides to hold an end-of-the-world rave party on the appropriately named Garbage Hill. That is after he fulfills his sexual quest of sleeping with 2,000 men. And his choice for the magic number is schizo Happy (Aftanas), who hears alien voices on his radio urging him to give in. But the path to sexual conquest does not run smooth as Sabu has a stalker/rival in pierced punk Spanky (Godson). Sometimes slick, sometimes outrageous, sometimes surreal and just plain weird. **75m/C VHS, DVD.** *CA* Jeremie Yuen, Craig Aftanas, Clayton Godson; *D:* Noam Gonick; *W:* Noam Gonick; *C:* Paul Suderman.

Hey! Hey! USA! 🦴 1/2 **1938** Ocean liner porter Benjamin Twist (Hays) masquerades as an education expert for bored millionaire's son Bertie (Bupp) and discovers gangster Bugs (Kennedy) is a stowaway aboard ship. Twist winds up in Chicago when Bertie is kidnapped and he's asked to deliver the ransom, which involves Bugs and rival gangsters. **89m/B DVD.** *GB* Will Hay, Edgar Kennedy, David Burns, Edmon Ryan, Tommy Bupp, Fred Duprez, Tommy Bupp, Paddy Reynolds; *D:* Marcel Varnel; *W:* Val Guest, Marriott Edgar, J.O.C. Orton; *C:* Arthur Crabtree; *M:* R. E. Dearing.

Hey There, It's Yogi Bear 🦴🦴 **1964** When Yogi Bear comes out of winter hibernation to search for food, he travels to the Chizzling Brothers Circus. The first feature-length cartoon to come from the H-B Studios. **98m/C VHS.** *D:* Joseph Barbera, William Hanna; *W:* Joseph Barbera, William Hanna; *M:* Marty Paich; *V:* Daws Butler, James Darren, Mel Blanc, J. Pat O'Malley, Julie Bennett.

Hi-De-Ho 🦴🦴 1/2 **1935** The great Cab Calloway and his red hot jazz are featured in this film, which has the band caught between rival gangsters. The plot is incidental to the music, anyway. ♫Hi-De-Ho; I Got A Gal Named Nettie; Little Old Lady From Baltimore; A Rainy Sunday. **60m/B VHS, DVD.** Cab Calloway, Ida James; *D:* Josh Binney.

Hi Diddle Diddle 🦴🦴 1/2 *Diamonds and Crime; Try and Find It* **1943** Topsy-turvy comedy features young lovers who long for conventional happiness. Instead they are cursed with con-artist parents who delight in crossing that law-abiding line. **72m/B VHS, DVD.** Adolphe Menjou, Martha Scott, Dennis O'Keefe, Pola Negri; *D:* Andrew L. Stone.

Hi, Good Lookin'! 🦴 1/2 **1944** A radio station employee pretends to be a bigshot executive to help a pretty girl become a singer. Ozzie Nelson and His Orchestra are featured. **62m/B VHS.** Harriet Hilliard Nelson, Eddie Quillan, Kirby Grant, Roscoe Karns, Fuzzy Knight, Milburn Stone, Betty Kean; *D:* Edward Lilley; *W:* Bradford Ropes, Paul Girard Smith, Claudie Blakley; *C:* Jerome Ash.

Hi-Jacked 🦴 **1950** When a parolee trucker's cargo is stolen, he inevitably becomes a suspect and must set out to find the true culprits. **66m/B VHS.** Jim Davis, Paul Cavanagh, Marsha Jones, Sid Melton, David Bruce, Ralph Sanford, Iris Adrian, George Eldredge; *D:* Sam Newfield; *W:* Orville H. Hampton, Fred Myton, Raymond L. Schrock; *C:* Philip Tannura; *M:* Paul Dunlap.

Hi-Life 🦴🦴 1/2 **1998 (R)** Talky, Christmastime, Manhattan-set ensemble comedy finds compulsive gambler and out of work actor Jimmy (Stoltz) owing bookie Fatty (Durning) $900. To get the money, he tells girlfriend Susan (Kelly) it's to finance an abortion for his slutty sis Maggie (Hannah). Then Maggie's ex-boyfriend Ray (Scott) gets involved and Fatty's associate Miner (Reigart) and numerous other players who all wind up at the Hi-Life Bar and discover Jimmy's scams. **82m/C VHS, DVD.** Eric Stoltz, Moira Kelly, Daryl Hannah, Campbell Scott, Peter Riegert, Katrin Cartlidge, Charles Durning, Saundra Santiago, Anne DeSalvo, Bruce MacVittie, Tegan West; *D:* Roger Hedden; *W:* Roger Hedden; *C:* John Thomas; *M:* David Lawrence.

The Hi-Lo Country 🦴🦴 1/2 **1998 (R)** For years, Sam Peckinpah wanted to make this movie. It took Martin Scorsese to resurrect the project and to secure Walon Green to adapt the 1961 Max Evans novel for the screen. Pete Calder (Crudup) returns to New Mexico from WWII. While waiting for buddy Big Boy Matson (Harrelson) to return from the Marines, Pete falls for Mona (Arquette), a saucy woman whose husband works for the area's biggest rancher, Jim Love (Elliott). When Big Boy does return, it becomes obvious that he and Mona are hot for each other, so Pete bows out. Big Boy is the last real cowboy (a favorite Peckinpah theme), who loves the land, fears no one, and knows his times are coming to an end. Director Frears may not completely understand the American mythic West, but thanks to Oliver Stapleton's cinematography, the film has a look close to what a Peckinpah or a Ford might have given it. **114m/C VHS, DVD.** Woody Harrelson, Patricia Arquette, Billy Crudup, Penelope Cruz, Sam Elliott, Cole Hauser, Darren E. Burrows, Jacob Vargas, James Gammon, Lane Smith, Katy Jurado, John Diehl, Enrique Castillo, Rosaleen Linehan; *D:* Stephen Frears; *W:* Walon Green; *C:* Oliver Stapleton; *M:* Carter Burwell.

Hi, Mom! 🦴🦴🦴 *Confessions of A Peeping John; Blue Manhattan* **1970 (R)** DePalma's follow-up to "Greetings" finds amateur pornographer/movie maker De Niro being advised by a professional in the field (Garfield) of sleazy filmmaking. De Niro films the residents of his apartment building and eventually marries one of his starlets. One of De Palma's earlier and better efforts with De Niro playing a crazy as only he can. **87m/C VHS, DVD.** Robert De Niro, Charles Durnham, Allen (Goorwitz) Garfield, Lara Parker, Jennifer Salt, Gerrit Graham; *D:* Brian De Palma; *W:* Brian De Palma.

Hi-Riders 🦴 **1977 (R)** A revenge-based tale about large, mag-wheeled trucks and their drivers. **90m/C VHS.** Mel Ferrer, Stephen McNally, Neville Brand, Ralph Meeker; *D:* Greydon Clark.

Hidalgo 🦴🦴 1/2 **2004 (PG-13)** Inspired by real-life U.S. Calvary horseman Frank T. Hopkins (Mortensen)—meaning it takes liberties with the truth (which Hopkins himself has been accused of). Old-fashioned adventure story hows the devotion he had for his mixed-breed horse, Hidalgo, as they travel 3,000 miles in 1890 to the "Ocean of Fire" endurance race, going against thoroughbreds and the wild elements of Arabia per the invitation of Sheikh Riyadh (Sharif). Mortensen looks stunning riding his steed, the elegant Sharif stirs up wonderful memories of Lawrence of Arabia, and the visual effects of sandstorms, colossal locusts, and the competition are captivating; however, this kind of story has been told before, with more dramatic twists and turns. **135m/C VHS, DVD.** Viggo Mortensen, Omar Sharif, Louise Lombard, Said Taghmaoui, Peter Mensah, J.K. Simmons, Adoni Maropis, Floyd "Red Crow" Westerman, Zuleikha Robinson, Adam Alexi-Malle, Silas Carson, Harsh Nayyar, Elizabeth Berridge, Victor Talmadge, Frank Collison, Jerry Hardin, C. Thomas Howell, Malcolm McDowell; *D:* Joe Johnston; *W:* John Fusco; *C:* Shelly Johnson; *M:* James Newton Howard.

Hidden 🦴🦴🦴 1/2 *Cache* **2005 (R)** Georges Laurent (Auteuil) and his wife Anne (Binoche) are upper middle class professionals living a comfortable life with their young son in Paris when suddenly a disturbing surveillance video tape of their own home is left at their front door, followed by another and another. This invasion plunges Georges into a world of repressed memories and disquieting dreams as he tries to make sense of these events as well as his past. On the surface a whodunit mystery not unlike any other from the post modern era. However, this is in post-9/11 modern-age France, and the story unfolds as a metaphor for personal and societal responsibility to those previously held under thumb. **121m/C DVD.** Daniel Auteuil, Juliette Binoche, Annie Girardot, Maurice Benichou, Bernard Le Coq, Lester Makedonsky, Walid Afkir; *D:* Michael Haneke; *W:* Michael Haneke; *C:* Christian Berger. L.A. Film Critics '05: Foreign Film.

The Hidden 🦴🦴🦴 **1987 (R)** A seasoned cop (Nouri) and a benign alien posing as an FBI agent (MacLachlan) team up to track down and destroy a hyper-violent alien who survives by invading the bodies of humans, causing them to go on murderous rampages. Much acclaimed, high velocity action film with state-of-the-art special effects (at least for the time). Followed by a minor 1994 sequel with a different cast. **98m/C VHS, DVD.** Kyle MacLachlan, Michael Nouri, Clu Gulager, Ed O'Ross, Claudia Christian, Clarence Felder, Richard Brooks, William Boyett, Chris Mulkey; *D:* Jack Sholder; *W:* Bob Hunt, Jim Kouf; *C:* Jacques Haitkin; *M:* Michael Convertino.

The Hidden 2 🦴🦴 1/2 **1994 (R)** The hyper-violent alien of the 1987 movie returns. With its love of fast cars, high-caliber weapons, and heavy metal music, this body-possessing creature appears to be unstoppable. **91m/C VHS, DVD.** Raphael Sbarge, Kate Hodge, Michael Nouri; *D:* Seth Pinsker; *W:* Seth Pinsker; *M:* David McHugh.

Hidden Agenda 🦴🦴 1/2 **1990 (R)** A human rights activist and an American lawyer uncover brutality and corruption among the British forces in Northern Ireland. Slow-paced but strong performances. The Northern Irish dialect is sometimes difficult to understand as are the machinations on the British police system. Generally worthwhile. **108m/C VHS, DVD.** Frances McDormand, Brian Cox, Brad Dourif, Mai Zetterling, John Benfield, Des McAleer, Jim Norton, Maurice Roeves; *D:* Ken Loach; *W:* Jim Allen; *C:* Clive Tickner; *M:* Stewart Copeland. Cannes '90: Special Jury Prize.

Hidden Agenda 🦴🦴 **1999 (R)** Arriving in Berlin, American tourist Dillon learns his brother has been murdered. He decides to do some investigating on his own and winds up caught between CIA spies and the German secret police. **97m/C VHS, DVD.** Kevin Dillon, Christopher Plummer, Andrea Roth, Michael Wincott, J.T. Walsh; *D:* Iain Paterson; *W:* Iain Paterson; *C:* Thom Best; *M:* Harry Manfredini. **VIDEO**

Hidden Agenda 🦴🦴 1/2 **2001 (R)** Former NSA agent Jason Price (Lundgren) is still doing covert government work by making people vanish. His latest client is a mobster (Houde) but Price finds that a legendary hit man (Roy) has taken an unhealthy interest in his operation. **94m/C VHS, DVD.** Dolph Lundgren, Maxim Roy, Brigitte Paquette, Serge Houde, Patrick Kerton, Christian Paul; *D:* Marc S. Grenier; *W:* Les Weldon; *C:* Sylvain Brault. **VIDEO**

Hidden Assassin 🦴 *The Shooter* **1994 (R)** French hit woman Simone (Detmers) supposedly shoots the Cuban ambassador to the U.N. and escapes back to her home base in Prague, followed by Czech-born U.S. Marshal Mickey Dane (Lundgren). Mickey starts to doubt that Simone is the killer (she claims she's long retired and is being set up) and the duo try to find the truth amid lots of double-crosses. Doesn't make much sense in any case. **89m/C VHS, DVD.** Dolph Lundgren, Maruschka Detmers, Assumpta Serna, Gavan O'Herlihy, John Ashton, Simon Andreu; *D:* Ted Kotcheff; *W:* Meg Thayer, Billy Ray, Yves Andre Martin; *C:* Fernando Arguelles; *M:* Stefano Mainetti.

The Hidden Blade 🦴🦴 1/2 *Kakushi Ken: Oni No Tsume* **2004 (R)** Set in 1861, Katagiri (Nagase) is a lower-caste samurai who has a forbidden love for serving girl Kie (Matsu), who he rescues from domestic abuse. He's also troubled by being ordered to kill an old comrade, Hazama (Ozawa), who plotted against the Shogunate and has escaped from confinement. Based on the short stories of Shuhei Fujisawa. The Japanese title, "Hidden Blade: The Devil's Claw," refers to a unique sword maneuver. Japanese with subtitles. **132m/C DVD.** *JP* Masatoshi Nagase, Min Tanaka, Nenji Kobayashi, Ken Ogata, Takako Matsu, Hidetaka Yoshioka, Yukioshi Ozawa, Tomoko Obata, Reiko Takashima; *D:* Yoji Yamada; *W:* Yoji Yamada, Yishitaka Yamamoto; *C:* Mutsuo Naganuma; *M:* Isao Tomita.

Hidden City 🦴🦴 **1987** A film archivist and a statistician become drawn into a conspiracy when a piece of revealing film is spliced onto the end of an innocuous government tape. **112m/C VHS.** Charles Dance, Cassie Stuart, Alex Norton, Tusse Silberg, Bill Paterson; *D:* Stephen Poliakoff.

Hidden Enemy 🦴 1/2 **1940** During WWII, a scientist develops a new metal alloy that is stronger than steel yet lighter than aluminum. His nephew must protect his scientist/uncle from spies who would steal the formula to use against the Allies. **63m/B VHS.** Warren Hull, Kay Linaker, Wilhelm von Brinken, George Cleveland; *D:* Howard Bretherton.

Hidden Fears 🦴🦴 1/2 **1993** Maureen Dietz (Foster) carries the gruesome memories of her husband's murder with her. Years later she goes to the police with new evidence to reopen her husband's case. Only the killers find out and return to finish off the eyewitnesses, and she's next! Based on the novel "Exercise in Terror" by Kaminsky, who also wrote the screenplay. **90m/C VHS.** Meg Foster, Frederic Forrest, Wally Taylor, Bever-Leigh Banfield, Marc Macaulay, Patrick Cherry, Scott Hayes; *D:* Jean Bodon; *W:* Stuart Kaminsky.

Hidden Floor 🦴🦴 *Nebeonjjae cheung-Eoneunal kabjagi doobeonjjae; Forbidden Floor: 4 Horror Tales* **2006** Korean horror film by director Byung-ki and written by Il-hoon Won was clearly inspired by "Dark Water." A single mom and her child move to an apartment building which is increasingly obviously haunted by ghosts. **93m/C DVD.** *KN* Seohyeong Kim, Yoo-joung Kim; *D:* Il-soon Kwon; *W:* Il-han Yoo; *C:* Hoon-Gwang Kim; *M:* Bong-Joon Oh.

The Hidden Fortress 🦴🦴🦴 1/2 *Kakushi Toride No San Akunin; Three Rascals in the Hidden Fortress; Three Bad Men in the Hidden Fortress* **1958** Kurosawa's tale of a warrior who protects a princess from warring feudal lords. An inspiration for George Lucas' "Star Wars" series and deserving of its excellent reputation. In Japanese with English subtitles. **139m/B VHS, DVD.** *JP* Toshiro Mifune, Misa(ko) Uehara, Kamatari (Keita) Fujiwara, Susumu Fujita, Eiko Miyoshi, Takashi Shimura, Kichijiro Ueda, Koji Mitsui, Minoru Chiaki, Toshiko Higuchi, Shiten Ohashi; ***D:*** Akira Kurosawa; ***W:*** Akira Kurosawa, Shinobu Hashimoto, Ryuzo Kikushima, Hideo Oguni; ***C:*** Kazuo Yamazaki; ***M:*** Masaru Sato. Berlin Intl. Film Fest. '59: Director (Kurosawa).

Hidden Gold 1/2 **1933** Routine western for Mix, which has him going undercover to win the confidence of three outlaws and discover where they have hidden their loot. **57m/B VHS.** Tom Mix, Judith Barrie, Raymond Hatton; ***D:*** Arthur Rosson.

Hidden Guns **1956** Above-average tale of father-and-son lawmen out to reform a town and put the bad guys away. When dad is killed, son goes up against the village alone. A Greek chorus adds an interesting twist to the action. Erich von Stroheim Jr. is listed as assistant director. **66m/B VHS.** Bruce Bennett, Richard Arlen, John Carradine, Faron Young, Angie Dickinson, Guinn "Big Boy" Williams; ***D:*** Albert C. Gannaway.

Hidden in America 1/2 **1996 (PG-13)** Bill Januson (Bridges) has lost his autoplant job because of downsizing and his wife to cancer. His savings exhausted and his prospects bleak, Januson struggles to put food on the table for his two kids, who increasingly begin to suffer the effects of poverty. Produced in conjunction with the End Hunger Network, whose co-founder, Jeff Bridges, has a cameo. **96m/C VHS, DVD.** Beau Bridges, Bruce Davison, Jena Malone, Shelton Dane, Alice Krige, Josef Sommer, Frances McDormand; ***Cameos:*** Jeff Bridges; ***D:*** Martin Bell; ***W:*** Peter Silverman, Michael deGuzman; ***C:*** James R. Bagdonas; ***M:*** Mason Daring. **CABLE**

Hidden Obsession 1/2 **1992 (R)** Newscaster Ellen is taking a much needed vacation at an isolated cabin when she learns that a serial killer has escaped from a nearby prison. Luckily, she has a hunky police officer neighbor for protection. But though the escaped killer is captured, the killings go on—with Ellen as the next target. **92m/C VHS.** Heather Thomas, Jan-Michael Vincent, Nicholas Celozzi; ***D:*** John Stewart; ***W:*** David Reskin.

Hidden Places 1/2 **2006** Widowed mom Eliza (Penny) is struggling through the Depression on her father-in-law's farm when he suddenly dies. Eliza has to get in the orange crop or risk foreclosure on the debt-ridden property. Her Aunt Batty (Jones) says to have faith and when charming veteran Gabe (Gedrick) shows up, he may be the answer to their prayers. Gabe agrees to help out with the harvest and falling in love with the young widow may be his bonus. Based on the novel by Lynn Austin. **?m/C DVD.** Sydney Penny, Jason Gedrick, Shirley Jones, Barry Corbin, Tom Bosley, John Diehl; ***D:*** Yelena Lanskaya; ***W:*** Robert Tate Miller; ***C:*** James W. Wrenn; ***M:*** Roger Bellon. **CABLE**

The Hidden Room *Obsession* **1949** A doctor finds out about his wife's affair and decides to get revenge on her lover. He kidnaps him, imprisons him in a cellar, and decides to kill him—slowly. Tense melodrama. **98m/B VHS, DVD.** *GB* Robert Newton, Sally Gray, Naunton Wayne, Phil Brown, Olga Lindo, Russell Waters, James Harcourt, Allan Jeayes, Stanley Baker; ***D:*** Edward Dmytryk; ***W:*** Alec Coppel; ***C:*** C.M. Pennington-Richards; ***M:*** Nino Rota.

Hidden Valley **1932** Early Steele western in which everyone is fighting over a map that leads to hidden treasure in the valley. **60m/B VHS, DVD.** Bob Steele, Gertrude Messinger, Francis McDonald; ***D:*** Robert North Bradbury.

Hide 1/2 **2008 (R)** Part torture porn, part crime drama. Betty and Billy fancy themselves the modern-day Bonnie and Clyde until Billy is captured after gunning down an innocent victim during a bank robbery. An eventual prison transfer leads to Betty springing her lover but Billy has gotten remorseful over the years and tells Betty someone is violently targeting those close to him in revenge for their crimes. **93m/C DVD.** *CA* Rachel Miner, Christian Kane, Polly Shannon, Beth Grant; ***D:*** K.C. Bascombe; ***W:*** Greg Rosati; ***C:*** Pablo Schverdfinger; ***M:*** Eliane Katz. **VIDEO**

Hide and Go Shriek **1987 (R)** Several high school seniors are murdered one by one during a graduation party. Also available in an unrated, gorier version. **90m/C VHS, DVD.** Annette Sinclair, Brittain Frye, Rebunkah Jones; ***D:*** Skip Schoolnik.

Hide and Seek **1977** When a high school hacker converts his computer into a nuclear weapon, he finds that it has developed a mind of its own. **60m/C VHS.** *CA* Bob Martin, Ingrid Veninger, David Patrick; ***D:*** Rene Bonniere; ***W:*** Barry Wexler.

Hide and Seek **1980** A study of children living in the land that would soon become Israel. Although they play as normal children, life is particularly difficult. This adversity will lay the foundation for their Israeli citizenry. In Hebrew with English subtitles. **90m/C VHS.** Gila Almagor, Doron Tavory, Chaim Hadaya; ***D:*** Dan Wolman.

Hide and Seek 1/2 *Cord* **2000 (R)** Pregnant Ann (Hannah) is kidnapped by a crazy childless couple (Tilly and Gallo) and it's no kids' game when husband Jack (Greenwood) tries to find her. **100m/C VHS, DVD.** Daryl Hannah, Jennifer Tilly, Vincent Gallo, Bruce Greenwood, Johanna Black; ***D:*** Sidney J. Furie; ***W:*** Joel Hladecek, Yas Takata; ***M:*** Robert Carli. **VIDEO**

Hide and Seek **2005 (R)** Nine-year-old Emily (Fanning) witnesses her mother's bloody suicide. Her father (De Niro), a psychologist, decides to take the traumatized girl from bustling Manhattan to a peaceful, rural community to help her cope. Once settled in, it's pretty clear that Emily isn't coping very well. Her issues manifest in the form of an imaginary friend named Charlie, who does some rather scary things when he's angry. Stellar cast and high production values can't hide the fact that it's still a run-of-the-mill horror movie. Fanning sports the best child goth look since Christina Ricci's Wednesday Addams. **100m/C DVD.** *US* Robert De Niro, Dakota Fanning, Famke Janssen, Elisabeth Shue, Amy Irving, Dylan Baker, Melissa Leo, Robert John Burke, David Chandler, Molly Grant Kallins; ***D:*** John Polson; ***W:*** Ari Schlossberg; ***C:*** Darius Wolski; ***M:*** John Ottman.

Hide in Plain Sight **1980 (PG)** A distraught blue-collar worker searches for his children who disappeared when his ex-wife and her mobster husband are given new identities by federal agents. Caan's fine directorial debut is based on a true story. **96m/C VHS.** James Caan, Jill Eikenberry, Robert Viharo, Kenneth McMillan, Josef Sommer, Danny Aiello; ***D:*** James Caan.

Hide-Out 1/2 **1934** A man running from the law winds up at a small farm, falls in love, and becomes reformed by the good family that takes him in. Good supporting cast includes a very young Rooney. **83m/B VHS.** Robert Montgomery, Maureen O'Sullivan, Edward Arnold, Elizabeth Patterson, Mickey Rooney, Edward Brophy; ***D:*** Woodbridge S. Van Dyke.

Hideaway **1994 (R)** Hodge podge movie finds Hatch Harrison (Goldblum) brought back from the other side after suffering injuries from a near-fatal car accident. He returns with the ability to psychically connect with Vassago (Sisto), a sadistic serial killer of young girls. Coincidentally, Harrison has a teenage daughter, Regina (Silverstone), and Vassago has her lined up as his next victim. The visual effects of spirits floating down a cosmic vortex are entertaining, but plot originality must have been hidden away to make room for the nifty special effects. Based on a novel by Dean R. Koontz. **103m/C VHS, DVD.** Jeff Goldblum, Christine Lahti, Alicia Silverstone, Jeremy Sisto, Rae Dawn Chong; ***D:*** Brett Leonard; ***W:*** Andrew Kevin Walker, Neal Jimenez; ***C:*** Gale Tattersall; ***M:*** Trevor Jones.

The Hideaways 1/2 *From the Mixed-Up Files of Mrs. Basil E. Frankweiler* **1973 (G)** A 12-year-old girl and her younger brother run away and hide in the Metropolitan Museum of Art. The girl becomes enamored of a piece of sculpture and sets out to discover its creator. Based on the children's novel by E.L. Konigsburg. **105m/C VHS, DVD.** Richard Mulligan, George Rose, Ingrid Bergman, Sally Prager, Johnny Doran, Madeline Kahn; ***D:*** Fielder Cook.

Hideous 1/2 **1997 (R)** Eccentric collector's greatest prize is a seemingly petrified toxic waste mutant that's not so petrified afterall. It manages to come to life and even spawn little mutants to go on a killing spree. **82m/C VHS, DVD.** Jacqueline Lovell, Michael Citrinti, Rhonda Griffin, Mel Johnson Jr., Traci May, Jerry O'Donnell; ***D:*** Charles Band; ***W:*** Benjamin Carr; ***M:*** Richard Band.

Hideous Kinky 1/2 **1999 (R)** Julia (Winslet) is a free-spirited single mom who decides to leave London and take her two daughters, Bea and Lucy, to live in Morocco in 1972. She gets by on sales of homemade dolls and the occasional check from the girls' father. Julia believes that a conversion to the Sufi life will solve her problems, while Bea would rather they settle into a "normal" life. Julia meets, and has a passionate affair with, juggler and sometime con man Bilal, whom the girls adopt as a surrogate father figure. Winslet plays her character's mixture of naivete and motherly concern well, and looks good doing it, as does the whole movie. The Moroccan locales are brilliantly displayed. Character development and consistent narrative are sometimes lacking. **97m/C VHS, DVD.** *GB FR* Kate Winslet, Said Taghmaoui, Bella Riza, Carrie Mullan, Pierre Clementi, Abigail Cruttenden, Sira Stampe; ***D:*** Gilles Mackinnon; ***W:*** Billy Mackinnon; ***C:*** John de Borman; ***M:*** John Keane.

Hideous Sun Demon 1/2 *Blood on His Lips; Terror from the Sun; The Sun Demon* **1959** A physicist exposed to radiation must stay out of sunlight or he will turn into a scaly, lizard-like creature. Includes previews of coming attractions from classic sci-fi films. **75m/B VHS, DVD.** Robert Clarke, Patricia Manning, Nan Peterson, Patrick Whyte, Peter Similuk, Fred La Porta, Robert Garry, Del Courtney; ***D:*** Thomas Bontross, Robert Clarke; ***W:*** Doane R. Hoag, E. S. Seeley Jr.; ***C:*** Vilis Lapenieks, John Morrill, Stan Follis; ***M:*** John Seeley.

Hider in the House 1/2 **1990 (R)** In a peaceful neighborhood a family is about to spend an evening of terror when they discover a psychopath is hiding in the attic of their home. **109m/C VHS.** Michael McKean, Gary Busey, Mimi Rogers, Kurt Christopher Kinder, Candy Hutson, Elizabeth Ruscio, Bruce Glover; ***D:*** Michael Patrick.

Hiding Out **1987 (PG-13)** A young stockbroker testifies against the Mafia and must find a place to hide in order to avoid being killed. He winds up at his cousin's high school in Delaware, but can he really go through all these teenage troubles once again? **99m/C VHS, DVD.** Jon Cryer, Keith Coogan, Gretchen Cryer, Annabeth Gish, Tim Quill; ***D:*** Bob Giraldi; ***W:*** Jeff Rothberg, Joe Menosky; ***C:*** Daniel Pearl; ***M:*** Anne Dudley.

The Hiding Place **1975** True story of two Dutch Christian sisters sent to a concentration camp for hiding Jews during WWII. Film is uneven but good cast pulls it through. Based on the Corrie Ten Boom book and produced by Billy Graham's Evangelistic Association. **145m/C VHS.** Julie Harris, Eileen Heckart, Arthur O'Connell, Jeanette Clift; ***D:*** James F. Collier.

High & Low 1/2 *Tengoku To Jigoku* **1962 (R)** Fine Japanese film noir about a wealthy businessman who is being blackmailed by kidnappers who claim to have his son. When he discovers that they have mistakenly taken his chauffeur's son he must decide whether to face financial ruin or risk the life of a young boy. Based on an Ed McBain novel. In Japanese with English subtitles. **143m/B VHS, DVD.** *JP* Toshiro Mifune, Tatsuya Mihashi, Tatsuya Nakadai; ***D:*** Akira Kurosawa; ***W:*** Evan Hunter, Ryuzo Kikushima, Hideo Oguni, Akira Kurosawa; ***C:*** Asakazu Nakai, Takao Saito; ***M:*** Masaru Sato.

The High and the Mighty **1954** One of Wayne's most sought-after films finally makes it to DVD, as it took 10 years for Wayne's daughter-in-law to restore a negative found in a pool of water in a warehouse. Wayne is Dan Roman, who steps up to the situation on a trans-Pacific airline flight in deep trouble. In a device that'll be familiar to viewers of "Lost" many flashbacks give backstory on passengers and crew. Unfortunately, this serves mostly to slow down the action and suspense of their current situation. Excellent performance by an all-star cast cover for some of the more dated elements of the film, which was, after all, a precursor to the popular disaster flicks of the 70s. **148m/C DVD.** John Wayne, Claire Trevor, Laraine Day, Robert Stack, Jan Sterling, Phil Harris, Robert Newton, David Brian, Paul Kelly, Sidney Blackmer, Julie Bishop, John Howard, Wally Brown, William Campbell, Ann Doran, John Qualen, Paul Fix, Joy Kim, George Chandler, Douglas Fowley, Regis Toomey, Carl "Alfalfa" Switzer, William Hopper, William Schallert, Julie Mitchum; ***D:*** William A. Wellman; ***W:*** Ernest K. Gann; ***C:*** Archie Stout; ***M:*** Dimitri Tiomkin. Oscars '54: Orig. Dramatic Score; Golden Globes '55: Support. Actress (Sterling).

High Anxiety **1977 (PG)** Brooks tries hard to please in this low-brow parody of Hitchcock films employing dozens of references to films like "Psycho," "Spellbound," "The Birds," and "Vertigo." Tells the tale of a height-fearing psychiatrist caught up in a murder mystery. The title song performed a la Sinatra by Brooks is one of the film's high moments. Brooks also has a lot of fun with Hitchcockian camera movements. Uneven (What? Brooks?) but amusing tribute. **92m/C VHS, DVD.** Mel Brooks, Madeline Kahn, Cloris Leachman, Harvey Korman, Ron Carey, Howard Morris, Dick Van Patten; ***D:*** Mel Brooks; ***W:*** Mel Brooks, Ron Clark, Barry Levinson, Rudy DeLuca.

High Art **1998 (R)** A trio of women play romantic games in New York's art community. Ambitious magazine editor-in-training Syd (Mitchell) has a boyfriend, James (Mann), but feels something's missing. Noticing a leak in her apartment ceiling, Syd heads upstairs to confront her neighbor and meets Lucy Berliner (Sheedy), a once-celebrated, now-retired photographer with a heroin problem and an equally hooked girlfriend, Greta (Clarkson). Syd and Lucy begin a friendship that leads to an affair, while Syd also wants to revitalize Lucy's career. Ex-Brat Packer Sheedy's the real revelation with her standout performance. **102m/C VHS, DVD.** Radha Mitchell, Ally Sheedy, Patricia Clarkson, Tammy Grimes, Gabriel Mann, William Sage, David Thornton, Anh Duong; ***D:*** Lisa Cholodenko; ***W:*** Lisa Cholodenko; ***C:*** Tami Reiker; ***M:*** Craig (Shudder to Think) Wedren. Ind. Spirit '99: Actress (Sheedy); L.A. Film Critics '98: Actress (Sheedy); Natl. Soc. Film Critics '98: Actress (Sheedy); Sundance '98: Screenplay.

High Ballin' **1978 (PG)** Truckers Fonda and Reed team up with lady trucker Shaver to take on the gang trying to crush the independent drivers. **100m/C VHS.** *CA* Peter Fonda, Jerry Reed, Helen Shaver; ***D:*** Peter Carter; ***W:*** Paul F. Edwards.

High Command 1/2 **1937** To save his daughter from an ugly scandal, the British general of an isolated Colonial African outpost traps a blackmailer's killer. **84m/B VHS, DVD.** *GB* Lionel Atwill, Lucie Mannheim, James Mason; ***D:*** Thorold Dickinson.

High Country 1/2 *The First Hello* **1981 (PG)** Two misfits, one handicapped, the other an ex-con, on the run from society learn mutual trust as they travel through the Canadian Rockies. **101m/C VHS.** *CA* Timothy Bottoms, Linda Purl, George Sims, Jim Lawrence, Bill Berry; ***D:*** Harvey Hart.

High Crime **1973** A "French Connection"-style suspense story about the heroin trade. Features high-speed chases and a police commissioner obsessed with capturing the criminals. **91m/C VHS.** James Whitmore, Franco Nero, Fernando Rey; ***D:*** Enzo G. Castellari.

High Crimes 1/2 **2002 (PG-13)** Military courtroom thriller is only average but does have Freeman, who's always worth watching. He's reteamed with "Kiss the Girls" co-star Judd, who plays spunky California attorney Claire Kubik. Claire gets a big surprise when her contractor hubby Tom (Caviezel) is suddenly arrested by the FBI and sent to a military prison. Turns out Tom, then known as Ron Chapman, was in an elite Marine special unit and is accused of a 1988 civilian massacre in El Salvador. She looks to recovering alcoholic and ex-JAG lawyer Charlie Grimes (Freeman) for assistance but sinister plots are afoot. Based on the 1998 novel by Joseph Finder. **115m/C VHS, DVD.** *US* Ashley Judd, James (Jim) Caviezel, Morgan Freeman, Amanda Peet, Tom Bower, Adam Scott, Bruce Davison, Michael Gaston, Juan Carlos Hernandez, Jude Ciccolella, Michael Shannon; ***D:*** Carl Franklin; ***W:*** Yuri Zeltser, Cary Bickley; ***C:*** Theo van de Sande; ***M:*** Graeme Revell.

The High Crusade 1/2 **1992 (PG-13)** A group of 13th-century English crusaders are heading for the Holy Land when they're interrupted on their journey by an alien spacecraft. They overpower the space guys and take over the vessel, hoping it will take them to Jerusalem, but since the spacecraft's on autopilot, the knights wind up heading for the aliens' home planet instead. **100m/C VHS, DVD.** *GB GE* John Rhys-Davies, Michael Des Barres, Rick Overton; ***D:*** Holger Neuhauser.

High Desert Kill **1990 (PG)** A science-fiction tale that will keep you guessing. Aliens landing in the New Mexican desert want something totally unexpected, and a trio of friends will be the first to find out what it is. Writer Cook was also responsible for "The China Syndrome." **93m/C VHS.** Chuck Connors, Marc Singer, Anthony Geary, Micah Grant; ***D:*** Harry Falk; ***W:*** T.S. Cook. **CABLE**

High Fidelity **2000 (R)** Frears, Cusack, and the writing team from "Grosse Pointe Blank" successfully bring Nick Hornby's 1995 novel to the screen, transplanting it from London to Chicago in the process. Cusack is Rob, a stuck-in-adolescence record store owner who just broke up with Laura (Hjejle), his long-time, live-in love. This gets him to thinking about his Top Five All-Time Breakups. Cue flashbacks. It also sends him on some hilarious conversations with his employees: know-it-all Barry (Black) who wields his musical tastes like a weapon, and Dick (Louiso), who's bashful to the point of invisibility. Cusack does his usual fine job, but Black and Louiso take over whenever they're on screen. **113m/C VHS, DVD.** John Cusack, Todd Louiso, Jack Black, Iben Hjejle, Tim Robbins, Joan Cusack, Lisa Bonet, Catherine Zeta-Jones, Lili Taylor, Natasha Gregson Wagner, Sara Gilbert, Chris Rehmann, Ben Carr, Joelle Carter, Bruce Springsteen; ***D:*** Stephen Frears; ***W:*** John Cusack, D.V. DeVincentis, Steve Pink, Scott Rosenberg; ***C:*** Seamus McGarvey; ***M:*** Howard Shore.

High Frequency **1988** Two young men monitoring a satellite relay station witness the murder of a woman. Believing they know who the killer's next victim will be, they set out to warn her. Lack of development mars what could have been a tidy little thriller. **105m/C VHS.** *IT* Oliver Benny, Vincent Spano, Isabelle Pasco, Anne Canovos; ***D:*** Faliero Rosati.

High Gear **1933** Heartstring-tugger about a race car driver, his girlfriend and the orphan son of a driver killed in a crash. Try to guess the outcome. **65m/B VHS.** James Murray, Joan Marsh, Jackie Searl, Theodore von Eltz, Lee Moran, Gordon DeMain; ***D:*** Leigh Jason.

High Heels *Docteur Popaul; Scoundrel in White* **1972** A black comedy about a doctor who believes beauty is only skin deep and marries a plain woman. However, when he meets her beautiful sister, he begins to wonder. In French with English subtitles. **100m/C VHS.** *FR* Laura Antonelli, Jean-Paul Belmondo, Mia Farrow, Daniel Ivernel; ***D:*** Claude Chabrol.

High Heels *Tacones Lejanos* **1991 (R)** An outrageous combination murder-melodrama-comedy from Almodovar. Rebecca is a TV anchorwoman in Madrid whose flamboyant singer/actress mother has returned to the city for a concert. Rebecca happens to be married to one of her mother's not-so-ex-flames. When her husband winds up dead, Rebecca confesses to his murder during her newscast—but is she telling the truth or just covering up for mom? Mix in a drag queen/judge, a dancing chorus of women prison inmates, and a peculiar police detective, and see if the plot convolutions make sense. In Spanish with English subtitles. **113m/C VHS.** *SP* Victoria Abril, Marisa Paredes, Miguel Bose, Feodor Atkine, Bibi Andersen, Rocio Munoz; ***D:*** Pedro Almodovar; ***W:*** Pedro Almodovar; ***C:*** Alfredo Mayo; ***M:*** Ryuichi Sakamoto. Cesar '93: Foreign Film.

High Heels and Low Lifes **2001 (R)** Brit nurse Shannon (Driver) and American actress Frances (McCormack) overhear a plot to rob a London safe deposit box center and immediately go to the cops. When the cops seem uninterested, the girls decide to blackmail the crooks into giving them a cut. Nice premise and an enjoyable performance by Driver are wasted by Smith's flat direction, which misses almost all comic payoff opportunities in the script. **85m/C VHS, DVD.** *US GB* Minnie Driver, Mary McCormack, Kevin McNally, Mark Williams, Danny Dyer, Michael Gambon, Kevin Eldon, Len Collin, Darren Boyd, Julian Wadham; ***D:*** Mel Smith; ***W:*** Kim Fuller; ***C:*** Steven Chivers; ***M:*** Charlie Mole.

High Hopes **1988** A moving yet nasty satiric comedy about a pair of ex-hippies maintaining their counterculture lifestyle in Margaret Thatcher's England, as they watch the signs of conservative "progress" overtake them and their geriatric, embittered Mum. Hilarious and mature. **110m/C VHS.** *GB* Philip Davis, Ruth Sheen, Edna Dore, Philip Jackson, Heather Tobias, Lesley Manville, David Bamber; ***D:*** Mike Leigh; ***W:*** Mike Leigh; ***C:*** Roger Pratt; ***M:*** Rachel Portman, Andrew Dixon.

High Ice 1/2 **1980** Forest ranger and a lieutenant colonel are involved in a clash of wills over a rescue mission high in the snow-capped Washington state peaks. **97m/C VHS.** David Janssen, Tony Musante; ***D:*** Eugene S. Jones.

High Lonesome 1/2 **1950** Barrymore is a drifter in Big Bend country, suspected in a series of mysterious murders. While he is being held captive, the real killers—thought dead—return to exact revenge on those they hold responsible for the range war in which they were wounded. This was LeMay's only stint as a director. **80m/C VHS, DVD.** John Drew (Blythe) Barrymore Jr., Chill Wills, John Archer, Lois Butler, Kristine Miller, Basil Ruysdael, Jack Elam; ***D:*** Alan LeMay; ***W:*** Alan LeMay; ***C:*** William Howard Greene; ***M:*** Rudolph (Rudy) Schrager.

High Noon **1952** Landmark Western about Hadleyville town marshal Will Kane (Cooper) who faces four professional killers alone, after being abandoned to his fate by the gutless townspeople who profess to admire him. Cooper is the ultimate hero figure, his sheer presence overwhelming. Note the continuing use of the ballad written by Dimitri Tiomkin, "Do Not Forsake Me, Oh My Darlin'" (sung by Tex Ritter) to heighten the tension and action. ♫ High Noon (Do Not Forsake Me, Oh My Darlin'). **85m/B VHS, DVD.** Gary Cooper, Grace Kelly, Lloyd Bridges, Lon Chaney Jr., Thomas Mitchell, Otto Kruger, Katy Jurado, Lee Van Cleef, Harry (Henry) Morgan, Robert J. Wilke, Sheb Wooley; ***D:*** Fred Zinnemann; ***W:*** Carl Foreman; ***C:*** Floyd Crosby; ***M:*** Dimitri Tiomkin. Oscars '52: Actor (Cooper), Film Editing, Song ("High Noon (Do Not Forsake Me, Oh My Darlin')"), Orig. Dramatic Score; AFI '98: Top 100; Golden Globes '53: Actor—Drama (Cooper), Support. Actress (Jurado), Score, Natl. Film Reg. '89;; N.Y. Film Critics '52: Director (Zinnemann), Film.

High Noon 1/2 **2000 (PG-13)** Generally faithful but needless TV remake of the 1952 western classic. Stoic marshal Will Kane (Skerritt), having just married the Quaker Amy (Thompson), is about to give up his badge when he learns that outlaw Frank Miller (Madsen) will be coming in on the noon train with revenge on his mind. Everyone thinks Will should just skedaddle out of town and save them all some grief but, hey, he's a hero and has to do what's right! **93m/C VHS, DVD.** Tom Skerritt, Susanna Thompson, Reed Edward Diamond, Maria Conchita Alonso, Michael Madsen, Dennis Weaver, August Schellenberg; ***D:*** Rod Hardy; ***W:*** Carl Foreman, T.S. Cook; ***C:*** Robert McLachlan; ***M:*** Allyn Ferguson. **CABLE**

High Noon **2009** Phoebe McNamara (de Ravin) is trying to juggle her high-pressure job as a police hostage negotiator with her life as a single mother and caregiver to her own agoraphobic mother, Essie (Shepherd). So she's not interested when bar owner Duncan (Sergei) starts flirting. Then Phoebe gets threatening messages and realizes that dealing with a psycho (who's obsessed with the Gary Cooper movie "High Noon") means getting some help. Romantic suspense from Lifetime that's based on the book by Nora Roberts. **90m/C DVD.** emile de ravin, Ivan Sergei, Cybill Shepherd, Brian Markinson, Ty Olsson, Olivia Cheng, Patrick Sabongui, emile de ravin, Ty Olsson; ***D:*** Peter Markle; ***W:*** Terri Kopp; ***C:*** Joel Ransom; ***M:*** Stuart M. Thomas. **CABLE**

High Noon: Part 2 **1980** Majors attempts to fill Gary Cooper's shoes, as Marshal Kane returns a year after the events of the original "High Noon" to remove the corrupt marshal who replaced him. Subtitled "The Return of Will Kane." **96m/C VHS.** Lee Majors, David Carradine, Pernell Roberts, Katherine (Kathy) Cannon; ***D:*** Jerry Jameson. **TV**

High Plains Drifter 1/2 **1973 (R)** A surreal, violent western focusing on a drifter who defends a town from gunmen intent on meting out death. One of Eastwood's most stylistic directorial efforts, indebted to his "Man with No Name" days with Sergio Leone. Laser format is letterboxed and includes chapter stops and the original theatrical trailer. **105m/C VHS, DVD.** Clint Eastwood, Verna Bloom, Mitchell Ryan, Marianna Hill, Jack Ging, Stefan Gierasch; ***D:*** Clint Eastwood; ***W:*** Ernest Tidyman, Dean Riesner; ***C:*** Bruce Surtees; ***M:*** Dee Barton.

High Risk 1/2 **1981 (R)** Improbable action-adventure of four unemployed Americans who battle foreign armies, unscrupulous gunrunners, and jungle bandits in a harrowing attempt to steal $5 million from an expatriate American drug dealer living in the peaceful splendor of his Columbian villa. Interesting in its own run-on way. **94m/C VHS, DVD.** James Brolin, Anthony Quinn, Lindsay Wagner, James Coburn, Ernest Borgnine, Bruce Davison, Cleavon Little, Chick Vennera; ***D:*** Stewart Raffill; ***W:*** Stewart Raffill; ***C:*** Alex Phillips Jr.; ***M:*** Mark Snow.

High Road to China **1983 (PG)** A hard-drinking former WWI air ace is recruited by a young heiress who must find her father before his ex-partner takes over his business. Post-"Raiders of the Lost Ark" thrills and romance, but without that tale's panache. **105m/C VHS.** Bess Armstrong, Tom Selleck, Jack Weston, Robert Morley, Wilford Brimley, Brian Blessed; ***D:*** Brian G. Hutton; ***M:*** John Barry.

High Rolling in a Hot Corvette *High Rolling* **1977 (PG)** Two carnival workers leave their jobs and hit the road in search of adventure and excitement, eventually turning to crime. **82m/C VHS.** *AU* Joseph Bottoms, Greg Taylor, Judy Davis, Wendy Hughes; ***D:*** Igor Auzins.

High School Caesar **1960** A seedy teenage exploitation flick about a rich teenager, with no parental supervision, who starts his own gang to run his high school. **75m/B VHS, DVD.** Steve Stevens, Lowell Brown, Gary Vinson, Judy Nugent, Daria Massey, John Ashley; ***D:*** O'Dale Ireland; ***W:*** Ethelmae Wilson Page, Robert Slaven; ***C:*** Harry Birch; ***M:*** Nicholas Carras.

High School Confidential *Young Hellions* **1958** Teen punk Tamblyn transfers to Santo Bello high school from Chicago and causes havoc among the locals. He soon involves himself in the school drug scene and looks to be the top dog in dealing, but what no one knows is that he's really a narc! A must for midnight movie fans thanks to high camp values, "hep cat" dialogue and the gorgeous Van Doren as Tamblyn's sex-crazed "aunt." **85m/B VHS, DVD.** Russ Tamblyn, Jan Sterling, John Drew (Blythe) Barrymore Jr., Mamie Van Doren, Diane Jergens, Jerry Lee Lewis, Ray Anthony, Jackie Coogan, Charles Chaplin Jr., Burt Douglas, Michael Landon, Jody Fair, Phillipa Fallon, Robin Raymond, James Todd, Lyle Talbot, William Wellman Jr.; ***D:*** Jack Arnold; ***W:*** Robert Blees, Lewis Meltzer; ***C:*** Harold Marzorati.

High School High 1/2 **1996 (PG-13)** Idealistic teacher Richard Clark (Lovitz) leaves the private school world for notorious inner city Marion Barry High. This school is so bad it has its own cemetery (it's a parody, folks), but Clark is determined to get through to the kids. "Clockers" star Phifer shows up as a helpful student. Penned by David Zucker of "Airplane!" fame, so don't expect a "Mr. Holland's Opus." **86m/C VHS, DVD.** Jon Lovitz, Tia Carrere, Mekhi Phifer, Louise Fletcher, Malinda Williams; ***D:*** Hart Bochner; ***W:*** Pat Proft, David Zucker, Robert Locash; ***C:*** Vernon Layton; ***M:*** Ira Newborn.

High School Musical 1/2 **2006 (PG)** Bouncy musical with catchy tunes, made for the Disney Channel, finds high school basketball star Troy (Efron) falling for studious Gabriella (Hudgens) on vacation (they do karaoke together). When they realize they go to the same school, Troy is pressured to stay with the status quo—especially when he wants to try out for the school musical with Gabriella against the very ambitious Evans siblings. **98m/C DVD.** Zac Efron, Ashley Tilsdale, Lucas Grabeel, Bart Johnson, Monique Coleman, Vanessa Anne Hudgens, Alyson Reed, Corbin Bleu; ***D:*** Kenny Ortega; ***W:*** Peter Barosocchini; ***C:*** Gordon C. Lonsdale; ***M:*** David Lawrence. **CABLE**

High School Musical 2 1/2 **2007 (G)** Just as lively (if not as fresh) as its predecessor. Gabriella is hoping to enjoy the summer with Troy but he needs to save some cash for college. The Wildcats get jobs at the Lava Springs Country Club, which happens to be owned by the parents of scheming Sharpay and Ryan. Sharpay dangles basketball perks and other incentives for Troy to sing with her in the club talent contest, which leaves Gabriella feeling neglected, but none of it is anything that a few song-and-dance numbers can't solve. **111m/C DVD, Blu-ray Disc.** Zac Efron, Vanessa Anne Hudgens, Ashley Tisdale, Corbin Bleu, Lucas Brabeel, Monique Coleman; ***D:*** Kenny Ortega; ***W:*** Peter Barsocchini; ***C:*** Daniel Aranyo; ***M:*** David Lawrence. **CABLE**

High School Musical 3: Senior Year **2008 (G)** The Disney juggernaut churns out the third installment of the wildly popular and squeaky clean teen musical series in as many years, this time cashing in with the big-screen debut of Zac and Vanessa. It's the utopian high-school experience, complete with all of the trappings: the big game, spring musical, prom, graduation, and puppy-love angst, as Troy and Gabriela are facing the prospect of, gulp, being separated as they plan on attending different colleges. Tweens will go ga-ga despite the forgettable tunes, logic-defying plot, and utter lack of edge. **100m/C DVD.** *US* Zac Efron, Vanessa Anne Hudgens, Ashley Tisdale, Lucas Grabeel, Corbin Bleu, Monique Coleman, Bart Johnson, Olesya Rulin; ***D:*** Kenny Ortega; ***W:*** Peter Barsocchini; ***C:*** Daniel Aranyo; ***M:*** David Lawrence.

High School USA 1/2 **1984** A high-school class clown confronts the king of the prep-jock-bullies. Antics ensue in this flick that features many stars from '50s and '60s sitcoms. **96m/C VHS, DVD.** Michael J. Fox, Nancy McKeon, Bob Denver, Angela Cartwright, Elinor Donahue, Dwayne Hickman, Lauri Hendler, Dana Plato, Tony Dow, David Nelson; ***D:*** Rod Amateau; ***M:*** Miles Goodman. **TV**

High Season 1/2 **1988 (R)** A satire about a beautiful English photographer (Bisset) stranded on an idyllic Greek island with neither money nor inspiration, and the motley assembly of characters who surround her during the tourist season. **95m/C VHS.** *GB* Jacqueline Bisset, James Fox, Irene Papas, Sebastian Shaw, Kenneth Branagh, Robert Stephens, Lesley Manville; ***D:*** Clare Peploe; ***W:*** Mark Peploe, Clare Peploe; ***C:*** Chris Menges; ***M:*** Jason Osborn.

High Sierra **1941** Bogart is Roy "Mad Dog" Earle, an aging gangster whose last job goes bad, so he's hiding out from the police in the High Sierras with a dame and a dog. He's also juggling a soft spot for a down-on-their luck farm family that reminds him of home. Bogart's first starring role. Based on the novel by W.R. Burnett. Remade in 1955 as "I Died A Thousand Times." Also available colorized. **96m/B VHS, DVD.** Humphrey Bogart, Ida Lupino, Arthur Kennedy, Joan Leslie, Cornel Wilde, Henry Travers, Henry Hull, Jerome Cowan, Minna Gombell, Barton MacLane, Elisabeth Risdon, Alan Curtis, Donald

MacBride, Paul Harvey, Willie Best, Spencer Charters, George Meeker; *D:* Raoul Walsh; *W:* John Huston, W.R. Burnett; *C:* Gaetano Antonio "Tony" Gaudio; *M:* Adolph Deutsch.

High Society ♂♂♂ **1956** A wealthy man attempts to win back his ex-wife who's about to be remarried in this enjoyable remake of "The Philadelphia Story." ♫ High Society Calypso; Little One; Who Wants to Be a Millionaire?; True Love; You're Sensational; I Love You, Samantha; Now You Has Jazz; Well, Did You Evah?; Mind if I Make Love to You?. **107m/C VHS, DVD.** Frank Sinatra, Bing Crosby, Grace Kelly, Louis Armstrong, Celeste Holm, Sidney Blackmer, Louis Calhern; *D:* Charles Walters; *C:* Paul Vogel; *M:* Cole Porter.

High Spirits ♂♂ **1988 (PG-13)** An American inherits an Irish castle and a sexy 200-year-old ghost. A painful, clumsy comedy by the fine British director that was apparently butchered by the studio before its release. **99m/C VHS, DVD.** Daryl Hannah, Peter O'Toole, Steve Guttenberg, Beverly D'Angelo, Liam Neeson, Martin Ferrero, Peter Gallagher, Jennifer Tilly; *D:* Neil Jordan; *W:* Neil Jordan; *C:* Alex Thompson; *M:* George Fenton.

High Stakes ♂♂ *Melanie Rose* **1989 (R)** Kirkland stars as a prostitute who's battling the Mob and falling in love. Limited release in theatres but another fine performance from Kirkland. **102m/C VHS.** Sally Kirkland, Robert LuPone, Richard Lynch, Sarah Michelle Gellar, Kathy Bates, W.T. Martin, Eddie Earl Hatch, Betty Miller, Maia Danziger, Jesse Corti, Samantha Louca, Larry Block, June Stein, Michael Steinhardt, Maggie Warner, William Kennedy; *D:* Amos Kollek; *W:* Amos Kollek; *C:* Marc Hirschfeld; *M:* Bob Dylan, Mira Spektor.

High Stakes ♂♂ ½ *The Disappearance of Nora* **1993** Nora Fremont (Hamel) wakes up in the Nevada desert bloodied and bruised from a beating and suffering from amnesia. She makes it to Vegas where she meets Denton (Farina), who does casino security, and he agrees to help her find out who she is. But when her husband (Collins) comes to claim her, Nora's nightmare is really just beginning. **98m/C VHS, DVD.** Veronica Hamel, Dennis Farina, Stephen Collins, Stan Ivar, Bryan Cranston; *D:* Joyce Chopra; *W:* Tom Cole, Alan Ormsby; *C:* James Glennon; *M:* Mark Snow. **TV**

High Strung ♂ ½ **1991 (PG)** Writer Thane Furrows (Oedekerk) thinks his life can't get any worse since he's plagued by a nagging mom, pressuring boss, and an insurance salesman. Then mysterious voices and images (played by Carrey) tell him he'll die that night. Naturally, Thane tries to think of a way out of his predicament. You'll hope he dies sooner since the movie is so lame. Beware, Carrey has very little screen time in spite of the advertising. **96m/C VHS.** Steve Oedekerk, Steve Oedekerk, Thomas F. Wilson, Fred Willard, Jim Carrey; *D:* Roger Nygard; *W:* Steve Oedekerk, Robert Kuhn; *C:* Alan Oltman; *M:* Thomas Lieberman.

High Tension WOOF! *Haute tension* **2003 (R)** French splatter exploitation film finds college friends Marie (De France) and Alex (Maiwenn) spending the weekend at the isolated farmhouse of Alex's parents. Your standard gross killer (Nahon), who enjoys decapitation, kills Alex's family and kidnaps Alex so he can torture her at his leisure. Marie sets out to rescue her. There's a lot more gore and even more bad dubbing. Americans do these things much better. **91m/C DVD, UMD.** *FR* Cecile de France, Maiwenn Le Besco, Philippe Nahon, Franck Khalfoun, Andrei Finti, Oana Pellea, Marco Claudiu Pascu; *D:* Alexandre Aja; *W:* Alexandre Aja, Gregory Levasseur; *C:* Maxime Alexandre; *M:* Francois Eudes.

High Tide ♂♂♂ **1987 (PG-13)** A strong and strange drama once again coupling the star and director of "My Brilliant Career." A small-time rock 'n' roll singer who is stranded in a small, beach town fortuitously meets up with her previously abandoned teenage daughter. Acclaimed. **120m/C VHS.** *AU* Judy Davis, Jan Adele, Claudia Karvan, Colin Friels, John Clayton, Mark Hembrow, Frankie J. Holden, Monica Trapaga; *D:* Gillian Armstrong; *W:* Laura Jones; *C:* Russell Boyd; *M:* Peter Best, Ricky Fataar, Mark Moffatt. Australian Film Inst. '87: Actress (Davis); Natl. Soc. Film Critics '88: Actress (Davis).

High Velocity ♂ ½ **1976 (PG)** Lame adventure about two mercenaries involved in the challenge of a lifetime—rescuing a kidnapped executive from Asian terrorists. Filmed in Manila. **105m/C VHS.** Ben Gazzara, Paul Winfield, Britt Ekland, Keenan Wynn; *D:* Remi Kramer; *M:* Jerry Goldsmith.

High Voltage ♂♂ **1929** A fast-moving comedy adventure set in the High Sierras. **62m/B VHS, DVD.** Carole Lombard, William Boyd, Gwen Moore, Billy Bevan; *D:* Howard Higgin.

High Voltage ♂♂ **1998 (R)** Tough guy Johnny Clay (Sabato Jr.) winds up in unexpected trouble when he and his cohorts rob a bank that's laundering money for the Asian mob. Mob boss Cheung decides they need to be taught a lesson. **92m/C VHS, DVD.** Antonio Sabato Jr., Lochlyn Munro, William Zabka, George Kee Cheung, Amy Smart, James Lew, Antonio (Tony) Sabato, Shannon Lee; *D:* Isaac Florentine; *W:* Mike Mains; *C:* Philip D. Schwartz; *M:* Stephen (Steve) Edwards. **VIDEO**

Highball ♂♂♂ **1997 (R)** Newlyweds try to expand their social life by throwing a series of theme parties. Charmingly low-key indie. **90m/C VHS, DVD.** Justine Bateman, Peter Bogdanovich, Rae Dawn Chong, Christopher Eigeman, Annabella Sciorra, Ally Sheedy, Eric Stoltz, Catherine Kellner, Dean Cameron, Andrea Bowen; *D:* Noah Baumbach; *W:* Noah Baumbach; *C:* Steven Bernstein. **VIDEO**

Higher and Higher ♂♂ **1944** Bankrupt aristocrat conspires with servants to regain his fortune, and tries to marry his daughter into money. Sinatra's first big-screen role. ♫ You Belong in a Love Song; A Most Important Affair; The Music Stopped; Today I'm A Debutante; A Lovely Way To Spend An Evening; I Couldn't Sleep a Wink Last Night; You're On Your Own; I Saw You First; Disgustingly Rich. **90m/B VHS.** Frank Sinatra, Leon Errol, Michele Morgan, Jack Haley, Mary McGuire; *D:* Tim Whelan.

Higher Education ♂♂ **1988 (R)** Andy leaves his small town for a big city college and falls head over heels for a student and a teacher. He didn't know college could be so much fun. **83m/C VHS.** Kevin Hicks, Isabelle Mejias, Lori Hallier, Maury Chaykin, Richard Monette; *D:* John Sheppard.

Higher Ground ♂ ½ **1988** Bland TV fare with Denver as an unlikely FBI agent. Disillusioned fed Jim Clayton (Denver) quits the Bureau and takes buddy Rick's (Kove) offer to become a pilot for his Alaskan air freight business. However, Rick is in financial trouble and has been taking work from local bootlegger McClain (Masur). When Rick tries quitting, he ends up dead and Jim is out to get justice. **96m/C DVD.** John Denver, Martin Kove, Meg Wittner, Richard Masur, John Rhys-Davies, Brandon Marsh; *D:* Robert Day; *W:* Michael Eric Stein; *C:* Richard Leiterman; *M:* Lee Holdridge. **TV**

Higher Learning ♂♂ **1994 (R)** Racism, idealism, and the struggle for identity converge in this stylistically shot but rarely enlightening commentary on campus life and strife, focusing on three very different freshmen at fictional Columbus University—a bright track star (Ebbs) who questions the exploitation of black student athletes; a sheltered, sexually confused beauty from the 'burbs (Swanson); and a goony, paranoid loner who falls in with a group of skinheads (Rapaport). Singleton's honorable intention—to make a movie that makes a difference—is marred by cardboard supporting characters, a penchant for in-your-face irony, and a predictable, simplistic conclusion. **127m/C VHS, DVD.** Omar Epps, Kristy Swanson, Michael Rapaport, Laurence Fishburne, Jennifer Connelly, Ice Cube, Tyra Banks, Jason Wiles, Cole Hauser, Regina King, Colleen (Ann) Fitzpatrick; *D:* John Singleton; *W:* John Singleton; *C:* Peter Lyons Collister.

The Highest Honor ♂♂ ½ **1984 (R)** True story set during WWII of a friendship between an Australian army officer, captured while attempting to infiltrate Singapore, and a Japanese security officer. Too long, but gripping. **99m/C VHS.** *AU* John Howard, Atsuo Nakamura, Stuart Wilson, Michael Aitkens, Steve Bisley; *D:* Peter Maxwell.

Highlander ♂♂♂ **1986 (R)** A strange tale about an immortal 16th-century Scottish warrior who has had to battle his evil immortal enemy through the centuries. The feud comes to blows in modern-day Manhattan. Connery makes a memorable appearance as the good warrior's mentor. Spectacular battle and death scenes. A cult favorite which spawned a weak sequel and a TV series. Based on a story by Gregory Widen. **110m/C VHS, DVD.** Christopher Lambert, Sean Connery, Clancy Brown, Roxanne Hart, Beatie Edney, Alan North, Sheila Gish, Jon Polito; *D:* Russell Mulcahy; *W:* Gregory Widen, Peter Bellwood, Larry Ferguson; *C:* Gerry Fisher; *M:* Michael Kamen.

Highlander 2: The Quickening ♂ ½ *Highlander 2: Renegade Version* **1991 (R)** The saga of Connor MacLeod and Juan Villa-Lobos continues in this sequel set in the year 2024. An energy shield designed to block out the sun's harmful ultraviolet rays has left planet Earth in perpetual darkness, but there is evidence that the ozone layer has repaired itself. An environmental terrorist and her group begin a sabotage effort and are joined by MacLeod and Villa-Lobos in their quest to save Earth. Stunning visual effects don't make up for the lack of substance. The Renegade version is a director's cut, which has been reedited and contains some 19 additional minutes of footage. **90m/C VHS, DVD.** Christopher Lambert, Sean Connery, Virginia Madsen, Michael Ironside, John C. McGinley; *D:* Russell Mulcahy; *W:* Peter Bellwood; *C:* Phil Meheux; *M:* Stewart Copeland.

Highlander: Endgame ♂♂ ½ **2000 (R)** Fourth series installment ignores the two middle films but harkens back to the 1985 original. Lambert returns as immortal Connor MacLeod, teaming up with his equally immortal clansman, Duncan (TV "Highlander" Paul), to battle baddie Jacob Kell (Payne). Kell has a long-standing grudge against Connor and doesn't follow the rules of the "game." Numerous flashbacks could be confusing for newcomers but fans will find enjoyment and there is much action and swordplay. Story is so fast-paced that some subplots and characters are left in the dust for the exploits of the three main immortals. The video release contains 12 more minutes of footage and a new ending. **101m/C VHS, DVD.** Christopher Lambert, Adrian Paul, Bruce Payne, Lisa Barbuscia, Peter Wingfield, Jim Byrnes, Donnie Yen, Beatie Edney, Sheila Gish; *D:* Douglas Aarniokoski; *W:* Joel Soisson; *C:* Doug Milsome; *M:* Stephen Graziano.

Highlander: The Final Dimension ♂ ½ *Highlander 3: The Magician; Highlander 3: The Sorcerer* **1994 (R)** Immortal Conner MacLeod (Lambert) battles master illusionist Kane (Van Peebles), who seeks to rule the world. Aiding MacLeod is Alex Smith (Unger), a research scientist who discovers Kane was once buried beneath a mystical mountain along with three other immortal warriors some 300 years before. MacLeod returns to his old Scottish stomping grounds to prepare for battle. Lots of action and special effects, really dumb storyline and overacting—even for a fantasy film. Original theatrical release was PG-13 and 94 minutes; the director's cut has been re-edited and footage added. **99m/C VHS, DVD.** Christopher Lambert, Mario Van Peebles, Deborah Kara Unger, Mako; *D:* Andrew Morahan; *W:* Paul Ohl; *C:* Steven Chivers; *M:* J. Peter Robinson.

Highlander: The Gathering ♂♂ ½ **1992 (PG-13)** Re-edited episodes from the syndicated TV series finds good immortals Connor MacLeod (Lambert) and distant relative Duncan (Paul) battling against an evil immortal (Moll as a particularly nasty villain) and a misguided human (Vanity). Lots of sword-play and a little bit of romance (courtesy of Vandernoot). **98m/C VHS, DVD.** Christopher Lambert, Adrian Paul, Richard Moll, Vanity, Alexandra Vandernoot, Stan Kirsch; *D:* Thomas J. Wright, Ray Austin; *W:* Lorain Despres, Dan Gordon. **TV**

Highlander: The Source ♂ ½ **2007 (R)** The fifth sequel takes its cues from the syndicated TV series rather than the original films, although the parameters of the myth change once again to conform to the confines of mindless action. Duncan MacLeod (Paul) learns that the Source—the cosmic dimension that resulted in the first immortal—has been located. Only the mutated immortal (Solimeno) who guards the spot won't let anyone near without a fight. **86m/C DVD.** Adrian Paul, Jim Byrnes, Peter Wingfield, Thekla Reuten, Cristian Solimeno, Stephen Wight; *D:* Brett Leonard; *W:* Stephen Kelvin Watkins, Mark Bradley; *C:* Steve Arnold; *M:* George Kalis. **VIDEO**

Highpoint ♂ **1980 (PG)** When an unemployed man becomes the chauffeur of a wealthy family, he finds himself in the middle of a mysterious murder and part of an international CIA plot. Hard to figure what's happening in this one. **91m/C VHS.** *CA* Richard Harris, Christopher Plummer, Beverly D'Angelo, Kate Reid, Saul Rubinek; *D:* Peter Carter.

Highway ♂♂ **2001 (R)** Vegas pool cleaner Jack Hayes (Leto) decides to make make a quick getaway when he gets caught in bed with a mobster's wife. So he and best pal Pilot Kelson (Gyllenhaal) score some drugs and head out on the road, along with hitchhiking hooker Cassie (Blair). And they even have a destination—to attend a vigil for the recently deceased Kurt Cobain in Seattle. **97m/C VHS, DVD.** Jared Leto, Selma Blair, Jake Gyllenhaal, Kimberley Kates, Jeremy Piven, John C. McGinley; *D:* James Cox; *W:* Scott Rosenberg; *C:* Mauro Fiore. **VIDEO**

Highway Hitcher ♂♂ *The Pass* **1998 (R)** Comic strip salesman Charles Duprey (Forsythe) is in the midst of a mid-life crisis, including having his wife Shirley (Allen) leave him. Charles' friend Willie (McKean) convinces him to hit the road to Reno for a little R&R. On a backroad Charles crosses paths with Hunter (LeGros), who's having car trouble, and reluctantly offers him a ride. He should have trusted his instincts, since this is only the beginning of trouble. **93m/C VHS, DVD.** William Forsythe, James LeGros, Elizabeth Pena, Jamie Kennedy, Nancy Allen, Michael McKean, Jaason Simmons, John Doe; *D:* Kurt Voss; *W:* Kurt Voss; *C:* Denis Maloney; *M:* Vinnie Golia. **VIDEO**

The Highway Man ♂♂ **1999 (R)** Middleaged Frank Drake (McHattie) is running telephone scams and winds up getting framed by his nasty boss (Gossett) for fraud and then accused of murder. Into this mess strolls Ziggy (Harris), who thinks Frank is her daddy, along with her boyfriend/thief Walter (Priestly), who's just made a big score. It plays more like two separate stories that never really come together. **97m/C VHS, DVD.** Jason Priestley, Louis Gossett Jr., Stephen McHattie, Laura Harris, Callum Keith Rennie, Gordon Michael Woolvett, Bernie Coulson; *D:* Keoni Waxman; *W:* Richard Beattie.

Highway Patrolman ♂♂ *El Patrullero* **1991** Young Pedro Rojas (Sosa) has just graduated from the National Highway Patrol Academy and he and best friend Anibal (Bichir) have been assigned to the isolated roads of northern Durango. He quickly learns that most of the people he stops for minor violations are too poor to pay for licenses and fines. What Pedro does get is a wife, Griselda (Gutierrez), who's soon complaining about Pedro's meager wages. Pedro's resistance to bribery begins to weaken and he becomes more depressed as his ideals are destroyed and his rage increases. Spanish with subtitles. **104m/C VHS.** *MX* Roberto Sosa, Zaide Silvia Gutierrez, Bruno Bichir, Vanessa Bauche; *D:* Alex Cox; *W:* Lorenzo O'Brien; *C:* Miguel Garzon; *M:* Zander Schloss.

Highway 61 ♂♂ **1991 (R)** Shy barber Pokey Jones lives in the small Canadian town of Pickerel Falls and becomes a celebrity when he discovers the frozen corpse of an unknown young man in his backyard. Jackie Bangs, a rock roadie who's stolen her band's stash of drugs, finds herself stranded in the same small town. So begins a wild road trip. Lackluster direction undercuts much of the first-rate acting and amusing story quirks. **110m/C VHS, DVD.** Valerie Buhagiar, Don McKellar, Earl Pastko, Peter Breck, Art Bergmann; *D:* Bruce McDonald; *W:* Don McKellar.

Highway 13 ♂ ½ **1948** When a trucker witnesses an "accidental" death at the loading warehouse, he falls under suspicion. He then sets out to clear his name. **60m/B VHS.** Robert Lowery, Pamela Blake, Lyle Talbot, Michael Whalen, Maris Wrixon, Clem Bevans; ***D:*** William Berke.

Highway to Hell **1992 (R)** Bergen plays the devil in a horror-comedy about going to hell—even if you're not dead yet. Lowe and Swanson are newlyweds on their way to Las Vegas when they're stopped by a "hellcop," who kidnaps the bride and takes her to the netherworld to be the devil's new plaything. Her human hubby doesn't take kindly to this and goes to hell to rescue his bride. Campy flick is played for laughs and has some good special effects. **93m/C VHS.** Patrick Bergin, Adam Storke, Chad Lowe, Kristy Swanson, Richard Farnsworth, C.J. Graham, Lita Ford, Kevin Peter Hall, Pamela Gidley, Brian Helgeland; ***Cameos:*** Gilbert Gottfried; ***D:*** Ate De Jong.

Highwaymen **2003 (R)** Rennie (Caviezel) uses a fast car and a police scanner to get a bead on the serial killer who murdered his wife by running her down with a '72 El Dorado. Along for the ride is Molly (Mitra), the one woman to survive the attacks. Intriguing premise is run off the road by the short run-time, which doesn't leave much time to make the plot very cohesive. **80m/C DVD.** *US* James (Jim) Caviezel, Rhona Mitra, Frankie Faison, Gordon Currie, Colm Feore; ***D:*** Robert Harmon; ***W:*** Hans Bauer, Craig Mitchell; ***C:*** Rene Ohashi; ***M:*** Mark Isham.

Hijacking Catastrophe: 9/11, Fear and the Selling of America ½ **2004** Another in a series of Anti-Bush documentaries to come out in 2004. This one suggests a much larger and darker conspiracy behind the Bush administration's agenda post-9/11. Hermann Goering is quoted at the start, offering a frightening parallel that may or may not be too out there, depending on your party affiliation. Many partisan and non-partisan authorities are interviewed, notably Noam Chomsky and Norman Mailer. **68m/C DVD.** ***D:*** Jeremy Earp, Sut Jhally; ***C:*** David Rabinovitz; ***M:*** Thom Monahan.

Hijacking Hollywood **1997** Modest Hollywood satire finds naive Kevin Conroy (Thomas) using family ties to land a menial job with distant relative Michael Lawrence (Metcalf), a tyrannical producer. Kevin's supervisor is the petty Russell (Thompson), who enjoys sending the kid on useless errands. Kevin's one important task is to pick up film rushes at the airport and he tells hustling roommate Tad (Mandt) that if someone took the dailies, a production could be held hostage. Naturally, Tad is all for the idea. **91m/C VHS, DVD.** Henry Thomas, Scott Thompson, Mark Metcalf, Paul Hewitt, Art LaFleur, Neil Mandt; ***D:*** Neil Mandt; ***W:*** Jim Rossow, Neil Mandt; ***C:*** Anton Floquet.

Hilary and Jackie **1998 (R)** Based on the true story of cover girl cellist Jacqueline Du Pre (Watson) and her relationship with her sister Hilary (Griffiths). As Jackie takes the world of classical music by storm, Hilary gives up her musical ambitions and marries conductor Kiffer (Morrissey). The story switches perspectives between the two women after Jackie arrives at Hilary's doorstep and asks if she may sleep with her husband. Hilary reluctantly agrees, and there go all those stereotypes you had about girls who play classical music. The second half details Jackie's decline and eventual death from multiple sclerosis and the sisters' mutual bonds developed during her illness. Excellent performances and music, including some actual Du Pre performances, make this a pleaser for those who liked "Shine." **124m/C VHS, DVD.** *GB* Emily Watson, Rachel Griffiths, James Frain, David Morrissey, Charles Dance, Celia Imrie, Rupert Penry-Jones, Nyree Dawn Porter, Bill Paterson, Vernon Dobtcheff, Auriol Evans, Keeley Flanders; ***D:*** Anand Tucker; ***W:*** Frank Cottrell-Boyce; ***C:*** David C(lark) Johnson; ***M:*** Barrington Pheloung.

The Hill ½ **1965** British soldiers in a WWII North African military prison are subjected to the brutal discipline of the sadistic Staff Sgt. Williams (Hendry). One of the harshest punishments is the "Hill" a man-made sand wall that the men must climb in full gear. When one of the men dies, it provokes a confrontation between the prisoners, led by Connery, and Williams and his C.O. (Andrews). Harrowing, disturbing look at British Army life and discipline excels on the strength of taut script and great work by the fine cast. **121m/B VHS, DVD.** *GB* Sean Connery, Harry Andrews, Ian Hendry, Ian Bannen, Ossie Davis, Alfred Lynch, Jack Watson, Roy Kinnear, Michael Redgrave, Norman Bird, Neil McCarthy, Howard Goorney, Tony Caunter; ***D:*** Sidney Lumet; ***W:*** Ray Rigby, R.S. (Ray) Allen; ***C:*** Oswald Morris.

Hill Number One **1951** A dramatization of the story of Easter, featuring Dean in one of his first major roles as John the Baptist. **57m/B VHS, DVD.** James Dean, Michael Ansara, Leif Erickson, Ruth Hussey, Roddy McDowall; ***D:*** Arthur Presson. **TV**

Hill 24 Doesn't Answer **1955** Four Zionist soldiers defend a strategic entrance to Jerusalem. While at their posts, they reflect on their lives and devotion to the cause. Made in Israel, in English. The first Israeli feature film. **101m/B VHS.** *IS* Edward Mulhare, Haya Harareet, Michael Wager; ***D:*** Thorold Dickinson.

Hillbillies in a Haunted House **WOOF!** *Hillbillys in a Haunted House* **1967** Two country and western singers en route to the Nashville jamboree encounter a group of foreign spies "haunting" a house. Features Rathbone's last film performance. Sequel to "Las Vegas Hillbillies" (1966). Giant step down for everyone involved. **88m/C VHS, DVD.** Ferlin Husky, Joi Lansing, Don Bowman, John Carradine, Lon Chaney Jr., Basil Rathbone, Merle Haggard, Sonny James, Linda Ho, Molly Bee, George Barrows; ***D:*** Jean Yarbrough; ***W:*** Duke Yelton; ***C:*** Vaughn Wilkins; ***M:*** Hal Borne.

Hillbilly Blitzkrieg *Enemy Round-Up* **1942** Two soldiers are sent to the boonies to guard a top-secret missile site from enemy agents. Come-to-life comic strip characters Snuffy Smith, Barney Google and Spark Plug join in the antics. **63m/B VHS, DVD.** Bud Duncan, Cliff Nazarro, Edgar Kennedy, Doris Linden, Lucien Littlefield, Alan Baldwin; ***D:*** Roy Mack.

The Hills Have Eyes ½ **2006 (R)** Unnecessary remake of Wes Craven's 1977 lunatic-fest. Not much has been altered in way of the storyline—family stranded in the desert with a pack of inbred killers on their tail, but this time around there's an actual budget. Most of it's blown on fake blood. Slick and humorless, desperate to cash in on the (hopefully) short-lived sadism genre resurrected by Rob Zombie. Thanks, Rob. **107m/C DVD, UMD.** *US* Aaron Stanford, Emilie de Ravin, Vinessa Shaw, Kathleen Quinlan, Ted Levine, Desmond Askew, Dan Byrd, Tom Bower, Billy Drago, Robert Joy, Michael Bailey Smith, Laura Ortiz; ***D:*** Alexandre Aja; ***W:*** Gregory Levasseur; ***C:*** Maxime Alexandre; ***M:*** Tomandandy.

The Hills Have Eyes **WOOF!** **1977 (R)** Desperate family battles for survival and vengeance against a brutal band of inbred hillbilly cannibals. Craven gore-fest followed by Hills II. **83m/C VHS, DVD.** Susan Lanier, Robert Houston, Martin Speer, Dee Wallace, Russ Grieve, John Steadman, James Whitworth, Michael Berryman, Virginia Vincent, Janus Blythe; ***D:*** Wes Craven; ***W:*** Wes Craven; ***C:*** Eric Saarinen; ***M:*** Don Peake.

The Hills Have Eyes 2 **2007 (R)** The unnecessary sequel to the unnecessary 2006 remake (not to be confused with 1984's unnecessary sequel to the gory 1977 original). The inbred mutant cannibal Carter clan were unfortunately not quite wiped out and are hiding in some New Mexico caves just waiting to pick off the members of a National Guard patrol and feed on their intestines. The Craven father and son screenwriting team isn't showing us anything we haven't seen before—or want to see again. **89m/C DVD, Blu-ray Disc.** *US* Flex Alexander, Jacob Vargas, Michael Bailey Smith, Lee Thompson Young, Michael McMillian, Jessica Stroup, Daniella Alonso, Eric Edelstein; ***D:*** Martin Weisz; ***W:*** Wes Craven, Jonathan Craven; ***C:*** Sam McCurdy; ***M:*** Trevor Morris.

The Hills Have Eyes, Part 2 **1984** Craven reprises Hills with Eyes number one to ill effect. Ignorant teens disregard warnings of a "Hills Have Eyes" refugee, and go stomping into the grim reaper's proving grounds. Predictably bad things happen. **86m/C VHS, DVD.** Michael Berryman, Kevin Blair Spirtas, John Bloom, Janus Blythe, John Laughlin, Tamara Stafford, Peter Frechette; ***D:*** Wes Craven; ***W:*** Wes Craven; ***C:*** David Lewis.

The Hills of Home *Master of Lassie* **1948 (G)** Warm sentimental tale about a Scottish doctor and his beloved pet collie. One of the better films in the "Lassie" series. **97m/C VHS.** Edmund Gwenn, Donald Crisp, Tom Drake, Janet Leigh; ***D:*** Fred M. Wilcox; ***W:*** William Ludwig.

Hills of Oklahoma **1950** Allen stars as the leader of a cattlemen's association who decides not to deal with dishonest meatpacker Keane, so he drives his herd across the desert to a slaughterhouse run by an honest businesswoman. Based on an original story by Cooper. **67m/B VHS.** Rex Allen, Elisabeth Fraser, Elisabeth Risdon, Fuzzy Knight, Roscoe Ates, Robert Emmett Keane, Trevor Bardette; ***D:*** R.G. Springsteen; ***W:*** Olive Cooper, Victor Arthur.

Hills of Utah ½ **1951** Autry finds himself in the middle of a feud between the local mine operator and a group of cattlemen, while searching for his father's murderer. **70m/B VHS.** Gene Autry, Pat Buttram, Denver Pyle; ***D:*** John English.

The Hillside Strangler ½ *The Case of the Hillside Stranglers* **1989** Crime-of-the-week drama about the investigation to apprehend the serial killer responsible for 10 deaths in 1977-78. **91m/C VHS.** Richard Crenna, Dennis Farina, Billy Zane, Tony Plana, James Tolkan, Tasia Valenza; ***D:*** Steven Gethers. **TV**

The Hillside Strangler ½ **2004 (R)** Okay dramatization of the serial murder cases that occurred over a 14-month period in California in 1977-78 and were originally thought to have been the work of one man. Instead, the crimes were committed by cousins Kenneth Bianchi (Howell) and Angelo Buono (Turturro) after their try at running an escort service went bad and Bianchi strangled one of the hookers. Flick ignores the police investigation in favor of showing the murders. Both lead actors are gung-ho about their roles but this is hardly Oscar-worthy material. **97m/C DVD.** Nicholas Turturro, C. Thomas Howell, Allison Lange, Lin Shaye, Aimee Brooks, Julia Lee; ***D:*** Chuck Parello; ***C:*** John Pirozzi.

Himalaya *Himalaya - L'Enfance d'un Chef; Himalaya - The Youth of a Chief; Caravan* **1999** The age-old struggle of generations deciding between tradition and progress plays itself out once more against the spectacular scenery of the Tibetan mountains. Although the story is nothing new, the film gives a detailed look into a traditional lifestyle that is fast dying out, using non-professional actors, location shooting, and not an ounce of special effects. A bit of the film's grandeur is lost on the small screen, but it is still breathtaking. **104m/C VHS, DVD.** *FR SI GB* Thinlen Lhondup, Karma Wangiel, Lhakpa Tsamchoe; ***D:*** Eric Valli; ***W:*** Eric Valli, Olivier Dazat; ***C:*** Eric Guichard, Jean-Paul Meurisse; ***M:*** Bruno Coulais.

Himatsuri *Fire Festival* **1985** An acclaimed film detailing the conflicts between man and nature, as a lumberjack in a Japanese forest believes he's the protector of the mountains through his divine relationship with the ancient gods. Outraged by the destruction, pollution, and commercial exploitation of the land he turns to violence. In Japanese with English subtitles. **120m/C VHS.** *JP* Kinya Kitaoji, Kwako Taichi, Ryota Nakamoto, Norihei Miki; ***D:*** Mitsuo Yanagimachi; ***W:*** Kenji Nakagami; ***C:*** Masaki Tamura; ***M:*** Toru Takemitsu.

The Hindenburg **1975 (PG)** A dramatization of what might have happened on the fateful night the Hindenburg exploded. Scott plays an investigator who is aware that something is up, and has numerous suspects to interrogate. The laser edition features widescreen format, digital Stereo Surround, the original trailer, and chapter stops. **126m/C VHS, DVD.** George C. Scott, Anne Bancroft, William Atherton, Roy Thinnes, Gig Young, Burgess Meredith, Charles Durning, Richard Dysart; ***D:*** Robert Wise; ***W:*** Nelson Gidding, Richard Levinson, William Link; ***C:*** Robert L. Surtees; ***M:*** David Shire. Oscars '75: Sound FX Editing, Visual FX.

Hindsight **1997** Ah, Hollywood. Joanne (Shower), the bored wife of studio exec Vincent (Law), is having an affair with younger, not-too-bright, aspiring actor Jason (Steadman). Joanne's finally agreed to run off when Jason happens to meet party girl Cassandra (Pass). Thanks to her studio connections, Jason soon has an important agent (Forster) and a studio deal that leaves Joanne in the back lot. But Cassandra is a wild woman with an agenda that doesn't bode well for our selfish himbo. **93m/C VHS.** Ken Steadman, Cyndi Pass, Kathy Shower, John Phillip Law, Robert Forster; ***D:*** John Bowen; ***W:*** Steve Tymon; ***C:*** Keith Holland; ***M:*** Jimmy Hodges. **VIDEO**

Hip Hip Hurrah! **1987** At the end of the 19th-century, a group of famous painters travel each summer to the northernmost cape of Skagen in Denmark to capture the beauty around them. The most talented of their group is Soren Kroyer (Skarsgard) who has a beautiful wife, Marie (Vieth), and a mistress Lille (Brondum). But his bright surface has a tragic core—Soren's mother was mad, he was born to her in an insane asylum, and he feels his own sanity is slipping away as the very light dims around him. Danish with subtitles. **110m/C VHS.** *DK* Stellan Skarsgard, Lene Brondum, Pia Vieth, Helge Jordal; ***D:*** Kjell Grede; ***W:*** Kjell Grede.

Hip Hop 4 Life **2002 (PG-13)** Devon is an eloquent wordsmith at the crossroads of life: pursue college or battle rap his way to the top? Despite his girlfriend and father pushing for college, Devon's dreams of becoming an mc drive him to the stage. Half-baked storyline begins to drag quickly, but to its credit, the film avoids the cliched misogyny and profanity that so many urban dramas cling to. Rough enough to keep younger audiences watching, but nice enough to satisfy the older crowd. Features a slew of Cleveland, Ohio's lesser-known, but decent, rap acts contributing stage time. **98m/C VHS, DVD.** Michael Bell, Q-Nice, Danielle Green; ***D:*** David Velo Stewart; ***W:*** David Velo Stewart. **VIDEO**

Hips, Hips, Hooray ½ **1934** Two supposed "hot shot" salesmen are hired by a cosmetic company to sell flavored lipstick. This lavish musical comedy is one of Wheeler and Woolsey's best vehicles. ♫Tired of It All; Keep Romance Alive; Keep On Doin' What You're Doin'. **68m/B VHS.** Robert Woolsey, Bert Wheeler, Ruth Etting, Thelma Todd, Dorothy Lee; ***D:*** Mark Sandrich.

Hired Hand ½ **1971** Two drifters settle on a farm belonging to one of their wives, only to leave again seeking to avenge the murder of a friend. TV prints include Larry Hagman in a cameo role. **93m/C VHS, DVD.** Peter Fonda, Warren Oates, Verna Bloom, Severn Darden, Robert Pratt; ***Cameos:*** Larry Hagman; ***D:*** Peter Fonda; ***W:*** Alan Sharp; ***C:*** Vilmos Zsigmond; ***M:*** Bruce Langhorne.

Hired to Kill ½ *The Italian Connection* **1973 (R)** A pair of Mafia hoods plot against each other over a $6 million drug shipment. **90m/C VHS.** Henry Silva, Woody Strode, Adolfo Celi, Mario Adorf; ***D:*** Fernando Di Leo; ***W:*** Fernando Di Leo; ***C:*** Franco Villa; ***M:*** Armando Trovajoli.

Hired to Kill ½ **1991 (R)** The granite-hewn Thompson plays a male-chauvinist commando grudgingly leading a squad of beautiful mercenary-ettes on an international rescue mission. Not as bad as it sounds (mainly because the ladies aren't complete bimbos), but between senseless plotting, gratuitous catfights, and a love scene indistinguishable from rape, there's plenty to dislike. **91m/C VHS, DVD.** Brian Thompson, George Kennedy, Jose Ferrer, Oliver Reed, Penelope Reed, Michelle Moffett, Barbara Lee (Niven) Alexander, Jordanna Capra; ***D:*** Nico Mastorakis, Peter Rader; ***W:*** Nico Mastorakis.

Hiroshima **1995 (PG)** Haunting depiction re-reates the circumstances surrounding the dropping of the first atomic bomb in 1945. Juxtaposes scenes between the U.S., Japan, and their leaders—President Truman (Welsh) and Emperor Hirohito

(Umewaka)—with the development of the Manhattan Project, the bombing itself, and its consequences. Filmed primarily in B&W, with newsreel and contemporary witness interviews in color; Japanese sequences are subtitled in English. Filmed on location in Montreal and Tokyo. **180m/C VHS, DVD.** *JP CA* Kenneth Welsh, Naohiko Umewaka, Wesley Addy, Richard Masur, Hisashi Igawa, Ken Jenkins, Jeffrey DeMunn, Leon Pownall, Saul Rubinek, Timothy West, Koji Takahashi, Kazuo Kato; ***D:*** Roger Spottiswoode, Koreyoshi Kurahara; ***W:*** John Hopkins, Toshiro Ishido; ***C:*** Pierre Mignot, Shohei Ando. **CABLE**

Hiroshima Maiden **1988** An American family gains new perspective when they meet a young survivor of the atomic bomb. Based on true stories of Japanese women who stayed with Americans while undergoing surgery to minimize their scars. Originally aired on PBS as part of the "Wonderworks" family movie series. **58m/C VHS.** Susan Blakely, Richard Masur, Tamlyn Tomita; ***D:*** Joan Darling.

Hiroshima, Mon Amour 🦴🦴🦴🦴
1959 Presented in a complex network of flashbacks this profoundly moving drama explores the shadow of history over the personal lives of a lonely French actress (Riva), who's working in Hiroshima, and the Japanese architect (Okada) with whom she's having an affair. She has suffered during the war in occupied France, while he has survived the city's bombing—and their pasts deeply affect their present. Resnais' first feature film and highly influential; adapted by Marguerite Duras from her book. Japanese with subtitles. **88m/B DVD.** *JP FR* Emmanuelle Riva, Eiji Okada, Bernard Fresson, Stella Dassas, Pierre Barbaud; ***D:*** Alain Resnais; ***W:*** Marguerite Duras; ***C:*** Sacha Vierny, Michio Takahashi; ***M:*** Georges Delerue, Giovanni Fusco. N.Y. Film Critics '60: Foreign Film.

Hiroshima: Out of the Ashes 🦴🦴🦴 **1990 (PG)** The terrible aftermath of the bombing of Hiroshima, August, 1945, as seen through the eyes of American and Japanese soldiers, the Japanese people, and a priest. Carefully detailed and realistic, creates an amazing emotional response. Don't miss the scene in which Nelson and his buddy find themselves surrounded by Japanese—the enemy—only to realize that their "captors" have been blinded by the blast. Created as an homage for the 45th anniversary of the bombing. **98m/C VHS.** Max von Sydow, Judd Nelson, Mako, Tamlyn Tomita, Stan(ford) Egi, Sab Shimono, Noriyuki "Pat" Morita, Kim Miyori; ***D:*** Peter Werner.

His Bodyguard 🦴🦴 ½ **1998 (PG-13)** A deaf young man (Natale) is witness to a break-in at the pharmaceutical lab that his family owns, where thieves steal a secret experimental drug. Jenny Farrell (Kapture), the head of lab security, is assigned to protect him from the perpetrators and the two end up running from the bad guys and getting quite friendly. **88m/C VHS.** Mitzi Kapture, Robert Guillaume, Anthony Natale, Vanessa Vaughan, Michael Copeman, Robin Gammell; ***D:*** Artie Mandelberg; ***W:*** Emma Samms. **CABLE**

His Brother's Ghost 🦴🦴 **1945** When Fuzzy is rubbed out by bandits, Billy Carson (no longer called Billy the Kid thanks to mothers' protestations) convinces his twin brother to impersonate him in order to make the bandits believe they are the victims of hocus pocus from the otherworld. Crabbe—who dressed noir before it was chic—made this during his post sci-fi western period, when he slugged it through some 50 low-rent oaters (usually under the direction of Newfield at PRC studios). **54m/C VHS.** Buster Crabbe, Al "Fuzzy" St. John, Charles "Blackie" King, Bud Osborne, Karl Hackett, Arch (Archie) Hall Sr.; ***D:*** Sam Newfield.

His Butler's Sister 🦴🦴 **1944** Bachelor composer Charles Gerard (Tone) lives a sybarite's life in his Manhattan penthouse, which is run by his butler Martin Murphy (O'Brien). When Murphy's stepsister Ann Carter (Durbin) arrives unexpectedly, she's delighted to hear who Murphy works for because she's a singer and wants an audition—an absolute taboo in Gerard's household. So she fools him into thinking she's the new maid until she can get her big break. Nothing new but Durbin does get to work her pretty pipes. ♫Nessun Dorma; In the Spirit of the Moment; When You're Away; Is It True What They Say About Dixie?. **87m/B VHS, DVD.** Deanna Durbin, Franchot Tone, Pat O'Brien, Evelyn Ankers, Akim Tamiroff, Alan Mowbray, Frank Jenks, Walter Catlett, Hans Conried, Florence Bates, Roscoe Karns, Franklin Pangborn; ***D:*** Frank Borzage; ***W:*** Samuel Hoffenstein, Bety Reinhardt; ***C:*** Elwood "Woody" Bredell; ***M:*** Hans J. Salter.

His Double Life 🦴🦴 ½ **1933** When a shy gentleman's valet dies, his master assumes the dead man's identity and has a grand time. From the play "Buried Alive" by Arnold Bennett. Remade in 1943 as "Holy Matrimony." **67m/B VHS, DVD.** Roland Young, Lillian Gish, Montagu Love; ***D:*** Arthur Hopkins.

His Fighting Blood 🦴 ½ **1935** Tom Elliott joins the Mounties but his first assignment is to bring in the Marsden gang and his brother Phil is a member. Based on a James Oliver Curwood story. **63m/B VHS, DVD.** Kermit Maynard, Polly Ann Young, Paul Fix, Ted Adams, Ben Hendricks Jr., Charles "Blackie" King, Joseph Girard, Frank LaRue; ***D:*** John English; ***W:*** Joseph O'Donnell; ***C:*** Jack Greenhalgh.

His First Command 🦴 ½ **1929** An early talkie wherein a playboy falls in love with the daughter of a cavalry officer, and enlists in order to win her affections. **60m/B VHS.** William Boyd, Dorothy Sebastian, Gavin Gordon; ***D:*** Gregory La Cava.

His First Flame 🦴🦴🦴 **1926** A classic Langdon silent romantic comedy. **62m/B VHS, DVD.** Harry Langdon, Vernon Dent, Natalie Kingston; ***W:*** Frank Capra.

His Girl Friday 🦴🦴🦴🦴 **1940** Classic, unrelentingly hilarious war-between-the-sexes comedy. Cynical newspaper editor Walter Burns (Grant) wants to get a big scoop on political corruption, which involves convincing star reporter (and ex-wife) Hildy Johnson (Russell), to come back to work and put off her marriage to dull Bruce Baldwin (Bellamy). Hildy can't resist covering a good story, even when it mean helping a condemned man (Qualen) escape the law. One of Hawks's most furious and inventive screen combats in which women are given uniquely equal (for Hollywood) footing, with staccato dialogue and wonderful performances. Based on the Hecht-MacArthur play "The Front Page," which was filmed in 1931, remade in 1974, and again in 1988 (as "Switching Channels"). **92m/B VHS, DVD.** Cary Grant, Rosalind Russell, Ralph Bellamy, Gene Lockhart, John Qualen, Porter Hall, Roscoe Karns, Abner Biberman, Cliff Edwards, Billy Gilbert, Helen Mack, Ernest Truex, Clarence (C. William) Kolb, Frank Jenks; ***D:*** Howard Hawks; ***W:*** Charles Lederer; ***C:*** Joseph Walker; ***M:*** Morris Stoloff. Natl. Film Reg. '93.

His Greatest Gamble 🦴 ½ **1934** Tearjerker. Philip Eden (Dix) escapes from prison after 15 years when he learns his estranged daughter, Alice (Wilson), has become a neurotic wimp under the thumb of her vengeful mother, Florence (O'Brien-Moore). And that's no way to treat daddy's little girl. **72m/B VHS.** Richard Dix, Dorothy Wilson, Bruce Cabot, Erin O'Brien-Moore, Shirley Grey, Leonard Carey; ***D:*** John S. Robertson; ***W:*** Sidney Buchman, Harry Hervey; ***C:*** Ted Tetzlaff.

His Kind of Woman 🦴🦴🦴 **1951** Sleazy, campy crime drama that turns out to be compelling fun. Unlucky gambler Dan Milner (Mitchum) accepts a big payday for an unknown job that takes him to a Mexican resort. He gets an eyeful of chanteuse Lenore (Russell) and the hot twosome hook-up, even though her married boyfriend, Mark (Price), is also hanging around. Then Dan learns his job is to be the fall guy for racketeer Nick Ferraro (Burr), who wants to get back into the States, and he doesn't go for the idea. **120m/B VHS, DVD.** Robert Mitchum, Jane Russell, Vincent Price, Tim Holt, Charles McGraw, Raymond Burr, Jim Backus, Marjorie Reynolds; ***D:*** John Farrow; ***W:*** Frank Fenton, Jack Leonard; ***C:*** Harry Wild; ***M:*** Leigh Harline.

His Majesty O'Keefe 🦴🦴 ½ **1953** Lancaster stars as a South Seas swashbuckler dealing in the lucrative coconut-oil trade of the mid-1800s. The natives see him as a god and allow him to marry a beautiful maiden. When his reign is threatened by unscrupulous traders, Lancaster springs into action to safeguard his kingdom. Based on a real-life American adventurer, this was the first movie ever filmed in the Fiji Islands. **92m/C VHS.** Burt Lancaster, Joan Rice, Benson Fong, Philip Ahn, Grant Taylor; ***D:*** Byron Haskin.

His Majesty, the American 🦴🦴 ½
1919 William Brooks (Fairbanks) is a young man whose heritage is unknown to him. It turns out he's an heir to a small European kingdom. When Brooks arrives in Alaine he discovers the war minister is trying to overthrow the present king. With his usual dash, our hero saves the day and also wins the hand of a beautiful princess. First picture released by United Artists studios, formed by Fairbanks, Mary Pickford, Charles Chaplin, and D.W. Griffith. **100m/B VHS.** Douglas Fairbanks Sr., Marjorie Daw, Lillian Langdon, Frank Campeau; ***D:*** Joseph Henabery.

His Name Was King **WOOF!** *Lo Chiamavano King* **1971** A man goes after the gang who murdered his brother and raped his young wife in the old West. **90m/C VHS.** *IT* Klaus Kinski, Anne Puskin, Richard Harrison; ***D:*** Giancarlo Romitelli; ***W:*** Renato Savino; ***C:*** Guglielmo Mancori; ***M:*** Luis Bacalov.

His Picture in the Papers 🦴🦴
1916 An early silent comedy wherein the robust, red-meat-eating son of a health food tycoon must get his father's permission to marry by getting his picture favorably in the paper for advertising's sake. **68m/B VHS.** Douglas Fairbanks Sr., Clarence Handysides, Rene Boucicault, Jean Temple, Charles Butler, Homer Hunt, Loretta Blake, Helena Rupport; ***D:*** John Emerson; ***W:*** John Emerson, Anita Loos.

His Private Secretary 🦴 ½ **1933** Wayne plays the jet-setting son of a wealthy businessman who wants his boy to settle down. And he does—after he meets the minister's beautiful daughter. **68m/B VHS, DVD.** John Wayne, Evalyn Knapp, Alec B. Francis, Reginald Barlow, Natalie Kingston, Arthur Hoyt, Al "Fuzzy" St. John; ***D:*** Philip H. (Phil, P.H.) Whitman.

His Secret Life 🦴🦴🦴 *Fate Ignoranti; Blind Fairies; Ignorant Fairies* **2001 (R)** Antonia (Buy) is devastated when her husband Massimo (Renzi) is killed in a car accident. But her grief turns to shock when she accidentally discovers he was having a longtime affair. She goes to confront her husband's mistress and learns it's a mister—Michele (Accorsi), who resents Antonia's interference in his life. But Antonia is desperate to learn about her husband's secret life and other love and they are finally drawn together by their mutual bereavement and curiosity. Italian with subtitles. **105m/C VHS, DVD.** *FR IT* Margherita Buy, Stefano Accorsi, Serra Yilmaz, Andrea Renzi, Erika Blanc, Gabriel Garko, Rosario De Cicco, Lucrezia Valia, Koray Candemir; ***D:*** Ferzan Ozpetek; ***W:*** Ferzan Ozpetek, Gianni Romoli; ***C:*** Pasquale Mari; ***M:*** Andrea Guerra.

His Wife's Lover 🦴🦴🦴 *Zayn Vaybs Lubovnik* **1931** An actor disguised as an old man wins the heart of a lovely young woman. He decides to test her fidelity by reverting to his handsome young self and attempting to seduce her. An enchanting comedy in Yiddish with English subtitles. **77m/B VHS.** Ludwig Satz, Michael Rosenberg, Isadore Cashier, Lucy Levine; ***D:*** Sidney Goldin.

The History Boys 🦴🦴 ½ **2006 (R)** Bennett adapted his own play, which also features the same cast and director and may seem more stagebound than cinematic. In 1983, at a Sheffield grammar school, eight senior boys are being specially tutored in history for a chance to pass the entrance exams to Oxford and Cambridge. To this end, the headmaster (Merrison) has brought in recent Oxford history grad Irwin (Campbell Moore) to tailor their studies, much to the dismay of portly general studies teacher Hector (Griffiths), who prefers a broader method of learning, and tart-tongued longtime teacher Dorothy (de la Tour). Except for class stud Dakin (Cooper) and the Jewish Posner (Barnett), who has a crush on him, the boys serve as background while the grownups show off. But Bennett can write some very good monologues. **109m/C DVD.** *US GB* Richard Griffiths, Frances de la Tour, James Corden, Samuel Anderson, Stephan Campbell Moore, Samuel Barnett, Dominic Cooper, Jamie Parker, Sacha Dhawan, Russell Tovey, Georgia Taylor, Andrew Knott, Clive Merrison, Penelope Wilton, Adrian Scarborough; ***D:*** Nicholas Hytner; ***W:*** Alan Bennett; ***C:*** Andrew Dunn; ***M:*** George Fenton.

History Is Made at Night 🦴🦴🦴
1937 A wife seeks a divorce from a jealous husband while on an Atlantic cruise; she ends up finding both true love and heartbreak in this story of a love triangle at sea. **98m/B VHS.** Charles Boyer, Jean Arthur, Leo Carrillo, Colin Clive; ***D:*** Frank Borzage; ***C:*** Gregg Toland.

The History of Mr. Polly 🦴🦴 ½
2007 Victorian everyman Alfred Polly (Evans) finds himself desperately unhappy since he's stuck with a nagging wife (Duff) and a failing business. So he decides to take drastic action to transform himself from a downtrodden loser into a hero. Based on a novel by H.G. Wells. **93m/C DVD.** *GB* Lee Evans, Anne-Marie Duff, Julie Graham, Richard Coyle, Roger Lloyd-Pack, Trevor Cooper; ***D:*** Gilles Mackinnon; ***W:*** Adrian Hodges; ***C:*** Nigel Willoughby; ***M:*** James Edward Barker, Tim Despic. **TV**

History of the World: Part 1 🦴🦴
1981 (R) More misses than hits in this Brooks parody of historic epics. A bluntly satiric vision of human evolution, from the Dawn of Man to the French Revolution told in an episodic fashion. Good for a few laughs. **90m/C VHS, DVD.** Mel Brooks, Dom DeLuise, Madeline Kahn, Harvey Korman, Cloris Leachman, Gregory Hines, Pamela Stephenson, Paul Mazursky, Bea Arthur, Fritz Feld, John Hurt, Jack Carter, John Hillerman, John Gavin, Barry Levinson, Ron Carey, Howard Morris, Sid Caesar, Jackie Mason, Charlie Callas, Henny Youngman, Hugh Hefner; ***D:*** Mel Brooks; ***W:*** Mel Brooks; ***C:*** John Morris, Woody Omens; ***M:*** Shecky Greene; ***Nar:*** Orson Welles.

A History of Violence 🦴🦴🦴 **2005 (R)** Unassuming small-town diner owner and family man Tom Stall foils a robbery, killing the hold-up men, and becomes a hero. This new status brings the unwanted attention of a trio of men who claim to be from Tom's past. And a very violent past it turns out to be. Cronenberg, with the exceptional help of a great cast, deftly and cleverly plays with the notion of identity and reality, while he takes a jab at the audience's knowledge of and expectations for action movies and their conventions. It's all very cool and engrossing, but he makes you squirm a little for enjoying the ride. **96m/C DVD, Blu-ray Disc.** *US* Viggo Mortensen, Maria Bello, William Hurt, Stephen McHattie, Peter MacNeill, Ed Harris, Ashton Holmes, Heidi Hayes; ***D:*** David Cronenberg; ***W:*** Josh Olson; ***C:*** Peter Suschitzky; ***M:*** Howard Shore. L.A. Film Critics '05: Support. Actor (Hurt); N.Y. Film Critics '05: Support. Actor (Hurt), Support. Actress (Bello); Natl. Soc. Film Critics '05: Director (Cronenberg), Support. Actor (Harris).

Hit! 🦴🦴 **1973 (R)** When the 15-year-old daughter of a government agent dies of a drug overdose, he deals his revenge to top French heroin traffickers. **135m/C VHS.** Billy Dee Williams, Richard Pryor, Gwen Welles, Paul Hampton, Warren Kemmerling, Sid Melton; ***D:*** Sidney J. Furie; ***W:*** Alan R. Trustman, David M. Wolf; ***M:*** Lalo Schifrin.

The Hit 🦴🦴 ½ **1985 (R)** A feisty young hooker gets mixed-up with two strong-armed hired killers as they escort an unusual stoolpigeon from his exile in Spain to their angry mob bosses. Minor cult-noir from the director of "My Beautiful Launderette" and "Dangerous Liaisons." **105m/C VHS, DVD.** *GB* Terence Stamp, John Hurt, Laura Del Sol, Tim Roth, Fernando Rey, Bill Hunter; ***D:*** Stephen Frears; ***W:*** Peter Prince; ***C:*** John A. Alonzo; ***M:*** Eric Clapton.

The Hit 🦴 ½ **2001** A not-very-thrilling thriller that finds Baltimore reporter Keith (Caulfield) furious when he learns of wife Sonia's (Pacula) infidelity. He gets drunk and arranges a contract hit on her but, after sobering up, realizes that's a little extreme and tries to call the whole thing off. Of course, Keith discovers he can't. Oh, and Lithuania fills in for Baltimore as a location site. **86m/C VHS, DVD.** Maxwell Caulfield, Joanna Pacula, Christine Elise, Lucky Vanous; ***D:*** Vincent Monton; ***W:*** Vincent Monton; ***C:*** Raphael Smadja. **VIDEO**

The Hit 🦴🦴 **2006** Rising record exec Hen (Underwood) wants to unite all rival rap labels under one black-owned company that will also be a community power. But he crosses the mob, bent on shutting down Hen's efforts. **97m/C DVD.** Blair Underwood, DeRay Davis, Ernest Harden Jr., James Russo, Michelle Flowers, Nicki Norris; ***D:*** Ryan Combs; ***W:*** Ryan Combs; ***C:*** Daniel Moder; ***M:*** Chris Winston. **VIDEO**

Hit & Run 🦴 *Revenge Squad* **1982** David Marks, a Manhattan cab driver, is haunted by recurring flashbacks of a freak hit-and-run accident in which his wife was struck down on a city street. **96m/C VHS.** Paul Perri, Claudia Cron; ***D:*** Charles Braverman; ***M:*** Brad Fiedel.

Hit and Runway 🦴🦴 **2001 (R)** Alex (Parducci) works at his family's restaurant, although he really wants to be a screenwriter. He comes up with the idea for a movie for a big action star named Jagger Stevens (Richards), although Alex has no writing talent at all. So, Alex turns to playwright Elliot (Jacobson), whom he meets at the restaurant, for professional help. In return, Alex promises to help Elliot win the body of cute waiter Joey (Smith). It's all cute and predictable. **90m/C VHS, DVD.** *US* Michael Parducci, Peter Jacobson, Kerr Smith, Judy Prescott, J.K. Simmons, Teresa De Priest, Hoyt Richards, John Fiore, Steve Singer; ***D:*** Christopher Livingston; ***W:*** Christopher Livingston, Jaffe Cohen; ***C:*** David Tumblety; ***M:*** Frank Piazza.

Hit Lady 🦴🦴 **1974** An elegant cultured woman becomes a hit lady for the syndicate in this predictable, yet slick gangster movie. **74m/C VHS, DVD.** Yvette Mimieux, Dack Rambo, Clu Gulager, Keenan Wynn; ***D:*** Tracy Keenan Wynn; ***W:*** Yvette Mimieux; ***M:*** George Aliceson Tipton. **TV**

The Hit List 🦴🦴 **1988 (R)** A regular guy fights back brutally when his wife and child are mistakenly kidnapped by the Mafia. Fast-paced action makes up for thin plot. **87m/C VHS.** Jan-Michael Vincent, Leo Rossi, Lance Henriksen, Charles Napier, Rip Torn; ***D:*** William Lustig; ***W:*** Peter Brosnan.

The Hit List 🦴🦴 ½ **1993 (R)** Charles Pike (Fahey) is a professional hitman working for attorney Peter Mayhew (Coburn) to wipe out drug lords. Then Mayhew gives Pike a new assignment. He introduces him to sexy widow Jordan Henning (Butler), who wants Pike to kill the man who murdered her husband. Pike finds himself mixing business with pleasure in a deadly combination that sees him dodging crooked cops and trained assassins. **97m/C VHS.** Jeff Fahey, Yancy Butler, James Coburn; ***D:*** William Webb; ***W:*** Reed Steiner.

The Hit Man 🦴🦴 *Il Sicario* **1960** A crime drama that profiles the crisis of a man unfit to commit murder but who does for a price. **100m/B VHS.** Andrea Checchi, Sergio Fantoni, Pietro Germi, Sylva Koscina, Belinda Lee, Alberto Lupo; ***D:*** Damiano Damiani; ***W:*** Damiano Damiani, Cesare Zavattini; ***C:*** Pier Ludovico Pavoni; ***M:*** Roberto Nicolosi.

Hit Me 🦴🦴 ½ **1996 (R)** Bleak neo-noir based on Jim Thompson's novel "A Swell-Looking Babe." Sonny (Koteas) is a thirty-something bellhop at the downscale Stillwell hotel who goes home to a scuzzy apartment and the responsibilities of caring for his retarded brother Leroy (Leggett). His first slip is falling for troubled guest Monique (Marsac)—the femme fatale of the flick. And then Sonny makes an even bigger mistake by agreeing to help his "friend" Del (Ramsay) rob the hotel's safe deposit boxes of cash intended for a big poker game. **125m/C VHS, DVD.** Elias Koteas, Laure Marsac, Bruce Ramsay, Jay Leggett, Kevin J. O'Connor, Philip Baker Hall, J.C. Quinn, Haing S. Ngor, William H. Macy; ***D:*** Steven Shainberg; ***W:*** Denis Johnson; ***C:*** Mark J. Gordon.

Hit Men 🦴 ½ *La Mala Ordina; Manhunt; Black Kingpin* **1973** Double crosses and gun battles highlight this tale of inner-city crime. **90m/C VHS.** *IT* Henry Silva, Mario Adorf, Woody Strode, Adolfo Celi, Luciana Paluzzi, Franco Fabrizi, Femi Benussi, Peter Berling, Cyril Cusack, Sylva Koscina; ***D:*** Fernando Di Leo; ***W:*** Fernando Di Leo, Augusto Finochi; ***C:*** Franco Villa; ***M:*** Armando Trovajoli.

Hit the Deck 🦴 ½ **1955** Second-rate studio musical about sailors on leave and looking for romance. Based on the 1927 Broadway musical. ♫ Sometimes I'm Happy; Hallelujah; Why, Oh Why; Keeping Myself For You; More Than You Know; I Know That You Know; Lucky Bird. **112m/C VHS.** Jane Powell, Tony Martin, Debbie Reynolds, Walter Pidgeon, Vic Damone, Gene Raymond, Ann Miller, Russ Tamblyn, J. Carrol Naish, Kay Armen, Richard Anderson; ***D:*** Roy Rowland; ***C:*** George J. Folsey.

Hit the Dutchman 🦴🦴 **1992 (R)** Routine gangster flick about Dutch Schultz trying to rise to the top of the New York crime community—with or without the help of underworld pals Legs Diamond and Lucky Luciano. An unrated version is also available. **116m/C VHS.** Bruce Nozick, Sally Kirkland, Will Kempe, Jenny (Jennifer) McShane; ***D:*** Menahem Golan.

Hit the Ice 🦴🦴 **1943** Newspaper photographers Bud and Lou are mistaken as gangsters in Chicago and the usual complications ensue. Includes an appearance by Johnny Long & His Orchestra. ♫ I'm Like A Fish Out Of Water; Happiness Bound; I'd Like to Set You to Music; Slap Polka. **89m/C VHS, DVD.** Bud Abbott, Lou Costello, Patric Knowles, Elyse Knox, Ginny Simms; ***D:*** Charles Lamont.

Hit the Saddle 🦴🦴 **1937** The Three Mesquiteers track down a gang involved in capturing wild horses in protected areas although one of three is more interested in the charms of a dance hall girl (played by starlet Rita Cansino who would soon become Rita Hayworth). **54m/B VHS.** Robert "Bob" Livingston, Ray Corrigan, Max Terhune, J(ohn) P(aterson) McGowan, Yakima Canutt, Rita Hayworth; ***D:*** Mack V. Wright.

Hit Woman: The Double Edge 🦴🦴 ½ **1993 (R)** Lucci plays a dual role as an FBI agent and the look-alike killer-for-hire that she's tracking. Originally made for TV; the video version contains additional footage that earned the "R" rating. **92m/C VHS.** Susan Lucci, Robert Urich, Michael Woods, Robert Prosky; ***D:*** Stephen Stafford; ***W:*** Alan Oltman, Joe Reb Moffly; ***C:*** Gideon Porath; ***M:*** Gerald Gouriet. **TV**

Hitch 🦴🦴 ½ **2005 (PG-13)** The charming Smith tackles romantic comedy to amiable effect as the title character. Alex "Hitch" Hitchens is a professional dating doctor, the hero of schlubs everywhere. This time his client is shy, hefty accountant Albert (James), who's in love with Allegra (Valletta), a wealthy beauty far out of his league. While Hitch works on Albert, he's also falling for cynical gossip columnist Sara (Mendes) but his every smooth move turns disastrous in her hot babe presence. Everyone pulls their weight and looks like they're having fun. So should the audience. **119m/C DVD, Blu-ray Disc, UMD.** *US* Will Smith, Eva Mendes, Amber Valletta, Michael Rapaport, Adam Arkin, Kevin James, Julie Ann Emery; ***D:*** Andy Tennant; ***W:*** Kevin Bisch; ***C:*** Andrew Dunn; ***M:*** George Fenton.

The Hitch-Hiker 🦴🦴🦴 **1953** Two young men off on the vacation of their dreams pick up a psychopathic hitchhiker with a right eye that never closes, even when he sleeps. Taut suspense makes this flick worth seeing. **71m/B VHS, DVD.** Edmond O'Brien, Frank Lovejoy, William Talman, Jose Torvay; ***D:*** Ida Lupino; ***W:*** Ida Lupino, Daniel Mainwaring, Lucille Fletcher, Robert L. Joseph; ***C:*** Nicholas Musuraca; ***M:*** Leith Stevens. Natl. Film Reg. '98.

Hitched 🦴🦴 **2001** Housewife Eve (Lee) doesn't suspect that her salesman hubby Ed (Hall) is cheating on her. But then he winds up in the hospital after a drunk-driving accident that also involved his lady friend of the moment. So Eve decides to get even by shackling him in their soundproof basement and filing a missing person's report. Detective Cary Grant (Carter) is immediately smitten and makes his move on Eve but gets confused when Ted reappears and Eve goes missing. **89m/C VHS, DVD.** Sheryl Lee, Anthony Michael Hall, Alex Carter; ***D:*** Wesley Strick; ***W:*** Wesley Strick; ***C:*** Jonathan Freeman; ***M:*** Randy Miller. **CABLE**

The Hitcher 🦴🦴 ½ **1986 (R)** A young man picks up a hitchhiker on a deserted stretch of California highway only to be tormented by the man's repeated appearances: is he real or a figment of his imagination? Ferociously funny, sadomasochistic comedy with graphic violence. **98m/C VHS, DVD.** Rutger Hauer, C. Thomas Howell, Jennifer Jason Leigh, Jeffrey DeMunn, John M. Jackson, Billy Green Bush; ***D:*** Robert Harmon; ***W:*** Eric Red; ***C:*** John Seale; ***M:*** Mark Isham.

The Hitcher 🦴 ½ **2007 (R)** Bean can't out-spook Rutger Hauer's title character from the 1986 original as this remake gets gutted (and not in a scary way) into generic action-horror. Jim (Knighton) and girlfriend Grace (Bush) are traveling that lonely desert highway, only to have repeated run-ins with psychopath John Ryder. Many of the original's set action pieces are recreated but, except for the addition of the nubile Bush, the '86 version is a lot more terrifying (if not as loud). **83m/C DVD, HD DVD.** *US* Sean Bean, Sophia Bush, Zachery Knighton, Neal McDonough; ***W:*** Jake Wade Wall, Eric Bernt; ***C:*** Dave Meyers, James Hawkinson; ***M:*** Steve Jablonsky.

The Hitcher 2: I've Been Waiting 🦴🦴 **2003 (R)** Jim Halsey (Howell reprises his role from the 1986 film) goes back to West Texas to confront his fear of the past accompanied by his girlfriend Maggie (Wuhrer). They travel the same stretch of desolate road and—surprise!—encounter a psycho hitchhiker, Jake (Busey, who certainly looks the part). **93m/C VHS, DVD.** C. Thomas Howell, Kari Wuhrer, Jake Busey; ***D:*** Louis Morneau; ***W:*** Molly Meeker, Charles Meeker, Leslie Scharf; ***C:*** George Mooradian; ***M:*** Joe Kraemer. **VIDEO**

Hitchhikers WOOF! **1972 (R)** Trash film about a bunch of scantily clad female hitchhikers who rob the motorists who stop to pick them up. Keep right on going when you spot this roadkill. **90m/C VHS.** Misty Rowe, Norman Klar, Linda Avery; ***D:*** Ferd Sebastian.

The Hitchhiker's Guide to the Galaxy 🦴🦴🦴 **1981** The six-episode BBC TV adaptation of Douglas Adams's hilarious science-fiction books. Features the intergalatic Ford Prefect, sent to Earth to update its planetary listing in the Hitchhiker's Guide; hapless hero Arthur Dent, a typical Englishman caught up in space mayhem; and an odd assortment of aliens, including Marvin the Paranoid Android. The show's sheer cheesiness is part of the charm. **194m/C VHS, DVD.** *GB* Simon Jones, David Dixon, Sandra Dickinson, Mark Wing-Davey; ***D:*** Alan Bell; ***W:*** Douglas Adams. **TV**

The Hitchhiker's Guide to the Galaxy 🦴🦴🦴 **2005 (PG)** Douglas Adams' absurdist sci-fi classic finally makes it to the big screen. When the Earth is demolished, Arthur Dent (Freeman) hitches a ride off the planet with Ford Prefect (Def), a writer for the HGTG, a Fodors-esque guidebook to the universe. Arthur and Ford fall in with Zaphod Beeblebrox (Rockwell), the sublimely dense President of the Galaxy, and his girlfriend, Trillian (Deschanel), in their quest to find the Ultimate Question to life, the universe, and everything. The script's slavish devotion to Adams' text weighs down certain scenes, making them sound more like audiobook recitations, but Jennings does a praiseworthy job of bringing the author's eccentric vision to life. The cast is uniformly strong, particularly Rockwell, who gleefully chews the scenery as two-headed egotist Zaphod. **110m/C DVD, UMD.** *GB US* Martin Freeman, Mos Def, Sam Rockwell, Zooey Deschanel, John Malkovich, Bill Nighy, Warwick Davis, Simon Jones, Anna Chancellor, Albie Woodington, Jason Schwartzman, Dominique Jackson, Jack Stanley; ***D:*** Garth Jennings; ***W:*** Douglas Adams, Karey Kilpatrick; ***C:*** Igor Jadue-Lillo; ***M:*** Joby Talbot; ***V:*** Alan Rickman, Thomas Lennon, Helen Mirren, Stephen Fry, Richard Griffiths, Ian McNeice.

Hitler 🦴🦴 ½ *Women of Nazi Germany* **1962** The true story of the infamous Nazi dictator's rise to power and his historic downfall. **103m/B VHS.** Richard Basehart, Maria Emo, Cordula Trantow; ***D:*** Stuart Heisler.

Hitler: Dead or Alive 🦴🦴 **1943** Three ex-cons devise a scheme to gain a million-dollar reward for capturing Adolf Hitler in this low-budget production. **64m/B VHS, DVD.** Ward Bond, Dorothy Tree, Bruce Edwards, Warren Hymer, Paul Fix, Russell Hicks, Bobby Watson; ***D:*** Nick Grinde.

Hitler: The Last Ten Days 🦴🦴 **1973 (PG)** Based on an eyewitness account, the story of Hitler's last days in an underground bunker gives insight to his madness. **106m/C VHS, DVD.** Alec Guinness, Simon Ward, Adolfo Celi, Phyllida Law, Diane Cilento, Gabriele Ferzetti, Eric Porter, Doris Kunstmann, Joss Ackland, John Bennett, John Barron, Barbara Jefford, Julian Glover, Michael Goodliffe, Mark Kingston, Philip Stone; ***D:*** Ennio de Concini; ***W:*** Ennio de Concini; ***C:*** Ennio Guarnieri; ***M:*** Mischa Spoliansky.

Hitler: The Rise of Evil 🦴🦴 **2003** General overview of the insecure but ambitious Hitler (Carlyle) during his rise to power. He goes from World War I soldier to member of the nationalistic German Worker's Party and leader of the Nazi Party. Filmed on location in Vienna and Prague. **186m/C DVD.** Robert Carlyle, Stockard Channing, Liev Schreiber, Peter O'Toole, Jena Malone, Julianna Margulies, Matthew Modine, Peter Stormare, Chris Larkin; ***D:*** Christian Duguay; ***W:*** John Pielmeier, G. Ross Parker; ***C:*** Pierre Gill; ***M:*** Normand Corbeil. **TV**

Hitler's Children 🦴🦴🦴 **1943** Two young people, a German boy and an American girl, are caught in the horror of Nazi Germany. He's attracted to Hitler's rant, she's repelled. Exploitative yet engrossing. **83m/B VHS.** Tim Holt, Bonita Granville, Otto Kruger, H.B. Warner, Irving Reis, Hans Conried, Lloyd Corrigan; ***D:*** Edward Dmytryk.

Hitler's Daughter 🦴 **1990 (R)** Made for TV movie following the trials and tribulations of the illegitimate daughter of Adolf Hitler. She's all grown up now...and wants to rule the United States. She secures a position of power during an election and now Nazi-hunters must figure out her identity before she takes over the world! **88m/C VHS.** Kay Lenz, Veronica Cartwright, Melody Anderson, Patrick Cassidy, Carolyn Dunn, Lindsay Merrithew, George R. Robertson; ***D:*** James A. Contner. **TV**

The Hitman 🦴🦴 **1991 (R)** Norris plays a cop undercover as a syndicate hit man in Seattle, where he cleans up crime by triggering a three-way mob bloodbath between beastly Italian mafiosi, snooty French-Canadian hoods, and fanatical Iranian scum. But he teaches a black kid martial arts, so you know he's politically correct. Action addicts will give this a passing grade; all others need not apply. **95m/C VHS, DVD.** Chuck Norris, Michael Parks, Al Waxman, Alberta Watson, Salim Grant, Ken Pogue, Marcel Sabourin, Bruno Gerussi, Frank Ferrucci; ***D:*** Aaron Norris; ***C:*** Joao Fernandes.

Hitman WOOF! **2007 (R)** Just like the videogame on which the film is based, orphaned kids are recruited by a top-secret organization that trains them as assassins. Grown, the killers are all bald with their heads tattooed with large bar codes, and they roam around the rest of the world with large guns, knocking off whomever needs knocking off. One of these guys, known only as "47" (Olyphant), is on task to murder Russian President Belicoff (Thomsen), which he does with brutal (and predictable) violence. But when Belicoff later shows up alive on television, 47 realizes he's been had, and now he's running from police, Interpol, and worse yet, a handful of his old cronies. Somehow gorgeous Nika (Kurylenko) gets tossed into the mix and is on the lam with 47. She lends some eye-candy and a touch of humanity, but that's about it. The violence is over the top, the plot is less than thin, and the acting perfunctory at best. **100m/C DVD.** *US* Timothy Olyphant, Olga Kurylenko, Dougray Scott, Robert Knepper, Ulrich Thomsen, Henry Ian Cusack, Michael Offei; ***D:*** Skip Woods, Xavier Gens; ***C:*** Laurent Bares; ***M:*** Geoff Zanelli.

Hitman's Journal 🦴🦴 *18 Shades of Dust* **1999 (R)** Vincent Dianni (Aiello) is a mob enforcer for Don Cucci and his son Tommy (Forsythe). But when info leaked to the feds gets the Don life in prison, Vincent comes under suspicion as the squealer. All Vincent wants to do is quietly retire but first he has to square things with his bosses. **95m/C VHS, DVD.** Danny Aiello, William Forsythe, Polly Draper, Vincent Pastore, Aida Turturro; ***D:*** Danny Aiello III. **VIDEO**

Hitman's Run ✓✓ **1999 (R)** Former Mafia hitman Roberts has double-crossed his bosses and is now in the FBI's Witness Protection Program. However, his safety is hardly guaranteed. **93m/C VHS, DVD.** Eric Roberts, Damian Chapa, Esteban Louis Powell; ***D:*** Mark L. Lester; ***W:*** Eric Barker; ***C:*** Zoltan David; ***M:*** Roger Bellon. **VIDEO**

The Hitter ✓✓ **1979 (R)** A former prize-fighter, his girlfriend, and a washed-up promoter are all on the run in this adventure tale. **94m/C VHS.** Ron O'Neal, Adolph Caesar, Sheila Frazier; ***D:*** Christopher Leitch.

Hittin' the Trail ✓ **1937** The Good Cowboy is mistaken for a murdering varmint, and must prove his innocence. **57m/B VHS, DVD.** Tex Ritter, Charles "Blackie" King, Ray Whitley, The Range Ramblers; ***D:*** Robert North Bradbury.

Hitz ✓ 1/2 *Judgment* **1989 (R)** In a Los Angeles barrio, Musico, a Loco gang member, kills two rival gang members. Arrested and convicted when a young boy named Pepe is coerced into testifying against him, Musico is killed in the courtroom. But the violence doesn't stop. The judge, who wants to reform the juvenile court system, tries to protect Pepe, and both are targeted for death by the Loco gang. **90m/C VHS.** Elliott Gould, Emilia Crow, Karen Black, Cuba Gooding Jr.; ***D:*** William Sachs; ***W:*** William Sachs; ***C:*** Kelly Johnson, Shelly Johnson; ***M:*** Garry Schyman.

The Hive ✓✓ **2008** Tries to be more than your typical creature feature but you can only do so much with killer ants. Exterminators Len (Weber) and Bill (Wopat) are dispatched by their company to eradicate a mass of flesh-eating ants in the jungles of Ben Tao, Thailand. Entomologist Claire (Healy) has discovered that the hive displays a disturbing collective intelligence. The team is actually captured by the ants and learn about their origin and intentions from the hive queen herself. Let's just say no one is going to be stepping on these babies anytime soon! **90m/C DVD.** Tom Wopat, Elizabeth Healey, Kal Weber, Jessica Reavis, Mark Ramsey; ***D:*** Peter Manus; ***W:*** T.S. Cook; ***C:*** Kittiwat Sawmaret; ***M:*** Mark Ryder, Charles Olins. **CABLE**

H.M. Pulham Esquire ✓✓ **1941** His 25th Harvard reunion (and an encounter with an old flame) has stuffy Bostonian Harry Pulham (Young) contemplating his conventional life. The scion of a wealthy family remembers the one time he went against society's strictures by falling for Iowa-born Marvin (Lamarr) when they worked together in New York. With his father disapproving of their romance, Harry scuttles home to marry suitable Kay (Hussey) while Marvin goes on to a successful career. Lamarr's heavy Viennese accent is distracting but so is her beauty. Adapted from the John P. Marquand novel. **119m/B DVD.** Robert Young, Hedy Lamarr, Ruth Hussey, Charles Coburn, Van Heflin, Fay Holden, Bonita Granville, Leif Erickson; ***D:*** King Vidor; ***W:*** King Vidor, Elizabeth Hill; ***C:*** Ray June; ***M:*** Bronislau Kaper.

The Hoax ✓✓ **2006 (R)** In 1971, egocentric writer Clifford Irving's (Gere) dreams collapse when his book deal falls through. To bolster his bruised ego, Irving tells his publisher (Davis) that his new tome will be a sensation—and then has to come up with an idea. With the help of loyal researcher Dick Suskind (Molina), Irving schemes to sell a bogus autobiography of recluse Howard Hughes and greed wins out over corporate suspicions before Irving's scam is exposed. Hallstrom and his cast do well but this long-forgotten hoax has to work hard to attract the interest of a casual viewer. **115m/C DVD.** *US* Richard Gere, Alfred Molina, Hope Davis, Marcia Gay Harden, Stanley Tucci, Julie Delpy; ***D:*** Lasse Hallstrom; ***W:*** William Wheeler; ***C:*** Oliver Stapleton; ***M:*** Carter Burwell.

The Hobbit ✓✓✓ **1978** An animated interpretation of J.R.R. Tolkien's novel of the same name. The story follows Bilbo Baggins and his journeys in Middle Earth and encounters with the creatures who inhabit it. He joins comrades to battle against evil beings and creatures. **76m/C VHS, DVD.** ***D:*** Arthur Rankin Jr., Jules Bass; ***M:*** Maury Laws; ***V:*** Cyril Ritchard, Brother Theodore, Paul Frees, Donald E. Messick, Hans Conried, Thurl Ravenscroft, Orson Bean, John Huston, Otto Preminger, Richard Boone. **TV**

Hobgoblins ✓ **1987** Little creatures escape from a studio vault and wreak havoc. **92m/C VHS, DVD.** Jeffrey Culver, Tom Bartlett; ***D:*** Rick Sloane.

Hobo's Christmas ✓✓ **1987** A man who left his family to become a hobo comes home for Christmas 25 years later. Hughes turns in a delightful performance as the hobo. **94m/C VHS.** Barnard Hughes, William Hickey, Gerald McRaney, Wendy Crewson; ***D:*** Will MacKenzie. **TV**

Hobson's Choice ✓✓✓ **1953** A prosperous businessman in the 1890s tries to keep his daughter from marrying, but the strong-willed daughter has other ideas. **107m/B VHS.** *GB* Charles Laughton, John Mills, Brenda de Banzie; ***D:*** David Lean; ***C:*** Jack Hildyard; ***M:*** Malcolm Arnold. British Acad. '54: Film.

Hobson's Choice ✓✓ **1983** Remake of the old family comedy about a crusty, penny-pinching businessman whose head-strong daughter proves to him she'll not become an old maid. Instead she marries one of his employees. Not bad, but not as good as the original. **95m/C VHS.** Jack Warden, Sharon Gless, Richard Thomas, Lillian Gish; ***D:*** Gilbert Cates. **TV**

Hockey Night ✓✓ 1/2 **1984** A movie for pre- and early teens in which a girl goalie makes the boys' hockey team. **77m/C VHS, DVD.** *CA* Megan Follows, Rick Moranis, Gail Youngs, Martin Harburg, Henry Ramer; ***D:*** Paul Shapiro.

Hocus Pocus ✓✓ 1/2 **1993 (PG)** The divine Miss M is back, but this time she's not so sweet. Midler, Najimy, and Parker are 17th century witches accidentally conjured up in the 20th century, appropriately enough on Halloween in Salem, Massachusetts. Seems they were hung 300 years back and they take their revenge in some surprisingly gruesome ways, given the Disney label. They rant, they rave, they sing (only once), they fly. See this one for the three stars who make up for the lack of substance with their comedic talents. **95m/C VHS, DVD.** Bette Midler, Kathy Najimy, Sarah Jessica Parker, Thora Birch, Doug Jones, Omri Katz, Vinessa Shaw, Stephanie Faracy, Charles Rocket; ***Cameos:*** Penny Marshall, Garry Marshall; ***D:*** Kenny Ortega; ***W:*** Neil Cuthbert, Mick Garris; ***M:*** John Debney.

Hoffa ✓✓✓ **1992 (R)** The story of union organizer James R. Hoffa, who oversaw the rise of the Teamsters, a labor union composed mostly of truck drivers, from its fledgling infancy during the Great Depression to a membership of two million by the 1970s. Powerful performances by Nicholson in the title role and DeVito, who plays a union aide, a fictitious composite of several men who actually served Hoffa. This almost affectionate biographical treatment stands out in contrast from a career bristling with tension and violence. Proceeds through a series of flashbacks from the day Hoffa disappeared, July 30, 1975. **140m/C VHS, DVD.** Jack Nicholson, Danny DeVito, Armand Assante, J.T. Walsh, Frank Whaley, Kevin Anderson, John P. Ryan, Robert Prosky, Natalija Nogulich, Nicholas Pryor, John C. Reilly, Karen Young, Cliff Gorman, Paul Guilfoyle, Jennifer Nicholson, Richard Schiff; ***D:*** Danny DeVito; ***W:*** David Mamet; ***C:*** Stephen Burum; ***M:*** David Newman.

Hoffman ✓ 1/2 **1970** Lonely, middle-aged business Benjamin Hoffman (Sellers) has a yen for his secretary Janet (Cusack). When he discovers her boyfriend Tom (Mitchell) is involved in some illegal activities, Hoffman blackmails her into spending the weekend with him. Very minor Sellers and not very funny. Gebler adapted from his own novel. **113m/C VHS, DVD.** *GB* Peter Sellers, Sinead Cusack, Jeremy Bulloch; ***D:*** Alvin Rakoff; ***W:*** Ernest Gebler; ***C:*** Gerry Turpin; ***M:*** Ron Grainer.

Hog Wild ✓ 1/2 **1980 (PG)** A clique of high school nerds exact revenge on bullies from the local mean motorcycle gang, and a girl is torn between the two factions. **97m/C VHS.** *CA* Patti D'Arbanville, Tony Rosato, Michael Biehn; ***D:*** Les Rose.

Hogfather ✓✓ 1/2 **2006** Adapted from the 20th book in Terry Pratchett's Discworld series, this is a more-or-less stand-alone Christmas story. It's the night before Hogswatch, the mid-winter festival where the Hogfather delivers presents to the kiddies. But the wraith-like Auditors have decided that Discworld's humans are destroying their perfect vision of the universe. They want assassin Mr. Teatime to eliminate Hogfather and destroy the idea of hope in the world. But Death decides to take over for the missing Hogfather while his granddaughter Susan investigates. **189m/C DVD.** *GB* David Jason, Joss Ackland, Marc Warren, David Warner, Michelle Dockery; ***D:*** Vadim Jean; ***W:*** Vadim Jean; ***C:*** Gavin Finney, Jan Pester; ***M:*** David A. Hughes; ***V:*** Ian Richardson. **TV**

The Holcroft Covenant ✓✓ **1985 (R)** Based upon the complex Robert Ludlum novel. Details the efforts of a man trying to release a secret fund that his Nazi father humanistically set up to relieve the future sufferings of Holocaust survivors. Confusing, and slow, but interesting, nonetheless. **112m/C VHS, DVD.** *GB* Michael Caine, Victoria Tennant, Anthony Andrews, Lilli Palmer, Mario Adorf, Michael (Michel) Lonsdale; ***D:*** John Frankenheimer; ***W:*** Edward Anhalt, John Hopkins, George Axelrod.

Hold 'Em Jail ✓✓ 1/2 **1932** Some good laughs with Wheeler and Woolsey starting a competitive football team at Kennedy's Bidemore Prison. **65m/B VHS.** Bert Wheeler, Robert Woolsey, Edgar Kennedy, Betty Grable, Edna May Oliver; ***D:*** Norman Taurog.

Hold Me, Thrill Me, Kiss Me ✓✓ 1/2 **1993 (R)** "Offbeat" barely begins to describe this comedy about a hapless loser who finds true love. Eli (Parrish) has escaped marriage to a rich girl named Twinkle (Young), unfortunately it took a little shooting to do it and now Eli's hiding out in a tacky pink trailer park where Sabra (Naschak), an insatiable stripper with a fondness for sex toys, immediately goes after Eli's bod. But he falls for her naive (and virginal) sister, Dannie (Shelly). Hershman manages to keep all the free-wheeling goings on under control. Film debut of former model Parrish; directorial debut feature of Hershman. **92m/C VHS.** Max Parrish, Adrienne Shelly, Andrea Naschak, Sean Young, Diane Ladd, Bela Lehoczky, Ania Suli; ***Cameos:*** Timothy Leary; ***D:*** Joel Hershman; ***W:*** Joel Hershman; ***C:*** Kent Wakeford; ***M:*** Gerald Gouriet.

Hold That Ghost ✓✓✓ *Oh, Charlie* **1941** Abbott and Costello inherit an abandoned roadhouse where the illicit loot of its former owner, a "rubbed out" mobster, is supposedly hidden. **86m/B VHS, DVD.** Bud Abbott, Lou Costello, Joan Davis, Richard Carlson, Mischa Auer, The Andrews Sisters, Shemp Howard, Evelyn Ankers, Nestor Paiva; ***D:*** Arthur Lubin; ***W:*** Robert Lees, Frederic Rinaldo, John Grant; ***C:*** Elwood "Woody" Bredell; ***M:*** Hans J. Salter.

Hold the Dream ✓✓ 1/2 **1986** Barbara Taylor Bradford's sequel to "A Woman of Substance." Kerr plays the adult Emma Harte while Seagrove, who played young Emma in the original miniseries, now plays her granddaughter Paula, who has been chosen to take over the family's retailing empire. But will her ambitions clash with her romantic possibilities? **200m/C VHS, DVD.** Jenny Seagrove, Deborah Kerr, Claire Bloom, James Brolin, Stephen Collins, Nicholas Farrell, Nigel Havers, John Mills, Liam Neeson, Valentine Pelka; ***D:*** Don Sharp; ***C:*** John Coquillon; ***M:*** Barrie Guard. **TV**

Hold Your Man ✓✓✓ **1933** Great star vehicle that turns from comedy to drama with Harlow falling for hustler Gable. Harlow and Gable are at their best in this unlikely story of a crooked couple. Direction drags at times, but snappy dialogue and the stars' personalities more than make up for it. **86m/B VHS.** Jean Harlow, Clark Gable, Stuart Erwin, Dorothy Burgess, Garry Owen, Paul Hurst, Elizabeth Patterson, Laura La Plante; ***D:*** Sam Wood; ***W:*** Anita Loos, Howard Emmett Rogers.

Holding Trevor ✓ 1/2 **2007 (R)** Disaffected 20-somethings try to find meaning in their L.A. lives. Trevor dutifully takes his heroin-addicted boyfriend Darrell to the hospital when he overdoses again. Once he finds out Darrell will be okay, Trevor decides he's done with the drama and turns to intern Ephram for stability. But when Trevor and his friends, alcoholic Andie and promiscuous Jake, decide to throw a party, it turns out to be an unexpectedly dramatic affair. **88m/C DVD.** Brent Gorski, Eli Ktanski, Melissa Searing, Jay Brannan; ***D:*** Christopher Wyllie, Rosser Goodman; ***W:*** Brent Gorski; ***C:*** Kara Stephens.

The Hole ✓✓ *The Last Dance; Dong* **1998** Originally conceived as an entry for a French TV series of end-of-the-millennium dramas, this award-winning film crosses several genres and might not be immediately accessible to most. Seven days before the end of the 21st century the rain simply will not let up, and a new virus is causing odd mutations in behavior (and sometimes bodies). Despite evacuation orders the tenants of one run down apartment building stay, and indulge in stockpiling toilet paper, performing odd musical numbers, and pretending to be roaches. If you like weird, drawn-out art films, this is for you. **95m/C DVD.** *FR* Kang-sheng Lee, Tien Miao, Kuei-Mei Yang, Hui-Chin Lin, Hsiang-Chu Tong; ***D:*** Ming-liang Tsai; ***W:*** Ming-liang Tsai, Pi-ying Yang; ***C:*** Pen-jung Liao; ***M:*** Grace Chang.

The Hole ✓ 1/2 **2001** Teen psycho-drama offers cheap thrills. A terrified Liz (Birch) is discovered to be the only survivor of four students who have been missing for 18 days. Liz talks to psychologist Philippa Horwood (Davidtz) as flashbacks reveal the nightmare. Liz has a crush on Mike (Harrington), which she revealed to confidante Martin (Brocklebank), who has an unrequited crush on her. Seeking to escape a school trip, Liz persuades Martin to let her and Mike and their friends Geoff (Fox) and Frankie (Knightley) spend the time in a disused WWII underground steel bunker he's discovered. Only jealous Martin locks them in. Or does he? Liz's story is full of holes and the police investigation offers another theory of what happened. Based on the novel "After the Hole" by Guy Burt. **102m/C VHS, DVD.** *GB* Thora Birch, Desmond Harrington, Embeth Davidtz, Daniel Brocklebank, Keira Knightley, Steven Waddington, Laurence Fox; ***D:*** Nick Hamm; ***W:*** Ben Court, Caroline Ip; ***C:*** Denis Crossan; ***M:*** Clint Mansell.

A Hole in One ✓✓ **2004** It's not about golf. Anna (Williams) is a sweet but troubled small-town girl in the 1950s whose boyfriend is the pathologically jealous and violent Billy (Aday). Emotionally fragile, Anna becomes convinced that the way out of her troubles is to undergo that ice pick cure-all—a lobotomy—at the hands of crackpot Dr. Ashton (Raymond). Billy ropes in diffident employee Tom (Guinee) to pose as a rival doc and dissuade Anna but the twosome end up falling in love. **97m/C DVD.** Michelle Williams, Meat Loaf Aday, Tim Guinee, Bill Raymond, Wendell Pierce; ***D:*** Richard Ledes; ***W:*** Richard Ledes; ***C:*** Stephen Kazmierski; ***M:*** Stephen Trask.

A Hole in the Head ✓✓ 1/2 **1959** A comedy-drama about a shiftless but charming lout who tries to raise money to save his hotel from foreclosure and learn to be responsible for his young son. Notable for the introduction of the song "High Hopes." ♫High Hopes; All My Tomorrows. **120m/C VHS, DVD.** Frank Sinatra, Edward G. Robinson, Thelma Ritter, Carolyn Jones, Eleanor Parker, Eddie Hodges, Keenan Wynn, Joi Lansing; ***D:*** Frank Capra; ***W:*** Arnold Schulman; ***C:*** William H. Daniels. Oscars '59: Song ("High Hopes").

Hole in the Sky ✓✓ 1/2 *The Ranger, The Cook and a Hole in the Sky* **1995 (PG)** Teenaged Mac (O'Connell) is working for the Montana forestry service in the summer of 1919 under the tutelage of taciturn legend Bill Bell (a mustache-less Elliott). Mac learns some lessons about growing up, first love, card-playing—and never to rile the camp cook. Based on an autobiographical story by Norman MacLean. Made for TV; filmed on location in British Columbia. **94m/C VHS, DVD.** Sam Elliott, Jerry O'Connell, Ricky Jay, Molly Parker; ***D:*** John Kent Harrison; ***W:*** Robert W. Lenski. **TV**

The Holes ✓✓ 1/2 *Les Gaspards* **1972 (PG)** A Parisian book shop owner's daughter vanishes along with other local citizens and American tourists, and he decides to investigate when the police won't. In French with subtitles. **92m/C VHS, DVD.** *FR* Philippe Noiret, Charles Denner, Michel Serrault, Gerard Depardieu; ***D:*** Pierre Tchernia; ***W:*** Pierre Tchernia, Rene Goscinny; ***C:*** Jean Tournier; ***M:*** Gerard Calvi.

Holes 🦴🦴🦴 ½ **2003 (PG)** Poor Stanley Yelnats VI. As a result of a family curse, he's just been convicted of a crime he didn't commit and sent to a juvenile facility in the middle of the Texas desert. While there, he's met with a nasty overseer, Mr. Sir (Voight, at his best), a proverb-spouting counselor (Nelson), and scariest of all, the Warden (Weaver) an intimidating figure who makes the kids dig holes in the desert to "build character." She's really looking for an Old West outlaw's treasure, and her ancestors' past may be connected to Stanley's family. Faithfully adapted by Sachar, from his own award-winning children's book, the movie keeps all the elements that make the book so popular with the early adolescent crowd: it doesn't talk down to the audience, it has an involving, complex plot, the characters are not caricatures, and it handles real issues with honesty. You won't find that in many movies aimed at any age nowadays. **111m/C VHS, DVD.** *US* Sigourney Weaver, Jon Voight, Patricia Arquette, Shia LaBeouf, Tim Blake Nelson, Dule Hill, Henry Winkler, Nathan Davis, Khleo Thomas, Jake M. Smith, Byron Cotton, Brendan Jefferson, Miguel Castro, Max Kasch, Noah Poletiek, Rick Fox, Scott Plank, Roma Maffia, Eartha Kitt, Siobhan Fallon Hogan; ***D:*** Andrew Davis; ***W:*** Louis Sachar; ***C:*** Stephen St. John; ***M:*** Joel McNeely.

Holiday 🦴🦴🦴 ½ *Free to Live; Unconventional Linda* **1938** The classically genteel screwball comedy about a rich girl who steals her sister's fiance. A yardstick in years to come for sophisticated, urbane Hollywood romanticism. Based on the play by Philip Barry who later wrote "The Philadelphia Story." **93m/B VHS, DVD.** Cary Grant, Katharine Hepburn, Doris Nolan, Edward Everett Horton, Ruth Donnelly, Lew Ayres, Binnie Barnes; ***D:*** George Cukor; ***W:*** Donald Ogden Stewart, Sidney Buchman.

The Holiday 🦴🦴 ½ **2006 (PG-13)** Chick romance lite. LA careerist Amanda (Diaz) has just discovered her boyfriend (Burns) cheating; London journalist Iris (Winslet) loves Jasper (Sewell), who's just announced his engagement. Naturally, Christmas joy is the furthest thing from their minds, until, thanks to an Internet site, the two women decide to swaps digs for the holidays. Iris gets Beverly Hills luxury and Amanda gets cozy, snowy English countryside cottage. At least the cottage is soon adorned with Iris's oh-so-attractive brother Graham (Law). Back in LA, Iris is stuck with goofy romancer Miles (Black). Well, three out of four attractive, charming characters is pretty good and Black is at least low-key (although that crazy gleam in his eye should give Iris pause). Happy holidays to all. **135m/C DVD, Blu-ray Disc.** *US* Cameron Diaz, Kate Winslet, Jude Law, Jack Black, Eli Wallach, Edward Burns, Rufus Sewell, Shannyn Sossamon, Bill Macy, Shelley Berman, Kathryn Hahn, John Krasinski; ***D:*** Nancy Meyers; ***W:*** Nancy Meyers; ***C:*** Dean Cundey; ***M:*** Hans Zimmer.

Holiday Affair 🦴🦴 ½ **1949** Hollywood yuletide charmer about a pretty widow being courted by two very different men. **86m/B VHS.** Robert Mitchum, Janet Leigh, Griff Barnett, Wendell Corey, Esther Dale, Henry O'Neill, Harry (Henry) Morgan, Larry J. Blake; ***D:*** Don Hartman.

Holiday Affair 🦴🦴 ½ **1996** Remake of the 1949 film finds Manhattan department store clerk Steve Mason (Elliott) intrigued by widowed mom Jodie Ennis (Gibb). Although she inadvertently gets him fired, Steve still expresses interest in Jodie and her son. But Jodie's accepted the marriage proposal of regular guy boyfriend Paul (Irwin) because he offers her security. It's up to Jodie's son Timmy (Blanck) and some Christmastime truthfulness to get Jodie to see the light. **93m/C VHS.** David James Elliott, Cynthia Gibb, Curtis Blanck, Tom Irwin, Al Waxman, Patricia Hamilton, Victor Ertmanis, Pam Hyatt; ***D:*** Alan Myerson; ***M:*** Lee Holdridge. **CABLE**

Holiday Heart 🦴🦴 **2000 (R)** Macho big man Rhames may not be the first actor to spring to mind to play a drag queen but he does a fine job in this melodramatic adaptation of the play by West. Holiday Heart (Rhames) comes to the rescue of ex-addict Wanda (Woodard) who has a 12-year-old daughter, Niki (Reynolds), and lousy taste in men. Wanda just can't make that final break with her dealer boyfriend Silas (Williamson), even though it leads to her sliding back into crack addiction and means that Heart has to draw on his maternal skills to give Niki a stable home. **97m/C VHS, DVD.** Ving Rhames, Alfre Woodard, Mykelti Williamson, Jesika Reynolds; ***D:*** Robert Kevin Townsend; ***W:*** Cheryl L. West; ***C:*** Jan Kiesser; ***M:*** Stephen James Taylor. **CABLE**

Holiday Hotel 🦴🦴 **1977 (R)** A group of wild French vacationers let loose at their favorite little resort hotel along the Brittany coast. Available in French with English subtitles or dubbed into English. **109m/C VHS.** *FR* Sophie Barjac, Daniel Ceccaldi; ***D:*** Michael (Michel) Lang.

Holiday in Handcuffs 🦴🦴 ½ **2007** Struggling waitress Trudie (Hart) goes a little nuts when dumped by her boyfriend right before the holidays. Desperate to make Christmas perfect and have her family believe that everything is going her way, Trudie kidnaps customer Clay (Lopez) and takes him home with her to pass off as her new beau. Rather than calling the cops, Clay eventually decides to go along and you know what happens next in this ABC Family movie. **90m/C DVD.** Melissa Joan Hart, Mario Lopez, June Lockhart, Markie Post, Timothy Bottoms, Kyle Howard, Vanessa Evigan; ***D:*** Ron Underwood; ***W:*** Sara Endsley; ***C:*** Derick Underschultz; ***M:*** Danny Lux. **CABLE**

Holiday in Havana 🦴🦴 **1949** Desi Arnaz is back in Cuba winning hearts and dance contests. Watch only for Desi's presence. ♫Holiday in Havana; The Arnaz Jam; Straw Hat Song; Rhumba Rumbero; Copacobana; Made For Each Other; I'll Take Romance. **73m/B VHS.** Desi Arnaz Sr., Lolita Valdez, Mary Hatcher, Ann Doran; ***D:*** Jean Yarbrough.

Holiday in Mexico 🦴🦴 ½ **1946** Pidgeon plays the U.S. ambassador to Mexico whose teenage daughter (Powell) tries to run his life along with his household. He falls for a singer while she develops a crush on an older, respected pianist (Iturbi playing himself). Lots of lively production numbers featuring Xavier Cugat and his orchestra. ♫I Think Of You; Walter Winchell Rhumba; Yo Te Amo Mucho—And That's That; And Dreams Remain; Holiday in Mexico; Ave Maria; Les Filles de Cadiz; Italian Street Song; Polonaise in A Flat Major. **127m/C VHS.** Walter Pidgeon, Jane Powell, Ilona Massey, Jose Iturbi, Roddy McDowall, Xavier Cugat, Hugo Haas; ***D:*** George Sidney; ***W:*** Isobel Lennart; ***C:*** Harry Stradling Sr.; ***M:*** Georgie Stoll.

Holiday Inn 🦴🦴🦴 **1942** Fred Astaire and Bing Crosby are rival song-and-dance men who decide to work together to turn a Connecticut farm into an inn, open only on holidays. Remade in 1954 as "White Christmas." ♫White Christmas; Be Careful, It's My Heart; Plenty to Be Thankful For; Abraham, Abraham; Let's Say It With Firecrackers; I Gotta Say I Love You Cause I Can't Tell A Lie; Let's Start the New Year Right; Happy Holidays; Song of Freedom. **101m/B VHS, DVD.** Bing Crosby, Fred Astaire, Marjorie Reynolds, Walter Abel, Virginia Dale; ***D:*** Mark Sandrich. Oscars '42: Song ("White Christmas").

Holiday Rhythm 🦴 ½ **1950** A TV promoter is knocked out and dreams of a worldwide trip full of entertainment, comedy, and insanity. **61m/B VHS.** Mary Beth Hughes, Tex Ritter, David Street, Donald MacBride; ***D:*** Jack Scholl; ***W:*** Lee Wainer; ***C:*** Benjamin (Ben H.) Kline; ***M:*** Bert Shefter.

The Hollow 🦴 ½ **2004 (R)** Updated remake of the classic Legend of Sleepy Hollow. Ian (Zegers), who is the great-great-grandson of Ichabod Crane, moves to town. Once he learns of his lineage, chaos ensues for the teens of Sleepy Hollow on Halloween eve, and it's up to Ian to settle the score with the Headless Horseman. Love interest Karen (Cuoco), nemesis Brody (Carter) and Claus Van Ripper (Keach) are among the cast. Strangely enough this film first aired on the ABC Family channel in 2004, though the violence would preclude many families from watching it. **82m/C DVD.** Kevin Zegers, Kaley Cuoco, Nick Carter, Ben Scott, Stacy Keach, Judge Reinhold, Nicholas Turturro, Eileen Brennan; ***D:*** Kyle Newman; ***W:*** Hans Rodionoff; ***C:*** Scott Kevan; ***M:*** Todd Haberman. **CABLE**

Hollow City 🦴🦴 *Na Cidade Vazia; In the Empty City* **2004** A group of children, fleeing the Angolan civil war, are taken to the capitol of Luanda by a nun. Young N'Dala (Roldan) leaves the group to explore the city and he meets a variety of characters who seek to influence his life. Portuguese with subtitles. **90m/C DVD.** *PT* Joao Roldan, Custado Francisco, Carlao Machado; ***D:*** Maria Joao Ganga; ***W:*** Maria Joao Ganga; ***C:*** Jacques Besse; ***M:*** Manu Dibango, Ne Goncalves.

Hollow Gate **1988** Trick or Treat?? Four kids find out when they run into a guy with hungry dogs. **90m/C VHS, DVD.** Katrina Alexy, Richard Dry, Patricia Jacques, Addison Randall; ***D:*** Ray Di Zazzo; ***W:*** Ray Di Zazzo; ***C:*** Vojislav Mikulic; ***M:*** John Gonzales.

Hollow Man 🦴🦴 **2000 (R)** Scientist Caine (Bacon) heads a team that discovers the ability to make humans invisible. He decides to test it on himself and the process works, in fact it's irreversible, and his newfound power has unexpected side effects when he gives into his worst impulses and terrorizes his colleagues, including ex-girlfriend Linda (Shue) and her new beau (Brolin). Stunning visual effects can't hide script's lack of imagination and creepy sexual kink. Degenerates into body-count slasher flick as the intriguing moral questions are dropped in favor of cheap scares. **114m/C VHS, DVD, Blu-ray Disc, UMD.** Kevin Bacon, Elisabeth Shue, Josh Brolin, William Devane, Kim Dickens, Greg Grunberg, Mary Jo Randle, Joey Slotnick; ***D:*** Paul Verhoeven; ***W:*** Andrew Marlowe; ***C:*** Jost Vacano; ***M:*** Jerry Goldsmith.

Hollow Man 2 🦴 ½ **2006 (R)** Volunteer soldier/assassin Michael Griffin (Slater) goes mad when he becomes invisible thanks to a research project. He needs certain drugs to stay alive so Michael goes after scientist Maggie Dalton (Regan), who's being protected by cop Frank Turner (Facinelli). Slater has little actual screen time since his character's invisible and does mostly voice work. **91m/C DVD.** Christian Slater, Peter Facinelli, Laura Regan, David McIlwraith, Sarah Deakins, William Macdonald; ***D:*** Claudio Fah; ***W:*** Joel Soisson; ***C:*** Peter Wunstorf; ***M:*** Marcus Trump. **VIDEO**

Hollow Point 🦴🦴 **1995 (R)** After FBI agent Diane Norwood (Carrere) and DEA agent Max Perish (Griffith) get in each other's way, they reluctantly team up to bring down crime kingpin Oleg Krezinsky (Hemblen). Only Krezinsky and his partner Livingston (Lithgow) learns she's a fed and hire assassin Lawton (Sutherland) to teach her a lesson. **103m/C VHS, DVD.** Thomas Ian Griffith, Tia Carrere, John Lithgow, Donald Sutherland, David Hemblen; ***D:*** Sidney J. Furie; ***C:*** David Franco; ***M:*** Brahm Wenger.

Hollow Reed 🦴🦴🦴 *Believe Me* **1995** Heart-wrenching, though not maudlin, drama revolves around nine-year-old Oliver Wyatt (Bould). His parents, Martyn (Donovan) and Hannah (Richardson), have bitterly divorced after Martyn finally acknowledges his homosexuality and moves in with his lover, Tom (Hart). Hannah's new live-in boyfriend Frank (Flemyng) turns out to be abusive towards Oliver, who's reluctant to say anything to destroy his mother's new happiness. But when Martyn discovers what's happening, he instigates a custody battle for his son that has everyone at each other's throats, with the terrified Oliver caught in the crossfire. Compelling performances. **105m/C VHS.** *GB* Martin Donovan, Joely Richardson, Ian Hart, Jason Flemyng, Sam Bould, Edward Hardwicke, Annette Badland, Douglas Hodge; ***D:*** Angela Pope; ***W:*** Paula Milne; ***C:*** Remi Adefarasin; ***M:*** Anne Dudley.

Holly 🦴🦴 **2007 (R)** American ex-pat gambler Patrick (Livingston) is working in Phnom Penh when he's contacted by criminal buddy Freddie (Penn) to move stolen artifacts across the border. Patrick's motorcycle breaks down in a red-light district and he spends the night in one of the brothels, which is where he meets 12-year-old Holly (Nguyen). She's been sold by her Vietnamese family into the sex trade and the madam is just waiting for the right customer so she can sell the girl's virginity for a high price. Spending (platonic) time with the damaged Holly gives Patrick the urge to rescue her. English, Khmer, and Vietnamese with subtitles. **114m/C DVD.** Ron Livingston, Christopher Penn, Udo Kier, Virginie Ledoyen, Thuy Nguyen; ***D:*** Guy Moshe; ***W:*** Guy Moshe, Guy Jacobsen; ***C:*** Yaron Orbach; ***M:*** Ton That Tiet.

Hollywood after Dark 🦴 **1965** McClanahan plays a young starlet trying to make it big in Hollywood. Pure exploitation schlock. Not released theatrically until 1968. **74m/C VHS.** Anthony (Tony) Vorno, Rue McClanahan, Paul Bruce, Ernest Macias, John Barrick; ***D:*** John Patrick Hayes; ***W:*** John Patrick Hayes; ***C:*** Vilis Lapenieks; ***M:*** Bill Marx.

Hollywood Boulevard 🦴🦴 ½ **1976 (R)** Behind-the-scenes glimpse of shoestring-budget movie making offers comical sex, violence, sight gags, one-liners, comedy bits, and mock-documentary footage. Commander Cody and His Lost Planet Airmen are featured. **93m/C VHS, DVD.** Candice Rialson, Mary Woronov, Rita George, Jonathan Kaplan, Jeffrey Kramer, Dick Miller, Paul Bartel, Charles B. Griffith, Richard Doran; ***D:*** Joe Dante, Allan Arkush; ***W:*** Patrick Hobby; ***C:*** Jamie Anderson; ***M:*** Andrew Stein.

Hollywood Boulevard 2 🦴 **1989 (R)** A "B" movie studio finds its top actresses being killed off and terror reigns supreme as the mystery grows more intense. Could that psycho-bimbo from outer space have something to do with it? **82m/C VHS.** Ginger Lynn Allen, Kelly Monteith, Eddie Deezen, Ken Wright, Steve Vinovich, Mindi Miller; ***D:*** Steve Barnett.

Hollywood Canteen 🦴🦴🦴🦴 **1944** Star-studded extravaganza with just about every Warner Bros. lot actor in this tribute to love and nationalism. Lovesick G.I. Hutton falls for Leslie, wins a date with her in a phony raffle set up at the Hollywood Canteen, and the sparks fly right away. But he thinks she tricked him as he boards his train and she's not there to see him off. Lame story is redeemed by the talented cast and wonderful musical numbers which make this picture fly with charm and style. Before production began there were arguments over "unpatriotic" actors—labeled as such due to their lack of participation in this, and other similar movies produced at the time. ♫Don't Fence Me In; Sweet Dreams, Sweetheart; You Can Always Tell A Yank; We're Having a Baby; What Are You Doin' the Rest of Your Life; The General Jumped At Dawn; Gettin' Corns For My Country; Voodoo Moon; Tumblin' Tumbleweeds. **124m/B VHS.** Robert Hutton, Dane Clark, Janis Paige, Jonathan Hale, Barbara Brown, James Flavin, Eddie Marr, Ray Teal, Bette Davis, Joan Leslie, Jack Benny, Jimmy Dorsey, Joan Crawford, John Garfield, Barbara Stanwyck, Ida Lupino, Eddie Cantor, Jack Carson, Eleanor Parker, Alexis Smith, S.Z. Sakall, Peter Lorre, Sydney Greenstreet, Helmut Dantine; ***D:*** Delmer Daves; ***W:*** Delmer Daves.

Hollywood Cavalcade 🦴🦴 ½ **1939** This Technicolor Fox drama is basically the Hollywoodized story of director Mack Sennett and actress Mabel Normand. Silent screen director Michael Linnett Connors (Ameche) discovers Molly Adair (Faye) and offers her a sweet movie deal, making her a comic star in her first film opposite Buster Keaton (playing himself). Molly loves Connors but he's too wrapped up in his career to notice so she eventually marries co-star Nicky Hayden (Curtis). Connors notices that and fires them both. While their careers rise, Connors's goes on the skids until Molly offers him another chance. A number of Sennett's (who also appears) original silent stars have cameos. **100m/C DVD.** Alice Faye, Don Ameche, Alan Curtis, J. Edward Bromberg, Stuart Erwin, Donald Meek, Jed Prouty, Russell Hicks, Irving Cummings; ***D:*** Irving Cummings; ***W:*** Ernest Pascal; ***C:*** Ernest Palmer, Allen Davey.

Hollywood Chainsaw Hookers 🦴🦴 **1988 (R)** A campy, sexy, very bloody parody about attractive prostitutes who dismember their unsuspecting customers. **90m/C VHS, DVD.** Linnea Quigley, Gunnar Hansen, Jay Richardson, Michelle (McClellan) Bauer, Dawn Wildsmith, Dennis Mooney, Jerry Fox; ***D:*** Fred Olen Ray; ***W:*** Fred Olen Ray, T.L. Lankford; ***C:*** Scott Ressler; ***M:*** Michael Perilstein.

Hollywood Chaos 🦴 ½ **1989** Director Ballantine's stars quit his production before it even starts, so he gets the next best thing—star look-alikes. However, his problems are just beginning. One of his new "stars" is kidnapped, and his reclusive stage manager is hunted as the object of desire for a female motorcycle gang. **90m/C VHS.** Carl Ballantine, Tricia Leigh Fisher, Kathleen Freeman; ***D:*** Sean McNamara.

Hollywood Confidential 1997 **(R)** TV movie stars Olmos as former LAPD cop Stan Navarro, who now runs a struggling detective agency specializing in the seamier sides of Hollywood. His latest cases involve getting dirt on a studio acting coach, seeing if a bartender at the newest hotspot is skimming the receipts, and "persuading" the mistress of a well-known director to take a hike. **90m/C VHS, DVD.** Edward James Olmos, Anthony Yerkovich, Rick Aiello, Richard T. Jones, Charlize Theron, Angela Alvarado, Christina Harnos, Thomas Jane, Amanda Pays; ***D:*** Reynaldo Villalobos; ***W:*** Anthony Yerkovich; ***C:*** Reynaldo Villalobos; ***M:*** Marc Bonilla. **TV**

Hollywood Cop 1/2 1987 **(R)** A tough cop in Hollywood goes up against the mob for the sake of a kidnapped boy. **101m/C VHS.** Jim Mitchum, David Goss, Cameron Mitchell, Troy Donahue, Aldo Ray; ***D:*** Amir Shervan.

Hollywood Cowboy *Wings Over Wyoming* **1937** A western involving gangsters, airplanes, and the movies. Movie cowboy Jeff Carson (O'Brien) is on vacation when he stumbles across Chicago gangster Kramer (Middleton) and his goons. Kramer is trying to expand his territory into Wyoming by running a cattlemen's protection racket using a plane buzzing grazing land to run off the cows. When Kramer threatens rancher Violet Butler (Esburne) and her niece Joyce (Parker), whom Carson is sweet on, he uses the skills he's learned in the movies to become a real hero instead of just a reel hero. **62m/B DVD.** George O'Brien, Cecilia Parker, Charles Middleton, Lee Shumway, Frank Milan, Maude Esburne, Joe Caits; ***D:*** Ewing Scott; ***W:*** Ewing Scott, Daniel Jarrett; ***C:*** Frank B. Good.

The Hollywood Detective 1989 **(PG)** An average TV movie that spoofs "Kojak." A TV detective tries it out for real, and gets into troubles for which he can't pause "for a message from our sponsor." **88m/C VHS.** Telly Savalas, Helene Udy, George Coe, Joe Dallesandro, Tom Reese; ***D:*** Kevin Connor. **TV**

Hollywood Dreams 1/2 1994 **(R)** Starlet on the Hollywood casting couch saga of a midwestern gal that comes to California with dreams of making it big. **90m/C VHS, DVD.** Kelly Cook, Danny Smith, Debra Beatty; ***D:*** Ralph Portillo.

Hollywood Ending 2002 **(PG-13)** Allen continues two recent disturbing trends: making mediocre comedies, and making creepy casting choices when picking his female leads. This time he's Val Waxman, a a down-on-his-luck, nuerotic director about ten years past his prime with a hot ex-wife, Ellie (Leoni) who's engaged to a smarmy studio head (Williams). He's also managed to snag a hot dim-bulb wannabe-actress girlfriend (Messing). When Ellie uses her connections to get Val a job directing an "Ode to New York" pic, his hypochodriac tendencies go into haywire and he goes blind. Woody's made some great comedies in the past, and if this was 10-15 years ago, this one might've been great, too. But his overwhelmingly annoying screen persona, and the missed execution of some pretty good setups, this one goes to the forgettable file. Leoni, Williams, and Rydell do well with what they're given. **114m/C VHS, DVD.** *US* Woody Allen, Tea Leoni, Treat Williams, Debra Messing, George Hamilton, Tiffani(-Amber) Thiessen, Mark Rydell, Isaac Mizrahi, Marian Seldes, Peter Gerety, Greg Mottola, Mark Webber, Lu Yu, Barney Cheng, Jodie Markell; ***D:*** Woody Allen; ***W:*** Woody Allen; ***C:*** Wedigo von Schultzendorff.

Hollywood Harry *Harry's Machine* **1986 (PG-13)** A private-eye mystery/parody, about an inept detective who searches for a missing porn actress. **99m/C VHS.** Robert Forster, Kathrine (Kate) Forster, Joe Spinell, Shannon Wilcox; ***D:*** Robert Forster; ***W:*** Curt Allen.

Hollywood Heartbreak 1989 It's heartbreak in tinseltown for a young writer who's trying to pitch his movie script but winds up defending himself from slimy agents and persistent starlets. Another entry for Bartlett's familiar plotlines. **90m/C VHS.** Mark Moses, Carol Mayo Jenkins, Ron Karabatsos, Richard Romanus, James LeGros; ***D:*** Lance Dickson.

Hollywood High 1977 **(R)** Four attractive teen couples converge on the mansion of an eccentric silent-film star for an unusual vacation experience in this teenage skin flick. Followed by a sequel. **81m/C VHS.** Marcy Albrecht, Sherry Hardin, Rae Sperling, Susanne Kevin Mead; ***D:*** Patrick Wright.

Hollywood High, Part 2 1981 **(R)** Ignored by their boyfriends for the lure of sun and surf, three comely high school students try their best to regain their interest. **86m/C VHS.** April May, Donna Lynn, Camille Warner, Lee Thomburg; ***D:*** Caruth C. Byrd.

Hollywood Homicide 2003 **(PG-13)** In 2003, director Shelton released the hard-edged corrupt cop film "Dark Blue." And then this buddy cop comedy. The first works, this doesn't (much), although the premise had possibilities. Veteran L.A. homicide detective Joe Gavilan (Ford) has three exwives, a couple of kids he never sees, money troubles thanks to his off-duty job peddling real estate, and an Internal Affairs investigator (Greenwood) dogging him. His dewy partner, K.C. Calden (Hartnett) isn't sure he even wants to be a detective—he'd rather be an actor. Meanwhile, he moonlights as a yoga instructor. Their on-and-off duty jobs collide as they investigate multiple homicides at a rap club. Ford's relaxed and grumpy; Hartnett's naive and cute but they don't have much rapport and the story's generally weak. **111m/C VHS, DVD.** *US* Harrison Ford, Josh Hartnett, Lena Olin, Master P, Bruce Greenwood, Keith David, Isaiah Washington IV, Lolita (David) Davidovich, Martin Landau, Dwight Yoakam, Kurupt, Lou Diamond Phillips, Gladys Knight, Meredith Scott Lynn, James MacDonald, Clyde Kusatsu, Frank Sinatra Jr., Smokey Robinson, Robert Wagner; ***Cameos:*** Eric Idle; ***D:*** Ron Shelton; ***W:*** Ron Shelton, Robert Souza; ***C:*** Barry Peterson; ***M:*** Alex Wurman.

Hollywood Hot Tubs 1984 **(R)** Teen sex romp has adolescent picking up some extra cash and a lot of fun repairing the hot tubs of the rich and famous. **103m/C VHS.** Donna McDaniel, Michael Andrew, Katt Shea, Paul Gunning, Edy Williams, Jewel Shepard; ***D:*** Chuck Vincent.

Hollywood Hot Tubs 2: Educating Crystal 1989 **(R)** A softcore comedy about a well-tanned ingenue learning about business in Hollywood during numerous hot tub trysts. **103m/C VHS.** Jewel Shepard, Patrick Day, Remy O'Neill, David Tiefen, Bart Braverman; ***D:*** Ken Raich.

Hollywood Hotel 1/2 1937 Singer/saxophonist Ronnie Bowers (Powell) wins a talent contest with a prize of a Hollywood film contract. When diva Mona (Lola Lane) refuses to attend her movie premiere, Ronnie escorts her stand-in Virginia (Rosemary Lane) and they fall in love. Ronnie learns he's dubbing the singing for actor Alex (Mowbray) in a film with Mona, but when Alex is supposed to sing on Louella Parson's radio program, Ronnie refuses to go along. Thanks to some showbiz maneuvers, Ronnie goes on the show himself and becomes a hit. The Berkeley-directed musical features Johnny Mercer's industry anthem "Hooray for Hollywood." **100m/B DVD.** Dick Powell, Rosemary Lane, Lola Lane, Alan Mowbray, Hugh Herbert, Ted Healy, Glenda Farrell, Mabel Todd, Lee Dixon; ***D:*** Busby Berkeley; ***W:*** Richard Macaulay, Jerry Wald, Johnnie Davis; ***C:*** George Barnes, Charles Rosher.

Hollywood in Trouble 1987 A bumbling middle-aged fool decides to break into the wacky movie-making business. **90m/C VHS.** Vic Vallard, Jean Levine, Jerry Tiffe, Pamela Dixon, Jerry Cleary; ***D:*** Joseph Merhi; ***W:*** Joseph Merhi; ***C:*** Bob Vose.

Hollywood, Je T'Aime *Hollywood, I Love You* **2009** Gay Frenchman Jerome Beaunez (Debets) goes on a solo Christmas vacation to L.A., vaguely deciding to try his luck as an actor in Hollywood to escape the romantic heartbreak of his life in Paris (those scenes are set in black-and-white). He makes a number of tourist mistakes, bewilderingly goes to auditions, and is taken under the wing of Silverlake drag queen Norma Desire (Airington) before realizing there's no place like home. The supporting characters are more colorful than the lead, who's at least likeable. English and French with subtitles. **95m/C DVD.** Eric Debets, Jonathan Blanc, Chad Allen, Michael Arlington, Diarra Kilpatrick; ***D:*** Jason Bushman; ***W:*** Jason Bushman; ***C:*** Alison Kelly; ***M:*** Timo Chen.

Hollywood Kills 1/2 2006 Horrible showbiz horror. Four struggling actors become pawns in a reclusive director/producer's sick games. He 'casts' them in a horror reality film that proves deadly. **90m/C DVD.** Dominic Keating, Zack (Zach) Ward, Happy Mahaney, Angela DiMarco, Matthew Scollon, Gillian Shure; ***D:*** Sven Pape; ***W:*** Nicholas Brandt; ***C:*** Dave Cramer; ***M:*** Gerhard Daum.

The Hollywood Knights 1980 **(R)** Cheap imitation of "American Graffiti" is not without its funny moments. Beverly Hills teens, lead by Newbomb Turk (Wuhl), are displeased that their hangout—Tubby's Drive-in—is being shut down by those no-fun adults. So they decide to retaliate. Set on Halloween Night, 1965. **91m/C VHS, DVD.** Robert Wuhl, Michelle Pfeiffer, Tony Danza, Fran Drescher, Leigh French, Gary (Rand) Graham, James Jeter, Stuart Pankin, Gailard Sartain, Mike Binder, T.K. Carter, Moosie Drier, Debra Feuer, Garry Goodrow, Joyce Hyser, Roberta Wallach, Doris Hargrave, Walter Janovitz, Art LaFleur, Glenn Withrow, Sandy Helberg; ***D:*** Floyd Mutrux; ***W:*** Floyd Mutrux; ***C:*** William A. Fraker.

Hollywood Man 1976 **(R)** A Hollywood actor wants to make his own film but when his financial support comes from the mob there's trouble ahead. **90m/C VHS.** William (Bill) Smith, Don Stroud, Jennifer Billingsley, Mary Woronov; ***D:*** Jack Starrett.

Hollywood Mystery 1/2 *Hollywood Hoodlum* **1934** A publicity agent stops at nothing to promote his would-be starlet girlfriend. **53m/B VHS, DVD.** June Clyde, Frank Albertson, Joe Crespo; ***D:*** B. Reeves Eason.

Hollywood North 1/2 2003 **(R)** Amusing satire on Canadian filmmaking when the government offered tax incentives for films made in Canada. Novice film producer Bobby Meyers (Modine) is trying to raise money to film a classic Canadian novel. But he needs a name actor and winds up with gun-toting paranoid Michael (Bates). Things just get worse—he's stuck with oversexed actress Gillian (Tilly), and numerous script changes turn Bobby's vision into something unrecognizable. All the while his trials are being documented by director Sandy (Unger). **89m/C VHS, DVD.** *CA* Matthew Modine, Alan Bates, Deborah Kara Unger, Jennifer Tilly, Alan Thicke, John Neville, Kim Coates, Clare Coulter, Joe Cobden, Saul Rubinek, Lindy Booth; ***D:*** Peter O'Brian; ***W:*** Barry Healey, John Hunter, Tony Johnston; ***C:*** Barry Stone; ***M:*** Terence Gowan, Blair Packham.

Hollywood or Bust 1/2 1956 The zany duo take their act on the road as they head for Tinsel Town in order to meet Lewis' dream girl Ekberg. This was the last film for the Martin & Lewis team and it's not the swan song their fans would have hoped for. **95m/C VHS.** Dean Martin, Jerry Lewis, Anita Ekberg, Pat(ricia) Crowley, Maxie "Slapsie" Rosenbloom, Willard Waterman; ***D:*** Frank Tashlin.

Hollywood Party 1/2 1934 Durante plays a film star who decides to throw a Hollywood bash. Any plot is incidental as it is mainly an excuse to have numerous stars of the day appear in brief comic bits or musical numbers. Mickey Mouse and the Big Bad Wolf of Disney fame also appear in color animated footage combined with live action. Numerous MGM directors worked on parts of the film but Dwan was given the task of trying to pull the various scenes together (he is uncredited onscreen). ♫Hollywood Party; Hello; Reincarnation; I've Had My Moments; Feeling High; Hot Chocolate Soldiers. **72m/B VHS.** Jimmy Durante, Stan Laurel, Oliver Hardy, Lupe Velez, Ted Healy, Moe Howard, Curly Howard, Larry Fine, Robert Young, Charles Butterworth, Polly Moran, George Givot, Tom Kennedy, Arthur Treacher; ***D:*** Allan Dwan, Richard Boleslawski; ***W:*** Howard Dietz, Arthur Kober; ***C:*** James Wong Howe; ***V:*** Walt Disney, Billy Bletcher.

Hollywood Revue of 1929 **1929** Whether or not the film is actually good is irrelevant (tastes obviously change) since it's a time capsule of the era's stars and popular bits. It was the first talkie showcase from MGM for a number of their previously silent stars, including comedians Laurel & Hardy and Buster Keaton, a dancing and singing Joan Crawford, and Norma Shearer and John Gilbert doing a Shakespeare spoof. There's also a big 'Singin' in the Rain' song and dance number. **118m/C DVD.** ***D:*** Charles Reisner; ***W:*** Al Boasberg, Robert Hopkins; ***C:*** John Arnold, Maximilian Fabian, Irving Reis.

Hollywood Safari 1/2 1996 **(PG)** Jane (Boone) and Troy (Leisure) Johnson train animals for the movies. But Kensho the mountain lion escapes into the woods after a transport accident and is eventually captured by the police who think it's the wild cat that recently attacked a local teen. The Johnsons try to prevent the sheriff's deputy (Savage) from having Kensho killed before they can prove their claims, but their best defense would be to find the renegade cougar. It's a pleasant enough time-waster, with Muddy, the Johnson's dog, providing some fine heroics. **89m/C VHS, DVD.** John Savage, Ted Jan Roberts, David Leisure, Debbie Boone, Ken Tigar, Don "The Dragon" Wilson; ***D:*** Henri Charr; ***W:*** Robert Newcastle; ***C:*** Guido Verweyen. **VIDEO**

Hollywood Shuffle 1/2 1987 **(R)** Townsend's autobiographical comedy about a struggling black actor in Hollywood trying to find work and getting nothing but stereotypical roles. Written, directed, financed by Townsend, who created this often clever and appealing film on a $100,000 budget. **81m/C VHS, DVD.** Robert Kevin Townsend, Anne-Marie Johnson, Starletta DuPois, Helen Martin, Keenen Ivory Wayans, Damon Wayans, Craigus R. Johnson, Eugene Robert Glazer; ***D:*** Robert Kevin Townsend; ***W:*** Robert Kevin Townsend, Keenen Ivory Wayans; ***C:*** Peter Deming; ***M:*** Patrice Rushen, Udi Harpaz.

The Hollywood Sign 2001 **(R)** Tom Greener (Berenger) and Kage Mulligan (Reynolds) have seen their acting careers fade away as has that of veteran actor Floyd Benson (Steiger). The three get together to drink and talk at the foot of the Hollywood sign where they happen to stumble across the body of a dead gangster. Doing some investigating, the trio discover a plot to steal millions from a Vegas casino. They include Tom's girlfriend Paula (Kim) in their plan to get the money, finance Paula's script, and jump start their careers. **93m/C VHS, DVD.** *US GE NL* Rod Steiger, Burt Reynolds, Tom Berenger, Jacqueline Kim, Al Sapienza, David Proval; ***Cameos:*** Garry Marshall; ***D:*** Soenke Wortmann; ***W:*** Leon de Winter; ***C:*** Wedigo von Schultzendorff; ***M:*** Peter Wolf.

Hollywood Stadium Mystery **1938** A boxer turns up dead before a big match and a D.A. investigates. Performances hold this one up, especially by Hamilton who later played Commissioner Gordon on TV's "Batman." **66m/B VHS, DVD.** Neil Hamilton, Evelyn Venable, Jimmy Wallington, Barbara Pepper, Lucien Littlefield, Lynne Roberts, Charles Williams, James Spottswood, Reed Hadley, Smiley Burnette; ***D:*** David Howard.

The Hollywood Strangler Meets the Skid Row Slasher **WOOF!** *The Model Killer* **1979 (R)** Voiced-over narration, canned music, and an unfathomable plot are but a few of this would-be fright fest's finer points. Uninhibited by any narrative connection, two terrors strike fear in the heart of Tinseltown. While a psycho photographer cruises L.A. taking pictures of models he subsequently strangles, a woman working in a bare-bums magazine store takes a stab (with a knife) at lowering the city's derelict population. There's a word for this sort of dribble, and it isn't versimilitude. Steckler used an alias (not surprisingly) for this one—Wolfgang Schmidt. **72m/C VHS.** Pierre Agostino, Carolyn Brandt, Forrest Duke, Chuck Alford; ***D:*** Ray Dennis Steckler, Ray Dennis Steckler.

Hollywood Vice Sqaud 1986 **(R)** Explores the lives of Hollywood police officers and the crimes they investigate. Contains three different storylines involving prostitution, child pornography, and organized crime. The film can't decide to be a comedy send-up of crime stories or a drama and is also crippled by a poor script. Written by the real-life chief of the Hollywood Vice Squad. **90m/C VHS, DVD.** Trish Van Devere, Ronny Cox, Frank Gorshin, Leon Isaac Kennedy, Carrie Fisher, Ben Frank, Robin Wright Penn; ***D:*** Penelope Spheeris; *W:* James J. Docherty; *M:* Michael Convertino.

Hollywood Zap WOOF! 1986 (R) Two losers, one a Southern orphan, the other a video game nut, hit Hollywood and engage in antics that are meant to be funny, but are actually tasteless. **85m/C VHS.** Ben Frank, Ivan E. Roth, De Waldron, Annie Gaybis, Chuck "Porky" Mitchell; *D:* David M. Cohen; *W:* David M. Cohen.

Hollywoodland 1/2 **2006 (R)** Low-rent detective Louis Simo (Brody) is hired by the mother (Smith) of actor George Reeves (Affleck) to investigate his suspicious death. In 1959, middle-aged Reeves allegedly shot himself in his bedroom—probably because of his failing career and his frustration at being typecast as TV's Superman. But Louis isn't so sure; George had dumped his longtime lover, fading beauty Toni Mannix (Lane), for young starlet Leonore (Tunney). Maybe Toni's protective tough hubby Eddie (Hoskins), an MGM exec, arranged something. Louis' poking around doesn't sit well with those in power and if he's not careful he may end up like Reeves. The self-aware Lane is the cast standout, though Affleck is comfortably capable while Brody is overly twitchy. **126m/C DVD, HD DVD.** *US* Adrien Brody, Diane Lane, Ben Affleck, Bob Hoskins, Lois Smith, Robin Tunney, Jeffrey DeMunn, Brad William Henke, Dash Mihok, Molly Parker, Kathleen Robertson, Joe Spano; *D:* Allen Coulter; *W:* Paul Bernbaum; *C:* Jonathan Freeman; *M:* Marcelo Zarvos.

Hollywood's New Blood **1988** Young actors making a movie are haunted by a film crew from hell. **90m/C VHS.** Bobby Johnston, Francine Lapensee; *D:* James Shyman.

Holocaust 1/2 **1978** The war years of 1935 to 1945 are relived in this account of the Nazi atrocities, focusing on the Jewish Weiss family, destroyed by the monstrous crimes, and the Dorf family, Germans who thrived under the Nazi regime. Highly acclaimed riveting miniseries with an exceptional cast. Won eight Emmys. **475m/C VHS.** Michael Moriarty, Fritz Weaver, Meryl Streep, James Woods, Joseph Bottoms, Tovah Feldshuh, David Warner, Ian Holm, Michael Beck, Marius Goring; *D:* Marvin J. Chomsky. **TV**

Holocaust Survivors... Remembrance of Love *Remembrance of Love* **1983** A concentration camp survivor and his daughter attend the 1981 World Gathering of Holocaust Survivors in Tel-Aviv and both find romance. **100m/C VHS.** Kirk Douglas, Pam Dawber, Chana Eden, Yoram Gal, Robert Clary; *D:* Jack Smight; *M:* William Goldstein. **TV**

Hologram Man **1995 (R)** Futuristic thriller finds psycho/terrorist Slash Gallagher (Lurie) captured by rookie cop Kurt Decoda (Lara). His prison term is to be served in Holographic Stasis, which means his mind is stored on a computer. Slash's gang manges to break his mind out of the computer but since his body is destroyed, Slash roams as a powerful electro-magnetic hologram. And it's up to cop Decoda to get Slash back. **96m/C VHS, DVD.** Joe Lara, Evan Lurie, William Sanderson, Tommy (Tiny) Lister, Michael Nouri, John Amos; *D:* Richard Pepin; *W:* Evan Lurie; *M:* John Gonzalez.

Holt of the Secret Service **1942** Secret service agent runs afoul of saboteurs and fifth-columnists in this 15-episode serial. **290m/B VHS, DVD.** Jack Holt, Evelyn Brent, C. Montague Shaw, Tristram Coffin, John Ward, George Chesebro; *D:* James W. Horne.

Holy Girl *La Nina Santa; The Holy Child* **2004 (R)** Martel's second feature film, in Spanish with English subtitles, explores themes of sexual power, shame and longing through the comings and goings and chance encounters of doctors and hotel staff during an otolaryngologists (ear, nose, & throat specialists) conference. At the center is the hotel manager's teenage and very Catholic daughter who is discovering the vulnerability and power of her own sexuality. The story unfolds in a not-so-orderly fashion but patience finds an intricate and startling conclusion. **106m/C DVD.** *AR NL SP IT* Mercedes Moran, Carlo Belloso, Alejandro Urdapilleta, Maria Alche, Julieta Zylberberg; *D:* Lucretia Martel; *W:* Lucretia Martel; *C:* Felix Monti; *M:* Andres Gerszenzon.

The Holy Innocents *Los Santos Inocentes* **1984 (PG)** A peasant family is torn asunder by their feudal obligations to their patrons. Set in the 1960s in Franco's Spain. In Spanish with English subtitles. **108m/C VHS.** *SP* Alfredo Landa, Francisco Rabal; *D:* Mario Camus. Cannes '84: Actor (Landa), Actor (Rabal).

Holy Man **1998 (PG)** This satire of home shopping networks is supposed to shell American consumerism, but ends up shooting itself in the foot instead. Murphy is G, a New Age-babble spouting wise man who is used by home shopping execs Goldblum and Preston to boost flagging sales. G lectures about the joy of spiritual over material happiness, but sales soar anyway. Misuses Murphy's wisecracking ability in what could have been a good premise, and reduces his character to a sight gag. **113m/C VHS, DVD.** Eddie Murphy, Jeff Goldblum, Kelly Preston, Robert Loggia, Jon Cryer, Eric McCormack, Marc Macaulay, Sam Kitchin, Robert Small, Morgan Fairchild; *D:* Stephen Herek; *W:* Tom Schulman; *C:* Adrian Biddle; *M:* Alan Silvestri.

Holy Matrimony 1/2 **1994 (PG-13)** Mild-mannered and pleasant comedy in spite of its potentially salacious plot. Thieves Peter (Donovan) and Havana (Arquette) take off to Canada to hide out in the Hutterite religious community where Peter grew up and where he's welcomed as the prodigal son. Peter hides their stolen loot but neglects to pass the word on before he's killed in an accident. Wanting to stay and search for the money, Havana uses the colony's reliance on biblical law to marry Peter's brother, Zeke (Gordon-Levitt). Only problem is Zeke is 12 and doesn't even like girls. Strictly brother-sister affection develops between the two. Amusing performances by both. **93m/C VHS, DVD.** Patricia Arquette, Joseph Gordon-Levitt, Armin Mueller-Stahl, Tate Donovan, John Schuck, Lois Smith, Courtney B. Vance, Jeffrey Nordling, Richard Riehle; *D:* Leonard Nimoy; *W:* David Weisberg, Douglas S. Cook; *C:* Bobby Bukowski; *M:* Bruce Broughton.

Holy Smoke **1999 (R)** Free-spirited Ruth (Winslet) travels to India and finds would-be spiritual enlightenment with an Indian guru. Her behavior terrifies her parents and her mother (Hamilton) manages to lure Ruth back home to Australia. They've hired American cult specialist, macho PJ Waters (Keitel), to rescue and deprogram her. Isolated in the Australian bush, the balance of power between Ruth and PJ begins to shift as sexual obsession takes hold. Complex characters but the strident storytelling gets annoying and some scenes seem staged for needless shock value. Based on the novel by the Campion sisters. **114m/C VHS, DVD.** *AU* Harvey Keitel, Kate Winslet, Julie Hamilton, Tim Robertson, Sophie Lee, Pam Grier, Paul Goddard, Daniel Wyllie; *D:* Jane Campion; *W:* Jane Campion, Anna Campion; *C:* Dion Beebe; *M:* Angelo Badalamenti.

The Holy Terror **1937** A Naval Air officer's daughter, Jane (Withers), unwittingly uncovers a group of spies while she entertains the troops with her musical shows. **68m/B VHS.** Jane Withers, Tony Martin, Leah Ray, El Brendel, Joe E. Lewis, Joan Davis; *D:* James Tinling; *W:* Lou Breslow, John Patrick.

Holy Terror **1965** The story of Florence Nightingale, who shocked Victorian society by organizing a nursing staff to aid British soldiers in the Crimean War, is told in this presentation from "George Schaefer's Showcase Theatre." **76m/C VHS.** Julie Harris, Denholm Elliott, Torin Thatcher, Kate Reid; *D:* George Schaefer. **TV**

Homage **1995 (R)** Archie's (Whaley) an emotionally disturbed mathematical nerd who needs a break from academia and persuades widowed ex-teacher Katherine Samuel (Danner) to hire him as caretaker for her New Mexico ranch. The duo achieve a strange serenity that shatters when Katherine's TV star daughter, self-absorbed Lucy (Lee), arrives seeking shelter because of her drug and drinking problems. A nasty triangle ensues as Lucy makes the mistake of sexually enticing, then rejecting, the needy Archie. In fact, the mistake's fatal. Based on Medoff's play "The Homage That Follows." **100m/C VHS, DVD.** Frank Whaley, Blythe Danner, Sheryl Lee, Bruce Davison, Danny Nucci; *D:* Ross Kagen Marks; *W:* Mark Medoff; *C:* Tom Richmond; *M:* W.G. Snuffy Walden.

Hombre **1967** A white man in the 1880s, raised by a band of Arizona Apaches, is forced into a showdown. In helping a stagecoach full of settlers across treacherous country, he not only faces traditional bad guys, but prejudice as well. Based on a story by Elmore Leonard. **111m/C VHS, DVD.** Paul Newman, Fredric March, Richard Boone, Diane Cilento, Cameron Mitchell, Barbara Rush, Martin Balsam; *D:* Martin Ritt; *W:* Harriet Frank Jr., Irving Ravetch; *C:* James Wong Howe.

Hombres Armados *Men with Guns* **1997 (R)** Fiercely independent filmmaker John Sayles' men with guns are not characters; they're an inevitable force like time or the weather that the characters have learned to accept. Set in a fictional Latin American country, story follows a well-to-do physician (Luppi) who trains doctors to work in the countryside among the local Mayan Indians. What he doesn't realize is that a civil war is engulfing his country, the Indians are practically enslaved, and his students have been murdered by the government that trained them. He picks up a ragged bunch of stragglers whose lives have been shattered by ever-present soldiers from either side of the war. Together they trudge through the jungle, searching for a place devoid of war or politics. Sayles based his idea on the 36-year-long civil war in Guatemala, which began in 1960. Spanish with subtitles. **128m/C VHS, DVD.** Federico Luppi, Damian Delgado, Dan Rivera Gonzalez, Tania Cruz, Damian Alcazar, Iguandili Lopez, Nandi Luna Ramirez, Rafael De Quevedo, Mandy Patinkin, Kathryn Grody, Roberto Sosa; *D:* John Sayles; *W:* John Sayles; *C:* Slawomir Idziak; *M:* Mason Daring.

Hombres Complicados **1997** Petty crook Roger (De Pauw) can't pay his debts to a group of gangsters. So he convinces gullible brother Bruno (Roofthooft) that they should use the small inheritance left to them by their mother to take a bonding road trip. Roger wants to buy some time until he can come up with a get-rich-quick scheme but, as usual in his sad-sack life, Roger's scheming leads to some bizarre happenings. Flemish and French with subtitles. **83m/C VHS.** *BE* Josse De Pauw, Dirk Roofthooft, Lies Pauwels; *D:* Dominique Deruddere; *W:* Dominique Deruddere, Marc Didden; *C:* Willy Stassen.

Home 1/2 **2005** Roommates Susan and Rose throw a party in their Brooklyn brownstone one hot summer night. Bobby shows up in hopes of re-connecting with his ex Harper, who's more interested in making a play for Rose's crush, Tommy. So Bobby gets to know Susan until HER ex shows up. Frankly, this is a pretty dull gathering although the situations and conversations will sound familiar. **91m/C DVD.** Nicol Zanzarella, E. Jason Liebrecht, Erin Stacey Visslailli, Minerva Scelza, T. Stephen Neave, Bradley Spinelli; *D:* Matt Seitz; *W:* Matt Seitz; *C:* Jonathan Wolff.

Home 1/2 **2008** Pennsylvania farm wife Inga (Harden) is recovering from breast cancer and her illness has caused fissures in her marriage to the distant Herman (Gaston). Inga is also worried how her illness has affected her eight-year-old daughter Indigo (Scheel, Harden's own daughter). When Inga learns an elderly neighbor (Seldes) wishes to sell her house, she fantasizes about buying and restoring the property, which reminds her of her childhood home and her relationship with her own mother, who died from cancer. **84m/C DVD.** Marcia Gay Harden, Michael Gaston, Marian Seldes, Eulala Scheel; *D:* Mary Haverstick; *W:* Mary Haverstick; *C:* Richard Rutkowski; *M:* Michele Mercure.

Home Alone **1990 (PG)** Eight-year-old Kevin is accidentally left behind when his entire (and large) family makes a frantic rush for the airport. That's the plausible part. Alone and besieged by burglars, Culkin turns into a pint-sized Rambo defending his suburban castle with the wile and resources of a boy genius with perfect timing and unlimited wherewithal. That's the implausible part. Pesci and Stern, the targets of Macauley's wrath, enact painful slapstick with considerable vigor, while Candy has a small but funny part as the leader of a polka band traveling cross-country with mom O'Hara. The highest-grossing picture of 1990, surpassing "Ghost" and "Jaws." **105m/C VHS, DVD.** Macaulay Culkin, Catherine O'Hara, Joe Pesci, Daniel Stern, John Heard, Roberts Blossom, John Candy, Billie Bird, Angela Goethals, Devin Ratray, Kieran Culkin; *D:* Chris Columbus; *W:* John Hughes; *C:* Julio Macat; *M:* John Williams.

Home Alone 2: Lost in New York 1/2 **1992 (PG)** In an almost exact duplication of the original blockbuster, the harebrained McCallister family leaves Kevin behind in the shuffle to start their Florida vacation. Boarding the wrong plane, Kevin lands in NYC, where wonder of wonders, he meets crooks Pesci and Stern, prison escapees who somehow survived the torture meted out in the first film. And they want revenge. Loaded with cartoon violence and shameless gag replicas from HA1, mega-hit still produces genuine laughs and manages to incorporate fresh material. Culkin is as adorable as ever, with supporting cast all delivering fine performances. Filmed in New York City. **120m/C VHS, DVD.** Macaulay Culkin, Joe Pesci, Daniel Stern, Catherine O'Hara, John Heard, Tim Curry, Brenda Fricker, Devin Ratray, Hillary Wolf, Eddie Bracken, Dana Ivey, Rob Schneider, Kieran Culkin, Gerry Bamman, Donald Trump; *D:* Chris Columbus; *W:* John Hughes; *C:* Julio Macat; *M:* John Williams.

Home Alone 3 **1997 (PG)** Regardless of the new faces, the story and cartoon violence seems all too familar. Linz (taking over for the teenaged Culkin) is stricken with the chicken pox but able to booby trap his suburban house with to foil the plans of international criminals trying to recover a microchip stashed in a toy car. Film fails to carry the charm of its predecessors and sends the wrong messages: it's okay for parents to leave underaged kids home by themselves and electrocuting people is fun. Writer Hughes should be left home alone to rethink his skills as a screenwriter. **102m/C VHS, DVD.** Alex D. Linz, Kevin Kilner, Olek Krupa, Rya Kihlstedt, Lenny Von Dohlen, David Thornton, Haviland (Haylie) Morris, Marian Seldes, Scarlett Johansson, Christopher Curry, Baxter Harris, Seth Smith; *D:* Raja Gosnell; *W:* John Hughes; *C:* Julio Macat; *M:* Nick Glennie-Smith.

The Home and the World 1/2 *Ghare Baire* **1984** Another masterpiece from India's Ray, this film deals with a sheltered Indian woman who falls in love with her husband's friend and becomes politically committed in the turmoil of 1907-08. Based on Rabindranath Tagore's novel. In Bengali with English subtitles. **130m/C VHS.** *IN* Victor Banerjee, Soumitra Chatterjee; *D:* Satyajit Ray.

Home at Last **1988** An orphan in turn of the century New York finds himself shipped to Nebraska on an orphan train. There he works on the farm of his adopted family, whose own son has died. The boy finds that he must adjust to a new lifestyle as well as strive to be accepted as someone other than a replacement for the couple's son. From the "Wonderworks" series. **58m/C VHS, DVD.** Adrien Brody, Frank Converse, Caroline Lagerfelt, Sascha Radetsky.

A Home at the End of the World 1/2 **2004 (R)** Cunningham adapted his 1990 novel, but the beauty of his prose gets lost in the transition. Sweet-but-awkward Bobby Morrow (Farrell) meets shy outsider Jonathan Glover (Roberts) in 1967 Cleveland. When Bobby is orphaned, he moves in with the Glovers (Spacek, Frewer) and stays with them even after Jonathan takes off for gay life in the New York. Bobby later follows and then bunks with Jonathan and his older, platonic roommate Clare (Wright Penn). Jonathan is in love with Bobby but it's Clare who seduces him and gets pregnant. When the threesome move out of the city and try to raise the baby together, Clare soon realizes that the emotional intimacy between the two men leaves no room for her. Farrell is tender, but the storytelling is disjointed and the ending somewhat abrupt. Farrell's controversial frontal nude scene, allegedly cut for being distracting, was not restored for the DVD release. **95m/C VHS, DVD.** *US* Colin Farrell, Robin Wright Penn, Dallas Roberts, Sissy Spacek, Matt Frewer, Erik

Smith, Harris Allan, Andrew Chalmers, Ryan Donowho; *D:* Michael Mayer; *W:* Michael Cunningham; *C:* Enrique Chediak; *M:* Duncan Sheik.

Home Before Midnight 1/2 **1984** A young songwriter falls in love with a 14-year-old, is discovered, and is subsequently charged with statutory rape. **115m/C VHS, DVD.** James Aubrey, Alison Elliott; *D:* Pete Walker.

Home for Christmas 1/2 **1990** An elderly homeless man, with the love of a young girl, teaches a wealthy family the spirit of Christmas. **96m/C VHS.** Mickey Rooney, Joel Kaiser; *D:* Peter McCubbin.

Home for Christmas 1/2 *Little Miss Millions* **1993 (PG)** A 12-year-old has run away from her wicked stepmom who hires a bounty hunter to bring her back—for a half a million bucks. Only when he finds the girl stepmom doesn't want to pay up and she tells anyone who will listen that the bounty hunter actually kidnapped the girl. Bounty hunter turns to friends, including the 12-year-old who isn't a fool and knows stepmom is a lying witch, for help. **90m/C VHS, DVD.** Howard Hesseman, Anita Morris, Jennifer Love Hewitt, James Avery, Steve Landesberg, Terri Treas, Deanna (Dee) Booher; *D:* Jim Wynorski; *W:* Jim Wynorski, R.J. Robertson; *C:* Zoran Hochstatter; *M:* Joel Goldsmith.

Home for the Holidays *Deadly Desires* **1972** Four daughters are called home on Christmas by their father who is convinced that his second wife is trying to poison him. **74m/C VHS.** Eleanor Parker, Walter Brennan, Sally Field, Jessica Walter, Julie Harris; *D:* John Llewellyn Moxey. **TV**

Home for the Holidays 1/2 **1995 (PG-13)** Frantic dysfunctional family saga finds eldest daughter Claudia Larson (Hunter) on her way to Baltimore to spend Thanksgiving with her family. Frazzled Claudia must deal with badly bewigged mom Adele (Bancroft), genial dad Henry (Durning), and her siblings—frenzied gay brother Tommy (Downey Jr.) and self-righteous sister Joanne (Stevenson), as well as screwy Aunt Glady (Chaplin) and Tommy's handsome friend Leo Fish (McDermott). Yes, there are moments of deja vu about your very own family holidays but the film seems badly paced and ultimately irritating. Adapted from a short story by Chris Radant. **103m/C VHS, DVD.** Holly Hunter, Anne Bancroft, Charles Durning, Robert Downey Jr., Dylan McDermott, Cynthia Stevenson, Geraldine Chaplin, Steve Guttenberg, Claire Danes, David Strathairn, Austin Pendleton; *D:* Jodie Foster; *W:* W.D. Richter; *C:* Lajos Koltai; *M:* Mark Isham.

Home Free All 1/2 **1984** A Vietnam vet turned revolutionary, turned writer, tries to reacquaint himself with childhood friends only to find one has joined the mob and another is settled in suburbia and none of them are dealing well with adulthood. **92m/C VHS.** Allan Nicholls, Roland Caccavo, Maura Ellyn, Shelley Wyant, Lucille Rivim; *D:* Stuart Bird.

Home Fries **1998 (PG-13)** Things go from bad to worse for pregnant fast-food cashier, Sally (Drew Barrymore), as she learns that the father of her child is not only married, but dead! The catch is that the philanderer's stepsons are responsible and believe that Sally may have overheard their dastardly deed on her drive-through headset. Brother Dorian (Luke Wilson) takes a job at the Burger-Matic to find out just what Sally knows, but predictably falls in love with her instead. Tries to be a quirky dark comedy in a sweet love story, but the result is a bad mix of bleak humor and saccarine-sweet puppy love. Barrymore's cute and convincing performance manages to keep the whole thing from spoiling. Unfortunately, first-time director Parisot leaves the audience thinking, "this isn't what I ordered." **94m/C VHS, DVD.** Drew Barrymore, Luke Wilson, Catherine O'Hara, Jake Busey, Shelley Duvall, Kim Robillard, Daryl (Chill) Mitchell, Lanny Flaherty, Chris Ellis, Edward "Blue" Deckert; *D:* Dean Parisot; *W:* Vince Gilligan; *C:* Jerzy Zielinski; *M:* Rachel Portman.

Home from the Hill **1960** A solemn, brooding drama about a southern landowner and his troubled sons, one of whom is illegitimate. This one triumphs because of casting. **150m/C VHS, DVD.** Robert Mitchum, George Peppard, George Hamilton, Eleanor Parker, Everett Sloane, Luana Parker, Constance Ford; *D:* Vincente Minnelli; *W:* Harriet Frank Jr., Irving Ravetch; *C:* Milton Krasner. Natl. Bd. of Review '60: Actor (Mitchum).

The Home Front 1/2 *The Scoundrel's Wife* **2002 (R)** During World War II, Camille (O'Neal), a Louisiana widow with two kids, Blue (McCullough) and Florida (Chabert), takes a job as an assistant to an exiled German doctor. They are both outcasts, she because of an incident years before involving her husband, and he because he is German. When German U-boats begin attacking ships in the harbor, they both fall under suspicion. Complicating matters is Florida's romance with a Nazi-hunting Coast Guard ensign. A little disjointed, and the conclusion isn't exactly believable, but the movie looks good, and has a great sense of the time and place. It should, as director/writer Pitre based it on stories he heard growing up in the same town in which the tale is set. **102m/C VHS, DVD.** Tatum O'Neal, Julian Sands, Tim Curry, Lacey Chabert, Eion Bailey, Rudolf Martin, Patrick McCullough; *D:* Glen Pitre; *W:* Glen Pitre, Michelle Benoit; *C:* Uta Briesewitz; *M:* Ernest Troost.

Home in Oklahoma **1947** A boy will be swindled out of his inheritance and a killer will escape justice until Roy comes to the rescue. Standard series fare. **72m/B VHS, DVD.** Roy Rogers, Dale Evans, George "Gabby" Hayes, Carol Hughes; *D:* William Witney.

Home Is Where the Hart Is **1988 (PG-13)** A rich 103-year-old is kidnapped by a nurse wanting to marry him and become heir to his estate. It's up to his sons, all in their 70s, to rescue him. **94m/C VHS.** Martin Mull, Leslie Nielsen, Valri Bromfield, Stephen E. Miller, Eric Christmas, Ted Stidder; *D:* Rex Bromfield; *W:* Rex Bromfield.

Home Movie 1/2 **2008 (R)** Shrink Clare Poe (McClain) and her minister husband David (Pasdar) move their two children into an isolated home and quickly come to realize that their offspring are deeply disturbed. Clare uses a video camera in her work and tries to document all the awful things they do instead of getting them some serious help since she's completely ineffectual. Dad drinks and goofs around because he was abused as a child and can't cope. The parents act so stupidly that you root for their vicious little brats. **80m/C DVD.** Cady McClain, Adrian Pasdar, Austin Williams, Amber Joy Williams; *D:* Christopher Denham; *W:* Christopher Denham; *C:* William M. Miller; *M:* Ryan Shore.

Home Movies 1/2 **1979 (PG)** Brian DePalma and his film students at Sarah Lawrence College devised this loose, sloppy comedy which hearkens back to DePalma's early films. Tells the story of a nebbish who seeks therapy to gain control of his absurdly chaotic life. **89m/C VHS, DVD.** Kirk Douglas, Nancy Allen, Keith Gordon, Gerrit Graham, Vincent Gardenia, Mary Davenport; *D:* Brian De Palma; *W:* Brian De Palma; *C:* James L. Carter; *M:* Pino Donaggio.

Home of Angels 1/2 **1994** Billy sneaks his granddad out of his nursing home in Philadelphia and together the twosome begin a perilous journey back to Billy's home in Long Island, New York so they can have a family Christmas. They're aided by a homeless man when they run into trouble with a street gang. **90m/C VHS.** Lance Robinson, Abe Vigoda, Sherman Hemsley, Joe Frazier; *D:* Nick Stagliano.

A Home of Our Own **1975** An American priest sets up a home in Mexico for orphan boys and changes their lives for the better. A true story of Father William Wasson. **100m/C VHS.** Pancho Cordova, Pedro Armendariz Jr., Carmen Zapata, Enrique Novi, Richard Angarola, Jason Miller; *D:* Robert Day; *W:* Blanche Hanalis; *C:* Jacques "Jack" Marquette; *M:* Laurence Rosenthal.

A Home of Our Own 1/2 **1993 (PG-13)** Semi-autobiographical tearjerker based on screenwriter Duncan's childhood. Widowed and poor mother of six (Bates) is fired from her job at a Los Angeles potato chip factory, packs up the tribe and heads for a better life and a home to call their own. They end up in Idaho, in a ramshackle house owned by lonely Mr. Moon (Oh) and what follows is a winter of discontent. Bates provides an intense performance as a poor but proud woman with a tough exterior. Furlong provides the story's narration as the eldest son. A story of spiritual triumph, this one is sure to make your heart weep. **104m/C VHS, DVD.** Kathy Bates, Edward Furlong, Soon-Teck Oh, Amy Sakasitz, Tony Campisi; *D:* Tony Bill; *W:* Patrick Duncan; *C:* Jean Lepine; *M:* Michael Convertino.

Home of the Brave **1949** A black soldier is sent on a top secret mission in the South Pacific, but finds that he must battle with his white comrades as he is subjected to subordinate treatment and constant racial slurs. Hollywood's first outstanding statement against racial prejudice. **86m/B VHS.** Lloyd Bridges, James Edwards, Frank Lovejoy, Jeff Corey, Douglas Dick, Steve Brodie, Cliff Clark; *D:* Mark Robson; *W:* Carl Foreman; *C:* Robert De Grasse; *M:* Dimitri Tiomkin.

Home of the Brave **2006 (R)** Iraqi war vets from the same National Guard unit return home to Spokane and have trouble readjusting to civilian life in Winkler's conventional drama. Medic Will Marsh (Jackson) turns to alcohol and lashing out at his wife (Rowell) and son (Jones). Single mom Vanessa (Biel) lost a hand and discovers her prosthesis makes everyone uncomfortable while Tommy (Presley) can't get past the death of his best friend. Actors do as well as can be expected with the cliched material. **105m/C DVD, Blu-ray Disc.** *US* Samuel L. Jackson, Jessica Biel, Curtis "50 Cent" Jackson, Sam Jones III, Victoria Rowell, Chad Michael Murray, Christina Ricci, Brian Presley; *D:* Irwin Winkler; *W:* Mark Friedman; *C:* Tony Pierce-Roberts; *M:* Stephen Endelman.

Home on the Range 1/2 **2004 (PG)** Disney kicks this 2-D cartoon old-school style—which would be great if there was anything new, fresh, or very funny going on. Three gal cow pals (Barr, Dench, and Tilly) trying to save their farm from foreclosure go after the bounty on the evil rustler Alameda Slim (Quaid). Lots of hyped-up action and gags will keep the kids amused; however, it wants oh-so-much to mimic the classic Looney Tunes but, like Daffy to Bugs, it just doesn't measure up. Oscar winner Alan Menken produces some pleasant if not memorable music with singers k.d. lang, Bonnie Raitt, and Tim McGraw. **75m/C VHS, DVD.** *US D:* John Sanford, Will Finn; *W:* John Sanford, Will Finn, Samm Levine, Michael LaBash, Mark Kennedy, Robert Lence; *C:* H. Lee Peterson; *M:* Alan Menken; *V:* Roseanne, G.W. Bailey, Steve Buscemi, Judi Dench, Randy Quaid, Lance LeGault, Charles Haid, Cuba Gooding Jr., Joe Flaherty, Carole Cook, Charles Dennis, Marshall Efron, Charlie Dell, Richard Riehle, Jennifer Tilly, Patrick Warburton, Mark Walton, Estelle Harris, Dennis Weaver, Edie McClurg, Samm Levine, Gov. Ann Richards.

Home Remedy **1988** An introverted New Jersey bachelor's isolated lifestyle is invaded by a flirtatious housewife and her jealous husband. **92m/C VHS.** Seth Barrish, Maxine Albert; *D:* Maggie Greenwald.

Home Room **2002 (R)** Philipps and Christensen shine in this riveting story of two girls on opposite end of the high school social spectrum who survive a Columbine-type massacre. Popular, affluent Deanna (Christensen) was seriously injured in the attack and is hospitalized. Alienated loner Alicia (Philipps) was near the perpetrator when he was killed, and is believed to be somehow involved. When Alicia is forced to visit Deanna in the hospital, the two eventually form a friendship and learn to cope with the aftermath of the incident. The two leads are excellent, with a breakout performance by Philipps, and the film wisely sticks to the story of their unlikely friendship, pushing other plotlines to the background. **133m/C VHS, DVD.** Busy Philipps, Erika Christensen, Victor Garber, Raphael Sbarge, Ken Jenkins, Holland Taylor, Arthur Taxier, James Pickens Jr., Constance Zimmer, Richard Gilliland, Roxanne Hart, Agnes Bruckner, Nathan West, Ben Gould, Jenette Goldstein, Vernee Watson-Johnson; *D:* Paul F. Ryan; *W:* Paul F. Ryan; *C:* Mike Shapiro; *M:* Rebecca Baehler.

Home Sick 1/2 **2008** A young girl goes home to meet her friends and party when some nutjob with a suitcase full of razor blades walks in and forces them all to name someone they hate while cutting himself. One guy doesn't take it seriously and names everyone there, and the bloodbath begins. You'd think someone would've beat the crap out of the kid who named everyone but between getting high and being murdered they're a little bit distracted. **89m/C DVD.** Lindley Evans, Bill Moseley, Tiffany Shepis, William M. Akers, Forrest Pitts, Brandon Carroll, Tom Towler, Matt Lero, Jeff Dylan Graham, L.C. Holt, Patrick Engel, Shaina Fewell; *D:* Adam Wingard; *W:* E.L. Katz; *C:* Andor Becsi, Michael 'Bear' Praytor; *M:* Zombi. **VIDEO**

Home Sweet Home 1/2 **1914** Suggested by the life of John Howard Payne (actor, poet, dramatist, critic, and world-wanderer) who wrote the title song amid the bitterness of his sad life. Silent with musical score. **62m/B VHS.** Lillian Gish, Dorothy Gish, Henry B. Walthall, Mae Marsh, Blanche Sweet, Donald Crisp, Robert "Bobbie" Harron; *D:* D.W. Griffith.

Home Sweet Home 1/2 *Slasher in the House* **1980** A murdering psychopath escapes from the local asylum, and rampages through a family's Thanksgiving dinner. **84m/C VHS.** Jake Steinfeld, Sallee Elyse, Peter DePaula; *D:* Nettie Pena.

Home Sweet Home **1982** Postman Stan fancies himself a ladies man, but his wife has left him. So Stan decides to assuage his loneliness by seducing his co-workers' wives. Black comedy look at British social classism. **90m/C VHS, DVD.** *GB* Eric Richard, Timothy Spall, Tim Barker, Su Elliot, Frances Barber, Kay Stonham; *D:* Mike Leigh; *W:* Mike Leigh. **TV**

Home Team 1/2 **1998 (PG)** Gambling addict and ex-con Henry Butler (Guttenberg) is required to perform community service as part of his parole. Since he's a former soccer coach, he finds a job at a boys' home where administor Karen (Lorain) figures a soccer team will teach the kids teamwork and sportsmanship. Familiar plot but that's not necessarily bad. **94m/C VHS, DVD.** Steve Guttenberg, Sophie Lorain, Ryan Slater, Johnny Morina; *D:* Allan Goldstein; *C:* Barry Gravelle. **CABLE**

Home to Danger 1/2 **1951** Ordinary (and short) crime drama finds Barbara (Anderson) returning home when her estranged father's will leaves her a wealthy woman. It also leaves her the target of a killer. **66m/B DVD.** *GB* Rona Anderson, Stanley Baker, Alan Wheatley, Guy Rolfe, Francis Lister; *D:* Terence Fisher; *W:* Francis Edge, John Temple-Smith; *C:* Reg Wyer; *M:* Malcolm Arnold.

Home to Stay **1979** A farmer who has suffered a stroke is fighting off repeated lapses into senility. His son and daughter have conflicting interests as to whether he should be committed to a nursing home. **74m/C VHS.** Henry Fonda, Frances Hyland, Michael McGuire; *D:* Delbert Mann; *M:* Hagood Hardy. **TV**

Home Town Story **1951** A politician is convinced big business is behind his election loss. Fair drama. Watch for Monroe in a bit part. **61m/B VHS, DVD.** Jeffrey Lynn, Donald Crisp, Marjorie Reynolds, Alan Hale Jr., Marilyn Monroe, Barbara Brown, Melinda Plowman; *D:* Arthur Pierson.

Homebodies **1974 (PG)** Six senior citizens, disgusted when they learn that they will be callously tossed out of their home, become violent murderers in their shocking attempt to solve their problem. An odd little film made in Cincinnati. **96m/C VHS.** Ruth McDevitt, Linda Marsh, William Hansen, Peter Brocco, Frances Fuller; *D:* Larry Yust.

Homeboy 1/2 *Black Fist* **1975** A Black boxer owes his career to the mob. When he tries to break free his wife is murdered—and he seeks revenge. **93m/C VHS, DVD.** Richard Lawson, Dabney Coleman, Philip Michael Thomas; *D:* Timothy Galfas, Richard Kaye; *W:* Tim Kelly; *C:* William Larrabure; *M:* Ed Townsend.

Homeboy **1988 (R)** A small-time club boxer who dreams of becoming middleweight champ is offered his big break, but the opportunity is jeopardized by his dishonest manager's dealings. Never released theatrically. **118m/C VHS.** Mickey Rourke, Christopher Walken, Debra Feuer, Kevin Conway, Antony Alda, Ruben Blades; ***D:*** Michael Seresin; ***M:*** Eric Clapton, Michael Kamen.

Homeboys **1992** Two East L.A. brothers find themselves on opposite sides of the law in this quickie designed to cash in on gang violence and ghetto dramas. **91m/C VHS.** Todd Bridges, David Garrison, Ron Odriozola, Ken Michaels; ***D:*** Lindsay Norgard.

Homecoming **1928** Two German prisoners of war escape from a Siberian lead mine. One reaches home first and has an affair with his comrade's wife. Silent. **74m/B VHS.** *GE* Dita Parlo, Lars Hanson, Gustav Froehlich; ***D:*** Joe May.

Homecoming **1948** Average soap opera starring Gable and Turner set amidst the trenches of WW II. Gable plays a selfish doctor who leaves behind his wife and colleague to enlist in the Medical Corps as a major. Turner is the battlefield nurse who forever changes his life. Film is hindered by a story which is far below the talents of the excellent cast. Although voted by the New York Critics as one of the ten worst movies of 1948, the public loved it. Based on the story "The Homecoming of Ulysses" by Sidney Kingsley. **113m/B VHS.** Clark Gable, Lana Turner, Anne Baxter, John Hodiak, Ray Collins, Gladys Cooper, Cameron Mitchell, Art Baker, Lurene Tuttle; ***D:*** Mervyn LeRoy; ***W:*** Paul Osborn, Jan Lustig.

Homecoming 1/2 **1996 (PG)** Mentally ill mother abandons her four children at a Connecticut shopping mall in the care of 13-year-old eldest daughter Dicey (Peterson). The children slowly make their way to a relative's (Bedelia) home in Bridgeport, but when she proves equally uncaring Dicey decides to continue the family trek to their maternal grandmother Ab's (Bancroft) house in Chrisfield, Maryland. No surprise when crazy grandma doesn't want them either but this time Dicey is determined to make them all a home. Based on the Newbery Medal-winning children's novel by Cynthia Voight. **105m/C VHS, DVD.** Anne Bancroft, Kimberlee Peterson, Bonnie Bedelia, Trever O'Brien, Hanna Hall, William Greenblatt; ***D:*** Mark Jean; ***W:*** Mark Jean, Christopher Carlson; ***C:*** Toyomichi Kurita; ***M:*** W.G. Snuffy Walden. **CABLE**

Homecoming **2009** Predictable psycho dreck with stupid characters. High school honey Shelby (Barton) is in total denial that her bland jock boyfriend Mike (Long) dumped her when he went off to college. Now it's Christmas vacation and Matt comes back to their small hometown with his new squeeze, dull-but-wealthy Elizabeth (Stroup). Low-class Shelby is not pleased and when Elizabeth is accidentally injured, Shelby holds her captive in her rundown house outside of town. Elizabeth makes lame escape attempts and Shelby gets increasingly violent. **90m/C DVD.** *US* Mischa Barton, Jessica Stroup, Matt Long, Michael Landes; ***D:*** Morgan J. Freeman; ***W:*** Katie Fetting, Jake Goldberger, Frank Hannah; ***C:*** Stephen Kazmierski; ***M:*** Jack Livesey.

Homecoming: A Christmas Story 1/2 **1971** Heart-tugger that inspired the television series "The Waltons." A depression-era Virginia mountain family struggles to celebrate Christmas although the whereabouts and safety of their father are unknown. Adapted from the autobiographical novel by Earl Hamner Jr. **98m/C VHS, DVD.** Richard Thomas, Patricia Neal, Edgar Bergen, Cleavon Little, Ellen Corby; ***D:*** Fielder Cook. **TV**

Homegrown 1/2 **1997 (R)** Engaging comedy-noir has three dense Norther California pot growers (Thornton, Azaria, Phillippe) witness their Boss's (Lithgow) murder. Seeing this as a bad omen, they take off, with the crop, to the operation's packaging department (Lynch) and decide to carry on as if the boss is still alive. Amid many cameos (Danson, Curtis) they set up a big deal with a seemingly laid-back wholesaler (Bon Jovi). **101m/C VHS, DVD.** Billy Bob Thornton, Hank Azaria, Ryan Phillippe, Kelly Lynch, Jon Bon Jovi, John Lithgow, Jon Tenney, Matt Clark; ***Cameos:*** Ted Danson, Jamie Lee Curtis, Judge Reinhold; ***D:*** Stephen Gyllenhaal; ***W:*** Stephen Gyllenhaal, Nicholas Kazan; ***C:*** Greg Gardiner; ***M:*** Trevor Rabin.

Homer and Eddie **1989 (R)** A witless road comedy with Goldberg as a dying sociopath and a mentally retarded Belushi. They take off cross-country to make a little trouble, learn a little about life, and create a less than entertaining movie. **100m/C VHS.** Whoopi Goldberg, James Belushi, Karen Black; ***D:*** Andrei Konchalovsky; ***W:*** Patrick Cirillo; ***C:*** Lajos Koltai; ***M:*** Eduard Artemyev.

Homesteaders of Paradise Valley 1/2 **1947** The Hume brothers oppose Red Ryder and a group of settlers building a dam in Paradise Valley. **54m/B VHS, DVD.** Allan "Rocky" Lane, Robert (Bobby) Blake, Martha Wentworth, Ann E. Todd, Gene Roth, John James, George Chesebro, Edythe Elliott, Milton Kibbee, Tom London; ***D:*** R.G. Springsteen; ***W:*** Earle Snell; ***C:*** Alfred S. Keller.

Hometown Boy Makes Good 1/2 **1993 (R)** Smalltown boy Boyd Geary moved to the big city to go to medical school. But what he never told his proud mom was that he dropped out and doesn't have the successful psychiatry practice she thinks he has, instead he's a barely surviving waiter. But when Boyd travels back home to confess to mom, the local mayor makes him an offer to set up his own practice and won't take no for an answer. **88m/C VHS.** Anthony Edwards, Grace Zabriskie, Cynthia Bain; ***D:*** David Burton Morris; ***W:*** Allen Rucker; ***M:*** Barry Goldberg.

Hometown Legend 1/2 **2002 (PG)** The local high school football team in Rachel Sawyer's (Chabert) Alabama hometown hasn't won a game in 12 years—ever since then-coach Buster Schuler's (O'Quinn) son died on the playing field. Rachel figures it wouldn't hurt to pray for a miracle and her prayers are answered when Coach Schuler returns and agrees to coach the team again. **106m/C VHS, DVD.** Terry O'Quinn, Lacey Chabert, Nick Cornish, Kirk B.R. Woller, Ian Bohen; ***D:*** James Anderson; ***W:*** Shawn Hoffman, Michael Patwin; ***C:*** Mark Petersen; ***M:*** Dan Haseltine. **VIDEO**

Hometown U.S.A. WOOF! **1979 (R)** Set in L.A. in the late '50s, this teenage cruising movie is the brainchild of director Baer, better known as Jethro from that madcap TV series "The Beverly Hillbillies." **97m/C VHS, DVD.** Brian Kerwin, Gary Springer, David Wilson, Cindy Fisher, Sally Kirkland; ***D:*** Max Baer Jr.

Homeward Bound **1980 (G)** A dying teenager tries to reunite his long-estranged father and grandfather. **96m/C VHS.** David Soul, Moosie Drier, Barnard Hughes; ***D:*** Richard Michaels. **TV**

Homeward Bound 2: Lost in San Francisco 1/2 **1996 (G)** House pets Chance, the feisty bulldog (Fox), Sassy the sophisticated feline (Field), and Shadow the sage golden retriever (Waite) find themselves on the loose again, this time in the tough streets of San Francisco. The animals escape from the airport as the family departs for a Canadian holiday, and on their way back home, encounter some tough mutts—a gang of streetwise dogs, (most notably comedian Sinbad as Riley) and, of course, some dog nappers. Chance even finds romance along the way with Delilah (Gugino). Not too scary for the little ones, flick carries the same charm of the first adventure. **88m/C VHS, DVD.** Robert Hays, Kim Greist, Veronica Lauren, Kevin Timothy Chevalia, Michael Rispoli, Max Perlich; ***D:*** David R. Ellis; ***W:*** Julie Hickson, Chris Hauty; ***C:*** Jack Conroy; ***V:*** Michael J. Fox, Sally Field, Ralph Waite, Al Michaels, Tommy Lasorda, Bob Uecker, Jon Polito, Adam Goldberg, Sinbad, Carla Gugino.

Homeward Bound: The Incredible Journey **1993 (G)** Successful remake of the 1963 Disney release "The Incredible Journey." Two dogs and a cat once again try to find their way home after their family relocates, armed with greater depth of character than the original. Hard not to shed a tear for the brave animal trio who develop a trusting bond through assorted misadventures. Based on the novel by Sheila Burnford. Superior family fare. **85m/C VHS, DVD.** Robert Hays, Kim Greist, Jean Smart, Benj Thall, Veronica Lauren, Kevin Timothy Chevalia; ***D:*** Duwayne Dunham; ***W:*** Linda Woolverton, Caroline Thompson; ***C:*** Reed Smoot; ***M:*** Bruce Broughton; ***V:*** Don Ameche, Michael J. Fox, Sally Field.

Homework **1982 (R)** Young man's after-school lessons with a teacher are definitely not part of the curriculum. Yawning sexploitation. **90m/C VHS, DVD.** Joan Collins, Michael Morgan, Betty Thomas, Shell Kepler, Wings Hauser, Lee Purcell; ***D:*** James Beshears.

Homework *La Tarea* **1990** Film student Virginia (Rojo) decides to record her prearranged meeting with her ex-lover Marcelo (Alonso). When Marcelo discovers that their sexual tryst has been videotaped, he eventually decides to help Virginia with her work. Spanish with subtitles. **85m/C VHS, DVD.** *MX* Maria Rojo, Jose Alonso; ***D:*** Jaime Humberto Hermosillo; ***W:*** Jaime Humberto Hermosillo; ***C:*** Toni Kuhn.

Homewrecker **1992 (PG-13)** Benson stars as a scientist who invents a computer, with a female voice, as the ultimate domestic worker. Only the computer turns possessive and against Benson's estranged wife. **88m/C VHS.** Robby Benson, Sydney Walsh, Sarah Rose Karr; ***D:*** Fred Walton; ***W:*** Eric Harlacher; ***V:*** Kate Jackson.

Homicidal **1961** Castle's "Psycho" imitation makes a belated debut on home video. He takes all the key elements of Hitchcock's original and reshuffles them: the big old house with the steep staircase, the creepy invalid older woman, a troubled young man, the blonde who's up to something, the cheap hotel, the vaguely threatening cops, the unexpectedly graphic knife violence, the young couple who investigates. And a central gimmick which is cheesily transparent; most viewers will tumble to it early on and that's part of the fun, too. With enthusiastic overacting from all the leads, the whole thing becomes a minor camp masterpiece. **87m/B DVD.** Glenn Corbett, Patricia Breslin, Alan Bunce, James Westerfield; ***D:*** William Castle; ***W:*** Robb White; ***C:*** Burnett Guffey; ***M:*** Hugo Friedhofer.

Homicidal Impulse 1/2 *Killer Instinct* **1992 (R)** When Assistant D.A. Tim Casey has an affair with his boss' ambitious niece he doesn't realize the danger he's in. His lover decides to kill her uncle so boyfriend Tim will get his job. Some women will do anything for love. Also available in an unrated version. **84m/C VHS.** Scott Valentine, Vanessa Angel, Talia Balsam, Brian Cousins; ***D:*** David Tausik; ***W:*** David Tausik; ***C:*** Janusz Kaminski; ***M:*** Nigel Holton.

Homicide 1/2 **1991 (R)** Terrific police thriller with as much thought as action; a driven detective faces his submerged Jewish identity while probing an anti-Semitic murder and a secret society. Playwright/filmmaker Mamet creates nail-biting suspense and shattering epiphanies without resorting to Hollywood glitz. Rich (often profane) dialogue includes a classic soliloquy mystically comparing a lawman's badge with a Star of David. **100m/C VHS.** Joe Mantegna, William H. Macy, Natalija Nogulich, Ving Rhames, Rebecca Pidgeon; ***D:*** David Mamet; ***W:*** David Mamet; ***C:*** Roger Deakins.

Homicide: The Movie **2000 (PG-13)** Rather a disappointment for fans of the intelligent NBC cop series but at least the TV movie tied up some loose ends. Giardello (Kotto) is gunned down at a rally where he's campaigning for mayor of Baltimore. While G hovers between life and death, the tragedy brings Pembleton (Braugher) back to town and gets Giardello's old squad—some of whom have retired or been re-assigned—back to work on his case. A somewhat surreal ending has cameos by cast members from previous seasons. **89m/C VHS, DVD.** Yaphet Kotto, Andre Braugher, Kyle Secor, Richard Belzer, Giancarlo Esposito, Peter Gerety, Clark Johnson, Zeljko Ivanek, Michael Michele, Reed Edward Diamond, Michelle Forbes, Isabella Hofmann, Melissa Leo, Callie (Calliope) Thorne, Jon Seda, Max Perlich, Jason Priestley, Daniel Baldwin, Ned Beatty, Jon Polito, Toni Lewis; ***D:*** Jean De Segonzac; ***W:*** Eric Overmyer, Tom Fontana, James Yoshimura; ***C:*** Jean De Segonzac; ***M:*** Douglas J. Cuomo. **TV**

Hondo **1953** In 1874, whites have broken their treaty with the Apache nation who are now preparing for war. Cavalry dispatch rider Hondo Lane (Wayne) encounters Angie (Page) and her young son at an isolated ranch and warns her of the danger but she refuses to leave. After various Indian attacks, Hondo persuades Angie (they've fallen in love) to leave for California with him. Based on the story "The Gift of Cochise" by Louis L'Amour. **84m/C VHS, DVD.** John Wayne, Geraldine Page, Ward Bond, Michael Pate, James Arness, Rodolfo Acosta, Leo Gordon, Lee Aaker, Paul Fix; ***D:*** John Farrow; ***W:*** James Edward Grant; ***C:*** Robert Burks, Archie Stout; ***M:*** Hugo Friedhofer, Emil Newman.

Honey 1/2 **1981** Attractive writer pays an unusual visit to the home of a distinguished publisher. Brandishing a pistol, she demands that he read aloud from her manuscript. As he reads, a unique fantasy unfolds, a dreamlike erotic tale that may be the writer's own sexual awakening. Or maybe not. **89m/C VHS.** *IT SP* Clio Goldsmith, Fernando Rey, Catherine Spaak; ***D:*** Gianfranco Angelucci.

Honey **2003 (PG-13)** Honey Daniels (Alba) shakes her tail feathers as a hip-hop dancer with a heart of gold. Honey is plucked out of clubland obscurity by slimy music director Michael Ellis (Moscow) and her career as a video choreographer skyrockets. Alba shines as Honey shows a lot of bare midriffs, romances the local good-guy barber (Phifer), and tries to prevent two local kids from falling in with the wrong crowd. Energetic dancing and hip-hop soundtrack couldn't prevent the formulaic cliches from popping up (does every dance movie need to put on a show to save the kids?). Could also be called "Save the Last Electric Boogaloo Flashdance." Cameos by Jadakiss, Ginuwine and Missy Elliott. **94m/C VHS, DVD.** *US* Jessica Alba, Mekhi Phifer, Joy Bryant, Lil' Romeo, David Moscow, Lonette McKee, Zachary Isaiah Williams, Laurie Ann Gibson, Anthony Sherwood; ***Cameos:*** Missy Elliott; ***D:*** Bille Woodruff; ***W:*** Alonzo Brown, Kim Watson; ***C:*** John R. Leonetti; ***M:*** Mervyn Warren.

Honey & Ashes *Miel et Cendres* **1996** Three women in Islamic Tunisia try to overcome their patriarchal society and control their own lives with bitter consequences. Leila flees to the city when her father disapproves of the boy she loves; Naima may be a successful doctor but she still can't avoid a pre-arranged marriage; and Amina suffers constant abuse from her husband. French and Arabic with subtitles. **80m/C VHS, DVD.** *SI* Nozha Khouadra, Amel Hedhili, Samia Mzali, Lara Chaouachi, Naji Najeh, Slim Larnaout, Jamel Sassi; ***D:*** Nadia Fares; ***W:*** Nadia Fares, Yves Kropf; ***C:*** Ismael Ramirez; ***M:*** Slim Larnaout, Jean-Francois Bovard, Mami Azairez.

Honey, I Blew Up the Kid 1/2 **1992 (PG)** Screwball suburban inventor Moranis reverses his shrinking process and this time manages to enlarge his two-year-old into a 112-foot giant who gets bigger every time he comes in contact with electricity. Yikes! Loaded with great special effects, this is a charming and funny film that's fit for the whole family. Sequel to "Honey I Shrunk the Kids." **89m/C VHS, DVD.** Rick Moranis, Marcia Strassman, Robert Oliveri, Daniel Shalikar, Joshua Shalikar, Lloyd Bridges, John Shea, Keri Russell, Gregory Sierra, Julia Sweeney, Kenneth Tobey, Peter Elbling; ***D:*** Randal Kleiser; ***W:*** Thom Eberhardt, Garry Goodrow; ***M:*** Bruce Broughton.

Honey, I Shrunk the Kids 1/2 **1989 (G)** The popular Disney fantasy about a suburban inventor. His shrinking device accidentally reduces his kids to 1/4 inch tall, and he subsequently throws them out with the garbage. Now they must journey back to the house through the jungle that was once the back lawn. Accompanied by "Tummy Trouble," the first of a projected series of Roger Rabbit Maroon Cartoons. Followed by "Honey, I Blew Up the Kids." **101m/C VHS, DVD.** Rick Moranis, Matt Frewer, Marcia Strassman, Kristine Sutherland, Thomas Wilson Brown, Jared Rushton, Amy O'Neill, Robert Oliveri; ***D:*** Joe Johnston, Rob Minkoff; ***W:*** Ed Naha, Tom Schulman, Stuart Gordon; ***C:*** Hiro Narita; ***M:*** James Horner; ***V:*** Charles Fleischer, Kathleen Turner, Lou Hirsch, April Winchell.

The Honey Pot 1/2 *It Comes Up Murder; Anyone for Venice?; Mr. Fox of Venice* **1967** A millionaire feigns death to see the reaction of three of his former lovers. Amusing black comedy with fine performances from all. Based on Moliere's "Volpone."

131m/C VHS. Rex Harrison, Susan Hayward, Cliff Robertson, Capucine, Edie Adams, Maggie Smith, Adolfo Celi; ***D:*** Joseph L. Mankiewicz; ***W:*** Joseph L. Mankiewicz; ***M:*** John Addison.

Honey, We Shrunk Ourselves 🦴🦴 ½ **1997 (PG)** Scientist Wayne Szalinsky (Moranis) manages to shrink himself, his wife, his brother, and his sister-in-law. The kids just think their parents are out of town for the weekend (so they go nuts). The third in the "Honey" series, this one was released directly to video. Though adults may find it dull, it was made with the kids in mind. **76m/C VHS.** Rick Moranis, Stuart Pankin, Robin Bartlett, Eve Gordon, Bug Hall; ***D:*** Dean Cundey; ***W:*** Karey Kirkpatrick, Nell Scovell, Joel Hodgson; ***C:*** Raymond N. Stella. **VIDEO**

Honeybaby 🦴🦴 **1974 (PG)** A smooth international soldier of fortune and a bright, sexy American interpreter are entangled in Middle-Eastern turbulence when they must rescue a politician kidnapped by terrorists. **94m/C VHS.** Calvin Lockhart, Diana Sands; ***D:*** Michael A. Schultz.

Honeyboy 🦴 ½ **1982** Estrada tries to win fame, fortune, and a ticket out of the barrio as an up-and-coming boxer. Outstanding fight scenes, but little else in this drama of the boxing scene. **100m/C VHS.** Erik Estrada, Morgan Fairchild, James McEachin, Robert Costanzo, Yvonne Wilder; ***D:*** John Berry. **TV**

Honeydripper 🦴🦴 **2007 (PG-13)** Sayles rarely is predictable, but this time the showbiz story seems all too familiar. In rural 1950s Alabama, Tyrone Purvis (Glover) is going to lose his debt-ridden roadhouse, the Honeydripper, unless he can come up with a surefire way to make money. He decides to advertise that local legend Guitar Sam will appear on Saturday night, though he hasn't actually booked the performer. Riding the rails into town to save the day is young blues upstart Sonny Blake (Clark), who brings along his solid wood-body electric guitar. **123m/C DVD.** *US* Danny Glover, Lisa Gay Hamilton, Yaya DaCosta, Charles S. Dutton, Gary Clark Jr., Vondie Curtis-Hall, Stacy Keach, Mable John; ***D:*** John Sayles; ***W:*** John Sayles; ***C:*** Dick Pope; ***M:*** Mason Daring.

Honeymoon 🦴🦴 **1987** A young French woman visiting New York learns she will be deported when her boyfriend is arrested for drug-smuggling. To stay, she is set up in a marriage of convenience and told her new husband will never see or bother her. But hubby has other plans! **96m/C VHS.** John Shea, Nathalie Baye, Richard Berry, Peter Donat; ***D:*** Patrick Jamain; ***W:*** Philippe Setbon.

Honeymoon Academy 🦴🦴 *For Better or For Worse* **1990 (PG-13)** Newly married man has lots to learn in this comic outing. His new wife never told him about her unusual line of business—as an undercover agent! **94m/C VHS.** Robert Hays, Kim Cattrall, Leigh Taylor-Young, Charles Rocket, Doris Roberts, Gordon Jump, Jonathan Banks; ***D:*** Gene Quintano; ***W:*** Gene Quintano; ***M:*** Robert Folk.

Honeymoon Horror 🦴 **1982** Stranded on an island, three honeymooning couples soon realize their romantic retreat is a nightmare. A crazy man with an axe is tracking them down. Minimally effective. **90m/C VHS.** Cheryl Black, William F. Pecchi, Bob Wagner; ***D:*** Harry Preston; ***W:*** Harry Preston; ***C:*** David Pinkston; ***M:*** Ron Di Lulio.

Honeymoon in Vegas 🦴🦴 ½ **1992 (PG-13)** Romantic comedy turns frantic after Cage loses his fiancee to Caan in a high stakes Vegas poker game. Cage displays lots of talent for manic comedy as the distraught young groom-to-be who encounters numerous obstacles on his way to the altar. Lightweight and funny, featuring a bevy of Elvis impersonators in every size, shape, and color and new versions of favorite Elvis tunes. Look for former UNLV basketball coach Jerry Tarkanian as one of Caan's gambling buddies. **95m/C VHS, DVD.** James Caan, Nicolas Cage, Sarah Jessica Parker, Noriyuki "Pat" Morita, John Capodice, Robert Costanzo, Anne Bancroft, Peter Boyle, Seymour Cassel, Tony Shalhoub, Ben Stein, Angela Pietropinto; ***D:*** Andrew Bergman; ***W:*** Andrew Bergman; ***C:*** William A. Fraker; ***M:*** David Newman.

Honeymoon Killers 🦴🦴🦴 *The Lonely Hearts Killers* **1970 (R)** A grim, creepy dramatization of a true multiple-murder case wherein an overweight woman and slimy gigolo living on Long Island seduce and murder one lonely woman after another. Independently made and frankly despairing. **103m/C VHS, DVD.** Tony LoBianco, Shirley Stoler, Mary Jane Higby, Dortha Duckworth, Doris Roberts, Marilyn Chris, Kip McArdle, Mary Breen, Barbara Cason, Ann Harris, Guy Sorel; ***D:*** Leonard Kastle; ***W:*** Leonard Kastle; ***C:*** Oliver Wood.

Honeymoon Lodge 🦴🦴 **1943** Bob (Bruce) and Carol (Vincent) Sterling make a last attempt to save their marriage by recreating their mountain resort honeymoon. Instead, they meet old flames Lorraine (Hilliard) and Big Boy (Cameron) and jealousy rears its ugly head. Hilliard also gets a chance to work with hubby Ozzie Nelson and His Orchestra. **63m/B VHS.** David Bruce, June Vincent, Rod Cameron, Franklin Pangborn, Harriet Hilliard Nelson; ***D:*** Edward Lilley; ***W:*** Clyde Bruckman; ***C:*** Paul Ivano.

The Honeymoon Machine 🦴🦴 ½ **1961** A lightweight comedy about two American sailors and a computer scam. McQueen and Mullaney hook up with computer expert Hutton to use their ship's computer to beat the gambling odds at an Italian casino. Their commander misinterprets the signals and thinks the ship is being attacked. Fast paced and the computer angle was new territory in '61. **87m/C VHS.** Steve McQueen, Jack Mullaney, Jim Hutton, Dean Jagger, Paula Prentiss, Brigid Bazlen, Jack Weston; ***D:*** Richard Thorpe; ***W:*** George Wells; ***C:*** Joseph LaShelle; ***M:*** Leigh Harline.

The Honeymooners 🦴🦴 **2003** Modest romantic comedy. When David is jilted at the altar, he gets drunk and decides to go on his honeymoon anyway. He meets Claire, who's just been fired and whose married lover keeps breaking his promises. She's anxious to get out of Dublin and David's too drunk to drive, so he pays her to take him to his brand-new cottage in Donegal where they can both recover from being betrayed. **86m/C DVD.** *IR GB* Jonathan Byren, Justine Mitchell, Alex Reid, Conor Mullen; ***D:*** Karl Golden; ***W:*** Karl Golden; ***C:*** Darran Tiernan; ***M:*** Niall Byrne.

The Honeymooners 🦴🦴 **2005 (PG-13)** The classic '50s TV series, which starred Jackie Gleason and Art Carney, is given an update—but why bother? Bus driver Ralph Kramden (Cedric the Entertainer) involves best pal, sewer worker Ed Norton (Epps), in various get-rich-quick schemes that always go wrong, exasperating both Ralph's wife Alice (Union) and Ed's wife Trixie (Hall). At least this time Ralph wants to give Alice the moon instead of sending her there, but the story should have been left in the TV vault where it belonged. **90m/C DVD.** *US* Cedric the Entertainer, Mike Epps, Gabrielle Union, Regina Hall, John Leguizamo, Jon Polito, Eric Stoltz, Carol Woods, Ajay Naidu, Kim Chan; ***D:*** John Schultz; ***W:*** Don Rhymer, Barry W. Blaustein, David Sheffield, Danny Jacobson; ***C:*** Shawn Maurer; ***M:*** Richard Gibbs.

Honeysuckle Rose 🦴🦴 ½ *On the Road Again* **1980 (PG)** A road-touring country-Western singer whose life is a series of one night stands, falls in love with an adoring young guitar player who has just joined his band. This nearly costs him his marriage when his wife, who while waiting patiently for him at home, decides she's had enough. Easygoing performance by Nelson, essentially playing himself. **120m/C VHS, DVD.** Willie Nelson, Dyan Cannon, Amy Irving, Slim Pickens, Joey Floyd, Charles Levin, Priscilla Pointer; ***D:*** Jerry Schatzberg; ***W:*** William D. Wittliff, John Binder, Carol Sobieski; ***M:*** Willie Nelson, Richard Baskin. Golden Raspberries '80: Worst Support. Actress (Irving).

Hong Kong Nights 🦴🦴 ½ **1935** Two agents attempt to break up a Chinese smuggling ring run by an unscrupulous madman. Good, action-packed low-budget film. **59m/B VHS.** Tom Keene, Wera Engels, Warren Hymer, Tetsu Komai, Cornelius Keefe; ***D:*** E. Mason Hopper.

Hong Kong 1941 🦴🦴 ½ **1984** Yip Kim Fay (Yun-Fat) arrives in Hong Kong on the eve of war in 1941 and befriends peasant Wong Hak Keung (Man). Fay and Keung plan to leave Hong Kong with Keung's girlfriend, Ah Nam (Yip), but fall victim to the Japanese invasion. An early role for Yun-Fat, who's the romantic hero here rather than the action star he later became. Chinese with subtitles. **118m/C VHS, DVD.** *HK* Cecilia Yip, Alex Man, Chow Yun-Fat; ***D:*** Po-Chih Leung; ***W:*** Koon-Chung Chan.

Hong Kong '97 🦴🦴 **1994 (R)** On the eve of China's takeover of Hong Kong from Great Britain, special agent Reg Cameron (Patrick) murders a Chinese general. With a $10 million bounty on his head, Cameron tries to escape with his partners and girlfriend in tow. Lots of action, good use of Hong Kong setting. **91m/C VHS.** Robert Patrick, Ming Na, Brion James, Tim Thomerson; ***D:*** Albert Pyun.

Honky 🦴 ½ **1971 (R)** An innocent friendship between a black woman and a white man develops into a passionate romance that has the whole town talking. **92m/C VHS.** Brenda Sykes, John Neilson, Maria Donzinger; ***D:*** William A. Graham; ***M:*** Quincy Jones.

Honky Tonk 🦴🦴🦴 **1941** A western soap opera in which ne'er do well Clark marries Lana and tries to live a respectable life. In this, the first of several MGM teamings between Gable and Turner, the chemistry between the two is evident. So much so in fact that Gable's then wife Carole Lombard let studio head Louis B. Mayer know that she was not at all thrilled. The public was pleased however, and made the film a hit. **106m/B VHS.** Clark Gable, Lana Turner, Frank Morgan, Claire Trevor, Marjorie Main, Albert Dekker, Chill Wills, Henry O'Neill, John Maxwell, Morgan Wallace, Betty Blythe, Francis X. Bushman, Veda Ann Borg; ***D:*** Jack Conway.

Honky Tonk Freeway 🦴 **1981 (PG)** An odd assortment of people become involved in a small town Mayor's scheme to turn a dying hamlet into a tourist wonderland. You can find better things to do with your evening than watch this accident. **107m/C VHS, DVD.** Teri Garr, Howard Hesseman, Beau Bridges, Hume Cronyn, William Devane, Beverly D'Angelo, Geraldine Page; ***D:*** John Schlesinger; ***W:*** Edward Clinton; ***C:*** John Bailey; ***M:*** Elmer Bernstein, Steve Dorff.

Honkytonk Man 🦴🦴 **1982 (PG)** Unsuccessful change-of-pace Eastwood vehicle set during the Depression. Aging alcoholic country singer tries one last time to make it to Nashville, hoping to perform at the Grand Ole Opry. This time he takes his nephew (played by Eastwoood's real-life son) with him. **123m/C VHS, DVD.** Clint Eastwood, Kyle Eastwood, John McIntire, Alexa Kenin, Verna Bloom; ***D:*** Clint Eastwood; ***W:*** Clancy Carlile; ***C:*** Bruce Surtees; ***M:*** Steve Dorff.

Honkytonk Nights 🦴 **1978 (R)** A honky-tonkin' romp through an evening in a country/western bar, featuring legendary topless dancer Carol Doda, Georgina ("Devil in Mrs. Jones") Spelvin, and the music of The Hot Licks (minus front man Dan Hicks). **90m/C VHS.** Carol Doda, Georgina Spelvin, Ramblin' Jack Elliot; ***D:*** Charles De Santos.

Honolulu 🦴🦴 ½ **1939** A screwball comedy with Powell providing the musical numbers. Young takes on the dual role of a Hollywood star who meets his exact double, a Hawaii plantation owner. They decide to switch identities to give their lives a little oomph. The star sails to Hawaii, falling for fellow passenger Powell, only to discover he's expected to get married upon his arrival in Honolulu. Anderson and Burns and Allen provide the comic relief. ♫The Leader Doesn't Like Music; This Night Was Made For Dreaming; Honolulu; Hymn To The Sun. **83m/B VHS.** Robert Young, Eleanor Powell, George Burns, Gracie Allen, Rita Johnson, Eddie Anderson, Clarence (C. William) Kolb; ***D:*** Edward Buzzell; ***W:*** Frank Partos, Herbert Fields; ***M:*** Franz Waxman.

Honor 🦴 ½ **2006 (R)** Standard martial arts showdown between two neighborhood friends, Raymond (Wong) and Gabriel (Barry), who wind up on dueling gangs when a vicious police conflict sends Raymond to the slammer and Gabriel to the military and an overseas war. After returning home, it's a natural end game for the now more callous pair. **85m/C DVD.** Jason Barry, Russell Wong, Roddy Piper, Remy Bonjasky, Linda Park; ***D:*** David Worth; ***W:*** Larry Felix Jr. **VIDEO**

Honor Among Thieves 🦴 ½ *Farewell, Friend; Adieu, l'ami* **1968 (R)** Two former mercenaries reteam for a robbery that doesn't come off as planned. Not as fast paced as others in Bronson canon. **115m/C VHS, DVD.** *FR IT* Charles Bronson, Alain Delon, Brigitte Fossey, Olga Georges-Picot, Bernard Fresson; ***D:*** Jean Herman; ***W:*** Sebastien Japrisot; ***C:*** Jean-Jacques Tarbes; ***M:*** Francois de Roubaix.

Honor and Glory 🦴🦴 **1992 (R)** Tracy Pride, an FBI agent and martial arts expert, teams up with an Interpol agent, who doubles as a TV anchorwoman, to stop an international banker from getting his greedy hands on the key to a nuclear arsenal. These fighting gals are up against a team of assassins but they can more than handle themselves. **90m/C VHS.** Cynthia Rothrock, Donna Jason, Chuck Jeffreys, Gerald Klein, Robin Shou, Richard Yuen; ***D:*** Godfrey Ho; ***W:*** Herb Borkland.

Honor of the Range 🦴🦴 **1934** The good sheriff's lady is whisked away by his evil twin brother and the sheriff must go undercover to get her back. Odd plot twists for a seemingly normal western. **60m/B VHS, DVD.** Ken Maynard, Cecilia Parker, Fred Kohler Sr.; ***D:*** Ken Maynard.

Honor Thy Father 🦴🦴 **1973** The everyday life of a real-life Mafia family as seen through the eyes of Bill Bonanno, the son of mob chieftain Joe Bonanno. Adapted from the book by Gay Talese. **97m/C DVD.** Raf Vallone, Richard S. Castellano, Brenda Vaccaro, Joseph Bologna; ***D:*** Paul Wendkos; ***M:*** George Duning. **TV**

Honor Thy Father and Mother: The True Story of the Menendez Brothers 🦴🦴 ½ **1994** First Amy Fisher won the true-sleaze-on-TV award and now its the turn of Lyle and Erik Menendez. Accused of the gruesome 1989 shotgun murders of their wealthy parents, the trial provided numerous sordid details, including alleged sexual abuse of the brothers by both parents. (Both Menendez trials ended in hung juries and will be retried). Composite characters and compressed time sequences play fast and loose with the facts of the case. Based on public records and on the book "Blood Brothers," by reporters John Johnson and Ronald L. Soble. **90m/C VHS.** Billy Warlock, David Beron, Jill Clayburgh, James Farentino, Susan Blakely, Erin Gray, Elaine Joyce, John Beck, John David Conti, Stanley Kamel; ***D:*** Paul Schneider; ***W:*** Michael J. Murray. **TV**

Hooch 🦴 ½ **1976 (PG)** Comedy about three members of the New York Mafia who get some unexpected southern hospitality when they try to muscle in on a southern family's moonshine operation. **96m/C VHS.** Gil Gerard, Erika Fox, Melody Rogers, Danny Aiello, Mike Allen, Raymond Serra; ***D:*** Edward Andrew (Santos Alcocer) Mann.

Hooded Angels 🦴🦴 *Glory Glory* **2000 (R)** Westrogen features six women out for revenge after enduring mistreatment by a gang of renegade soldiers shortly after the Civil War. Male posse, led by brothers Bauer and Johansson, don't realize their outlaws are female at first but they learn these ladies give as good as they get. **95m/C VHS, DVD.** Amanda Donohoe, Steven Bauer, Paul Johansson, Chantel Stander, Gary Busey, Juliana Venter; ***D:*** Paul Matthews; ***W:*** Paul Matthews; ***C:*** Vincent Cox.

The Hooded Terror *Sexton Blake and the Hooded Terror* **1938** A merciless group of murderers take on a G-man. **70m/B VHS.** *GB* George Curzon, Tony Sympson, Charles Oliver, David Farrar, Tod Slaughter, Greta Gynt; ***D:*** George King; ***W:*** A.R. Rawlinson; ***C:*** Hone Glendinning.

The Hoodlum 🦴🦴 **1951** A criminal does his best to rehabilitate and, with a little help from his brother, is able to hold a steady job. However the crime bug dies hard and when he spots an armored car, he just can't resist the temptation. Tierney's real brother, Edward, plays his screen brother. **61m/B VHS, DVD.** Lawrence Tierney, Allene Roberts, Marjorie (Reardon) Riordan, Lisa Golm, Edward Tierney; ***D:*** Max Nosseck.

Hoodlum 🦴🦴 ½ *Gangster; Hoods* **1996 (R)** Highly fictionalized tale of '30s gangster "Bumpy" Johnson (Fishburne, reprising his role from "The Cotton Club"), who refuses to allow Dutch Schultz (Roth) and

Lucky Luciano (Garcia) to muscle into the Harlem numbers rackets. Duke makes the proceedings nice to look at, and does well by the eclectic cast, but the uneven screenplay occasionally lets everybody down, especially during the cheesy time-passage montage (complete with Tommy Gun fire and flipping calendar pages). Roth is ruthless as ever and Garcia is smooth as ever. But it's definitely Fishburne's show, as he explores Johnson's professional triumphs and the personal toll they take. Fishburne previously worked with director Duke on "Deep Cover." Singer Michael McCary from Boyz II Men makes his film debut as an explosives expert. **130m/C VHS, DVD.** Laurence Fishburne, Tim Roth, Andy Garcia, Vanessa L(ynne) Williams, Cicely Tyson, Clarence Williams III, William Atherton, Chi McBride, Richard Bradford, Loretta Devine, Queen Latifah, Paul Benjamin, Mike Starr, Beau Starr, Joe Guzaldo, Ed O'Ross; ***D:*** Bill Duke; ***W:*** Chris Brancato; ***C:*** Frank Tidy; ***M:*** Elmer Bernstein.

Hoodlum & Son ½ **2003 (PG-13)** Charlie's a 1930s gangster who neglects his ten-year-old trouble-prone son Archie. The kid then gets in dad's way when he's trying to do a job for mob boss Benny and collect on a debt. Stolen money and a beautiful widow also figure in to the good-natured plot. Shot (though not set) in South Africa. **92m/C DVD.** *GB* T. W. (Ted) King, Ron Perlman, Myles Jeffrey, Mia Sara, Robert Vaughn; ***D:*** Ashley Way; ***W:*** Ashley Way; ***C:*** Buster Reynolds; ***M:*** Mark Thomas.

Hoodlum Empire **1952** A senator enlists the aid of a former gangster, now a war hero, in his battle against the syndicate. Loosely based on the Kefauver investigations of 1950-51. **98m/B VHS.** Brian Donlevy, Claire Trevor, Forrest Tucker, Vera Hruba Ralston, Luther Adler, John Russell, Gene Lockhart, Grant Withers, Taylor Holmes, Roy Barcroft, Richard Jaeckel; ***D:*** Joseph Kane.

The Hoodlum Priest **1961** Biography of the Rev. Charles Dismas Clark (Murray), a Jesuit priest who dedicated his life to working with juvenile delinquents and ex-cons in St. Louis. Dullea made his screen debut as Billy Lee Jackson, a thief who finds the straight and narrow is a hard road with more detours than he can handle. Fine performances with Murray co-scripting under the pseudonym Don Deer. **101m/B VHS, DVD.** Don Murray, Keir Dullea, Larry Gates, Logan Ramsey, Cindi Wood; ***D:*** Irvin Kershner; ***W:*** Don Murray, Joseph Landon; ***C:*** Haskell Wexler.

Hoodoo Ann **1916** The story of Hoodoo Ann, from her days in the orphanage to her happy marriage. Silent. **27m/B VHS, DVD.** Mae Marsh, Robert "Bobbie" Harron, Wilbur Higby, William H. Brown, Loyola O'Connor, Mildred Harris, Elmo Lincoln, Anna Dodge, Charles Lee, Carl Stockdale; ***D:*** Lloyd Ingraham; ***W:*** D.W. Griffith.

Hoods ½ **1998 (R)** Mob comedy features a bunch of pros that make it worth watching. Smalltime mobster Martinelli (Mantegna) suffers a midlife crisis on his 50th birthday when he learns that his floozy girlfriend (Tilly) is cheating on him and his aging father wants him to whack someone named Carmine—who turns out to be a nine-year-old boy. **92m/C VHS, DVD.** Joe Mantegna, Kevin Pollak, Joe Pantoliano, Jennifer Tilly; ***D:*** Mark Malone; ***W:*** Mark Malone; ***C:*** Tobias Schliessler; ***M:*** Anthony Marinelli.

Hoodwinked **2005 (PG)** "Rashamon" meets the brothers Grimm as the Weinsteins introduce the kiddies to police procedurals and action flicks by way of "The Thin Man" and extreme sports. Red Riding Hood (Hathaway), Granny (Close), the Wolf (Warburton), and the Woodsman (Belushi) all get to tell their side of the famous story when the cops bust in on the proceedings. Plenty of references to genres and movies old and new ensure that adults will enjoy this one as much as, if not more than, the kids. Somewhat clunky animation is the only flaw. **89m/C DVD.** *US* ***D:*** Cory Edwards; ***W:*** Cory Edwards, Todd Edwards, Tony Leech; ***M:*** Todd Edwards; ***V:*** Anne Hathaway, Glenn Close, James Belushi, Patrick Warburton, Anthony Anderson, David Ogden Stiers, Xzibit, Chazz Palminteri, Andy Dick, Cory Edwards, Benjy Gaither.

Hoodwinked Too! Hood vs. Evil *Hoodwinked 2: Hood vs. Evil* **2010 (PG)** A teenaged Red Riding Hood is training with the covert Sister Hoods when she and the Wolf are called in to investigate the disappearance of Hansel and Gretel. **m/C DVD.** Cory Edwards; ***D:*** Mike Disa; ***W:*** Cory Edwards, Todd Edwards, Tony Leech; ***M:*** Murray Gold; ***V:*** Hayden Panettiere, Patrick Warburton, Glenn Close, David Ogden Stiers, Andy Dick, Martin Short, Brad Garrett, Joan Cusack, Bill Hader, Amy Poehler.

Hook **1991 (PG)** Although he said he was never gonna to do it, Peter Pan has grown up. Uptight Peter Banning places work before family and has forgotten all about Neverland and the evil Captain Hook, until Hook kidnaps the Banning kids and takes them to Neverland. With the help of Tinkerbell, her magic pixie dust, and happy thoughts, Peter rescues his kids and rediscovers his youth while visiting with the Lost Boys. The sets and special effects are spectacular; the direction less so. Big-budget fantasy lacks the charm it needs to really fly. Still, kids seem to love it. You'll have to look hard to spot pirates Crosby and Close. Futurizes the J.M. Barrie classic. **142m/C VHS, DVD.** Dustin Hoffman, Robin Williams, Julia Roberts, Bob Hoskins, Maggie Smith, Charlie Korsmo, Caroline Goodall, Amber Scott, Phil Collins, Arthur Malet, Dante Basco, Gwyneth Paltrow, Glenn Close, David Crosby; ***D:*** Steven Spielberg; ***W:*** Nick Castle; ***C:*** Dean Cundey; ***M:*** John Williams.

Hook, Line and Sinker **1930** A couple of insurance investigators try to help a young woman restore a hotel, and they find romance and run-ins with crooks. Directed by Cline, who later directed W.C. Fields in "The Bank Dick," "My Little Chickadee," and "Never Give a Sucker an Even Break." **75m/B VHS, DVD.** Bert Wheeler, Robert Woolsey, Dorothy Lee, Jobyna Howland, Ralf Harolde, Natalie Moorhead, George F. Marion Sr., Hugh Herbert; ***D:*** Edward F. (Eddie) Cline; ***W:*** Rod Amateau.

The Hooked Generation **1969 (R)** A group of drug pushers kidnap defenseless victims, rape innocent girls, and even murder their own Cuban drug contacts (and all without the aid of a cohesive plot). Many gory events precede their untimely deaths; few will be entertained. **92m/C VHS, DVD.** Jeremy Slate, Steve Alaimo; ***D:*** William Grefe; ***W:*** William Grefe; ***C:*** Gregory Sandor; ***M:*** Chris Martell.

Hoop Dreams **1994 (PG-13)** Exceptional documentary follows two inner-city basketball phenoms' lives through high school as they chase their dreams of playing in the NBA. We meet Arthur Agee and William Gates as they prepare to enter St. Joseph, a predominantly white Catholic school that has offered them partial athletic scholarships. The coach tabs Gates as the "next Isiah Thomas," alluding to the school's most famous alum. There's plenty of game footage, but the more telling and fascinating parts of the film deal with the kids' families and home life. Both players encounter dramatic reversals of fortune on and off the court, demonstrating the incredibly long odds they face. **169m/C VHS, DVD.** Arthur Agee, William Gates; ***D:*** Steve James; ***C:*** Peter Gilbert. Directors Guild '95: Feature Doc. (James); L.A. Film Critics '94: Feature Doc.; MTV Movie Awards '95: New Filmmaker (James); Natl. Bd. of Review '94: Feature Doc., Natl. Film Reg. '05;; N.Y. Film Critics '94: Feature Doc.; Natl. Soc. Film Critics '94: Feature Doc.; Sundance '94: Aud. Award.

Hooper ½ **1978 (PG)** Lightweight behind-the-scenes satire about the world of movie stuntmen. Reynolds is a top stuntman who becomes involved in a rivalry with an up-and-coming young man out to surpass him. Dated good-ole-boy shenanigans. **94m/C VHS, DVD.** Burt Reynolds, Jan-Michael Vincent, Robert Klein, Sally Field, Brian Keith, John Marley, Adam West; ***D:*** Hal Needham; ***W:*** Bill Kerby, Thomas (Tom) Rickman; ***C:*** Bobby Byrne; ***M:*** Bill Justis.

Hoopla **1933** Bow's last film has her portraying the seductive older woman in a number of scanty outfits. Carnival femme Lou (Bow) seduces teen Chris (Cromwell) and makes him a man. Climax (not that kind!) takes place at the Chicago World's Fair. Adapted from the Kenyon Nicholson play "The Barker." **85m/B VHS.** Clara Bow, Richard Cromwell, Preston Foster, Herbert Mundin, James Gleason, Minna Gombell, Florence Roberts, Roger Imhof; ***D:*** Frank Lloyd; ***W:*** Joseph Moncure March, Bradley King; ***C:*** Ernest Palmer; ***M:*** Louis De Francesco.

Hoosier Schoolboy ½ **1937** Pure free-flowing sap. Shockey (Rooney) is a poor smalltown student, subjected to constant ridicule because his dad (Shields) is a shell-shocked drunk. New teacher Mary (Nagel) sets out to help them both but there's more tragedy to come because of a local strike. **62m/B DVD.** Mickey Rooney, Anne Nagel, Frank Shields, Dorothy Vaughan, William (Bill) Gould, Edward Pawley; ***D:*** William Nigh; ***W:*** Robert Lee Johnson; ***C:*** Paul Ivano.

Hoosiers **1986 (PG)** In Indiana, where basketball is the sport of the gods, a small town high school basketball team gets a new, but surprisingly experienced coach. He makes the team, and each person in it, better than they thought possible. Classic plot rings true because of Hackman's complex and sensitive performance coupled with Hopper's touching portrait of an alcoholic basketball fanatic. **115m/C VHS, DVD, Blu-ray Disc, UMD.** Gene Hackman, Barbara Hershey, Dennis Hopper, David Neidorf, Sheb Wooley, Fern Parsons, Brad Boyle, Steve Hollar, Brad Long; ***D:*** David Anspaugh; ***W:*** Angelo Pizzo; ***C:*** Fred Murphy; ***M:*** Jerry Goldsmith. L.A. Film Critics '86: Support. Actor (Hopper), Natl. Film Reg. '01.

Hoot ½ **2006 (PG)** Mild eco-tale based on Carl Hiaasen's young-adult novel. Young teen Roy (Lerman) is the new kid at his Coconut Cove, Florida, school. After tangling with a bully, Roy is grateful to befriend tomboy Beatrice (Larson) and runaway Mullet Fingers (Linley). Mullet spends his time sabotaging a construction site that is the habitat of the endangered burrowing owl (which is small and cute while the corporation destroying it is big and greedy). Naturally, Roy decides to help out (the owls of course). **90m/C DVD.** *US* Luke Wilson, Logan Lerman, Tim Blake Nelson, Brie Larson, Cody Linley, Neil Flynn, Clark Gregg, Kiersten Warren, Jessica Cauffiel, Dean Collins, Robert Wagner, Eric Phillips, Jimmy Buffett, John Archie, Kin Shriner; ***D:*** Will Shriner; ***W:*** Will Shriner; ***C:*** Michael Chapman; ***M:*** Phil Marshall, Michael Utley, Mac McAnally.

Hootch Country Boys *Redneck County; The Great Lester Boggs* **1975 (PG)** A film packed with moonshine, sheriffs, busty country girls, and chases. **90m/C VHS, DVD.** Alex Karras, Scott MacKenzsie, Dean Jagger, Willie Jones, Bob Ridgely, Susan Denbo, Bob Ginnaven, David Haney; ***D:*** Harry Z. Thomason.

Hopalong Cassidy *Hopalong Cassidy Enters* **1935** In this first of a long series of "Hopalong Cassidy" films, Hoppy and his pals intervene in a brewing range war. A gang of rustlers is helped by a two-timing foreman who's playing both sides off each other. After a career in silent films, Boyd was pretty much washed up before taking on the role of Cassidy. He was originally asked to play the villain and declined, but agreed to be the good guy if the character was cleaned up. "Gabby" Hayes' stock character was killed off in this episode, but was brought back for later installments. **60m/B VHS, DVD.** William Boyd, James Ellison, Paula Stone, Robert Warwick, Charles Middleton, Frank McGlynn, Kenneth Thomson, George "Gabby" Hayes, James Mason, Franklyn Farnum, Doris Schroeder; ***D:*** Howard Bretherton; ***C:*** Archie Stout.

Hopalong Cassidy: Borrowed Trouble ½ **1948** Hoppy must save a righteous teacher from the clutches of kidnappers who plan to place a saloon right next to the school. **61m/B VHS, DVD.** William Boyd, Andy Clyde, Rand Brooks, Elaine Riley, John Kellogg, Helen Chapman; ***D:*** George Archainbaud.

Hopalong Cassidy: Dangerous Venture **1948** "Dangerous Venture" was one of Hoppy's last ventures, produced the final year of the series' 13-year tenure. Hoppy and the gang hunt for Aztec ruins in the great Southwest, and have to deal with renegade Indians and a band of treacherous looters along the way. **55m/B VHS, DVD.** William Boyd, Andy Clyde, Rand Brooks; ***D:*** George Archainbaud; ***W:*** Doris Schroeder; ***C:*** Mack Stengler; ***M:*** David Chudnow.

Hopalong Cassidy: False Paradise **1948** Another late Hopalong has the noir-clad cowboy rushing to the aid of a girl and her dad when control of their ranch is threatened by swindlers with false mining claims. **59m/B VHS.** William Boyd, Andy Clyde, Rand Brooks; ***D:*** George Archainbaud.

Hopalong Cassidy: Hoppy's Holiday **1947** Boyd—the only celluloid incarnation of Clarence Mulford's pulp hero—plays the Hopster yet again. This time, the non-drinking, non-smoking (what does he do for kicks?) hero and a passel of Bar-20 cowboys visit Mesa City for some well-earned R and R, but find themselves caught in a web of corruption. **60m/B VHS, DVD.** William Boyd, Andy Clyde, Rand Brooks, Jeff Corey; ***D:*** George Archainbaud.

Hopalong Cassidy: Renegade Trail **1939** Hoppy comes to the aid of both a small town sheriff and a widow. **61m/B VHS.** William Boyd, George "Gabby" Hayes, Russell Hayden, Charlotte Wynters, Russell Hopton, Sonny Bupp, Jack Rockwell, Roy Barcroft, John Merton, Robert F. (Bob) Kortman; ***D:*** Lesley Selander.

Hopalong Cassidy Returns ½ **1936** In the seventh entry in the "Hopalong Cassidy" series, Hoppy (Boyd) faces a lady outlaw, Lilli Marsh (Brent), who, of course, falls hard for our stalwart hero. If this is not one of the best in the series, it maintains the high production standards, and it contains the debut of series regular Morris Ankrum as a villain. **74m/B DVD.** William Boyd, George "Gabby" Hayes, Evelyn Brent, Morris Ankrum, William Janney; ***D:*** Nate Watt; ***W:*** Doris Schroeder; ***C:*** Archie Stout.

Hopalong Cassidy: Riders of the Deadline **1943** Hoppy turns into a baddie in this episode in order to infiltrate a treacherous gang and apprehend their leader. **70m/B VHS, DVD.** William Boyd, Andy Clyde, Jimmy Rogers, Robert Mitchum; ***D:*** Lesley Selander.

Hopalong Cassidy: Silent Conflict **1948** Lucky is tricked and hypnotized by a traveling medicine man who commands him to rob and kill Hoppy. **61m/B VHS, DVD.** William Boyd, Andy Clyde, Rand Brooks; ***D:*** George Archainbaud.

Hopalong Cassidy: Sinister Journey **1948** Mysterious accidents are plaguing a railroad where an old friend of Hoppy's works, so Hoppy, California, and Lucky take railroad jobs to find out what gives. **58m/B VHS, DVD.** William Boyd, Andy Clyde, Rand Brooks; ***D:*** George Archainbaud.

Hopalong Cassidy: The Dead Don't Dream **1948** Hoppy's sidekick Lucky decides to get married, but happily-ever-afterdom is threatened when the father of Mrs. Lucky-to-be is murdered. When Hoppy sets out to find the killer, he finds himself suspected of the dastardly deed. **55m/B VHS, DVD.** William Boyd, Andy Clyde, Rand Brooks, John Parrish; ***D:*** George Archainbaud.

Hopalong Cassidy: The Devil's Playground **1946** Strange things are afoot in a peaceful valley adjacent to a desolate, forbidding wasteland. When Hoppy and a young woman set out across the wasteland to make a gold delivery, they encounter a band of desperados and begin to unravel the secrets of a dishonest political ring. **65m/B VHS, DVD.** William Boyd, Andy Clyde, Rand Brooks, Elaine Riley; ***D:*** George Archainbaud.

Hopalong Cassidy: The Marauders **1947** After seeking shelter in an abandoned church one rainy night, Hoppy and the boys must defend the kirk when it is threatened by a marauder and his gang. **64m/B VHS, DVD.** William Boyd, Andy Clyde, Rand Brooks; ***D:*** George Archainbaud.

Hopalong Cassidy: Unexpected Guest 🦴🦴 1/2 **1947** When a small fortune is left to a California family, the head count starts to dwindle, and Hoppy aims to find out why. **59m/B VHS, DVD.** William Boyd, Andy Clyde, Rand Brooks, Una O'Connor; ***D:*** George Archainbaud.

Hope 🦴🦴 1/2 **1997** Thirteen-year-old Lily Kate Burns (Malone) is living in the small southern town of Hope in 1962. Her mother's had a severe stroke and the only family she has to turn to are racist Uncle Ray (Walsh) and fragile Aunt Emma (Lahti). Amidst the town's segregation and fears about the Cuban Missile Crisis, Lily Kate is also more open to befriending new town residents than her elders, including visiting black preacher Jediah (Sams). Hawn's directorial debut. **100m/C VHS.** Mary Ellen Trainor, Christine Lahti, Jena Malone, J.T. Walsh, Jeffrey D. Sams, Catherine O'Hara; ***D:*** Goldie Hawn; ***W:*** Kerry Kennedy. **CABLE**

Hope and Glory 🦴🦴🦴 1/2 **1987 (PG-13)** Boorman turns his memories of WWII London into a complex and sensitive film. Father volunteers, and mother must deal with the awakening sexuality of her teenage daughter, keep her son in line, balance the ration books, and try to make it to the bomb shelter in the middle of the night. Seen through the boy's eyes, war creates a playground of shrapnel to collect and wild imaginings come true. Nice companion film to "Empire of the Sun" and "Au Revoir Les Enfants," two more 1987 releases that explore WWII from the recollections of young boys. **97m/C VHS, DVD.** *GB* Sebastian Rice-Edwards, Geraldine Muir, Sarah Miles, Sammi Davis, David Hayman, Derrick O'Connor, Susan Wooldridge, Jean-Marc Barr, Ian Bannen, Jill Baker, Charley Boorman, Annie Leon, Katrine Boorman, Gerald James, Amelda Brown, Colin Higgins; ***D:*** John Boorman; ***W:*** John Boorman; ***C:*** Philippe Rousselot; ***M:*** Peter Martin. British Acad. '87: Film, Support. Actress (Wooldridge); Golden Globes '88: Film—Mus./Comedy; L.A. Film Critics '87: Director (Boorman), Film, Screenplay; Natl. Soc. Film Critics '87: Cinematog., Director (Boorman), Film, Screenplay.

Hope Floats 🦴🦴 1/2 **1998 (PG-13)** Former small town Texas beauty queen Birdee Pruitt (Bullock) finds out her husband Bill (Pare) is having an affair with her best friend (Arquette) live on TV, thanks to a tabloid talk show expose. Completely humiliated, she takes her daughter Bernice (Whitman) and heads home to her own rather spaced-out mom Ramona (Rowlands). She's trying to gain some perspective on her life—and maybe, slowly, find a new love with the help of handsome cowpoke Justin (Connick Jr.) Movie is sweet, sentimental, obvious, and has an appealing cast and a happy ending. Perfect girlfriend fare. **114m/C VHS, DVD.** Sandra Bullock, Harry Connick Jr., Gena Rowlands, Mae Whitman, Cameron Finley, Michael Pare, Rosanna Arquette, Kathy Najimy, Bill Cobbs; ***D:*** Forest Whitaker; ***W:*** Steven Rogers; ***C:*** Caleb Deschanel; ***M:*** Dave Grusin.

Hope Ranch 🦴🦴 **2002 (PG-13)** J.T Hope (Boxleitner), an ex-cop and Marine, runs a ranch designed to rehabilitate juvenile delinquents. When three street-wise but troubled kids arrive, J.T. and his staff are put to the test. Uplifting family fare blends action and message smoothly. Produced for the Animal Planet network. **100m/C VHS, DVD.** Bruce Boxleitner, Lorenzo Lamas, Barry Corbin, Gail O'Grady, Laura Johnson, Richard Lee Jackson, Brian Gross, J.D. Pardo, Isabell Howell, Brad Hawkins; ***D:*** Rex Piano; ***W:*** C. Thomas Howell, Jim Snider; ***C:*** Howard Wexler; ***M:*** Bruce Lynch. **CABLE**

Hoppity Goes to Town 🦴🦴 *Mr. Bug Goes to Town* **1941** Full-length animated feature from the Max Fleischer studios tells the story of the inhabitants of Bugville, who live in a weed patch in New York City. **77m/C VHS, DVD.** ***D:*** Dave Fleischer; ***M:*** Frank Loesser, Hoagy Carmichael.

Hoppy Serves a Writ 🦴🦴 **1943** In this last of the series to be based on the writings of the original author, Texas sheriff Cassidy tries to bring a gang of outlaws to justice. Look for a young Robert Mitchum as one of the villains. **67m/B VHS, DVD.** William Boyd, Andy Clyde, Jay Kirby, Victor Jory, George Reeves, Hal Taliaferro, Robert Mitchum, Byron Foulger, Earle Hodgins, Roy Barcroft; ***D:*** George Archainbaud.

Hopscotch 🦴🦴🦴 **1980 (R)** A C.I.A. agent drops out when his overly zealous chief demotes him to a desk job. When he writes a book designed to expose the dirty deeds of the CIA, he leads his boss and KGB pal on a merry chase. Amiable comedy well-suited for Matthau's rumpled talents. **107m/C VHS, DVD.** Walter Matthau, Glenda Jackson, Ned Beatty, Sam Waterston, Herbert Lom; ***D:*** Ronald Neame.

Horatio Hornblower 🦴🦴🦴 **1999** Adventure on the high seas in these adaptations of C.S. Forester's popular novels, which are set in the late 18th-century. Hornblower (Gruffudd) is a young recruit who rises through the ranks of the King's Navy as the British battle the French. "The Duel" provides the introduction to Hornblower and his mentor, Captain Pellew (Lindsay). "The Fire Ships" has Hornblower preparing for his lieutenant's exam. "The Duchess and the Devil" finds Hornblower escorting the Duchess of Wharfedale (Lunghi) to England with important naval dispatches. "The Wrong War" finds the Brits preparing a coup against the French Republican government. **400m/C VHS, DVD.** *GB* Ioan Gruffudd, Robert Lindsay, Denis Lawson, Cherie Lunghi, Anthony Sher, Samuel West, Andrew Tiernan, Ronald Pickup; ***D:*** Andrew Grieve; ***W:*** Russell Lewis, Mike Cullen, Patrick Harbinson; ***C:*** Alec Curtis, Neve Cunningham. **TV**

Horatio Hornblower: The Adventure Continues 🦴🦴🦴 **2001** The adventures of young British naval officer Hornblower (Gruffud) continue with two linked stories: "Mutiny" and "The Retribution." Horatio recounts to his mentor, Captain Pellew (Lindsay), the reasons for his imprisonment on mutiny charges after confining his insane captain (Warner) to his quarters to prevent his sending the crew into a suicidal battle. But Hornblower must also lead a force to recapture an enemy fort. Based on C.S. Forrester's novel, "Lieutenant Hornblower." **200m/C VHS, DVD.** *GB* Ioan Gruffudd, Robert Lindsay, David Warner, Jamie Bamber, Paul McGann, Nicholas Jones, Philip Glenister, David Rintoul; ***D:*** Andrew Grieve; ***C:*** Chris O'Dell; ***M:*** John Keane. **TV**

Horizons West 🦴🦴 1/2 **1952** Two brothers go their separate ways after the Civil War. One leads a peaceful life as a rancher but the other, corrupted by the war, engages in a violent campaign to build his own empire. Ryan's outstanding performance eclipses that of the young Hudson. **81m/C VHS.** Robert Ryan, Julie Adams, Rock Hudson, Raymond Burr, James Arness, John McIntire, Dennis Weaver, Frances Bavier; ***D:*** Budd Boetticher; ***M:*** Henry Mancini.

The Horizontal Lieutenant 🦴🦴 1/2 **1962** Hutton and Prentiss team up again in this moderately funny romantic-comedy about an officer's escapades during WWII. Based on the novel "The Bottletop Affair" by Gordon Cotler. **90m/C VHS, DVD.** Jim Hutton, Paula Prentiss, Jack Carter, Jim Backus, Charles McGraw, Miyoshi Umeki; ***D:*** Richard Thorpe; ***W:*** George Wells.

The Horn Blows at Midnight 🦴🦴🦴 **1945** A band trumpeter falls asleep and dreams he's a bumbling archangel, on Earth to blow the note bringing the end of the world. But a pretty girl distracts him, and...A wild, high-gloss, well-cast fantasy farce, uniquely subversive in its lighthearted approach to biblical Doomsday. Benny made the film notorious by acting ashamed of it in his later broadcast routines. **78m/B VHS.** Jack Benny, Alexis Smith, Dolores Moran, Allyn Joslyn, Reginald Gardiner, Guy Kibbee, John Alexander, Margaret Dumont; ***D:*** Raoul Walsh.

Hornet's Nest 🦴🦴 1/2 **1970** Captain Turner (Hudson) is the lone survivor of an Army commando unit which parachuted into the Italian countryside in an effort to blow up a dam being held by the Nazis. He's rescued by a group of boys, the survivors of a German massacre of their nearby town. Turner wants the boys to help him blow up the dam—and they want his help in getting revenge on the Nazis who have occupied their homes. **110m/C VHS.** Rock Hudson, Sylva Koscina, Sergio Fantoni, Jacques Sernas, Giacomo "Jack" Rossi-Stuart, Andrea Bosic, Gerard Herter, Tom Felleghi; ***D:*** Phil Karlson; ***W:*** S.S. Schweitzer.

The Horrible Dr. Bones 🦴🦴 **2000 (R)** Dr. Bones (Igus) is a record producer who gives the young Urban Protectors band their big break, but it turns out that he's exploiting them in a supernatural scheme involving human sacrifice and zombies. The plotting is amateurish. Some of the effects have shock value. The low-budget horror doesn't rise much above the studio's bare-bones production. **72m/C DVD.** Darrow Igus, Larry Bates, Sarah Scott, Rhonda Claebaut, Nathaniel Lamar; ***D:*** Art Carnage; ***W:*** Raymond Forchon; ***C:*** Adolfo Bartoli.

The Horrible Dr. Hichcock 🦴🦴 1/2 *L'Orribile Segreto del Dr. Hichcock* **1962** A sicko doctor, who accidentally killed his first wife while engaged in sexual antics, remarries to bring the first missus back from the dead using his new wife's blood. Genuinely creepy. Sequelled by "The Ghost." **76m/C VHS, DVD.** *IT* Robert Flemyng, Barbara Steele, Silvano Tranquilli, Harriet Medin, Ernesto Gastaldi, Maria Teresa Vianello; ***D:*** Riccardo Freda; ***W:*** Perry (Ernesto Gastaldi) Julyan; ***C:*** Raffaele Masciocchi; ***M:*** Roman Vlad.

The Horror Chamber of Dr. Faustus 🦴🦴🦴 1/2 *Eyes without a Face; Les Yeux sans Visage; Occhi senza Volto* **1959** A wickedly intelligent, inventive piece of Grand Guignol about a mad doctor who kills young girls so he may graft their skin onto the face of his accidentally mutilated daughter. In French with English subtitles. **84m/B VHS, DVD.** *FR* Alida Valli, Pierre Brasseur, Edith Scob, Francois Guerin, Juliette Mayniel, Alex(andre) Rignault, Claude Brasseur, Charles Blavette; ***D:*** Georges Franju; ***W:*** Jean Redon; ***C:*** Eugen Shufftan; ***M:*** Maurice Jarre.

Horror Express 🦴🦴 1/2 *Panic on the Trans-Siberian Express; Panico en el Transiberiano; Panic in the Trans-Siberian Train* **1972 (R)** A creature from prehistoric times, that was removed from its tomb, is transported on the Trans-Siberian railroad. Passengers suddenly discover strange things happening—such as having their souls sucked out of them. **88m/C VHS, DVD.** *SP GB* Christopher Lee, Peter Cushing, Telly Savalas, Alberto De Mendoza, Silvia Tortosa, Julio Pena, Angel Del Pozo, Helga Line, Jorge (George) Rigaud, Jose Jaspe; ***D:*** Eugenio (Gene) Martin; ***W:*** Julian Zimet, Arnaud d'Usseau; ***C:*** Alejandro Ulloa.

Horror Hospital 🦴 *Computer Killers; Doctor Blood Bath* **1973 (R)** Patients are turned into zombies by a mad doctor in this hospital where no anesthesia is used. Those who try to escape are taken care of by the doctor's guards. **91m/C VHS, DVD.** *GB* Michael Gough, Robin Askwith, Vanessa Shaw, Ellen Pollock, Skip Martin, Dennis Price; ***D:*** Antony Balch; ***W:*** Antony Balch, Alan Watson; ***C:*** David McDonald.

Horror Hotel 🦴🦴 1/2 *The City of the Dead* **1960** A young witchcraft student visits a small Massachusetts town which has historic ties to witch burnings and discovers a new, and deadly, coven is now active. Well done and atmospheric. **76m/B VHS, DVD.** *GB* Christopher Lee, Patricia Jessel, Betta St. John, Dennis Lotis, Venetia Stevenson, Valentine Dyall; ***D:*** John Llewellyn Moxey; ***W:*** George L. Baxt; ***C:*** Desmond Dickinson.

Horror House on Highway 5 **WOOF! 1986** Someone in a Nixon mask kills people in this extremely cheap dud. **90m/C VHS, DVD.** Phil Therrien, Max Manthey, Susan Leslie; ***D:*** Richard Casey; ***W:*** Richard Casey; ***C:*** David Golia.

Horror Island 🦴 1/2 **1941** Down on his luck entrepreneur, Bill Martin (Foran), who's always game for a get-rich-quick scheme, stumbles onto a shabby island thought to be the hiding place of a pirate's treasure. With the help of his sidekick, "Stuff" (Knight), he launches an island adventure business, but with his first group of patrons he discovers the island also conceals a phantom, murder and intrigue. Alleged to be the least expensive of Universal's 1940s horror films. **61m/B DVD.** Dick Foran, Leo Carrillo, Peggy Moran, Fuzzy Knight, John Eldredge; ***D:*** George Waggner; ***C:*** Elwood "Woody" Bredell; ***M:*** Hans J. Salter.

The Horror of Dracula 🦴🦴🦴 1/2 *Dracula* **1958** The first Hammer Dracula film, in which the infamous vampire is given a new, elegant and ruthless persona, as he battles Prof. Van Helsing after coming to England. Possibly the finest, most inspired version of Bram Stoker's macabre chestnut, and one that single-handedly revived the horror genre. **82m/C VHS, DVD.** *GB* Peter Cushing, Christopher Lee, Michael Gough, Melissa Stribling, Carol Marsh, John Van Eyssen, Valerie Gaunt, Charles Lloyd-Pack, Miles Malleson; ***D:*** Terence Fisher; ***W:*** Jimmy Sangster; ***C:*** Jack Asher; ***M:*** James Bernard.

The Horror of Frankenstein 🦴🦴 **1970** Spoof of the standard Frankenstein story features philandering ex-med student Baron Frankenstein, whose interest in a weird and esoteric branch of science provides a shocking and up-to-date rendition of the age-old plot. Preceded by "Frankenstein Must Be Destroyed" and followed by "Frankenstein and the Monster from Hell." **93m/C VHS, DVD.** *GB* Ralph Bates, Kate O'Mara, Dennis Price, David Prowse, Veronica Carlson, Joan Rice, Bernard Archard, Graham James; ***D:*** Jimmy Sangster; ***W:*** Jimmy Sangster, Jeremy Burnham; ***C:*** Moray Grant.

Horror of Party Beach **WOOF!** *Invasion of the Zombies* **1964** Considered to be one of the all-time worst films. Features a mob of radioactive seaweed creatures who eat a slew of nubile, surf-minded teenagers. ♫Zombie Stomp. **71m/C VHS, DVD.** John Scott, Alice Lyon, Allen Laurel, Marilyn Clarke, Augustin Mayer, Eulabelle Moore; ***D:*** Del Tenney; ***W:*** Richard Hilliard; ***C:*** Richard Hilliard; ***M:*** Bill Holmes.

Horror of the Blood Monsters **WOOF!** *Vampire Men of the Lost Planet; Horror Creatures of the Prehistoric Planet; Creatures of the Prehistoric Planet; Creatures of the Red Planet; Flesh Creatures of the Red Planet; The Flesh Creatures; Space Mission of the Lost Planet* **1970 (PG)** John Carradine made a career out of being in bad movies, and this one competes as one of the worst. This is an editor's nightmare, made up of black & white film spliced together and colorized. Vampires from outer space threaten to suck all the blood from the people of Earth. **85m/C VHS, DVD.** *PH* John Carradine, Robert Dix, Vicki Volante, Jennifer Bishop; ***D:*** Al Adamson, George Joseph.

Horror of the Zombies 🦴 *El Buque Maldito* **1974 (R)** Bikinied models are pursued by hooded zombies on board a pleasure yacht...the horror. Effete final installment in the "blind dead" trilogy; see also "Tombs of the Blind Dead" and "Return of the Evil Dead." **90m/C VHS, DVD.** *SP* Maria Perschy, Jack Taylor; ***D:*** Armando de Ossorio; ***W:*** Armando de Ossorio.

Horror Rises from the Tomb 🦴🦴 *El Espanto Surge de la Tumba* **1972** A 15th century knight and his assistant are beheaded for practicing witchcraft. Five hundred years later, they return to possess a group of vacationers and generally cause havoc. **89m/C VHS, DVD.** *SP* Paul Naschy, Vic Winner, Emma Cohen, Helga Line, Cristina Suriani; ***D:*** Carlos Aured; ***W:*** Paul Naschy.

The Horror Show 🦴 *House 3* **1989 (R)** Serial killer fries in electric chair, an event that really steams him. So he goes after the cop who brought him in. Standard dead guy who won't die and wants revenge flick. **95m/C VHS, DVD.** Brion James, Lance Henriksen, Rita Taggart, Dedee Pfeiffer, Aron Eisenberg, Matt Clark, Thom Bray, Terry Alexander, David Oliver; ***D:*** James Isaac; ***W:*** Alan Smithee, Leslie Bohem; ***C:*** Mac Ahlberg.

Horrors of Burke & Hare 🦴 **1971** A gory tale about the exploits of a bunch of 19th-century grave robbers. **94m/C VHS.** Derren Nesbitt, Harry Andrews, Yootha Joyce; ***D:*** Vernon Sewell.

Horrors of Malformed Men 🦴🦴 *Edogawa Rampo taizen: Kyofu kikei ningen; Horror of a Deformed Man* **1969** Based loosely on the works of Edogawa Rampo (Japanese mystery/horror writer and fan of Edgar Allan Poe), this exploitation film from the 60s is still supposed to be banned in its native Japan. A young amnesiac determined to find his lost father escapes from an asylum only to see his spitting image in the local newspaper. He assumes the man's identity and travels to Panorama Island to find out their connection, and discovers an insane scientist obsessed with curing his disfigured wife. The byproducts of his experiment are horrifying malformed creatures some more beast than man. **99m/C DVD.** *JP* Teruo Yoshida, Teruko Yumi, Asao Koike; ***W:*** Teru Ishii, Edogawa Rampo, Masahiro Kakefuda; ***C:*** Shigeru Akatsuka; ***M:*** Masao Yagi.

Horrors of Spider Island *It's Hot in Paradise; Ein Toter Hing im Netz; A Corpse Hangs in the Web* **1959** D'Arcy is a Hollywood talent scout who sniffs a goldmine in a team of young female dancers whom he schedules to perform for him in Singapore. Their transport plane crashes in the Pacific Ocean and he and the girls are forced to take refuge on an uncharted isle. Upon landing there they discover it is infested with giant crab-sized spiders. Lots of potential for both shock and arousal, which was probably why it was originally released in both "horror" and "girlie" versions. D'Arcy later admitted to taking over for director Bottger and adding all the horror sequences himself. Dubbed from the German. **77m/C VHS, DVD.** *GE* Alexander D'Arcy, Ursula Lederstger, Barbara Valentin, Harold Maresch, Helga Franck; ***D:*** Fritz Bottger; ***W:*** Fritz Bottger.

Horrors of the Red Planet *The Wizard of Mars* **1964** Cheapo epic sees astronauts crash on Mars, meet its Wizard, and stumble into a few Oz-like creatures. Technically advised by Forrest J. Ackerman. **81m/C VHS.** John Carradine, Roger Gentry, Vic McGee; ***D:*** David L. Hewitt.

The Horse 1/2 *Horse, My Horse* **1982** A moving, mature Turkish film about a father and son trying to overcome socioeconomic obstacles and their own frailties in order to make enough money to send the boy to school. In Turkish with English subtitles. **116m/C VHS, DVD.** *TU* Genco Erkal; ***D:*** Ali Ozgenturk; ***W:*** Isil Ozgenturk; ***C:*** Kenan Ormanlar; ***M:*** Okay Temiz.

Horse Feathers 1/2 **1932** Huxley College has to beef up its football team to win the championship game which has been rigged by local gamblers in the opposition's favor, and the corrupt new college president (Groucho) knows just how to do it. Features some of the brothers' classic routines, and the songs "Whatever It Is, I'm Against It" and "Everyone Says I Love You." **67m/B VHS, DVD.** Groucho Marx, Chico Marx, Harpo Marx, Zeppo Marx, Thelma Todd, David Landau, Nat Pendleton; ***D:*** Norman Z. McLeod; ***W:*** Bert Kalmar, S.J. Perelman, Harry Ruby; ***C:*** Ray June; ***M:*** Harry Ruby.

A Horse for Danny 1/2 **1995 (G)** Horse trainer Eddie (Urich), dogged by bad luck, and his 11-year-old niece Danny (Sobieski), come across a thoroughbred named Tom Thumb, who may be their chance at racing's winners circle. TV movie. **92m/C VHS, DVD.** Robert Urich, Leelee Sobieski, Ron Brice, Karen Carlson, Gary Basaraba; ***D:*** Dick Lowry; ***C:*** Steven Fierberg.

The Horse in the Gray Flannel Suit 1/2 **1968 (G)** Disney comedy portrays an advertising executive who links his daughter's devotion to horses with a client's new ad campaign. **114m/C VHS, DVD.** Dean Jones, Ellen Janov, Fred Clark, Diane Baker, Lloyd Bochner, Kurt Russell; ***D:*** Norman Tokar; ***W:*** Louis Pelletier; ***M:*** George Bruns.

The Horse of Pride 1/2 *Le Cheval D'Orgeuil* **1980** Chabrol takes a telling look at the everyday life of the peasants of Breton—both their pleasures and their sorrows. In French with English subtitles. French script booklet available. **118m/C VHS.** *FR* Jacques Dufilho, Francois Cluzet; ***D:*** Claude Chabrol.

The Horse Soldiers 1/2 **1959** An 1863 Union cavalry officer is sent 300 miles into Confederate territory to destroy a railroad junction and is accompanied by a fellow officer who is also a pacifist doctor. Based on a true Civil War incident. **114m/C VHS, DVD.** John Wayne, William Holden, Hoot Gibson, Constance Towers, Russell Simpson, Strother Martin, Anna Lee, Judson Pratt, Denver Pyle, Jack Pennick, Althea Gibson, William Forrest, Willis Bouchey, Bing (Neil) Russell, Ken Curtis, O.Z. Whitehead, Walter Reed, Hank Worden, Carleton Young, Cliff Lyons; ***D:*** John Ford; ***W:*** John Lee Mahin, Martin Rackin; ***C:*** William Clothier; ***M:*** David Buttolph.

The Horse Thief *Daoma Zei* **1987** Noted as the first movie from the People's Republic of China to be released on video, this epic tells the tale of Norbu, a man who, exiled from his people for horse thievery, is forced to wander the Tibetan countryside with his family in search of work. His son dies while he is in exile, and he, a devout Buddhist, is ultimately forced to accept tribal work in a ritual exorcism, after which he pleads to be accepted back into his clan. Beautiful and image-driven, offering a rare glimpse into the Tibet you won't see in travel brochures. Filmed on location with locals as actors. In Mandarin with English subtitles. **88m/C VHS.** *CH* Daiba, Jiji Dan, Drashi, Gaoba, Jamco Jayang, Rigzin Tseshang; ***D:*** Tian Zhuangzhuang; ***W:*** Rui Zhang; ***C:*** Fei Zhao, Hou Yong; ***M:*** Xiao-Song Qu.

The Horse Whisperer 1/2 **1997 (PG-13)** After her teenaged daughter Grace (Johansson) is injured in a riding accident, determined mom Annie (Thomas), believeing that the girl's recovery is tied to the horse's, takes child and horse to Montana to seek the help of horse healer Tom (Redford) in the big-screen adaptation of the Nicholas Evans novel. While there, chilly New York editor Annie warms up to Tom and the possibility of love. Like "The Bridges of Madison County," this adaptation removes the overwrought syrupy melodrama of its source novel to concentrate on mature themes like fidelity, trust, and fate. Fine performances by all (although Redford could be seen as a bit self-indulgent at times) and the beautiful Montana backdrop make up for the lack of sustained dramatic impact, which is probably due to the almost three-hour run time and some dramatic changes from the book. **168m/C VHS, DVD.** Robert Redford, Kristin Scott Thomas, Scarlett Johansson, Sam Neill, Chris Cooper, Dianne Wiest, Cherry Jones, Jeannette Nolan, Don Edwards, Ty Hillman, Kate (Catherine) Bosworth, Steve Frye; ***D:*** Robert Redford; ***W:*** Eric Roth, Richard LaGravenese; ***C:*** Robert Richardson; ***M:*** Thomas Newman.

The Horse Without a Head 1/2 **1963** Stolen loot has been hidden in a discarded toy horse which is now the property of a group of poor children. The thieves, however, have different plans. Good family fare from the Disney TV show. **89m/C VHS.** Jean-Pierre Aumont, Herbert Lom, Leo McKern, Pamela Franklin, Vincent Winter; ***D:*** Don Chaffey. **TV**

The Horseman on the Roof 1/2 *Le Hussard sur le Toit* **1995 (R)** Lavish costume drama set in Provence in the 1830s, during a cholera epidemic. Italian officer/revolutionary Angelo (Martinez) is on the run and eventually meets up with beautiful Pauline de Theus (Binoche), who hides him in a quarantined French village. Pauline's in search of her husband and Angelo reluctantly agrees to help her. Together they manage to escape a military cordon and travel to another plague town. There's lots of riding through the countryside and hiding out and not much actually happens. Nice scenery, attractive stars. Based on the 1951 novel by Jean Giono. French with subtitles; originally released at 135 minutes. **119m/C VHS, DVD.** *FR* Olivier Martinez, Juliette Binoche, Francois Cluzet, Isabelle Carre, Jean Yanne, Claudio Amendola, Pierre Arditti; ***Cameos:*** Gerard Depardieu; ***D:*** Jean-Paul Rappeneau; ***W:*** Jean-Paul Rappeneau, Jean-Claude Carriere, Nina Companeez; ***C:*** Thierry Arbogast; ***M:*** Jean-Claude Petit. Cesar '96: Cinematog., Sound.

Horsemasters **1961** A group of young riders enter a special training program in England to achieve the ultimate equestrian title of horsemaster, with Annette having to overcome her fear of jumping. Originally a two-part Disney TV show, and released as a feature film in Europe. **85m/C VHS.** Tommy Kirk, Annette Funicello, Janet Munro, Tony Britton, Donald Pleasence, Jean Marsh, John Fraser, Millicent Martin; ***D:*** William Fairchild. **TV**

The Horsemen 1/2 **1970 (PG)** An Afghani youth enters the brutal buzkashi horse tournament to please his macho-minded father. Beautifully shot in Afghanistan and Spain by Claude Renoir. **109m/C VHS, DVD.** Omar Sharif, Leigh Taylor-Young, Jack Palance, David De, Peter Jeffrey; ***D:*** John Frankenheimer; ***W:*** Dalton Trumbo; ***M:*** Georges Delerue.

Horsemen 1/2 **2009 (R)** Gory and slapdash horror-thriller. Forensic dentist Aidan Breslin (Quaid) realizes that a series of mutilated corpses is related to the biblical passage about the 'Four Horsemen of the Apocalypse.' The domestic scenes with Breslin's estranged sons (and a good performance by Quaid) at least offer something slightly different. **88m/C DVD.** Dennis Quaid, Ziyi Zhang, Lou Taylor Pucci, Clifton (Gonzalez) Collins Jr., Liam James, Peter Stormare, Patrick Fugit, Eric Balfour; ***D:*** Jonas Akerlund; ***W:*** David Callaham; ***C:*** Eric Broms; ***M:*** Jan A.P. Kaczmarek.

The Horseplayer 1/2 **1991 (R)** A loner is drawn into a mysterious triangle of decadence and desire in this riveting psycho-thriller. **89m/C VHS.** Brad Dourif, Sammi Davis, Michael (M.K.) Harris, Vic Tayback; ***D:*** Kurt Voss.

The Horse's Mouth *The Oracle* **1958** An obsessive painter discovers that he must rely upon his wits to survive in London. A hilarious adaptation of the Joyce Cary novel. **93m/C VHS, DVD.** *GB* Alec Guinness, Kay Walsh, Robert Coote, Renee Houston, Michael Gough; ***D:*** Ronald Neame; ***W:*** Alec Guinness; ***C:*** Arthur Ibbetson; ***M:*** Kenneth V. Jones. Natl. Bd. of Review '58: Support. Actress (Walsh).

Horsey **1999** Young Delilah makes no apologies for any of her passions—those of her art or the men or women she chooses to love. Then she starts a relationship with volatile Ryland Yale, a rock 'n' roller with a heroin addiction who still manages to fill all Delilah's emotional and physical needs. But is Delilah ready to deal with what Ryland will cost her? **93m/C VHS, DVD.** Holly Ferguson, Todd Kerns, Ryan Robbins, Victoria Deschanel; ***D:*** Kirsten Clarkson; ***W:*** Kirsten Clarkson; ***C:*** Glen Winter; ***M:*** Helen Keller.

Horton Foote's Alone 1/2 *Alone* **1997** John Webb (Cronyn) is an elderly Texas farmer, lost after the death of his wife of 52 years. His nephews (Forrest, Cooper) want him to sell his land to an interested oil company and his daughters (Miles, Hart) want to cry on his shoulder. Then Webb's former tenant farmer (Jones) comes back to visit and is the only one to ask the old man what he wants to do. **107m/C VHS, DVD.** Hume Cronyn, James Earl Jones, Chris Cooper, Frederic Forrest, Joanna Miles, Roxanne Hart, Shelley Duvall, Hallie Foote, Ed Begley Jr., David Selby, Piper Laurie; ***D:*** Michael Lindsay-Hogg; ***W:*** Horton Foote; ***C:*** Jeffrey Jur; ***M:*** David Shire. **CABLE**

The Hospital 1/2 **1971 (PG)** Cult favorite providing savage, unrelentingly sarcastic look at the workings of a chaotic metropolitan hospital beset by murders, witchdoctors, madness, and plain ineptitude. Scott's suicidal chief surgeon Herbert Bock, who falls in love with free-spirited Barbara Drummond (Riggs), a patient's daughter. **101m/C VHS, DVD.** George C. Scott, Diana Rigg, Barnard Hughes, Stockard Channing, Nancy Marchand, Richard Dysart, Stephen Elliott, Rehn Scofield, Katherine Helmond, Roberts Blossom; ***D:*** Arthur Hiller; ***W:*** Paddy Chayefsky; ***C:*** Victor Kemper. Oscars '71: Story & Screenplay; Berlin Intl. Film Fest. '72: Silver Prize; British Acad. '72: Screenplay; Golden Globes '72: Screenplay, Natl. Film Reg. '95;; Writers Guild '71: Orig. Screenplay.

Hospital Massacre WOOF! *X-Ray; Ward 13; Be My Valentine, Or Else* **1981 (R)** Psychopathic killer is loose in a hospital. Seems he holds a grudge against the woman who laughed at his valentine when they were children 20 years earlier, and too bad for her that she just checked in as a patient. Former "Playboy" and Hefner playmate Benton frolics in dangerous health care situation presented by the Cannon organization. **89m/C VHS.** Barbi Benton, Jon Van Ness, Charles (Chip) Lucia; ***D:*** Boaz Davidson; ***W:*** Marc Behm.

Hospital of Terror *Nurse Sherri; Terror Hospital; Beyond the Living* **1978 (R)** A transmigratory religious fanatic who died on the operating table manages to possess a nurse (Jacobson) before he kicks the bucket, and once in his candystripe incarnation, vents his spleen on the doctors who botched his operation. It's got a little more plasma than Adamson's "AstroZombies," considered by many to be a world-class boner. **88m/C VHS, DVD.** Jill Jacobson, Geoffrey Land, Marilyn Joi, Mary Kay Pass, Prentiss Moulden, Clayton Foster; ***D:*** Al Adamson.

The Host *Gwoemul* **2006 (R)** An overgrown mutant tadpole is on a man-eating bender along the Han River in South Korea, but that's not the most peculiar thing going on in this genre-stomping thriller. The family of one of the monsters would-be victims, high-schooler Park Hyeon-seo (Ko A-sung), is kookier than the monster. The story simultaneously lampoons and exploits the monster-on-the-loose genre to great effect. Fantastic visual effects, oddly juxtaposed humor and a super-stylie monster... it doesn't get much better. **119m/C DVD, Blu-ray Disc, HD DVD.** *KN* Du-na Bae, Kang-ho Song, Hie-bon Byeon, Hae-il Park, Ah-sung Ko; ***D:*** Joon-ho Bong; ***W:*** Joon-ho Bong, Chul-hyan Baek; ***C:*** Hyung-ku Kim; ***M:*** Byung-woo Lee.

The Hostage 1/2 **1967 (PG)** A young teenager is witness to a gruesome and clandestine burial. The two murderers responsible take it upon themselves to see that their secret is never told. **84m/C VHS, DVD.** Don O'Kelly, Harry Dean Stanton, John Carradine, Danny Martins; ***D:*** Russell S. Doughten Jr.

Hostage 1/2 **1987 (R)** Arab terrorists hijack a plane and the passengers start to fight back. Filmed in South Africa. **94m/C VHS.** Karen Black, Kevin McCarthy, Wings Hauser; ***D:*** Hanro Mohr; ***M:*** Brad Fiedel.

Hostage **1992 (R)** British Secret Service agent John Rennie is fed up after a difficult mission in Argentina. He thinks he can walk away clean but his superiors beg to differ. He's marked for murder but Rennie has a dangerous plan that could guarantee his safety—only if he returns to Argentina to set things in motion. Based on the novel "No Place to Hide" by Ted Allbeury. **100m/C VHS.** Sam Neill, Talisa Soto, James Fox; ***D:*** Robert W. Young.

Hostage 1/2 **2005 (R)** Burnt-out hostage negotiator (Willis) retreats to the suburbs hoping for calm, only to find himself pulled into the middle of a deadly crisis. Three delinquents take over the house of an underworld accountant (Pollack), whose shadowy employers then kidnap Willis's family, forcing him to retrieve their vital info hidden inside. Very violent, exciting, and grim melodrama with a dizzying number of twists and turns. Ben Foster is memorably sick as the psycho leader of the young thugs. **113m/C DVD.** *US* Bruce Willis, Kevin Pollak, Ben Foster, Jonathan Tucker, Jimmy Bennett, Tina Lifford, Kim Coates, Serena Scott Thomas, Marshall Allman, Michelle Horn, Robert Knepper, Rumer Willis, Marjean Holden, Johnny Messner, Glenn Morshower, Chad Smith; ***D:*** Florent Emilio Siri; ***W:*** Doug Richardson; ***C:*** Giovanni Fiore Coltellacci; ***M:*** Alexandre Desplat.

Hostage for a Day 1/2 **1994** Married to a shrew, toiling for an overbearing father-in-law, and suffering a midlife crisis, Wendt decides to fake his own kidnapping, take the ransom money, and head off for a better life. A series of comedic complications abound. Candy's directorial debut. Made for TV. **92m/C VHS.** George Wendt, John Vernon, Robin Duke, Peter Torokvei, Don Lake, Frank Moore, John Hemphill, Christopher Templeton; ***Cameos:*** John Candy; ***D:*** John Candy; ***W:*** Peter Torokvei, Robert Crane, Kari Hildebrand; ***M:*** Ian Thomas. **TV**

Hostage High *Detention: The Siege at Johnson High* **1997 (R)** Jason Copeland (Schroeder) returns to his former high school with a gun in order to take revenge on the teachers who failed him. The students, including Aaron (Prinze Jr.), he holds hostage inside the building have entirely different tactics for negotiation from the adults who are outside. Based on a true story. **93m/C VHS, DVD.** Rick Schroder, Henry Winkler, Freddie Prinze Jr., Ren Woods, Katie Wright, Alexis Cruz, Patrick Malone; ***D:*** Michael W. Watkins; ***W:*** Larry Golin; ***C:*** Bill Roe; ***M:*** Brian Adler. **TV**

Hostage Hotel 2000 (R) Ex-cop Logan McQueen (Reynolds) tries to outmaneouver a kidnapper who's holding a congressman's daughter and McQueen's old partner hostage in an abandoned old hotel. **95m/C VHS, DVD.** Burt Reynolds, Charles Durning, Keith Carradine, David Rasche; ***D:*** Hal Needham; ***W:*** Nicholas Factor. **CABLE**

The Hostage Tower **1980 (PG)** In France, a group of international crime figures capture the visiting U.S. president's mother, hold her hostage in the Eiffel Tower and demand $30 million in ransom. **97m/C VHS.** Peter Fonda, Maud Adams, Britt Ekland, Billy Dee Williams, Keir Dullea, Douglas Fairbanks Jr., Rachel Roberts, Celia Johnson; ***D:*** Claudio Guzman. **TV**

Hostages *Under Siege* **1980** A gang of criminals kidnap a family on vacation at a Caribbean island. **93m/C VHS.** *MX SP* Hugo Stiglitz, Marisa Mell, Francisco Rabal, Stuart Whitman; ***D:*** Rene Cardona Jr.; ***W:*** Rene Cardona Jr.; ***C:*** Leopoldo Villasenor; ***M:*** Manuel De Sica.

Hostages **1993 (R)** Harrowing docudrama about the Beirut hostage crisis combines acutal news footage with scenes of the prisoners and their families. Under desperate conditions hostages John McCarthy, Brian Keenan, Terry Anderson, Thomas Sutherland, Frank Reed, and Terry Waite try to hold on to their sanity and humanity as their families struggle for their release. Filmed on location in England, Israel, and Lebanon. **90m/C VHS.** Colin Firth, Ciaran Hinds, Jay O. Sanders, Josef Sommer, Harry Dean Stanton, Kathy Bates, Natasha Richardson, Conrad Asquith; ***D:*** David Wheatley; ***W:*** Bernard MacLaverty. **CABLE**

Hostel **2006 (R)** Just another brick in the faux-snuff genre wall. This time around some hot-to-trot American dudes are led to a Slovakian hostel after several splurges into red-light debauchery and uninhibited misogyny. (They probably got distracted on the way to the history museums.) Much to their chagrin, they find that the Russian mafia has converted their lodging quarters into a pleasuredome for sickos looking to get their sadism on. Since our heroes have been developed as mindless hornballs, we're expected to almost cheer their pain and agony. The creators try, rather unsuccessfully, to disguise the charade as a parody of the snuff and torture films it actually reproduces. **95m/C DVD, Blu-ray Disc, UMD.** *US* Jay Hernandez, Derek Richardson, Jan Vlasak, Eythor Gudjonsson, Barbara Nedeljakova, Jana Kaderabkova, Jennifer Lim, Lubomir Bukovy, Petr Janis, Josef Bradna, Keiko Seiko, Rick Hoffman; ***D:*** Eli Roth; ***W:*** Eli Roth; ***C:*** Milan Chadima; ***M:*** Nathan Barr.

Hostel: Part 2 **2007 (R)** You can add (or subtract) your own bones to the rating, depending on your appetite for torture porn. Roth out-does the gross and gore of his original, and switches his victims to the female gender, also making them slightly more sympathetic. American tourists Beth (German), Whitney (Phillips), and Lorna (Matarazzo) wind up at a Slovakian hostel where scummy businessmen pay top dollar to turn their snuff fantasies into reality, with Sasha (Knazko) the operational mastermind (and ripe for leading further sequels). **94m/C DVD, Blu-ray Disc.** *US* Lauren German, Bijou Phillips, Heather Matarazzo, Vera Jordanova, Roger Bart, Richard Burgi, Stanislav Ianevski, Jay Hernandez, Jordan Ladd, Edwige Fenech, Milan Knazko; ***D:*** Eli Roth; ***W:*** Eli Roth; ***C:*** Milan Chadima; ***M:*** Nathan Barr.

Hostile Guns 1/2 **1967** A law man discovers a woman he once loved is now an inmate he is transporting across the Texas badlands. Routine with the exception of cameos by veteran actors. Based on a story by Sloan Nibley and James Edward Grant. **91m/C VHS.** George Montgomery, Yvonne De Carlo, Tab Hunter, John Russell; ***Cameos:*** Brian Donlevy, Richard Arlen, Fuzzy Knight, Donald (Don "Red") Barry; ***D:*** R.G. Springsteen; ***W:*** Steve Fisher, Sloan Nibley.

Hostile Intent **1997 (R)** Computer whiz Mike Cleary (Lowe) has designed a new program to counter a computer chip that will allow the government access to everyone's computer. Naturally, this does not make the feds happy and when Mike and his team are off in the woods playing wargames for relaxation, someone is using real bullets to pick off the workers. **90m/C VHS, DVD.** Rob Lowe, John Savage, Sofia Shinas, James Kidnie; ***D:*** Jonathan Heap; ***W:*** Manny Coto; ***C:*** Gerald R. Goozie; ***M:*** Christophe Beck. **VIDEO**

Hostile Intentions **1994 (R)** Three girlfriends head for a weekend of fun in the sun in Tijuana and find themselves turned into fugitives through a series of misunderstandings. In order to get home, they must risk a night border crossing with a group of illegal immigrants. **90m/C VHS.** Tia Carrere, Lisa Dean Ryan, Tricia Leigh Fisher, Carlos Gomez, Rigg Kennedy; ***D:*** Catherine Cyran; ***W:*** Catherine Cyran; ***C:*** Azusa Ohno; ***M:*** Marcos Loya.

Hostile Takeover 1/2 *Office Party* **1988 (R)** A mild-mannered accountant finally cracks and takes his co-workers hostage. He faces the police in a tense showdown. **93m/C VHS.** David Warner, Michael Ironside, Kate Vernon, Jayne (Jane) Eastwood; ***D:*** George Mihalka.

Hostile Waters 1/2 **1997 (PG)** Based on Soviet accounts of an October 1986 incident that nearly set off a nuclear holocaust. A Russian and a U.S. sub play a game of cat-and-mouse 500 miles east of Bermuda. There's a collision and a fire aboard the Soviet sub threatens their cargo of thermonuclear missiles. Soviet captain Igor Britanov (Hauer) tries to control the situation while the U.S. skipper (Sheen) tries to figure out just what's going on. **92m/C VHS, DVD.** Rutger Hauer, Martin Sheen, Colm Feore, Rob Campbell, Harris Yulin, Max von Sydow, Regina Taylor, John Rothman; ***D:*** David Drury; ***W:*** Troy Kennedy-Martin; ***C:*** Alec Curtis; ***M:*** David Ferguson. **CABLE**

Hot Blood **1989** Two bank robbers take an innocent woman hostage and thrust her in the midst of a huge family battle. Another lukewarm entry from the director of "The Arrogant." **89m/C VHS.** Sylvia Kristel, Alicia Moro, Aldo Sambrel, Gaspar Cano; ***D:*** Philippe Blot.

Hot Blooded *Hit & Run; Red Blooded American Girl 2* **1998 (R)** Trent Colbert (Winters) is a naive college freshman driving back to his family at Thanksgiving. Pulling into a truck stop he's makes the mistake of offering alluring hooker Miya (Wuhrer) a ride. But Miya's a twisted soul and all this means for the libidinous Trent is trouble. **95m/C VHS, DVD.** Kari Wuhrer, Kristoffer Ryan Winters, David Keith, Burt Young; ***D:*** David Blyth; ***W:*** Nicolas Stiliadis; ***C:*** Edgar Egger; ***M:*** Paul Zaza. **VIDEO**

Hot Box WOOF! **1972 (R)** A Filipino-shot, low budget woofer. Prison flick about women who break out and foment a revolution. **85m/C VHS.** Andrea Cagan, Margaret Markov, Rickey Richardson, Laurie Rose; ***D:*** Joe Viola; ***W:*** Joe Viola, Jonathan Demme.

Hot Bubblegum *Shifshuf Naim* **1981 (R)** Three teenagers discover sex, the beach, rock 'n' roll, sex, drag racing, and sex. Hebrew with subtitles. **94m/C VHS.** *IS* Jonathan Sagalle, Zachi Noy, Yftach Katzur; ***D:*** Boaz Davidson; ***W:*** Boaz Davidson, Eli Tavor; ***C:*** Amnon Salomon.

The Hot Chick **2002 (PG-13)** Snotty high school queen Jessica (MacAdams) magically switches bodies with 30-ish shlub Clive (Schneider) and finds the true meaning of "bad hair day." As you'd expect from a movie starring and co-written by Schneider and produced by Adam Sandler, it does take a few dips in the gutter, but manages to have heart, much like Sandler's surprising "Wedding Singer" a few years back. Strings together enough laughs to make you forget "Like Father, Like Son" ever happened. **101m/C VHS, DVD.** *US* Rob Schneider, Anna Faris, Matthew Lawrence, Eric Christian Olsen, Robert Davi, Melora Hardin, Alexandra Holden, Rachel McAdams, Fay Hauser, Tamera Mowry, Tia Mowry, Lee Garlington, Michael O'Keefe; ***Cameos:*** Adam Sandler; ***D:*** Tom Brady; ***W:*** Tom Brady; ***C:*** Tim Suhrstedt; ***M:*** John Debney.

Hot Child in the City **1987** A country girl goes to Los Angeles and searches through the city's fleshpots for her sister's killer. Music by Nick Glider, Lou Reed, Billy Idol, and Fun Boy Three. **85m/C VHS.** Leah Ayres Hendrix, Shari Shattuck, Geof Pryssir; ***D:*** John Florea; ***M:*** W. Michael Lewis.

Hot Chocolate **1992 (PG-13)** Derek is a sultry Texas tycoon who wants to buy out the French chocolate factory run by Hays. After getting a look at her, work isn't all that's on his mind. **93m/C VHS.** Bo Derek, Robert Hays, Howard Hesseman, Vincent Cassel, Francois Marthouret, Amidou; ***D:*** Josee Dayan; ***W:*** Maryedith Burrell, Ginny Cerrella; ***C:*** Jean-Pierre Aliphat; ***M:*** John Goldstein.

Hot Dog... The Movie! 1/2 **1983 (R)** There's an intense rivalry going on between an Austrian ski champ and his California challenger during the World Cup Freestyle competition in Squaw Valley. Snow movie strictly for teens or their equivalent. **96m/C VHS, DVD.** David Naughton, Patrick Houser, Shannon Tweed, Tracy N. Smith; ***D:*** Peter Markle; ***M:*** Peter Bernstein.

Hot Fuzz **2007 (R)** Wright and Pegg, the lads who revitalized the zombie genre with "Shaun of the Dead", offer this decidedly English take on the over-the-top Hollywood action genre. Constable Nick Angel (Pegg) is the best cop in London, but when his over-achieving starts making the force look bad, he's transferred to the quiet village of Sandford and saddled with a lump of a partner, Danny Butterman (Frost). However, once Angel discovers the secret behind Sandford's surprisingly high "accident" rate, he and Danny team up Riggs and Murtaugh-style to take down the town fathers, vicar and all. Such a smart premise, and Pegg sells every moment, but it veers off into parody occasionally due to some regrettably broad supporting players. **121m/C DVD, HD DVD.** *GB US* Simon Pegg, Nick Frost, Jim Broadbent, Paddy Considine, Timothy Dalton, Billie Whitelaw, Edward Woodward, Rafe Spall, Olivia Colman, Paul Freeman, Martin Freeman, Bill Nighy, Steve Coogan, Cate Blanchett, Peter Jackson, Kevin Eldon, Stuart Wilson; ***D:*** Edgar Wright; ***W:*** Simon Pegg, Edgar Wright; ***C:*** Jess Hall; ***M:*** David Arnold.

Hot Lead **1951** Typical Holt oater which has the cowpoke and his sidekick Martin trying to avenge the death of a close friend who was killed by a gang of train robbers. **60m/B VHS.** Tim Holt, Joan Dixon, Ross Elliott, John Dehner; ***D:*** Stuart Gilmore.

Hot Lead & Cold Feet **1978 (G)** Twin brothers (one a gunfighter, the other meek and mild) compete in a train race where the winner will take ownership of a small western town. Dale not only plays both brothers, but also their tough father. Standard Disney fare. **89m/C VHS, DVD.** Jim Dale, Don Knotts, Karen Valentine; ***D:*** Robert Butler; ***W:*** Arthur Alsberg; ***M:*** Buddy (Norman Dale) Baker.

The Hot Line 1/2 *The Day the Hot Line Got Hot; Le Rouble a Deux Faces; El Rublo de las dos Caras* **1969** The world's two superpowers become befuddled when the hot line connecting Washington and Moscow breaks down. Taylor's final film. **87m/C VHS.** Robert Taylor, Charles Boyer, George Chakiris, Dominique Fabre, Gerard Tichy; ***D:*** Etienne Perier.

Hot Millions **1968** Hysterical comedy about high-class swindling operation with Ustinov as a refined embezzler. Excellent cast and sharp script. Although it didn't do well at the boxoffice, this amusing romp became one of the biggest sleepers of the year. **106m/C VHS.** *GB* Peter Ustinov, Maggie Smith, Karl Malden, Bob Newhart, Robert Morley, Cesar Romero, Melinda May, Ann Lancaster, Margaret Courtenay, Lynda Baron, Billy Milton, Peter Jones, Raymond Huntley, Kynaston Reeves; ***D:*** Eric Till; ***W:*** Ira Wallach, Peter Ustinov; ***C:*** Ken Higgins.

Hot Money **1979** A small-town drama about an ex-con who poses as an assistant sheriff and plots a million-dollar robbery during the town's 4th of July parade. Made shortly before Welles' death, and kept on the shelf for more than five years. **78m/C VHS.** Orson Welles, Michael Murphy, Bobby "Boris" Pickett, Michelle Finney; ***W:*** Joel Cohen, Neil Cohen; ***M:*** Rob McConnell.

Hot Moves **1984 (R)** Four high school boys make a pact to lose their virginity before the end of the summer. **89m/C VHS.** Michael Zorek, Adam Silbar, Jill Schoelen, Deborah Richter, Monique Gabrielle, Tami Holbrook, Virgil Frye; ***D:*** Jim Sotos.

Hot Potato **1976 (PG)** Black Belt Jones rescues a senator's daughter from a megalomaniacal general, by using skull-thwacking footwork. **87m/C VHS.** Jim Kelly, George Memmoli, Geoffrey Binney; ***D:*** Oscar Williams.

Hot Pursuit 1/2 **1984 (PG)** A woman who has been framed for murder runs from the law and a relentless hitman. **94m/C VHS, DVD.** Mike (Michael) Preston, Dina Merrill, Kerrie Keane; ***D:*** Kenneth Johnson; ***W:*** Kenneth Johnson; ***C:*** John McPherson; ***M:*** Joseph Harnell.

Hot Pursuit 1/2 **1987 (PG-13)** A prep-school bookworm resorts to Rambo-like tactics in tracking down his girlfriend and her family after being left behind for a trip to the tropics. **93m/C VHS, DVD.** Monte Markham, Shelley Fabares, Ben Stiller, John Cusack, Robert Loggia, Jerry Stiller, Wendy Gazelle; ***D:*** Steven Lisberger; ***W:*** Steven W. Carabatsos; ***C:*** Frank Tidy; ***M:*** Joseph Conlan.

Hot Resort 1/2 **1985 (R)** Young American lads mix work and play when they sign on as summer help at an island resort. Typical teen sex fantasy. **92m/C VHS.** Bronson Pinchot, Tom Parsekian, Michael Berz, Linda Kenton, Frank Gorshin; ***D:*** John Robins; ***W:*** John Robins, Boaz Davidson.

The Hot Rock *How to Steal a Diamond in Four Easy Lessons* **1970 (PG)** A motley crew of bumbling thieves conspire to steal a huge, priceless diamond; a witty, gritty comedy that makes no moral excuses for its characters and plays like an early-'70s crime thriller gone awry. Adapted from the novel by Donald E. Westlake. The sequel, 1974's "Bank Shot," stars George C. Scott in the role created by Redford. **97m/C VHS, DVD.** Robert Redford, George Segal, Ron Leibman, Zero Mostel, Moses Gunn, William Redfield, Charlotte Rae, Topo Swope; ***M:*** Quincy Jones.

Hot Rod *Rebel of the Road* **1979** A young California hotrodder battles the evil sponsor of a drag race championship. **97m/C VHS.** Gregg Henry, Robert Culp, Pernell Roberts, Robin Mattson, Grant Goodeve; ***D:*** George Armitage.

Hot Rod **2007 (PG-13)** Twenty-seven year old moped-riding stuntman-wannabe Rod Kimble (Samberg) lives at home with mom Marie (Spacek) and stepdad Frank (McShane). Rod's real dad, now dead, is a legend as a former Evel Kneivel second-hand man who is said to have performed all of Evel's stunts himself in order to test the bikes. Rod dreams of making his father proud; meanwhile he and stepdad go at it like archrivals, and Rod's always on the losing side of their jousts. Rod sees his chance when they learn that Frank needs a $50,000 heart transplant—money they don't have. He'll raise the money by jumping over 15 buses on his moped, fix Frank's heart, and then beat him to a pulp. Loaded with goofy gags, and aimed at "Napoleon Dynamite," "Saturday Night Live" (several of the film's cast are from SNL,) and Will Ferrell fans, but never nails the landing. Has some moments, but that's about it. **88m/C DVD, HD DVD.** *US* Isla Fisher, Andy Samberg, Jorma Taccone, Bill Hader, Sissy Spacek, Ian McShane, Will Arnett, Chris Parnell, Brittney Irvin, Danny McBride; ***D:*** Akiva Shaffer; ***W:*** Pam Brady; ***C:*** Andrew Dunn; ***M:*** Trevor Rabin.

Hot Rod Girl *Hot Car Girl* **1956** A concerned police officer (Conners) organizes supervised drag racing after illegal drag racing gets out of hand in his community. **75m/B VHS, DVD.** Lori Nelson, Chuck Connors, John Smith; ***D:*** Leslie Martinson; ***W:*** John McGreevey; ***C:*** Sam Leavitt.

Hot Saturday **1932** Small-town bank clerk Ruth (Carroll) has a reputation for being fast. She and some friends are invited for a Saturday shindig at the home of notorious playboy Romer Sheffield (Grant) and Ruth winds up spending quality alone time (platonically) with their host. Gossip is rampant, Ruth loses her job and her straight arrow beau Bill (Scott), but Romer steps in to set the record straight and offer Ruth an out. **72m/B DVD.** Nancy Carroll, Cary Grant, Randolph Scott, Edward (Eddie) Woods, William Collier Sr., Jane Darwell, Lillian Bond; ***D:*** William A. Seiter; ***W:*** Seton I. Miller; ***C:*** Arthur L. Todd.

Hot Shot 1/2 **1986 (PG)** An inspirational tale involving a young soccer player who goes to great lengths to take training from a soccer star, played—of course—by Pele. **90m/C VHS, DVD.** Pele, Jim Youngs, Billy Warlock, Weyman Thompson, Mario Van Peebles, David Groh; ***D:*** Rick King.

Hot Shots! **1991 (PG-13)** Another entry from "The Naked Gun" team of master movie parodists, this has lots of clever sight gags but the verbal humor often plummets to the ground. Spoofs "Top Gun" and similar gung-ho air corps adventures but doesn't forget other popular films including "Dances with Wolves" and "The Fabulous Baker Boys." Sheen is very funny as ace fighter pilot Sean "Topper" Harley who's to avenge the family honor. Great when you're in the mood for laughs that don't require thought. **83m/C VHS, DVD.** Charlie Sheen, Cary Elwes, Valeria Golino, Lloyd Bridges, Kevin Dunn, Jon Cryer, William O'Leary, Kristy Swanson, Efrem Zimbalist Jr., Bill Irwin, Heidi Swedberg, Judith Kahan, Pat Proft; ***Cameos:*** Charles Barkley, Bill Laimbeer; ***D:*** Jim Abrahams; ***W:*** Pat Proft, Jim Abrahams; ***C:*** Bill Butler; ***M:*** Sylvester Levay.

Hot Shots! Part Deux 1/2 **1993 (PG-13)** Second "Hot Shots" outing doesn't live up to the first, but it's not bad either. Admiral Tug Benson (Bridges) is elected President (yes, of the U.S.) and calls on Sheen's newly pumped-up Topper to take on Saddam Hussein Rambo-style. Love interest Ramada (Golino), returns but this time she's competing with Michelle (Bakke), a sexy CIA agent. Crenna spoofs his role in the "Rambo" films as Sheen's mentor; look for real-life dad Martin in a take-off of "Apocalypse Now." Shtick flies as fast and furious as the bodies, with Bridges getting a chance to reprise his glory days of "Sea Hunt." Don't miss the credits. **89m/C VHS, DVD.** Charlie Sheen, Lloyd Bridges, Valeria Golino, Brenda Bakke, Richard Crenna, Miguel Ferrer, Rowan Atkinson, Jerry Haleva, Mitchell Ryan, Gregory Sierra, Ryan Stiles, Michael Colyar; ***Cameos:*** Martin Sheen, Bob Vila; ***D:*** Jim Abrahams; ***W:*** Pat Proft, Jim Abrahams; ***M:*** Basil Poledouris.

Hot Spell 1/2 **1958** In an attempt to repair her marriage and unify her family, a mother plans a reunion-birthday party for her husband. Despair reigns in this sultry, Southern melodrama. **86m/B VHS.** Shirley Booth, Anthony Quinn, Shirley MacLaine, Earl Holliman, Eileen Heckart; ***D:*** Daniel Mann; ***C:*** Loyal Griggs; ***M:*** Alex North.

The Hot Spot 1/2 **1990 (R)** An amoral drifter arrives in a small Texas town and engages in affairs with two women, including his boss's over-sexed wife and a young woman with her own secrets. Things begin to heat up when he decides to plot a bank robbery. Based on Charles Williams' 1952 novel "Hell Hath No Fury." **120m/C VHS, DVD.** Don Johnson, Virginia Madsen, Jennifer Connelly, Charles Martin Smith, William Sadler, Jerry Hardin, Barry Corbin, Leon Rippy, Jack Nance; ***D:*** Dennis Hopper; ***W:*** Charles Williams, Nona Tyson; ***C:*** Ueli Steiger; ***M:*** Jack Nitzsche.

Hot Stuff **1980 (PG)** Officers on a burglary task force decide the best way to obtain convictions is to go into the fencing business themselves. **91m/C VHS.** Dom DeLuise, Jerry Reed, Suzanne Pleshette, Ossie Davis; ***D:*** Dom DeLuise; ***W:*** Donald E. Westlake, Michael Kane.

Hot Summer *Heisser Sommer* **1968** A group of high school girls and boys meet on their way to a Baltic Sea vacation and begin their own version of the war between the sexes, especially since there's one more girl than boy. Then Kai (Schoel) and Brit (Doerk) decide they're in love, causing trouble for everyone else. Goofy teen romp starring pop stars Schoebel and Doerk that was the East German version of the '60s American beach movie. German with subtitles. **91m/C VHS, DVD.** *GE* Frank Schobel, Chris Doerk, Madeleine Lierck, Hanns-Michael Schmidt, Regine Albrecht; ***D:*** Joachim Hasler.

Hot Summer in Barefoot County **1974 (R)** A state law enforcement officer on the search for illegal moonshiners finds more than he bargained for. **90m/C VHS.** Sherry Robinson, Tonia Bryan, Dick Smith; ***D:*** Will Zens.

Hot T-Shirts **WOOF!** **1979 (R)** A small town bar owner needs a boost for business, finding the answer in wet T-shirt contests. Softcore trash. **86m/C VHS.** Ray Holland, Stephanie Lawlor, Pauline Rose, Corinne Alphen; ***D:*** Chuck Vincent.

Hot Tamale 1/2 **2006 (R)** Amusing action-comedy finds naive musician Harlan Woodriff (Spelling) traveling from Wyoming to LA so he can play in a salsa band. Along the way, a con man (Priestley) hides some stolen diamonds in Harlan's car. In LA, Harlan meets sexy neighbor Tuesday (Baird) while unwittingly being targeted by thugs after the loot. **98m/C DVD.** Jason Priestley, Carmen Electra, Mike Starr, Beth Grant, Randy Spelling, Diora Baird, Matt Cedeno; ***D:*** Michael Damian; ***W:*** Michael Damian, Janeen Damian; ***C:*** Fred Iannone; ***M:*** Mark Thomas.

Hot Target **1985 (R)** An ideal mother becomes obsessed with the stranger who seduced her, even after she finds out he's a thief planning to rob her home. **93m/C VHS, DVD.** *NZ* Simone Griffeth, Steve Marachuk; ***D:*** Denis Lewiston.

Hot Times **1974 (R)** Low-budget comedy about a high school boy who, after striking out with the high school girls, decides to go to New York and have the time of his life. **80m/C VHS.** Gail Lorber, Amy Farber, Henry Cory; ***D:*** Jim McBride; ***W:*** Jim McBride.

Hot Tip **1935** Restaurant owner Jimmy McGill (James Gleason) is a sucker for the ponies but promises his wife Belle (Pitts) that he'll stop gambling. Until future son-in-law Ben (Gleason's real-life son Russell) gets into a jam after losing at the track and needs some quick cash. **70m/B VHS.** James Gleason, Zasu Pitts, Russell Gleason, Margaret Callahan, J.M. Kerrigan; ***D:*** Ray McCarey; ***W:*** Olive Cooper, Hugh Cummings, Louis Stevens; ***C:*** Jack MacKenzie.

Hot to Trot! **1988 (PG)** A babbling idiot links up with a talking horse in an updated version of the "Francis, the Talking Mule" comedies, by way of Mr. Ed. The equine voice is provided by Candy. Some real funny guys are wasted here. **90m/C VHS.** Bob(cat) Goldthwait, Dabney Coleman, Virginia Madsen, Jim Metzler, Cindy Pickett, Tim Kazurinsky, Santos Morales, Barbara Whinnery, Garry Kluger; ***D:*** Michael Dinner; ***W:*** Charlie Peters; ***M:*** Danny Elfman; ***V:*** John Candy.

Hot Touch **WOOF!** **1982** An art forger with a large heist is besieged by a slashing maniac, and must discover the culprit. **92m/C VHS.** Wayne Rogers, Samantha Eggar, Marie-France Pisier, Melvyn Douglas; ***D:*** Roger Vadim; ***W:*** Peter Dion; ***C:*** Francois Protat; ***M:*** Andre Gagnon.

Hot Tub Time Machine **2010** A group of bored, middle-aged buddies have lost their mojo. But thanks to vodka, Red Bull, and a hot tub they travel back in time 20 years and rediscover their young and stupider selves. **m/C DVD.** John Cusack, Rob Corddry, Craig Robinson, Crispin Glover, Sebastian Stan, Chevy Chase, Lizzy Caplan, Lyndsy Fonseca; ***D:*** Steve Pink; ***W:*** Josh Heald.

Hot Under the Collar 1/2 **1991 (R)** Jerry is a weasel who tries to seduce the luscious Monica by using hypnosis. But his plans backfire and instead Monica enters a convent and takes a vow of chastity. This isn't going to stop Jerry, he tries posing as a priest and even dressing as a nun in order to get her out. Things get even more complicated when a mobster, looking for a fortune in stolen diamonds, sneaks into the convent. **87m/C VHS.** Richard Gabai, Angela Visser, Daniel Friedman, Melinda (Mindy) Clarke, Tane McClure; ***D:*** Richard Gabai.

Hotel 1/2 **1967 (PG)** A pale rehash of the "Grand Hotel" formula about an array of rich characters interacting in a New Orleans hotel. From the Arthur Hailey potboiler; basis for the TV series. **125m/C VHS.** Rod Taylor, Catherine Spaak, Karl Malden, Melvyn Douglas, Merle Oberon, Michael Rennie, Richard Conte, Kevin McCarthy; ***D:*** Richard Quine; ***W:*** Wendell Mayes; ***C:*** Charles B(ryant) Lang Jr.

Hotel **2001 (R)** Using a Dogme 95 approach, Director Figgis gathers a bunch of celebs and lets them aimlessly make things up as they go along. Follows the filming of John Webster's play "The Duchess of Malfi" by an English production crew at a hotel in Venice, Italy that has call girls, a murderer, and cannibalistic hotel staffers lurking about while the entire fiasco is caught on film by a brash documentarian. Fans of Figgis' work or the Dogme movement will want to check in on this one. **112m/C VHS, DVD.** *GB IT* Rhys Ifans, John Malkovich, Saffron Burrows, Salma Hayek, Max Beesley, Lucy Liu, Julian Sands, David Schwimmer, Jason Isaacs; ***D:*** Mike Figgis; ***W:*** Mike Figgis; ***C:*** Patrick Alexander Stewart; ***M:*** Mike Figgis, Anthony Marinelli.

Hotel America *Hotel des Ameriques* **1981** Techine's drama meanders to little purpose and often less interest despite its leads. Layabout Gilles (Dewaere) is sponging off his mother Elise (Haudepin), who owns a small hotel. Helene (Deneuve), depressed after her lover's accidental death, is high from popping pills and nearly runs Gilles down in the street. They begin a haphazard relationship that lessens Helene's depression but Gilles is jealous of her architect lover's renown and pushes her away to pine for self-absorbed musician Bernard (Chicot) instead. French with subtitles. **95m/C DVD.** *FR* Catherine Deneuve, Patrick Dewaere, Etienne Chicot, Sabine Haudepin, Dominque Lavanant, Josiane Balasko, Jean-Louis Vitrac; ***D:*** Josiane Balasko, Andre Techine; ***W:*** Josiane Balasko, Andre Techine, Gilles Taurand; ***C:*** Bruno Nuytten; ***M:*** Philippe Sarde.

Hotel Colonial 1/2 **1988 (R)** A young Italian idealist ventures to Columbia to retrieve the body of his brother, who reportedly killed himself. Once there, he finds the dead man is not his brother, and decides to investigate. **103m/C VHS.** *IT* Robert Duvall, John Savage, Rachel Ward, Massimo Troisi; ***D:*** Cinzia Torrini; ***W:*** Ira Barmak, Enzo Monteleone; ***M:*** Pino Donaggio.

Hotel de Love 1/2 **1996 (R)** Seventeen-year-old fraternal twin brothers Rick (Young) and Stephen Dunne (Bossell) both fall for beautiful Melissa (Burrows) and she has a short-lived romance with the more-aggressive Rick. Ten years later, mopey stockbroker Stephen shows up at the tacky theme honeymoon hotel Rick now manages and who should show up (besides the twins bickering parents) but Melissa and her fiance Norman (O'Brien). So the twins renew their competition while Melissa decides if Norman is the right guy for her, Mrs. Dunne gets mash notes from a secret admirer, and fortuneteller Alison (Grandison), who happens to be Rick's ex-girlfriend, offers romantic advice to Stephen. **93m/C VHS.** *AU* Aden Young, Simon Bossell, Saffron Burrows, Julia Blake, Ray Barrett, Pippa Grandison, Alan Hopgood, Peter O'Brien; ***D:*** Craig Rosenberg; ***W:*** Craig Rosenberg; ***C:*** Stephen Windon; ***M:*** Brett Rosenberg.

Hotel du Lac **1986** Adaptation of the Anita Brookner novel about a woman writer languishing at a Swiss lakefront hotel. **75m/C VHS.** *GB* Anna Massey, Denholm Elliott, Googie Withers; ***D:*** Giles Foster; ***M:*** Carl Davis. **TV**

Hotel for Dogs 1/2 **2009 (PG)** Orphaned teenager Andi and her younger brother Bruce are living in a new foster home with a strict no pets rule, which means Andi has to find a place for their beloved dog Friday. When they spot an abandoned hotel nearby, it becomes the perfect solution not only for Friday but also dozens of neighborhood strays (as long as the neighbors don't find out). Despite star-filled supporting roles by the likes of Don Cheadle, Matt Dillon and Lisa Kudrow, the numerous trained dogs are the best part of this woofer (no canine bias by the Hound!). Purely a kids' movie with ample silly sweetness courtesy of the dogs. Based on the novel by Lois Duncan. **100m/C DVD.** *US* Emma Roberts, Jake T. Austin, Lisa Kudrow, Don Cheadle, Kevin Dillon, Kyla Pratt, Troy Gentile, Johnny Simmons, Robine Lee; ***D:*** Thor Freudenthal; ***W:*** Jeff Lowell, Robert Schooley, Mark McCorkle; ***C:*** Michael Grady; ***M:*** John Debney.

Hotel Imperial **1927** Set in 1917 Budapest, six Hungarian soldiers ride into a frontier town and find it occupied by Russians. Hall plays Lieutenant Almasy, who takes refuge in the Hotel Imperial. Orchestra scored. **84m/B VHS, DVD.** Pola Negri, James Hall, George Siegmann, Max Davidson; ***D:*** Mauritz Stiller.

The Hotel New Hampshire **1984 (R)** The witless, amoral adaptation of John Irving's novel about a very strange family's adventures in New Hampshire, Vienna and New York City, which include gang rape, incest, and Kinski in a bear suit. **110m/C VHS, DVD.** Jodie Foster, Rob Lowe, Beau Bridges, Nastassja Kinski, Wallace Shawn, Wilford Brimley, Amanda Plummer, Anita Morris, Matthew Modine, Lisa Banes, Seth Green, Jennifer (Jennie) Dundas Lowe; ***D:*** Tony Richardson; ***W:*** Tony Richardson; ***C:*** David Watkin.

Hotel Paradiso 1/2 **1966** Slightly amusing bedroom farce has timid Guinness trying to carry on affair with Italian sexpot Lollibrigida. Guinness fans won't be disappointed, although it's not a top-rate production. Based on the play "L'Hotel du Libre Echange" by Georges Feydeau and Maurice Desvalliers. **100m/C VHS.** *GB* Alec Guinness, Gina Lollobrigida, Akim Tamiroff, Marie Bell, Derek Fowlds; ***D:*** Peter Glenville; ***W:*** Peter Glenville, Jean-Claude Carriere.

Hotel Reserve **1944** A Nazi spy is reportedly afoot in a French resort during WWII, and tension mounts as the guests attempt to flush him out. Critical response to this film is wildly split; some find it obvious, while others call it well-done and suspenseful. Based on the novel "Epitaph for a Spy" by Eric Ambler. **79m/B VHS.** *GB* James Mason, Lucie Mannheim, Raymond Lovell, Julien Mitchell, Martin Miller, Herbert Lom, Frederick Valk, Valentine Dyall, Patricia Medina; ***D:*** Victor Hanbury, Lance Comfort, Max Greene.

Hotel Room 1/2 *David Lynch's Hotel Room* **1993** A trilogy of stories set in the same drab New York hotel room in three different time periods. "Getting Rid of Robert," set in 1992, has three girlfriends swilling champagne and discussing Sasha's slick, movie exec boyfriend whom she wants to dump. "Tricks," set in 1969, features Darlene, a bored, druggy prostitute; her client, Moe; and the sudden appearance of Moe's talkative friend, Lou. "Blackout" is set in 1936 and features a young husband trying to cope with the madness of his beautiful wife. Unfortunately, all three stories are rambling and lacking in energy. **100m/C VHS.** Deborah Kara Unger, Mariska Hargitay, Chelsea Field, Griffin Dunne, Glenne Headly, Harry Dean Stanton, Freddie Jones, Crispin Glover, Alicia Witt, Clark Heathcliffe Brolly, Camilla Overbye Roos; ***D:*** James Signorelli, David Lynch; ***W:*** Barry Gifford, Jay McInerney; ***M:*** Angelo Badalamenti. **CABLE**

Hotel Rwanda 1/2 **2004 (PG-13)** Cheadle gives a remarkable performance in a drama that covers a too-little-known episode in recent history. In 1994 Rwanda, a former Belgian colony, members of the Hutu tribe killed some 800,000 members of the once-dominant Tutsi tribe. Paul Rusesabagina (Cheadle) is a Hutu, who manages a four-star hotel in Kigali. When the genocide begins, he fears for his own family since his wife, Tatiana (Okonedo), is a Tutsi. Unable to escape or to get any help, Paul decides his safety depends on business as usual (and bribing the military) even as he comes to shelter some 1,200 refugees within the hotel. Film focuses on Paul and not on what is happening in Rwanda in general. Without some historical background, the general viewer will likely be somewhat confused. **110m/C DVD.** *GB IT SA* Don Cheadle, Sophie Okonedo, Joaquin Rafael (Leaf) Phoenix, Nick Nolte, Desmond Dube, David O'Hara, Jean Reno, Cara Seymour; ***D:*** Terry George; ***W:*** George Pearson; ***C:*** Robert Fraisse, Naomi Geraghty; ***M:*** Andrea Guerra, Rupert Gregson-Williams.

Hothead **1963** Angry teenaged punk blames all his troubles on his dead-beat dad and takes it out on a boozy transient. Along the way his story intersects with that of a young hooker and a runaway husband. **74m/B DVD.** Barbara Joyce, Steve Franklin, Robert Glen, John Delgar; ***D:*** Edward Andrew (Santos Alcocer) Mann; ***W:*** Milton Mann; ***C:*** Edward Nicholson.

Hothead *Coup de Tete* **1978** A heedless, impulsive soccer player's behavior gets him cut from the team, fired from his mill job, and booted out of his favorite bar. In French with English subtitles or dubbed. **98m/C VHS.** *FR* Patrick Dewaere, Jean Bouise, Michel Aumont, France Dougnac; ***D:*** Jean-Jacques Annaud; ***W:*** Francis Veber. Cesar '80: Support. Actor (Bouise).

Hotline 🦴🦴 **1982** After taking a job answering phones at a crisis center, a woman becomes the next target of a psychotic killer. **96m/C VHS.** Lynda Carter, Steve Forrest, Granville Van Dusen, Monte Markham, James Booth; ***D:*** Jerry Jameson. **TV**

H.O.T.S. 🦴 *T & A Academy* **1979 (R)** A sex-filled sorority rivalry film, starring a slew of ex-Playboy Playmates in wet shirts. Screenplay co-written by exploitation star Caffaro. **95m/C VHS, DVD.** Susan Kiger, Lisa London, Kimberly Cameron, Danny Bonaduce, Steve Bond; ***D:*** Gerald Seth Sindell; ***W:*** Cheri Caffaro, Joan Buchanan; ***C:*** Harvey Genkins; ***M:*** David Davis.

The Hottest State 🦴🦴 **2006 (R)** Sarah Garcia (Moreno), a young girl with dreams of the big city, sets out for New York to begin her singing career. Enter romantic William Harding (Webber), an aspiring actor transplanted from Texas. They fall in love, and then as often happens with young love, someone gets dumped. But Harding can't seem to move on, pining and yearning insufferably for his lost love, and in doing so annoys everyone around him. Mom Jesse (Linney) offers sympathy, but it's not until distant dad (Hawke) shows up that the lovesick puppy gets some clarity and maturity about the situation. Hawke serves as writer/director/actor in this self-indulgent and overly talky bit about young (and unrequited) love based on Hawke's own semi-biographical novel of the same name. **117m/C DVD.** *US* Mark Webber, Catalina Sandino Moreno, Laura Linney, Michelle Williams, Sonia Braga, Jesse Harris, Ethan Hawke; ***D:*** Ethan Hawke; ***W:*** Ethan Hawke; ***C:*** Christopher Norr; ***M:*** Jesse Harris.

The Hottie and the Nottie 🦴 **2008 (PG-13)** Despite Hilton's blonde banality this comedy isn't quite as bad as you might expect. Geeky Joel fell in love with Cristabel when they were kids. Now an adult, he's come to L.A. to pursue romance. Only problem is Cristabel (Hilton) won't put out until Joel (Moore) finds her incredibly ugly best friend June (Lakin) a boyfriend. June's a decent gal in need of a makeover and you have to wonder why Cristabel didn't think of that herself. Maybe because once June's inner beauty is reflected outwardly, Joel's attentions waver. **91m/C DVD.** Paris Hilton, Christine Lakin, Joel David Moore, Johann Urb, Adam Kulbersh; ***D:*** Tom Putnam; ***W:*** Heidi Ferrer; ***C:*** Alex Vendler; ***M:*** David E. Russo. Golden Raspberries '08: Worst Actress (Hilton).

Hotwire 🦴 1/2 **1980** Tired comedy about the unscrupulous side of the car repossession racket. **92m/C VHS.** George Kennedy, Strother Martin, Lawrence (Larry) Dobkin; ***D:*** Frank Q. Dobbs; ***W:*** Frank Q. Dobbs; ***C:*** Robert Bethard; ***M:*** John Gary Smith, Danny Ward.

Houdini 🦴🦴 1/2 **1953** Historically inaccurate but entertaining biopic of the infamous magician and escapologist. Chronicles his rise to stardom, his efforts to contact his dearly departed mother through mediums (a prequel to "Ghost"?), and his heart-stopping logic-defying escapes. First screen teaming of Leigh and Curtis, who had already been married for two years. **107m/C VHS, DVD.** Tony Curtis, Janet Leigh, Torin Thatcher, Angela (Clark) Clarke, Stefan Schnabel, Ian Wolfe, Sig Rumann, Michael Pate, Connie Gilchrist, Mary Murphy, Tor Johnson; ***D:*** George Marshall; ***W:*** Philip Yordan; ***C:*** Ernest Laszlo; ***M:*** Roy Webb.

Houdini 🦴🦴 1/2 **1999** New York Jewish youth Erich Weiss transforms himself into vaudeville magician/illusionist Harry Houdini (Schaech) and marries Bess (Edwards), who becomes his assistant. Houdini soon becomes a famed escape artist, pushing himself into ever-more dangerous stunts. After his beloved mother's death, Houdini then goes on a crusade to expose fake spiritualists who had promised him contact with her. **94m/C VHS.** Johnathon Schaech, Stacy Edwards, Grace Zabriskie, Paul Sorvino, Rhea Perlman, George Segal, David Warner, Mark Ruffalo, Ron Perlman, Judy Geeson; ***D:*** Pen Densham; ***W:*** Pen Densham; ***C:*** Gordon C. Lonsdale; ***M:*** Don Harper. **CABLE**

The Houdini Serial 🦴 *The Master Mystery* **1920** Quentin Locke (Houdini) is a Justice Department agent investigating a powerful crime cartel in this silent chapter serial. The cartel is protected by a "robot" armed with a deadly gas weapon and at the end of each chapter Locke is trapped in some perilous situation from which he is able to astonishingly escape. While the plot is rather tedious, Houdini's performance is an absolute delight. **?m/B DVD.** Harry Houdini, Marguerite Marsh, Ruth Stonehouse, Edna Britton, William Pike, Charles Graham; ***D:*** Harry Grossman, Burton King; ***W:*** Arthur B. Reeve, Charles Logue.

The Hound of London 🦴🦴 1/2 *Sherlock Holmes in The Hound of London* **1993** Inspector Lestrade brings Sherlock Holmes (Macnee) his latest case, a double murder that has taken place at the Strand Theatre. And among the suspects is the only woman Holmes has ever admired, the lovely Irene Adler. Eccentric characters, a sword duel, backstage mischief, and Holmes and Watson together once more. Based on the play by Craig Bowlsby. **72m/C VHS.** *CA* Patrick Macnee, John Scott-Paget, Colin Skinner, Jack McCreath, Carolyn Wilkinson, Sophia Thornley, Drew Kemp, Ned Lemley, Craig Bowlsby; ***D:*** Gil Letourneau, Peter Reynolds-Long; ***W:*** Craig Bowlsby.

The Hound of the Baskervilles 🦴🦴🦴 **1939** The curse of a demonic hound threatens descendants of an English noble family until Holmes and Watson solve the mystery. **80m/B VHS, DVD.** *GB* Basil Rathbone, Nigel Bruce, Richard Greene, John Carradine, Wendy Barrie, Lionel Atwill, E.E. Clive; ***D:*** Sidney Lanfield.

The Hound of the Baskervilles 🦴🦴 1/2 **1959** Cushing's not half bad as Sherlock Holmes as he investigates the mystery of a supernatural hound threatening the life of a Dartmoor baronet. Dark and moody. **86m/C VHS, DVD.** *GB* Peter Cushing, Christopher Lee, Andre Morell; ***D:*** Terence Fisher; ***W:*** Peter Bryan; ***C:*** Jack Asher; ***M:*** James Bernard.

The Hound of the Baskervilles WOOF! **1977** Awful spoof of the Sherlock Holmes classic with Cook as Holmes and Moore as Watson (and Holmes' mother). Even the cast can't save it. **84m/C VHS, DVD.** Dudley Moore, Peter Cook, Denholm Elliott, Joan Greenwood, Spike Milligan, Jessie Matthews, Roy Kinnear; ***D:*** Paul Morrissey; ***W:*** Dudley Moore, Peter Cook, Paul Morrissey; ***C:*** Dick Bush; ***M:*** Dudley Moore.

The Hound of the Baskervilles 🦴🦴 **1983** Another remake of the Sherlock Holmes story which finds the great detective investigating the murder of Sir Charles Baskerville and a mysterious haunted moor. **100m/C VHS, DVD.** *GB* Ian Richardson, Donald Churchill, Martin Shaw, Nicholas Clay, Denholm Elliott, Brian Blessed, Ronald Lacey; ***D:*** Douglas Hickox; ***W:*** Charles Edward Pogue; ***C:*** Ronnie Taylor; ***M:*** Michael Lewis.

The Hound of the Baskervilles 🦴🦴 1/2 **2000** Frewer takes on the role of Sherlock Holmes, emphasizing the character's cynical humor as well as his sometimes insufferable intelligence. Welsh ably backs him up as Watson and this version closely follows the Conan Doyle story. Sir Henry Baskerville (London) has inherited an estate with a curse and a devilish hound that terrorizes the moors. Holmes investigates. **90m/C VHS, DVD.** *CA* Matt Frewer, Kenneth Welsh, Jason London, Emma Campbell, Robin Wilcock, Arthur Holden, Leni Parker, Gordon Masten; ***D:*** Rodney Gibbons; ***W:*** Joe Wiesenfeld; ***C:*** Eric Cayla; ***M:*** Marc Ouellette. **CABLE**

The Hound of the Baskervilles 🦴🦴🦴 **2002** The umpteenth version of the Sherlock Holmes story about an inheritance and a vicious dog out on the moors is distinguished by its cast with Roxburgh's Holmes and Hart's Watson ably playing off each other. **100m/C VHS, DVD.** *GB* Richard Roxburgh, Ian Hart, Matt(hew) Day, Richard E. Grant, Neve McIntosh, John Nettles, Geraldine James, Ron Cook, Danny (Daniel) Webb; ***D:*** David Attwood; ***W:*** Allan Cubitt; ***C:*** James Welland; ***M:*** Robert (Rob) Lane. **TV**

Hounddog 🦴 1/2 **2008 (R)** Grimy fairy tale set in a 1950's ramshackled Southern town, home to high-spirited 14-year-old tomboy Lewellen (Fanning), who has a rotten family and a budding Elvis obsession. Most of her time is taken up at the local swimming hole with her best friend Buddy, as the two begin teaching each other the differences between boys and girls. Lewellen's glow quickly fades after an older boy takes advantage of her curiosity, leaving her silent and afraid. Somehow revived by a mysterious midnight snake infestation, she again turns to Elvis to save her soul. Unfortunately, most of Fanning's mature performance, in which she proves she's more Jodie Foster than Lindsay Lohan, is lost on Southern cliches and aimless coming-of-age nonsense. Despite the controversy, the rape scene is restrained and brief. **93m/C DVD.** *US* Dakota Fanning, Piper Laurie, David Morse, Afemo Omilami, Cody Hanford, Robin Wright Penn, Jill Scott, Christoph Sanders; ***D:*** Deborah Kampmeier; ***W:*** Deborah Kampmeier; ***C:*** Edward Lachman, Jim Denault.

Hour of Decision 🦴 1/2 **1957** When a newspaper columnist turns up dead, a reporter investigates the murder. Things get hairy when he finds the prime suspect is his own wife. **81m/B VHS.** *GB* Jeff Morrow, Hazel Court, Lionel Jeffries, Anthony Dawson, Mary Laura Wood; ***D:*** C.M. Pennington-Richards.

Hour of the Assassin 🦴 1/2 **1986 (R)** A mercenary is hired to assassinate a South American ruler, and a CIA operative is sent to stop him. Shot in Peru. **96m/C VHS.** Erik Estrada, Robert Vaughn; ***D:*** Luis Llosa.

Hour of the Gun 🦴🦴 **1967** Western saga chronicles what happens after the gunfight at the OK Corral. Garner plays the grim Wyatt Earp on the trail of vengeance after his brothers are killed. Robards is excellent as the crusty Doc Holliday. **100m/C VHS, DVD.** James Garner, Jason Robards Jr., Robert Ryan, Albert Salmi, Charles Aidman, Steve Ihnat, Jon Voight, Robert Phillips; ***D:*** John Sturges; ***W:*** Edward Anhalt; ***M:*** Jerry Goldsmith.

The Hour of the Star 🦴🦴🦴 1/2 *A Hora Da Estrela* **1985** The poignant, highly acclaimed feature debut by Amaral, about an innocent young woman moving to the city of Sao Paulo from the impoverished countryside of Brazil, and finding happiness despite her socioeconomic failures. Based on Clarice Lispector's novel. In Portuguese with English subtitles. **96m/C VHS, DVD.** *BR* Marcelia Cartaxo; ***D:*** Suzana Amaral. Berlin Intl. Film Fest. '85: Actress (Cartaxo).

Hour of the Wolf 🦴🦴🦴 1/2 *Vargtimmen* **1968** An acclaimed, surreal view into the tormented inner life of a painter as he and his wife are isolated on a small northern island. In Swedish with English subtitles. **89m/B VHS, DVD.** *SW* Max von Sydow, Liv Ullmann, Ingrid Thulin, Erland Josephson, Gertrud Fridh, Gudrun Brost, Georg Rydeberg, Naima Wifstrand, Bertil Anderberg, Ulf Johansson; ***D:*** Ingmar Bergman; ***W:*** Ingmar Bergman; ***C:*** Sven Nykvist; ***M:*** Lars Johan Werle. Natl. Bd. of Review '68: Actress (Ullmann); Natl. Soc. Film Critics '68: Director (Bergman).

Hourglass 🦴🦴 **1995 (R)** Fashion industry honcho Michael Jardine (Howell) risks his reputation and his life when he becomes involved with deadly, revenge-minded seductress Dara (Shinas), who blames the Jardines for her father's suicide. Another in a long line of be careful who you sleep with movies. **91m/C VHS.** C. Thomas Howell, Sofia Shinas, Ed Begley Jr., Timothy Bottoms, Anthony Clark; ***D:*** C. Thomas Howell; ***W:*** C. Thomas Howell, Darren Dalton; ***C:*** John Lambert; ***M:*** Chris Saranec.

The Hours 🦴🦴🦴 1/2 **2002 (PG-13)** In 1923 Virginia Woolf (Kidman) is recovering from a mental collapse while writing her novel "Mrs. Dalloway." In the 1950s, Laura Brown (Moore) is reading said novel, and in 2001, Clarissa (Streep) eerily embodies Woolf's character Dalloway. All three are facing questions of fulfillment in their lives and examining whether it's worth living, and all have issues with their own sexuality and the current men in their lives. Parallel gestures and words from era to era wonderfully enhance the illusion the three are indeed one. Many felt Cunningham's Pulitzer Prize-winning novel would not translate well to the screen, but Hare's screenplay and Daldry's direction superbly present this quilt of tales. **114m/C VHS, DVD.** *US* Nicole Kidman, Julianne Moore, Meryl Streep, Stephen (Dillon) Dillane, Miranda Richardson, John C. Reilly, Ed Harris, Allison Janney, Claire Danes, Jeff Daniels, Toni Collette, Eileen Atkins, Jack Rovello, Margo Martindale, Linda Bassett; ***D:*** Stephen Daldry; ***W:*** David Hare; ***C:*** Seamus McGarvey; ***M:*** Philip Glass. Oscars '02: Actress (Kidman); British Acad. '02: Actress (Kidman), Score; Golden Globes '03: Actress—Drama (Kidman), Film—Drama; L.A. Film Critics '02: Actress (Moore); Natl. Bd. of Review '02: Film; Writers Guild '02: Adapt. Screenplay.

The Hours and Times 🦴🦴🦴 **1992** A concise drama based on one point of fact used to quietly evoke differences in class, talent, sexual orientation, and unrequited love. The fact is that in the spring of 1963 Brian Epstein, the Beatles brilliant homosexual manager, shared a four-day Barcelona vacation with John Lennon. Director Munch speculates that the sophisticated Epstein was hopelessly in love with the younger, working-class Lennon who is friendly but unresponsive to the courtship. A tender and rueful depiction of friendship longing to be something more. **60m/B VHS, DVD.** David Angus, Ian Hart, Stephanie Pack, Robin McDonald, Sergio Moreno, Unity Grimwood; ***D:*** Christopher Munch; ***W:*** Christopher Munch. Sundance '92: Special Jury Prize.

House 🦴🦴🦴 **1986 (R)** Horror novelist Roger Cobb (Katt) moves into his dead aunt's supposedly haunted house only to find that the monsters don't necessarily stay in the closets. His worst nightmares come to life as he writes about his Vietnam experiences and is forced to relive the tragic events, but these aren't the only visions that start springing to life. It sounds depressing, but is actually a funny, intelligent "horror" flick. Followed by several lesser sequels. **93m/C VHS, DVD.** William Katt, George Wendt, Richard Moll, Kay Lenz, Michael Ensign, Mary Stavin, Susan French; ***D:*** Steve Miner; ***W:*** Ethan Wiley; ***C:*** Mac Ahlberg; ***M:*** Harry Manfredini.

House 2: The Second Story 🦴 **1987 (PG-13)** The flaccid sequel to the haunted-house horror flick concerns two innocent guys who move into the family mansion and discover Aztec ghosts. Has none of the humor which helped the first movie along. **88m/C VHS, DVD.** John Ratzenberger, Arye Gross, Royal Dano, Bill Maher, Jonathan Stark, Lar Park-Lincoln, Amy Yasbeck, Devin Devasquez; ***D:*** Ethan Wiley; ***W:*** Ethan Wiley; ***C:*** Mac Ahlberg.

House 4: Home Deadly Home 🦴 1/2 **1991 (R)** Another bad real estate epic on a par with the other unusually inept "House" efforts. When her husband (Katt) is killed in an auto accident, a young woman and her daughter move into a mysterious old house. Terror begins to confront them at every turn, threatening to destroy them both. We can only hope. **93m/C VHS.** Terri Treas, Scott Burkholder, Melissa Clayton, William Katt, Ned Romero; ***D:*** Lewis Abernathy.

House Across the Bay 🦴🦴 1/2 **1940** Raft, an imprisoned nightclub owner, finds that he is being duped by his attorney who's eager to get his hooks into the lingerie-clad prisoner's wife. But prison isn't going to stop the bitter husband from getting his revenge. **88m/B VHS.** George Raft, Walter Pidgeon, Joan Bennett, Lloyd Nolan, Gladys George; ***D:*** Archie Mayo.

House Arrest 🦴 1/2 **1996 (PG)** Another tired kids-think-they-know-best formula film. When Grover Beindorf (Howard) and his younger sister learn that their constantly fighting parents (Curtis and Pollak) are separating, they lock them in the basement so they'll be forced to sort things out. Word gets around and some school pals kidnap their problem parents and stash them in the basement with the Beindorfs. Most of the movie was actually shot in a basement; watch for Curtis hanging upside down in a laundry chute "True Lies" style. **107m/C VHS, DVD.** Jamie Lee Curtis, Kevin Pollak, Christopher McDonald, Jennifer Tilly, Caroline Aaron, Wallace Shawn, Sheila McCarthy, Ray Walston, Kyle Howard, Amy Sakasitz, Jennifer Love Hewitt; ***D:*** Harry Winer; ***W:*** Michael Hitchcock; ***C:*** Ueli Steiger; ***M:*** Bruce Broughton.

The House Bunny 2008 (PG-13) Playboy Bunny Shelly (Faris) is tossed from the mansion after turning the ripe old age of 27 (which is like 59 in Playboy years, she's told). Oblivious to the outside world, she wanders the streets like some Pinocchio Barbie until the geeky sorority girls of Zeta Alpha Zeta take her in as "house mom." Shelly slowly convinces the girls to get makeovers and let their hair down, transforming the ugly ducklings into tarted-up swans. Meanwhile, to win over sweet, brainy co-ed Oliver (Hanks), the girls help Shelly undergo her own makeover via books and less hairspray. Brainless and shallow (shocking!). Faris's considerable comic talents deserve more than what she's given to work with here. She really needs a new agent. **97m/C DVD, Blu-ray Disc.** *US* Anna Faris, Colin Hanks, Emma Stone, Kat Dennings, Katharine McPhee, Rumer Willis, Tyson Ritter, Kiely Williams, Dana Min Goodman, Monet Mazur, Christopher McDonald, Kimberly Makkouk, Beverly D'Angelo, Charles Robinson, Jonathan Loughran; ***Cameos:*** Hugh Hefner; ***D:*** Fred Wolf; ***W:*** Karen McCullah Lutz, Kirsten Smith; ***C:*** Shelly Johnson; ***M:*** Waddy Wachtel.

The House by the Cemetery *Quella Villa Accanto Al Cimitero* 1983 (R) When a family moves into a house close to a cemetery, strange things start to happen to them. **84m/C VHS, DVD.** *IT* Katherine (Katriona) MacColl, Paolo Malco, Giovanni Frezza; ***D:*** Lucio Fulci; ***W:*** Lucio Fulci, Dardano Sacchetti; ***C:*** Sergio Salvati; ***M:*** Walter Rizzati.

House Calls 1978 (PG) A widowed surgeon turns into a swinging bachelor until he meets a witty but staid English divorcee. Wonderful dialogue. Jackson is exceptional. Made into a short-lived TV series. **98m/C VHS, DVD.** Walter Matthau, Glenda Jackson, Art Carney, Richard Benjamin, Candice Azzara; ***D:*** Howard Zieff; ***W:*** Charles Shyer; ***M:*** Henry Mancini.

A House Divided 1/2 2000 (R) Amanda (Beals) is the beloved only child of wealthy Georgia plantation owner David Dickson (Waterson) and is named as his heir when her father dies. But when Dickson's estranged brother (White) contests the will, family secrets come to light, includig the devastating fact that Amanda's real mother is Julia (Hamilton), who was one of Dickson's slaves. And although it may be 1874, race is still definitely an issue. Based on a true court case described in the book "Woman of Color, Daughter of Privilege" by Kent Anderson Leslie. **99m/C VHS.** Sam Waterston, Jennifer Beals, Lisa Gay Hamilton, Timothy Daly, Ron White, Shirley Douglas, Sean McCann, Gerard Parkes, Colin Fox; ***D:*** John Kent Harrison; ***W:*** Paris Qualles; ***C:*** Kees Van Oostrum; ***M:*** Lawrence Shragge. **CABLE**

The House in Marsh Road 1960 A faithless husband decides to rid himself of She Who Must Be Obeyed, but his wife's ghost-friend intervenes. **70m/B VHS.** *GB* Tony Wright, Patricia Dainton, Sandra Dorne, Derek Aylward, Sam Kydd; ***D:*** Montgomery Tully.

A House in the Hills 1993 (R) A struggling actress is housesitting at a luxurious estate and innocently lets in the exterminator. Except he's an ex-con looking for revenge on the home's current occupant (whom the actress is pretending to be) and may just exterminate her instead. **91m/C VHS.** Helen Slater, Michael Madsen, Jeffrey Tambor, James Laurenson, Elyssa Davalos, Toni Barry; ***D:*** Ken Wiederhorn; ***W:*** Ken Wiederhorn; ***C:*** Josep Civit; ***M:*** Richard Einhorn.

The House Next Door 2001 Lori (Cook) and Tom (Harrison) Peterson move into their dream house, meeting next-door neighbors Helen (Russell) and Carl (Russo) Schmidt. Carl seems rowdy but friendly but Lori comes to realize that he's a wife-beater and when Helen disappears she suspects the worse. Tom doesn't take his wife seriously and leaves on a business trip, with Lori's friend Monica (Young) coming to visit. So Lori persuades Monica to help her investigate Carl. **93m/C VHS, DVD.** A.J. Cook, James Russo, Theresa Russell, Sean Young, Frederic Forrest, Matthew Harrison; ***D:*** Joey Travolta; ***W:*** John Benjamin Martin; ***C:*** Pieter Stathis; ***M:*** John Sereda. **VIDEO**

House of Angels *Anglagard; Colin Nutley's House of Angels* 1992 (R) Charming comedy, with some serious overtones, about what happens to the gossipy inhabitants of a small Swedish village when two free-spirited newcomers come to stay. Fanny and her friend Zac, who are cabaret performers, show up at the funeral of eccentric Erik, who turns out to be the grandfather Fanny never knew. With her outrageous clothes and attitude, Fanny has most of the neighbors scandalized but what the generous Fanny wants is some information about her past, including who her father might be. What the neighbors want is for Fanny and Zac to leave as quickly as possible. In Swedish with English subtitles. **119m/C VHS.** *SW* Helena Bergstrom, Rikard Wolff, Sven Wollter, Jakob Eklund, Viveka Seldahl, Ernst Gunther, Reine Brynolfsson, Per Oscarsson; ***D:*** Colin Nutley; ***W:*** Susanne Falck.

House of Bamboo 1/2 1955 A ruthless gang in Tokyo is holding up U.S. ammunition trains and will stop at nothing to cover their tracks, including killing their own. Stack is an undercover cop who infiltrates the gang, led by Ryan's vicious crime boss. Although Ryan does not disappoint, Stack's not at his best, and love scenes between him and Shirley Yamaguchi are stilted and uncomfortable to watch. The real star in this remake of "The Street with No Name" (1948) is the Cinemascope view of post war Japan and the finale in a Tokyo amusement park. **102m/C DVD.** Robert Ryan, Robert Stack, Yoshiko (Shirley) Yamaguchi, Cameron Mitchell, Brad Dexter, Sessue Hayakawa, Biff (Elliott) Elliot, Harry Carey Jr., John Doucette, Barry Coe, DeForest Kelley; ***D:*** Samuel Fuller; ***W:*** Harry Kleiner; ***C:*** Joe MacDonald; ***M:*** Leigh Harline.

House of Cards 1990 Depicts the political machinations of Machiavellian Tory whip Francis Urquhart (Richardson), who schemes to bring down the present government so that he can become the next Prime Minister. And there's absolutely nothing "F.U." (as he's appropriately known) won't do to achieve power. Followed by "To Play the King" and "The Final Cut"; based on the novel Michael Dobbs. On two cassettes. **200m/C VHS, DVD.** *GB* Miles Anderson, David Lyon, Malcolm Tierney, Nicholas Selby, James Villiers, Diane Fletcher, Ian Richardson, Susannah Harker; ***D:*** Paul Seed; ***W:*** Andrew Davies; ***C:*** Ian Punter, Jim Fyans; ***M:*** Jim Parker.

House of Cards 1/2 1992 (PG-13) Precocious six-year-old Sally (Menina) suddenly stops talking after her father is killed in an accident at an archeological site in Mexico. Mom Ruth (Turner) fights to bring her daughter out of her fantasy world and seeks medical advice from a psychiatrist (a sympathetic Jones) but ignores it when it clashes with her own theories. The ethereal Menina, in her acting debut, gives the best performance in this weakly plotted and confusing family saga. **109m/C VHS, DVD.** Kathleen Turner, Asha Menina, Tommy Lee Jones, Shiloh Strong, Esther Rolle, Park Overall, Michael Horse, Anne Pitoniak; ***D:*** Michael Lessac; ***W:*** Michael Lessac; ***C:*** Victor Hammer.

House of D 2004 (PG-13) First time writer/director Duchovny is Tom Warshaw. He recounts for his son the events of his own early adolescence that shaped his life. In the early '70s, young Tommy has recently lost his father, his mother is suffering from depression, his best friend is Pappas, the retarded janitor at his school, he gets life advice from an inmate at the nearby Women's House of Detention, and he is just now noticing girls, particularly neighbor Melissa. This last development leads a jealous Pappas to petty theft to win back Tommy's friendship. Cloying, overly sentimental, and shamelessly sappy, this tale works much better as nostalgia for the carefree Greenwich Village Duchovny grew up in than the coming of age fable he obviously intended. **96m/C DVD.** *US FR* David Duchovny, Anton Yelchin, Erykah Badu, Robin Williams, Zelda Williams, Magali Amadei, Tea Leoni, Frank Langella, Harold Cartier, Orlando Jones, Alice Drummond; ***D:*** David Duchovny; ***W:*** David Duchovny; ***C:*** Michael Chapman; ***M:*** Geoff Zanelli.

House of Dark Shadows 1970 (PG) Gory, intense feature-film version of the gothic TV daytime soap "Dark Shadows." Released from his coffin by a handyman seeking treasure, 150-year-old vampire Barnabas Collins (Frid) avails himself of the hospitality of his descendents and moves into a house on their property. As a series of vampire attacks plague the area, Barnabas finds himself involved with a love-smitten doctor who wants to cure him (Hall) and a young girl who resembles his lost love, Josette (Scott). A violent and exciting film, long on shocks but short on continuity and character development. **97m/C VHS.** Jonathan Frid, Joan Bennett, Grayson Hall, Kathryn Leigh Scott, Roger Davis, Nancy Barrett, John Karlen, Thayer David, Louis Edmonds; ***D:*** Dan Curtis; ***W:*** Sam Hall, Gordon Russell; ***C:*** Arthur Ornitz.

House of Darkness 1/2 1948 Psycho-thriller opens with a narrative by composer Melachrino explaining how the inspiration for a symphony came from his visit to a haunted house. Greedy Francis Merryman (Harvey) wants to inherit his stepbrother John's (Archdale) lavish mansion. Knowing John has a severe heart condition, Francis smashes John's prized violin, which brings on a fatal attack. Driven to paranoia and madness by his actions, Francis thinks he hears violin music (and possibly sees John's ghost). Director Mitchell's last film. **77m/B DVD.** *GB* Laurence Harvey, John Stuart, Lesley Brook, Lesley Osmond, Alexander Archdale, Grace Arnold, George Melachrino, John Teed; ***D:*** Oswald Mitchell; ***W:*** John Gilling; ***C:*** Cyril Bristow.

House of Death *Death Screams* 1982 (R) The ex-Playmate of the Year runs in hysterical fear from a knife-wielding lunatic. **88m/C VHS.** Susan Kiger, William T. Hicks, Jody Kay, Martin Tucker, Jennifer Chase; ***D:*** David Nelson; ***W:*** Paul Elliott; ***C:*** Darrell Cathcart; ***M:*** Dee Barton.

The House of Dies Drear 1/2 1988 A modern-day African American family moves into an old house that turns out to be haunted by the ghost of a long dead abolitionist. The family is transported back to the days of slavery as they interact with the ghost. Based on the story by Virginia Hamilton. Aired on PBS as part of the "Wonderworks" family movie series. **107m/C VHS, DVD.** Howard E. Rollins Jr., Moses Gunn, Shavar Ross, Gloria Foster, Clarence Williams III; ***D:*** Allan Goldstein.

House of Dracula 1945 Sequel to "House of Frankenstein" features several of the Universal monsters. Overly ambitious story gets a bit hokey, but it's entertaining, nonetheless. **67m/B VHS, DVD.** Lon Chaney Jr., Martha O'Driscoll, John Carradine, Lionel Atwill, Onslow Stevens, Glenn Strange, Jane Adams, Ludwig Stossel; ***D:*** Erle C. Kenton; ***W:*** Edward T. Lowe; ***C:*** George Robinson.

House of Dreams 1964 Berry is a blocked writer coping with domestic difficulties whose dreams reveal a disturbing future. Contains a bit part for Goodnow, now a CNN talking head. **80m/B VHS.** Robert Berry, Pauline Elliott, Charlene Bradley, Lance Bird, David Goodnow; ***D:*** Robert Berry.

The House of Eliott 1/2 1992 BBC miniseries set in 1920s London finds the orphaned Beatrice and Evangeline Eliott struggling to begin their fashion business as couturiers to the rich and influential, which eventually leads to their founding of the House of Eliott. Lots of romance and intrigue along the way. Boxed set of six cassettes. **600m/C VHS, DVD.** *GB* Stella Gonet, Louise Lombard, Aden (John) Gillett, Richard Lintern.

House of Errors 1/2 1942 Two deliverymen pose as reporters to safeguard a prototype machine gun from the bad guys. Contrived plot consisting of outdated comic routines. This was Marsh's last film. **63m/B VHS.** Roy Butler, Vernon Dent, Harry Langdon, Charles R. Rogers, Marian Marsh, Ray Walker, Betty Blythe, John Holland, Monte (Monty) Collins Jr., Guy Kingsford; ***D:*** Bernard B. Ray; ***W:*** Ewart Adamson, Eddie Davis; ***M:*** Lee Zahler.

House of Fear 1/2 1945 Holmes and Watson investigate the murders of several members of the Good Comrades Club, men who were neither good nor comradely. **69m/B VHS, DVD.** Basil Rathbone, Nigel Bruce, Dennis Hoey, Aubrey Mather, Paul Cavanagh, Gavin Muir; ***D:*** Roy William Neill.

House of Flying Daggers *Shimian Maifu* 2004 Zhang continues his interest in swordplay and chivalry following 2002's "Hero." Set in 859 A.D., during a period of unrest in the Tang Dynasty, the film follows three main characters. Police captains Leo (Lau) and Jin (Kaneshiro) are assigned to uncover the leader of the Flying Daggers, an anti-government rebel group. An elaborate set piece introduces beautiful blind dancer Mei (Zhang), the apex of the triangle. Jin poses as a sympathizer and hopes Mei will lead him to the rebel headquarters but doesn't expect to fall in love with her. A bamboo forest scene is among the film's action highlights. Mandarin with subtitles. Film is dedicated to actress Anita Mui who died from cancer before filming her role. **120m/C VHS, DVD, Blu-ray Disc, UMD.** *CH HK* Takeshi Kaneshiro, Andy Lau, Zhang Ziyi, Song Dandan; ***D:*** Yimou Zhang; ***W:*** Yimou Zhang, Feng Li, Bin Wang; ***C:*** Xiaoding Zhao; ***M:*** Shingeru Umebayashi.

House of Fools *Dom Durakov* 2002 (R) Janna (Vysotsky) is a young psychiatric patient in an old mansion located near the border of Chechnya. The cheerful Janna believes herself to be the fiancee of Canadian singer Bryan Adams (who appears as himself in the young woman's fantasies). The everyday activities of the childlike patients are disrupted when the fighting between the Russians and the Chechens comes closer. The staff flee and the doctor (Bagdonas) leaves to find buses to evacuates his patients. Meanwhile, the inmates are left to fend for themselves—and are soon joined by a group of Chechen soldiers, including handsome Akhmed (Isalmov) who Janna falls in love with. The film was inspired by an incident that happened in 1996. Russian with subtitles. **104m/C VHS, DVD.** *RU FR* Julia Vysotsky, Sultan Iskamov, Bryan Adams, Vladas Bagdonas, Stanislav Varkki, Marina Politseimako; ***D:*** Andrei Konchalovsky; ***W:*** Andrei Konchalovsky; ***C:*** Sergei Kozlov; ***M:*** Eduard Artemyev.

House of Frankenstein 1/2 1944 An evil scientist (Karloff) escapes from prison, and, along with his hunchback manservant, revives Dracula, Frankenstein's monster, and the Wolfman to carry out his dastardly deeds. An all-star cast helps this horror fest along. **71m/B VHS, DVD.** Boris Karloff, J. Carrol Naish, Lon Chaney Jr., John Carradine, Elena Verdugo, Anne Gwynne, Lionel Atwill, Peter Coe, George Zucco, Glenn Strange, Sig Rumann; ***D:*** Erle C. Kenton; ***W:*** Edward T. Lowe; ***C:*** George Robinson.

House of Fury *Jing Mo Gaa Ting* 2005 Yue (Anthony Wong) is a former secret agent turned chiropractor who annoys his rebellious children with far-fetched tales of the good old days. That is until they're proven true when an old nemesis kidnaps their father, and the family is required to rescue him. Fortunately he's trained them in kung fu since early childhood. Suspending disbelief helps. **102m/C DVD, Blu-ray Disc, UMD.** *HK* Anthony Wong Chau-Sang, Stephen Fung, Charlene (Cheuk-Yin) Choi, Gillian (Yan-Tung) Chung, Michael Wong, Daniel Wu, Winnie Leung, Ma Wu, Jon Foo, Philip Ng; ***D:*** Stephen Fung; ***W:*** Stephen Fung, Yui Fai Lo.

House of Games 1987 (R) The directorial debut of playwright Mamet is a tale about an uptight female psychiatrist who investigates the secret underworld of con-artistry and becomes increasingly involved in an elaborate con game. She's led along her crooked path by smooth-talking con-master Mantegna. A taut, well plotted psychological suspense film with many twists and turns. Stylishly shot, with dialogue which has that marked Mamet cadence. Most of the leads are from Mamet's theatre throng (including his wife, Crouse). **102m/C VHS, DVD.** Joe Mantegna, Lindsay Crouse, Lilia Skala, J.T. Walsh, Meshach Taylor, Ricky Jay, Mike Nussbaum, Willo Hausman; ***D:*** David Mamet; ***W:*** David Mamet; ***C:*** Juan Ruiz-Anchia; ***M:*** Alaric Jans.

House of Horrors 1/2 1946 Deformed murderer "The Creeper" (Hatton) is used by a mad sculptor in a twisted revenge plot. Marcel De Lange (Kosleck) believes his work has been vilely abused by art critics so he uses his friend's homicidal urges to get rid of anyone who stands in his way. **76m/B VHS.** Martin Kosleck, Rondo Hatton, Robert Lowery, Virginia Grey, Bill Goodwin, Alan Napier, Joan Shawlee, Howard Freeman; ***D:*** Jean Yarbrough; ***W:*** George Bricker.

House of Mirth 2000 (PG-13) The treacherous world of high society is the backdrop for savvy social climber Lily Bart

(Anderson), who seeks to match her wits with an eligible bachelor's money in early 20th-century N.Y.C. Stoltz plays friend Selden who is not quite up to snuff financially for Lily, and Aykroyd, a well-heeled and seemingly well-meaning married "friend" who offers her investment advice...but at a hefty price. To make matter worse, a high-profile social maven (Linney) uses Lily to distract her husband from her own infidelities which puts Lily's reputation in jeopardy. With powerful friends lining up against her and her gambling debts piling up, the innocent Lily soon finds her once promising social position compromised. Disturbing but involving story made all the more so by Anderson's performance. Based on the novel by Edith Wharton. **140m/C VHS, DVD.** *GB US* Gillian Anderson, Eric Stoltz, Dan Aykroyd, Eleanor Bron, Terry Kinney, Anthony LaPaglia, Laura Linney, Jodhi May, Elizabeth McGovern; ***D:*** Terence Davies; ***W:*** Terence Davies; ***C:*** Remi Adefarasin.

House of Mystery **1934** For a shot at some priceless jewels stolen by the host from a Hindu princess, several guests gather for a weekend in a spine-tingling mansion. A creepy curse keeps them looking over their shoulders. **62m/C VHS, DVD.** Ed Lowry, Verna Hillie, Brandon Hurst, George "Gabby" Hayes; ***D:*** William Nigh.

House of Mystery ½ *At the Villa Rose* **1941** Splendid British remake of 1934 film in which the detective does some true sleuthing to catch the culprits. An old widow is killed for her jewels, but the murderers can't locate the goods. After they try a series of fiendish plans to retrieve them, the detective must work to stop the crooks. **61m/B VHS.** *GB* Kenneth Kent, Judy Kelly, Peter Murray Hill, Walter Rilla, Ruth Maitland; ***D:*** Walter Summers.

House of 9 **2005 (R)** So how familiar does this sound? Nine strangers wake up trapped in a creepy mansion without any idea how they got there. A voice tells them that only one will survive and that last person gets five million bucks for their trouble. Not as grisly as "Saw" or "Cube" but still nasty. **86m/C DVD.** *GB* Dennis Hopper, Hippolyte Girardot, Peter Capaldi, Raffaello Degruttola, Kelly Brook, Ashley Walters, Susie Amy, Morven Christie, Julienne Davis; ***D:*** Stephen R. Monroe; ***W:*** Philippe Vidal; ***C:*** Damian Bromley; ***M:*** Mark Ryder.

House of 1000 Corpses **WOOF!** **2003 (R)** Disjointed and thoroughly confusing homage to horror films akin to "The Texas Chainsaw Massacre." Director Zombie has an honest affection for the films he references and recreates. Unfortunately, his movie is a hodge-podge of stories with no clear direction. It's stylish enough to be a popular cult film, but it lacks tangible scares or real drama. None of the episodes really fit together in this failure paved by good intentions. Hype may lead you to think this will be a gorefest. It isn't. **88m/C VHS, DVD, Blu-ray Disc.** *US* Sid Haig, Bill Moseley, Karen Black, Sheri Moon Zombie, Chris Hardwick, Erin Daniels, Dennis Fimple, Jennifer Jostyn, Walton Goggins, Tom Towler, Michael J. Pollard, Harrison Young; ***D:*** Rob Zombie; ***W:*** Rob Zombie; ***C:*** Tom Richmond, Alex Poppas; ***M:*** Rob Zombie, Scott Humphrey.

The House of 1000 Dolls *Haus Der Tausend Freuden* **1967** Doleful, not dollful, exploitation thriller as magician Price drugs young girls and sells them to slavery rings. An international production set in Tangiers; dialogue is dubbed. **79m/C VHS.** *GE SP GB* Vincent Price, Martha Hyer, George Nader, Ann Smyrner, Maria Rohm; ***D:*** Jeremy Summers.

House of Psychotic Women **WOOF!** *Los Ojos Azules de la Muneca Rota; Blue Eyes of the Broken Doll* **1973 (R)** Naschy, Spain's premier horror movie star, plays a studly drifter who winds up in the home of three sisters, one with an artifical arm, one confined to a wheelchair and the other a nymphomaniac. No problemo thinks the hirsute Spaniard, until a series of bizarre murders—in which the victims eyes are ripped out—spoils his fun. Naschy, who usually sprouts fur and fangs, actually doesn't turn into a werewolf. Catchy but inappropriate score. A must for Naschy/bad movie fans. **87m/C VHS.** *SP* Paul Naschy, Maria Perschy, Diana Lorys, Eva Leon, Ines Morales, Tony Pica; ***D:*** Carlos Aured; ***W:*** Paul Naschy; ***C:*** Francisco Sanchez.

House of Saddam ½ **2008** HBO miniseries depicting power-mad Saddam Hussein's (Naor) rise and fall through his reliance on family ties to keep his country under control. His paranoia and megalomania aren't attractive traits and there's no one else to root for either as the biography focuses on the Iraqi side of the various conflicts that lead to the American invasion. **260m/C DVD.** Igal Naor, Shohreh Aghdashloo, Said Taghmaoui, Makram Khoury, Uri Gavriel, Philip Arditti, Christine Stephen-Daly; ***D:*** Alex Holmes, Jim O'Hanlon; ***W:*** Alex Holmes, Stephen Butchard; ***C:*** Florian Hoffmeister; ***M:*** Samuel Sim. **CABLE**

House of Sand *Casa de Areia* **2005 (R)** In 1910, Aurea (Torres) and her mother Maria (Montenegro, Torres' real-life mom) are transplanted to the oblivion of northern Brazil by Aurea's delusioned husband, who is intent on turning the barren land into a farm. She quickly finds her pregnant self widowed and stranded, but she is befriended by Massu (Moldia), a former slave from a nearby settlement who helps the women make their way. The story unfolds over three generations (Torres and Motenegro eventually shift roles, with Montenegro as Aurea and Torres as daughter Maria) as the house slowly fills with sand, symbolizing the effects of gradual but inevitable passage of time. Not much happens save the occasional opportunity for escape from the desolate desert life, but for those with patience, it's a visual and dramatic treat. Portuguese with English subtitles. **115m/C DVD.** *BR* Fernanda Montenegro, Fernanda Torres, Ruy Gerra, Luiz Melodia, Emiliano Queiroz, Enrique Diaz; ***D:*** Andrucha Waddington; ***W:*** Elena Soarez; ***C:*** Ricardo Della Rosa; ***M:*** Joao Barone.

House of Sand and Fog ½ **2003 (R)** Kathy (Connolly) is a recovering alcoholic whose husband recently left her. Because of a bureaucratic mix-up, she finds her house has been auctioned off from beneath her to Colonel Massoud Behrani (Kingsley), a former Iranian officer desperate to live the American dream. What follows is the conflict and struggle between the two, neither of which are evil or wrong in their viewpoints. Superb acting all around, combined with an interesting story. Based on the best-selling novel by Andre Dubus III. **126m/C VHS, DVD.** *US* Jennifer Connelly, Ben Kingsley, Ron Eldard, Shohreh Aghdashloo, Frances Fisher, Kim Dickens, Jonathan Ahdout, Navi Rawat, Carlos Gomez; ***D:*** Vadim Perelman; ***W:*** Vadim Perelman, Shawn Otto; ***C:*** Roger Deakins; ***M:*** James Horner. Ind. Spirit '04: Support. Actress (Aghdashloo); L.A. Film Critics '03: Support. Actress (Aghdashloo); N.Y. Film Critics '03: Support. Actress (Aghdashloo).

The House of Secrets **1937** A Yank travels to Britain to collect an inheritance and stays in a dusty old mansion filled with an odd assortment of characters. **70m/B VHS, DVD.** Leslie Fenton, Muriel Evans, Noel Madison, Sidney Blackmer, Morgan Wallace, Holmes Herbert; ***D:*** Roland D. Reed.

The House of Seven Corpses **1973 (PG)** A crew attempts to film a horror movie in a Victorian manor where seven people died in a variety of gruesome manners. Things take a turn for the ghoulish when a crew member becomes possesed by the house's evil spirits. Good, low budget fun with a competent "B" cast. Filmed in what was the Utah governor's mansion. **90m/C VHS, DVD.** John Ireland, Faith Domergue, John Carradine, Carole Wells; ***D:*** Paul Harrison; ***W:*** Paul Harrison, Thomas J. Kelly.

House of Shadows ½ *La Casa de las Sombras* **1976** A 20-year-old murder comes back to haunt the victim's friends in this tale of mystery and terror. **90m/C VHS.** *AR* John Gavin, Yvonne De Carlo, Leonor Manso; ***D:*** Richard Wulicher.

House of Strangers ½ **1949** Conte, in a superb performance, swears vengeance on his brothers, whom he blames for his father's death. Robinson, in a smaller part than you'd expect from his billing, is nevertheless excellent as the ruthless banker father who sadly reaps a reward he didn't count on. Based on Philip Yordan's "I'll Never Go There Again." **101m/B VHS, DVD.** Edward G. Robinson, Susan Hayward, Richard Conte, Luther Adler, Efrem Zimbalist Jr., Debra Paget; ***D:*** Joseph L. Mankiewicz; ***W:*** Philip Yordan; ***C:*** Milton Krasner. Cannes '49: Actor (Robinson).

House of Terror *The Five at the Funeral; Scream Bloody Murder* **1972** A woman and her boyfriend plot to kill her rich boss, while they too are being stalked by some undefined horror. **91m/C VHS.** Jennifer Bishop, Arell Blanton, Jacquelyn Hyde; ***D:*** Sergei Goncharoff.

The House of the Arrow **1953** Investigating the murder of a French widow, who was killed by a poisoned arrow, a detective must sort through a grab bag of potential suspects. Superior adaptation of the A.E.W. Mason thriller. **73m/B VHS.** *GB* Oscar Homolka, Yvonne Furneaux, Robert Urquhart; ***D:*** Michael Anderson Sr.

House of the Black Death ½ *Blood of the Man Devil; Night of the Beast* **1965** Horror titans Chaney and Carradine manage to co-star in this as warring warlocks, yet they share no scenes together! Chaney is the evil warlock (the horns are a giveaway) holding people hostage in the title edifice. **89m/B VHS.** Lon Chaney Jr., John Carradine, Katherine Victor, Tom Drake, Andrea King; ***D:*** Harold Daniels, Reginald LeBorg.

House of the Damned ½ **1971** A young woman, a mental hospital, a murdered father, a priceless gold statue—mix together and you get a mystery horror movie. A woman tries to solve her father's murder. **89m/C VHS.** Donald Pleasence, Michael Dunn; ***D:*** Gonzalo Suarez.

House of the Dead *Alien Zone* **1978** Man is trapped inside a haunted house. Scary. **100m/C VHS.** John Ericson, Charles Aidman, Bernard Fox, Ivor Francis; ***D:*** Sharron Miller; ***W:*** David O'Malley; ***C:*** Ken Gibb; ***M:*** Stan Worth.

House of the Dead **WOOF!** **2003 (R)** Cinematic trainwreck Uwe Boll attempts to make the filmmakers behind "Super Mario Brothers" feel better about themselves by directing one of the worst video game movies ever (and that's saying something). Four actors you could care less about travel to a remote island for the lamest rave ever captured on film (it has a baked goods tent... honestly) and, surprise, surprise, hordes of the undead start chomping on the extras. B-movie mainstays like Jurgen Prochnow and Clint Howard sleepwalk past the camera occasionally, but the real star is Boll's near-legendary technical ineptitude. Take a shot every time you notice a glaring gaffe and, trust us, you'll be dead long before the movie's over. **90m/C VHS, DVD, UMD.** *GE CA US* Jonathan Cherry, Tyron Leitso, Clint Howard, Ellie Cornell, Will Sanderson, Sonya Salomaa, Michael Eklund, David Palffy, Jurgen Prochnow, Erica Durance, Anthony Harrison, Ona Grauer, Enuka Okuma, Kira Clavell; ***D:*** Uwe Boll; ***W:*** Mark Altman, David Parker; ***C:*** Mathias Neumann; ***M:*** Reinhard Besser, Oliver Lieb.

House of the Dead 2: Dead Aim ½ **2005 (R)** Tongue-in-cheek horror about a college prof (Haig) whose experiments unleash a zombie infestation on campus. A couple of scientists try to find a cure before the bomb-happy military decides to solve the problem by blowing up the area. **95m/C DVD.** Emmanuelle Vaugier, Edward Quinn, Kirk "Sticky Fingaz" Jones, Victoria Pratt, Sid Haig, Steve Monroe; ***D:*** Michael Hurst; ***W:*** Michael Roesch; ***C:*** Raymond N. Stella; ***M:*** Joe Kraemer. **VIDEO**

The House of the Devil **2009 (R)** Retro horror homage set in the 1980s as college sophomore Samantha (Donahue) takes a babysitting job for a strange family. Samantha soon realizes that weirdoes Mr. And Mrs. Ulman, who live in a creepy Victorian mansion out in the woods, hired her not to watch young children, but instead, the father's aged mother on the night of the total lunar eclipse. Refreshingly free of the sadistic torture that mars so many modern horror flicks, relying instead on good old-fashioned suspense. Genuinely scary stuff, understanding that it's not what you see, but what you don't see. **95m/C DVD.** *US* Jocelin Donahue, AJ Bowen, Dee Wallace, Tom Noonan, Mary Woronov, Greta Gerwig; ***D:*** Ti West, Tom Noonan; ***W:*** Ti West, Tom Noonan; ***C:*** Eliot Rockett; ***M:*** Tom Noonan, Jeff Grace.

House of the Living Dead *Doctor Maniac* **1973 (PG)** Brattling Manor harbors a murderous and flesh-eating secret ready to lure the unsuspecting. Don't you be one. **87m/C VHS.** *SA* Mark Burns, Shirley Anne Field, David Oxley; ***D:*** Ray Austin.

House of the Long Shadows ½ **1982 (PG)** Comedy mixes with gore, as four of the horror screen's best leading men team up for the first time, although they have only minor roles. Might have been a contender, but Arnaz is miscast as author who stays in spooky house on a bet with Todd. Some wit but not enough. Based on the play "Seven Keys to Baldpate" by George M. Cohan (and novel by Earl Derr Biggers). **96m/C VHS.** *GB* Vincent Price, Christopher Lee, Peter Cushing, John Carradine, Desi Arnaz Jr., Sheila Keith, Richard Todd; ***D:*** Pete Walker; ***W:*** Michael Armstrong; ***C:*** Norman G. Langley.

House of the Rising Sun ½ **1987** A Los Angeles reporter goes under cover for a story on an exclusive brothel only to discover the owner is a psychopath who has very permanent ways of dealing with troublesome employees. **86m/C VHS.** John York, Bud Davis, Deborah Wakeham, Frank Annese; ***D:*** Greg Gold; ***M:*** Tina Turner, Bryan Ferry.

The House of the Seven Gables ½ **1940** Nathaniel Hawthorne's brooding novel about greed and a family curse. Jaffrey Pyncheon (Sanders) frames his brother Clifford (Price) for the murder of their father so that he can search in peace for the fortune Jaffrey believes is hidden somewhere in the family mansion, Seven Gables. But, eventually, Clifford gets out of prison and returns to claim his birthright. The studio built an exact duplicate of the original Salem house. **89m/B VHS.** George Sanders, Vincent Price, Margaret Lindsay, Dick Foran, Nan Grey, Cecil Kellaway, Alan Napier; ***D:*** Joe May; ***W:*** Harold Greene; ***C:*** Milton Krasner.

The House of the Spirits **1993 (R)** Star-studded adaptation of the novel by Isabel Allende is a multi-generational saga following the fortunes of the powerful Trueba family. The ambitious Esteban (Irons) marries the clairvoyant Clara (Streep), exploits the peasants on his property, and becomes a conservative senator. Their rebellious daughter Blanca (Ryder) falls for rabble-rousing peasant Pedro (Banderas), and the country undergoes a bloody revolution. Magical realism of the novel is lost in screen melodrama, with the international cast ill-served by tepid direction. The child Clara is played by Streep's daughter, Mary Willa (listed in the credits as Jane Gray). **109m/C VHS, DVD.** Meryl Streep, Jeremy Irons, Glenn Close, Winona Ryder, Antonio Banderas, Armin Mueller-Stahl, Vanessa Redgrave, Sarita Choudhury, Maria Conchita Alonso, Vincent Gallo, Miriam Colon, Jan Niklas, Teri Polo, Jane Gray; ***D:*** Bille August; ***W:*** Bille August; ***C:*** Jorgen Persson; ***M:*** Hans Zimmer.

House of the Yellow Carpet ½ **1984** A couple try to sell an ancient Persian carpet heirloom, and in doing so transgress some unwritten mystical law. Havoc ensues. **90m/C VHS.** Roland Josephson, Beatrice Romand; ***D:*** Carlo Lizzani.

House of Traps *Chong xiao lou; Chung siu lau* **1981** In this last film reuniting director Chang Cheh and (most of) the cast of the "5 Deadly Venoms," a rebellious nephew wishes to usurp his uncle's throne. All of the people conspiring with him (along with all the goods and treasure he has stolen) are placed in a pagoda loaded with death traps. When the judge investigating the case is murdered, a group of avengers set out to recover the treasure and put an end to the rebellion. **95m/C DVD.** *HK* Feng Lu, Li Wang, Tien Hsiang Lung, Chien Sun, Siu-hou Chin, Philip Kwok, Ke Chu, Sheng Chiang, Tien-chi Ni; ***D:*** Cheh Chang; ***W:*** Cheh Chang, Kuang Ni; ***C:*** Hui-chi Tsao; ***M:*** Eddie Wang.

The House of Usher *Edgar Allen Poe's House of Usher; The Fall of the House of Usher* **1988 (R)** Some serious overacting by Reed (as Roderick) and Pleasence (as his balmy brother) almost elevate this Poe retread to "so bad it's good" status, and there are a few admirably grisly moments. But, without other camp virtues, it's merely dreary. Adapted by Michael J. Murray and filmed in South Africa. **92m/C VHS.** *SA* Oliver Reed, Donald Pleasence, Romy Windsor, Rufus Swart, Norman Coombes, Anne Stradi; ***D:*** Alan Birkinshaw; ***W:*** Michael J. Murray; ***C:*** Yossi Wein; ***M:*** Gary Chang.

The House of Usher 🦴 1/2 **2006 (R)** Jill arrives at Usher House, which comes complete with a sinister housekeeper, to attend the funeral of her friend Maddy. She also encounters Roderick, her former lover and Maddy's twin brother, who's suffering the same inherited illness that claimed his sister's life. Jill becomes drawn to Rick once again, despite menacing warnings and curiosity that could get her killed. Another very loose adaptation of the famed Poe story. **81m/C DVD.** Izabella Miko, Austin Nichols, Beth Grant, Danielle McCarthy, Stephen Fischer; ***D:*** Hayley Cloake; ***W:*** Colin Chang; ***C:*** Eric Trageser. **VIDEO**

House of Wax 🦴🦴🦴 **1953 (PG)** A deranged sculptor (Price, who else?) builds a sinister wax museum which showcases creations that were once alive. A remake of the early horror flick "Mystery of the Wax Museum," and one of the '50s most popular 3-D films. This one still has the power to give the viewer the creeps, thanks to another chilling performance by Price. Look for a very young Charles Bronson, as well as Carolyn "Morticia Addams" Jones as a victim. **88m/C VHS, DVD.** Vincent Price, Frank Lovejoy, Carolyn Jones, Phyllis Kirk, Paul Cavanagh, Charles Bronson, Paul Picerni, Angela (Clark) Clarke; ***D:*** Andre de Toth; ***W:*** Crane Wilbur; ***C:*** Bert Glennon; ***M:*** David Buttolph.

House of Wax 🦴 1/2 **2005 (R)** Based on, but not very faithful to, the creepy 1953 3-D horror flick that starred Vincent Price. In this dismal dumbed-down remake, your usual gang of stupid college students are stranded by car trouble on their way to a football game. They wind up in the very small town of Ambrose and make the mistake of seeking help from the curator of a strange museum, Trudy's House of Wax, filled with wax figures that seem suspiciously lifelike. Said students include Hilton (making her legit film debut) who everyone will be happy to see encased in wax, which should actually make her more lifelike. **113m/C DVD, Blu-ray Disc, UMD, HD DVD.** *US AU* Elisha Cuthbert, Chad Michael Murray, Brian Van Holt, Jared Padalecki, Jon Abrahams, Robert Ri'chard, Paris Hilton; ***D:*** Jaume Collet-Serra; ***W:*** Carey Hayes, Chad Hayes; ***C:*** Stephen Windon; ***M:*** John Ottman. Golden Raspberries '05: Worst Support. Actress (Hilton).

House of Whipcord **WOOF!** **1975** Beautiful young women are kidnapped and tortured in this British gore-o-rama. Awful and degrading. **102m/C VHS, DVD.** *GB* Barbara Markham, Patrick Barr, Ray Brooks, Penny Irving, Anne Michelle, Ivor Salter, Robert Tayman; ***D:*** Pete Walker; ***W:*** David McGillivray; ***C:*** Peter Jessop; ***M:*** Stanley Myers.

The House of Yes 🦴🦴 **1997 (R)** Thanksgiving certainly brings out the worst in families although the Pascal clan is dysfunction personified. Marty (Hamilton) brings home fiancee Lesley (Spelling) to meet his eccentric mom (Bujold) and siblings. Younger brother Anthony's (Prinze) a dropout with no direction and Marty's twin sister Jackie-O (Parker) is bonkers. She's recreated herself as Jackie Kennedy Onassis and has had a very intimate relationship with Marty that Lesley probably doesn't know about. **90m/C VHS, DVD.** Parker Posey, Josh Hamilton, Tori Spelling, Freddie Prinze Jr., Genevieve Bujold, Rachael Leigh Cook; ***D:*** Mark S. Waters; ***W:*** Mark S. Waters; ***C:*** Michael Spiller; ***M:*** Jeff Rona.

The House on Carroll Street 🦴 1/2 **1988 (PG)** New York 1951, the middle of the McCarthy era. A young woman overhears a plot to smuggle Nazi war criminals into the U.S. She's already lost her job because of accusations of subversion, and it's not easy persuading FBI agent Daniels that she knows what she's talking about. Contrived plot and melodramatic finale help sink this period piece. **111m/C VHS, DVD.** Kelly McGillis, Jeff Daniels, Mandy Patinkin, Jessica Tandy; ***D:*** Peter Yates; ***W:*** Walter Bernstein; ***C:*** Michael Ballhaus; ***M:*** Georges Delerue.

The House on Chelouche Street 🦴🦴 1/2 **1973** In Tel-Aviv, during the summer of 1946, 15-year-old Sami, an Egyptian immigrant, tries to help support his mother and family during the upheavals of Palestine under the British mandate. A well thought-out story detailing the struggles of a North African Jewish family before the creation of the country of Israel. In Hebrew with English subtitles. **111m/C VHS.** *IS* Gila Almagor, Michal Bat-Adam, Shai K. Ophir; ***D:*** Moshe Mizrahi.

The House on Garibaldi Street 🦴🦴 1/2 **1979** Spy drama about the capture of Nazi war criminal Adolph Eichmann in Argentina and his extradition to Israel for trial. Based on the book by Isser Harel. **96m/C VHS.** Chaim Topol, Nick Mancuso, Martin Balsam, Janet Suzman, Leo McKern, Charles Gray, Alfred Burke; ***D:*** Peter Collinson; ***M:*** Charles Bernstein. **TV**

House on Haunted Hill 🦴🦴 1/2 **1958** A wealthy man throws a haunted house party and offers $10,000 to anyone who can survive the night there. Vintage cheap horror from the master of the macabre Castle. Remembered for Castle's in-theatre gimmick of dangling a skeleton over the audiences' heads in the film's initial release. **75m/B VHS, DVD.** Vincent Price, Carol Ohmart, Richard Long, Alan Marshal, Carolyn Craig, Elisha Cook Jr., Julie Mitchum, Howard Hoffman; ***D:*** William Castle; ***W:*** Robb White; ***C:*** Carl Guthrie; ***M:*** Von Dexter.

House on Haunted Hill 🦴🦴 1/2 **1999 (R)** This remake of William Castle's 1958 B-movie doesn't reach too far above its predecessor. In an homage to original star Vincent Price, Geoffrey Rush plays mincing amusement park tycoon Stephen Price, who invites a few friends over for his wife Evelyn's (Janssen) birthday. However, he invites them to a haunted former insane asylum, and offers them a million bucks if they can stick it out for the entire night. Stephen and the scheming Evelyn have a few tricks rigged for the guests, who all end up having some connection to the horrors that went on in the house in the bad old days. Soon, however, actual supernatural creepiness starts thinning the ranks of the guests. Unashamedly bloody and cheesy. **96m/C VHS, DVD.** Geoffrey Rush, Famke Janssen, Taye Diggs, Peter Gallagher, Chris Kattan, Ali Larter, Bridgette Wilson-Sampras, Max Perlich, Jeffrey Combs; ***D:*** William Malone; ***W:*** Dick Beebe; ***C:*** Rick Bota; ***M:*** Don Davis.

House on 92nd Street 🦴🦴🦴 **1945** Documentary-style thriller finds federal investigator George Briggs (Nolan) contacted by German-American student Bill Dietrich (Eythe), who's been sought out by Nazi spies. Briggs encourages Dietrich to play along and report their nefarious activities to the feds. What Dietrich discovers is that a scientist, working on the atomic bomb project, is actually a Nazi agent. Lots of atmosphere and action, with director Hathaway incorporating newsreel footage to highlight the true-to-life feel. Title refers the the house where the head of the Nazi spies resides. **89m/B VHS, DVD.** William Eythe, Lloyd Nolan, Signe Hasso, Gene Lockhart, Leo G. Carroll, William Post Jr., Harry Bellaver; ***D:*** Henry Hathaway; ***W:*** Barre Lyndon, John Monks Jr., Charles G. Booth; ***C:*** Norbert Brodine; ***M:*** David Buttolph. Oscars '45: Story.

The House on Skull Mountain 🦴 1/2 **1974 (PG)** The four surviving relatives of a deceased voodoo priestess are in for a bumpy night as they gather at the House on Skull Mountain for the reading of her will. **85m/C VHS.** Victor French, Janee Michelle, Mike Evans, Jean Durand; ***D:*** Ron Honthaner.

The House on Sorority Row 🦴 1/2 *House of Evil; Seven Sisters* **1983** Less-than-harrowing story of what happens when seven sorority sisters have a last fling and get back at their housemother at the same time. **90m/C VHS, DVD.** Eileen Davidson, Kate McNeil, Robin Meloy, Lois Kelso Hunt, Christopher Lawrence, Janis Zido; ***D:*** Mark Rosman; ***W:*** Mark Rosman; ***C:*** Tim Suhrstedt; ***M:*** Richard Band.

The House on Straw Hill 🦴 1/2 *Expose; Trauma* **1976 (R)** A successful novelist is intrigued by an attractive woman who lives in an isolated farmhouse. Her presence inspires gory hallucinations, lust, and violence. **84m/C VHS.** *GB* Udo Kier, Linda Hayden, Fiona Richmond, Karl Howman, Patsy Smart; ***D:*** James Kenelm Clarke; ***W:*** James Kenelm Clarke; ***C:*** Denis Lewiston.

House on the Edge of the Park **WOOF!** *La Casa Nel Parco* **1984** A frustrated would-be womanizer takes revenge on a parade of women during an all-night party. **91m/C VHS, DVD.** *IT* David A(lexander) Hess, Annie Belle, Lorraine (De Sette) De Selle; ***D:*** Ruggero Deodato.

The House on Todville Road 🦴 **1995 (R)** Fact-based story about a dangerous cult and its followers. **94m/C VHS.** David Harrod, Terri Harrel, Lisa Marie Newmyer; ***D:*** Robert Burge; ***W:*** Robert Burge; ***C:*** Eric Scott; ***M:*** David Connor.

The House on Tombstone Hill 🦴 1/2 **1992** An old, abandoned mansion seems like a good investment to a group of friends. Wrong! The original owner is still around and doesn't like strangers coming to visit. **95m/C VHS, DVD.** Doug Gibson, John Dayton (J.D.) Cerna, Sarah Newhouse; ***D:*** J. Reifel; ***W:*** J. Reifel.

House Party 🦴🦴🦴 **1990 (R)** Lighthearted, black hip-hop version of a '50s teen comedy with rap duo Kid 'n' Play. After his father grounds him for fighting, a high-schooler attempts all sorts of wacky schemes to get to his friend's party. Sleeper hit features real-life music rappers and some dynamite dance numbers. **100m/C VHS, DVD.** Christopher Reid, Christopher Martin, Martin Lawrence, Tisha Campbell, Paul Anthony, A.J. (Anthony) Johnson, Robin Harris; ***D:*** Reginald (Reggie) Hudlin; ***W:*** Reginald (Reggie) Hudlin; ***C:*** Peter Deming; ***M:*** Marcus Miller. Sundance '90: Cinematog.

House Party 2: The Pajama Jam 🦴🦴 1/2 **1991 (R)** Rap stars Kid 'N' Play are back in this hip-hop sequel to the original hit. At Harris University Kid 'N' Play hustle up overdue tuition by holding a campus "jammie jam jam." A stellar cast shines in this rap-powered pajama bash. **94m/C VHS, DVD.** Christopher Reid, Christopher Martin, Tisha Campbell, Iman, Queen Latifah, Georg Stanford Brown, Martin Lawrence, Eugene Allen, George Anthony Bell, Kamron, Tony Burton, Helen Martin, William Schallert; ***D:*** Doug McHenry, George Jackson; ***W:*** Rusty Cundieff, Daryl G. Nickens; ***M:*** Vassal Benford.

House Party 3 🦴 **1994 (R)** Kid is engaged to be married and Play tries to set up a blowout bachelor party. The duo are also working on their record producer careers by trying to sign a feisty female rap group (real life TLC). Strikes out early for easy profanity while never coming within spitting distance of first two flicks. **93m/C VHS, DVD.** Christopher Reid, Christopher Martin, Angela Means, Tisha Campbell, Bernie Mac, Barbara (Lee) Edwards, Michael Colyar, David Edwards, Betty Lester, Chris Tucker; ***D:*** Eric Meza; ***W:*** Takashi Bufford; ***M:*** David Allen Jones.

The House that Bled to Death 🦴 **1981** Strange things happen to a family when they move into a run-down house where a murder occurred years before. A part of the BBC's "Hammer House of Horror" TV series. **60m/C VHS, DVD.** *GB* Nicholas Ball, Rachel Davies, Brian Croucher, Pat Maynard, Emma Ridley; ***D:*** Tom Clegg, Francis Megahy. **TV**

The House that Dripped Blood 🦴🦴 1/2 **1971 (PG)** A Scotland Yard inspector discovers the history of an English country house while investigating an actor's disappearance. Four horror tales comprise the body of this omnibus creeper, following the successful "Tales from the Crypt" mold. Duffell's debut as director. **101m/C VHS, DVD.** *GB* Christopher Lee, Peter Cushing, Jon Pertwee, Denholm Elliott, Ingrid Pitt, John Bennett, Tom Adams, Joss Ackland, Chloe Franks; ***D:*** Peter Duffell; ***W:*** Robert Bloch.

The House that Vanished 🦴 *Scream and Die; Psycho Sex Fiend* **1973 (R)** Semi-exploitative fare about a beautiful young model who witnesses a murder in a house but later can't find the place. Her boyfriend is skeptical. **84m/C VHS.** *GB* Andrea Allan, Karl Lanchbury, Judy Matheson, Maggie Walker, Alex Leppard; ***D:*** Joseph (Jose Ramon) Larraz.

House Where Evil Dwells 🦴 1/2 **1982 (R)** An American family is subjected to a reign of terror when they move into an old Japanese house possessed by three deadly samurai ghosts. The setting doesn't upgrade the creepiness of the plot. Based on a novel by James Hardiman. **88m/C VHS, DVD.** Edward Albert, Susan George, Doug McClure, Amy Barrett, Mako Hattori, Toshiya Maruyama, Henry Mitowa, Tsuyako Okajima, Tsuiyuki Sasaki; ***D:*** Kevin Connor; ***W:*** Robert Subotsky; ***C:*** Jacques Haitkin.

A House Without a Christmas Tree 🦴🦴 1/2 **1972** A frustrated middle-aged man denies his young daughter her one desire—a Christmas tree. Charming TV holiday fare. **90m/C VHS.** Kathryn Walker, Alexa Kenin, Jason Robards Jr., Lisa Lucas, Mildred Natwick; ***D:*** Paul Bogart; ***V:*** Patricia Hamilton. **TV**

Houseboat 🦴🦴 1/2 **1958** Widower Grant with three precocious kids takes up residence on a houseboat with Italian maid Loren who is actually a socialite, incognito. Naturally, they fall in love. Light, fun Hollywood froth. **110m/C DVD.** Cary Grant, Sophia Loren, Martha Hyer, Eduardo Ciannelli, Murray Hamilton, Harry Guardino; ***D:*** Melville Shavelson; ***W:*** Melville Shavelson, Jack Rose; ***M:*** George Duning.

Houseguest 🦴🦴 **1994 (PG)** Dumb comedy about mistaken identity finds hard luck dreamer Kevin Franklin (Sinbad) on the run from loan sharks. Fortunately, while trying to make a getaway at the airport, he's mistaken for the childhood buddy (who's also an eminent dentist prompting some hygiene humor) of family guy/lawyer Gary Young (Hartman), who opens his suburban home to his long lost pal. Street smart Kevin naturally manages to solve every dysfunctional family problem that arises while avoiding some inept Mafia thugs. Everyone is oh-so-good-natured but there's nothing new to hold much interest. **109m/C VHS, DVD.** Sinbad, Phil Hartman, Jeffrey Jones, Kim Greist, Stan Shaw, Tony Longo, Mason Adams, Paul Ben-Victor, Chauncey Leopardi, Ron Glass, Talia Seider, Kim Murphy; ***D:*** Randall Miller; ***W:*** Michael J. Di Gaetano, Laurence Gay; ***C:*** Jerzy Zielinski; ***M:*** John Debney.

Household Saints 🦴🦴🦴 **1993 (R)** Chronicling one family from post-WWII Little Italy through the 1970s, this is a quirky little story about sausage, religion, women, and families (not necessarily in that order). Joseph (D'Onofrio) wins his bride (Ullman) in a pinochle game, much to his superstitious Catholic mother's (Malina) chagrin. The product of that union is a slightly obsessive girl (Taylor), who sees visions and wants to be a saint. Interesting study of Italian-American families, and the roles religion and food play in the culture of Little Italy. **124m/C VHS.** Tracey Ullman, Vincent D'Onofrio, Lili Taylor, Judith Malina, Michael Rispoli, Victor Argo, Michael Imperioli, Rachael Bella, Illeana Douglas, Joe Grifasi, Sebastien Roche; ***D:*** Nancy Savoca; ***W:*** Nancy Savoca, Richard Guay; ***C:*** Bobby Bukowski; ***M:*** Stephen Endelman. Ind. Spirit '94: Support. Actress (Taylor).

The Householder 🦴🦴 *Gharbar* **1963** An early Merchant-Ivory collaboration featuring a young Indian schoolteacher whose widowed mother arranges his marriage to a woman he doesn't know. The immature couple find their adjustment to marriage fraught with, sometimes amusing, complications. **101m/B VHS, DVD.** *IN* Shashi Kapoor, Leela Naidu, Durga Khote; ***D:*** James Ivory; ***W:*** Ruth Prawer Jhabvala.

The Housekeeper 🦴🦴 *A Judgement in Stone* **1986 (R)** Tushingham's portrayal of a deranged housekeeper brings this movie to life even as she kills off her employers. **97m/C VHS.** *CA* Rita Tushingham, Ross Petty, Jackie Burroughs, Tom Kneebone, Shelly Peterson, Jessica Steen, Jonathan Crombie; ***D:*** Ousama Rawi.

The Housekeeper 🦴🦴 *Une Femme de Menage* **2002 (R)** When his wife (Breillat) walks out on him after 15 years, middle-aged

Jacques (Bacri) can't manage to keep his Paris apartment clean, so he hires young and energetic Laura (Dequenne) as a housekeeper. Soon she is taking on more domestic responsibilities and Jacques grows increasingly used to her presence, even when she shows up in his bed. Laura assumes they have a relationship and Jacques even agrees to take her along on a summer holiday, but soon their differences are making themselves very clear. Based on the novel by Christian Oster. French with subtitles. **86m/C DVD.** *FR* Jean-Pierre Bacri, Emilie Dequenne, Brigitte Catillon, Jacques Frantz, Catherine Breillat, Axelle Abbadie; ***D:*** Claude Berri; ***W:*** Claude Berri; ***C:*** Eric Gautier; ***M:*** Frederic Botton.

Housekeeping **1987 (PG)** A quiet but bizarre comedy by Forsyth (his first American film). A pair of orphaned sisters are cared for by their newly arrived eccentric, free-spirited aunt in a small and small-minded community in Oregon in the 1950s. Conventional townspeople attempt to intervene, but the sisters' relationship with their offbeat aunt has become strong enough to withstand the coercion of the townspeople. May move too slowly for some viewers. Based on novel by Marilynne Robinson. **117m/C VHS.** Christine Lahti, Sarah Walker, Andrea Burchill; ***D:*** Bill Forsyth; ***W:*** Bill Forsyth; ***C:*** Michael Coulter; ***M:*** Michael Gibbs.

Housemaster ½ **1938** In a British boys' school the housemaster is kind and understanding of his sometimes-unruly charges. The stern new headmaster is not, and the students conspire against him. An okay but dated comedy, featuring characters with names like Bimbo and Button. Based on "Bachelor Born" by Ian Hay, a London stage hit at the time. **95m/B VHS.** Otto Kruger, Diana Churchill, Phillips Holmes, Rene Ray, Walter Hudd, George L. Baxt, Cecil Parker, Michael Shepley, Jimmy Hanley, Rosamund Barnes; ***D:*** Herbert Brenon.

Housesitter ½ **1992 (PG)** Newton Davis (Martin), an architect/dreamer, builds his high school sweetheart (Delany) a beautiful house and surprises her with a marriage proposal. She says no, so he has a one-night stand with Gwen (Hawn), who moves into his empty house and assumes the position of Davis's wife, unbeknownst to him. Gwen spins whopper lies and soon has the entire town, including Davis's parents and ex-girlfriend, believing her wacky stories. This romantic screwball comedy is a delight, not only because of Martin and Hawn, but also because of the array of other characters who complicate the stories they spin. **102m/C VHS, DVD.** Steve Martin, Goldie Hawn, Dana Delany, Julie Harris, Donald Moffat, Peter MacNichol, Richard B. Shull, Laurel Cronin, Christopher Durang; ***D:*** Frank Oz; ***W:*** Mark Stein, Brian Grazer; ***C:*** John A. Alonzo; ***M:*** Miles Goodman.

Housewife *Bone; Beverly Hills Nightmare; Dial Rat for Terror* **1972 (R)** Bone (Kotto) is a vengeful black man, who holds an unhappily married Beverly Hills couple (Duggan and Van Patten) hostage in their home. **96m/C VHS, DVD.** Yaphet Kotto, Andrew Duggan, Joyce Van Patten, Jeannie Berlin; ***D:*** Larry Cohen; ***W:*** Larry Cohen; ***C:*** George Folsey Jr.; ***M:*** Gil Melle.

How About You ½ **2007** Widowed Kate Harris (Brady) operates a financially-shaky Irish retirement home. Her feisty younger sister Ellie (Atwill) comes to help out and Kate must leave her in charge over the Christmas holidays when their mother becomes ill. The four most difficult residents (two alcoholics and two spinster sisters) are left in Ellie's less-than-tender care and they all find something to learn about each other. Less twee than might be indicated (probably because the cast is terrific). Based on a short story by Maeve Binchy. **90m/C DVD.** Hayley Atwell, Vanessa Redgrave, Joss Ackland, Imelda Staunton, Brenda Fricker, Orla Brady, Joan O'Hara; ***D:*** Anthony Byrne; ***W:*** Jean Pasley; ***C:*** Des Whelan; ***M:*** Niall Byrne.

How Come Nobody's On Our Side? **1973 (PG)** Two out-of-work stuntmen try astrology to find the best time to make some easy money smuggling marijuana out of Mexico. **84m/C VHS.** Adam Roarke, Larry Bishop, Alexandra Hay, Rob Reiner, Penny Marshall; ***W:*** Leigh Chapman.

How Funny Can Sex Be? **1976 (R)** Eight risque sketches about love and marriage Italian style. **97m/C VHS.** *IT* Giancarlo Giannini, Laura Antonelli, Dulio Del Prete; ***D:*** Dino Risi.

How Green Was My Valley **1941** Compelling story of the trials and tribulations of a Welsh mining family, from the youthful perspective of the youngest child (played by a 13-year-old McDowall). Spans 50 years, from the turn of the century, when coal mining was a difficult but fair-paying way of life, and ends, after unionization, strikes, deaths, and child abuse, with the demise of a town and its culture. Considered by many to be director Ford's finest work. When WWII prevented shooting on location, producer Zanuck built a facsimile Welsh valley in California (although Ford, born Sean Aloysius O'Fearna, was said to have been thinking of his story as taking place in Ireland rather than Wales). Based on the novel by Richard Llewellyn. **118m/C VHS, DVD.** Walter Pidgeon, Maureen O'Hara, Donald Crisp, Anna Lee, Roddy McDowall, John Loder, Sara Allgood, Barry Fitzgerald, Patric Knowles, Rhys Williams, Arthur Shields, Ann E. Todd, Mae Marsh; ***D:*** John Ford; ***W:*** Philip Dunne; ***C:*** Arthur C. Miller; ***M:*** Alfred Newman; ***Nar:*** Irving Pichel. Oscars '41: B&W Cinematog., Director (Ford), Picture, Support. Actor (Crisp), Natl. Film Reg. '90;; N.Y. Film Critics '41: Director (Ford).

How Harry Became a Tree ½ *Bitter Harvest* **2001 (R)** Harry, an embittered farmer (Meany) declares war on the most powerful man in town, who happens to be the town matchmaker. In order to marry off his dim but handsome son, Harry finds himself again indebted to his nemesis, which only fuels his anger and proves he is his own worst enemy. Engaging Irish drama with a dark comedic edge. **100m/C DVD.** *IR IT GB FR* Colm Meaney, Adrian Dunbar, Cillian Murphy, Kerry Condon, Pat Laffan; ***D:*** Goran Paskalyevic; ***W:*** Goran Paskalyevic, Christine Gentet, Stephen Walsh; ***C:*** Milan Spasic; ***M:*** Stefano Arnaldi.

How High ½ **2001 (R)** Genial stoner comedy finds tokers Silas (Method Man) and Jamal (Redman) smoking some extra-potent "smart" ganja that magically gets them into Harvard. There the laid back homeboys clash with uptight Dean Cain (Babatunde) but find time for some fine chicks. **93m/C VHS, DVD.** Method Man, Redman, Obba Babatunde, Chuck Davis, Anna Maria Horsford, Fred Willard, Lark Voorhies, Essence Atkins, Jeffrey Jones, Mike Epps, Hector Elizondo, Chris Elwood, Spalding Gray, Tracey Walter, Louis Freese, Al Shearer; ***D:*** Jesse Dylan; ***W:*** Dustin Lee Abraham; ***C:*** Francis Kenny; ***M:*** Rockwilder.

How I Got into College **1989 (PG-13)** A slack, uninspired satire about doofus high school senior Marion Browne (Parker) who is eager to attend the same college as brainy Jessica (Boyle). But both run into problems from the snooty college recruiter (Rocket). More interesting for what the cast went on to do in the nineties. **87m/C VHS, DVD.** Corey Parker, Lara Flynn Boyle, Christopher Rydell, Anthony Edwards, Phil Hartman, Brian Doyle-Murray, Nora Dunn, Finn Carter, Charles Rocket; ***D:*** Savage Steve Holland; ***W:*** Terrel Seltzer; ***C:*** Robert Elswit; ***M:*** Joseph Vitarelli.

How I Killed My Father *Comment J'ai Tue Mon Pere* **2003** No fathers were actually killed in the making of this film. Grim, dry melodrama about a man whose life is upset when the father who deserted him as a boy reappears in his life. Jean-Luc (Berling) is an aloof doctor with a seemingly perfect life but very little passion for his work or his family, and he's afraid of having children. Enter his father, Maurice (Bouquet), who storms back in and starts to wear away at his son's appearance of perfection. The result is a metaphorical tug-of-war between the two men. Fontaine's direction is both effective and ruthless as she questions the nature of the relationship between father and son, but it's occasionally heavy-handed and predictable, giving the sense that the characters are doomed before they get a chance to start. **100m/C DVD.** *FR SP* Michel Bouquet, Charles Berling, Natacha Regnier, Amira Casar, Hubert Kounde, Stephane Guillon; ***D:*** Anne Fontaine; ***W:*** Anne Fontaine, Jacques Fieschi; ***C:*** Jean-Marc Fabre; ***M:*** Jocelyn Pook.

How I Learned to Love Women **1966** A British comedy of errors involving a car-loving youth who learns about women and love. **95m/C VHS.** *IT FR GE* Michele Mercier, Nadja Tiller, Romina Power, Robert Hoffman, Anita Ekberg; ***D:*** Luciano Salce; ***C:*** Erico Menczer; ***M:*** Ennio Morricone.

How I Spent My Summer Vacation **1997** Squabbling college sweethearts Perry (Lea) and Stephanie (Davis) have decided their battles have blighted their romance and they split up right before their senior year. Perry moves into an apartment with a couple of buddies and pines for his ex, who's independently getting on with her life, although the dating scene turns out to be trying for them both. Sweetly amusing debut for writer/director Fisher. **75m/C VHS, DVD.** RonReaco Lee, Deanna Davis, E. Roger Mitchell, Mike Ngaujah, Jade Janise Dixon; ***D:*** John Fisher; ***W:*** John Fisher; ***C:*** Charles Mills; ***M:*** Johnny Barrow.

How I Won the War **1967 (PG)** An inept officer must lead his battalion out of England into the Egyptian desert to conquer a cricket field. Indulgent, scarcely amusing Richard Lester comedy; Lennon, in a bit part, provides the brightest moments. **111m/C VHS, DVD.** *GB* Roy Kinnear, John Lennon, Michael Crawford, Michael Hordern; ***D:*** Richard Lester; ***W:*** Charles Wood; ***C:*** David Watkin; ***M:*** Ken Thorne.

How Many Miles to Babylon? **1982** During WWI, two young men become friends despite their different backgrounds. But one is court-martialed for desertion, and the other is supposed to oversee his execution. **106m/C VHS.** *GB* Daniel Day-Lewis, Christopher Fairbank; ***D:*** Moira Armstrong. **TV**

How Much Do You Love Me? *Combien Tu M'Aimes?* **2005** Downtrodden, ordinary office worker Francois (Campan) tells gorgeous hooker Daniela (Bellucci) that he's won the lottery and invites her to live with him and help him spend his windfall. Naturally, she agrees despite her threatening gangster boyfriend Charly (Depardieu) and the fact that Francois' heart condition flairs up when he gets too, uh, stimulated. French with subtitles. **95m/C DVD.** *FR* Monica Bellucci, Gerard Depardieu, Jean-Pierre Darroussin, Bernard Campan; ***D:*** Bernard Blier; ***W:*** Bernard Blier; ***C:*** Francois Catonne.

How She Move ½ **2008 (PG-13)** Talented dancer Raya (Wesley) returns to her inner-city Toronto neighborhood from private school after her sister dies of a drug overdose. Desperate for a new route out, she uses her dance talents to earn a spot in an all-male dance troupe, where she must constantly prove herself to be as good as the boys. Films's grit, depth, and excellent choreography make it a cut above the average hip-hop dance movie. **94m/C DVD.** *CA* Melanie Nicholls-King, Rutina Wesley, Tre Armstrong, Dwain Murphy, Brennan Gademans, Shawn Desman, Kevin Duhaney; ***D:*** Ian Iqbal Rashid; ***W:*** Annmarie Morais; ***C:*** Andre Pienaar; ***M:*** Andrew Lockington.

How Stella Got Her Groove Back **1998 (R)** Underneath the flawless physique and upscale way of life, fortyish single mom Stella (Bassett) is sad; too much work and no love life is to blame. Coaxed by her best friend Delilah (Goldberg), Stella takes a trip to Jamaica where she falls in love with 20-year-old islander Winston (Diggs in his film debut). A flipside to the May-December romance that is purely more gloss (picturesque shots of the Carribean landscape) than grit. Bassett glows in a tailor-made role and muscular hunk Diggs is a find, but perfection in casting can't rescue this hollow romance that woefully missteps after a promising beginning. Based on the novel by Terry McMillan. **124m/C VHS, DVD.** Angela Bassett, Whoopi Goldberg, Taye Diggs, Regina King, Suzzanne Douglass, Richard Lawson, Michael J. Pagan, Barry (Shabaka) Henley, Sicily; ***D:*** Kevin Rodney Sullivan; ***W:*** Ronald Bass, Terry McMillan; ***C:*** Jeffrey Jur; ***M:*** Michel Colombier.

How Sweet It Is! **1968** Typical American family takes a zany European vacation. Looks like a TV sitcom and is about as entertaining. National Lampoon's version is a lot more fun. **99m/C VHS.** James Garner, Debbie Reynolds, Maurice Ronet, Paul Lynde, Erin Moran, Marcel Dalio, Terry-Thomas, Jenie Jackson; ***D:*** Jerry Paris; ***W:*** Jerry Belson; ***C:*** Lucien Ballard.

How Tasty Was My Little Frenchman *Como Era Gostoso O Meu Frances* **1971** French explorer is captured by a cannibal tribe in the jungles of Brazil. He's treated very well and attempts to learn tribal customs to avoid his fate—he's going to be the main course in a ceremonial dinner. French and Tupi with subtitles. **80m/C VHS, DVD.** *BR* Arduino Colasanti, Ana Maria Magalhaes, Ital Natur, Eduardo Embassahy; ***D:*** Nelson Pereira dos Santos.

How the Garcia Girls Spent Their Summer **2005 (R)** During a sweltering summer in an Arizona border town, Dona Genoveva (Gallardo), the 70-year-old matriarch of the Garcia family, buys a car and announces she's going to learn to drive, with gardener Don Pedro (Cervera Jr.) happy to offer lessons. Her middle-aged divorced daughter Lolita (Pena) breaks off an affair with a married man (Bauer) only to become interested in fellow butcher shop employee Jose (Najera). And Lolita's 17-year-old daughter Blanca (Ferrera) is discovering first love with Sal (Minaya), a boy with a bad reputation. English and Spanish with subtitles. **128m/C DVD.** Lucy Gallardo, Elizabeth Pena, America Ferrera, Steven Bauer, Leo Minaya, Jorse Cervera Jr., Rick Najera; ***D:*** Georgina Garcia Riedel; ***W:*** Georgina Garcia Riedel; ***C:*** Tobias Datum.

How the West Was Fun ½ **1995** The Olsen gals are visiting great godmother Natty's dude ranch, which is in financial difficulty, and must outsmart her greedy son Bart (Mull), a land grabber who wants to turn the ranch into an environmentally unfriendly western theme park. Made for TV. **93m/C VHS, DVD.** Mary-Kate Olsen, Ashley (Fuller) Olsen, Martin Mull, Michele Greene, Patrick Cassidy, Leon Pownall, Margaret "Peg" Phillips; ***D:*** Stuart Margolin; ***M:*** Richard Bellis. **TV**

How the West Was Won **1963 (G)** A panoramic view of the American West, focusing on the trials, tribulations and travels of three generations of one family, set against the background of wars and historical events. Particularly notable for its impressive cast list and expansive western settings. **165m/C VHS, DVD, Blu-ray Disc.** John Wayne, Carroll Baker, Lee J. Cobb, Spencer Tracy, Gregory Peck, Karl Malden, Robert Preston, Eli Wallach, Henry Fonda, George Peppard, Debbie Reynolds, Carolyn Jones, Richard Widmark, James Stewart, Walter Brennan, Andy Devine, Raymond Massey, Agnes Moorehead, Harry (Henry) Morgan, Thelma Ritter, Russ Tamblyn; ***D:*** John Ford, Henry Hathaway, George Marshall; ***W:*** James R. Webb; ***C:*** Milton Krasner, Charles B(ryant) Lang Jr. Oscars '63: Film Editing, Sound, Story & Screenplay, Natl. Film Reg. '97.

How to Be ½ **2008** Dumped by his girlfriend and forced to move back in with his parents, depressed London supermarket clerk and would-be musician Art (Pattinson) hires a self-help author to be his life coach. Navel-gazing aimlessness. **85m/C DVD.** *GB* Robert Pattinson, Rebecca Pidgeon, Powell Jones, Jeremy Hardy, Michael Irving, Alisa Arnah, Mike Pearce, Johnny White; ***D:*** Oliver Irving; ***W:*** Oliver Irving; ***C:*** Paul Swann; ***M:*** Joe Hastings.

How to be a Serial Killer **2008** Genial serial killer Mike Wilson has developed his own ten-step program and seminar, including ethics, killing methods, body disposal, and balancing your work and personal life. Mike needs an apprentice so he takes on vulnerable video store clerk Bart to test his theories. **91m/C DVD.** Laura Regan, George Wyner, Dameon Clarke, Matthew Gray; ***D:*** Luke Ricci; ***W:*** Luke Ricci; ***C:*** H. Michael Otano; ***M:*** Nicholas O'Toole.

How to Be a Woman and Not Die in the Attempt *How to Be a Woman and Not Die Trying; Como ser Mujer y No Morir en El* **1991** Carmen has just turned 42, is married to her third husband, and is raising three children. She's also very serious about her journalistic career on the local paper. So, she's a modern woman with too much to do and too little time, trying to juggle her home and her work and still keep a sense of humor. Based on the novel by Carmen Rico-Godoy. Spanish with subtitles. **96m/C VHS, DVD.** *SP* Carmen Maura, Antonio Resines; ***D:*** Ana Belen; ***W:*** Carmen Rico Godoy; ***C:*** Juan Amoros.

How to Beat the High Cost of Living 1/2 **1980 (PG)** Three suburban housewives decide to beat inflation by taking up robbery, and they start by planning a heist at the local shopping mall. Comedic talent can't salvage whipped script and direction. **105m/C VHS, DVD.** Jessica Lange, Susan St. James, Jane Curtin, Richard Benjamin, Eddie Albert, Dabney Coleman, Fred Willard, Cathryn Damon, Art Metrano; ***D:*** Robert Scheerer.

How to Break Up a Happy Divorce **1976** A divorced woman starts a vigorous campaign to win her ex-husband back by dating another man to make him jealous. Lightweight comedy. **74m/C VHS.** Barbara Eden, Hal Linden, Peter Bonerz, Marcia Rodd, Harold Gould; ***D:*** Jerry Paris. **TV**

How to Commit Marriage 1/2 **1969 (PG)** Hope and Wyman have been married for 20 years when they decide to divorce—just when their daughter (Cameron) decides to marry her college boyfriend (Matheson). His father (Gleason) tries to stop the wedding, fails, but sticks around to cause more trouble. Subplots involve the divorced duo's new loves and the fact that they're about to become grandparents but the comedy is completely uninspired. **96m/C VHS, DVD.** Bob Hope, Jane Wyman, Jackie Gleason, Joanna Cameron, Tim Matheson, Bea Arthur, Leslie Nielsen, Tina Louise, Paul Stewart, Prof. Irwin Corey; ***D:*** Norman Panama; ***W:*** Ben Starr, Michael Kanin; ***C:*** Charles B(ryant) Lang Jr.; ***M:*** Joseph J. Lilley.

How to Deal 1/2 **2003 (PG-13)** High schooler Halley (Moore) decides love is a crock when she hits some speed bumps on the road of life. Her parents split when DJ dad Len (Gallagher) has a midlife crisis and romances a younger woman. Bitter mom Lydia (Janney) copes by getting involved with the wedding plans of older daughter Ashley (Garrison), whose fiance (Astin) seems dominated by his wealthy parents. Then Halley's best friend Scarlett (Holden) finds out she's preggers after her boyfriend is killed in an accident. So Halley is none too receptive to romance when sensitive hunk Macon (Ford) comes around. Adapted from the young adult novels "Someone Like You" and "That Summer" by Sarah Dessen. **101m/C VHS, DVD.** *US* Mandy Moore, Allison Janney, Peter Gallagher, Trent Ford, Alexandra Holden, Dylan Baker, MacKenzie Astin, Connie Ray, Nina Foch, Sonja Smits, Mary Catherine Garrison; ***D:*** Clare Kilner; ***W:*** Neena Beber; ***C:*** Eric Alan Edwards; ***M:*** David Kitay.

How to Eat Fried Worms 1/2 **2006 (PG)** New kid in school tries to put the class bully in his place by meeting the challenge of eating 10 worms—each served up in increasingly creative but decidedly unappetizing ways—in one day without ralphing. The 1973 kid-lit classic of the same name by Thomas Rockwell is sliced and diced to fit its over-the-top big-screen rendering (really, what kids know their way around a kitchen like these do?). But with decent performances by the kiddie cast, it's big-time gross-out fun for the younguns, tied up with a positive (if equally barf-inducing) message about standing up for yourself—if you can get to the end without wretching, that is. **98m/C DVD.** *US* Luke Benward, Hallie Kate Eisenberg, Alexander Gould, James Rebhorn, Adam Hicks, Austin Rogers, Tom Cavanagh, Kimberly Williams; ***D:*** Bob Dolman; ***W:*** Bob Dolman; ***C:*** Richard Rutkowski; ***M:*** Mark Mothersbaugh, Bob Mothersbaugh.

How to Eat Your Watermelon in White Company (and Enjoy It) 1/2 **2005** Full-bodied documentary paying tribute to the life and times of Melvin Van Peebles, the famed black filmmaker most noted for 1971's "Sweet Sweetback's Baadasssss Song." Van Peebles was also an Air Force navigator, cable car operator, novelist in two languages, composer, recording artist, and floor trader at the American Stock Exchange. Title comes from an essay written by Van Peebles. **85m/C DVD.** *US* ***D:*** Joe Angio; ***C:*** Michael Solomon, Joe Angio; ***M:*** Jeremy Parise.

How to Frame a Figg 1/2 **1971 (G)** Bookkeeper Hollis A. Figg (Knotts) is working at Dalton's corrupt city hall where he's setup to be the patsy in the fradulent doings of the mayor and city council. But his best friends Prentiss (Welker) and Ema Letha (Joyce) set out to prove the bumbler's innocence. **103m/C VHS, DVD.** Don Knotts, Elaine Joyce, Frank Welker, Joe Flynn, Edward Andrews, Yvonne Craig, Parker Fennelly, Fay DeWitt; ***D:*** Alan Rafkin; ***W:*** George Tibbles; ***C:*** William Margulies; ***M:*** Vic Mizzy.

How to Get Ahead in Advertising **1989 (R)** A cynical, energetic satire about a manic advertising idea man who becomes so disgusted with trying to sell a pimple cream that he quits the business. Ultimately he grows a pimple of his own that talks and begins to take over his life. Acerbic and hilarious. **95m/C VHS, DVD.** *GB* Richard E. Grant, Rachel Ward, Susan Wooldridge, Mick Ford, Richard Wilson, John Shrapnel, Jacqueline Tong; ***D:*** Bruce Robinson; ***W:*** Bruce Robinson; ***C:*** Peter Hannan; ***M:*** David Dundas, Rick Wentworth.

How to Go Out on a Date in Queens **2006 (R)** Interesting cast, lame story involving three romantic crises set in a Queens restaurant called Mandatori's. Self-proclaimed dating expert Stan (Drillinger) sets up a double date with his widowed friend Artie (Estes) that turns into a disaster. Bookie Johnny (Alexander) finds out that he owes a lot of money to the Russian mob and must blow town just as his gal Ann Marie (Dunford) tells him she's pregnant. And assistant manager Elizabeth (Lynn) is sure her boyfriend Frankie (Morales) is going to propose but he wants to use their life savings to bet on the Super Bowl. **90m/C DVD.** Robert Estes, Jason Alexander, Esai Morales, Brian Drillinger, Kimberly Williams, Christine Dunford, Meredith Scott Lynn, Ron Perlman, Alison Eastwood, Enrique Murciano, Bjorn Johnson, Michelle Danner; ***D:*** Michelle Danner; ***W:*** Richard Vetere; ***C:*** Jens Sturup; ***M:*** Shark.

How to Kill 400 Duponts *Arriva Dorellik* **1968** Bumbling Scotland Yard detective is off to France to stop a master criminal from trying to kill off the rich Dupont family. Why? So he'll be the only one left with any claim to the remaining family fortune. **98m/C VHS.** *IT* Terry-Thomas, Johnny Dorelli, Margaret Lee, Rosella Como, Riccardo Garrone; ***D:*** Steno; ***W:*** Franco Castellano; ***C:*** Mario Capriotti; ***M:*** Franco Pisano.

How to Kill Your Neighbor's Dog **2001 (R)** Critically acclaimed playwright Peter McGowen (Branagh) has fallen on hard times after a string of flops and is feeling the pressure from his sunny-natured wife Melanie (Wright Penn) to have kids. He's trying to fix his latest work but his neighbor's incessantly barking dog keeps him awake nights. The grouch also finds he must befriend a neighbor's daughter, Amy (Hofrichter), because he needs a model for the child role in his play, although Amy's presence does some not entirely unexpected reexamination of Peter and Melanie's marriage. Branagh is amusingly sharp-tongued but the film has a squishy center. **108m/C VHS, DVD.** Kenneth Branagh, Robin Wright Penn, Jared Harris, Suzi Hofrichter, Johnathon Schaech, Peter Riegert, Lynn Redgrave; ***D:*** Michael Kalesniko; ***W:*** Michael Kalesniko; ***C:*** Hubert Taczanowski; ***M:*** David Robbins.

How to Lose a Guy in 10 Days **2003 (PG-13)** Andie (Hudson) is a columnist who needs to date Ben (McConaughey) and then be so obnoxious that he will dump her in 10 days so she can write an article about it for Composure magazine. Ben has placed a bet with his colleagues that he can get any woman to fall in love with him in 10 days so he can get an account he wants. So while Andie is being the needy, clingy narcissic woman from hell, Ben patiently puts up with it for his own reasons. It's a universal rule that such contrivances in a romantic comedy guarantee that the two will genuinely fall in love. Unfortunately, the laughs are far too sparse and both characters too distasteful in their deceit for you to care. **112m/C VHS, DVD.** *US* Kate Hudson, Matthew McConaughey, Adam Goldberg, Michael Michele, Shalom Harlow, Bebe Neuwirth, Robert Klein, Kathryn Hahn, Thomas Lennon, Annie Parisse; ***D:*** Donald Petrie; ***W:*** Kristen Buckley, Brian Regan, Burr Steers; ***C:*** John Bailey; ***M:*** David Newman.

How to Lose Friends & Alienate People 1/2 **2008 (R)** Smart aleck British writer Sydney Young (Pegg) struggles to fit in at his new job in a high-profile New York magazine. Constantly irritating his boss Lawrence (Huston) and eventually blowing a connection with one of Hollywood's most powerful publicists Eleanor Johnson (Anderson), Sydney can't go ten minutes without ruining someone's day. Unfortunately, Johnson represents Sophie Maes (Fox), an up-and-coming starlet who also happens to be the object of Sydney's lustful affection, leaving co-worker Alison (Dunst), who's in love with their boss, as his only hope in the Big Apple. Pegg is great, as usual, but miscast as a romantic lead, again. Funny in places, but the movie suffers from tone problems, unable to decide if it wants be a gooey romantic comedy or a vicious satire. Based on the 2001 memoir by Toby Young, who briefly worked for "Vanity Fair." **110m/C DVD.** *GB* Simon Pegg, Kirsten Dunst, Megan Fox, Jeff Bridges, Gillian Anderson, Danny Huston, Max Minghella, Miriam Margolyes; ***D:*** Robert B. Weide; ***W:*** Peter Straughan; ***C:*** Oliver Stapleton; ***M:*** David Arnold.

How to Lose Your Lover 1/2 *50 Ways to Leave Your Lover* **2004** Owen (Schneider) lives in L.A. and writes trashy celebrity biographies. He decides to break free and move to New York to find intellectual fulfillment. So he won't be tempted to return, Owen crudely breaks all ties to friends and family. Of course, just as he's leaving, he meets the girl of his dreams, Val (Westfeldt), and decides to put her through various romantic trials to see if it could be true love. Val should personally put Owen on that plane instead. **95m/C DVD.** Paul Schneider, Jennifer Westfeldt, Poppy Montgomery, Tori Spelling, Fred Willard; ***D:*** Joran Hawley; ***W:*** Joran Hawley; ***C:*** Dino Parks; ***M:*** Stephen Trask.

How to Make a Doll **1968** Lewis' sex farce about an extremely shy professor whose ineptness with women inspires him to invent android females to satisfy his sexual needs. **81m/C VHS.** Robert S. Woods, Bobbi West, Jim Vance, Patricia Rhea; ***D:*** Herschell Gordon Lewis; ***W:*** Herschell Gordon Lewis, Bert Ray.

How to Make a Monster **1958** In-joke from the creators of youth-oriented '50s AIP monster flicks; a mad makeup man's homebrew greasepaint brainwashes the actors. Disguised as famous monsters, they kill horror-hating movie execs. Mild fun if—and only if—you treasure the genre. Conway repeats his role as Teenage Frankenstein, but the studio couldn't get Michael Landon for the Teenage Werewolf. **73m/B VHS.** Robert H. Harris, Paul Brinegar, Gary Conway, Gary Clarke, Malcolm Atterbury, Dennis Cross, John Ashley, Morris Ankrum, Walter Reed, Heather Ames; ***D:*** Herbert L. Strock.

How to Make a Monster **2001 (R)** Computer game company hires three ambitious programmers to finish a game and bring it to market in four weeks. A telemetry suit is used to render a 3-D version of the game's villain but a power-surge brings the program to life. Now the game's killer cyborg (AKA the telemetry suit) goes after the threesome, thinking they're players in the game. Basically takes only the title from the 1958 A.I.P. flick. **90m/C VHS, DVD.** Steven Culp, Clea DuVall, Jason Marsden, Tyler Mane, Julie Strain, Karim Prince; ***D:*** George Huang; ***W:*** George Huang; ***C:*** Steven Finestone; ***M:*** David Reynolds. **CABLE**

How to Make an American Quilt 1/2 **1995 (PG-13)** Slow-moving take on female friendship and marriage revolves around perennial grad student Finn (the mopey Ryder), who is frantic to both finish her third attempted thesis and to answer a marriage proposal from practically perfect beau Sam (Mulroney). She takes a summer refuge with her grandmother (Burstyn), where a variety of family friends work on her wedding quilt as they tell stories of loves lost and won. Lots of (somewhat overextended) flashbacks and with so many characters, naturally some get the short end of the script. Based on the novel by Whitney Otto. **109m/C VHS, DVD.** Winona Ryder, Ellen Burstyn, Anne Bancroft, Lois Smith, Jean Simmons, Kate Nelligan, Maya Angelou, Alfre Woodard, Dermot Mulroney, Kate Capshaw, Rip Torn, Derrick O'Connor, Loren Dean, Samantha Mathis, Joanna Going, Tim Guinee, Johnathon Schaech, Claire Danes, Jared Leto, Esther Rolle, Melinda Dillon, Alicia (Lecy) Goranson, Maria Celedonio, Mykelti Williamson; ***D:*** Jocelyn Moorhouse; ***W:*** Jane Anderson; ***C:*** Janusz Kaminski; ***M:*** Thomas Newman.

How to Marry a Millionaire 1/2 **1953** Three models pool their money and rent a lavish apartment in a campaign to trap millionaire husbands. Clever performances by three lead women salvage a vehicle intended primarily to bolster Monroe's career. The opening street scene, with the accompanying theme music, was a state-of-the-art achievement of screen and sound in the one of the first movies to be filmed in CinemaScope ("The Robe" was the first). Remake of "The Greeks Had a Word for Them." **96m/C VHS, DVD.** Charlotte Austin, Lauren Bacall, Marilyn Monroe, Betty Grable, William Powell, David Wayne, Cameron Mitchell; ***D:*** Jean Negulesco; ***W:*** Nunnally Johnson; ***C:*** Joe MacDonald; ***M:*** Alfred Newman.

How to Murder Your Wife **1964** While drunk, a cartoonist marries an unknown woman and then frantically tries to think of ways to get rid of her—even contemplating murder. Frantic comedy is tailored for Lemmon. **118m/C VHS, DVD.** Jack Lemmon, Terry-Thomas, Virna Lisi, Eddie Mayehoff, Sidney Blackmer, Claire Trevor, Mary Wickes, Jack Albertson; ***D:*** Richard Quine; ***W:*** George Axelrod; ***C:*** Harry Stradling Sr.

How to Pick Up Girls **1978** Comic tale based on Eric Weber's bestseller follows the exploits of a small-town boy who moves to New York City and finds the secret to picking up women. Made for television. **93m/C VHS.** Desi Arnaz Jr., Bess Armstrong, Fred McCarren, Polly Bergen, Richard Dawson, Alan King, Abe Vigoda, Deborah Raffin; ***D:*** Bill Persky. **TV**

How to Rob a Bank **2007** Tedious crime caper that tries too hard to be clever. Jinx (Stahl) and Jessica (Christensen) are trapped in a bank vault during a robbery they may or may not be a part of. The bank robbers are holding hostages in the lobby, the cops are outside, and the guy (Carradine) who planned the heist is none too pleased that things have gone wrong. **81m/C DVD.** Nick Stahl, Erika Christensen, Gavin Rossdale, David Carradine, Terry Crews, Leo Fitzpatrick, Adriano Aragon; ***D:*** Andrew Jenkins; ***W:*** Andrew Jenkins; ***C:*** Joseph Meade; ***M:*** Didier Rachou.

How to Seduce a Woman WOOF! **1974** A playboy attempts to bed five supposedly unattainable women. **108m/C VHS.** Angus Duncan, Marty Ingels, Lillian Randolph; ***D:*** Charles Martin; ***W:*** Charles Martin; ***C:*** William Cronjager; ***M:*** Stu Phillips.

How to Steal a Million *How to Steal a Million Dollars and Live Happily Ever After* **1966** Sophisticated comedy-crime caper involving a million-dollar heist of a sculpture in a Paris art museum. Hepburn and O'Toole are perfectly cast as partners in crime and Griffith gives a good performance as Hepburn's art-forging father. A charming, lightweight script and various Parisian locales combine for fun, above-average fluff. Based on the story "Venus Rising" by George Bradshaw. **127m/C VHS, DVD.** Audrey Hepburn, Peter O'Toole, Eli Wallach, Hugh Griffith, Charles Boyer, Fernand Gravey, Marcel Dalio, Jacques Marin; ***D:*** William Wyler; ***W:*** Harry Kurnitz; ***C:*** Charles B(ryant) Lang Jr.; ***M:*** John Williams.

How to Stuff a Wild Bikini **1965** Tired next to last feature in the overlong tradition of Frankie and Annette doing the beach thing, featuring a pregnant Funicello (though this is hidden and not part of the plot). Avalon actually has only a small role as the jealous boyfriend trying to see if Annette will remain faithful while he's away on military duty. Keaton is the witch doctor who helps Frankie keep Annette true. "Playboy" playmates wander about in small swimsuits, garage band extraordinare "The Kingsmen" play themselves, and Brian Wilson of the "Beach Boys" drops by. Followed by "Ghost in the Invisible Bikini," the only movie in the series that isn't on video. ♫ After the Party; Better Be Ready; Follow Your Leader; Give Her Lovin'; How About Us?; How to Stuff a Wild Bikini; I'm the Boy Next Door; Madison Avenue; The Perfect Boy. **90m/C VHS, DVD.** Annette Funicello, Dwayne Hickman, Frankie Avalon, Beverly Adams, Buster Keaton, Harvey Lembeck, Mickey Rooney, Brian Donlevy, Jody McCrea, John Ashley, Marianne Gaba, Len Lesser, Irene Tsu, Bobbi Shaw, Luree Holmes; ***D:*** William Asher; ***W:*** William Asher, Leo Townsend; ***C:*** Floyd Crosby; ***M:*** Les Baxter.

How to Succeed in Business without Really Trying 1/2 **1967** Classic musical comedy about a window-washer who charms his way to the top of a major company. Robert Morse repeats his Tony winning Broadway role. Loosely based on a non-fiction book of the same title by Shepherd Mead, which Morse purchases on his first day of work. Excellent transfer of stage to film, with choreography by Moreda expanding Bob Fosse's original plan. Dynamite from start to finish. ♫ I Believe In You; The Company Way; Coffee Break; The Brotherhood of Man; A Secretary Is Not A Toy; Grand Old Ivy; Been A Long Day; Rosemary; Finch's Frolic. **121m/C VHS, DVD.** Robert Morse, Michele Lee, Rudy Vallee, Anthony Teague, George Fenneman, Maureen Arthur; ***D:*** David Swift; ***W:*** David Swift, Abe Burrows; ***C:*** Burnett Guffey; ***M:*** Frank Loesser.

How to Succeed with Girls **1964** Marginally funny comedy about pious wax salesman (Leder) with a secret fantasy life who unwittingly enlists the aid of his wife's lover (Schrier) to help him overcome his shyness. Several fantasy sequences (in color; the rest of the film is B&W) include an Arabian harem, an old West saloon, and a science laboratory. Brubaker's secretary (Mathes) was Playboy's Miss June 1962. Pete's girlfriend (McClanahan of TV's "Golden Girls") is credited as either Patty Leigh or Helen Goodman. **83m/C VHS.** Marissa Mathes, Rue McClanahan, Paul Leder, Leon Schrier; ***D:*** Edward A. Biery.

How to Train Your Dragon **2010** Viking teen Hiccup lives on an island where fighting dragons is a way of life. However, when Hiccup finds and befriends an injured dragon he upsets his family and tribe. Based on the book by Cressida Cowell. **m/C DVD.** ***D:*** Christopher Sanders, Dean DeBlois; ***W:*** Christopher Sanders, Dean DeBlois; ***M:*** John Powell; ***V:*** Jay Baruchel, Gerard Butler, America Ferrera, Jonah Hill, Christopher Mintz-Plasse, Craig Ferguson, Kristen Wiig.

How U Like Me Now? **1992 (R)** Comedy set on Chicago's south side focuses on Thomas, an attractive but unmotivated guy with low earning potential, and his girl Valerie, a pretentious overachiever who wants much more than he's able to offer. Robert's second directorial effort offers a fresh look at African Americans on film with plenty of lively supporting characters and witty dialogue. Filmed on a $600,000 budget. **109m/C VHS, DVD.** Darnell Williams, Salli Richardson, Daniel Gardner, Raymond Whitefield, Debra Crable, Jonelle Kennedy, Byron Stewart, Charnele Brown, Daryll Roberts; ***D:*** Daryll Roberts; ***W:*** Daryll Roberts; ***M:*** Kahil El Zabar, Chuck Webb.

How You Look to Me **2005 (R)** William Marshall (Romans), the son of a wealthy Kentucky horse racing family, reluctantly heads back to graduate school to prevent being cut off financially. He falls for classmate Jane Webb (Allen), who's not interested in a wannabe playboy, and is encouraged to find his potential by his writing teacher, Professor Driskoll (Langella). Shot on location at Churchill Downs. **101m/C DVD.** Laura Allen, Frank Langella, Bruce Marshall Romans, Kevin Butler, David S. Jung; ***D:*** J. Miller Tobin; ***W:*** Bruce Marshall Romans; ***C:*** Michael Caporale; ***M:*** Veigar Margeirsson. **VIDEO**

Howard the Duck **1986 (PG)** Big-budget Lucasfilm adaptation of the short-lived Marvel comic book about an alien, resembling a cigar-chomping duck, who gets sucked into a vortex, lands on Earth and saves it from the Dark Overlords. While he's at it, he befriends a nice young lady in a punk rock band and starts to fall in love. A notorious boxoffice bomb and one of the '80s' worst major films, although it seems to work well with children, given the simple storyline and good special effects. **111m/C VHS.** Lea Thompson, Jeffrey Jones, Tim Robbins, Elizabeth Sagal, Thomas Dolby, Paul Guilfoyle, Dominique Davalos, Holly Robinson, Tommy Swerdlow, Richard Edson, Miguel (Michael) Sandoval, David Paymer; ***D:*** Willard Huyck; ***W:*** Willard Huyck, Gloria Katz; ***C:*** Richard H. Kline; ***M:*** John Barry, Sylvester Levay; ***V:*** Chip Zien, Richard Kiley. Golden Raspberries '86: Worst Picture, Worst Screenplay.

Howard's End **1992 (PG)** E.M. Forster's 1910 novel about property, privilege, class differences, and Edwardian society is brought to enchanting life by the Merchant Ivory team. A tragic series of events occurs after two impulsive middle-class sisters, Margaret (Thompson) and Helen (Bonham Carter), become involved with the working class Basts (West, Duffett), and the wealthy Wilcox family (Hopkins, Redgrave). Tragedy aside, this is a visually beautiful effort with subtle performances where a glance or a gesture says as much as any dialog. The winner of numerous awards and wide critical acclaim. Thompson is especially notable as the compassionate Margaret, while Hopkins plays the repressed English gentleman brilliantly. **143m/C VHS, DVD.** *GB* Anthony Hopkins, Emma Thompson, Helena Bonham Carter, Vanessa Redgrave, James Wilby, Samuel West, Jemma Redgrave, Nicola Duffett, Prunella Scales, Joseph Bennett; ***Cameos:*** Simon Callow; ***D:*** James Ivory; ***W:*** Ruth Prawer Jhabvala; ***C:*** Tony Pierce-Roberts; ***M:*** Richard Robbins. Oscars '92: Actress (Thompson), Adapt. Screenplay, Art Dir./Set Dec.; British Acad. '92: Actress (Thompson); Golden Globes '93: Actress—Drama (Thompson); L.A. Film Critics '92: Actress (Thompson); Natl. Bd. of Review '92: Actress (Thompson), Director (Ivory), Film; N.Y. Film Critics '92: Actress (Thompson); Natl. Soc. Film Critics '92: Actress (Thompson).

The Howards of Virginia 1/2 *Tree of Liberty* **1940** A lavish Hollywood historical epic, detailing the adventures of a backwoodsman and the rich Virginia girl he marries as their families become involved in the Revolutionary War. **117m/B VHS, DVD.** Cary Grant, Martha Scott, Cedric Hardwicke, Alan Marshal, Richard Carlson, Paul Kelly, Irving Bacon, Tom Drake, Anne Revere, Ralph Byrd, Alan Ladd; ***D:*** Frank Lloyd.

The Howling **1981 (R)** A pretty TV reporter takes a rest at a clinic and discovers slowly that its denizens are actually werewolves. Crammed with inside jokes, this horror comedy pioneered the use of the body-altering prosthetic makeup (by Rob Bottin) now essential for on-screen man-to-wolf transformations. At last count, followed by six sequels. **91m/C VHS, DVD.** Dee Wallace, Patrick Macnee, Dennis Dugan, Christopher Stone, Belinda Balaski, Kevin McCarthy, John Carradine, Slim Pickens, Elisabeth Brooks, Robert Picardo, Dick Miller, Kenneth Tobey, Meshach Taylor; ***Cameos:*** John Sayles, Roger Corman, Forrest J Ackerman; ***D:*** Joe Dante; ***W:*** John Sayles, Terence H. Winkless; ***C:*** John Hora; ***M:*** Pino Donaggio.

Howling 2: Your Sister Is a Werewolf *Howling 2: Stirba—Werewolf Bitch* **1985 (R)** A policeman (the brother of one of the first film's victims) investigates a Transylvanian werewolf-ridden castle and gets mangled for his trouble. Followed by four more sequels. **91m/C VHS, DVD.** *FR IT* Sybil Danning, Christopher Lee, Annie McEnroe, Marsha A. Hunt, Reb Brown, Ferdinand "Ferdy" Mayne, Judd Omen, Jimmy Nail; ***D:*** Philippe Mora; ***W:*** Gary Brandner, Robert Sarno; ***C:*** Geoffrey Stephenson.

Howling 3: The Marsupials *The Marsupials: Howling 3* **1987 (PG-13)** Australians discover a pouch-laden form of lycanthrope. Third "Howling" (surprise), second from Mora and better than his first. **94m/C VHS, DVD.** *AU* Barry Otto, Imogen Annesley, Dasha Blahova, Max Fairchild, Ralph Cotterill, Leigh Biolos, Frank Thring Jr., Michael Pate; ***D:*** Philippe Mora; ***W:*** Philippe Mora; ***C:*** Louis Irving; ***M:*** Allan Zavod.

Howling 4: The Original Nightmare **1988 (R)** A woman novelist hears the call of the wild while taking a rest cure in the country. This werewolf tale has nothing to do with the other sequels. **94m/C VHS.** Romy Windsor, Michael T. Weiss, Antony (Tony) Hamilton, Susanne Severeid, Lamya Derval, Dennis Folbigge; ***D:*** John Hough.

Howling 5: The Rebirth **1989 (R)** The fifth in the disconnected horror series, in which a varied group of people stranded in a European castle are individually hunted down by evil. **99m/C VHS, DVD.** Philip Davis, Victoria Catlin, Elizabeth She, Ben Cole, William Shockley; ***D:*** Neal Sundstrom; ***C:*** Arledge Armenaki.

Howling 6: The Freaks 1/2 **1990 (R)** Hideous werewolf suffers from multiple sequels, battles with vampire at freak show, and discovers that series won't die. Next up: "Howling 7: The Nightmare that Won't Go Away." **102m/C VHS.** Brendan Hughes, Michelle Matheson, Sean Gregory Sullivan, Antonio Fargas, Carol Lynley, Jered Barclay, Bruce Payne; ***D:*** Hope Perello.

The Howling: New Moon Rising 1/2 *Howling 7* **1995 (R)** Small desert town is plagued by a series of terrifying murders believed to be the work of a werewolf, whose victims then join his vicious pack. **92m/C VHS.** Clive Turner, John Ramsden, Ernest Kester, Elizabeth She, Jacqueline Armitage, Romy Windsor; ***D:*** Clive Turner; ***W:*** Clive Turner.

Howl's Moving Castle 1/2 *Hauru no ugoku shiro* **2004 (PG)** More eye-popping anime from Miyazaki. Young wizard Howl (Bale) and his moveable castle travel around the countryside to avoid his enemy, the Witch of the Waste (Bacall). When Howl rescues Sophie (Mortimer) from thugs, the jealous Witch turns her into an old woman (now voiced by Simmons). Sophie appoints herself the castle housekeeper and encounters various strange characters and many adventures. There's a lot of plot but it's the visuals that will keep attention riveted. Adapted from Diana Wynne Jones' 2000 fantasy novel. There is also a Japanese-language version. **120m/C DVD.** *JP* ***D:*** Hayao Miyazaki; ***W:*** Hayao Miyazaki; ***C:*** Atsushi Okui; ***M:*** Joe Hisaishi; ***V:*** Emily Mortimer, Jean Simmons, Christian Bale, Lauren Bacall, Blythe Danner, Josh Hutcherson, Billy Crystal, Jena Malone, Liliana Mumy. L.A. Film Critics '05: Orig. Score; N.Y. Film Critics '05: Animated Film.

H.P. Lovecraft's Necronomicon: Book of the Dead *Necronomicon* **1993 (R)** Trilogy of stories: Payne encounters a demon who resurrects his late wife and son in "The Drowning"; "The Cold" finds a reporter investigating a series of murders and uncovers crazed doctor Warner, who's discovered the secret to immortality; and a female cop discovers a subterranean alien in "Whispers." Combs serves as narrator, Lovecraft. **96m/C VHS.** Bruce Payne, Belinda Bauer, Bess Meyer, David Warner, Signy Coleman, Richard Lynch, Dennis Christopher, Jeffrey Combs, Maria Ford, Don Calfa; ***D:*** Brian Yuzna, Shusuke (Shu) Kaneko, Christophe Gans; ***W:*** Brian Yuzna, Christophe Gans, Brent Friedman, Kazunori Ito; ***C:*** Russ Brandt; ***M:*** Joseph LoDuca, Daniel Licht.

Huck and the King of Hearts 1/2 **1993 (PG)** When a cardshark and his young friend Huck travel the country searching for Huck's long-lost grandfather, they find adventure everywhere from Hannibal, Missouri to L.A. to Vegas. Loose, contemporary adaptation of Mark Twain's "The Adventures of Huckleberry Finn." **103m/C VHS, DVD.** Chauncey Leopardi, Graham Greene, Dee Wallace, Joe Piscopo, John Astin, Gretchen Becker; ***D:*** Michael Keusch; ***W:*** Christopher Sturgeon; ***M:*** Chris Saranec.

Huckleberry Finn **1974 (G)** The musical version of the Mark Twain story about the adventures a young boy and a runaway slave encounter along the Mississippi River. **114m/C VHS.** Jeff East, Paul Winfield, Harvey Korman, David Wayne, Arthur O'Connell, Gary Merrill, Natalie Trundy, Lucille Benson; ***D:*** J. Lee Thompson.

Huckleberry Finn 1/2 **1975 (G)** Whitewashed version of the Twain classic features post Opie Howard as the incredible Huck and Dano as the sharp witted short storyist. Stars four members of the Howard clan. Made for TV. **74m/C VHS.** Ron Howard, Donny Most, Royal Dano, Antonio Fargas, Jack Elam, Merle Haggard, Rance Howard, Jean Howard, Clint Howard, Shug Fisher, Sarah Selby, Bill Erwin; ***D:*** Robert Totten. **TV**

Huckleberry Finn 1/2 **1981** A version of the classic Mark Twain novel about the adventures a young boy and a runaway slave encounter as they travel down the Mississippi River. **72m/C VHS.** ***V:*** Timothy Gibbs.

The Hucksters **1947** Account of a man (Gable) looking for honesty and integrity in the radio advertising world and finding little to work with. All performances are excellent; but Greenstreet, as the tyrannical head of a soap company, is a stand out. Deborah Kerr's American debut. Based on the novel by Frederic Wakeman. **115m/B VHS.** Clark Gable, Deborah Kerr, Sydney Greenstreet, Adolphe Menjou, Ava Gardner, Keenan Wynn, Edward Arnold; ***D:*** Jack Conway; ***W:*** Edward Chodorov, Luther Davis, George Wells; ***C:*** Harold Rosson; ***M:*** Lennie Hayton.

Hud **1963** Newman is a hard-driving, hard-drinking, woman-chasing young man whose life is a revolt against the principles of stern father Douglas. Neal is outstanding as the family housekeeper. Excellent photography. Based on the Larry McMurtry novel "Horseman, Pass By." **112m/B VHS, DVD.** Paul Newman, Melvyn Douglas, Patricia Neal, Brandon de Wilde, John Ashley; ***D:*** Martin Ritt; ***W:*** Irving Ravetch, Harriet Frank Jr.; ***C:*** James Wong Howe; ***M:*** Elmer Bernstein. Oscars '63: Actress (Neal), B&W Cinematog., Support. Actor (Douglas); British Acad. '63: Actress (Neal); Natl. Bd. of Review '63: Actress (Neal), Support. Actor (Douglas); N.Y. Film Critics '63: Actress (Neal), Screenplay.

Hudson Hawk **1991 (R)** A big-budget star vehicle with little else going for it. Willis plays a master burglar released from prison, only to find himself trapped by the CIA into one last theft. Everyone in the cast tries to be extra funny, resulting in a disjointed situation where no one is. Weakly plotted, poorly paced. **95m/C VHS, DVD.** Bruce Willis, Danny Aiello, Andie MacDowell, James Coburn, Sandra Bernhard, Richard E. Grant, Frank Stallone; ***D:*** Michael Lehmann; ***W:*** Steven E. de Souza, Daniel Waters; ***C:*** Dante Spinotti; ***M:*** Michael Kamen, Robert Kraft. Golden Raspberries '91: Worst Picture, Worst Director (Lehmann), Worst Screenplay.

The Hudsucker Proxy **1993 (PG)** In an effort to scare off would-be investors in a public stock offering dim bulb mail-boy Robbins is installed as the Prez of Hudsucker Industries (in 1958) by Board Director Newman after corporate magnate Hudsucker (Durning) takes a swan dive from the 44th floor. First truly mainstream effort from the maverick Coen brothers is peppered with obscure references to numerous points on the historical map of cinematic style, and trots out an equally old but instantly recognizable story. Will delight Coen fans, but may be too dark for others. Destined to keep art history profs busy for decades. **115m/C VHS, DVD.** Tim Robbins, Paul Newman, Jennifer Jason Leigh, Charles Durning, John Mahoney, Jim True-Frost, Bill Cobbs, Bruce Campbell, Steve Buscemi; ***Cameos:*** Peter Gallagher; ***D:*** Joel Coen; ***W:*** Ethan Coen, Joel Coen, Sam Raimi; ***C:*** Roger Deakins; ***M:*** Carter Burwell.

Hue and Cry **1947** Nobody believes a young boy when he discovers crooks are sending coded messages in a weekly children's magazine. A detective writer finally believes his story and they set off to capture the crooks. **82m/B VHS.** *GB* Alastair Sim, Jack Warner, Frederick Piper, Jack Lambert, Joan Dowling; ***D:*** Charles Crichton.

Hugh Hefner: Once Upon a Time **1992 (R)** Fascinating look at the "Bunny" king and Playboy Enterprises. His celebrated life of isolation and excess at the Playboy mansions is portrayed as is the founding of "Playboy" magazine in 1953 and the Playboy clubs (with their notorious Bunnies). Includes interviews, home movies, and photographs. Admiring yet not without a few sharp edges. **91m/C VHS, DVD.** Hugh Hefner; ***D:*** Robert Heath; ***Nar:*** James Coburn.

Hughes & Harlow: Angels in Hell 1977 (R) The story of the romance that occurred between Howard Hughes and Jean Harlow during the filming of "Hell's Angels" in 1930. **94m/C VHS.** Lindsay Bloom, Victor Holchak, David McLean, Royal Dano, Adam Roarke, Linda Cristal; ***D:*** Larry Buchanan.

Hugo Pool 1/2 1997 (R) Pool cleaner Hugo Dugay (Milano) has to clean the pools of 44 backyard eccentrics. Reluctantly, she must enlist the aid of her gambler mom (Moriarty) and drug addict father (McDowell). Bizarre characters abound, including Downey Jr. overacting as Hungarian film director Franz Mazur, whose accent changes with each line. Most interesting is Dempsey as ALS-afflicted Floyd Galen. The romance between Floyd and Hugo supplies the most sensitive and well-acted sequences. Disappointing, long-anticipated outing from director Downey Sr. (this is his first directorial effort in six years) who shared writing duties with wife Laura, who died of ALS in 1994. **92m/C VHS, DVD.** Alyssa Milano, Patrick Dempsey, Robert Downey Jr., Malcolm McDowell, Cathy Moriarty, Sean Penn, Richard Lewis, Chuck Barris; ***D:*** Robert Downey; ***W:*** Laura Downey; ***C:*** Joe Montgomery; ***M:*** Danilo Perez.

Hugo the Hippo 1976 (G) Animated musical about a forlorn baby hippo who struggles to survive in the human jungle of old Zanzibar. **90m/C VHS.** ***D:*** William Feigenbaum; ***W:*** William Feigenbaum, Thomas Baum; ***M:*** Burt Keyes; ***V:*** Paul Lynde, Burl Ives, Robert Morley, Marie Osmond.

Hula 1/2 1928 Unflappable flapper Bow and her gang frolic on a Pacific island. **64m/B VHS.** Clara Bow, Clive Brook, Patricia Dupont, Arnold Kent, Agaslino Borgato; ***D:*** Victor Fleming.

Hula Girls *Hula garu* 2006 Based on the true story of the rural Japanese coal mining town of Iwaki in 1965. After the Korean War, demand for coal has plummeted, and Iwaki is dying. To rescue their city the natives decide to rebuild as a tourist town with a Hawaiian themed spa resort using the hot springs that were the bane of the mine. But this means they need Hula girls, and Japan is still pretty conservative. One of the female characters is based on famous hula dancer Kaleinani Hayakawa who founded a hula school in Japan, and also did the choreography for the film. **120m/C DVD.** *JP* Etsushi Toyokawa, Yu Aoi, Ittoku Kishibe, Yasuko Matsuyuki, Shizuyo Yamazaki, Eri Tokunaga, Junko Fuji; ***D:*** Sang-il Lee; ***W:*** Sang-il Lee, Daisuke Habara; ***C:*** Hideo Yamamoto; ***M:*** Jake Shimabakuro.

Hulk 1/2 2003 (PG-13) Hulk SMASH! Hulk explore Oedipal relationship. Hulk confused! Scientist Bruce Banner (Bana) gets zapped by gamma rays during an experiment gone wrong, and finds out that it's harder than ever to control his temper. Ang Lee classes up the summer superhero blockbuster genre by going beyond the special effects and action (but he doesn't leave 'em behind, either) to explore Banner's troubled relationships with girlfriend/colleague Betty (Connolly) and wacked-out former scientist dad David (Nolte). The extra depth may be jarring for the target fan-boy audience, but it should play better to people looking for a little thought with their thrills. Solid performances by Bana, Connolly, and Elliot as Betty's aloof, gung-ho military man father help Lee pull off the more angst-ridden moments. **138m/C VHS, DVD, HD DVD.** *US* Eric Bana, Jennifer Connelly, Josh(ua) Lucas, Sam Elliott, Nick Nolte, Paul Kersey, Cara Buono, Mike Erwin, Celia Weston; ***Cameos:*** Lou Ferrigno, Stan Lee; ***D:*** Ang Lee; ***W:*** James Schamus, Michael France, John Turman; ***C:*** Frederick Elmes; ***M:*** Danny Elfman.

Hullabaloo over Georgie & Bonnie's Pictures 1/2 1978 A young maharajah has inherited a priceless collection of Indian miniature paintings he doesn't appreciate and which his greedy sister is anxious for him to sell. They're beseiged by art dealers and collectors who learn about the treasure trove and will do anything to possess it. Among them are the British Ashcroft, who wants the art for the British Museum, and competing American collector Pine. **85m/C VHS, DVD.** *GB* Victor Banerjee, Aparna Sen, Larry Pine, Saeed Jaffrey, Peggy Ashcroft; ***D:*** James Ivory; ***W:*** Ruth Prawer Jhabvala; ***C:*** Walter Lassally. **TV**

Human Beasts 1980 Jewel robbers face a tribe of hungry cannibals. **90m/C VHS.** *SP JP* Paul Naschy, Eiko Nagashima; ***D:*** Paul Naschy; ***W:*** Paul Naschy.

Human Bomb 1/2 1997 (PG-13) After her husband dies, Marcia Weller (Kensit) moves to Germany to be near her mother. Marcia's only been at her new teaching job a few days when she and her class of third-graders are taken hostage by a masked gunman. Captain Gerhardt (Prochnow) is brought in to resolve the crisis, but the terrorist won't negogiate, so Gerhardt must come up with a rescue plan before the bomber decides to carry out his threats. **93m/C VHS.** Patsy Kensit, Jurgen Prochnow, Dorian Healy, Richard Moore; ***D:*** Anthony Page.

The Human Comedy 1/2 1943 A small-town boy experiences love and loss and learns the meaning of true faith during WWII. Straight, unapologetically sentimental version of the William Saroyan novel. **117m/B VHS.** Mickey Rooney, Frank Morgan, James Craig, Fay Bainter, Ray Collins, Donna Reed, Van Johnson, Barry Nelson, Robert Mitchum, Jackie "Butch" Jenkins; ***D:*** Clarence Brown; ***W:*** William Saroyan; ***C:*** Harry Stradling Sr. Oscars '43: Story.

The Human Condition: A Soldier's Prayer 1961 A Japanese pacifist escapes from his commanders and allows himself to be captured by Russian troops, hoping for better treatment as a P.O.W. The final part of the trilogy preceded by "The Human Condition: No Greater Love" and "The Human Condition: Road to Eternity." In Japanese with English subtitles. **190m/B VHS, DVD.** *JP* Tatsuya Nakadai, Michiyo Aratama, Yusuke Kawazu, Tamao Nakamura, Chishu Ryu, Taketoshi Naito, Reiko Hitomi, Kyoko Kishida, Keijiro Morozumi, Koji Kiyomura, Nobuo Kaneko, Fujio Suga; ***D:*** Masaki Kobayashi.

The Human Condition: No Greater Love 1958 First of a three-part series of films. A pacifist is called into military service and subsequently sent to a run a military mining camp. A gripping look at one man's attempt to retain his humanity in the face of war. Followed by "The Human Condition: Road to Eternity" and "The Human Condition: A Soldier's Prayer." In Japanese with English subtitles. **200m/B VHS, DVD.** *JP* Tatsuya Nakadai, Michiyo Aratama, So Yamamura, Eitaro (Sakae, Saka Ozawa) Ozawa, Akira Ishihama, Chikage Awashima, Ineko Arima, Keiji Sada, Shinji Nambara, Seiji Miyaguchi, Toru Abe, Masao Mishima, Eijiro Tono, Yasushi Nagata, Yoshio Kosugi; ***D:*** Masaki Kobayashi; ***W:*** Masaki Kobayashi, Zenzo Matsuyama; ***C:*** Yoshio Miyajima; ***M:*** Chuji Kinoshita.

The Human Condition: Road to Eternity *No Greater Love; Ningen No Joken* 1959 A Japanese pacifist is on punishment duty in Manchuria where he is beaten by sadistic officers who try to destroy his humanity. The second part of the trilogy, preceded by "The Human Condition: No Greater Love" and followed by "The Human Condition: A Soldier's Prayer." In Japanese with English subtitles. **180m/B VHS, DVD.** *JP* Tatsuya Nakadai, Michiyo Aratama, Kokinji Katsura, Jun Tatara, Michio Minami, Keiji Sada, Minoru Chiaki, Ryohei Uchida, Kan Yanagidani, Kenjiro Uemura, Yusuke Kawazu, Susumu Fujita; ***D:*** Masaki Kobayashi; ***W:*** Masaki Kobayashi, Zenzo Matsuyama; ***C:*** Yoshio Miyajima; ***M:*** Chuji Kinoshita.

The Human Contract 2008 (R) Pinkett Smith makes her screenwriting and directing debut. Uptight businessman Julian (Clarke) allows his life to be turned upside down when he meets beautiful Michael (Vega), a woman who believes in abandon rather than control. **107m/C DVD.** Jason Clarke, Paz Vega, Idris Elba, Steven Brand, Joanna Cassidy, Ted Danson, T.J. Thyne, Jada Pinkett Smith; ***D:*** Jada Pinkett Smith; ***W:*** Jada Pinkett Smith; ***C:*** Darren Genet; ***M:*** Anthony Marinelli.

Human Desire 1/2 1954 Femme fatale Grahame and jealous husband Crawford turn out the lights on Crawford's boss (seems there's some confusion about how Miss Gloria managed to convince the guy to let her hubby have his job back). Ford's wise to them but plays see no evil because he's gone crackers for Grahame, who by now has decided she'd like a little help to rid herself of an unwanted husband. Bleak, melodramatic, full of big heat, its Lang through and through. Based on the Emile Zola novel "La Bete Humaine," which inspired Renoir's 1938 telling as well. **90m/B VHS.** Glenn Ford, Gloria Grahame, Broderick Crawford, Edgar Buchanan, Kathleen Case; ***D:*** Fritz Lang; ***C:*** Burnett Guffey.

Human Desires 1997 (R) A lingerie beauty contest provides a bevy of beauties for P.I. Dean Thomas (Noble) to investigate when one of them turns up dead. The death is ruled a suicide but a fellow contestant thinks it was murder and Thomas is around to check things out—very closely. **95m/C VHS, DVD.** Shannon Tweed, Christian Noble, Dawn Ann Billings, Duke Stroud; ***D:*** Ellen Earnshaw; ***W:*** Todd Smith; ***C:*** Carl Oakwood; ***M:*** Ed Korvin.

The Human Duplicators 1/2 1964 Kiel is an alien who has come to Earth to make androids out of important folk, thus allowing the "galaxy beings" to take over. Cheap stuff, but earnest performances make this more fun than it should be. **82m/C VHS.** George Nader, Barbara Nichols, George Macready, Dolores Faith, Hugh Beaumont, Richard Kiel, Richard Arlen; ***D:*** Hugo Grimaldi.

Human Experiments 1979 (R) Psychiatrist in a women's prison conducts a group of experiments in which he destroys the "criminal instinct" in the inmates through brute fear. **82m/C VHS.** Linda Haynes, Jackie Coogan, Aldo Ray; ***D:*** Gregory Goodell.

The Human Factor 1/2 1975 (R) Kennedy stars as a computer expert who tracks down his family's murderers using technology. Bloody and violent. **96m/C VHS, DVD.** *GB IT* George Kennedy, John Mills, Raf Vallone, Rita Tushingham, Barry Sullivan, Arthur Franz; ***D:*** Edward Dmytryk; ***M:*** Ennio Morricone.

The Human Factor 1/2 1979 (R) Unexciting spy caper has a British Secret Service agent (Williamson) betraying his country in order to aid a friend. As a result of his actions an innocent man is killed and Williamson is forced to defect to the Soviet Union. Based on a novel by Graham Greene. **115m/C VHS.** *GB* Nicol Williamson, Richard Attenborough, John Gielgud, Derek Jacobi, Robert Morley, Ann Todd, Richard Vernon, Iman; ***D:*** Otto Preminger; ***W:*** Tom Stoppard.

Human Gorilla *Behind Locked Doors* 1948 A thriller involving a mad scientist, an insane asylum, a reporter, and various other mysterious trappings. **58m/B VHS, DVD.** Richard Carlson, Lucille Bremer, Tor Johnson; ***D:*** Budd Boetticher; ***W:*** Eugene Ling, Malvin Wald; ***C:*** Guy Roe.

Human Hearts 1922 A creaky old silent starring "Phantom of the Opera" leading lady Philbin. A family is torn apart by a con man and his femme fatale. **99m/B VHS.** House Peters Sr., Russell Simpson, Mary Philbin; ***D:*** King Baggot; ***W:*** George C. Hull; ***C:*** Victor Milner, Oscar Day.

Human Lanterns *Ren pi deng long; Human Skin Lanterns; Yun pei dung lung* 1982 Lung Shu-ai (Tony Liu) and Tan Fu (Kuan Tai Chen) are rival martial artists, and they stop at nothing to one-up each other, including their village's annual lantern show. When Lung hires a mysterious craftsman known for making the best lanterns around to compete, a strange furry skull-faced demon begins kidnapping the village's women, all of whom turn up dead and skinned. Needless to say the rivals blame each other while everyone else tries to figure out what's going on. **95m/C DVD.** *HK* Tony Liu, Kuan Tai Chen, Lieh Lo, Linda Chu, Hsiu Chun Lin, Meng Lo, Chien Sun; ***D:*** Chung Sun; ***W:*** Chung Sun, Kuang Ni; ***C:*** An-Shun Tsao; ***M:*** Stephen Shing, Chun-Hou So.

The Human Monster 1/2 *Dark Eyes of London* 1939 Scotland Yard inspector investigates five drownings of the blind patients a phony Dr. Orloff (Lugosi) is exploiting for insurance money. Superior Lugosi effort that's modestly violent and tasteless. Based on the Edgar Wallace novel. **73m/B VHS, DVD.** *GB* Bela Lugosi, Hugh Williams, Greta Gynt; ***D:*** Walter Summers; ***W:*** Walter Summers.

Human Nature 1/2 2002 (R) Offbeat and charming screwball comedy stars Arquette as Lila, a sweet kid with a hairy problem—extreme hirsutism—which forces her to become a reclusive nature writer living in the woods. Her sex drive finally forces her back to civilization, where she finds a sympathetic electrologist (Perez) who sets her up with repressed scientist Nathan (Robbins). As a result of his uber-repressed upbringing, Nathan is on a quest to teach mice good table manners, but when the couple finds a woods-dwelling wildman (Ifans), he has something new to experiment on and tries to teach nature-boy to be civilized, despite his raging libido. Eccentric feature debut of Gallic director Gondry is a quirky study of three characters at odds with their own true nature and trying to fit into a judgmental society. In keeping with the offbeat humor of writer/co-producer Kaufman's "Being John Malkovich." **96m/C VHS, DVD.** *US FR* Tim Robbins, Rhys Ifans, Patricia Arquette, Miranda Otto, Robert Forster, Mary Kay Place, Miguel (Michael) Sandoval, Toby Huss, Peter Dinklage, Rosie Perez; ***D:*** Michel Gondry; ***W:*** Charlie Kaufman; ***C:*** Tim Maurice-Jones; ***M:*** Graeme Revell. Natl. Bd. of Review '02: Screenplay.

The Human Shield 1992 (R) A man risks his life on a mission to save his brother during the Persian Gulf War. **88m/C VHS.** Michael Dudikoff, Tommy Hinkley, Steve Inwood; ***D:*** Ted Post.

The Human Stain 2003 (R) Anthony Hopkins is a professor in the middle of a racial controversy who's passing as a white Jew and Nicole Kidman is the sorrowful, down-on-her-luck janitor with whom he becomes involved in Benton's watered-down adaptation of Philip Roth's 2000 novel. The book is an angry expose of America's struggles with issues of race, age, and sexuality, but the film falls short of conveying that anger. Excellent cast does what it can to compensate. **106m/C VHS, DVD.** *US* Anthony Hopkins, Nicole Kidman, Ed Harris, Gary Sinise, Wentworth Miller, Harry J. Lennix, Anna Deavere Smith, Jacinda Barrett, Phyllis Newman, Kerry Washington, Margo Martindale, Ron Canada, Mili Avital, Mimi Kuzyk; ***D:*** Robert Benton; ***W:*** Nicholas Meyer; ***C:*** Jean-Yves Escoffier; ***M:*** Rachel Portman.

Human Traffic 1/2 1999 (R) It's kinda like "Groove" only these club kids are spending their oblivious weekend in Cardiff, Wales. They have various personal dilemmas that they try to overcome by taking E and dancing the hours away and they're all one step away from insufferable. Writer/director Kerrigan was just 25 when he recorded his debut film so he's got time to grow up. Or maybe the Hound is just getting old. **84m/C VHS, DVD.** *GB* John Simm, Lorraine Pilkington, Shaun Parkes, Nicola Reynolds, Danny Dyer, Dean Davies; ***D:*** Justin Kerrigan; ***W:*** Justin Kerrigan; ***C:*** David Bennett; ***M:*** Matthew Herbert, Rob Mellow.

Human Trafficking 1/2 2005 Kate Morozov (Sorvino) and Bill Meehan (Sutherland) are agents for Immigrations and Customs Enforcement. They're trying to bring down Russian gangster Sergei (Carlyle) who poses as the owner of a modeling agency while actually running a sex-slave ring, bringing in desperate young women from Eastern Europe to work for him. Tawdry and moralizing but still compelling. Montreal substitutes for Washington, D.C. **180m/C DVD.** *US CA* Mira Sorvino, Donald Sutherland, Robert Carlyle, Remy Girard, Isabelle Blais, Vlasta Vrana, Celine Bonnier; ***D:*** Christian Duguay; ***W:*** Carol Doyle, Agatha Dominik; ***C:*** Christian Duguay; ***M:*** Normand Corbeil. **CABLE**

Humanity *L'Humanite* 1999 Overly long and raw look at a few days in the life naive cop Pharon De Winter (Schotte), who suffers from an overabundance of empathy for the pain of others. His latest assignment is certain to plunge Pharon into despair as he investigates the rape and murder of an 11-year-old girl. Pharon is also hopelessly attracted to his young neighbor Domino (Caneele), whose sexual interludes with boyfriend Joseph (Tullier) leave nothing to the viewers' imagination. French with subtitles. **142m/C VHS, DVD.** *FR* Emmanuel Schotte, Severine Caneele, Philippe Tullier, Ghislain Ghesquiere, Ginette Allègre; *D:* Bruno Dumont; *W:* Bruno Dumont; *C:* Yves Cape; *M:* Richard Cuvillier. Cannes '99: Actor (Schotte), Actress (Caneele), Grand Jury Prize.

Humanoid Defender **1985** A scientist and an android rebel against the government that wants to use the android as a warfare prototype. **94m/C VHS.** Terence Knox, Gary Kasper, Aimee (Amy) Eccles, William Lucking; *D:* William Lucking. **TV**

Humanoids from the Deep **WOOF!** *Monster* **1980 (R)** Mutated salmon-like monsters rise from the depths of the ocean and decide to chomp on some bikinied babes. Violent and bloody. **81m/C VHS, DVD.** Doug McClure, Ann Turkel, Vic Morrow, Cindy Weintraub, Anthony Penya, Denise Balik, Hoke Howell, Meegan King, Rob Bottin; *D:* Barbara Peeters; *W:* Frank Arnold, Frederick James, Martin B. Cohen; *C:* Daniel Lacambre; *M:* James Horner.

Humanoids from the Deep *Roger Corman Presents: Humanoids from the Deep* **1996 (R)** Remake of the 1980 Corman culter finds fishery manager Wade Parker (Carradine) and researcher Dr. Drake (Samms) dealing with a coastal town's battle against killers whose DNA has been genetically combined with that of fish. When the fish monsters escape the lab, their mutations are further altered by toxic waste and they go on a rampage. **90m/C VHS, DVD.** Robert Carradine, Emma Samms, Mark Rolston, Clint Howard, Kaz Garas, Warren Burton, Bert Remsen; *D:* Jeff Yonis; *W:* Jeff Yonis; *C:* Christopher Baffa; *M:* Christopher Lennertz. **CABLE**

Humble Pie *American Fork* **2007** Melancholy rules in this quirky comedy. Grocery store clerk Tracy Orbison has a huge heart and a binge-eating body to match. Mom Agnes is bitter and nagging and his sister Peggy is more than a little odd, while dad is long gone. His life gets a shake-up (in a low-key way) when Tracy decides to take acting classes with vain teacher Truman Hope and learns to stand up for himself. **84m/C DVD.** Hubbel Palmer, Kathleen Quinlan, Mary Lynn Rajskub, William Baldwin, Vincent Caso, Nick Lashaway, Bruce McGill; *D:* Chris Bowman; *W:* Hubbel Palmer; *C:* Douglas Chamberlain; *M:* Bobby Johnston.

Humboldt County 1/2 **2008 (R)** A failing grade leads to stodgy medical student Peter getting drunk in a club where he attracts the attention of singer Bogart. He later wakes up in a northern California community of hippies and pot farmers who live off-the-grid. Peter is offered a place to stay by Jack and his wife Rosie, whose son Max runs the family's business. Peter decides to hang out and then gets involved in a family conflict when Max plans a big score that could bring too much interest from the DEA. **97m/C DVD.** Fairuza Balk, Brad Dourif, Frances Conroy, Chris Messina, Jeremy Strong, Madison Davenport, Peter Bogdanovich; *D:* Darren Grodsky, Danny Jacobs; *W:* Darren Grodsky, Danny Jacobs; *C:* Ernest Holtzman; *M:* Izler.

Humongous **WOOF!** **1982 (R)** Brain-dead bevy of teens shipwreck on an island where they encounter a deranged mutant giant who must kill to survive. You'll be rooting for the monster. **93m/C VHS.** *CA* Janet (Johnson) Julian, David Wallace, Janit Baldwin, Joy Boushel, Page Fletcher; *D:* Paul Lynch; *W:* William Gray; *C:* Brian R.R. Hebb.

Humoresque 1/2 **1946** Talented but struggling young musician Paul Boray (Garfield) finds a patron in the married, wealthy, and older Helen Wright (Crawford). His appreciation is not as romantic as she hoped. Stunning performance from Crawford, with excellent supporting cast (Levant supplies the witty comebacks), including a young Robert Blake as a young Paul. Fine music sequences (Isaac Stern dubbed the violin), and lush production values. **123m/B VHS, DVD.** Joan Crawford, John Garfield, Oscar Levant, J. Carrol Naish, Joan Chandler, Tom D'Andrea, Peggy Knudsen, Ruth Nelson, Craig Stevens, Paul Cavanagh, Richard Gaines, John Abbott, Robert (Bobby) Blake; *D:* Jean Negulesco; *W:* Clifford Odets, Zachary Gold; *C:* Ernest Haller; *M:* Franz Waxman.

Humpday 1/2 **2009 (R)** Best pals in college, Ben and Andrew have drifted apart over the last decade. Ben has a job, wife, and home in Seattle while Andrew has lived the life of a deliberately scruffy vagabond artist. When Andrew suddenly turns up, they fall back into their macho male-bonding pretensions. Andrew takes Ben to a bohemian party where they hear about Humpfest, an experimental homemade porn film festival and, during their drunken evening, they vow to enter the contest with the two straight men having sex together on camera. Male bluster makes them determined not to wimp out despite their increasing discomfort, but how is Ben going to explain such shenanigans to his exasperated wife Anna? **94m/C DVD.** *US* Mark Duplass, Joshua Leonard, Alycia Delmore, Trina Willard, Lynn Shelton; *D:* Lynn Shelton; *W:* Lynn Shelton; *C:* Benjamin Kasulke; *M:* Vinny Smith.

The Hunchback 1/2 **1997** Cable version of Victor Hugo's ever-popular "The Hunchback of Notre Dame." In 15th-century Paris, hunchbanked Notre Dame bell-ringer Quasimodo (Patinkin) loves spirited and kind gypsy Esmeralda (Hayek), who's the lustful obsession of evil archdeacon Frollo (Harris). Properly melodramatic, with Harris stealing the film as the cold cleric. **98m/C VHS.** Mandy Patinkin, Richard Harris, Salma Hayek, Jim Dale, Edward Atterton; *D:* Peter Medak; *W:* John Fasano; *C:* Elemer Ragalyi; *M:* Ed Shearmur. **CABLE**

The Hunchback of Notre Dame **1923** The first film version of Victor Hugo's novel about the tortured hunchback bellringer of Notre Dame Cathedral, famous for the contortions of Lon Chaney's self-transformations via improvised makeup. Also available at 68 minutes. **100m/B VHS, DVD.** Lon Chaney Sr., Patsy Ruth Miller, Norman Kerry, Ernest Torrence, Kate Lester, Brandon Hurst; *D:* Wallace Worsley II; *W:* Edward T. Lowe; *C:* Tony Kornman, Robert S. Newhard.

The Hunchback of Notre Dame **1939** Best Hollywood version of the Victor Hugo classic, infused with sweep, sadness, and an attempt at capturing a degree of spirited, Hugoesque detail. Laughton is Quasimodo, a deformed Parisian bellringer, who provides sanctuary to young gypsy Esmeralda (O'Hara) accused by church officials of being a witch. The final scene of the townspeople storming the cathedral remains a Hollywood classic. Great performances all around; the huge facade of the Notre Dame cathedral was constructed on a Hollywood set for this film. Remake of several earlier films, including 1923's Lon Chaney silent, and followed by several remakes for both the big screen (included an animated Disney version) and for TV. **117m/B VHS, DVD.** Charles Laughton, Maureen O'Hara, Edmond O'Brien, Cedric Hardwicke, Thomas Mitchell, George Zucco, Alan Marshal, Walter Hampden, Harry Davenport, Curt Bois, George Tobias, Rod La Rocque; *D:* William Dieterle; *W:* Sonya Levien, Bruno Frank; *C:* Joseph August; *M:* Alfred Newman.

The Hunchback of Notre Dame 1/2 *Notre Dame de Paris* **1957 (PG)** Slow retelling of the Victor Hugo novel, filmed entirely in France in CinemaScope. Quinn's the tragic Quasimodo with bombshell Lollobrigida appropriatley hot-blooded as gypsy Esmerelda. **104m/C VHS, DVD.** *FR* Anthony Quinn, Gina Lollobrigida, Alain Cuny, Jean Danet, Robert Hirsch, Jean Tissier; *D:* Jean Delannoy; *W:* Jacques Prevert, Jean Aurenche; *C:* Michel Kelber; *M:* Georges Auric.

The Hunchback of Notre Dame *Hunchback* **1982 (PG)** It's not often that a classic novel is remade into a classic movie that's remade into a made-for-TV reprise, and survives its multiple renderings. But it's not often a cast so rich in stage trained actors is assembled on the small screen. Hopkins gives a textured, pre-Hannibal Lecter interpretation of Quasimodo, the Hunchback in Hugo's eponymous novel. Impressive model of the cathedral by production designer John Stoll. **102m/C VHS.** Anthony Hopkins, Derek Jacobi, Lesley-Anne Down, John Gielgud, Tim Pigott-Smith, Rosalie Crutchley, Robert Powell; *D:* Michael Tuchner.

The Hunchback of Notre Dame **1996 (G)** Animated/musical version of Victor Hugo's story about deformed bellringer Quasimodo (Hulce) and his love for the beautiful gypsy Esmerelda (Moore). The original isn't exactly fun fare but you expect Disney to find a way to leave everybody humming (and happy). The sweeping music was provided by "Pocahontas" tunesmiths Menken and Schwartz. Comic relief is supplied by three gargoyles, companions to Quasimodo, who are voiced wonderfully by Alexander, Kimbrough and Wickes. Wickes, 85, died six weeks after voicing her role. Looks like another boatload of boxoffice, merchandising, and video sale cash is making its way into old Walt's vaults. **91m/C VHS, DVD.** *D:* Kirk Wise, Gary Trousdale; *W:* Irene Mecchi, Tab Murphy, Jonathan Roberts, Bob Tzudiker, Noni White; *M:* Stephen Schwartz, Alan Menken; *V:* Tom Hulce, Demi Moore, Kevin Kline, Tony Jay, Charles Kimbrough, Jason Alexander, Mary Wickes, David Ogden Stiers.

Hundra **1985** A warrior queen vows revenge when her all-female tribe is slain by men. Nothing can stop her fierce vendetta—except love. **96m/C VHS, DVD.** *IT* Laurene Landon, John Gaffari, Ramiro Oliveros, Marissa Casel; *D:* Matt Cimber; *M:* Ennio Morricone.

A Hungarian Fairy Tale *Hol Volt, Hol Nem Volt* **1987** Political satire meets fantasy in a magical tale of a fatherless young boy searching for a surrogate dad. Unusual characters as well as an homage to Mozart's "The Magic Flute." In Hungarian with English subtitles. **97m/B VHS.** *HU* Arpad Vermes, Maria Varga, Frantisek Husak, Eszter Csakanyi, Szilvia Toth, Judith Pogany, Geza Balkay; *D:* Gyula Gazdag.

Hungarian Rhapsody **1978** In 1911, a Hungarian nobleman joins the ranks of the rebelling peasants in order to oppose his brother, who represents aristocratic repression. One of Jancso's clearest political films, and one that continues the filmmaker's experiments with long, uncut sequences and dynamic mise-en-scene. In Hungarian with English subtitles. **101m/C VHS.** *HU* Gyorgy Cserhalmi, Lajos Balaszovits, Gabor Koncz, Bertalan Solti; *D:* Miklos Jancso.

Hunger *Sult* **1966** In the late 1800s, a starving Norwegian writer, unable to sell his work, rejects charity out of pride, and retains his faith in his talent. Based on a novel "Sult" by Knut Hamsun. In Danish with English subtitles. **115m/B VHS, DVD.** *DK* Per Oscarsson, Gunnel Lindblom; *D:* Henning Carlsen; *W:* Henning Carlsen. Cannes '66: Actor (Oscarsson); Natl. Soc. Film Critics '68: Actor (Oscarsson).

The Hunger **1983 (R)** A beautiful 2000-year-old vampire needs new blood when she realizes that her current lover, Bowie, is aging fast. Visually sumptuous but sleepwalking modern vampire tale, complete with soft-focus lesbian love scenes between Deneuve and Sarandon. **100m/C VHS, DVD.** Catherine Deneuve, David Bowie, Susan Sarandon, Cliff DeYoung, Ann Magnuson, Dan Hedaya, Willem Dafoe, Beth Ehlers, Suzanne Bertish, Rufus Collins, James Aubrey; *D:* Tony Scott; *W:* Michael Thomas, Ivan Davis; *C:* Stephen Goldblatt, Tom Mangravite; *M:* Denny Jaeger, Michel Rubini.

Hunk **1987 (PG)** A computer nerd sells his soul to the devil for a muscular, beach-blonde physique. Answers the question, "Was it worth it?" **102m/C VHS, DVD.** John Allen Nelson, Steve Levitt, Deborah Shelton, Rebecca Bush, James Coco, Avery Schreiber; *D:* Lawrence Bassoff; *W:* Lawrence Bassoff; *C:* Bryan England.

The Hunley 1/2 **1999** Based on the true story of the Confederate submarine that was used to defend Charleston harbor against Union forces in 1864. The experimental craft has already claimed the lives of two crews but General Beauregard (Sutherland) is desperate to break the blockade of the city and gives command to Lt. George E. Dixon (Assante), an engineer. As usual, Dixon's crew is a ragged bunch of misfits but Dixon perseveres. **120m/C VHS.** Armand Assante, Donald Sutherland, Alex Jennings, Sebastien Roche, Michael Dolan, Chris Bauer, Michael Stuhlbarg, Jack Baun, Kevin Robertson; *D:* John Gray; *W:* John Gray; *C:* John Thomas; *M:* Randy Edelman. **CABLE**

The Hunt *La Caza* **1965** A teenage boy accompanies three Spanish Civil War veterans on what is supposed to be a friendly rabbit hunt. Things turn violent, however, when old rivalries and tensions begin to surface. In Spanish with English subtitles. **87m/B VHS, DVD.** *SP* Alfredo Mayo, Ismael Merlo, Jose Maria Prada, Emilio Gutierrez-Caba, Fernando Sanchez Polack; *D:* Carlos Saura.

The Hunt for Eagle One: Crash Point **2006 (R)** Routine military action pic. The Strike Force team returns when terrorists steal an anti-hijack device. Lt. Matt Daniels (Dacascos) and his crew must get the device back and also prevent the bad guys from crashing a jetliner into a military base. **86m/C DVD.** Mark Dacascos, Theresa Randle, Gary Kasper, Rutger Hauer, Zach McGowan, Joe Suba, Jeff Fahey; *D:* Henry Crum; *W:* Michael Henry Carter; *C:* Andrea V. Rossotto; *M:* Mel Lewis. **VIDEO**

The Hunt for Red October **1990 (PG)** Based on Tom Clancy's blockbuster novel, a high-tech Cold War yarn about a Soviet nuclear sub (commanded by Connery) turning rogue and heading straight for U.S. waters, as both the U.S. and the U.S.S.R. try to stop it. Complicated, ill-plotted potboiler that succeeds breathlessly due to the cast and McTiernan's tommy-gun direction. Introduces the character of CIA analyst Jack Ryan (Baldwin) who returns in "Patriot Games," though in the guise of Harrison Ford. **137m/C VHS, DVD.** Sean Connery, Alec Baldwin, Richard Jordan, Scott Glenn, Joss Ackland, Sam Neill, James Earl Jones, Peter Firth, Tim Curry, Courtney B. Vance, Jeffrey Jones, Fred Dalton Thompson; *D:* John McTiernan; *W:* Larry Ferguson, Donald Stewart; *C:* Jan De Bont; *M:* Basil Poledouris. Oscars '90: Sound FX Editing.

The Hunt for the Night Stalker *Manhunt: The Search for the Night Stalker* **1991 (PG-13)** Another one of those True-Detective quickies so beloved by network TV, following two hardworking L.A. cops who tracked down satanic serial killer Richard Ramirez in the mid-1980s. It originally aired (under the title "Manhunt: The Search for the Night Stalker") on the date of the killer's death-sentence verdict; the videotape lacks that particular timely sparkle. **95m/C VHS.** Richard Jordan, A. Martinez, Lisa Eilbacher, Julie Carmen, Alan Feinstein; *D:* Bruce Seth Green. **TV**

Hunt the Man Down 1/2 **1950** An innocent man is charged with murder, and a public defender must find the real killer before time runs out. **68m/B VHS, DVD.** Gig Young, Lynne Roberts, Gerald Mohr; *D:* George Archainbaud.

Hunted **1988 (PG)** WWII prisoner attempts to escape from demented officer who seems to enjoy bugging him. Hunted by the MPs, he relies on unorthodox guide to sustain feature length footage. **75m/C VHS.** Andrew Buckland, Richard Carlson, Ron Smerczak, Mercia Van Wyk; *D:* David Lister.

The Hunted 1/2 **1994 (R)** American businessman in Japan meets, beds, and witnesses the assassination of a mysterious woman and is forced on the run by the modern-day ninja clan that committed the crime. Only a notch above the low-budget, badly dubbed martial arts flicks of the '70s, this shameless bloodfest features unintentionally campy performances by Lambert and Lone and lots of silly dialogue. Beware, the cliches pile up as quickly as the bodies. **110m/C VHS, DVD.** Christopher Lambert, John Lone, Joan Chen, Yoshio Harada, Yoko Shimada, Mari Natsuki, Tak Kubota; *D:* J.F. Lawton; *W:* J.F. Lawton; *C:* Jack Conroy; *M:* Motofumi Yamaguchi.

The Hunted **1998 (R)** Insurance investigator Samantha Clark (Amick) needs to recover $12 million from a crash site in the Pacific Northwest. She meets reclusive Doc (Hamlin), who offers to help her out and then discovers she's become the prey in a deadly hunt. **96m/C VHS.** Harry Hamlin, Madchen Amick, Hannes Jaenicke; *D:* Stuart Cooper; *W:* Bennett Cohen, David Ives; *C:* Curtis Petersen. **VIDEO**

The Hunted **2003 (R)** "First Blood" meets "The Fugitive" in Friedkin's newest chase thriller. Ex-Special Forces member Hallam (Del Toro) comes back from Kosovo severely messed up and heads to the Oregon woods, fileting hunters who use high-powered scopes to stalk their prey. Apparently he's joined PETA's paramilitary wing. Jones is Bonham, the man who trained him in the arts of stalking, killing, and surviving, and must now stop him. He's teamed with female FBI agent Durrell (Nielsen), who doesn't realize she's brought a gun to knife fight. She (as well as plot) is basically window dressing, as Friedkin is clearly more concerned with the grunt-inducing mano-a-mano action scenes and car chases. It's a good thing they're well done, because the meditation of the good and evil that men do doesn't cut it. **94m/C VHS, DVD.** *US* Tommy Lee Jones; Benicio Del Toro, Connie Nielsen, Leslie Stefanson, John Finn, Jose Zuniga, Ron Canada, Mark Pellegrino, Lonny (Lonnie) Chapman, Rex Linn, Eddie Velez; ***D:*** William Friedkin; ***W:*** David Griffiths, Peter Griffiths, Art Monterastelli; ***C:*** Caleb Deschanel; ***M:*** Brian Tyler.

The Hunted Lady 🦴 1/2 **1977** In this TV pilot, Mills is an undercover policewoman who is framed by the mob. Tired and predictable. **100m/C VHS.** Donna Mills, Robert Reed, Lawrence Casey, Andrew Duggan, Will Sampson, Alan Feinstein; ***D:*** Richard Lang. **TV**

Hunter 🦴 1/2 **1973** Unsuccessful TV pilot in which a government agent uncovers an enemy brainwashing scam. **90m/C VHS.** John Vernon, Steve Ihnat, Fritz Weaver, Edward Binns, Sabrina Scharf, Barbara Rhoades; ***D:*** Leonard Horn. **TV**

Hunter 🦴 **1976** An attorney is falsely accused of a crime and imprisoned. Released after eight years, he sets out to even the score with the mysterious millionaire who set him up. **120m/C VHS.** James Franciscus, Linda Evans, Broderick Crawford, Ned Beatty; ***D:*** Tom Gries. **TV**

The Hunter 🦴🦴 1/2 **1980 (PG)** Action drama based on the real life adventures of Ralph (Papa) Thorson, a modern day bounty hunter who makes his living by finding fugitives who have jumped bail. McQueen's last. **97m/C VHS, DVD.** Steve McQueen, Eli Wallach, Kathryn Harrold, LeVar Burton; ***D:*** Buzz Kulik; ***W:*** Peter Hyams; ***C:*** Fred W. Koenekamp; ***M:*** Charles Bernstein.

Hunter in the Dark 🦴🦴 **1980** Set in 18th-century Japan, where power, betrayal, and corruption are the dark side of the samurai world. Tanuma is a powerful shogunate minister who becomes involved with Gomyo, the leader of a secret underworld organization of thieves and murderers with a violent honor code. In Japanese with English subtitles. **138m/C VHS.** *JP* Tatsuya Nakadai, Tetsuro Tamba, Sonny Chiba; ***D:*** Hideo Gosha.

The Hunters 🦴🦴 1/2 **1958** A motley crew of pilots learn about each other and themselves in this melodrama set during Korean war. Incredible aerial photography sets this apart from other films of the genre. **108m/C VHS, DVD.** Robert Mitchum, Robert Wagner, Richard Egan, May Britt, Lee Philips, John Gabriel, Stacy Harris, John Doucette, Jay Jostyn, Leon Lontoc, Ralph Manza, Alena Murray, Robert Reed, Victor Sen Yung, Candace Lee; ***D:*** Dick Powell; ***W:*** Wendell Mayes; ***C:*** Charles G. Clarke; ***M:*** Paul Sawtell. Natl. Film Reg. '03.

Hunter's Blood 🦴 1/2 **1987 (R)** Five urbanites plunge into the Southern wilderness to hunt deer, and are stalked by maniacal hillbillies. **102m/C VHS.** Sam Bottoms, Kim Delaney, Clu Gulager, Mayf Nutter, Eugene Robert Glazer; ***D:*** Robert C. Hughes; ***W:*** Emmett Alston.

Hunter's Moon 🦴🦴 1/2 **1997 (R)** Reynolds plays a very bad guy (very well) as a Depression era, Kentucky backwoods moonshiner who has no intention of letting his lovely daughter, Flo (Du Mond), fall for a city boy (Carradine) who's trying to make a new life for himself. **104m/C VHS, DVD.** Burt Reynolds, Keith Carradine, Hayley Du Mond, Ann Wedgeworth, Pat Hingle, Brion James, Charles Napier; ***D:*** Richard Weinman; ***W:*** Richard Weinman, L. Ford Neale, John Huff, William Kemper; ***C:*** Suki Medencevic.

Hunters of the Golden Cobra 🦴 **1982 (R)** Two American soldiers plot to recover the priceless golden cobra from the Japanese general who stole the prized relic during the last days of WWII. **95m/C VHS.** David Warbeck, Almanta Suska, Alan Collins, John Steiner; ***D:*** Anthony M. Dawson.

The Hunting 🦴🦴 **1992 (R)** A married woman falls for a ruthless businessman and is drawn into a web of blackmail and murder in this low-budget erotic thriller. **97m/C VHS.** John Savage, Kerry Armstrong, Guy Pearce, Rebecca Rigg; ***D:*** Frank Howson; ***W:*** Frank Howson.

The Hunting of the President 🦴🦴 **2004** Documentary about the extreme Right's attempts to smear and destroy the presidency of Bill Clinton. Covers events from Whitewater-gate to the impeachment proceedings. Partisan slam against Starr and company co-written and directed by Thomason, a close friend of the Clintons. In the year of partisan political docs, acceptance will depend on party affiliation and ideology. Techniques used are overly arch and comic at times. **88m/C VHS, DVD.** ***D:*** Nickolas Perry, Harry Z. Thomason; ***W:*** Nickolas Perry, Harry Z. Thomason; ***C:*** Jim Roberson; ***M:*** Bruce Miller.

The Hunting Party 🦴 1/2 **2007 (R)** What could be funnier than a couple of journalists tromping through postwar Bosnia hunting a war criminal? Simon Hunt (Gere) is a former big-time television reporter, fallen from grace after an on-camera meltdown. Now a freelancer covering tragedies around the globe, he and his journalist buddies improbably find themselves mistaken as a hit squad on the lookout for a brutal war criminal, Bosnian Serb leader Radovan Karadzic (Kerekes). Based on Scott Anderson's 2000 article in "Esquire" magazine about five journalists who found themselves in just that situation, although sans the goofy and madcap tone. Doesn't work as a war comedy, as the story just doesn't translate, particularly with oddly-cast Gere. **104m/C DVD.** *US* Richard Gere, Terrence Howard, Jesse Eisenberg, Diane Kruger, James Brolin, Dylan Baker, Ljubomir Kerekes; ***D:*** Richard Shepard; ***W:*** Richard Shepard; ***C:*** David Tattersall; ***M:*** Rolfe Kent.

Hurlyburly 🦴🦴 **1998 (R)** Casting agents Eddie (Penn) and Mickey (Spacey) share a Hollywood apartment with out-of-work actor Phil (Palminteri). Eddie uses cocaine almost constantly, Phil has just been dumped by his wife, and Mickey (Spacey), although more low key, is himself ready to explode. They're all desperate to be huge "Hollywood" successes. Plot pretty much consists of the men venting their spleens and treating women like crap, particularly Bonnie (Ryan), a slutty exotic dancer traded between the boys. Snappy dialogue-happy script might have worked on the stage, but here, with the camera in close, the mean spirit becomes tiring very quickly. Paquin shows confidence in her first adult role, as a drifter girl-toy. **122m/C VHS, DVD.** Sean Penn, Kevin Spacey, Chazz Palminteri, Meg Ryan, Robin Wright Penn, Anna Paquin, Garry Shandling; ***D:*** Tony Drazan; ***W:*** David Rabe; ***C:*** Gu Changwei; ***M:*** David Baerwald.

The Hurricane 🦴🦴🦴 **1937** A couple on the run from the law are aided by a hurricane and are able to build a new life for themselves on an idyllic island. Filmed two years before the Academy's "special effects" award came into being, but displaying some of the best effects of the decade. Boringly remade in 1979. **102m/B VHS, DVD.** Jon Hall, Dorothy Lamour, Mary Astor, Sir C. Aubrey Smith, Raymond Massey, Thomas Mitchell, John Carradine; ***D:*** John Ford; ***W:*** Oliver H.P. Garrett, Dudley Nichols; ***C:*** Bert Glennon, Paul Eagler, Archie Stout; ***M:*** Alfred Newman. Oscars '37: Sound.

Hurricane 🦴 **1974** TV's answer to the disaster movie craze of the early 1970s. Realistic hurricane footage and an adequate cast cannot save this catastrophe. **78m/C VHS, DVD.** Larry Hagman, Martin Milner, Jessica Walter, Barry Sullivan, Will Geer, Frank Sutton; ***D:*** Jerry Jameson. **TV**

Hurricane WOOF! *Forbidden Paradise* **1979 (PG)** And the wind cried, "turkey." Robards is the governor of a tropical island beset with environmental and personal concerns. Virginal daughter Farrow falls for hunky native, standard colonial power/indigenous people complications ensue, vital explanatory footage is cut, and overacting reaches epidemic heights. Then too late the big wind blows in, leveling the place. Expensive (most of the $22 million must have gone to catering) and essentially misdirected remake of the 1937 semi-classic. **120m/C VHS, DVD.** Mia Farrow, Jason Robards Jr., Trevor Howard, Max von Sydow, Timothy Bottoms, James Keach; ***D:*** Jan Troell; ***C:*** Sven Nykvist; ***M:*** Nino Rota.

The Hurricane 🦴🦴🦴 *Lazarus and the Hurricane* **1999 (R)** Moving, albeit truncated account of the true story of middleweight boxing champ Rubin "Hurricane" Carter (Washington—in peak physical and professional form), who was falsely accused and convicted of murder and who spent 20 years in prison. Anchored by a transcendent performance by Washington, pic came under fire for its liberal rearrangement of the facts behind the case. If you want a full lowdown on the case, read one of several books written about this unique court battle by Carter himself ("The Sixteenth Round") or "Lazurus and the Hurricane," which served as the basis for the film; but if you want to see acting that can lift one to a higher spirtual plane, give "The Hurricane" a look. Carter was immortalized in Bob Dylan's 1976 protest song, "Hurricane." **125m/B VHS, DVD, HD DVD.** Denzel Washington, Vicellous Shannon, Deborah Kara Unger, Liev Schreiber, John Hannah, David Paymer, Dan Hedaya, Debbi (Deborah) Morgan, Clancy Brown, Harris Yulin, Vincent Pastore, Rod Steiger; ***D:*** Norman Jewison; ***W:*** Armyan Bernstein, Dan Gordon; ***C:*** Roger Deakins; ***M:*** Christopher Young. Golden Globes '00: Actor—Drama (Washington).

Hurricane Express 🦴🦴 **1932** Twelve episodes of the vintage serial, in which the Duke pits his courage against an unknown, powerful individual out to sabotage a railroad. **223m/B VHS, DVD.** John Wayne, Joseph Girard, Conway Tearle, Shirley Grey; ***D:*** J(ohn) P(aterson) McGowan, Armand Schaefer.

Hurricane Season **2008** A year after Hurricane Katrina, Louisiana high school basketball coach Al Collins assembles a team of players who previously attended five different schools to work towards the state championship. **m/C DVD.** *US* Forest Whitaker, Taraji P. Henson, Isaiah Washington IV, Bow Wow, Khleo Thomas, Michael Gaston, Irma P. Hall, China McClain, Lil Wayne; ***D:*** Tim Story; ***W:*** Robert Eisele; ***C:*** Larry Blanford.

Hurricane Smith 🦴🦴 **1992 (R)** Weathers stars as a roughneck Texan who travels to Australia's Gold Coast in search of his missing sister. While in the land of Oz, he gets entangled in a Mafia-style drug and prostitution ring around the "Surfer's Paradise" section of the Gold Coast. Packed with mind-blowing stunts and a good performance from Weathers, this fast-paced action thriller won't disappoint fans of this genre. **86m/C VHS.** Carl Weathers, Jurgen Prochnow, Tony Bonner, Cassandra Delaney; ***D:*** Colin Budds.

Hurricane Streets 🦴🦴 1/2 *Hurricane* **1996** Freeman's directorial debut centers on a group of young teenagers getting into trouble in lower Manhattan. 15-year-old Marcus (Sexton) is on the edge—his dad is dead, his mother's in jail, he's being ineffectually looked after by his working grandma, and the authorities are already eyeing this petty thief. He hangs with three buddies, one of whom, Chip (Frank), wants to start them stealing cars. Meanwhile, Marcus falls for 14-year-old Melena (Vega), whose father is both possessive and abusive, and tries to plan an escape for them both. **89m/C VHS.** Terry Alexander, Brendan Sexton III, Isidra Vega, David Roland Frank, L.M. Kit Carson, Jose Zuniga, Lynn Cohen, Edie Falco, Shawn Elliot, Heather Matarazzo; ***D:*** Morgan J. Freeman; ***W:*** Morgan J. Freeman; ***C:*** Enrique Chediak. Sundance '97: Cinematog., Director (Freeman), Aud. Award.

Hurry, Charlie, Hurry 🦴 **1941** Husband gets in trouble when he bows out of a trip with his social-climber wife when he tells her he must travel to Washington to see the Vice President. **65m/B VHS.** Leon Errol, Mildred Coles, Kenneth Howell, Cecil Cunningham, George Watts, Noble Johnson; ***D:*** Charles E. Roberts; ***W:*** Paul Girard Smith; ***C:*** Nicholas Musuraca.

Hurry Up or I'll Be Thirty 🦴🦴 **1973** A Brooklyn bachelor celebrates his 30th birthday by becoming morose, depressed, and enraged. His friends try to help; they fail, but he finds love anyway. For those seeking a better life through celluloid. **87m/C VHS, DVD.** Danny DeVito, John Lefkowitz, Steve Inwood, Linda DeCoff, Ronald Anton, Maureen Byrnes, Francis Gallagher; ***D:*** Joseph Jacoby.

Hurt 🦴 1/2 **2009 (R)** When Helen's husband Robert is killed in a car crash, she and her two teenaged children are forced by financial circumstances to move in with her strange brother-in-law Darryl, who lives in an Arizona junkyard. Artistic son Conrad readily adjusts but popular Lenore is upset. Then young, orphaned Sarah moves in as well, after telling the family that Robert promised to protect her from her own abusive family. However, Sarah isn't as innocent as she seems. **97m/C DVD.** Melora Walters, William Mapother, Sofia Vassilieva, Jackson Rathbone, Johanna Braddy; ***D:*** Barbara Stepansky; ***W:*** Barbara Stepansky, Alison Lea Bingeman; ***C:*** Ralph Kachele; ***M:*** Dana Niu. **VIDEO**

The Hurt Locker 🦴🦴🦴 **2008 (R)** Set in Baghdad in 2004, Bigelow's unconventional Iraq war film offers disorienting anxiety and fear centering on a three-man Army bomb-disposal unit. Staff Sgt. William James (Renner, in an effortlessly breakout performance) arrives to take the place of his deceased predecessor with 38 days left in the unit's rotation. Vulnerable Specialist Owen Eldridge (Geraghty) and by-the-book professional Sgt. J.T. Sanborn (Mackie) aren't sure they'll make it since the new guy is a wild card—an adrenaline cowboy consumed by his work. There's mutual distrust between the American occupiers and Iraqi citizens, but Bigelow isn't interested in the rights or wrongs of the conflict itself as much as the small, sometimes terrifying moments. Military "experts" can squawk all they want about technical accuracy (this is hardly the first war film to take artistic liberties), but the film succeeds in providing 'twisting your guts' tension. Based on screenwriter Boal's embedded reports from his time in Baghdad. **131m/C DVD.** *US* Jeremy Renner, Anthony Mackie, Brian Geraghty, Guy Pearce, Ralph Fiennes, David Morse, Evangeline Lilly, Christian Camargo, Christopher Sayegh, Nabil Koni; ***D:*** Kathryn Bigelow; ***W:*** Mark Boal; ***C:*** Barry Ackroyd; ***M:*** Marco Beltrami, Buck Sanders. Oscars '09: Director (Bigelow), Film, Film Editing, Orig. Screenplay, Sound, Sound FX Editing; British Acad. '09: Cinematog., Director (Bigelow), Film, Orig. Screenplay, Sound; Directors Guild '09: Director (Bigelow); Writers Guild '09: Orig. Screenplay.

Husbands 🦴🦴 1/2 **1970 (PG-13)** When Stuart (Rowlands) dies suddenly of a heart attack, his three equally middleaged buddies—Harry (Gazzara), Archie (Falk), and Gus (Cassavettes)—are reluctantly confronted with their own mortality. These suburban married men decide to cut loose and go on a spree, with Harry even persuading his buddies they should carry their frantic merriment across the pond in a trip to London. Meanders on a bit too long, thanks to Cassavettes usual reliance on improv and reluctance to edit. **140m/C VHS.** Ben Gazzara, Peter Falk, John Cassavetes, Jenny Runacre, David Rowlands, Jenny Lee Wright, Noelle Kao; ***D:*** John Cassavetes; ***W:*** John Cassavetes; ***C:*** Victor Kemper.

Husbands and Lovers 🦴🦴 **1991 (R)** Controversial and confusing film focuses on a couple's untraditional marriage. Stephen (Sands) and Alina (Pacula) have agreed to be totally honest with each other and when Alina decides to take a lover, Stephen agrees on the condition that she report back to him every intimate detail of her affair. In the confusion and excitement of this kinky love triangle, everyone starts losing control as sexual boundaries are pushed to the limit. Also available in an unrated version. **91m/C VHS.** Julian Sands, Joanna Pacula, Tcheky Karyo; ***D:*** Mauro Bolognini; ***W:*** Sergio Bazzini; ***M:*** Ennio Morricone.

Husbands and Wives 🦴🦴🦴 1/2 **1992 (R)** Art imitates life as Allen/Farrow relationship dissolves onscreen (and off) and Woody becomes involved with young student. Mature, penetrating look at modern pair bonding and loneliness offers more painful honesty and sadness than outright laughs, though still retains essential Allen charm. Stylistically burdened by experiment with pseudo-documentary telling of tale and spasmodic hand-held cameras that annoy more than entertain. Excellent, intriguing cast, notably Davis as the overwhelming, overbearing wife/friend. Trailers became unintentionally funny in light of the highly publicized personal problems of Allen and Farrow. **107m/C VHS, DVD.** Woody Allen, Mia Farrow, Judy Davis, Sydney Pollack, Liam Neeson, Juliette Lewis, Lysette Anthony, Blythe Danner; ***D:*** Woody Allen; ***W:*** Woody Allen; ***C:*** Carlo Di Palma. British Acad. '92: Orig. Screenplay; L.A. Film Critics '92: Support. Actress (Davis); Natl. Bd. of Review '92: Support. Actress (Davis); Natl. Soc. Film Critics '92: Support. Actress (Davis).

Husbands, Wives, Money, and Murder 🦴 **1986** A couple is pushed over the edge by a nosey census taker and then must dispose of the consequences. **92m/C VHS.** Garrett Morris, Greg Mullavey, Meredith MacRae, Timothy Bottoms; ***D:*** Bruce Cook Jr.

Hush 🦴 **1/2** *Kilronan; Bloodline* **1998 (PG-13)** Stinky thriller stars Paltrow as a working-class gal who marries wealthy dreamboat Jackson (Schaech) and moves to his family's Kentucky estate, Kilronan. There, smother-in-law Lange camps it up (albeit unknowingly) as she turns psycho on the pregnant bride while coming on to her dim-witted son who doesn't have a clue. Apparently, neither did filmmaker Darby, whose film was held from release pending two years of pasting Band-Aids on this gaping wound of a movie. Foch's crusty grandmother is the sole highlight of this horror of a film. **96m/C VHS, DVD.** Gwyneth Paltrow, Jessica Lange, Johnathon Schaech, Nina Foch, Debi Mazar, Kaiulani Lee, David Thornton, Hal Holbrook; ***D:*** Jonathan Darby; ***W:*** Jonathan Darby, Jane Rusconi; ***C:*** Andrew Dunn; ***M:*** Christopher Young.

Hush, Hush, Sweet Charlotte 🦴🦴🦴 **1965** A fading southern belle finds out the truth about her married lover's murder when the case is reopened 37 years later by her cousin in an elaborate plot to drive her crazy. Grisly, superbly entertaining Southern Gothic horror tale, with vivid performances from the aging leads. **134m/B VHS, DVD.** Bette Davis, Olivia de Havilland, Joseph Cotten, Agnes Moorehead, Mary Astor, Bruce Dern, Cecil Kellaway, Victor Buono; ***D:*** Robert Aldrich; ***W:*** Lukas Heller, Henry Farrell; ***C:*** Joseph Biroc. Golden Globes '65: Support. Actress (Moorehead).

Hush Little Baby 🦴 **1/2 1993** Susan Nolan (Meldrum), with a husband and family of her own, is shocked when the biological mother she had thought was dead tries to contact her. Turns out that Edie Landers (Ladd) is another of those female psychos who were so popular in suspense films of the late '80s and '90s. This made-for-TV variation connects the dots competently enough. **91m/C DVD.** Diane Ladd, Wendel Meldrum, Geraint Wyn Davies, Ilya Woloshyn, Ingrid Veninger; ***D:*** Jorge Montesi. **TV**

Hussy 🦴 **1980 (R)** Hooker and her boyfriend find themselves trapped in a web of gangsters and drugs. **95m/C VHS, DVD.** *GB* Helen Mirren, John Shea, Jenny Runacre; ***D:*** Matthew Chapman; ***W:*** Matthew Chapman; ***M:*** George Fenton.

The Hustle 🦴🦴 **1975 (R)** Gritty urban adventure with Reynolds as an L.A. detective investigating a young call girl's death. He becomes romantically entangled with high-priced call girl Deneuve. **120m/C VHS, DVD.** Burt Reynolds, Catherine Deneuve; ***D:*** Robert Aldrich; ***C:*** Joseph Biroc.

Hustle 🦴 **1/2 2004** Slight, sometimes laughable, story of Pete Rose's banishment from Major League Baseball as a result of his gambling on games his team was playing. Traces the beginnings and escalation of his gambling problem and the investigation that brought him down. Sizemore's ridiculous portrayal of Rose does nothing to help the situation. **90m/C DVD.** Tom Sizemore, Dash Mihok, Melissa Di Marco, George DiCenzo, Paul Fauteux; ***D:*** Peter Bogdanovich; ***W:*** Christian Darren; ***C:*** James Gardner; ***M:*** Lou Natale. **CABLE**

Hustle & Flow 🦴🦴🦴 **2005 (R)** After reuniting with an old buddy who's a sound engineer, Djay, an aging pimp (Howard), decides to go after a dream he let slide and use his talent as a wordsmith to make rap songs. The plan includes giving the demo to Skinny Black (Ludacris) a big-time rap star who Djay claims to know. The film's heart is in the second act where they create a makeshift recording studio and enlist a hooker to sing backup, daring to move beyond their current situations into one dreams are made of. Easy to see why this won the Audience Award at the 2005 Sundance Film Festival, earning Singleton and Allain a hefty distribution deal. **114m/C DVD, Blu-ray Disc, UMD, HD DVD.** *US* Terrence Howard, Taryn Manning, Taraji P. Henson, Paula Jai Parker, Elise Neal, Isaac Hayes, DJ Qualls, Ludacris, Anthony Anderson; ***D:*** Craig Brewer; ***W:*** Craig Brewer; ***C:*** Amy Vincent; ***M:*** Scott Bomar. Oscars '05: Song ("It's Hard Out Here for a Pimp"); Natl. Bd. of Review '05: Breakthrough Perf. (Howard); Broadcast Film Critics '05: Song ("Hustle and Flow").

The Hustler 🦴🦴🦴🦴 **1961** The original story of Fast Eddie Felsen and his adventures in the seedy world of professional pool. Newman plays the naive, talented and self-destructive Felsen perfectly, Laurie is oustanding as his lover, and Gleason epitomizes the pool great Minnesota Fats. Rivetingly atmospheric, and exquisitely photographed. Parent to the reprise "The Color of Money," made 25 years later. **134m/B VHS, DVD.** Paul Newman, Jackie Gleason, Piper Laurie, George C. Scott, Myron McCormick, Murray Hamilton, Michael Constantine, Jake LaMotta, Vincent Gardenia; ***D:*** Robert Rossen; ***W:*** Robert Rossen; ***C:*** Eugen Shufftan. Oscars '61: Art Dir./Set Dec., B&W, B&W Cinematog.; British Acad. '61: Actor (Newman), Film; Natl. Bd. of Review '61: Support. Actor (Gleason), Natl. Film Reg. '97;; N.Y. Film Critics '61: Director (Rossen).

Hustler Squad 🦴 **1976 (R)** U.S. Army major and Philippine guerrilla leader stage a major operation to help rid the Philippines of Japanese Occupation forces: they have four combat-trained prostitutes infiltrate a brothel patronized by top Japanese officers. Verrrrry clever. **98m/C VHS, DVD.** John Ericson, Karen Ericson, Lynda Sinclaire, Nory Wright; ***D:*** Ted V. Mikels.

Hustler White 🦴🦴 **1996** Outrageous underground actor/filmmaker LaBruce stars as pretentious German writer Jurgen Anger, who comes to Hollywood to research the gay scene for a book. Cruising Santa Monica Boulevard he becomes obsessively intrigued by local hustler Montgomery Ward (Ward), who serves as a tour guide to the city's sexual kinks. Yes, it's racy, but it's also not as hardcore as the subject matter might imply. **80m/C VHS, DVD.** Tony Ward, Bruce La Bruce; ***D:*** Rick Castro, Bruce La Bruce; ***W:*** Rick Castro, Bruce La Bruce; ***C:*** James Carman.

Hustling 🦴🦴🦴 **1975** A reporter writing a series of articles on prostitution in New York City takes an incisive look at their unusual and sometimes brutal world. Notable performance by Remick as the reporter and Clayburgh as a victimized hooker. Made for TV and based on a novel by Gail Sheehy. **96m/C VHS, DVD.** Jill Clayburgh, Lee Remick, Alex Rocco, Monte Markham; ***D:*** Joseph Sargent. **TV**

Hybrid 🦴 **1/2 1997 (R)** Another bleak apocalyptic future flick, which finds a handful of survivors stumbling across a remote desert lab where they decide to take shelter. Big mistake since the lab still houses a living alien hybrid that's bent on reproduction and destruction. **87m/C VHS, DVD.** Brinke Stevens, Tim Abell, John Barrymore III; ***D:*** Fred Olen Ray; ***W:*** Sean O'Bannon; ***C:*** James Lawrence Spencer; ***M:*** Jeff Walton.

Hybrid 🦴 **2007** Low-budget horror hokum. After being blinded in an explosion, Aaron (Monteith) comes under the care of Dr. Andrea Hewitt (Bateman), whose latest medical experiment involves cross-species transplants. Hewitt uses a wolf's eyes to replace Aaron's and suddenly he has exceptional night vision, acute hearing, a taste for raw meat, and a desire to hunt prey. Native American Lydia (Korey) has learned to control her own feral instincts with the help of a shaman (Tootoosis) but Hewitt's colleagues think Aaron should just be destroyed. Won't be easy—don't they know wolves hunt in packs? **90m/C DVD.** Cory Monteith, Justine Bateman, Gordon Tootoosis, Gordon Tanner, Tinsel Korey, Aaron Hughes, Brett Sorensen; ***D:*** Yelena Lanskaya; ***W:*** Arne Olsen; ***C:*** Barry Gravelle; ***M:*** Terry Frewer. **TV**

Hydra 🦴 **1/2 2009** Chomp! A quartet of super-rich men travel to a remote island to hunt human prisoners but the island is already inhabited by the multi-headed mythical dragon/snake monster of the title. And it has its own plans for them. **103m/C DVD.** Polly Shannon, Alex McArthur, George Stults, Roark Critchlow, Texas Battle, Dawn Olivieri, James Wlcek, Michael Shamus Wiles; ***D:*** Andrew Prendergast; ***W:*** Peter Sullivan; ***M:*** Gregory Tripi. **CABLE**

Hyena of London 🦴🦴 **1962** A doctor steals the hyena of London's corpse and injects the rabid protoplasm into his own brain with deadly results. **?m/C VHS.** Tony Kendall, Bernard Price, Alan Collins, Claude Dantes; ***D:*** Gino Mangini; ***W:*** Gino Mangini.

Hyper-Sapien: People from Another Star 🦴 **1/2 1986 (PG)** Two cuddly aliens run away from home, are befriended by a lonely farmboy, and are chased all over the wilds of Wyoming. **93m/C VHS.** Sydney Penny, Keenan Wynn, Gail Strickland, Ricky Paull Goldin, Peter Jason, Talia Shire; ***D:*** Peter Hunt; ***W:*** Richard Adcock, Christopher Blue.

Hyper Space 🦴 **1/2** *Black Forest: Rage in Space* **1989** Six people awaken from cryogenic sleep to discover that their spaceship has become marooned lightyears from earth and only a single passenger shuttle is available to get someone home. Naturally, everyone wants that one chance. **90m/C VHS, DVD.** Richard Norton, Don Stroud, Lynn-Holly Johnson, James Van Patten, Ron O'Neal, Rebecca Cruz; ***D:*** David Huey; ***W:*** Richard Dominguez; ***C:*** Roger Olkowski.

The Hypothesis of the Stolen Painting 🦴🦴 *L'Hypothese du Tableau Vole* **1978** An art collector guides an interviewer around six paintings by Frederic Tonnerre, an academic 19th century painter, in an attempt to solve the mysterious disappearance of a seventh painting. The film presents the paintings as tableaux vivants in which the actors hold poses as they are examined. Based on the novel "Baphomet" by Pierre Klossowski. In French with English subtitles. **87m/B VHS.** ***D:*** Raul Ruiz; ***W:*** Raul Ruiz.

Hysteria 🦴 **1/2 1964 (PG)** When an American becomes involved in an accident and has amnesia, a mysterious benefactor pays all his bills and gives the man a house to live in. But a series of murders could mean he's the murderer—or the next victim. **85m/B VHS.** *GB* Robert Webber, Sue Lloyd, Maurice Denham; ***D:*** Freddie Francis; ***W:*** Jimmy Sangster; ***M:*** Don Banks.

Hysterical 🦴🦴 **1983 (PG)** Odd little attempt at a horror flick parody features the Hudson Brothers and involves a haunted lighthouse occupied by the vengeful spirit of a spurned woman. Late-night fun. **86m/C VHS, DVD.** Brett Hudson, Bill Hudson, Mark Hudson, Cindy Pickett, Richard Kiel, Julie Newmar, Bud Cort; ***D:*** Chris Bearde; ***W:*** Trace Johnston, Brett Hudson, Bill Hudson, Mark Hudson; ***C:*** Thomas Del Ruth; ***M:*** Robert Alcivar.

Hysterical Blindness 🦴🦴 **1/2 2002** It's 1987 in Bayonne, New Jersey where Debby (Thurman) and her best friend Beth (Lewis) like to hang out at the local bar and pick up guys. Despite her looks, Debby, who lives with her waitress mom Virginia (Rowlands), comes off as so needy that she can't find anything more stable than a one-night stand. Meanwhile, Beth neglects her young daughter for non-committal barender Bobby (de Sando) and Viriginia gets a second chance with nice-guy customer Nick (Gazzara). Overly familiar and somewhat shrill; the best reason to watch are veterans Rowlands and Gazzara. Cahill adapted from her play. **99m/C VHS, DVD.** Uma Thurman, Juliette Lewis, Gena Rowlands, Ben Gazzara, Justin Chambers, Anthony De Sando, Jolie Peters; ***D:*** Mira Nair; ***W:*** Laura Cahill; ***C:*** Declan Quinn; ***M:*** Lesley Barber. **CABLE**

I, a Woman 🦴🦴 *Jag, en Kvinna* **1966** Siv (Persson) is a seductive young nurse who likes to have sex with every man she meets—and then leave them after they fall in love with her. Based on the novel by the pseudononomous Siv Holm. Dubbed. **90m/B VHS, DVD.** *SW* Essy Persson, Jorgen Reenberg, Preben Mahrt; ***D:*** Mac Ahlberg; ***W:*** Peer Guldbrandsen; ***C:*** Mac Ahlberg.

I Accidentally Domed Your Son 🦴🦴 **2004 (R)** Uneven urban comedy has four friends trying to score some pot from the local kingpin's son. When the kid ends up dead, the over-protective boss sends his killers after the guys, so they head underground to try to change their appearance and get away. Fans of the genre and star Kurupt may be the only ones pleased by this one. **89m/C VHS, DVD.** Ryan Combs, Tony Cox, Kurupt, Pedro (Pete) Pano; ***D:*** Ryan Combs; ***W:*** Ryan Combs. **VIDEO**

I Accuse My Parents 🦴 **1/2 1945** Juvenile delinquent tries to blame a murder and his involvement in a gang of thieves on his mom and dad's failure to raise him properly. **70m/B VHS, DVD.** Mary Beth Hughes, Robert Lowell, John Miljan, Edward Earle, Patricia Knox, George Meeker, George Lloyd; ***D:*** Sam Newfield; ***W:*** Marjorie Dudley; ***C:*** Robert E. Cline; ***M:*** Lee Zahler.

I Am a Camera 🦴🦴🦴 **1955** A young English writer develops a relationship with a reckless young English girl in Berlin during the 1930s. Based on the Berlin stories by Christopher Isherwood, later musicalized as "Cabaret." **99m/B VHS.** *GB* Julie Harris, Shelley Winters, Laurence Harvey, Patrick McGoohan; ***D:*** Henry Cornelius; ***C:*** Guy Green; ***M:*** Malcolm Arnold.

I Am a Fugitive from a Chain Gang 🦴🦴🦴🦴 *I Am a Fugitive From the Chain Gang* **1932** WWI veteran Muni returns home with dreams of traveling across America. After a brief stint as a clerk, he strikes out on his own. Near penniless, Muni meets up with a tramp who takes him to get a hamburger. He becomes an unwilling accomplice when the bum suddenly robs the place. Convicted and sentenced to a Georgia chain gang, he's brutalized and degraded, though he eventually escapes and lives the life of a criminal on the run. Based on the autobiography by Robert E. Burns. Brutal docu-details combine with powerhouse performances to create a classic. Timeless and thought-provoking. **93m/B VHS, DVD.** Paul Muni, Glenda Farrell, Helen Vinson, Preston Foster, Edward Ellis, Allen Jenkins; ***D:*** Mervyn LeRoy; ***W:*** Howard J. Green. Natl. Film Reg. '91.

I Am Cuba 🦴🦴 *Soy Cuba; Ja Cuba* **1964** Agitprop Russian-Cuban co-production illustrates different aspects of the Cuban revolution from the toppling of Batista's decadent Havana to idealistic soldiers and student revolutionaries. Lots of oratory and deliberate artificiality combined with cinematographer Urusevky's stunning high-contrast photography. Spanish and Russian with subtitles. **141m/B VHS, DVD.** *CU RU* Luz Maria Collazo, Jose Gallardo, Sergio Corrieri, Jean Bouise, Raul Garcia, Celia Rodriguez; ***D:*** Mikhail Kalatozov; ***W:*** Yevgeny Yevtushenko, Enrique Pineda Barnet; ***C:*** Sergei Urusevsky; ***M:*** Carlos Farinas.

I Am Curious (Yellow) 🦴🦴 **1/2** *Jag ar nyfiken-gul; Jag ar nyfiken-en film i gult* **1967** A woman sociologist is conducting a sexual survey on Swedish society, which leads her to have numerous sexual encounters in all sorts of places. Very controversial upon its U.S. release because of the nudity and sexual content but tame by today's standards. Followed by "I Am Curious (Blue)" which was filmed at the same time. In Swedish with English subtitles. **95m/B VHS, DVD.** *SW* Lena Nyman, Peter Lindgren, Borje Ahlstedt, Marie Goranzon, Magnus Nilsson; ***D:*** Vilgot Sjoman; ***W:*** Vilgot Sjoman; ***M:*** Bengt Ernryd.

I Am David 🦴🦴 **2004 (PG)** Unlikely adventure story follows the travails of a 12-year-old orphan named David (Tibber), who escapes from a 1952 Stalinist labor camp in Bulgaria and makes his way across Greece, Italy, and Switzerland to safety in Denmark. He gets really lucky—first his nice camp friend Johannes (Caviezel) helps him, then nice Italian Roberto (De Vito), and then nice Swiss grandmother Sophie (Plowright). Based on the novel "North to Freedom" by Anne Holm. **95m/C VHS, DVD.** *US* Ben Tibber, Joan Plowright, James (Jim) Caviezel, Maria Bonnevie, Paco Reconti, Hristo Naumov

Shopov, Alessandro Sperduti, Viola Carinci, Silvia De Santis; *D:* Paul Feig; *M:* Stewart Copeland.

I Am Frigid... Why? 🦴🦴 *Je Suis Frigide...Pourquoi?; She Should Have Stayed in Bed; Comment le Desir Vient aux Filles* **1972** Eighteen-year-old Doris is the gardener's daughter. She is raped by Eric Chambon, the estate owner's son, and is then sent to boarding school to hush up the scandal. But Doris can't forget and befriends an older woman who runs an expensive call girl operation in Paris. Doris joins her other girls and one of her clients turns out to be Eric's father. French with subtitles. **90m/C VHS.** *FR* Joelle Coeur, Sandra Julien, Anne Kerylen, Stephane Machanovitch, Marie-Georges Pascal, Thierry Murzeau, Jean-Luc Terrade, Virginie Vignon; *D:* Max Pecas; *W:* Max Pecas; *C:* Robert Lefebvre; *M:* Derry Hall.

I Am Legend 🦴🦴🦴 **2007 (PG-13)** Third adaptation of Richard Matheson's 1954 classic novel, following "The Last Man on Earth" and "The Omega Man," about Robert Neville (Smith), a scientist who is the last man standing after a massive plague wipes out the entire world population. However, after three years of biological research and wandering the desolate streets of Manhattan with his dog, he discovers he may not be alone. Will Smith holds his own, with some big special effects carrying the rest. Entertaining as it is, apparently logic and coherency were lost in the plague as well. **100m/C DVD, Blu-ray Disc.** *US* Will Smith, Dash Mihok, Salli Richardson, Alice Braga, Charlie Tahan, Willow Smith; *D:* Francis Lawrence; *W:* Mark Protosevich, Akiva Goldsman; *C:* Andrew Lesnie; *M:* James Newton Howard.

I Am Omega 🦴 **2007** Sci Fi Channel horror that's a rip-off of "I Am Legend." L.A. has been overrun with cannibal survivors of a plague and non-infected Renchard (Dacascos) is setting bombs to blow up the city, apparently in an effort to stop the contagion (or maybe he just likes things to go boom). Brianna (Wiggins), another non-infected survivor, shows up claiming to know about a cure and wanting to get to Antioch, a town the non-infected have allegedly made their own. Two soldiers then come along with bad intentions. Low-budget and with plot holes bigger than the explosions Renchard likes. **90m/C DVD.** Mark Dacascos, Jennifer Lee Wiggins, Ryan Llody, Geoff Mead; *D:* Griff Furst; *W:* Geoff Mead; *C:* Alexander Yellen; *M:* David Raiklen. **CABLE**

I Am Sam 🦴 ½ **2001 (PG-13)** Single father Penn has the mental capacity of a seven-year-old which makes authorities question his ability to raise young daughter Fanning. Pfeifer's the hard-edged lawyer who comes to his aid and becomes a better person for it. Overly sentimental and sweet, with not much new to offer except the obvious talent of Fanning. **93m/C VHS, DVD.** Sean Penn, Michelle Pfeiffer, Dakota Fanning, Dianne Wiest, Loretta Devine, Richard Schiff, Laura Dern, Brad Allan Silverman, Stanley DeSantis, Doug Hutchison, Joseph Rosenberg, Mary Steenburgen; *D:* Jessie Nelson; *W:* Jessie Nelson, Kristine Johnson; *C:* Elliot Davis; *M:* John Powell.

I Am the Cheese 🦴🦴 **1983** An institutionalized boy undergoes psychiatric treatment; with the aid of his therapist (Wagner) he relives his traumatic childhood and finds out the truth about the death of his parents. A bit muddled, but with its moments. Adapted from a Robert Cormier teen novel. **95m/C VHS, DVD.** Robert MacNaughton, Hope Lange, Don Murray, Robert Wagner, Sudie Bond, Cynthia Nixon, John Fiedler; *D:* Robert Jiras; *M:* Jonathan Tunick.

I Am the Law 🦴🦴🦴 **1938** Robinson is given the task of stopping gangster activity in the city. Although regularly a law professor, he is made special prosecutor and starts canvassing for people to testify. His witnesses become murder victims as an enemy on the inside attempts to thwart the game plan. Robinson is dismissed from the case but continues to pursue justice in streetclothes. Fine performances but somewhat predictable. **83m/B VHS.** Edward G. Robinson, Otto Kruger, John Beal, Barbara O'Neil, Wendy Barrie, Arthur Loft, Marc Lawrence, Charles Halton; *D:* Alexander Hall; *W:* Jo Swerling.

I Beheld His Glory **1953** Story based on the experience of Cornelius, the Roman centurion who guarded Christ's tomb. **53m/C VHS, DVD.** George Macready, Robert Wilson, Virginia Wave; *D:* John T. Coyle; *W:* Arthur T. Horman; *C:* Frederick E. West; *M:* Irving Gertz.

I Bombed Pearl Harbor 🦴🦴 **1960** Mifune stars in this epic that shows events of WWII through Japanese eyes. Dramatic battle scenes boast the most ships destroyed per minute of film. Dubbed from Japanese. **98m/C VHS.** *JP* Toshiro Mifune, Yosuke Natsuki, Makoto Sato, Misa(ko) Uehara; *D:* Shue Matsubayashi; *W:* Shinobu Hashimoto, Takeo Kunihiro; *C:* Kazuo Yamada; *M:* Ikuma Dan.

I Bury the Living 🦴🦴🦴 **1958** A cemetery manager sticks pins in his map of a graveyard and people mysteriously start to die. Well-done suspense film. **76m/B VHS, DVD.** Richard Boone, Theodore Bikel, Peggy Maurer, Herbert Anderson, Howard Smith, Robert Osterloh, Russ Bender, Matt Moore, Ken Drake, Glenn Vernon, Lynn Bernay, Cyril Delevanti; *D:* Albert Band; *W:* Louis Garfinkle; *C:* Frederick Gately; *M:* Gerald Fried.

I Can Do Bad All By Myself 🦴🦴 ½ *Tyler Perry's I Can Do Bad All By Myself* **2009 (PG-13)** Tyler Perry's Madea franchise continues, but this time Madea (Perry) offers up some laughs and then steps aside, allowing the real story to develop. Don't expect any surprises, though. In this installment, Madea finds three teens robbing her home, and after learning that their druggy mom is dead and grandma is missing, she sends them to live with hard-drinking, tough-living nightclub singer Aunt April. April's life and outlook are transformed with the help of church lady Miss Wilma (Knight) and a nightclub owner (Blige), who both belt out powerful vocal performances. It's never in doubt that April will embrace her lessons in caring and generosity, but fans of Perry will absolutely love the journey. **113m/C DVD.** *US* Tyler Perry, Taraji P. Henson, Gladys Knight, Brian White, Adam Rodriguez, Hope Olaide Wilson, Mary J. Blige, Marvin Winans, Kwesi Boakye, Frederick Siglar; *D:* Tyler Perry; *W:* Tyler Perry; *C:* Alexander Grusynski.

I Can't Escape 🦴🦴 **1934** A man attempts to piece his life back together after serving time for a crime he didn't commit. To prove himself to his girlfriend, he tries to break up an illegal stock scam. **60m/B VHS.** Onslow Stevens, Lila Lee, Russell Gleason, Otis Harlan, Hooper Atchley, Clara Kimball Young; *D:* Otto Brower.

I Can't Sleep 🦴🦴 *J'ai Pas Sommeil* **1993** Serial killers, French style. Gay, black Camille (Courcet), an immigrant from Martinique, and his white lover Raphael (Dupont) live in a Paris hotel and murder elderly women. Though they also rob them, the motive for their horrific crimes is vague (seemingly even to themselves). Not much actually happens—Camille visits his brother, who longs to return home, and their status as outsiders is juxtaposed against another immigrant, Daiga (Golubeva) from Lithuania, who takes little interest in the crimes but unwittingly crosses paths with Camille. Atmospheric if nothing else. Based on the 1987 "Granny Killer" slayings of 20 women. French with subtitles. **110m/C VHS, DVD.** *FR* Richard Courcet, Vincent Dupont, Yekaterina (Katia) Golubeva, Alex Descas, Beatrice Dalle, Laurent Grevill; *D:* Claire Denis; *W:* Claire Denis, Jean-Pol Fargeau; *C:* Agnes Godard; *M:* Jean Murat.

I Capture the Castle 🦴🦴 ½ **2002 (R)** First, the R rating is dumb—it's for a bit of nudity that wouldn't shock a country vicar. Second, the film is based on the book by Dodie Smith (who wrote "101 Dalmatians") and is a coming-of-age tale set in 1936 in the Suffolk countryside. The Mortmains rent a small crumbling castle and times are hard. Dad James (Nighy) ignores his family and hides away to "write," leaving flaky second wife Topaz (Fitzgerald) to cope. Cassandra (Garai) is 17, smart, and pretty but overshadowed by her ambitious, beautiful older sister Rose (Bryne) who is determined to marry well. She gets her chance when two wealthy American brothers, Simon (Thomas) and Neil (Blucas), arrive to claim their inheritance, which includes the castle. Quite a romantic tangle ensues. Fine acting, particularly by Garai who gives the story its point of view. **113m/C VHS, DVD.** *GB* Romola Garai, Rose Byrne, Henry Thomas, Marc Blucas, Bill Nighy, Tara Fitzgerald, Sinead Cusack, Henry Cavill, James Faulkner, Sarah Woodward; *D:* Tim Fywell; *W:* Heidi Thomas; *C:* Richard Greatrex; *M:* Dario Marianelli. L.A. Film Critics '03: Support. Actor (Nighy).

I Come in Peace 🦴🦴 *Dark Angel* **1990 (R)** A tough, maverick Texas cop embarks on a one-way ride to Nosebleed City when he attempts to track down a malevolent alien drug czar who kills his victims by sucking their brains. Mindless thrills. **92m/C VHS.** Dolph Lundgren, Brian Benben, Betsy Brantley, Jesse Vint, Michael J. Pollard; *D:* Craig R. Baxley; *M:* Jan Hammer.

I Confess 🦴🦴 ½ **1953** Interesting but overly serious mid-career Hitchcock, adapted from Paul Anthelme's 1902 play, "Our Two Consciences." Father Michael Logan (Clift) is a young curate in Quebec, who hears the murder confession of Otto Keller (Hasse). Keller knows Father Logan can tell no one because of the sanctity of the confessional, even when Logan himself comes under suspicion for the crime. Unfortunately, the resolution to the conflict is not up to the master's usual standards. **95m/B VHS, DVD.** Montgomery Clift, Anne Baxter, Karl Malden, Brian Aherne, O.E. Hasse, Dolly Haas, Roger Dann; *D:* Alfred Hitchcock; *W:* William Archibald, George Tabori; *C:* Robert Burks; *M:* Dimitri Tiomkin.

I Conquer the Sea 🦴 ½ **1936** Two brothers, who works as whalers, cast their affection on the same woman. Drowns in its own melodrama. **68m/B VHS.** Steffi Duna, Dennis Morgan, Douglas Walton, George Cleveland, Johnny Pirrone; *D:* Victor Halperin.

I Could Go on Singing 🦴🦴 ½ **1963** An aging American songstress, on a tour in Britain, becomes reacquainted with her illegitimate son and his British father, but eventually goes back to the footlights. Garland's last film. Songs include "By Myself" and "It Never Was You." A must for Garland fans. Letterboxed. **99m/C VHS, DVD.** Judy Garland, Dirk Bogarde, Jack Klugman, Aline MacMahon; *D:* Ronald Neame.

I Could Never Be Your Woman 🦴 ½ **2006 (PG-13)** Not terribly romantic or funny although Pfeiffer is as gorgeous as ever. Divorced and frazzled, 40-something TV sitcom producer Rosie (Pfeiffer) is shocked when she falls for the show's newest cast member, the years-younger Adam (Rudd). Meanwhile, Rosie's teen daughter Izzy (Ronan) is in the throes of first love. Thrown into the mix—and an uneasy addition—is Ullman's Mother Nature, who appears as Rosie's conscience, offering unsolicited and unwelcome romantic advice. **97m/C DVD.** Michelle Pfeiffer, Paul Rudd, Stacey Dash, Tracey Ullman, Fred Willard, Henry Winkler, Sally Kellerman, Jon Lovitz, Saoirse Ronan, Sarah Alexander, Brittany Benson, Jed Bernard; *D:* Amy Heckerling; *W:* Amy Heckerling; *C:* Brian Tufano.

I Cover the Waterfront 🦴🦴 ½ **1933** A reporter is assigned to write about a boatman involved in a fishy scheme to smuggle Chinese immigrants into the country wrapped in shark skins. While trying to get the story, the journalist falls in love with the fisherman's daughter. Torrance passed away before its release. **70m/B VHS, DVD.** Claudette Colbert, Ben Lyon, Ernest Torrence, Hobart Cavanaugh; *D:* James Cruze.

I Died a Thousand Times 🦴🦴 **1955** Aging gangster Mad Dog Earle (pushup prince Palance) plans one last death-defying heist while hiding from police in the mountains. Meanwhile, the hard boiled gangster softens a bit thanks to surgery-needing girlfriend, but moll Winters doesn't seem to think that three's company. A low rent "High Sierra." From the novel by W.R. Burnett. **109m/C VHS.** Jack Palance, Shelley Winters, Lori Nelson, Lee Marvin, Earl Holliman, Lon Chaney Jr., Howard St. John; *D:* Stuart Heisler; *W:* W.R. Burnett.

I Dismember Mama **WOOF!** *Poor Albert and Little Annie* **1974 (R)** Classless story of an asylum inmate who escapes to kill his mother. Although he hates women, he likes little girls as evidenced by his nine-year-old love interest. Notably lacking in bloody scenes. **81m/C VHS.** Zooey Hall, Joanne Moore Jordan, Greg Mullavey, Marlene Tracy, Geri Reischl, Frank Whiteman; *D:* Paul Leder; *W:* William W. Norton Sr.; *C:* Andreas Mannkopff; *M:* Herschel Burke Gilbert.

I Do 🦴 ½ *Prete-Moi ta Main* **2006** Overplayed and obvious romantic comedy. Middle-aged Luis (Chabat) is happily single since his over-protective mother and multiple sisters care for him. But when they finally insist he get married, Luis decides to hire a fiance to charm them and then leave him at the altar. Emma's (Gainsbourg) a hit, but when she dumps Luis, his family insist he win back the perfect woman. The original French title translates to "lend me your hand." French with subtitles. **90m/C DVD.** *FR* Alain Chabat, Charlotte Gainsbourg, Bernadette LaFont, Gregoire Oestermann, Wladimir Yordanoff; *D:* Eric Lartigau; *W:* Laurent Zeitoun, Laurent Tiraud, Philippe Mechelen, Gregoire Vigeron; *C:* Regis Blondeau; *M:* Erwann Kermorvant.

I Don't Buy Kisses Anymore 🦴🦴 ½ **1992 (PG)** Heartwarming story starring Alexander and Peeples as two mismatched lovers who end up realizing that they're made for each other. Alexander plays Bernie Fishbine, an overweight Jewish shoe store owner who falls for a psychology graduate student (Peeples). Little does he know, but Peeples is studying him for her term paper, appropriately titled "The Psychological Study of an Obese Male." Alexander gives a great performance, as do Kazan and Jacobi who play Bernie's parents. **112m/C VHS, DVD.** Jason Alexander, Nia Peeples, Lainie Kazan, Lou Jacobi, Eileen Brennan, Larry Storch, Arleen (Arlene) Sorkin; *D:* Robert Marcarelli; *W:* Jonnie Lindsell; *C:* Michael Ferris; *M:* Cobb Bussinger. **TV**

I Don't Give a Damn 🦴🦴 **1988 (R)** An embittered wounded soldier returns home to his loved ones, rejects them, and becomes more and more uninterested in life itself. Subtitled. **94m/C VHS.** *IS* Ika Sohar, Anat Waxman; *D:* Shmuel Imberman.

I Don't Kiss 🦴🦴 *J'embrasse Pas* **1991** An episodic pic about Pierre (Blanc), a young man from the country who has dreams of finding success as an actor in Paris. But he soon finds himself making a living as a hustler with only fellow prostie Ingrid (Beart) offering genuine friendship. French with subtitles. **116m/C DVD.** *FR* Manuel Blanc, Emmanuelle Beart, Philippe Noiret, Helene Vincent, Ivan Desny, Roschdy Zem, Jacques Nolot, Christophe Bernard; *D:* Andre Techine; *W:* Jacques Nolot; *C:* Thierry Arbogast; *M:* Philippe Sarde.

I Don't Want to Be Born 🦴 *The Devil Within Her* **1975 (R)** It's got all the right ingredients for overnight camp: a spurned dwarf, a large, howling baby-thing, slice and dice murder and mayhem, and Collins. It could've been so bad. Instead, this "Rosemary's Baby" rehash is just stupid bad. **90m/C VHS.** *GB* Joan Collins, Eileen Atkins, Donald Pleasence, Ralph Bates, Caroline Munro; *D:* Peter Sasdy.

I Don't Want to Talk About It 🦴🦴 ½ *De Eso No Se Habla* **1994** Fable set in a small South American town in the '30s. The widowed Leonor (Brando) is the community leader, a woman determined to see that her daughter Charlotte (Podesta) be as happy and accomplished as possible. Leonor refuses to acknowledge Charlotte is a dwarf and size is never permitted to be mentioned in her presence. Her zealous protectiveness is challenged by worldly and charming newcomer Ludovico (Mastroianni) who becomes entranced by Charlotte. Mastroianni is masterly as always but the moody film proves slight. Based on story by Julio Llinas. Spanish with subtitles. **102m/C VHS.** *AR* Marcello Mastroianni, Luisina Brando, Alejandra Podesta; *D:* Maria-Luisa Bemberg; *W:* Maria-Luisa Bemberg, Jorge Goldenberg.

I Dood It 🦴🦴 *By Hook or By Crook* **1943** Young tailor's assistant Skelton falls hard for young actress Powell working near his shop. She agrees to date, and eventually marry him, but only to spite her boyfriend who has just run off with another woman. All's well however, when Skelton stumbles across a spy ring, is hailed a hero and helps Powell realize she really loves him. ♫ Star Eyes; Taking a Chance on Love; Jericho; One O'Clock Jump; So Long Sarah Jane; Hola E Pae; Swing the Jinx Away. **102m/B VHS.** Red Skelton, Eleanor Powell, Richard Ainley, Patricia Dane, Sam Levene, Thurston Hall, Lena Horne, Butterfly McQueen; ***D:*** Vincente Minnelli.

I Downloaded a Ghost 1/2 **2004 (PG)** Amusing family-oriented Halloween TV movie. Misfit 12-year-old Stella (Page) wants to create the ultimate spooky haunted house for Halloween and repeatedly uses a ghost-oriented website for some tips. This leads to Stella accidentally contacting a ghost (who needs to make amends) who travels into her world. Now, unless she and her best pal Albert (Kaney) can help him, they've just made a new friend who they really don't want hanging around. **90m/C DVD.** *CA* Ellen Page, Michael Kaney, Carlos Alazraqui, Gary Hudson, Barbara Alyn Woods, Vincent Corazza, Tim Progosh, Kirsty Mitchell; ***D:*** Kelly Sandefur; ***W:*** Jeff Phillips; ***C:*** Ken Krawczyk; ***M:*** Tim Jones. **TV**

I Dream of Jeannie **1952** The third and worst bio of Stephen Foster has Foster as a bookkeeper-cum-songwriter alternating between writing tunes and chasing Lawrence. When she dumps him, he goes into a funk. Will he be able to complete the title song? The suspense will kill you. Lots of singing, but not much else. **90m/C VHS, DVD.** Ray Middleton, Bill (William) Shirley, Muriel Lawrence, Lynn Bari, Rex Allen; ***D:*** Allan Dwan.

I Dream Too Much **1935** A musical vehicle for opera star Pons, as a French singer who marries an American composer played by Fonda. Songwriter falls into wife's shadow after pushing her into a singing career; she then raises his spirits a couple of octaves by helping him sell a musical comedy. Went into production after a rival company, Columbia, launched opera singer Grace Moore's acting career. Ball later bought this studio, where she was given her second starring role. ♫ The Jockey on the Carousel; I'm the Echo; I Got Love; I Dream Too Much; Bell Song; Caro Nome. **90m/B VHS.** Lily Pons, Henry Fonda, Eric Blore, Lucille Ball, Mischa Auer, Scotty Beckett; ***D:*** John Cromwell; ***M:*** Max Steiner.

I Dreamed of Africa 1/2 **2000 (PG-13)** Okay the scenery is beautiful (it was filmed in Kenya), including blonde Basinger, but the story is predictable and trite despite being based on the autobiography of Italian socialite Kuki Gallmann. Gallmann (Basinger) trades in her designer duds for safari khaki when she, her young son, Emanuele (Aiken), and her second husband, Paolo (Perez), decide they need a fresh start. The somewhat irresponsible Paolo likes to go big game hunting with his friends, leaving Kuki alone, and she eventually becomes a conservationist after some personal tragedies. Most of the roles, except Basinger's, are one-dimensional. **114m/C VHS, DVD.** Kim Basinger, Vincent Perez, Eva Marie Saint, Daniel Craig, Lance Reddick, Liam Aiken, Garrett Strommen; ***D:*** Hugh Hudson; ***W:*** Paula Milne, Susan Shilliday; ***C:*** Bernard Lutic; ***M:*** Maurice Jarre.

I Dreamt Under the Water 1/2 *J'ai Reve Sous L'eau* **2007** Bisexual Antonin (Benhamdine) is unrequitedly in love with bandmate Alex (Victor), who dies of a heroin overdose. In despair, Antonin indulges himself in the degrading side of Paris nightlife and starts turning tricks, with only his client Baptiste (Nazzal) offering any concern. However, Antonin can't help himself and he gets involved with unstable Juliette (Ducey), who turns out to be another junkie. French with subtitles. **95m/C DVD.** *FR* Caroline Ducey, Christine Boisson, Hubert Benhamadine, Hicham Nazzal, Franck Victor; ***D:*** Hormoz; ***W:*** Hormoz, Philippe Arrizabalaga; ***C:*** Sabastien Joffard.

I Drink Your Blood 1/2 **1971 (R)** Hippie satanists looking for kicks spike an old man's drink with LSD. To get revenge, the old codger's grandson sells the nasty flower children meat pies injected with the blood of a rabid dog. The hippies then turn into cannibalistic maniacs, infecting anyone they bite. From the man responsible for "I Spit on Your Grave"; originally played on a double bill with "I Eat Your Skin." **83m/C VHS, DVD.** Bhasker, Jadine Wong, Ronda Fultz, Elizabeth Marner-Brooks, George Patterson, Riley Mills, Iris Brooks, John Damon, Bruno Damon; ***D:*** David E. Durston; ***W:*** David E. Durston; ***C:*** Jacques Demarecaux; ***M:*** Clay Pitts.

I Eat Your Skin **WOOF!** *Voodoo Blood Bath; Zombie; Zombies* **1964** Cannibalistic zombies terrorize a novelist and his girlfriend on a Caribbean island. Blood and guts, usually shown on a gourmet double bill with "I Drink Your Blood." **82m/B VHS, DVD.** William Joyce, Heather Hewitt, Betty Hyatt Linton, Robert Stanton, Dan Stapleton; ***D:*** Del Tenney; ***W:*** Del Tenney; ***C:*** Francois Farkas; ***M:*** Lon Norman.

I Got Five on It **2005** Absurd partying flick begins with Jimmy (Bridges) behind bars for buying dope, leaving his three spacey pals to fend for themselves. As they scavenge about town to score weed, trouble seems to be all they can find, even after Jimmy returns. **76m/C DVD.** Todd Bridges, Jose Rosette, Chris Angelo, Carl Washington; ***D:*** Eduardo Quiroz, Jose Quiroz; ***W:*** Eduardo Quiroz, Jose Quiroz. **VIDEO**

I Got the Hook-Up 1/2 **1998 (R)** Inner-city hustlers Black (Master P) and Blue (Johnson) have their own "department store" in a vacant lot where they sell various goods of dubious quality and origin. When a truckload of cell phones is mistakenly delivered to them, it ushers them into a new business venture. All hell breaks loose when a thug (Lister) has a money pick-up go bad because of the defective phones. Sporadically amusing comedy plays gang violence and misogyny for laughs, while the leads do nothing to make their characters interesting or even likable. **93m/C VHS, DVD.** Mark Zuelzke, A.J. (Anthony) Johnson, Gretchen Palmer, Frantz Turner, Tommy (Tiny) Lister, Helen Martin, John Witherspoon, Harrison White, Ice Cube, Anthony Boswell, Lola Mae; ***D:*** Michael Martin; ***W:*** Mark Zuelzke; ***C:*** Antonio Calvache; ***M:*** Tommy Coster, Brad Fairman.

I Hate Blondes 1/2 *Odio le Bionde* **1983** A group of criminals use a ghostwriter's burglaring stories as instructional manuals. The writer becomes involved with the gang. Relies heavily on visual humor. Notable among the comedy scenes is the author's search for jewels at a get-together. **90m/C VHS.** *IT* ***D:*** Giorgio Capitani, Giorgio Capitani.

I Hate Valentine's Day 1/2 **2009 (PG-13)** Vardalos' appeal comes from her everywoman qualities but she keeps undermining it by trying too hard to be the center of flattering attention. Brooklyn flower shop owner Genevieve is the one everyone turns to for romantic advice despite her stupid rule that she only dates a guy five times so the romantic infatuation will last (she says she's not interested in a relationship). Then along comes hunky new neighbor Greg (Corbett), they hit it off really well, and Genevieve starts rethinking her situation. **89m/C DVD.** Nia Vardalos, John Corbett, Zoe Kazan, Gary Wilmes, Mike Starr, Judah Friedlander, Rachel Dratch, Jay O. Sanders, Stephen Guarino, Amir Arison; ***D:*** Nia Vardalos; ***W:*** Nia Vardalos; ***C:*** Brian Przypek; ***M:*** Keith Power.

I Heard the Owl Call My Name 1/2 **1973** Poignant story of an Anglican priest who is relocated to an Indian fishing village on the ouskirts of Vancouver, British Columbia. Based on a Margaret Craven book. **74m/C** Tom Courtenay, Dean Jagger, Paul Stanley; ***D:*** Daryl Duke. **TV**

I Heart Huckabees **2004 (R)** Director Russell's existential comedy has a cast willing to take chances with material that is too clever for its own good—and a viewers' enjoyment. Environmentalist/poet Albert (Schwartzman), fighting giant retail chain Huckabees, takes his search for enlightenment to the offices of existential detectives Bernard and Vivian Jaffe (Hoffman, Tomlin), who believe everything in life is connected. Albert thinks his nemesis is Huckabee's golden exec Brad Stand (Law) and Brad's gorgeous spokesmodel girlfriend Dawn (Watts) until they also become the Jaffes' clients. Then Albert befriends Tommy Corn (Wahlberg), a firefighter, who has become involved with French nihilist Caterine (Huppert), who believes everything is meaningless and...okay, things get even more convoluted, although Tomlin and Hoffman, at least, seem to be having a grand time. **105m/C VHS, DVD.** Jason Schwartzman, Isabelle Huppert, Dustin Hoffman, Lily Tomlin, Jude Law, Mark Wahlberg, Naomi Watts; ***D:*** David O. Russell; ***W:*** David O. Russell, Jeff Baena; ***C:*** Peter Deming.

I Hope They Serve Beer in Hell **2009 (R)** With friends like these... Based on the true life stories of Tucker Max (Czuchry), who has his best bud Dan (Stults) lying to fiancee Kristy (Pratt) so Tucker can take Dan to an impromptu bachelor party at a strip club where things invariably go out of control. Disinvited from the wedding (and the friendship), Tucker has to figure out a way to get back into everyone's good graces. Unfortunately, main character Tucker is completely unlikable and narcissistic-to-the-nth degree and succeeds in making a supposed raunchy romp quite unfunny. **105m/C DVD.** *US* Matt Czuchry, Marika Dominczyk, Geoff Stults, Jesse Bradford, Keri Lynn Pratt; ***D:*** Bob Grosse; ***W:*** Tucker Max, Nils Parker; ***C:*** Suki Medencevic; ***M:*** James L. Venable.

I Killed Rasputin 1/2 **1967** The "Mad Monk" who rose to power before the Russian Revolution lost his life in a bizarre assassination by Felix Youssoupoff. Film deals with the friendship between the men that ended in betrayal. Well-intentioned, but overwrought. Dubbed. **95m/C VHS.** *FR IT* Geraldine Chaplin, Gert Frobe, Peter McEnery; ***D:*** Robert Hossein; ***M:*** Don Banks.

I Killed That Man 1/2 **1942** A prisoner scheduled to die in the electric chair is given an early ticket out when he is found poisoned. Evidence points to an unusual group of suspects. Effective low-budget thriller offers a few unexpected surprises. **72m/B VHS, DVD.** Ricardo Cortez, Joan Woodbury, Iris Adrian, George Pembroke, Herbert Rawlinson, Pat Gleason, Ralf Harolde, Jack Mulhall, Vince Barnett, Gavin Gordon, John Hamilton; ***D:*** Phil Rosen.

I Know What You Did Last Summer **1997 (R)** Four teens get involved in a fatal hit-and-run accident and think they've managed to keep it a secret. Good girl Julie (Hewitt), beauty queen Helen (Gellar), arrogant jock Barry (Philippe), and regular guy Ray (Prinze) make a pact to take the secret to their graves, which may be sooner than they thought. One year later, the quartet receive letters which give the movie its title and set them against each other. After a few youngsters are made into bait on rather large fishing hooks, they band together to stop the bloodthirsty killer. Hint: It's not Mrs. Paul. Another quality slasher throwback written by Kevin Williamson, the man who made you "Scream." **100m/C VHS, DVD.** Jennifer Love Hewitt, Sarah Michelle Gellar, Ryan Phillippe, Freddie Prinze Jr., Muse Watson, Anne Heche, Bridgette Wilson-Sampras, Johnny Galecki, Dan Albright; ***D:*** Jim Gillespie; ***W:*** Kevin Williamson; ***C:*** Denis Crossan; ***M:*** John Debney.

I Know Where I'm Going **1945** A young woman (Hiller), who believes that money brings happiness, is on the verge of marrying a rich old man, until she meets a handsome naval officer (Livesey) and finds a happy, simple life. Early on the female lead appears in a dream sequence filmed in the mode of surrealist painter Salvador Dali and avant garde director Luis Bunuel. Scottish setting and folk songs give a unique flavor. Brown provides a fine performance as a native Scot. **91m/B VHS, DVD.** *GB* Roger Livesey, Wendy Hiller, Finlay Currie, Pamela Brown, George Carney, Walter Hudd; ***D:*** Michael Powell, Emeric Pressburger; ***W:*** Michael Powell, Emeric Pressburger; ***C:*** Erwin Hillier; ***M:*** Allan Gray.

I Know Who Killed Me **2007 (R)** Upper middle class high school student Aubrey Fleming (Lohan) goes missing. Her distraught parents (Ormond and McDonough) cooperate with the police but have little insight into the disappearance. When Aubrey's found beside a rural road near death and mutilated in the M.O. of a local serial killer, the case seems pretty simple, until Aubrey awakes and thinks she's actually stripper Dakota Moss, who is the subject of a story Aubrey was writing for a class. Flashbacks, dream sequences and semi-plausible cinematic gimmicks bring this to a tidy conclusion, with unfortunate results. With her career in shambles, this might be your last chance to see Lohan (outside a courthouse) for a while. **108m/C DVD, Blu-ray Disc.** *US* Lindsay Lohan, Julia Ormond, Neal McDonough, Garcelle Beauvais, Brian Geraghty, Spencer Garrett, Gregory Itzin, Rodney Rowland, Paula Marshall, Eddie Steeples, Kenya Moore, Donovan Scott, Bonnie Aarons, Thomas Tofel, David Figlioni, Michael (Mike) Papajohn, Michelle Page; ***D:*** Chris Sivertson; ***W:*** Jeffrey Hammond; ***C:*** John R. Leonetti; ***M:*** Joel McNeely. Golden Raspberries '07: Worst Picture, Worst Actress (Lohan), Worst Director (Sivertson), Worst Screenplay, Worst Remake.

I Know Why the Caged Bird Sings **1979** A black writer's memories of growing up in the rural South during the 1930s. Strong performances from Rolle and Good. Based on the book by Maya Angelou. **100m/C VHS.** Diahann Carroll, Ruby Dee, Esther Rolle, Roger E. Mosley, Paul Benjamin, Constance Good; ***D:*** Fielder Cook. **TV**

I Like Bats **1985** Can a psychiatrist help a vampire become a human? Polish dialogue with English subtitles. **90m/C VHS.** Katarzyna Walter, Marek Barbasiewicz, Malgorzata Lorentowicz; ***D:*** Grzegorz Warchol; ***W:*** Grzegorz Warchol; ***C:*** Krysztof Pakulski; ***M:*** Zbigniew Preisner.

I Like It Like That **1994 (R)** Chaotic family life and loves in the Bronx are the setting for this tale of a Cinderella in the record industry. Strong-willed black-Latina Lisette (Velez) has been married for 10 years to macho Latin, Chino (Seda), who has a wandering eye. When Chino is jailed for looting during a blackout, Lisette, needing to support their three kids, talks her way into a job with WASP record promoter Stephen Price (Dunne). When local gossips make it seem Lisette is having an affair, the newly sprung Chino retaliates by turning to lusty Magdalena (Vidal). Lisette, meanwhile, gathers support from her transvestite brother and proves to have inner resources previously unnoticed. Great Latino soundtrack illuminates the complications. Modest-budget sleeper quickly exited the theatre but proves to be a strong debut for director/writer Martin, reputed to be the first African-American woman to be given the reins by a major studio. **106m/C VHS, DVD.** Lauren Velez, Jon Seda, Lisa Vidal, Jesse Borrego, Griffin Dunne, Rita Moreno, Tomas Melly, Desiree Casado, Isaiah Garcia; ***D:*** Darnell Martin; ***W:*** Darnell Martin; ***C:*** Alexander Grusynski; ***M:*** Sergio George.

I Like to Play Games 1/2 **1995 (R)** Michael is looking for a woman who enjoys playing sexual games—and he seems to have the perfect partner in Suzanne. But just how far will their kinks take them? Also available unrated. **95m/C VHS, DVD.** Lisa Boyle, Ken Steadman; ***D:*** Moctezuma Lobato; ***W:*** David Keith Miller; ***C:*** Kim Haun; ***M:*** Herman Beeftink.

I Live in Fear *Record of a Living Being; Kimono No Kiroku* **1955** Nakajima, an elderly, wealthy owner of a foundry, becomes increasingly fearful of atomic war and the threats to his family's safety. He tries to persuade them to leave Japan and move with him to Brazil but they fear the family will be ruined financially. Nakajima then burns down his foundry to force his children to move but instead they go to court and have him declared mentally incompetent. He is placed in an institution where he finds peace in the delusion that he has escaped to another planet and that the Earth has indeed suffered a nuclear holocaust. Provocative look at the fear of atomic warfare and radiation. In Japanese with English subtitles. **105m/C VHS.** *JP* Toshiro Mifune, Takashi Shimura, Eiko Miyoshi, Haruko Togo; ***D:*** Akira Kurosawa; ***W:*** Akira Kurosawa, Shinobu Hashimoto, Hideo Oguni; ***C:*** Asakazu Nakai; ***M:*** Fumio Hayasaka.

I Live in Grosvenor Square *A Yank In London* **1946** An American soldier in Great Britain falls in love with a major's fiancee. Entertaining if a bit drawn out. **106m/B VHS.** *GB* Anna Neagle, Rex Harrison, Dean Jagger, Robert Morley, Jane Darwell; ***D:*** Herbert Wilcox.

I Live My Life 1/2 **1935** Stylish glossy flick with Crawford playing a bored New York debutante who travels to Greece and meets a dedicated archaelogist (Aherne). A love/hate relationship ensues in this typical Crawford vehicle where she is witty and parades around in sophisticated fashions, but there is little substance here. **92m/B VHS.** Joan Crawford, Brian Aherne, Frank Morgan, Aline MacMahon, Eric Blore, Fred Keating, Jessie Ralph, Arthur Treacher, Frank Conroy, Sterling Holloway, Vince Barnett, Hedda Hopper, Lionel Stander; ***D:*** Woodbridge S. Van Dyke; ***W:*** Joseph L. Mankiewicz, Gottfried Reinhardt, Ethel B. Borden; ***C:*** George J. Folsey.

I Live with Me Dad 1/2 **1986** A vagrant drunk and his son fight the authorities for the right to be together. **86m/C VHS.** *AU* Peter Hehir, Haydon Samuels; ***D:*** Paul Maloney.

I Love a Bandleader 1/2 **1945** Housepainter Phil Burton (Harris) gets amnesia and imagines he's the leader of a swing band. He also falls in love with Ann (Brooks) who's determined to get him back on the bandstand when Phil's memory returns and he goes back to his old boring life. **70m/B VHS.** Phil Harris, Leslie Brooks, Eddie Anderson, Walter Catlett; ***D:*** Del Lord; ***W:*** Paul Yawitz; ***C:*** Franz Planer; ***M:*** Walter Kent.

I Love Budapest **2001** Teenaged Aniko leaves her village to have a better life in Budapest. She gets a factory job and becomes smitten with security guard Miki. Aniko's new friend, the more sophisticated Moni, gets her boyfriend Krisztian to offer Miki a better job to impress Aniko. The problem is the job is part of Krisztian's underground criminal world, which will effect everyone's relationships. Hungarian with subtitles. **85m/C VHS, DVD.** *HU* Gabriella Hamor, Sandor Csanyi, Martina Kovacs, Tomas Lengyel; ***D:*** Agnes Incze; ***W:*** Agnes Incze; ***C:*** Gergely Poharnok; ***M:*** Laszlo Fogarasi.

I Love Melvin 1/2 **1953** Reynolds wants to be a Tinseltown goddess, and O'Connor just wants Reynolds; so he passes himself off as chief lenseman for a famous magazine and promises her a shot at the cover of "Look." Seems he has a little trouble on the follow through. Choreographed by Robert Alton, it's got a best ever football ballet (with Reynolds as pigskin). ♫ A Lady Loves; Saturday Afternoon Before The Game; I Wanna Wander; We Have Never Met As Of Yet; Life Has Its Funny Little Ups And Downs; Where Did You Learn To Dance?; And There You Are. **77m/C VHS.** Donald O'Connor, Debbie Reynolds, Una Merkel, Richard Anderson, Jim Backus, Allyn Joslyn, Les Tremayne, Noreen Corcoran, Robert Taylor, Howard Keel, Helen Winston; ***D:*** Don Weis.

I Love My... Wife **1970 (R)** A medical student plays doctor with hospital nurses when he and his wife stop having sex during her pregnancy. The marriage becomes more strained when their son is born and his mother-in-law moves in. A comedy without the proper dosage of laughs. **98m/C VHS.** Elliott Gould, Brenda Vaccaro, Angel Tompkins; ***D:*** Mel Stuart.

I Love N.Y. **1987** A young metropolitan couple struggles to find true love amidst disapproving parents and doubting friends. Choppy direction and poor writing contribute to its failure. **100m/C VHS, DVD.** Scott Baio, Kelley Van Der Velden, Christopher Plummer, Jennifer O'Neill, Jerry Orbach, Virna Lisi; ***D:*** Alan Smithee; ***M:*** Bill Conti.

I Love Trouble 1/2 **1994 (PG)** Veteran reporter Peter Brackett (sexy veteran Nolte) and ambitious cub reporter Sabrina Petersen (young and sexy Roberts) are competitors working for rival Chicago newspapers. When they begin to secretly exchange information on a big story, they find their lives threatened and their rivalry turning to romance. Some action, simplistic retro script, one big star, one sorta big star, and you've got the perfect movie package for the Prozac decade. Written, produced and directed by husband/wife team Meyers and Shyer. **123m/C VHS, DVD.** Dan E. Butler, Kelly Rutherford, Olympia Dukakis, Marsha Mason, Eugene Levy, Charles Martin Smith, Paul Gleason, Jane Adams, Lisa Lu, Nora Dunn, Clark Gregg, Kevin Breznahan, Dorothy Lyman, Keith Gordon, Joseph (Joe) D'Onofrio, Barry Sobel, Frankie Faison, Stuart Pankin, Megan Cavanagh, Jessica Lundy, Nestor Serrano, Robin Duke, Julia Roberts, Nick Nolte, Saul Rubinek, Robert Loggia, James Rebhorn; ***D:*** Charles Shyer; ***W:*** Nancy Meyers, Charles Shyer; ***C:*** John Lindley; ***M:*** David Newman.

I Love You 1/2 **1981 (R)** Man down on his luck mistakenly assumes that a woman he meets is a hooker. She plays along, only to find that they are becoming emotionally involved. Pretentious cat-and-mouse game. **104m/C VHS.** *BR* Sonia Braga, Paulo Cesar Pereio, Vera Fischer, Tarcisio Meira; ***D:*** Arnaldo Jabor.

I Love You Again 1/2 **1940** A classic screwball comedy with Powell and Loy working together (wonderfully) in something other than their "Thin Man" series. Powell is a gloomy businessman who's about to be divorced by Loy. But after an accident it turns out Powell had been suffering from amnesia and has now regained his memory (which he keeps a secret). It seems Mr. Respectable used to be a con man and he decides to revert to his criminal ways. He also doesn't remember Loy but falls instantly in love with her and must decide what kind of life he wants. Witty dialog, amusing situations, fine direction. **97m/B VHS, DVD.** William Powell, Myrna Loy, Frank McHugh, Edmund Lowe; ***D:*** Woodbridge S. Van Dyke.

I Love You, Alice B. Toklas! 1/2 *Kiss My Butterfly* **1968** A straight uptight lawyer decides to join the peace and love generation in this somewhat maniacal satire of the hippie culture. Pretty dated now. Authored by Paul Mazursky and Larry Tucker. Incidentally, the title's Alice B. Toklas was actually the lifemate of "Lost Generation" author Gertrude Stein. **94m/C VHS, DVD.** Peter Sellers, Jo Van Fleet, Leigh Taylor-Young, Joyce Van Patten, David Arkin, Herb Edelman, Salem Ludwig; ***D:*** Hy Averback; ***W:*** Paul Mazursky, Larry Tucker; ***C:*** Philip Lathrop; ***M:*** Elmer Bernstein.

I Love You All 1/2 *Je Vous Aime* **1980** Deneuve relives experiences with three former lovers—a composer, a well-intentioned nobody, and a rock star—as she enters into a relationship with a widower. **103m/C VHS.** *FR* Catherine Deneuve, Jean-Louis Trintignant, Gerard Depardieu, Serge Gainsbourg; ***D:*** Claude Berri; ***W:*** Claude Berri; ***C:*** Etienne Becker; ***M:*** Serge Gainsbourg.

I Love You Baby **2001** Absurd romantic comedy with an implausible premise (even for the genre) and a mis-cast leading actor in Sanz, who seems too old matched against his co-stars. Marcos (Sanz) has hooked up with Daniel (Magill). They're happy until a mirror ball falls on Marcos's head in a disco and he wakes up thinking he's straight. So he falls for Marisol (Scanda) and they settle down together. Meanwhile Daniel will do anything to get his boyfriend back. Spanish with subtitles. **110m/C DVD.** *SP* Jorge Sanz, Santiago Magill, Tiare Scanda, Veronica Forque, Boy George; ***D:*** Alfonso Albacete, David Menkes; ***W:*** Alfonso Albacete, David Menkes, Lucia Etxeberria; ***C:*** Gonzalo Fernandez-Berridi; ***M:*** Paco Ortega, Miguel Angel Collado.

I Love You, Beth Cooper 1/2 **2009 (PG-13)** During his graduation speech, ubernerdy high school valedictorian Denis Cooverman (Rust) publicly declares his love for popular cheerleader Beth Cooper (Panettiere). Intrigued, somewhat bored, and having just dumped her loser macho boyfriend, Beth and her two best friends wind up at Denis' and proceed to show him that his dream girl is not the right one for him at all during an evening of rather brutal humiliations. A rehash of teen cliches based on the novel by Doyle, who also wrote the screenplay. **102m/C DVD.** *US* Hayden Panettiere, Shawn Roberts, Lauren Storm, Lauren London, Paul Rust, Jack Carpenter, Alan Ruck, Cynthia Stevenson; ***D:*** Chris Columbus; ***W:*** Larry Doyle; ***C:*** Phil Abraham; ***M:*** Christophe Beck.

I Love You, Don't Touch Me! 1/2 **1997 (R)** Katie (Schafel) is a smart-mouthed, 25-year-old would-be singer in L.A., who also happens to be a virgin. She wants everything to be perfect her first time but all the guys she meets are just wrong. Her best friend Ben (Whitfield) would like to be the one, but Katie just can't see him in a romantic like. Then Katie finally gets involved with an older composer (Webber) who takes an interest in her career and all the romantic complications just get worse. **85m/C VHS, DVD.** Maria Schaffel, Mitchell Whitfield, Michael (M.K.) Harris, Nancy Sorel, Meredith Scott Lynn, Darryl Theirse; ***D:*** Julie Davis; ***W:*** Julie Davis; ***C:*** Mark Putnam.

I Love You, Goodbye **1974** A frustrated housewife, fed up with the constant role of wife and mother, leaves her family in an effort to find a more challenging and fulfilling life. A good performance by Lange compensates for some of its muddledness. **74m/C VHS.** Hope Lange, Earl Holliman, Michael Murphy, Patricia Smith, Mary Murphy; ***D:*** Sam O'Steen; ***W:*** Diana Gould; ***C:*** Andrew Jackson; ***M:*** Billy Goldenberg. **TV**

I Love You, I Love You Not 1/2 **1997 (PG-13)** The Holocaust becomes a metaphor for one teen's survival of her first painful romance. Daisy (Danes) is a Jewish student at a snobby and anti-Semetic Manhattan prep school, where she falls in love with the ultimate gentile, Ethan (Law) in a "Kids" meets "The Way We Were" spin. Moreau is Nana, Daisy's grandmother and a Holocaust survivor, whom Daisy visits every weekend. The two share their painful stories (Danes also plays Nana as a young girl). Danes does what she does best as a misunderstood teen coming of age. Moreau shines in her role as the beloved grandmother. What misfires is the trite handling of the serious subject matter as Daisy's romance scores far more screen time than Nana's suffering. Hopkins, an established casting director, makes his feature debut. **92m/C VHS, DVD.** *FR GE GB* Claire Danes, Jeanne Moreau, Jude Law, James Van Der Beek, Robert Sean Leonard, Kris Park, Lauren Fox, Emily Burkes-Nossiter, Carrie Slaza; ***D:*** Billy Hopkins; ***W:*** Wendy Kesselman; ***C:*** Maryse Alberti; ***M:*** Gil Goldstein.

I Love You, Man *Let's Make Friends* **2009 (R)** Peter (Rudd) discovers proposing to his girlfriend might have been the easiest part of getting married. Now he has to find a male friend to be his best man and embarks on a series of "man dates" to find Mr. Right in time for his wedding. Formulaic but funny, thanks mainly to the excellent performances by Rudd and Segel, who strike a perfect mix and complement each other's comedic strong suit a la the original buddy movie, "The Odd Couple." Full of the apparently requisite gross-out and sex jokes that the young, male target audience won't mind but may be a little much for their dates. Another solid entry in the booming "bromance" category. **105m/C DVD.** *US* Paul Rudd, Jason Segel, Jon Favreau, Rashida Jones, Adam Samberg, Jaime Pressly, J.K. Simmons, Jane Curtin; ***D:*** John Hamburg; ***W:*** John Hamburg, Larry Levin; ***C:*** Lawrence Sher; ***M:*** Theodore Shapiro.

I Love You Phillip Morris **2010 (R)** Based on a true story and the novel by Steve McVicker. Steven Russell goes from law-abiding family man to charming gay con man, which eventually lands him in prison. He falls in love with cellmate Phillip Morris and they set up a home together when they're released but Steven just can't let go of his criminal ways. **100m/C DVD.** Jim Carrey, Ewan McGregor, Leslie Mann, Rodrigo Santoro; ***D:*** Glenn Ficarra, John Requa; ***W:*** Glenn Ficarra, John Requa; ***C:*** Xavier Perez Grobet; ***M:*** Nick Urata.

I Love You Rosa 1/2 **1972** Rosa, a young Jewish widow, wrestles big time with old world values. Required by custom to marry her dearly departed's eldest brother, she's not enamored with her newly betrothed. Not that he's not a nice guy; he seems to plan to take his marital duties very seriously. It's just that he's a tad youthful (11 years old, to be exact). Much rabbi consulting and soul searching. **90m/C VHS.** Michal Bat-Adam, Gabi Oterman, Joseph Shiloah; ***D:*** Moshe Mizrahi; ***W:*** Moshe Mizrahi.

I Love You to Death 1/2 **1990 (R)** Dry comedy based on a true story, concerns a woman who tries to kill off her cheating husband. Lots of stars, but they never shine. Hurt and Reeves are somewhat amusing as drugged up hit men who struggle with the lyrics to the National Anthem. Watch for director Kasdan as Devo's lawyer. Cates, Kline's real-life wife, has an unbilled part as one of his one-night stands. **110m/C VHS, DVD.** Jack Kehler, Kevin Kline, Tracey Ullman, Joan Plowright, River Phoenix, William Hurt, Keanu Reeves, James Gammon, Victoria Jackson, Miriam Margolyes, Heather Graham; ***Cameos:*** Phoebe Cates; ***D:*** Lawrence Kasdan; ***W:*** John Kostmayer; ***C:*** Owen Roizman; ***M:*** James Horner.

I Love Your Work **2003 (R)** Goldberg tries to highlight the glamour and fake fabulousness of modern Hollywood celebrity, not always successfully, but at times interestingly. Loft-dwelling Gray Evans (Ribisi) and his wife Mia Lang (Potente) are famous, paparazzi-stalked actors living in Los Angeles. Gray's navel-gazing and paranoia turn into obsession with a young artist who reminds him of his pre-fame days. May be tedious for those not well-versed in the L.A. vibe. **111m/C DVD.** *US* Marisa Coughlan, Judy Greer, Shalom Harlow, Jared Harris, Joshua Jackson, Nicky Katt, Jason Lee, Franka Potente, Giovanni Ribisi, Christina Ricci, Vince Vaughn; ***Cameos:*** Elvis Costello; ***D:*** Adam Goldberg; ***W:*** Adam Goldberg, Adrian Butchart; ***C:*** Mark Putnam; ***M:*** Adam Goldberg, Steven Drozd.

I, Madman **1989 (R)** A novel-loving horror actress is stalked by the same mutilating madman that appears in the book she's presently reading. We call that bad luck. **90m/C VHS, DVD.** Jenny Wright, Clayton Rohner, William Cook; ***D:*** Tibor Takacs; ***W:*** David Chaskin; ***C:*** Bryan England.

I Married a Centerfold **1984** Fluff about a young man's amorous pursuit of a model. **100m/C VHS, DVD.** Teri Copley, Timothy Daly, Diane Ladd, Bert Remsen, Anson Williams; ***D:*** Peter Werner. **TV**

I Married a Dead Man *J'ai Epouse une Ombre; I Married a Shadow* **1982** When the train she's travelling on is involved in a terrible crash, abandoned, pregnant Helene (Baye) decides to assume the identity of a wealthy young woman who was killed in the wreck. But soon Helene is receiving anonymous threats from someone who knows who she really is. Based on a book by Cornell Woolrich and also filmed as "No Man of Her Own" (1950) and "Mrs. Winterbourne" (1996). French with subtitles. **110m/C VHS.** *FR* Nathalie Baye, Richard Bohringer, Victoria Abril, Francis Huster, Madeleine Robinson, Guy Trejan, Humbert Balsan, Veronique Genest; ***D:*** Robin Davis; ***W:*** Patrick Laurent; ***C:*** Bernard Zitzermann; ***M:*** Philippe Sarde.

I Married a Monster 1/2 **1998 (PG-13)** Update of the 1958 sci-fi film "I Married a Monster from Outer Space." The title tells the story—small town newlywed (Walters) finds out her hubby (Burgi) has been possessed by an alien intent on procreating its dying race. **90m/C VHS.** Susan Walters, Richard Burgi, Richard Herd, Barbara Niven; ***D:*** Nancy Malone; ***W:*** Duane Poole. **TV**

I Married a Monster from Outer Space 1/2 **1958** The vintage thriller about a race of monster-like aliens from another planet who try to conquer earth. Despite its head-shaking title, an effective '50s sci-fi creeper. **78m/B VHS, DVD.** Tom Tryon, Gloria Talbott, Maxie "Slapsie" Rosenbloom, Mary Treen, Ty Hardin, Ken Lynch, John Eldridge, Jean-Phillippe Carson, Alan Dexter; ***D:*** Gene Fowler Jr.; ***W:*** Louis Vittes; ***C:*** Haskell Boggs.

I Married a Vampire **1987** A country girl in the city is romanced and wed by a dashing vampire. Troma-produced hyper-camp. **85m/C VHS.** Rachel Gordon, Brendan Hickey, Ted Zalewski, Deborah Carroll, Temple Aaron; ***D:*** Jay Raskin; ***W:*** Jay Raskin; ***C:*** Oren Rudavsky.

I Married a Witch **1942** Jennifer (Lake) and her father Daniel (Kellaway) are burned at the stake during the Salem witch trials but not before cursing their persecutors, the Wooley family, vowing that no male of the line will ever find happiness. When Jennifer and Daniel are accidentally freed from their burial place centuries later, Jennifer locates Wallace Wooley (March) and tries to get him to fall in love with her so that she can remain on the mortal plane. Wonderfully played fantasy/comedy. **77m/B VHS.** Veronica Lake, Fredric March, Susan Hayward, Robert Benchley, Cecil Kellaway, Elizabeth Patterson, Robert Warwick, Eily Malyon, Mary Field, Nora Cecil, Emory Parnell, Helen St. Rayer, Aldrich Bowker, Emma Dunn, Harry Tyler, Ralph Peters, Ann Carter; ***D:*** Rene Clair; ***W:*** Robert Pirosh, Marc Connelly; ***C:*** Ted Tetzlaff; ***M:*** Roy Webb.

I Married a Woman **1956** Advertising executive marries beautiful blonde woman, but finds it very difficult to balance his career and marriage. Low on laughs. Shot in black and white, but includes a fantasy scene in color that features John Wayne. Pay attention to see young Angie

Dickinson. **84m/B VHS.** George Gobel, Diana Dors, Adolphe Menjou, Nita Talbot, William Redfield, Jessie Royce Landis, Steve (Stephen) Dunne, John McGiver, Steve Pendleton, Angie Dickinson; ***Cameos:*** John Wayne; ***D:*** Hal Kanter; ***W:*** Goodman Ace; ***C:*** Lucien Ballard; ***M:*** Cyril Mockridge.

I Married an Angel ½ **1942** The last MacDonald/Eddy film. A playboy is lured away from his usual interests by a beautiful angel. Adapted from Rodgers and Hart Broadway play. Strange and less than compelling. ♫ I Married An Angel; I'll Tell the Man in the Street; Spring is Here; Tira Lira La; A Twinkle in Your Eye; Aloha Oe; Caprice Viennoise; Chanson Boheme; Anges Purs. **84m/C VHS.** Jeanette MacDonald, Nelson Eddy, Binnie Barnes, Edward Everett Horton, Reginald Owen, Mona Maris, Janis Carter, Inez Cooper, Douglass Dumbrille, Leonid Kinskey, Marion Rosamond, Anne Jeffreys, Marek Windheim, Veda Ann Borg; ***D:*** Woodbridge S. Van Dyke; ***W:*** Anita Loos; ***M:*** Richard Rodgers, Lorenz Hart.

I Met a Murderer ½ **1939** A man kills his nagging wife after a bitter argument and flees from her vengeful brother. Fine fugitive drama with a number of interesting twists. **79m/B VHS.** James Mason, Pamela Kellino, Sylvia Coleridge, William Devlin, Esma Cannon, James Harcourt; ***D:*** Roy Kellino; ***W:*** Roy Kellino; ***C:*** Roy Kellino.

I, Mobster ½ **1958** Cochran tells a Senate Sub-Committee of his rise in the ranks of the Underworld—from his humble beginning as a bet collector for a bookie to his position as kingpin of the crime syndicate. **80m/B VHS, DVD.** Steve Cochran, Lita Milan, Robert Strauss, Celia Lovsky; ***D:*** Roger Corman; ***C:*** Floyd Crosby.

I, Monster **1971** The character names may have changed but this is still Robert Louis Stevenson's "Dr. Jekyll and Mr. Hyde." Lee tackles the title characters with his usual sinister savoir faire as Dr. Marlowe, who is obsessed with the nature of the id, the ego, and the superego and whether they can be separated within an individual. He injects himself with his secret formula and is transformed into Mr. Blake, who prowls the seedy sections of Victorian London to satisfy his violent desires. Frequent co-star Cushing shows up as a suspicious colleague. **74m/C VHS, DVD.** *GB* Christopher Lee, Peter Cushing, Mike Raven, George Merritt, Richard Hurndall, Kenneth J. Warren, Michael Des Barres, Susan Jameson; ***D:*** Stephen Weeks; ***W:*** Milton Subotsky; ***C:*** Moray Grant; ***M:*** Carl Davis.

I Never Promised You a Rose Garden **1977 (R)** A disturbed 16-year-old girl spirals down into madness and despair while a hospital psychiatrist struggles to bring her back to life. Based on the Joanne Greenberg bestseller. Compelling and unyielding exploration of the clinical treatment of schizophrenia. **90m/C VHS, DVD.** Kathleen Quinlan, Bibi Andersson, Sylvia Sidney, Diane Varsi, Dennis Quaid, Jeff Conaway; ***D:*** Anthony Page; ***W:*** Gavin Lambert, Lewis John Carlino; ***C:*** Bruce Logan; ***M:*** Paul Chihara.

I Never Sang for My Father ½ **1970 (PG)** A devoted son must choose between caring for his cantankerous but well-meaning father, and moving out West to marry the divorced doctor whom he loves. While his mother wants him to stay near home, his sister, who fell out of her father's favor by marrying out of the family faith, argues that he should do what he wants. An introspective, stirring story based on the Robert Anderson play. **90m/C VHS.** Gene Hackman, Melvyn Douglas, Estelle Parsons, Dorothy Stickney; ***D:*** Gilbert Cates; ***W:*** Robert Anderson. Writers Guild '70: Adapt. Screenplay.

I Now Pronounce You Chuck and Larry **2007 (PG-13)** In an effort to game the benefits system two Brooklyn firefighters pose as gay life partners. Larry's (James) spouse has died and he must name a new beneficiary, so of course he turns to his womanizing buddy Chuck (Sandler), who owes him one for saving his life. They have to make the whole gay couple thing believable, pulling out all of the cringe-worthy stereotypical gags while they're at it. Once their scam comes under suspicion they have to up the ante, which proves difficult while being represented by super hot (female) lawyer Alex (Biel). If you chuckle at bum jokes, or want to see Biel in a PVC catwoman costume, this is the movie to see. **115m/C DVD, HD DVD.** *US* Adam Sandler, Kevin James, Jessica Biel, Ving Rhames, Steve Buscemi, Dan Aykroyd, Nicholas Turturro, Dennis Dugan, Allen Covert, Richard Chamberlain, Rob Schneider, Rachel Dratch, Mary Pat Gleason, Rob Corddry, Nick Swardson, Jonathan Loughran, Chandra West, Blake Clark, Richard Kline; ***D:*** Dennis Dugan; ***W:*** Barry Fanaro, Alexander Payne, Jim Taylor, Brooks Arthur; ***C:*** Dean Semler; ***M:*** Rupert Gregson-Williams.

I Only Want You to Love Me *Ich Will Doch Nur, Dass Ihr Mich Liebt* **1976** Peter's (Zeplichal) been denigrated by his family his entire life, so he decides to move with his wife (Aberle) to Munich and show them he can make something of himself. But his desires become compulsions and he falters under the strain of work and marriage, leading to a terrifying crackup. A true story, based on the book "Life Sentence" by Klaus Antes and Christine Eberhardt. Originally produced for TV; German with subtitles. **104m/C VHS.** *GE* Vitus Zeplichal, Elke Aberle, Ernie Mangold, Joanna Hofe, Alexander Allerson; ***D:*** Rainer Werner Fassbinder; ***W:*** Rainer Werner Fassbinder; ***C:*** Michael Ballhaus; ***M:*** Peer Raben.

I Ought to Be in Pictures **1982 (PG)** After hitchhiking from New York to Hollywood to break into the movies, a teenage actress finds her father, a screenwriter turned alcoholic-gambler. Late, desperately unfunny Neil Simon outing, adapted from a Simon play. **107m/C VHS.** Walter Matthau, Ann-Margret, Dinah Manoff, Lance Guest, Michael Dudikoff; ***D:*** Herbert Ross; ***W:*** Neil Simon; ***M:*** Marvin Hamlisch.

I Posed for Playboy **1991 (R)** Three women—one a college co-ed, one a stockbroker, and one a 37-year-old mother—quench their private passions by posing for "Playboy" magazine. Made for TV with additional footage added to give it an "R" rating. **98m/C VHS.** Lynda Carter, Michele Greene, Amanda Peterson, Brittany York; ***D:*** Stephen Stafford. **TV**

I Promise to Pay **1937** Working stiff Eddie Lang (Morris) borrows money from Richard Farra (Carrillo) to take his family on vacation. Apparently Eddie didn't understand what a loan shark was and gets into serious trouble when he can't meet the payments. **68m/B VHS.** Chester Morris, Leo Carrillo, Helen Mack, Thomas Mitchell, Thurston Hall, John Gallaudet; ***D:*** David Ross Lederman; ***W:*** Lionel Houser, Mary C. McCall; ***C:*** Lucien Ballard.

I Really Hate My Job ½ **2007** Some days, don't we all. Five women all hold down mundane, low-paying jobs at the same London restaurant while dreaming of better opportunities ahead. They struggle through a somewhat atypical series of mishaps during their evening shift, with things going wrong at the worst possible times. **89m/C DVD.** *GB* Neve Campbell, Shirley Henderson, Alexandra Maria Lara, Oana Pellea, Danny Huston, Barry Morse; ***D:*** Oliver Parker; ***W:*** Jennifer Higgie; ***C:*** Tony Miller; ***M:*** Charlie Mole.

I Remember Mama ½ **1948** A true Hollywood heart tugger chronicling the life of a Norwegian immigrant family living in San Francisco during the early 1900s. Dunne triumphs as the mother, with a perfect Norwegian accent, and provides her family with wisdom and inspiration. A kindly father and four children round out the nuclear family. A host of oddball characters regularly pop in on the household—three high-strung aunts and an eccentric doctor who treats a live-in uncle. Adapted from John Van Druten's stage play, based on Kathryn Forbes memoirs, "Mama's Bank Account"; a TV series ran from 1946-57. **95m/B VHS, DVD.** Irene Dunne, Barbara Bel Geddes, Oscar Homolka, Ellen Corby, Cedric Hardwicke, Edgar Bergen, Rudy Vallee, Barbara O'Neil, Florence Bates; ***D:*** George Stevens; ***W:*** DeWitt Bodeen. Golden Globes '49: Support. Actress (Corby).

I, Robot **2004 (PG-13)** Very loose adaptation of Asimov's seminal 1950 sci-fi collection of short stories has action-hero Smith as Chicago detective Del Spooner, who's investigating the murder of robotic pioneer, Dr. Alfred Lanning (Cromwell). It's 2035, and robots are as common a household appliance as a toaster, and supposedly just as safe. But Spooner thinks those 'bots have minds (and plans) of their own and that one of them offed the good doctor. When Spooner persists in his theory that a robot committed the crime, he gets bumped from the force, which doesn't stop his investigation. The robots are creepily cool but there's no shock of the new in this crime caper. **115m/C DVD, UMD.** *US* Will Smith, Bridget Moynahan, Bruce Greenwood, Chi McBride, Alan Tudyk, James Cromwell, Shia LaBeouf, Adrian L. Ricard; ***D:*** Alex Proyas; ***W:*** Akiva Goldsman, Jeff Vintar; ***C:*** Simon Duggan; ***M:*** Marco Beltrami.

I See a Dark Stranger *The Adventuress* **1946** Cynical yet whimsical postwar British spy thriller about an angry Irish lass who agrees to steal war plans for the Nazis in order to battle her native enemies, the British—then she falls in love with a British officer. A sharply performed, decidedly jaded view of nationalism and wartime "heroism." **112m/B VHS, DVD.** *GB* Deborah Kerr, Trevor Howard, Raymond Huntley; ***D:*** Frank Launder.

I-See-You.Com ½ **2006** And I really wish I hadn't. After single parents Harvey and Lydia marry, they discover they can't make ends meet with their blended families. Entrepreneurial teenager Colby buys some webcams and installs them around the house (without his family's knowledge), uploads the footage to the Internet, and makes them a reality show sensation. Only their 15 minutes of fame proves to be a problem. **94m/C DVD.** Beau Bridges, Rosanna Arquette, Mathew Botuchis, Shiri Appleby, Dan Castellaneta, Doris Roberts, Hector Elizondo, Victor Alfieri, Baelyn Neff, Tracee Ellis Ross; ***D:*** Eric Steven Stahl; ***W:*** Eric Steven Stahl, Sean McLain; ***C:*** Ricardo Jacques Gale; ***M:*** Kevin Kiner.

I Sent a Letter to My Love **1981** An aging spinster, faced with the lonely prospect of the death of her paralyzed brother, places a personal ad for a companion in a local newspaper, using a different name. Unknown to her, the brother is the one who answers it, and they begin a romantic correspondence. Well-acted, touching account of relationships that change lives, but it takes its time in telling the story. **102m/C VHS.** *FR* Simone Signoret, Jean Rochefort, Delphine Seyrig; ***D:*** Moshe Mizrahi; ***W:*** Moshe Mizrahi, Gerard Brach; ***C:*** Ghislan Cloquet.

I Served the King of England ½ *Obsluhoval Jsem Anglickeho Krale* **2007 (R)** Well-acted portrayal of the life of Jan Dite (Barnev), a waiter in Prague's finest hotel restaurant with aspirations of wealth during a time when Czechoslovakia was controlled by Germany and later the Soviet Union. An older Dite (Kaiser) flashes back to his younger days - the dissident gets out of prison and is so seduced by his desire for material success that he weds Aryan Liza (Jentsch) and has no hesitation using wealth looted from Jewish households to purchase the hotel he has worked in. Dite's relatively unremarkable life provides a perfect backdrop for a satirical jab at Nazis and Commies alike. Put on your thinking cap to extract the many-layered dark humor from this one, but in the end what's better than disarming tyrants with brainy laughter? In Czech with English subtitles. **120m/C DVD.** *CZ* Oldrich Kaiser, Julia Jentsch, Marin Huba, Jiri Labus, Ivan Barnev, Marian Lasica, Josef Abrham, Jaromir Dulava; ***D:*** Jiri Menzel; ***W:*** Jiri Menzel; ***C:*** Jaromir Sofr; ***M:*** Ales Brezina.

I Shot a Man in Vegas ½ **1996 (R)** Low-budget variation of "Rashomon." Drinking buddies Johnny (Cubitt) and Grant (Stockwell) wind up in a back alley brawl and Johnny takes a bullet, supposedly shot dead by Grant. Only their friends, Gale (Garofalo), Martin (Drillinger), and Amy (Lippman), who witnessed the fight all saw it differently. So they decide to stash the corpse in their car trunk and head out across the desert to California. There's a last-minute revelation and a big finale but the strain shows. **84m/C VHS.** John Stockwell, Janeane Garofalo, Brian Drillinger, Noelle Lippman, David Cubitt; ***D:*** Keoni Waxman; ***W:*** Keoni Waxman; ***C:*** Steven Finestone.

I Shot Andy Warhol **1996 (R)** Based on a true story, this black comedy focuses on the 15 minutes of fame achieved by Valerie Solanas, the woman who shot pop artist Andy Warhol for ignoring her in 1968. Taylor manages to recreate the more unpleasant aspects of Solanas without making her completely unsympathetic. Writer/director Harron, making her feature film debut, does a wonderful job of recreating the drugged-out world Warhol and his cohorts inhabited. Her script succeeds by attempting to understand Solanas's actions, while not excusing or sensationalizing them. Features music by former Velvet Underground member, John Cale. **100m/C VHS, DVD.** Lili Taylor, Jared Harris, Stephen Dorff, Martha Plimpton, Donovan Leitch, Tahnee Welch, Michael Imperioli, Lothaire Bluteau, Anna Thomson, Peter Friedman, Jill(ian) Hennessey, Craig Chester, James Lyons, Reginald Rodgers, Jamie Harrold, Edoardo Ballerini, Lynn Cohen, Myriam Cyr, Isabel Gillies, Eric Mabius; ***D:*** Mary Harron; ***W:*** Mary Harron, Daniel Minahan; ***C:*** Ellen Kuras; ***M:*** John Cale.

I Shot Billy the Kid ½ **1950** Billy the Kid decides to turn over a new leaf and live a decent life. The cards are stacked against him though: He's killed a man for nearly every year of his life, and old habits are hard to break. **58m/B VHS, DVD.** Donald (Don "Red") Barry, Robert Lowery, Tom Neal, Jack Perrin; ***D:*** William Berke.

I Shot Jesse James **1949** In his first film, director Fuller breathes characteristically feverish, maddened fire into the story of Bob Ford (Ireland) after he killed the notorious outlaw. An essential moment in Fuller's unique, America-as-tabloid-nightmare canon, and one of the best anti-westerns ever made. **83m/B VHS, DVD.** John Ireland, Barbara Britton, Preston Foster, Reed Hadley; ***D:*** Samuel Fuller; ***W:*** Samuel Fuller.

I Spit on Your Corpse **WOOF!** *Girls for Rent* **1974 (R)** A vicious female hired killer engages in a series of terrorist activities. Stars Spelvin in a non-pornographic role. **90m/C VHS, DVD.** Georgina Spelvin, Susan McIver, Kent Taylor, Rosalind Miles, Preston Pierce, Robert "Bob" Livingston; ***D:*** Al Adamson.

I Spit on Your Grave **WOOF!** *Day of the Woman* **1977 (R)** Woman vacationing at a Connecticut lake house (on the Housatonic River) is brutally attacked and raped by four men. Left for dead, she recovers and seeks revenge. Not to be confused with the 1962 film of the same title, this one is worth zero as a film; lots of violent terror and gory death, totally irresponsibly portrayed. Also available in a 102-minute version. **98m/C VHS, DVD.** Camille Keaton, Eron Tabor, Richard Pace, Anthony Nichols, Gunter Kleeman, Alexis Magnotti; ***D:*** Mier Zarchi; ***W:*** Mier Zarchi; ***C:*** Yuri Haviv.

I Spy **2002 (PG-13)** Bland adaptation of the Robert Culp/Bill Cosby TV series falls short of the cool vibe of the original. Second-banana spy Alex Scott (Wilson) is teamed up with heavyweight boxing champion Kelly Robinson (Murphy) to catch illegal arms dealer Gundars (McDowell), who has stolen a prototype stealth fighter from the U.S. government. Along the way, the duo engage in familiar buddy picture jokiness, and Kelly helps Alex woo mysterious spygirl Rachel (Janssen). Gary Cole is a scene stealer as faux-Spanish superagent Carlos. **96m/C VHS, DVD.** *US* Eddie Murphy, Owen Wilson, Famke Janssen, Malcolm McDowell, Gary Cole, Phill Lewis, Viv Leacock; ***D:*** Betty Thomas; ***W:*** Cormac Wibberley, Marianne S. Wibberley, Jay Scherick, David Ronn; ***C:*** Oliver Wood; ***M:*** Richard Gibbs.

I Stand Alone *Seul contre tous* **1998 (R)** Loud and RE-PUL-SIVE drama has unemployed butcher Chevalier (Nahon) descending into madness at warp speed when he can't find work. The brutal approach Noe takes distracts, rather than intrigues, as the "hero" is such a low-life loser. His hate-filled narration is accompanied by wild camera moves and loud gun-shot booms ending each scene. A 30-second warning plastered before the film's grisly climax is not only unique but warranted when the least of Chevalier's crimes is maliciously kicking his pregnant girlfriend in the stomach. Considered a continuation to Noe's 1991 short feature entitled "Carne." French with English subtitles. **93m/C VHS.** Philippe Nahon, Blandine Lenoir, Frankye Pain, Martine Audrain; ***D:*** Gaspar Noe; ***W:*** Gaspar Noe; ***C:*** Dominique Colin.

I Stand Condemned 1/2 *Moscow Nights* **1936** A Russian officer is tricked into borrowing money from a spy and is condemned for treason. He's saved when a girl who loves him gives herself to a profiteer. Worth seeing only for young Olivier's performance. **90m/B VHS.** *GB* Laurence Olivier, Penelope Dudley Ward, Robert Cochran; ***D:*** Anthony Asquith.

I Still Know What You Did Last Summer **1998 (R)** You know what the real problem with teenagers is? It's not the loud music or the messy room; it's that they can't finish off psycho-killers who show up annually on a major holiday to wield the axe they've been grinding for the rest of the year. Perky survivor Julie James (Hewitt) and new best friend Karla (Brandy) win a vacation in the Bahamas, and take boyfriends Tyrell (Phifer) and Will (Settle) along for some fun in the monsoon. Along with the hurricane, the kids must cope with fish stick guy/killer Ben Willis, who's still pretty cranky. The scares come at such a regular interval, and sometimes with such a lame premise, that the viewer becomes numb to them. The young cast, especially the wet t-shirt adorned Hewitt, help to keep it afloat, however. **100m/C VHS, DVD.** Jack Black, Jennifer Love Hewitt, Freddie Prinze Jr., Brandy Norwood, Mekhi Phifer, Muse Watson, Matthew Sattle, Bill Cobbs, Jeffrey Combs, John Hawkes, Jennifer Esposito; ***D:*** Danny Cannon; ***W:*** Trey Callaway; ***C:*** Vernon Layton; ***M:*** John (Gianni) Frizzell.

I Take This Oath **1940** A cop is shocked to discover that his uncle is a wanted mobster, responsible for the death of a man. Hackneyed plot. **64m/B VHS, DVD.** Gordon Jones, Joyce Compton, Craig Reynolds, J. Farrell MacDonald, Robert E. Homans, Veda Ann Borg; ***D:*** Sam Newfield.

I Take This Woman **1940** Lonely Dr. Karl Decker (Tracy) saves beautiful Georgi Gragore (Lamarr) from a shipboard suicide attempt after Georgi discovers her married lover Phil (Taylor) hasn't divorced his wife (Barrie) as promised. A smitten Decker, who works with the poor, eventually persuades Georgi to marry him and he trades in his clinic work for an uptown practice to support her in style. But Georgi (who possibly sees the older Karl as more father figure than husband material) can't get Phil out of her heart. **98m/B DVD.** Spencer Tracy, Hedy Lamarr, Kent Taylor, Verree Teasdale, Mona Barrie, Laraine Day, Paul Cavanagh, Louis Calhern, Jack Carson, Marjorie Main; ***D:*** W.S. Van Dyke; ***W:*** James Kevin McGuinness; ***C:*** Harold Rosson; ***M:*** Bronislau Kaper, Artur Guttmann.

I, the Jury **1982 (R)** A remake of the 1953 Mike Hammer mystery in which the famed PI investigates the murder of his best friend. Assante mopes around as Hammer and looks out of place in this slowed-down version. **111m/C VHS.** Armand Assante, Barbara Carrera, Laurene Landon, Alan King, Geoffrey Lewis, Paul Sorvino, Jessica James, Leigh Anne Harris, Lynette Harris; ***D:*** Richard T. Heffron; ***W:*** Larry Cohen; ***M:*** Bill Conti.

I, the Worst of All *Yo, la Peor de Todas* **1990** Portrayal of 17th-century Mexican poet, Sister Juana Ines del la Cruz (Serna). She develops a passionate but chaste friendship with Maria Luisa (Sanda), the wife of the Spanish viceroy in Mexico, and writes love poems to her. However, the newly appointed archbishop (Murua) is a religious fanatic who condemns Juana's work, burns her books, and proceeds to persecute her. Adapted from the novel, "The Traps of Faith," by Octavio Paz. Spanish with subtitles. **105m/C VHS, DVD.** *SP* Assumpta Serna, Dominique Sanda, Lautaro Murua, Hector Alterio; ***D:*** Maria-Luisa Bemberg; ***W:*** Maria-Luisa Bemberg, Antonio Larreta; ***C:*** Felix Monti; ***M:*** Luis Maria Serra.

I Think I Do **1997** Gay Bob (Arquette) has always had an unrequited crush on college roomie, Brendan (Maelen). Five years after graduation, the duo meet up at the wedding of mutual friends, Carol (Velez) and Matt (Harrold). Bob's brought along his boyfriend, Sterling (Watkins), and doesn't know that Brendan has come out and is anticipating their reunion. It seems no one's sure about any of their romantic entanglements and someone's bound to be disappointed. **92m/C VHS, DVD.** Alexis Arquette, Christian Maelen, Maddie Corman, Guillermo Diaz, Lauren Velez, Jamie Harrold, Marianne Hagan, Tuc Watkins, Marni Nixon, Dechen Thurman; ***D:*** Brian Sloan; ***W:*** Brian Sloan; ***C:*** Milton Kam; ***M:*** Gerry Gershman.

I Think I Love My Wife **2007 (R)** Redo of Eric Rohmer's 1972 French film "Chloe in the Afternoon." Rock directs and stars as bored, frustrated middle-class hubby Richard Cooper, who's not getting any loving from his beautiful wife Brenda (Torres), leaving him vulnerable to the wanton charms of Nikki (Washington), the ex of an old pal. Richard's conscience won't quite let him actually indulge (all the guilt, none of the pleasure). Rock does manage some humorous takes on modern marriage and Washington is smokin' hot. **94m/C DVD.** *US* Chris Rock, Kerry Washington, Gina Torres, Steve Buscemi, Edward Herrmann, Michael K. Williams, Wendell Pierce, Cassandra Freeman, Welker White; ***D:*** Chris Rock; ***W:*** Chris Rock, Louis CK; ***C:*** William Rexer; ***M:*** Marcus Miller.

I, Vampiri 1/2 *The Devil's Commandment; Lust of the Vampires* **1956** Original vampire film which started the classic Italian horror cycle. A gorgeous Countess needs blood to stay young, otherwise she reverts to a 200-year-old vampire. **81m/B VHS, DVD.** *IT* Gianna Maria Canale, Carlo D'Angelo, Dario Michaelis, Wandisa Guida, Renato Tontini; ***D:*** Riccardo Freda; ***W:*** Riccardo Freda, Piero Regnoli; ***C:*** Mario Bava; ***M:*** Franco Mannino, Roman Vlad.

I Vitelloni 1/2 *The Young and the Passionate; Vitelloni; Spivs* **1953** Fellini's semi-autobiographical drama, argued by some to be his finest work. Five young men grow up in a small Italian town. As they mature, four of them remain in Romini and limit their opportunities by roping themselves off from the rest of the world. The characters are multi-dimensional, including a loafer who is supported by his sister and a young stud who impregnates a local woman. The script has some brilliant insights into youth, adulthood and what's in between. **104m/B VHS, DVD.** *IT* Alberto Sordi, Franco Interlenghi, Franco Fabrizi, Leopoldo Trieste, Riccardo Fellini; ***D:*** Federico Fellini; ***W:*** Federico Fellini, Ennio Flaiano; ***C:*** Carlo Carlini, Otello Martelli; ***M:*** Nino Rota.

I Wake Up Screaming *Hot Spot* **1941** An actress' promoter is accused of her murder. Entertaining mystery with a surprise ending. Remade as "Vicki." **82m/B VHS, DVD.** Betty Grable, Victor Mature, Carole Landis, Laird Cregar, William Gargan, Alan Mowbray, Allyn Joslyn, Elisha Cook Jr., Chick Chandler, Cyril Ring, Morris Ankrum, Charles Lane, May (Mae) Beatty, Frank Orth; ***D:*** H. Bruce Humberstone; ***W:*** Steve Fisher, Dwight Taylor; ***C:*** Edward Cronjager; ***M:*** Cyril Mockridge.

I Walk the Line 1/2 **1970 (PG-13)** Tennessee sheriff Henry Tawes (Peck) is known for his inflexible upholding of the law and his moral character. But even he can't resist the tawdry charms of wild nymphet Alma (Weld), the daughter of local moonshiner Carl McCain (Meeker). Tawes crosses all lines to be with Alma, even leaving his family and ignoring McCain's crimes with tragic consequences. Johnny Cash sings the title track. **95m/C DVD.** Gregory Peck, Tuesday Weld, Ralph Meeker, Estelle Parsons, Charles Durning, Lonny (Lonnie) Chapman; ***D:*** John Frankenheimer; ***W:*** Alvin Sargent; ***C:*** David M. Walsh; ***M:*** Bobby Johnston.

I Walked with a Zombie 1/2 **1943** The definitive and eeriest of the famous Val Lewton/Jacques Tourneur horror films. Dee, a young American nurse, comes to Haiti to care for the catatonic matriarch of a troubled family. Local legends bring themselves to bear when the nurse takes the ill woman to a local voodoo ceremony for "healing." Superb, startling images and atmosphere create a unique context for this serious "Jane Eyre"-like story; its reputation has grown through the years. **69m/B VHS, DVD.** Frances Dee, Tom Conway, James Ellison, Christine Gordon, Edith Barrett, Darby Jones, Sir Lancelot; ***D:*** Jacques Tourneur; ***W:*** Curt Siodmak, Ardel Wray; ***C:*** J. Roy Hunt; ***M:*** Roy Webb.

I Wanna Be a Beauty Queen **1985** Divine hosts the "Alternative Miss World" pageant featuring all sorts of bizarre contestants. **81m/C VHS.** Divine, Nell Campbell, Andrew Logan; ***D:*** Richard Gayer; ***M:*** Peter Logan.

I Wanna Hold Your Hand 1/2 **1978 (PG)** Teenagers try to crash the Beatles' appearance on the Ed Sullivan show. **104m/C VHS, DVD.** Nancy Allen, Bobby DiCicco, Wendie Jo Sperber, Marc McClure, Susan Kendall Newman, Theresa Saldana, Eddie Deezen, William Jordan; ***D:*** Robert Zemeckis; ***W:*** Robert Zemeckis.

I Want Candy **2007 (R)** Juvenile Brit sex comedy. Joe (Riley) and Baggy (Burke) are two struggling film students in Leatherhead, England, who have been working on a feature-length script for their graduation thesis, only to learn they are supposed to film a several-minute short. They decide to flog their script in London but Doug (Marsan) the producer is only interested if they turn it into a porno and cast adult star Candy Fiveways (Electra). The boys manage to get Candy to agree but the only place they have to film is in Joe's parents' house, which makes the sex scenes (including one with a pear) a little awkward. More nudge-nudge, wink-wink than sleazy. **86m/C DVD.** *GB* Tom Riley, Tom Burke, Carmen Electra, Michelle Ryan, Eddie Marsan, Mackenzie Crook, Philip Jackson, John Standing, Felicity Montagu; ***D:*** Stephen Surjik; ***W:*** Peter Hewitt, Phil Hughes; ***C:*** Crighton Bone; ***M:*** Murray Gold.

I Want Someone to Eat Cheese With 1/2 **2006** Garlin adapts his one-man stage show into a full-length movie about overeating comedian James (Garlin), who's trying to find love while still living at home with his mother (Kolb). His best options are a sweet but weird schoolteacher (Hunt) or a possibly crazy ice cream store worker (Silverman). Self-deprecating but sweet, Garlin's debut relies on the improvisation skills of his cast to flesh out a thin but charming story. **80m/C DVD.** *US* Jeff Garlin, Sarah Silverman, Bonnie Hunt, Amy Sedaris, Wallace (Wally) Langham, Joey Slotnick, Richard King, Gina Gershon, Mina Kolb, David Pasquesi; ***D:*** Jeff Garlin; ***W:*** Jeff Garlin; ***C:*** Pete Biagi; ***M:*** Rob Kolson.

I Want to Go Home 1/2 *Je Veux Rentrer a la Maison* **1989** Crass comedy about culture shock and family ties. Cranky Cleveland cartoonist Joey Wellman (Green) agrees to attend an exhibition of his work in Paris in an effort to reunite with his estranged daughter Elsie (Benson), who's studying at the Sorbonne. Elsie is ashamed of her dad but the scholar she's trying to impress, Christian Gauthier (Depardieu), is a big fan of American comic books and is thrilled to befriend Joey, who can't adjust to French culture. Joey's cartoon cat characters pop up in animated thought balloons to offer their own comments. English and French with subtitles. **100m/C DVD.** *FR* Adolph Green, Gerard Depardieu, Linda Lavin, Geraldine Chaplin, Micheline Presle, John Aston, Laura Benson; ***D:*** Alain Resnais; ***W:*** Jules Feiffer; ***C:*** Charlie Van Damme; ***M:*** John Kander.

I Want to Live! **1958** Based on a scandalous true story, Hayward gives a riveting, Oscar-winning performance as a prostitute framed for the murder of an elderly woman and sentenced to death in the gas chamber. Producer Walter Wanger's seething indictment of capital punishment. **120m/B VHS, DVD.** Susan Hayward, Simon Oakland, Theodore Bikel, Virginia Vincent, Wesley Lau; ***D:*** Robert Wise; ***W:*** Nelson Gidding, Don Mankiewicz; ***C:*** Lionel Lindon; ***M:*** Johnny Mandel. Oscars '58: Actress (Hayward); Golden Globes '59: Actress—Drama (Hayward); N.Y. Film Critics '58: Actress (Hayward).

I Want What I Want **1972 (R)** A young Englishman wants a sex-change, lives as a woman, falls in love, complications ensue. Not as shocking to watch as it might seem, but more a melodramatic genderbender. **91m/C VHS.** *GB* Anne Heywood, Harry Andrews, Jill Bennett; ***D:*** John Dexter.

I Want You 1/2 **1951** Small-town life in Greenhill is disturbed for various citizens by the gathering storm of the Korean War. WWII vet Martin Greer (Andrews) is uncertain about re-enlisting while his wife Nancy (McGuire) is totally against the idea. Young Jack (Granger) doesn't want to leave his girl and family while his dad (Keith) tries to instill some patriotic fervor in his son, while George's (Milner) father (Baldwin) doesn't want to let him go. Dated but not unaffecting. **102m/B VHS.** Dana Andrews, Dorothy McGuire, Farley Granger, Peggy Dow, Robert Keith, Mildred Dunnock, Martin Milner, Walter Baldwin, Jim Backus, Ray Collins; ***D:*** Mark Robson; ***W:*** Irwin Shaw; ***C:*** Harry Stradling Sr.; ***M:*** Leigh Harline.

I Want You **1998 (R)** Smokey (Mitevska) and her mute brother Honda (Petrusic) are Central European refugees in the British seaside town of Haven. Honda is shyly entranced by Helen (Weisz), who is trying to deal with her old boyfriend, paroled con Martin (Nivola). Martin becomes increasingly violent towards Helen and Hondo comes to her rescue, but there's more to her relationship with Martin than Helen wants to admit. Winterbottom often flirts with the darker side of human nature and does so again in this rather thinly plotted Brit noir. **87m/C VHS.** *GB* Rachel Weisz, Luka Petrusic, Alessandro Nivola, Labina Mitevska, Ben Daniels, Carmen Ejogo, Graham Crowden, Geraldine O'Rawe, Des McAleer, Phyllida Law, Mary MacLeod; ***D:*** Michael Winterbottom; ***W:*** Eoin McNamee; ***C:*** Slawomir Idziak; ***M:*** Adrian Johnston.

I Was a Communist for the FBI **WOOF!** **1951** Pure paranoid propaganda made when Hollywood was running scared of Joe McCarthy and his communists-under-the-bed witch hunt. Pittsburgh steelworker Matt (Lovejoy) is recruited by the feds to infiltrate his labor union, which is just a Communist front, despite the trouble it causes since his family think he's a pinko. Matt also opens the eyes of naive teacher Dorothy (Merrick), saving her from the evil clutches of red recruiters. Based on a "Saturday Evening Post" article. **82m/B DVD.** Frank Lovejoy, Dorothy Hart, Phil Carey, Richard Webb, James Millican, Paul Picerni; ***D:*** Gordon Douglas; ***W:*** Crane Wilbur; ***C:*** Edwin DuPar.

I Was a Male War Bride **1949** Hilarious WWII comedy. French officer Grant falls in love with and marries WAC lieutenant Sheridan in occupied Europe. Planning to leave the continent and settle down in the U.S., the couple hits a roadblock of red tape and Grant must cross-dress in order to accompany his bride on the troop ship taking her home. Worth watching for Grant's performance alone. Based on the novel by Henri Rochard. **105m/B VHS, DVD.** Cary Grant, Ann Sheridan, Randy Stuart, Kenneth Tobey, William Neff, Marion Marshall; ***D:*** Howard Hawks; ***W:*** Charles Lederer, Leonard Spigelgass, William Neff; ***M:*** Cyril Mockridge.

I Was a Teenage TV Terrorist **WOOF!** *Amateur Hour* **1987** Two teenagers pull on-the-air pranks at the local cable television, blaming it all on an imaginary terrorist group. Poorly acted, cheaply made, and pointless. **85m/C VHS.** Adam Nathan, Julie Hanlon, John MacKay; ***D:*** Stanford Singer; ***W:*** Stanford Singer, Kevin McDonough; ***C:*** Lisa Rinzler; ***M:*** Cengiz Yaltkaya.

I Was a Teenage Werewolf 1/2 **1957** "Rebel Without a Cause" meets "The Curse of the Werewolf" in this drive-in rock 'n' roll horror. Troubled teen Tony (Landon in his first film appearance) suffers from teen angst and low production values, falling victim to shrink Dr. Brandon (Bissell). The doc's been exploring hypnosis and regression therapy that, when practiced on Tony, turn him positively prehistoric. Misconstrued and full of terrible longings, the hairy highschooler goes on a rampage despite the loyal love of girfriend Arlene (Lime). Directorial debut of Fowler. **70m/B VHS.** Michael Landon, Yvonne Lime, Whit Bissell, Tony Marshall, Dawn Richard, Barney (Bernard) Phillips, Ken Miller, Cindy Robbins, Michael Rougas, Robert E. (Bob) Griffin, Joseph Mell, Malcolm Atterbury, Eddie Marr, Vladimir Sokoloff, Louise Lewis, S. John Launer, Guy Williams, Dorothy Crehan; ***D:*** Gene Fowler Jr.; ***W:*** Aben Kandel; ***C:*** Joseph LaShelle; ***M:*** Paul Dunlap.

I Was a Teenage Zombie **1987** Spoof of high school horror films features a good zombie against a drug-pushing zombie. Forget the story and listen to the music by Los Lobos, the Fleshtones, the Waitresses, Dream Syndicate, and Violent Femmes. **92m/C VHS, DVD.** Michael Rubin, Steve Mc-

Coy, Cassie Madden, Allen Rickman; ***D:*** John E. Michalakis; ***W:*** George Seminara, Steve McCoy; ***C:*** Peter Lewnes; ***M:*** Jonathan Roberts, Craig Seeman.

I Was a Zombie for the FBI 🦴 1/2 **1982** Intelligence agency toughens its hiring criteria. Much McCarthyian mirth. **105m/B VHS, DVD.** James Raspberry, Larry Raspberry, John Gillick, Christina Wellford, Anthony Isbell, Laurence Hall, Rick Crowe; ***D:*** Maurice Penczner; ***W:*** Maurice Penczner, John Gillick; ***C:*** Rick Dupree.

I Was an American Spy 🦴🦴 1/2 **1951** Entertainer Claire Phillips (Dvorak) becomes a spy during the Japanese occupation of Manila after her American soldier husband is killed. She opens a nightclub to get info that she passes on to guerilla fighter Boone (Evans) but is eventually caught and imprisoned. Can she be rescued before her scheduled execution? Based on a true story. **84m/B DVD.** Ann Dvorak, Douglas Kennedy, Gene Evans, Richard Loo, Philip Ahn; ***D:*** Lesley Selnder; ***W:*** Samuel Roeca; ***C:*** Harry Neumann; ***M:*** Edward Kay.

I Was Born But... 🦴🦴🦴 *Umarete Wa Mita Keredo* **1932** Two young brothers (Sugahara and Tokkankozo) are the leaders of the neighborhood gang of kids. Their office clerk father (Saito), who is trying to advance his position by playing up to the boss, insists the boys accompany him to his boss' house for a visit. The sons are embarassed by their father's ingratiating behavior, especially when they realize that the boss' son is a minor member of their gang. In retaliation, the brothers decide to go on a hunger strike. Charming social satire. Japanese with subtitles. **89m/B VHS.** *JP* Tatsuo Saito, Hideo Sugahara, Tokkankozo, Mitsuko Yoshikawa, Takeshi Sakamoto; ***D:*** Yasujiro Ozu; ***W:*** Akira Fushimi, Geibei Ibushiya; ***C:*** Hideo Shigehara.

I Was Framed 🦴 1/2 **1942** Newspaperman Ken Marshall (Ames) has the goods on a crooked politician running for governor, but before he can print the story, he's knocked unconscious and placed behind the wheel of a car, which is then sent speeding down a road to collide with another car—killing three people. Marshall is sent to jail, but escapes and assumes a new identity for several years until a former prison cellmate shows up and attempts to blackmail him. **61m/B DVD.** Tod Andrews, Julie Bishop, Regis Toomey, John Harmon; ***D:*** David Ross Lederman; ***W:*** Jerome Odlum; ***C:*** Ted D. McCord.

I Was Nineteen 🦴🦴 *Ich War Neunzehn* **1968** Gregor Hecker left Germany with his parents as a eight-year-old. Now, at the end of WWII, he's returning at 19 in the uniform of a Russian Lieutenant and isn't sure of his identity anymore. Based on the diary kept by German filmmaker Wolf when he was in the Russian Army. German with subtitles. **115m/B VHS.** *GE* Jaecki Schwarz, Wassili Liwanow, Alexej Ejboshenko; ***D:*** Konrad Wolf.

I Went Down 🦴🦴🦴 **1997 (R)** The title of this dark comedy about Irish gangsters has many meanings, including a quote from Plato. Not too many caper movies can boast of a plug from the father of Western philosophy, but luckily director Breathnach and writer McPherson don't take anything too seriously. Their heroes are hapless Git (McDonald) and hair-trigger Bunny (Gleeson), a duo who show you what Laurel and Hardy might look like if they were cast as the hit men in "Pulp Fiction." Ordered by big boss Tom French (Doyle) to bring in Frank Grogan (Caffrey), a man who swindled him out of big bucks and also slept with his wife, they fumble through bad directions and a missed meeting with a sinister fellow called "The Friendly Face," but manage to nab Grogan anyway. The two then attempt to deliver the extremely gabby Grogan to French, leading to a showdown between all four men. More character and dialogue driven than action oriented, this went down as the highest grossing independent Irish film after its theatrical release. **105m/C VHS.** *IR GB* Brendan Gleeson, Peter McDonald, Tony Doyle, Peter Caffrey, Donal O'Kelly, Antoine Byrne; ***D:*** Paddy Breathnach; ***W:*** Conor McPherson; ***C:*** Cian de Buitlear; ***M:*** Dario Marianelli.

I Will Fight No More Forever 🦴🦴🦴 **1975** A vivid recounting of the epic true story of the legendary Chief Joseph who led the Nez Perce tribe on a 1600-mile trek to Canada in 1877. Disturbing and powerful. **100m/C VHS, DVD.** James Whitmore, Ned Romero, Sam Elliott; ***D:*** Richard T. Heffron. **TV**

I Will, I Will for Now 🦴🦴 **1976 (R)** Tacky sex clinic comedy with Keaton and Gould trying to save their marriage through kinky therapy. **109m/C VHS.** Diane Keaton, Elliott Gould, Paul Sorvino, Victoria Principal, Robert Alda, Warren Bellinger; ***D:*** Norman Panama; ***W:*** Norman Panama; ***C:*** John A. Alonzo.

I Witness 🦴🦴 **2003 (R)** Greed and corruption lead to a single culprit in three separate crimes: 27 people are found dead in a collapsed tunnel at a Mexican border town, two American college boys on holiday go missing and are later found murdered, and human rights observer James (Daniels) is monitoring a union election taking place at a chemical plant owned by a multinational corporation. Spader is typecast as an oily rep who keeps those third-world wheels greased and turning for the sake of the American economy. **95m/C DVD.** Jeff Daniels, James Spader, Portia de Rossi, Clifton (Gonzalez) Collins Jr., Wade Andrew Williams, Jordi Caballero; ***D:*** Rowdy Herrington; ***W:*** Colin Greene, Robert Ozn; ***C:*** Michael G. Wojciechowski; ***M:*** David Kitay.

I Wonder Who's Killing Her Now? 🦴🦴 *Kill My Wife... Please!* **1976 (PG)** Scuzzy husband pays to have his wife murdered for the insurance money, then changes his mind. On-again, off-again comedy. **87m/C VHS, DVD.** Bob (Robert) Dishy, Joanna Barnes, Bill Dana, Vito Scotti, Severn Darden, Harvey Jason, Richard Libertini, Noriyuki "Pat" Morita; ***D:*** Steven Hilliard Stern; ***W:*** Mickey Rose; ***C:*** Richard H. Kline; ***M:*** Patrick Williams.

I Wouldn't Be in Your Shoes 🦴 1/2 **1948** Down-and-out dance duo Tom (Castle) and Ann (Knox) find some much-needed money—but it gets them into a heap of trouble when they're simultaneously found with the cash and a local recluse is found dead—with prints from Tom's dancing shoes near the murder scene. It looks like an open-and-shut case, but Ann has to unravel the mystery before Tom's execution date. **70m/B DVD.** Don Castle, Elyse Knox, Regis Toomey, Charles D. Brown; ***D:*** William Nigh; ***W:*** Cornell Woolrich, Steve Fisher; ***C:*** Mack Stengler; ***M:*** Edward Kay.

Ibiza Dream 🦴🦴 *El Sueno de Ibiza* **2002** The island of Ibiza has the rep of being a party-time vacation resort but in this case the dreams of three friends go unfulfilled. Nacho (Collado) has returned from India determined to open a center for meditation. He enlists his childhood friends Chica (Dominguez), a nurse, and beach bum Cacho (Marin) to help him out, hoping it will strengthen their friendship. The center opens but the friends find themselves further apart than ever. Spanish with subtitles. **98m/C VHS, DVD.** *SP* Paco Marin, Adriana Dominguez, Adria Collado; ***D:*** Igor Fioravanti; ***W:*** Igor Fioravanti; ***C:*** Miguel Leal; ***M:*** Jose Padilla.

Ice 🦴🦴 1/2 **1993 (R)** Charley and Ellen Reed are thieves whose latest heist is $60 million in diamonds from mob boss Vito Malta. There's trouble when they try to fence the goods and Ellen is left with the merchandise and on the run from Malta's henchmen. **91m/C VHS, DVD.** Traci Lords, Phillip Troy, Zach Galligan, Jorge (George) Rivero, Michael Bailey Smith, Jamie Alba, Jean Pflieger, Floyd Levine; ***D:*** Brook Yeaton; ***W:*** Sean Dash.

Ice Age 🦴🦴🦴 **2002 (PG)** Director Wedge (also the voice of Scrat the squirrel) crafts a smart, sophisticated and touching animated comedy/adventure about a group of prehistoric beasts who find a human baby and then try to restore the tyke to his tribe. During the long march south during an ice age, the cuddly Manfred the Mammoth (Romano) and Sid the Sloth (the already animated Leguizamo) are joined by Diego the scheming Sabertooth Tiger (Leary) whose bond is solidified after the two save Diego's life. Amazing computer-animation technology and artistry are top-notch. Characters are likeable but sometimes spew overly glib dialogue. Although not quite of the same caliber story-wise, this one fits right in with "Shrek," "Monsters, Inc." and "Toy Story." **81m/C VHS, DVD, Blu-ray Disc, UMD.** *US* ***D:*** Chris Wedge; ***W:*** Michael Berg, Michael J. Wilson, Peter Ackerman; ***M:*** David Newman; ***V:*** John Leguizamo, Denis Leary, Ray Romano, Goran Visnjic, Jack Black, Cedric the Entertainer, Stephen (Steve) Root, Tara Strong, Diedrich Bader, Alan Tudyk, Lorri Bagley, Jane Krakowski, Chris Wedge.

Ice Age: Dawn of the Dinosaurs 🦴🦴 1/2 **2009 (PG)** Animated 3-D sequel is content to coast along on the strengths of the previous two films. Anxiety-ridden Manny and fun-loving Ellie are awaiting the birth of their baby mammoth, which causes jealousy in sloth Sid who decides he needs a family of his own. So he adopts three dinosaur eggs but momma T-Rex is none too pleased and leaves her subterranean tropical jungle world to retrieve her offspring—taking Sid back with her. This means the rest of the crew, including saber-toothed tiger Diego who fears he's been domesticated, go on a rescue mission. Underground, they meet swashbuckling (and crazy) one-eyed weasel Buck and his albino dino nemesis. Meanwhile, squirrel/rat Scrat must guard his beloved acorn from a flirtatious rival, Scratte. **94m/C DVD.** *US* John Leguizamo; ***D:*** Carlos Saldanha; ***W:*** Michael Berg, Peter Ackerman, Mike Reiss, Yoni Brenner; ***M:*** John Powell; ***V:*** Ray Romano, Queen Latifah, Denis Leary, Chris Wedge, Simon Pegg, Seann William Scott, Josh Peck, Bill Hader.

Ice Age: The Meltdown 🦴🦴 1/2 **2006 (PG)** Okay, so global warming gets its licks in but this is hardly an environmental diatribe. Anyway, the glaciers are melting, the water is rising, and the animals are on the move to higher, drier ground. Manny (Romano) believes he's the last wooly mammoth left until he meets flirty Ellie (Queen Latifah), who thinks she's actually a possum like her two foster brothers (Scott & Peck). Fast-talking Sid (Leguizamo) and grumpy Diego (Leary) are part of the mix as is acorn-chasing, scene-stealing Scrat. The animation still rocks even if the adventures are a mild retread. **90m/C DVD, Blu-ray Disc.** *US* ***D:*** Carlos Saldanha; ***W:*** Peter Gaulke, Gerry Swallow, Jim Hecht; ***C:*** Harry Hitner; ***M:*** John Powell; ***V:*** Ray Romano, John Leguizamo, Denis Leary, Seann William Scott, Josh Peck, Queen Latifah, Will Arnett, Jay Leno, Joseph Bologna, Renee Taylor, Stephen (Steve) Root, Mindy Sterling, Alan Tudyk, Clea Lewis.

Ice Castles 🦴🦴 **1979 (PG)** A young figure skater's Olympic dreams are dimmed when she is blinded in an accident, but her boyfriend gives her the strength, encouragement, and love necessary to perform a small miracle. Way too schmaltzy. **110m/C VHS, DVD.** Robby Benson, Lynn-Holly Johnson, Tom Skerritt, Colleen Dewhurst, Jennifer Warren, David Huffman; ***D:*** Donald Wrye; ***W:*** Donald Wrye, Gary L. Bain; ***C:*** Bill Butler; ***M:*** Marvin Hamlisch.

Ice Cream Man 🦴 **1995 (R)** Quite disgusting horror tale of a dweeby, demented ice cream man who delivers gore and death along with his frozen treats. **96m/C VHS, DVD.** Clint Howard, Sandahl Bergman, Olivia Hussey, Lee Majors II, David Naughton, Jan-Michael Vincent, David Warner, Steve Garvey; ***D:*** Norman Apstein.

The Ice Flood 🦴🦴 **1926** Silent family type comedy of a son who proves to the old man that he wrote the book on life, wagering the successful supervision of dad's lumberjacks. **63m/B VHS.** Kenneth Harlan, Viola Dana; ***D:*** George B. Seitz.

Ice Follies of 1939 🦴🦴 **1939** The marriage of skating team Mary (Crawford) and Larry (Stewart) is in trouble when she gets a Hollywood film contract and he can't make it on his own. Egged on by Mary, producer Tolliver (Stone) offers Larry the chance to produce an ice revue extravaganza. The only highlight (besides watching Crawford) is the finale—a Technicolor Cinderella fantasy performed by the International Ice Follies. **82m/B DVD.** Joan Crawford, James Stewart, Lewis Stone, Lionel Stander, Lew Ayres; ***D:*** Reinhold Schunzel; ***W:*** Florence Ryerson, Edgar Allen Woolf, Leonard Praskins; ***C:*** Joseph Ruttenberg, Oliver Marsh; ***M:*** Roger Edens.

The Ice Harvest 🦴🦴 1/2 **2005 (R)** It's Christmas Eve in Wichita, and mob lawyer Charlie (Cusack) still has a pretty long to-do list. But things got complicated when he and his partner Vic (Thornton) skimmed $2.2 million from crime lord Bill Guerrard (Quaid). Now, in the midst of an ice storm, Charlie has to dodge Bill's hit man Roy (Starr), withstand the dangerous charms of topless bar manager/femme fatale Renata (Nielson), baby-sit his drunken brother-in-law Pete (a hilariously over-the-top Platt), and finish his shopping. A lovely bit of screwball comedic film noir, but with a director like Ramis, things should have been funnier. **88m/C DVD.** *US* John Cusack, Billy Bob Thornton, Connie Nielsen, Randy Quaid, Oliver Platt; ***D:*** Harold Ramis; ***W:*** Richard Russo, Robert Benton; ***C:*** Alar Kivilo; ***M:*** David Kitay.

Ice House 🦴🦴 **1989** A sophisticated young lady flees Texas for Hollywood, searching for a better life. When her ex-lover shows up and wants her to go back, the lackless turmoil begins. Pairs real-life couple Gilbert and Brinkman. **81m/C VHS.** Melissa Gilbert, Bo Brinkman, Andreas Manolikakis, Buddy Quaid; ***D:*** Bo Brinkman, Eagle Pennell; ***W:*** Bo Brinkman.

The Ice House 🦴🦴🦴 **1997** Chilling TV adaptation of Minette Walters' first mystery. Ten years ago Phoebe Maybury's (Downie) abusive husband David disappeared. Locally condemned as a murderess, she and her friends Diana (Barber) and Anne (Aldridge) have been shunned by their small-minded community. Now a body has been discovered in an ice house located on Maybury property. Is it David? Inspector Walsh (Redgrave), who couldn't prove anything against Phoebe before, certainly thinks so, but his on-the-edge associate Sgt. McLoughlin (Craig) isn't so certain. **180m/C VHS, DVD.** *GB* Daniel Craig, Penny Downie, Corin Redgrave, Kitty Aldridge, Frances Barber; ***D:*** Tim Fywell; ***W:*** Elizabeth (Lizzie) Mickery.

Ice Men 🦴🦴 **2004** Uptight Vaughn (Cummins) decides to throw a birthday party for buddy Bryan (Hewlett) at the lakeside cabin he's inherited. He also invites Jon (Spottiswood) and Steve (Thomas) for a weekend of hunting and drinking. Unfortunately, there's some uninvited guests as well: Vaughn's drunken black sheep brother Trevor (Tracey) and his ex-girlfriend Renee (Ledford), who both cause problems. Some sexual shenanigans and revealed secrets don't make for relaxation either, although the plot tends to meander. **108m/C DVD.** *CA* Martin Cummins, David Hewlett, Greg Spottiswood, Ian Tracey, James Thomas, Brandy Ledford; ***D:*** Thom Best; ***W:*** Michael Lewis MacLennan; ***C:*** Gavin Smith; ***M:*** Michael Shields, Russell Broom.

Ice Palace 🦴🦴 **1960** Two rugged adventurers maintain a lifelong rivalry in the primitive Alaskan wilderness, their relationship dramatizing the development of the 49th state. Silly but entertaining. Based on Edna Ferber's novel. **143m/C VHS.** Richard Burton, Robert Ryan, Carolyn Jones, Shirley Knight, Martha Hyer, Jim Backus, George Takei; ***D:*** Vincent Sherman; ***C:*** Joseph Biroc; ***M:*** Max Steiner.

Ice Pawn 🦴🦴 **1992** Alex Dalton may finally get to realize his dream of becoming a gold medal ice skater if he can beat Misha, his Russian rival. He soon finds out that Misha isn't his only problem, as he unknowingly becomes a pawn in a game of corruption and greed that could totally ruin his career. **102m/C VHS.** Paul Cross, Dan Haggerty, Robert Budaska, Chris Thomas; ***D:*** Barry Samson; ***W:*** Paul Cross.

Ice Pirates 🦴 1/2 **1984 (PG)** Space pirates in the far future steal blocks of ice to fill the needs of a thirsty galaxy. Cool plot has its moments. **91m/C VHS, DVD.** Robert Urich, Mary Crosby, Michael D. Roberts, John Matuszak, Anjelica Huston, Ron Perlman, John Carradine, Robert Symonds; ***D:*** Stewart Raffill; ***W:*** Stewart Raffill; ***M:*** Bruce Broughton.

Ice Princess 🦴🦴 1/2 **2005 (G)** Casey Carlyle (Trachtenberg) is a high school science whiz kid who needs a stellar science project to get into Harvard. She decides to analyze the science of figure skating by observing a bunch of local elite skaters at a nearby rink. Casey is not satisfied with simply observing, so she straps on a pair of skates and starts taking lessons. She soon realizes that she has a natural talent for it, but her feminist mother (Joan Cusack) disapproves.

While the movie holds no surprises, it's still enjoyable for the target audience. Go figure. **92m/C VHS, DVD.** *US* Michelle Trachtenberg, Joan Cusack, Kim Cattrall, Hayden Panettiere, Trevor Blumas, Kirsten Olson, Connie Ray, Juliana Cannarozzo; ***Cameos:*** Brian Boitano, Michelle Kwan; ***D:*** Tim Fywell; ***W:*** Hadley Davis, Meg Cabot; ***C:*** David Hennings; ***M:*** Christophe Beck.

The Ice Rink ✐✐ *La Patinoire* **1999** A director (Novembre) decides to make a movie about the romance between a French ice skater (Chaplin) and an American hockey player (Campbell) that is to be filmed on an ice skating rink. However, most of the cast and crew can't skate, the ice keeps melting, the supporting hockey players are Lithuanian and don't speak French, the two leads are having a torrid (and disruptive) affair, and that's just the beginning. A generally playful look at the tribulations of making a movie. French with subtitles. **80m/C VHS, DVD.** *FR* Tom Novembre, Marie-France Pisier, Bruce Campbell, Dolores Chaplin, Mireille Perrier, Jean-Pierre Cassel; ***D:*** Jean-Philippe Toussaint; ***W:*** Jean-Philippe Toussaint; ***C:*** Jean-Francois Robin.

The Ice Runner ✐✐ 1/2 **1993 (R)** Low-key Cold War thriller, filmed in 1991, about a U.S. spy who escapes from the Soviet gulag. Jeffrey West (Albert) gets caught in a botched payoff to a Soviet minister and when the diplomats wash their hands of him a rigged trial has West sentenced to 12 years hard labor. A convenient train wreck lets him assume a different prisoner's name which gets him to a minimum security camp under the eyes of a suspicious commander. Now West needs to escape and cross 39 miles of icy tundra separating his Russian prison from American freedom. **116m/C VHS, DVD.** Edward Albert, Eugene (Yevgeny) Lazarev, Olga Kabo, Victor Wong, Alexander Kuznitsov, Basil Hoffman, Bill Bordy, Sergei Ruban; ***D:*** Barry Samson; ***W:*** Joyce Warren, Clifford Coleman, Joshua Stallings.

Ice Spiders ✐✐ 1/2 **2007 (R)** Pure camp and gore from the Sci-Fi Channel. Olympic ski hopefuls head to a remote resort in Utah where Dash (Muldoon) is the head instructor. He has the hots for Dr. April (Williams), who works at a secret government lab where they're doing military experiments on gigantic spiders with ravenous appetites who get loose and don't mind the cold as they go looking for their next meal. **86m/C DVD.** Patrick Muldoon, Vanessa Williams, Thomas Calabro, Stephen J. Cannell, David Millbern, Noah Bastien, Carleigh King; ***D:*** Tibor Takacs; ***W:*** Eric Miller; ***C:*** Barry Gravelle. **CABLE**

Ice Station Zebra ✐✐ 1/2 **1968 (G)** A nuclear submarine races Soviet seamen to find a downed Russian satellite under a polar ice cap. Suspenseful Cold War adventure based on the novel by Alistair MacLean. **148m/C VHS, DVD.** Rock Hudson, Ernest Borgnine, Patrick McGoohan, Jim Brown, Lloyd Nolan, Tony Bill; ***D:*** John Sturges; ***W:*** Douglas Heyes, W.R. Burnett; ***C:*** Daniel F. Fapp; ***M:*** Michel Legrand.

The Ice Storm ✐✐✐ 1/2 **1997 (R)** Excellent family drama/period piece (the 1970s!) directed by Ang Lee and based on the book by Rick Moody. Kline plays a husband and father too self-absorbed to notice his marriage (to Allen) unraveling into crisis, and his children (Maguire and Ricci) mimicking the sordid behavior that surrounds them. Skillfully fuses together a frank, unsympathetic look at family psychology, while also making a comment on the social situation of the early 1970s. Flirts with being overpoweringly negative and moody, but is elevated by Lee's insight and direction. Excellent job by the entire cast, especially Weaver, frighteningly dead-on as an emotionally reckless wife and mother, and Hann-Byrd and Wood as her eerie sons. **113m/C VHS, DVD.** Kevin Kline, Sigourney Weaver, Joan Allen, Christina Ricci, Tobey Maguire, Elijah Wood, Katie Holmes, Henry Czerny, Adam Hann-Byrd, David Krumholtz, Jamey Sheridan, Maia Danziger, Kate Burton, John Benjamin Hickey, Allison Janney, Byron Jennings; ***D:*** Ang Lee; ***W:*** James Schamus; ***C:*** Frederick Elmes; ***M:*** Mychael Danna. British Acad. '97: Support. Actress (Weaver).

L'Iceberg ✐ 1/2 *The Iceberg* **2005** Slight comedy features much physical humor, little dialogue, and is overly cute. Manager Fiona gets locked in the restaurant's walk-in freezer. Barely alive when she's rescued the next day, Fiona returns home to discover her husband and children didn't even notice her missing. She develops an obsession with everything frozen and cold, so she hides out in a frozen food delivery truck and leaves to make a new home for herself on an iceberg. French with subtitles. **84m/C DVD.** *BE* Fiona Gordon, Dominique Abel, Bruno Romy, Philippe Martz; ***D:*** Fiona Gordon, Dominique Abel, Bruno Romy; ***W:*** Fiona Gordon, Dominique Abel, Bruno Romy; ***C:*** Sebastien Koeppel; ***M:*** Jacques Luley.

Icebox Murders **WOOF!** **1982** A crazed, motiveless, faceless killer hangs his victims in a walk-in freezer. Store this one. **90m/C VHS.** *SP* Jack Taylor, Mirta Miller; ***D:*** Francisco Rodriguez Gordillo; ***W:*** Francisco Prosper; ***C:*** R(aul) P. Cubero; ***M:*** Gregorio Garcia Segura.

Iced ✐ **1988** Wild fun turns to horror on a ski trip as a group of college friends are hunted by a maniac on the loose. It's all downhill. **86m/C VHS.** Debra Deliso, Doug Stevenson, Ron Kologie, Elizabeth Gorcey, Alan Johnson; ***D:*** Jeff Kwitny.

Iceland ✐✐ **1942** Labored romance of an Iceland girl and a Marine with plenty of skating thrown in for good measure. Skating and singing interludes are the best part of an otherwise average film. ♫You Can't Say No to a Soldier; There Will Never Be Another You; Lover's Knot; Let's Bring New Glory to Old Glory; I Like a Military Tune. **79m/B VHS.** Sonja Henie, John Payne, Jack Oakie, Felix Bressart, Osa Massen, Fritz Feld; ***D:*** H. Bruce Humberstone; ***W:*** Robert Ellis, Helen Logan.

Iceman ✐✐✐ **1984 (PG)** A frozen prehistoric man is brought back to life, after which severe culture shock takes hold. Underwritten but nicely acted, especially by Lone as the primal man. **101m/C VHS, DVD.** *CA* Timothy Hutton, Lindsay Crouse, John Lone, David Strathairn, Josef Sommer, Danny Glover; ***D:*** Fred Schepisi; ***W:*** Chip Proser; ***C:*** Ian Baker; ***M:*** Bruce Smeaton.

The Iceman Cometh ✐✐✐ **1960** A recording of CBS' live version (flubs and all) of Eugene O'Neill's searing drama. Traveling salesman Hickey (Robards) comes to visit his old pals, the no-hopers who populate Harry Hope's (Pelly) Greenwich Village saloon, circa 1912. But something's changed about the glad-handing Hickey as he seeks to strip the bar's denizens of all their so-called pipe dreams. This is the role that made Robards a star in a 1956 off-Broadway revival; he would eventually embody many of O'Neill's characters. Originally shown in kinescope. **210m/B DVD.** Jason Robards Jr., Myron McCormick, Tom Pedi, James Broderick, Robert Redford, Ronald Radd, Roland Winters, Michael Strong, Sorrell Booke, Hilda Brawner, Julie Bovasso, Joan Copeland, Farrell Pelly, Harrison Dowd; ***D:*** Sidney Lumet. **TV**

The Iceman Cometh ✐✐ 1/2 **1973** American Film Theater version of the Eugene O'Neill play with Marvin starring as salesman Hickey, who's found an unsettling peace of mind after—it's slowly revealed to the drunks of Harry Hope's bar—committing a terrible crime. However, it's Ryan who steals the picture as former anarchist Larry, a man simply waiting to die. Ryan was ill with terminal cancer, as was March (who plays Harry Hope); this would be the last appearance for both men. **239m/C DVD.** Lee Marvin, Fredric March, Robert Ryan, Jeff Bridges, Martyn Green, George Voskovec, Moses Gunn, Tom Pedi, Evans Evans, Bradford Dillman, Sorrell Booke, John McLiam, Hildy Brooks, Clifton James; ***D:*** John Frankenheimer; ***W:*** Thomas Quinn Curtiss; ***C:*** Ralph Woolsey.

Ichi the Killer ✐✐ *Koroshiya Ichi* **2001** Based on the comic of the same name, this film centers around Kakihara, a sadistic yakuza killer in Shinjuku. His boss Anjo has disappeared, so Kakihara kidnaps a rival boss to torture the information of Anjo's whereabouts from him. A hostess from a club later informs him that his boss is dead, slain by a mysterious superhuman killer known only as Ichi. Unable to find the pain he craves (Kakihara is also a masochist) that he used to get from his boss, Kakihara sets out to find the murderer in a quest to assuage his needs, and find out why Anjo was killed. Director Takashi Miike is known for over the top films, and Ichi is truly one of those. **128m/C DVD.** *JP* Tadanobu Asano, Shinya Tsukamoto, Paulyn Sun, Susumu Terajima, Shun Sugata, Jun Kunimura, Nao Omori, Toru Tezuka, Yoshiki Arizano, Kiyohiko Shibukawa, Satoshi Nizuma, Suzuki Matsuo, Hiroyuki Tanaka, Moro Morooka, Houka Kinoshita, Hirohoshi Kobayashi, Mai Goto, Rio Aoki, Yuki Kazamatsuri; ***D:*** Takashi Miike; ***W:*** Hideo Yamamoto, Sakichi Sato; ***C:*** Hideo Yamamoto; ***M:*** Seiichi Yamamoto, Karera Musication.

The Icicle Thief ✐✐✐ *Ladri di Saponette* **1989** "The Naked Gun" for the art-house crowd. As a stark, black-and-white neo-realist tragedy airs on TV, bright color commercials disrupt the narrative. Soon ads invade the the movie itself, and the film's director jumps into his picture to fix the damage. Study up on your postwar Italian cinema and this'll seem hilarious; otherwise the real fun doesn't kick in until the halfway point. In Italian with English subtitles. **93m/C VHS.** *IT* Maurizio Nichetti, Cateria Sylos Labini, Claudio G. Fava, Renato Scarpa, Heidi Komarek; ***D:*** Maurizio Nichetti; ***W:*** Maurizio Nichetti; ***C:*** Mario Battistoni; ***M:*** Manuel De Sica.

Icy Breasts ✐✐✐ **1975** A French psychiatrist tries to prevent his beautiful but psychotic patient from continuing her murdering spree. Dubbed. **105m/C VHS, DVD.** *FR* Alain Delon, Mireille Darc; ***D:*** Georges Lautner.

I'd Climb the Highest Mountain ✐✐✐ **1951** Sincere, sentimental piece of Americana about a country preacher (Lundigan) and his city wife (Hayward) as they adjust to life in a small town in Southern hill country. Filmed on location in Georgia. Film was a big hit, especially in the South. Based on the novel by Corra Harris. **88m/C VHS.** Susan Hayward, William Lundigan, Rory Calhoun, Gene Lockhart, Ruth Donnelly, Barbara Bates, Lynn Bari, Alexander Knox; ***D:*** Henry King; ***W:*** Lamar Trotti.

I'd Give My Life ✐ 1/2 **1936** A gangster's ex-wife is presently married to the governor. He tries to use their honest but framed son to blackmail her. **73m/B VHS.** Guy Standing, Frances Drake, Tom Brown, Janet Beecher; ***D:*** Edwin L. Marin.

Idaho ✐ 1/2 **1943** On a mission to close down houses of ill repute, Rodgers teams up with Autry's old sidekick Burnette. **70m/B VHS, DVD.** Roy Rogers, Harry Shannon, Virginia Grey, Smiley Burnette, Ona Munson; ***D:*** Joseph Kane.

Idaho Transfer **WOOF!** *Deranged* **1973 (PG)** Fonda's second directorial effort; Carradine's first screen appearance. An obnoxious group of teens travel through time to Idaho in the year 2044. Environmental wasteland story is dull and confused. **90m/C VHS, DVD.** Keith Carradine, Kelley Bohanan; ***D:*** Peter Fonda.

An Ideal Husband ✐✐ 1/2 **1947** Adventuress Laura Cheveley (Goddard) slithers back into the life of former schoolmate Gertrude Chiltern (Wynyard) with the intention of blackmailing her husband Robert (Williams). Robert is a rising politician, known for his honesty, but he committed a financial indiscretion in his youth that Laura is happy to exploit. Elegantly witty version of the Oscar Wilde play; remade in 1999. **96m/C DVD.** *GB* Paulette Goddard, Hugh Williams, Diana Wynyard, Michael Wilding, Sir C. Aubrey Smith, Glynis Johns, Constance Collier; ***D:*** Alexander Korda; ***W:*** Lajos Biro; ***C:*** Georges Perinal; ***M:*** Arthur Benjamin.

An Ideal Husband ✐✐✐ **1999 (PG-13)** Victorian comedy of manners adapted from the play by Oscar Wilde. The very proper Lady Gertrud Chiltern (Blanchett) discovers that her husband, Sir Robert (Northam), a member of Parliament, attained their fortune and power through questionable means. Robert is being blackmailed over a shady business deal by Gertrud's loathed ex-school mate, Laura Cheveley (Moore). Cynical social butterfly, Lord Arthur Goring (Everett), is drawn into the fray because of his friendship with Chiltern. It's rather exaggerated and very witty, as one would expect of Wilde. **96m/C VHS, DVD.** *GB* Cate Blanchett, Jeremy Northam, Minnie Driver, Rupert Everett, Julianne Moore, Jeroen Krabbe, Lindsay Duncan, Peter Vaughan, John Wood, Marsha Fitzalan, Benjamin Pullen; ***D:*** Oliver Parker; ***W:*** Oliver Parker; ***C:*** David C(lark) Johnson; ***M:*** Charlie Mole. Natl. Bd. of Review '99: Support. Actress (Moore).

Identification of a Woman ✐✐ *Identificazione di una Donna* **1982** Niccolo (Milian) is a middle-aged film director who is searching for the perfect female image as the focus for his new movie. But his personal search alienates the flesh-and-blood women already in his life. Lots of visuals give the film a slow, dreamlike quality. Italian with subtitles. **131m/C VHS.** *IT* Tomas Milian, Christine Boisson, Daniela Silverio, Sandra Monteleoni; ***D:*** Michelangelo Antonioni; ***W:*** Michelangelo Antonioni, Gerard Brach; ***C:*** Carlo Di Palma; ***M:*** John Foxx.

Identity ✐✐ 1/2 **2003 (R)** See if this premise sounds familiar—ten strangers, an ex-cop turned chauffeur; his movie star passenger; a family with a wounded wife; a newlywed couple; a cop transporting a prisoner; and an ex-hooker are brought together (because of a severe rainstorm) at a desolate motel run by a creepy clerk. One by one they start to die in various icky and/or disturbing ways. A possibly-connected subplot involves a man on death row getting a last-minute, late-night hearing. Well-executed, if unspectacular, suspenser provides a satisfyingly twisty thrill. **90m/C VHS, DVD, Blu-ray Disc.** *US* John Cusack, Rebecca De Mornay, Ray Liotta, Jake Busey, Amanda Peet, Clea DuVall, William Lee Scott, John C. McGinley, Leila Kenzle, Bret Loehr, John Hawkes, Pruitt Taylor Vince, Alfred Molina, Matt Letscher, Carmen Argenziano, Marshall Bell, Holmes Osborne, Frederick Coffin; ***D:*** James Mangold; ***W:*** Michael Cooney; ***C:*** Phedon Papamichael; ***M:*** Alan Silvestri.

Identity Crisis ✐ **1990 (R)** Campy fashion maven and flamboyant rapper switch identities causing much tedious overacting. Lifeless murder comedy from father and son Van Peebles. **98m/C VHS, DVD.** Mario Van Peebles, Ilan Mitchell-Smith, Nicholas Kepros, Shelly Burch, Richard Clarke; ***D:*** Melvin Van Peebles.

Identity Unknown ✐✐ 1/2 **1945** Shell-shocked veteran goes AWOL to discover who he is, meeting grieving relatives along the way. Interesting premise is sometimes moving. **70m/B VHS, DVD.** Richard Arlen, Cheryl Walker, Roger Pryor, Bobby Driscoll; ***D:*** Walter Colmes.

Idiocracy ✐✐ **2006 (R)** Mike Judge's "Office Space" became a cult hit after being rudely dumped during its studio release, and this satirical flick may obtain the same status. Everyman soldier Joe (Wilson) and hooker Rita (Rudolph) are selected by the Pentagon to take part in a hibernation experiment. Thanks to a snafu, they wake up 500 years later in an America so completely dumbed-down that they are now the smartest couple alive, with Joe given a presidential appointment to turn this mess around. The ultimate "what if" movie, with Wilson at his clueless, curious best. **84m/C DVD.** *US* Luke Wilson, Maya Rudolph, Dax Shepard, Terry Crews, David Herman, Justin Long, Thomas Haden Church, Stephen (Steve) Root; ***D:*** Mike Judge; ***W:*** Mike Judge, Etan Cohen; ***C:*** Tim Suhrstedt; ***M:*** Theodore Shapiro; ***V:*** Earl Mann.

The Idiot ✐✐✐✐ **1951** Dostoevski's Russian novel is transported by Kurosawa across two centuries to post-war Japan, where the madness and jealousy continue to rage. In Japanese with English subtitles. **166m/B VHS.** Toshiro Mifune, Masayuki Mori, Setsuko Hara, Yoshiko Kuga, Takashi Shimura; ***D:*** Akira Kurosawa.

Idiot Box ✐✐ **1997** Crazy youth comedy about lazy, brainless Kev (Mendelsohn) and Mick (Sims) who spend most of their unemployed time watching violent cop shows on TV and drinking beer. It's from the "idiot box" that the dim duo get the idea that they've learned enough to rob a bank, but it just so happens that a pair of crooks, who wear clown masks, are already on a bank crime spree. Naturally, both sets of robbers choose the same bank as their target and the cops just happen to be waiting. **83m/C VHS, DVD.** *AU* Ben Mendelsohn, Jeremy Sims, John Polson, Robyn Loau, Graeme Blundell, Deborah Kennedy, Stephen Rae, Andrew S. Gilbert, Amanda Muggleton, Paul Gleeson, Susie Porter;

D: David Caesar; *W:* David Caesar; *C:* Joseph Pickering; *M:* Tim Rogers, Nick Launay.

The Idiots *Idioterne* **1999 (R)** Von Trier uses the stripped back camerawork of Dogma 95 to tell an annoying, pointless story involving a commune-like group of middle-class drop-outs around Copenhagen who spend their time deliberately acting like idiots in public places. They're trying to get in touch with their wounded inner child while you'll want to slap some sense into them. Film provoked controversy because of a group sex scene that (at least) borders on porn. Danish with subtitles. **115m/C VHS, DVD.** *DK* Bodil Jorgensen, Jens Albinus, Louise Hassing, Troels Lyby, Nikolaj Lie Kaas, Henrik Prip, Luis Mesonero, Louise Mieritz, Knud Romer Jorgensen, Trine Michelsen; *D:* Lars von Trier; *W:* Lars von Trier; *C:* Lars von Trier.

Idiot's Delight **1939** At an Alpine hotel, a song and dance man meets a gorgeous Russian countess who reminds him of a former lover. Incredibly, Gable sings and dances through "Puttin' on the Ritz," the film's big highlight. Based on the Pulitzer Prize-winning play by Robert Sherwood. **107m/B VHS.** Clark Gable, Norma Shearer, Burgess Meredith, Edward Arnold, Charles Coburn, Joseph Schildkraut; *D:* Clarence Brown; *C:* William H. Daniels.

Idle Hands 1/2 **1999 (R)** Pothead slacker Anton (Sawa) finds that his very idle hand is possessed by a demon, making him do things he doesn't want to do, like get up off the couch and kill his friends Mick (Green) and Pnub (Henson). When Anton cuts off the offending appendage, it's free to terroroze his girlfriend Molly (Alba). With the help of a Druid priestess (Fox) and his now undead friends, Anton must stop the hand from taking Molly's soul to Hell. Even if the release hadn't coincided with the Littleton tragedy, this tasteless horror-comedy wouldn't be funny. Relentless overacting tries to cover up for a lame script filled with pot jokes and gory high school slasher conventions. Green and Henson are the only bright spots. **90m/C VHS, DVD.** Devon Sawa, Seth Green, Elden (Ratliff) Henson, Jessica Alba, Christopher Hart, Vivica A. Fox, Jack Noseworthy, Sean M. Whalen, Nicholas Sadler, Fred Willard, Katie Wright, Connie Ray; *D:* Rodman Flender; *W:* Terri Hughes, Ron Milbauer; *C:* Christopher Baffa; *M:* Graeme Revell.

Idlewild **2006 (R)** OutKast bandmates star in a genre-bending tale of two buddies in 1930s Georgia, creating an anachronistic but entertaining jumble of eye- and ear-candy. Percival (Benjamin), a mortician by day, reserved piano player by night, and Rooster (Patton), a club-owning family man and musician in his own right, escape their ho-hum lives at Church, a lively speakeasy that encapsulates the flick's mash-up of jazz-era nostalgia with a contemporary vibe. Soon love and murder and lots of stars making cameos come to town for a mix of lavish production numbers and murder. It's all as gutsy and confusing as it sounds. **120m/C DVD.** *US* Andre Benjamin, Antwan Andre Patton, Paula Patton, Terrence Howard, Malinda Williams, Macy Gray, Ben Vereen, Ving Rhames, Faizon Love; *D:* Bryan Barber; *W:* Bryan Barber; *C:* Pascal Rabaud; *M:* John Debney.

The Idol Dancer 1/2 **1920** Romance and adventure in the South Seas with a drunken American beachcomber inspired by love to change his ways. There's also a native uprising for added excitement. Minor Griffith but nice Nassau scenery. **93m/B VHS.** Richard Barthelmess, Clarine Seymour, Creighton Hale, George MacQuarrie, Kate Bruce, Anders Randolf, Walter James, Thomas Carr; *D:* D.W. Griffith.

Idolmaker 1/2 **1980 (PG)** A conniving agent can make a rock star out of anyone. Well-acted fluff with Sharkey taking a strong lead. The first film by hack-meister Hackford and somewhat based on true-life teen fab Fabian. **119m/C VHS, DVD.** Ray Sharkey, Tovah Feldshuh, Peter Gallagher, Paul Land, Joe Pantoliano, Maureen McCormick, John Aprea, Richard Bright, Olympia Dukakis, Steven Apostlee Peck; *D:* Taylor Hackford; *C:* Adam Holender; *M:* Jeff Barry. Golden Globes '81: Actor—Mus./Comedy (Sharkey).

If... **1969 (R)** Three unruly seniors at a British boarding school refuse to conform. A popular, anarchic indictment of staid British society, using the same milieu as Vigo's "Zero de Conduite," with considerably more violence. The first of Anderson and McDowell's trilogy, culminating with "O Lucky Man!" and "Britannia Hospital." In color and black and white. **111m/C VHS, DVD.** *GB* Malcolm McDowell, David Wood, Christine Noonan, Richard Warwick, Robert Swann, Arthur Lowe, Mona Washbourne, Graham Crowden, Hugh Thomas, Guy Rose, Peter Jeffrey, Geoffrey Chater, Mary MacLeod, Anthony Nicholls, Ben Aris, Charles Lloyd-Pack, Rupert Webster, Brian Pettifer, Sean Bury, Michael Cadman; *D:* Lindsay Anderson; *W:* David Sherwin; *C:* Miroslav Ondricek; *M:* Marc Wilkinson. Cannes '69: Film.

If Ever I See You Again **1978 (PG)** The creator of "You Light Up My Life" stars in the sentimental melodrama. Two adolescent lovers meet again years later and try to rekindle old passions. Done with as much skill as "Light" minus a hit song. **105m/C VHS.** Joseph Brooks, Shelley Hack, Jerry Keller, Jimmy Breslin; *D:* Joseph Brooks; *W:* Joseph Brooks; *M:* Joseph Brooks.

If I Die Before I Wake WOOF! **1998 (R)** Suburban family become the grisly victims of three intruders who enjoy terrorizing, torturing, and killing until teenaged LoriBeth (Jones), who has been hiding from the bad guys, gets revenge. Ick, ick, ick. **77m/C VHS, DVD.** Michael (Mick) McCleery, Muse Watson, Stephanie Jones, Anthony Nicosia; *D:* Brian Katkin; *W:* Brian Katkin; *C:* Zoran Hochstatter; *M:* Thomas Morse. **VIDEO**

If I Had My Way **1940** When their best friend Fred is killed in an accident, buddies Buzz (Crosby) and Axel (Brendel) vow to take his teenaged daughter Patricia (Jean) to find her relatives in New York. Joe (Dodd) and his wife Marian (Bryant) are a couple of kind-hearted but penniless vaudevillians and Buzz is horrified when Axel uses Patricia's inheritance to buy a failing restaurant. So he decides to make lemonade out of lemons and convert the eatery into a nightclub in hopes of providing for the family. **82m/B DVD.** Bing Crosby, Gloria Jean, El Brendel, Claire Dodd, Nana Bryant, Charles Winninger, Allyn Joslyn, Donald Woods, William Conselman, James V. Kern; *D:* David Butler; *C:* George Robinson; *M:* Charles Previn.

If I Were King **1938** Colman, of the impeccable diction, stars as swashbuckling 15th-century French poet Francois Villon, who matches wits with King Louis XI (Rathbone), and falls in love with aristocratic Katherine de Vaucelles (Dee). He even manages to save Paris by leading a peasant army against the invading Burgundians. Probably the best scenes are the witty repartee between Colman and Rathbone, each trying to best the other. Also filmed as 1927's "The Beloved Rogue" (with John Barrymore) and the operetta "The Vagabond King." **102m/B VHS.** Ronald Colman, Basil Rathbone, Frances Dee, Henry Wilcoxon, C.V. France, Ellen Drew, Sidney Toler, Heather Thatcher, Stanley Ridges; *D:* Frank Lloyd; *W:* Preston Sturges; *C:* Theodor Sparkuhl; *M:* Richard Hageman.

If I Were Rich *Cash; For Love or Money* **1933** Gwenn is arranging a meeting at his home for a group of financiers he hopes will back a scheme to save his ailing business. Meanwhile he has to dodge bill collectors and others determined to ruin his plans. **63m/B VHS.** *GB* Edmund Gwenn, Wendy Barrie, Robert Donat, Clifford Heatherley; *D:* Zoltan Korda.

If I'm Lucky **1946** Bandleader Earl Gordon (James) gets a gig working for a corrupt political campaign by playing concerts to lure in voters. The politicos decide that the band's squeaky clean singer, Allen Clark (Como), would be a better promoter than their own candidate. But when Allen doesn't want to go along, the politicians threaten to ruin everyone's reputations. A remake of 1935's "Thanks a Million." **80m/B DVD.** Perry Como, Vivian Blaine, Harry James, Carmen Miranda, Phil Silvers, Edgar Buchanan, Reed Hadley; *D:* Lewis Seiler; *W:* Helen Logan, George Bricker, Robert Ellis, Snag Werris, Snag Werris; *C:* Glen MacWilliams; *M:* Emil Newman.

If It's a Man, Hang Up 1/2 **1975** A model is terrified by harrowing telephone calls from a stranger. **71m/C VHS.** Tom Conti, David Gwillim, Carol Lynley, Gerald Harper; *D:* Shaun O'Riordan; *W:* Brian Clemens.

If It's Tuesday, This Must Be Belgium **1969 (G)** A fast-paced, frantic, and funny look at a group of Americans on a whirlwind European tour. The group does a nine-country, 18-day bus tour with clashing, comic personalities and lots of romantic possibilities. Remade in 1987 for TV. **99m/C VHS.** Suzanne Pleshette, Ian McShane, Mildred Natwick, Norman Fell, Michael Constantine, Peggy Cass, Murray Hamilton, Marty Ingels, Sandy Baron, Pamela Britton, Luke Halpin; *D:* Mel Stuart.

If Looks Could Kill **1986 (R)** Would-be film noir about a man spying on a female embezzler and falling in love. **90m/C VHS.** Alan Fisler, Tim Gail, Kim Lambert, Jeanne Marie; *D:* Chuck Vincent.

If Looks Could Kill 1/2 **1991 (PG-13)** TV stud Grieco makes film debut as a high school class cutup who travels to France with his class to parlez vous for extra credit. Mistaken for a CIA agent, he stumbles into a plot to take over all the money in the whole wide world, and much implausible action and eyelash batting follows. Extra kibbles for supporting characterizations. Oh, and don't be put off by the fact that the Parisian scenes were shot in Montreal. **89m/C VHS.** Richard Grieco, Linda Hunt, Roger Rees, Robin Bartlett, Gabrielle Anwar, Roger Daltrey, Geraldine James, Carole (Raphaelle) Davis; *D:* William Dear; *W:* Fred Dekker; *M:* David Foster.

If Lucy Fell **1995 (R)** Schaeffer serves as writer/director/star of this predictable 90s-style romantic comedy. Ludicrous premise has psychotherapist Lucy (Parker) bent on realizing a 10-year-old pact with longtime friend Joe (Schaeffer) that stipulates they both jump off the Brooklyn Bridge if neither one has found true love by age 30. With the big birthday approaching, Lucy takes a desperate shot with eccentric painter Bwick (Stiller), while Joe finally goes for the object of his desire, asking beautiful neighbor Jane (MacPherson) to a showing of his paintings. Highlights come in the casting, with Parker a solid and energetic neurotic and MacPherson showing that there's something beyond her more obvious talents. **92m/C VHS, DVD.** Sarah Jessica Parker, Eric Schaeffer, Ben Stiller, Elle Macpherson, James Rebhorn, Dominic Chianese; *D:* Eric Schaeffer; *W:* Eric Schaeffer, Tony Spiridakis; *C:* Ron Fortunato; *M:* Amanda Kravat, Charles Pettis.

If Only 1/2 **2004 (PG-13)** Sappy romantic drama finds perky American Samantha Andrews (Hewitt) studying music in London. She and her British businessman boyfriend Ian (Nicholls) are constantly at odds and finally break up. Samantha is immediately killed in a car accident before Ian can come to his senses and reunite with her. But when Samantha appears the next morning, Ian realizes he's reliving their last day together. However, the more he tries to change the outcome, the more inevitable it seems. **92m/C DVD.** *GB* Jennifer Love Hewitt, Paul Nicholls, Tom Wilkinson, Diana Hardcastle, Lucy Davenport; *D:* Gil Junger; *W:* Christian Welsh; *C:* Giles Nuttgens; *M:* Adrian Johnston.

If These Walls Could Talk 1/2 **1996 (R)** Covers four decades, from the '50s to the present, telling the stories of three women and the different ways they deal with unexpected pregnancies. "1952" finds recently widowed nurse Claire (Moore) discovering she's pregnant—and it's not her late husband's. In some graphic scenes she tries to end the pregnancy herself with a knitting needle and later through a back-alley abortion. Happily married Barbara (Spacek) already has four children in "1974" and has just returned to college. Then she discovers she's pregnant again. Abortion's an option but does Barbara want one? Finally, college student Christine (Heche) gets pregnant by her married professor in "1996" and reluctantly opts for an abortion at a family planning clinic, which is besieged by pro-lifers and on the edge of some violent confrontations. **109m/C VHS, DVD.** Demi Moore, Catherine Keener, Jason London, Shirley Knight, Kevin Cooney, CCH Pounder, Robin Gammell, Sissy Spacek, Xander Berkeley, Joanna Gleason, Harris Yulin, Anne Heche, Jada Pinkett Smith, Cher, Diana Scarwid, Lindsay Crouse, Lorraine Toussaint, Rita Wilson, Eileen Brennan, Craig T. Nelson; *D:* Cher, Nancy Savoca; *W:* Nancy Savoca, Susan Manus, I. Marlene King; *C:* Ellen Kuras, Bobby Bukowski, John Stanier; *M:* Cliff Eidelman. **CABLE**

If These Walls Could Talk 2 1/2 **2000 (R)** Anthology features the stories of three lesbian couples in America. "1961" shows the sedate lives of retired schoolteachers Edith (Redgrave) and Abby (Seldes), who have lived together for decades. But when Abby suddenly dies, Edith discovers she will be dispossessed by Abby's greedy nephew. "1972" finds Linda (Williams) living with a group of lesbian feminists who disapprove of butch-femme couples. But Linda is still drawn to the butch Amy (Sevigny), who refuses to apologize for how she chooses to live. "2000" has thirtysomething couple Fran (Stone) and Kal (DeGeneres) deciding to have a baby and having some comical problems with the sperm issue. **96m/C VHS, DVD.** Vanessa Redgrave, Marian Seldes, Paul Giamatti, Elizabeth Perkins, Michelle Williams, Chloe Sevigny, Nia Long, Natasha Lyonne, Heather McComb, Sharon Stone, Ellen DeGeneres, Regina King, Kathy Najimy, Mitchell Anderson, George Newbern, Amy Carlson; *D:* Jane Anderson, Martha Coolidge, Anne Heche, Alex Sichel; *W:* Jane Anderson, Sylvia Sichel, Anne Heche; *C:* Paul Elliott, Robbie Greenberg, Peter Deming; *M:* Basil Poledouris. **CABLE**

If They Tell You I Fell 1/2 *Si Te Dicen Que Cai; Aventis* **1989** The corpse of a man famous from the Spanish Civil War and in local folk stories (called "aventis") is found by a doctor and nurse and spawns revelations that clash with the tall tales. Based on Juan Marse's 1976 novel, spans several decades in muddled flashbacks with actors taking on multiple roles. Spanish, with English subtitles. **120m/C VHS, DVD.** Victoria Abril, Antonio Banderas, Juan Diego Botto, Maria Botto, Marc Barahoma, Javier Gurruchaga, Lluis Homar, Guillermo Montesinos, Margarita Calahorra, Jose Cerro, Pep Cruz, Teresa Cunille, Cesareo Estebanez, Luis Giralte, Aitor Merino, Joan Miralles, Montserrat Salvador, Jorge Sanz, Rosa Morata, Ariadna Novarro, Ferran Rane, Merce Sans, Carlos Tristancho; *D:* Vicente Aranda; *W:* Vicente Aranda, Juan Marse; *C:* Juan Amoros; *M:* Jose Nieto. **VIDEO**

If Things Were Different 1/2 **1979** Feisty woman struggles to hold her family together after her husband is hospitalized with a nervous breakdown. **96m/C VHS.** Suzanne Pleshette, Tony Roberts, Arte Johnson, Chuck McCann, Don Murray; *D:* Robert Lewis.

If You Could Only Cook 1/2 **1936** Down-and-out Joan (Arthur) is looking for work when she meets Jim (Marshall) on a park bench and assumes he needs a job too. Jim is actually an auto exec who's fed up with his board of directors and thinks it would be fun to play hooky for awhile. He agrees to Joan's idea to pretend to be a married so they can apply for the cook and butler positions at mobster (and gourmet) Mike Rossini's (Carrillo) mansion. Confusion follows. **70m/B DVD.** Jean Arthur, Herbert Marshall, Leo Carrillo, Lionel Stander, Frieda Inescort, Alan Edwards, Herbert Marshall; *D:* William A. Seiter; *W:* Howard J. Green, Gertrude Purcell; *C:* John Stumar.

If You Could See What I Hear 1/2 **1982 (PG)** Irritatingly upbeat true-life story of blind singer-musician, Tom Sullivan. Covers his life from college days to marriage. Sophomoric comedy centers around the hero's irresponsible, and often life-endangering, behavior. **103m/C VHS.** *CA* Marc Singer, R.H. Thomson, Sarah Torgov, Shari Belafonte; *D:* Eric Till. Genie '83: Support. Actor (Thomson).

If You Don't Stop It... You'll Go Blind 1/2 **1977 (R)** A series of gauche and tasteless vignettes from various little-known comedians. **80m/C VHS.** Pat McCormick, George Spencer, Patrick Wright; *D:* I. Robert Levy, Keefe Brasselle.

If You Knew Susie **1948** Two retired vaudeville actors find a letter from George Washington which establishes them as descendants of a colonial patriot and the heirs to a $7 billion fortune. ♫ If You Knew Susie; My Brooklyn Love Song; What Do I Want With Money?; We're Living the Life We Love; My, How the Time Goes By. **90m/B VHS.** Eddie Cantor, Joan Davis, Allyn Joslyn,

Charles Dingle, Charles Halton; *D:* Gordon Douglas.

If You Only Knew **2000** Struggling New York writer (are there any other kind?) Parker (Schaech) falls for painter Samantha (Eastwood) when he answers her ad for someone to share her loft. She has no problem rooming with a guy—as long as he's gay. So Parker moves in and finds the pretense an increasing struggle. Formulaic but Eastwood is a real charmer. **111m/C VHS, DVD.** Johnathon Schaech, Alison Eastwood, Gabrielle Anwar, James LeGros, Lainie Kazan, Paul Sampson, Frank Vincent, Annie Corley, Miguel A. Nunez Jr., Gabrielle Anwar, David Snedeker; *D:* David Snedeker.

Igby Goes Down **2002 (R)** Steers's directorial debut is a smart, dark comedy. Modern-day Holden Caufield Igby (Culkin) rebels against his privileged upbringing, dropping out of countless prep and, finally, military schools. Adrift, Igby heads to the boho pad of his rich godfather (Goldblum) and his beautiful, drug-addled girlfriend (Peet) and is initiated into their degenerate "arty" scene. While in a questionable relationship with Peet, Igby falls for soulful college dropout Sookie Sapperstein (Danes) who's also the target of his slick older brother Oliver's (Phillippe) affection. The matriarch of Igby's dysfunctional family is Sarandon, in a humorously unlikable role. Thoughtful, satiric view of the emptiness of the American Dream. **98m/C VHS, DVD.** *US* Kieran Culkin, Ryan Phillippe, Susan Sarandon, Claire Danes, Jeff Goldblum, Amanda Peet, Jared Harris, Rory Culkin, Cynthia Nixon, Eric Bogosian; *D:* Burr Steers; *W:* Burr Steers; *C:* Wedigo von Schultzendorff; *M:* Uwe Peterson.

Ignition **1/2 2001 (R)** The U.S. Army is preparing a major rocket launch just as Federal Judge Faith Matheson (Olin) begins a corruption and treason trial that involves the military. Is it any surprise that there are links between the launch and her case? When Faith is threatened, she turns to former Marine helicopter pilot Conor Gallagher (Pullman) for help. **95m/C VHS, DVD.** *US CA* Lena Olin, Bill Pullman, Colm Feore, Nicholas Lea, Peter Kent, Michael Ironside, Roger Dunn, Scott Hylands, Benjamin Ratner; *D:* Yves Simoneau; *W:* William Davies; *C:* Jonathan Freeman.

Igor **2008 (PG)** Looney and colorful animated tale about Igor (Cusack), the hunchbacked assistant to mad scientist Dr. Glickenstein (Cleese) who secretly longs to be a scientist himself. In the hopes of winning the Evil Science Fair, Igor builds his own female monster, Eva (Shannon), who turns out to be a sweet, gentle giant. After learning of Igor's creation, even more evil than most evil scientists, Dr. Schadenfreude (Izzard) tries to steal Eva and take the credit. At Igor's side are best friends Scamper (Buscemi), a road-kill rabbit on two feet, and clueless Brain (Hayes), a literal brain floating in a jar with eyes. Not nearly as witty or technically sharp as Pixar's CGI releases, but nonetheless, pulls off an entertaining gothic fable in the vein of a Tim Burton cartoon. **86m/C DVD, Blu-ray Disc.** *US* *D:* Anthony Leondis; *W:* Chris McKenna; *M:* Patrick Doyle; *V:* John Cusack, Steve Buscemi, John Cleese, Sean P. Hayes, Molly Shannon, Jennifer Coolidge, Eddie Izzard, Jay Leno, Arsenio Hall, Christian Slater, James Lipton.

Igor & the Lunatics **1985 (R)** Tasteless tale of a cannibal cult leader released from prison who picks up where he left off. **79m/C VHS, DVD.** Joseph Eero, Joe Niola, T.J. Michaels; *D:* Billy Parolini.

Iguana **1989** The videocassette box art makes this look like a horror movie, but it's really a stiff, solemn period drama about a deformed sailor with lizardlike features. After a life of mistreatment he reigns mercilessly over a handful of island castaways. An international coproduction with mostly English dialogue, some Spanish and Portuguese with subtitles. **88m/C VHS, DVD.** *SI IT* Everett McGill, Michael Madsen, Joseph Culp, Fabio Testi; *D:* Monte Hellman; *W:* Monte Hellman, Jaime Comas Gil, Steven Gaydos; *C:* Josep Civit.

Ike **1/2** *Ike: The War Years* **1979** Duvall is top brass in this epic biography tracing Eisenhower's career during WWII. Originally a six-hour miniseries. **291m/C VHS.** Robert Duvall, Lee Remick, Darren McGavin, Dana Andrews, Laurence Luckinbill; *D:* Melville Shavelson. **TV**

Ike: Countdown to D-Day **1/2 2004 (PG)** Selleck shaves off the signature mustache—and the rest of his hair—to star in this low-key (meaning no battle scenes) biopic of Gen. Dwight D. Eisenhower that gives a behind-the-scenes account of the war-room planning for the pivotal D-Day invasion. **89m/C VHS, DVD.** Tom Selleck, James Remar, Timothy Bottoms, Gerald McRaney, Ian Mune, Bruce Phillips, John Bach, Nick Blake, Kevin J. Wilson, Christopher Baker, George Shevtsov, Gregor McLennan, Paul Gittins, Craig Hall, Stephen Brunton, Paul Barrett, Mickey Rose, Carole Seay; *D:* Robert Harmon; *W:* Lionel Chetwynd; *C:* David Gribble; *M:* Jeff Beal. **TV**

Ikiru *To Live; Doomed; Living* **1952** When a clerk finds out he is dying of cancer, he decides to build a children's playground and give something of himself back to the world. Highly acclaimed, heartbreaking drama from the unusually restrained Kurosawa; possibly his most "eastern" film. In Japanese with English subtitles. **134m/B VHS, DVD.** *JP* Takashi Shimura, Nobuo Kaneko, Kyoko Seki, Miki Odagari, Yunosuke Ito; *D:* Akira Kurosawa; *W:* Akira Kurosawa, Shinobu Hashimoto, Hideo Oguni; *C:* Asakazu Nakai; *M:* Fumio Hayasaka.

Il Bell'Antonio **1/2** *Handsome Antonio* **1960** The boastful Antonio has a reputation as a womanizer but when he finally marries, to a lovely young woman, he faces the loss of his libido. Satire of machismo, marriage, and Catholicism. In Italian with English subtitles. **115m/C VHS.** *IT* Marcello Mastroianni, Claudia Cardinale, Pierre Brasseur, Tomas Milian, Rina Morelli; *D:* Mauro Bolognini; *W:* Pier Paolo Pasolini, Gino Vissentini; *C:* Armando Nannuzzi; *M:* Piero Piccioni.

Il Bidone *The Swindle* **1955** Three Italian conmen pull capers in Rome trying to make a better life for themselves. Dark overtones permeate one of Fellini's lesser efforts. Good cast can't bring up the level of this film. In Italian with English subtitles. **92m/C VHS, DVD.** *IT* Broderick Crawford, Giulietta Masina, Richard Basehart, Franco Fabrizi; *D:* Federico Fellini; *W:* Federico Fellini, Tullio Pinelli, Ennio Flaiano; *C:* Otello Martelli; *M:* Nino Rota.

Il Divo **2008** Complicated political bio of seven-time Italian Prime Minister Giulio Andreotti. Pic focuses on his seventh election in the 1990s to his later trial for corruption and conspiracy with the Mafia in a series of political assassinations, including that of political rival Aldo Moro by the Red Brigade. (Andreotti was first convicted and then later acquitted.) Italian with subtitles. **110m/C DVD.** *IT* Toni Servillo, Anna Bonaiuto, Guilio Bosetti, Flavio Bucci, Carlo Buccirosso, Giorgio Colangeli; *D:* Poalo Sorrentino; *W:* Poalo Sorrentino; *C:* Luca Bigazzi; *M:* Teho Teardo.

Il Grido *The Cry; The Outcry* **1957** A jilted husband takes his young daughter from village to village in search of the woman who deserted them for another man. Set in the desolate Po Valley of director Antonioni's childhood. In Italian with English subtitles. **116m/B VHS, DVD.** *IT* Steve Cochran, Alida Valli, Dorian Gray, Betsy Blair, Gabriella Pallotta; *D:* Michelangelo Antonioni; *W:* Michelangelo Antonioni, Ennio de Concini; *C:* Gianni Di Venanzo; *M:* Giovanni Fusco.

Il Sorpasso **1/2 1963** A braggart, who has failed at everything, spends all his time traveling around Italy in his sportscar. He takes a repressed law student under his wing and decides to teach him how to have fun. In Italian with English subtitles. **116m/B VHS.** *IT* Vittorio Gassman, Jean-Louis Trintignant; *D:* Dino Risi.

I'll Be Home for Christmas **1/2 1998 (PG)** Snotty college kid Jake (Thomas) wants to teach his Dad a lesson by boycotting Christmas and stealing away to Mexico with his girlfriend (Biel). Jake thinks his Dad remarried too soon after his mother's death, but is bribed home with his Dad's prized Porshe (now there's a lesson for the kids) if he can arrive for Christmas Eve dinner. A series of absurd mishaps ensue (almost all of which occur because Jake is a lying, cheating jerk) as he makes his away cross-country while glued inside of a Santa suit. The characters are superficial and at times downright annoying. This run of the mill holiday stinker will likely only appeal to Thomas' legion of teenage groupies. **86m/C VHS, DVD.** Jonathan Taylor Thomas, Jessica Biel, Adam LaVorgna, Gary Cole, Eve Gordon, Sean O'Bryan, Andrew Lauer; *D:* Arlene Sanford; *W:* Harris Goldberg, Tom Nursall; *C:* Hiro Narita; *M:* John Debney.

I'll Be Seeing You **1/2 1944** Not exactly your typical Christmas fare, although the schmaltz is laid on as thickly as icing on cookies. Mary (Rogers) meets Zachary (Cotten) on a train as she's traveling to Texas to spend the holidays with her family. They've both got secrets: she's on a good behavior furlough from the pen where she's serving time for manslaughter, and he's a shell-shocked soldier on leave from the psych ward. Mary takes Zach home for a family Xmas and they fall in love but she doesn't want to make his shaky hold on his sanity worse by admitting she's going back to jail. 17-year-old Temple plays curious cousin Barbara. Adapted from the radio play "Double Furlough" by Charles Martin. **83m/B VHS, DVD.** Ginger Rogers, Joseph Cotten, Shirley Temple, Spring Byington, Tom Tully, Chill Wills, John Derek; *D:* William Dieterle; *W:* Marion Parsonnet; *C:* Gaetano Antonio "Tony" Gaudio; *M:* Daniele Amfitheatrof.

I'll Be There **1/2 2003 (PG-13)** Aging pop idol (Ferguson) sobers up and discovers he has a teenage daughter (Church). The two start to develop a relationship in spite of Mother's reservations. Of course, the kid can sing and catches the attention of Dad's slimy manager. Church's acting has a way to go to catch up to her singing, but she's better than Britny or Mariah (at both). Scottish comic Ferguson seems to have taken on more (co-writing/directing/acting) than he can currently handle, but gets points for effort. **104m/C VHS, DVD.** *US* Craig Ferguson, Jemma Redgrave, Joss Ackland, Charlotte Church, Ralph Brown, Ian McNeice, Imelda Staunton, Anthony Head; *D:* Craig Ferguson; *W:* Craig Ferguson, Philip McGrade; *C:* Ian Wilson; *M:* Trevor Jones.

I'll Be Yours **1/2 1947** Small-town Louise Ginglebusher (Durbin) moves to New York and becomes an usher at the Buckingham Theatre (a fictional Radio City Music Hall). She gets involved with millionarie, J. Conrad Nelson (Menjou), and struggling lawyer, George Prescott (Drake). She falls for George and tries to help him get a job with Nelson by telling Nelson that they have just gotten married. Bendix plays the sympathetic coffee shop owner. Remake of 1935's "The Good Fairy," which was also a play by Ferenc Molnar. ♫ It's Dreamtime; Cobbleskill School Song; Granada; Sari Waltz. **94m/B VHS.** Deanna Durbin, Tom Drake, Adolphe Menjou, William Bendix, Walter Catlett, Franklin Pangborn; *D:* William A. Seiter; *W:* Preston Sturges; *C:* Hal Mohr; *M:* Frank Skinner.

I'll Believe You **1/2 2007 (PG)** Genial Dale Sweeney is the late-night host of a low-rated radio show in Melbourne, Florida that's devoted to UFO sightings and conspiracy theories. Threatened with cancellation, Dale decides he needs one legitimate alien encounter to save his job and maybe one of his strange callers is actually from another world. **81m/C DVD.** David Alan Basche, Patrick Warburton, Patrick Gallo, Fred Willard, Doc Dougherty, Thomas Gibson, Mo Rocca, Chris Elliott, Cece Pleasants, Paul Sullivan; *D:* Paul Sullivan; *W:* Ted Sullivan, Sean McPharlin, Gregory Lee, Paul Sullivan; *C:* John Mans; *M:* J.J. McGeehan. **VIDEO**

I'll Bury You Tomorrow **1/2 2002** Low-budget indie horror is a true creepfest. Beech Funeral Home attracts whack jobs, including new assistant mortician Delores (Chlanda), who keeps a big secret in a steamer trunk. This is discovered by fellow employee Jake (Murdock), who is into illegal organ donations. So he tries blackmailing Delores into helping him, which is a really bad idea. **119m/C DVD.** Zoe Daelman Chlanda, Jerry Murdock, Bill Corry, Katherine O'Sullivan, Kristen Overdurf, Renee West, Alan Rowe Kelly, Tom Burns; *D:* Alan Rowe Kelly; *W:* Alan Rowe Kelly; *C:* Tom Cadawas, Gary Malick; *M:* Tom Burns.

I'll Cry Tomorrow **1955** Hayward brilliantly portrays actress Lillian Roth as she descends into alcoholism and then tries to overcome her addiction. Based on Roth's memoirs. ♫ Sing You Sinners; When The Red Red Robin Comes Bob Bob Bobbin' Along; Happiness Is Just a Thing Called Joe; Vagabond King Waltz. **119m/B VHS.** Susan Hayward, Richard Conte, Eddie Albert, Jo Van Fleet, Margo, Don Taylor, Ray Danton, Veda Ann Borg; *D:* Daniel Mann; *M:* Alex North. Oscars '55: Costume Des. (B&W); Cannes '56: Actress (Hayward).

I'll Do Anything **1/2 1993 (PG-13)** Hollywood satire finds unemployed actor Matt (Nolte) suddenly forced to care for his six-year-old daughter Jeannie (Wright), whom he hasn't seen in three years. Matt also finally gets a job—as a chauffeur to an obnoxious producer (well played by Brooks) whose company winds up making the manipulative demon Jeannie into a hot child star. Great work by Kavner as the owner of a test-screening service who romances Brooks. Originally intended as a musical, the test screenings were so disastrous that the numbers were axed. What's left is less jerky than expected; Brooks reportedly based his character in part on mega-mogul Joel Silver. **115m/C VHS, DVD.** Nick Nolte, Albert Brooks, Julie Kavner, Whittni Wright, Joely Richardson, Tracey Ullman; *D:* James L. Brooks; *W:* James L. Brooks; *C:* Michael Ballhaus; *M:* Hans Zimmer.

I'll Get You *Escape Route* **1953** An FBI agent goes to England on the trail of a kidnapping ring. **79m/B VHS, DVD.** George Raft, Sally Gray, Clifford Evans; *D:* Seymour Friedman.

I'll Name the Murderer **1936** Suspense film in which a gossip columnist starts his own investigation into the murder of a club singer. **66m/B VHS, DVD.** Ralph Forbes, Marion Shilling; *D:* Bernard B. Ray.

I'll Never Forget What's 'Isname **1967** To some tastes, this overwrought and long-unseen comedy from the swinging '60s will be completely dated with characters whose mindsets are totally alien. Protagonist Andrew Quint (Reed) is a piggish young ad executive who tries to leave his even more piggish boss (Welles), and his two mistresses, though he's not sure he wants to divorce his wife. Why? He wants to go back to do something meaningful with his life, something like working for a literary magazine. It's actually a long midlife crisis (though the phrase did not exist when the film was made) that set standards for frankness in its sexual material. **99m/C DVD.** Oliver Reed, Orson Welles, Carol White, Marianne Faithfull, Michael Hordern, Frank Finlay; *D:* Michael Winner; *W:* Peter Draper; *C:* Otto Heller; *M:* Francis Lai.

I'll Never Forget You *The House in the Square* **1951** American atomic physicist Peter Standish (Power) has inherited a London house. His friend Roger (Rennie) tells him about an American ancestor who lived there in the 18th century. According to Standish's theory of time and space, he should be able to switch places and—with the help of a lightning strike—Peter wakes up in the past, engaged to Kate (Campbell). Too bad Peter actually falls in love with her younger sister Helen (Blyth). Another storm eventually propels Peter back to the 20th century, but can his love transcend time as well? Some scenes are filmed in Technicolor. Adapted from the play by John Baldeston and previously filmed in 1933 as "Berkeley Square." **89m/B DVD.** *GB* Tyrone Power, Michael Rennie, Ann Blyth, Beatrice Campbell, Dennis Price, Kathleen Byron, Raymond Huntley; *D:* Roy Ward Baker; *W:* Ranald MacDougall; *C:* Georges Perinal; *M:* William Alwyn.

I'll Remember April **1/2 1999** In the days following the bombing of Pearl Harbor rumors abound that Japanese submarines are patrolling the Pacific and four 10-year-old California boys like to pretend they are Marines in search of the Japanese enemy. Imagine their surprise when they discover a Japanese soldier who washed up on the beach and is hiding out in their clubhouse. They keep him their prisoner while trying to decide what to do but when the soldier rescues one of the boys from drowning, the boys decide that they have to save him. **90m/C VHS, DVD.** Haley Joel Osment, Trevor Morgan, Richard Taylor Olson, Yuki Tokuhiro, Mark Harmon, Pam Dawber, Noriyuki "Pat" Morita, Yuji Okumoto, Troy Evans, Paul Dooley; ***D:*** Bob (Benjamin) Clark; ***W:*** Mark Sanderson; ***C:*** Stephen M. Katz; ***M:*** Paul Zaza.

I'll See You in My Dreams 🦴🦴 1/2 **1951** Hokey but fun musical biography of songwriter Gus Kahn (Thomas) and his wife Grace LeBoy (Day). Kahn gets his start in Ziegfeld shows but loses both his career and wife after the 1929 crash. However, she soon returns and everything ends happily ever after. ♫ Ain't We Got Fun; Ukelele Lady; The One I Love Belongs To Somebody Else; I'll See You In My Dreams; It Had To Be You; Swingin' Down the Lane; My Buddy; Makin' Whoopee!; Yes Sir, That's My Baby. **109m/B VHS, DVD.** Danny Thomas, Doris Day, Frank Lovejoy, Patrice Wymore, James Gleason, Mary Wickes, Jim Backus, Minna Gombell, William Forrest; ***D:*** Michael Curtiz; ***W:*** Melville Shavelson, Jack Rose.

I'll Sleep When I'm Dead 🦴🦴🦴 **2003 (R)** Will Graham (Owen) thinks he has escaped the horrors of urban life for the great outdoors. Unfortunately, his hipster drug-dealing younger brother (Rhys Meyers) has been found dead from an apparent suicide. Shady businessman Boad (McDowell) took a nasty fancy to him and, with the help of his stooges, raped him quite brutally. Now Will has to return to London and make the bad men pay. Extra dark and mean contemporary noir from Hodges looks and acts like a remake of his classic "Get Carter," with Clive Owen ably filling Michael Caine's shoes (unlike a certain American action star). Story is a bit muddled and confusing at times, but the onslaught of action makes up for it. The rape scene is one of the most agonizing sequences you'll see. Not for the faint of heart. **102m/C DVD.** *US GB* Clive Owen, Charlotte Rampling, Malcolm McDowell, Jamie Foreman, Ken Stott, Sylvia Syms, Geoff Bell, Desmond Baylis, Kirris Riviere, Brian Croucher, Ross Boatman, Marc O'Shea; ***D:*** Mike Hodges; ***W:*** Trevor Preston; ***C:*** Mike Garfath; ***M:*** Simon Fisher Turner.

I'll Take Sweden 🦴🦴 1/2 **1965** Overprotective father Hope disapproves of teenaged daughter Weld's guitar-playing boyfriend (Avalon). So to keep her out of harm's way he finagles a company transfer to Sweden. Dad falls for an interior decorator (Merrill) while Weld gets involved with a Swedish playboy (Slate). Deciding Avalon is the lesser of two evils, Hope schemes to get the two back together. **96m/C VHS, DVD.** Bob Hope, Tuesday Weld, Frankie Avalon, Dina Merrill, Jeremy Slate, Walter Sande, John Qualen, Roy Roberts, Maudie Prickett; ***D:*** Fred de Cordova; ***W:*** Arthur Marx, Bob Fisher, Nat Perrin; ***C:*** Daniel F. Fapp.

I'll Take You There 🦴🦴 **1999 (R)** Lightweight, somewhat schizophrenic romantic comedy-road flick-drama has despondent Bill (Rogers) trying to recover from a failed relationship. His sister sets him up with old school friend Bernice (Sheedy), but he viciously insults her on the date. She shows up a few days later, and kidnaps him on a road trip that begins with the heist of a prom dress. More outlandish events ensue, but the unbelievable plot almost sinks the whole enterprise. Solid work by a strong cast mostly save the day. **93m/C VHS, DVD.** Ally Sheedy, Reg Rogers, Lara Harris, John Pyper-Ferguson, Alice Drummond, Alan North, Ben Vereen, Adrienne Shelly; ***D:*** Adrienne Shelly; ***W:*** Adrienne Shelly; ***C:*** Vanja Cernjul; ***M:*** Andrew Hollander.

Illegal 🦴🦴 1/2 **1955** Crime melodrama stars Robinson as an attorney who risks all to acquit his assistant of murder. Early Mansfield appearance. Remake of "The Mouthpiece." **88m/B VHS, DVD.** Edward G. Robinson, Nina Foch, Hugh Marlowe, Jayne Mansfield, Albert Dekker, Ellen Corby, DeForest Kelley, Howard St. John; ***D:*** Lewis Allen; ***W:*** W.R. Burnett.

Illegal Affairs 🦴 **1996** The kind of film that almost makes you feel sorry for lawyers. The sleazy firm of Grimes and Peterson specializes in divorce cases—and seem personally responsible for any number of them on account of adultery. **87m/C VHS, DVD.** Jay Richardson, Monique Parent, Christian Noble; ***D:*** Michael Paul Girard; ***W:*** Michael Paul Girard; ***C:*** Denis Maloney; ***M:*** Miriam Cutler. **VIDEO**

Illegal Entry: Formula for Fear 🦴 1/2 **1993** Tracie's scientist father has invented a formula that could change the world. When he's murdered the formula falls into her unsuspecting hands. Tracie might not know what she has but that doesn't stop some very ruthless efforts to get the information others want. **88m/C VHS.** Sabryn Gene't, Barbara Lee (Niven) Alexander, Gregory Vignolle, Arthur Roberts, Carol Hoyt; ***D:*** Henri Charr; ***W:*** John B. Pfeifer.

Illegal in Blue 🦴🦴 **1995 (R)** Chris (Gauthier) the cop falls for sultry blues singer Kari (Dash) and then realizes she could be a suspect in the murder he's investigating. Will libido win out over loyalty to the job? Also available unrated. **94m/C VHS.** Dan Gauthier, Stacey Dash, Louis Giambalvo, Michael Durrell, David Groh; ***D:*** Stu Segall; ***W:*** Noel Hynd; ***M:*** Stephen (Steve) Edwards.

Illegal Tender 🦴 1/2 **2007 (R)** Twenty-one-year-old Wilson (Gonzalez) enjoys his upper-middle class lifestyle until his mother (De Jesus) informs him that his dead father was a drug dealer and hands him a gun. Turns out they need to defend themselves from his father's murderer, who's still after them and the money Dad stole. Wilson is mostly adequate as the reluctant heir to his father's legacy but is overshadowed by De Jesus's two-gun Pam Grier-style performance. You'll find yourself wishing you saw more of Mom and a lot less of Wilson. John Singleton produced what is, essentially, a blaxploitation film gone Latino (Laxploitation?). Nothing really distinguishes it from any other mediocre B-movie revenge flick. **107m/C DVD.** *US* Wanda De Jesus, Rick Gonzalez, Dania Ramirez, Antonio Ortiz, Manny Perez, Tego Calderon; ***D:*** Franc Reyes; ***W:*** Franc Reyes; ***C:*** Frank Byers; ***M:*** Hector Pereira.

Illegally Yours 🦴 **1987 (PG)** Miscast comedy about a college student serving on the jury in trial of old girlfriend. Bring down the gavel on this one. **94m/C VHS, DVD.** Rob Lowe, Colleen Camp, Kenneth Mars; ***D:*** Peter Bogdanovich.

Illicit 🦴🦴 **1931** In love, Stanwyck fears that marrying Rennie will only ruin their wonderful relationship. Two years after their marriage her fears are realized when each searches for happiness with a past lover. A melodramatic performance that doesn't quite hit its mark. Remade two years later as "Ex-Lady" with Bette Davis in the lead. Based on the play by Edith Fitzgerald and Robert Riskin. **76m/B VHS.** Barbara Stanwyck, Ricardo Cortez, Natalie Moorhead, Charles Butterworth, Joan Blondell, Claude Gillingwater; ***D:*** Archie Mayo; ***W:*** Harvey Thew.

Illicit Behavior 🦴🦴 1/2 **1991 (R)** A dangerous manipulative woman (Severance) is out to claim a $2 million inheritance in this intricate and seductive police thriller. Included among her victims are her husband; a Hollywood vice cop suspended for use of excessive force; his partner; her husband's internal affairs adversary; and her own psychiatrist. Also available in an uncut, unrated version. **101m/C VHS.** Joan Severance, Robert Davi, James Russo, Jack Scalia, Kent McCord; ***D:*** Worth Keeter.

Illicit Dreams 🦴 1/2 **1994** A lonely housewife fantasizes about a dream lover who then becomes real. Too bad her possessive and vicious tycoon hubby would rather kill than lose her. **93m/C VHS.** Michelle Johnson, Stella Stevens, Joseph Cortese, Shannon Tweed, Andrew Stevens; ***D:*** Andrew Stevens; ***W:*** Karen Kelly; ***C:*** Christian Sebaldt; ***M:*** Claude Gaudette.

Illtown 🦴🦴 1/2 **1996** A happy trio of yuppy-ish Florida drug dealers, led by Rapaport's Dante, land in their own inferno when Dante's former business partner Gabriel (Trese), emerges from jail hell-bent on revenge. Danza plays the evil, effeminate underworld boss while Hayes takes the high road as the saintly detective. Abundance of metaphors aside and amid all the violence, the sluggish narrative style, with everything thrown in from dream sequences and flashbacks to dissolves and slow motion, is more effective at setting a mood than telling a story. Effective score and powerful performances, beautifully filmed by Denault, make a stylish pic that sacrifices substance. **103m/C VHS.** Michael Rapaport, Lili Taylor, Adam Trese, Kevin Corrigan, Paul Schulze, Angela Featherstone, Saul Stein, Tony Danza, Isaac Hayes; ***D:*** Nick Gomez; ***W:*** Nick Gomez; ***C:*** Jim Denault; ***M:*** Brian Keane.

Illuminata 🦴🦴 **1998 (R)** Comedy-drama about a struggling theatre troupe in turn-of-the-century New York. Tuccio (Turturro) is the company's playwright—in love with manager/leading lady, Rachel (Turturro's wife Borowitz), and worried about the reception for his new work. Also involved are self-centered aging diva Celimene (Sarandon), theatre owner Astergourd (D'Angelo), foppish critic Bevalaqua (Walken) and the unlikely object of his affections, the troupe's clown, Marco (Irwin), among many others. Adapted from the play by Brandon Cole. **111m/C VHS, DVD.** John Turturro, Katherine Borowitz, Christopher Walken, Susan Sarandon, Beverly D'Angelo, Bill Irwin, Rufus Sewell, Georgina Cates, Ben Gazzara, Donal McCann, Aida Turturro, Matthew Sussman, Leo Bassi; ***D:*** John Turturro; ***W:*** John Turturro, Brandon Cole; ***C:*** Harris Savides; ***M:*** William Bolcom, Arnold Black.

Illumination 🦴🦴 *Illuminacja* **1973** Cryptic drama about a young scientist who believes that rational analysis can solve every crisis. Until he must confront the accidental death of a close friend and his problematic affair with an older woman. Intercutting of documentary material can prove disconcerting. Polish with subtitles. **91m/C VHS.** *PL* Stanislaw Latallo, Monika Denisiewicz-Olbrzychska, Malgorzata Pritulak, Edward Zebrowski; ***D:*** Krzysztof Zanussi; ***W:*** Krzysztof Zanussi; ***C:*** Edward Klosinski; ***M:*** Wojciech Kilar.

The Illusion Travels by Streetcar 🦴🦴🦴 *La Illusion Viaja en Tranvia* **1953** Odd but enchanting story of two men who restore a streetcar, only to find that it will not be used by the city. In a gesture of defiance, they steal the streetcar and take it for one last ride, picking up an interesting assortment of characters along the way. In Spanish with English subtitles. Not released in the U.S. until 1977. **90m/B VHS.** *MX* Lilia Prado, Carlos Navarro, Domingo Soler, Fernando Soto Mantequilla, Agustin Isunza, Miguel Manzano; ***D:*** Luis Bunuel.

The Illusionist 🦴🦴 1/2 **2006 (PG-13)** Eisenheim (Norton) is a wildly popular magician in 1900 Vienna where he is reunited with his childhood love, the aristocratic Sophie (Biel). She's now engaged to suspicious Crown Prince Leopold (Sewell) who sics police chief Inspector Uhl (Giamatti) on Eisenheim in an effort to debunk his illusions. You won't find anyone pulling doves out of their sleeves to the tune of "Final Countdown" in Burger's icy turn-of-the-century romance, but there's still a lot to like, particularly the always-intriguing Norton and Giamatti. Unfortunately, no illusion can make the audience believe there's any spark between Eisenheim and Sophie, which is mostly the fault of the lovely, though vacant, Ms. Biel. **110m/C DVD.** *US* Edward Norton, Jessica Biel, Rufus Sewell, Paul Giamatti, Eddie Marsan, Aaron Johnson; ***D:*** Neil Burger; ***W:*** Neil Burger; ***C:*** Dick Pope; ***M:*** Philip Glass.

Illusions 🦴🦴 **1991 (R)** Jan (Locklear) is trying to recover from a nervous breakdown and improve her crumbling marriage when her husband's sexy sister arrives and things start to heat up. Jan thinks her husband and sister-in-law are just a little too close, but when she lets her landlord in on her suspicions, he reacts quite strangely. Will Jan have another nervous breakdown? Mysterious with lots of plot twists. Based on Colley's play "I'll Be Back Before Midnight." **95m/C VHS.** Robert Carradine, Heather Locklear, Emma Samms, Ned Beatty; ***D:*** Victor Kulle; ***W:*** Peter Colley.

The Illustrated Man 🦴🦴🦴 **1969 (PG)** A young drifter meets a tattooed man. Each tattoo causes a fantastic story to unfold. A strange, interesting, but finally limited attempt at literary sci-fi. Based on the story collection by Ray Bradbury. **103m/C VHS, DVD.** Rod Steiger, Claire Bloom, Robert Drivas, Don Dubbins; ***D:*** Jack Smight; ***M:*** Jerry Goldsmith.

Ilsa, Harem Keeper of the Oil Sheiks WOOF! **1976 (R)** The naughty Ilsa works for an Arab sheik in the slave trade. More graphic violence and nudity. Plot makes an appearance. **90m/C VHS, DVD.** Dyanne Thorne, Max (Michael) Thayer, Victor Alexander, Elke Von, Sharon Kelly, Haji, Tanya Boyd, Marilyn Joy, Bobby Woods; ***D:*** Don Edmonds; ***W:*** Langton Stafford; ***C:*** Dean Cundey, Glenn Roland.

Ilsa, She-Wolf of the SS WOOF! **1974 (R)** The torture-loving Ilsa runs a medical camp for the Nazis. Plot is incidental to nudity and violence. **45m/C VHS, DVD.** Dyanne Thorne, Greg Knoph, Sharon Kelly, Uschi Digart, Sandy Richman; ***D:*** Don Edmonds; ***W:*** Jonah Royston.

Ilsa, the Tigress of Siberia WOOF! *The Tigress* **1979** Everyone's favorite torturer has been working her wiles on political prisoners in Russia. After escaping to Canada, her past threatens to catch up with her. As usual, no plot, violence. **85m/C VHS.** Dyanne Thorne, Michel Morin, Jean-Guy Latour, Michael Mallot, Tony Angelo, Terry Coady, Joe Mattia, Sonny Forbes, Greg Giants, Howard Maurer; ***D:*** Jean LaFleur; ***W:*** Marven McGara; ***C:*** Richard Ciupka.

Ilsa, the Wicked Warden WOOF! *Ilsa, the Absolute Power; Greta the Mad Butcher* **1978 (R)** Ilsa is now a warden of a woman's prison in South America, behaving just as badly as she always has, until the prisoners stage an uprising. Lots of skin, no violence, no acting. Also: no plot. **90m/C VHS, DVD.** Dyanne Thorne, Lina Romay, Tania Busselier, Howard Maurer, Jess (Jesus) Franco; ***D:*** Jess (Jesus) Franco; ***W:*** Erwin C. Dietrich, Jess (Jesus) Franco; ***C:*** Ruedi Kuttel; ***M:*** Walter Baumgartner.

I'm All Right Jack 🦴🦴🦴 **1959** Sellers plays a pompous communist union leader in this hilarious satire of worker-management relations. Based on Alan Hackney's novel "Private Life." **101m/B VHS, DVD.** Peter Sellers, Ian Carmichael, Terry-Thomas, Victor Maddern; ***D:*** John Boulting. British Acad. '59: Actor (Sellers), Screenplay.

I'm Dancing as Fast as I Can 🦴🦴 **1982 (R)** A successful TV producer hopelessly dependent on tranquilizers tries to stop cold turkey. Good story could be better; based on Barbara Gordon's memoirs. **107m/C VHS, DVD.** Jill Clayburgh, Nicol Williamson, Dianne West, Joe Pesci, Geraldine Page, John Lithgow, Daniel Stern; ***D:*** Jack Hofsiss; ***W:*** David Rabe; ***C:*** Jan De Bont.

I'm Dangerous Tonight 🦴 1/2 **1990 (R)** Wallflower Amick (Shelley the Waitress in "Twin Peaks") turns into party monster when she dons red dress made from evil ancient Aztec cloak. Many dead soldiers when this girl parties. Based on a Cornell Woolrich short story, it's another in a series of ever more disappointing entries from Hooper, whose cult fave "The Texas Chainsaw Massacre" had low as they come production values, but far better scares. **92m/C VHS.** Madchen Amick, Corey Parker, R. Lee Ermey, Mary Frann, Dee Wallace, Anthony Perkins, Natalie Schafer, William Berger; ***D:*** Tobe Hooper; ***W:*** Alice Wilson. **CABLE**

I'm from Arkansas 🦴 **1944** The little town of Pitchfork, Arkansas, goes nuts when a pig gives birth to ten piglets. **68m/B VHS.** El Brendel, Slim Summerville, Iris Adrian, Harry Harvey, Bruce Bennett; ***D:*** Lew Landers.

I'm Going Home 🦴🦴🦴 *Je Rentre a la Maison* **2000** Distinguished, elderly actor Gilbert Valence (Piccoli) is dealt a devastating blow when his wife, daughter, and son-in-law are killed in a car accident. Coping with dignity, he looks after his young grandson and works in the theatre (playing Prospero in "The Tempest"). His agent urges Valance to take his first role in an English-language film directed by an American (Malkovich) and he struggles mightily to cope with his part. Title refers to Valance's simple statement when he realizes that his time is past. French with subtitles. **90m/C VHS, DVD.** *PT FR* Michel Piccoli, Catherine Deneuve, John Malkovich, Leonor Silveira, Antoine Chappey, Leonor Baldaque, Jean Koeltgen; ***D:*** Manoel de Oliveira; ***W:*** Manoel de Oliveira; ***C:*** Sabine Lancelin.

I'm Gonna Git You Sucka 🦴🦴🦴 **1988 (R)** Parody of "blaxploitation" films popular during the '60s and '70s. Funny and laced with out-right bellylaughs. A number of stars who made "blaxploitation" films, including Jim Brown, take part in the gags. **89m/C VHS, DVD.** Keenen Ivory Wayans, Bernie Casey, Steve James, Isaac Hayes, Jim Brown, Ja'net DuBois, Dawnn Lewis, Anne-Marie Johnson, John Vernon, Antonio Fargas, Eve Plumb, Clu Gulager, Kadeem Hardison, Damon Wayans, Gary Owens, Clarence Williams III, David Alan Grier, Kim Wayans, Robin Harris, Chris Rock, Jester Hairston, Eugene Robert Glazer, Peggy Lipton, Robert Kevin Townsend; ***D:*** Keenen Ivory Wayans; ***W:*** Keenen Ivory Wayans; ***C:*** Tom Richmond; ***M:*** David Michael Frank.

I'm Losing You ✂✂ **1998 (R)** Confusing story with too many shocks and no point of view, which wastes a good cast. TV producer Perry Krohn (Langella) learns that he is dying of cancer. His wife, Diantha (Jens), takes the news badly, as do his wayward children Bertie (McCarthy) and Rachel (Arquette). But it seems everyone has a doomladen revelation to deal with. Wagner adapts from his own novel. **102m/C VHS, DVD.** Frank Langella, Salome Jens, Rosanna Arquette, Andrew McCarthy, Amanda Donohoe, Elizabeth Perkins, Gina Gershon, Buck Henry, Ed Begley Jr.; ***D:*** Bruce Wagner; ***W:*** Bruce Wagner; ***C:*** Rob Sweeney; ***M:*** Daniel Catan.

I'm No Angel ✂✂✂ **1933** "Beulah, peel me a grape." Well, you'd be hungry too if you spent your time eyeing playboy Grant as West does. She's a circus floozy who's prone to extorting money from her men (after hashing over their shortcomings with her seen-it-all-maid, the aforementioned Beulah). However, after wooing Grant, she sues for breach of promise. This leads to a comic courtroom scene with Grant bringing in all West's exlovers as witnesses. Grant's second film with West, following "She Done Him Wrong." **88m/B VHS, DVD.** Mae West, Cary Grant, Gregory Ratoff, Edward Arnold, Ralf Harolde, Kent Taylor, Gertrude Michael, Russell Hopton, Dorothy Peterson, William B. Davidson, Gertrude Howard, Hattie McDaniel; ***D:*** Wesley Ruggles; ***W:*** Lowell Brentano, Mae West; ***C:*** Leo Tover; ***M:*** Harvey Brooks.

I'm Not Rappaport ✂✂ **1996 (PG-13)** Matthau does some comic grump schtick as irascible, unrepentent 81-year-old New York Jewish radical Nat. He likes to vent his considerable opinions in Central Park and carries on a grumbling friendship with fellow octogenarian Midge (Davis), who stills works as a building superintendent, tending an equally ancient boiler. But Nat's fed-up daughter Clara (Irving) is threatening to put him in a home and Midge seems likely to lose his job when the boiler is scheduled for replacement. Gardner's 1986 stage play tends to show its weaknesses on the big screen. **135m/C VHS, DVD.** Walter Matthau, Ossie Davis, Amy Irving, Martha Plimpton, Craig T. Nelson, Boyd Gaines, Guillermo Diaz, Elina Lowensohn, Ron Rifkin; ***D:*** Herb Gardner; ***W:*** Herb Gardner; ***C:*** Adam Holender; ***M:*** Gerry Mulligan.

I'm Not Scared ✂✂ *Io Non Ho Paura* **2003 (R)** 10-year-old Michele (Christiana) lives in a remote and poor village in southern Italy. As he pokes around an abandoned house one hot summer day, he discovers a trapdoor that leads to a pit where a traumatized kidnapped boy, Filippo (Di Pierro), is being held prisoner. Michele's afraid to tell his parents-rightly so as it becomes clear his father (Abbrescia) is involved-but he also can't abandon Filippo, returning to him again and again with food and water. Just what Michele does do becomes the crux of this disturbing thriller. Based on the novel by co-screenwriter Ammaniti. Italian with subtitles. **110m/C DVD.** *GB IT SP* Aitana Sanchez-Gijon, Diego Abatantuono, Dino Abbrescia, Giorgio Careccia, Giuseppe Cristiano, Mattia Di Perro; ***D:*** Gabriele Salvatores; ***W:*** Francesca Marciano, Niccolo Ammaniti; ***C:*** Italo Petriccione; ***M:*** Pepo Scherman, Ezio Bosso.

I'm Not There ✂✂✂ **2007 (R)** Sort of a symbolist musical history pic loaded with real-life clips and acted by no less than six separate actors and actresses representing different identities of poet/musician/revolutionary Bob Dylan. There's 11-year-old Woody (Franklin) who hops trains and tells far-fetched stories; Jack Rollins (Bale) personifies Dylan's first look at fame in folk-song roots; Jude (Blanchett) represents Dylan's shift to electric rock, a divisive move that alienated many of his fans. Richard Gere shows up as Billy, a personification of Dylan exiled in Missouri. Arthur (Whishaw), yet another Dylan, narrates and brings the sequences somewhat into focus. It's long and rambling and dreamlike, but Dylan fans will delight at the many references that their less-obsessed friends will miss. **135m/C DVD.** *GE US* Christian Bale, Heath Ledger, Cate Blanchett, Ben Whishaw, Marcus Carl Franklin, Richard Gere, Charlotte Gainsbourg, Julianne Moore, Michelle Williams, David Cross, Bruce Greenwood, Lisa Bronwyn Moore; ***D:*** Todd Haynes; ***W:*** Todd Haynes, Oren Moverman; ***C:*** Edward Lachman. Golden Globes '08: Support. Actress (Blanchett); Ind. Spirit '08: Support. Actress (Blanchett).

I'm Reed Fish ✂✂ **2006 (PG)** Reed Fish (Baruchel), a talk jock on the small local radio station in Mud Meadows, is about to marry his high school sweetheart, Kate (Bledel). But Reed questions his carefully planned-out world when former school chum/aspiring musician Jill (Fisk) blows back into town. Reed decides to quit his job and make a movie about his life. Yeah, this quirky comedy is based on the life of screenwriter—wait for it—Reed Fish. **93m/C DVD.** Jay Baruchel, Alexis Bledel, Schuyler Fisk, DJ Qualls, Shiri Appleby, Katey Sagal, Victor Rasuk, Chris Parnell, A.J. Cook; ***D:*** Zackary Adler; ***W:*** Reed Fish; ***C:*** Douglas Chamberlain; ***M:*** Roddy Bottum.

I'm the Girl He Wants to Kill ✂ 1/2 **1974** A woman sees a murder committed, and the murderer sees her. Now he's after her. **71m/C VHS.** Robert Lang, Julie Sommars, Anthony Steel; ***D:*** Shaun O'Riordan; ***W:*** Brian Clemens.

I'm the One You're Looking For ✂✂ 1/2 **1988** A famous model obsessively combs Barcelona for the man who raped her. Suspenseful thriller based on a short story by Gabriel Garcia Marquez. In Spanish with English subtitles. **85m/C VHS.** *SP* Patricia Adriani, Chus (Maria Jesus) Lampreave, Ricard Borras, Toni Canto, Angel Alcazar, Marta Fedz, Frank Muro, Miriam DeMaeztu; ***D:*** Jaime Chavarri.

I'm with Lucy ✂✂ 1/2 **2002 (R)** Cutesy romantic comedy. Lucy (Potter) gets publicly dumped by her boyfriend but still believes her soulmate is out there somewhere. So she goes on five blind dates (Hannah, Bernal, LaPaglia, Thomas, Boreanaz) but can only see her would-be suitors' flaws and not their good points. Still, it all comes out right in the end. **90m/C VHS, DVD.** Monica Potter, John Hannah, Gael Garcia Bernal, Anthony LaPaglia, Henry Thomas, David Boreanaz, Julianne Nicholson, Harold Ramis, Julie Christie; ***D:*** Jon Sherman; ***W:*** Eric Pomerance; ***C:*** Tom Richmond; ***M:*** Stephen Endelman.

The Image ✂✂ 1/2 **1989** Anchorman Finney, the unscrupulous czar of infotainment, does a little soul delving when a man he wrongly implicated in a savings and loan debacle decides to check into the hereafter ahead of schedule. Seems the newsmonger's cut a few corners en route to the bigtime, and his public is mad as hell and..oops, wrong movie (need we say there are not a few echoes of "Network"?). Finney's great. **91m/C VHS, DVD.** Albert Finney, John Mahoney, Kathy Baker, Swoosie Kurtz, Marsha Mason, Spalding Gray; ***D:*** Peter Werner; ***M:*** James Newton Howard. **CABLE**

Image of Death ✂ **1977** Woman plots to take the life of an old school chum, assume her identity, and then blow up the Capitol. **83m/C VHS.** Cathy Paine, Cheryl Waters, Tony Banner, Barry Pierce, Sheila Helpmann, Penne Hackforth-Jones; ***D:*** Kevin James Dobson.

Image of Passion ✂ **1986** Weak account of male stripper/lovely advertising executive romance. **90m/C VHS.** James Horan, Susan Damante-Shaw, Edward Bell; ***D:*** Susan Orlikoff-Simon.

Imagemaker ✂ 1/2 **1986 (R)** Uneven story of a presidential media consultant who bucks the system and exposes corruption. **93m/C VHS.** Michael Nouri, Jerry Orbach, Jessica Harper, Farley Granger; ***D:*** Hal Wiener.

Images ✂ **1972 (R)** Minor Altman is a confusing mish-mash with the scenery more dramatic than the flick. Hugh (Auberjonois) has taken his anxiety-ridden wife Cathryn (York) for a weekend at their country retreat on the Irish coast. Cathryn is having hallucinations about dead lovers but Hugh doesn't seem to realize his wife is going nuts until it's too late. **101m/C DVD.** Susannah York, Rene Auberjonois, Marcel Bozzuffi, Hugh Millais, Cathryn Harrison; ***D:*** Robert Altman; ***W:*** Robert Altman; ***C:*** Vilmos Zsigmond; ***M:*** John Williams.

The Imaginarium of Doctor Parnassus ✂✂ **2009 (PG-13)** Traveling showman Dr. Parnassus (Plummer) made a very long ago deal with the devil (Waits) for immortality but barters his teenage daughter Valentina's (Cole) soul in exchange. That is, unless he can deliver five other souls to an alternate world of the imagination that's entered through a looking glass (shades of Lewis Carroll). When Tony (Ledger et al) is saved from suicide by the travelers, Parnassus sees him as being a possible way to win the bet. Since Heath Ledger died during production, director Gilliam had actors Depp, Law, and Farrell play variations of the same character to melancholy effect. It's fool-the-eye, existential smoke and mirrors from Gilliam's obviously overloaded and exhausting imagination. **122m/C DVD.** *GB CA* Christopher Plummer, Heath Ledger, Johnny Depp, Jude Law, Colin Farrell, Tom Waits, Lily Cole, Verne Troyer, Andrew Garfield; ***D:*** Terry Gilliam; ***W:*** Terry Gilliam, Charles McKeown; ***C:*** Nicola Pecorini; ***M:*** Mychael Danna, Jeff Danna.

Imaginary Crimes ✂✂✂ **1994 (PG)** Ray Weiler (Keitel) is a well-meaning salesman with dreams much bigger than his reach. After the death of his wife (Lynch), Ray tries to raise his two daughters, Sonya (Balk) and Greta (Moss). But gifted high school senior (in 1962) Sonya is resentful of being her sister's maternal anchor and having her father's schemes come to nothing even as she acknowledges how much Ray cares and how he wants to improve their lives. Remarkable performances by Keitel and Balk. From the novel by Sheila Ballantyne. **106m/C VHS, DVD.** Harvey Keitel, Fairuza Balk, Kelly Lynch, Vincent D'Onofrio, Elisabeth (Elissabeth, Elizabeth, Liz) Moss, Diane Baker, Christopher Penn, Seymour Cassel, Annette O'Toole; ***D:*** Tony Drazan; ***W:*** Kristine Johnson, Davia Nelson; ***C:*** John Campbell; ***M:*** Stephen Endelman.

Imaginary Heroes ✂✂ **2005 (R)** Painfully cliche-ridden story of a dysfunctional, angst-ridden suburban family. When her superjock son kills himself, Sandy (Weaver) descends into a weed-smoking haze while the rest of her family struggles to deal with Matt's death as well as their own problems. Drugs, anger, bisexual experimentation, eating disorders, and cancer scares ensue. Writer/director Harris piles on the plot twists and tragedies to remind you of how bad these people have it. Weaver and Hirsch (as younger son Tim) are convincing, but the film's combination of grief-stricken melodrama and wry irony is awkward and contrived, and the movie just ends up feeling like a cheap knock-off of many superior films. **112m/C DVD.** *US* Sigourney Weaver, Emile Hirsch, Jeff Daniels, Michelle Williams, Kip Pardue, Deirdre O'Connell, Ryan Donowho, Jay Paulson, Suzanne Santo; ***D:*** Daniel P. "Dan" Harris; ***W:*** Daniel P. "Dan" Harris; ***C:*** Tim Orr; ***M:*** John Ottman, Deborah Lurie.

Imagine Me & You ✂ 1/2 **2006 (R)** In this London-set confection, Rachel (Perabo) is walking up the aisle to marry longtime sweetie Heck (Goode) when she catches the eye of attractive florist Luce (Headey). Newlywed Rachel and Luce are then repeatedly thrown together and soon admit to their mutual attraction. Heck eventually realizes that something is amiss in his marriage even as Luce despairs at being the other woman. Bland and boring, despite, or maybe because of, the attractive cast. **93m/C DVD.** *US* Piper Perabo, Lena Headey, Matthew Goode, Celia Imrie, Anthony Head, Darren Boyd, Eva Birthistle, Bo Jackson, Sue Johnston, Sharon Horgan; ***D:*** Ol Parker; ***W:*** Ol Parker; ***C:*** Benjamin Davis; ***M:*** Alex Heffes.

Imagine That ✂✂ 1/2 *Nowhereland* **2009 (PG)** Murphy as family man. Evan Danielson is a workaholic investment advisor who discovers his bonding with his adorable seven-year-old daughter Olivia (Shahidi) leads literally to an unexpected payoff. Olivia's imaginary world (that is accessed through her security blanket Goo-Gaa) consists of three princesses, a queen, and a dragon that provide exceptionally accurate financial advice. Of course, Evan has to make a fool of himself (to placate Olivia's invisible playmates) and his business rival—fake Native American Johnny Whitefeather (Church)—is jealous and suspicious of Evan's sudden success. **107m/C DVD.** *US* Eddie Murphy, Nicole Ari Parker, Thomas Haden Church, Vanessa Williams, Ronny Cox, Yara Shahidi, Martin Sheen; ***D:*** Karey Kirkpatrick; ***W:*** Edward Solomon, Chris M. Theson; ***C:*** John Lindley; ***M:*** Mark Mancina.

Imagining Argentina ✂✂ **2004 (R)** In 1970s Argentina, Banderas is Carlos Rueda, a childrens' theater director whose journalist wife (Thompson) has disappeared after trying to investigate the fate of thousands of people who have been taken away by government agents. He soon discovers psychic abilities and is able to tell the fates of many of the victims, but is only able to divine obscure clues to his wife's disappearance. The introduction of the pshychic element is jarring to the political and personal story of the toll of totalitarian persecution, and derails the entire production. **108m/C DVD.** Antonio Banderas, Emma Thompson, Ruben Blades, Maria Canals, Claire Bloom, John Wood; ***D:*** Christopher Hampton; ***W:*** Christopher Hampton; ***C:*** Guillermo Navarro; ***M:*** George Fenton.

Imitation of Life ✂✂ 1/2 **1934** Fannie Hurst novel tells the story of widowed Beatrice Pullman (Colbert) who uses maid Delilah's (Beaver) recipe for pancakes in order to have the women open a restaurant, which becomes a success. Both mothers suffer at the hands of their willfull teenaged daughters. Delilah's lightskinned daughter Peola (Washington) breaks away from her mother so she can continue to pass for white and Bea's daughter Jessie (Hudson) has a serious crush on her mother's beau, Stephen (William). Weepie was also successfully filmed in 1959. **106m/B VHS.** Claudette Colbert, Louise Beavers, Rochelle Hudson, Fredi Washington, Warren William, Ned Sparks, Alan Hale; ***D:*** John M. Stahl; ***W:*** Preston Sturges, William Hurlbut; ***C:*** Merritt B. Gerstad. Natl. Film Reg. '05.

Imitation of Life ✂✂✂ **1959** Remake of the successful 1934 Claudette Colbert outing of the same title, and based on Fanny Hurst's novel, with a few plot changes. Turner is a single mother, more determined to achieve acting fame and fortune than function as a parent. Her black maid, Moore, is devoted to her own daughter (Kohner), but loses her when the girl discovers she can pass for white. When Turner discovers that she and her daughter are in love with the same man, she realizes how little she knows her daughter, and how much the two of them have missed by not having a stronger relationship. Highly successful at the boxoffice. **124m/C VHS, DVD.** Lana Turner, John Gavin, Troy Donahue, Sandra Dee, Juanita Moore, Susan Kohner; ***D:*** Douglas Sirk; ***C:*** Russell Metty. Golden Globes '60: Support. Actress (Kohner).

Immediate Family ✂✂ 1/2 **1989 (PG-13)** Childless couple contact a pregnant, unmarried girl and her boyfriend in hopes of adoption. As the pregnancy advances, the mother has doubts about giving up her baby. A bit sugar-coated in an effort to woo family trade. **112m/C VHS, DVD.** Glenn Close, James Woods, Kevin Dillon, Mary Stuart Masterson, Linda Darlow, Jane Greer, Jessica James, Mimi Kennedy; ***D:*** Jonathan Kaplan; ***W:*** Barbara Benedek; ***M:*** Brad Fiedel. Natl. Bd. of Review '89: Support. Actress (Masterson).

The Immigrant ✂✂✂ 1/2 **1917** Chaplin portrays a newly arrived immigrant who falls in love with the first girl he meets. Silent with musical soundtrack added. **20m/B VHS, DVD.** Charlie Chaplin, Edna Purviance, Eric Campbell, Kitty Bradbury; ***D:*** Charlie Chaplin; ***W:*** Charlie Chaplin. Natl. Film Reg. '98.

The Immoral One ✂ 1/2 *Confessions of a Prostitute; L'Immorale* **1980** Lamo is suffering from amnesia. Fortunately, she's apparently taped her life story for a book deal and can learn all the sordid details. And sordid they are since she was a prostitute in Paris, involved with both men and women, and with a blackmailing madam. **90m/C VHS.** *FR* Sylvia Lamo, Yves Jouffroy, Isabelle Legentil; ***D:*** Claude Mulot; ***W:*** Claude Mulot.

The Immortal 2001 The pilot to a short-lived syndicated TV show that was more camp than action. Lamas is the title character who has a 400-year history of detecting and destroying demons who are plaguing the world. **m/C VHS, DVD.** Lorenzo Lamas, Steve Braun, April Telek. **TV**

Immortal 1/2 *Immortal Ad Vitam* **2004 (R)** Writer/director Bilal uses CGI and blue screen to depict a devastated New York in 2095 in this visually arresting but completely confusing (and very loose) adaptation of two of his graphic novels. An interstellar pyramid invisibly hovers over the city, housing several Egyptian gods, including Horus (Pollard), who is about to lose his immortality. He has seven days to find a human vessel to host his spirit long enough so that he may impregnate a mate who will give birth to a new immortal. Horus chooses the rebellious Alcide Nikopol (Kretschmann) and the blue-haired Jill (Hardy), only there are a lot of complications to overcome, including the fact that Jill isn't exactly human. **102m/C DVD, Blu-ray Disc.** *GB FR IT* Linda Hardy, Thomas Pollard; ***D:*** Enki Bilal; ***W:*** Enki Bilal, Joe Sheridan, Serge Lehman; ***C:*** Pascal Gennesseaux; ***M:*** Goran Vejvoda.

Immortal Bachelor 1/2 **1980 (PG)** Good cast can't overcome the silliness of this one. A juror daydreams about the dead husband of a cleaning woman on trial for killing her adulterous spouse. She decides the dead man seems a lot more exciting than her own dull and tiresome husband. **94m/C VHS.** *IT* Giancarlo Giannini, Monica Vitti, Claudia Cardinale, Vittorio Gassman; ***D:*** Marcello Fondato; ***C:*** Pasqualino De Santis.

Immortal Battalion *The Way Ahead* **1944** Entertaining wartime psuedo-documentary follows newly recruited soldiers as they are molded from an ordinary group of carping civilians into a hardened battalion of fighting men by Niven. Some prints run to 116 minutes. **89m/B VHS, DVD.** *GB* David Niven, Stanley Holloway, Reginald Tate, Raymond Huntley, William Hartnell, James Donald, Peter Ustinov, John Laurie, Leslie Dwyer, Hugh Burden, Jimmy Hanley, Leo Genn, Renee Asherson, Mary Jerrold, Tessie O'Shea, Raymond Lovell, A.E. Matthews, Jack Watling; ***D:*** Carol Reed; ***W:*** Eric Ambler, Peter Ustinov; ***C:*** Guy Green; ***M:*** William Alwyn.

Immortal Beloved **1994 (R)** The death of Ludwig van Beethoven prompts his loyal secretary to seek the identity of a mystery love to whom the composer has bequeathed his estate. While Beethoven's genius is awesome and his music breathtaking, his lovelife is neither, and the ensuing confessions of the maestro's former loves only get in the way of flashbacks that hint at his torment and triumph. Oldman is darkly intense, and a scene in which the aged Beethoven remembers his terrifying childhood amid the strains of "Ode to Joy" is simply stunning, but an unfocused script undoes what might have been a fine tribute to the master. The London Symphony Orchestra and soloists Murray Perahia, Emanuel Ax, and Yo Yo Ma contributed to the splendid soundtrack. **121m/C VHS, DVD, Blu-ray Disc.** Gary Oldman, Jeroen Krabbe, Isabella Rossellini, Johanna Ter Steege, Marco Hofschneider, Miriam Margolyes, Barry Humphries, Valeria Golino, Christopher Fulford; ***D:*** Bernard Rose; ***W:*** Bernard Rose; ***C:*** Peter Suschitzky.

Immortal Combat 1/2 **1994 (R)** An army of men trained in ninja and guerilla warfare have seemingly immortal powers. Can our two violent heroes find an equally destructive way to stop the killing? **109m/C VHS, DVD.** Roddy Piper, Sonny Chiba, Tommy (Tiny) Lister, Meg Foster; ***D:*** Daniel Neira; ***W:*** Daniel Neira, Robert Crabtree; ***C:*** Henner Hofmann.

Immortal Sergeant 1/2 **1943** After the battle death of the squad leader, an inexperienced corporal takes command of North African troops during WWII. Fonda gives a strong performance. Based on a novel by John Brody. **91m/B VHS, DVD.** Henry Fonda, Thomas Mitchell, Maureen O'Hara, Allyn Joslyn, Reginald Gardiner, Melville Cooper, Morton Lowry, Peter Lawford, John Banner, Bud Geary, James Craven; ***D:*** John M. Stahl; ***W:*** Lamar Trotti; ***C:*** Clyde De Vinna, Arthur C. Miller; ***M:*** David Buttolph.

Immortal Sins **1991 (R)** Michael and Susan inherited an old Spanish Castle, complete with its own curse, which comes in the form of a seductive women that has haunted families for centuries. **80m/C VHS.** Cliff DeYoung, Maryam D'Abo; ***W:*** Thomas McKelvey Cleaver.

Immortality *The Wisdom of Crocodiles* **1998 (R)** The vampire myth undergoes yet another postmodern twist. Steven Grlscz (Law) is a medical researcher, living in London, who stops Maria (Fox) from committing suicide and then sets out to seduce her. When he's convinced she's in love with him, he kills her and takes her blood. His next would-be victim is Anne (Lowensohn), but she's reluctant to commit to Steven and soon he becomes ill, which leads him to confess to Anne that his bloodsucking tendencies can only be satiated when he believes his victims love him. While Law is a charming seducer, he fails to chill as a vampire killer. **98m/C VHS, DVD.** *GB* Jude Law, Elina Lowensohn, Timothy Spall, Kerry Fox, Jack Davenport, Colin Salmon; ***D:*** Po-Chih Leung; ***W:*** Paul Hoffman; ***C:*** Oliver Curtis; ***M:*** John Lunn, Orlando Gough.

The Immortalizer **1989 (R)** A mad doctor transfers people's brains into young bodies for a price, although it's not as simple as it sounds. **85m/C VHS.** Ron Kay, Chris Crone, Melody Patterson, Clarke Lindsley, Bekki Armstrong; ***D:*** Joel Bender.

The Immortals **1995 (R)** Nightclub owner Jack (Roberts) recruits eight terminally ill criminals in an elaborate heist that calls for simultaneously hitting targets citywide. But when they compare notes, the team fear a doublecross. **92m/C VHS, DVD.** Louis Lombardi, Eric Roberts, Tia Carrere, William Forsythe, Joe Pantoliano, Clarence Williams III, Tony Curtis, Chris Rock, Kieran Mulroney, Kevin Bernhardt; ***D:*** Brian Grant; ***W:*** Kevin Bernhardt; ***C:*** Anthony B. Richmond.

Impact **1949** A woman and her lover plan the murder of her rich industrialist husband, but the plan backfires. More twists and turns than a carnival ride. **111m/B VHS, DVD.** Brian Donlevy, Ella Raines, Charles Coburn, Helen Walker, Anna May Wong, Philip Ahn, Art Baker, Tony Barrett, Harry Cheshire, Lucius Cooke, Joel Friedkin, Sheilah Graham, Tom Greenway, Hans Herbert, Linda Johnson, Joe (Joseph) Kirk, Clarence (C. William) Kolb, Mary Landa, Mae Marsh; ***D:*** Arthur Lubin; ***W:*** Dorothy Reid, Jay Dratler; ***C:*** Ernest Laszlo; ***M:*** Michel Michelet.

Impact Point 1/2 **2008 (R)** Popular pro beach volleyball player Kelly Reyes (Keller) has only cared about her game until mysterious reporter Holden (Green) shows up. A series of bizarre events threaten to derail her career and then things turn even more sinister. **85m/C DVD.** Melissa Keller, Linden Ashby, Joe Manganiello, Brian Austin Green, Eddie Alfano; ***D:*** Hayley Cloake; ***W:*** Brett Merryman; ***C:*** Thomas M. Harting; ***M:*** Steven Stern. **VIDEO**

The Imperial Japanese Empire **1985** Epic of the WWII Pacific seen through Japanese eyes. **130m/C VHS.** *JP* Tetsuro Tamba, Tomokazu Miura, Teruhiko Saigo, Teruhiko Aoi, Saburo Shinoda, Keiko Sekine, Masako Natsume, Akiko Kana.

Imperial Venus *Venere Imperiale* **1963 (PG)** Biography of Napoleon's sister, Paolina Boneparte—with particular focus on her many loves, lusts and tribulations. **121m/C VHS, DVD.** *FR IT* Gina Lollobrigida, Stephen Boyd, Raymond Pellegrin; ***D:*** Jean Delannoy; ***W:*** Jean Delannoy; ***C:*** Gabor Pogany; ***M:*** Angelo Francesco Lavagnino.

Implicated **1998 (R)** Tom (McNamara) asks his new girlfriend Ann (Locane) to help him out by babysitting his boss' young daughter, Katie. But Ann soon realizes that Tom's kidnapped Katie and they're both pawns in an elaborate scheme that has gone out of control. Based on the book "Wishful Thinking" by Frank Wyka. **95m/C VHS.** Amy Locane, William McNamara, Frederic Forrest, Priscilla Barnes; ***D:*** Irving Belateche; ***W:*** Webb Millsaps, Irving Belateche. **VIDEO**

Impolite 1/2 **1992** After getting on the wrong side during a police corruption story, alcoholic reporter Jack (Wisden) has been demoted to writing obits. When he gets a tip that rich and powerul O'Rourke (an uncredited Plummer who also plays the character's twin brother, a priest) has died, Jack decides to investigate the rumor by interviewing the strange group who surrounded O'Rourke. **90m/C VHS, DVD.** *CA* Robert Wisden, Kevin McNulty, Stuart Margolin, Jill Teed, Susan Hogan, Christopher Plummer; ***D:*** David Hauka; ***W:*** Michael McKinley; ***C:*** Robert McLachlan; ***M:*** Braun Farnon, Robert Smart.

The Importance of Being Earnest **1952** Fine production of classic Oscar Wilde comedy-of-manners. Cast couldn't be better or the story funnier. **95m/C VHS, DVD.** Michael Redgrave, Edith Evans, Margaret Rutherford, Michael Denison, Joan Greenwood, Dorothy Tutin; ***D:*** Anthony Asquith; ***W:*** Anthony Asquith; ***C:*** Desmond Dickinson; ***M:*** Benjamin Frankel.

The Importance of Being Earnest **2002 (PG)** Jack Worthing (Firth) has invented a brother, Earnest, in order to leave the dull country and visit lovely Gwendolyn (O'Connor), the daughter of the formidable Lady Bracknell (Dench), in London. His best friend Algernon Montcrieff (Everett), who is Gwendolyn's cousin, also has a make-believe chum named Bunbury to get Algy out of boring situations. Then Algy decides to pose as Earnest in order to woo Jack's country ward, Cecily (Witherspoon). But when everyone ends up together, chaos threatens. Based on the play by Oscar Wilde and filled with bon mots, director Parker felt compelled to "open up" the production, which only works some of the time. But the performances are all delightful and Witherspoon manages her English accent quite nicely. **100m/C VHS, DVD.** *US GB* Colin Firth, Rupert Everett, Frances O'Connor, Reese Witherspoon, Judi Dench, Tom Wilkinson, Anna Massey, Edward Fox, Patrick Godfrey, Charles Kay, Finty Williams; ***D:*** Oliver Parker; ***W:*** Oliver Parker; ***C:*** Tony Pierce-Roberts; ***M:*** Charlie Mole.

The Imported Bridegroom **1989** A comedy set at the turn of the century about a man who returns to Poland in order to find his daughter a proper husband. **93m/C VHS.** Eugene Troobnick, Avi Hoffman, Greta Cowan, Annette Miller; ***D:*** Pamela Berger; ***W:*** Pamela Berger.

The Impossible Spy **1987** True story of Elie Cohen, an unassuming Israeli who doubled as a top level spy in Syria during the 1960s. Cohen became so close to Syria's president that he was nominated to become the Deputy Minister of Defense before his double life was exposed. Well-acted spy thriller and is worth a look for espionage fans. **96m/C VHS, DVD.** *GB* John Shea, Eli Wallach, Michal Bat-Adam, Rami Danon, Sasson Gabray, Chaim Girafi; ***D:*** Jim Goddard; ***M:*** Richard Hartley. **CABLE**

The Impossible Years **1968** Unattractive, leering sex farce about psychiatrist Nivens who has problems with his own young daughter. Dismal adaptation of the hit Broadway play by Bob Fisher and Arthur Marx. **97m/C VHS.** David Niven, Lola Albright, Chad Everett, Ozzie Nelson, Christina Ferrare, Jeff Cooper, John Harding; ***D:*** Michael Gordon; ***W:*** George Wells.

The Imposters *Ship of Fools* **1998 (R)** Its the 1930s, and third-rate actors Arthur and Maurice (Tucci and Platt, respectively) are out of work. Inadvertently forced into hiding on a cruise ship, they encounter a virtual ship of fools while slinking around in an array of costumes. The wacky story unfolds as the stowaways run into various characters: the Nazi-like, crop-wielding head steward (Scott), a gay Scottish wrestler (Connolly), an anarchist bomber from an unnamed Eastern European nation (Shalhoub), his country's deposed queen (Rossellini), and a pair of murderous con artists posing as French tourists. Written and directed by Tucci, pic reunites much of the cast from Tucci and Scott's "Big Night." Unfortunately, they weren't as successful this time. Too much free-reign hamming by the big-name indie cast sinks this homage to Buster Keaton and the Marx Brothers. **101m/C VHS, DVD.** Stanley Tucci, Oliver Platt, Elizabeth Bracco, Steve Buscemi, Billy Connolly, Allan Corduner, Hope Davis, Dana Ivey, Allison Janney, Richard Jenkins, Matt McGrath, Alfred Molina, Isabella Rossellini, Campbell Scott, Tony Shalhoub, Lili Taylor, Lewis J. Stadlen, Woody Allen; ***D:*** Stanley Tucci; ***W:*** Stanley Tucci; ***C:*** Ken Kelsch; ***M:*** Gary DeMichele.

The Impostor 1/2 **1984** Improbable tale of a con artist/ex-con who impersonates a high school principal in order to regain his estranged girlfriend, who works as a teacher. Complications ensue when he tackles the school's drug problems. **95m/C VHS.** Anthony Geary, Billy Dee Williams, Lorna Patterson; ***D:*** Michael Pressman. **TV**

Impostor **2002 (PG-13)** When a movie is shelved for a year and a half, there's usually a reason. Earth in 2079 is dystopian and paranoid, and the neon-blue cave lighting makes it difficult to see. Which is not a huge loss. Talented cast is reduced to a collection of archetypes, including the usually solid Sinise as an elite military scientist accused of fighting (as a replicant) for the wrong team, namely, the sinister aliens who are laying waste to our earth. Citizens are monitored via spinal identification chips, yet a hooded sweatshirt and sunglasses are enough to shield public enemy #1 from detection. Tired sci-fi themes of soul and identity are not enough to keep things interesting. Adapted (and yawningly stretched) from a short story by perennial sci-fi source Philip K. Dick. **96m/C VHS, DVD.** *US* Gary Sinise, Madeleine Stowe, Vincent D'Onofrio, Tony Shalhoub, Mekhi Phifer, Tim Guinee, Lindsay Crouse, Gary Dourdan, Erica Gimpel, Elizabeth Pena; ***D:*** Gary Fleder; ***W:*** Ehren Kruger, David N. Twohy, Caroline Case; ***C:*** Robert Elswit; ***M:*** Mark Isham.

Impostors **1980** A comedy centering on the romantic problems between a self-indulgent young man and the woman who cheats on him. **110m/C VHS.** Ellen McElduff, Charles Ludlam, Michael J. Burg, Peter Evans; ***D:*** Mark Rappaport; ***W:*** Mark Rappaport; ***C:*** Fred Murphy.

Impromptu **1990 (PG-13)** A smart, sassy, romantic comedy set in 1830s Europe among the era's artistic greats—here depicted as scalawags, parasites and early beatniks. The film's ace is Davis in a lusty, dynamic role as mannish authoress George Sand, obsessively in love with the dismayed composer Chopin. Though he's too pallid a character for her attraction to be credible, a great cast and abundant wit make this a treat. Beautiful score featuring Chopin and Liszt. Film debut of stage director Lapine; screenplay written by his wife, Sarah Kernochan. **108m/C VHS, DVD.** Judy Davis, Hugh Grant, Mandy Patinkin, Bernadette Peters, Julian Sands, Ralph Brown, Georges Corraface, Anton Rodgers, Emma Thompson, Anna Massey, John Savident, Elizabeth Spriggs; ***D:*** James Lapine; ***W:*** Sarah Kernochan; ***C:*** Bruno de Keyzer. Ind. Spirit '92: Actress (Davis).

Improper Channels **1982 (PG)** Mediocre comedy about a couple trying to recover their daughter after being accused of child abuse. **91m/C VHS.** Monica Parker, Alan Arkin, Mariette Hartley; ***D:*** Eric Till; ***W:*** Adam Arkin.

Improper Conduct **1994 (R)** Ad agency employee is sexually harassed by her boss but loses her court case. Her sister decides to get revenge by getting hired and setting the slimeball up for a fall. **95m/C VHS.** Steven Bauer, Lee Ann Beaman, John Laughlin, Kathy Shower, Tahnee Welch, Nia Peeples, Stuart Whitman, Adrian Zmed, Patsy Pease; ***D:*** Jag Mundhra; ***W:*** Carl Austin.

Impulse 1/2 **1955** When his wife leaves for a visit with her mother, a young man is thrust into cahoots with gangsters, and wrapped up in an affair with another woman. **81m/B VHS.** *GB* Arthur Kennedy, Constance Smith, Joy Shelton; ***D:*** Cy Endfield; ***W:*** Cy Endfield.

Impulse **WOOF!** *Want a Ride, Little Girl?; I Love to Kill* **1974 (PG)** Shatner, a crazed killer, is released from prison and starts to kill again in this low-budget, predictable, critically debased film about child-molesting. **85m/C VHS, DVD.** William Shatner, Ruth Roman, Harold Sakata, Kim Nicholas, Jennifer Bishop, James Dobson; ***D:*** William Grefe; ***W:*** Tony Crechales; ***C:*** Edwin Gibson; ***M:*** Lewis Perles.

Impulse **1984 (R)** Small town residents can't control their impulses, all because of government toxic waste in their milk. A woman worried about her mother's mental health returns to town with her doctor boyfriend to discover most of the inhabitants are quite mad. Starts strong but... **95m/C VHS, DVD.** Tim Matheson, Meg Tilly, Hume Cronyn, John Karlen, Bill Paxton, Amy Stryker, Claude Earl Jones, Sherri Stoner; ***D:*** Graham Baker; ***W:*** Don Carlos Dunaway, Nicholas Kazan; ***C:*** Thomas Del Ruth; ***M:*** Paul Chihara.

Impulse ½ **1990 (R)** A beautiful undercover vice cop poses as a prostitute, and gives in to base desires. Russell gives a fine performance in this underrated sleeper. **109m/C VHS.** Theresa Russell, Nicholas Mele, Eli Danker, Charles McCaughan, Jeff Fahey, George Dzundza, Alan Rosenberg, Lynne Thigpen, Shawn Elliott; ***D:*** Sondra Locke; ***W:*** John DeMarco, Leigh Chapman; ***M:*** Michel Colombier.

Impulse **2008 (R)** Utterly preposterous, not-so-erotic thriller. Clair (Ford) is an advertising manager, married to older psychologist Jonathan (Macfayden). Wanting to spice up their love life, Clair suggests a hotel fantasy while she's on a business trip. Clair's happily surprised when Jonathan picks her up in the bar, only to find out that the man in bed with her is not her husband but a lookalike named Simon. Upset when Clair suddenly rejects him without explanation, Simon begins stalking her. **101m/C DVD.** Angus MacFadyen, Ingrid Torrance, Willa Ford; ***D:*** Charles Kanganis; ***W:*** Charles Kanganis; ***C:*** Gordon Verheul; ***M:*** Stu Goldberg. **VIDEO**

Impure Thoughts **1986 (PG)** Four friends meet in the afterlife and discuss their Catholic school days. Odd premise never catches fire. **87m/C VHS.** Brad Dourif, Lane Davies, John Putch, Terry Beaver; ***D:*** Michael A. Simpson.

iMurders **2008** A serial killer targets a group of friends who chat nightly on a social network. A couple of FBI agents show up before the group realizes they're losing members to more than boredom and the crime relates back to a secret in someone's past. Actually the movie makes little to no sense with characters popping in and out for no discernable reason. **98m/C DVD.** Terri Colombino, Frank Grillo, Joanne Baron, Gabrielle Anwar, Billy Dee Williams, Tony Todd, Brooke Lewis, Wilson Jermaine Heredia, Shannon Ivey, Charles Durning, William Forsythe, Margaret Colin, Justin Deas; ***D:*** Robbie Bryan; ***W:*** Robbie Bryan, Ken Del Vecchio; ***C:*** Hiroo Takaoka. **VIDEO**

In a Class of His Own ½ **1999** School janitor Rich Donato (Phillips) is an ex-teen bad boy who has formed a close relationship with both the teachers and the students at the high school where he works. However, in order to keep his job, he learns he must pass his GED and this isn't an easy task. When his wife appeals for help, Rich finds himself becoming a school project. Based on a true story. **94m/C VHS, DVD.** Lou Diamond Phillips, Cara Buono, Joan Chen, Nathaniel DeVeaux; ***D:*** Robert Munic; ***W:*** Robert Munic; ***C:*** Ron Stannett; ***M:*** Sharon Farber. **CABLE**

In a Day **2006** Ashley (Pilkington) is waiting at a London bus stop when a crazy stranger throws coffee all over her. Michael (Robertson), whom Ashley recognizes as a frequent customer at the sandwich shop where she works, comes to her aid and persuades her to let him make things better with a gourmet lunch and a makeover though Ashley wants to know what he wants in return. **81m/C DVD.** *GB* Lorraine Pilkington, Finlay Robertson, Rose Keegan, Jake Broder, Nolan Hemmings; ***D:*** Evan Richards; ***W:*** Evan Richards; ***C:*** Gareth Pritchard; ***M:*** George M. Young.

In a Glass Cage ½ *Tras el Cristal* **1986** A young boy who was tortured and sexually molested by a Nazi official seeks revenge. Years after the war, he shows up at the Nazi's residence in Spain and is immediately befriended by his tormentor's family. Confined to an iron lung, the official is at the mercy of the young man who tortuously acts out the incidents detailed in the Nazi's journal. Suspenseful and extremely graphic, it's well crafted and meaningful but may be just too horrible to watch. Sexual and violent acts place it in the same league as Pasolini's infamous "Salo, or The 120 Days in Sodom." Definitely not for the faint of heart. In Spanish with English subtitles. **110m/C VHS, DVD.** *SP* Gunter Meisner, David Sust, Marisa Paredes, Gisela Echevarria; ***D:*** Agustin Villaronga; ***W:*** Agustin Villaronga.

In a Lonely Place ½ **1950** Bogart is outstanding as Dixon Steele, a hard-drinking and volatile Hollywood screenwriter, who becomes the prime suspect in the murder of a hat-check girl, last seen alive leaving his apartment. New neighbor Laurel Gray (Grahame) alibis the guy because she doesn't think he's a killer and he's grateful. Enough so to begin a romance with the cool beauty. But the investigating detectives still have the writer on their A-list and his paranoia kicks in. Dix begins to question Laurel's loyalty and violently over-reacts to his suspicions. Offbeat, yet superb film noir, expertly directed by Ray. Based on the novel by Dorothy B. Hughes. Ray's disintegrating marriage to Grahame seemingly played out onscreen; they split after filming. **93m/B VHS, DVD.** Humphrey Bogart, Gloria Grahame, Frank Lovejoy, Carl Benton Reid, Art Smith, Jeff Donnell; ***D:*** Nicholas Ray; ***W:*** Andrew Solt; ***C:*** Burnett Guffey. Natl. Film Reg. '07.

In a Moment of Passion ½ **1993 (R)** A two-bit actor wants to be a star—in the worst way possible. So he kills off the lead actor of a new film, takes his place, and proceeds to eliminate any obstacle that gets in his way. The problem comes in when an aspiring actress falls for the actor and then figures out what's going on. **100m/C VHS.** Maxwell Caulfield, Chase Masterson, Vivian Schilling, Julie Araskog, Joe Estevez, Robert Z'Dar, Zbigniew Kaminski; ***Cameos:*** Jeff Conaway; ***W:*** Charles Haigh.

In a Savage Land ½ **1999** Interesting premise gets a laughable execution. Prim married anthropologists Philip (Donovan) and Evelyn (Stange) Spence travel to the South Seas in the late 1930s to study native society and find their marriage quickly unraveling. Philip refuses to acknowledge the sexuality and importance of the tribe's women, so Evelyn decides to take advantage (in more than one way) of pearl merchant Mick (Sewell) to continue her studies in another village. Pretty scenery courtesy of the Trobriand Islands is the only high point. **116m/C VHS.** *AU* Martin Donovan, Rufus Sewell, Maya Stange; ***D:*** Bill Bennett; ***W:*** Bill Bennett, Jennifer Bennett; ***C:*** Danny Ruhlmann; ***M:*** David Bridie. Australian Film Inst. '99: Sound, Score.

In a Shallow Grave **1988 (R)** Shallow treatment of James Purdy's novel about a WWII veteran, badly disfigured in combat at Guadalcanal, who returns to Virginia in an attempt to return to the life he once had with the woman he still loves. Handsome Biehn plays the disfigured vet, Mueller's his ex-fiancee, and Dempsey's the drifter who adds a bisexual hypotenuse to the love triangle. Pokey American Playhouse coproduction. **92m/C VHS.** Michael Biehn, Maureen Mueller, Patrick Dempsey, Michael Beach, Thomas Boyd Mason; ***D:*** Kenneth Bowser; ***W:*** Kenneth Bowser.

In a Stranger's Hand ½ **1992** Urich stars a respected businessman who happens to find a doll which belongs to a kidnapped young girl. The police have their suspicions but Urich teams up with the child's mother to find the girl and winds up uncovering a child-selling ring. **93m/C VHS, DVD.** Robert Urich, Megan Gallagher, Brett Cullen, Vondie Curtis-Hall, Dakin Matthews, Alan Rosenberg, Maria O'Brien; ***D:*** David Greene. **TV**

In a Year of 13 Moons *In a Year with 13 Moons; In Einem Jahr Mit 13 Monden* **1978** Notorious Fassbinder tale of Erwin who becomes Elvira and is subjected to a series of humiliating relationships with men. Finally, with the aid of his/her ex-wife and a prostitute, Elvira looks into the past in an effort to resolve the present. Alternatingly depressing and pretentious. German with subtitles. **119m/C VHS, DVD.** *GE* Volker Spengler, Ingrid Caven, Gottfried John, Elisabeth Trissenaar, Eva Mattes, Gunther Kaufman; ***D:*** Rainer Werner Fassbinder; ***W:*** Rainer Werner Fassbinder; ***C:*** Rainer Werner Fassbinder; ***M:*** Peer Raben.

In America **2002 (PG-13)** After their 2-year old son dies from a brain tumor, Johnny (Considine) and Sarah (Morton) Sheridan leave Ireland with their family and head for America. The family deals with poverty and personal struggles while trying to create a better life. Real life sisters Sarah and Emma Bolger steal every scene they're in as the young Sheridans, not an easy task with this top-notch group. Honsou stands out as a dying artist neighbor. Based on the experiences of director Jim Sheridan, who co-wrote with daughters Kirsten and Naomi. Well-paced and uplifting. **103m/C VHS, DVD.** *IR GB* Paddy Considine, Samantha Morton, Sarah Bolger, Emma Bolger, Djimon Hounsou; ***D:*** Jim Sheridan; ***W:*** Jim Sheridan, Naomi Sheridan, Kirsten Sheridan; ***C:*** Declan Quinn; ***M:*** Gavin Friday, Maurice Seezer. Ind. Spirit '04: Cinematog., Support. Actor (Hounsou).

In an Old Manor House ½ **1984** Residents of an old house are tormented by the vindictive ghost of a murdered adultress whose husband didn't approve of the, uh, affection she showed his son from a previous marriage. Based on the play by Stanislaw Witkiewicz. In Polish with English subtitles. **90m/C VHS.** *PL* ***D:*** Jerzy Kotkowski.

In and Out **1997 (PG-13)** See what an Oscar can do? When Tom Hanks thanked, and inadvertently outed, his high school drama teacher during his Academy Awards speech (for "Philadelphia"), it lead to this feature. Popular high school English teacher Howard Brackett (Kline) has his sexuality come into question on the eve of his wedding thanks to a former-student-turned-movie-star (Dillon). As a media circus converges on the small town, Howard is forced to examine his sexuality by openly gay reporter Selleck (out to prove Howard's gay), his mother Reynolds (who wants the wedding to go on regardless of his orientation) and his tightly wound fiancee Cusack (who wants to put a serious hurtin' on Barbra Striesand). All-around excellent performances, especially by Kline and Cusack. **92m/C VHS, DVD.** Kevin Kline, Joan Cusack, Matt Dillon, Debbie Reynolds, Wilford Brimley, Bob Newhart, Tom Selleck, Deborah Rush, Lewis J. Stadlen, J. Smith-Cameron, Zak Orth, Gregory Jbara, Shalom Harlow, Kate McGregor-Stewart, Shawn Hatosy, Lauren Ambrose, Alexandra Holden; ***D:*** Frank Oz; ***W:*** Paul Rudnick; ***C:*** Rob Hahn; ***M:*** Marc Shaiman. N.Y. Film Critics '97: Support. Actress (Cusack); Broadcast Film Critics '97: Support. Actress (Cusack).

In Between ½ **1992 (PG-13)** When Margo, Jack, and Amy wake up they expect it to be another average day. Instead, these three strangers find themselves together in a peculiar house. An angel informs them that the house is a way station between life and the hereafter. The three must look at their pasts, imagine their futures, and decide whether to return to their old lives or accept death and go on to an afterlife. **92m/C VHS.** Wings Hauser, Robin Mattson, Alexandra Paul, Robert Forster; ***D:*** Thomas Constantinides; ***W:*** Thomas Constantinides; ***C:*** Irv Goodnoft; ***M:*** Alfred Owens.

In Bruges ½ **2008 (R)** Ray (Farrell) and Ken (Gleeson), two Irish hitmen, are sent to the picturesque medieval berg of Bruges, Belgium, to hide out following a partially botched job that targeted a priest but accidentally offed a young boy, hardly a premise for comedy. But writer/director McDonagh's debut mostly hits the mark with this pitch-black fish-out-of-water tale of tough guys laying low in the quaint town, a feat made impossible by their involvement with a local hottie and a filmmaking dwarf and the arrival of their cool boss (Fiennes). Snappy repartee and postcard scenery offset an abundance of inner torment and blood, and it's all almost too hip for its own good, but Farrell and Gleeson are terrific. **107m/C DVD.** *GB* Colin Farrell, Brendan Gleeson, Ralph Fiennes, Clarence Poesy, Jeremie Renier, Thekla Reuten, Jordan Prentice; ***D:*** Martin McDonagh; ***W:*** Martin McDonagh; ***C:*** Eigil Bryld; ***M:*** Carter Burwell. British Acad. '08: Orig. Screenplay; Golden Globes '09: Actor—Mus./Comedy (Farrell).

In Celebration **1975 (PG)** Three successful brothers return to the old homestead for their parents' 40th wedding celebration. Intense drama but somewhat claustrophobic. Based on a play by David Storey. **131m/C VHS, DVD.** *GB CA* Alan Bates, James Bolam, Brian Cox, Constance Chapman, Gabrielle Daye, Bill Owen; ***D:*** Lindsay Anderson; ***W:*** David Storey; ***C:*** Dick Bush.

In Cold Blood ½ **1967** Truman Capote's supposedly factual novel provided the basis for this hard-hitting docu-drama about two ex-cons who ruthlessly murder a Kansas family in 1959 in order to steal their non-existent stash of money. Blake is riveting as one of the killers. **133m/B VHS, DVD.** Robert (Bobby) Blake, Scott Wilson, John Forsythe, Paul Stewart, Gerald S. O'Loughlin, Jeff Corey, Will Geer, James Flavin, John Gallaudet, John Collins, Charles McGraw, John McLiam; ***D:*** Richard Brooks; ***W:*** Richard Brooks; ***C:*** Conrad L. Hall; ***M:*** Quincy Jones. Natl. Bd. of Review '67: Director (Brooks), Natl. Film Reg. '08.

In Cold Blood **1996** Tv miniseries version of the Truman Capote true crime classic, which follows the 1959 murders of the four members of the Clutter family in Holcomb, Kansas by ex-cons Dick Hickock (Edwards) and Perry Smith (Roberts). The TV version covers more of the background of both the killers and the Holcombs, the relentless hunt by Al Dewey (Neill) of the Kansas Bureau of Investigation, and the duo's time on death row. **180m/C VHS, DVD.** Anthony Edwards, Eric Roberts, Sam Neill, Kevin Tighe, Gillian Barber, Robbie Bowen, Margot Finley, Bethel Leslie, Gwen Verdon, Stella Stevens, L.Q. Jones, Louise Latham, Campbell Lane, Leo Rossi; ***D:*** Jonathan Kaplan; ***W:*** Benedict Fitzgerald. **TV**

In Country ½ **1989 (R)** Based on Bobbie Ann Mason's celebrated novel, the story of a young Kentucky high schooler (perfectly played by Lloyd) and her search for her father, killed in Vietnam. Willis plays her uncle, a veteran still struggling to accept his own survival, and crippled with memories. Moving scene at the Vietnam Veterans Memorial. **116m/C VHS, DVD.** Bruce Willis, Emily Lloyd, Joan Allen, Kevin Anderson, Richard Hamilton, Judith Ivey, Peggy Rea, John Terry, Patricia Richardson, Jim Beaver; ***D:*** Norman Jewison; ***W:*** Frank Pierson, Cynthia Cidre; ***C:*** Russell Boyd; ***M:*** James Horner.

The In Crowd **1988 (PG)** A bright high school student gets involved with a local TV dance show circa 1965, and must choose between uncertain fame and an Ivy League college. A fair nostalgic look at the period. Leitch is the son of psychedelic folk singer Donovan. **96m/C VHS.** Donovan Leitch, Jennifer Runyon, Scott Plank, Joe Pantoliano; ***D:*** Mark Rosenthal; ***W:*** Mark Rosenthal.

The In Crowd **2000 (PG-13)** Having been cured of her "erotomania," pretty, young Adrien (Heuring) is released from a psychiatric hospital, and, on the advice of her doctor, gains employment for the summer at a seaside country club. There Adrien is confronted by the in crowd, which is led by the ultra bitchy (what other name would suffice?) Brittany (Ward), who, with clearly ulterior motives, befriends the lovely Adrien. As Adrien is introduced to the ways of the privileged, things become stranger and stranger as our heroine discovers some unpleasant things about her new acquaintance. **98m/C VHS, DVD.** Susan Ward, Lori Heuring, Matthew Settle, Nathan Bexton, Tess Harper, Laurie Fortier, Kim Murphy; ***D:*** Mary Lambert; ***W:*** Mark Gibson, Philip Halprin; ***C:*** Tom Priestley; ***M:*** Jeff Rona.

In Custody *Hifazaat* **1994 (PG)** Producer Merchant makes his feature directorial debut with this dreamy tale of small-town teacher Deven (Puri) who's urged by a publishing friend to interview Nur (Kapoor), the greatest living poet in the disappearing Urdu language. The worshipful Deven is dismayed to find his idol a wreck, surrounded by sycophants and a shrewish second wife who's plagiarizing her husband's work, and soon finds himself hopelessly entangled in the writer's life. Unabashedly literary (the poetry recited is by Faiz Ahmed Faiz) with a star cast. Based on the 1987 novel by Anita Desai. Urdu with subtitles. **123m/C VHS, DVD.** *IN* Shashi Kapoor, Om Puri, Shabana Azmi, Sushma Seth, Neena Gupta, Ajay Sahni, Tinnu Anand; ***D:*** Ismail Merchant; ***W:*** Anita Desai, Shahrukh Husain; ***C:*** Larry Pizer; ***M:*** Zakir Hussain, Ustad Sultan Khan.

In Dangerous Company **1988 (R)** Beautiful babe balances beaux and battles abound. A brow lowering experience. **92m/C VHS.** Tracy Scoggins, Cliff DeYoung, Chris Mulkey, Henry Darrow, Steven Keats, Richard Portnow; ***D:*** Ruben Preuss; ***W:*** Mitch Brown; ***C:*** James L. Carter.

In Dark Places **1997 (R)** Seductive artist Chapelle (Severance) visits long-estranged brother Chazz (Kestner) with more than familial feelings on her mind. As things between them heat up, Chazz loses his girl, best friend, and job before discovering his sister's true agenda. This one actually has a story to go along with the eroticism. **96m/C VHS.** Joan Severance, Bryan Kestner, John Vargas, Suzanne Turner; ***D:*** James Burke.

In Desert and Wilderness ½
1973 Two kidnapped children escape and are thrust into the wilds of Africa, where they must survive with wits and courage. Based on a novel by Nobel prize-winning author Henyk Sienkiewicz. In Polish with English subtitles. **144m/C VHS.** *PL* Monika Rosca, Tomasz Medrzak, Emos Bango, Malija Mekki, Edmund Fetting; ***D:*** Wladyslaw Slesicki; ***W:*** Wladyslaw Slesicki; ***C:*** Boguslaw Lambach; ***M:*** Andrzej Korzynski.

In Desert and Wilderness *W Pustyni i W Puszczy* **2001** Children's adventure story has problems for what should be its target audience since it is in Polish with subtitles—maybe the stunning visuals will interest the kids. Set in North Africa at the end of the 19th century, Stas and Nel are children of engineers working on the Suez Canal. They are kidnapped by rebels but escape from their captors, along with two African children, Mea and Kali, who were slaves. Their journey across the beautiful but desolate country is fraught with hardship and unexpected adventures. Based on the novel by Henryk Sienkiewicz. **111m/C VHS, DVD.** *PL* Adam Fidusiewicz, Karolina Sawka, Lingile Shongwe, Mzwandile Ngubeni, Krzystof Kowalewski, Krzysztof Kolberger; ***D:*** Gavin Hood; ***W:*** Gavin Hood; ***C:*** Paul Gilpin; ***M:*** Krzesinir Debski.

In Dreams ½ *Blue Vision* **1998 (R)** Bening is a small town wife and mother with a psychic connection to twisted child killer Downey, causing her to dream of his gruesome crimes before he commits them. After she dreams that her daughter is killed, her life begins to unravel, causing those around her to suspect her of insanity. Draws its chills from a more cerebral standpoint, so fans of big action may want to pass. The unnerving dream sequences are suitable murky and ominous thanks to cinematographer Darius Khondji, who also filmed "Seven." **99m/C VHS, DVD.** Annette Bening, Robert Downey Jr., Aidan Quinn, Stephen Rea, Paul Guilfoyle, Dennis Boutsikaris, Pamela Payton-Wright, Margo Martindale, Prudence Wright Holmes, Katie Sagona, Krystal Benn; ***D:*** Neil Jordan; ***W:*** Neil Jordan, Bruce Robinson; ***C:*** Darius Khondji; ***M:*** Elliot Goldenthal.

In Enemy Hands *U-Boat* **2004** Germans take an American submarine crew captive during WWII but the POWs face greater threats from a meningitis outbreak and a U.S. vessel posed to attack. **98m/C VHS, DVD.** Til Schweiger, Thomas Kretschmann, Connor Donne, Matt Lindquist, Andy Gatjen, Rene Heger, Alex Prusmack, Sascha Rosemann, Sven-Ole Thorsen, Scott Caan, Clark Gregg, A.J. Buckley, William H. Macy, Jeremy Sisto, Ian Somerhalder, Carmine D. Giovinazzo, Sam Huntington, Lauren Holly, Xander Berkeley, Chris Ellis, James Burke, Roy Werner, Connor Donne, Matt Lindquist, Andy Gatjen, Rene Heger, Alex Prusmack, Sascha Rosemann, Justin Thomson, Braden R. Morgan, Patrick Gallagher, Tom DeGrezia, William Gregory Lee, Doug Biolchini; ***D:*** Tony Giglio; ***W:*** Tony Giglio, John Hartmann, John E. Deaver; ***C:*** Gerry Lively; ***M:*** Steven Bremson. **VIDEO**

In for Treatment **1982** A terminally ill cancer patient, lost in the bureaucracy of the hospital, fights to rediscover the joy of life. Strong and disturbing story. In Dutch with English subtitles. **92m/C VHS.** *NL* Helmut Woudenberg, Frank Groothof, Hans Man Int Veld; ***D:*** Eric Van Zuylen, Marja Kok.

In God We Trust WOOF! **1980 (PG)** Bleech. Monumentally unfunny comedy about innocent monk, Brother Ambrose (Feldman), who travels to Hollywood to raise money to save his monastery. He winds up getting involved with crooked TV evangelist Armageddon T. Thunderbird (Kaufman). Pryor plays G.O.D. **97m/C VHS.** Marty Feldman, Andy Kaufman, Richard Pryor, Peter Boyle, Louise Lasser, Wilfrid Hyde-White, Severn Darden; ***D:*** Marty Feldman; ***W:*** Marty Feldman, Chris Allen; ***C:*** Charles Correll; ***M:*** John Morris.

In God's Hands **1998 (PG-13)** Dude! Check it out! Three surfers (Dorian, George, and Liu) travel the world looking for (what else?) the perfect wave. Disjointed, plot-deprived, but beautifully shot flick has the trio busting out of prison (why they're there is never explained) to begin their quest. Moving from Madagascar to Bali to Hawaii, one finds love with a girl from Ipanema (!), another contracts malaria, and the other succumbs to the surf. What happens to whom doesn't really matter, because as actors, they're really great surfers. Besides, the "story" is just connective tissue for the killer surfing scenes. Gnarly. **98m/C VHS, DVD.** Patrick Shane Dorian, Matt George, Matty Liu, Brion James, Shaun Thompson, Maylin Pultar, Bret Michaels, Brian L. Keaulana, Darrick Doerner; ***D:*** Zalman King; ***W:*** Zalman King, Matt George; ***C:*** John Aronson.

In Gold We Trust ½ **1991** Vincent leads an elite battalion of fighters against a group of rogue American MIAs (!) laying waste to the Vietnamese countryside. **89m/C VHS.** Jan-Michael Vincent, Sam Jones; ***D:*** P. (Philip) Chalong; ***M:*** Hummie Mann.

In Good Company **2004 (PG-13)** Writer-director Weitz scores with this wry commentary on the effect of corporate politics on the modern family. Seasoned ad-exec Dan Foreman (Quaid) arrives at work to discover he's been demoted to make room for his new boss, 26-year-old Carter Duryea (Grace). Carter is the golden boy of the office's new corporate owners, but his work success barely masks his unfulfilling personal life. Carter finds himself drawn to family-man Dan, particularly Dan's fetching daughter Alex (Johansson), and the two men reluctantly teach each other about the vagaries of workplace ethics. Lapses into sentimentality and the end comes a bit easy, but strong performances by Quaid and Grace save the day. **131m/C DVD, HD DVD.** *US* Dennis Quaid, Topher Grace, Scarlett Johansson, Marg Helgenberger, David Paymer, Clark Gregg, Philip Baker Hall, Selma Blair, Frankie Faison, Ty Burrell, Kevin Chapman, Amy Aquino, Zena Grey, Colleen Camp; ***D:*** Paul Weitz; ***W:*** Paul Weitz; ***C:*** Remi Adefarasin; ***M:*** Stephen Trask.

In Harm's Way **1965** Overdone story about two naval officers and their response to the Japanese attack at Pearl Harbor. Even the superb cast members (and there are plenty of them) can't overcome the incredible length and overly intricate plot. **165m/B VHS, DVD.** John Wayne, Kirk Douglas, Tom Tryon, Patricia Neal, Paula Prentiss, Brandon de Wilde, Burgess Meredith, Stanley Holloway, Henry Fonda, Dana Andrews, Franchot Tone, Jill Haworth, George Kennedy, Carroll O'Connor, Patrick O'Neal, Slim Pickens, Bruce Cabot, Larry Hagman, Hugh O'Brian, Jim Mitchum, Barbara Bouchet, Stewart Moss, Tod Andrews; ***D:*** Otto Preminger; ***W:*** Wendell Mayes; ***C:*** Loyal Griggs; ***M:*** Jerry Goldsmith. British Acad. '65: Actress (Neal).

In Hell *The Savage* **2003 (R)** An American engineer working in Russia, Kyle LeBlanc (Van Damme) kills his wife's murderer and is convicted and sent to a remote prison run by corrupt officials. The warden likes to organize and take bets on fights between the prisoners and Kyle soon turns himself into a champion in order to survive. Now, he's pitted against his most vicious opponent—Valya (Smith). **98m/C VHS, DVD.** Jean-Claude Van Damme, Michael Bailey Smith, Lawrence Taylor, Marnie Alton, Malakai Davidson, Billy Reick; ***D:*** Ringo Lam; ***W:*** Eric James Virgets; ***C:*** John Aronson; ***M:*** Alexander Bubenheim. **VIDEO**

In Her Line of Fire ½ **2006 (R)** Vice President Walker's (Keith) jet crashes on a South American island dominated by insurgents who hold the Yankee dog for ransom. Having evaded capture, Walker's sinewy secret service agent Lynn Delaney (Hemingway) and press secretary Sharon Serrano (Bennett) devise their own rescue plan. The two are lesbians who kinda have a maybe thing going on but romance is put on hold until they free their boss. **88m/C DVD.** Mariel Hemingway, Jill Bennett, David Keith, David Millbern, Sydney Jackson; ***D:*** Brian Trenchard-Smith; ***W:*** Paula Goldberg, Anna Lorenzo; ***C:*** Neil Cervino; ***M:*** David Reynolds. **CABLE**

In Her Shoes **2005 (PG-13)** Despite its sometimes-embarrassing stereotypes and implausible situations, sappy but fun chick-flick works as a story of two very different sisters navigating the bonds of family. Rose (Colette) seemingly has life buttoned up, while Maggie (Diaz) is a mess who shows up homeless and drunk at Rose's door. Maggie manages to continually screw things up and Rose finally tosses her out. Maggie ends up at long-lost grandma Ella's door, where she rather comically falls in with Ella's senior friends as relationships eventually get mended. **129m/C DVD.** *US* Cameron Diaz, Toni Collette, Shirley MacLaine, Mark Feuerstein, Ken Howard, Candice Azzara, Francine Beers, Norman Lloyd, Jerry Adler, Brooke Smith, Richard Burgi, Anson Mount; ***D:*** Curtis Hanson; ***W:*** Susannah Grant; ***C:*** Terry Stacey; ***M:*** Mark Isham.

In His Father's Shoes ½ **1997 (PG)** After his father (Gossett) dies, 15-year-old Clay (Ri'chard) takes a literal journey of self-discovery. Slipping on a pair of his dad's old wingtips, the teen is transported back to the '60s to revisit his father's past, and then further back to his grandfather's (Gossett again) day. Clay learns his granddad was a hard-working man who gave up his own dreams to support his family, which later caused a generational rift. Touching drama. **105m/C VHS, DVD.** Louis Gossett Jr., Robert Ri'chard, Rachael Crawford; ***D:*** Vic Sarin; ***W:*** Gary Gelt; ***C:*** Michael Storey; ***M:*** John Welsman. **CABLE**

In His Life: The John Lennon Story ½ **2000** Focuses on seven years in the life of John Lennon—from the purchase of his first guitar to the Beatles arrival in America. Flashbacks show a teenage John (McQuillian) in 1957 Liverpool teaming up with art school pal Stu Sutcliffe (Williams) and meeting Paul (McGowan) and George (Rice-Oxley). There's the trip to Hamburg, the group's meeting with eventual manager Brian Epstein (Glover), Ringo (Ealey) becoming the band's drummer, and the first recordings. Skims the surface but, of course, the music is excellent. **87m/C VHS, DVD.** Phillip McQuillan, Daniel McGowan, Mark Rice-Oxley, Lee Williams, Jamie Glover, Scot Williams, Blair Brown, Kristian Ealey, Christine Kavanagh, Gillian Kearney, Palina Jonsdottir; ***D:*** David Carson; ***W:*** Michael O'Hara; ***C:*** Lawrence Jones; ***M:*** Dennis McCarthy. **TV**

In Hot Pursuit ½ *Polk County Pot Plane* **1977** Convicted for drug smuggling, two young men stage a daring but not too exciting escape from a southern prison. **90m/C VHS.** Bob Watson, Debbie Washington; ***D:*** Jim West.

The In-Laws **1979 (PG)** A wild comedy with Falk, who claims to be a CIA agent, and Arkin, a dentist whose daughter is marrying Falk's son. The fathers foil a South American dictator's counterfeiting scheme in a delightfully convoluted plot. **103m/C VHS, DVD.** Peter Falk, Alan Arkin, Richard Libertini, Nancy Dussault, Penny Peyser, Arlene Golonka, Michael Lembeck, Ed Begley Jr., Rosanna Desoto, Art Evans; ***D:*** Arthur Hiller; ***W:*** Andrew Bergman; ***M:*** John Morris.

The In-Laws ½ **2003 (PG-13)** According to Douglas and Brooks this isn't really a remake of the 1979 Peter Falk/Alan Arkin comedy. They're right. That one was funny. Douglas is the groom's (Reynolds) dad, a CIA operative on the trail of a French weapons dealer and Brooks is the bride's neurotic podiatrist pop, who's shanghaied for the mission and becomes the object of the bad guy's affections. The tedious script avoids laughter at every turn, while Brooks and Douglas never seem to click as a comic duo. Bergen is amusing in her too few scenes as Douglas's New Age ex, while Reynolds does well with what little he's given to do. **98m/C VHS, DVD.** *US* Michael Douglas, Albert Brooks, Candice Bergen, Robin Tunney, Ryan Reynolds, Lindsay Sloane, David Suchet, Maria Ricossa, Russell Andrews; ***D:*** Andrew Fleming; ***W:*** Nat Mauldin, Edward Solomon; ***C:*** Alexander Grusynski; ***M:*** Jocelyn Pook.

In Like Flint ½ **1967** Sequel to "Our Man Flint" sees our dapper spy confronting an organization of women endeavoring to take over the world. Spy spoofery at its low-level best. **107m/C VHS, DVD.** James Coburn, Lee J. Cobb, Anna Lee, Andrew Duggan, Jean Hale; ***D:*** Gordon Douglas; ***W:*** Hal Fimberg; ***C:*** William H. Daniels; ***M:*** Jerry Goldsmith.

In Love and War ½ **1991 (R)** Woods plays Navy pilot Jim Stockdale, whose plane was grounded over hostile territory and who endured nearly eight years of torture as a POW. Meanwhile, wife Sybil is an organizer of POW wives back in the States. Low octane rendering of the US Navy Commander's true story. Aaron earlier directed "The Miracle Worker," and you may recognize Ngor from "The Killing Fields." **96m/C VHS, DVD.** James Woods, Jane Alexander, Haing S. Ngor, Concetta Tomei, Richard McKenzie, James Pax; ***D:*** Paul Aaron; ***W:*** Carol Schreder.

In Love and War ½ **1996 (PG-13)** Tells the story of 19-year-old Ernest Hemingway's (O'Donnell) romance with 27-year-old Red Cross nurse Agnes (Bullock) while both were stationed in Italy during WWI. This romance later served as the basis for Hemingway's novel "A Farewell to Arms." Here's a thought. Read the book instead. The boyish O'Donnell is so miscast as testosterone-junkie Hemingway, the only analogy would be having Sylvester Stallone play Truman Capote. The lack of passion and chemistry between the two stars is unsettling, and the action is just plain clunky. Bullock looks great in a nurse's uniform, though. Adapted from "Hemingway in Love and War: The Lost Diary of Agnes Von Kurowsky" by Henry Villard and James Nagel. **115m/C VHS, DVD.** Chris O'Donnell, Sandra Bullock, MacKenzie Astin, Ingrid Lacey, Emilio Bonucci, Margot Steinberg, Colin Stinton, Ian Kelly, Richard Blackburn; ***D:*** Richard Attenborough; ***W:*** Allan Scott, Anna Hamilton Phelan, Clancy Sigal, Dimitri Villard; ***C:*** Roger Pratt; ***M:*** George Fenton.

In Love and War ½ **2001** British commando Eric Newby (Blue) is captured by the Italian army in 1942 and held as a POW until the Italian Armistice in 1943. He is released just before the advancing German forces and is rescued by a group of anti-fascist farmers, including lovely Wanda (Bobulova). They fall in love but Eric is betrayed and Wanda risks her life to warn him so he can escape. But can he bear to leave her behind? Based on Newby's autobiography "Love and War in the Apennines." **98m/C VHS, DVD.** Callum Blue, Barbara Bobulova, Peter Bowles, Nick Reding, John Warnaby, Toby Jones, Robert Weatherby, Nicholas Gallagher; ***D:*** John Kent Harrison; ***W:*** John Mortimer; ***C:*** Giovanni Fiore Coltellacci; ***M:*** Nicola Piovani. **TV**

In Love We Trust *Zuo You* **2007** Mei Zhu and Xiao Lu are divorced and both have remarried with Mei Zhu having custody of their five-year-old daughter Hehe. When they learn that Hehe is dying from leukemia, the doctor informs them that the best chance for Hehe's survival is for Mei Zhu and Xiao Lu to have another child (via in-vitro fertilization) and use the baby's umbilical cord blood for a transplant. Naturally, this is a shock to both their spouses but Mei Zhu becomes obsessed with doing anything that will save her child, regardless of the upset to everyone's lives. Mandarin with subtitles. **115m/C DVD.** *CH* Weiwei Liu, Jia-yi Zhang, Nan Yu, Taisheng Chen, Chuqian Zhang; ***D:*** Xiaoshuai Wang; ***W:*** Xiaoshuai Wang; ***C:*** Di Wu; ***M:*** Wei Dou.

In Love with an Older Woman **1982** Ritter takes fewer pratfalls than usual in this film; after all, it's a romantic comedy. Adapted from "Six Months with an Older Woman," the novel by David Kaufelt. **100m/C VHS.** John Ritter, Karen Carlson, Jamie Rose, Robert Mandan, Jeff Altman, George Murdock; ***D:*** Jack Bender. **TV**

In Memoriam ½ **1976** Tragic and gripping drama about one man's ability, albeit too late, to cope with his unforgettable past. Based on a story by Adolfo Bioy Casares. In Spanish with English subtitles. **96m/C VHS.** *SP* Geraldine Chaplin, Jose Luis Gomez; ***D:*** Enrique Braso.

In My Country *Country of My Skull* **2004 (R)** High-minded, well-intentioned, and oh-so-serious neocolonial drama. Based on the memoir "Country of My Skull" by Afrikaans poet Antjie Krog, a personal account of the 1996 Truth and Reconciliation Commission, investigating human rights abuses under apartheid. Washington Post reporter Langston Whitfield (Jackson) covers the hearings and meets poet/journalist Anna Malan (Binoche), who's doing daily radio broadcasts about the event. They each have their prejudices; they argue and, no surprise, find romance. The strongest moments are actually between Whitfield and his interviewee, Col. De Jager (Gleeson), a brutal cop who tries to explain his actions. Binoche seems merely bewildered. **100m/C DVD.** *US GB IR* Samuel L. Jackson, Juliette Binoche, Brendan Gleeson, Menzi "Ngubs" Ngubane, Sam Ngakane, Aletta Bezuidenhout, Lionel Newton, Langley Kirkwood, Owen Sejake, Harriet Manamela, Louis Van Niekirk, Jeremiah Ndlovu, Fiona Ramsay, Charley Boorman; ***D:*** John Boorman; ***W:*** Ann Peacock; ***C:*** Seamus Deasy.

In 'n Out ½ **1986** An American loser ventures to Mexico to recover a long-lost inheritance, meeting with mildly comic obstacles along the way. **85m/C VHS.** Sam Bottoms, Pat Hingle; ***D:*** Ricardo Franco; ***W:*** Ricardo Franco; ***C:*** Juan Ruiz Anchia; ***M:*** T-Bone Burnett.

In Name Only ½ **1939** Somber drama about a heartless woman who marries for wealth and prestige and holds her husband to a loveless marriage. Based on "Memory of Love" by Bessie Brewer. **102m/B VHS.** Carole Lombard, Cary Grant, Kay Francis, Charles Coburn; ***D:*** John Cromwell.

In Old Caliente ½ **1939** Rogers battles the bad guys in the frontier town of Caliente. **60m/B VHS, DVD.** Roy Rogers, Lynne Roberts, George "Gabby" Hayes, Jack La Rue, Katherine DeMille, Frank Puglia, Harry Woods; ***D:*** Joseph Kane; ***W:*** Gerald Geraghty, Norman Houston; ***C:*** William Nobles.

In Old California ½ **1942** Plucky story of a young Boston pharmacist who searches for success in the California gold rush and runs into the local crime boss. Also available colorized. **88m/B VHS, DVD.** John Wayne, Patsy Kelly, Binnie Barnes, Albert Dekker, Charles Halton; ***D:*** William McGann.

In Old Cheyenne ½ **1941** Bank holdups, cattle rustling, fist fights, and even car crashes mix with some good ol' guitar plunking in this western. **60m/B VHS, DVD.** Roy Rogers, George "Gabby" Hayes, Joan Woodbury, J. Farrell MacDonald, Sally Payne, George Rosener, Wally Wales; ***D:*** Joseph Kane; ***W:*** Olive Cooper; ***C:*** William Nobles.

In Old Chicago **1937** The O'Leary family travels to Chicago to seek their fortune, with mom working as a washerwoman to support her sons. Brothers Power and Ameche become power-broking rivals and when mom comes to break up a brawl between the two, she neglects to properly restrain the family cow. This leads to the great Chicago fire of 1871, supposedly started when the cow kicks over a latern and sets the barn ablaze. The city burns down in a spectacular 20-minute sequence. Based on the story "We the O'Learys" by Niven Busch. **115m/B VHS, DVD.** Tyrone Power, Alice Faye, Don Ameche, Alice Brady, Andy Devine, Brian Donlevy, Phyllis Brooks, Tom Brown, Sidney Blackmer, Gene Reynolds, Berton Churchill, Bobs Watson; ***D:*** Henry King; ***W:*** Lamar Trotti, Sonya Levien. Oscars '37: Support. Actress (Brady).

In Old Colorado ½ **1941** Ankrum and his cronies try to stir up trouble over water rights, but Boyd and his pals ride to the rescue. **67m/B VHS, DVD.** William Boyd, Russell Hayden, Andy Clyde, Margaret (Maggie) Hayes, Morris Ankrum, Sarah Padden, Cliff Nazarro, Stanley Andrews, James Seay, Morgan Wallace; ***D:*** Howard Bretherton.

In Old Kentucky ½ **1935** The Shattucks and the Martingales are fussing, feuding race horse owners. Steve Tapley (Rogers) is the Shattucks' trainer but gets fired for helping out crazy old coot Ezra Martingale (Sellon). So Steve decides to train the Martingale's horse Greyboy to run against the Shattucks' horse Emperor in a big race. Rogers' last released film. **86m/B DVD.** Will Rogers, Dorothy Wilson, Charles Sellon, Louise Henry, Russell Hardie, Charles Richman, Alan Dinehart, Esther Dale, Gladys Lehman; ***D:*** George Marshall; ***W:*** Sam Hellman; ***C:*** L.W. O'Connell; ***M:*** Arthur Lange.

In Old Montana **1939** A Cavalry lieutenant tries to settle a cattleman vs. sheepherding war. **60m/B VHS.** Fred Scott, Jeanne Carmen, Harry Harvey, John Merton; ***D:*** Bernard B. Ray.

In Old New Mexico *The Cisco Kid in Old New Mexico* **1945** The Cisco Kid and Pancho reveal the murderer of an old woman—a mysterious doctor who was after an inheritance. **60m/B VHS.** Duncan Renaldo, Martin Garralaga, Gwen Kenyon, Norman Willis, Lee White, Ken Terrell; ***D:*** Phil Rosen; ***W:*** Betty Burbridge; ***C:*** Arthur Martinelli; ***M:*** David Chudnow.

In Old Santa Fe ½ **1934** Cowboy star Maynard's best western, and the first film ever with Autry and Burnette. Maynard is framed for murder and his pals save him. **60m/B VHS.** Ken Maynard, Gene Autry, Smiley Burnette, Evalyn Knapp, George "Gabby" Hayes, Kenneth Thomson, Wheeler Oakman, George Chesebro; ***D:*** David Howard, Joseph Kane.

In Person ½ **1935** Spry comedy about a movie star who disguises herself to take a vacation incognito and falls in love with a country doctor who is unaware of her identity. ♫ Don't Mention Love To Me; Out of Sight, Out of Mind; Got a New Lease on Life. **87m/B VHS.** Ginger Rogers, George Brent, Alan Mowbray, Grant Mitchell; ***D:*** William A. Seiter; ***M:*** Oscar Levant.

In Praise of Love *Eloge de L'Amour; Eulogy of Love* **2001** The aged New Wave pioneer has made a generally incomprehensible, didactic, visually interesting film that will be mostly of interest to Godard completists. Director Edgar (Putzulu) is in the process of casting his latest production (which is about the stages of love) but discovers the young woman, Berthe, he wants for his lead has committed suicide. The film then flashes back a couple of years to Edgar interviewing an elderly couple who fought in the Resistance and who are thinking of selling their story for an American film. Their granddaughter, who turns out to be Berthe, is present at the interview. French with subtitles. **98m/C VHS, DVD.** *FR SI* Bruno Putzulu, Cecile Camp, Jean Davy, Francoise Verney, Audrey Klebaner, Jeremy Lippman, Claude Baigneres; ***D:*** Jean-Luc Godard; ***W:*** Jean-Luc Godard; ***C:*** Christophe Pollock, Julien Hirsch.

In Praise of Older Women **1978** Berenger is just right as a young Hungarian who is corrupted by WWII and a large number of older women. Based on a novel by Stephen Vizinczey. **110m/C VHS, DVD.** *CA* Karen Black, Tom Berenger, Susan Strasberg, Helen Shaver, Alexandra Stewart; ***D:*** George Kaczender.

In Pursuit **2000 (R)** Attorney Rick Alvarez (Baldwin) is accused of murdering his lover Katherine's (Schiffer) rich husband (Stockwell) and goes on the lam to Mexico. Routine thriller. **91m/C VHS, DVD.** Daniel Baldwin, Claudia Schiffer, Coolio, Sarah Lassez, Dean Stockwell; ***D:*** Peter Pistor; ***W:*** Peter Pistor, John Penney; ***C:*** Richard Crudo. **VIDEO**

In Pursuit of Honor ½ **1995 (PG-13)** Based on the true story of five American cavalry soldiers who find themselves being phased out in the 1935 Army. Ordered by General Douglas MacArthur to destroy their horses, they instead try to outrun an elite tank division to get some 400 horses to safety in Canada. Rugged performances and the violence towards the horses is aptly disturbing. Filmed on location in Australia and New Zealand. **110m/C VHS, DVD.** Don Johnson, Craig Sheffer, Gabrielle Anwar, Bob Gunton, Rod Steiger, James B. Sikking, John Dennis Johnston, Robert Coleby; ***D:*** Ken Olin; ***W:*** Dennis Lynton Clark; ***C:*** Stephen Windon; ***M:*** John Debney. **CABLE**

In Search of a Golden Sky **1984 (PG)** Following their mother's death, a motley group of children move in with their secluded cabin-dwelling uncle, much to the righteous chagrin of the welfare department. **94m/C VHS.** Charles Napier, George "Buck" Flower, Cliff Osmond; ***D:*** Jefferson (Jeff) Richard.

In Search of Anna **WOOF!** **1979** When a convict is released from jail, he hits the road with a flighty model in search of the girlfriend who corresponded with him in prison. There auto be a law. **90m/C VHS.** *AU* Judy Morris, Richard Moir, Chris Hayward, Bill Hunter; ***D:*** Esben Storm.

In Search of the Castaways **1962** Stirring adventure tale of a teenage girl and her younger brother searching for their father, a ship's captain lost at sea years earlier. Powerful special effects and strong cast make this a winning Disney effort. Based on a story by Jules Verne. **98m/C VHS, DVD.** *GB* Hayley Mills, Maurice Chevalier, George Sanders, Wilfrid Hyde-White, Michael Anderson Jr.; ***D:*** Robert Stevenson.

In Self Defense ½ **1993 (PG)** Purl is supposed to be protected from the killer she testified against but it doesn't quite work out that way. **94m/C VHS.** Linda Purl, Yaphet Kotto, Billy Drago; ***D:*** Bruce Seth Green; ***M:*** Patrick Gleeson.

In Society ½ **1944** The duo play dim-witted plumbers who are mistakenly invited to a high society party, where they promptly create catastrophe. **84m/B VHS, DVD.** Bud Abbott, Lou Costello, Marion Hutton, Kirby Grant, Ann Gillis, Arthur Treacher, Thomas Gomez, Steven Geray, Margaret Irving, Thurston Hall; ***Cameos:*** Sid Fields; ***D:*** Jean Yarbrough; ***W:*** Sid Fields, Hal Fimberg, Edmund Hartmann, John Grant.

In the Aftermath: Angels Never Sleep ½ **1987** Mix of animation and live-action in this post-nuclear wasteland tale never quite works. **85m/C VHS.** Tony Markes, Rainbow Dolan; ***D:*** Carl Colpaert.

In the Arms of My Enemy ½ *Voleurs de Chevaux; Horse Thieves* **2007** An eastern western. In the early 1800s, brothers Jakub (Jolivet) and Valdimir (Leprince-Ringuet) escape their lives of poverty by joining the vicious Cossack army. Meanwhile, gypsy brothers Roman (Colin) and Elias (Dupont) are horse thieves and their lives intersect when Vladimir is killed by Roman, who's stealing their horses. Now a vengeful Jakub is after him. Little dialogue, lots of violence. French with subtitles. **87m/C DVD.** *FR BE CA* Gregoire Colin, Gregoire Leprince-Ringuet, Adrien Jolivet, Francois-Rene Dupont; ***D:*** Micha Wald; ***W:*** Micha Wald; ***C:*** Jean-Paul de Zaeytijd; ***M:*** Stephan Micus, Johann Johannsson, Jef Mercelis.

In the Army Now **1994 (PG)** Pauly dude gets his head shaved, man. Service comedy about a slacker who joins the Army hoping to cash in on military benefits but who winds up in combat instead. Shore drops the Valley Guy shtick and ventures into the land of action when he gets sent on a mission to the Sahara. Strictly for Shore's fans. **92m/C VHS, DVD.** Pauly Shore, Esai Morales, Lori Petty, David Alan Grier, Ernie Hudson, Andy Dick; ***D:*** Daniel Petrie Jr.; ***W:*** Daniel Petrie Jr., Ken Kaufman, Fax Bahr, Stu Krieger, Adam Small; ***M:*** Robert Folk.

In the Bedroom ½ **2001 (R)** Spacek and Wilkinson are a middle age couple who lose their son to violence. The numbing grief, paralyzing emotional swirl, and long-simmering but long-denied marital resentments that follow combine to drastically alter their marriage and lives. Field's impressive, if gut-wrenching directorial debut shows trust for the script and in the actors by not overplaying the obvious emotional moments, or the dramatic twists. This trust is rewarded with exceptional performances by Spacek, Wilkinson, and Tomei (in her best performance to date), and by a film that doesn't miss a chance to be subtle when it's called for, or explosive when it's needed. **131m/C VHS, DVD.** Sissy Spacek, Tom Wilkinson, Nick Stahl, Marisa Tomei, William Mapother, William Wise, Celia Weston, Karen Allen; ***D:*** Todd Field; ***W:*** Todd Field, Rob Festinger; ***C:*** Antonio Calvache; ***M:*** Thomas Newman. Golden Globes '02: Actress—Drama (Spacek); Ind. Spirit '02: Actor (Wilkinson), Actress (Spacek), First Feature; L.A. Film Critics '01: Actress (Spacek), Film; Natl. Bd. of Review '01: Director (Field), Screenplay; N.Y. Film Critics '01: Actor (Wilkinson), Actress (Spacek), First Feature; Broadcast Film Critics '01: Actress (Spacek).

In the Blood **2006** Campy, low-budget gay horror played, uh, straight. A serial killer is attacking pretty blonde co-eds, which has pretty, blonde Jessica (Flynn) freaked out. Especially since her sexually confused brother Cassidy (Hanes) keeps having vague visions of her bloody corpse, which are followed by his suffering wicked nose bleeds. It seems Cassidy could get a much clearer image (and stop his blood loss) if he would just come out of the closet. **82m/C DVD.** Carlos Valencia, Tyler Hanes, James Katherine Flynn, Graeme Malcolm, Robert Dionne, Alison Fraser; ***D:*** Lou Peterson; ***W:*** Lou Peterson; ***C:*** Aaron Medick; ***M:*** Sasha Gordon. **VIDEO**

In the Cold of the Night **1989 (R)** Another drowsy entry into the "to sleep perchance to have a nightmare genre." A photographer with a vivid imagination dreams he murders a woman he doesn't know, and when said dream girl rides into his life on the back of a Harley, Mr. Foto's faced with an etiquette quandary: haven't they met before? Cast includes Hedren (Hitchcock's Marnie and Melanie Griffith's mother). **112m/C VHS, DVD.** Jeff Lester, Adrienne Sachs, Shannon Tweed, David Soul, John Beck, Tippi Hedren, Marc Singer; ***D:*** Nico Mastorakis; ***W:*** Nico Mastorakis; ***C:*** Andreas Bellis.

In the Company of Men **1996 (R)** A couple of dissatisfied Yuppies, Chad (Eckhart) and Howard (Malloy), are sent on a six-week job out of town by their home office. Grumbling about the lack of control in their lives (and blaming it on women), Chad formulates a nasty plan (to which Howard eventually agrees)—they'll deliberately get involved with the same girl, secretary Christine (Edwards), string her along, and then abandon her when their job is done. But Chad actually has his own agenda and bigger corporate ideas in mind. Think misogynistic satire. **93m/C VHS, DVD.** Matt Malloy, Aaron Eckhart, Stacy Edwards, Mark Rector, Jason Dixie, Emily Cline, Michael Martin, Chris Hayes; ***D:*** Neil LaBute; ***W:*** Neil LaBute; ***C:*** Anthony P. Hettinger; ***M:*** Ken Williams. Ind. Spirit '98: Debut Perf. (Eckhart); Ind. Spirit '99: First Screenplay; Sundance '97: Filmmakers Trophy.

In the Company of Spies ½ **1999 (PG-13)** CIA operative Brown is captured and tortured by the North Koreans while his bosses back in Washington try to protect national security. Retired operative Berenger is called back to active service to retrieve the agent and the information in his possession. **102m/C VHS.** Tom Berenger, Clancy Brown, Elizabeth Arlen, Ron Silver, Alice Krige, Arye Gross, Al Waxman, Len Cariou, David McIlwraith; ***D:*** Tim Matheson; ***W:*** Roger Towne; ***C:*** Roy Wagner; ***M:*** Don Davis. **CABLE**

In the Country Where Nothing Happens *En el Pais de No Pasa Nada* **1999** Corrupt businessman Enrique is kidnapped but, thanks to a videotape, wife Elena discovers he has a young lover, Rita. Instead of getting angry, Elena befriends Rita and they both decide Enrique isn't worth the bother of rescuing, so he's left to deal with his inept kidnappers on his own. Spanish with subtitles. **92m/C VHS, DVD.** *MX* Fernando Lujan, Julieta Egurrola, Maria (Isasi-Isasmendi) Isasi, Alvaro Guerrero, Zaide Silvia Gutierrez; ***D:*** Maricarmen de Lara; ***W:*** Maricarmen de Lara, Laura Sosa; ***C:*** Arturo de la Rosa.

In the Custody of Strangers **1982** A teenager's parents refuse to help when he is arrested for being drunk and he ends up spending the night in jail. Realistic handling of a serious subject. Real-life father and son Sheen and Estevez play father and son. **100m/C VHS.** Martin Sheen, Jane Alexander, Emilio Estevez, Kenneth McMillan, Ed Lauter, Matt Clark, John Hancock; ***D:*** Robert Greenwald. **TV**

In the Cut **2003 (R)** Meg Ryan, in an attempt to break out of her sweet, blond, comic romance roles takes on the part of a sexually repressed teacher who engages in an affair with a suspected serial killer. The sex scenes are appropriately steamy, but a weak plot and so-so acting conspire to undercut the suspense. Based on the Susanna Moore novel. **113m/C VHS, DVD.** *US AU* Meg Ryan, Mark Ruffalo, Jennifer Jason Leigh, Kevin Bacon, Nick Damici, Sharrieff Pugh; ***D:*** Jane Campion; ***W:*** Jane Campion, Susanna Moore; ***C:*** Dion Beebe; ***M:*** Hilmar Orn Hilmarsson.

In the Days of the Thundering Herd & the Law & the Outlaw **1914** In the first feature, a pony express rider sacrifices his job to accompany his sweetheart on a westward trek to meet her father. In the second show, a fugitive falls in love with a rancher's daughter and risks recognition. **76m/B VHS.** Tom Mix, Myrtle Stedman; ***D:*** Colin Campbell.

In the Dead of Space ☙ 1/2 **1999 (R)** Confusing sci fier has the space station Tesla becoming the target of saboteurs, who are determined to crash the ship into Los Angeles. **85m/C VHS, DVD.** Michael Pare, Lisa Bingley, Tony Curtis Blondell; ***D:*** Eli Necakov. **VIDEO**

In the Deep Woods ☙☙ **1991** Children's author Joanna Warren (Arquette) gets too close to mayhem when a childhood friend is murdered by the Deep Woods Killer. A mysterious private detective (Perkins) is on the killer's trail but when Joanna comes into the picture will she be a suspect or a victim? Based on the book by Nicholas Conde. **96m/C VHS, DVD.** Rosanna Arquette, Anthony Perkins, Will Patton, D.W. Moffett, Christopher Rydell, Harold Sylvester, Kimberly Beck; ***D:*** Charles Correll; ***W:*** Robert Nathan, Robert Rosenbaum; ***C:*** James Glennon.

In the Doghouse ☙☙ **1998 (PG)** A valuable movie pooch is dognapped just before the start of his next film and his owners are out to discover whodunnit. **90m/C VHS.** Matt Frewer, Rhea Perlman, Trevor Morgan; ***D:*** George Miller; ***W:*** Paul Bernbaum; ***M:*** Richard Band. **VIDEO**

In the Electric Mist ☙ 1/2 **2008 (R)** Generally disappointing adaptation of the James Lee Burke novel "In the Electric Mist with Confederate Dead," which features his veteran detective Dave Robicheaux. Robicheaux (Jones) thinks a series of murders are linked to New Orleans mobster Balboni (Goodman). But he has other problems: back in New Iberia, the star (Sarsgaard) of a Civil War film shooting in the area claims he found the corpse of a black man in a swamp and there are reports of ghostly Confederate soldiers making an appearance. Corruption and long-buried secrets surface to threaten Robicheaux's own family. It helps to be familiar with the mystery series to understand the characters, and the various plot threads don't hang together very well. **102m/C DVD.** Tommy Lee Jones, John Goodman, Peter Sarsgaard, Kelly Macdonald, Mary Steenburgen, Justina Machado, Ned Beatty, James Gammon, Pruitt Taylor Vince, Levon Helm, Buddy Guy; ***D:*** Bertrand Tavernier; ***W:*** Jerzy Kromolowski; ***C:*** Bruno de Keyzer; ***M:*** Marco Beltrami.

In the Flesh ☙☙ **1997** Closeted Atlanta police detective Philip (Corbin) is working an undercover drug operation that puts him in a gay bar. Which is where he meets Oliver (Ritter), a student by day/hustler by night. When Oliver witnesses a murder, it's Philip who provides him with an alibi, a place to stay, and a new relationship, even though it nearly destroys his own career. But then it seems Philip and Oliver have other connections besides sex. **105m/C VHS, DVD.** Dane Ritter, Ed Corbin, Roxzane T. Mims, Adrian Roberts; ***D:*** Ben Taylor; ***W:*** Ben Taylor; ***C:*** Brian Gurley; ***M:*** Eddie Horst.

In the Gloaming ☙☙☙ **1997 (PG)** Twentysomething Danny (Leonard) bitterly returns home to his suburban, wealthy, emotionally cold family because he is dying of AIDS. He and mother Janet (Close) renew their strained family ties but his businessman dad (Strathairn) doesn't know how to cope except with distance, and his sullen sister Anne (Fonda) is resentful. Wrenching story with fine work by all, including Goldberg in the small role of live-in nurse, Myrna. Based on a short story by Alice Elliot Dark. Reeve's directorial debut. **60m/C VHS, DVD.** Robert Sean Leonard, Glenn Close, David Strathairn, Bridget Fonda, Whoopi Goldberg; ***D:*** Christopher Reeve; ***W:*** Will Scheffer; ***C:*** Frederick Elmes; ***M:*** Dave Grusin. **CABLE**

In the Good Old Summertime ☙☙☙ **1949** This pleasant musical version of "The Shop Around the Corner" tells the story of two bickering co-workers who are also anonymous lovelorn pen pals. Minnelli made her second screen appearance at 18 months in the final scene. ♫I Don't Care; Meet Me Tonight In Dreamland; Play That Barbershop Chord; In the Good Old Summertime; Put Your Arms Around Me Honey; Wait Till the Sun Shines Nellie; Chicago; Merry Christmas. **104m/C VHS, DVD.** Judy Garland, Van Johnson, S.Z. Sakall, Buster Keaton, Spring Byington, Liza Minnelli, Clinton Sundberg; ***D:*** Robert Z. Leonard; ***C:*** Harry Stradling Sr.

In the Heat of Passion ☙ 1/2 **1991 (R)** A low-budget ripoff of "Body Heat" and "Fatal Attraction" starring Kirkland as a married woman who involves a much younger man in a very steamy affair that leads to murder. This movie wants to be a thriller, but is little more than a soft-core sex flick. Also available in an unrated version that contains explicit footage. **84m/C VHS.** Sally Kirkland, Jsu Garcia, Jack Carter, Michael Greene; ***D:*** Rodman Flender; ***W:*** Rodman Flender.

In the Heat of Passion 2: Unfaithful ☙ 1/2 **1994 (R)** Philip Donovan (Bostwick) is having an affair with his stepdaughter Casey (Hill) and the duo murder hapless wife/mother (Down) to get her money. But it seems someone else knows about their crime. **88m/C VHS.** Barry Bostwick, Teresa Hill, Lesley-Anne Down, Michael Gross; ***D:*** Catherine Cyran.

In the Heat of the Night ☙☙☙ 1/2 **1967** A wealthy industrialist in a small Mississippi town is murdered. A black homicide expert is asked to help solve the murder, despite resentment on the part of the town's chief of police. Powerful script with underlying theme of racial prejudice is served well by taut direction and powerhouse performances. Poitier's memorable character Virgil Tibbs appeared in two more pictures, "They Call Me Mister Tibbs" and "The Organization." **109m/C VHS, DVD.** Sidney Poitier, Rod Steiger, Warren Oates, Lee Grant; ***D:*** Norman Jewison; ***W:*** Stirling Silliphant; ***C:*** Haskell Wexler; ***M:*** Quincy Jones. Oscars '67: Actor (Steiger), Adapt. Screenplay, Film Editing, Picture, Sound; British Acad. '67: Actor (Steiger); Golden Globes '68: Actor—Drama (Steiger), Film—Drama, Screenplay, Natl. Film Reg. '02;; N.Y. Film Critics '67: Actor (Steiger), Director (Nichols), Film; Natl. Soc. Film Critics '67: Actor (Steiger), Cinematog.

In the Kingdom of the Blind the Man with One Eye Is King ☙☙ **1994 (R)** The title doesn't seem to mean anything and you may feel the same way about this standard crime drama, despite a strong cast. Mobster Tony (Petersen) gets police assistance from detective Al (Vallelonga) in discovering who murdered a mob boss' brother. **99m/C VHS.** Nick Vallelonga, William L. Petersen, Michael Biehn, Paul Winfield, James Quarter; ***D:*** Nick Vallelonga; ***W:*** Nick Vallelonga.

In the Lake of the Woods ☙☙ 1/2 **1996** Senatorial candidate John Waylan (Strauss) finds his political campaign crashing down when a journalist reveals his part in a Vietnam massacre of civilians. He and wife Kathy (Quinlan) retire to a lakeside cottage to lick their wounds and repair their tattered marriage. But Kathy finds it difficult to reach her distant and increasingly disturbed husband, who's having wartime flashbacks. Then Kathy disappears and the local police, as well as Kathy's sister, suspect that John killed her. Very disturbing TV movie, adapted from the novel by Tim O'Brien. **90m/C VHS.** Peter Strauss, Kathleen Quinlan, Peter Boyle, Richard Anderson, Ken Pogue, Nancy Sorel; ***D:*** Carl Schenkel; ***W:*** Philip Rosenberg; ***C:*** Dietrich Lohmann; ***M:*** Don Davis.

In the Land of Women ☙☙ **2006 (PG-13)** Sensitive 26-year-old aspiring screenwriter Carter Webb (Brody) escapes a failed relationship and a nowhere career in L.A. to visit his grouchy ailing grandma, Phyllis (Dukakis), in Michigan. Carter then becomes involved in the lives of neighbors Sarah (Ryan) and Lucy (Stewart) Hardwicke. Sarah's just been diagnosed with breast cancer and has a troubled marriage, while 16-year-old Lucy is acting like an obnoxious brat. Carter becomes the confidante of each, which leads to some emotional fireworks, although the pic is so low-key and familiar it's hard to get involved. Kasdan, making his feature debut, is the son of director Lawrence and younger brother of director Jake. **97m/C DVD.** *US* Adam Brody, Kristen Stewart, Meg Ryan, Olympia Dukakis, Makenzie Vega, Elena Anaya, Gregg Henry, JoBeth Williams, Dustin Milligan, Ginnifer Goodwin, Clark Gregg, Gina Mantegna; ***D:*** Jonathan Kasdan; ***W:*** Jonathan Kasdan; ***C:*** Paul Cameron; ***M:*** Stephen Trask.

In the Line of Duty: A Cop for the Killing ☙☙ *A Cop for the Killing* **1990 (R)** Undercover L.A. narcotics squad is about to bust the city's biggest drug lord when their sting operation goes bad and one of the team is brutally murdered. So, squad leader Ray Wiltern (Farentino) decides to get even. One in a series of TV movies under the "In the Line of Duty" banner. **95m/C VHS.** James Farentino, Steven Weber, Charles Haid, Tony Crane, Harold Sylvester, Dan Lauria, Tony Plana; ***D:*** Dick Lowry; ***W:*** Philip Rosenberg; ***C:*** Frank Beascoechea; ***M:*** Mark Snow. **TV**

In the Line of Duty: Ambush in Waco ☙☙ 1/2 *Ambush in Waco* **1993 (R)** Insta-TV movie made by NBC even before the fire which engulfed the Texas compound and ended the standoff between self-proclaimed "prophet" David Koresh and the federal government. Daly does well as the manipulative, charasmatic Branch Davidian cult leader whose stockpiling of illegal weapons lead to an investigation by the Bureau of Alcohohol, Tobacco and Firearms and a botched raid which caused the ultimately fatal siege. Filmed on location outside Tulsa, Oklahoma. **93m/C VHS, DVD.** Timothy Daly, Dan Lauria, William O'Leary; ***D:*** Dick Lowry; ***W:*** Phil Penningroth. **TV**

In the Line of Duty: The FBI Murders ☙☙☙ *The FBI Murders* **1988** A fact-based chiller about the bloody 1986 shootout between Miami FBI agents and a pair of violent killers (Soul and Gross playing against type). **95m/C VHS, DVD.** David Soul, Michael Gross, Ronny Cox, Bruce Greenwood, Doug Sheehan, Teri Copley; ***D:*** Dick Lowry; ***W:*** Tracy Keenan Wynn. **TV**

In the Line of Fire ☙☙☙ 1/2 **1993 (R)** Aging Secret Service agent Frank Horrigan (Eastwood) meets his match in a spooky caller, ex-CIA assassin Mitch Leary (Malkovich), who threatens his honor and the president in an exciting, fast-paced cat and mouse game. Terrific performance by Eastwood includes lots of dry humor and an unscripted emotional moment, but is nearly overshadowed by Malkovich's menacing bad guy. Russo is agent Lily Raines, who begins a charmingly tentative romance with Horrigan. Eerie special effects add to the mood. The Secret Service cooperated and most scenes are believable, with a few Hollywood exceptions; the end result clearly pays homage to the agents who protect our presidents. **128m/C VHS, DVD, Blu-ray Disc.** Clint Eastwood, John Malkovich, Rene Russo, Dylan McDermott, Gary Cole, Fred Dalton Thompson, John Mahoney, Gregory Alan Williams, John Heard, Tobin Bell, Clyde Kusatsu, Steve Hytner, Bob Schott, Eric Bruskotter, Joshua Malina, Steve Railsback; ***D:*** Wolfgang Petersen; ***W:*** Jeff Maguire; ***C:*** John Bailey; ***M:*** Ennio Morricone.

In the Loop ☙☙ **2009** In this British political satire, fumbling development minister Simon Foster (Hollander) gives a radio interview that sends communications minister Malcolm Tucker (Capaldi) apoplectic because the British government is trying to downplay its involvement with the Americans in the imminent invasion of Iraq. Timid Simon is thrust into a media frenzy where his every utterance is analyzed. It's decided he can do less damage by getting shuttled off to Washington, where the Americans decide to use Simon for their own ends. **105m/C DVD.** *GB* Tom Hollander, Peter Capaldi, Gina McKee, James Gandolfini, Chris Addison, Anna Chlumsky, Paul Higgins, Mimi Kennedy, David Rasche, Steve Coogan, Alex MacQueen; ***D:*** Armando Iannucci; ***W:*** Armando Iannucci, Jesse Armstrong, Simon Blackwell, Tony Roche; ***C:*** Jaimie Cairney; ***M:*** Adem Ilhan.

In the Middle of Nowhere ☙☙ *En Medio de la Nada* **1993** Sounds vaguely like a Mexican version of "Petrified Forest." A quiet highway restaurant, run by a former union leader, his wife, and his son is invaded by three fugitives: a wounded criminal, his brother, and his mistress. They are being pursued by the woman's powerful husband. They hold the family as hostages until the inevitable confrontation but may be in for a surprise about who will confront whom. Spanish with subtitles. **89m/C VHS, DVD.** *MX* Gabriela Roel, Blanca Guerra, Manuel Ojeda, Alonso Echanove; ***D:*** Hugo Rodriguez; ***W:*** Hugo Rodriguez, Marina Stavenhagen; ***C:*** Guillermo Granillo.

In the Mix **WOOF! 2005 (PG-13)** This one's a straight-up vehicle for recording artist Usher. If that just made you wonder "Who?" stop here. Darrell (Usher) is a New York City DJ/chick magnet who, as a result of a family friendship, must step in as body guard to a Jersey mobster's daughter, Dolly (Chriqui). A romantic flame ignites between the two. With nowhere else to go, the film becomes a handful of mafia and racial jokes. **97m/C DVD.** *US* Usher Raymond, Chazz Palminteri, Emmanuelle Chriqui, Robert Davi, Robert Costanzo, Geoff Stults, K.D. Aubert, Kevin Hart, Matt Gerald, Anthony Fazio; ***D:*** Ron Underwood; ***W:*** Jacqueline Zambrano; ***C:*** Clark Mathis; ***M:*** Aaron Zigman.

In the Money ☙ **1934** Veteran vaudevillian "Skeets" Gallagher introduces a muddled mass of acts, including a poor imitator of boxing great Gene Tunney, a mad scientist who talks to rabbits and writes rubber checks, and a limp-wristed lisper. **66m/B VHS.** Lois Wilson, Warren Hymer, Arthur Hoyt, Frank "Junior" Coghlan, Louise Beavers; ***D:*** Frank Strayer.

In the Mood ☙☙ 1/2 **1987 (PG-13)** Based on fact, this is the story of teenager Sonny Wisecarver, nicknamed "The Woo Woo Kid," who in 1944, seduced two older women and eventually landed in jail after marrying one of them. Look for Wisecarver in a cameo role as a mailman in the film. **98m/C VHS.** Patrick Dempsey, Beverly D'Angelo, Talia Balsam, Michael Constantine, Betty Jinnette, Kathleen Freeman, Peter Hobbs, Edith Fellows; ***Cameos:*** Ellsworth Wisecarver; ***D:*** Phil Alden Robinson; ***W:*** Phil Alden Robinson; ***M:*** Ralph Burns.

In the Mood for Love ☙☙ 1/2 **2000 (PG)** Romantic melodrama set in the Shanghai community of Hong Kong in 1962. Newspaper editor Chow (Leung Chiu-Wai) and his wife have just moved into a new apartment across the hall from Li-zhen (Cheung) and her husband. Both their respective spouses are away from home a great deal, traveling on business, so the lonely duo begin a tentative friendship. Then Chow begins to suspect his wife is having an affair and it quickly becomes apparent that it's with Li-zhen's husband. Gorgeous to look at, melancholy in tone, if somewhat oblique. Chinese with subtitles. **98m/C VHS, DVD.** *HK* Tony Leung Chiu-Wai, Maggie Cheung, Rebecca Pan, Lai Chen, Siu Ping-Lam; ***D:*** Wong Kar-Wai; ***W:*** Wong Kar-Wai; ***C:*** Christopher Doyle, Mark Lee Ping-Bin; ***M:*** Michael Galasso, Shingeru Umebayashi. Cannes '00: Actor (Leung Chiu-Wai); N.Y. Film Critics '01: Cinematog., Foreign Film.

In the Mouth of Madness ☙☙ **1995 (R)** Standard horror flick pays homage to or pokes fun at Stephen King (you decide) with story of successful horror novelist whose fans become a bit too engrossed in his stories—seems his readers tend to slip into dementia and carry out the grisly acts depicted within the pages. Neill plays an insurance investigator who must track down the missing author while combating the psychotic, axe-wielding residents of the seemingly quiet east coast hamlet where the author resides. Worth a look for the above-average special effects and makeup provided by Industrial Light and Magic (ILM). **95m/C VHS, DVD.** Sam Neill, Jurgen Prochnow, Julie Carmen, Charlton Heston, David Warner, John Glover, Bernie Casey, Peter Jason, Frances Bay, Wilhelm von Homburg; ***D:*** John Carpenter; ***W:*** Michael De Luca; ***C:*** Gary B. Kibbe; ***M:*** John Carpenter, Jim Lang.

In the Name of the Father ☙☙☙ 1/2 **1993 (R)** Compelling true story of Gerry Conlon and the Guildford Four, illegally imprisoned in 1974 by British officials after a tragic IRA bombing near London. The British judicial system receives a black eye, but so does the horror and cruelty of IRA terrorism. Politics and family life in a prison cell share the focus, as Sheridan captures superior performances from Day-Lewis and Postlethwaite (beware the thick Belfast brogue). Thompson was accused of pro-IRA sympathies in the British press for her role as the lawyer who believed in Conlon's innocence. Adapted from "Proved Innocent," Conlon's prison memoirs; reunites Sheridan and Day-Lewis after "My Left Foot." Includes original songs by U2's Bono, with a haunting theme sung by Sinead O'Connor. **127m/C VHS, DVD.** *GB IR* Daniel Day-Lewis, Pete Postlethwaite, Emma Thompson, John Lynch, Corin Redgrave, Beatie Edney, John Benfield, Paterson Joseph, Marie Jones, Gerard McSorley, Frank Harper, Mark Sheppard, Don Baker, Britta Smith, Aidan Grennell, Daniel Massey, Bosco Hogan; ***D:*** Jim Sheridan; ***W:*** Jim Sheridan, Terry George; ***C:*** Peter Biziou; ***M:*** Trevor Jones, Bono, Sinead O'Connor. Berlin Intl. Film Fest. '94: Golden Berlin Bear.

In the Name of the King: A Dungeon Siege Tale WOOF! **2008 (PG-13)** It's just like "Lord of the Rings"... only much, much worse. German schauenfreude-specialist Uwe Boll is at it again with yet another video game adaptation, this time with his biggest budget ever. But money doesn't mean a thing if you don't have the talent to spend it wisely, and Boll squanders his wad on unconvincing FX and Peter Jackson-esque helicopter shots. In ye olden times, a man named Farmer (Statham, who is, guess what... a farmer) rallies a nation to defend Burt Reynolds' kingdom (King Bandit the IV) against evil wizard and not-so-goodfella Ray Liotta. The rest is a mish-mash of boring battles, orc knock-offs, and inexplicable ninjas. What in the name of the king was Boll thinking? **124m/C DVD, Blu-ray Disc.** *GE CA* Jason Statham, John Rhys-Davies, Ray Liotta, Leelee Sobieski, Matthew Lilliard, Burt Reynolds, Ron Perlman, Claire Forlani, Kristanna Loken, Will Sanderson, Brian White, Mike Dopud; ***D:*** Uwe Boll; ***W:*** Doug Taylor; ***C:*** Mathias Neumann; ***M:*** Jessica de Rooij, Henning Lohner. Golden Raspberries '08: Worst Director (Boll).

In the Name of the Pope-King 🦴🦴🦴 **1985** An acclaimed historical epic about the politics and warfare raging around the 1867 Italian wars that made the Pope the sole ruler in Rome. In Italian with English subtitles. **115m/C VHS.** Nino Manfredi, Danilo Mattei, Carmen Scarpitta, Giovannella Grifea, Carlo Bagno; ***D:*** Luigi Magni.

In the Navy 🦴🦴 1/2 *Abbott and Costello in the Navy* **1941** Abbott and Costello join the Navy in one of four military-service comedies they cranked out in 1941 alone. The token narrative involves about a singing star (Powell) in uniform to escape his female fans, but that's just an excuse for classic A & C routines. With the Andrews Sisters. ♫ Starlight, Starbright; You're Off To See The World; Hula Ba Lua; Gimme Some Skin; A Sailor's Life For Me; We're In The Navy; Anchors Aweigh (instrumental); You're A Lucky Fellow, Mr. Smith (instrumental). **85m/B VHS, DVD.** Lou Costello, Bud Abbott, Dick Powell, The Andrews Sisters; ***D:*** Arthur Lubin; ***W:*** Arthur T. Horman, John Grant; ***C:*** Joseph Valentine.

In the Pit 🦴🦴 1/2 *En el Hoyo* **2006** Rulfo filmed a single crew, who were building the second level of Mexico City's Periferico freeway, from March 2003 to December 2005. He focuses primarily on the distinctly different attitudes of two workers: Shorty's live-and-let-live philosophy and El Grande's disgust with corruption and the lack of credit given the working man. Spanish with subtitles. **84m/C DVD.** *MX* ***D:*** Juan Carlos Rulfo; ***C:*** Juan Carlos Rulfo; ***M:*** Leonardo Heiblum.

In the Presence of Mine Enemies 🦴🦴 1/2 **1997 (PG-13)** Remake of Rod Serling's 1960 script for "Playhouse 90." Rabbi Adam Heller (Mueller-Stahl) and his daughter Rachel (Lowensohn) are living in the Warsaw ghetto in 1942, trying to deal with Nazi oppression. But the Rabbi's faith is put the test when his son Paul (McKellar), who's escaped from the Treblinka labor camp, returns for vengeance and Rachel becomes the sexual victim of a vicious German officer (Dance). **100m/C VHS, DVD.** Armin Mueller-Stahl, Elina Lowensohn, Don McKellar, Charles Dance, Chad Lowe; ***D:*** Joan Micklin Silver; ***W:*** Rod Serling. **CABLE**

In the Realm of the Senses 🦴🦴🦴 *Ai No Corrida* **1976 (NC-17)** Taboo-breaking story of a woman and man who turn their backs on the militaristic rule of Japan in the mid-1930s by plunging into an erotic and sensual world all their own. Striking, graphic work that was seized by U.S. customs when it first entered the country. Violent with explicit sex, and considered by some critics as pretentious, while others call it Oshima's masterpiece. In Japanese with English subtitles. **105m/C VHS, DVD.** *JP FR* Tatsuya Fuji, Eiko Matsuda, Aio Nakajima, Meika Seri; ***D:*** Nagisa Oshima; ***W:*** Nagisa Oshima; ***C:*** Hideo Ito; ***M:*** Minoru Miki.

In the Realms of the Unreal 🦴🦴🦴 1/2 **2004** Rich documentary study of the life of outsider artist Henry Darger, who lived most of his life as a harmless oddball janitor. When he died in 1973, his neighbors discovered a huge cache of paintings and writings showing a bizarre, oceanic imaginary world. If you can get beyond Darger's obsession with naked hermaphroditic little girls, and that's not so easy, film is an awesome exploration of the power of the human mind. One of a kind. **82m/C DVD.** *US*

In the Region of Ice 🦴🦴🦴 **1976** Award-winning short reveals the complexities of the relationship between a nun and a disturbed student. **38m/B VHS.** Fionnula Flanagan, Peter Lempert; ***D:*** Peter Werner.

In the Secret State 🦴🦴 **1985** Inspector Strange finds himself faced with the apparent suicide of a colleague on the day of his own retirement from the force. His private investigation into the case finds him mired in murder and espionage. **107m/C VHS.** *GB* Frank Finlay, Matthew Marsh, Thorley Walters; ***D:*** Christopher Morahan; ***W:*** Brian Phelan; ***C:*** Nat Crosby; ***M:*** Richard Harvey. **TV**

In the Shadow of Kilimanjaro WOOF! **1986 (R)** A pack of hungry baboons attacks innocent people in the wilderness of Kenya. Based on a true story but the characters are contrived and just plain stupid at times. Quite gory as well. Filmed on location in Kenya. **105m/C VHS.** *GB* John Rhys-Davies, Timothy Bottoms, Michele Carey, Irene Miracle, Calvin Jung, Donald Blakely; ***D:*** Raju Patel.

In the Shadow of the Moon 🦴🦴🦴 1/2 **2007 (PG)** Using original (and some never-before-seen) footage, this exceptional documentary examines the triumphs and failures of America's race to the moon, from the beginnings of the Apollo program to its end in 1972. Movie focuses on the astronauts who were on the missions, capturing the wonder and unique perspective of the men who looked at Earth from the surface of another world. Notably absent is the legendary (and incredibly private) Neil Armstrong. Through interviews and remastered footage, Sington creates a compelling, moving film about a time when humanity reached for the skies and technology equaled hope for the future. **100m/C DVD.** ***D:*** David Sington; ***C:*** Clive North; ***M:*** Philip Sheppard.

In the Shadows 🦴🦴 1/2 *Under Heaven* **1998 (R)** Modern update of Henry James' 1902 novel "The Wings of the Dove." Lonely, wealthy divorcee Eleanor (Richardson) is dying from cancer and needs a caregiver. Cynthia (Parker) moves in along with her weak-willed boyfriend Buck (Young), who passes himself off as Cynthia's brother and takes a job as a gardener. Avaricious Cynthia decides Buck should make Eleanor fall in love and marry him, so they can inherit her fortune. Of course this menage is made for misery. **115m/C VHS, DVD.** Joely Richardson, Molly Parker, Aden Young; ***D:*** Meg Richman; ***W:*** Meg Richman; ***C:*** Claudio Rocha; ***M:*** Marc Olsen.

In the Shadows 🦴🦴 **2001 (R)** New York hitman Eric O'Byrne (Modine) is sent to Miami to kill veteran Hollywood stunt coordinator Lance Huston (Caan) in retaliation for an accident that killed stuntman Jimmy (Brancato), a mobster's nephew. But before he died, Jimmy managed to steal money and drugs from an undercover FBI agent (Gooding Jr.) who's posing as a dealer. So both the mob and the feds want to reclaim their property. And then Eric goes and falls for the doctor daughter (Adams) of his target just to complicate things further. **104m/C VHS, DVD.** James Caan, Joey Lauren Adams, Matthew Modine, Cuba Gooding Jr., Lillo Brancato, Jeffrey Chase; ***D:*** Ric Roman Waugh; ***W:*** Ric Roman Waugh; ***C:*** Chuck Cohen; ***M:*** Adam Gorgoni.

In the Soup 🦴🦴 1/2 **1992 (R)** Adolpho is a naive New York filmmaker barely scraping by. He decides to sell his script in a classified ad which is answered by the fast-talking Joe, a would-be film producer who's true profession is as a con artist. The two then try numerous (and humorous) ways to raise the money to begin filming. Also available colorized. **93m/B VHS, DVD.** Steve Buscemi, Seymour Cassel, Jennifer Beals, Will Patton, Pat Moya, Stanley Tucci, Sully Boyar, Rockets Redglare, Elizabeth Bracco, Ruth Maleczech, Debi Mazar, Steven Randazzo, Francesco Messina; ***Cameos:*** Jim Jarmusch, Carol Kane; ***D:*** Alexandre Rockwell; ***W:*** Tim Kissell, Alexandre Rockwell; ***C:*** Phil Parmet; ***M:*** Mader. Sundance '92: Grand Jury Prize.

In the Spider's Web 🦴 **2007** The only reason to see this mess is to watch Henriksen in one of his whacko roles. A group of backpackers are traveling in a remote area of India when one is bitten by a poisonous spider. The others carry their stricken friend to the closest village where American physician Dr. Lecorpus (guess who) lives. The villagers actually worship the lethal arachnids at a nearby temple. Turns out a spider bite is the least of the friends' worries. **90m/C DVD.** Lance Henriksen, Michael Rogers, Emma Catherwood, Cian Barry, Michael Smiley, Lisa Livingstone, Jane Perry, Sohrab Ardeshir; ***D:*** Terry Winsor; ***W:*** Gary Dauberman; ***M:*** Charles Olins, Mark Ryder. **TV**

In the Spirit 🦴🦴 1/2 **1990 (R)** New Age couple move from Beverly Hills to New York, where they meet an air-headed mystic and are forced to hide from a murderer. Falk gives solid performance in sometimes rocky production. Berlin is the real-life daughter of May. **94m/C VHS.** Elaine May, Marlo Thomas, Jeannie Berlin, Peter Falk, Melanie Griffith, Olympia Dukakis, Chad Burton, Thurn Hoffman, Michael Emil, Christopher Durang, Laurie Jones; ***D:*** Sandra Seacat; ***W:*** Jeannie Berlin, Laurie Jones; ***C:*** Dick Quinlan; ***M:*** Patrick Williams.

In the Steps of a Dead Man 🦴 1/2 **1974** A family grieving for a fallen soldier is earmarked for evil by a young man who bears an uncanny resemblance to the dead man. A friend of the family has her suspicions and must find out the truth before something terrible happens. **71m/C VHS.** Skye Aubrey, John Nolan; ***D:*** Shaun O'Riordan; ***W:*** Brian Clemens.

In the Time of the Butterflies 🦴🦴 1/2 **2001 (PG-13)** Based on the novel by Julia Alvarez, which was inspired by the true story of the three Mirabal sisters (collectively known as Las Mariposas) who fought against the Trujillo dictatorship in the Dominican Republic. After their father is murdered, Minerva (Hayek) persuades her sisters Mate (Maestro) and Patria (Cavazos) to join with the rebels in overthrowing the government to ultimately tragic consequences for the women. **92m/C VHS, DVD.** Salma Hayek, Lumi Cavazos, Mia Maestro, Edward James Olmos, Marc Anthony, Pilar Padilla, Demian Bichir, Fernando Becerril; ***D:*** Mariano Barroso; ***W:*** Judy Klass, David Klass; ***C:*** Xavier Perez Grobet; ***M:*** Van Dyke Parks. **CABLE**

In the Valley of Elah 🦴🦴🦴 **2007 (R)** Retired army sergeant and Vietnam vet Hank Deerfield (Jones) and wife Joan (Sarandon) learn that their soldier son is actually back from Iraq, but they haven't yet heard from him. Hank goes looking and finds that his son has been killed, not in the line of duty but stateside at his New Mexico base—and drugs may be involved. Army investigators and local police are anything but helpful, until Hank hooks up with detective Emily Sanders (Theron). Then the pieces begin to fall into place and Hank delves into his son's experience in the Middle East. Part exploration into the senselessness of war and part exploration into the depths of pain a family can encounter when losing a son to the terror and tragedy that comes with, and out of, fighting. Gritty and raw, Jones' intensity makes it all work. **121m/C DVD.** *US* Tommy Lee Jones, Charlize Theron, Susan Sarandon, Jason Patrick, Jonathan Tucker, James Franco, Barry Corbin, Josh Brolin, Frances Fisher, Wes Chatham, Jake McLaughlin, Victor Wolf, Devin Brochu; ***D:*** Paul Haggis; ***W:*** Paul Haggis; ***C:*** Roger Deakins; ***M:*** Mark Isham.

In the Weeds 🦴 **2000 (R)** A series of obvious situations (and obvious characters) render this ensemble comedy unfit for human consumption. Spend an evening shift with the wait staff at an upscale Manhattan eatery as their obnoxious boss castigates them, they avoid the psychotic chef, deal with rude diners, and whine about their lives. **90m/C DVD.** Molly Ringwald, Joshua Leonard, Eric Bogosian, John Paul (J.P.) Pitoc, Ellen Pompeo, Michael B. Silver, Sam Harris, Kirk Acevedo, Bonnie Root, Peter Riegert, Bridget Moynahan; ***D:*** Michael Rauch; ***W:*** Michael Rauch; ***C:*** Horacio Marquinez; ***M:*** Douglas J. Cuomo.

In the White City 🦴🦴🦴 *Dans la Ville Blanche* **1983** A sailor jumps ship in Lisbon and uses a movie camera to record himself and his search through the twisted streets and alleys of the city for something or someone to connect to. In French, Portuguese, and German with English subtitles. **108m/C VHS.** *PT SI* Bruno Ganz, Teresa Madruga, Julia Vonderlinn, Jose Carvalho; ***D:*** Alain Tanner; ***W:*** Alain Tanner; ***C:*** Acacio De Almeida; ***M:*** Jean-Luc Barbier.

In the Winter Dark 🦴🦴 **1998** The isolation of a remote valley community (filmed in Australia's Blue Mountains) is enhanced by the discovery of a woman's body and the slaughter of livestock. Maurice (Barrett) and Ida (Blethyn) have scratched out a farm living but personally never recovered from the death of their baby son long before. Outcast Laurie (Roxburgh) spends his time drifting through the countryside while pregnant Ronnie (Otto) has been abandoned by her lover. The four are brought together by death and what (or who) might be causing it. Based on the novel by Tim Winton. **92m/C VHS.** *AU* Ray Barrett, Brenda Blethyn, Richard Roxburgh, Miranda Otto; ***D:*** James Bogle; ***W:*** James Bogle, Peter Rasmussen; ***C:*** Martin McGrath; ***M:*** Peter Cobbin.

In This House of Brede 🦴🦴🦴 **1975** A sophisticated London widow turns her back on her worldly life to become a cloistered Benedictine nun. Rigg is outstanding as the woman struggling to deal with the discipline of faith. Based on the novel by Rumer Godden. **105m/C VHS, DVD.** Diana Rigg, Pamela Brown, Gwen Watford, Denis Quilley, Judi Bowker; ***D:*** George Schaefer; ***M:*** Peter Matz. **TV**

In This Our Life 🦴🦴 1/2 **1942** Histrionic melodrama handled effectively by Huston about a nutsy woman who steals her sister's husband, rejects him, manipulates her whole family and eventually leads herself to ruin. Vintage star vehicle for Davis, who chews scenery and fellow actors alike. Adapted by Howard Koch from the Ellen Glasgon novel. **101m/B VHS.** Bette Davis, Olivia de Havilland, Charles Coburn, Frank Craven, George Brent, Dennis Morgan, Billie Burke, Hattie McDaniel, Lee Patrick, Walter Huston, Ernest Anderson; ***D:*** John Huston; ***M:*** Max Steiner.

In This World 🦴🦴 1/2 *M1187511* **2003 (R)** Torabi and Enayatullah star as themselves as the film recounts their journey as Afghan refugees from Pakistan to London. Winterbottom's most political film is powerful and effectively balances the personal issues and travails of its characters with the larger issues it illustrates. The lack of a script (they used mostly outlines) hurts the film in the end, but the performances of the mostly non-professional cast balance that weakness. Shot in documentary style on digital video. **88m/C DVD.** *GB* Jamal Udin Torabi, Enayatullah, Imran Paracha, Hiddayatullah, Jamau, Wakeel Khan, Lal Zarin, Mirwais Torabi, Amanullah Torabi; ***D:*** Michael Winterbottom; ***W:*** Tony Grisoni; ***C:*** Marcel Zyskind; ***M:*** Dario Marianelli. British Acad. '03: Foreign Film.

In Too Deep 🦴 1/2 **1990 (R)** A rock star and a beautiful woman are physically drawn to one another in spite of the fact that any contact between them could have disasterous results. **106m/C VHS.** Hugo Race, Santha Press, Rebekah Elmaloglou, John Flaus, Dominic Sweeney; ***D:*** Colin South.

In Too Deep 🦴🦴 **1999 (R)** Omar Epps and LL Cool J rise above the tired formula in this by-the-book undercover cop/paranoid drug dealer crime drama. Young Cincinnati cop Jef Cole (Epps) is working undercover in a drug ring run by a none-too-humble crime lord who calls himself God (LL Cool J). As he tries to gain the confidence of God, Cole becomes so deeply mired in the gangster life that his commander Boyd (Tucci) begins to question his loyalty. Epps does an excellent job conveying the tension in his character's position, although the script is totally devoid of any kind of plot twist to help him out. Also shining in minor parts are Pam Grier as a veteran detective and Nia Long as the standard issue love interest. **104m/C VHS, DVD.** Omar Epps, Stanley Tucci, LL Cool J, Pam Grier, Veronica Webb, Nia Long, David Patrick Kelly, Hill Harper, Kirk "Sticky Fingaz" Jones; ***D:*** Michael Rymer; ***W:*** Paul Aaron, Michael Henry Brown; ***C:*** Ellery Ryan; ***M:*** Christopher Young.

In Tranzit 🦴 1/2 **2007** Intriguing premise (supposedly based on fact) but obvious execution. In the aftermath of WWII, some 50 German POWs in Russian hands are sent to a female-run Soviet prison camp. The commander has been informed that some prisoners were SS officers and they need to find out just who, but circumstances aren't exactly what they seem. **113m/C DVD.** *GB RU* Thomas Kretschmann, Vera Farmiga, Daniel Bruhl, Nathalie Press, John Malkovich, Ingeborga Dapkounaite; ***D:*** Tom Roberts; ***W:*** Natalia Portnova, Simon van der Borgh; ***C:*** Sergei Astakhov; ***M:*** Dan (Daniel) Jones.

In Trouble WOOF! 1967 Hard-to-follow and frequently aimless story of a pregnant girl who invents a fake rape story that her dull-witted brothers take seriously, embarking on a cross-country search for the culprit. **82m/C VHS.** *CA* Julie LaChapelle, Katherine Mousseau, Daniel Pilon; ***D:*** Gilles Carle.

In Which We Serve 🦴🦴🦴 1/2 **1943** Much stiff upper-lipping in this classic that captures the spirit of the British Navy during WWII. The sinking of the destroyer HMS Torrin during the Battle of Crete is told via flashbacks, with an emphasis on realism that was unusual in wartime flag-wavers. Features the film debuts of Johnson and Attenborough, and the first Lean directorial effort. Coward received a special Oscar for his "outstanding production achievement," having scripted, scored, codirected, and costarred. **114m/B VHS, DVD.** *GB* Noel Coward, John Mills, Bernard Miles, Celia Johnson, Kay Walsh, James Donald, Richard Attenborough, Michael Wilding, George Carney, Gerald Case, John Varley; ***D:*** David Lean, Noel Coward; ***W:*** Noel Coward; ***C:*** Ronald Neame; ***M:*** Noel Coward. N.Y. Film Critics '42: Film.

In Your Dreams 🦴🦴 **2007** Unhappy Albert Ross suffers an accident and suddenly can see the future in his dreams, including a sexy girl named Olivia who's interested in him. But first Albert teams up with amateur sleuth Georgie to figure out why his dreams (good and bad) are coming true and if he can prevent one particular vision in which someone dies. **90m/C DVD.** *GB* Dexter Fletcher, Linda Hamilton, Parminder K. Nagra, Susan George, Elize du Toit, Robert Portal, Beatie Edney; ***D:*** Gary Sinyor; ***W:*** Gary Sinyor; ***C:*** Jean-Philippe Gossart; ***M:*** David A. Hughes.

In Your Face 🦴 1/2 *Abar, the First Black Superman* **1977 (R)** Little known blaxploitation film about a black family harrassed in a white suburb. A black motorcycle gang comes to their rescue. **90m/C VHS, DVD.** J. Walter Smith, Tobar Mayo, Roxie Young, Tina James; ***D:*** Frank Packard.

InAlienable 🦴 1/2 **2008** Cheesy morality tale (with a lot of familiar faces) wrapped in a sci-fi story. Scientist Eric Norris (Hatch) has an alien parasite growing inside him and he fights to protect what he comes to see as a surrogate offspring for his son, who died years before. Turns into a courtroom debate on whether the alien can be considered a human being with rights or if it should be destroyed as a threat to mankind. **105m/C DVD.** Richard Hatch, Walter Koenig, Courtney Peldon, Erik Avari, Marina Sirtis, Jay Acovone, Alan Ruck, Judy Levitt; ***D:*** Robert Dyke; ***W:*** Walter Koenig; ***C:*** Jonathan Hall; ***M:*** Justin Durban. **VIDEO**

Incantato 🦴 1/2 *Enchanted; Il Cuore Altroe; The Heart Is Elsewhere* **2003** Meek Nello is a 35-year-old classics teacher in 1920s Rome. He's sent to Bologna by his exasperated father in hopes that a change of scene will finally lead Nello into marriage. Nello meets society beauty Angela and thinks he has a chance because she has been recently blinded in an accident and hasn't resumed her wild ways. But Angela is just leading the poor schlub on. Italian with subtitles. **107m/C DVD.** *IT* Neri Marcore, Vanessa Incontrada, Guilio Bosetti, Nino D'Angelo, Sandra Milo, Giancarlo Giannini; ***D:*** Pupi Avati; ***W:*** Pupi Avati; ***C:*** Pasquale Rachini; ***M:*** Riz Ortolani.

Incendiary 🦴🦴 **2008** Williams is the nameless London working-class mother of a young son whose marriage to a bomb disposal expert is in trouble. So she starts up with charming if slightly sleazy journalist Jasper (McGregor) and while they are canoodling one afternoon, terrorists set off a bomb in a soccer stadium and her husband and son are killed. Her husband's friend Terrence (Macfadyen) is taking part in the investigation, and takes a very personal interest in the new widow, who manages to learn that one of the bomber's wives, the mother of a young son, works nearby. Story doesn't hold together particularly well and some of the narration is risible but Williams is watchable no matter what. **100m/C DVD.** *GB* Michelle Williams, Ewan McGregor, Matthew MacFadyen, Nicholas Greaves, Sidney Johnston, Sasha Behar, Usman Khokhar; ***D:*** Sharon Maguire; ***W:*** Sharon Maguire; ***C:*** Benjamin Davis; ***M:*** Shingeru Umebayashi.

Inception 2010 When the human mind can dream ideas into existence, the world becomes a very dangerous place. Writer/director Christopher Nolan's sci fi pic sounds intriguing if nothing else since it's a mystery as to what's actually going on. **m/C DVD.** *US* Leonardo DiCaprio, Ken(saku) Watanabe, Ellen Page, Joseph Gordon-Levitt, Marion Cotillard, Thomas (Tom) Hardy, Cillian Murphy, Tom Berenger, Michael Caine, Lukas Haas; ***D:*** Christopher Nolan; ***W:*** Christopher Nolan; ***C:*** Wally Pfister; ***M:*** Hans Zimmer.

The Incident 🦴🦴 1/2 **1967** A gritty, controversial (at-the-time) drama about two abusive thugs who take over a New York subway car late at night, humiliating and terrorizing each passenger in turn. Film debut for Sheen and Musante as the thugs. **99m/B VHS.** Martin Sheen, Tony Musante, Beau Bridges, Ruby Dee, Jack Gilford, Thelma Ritter, Brock Peters, Ed McMahon, Gary Merrill, Donna Mills, Jan Sterling, Mike Kellin, Bob Bannard, Diana Van Der Vlis, Victor Arnold, Robert Fields; ***D:*** Larry Peerce; ***W:*** Charles Fox, Nicholas E. Baehr; ***C:*** Gerald Hirschfeld; ***M:*** Charles Fox.

The Incident 🦴🦴🦴 **1989** Political thriller set during WWII in Lincoln Bluff, Colorado. Matthau is excellent in his TV debut as a small-town lawyer who must defend a German prisoner of war accused of murder at nearby Camp Bremen. An all-star cast lends powerful performances to this riveting made for TV drama. **95m/C VHS, DVD.** Walter Matthau, Susan Blakely, Harry (Henry) Morgan, Robert Carradine, Barnard Hughes, Peter Firth, William Schallert; ***D:*** Joseph Sargent. **TV**

Incident at Channel Q 🦴 1/2 **1986** A heavy-metal rock musical about a suburban neighborhood declaring war on a chain-and-leather deejay. **85m/C VHS.** Steve Mitchell, Joe Janus, David Dreisin, Al Corley; ***D:*** Storm Thorgerson.

Incident at Deception Ridge 🦴🦴 1/2 **1994 (R)** After five years in prison, Jack Bolder (O'Keefe) is finally a free man, and headed for Seattle by bus. Unfortunately, also aboard is weasely bank manager Jack Davis (Begley Jr.) who's bolted with the ransom money for his kidnapped wife, Helen (Purl). Now Helen is left at the mercy of her kidnappers, who've discovered where their money is and decide to go after it—no matter who gets in their way. Filmed in Vancouver, British Columbia. **94m/C VHS.** Michael O'Keefe, Ed Begley Jr., Linda Purl, Miguel Ferrer, Colleen Flynn, Michelle Johnson, Ian Tracey; ***D:*** John McPherson; ***W:*** Ken Hixon, Randy Kornfield; ***C:*** David Geddes. **CABLE**

Incident at Loch Ness 🦴🦴🦴 1/2 **2004 (PG-13)** Famously difficult German director Werner Herzog is followed by a documentary crew ala "Burden of Dreams" as he tries to film his meditation on humanity's obsession with the Loch Ness monster. Whole production is wonderfully tongue-in-cheek mockumentary within a mockumentary. Game and lively cast pokes unrelenting fun at themselves and the task at hand in this humorous exploration of filmmaking and unmaking. Though nodding to such films as "Waiting for Guffman" and "Blair Witch Project," film is thoroughly and enjoyably one of a kind. **90m/C DVD.** *US* ***D:*** Zak Penn; ***C:*** John Bailey; ***M:*** Henning Lohner.

Incident at Oglala: The Leonard Peltier Story 🦴🦴🦴 **1992 (PG)** Offers a detailed account of the violent events leading to the murder of two FBI agents in Oglala, South Dakota in 1975. American Indian activist Leonard Peltier was convicted of the murders and is presently serving two consecutive life sentences, but he's cited as a political prisoner by Amnesty International. The documentary examines the highly controversial trial and the tensions between the government and the Oglala Nation stemming back to the Indian occupation of Wounded Knee in 1973. Director Apted is sympathetic to Peltier and offers reasons why he should be allowed a retrial; he examined similar incidents in his film "Thunderheart." **90m/C VHS, DVD.** ***D:*** Michael Apted; ***M:*** John Trudell, Jackson Browne; ***Nar:*** Robert Redford.

Incognito 🦴 1/2 **1997 (R)** Art forger Harry Donovan (Patric) is approached by a couple of British art dealers and a Japanese broker to forge a Rembrandt for a Japanese client. He checks out the painter's style by traveling to Amsterdam and Paris, where he falls for art expert Marieke (Jacob). Harry forges the painting and then gets doublecrossed and caught up in murder. Convoluted plot; lots of cliches. Original director Peter Weller was replaced by Badham after two weeks of filming. **107m/C VHS, DVD.** Jason Patric, Irene Jacob, Rod Steiger, Thomas Lockyer, Simon Chandler, Michael Cochrane, Ian Richardson, Pip Torrens, Togo Igawa; ***D:*** John Badham; ***W:*** Jordan Katz; ***C:*** Denis Crossan; ***M:*** John Ottman.

Incognito 🦴🦴 **1999** After exec Erin Courtland (Dean) is raped by Derek Scanlon (Morris), he eludes prosecution and begins stalking her. So Erin's wealthy daddy (Glass) hires bodyguard Jake Hunter (Jones) to protect his little girl. **95m/C DVD.** Allison Dean, Richard T. Jones, Phil Morris, Ron Glass, Vanessa Williams, Joan Pringle, Roger Guenveur; ***D:*** Julie Dash; ***W:*** Shirley Pierce; ***C:*** David West. **CABLE**

An Inconvenient Truth 🦴🦴🦴 1/2 **2006 (PG)** Former Vice President Al Gore speaks out on his personal cause—the dangers of global warming. Guggenheim follows Gore on the lecture circuit as he tries to raise awareness and state his case in an effective (and alarming) multimedia presentation that he has been giving, with a certain confident and professorial charm, since 1989. **100m/C DVD.** *US* ***D:*** Davis Guggenheim; ***C:*** Davis Guggenheim, Bob Richman; ***M:*** Michael Brook. Oscars '06: Feature Doc., Song ("I Need to Wake Up").

An Inconvenient Woman 🦴🦴 **1991** When an older married man has an affair with a young seductress, there's suicide, murder, a nasty gossip columnist, a reporter, a knowing society wife, and a lot of cover-ups among the rich and famous. Miniseries from the novel by Dominick Dunne and based on the Alfred Bloomingdale scandal. **126m/C VHS.** Rebecca De Mornay, Jason Robards Jr., Jill Eikenberry, Peter Gallagher, Roddy McDowall, Chad Lowe; ***D:*** Larry Elikann; ***W:*** John Pielmeier; ***M:*** Craig Safan. **TV**

The Incredible Hulk 🦴🦴 1/2 **1977** Bixby is a scientist who achieves superhuman strength after he is exposed to a massive dose of gamma rays. But his personal life suffers, as does his wardrobe. Ferrigno is the Hulkster. Pilot for a TV series; based on the Marvel Comics character. **94m/C VHS, DVD.** Bill Bixby, Susan Sullivan, Lou Ferrigno, Jack Colvin; ***D:*** Kenneth Johnson. **TV**

The Incredible Hulk 🦴🦴 1/2 **2008 (PG-13)** Hulk SMASH! A re-do for the Hulk franchise, with the studio hoping to get off to a better start than Ang Lee's, dare we say, overly thoughtful "Hulk." The story's more or less the same—mild-mannered scientist Bruce Banner (now played by Norton) inherits the wild-mannered Hulk gene from his old man and falls in love with Betty Ross (Tyler). Betty's military father, General Thaddeus "Thunderbolt" Ross (Hurt), has a devious plan to breed a whole infantry of Hulk soldiers, and makes the mistake of testing his scheme out on blood-thirsty Marine Emil Blonsky (Roth). Very little to think or care about, but lots of fun with the usual CGI overloading all of the action. **112m/C DVD.** *US* Edward Norton, Tim Roth, Liv Tyler, William Hurt, Tim Blake Nelson, Ty Burrell, Christina Cabot, Peter Mensah, Robert Downey Jr.; ***D:*** Louis Leterrier; ***W:*** Zak Penn; ***C:*** Peter Menzies Jr.; ***M:*** Craig Armstrong.

The Incredible Hulk Returns 🦴 1/2 **1988** The beefy green mutant is back and this time he wages war against a Viking named Thor. Very little substance in this made for TV flick, so be prepared to park your brain at the door. Followed by "The Trial of the Incredible Hulk." **100m/C VHS, DVD.** Bill Bixby, Lou Ferrigno, Jack Colvin, Lee Purcell, Charles Napier, Steve Levitt; ***D:*** Nicholas J. Corea. **TV**

The Incredible Journey 🦴🦴 1/2 **1963** A labrador retriever, bull terrier and Siamese cat mistake their caretaker's intentions when he leaves for a hunting trip, believing he will never return. The three set out on a 250 mile adventure-filled trek across Canada's rugged terrain. Entertaining family adventure from Disney taken from Sheila Burnford's book. **80m/C VHS.** ***D:*** Fletcher Markle.

The Incredible Journey of Dr. Meg Laurel 🦴🦴🦴 **1979** A young doctor returns to her roots to bring modern medicine to the Appalachian mountain people during the 1930s. Features Wagner in a strong performance. **143m/C VHS.** Lindsay Wagner, Jane Wyman, Dorothy McGuire, James Woods, Gary Lockwood; ***D:*** Guy Green. **TV**

The Incredible Journey of Mary Bryant 🦴🦴 1/2 *Mary Bryant* **2005 (R)** Mary (Garai) is convicted of theft in 1786 and becomes one of the first British convicts transported to Australia's Botany Bay colony. She marries fellow convict Will Bryant (O'Loughlin) but when the colony faces starvation, Mary wants to save her family by escaping and reaching safety in the Dutch colony of Timor. True story was originally broadcast as an Australian miniseries. **185m/C DVD.** *AU* Romola Garai, Alex O'Loughlin, Jack Davenport, Sam Neill, Tony (Anthony) Martin; ***D:*** Peter Andrikidis; ***W:*** Peter Berry; ***C:*** Joseph Pickering; ***M:*** Iva Davies. **TV**

Incredible Melting Man WOOF! 1977 (R) Two transformations change an astronaut's life after his return to earth. First, his skin starts to melt, then he displays cannibalistic tendencies. Hard to swallow. Special effects by Rick Baker. Look for director Jonathan Demme in a bit part. Gross-out remake of 1958's "First Man Into Space." **85m/C VHS.** Alex Rebar, Burr de Benning, Cheryl "Rainbeaux" Smith; ***Cameos:*** Jonathan Demme; ***D:*** William Sachs.

The Incredible Mrs. Ritchie 🦴🦴 *L'Incroyable Mme. Ritchie* **2003 (PG-13)** Sentimental "After-school-Special"influenced drama has troubled kid Charlie fall in with the wrong crowd, get in trouble, and find himself helping an eccentric old lady in her garden as punishment. This is one of those sappy dramas in which everyone who is not a part of Charlie's dysfunctional family is gentle, quirky, insightful, and always right. Of course, everone in his family is none of these things, and desperately in need of these kinds of people to point out what they were doing wrong and help them mend their ways. As if that wasn't bad enough, there's a puppy drowning. **102m/C VHS, DVD.** *CA* Kevin Zegers, Gena Rowlands, James Caan, Brenda James, Leslie Hope, Justin Chatwin; ***D:*** Paul Johansson; ***W:*** Paul Johansson; ***C:*** Paul Sarossy. **TV**

The Incredible Mr. Limpet 🦴🦴 **1964** Limp comedy about a nebbish bookkeeper who's transformed into a fish, fulfilling his aquatic dreams. Eventually he falls in love with another fish, and helps the U.S. Navy find Nazi subs during WWII. Partially animated, beloved by some, particularly those under the age of seven. Based on Theodore Pratt's novel. **99m/C VHS, DVD.** Don Knotts, Jack Weston, Carole Cook, Andrew Duggan, Larry Keating, Elizabeth McRae; ***D:*** Arthur Lubin; ***W:*** Jameson Brewer.

The Incredible Petrified World WOOF! 1958 Divers are trapped in an underwater cave when volcanic eruptions begin. Suffocating nonsense. **78m/B VHS, DVD.** John Carradine, Allen Windsor, Phyllis Coates, Lloyd Nelson, George Skaff; *D:* Jerry Warren.

The Incredible Rocky Mountain Race 🦴🦴 **1977** The townspeople of St. Joseph, fed up with Mark Twain's destructive feud with a neighbor, devise a shrewd scheme to rid the town of the troublemakers by sending them on a road race through the West. Comedy starring the F-Troop. **97m/C VHS.** Christopher Connelly, Forrest Tucker, Larry Storch, Mike Mazurki; *D:* James L. Conway. **TV**

The Incredible Sarah 🦴🦴 **1976 (PG)** A limp adapted stage biography from "Reader's Digest" of the great actress Sarah Bernhardt. Jackson chews scenery to no avail. **105m/C VHS.** Glenda Jackson, Daniel Massey, Yvonne Mitchell, Douglas Wilmer; *D:* Richard Fleischer; *M:* Elmer Bernstein.

The Incredible Shrinking Man 🦴🦴🦴 ½ **1957** Adapted by Richard Matheson from his own novel, the sci-fi classic is a philosophical thriller about a man who is doused with radioactive mist and begins to slowly shrink. His new size means that everyday objects take on sinister meaning and he must fight for his life in an increasingly hostile, absurd environment. A surreal, suspenseful allegory with impressive special effects. Endowed with the tension usually reserved for Hitchcock films. **81m/B VHS, DVD.** Grant Williams, Randy Stuart, April Kent, Paul Langton, Raymond Bailey, William Schallert, Frank Scanell, Billy Curtis; *D:* Jack Arnold; *W:* Richard Matheson; *C:* Ellis W. Carter. Natl. Film Reg. '09.

The Incredible Shrinking Woman 🦴🦴 ½ **1981 (PG)** "...Shrinking Man" spoof and inoffensive social satire finds household cleaners producing some strange side effects on model homemaker Tomlin, slowly shrinking her to doll-house size. She then encounters everyday happenings as big tasks and not so menial. Her advertising exec husband has a hand in the down-sizing. Sight gags abound but the cuteness wears thin by the end. **89m/C VHS.** Lily Tomlin, Charles Grodin, Ned Beatty, Henry Gibson; *D:* Joel Schumacher; *W:* Jane Wagner.

The Incredible Two-Headed Transplant WOOF! **1971 (PG)** Mad scientist Dern has a criminal head transplanted on to the shoulder of big John Bloom and the critter runs amuck. Low-budget special effects guaranteed to give you a headache or two. Watch for Pat "Marilyn Munster" Priest in a bikini. **88m/C VHS, DVD.** Bruce Dern, Pat Priest, Casey Kasem, Albert Cole, John Bloom, Berry Kroeger; *D:* Anthony M. Lanza; *W:* John Lawrence, James Gordon White; *C:* Glen Gano, Paul Hipp, Jack Steely; *M:* John Barber.

The Incredibles 🦴🦴🦴 ½ **2004 (PG)** Pixar's final feature as a Disney partner ends the relationship on a high note with this story of a retired superhero family and their difficulties adjusting to "normal" life. Bob Parr (Nelson) is the former Mr. Incredible, who, because of multiple lawsuits, has been forced, along with all other costumed heroes, including wife Helen (Hunter) and best friend Lucius (Jackson), into the Hero Relocation Program. He's stuck in a soul-sucking corporate job where he can't save anyone, he misses the old crimefighting days, and his kids Dash and Violet aren't allowed to use their powers. That is, until someone from Mr. Incredible's past returns to endanger them all. Director/writer Bird's script is smart, funny, and insightful. There's plenty for the kids to enjoy, to be sure, but Bird makes some pointed and poignant observations about marriage, middle class values, and the rise of mediocrity in a self-esteem obsessed society. No wonder the screenplay was nominated for an Oscar. **115m/C VHS, DVD, Blu-ray Disc, UMD.** *US D:* Brad Bird; *W:* Brad Bird; *C:* Janet Lucroy, Patick Lin, Andrew Jimenez; *M:* Michael Giacchino; *V:* Craig T. Nelson, Holly Hunter, Samuel L. Jackson, Jason Lee, Wallace Shawn, Sarah Vowell, Spencer Fox, Brad Bird, Elizabeth Pena, Dominique Louis. Oscars '04: Animated Film, Sound FX Editing.

Incredibly Strange Creatures Who Stopped Living and Became Mixed-Up Zombies WOOF! *The Teenage Psycho Meets Bloody Mary; The Incredibly Strange Creatures* **1963** The infamous, super-cheap horror spoof that established Sheckler (for whom Cash Flagg is a pseudonym), about a carny side show riddled with ghouls and bad rock bands. Assistant cinematographers include the young Laszlo Kovacs and Vilmos Zsigmond. A must-see for connoisseurs of cult and camp. **90m/C VHS, DVD.** Ray Dennis Steckler, Carolyn Brandt, Brett O'Hara, Atlas King, Sharon Walsh, Toni Camel, Erina Enyo; *D:* Ray Dennis Steckler; *W:* Gene Pollock, Robert Silliphant; *C:* Laszlo Kovacs, Vilmos Zsigmond, Joseph Mascelli; *M:* Andre Brummer.

The Incredibly True Adventure of Two Girls in Love 🦴🦴 ½ **1995 (R)** Gentle low-budget romantic comedy about first love between two high school girls. Tomboyish working-class Randy (Holloman) lives with her lesbian aunt and works part-time at the local gas station where she spots the rich and beautiful Evie (Parker), one of the popular girls in school. Some sparks fly but Evie's confused, though she's willing to be wooed and, later, defend her new relationship. The issue of race (Randy's white, Evie's black) is only briefly alluded to—more is made of the differences between the girls' social classes and their vulnerability. Directorial debut for Maggenti. **95m/C VHS, DVD.** Laurel Holloman, Nicole Ari Parker, Kate Stafford, Stephanie Berry; *D:* Maria Maggenti; *W:* Maria Maggenti.

Incubus 🦴🦴 **1965** One of the very few films made in the artificial language of Esperanto (so it's subtitled in English). Beautiful Kia (Ames) and Amael (Hardt) are sisters who retain their youth and beauty by sucking the life out of the corrupted souls who visit a supposedly magic well. Then Kia discovers the uncorrupted soldier Mark (Shatner) and falls big time. But her succubis sis doesn't like what's going on and casts a spell that calls an incubus to wreak havoc. Creepily atmospheric with striking cinematography by Hall. **76m/B VHS, DVD.** William Shatner, Allyson Ames, Eloise Hardt, Ann Atmar, Robert Fortier, Milos Milos; *D:* Leslie Stevens; *W:* Leslie Stevens; *C:* Conrad L. Hall; *M:* Dominic Frontiere.

Incubus WOOF! **1982 (R)** A doctor and his teenaged daughter settle in a quiet New England community, only to encounter the incubus, a terrifying, supernatural demon who enjoys sex murders. Offensive trash. **90m/C VHS, DVD.** *CA* John Cassavetes, Kerrie Keane, Helen Hughes, Erin Flannery, John Ireland, Duncan McIntosh; *D:* John Hough; *W:* George Franklin; *C:* Conrad L. Hall, Albert J. Dunk; *M:* Stanley Myers.

Incubus 🦴 **2005** Getting stranded in the middle of nowhere never seems to end well. When Jay (Reid) and her college pals have a car accident, they find refuge in an ominous looking (for a reason!) building that is, indeed, filled with lots of dead folks and a killer in a coma who can enter people's minds as they sleep. No, he is NOT named Freddy but rather, um, cleverly "The Sleeper." Once in their dreams they themselves begin hunting one another so Jay tries really, really super hard not to snooze, as does the unfortunate viewer. **89m/C DVD.** Tara Reid, Akemnji Ndifernyan, Alice O'Connell, Russell Carter II, Christian Brassington; *D:* Anya Camilleri; *W:* Gary Humphreys. **VIDEO**

Indecency 🦴🦴 **1992 (PG-13)** Ellie (Beals) is still recovering from a mental breakdown when she goes to work for Marie (Clarkson) at her ad agency. There Ellie must deal with manipulative associate Nia (Davis) and Marie's charming, estranged husband Mick (Remar), who draws the fragile Ellie into an affair. Then Marie commits suicide—or maybe it was murder. **88m/C VHS.** Jennifer Beals, James Remar, Sammi Davis, Barbara Williams, Christopher John Fields, Ray McKinnon; *D:* Marisa Silver; *W:* Amy Holden Jones, Holly Goldberg Sloan, Alan Ormsby.

Indecent Behavior 🦴🦴 **1993 (R)** Tweed is a sex therapist who's accused of murder when one of her clients overdose's on the latest designer drug. Hudson, who plays the genre's hard-boiled cop figure, gets very personally involved investigating the allegations, which really upsets Tweed's hubby, Vincent. Also available in an unrated version. **93m/C VHS.** Shannon Tweed, Gary Hudson, Jan-Michael Vincent, Michelle Moffett, Lawrence-Hilton Jacobs, Penny Peyser; *D:* Lawrence Lanoff.

Indecent Behavior 2 🦴 ½ **1994 (R)** Sex therapist Rebecca is targeted for blackmail as she finds out all sorts of unhealthy things about her patients. Meanwhile, she's practicing her technique with a fellow therapist. Also available unrated. **96m/C VHS, DVD.** Shannon Tweed, James Brolin, Chad McQueen, Elizabeth Sandifer, Craig Stepp, Rochelle Swanson; *D:* Carlo Gustaff.

Indecent Behavior 3 🦴 **1995 (R)** Sex therapist becomes the obsessed object of desire for a decidedly deadly client. Also available unrated. **90m/C VHS.** Shannon Tweed, Sam Hennings, Colleen T. Coffey, Doug Jeffery, Beau Billingslea, Laura Rogers; *D:* Kelley Cauthen; *W:* Hel Styverson.

An Indecent Obsession 🦴🦴 ½ **1985** Colleen McCullough's bestseller about WWII Australian soldiers recuperating in a field hospital mental ward. Hughes plays the nurse everyone's in love with. **100m/C VHS.** *AU* Wendy Hughes, Gary Sweet, Richard Moir, Jonathan Hyde, Bill Hunter, Bruno Lawrence; *D:* Lex Marinos; *W:* Denise Morgan.

Indecent Proposal 🦴🦴 ½ **1993 (R)** High-gloss movie that had couples everywhere discussing the big question: Would you let your wife sleep with a billionaire in exchange for a million bucks? Probably, if all were as goodlooking as the weathered, yet ever gorgeous Redford. Moore and Harrelson are the financially down on their luck, but happy, couple who venture to Vegas on a last-ditch gambling effort. Surreally slick direction from Lyne, but an ultimately empty film that explores the values of marriage in a terribly angst-ridden fashion. Based on the novel by Jack Engelhard. Proof that average movies can make a killing at the boxoffice, landing in sixth place for 1993. **119m/C VHS, DVD.** Robert Redford, Demi Moore, Woody Harrelson, Seymour Cassel, Oliver Platt, Billy Bob Thornton, Rip Taylor, Billy Connolly, Joel Brooks, Sheena Easton, Herbie Hancock; *D:* Adrian Lyne; *W:* Amy Holden Jones; *C:* Howard Atherton; *M:* John Barry. MTV Movie Awards '94: Kiss (Demi Moore/Woody Harrelson); Golden Raspberries '93: Worst Picture, Worst Support. Actor (Harrelson), Worst Screenplay.

Independence Day 🦴🦴 *Follow Your Dreams* **1983 (R)** Uneven romantic drama about a small-town photographer, yearning for the big city, who falls in love with a racing car enthusiast, whose sister is a battered wife. Strong cast, particularly Wiest as the abused wife, is left occasionally stranded by a script reaching too hard for social significance. **110m/C VHS.** Kathleen Quinlan, David Keith, Frances Sternhagen, Dianne Wiest, Cliff DeYoung, Richard Farnsworth, Josef Sommer, Cheryl "Rainbeaux" Smith; *D:* Robert Mandel; *M:* Charles Bernstein.

Independence Day 🦴🦴🦴 **1996 (PG-13)** The biggest of the new wave of disaster flicks paying tribute to the Irwin Allen celebrity-fests of the '70s finds an alien armada descending on Earth to create some fireworks on the July 4th weekend. The fate of the world rests in the hands of an unlikely band of Earthlings led by President Whitmore (Pullman), a computer expert (Goldblum), and a Marine fighter pilot (Smith). Special effects, despite forgoing some of the more expensive newer technology, don't disappoint. Strong (if not A-list) cast and plenty of action. Devlin and Emmerich wrote the script while promoting "Stargate," after a reporter asked Emmerich if he believed in aliens. **135m/C VHS, DVD, UMD.** Bill Pullman, Will Smith, Jeff Goldblum, Judd Hirsch, Margaret Colin, Randy Quaid, Mary McDonnell, Robert Loggia, Brent Spiner, James Rebhorn, Vivica A. Fox, James Duval, Harry Connick Jr., Harvey Fierstein, Richard Speight Jr., Adam Baldwin, Bill Smitrovich, Mae Whitman, Kiersten Warren, Giuseppe Andrews, Devon Gummersall, Leland Orser, Raphael Sbarge, Bobby Hosea, Dan Lauria, Robert Pine, John Capodice, Lyman Ward; *D:* Roland Emmerich; *W:* Dean Devlin, Roland Emmerich; *C:* Karl Walter Lindenlaub; *M:* David Arnold. Oscars '96: Visual FX; MTV Movie Awards '97: Kiss (Vivica A. Fox/Will Smith).

The Independent 🦴🦴 **2000** Affectionate spoof of low-budget, schlock cinema. Morty Fineman (Stiller) has directed more than 400 "B" movies, which has made him a legend in certain circles. His latest project has gone bust, leaving him facing bankruptcy once again, but he's sure he has a hit with his next idea—the rights to the life story of serial killer William Henry Ellis (Hankin). Now Morty just has to convince his exasperated, estranged daughter Paloma (Garofalo) to help him raise the cash for his new opus. Faux trailers from some of Morty's epics and interviews with various co-workers, admirers, and cast are among the inspired bits. **93m/C VHS, DVD.** Jerry Stiller, Janeane Garofalo, Max Perlich, Larry Hankin, Ginger Lynn Allen, Billy Burke, Andy Dick, Fred (John F.) Dryer, Ethan (Randall) Embry, Jonathan Katz, John (Johnny Rotten) Lydon, Anne Meara; ***Cameos:*** Ben Stiller, Fred Williamson, Karen Black, Peter Bogdanovich, Nick Cassavetes, Roger Corman, Ron Howard, Ted (Edward) Demme; *D:* Stephen Kessler; *W:* Stephen Kessler, Mike Wilkins; *C:* Amir Hamed; *M:* Ben Vaughn.

The Indestructible Man 🦴 **1956** Chaney, electrocuted for murder and bank robbery, is brought back to life by a scientist. Naturally, he seeks revenge on those who sentenced him to death. Chaney does the best he can with the material. **70m/B VHS, DVD.** Ross Elliott, Ken Terrell, Robert Shayne, Lon Chaney Jr., Marian Carr, Max (Casey Adams) Showalter; *D:* Jack Pollexfen; *W:* Sue Bradford, Vy Russell; *C:* John L. "Jack" Russell; *M:* Albert Glasser.

The Indian 🦴🦴 ½ **2007 (PG-13)** Skip is dying and needs a transplant. His most likely match is his teenaged son Danny, whom he abandoned years before. So Skip hires beautiful mechanic Shelby to manipulate Danny into helping restore a 1917 Indian motorcycle, hoping the developing bond between the three of them will save his life. **91m/C DVD.** Matt Dallas, Sal Landi, Alison Haislip, Jane Higginson, Angela Lanza, Richard Portnow, Robert Miano; *D:* James R. Gorrie; *W:* James R. Gorrie; *C:* David Palmieri; *M:* Frederik Wiedmann. **VIDEO**

The Indian Fighter 🦴🦴🦴 **1955** Exciting actioner has Douglas as a scout hired to lead a wagon train to Oregon in 1870. The train must past through dangerous Sioux territory and Douglas tries to make peace with the Sioux leader but a secret Indian gold mine and romance cause friction and keep things lively. **88m/C VHS, DVD.** Kirk Douglas, Elsa Martinelli, Walter Abel, Walter Matthau, Diana Douglas, Lon Chaney Jr., Eduard Franz, Alan Hale Jr., Elisha Cook Jr., Harry Landers; *D:* Andre de Toth; *W:* Ben Hecht, Robert L. Richards.

The Indian in the Cupboard 🦴🦴 ½ **1995 (PG)** On his ninth birthday, Omri receives a three-inch plastic indian named Little Bear and an old wooden medicine cabinet. (Guess they were out of Power Rangers.) When placed in the cabinet, Little Bear magically comes to life, taking Omri on adventures and teaching him important lessons. Blue screen techniques allow them to appear together on-screen although they were actually shot together only once. Based on the best-selling children's book by Lynne Reid Banks. **97m/C VHS, DVD.** Michael (Mike) Papajohn, Hal Scardino, Litefoot, Lindsay Crouse, Richard Jenkins, Rishi Bhat, David Keith; *D:* Frank Oz; *W:* Melissa Mathison; *C:* Russell Carpenter; *M:* Miles Goodman.

Indian Paint 🦴🦴 **1964** A pleasant children's film about an Indian boy's love for his horse and his rite of passage. Silverheels was Tonto on TV's "The Lone Ranger," while Crawford was the "Rifleman's" son. **90m/C VHS.** Jay Silverheels, Johnny Crawford, Pat Hogan, Robert Crawford Jr., George Lewis; *D:* Norman Foster.

The Indian Runner 🦴🦴 ½ **1991 (R)** Penn's debut as a writer-director tells the story of two brothers in Nebraska during the late '60s, who are forced to change their lives with the loss of their family farm. Joe is a good cop and family man who can't deal with the rage of his brother Frank, who has just returned from Vietnam and is turning to a life of crime. Penn does a decent job of representing the struggle between the responsible versus the rebellious side of human nature. Quiet and very stark. Based on the song "Highway Patrolman" by Bruce Springsteen.

127m/C VHS, DVD. David Morse, Viggo Mortensen, Sandy Dennis, Charles Bronson, Valeria Golino, Patricia Arquette, Dennis Hopper, Benicio Del Toro; ***D:*** Sean Penn; ***W:*** Sean Penn.

The Indian Scarf **1963** Heirs to a dead man's fortune are being strangled one by one at the benefactor's country estate. An Edgar Wallace suspense tale. **85m/C VHS.** *GE* Heinz Drache, Gisela Uhlen, Klaus Kinski; ***D:*** Alfred Vohrer.

Indian Summer **1993 (PG-13)** Yet another addition to the growing 30-something nostalgia genre. Delete the big house, add a crusty camp director (Arkin), change the characters' names (but not necessarily their lives) and you feel like you're experiencing deja vu. This time seven friends and the requisite outsider reconvene at Camp Tamakwa, the real-life summer camp to writer/director Binder. The former campers talk. They yearn. They save Camp Tamakwa and experience personal growth. A must see for those who appreciate listening to situational jokes that are followed by "I guess you had to be there." **108m/C VHS, DVD.** Alan Arkin, Matt Craven, Diane Lane, Bill Paxton, Elizabeth Perkins, Kevin Pollak, Sam Raimi, Vincent Spano, Julie Warner, Kimberly Williams, Richard Chevolleau; ***D:*** Mike Binder; ***W:*** Mike Binder; ***M:*** Miles Goodman.

The Indian Tomb 1/2 *The Mission of the Yogi; The Tiger of Eschanapur* **1921** Silent film fare in two parts. Ayan (Veidt) is the Maharajah of Eschanapur. But all his wealth and power has not prevented Ayan's wife, Princess Savitri, from falling in love with British officer MacAllan. Ayan plots to built a massive tomb to imprison the woman who betrayed him but yogi Ramigani prophesizes that such revenge will destroy the prince's life. Huge budget (for the time) and lavish spectacle, which was all created at director May's German studio. Adapted from the novel by Thea von Haubou. **212m/B VHS, DVD.** *GE* Conrad Veidt, Paul Richter, Olaf Fonss, Mia May, Bernhard Goetzke, Lya de Putti, Erna Morena; ***D:*** Joe May; ***W:*** Fritz Lang; ***C:*** Werner Brandes.

The Indian Tomb *Das Indische Grabmal* **1959** Sequel to "The Tiger of Eschnapur" finds Harald Berger (Hubschmid) and Seetha (Paget) managing to elude Chandra's soldiers until Seetha's faith in her gods results in her capture and his apparent death. Berger's partner Dr. Rhode (Holm) and Berger's sister Irene (Bethmann) discover they're in the hands of a madman when Chandra lies about Berger's whereabouts. Along the way is another knockout exotic dance (with Ms. Paget in an even more revealing costume), encounters with a horde of lepers locked away in the catacombs, and a full-scale palace revolt. **102m/C DVD.** *GE* Debra Paget, Paul (Christian) Hubschmid, Walter Reyer, Sabine Bethmann; ***D:*** Fritz Lang; ***W:*** Werner Jorg Luddecke; ***C:*** Richard Angst; ***M:*** Michel Michelet.

Indian Uprising **1951** An army captain tries to keep local settlers from causing trouble with Geronimo and his people when gold is discovered on their territory. **75m/C VHS.** George Montgomery, Audrey Long, Carl Benton Reid, John Baer, Joseph (Joe) Sawyer; ***D:*** Ray Nazarro.

Indiana Jones and the Kingdom of the Crystal Skull 1/2 **2008 (PG-13)** Lucas and Spielberg again team up to bring Harrison Ford back in the fedora in a hugely hyped return that lives up to its adventurous roots, but suffers from the vices of its day. The Soviets are hot on Indy's trail as they both race deep into the Amazon to recover a legendary crystal skull with potentially extraterrestrial powers. Indy's joined by a young greaser named Mutt Williams (LaBeouf), who shares Jones's thrill for danger and possibly his gene structure. The thrill and excitement are constant, but suffer from a CGI overload and a series of lapses in credibility in the second half. Allen is back as Indy's long-lost love and LaBeouf brings a renewed spirit of youth to the journey (and likely a renewed boom in lunchbox and Lego sales for a second generation of Indy fans). **122m/C DVD.** *US* Harrison Ford, Shia LaBeouf, Karen Allen, Cate Blanchett, Ray Winstone, Jim Broadbent, John Hurt, Andrew Divoff, Igor Jijikine, Neil Flynn, Ernie Reyes Jr.; ***D:*** Steven Spielberg; ***W:*** David Koepp; ***C:*** Janusz Kaminski; ***M:*** John Williams. Golden Raspberries '08: Worst Sequel/Prequel.

Indiana Jones and the Last Crusade **1989 (PG)** In this, the third and last (?) Indiana Jones adventure, the fearless archaeologist is once again up against the Nazis in a race to find the Holy Grail. Connery is perfectly cast as Indy's father; opening sequence features Phoenix as a teenage Indy and explains his fear of snakes and the origins of the infamous fedora. Returns to the look and feel of the original with more adventures, exotic places, dastardly villains, and daring escapes than ever before; a must for Indy fans. **126m/C VHS, DVD.** Harrison Ford, Sean Connery, Denholm Elliott, Alison Doody, Julian Glover, John Rhys-Davies, River Phoenix, Michael Byrne, Alex Hyde-White; ***D:*** Steven Spielberg; ***W:*** Jeffrey Boam; ***C:*** Douglas Slocombe; ***M:*** John Williams.

Indiana Jones and the Temple of Doom **1984 (PG)** Daredevil archaeologist Indiana Jones is back. This time he's on the trail of the legendary Ankara Stone and a ruthless cult that has enslaved hundreds of children. More gore and violence than the original; Capshaw's whining character is an irritant, lacking the fresh quality that Karen Allen added to the original. Enough action for ten movies, special effects galore, and the usual booming Williams score make it a cinematic roller coaster ride, but with less regard for plot and pacing than the original. Though second in the series, it's actually a prequel to "Raiders of the Lost Ark." Followed by "Indiana Jones and the Last Crusade." **118m/C VHS, DVD.** Harrison Ford, Kate Capshaw, Ke Huy Quan, Amrish Puri; ***D:*** Steven Spielberg; ***W:*** Willard Huyck, Gloria Katz; ***C:*** Douglas Slocombe; ***M:*** John Williams. Oscars '84: Visual FX.

Indictment: The McMartin Trial **1995 (R)** Woods stars as attorney Danny Davis, who has the unenviable task of providing a defense in the notorious McMartin child molestation trial. In 1983, Manhattan Beach, California was rocked by reports that some 60 preschoolers had been abused at a day-care center. Seven defendants were accused thanks to lurid videotaped interviews with the children. The trial lasted six years (the longest and most expensive on record) and all charges were eventually dismissed. It's clear from this telepic that public hysteria and media hype lead to a grave miscarriage of justice that put the legal system on trial as well. **132m/C VHS, DVD.** James Woods, Henry Thomas, Mercedes Ruehl, Shirley Knight, Sada Thompson, Mark Blum, Alison Elliott, Chelsea Field, Richard Bradford, Lolita (David) Davidovich; ***D:*** Mick Jackson; ***W:*** Abby Mann, Myra Mann; ***C:*** Rodrigo Garcia; ***M:*** Peter Melnick.

Indio **1990 (R)** A Marine-trained half-breed takes it on himself to save the Amazon rain forest. Not a peaceful demonstrator, his tactics are violent ones. **94m/C VHS.** Marvin Hagler, Francesco Quinn, Brian Dennehy; ***D:*** Anthony M. Dawson.

Indio 2: The Revolt **1992 (R)** Greedy developers are cutting a highway into the Amazon jungle, destroying everything in their path. All is not lost though, because U.S. Marine Sgt. Iron is on top of things, continuing his struggle to unite the Amazon tribes and save the rainforest, no matter what it takes. **104m/C VHS.** Marvin Hagler, Charles Napier; ***M:*** Pino Donaggio.

Indiscreet 1/2 **1931** Empty-headed romantic comedy about a fashion designer whose past catches up with her when her ex-lover starts romancing her sister. No relation to the classic 1958 film with Cary Grant and Ingrid Bergman. ♫ Come To Me; If You Haven't Got Love. **81m/B VHS, DVD.** Gloria Swanson, Ben Lyon, Barbara Kent; ***D:*** Leo McCarey.

Indiscreet **1958** A charming American diplomat in London falls in love with a stunning actress, but protects himself by saying he is married. Needless to say, she finds out. Stylish romp with Grant and Bergman at their sophisticated best. Adapted by Norman Krasna from his stage play "Kind Sir." **100m/C VHS, DVD.** Cary Grant, Ingrid Bergman, Phyllis Calvert; ***D:*** Stanley Donen; ***W:*** Norman Krasna; ***C:*** Frederick A. (Freddie) Young; ***M:*** Richard Rodney Bennett.

Indiscreet 1/2 **1988 (PG)** Indistinctive made for TV rehash of the charming 1958 Grant/Bergman romantic comedy in which a suave American falls for an English actress. Both versions derive from the play "Kind Sir" by Norman Krasna, but this one suffers by comparison. **94m/C VHS.** Robert Wagner, Lesley-Anne Down, Maggie Henderson, Robert McBain, Jeni Barnett; ***D:*** Richard Michaels. **TV**

Indiscreet 1/2 **1998 (R)** Private eye Michael Nash (Perry) is hired by a suspicious millionaire to follow his wife, Eve (Reuben). When Nash winds up saving the desperately unhappy Eve from suicide, the two begin an affair. Then her husband is murdered and the cops find Nash a very handy suspect. **101m/C VHS.** Luke Perry, Gloria Reuben, Peter Coyote, Adam Baldwin; ***D:*** Marc Bienstock; ***W:*** Vladimir Nemirovsky.

Indiscretion of an American Wife *Indiscretion; Terminus Station; Terminal Station Indiscretion* **1954** Set almost entirely in Rome's famous Terminal Station, where an ill-fated couple say goodbye endlessly while the woman tries to decide whether to join her husband in the States. Trimmed down from 87 minutes upon U.S. release. **63m/C VHS, DVD.** *IT* Jennifer Jones, Montgomery Clift, Richard Beymer; ***D:*** Vittorio De Sica; ***W:*** Truman Capote; ***C:*** Oswald Morris.

Indochine **1992 (PG-13)** Soapy melodrama follows the fortunes of Eliane (Deneuve), a Frenchwoman born and reared in Indochina, from 1930 to the communist revolution 25 years later. She contends with the changes to her country as well as her adopted daughter as she grows up and becomes independent. Deneuve's controlled performance (and unchanging beauty) is eminently watchable. Filmed on location in Vietnam with breathtaking cinematography by Francois Catonne. In French with English subtitles. **155m/C VHS, DVD.** *FR* Catherine Deneuve, Linh Dan Pham, Vincent Perez, Jean Yanne, Dominique Blanc, Henri Marteau, Carlo Brandt, Gerard Lartigau; ***D:*** Regis Wargnier; ***W:*** Erik Orsenna, Louis Gardel, Catherine Cohen, Regis Wargnier; ***C:*** Francois Catonne; ***M:*** Patrick Doyle. Oscars '92: Foreign Film; Cesar '93: Actress (Deneuve), Art Dir./Set Dec., Cinematog., Sound, Support. Actress (Blanc); Golden Globes '93: Foreign Film; Natl. Bd. of Review '92: Foreign Film.

Inevitable Grace 1/2 **1994** Strictly amateur attempt at neo-noir for fledgling director Canawati. Wealthy Adam Cestare (Caulfield) becomes enamoured with young psychiatrist Lisa Kelner (Knights), who's treating his hysterical wife, Veronica (Nicholson, daughter of Jack). Naturally, Adam turns out to have more than a few screws loose himself and Lisa finds herself the object of his obsession. **104m/C VHS.** Maxwell Caulfield, Stephanie Knights, Jennifer Nicholson, Tippi Hedren, Andrea King, Taylor Negron; ***Cameos:*** Samantha Eggar; ***D:*** Alex Canawati; ***W:*** Alex Canawati; ***C:*** Christian Sebaldt; ***M:*** Christopher Whiffen.

Infamous **2006 (R)** The other Truman Capote movie, which was filmed at the same time as the more successful (both financially and artistically) "Capote." Englishman Jones is at least physically more suited to the role of the fey author, who revels in his Gotham society milieu. Still, you've got Truman and his best friend Harper Lee (an understated Bullock) traipsing off to Kansas to work on his true-crime story. Daniels is solid as lawman Alvin Dewey while Craig (the new James Bond) is a mixed blessing as killer Perry Smith; he's physically wrong and overwhelming for the part but you still can't take your eyes off him. Without that the same could be said of McGrath's glossy film. **118m/C DVD.** *US* Toby Jones, Sandra Bullock, Daniel Craig, Lee Pace, Peter Bogdanovich, Jeff Daniels, Hope Davis, Sigourney Weaver, Isabella Rossellini, Juliet Stevenson, Gwyneth Paltrow, John Benjamin Hickey; ***D:*** Douglas McGrath; ***W:*** Douglas McGrath; ***C:*** Bruno Delbonnel; ***M:*** Rachel Portman.

Infamous Crimes *Philo Vance Returns* **1947** Philo investigates the murders of a playboy and his girlfriends. One of the last of the series whose character was based on the S.S. Van Dine stories. **64m/B VHS.** William Wright, Terry Austin, Leon Belasco, Clara Blandick, Iris Adrian, Frank Wilcox; ***D:*** William Beaudine.

Infected 1/2 **2008** Ben (Bellows) and Lisa (Roy) are working at a Boston newspaper when an informant of Lisa's says a big bad corporation is actually a front for an alien plague (the precursor to an invasion) and the toxins are delivered to humans through—wait for it!—designer bottled vitamin water! See—all those environmentalists were right about it being bad for you! But maybe not as bad as this SciFi Channel effort, which is boring. **84m/C DVD.** Gil Bellows, Maxim Roy, Judd Nelson, Isabella Rossellini, Jesse Todd; ***D:*** Adam Weissman; ***W:*** Joshua Hale Failkov, Mark Wheaton; ***C:*** Daniel Villeneuve; ***M:*** Ned Bouhalassa. **CABLE**

Infernal Affairs *Mogan Do; Wu jian dao* **2002 (R)** Claustrophobic cat-and-mouse, cops-and-robbers noir. Lau (Lau) is a Triad member who's sent by his boss Hon Sam (Tsang) to the police academy so he can become a deep cover mole. Chan (Leung Chui-wai) is a cop whose boss, Supt. Wong (Wong), has sent him into the mob as a police informer. Each boss knows he has a mole and each mole knows it's only a matter of time before a slip-up will prove fatal. Lau is sent by Internal Affairs to investigate the Triad mole while Chan is told to find out who the police stoolie is. Talk about your identity crisis! Cantonese with subtitles. There's also a prequel and a sequel. **100m/C DVD.** Tony Leung Chiu-wai, Andy Lau, Anthony Wong, Eric Tsang, Lam Ka-tung, Ng Ting-yip, Wan Chi-keung, Sammi Cheng; ***D:*** Wai Keung (Andrew) Lau; ***W:*** Felix Chong; ***C:*** Lai Yui-fai Lang; ***M:*** Chan Kwong-wing.

Infernal Affairs 2 1/2 *Infernal Affairs II; Mou gaan dou II; Wu jian dao 2* **2003** In this prequel, a Triad boss is murdered and his son takes over the empire before all out war is declared. Meanwhile Yan (now played by Shawn Yue), has just been thrown out of the police academy for violating the rules, and then quickly drafted to infiltrate the Triads undercover when it's discovered that he's the new boss's half-brother. **119m/C DVD.** *HK* Anthony Wong Chau-Sang, Eric Tsang, Carina Lau, Frances Ng, Edison Chen, Peter Ngor, Arthur Wong, Teddy Chan, Roy Cheung, Chapman To, Shawn Yue, Jun Hu, Tung Cho 'Joe' Cheung, Henry Fong, Chung-yue Chiu, Phorjeat Keanpetch, Shipin Ye, Ping Hui Tay, Alexander Chan, Chi Keung Wan; ***D:*** Wai Keung (Andrew) Lau, Siu Fai Mak; ***W:*** Felix Chong, Siu Fai Mak; ***C:*** Wai Keung (Andrew) Lau, Man-Ching Ng; ***M:*** Kwong Wing Chan.

Infernal Affairs 3 *Mou gaan dou III: Jung mik mou gaan; Infernal Affairs III; Infernal Affairs: End Inferno 3; Wu jian dao III: Zhong ji wu jian* **2003** Picking up where the first film left off, Ming (Andy Lau) is cleared of all charges of killing a fellow officer, and is somehow inexplicably promoted to Internal Affairs. He discovers a corrupt cop who may be a Triad mole, and tries to expose him while covering up the fact that he used to be one himself. Unfortunately the aforementioned mole has the same idea about Ming. **118m/C DVD.** *HK* Anthony Wong Chau-Sang, Eric Tsang, Carina Lau, Chi Keung Wan, Andy Lau, Leon Lai, Daoming Chen, Tony Leung Chiu-Wai, Kelly Chen, Sammi Cheng, Chapman To, Waise Lee, Ka-tung Lam, Ting Yip Ng, Huang Zhi Zhong; ***D:*** Wai Keung (Andrew) Lau, Siu Fai Mak; ***W:*** Siu Fai Mak, Felix Chong; ***C:*** Man-Ching Ng; ***M:*** Kwong Wing Chan.

The Infernal Trio 1/2 *Le Trio Infernal* **1974** An attorney comes up with a plan involving two sisters (who are his lovers) which will make them both wealthy; but it will also make them both murderers. Sophisticated black comedy based on a true story. In French with English subtitles or dubbed. **100m/C VHS.** *FR IT* Romy Schneider, Michel Piccoli, Mascha Gonska; ***D:*** Francis Girod.

Inferno **1980 (R)** Uneven occult horror tale about a young man who arrives in New York to investigate the mysterious circumstances surrounding his sister's death. Dubbed. **106m/C VHS, DVD.** *IT* Leigh McCloskey, Elenora Giorgi, Irene Miracle, Sacha (Sascha) Pitoeff; ***D:*** Dario Argento; ***W:*** Dario Argento; ***C:*** Romano Albani; ***M:*** Keith Emerson.

Inferno **1998 (PG-13)** A massive fireball is

headed straight toward Earth. **90m/C VHS.** James Remar, Stephanie Niznik, Daniel von Bargen, Anthony Starke, Kathryn Morris, Frederic Lehne, Jonathan LaPaglia, Ian Barry; ***W:*** Bruce Taylor, Roderick Taylor; ***C:*** Jacques Haitkin; ***M:*** Joel Goldsmith, K. Alexander (Alex) Wilkinson.

Inferno ½ **1999 (R)** Jack Conley awakens in the middle of the desert with no idea who he is or what's happened to him. Taken in by a reclusive artist, Jack suffers violent flashbacks as he tries to piece together his identity, only remembering that he had a lot of money in his possession and it's gone. Then two of Jack's former associates track him down and he learns the dangerous truth about himself. **94m/C VHS, DVD.** Ray Liotta, Gloria Reuben, Armin Mueller-Stahl; ***D:*** Harley Cokliss; ***C:*** Stephen McNutt; ***M:*** Fred Mollin. **VIDEO**

Inferno ½ **2001** Darcy Hamilton (Gunn) is an expert firejumper who leads her team in controlling a forest fire that Darcy suspects was arson. A second blaze erupts and heads for the nearest town and the local fire chief accuses Darcy's daughter and her boyfriend of being fire bugs. Now Darcy not only has to fight the fire but prove her daughter's innocence. **91m/C VHS, DVD.** Janet Gunn, Jeff Fahey, Dean Stockwell; ***D:*** Dusty Nelson; ***M:*** Jeff Marsh.

Inferno in Paradise **1988** Mucho macho firefighter and bimbous gal pal photographer get hot while trailing a murderous pyromaniac. More like purgatory in the living room (that is, unless you thought Forsyth's earlier "Chesty Anderson, US Navy" was divine comedy). **115m/C VHS.** Richard Young, Betty Ann Carr, Jim Davis, Andy Jarrell, Dennis Chun; ***D:*** Ed Forsyth.

Infestation ½ **2009 (R)** Funny and fast-paced horror comedy that finds slacker Cooper waking up cocooned in webbing as the next meal for huge, mutant flesh-eating bugs. Freeing himself, Cooper also unwraps those around him and the would-be meals decide to fight back by going after the queen of the bugs and saving the world! **93m/C DVD.** Christopher Marquette, Brooke Nevin, Ray Wise, Wesley Thompson, Deborah Geffner, Kinsey Packard, E. Quincy Sloan; ***D:*** Kyle Rankin; ***C:*** Thomas Ackerman; ***M:*** Steve Gutheinz. **VIDEO**

Infested: Invasion of the Killer Bugs **2002 (R)** It's a boomer reunion with bugs! Yuppie friends gather for a funeral and have their reminiscing disturbed by mutant flies that transform their victims into zombies. This one is meant to be cheesy. **84m/C VHS, DVD.** Zach Galligan, Amy Jo Johnson, Robert Duncan McNeill, Mark Margolis, Lisa Ann Hadley, Daniel H. Jenkins; ***D:*** Josh Olson; ***W:*** Josh Olson; ***C:*** M. David Mullen; ***M:*** Rodney Whittenberg. **VIDEO**

The Infiltrator ½ **1995 (R)** Based on the true story of Yaron Svoray (Platt), an Israeli journalist and the son of Holocaust survivors, whose latest assignment is to go to Berlin and investigate the rising Neo-Nazi movement. Eventually, Svoray manages to meet leaders of the Nationalist Front and then finds himself enmeshed in a worldwide political network. Based on the book "In Hitler's Shadow" by Yaron Svoray and Nick Taylor. **102m/C VHS.** Oliver Platt, Arliss Howard, Peter Riegert, Alan King, Tony Haygarth, Michael Byrne, Julian Glover, Alex Kingston; ***D:*** John MacKenzie; ***W:*** Guy Andrews; ***M:*** Hal Lindes. **CABLE**

Infinity ½ **1996 (PG)** Based on memoirs covering the early years of Nobel Prize-winning physicist Richard Feynman (Broderick) and his romance with aspiring artist Arline Greenbaum (Arquette). They marry despite the fact that Arline is diagnosed with tuberculosis, at this time in the '30s a contagious and incurable disease. Richard's recruited to work on the Manhattan Project at Los Alamos, New Mexico, and the narrative travels between his scientific endeavors and Arline's worsening illness in an Albuquerque hospital. Problem is it's neither a character study or a love story but a weak combo. Directing debut of Broderick; screenplay is written by his mother. **119m/C VHS, DVD.** Matthew Broderick, Patricia Arquette, James LeGros, Peter Riegert, Dori Brenner, Peter Michael Goetz, Zeljko Ivanek; ***D:*** Matthew Broderick; ***W:*** Patricia Broderick; ***C:*** Toyomichi Kurita; ***M:*** Bruce Broughton.

The Informant **1997 (R)** In 1983, ex-IRA soldier Gingy McAnally (Brophy) has been tracked down by his cohorts and blackmailed (with threats to his family) into assassinating a Belfast judge. Recognized by British army officer Ferris (Elwes), Gingy is quickly arrested and interrogated by ruthless inspector Rennie (Dalton), who puts the pressure on Gingy to give up his comrades in exchange for immunity. Moved to a safe house, hapless Gingy has to live with being an informant and stay alive long enough to testify. Based on the novel "Field of Blood" by Gerald Seymour. **106m/C VHS.** *IR* Anthony Brophy, Timothy Dalton, Cary Elwes, Sean McGinley, Maria Lennon, John Kavanagh, Frankie McCafferty, Stuart Graham; ***D:*** Jim McBride; ***W:*** Nicholas Meyer; ***C:*** Alfonso Beato.

The Informant! **2009 (R)** Damon gained 30 pounds and a goofy mustache in this seriously nutzoid tale that's based on a true story. In 1992, Mark Whitacre (Damon) turns whistleblower when he exposes multinational agri-giant Archer Daniels Midland's price-fixing schemes to the FBI. Whitacre wears a wire and collects documents to make their case, but the feds discover Whitacre's hands aren't exactly clean. Then the pressure from doing undercover work causes Whitacre to crack (although he doesn't seem very stable to begin). Adapted from the nonfiction book by Kurt Eichenwald. **108m/C DVD.** *US* Matt Damon, Scott Bakula, Melanie Lynskey, Patton Oswalt, Joel McHale; ***D:*** Steven Soderbergh; ***W:*** Scott Burns; ***M:*** Marvin Hamlisch.

The Informer ½ **1929** Hanson wants to flee Ireland's poverty for America, using the reward money he gets for turning in an IRA comrade. But things don't turn out as planned and instead he's haunted by the guilt of his betrayal. Based on the novel by Liam O'Flaherty and filmed to much greater effect by John Ford in 1935. **83m/B VHS.** *GB* Lars Hanson, Lya de Putti, Warwick Ward, Dennis Wynham; ***D:*** Arthur Robison; ***W:*** Benn W. Levy, Rolfe E. Vanlo.

The Informer **1935** Based on Liam O'Flaherty's novel about the Irish Sinn Fein Rebellion of 1922, it tells the story of a hard-drinking Dublin man (McLaglen) who informs on a friend (a member of the Irish Republican Army) in order to collect a 20-pound reward. When his "friend" is killed during capture, he goes on a drinking spree instead of using the money, as planned, for passage to America. Director Ford allowed McLaglen to improvise his lines during the trial scene in order to enhance the realism, leading to excruciating suspense. Wonderful score. **91m/B VHS, DVD.** Victor McLaglen, Heather Angel, Wallace Ford, Margot Grahame, Joseph (Joe) Sawyer, Preston Foster, Una O'Connor, J.M. Kerrigan, Donald Meek; ***D:*** John Ford; ***W:*** Dudley Nichols; ***M:*** Max Steiner. Oscars '35: Actor (McLaglen), Director (Ford), Screenplay, Score; N.Y. Film Critics '35: Director (Ford), Film.

The Informers **2009 (R)** Hedonism in 1980s L.A. courtesy of a Bret Easton Ellis novel and screenplay. Movie honcho William (Thornton) is having an affair with newscaster Cheryl (Ryder) as wife Laura (Basinger) pops pills. Their son Graham (Foster) deals drugs and parties with his pretty friends. Working-class Jack (Renfro in his last role) gets disastrously involved in a kidnapping scheme orchestrated by his perverted surrogate father Peter (Rourke) and the shallowness just keeps getting more apparent. Disturbing, generally unlikeable characters and situations (especially those involving Rourke) make this a waste. **100m/C DVD.** *US* Billy Bob Thornton, Kim Basinger, Mickey Rourke, Winona Ryder, Jon Foster, Amber Heard, Austin Nichols, Lou Taylor Pucci, Chris Isaak, Rhys Ifans, Bryan Metro; ***D:*** Gregor Jordan; ***W:*** Bret Easton Ellis, Nicholas Jarecki; ***C:*** Petra Korner; ***M:*** Christopher Young.

Infra-Man WOOF! *The Super Inframan; The Infra Superman* **1976 (PG)** If you're looking for a truly bad, hokey flick, this could be it. Infra-man is a superhero who must rescue the galaxy from the clutches of the evil Princess Dragon Mom and her army of prehistoric monsters. Outlandish dialogue (delivered straight) combines with horrible special effects and costumes to create what may well be one of the best camp classics to date. Poorly dubbed in English. **92m/C VHS, DVD.** *HK* Li Hsiu-hsien, Wang Hsieh, Yuan Man-tzu, Terry Liu, Tsen Shu-yi, Huang Chien-lung, Lu Sheng; ***D:*** Shan Hua; ***W:*** Kuang Ni.

The Inglorious Bastards *Quel Maldetto Treno Blindato* **1978** Resembles "The Dirty Dozen" only with less prisoners (and a lesser cast). In 1944, five American soldiers facing time in a military prison escape custody to head for the Swiss border. Having accidentally foiled an Allied plan for stopping a German train carrying an advanced rocket, the quintet must step in and complete the mission, which means a lot of fighting and blowing things up. An in-name-only remake by Quentin Tarantino (with a deliberately misspelled title) was done in 2009. **89m/C DVD.** *IT* Bo Svenson, Fred Williamson, Peter Hooten, Michael Pergolani, Jackie Basehart, Raimund Harmstorf, Ian Bannen; ***D:*** Enzo G. Castellari; ***W:*** Sandro Continenza, Sergio Grieco, Laura Toscano; ***C:*** Giovanni Bergamini; ***M:*** Francesco De Masi.

Inglourious Basterds **2009 (R)** Tarantino's sorta remake of the 1978 Italian-produced action pic set in WWII. American Lt. Aldo Raine (Pitt) puts together a squad of Jewish soldiers to attack the Nazis in brutal guerrilla raids. Meanwhile, teenager Shosanna (Laurent) has witnessed her family's extermination by the Nazis and vows revenge. All are pursued by an icily charming SS officer (Waltz, in a brilliant performance). Ten years in the making, the screenplay shows off Tarantino's legendary ear for dialogue, and he does a fantastic job of building tension and atmosphere. Pacing is a bit of a problem, and those who are looking for non-stop action will be disappointed. The violence, when it does show up, is swift and graphic. All of Tarantino's strengths and weaknesses are on full display, giving plenty of ammo to both his admirers and detractors. **153m/C DVD.** *US* Brad Pitt, Diane Kruger, Melanie Laurent, Christoph Waltz, Samm Levine, B.J. Novak, Eli Roth, Daniel Bruhl, Til Schweiger, Mike Myers, Cloris Leachman, Michael Fassbender, Maggie Cheung, Rod Taylor, Gedeon Burkhard, Omar Doom, August Diehl, Julie Dreyfus, Martin Wuttke, Michael Bacall, Bo Svenson, Jacky Ido, Denis Menochet, Sylvester Groth, Anne-Sophie Franck; ***D:*** Quentin Tarantino; ***W:*** Quentin Tarantino; ***C:*** Robert Richardson; ***Nar:*** Samuel L. Jackson. Oscars '09: Support. Actor (Waltz); British Acad. '09: Support. Actor (Waltz); Golden Globes '10: Support. Actor (Waltz); Screen Actors Guild '09: Support. Actor (Waltz), Cast.

Inherit the Wind **1960** Powerful courtroom drama, based on the Broadway play, is actually a fictionalized version of the infamous Scopes "Monkey Trial" of 1925. Tracy is the defense attorney for the schoolteacher on trial for teaching Darwin's Theory of Evolution to a group of students in a small town ruled by religion. March is the prosecutor seeking to put the teacher behind bars and restore religion to the schools. **128m/B VHS, DVD.** Spencer Tracy, Fredric March, Florence Eldridge, Gene Kelly, Dick York, Donna Anderson, Harry (Henry) Morgan, Elliott Reid, Philip Coolidge, Claude Akins, Noah Beery Jr., Norman Fell; ***D:*** Stanley Kramer; ***W:*** Nedrick Young, Harold Jacob Smith; ***C:*** Ernest Laszlo; ***M:*** Ernest Gold. Berlin Intl. Film Fest. '60: Actor (March).

Inherit the Wind ½ **1999 (PG)** Adaptation of the 1955 play by Jerome Lawrence and Robert E. Lee, previously filmed in 1960 and based on the 1925 Scopes Monkey Trial. Tennessee science teacher Bertram Cates (Tom Everett Scott) is being prosecuted for teaching evolution. Agnostic attorney Henry Drummond (Lemmon) comes to town to defend Cates against respected, conservative prosecutor Matthew Harrison Brady (George C. Scott) who wants to keep religious teachings in the school. **113m/C VHS.** Jack Lemmon, George C. Scott, Tom Everett Scott, Piper Laurie, Beau Bridges, John Cullum, Kathryn Morris, Lane Smith, Brad Greenquist, David Wells, Royce D. Applegate, Dirk Blocker, Russ Tamblyn, Steve Monroe; ***D:*** Daniel Petrie; ***W:*** Nedrick Young, Harold Jacob Smith; ***C:*** James Bartle; ***M:*** Laurence Rosenthal. **CABLE**

Inheritance *Uncle Silas* **1947** Victorian-era melodrama of a young heiress endangered by her guradian, who plots to murder his charge for her inheritance. Chilling and moody story based on a novel by Sheridan Le Fanu. **103m/B VHS.** *GB* Jean Simmons, Katina Paxinou, Derrick DeMarney, Derek Bond; ***D:*** Charles Frank.

The Inheritance ½ *L'Eredita Ferramonti* **1976 (R)** Wealthy partiarch becomes sexually involved with scheming daughter-in-law. Tawdry tale is nonetheless engaging. **121m/C VHS, DVD.** *IT* Anthony Quinn, Fabio Testi, Dominique Sanda; ***D:*** Mauro Bolognini; ***W:*** Sergio Bazzini; ***C:*** Ennio Guarnieri; ***M:*** Ennio Morricone. Cannes '76: Actress (Sanda).

The Inheritance *Arven* **1976** Christoffer (Thomsen) is bullied by his manipulative mother Annelise (Norby) to take over the family's near-bankrupt steel company in Copenhagen after his father commits suicide. Doing this means making hard decisions, both personally and professionally, that torment Christoffer and cause serious problems within his family. Danish and Swedish with subtitles. **115m/C DVD.** *CZ* Ulrich Thomsen, Ghita Norby, Lisa Welinder, Lars Brygmann, Karina Skands; ***D:*** Per Fly; ***W:*** Per Fly, Kim Leona; ***C:*** Harald Gunnar Paalgard.

The Inheritor **1990 (R)** Set in a small New England town, this mystery centers on the death of a young woman and her sister's attempts to uncover the murderer. The local celebrity, a writer, seems to be at the heart of the mystery and the sister finds herself growing interested. Keeps you guessing. **83m/C VHS.** Dan Haggerty; ***D:*** Brian Savegar.

The Inheritors ½ **1982** Not-too-subtle tale of a young German boy who becomes involved with a Nazi youth group as his home life deteriorates. Heavy-going anti-fascism creates more message than entertainment. In German with English subtitles or dubbed. **89m/C VHS, DVD.** *GE* Nikolas Vogel, Roger Schauer, Klaus Novak, Johanna Tomek; ***D:*** Walter Bannert; ***W:*** Walter Bannert.

The Inheritors *Die Siebtelbauern* **1998 (R)** Seven peasants in 1930s rural Austria unexpectedly inherit the farm they've been working from its misanthropic owner, who was murdered by an elderly peasant woman. The foreman (Pruckner) tries to bully the others to sell the farm to the neighboring gentry, Danniger (Wildgruber). When they refuse, the twosome try to sabotage the property, which leads to the foreman's death and places the peasants in the murderous path of the intolerant locals. German with subtitles. **94m/C VHS, DVD.** *GE* Tito Pruckner, Ulrich Wildgruber, Simon Schwarz, Sophie Rois, Lars Rudolph, Julia Gschnitzer; ***D:*** Stefan Ruzowitzky; ***W:*** Stefan Ruzowitzky; ***C:*** Peter von Haller.

Inhibition **1976** A beautiful heiress has lots of sex with different people in exotic locales. Softcore soap. **90m/C VHS.** *IT* Claudine Beccaire, Ilona Staller; ***D:*** Paolo Poeti; ***W:*** Adriano Belli; ***C:*** Giancarlo Ferrando; ***M:*** Guido de Angelis, Maurizio de Angelis.

Inhumanity **2000** Serial killer thriller is indescribably inept. Though the lead performances are mostly all right, supporting work is amateur. The film is padded with shots of traffic and buildings in Dallas. Lighting, writing, and directing are substandard. **90m/C DVD.** Todd Bridges, Faizon Love, Carl Jackson, Georgia Foy, Billy Davis; ***D:*** Carl Jackson; ***W:*** Carl Jackson; ***C:*** Kurt Ugland; ***M:*** Damon Criswell.

Inhumanoid WOOF! *Roger Corman Presents: Inhumanoid; Circuit Breaker* **1996 (R)** Violent sci-fier focusing on an android's unexpected obsession with his creator's wife. The lady doesn't share the passion (and the scientist isn't too happy either). Made for cable. **86m/C VHS.** Richard Grieco, Corbin Bernsen, Lara Harris, Edie McClurg, Robin Gammell; ***D:*** Victoria Muspratt; ***W:*** Victoria Muspratt; ***C:*** John Aronson; ***M:*** Marco Beltrami. **CABLE**

The Initiation **1984 (R)** Trying to rid herself of a troublesome nightmare, a coed finds herself face-to-face with a psycho. Gory campus slaughterfest. **97m/C VHS, DVD.** Vera Miles, Clu Gulager, James Read, Daphne Zuniga; ***D:*** Larry Stewart.

Initiation of Sarah **1978** College freshman joins a sorority, undergoes abusive initiation, and gains a supernatural revenge.

"Carrie" rip-off. **100m/C VHS.** Kay Lenz, Shelley Winters, Kathryn Crosby, Morgan Brittany, Tony Bill, Tisa Farrow, Robert Hays, Morgan Fairchild; ***D:*** Robert Day. **TV**

The Initiation of Sarah ½ **2006** Dull ABC Family remake of the 1978 TV frightener. Fraternal twin sisters, nonconformist Sarah (Boorem) and insecure Lindsey (Glau), are freshmen at Temple Hill University. Their domineering mother Trina (Fairchild) is determined that they pledge her old sorority Alpha Nu Gamma, who happen to be a coven of witches. They need a virgin blood sacrifice to keep their mojo working and Sarah seems to be the chosen one. However, Sarah prefers Pi Epsilon Delta (also witches, only good ones) and making out with boyfriend Finn (Ziff), so that whole virgin thing may be moot. **90m/C DVD.** Mika Boorem, Summer Glau, Morgan Fairchild, Joanna Garcia, Jennifer Tilly, Tessa Thompson, Ben Ziff; ***D:*** Stuart Gillard; ***W:*** Daniel Berendsen; ***C:*** Manfred Guthe; ***M:*** John Van Tongeren.

Inkheart **2009 (PG)** As a "silvertongue," Mo (Fraser) has the power to bring book characters to life simply by reading aloud. He travels the world with teenaged daughter, Meggie (Bennett), as a professional book buyer in search of an exceptionally rare medieval tale that wreaked havoc on their lives. Years earlier, while reading that book Mo unleashed the nefarious characters Dustfinger (Bettany) and Capricorn (Serkis) while accidentally banishing his wife into the book, because when a silvertongue draws a character out someone must be sent in. As he tries to bring her back and return Dustfinger and Capricorn to their dusty pages, Capricorn employs all manner of magical powers to interfere and conquer the world. Based on the novel by Cornelia Funke, the special effects are thrilling but the complicated story struggles on the big screen. **105m/C DVD.** *US* Brendan Fraser, Eliza Bennett, Paul Bettany, Andy Serkis, Helen Mirren, Sienna Guillory, Rafi Gavron, Jim Broadbent; ***D:*** Iain Softley; ***W:*** David Lindsay-Abaire; ***C:*** Roger Pratt; ***M:*** Javier Navarrete.

The Inkwell ½ **1994 (R)** Quiet teenager Drew Tate finds first love when his family spends their vacation with relatives on Martha's Vineyard. Drew is drawn into the party atmosphere of the Inkwell, the area where affluent black professionals have summered for decades. Meanwhile, political differences between Drew's former Black Panther father and his conservative uncle threaten family harmony. Everything about the film has a sugary aura, with conflicts handled tastefully. Rich directs broadly, leading to some overacting. Film is set in 1976. **112m/C VHS, DVD.** Larenz Tate, Joe Morton, Phyllis Stickney, Jada Pinkett Smith; ***D:*** Matty Rich; ***W:*** Paris Qualles, Trey Ellis; ***C:*** John L. (Ndiaga) Demps Jr.; ***M:*** Terence Blanchard.

Inland Empire **2006 (R)** Lynch has taken his film experiments to a whole new level of weirdness with this digital-video effort. Nikki (Dern) is a married actress who is warned by her sinister new neighbor (Zabriskie), who may be a Polish Gypsy, that she shouldn't take the part in a new film because bad things will happen, but she doesn't listen. Nikki and married co-star Devon (Theroux) are playing characters (Sue and Billy) that have an affair, which leaks over into their real lives. And then they find out that their film is a remake of a Polish movie where the two leads were murdered. Giant talking rabbits and Polish hookers are also involved and there's something about an alternate reality—or maybe Lynch'. **172m/C DVD.** *US PL FR* Laura Dern, Justin Theroux, Jeremy Irons, Harry Dean Stanton, Grace Zabriskie, Peter J. Lucas, Diane Ladd, Julia Ormond, Ian Abercrombie, Laura Elena Harring; ***D:*** David Lynch; ***W:*** David Lynch; ***C:*** Odd Geir Saether; ***V:*** Scott Coffey, Naomi Watts.

Inn of Temptation *Hot Sex in Bangkok* **1973** A bunch of bowling buddies take off for Bangkok on an impulsive weekend, and meet lots of Oriental women. **72m/C VHS.** Michael Jacot, Claude Martin; ***D:*** Erwin C. Dietrich; ***W:*** Erwin C. Dietrich; ***C:*** Peter Baumgartner; ***M:*** Walter Baumgartner.

Inn of the Damned ½ **1974** Detective looks into an inn where no one ever gets charged for an extra day; they simply die. Anderson is watchable. **92m/C VHS, DVD.** *AU* Alex Cord, Judith Anderson, Tony Bonner, Michael Craig, John Meillon; ***D:*** Terry Burke.

The Inn of the Sixth Happiness **1958** Inspiring story of Gladys Aylward, an English missionary in 1930s' China, who leads a group of children through war-torn countryside. Donat's last film. **158m/C VHS, DVD.** Ingrid Bergman, Robert Donat, Curt Jurgens; ***D:*** Mark Robson; ***C:*** Frederick A. (Freddie) Young; ***M:*** Malcolm Arnold. Natl. Bd. of Review '58: Actress (Bergman).

Inn on the River ½ **1962** Scotland Yard investigates a series of murders taking place on the waterfront by the "Shark's" gang. Remake of "The Return of the Frog." **95m/C VHS.** *GE* Klaus Kinski, Joachim Fuchsberger, Brigitte Grothum, Richard Much; ***D:*** Alfred Vohrer.

The Inner Circle ½ **1946** A private detective, framed for murder by his secretary, has a limited amount of time to find the real murderer. Confusing. **57m/B VHS, DVD.** Adele Mara, Warren Douglas, William Frawley, Ricardo Cortez, Virginia Christine; ***D:*** Philip Ford.

The Inner Circle **1991 (PG-13)** Ivan Sanshin is a meek, married man working as a movie projectionist for the KGB in 1935 Russia. Sanshin is taken by the KGB to the Kremlin to show movies, primarily Hollywood features, to leader Joseph Stalin, a job he cannot discuss with anyone, even his wife. Under the spell of Stalin's personality, Sanshin sees only what he's told and overlooks the oppression and persecution of the times. Based on the life of the projectionist who served from 1935 until Stalin's death in 1953. Filmed on location at the Kremlin. **122m/C VHS.** Tom Hulce, Lolita (David) Davidovich, Bob Hoskins, Alexandre Zbruev, Maria Baranova, Feodor Chaliapin Jr., Bess Meyer; ***D:*** Andrei Konchalovsky; ***W:*** Andrei Konchalovsky, Anatoli Usov; ***M:*** Eduard Artemyev.

Inner Sanctum **1948** Adequate tale of a young girl accosted by a gypsy who claims that tragedy awaits her. Based on a radio show of the same name. **62m/B VHS, DVD.** Chuck Russell, Mary Beth Hughes, Lee Patrick, Nana Bryant; ***D:*** Lew Landers.

Inner Sanctum WOOF! **1991 (R)** Cheating husband hires sensuous nurse to tend invalid wife. You can guess the rest; in fact, you have to because the plot ultimately makes no sense. Available in R-rated and sex-drenched unrated editions. **87m/C VHS, DVD.** Tanya Roberts, Margaux Hemingway, Joseph Bottoms, Valerie Wildman, William Butler, Brett (Baxter) Clark; ***D:*** Fred Olen Ray.

Inner Sanctum 2 ½ **1994 (R)** Jennifer Reed (Swope) had a breakdown and killed her husband in the first film. Now under a doctor's (Warner) care, Jennifer is under siege from her brother-in-law's (Nouri) evil plot to send her over the edge again and claim her fortune. As if that's not enough, Jennifer's also being stalked by a murderer. Also available in an unrated version. **90m/C VHS.** Michael Nouri, Tracy Brooks Swope, Sandahl Bergman, David Warner, Jennifer Ciesar, Margaux Hemingway; ***D:*** Fred Olen Ray; ***W:*** Sherman Scott; ***M:*** Chuck Cirino.

Innerspace ½ **1987 (PG)** A space pilot, miniaturized for a journey through a lab rat a la "Fantastic Voyage," is accidentally injected into a nebbish supermarket clerk, and together they nab some bad guys and get the girl. Award-winning special effects support some funny moments between micro Quaid and nerdy Short, with Ryan producing the confused romantic interest. **120m/C VHS, DVD.** Dennis Quaid, Martin Short, Meg Ryan, Kevin McCarthy, Fiona Lewis, Henry Gibson, Robert Picardo, John Hora, Wendy Schaal, Orson Bean, Chuck Jones, William Schallert, Dick Miller, Vernon Wells, Harold Sylvester, Kevin Hooks, Kathleen Freeman, Kenneth Tobey; ***D:*** Joe Dante; ***W:*** Jeffrey Boam, Chip Proser; ***M:*** Jerry Goldsmith. Oscars '87: Visual FX.

Innocence ½ **2000 (R)** Sweet tale of lasting love has postwar teenaged Belgian lovers meeting again 45 years later in Australia. Andreas is an affable widower who finds out his long-lost love, Claire, is living in his town and looks her up. Claire is still married, but soon the old feelings are rekindled between the two and they begin an affair. Film deals honestly and beautifully with the endurance of true love, and how the routines and expectations of everyday life are affected by it. The role of Andreas was originally written for Kaye, but illness forced him to take a smaller, supporting role. **96m/C VHS, DVD.** *AU AU* Julia Blake, Charles "Bud" Tingwell, Terry Norris, Robert Menzies, Chris Haywood, Norman Kaye, Joey Kennedy, Marta Dusseldorp, Kristien Van Pellicom, Kenny Aernouts; ***D:*** Paul Cox; ***W:*** Paul Cox; ***C:*** Tony Clark; ***M:*** Paul Grabowsky.

Innocence Unprotected ½ **1968** A film collage that contains footage from the 1942 film "Innocence Unprotected," the story of an acrobat trying to save an orphan from her wicked stepmother, newsreels from Nazi-occupied Yugoslavia, and interviews from 1968 with people who were in the film. Confiscated by the Nazis during final production, "Innocence Unprotected" was discovered by director Makavejev, who worked it into the collage. Filmed in color and black and white; in Serbian with English subtitles. **78m/C VHS.** *YU* Dragoljub Aleksic, Ana Milosavljevic, Vera Jovanovic; ***D:*** Dusan Makavejev; ***W:*** Dusan Makavejev.

The Innocent *L'Innocente* **1976** Visconti's final film is a stately costume drama adapted from Gabriele D'Annunzio's 1892 novel. Aristocrat Tullio (Giannini) is openly carrying on an affair with manipulative Teresa (O'Neill) and expects his wife Guilliana (Antonelli) not only to understand but to help him when he returns to her. However, he's not so understanding when he discovers Guilliana had her own lover and is now pregnant. Italian with subtitles. **112m/C DVD.** *IT* Giancarlo Giannini, Laura Antonelli, Jennifer O'Neill, Massimo Girotti, Marc Porel, Rina Morelli; ***D:*** Luchino Visconti; ***W:*** Suso Cecchi D'Amico, Enrico Medioli; ***C:*** Pasqualino De Santis; ***M:*** Franco Mannino.

The Innocent ½ **1993 (R)** Cold War thriller has naive British engineer Leonard Markham (Scott) sent to Berlin in 1955 by Brits who are warily cooperating with the U.S. forces. He's turned over to CIA operator Bob Glass (Hopkins) and asked to intercept communications between East Germany and the Soviet Union. Glass continually warns Markham not to trust anyone, including Maria (Rossellini), the married German woman with whom he begins an affair. Failure to build necessary suspense and performances leads to disappointing one-note display. Based on the novel by McEwan. **97m/C VHS, DVD.** *GE GB* Anthony Hopkins, Campbell Scott, Isabella Rossellini, Hart Bochner, James Grant, Jeremy Sinden, Ronald Nitschke; ***D:*** John Schlesinger; ***W:*** Ian McEwan; ***M:*** Gerald Gouriet.

Innocent Blood **1992 (R)** A mediocre modern-day vampire/gangster combo with the beautiful (though red-eyed) Parillaud as the woman with a taste for someone "Italian." Unfortunately, she doesn't finish off her latest meal—mobster Loggia—who finds being undead very useful to his vicious work. LaPaglia plays the bewildered, love-struck cop involved with the vamp. Parillaud appears nude in several scenes and the gore and violence are stomach-turning. **112m/C VHS, DVD.** Anne Parillaud, Anthony LaPaglia, Robert Loggia, David Proval, Don Rickles, Rocco Sisto, Kim Coates, Chazz Palminteri, Angela Bassett, Tom Savini, Frank Oz, Forrest J Ackerman, Sam Raimi, Dario Argento, Linnea Quigley; ***D:*** John Landis; ***W:*** Michael Wolk; ***C:*** Mac Ahlberg; ***M:*** Ira Newborn.

Innocent Lies ½ **1995 (R)** In 1938, British policeman Alan Cross (Dunbar) heads for an island off the French coast to look into the suicide of a colleague who was investigating the expatriate Graves family. There are family tensions, skeletons in the closet, and some Nazi-sympathizers all mixed together in an old-fashioned but satisfying stew. **88m/C VHS, DVD.** *FR GB* Adrian Dunbar, Stephen Dorff, Gabrielle Anwar, Joanna Lumley; ***D:*** Patrick Dewolf; ***W:*** Kerry Crabbe, Patrick Dewolf; ***C:*** Patrick Blossier; ***M:*** Alexandre Desplat.

An Innocent Man ½ **1989 (R)** Uneven story of Selleck, an ordinary family man and airline mechanic, framed as a drug dealer and sent to prison. **113m/C VHS, DVD.** Tom Selleck, F. Murray Abraham, Laila Robins, David Rasche, Richard Young, Badja (Medu) Djola; ***D:*** Peter Yates; ***W:*** Larry Brothers; ***M:*** Howard Shore.

Innocent Prey **1988 (R)** When a woman finally summons the courage to bid hasta la vista to her abusive husband, it turns out he's not so quick to say ciao. Definitely not a highlight in Balsam's career. **88m/C VHS.** *AU* P.J. Soles, Martin Balsam, Kit Taylor, Grigor Taylor, John Warnock, Susan Stenmark, Richard Morgan; ***D:*** Colin Eggleston.

The Innocent Sleep ½ **1995 (R)** Adequate thriller that stays true to genre cliches. Homeless drunk Alan Terry (Graves) witnesses an execution (by hanging) from London's Tower Bridge, near where he's bedded down. He's spotted but manages to escape. When he tries to report the crime, Terry realizes that one of the killers is police investigator Matheson (Gambon). Terry then goes to tabloid journalist Billie Hayman (Sciorra) for help but her probing into the death leads to even more danger. **96m/C VHS, DVD.** *GB* Rupert Graves, Annabella Sciorra, Michael Gambon, Franco Nero, Graham Crowden, John Hannah; ***D:*** Scott Michell; ***W:*** Ray Villis; ***C:*** Alan Dunlop; ***M:*** Mark Ayres.

Innocent Sorcerers *Niewinni Czarodzieje* **1960** Ironic comedy about aimless '60s Polish youth that finds a young doctor having trouble committing himself to his superficial girlfriend and coping with the problems of his cynical friends. Polish with subtitles. **86m/B VHS, DVD.** *PL* Tadeusz Lomnicki, Zbigniew Cybulski, Roman Polanski, Krystyna Stypulkowska, Jerzy Skolimowski; ***D:*** Andrzej Wajda; ***W:*** Jerzy Skolimowski, Andrzej Wajda; ***M:*** Krzysztof Komeda.

Innocent Victim *The Tree of Hands* **1990 (R)** Convoluted tale of revenge and madness. Bacall plays a mad grandmother who kidnaps a boy to take the place of her dead grandson. The kidnapped boy's stepfather then is accused of murdering him, and starts murdering others to get the boy back. **100m/C VHS.** Lauren Bacall, Helen Shaver, Paul McGann, Peter Firth; ***D:*** Giles Foster.

Innocent Voices *Voces inocentes* **2004 (R)** In the 1980's, Chava (Padilla) is the 11-year-old man of the family, trying to help his mother Kella (Varela) and his siblings survive during El Salvador's protracted civil war. Things are going to get worse since 12 is the legal age for conscription into the right-wing government's army. The horrifying and bewildering events are seen through Chava's eyes and are based on the experiences of co-writer Torres. Spanish with subtitles. **120m/C DVD.** Leonor Varela, Jose Maria Yazpik, Ofelia Medina, Daniel Gimenez Cacho, Jesus Ochoa, Carlos Padilla, Gustavo Munoz; ***D:*** Luis Mandoki; ***W:*** Oscar Torres; ***C:*** Juan Ruiz-Anchia; ***M:*** Andre Abujarrura.

The Innocents ½ **1961** Incredibly creepy version of Henry James' "The Turn of the Screw." Minister's daughter, Miss Giddens (Kerr), is hired by Redgrave (known only as "The Uncle") as governess to young Flora (Franklin) and her brother Miles (Stephens) at his country estate. Miss Giddens begins to see the specters of a man and a woman and is told her descriptions match that of former estate manager Peter Quint and the last governess, his mistress, whose influence on the children was thought to be malevolent. Indeed, Miss Giddens believes the children are possessed by evil—but is it true or a product of her own hysteria? **85m/B VHS, DVD.** *GB* Deborah Kerr, Michael Redgrave, Pamela Franklin, Martin Stephens, Peter Wyngarde, Megs Jenkins, Clytie Jessop, Isla Cameron, Eric Woodburn; ***D:*** Jack Clayton; ***W:*** Truman Capote, William Archibald, John Mortimer; ***C:*** Freddie Francis; ***M:*** Georges Auric.

Innocents ½ *Dark Summer* **2000** Boring thriller about French cellist Gerard (Anglade) who gets involved with beautiful Megan (Nielsen) and her disturbed younger sister, Dominique (Kirshner). After the sisters' father (Langella) dies, the trio head to Seattle to tell mom (Archer) she's now a widow. The road trip takes a turn for the worst when a judge (Culp) gets killed and Gerard gets blamed. Never does make much sense. **90m/C VHS, DVD.** *CA* Jean-Hugues Anglade, Connie Nielsen, Mia Kirshner, Robert Culp, Anne Archer, Keith David, Joseph Culp; ***Cameos:*** Frank Langella; ***D:*** Gregory Marquette; ***W:*** Gregory Marquette; ***C:*** Bruce Worrall; ***M:*** Michel Colombier.

The Innocents Abroad 🦴🦴 1/2 **1984** Entertaining adaptation of Mark Twain's novel about a group of naive Americans cruising the Mediterranean. Ensemble cast offers some surprising performances. Originally produced for PBS. **116m/C VHS.** Craig Wasson, Brooke Adams, David Ogden Stiers; ***D:*** Luciano Salce; ***W:*** Alfredo Silveri; ***C:*** Erico Menczer; ***M:*** William Perry.

Innocents in Paris 🦴🦴 1/2 **1953** A group of seven Britons visit Paris for the first time. A bit long but enough ooo-la-la to satisfy. **89m/B VHS.** *GB* Alastair Sim, Laurence Harvey, Jimmy Edwards, Claire Bloom, Margaret Rutherford; ***D:*** Gordon Parry.

Innocents with Dirty Hands 🦴🦴 *Les Innocents aux Mains Sales; Dirty Hands* **1976** A woman and her lover conspire to murder her husband. A must for fans of the sexy Schneider. Cinematography provides moments that are both interesting and eerie. **102m/C VHS, DVD.** *FR* Rod Steiger, Romy Schneider, Paul(o) Giusti, Jean Rochefort, Hans-Christian Blech; ***D:*** Claude Chabrol.

The Inquiry 🦴🦴 1/2 **1987** A new twist on the resurrection of Christ. Carradine senses a cover-up when he's sent from Rome to investigate the problem of Christ's missing corpse. He retraces Christ's final days to solve the case in this interesting, offbeat film. Dubbed. **107m/C VHS.** *IT* Keith Carradine, Harvey Keitel, Phyllis Logan, Angelo Infanti, Lina Sastri; ***D:*** Damiano Damiani.

Inquisition 🦴 1/2 **1976** Naschy is a 16th century witch hunting judge who finds himself accused of witchcraft. **85m/C VHS.** *SP* Paul Naschy, Daniela Giordano, Juan Gallardo, Monica Randall; ***D:*** Paul Naschy; ***W:*** Paul Naschy.

Insanitarium 🦴🦴 **2008 (R)** Ooh, blood, gore and flesh-eating psychos! How much fun is that? Well, more than you might expect from Buhler's directorial debut, which doesn't take itself too seriously. Lily (Sanchez) is institutionalized after a suicide attempt and when her equally troubled brother Jack (Metcalfe) can't contact her, he decides to get himself committed as well. He discovers the real loon is doc-in-charge Gianetti (Stomare), who's been experimenting on his patients with a drug "therapy" that turns them into gleeful, blood-thirsty cannibals. **89m/C DVD.** Jesse Metcalfe, Lisa Arturo, Armin Shimerman, Carla Gallo, Kevin Sussman, Kiele Sanchez, Peter Stomare; ***D:*** Jeff Buhler; ***W:*** Jeff Buhler; ***C:*** Robert Hauer; ***M:*** Paul D'Amour. **VIDEO**

Insanity 🦴 *Striptease* **1976** A film director becomes violently obsessed with a beautiful actress. **101m/C VHS, DVD.** *SP* Terence Stamp, Fernando Rey, Corinne Clery; ***D:*** German Lorente; ***W:*** German Lorente; ***C:*** Antonio Ballesteros; ***M:*** Francis Lai.

The Insatiable 🦴🦴 **2006** Shy Harry (Flanery) witnesses a murder by beautiful vampire Tatiana (Ayanna). Since no one believes his story, Harry decides to track her down before she can strike again. But when he gets up close and personal, Harry can't kill Tatiana. Instead he puts her in a cage in his basement, trying to figure out what to do. But she'll die without fresh blood, so Harry has to find a way to keep her fed and satisfied. **103m/C DVD.** Sean Patrick Flanery, Charlotte Ayanna, Michael Biehn, Josh Hopkins, Boyd Kestner, Jon Huertas, Brad Rowe; ***D:*** Chuck Konzelman, Cary Solomon; ***W:*** Chuck Konzelman, Cary Solomon; ***C:*** Mike Washlesky; ***M:*** Christopher Tin. **VIDEO**

The Insect Woman 🦴🦴🦴 *The Insect; Nippon Konchuki* **1963** Chronicles 45 years in the life of a woman who must work with the diligence of an ant in order to survive. Thoughtfully reflects the exploitation of women and the cruelty of human nature in Japanese society. Beautiful performance from Hidari, who ages from girlhood to middle age. In Japanese with English subtitles. **123m/B VHS.** *JP* Sachiko Hidari, Jitsuko Yoshimura, Hiroyuki Nagaes, Sumie Sasaki; ***D:*** Shohei Imamura.

Insecticidal 🦴 **2005 (R)** Oy. A science experiment by sorority girl Cami in insect intelligence goes wrong and giant mutant insects attack the sorority house. Girls run around in their scanties being bugged by really bad CGI. **81m/C DVD.** Meghan Heffern, Rhonda Dent, Samantha McLeod, Vicky Huang; ***D:*** Jeffrey Scott Lando; ***W:*** Jeff O'Brien; ***C:*** Pieter Stathis; ***M:*** Chris Nickel. **VIDEO**

Inseminoid WOOF! *Horror Planet* **1980 (R)** Alien creature needs a chance to breed before moving on to spread its horror. When a group of explorers disturbs it, the years of waiting are over, and the unlucky mother-to-be will never be the same. Graphic and sensationalistic, capitalizing on the popularity of "Aliens." **93m/C VHS, DVD.** *GB* Robin Clarke, Jennifer Ashley, Stephanie Beacham, Judy Geeson, Stephen Grives, Victoria Tennant; ***D:*** Norman J. Warren; ***W:*** Gloria Maley, Nick Maley; ***C:*** John Metcalfe; ***M:*** John Scott.

Inserts 🦴 **1976 (R)** A formerly successful director has been reduced to making porno films in this pretentious, long-winded effort set in a crumbling Hollywood mansion in the 1930s. Affected, windbaggish performances kill it. **99m/C VHS, DVD.** *GB* Richard Dreyfuss, Jessica Harper, Veronica Cartwright, Bob Hoskins; ***D:*** John Byrum; ***W:*** John Byrum.

Inside 🦴🦴🦴 **1996 (R)** Harrowing anti-apartheid drama finds university professor and white Afrikaaner Peter Martin Strydom (Stoltz) being held in a Johannesburg government prison. He's being interrogated by Col. Kruger (Hawthorne), head of the prison security force, supposedly for conspiracy against the South African regime. Tortured, Strydom's will begins to break as the drama flashes forward ten years, with Colonel Kruger now subjected to interrogration by a nameless black questioner (Gossett Jr.) investigating human rights crimes, including Strydom's fate. **94m/C VHS, DVD.** Eric Stoltz, Nigel Hawthorne, Louis Gossett Jr.; ***D:*** Arthur Penn; ***W:*** Bima Stagg; ***C:*** Jan Weincke; ***M:*** Robert Levin. **CABLE**

Inside 🦴 1/2 **2006** Reclusive Alex (D'Agosto) likes to spy on people. He follows folks to observe their daily routines and becomes extremely interested in Alice (White) and Mark (Kilner) Smith because of the sadness they project. Alex goes too far and is caught in their home but the Smiths don't call the cops. Seems their only child—a son—has died and Alex looks like him. They start to bond (Alex's own parents are dead) and when he's in a car accident, the Smiths take him in to recover. Only the grieving Alice is now convinced that Alex IS her son returned from the grave and won't ever let him leave. Despite Meester's prominence on the box art, she only has a small role as a kleptomaniac, would-be friend of Alex's. **103m/C DVD.** Nicholas D'Agosto, Kevin Kilner, Leighton Meester, Cheryl White; ***D:*** mahler Jeff; ***W:*** mahler Jeff; ***C:*** Michael Marius Pessah; ***M:*** Jason Brandt. **VIDEO**

Inside Daisy Clover 🦴🦴 1/2 **1965** Wood is the self-sufficient, junior delinquent waif who becomes a teenage musical star and pays the price for fame in this Hollywood saga set in the 1930s. Discovered by tyrannical studio head Plummer, Daisy is given her big break and taken under his wing for grooming as Swan Studio's newest sensation. She falls for fellow performer, matinee idol Redford, who has some secrets of his own, and eventually has a breakdown from the career pressure. Glossy melodrama is filled with over-the-top performances but its sheer silliness makes it amusing. **128m/C VHS.** Natalie Wood, Christopher Plummer, Robert Redford, Ruth Gordon, Roddy McDowall, Katharine Bard; ***D:*** Robert Mulligan; ***W:*** Gavin Lambert; ***C:*** Charles B(ryant) Lang Jr.; ***M:*** Andre Previn. Golden Globes '66: Support. Actress (Gordon).

Inside Deep Throat 🦴🦴🦴 **2005 (NC-17)** Respectable documentary about the landmark porno blockbuster "Deep Throat." Mixes old and new interviews, newsreel footage, and, yes, full-on, full-frontal clips to tell the story of an enterprising hairdresser, Gerard Damiano, who dared to make a porno "film," not a porno "flick." He set out to build a story, create some characters, and inject some (admittedly pretty dumb) humor. He wasn't marketing to the old men in raincoats out for a quick peep, but aiming at couples looking to goose their relationship. It worked. Made for only $25,000, it went on to become the most profitable movie in history, grossing over $600 million. Since Universal produced the documentary, we're thankfully spared gratuitous reenactments. **90m/C** *US* ***D:*** Fenton Bailey, Randy Barbato; ***W:*** Fenton Bailey, Randy Barbato; ***C:*** Teodoro Maniaci, David Kempner; ***M:*** David Steinberg.

Inside Edge 🦴🦴 **1992 (R)** Urban crime thriller is a complex yet surprisingly uninteresting story of a police officer who falls for the girlfriend of the drug lord he is chasing. Filled with the standard genre violence. **84m/C VHS.** Michael Madsen, Richard Lynch, Rosie Vela, Tony Peck, Conrad Dunn, Branscombe Richmond; ***D:*** Warren Clark; ***W:*** William Tannen.

Inside Information 🦴 **1934** With Tarzan's (the Police Dog, not The Apeman) help, a cop searches out the leader of a ring of jewel thieves. **51m/B VHS.** Rex Lease, Marion Shilling, Philo (Philip, P.H., P.M.) McCullough, Henry Hall, Charles "Blackie" King, Jean Porter, Victor Potel, Henry Roquemore, Robert F. "Bob" Hill; ***D:*** Robert F. "Bob" Hill; ***W:*** Victor Potel, Betty Laidlaw, Robert Lively; ***C:*** George Meehan Jr.

The Inside Man 🦴🦴 1/2 **1984** Double agents struggle to find a submarine-detecting laser device. Based on true incidents in which a soviet sub ran aground in Sweden. Made in Sweden; dubbed. **90m/C VHS, DVD.** *SW* Dennis Hopper, Hardy Kruger, Gosta Ekman Jr., David Wilson; ***D:*** Tom Clegg; ***W:*** Alan Plater; ***C:*** Jorgen Persson; ***M:*** Stefan Nilsson.

Inside Man 🦴🦴🦴 **2006 (R)** Lee spins the conventional in this over-extended, gabby but well-played crime thriller. Dalton Russell (Owen) and his gang enter a Manhattan bank, apparently to rob the vault. They take hostages but aren't in a hurry to negotiate with slick detective Keith Frazier (Washington). Frazier suspects more is up when icy fixer Madeline White appears, at nervous bank chairman Arthur Case's (Plummer) request, saying Russell must be prevented at any cost from obtaining the contents of a particular safety deposit box. Many twists and turns follow to a satisfying conclusion. **129m/C DVD, HD DVD.** *US* Denzel Washington, Clive Owen, Jodie Foster, Christopher Plummer, Willem Dafoe, Chiwetel Ejiofor, Peter Gerety, Daryl (Chill) Mitchell, Kim Director, Marcia Jean Kurtz, Waris Ahluwalia, Amir Ali Said; ***D:*** Spike Lee; ***W:*** Russell Gewirtz; ***C:*** Matthew Libatique; ***M:*** Terence Blanchard.

Inside Monkey Zetterland 🦴🦴 **1993 (R)** Monkey Zetterland (Antin) is a screenwriter and former actor with an eccentric family. His actress mother is neurotically insecure and a nag; his father is an aging hippie who only shows up at Thanksgiving; his lesbian sister Grace is trying to get over a failed relationship; and his brother Brent is totally self-absorbed. Add to this menage his equally lunatic friends: Imogene, the compulsive talker and exhibitionist; his vicious girlfriend Daphne; and frightening married couple Sophie and Sasha. Meanwhile, Monkey tries to survive amidst the chaos. Interesting cast but lots of camera tricks do not a successful film make and the effort to be hip is all too apparent. **92m/C VHS, DVD.** Steve Antin, Patricia Arquette, Sandra Bernhard, Sofia Coppola, Tate Donovan, Katherine Helmond, Bo Hopkins, Debi Mazar, Martha Plimpton, Rupert Everett, Ricki Lake, Lance Loud, Frances Bay, Luca Bercovici; ***D:*** Jefery Levy; ***W:*** John Boskovich, Steve Antin; ***C:*** Christopher Taylor; ***M:*** Rick Cox, Jeff Elmassian.

Inside Moves 🦴🦴 1/2 **1980 (PG)** A look at handicapped citizens trying to make it in everyday life, focusing on the relationship between an insecure, failed suicide and a volatile man who is only a knee operation away from a dreamed-about basketball career. **113m/C VHS.** John Savage, Diana Scarwid, David Morse, Amy Wright; ***D:*** Richard Donner; ***W:*** Valerie Curtin, Barry Levinson; ***M:*** John Barry.

Inside Out 🦴🦴 1/2 *The Golden Heist; Hitler's Gold* **1975 (PG)** An ex-GI, a jewel thief and a German POW camp commandant band together to find a stolen shipment of Nazi gold behind the Iron Curtain. To find the gold, they help a Nazi prisoner who knows the secret to break out of prison. Good action caper. **97m/C VHS.** *GB* Telly Savalas, Robert Culp, James Mason, Aldo Ray, Doris Kunstmann; ***D:*** Peter Duffell.

Inside Out 🦴🦴 1/2 **1991 (R)** Hiding in his apartment from a world which terrifies him, Jimmy doesn't feel he's missing much—since he has the necessary women and bookies come to him. He soon finds he's not quite as safe as he thought, and the only way out is "out there." Fine performance from Gould, suspenseful pacing. **87m/C VHS.** Elliott Gould, Jennifer Tilly, Howard Hesseman, Beah Richards, Timothy Scott, Sandy McPeak, Dana Elcar, Meshach Taylor, Nicole Norman; ***D:*** Robert Taicher; ***W:*** Robert Taicher.

Inside Out 🦴 1/2 **2005 (R)** Bored in the 'burbs. Neighbors suffer ennui until a mysterious single guy, shrink Dr. Peoples, moves in and antagonizes everyone with his peculiarities. Then the new guy gets suspected of murder. Dull, including the last-minute revelation. **95m/C DVD.** Eriq La Salle, Steven Weber, Kate Walsh, Russell Wong, Nia Peeples, Tim Maculan, Tim Maculan, Tyler Posey; ***D:*** David Ogden; ***W:*** David Ogden; ***C:*** Steven Douglas Smith; ***M:*** Jamie Christopherson.

Inside Paris 🦴🦴 1/2 *Dans Paris* **2006** Depressed, heartbroken Paul (Duris) moves into his father's apartment after a breakup and immediately confines himself to bed. His father (Marchand), himself divorced, worries that Paul's depression will have tragic results, while Paul's brother Jonathan (Garrel) goofs his way through life and his brother's trauma. All three men struggle to find common ground and understanding in light of Paul's ongoing depression. Tone alternates between fanciful and somber as characters break into song and jump into rivers. For fans of French cinema. **93m/C DVD.** *FR* Louis Garrel, Guy Marchand, Joana Preiss, Romain Duris, Alice Butaud; ***D:*** Christophe Honore; ***W:*** Christophe Honore; ***C:*** Jean-Louis Vialard; ***M:*** Alexandre Beaupain.

Inside the Law 🦴🦴 **1942** A gang of crooks takes over a bank and must stay "inside the law" and resist their natural inclinations. Lots of comic situations. **65m/B VHS, DVD.** Wallace Ford, Frank Sully, Harry Holman, Luana Walters, Lafe (Lafayette) McKee, Danny Duncan, Earle Hodgins; ***D:*** Hamilton MacFadden.

Inside the Lines 🦴🦴 **1930** A WWI tale of espionage and counter-espionage. **73m/B VHS, DVD.** Betty Compson, Montagu Love, Mischa Auer, Ralph Forbes, Ivan Simpson, Wilhelm von Brinken, Reginald Sharland, Betty Carter, Evan Thomas; ***D:*** Roy Pomeroy; ***W:*** Ewart Adamson; ***C:*** Nicholas Musuraca; ***M:*** Roy Webb.

Inside the Third Reich 🦴🦴 1/2 **1982** Miniseries detailing the rise to power within the Third Reich of Albert Speer, top advisor to Hitler. Based on Speer's rather self-serving memoirs. **250m/C VHS.** Derek Jacobi, Rutger Hauer, John Gielgud, Blythe Danner, Maria Schell, Ian Holm, Trevor Howard, Randy Quaid, Viveca Lindfors, Robert Vaughn, Stephen Collins, Elke Sommer, Renee Soutendijk; ***D:*** Marvin J. Chomsky. **TV**

The Insider 🦴🦴🦴 1/2 **1999 (R)** Riveting and controversial film that caused a real-life snit at "60 Minutes" over the facts and portrayals in the story. After Jeffrey Wigand (Crowe) is fired from his top-level tobacco company job, he turns whistleblower, claiming his former employers lied about the dangers of cigarettes. Veteran "60 Minutes" producer Lowell Bergman (Pacino) and newsman Mike Wallace (Plummer) pursue the story—only to be shot down by their own network. The fallout causes ethical consequences for all involved. Performances are outstanding—from the chameleon Crowe to the relatively subdued Pacino and the slyly pompous Plummer. Based on a "Vanity Fair" magazine article. **157m/C VHS, DVD.** Russell Crowe, Al Pacino, Christopher Plummer, Gina Gershon, Philip Baker Hall, Diane Venora, Lindsay Crouse, Debi Mazar, Stephen Tobolowsky, Colm Feore, Bruce McGill, Michael Gambon, Rip Torn, Lynne Thigpen, Hallie Kate Eisenberg, Michael Paul Chan, Wings Hauser, Pete Hamill, Nestor Serrano, Michael Moore; ***D:*** Michael Mann; ***W:*** Michael Mann, Eric Roth; ***C:*** Dante Spinotti; ***M:*** Graeme Revell. L.A. Film Critics '99: Actor (Crowe), Cinematog., Film, Support. Actor (Plummer); Natl. Bd. of Review '99: Actor (Crowe); Natl. Soc. Film Critics '99: Actor (Crowe), Support. Actor (Plummer); Broadcast Film Critics '99: Actor (Crowe).

Insignificance 🦴🦴🦴 **1985** A film about an imaginary night spent in a New York hotel by characters who resemble Marilyn Monroe, Albert Einstein, Joe McCarthy, and Joe

DiMaggio. Entertaining and often amusing as it follows the characters as they discuss theory and relativity, the Russians, and baseball among other things. **110m/C VHS, DVD.** *GB* Gary Busey, Tony Curtis, Theresa Russell, Michael Emil, Will Sampson; ***D:*** Nicolas Roeg; ***W:*** Terry Johnson; ***C:*** Peter Hannan; ***M:*** Hans Zimmer.

Insomnia ☙☙☙ **1997** After a young girl is murdered in northern Norway, Oslo detective Jonas Engstrom (Skarsgard) and his partner Erik Vik (Ousdal) are called in to solve the crime, aided by local cop Hilde Hagen (Armand). Engstrom accidentally shoots and kills his partner during a stakeout in the fog and attempts to cover up one killing while uncovering another. He begins to unravel when his conscience and the unrelenting sun cause not only insomnia, but a moral breakdown. His nerves jangle as he comes under suspicion from Hilde. He is also forced into a face-to-face climax with the killer, who witnessed the shooting. Excellent feature debut for Norwegian director Erik Skjoldbjaerg. **97m/C VHS, DVD.** *NO* Stellan Skarsgard, Sverre Anker Ousdal, Maria Bonnevie, Bjorn Floberg, Gisken Armand, Marianne O. Ulrichsen, Maria Mathiesen; ***D:*** Erik Skjoldbjaerg; ***W:*** Nikolaj Frobenius; ***C:*** Erling Thurmann-Andersen; ***M:*** Geir Jenssen.

Insomnia ☙☙☙ 1/2 **2002 (R)** American remake of a 1997 Norwegian films finds veteran police detective Will Dormer (Pacino), under Internal Affairs investigation back home, sent to a small Alaskan town to investigate the murder of a 17-year-old girl. Primary suspect Walter Finch (Williams) plays a game of psychological chicken after witnessing a moment of Dormer's increasing weakness. Pacino, in service to an excellent script, gives an outstanding performance as the guilt-ridden, exhausted supercop, and Swank impresses (again) as the idol-worshipping but self-assured local deputy. "Memento" helmer Nolan proves there doesn't have to be a letdown after a breakout, groundbreaking hit. **116m/C VHS, DVD.** *US* Al Pacino, Robin Williams, Hilary Swank, Maura Tierney, Martin Donovan, Nicky Katt, Paul Dooley, Jonathan Jackson, Katharine Isabelle, Larry Holden, Crystal Lowe, Tasha Simms; ***D:*** Christopher Nolan; ***W:*** Hillary Seitz; ***C:*** Wally Pfister; ***M:*** David Julyan.

Inspector Clouseau ☙☙ **1968 (G)** The bumbling French detective (Arkin) goes to England to help break up a daring robbery ring that uses Clouseau masks to hide their identity. Arkin gives it a fine effort, but he's no Peter Sellers. This makes the absence of the usual band of comic foils like Cato, Dreyfus, and Hercule (as well as director Blake Edwards) that much more glaring. The same writing team remains, but maybe they needed Sellers as their muse, because the entire script falls flat. **98m/C VHS, DVD.** Alan Arkin, David Bauer, Patrick Cargill, Anthony Ainley, Delia Boccardo, Barbara Dana, Frank Finlay, Barry Foster, Beryl Reid, John Bindon, Tutte Lemkow, Bud Yorkin; ***W:*** Frank Waldman, Tom Waldman; ***C:*** Arthur Ibbetson; ***M:*** Ken Thorne.

Inspector Gadget ☙☙ **1999 (PG)** Go-go gadget script rewrite! The popular cartoon character goes live-action with Broderick in the title role. Blown to pieces by the evil Dr. Claw (Everett), a naive security guard is put back together by scientist Brenda Bradford (Fisher) with a vast array of graft-ed-on gizmos. Gadget becomes the world's top detective and discovers that Claw also murdered Brenda's father. In his battle against Claw, he is forced to fight his evil robot twin in order to clear his own name. The computer generated effects are eye-catching but far too brief, and Broderick is forced to react lamely to them most of the time. **77m/C VHS, DVD.** Matthew Broderick, Rupert Everett, Joely Fisher, Michelle Trachtenberg, Dabney Coleman, Andy Dick, Michael G. (Mike) Hagerty, Rene Auberjonois, Frances Bay; ***D:*** David Kellogg; ***W:*** Kerry Ehrin, Zak Penn; ***C:*** Adam Greenberg; ***M:*** John Debney; ***V:*** Don Adams, D.L. Hughley.

Inspector Gadget 2 ☙☙ **2002 (G)** A female agent called G2 is competing with Inspector Gadget (Stewart) to stop Claw from using a time-freezing device to rob a bank. **88m/C VHS, DVD.** French Stewart, Elaine Hendrix, Caitlin Wachs, Tony (Anthony) Martin, Mark Mitchell, Sigrid Thornton, Bruce Spence; ***D:*** Alex Zamm; ***W:*** Alex Zamm. **VIDEO**

Inspector Gadget's Biggest Caper Ever ☙☙ 1/2 **2005** Bionic detective Gadget must stop a flying dinosaur, under the control of the evil Dr. Claw, from destroying Metro City. Animated adventure has some slow patches but should still satisfy Gadget's kiddie fans. **70m/C VHS, DVD.** ***W:*** Phil Harnage; ***V:*** Maurice LaMarche, Bernie Mac, Tegan Moss, Ezekiel Norton, Brian Drummond. **VIDEO**

The Inspector General ☙☙☙ *Happy Times* **1949** Classic Kaye craziness of mistaken identities with the master comic portraying a carnival medicine man who is mistaken by the villagers for their feared Inspector General. If you like Kaye's manic performance, you'll enjoy this one. ♫The Gypsy Drinking Song; Onward Onward; The Medicine Show; The Inspector General; Lonely Heart; Soliloquy For Three Heads; Happy Times; Brodny. **103m/C VHS, DVD.** Danny Kaye, Walter Slezak, Barbara Bates, Elsa Lanchester, Gene Lockhart, Walter Catlett, Alan Hale; ***D:*** Henry Koster; ***W:*** Harry Kurnitz, Philip Rapp; ***C:*** Elwood "Woody" Bredell; ***M:*** Johnny Green. Golden Globes '50: Score.

The Inspector General ☙☙ 1/2 **1952** The filmed performance of Gogol's great play by the Moscow Art Theatre, wherein a provincial town panics when they mistake a wandering moron for the Inspector come to check up on them. In Russian with English subtitles. **128m/B VHS.** *RU* Yuri Tolubeyev, Igor Gobachyov, Anatasiya Georgiyevskaya, Tama Nosova; ***D:*** Vladimir Petrov; ***W:*** Vladimir Petrov; ***C:*** Yuri Yekelchik; ***M:*** Nikolai Timofeyev.

Inspector Hornleigh ☙☙ 1/2 **1939** A pair of bumbling detectives arrive on the scene when a Chancellor's fortune is stolen. Fine comedy, although the Scottish and British accents can be rather thick now and again. **76m/B VHS.** *GB* Gordon Harker, Alastair Sim, Miki Hood, Wally Patch, Steven Geray, Edward Underdown, Hugh Williams, Gibb McLaughlin; ***D:*** Eugene Forde.

Inspector Lynley Mysteries: A Great Deliverance ☙☙ 1/2 **2001** Inspector Thomas Lynley (Parker) just so happens to also be the eighth Earl of Asherton. His new partner is working-class Barbara Havers (Small), who deeply resents what she sees as Lynley's privileged life and she's not the only one. Still, Lynley is very good at his job and their first case together is a rural murder where a farmer is found decapitated and his traumatized daughter is the primary suspect. Based on the mysteries by Elizabeth George. **160m/C VHS, DVD.** *GB* Nathaniel Parker, Sharon Small, Anthony Calf, Amanda Ryan, Paul Brennan, Emma Fielding; ***D:*** Richard Laxton; ***W:*** Elizabeth (Lizzie) Mickery; ***C:*** Jonathan Bloom; ***M:*** Robert Lockhart. **TV**

The Inspectors ☙ 1/2 **1998** Remarkably dull thriller about postal inspectors Silverman and Gossett Jr., who are tracking a mail bomber. **91m/C VHS, DVD.** Louis Gossett Jr., Jonathan Silverman; ***D:*** Brad Turner; ***W:*** Bruce Zimmerman; ***C:*** Albert J. Dunk; ***M:*** Terry Frewer. **CABLE**

The Inspectors 2: A Shred of Evidence ☙☙ **2000** Con man is using the mail to assume other identities and must be stopped by our two intrepid postal inspectors. Standard made-for-TV suspense. **95m/C DVD.** Louis Gossett Jr., Jonathan Silverman, Michael Madsen; ***D:*** Brad Turner; ***W:*** Bruce Zimmerman; ***C:*** Albert J. Dunk; ***M:*** Terry Frewer. **CABLE**

Instant Justice ☙ 1/2 *Marine Issue* **1986 (R)** A professional Marine jeopardizes his military career by avenging his sister's murder, vigilante style. Exclusive action. **101m/C VHS.** *GB* Michael Pare, Tawny Kitaen, Charles Napier; ***D:*** Craig T. Rumar.

Instant Karma ☙ 1/2 **1990** Would be comedy depicts young man's far fetched attempts to score babewise. Ask no more what happened to erstwhile teen heart throb Cassidy: he suffers from a major bout of bad karma. **94m/C VHS.** Craig Sheffer, Chelsea Noble, David Cassidy, Alan Blumenfeld, Glen Hirsch, Marty Ingels, Orson Bean; ***D:*** Roderick Taylor.

Instinct ☙☙ **1999 (R)** Primatologist Ethan Powell (Hopkins) has been in the African jungle studying gorillas a little too long, and has turned apeman, killing poachers threatening his primate friends. Since he's been returned to the U.S. and incarcerated in a Miami prison ward for the insane, he's taken a vow of silence. Theo Caulder (Gooding) is an ambitious shrink who's sent to see if Powell is still (or ever was) a clinical whacko. Hopkins mainly gets to chew the scenery and leave Gooding wide-eyed in his wake. "Suggested" by the novel "Ishmael" by Daniel Quinn. **123m/C VHS, DVD.** Anthony Hopkins, Cuba Gooding Jr., Donald Sutherland, George Dzundza, Maura Tierney, John Ashton, Paul Bates, John Aylward; ***D:*** Jon Turteltaub; ***W:*** Gerald Di Pego; ***C:*** Philippe Rousselot; ***M:*** Danny Elfman.

Instinct to Kill ☙☙ **2001 (R)** Abused wife Tess (Crider) helps put her husband Jim (Abell) in prison after discovering he's a killer. But when he escapes, Tess hires martial arts expert J.T. Dillon (Dacascos) to teach her how to defend herself and waits for her hubby to come after her. Based on the novel "The Perfect Husband" by Lisa Gardner. **92m/C VHS, DVD.** Missy (Melissa) Crider, Tim Abell, Mark Dacascos, Kadeem Hardison; ***D:*** Gustavo Graef-Marino; ***W:*** Randall Frakes. **VIDEO**

Institue Benjamenta or This Dream People Call Human Life ☙☙ **1995** The Brothers Quay's first live-action feature is a surreal nightmareish fairytale based on the 1905 novel "Jakob von Gunten" by Robert Waiser. Jakob (Rylance) arrives at the secluded Institute Benjamenta, which is run by Lisa (Krige) and her brother Johannes (John), to train as a servant. He becomes a favorite of the enigmatic duo and tries to decide what is real and what isn't. Eccentric and wonderfully photographed by Knowland. **105m/B VHS, DVD.** *GB* Mark Rylance, Alice Krige, Gottfried John; ***D:*** Stephen Quay, Timothy Quay; ***W:*** Stephen Quay, Timothy Quay, Allan Passes; ***C:*** Nicholas D. Knowland; ***M:*** Lech Jankowski.

The Instructor ☙ **1983** The head of a karate school proves the value of his skill when threatened by the owner of a rival school. **91m/C VHS.** Don Bendell, Bob Chaney, Bob Saal, Lynday Scharnott; ***D:*** Don Bendell.

The Insurgents ☙☙ 1/2 **2006 (R)** Thought-provoking look at post-9/11 paranoia and homegrown terrorism. A radical author persuades a small-time crook, an ex-hooker, and an angry Iraq War vet to become a terrorist cell, build a truck bomb, and detonate it on U.S. soil. **85m/C DVD.** John Shea, Henry Simmons, Juliette Marquis, Michael Mosley, Mary Stuart Masterson; ***D:*** Scott Dacko; ***W:*** Scott Dacko; ***M:*** Ben Butler, Mariò Grigorov, Learan Kahanov.

Intacto ☙☙ **2001 (R)** Samuel Berg (von Sydow) has survived the Nazi death camps and believes that he not only possesses good luck but runs a remote Spanish casino where the patrons bet their good luck against his own in a version of Russian roulette. When Sam steals the luck of his one-time confidante (and earthquake survivor) Federico (Poncela), the man goes looking for a protege to pit against his former boss and eventually finds Tomas (Sbaraglia), the only person to survive a plane crash. But Tomas is also a bank robber trailed by police officer Sara (Lopez), who survived a car crash. So luck gets pitted against luck—winner takes all. English and Spanish with subtitles. **108m/C VHS, DVD.** *SP* Max von Sydow, Leonardo Sbaraglia, Eusebio Poncela, Monica Lopez, Antonio Dechent, Paz Gomez; ***D:*** Juan Carlos Fresnadillo; ***W:*** Juan Carlos Fresnadillo, Andres M. Koppel; ***C:*** Xavier Jimenez; ***M:*** Lucio Godoy.

The Intended ☙☙ **2002 (R)** Period melodrama set in steamy 1920s Indochina. Ambitious young surveyor (Feild) heads upriver with his older fiancee (McTeer) in hopes of starting a new life at a colonial trading post. Of course, all is not right when they arrive. They find the post run by scary militant widow Fricker, surrounded by a freakshow of family and hangers-on. Her son, a disgustingly oily slacker (Maudsley), is angry when mommy decides to pass control over to a nephew instead of him and starts scheming. While Maudsley's unhinged nanny (Dukakis) creepily fawns over him, he casts a greedy eye towards McTeer. Wonderfully twisted over-the-top horror show reminds at times of Old Dark House thrillers of the '30s, minus the knowing, tongue-in-cheek humor. Takes itself way too seriously, but it's good fun for fans of unintentional camp. **110m/C DVD.** *GB DK* Janet McTeer, J.J. Feild, Olympia Dukakis, Brenda Fricker, Tony Maudsley, David Bradley, Philip Jackson, Robert Pugh; ***D:*** Kristian Levring; ***W:*** Kristian Levring; ***C:*** Jens Schlosser; ***M:*** Matthew Herbert.

Interceptor ☙☙ **1992 (R)** Hijackers attempt to steal a Stealth Bomber in this action-adventure saga which features virtual reality computer-generated imagery in its combat sequences. **92m/C VHS, DVD.** Jurgen Prochnow, Andrew Divoff, Elizabeth Morehead; ***D:*** Michael Cohn; ***W:*** John Brancato, Michael Ferris; ***M:*** Richard (Rick) Marvin.

Interceptor Force ☙☙ **1999 (R)** The Interceptors are a top-secret group of soldiers trained for encounters with aliens. Their latest assignment involves a UFO in a remote community and a species that's capable of morphing into any form. And if they can't clean up the mess in 24 hours, the military will nuke the region. **91m/C VHS, DVD.** Olivier Gruner, Brad Dourif, Glenn Plummer, Ernie Hudson, Ken Olandt, Angel Boris, Holly Fields; ***D:*** Phillip J. Roth; ***W:*** Phillip J. Roth, Martin Lazarus. **VIDEO**

Interceptor Force 2 ☙ **2002 (R)** In the near future an elite team of soldiers, led by stone-faced Sean Lambert (Gruner), combat a shape-shifting female alien that has taken over a Russian nuclear plant and is threatening a nuclear winter. Things get personal when the alien learns it was Lambert who killed her mate (in the first bad pic). A Sci-Fi Channel original. **89m/C DVD.** Olivier Gruner, Roger R. Cross, Elizabeth (Ward) Gracen, Nigel Bennett, Adrienne Wilkinson, Eve Scheer; ***D:*** Phillip J. Roth; ***W:*** Patrick Phillips; ***C:*** Todd Barron; ***M:*** Tony Riparetti. **CABLE**

Interface ☙ 1/2 **1984** A computer game gets out of hand at a university, turning the tunnels beneath the campus into a battleground of good and evil. **88m/C VHS.** John Davies, Laura Lane, Matthew Sacks; ***D:*** Andy Anderson; ***W:*** Roger Pistole; ***M:*** David Hoey, Steven Jay Hoey.

Interiors ☙☙☙ 1/2 **1978 (R)** Ultra serious, Bergmanesque drama about three neurotic adult sisters, coping with the dissolution of their family. When Father decides to leave mentally unbalanced mother for a divorcee, the daughters are shocked and bewildered. Depressing and humorless, but fine performances all the way around, supported by the elegant camera work of Gordon Willis. **95m/C VHS, DVD.** Diane Keaton, Mary Beth Hurt, E.G. Marshall, Geraldine Page, Richard Jordan, Sam Waterston, Kristin Griffith, Maureen Stapleton; ***D:*** Woody Allen; ***W:*** Woody Allen; ***C:*** Gordon Willis. British Acad. '78: Support. Actress (Page); L.A. Film Critics '78: Support. Actress (Stapleton).

Interlocked ☙ 1/2 *A Bold Affair* **1998 (R)** Another psycho-babe thriller. Pregnant Emily Anderson (Ferguson) and happy hubby Michael (Trachta) befriend Eva (Harrison), which turns into trouble. Harrison and Trachta previously worked together on TV soap "The Bold & the Beautiful." **94m/C VHS, DVD.** Jeff Trachta, Schae Harrison, Sandra Ferguson, George Alvarez, Bruce Kirby; ***D:*** Rick Jacobson; ***W:*** Al Sophianopoulos; ***C:*** Jesse Weathington. **VIDEO**

Intermezzo ☙☙☙ *Interlude* **1936** Married violinist Ekman meets pianist Bergman and they fall in love. He deserts his family to tour with Bergman, but the feelings for his wife and children become too much. When Bergman sees their love won't last, she leaves him. Shakily, he returns home and as his daughter runs to greet him, she is hit by a truck and he realizes that his family is his true love. One of the great grab-your-hanky melodramas. In Swedish with English subtitles. 1939 English re-make features Bergman's American film debut. **88m/B VHS, DVD.** *SW* Gosta Ekman, Inga Tidblad, Ingrid Bergman, Erik "Bullen" Berglund, Anders Henrikson, Hasse (Hans) Ekman, Britt Hagman, Hugo Bjorne; ***D:*** Gustaf Molander; ***W:*** Gustaf Molander, Gosta Stevens; ***C:*** Ake Dahlqvist; ***M:*** Heinz Provost.

Intermezzo ☙☙☙ *Intermezzo: A Love Story* **1939** Fine, though weepy, love story of a renowned, married violinist who has an affair with his stunningly beautiful protege (Bergman), but while on concert tour realizes that his wife and children hold his heart, and he returns to them. A re-make of the 1936 Swedish film, it's best known as Bergman's American debut. Howard's violin playing was dubbed by Toscha Seidel. **70m/B VHS, DVD.** *IT* Ingrid Bergman, Leslie Howard, Edna Best, Ann E. Todd; ***D:*** Gregory Ratoff; ***C:*** Gregg Toland; ***M:*** Max Steiner.

Intern ½ **2000** Satire on the fashion industry is filled with insider chit-chat and cameos from fashionistas and designers, takes a lot of well-placed digs, and is finally as superficial and throw away as the world it depicts. Naive Jocelyn (Swain) is an intern at fashion magazine Skirt who is desperate to fit in. But everyone is more paranoid and mean-spirited than usual because there's an insider giving the rag's best ideas to archrival Vogue. **93m/C VHS, DVD.** Dominique Swain, Benjamin Pullen, Peggy Lipton, Joan Rivers, David Deblinger, Dwight Ewell, Billy Porter, Anna Thomson, Paulina Porizkova, Kathy Griffin; ***D:*** Michael Lange; ***W:*** Caroline Doyle, Jill Kopelman; ***C:*** Rodney Charters; ***M:*** Jimmy Harry.

Internal Affairs ½ **1990 (R)** Wild, sexually charged action piece about an Internal Affairs officer for the L.A.P.D. (Garcia) who becomes obsessed with exposing a sleazy, corrupt street cop (Gere). Drama becomes illogical, but boasts excellent, strung out performances, especially Gere as the creepy degenerate you'd love to bust. **114m/C VHS, DVD.** Elijah Wood, Arlen Dean Snyder, Faye Grant, John Capodice, Xander Berkeley, John Kapelos, Richard Gere, Andy Garcia, Laurie Metcalf, Ron Vawter, Marco Rodriguez, Nancy Travis, William Baldwin, Richard Bradford, Annabella Sciorra, Michael Beach, Mike Figgis; ***D:*** Mike Figgis; ***W:*** Henry Bean; ***C:*** John A. Alonzo; ***M:*** Brian Banks, Mike Figgis.

The International **2009 (R)** Interpol agent Louis Salinger (Owen) and Manhattan ADA Eleanor Whitman (Watts) uncover myriad illegal activities at one of the world's most powerful financial institutions, sending them on a death-defying global chase to expose the truth. Flick takes enough liberties to make Dick and W proud while going for the international espionage vibe, a la Jason Bourne, but with a timely financial twist. Ultimately doesn't offer enough to differentiate itself from the superior Bourne series and follows a predictable, paint-by-numbers approach. A lowlight on the considerable resumes of Owen and Watts. **118m/C DVD.** *US GE* Clive Owen, Naomi Watts, Armin Mueller-Stahl, Brian F. O'Byrne, Ulrich Thomsen, Jack McGee, James Rebhorn; ***D:*** Tom Tykwer; ***W:*** Eric Singer; ***C:*** Frank Griebe; ***M:*** Tom Tykwer, Reinhold Heil, Johnny Klimek.

International Crime **1937** Radio hero The Shadow solves a tough crime in this adventure film. **62m/B VHS, DVD.** Rod La Rocque, Astrid Allwyn, Wilhelm von Brinken; ***D:*** Charles Lamont.

International House ½ **1933** A wacky Dada-esque Hollywood farce about an incredible array of travelers quarantined in a Shanghai hotel where a mad doctor has perfected television. Essentially a burlesque compilation of skits, gags, and routines. Guest stars Rudy Vallee, Baby Rose Marie, and Cab Calloway appear on the quaint "TV" device, in musical sequences. ♫Tea Cup; Thank Heaven For You; My Bluebirds are Singing the Blues; Reefer Man. **72m/B VHS, DVD.** W.C. Fields, Peggy Hopkins Joyce, Rudy Vallee, George Burns, Cab Calloway, Sari Maritza, Gracie Allen, Bela Lugosi, Sterling Holloway, Baby Rose Marie; ***D:*** Edward Sutherland.

International Lady ½ **1941** Sexy musician Carla (Massey) travels the world performing and spying for the Germans in the early days of WWII. Brent and Rathbone are the American and British agents sent to capture the spy. Things get complicated when Brent falls for her. Romantic spy thriller has its lighter moments. **102m/B VHS.** Ilona Massey, George Brent, Basil Rathbone, George Zucco, Gene Lockhart, Clayton Moore, Charles D. Brown, Marjorie Gateson, Gordon DeMain, Leyland Hodgson, Martin Kosleck, Jack Mulhall, Frederick Worlock, William Forrest, Marten Lamont, Selmer Jackson; ***D:*** Tim Whelan; ***W:*** Howard Estabrook; ***C:*** Hal Mohr; ***M:*** Lucien Moraweck.

International Velvet ½ **1978 (PG)** Why did they bother? This dismal and long overdue sequel to "National Velvet," finds the adult Velvet, with live-in companion (Plummer), grooming her orphaned niece (O'Neal) to become an Olympic champanion horsewoman. O'Neal's way out of her league although Plummer and Hopkins give good performances and the sentiment is kept at a trot. **126m/C VHS.** *GB* Tatum O'Neal, Anthony Hopkins, Christopher Plummer; ***D:*** Bryan Forbes.

Internecine Project ½ **1973 (PG)** Stylistic espionage tale with Coburn's English professor acting as the mastermind behind an unusual series of murders where industrial spies kill each other, so Coburn can garner a top government job in D.C. Unexpected ending is worth the viewing. Based on Mort Elkind's novel. **89m/C VHS, DVD.** *GB* James Coburn, Lee Grant, Harry Andrews, Keenan Wynn; ***D:*** Ken Hughes; ***W:*** Barry Levinson; ***C:*** Geoffrey Unsworth.

Internes Can't Take Money ½ **1937** With the help of McCrea and gangster Nolan, widow Stanwyck is desperately trying to find the daughter her bank robber husband hid before he died. Young doctor McCrea must save the life of another gangster who knows the whereabouts of the toddler. The first film featuring writer Max Brand's Dr. Kildare characters, which later became part of a series starring Lew Ayres and Laraine Day. **79m/B VHS.** Barbara Stanwyck, Joel McCrea, Lloyd Nolan, Stanley Ridges, Lee Bowman, Irving Bacon; ***D:*** Alfred Santell; ***W:*** Rian James, Theodore Reeves; ***C:*** Theodor Sparkuhl; ***M:*** Gregory Stone.

Internet Dating ½ **2008** Lonely, unprepossessing single guy Mikey creates a false profile on an Internet dating service claiming to be a professional basketball player. Imagine how many doors get slammed in his face when he shows up and his would-be date gets a look at him. **86m/C DVD.** Katt Micah Williams, Clifton Powell, Master P, Lil' Romeo, Reynaldo Rey, Liana Mendoza, Jessica Meza; ***D:*** Master P; ***W:*** Master P; ***M:*** Ramon Balcazar. **VIDEO**

The Interns ½ **1962** Finessed hospital soaper about interns on the staff of a large city hospital, whose personal lives are fraught with trauma, drugs, birth, death, and abortion. Good performances and direction keep this medical melodrama moving in a gurney-like manner. Followed by the "The New Interns" and the basis for a TV series. Adapted from a novel by Richard Frede. **120m/C VHS.** Angela (Clark) Clarke, Cliff Robertson, James MacArthur, Michael Callan, Nick Adams, Stefanie Powers, Suzy Parker, Buddy Ebsen, Telly Savalas, Haya Harareet; ***D:*** David Swift; ***W:*** Walter Newman, David Swift; ***C:*** Russell Metty; ***M:*** Leith Stevens.

Interpol Connection ½ **1992** International drug dealer Law Tak is being pursued by Hong Kong narcotics officer Ko Pang, international police officer Cynthia, and bumbling Philippine cop KingKong. The cop trio reluctantly decide to work together to bring down the bad guy. Dubbed into English. **91m/C VHS.** *HK* Robin Shou, Yukari Oshima, Philip Ko; ***D:*** Philip Ko.

The Interpreter ½ **2005 (PG-13)** White, native African U.N. interpreter Sylvia Broome (Kidman) accidently overhears a plot to kill the corrupt and murderous president of a small African country, a man with whom her family has a past. Tobin Keller (Penn) is the burned-out, recently-widowed Secret Service agent assigned to investigate her claim and, if necessary, protect her as a possible witness. Pollack's taut thriller is well-paced and full of twists and revelations that succeed in keeping the resolution in doubt right up to the end. Kidman and Penn are excellent, as is Keener in the thankless role of Keller's level-headed partner. **128m/C DVD, HD DVD.** *US* Nicole Kidman, Sean Penn, Catherine Keener, Jesper Christensen, Yvan Attal, Michael Wright, Earl Cameron, George Harris, Tsai Chin, Clyde Kusatsu, Hugo Speer, Maz Jobrani, Eric Keenleyside, Christopher Evan Welch, David Zayas, Sydney Pollack, Curtiss Cook, Byron Utley; ***D:*** Sydney Pollack; ***W:*** Charles Randolph, Scott Frank, Steven Zaillian; ***C:*** Darius Khondji; ***M:*** James Newton Howard.

The Interrogation *Przesluchanie* **1982** Grueling depiction of Stalin-era Poland proves that nobody makes anticommunist movies better than those who knew tyranny firsthand. A 1950s cabaret starlet is arrested on false charges and endures years of torment in custody. Banned under Polish martial law in 1982, it circulated illegally in the country until 1989. Janda won an award at Cannes for her transformation from showgirl floozy to defiant heroine. In Polish with English subtitles. **118m/C VHS.** *PL* Krystyna Janda, Janusz Gajos, Adam Ferency, Agnieszka Holland, Anna Romantowska; ***D:*** Richard Bugajski; ***W:*** Richard Bugajski, Janusz Dymek; ***C:*** Jacek Petrycki.

Interrupted Journey ½ **1949** A married man runs away to start a new life with another woman. When she is killed in a train accident, he becomes the prime suspect in her murder. Lots of action and speed, but a disappointing ending. **80m/B VHS.** *GB* Richard Todd, Valerie Hobson; ***D:*** Daniel Birt.

Interrupted Melody **1955** True story of opera diva Marjorie Lawrence's courageous battle with polio and her fight to appear once more at the Metropolitan Opera. Parker was nominated for an Oscar in her excellent portrayal of the Australian singer who continues her career despite her handicap. Vocals dubbed by opera star Eileen Farrell. Based on the book by Marjorie Lawrence. **106m/C VHS.** Glenn Ford, Eleanor Parker, Roger Moore, Cecil Kellaway, Evelyn Ellis, Walter Baldwin; ***D:*** Curtis Bernhardt; ***W:*** William Ludwig, Sonya Levien; ***C:*** Paul Vogel. Oscars '55: Story & Screenplay.

Intersection ½ **1993 (R)** Successful architect Vincent (Gere) is torn between his aloof wife/partner, Sally (Stone), and a sexy journalist mistress, Olivia (Davidovitch). Whom to choose? Since he's a completely self-involved boor, you won't care either way. Another retooling of a French film ("Les Choses de la Vie") as a Hollywood star vehicle that doesn't work. Lousy dialogue doesn't help. Does boast some nice location shots of Vancouver, B.C. **98m/C VHS, DVD.** Richard Gere, Sharon Stone, Lolita (David) Davidovich, Martin Landau, David Selby, Jenny (Jennifer) Morrison; ***D:*** Mark Rydell; ***W:*** Marshall Brickman, David Rayfiel; ***C:*** Vilmos Zsigmond; ***M:*** James Newton Howard. Golden Raspberries '94: Worst Actress (Stone).

Interstate **2007** Montreal DJ Edgar (Fernandez), who proves to be amazingly stupid, is driving across the U.S. to meet his girlfriend in L.A. He can't pay for the repairs after having car trouble, so Edgar starts hitching. He's picked up by speed freak Allan (Pena), but soon Edgar is alone with the car. Not having had enough trouble, Edgar picks up his own hitchers, skanky weird sisters Veronica (Ackerman) and Gloria (Stanford). Veronica slips Edgar some acid and they wind up in a seedy interstate motel where Veronica tries out her blackmail scheme only it's not over for Edgar yet. **89m/C DVD.** Shiloh Fernandez, Alexandra Ackerman, Jodi Stanford, Walter Pena, Chase Mallen; ***D:*** Marc-Andre Samson; ***W:*** Marc-Andre Samson; ***C:*** Pascal Chappuis; ***M:*** David Bawal, Daniel Fowler. **VIDEO**

Interstate 60 **2002 (R)** Weird road trip down a highway that doesn't exist. College grad Neil (Marsden) is being pressured to follow his dad into the law but thinks he may want to become an artist instead. After an accidental conk on the head, Neil's perceptions are skewed—his dream girl talks to him from billboards and he meets the oddball O.C. (Oldman), who persuades Neil to take a trip in his new convertible on (nonexistant) Interstate 60 to deliver a mysterious package. **112m/C VHS, DVD.** James Marsden, Gary Oldman, Chris Cooper, Amy Smart, Christopher Lloyd, Ann-Margret; ***Cameos:*** Kurt Russell, Michael J. Fox; ***D:*** Bob Gale; ***W:*** Bob Gale; ***C:*** Denis Maloney; ***M:*** Christophe Beck.

Interval **1973 (PG)** A middle-aged, globe-trotting woman becomes involved with a young American painter while running from her past. Oberon, 62 at the time, produced and played in this, her last film. Filmed in Mexico. **84m/C VHS.** Merle Oberon, Robert Wolders; ***D:*** Daniel Mann.

The Interview **1998** Eddie Fleming (Weaving) is a seemingly ordinary bloke who is rudely awakened when armed police burst into his apartment and haul him off for questioning. His interrogators are tenacious Detective Steele (Martin) and his younger partner, Prior (Jeffery). It slowly becomes clear that the cops are interested in a serial killer and that Fleming isn't the only one under investigation. It seems the two detectives are being watched by an internal affairs unit who are suspicious of Steele himself. And maybe Fleming isn't quite as innocent as he protests. **101m/C VHS, DVD.** *AU* Hugo Weaving, Tony (Anthony) Martin, Aaron Jeffery, Paul Sonkkila, Michael Caton, Peter McCauley; ***D:*** Craig Monahan; ***W:*** Craig Monahan, Gordon Davie; ***C:*** Simon Duggan; ***M:*** David Hirschfelder. Australian Film Inst. '98: Actor (Weaving), Film, Orig. Screenplay.

Interview ½ **2007 (R)** A White House scandal is breaking, but ace political reporter Pierre (Buscemi) is stuck in Manhattan profiling beautiful but vacuous starlet Katya (Miller). He waits an hour for the unapologetic diva, and once she shows up he's had enough and they argue. Name-calling ensues and the interview ends with Katya running outside, Pierre on her heels. He's injured and she insists he come to her nearby loft for a cold compress. Here the two posture, drink, flirt and eventually reveal their darkest truths to each other. As in life, both characters are more complex than one initially assumes. Script, camera work and editing are top notch. **83m/C DVD.** *US* Steve Buscemi, Sienna Miller; ***D:*** Steve Buscemi; ***W:*** Steve Buscemi, David Schechter; ***C:*** Thomas Kist; ***M:*** Evan Lurie.

Interview with the Assassin ½ **2002 (R)** Ron Kobeleski (Haggerty) is an unemployed video cameraman who needs cash, so Ron agrees when his loner neighbor Walter Ohlinger (Barry) wants to hire him to record a confession. What ex-Marine Walter confesses to is being the second gunman on the grassy knoll in Dallas and the one who actually fired the fatal shot killing President Kennedy. His story turns out to have enough truth that Ron accompanies Walter to Dallas for a re-enactment. But just what did the people who hired Walter want? Character actor Barry is formidable as the ambiguous assassin. **85m/C VHS, DVD.** Raymond J. Barry, Dylan Haggerty, Darrell Sandeen, Kate Williamson; ***D:*** Neil Burger; ***W:*** Neil Burger; ***C:*** Richard Rutkowski.

Interview with the Vampire **1994 (R)** Portrayal of the elegantly decadent world of vampires and their prey, which features the perverse Lestat (Cruise) who decides to make 18th-century New Orleans aristocrat Louis (Pitt) his latest recruit. Only problem is Louis is horrified by his blood-sucking nature and whines about it for 200 years (it does get tedious). Lestat even makes a child-vampire, Claudia (Dunst), for their own very dysfunctional family but this doesn't turn out well. Director Jordan brings some much needed humor to the dark mix along with some overdone gore. The first book in Anne Rice's "The Vampire Chronicles" was a 17-year film project beset by controversy, including the casting of Cruise (who looks nothing like Rice's description of the character, although Pitt does), leading to an outcry among the cult book's fans though Rice finally came around. Slater replaced the late River Phoenix as the interviewer. **123m/C VHS, DVD.** Tom Cruise, Brad Pitt, Kirsten Dunst, Christian Slater, Antonio Banderas, Stephen Rea, Domiziana Giordano; ***D:*** Neil Jordan; ***W:*** Anne Rice; ***C:*** Philippe Rousselot; ***M:*** Elliot Goldenthal. MTV Movie Awards '95: Male Perf. (Pitt), Breakthrough Perf. (Dunst), Most Desirable Male (Pitt).

Intervista *Federico Fellini's Intervista* **1987** A pseudo-documentary look at director Fellini's love of the movies, "Intervista" is a mixture of recollection, parody, memoir, satire, self-examination and fantasy. Fellini himself is the master of ceremonies in this joyous celebration of the studio community that features actors, actresses, bit players, make-up artists, scene painters, publicity agents, technicians, and gate-crashers. The high point of the film arrives with the stars of "La Dolce Vita" re-screening the Fellini masterpiece at Ekberg's country villa. It's a special moment of fantasy vs. reality in this glorious tribute to cinema history. In Italian with English subtitles. **108m/C VHS, DVD.** *IT* Marcello Mastroianni, Anita Ekberg, Sergio Rubini, Lara Wendel, Antonio Cantafora, Antonella Ponziani, Maurizio Mein, Paola Liguori, Nadia Ottaviani, Federico Fellini; ***D:*** Federico Fellini; ***W:*** Federico Fellini, Gianfranco Angelucci; ***C:*** Tonino Delli Colli; ***M:*** Nicola Piovani.

Interzone 🦴 1/2 **1988** Humans battle mutants in a post-holocaust world. **97m/C VHS.** Beatrice Ring, Teagan Clive, John Armstead, Bruce Abbott; ***D:*** Deran Sarafian, Deran Sarafian; ***W:*** Deran Sarafian; ***C:*** Gianlorenzo Battaglia; ***M:*** Stefano Mainetti.

Intimacy 🦴🦴 **2000** Furtive and explicit; the first English-language pic from director Chereau. Jay (Rylance), who's walked away from his wife and kids, is managing a bar and living in a basement hovel. Unhappily married Claire (Fox) has sexual trysts with Jay every Wednesday afternoon, although neither seem interested in learning anything about one another. Then Jay decides to follow Claire and discovers she's married and an amateur actress; Jay then befriends Claire's taxi-driving husband, Andy (Spall). When Claire finds out, she skips her trysts and Jay becomes resentful, leading to more emotional upheavals. Based on two stories by Hanif Kureishi. **119m/C DVD.** *GB FR* Mark Rylance, Kerry Fox, Timothy Spall, Alastair Galbraith, Marianne Faithfull, Susannah Harker, Philippe Calvario, Rebecca Palmer, Fraser Ayres; ***D:*** Patrice Chereau; ***W:*** Patrice Chereau, Anne-Louise Trividic; ***C:*** Eric Gautier; ***M:*** Eric Neveux.

Intimate Affairs 🦴 1/2 *Investigating Sex* **2001 (R)** In 1929, academician Edgar (Mulroney) is determined to take a clinical, psychological approach to examining the heterosexual male libido. He hires two attractive women, Alice (Campbell) and Zoe (Tunney), as stenographers, but his approach soon goes awry as his subjects don't cooperate as expected. **101m/C DVD.** Dermot Mulroney, Neve Campbell, Robin Tunney, Alan Cumming, Nick Nolte, Til Schweiger, John Light, Julie Delpy, Terrence Howard, Jeremy Davies, Tuesday Weld; ***D:*** Alan Rudolph; ***W:*** Alan Rudolph, Michael Henry Wilson; ***C:*** Florian Ballhaus; ***M:*** Ulf Skogsbergh.

Intimate Betrayal 🦴 1/2 **1996 (R)** Mack (Brown) is surprised when ex-friend Charlie (Edson) crashes his bachelor party. Charlie still wants the bride-to-be, Katie (Hecht), and has hired a hooker, Shelley (Conaway), to seduce Mack and then tell Katie all the dirty details. The wedding's off, Charlie makes his play, Shelley confesses the scam, blah, blah, blah. Neither of these guys is worth the time. **90m/C VHS.** Dwier Brown, Richard Edson, Cristi Conaway, Jessica Hecht; ***D:*** Andrew Behar; ***W:*** Sara Sackner; ***C:*** Hamid Shams; ***M:*** Peter Fish.

Intimate Contact 🦴🦴🦴 **1987 (PG)** Top executive discovers he has AIDS after a business trip fling. Powerful drama as he and his wife try to cope. Excellent, understated performances from Massey and Bloom. **140m/C VHS.** *GB* Claire Bloom, Daniel Massey, Abigail Cruttenden, Mark Kingston, Sylvia Syms, Sally Jane Jackson; ***D:*** Waris Hussein; ***W:*** Alma Cullen. **CABLE**

Intimate Deception 🦴🦴 **1996** Artist Charles Michaels is in a crumbling marriage and having dreams about a murder that took place in his past. Into his confused life comes new neighbor John and beautiful model Tina and neither meeting is a coincidence. **96m/C VHS.** George Saunders, Lisa Boyle, Dan Frank, Nicole Gian; ***D:*** George Saunders; ***W:*** George Saunders.

Intimate Lighting 🦴🦴 1/2 *Intimni Osvetleni* **1965** Professional cello player takes his fiancee to a provincial town to meet his friend, the local orchestra director. Slice of life comedy enjoys the simple pleasures of sharing food, music, and reminiscences, all tinged with melancholy. Czech with subtitles. **73m/B VHS.** *CZ* Zdenek Bezusek, Vera Kresadlova, Jan Vostrcil, Karel Blazek, Jaroslava Stedra, Vlastimila Vlkova; ***D:*** Ivan Passer; ***W:*** Ivan Passer, Jaroslav Papousek, Vaclav Sasek; ***C:*** Miroslav Ondricek, Jan Strecha; ***M:*** Oldrich Korte.

Intimate Power 🦴🦴 1/2 **1989 (R)** True story of French schoolgirl sold into slavery to an Ottoman sultan who becomes the harem queen. She bears an heir and begins to teach her son about his people's rights, in the hope that he will bring about reform in Turkey where he grows up to be a sultan. Good cast supports the exotic storytelling in this cable drama. **104m/C VHS, DVD.** F. Murray Abraham, Maud Adams, Amber O'Shea; ***D:*** Jack Smight. **CABLE**

Intimate Relations 🦴🦴 1/2 **1995 (R)** Fifties family dsyfunction—British style. Harold Guppy (Graves) is an orphaned merchant marine who winds up in an English coastal town where he takes rooms with the seemingly respectable Beasleys. Stanley Beasley (Walker) is a quiet nonentity whose life is run by homemaker extraordinaire Marjorie (Walters), with 14-year-old daughter Joyce (Sadler) rounding out the family. The needy Harold fits in fine, especially to the sexually hungry Marjorie who's soon offering her boarder unexpected services. But young Joyce won't be left out and then there's a blackmailing tug of war between the threesome. Based on the true story of a crime of passion that shocked Great Britain. **105m/C VHS.** *GB* Julie Walters, Rupert Graves, Laura Sadler, Matthew (Matt) Walker, Holly Aird, Les Dennis, Liz McKechnie; ***D:*** Philip Goodhew; ***W:*** Philip Goodhew; ***C:*** Andres Garreton; ***M:*** Lawrence Shragge. Montreal World Film Fest. '95: Actor (Graves).

Intimate Story 🦴🦴 1/2 **1981** Intimate story of a husband and wife trying unsuccessfully to have a baby, amid the lack of privacy in a Kibbutz. Each blames the other for the problem and tries to escape the problems by focusing on personal fantasies. In Hebrew with English subtitles. **95m/C VHS.** *IS* Chava Alberstein, Alex Peleg; ***D:*** Israeli Nadav Levitan.

Intimate Stranger 🦴 1/2 **1991 (R)** Sexy, would-be rock star by day, Harry sets out in search of a steadier source of income. Rather than wait on tables all day, she chooses instead to become a phone-sex girl. This turns out to be an unwise career move, as she promptly finds herself the target of a phone-psycho who just can't take "no" for an answer. Will Debbie be able to shake this loser, or will he put a permanent end to her life-long dreams? **96m/C VHS.** Deborah Harry, James Russo, Tim Thomerson, Paige French, Grace Zabriskie; ***D:*** Allan Holzman. **TV**

Intimate Strangers 🦴🦴 1/2 **1977** Taut expose on battering and its effects on the family. Weaver and Struthers outshine the material, but the finest performance is a cameo by Douglas as Weaver's irascible aged father. **96m/C VHS.** Dennis Weaver, Sally Struthers, Quinn Cummings, Tyne Daly, Larry Hagman, Rhea Perlman; ***Cameos:*** Melvyn Douglas; ***D:*** John Llewellyn Moxey. **TV**

Intimate Strangers 🦴🦴🦴 1/2 *Confidences trop intimes* **2004 (R)** French suspense thriller in the vein of Alfred Hitchcock. William Faber (Luchini) is visited in his office by a beautiful woman named Anna (Bonnaire), who begins to unload her personal problems, mistaking him for a therapist. William, who is actually a tax consultant, is bewildered but also drawn into Anna's world. Stylish and sophisticated flick excellent makes use of two very talented and mesmerizing leads. **104m/C VHS, DVD.** Sandrine Bonnaire, Fabrice Luchini, Michel Duchaussoy, Anne Brochet, Gilbert Melki, Helene Surgere, Urbain Cancellier, Laurent Gamelon; ***D:*** Patrice Leconte; ***W:*** Patrice Leconte, Jerome Tonnerre; ***C:*** Eduardo Serra; ***M:*** Pascal Esteve.

Into Temptation 🦴🦴 1/2 **2009 (R)** Father John Burlien (Sisto) is hearing confessions when abused call girl Linda (Chenoweth) tells him she's going to commit suicide. Hoping to save her, the priest plunges into a morass of Catholic sin and guilt (over celibacy and his vocation) when he checks out the seedier environs of Minneapolis hoping to find Linda before it's too late. Things don't play out as you might imagine. **95m/C DVD.** Jeremy Sisto, Kristin Chenoweth, Brian Baumgartner, Amy Matthews, Bruce A. Young; ***D:*** Patrick Coyle; ***W:*** Patrick Coyle; ***C:*** David Doyle; ***M:*** Russell Holsapple. **VIDEO**

Into the Arms of Strangers 🦴 1/2 **2007** Several years ago, Andy Barker (Carey) suffered brain damage and memory loss in a car accident. Now some memories are re-surfacing and they seem to have something to do with his hometown. So Andy insists that he and wife Erin (Wade) move back (over her objections), but he soon realizes that he doesn't like what he's finding out. **101m/C DVD.** Ron Carey, April Wade, Juliana Dever, Alison Haislip, Justin Lawrence, Robert T. Bruce, Mark Shady, Lee Perkins; ***D:*** Chris Harris; ***W:*** Chris Harris, Andrew Putnam-Nelson; ***C:*** Chris Harris; ***M:*** Luke McQueen. **VIDEO**

Into the Badlands 🦴🦴 **1992 (R)** Mild thriller presents three suspense tales in "Twilight Zone" fashion, linked by the appearance of a mysterious Man in Black. No, it's not Johnny Cash, but Dern as a sinister bounty hunter in the old west, who inspires strange events on the trail. **89m/C VHS, DVD.** Bruce Dern, Mariel Hemingway, Helen Hunt, Dylan McDermott, Lisa Pelikan, Andrew (Andy) Robinson; ***D:*** Sam Pillsbury; ***W:*** Dick Beebe, Marjorie David, Gordon Dawson. **CABLE**

Into the Blue 🦴🦴 1/2 **1997** Harry Barnett (Thaw) is a bankrupt businessman now working as a caretaker at a friend's estate on the Greek isle of Rhodes. He has a one-nighter with young Englishwoman Heather Mallender (Cruttenden) and when she mysteriously disappears, Harry becomes a suspect. Then he learns she was investigating the drowning death of her sister, which involves people Harry knows, and he returns to London to try and sort out the mess he's in. **120m/C VHS.** *GB* John Thaw, Abigail Cruttenden, Miles Anderson, Michael Culkin, Celia Imrie; ***D:*** Jack Gold. **TV**

Into the Blue 🦴🦴 **2005 (PG-13)** Sam (Alba) works for an entertainment venture, bobbing about in a bikini and feeding sharks all day. Jared (Walker) has a similar affinity to water, earning his keep as a scuba instructor. Together they hunt for buried treasure, instead finding a cocaine stash buried at the bottom of the ocean in a crashed plane. Of course, the drug dealers aren't too happy to have them sniffing around the goods. Amazingly, there is a bit of a plot behind what first appears to be a video swimsuit catalog. Sure, attractive young people in bathing suits are the focus, but flick surprises with a decent dose of adventure, action, suspense, and some interesting underwater scenes. **110m/C DVD, Blu-ray Disc, UMD.** *US* Paul Walker, Jessica Alba, Scott Caan, Ashley Scott, Josh Brolin, James Frain, Tyson Beckford; ***D:*** John Stockwell; ***W:*** Matt Johnson; ***C:*** Shane Hurlbut; ***M:*** Paul Haslinger.

Into the Blue 2: The Reef 🦴 **2009** Scuba divers Sebastian (Carmack) and Dani (Vandervoort) are hired by suspicious Eurotrash couple Azra (Thomason) and Carlton (Anders) to search a dangerous Hawaiian reef for Christopher Columbus' lost treasure ship. But really the duo are interested in some cargo that smugglers were forced to abandon. Low-rent and uninteresting with two bland, blonde, albeit hard-bodied, leads. **92m/C DVD.** Chris Carmack, Marsha Thomason, David Anders, Mircea Monroe, Laura Vandervoort, Michael Graziadel; ***D:*** Stephen Herek; ***W:*** Mitchell Kapner; ***C:*** Thomas Yatsko; ***M:*** Robert Duncan. **VIDEO**

Into the Darkness 🦴 1/2 **1986** In the world of fashion models, a maniacal, demented killer stalks his prey. **90m/C VHS.** John Saint Ryan, Donald Pleasence, Ronald Lacey; ***D:*** David Kent-Watson; ***W:*** John Saint Ryan.

Into the Fire 🦴 **1988 (R)** Thriller about a young drifter who, against the backdrop of a Canadian winter, happens upon a roadside lodge and diner, where he gets involved in sex and murder. Title gives a good idea of what to do with this one. **88m/C VHS, DVD.** *CA* Susan Anspach, Art Hindle, Olivia D'Abo, Lee Montgomery; ***D:*** Graeme Campbell.

Into the Fire 🦴 **2005** Ernest, overwrought, and depressing drama examines the crack up of police lieutenant Walter Hartwig Jr. (Flanery) who's with the NYC Harbor Patrol. Bad times ensue when a jumbo jet crashes into the ocean before it can land at Kennedy Airport and Walter searches for survivors. Walter has family issues (including a sister who drowned) that lead him to try to comfort distraught June (Williams) and Catrina (Kanakaredes). **90m/C DVD.** *US* Melina Kanakaredes, JoBeth Williams, Sean Patrick Flanery, Ron McLarty, Lydia Grace Jordan, Ed Lauter, Pablo Schreiber, Talia Balsam; ***D:*** Michael Phelan; ***W:*** Michael Phelan; ***C:*** Christopher Norr; ***M:*** Steve O'Reilly, Matt Anthony, Steve O'Reilly.

Into the Homeland 🦴🦴 **1987** Seasoned ex-cop (Boothe) infiltrates a white supremacist group which had kidnapped his teenage daughter. Failed "message" about neo-nazi ethics, but good confrontation between Boothe and his son (Howell) make this so-so viewing. **95m/C VHS.** Powers Boothe, C. Thomas Howell, Paul LeMat; ***D:*** Leslie Linka Glatter. **CABLE**

Into the Night 🦴🦴 **1985 (R)** Campy, off-beat thriller about a middle-aged, jilted deadbeat (Goldblum), who meets a beautiful woman (Pfeiffer) when she suddenly drops onto the hood of his car, with a relentless gang of Iranians pursuing. During their search through L.A. and other parts of California for the one person who can help her out of this mess, a whole crew of Hollywood directors make cameo appearances, making this a delight for film buffs, but occasionally tedious for general audiences. B.B. King sings the title song. **115m/C VHS, DVD.** Jeff Goldblum, Michelle Pfeiffer, David Bowie, Carl Perkins, Richard Farnsworth, Dan Aykroyd, Paul Mazursky, Roger Vadim, Irene Papas, Bruce McGill, Vera Miles, Clu Gulager, Don Steel, Kathryn Harrold; ***Cameos:*** Jim Henson, Paul Bartel, David Cronenberg, Jack Arnold, Jonathan Demme, Lawrence Kasdan, Amy Heckerling, Donald Siegel, Richard Franklin, Colin Higgins, Andrew Marton; ***D:*** John Landis; ***W:*** Ron Koslow; ***M:*** Ira Newborn.

Into the Sun 🦴 1/2 **1992 (R)** Hall plays a Hollywood star who encounters real-life danger while hanging out with an Air Force pilot (Pare) to prepare for an upcoming role. Spectacular aerial scenes steal the show, which isn't hard to do in this lackluster movie. **101m/C VHS.** Anthony Michael Hall, Michael Pare, Terry Kiser, Deborah Maria Moore; ***D:*** Fritz Kiersch; ***W:*** John Brancato, Michael Ferris.

Into the West 🦴🦴🦴 **1992 (PG)** Enchanting horse tale set amid the mystic isle of Eire. Brooding, drunken Riley (Byrne), once the leader of a band of travelers (the Irish version of gypsies), leaves the road after his wife's death and settles in a Dublin slum with his two boys. The boys are enraptured when their grandfather turns up with a beautiful white horse, but their happiness is shattered when the police take it away. Boys and horse eventually escape in a wild ride across Ireland and into the west. Spiritual and mythic, with an awe-inspiring performance by the horse. Fitzgerald and Conroy make a run at best performances by kids, while Byrne is convincingly sodden and sulky. Meany and Barkin shine in small parts as sibling travellers. **97m/C VHS, DVD.** *IR* Gabriel Byrne, Ellen Barkin, Ciaran Fitzgerald, Ruaidhri Conroy, David Kelly, Colm Meaney; ***D:*** Mike Newell; ***W:*** Jim Sheridan; ***M:*** Patrick Doyle.

Into the Wild 🦴🦴🦴 **2007 (R)** Director Sean Penn tells the true story of Christopher McCandless' (Hirsch) heady journey from 22-year-old middle class college grad to a state of romanticized independence in wild and free Alaska, where McCandless finds the wilderness as brutally indifferent to his high-minded ideals as it is stunningly beautiful. Adapted from Jon Krakauer's book of the same name, the film follows McCandless from Virginia through the American West, where he dons the moniker "Alexander Supertramp." Scenes cut between his journey, his last weeks in the wild, and his personal journal entries to effectively paint a picture of McCandless' thoughts and motivations as he tries to drop off the grid. Quintessential American film for adventurers and non-adventurers alike. **140m/C DVD, HD DVD.** *US* Emile Hirsch, Marcia Gay Harden, William Hurt, Jena Malone, Catherine Keener, Vince Vaughn, Kristen Stewart, Hal Holbrook, Brian Dierker; ***D:*** Sean Penn; ***W:*** Sean Penn; ***C:*** Eric Gautier; ***M:*** Michael Brook, Edward Vedder, Kaki King. Golden Globes '08: Song ("Guaranteed").

Into Thin Air 🦴🦴🦴 **1985** A mother searches tirelessly for her college bound son who disappeared on a cross-country drive. Well-done TV drama with a good performance from Burstyn. **100m/C VHS, DVD.** Ellen Burstyn, Robert Prosky, Sam Robards, Tate Donovan, Caroline McWilliams, Nicholas Pryor, John Dennis Johnston; ***D:*** Roger Young; ***W:*** George Rubio, Larry Cohen; ***M:*** Brad Fiedel. **TV**

Into Thin Air: Death on Everest 🦴🦴 **1997** Based on the book by Jon Krakauer (played in the telepic by McDonald) about the tragic May, 1996 climbing expedition to Mount Everest that resulted in the deaths of eight climbers. **90m/C VHS, DVD.** Peter Horton, Christopher McDonald, Nathaniel Parker, Richard Jenkins; ***D:*** Robert Markowitz; ***W:*** Robert J. Avrech. **TV**

Intolerable Cruelty ✐✐ 1/2 **2003 (PG-13)** The Coens are back with another impeccably cast and written comedy. This time they tackle the genre of screwball comedy, with the formidable help of stars Clooney and Zeta-Jones. He is Miles Massey, an unbeatable divorce attorney, and she's Marilyn Rexroth, a gold-digging serial divorcee. They meet when Miles is hired by Marilyn's soon-to-be-ex, Rex, who's been caught cheating but doesn't want to pay up. When Miles beats her out of her settlement, they begin a dance of mutual attraction and escalating acts of-...well, you know. In addition to the genuine movie-star spark of the leads, plenty of hilarious supporting characters inhabit the Coens' over-the-top L.A. landscape. Film's fascination with the characters' charming amorality results in great moments, but contributes to a weak ending by draining the warmth that the romance portion requires. **100m/C VHS, DVD.** *US* George Clooney, Catherine Zeta-Jones, Geoffrey Rush, Cedric the Entertainer, Edward Herrmann, Richard Jenkins, Billy Bob Thornton, Paul Adelstein, Irwin Keyes, Julia Duffy, Tom Aldredge, Jonathan Hadary, Stacey Travis, Royce D. Applegate; ***D:*** Joel Coen; ***W:*** Joel Coen, Ethan Coen, Robert Ramsey, Matthew Stone; ***C:*** Roger Deakins; ***M:*** Carter Burwell.

Intolerance ✐✐✐✐ **1916** Griffith's largest film in every aspect. An interwoven, four-story epic about human intolerance, with segments set in Babylon, ancient Judea, and Paris. One of the cinema's grandest follies, and greatest achievements. Silent with music score; B&W with some restored color footage. **175m/B VHS, DVD.** Lillian Gish, Mae Marsh, Constance Talmadge, Bessie Love, Elmer Clifton, Erich von Stroheim, Eugene Pallette, Seena Owen, Alfred Paget; ***D:*** D.W. Griffith; ***W:*** D.W. Griffith, Tod Browning; ***C:*** Billy (G.W.) Bitzer, Karl Brown. Natl. Film Reg. '89.

Intrigue ✐✐ 1/2 **1990 (PG)** Former CIA agent (Loggia) defects to the KGB, but wants to return to the U.S. when he realizes he has a progressive illness. Underground agent and old buddy (Glenn) is recruited with orders to smuggle his former colleague out. Tension continues throughout as murder comes along with the orders. Loads of suspense and twist ending in this nail-biter. **96m/C VHS.** Scott Glenn, Robert Loggia, William Atherton, Martin Shaw, Cherie Lunghi, Eleanor Bron; ***D:*** David Drury. **TV**

Intrigue and Love ✐✐ *Kabale und Liebe* **1959** Luise, who's the daughter of the town musician, is in love with Ferdinand, the son of President von Walter. Von Walter wants his son to marry the Duke's mistress, in order to increase his own influence. Finding their romance impossible, the lovers come up with a drastic solution. Based on the drama by Friedrich Schiller. German with subtitles. **109m/B VHS.** *GE* Otto Mellies, Karola Ebeling, Wolf Kaiser, Marion Van de Kamp, Willi Schwabe; ***D:*** Martin Hellberg; ***W:*** Martin Hellberg; ***C:*** Karl Plintzner; ***M:*** Wilhelm Neef.

Introducing Dorothy Dandridge ✐✐✐ **1999 (R)** Beautiful, sexy singer/actress Dorothy Dandridge (Berry) was the first African-American woman to be nominated for a best actress Oscar for her title role in 1955's "Carmen Jones." Ten years later, at the age of 42, she was dead from an overdose of antidepressants after suffering a lifetime of tragedies—an abusive childhood, two failed marriages, a brain-damaged child, tumultuous affairs, limited career choices, and bad financial decisions. Based on the book by Dandridge's loyal manager, Earl Mills. **115m/C VHS, DVD.** Halle Berry, Brent Spiner, Obba Babatunde, Loretta Devine, Cynda Williams, LaTanya Richardson Jackson, Tamara Taylor, Klaus Maria Brandauer, D.B. Sweeney, William Atherton; ***D:*** Martha Coolidge; ***W:*** Scott Abbott, Shonda Rhimes; ***C:*** Robbie Greenberg; ***M:*** Elmer Bernstein. **CABLE**

Introducing the Dwights ✐✐ 1/2 *Clubland* **2007 (R)** Jean Dwight (Blethyn) and grown sons Tim (Chittenden) and Mark (Wilson) live in Sydney, Australia, where Jean laments her lost career as a comedienne, which she left behind in her native England after relocating with ex-husband and one-hit-wonder musician John (Holden). Self-absorbed Jean works in a cafeteria by day while attempting to resurrect her comedy career by night, leaving little room for helping the boys sort out adulthood. Mark, brain damaged at birth, is addled and precocious. Tom, overcoming his shyness enough to pursue romance with blonde beauty Jill (Booth), sparks conflicts. Feel-good comedy drama strikes a good balance. **105m/C DVD.** *AU* Brenda Blethyn, Frankie J. Holden, Rebecca Gibney, Philip Quast, Russell Dykstra, Khan Chittenden, Emma Booth, Katie Wall; ***D:*** Cherie Nowlan; ***W:*** Keith Thompson; ***C:*** Mark Wareham; ***M:*** Martin Armiger.

Intruder ✐✐ *Les Passagers* **1976** A man and his stepson are terrorized by a stranger in a panel truck as they travel from Rome to Paris. Adapted from a novel by Dean R. Koontz. **98m/C VHS.** *FR* Jean-Louis Trintignant, Mireille Darc, Adolfo Celi, Bernard Fresson; ***D:*** Serge Leroy; ***W:*** Christopher Frank; ***M:*** Claude Bolling.

Intruder ✐✐ **1988 (R)** A psychotic killer stalks an all-night convenience store shopping for fresh meat (customers beware). Slasher movie fans should get a kick out of the plot twist at the end. **90m/C VHS, DVD.** Elizabeth Cox, Renee Estevez, Alvy Moore; ***D:*** Scott Spiegel; ***W:*** Lawrence Bender.

The Intruder ✐✐✐ *L'Intrus* **2004** Spurred on by a mild heart attack, Louis Trebor (Subor), a troubled and aging loner living in a forest near the French-Swiss border, sets out on a journey to bring meaning to his self-serving life. He first arranges a black market heart transplant then travels to South Korea to purchase a boat, which he sails to a remote island near Tahiti were he lived and fathered a son many years prior. As his health begins to deteriorate, his dreams, visions, memories and reality all blur to create a metaphor for Louis's inner turmoil. Denis creates a stunning piece dripping with impressionistic imagery. **130m/C DVD.** Michel Subor, Beatrice Dalle, Gregoire Colin, Florence Loiret-Caille, Yekaterina (Katia) Golubeva; ***D:*** Claire Denis; ***W:*** Claire Denis, Jean-Pol Fargeau; ***C:*** Agnes Godard; ***M:*** S. A. Staples.

Intruder in the Dust ✐✐✐ 1/2 **1949** A small southern community develops a lynch mob mentality when a black man is accused of killing a white man. Powerful, but largely ignored portrait of race relations in the South. Solid performances from the whole cast; filmed in Mississippi. Adapted from a novel by William Faulkner. **87m/B VHS.** David Brian, Claude Jarman Jr., Juano Hernandez, Porter Hall, Elizabeth Patterson; ***D:*** Clarence Brown; ***C:*** Robert L. Surtees.

Intruder Within ✐ **1981** Half-baked thriller about crew on an isolated oil rig in Antarctica who, while drilling, unearth a nasty creature that goes around terrorizing the frost-bitten men and occasional stray woman. **91m/C VHS.** Chad Everett, Joseph Bottoms, Jennifer Warren; ***D:*** Peter Carter. **TV**

Intruders ✐✐ **1992** Follows the story of three people who have unexplained lapses of time in their lives which they eventually believe are connected to visits by aliens. The three are brought together by a skeptical psychiatrist. The aliens are your typical bugged-eyed, white-faced spooks but part of the film is genuinely unsettling. **162m/C VHS.** Richard Crenna, Mare Winningham, Susan Blakely, Ben Vereen, Steven Berkoff, Daphne Ashbrook; ***D:*** Dan Curtis.

Intruso ✐✐ 1/2 *Intruder* **1993** Gloomy story set in a coastal city in northern Spain. Luisa (Abril) spots her destitute ex-husband Angel (Arias) and persuades him to stay with her and her new family, husband Ramiro (Valero)—once Angel's good friend—and their two young children. Angel turns out to be terminally ill and decides to wreak vengeance on Ramiro by reclaiming Luisa for himself. In Spanish with English subtitles. **85m/C VHS.** *SP* Victoria Abril, Imanol Arias, Antonio Valero; ***D:*** Vicente Aranda; ***W:*** Vicente Aranda, Alvaro del Amo.

Inugami ✐✐✐ **2001** Inugami (literal translation "dog spirit") are familiar spirits created by burying a dog up to his neck and letting it starve to death. Their owners receive wealth and success, at the expense of being shunned by other people. But the Inugami are fickle, and if their owners offend them they will turn on them instead of their enemies. Akira Nutahara is a young grade-school teacher who gets transferred to a school in a remote mountain village. There he falls in love with lonely spinster and paper maker Miki Bonomiya. It isn't long before he discovers the Bonomiya family is shunned due to their connection to the Inugami, and because of other, darker family secrets. **106m/C DVD.** *JP* Yuki Amami, Atsuro Watabe, Kenichi Yajima, Keiko Awaji, Koichi Sato, Eugene Harada, Shiho Fujimara, Kazuhiro Yamaji, Kanako Fukaura, Shion Machida, Masato Irie, Makoto Tagashi, Torahiko Yamada, Miyu Watase; ***D:*** Masato Harada; ***W:*** Masato Harada, Masako Bando; ***C:*** Junichi Fujisawa; ***M:*** Takatsugu Muramatsu.

Invader ✐✐ **1991 (R)** When a news reporter is sent to cover a mysterious massacre, he begins to realize that the culprits are vicious aliens thirsty for blood...and now they're after him! **95m/C VHS, DVD.** Hans Bachman, A. Thomas Smith, Rich Foucheux, John Cooke, Robert Diedermann, Allison Sheehy, Ralph Bluemke; ***D:*** Phillip Cook.

The Invader ✐✐ 1/2 **1996** Schoolteacher Annie (Young) discovers she's pregnant by a mystery man (Cross), who turns out to be an alien from a dying race—and Annie's child may be their salvation. Only her ex-cop boyfriend (Baldwin) is on their trail as is an intergalactic bounty hunter (Mancuso). This one is on the romance rather than the action side. **97m/C VHS, DVD.** Sean Young, Ben Cross, Nick Mancuso, Daniel Baldwin; ***D:*** Mark Rosman; ***W:*** Mark Rosman; ***C:*** Gregory Middleton; ***M:*** Todd Hayen. **VIDEO**

The Invaders ✐✐ *Erik the Conqueror; Gli Invasori; La Ruee Des Vikings; Fury of the Vikings* **1963** Two Viking brothers battle each other and the Britons. **88m/C VHS.** *FR IT* Cameron Mitchell, George Ardisson, Andrea Checchi, Francoise Christophe, Joe Robinson; ***D:*** Mario Bava; ***M:*** Les Baxter.

The Invaders ✐✐ 1/2 **1995** TV mini is an updated continuation of the 1967 sci-fi series that finds the pollution-loving aliens gradually conquering Earth by allowing humans to destroy their own ecosystem (which we're so good at anyway). Bewildered hero Nolan Wood (Bakula) is trying to get everyone to believe in the alien invasion but since he's just gotten out of prison, it's an uphill climb. Still, the aliens (lead by effectively evil Thomas) would like to permanently shut Nolan up. Thinnes, who starred in the original series, briefly reprises his role as David Vincent. **180m/C VHS.** Scott Bakula, Richard Thomas, DeLane Matthews, Terence Knox, Elizabeth Pena, Raoul Trujillo, Richard Belzer, Jon Polito, Roy Thinnes, Jon Cypher, Todd Susman, Jack Kehler, Elinor Donahue; ***D:*** Paul Shapiro; ***W:*** James Dott; ***C:*** Alar Kivilo; ***M:*** Joseph Vitarelli.

Invaders from Mars ✐✐ 1/2 **1953** Young boy cries "martian" in this sci-fi cheapy classic. He can't convince the townspeople of this invasion because they've already been possessed by the alien beings. His parents are zapped by the little green things first, making this perhaps an allegory for the missing Eisenhower/Stepford years. Includes previews of coming attractions from classic science-fiction films. Remade in 1986 by Tobe Hooper. **78m/C VHS, DVD.** Helena Carter, Arthur Franz, Jimmy Hunt, Leif Erickson, Hillary Brooke, Morris Ankrum, Lock Martin; ***D:*** William Cameron Menzies; ***W:*** Richard Blake, John Tucker Battle; ***C:*** John Seitz; ***M:*** Raoul Kraushaar.

Invaders from Mars ✐ 1/2 **1986 (PG)** A high-tech remake of Menzies' 1953 semi-classic about a Martian invasion perceived only by one young boy and a sympathetic (though hysterical) school nurse, played by mother and son Black and Carson. Instant camp. **102m/C VHS, DVD.** Hunter Carson, Karen Black, Louise Fletcher, Laraine Newman, Timothy Bottoms, Bud Cort, Dale Dye; ***D:*** Tobe Hooper; ***W:*** Dan O'Bannon, Don Jakoby; ***C:*** Daniel Pearl; ***M:*** Sylvester Levay, David Storrs, Christopher Young.

Invasion ✐✐ 1/2 **1965** A hospital opens its doors to an accident victim, and his attractive female visitors don't seem sympathetic to the idea of a long hospital stay. Turns out he's an escaped alien prisoner, and the alien babes, intent on intergalactic extradition, place a force field around the hospital and demand his return. Early effort of director Bridges, who later did "The Shooting Party." Interesting, creepy, atmospheric, with very cool camera moves. **82m/B VHS.** *GB* Edward Judd, Yoko Tani, Valerie Gearon, Lyndon Brook, Tsai Chin, Barrie Ingham; ***D:*** Alan Bridges.

Invasion! ✐✐ 1/2 *Top of the Food Chain* **1999 (PG-13)** Deliberately tacky and frequently amusing spoof of alien invasion flicks. Atomic scientist Dr. Karel Lamonte (Scott) comes to the town of Exceptional Vista just after the local TV tower is hit by a big meteor. It's hard to tell if aliens have invaded since the townspeople are so weird to begin with, but they have. And they turn out to be the cannibalistic kind who take to munching on the locals. Oh, and it turns out that TV is the key to the aliens' destruction. **99m/C VHS, DVD.** *CA* Campbell Scott, Fiona Loewi, Tom Everett Scott, Hardee T. Lineham, Bernard Behrens, Nigel Bennett, Peter Donaldson, Robert Bockstael, Lorry Ayers, Ron Gabriel, James Allodi, Maggie Butterfield, Kathryn Kirkpatrick; ***D:*** John Paizs; ***W:*** Phil Bedard, Larry Lalonde; ***C:*** Bill Wong; ***M:*** David Krystal.

The Invasion ✐ 1/2 **2007 (PG-13)** In this "Body Snatchers" for the 21st century, Kidman and friends must fight infection by an alien species that takes hold while people are asleep, leaving zombies with no individual thought and no conflict. The only way to prevent the infection is to stay awake, which leads to sleep-deprived paranoia as they struggle to fight the alien menace. Never manages to settle on a consistent theme or tone, as director Hirschbiegel's original version was extensively reshot and recut by the Wachowski/McTeigue team. The end result is a movie that doesn't make any sense, switches from moody thriller to absurd high-impact actioner with no warning, and lacks any standout performances to redeem it. The worst of many versions of the classic "Invasion of the Body Snatchers" story. **93m/C DVD, Blu-ray Disc, HD DVD.** *US* Nicole Kidman, Daniel Craig, Jeremy Northam, Jackson Bond, Jeffrey Wright, Veronica Cartwright, Malin Akerman, John M. Jackson, Josef Sommer, Celia Weston, Jeff Wincott, Alexis Raben, Roger Rees; ***D:*** Oliver Hirschbiegel; ***W:*** David Kajganich; ***C:*** Rainer Klausmann; ***M:*** John Ottman.

Invasion: Earth ✐✐ 1/2 **1998** Britain's Royal Air Force and U.S. Air Force officers discover that two alien races have invaded earth and only one of them is amenable to letting the current inhabitants remain. British sci-fi miniseries on 3 cassettes. **270m/C VHS.** *GB* Fred Ward, Maggie O'Neill, Phyllis Logan, Vincent Regan; ***D:*** Richard Laxton, Patrick Lau. **TV**

Invasion Earth: The Aliens Are Here! ✐ **1987** A cheap spoof of monster movies, as an insectoid projectionist takes over the minds of a movie audience. Clips of Godzilla, Mothra and other beasts are interpolated. **84m/C VHS, DVD.** Janice Fabian, Christian Lee; ***D:*** George Maitland.

Invasion Force ✐ **1990** A terrorist army parachutes into a remote region where a film crew is preparing to set up for an action movie. The moviemakers must scare away the terrorists with their smokepots and blanks. Sounds promising, but proves to be as empty as the movie props used to scare the terrorists. **93m/C VHS.** Richard Lynch, David "Shark" Fralick, Renee Cline, Douglas Harter, Graham Times, Angie Synodis; ***D:*** David A. Prior.

The Invasion of Carol Enders ✐ 1/2 **1974** A woman, almost killed by a prowler, awakens with an expanded consciousness, and tries to convince her husband that her near death wasn't an accident. **72m/C VHS.** Meredith Baxter, Christopher Connelly, Charles Aidman; ***D:*** Burt Brinckerhoff; ***W:*** Gene R. Kearney; ***M:*** Robert Colbert.

The Invasion of Johnson County ✐✐ **1976** TV movie based on the events of the Johnson County War in 1892. Bostonian Sam Lowell (Bixby) heads to Wyoming and joins with a group of homesteaders who are fighting off cattle barons determined to stop the interlopers from settling in. **100m/C DVD.** Bill Bixby, Bo Hopkins, John Hillerman, Billy Green Bush, Stephen Elliott, M. Emmet Walsh, Lee De Broux; ***D:*** Jerry Jameson; ***W:*** Nicholas E. Baehr; ***C:*** Rexford Metz; ***M:*** Peter Carpenter, Mike Post. **TV**

Invasion of Privacy 🦴🦴 **1992 (R)** Alex is a psycho prison inmate obsessed with high profile journalist, Hilary. When Hilary interviews Alex for a magazine cover story, his obsession only grows stronger. Then Alex gets paroled and goes to work for Hilary. When he discovers Hilary isn't interested in him, Alex turns his fantasies to her daughter, who has no notion what she's getting into. An unrated version is also available. **95m/C VHS.** Robby Benson, Jennifer O'Neill, Lydie Denier, Ian Ogilvy, John Agar; ***D:*** Kevin Meyer; ***W:*** Kevin Meyer. **CABLE**

Invasion of Privacy 🦴🦴 **1996 (R)** Some hot-button topics take the thriller route. When Theresa (Avital) becomes pregnant, she discovers her boyfriend Josh (Schaech) is seriously unbalanced. She decides on an abortion but retreats for some quiet time to an isolated lakeside cabin. Mistake—the expectant dad shows up and holds her prisoner until Theresa is too far along to terminate the pregnancy. When Josh finally releases her, Theresa heads for the cops and charges him with kidnapping. He gets a hot female lawyer (Rampling), who turns the media attention into making him a cause celebre for parental rights. Once the baby is born, Josh is also detemined to gain custody—by whatever means necessary. **94m/C VHS.** Johnathon Schaech, Mili Avital, David Keith, Charlotte Rampling, Naomi Campbell, R.G. Armstrong; ***D:*** Anthony Hickox; ***W:*** Larry Cohen; ***C:*** Peter Wunstorf; ***M:*** Angelo Badalamenti.

Invasion of the Animal People WOOF! *Terror in the Midnight Sun; Space Invasion of Lapland; Horror in the Midnight Sun; Space Invasion from Lapland* **1962** Hairy monster from outer space attacks Lapland. Narrated by Carradine, the only American in the cast. Pretty silly. **73m/B VHS, DVD.** *SW* Robert Burton, Barbara Wilson, John Carradine; ***D:*** Jerry Warren, Virgil W. Vogel; ***W:*** Arthur C. Pierce; ***C:*** Hilding Bladh; ***M:*** Harry Arnold, Allan Johansson.

Invasion of the Bee Girls 🦴🦴🦴 *Graveyard Tramps* **1973** California girls are mysteriously transformed into deadly nymphomaniacs in this delightful campy science fiction romp. Written by Meyer who later directed "Star Trek II: The Wrath of Khan." **85m/C VHS, DVD.** William (Bill) Smith, Anitra Ford, Cliff Osmond, Victoria Vetri, Wright King, Ben Hammer, Cliff Emmich, Anna Aries, Tom Pittman; ***D:*** Denis Sanders; ***W:*** Nicholas Meyer; ***C:*** Gary Graver; ***M:*** Charles Bernstein.

Invasion of the Blood Farmers WOOF! **1972 (PG)** In a small New York town, members of an ancient Druidic cult murder young women, taking their blood in the hope of finding the precise, rare blood type to keep their queen alive. A real woofer. **86m/C VHS, DVD.** Norman Kelley, Tanna Hunter, Bruce Detrick, Jack Neubeck, Cythia Fleming, Paul Craig Jennings; ***D:*** Ed Adlum; ***W:*** Ed Adlum, Ed Kelleher.

Invasion of the Body Snatchers 🦴🦴🦴🦴 *Sleep No More* **1956** The one and only post-McCarthy paranoid sci-fi epic, where a small California town is infiltrated by pods from outer space that replicate and replace humans. A chilling, genuinely frightening exercise in nightmare dislocation. Based upon a novel by Jack Finney. Remade in 1978. **80m/B VHS, DVD.** Kevin McCarthy, Dana Wynter, Carolyn Jones, King Donovan, Larry Gates, Jean Willes, Whit Bissell, Richard Deacon, Pat O'Malley, Sam Peckinpah, Donald Siegel, Dabbs Greer, Whit Bissell; ***D:*** Donald Siegel; ***W:*** Daniel Mainwaring, Sam Peckinpah; ***C:*** Ellsworth Fredericks; ***M:*** Carmen Dragon. Natl. Film Reg. '94.

Invasion of the Body Snatchers 🦴🦴🦴 1/2 **1978 (PG)** One of the few instances where a remake is an improvement on the original, which was itself a classic. This time, the "pod people" are infesting San Francisco, with only a small group of people aware of the invasion. A ceaselessly inventive, creepy version of the alien-takeover paradigm, with an intense and winning performance by Sutherland. Features cameos by Don Siegel and Kevin McCarthy from the original, as well as an uncredited appearance by Robert Duvall. **115m/C VHS, DVD.** Donald Sutherland, Brooke Adams, Veronica Cartwright, Leonard Nimoy, Jeff Goldblum, Kevin McCarthy, Donald Siegel, Art Hindle, Robert Duvall; ***D:*** Philip Kaufman; ***W:*** W.D. Richter; ***C:*** Michael Chapman.

Invasion of the Body Stealers WOOF! *Thin Air; The Body Stealers* **1969 (PG)** Aliens are thought to be the captors when sky-divers begin vanishing in mid-air. Uneven sci-fi with nothing going for it. **115m/C VHS.** *GB* George Sanders, Maurice Evans, Patrick Allen; ***D:*** Gerry Levy.

Invasion of the Girl Snatchers WOOF! **1973** Aliens from another planet, in cahoots with a cult kingpin, subdue young earth girls and force them to undergo bizarre acts that may just rob them of their dignity. Save a bit of your own dignity by staying away. Cheap look, cheap feel, cheap thrills. **90m/C VHS.** Elizabeth Rush, Ele Grigsby, David Roster; ***D:*** Lee Jones.

Invasion of the Saucer Men 🦴 *Hell Creatures; Spacemen Saturday Night* **1957** Suburban teenagers (Terrell, Castillo) are detained by a little green man at lovers lane. When they return with police to the scene, only the corpse of the town drunk (Gorshin) remains. Fortunately, the dead man's roommate (Osborn) believes them but the trio must convince authorities before the alien creatures multiply and take over the world. **69m/B VHS.** Steven Terrell, Gloria Castillo, Frank Gorshin, Lyn Osborn, Ed Nelson, Angelo Rossitto, Raymond Hatton, Russ Bender, Paul Blaisdell, Kelly Thordsen; ***D:*** Edward L. Cahn; ***W:*** Al Martin; ***C:*** Frederick E. West; ***M:*** Ronald Stein.

Invasion of the Space Preachers 🦴🦴 *Strangest Dreams: Invasion of the Space Preachers* **1990** Hideous creatures from outer space arrive on Earth with plans for conquest. Led by the seemingly human Reverend Lash, they prey on the innocent and trusting, fleecing God-fearing folk out of their hard earned cash! **100m/C VHS.** Jim Wolfe, Guy Nelson, Eliska Hahn, Gary Brown, Jesse Johnson, John Riggs, Jimmie Walker; ***D:*** Daniel Boyd; ***W:*** Daniel Boyd; ***C:*** Bill Hogan; ***M:*** Michael Lipton.

Invasion of the Star Creatures WOOF! **1963** Barely good for a giggle, this sci-fi comedy is a clunker in every possible way. A couple of dimwit army privates get separated from their patrol while investigating a mysterious crater. They are captured by VegeMonsters, taken to a spaceship hidden in a cave, and find the aliens are your typical Amazonian babes who just need a little earthly smooching to get over that whole invasion thing. Ewwwww. **70m/B DVD.** Frankie Ray, Robert Ball, Gloria Victor, Dolores Reed, Mark Ferris; ***D:*** Bruno VeSota; ***W:*** Jonathan Haze; ***C:*** Basil Bradbury; ***M:*** Jack Cookerly, Elliott Fisher.

Invasion of the Vampires 🦴 *La Invasion de Los Vampiros* **1961** Burrito bat fest has Count Frankenhausen doing his vampire thing in a small, 16th century village. Atmospheric sets are highlight. Not a good substitute for No Doze. **78m/B VHS.** *MX* Carlos Agosti, Rafael Etienne, Bertha Moss, Tito Junco, Erna Martha Bauman, Fernando Soto Mantequilla, Enrique Garcia Alvarez, David Reynoso; ***D:*** Miguel Morayta; ***W:*** Miguel Morayta.

Invasion of the Zombies 🦴 **1961** Bare-fisted wrestler Santo faces of brace of zombies in order to prove that men with short necks can hug other men and still be mucho macho. **85m/B VHS.** *MX* Santo; ***D:*** Benito Alazraki.

Invasion U.S.A. 🦴 1/2 **1952** Cheap Red Scare movie using tons of stock footage showing actual bombings and air battles. O'Herlihy is a stranger who visits a New York bar and convinces the patrons that the H-bomb has been unleashed on America, while Mohr romances Castle. Full of propaganda and overacting. Based on a story by Robert Smith and Franz Spencer. **73m/B VHS, DVD.** Gerald Mohr, Peggy Castle, Dan O'Herlihy, Robert Bice, Tom Kennedy, Phyllis Coates, Erik Blythe, Wade Crosby, William Schallert, Noel Neill; ***D:*** Alfred E. Green; ***W:*** Robert Smith; ***C:*** John L. "Jack" Russell; ***M:*** Albert Glasser.

Invasion U.S.A. 🦴 **1985 (R)** A mercenary defends nothing less than the entire country against Russian terrorists landing in Florida and looking for condos. A record-setting amount of people killed. Count them—it's not like you'll miss anything important. Norris is a bit less animated than a wooden Indian, and the acting is more painful to endure than the violence. Glasnost saved the movie industry from additional paranoia movies of this kind. **108m/C VHS, DVD.** Chuck Norris, Richard Lynch, Melissa Prophet, Alex Colon, Billy Drago; ***D:*** Joseph Zito; ***W:*** James Bruner; ***C:*** Joao Fernandes; ***M:*** Jay Chattaway.

Inventing the Abbotts 🦴🦴 **1997 (R)** Appealing cast populates this sleepy, bittersweet coming-of-age story set in small town Illinois in 1957. Alice (Going), Eleanor (Connelly) and Pamela (Tyler) are the lovely daughters of wealthy Lloyd Abbott (Patton) who's determined that they'll marry well despite the temptations offered by the two working-class Holt boys. Surly stud Jacey (Crudup) holds a grudge against Lloyd for possibly cheating his deceased father in a business deal and causing whispers about his schoolteacher mother Helen's (Baker) reputation, while sweet-natured younger brother Doug (Phoenix) has his romantic ideals fixed on Pamela, who loves him in return. Not memorable, but not a complete waste of time, either. Based on the story by Sue Miller. **110m/C VHS, DVD.** Billy Crudup, Joaquin Rafael (Leaf) Phoenix, Liv Tyler, Will Patton, Kathy Baker, Jennifer Connelly, Joanna Going, Barbara Williams; ***D:*** Pat O'Connor; ***W:*** Ken Hixon; ***C:*** Kenneth Macmillan; ***M:*** Michael Kamen.

The Invention of Lying 🦴🦴 1/2 *This Side of the Truth* **2009 (PG-13)** Jobless filmmaker Mark Bellison (Gervais) lives in a rather drab world where lying, in all its forms (embellishment, flattery, storytelling, religion, and presumably politics) has yet to be discovered. During the course of a particularly bad day, Mark discovers that the untruth can set you free. Interesting and funny concept takes on some big issues in an amusing way, but falters after a brilliant opening. Gervais leavens some potentially offensive (to some) and cringe-worthy spots with genuine warmth and, well, honesty. **99m/C DVD.** *US* Ricky Gervais, Jennifer Garner, Fionnula Flanagan, Rob Lowe, Jonah Hill, Tina Fey, Christopher Guest, Jason Bateman, Jeffrey Tambor, Louis CK, Stephanie March, Philip Seymour Hoffman, Nathan Corddry, Conner Rayburn, Edward Norton; ***D:*** Ricky Gervais, Matt Robinson; ***W:*** Ricky Gervais, Matt Robinson; ***C:*** Tim Suhrstedt; ***M:*** Tim Atack; ***Nar:*** Patrick Stewart.

Investigation 🦴🦴 1/2 **1979** A Frenchman plans to murder his wife so he can marry his pregnant mistress, guaranteeing an heir. Subtle study of small town people so concerned with their own welfare that the dirty deeds of the lead character might be overlooked. Fine performances and story development make this worth investigating. In French with English subtitles. **116m/C VHS.** *FR* Victor Lanoux, Valerie Mairesse; ***D:*** Etienne Perier.

The Inveterate Bachelor 🦴🦴 1/2 *I Zitelloni* **1958** Young sales clerk Marcello ignores the advice of 'Professor' Luigi and decides to marry his landlady's beautiful daughter. But he's soon driven crazy by his new wife and mother-in-law and is arrested for murder. Don't believe everything you see—this is a comedy. Italian with subtitles. **98m/B DVD.** *IT* Vittorio De Sica, Walter Chiari, Rina Morelli, Maria Luz Galicia, Mario Riva; ***D:*** Giorgio Bianchi; ***W:*** Silvio Amadio, Antonio Amurri; ***C:*** Manuel Berenguer; ***M:*** Italo Greco.

Invictus 🦴🦴🦴 **2009 (PG-13)** Director Eastwood tells the true story of political prisoner-turned-President Nelson Mandela (Freeman), who in an effort to unite South Africa after years of apartheid joins with the captain (Damon) of the country's underdog rugby team to try to win the 1995 World Cup. Freeman and Damon are solid as two men from very different worlds working towards a common goal. And, as usual, Eastwood delivers—in this case, with the compelling tale of how a sport can pull together people for the greater good—though glossing over much of the historical figures and times. Adapted from the 2008 book by John Carlin "Playing the Enemy: Nelson Mandela and the Game That Made a Nation." **134m/C DVD.** Morgan Freeman, Matt Damon, Robert Hobbs, Langley Kirkwood, Grant Roberts; ***D:*** Clint Eastwood; ***W:*** Anthony Peckham; ***C:*** Tom Stern; ***M:*** Steve Juliani.

Invincible 🦴🦴 **2001 (PG-13)** Herzog's stylized and operatic exploration of a true story is his first dramatic feature in 10 years. In 1932, naive Polish blacksmith Zishe (Ahola) is hired as a strongman to perform at the Palace of the Occult in Berlin, which is owned by showman Hanussen (Roth), who outfits Zishe to resemble German hero Siegfried. Hanussen wishes to be a significant player in the emerging Nazi party but when Zishe reveals himself to be Jewish, he takes it in stride and revels in Zishe's money-making abilities as a "new Samson." But politics and entertainment prove to be a volatile mix. **135m/C VHS, DVD.** *GB GE* Tim Roth, Jouko Ahola, Anna Gourari, Max Raabe, Udo Kier, Jacob Wein, Gustav Peter Wohler; ***D:*** Werner Herzog; ***W:*** Werner Herzog; ***C:*** Peter Zeitlinger; ***M:*** Hans Zimmer, Klaus Badelt.

Invincible 🦴🦴🦴 **2006 (PG)** True-ish story of not-quite over-the-hill South Philly substitute teacher and part-time bartender Vince Papale (Wahlberg), who gives it a go when new Philadelphia Eagles coach Dick Vermeil (Kinnear) holds open tryouts. Of course the otherwise down-and-out Papale makes the team, much to the delight of his football-crazy buds and the dismay of other players. Papale's on-screen gridiron accomplishments are a Disneyfied exaggeration of his real-life experience, but just try not to root for another underdog sports hero. Exceptional cinematography and cool soundtrack make up for any schmaltz. **104m/C DVD, Blu-ray Disc.** *US* Mark Wahlberg, Greg Kinnear, Elizabeth Banks, Kevin Conway, Michael Rispoli, Kirk Acevedo, Michael Nouri, Jack Kehler, Lola Glaudini, Paige Turco, Michael Kelly; ***D:*** Ericson Core; ***W:*** Brad Gann; ***C:*** Ericson Core; ***M:*** Mark Isham.

Invincible Barbarian WOOF! **1983** A young man leads a tribe of amazing Amazon warriors in a sneak attack against the tribe that annihilated his native village. One of those movies that presumes "primitivism" can be recreated through bad acting. **92m/C VHS.** *IT* Diana Roy, David Jenkins; ***D:*** Franco Prosperi; ***W:*** Piero Regnoli; ***C:*** Pasquale Fanetti; ***M:*** Roberto Pregadio.

The Invincible Gladiator 🦴 1/2 *Il Gladiatore Invincible* **1962** A cut above the usual gladiator pics because star Harrison is fun to watch. Rezius (Harrison) is recruited by evil regent Rabirius (Anchoriz) to wipe out some annoying bandits. Imagine his surprise when Rezius figures out they're lead by babe Sira (Boni), the sister of the boy king whom Rabirius wants dead. Rezius winds up back in the arena fighting for the good guys. Dubbed. **90m/C DVD.** *IT SP* Richard Harrison, Luisella Boni, Leo Anchoriz, Joseph Marco, Livio Lorenzon, Ricardo Canales; ***D:*** Alberto De Martino, Antonio Momplet; ***W:*** Alberto De Martino, Antonio Momplet; ***C:*** Eloy Mella; ***M:*** Carlo Franci, Carlo Franci.

The Invincible Gladiator 🦴 1/2 *Il Gladiatore Invincible* **1963** A gladiator who saves the evil man ruling a land for a boy-king is given command of an army. He eventually leads the army in revolt when the evil man tries to take over the throne. Plodding with stock characters. **96m/C VHS, DVD.** *IT SP* Richard Harrison, Isabel Corey, Livio Lorenzon; ***D:*** Frank Gregory.

Invincible Gladiators WOOF! **1964** The sons of Hercules labor to aid a prince whose bride had been kidnapped by an evil queen. Laborious to watch. **87m/C VHS, DVD.** Richard Lloyd, Claudia Lange; ***D:*** Robert (Roberto) Mauri.

Invincible Mr. Disraeli 🦴🦴 1/2 **1963** Presentation from "George Schaefer's Showcase Theatre" deals with the life and career of Benjamin Disraeli, novelist, philosopher, first Earl of Beaconsfield, statesman, and Prime Minister. Basically a tribute. **76m/C VHS.** Trevor Howard, Greer Garson, Hurd Hatfield, Kate Reid; ***D:*** George Schaefer. **TV**

The Invincible Six 🦴🦴 *The Heroes* **1968** An unlikely band of thieves running from the law winds up protecting a small village from marauding bandits. Plenty of action, as you would expect when thieves take on bandits, but with no scene-stealers or sympathetic characters the story lacks interest. Unremarkable choreography by ballet great Rudolf Nureyev. Filmed in Iran. **96m/C VHS.** Stuart Whitman, Elke Sommer, Curt Jurgens, Jim Mitchum, Ian Ogilvy; *D:* Jean Negulesco.

Invisible **2006** An improvised, bare bones indie that turns from marital drama to psychos in the woods. Joe and Jane squabble all the way to their secluded cabin. Just as they finally relax, they encounter a couple of crazies who insist that Jane is their long-lost mother. **86m/C DVD.** James Tupper, Kit Pongetti, David Mongentale, Joe Mellis; *D:* Adam Watstein; *W:* Adam Watstein; *C:* Adam Watstein, Tim Nuttall; *M:* Steve Bias.

The Invisible 1/2 **2007 (PG-13)** Supernatural mystery of no particular distinction. Unhappy teen Nick Powell (Chatwin) is beaten by bad seed Annie (Levieva) and she dumps his body in the woods, but he's not dead. Now Nick's spirit is hovering around, hoping he's found before he does become a homicide case. although he can't do anything useful like spirit writing or move objects. Based on the 2002 Swedish film (and novel) "Den Osynlige." **97m/C DVD, Blu-ray Disc.** *US* Justin Chatwin, Marcia Gay Harden, Christopher Marquette, Alex O'Loughlin, Margarita Levieva, Callum Keith Rennie, Michelle Harrison, Ryan Kennedy, Serge Houde; *D:* David S. Goyer; *W:* Mick Davis, Christine Roum; *C:* Gabriel Beristain; *M:* Marco Beltrami.

Invisible Adversaries **1977** A photographer uncovers an extra-terrestrial plot to cause excessive aggression in humans. She and her lover attempt to hold on to their crumbling humanity. Movies like this make you mad enough to tear something up. Enjoyed a meek cult following. In German with English subtitles. **112m/C VHS.** *AT* Susanne Widl, Peter Weibel; *D:* Valie Export.

Invisible Agent **1942** Hall plays an agent using the secret formula to outwit the Nazis in this third sequel to "The Invisible Man." Especially enjoyable for the kids. Based on characters suggested in H.G. Wells' "The Invisible Man." **83m/B VHS, DVD.** Ilona Massey, Jon Hall, Peter Lorre, Cedric Hardwicke, J. Edward Bromberg, Albert Basserman, John Litel, Holmes Herbert; *D:* Edwin L. Marin; *W:* Curt Siodmak.

The Invisible Avenger *Bourbon St. Shadows* **1958** Based on the vintage radio character "The Shadow." A detective who can make himself invisible investigates the murder of a New Orleans jazz musician. The mysterious element successful on radio is lost on film, and only the Shadow knows why. **60m/B VHS, DVD.** Richard Derr, Marc Daniels, Helen Westcott, Jeanne Neher; *D:* John Sledge, Ben Parker.

The Invisible Boy 1/2 **1957 (G)** Science fiction story about a young boy and his robot (Robby the Robot from "Forbidden Planet"). Kids will enjoy this adventure as told through the viewpoint of the child. Based on a story by Edmund Cooper. **89m/B VHS.** Richard Eyer, Diane Brewster, Philip Abbott, Harold J. Stone, Robert H. Harris; *D:* Herman Hoffman; *W:* Cyril Hume; *C:* Harold E. Wellman; *M:* Les Baxter.

Invisible Child **1999** Annie (Wilson) is a wife and mother who believes she has three children—only the third happens to be invisible. Her husband and kids go along with her delusions with the hope of keeping the family together but then Annie decides to hire nanny Gillian (Bergen) to help out. Since no reason is given for Annie's delusions, this film is just silly. **93m/C VHS, DVD.** Rita Wilson, Victor Garber, Tushka Bergen, Mae Whitman, David Dorfman; *D:* Joan Micklin Silver; *W:* David Field; *C:* Ken Kelsch; *M:* Victoria Dolceamore. **CABLE**

Invisible Circus 1/2 **2000 (R)** Coming-of-age drama set in 1976 of a young woman, Phoebe (Brewster), who treks through Europe in an attempt to solve the mystery of her older sister Faith (Diaz), a radical hippie who died there seven years ago. Her Nancy Drew-like sleuthing leads her to the big, bad Wolf (Eccleston) in Paris, Faith's old boho boyfriend, now a bourgeois married. Somewhat unlikely tales emerge about Faith's dealings with German terrorists gone bad and bring Phoebe closer to the truth and danger. Story told much like many a late 1960s memory, in confusing flashback fashion, and lacks adequate pacing. Brewster has inspired moments, along with Danner as the girls' mother, while Diaz seems an unlikely terrorist. Based on the novel by Jennifer Egan. **98m/C VHS, DVD.** *US* Cameron Diaz, Jordana Brewster, Christopher Eccleston, Blythe Danner, Patrick Bergin, Moritz Bleibtreu, Isabelle Pasco; *D:* Adam Brooks; *W:* Adam Brooks; *C:* Henry Braham; *M:* Nick Laird-Clowes.

Invisible Dad **1997 (PG)** Doug Baily's dad invents a machine that makes him invisible and uses it to foil the evil designs of a co-worker. Unfortunately, the machine isn't perfect, and Mr. Baily tends to reappear at inopportune moments. When Doug discovers his dad is in danger, he figures it's time to help out. **90m/C VHS, DVD.** Daran Noris, William Meyers, Mary Elizabeth McGlynn, Charles Dierkop, Karen Black; *D:* Fred Olen Ray; *W:* Steve Latshaw; *C:* Gary Graver; *M:* Jeff Walton. **VIDEO**

The Invisible Dr. Mabuse *The Invisible Horror; Die Unsichtbaren Krallen des Dr. Mabuse* **1962** Possibly the best of the Dr. Mabuse series sees the mad scientist using an invisibility agent in an attempt to take over the world. Preiss also played the title villian in Fritz Lang's "The Thousand Eyes of Dr. Mabuse." **89m/B VHS.** *GE* Lex Barker, Karin Dor, Siegfried Lowitz, Wolfgang Preiss, Rudolf Fernau; *D:* Harald Reinl.

The Invisible Ghost 1/2 **1941** A man carries out a series of grisly stranglings while under hypnosis by his insane wife. Typically bad low-budget exploiter about a fun-lovin' crazy couple bringing down property values in the neighborhood. **70m/B VHS, DVD.** Bela Lugosi, Polly Ann Young, John McGuire, Clarence Muse, Betty Compson; *D:* Joseph H. Lewis; *W:* Helen Martin, Al Martin; *C:* Marcel Le Picard.

Invisible Invaders **1959** Short, cheap, and silly aliens-try-to-take-over-the-earth flick. This time they're moonmen who use the bodies of dead earthlings (ugh) to attack the living until Agar can save the day. Carradine has a brief role as a formerly dead scientist. **67m/B VHS, DVD.** John Agar, Robert Hutton, Hal Torey, Jean Byron, Philip Tonge, John Carradine; *D:* Edward L. Cahn; *W:* Samuel Newman; *C:* Maury Gertsman.

The Invisible Kid **1988** A shy teen manages to make himself invisible, a feat which ironically permits him to get people to notice him. Now he can visit places he's only dreamed of, including the girls' locker room. For those who have dreamed about girls' locker rooms. **95m/C VHS.** Karen Black, Jay Underwood, Chynna Phillips, Wallace (Wally) Langham, Brother Theodore; *D:* Avery Crounse; *W:* Avery Crounse.

The Invisible Killer 1/2 **1940** Someone is killing folks by sending poison through telephone lines. A detective and a reporter team up to find the scoundrel by setting up an answering machine that automatically plays back messages to the caller. Bad connection of events leads to a static resolution. **61m/B VHS, DVD.** Grace Bradley, Roland (Walter Goss) Drew, William "Billy" Newell, David Oliver; *D:* Sam Newfield.

The Invisible Man **1933** The vintage horror-fest based on H. G. Wells' novella about scientist Jack Griffin (Rains) whose formula for invisibility slowly drives him insane. His mind definitely wandering, Jack plans to use his recipe to rule the world. Rains' first role; though his body doesn't appear until the final scene, his voice characterization is magnificent. The visual detail is excellent, setting standards that are imitated because they are difficult to surpass; with special effects by John P. Fulton and John Mescall. **71m/B VHS, DVD.** Claude Rains, Gloria Stuart, Dudley Digges, William Harrigan, Una O'Connor, E.E. Clive, Dwight Frye, Henry Travers, Holmes Herbert, John Carradine, Walter Brennan; *D:* James Whale; *W:* R.C. Sherriff; *C:* Arthur Edeson; *M:* W. Franke Harling. Natl. Film Reg. '08.

The Invisible Man Returns **1940** Price stars as the original invisible man's brother. Using the same invisibility formula, Price tries to clear himself after being charged with murder. He reappears at the worst times, and you gotta love that floating gun. Fun sequel to 1933's classic "The Invisible Man." **81m/B VHS, DVD.** Cedric Hardwicke, Vincent Price, John Sutton, Nan Grey; *D:* Joe May; *W:* Lester Cole, Curt Siodmak; *C:* Milton Krasner.

The Invisible Maniac **WOOF!** **1990 (R)** A crazy voyeur perfects a serum for invisibility and promptly gets a job as a physics teacher in a high school. There he leers at girls taking showers and slaughters students when he is caught. For voyeurs. Get outta here, you maniac. Rifkin used the pseudonym Rif Coogan. **87m/C VHS.** Noel Peters, Shannon Wilsey, Melissa Moore, Robert Ross, Rod Sweitzer, Eric Champnella, Kalei Shellabarger, Gail Lyon, Debra Lamb; *D:* Adam Rifkin; *W:* Adam Rifkin; *C:* James Bay; *M:* Marc David Decker.

The Invisible Man's Revenge 1/2 **1944** Left for dead on a safari five years before, Robert Griffin (Hall) seeks revenge against wealthy English couple Lady Irene (Sondergaard) and Sir Jasper (Matthews) Herrick by taking over their estate and marrying their daughter, Julie (Akers). He's aided by scientist Peter Drury (Carradine) who renders Griffin invisible. Only problem is he doesn't stay that way. Fifth in Universal's "Invisible Man" film series. **78m/B VHS, DVD.** Jon Hall, John Carradine, Gale Sondergaard, Lester Matthews, Evelyn Ankers, Alan Curtis, Leon Errol, Doris Lloyd; *D:* Ford Beebe; *W:* Bertram Millhauser; *C:* Milton Krasner; *M:* Hans J. Salter.

Invisible Mom 1/2 **1996 (PG)** Dad (Livingston) invents an invisibility potion that his 10-year-old son decides will make him popular at school. Too bad Mom (Wallace Stone) accidentally swallows the concoction instead. **80m/C VHS, DVD.** Justin Berfield, Mary Woronov, Mickey Dolenz, Dee Wallace, Barry Livingston, Trenton Knight, Russ Tamblyn, Stella Stevens; *D:* Fred Olen Ray; *W:* William Martell, Sean O'Bannon; *C:* Gary Graver; *M:* Jeff Walton.

Invisible Mom 2 **1999 (PG)** Newly adopted 12-year-old discovers his mom can literally disappear and has to deal with cousins trying to get in on his good fortune. Harmless family fare may entertain fans of the original, or the not-too-discerning pre-adolescent. **m/C VHS.** Dee Wallace, Justin Berfield, Barry Livingston, Mickey Dolenz, Mary Woronov; *D:* Fred Olen Ray; *W:* Sean O'Bannon; *C:* Jesse Weathington. **VIDEO**

The Invisible Monster *Slaves of the Invisible Monster* **1950** Special investigators Lane Carlson and Carol Richards battle a mad scientist ready to take over the world with his invisible army. Twelve episodes of the original serial edited onto two cassettes. **167m/B VHS.** Richard Webb, Aline Towne, Lane Bradford, Stanley Price, John Crawford, George Meeker; *D:* Fred Brannon.

The Invisible Ray 1/2 **1936** For a change, this horror film features Lugosi as the hero, fighting Karloff, a scientist who locates a meteor that contains a powerful substance. Karloff is poisoned and becomes a murdering megalomaniac. Watching Karloff and Lugosi interact, and the great special effects—including a hot scene where a scientist bursts into flames—helps you ignore a generally hokey script. **82m/B VHS, DVD.** Boris Karloff, Bela Lugosi, Frances Drake, Frank Lawton, Beulah Bondi, Walter Kingsford; *D:* Lambert Hillyer; *W:* John Colton; *C:* George Robinson.

The Invisible Strangler 1/2 *The Astral Factor* **1976 (PG)** A death-row murderer can make himself invisible and rubs out witnesses who helped put him away; woman risks her life to expose him when the police fail to see the problem. Very violent collection of brutal scenes. Not released theatrically until 1984. **85m/C VHS, DVD.** Robert Foxworth, Stefanie Powers, Elke Sommer, Sue Lyon, Leslie Parrish, Marianna Hill; *D:* John Florea; *W:* Arthur C. Pierce; *C:* Alan Stensvold; *M:* Richard Hieronymous, Alan Oldfield.

Invisible Stripes 1/2 **1939** Cliff (Raft) and Chuck (Bogart) just got out of the pen. Cliff is determined to go straight but Chuck goes right back to his criminal ways. Cliff's kid brother Tim (Holden) needs dough to marry sweetheart Peggy (Bryan) and Cliff (who has job problems as an ex-con) winds up pulling some heists with Chuck. Chuck then hides out at Tim's, who is arrested for harboring a fugitive, and Cliff makes a deal with the cops. It doesn't end well. **82m/B DVD.** George Raft, Humphrey Bogart, William Holden, Jane Bryan, Paul Kelly, Marc Lawrence, Flora Robson, Lee Patrick, Joe Downing; *D:* Lloyd Bacon; *W:* Warren Duff; *C:* Ernest Haller; *M:* Heinz Roemheld.

The Invisible Terror **1963** A maniac steals a mad scientist's invisibility formula and uses it on a number of innocent victims. **102m/C VHS.** *GE* Herbert Stass, Ellen Scheirs; *D:* Raphael Nussbaum; *W:* Raphael Nussbaum; *C:* Michael Marszalek.

Invisible: The Chronicles of Benjamin Knight 1/2 **1993 (R)** Scientist Benjamin Knight is rendered invisible during a terrible laboratory accident. His only hope of regaining his visible form is a desperate search by Knight and his fellow scientists for just the right chemical antidote. **80m/C VHS.** Brian Cousins, Jennifer Nash, Michael DellaFemina, Curt Lowens, David Kaufman, Alan Oppenheimer, Aharon Ipale; *D:* Joakim (Jack) Ersgard; *W:* Earl Kenton.

The Invisible Woman **1940** Above average comedy about zany professor Gibbs (Barrymore) discovering the secret of invisibility and making luscious model Kitty (Bruce) transparent during his experiments. She tries some romance with Richard (Howard), the guy who financed the invention, and then gets involved with crooks who want to steal the machine for their own illicit gain. A very likeable movie with a good cast. Based on a story by Curt Siodmak and Joe May, the same team that wrote "The Invisible Man Returns." **73m/B VHS, DVD.** John Barrymore, Virginia Bruce, John Howard, Charlie Ruggles, Oscar Homolka, Margaret Hamilton, Donald MacBride, Edward Brophy, Shemp Howard, Charles Lane, Thurston Hall; *D:* Edward Sutherland; *W:* Robert Lees, Frederic Rinaldo, Gertrude Purcell; *C:* Elwood "Woody" Bredell.

The Invisibles 1/2 **1999** Likeable actors in unlikeable roles and a rather pretentious script. Rock star Jude (Goorjian) and supermodel Joy (De Rossi) share more than a romance, they share a heroin habit. So they take off for a Paris flat to kick drugs (what's wrong with going into rehab?). They're spoiled and childish and not much happens that you'll care about. **89m/C VHS, DVD.** Michael Goorjian, Portia de Rossi, Terry Camillieri, Jonathan Segel; *D:* Noah Stern; *W:* Noah Stern; *C:* Robert Humphreys; *M:* Jonathan Segel.

Invitation 1/2 **1951** Ellen (McGuire) is dying of a heart condition and her wealthy father Simon (Calhern) decides it would make his little girl happy to be married. So he pays playboy Dan (Johnson) to woo and wed her. However, Dan has dumped Maud (Roman) to do so and she gets back at him by not-so-subtly hinting to Ellen that her new husband was bought and paid for. This news devastates Ellen but Dan is now actually in love with his wife and must convince her of that fact. The lovely, classy McGuire steals the picture. **85m/B DVD.** Dorothy McGuire, Van Johnson, Ruth Roman, Louis Calhern, Ray Collins, Michael Chekhov; *D:* Gottfried Reinhardt; *W:* Paul Osborn; *C:* Ray June; *M:* Bronislau Kaper.

The Invitation **2003 (R)** Clunky thriller has wealthy writer Roland Levy (Henriksen) inviting six friends to his island for what turns out to be a deadly dinner invitation. Seems after a near-death experience, Roland poisons his guests so they can too can experience the bliss he felt. He promises the antidote—if they'll reveal their deepest, darkest secrets. **85m/C VHS, DVD.** Lance Henriksen, Christopher Shyer, Sarah Jane Redmond, Stefanie von Pfetten, Doug O'Keefe, Fred Henderson; *D:* Patrick Bermel; *W:* Patrick Bermel; *C:* Barney Donlevy; *M:* Michael Richard Plowman. **VIDEO**

Invitation au Voyage 1/2 **1982 (R)** Follows the journey of a twin who refuses to accept the death of his sister, a rock singer. The obsession is played fairly well, but it's a no-twin situation, even though the guy can't admit it. Perversity is played to the point of overkill. From the novel "Moi, Ma Soeur Images," by Jean Bany. In French with English subtitles. **90m/C VHS.** *FR* Laurent Malet, Nina Scott, Aurore Clement, Mario Adorf; ***D:*** Peter Del Monte.

Invitation to a Gunfighter 🦴🦴 **1964** Small town politics change when a paid assassin ambles into town and creates a lot of talk among the neighbors. Like a long joke in which the teller keeps forgetting the important details, the plot grows confusing though it's not complicated. Brynner is interesting as an educated, half-black/half-creole, hired gun. **92m/C VHS, DVD.** Yul Brynner, George Segal, Strother Martin, William Hickey, Janice Rule, Mike Kellin, Pat Hingle, John Alonzo; ***D:*** Richard Wilson.

Invitation to Hell **WOOF!** **1982** Tormented maiden has a devil of a time discovering a secret power that can enable her to gracefully decline a satanic summoning. The cliched evil is tormenting. **100m/C VHS, DVD.** Becky Simpson, Joseph Sheahan, Colin Efford; ***D:*** Michael J. Murphy; ***W:*** Carl Humphrey; ***M:*** Terence Mills.

Invitation to Hell 🦴 ½ **1984** "Faust" meets "All My Children" in celluloid suburbia. Never Emmied Lucci is the devil's dirty worker, persuading upwardly mobile suburbanites to join a really exclusive country club in exchange for a little downward mobility. Urich, a space scientist, and family are new in town, and soul searching Lucci's got her devil vixen sights set on space jock and brood. Bound to disappoint both fans of Craven's early independent work ("Last House on the Left") and his later high gloss ("Nightmare on Elm Street") formulas. Made for the small screen. **100m/C VHS, DVD.** Susan Lucci, Robert Urich, Joanna Cassidy, Kevin McCarthy, Patty McCormack, Joe Regalbuto, Soleil Moon Frye, Barret Oliver; ***D:*** Wes Craven. **TV**

Invitation to the Dance 🦴🦴 ½ **1956** Three classic dance sequences, "Circus," "Ring Around the Rosy," and "Sinbad the Sailor." For dance lovers, featuring excellent performances by Kelly. **93m/C VHS.** Gene Kelly, Igor Youskevitch, Tamara Toumanova; ***D:*** Gene Kelly. Berlin Intl. Film Fest. '56: Golden Berlin Bear.

Invitation to the Wedding 🦴🦴 **1973 (PG)** When the best friend of a bridegroom falls in love with the bride, he stops at nothing to halt the wedding. Not exactly the Gielgud movie of the year, but there are some excellent scenes between him and Richardson. **89m/C VHS.** John Gielgud, Ralph Richardson, Paul Nicholas, Elizabeth Shepherd; ***D:*** Joseph Brooks; ***M:*** Joseph Brooks.

Iowa 🦴 **2005** Low-budget indie that's an overly-familiar tale of drug addiction and crime. Esper (Farnsworth) and his girlfriend Donna (Foster) begin manufacturing crystal meth so they can get the money to hightail it out of their Iowa hometown. Instead, they become addicts. Esper also has a problem with his floozy mom (Arquette) and her psychotic cop boyfriend (Weiss) who are after an inheritance due from Esper's late dad. **97m/C DVD.** Matt Farnsworth, Dianne Foster, Michael T. Weiss, Rosanna Arquette, John Savage, Muse Watson; ***D:*** Matt Farnsworth; ***W:*** Matt Farnsworth; ***C:*** Andy Parke, John Houghton; ***M:*** Elia Cmiral. **VIDEO**

The Ipcress File 🦴🦴🦴 **1965** The first of the Harry Palmer spy mysteries that made Caine a star. Based upon the bestseller by Len Deighton, it features the flabby, nearsighted spy investigating the kidnapping of notable British scientists. Solid scenes, including a scary brainwashing session, and tongue-firmly-in-British-cheek humor. Lots of camera play to emphasize Caine's myopia. Two sequels: "Funeral in Berlin" and "Billion Dollar Brain." **108m/C VHS, DVD.** *GB* Michael Caine, Nigel Green, Guy Doleman, Sue Lloyd, Gordon Jackson; ***D:*** Sidney J. Furie; ***W:*** Bill Canaway, James Doran; ***C:*** Otto Heller; ***M:*** John Barry. British Acad. '65: Film.

Iphigenia 🦴🦴🦴 **1977** Based on the classic Greek tragedy by Euripides, this story concerns the Greek leader Agamemnon, who plans to sacrifice his lovely daughter, Iphigenia, to please the gods. Mere mortals protest and start a save-the-babe movement, but Euripides' moral—you can't please 'em all—is devastatingly realized. Fine adaptation that becomes visually extravagant at times, with an equally fine musical score. In Greek with English subtitles. **130m/C VHS.** *GR* Irene Papas, Costa Kazakos, Tatiana Papamoskou, Costas Carras, Christos Tsangas, Panos Michalopoulas; ***D:*** Michael Cacoyannis; ***W:*** Michael Cacoyannis; ***C:*** Yorgos Arvanitis; ***M:*** Mikis Theodorakis.

I.Q. 🦴🦴 ½ **1994 (PG)** Albert Einstein (the irascible Matthau) thinks his co-ed niece (Ryan) is in need of a little romance, so he engineers a plan to get her into the arms of Robbins, a local auto mechanic. Robbins and Ryan are comfortable in their comic roles, although they're both above the material. Matthau shines as the famous physicist. Plot gets a little farfetched with its central contrivance of making Robbins look like a brilliant scientist, which leaves second half of story flat. However, chemistry between leads is undeniable and you can't help but cheer on the inevitable. Visually pleasing with Ryan costumed in cool, elegant '50s fashions. Filmed in Princeton, New Jersey. **95m/C VHS, DVD.** Tim Robbins, Meg Ryan, Walter Matthau, Lou Jacobi, Gene Saks, Joseph Maher, Stephen Fry, Tony Shalhoub, Frank Whaley; ***D:*** Fred Schepisi; ***W:*** Michael Leeson, Andy Breckman; ***C:*** Ian Baker; ***M:*** Jerry Goldsmith.

Ira & Abby 🦴🦴 **2006 (R)** Jewish Ira (Messina) is the neurotic, underachieving son of two analysts (Klein, Light) while shiksa Abby (Westfeldt) is a free spirit, thanks to her hipster parents (Willard, Conroy). They impulsively get married but discover exes and in-laws, affairs and insecurities, and too many therapists cause them lots of trouble. Manhattan looks great, the parents are great, but the flick is Woody Allen-lite via an episode of "Dharma & Greg" with swearing and overt sexual content. **105m/C DVD.** Jennifer Westfeldt, Judith Light, Jason Alexander, Fred Willard, Chris Messina, Frances Conroy, Robert Klein, Darrell Hammond, Chris Parnell; ***D:*** Robert Cary; ***W:*** Jennifer Westfeldt; ***C:*** Harlan Bosmajian; ***M:*** Marcelo Zarvos.

Iran: Days of Crisis 🦴🦴 ½ **1991** An insightful cable miniseries recounts America's humiliation at the hands of Iranian radicals in 1979, told from the vantage of a U.S. embassy official married to a Tehran woman. Former Carter administration aides Hamilton Jordan and Gerald Rafshoon devised the docudrama, which spares neither them nor their president in showing how bungled and shortsighted policies led to 52 Americans held hostage for over a year. **185m/C VHS.** Arliss Howard, Alice Krige, George Grizzard, Jeff Fahey, Tony Goldwyn, Ronald Guttman, Valerie Kaprisky, Daniel Gelin; ***D:*** Kevin Connor. **CABLE**

Irezumi 🦴🦴🦴 *Spirit of Tattoo* **1983** A Japanese woman has her body elaborately tattooed to please her lover. Things start off well enough. He's an inept lover, so she has directions tattooed, but then he discovers a "Dear John" letter on her foot just as she gives him the boot. Actually proves an interesting study in obsession and eroticism, with the tattoos drawing the lovers deeper and deeper until they get under each other's skin. In Japanese with English subtitles. **88m/C VHS.** *JP* Tomisaburo Wakayama, Yusuke Takita, Masayo Utsunomiya, Masaki Kyomoto, Taihi Tomoyama; ***D:*** Yoichi Takabayashi; ***W:*** Chiho Katsura; ***C:*** Hideo Fujii; ***M:*** Masaru Sato.

Irina Palm 🦴🦴 **2007 (R)** Provincial middle-aged widow Maggie (Faithfull) is happy to care for her seriously ill grandson Olly (Burke) and play bridge with her girlfriends. Olly's parents learn about an experimental new treatment but it's impossibly expensive and Maggie decides to get a job in London but is constantly rejected until she answers an advert at a Soho sex club. When she learns what she'll be paid, Maggie accepts the job—using the professional name Irina Palm, which hints at her sexual specialty—and is an unexpected success. However, her son Tom (Bishop) is soon wondering why his mother is so secretive. **103m/C DVD.** *FR BE* Marianne Faithfull, Miki (Predrag) Manojlovic, Kevin Bishop, Siobhan Hewlett, Jenny Agutter, Corey Burke, Dorka Gryllus; ***D:*** Sam Garbarski; ***W:*** Philippe Blasband, Martin Herron; ***C:*** Christophe Beaucarne; ***M:*** Ghinzu.

Iris 🦴🦴 *Out of Time* **1989** Drama follows the passionate and tragic life of New Zealand writer Iris Wilkinson, an international novelist, poet, and journalist. Wilkinson achieved a great deal of acclaim as a writer, but suffered many personal tragedies, and eventually took her own life at age 33. Well intentioned but clunky treatment of powerful subject matter. **90m/C VHS.** *NZ* Philip Holder, John Bach, Donough Rees, David Ashton, Helen Morse; ***D:*** Tony Issac; ***W:*** Keith Aberdein; ***C:*** James Bartle; ***M:*** John Charles.

Iris 🦴🦴🦴 **2001 (R)** Enduring love story between novelist/philosopher Iris Murdoch and her husband John Bayley from their days at Oxford in the 1950s to Murdoch's long decline from Alzheimer's and death in 1999. Winslet and Bonneville play the young duo while Dench and Broadbent play the mature marrieds. The ladies have the showier roles, especially Winslet, since the young Iris was a sexual free-spirit and disdained conventional morality while John comes across as shy and rather awed by Murdoch's talents. Based on Bayley's memoirs "Iris: A Memoir" and "Elegy for Iris." **90m/C VHS, DVD.** *GB US* Judi Dench, Jim Broadbent, Kate Winslet, Hugh Bonneville, Penelope Wilton, Juliet Aubrey, Timothy West, Samuel West, Eleanor Bron; ***D:*** Richard Eyre; ***W:*** Richard Eyre, Charles Wood; ***C:*** Roger Pratt; ***M:*** James Horner. Oscars '01: Support. Actor (Broadbent); British Acad. '01: Actress (Dench); Golden Globes '02: Support. Actor (Broadbent); L.A. Film Critics '01: Support. Actor (Broadbent), Support. Actress (Winslet); Natl. Bd. of Review '01: Support. Actor (Broadbent).

Iris Blond 🦴🦴 ½ **1998 (R)** Bittersweet romantic comedy about a sadsack piano player named Romeo (Verdone), who's pushing 50 and is unlucky in love. Having been cuckholded by his girlfriend, Romeo asks a fortuneteller (Fumo) for some help. She tells him his future resides with a singer who has the name of a flower. Naturally, Romeo picks the wrong chick (Ferrerol), only to soon meet red-hot maneater, Iris (Gerini). Eventually things work out as they should. French and Italian with subtitles. **100m/C VHS.** *IT* Carlo Verdone, Andrea Ferreol, Claudia Gerini, Nuccia Fumo; ***D:*** Carlo Verdone; ***W:*** Carlo Verdone, Francesca Marciano, Pasquale Plastino; ***C:*** Giuseppe Di Biase.

The Iris Effect 🦴🦴 **2004 (R)** Confusing thriller. Sarah Hathaway's (Archer) troubled son Thomas disappeared 10 years ago. Unexpectedly, Sarah sees an art catalog that contains paintings similar to those Thomas did, so she travels to St. Petersburg, Russia, to find the art gallery and the artist—which isn't Thomas. Or is it? Something strange is happening as Sarah is followed by a mute street kid (Alan) who seems to know a lot about her son. **90m/C DVD.** Anne Archer, Agnes Bruckner, Mia Kirshner, Kip Pardue, Gregory Hlady, Devon Alan, Yuri Kolokol; ***D:*** Nikolai Lebedev; ***W:*** Kam Miller; ***C:*** Irek Hartowicz; ***M:*** Alexey Rybnikov. **VIDEO**

Irish Cinderella 🦴🦴 **1922** A silent version of the Cinderella legend set in Ireland, with thematic stress on Irish politics and patriotism. **72m/B VHS.** Pattie MacNamara.

Irish Jam 🦴🦴 **2005** Con man Jimmy (Griffin) has a tough life in L.A. and sees a small Irish town's poetry contest as a way out. After lifting some rap lyrics he wins the grand prize and becomes the town's new pub owner, not knowing the locales concocted the whole thing to keep a filthy rich developer at bay. Usual "worlds colliding" confusion plus an unlikely romance with a lonely widowed mother. **90m/C DVD.** Eddie Griffin, Anna Friel, Kevin McNally, Mo'Nique Imes; ***D:*** John Eyres; ***W:*** John Eyres, Max Myers. **VIDEO**

Irish Luck 🦴🦴 **1939** A bellhop turns detective to figure out the mysterious happenings in his hotel. Becomes terminally cute by playing on a luck o' the Irish theme. **58m/B VHS, DVD.** Frankie Darro, Dick Purcell, Sheila Darcy, Grant Withers; ***D:*** Howard Bretherton.

The Irishman 🦴🦴 ½ **1978** Set in 1920s Australia, the tale of a proud North Queensland family and their struggles to stay together. The Irish immigrant father is a teamster whose horse-drawn wagons are threatened by progress. His fight to preserve old ways is impressive, but gives way to sentimentality. **108m/C VHS, DVD.** *AU* Lou Brown, Michael Craig, Simon Burke, Robyn Nevin, Bryan Brown; ***D:*** Donald Crombie; ***W:*** Donald Crombie; ***C:*** Peter James; ***M:*** Charles Marawood.

Irma La Douce 🦴🦴 ½ **1963** A gendarme pulls a one-man raid on a back-street Parisian joint and falls in love with one of the hookers he arrests. Lemmon is great as a well-meaning, incompetent boob, and MacLaine gives her all as the hapless hooker. A plodding pace, however, robs it of the original's zip, though it was a boxoffice smash. Broadway musical is lost without the music. **144m/C VHS, DVD.** Jack Lemmon, Shirley MacLaine, Herschel Bernardi; ***D:*** Billy Wilder; ***W:*** Billy Wilder, I.A.L. Diamond; ***M:*** Andre Previn. Oscars '63: Adapt. Score; Golden Globes '64: Actress—Mus./Comedy (MacLaine).

Irma Vep 🦴🦴 **1996** Satiric tweaking of French filmmaking begins with has-been director Rene Vidal (Leaud) hiring Hong Kong star Maggie Cheung to take the lead role of Irma Vep in a remake of the 1915 silent French classic "Les Vampires." But from the moment the actress arrives in Paris, it's one disaster after another. Cheung has trouble with the language barrier, Vidal is having a breakdown, lesbian costumer Zoe (Richard) is instantly smitten by Cheung and has her interest humiliatingly conveyed to everyone on the production. Then there's Jose Murano (Castel), a snobbish auteur who replaces Vidal and believes the Chinese actress can't play a French thief, not knowing that Cheung has become obsessed with her role and is practicing stealing from other hotel guests. English and French with subtitles. **96m/C VHS, DVD.** *FR* Maggie Cheung, Jean-Pierre Leaud, Nathalie Richard, Bulle Ogier, Lou Castel, Antoine Basler, Nathalie Boutefeu, Arsinee Khanjian, Alex Descas; ***D:*** Olivier Assayas; ***W:*** Olivier Assayas; ***C:*** Eric Gautier.

Iron & Silk 🦴🦴 ½ **1991 (PG)** A young American searches for himself while he teaches English and learns martial arts in mainland China. Based on the true story of Salzman's travels. His studies of martial arts and Chinese culture provide a model for his students in their studies of American language and culture. Beautiful photography. Fine performances. **94m/C VHS, DVD.** Mark Saltzman, Pan Qingfu, Jeanette Lin Tsui, Vivian Wu; ***D:*** Shirley Sun; ***W:*** Mark Saltzman, Shirley Sun; ***M:*** Michael Gibbs.

Iron Angel 🦴 ½ **1964** During the Korean War a squadron sets out to silence North Korean guns. They do. Judging by their eternal bickering they must have put the enemy to sleep. **84m/B VHS.** Jim Davis, Margo Woode, Donald (Don "Red") Barry, L.Q. Jones; ***D:*** Ken Kennedy; ***W:*** Ken Kennedy.

Iron Cowboy 🦴🦴 **1968** Actor finds romance with film editor while audience stifles yawns. Filmed on the set of "Blue," this pre-"Deliverance" Reynolds comedy never made it to the theaters. (Smithee is actually director Jud Taylor.) **86m/C VHS.** Burt Reynolds, Barbara Loden, Terence Stamp, Noam Pitlik, Ricardo Montalban, Patricia Casey, Jane Hampton, Joseph V. Perry; ***D:*** Alan Smithee.

The Iron Crown 🦴🦴 **1941** A 13th-century legend inspired this sometime violent spectacle involving the title totem, a symbol of justice ignored by a powerful king at his peril. There's wonderful pagentry and a notable Tarzan imitator, but the pace is terribly slow. Italian dialogue with English subtitles. **100m/C VHS.** Massimo Girotti, Elisa Cegani, Rina Morelli, Osvaldo Valenti, Primo Carnera, Gino Cervi, Luisa Ferida; ***D:*** Alessandro Blasetti; ***W:*** Renato Castellani; ***C:*** Mario Craveri; ***M:*** Alessandro Cicognini.

The Iron Duke 🦴🦴 ½ **1934** Fair to middlin' historical account of the life of the Duke of Wellington, victor over Napoleon at Waterloo. **88m/B VHS.** *GB* George Arliss, Gladys Cooper, A.E. Matthews, Emlyn Williams, Felix Aylmer; ***D:*** Victor Saville.

Iron Eagle 🦴🦴 ½ **1986 (PG-13)** A teenager teams with a renegade fighter pilot to rescue the youth's father from captivity in the Middle East. Predictable but often exciting. Followed by two sequels. **117m/C VHS, DVD.** Louis Gossett Jr., Jason Gedrick, Tim Thomerson, David Suchet, Larry B. Scott, Caroline Lagerfelt, Jerry Levine, Michael Bowen, Robbie (Reist) Rist, Bobby Jacoby, Melora Hardin; ***D:*** Sidney J. Furie; ***W:*** Kevin Elders, Sidney J. Furie; ***M:*** Basil Poledouris.

Iron Eagle 2 1988 (PG) Lower-budget extended adventures of a maverick fighter pilot after he is reinstated in the Air Force. This time he links with an equally rebellious commie fighter and blasts away at nuke-happy Ivan. Yahoo fun for all overt Yankees! Followed by "Aces: Iron Eagle 3." Available in Spanish. **102m/C VHS, DVD.** *CA IS* Louis Gossett Jr., Mark Humphrey, Stuart Margolin, Alan Scarfe, Maury Chaykin, Sharon H. Brandon; ***D:*** Sidney J. Furie; ***W:*** Sidney J. Furie, Kevin Elders; ***C:*** Alan Dostie; ***M:*** Amin Bhatia.

Iron Eagle 4 ½ **1995 (PG-13)** Series has gotten old and tired though Gossett Jr. shows professionalism in his father figure role of retired Air Force General "Chappy" Sinclair. He's running the Iron Eagle Flight School—a training center/holding cell for troubled teens—along with pilot Doug Masters (Cadieux). Masters and his would-be pilots discover suspicious activities at a local air base, leading to biological weapons and an Air Force conspiracy. **95m/C VHS, DVD.** *CA* Louis Gossett Jr., Jason Cadieux, Al Waxman, Joanne Vannicola, Rachel Blanchard, Sean McCann, Ross Hill, Karen Gayle; ***D:*** Sidney J. Furie; ***W:*** Michael Stokes; ***C:*** Curtis Petersen; ***M:*** Paul Zaza.

The Iron Giant ½ **1999 (PG)** After a giant robot falls from the sky and frightens a small town, only a young boy is willing to befriend the iron man. With his new friend, he teaches the townspeople a lesson about being afraid of what is different. Jennifer Aniston provides the voice for the boy's mother, and Harry Connick Jr. that of the town beatnik. Great animation and story propel this tale above the level of most kiddie fare. Based on the 1968 children's book by Ted Hughes, which was also used for a 1989 concept album by Pete Townshend. **86m/C VHS, DVD.** ***D:*** Brad Bird; ***W:*** Tim McCanlies; ***M:*** Michael Kamen; ***V:*** Vin Diesel, Eli Marienthal, Jennifer Aniston, Harry Connick Jr., John Mahoney, M. Emmet Walsh, Cloris Leachman, James Gammon, Christopher McDonald.

The Iron Horse **1924** Davy Brandon is a frontiersman and scout who learned about western trails from his surveyor father. His childhood sweetheart Miriam is traveling with her fiance Jesson, who is working on the route for the new transcontinental railway. Davy says he knows a shortcut but a jealous Jesson (who's been bribed by land speculators) tries to kill him. There's lots more action (and Abraham Lincoln!) before the railroad is finished and the sweethearts reunited. Ford's epic western was filmed on location and was his first major studio success. **119m/B DVD.** George O'Brien, Madge Bellamy, Cyril Chadwick, Fred Kohler Jr., Charles Edward Bull, Gladys Hullette; ***D:*** John Ford; ***W:*** Charles Kenyon, John Russell, Charles Denton; ***C:*** George Schneiderman.

Iron Horsemen *J.C* **1971 (R)** A motorcycle gang leader has a prophetic vision while tripping on LSD, and returns to his former town to challenge its religious establishment. **97m/C VHS.** William F. McGaha, Hannibal Penny, Joanna Moore, Burr de Benning, Slim Pickens, Pat Delaney; ***D:*** William F. McGaha.

The Iron Ladies ½ *Satree Lex* **2000** The true story of a 1996 Thai volleyball team that made it to national competition. When the governor asks the coach to assemble a dream team to compete in volleyball, the addition of a transvestite and a drag queen so offend the team all of them quit except for one guy. So the coach rounds the team out with assorted gays, drag queens, transvestites, and a transsexual. Definitely a new take on the underdog sports comedy genre, and Thailand's second-highest grossing film. **104m/C DVD.** *TH* Jesdaporn Pholdee, Sahaphap Tor, Ekachai Buranapanit, Giorgio Maiocchi, Chaicham Nimpulsawasdi, Kokkorn Benjathikoon, Shiriohona Hongsopon, Phomsit Sitthijamroenkhun, Sutthipong Sitthijamroenkhun, Anucha Chatkaew; ***D:*** Youngyooth Thongkonthun; ***W:*** Youngyooth Thongkonthun, Visuttchai Boonyakarnjawa, Jira Maligool; ***C:*** Jira Maligool.

The Iron Ladies 2 ½ *Satree lek 2; The Iron Ladies 2: Before and After; The Iron Ladies II: The Early Years* **2003** Both a sequel and a prequel, the film begins with the background stories of how the various Iron Ladies met. Fast-forward to the present after their success in the first film, and one of the teammates has joined up with a promoter attempting to copy the Iron Ladies. Sensing he is dishonest, the group splits, but they ponder a reunion when they learn the promoter's copycat team is going to be captained by an infamous homophobe. **100m/C DVD.** *TH* Anucha Chatkaew, Shiriohona Hongsopon, Chaicham Nimpulsawasdi, Phomsit Sitthijamroenkhun, Sutthipong Sitthijamroenkhun, Sahaphap Tor, Sujira Arunpipat, Kokkorn Benjathikoon, Surapun Chatkaew, Giorgio Maiocchi, Peter Maiocchi, Jesdaporn Pholdee, Aphichart Vongkavee, Hathairat Jaroenchaichana; ***D:*** Youngyooth Thongkonthun; ***W:*** Youngyooth Thongkonthun; ***C:*** Jira Maligool, Sayombhu Mukdeeprom.

The Iron Major ½ **1943** Frank Cavanaugh, a famous football coach, becomes a hero in WWI. Standard flag-waving biography to increase morale back home, but fairly well-made. **85m/B VHS.** Pat O'Brien, Ruth Warrick, Robert Ryan, Leon Ames, Russell Wade, Bruce Edwards; ***D:*** Ray Enright.

Iron Man **2008 (PG-13)** Sadly not based on the Black Sabbath song, this big-screen version of Marvel Comics' B-list armored avenger is one of the better movies to emerge from the bloated, nerd-fed superhero genre. Billionaire weapons-maker/media playboy Tony Stark (Downey) builds an amazing suit of armor to help him escape from terrorists and decides to make a go of it as a card-carrying hero, much to the confusion of his flirty assistant (Paltrow) and chagrin of his business partner (Bridges). There's some great FX and sharp dialogue, but 95 percent of the movie's appeal comes from Downey, who brings a ridiculous charm and energy to the whole affair. On the flip side, the plot is paper-thin and you saw all the best bits in the trailer. Not exactly iron, but solid summer fun, nonetheless. **126m/C DVD.** Robert Downey Jr., Gwyneth Paltrow, Terrence Howard, Jeff Bridges, Samuel L. Jackson, Shaun Toub, Leslie Bibb, Bill Smitrovich, Clark Gregg, Tim Guinee, Faran Tahir, Ahmed Ahmed, Joshua Harto, Peter Billingsley, Jon Favreau, Sayed Badreya; ***D:*** Jon Favreau; ***W:*** Mark Fergus, Art Marcum, Mat Holloway, Hawk Ostby; ***C:*** Matthew Libatique; ***M:*** Ramin Djawadi; ***V:*** Paul Bettany.

Iron Man 2 **2010** In the Marvel Comics sequel, billionaire industrialist/inventor Tony Stark (Downey Jr.) has a business rival (Rockwell) and the government to deal with while his alter-ego Iron Man has trouble with the villainous Whiplash (Rourke) and the seductive Black Widow (Johansson). Don Cheadle replaces Terrence Howard as Stark's bud Col. James Rhodes. **117m/C DVD.** *US* Robert Downey Jr., Gwyneth Paltrow, Don Cheadle, Mickey Rourke, Scarlett Johansson, Sam Rockwell, Samuel L. Jackson, Kate Mara, Leslie Bibb, Olivia Munn, John Slattery, Clark Gregg, Garry Shandling, Tim Guinee, Helena Mattsson, Jon Favreau; ***D:*** Jon Favreau; ***W:*** Justin Theroux; ***C:*** Matthew Libatique; ***M:*** John Debney; ***V:*** Paul Bettany.

The Iron Mask ½ **1929** Early swashbuckling extravaganza with a master swordsman defending the French king from a scheme involving substitution by a lookalike. Still fairly exciting, thanks largely to director Dwan's flair. Based on Alexandre Dumas's "Three Musketeers" and "The Man in the Iron Mask" with talking sequences. **103m/B VHS, DVD.** Douglas Fairbanks Sr., Nigel de Brulier, Marguerite de la Motte, Ullrich Haupt, William "Billy" Bakewell; ***D:*** Allan Dwan; ***W:*** Douglas Fairbanks Sr.; ***C:*** Henry Sharp.

Iron Maze ½ **1991 (R)** A fascinating notion forms the center of this dramatic scrapheap; the classic Japanese "Rashomon" plot shifted to a rusting Pennsylvania steel town. When a Tokyo businessman is found bludgeoned, witnesses and suspects (including his American-born wife) tell contradictory stories. It's too convoluted and contrived to work, with a hollow happy ending tacked on. Oliver Stone helped produce. **102m/C VHS, DVD.** Jeff Fahey, Bridget Fonda, Hiroaki Murakami, J.T. Walsh, Gabriel Damon, John Randolph, Peter Allas; ***D:*** Hiroaki Yoshida; ***W:*** Tim Metcalfe; ***C:*** Morio Saegusa; ***M:*** Stanley Myers.

The Iron Mistress **1952** Lots of action but hardly a historically accurate bio of frontiersman Jim Bowie. Bowie (Ladd) comes to New Orleans to run the family's lumber business and is made a fool of by Creole beauty Judalon (Mayo), who's stringing along several beaus. Bowie turns to gambling to get the money to woo Judalon, who marries another man (Kjellin) anyway. However, the femme still has Bowie in her clutches, which leads to his design of the titular double-edged knife. **109m/C DVD.** Alan Ladd, Virginia Mayo, Alf Kjellin, Joseph Calleia, Anthony Caruso, Phyllis Kirk, Douglas Dick; ***D:*** Gordon Douglas; ***W:*** James R. Webb; ***C:*** John Seitz; ***M:*** Max Steiner.

Iron Monkey ½ *Siunin Wong Fei-hung Tsi Titmalau; Shao Nian Huang Fei Hong Zhi Tie Ma Liu; Iron Monkey: The Young Wong Fei-hung* **1993 (PG-13)** Historical fantasy martial arts is built around the Iron Monkey (Rongguang Yu), a Robin-Hood figure who defeats whole armies of opponents and can leap tall buildings in a single bound. The humor and outstanding choreography of the fight scenes put this one a cut above the usual martial arts action flick. **87m/C VHS, DVD.** *HK* Rongguang Yu, Donnie Yen, Yam Sai-kun, Tsing-ying Wong; ***D:*** Wooping Yuen; ***W:*** Tseng Pik-Yin, Tsui Hark, Tai-Muk Lau, Cheung Tan, Pik-yin Tang; ***C:*** Arthur Wong Ngok Tai; ***M:*** James L. Venable.

Iron Mountain Trail ½ **1953** Postal inspector Allen is sent to California to see what's holding up mail delivery. He discovers a couple of nefarious types and he and his horse Koko put them in their place. **54m/B VHS.** Rex Allen, Slim Pickens, Roy Barcroft, Grant Withers, Nan Leslie, Forrest Taylor; ***D:*** William Witney; ***W:*** Gerald Geraghty; ***C:*** Bud Thackery; ***M:*** Stanley Wilson.

Iron Thunder ½ **1989** Liberty is in peril and only much kicking and pec flexing will make the world a kinder gentler place. A thundering bore. **85m/C VHS.** Anthony "Amp" Elmore, George M. Young, Julius Dorsey; ***D:*** Anthony "Amp" Elmore.

The Iron Triangle **1989 (R)** A U.S. officer taken prisoner by the Viet Cong forms a bond with one of his captors. Film lends the viewer an opportunity to see things from the other sides perspective. **94m/C VHS.** Beau Bridges, Haing S. Ngor, Liem Whatley; ***D:*** Eric Weston; ***W:*** John Bushelman.

Iron Warrior **1987 (R)** A barbarian hacks his way through a fantastical world to get to a beautiful princess. **82m/C VHS.** Miles O'Keeffe, Savina Gersak, Tim Lane; ***D:*** Al (Alfonso Brescia) Bradley; ***W:*** Al (Alfonso Brescia) Bradley.

Iron Will ½ **1993 (PG)** Okay Disney family movie based on a true story. Will Stoneman is a 17-year-old farm kid from South Dakota. It's 1917 and because of his father's death there's no money to send Will to college. So he decides to enter the 500 mile winner-take-all dog sled race, with its $10,000 prize. Lots of obstacles, several villains, but Will perseveres. **109m/C VHS, DVD.** MacKenzie Astin, Kevin Spacey, David Ogden Stiers, August Schellenberg, George Gerdes, John Terry; ***D:*** Charles Haid; ***W:*** John Michael Hayes, Jeffrey Arch, Djordje Milicevic; ***M:*** Joel McNeely.

Ironclads ½ **1990** Memorable dramatization of the five-hour naval battle between the Confederate's Merrimac and the Union's Monitor during the Civil War. The special effects are the only thing worth watching in this overlong tale that includes standard subplots of loyalty, lost loves, and death from war. **94m/C VHS.** Virginia Madsen, Alex Hyde-White, Reed Edward Diamond, E.G. Marshall, Fritz Weaver, Philip Casnoff; ***D:*** Delbert Mann.

Ironheart ½ **1992** Slimy Milverstead and his henchman meet lovely young women at dance clubs, drug them, and sell them into slavery. But the trouble really starts when they kill a cop and his former partner, John Keem (Lee), lashes out with his blazing martial arts skill to still the perpetrators. **92m/C VHS.** Britton Lee, Bolo Yeung, Richard Norton, Karman Kruschke; ***D:*** Robert Clouse; ***W:*** Lawrence Riggins.

Ironmaster **1982** When a primitive tribesman is exiled from his tribe, he discovers a mysteriously power-filled iron staff on a mountainside. **98m/C VHS.** *IT FR* George Eastman, Pamela Field, Danilo Mattei, Jacques Herlin; ***D:*** Umberto Lenzi; ***W:*** Umberto Lenzi, Lea Martino; ***C:*** Giancarlo Ferrando; ***M:*** Guido de Angelis, Maurizio de Angelis.

Ironweed **1987 (R)** Grim and gritty drama about bums living the hard life in Depression-era Albany. Nicholson excels as a former ballplayer turned drunk bothered by visions of the past, and Streep is his equal in the lesser role of a tubercular boozer. Waits also shines. Another grim view from "Pixote" director Babenco. Kennedy scripted based on his Pulitzer Prize-winning tragedy. **135m/C VHS.** Jack Nicholson, Meryl Streep, Tom Waits, Carroll Baker, Michael O'Keefe, Fred Gwynne, Diane Venora, Margaret Whitton, Jake Dengel, Nathan Lane, James Gammon, Joe Grifasi, Bethel Leslie, Ted Levine, Frank Whaley; ***D:*** Hector Babenco; ***W:*** William Kennedy; ***M:*** John Morris. L.A. Film Critics '87: Actor (Nicholson); N.Y. Film Critics '87: Actor (Nicholson).

Irreconcilable Differences ½ **1984 (PG)** When her Beverly Hills parents spend more time working and fretting than giving hugs and love, a ten-year-old girl sues them for divorce on the grounds of "irreconcilable differences." The media has a field day when they hear that she would rather go live with the maid. Well cast, with well-developed characterizations. The script, by the creators of "Private Benjamin," is humanely comic rather than uproariously funny. **112m/C VHS.** Ryan O'Neal, Shelley Long, Drew Barrymore, Sam Wanamaker, Allen (Goorwitz) Garfield, Sharon Stone, Luana Anders; ***D:*** Charles Shyer; ***W:*** Charles Shyer, Nancy Meyers.

Irresistible ½ **2006** Sophie Harley (Sarandon) is convinced she's being stalked by her husband Craig's (Neill) beautiful coworker Mara (Blunt) because she wants Sophie's life for herself. But the truth will shock Sophie even more. Formulaic psychothriller redeemed by expert cast. **109m/C DVD.** *AU* Susan Sarandon, Sam Neill, Emily Blunt, Charles "Bud" Tingwell, William McInnes; ***D:*** Ann Turner; ***W:*** Ann Turner; ***C:*** Martin McGrath; ***M:*** David Hirschfelder. **VIDEO**

Irresistible Impulse ½ **1995** Sleazy real estate agent Jeffrey allows himself to become entangled in a wild scheme with bad girl Beaman. **107m/C VHS.** Doug Jeffery, Lee Anne Beavan; ***D:*** Jag Mundhra.

Irreversible ½ **2002** The rape scene is nine minutes long. If you're still willing to sit through this abrasive flick after knowing that, here's the story (which is told backwards). Marcus (Cassel) and Pierre (Dupontel) are being led away from a gay S&M club where a murder has occurred. They have sought revenge for what happened to Marcus's lover Alex (Bellucci). Earlier, Marcus fought with Alex at a party and she leaves alone—to be brutalized into a coma by a thug (Prestia) in an underground pedestrian tunnel. Then we see the trio, Pierre is an old friend of Alex's and is jealous of Marcus, going to the party and expecting to have fun. Everyone's destined to be disappointed. French with subtitles. **99m/C VHS, DVD.** *FR* Monica Bellucci, Vincent Cassel, Albert Dupontel, Jo Prestia, Philippe Nahon; ***D:*** Gaspar Noe; ***W:*** Gaspar Noe; ***C:*** Gaspar Noe; ***M:*** Thomas Bangalter.

Is Anybody There? ½ **2008 (PG-13)** And the answer would be 'not anymore.' Elderly traveling magician Clarence Parkinson (Caine) has ended up at a rundown seaside retirement home. Despite his general grumpiness, Clarence befriends lonely 10-year-old Edward (Milner), the son of the home's harried owners. Clarence starts teaching Edward magic tricks but the magic Clarence would like is a chance to visit his late wife's grave before his dementia takes control of his life—and Edward wants to help. Notable, vanity-free performance by Caine. **94m/C DVD.** *GB* Michael Caine, Bill Milner, Anne-Marie Duff, David Morrissey, Rosemary Harris, Peter Vaughan, Elizabeth Spriggs; ***D:*** John Crowley; ***W:*** Peter Harness; ***C:*** Rob Hardy; ***M:*** Joby Talbot.

Is Money Everything? **1923** Man goes to the big city, becomes a success, and then has an affair with a married woman. **58m/B VHS.** Norman Kerry, Miriam Cooper, Martha Mansfield, William Bailey, Andrew Hicks, John Sylvester, Lawrence Brooke; ***D:*** Glen Lyons; *W:* Glen Lyons; *C:* Alvin Knechtel.

Is Paris Burning? 🦴🦴🦴 *Paris Brule-t-il?* **1966** A spectacularly star-studded but far too sprawling account of the liberation of Paris from Nazi occupation. The script, in which seven writers had a hand, is based on Larry Collins and Dominique Lapierre's best-seller. **173m/C VHS, DVD.** *FR* Jean-Paul Belmondo, Charles Boyer, Leslie Caron, Jean-Pierre Cassel, George Chakiris, Claude Dauphin, Alain Delon, Kirk Douglas, Glenn Ford, Gert Frobe, Daniel Gelin, E.G. Marshall, Yves Montand, Anthony Perkins, Claude Rich, Simone Signoret, Robert Stack, Jean-Louis Trintignant, Pierre Vaneck, Orson Welles, Bruno Cremer, Suzy Delair, Michael (Michel) Lonsdale; *D:* Rene Clement; *W:* Gore Vidal, Francis Ford Coppola; *C:* Marcel Grignon; *M:* Maurice Jarre.

Is There Life Out There? 🦴🦴 1/2 **1994** Wife, mother, and waitress Lily Marshall (McEntire) decides it's time to do something for herself—so she goes to work on her college degree. But there's unexpected family resentments, a breast cancer scare, and the interest of a young teaching assistant to turn her head away from her studies. Filmed in Nashville, Tennessee. Based on a song by McEntire; made for TV. **92m/C VHS, DVD.** Reba McEntire, Keith Carradine, Mitchell Anderson, Donald Moffat, Genia Michaela; *D:* David Hugh Jones; *W:* Dalene Young. **TV**

Is There Sex After Death? 🦴🦴🦴 **1971 (R)** Often funny satire on the sexual revolution is constructed as a behind-the-scenes view of the porn film world. Odd cast includes Henry and Warhol superstar Woodlawn. Originally rated "X." **97m/C VHS, DVD.** Buck Henry, Alan Abel, Marshall Efron, Holly Woodlawn, Earl Doud; *D:* Alan Abel, Jeanne Abel.

Isaac Asimov's Nightfall 🦴🦴 *Nightfall* **2000 (R)** The planet Aeon has six suns and has never experienced night. But with an eclipse approaching, religious cultists are predicting catastrophe. Scientist Carradine tries to allay the population's fear. Low-budget and bland adaptation of Asimov's 1941 short story. **85m/C VHS, DVD.** David Carradine, Jennifer Burns, Joseph Hodge; *D:* Gwyneth Gibby; *W:* Gwyneth Gibby, John W. Corrington, Michael B. Druxman; *C:* Abhik Mukhopadhyay; *M:* Nicolas Tenbroek, Brad Segal. **VIDEO**

Isadora 🦴🦴🦴 *The Loves of Isadora* **1968** A loose, imaginative biography of Isadora Duncan, the cause celebre dancer in the 1920s who became famous for her scandalous performances, outrageous behavior, public love affairs, and bizarre, early death. Redgrave is exceptional in the lead, and Fox provides fine support. Restored from its original 131-minute print length by the director. **138m/C VHS.** *GB* Vanessa Redgrave, Jason Robards Jr., James Fox, Ivan Tchenko, John Fraser, Bessie Love, Cynthia Harris, Libby Glenn, Tony Vogel, Wallace (Wallas) Eaton, John Quentin, Nicholas Pennell, Ronnie Gilbert, Alan Gifford, Christian Duvaleix; *D:* Karel Reisz; *W:* Melvyn Bragg, Clive Exton; *C:* Larry Pizer; *M:* Maurice Jarre. Cannes '69: Actress (Redgrave); Natl. Soc. Film Critics '69: Actress (Redgrave).

Ishtar 🦴🦴 **1987 (PG-13)** Two astoundingly untalented performers have a gig in a fictional Middle Eastern country and become involved in foreign intrigue. A big-budget box-office bomb produced by Beatty offering few laughs, though it's not as bad as its reputation. Considering the talent involved, though, it's a disappointment, with Beatty and Hoffman laboring to create Hope and Crosby chemistry. Anyone for a slow night? **107m/C VHS.** Dustin Hoffman, Warren Beatty, Isabelle Adjani, Charles Grodin, Jack Weston, Tess Harper, Carol Kane, Matt Frewer; *D:* Elaine May; *W:* Elaine May; *C:* Vittorio Storaro; *M:* Dave Grusin. Bahjawa. Golden Raspberries '87: Worst Director (May).

The Island 🦴🦴🦴 1/2 *Hadaka No Shima; Naked Island* **1961** Poetic examination of a peasant family's daily struggle for existence on a small island. No dialogue in this slow but absorbing work by one of Japan's master directors. **96m/B VHS.** *JP* Nobuko Otowa, Taiji Tonoyama, Shinji Tanaka, Masanori Horimoto; *D:* Kaneto Shindo.

The Island WOOF! **1980 (R)** New York reporter embarks on a Bermuda triangle investigation, only to meet with the murderous but sterile descendants of 17th century pirates on a deserted island. Caine is designated as stud service for the last remaining fertile woman. Almost surreal in its badness. Adapted by Benchley from his novel. **113m/C VHS.** Michael Caine, David Warner, Angela Punch McGregor, Frank Middlemass, Don Henderson; *D:* Michael Ritchie; *W:* Peter Benchley; *C:* Henri Decae; *M:* Ennio Morricone.

The Island 🦴🦴 1/2 **2005 (PG-13)** In 2019, folks at the sterile, white-uniform-only, underground community believe that they've been spared from a cataclysmic disaster and await a lottery pick that's supposedly a ticket to "The Island," the last uncontaminated place on the planet. Among the placid group is troublemaker Lincoln Six Echo (McGregor), who discovers they're clones created by evil scientist Merrick (Bean) to serve as donors for their human counterparts. Lincoln flees with fellow resident Jordan Two Delta (Johansson) but Merrick's henchman Laurent (Hounsou) isn't far behind. Initially intriguing plot becomes a typical Bay blow'em up, kill'em all action fest. Interesting (at least to the original's producer) similarity to "Parts: The Clonus Horror" adds another dimension to all the cloning around, and became fodder for some controversy. Partially filmed in Detroit. **136m/C DVD, UMD.** *US* Ewan McGregor, Scarlett Johansson, Djimon Hounsou, Steve Buscemi, Michael Clarke Duncan, Shawnee Smith, Sean Bean, Ethan Phillips, Max Baker, Kim Coates; *D:* Michael Bay; *W:* Caspian Tredwell-Owen, Alex Kurtzman, Roberto Orci; *C:* Mauro Fiore; *M:* Steve Jablonsky.

The Island at the Top of the World 🦴🦴 1/2 **1974 (G)** A rich Englishman, in search of his missing son, travels to the Arctic Circle in 1908. The rescue party includes an American archeologist, a French astronaut, and an Eskimo guide. Astonishingly, they discover an unknown, "lost" Viking kingdom. This Jules Verne-style adventure doesn't quite measure up, but kids will like it. **93m/C VHS, DVD.** David Hartman, Donald Sinden, Jacques Marin, Mako, David Gwillim; *D:* Robert Stevenson; *W:* John Whedon; *C:* Frank Phillips; *M:* Maurice Jarre.

Island Claw WOOF! *Night of the Claw* **1980** A group of marine biologists experimenting on a tropical island discover the "Island Claw," who evolved as the result of toxic waste seeping into the ocean. A festering, oozing woofer. **91m/C VHS.** Barry Nelson, Robert Lansing; *D:* Hernan Cardenas.

Island in the Sky 🦴🦴🦴 **1953** When a transport plane crashes in an isolated area of Labrador, the captain (Wayne) must keep his crew alive long enough for them to be rescued. Long-awaited release has all the rugged manliness you'd expect of a Wayne flick. Faithful adaptation successfully conveys the increasing desperation and sense of doom of the crew and the would-be rescuers. **109m/B DVD.** John Wayne, Lloyd Nolan, Walter Abel, James Arness, Andy Devine, Allyn Joslyn, Jimmy Lydon, Harry Carey Jr., Hal Baylor, Sean McClory, Wally Cassell, Gordon Jones, Frank Fenton, Regis Toomey, Paul Fix, George Chandler, Louis Jean Heydt, Darryl Hickman, Mike Connors, Carl "Alfalfa" Switzer, Ann Doran, Fess Parker; *D:* William A. Wellman; *W:* Ernest K. Gann; *C:* Archie Stout; *M:* Emil Newman.

Island in the Sun 🦴🦴 **1957** Racial tension pulls apart the lives of the residents of a Caribbean island. Good cast, but a very poor adaptation of Alec Waugh's novel. Marvelous location shots. **119m/C VHS, DVD.** James Mason, Joan Fontaine, Dorothy Dandridge, John Williams, Harry Belafonte; *D:* Robert Rossen; *C:* Frederick A. (Freddie) Young; *M:* Malcolm Arnold.

Island Monster 🦴 1/2 *Monster of the Island* **1953** Deals with ruthless, kidnapping drug-smugglers led by "monster" Karloff, and the efforts to bring them to justice. **87m/B VHS, DVD.** *IT* Boris Karloff, Renata Vicario, Franca Marzi; *D:* Robert Bianchi Montero.

Island of Blood 🦴 1/2 **1982** Buckets of blood abound on a remote island when a film crew's beset by berserk butcher. **84m/C VHS.** Gary Phillips, Rick Dean, Jim Williams, Dean Richards; *D:* William T. Naud; *W:* William T. Naud; *C:* Thomas E. Spalding; *M:* Joel Goldsmith.

Island of Desire 🦴 *Saturday Island* **1952** An Army nurse, a doctor, and a young Navy Adonis are trapped on a deserted island. Not surprisingly, a love triangle develops. **93m/C VHS.** *GB* Tab Hunter, Linda Darnell, Donald Gray; *D:* Stuart Heisler.

The Island of Dr. Moreau 🦴🦴 1/2 **1977 (PG)** This remake of the "Island of the Lost Souls" (1933) is a bit disappointing but worth watching for Lancaster's solid performance as the scientist who has isolated himself on a Pacific island in order to continue his chromosome research—he can transform animals into near-humans and humans into animals. Neat-looking critters. Adaptation of the H.G. Wells novel of the same title. **99m/C VHS, DVD.** Burt Lancaster, Michael York, Nigel Davenport, Barbara Carrera, Richard Basehart, Nick Cravat; *D:* Don Taylor; *W:* John Herman Shaner, Al Ramrus; *C:* Gerry Fisher.

The Island of Dr. Moreau 🦴 1/2 **1996 (PG-13)** What were they thinking? Not even the frightening "manimals" could prevent the unintentional laughs from this abomination of the horrifying 1896 H.G. Wells novel. Brando's enormous presence as the mad scientist Moreau walks a tight rope between puzzling and campy, especially as he explains his ghastly DNA experiments on a remote Pacific to a miscast Thewlis. A wasted Kilmer is the doctors's right-hand hybrid who often seems to be acting in a different movie. Filming hit some big rocks when "creative differences" caused original director Richard Stanley to be replaced and Rob Morrow (originally the lawyer) to ask for his release. Previously filmed under the same title in 1977 and (terrifically) as "Island of Lost Souls" in 1933. **91m/C VHS, DVD.** Marlon Brando, Val Kilmer, David Thewlis, Fairuza Balk, Marco Hofschneider, Temuera Morrison, Ron Perlman; *D:* John Frankenheimer; *W:* Richard Stanley, Ron Hutchinson; *C:* William A. Fraker; *M:* Gary Chang.

Island of Lost Girls WOOF! *Kommissar X - Drei Goldene Schlangen; Three Golden Serpents* **1968 (R)** Young women are taken to an unknown location in the Far East to be sold as part of a white slave ring. **85m/C VHS.** *IT GE* Brad Harris, Tony Kendall, Monica Pardo, Herbert (Fuchs) Fux; *D:* Robert (Roberto) Mauri; *W:* Manfred Kohler, Gianfranco Parolini; *C:* Francesco Izzarelli; *M:* Francesco De Masi.

Island of Lost Souls 🦴🦴🦴 1/2 **1932** Horrifying adaptation of H.G. Wells's "The Island of Dr. Moreau" was initially banned in parts of the U.S. because of its disturbing contents. Dr. Moreau (Laughton) is a mad scientist who lives on a remote island and is obsessed with making men out of jungle animals. When shipwreck survivor Edward Parker (Arlen) gets stranded on the island, little does he know that Moreau wants to mate him with Lota (Burke), the Panther Woman, to produce the first human-animal child. As unsettling today as it was in the '30s. Lugosi has the notable role of the hybrid "Sayer of the Law" while Burke beat out more than 60,000 young women in a nationwide search to play the Panther Woman, winning the role because of her "feline" look. Remade as "The Island of Dr. Moreau" in both 1977 and 1996. **71m/B VHS, DVD.** Charles Laughton, Bela Lugosi, Richard Arlen, Leila Hyams, Kathleen Burke, Stanley Fields, Robert F. (Bob) Kortman, Arthur Hohl; ***Cameos:*** Alan Ladd, Randolph Scott, Buster Crabbe; *D:* Erle C. Kenton; *W:* Philip Wylie, Waldemar Young; *C:* Karl Struss.

Island of Terror 🦴🦴🦴 *Night of the Silicates; The Creepers* **1966** First-rate science fiction chiller about an island overrun by shell-like creatures that suck the bones out of their living prey. Good performances and interesting twists make for prickles up the spine. **90m/C VHS.** *GB* Peter Cushing, Edward Judd, Carole Gray, Sam Kydd, Niall MacGinnis; *D:* Terence Fisher.

Island of the Blue Dolphins 🦴🦴 1/2 **1964** Based on a popular children's book by Scott O'Dell, this is a true story of a young Native American girl who, with her brother, are stranded on a deserted island when their people accidentally leave them. When the boy is killed, the girl learns to survive by her skills and by befriending the leader of a pack of wild dogs. Good family fare. **99m/C VHS.** Celia Kaye, Larry Domasin, Ann Daniel, George Kennedy; *D:* James B. Clark; *W:* Ted Sherdeman; *C:* Leo Tover; *M:* Paul Sawtell.

Island of the Burning Doomed 🦴🦴 1/2 *Island of the Burning Damned; Night of the Big Heat* **1967** A brutal heat wave accompanies invading aliens in this British-made outing. Lee and Cushing carry the picture. **94m/C VHS, DVD.** *GB* Christopher Lee, Peter Cushing, Patrick Allen, Sarah Lawson, Jane Merrow; *D:* Terence Fisher.

Island of the Dead 🦴🦴 **2000 (R)** Now here's a storyline sure to be entertaining. One business tycoon, one policewoman, one prison warden, and three convicts are all trapped on a island burial ground. Just when the dead (in the form of maggots and killer flies) decide to rise up and strike a little terror. **91m/C VHS, DVD.** Malcolm McDowell, Talisa Soto, Bruce Ramsay, Mos Def; *D:* Tim Southam; *W:* Peter Koper, Tim Southam. **VIDEO**

Island of the Lost 🦴 1/2 **1968** An anthropologist's family must fight for survival when they become shipwrecked on a mysterious island. **92m/C VHS, DVD.** *GB* Richard Greene, Luke Halpin, Mart Hulswit, Jose De Vega, Robin Mattson, Irene Tsu, Sheilah Wells; *D:* John Florea, Ricou Browning; *W:* Richard Carlson, Ivan Tors; *C:* Howard Winner; *M:* George Bruns.

The Island on Bird Street 🦴🦴 1/2 **1997 (PG-13)** Eleven-year-old Jewish Alex (Kiziuk) is forced to live in the Warsaw ghetto with his father Stefan (Bergin) and great-uncle Boruch (Warden). When the Gestapo round up the inhabitants to send them to concentration camps, Alex manages to elude capture. Inspired by his favorite book, "The Adventures of Robinson Crusoe," he hides out in an abandoned building on Bird Street with only his pet mouse Snow for company. Alex struggles with daily survival as he awaits his father's promised return. Based on the autobiographical children's book by Uri Orlev. **102m/C DVD.** *GB DK GE* Patrick Bergin, Jack Warden, Soeren Kragh-Jacobsen, Jordan Kiziuk; *W:* John Goldsmith, Tony Grisoni; *C:* Ian Wilson; *M:* Zbigniew Preisner.

Island Trader 🦴 **1971** Young lad battles pirates and a crooked tug captain who seek hidden gold that he knows about. **95m/C VHS.** John Ewart, Ruth Cracknell, Eric Oldfield; *D:* Harold Rubie.

The Islander 🦴 **1988** Sixteen-year-old Inga comes of age among the commercial fishermen of Lake Michigan. **99m/C VHS.** Kit Wholihan, Jeff Weborg, Celia Klehr, Jacob Mills, Julie Johnson, Mary Ann McHugh, Michael Rock, Sheri Parish; *D:* Phyllis Berg-Pigorsch.

Islander 🦴🦴 **2006 (R)** Lobster fisherman Eben Cole lives in a tight-knit community on a small island off the Maine coast. A tragedy leads to Eben's 5-year imprisonment and he returns to find himself shunned as other fisherman now consider him bad luck. Eben tries to rebuild his life, getting a second chance at what he does best from elderly trawler Popper. **100m/C DVD.** Amy Jo Johnson, Philip Baker Hall, Judy Prescott, Ron Canada, Larry Pine, Thomas Hildreth, Mark Kiely, Emma Ford; *D:* Ian McCrudden; *W:* Thomas Hildreth; *C:* Dan Coplan; *M:* Billy Mallery.

Islands 🦴🦴 **1987** Drama about a middle-aged ex-hippie and a young rebellious punk who clash during a summer together on a secluded island. **55m/C VHS.** Louise Fletcher; *D:* Rene Bonniere. **TV**

Islands in the Stream 🦴🦴 1/2 **1977 (PG)** Based on Ernest Hemingway's novel, this film is actually two movies in one. An American painter/sculptor, Thomas Hudson, lives a reclusive life on the island of Bimini shortly before the outbreak of WWII. The first part is a sensitive story of a broken family and the coming of the artist's three sons to live with their father after a four-year separation. The second part is a second rate action-adventure. **105m/C VHS, DVD.** George C. Scott, David Hemmings, Claire Bloom, Susan Tyrrell, Gilbert Roland; *D:* Franklin J. Schaffner; *C:* Fred W. Koenekamp; *M:* Jerry Goldsmith.

The Isle 🦴🦴 *Seom* **2001** For those who like their arthouse features on the kinky side. The isle is a series of small huts anchored in a river that's part of a remote fishing area. But the male guests don't just come for the fishing—they bring their own female company or take what's offered by mute manager Hee-Jin. She becomes obsessed with Hyun-Shik, an ex-cop who murdered his unfaithful lover and who's hiding out while contemplating suicide. She saves him, protects him from the police, and shares a very intimate relationship with the unstable man. Korean with subtitles. **89m/C VHS, DVD.** *KN* Suh Jung, Yoo-Suk Kim, Sung-Hee Park; ***D:*** Ki-Duk Kim; ***W:*** Ki-Duk Kim; ***C:*** Seo-Shik Hwang; ***M:*** Sang-Yun Jeon.

Isle of Forgotten Sins *Monsoon* **1943** Deep sea divers and an evil ship's captain vie for treasure. Good cast and direction but unremarkable material. **82m/B VHS, DVD.** John Carradine, Gale Sondergaard, Sidney Toler, Frank Fenton, Veda Ann Borg; ***D:*** Edgar G. Ulmer.

Isle of Secret Passion **1982** A romance novel comes to video life as two lovers thrash out their problems on a Greek island. **90m/C VHS.** Patch MacKenzie, Michael MacRae, Zohra Lampert; ***D:*** Herbert Stein.

Isle of the Dead 1/2 **1945** A Greek general is quarantined with seemingly all manner of social vermin on a plague-infested island in the early 1900s. The fear is that vampires walk among them. Characteristically spooky Val Lewton production with some original twists. **72m/B VHS, DVD.** Boris Karloff, Ellen Drew, Marc Cramer, Katherine Emery, Helen Thimig, Alan Napier, Jason Robards Sr., Skelton Knaggs; ***D:*** Mark Robson; ***W:*** Josef Mischel, Ardel Wray; ***C:*** Jack MacKenzie; ***M:*** Leigh Harline.

Isn't Life Wonderful **1924** Inga's (Dempster) a Polish war orphan who struggles to provide for her family in post-WWI Germany. It means giving up her dream to marry former soldier, Paul (Hamilton), but he has a secret plan to reunite them. Filmed on location. **118m/B VHS.** Carol Dempster, Neil Hamilton, Lupino Lane, Hans von Schlettow; ***D:*** D.W. Griffith; ***W:*** D.W. Griffith.

Isn't She Great **2000 (R)** Irreverant biopic about the queen of '60s trash novels, Jacqueline Susann (Midler), and her hungry quest for flashy fame. Lane plays her ever-loyal husband and manager, Irving Mansfield. Susann's life was no bed of roses as she fought a long battle with breast cancer and had an austistic child, although she never let her personal tragedies become public fodder. Midler gives an overripe performance while Channing (as best friend Florence) proves to be the true scene-stealer. Unfortunately, the film is even more shallow than a Susann novel and lot less fun. Based on a memoir by Susann's editor, Michael Korda. **96m/C VHS, DVD.** Bette Midler, Nathan Lane, Stockard Channing, David Hyde Pierce, John Cleese, John Larroquette, Amanda Peet, Lisa Bronwyn Moore, Dina Spybey; ***D:*** Andrew Bergman; ***W:*** Paul Rudnick; ***C:*** Karl Walter Lindenlaub; ***M:*** Burt Bacharach.

Istanbul 1/2 **1957** Adventurer Jim Brennan (Flynn) finds a fortune in smuggled diamonds, which he hides in a hotel room. Unfortunately, he's deported before he can retrieve the gems and it takes him five years to make it back to Istanbul. Then he's hounded by the original smugglers who want their gems back and discovers his lost love Stephanie (Borchers). Cole croons a couple of songs in his role as a lounge singer. Remake of 1947's "Singapore." ♫When I Fall In Love; I Was a Little Too Lonely. **85m/C VHS.** Errol Flynn, Cornell Borchers, John Bentley, Torin Thatcher, Leif Erickson, Peggy Knudsen, Martin Benson, Nat King Cole, Werner Klemperer; ***D:*** Joseph Pevney; ***W:*** Seton I. Miller, Barbara Gray; ***C:*** William H. Daniels.

Istanbul **1985 (R)** An American charms a Belgian student into taking part in a kidnap scheme. **90m/C VHS.** *FR* Brad Dourif, Dominique Deruddere, Ingrid De Vos, Francois Beukelaers; ***D:*** Marc Didden.

Istanbul *Istanbul, Keep Your Eyes Open* **1990 (PG-13)** Believing he has stumbled upon the best story of his career, a journalist soon discovers that he has been pulled into a world of guns and violence. **88m/C VHS.** *TU SW* Robert Morley, Timothy Bottoms, Twiggy; ***D:*** Mats Arehn.

The Ister **2004** Rookie writers/directors Barison and Ross document their thought-provoking five-year trek up the 2,000-mile-long Danube River (ancient Greek name "The Ister") from its mouth in the Black Sea to its origin in Germany's Black Forest. Along the way, the Australian philosophy students visit with prominent European philosophers who discuss the 1942 lecture of German existentialist Martin Heidegger (their inspiration and author of "Time and Being") while capturing such images as an ancient Greek city, war-torn Serbian towns, and the Mauthausen-Gusen concentration camp. **189m/C DVD.** ***D:*** Daniel Ross, David Barison; ***C:*** Daniel Ross, David Barison.

It 1/2 **1927** The film that established Bow as a prominent screen siren. Betty Lou (Bow) is a saucy lingerie sales clerk who sets her sights on department store owner Cyrus (Moreno), despite the fact that he has a fiancee. Adapted by Elinor Glyn from her own story; Glyn also makes an appearance. **71m/B VHS, DVD.** Clara Bow, Antonio Moreno, Jacqueline Gadsdon, William Austin, Gary Cooper, Julia Swayne Gordon; ***D:*** Clarence Badger, Josef von Sternberg; ***W:*** Hope Loring, Louis D. Lighton; ***C:*** Kinley Martin. Natl. Film Reg. '01.

It Ain't Hay 1/2 **1943** Grover (Abbott) and buddy Wilbur (Costello) accidentally kill their friend King O'Hara's (Kellaway) horse, so they steal a horse from the racetrack. Only the horse turns out to be a champion racer. Remake of the 1935 film "Princess O'Hara" and based on a Damon Runyon story. **79m/B VHS.** Bud Abbott, Lou Costello, Cecil Kellaway, Grace McDonald, Eugene Pallette, Shemp Howard, Eddie Quillan; ***D:*** Erle C. Kenton; ***W:*** Allen Boretz, John Grant; ***C:*** Charles Van Enger.

It Always Rains on Sunday 1/2 **1947** Slice-of-life snapshot of several lives intertwining on a rainy Sunday in post-war London. Tommy Swann (McCallum) has just escaped from prison and hopes to hide out with ex Rose (Withers), but she's moved on and is now married. Tommy's arrival brings up Rose's own unhappiness, and the family is thrown into turmoil. **92m/B DVD.** Googie Withers, Edward Chapman, Susan Shaw, Patricia Plunkett, David Lines, Sydney Tafler, Betty Ann Davies, John Slater, Jane Hylton, Meier Tzelniker, John McCallum, Jimmy Hanley, John Carol, Alfie Bass, Jack Warner; ***D:*** Robert Hamer; ***W:*** Henry Cornelius; ***C:*** Douglas Slocombe; ***M:*** Georges Auric.

It Came from Beneath the Sea **1955** A giant octopus arises from the depths of the sea to scour San Francisco for human food. Ray Harryhausen effects are special. **80m/B VHS, DVD.** Kenneth Tobey, Faith Domergue, Ian Keith, Donald Curtis; ***D:*** Robert Gordon.

It Came from Outer Space **1953** Aliens take on the form of local humans to repair their spacecraft in a small Arizona town. Good performances and outstanding direction add up to a fine science fiction film. Based on the story "The Meteor" by Ray Bradbury, who also wrote the script. Originally filmed in 3-D. **81m/B VHS, DVD.** Richard Carlson, Barbara Rush, Charles Drake, Russell Johnson, Kathleen Hughes; ***D:*** Jack Arnold; ***W:*** Harry Essex, Ray Bradbury; ***C:*** Clifford Stine; ***M:*** Henry Mancini, Herman Stein, Irving Gertz.

It Came from Outer Space 2 1/2 **1995 (PG-13)** Poorly updated cable version of the sci-fi film finds photographer Jack Putnam (Kerwin) heading home to his isolated desert community. A freakish blue lightning storm causes big changes amongst the desert dwellers who are sucked into a glowing ground mass and re-emerge possessed by shape-shifting aliens, who need the human bodies to rebuild their crashed space ship. Based on a story by Ray Bradbury and the 1953 screenplay by Harry Essex. **85m/C VHS.** Brian Kerwin, Elizabeth Pena, Bill McKinney, Jonathan Carrasco, Adrian Sparks, Howard Morris, Mickey Jones, Lauren Tewes; ***D:*** Roger Duchowny; ***W:*** Jim Wheat, Ken Wheat; ***M:*** Shirley Walker. **CABLE**

It Came from the Sky **1998 (R)** Eccentric strangers Jarvis Moody (Lloyd) and his girlfriend Pepper (Bleeth) invade the lives of bitter Donald (Ritter), his long-suffering wife Alice (Williams), and their brain-damaged teenage son (Zegers). Has fate sent the strange duo to intervene for good or is disaster about to strike? **92m/C VHS, DVD.** John Ritter, Christopher Lloyd, Yasmine Bleeth, JoBeth Williams, Kevin Zegers; ***D:*** Jack Bender.

It Came Upon a Midnight Clear 1/2 **1984** A heavenly miracle enables a retired (and dead) New York policeman to keep a Christmas promise to his grandson. **96m/C VHS, DVD.** Mickey Rooney, Scott Grimes, George Gaynes, Annie Potts, Lloyd Nolan, Barrie Youngfellow; ***D:*** Peter H. Hunt; ***C:*** Dean Cundey. **TV**

It Conquered the World 1/2 **1956** Vegetable critters from Venus follow a probe satellite back to Earth and drop in on scientist Van Cleef, who'd been their intergalactic pen pal (seems he thought a Venusian invasion would improve the neighborhood). Their travelling companions, little bat creatures, turn earth dwellers into murderous zombies, and it starts to look like the Venusians are trying to make earth their planetary exurbia. Early vintage zero-budget Corman, for schlock connoisseurs. Remade for TV as "Zontar, the Thing from Venus." **68m/B VHS.** Peter Graves, Beverly Garland, Lee Van Cleef, Sally Fraser, Charles B. Griffith, Russ Bender, Jonathan Haze, Dick Miller, Karen Kadler, Paul Blaisdell; ***D:*** Roger Corman; ***W:*** Lou Rusoff, Charles B. Griffith; ***C:*** Frederick E. West; ***M:*** Ronald Stein.

It Could Happen to You 1/2 **1937** Stepbrothers raised by a gentle immigrant take different paths in life. When one ends up killing someone during a botched robbery, the other—a lawyer—defends him. Standard '30s morality play. **64m/B VHS.** Alan Baxter, Andrea Leeds, Owen Davis Jr., Astrid Allwyn, Walter Kingsford, Al Shean; ***D:*** Phil Rosen.

It Could Happen to You **1939** A drunken advertising executive is charged with murder after a dead nightclub singer is found in his car. His wife sets out to clear him. **64m/C VHS.** Stuart Erwin, Gloria Stuart, Raymond Walburn, Douglas Fowley, June Gale, Paul Hurst, Richard Lane; ***D:*** Alfred Werker.

It Could Happen to You 1/2 *Cop Tips Waitress $2 Million* **1994 (PG)** NYC cop Charlie Lang (Cage) doesn't have any change to leave coffee shop waitress Yvonne (Fonda) a tip, so he promises to split his lottery ticket with her. When he nets $4 million, he makes good on the promise, much to the chargrin of his upwardly mobile wife (Perez). Capra-corn for the X-crowd is pleasant dinnertime diversion as Cage and Perez shine as henpecked nice guy and the wife committed to making him miserable. Don't look for the diner on your next trip to NYC; it was specially built in TriBeCa and dismantled after the shoot. **101m/C VHS, DVD.** Bridget Fonda, Nicolas Cage, Rosie Perez, Red Buttons, Isaac Hayes, Seymour Cassel, Stanley Tucci, J.E. Freeman, Richard Jenkins, Ann Dowd, Wendell Pierce, Angela Pietropinto, Vincent Pastore, Peter Jacobson; ***D:*** Andrew Bergman; ***W:*** Andrew Bergman, Jane Anderson; ***C:*** Caleb Deschanel; ***M:*** Carter Burwell.

It Couldn't Happen Here **1988 (PG-13)** Fans of the techno-pop duo The Pet Shop Boys can test their loyalty by enduring this feature music-video that actually played a few theatres. The dour pair journey across a surreal England, encountering a sinister blind priest, a philisophical ventriloquist's dummy, and more. Songs, sometimes presented only as muted incidental music, include the title track, "West End Girls," "It's a Sin," and "Always on My Mind." **87m/C VHS.** *GB* Neil Tennant, Chris Lowe, Joss Ackland, Neil Dickson, Carmen (De Sautoy) Du Sautoy, Gareth Hunt; ***D:*** Jack Bond.

It Had to Be You 1/2 **2000 (PG)** Elementary school teacher Anna (Henstridge) is engaged to marry advertising exec David (Healy). Ex-cop Charlie (Vartan) is engaged to busy editor Claire (Parker). Both find themselves staying at the Plaza Hotel—without their fiancees who have opted to work—planning their mutual weddings. As Charlie and Anna discuss flowers and entertainment, it becomes clear that the duo are marrying the wrong people. But what will they do about it? Charming and lightweight romantic comedy. **95m/C VHS, DVD.** Natasha Henstridge, Michael Vartan, Joelle Carter, David Healy, Frankie Muniz, Phyllis Newman, Faith Prince, Olivia D'Abo, G. Anthony "Tony" Sirico; ***D:*** Steven Feder; ***W:*** Steven Feder; ***C:*** Ken Kelsch; ***M:*** Luis Bacalov.

It Happened at Nightmare Inn *A Candle for the Devil; Nightmare Hotel* **1970** Average thriller in which Geeson travels to Spanish inn and confronts two mad sisters who run the hotel. **95m/C VHS, DVD.** *SP* Judy Geeson, Aurora Bautista, Esperanza Roy, Victor Alcocer, Lone Fleming; ***D:*** Eugenio (Gene) Martin.

It Happened at the World's Fair 1/2 **1963** Fun and light romance comedy has Elvis and a companion (O'Brien) being escorted through the Seattle World's Fair by a fetching Chinese girl. ♫I'm Falling In Love Tonight; They Remind Me Too Much Of You; Take Me To The Fair; Relax; How Would You Like To Be; Beyond the Bend; One Broken Heart For Sale; Cotton Candy Land; A World Of Our Own. **105m/C VHS, DVD.** Elvis Presley, Joan O'Brien, Gary Lockwood, Kurt Russell, Edith Atwater, Yvonne Craig; ***D:*** Norman Taurog.

It Happened in Brooklyn **1947** Former sailor with blue eyes bunks with janitor with big nose in Brooklyn. Sailor and cronies encounter many musical opportunities. Lots of songs and falling in love, little entertainment. **104m/B VHS.** Frank Sinatra, Kathryn Grayson, Jimmy Durante, Peter Lawford, Gloria Grahame; ***D:*** Richard Whorf.

It Happened in Hollywood **1937** Fading silent western stars Tim (Dix) and Gloria (Wray) try to make the transition to sound but Tim's drawl is dubbed unappealing. Gloria is more successful but she doesn't like working without her old partner. Meanwhile, Tim has gone broke but tries to keep up appearances when a sick child, who idolizes the white-hatted cowboy, makes a surprise appearance at his ranch. **67m/B DVD.** Richard Dix, Fay Wray, Victor Kilian, Franklin Pangborn, Charles Arnt, Granville Bates; ***D:*** Harry Lachman; ***W:*** Ethel Hill, Samuel Fuller, Harvey Fergusson; ***C:*** Joseph Walker.

It Happened in New Orleans 1/2 *Rainbow on the River* **1936** A young boy is cared for by a former slave in post-Civil War New Orleans until his Yankee grandmother claims him and takes him to New York. The boy is resented by his family but manages to overcome their hostilities. **86m/B VHS.** Bobby Breen, May Robson, Alan Mowbray, Benita Hume, Charles Butterworth, Louise Beavers, Henry O'Neill, Marilyn Knowlden; ***D:*** Kurt Neumann; ***W:*** Harry Chandlee, William Hurlbut; ***C:*** Charles E. Schoenbaum; ***M:*** Karl Hajos, Hugo Riesenfeld.

It Happened in the Park 1/2 **1956** A rare film exercise for De Sica, wherein the patrons of the Villa Borghese parks are surveyed for a 24-hour period. In French with English dialogue. **72m/B VHS.** *FR* ***D:*** Vittorio De Sica.

It Happened on 5th Avenue 1/2 **1947** Mysterious hobo Aloyious T. McKeever (Moore) makes his home in the vacant 5th Ave. mansion of wealthy Michael O'Connor (Ruggles), who's gone south for the winter. It's Christmas and McKeever plays Santa to evicted war veteran Jim Bullock (DeFore) and his friends. Runaway Trudy O'Connor (Storm) returns home and lets everyone stay, but then her father shows up. Michael decides to pass himself off as the new butler so he can figure out what's going on but when the inhabitants realize who he is, they hope he'll remember what happened to that guy Scrooge and change his hard-hearted ways. **116m/B DVD.** Victor Moore, Don DeFore, Gale Storm, Charlie Ruggles, Ann Harding, Alan Hale Jr., Eddie Ryan, Edward Brophy, Grant Mitchell, Dorothea Kent, Cathy Carter; ***D:*** Roy Del Ruth; ***W:*** Everett Freeman; ***C:*** Henry Sharp; ***M:*** Edward Ward.

It Happened One Night **1934** Classic Capra comedy about an antagonistic couple determined to teach each other about life. Colbert is an unhappy heiress who runs away from her affluent home in search of contentment. On a bus she meets newspaper reporter Gable, who teaches her how "real" people live. She returns the favor in this first of the 1930s screwball comedies.

The plot is a framework for an amusing examination of war between the sexes. Colbert and Gable are superb as affectionate foes. Remade as the musicals "Eve Knew Her Apples" and "You Can't Run Away From It." **105m/B VHS, DVD.** Clark Gable, Claudette Colbert, Roscoe Karns, Walter Connolly, Alan Hale, Ward Bond; ***D:*** Frank Capra; ***W:*** Robert Riskin; ***C:*** Joseph Walker. Oscars '34: Actor (Gable), Actress (Colbert), Adapt. Screenplay, Director (Capra), Picture; AFI '98: Top 100, Natl. Film Reg. '93.

It Happened Tomorrow ✗✗ 1/2 **1944** Now-familiar plotline will remind TV viewers of "Early Edition." Whimsical fantasy finds obituary writer Larry Stevens (Powell) receiving the next day's newspaper from his paper's librarian (Philliber). Stevens uses his knowledge of coming events to get some major scoops, win at the track, and impress beautiful spiritualist Sylvia (Darnell). Then, he reads his own obituary and tries to avoid his fate. **84m/B VHS.** Dick Powell, Linda Darnell, Jack Oakie, John Philliber, Edgar Kennedy, Edward Brophy, Sig Rumann, George Cleveland, Paul Guilfoyle, Eddie Acuff; ***D:*** Rene Clair; ***W:*** Rene Clair, Dudley Nichols; ***C:*** Archie Stout.

It Happens Every Spring ✗✗✗ 1/2 **1949** Chemistry professor Vernon Simpson (Milland) is working on a bug repellant for trees and accidentally invents a potion that repels any kind of wood that it comes in contact with. Since he needs some big bucks to pop the question to his sweetie Deborah (Peters), Vernon, who also loves baseball, gets a tryout as a pitcher with a major league team and uses the solution on the baseballs he pitches. Naturally, it's strikeout time and the prof becomes a pitching phenom. Now, if he can only keep his little secret. Wacky baseball footage is a highlight. **87m/B VHS.** Ray Milland, Jean Peters, Paul Douglas, Ed Begley Sr., Ted de Corsia, Ray Collins, Jessie Royce Landis, Alan Hale Jr., Gene Evans; ***D:*** Lloyd Bacon; ***W:*** Valentine Davies; ***M:*** Leigh Harline.

It Means That to Me ✗✗ *Me Faire ca a Moi* **1960** Espionage thriller in which Constantine plays a reporter who's hired by the government to transport top secret microfilm. **88m/B VHS.** *FR* Eddie Constantine, Jean-Louis Richard, Rita Cadillac, Henri Cogan, Bernadette LaFont; ***D:*** Pierre Grimblat; ***W:*** Pierre Grimblat; ***C:*** Michel Kelber; ***M:*** Michel Legrand.

It Might Get Loud ✗✗ 1/2 **2009 (PG)** Slick documentary that acknowledges the ties between three generations of electric guitar rock music virtuosos: "Led Zeppelin"'s Jimmy Page, "U2"'s The Edge, and Jack White of the "White Stripes" (and numerous side projects). Director Guggenheim gets the three together for the first time at an L.A. soundstage jam session and then profiles them individually (in London, Dublin, and Tennessee), including how the guitarists developed their signature styles. Numerous performance clips and concert footage are included. **97m/C DVD.** *US* Jimmy Page, Edge, Jack White; ***D:*** Davis Guggenheim; ***C:*** Erich Roland, Guillermo Navarro.

It Rained All Night the Day I Left ✗✗ **1978 (R)** Two drifters find their fortunes change when they are hired by a wealthy widow. Interesting romance adventure. **100m/C VHS.** Louis Gossett Jr., Sally Kellerman, Tony Curtis; ***D:*** Nicolas Gessner.

It Runs in the Family ✗✗ 1/2 **2003 (PG-13)** The curiosity factor is at least high, even if the family drama seems familiar. Michael Douglas co-stars with father Kirk, as well as mom Diana (Kirk's first wife), and Cameron, the son from his first marriage. They're the Grombergs, a Jewish upper-middle class professional family living in Manhattan. Alex (Michael) is a lawyer; dad Mitchell (Kirk) founded the firm. Alex's marriage to Rebecca (Peters) is strained and their older son Asher (Cameron) is troubled. Only Mitchell and wife Evelyn (Diana) seem to have found a measure of peace despite Mitchell's still recovering from a stroke. There's a lot of bickering until the true meaning of family comes through. **101m/C VHS, DVD.** *US* Michael Douglas, Kirk Douglas, Diana Douglas, Cameron Douglas, Rory Culkin, Bernadette Peters, Michelle Monaghan, Geoffrey Arend, Sarita Choudhury, Annie Golden, Irene Gorovaia, Mark Hammer, Audra McDonald; ***D:*** Fred Schepisi; ***W:*** Jesse Wigutow; ***C:*** Ian Baker; ***M:*** Paul Grabowsky.

It Seemed Like a Good Idea at the Time ✗✗ *Good Idea* **1975** Newley is an artist whose gold-digging wife leaves him for a dim rich guy. Of course he embarks on a covoluted scheme to get her back. Canadian producton wastes a decent cast and premise with undervelped writing. Candy's feature premiere, which got him a sequel, "Find the Lady." **106m/C VHS, DVD.** *CA* Anthony Newley, Stefanie Powers, Isaac Hayes, Lloyd Bochner, John Candy, Yvonne De Carlo, Henry Ramer, Lawrence Dane; ***D:*** John Trent; ***W:*** David Main, Claude Harz; ***C:*** Harry Makin; ***M:*** William McCauley.

It Should Happen to You ✗✗✗ **1954** An aspiring model attempts to boost her career by promoting herself on a New York City billboard. The results, however, are continually surprising. Fine comedy teamwork from master thespians Holliday and Lemmon in this, the latter's first film. **87m/B VHS, DVD.** Judy Holliday, Jack Lemmon, Peter Lawford; ***D:*** George Cukor; ***W:*** Ruth Gordon, Garson Kanin; ***C:*** Charles B(ryant) Lang Jr.

It Started in Naples ✗✗✗ **1960** Good performances by both Gable and Loren in this comedy-drama about an American lawyer in Italy who, upon preparing his late brother's estate, finds that his brother's nephew is living with a stripper. A custody battle ensues, but love wins out in the end. Loren is incredible in nightclub scenes. **100m/C VHS, DVD.** Clark Gable, Sophia Loren, Marietto, Vittorio De Sica, Paolo Carlini, Claudio Ermelli, Giovanni Filidoro; ***D:*** Melville Shavelson; ***W:*** Melville Shavelson, Jack Rose.

It Started with a Kiss ✗✗ 1/2 **1959** Reynolds plays a showgirl who impulsively marries an Air Force sargeant (Ford). When he's transfered to Spain they try to make a go of their hasty marriage among numerous comic complications. Flimsy farce with likeable leads. **104m/C VHS.** Debbie Reynolds, Glenn Ford, Eva Gabor, Gustavo Rojo, Fred Clark, Edgar Buchanan, Robert Warwick, Harry (Henry) Morgan, Frances Bavier; ***D:*** George Marshall.

It Started with Eve ✗✗✗ **1941** Funny comedy about grumpy old millionaire Jonathan Reynolds (Laughton) whose dying wish is to meet the young lady his son Johnny (Cummings) is to wed. Unfortunately, the bride-to-be is unavailable, so Johnny finds a replacement in hatcheck girl Anne (Durbin). Of course, Anne steals the old man's heart and he miraculously makes a full-blown recovery, which means big trouble for Johnny. Remade in 1964 as "I'd Rather Be Rich." Based on the story "Almost An Angel" by Hans Kraly. ♫ Clavelitos; Going Home. **92m/B VHS, DVD.** Deanna Durbin, Charles Laughton, Robert Cummings, Guy Kibbee, Margaret Tallichet, Catherine Doucet, Walter Catlett, Charles Coleman, Clara Blandick; ***D:*** Henry Koster; ***W:*** Norman Krasna, Leo Townsend; ***C:*** Rudolph Mate; ***M:*** Hans J. Salter.

It Takes a Thief ✗✗ *The Challenge* **1959** Tough cookie Jayne's a buxom gangstress who does the hokey pokey with her criminal minions. A former lover who's been released from the big house seems to think she's been minding the mint for him. Au contraire. **93m/B VHS, DVD.** *GB* Jayne Mansfield, Anthony Quayle, Carl Mohner, Peter Reynolds, John Bennett, Barbara Mullen, Robert Brown, Dermot Walsh, Patrick Holt; ***D:*** John Gilling; ***W:*** John Gilling; ***C:*** Gordon Dines; ***M:*** Bill McGuffie.

It Takes Two ✗✗ **1988 (PG-13)** A young man spends his last ten days of bachelorhood cruising down Texas highways with a beautiful car saleswoman. Meanwhile, back at the altar, his bride waits patiently. Upbeat with some genuinely funny moments. From the director of "Pass the Ammo." **79m/C VHS.** George Newbern, Leslie Hope, Kimberly Foster, Barry Corbin, Anthony Geary; ***D:*** David Beaird; ***W:*** Thomas Szollosi, Richard Christian Matheson; ***C:*** Peter Deming; ***M:*** Carter Burwell.

It Takes Two ✗ **1995 (PG)** Vapid sugary comedy finds the nine-year-old Olsen twins playing a duo from opposite sides of the tracks who change identities in an effort to get their respective adults (Guttenberg and Alley) together. See "The Parent Trap" instead. **100m/C VHS, DVD.** Ashley (Fuller) Olsen, Mary-Kate Olsen, Kirstie Alley, Steve Guttenberg, Philip Bosco, Jane Sibbett, Lawrence Dane, Gerard Parkes; ***D:*** Andy Tennant; ***W:*** Deborah Dean Davis; ***C:*** Kenneth Zunder; ***M:*** Sherman Foote, Ray Foote.

It! The Terror from Beyond Space ✗✗ 1/2 *It! The Vampire from Beyond Space* **1958** The sole survivor of a Martian expedition is believed to have murdered his colleagues. He's arrested and brought back to Earth via space ship. En route, a vicious alien, the actual culprit, is discovered on board and begins killing the crew members. A fun science fiction thriller which, 20 years later, would provide Ridley Scott with the plot for "Alien." **68m/B VHS, DVD.** Marshall Thompson, Shawn Smith, Kim Spalding, Ann Doran, Dabbs Greer, Paul Langton, Ray Corrigan; ***D:*** Edward L. Cahn; ***W:*** Jerome Bixby; ***C:*** Kenneth Peach Sr.; ***M:*** Paul Sawtell, Bert Shefter.

It Waits WOOF! **2005** And you'll wish it hadn't. Silly spooker finds alcoholic forest ranger Danielle (Vincent, she of the bouncy breasts and tight tank tops) goes into the woods after the creature that has ripped apart her boyfriend. It turns out to be a Native American spirit that was entombed in a cave until some stupid college kids released it. **88m/C DVD.** Cerina Vincent, Dominic Zamprogna, Eric Schweig; ***D:*** Stephen R. Monroe; ***W:*** Richard Christian Matheson, Thomas Szollosi, Stephen J. Cannell; ***C:*** Jon Joffin; ***M:*** Corey A. Jackson. **VIDEO**

The Italian **1915** The story of an Italian immigrant family living in the slums of New York during the turn of the century. **78m/B VHS.** George Beban, Clara Williams, Leo Wills, J. Frank Burke, Fanny Midgley; ***D:*** Reginald Barker; ***W:*** Thomas Ince. Natl. Film Reg. '91.

The Italian ✗✗ *Italianetz* **2005 (PG-13)** Tough story based on a true incident and best seen by adults despite its MPAA rating. Six-year-old Vanya (solemnly appealing Spiridonov) has been deposited in a bleak Russian orphanage by his mother. His luck is apparently changing when a rich Italian couple offer to buy him from the home's corrupt adoption broker, known only as Madam (Kuznetsova). While waiting for the red tape to untangle, Vanya decides he wants to find his birth mom and, armed with an old address from his stolen files, he hits the road pursued by Madam and her lackey, who don't want to lose a sale. Russian with subtitles. **99m/C DVD.** *RU* Kolya Spiridonov, Denis Moiseenko, Sasha Syrotkin, Olga Shuvalova, Dima Zemlyanko, Maria Kuznetsova, Yuri Itskov; ***D:*** Andrei Kravchuk; ***W:*** Andrei Romanov; ***C:*** Alexander Burov; ***M:*** Alexander Kneiffel.

Italian for Beginners ✗✗ 1/2 *Italiensk for Begyndere* **2001 (R)** Director Scherfig is the first woman to use the strict Dogma 95 filmmaking rules (hand-held cameras, natural light, live music, no studios scenes, no costumes, and no special effects) of her Danish colleagues. She's also the first to try to do a romantic comedy in the Dogma style, and she pulls it off nicely. Her tale brings together six quirky lonelyhearts: Andreas (Berthlesen), newly widowed minister; Hall-Finn (Kaalund), a soccer-obsessed restaurant manager; his best friend Jorgen (Gantzler), who's convinced he's impotent; Olympia (Stovelbaek), who likes Andreas and cares for her abusive, ill father; Karen (Jorgensen) who cuts Hal-Finn's hair and cares for her alcoholic shrew of a mother; and Giulia (Jensen), an Italian waitress with a crush on Jorgen, in a Conversational Italian class. The seemingly lightweight plot is anchored by insight into everyday misery and hurt amid the giddy matchmaking and likeable characters. **112m/C VHS, DVD.** *DK* Anders W. Berthelsen, Peter Gantzler, Anette Stovelbaek, Ann Eleonora Jorgensen, Lars Kaalund, Sara Indrio Jensen; ***D:*** Lone Scherfig; ***W:*** Lone Scherfig; ***C:*** Jorgen Johansson.

The Italian Job ✗✗ 1/2 **1969 (G)** Caine and Coward pair up to steal $4 million in gold by causing a major traffic jam in Turin, Italy. During the jam, the pair steals the gold from an armored car. Silliness and chases through the Swiss mountains ensue, culminating in a hilarious ending. **99m/C VHS, DVD.** *GB* Michael Caine, Noel Coward, Benny Hill, Raf Vallone, Tony Beckley, Rossano Brazzi, Margaret Blye; ***D:*** Peter Collinson; ***M:*** Quincy Jones.

The Italian Job ✗✗✗ **2003 (PG-13)** Typically cool crew of expert theives, led by Charlie (Wahlberg), pulls off a heist of $35 million worth of gold bars in Venice, only to be doublecrossed by crewmember Steve (Norton), who kills Charlie's mentor John (Sutherland) and leaves the rest for dead. When the group find Steve a year later in L.A., John's daughter Stella (Theron), an exceptional safecracker in her own right, joins the gang for revenge. Amiable caper flick succeeds on the multiple strengths of understated cool, superbly orchestrated action, pitch-perfect humor, and an excellent cast doing a great job. Green, as computer geek Lyle, stands out, while Wahlberg boosts his leading man appeal. Remake of the 1969 Michael Caine vehicle copies original's use of Mini Coopers, but not much else. **111m/C VHS, DVD, Blu-ray Disc, UMD, HD DVD.** *US* Mark Wahlberg, Edward Norton, Charlize Theron, Mos Def, Seth Green, Jason Statham, Donald Sutherland, Christina Cabot, Franky G., Olek Krupa; ***D:*** F. Gary Gray; ***W:*** Wayne Powers, Donna Powers; ***C:*** Wally Pfister; ***M:*** John Powell.

Italian Movie ✗✗ **1993** First-generation Italian immigrant Leonardo decides to become a male escort to pay off his gambling debts and support his large family but things get quite complicated. **95m/C VHS, DVD.** Michael DellaFemina, Rita Moreno, James Gandolfini, Caprice Benedetti; ***D:*** Roberto Monticello.

The Italian Stallion ✗ *The Party at Kitty and Stud's* **1973** Stallone plays a man with only one thing on his mind...sex! **90m/C VHS, DVD.** Sylvester Stallone, Henrietta Holm; ***D:*** Morton Lewis; ***W:*** Morton Lewis; ***C:*** Rolph Laube; ***M:*** Kay Leodel.

Italian Straw Hat ✗✗✗ *Un Chapeau de Paille d'Italie* **1927** Classic silent about the chain of errors that ensues when a man's horse eats a woman's hat. His vast, unending struggle to replace the hat is the source of continual comedy. From Eugene Labiche's play. **114m/B VHS.** *FR* Albert Prejean, Olga Tschekowa; ***D:*** Rene Clair.

It's a Big Country ✗ 1/2 **1951** And apparently it's very boring too if you go by these eight inconsistent vignettes that are set throughout the then-48 states. A professor lectures a fellow train passenger about USA diversity to link the tales together. The best is the tongue-in-cheek humor of Cooper's laconic cowboy as he tackles the stereotypes of Texas and the worst is the overextended story of a boy whose immigrant father refuses to believe he needs to get glasses for school. **89m/B DVD.** William Powell, James Whitmore, Gary Cooper, Ethel Barrymore, Keenan Wynn, George Murphy, Gene Kelly, Janet Leigh, S.Z. Sakall, Van Johnson, Keefe Brasselle, Marjorie Main, Fredric March, Robert Hyatt, Nancy Davis; ***D:*** William A. Wellman, Clarence Brown, Richard Thorpe, Charles Vidor, John Sturges, Don Weis; ***W:*** Allen Rivkin, Dorothy Kingsley, William Ludwig, George Wells, Dore Schary, Helen Deutsch, Isobel Lennart; ***C:*** John Alton, William Mellor, Joseph Ruttenberg, Ray June; ***M:*** Charles Wolcott, Adolph Deutsch, Bronislau Kaper, David Rose, David Raskin, Lennie Hayton.

It's a Boy Girl Thing ✗✗ 1/2 **2006 (PG-13)** Good girl brainiac Nell (Armstrong) and high school QB Woody (Zegers) grew up next door to each other and are lifelong enemies. Thanks to one of those goofy movie contrivances, they wake up one morning in each other's bodies. After dealing with their different—ah—equipment, the antagonistic duo first try to trash each other's reputations and then realize they have to work together to get back to normal. There's more juvenile raunch than you might expect, but the leads are likeable and it's good for a giggle. **95m/C DVD.** *GB* Samaire Armstrong, Kevin Zegers, Sherry Miller, Robert Joy, Maury Chaykin, Sharon Osbourne, Mpho Koaho, Brooke D'Orsay, Emily Hampshire; ***D:*** Nick Hurran; ***W:*** Geoff Deane; ***C:*** Steve Danyluk; ***M:*** Christian Henson.

It's a Date ✗✗ **1940** A mother and daughter, both actresses, continually get their professional and romantic lives intertwined. It begins when Durbin (the daughter) is offered Kay's (the mother) Broadway role. It continues in Hawaii where the man that

Kay is in love with tries to court Durbin. As it's a comedy, of course, all is put right in the end. ♫ Musetta's Waltz; Ave Maria; Loch Lomond; Love Is All; It Happened in Kaloha; Rhythm of the Islands; Hawaiian War Chant. **103m/B VHS.** Deanna Durbin, Kay Francis, Walter Pidgeon, Samuel S. Hinds, S.Z. Sakall, Henry Stephenson, Charles Lane, Leon Belasco; ***D:*** William A. Seiter; ***W:*** Norman Krasna; ***C:*** Joseph Valentine.

It's a Dog's Life 🦴🦴 1/2 *The Bar Sinister* **1955** The hero and narrator of this story is a wily bull terrier called Wildfire. Wildfire is a tough dog on the mean streets of the Bowery in turn-of-the-century New York. His master has him in dog fights in the local saloon but eventually abandons him. Wildfire is then taken in by the kindly employee of the rich and dog-hating Jagger but naturally manages to win the codger over. Based on the short story "The Bar Sinister" by Richard Harding Davis. **87m/C VHS.** Jeff Richards, Edmund Gwenn, Dean Jagger; ***D:*** Herman Hoffman; ***W:*** John Michael Hayes; ***M:*** Elmer Bernstein.

It's a Gift 🦴🦴🦴 1/2 **1934** A grocery clerk moves his family west to manage orange groves in this classic Fields comedy. Several inspired sequences. The supporting cast shines too. A real find for the discriminating comedy buff. Remake of the silent "It's the Old Army Game." **71m/B VHS, DVD.** W.C. Fields, Baby LeRoy, Kathleen Howard, Jean Rouveral, Julian Madison, Tammany Young, Tommy Bupp; ***D:*** Norman Z. McLeod; ***W:*** Jack Cunningham; ***C:*** Henry Sharp.

It's a Great Feeling 🦴🦴 1/2 **1949** Another Carson and Day team-up where Carson plays a camera-hogging show-off whom no one wants to direct. He's such an industry piranha that he ends up directing himself! He cons Day, a waitress and would-be actress, by promising her a part in his new film. Some executives hear her sing before she heads back home to Wisconsin, fed up with Hollywood. They make Carson track her down to star in the new picture, but when he arrives she is at the altar with her high school sweetheart. **85m/C VHS.** Dennis Morgan, Doris Day, Jack Carson, Bill Goodwin, Errol Flynn, Gary Cooper, Joan Crawford, Ronald Reagan, Sydney Greenstreet, Danny Kaye, Eleanor Parker, Edward G. Robinson, Jane Wyman; ***D:*** David Butler.

It's a Great Life 🦴 1/2 **1929** It's also a pretty lousy movie. The only talkie-era film for the Duncan sisters, who play sisters working at a department store. They get fired and start a vaudeville act but split up when Babe marries piano player Jimmy whom sister Casey can't stand. The sisters eventually reunite when they're a flop on their own. Includes two-color sequences. Since the film wasn't successful the Duncans returned to vaudeville themselves. **93m/C DVD.** Rosetta Duncan, Vivian Duncan, Lawrence Gray, Jed Prouty, Benny Rubin; ***D:*** Sam Wood; ***W:*** Al Boasberg, Willard Mack; ***C:*** J. Peverell Marley.

It's a Great Life 🦴🦴 1/2 **1943** Blondie wants Dagwood to buy a house but instead he buys a horse. He's scheming to impress a client of Mr. Dither's by participating in a fox hunt. Blondie comes to the rescue. 13th entry in series. **75m/B VHS.** Penny Singleton, Arthur Lake, Larry Simms, Hugh Herbert, Jonathan Hale, Danny Mummert, Alan Dinehart, Irving Bacon, Douglas Leavitt, Marjorie Ann Mutchie; ***D:*** Frank Strayer; ***W:*** Karen De Wolf, Connie Lee.

It's a Joke, Son! 🦴🦴 **1947** Follows the fictional politician, Senator Claghorn from the Fred Allen radio show, during his first run for the U.S. Senate. **67m/B VHS, DVD.** Kenny Delmar, Una Merkel; ***D:*** Ben Stoloff.

It's a Mad, Mad, Mad, Mad World 🦴🦴 **1963** Overblown epic comedy with a cast of notables desperately seeking the whereabouts of stolen money. Ultimately exhausting film undone by its length and overbearing performances. **155m/C VHS, DVD.** Spencer Tracy, Sid Caesar, Milton Berle, Ethel Merman, Jonathan Winters, Jimmy Durante, Buddy Hackett, Mickey Rooney, Phil Silvers, Dick Shawn, Edie Adams, Dorothy Provine, Buster Keaton, Terry-Thomas, Moe Howard, Larry Fine, Joe DeRita, Jim Backus, William Demarest, Peter Falk, Leo Gorcey, Edward Everett Horton, Joe E. Brown, Carl Reiner, Zasu Pitts, Eddie Anderson, Jack Benny, Jerry Lewis, Norman Fell, Stan Freberg, Don Knotts; ***D:*** Stanley Kramer; ***W:*** William Rose, Tania Rose; ***C:*** Ernest Laszlo; ***M:*** Ernest Gold. Oscars '63: Sound FX Editing.

It's a Pleasure 🦴🦴 1/2 **1945** Henie in Technicolor splendor. Ice skater Chris wants to help out hockey player Don Martin (O'Shea) who gets thrown out of the league for punching out a ref. He becomes her skating partner and they get married but Don's also an alcoholic and is soon bringing Chris problems on and off the ice. When she gets a shot at stardom, is he man enough to let her go? **90m/C DVD.** Sonja Henie, Michael O'Shea, Bill Johnson, Marie McDonald, Gus Schilling, Arthur Loft; ***D:*** William A. Seiter; ***W:*** Elliot Paul, Lynn Starling; ***C:*** Ray Rennahan; ***M:*** Arthur Lange.

It's a Wonderful Life 🦴🦴🦴🦴 **1946** American classic about a man saved from suicide by a considerate angel, who then shows the hero how important he's been to the lives of loved ones. Corny but inspirational and heartwarming, with an endearing performance by Travers as angel Clarence. Stewart and Reed are typically wholesome. Perfect film for people who want to feel good, joyfully teetering on the border between Hollywood schmaltz and genuine heartbreak. Available colorized. Also available in a 160-minute Collector's Edition with original preview trailer, "The Making of 'It's a Wonderful Life,'" and a new digital transfer from the original negative. **125m/B VHS, DVD.** Carl "Alfalfa" Switzer, James Stewart, Donna Reed, Henry Travers, Thomas Mitchell, Lionel Barrymore, Samuel S. Hinds, Frank Faylen, Gloria Grahame, H.B. Warner, Ellen Corby, Sheldon Leonard, Beulah Bondi, Ward Bond, Frank Albertson, Todd Karns, Mary Treen, Charles Halton; ***D:*** Frank Capra; ***W:*** Frances Goodrich, Albert Hackett, Jo Swerling; ***C:*** Joseph Biroc, Joseph Walker; ***M:*** Dimitri Tiomkin. AFI '98: Top 100; Golden Globes '47: Director (Capra), Natl. Film Reg. '90.

It's Alive! 🦴 **1968** Slow-moving dud about a farmer feeding passersby to the area's cave-dwelling lizard man. The ping pong ball-eyed monster puts in a belated appearance that's not worth the wait. **80m/C VHS, DVD.** Tommy Kirk, Shirley Bonne, Bill (Billy) Thurman, Annabelle MacAdams, Corveth Osterhouse; ***D:*** Larry Buchanan; ***W:*** Larry Buchanan; ***C:*** Robert Alcott.

It's Alive 🦴🦴🦴 **1974 (PG)** Cult film about a mutated baby, born to a normal Los Angeles couple, who escapes and goes on a bloodthirsty, murderous rampage. It's a sight to behold. Fantastic score by Bernard Herrmann makes this chilling film a memorable one. **91m/C VHS, DVD.** John P. Ryan, Sharon Farrell, Andrew Duggan, Guy Stockwell, James Dixon, Michael Ansara, William Wellman Jr., Shamus Locke; ***D:*** Larry Cohen; ***W:*** Larry Cohen; ***C:*** Fenton Hamilton; ***M:*** Bernard Herrmann.

It's Alive 2: It Lives Again **WOOF!** *It Lives Again* **1978 (R)** In this sequel to "It's Alive," the original hellspun baby meets up with two more of the same and all three terrorize the city, murdering everyone they can find. Truly horrendous. **91m/C VHS, DVD.** Frederic Forrest, Kathleen Lloyd, John P. Ryan, Andrew Duggan, John Marley, Eddie Constantine, James Dixon, Bobby Ramsen; ***D:*** Larry Cohen; ***W:*** Larry Cohen; ***C:*** Fenton Hamilton.

It's Alive 3: Island of the Alive 🦴 *Island of the Alive* **1987 (R)** The second sequel to the tongue-in-cheek horror film, in which the infant mutant of the previous films has been left with other mutations to spawn on a desert island. **94m/C VHS, DVD.** Michael Moriarty, Karen Black, Laurene Landon, Gerrit Graham, James Dixon, Neal Israel, MacDonald Carey; ***D:*** Larry Cohen; ***W:*** Larry Cohen; ***C:*** Daniel Pearl; ***M:*** Laurie Johnson.

It's All About Love 🦴 **2003** Danish director Vinterberg, one of the founders of Dogme 95, tries on a futuristic romantic thriller with dismal results. John (Phoenix) arrives in New York to sign final divorce papers with his estranged wife Elena (Danes), an ice-skating superstar. Elena is in some kind of mysterious trouble and the twosome elude her flunkies to be together, later learning that Elena has been cloned for insurance purposes. They then go on the run. And Penn is around as John's brother who muses while constantly flying around the world (and no, it doesn't make any sense). Both American leads have really bad, allegedly Polish, accents and although it's supposed to be New York it was filmed in a Swedish movie studio. **104m/C DVD.** *US* Joaquin Rafael (Leaf) Phoenix, Claire Danes, Sean Penn, Douglas Henshall, Alun Armstrong, Margo Martindale, Mark Strong, Geoffrey Hutchings; ***D:*** Thomas Vinterberg; ***C:*** Anthony Dod Mantle; ***M:*** Zbigniew Preisner.

It's All Gone, Pete Tong **WOOF!** **2004 (R)** "Pete Tong" is a Cockney rhyming slang for 'wrong.' Frankie Wilde (Kaye) is a DJ with a major coke habit and the club world at his feet when, after years of audio at excessive levels, he loses his hearing. Dropping out of sight he hires a beautiful deaf woman to teach him lip-reading and learns the properties of vibration from a flamenco dancer, all to eventually reclaim his King of the Club DJ status. Too little hilarity and an unfocused script. **88m/C DVD.** *GB CA* Paul Kaye, Beatriz Batarda, Mike Wilmot, Paul J. Spence, Kate Magowan, Dave Lawrence; ***D:*** Michael Dowse; ***W:*** Michael Dowse; ***C:*** Balasz Bolygo; ***M:*** Graham Massey.

It's All True 🦴🦴 **1993 (G)** A look at auteur Welles' ill-fated WWII filmmaking project. Welles served as a special cultural ambassador to South America and, in 1942, began a documentary covering the area's complex political and social issues. Includes footage from "Four Men on a Raft," Welles' recreation about the peasant fishermen of Brazil; surviving excerpts from "The Story of Samba," a Technicolor musical about Carnaval in Rio de Janeiro; and footage from "My Friend Bonito," set against a backdrop of bullfighting in Mexico. **85m/C VHS, DVD.** ***D:*** Richard Wilson, Bill Krohn, Myron Meise, Orson Welles; ***W:*** Richard Wilson, Bill Krohn, Myron Meise; ***C:*** Gary Graver, George Fanto; ***M:*** Jorge Arriagada; ***Nar:*** Miguel Ferrer.

It's Always Fair Weather 🦴🦴 **1955** Three WWII buddies meet again at a 10-year reunion and find that they don't like each other very much. A surprisingly cynical film. Director Donen produced "Seven Brides for Seven Brothers" the previous year. ♫ Stillman's Gym; March, March; Why Are We Here? (Blue Danube); Music Is Better Than Words; Once Upon A Time; The Time For Parting; I Like Myself; Baby You Knock Me Out; Thanks A Lot But No Thanks. **102m/C VHS, DVD.** Gene Kelly, Cyd Charisse, Dan Dailey, Michael Kidd; ***D:*** Stanley Donen; ***W:*** Betty Comden, Adolph Green; ***M:*** Betty Comden, Adolph Green, Andre Previn.

It's Called Murder, Baby 🦴 **1982 (R)** The famed porn star gives the viewer a lesson in English vocabulary in this tale of a blackmailed movie queen. **94m/C VHS.** John Leslie, Cameron Mitchell, Lisa Trego; ***D:*** Sam Weston.

It's Complicated 🦴🦴 1/2 **2009 (R)** Meyers' comfortable film is probably best appreciated by a specific and generally neglected audience—middle-aged (and older) women looking to relax into a dazzling, if shallow, world of consumerism and romantic possibilities. Radiant Santa Barbara bakery/restaurant owner Jane Adler (Streep) has been divorced from Jake (Baldwin) for 10 years, thanks to his cheating and subsequent marriage to younger, pouty beauty Agness (Bell). They maintained a civilized relationship for the sake of their three now-grown kids and it's the kids' lives (and too much alcohol) that brings Jane and Jake closer together than expected. As Jane rather gleefully exclaims to her gal pals, she's now the 'other woman.' Of course the smarmily charming Jake is suddenly not Jane's only suitor as she hires gentlemanly architect Adam (Martin) for a kitchen re-do and some wooing of his own. Oh, romance among actual adults! Even though they may not act like it. **118m/C DVD.** *US* Meryl Streep, Alec Baldwin, Steve Martin, John Krasinski, Zoe Kazan, Hunter Parrish, Lake Bell, Rita Wilson, Mary Kay Place, Nora Dunn, Alexandra Wentworth, Caitlin Fitzgerald; ***D:*** Nancy Meyers; ***W:*** Nancy Meyers; ***C:*** John Toll; ***M:*** Hans Zimmer, Hector Pereira.

It's Good to Be Alive 🦴🦴 1/2 **1974** The true story of how Brooklyn Dodgers' catcher Roy Campanella learned to face life after an automobile accident left him a quadriplegic. Good performances. **100m/C VHS, DVD.** Ramon Bieri, Joe De Santis, Paul Winfield, Ruby Dee, Louis Gossett Jr.; ***D:*** Michael Landon; ***M:*** Michel Legrand. **TV**

It's in the Bag 🦴🦴 1/2 *The Fifth Chair* **1945** A shiftless flea circus owner sells chairs he has inherited, not knowing that a fortune is hidden in one of them. **87m/B VHS.** Fred Allen, Don Ameche, Jack Benny, William Bendix, Binnie Barnes, Robert Benchley; ***D:*** Richard Wallace.

It's In the Water 🦴🦴 **1996** Small, conservative Azalea Springs, Texas is rocked by the opening of an AIDS hospice. The homophobia outrages society wife Alex, who begins working at the hospice alongside best friend (soon to be more) Grace. Then a rumor starts that the local drinking water turns you gay and things really get wild. Fast-moving and funny. **100m/C VHS, DVD.** Keri Jo Chapman, Teresa Garrett, Barbara Lasater, Larry Randolph; ***D:*** Kelli Herd.

It's Love Again 🦴🦴 1/2 **1936** A street-wise chorus girl poses as a fictional socialite in a light music-hall comedy. ♫ It's Love Again; Heaven In Your Arms. **83m/B VHS.** *GB* Jessie Matthews, Robert Young, Sonnie Hale; ***D:*** Victor Saville.

It's My Party 🦴🦴 1/2 **1995 (R)** When L.A. architect Nick Stark (Roberts) learns that he's developed untreatable brain lesions from AIDS that will essentially leave him helpless, he decides to throw himself a monumental farewell bash before taking a drug overdose. Friends and family all turn up as does, awkwardly enough, Brandon Theis (Harrison), Nick's former live-in who couldn't handle his HIV-positive diagnosis but would like a last reapproachment. Fine, sympathetic performances, espcially by the two leads, and yes, it's a weepie. Based on a true story. **120m/C VHS, DVD.** Eric Roberts, Gregory Harrison, Marlee Matlin, Lee Grant, George Segal, Bronson Pinchot, Bruce Davison, Devon Gummersall, Roddy McDowall, Margaret Cho, Paul Regina, Olivia Newton-John, Christopher Atkins, Dennis Christopher, Ron Glass, Eugene Robert Glazer; ***D:*** Randal Kleiser; ***W:*** Randal Kleiser; ***C:*** Bernd Heinl; ***M:*** Basil Poledouris.

It's My Turn 🦴🦴 **1980 (R)** A mathematics professor (Clayburgh) struggles in her relationship with live-in lover (Grodin) who sells real-estate in Chicago. She meets retired baseball player (Douglas) and falls in love. "Ho-hum" just about describes the rest. **91m/C VHS.** Jill Clayburgh, Michael Douglas, Charles Grodin, Beverly Garland, Steven Hill, Dianne Wiest, Daniel Stern; ***D:*** Claudia Weill; ***W:*** Eleanor Bergstein; ***C:*** Bill Butler.

It's My Turn, Laura Cadieux 🦴🦴 *C't'a Ton Tour, Laura Cadieux* **1998** One a week several women meet at the same doctor's office as they've done for the past 15 years. The social aspects far outweigh the medical benefits for the women as they gossip and talk about their restricted lives. But one week a series of misunderstandings unfold when Madame Therrien believes her friend Laura Cadieux's son has gone missing. Based on the novel by Michel Tremblay. French with subtitles. **92m/C VHS.** *CA* Ginette Reno, Donald Pilon, Pierrette Robitaille, Denise Dubois, Samuel Landry, Adele Reinhardt; ***D:*** Denise Filiatrault; ***W:*** Denise Filiatrault; ***C:*** Daniel Jobin; ***M:*** Francois Dompierre.

It's Not the Size That Counts **WOOF!** *Percy's Progress* **1974** After the Earth's drinking water is contaminated, Lawson is the only man on Earth not to be struck by impotency. Limp sequel to "Percy," the British comedy about the first man to receive a penis transplant. Promising comedy doesn't deliver. **90m/C VHS.** Leigh Lawson, Elke Sommer, Denholm Elliott, Vincent Price, Judy Geeson, Milo O'Shea, Julie Ege, George Coulouris, Bernard Lee; ***D:*** Ralph Thomas; ***W:*** Harry H. Corbett, Sid Colin, Ian La Frenais; ***C:*** Tony Imi; ***M:*** Tony Macaulay.

It's Pat: The Movie **WOOF!** **1994 (PG-13)** This movie is so bad, let's pray it sounds the death knell to big-screen versions of "Saturday Night Live" sketch characters—who possessed little humor to begin with. For what it's worth, the androgynous Pat (Sweeney) falls for the equally gender-suspect Chris (Foley, from Canada's version of SNL, "Kids in the Hall") and all sorts of embarrassing situations arise. Pat's quest to find Pat's self is sketch material stretched see-through thin. **78m/C VHS, DVD.** Julia Sweeney, Dave Foley, Charles Rocket, Kathy Griffin, Julie Haydon, Tim Meadows, Arleen (Arlene) Sorkin; ***Cameos:*** Sally Jesse Raphael, Kathy Najimy; ***D:*** Adam Bernstein; ***W:*** Julia Sweeney, Jim Emerson, Stephen Hibbert.

It's the Old Army Game **1926** Classic Fields gags in three of his best Ziegfeld Follies sketches: "The Drug Store," "A Peaceful Morning," and "The Family Flivver." The beautiful Brooks serves as his comic foil. **75m/B VHS.** W.C. Fields, Louise Brooks, Blanche Ring, William Gaxton; ***D:*** Edward Sutherland.

It's the Rage 🦴🦴 1/2 *All the Rage* **1999 (R)** Glib ensemble comedy about the collision of guns and anger, with an interesting cast. Warren (Daniels) shoots an intruder who turns out to be his business partner, who may have been fooling around with Warren's prim wife, Helen (Allen). His lawyer, Tim (Braugher), has just been given a gun by his boyfriend (Schwimmer), and he has another client (Paquin) whose brother (Ribisi) is trigger-happy. Meanwhile, Helen takes a job with paranoid billionaire, Mr. Morgan (Sinise), while Warren's being investigated by a couple of detectives (Forster, Woodbine) for whom guns are job accessories. Reddin scripted from his play. **97m/C VHS, DVD.** Jeff Daniels, Joan Allen, Andre Braugher, David Schwimmer, Anna Paquin, Giovanni Ribisi, Gary Sinise, Josh Brolin, Robert Forster, Bokeem Woodbine; ***D:*** James D. Stern; ***W:*** Keith Reddin; ***C:*** Alex Nepomniaschy; ***M:*** Mark Mothersbaugh.

Itty Bitty Titty Committee 🦴 1/2 **2007** Recent high school grad Anna (Diaz) has just been dumped by her first girlfriend and is working a monotonous job with no direction to her life. Then she meets guerilla grrl Sadie (Vicius) and her group of radical femmes who stage public art protests. Anna joins in, but the eventual romance between her and Sadie upsets a delicate balance within the group. **87m/C DVD.** Melonie Diaz, Nicole Vicius, Carly Pope, Guinevere Turner, Jenny Shimizu, Deak Evgenikos, Lauren Mollica, Daniela Sea, Melanie Myron; ***D:*** Jamie Babbit; ***W:*** Tina Mabry, Abigail Shafran; ***C:*** Christine A. Maier.

Ivan and Abraham 🦴🦴 **1994** Abraham (Alexandrovitch) is a nine-year-old Jewish boy, living on a shetl in 1930s eastern Poland, with his best friend being the family's 14-year-old Christian apprentice Ivan (Iakovlev). The boys sense the increasing family tensions and escape into the nearby forest, only to find politics and prejudice sweeping over them all. In Yiddish, Russian, Polish, and Romany, with English subtitles. **105m/B VHS.** Roma Aleksandrovitch, Sacha Iakovlev, Vladimir Machkov, Maria Lipkina, Rolan Bykov, Daniel Olbrychski; ***D:*** Yolande Zauberman; ***W:*** Yolande Zauberman; ***C:*** Jean-Marc Fabre.

Ivan the Terrible, Part 1 🦴🦴🦴🦴 *Ivan Groznyi* **1944** Contemplative epic of Russia's first czar is a classic, innovative film from cinema genius Eisenstein. Visually stunning, with a fine performance by Cherkassov. Ivan's struggles to preserve his country is the main concern of the first half of Eisenstein's masterwork (which he originally planned as a trilogy). In Russian with English subtitles. **100m/B VHS, DVD.** *RU* Nikolai Cherkassov, Lyudmila Tselikovskaya, Serafina Birman, Piotr Kadochnikev; ***D:*** Sergei Eisenstein; ***W:*** Sergei Eisenstein; ***C:*** Eduard Tisse; ***M:*** Sergei Prokofiev.

Ivan the Terrible, Part 2 🦴🦴🦴 1/2 *Ivan the Terrible, Part 2: The Boyars' Plot; Ivan Groznyi 2* **1946** Landed gentry conspire to dethrone the czar in this continuation of the innovative epic. More stunning imagery from master Eisenstein, who makes no false moves in this one. Slow going, but immensely rewarding. Russian dialogue with English subtitles; contains color sequences. **87m/B VHS, DVD.** *RU* Nikolai Cherkassov, Lyudmila Tselikovskaya, Serafina Birman, Piotr Kadochnikev; ***D:*** Sergei Eisenstein; ***W:*** Sergei Eisenstein; ***C:*** Eduard Tisse, Andrei Moskvin; ***M:*** Sergei Prokofiev.

Ivanhoe 🦴🦴🦴 **1952** Knights fight each other and woo maidens in this chivalrous romance derived from the Sir Walter Scott classic. Taylor is suitably noble, while Sanders is familiarly serpentine. Remade in 1982. **107m/C VHS, DVD.** Robert Taylor, Elizabeth Taylor, Joan Fontaine, George Sanders, Finlay Currie, Felix Aylmer; ***D:*** Richard Thorpe; ***W:*** Marguerite Roberts, Noel Langley; ***C:*** Frederick A. (Freddie) Young; ***M:*** Miklos Rozsa.

Ivanhoe 🦴🦴 1/2 **1982** A version of Sir Walter Scott's classic novel of chivalry and knighthood in 12th-century England. Remake of the 1953 film classic. **142m/C VHS.** Anthony Andrews, James Mason, Lysette Anthony, Sam Neill, Olivia Hussey, Michael Hordern, Julian Glover, George Innes, Ronald Pickup, John Rhys-Davies, Chloe Franks; ***D:*** Douglas Camfield. **TV**

Ivanhoe 🦴🦴🦴 **1997** TV miniseries version of Sir Walter Scott's epic tale of knights, chivalry, romance, and daring. Saxon knight Wilfred of Ivanhoe (Waddington), having fought for Richard the Lionheart (Edwards) during the Crusades, returns to England to battle the scheming Prince John (Brown) and sinister Grand Master of the Templars, Lucas De Beaumanoir (Lee) in order to regain his honor. His childhood sweetheart, Saxon heiress Rowena (Smurfit), is betrothed to another but Ivanhoe's also drawn to Jewish healer Rebecca (Lynch) as is scheming Knight Templar, Sir Brian Bois-Guilbert (Hinds). Lots of action. On six cassettes. **292m/C VHS, DVD.** *GB* Steven Waddington, Susan Lynch, Ciaran Hinds, Victoria Smurfit, Ralph Brown, Rory Edwards, Ronald Pickup, David Horovitch, Trevor Cooper, Valentine Pelka, Nick Brimble, Jimmy Chisholm, Christopher Lee, Aden (John) Gillett, James Cosmo, Sian Phillips, Ciaran Madden; ***D:*** Stuart Orme; ***W:*** Deborah Cook; ***C:*** Clive Tickner; ***M:*** Colin Towns. **TV**

I've Always Loved You 🦴🦴 1/2 *Concerto* **1946** The drama of love and jealousy explored in an extravagant production filled with classical music. **117m/C VHS.** Philip Dorn, Catherine McLeod; ***D:*** Frank Borzage; ***C:*** Gaetano Antonio "Tony" Gaudio.

I've Been Waiting for You 🦴🦴 1/2 **1998 (PG-13)** California teen Sarah Zoltanne (Chalke), who has an interest in the occult, moves with her family to a New England town. Her fellow teens begin to believe that she's a witch out for revenge on the descendents of the townspeople who burned another witch, who had the same name. Then on Halloween, Sarah begins to see events beyond her knowledge or control. Based on the novel "Gallows Hill" by Lois Duncan. **90m/C VHS, DVD.** Sarah Chalke, Soleil Moon Frye, Markie Post, Christian Campbell, Tom Dugan; ***D:*** Christopher Leitch; ***W:*** Duane Poole. **TV**

I've Heard the Mermaids Singing 🦴🦴🦴 **1987** Independent Canadian semi-satiric romantic comedy details the misadventures of a klutzy woman who suddenly obtains a desirable job in an art gallery run by a lesbian on whom she develops a crush. Good-natured tone helped considerably by McCarthy's winning performance. **81m/C VHS, DVD.** *CA* Sheila McCarthy, Paule Baillargeon, Ann-Marie MacDonald, John Evans; ***D:*** Patricia Rozema; ***M:*** Mark Korven. Genie '88: Actress (McCarthy), Support. Actress (Baillargeon).

I've Loved You So Long 🦴🦴🦴 *Il Y a Longtemps Que Je T'aime* **2008 (PG-13)** A quiet slice of life family drama from debuting director Claudel that features outstanding (but not showy) work from the female leads. Careworn and self-contained Juliette (Scott Thomas) has just moved in with her anxious younger sister Lea (Zylberstein) and her family. Everyone seems wary of each other but Claudel only lets the past be revealed in snippets: Juliette's estrangement is because she's spent 15 years in prison for murder. That fact is something no one cares to broadcast to curious friends in their provincial town. Both sisters slowly learn to trust while Juliette also struggles to make a full life for herself. French with subtitles. **115m/C DVD.** *FR GE* Elsa Zylberstein, Laurent Grevill, Frederic Pierrot, Kristin Scott Thomas, Serge Hazanavicius, Lise Segur, Jean-Claude Arnaud, Mouss Zouheyri; ***D:*** Philippe Claudel; ***W:*** Philippe Claudel; ***C:*** Jerome Almeras; ***M:*** Jean-Louis Aubert. British Acad. '09: Foreign Film.

The Ivory Handled Gun 🦴🦴 **1935** The Wolverine Kid wants Buck Ward (Jones) dead because the Kid's father, John Plunkett, was rejected by Buck's mother in favor of Buck's dad, Bill, who killed the interloper in a fight. Bill also happens to be in possession of one of Plunkett's ivory-handed guns and the Kid wants that back as well. In chapter 2 of "Gordon of Ghost City," Gordon and Mary Gray are observed by a mysterious, threatening figure and Mary gets caught in a stampede. **81m/B VHS.** Buck Jones, Charlotte Wynters, Walter Miller, Frank Rice, Carl Stockdale, Joseph Girard, Madge Bellamy; ***D:*** Ray Taylor.

Ivory Hunters 🦴🦴 1/2 *The Last Elephant* **1990** Conservationists team up to thwart a massacre of elephants by poachers. Predictable made-for-cable entertainment co-produced by the National Audubon Society. **94m/C VHS.** John Lithgow, Isabella Rossellini, James Earl Jones, Tony Todd, Olek Krupa; ***D:*** Joseph Sargent; ***W:*** Richard Guttman, Bill Bozzone; ***M:*** Charles Bernstein. **CABLE**

Ivory Tower 🦴🦴 **1997** Anthony Daytona (Van Horn) is a hotshot marketing exec in charge of launching a new computer product. But then his new boss arrives and suddenly not only the project but Anthony's career and the company itself is in jeopardy. **107m/C VHS, DVD.** Patrick Van Horn, James Wilder, Kari Wuhrer, Michael Ironside, Donna Pescow, Keith Coogan, Ian Buchanan; ***D:*** Darin Ferriola; ***W:*** Darin Ferriola; ***C:*** Maida Sussman.

Izzy & Moe 🦴🦴 1/2 **1985** Carney and The Great One are reunited for the last time on screen as former vaudevillians who become federal agents and create havoc amid speak-easies and bathtub gin during Prohibition. Based on true stories. **92m/C VHS, DVD.** Jackie Gleason, Art Carney, Cynthia Harris, Zohra Lampert, Drew Snyder, Dick Latessa; ***D:*** Jackie Cooper. **TV**

J. Edgar Hoover 🦴🦴 **1987** Cable adaptation from "My 30 years in Hoover's FBI" by William G. Sullivan and William S. Brown. Biographical drama deals with Hoover's 55-year career with the government. Included are his FBI days. **110m/C VHS.** Treat Williams, Rip Torn, David Ogden Stiers, Andrew Duggan, Art Hindle, Louise Fletcher; ***D:*** Robert E. Collins. **CABLE**

J-Men Forever! 🦴🦴🦴 **1979 (PG)** A spoof on early sci-fi/spy serials in which an alien takeover is attempted via rock-n-roll (your parents warned you). Employs an amusing technique of dubbing footage from dozens of Republic dramas intercut with new film featuring the "Firesign Theater" crew. **73m/B VHS, DVD.** Peter Bergman, Phil(ip) Proctor; ***D:*** Richard Patterson.

Jabberwocky 🦴🦴 1/2 **1977 (PG)** Pythonesque chaos prevails in the medieval cartoon kingdom of King Bruno the Questionable, who rules with cruelty, stupidity, lust and dust. Jabberwocky is the big dragon mowing everything down in its path until hero Palin decides to take it on. Uneven, but real funny at times. **104m/C VHS, DVD.** *GB* Michael Palin, Eric Idle, Max Wall, Deborah Fallender, Terry Jones, John Le Mesurier, Annette Badland, Warren Mitchell, Harry H. Corbett, David Prowse, Neil Innes; ***D:*** Terry Gilliam; ***W:*** Charles Alverson, Terry Gilliam; ***C:*** Terry Bedford; ***M:*** De Wolfe.

J'accuse! 🦴🦴🦴 1/2 *I Accuse!* **1919** Filmed before the WWI armistice, director (and soldier) Gance was able to use actual footage of trench warfare in his anti-war, love-triangle melodrama that features some stunning scenes. Francois Laurin (Severi-Mars) is married to the younger Edith (Dauvray), a marriage forced on her by her father (Desjardins). She loves, and is loved by, poet Jean Diaz (Joube), who is a pacifist until Marie is captured by German soldiers. Diaz enlists and winds up in the trenches where he and Laurin become friends. Much heartbreak follows as Diaz goes mad and has visions of dead soldiers rising out of their graves. **166m/B DVD.** *FR* Romuald Joube, Maryse Dauvray, Severin Mars, Maxime Desjardins, Angele Guys; ***D:*** Abel Gance; ***W:*** Abel Gance; ***C:*** Marc Bujard, Leonce-Henri Burel, Maurice Foster.

J'Accuse 🦴🦴🦴 *I Accuse; That They May Live* **1937** A Frenchman creates a device he believes will stop the war but it is confiscated by the government and used as part of the national defense. Subsequently, he goes mad. Gance (known for his 1927 "Napoleon"), remade his 1919 silent film, retelling the powerful anti-war message with great sensitivity. Banned in Nazi Germany. **125m/B VHS.** *FR* Victor Francen, Jean Max, Deltaire, Renee Devillers; ***D:*** Abel Gance.

Jack 🦴🦴 1/2 **1996 (PG-13)** Ten-year-old Jack Powell (Williams) suffers from a rare genetic disorder that causes him to age at four times the normal rate so he looks like a 40-year-old. His family, fearing ridicule, has kept him isolated but since Jack's so lonely, they finally agree to let him attend school. This new fourth grader isn't the only one with a lot to learn. **111m/C VHS, DVD.** Robin Williams, Bill Cosby, Diane Lane, Brian Kerwin, Fran Drescher, Michael McKean, Jennifer Lopez, Don Novello, Todd Bosley; ***D:*** Francis Ford Coppola; ***W:*** James DeMonaco, Gary Nadeau; ***C:*** John Toll; ***M:*** Michael Kamen.

Jack Ahoy 🦴 1/2 **1934** Jack Hulbert plays an incompetent sailor set on impressing his country and the admiral's daughter by finding the British submarine that was stolen by the Chinese. Froth with song and dance for the jaunty at heart. **70m/B VHS.** Jack Hulbert, Nancy O'Neil, Alfred Drayton; ***D:*** Leslie Arliss, Walter Ford; ***W:*** Gerald Fairlie. **VIDEO**

Jack and His Friends 🦴🦴 **1992 (R)** Comic satire of the tribulations of Jack the shoe salesman (Garfield), who is shown the front door by his unfaithful wife. Beset by grief, he drives the streets aimlessly until he is kidnapped by a young couple (Rockwell and Reyes) on the run from the law, who force Jack to take them to his summer house where they all try to decide what to do with their lives. **93m/C VHS.** Allen (Goorwitz) Garfield, Sam Rockwell, Judy Reyes; ***D:*** Bruce Ornstein.

Jack and Jill vs. the World 🦴🦴 **2008 (PG-13)** Predictable mix of romantic comedy with some tears thrown in. Control freak Jack (Prinze) is a New York ad exec who meets cute but naive newcomer Jill (Manning). Soon they are friends with benefits, negotiating their relationship with a generally light-hearted nine-rule manifesto. Except Jill breaks the honesty rule in a big way when she doesn't tell Jack that she has cystic fibrosis. **87m/C DVD.** Freddie Prinze Jr., Taryn Manning, Peter Stebbings, Kelly Rowan, Vanessa Parise, Hannah Lochner, Robin Dunne, Charles Martin Smith, Robert Forster; ***D:*** Vanessa Parise; ***W:*** Vanessa Parise; ***C:*** Manfred Guthe; ***M:*** Jeremy Parise.

Jack and Sarah 🦴🦴 1/2 **1995 (R)** Widowed London lawyer (Grant) hires American waitress (Mathis), to help raise his infant daughter Sarah. Complications arise because Amy has no child rearing skills and Jack's parents and in-laws disapprove of the whole situation. Performances are nice (especially the scene-stealing infants), and there's some fine moments combining tragedy with romance, but the plot is a little thin and the whole film is slow moving (it takes more than half the movie to get the three protagonists in place). An edited version is rated PG. **110m/C VHS, DVD.** *GB* Richard E. Grant, Samantha Mathis, Ian McKellen, Judi Dench, Cherie Lunghi, Eileen Atkins, Imogen Stubbs; ***D:*** Tim Sullivan; ***W:*** Tim Sullivan; ***C:*** Jean-Yves Escoffier; ***M:*** Simon Boswell.

Jack & the Beanstalk 🦴🦴 **1952** While baby-sitting, Lou falls asleep and dreams he's Jack in this spoof of the classic fairy tale. **78m/C VHS, DVD.** Bud Abbott, Lou Costello, Buddy Baer, Dorothy Ford, Barbara Brown, William Farnum; ***D:*** Jean Yarbrough; ***W:*** Nathaniel Curtis; ***C:*** George Robinson; ***M:*** Heinz Roemheld.

Jack & the Beanstalk 🦴🦴🦴 **1983** From the "Faerie Tale Theatre" comes this classic tale of Jack, who sells his family's cow for five magic beans, climbs the huge beanstalk that sprouts from them, and encounters an unfriendly giant. **60m/C VHS, DVD.** Dennis Christopher, Katherine Helmond, Elliott Gould, Jean Stapleton, Mark Blankfield; ***D:*** Lamont Johnson.

Jack and the Beanstalk: The Real Story 🦴 1/2 *Jim Henson's Jack and the Beanstalk* **2001** Attenuated and dull take on the familiar fairytale finds Modine's Jack a modern-day descendant of the Jack who stole the golden goose. That's how his family built an empire but it's payback time and Jack needs to climb that beanstalk and make reparations for his ancestor's crimes. **184m/C VHS, DVD.** Matthew Modine, Vanessa Redgrave, Mia Sara, Jon Voight, Daryl Hannah, Richard Attenborough; ***D:*** Brian Henson; ***W:*** James V. Hart, Brian Henson. **TV**

Jack Be Nimble **1994 (R)** Siblings Jack (Arquette) and Dora (Kennedy) were separated as children and adopted by different families. Jack's family turns out to be sadistic and he suffers much abuse, until he enacts a violent revenge; Dora begins to hear voices and soon realizes it's Jack crying out to her. The duo finally reunite but between Jack's rage and Dora's telepathic abilities, life takes on further bizarre twists. Much psychological terror rather than gore. **93m/C VHS, DVD.** *NZ* Alexis Arquette, Sarah Smuts-Kennedy, Bruno Lawrence; ***D:*** Garth Maxwell; ***W:*** Garth Maxwell; ***C:*** Donald Duncan; ***M:*** Chris Neal.

Jack Brown, Genius **1994 (PG-13)** Offbeat fantasy, written by Peter Jackson and Fran Walsh, concerns a medieval monk named Elmer (Devenie) who tried to fly (shades of Icarus) and wound up killing himself instead. Somehow Elmer briefly gets his spirit out of Hell and into the modern mind of inventor Jack Brown (Balme). Now he has to get Jack to invent a contraption that will allow man himself to fly so Elmer's soul can get into Heaven instead. **90m/C DVD.** *NZ* Timothy Balme, Stuart Devenie, Marton Csokas, Nicola Murphy, Edward Campbell; ***D:*** Tony Hiles; ***W:*** Peter Jackson, Fran Walsh; ***C:*** Allen Guilford; ***M:*** Michelle Scullion.

The Jack Bull 1/2 **1999 (R)** Cusack's father adapted a 19th-century German novel, "Michael Kohlhaas" by Heinrich Von Kleist, into a 19th-century American western, set in Wyoming. Myrl Redding (Cusack) is a peaceful horse trader who demands justice when wealthy landowner Henry Ballard (Jones) beats two of Redding's horses and their Indian caretaker. Since Ballard has the local law in his pocket, Redding gets no satisfaction. Becoming obsessed, he decides to form a vigilante posse to get Ballard to pay for his actions. **120m/C VHS, DVD.** John Cusack, L.Q. Jones, John Goodman, Rodney A. Grant, Miranda Otto, John C. McGinley, John Savage, Jay O. Sanders, Scott Wilson, Drake Bell, Glenn Morshower, Ken Pogue; ***D:*** John Badham; ***W:*** Richard (Dick) Cusack; ***C:*** Gale Tattersall; ***M:*** Lennie Niehaus. **CABLE**

Jack Frost **1997 (R)** Convicted serial killer Jack Frost (McDonald) mutates after accidental exposure to an experimental liquid DNA, becomes a killer snowman, and terrorizes a town preparing for the annual Snowman Festival. Snickering seasonal gore with a killer who uses icicles and a carrot nose to dispatch some of his latest victims. **89m/C VHS, DVD.** Scott McDonald, Christopher Allport, F. William Parker; ***D:*** Michael Cooney; ***W:*** Michael Cooney; ***C:*** Dean Lent. **VIDEO**

Jack Frost **1998 (PG)** As emotionally realistic and cool as soap flake snow, alleged family feature has Keaton playing Jack Frost, a struggling musician who spends too much time away from wife Gabby (Preston) and son Charlie (Cross). He decides to blow off a Christmas Day gig to spend more time with the family, only to be killed on his way to their mountain cabin. One year later, forlorn Charlie makes a snowman, dresses it in his dead dad's duds, and blows a note on Jack's harmonica. Bingo! Now his dead father is back to life as a creepy-looking talking snowman! Keaton tries his best with the lame material; but with the use of four confused screenwriters, he didn't have a snowball's chance. Additional warning: Keaton sings. Not to be confused with the straight-to-video release of the same name about a murderous deranged talking snowman. **95m/C VHS, DVD.** Michael Keaton, Kelly Preston, Joseph Cross, Mark Addy, Eli Marienthal, Dweezil Zappa, Henry Rollins, Andrew (Andy) Lawrence, Ahmet Zappa, Jeff Cesario; ***D:*** Troy Miller; ***W:*** Mark Steven Johnson, Steven L. Bloom, Jonathan Roberts, Jeff Cesario; ***C:*** Laszlo Kovacs; ***M:*** Trevor Rabin.

Jack Frost 2: Revenge of the Mutant Killer Snowman **WOOF!** **2000 (R)** Snowy horror is returned to his evil ways by a lab accident that also makes him impervious to heat, bullets, and antifreeze. So Jack decides to get revenge on Sheriff Sam (who defeated him previously), who just happens to be on vacation in a tropical paradise. But Chilly Boy doesn't have to worry about that. **91m/C VHS, DVD.** Christopher Allport, David Allan Brooks, Chip Heller, Eileen Seeley, Adrienne Barbeau; ***D:*** Michael Cooney; ***W:*** Michael Cooney. **VIDEO**

Jack Higgins' Midnight Man 1/2 *Midnight Man* **1996 (R)** Ex-terrorist Sean Dillon (Lowe) is reluctantly recruited by British intelligence to thwart a plot to kill Princes Harry and William in a scheme to overthrow the monarchy. Only Dillon soon realizes his target is a dangerous ex-colleague and a band of fanatics. Based on the Higgins novel "Eye of the Storm." **104m/C VHS.** Rob Lowe, Kenneth Cranham, Deborah Maria Moore, Michael Sarrazin, Hannes Jaenicke, Daphne Cheung, Jim Duggan; ***D:*** Lawrence Gordon-Clark; ***W:*** Jurgen Wolff; ***C:*** Ken Westbury; ***M:*** Leon Aronson. **CABLE**

Jack Higgins' On Dangerous Ground *On Dangerous Ground* **1995 (R)** A major miscast ruins thriller writer Higgins's chances in this cable movie. Ex-IRA assassin and all-around terrorist Sean Dillon (Lowe) nows works for a British intelligence agency, headed by Brigadier Ferguson (Cranham). A secret agreement documenting a WWII deal between Lord Mountbatten and Mao Tse-tung has come to murky light and could exacerbate the tensions between China and Britain over Hong Kong. Dillon not only is expected to retrieve the document but also prevent an assassination attempt while the U.S. prez visits England. Lowe's way too lightweight for the Dillon role and manages to throw what should have been a good action yarn completely off-balance. **105m/C VHS.** *CA GB LU* Rob Lowe, Kenneth Cranham, Jurgen Prochnow, Deborah Maria Moore, Ingeborga Dapkounaite, Daphne Cheung, Richard Rees, Claude Blanchard; ***D:*** Lawrence Gordon-Clark; ***W:*** Christopher Wickens; ***C:*** Ken Westbury; ***M:*** Leon Aronson. **CABLE**

Jack Higgins' The Windsor Protocol 1/2 *The Windsor Protocol* **1997 (R)** The sequel to "Jack Higgins' Thunder Point" finds ex-terrorist Sean Dillon (MacLachlan), now working for British Intelligence, still trying to recover The Windsor Protocol, a Nazi-era document that has recently come to light and involves present-day Nazi sympathizers, money, power, and both the U.S. and British governments. **96m/C VHS.** Kyle MacLachlan, Alan Thicke, Macha Grenon, John Colicos, Chris Wiggins; ***D:*** George Mihalka; ***W:*** David Preston, Stephen Zoller; ***C:*** Peter Benison; ***M:*** Stanislas Syrewicz. **CABLE**

Jack Higgins' Thunder Point 1/2 *Thunder Point* **1997 (R)** MacLachlan takes over from Rob Lowe as ex-IRA terrorist Sean Dillon and the casting still stinks. (Doesn't anybody read Higgins' books!) A treasure diver finds The Windsor Protocol, a Hitler directive that also contains info on hidden funds that neo-Nazis hope to use to resurrect the Reich. Dillon's hired to find the document but it eventually does winds up in the hands of Nazi sympathizers, leading to the sequel "Jack Higgins' The Windsor Protocol." **95m/C VHS.** Kyle MacLachlan, Michael Sarrazin, Kenneth Welsh, Pascale Bussieres, Chris Wiggins, John Colicos, Cedric Smith; ***D:*** George Mihalka; ***W:*** Morrie Ruvinsky; ***C:*** Peter Benison; ***M:*** Stanislas Syrewicz. **CABLE**

The Jack Knife Man **1920** Sentimental silent treatment of the relationship between a boy and a man. A new mother close to death hands over her bundle of joy to a kindly old river man, and the two bond in a familial way despite incessant adversity. Made the year following Vidor's debut as a feature film director. **70m/B VHS.** Fred Turner, Harry Todd, Bobby Kelso, Willis Marks, Lillian (Lillianne, Lyllian) Leighton, James Corrigan; ***D:*** King Vidor; ***W:*** William Parker.

Jack London 1/2 *The Adventures of Jack London; The Life of Jack London* **1944** Dramatizes London's most creative years during his careers as oyster pirate, prospector, war correspondent and author. Based on "The Book of Jack London" by Charmian London. **94m/B VHS, DVD.** Michael O'Shea, Susan Hayward, Harry Davenport, Virginia Mayo, Frank Craven; ***D:*** Alfred Santell.

Jack London's The Call of the Wild 1/2 *The Call of the Wild: Dog of the Yukon* **1997 (PG)** Adaptation of Jack London's 1903 adventure story is told from the view of Buck, an intelligent St. Bernard-Labrador mix who's kidnapped from his California home. He's sold in the Yukon and eventually winds up with prospector John Thornton (Hauer) but Buck is increasingly drawn to running free. **90m/C VHS, DVD.** Rutger Hauer, Luc Morrissette, Bronwyn Booth; ***D:*** Peter Svatek; ***W:*** Graham Ludlow; ***C:*** Sylvain Brault; ***M:*** Alan Reeves; ***Nar:*** Richard Dreyfuss. **CABLE**

Jack-O 1/2 **1995 (R)** Halloween nightmares in the small town of Oakmoor Crossing. When warlock Walter Machen (Carradine) was hung 100 years before, he invoked a demon creature to take his revenge. Now partyers, fooling around in the local cemetery, have stumbled onto horrific Jack-O's remains and manage to once again unleash the evil within. Cheesy grade-Z horror features old footage of deceased actors Carradine and Mitchell incorporated into what little plot there is. **90m/C VHS, DVD.** Linnea Quigley, Ryan Latshaw, Cameron Mitchell, John Carradine, Dawn Wildsmith, Brinke Stevens; ***D:*** Steve Latshaw; ***W:*** Patrick Moran; ***C:*** Maxwell J. Beck; ***M:*** Jeff Walton.

Jack O'Lantern **2004 (R)** Inept, miniscule-budgeted horror flick finds Jack (Watkins) still suffering nightmares a year after a deadly car crash. Only his nightmares are now resulting in murder. Oh, and the monster has a Jack o'lantern for a head. **94m/C VHS, DVD.** David R. Watkins, Kevin L. Powers, Tracy Yarkoni, Justice Leak, Brian Avenet-Bradley, Ron McLellen, Sacha A. Dzuba; ***D:*** Ron McLellen; ***W:*** Ron McLellen; ***M:*** Sacha A. Dzuba. **VIDEO**

Jack the Bear 1/2 **1993 (PG-13)** Exercise in misery centers on a father and his two sons, trying to pick up the pieces after the death of wife and mother Marcovicci. Dad DeVito is the host of a late-night horror show who's cuddly as a bear—when he's not drinking. While the talent and circumstances might have been enough to create a sensitive study, the emotion is completely overwrought by contrived plot twists, including a kidnapping by the local Nazi. TV's "thirtysomething" director Herskovitz creates an effect not unlike a cement block being dropped on a card house. Point made, but so much for subtlety. Based on a novel by Dan McCall. **98m/C VHS, DVD.** Danny DeVito, Robert J. Steinmiller Jr., Miko Hughes, Gary Sinise, Art LaFleur, Andrea Marcovicci, Julia Louis-Dreyfus, Reese Witherspoon; ***D:*** Marshall Herskovitz; ***W:*** Steven Zaillian; ***C:*** Fred Murphy; ***M:*** James Horner.

Jack the Giant Killer **1962 (G)** A young farmer joins a medieval princess on a journey to a distant convent. Along the way, they combat an evil wizard, dragons, sea monsters, and other mystical creatures, and are assisted by leprechauns, a dog, and a chimp. Generally considered a blatant rip-off of "The Seventh Voyage of Sinbad," the film nonetheless delivers plenty of fun and excitement. Jim Danforth of "Gumby" fame provided the stop-motion animation. **95m/C VHS, DVD.** Kerwin Mathews, Judi Meredith, Torin Thatcher, Walter Burke, Roger Mobley, Barry Kelley, Don Beddoe, Anna Lee, Robert Gist; ***D:*** Nathan "Jerry" Juran; ***W:*** Nathan "Jerry" Juran, Orville H. Hampton; ***C:*** David S. Horsley; ***M:*** Paul Sawtell, Bert Shefter.

Jack the Ripper **1960** An American detective joins Scotland Yard in tracking down the legendary and elusive Jack the Ripper. More gory than most. The last scene is in color. **88m/B VHS, DVD.** *GB* Lee Patterson, Betty McDowall, Barbara Burke, John Le Mesurier, George Rose; ***D:*** Monty Berman, Robert S. Baker; ***M:*** Stanley Black.

Jack the Ripper *Der Dirnenmoerder von London* **1976 (R)** The inimitable Kinski assumes the role of the most heinous criminal of modern history—Jack the Ripper. **82m/C VHS, DVD.** *SI GE* Klaus Kinski, Josephine Chaplin, Herbert (Fuchs) Fux, Ursula von Wiese, Lina Romay, Andreas Mannkopff; ***D:*** Jess (Jesus) Franco; ***W:*** Jess (Jesus) Franco; ***C:*** Peter Baumgartner.

Jack the Ripper **1988** Another retelling of the life of the legendary serial killer. Caine is the Scotland Yard inspector who tracks down the murderer. Ending is based on recent evidence found by director/co-writer Wickes. Extremely well done TV film. **200m/C VHS.** Michael Caine, Armand Assante, Ray McNally, Susan George, Jane Seymour, Lewis Collins, Ken Bones; ***D:*** David Wickes; ***W:*** David Wickes. **TV**

The Jackal 1/2 **1997 (R)** The plot has more holes than Swiss cheese but thanks to a pro cast this film manages to be at least a workmanlike thriller. Willis stars as a killer-for-hire known only as "The Jackal." His latest employer, a Russian gangster, wants revenge for FBI interference in his business, and the Jackal's target is apparently the FBI's Director. Few know what the Jackal looks like and the most available is Declan Mulqueen (Gere), an IRA gunman imprisoned in the U.S. He's given a deal by good FBI guy Preston (Poitier) and the hunt is on. Unfortunately, the Jackal's elaborate preparations don't raise the tension, though they do provide some gross-out moments. The end game (in the D.C. subway) between the Jackal and Mulqueen provides a satisfying conclusion and Willis does excell as the ice-cold killer. Started off as a heavily reworked version of the 1973 assassination thriller "The Day of the Jackal" but most of the associations have been cut. **124m/C VHS, DVD.** Bruce Willis, Richard Gere, Sidney Poitier, Diane Venora, Mathilda May, Stephen Spinella, John Cunningham, J.K. Simmons, Tess Harper, Richard Lineback, Jack Black, David Hayman, Steve Bassett; ***D:*** Michael Caton-Jones; ***W:*** Chuck Pfarrer; ***C:*** Karl Walter Lindenlaub; ***M:*** Carter Burwell.

The Jackals **1967** Six bandits threaten miner Price and his granddaughter in order to get his gold. Set in South Africa. **105m/C VHS, DVD.** Vincent Price, Diana Ivarson, Robert Gunner, Bob Courtney, Patrick Mynhardt; ***D:*** Robert D. Webb; ***W:*** W.R. Burnett.

Jackass Number Two **2006 (R)** With the TV series iced, the Jackass posse is back with four years' worth of new gags, stunts, and bad ideas. There's less talk, more shock and if you're familiar with the curiously charismatic Knoxville, you'll know what to expect—men are stupid and eager to risk their body parts in even more insane contests. By the way, the title is not just an indication that it's a sequel, it's a literal warning of what to expect. **95m/C DVD.** *US* Johnny Knoxville, Bam Margera, Chris Pontius, Ryan Dunn, Steve-O, Dave England, Preston Lacy, Ehren McGhehey; ***D:*** Jeff Tremaine; ***W:*** Preston Lacy, Sean Cliver; ***C:*** Dimitry Elyashkavich, Lance Bangs, Rick Kosick.

Jackass: The Movie **2002 (R)** The ultimate critic-proof movie. Those who love the TV show will also love the fact that these guys can swear and be as gross as they wanna be, and indulge in even bigger, dumber, if not always more elaborate stunts. Those who think the whole thing is stupid and childish will continue to think so. In case you don't know the drill, Johnny Knoxville and his crew perform homemade or made-up stunts to a) get laughs, b) get a reaction out of people, c) gross out bystanders, d) see if they can be done, and e) all of the above. Watch it to bring out your inner 12-year-old with ADHD. **87m/C VHS, DVD.** Johnny Knoxville, Bam Margera, Steve "Steve-O" Glover, Chris Pontius, Ryan Dunn, Jason "Wee Man" Acuna; ***D:*** Jeff Tremaine; ***C:*** Dimitry Elyashkavich.

The Jacket 1/2 **2005 (R)** A gulf vet (Brody) is falsely convicted of murder. Having no memory of the crime, he's sentenced to a mental institution instead of prison. The chief psychiatrist's therapy consists of drugs, a straitjacket, and sensory deprivation in a morgue drawer. Vet's reaction to this is, of course, to time-travel, allowing him to confront the ghosts of his present in the future and effect changes for the general good of all. Interesting premise, but handled with a lead foot and little originality. Think "Jacob's Ladder" meets "Twelve Monkeys" meets "One Flew Over the Cuckoo's Nest." Fairly entertaining with good performances by solid cast. **102m/C DVD.** *US* Adrien Brody, Keira Knightley, Kris Kristofferson, Jennifer Jason Leigh, Kelly Lynch, Brad Renfro, Daniel Craig, MacKenzie Phillips; ***D:*** John Maybury; ***W:*** Massy Tadjedin; ***C:*** Peter Deming; ***M:*** Brian Eno.

Jackie Brown **1997 (R)** Tarantino finally climbs back into the director's chair with his leisurely but satisfying adaptation of Elmore Leonard's "Rum Punch." No, it's not "Pulp Fiction," but it could do for Pam Grier what "Pulp" did for John Travolta. Grier stars as out-of-luck-and-options stewardess Jackie Brown, who runs money to Mexico for ruthless arms dealer Ordell (Jackson). Busted on one of her errands, she comes up with an intricate plan to get out from under, hopefully with the money and without getting caught or killed. Slower and less bloody than Quentin fans are used to, but as usual, he gets killer performances from everybody. Cool dialogue and chronological shifts are again key ingredients, along with a hightened sense of character development. Fonda and De Niro make the most of small (but crucial) roles, but it's Forster (another '70s whatever-happened-to refugee) who provides the standout performance. The look and feel of the movie reflects the dingy world it inhabits, as well as Tarantino's love of '70s blaxploitation flicks. **155m/C VHS, DVD.** Pam Grier, Robert Forster, Samuel L. Jackson, Robert De Niro, Bridget Fonda, Michael Keaton, Michael Bowen, Chris Tucker, Lisa Gay Hamilton, Tommy (Tiny) Lister, Hattie Winston, Aimee Graham, Sid Haig; ***D:*** Quentin Tarantino; ***W:*** Quentin Tarantino; ***C:*** Guillermo Navarro; ***M:*** Mary Ramos, Michelle Kuznetsky.

Jackie Chan's First Strike ✪✪✪ *First Strike; Police Story 4* **1996 (PG-13)** Plot, schmot. The human hurricane that is Jackie Chan is once again amazing in this kung-fu comedy homage to '60s James Bond movies. Half Bruce Lee and half Charlie Chaplin, Chan reprises the role of the Hong Kong supercop named Jackie, who is this time loaned out by his superior officer "Uncle Bill" (Tung) to the CIA. He is sent to the Ukraine to spy on a beautiful young woman involved in smuggling nuclear weapons along with rogue CIA agent Tsui (Lou). He follows the villains to Australia, where he secures justice, peace, and sharp blows to the head. Enough about the plot. Listen to this! He holds bad guys at bay by whirling an aluminum stepladder like it was a drum major's baton! He kicks somebody off of a second story ledge while on stilts! He sings and dances while wearing koala bear underwear! Dubbed in English. **87m/C VHS, DVD.** *HK* Jackie Chan, Bill Tung, Jackson Lou, Annie (Chen Chun) Wu, Jouri (Yuri) Petrov, Grishajeva Nonna; ***D:*** Stanley Tong; ***W:*** Stanley Tong, Greg Mellott, Nick Tramontane, Elliot Tong; ***C:*** Jingle Ma; ***M:*** J. Peter Robinson.

Jackie Chan's Who Am I ✪✪ 1/2 *Who Am I; Ngo Hai Sui* **1998 (PG-13)** Jackie (Chan) is recruited by the CIA to join a team of commandos leading a raid on a secret weapons research lab in South Africa. The team hijack a piece of highly explosive experimental material and are betrayed by their leader. Only Jackie survives but he's got amnesia. When he finally returns home, he's still wondering who he is—an important question since he's being pursued by the bad guys who want him to stay dead. **108m/C VHS, DVD.** *HK* Jackie Chan, Ed Nelson, Ron Smerczak, Michelle Ferre, Mirai Yamamoto; ***D:*** Jackie Chan, Benny Chan; ***W:*** Jackie Chan, Lee Reynolds, Susan Chan; ***C:*** Hang-Seng Poon; ***M:*** Nathan Wang.

Jackie, Ethel, Joan: The Kennedy Women ✪✪ 1/2 *Jackie, Ethel, Joan: Women of Camelot* **2001** TV miniseries focuses on the Kennedy wives: Jackie (Hennessy), Ethel (Holly), and Joan (Stefanson) rather than on their husbands and the toll that politics and the spotlight took on them as individuals. Sudser follows the period from 1960 to 1980; based on the bestseller by J. Randy Taraborrelli. **172m/C VHS, DVD.** Jil-l(ian) Hennessey, Lauren Holly, Leslie Stefanson, Daniel Hugh-Kelly, Robert Knepper, Matt Letscher, Harve Presnell, Charmion King, Thom Christopher; ***D:*** Larry Shaw; ***W:*** David Stevens; ***C:*** Frank Byers; ***M:*** Martin Davich. **TV**

The Jackie Robinson Story ✪✪✪ **1950** Chronicles Robinson's rise from UCLA to his breakthrough as the first black man to play baseball in the major league. Robinson plays himself; the film deals honestly with the racial issues of the time. **76m/B VHS, DVD.** Jackie Robinson, Ruby Dee, Minor Watson, Louise Beavers, Richard Lane, Harry Shannon, Joel Fluellen, Ben Lessy; ***D:*** Alfred E. Green; ***W:*** Arthur Mann, Lawrence Taylor; ***C:*** Ernest Laszlo; ***M:*** David Chudnow.

Jackie's Back ✪✪ 1/2 **1999 (R)** Mockumentary follows the stumbling comeback of forgotten pop diva, Jackie Washington (Lewis). Spoiled and temperamental, Jackie is followed by a supersilicious British doumentary filmmaker, Edward Whatsett St. John (Curry), as she prepares for a big concert as everything is in chaos around her. Flashbacks reflect on Jackie's early career. **91m/C VHS, DVD.** Jenifer Lewis, Tim Curry, Tangie Ambrose, Whoopi Goldberg, David Hyde Pierce, Tom Arnold, Julie Hagerty, JoBeth Williams, Dolly Parton, Grace Slick, Liza Minnelli; ***D:*** Robert Kevin Townsend; ***W:*** Mark Brown, Dee La Duke; ***C:*** Charles Mills; ***M:*** Marc Shaiman. **CABLE**

Jacknife ✪✪✪ **1989 (R)** The well-crafted story of a Vietnam veteran who visits his old war buddy and tries to piece together what's happened to their lives since their homecoming. During his visit he encounters anger and hostility from the other veteran, and tenderness from his friend's sister. A masterfully acted, small-scale drama, adapted by Stephen Metcalfe from his play. **102m/C VHS, DVD.** Robert De Niro, Kathy Baker, Ed Harris, Loudon Wainwright III, Charles S. Dutton; ***D:*** David Hugh Jones; ***W:*** Stephen Metcalfe; ***M:*** Bruce Broughton.

Jacko & Lise ✪✪ **1982 (R)** A French lad falls in love with a young girl, and abandons his previously decadent lifestyle to win her. Available with English subtitles or dubbed. **92m/C VHS.** *FR* Laurent Malet, Annie Girardot; ***D:*** Walter Bal.

The Jackpot ✪✪ **1950** An average Joe wins a bushel of money from a radio quiz show but can't pay the taxes. Maybe that was funny before the age of read-my-lips economics, but the all-star cast doesn't deliver on its promise. Lang, noted for mostly mediocre pictures, went on to direct "The King and I." **87m/C VHS.** James Stewart, Natalie Wood, Barbara Hale, James Gleason, Fred Clark, Patricia Medina; ***D:*** Walter Lang; ***C:*** Joseph LaShelle.

Jackpot ✪✪ **2001 (R)** Brothers Mark and Michael Polish follow up their critically lauded debut "Twin Falls Idaho" with this road tale of karaoke and crackpots. Sunny Holiday (Gries) is an aspiring country singer riding the back roads of the remote West with his manager Les (Morris), trying to break into Nashville via the untraveled karaoke route. Neither one seems to realize the futility of his dreams, but Bobbi (Hannah), the wife he's abandoned with their young child, does. The "Jackpot" of the title is his dream of making it big, the way he hopes to support his family (he sends them a lottery ticket each week in lieu of child support) and the name of the Nevada town where he hopes to be discovered. Tries way too hard to be arty in a folksy "look at these eccentric characters" way, but it's not without its own weird charm. **100m/C VHS, DVD.** *US* Jon(athan) Gries, Garrett Morris, Daryl Hannah, Peggy Lipton, Adam Baldwin, Mac Davis, Crystal Bernard, Anthony Edwards; ***D:*** Michael Polish; ***W:*** Michael Polish, Mark Polish; ***C:*** M. David Mullen; ***M:*** Stuart Matthewman; ***V:*** Patrick Bauchau.

Jack's Back ✪✪✪ **1987 (R)** When a lunatic is killing Los Angeles prostitutes Jack-the-Ripper style, twin brothers get mistakenly involved (Spader in both roles). One of the brothers is accused of the murders and it is up to the other either to clear his name or to provide the final evidence of guilt. A well-thought out story with enough twists and turns for any suspense buff. **97m/C VHS.** James Spader, Cynthia Gibb, Rod Loomis, Rex Ryon, Robert Picardo, Jim Haynie, Chris Mulkey, Danitza Kingsley, Wendell Wright; ***D:*** Rowdy Herrington; ***W:*** Rowdy Herrington; ***C:*** Shelly Johnson.

Jackson County Jail ✪✪ 1/2 **1976 (R)** While driving cross-country, a young woman is robbed, imprisoned, and raped by a deputy, whom she kills. Faced with a murder charge, she flees, with the law in hot pursuit. Also known by its later remade-for-TV name, "Outside Chance," this is a minor cult film. **84m/C VHS, DVD.** Yvette Mimieux, Tommy Lee Jones, Robert Carradine, Severn Darden, Howard Hesseman, Mary Woronov, Ed Marshall, Cliff Emmich, Betty Thomas; ***D:*** Michael Miller; ***W:*** Donald Stewart; ***C:*** Bruce Logan; ***M:*** Loren Newkirk.

The Jacksons: An American Dream ✪✪ 1/2 **1992** Miniseries covering the career of the Jackson 5, the working-class family from Gary, Indiana, who became a celebrated show business success. The series begins with the courtship of Joseph and Katherine Jackson and ends with the group's farewell tour in 1984, covering both family and career turmoils. Simplistic, glossy biography. **225m/C VHS, DVD.** Lawrence-Hilton Jacobs, Angela Bassett, Wylie Draper, Angel Vargas, Jacen Wilkerson, Terrence Howard, Jason Weaver, Jermaine Jackson II, Billy Dee Williams, Vanessa L(ynne) Williams, Holly Robinson, Margaret Avery; ***D:*** Karen Arthur. **TV**

Jacob ✪✪ 1/2 **1994** Jacob (Modine), second son of Isaac (Ackland), tricks his father into giving him the blessing meant for eldest son Esau (Bean). Jacob is forced to run away to his Uncle Laban (Giannini), where he promptly falls in love with his cousin Rachel (Boyle). But Laban tricks Jacob into marrying eldest daughter Leah (Aubrey), before allowing his marriage to Rachel. Finally, Jacob settles on his own land with his wives and children (who will become the tribes of Israel). Dignified retelling of the biblical story; filmed on location in Morocco. **120m/C VHS, DVD.** Matthew Modine, Lara Flynn Boyle, Sean Bean, Juliet Aubrey, Giancarlo Giannini, Joss Ackland, Irene Papas, Christoph Waltz; ***D:*** Peter Hall; ***W:*** Lionel Chetwynd; ***M:*** Marco Frisina. **CABLE**

Jacob Have I Loved **1988** A teenage girl struggles to overcome her jealousy of her twin sister and find her own place in life as she comes of age on a Chesapeake island. Based on the book by Katherine Paterson. Part of the "Wonderworks" family movie series from PBS. **57m/C VHS, DVD.** Bridget Fonda, Jenny Robertson, John Kellogg; ***D:*** Victoria Hochberg.

Jacob the Liar ✪✪ *Jakob der Lugner* **1974 (PG-13)** When Jacob Heim is stopped for being out of the Jewish ghetto after curfew, he is sent to see the police commander. On the police radio, he hears that the Red Army is advancing and he returns to the ghetto to pass along the news, pretending that he heard it on his own hidden radio. Soon, Jacob is inventing news reports to give his fellow Jews hope. German with subtitles. A sentimental American remake came out in 1999. **101m/C VHS, DVD.** *GE* Armin Mueller-Stahl, Vlastimil Brodsky, Erwin Geschonneck, Henry Hubchen, Blanche Kommerell, Manuela Simon; ***D:*** Frank Beyer; ***W:*** Jurek Becker; ***C:*** Gunter Marczinkowski.

Jacob Two Two Meets the Hooded Fang ✪✪ 1/2 **1999** Edgy kids fantasy based on the book by Mordecai Richler. Jacob (Morrow) is nicknamed Jacob Two Two because he repeats everything since no one every listens to him the first time he says something. Because of this Jacob gets into unexpected trouble when shopping at the corner store, runs into the store basement, and knocks himself out in the darkness. Jacob dreams he's now on trial and is sentenced to Slimers' Island, which is run by a bizarre creature called the Hooded Fang (Busey) and his equally strange henchmen. **96m/C VHS, DVD.** *CA* Max Morrow, Gary Busey, Miranda Richardson, Ice-T, Mark McKinney, Maury Chaykin; ***D:*** George Bloomfield; ***W:*** Tim Burns; ***C:*** Gerald Packer; ***M:*** Jono Grant.

Jacob's Ladder ✪✪ 1/2 **1990 (R)** A man struggles with events he experienced while serving in Vietnam. Gradually, he becomes unable to separate reality from the strange, psychotic world into which he increasingly lapses. His friends and family try to help him before he's lost forever. Great story potential is flawed by too many flashbacks, leaving the viewer more confused than the characters. **116m/C VHS, DVD.** Tim Robbins, Elizabeth Pena, Danny Aiello, Matt Craven, Pruitt Taylor Vince, Jason Alexander, Patricia Kalember, Ving Rhames, Eriq La Salle, Macaulay Culkin, Lewis Black; ***D:*** Adrian Lyne; ***W:*** Bruce Joel Rubin; ***C:*** Jeffrey L. Kimball; ***M:*** Maurice Jarre.

Jacqueline Bouvier Kennedy ✪ 1/2 **1981** Biography of the former First Lady, from her childhood to "Camelot," the glorious years with JFK in the White House. Smith bears a physical resemblance to Jackie, but this drama is far too glossy. **150m/C VHS.** Jaclyn Smith, James Franciscus, Rod Taylor, Donald Moffat, Dolph Sweet, Stephen Elliott, Claudette Nevins; ***D:*** Steven Gethers; ***M:*** Billy Goldenberg. **TV**

Jacquot ✪✪ *Jacquot de Nantes* **1991 (PG)** Director Varda offers a loving tribute to her husband, filmmaker Jacques Demy. Based on the memoirs of her husband's childhood as a boy obsessed with movies, Varda re-stages scenes and also uses clips from various Demy films to illustrate her points. In French with English subtitles. **118m/C VHS.** *FR* Philippe Maron, Edouard Joubeaud, Laurent Monnier, Brigitte de Villepoix, Daniel Dublet; ***D:*** Agnes Varda; ***W:*** Agnes Varda; ***C:*** Patrick Blossier; ***M:*** Joanne Bruzdowicz.

Jada ✪ 1/2 **2008 (PG)** Uninspired though well-meaning drama about a woman's faith in troubled times. After Jada's husband dies, she and her two teenage children are forced to move into the gang-run projects. Jada turns to the church for guidance and to helpful ex-con Simon as well. **89m/C DVD.** Siena Goines, Rockmond Dunbar, Jennifer Freeman, Jason Weaver, Clifton Powell; ***D:*** Robert Johnson; ***W:*** Daniel Chavez; ***C:*** Christopher Gosch. **VIDEO**

Jade ✪ 1/2 **1995 (R)** Sleazy whodunnit scraped from the bottom of the Eszterhas barrel (and it's a deep one) has hot-shot San Francisco Assistant D.A. David Corelli (Caruso) tracking a trail of pubic hairs across San Francisco. Seems he's caught up in the murder of a millionaire that points to his ex-lover, psychologist Katrina Gavin (Fiorentino), as the killer. Oh yeah, she's also a kinky call girl of choice to California's rich and famous, and happens to be married to Corelli's best friend (Palminteri). Psycho-thriller with little of either injects lots of lurid details (and a car chase scene that Friedkin has done much better elsewhere) in an attempt to curtail boredom; it doesn't work. Combine it with "Showgirls" for the No Self-Respect Film Festival, then go to confession. **94m/C VHS, DVD.** David Caruso, Linda Fiorentino, Chazz Palminteri, Michael Biehn, Richard Crenna, Kenneth King, Angie Everhart; ***D:*** William Friedkin; ***W:*** Joe Eszterhas; ***C:*** Andrzej Bartkowiak; ***M:*** James Horner.

The Jade Mask ✪ 1/2 **1945** Chan discovers a murderer and his wife use puppets and masks to make it appear their victims are still alive. Another in the detective series with nothing noteworthy about it. Luke, the brother of actor Keye Luke, takes on the role of Chan's Number Four son. **66m/B VHS, DVD.** Sidney Toler, Mantan Moreland, Edwin Luke, Janet Warren, Hardie Albright, Edith Evanson; ***D:*** Phil Rosen.

Jaded ✪✪ 1/2 **1996 (R)** Seemingly innocent Meg (Gugino) is befriended by a couple of uninhibited babes (Kihlstedt, Thompson) at the local bar and goes with them to a party where she's sexually assaulted. The two women are accused of rape and the case goes to trial but Meg's past secrets come to light and things don't seem so cut-and-dried anymore. The box art is the real tease since the film isn't the erotic thriller it might appear to be. **95m/C VHS, DVD.** Carla Gugino, Anna Thomson, Rya Kihlstedt, Christopher McDonald, Lorraine Toussaint; ***D:*** Caryn Krooth. **VIDEO**

Jadup and Boel ✪ 1/2 **1981** Jadup, the respected mayor of a small East German town in the 1970s, is haunted by his memories of WWII after someone finds a Marxist pamphlet in an abandoned building. He gave the pamphlet to teenaged refugee Boel, who vanished after refusing to name her rapist (despite Jadup's harsh interrogation of her), amidst fears that the crime would lead back to Russian soldiers billeted in the town. German with subtitles. **100m/C DVD.** *GE* Kurt Bowe, Katrin Knappe, Gudrun Ritter, Kathe Reichel, Timo Jakob, Franciszek Pieckza, Michael Gwisdek; ***D:*** Rainer Simon; ***W:*** Rainer Simon; ***C:*** Roland Dressel; ***M:*** Reiner Bredemeyer.

JAG ✪✪ 1/2 **1995** TV pilot episode features Navy pilot-turned-lawyer Lt. Harmon Rabb, Jr. (Elliott) assigned to investigate the case of a young female pilot who disappears from an aircraft carrier. Seems some of her fellow sailors resented having women on board so was it an accident or murder? JAG stands for the office of the Judge Advocate General, whose Navy lawyers serve as investigators, prosecutors, and defense attorneys. **94m/C VHS.** David James Elliott, Andrea Parker, Terry O'Quinn, John Roselius, Katie Rich,

Scott Jaeck, Patrick Laborteaux, Cliff DeYoung, Kevin Dunn; *D:* Donald P. Bellisario; *W:* Donald P. Bellisario; *C:* Thomas Del Ruth; *M:* Bruce Broughton. **TV**

The Jagged Edge 1/2 **1985 (R)** The beautiful wife of successful newspaper editor, Jack Forester, is killed and the police want to point the guilty finger at Jack. Attorney Teddy Barnes is brought in to defend him and accidentally falls in love. Taut murder mystery will keep you guessing "whodunit" until the very end. **108m/C VHS, DVD.** Jeff Bridges, Glenn Close, Robert Loggia, Peter Coyote, John Dehner, Leigh Taylor-Young, Lance Henriksen, James Karen, Karen Austin, Michael Dorn, Guy Boyd, Marshall Colt, Louis Giambalvo; *D:* Richard Marquand; *W:* Joe Eszterhas; *C:* Matthew F. Leonetti; *M:* John Barry.

Jaguar 1956 Three men leave their homes in Niger in order to find jobs in the cities. When they return to their village, they bring back with them their experiences. **93m/C VHS.** Sabu, Mike Connors, Jay Novello, Barton MacLane; *D:* George Blair; *W:* John Fenton Murray, Benedict Freedman; *C:* Bud Thackery; *M:* Van Alexander.

Jaguar Lives **1979 (PG)** A high-kicking secret agent tracks down bad boy drug kings around the world. **91m/C VHS.** Joe Lewis, Barbara Bach, Christopher Lee, Woody Strode, Donald Pleasence, Joseph Wiseman, John Huston, Capucine; *D:* Ernest Pintoff.

Jail Bait 1/2 *Hidden Face* **1954** Early Wood film about a group of small-time crooks who are always in trouble with the law; they blackmail a plastic surgeon into using his talents to help them ditch the cops. Not as "bad" as Wood's "Plan 9 From Outer Space," but still bad enough for camp fans to love (check the cheesy score leftover from an equally cheesy Mexican mad-scientist flick). **80m/B VHS, DVD.** Timothy Farrell, Clancy Malone, Lyle Talbot, Steve Reeves, Herbert Rawlinson, Dolores Fuller, Theodora Thurman, Conrad Brooks, Mona McKinnon; *D:* Edward D. Wood Jr.; *W:* Edward D. Wood Jr., Alex Gordon; *C:* William C. Thompson.

Jail Party **2004** Urban spoof tries to put the funny into ex-con Yusef Porter's (Sharp) desire to flee his Atlanta 'hood in search of a better life with girlfriend Elise (Terry) after his prison time wraps up. Things go expectedly sour at his homecoming party when his past, naturally, catches up to him. **90m/C DVD.** Shane Sharp, Richard Player, Trina Braxton, Antonette Terry, Rashaun Murdaugh; *D:* Bernie Calloway; *W:* Redd Claiborne, Donnie Leapheart, Jason Upson. **VIDEO**

Jailbait *Streetwise* **1993 (R)** A cop gets involved with an alleged murder witness, a teenaged runaway named Kyle. What they discover is an international crime syndicate that kidnaps runaways to exploit as sex slaves. Now they know too much. An unrated version is also available. **100m/C VHS.** C. Thomas Howell, Renee Humphrey; *D:* Rafal Zielinski; *W:* Robert Vincent O'Neil.

Jailbait! **2000 (R)** Popular high school jock Adam (Mundy), who's 18, cheats on his girlfriend and gets wrong side of the tracks 16-year-old Gynger (Purrott) preggers leading to a charge of statutory rape. Satire on teen sex, political platforms, and society. First original movie made for MTV. **94m/C VHS, DVD.** Kevin Mundy, Mo Gaffney, Alycia Purrott, Melody Johnson, Matt Frewer, Mary Gross, Reagan Pasternak; *D:* Allan Moyle. **CABLE**

Jailbait: Betrayed By Innocence 1/2 **1986 (R)** A man is on trial for statutory rape. **90m/C VHS, DVD.** Barry Bostwick, Lee Purcell, Paul Sorvino, Cristen Kauffman, Isaac Hayes; *D:* Elliot Silverstein. **TV**

Jailbird Rock 1/2 **1988** We'd like to tell you that this isn't really a sweet-young-thing-in-prison musical, but it is. When Antin shoots her stepfather (he told her to turn that damn noise down?) she tries to bring down the Big House with song and dance. No kidding. **90m/C VHS.** Robin Antin, Valchie Gene Richards, Robin Cleaver, Rhonda Aldrich, Jacquelyn Houston, Debra Laws, Erica Jordan, Perry Lang, Ronald Lacey; *D:* Phillip Schuman; *W:* Edward Kovach, Carole Stanley; *C:* Leonardo Solis; *M:* Rick Nowecs.

Jailbird's Vacation 1/2 *Les Grandes Gueules* **1965** From the director of the classic "An Occurrence at Owl Creek Bridge," comes this comedy-drama about a sawmill owner dealing with two ex-convicts hired as lumberjacks. They want to get revenge on the bum who put them away. French with subtitles. **125m/C VHS.** *FR* Lino Ventura, Andre Bourvil, Marie DuBois; *D:* Robert Enrico.

Jailbreakers **1994 (R)** Another remake from Showtime's "Rebel Highway" series that takes little but the title from the 1960 A.I.P. flick. Cheerleader Angel (Doherty) falls for bad boy Tony (Sabato Jr.) and gets busted by the cops while they're out on a little crime spree. He goes to prison, she and her family must leave town. But boy can't get girl out of his head and he busts out of the big house to reunite with his true love. Then the crazy kids hit the road for the Mexican border. **76m/C VHS, DVD.** Shannen Doherty, Antonio Sabato Jr., Adrienne Barbeau, Adrien Brody, Vince Edwards, George Gerdes; *D:* William Friedkin; *W:* Debra Hill, Gigi Vorgan; *C:* Cary Fisher; *M:* Hummie Mann. **CABLE**

Jailbreakin' *The Ballad of Billie Blue* **1972** A faded country singer and a rebellious youth team up to break out of jail. **90m/C VHS.** Jason Ledger, Marty Allen, Ray Danton, Sherry Bain, Sherry Miles, Erik Estrada; *D:* Ken Osborne.

Jailhouse Rock **1957 (G)** While in jail for manslaughter, teenager Vince Everett (Presley) learns to play the guitar. After his release, he slowly develops into a top recording star. Probably the only film that captured the magnetic power of the young Elvis Presley; an absolute must for fans. Also available in a colorized version. ♫Jailhouse Rock; Treat Me Nice; Baby, I Don't Care; Young and Beautiful; Don't Leave Me Now; I Wanna Be Free; One More Day. **96m/B VHS, DVD, Blu-ray Disc, HD DVD.** Elvis Presley, Judy Tyler, Vaughn Taylor, Dean Jones, Mickey Shaughnessy, William Forrest, Glenn Strange, Jennifer Holden, Anne Neyland; *D:* Richard Thorpe; *W:* Guy Trosper; *C:* Robert J. Bronner; *M:* Jeff Alexander. Natl. Film Reg. '04.

Jakarta 1/2 **1988 (R)** Before gaining fame on the popular t.v. series "Law and Order," actor Chris Noth was action hero material. Sadly without much success in this dud. A love-hardened CIA operative (Noth) is whisked away to Jakarta for reasons unknown, only to find his thought-to-be-dead lover still alive and caught in a deadly game of espionage. **94m/C VHS.** Christopher Noth, Sue Francis Pai, Ronald Hunter; *D:* Charles Kaufman.

Jake Speed 1/2 **1986 (PG)** Comic-book mercenary Jake and his loyal associate Remo rescue a beautiful girl from white slave traders. Supposedly a parody of the action adventure genre. **93m/C VHS, DVD.** Wayne Crawford, John Hurt, Karen Kopins, Dennis Christopher; *D:* Andrew Lane; *W:* Wayne Crawford; *C:* Bryan Loftus; *M:* Mark Snow.

Jakob the Liar **1999 (PG-13)** Robin Williams reins in his usual manic personality in this touching tale set during the Holocaust. Jakob (Williams) is a Jew confined to the Polish ghetto by the Nazis. After he hears a radio broadcast describing German defeats while in a Nazi commandant's office, he relates the news to his friend Mischa (Schreiber). This leads to rumors that he owns a contraband radio, which is an offense punishable by death. He sees the excitement and hope that his news has brought and begins to make up new stories to encourage his oppressed community. Finally, the men become courageous enough to start a resistance movement, with Jakob as the leader. The realities of the Holocaust are shown with no attempt to sugarcoat them, and the performances are excellent all around. **114m/C VHS, DVD.** Robin Williams, Armin Mueller-Stahl, Alan Arkin, Bob Balaban, Michael Jeter, Liev Schreiber, Hannah Taylor Gordon, Nina Siemaszko, Mathieu Kassovitz, Mark Margolis; *D:* Peter Kassovitz; *W:* Peter Kassovitz, Didier Decoin; *C:* Elemer Ragalyi; *M:* Ed Shearmur.

Jalsaghar *The Music Room* **1958** Bisambhar Roy is the last in his aristocratic line and has inherited nothing but debts. But his position in society demands a certain style and he pawns family heirlooms in order to host expensive private concerts, even after tragedy strikes his family. Bengali with subtitles. **100m/B VHS, DVD.** *IN* Chhabi Biswas, Padma Devi, Tulsi Lahiri, Pinaki Sen Gupta, Kali Sarkar; *D:* Satyajit Ray; *W:* Satyajit Ray; *C:* Subrata Mitra; *M:* Satyajit Ray.

Jam **2006** That's jam as in traffic, not food product, or Phish concert. Sitcom characters and situations abound as 15 weary souls are trapped in their cars after an accident on a mountain road. It's Father's Day—so everyone can exchange trite stories. A woman goes into labor (ah, that old chestnut!). There's a couple of bumbling crooks and even a kitchen sink 'cause someone's driving a camper. **91m/C DVD.** Jeffrey Dean Morgan, William Forsythe, Gina Torres, Amanda Detmer, Jonathan Silverman, Marianne Jean-Baptiste, Dan Byrd, David DeLuise, Elizabeth Bogush, Tess Harper, Alex Rocco, Christopher Amitrano, Christopher Amitrano, Julie Claire, Amanda Foreman; *D:* Craig Sterling; *W:* Craig Sterling, Nicole Lonner; *C:* Jeff Venditti; *M:* Andy Kubiszewski. **VIDEO**

Jamaica Inn **1939** In old Cornwall, an orphan girl becomes involved with smugglers. Remade in 1982; based on the story by Daphne Du Maurier. **98m/B VHS, DVD.** *GB* Charles Laughton, Maureen O'Hara, Leslie Banks, Robert Newton; *D:* Alfred Hitchcock; *W:* Sidney Gilliat, Joan Harrison; *C:* Harry Stradling Sr.; *M:* Eric Fenby.

Jamaica Inn 1/2 **1982** Miniseries based on the old Daphne Du Maurier adventure about highwaymen and moor-lurking thieves in Cornwall. Remake of the 1939 Hitchcock film. **192m/C VHS, DVD.** Patrick McGoohan, Jane Seymour; *D:* Lawrence Gordon-Clark. **TV**

James and the Giant Peach **1996 (PG)** Terrific combo of live action and stop-motion animation highlights this adaptation of Roald Dahl's 1961 children's book. Orphaned James is sent to live with his wicked aunts. When magic "crocodile tongues," given to James by a hobo, spill at the base of a peach tree, one fruit grows to such a tremendous size that James crawls inside, meets six insect friends, and goes on numerous adventures, all the while trying to face his fears. Dahl's books are creepy and since the people who brought you "Nightmare Before Christmas" are also doing "James," expect the visuals to be astonishing but too scary for the little ones. **80m/C VHS, DVD.** *D:* Henry Selick; *C:* Pete Kozachik, Hiro Narita; *M:* Randy Newman; *V:* Paul Terry, Pete Postlethwaite, Joanna Lumley, Miriam Margolyes, Richard Dreyfuss, Susan Sarandon, David Thewlis, Simon Callow, Jane Leeves.

James Dean *The Legend* **1976** Dean's friend Bast wrote this behind-the-scenes look at the short life of the enigmatic movie star. **99m/C VHS, DVD.** Stephen McHattie, Michael Brandon, Candy Clark, Amy Irving, Brooke Adams, Dane Clark, Jayne Meadows, Meg Foster; *D:* William Bast, Robert Butler; *W:* William Bast; *M:* Billy Goldenberg. **TV**

James Dean 1/2 **2001** The original rebel without a cause gets a superficial biopic treatment that doesn't have much time to explore the appeal of the young legend who died at the age of 24. Dean's (Franco) troubles stem from his unhappy relationship with his distant father (Moriarty) and even his impressive acting talents can't save him from self-destruction. Film focuses on the making of "East of Eden" and Dean's romance with fragile actress Pier Angeli (Cervi). Franco does well in the title role. **95m/C VHS, DVD.** James Franco, Michael Moriarty, Valentina Cervi, Enrico Colantoni, Edward Herrmann, Barry Primus, Mark Rydell, Joanne Linville, John Pleshette; *D:* Mark Rydell; *W:* Israel Horovitz; *C:* Robbie Greenberg. **CABLE**

James Dean: Live Fast, Die Young *James Dean: Race with Destiny* **1997 (PG-13)** Lightweight biopic of legendary acting rebel with a cause Dean (Van Dien). Film finds Dean troubled when girlfriend Pier Angeli (Carrie Mitchum, Robert's granddaughter) marries another, and in trouble with studio boss Jack Warner (Connors) and director George Stevens (Mitchum). **105m/C VHS, DVD.** Casper Van Dien, Robert Mitchum, Mike Connors, Carrie Mitchum, Diane Ladd, Connie Stevens, Monique Parent, Casey Kasem, Joseph Campanella; *D:* Marti Rustam; *W:* Dan Sefton; *C:* Gary Graver, Irv Goodnoff. **TV**

James' Journey to Jerusalem *Massa'ot James Be'eretz Hakodesh* **2003** Idealistic James (Shibe) is a young African Christian who is sent on a pilgrimage to the promised land of Zion. Only the promise starts out tarnished when the innocent is thrown into a Tel Aviv jail by a cynical immigration official who thinks he's just another illegal. James gets bailed out by shady businessman Shimi (Daw) to be used as cheap labor and he begins to learn—and work—the system, which leads James into some very secular temptation. English, Zulu, and Hebrew with subtitles. **87m/C DVD.** Siyabonga Melongisi Shibe, Salim Dau, Arie Elias, Sandra Schonwald, Hugh Masebenza, Gregory Tal; *D:* Ra'anan Alexandrowicz; *W:* Ra'anan Alexandrowicz, Sami Duenias; *C:* Shark (Sharon) De Mayo; *M:* Ehud Banay.

James Joyce: A Portrait of the Artist as a Young Man **1977** A moving, lyrical adaptation of the author's autobiography, told through the character of Stephen Dedalus. Joyce's characterizations, words, and scenes are beautifully translated to the medium of film. Excellent casting. **93m/C VHS.** John Gielgud, T.P. McKenna, Bosco Hogan; *D:* Joseph Strick.

James Joyce's Women **1985 (R)** Adapted from her one-woman stage show as well as produced by Flanagan, this acclaimed film features enacted portraits of three real-life Joyce associates, including his wife (Nora Barnacle) and three of his famous characters. **91m/C VHS.** Fionnula Flanagan, Timothy E. O'Grady, Chris O'Neill; *D:* Michael Pearce; *W:* Fionnula Flanagan.

Jamon, Jamon *Ham Ham* **1993** Comedic melodrama satirizing various aspects of the Spanish character, including machismo, sex, and food. A small Spanish town is dominated by two businesses—an underwear factory and a brothel—both run by strong-minded women. The brothel's Carmen and the factory's Conchita clash when Carmen's daughter, Silvia, becomes pregnant by Conchita's son, Manuel. Conchita's appalled and hires stud Raul to seduce Silvia—only to fall for him herself. Oh yes, Raul attributes his sexual prowess to a steady diet of ham and garlic. In Spanish with English subtitles. **95m/C VHS.** *SP* Penelope Cruz, Anna Galiena, Javier Bardem, Stefania Sandrelli, Juan Diego, Jordi Molla; *D:* Bigas Luna; *W:* Bigas Luna, Cuca Canals; *C:* Jose Luis Alcaine; *M:* Nicola Piovani.

Jane & the Lost City 1/2 **1987 (PG)** A British farce based on the age-old, barely dressed comic-strip character, Jane, as she stumbles on ancient cities, treasures, villains, and blond/blue-eyed heroes. Low-budget camp fun. **94m/C VHS, DVD.** *GB* Kristen Hughes, Maud Adams, Sam Jones; *D:* Terry Marcel; *W:* Mervyn Haisman; *C:* Paul Beeson; *M:* Harry Robertson.

The Jane Austen Book Club **2007 (PG-13)** Why yes, this is a chick flick, and unabashedly so. A group of Jane Austen devotees gather monthly to discuss six Jane Austen books, but end up revealing themselves in the process. The characters are not unlike Austen's, albeit living in the dizzying pace of the modern world. There's Bernadette (Baker), a wise and carefree divorcee; free-spirit dog-breeder Jocelyn (Bello); Sylvia (Brenneman), whose 20-plus-year marriage has abruptly ended, and her lesbian daughter (Grace); uptight teacher Prudie (Blunt); and a token man, software geek Grigg (Dancy). Austen's spirit floats (figuratively) in and out of the clubber's lives, losses, and romances as they navigate the passages Austen penned two centuries ago. **106m/C DVD, Blu-ray Disc.** *US* Kathy Baker, Maria Bello, Emily Blunt, Amy Brenneman, Maggie Grace, Hugh Dancy, Lynn Redgrave, Jimmy Smits, Marc Blucas, Kevin Zegers, Nancy Travis, Parisa Fitz-Henley; *D:* Robin Swicord; *W:* Robin Swicord; *C:* John Toon; *M:* Aaron Zigman.

Jane Austen in Manhattan 1/2 **1980** Two acting-teachers vie to stage a long-lost play written by a youthful Jane

Austen. Dreary, despite the cast. Hodiak is the real-life daughter of Baxter. **108m/C VHS, DVD.** Anne Baxter, Robert Powell, Michael Wager, Sean Young, Kurt Johnson, Katrina Hodiak; ***D:*** James Ivory; ***W:*** Ruth Prawer Jhabvala.

Jane Doe 1/2 **1983** Valentine plays a young amnesia victim who is linked to a series of brutal slayings. Quite suspenseful for a TV movie. **100m/C VHS, DVD.** Karen Valentine, William Devane, Eva Marie Saint, Stephen E. Miller, Jackson Davies; ***D:*** Ivan Nagy. **TV**

Jane Doe *Pictures of Baby Jane Doe* **1996 (R)** Jane Doe (Flockhart) is a drug addict who's getting seriously involved with shy writer Horace (Peditto). Only her addictions begin to cause some serious trouble for this odd couple. Adapted from a play. **92m/C VHS, DVD.** Calista Flockhart, Elina Lowensohn, Joe Ragno, Christopher Peditto; ***D:*** Paul Peditto; ***W:*** Paul Peditto.

Jane Eyre **1934** Stiff, early version of Charlotte Bronte's classic gothic romance. English orphan grows up to become the governess of a mysterious manor. Notable as the first talkie version. Remade several times. **67m/B VHS, DVD.** Virginia Bruce, Colin Clive, Beryl Mercer, Jameson Thomas, Aileen Pringle, David Torrence, Clarissa Selwynne, Anne Howard; ***D:*** Christy Cabanne; ***W:*** Adele Comandini; ***C:*** Robert Planck; ***M:*** Mischa Bakaleinikoff.

Jane Eyre **1944** Excellent adaptation of the Charlotte Bronte novel about the plain governess with the noble heart and her love for the mysterious and tragic Mr. Rochester. Fontaine has the proper backbone and yearning in the title role but to accommodate Welles' emerging popularity the role of Rochester was enlarged. Excellent bleak romantic-Gothic look. Taylor, in her third film role, is seen briefly in the early orphanage scenes. **97m/B VHS, DVD.** Joan Fontaine, Orson Welles, Margaret O'Brien, Peggy Ann Garner, John Sutton, Sara Allgood, Henry Daniell, Agnes Moorehead, Aubrey Mather, Edith Barrett, Barbara Everest, Hillary Brooke, Elizabeth Taylor; ***D:*** Robert Stevenson; ***W:*** John Houseman, Aldous Huxley, Robert Stevenson; ***C:*** George Barnes; ***M:*** Bernard Herrmann.

Jane Eyre **1983** Miniseries based on the famed Charlotte Bronte novel about the maturation of a homeless English waif, her love for the tormented Rochester, and her quest for permanent peace. **239m/C VHS, DVD.** *GB* Timothy Dalton, Zelah Clarke; ***D:*** Julian Amyes. **TV**

Jane Eyre **1996 (PG)** Zeffirelli creates an eloquent yet spare interpretation of Charlotte Bronte's 1847 masterpiece, about a meek governess and her mysterious employer, in its fourth film incarnation. Everything about it, from the lighting to the score, is muted and somber. Still a beautiful film, it seems to lack a certain passion that earlier versions (especially the 1944 classic) brought to the screen. Strong performances all around, including Oscar-winner Paquin and French star Gainsbourg as the younger and older Jane, and Hurt as the tormented Rochester. **116m/C VHS, DVD.** William Hurt, Anna Paquin, Charlotte Gainsbourg, Joan Plowright, Elle Macpherson, Geraldine Chaplin, Fiona Shaw, John Wood, Amanda Root, Maria Schneider, Josephine Serre, Billie Whitelaw; ***D:*** Franco Zeffirelli; ***W:*** Franco Zeffirelli, Hugh Whitemore; ***C:*** David Watkin; ***M:*** Alessio Vlad, Claudio Capponi.

Jane Eyre 1/2 **1997** Charlotte Bronte's dark romance between meek-yet-strong-willed governess Jane (Morton) and her tormented-yet-dashing employer, Mr. Rochester (Hinds). This version dispenses quickly with many of the subplots to concentrate on the main duo. **108m/C VHS, DVD.** *GB* Samantha Morton, Ciaran Hinds, Gemma Jones, Abigail Cruttenden, Richard Hawley; ***D:*** Robert M. Young; ***W:*** Kay Mellor; ***M:*** Richard Harvey. **CABLE**

Jane Eyre 1/2 **2006** Yet another version (from the BBC) of Charlotte Bronte's novel, complete with gothic romance, naive but undaunted governess Jane (Wilson, properly plain), and secretive aristocrat Edward Rochester (Stephens, more grumpy than brooding). Well done but unnecessary; didn't Charlotte write anything else worth filming? **247m/C DVD.** *GB* Toby Stephens, Francesca Annis, Christina Cole, Tara Fitzgerald, Ruth Wilson, Claudia Coulter, Pam Ferris, Andrew Buchan; ***D:*** Susanna White; ***W:*** Sandy Welch; ***C:*** Mike Eley; ***M:*** Robert (Rob) Lane. **TV**

Janice Beard **1999** Eccentric comedy about a social misfit that's overwhelmed by whimsey. Janice (Walsh) moves from her Scottish town to London in hopes of making enough money to help her agoraphobic mother Mimi (Voe). Living in her own fantasy world (she videotapes letters to her mother that are mostly fabrications of how swell things are going), Janice gets a temp job at a car manufacturing company and gets unwittingly involved in corporate espionage with sneaky office assistant Sean (Ifans). Walsh is endearing but the office antics get tedious. **80m/C DVD.** *GB* Eileen Walsh, Rhys Ifans, Patsy Kensit, Sandra Voe, David O'Hara, Frances Gray; ***D:*** Clare Kilner; ***W:*** Clare Kilner, Ben Hopkins; ***C:*** Richard Greatrex, Peter Thwaites; ***M:*** Paul Carr.

Janky Promoters **2009** Two shady concert promoters from Modesto get into trouble when they try to book a superstar rapper into a local venue. **m/C DVD.** *US* Ice Cube, Mike Epps, Darris Love, Julio Oscar Mechoso, Glenn Plummer; ***D:*** Marcus Raboy; ***W:*** Ice Cube; ***C:*** Tom Priestly Jr.

The January Man **1989 (R)** An unorthodox cop, previously exiled by a corrupt local government to the fire department, is brought back to the force in New York City to track down a serial killer. Written by the "Moonstruck" guy, Shanley, who apparently peaked with the earlier movie. **97m/C VHS, DVD.** Kevin Kline, Susan Sarandon, Mary Elizabeth Mastrantonio, Harvey Keitel, Rod Steiger, Alan Rickman, Danny Aiello; ***D:*** Pat O'Connor; ***W:*** Pat O'Connor, John Patrick Shanley; ***C:*** Jerzy Zielinski; ***M:*** Marvin Hamlisch.

Japan Japan 1/2 **2007** A brief look at the life of aimless teen Imri who moves to Tel Aviv and idly fantasizes about emigrating to Japan despite his misconceptions about the country. There's a rather confusingly random, improvised feel and writer/director Shamriz likes to break the fourth wall and have his actors speak directly to the camera and audience. Hebrew with subtitles. **67m/C DVD.** *IS* Imri Kahn, Amnon Friedman, Irit Gidron, Neema Yuria; ***D:*** Lior Shamriz; ***W:*** Lior Shamriz; ***C:*** Lior Shamriz.

Japanese Story **2003 (R)** Headstrong Sandy (Collette) is a geologist by trade and part owner of a software firm who is obliged to entertain a potential client, Hiromitsu (Tsunashima), an uptight Japanese businessman looking to experience the Australian landscape. Despite her objections he insists that they drive into the desert where they end up stranded for a night amid the harsh elements. Their struggle to endure brings them closer but their eventual affair (he's married) is marred by a dramatic plot twist midstream that shakes Sandy to her core. Gorgeous scenery provides a striking backdrop for Brooks' passionate piece while Collette displays great depth as a woman challenged by a gamut of emotions. **105m/C DVD.** *AU* Toni Collette, Matthew Dyktynski, Lynette Curran, John Howard, Gotaro Tsunashima, Yukimo Tanaka, Kate Atkinson, Bill Young, George Shevtsov, Justine Clarke; ***D:*** Sue Brooks; ***W:*** Alison Tilson; ***C:*** Ian Baker; ***M:*** Elizabeth Drake.

The Jar **1984** A recluse discovers a disgusting creature in a jar. He keeps it, only to discover that it is out to kill him. **90m/C VHS.** Gary Wallace, Karen Sjoberg; ***D:*** Bruce Toscano; ***W:*** George Bradley.

Jarhead 1/2 **2005 (R)** Solid adaptation of Anthony Swofford's memoir is not so much an anti-war film as an absence-of-war film. Gyllenhaal is excellent as "Swoff," a Marine recruit trained as a sniper and sent to fight in the first Gulf War. Only when he gets there, there's no fighting, just waiting and preparing. Mendes' deft touch is put to good use in showing the frustration and boredom of the Marines, using other war movies as touchstones and keeping politics in the background while focusing on the characters. The drawback of this approach is that the audience becomes just as frustrated as the soldiers with all the inaction. **122m/C DVD, UMD, HD DVD.** *US* Jake Gyllenhaal, Peter Sarsgaard, Lucas Black, Brian Geraghty, Jacob Vargas, Laz Alonso, Evan Jones, Ivan Fenyo, Chris Cooper, Dennis Haysbert, Scott MacDonald, Jamie Foxx, Jamie Martz, Kareem Grimes, Peter Gail, Jocko Sims, John Krasinski; ***D:*** Sam Mendes; ***W:*** William Broyles Jr.; ***C:*** Roger Deakins; ***M:*** Thomas Newman.

Jason and the Argonauts **1963 (G)** Jason, son of the King of Thessaly, sails on the Argo to the land of Colchis, where the Golden Fleece is guarded by a seven-headed hydra. Superb special effects and multitudes of mythological creatures; fun for the whole family. **104m/C VHS, DVD.** *GB* Todd Armstrong, Nancy Kovack, Gary Raymond, Laurence Naismith, Nigel Green, Michael Gwynn, Honor Blackman, Niall MacGinnis, Douglas Wilmer, Jack (Gwyllam) Gwillim; ***D:*** Don Chaffey; ***W:*** Jan Read, Beverley Cross; ***C:*** Wilkie Cooper; ***M:*** Bernard Herrmann.

Jason and the Argonauts 1/2 **2000** Elaborate retelling of the Greek myth of Jason and his quest for the golden fleece. Young Prince Jason (London) has had his heritage usurped by his evil Uncle Pelias (Hopper in braids), who has killed Jason's father and taken his throne. In order to reclaim it, Jason must retrieve the magical golden fleece from distant Colchis and bring it to Pelias. So Jason assembles the usual motley crew of would-be heroes and sets sail on the Argos for uncharted waters and numerous adventures. TV saga with lots of action and some good special effects. **179m/C VHS, DVD.** Jason London, Dennis Hopper, Angus MacFadyen, Olivia Williams, Brian Thompson, Adrian Lester, Derek Jacobi, Jolene Blalock, Frank Langella, Natasha Henstridge, Ciaran Hinds, Kieran O'Brien, Charles Cartmell; ***D:*** Nick Willing; ***W:*** Matthew Faulk, Mark Skeet; ***C:*** Sergei Kozlov; ***M:*** Simon Boswell. **TV**

Jason Goes to Hell: The Final Friday **WOOF!** **1993 (R)** The supposed last, at least so far, in the "Friday the 13th" gore series. Only through the bodies—dead or alive—of his Vorhees kin can supernatural killer Jason be reborn, and only at their hands can he truly die. One can only hope that this is finally true. An unrated, even gorier, version is also available. **89m/C VHS, DVD.** Kane Hodder, John D. LeMay, Kari Keegan, Steven Williams, Steven Culp, Erin Gray, Richard Gant, Leslie Jordan, Billy Green Bush, Rusty Schwimmer, Allison Smith, Julie Michaels; ***D:*** Adam Marcus; ***W:*** Dean Lorey, Jay Huguely-Cass; ***M:*** Harry Manfredini.

Jason X **2001 (R)** This time it's Jason in space. The tenth installment of the "Friday the 13th" franchise is set in 2455, when Earth has been abandoned because of toxic damage. An archeological expedition discovers the cryogenically frozen Jason and a young woman and brings them back to their spaceship. Of course, if they'd just leave him on Earth with no one to kill, he'd die a horrible existential death that'd be really cool to see. Unfortunately, there's a passel of horny med students that needs killin' so here we go again. The space setting does give the series a bunch of new franchises to rip off, but that doesn't really help. **93m/C VHS, DVD.** *US* Lexa Doig, Lisa Ryder, Kane Hodder, Jonathan Potts, Chuck Campbell, Peter Mensah, Melyssa Ade, Melody Johnson, Dov Tiefenbach, David Cronenberg, Derwin Jordan; ***D:*** James Isaac; ***W:*** Todd Farmer; ***C:*** Derick Underschultz; ***M:*** Harry Manfredini.

Jason's Lyric **1994 (R)** A romantic triangle, sibling rivalry, family bonds, and neighborhood violence all set on the wrong side of the Houston tracks. Jason (Payne) is the responsible young man who works hard and helps out his mom; younger brother Joshua (Woodbine) has just gotten out of jail and is headed straight for more trouble. Between the two is Lyric (Pinkett), a soulfood waitress whose bad news half-brother Alonzo (Treach) is naturally one of Joshua's homies. Good-looking but ultimately empty storytelling. **119m/C VHS, DVD.** Allen Payne, Bokeem Woodbine, Jada Pinkett Smith, Suzzanne Douglass, Forest Whitaker, Treach; ***D:*** Doug McHenry; ***W:*** Bobby Smith Jr.; ***M:*** Matt Noble.

Jasper, Texas 1/2 **2003** Dramatization of the 1998 hate crime that shook the small Texas town. When black James Byrd Jr. dies after being chained to the back of a pickup truck and dragged for three miles, the town's citizens find themselves at the center of a nationwide political and media frenzy. It's up to Sheriff Billy Rowles (Voight) and Jasper's first black mayor, R.C. Horn (Gossett Jr.) to portray the murder as an isolated incident, but the subsequent trial force the townsfolk to take a hard look at their community. Some Hollywood platitudes remain but the story is neither white-washed nor sensationalized. **120m/C DVD.** Jon Voight, Louis Gossett Jr., Joe Morton, Emily Yancy, Bokeem Woodbine, Blu Mankuma, Karen Robinson, Ron White, Eugene Clark; ***D:*** Jeff Byrd; ***W:*** Jonathan Estrin; ***C:*** Ousama Rawi. **CABLE**

Java Head **1935** Young Chinese wife commits suicide so her husband can marry an English girl. Set in mid-1800s England. Based on the novel by Joseph Hergesheimer. **70m/B VHS.** *GB* Anna May Wong, Elizabeth Allan, John Loder, Edmund Gwenn, Ralph Richardson, George Curzon; ***D:*** J. Walter Ruben.

Jawbreaker **1998 (R)** Writer-director Darren Stein steals the plot from "Heathers" and adds a dash of S&M for this black comedy about high school clique queens. Courtney (McGowan) is the leader of a group of glam princesses who accidentally kill one of their own during a mock kidnapping. Fellow beautiful people Julie (Gayheart) and Marcie (Benz) help her cover up, but class nerd Fern (Greer) is a witness. Further complicating things are nosy detective Vera Cruz (Grier) and the upcoming prom, which provides a "Carrie" style finale. Although the movie treads familiar ground, McGowan's performance keeps it interesting. Cameo by rocker Marilyn Manson, billed as Brian Warner. **87m/C VHS, DVD.** Rose McGowan, Rebecca Gayheart, Julie Benz, Charlotte Roldan, Judy Greer, Chad Christ, Carol Kane, Pam Grier, William Katt, P.J. Soles, Jeff Conaway, Ethan Erickson; ***D:*** Darren Stein; ***W:*** Darren Stein; ***C:*** Amy Vincent.

Jaws 1/2 **1975 (PG)** Early directorial effort by Spielberg from the Peter Benchley potboiler. A tight, very scary, and sometimes hilarious film about the struggle to kill a giant great white shark that is terrorizing an eastern beach community's waters. The characterizations by Dreyfuss, Scheider, and Shaw are much more enduring than the shock effects. Memorable score. Sequelled by "Jaws 2" in 1978, "Jaws 3" in 1983, and "Jaws: The Revenge" in 1987. Look for Benchley as a TV reporter. **124m/C VHS, DVD.** Roy Scheider, Robert Shaw, Richard Dreyfuss, Lorraine Gary, Murray Hamilton, Carl Gottlieb, Peter Benchley; ***D:*** Steven Spielberg; ***W:*** Carl Gottlieb, Peter Benchley; ***C:*** Bill Butler; ***M:*** John Williams. Oscars '75: Film Editing, Sound, Orig. Score; AFI '98: Top 100; Golden Globes '76: Score, Natl. Film Reg. '01.

Jaws 2 1/2 **1978 (PG)** Unsatisfactory sequel to "Jaws." It's been four years since the man-eating shark feasted on the resort town of Amity; suddenly a second shark stalks the waters and the terror returns. Scheider—who must by now wonder at his tendancy to attract large aquatic carnivores with lunch on their minds—battles without his compatriots from the original. And we haven't seen the last of the mechanical dorsal fin yet; two more sequels follow. **116m/C VHS, DVD.** Roy Scheider, Lorraine Gary, Murray Hamilton, Joseph Mascolo, Jeffrey Kramer, Collin Wilcox-Paxton, Keith Gordon; ***D:*** Jeannot Szwarc; ***W:*** Carl Gottlieb, Howard Sackler; ***C:*** Michael C. Butler; ***M:*** John Williams.

Jaws 3 *Jaws 3-D* **1983 (PG)** Same monster, new setting: in a Sea World-type amusement park, a great white shark escapes from its tank and proceeds to cause terror and chaos. Little connection to the previous "Jaws" sagas. Followed by one more sequel, "Jaws: The Revenge." **98m/C VHS, DVD.** Dennis Quaid, Bess Armstrong, Louis Gossett Jr., Simon MacCorkindale, Lea Thompson, John Putch; ***D:*** Joe Alves; ***W:*** Richard Matheson, Carl Gottlieb; ***C:*** James A. Contner; ***M:*** John Williams.

Jaws of Death *Mako: The Jaws of Death* **1976** "Jaws"-like saga of shark terror. Jaeckel illogically strikes out to protect his "friends," the sharks. **91m/C VHS, DVD.** Richard Jaeckel, Harold Sakata, Jennifer Bishop, John Chandler, Buffy Dee; ***D:*** William Grefe.

Jaws of Justice 1/2 **1933** A Canadian Mountie and his trusty German shepherd track down outlaws in the Canadian Northwest. **55m/B VHS.** Richard Terry, Lafe (Lafayette) McKee; ***D:*** Spencer Gordon Bennett; ***W:*** Joseph Anthony Roach; ***C:*** Edward Snyder.

Jaws of Satan WOOF! *King Cobra* **1981 (R)** Weaver is terrorized by a slimy snake who is, in actuality, the Devil. Not released for two years after it was filmed, and generally considered a bomb of the first caliber. Unfortunate work for usually worthwhile Weaver. **92m/C VHS.** Fritz Weaver, Gretchen Corbett, Jon Korkes, Norman Lloyd, Christina Applegate; ***D:*** Bob Claver; ***C:*** Dean Cundey.

Jaws: The Revenge **1987 (PG-13)** The third sequel, in which Mrs. Brody is pursued the world over by a seemingly personally motivated Great White Shark. Includes footage not seen in the theatrical release. Each sequel in this series is progressively inferior to the original. **87m/C VHS, DVD.** Lorraine Gary, Lance Guest, Karen Young, Mario Van Peebles, Michael Caine, Judith Barsi, Lynn Whitfield; ***D:*** Joseph Sargent; ***W:*** Michael deGuzman; ***C:*** John McPherson; ***M:*** Michael Small.

Jay and Silent Bob Strike Back 1/2 **2001 (R)** The fifth in Smith's series of movies with ties to Red Bank, New Jersey, is a road movie as the boys go after Miramax studio (which produced the film) when it makes a movie based on the comic book characters that are based on them without their permission. It makes more sense (and is probably more enjoyable) if you've seen Smith's entire ouvre. Besides Jay (Mewes) and Silent Bob (Smith himself), many of the characters and jokes are from Smith's previous movies. Subplots and detours abound for our heroes, allowing Smith to effectively parody and lampoon recent summer blockbusters, his own stars, and Hollywood in general. **95m/C VHS, DVD, Blu-ray Disc.** *US* Kevin Smith, Jason Mewes, Jason Lee, Ben Affleck, Shannon Elizabeth, Eliza Dushku, Ali Larter, Jennifer Schwalbach Smith, Chris Rock, Will Ferrell, Brian O'Halloran, Seann William Scott, George Carlin, Carrie Fisher, Judd Nelson, Jon Stewart, Mark Hamill, Diedrich Bader, Renee Humphrey, Joey Lauren Adams, Dwight Ewell, Eli Marienthal, Marc Blucas; ***Cameos:*** Wes Craven, Gus Van Sant, Matt Damon, Shannen Doherty, Jason Biggs, James Van Der Beek, Alanis Morissette; ***D:*** Kevin Smith; ***W:*** Kevin Smith; ***C:*** Jamie Anderson; ***M:*** James L. Venable.

The Jayhawkers **1959** Chandler and Parker battle for power and women in pre-Civil War Kansas. **100m/C VHS.** Jeff Chandler, Fess Parker, Nicole Maurey, Henry Silva, Herbert Rudley, Frank De Kova, Don Megowan, Leo Gordon; ***D:*** Melvin Frank.

The Jayne Mansfield Story *Jayne Mansfield: A Symbol of the '50s* **1980** Recounts the blond bombshell's career from her first career exposure, through her marriage to a bodybuilder, to the famous car crash that beheaded her. **97m/C VHS, DVD.** Loni Anderson, Arnold Schwarzenegger, Raymond Buktenica, Kathleen Lloyd, G.D. Spradlin, Dave Shelley; ***D:*** Dick Lowry. **TV**

The Jazz Singer 1/2 **1927** A Jewish cantor's son breaks with his family to become a singer of popular music. Of historical importance as the first successful part-talkie; a very early Loy performance. With the classic line "You ain't heard nothing yet!" Remade several times. ♫ Toot, Toot, Tootsie Goodbye; Blue Skies; My Gal Sal; Waiting for the Robert E. Lee; Dirty Hands, Dirty Face; Mother, I Still Have You; Kol Nidre; Yahrzeit; My Mammy. **89m/B VHS, DVD.** Al Jolson, May McAvoy, Warner Oland, William Demarest, Eugenie Besserer, Myrna Loy; ***D:*** Alan Crosland; ***C:*** Hal Mohr. AFI '98: Top 100, Natl. Film Reg. '96.

The Jazz Singer WOOF! **1980 (PG)** Flat and uninteresting (if not unintentionally funny) remake of the 1927 classic about a Jewish boy who rebels against his father and family tradition to become a popular entertainer. Stick with the original, this is little more than a vehicle for Diamond to sing. ♫ America; You Baby Baby; Jerusalem; Love on the Rocks; Summer Love; On the Robert E. Lee; Louise; Songs of Life; Hello Again. **115m/C VHS, DVD.** Neil Diamond, Laurence Olivier, Lucie Arnaz, Catlin Adams, Franklin Ajaye, Ernie Hudson; ***D:*** Richard Fleischer; ***W:*** Herbert Baker, Stephen H. Foreman; ***C:*** Isidore Mankofsky; ***M:*** Leonard Rosenman, Neil Diamond. Golden Raspberries '80: Worst Actor (Diamond), Worst Support. Actor (Olivier).

Jazzman **1984** A comedy set in the late 1920s with a young musician forming a jazz band with two street musicians and a saxophonist who played in the czar's marching band. Their music is condemned as a product of bourgeois society but that doesn't stop them. In Russian with English subtitles. **80m/C VHS.** *RU* Igor Sklyar, Alexander Chorny; ***D:*** Karen Chakhnazarov.

J.D.'s Revenge 1/2 **1976 (R)** Attorney in training Glynn Turman is possessed by the spirit of a gangster who was murdered on Bourbon Street in the early 1940s and grisly blaxploitation results. Ever so slightly better than others of the genre. Shot in New Orleans, with a soundtrack by a then-unknown Prince. **95m/C VHS, DVD.** Louis Gossett Jr., Glynn Turman, Joan Pringle, David McKnight, James L. Watkins; ***D:*** Arthur Marks; ***W:*** Jaison Starkes; ***C:*** Harry J. May; ***M:*** Prince.

Je Tu Il Elle 1/2 *I You She He* **1974** A hyperactive young woman desperately seeking the answers to life gradually gains experience and maturity as she travels around France. The directorial debut of Ackerman. In French with English subtitles. **90m/B VHS.** *FR* Niels Arestrup, Claire Wauthion, Chantal Akerman; ***D:*** Chantal Akerman.

Jealousy **1984** Three dramatic episodes dealing with jealousy. Made for TV. **95m/C VHS.** Angie Dickinson, Paul Michael Glaser, David Carradine, Bo Svenson; ***D:*** Jeffrey Bloom. **TV**

Jealousy *Celos* **1999** Antonio (Giminez Cacho) and Carmen (Sanchez-Gijon) seem to be happily engaged and making wedding plans when Antonio finds an old photo of Carmen with another man. Although he has no reason to be suspicious, he begins to investigate Carmen's past and becomes consumed by a jealous obsession that threatens to tear the couple apart. Spanish with subtitles. **105m/C VHS, DVD.** *SP* Daniel Gimenez Cacho, Aitana Sanchez-Gijon, Maria Botto, Luis Tosar; ***D:*** Vicente Aranda; ***W:*** Vicente Aranda, Alvaro del Amo; ***C:*** Jose Luis Alcaine; ***M:*** Jose Nieto.

Jean de Florette 1/2 **1987 (PG)** The first of two films (with "Manon of the Spring") based on Marcel Pagnol's novel. A single spring in drought-ridden Provence, France is blocked by two scheming countrymen (Montand and Auteuil). They await the imminent failure of the farm nearby, inherited by a city-born hunchback, whose chances for survival fade without water for his crops. A devastating story with a heartrending performance by Depardieu as the hunchback. Lauded and awarded; in French with English subtitles. **122m/C VHS, DVD.** *FR* Gerard Depardieu, Yves Montand, Daniel Auteuil, Elisabeth Depardieu, Ernestine Mazurowna, Margarita Lozano, Armand Meffre; ***D:*** Claude Berri; ***W:*** Claude Berri, Gerard Brach; ***C:*** Bruno Nuytten; ***M:*** Jean-Claude Petit. British Acad. '87: Adapt. Screenplay, Film, Support. Actor (Auteuil); Cesar '87: Actor (Auteuil), Support. Actress (Beart).

Jeanne and the Perfect Guy *Jeanne et le Garcon Formidable* **1998** Jeanne (Ledoyen) is a hopeless romantic looking for her perfect love and having a lot of sex as she "auditions" her would-be Romeos. Then she meets Olivier (Demy) in the subway and decides he's the one. Only Olivier tells Jeanne that he has AIDS. Oh yeah, and it's a musical, with everyone breaking into song and dancing through the Parisian streets. It's gawky romanticism is strangely appealing and Ledoyen has a lot of charisma. French with subtitles. **98m/C VHS, DVD.** *FR* Virginie Ledoyen, Mathieu Demy, Frederic Gorny, Jacques Bonnaffe, Valerie Bonneton; ***D:*** Olivier Ducastel, Jacques Martineau; ***W:*** Olivier Ducastel, Jacques Martineau; ***C:*** Mathieu Poirot-Delpech; ***M:*** Philippe Miller.

Jeanne la Pucelle *Joan the Maid: The Battles; Joan the Maid: The Prisons; Jeanne la Pucelle: Les Batailles; Jeanne la Purcelle: Les Prisons* **1994** Rivette's ambitious two-part production on the life of Joan of Arc. The first section, "The Battles," follows Joan (Bonnaire) as she becomes convinced that God has spoken to her, and that only she can lead the Dauphin's soldiers and end the English siege of Orleans. "The Prisons" finds the Dauphin crowned King Charles VII and no longer needing Joan's aid—in fact she becomes a hindrance to his plans and is sold to the English for trial and execution. French with subtitles. **241m/C VHS, DVD.** *FR* Sandrine Bonnaire, Andre Marcon, Jean-Louis Richard, Jean-Pierre Lorit; ***D:*** Jacques Rivette; ***W:*** Christine Laurent, Pascal Bonitzer; ***C:*** William Lubtchansky; ***M:*** Jordi Savall.

Jeepers Creepers 1/2 **1939** Rogers is strictly sidekick material in this story. Hall discovers coal on the Weaver's property and proceeds to, underhandedly, acquire the land for himself. **69m/B VHS.** Thurston Hall, Leon Weaver, Frank Weaver, June "Elviry" Weaver, Loretta Weaver, Roy Rogers, Lucien Littlefield; ***D:*** Frank McDonald; ***W:*** Dorrell McGowan, Stuart E. McGowan; ***C:*** Ernest Miller.

Jeepers Creepers **2001 (R)** Uneven horror entry that slips from mocking trite slasher flicks to becoming a trite slasher flick itself. Trish (Phillips) and her brother Darry (Long) are driving home from college during spring break when they're almost run down by a dilapidated cargo hauler. Further on down the abandoned desolate road, they see the driver of the van dumping what looks to be squirming human bodies into a drain pipe near a creepy church. They turn around to see if anyone needs help. Well, no one needs help, but a horror movie needs victims and they've just volunteered. The storyline then degrades into demonic, prophecy-laden voodoo nonsense while trying to keep its tongue firmly in cheek. Creature effects and make-up take over in no time. **89m/C VHS, DVD.** *US* Gina Philips, Justin Long, Jonathan Breck, Patricia Belcher, Brandon Smith, Eileen Brennan; ***D:*** Victor Salva; ***W:*** Victor Salva; ***C:*** Don E. Fauntleroy; ***M:*** Bennett Salvay.

Jeepers Creepers 2 1/2 **2003 (R)** Sequel finds teen football players and cheerleaders stranded on a bus somewhere in the sticks, looking like the next batch of victims of the titular Creeper, who apparently didn't get dead enough in the original. While the stereotypical, cardboard cast chews on the uninspired dialogue within the doomed bus, grizzled local farmer Jack Taggart (Wise) prepares to do battle with the thing that ate his son some 23 years ago. Although pic furnishes this beast with more special effects, including wings, it loses some of the low tech charm of the original in the process. Apparently the extra money spent on amping up the monster came out of the wardrobe budget, as a host of well-developed football players frequently, and inexplicably, walk around shirtless. **103m/C VHS, DVD.** *US* Ray Wise, Jonathan Breck, Deaundre "Double D" Davis, Eric Nenninger, Nicki Aycox, Travis Schiffner, Lena Cardwell, Billy Aaron Brown, Drew Tyler Bell, Marieh Delfino; ***D:*** Victor Salva; ***W:*** Victor Salva; ***C:*** Don E. Fauntleroy; ***M:*** Bennett Salvay.

Jefferson in Paris 1/2 **1994 (PG-13)** Costume drama explores the impact Thomas Jefferson's (Nolte) five years in prerevolutionary Paris (as American ambassador to Versailles) had on his private life. Jefferson confronts the personal and political issues of slavery in America, as well as his feelings for Sally Hemings (Newton), a Monticello slave brought to Paris by Jefferson's daughter. The Jefferson-Hemings legend may or may not be true (more likely not, according to many historians), but it seems to be the central theme here. Merchant Ivory's trademark tasteful production values and earnest characters can't camouflage the fact that they're playing fast and loose with the historical facts. **139m/C VHS, DVD.** Nick Nolte, Greta Scacchi, Gwyneth Paltrow, Thandie Newton, Jean-Pierre Aumont, Seth Gilliam, Todd Boyce, James Earl Jones; ***D:*** James Ivory; ***W:*** Ruth Prawer Jhabvala; ***M:*** Richard Robbins.

Jeffrey 1/2 **1995 (R)** AIDS-fearing Jeffrey (Weber) decides to give celibacy a try until a trip to the gym brings Mr. Right into the picture. Steve (Weiss) is a hunk, but he happens to be HIV-positive, which prompts Jeffrey to do some serious soul-searching. Hence the message: AIDS sucks, but don't let it destroy life's joys. Musical fantasy numbers, phallic fireworks, and a game show are a bit crass and the high theatrics can get annoying, but wicked barbs and one-liners score lots of laughs. Scene-stealer Stewart is caustically funny as Jeffrey's flamboyantly effeminate best friend Sterling, who works as an interior decorator and dates a "Cats" chorus boy. Adapted from the Paul Rudnick play. **92m/C VHS, DVD.** Steven Weber, Patrick Stewart, Michael T. Weiss, Bryan Batt, Sigourney Weaver, Olympia Dukakis, Kathy Najimy, Nathan Lane; ***Cameos:*** Victor Garber, Christine Baranski; ***D:*** Christopher Ashley; ***W:*** Paul Rudnick; ***C:*** Jeffery Tufano; ***M:*** Stephen Endelman.

Jekyll **2007** A modern retelling of the Robert Louis Stevenson tale of the ultimate split personality. Using modern technology Dr. Tom Jackson (Nesbitt), the last descendent of Jekyll/Hyde, is determined to keep his dangerous alter ego under control. But he doesn't realize that someone else is monitoring him (or them, as the case may be). As usual, Hyde has a great deal more fun than his responsible other half. **300m/C DVD.** *GB* James Nesbitt, Gina Bellman, Denis Lawson, Michelle Ryan, Meera Syal, Fenella Woolgar; ***D:*** Douglas Mackinnon, Matt Lipsey; ***W:*** Steven Moffatt; ***C:*** Adam Suschitzky; ***M:*** Debbie Wiseman. **TV**

Jekyll and Hyde 1/2 **1990** Unmemorable remake of the Robert Louis Stevenson tale of a doctor whose scientific experiments lead to a horrifyingly violent split personality. Caine does have a good time with his dual role. Made for TV. **100m/C VHS, DVD.** Michael Caine, Cheryl Ladd, Joss Ackland, Ronald Pickup, Kim Thomson, Lionel Jeffries, Kevin McNally, Lee Montague, Diane Keen, David Schofield; ***D:*** David Wickes; ***W:*** David Wickes; ***C:*** Norman G. Langley. **TV**

Jekyll & Hyde... Together Again **1982 (R)** New Wave comic version of the classic story. This time, a serious young surgeon turns into a drug-crazed punk rocker after sniffing a mysterious powder. Mad scientist Blankfield fires and misfires, occasionally eliciting a snort. **87m/C VHS, DVD.** Mark Blankfield, Bess Armstrong, Krista Errickson, Tim Thomerson, Michael McGuire, Cassandra Peterson, Peter Brocco, Lin Shaye, Corinne Bohrer, George Wendt, Michael Ensign, Sam Whipple, Tony Cox, Art LaFleur; ***D:*** Jerry Belson; ***W:*** Jerry Belson, Monica Johnson, Michael Leeson, Harvey Miller; ***C:*** Philip Lathrop; ***M:*** Barry DeVorzon.

Jennifer 1/2 *Jennifer (The Snake Goddess)* **1978 (PG)** Elaboration of that old "Carrie" theme: a teenage girl outcast who likes snakes wreaks havoc on her catty classmates in this supernatural thriller. **90m/C VHS.** Lisa Pelikan, Bert Convy, Nina Foch, John Gavin, Wesley Eure, Jeff Corey; ***D:*** Brice Mack; ***W:*** Kay Cousins Johnson, Steve Krantz.

Jennifer 8 **1992 (R)** Mix of familiar genres results in a film about a burned-out cop moving to the suburbs where he finds the eighth victim of a serial killer and falls in love with the chief witness. Garcia is John Berlin, the cop who discovers the hand of the blind female victim, which leads him to her school and Helena Robertson (Thurman), another blind woman who may have the information he needs. Dark and mysterious atmosphere is dramatic, but plot lacks logic and sense of thrill. **127m/C VHS, DVD.** Andy Garcia, Uma Thurman, Lance Henriksen, Kathy Baker, Graham Beckel, Kevin Conway, John Malkovich; ***D:*** Bruce Robinson; ***W:*** Bruce Robinson.

Jennifer's Body **2009 (R)** Campy, messy (in many ways), self-referential teen horror comedy. Bitchy high school sex bomb/cheerleader Jennifer (Fox) gets transformed into a succubus-type demon who munches on the flesh of teenaged boys. Her best friend—sensible, smart Needy (Seyfried)—discovers Jennifer's bloody afterschool pursuits and decides to put a stop to the mayhem when Jennifer goes after Needy's sweetie, Chip (Simmons). **102m/C DVD.** *US* Megan Fox, Amanda Seyfried, Johnny Simmons, Adam Brody, J.K. Simmons, Amy Sedaris, Chris Pratt, Kyle Gallner, Allison Janney; ***D:*** Karyn Kusama; ***W:*** Diablo Cody; ***C:*** M. David Mullen; ***M:*** Theodore Shapiro.

Jenny **1970 (PG)** A loveless marriage of convenience between a draft-dodger and a film buff gets turned around as they fall in love despite themselves. **90m/C VHS.** Marlo Thomas, Alan Alda, Marian Hailey, Elizabeth Wilson, Vincent Gardenia, Charlotte Rae; ***D:*** George Bloomfield.

Jenny Lamour 🦴🦴 *Quai des Orfevres* **1947** A dark mystery thriller about a singer accused of murdering a man he thought was stealing his woman. Acclaimed genre piece, dubbed into English. **95m/B VHS, DVD.** *FR* Louis Jouvet, Suzy Delair, Bernard Blier, Simone Renant; ***D:*** Henri-Georges Clouzot.

Jenny's War 🦴🦴 **1/2 1985 (PG)** An unbelievable WWII adventure story of an American teacher (Cannon) who outwits the Gestapo and infiltrates a Nazi POW camp in search of her missing soldier son. Actually based on a true story. From the book by Jack Stoneley. **192m/C VHS.** Dyan Cannon, Elke Sommer, Robert Hardy, Nigel Hawthorne, Christopher Cazenove, Patrick Ryecart, Hartmut Becker; ***D:*** Steven Gethers; ***W:*** Steven Gethers. **TV**

Jeopardy 🦴🦴 **1/2 1953** Sunlit noirish thriller with an intriguingly crazed performance by Meeker and Stanwyck doing some vamping. While vacationing on a remote beach spot in Baja, Mexico, Doug Stilwin (Sullivan) gets trapped by a piling on a rotted pier with the tide coming in. Leaving their young son (Aaker) to comfort dad, mom Barb (Stanwyck) takes off in the car to get help. She's thankful to run into an American along the deserted road, except Lawson (Meeker) turns out to be a dangerous escaped con who takes her hostage and steals the car. Barb eventually persuades Lawson that she'll run away with him if only he'll rescue her hubby first. Ya know, sometimes crime does pay. **69m/C DVD.** Barbara Stanwyck, Ralph Meeker, Barry Sullivan, Lee Aaker; ***D:*** John Sturges; ***W:*** Mel Dinelli; ***C:*** Victor Milner; ***M:*** Dimitri Tomkin.

Jeremiah 🦴🦴 **1/2 1998** The prophet Jeremiah abandons his family and the woman he loves in order to proclaim God's message that the people of Judah must change their ways or be overcome by the Babylonians. He's deemed a traitor but the prophecy is fulfilled when Jerusalem is destroyed. **96m/C VHS, DVD.** Patrick Dempsey, Oliver Reed, Klaus Maria Brandauer; ***D:*** Harry Winer. **CABLE**

Jeremiah Johnson 🦴🦴🦴 **1972 (PG)** The story of a man (Redford) who turns his back on civilization, circa 1830, and learns a new code of survival (thanks to a trapper, played by Geer) in a brutal land of isolated mountains and hostile Indians. In the process, Jeremiah becomes part of the wilderness, eventually taking an Indian wife and adopting a son. When hostile Crow warriors kill them, he begins a one-man revenge mission, gaining legendary status as a warrior. Based on the novel "Mountain Man" by Vardis Fisher and the story "Crow Killer" by Raymond W. Thorp and Robert Bunker. A notable and picturesque movie, filmed in Utah. **107m/C VHS, DVD.** Robert Redford, Will Geer, Stefan Gierasch, Allyn Ann McLerie, Joaquin Martinez, Charles Tyner, Paul Benedict, Josh Albee, Delle Bolton; ***D:*** Sydney Pollack; ***W:*** Edward Anhalt, John Milius; ***C:*** Duke Callaghan; ***M:*** John Rubinstein.

Jeremy's Family Reunion 🦴 **2004** Jeremy is a young, successful, African American attorney in New York City. He and his attractive white fiancee, Lisa, attend Jeremy's annual family reunion in New Orleans, where his colorful kin embarrass Jeremy. The family show their disapproval of Jeremy's relationship and his city lifestyle, and Lisa flirts with the relatives—ultimately ending up in the bathroom with one. Unapologetically urban farce with unapologetically cheap story line and production values. **88m/C DVD.** Jedda Jones, Gavin Lewis, Chauvon Higgins, Nolan Powell; ***D:*** Abel Garcia; ***W:*** Abel Garcia. **VIDEO**

Jericho 🦴🦴 *Dark Sands* **1938** Jericho Jackson (Robeson) is a corporal in the black unit of the U.S.'s Expeditionary Forces in WWI France. After a fight with his sergeant leads to the man's accidental death, Jackson is court-martialed and sentenced to die. He manages to escape to North Africa and begin a new life but military authorities eventually discover his whereabouts. Despite the military drama, Robeson's vocal talents are still showcased. ♫ My Way; Golden River; Silent Night; Deep Desert; Shortnin' Bread. **77m/B VHS, DVD.** *GB* Paul Robeson, Henry Wilcoxon, Wallace Ford; ***D:*** Thornton Freeland.

Jericho 🦴 **1/2 2001 (PG-13)** When a robbery goes wrong in the town of Jericho, the three bandits—one of whom has suffered a serious head wound—leave a dead sheriff behind as they head out of town. The wounded thief is soon left to die but is found and nursed back to health by freed slave turned preacher Joshua (Coffee), who names the amnesiac "Jericho." As the two travel the countryside, bits and pieces of Jericho's past surface and he's drawn to his namesake town, where his past is finally revealed. The surprise ending feels tacked on rather than a part of the ordinary script but the two men's friendship is a bonus as is Coffee's affecting performance. **102m/C VHS, DVD.** Mark Valley, R. Lee Ermey, Leon Coffee, Lisa Stewart, Buck Taylor, Mark Collie; ***D:*** Merlin Miller; ***W:*** Robert Avard Miller; ***C:*** Jerry Holway; ***M:*** Mark Haffner. **VIDEO**

Jericho Fever 🦴🦴 **1/2 1993 (PG-13)** A group of terrorists assassinate Palestinian and Israeli negotiators engaged in peace talks in Mexico. Infected with a deadly disease they escape to the U.S., tracked by Israeli Mossad agents, a border patrolman, and two investigators from the Centers for Disease Control who want to stop the spread of the plague. **88m/C VHS.** Stephanie Zimbalist, Perry King, Branscombe Richmond, Alan Scarfe, Elyssa Davalos, Ari Barak; ***D:*** Sandor Stern; ***W:*** I.C. Rapoport; ***M:*** Cameron Allan.

Jericho Mansions 🦴🦴 **1/2 2003 (R)** Longtime apartment building super Leonard (Caan) becomes involved in a murder investigation when a tenant turns up dead. He's already having a rough time, with complaints from other tenants and a theft accusation. Director Sciamma takes a much cooler, smarter path to the surprise ending than most mystery/thriller tales these days. Caan is in fine form. **98m/C VHS, DVD.** James Caan, Jennifer Tilly, Genevieve Bujold, Maribel Verdu, Peter Keleghan, Bruce Ramsay, Susan Glover, Mark Camacho; ***D:*** Alberto Sciamma; ***W:*** Alberto Sciamma, Harriet Sand; ***C:*** Alastair Meux; ***M:*** Dan (Daniel) Jones. **VIDEO**

The Jericho Mile 🦴🦴 **1979** Drama about a track-obsessed convicted murderer who is given a chance at the Olympics. Powerful lead performance by Strauss. **97m/C VHS.** Peter Strauss, Roger E. Mosley, Brian Dennehy; ***D:*** Michael Mann. **TV**

The Jerk 🦴🦴 **1/2 1979 (R)** A jerk tells his rags-to-riches-to-rags story in comedic flashbacks, from "I was born a poor Black child," through his entrepreneurial success in his invention of the "Optigrab," to his inevitable decline. Only film in history with a dog named "Shithead." Martin's first starring role, back in his wild and crazy days; his ridiculous misadventures pay tribute to Jerry Lewis movies of the late '60s. Followed by a TV version released in 1984 as "The Jerk Too," with Mark Blankfield as the Jerk. **94m/C VHS, DVD, HD DVD.** Steve Martin, Bernadette Peters, Catlin Adams, Bill Macy, Jackie Mason, Carl Gottlieb, Mabel King, Richard Ward, M. Emmet Walsh, Dick O'Neill, Maurice Evans, Pepe Serna, Trinidad Silva, Lenny Montana; ***Cameos:*** Carl Reiner, Rob Reiner; ***D:*** Carl Reiner; ***W:*** Steve Martin, Carl Gottlieb, Michael Elias; ***C:*** Victor Kemper; ***M:*** Jack Elliott.

The Jerky Boys **WOOF! 1995 (R)** Quick! Let's make a Jerky Boys movie and exploit their popularity before everyone realizes what a lame, one-joke act it is! Too late, guys. In what passes for a plot, Johnny and Kamal prank call an irritable mob boss (Arkin), pretending to be Chicago hitmen in need of a hideout. The wiseguys soon figure out the truth, but the requisite dumb cop (Sullivan) pads the film by not catching on. All these "twists" serve only one purpose—to get our heroes to the next phone. Don't accept the charges for this one. **82m/C VHS.** Johnny Brennan, Kamal Ahmed, Alan Arkin, William Hickey, Alan North, James Lorinz, Brad Sullivan, Vincent Pastore, Ozzy Osbourne, Paul Bartel, Suzanne Shepherd; ***Cameos:*** Tom Jones; ***D:*** James Melkonian; ***W:*** Johnny Brennan, Kamal Ahmed, Rich Wilkes, James Melkonian.

Jerome 🦴🦴🦴 **1998** Well-acted indie with a compelling story that deserves a wider audience. After 15 soul-sucking years as a factory welder in California, Wade Hampton (Pillsbury) decides to just walk away from his life. He picks Jerome, Arizona as his destination because he's heard it has an artists' colony and Wade has secretly been making miniature metal sculptures. So Wade heads out on the highway and encounters restless hitchhiker, Jane (Malick), who has no destination in mind at all. The film is interspersed with interviews with people from Wade's past, so the viewer also anticipates trouble coming for the travelers as well. **91m/C VHS, DVD.** Wendie Malick, Drew Pillsbury, Scott McKenna, Beth Kennedy, James Keeley; ***D:*** Thomas Johnston, David Elton, Eric Tignini; ***W:*** Thomas Johnston, David Elton, Eric Tignini; ***C:*** Gina DeGirolamo.

Jerry and Tom 🦴🦴 **1998 (R)** Tom (Mantegna) is a veteran hitman breaking in an impatient protege, Jerry (Rockwell), on various assignments for a couple of old-time mobsters. The most important thing to remember is that it's just a job—nothing personal—but that kind of emotional vacuum isn't easy to maintain. Familiar story but it has the advantage of a talented cast and good direction. **97m/C VHS, DVD.** Joe Mantegna, Sam Rockwell, Maury Chaykin, Charles Durning, Peter Riegert, William H. Macy, Ted Danson; ***D:*** Saul Rubinek; ***W:*** Rick Cleveland; ***C:*** Paul Sarossy; ***M:*** David Buchbinder.

Jerry Maguire 🦴🦴🦴 **1/2 1996 (R)** Romantic sports comedy focuses on the off-field action and makes an agent the good guy. Risky business in an era of strikes, lockouts, and astronomical salaries, but writer/director Crowe manages to pull it off. Cruise is well-used as the title character in the story of a shark-like sports agent who sees the error of his ways and transforms into...a more moral sports agent. Somewhat regretting his momentary twinge of honor (which gets him fired from his ultra-huge agency), he allies himself with his obnoxious and least important client Rod Tidwell (Gooding Jr.), as well as Dorothy, an adoring young accountant (Zellweger) with a lovable young son (Lipnicki, making a strong bid for Culkin-like stardom). Famously well-researched, film sports great dialogue, talented leads, great supporting cast and a mega-star currently riding a wave of $100-million-plus films (talk about "Show me the money!"). Pop culture bonus points for coining 1996's most memorable catch phrase, which Crowe took from real life ex-Phoenix Cardinal Tim McDonald, and is now being used to sell everything from magazines to t-shirts. **135m/C VHS, DVD, UMD.** Tom Cruise, Cuba Gooding Jr., Renee Zellweger, Kelly Preston, Bonnie Hunt, Jerry O'Connell, Jay Mohr, Regina King, Glenn Frey, Jonathan Lipnicki, Todd Louiso, Mark Pellington; ***Cameos:*** Eric Stoltz; ***D:*** Cameron Crowe; ***W:*** Cameron Crowe; ***C:*** Janusz Kaminski; ***M:*** Nancy Wilson. Oscars '96: Support. Actor (Gooding); Golden Globes '97: Actor—Mus./Comedy (Cruise); MTV Movie Awards '97: Male Perf. (Cruise); Natl. Bd. of Review '96: Actor (Cruise); Screen Actors Guild '96: Support. Actor (Gooding); Broadcast Film Critics '96: Breakthrough Perf. (Zellweger), Support. Actor (Gooding).

Jersey Girl 🦴🦴 **1/2 1992 (PG-13)** Toby Mastellone (Gertz) is a bright single gal from the Jersey shore who wants something better in her life. Her hard-working dad (Bologna) has fixed her up with an apprentice plumber but she wants a Manhattan guy. And then Toby meets cute with Sal (McDermott), who seems just the ticket, but can you really take the Jersey out of the girl? **95m/C VHS, DVD.** Jami Gertz, Dylan McDermott, Joseph Bologna, Aida Turturro, Star Jasper, Sheryl Lee, Joseph Mazzello, Molly Price; ***D:*** David Burton Morris; ***W:*** Gina Wendkos; ***M:*** Stephen Bedell.

Jersey Girl 🦴🦴 **1/2 2004 (PG-13)** Big shot music PR man Ollie (Affleck) is widowed when wife Gertrude (Lopez) dies in childbirth and must raise his daughter Gertie (Castro) on his own. But this proves too challenging as he loses his job and is forced to crash with dear old dad (Carlin) in New Jersey. After seven years, he's still struggling with his loss. Celibate, he frequents the video shop for porno flicks where he meets the shoot-from-the-hip clerk, Maya (Tyler). Ah, and there the romance begins, along with the "should I be a good parent or have a great career" dilemma. Writer-director Smith's considerable comedic talents emerge unevenly in his foray into the dramatic-comedy genre. Granted, it's probably not what Smith's fans are used to, but it's still enjoyable. Castro is a fresh, sassy presence in her feature debut. **102m/C VHS, DVD.** *US* Ben Affleck, Jennifer Lopez, George Carlin, Liv Tyler, Raquel Castro, Stephen (Steve) Root, Mike Starr, Jason Biggs, S. Epatha Merkerson, Jennifer Schwalbach Smith, Jason Lee, Matt Damon, Paulie (Litowsky) Litt; ***Cameos:*** Will Smith; ***D:*** Kevin Smith; ***W:*** Kevin Smith; ***C:*** Vilmos Zsigmond; ***M:*** James L. Venable.

Jerusalem 🦴🦴 **1996 (PG-13)** Charismatic fundamentalist preacher Hellgum (Taube) travels to a small turn-of-the-century Swedish village preaching the end of the world and encouraging the people in his belief that all Christians should move to the Holy Land in order to build the new Jerusalem. He manages to convince the wealthy Karin (August) and to tempt young Gertrud (Bonnevie), whose fiance Ingmar (Friberg) is away trying to earn money so they can get married. Based on the novel by Selma Lagerlof who was inspired by Swedes who made a move to Palestine in 1900. Swedish with subtitles. **166m/C VHS.** *SW* Maria Bonnevie, Ulf Friberg, Lena Endre, Pernilla August, Olympia Dukakis, Max von Sydow, Sven-Bertil Taube; ***D:*** Bille August; ***W:*** Bille August; ***C:*** Jorgen Persson; ***M:*** Stefan Nilsson.

Jesse 🦴🦴 **1988 (PG)** A heroic nurse ministers to remote Death Valley residents, and state bureaucats hound her for practicing medicine without a license. Although based on a true case and well-acted, this made-for-TV drama just lacks import and impact. **94m/C VHS.** Lee Remick, Scott Wilson, Leon Rippy, Priscilla Lopez, Albert Salmi; ***D:*** Glenn Jordan; ***M:*** David Shire.

Jesse James 🦴🦴🦴 **1939** One of director King's best efforts is this Hollywood biography of the notorious outlaw. 24-year-old Power showed he was more than just his good looks in the title role but Fonda truly became a star in the role of brother Frank James. Screenwriter Johnson also focused more on the legend than the reality of the outlaw's career in post-Civil War Missouri. **105m/C VHS, DVD.** Henry Fonda, Tyrone Power, Randolph Scott, Henry Hull, Jane Darwell, Brian Donlevy, Charles Halton, John Carradine, Donald Meek, Slim Summerville; ***D:*** Henry King; ***W:*** Nunnally Johnson; ***C:*** George Barnes, William Howard Greene; ***M:*** Louis Silvers.

Jesse James at Bay 🦴🦴 **1941** Rogers is the do-good Jesse who's warring against some crooked railroad execs. Interesting perspective. **54m/B VHS, DVD.** Roy Rogers, George "Gabby" Hayes, Sally Payne; ***D:*** Joseph Kane.

Jesse James Meets Frankenstein's Daughter 🦴 **1/2 1965** The gunslinger and Frankenstein's granddaughter, Maria, meet up in the Old West in this wacky combination of western and horror genres. **95m/C VHS, DVD.** John Lupton, Cal Bolder, Narda Onyx, Steven Geray, Estelita, Jim Davis, William "Bill" Fawcett, Nestor Paiva, Rayford Barnes, Roger Creed; ***D:*** William Beaudine; ***W:*** Carl K. Hittleman; ***C:*** Lothrop Worth; ***M:*** Raoul Kraushaar.

Jesse James Rides Again 1947 Originally a serial, this feature depicts the further adventures of the West's most notorious outlaw. **181m/B VHS, DVD.** Clayton Moore, Linda Stirling, Roy Barcroft, Tristram Coffin; ***D:*** Fred Brannon, Thomas Carr.

Jesse James Under the Black Flag 🦴🦴 **1/2 1921** An interesting western/pseudo biography/flashback in which Coates and James Jr. (the outlaw's son) play themselves. As Coates attempts to gather information from Jesse's decendants, a stranger appears and falls for Jesse's granddaughter, who shuns him. He proceeds to read the Coates biography and the flashback begins, in the Jesse was really a good guy forced off the straight and narrow vein. **59m/B VHS.** Jesse James Jr., Franklin Coates, Diana Reed, Marguerite Hungerford; ***D:*** Franklin Coates.

The Jesse Owens Story 🦴🦴 **1984** The moving story of the four-time Olympic Gold medal winner's triumphs and misfortunes. **174m/C VHS, DVD.** Dorian Harewood, Debbi (Deborah) Morgan, Georg Stanford Brown, LeVar Burton, George Kennedy, Tom Bosley, Ben

Vereen; *D:* Richard Irving; *W:* Harold Gast. **TV**

Jesse Stone: Death in Paradise ✂✂ 1/2 *Death in Paradise; Robert B. Parker's Jesse Stone: Death in Paradise* **2006** Jesse (Selleck) is reluctantly seeing a shrink (Devane) to help him with his drinking problem but his bad habits don't interfere with his investigating skills. When the body of a pregnant teenage girl is found floating in a lake, he wants to know why no one reported her missing. Jesse's investigation soon leads him to a best-selling local author (Basaraba) and a Boston mob boss (Flynn). The third in the series of TV movies. Based on a novel by Robert B. Parker. **87m/C DVD.** Tom Selleck, Viola Davis, Kohl Sudduth, Stephen McHattie, William Devane, Edward Edwards, Gary Basaraba, Matthew F. Barr, Steve Flynn, John Diehl, Debra Christofferson, Orla Brady, Mae Whitman; *D:* Robert Harmon; *W:* J.T. Allen, Michael Brandman; *C:* David Gribble; *M:* Jeff Beal. **TV**

Jesse Stone: Night Passage ✂✂ 1/2 *Night Passage; Robert B. Parker's Jesse Stone: Night Passage* **2006** In this prequel, we see how Jesse Stone (Selleck), a former L.A. homicide detective with a drinking problem and an ex-wife he still loves, gets his last chance by taking on the job of police chief of Paradise. Town councilor Hasty Hardaway (Rubinek) thinks Stone will be easy to push around but he learns differently. Jesse is soon investigating the suspicious death of his recently retired predecessor, which leads to a money laundering scheme and mob ties. Second in the series of TV movies. Based on the book by Robert B. Parker. **89m/C DVD.** Tom Selleck, Viola Davis, Kohl Sudduth, Polly Shannon, Stephen McHattie, Saul Rubinek, Stephanie March, Stephen Baldwin, Mike Starr; *D:* Robert Harmon; *W:* Tom Epperson; *C:* David Gribble; *M:* Jeff Beal. **TV**

Jesse Stone: Sea Change ✂✂ 1/2 *Sea Change* **2007** In this fourth TV movie (based on the novel by Robert B. Parker), Paradise sheriff Jesse Stone (Selleck) is bored, brooding, and drinking too much. So bored that he recruits deputy Rose (Baker) and reopens a cold case—a bank robbery, shooting, and missing teller from 15 years ago. Then things heat up when a young local woman claims to have been raped aboard a visitor's yacht and some Boston thug is tailing Jesse with bad intent. **87m/C DVD.** Tom Selleck, Kathy Baker, William Devane, Rebecca Pidgeon, Sean Young, Saul Rubinek, Viola Davis, Kohl Sudduth, Nigel Bennett; *D:* Robert Harmon; *W:* Ronni Kern; *C:* Rene Ohashi; *M:* Jeff Beal. **TV**

Jesse Stone: Stone Cold ✂✂ 1/2 *Stone Cold; Robert B. Parker's Jesse Stone: Stone Cold* **2005** Jesse Stone (Selleck) is settling into his life as police chief of Paradise, a small New England fishing/tourist community. But his quiet, which is usually spent with a bottle of scotch, is disturbed by a series of murders—one of which hits too close to home. The first in a series of TV movies. Based on the book by Robert B. Parker. **87m/C DVD.** Tom Selleck, Viola Davis, Kohl Sudduth, Polly Shannon, Stephen McHattie, Jane Adams, Mimi Rogers; *D:* Robert Harmon; *W:* John Fasano, Michael Brandman; *C:* Rene Ohashi; *M:* Jeff Beal. **TV**

Jesse Stone: Thin Ice ✂✂ 1/2 *Thin Ice* **2009** In Selleck's fifth outing as Robert B. Parker's sheriff of smalltown Paradise, Jesse is hitting the booze a little harder than usual before two investigations occupy his time. First, his Boston buddy Capt. Healy (McHattie) is nearly murdered, and second, desperate Elizabeth Blue (Manheim) visits the town looking for her long-missing son. And as usual, Jesse's unorthodox policing has the town council threatening to suspend or fire him. **88m/C DVD.** Tom Selleck, Kathy Baker, Kohl Sudduth, Leslie Hope, Stephen McHattie, Camryn Manheim, William Sadler, Jessica Hecht, William Devane, Joanna Miles; *D:* Robert Harmon; *W:* Ronni Kern; *C:* Rene Ohashi; *M:* Jeff Beal. **TV**

The Jesse Ventura Story ✂ 1/2 **1999** Cheap quickie TV movie capitalizes on Ventura's unlikely career path. Smalltown boy Ventura becomes a Navy SEAL, a professional wrestler known as "The Body" (among other jobs), and eventually winds up in an upset victory as the governor of Minnesota. A dull, unauthorized whitewash that would probably bore even Ventura himself. **95m/C VHS, DVD.** Nils Allen Stewart, Nancy Sakovich, Thomas Brandise, Christopher Bondy, Nola Auguston; *D:* David S. Jackson; *W:* Patricia Jones, Donald Reiker; *C:* John Holosko; *M:* Richard Gibbs. **TV**

Jessi's Girls ✂ 1/2 *Wanted Women* **1975 (R)** In retaliation for the murder of her husband, an angry young woman frees three female prisoners, and they embark on a bloody course of revenge. Together, they track down the killers, and one by one, they fight to even the score. **86m/C VHS.** Sondra Currie, Regina Carrol, Jennifer Bishop, Rigg Kennedy; *D:* Al Adamson.

Jesus ✂✂ **1979 (G)** A supposedly authenticated life of Christ, using real artifacts. **118m/C VHS, DVD.** Brian Deacon; *D:* Peter Sykes, John Kirsh.

Jesus ✂✂ 1/2 **2000** Not completely reverential look at the life and teachings of Jesus (Sisto) from a historical, political, and religious viewpoint. Jesus is kind of a fun-loving 30-year-old who knows he has a destiny to fulfill. He and his parents (Bissett and Mueller-Stahl) struggle to deal with that as his followers seek the best course of resistance to Roman oppression, embodied by the political savvy Pontius Pilate (Oldman). The only truly disconcerting note is a slick Satan (Krabbe), who dresses like a contemporary wiseguy, and his temptation of Jesus in the wilderness. **174m/C VHS, DVD.** Jeremy Sisto, Jacqueline Bisset, Armin Mueller-Stahl, Debra Messing, Gary Oldman, Jeroen Krabbe, David O'Hara, G.W. Bailey, Thomas Lockyer, Luca Zingaretti, Stefania Rocca, Claudio Amendola; *D:* Roger Young; *W:* Suzette Couture; *C:* Raffaele Mertes; *M:* Patrick Williams. **TV**

Jesus Camp **2006 (PG-13)** Follows several children at an evangelical Christian summer camp that serves as a training ground for the youth to become advocates and assume leadership roles in a born-again religious revival. **84m/C DVD.** *D:* Heidi Ewing, Rachel Grady.

Jesus Christ, Superstar ✂✂✂ **1973 (G)** A rock opera that portrays, in music, the last seven days in the earthly life of Christ, as reenacted by young tourists in Israel. Outstanding musical score was the key to the success of the film, although Elliman and Anderson are standouts as, respectively, Mary Magdalene and Judas. Based on the stage play by Tim Rice and Andrew Lloyd Webber, film is sometimes stirring while exhibiting the usual heavy-handed Jewison approach. ♫Jesus Christ, Superstar; I Don't Know How To Love Him; What's The Buzz?; Herod's Song; Heaven On Their Minds; Strange Thing, Mystifying; Then We Are Decided; Everything's Alright; This Jesus Must Die. **108m/C VHS, DVD.** Ted Neeley, Carl Anderson, Yvonne Elliman, Josh Mostel, Barry Dennen, Bob Bingham, Larry T. Marshall; *D:* Norman Jewison; *W:* Melvyn Bragg; *C:* Douglas Slocombe; *M:* Andrew Lloyd Webber, Andre Previn, Herbert W. Spencer.

Jesus Christ Superstar ✂✂ 1/2 **2000** This new version updates the Tim Rice-Andrew Lloyd Webber rock opera for the MTV generation. The musical numbers have a rock video look and feel. The production is based on a stage version and so it doesn't feel or look like a real film. **112m/C VHS, DVD.** Glenn Carter, Jerome Pradon, Renee Castle, Rik Mayall; *D:* Nick Morris, Gale Edwards; *W:* Tim Rice, Andrew Lloyd Webber; *C:* Nicholas D. Knowland, Anthony Van Laast; *M:* Simon Lee, Tim Rice, Andrew Lloyd Webber.

Jesus of Montreal ✂✂✂ 1/2 *Jesus de Montreal* **1989 (R)** A vagrant young actor (stage-trained Canadian star Bluteau) is hired by a Montreal priest to produce a fresh interpretation of an Easter passion play. Taking the good book at its word, he produces a contemporized literal telling that captivates audiences, inflames the men of the cloth, and eventually wins the players' faith. Quebecois director Arcand (keep an eye out for him as the judge) tells a compelling, acerbically satirical and haunting story that never forces its Biblical parallels. In French with English subtitles. **119m/C VHS, DVD.** *FR CA* Gilles Pelletier, Lothaire Bluteau, Catherine Wilkening, Robert Lepage, Johanne-Marie Tremblay, Remy Girard, Marie-Christine Barrault; *D:* Denys Arcand; *W:* Denys Arcand; *C:* Guy Dufaux; *M:* Jean-Marie Benoit, Francois Dompierre, Yves Laferriere. Cannes '89: Special Jury Prize; Genie '90: Actor (Girard), Director (Arcand), Film, Support. Actor (Girard).

Jesus of Nazareth ✂✂ 1/2 **1928** A dramatic recreation of the life of Christ from the Annunciation through the Ascension. The film titles are taken from descriptive Biblical passages. **85m/B VHS.** Philip Van Loan, Anna Lehr, Charles McCaffrey; *W:* Jean Conover.

Jesus of Nazareth ✂✂✂ **1977** An all-star cast vividly portrays the life of Christ in this miniseries. Wonderfully directed and sensitively acted. **371m/C VHS, DVD.** Robert Powell, Anne Bancroft, Ernest Borgnine, Claudia Cardinale, James Mason, Laurence Olivier, Anthony Quinn; *D:* Franco Zeffirelli; *W:* Franco Zeffirelli, Anthony Burgess, Suso Cecchi D'Amico; *M:* Maurice Jarre. **TV**

Jesus' Son ✂✂ **1999 (R)** Crudup gives a fine performance as a sweet, passive, bungling druggie known only as FH (which stands for F***head). He falls for reckless heroin-addict Michelle (Morton), ODs, gets saved, gets dumped, gets in a car wreck, and eventually cleans up and finds some kind of peace working in an Arizona nursing home. There's really not much plot; it's the characters that carry things along. Film is set in the '70s and based on Dennis Johnson's 1992 collection of short stories. **109m/C VHS, DVD.** Billy Crudup, Samantha Morton, Denis Leary, Holly Hunter, Dennis Hopper, Jack Black, Will Patton, Greg Germann; *D:* Alison Maclean; *W:* Elizabeth Cuthrell, David Urrutia, Oren Moverman; *C:* Adam Kimmel; *M:* Joe Henry.

The Jesus Trip ✂ 1/2 **1971** Hunted motorcyclists take a young nun hostage in the desert. **86m/C VHS.** Robert Porter, Tippy Walker; *D:* Russ Mayberry.

Jet Benny Show **1986** A Buck Rogers/Star Wars-style spoof of Jack Benny's classic TV show. **76m/C VHS.** Steve Norman, Kevin Dees, Polly MacIntyre, Ted Luedemann; *D:* Roger Evans.

Jet Lag ✂✂ *Decalage Horaire* **2002 (R)** Lightweight romance finds beautician Rose (Binoche) stuck at Charles de Gaulle airport thanks to an unexpected strike. She is heading on a solo holiday away from her abusive boyfriend Sergio (Lopez). Also stuck is Felix (Reno), a former chef turned frozen-food businessman on his way to Munich. Rose loses her cell phone and asks to borrow Felix's. They wind up sharing the last available room in an airport hotel and compare lives. Felix cooks dinner for Rose, they argue, leave, get together again—it's creaky but watchable because of the two leads. French with subtitles. **81m/C VHS, DVD.** *FR GB* Juliette Binoche, Jean Reno, Sergi Lopez; *D:* Daniele Thompson; *W:* Daniele Thompson, Christopher Thompson; *C:* Patrick Blossier; *M:* Eric Serra.

Jet Li's Fearless ✂✂ *Fearless; Huo Yuan Jia* **2006 (PG-13)** Touted as Jet Li's final go at traditional Chinese martial arts (wushu) cinema. Li plays famed mainland fighter Huo Yuanjia in this elaborate bio, which begins in 1910, with flashbacks and flashforwards that document Yuanjia's childhood and gradual ascent to martial arts stardom. Yuanjia's initial arrogance costs him much and he must learn humility in order to achieve true harmony (or something like that). Director Yu wisely avoids wasting much time in between fight scenes and takes an almost purist approach with very little CGI and cable work. English and Chinese with subtitles. **103m/C DVD, HD DVD.** *CH HK* Jet Li, Shido Nakamura, Betty Sun, Yong Dong, Collin Chou, Nathan Jones, Yun Qu; *D:* Ronny Yu; *W:* Wang Bin, Chris Chow, Christine To, Li Feng; *C:* Hang-Seng Poon; *M:* Mei Linmao.

Jet Li's The Enforcer ✂✂ 1/2 *The Enforcer; My Father Is a Hero; Letter to Daddy; Gei Ba Ba de Xin* **1995** Chinese cop Li goes undercover to infiltrate a Hong Kong gang. His son (Miu) has been told dad is a crook but he has faith. When Li's wife dies, cop Mui brings the boy to Hong Kong and the kid (a fighting fiend just like his father) winds up helping dad with his police work. Dubbed from Cantonese. **100m/C VHS, DVD.** *HK* Jet Li, Anita (Yim-Fong) Mui, Damian Lau, Tse Miu, Rongguang Yu, Collin Chou; *D:* Corey Yuen.

Jet Over the Atlantic ✂ 1/2 **1959** Dangerous situation arises as a bomb is discovered aboard a plane en route from Spain to New York. **92m/B VHS.** Guy Madison, George Raft, Virginia Mayo, Brett Halsey; *D:* Byron Haskin.

Jet Pilot ✂✂ **1957** An American Air Force colonel (Wayne) in charge of an Alaskan Air Force base falls in love with a defecting Russian jet pilot (Leigh). They marry, but Wayne suspects Leigh is a spy planted to find out top U.S. secrets. He pretends to defect with her back to Russia to see what he can find out, but they again flee. Ludicrous plot is saved only by spectacular flying scenes, some performed by Chuck Yeager. Although this was filmed in 1950, it took seven more years to be released because producer Hughes couldn't keep his hands off it. **112m/B VHS, DVD.** John Wayne, Janet Leigh, Jay C. Flippen, Paul Fix, Richard Rober, Roland Winters, Hans Conried, Ivan Triesault; *D:* Josef von Sternberg; *C:* Winton C. Hoch.

Jetsons: The Movie ✂✂ **1990 (G)** The famous outer space family of '60s TV is given a new silver-screened life. George gets a promotion that puts him in charge of an asteroid populated by furry creatures. Ecological concerns are expressed; while this is rare for a cartoon, the story is overall typical. **82m/C VHS.** *D:* William Hanna, Joseph Barbera; *M:* John Debney; *V:* George O'Hanlon, Mel Blanc, Penny Singleton, Tiffany, Patric Zimmerman, Donald E. Messick, Jean Vander Pyl, Ronnie Schell, Patti Deutsch, Dana Hill, Russi Taylor, Paul Kreppel, Rick Dees.

The Jew ✂✂ **1996** Portrait of 18th century playwright Antonio Jose da Silva (Pinheiro), whose family was forcibly converted from their Jewish faith by the Catholic Church. Living in Lisbon, da Silva founded a puppet theatre for which he wrote comic operas. Eventually condemned for heresy, he was executed by the Inquisition in 1739. Explicit torture scenes. Portuguese with subtitles. **85m/C VHS.** *PT* Felipe Pinheiro, Dina Sfat, Mario Viegas, Edwin Luisi, Jose Neto; *D:* Jom Tob Azulay; *W:* Millor Fernandes, Billy Eckstine, Gilvan Pereira; *C:* Eduardo Serra.

Jew-Boy Levi ✂✂ *Viehjud Levi* **1999** It's 1935 in a German farming village where Lisbeth (Ebner) works at the local bar and is romanced by cattle trader Levi (Cathomas) each year when he passes through town. Only this year, a Nazi engineer and his men are in town to repair a tunnel and gradually the peace of the community is shattered by unreasoning hatred and Levi is found dead. German with subtitles. **90m/C VHS, DVD.** *GE* Bruno Cathomas, Bernd Michael Lade, Eva Mattes, Caroline Ebner, Georg Olschewski, Martina Gedeck; *D:* Didi Danquart; *W:* Didi Danquart, Martina Docker; *C:* Johann Feindt; *M:* Cornelius Schwehr.

The Jewel in the Crown ✂✂✂ **1984** Epic saga of the last years of British rule in India from 1942-47 concentrating on a controversial love affair between the Indian Hari Kumar and the English Daphne Manners, which profoundly affects the lives of many. Based on "The Raj Quartet" by Paul Scott. Originally shown on British TV, it aired in the U.S. on the PBS series "Masterpiece Theatre." An excellent miniseries that was shown in 14 segments. **750m/C VHS, DVD.** *GB* Charles Dance, Susan Wooldridge, Art Malik, Tim Pigott-Smith, Geraldine James, Peggy Ashcroft, Judy Parfitt; *D:* Christopher Morahan, Jim O'Brien; *M:* George Fenton. **TV**

The Jewel of the Nile ✂✂ 1/2 **1985 (PG)** Sequel to "Romancing the Stone" with the same cast but new director. Romance novelist Joan thought she found her true love in Jack but finds that life doesn't always end happily ever. After they part ways, Jack realizes that she may be in trouble and endeavors to rescue her from the criminal hands of a charming North African president. Of course, he can always check out this "jewel" at the same time. Chemistry is still there, but the rest of the film isn't quite up to the "Stone's" charm. **106m/C VHS, DVD, Blu-ray Disc.** Michael Douglas, Kathleen Turner, Danny DeVito, Avner Eisenberg, The Flying Karamazov Brothers, Spiros Focas, Holland Taylor; *D:* Lewis Teague; *W:* Mark Rosenthal, Larry Konner; *C:* Jan De Bont; *M:* Jack Nitzsche.

The Jeweller's Shop ✂✂ **1990** A highly spiritual tale of two married couples in Poland whose children meet and fall in love much later in Canada. Based on a play by Karol Wojtyla—who later became Pope Jean-Paul II. Adapted under strict Vatican supervision. **90m/C VHS.** Burt Lancaster, Ben Cross, Olivia Hussey; ***D:*** Michael Anderson Sr.; ***W:*** Jeff Andrus; ***C:*** Franco Di Giacomo; ***M:*** Michel Legrand.

Jewels ½ *Danielle Steel's Jewels* **1992** Sarah and her second husband the Duke of Whitfield—as a goodwill gesture after WWI—start buying jewelry from war survivors, which eventually leads to a successful jewelry store business. After William dies, Sarah struggles to keep control of her children and the family business. Classic soap-opera mini-series drama. **228m/C DVD.** Annette O'Toole, Anthony Andrews, Jurgen Prochnow, Sheila Gish, Simon Oates, Robert Wagner, Ursula Howells, Geoffrey Whitehead, Corinne Touzet; ***D:*** Roger Young; ***W:*** Shelley List, Jonathan Estrin; ***M:*** Patrick Williams. **CABLE**

Jezebel ½ **1938** Davis is a willful Southern belle who loses fiance Fonda through her selfish and spiteful ways in this pre-Civil War drama. When he becomes ill, she realizes her cruelty and rushes to nurse him back to health. Davis' role won her an Oscar for Best Actress, and certainly provided Scarlett O'Hara with a rival for most memorable female character of all time. **105m/B VHS, DVD.** Bette Davis, George Brent, Henry Fonda, Margaret Lindsay, Fay Bainter, Donald Crisp, Spring Byington, Eddie Anderson; ***D:*** William Wyler; ***W:*** Clements Ripley, Abem Finkel, John Huston, Robert Buckner; ***C:*** Ernest Haller; ***M:*** Max Steiner. Oscars '38: Actress (Davis), Support. Actress (Bainter), Natl. Film Reg. '09.

Jezebel's Kiss **1990 (R)** A sizzling young beauty returns to the town where she grew up and proceeds to destroy any man she pleases. **96m/C VHS, DVD.** Meg Foster, Malcolm McDowell, Meredith Baxter, Everett McGill, Katherine Barrese; ***D:*** Harvey Keith; ***W:*** Harvey Keith.

JFK ½ **1991 (R)** Highly controversial examination of President John F. Kennedy's 1963 assassination, from the viewpoint of New Orleans district attorney Jim Garrison. Hotly debated because of Stone's conspiracy theory, it sparked new calls to open the sealed government records from the 1977 House Select Committee on Assassinations investigation. Outstanding performances from all-star principal and supporting casts, stunning cinematography, and excellent editing. Even Garrison himself shows up as Chief Justice Earl Warren. Considered by some to be a cinematic masterpiece, others see it as revisionist history that should be taken with a grain of salt. Extended version adds 17 minutes. **189m/C VHS, DVD.** Dale Dye, Kevin Costner, Sissy Spacek, Kevin Bacon, Tommy Lee Jones, Laurie Metcalf, Gary Oldman, Michael Rooker, Jay O. Sanders, Beata Pozniak, Joe Pesci, Donald Sutherland, John Candy, Jack Lemmon, Walter Matthau, Ed Asner, Vincent D'Onofrio, Sally Kirkland, Brian Doyle-Murray, Wayne Knight, Tony Plana, Tomas Milian, Sean Stone; ***Cameos:*** Lolita (David) Davidovich, Frank Whaley, Jim Garrison; ***D:*** Oliver Stone; ***W:*** Oliver Stone, Zachary Sklar; ***C:*** Robert Richardson; ***M:*** John Williams. Oscars '91: Cinematog., Film Editing; Golden Globes '92: Director (Stone).

The JFK Conspiracy **1991** Did Lee Harvey Oswald act alone? Opinions of government officials, eyewitnesses, and director Oliver Stone, in addition to testimony, photographs, documents, and other evidence, address the perennial American question. Includes footage from the House Select Committee on Assassination. **98m/C VHS. TV**

JFK: Reckless Youth ½ **1993** Dempsey does a fine job as the young John F. Kennedy Jr. TV flick covers the first 30 years of his life and the family ties and influences that shape him up to his 1946 election to Congress. Based on the book by Nigel Hamilton. **183m/C DVD.** *US* Patrick Dempsey, Terry Kinney, Loren Dean, Robin Tunney, Diana Scarwid, Malachy McCourt, Claire Forlani, Yolanda Jilot, James Rebhorn, Natalie Radford, Stan Cahill, Andrew Lowery, Cedric Smith, Greg Spottiswood, Nikki de Boer, Barry Morse; ***D:*** Harry Winer; ***W:*** William Broyles Jr.; ***C:*** Jean Lepine; ***M:*** Cameron Allan. **TV**

Jigsaw *Gun Moll* **1949** Crime drama with a smattering of cameos by Hollywood favorites. A newspaper reporter is murdered. The dead man's friend, an assistant district attorney, seeks the punks responsible. They send in a seductress to keep the D.A. busy, but she too is murdered. Action and tension in a well-made flick. Based on a story by John Roeburt. **70m/B VHS, DVD.** Franchot Tone, Jean Wallace, Myron McCormick, Marc Lawrence, Winifred Lenihan, Betty Harper, Robert Gist; ***Cameos:*** Marlene Dietrich, Henry Fonda, Burgess Meredith, John Garfield; ***D:*** Fletcher Markle.

Jigsaw *Man on the Move* **1971** Missing persons lawman is lured into a cover-up more complex than he had bargained for. A tense drama originated as the pilot for a series. **100m/C VHS.** James Wainwright, Vera Miles, Richard Kiley, Andrew Duggan, Edmond O'Brien; ***D:*** William A. Graham. **TV**

Jigsaw **1990** A developer is found dead the day after his wedding. His widow and a cop team up to find out who, what, where, and why. Lukewarm Australian mystery export. **85m/C VHS.** Rebecca Gibney, Dominic Sweeney, Michael Coard; ***D:*** Marc Gracie; ***W:*** Marc Gracie; ***C:*** Jaems Grant; ***M:*** Dalmazio Babare.

Jigsaw ½ **1999 (R)** Convential neo-noir is weak in both plot and performances. Vicky (Ehm) asks her boyfriend, Jules (Corno), to pick up $5000 that's owed her. Vicky winds up dead and Jules is on the lam from both cops and drug dealers. **83m/C VHS, DVD.** *CA* William Corno, Erica Ehm, Edgar George; ***D:*** Paul Shoebridge. **VIDEO**

The Jigsaw Man **1984 (PG)** A British-Russian double agent is sent back to England to retrieve a list of Soviet agents which he hid there many years before. **90m/C VHS.** *GB* Michael Caine, Laurence Olivier, Susan George, Robert Powell, Charles Gray, David Patrick Kelly, Michael Medwin; ***D:*** Terence Young.

Jigsaw Murders **1989** A macho detective is out to solve a grisly murder, but the only available leads are a jigsaw puzzle and the victim's severed, tattooed lower limb. **98m/C VHS.** Chad Everett, Michelle Johnson, Yaphet Kotto; ***D:*** Jag Mundhra.

Jill the Ripper **2000 (R)** Alcoholic ex-cop Matt Wilson launches his own investigation after his brother is murdered. This takes him into a world of political corruption and kinky sex, circa 1977 in Boston. **94m/C VHS, DVD.** Dolph Lundgren, Danielle Brett; ***D:*** Anthony Hickox; ***W:*** Kevin Bernhardt, Gareth Wardell; ***C:*** David Pelletier; ***M:*** Steve Gurevitch, Thomas Barquee. **VIDEO**

Jim Thorpe: All American ½ *Man of Bronze* **1951** The life story of Thorpe, a Native American athlete who gained international recognition for his excellence in many different sports. A must for sports fans. **105m/B VHS.** Burt Lancaster, Phyllis Thaxter, Charles Bickford, Steve Cochran, Dick Wesson; ***D:*** Michael Curtiz; ***W:*** Douglas S. Morrow; ***M:*** Max Steiner.

Jiminy Glick in LaLa Wood ½ **2005 (R)** Obsequious smalltime entertainment critic Jiminy Glick (Short) and his clueless wife Dixie (Hooks) are in showbiz heaven at the Toronto Film Festival. Granted an exclusive interview with rising young star Ben DiCarlo (Pearson), Jiminy is wined and dined and catches the eye of fading diva Miranda Coolidge (Perkins). When Miranda is murdered, Jiminy inexplicably investigates. Short's grating Comedy Central character is unsuccessfully carried to the big screen, seemingly so Short will have a showcase for his dead-on David Lynch impersonation. The only other reason to take a look is Higgins's turn as Eurotrash snob Andre. **90m/C DVD.** *US CA* Martin Short, Jan Hooks, Elizabeth Perkins, John Michael Higgins, Linda Cardellini, Janeane Garofalo, Carlos Jacott, Corey Pearson, Aries Spears, Robert Trebor, Gary Anthony Williams, Larry Joe Campbell, Mo Collins, DeRay Davis, London Hansen, Jake Hoffman; ***Cameos:*** Kiefer Sutherland, Whoopi Goldberg, Steve Martin, Kevin Kline, Sharon Stone, Forest Whitaker, Susan Sarandon, Kurt Russell, Rob Lowe; ***D:*** Vadim Jean; ***W:*** Martin Short, Paul Flaherty; ***C:*** Mike J. Fox; ***M:*** David Lawrence.

Jimmy & Judy **2006 (R)** Social misfits Jimmy (Furlong) and Judy (Bella) turn into lover/losers on the lam after setting out from suburbia on one wild ride—of all which is naturally documented by video camera. Derivative drivel trying way too hard. **100m/C DVD.** Edward Furlong, Rachael Bella, William Sadler, James Eckhouse, A.J. Buckley, A. J. Buckley; ***D:*** Randall K. Rubin, Jon Schroder; ***W:*** Jon Schroder; ***C:*** Ben Kufrin; ***M:*** Benoit Grey.

Jimmy Hollywood ½ **1994 (R)** Wanna-be Hollywood actor Pesci has never acted in his life but longs for stardom—which he gets after he accidentally becomes a community vigilante. Burned-out sidekick Slater helps create the videotapes that will bring Jimmy his 15 minutes of fame. Although appropriately desperate, Pesci's role comes off as mostly shtick; two dogs in a row for the usually talented Levinson (after "Toys"). **118m/C VHS, DVD.** Joe Pesci, Christian Slater, Victoria Abril; ***Cameos:*** Barry Levinson, Rob Weiss; ***D:*** Barry Levinson; ***W:*** Barry Levinson; ***C:*** Peter Sova; ***M:*** Robbie Robertson.

Jimmy Neutron: Boy Genius ½ **2001 (G)** Huge-brained and grease-haired Jimmy Neutron is a retro geek hero for the new millennium in this bright and flashy computer animated feature. The child-inventor is young enough to think a sugar rush is the ultimate taboo but smart enough to have created a toaster-satellite that makes contact with an alien race. When said alien race respond by stealing all the parents in Retroville, Jimmy and his band of nerds endeavor to rescue them. Though mildly targeted at adults, it prefers gas gags to pop culture reference; even the new-wave songs are covered by kiddie bands. Frenetic pacing and onslaught of images may tire older (than teenage) viewers, although the animation is pleasant enough and there are some inventive lines that will go over the young-uns' heads. Short and Stewart are amusing as a pair of egg-shaped space invaders. **90m/C VHS, DVD.** *US* ***D:*** John A. Davis; ***W:*** David N. Weiss, J. David Stem, Steve Oedekerk, John A. Davis; ***M:*** John Debney; ***V:*** Debi Derryberry, Carolyn Lawrence, Rob Paulsen, Martin Short, Patrick Stewart, Megan Cavanagh, Mark DeCarlo, Jeff Garcia, Candi Milo, Andrea Martin.

The Jimmy Show ½ **2001 (R)** Average Jimmy O'Brien (Whaley) vents the frustrations of his humble daily life at open mike night at a comedy club. But his routine isn't about jokes—his monologues are painful confessions about thwarted dreams, which only get worse when his fed-up wife Annie (Gugino) leaves. Whaley's at his best in the club scenes but they tend to overwhelm the rest of film. **93m/C VHS, DVD.** Frank Whaley, Carla Gugino, Ethan Hawke, Lynn Cohen; ***D:*** Frank Whaley; ***W:*** Frank Whaley; ***C:*** Mike Mayers; ***M:*** Robert Whaley, Anthony Grimaldi.

Jimmy, the Boy Wonder ½ **1966** Goremeister Lewis' attempt at a "family" film turns out just as weird as expected. A young boy goes on a magical trip to find out who stopped time and meets an absent-minded astronomer, the evil Mr. Fig, and then discovers what happens at world's end. **?m/C VHS.** Dennis Jones, David Blight Jr., Nancy Jo Berg; ***D:*** Herschell Gordon Lewis; ***W:*** Hal Berg; ***C:*** Andy Romanoff.

Jimmy the Kid **1982 (PG)** A young boy becomes the unlikely target for an improbable gang of would-be crooks on a crazy, "fool-proof" crime caper. Kiddie comic caper. **95m/C VHS.** Gary Coleman, Cleavon Little, Fay Hauser, Ruth Gordon, Dee Wallace, Paul LeMat, Don Adams; ***D:*** Gary Nelson; ***W:*** Sam Bobrick.

Jimmy Zip **2000 (R)** Jimmy (Fletcher) is a pyromaniac abused runaway who gets a job working for drug dealing pimp Rick (Mulkey). He goes on a fireworks spree, which is how Jimmy meets down-and-out sculptor Horace (Gossett), who encourages him to channel his energies in more productive directions. But Jimmy fuels his new interests by stealing money from Rick, which puts him and girlfriend Sheila (Frantz) in a very dangerous position. **112m/C VHS, DVD.** *CA* Brendan Fletcher, Chris Mulkey, Robert Gossett, Adrienne Frantz, James Russo, Kim (Kimberly Dawn) Dawson; ***D:*** Robert McGinley; ***W:*** Robert McGinley; ***C:*** Christopher Tufty; ***M:*** Geoff Levin.

Jindabyne ½ **2006 (R)** Director Lawrence transports this Raymond Carver story from the Pacific Northwest to the mountainous southwest of Australia. Working-class buddies Stewart (Byrne), Carl (Howard), Rocco (Yiakmis), and Billy (Stone) go off for a weekend fishing trip. They quickly find a dead Aboriginal girl floating in the river and tie the body to a tree while they continue with their plans. When they finally report their discovery, all hell breaks loose: Stewart's wife Claire (Linney) is appalled at their callousness, there's the racial aspect (would they have left the body if she had been white?), and it turns out that the girl was murdered. Despite some strong performances, pic tends to be sluggish and underdeveloped. **123m/C DVD.** *AU* Gabriel Byrne, Laura Linney, John Howard, Stelios Yiakmis, Deborra-Lee Furness, Leah Purcell, Chris Haywood, Alice Garner, Simon Stone, Sean Rees-Memyss, Eva Lazzaro, Tatea Reilly; ***D:*** Ray Lawrence; ***W:*** Beatrix Christian; ***C:*** David Williamson; ***M:*** Paul Kelly, Dan Luscombe.

Jingle All the Way **1996 (PG)** Producer Chris Columbus grabs the reins of the slapstick and sentiment sleigh from mentor John Hughes in this farce of holiday capitalism. Any parent who has searched frantically for that Mighty Morphin' Cabbage Elmo will understand hapless Howard Langston (Schwarzenegger), a workaholic dad who was supposed to secure the coveted Turbo Man action figure for his son Jamie (Lloyd). Unfortunately, it slips his mind until Christmas Eve and all the Turbo Men have blasted off with more mindful parents. In his panic-stricken quest for the toy, he is confronted by a crazed postman (Sinbad) hunting Turbo Man, a pack of sleazy Santas, and a vicious reindeer attack. Meanwhile, Howard's slimy neighbor Ted (Hartman) is attempting to get into his wife Liz's (Wilson) stockings with great care. Although aimed at a younger audience, there's a definite lack of kids; which leaves it too grown-up for the kids and too childish for the adults. There is some satisfaction in seeing the Mall of America torn to shreds, however. Ho ho hum. **88m/C VHS, DVD.** Arnold Schwarzenegger, Phil Hartman, Sinbad, Rita Wilson, James Belushi, Robert Conrad, Martin Mull, Jake Lloyd, Harvey Korman, Laraine Newman; ***D:*** Brian Levant; ***W:*** Randy Kornfield; ***C:*** Victor Kemper; ***M:*** David Newman.

Jinxed **1982 (R)** Las Vegas night-club singer tries to convince a gullible blackjack dealer to murder her crooked boyfriend, but the plan backfires when the gangster electrocutes himself while taking a shower. Offscreen cast disputes were probably much more interesting than onscreen comedy. **104m/C VHS, DVD.** Bette Midler, Ken Wahl, Rip Torn; ***D:*** Donald Siegel; ***W:*** David Newman, Frank D. Gilroy; ***M:*** Miles Goodman.

Jit **1994** Unpretentious romantic comedy finds the easy-going U.K., who runs errands for his uncle in a Zimbabwe town, falling in love with the beautiful Sofi, who already has a boyfriend. But U.K. won't be stopped by this or Sofi's greedy father. "Jit" refers to the infectious local music, a fusion of traditional African rhythms and reggae-pop. **98m/C VHS.** Dominic Makuvachuma, Sibongile Nene, Faria Sevenzo, Winnie Ndemera; ***D:*** Michael Raeburn.

The Jitters **1988 (R)** The Chinese hopping vampire comes to America to make a bad movie on a different continent. The murdered dead turn into zombies and seek revenge on their killers. Maybe they should've sought revenge on the producers. **80m/C VHS.** Sal Viviano, Marilyn Tokuda, James Hong, Frank Dietz; ***D:*** John Fasano.

Jive Junction **1943** A group of patriotic teenagers convert a barn into a canteen for servicemen and name it "Jive Junction." **62m/B VHS.** Dickie Moore, Tina Thayer, Gerra Young, Johnny Michaels, Jan Wiley, Beverly Boyd, William (Bill) Halligan; ***D:*** Edgar G. Ulmer.

Jo Jo Dancer, Your Life Is Calling ½ **1986 (R)** Pryor directed and starred in this semi-autobiographical price-of-fame story of a comic, hospitalized for a drug-related accident, who must re-evaluate his life. A serious departure from

Pryor's slapstick comedies that doesn't quite make it as a drama; Pryor nevertheless deserves credit for the honesty he demonstrates in dealing with his real-life problems. **97m/C VHS, DVD.** Richard Pryor, Debbie Allen, Art Evans, Fay Hauser, Barbara Williams, Paula Kelly, Wings Hauser, Carmen McRae, Diahnne Abbott, Scoey Mitchell, Billy Eckstine, Virginia Capers, Dennis Farina; ***D:*** Richard Pryor; ***W:*** Richard Pryor, Rocco Urbisci; ***C:*** John A. Alonzo; ***M:*** Herbie Hancock.

Joan of Arc ½ **1948** A touching and devout look at the life of Joan of Arc. Perhaps unfortunately, the film is accurately based on the play by Maxwell Anderson, and adds up to too much talk and too little action. **100m/C VHS, DVD.** Ingrid Bergman, Jose Ferrer, John Ireland, Leif Erickson; ***D:*** Victor Fleming; ***C:*** Joseph Valentine. Oscars '48: Color Cinematog., Costume Des. (C).

Joan of Arc ½ **1999** Earnest biopic of legendary 15th-century French heroine, Joan of Arc (Sobieski). Joan is a peasant girl, born during France's Hundred Years War with England. She hears saints' voices telling her to help the Dauphin Charles (Harris) claim the French throne and drive out the English. Charles persuades Joan to proclaim herself the legendary Maid of Lorraine and raise an army to battle the Brits. But after her success, Joan is betrayed by the King, sold to the English, and put on trial for heresy. **240m/C VHS, DVD.** Leelee Sobieski, Neil Patrick Harris, Peter O'Toole, Robert Loggia, Jacqueline Bisset, Powers Boothe, Shirley MacLaine, Olympia Dukakis, Maury Chaykin, Jonathan Hyde, Maximilian Schell, Peter Strauss; ***D:*** Christian Duguay; ***W:*** Ronald Parker, Michael Miller; ***C:*** Pierre Gill; ***M:*** Asher Ettinger, Tony Kosinec. **TV**

Joan of Paris ½ **1942** A French resistance leader dies so that Allied pilots can escape from the Nazis. A well done, but obviously dated propaganda feature. **91m/B VHS.** Michele Morgan, Paul Henreid, Thomas Mitchell, Laird Cregar, May Robson, Alexander Granach, Alan Ladd; ***D:*** Robert Stevenson; ***W:*** Charles Bennett.

Joan Rivers: A Piece of Work 2010 Directors Stern and Sundberg follow a year in the life of 75-year-old Joan Rivers, who's been a trailblazing comedian for more than 40 years. The focus is on workaholic Rivers' concentration on her career and how to keep it going, including TV appearances and performing club gigs. **84m/C DVD.** *US* Joan Rivers, Melissa Rivers; ***D:*** Ricki Stern, Annie Sundberg; ***W:*** Ricki Stern; ***C:*** Charles Miller; ***M:*** Paul Brill.

The Job **2003 (R)** Hitwoman CJ (Hannah) has agreed to one last job before she leaves her violent life behind her. Only she has a crisis of conscience and finds it difficult to pull the trigger on the target—young wannabe gangster Troy (Renfro), who stole a drug shipment from the wrong people. However, if CJ doesn't follow through, it'll be her life on the line. **86m/C VHS, DVD.** Daryl Hannah, Brad Renfro, Dominique Swain, Eric Mabius, Alex Rocco; ***D:*** Kenny Golde; ***W:*** Kenny Golde; ***C:*** Scott Kevan. **VIDEO**

Jock Petersen *Petersen* **1974 (R)** A light-hearted story about a blonde hunk who enrolls in college, cavorting and seducing his way to questionable fame and fortune. **97m/C VHS.** Jack Thompson, Wendy Hughes; ***D:*** Tim Burstall.

Jocks ½ **1987 (R)** A whiz-kid tennis team competes in a pro meet in Las Vegas, and paints the town red. **90m/C VHS, DVD.** Christopher Lee, Perry Lang, Richard Roundtree, Scott Strader; ***D:*** Steve Carver; ***W:*** Jeff Buhai.

Joe ½ **1970 (R)** An odd friendship grows between a businessman and a blue-collar worker as they search together for the executive's runaway daughter. Thrust into the midst of the counter-culture, they react with an orgy of violence. **107m/C VHS, DVD.** Peter Boyle, Susan Sarandon, Dennis Patrick; ***D:*** John G. Avildsen; ***W:*** Norman Wexler; ***C:*** John G. Avildsen, Henri Decae; ***M:*** Bobby Scott.

Joe and Max **2002 (PG-13)** That would be heavyweight boxing champs Joe "the Brown Bomber" Louis and Max Schmeling. In 1936, Max defeats Joe in a title match, although the two become friends. Joe has to put up with his country's racism (the whites in the audience cheer for Schmeling) while Max has to endure the Nazi's using him as a symbol of Aryan superiority. In 1938, the tables are turned in a rematch at Yankee Stadium—this time it's Louis that's the people's choice and the victor. Not only does the film relate the duo's celebrity (and symbolism) but their alternating fortunes after WWII. Both leads do fine work, although Schweiger seems more comfortable in his role. **113m/C VHS, DVD.** *US GE* Til Schweiger, Leonard Roberts, Peta Wilson, Richard Roundtree, David Paymer, John Toles-Bey, Bruce Weitz; ***D:*** Steve James; ***W:*** Jason Horwitch; ***C:*** Bill Butler; ***M:*** Jeff Beal. **CABLE**

Joe Dirt **2001 (PG-13)** Spade plays the hapless, well-meaning personification of every trailer-trash joke you've ever heard or told. He sports a robo-mullet, earns his keep with degrading, sub-minimum wage jobs, drives a beat-up muscle car, and grooves to '70s arena-rock. He's also searching for his parents, who bailed on him during a trip to the Grand Canyon when he was eight. Too bad he isn't funny. Co-writers Spade and Wolf spend too much time on the heart strings and not enough on the funny bone, which results in an unholy hybrid of Jerry Springer and the Lifetime Network. Miller's shock-jock and Walken's crazed janitor add some genuine laughs to the proceedings, but not enough. **91m/C VHS, DVD, UMD.** *US* David Spade, Dennis Miller, Adam Beach, Christopher Walken, Jaime Pressly, Caroline Aaron, Fred Ward, Brittany Daniel, Kid Rock, Erik Per Sullivan, Megan Taylor Harvey; ***D:*** Dennie Gordon; ***W:*** David Spade, Fred Wolf; ***C:*** John R. Leonetti; ***M:*** Waddy Wachtel.

Joe Gould's Secret ½ **2000 (R)** Tucci directed, co-wrote, and stars as Joe Mitchell, famed "New Yorker" columnist who chronicled, among many others, the peculiar life of Greenwich Village eccentric Joe Gould in the 1940s. Gould (Holm) lived on the streets of New York for 26 years, regaling the intelligensia with wild stories and behavior while claiming to be writing the "Oral History of Our Time," which he said was two million words long and contained the fruits of 20,000 overheard conversations. The film quietly (except when Holm's Gould is onscreen) and effectively explores the relationship between Mitchell and Gould, and the reasons for Mitchell's fascination with his subject. **108m/C VHS, DVD.** Stanley Tucci, Ian Holm, Hope Davis, Patricia Clarkson, Steve Martin, Susan Sarandon, Celia Weston, Allan Corduner, Alice Drummond, Julie Halston, Hallee Hirsh, Ben Jones, John Tormey, David Wohl, Patrick Tovatt, Sarah Hyland; ***D:*** Stanley Tucci; ***W:*** Howard A. Rodman, Stanley Tucci; ***C:*** Maryse Alberti; ***M:*** Evan Lurie.

Joe Kidd ½ **1972 (PG)** A land war breaks out in New Mexico between Mexican natives and American land barons. Eastwood, once again portraying the "mysterious stranger," must decide with whom he should side, all the while falling in love with Garcia. Lackluster direction results in a surprisingly tedious western, in spite of the cast. One of Eastwood's lowest money grossers. **88m/C VHS, DVD.** Clint Eastwood, Robert Duvall, John Saxon, Don Stroud, Stella Garcia, James Wainwright, Paul Koslo, Gregory Walcott, Dick Van Patten, Lynn(e) Marta; ***D:*** John Sturges; ***W:*** Elmore Leonard; ***C:*** Bruce Surtees; ***M:*** Lalo Schifrin.

The Joe Louis Story **1953** The story of Joe Louis' rise to fame as boxing's Heavyweight Champion of the world. **88m/B VHS, DVD.** Coley Wallace, Paul Stewart, Hilda Simms, Albert "Poppy" Popwell; ***D:*** Robert Gordon; ***W:*** Robert Sylvester; ***C:*** Joseph Brun; ***M:*** George Bassman.

The Joe McDoakes Collection ½ **1942** Sixty-three one-reelers released by Warner Bros. from 1942-1956 that starred George O'Hanlon as frustrated everyman Joe McDoakes whose every plan, challenge, and ambition went wrong in a comedic way. **648m/B DVD.** George O'Hanlon, Phyllis Coates; ***D:*** Richard Bare; ***W:*** Richard Bare.

Joe Panther **1976 (G)** Family drama about a young Seminole Indian who stakes his claim in the Anglo world by wrestling alligators. Montalban plays a wise old chieftain who helps the youth handle the conflict between Indian and white societies. **110m/C VHS, DVD.** Brian Keith, Ricardo Montalban, Alan Feinstein, Cliff Osmond, A. Martinez, Robert Hoffman; ***D:*** Paul Krasny.

Joe Somebody **2001 (PG)** By-the-numbers dud feels like an after-school special with ten times the budget and half the brains or heart. Tim Allen again plays the allegedly likable Average Joe, only this time, his name is actually Joe. Trouble is, he doesn't look nerdy or ineffectual, even if he's wearing glasses and getting beat up in the parking lot. After Joe's daughter (Panettiere) witnesses his turn as punching bag for the office bully (Warburton), he slides into a depression. But after a visit from sure-to-be romantic interest Meg (Bowen), Joe decides he wants a rematch. He enlists the help of a faded martial arts guru (Belushi) and becomes popular, but his daughter and love interest like the old Joe better. Tries to have a moral message about rejecting violence while also giving a good dose of it. Joe's precocious, sage-like daughter makes the Olsen twins pleasant by comparison. **97m/C VHS, DVD.** *US* Tim Allen, Julie Bowen, Hayden Panettiere, Kelly Lynch, James Belushi, Patrick Warburton, Greg Germann, Robert Joy, Ken Marino; ***D:*** John Pasquin; ***W:*** John Scott Shepherd; ***C:*** Daryn Okada; ***M:*** George S. Clinton.

Joe the King **1999 (R)** Undistinguished coming of age pic, set in the mid-'70s, about a boy caught up in violence. Fourteen-year-old Joe (Fleiss) and his older brother Mike (Ligosh) are subjected to the constant drunken abuse of their father Bob (Henry) and the indifference of their overworked mother Theresa (Young). Joe begins stealing to get by but his crimes gradually becomes less than petty. A troubled student as well, Joe is befriended by guidance counselor Len (Hawke), whose attempts to help only result in a stint for Joe in a juvie center. Slow-paced and developmentally challenged. **101m/C VHS, DVD.** Noah Fleiss, Val Kilmer, Ethan Hawke, Karen Young, John Leguizamo, Austin Pendleton, Max Ligosh, James Costa; ***D:*** Frank Whaley; ***W:*** Frank Whaley; ***C:*** Mike Mayers; ***M:*** Robert Whaley, Anthony Grimaldi. Sundance '99: Screenplay.

Joe Torre: Curveballs Along the Way ½ **1997** Bio of manager Torre (Sorvino), who's hired by George Steinbrenner (Welsh) in 1996 to coach the New York Yankees. The Yanks actually start winning and Torre takes them all the way to the World Series (they win), but his triumph is marred by family heartbreak, as his brother Frank (Loggia) is in the hospital awaiting a heart transplant. Not bad for a quickie cable biopic, but only because the cast is outstanding. **90m/C VHS.** Paul Sorvino, Robert Loggia, Barbara Williams, Isaiah Washington IV, Gailard Sartain, Kenneth Welsh, Marilyn Chris; ***D:*** Sturla Gunnarsson; ***W:*** Philip Rosenberg; ***C:*** Mark Irwin. **CABLE**

Joe Versus the Volcano **1990 (PG)** Expressionistic goofball comedy about a dopey guy who, after finding out he has only months to live, contracts with a millionaire to leap into a volcano alive. Imaginative farce with great "Metropolis"-pastiche visuals that eventually fizzle out. Watch for Ryan in not one, but three roles, and mysterious symbolism throughout. Special effects courtesy of Industrial Light and Magic. **106m/C VHS, DVD.** Tom Hanks, Meg Ryan, Lloyd Bridges, Robert Stack, Amanda Plummer, Abe Vigoda, Dan Hedaya, Barry McGovern, Ossie Davis; ***D:*** John Patrick Shanley; ***W:*** John Patrick Shanley; ***C:*** Stephen Goldblatt; ***M:*** Georges Delerue.

Joe's Apartment **1996 (PG-13)** Fresh-from-Iowa Joe (O'Connell) comes to New York, finds a squalid apartment, and then discovers its other occupants are hordes of singing, joking cockroaches. Lucky for Joe, his unwelcome roommates are on his side, even helping out with his love life, when necessary. Gross but interesting, throw in Vaughn as a panty-wearing politician and you've got yourself a potential cult-movie favorite. Neat freaks probably won't enjoy it much. Flick took three years to finish as computer-animated roaches had to do all the dancing and singing. Feature directorial debut for writer Payson, who created the original 1992 live-action/animation MTV short. **82m/C VHS, DVD.** Jerry O'Connell, Megan Ward, Robert Vaughn, Jim Turner, Don Ho, Sandra "Pepa" Denton, Shiek Mahmud-Bey; ***D:*** John Payson; ***W:*** John Payson; ***C:*** Peter Deming; ***V:*** Billy West, Reginald (Reggie) Hudlin.

Joe's Bed-Stuy Barbershop: We Cut Heads ½ **1983** Lee's first film takes place inside a neighborhood landmark, the corner barbershop. Lee displays the social awareness and urban humor that he honed in his later, bigger films. **60m/C VHS.** Monty Ross, Morris Carnovsky, Stuart Smith, Tommy Redmond Hicks; ***D:*** Spike Lee; ***W:*** Spike Lee; ***C:*** Ernest R. Dickerson.

Joey ½ **1985 (PG)** Daddy, a former doo-wopper, looks back on his years of musical success as a waste of time. His son takes to the world of rock guitar with blind fervor. Their argument plays against the backdrop of the "Royal Doo-Wopp Show" at New York City's Radio Music Hall. Features multi-generational rock songs. **90m/C VHS, DVD.** Neill Barry, James Quinn, Ellen Hammill, Dan Grimaldi; ***D:*** Joseph Ellison; ***W:*** Ellen Hammill, Joseph Ellison; ***C:*** Oliver Wood; ***M:*** Jim Roberge.

Joey ½ **1998 (PG)** Young Billy (Croft) rescues a baby kangaroo (known as a joey) who was left behind when an evil hunter captures a group of kangaroos and hauls them off to Sydney for nefarious purposes. So Billy puts Joey in his backpack and heads off to the city to reunite the little family—aided by the rebellious daughter (McKenna) of the newly appointed U.S. ambassador (Begley). **96m/C VHS, DVD.** *AU* Jamie Croft, Alex McKenna, Ed Begley Jr., Rebecca Gibney, Ruth Cracknell, Harold Hopkins; ***D:*** Ian Barry; ***W:*** Stuart Beattie; ***C:*** David Burr; ***M:*** Roger Mason.

Joey Breaker **1993 (R)** Joey (cult-fave Edson) is a hot-shot Manhattan talent agent who's consumed by his job. A series of encounters (romantic and otherwise) expands his outlook, first among them with Cyan (Marley), a young Jamaican waitress. On his journey to possible enlightenment Joey also meets AIDS-stricken Fondren, who helps Joey see another side of life. Quirky with a reggae beat, small pic works large message with sense of humor and sincere performances. Dedicated to Fondren, who died of AIDS in 1992. Marley, daughter of late reggae superstar Bob, shares a tune on the soundtrack with brother Ziggy. Filmed in da Big Apple and St. Lucia, West Indies. **92m/C VHS.** Richard Edson, Gina Gershon, Philip Seymour Hoffman, Cedella Marley, Erik King, Fred Fondren, Lewis Black; ***D:*** Steven Starr; ***W:*** Steven Starr; ***C:*** Joe DeSalvo; ***M:*** Paul Aston.

John Adams ½ **2008** Enjoyment rests on whether you can buy Giamatti as the titular founding father and second president of the U.S. Based on the best-selling bio by David McCullough, Adams is intelligent, impatient, irascible, resentful, and deeply devoted to both his country and his wife, the equally resourceful Abigail (Linney). Most of the familiar historical figures are present and accounted for—George Washington (Morse), Benjamin Franklin (Wilkinson), and Thomas Jefferson (Dillane)—as well as such events as the Continental Congress and the Declaration of Independence, but Adams isn't particularly likeable and you'll probably find out more than you could ever want to know. **560m/C DVD.** Paul Giamatti, Laura Linney, David Morse, Tom Wilkinson, Stephen (Dillon) Dillane, Zeljko Ivanek, Danny Huston, Sarah Polley, Rufus Sewell, Justin Theroux; ***D:*** Tom Hooper; ***W:*** Kirk Ellis; ***C:*** Tak Fujimoto; ***M:*** Robert (Rob) Lane, Joseph Vitarelli. **CABLE**

John and Julie ½ **1955** Sweet story about two young friends, living in the English countryside in 1953, who decide to run away to London in order to witness the coronation of Queen Elizabeth II. They're hoping John's Uncle, a Royal Escort guard, will help them but first they have to get to the city, which involves a lot of complicated travelling plans. **82m/C VHS.** *GB* Colin Gibson, Lesley Dudley, Noelle Middleton, Moira Lister, Constance Cummings, Wilfrid Hyde-White, Sidney James, Joseph Tomelty, Megs Jenkins, Patric Doonan, Peter Sellers, John Stuart, Vincent Ball, Colin Gordon, Peter Jones, Katie Johnson, Cyril Smith, Andrew Cruikshank, Winifred Shotter, Richard Dimbleby, Wynfold Vaughn Thomas; ***D:*** William Fairchild; ***W:*** William Fairchild; ***C:*** Arthur Grant.

John and the Missus 1/2 **1987 (PG)** After the discovery of a copper mine threatens to destroy a nearby town, the Canadian government begins a relocation process. However, one man refuses to give up his generations-old home. Canadian Pinsent's directorial debut, adapting his own 1973 novel. **98m/C VHS.** *CA* Gordon Pinsent, Jackie Burroughs, Randy Follet, Jessica Steen; ***D:*** Gordon Pinsent. Genie '87: Actor (Pinsent).

John & Yoko: A Love Story **1985** Appalling TV version of the rock legend's life and marriage. With original Beatles tunes. **146m/C VHS.** Mark McGann, Kim Miyori, Kenneth Price, Peter Capaldi, Richard Morant, Philip Walsh; ***D:*** Sandor Stern. **TV**

John Carpenter Presents Vampires: Los Muertos 1/2 *Vampires: Los Muertos* **2002 (R)** It's mostly a yawner because it's so predictable. Vamp hunter Derek (Bon Jovi) loses his team to the bloodsuckers but hooks up with a rag tag crew, including Father Rodrigo (De La Fuente), to go a-hunting in Mexico. This time the head biter is a vampire babe (Jover). Pretty tame even in comparison to the first flick. **94m/C VHS, DVD.** Jon Bon Jovi, Christian de la Fuente, Arly Jover, Darius McCrary, Natasha Gregson Wagner, Diego Luna; ***D:*** Tommy Lee Wallace; ***W:*** Tommy Lee Wallace; ***C:*** Jack Lorenz; ***M:*** Brian Tyler.

John Carpenter's Ghosts of Mars *Ghosts of Mars* **2001 (R)** John Carpenter unashamedly fires up his B-movie machine to maximum cheese factor in this tale of space babes and zombies. Henstridge is a police lieutenant on the matriarchal Mars colony in 2025 sent to retrieve murderer "Desolation" Williams (Ice Cube). The job turns from get the bad guy to simple survival when long-dormant Martian warriors begin taking over the bodies of the Earth intruders, turning them into zombies. So do you think the bad guys and the good guys have to team up to win one for the humans? At its best during the action sequences, but probably a bad choice to follow "A Room with a View" for a Saturday night double feature. **98m/C VHS, DVD.** *US* Natasha Henstridge, Ice Cube, Clea DuVall, Pam Grier, Jason Statham, Joanna Cassidy, Rosemary Forsyth, Liam Waite, Richard Cetrone; ***D:*** John Carpenter; ***W:*** John Carpenter, Larry Sulkis; ***C:*** Gary B. Kibbe; ***M:*** John Carpenter.

John Carpenter's Vampires 1/2 *Vampires* **1997 (R)** Vatican-sponsored vampire hunter Jack Crow (Woods) leads his team of mercenaries into the American Southwest to battle master bloodsucker Valek (Griffith) and his hordes. After destroying a vampire hideout, Crow and company are ambushed at a post-stake party. The only survivors are Crow, his buddy Montoya (Baldwin), and a hooker (Lee) with a psychic link to the vampires. Satisfying horror-western packs plenty of action and gore (along with just enough humor) to hold attention until the inevitable showdown. Woods does a good job of toning down from his usual bug-eyed crazy to merely borderline disturbed here. Based on the novel "Vampires" by John Steakley. **108m/C VHS, DVD.** James Woods, Thomas Ian Griffith, Sheryl Lee, Daniel Baldwin, Tim Guinee, Maximilian Schell, Cary-Hiroyuki Tagawa, Mark Boone Jr., Tom Rosales; ***D:*** John Carpenter; ***W:*** John Carpenter, Don Jacoby; ***C:*** Gary B. Kibbe; ***M:*** John Carpenter.

John Cleese on How to Irritate People *How to Irritate People* **1968** Cleese, a master at causing irritation, demonstrates how to take care of all those annoying people who irritate you, including job interviewers, bank clerks, waiters, and salesmen. Monty Python alumni Palin and Chapman also join Cleese in the "Airline Pilots" sketch about bored pilots deliberately trying to terrify their passengers. **65m/C VHS, DVD.** John Cleese, Michael Palin, Graham Chapman, Connie Booth.

John Grisham's The Rainmaker 1/2 *The Rainmaker* **1997 (PG-13)** Yet another legal drama from the successful pen of John Grisham. Baylor (Damon) is a young lawyer whose job disappears when his firm is absorbed by a giant company. He fills his time giving legal advice to indigents and mooning over Kelly (Danes), a young abused wife. Then he takes on the case of a couple whose leukemia-stricken son was denied treatment by their insurance company, coincidentally represented by the firm that booted Baylor. Pre-"Jack," Coppola probably wouldn't have gone anywhere near such formulaic franchise fare, and if he did, he could've directed it in his sleep. As it is he creates a serviceable, if not spectacular, piece of entertainment. His main allies are Voight's insurance company mouthpiece and DeVito's ambulance chaser. Damon plays the hero with much less bravado than previous Grisham protagonists. **137m/C VHS, DVD.** Sonny Shroyer, Matt Damon, Claire Danes, Danny DeVito, Jon Voight, Danny Glover, Virginia Madsen, Mary Kay Place, Mickey Rourke, Johnny Whitworth, Teresa Wright, Dean Stockwell, Red West, Roy Scheider, Randy Travis, Andrew Shue; ***D:*** Francis Ford Coppola; ***W:*** Francis Ford Coppola, Michael Herr; ***C:*** John Toll; ***M:*** Elmer Bernstein.

John John in the Sky **2000 (PG-13)** Ten-year-old John John (Craft) is living with a lot of tension in 1968. His good ol' boy dad (Travis) is abusive and angry at the changes going on around him, especially the fact that his wife (Rosemont) wants to take her kid and flee to San Francisco to join a commune. And John John also doesn't know how to deal with the unwanted friendship of the disabled Zeola (Schwimmer). Title comes from the boy's dream to build his own airplane. Sometimes confusing story with its series of flashbacks and flash-forwards. **101m/C VHS, DVD.** Randy Travis, Christian Craft, Romy Rosemont, Rusty Schwimmer, Matt Letscher; ***D:*** Jefferson Davis; ***W:*** Keri Skogland, Jefferson Davis; ***C:*** Joel David; ***M:*** Christopher Ward.

John Loves Mary **1948** Wartime marriage dilemmas. Soldier John (Reagan) owes buddy Fred (Carson) bigtime for saving his life so he agrees to an in-name-only marriage to Fred's English girlfriend Lily (Field) so she can get to the States. But by the time that happens, fickle Fred has actually married another gal and John must keep his marriage a secret from his own fiancee, Mary (Neal), until he can get that Reno divorce. But John's waffling has left Mary believing that he doesn't love her anymore. **96m/B DVD.** Ronald Reagan, Patricia Neal, Jack Carson, Virginia Field, Edward Arnold, Wayne Morris, Katherine Alexander, Paul Harvey; ***D:*** David Butler; ***W:*** Henry Ephron, Phoebe Ephron; ***C:*** J. Peverell Marley; ***M:*** David Buttolph.

John Paul Jones 1/2 **1959** Big bio of the Revolutionary War naval hero ("I have not yet begun to fight!") who wins a lot of battles but can't convince Congress to maintain a strong navy at war's end. He's sent to win sea battles for the Empress Catherine the Great of Russia and then spends his last years in France. Great action scenes, otherwise tedious. **126m/C VHS.** Robert Stack, Charles Coburn, MacDonald Carey, Marisa Pavan, Jean-Pierre Aumont, Peter Cushing, Erin O'Brien, Bruce Cabot, David Farrar, Basil Sydney, John Crawford; ***Cameos:*** Bette Davis; ***D:*** John Farrow; ***W:*** John Farrow, Jesse Lasky Jr.; ***M:*** Max Steiner.

John Q **2002 (PG-13)** "Dog Day Afternoon" lite is essentially a two hour tirade against the U.S. health system (who can blame them?) which casts Washington as the title's everyman hero who's desperate and gutsy enough to bypass medical bureaucracy altogether to get his 10-year old son Mike (Smith) the heart transplant he desperately needs to live. John Quincy Archibald's plant has just cut his hours, and when his HMO gives him the run-around, he is forced to come up with the $75,000 for his son's operation. Unable to come up with it, John Q. takes over the ER and demands his son be placed at the top of the transplant list. Talented cast, including Duvall as the sympathetic police negotiator, Woods as the cynical doctor, and Liotta, as the boldly drawn police chief, is generally wasted on the sentimental and melodramatic one-note premise. **118m/C VHS, DVD.** *US* Denzel Washington, Robert Duvall, James Woods, Anne Heche, Eddie Griffin, Kimberly Elise, Shawn Hatosy, Ray Liotta, Daniel E. Smith, David Thornton, Ethan Suplee, Kevin Connolly, Paul Johansson, Troy Beyer, Obba Babatunde, Laura Elena Harring; ***D:*** Nick Cassavetes; ***W:*** James Kearns; ***C:*** Rogier Stoffers; ***M:*** Aaron Zigman.

John Tucker Must Die **2006 (PG-13)** Title character (Metcalfe) is the resident B.M.O.C. who uses his looks and status to triple-time the three hottest girls in school, who end up learning about his cheating ways. The hotties plot unsuccessfully for revenge until they enlist the help of the ugly-duckling new girl, Kate (Snow), and the requisite makeover-to-lure-the-jerk ensues. Pic backfires in its girl-power message by resorting to cliches about female sensitivity, self-image, and estrogen side-effects and never gets as mean as "Mean Girls" or as darkly original as "Heathers." **82m/C DVD.** *US* Jesse Metcalfe, Ashanti, Arielle Kebbel, Brittany Snow, Sophia Bush, Jenny McCarthy, Fulvio Cecere, Penn Badgley; ***D:*** Betty Thomas; ***W:*** Jeff Lowell; ***C:*** Anthony B. Richmond; ***M:*** Richard Gibbs.

Johnnie Gibson F.B.I. *Johnnie Mae Gibson: FBI* **1987** Supposedly based on a true story, the adventures of a beautiful, black FBI agent who falls in love with a man she's investigating. **96m/C VHS, DVD.** Howard E. Rollins Jr., Lynn Whitfield, William Allen Young, Richard Lawson; ***D:*** Bill Duke; ***M:*** Billy Goldenberg.

Johnny Angel **1945** Merchant Marine captain unravels mystery of his father's murder aboard a ship. Tense film noir. **79m/B VHS.** George Raft, Claire Trevor, Signe Hasso, Lowell Gilmore, Hoagy Carmichael; ***D:*** Edwin L. Marin.

Johnny Apollo 1/2 **1940** Upright college student Power keeps his nose clean until Dad's sent to jail for playing with numbers. Scheming to free his old man (Arnold) from the big house, he decides crime will pay for the stiff price tag of freedom. Predictable and melodramatic, but well directed. **93m/B VHS.** Tyrone Power, Dorothy Lamour, Lloyd Nolan, Edward Arnold, Charley Grapewin, Lionel Atwill, Marc Lawrence, Jonathan Hale, Russell Hicks, Selmer Jackson, Charles Trowbridge; ***D:*** Yves Allegret; ***W:*** Rowland Brown, Philip Dunne, Samuel G. Engel; ***C:*** Arthur C. Miller; ***M:*** Cyril Mockridge, Alfred Newman, Lionel Newman.

Johnny Appleseed **1986** True story of the legendary American who spent his life planting apple trees across the country. Comedy the entire family will enjoy from Shelly Duvall's "Tall Tales and Legends" cable series. **60m/C VHS.** Martin Short, Rob Reiner, Molly Ringwald. **CABLE**

Johnny B. 1/2 **2000 (R)** College dropout Johnny B. has become a smalltime hustler with no ambitions since the murder of his older brother. Then he learns his ex-girlfriend, who's also the mother of his young daughter, has gotten engaged to a successful lawyer. Now, Johnny has some tough decisions to make. **98m/C VHS, DVD.** Richard Brooks, Vonetta McGee, Richard Gant, Kent Masters King, Tempestt Bledsoe; ***D:*** Richard Brooks; ***W:*** Gwendolyn J. Lester; ***C:*** Pancho Gonzales.

Johnny Be Good **1988 (R)** A too-talented high school quarterback is torn between loyalty to his best friend and to his girlfriend amid bribery and schemings by colleges eager to sign him up. **91m/C VHS, DVD.** Anthony Michael Hall, Robert Downey Jr., Paul Gleason, Uma Thurman, John Pankow, Steve James, Seymour Cassel, Michael Greene, Marshall Bell, Deborah May; ***D:*** Bud Smith; ***W:*** Jeff Buhai; ***M:*** Jay Ferguson.

Johnny Belinda **1948** A compassionate physician cares for a young deaf mute woman and her illegitimate child. Tension builds as the baby's father returns to claim the boy. **103m/B VHS, DVD.** Jane Wyman, Lew Ayres, Charles Bickford, Agnes Moorehead, Jan Sterling; ***D:*** Jean Negulesco; ***M:*** Max Steiner. Oscars '48: Actress (Wyman); Golden Globes '49: Actress—Drama (Wyman), Film—Drama.

Johnny Belinda **1982** TV adaptation of the Elmer Harris weepie about a small town doctor who befriends an abused deaf girl. Remake of the 1948 film. **95m/C VHS.** Richard Thomas, Rosanna Arquette, Dennis Quaid, Candy Clark, Roberts Blossom, Fran Ryan; ***D:*** Anthony Page. **TV**

Johnny Come Lately 1/2 *Johnny Vagabond* **1943** An elderly editor helps out an ex-newspaperman with a police charge. The two then team up to expose political corruption despite threats from a rival newspaperman. **97m/B VHS.** James Cagney, Grace George, Marjorie Main, Marjorie Lord, Hattie McDaniel, Edward McNamara; ***D:*** William K. Howard.

Johnny Dangerously **1984 (PG-13)** A gangster spoof about Johnny Dangerously, who turned to crime in order to pay his mother's medical bills. Now, Dangerously wants to go straight, but competitive crooks would rather see him dead than law-abiding and his mother requires more and more expensive operations. Crime pays in comic ways. **90m/C VHS, DVD.** Michael Keaton, Joe Piscopo, Danny DeVito, Maureen Stapleton, Marilu Henner, Peter Boyle, Griffin Dunne, Glynnis O'Connor, Dom DeLuise, Richard Dimitri, Ray Walston, Dick Butkus, Alan Hale Jr., Bob Eubanks; ***D:*** Amy Heckerling; ***W:*** Norman Steinberg, Harry Colomby.

Johnny Eager **1942** Glossy crime melodrama starring Taylor as an unscrupulous racketeer and Turner as the daughter of D.A. Arnold who falls for him and ends up becoming a pawn in his schemes. Heflin won an Oscar for his outstanding performance as Taylor's alcoholic confidant. Excellent direction by LeRoy makes this a top-rate gangster film. Based on a story by James Edward Grant. **107m/B VHS.** Robert Taylor, Lana Turner, Edward Arnold, Van Heflin, Robert Sterling, Patricia Dane, Glenda Farrell, Barry Nelson, Henry O'Neill, Charles Dingle, Cy Kendall; ***D:*** Mervyn LeRoy; ***W:*** James Edward Grant, John Lee Mahin. Oscars '42: Support. Actor (Heflin).

Johnny English 1/2 **2003 (PG)** Johnny English (Atkinson) is a deskbound member of the espionage community who's promoted to active status due to some unfortunate circumstances that he caused. The klutz must then prevent an evil French businessman (Malkovich) from dethroning the Queen and taking over. Anglophiles, fans of Rowan Atkinson, and toilet/slapstick humor lovers will enjoy this stale crumpet, but there's not much here for anyone else Stateside. Atkinson manages to squeeze some laughs from a poor script with his supreme gift for physical comedy, however, and Malkovich gleefully throws himself over the top. Imbruglia, making her feature debut, is game, but doesn't have much to do. **86m/C VHS, DVD.** *GB US* Rowan Atkinson, John Malkovich, Natalie Imbruglia, Ben Miller, Kevin McNally, Tim Pigott-Smith, Douglas McFerran, Greg Wise, Oliver Ford Davies; ***D:*** Peter Howitt; ***W:*** Neal Purvis, Robert Wade, William Davies; ***C:*** Remi Adefarasin; ***M:*** Ed Shearmur.

Johnny Firecloud **1975** A modern Indian goes on the warpath when the persecution of his people reawakens his sense of identity. **94m/C VHS, DVD.** Victor Mohica, Ralph Meeker, Frank De Kova, Sacheen Little Feather, David Canary, Christina Hart; ***D:*** William Allen Castleman; ***W:*** Wilton Denmark; ***M:*** William Loose.

Johnny Frenchman **1946** Rival fishing groups battle it out, complicated by a romance across the water, but when World War II breaks out they join together. Featured in the cast are real fishermen and villagers from Cornwall, as well as authentic Free French Resistance fighters from WWII. **104m/B VHS.** *GB* Francoise Rosay, Tom Walls, Patricia Roc, Ralph Michael, Frederick Piper, Pierre Richard, Bill Blewitt, Carroll O'Connor, Paul Dupuis, James Harcourt, Richard George; ***D:*** Charles Frend; ***W:*** T.E.B. Clarke; ***C:*** Roy Kellino; ***M:*** Clifton Parker.

Johnny Got His Gun **1971 (R)** Dalton Trumbo's story of a young WWI veteran (Bottoms) who meets a bomb with his name on it and is rendered armless, legless, and more or less faceless, as well as deaf, dumb, and blind. Regarded as a vegetable and stuck in a lightless hospital utility room, he dreams and fantasizes about life before and after the bomb, and tries vainly to communicate with the staff. Wrenching and bleak anti-war diatribe made at the climax of the Vietnam War. **111m/C VHS.** Timothy Bottoms, Jason Robards Jr., Donald Sutherland, Diane Varsi, Kathy Fields, Donald (Don "Red") Barry, Peter Brocco, Judy Chaikin, Eric Christmas, Maurice Dallimore, Robert Easton, Eduard Franz, Anthony Geary, Edmund Gilbert, Ben Hammer, Wayne Heffley, Marsha Hunt, Joseph Kaufmann, Charles McGraw, Byron Morrow, David Soul; ***D:*** Dalton Trumbo; ***W:*** Dalton

Trumbo; *C:* Jules Brenner; *M:* Jerry Fielding. Cannes '71: Grand Jury Prize.

Johnny Guitar 1/2 **1953** Women strap on six-guns in Nicholas Ray's unintentionally hilarious, gender-bending western. A guitar-playing loner wanders into a small town feud between lovelorn saloon owner Crawford and McCambridge, the town's resident lynch mob-leading harpy. This fascinating cult favorite has had film theorists arguing for decades: is it a parody, a political McCarthy-era allegory, or Freudian exercise? The off-screen battles of the two female stars are equally legendary. Stick around for the end credits to hear Peggy Lee sing the title song. **116m/C VHS, DVD.** Joan Crawford, Ernest Borgnine, Sterling Hayden, Mercedes McCambridge, Scott Brady, Ward Bond, Royal Dano, John Carradine, Ben Cooper, Frank Ferguson, Paul Fix, Denver Pyle; *D:* Nicholas Ray; *W:* Philip Yordan; *C:* Harry Stradling Sr.; *M:* Victor Young. Natl. Film Reg. '08.

Johnny Handsome **1989 (R)** An ugly, deformed hood, after he's been double-crossed and sent to prison, volunteers for a reconstructive surgery experiment and is released with a new face, determined to hunt down the scum that set him up. A terrific modern B-picture based on John Godey's "The Three Worlds of Johnny Handsome." **96m/C VHS, DVD.** Mickey Rourke, Ellen Barkin, Lance Henriksen, Elizabeth McGovern, Morgan Freeman, Forest Whitaker, Scott Wilson, Blake Clark; *D:* Walter Hill; *W:* Ken Friedman; *M:* Ry Cooder.

Johnny Holiday 1/2 **1949** A heartwarming story about a fatherless boy, Johnny, who is dumped into reform school to prevent him from pursuing a life of crime with his small-time hood buddies. While there, he is befriended by Sargeant Walker, an ex-Calvary man who teaches him about life and becomes the father Johnny never had. **94m/B VHS.** Allen Martin Jr., William Bendix, Stanley Clements; *D:* Willis Goldbeck.

Johnny Mnemonic **1995 (R)** Robo-yuppie data courier Johnny (Reeves), has over extended the storage capacity in his head and must download his latest job before his brain turns to applesauce. Aided by an implant-enhanced bodyguard (Meyer), underground hacker rebels called LoTeks, and a former doctor (Rollins) battling a technology-induced epidemic, Johnny is on the run from the corporation that wants his head (literally). Freshman director Longo can't seem to get a handle on the plot and doesn't get much help from Gibson, who combined characters and scenarios from his other books. Action sequences and computer effects are appropriately spiffy, preventing a total system crash. **98m/C VHS, DVD.** Keanu Reeves, Dina Meyer, Ice-T, Takeshi "Beat" Kitano, Dolph Lundgren, Henry Rollins, Udo Kier, Barbara Sukowa, Denis Akayama; *D:* Robert Longo; *W:* William Gibson; *C:* Francois Protat; *M:* Brad Fiedel.

Johnny Nobody 1/2 **1961** A mysterious stranger murders a writer who has been taunting the residents of a quaint Irish town. A sleeper of a thriller, especially in the treatment of the town's reaction to this murder. **88m/B VHS.** *GB* William Bendix, Aldo Ray, Nigel Patrick, Yvonne Mitchell, Cyril Cusack; *D:* Nigel Patrick.

Johnny 100 Pesos **1993** Seventeen-year-old Johnny (Araiza) walks into a video store that is a front for an illegal currency exchange operation. He's the advance man for a quartet of criminals who are planning to rob the place but before they can escape with the cash, the police show up and the crooks take the store's inhabitants hostage. Now there's a standoff, with the media shamelessly broadcasting all events and the Chilean authorities struggling to control the escalating situation. Based on a true 1990 incident. Spanish with subtitles. **90m/C VHS, DVD.** Armando Araiza, Patricia Rivera, Willy Semler, Sergio Hernandez; *D:* Gustavo Graef-Marino; *W:* Gustavo Graef-Marino, Gerardo Caceres; *C:* Jose Luis Arredondo; *M:* Andres Pollak.

Johnny Reno 1/2 **1966** Laughable western that has U.S. Marshal Andrews trying to save an accused killer from lynching. Of interest for star-watching only. Based on a story by Steve Fisher, A.C. Lyles, and Andrew Craddock. **83m/C VHS, DVD.** Dana Andrews, Jane Russell, Lon Chaney Jr., John Agar, Lyle Bettger, Tom Drake, Richard Arlen, Robert Lowery; *D:* R.G. Springsteen; *W:* Steve Fisher.

Johnny Shiloh **1963** An underage youth becomes a heroic drummer during the Civil War. Originally a two-part Disney TV show. **90m/C VHS.** Kevin Corcoran, Brian Keith, Darryl Hickman, Skip Homeier; *D:* James Neilson. **TV**

Johnny Skidmarks **1997 (R)** Johnny (Gallagher) is a burned-out freelance crime-scene photographer who moonlights for blackmailers by shooting incriminating pics of prominent citizens in seedy motels. Then the blackmailers start winding up dead and Johnny checks out his photos to see if he can figure out who's doing the crime before he becomes the next target. **96m/C VHS, DVD.** Peter Gallagher, Frances McDormand, John Lithgow, Jack Black, Charlie Spradling; *D:* John Raffo; *W:* John Raffo, William Preston Robinson; *C:* Bernd Heinl; *M:* Brian Langsbard.

Johnny Stecchino **1992 (R)** A breathless, charming comedy about mistaken identity, with Benigni starring as both Dante, a mild-mannered Roman bus driver, and his double, a notorious Mafioso known as "Johnny Toothpick." Dante happens to meet a lovely woman who takes exceptional interest in him, even inviting him to visit her home in Palermo. The reason she's interested is that Dante is the exact double of her husband, who has ratted on his fellow mobsters and needs a patsy to take the fall. Benigni's expressive body language and sweetness of character is well-showcased. In Italian with English subtitles. **100m/C VHS.** *IT* Roberto Benigni, Nicoletta Braschi, Paolo Bonacelli, Ignazio Pappalardo, Franco Volpi; *D:* Roberto Benigni; *W:* Roberto Benigni, Vincenzo Cerami; *C:* Giuseppe Lanci; *M:* Evan Lurie.

Johnny Suede 1/2 **1992 (R)** Hip kid with big hair wanders the city seeking an identity via retro black suede elevator shoes. Sleepy surreal comedy walks Pitt through two romantic entanglements and a rendezvous with his own rock idol in his quest for musical talent and pop singer nirvana (not necessarily in that order). Candidate for induction into the David Lynch Movie Musuem of the Weird. **97m/C VHS, DVD.** Brad Pitt, Calvin Levels, Nick Cave, Wilfredo Giovanni Clark, Alison Moir, Peter McRobbie, Tina Louise, Michael Mulheren, Catherine Keener, Samuel L. Jackson; *D:* Tom DiCillo; *W:* Tom DiCillo; *M:* Jim Farmer.

Johnny Tiger 1/2 **1966** A teacher has his hands full when he arrives at the Seminole Reservation in Florida to instruct the Indian children. **100m/C VHS.** Robert Taylor, Geraldine Brooks, Chad Everett, Brenda Scott; *D:* Paul Wendkos.

Johnny Tremain & the Sons of Liberty **1958** The story of the gallant American patriots who participated in the Boston Tea Party. **85m/C VHS, DVD.** Sebastian Cabot, Hal Stalmaster, Luana Patten, Richard Beymer; *D:* Robert Stevenson.

Johnny 2.0 1/2 **1999 (PG-13)** Contrived thriller about a genetic scientist, Johnny Dalton (Fahey), who awakens from a 15-year coma and discovers his memory has been transplanted into a clone, Johnny 2.0. Now Dalton has six days to find his duplicate before the Corporation, the group behind the procedure, decides on termination. **95m/C VHS, DVD.** Jeff Fahey, Michael Ironside, Tahnee Welch; *D:* Neill Fearnley. **CABLE**

Johnny Was 1/2 **2005 (R)** Johnny Doyle (Jones) escapes his IRA past by hiding out in London's tough Brixton neighborhood, trapped between a pirate reggae radio station and a crack-dealing gangster. His life gets tougher when former mentor Flynn (Bergin) escapes from prison and is determined to derail the Irish peace process with a new bombing campaign. Good soundtrack but inept thriller. **90m/C DVD.** *GB IR* Vinnie Jones, Patrick Bergin, Roger Daltrey, Samantha Mumba, Lennox Lewis, Eriq La Salle; *D:* Mark Hammond; *W:* Brendan Foley; *C:* Mark Moriarty.

Johnny We Hardly Knew Ye 1/2 **1977** Well-made biographical drama recounts John F. Kennedy's first political campaign for local office in Boston in 1946. **90m/C VHS.** Paul Rudd, Kevin Conway, William Prince, Burgess Meredith, Tom Berenger, Brian Dennehy, Kenneth McMillan; *D:* Gilbert Cates. **TV**

Johnny's Girl 1/2 **1995** After her mom's death, a 16-year-old (Kirshner) moves to Anchorage, Alaska to live with her wayward dad (Williams). He's a kinda con man involved in shady deals, who tries to go legit in order to give his daughter a proper home. TV movie based on the novel by Kim Rich. **92m/C VHS.** Mia Kirshner, Treat Williams, Ron White, Gloria Reuben, Shirley Douglas, Janne Mortil; *D:* John Kent Harrison.

johns 1/2 **1996 (R)** A gritty, yet predictable tale of street hustling in L.A. redeemed by intense performances by its two lead actors. It's Christmas Eve and John (Arquette) has only one thing in mind: recover his stolen money and celebrate his birthday in style. On the way, he mentors crony Donnor (Haas), who's love for John blinds him to the rules of hustling, which can only lead to tragedy. Arquette's controlled performance is on target for the cynical male lead and Haas's doe-eyed look is perfect for the slightly dim-witted naivete his character revels in. Downfall comes when first-time director Silver fails to maintain actors' intensity with uneven editing and out of place symbolism. Still, not a bad first try. **96m/C VHS, DVD.** David Arquette, Lukas Haas, Arliss Howard, Keith David, Elliott Gould, Christopher Gartin, Joshua Schaefer, Wilson Cruz, Terrence Howard, Nicky Katt, Alanna Ubach; *D:* Scott Silver; *W:* Scott Silver; *C:* Tom Richmond; *M:* Charles D. Brown.

Johnson County War **2002** The Hammett brothers, Cain (Berenger), Harry (Perry), and Dale (Storke) struggle to protect their ranch against greedy cattle barons after their property and that of other homesteaders. And in this case, the "law" in the guise of trigger-happy Hunt Lawton (Reynolds) is on the side of the bad guys. Based on the novel "Riders of Judgment" by Frederic Manfred. The story of this 1890s Wyoming range war was also covered in the film "Heaven's Gate." **178m/C VHS, DVD.** Tom Berenger, Luke Perry, Adam Storke, Burt Reynolds, Rachel Ward, Michelle Forbes, Christopher Cazenove, Jack Conley, Fay Masterson, Blu Mankuma, Silas Weir Mitchell, Ken Pogue; *D:* David S. Cass Sr.; *W:* Larry McMurtry, Diana Ossana; *C:* Doug Milsome; *M:* Sheldon Mirowitz. **CABLE**

Johnson Family Vacation 1/2 **2004 (PG-13)** Slapdash road comedy will have viewers whining miles before the end, "Are we there yet?" At a crisp 97 minutes, that is no easy feat but one managed with uninspired, corny dialogue, and not one ounce of originality as the Johnson family, headed by patriarch Nate (Cedric the Entertainer) hit the road in search of a decent premise...er, family reunion in Missouri. Recently separated from wife Dorothy (Williams), Nate hopes the trip with their three children (Bow Wow, Knowles, and Soleil) will bring them closer together and hopefully snatch the coveted reunion "family of the year" trophy from regular winner Mack (Harvey), Nate's older bro. Cedric's natural charisma somewhat elevates this washed-out "Vacation." **97m/C DVD.** Cedric the Entertainer, Vanessa L(ynne) Williams, Bow Wow, Steve Harvey, Solange Knowles, Shannon Elizabeth, Aloma Wright, Shari Headley, Jennifer Freeman, Lee Garlington, Gabby Soleil, Philip Daniel Bolden, Rodney B. Perry, Christopher B. Duncan; ***Cameos:*** Kurupt; *D:* Christopher Erskin; *W:* Todd R. Jones, Earl Richey Jones; *C:* Shawn Maurer, Shawn Maurer; *M:* Richard Gibbs, Richard Gibbs.

A Joke of Destiny, Lying in Wait Around the Corner Like a Bandit *A Joke of Destiny* **1984 (PG)** A irreverent satire about a Minister of the Interior (Tognazzi, of "La Cage aux Folles" fame) who becomes trapped in his high-tech limousine before a vital press conference. An exaggerated vision of Italian bureaucracy. With English subtitles. **105m/C VHS.** *IT* Ugo Tognazzi, Piera Degli Esposti, Gastone Moschin, Renzo Montagnani, Valeria Golino; *D:* Lina Wertmuller; *W:* Lina Wertmuller.

The Jolly Boys' Last Stand **2000** Spider (Serkis) is leaving behind his loutish, hard-drinking mates, known as the Jolly Boys, after proposing to girlfriend Annie (Craig). His best man Des (Twomey) decides to make a pre-wedding video for the groom as a gift. Then Vinnie (Baron Cohen) also goes domestic, which throws the rest of the gang into a tizzy and the video turns into a group effort with unexpected results. Ragged (and amiable) debut for writer/director Payne that was shot in 1998. **88m/C DVD.** *GB* Andy Serkis, Sacha Baron Cohen, Milo Twomey, Rebecca Craig, Jo Martin; *D:* Christopher Payne; *W:* Christopher Payne; *C:* Will Jacob, Robin Cox; *M:* Jeremy Panufnik.

The Jolly Paupers 1/2 *Freylekhe Kabtsonim* **1938** A pre-war comedy made in Warsaw about two small-town Jews who try to achieve fame and fortune in the face of setbacks, community quarrels, and insanity. In Yiddish with English subtitles. **62m/B VHS.** Shimon Dzigan, Yisroel Shumacher, Max Bozyk, Menasha Oppenheim; *D:* Zygmund Turkow.

Jolson Sings Again **1949** This sequel to "The Jolson Story" brings back Larry Parks as the ebullient entertainer, with Jolson himself dubbing Parks's voice for the songs. Picking up where the other film ended, the movie chronicles Jolson's comeback in the 1940s and his tireless work with the USO overseas during WWII and the Korean War. ♫ After You've Gone; Chinatown, My Chinatown; Give My Regards to Broadway; I Only Have Eyes For You; I'm Just Wild About Harry; You Made Me Love You; I'm Looking Over a Four-Leaf Clover; Is It True What They Say About Dixie?; Ma Blushin' Rose. **96m/C VHS, DVD.** Larry Parks, William Demarest, Barbara Hale, Bill Goodwin; *D:* Henry Levin; *M:* George Duning.

The Jolson Story **1946** A smash Hollywood bio of Jolson, from his childhood to super-stardom. Features dozens of vintage songs from Jolson's parade of hits. Jolson himself dubbed the vocals for Parks, rejuvenating his own career in the process. ♫ Swanee; You Made Me Love You; By the Light of the Silvery Moon; I'm Sitting On Top of the World; There's a Rainbow Round My Shoulder; My Mammy; Rock-A-Bye Your Baby With a Dixie Melody; Liza; Waiting for the Robert E. Lee. **128m/C VHS, DVD.** Larry Parks, Evelyn Keyes, William Demarest, Bill Goodwin, Tamara Shayne, John Alexander, Jimmy Lloyd, Ludwig Donath, Scotty Beckett; *D:* Alfred E. Green; *M:* Morris Stoloff. Oscars '46: Sound, Scoring/Musical.

Jon Jost's Frameup *Frameup* **1993** Cocky ex-con Ricky Lee hooks up with dizzy waitress Beth Ann and they head out on a 3000-mile nightmare road trip to California. Free-form story shot in 10 days. **91m/C VHS.** Howard Swain, Nancy Carlin; *D:* Jon Jost; *W:* Jon Jost.

Jonah Hex **2010** Based on the DC Comics graphic novel. Having survived death, Jonah Hex (Brolin), a scarred, gunslinging bounty hunter, has ties to both the natural and supernatural worlds. If he wants to maintain his freedom though, he must agree to accept the military's job to stop voodoo practitioner Quentin Turnbull (Malkovich) from literally unleashing Hell and raising an army of the dead. **m/C DVD.** *US* Josh Brolin, John Malkovich, Megan Fox, Michael Shannon, Michael Fassbender, Aidan Quinn, David Patrick Kelly, Luke James Fleischmann, Julia Jones, Will Arnett; *D:* Jimmy Hayward; *W:* Mark Neveldine, Brian Taylor; *C:* Mitchell Amundsen; *M:* John Powell.

Jonah Who Will Be 25 in the Year 2000 1/2 *Jonas—Qui Aura 25 Ans en l'An 2000* **1976** A group of eight friends, former 60s radicals, try to adjust to growing older and coping with life in the 70s. The eccentric octet include a disillusioned journalist turned gambler, an unorthodox teacher, and a grocery store cashier who gives away food to the elderly. Wonderful performances highlight this social comedy. In French with English subtitles. **110m/C VHS.** *SI* Jean-Luc Bideau, Myriam Meziere, Miou-Miou, Jacques Denis, Rufus, Dominique Labourier, Roger Jendly, Miriam Boyer, Raymond Bussieres, Jonah; *D:* Alain Tanner; *W:* Alain Tanner; *C:* Renato Berta; *M:* Jean-Marie Senia. Natl. Soc. Film Critics '76: Screenplay.

Jonas Brothers: The 3D Concert Experience 1/2 **2009 (G)** Disney flick, showcasing the squeaky-clean pop trio, is tailor-made for the brothers' squealing young teen girl demographic. The performance part is taken mainly from their 2008 Anaheim, CA arena show (which is also where the 3D effects appear) with some brief New York appearances and the usual mayhem with Joe, Nick, and Kevin being chased by their rabid fans. Demi Lovato and Taylor Swift drop by to do a couple of songs. **76m/C DVD.** *US* Joe Jonas, Kevin Jonas, Nick Jonas; ***D:*** Bruce Hendricks; ***C:*** Mitchell Amundsen, Reed Smoot. Golden Raspberries '09: Worst Actor (Jonas), Worst Actor (Jonas, Jonas).

Jonathan Livingston Seagull 🦴🦴 1/2 **1973 (G)** Based on the best-selling novella by Richard Bach, this film quietly envisions a world of love, understanding, achievement, hope and individuality. **99m/C VHS.** James Franciscus, Juliet Mills; ***D:*** Hall Bartlett; ***M:*** Neil Diamond. Golden Globes '74: Score.

The Joneses 2010 (R) A fake family is commissioned by a marketing company to move into a suburban neighborhood and extol new luxury goods to the neighbors in an effort to make them popular. Only the fakes have as many issues as real families. **93m/C DVD.** *US* David Duchovny, Demi Moore, Amber Heard, Gary Cole, Chris(topher) Williams, Glenne Headley, Lauren Hutton; ***D:*** Derrick Borte; ***W:*** Derrick Borte; ***C:*** Yaron Orbach; ***M:*** Nick Urata.

Joni 🦴🦴 **1979 (G)** An inspirational story based on the real life of Tada (playing herself) who was seriously injured in a diving accident, and her conquering of the odds. A born-again feature film based on the book by Tada. **75m/C VHS.** Joni Eareckson Tada, Bert Remsen, Katherine De Hetre, Cooper Huckabee; ***D:*** James F. Collier.

Jory 🦴🦴 **1972 (PG)** A young man's father is killed in a saloon fight, and he must grow up quickly to survive. **96m/C VHS, DVD.** Robby Benson, B.J. Thomas, John Marley; ***D:*** Jorge Fons.

Joseph 🦴🦴 1/2 **1995** Following "Abraham" and "Jacob" comes the Old Testament story of young Joseph (Mercurio), beloved son of Jacob, who's sold into slavery by his envious older brothers. Joseph is bought by the Pharoah's chief steward, Potiphar (Kingsley), and, after a long series of tribulations, rises to become a power in Egypt, which unexpectedly leads Joseph to hold the fate of his long-lost family in his hands. Filmed in Morocco. **240m/C VHS, DVD.** Paul Mercurio, Ben Kingsley, Martin Landau, Lesley Ann Warren, Warren Clarke, Alice Krige, Dominique Sanda, Stefano Dionisi, Valeria Cavalli, Peter Eyre, Timothy Bateson, Jamie Glover, Michael Attwell; ***D:*** Roger Young; ***W:*** Lionel Chetwynd, James Carrington; ***C:*** Raffaele Mertes; ***M:*** Marco Frisina.

Joseph and the Amazing Technicolor Dreamcoat 🦴🦴🦴 **2000** Something more than a filmed stage presentation of the Webber-Rice musical, but something less than a real movie. It begins with a school assembly hall where the narrator (Friedman) bursts into song and tells the biblical story of Joseph (Osmond). Then the scene shifts to soundstages. The catchy songs often seem to be on the verge of morphing into "Cats" or "Phantom of the Opera." Overall, the production values are good and the sound is excellent. **78m/C VHS, DVD.** Donny Osmond, Richard Attenborough, Joan Collins, Maria Friedman; ***D:*** David Mallet, Steven Pimlott; ***C:*** Nicholas D. Knowland; ***M:*** Andrew Lloyd Webber, Tim Rice. **VIDEO**

Joseph Andrews 🦴🦴 **1977 (R)** This adaptation of a 1742 Henry Fielding novel chronicles the rise of Joseph Andrews from servant to personal footman (and fancy) of Lady Booby. **99m/C VHS, DVD.** *GB* Ann-Margret, Peter Firth, Jim Dale, Michael Hordern, Beryl Reid; ***D:*** Tony Richardson; ***W:*** Chris Bryant, Allan Scott; ***C:*** David Watkin; ***M:*** John Addison.

Josepha 🦴🦴🦴 **1982 (R)** A husband and wife, both actors, are forced to re-examine their relationship when the wife finds a new love while on a film location. In French with English subtitles. **114m/C VHS.** *FR* Miou-Miou, Claude Brasseur, Bruno Cremer; ***D:*** Christopher Frank.

The Josephine Baker Story 🦴🦴🦴 **1990 (R)** Biopic of exotic entertainer/activist Josephine Baker, an Afro-American woman from St. Louis who found superstardom in pre-WWII Europe, but repeated racism and rejection in the U.S. At times trite treatment turns her eventful life into a standard rise-and-fall showbiz tale, but a great cast and lavish scope pull it through. Whitfield recreates Baker's (sometimes topless) dance routines; Carol Dennis dubs her singing. Filmed on location in Budapest. **129m/C VHS, DVD.** Lynn Whitfield, Ruben Blades, David Dukes, Craig T. Nelson, Louis Gossett Jr., Kene Holliday, Vivian Bonnell; ***D:*** Brian Gibson; ***M:*** Ralph Burns. **CABLE**

Josh and S.A.M. 🦴🦴 **1993 (PG-13)** Road movie for youngsters with a twist: the driver can barely see over the dashboard. Josh and Sam are brothers whose parents are splitting. They cope by taking off on their own. Sam, meanwhile has been convinced by Josh that he's not a real boy at all, but rather a S.A.M.: Strategically Altered Mutant. Weber's directorial debut will appeal to young kids, but adults will see over the dashboard and through the transparent plot. **97m/C VHS.** Jacob Tierney, Noah Fleiss, Martha Plimpton, Joan Allen, Christopher Penn, Stephen Tobolowsky, Ronald Guttman; ***D:*** Billy Weber; ***W:*** Frank Deese; ***C:*** Don Burgess; ***M:*** Thomas Newman.

Josh Kirby...Time Warrior: Chapter 1, Planet of the Dino-Knights 🦴🦴 1/2 **1995 (PG)** Time-traveling 14-year-old Josh Kirby is accidently zapped to the 25th-century where fierce warriors ride dinosaurs and a madman is out to destroy the universe. The first tale in a fantasy series designed as an old-fashioned movie serial, complete with cliff-hanger ending. **88m/C VHS, DVD.** Corbin Allred, Jennifer Burns, Derek Webster, John De Mita; ***D:*** Ernest Farino; ***W:*** Ethan Reiff, Cyrus Voris, Paul Callisi.

Josh Kirby... Time Warrior: Chapter 2, The Human Pets 🦴🦴 1/2 **1995 (PG)** Josh and his friends now find themselves in the year 70,370—held hostage by the enormous Fatlings, who regard their human finds as pet-like action toys. **90m/C VHS, DVD.** Corbin Allred, Jennifer Burns; ***D:*** Frank Arnold; ***W:*** Ethan Reiff, Cyrus Voris, Paul Callisi.

Josh Kirby... Time Warrior: Chapter 3, Trapped on Toyworld 🦴🦴 1/2 **1995 (PG)** Josh is stranded away from his friends on the strange planet of Toyworld and must rely on the lifelike creations of a toy magnate to defend himself from the villainous Dr. Zoetrope. **90m/C VHS, DVD.** Corbin Allred, Jennifer Burns, Derek Webster, Sharon Lee Jones, Buck Kartalian, Barrie Ingham; ***D:*** Frank Arnold; ***W:*** Nick Paine.

Josh Kirby... Time Warrior: Chapter 4, Eggs from 70 Million B.C. 🦴🦴 1/2 **1995 (PG)** Josh and his pals finds themselves in a military compound that is under attack and encounter some very hungry alien worms. **93m/C VHS, DVD.** Corbin Allred, Jennifer Burns, Derek Webster, Gary Kasper, Barrie Ingham; ***D:*** Mark Manos.

Josh Kirby... Time Warrior: Chapter 5, Journey to the Magic Cavern 🦴🦴 1/2 **1996 (PG)** Josh and pals find themselves in the center of a planet where they are befriended by the weird Mushroom People who are under siege by a monster known as "the Muncher." **93m/C VHS, DVD.** Corbin Allred, Jennifer Burns, Derek Webster, Michael Hagiwara, Barrie Ingham; ***D:*** Ernest Farino; ***W:*** Ethan Reiff, Cyrus Voris.

Josh Kirby... Time Warrior: Chapter 6, Last Battle for the Universe 🦴🦴 1/2 **1996 (PG)** Josh is ready to get back to his own time but first he must survive a battle between long-feuding rivals of the timebelt. **90m/C VHS, DVD.** Corbin Allred, Jennifer Burns, Derek Webster, Barrie Ingham; ***D:*** Frank Arnold; ***W:*** Ethan Reiff, Cyrus Voris.

Joshua 🦴 *Black Rider* **1976 (R)** Western drama about a vigilante who tracks down the group of outlaws that killed his mother. **75m/C VHS, DVD.** Fred Williamson, Isela Vega; ***D:*** Larry Spangler.

Joshua 🦴🦴 1/2 **2002 (G)** Joshua (Goldwyn) is a stranger to the 19th-century midwestern community of Auburn. He rents a barn and sets himself up as a woodworker and all-around helpful guy. Seeing that the black community's church is damaged, Joshua sets out to rebuild it and soon has the entire town pitching in to help. But traditionalist priest Father Tardone (Abraham) is askance when townsfolk begin to think Joshua has miraculous powers. Spiritually uplifting without being preachy; based on the novel by Father Joseph Girzone. **90m/C VHS, DVD.** Tony Goldwyn, F. Murray Abraham, Kurt Fuller, Giancarlo Giannini, Stacy Edwards, Colleen Camp; ***D:*** Jon Purdy; ***W:*** Brad Mirman, Keith Giglio; ***C:*** Bruce Surtees; ***M:*** Michael W. Smith.

Joshua 🦴🦴🦴 **2007 (R)** New twist on the creepy-kid movie trades demon possession for subtle psychological twists and turns. Joshua (Kogan) is a tidy, disconnected child prodigy who goes from simply odd to creepy after the birth of his sister. Meanwhile, his mother Abby (Farmiga) descends into postpartum depression and dad Brad (Rockwell) struggles to hold his family together as pets die and Granny has an accident. Director Ratliff maintains suspense by never showing all his cards, but it leaves you with a question: is there a method to the madness, or is this just a series of events in the lives of some screwed-up people? **105m/C DVD.** *US* Sam Rockwell, Vera Farmiga, Dallas Roberts, Celia Weston, Michael McKean, Jacob Kogan; ***D:*** George Ratliff; ***W:*** George Ratliff, David Gilbert; ***C:*** Benoit Debie; ***M:*** Nico Muhly.

Joshua Then and Now 🦴🦴🦴 **1985 (R)** When a Jewish-Canadian novelist (Woods) is threatened by the breakup of his marriage to his WASPy wife, compounded by a gay scandal, he re-examines his picaresque history, including his life with his gangster father (Arkin). A stirring story that is enhanced by a strong performance by Woods, as well as a picturesque Canadian backdrop. Adapted by Mordecai Richler from his own novel. **102m/C VHS.** *CA* James Woods, Gabrielle Lazure, Alan Arkin, Michael Sarrazin, Chuck Shamata, Linda Sorensen, Alan Scarfe, Alexander Knox, Robert Joy, Ken Campbell; ***D:*** Ted Kotcheff; ***W:*** Mordecai Richler; ***M:*** Philippe Sarde. Genie '86: Support. Actor (Arkin), Support. Actress (Sorensen).

Josie and the Pussycats 🦴🦴 **2001 (PG-13)** This Josie and company have almost as many dimensions as the cartoon from whence they came. Simple plot has Josie's band looking for their big break when record company exec Wyatt Frame, looking for a new sound, spots our heroines and remakes them as teen sensations. Wyatt is partnered with Fiona (Posey, chewing scenery like a starving dog in an Alpo factory) in a scheme to use pop music to control the minds of teens. Basically harmless parody of the pop music biz chokes on its own product-placing hypocrisy, but gets by on the obvious charms of leads Cook, Reid, and Dawson. **99m/C VHS, DVD.** *US* Rachael Leigh Cook, Tara Reid, Rosario Dawson, Parker Posey, Alan Cumming, Gabriel Mann, Paulo Costanzo, Tom Butler, Missi Pyle, Carson Daly; ***Cameos:*** Seth Green, Breckin Meyer, Donald Adeosun Faison; ***D:*** Deborah Kaplan, Harry Elfont; ***W:*** Deborah Kaplan, Harry Elfont; ***C:*** Matthew Libatique; ***M:*** John (Gianni) Frizzell.

Jour de Fete 🦴🦴🦴 1/2 *The Big Day; Holiday* **1948** Tati's first film, dealing with a French postman's accelerated efforts at efficiency after viewing a motivational film of the American post service. Wonderful slapstick moments. In French with English subtitles. **79m/B VHS.** *FR* Jacques Tati, Guy Decomble, Paul Fankeur, Santa Relli; ***D:*** Jacques Tati; ***W:*** Henri Marquet, Jacques Tati; ***C:*** Jacques Mercanton; ***M:*** Jean Yatove.

Journey 🦴 **1972 (PG)** Violent story of a girl who is rescued from the Sagueney River and falls in love with her rescuer. Choosing to remain in the remote pioneer community of this "hero," she brings everyone bad luck and misery. **87m/C VHS.** *CA* Genevieve Bujold, John Vernon; ***D:*** Paul Almond.

Journey 🦴🦴 1/2 **1995 (PG)** Eleven-year-old Journey (Pomeranc) and his teenaged sister Cat (Dushku) are abandoned by their unhappy, restless mother Min (Tilly) at the home of her parents, Marcus (Robards) and Lottie (Fricker). Marcus is an amatuer photographer and Journey searches through the family photo albums to find reasons for his mother's leaving as he and his grandfather slowly build their relationship. Based on the book by Patricia MacLachlan. **98m/C VHS.** Max Pomeranc, Jason Robards Jr., Brenda Fricker, Eliza Dushku, Meg Tilly; ***D:*** Tom McLoughlin; ***W:*** Patricia MacLachlan; ***C:*** Kees Van Oostrum. **TV**

Journey Back to Oz 🦴🦴 1/2 **1971** Animated special features Dorothy and Toto returning to visit their friends in the magical land of Oz. **90m/C VHS, DVD.** ***D:*** Hal Sutherland; ***W:*** Fred Ladd, Norm Prescott; ***M:*** Walter Scharf, James Van Heusen; ***V:*** Liza Minnelli, Ethel Merman, Paul Lynde, Milton Berle, Mickey Rooney, Danny Thomas, Herschel Bernardi, Margaret Hamilton.

Journey Beneath the Desert 🦴🦴 *Antinea, l'Amante Della Citta Sepolta* **1961** Three engineers discover the lost-but-always-found-in-the-movies kingdom of Atlantis when their helicopter's forced down in the sunny Sahara. A poor hostess with a rotten disposition, the mean sub-saharan queen doesn't roll out the welcome mat for her grounded guests, so a beautiful slave babe helps them make a hasty exit. Dawdling Euro production with adequate visuals. **105m/C VHS.** *FR IT* Haya Harareet, Jean-Louis Trintignant, James Westmoreland, Amedeo Nazzari, Georges Riviere, Giulia Rubini, Gabriele Tinti, Gian Marie Volonte; ***D:*** Edgar G. Ulmer, Giuseppe Masini, Frank Borzage.

Journey for Margaret 🦴🦴🦴 **1942** Young and Day star as an expectant American couple living in London during WWII so Young can cover the war for a newspaper back home. After she loses her baby during an air raid, Day heads back to the States. Young stays in London where he meets two young orphans and takes them under his wing. He decides to take them back to the United States and adopt them, but problems arise. A real tearjerker and a good story that shows the war through the eyes of children. O'Brien's first film. Based on the book by William L. White. **81m/B VHS.** Robert Young, Laraine Day, Fay Bainter, Signe Hasso, Margaret O'Brien, Nigel Bruce, G.P. (Tim) Huntley Jr., William Severn, Doris Lloyd, Halliwell Hobbes, Jill Esmond; ***D:*** Woodbridge S. Van Dyke.

Journey into Fear 🦴🦴🦴 **1942** During WWII, an American armaments expert is smuggled out of Istanbul, but Axis agents are close behind. From the novel by Eric Ambler. **71m/B VHS.** Joseph Cotten, Dolores Del Rio, Orson Welles, Agnes Moorehead, Norman Foster; ***D:*** Norman Foster; ***C:*** Karl Struss.

Journey into Fear 🦴 1/2 *Burn Out* **1974** A remake of the 1942 Orson Welles classic about a geologist ensnared in Turkish intrigue and murder. **96m/C VHS.** *CA* Sam Waterston, Vincent Price, Shelley Winters, Donald Pleasence, Zero Mostel, Yvette Mimieux, Ian McShane; ***D:*** Daniel Mann; ***M:*** Alex North.

The Journey of August King 🦴🦴 1/2 **1995 (PG-13)** Adapted by Ehle from his own 1971 novel, set in 1815, about a runaway slave (Newton) protected by a lonely farmer against the landowner and posse tracking her down. August King (Patric), a widower on his way home from town, comes upon Annalees (Newton), prize possession of powerful slaveowner Olaf Singletary (Drake). August, a highly principled man, resists helping her at first, for fear of breaking the law and losing his farm and only remaining possessions. But he rises to higher moral ground, deciding to help her find freedom, whatever the consequences. Director Duigan ("Sirens") crafts a thoughtful, but not particularly suspenseful, period piece of early American history. Patric/Newton relationship reflects the gradual feel of the film. Drake booms as slaveowner. Includes brief brutal scene of slave torture. **91m/C VHS, DVD.** Jason Patric, Thandie Newton, Larry Drake, Sam Waterston; ***D:*** John Duigan; ***W:*** John Ehle; ***C:*** Slawomir Idziak; ***M:*** Stephen Endelman.

Journey of Honor 🦴🦴 1/2 **1991 (PG-13)** During a civil war in 17th century Japan, a nearly defeated Shogun sends his son,

Lord Mayeda, to Spain to buy guns from King Phillip III. Along the way he must fight shipboard spies and fierce storms, and once Mayeda arrives in Spain, he is confronted by the evil Duke Don Pedro. In defeating Don Pedro, Mayeda saves King Phillip, gets his guns, and wins the love of Lady Cecilia. To get revenge, Don Pedro plots to capture the Japanese ship and enslave everyone on board. Lots of action and fine acting. Based on a story by martial artist Sho Kosugi. **107m/C VHS.** Sho Kosugi, David Essex, Kane (Takeshi) Kosugi, Christopher Lee, Norman Lloyd, Ronald Pickup, John Rhys-Davies, Dylan Kussman, Toshiro Mifune; ***D:*** Gordon Hessler.

Journey of Hope 🦴🦴🦴 1/2 **1990 (PG)** Powerful drama about Kurdish family that sells its material possessions in hopes of emigrating legally to Switzerland, where life will surely be better. During the perilous journey, smugglers take their money and the family must attempt crossing the formidable slopes of the Swiss Mountains on foot. Based on a true story. In Turkish with English subtitles. **111m/C VHS.** *SI* Necmettin Cobanoglu, Nur Surer, Emin Sivas, Yaman Okay, Mathias Gnaedinger, Dietmar Schoenherr; ***D:*** Xavier Koller; ***W:*** Xavier Koller. Oscars '90: Foreign Film.

The Journey of Jared Price 🦴🦴 1/2 **2000** Sweet-natured but predictable gay coming of age tale. 19-year-old Jared (Spears) leaves Georgia for California and self-discovery, winding up in a youth hostel where he's befriended by Robert (Jacobson), who wants to be more than buddies. Jared eventually gets a job as a caretaker to elderly, blind Mrs. Haines (Craigg) and is soon pulled into a destructive relationship with the older Matthew (Tyler), Mrs. Haines son. **96m/C VHS, DVD.** Corey Spears, Josh Jacobson, Steve Tyler, Rocki Craigg; ***D:*** Dustin Lance Black; ***W:*** Dustin Lance Black; ***C:*** Tony Croll; ***M:*** Damon Intrabartolo.

The Journey of Natty Gann 🦴🦴🦴 1/2 **1985 (PG)** With the help of a wolf (brilliantly portrayed by a dog) and a drifter, a 14-year-old girl travels across the country in search of her father in this warm and touching film. Excellent Disney representation of life during the Great Depression. **101m/C VHS, DVD.** Meredith Salenger, John Cusack, Ray Wise, Scatman Crothers, Lainie Kazan, Verna Bloom; ***D:*** Jeremy Paul Kagan; ***W:*** Jeanne Rosenberg; ***C:*** Dick Bush; ***M:*** James Horner.

Journey Through Rosebud 🦴🦴 **1972** A draft-doging youth (Tabori) from San Francisco wanders onto a Sioux reservation just before Native American youths protest at Wounded Knee and the confrontation becomes violent. He complicates the situation by trying to befriend an alcoholic local (Forster) and his ex-wife (Racimo). Simplistic script and uneven performances add up to a wasted opportunity. **93m/C VHS.** Robert Forster, Eddie Little Sky, Kristopher Tabori, Victoria Racimo; ***D:*** Tom Gries.

The Journey to Kafiristan 🦴🦴 *Die Reise nach Kafiristan* **2001** In 1939, Zurich writer Annemarie Schwarzenbach (Hain) and Geneva ethnologist Ella Maillart (Petri) drive from Switzerland to a remote valley in Afghanistan. Ella's on a scientific expedition but Annemarie, just out of a drug rehab clinic, is out to test her emotional and sexual limits. Based on a true story. German with subtitles. **100m/C VHS, DVD.** *GE SI NL* Jeanette Hain, Nina Petri, Matthew Burton, Ozlen Soydan; ***D:*** Donatello Dubini, Fosco Dubini; ***W:*** Donatello Dubini, Fosco Dubini; ***C:*** Matthias Kaelin.

Journey to Spirit Island 🦴🦴 1/2 **1992 (PG)** A young Native American girl dreams of her ancestors who are buried on Spirit Island, an ancient burial ground. However, the island is now scheduled to be developed into a resort. With the help of three friends the girl tries to protect the land. Filmed in the Pacific Northwest. **93m/C VHS.** Brandon Douglas, Gabriel Damon, Tony Acierto, Nick Ramus, Marie Antoinette Rodgers, Tarek McCarthy; ***D:*** Laszlo Pal.

Journey to the Center of the Earth 🦴🦴🦴 **1959** A scientist and student undergo a hazardous journey to find the center of the earth and along the way they find the lost city of Atlantis. Based upon the Jules Verne novel. **132m/C VHS, DVD.** James Mason, Pat Boone, Arlene Dahl, Diane Baker, Thayer David, Alan Napier, Peter Ronson; ***D:*** Henry Levin; ***W:*** Charles Brackett, Robert Gunter, Walter Reisch; ***C:*** Leo Tover; ***M:*** Bernard Herrmann.

Journey to the Center of the Earth 1988 (PG) A young nanny and two teenage boys discover Atlantis while exploring a volcano. **83m/C VHS, DVD.** Nicola Cowper, Paul Carafotes, Ilan Mitchell-Smith; ***D:*** Rusty Lemorande; ***W:*** Rusty Lemorande, Kitty Chalmers.

Journey to the Center of the Earth 🦴🦴 **1999** Jules Verne's 1864 fantasy made its way to cable in this adventurous retelling. Geologist Theodore Lytton (Williams) is hired by wealthy Alice Hastings (Bergen) to find her husband, Casper (Brown), who disappeared seven years earlier during an expedition to a volcano in New Zealand. Lytton and his compatriots descend into deep caverns and discover a tunnel system leading to the planet's center and a new civilization that Hastings has usurped for his own greedy purposes. There's derring-do and even babes in animal-hide bikinis. **139m/C VHS, DVD.** Treat Williams, Jeremy London, Tushka Bergen, Hugh Keays-Byrne, Bryan Brown, Sarah Chadwick, Petra Yared, Tessa Wells; ***D:*** George Miller; ***W:*** Thomas Baum; ***C:*** John Stokes; ***M:*** Bruce Rowland. **CABLE**

Journey to the Center of the Earth 🦴🦴 1/2 **2008** Edward Dennison (Fonda) vanished four years ago while on an expedition to find an Alaskan passage leading into the center of the earth. His wealthy wife Martha (Pratt) hires anthropologist Jonathan Brock (Schroder) to find Edward, accompanied by his journalist nephew Abel (Grayhm) and Russian miner Sergei (Dopud) whose brother disappeared on the same journey. After discovering the passage, the four find it leads to an evolving prehistoric world and a primitive tribe that worships the now power-mad Edward. But a rival tribe could prove deadly to them all. Loose adaptation of the Jules Verne adventure. **89m/C DVD.** Rick Schroder, Victoria Pratt, Peter Fonda, Mike Dopud, Jonathan Brewer, Tim James, Steve Grahym; ***W:*** Thomas Baum; ***C:*** Philip Linzey; ***M:*** Rene Dupere. **TV**

Journey to the Center of the Earth 🦴🦴 1/2 **2008 (PG)** Volcanologist Trevor Anderson ventures to Iceland with some young charges to continue the research of his missing brother Max, whose notes in the margins of a tattered copy of Jules Verne's classic sci-fi fantasy novel help guide the group. Soon they're battling ancient flora and fauna in, you guessed it, the earth's core. Only problem is they have to find their way out or risk being trapped. The CGI is wild, with carnivorous plants, flying piranhas, dinosaurs and other creepy creatures, and affable Fraser keeps it all cheery, but the plot's a bit thin and the premise is, well, silly. Just enjoy the thrill-ride and don't think too much. **92m/C DVD.** *US* Brendan Fraser, Josh Hutcherson, Anita Briem; ***D:*** Eric Brevig; ***W:*** Michael D. Weiss, Jennifer Flackett, Marc Levin; ***C:*** Chuck Shuman; ***M:*** Andrew Lockington.

Journey to the Center of Time 🦴 1/2 **1967** A scientist and his crew are hurled into a time trap when a giant reactor explodes. **83m/C VHS, DVD.** Lyle Waggoner, Scott Brady, Gigi Perreau, Anthony Eisley; ***D:*** David L. Hewitt.

Journey to the End of the Night 🦴🦴 **2006 (R)** Rosso (Glenn) is a shady ex-pat American who owns a brothel in Sao Paulo, Brazil, that he runs with his gambler son Paul (Fraser). A drug deal is meant to get them out of the sex business and Rosso into a nicer life with his squeeze Angie (Sandino Moreno) and their young kid (who may actually be Paul's because Angie used to be a hooker). Paul is planning a doublecross but the deal starts going south when the drug mule dies and Rosso presses their Nigerian dishwasher Wemba (Mos Def) into service. Sleazy crime thriller that has its moments although it doesn't hang together. **98m/C DVD.** Scott Glenn, Brendan Fraser, Mos Def, Catalina Sandino Moreno, Alice Braga; ***D:*** Eric Eason; ***W:*** Eric Eason; ***C:*** Ulrich Burtin; ***M:*** Elia Cmiral.

Journey to the Far Side of the Sun 🦴🦴🦴 *Doppelganger* **1969 (G)** Chaos erupts in the Earth's scientific community when it is discovered that a second, identical Earth is on the other side of the Sun. Both planets end up sending out identical exploratory missions. The denouement is worth the journey. **92m/C VHS, DVD.** *GB* Roy Thinnes, Ian Hendry, Lynn Loring, Patrick Wymark, Loni von Friedl, Herbert Lom, Ed Bishop; ***D:*** Robert Parrish; ***W:*** Gerry Anderson; ***C:*** John Read; ***M:*** Barry Gray.

Journey to the Lost City 🦴 1/2 *Tiger of Bengal* **1958** Architect living in India happens upon a lost city, the rulership of which is being contested by two brothers. In the midst of fighting snakes and tigers, he falls in love with Paget, a beautiful dancer. This feature is actually a poorly edited hybrid of two Lang German adventures, "Der Tiger von Eschnapur" and "Das Indische Grabmal" merged for U.S. release. **95m/C VHS, DVD.** *FR IT GE* Debra Paget, Paul (Christian) Hubschmid, Walter Reyer, Claus Holm, Sabine Bethmann, Valeri Inkizhinov, Rene Deltgen, Luciana Paluzzi; ***D:*** Fritz Lang.

Journeys with George 🦴🦴 1/2 **2002** On the road with George W. Bush's 2000 presidential campaign, NBC News producer Alexandra Pelosi—daughter of California congresswoman Nancy Pelosi—offers a day-in-the-grinding-life view of a pool reporter captured via camcorder yet stops short of any meaty behind-the-scenes strategy sessions. Allows W to show off his easy-going manner while sidestepping any heavy topics. **76m/C VHS, DVD.** ***Cameos:*** George W. Bush, Tom Brokaw, Barbara Bush, George Bush, Howard Dean, Alexandra Pelosi, Erin Brockovich-Ellis, Jeb Bush, Laura Bush, Dick Cheney, Al Gore, John McCain; ***D:*** Alexandra Pelosi; ***W:*** Alexandra Pelosi; ***C:*** Alexandra Pelosi. **TV**

Joy House 🦴🦴 *The Love Cage; Les Felins* **1964** French playboy Marc (Delon) seduces the wife of an American mobster who sends his goons after him. Marc hides out by becoming the chauffeur to Barbara (Albright) at her chateau, which is also where he meets his employer's niece, Melinda (Fonda). Soon, Marc is part of a romantic triangle—or is it quartet since Barbara's lover, Vincent (Oumansky), is also living there. And don't forget the gangsters, who certainly haven't forgotten Marc. Complicated plot with no particular payoff. **98m/B VHS, DVD.** Jane Fonda, Alain Delon, Lola Albright, Andre Oumansky, Sorrell Booke; ***D:*** Rene Clement; ***W:*** Rene Clement; ***C:*** Henri Decae; ***M:*** Lalo Schifrin.

The Joy Luck Club 🦴🦴🦴 **1993 (R)** Universal themes in mother/daughter relationships are explored in a context Hollywood first rejected as too narrow, but which proved to be a modest sleeper hit. Tan skillfully weaves the plot of her 1989 best-seller into a screenplay which centers around young June's (Ming-Na) going-away party. Slowly the stories of four Chinese women, who meet weekly to play mah-jongg, are unraveled. Each vignette reveals life in China for the four women and the tragedies they survived, before reaching into the present to capture the relationships between the mothers and their daughters. Powerful, relevant, and moving. **136m/C VHS, DVD.** Tsai Chin, Kieu Chinh, France Nuyen, Rosalind Chao, Tamlyn Tomita, Lisa Lu, Lauren Tom, Ming Na, Michael Paul Chan, Andrew McCarthy, Christopher Rich, Russell Wong, Victor Wong, Vivian Wu, Jack Ford, Diane Baker; ***D:*** Wayne Wang; ***W:*** Amy Tan, Ronald Bass.

The Joy of Knowledge 🦴 1/2 *Le Gai Savoir* **1965** Godard's experimental use of language and image in a plotless narrative. Berto and Leaud sit together on a bare sound stage and are exposed to popular culture through images, word association, and conversation. In French with English subtitles. **96m/C VHS.** *FR* Juliet Berto, Jean-Pierre Leaud; ***D:*** Jean-Luc Godard; ***W:*** Jean-Luc Godard.

Joy of Living 🦴🦴🦴 **1938** Vintage screwball farce finds successful songstress Maggie (Dunne) the sole support of her n'er-do-well family. Maggie's aggressively courted by playboy Dan Brewster (Faribanks Jr.) and finally (after numerous silly complications) they fall in love. ♫You Couldn't Be Cuter; A Heavenly Party; What's Good About Goodnight; Just Let Me Look At You. **90m/B VHS.** Irene Dunne, Douglas Fairbanks Jr., Alice Brady, Guy Kibbee, Jean Dixon, Eric Blore, Lucille Ball, Warren Hymer, Billy Gilbert, Frank Milan; ***D:*** Tay Garnett; ***W:*** Graham Baker, Allan Scott, Gene Towne; ***C:*** Joseph Walker; ***M:*** Jerome Kern, Dorothy Fields.

Joy of Sex 🦴 **1984 (R)** An undercover narcotics agent is sent to Southern California's Richard M. Nixon High School to investigate the school's extracurricular activities. Typical teen sex flick; no relation to the book. **93m/C VHS.** Cameron Dye, Michelle Meyrink, Colleen Camp, Christopher Lloyd, Ernie Hudson, Lisa Langlois; ***D:*** Martha Coolidge; ***W:*** Kathleen Rowell.

Joy Ride 🦴🦴🦴 **2001 (R)** Released about the same time as fellow road thriller/horror entry "Jeepers Creepers," this superior outing benefits from better humor, pacing, and performances. Nice guy Lewis (Walker), a college freshman, offers to drive friend/potential squeeze Venna (Sobieski) back home from Colorado for the holidays. Unfortunately for Lewis, roguish brother Fuller (Zahn) calls Lewis to bail him out of jail in Utah and sticks around for the ride. Fuller instigates a CB radio prank in which Lewis, imitating a woman's voice, invites a trucker with the handle Rusty Nail to the hotel room next to theirs. The next day, the man in the room is found close to death in the middle of the road, and the trio has a very angry trucker on their tail. Taut countrywide chase thrills are reminiscent of Spielberg's "Duel." Great mixture of shocks and black humor. **96m/C VHS, DVD.** *US* Paul Walker, Steve Zahn, Leelee Sobieski, Jessica Bowman, Stuart Stone, Basil Wallace, Brian Leckner; ***D:*** John Dahl; ***W:*** J.J. (Jeffrey) Abrams, Clay Tarver; ***C:*** Jeffrey Jur; ***M:*** Marco Beltrami; ***V:*** Ted Levine.

Joy Ride 2: Dead Ahead 🦴 **2008** Truck driver Rusty Nails had found someone new to slaughter. Four friends traveling to Vegas get into trouble when their car breaks down. They find a seemingly abandoned farmhouse with a working vehicle in the barn and borrow it, not knowing it belongs to the trucker/psycho, who then comes after them. **91m/C DVD.** Nick Zano, Nicki Aycox, Kyle Schmid, Laura Jordan; ***D:*** Louis Morneau; ***W:*** James Johnston, Bennett Yellin; ***C:*** Robert New. **VIDEO**

Joy Ride to Nowhere 🦴 **1978 (PG)** Two young women steal a Cadillac with $2 million in the trunk and ride away with the owner hot on their tail. **86m/C VHS.** Leslie Ackerman, Sandy Serrano, Len Lesser, Ron Ross, Speed Stearns; ***D:*** Mel Welles; ***W:*** Mel Welles; ***C:*** Bill Davies.

Joy Sticks WOOF! **1983 (R)** Joy sticks in question are down at the arcade. Businessman wants to shut down local video game palace. Inhabitants just say no. **88m/C VHS, DVD.** Joe Don Baker, Leif Green, Jim Greenleaf, Scott McGinnis, Jon(athan) Gries; ***D:*** Greydon Clark.

Joyeux Noel 🦴🦴🦴 *Merry Christmas* **2005 (PG-13)** On Christmas Eve, during World War I in France, troops on both sides of the battlefield laid down their weapons in unified holiday spirit for a performance of "Silent Night" by a German soldier, and famed tenor named Sprink, along with his wife. Drinking, cheering, and even some soccer followed, right there in the trenches. This really happened, and it makes for the perfect centerpiece in this postmodern French Christmas miracle movie. WWI is a backdrop to the human turmoil faced by German, French, and Scottish troops at war. An almost ironically surreal melodrama that's just as sad as it is joyous. Nominated for Best Foreign Film Oscar. **110m/C DVD.** *FR GE GB BE RO* Diane Kruger, Benno Furmann, Guillaume Canet, Gary Lewis, Daniel Bruhl, Steven Robertson, Lucas Belvaux, Bernard Le Coq, Ian Richardson, Robin Laing, Suzanne Flon, Michel Serrault, Dany Boon, Alex Ferns, Frank Witter, Thomas Schmauser, Joachim Bissmeier; ***D:*** Christian Carion; ***W:*** Christian Carion; ***C:*** Walther Vanden Ende; ***M:*** Philippe Rombi.

Joyful Laughter 🦴🦴 *Risate di Gioia* **1960** The dreary life of an Italian movie bit player draws strength from Magnani's powerful emotions as she repeatedly comes near to success only to find disappointment. Set in

Rome. With English subtitles. **106m/B VHS.** *IT* Anna Magnani, Ben Gazzara, Carlo Pisacane, Fred Clark; ***D:*** Mario Monicelli; ***W:*** Suso Cecchi D'Amico, Agenore Incrocci; ***C:*** Leonida Barboni; ***M:*** Lelio Luttazzi.

Joyless Street 🦴🦴🦴 1/2 *Street of Sorrow; Die Freudlosse Gasse* **1925** Silent film focuses on the dismal life of the middle class in Austria during an economic crisis. Lovely piano score accompanies the film. **96m/B VHS, DVD.** *GE* Greta Garbo, Werner Krauss, Asta Nielson, Jaro Furth, Loni Nest, Max Kohlhase, Silva Torf, Karl Ettlinger, Ilka Gruning, Agnes Esterhazy, Alexander Musky, Valeska Gert; ***D:*** G.W. Pabst; ***W:*** Willj Haas; ***C:*** Guido Seeber, Curt Oertel, Walter Robert Lach.

Joyride 🦴 1/2 **1977 (R)** Mistreated by a union official, three friends steal a car for a joy ride and plummet into a life of crime. **91m/C VHS, DVD.** Desi Arnaz Jr., Robert Carradine, Melanie Griffith, Anne Lockhart; ***D:*** Joseph Ruben.

Joyride 🦴🦴 **1997 (R)** Three friends make the mistake of stealing a car that belongs to a beautiful blonde assassin, who'll stop at nothing to get her wheels back (her latest victim is stashed in the trunk). **92m/C VHS, DVD.** Tobey Maguire, Wilson Cruz, Amy Hathaway, Christina Naify, James Karen, Adam West, Benicio Del Toro, Judson Mills; ***D:*** Quinton Peeples; ***W:*** Quinton Peeples; ***C:*** S. Douglas Smith. **VIDEO**

JSA: Joint Security Area 🦴🦴🦴 1/2 *J.S.A. Joint Security Area; Gongdong gyeongbi guyeok JSA* **2000** A group of North and South Korean soldiers befriend each other when the troops from the South stray across the border into the North after getting lost one evening. Later invited to return, one of the men from the South ends up dead, and a Korean national raised in Switzerland (apparently this makes her a neutral party somehow) is asked to investigate the affair before it mushrooms into a war. **107m/C DVD.** *KN* Yeong-ae Lee, Byung-hun Lee, Kang-ho Song, Ha-Kyun Shin, Tae-woo Kim; ***D:*** Chan-wook Park; ***W:*** Chan-wook Park, Mu-yeong Lee, Seong-san Jeong, Sang-yeon Park, Hyeon-seok Kim; ***C:*** Sung-Bok Kim; ***M:*** Yeong-wook Jo, Jun-Seok Bang.

Ju Dou 🦴🦴🦴🦴 **1990 (PG-13)** Breathtaking story of an aging factory owner in search of an heir. He takes a third wife, but she finds caring in the arms of another man, when her husband's brutality proves too much. Beautiful color cinematography, excellent acting, and epic story. Oscar nominee for Best Foreign Film. In Chinese with English subtitles. **98m/C VHS, DVD.** *CH* Gong Li, Baotian Li, Li Wei, Zhang Yi, Zheng Jian; ***D:*** Yimou Zhang; ***W:*** Liu Heng; ***C:*** Gu Changwei, Yang Lun; ***M:*** Xia Ru-jin, Jiping Zhao.

Ju-On 2 🦴🦴 **2000** Pregnant horror movie actress Kyoko miscarries in a tragic road accident in front of the cursed house from the first "Ju-On" where she encounters the ghosts. Despite this she goes through with starring in the documentary a film crew is making about the house's curse, and the ghosts that dwell in it. You can pretty much guess what happens from here. Eventually she falls ill, and a doctor tells her that not only hasn't she miscarried, her pregnancy is progressing smoothly. Not as effective as the original, as it is marred by scenes of camp that seem entirely out of place, and too much time is spent recapping the events of the first film. Several scenes will inspire much confusion. **76m/C DVD.** *JP* Yuko Daike, Makoto Ashikawa, Kahori Fujii, Yurei Yanagi, Takako Fuji, Taro Suwa, Reita Serizawa, Kiriko Shimizu, Mayoko Saito, Dankan, Tomohiro Kaku, Ryota Koyama, Denden, Taizo Mizumura, Harumi Matsukaze, Takashi Matsuyama, Hue Rong Weng, Yuue, Miyako Nakatsuka, Kenta Ishikawa, Ganko Fuyu, Takemura Nagisa, Hayato Ichihara, Akihiro Toyotome, Shiori Yonezawa, Mashio Miyazaki; ***D:*** Takashi Shimizu; ***W:*** Takashi Shimizu; ***C:*** Nobuhito Kisuki; ***M:*** Gary Ashiya.

Ju-On: The Grudge 🦴 1/2 *The Grudge* **2003** This is the third in the Shimizu's Japanese horror series, following "Ju-On: The Curse" and "Jun-On 2: The Curse 2," which all revolve around (in a convoluted manner) a horrific event occurring in the same house. Social worker Rika (Okina) discovers her elderly patient mute, terrified, and alone. Then Rika finds a ghostly boy hiding in a closet—the victim of previous violence. Premise is that great rage leaves an evil presence behind, which drives new inhabitants mad and causes them to commit more acts of violence, leaving more evil behind. Or something like that. Lots of interlocking flashbacks and intermittent shocks. Best left to fanciers of Asian horror; Japanese with subtitles. The 2004 American remake, "The Grudge," holds no surprises. **92m/C VHS, DVD.** *JP* Misa(ko) Uehara, Megumi Okina, Misaki Ito, Yuya Ozeki, Takako Fuji; ***D:*** Takashi Shimizu; ***W:*** Takashi Shimizu; ***C:*** Tokusho Kikumura; ***M:*** Shiro Sato.

Ju-Rei: The Uncanny 🦴 1/2 **2004** In Japan V-Cinema (i.e. direct to video movies) is considered a viable and respected medium, whereas in the U.S. it's looked down on; this traditional yurei (vengeful ghost) film is definitely American-style release, which borrows heavily from "Ju-On" and "Ringu" and could almost be considered the low budget entry of either film series. Its only innovation is that it is filmed in ten chapters played in reverse order, telling the story from finish to start. **76m/C DVD.** *JP* Eriko Kazuto, Mirai Ueno, Chinatsu Wakatsuki; ***D:*** Kohi Shiraishi; ***W:*** Naoyuki Yokota.

Juarez 🦴🦴 **1939** A revolutionary leader overthrows the Mexican government and then becomes President of the country. Based on the true story of Benito Pablo Juarez. **132m/B VHS.** Paul Muni, John Garfield, Bette Davis, Claude Rains, Gale Sondergaard, Charles Halton; ***D:*** William Dieterle; ***C:*** Gaetano Antonio "Tony" Gaudio.

Jubal 🦴🦴 **1956** A rancher (Borgnine) seeks advice from a cowhand (Ford) about pleasing his wife, but another cowhand (Steiger) implies that Ford is "advising" Borgnine's wife, as well. A western take on "Othello." **101m/C VHS, DVD.** Glenn Ford, Rod Steiger, Ernest Borgnine, Felicia Farr, Charles Bronson, Valerie French, Noah Beery Jr.; ***D:*** Delmer Daves.

Jubilee Trail 🦴🦴 1/2 **1954** Wagon trail western follows the lives of a group of pioneers from New Orleans to California. A woman goes through a marriage, a baby, and her husband's death. Ralston has some good tunes in this lush picture. **103m/C VHS.** Vera Hruba Ralston, Joan Leslie, Forrest Tucker, John Russell, Ray Middleton, Pat O'Brien; ***D:*** Joseph Kane.

Jud 🦴 1/2 **1971 (PG)** Society's refusal to understand a young soldier returning from the Vietnam conflict leads him to violence and tragedy. Jennings' first film; music by Phillips of Creedence Clearwater Revival. **80m/C VHS.** Joseph Kaufmann, Robert Deman, Alix Wyeth, Norman Burton, Claudia Jennings, Maurice Sherbanee, Vic Dunlop, Bonnie Bittner; ***D:*** Gunther Collins; ***M:*** Stu Phillips.

Jud Suess 🦴🦴🦴 **1940** Classic, scandalous Nazi anti-Semitic tract about a Jew who rises to power under the duchy of Wuerttemberg by stepping on, abusing, and raping Aryans. A film that caused riots at its screenings and tragedy for its cast and crew, and the Third Reich's most notorious fictional expression of policy. In German with English subtitles. **100m/B VHS.** *GE* Ferdinand Marian, Werner Krauss, Heinrich George, Kristina Soderbaum, Eugene Klopfer; ***D:*** Veit Harlan.

Judas Kiss 🦴🦴 1/2 **1998 (R)** Coco (Gugino) and her lover Junior (Baker-Denny) kidnap New Orleans exec Ben Dyson (Wise), but during the crime Coco shoots a woman who turns out to be Patty Hornbeck (Penberthy), the wife of a powerful Senator (Holbrook). Assigned to the case are detective David Friedman (Rickman) and FBI agent Sadie Hawkins (Thompson) and their investigation uncovers some secrets, including the fact that Patty and the kidnapped Dyson were having an affair. Uneven crime drama with an interesting cast. **108m/C VHS.** Emma Thompson, Alan Rickman, Carla Gugino, Simon Baker, Hal Holbrook, Gil Bellows, Til Schweiger, Greg Wise, Lisa Eichhorn, Beverly Penberthy; ***D:*** Sebastian Gutierrez; ***W:*** Sebastian Gutierrez; ***C:*** James Chressanthis; ***M:*** Christopher Young.

The Judas Project: The Ultimate Encounter 🦴 1/2 **1994 (PG-13)** Religious fantasy finds Jesse battling corruption and pseudo-religious figures in a fight to save a violent and decaying world. But Jesse's destroyed by his own disciple, Jude. Sound familiar? (There's even a cruxifixion scene.) **98m/C VHS, DVD.** John O'Bannion, Ramy Zada, Richard Herd; ***D:*** James H. Barden; ***C:*** Bryan England.

Jude 🦴🦴🦴 *Jude the Obscure* **1996 (R)** Engrossing retelling of Thomas Hardy's depressing 1896 novel "Jude the Obscure," set in his fictional Wessex. Country stonemason Jude (Eccleston) hopes to improve his impoverished lot in life by becoming a student at Christminister University. But first he's distracted into an unwise marriage with lively Arabella (Griffiths), who soon leaves him, and then into an ill-fated romance with his capricious cousin Sue Brideshead (Winslet). Class and societal barriers prove impossible for the couple to overcome and lead to a shocking tragedy. Hardy's book was so badly received by critics that he never wrote another novel and stuck to poetry for the rest of his life. **123m/C VHS, DVD.** *GB* Christopher Eccleston, Kate Winslet, Liam Cunningham, Rachel Griffiths; ***D:*** Michael Winterbottom; ***W:*** Hossein Amini; ***C:*** Eduardo Serra; ***M:*** Adrian Johnston.

Jude the Obscure 🦴🦴 1/2 **1971** Thomas Hardy's last novel is a tragic, bleak story of mismatched lovers and blighted ambitions. Jude is a poor stonemason whose dream is to get a proper education and marry his beloved cousin. Failing to get into Oxford he is seduced by a farm girl, whom he marries and fathers a child by (a gnome-like creature named "Father Time"). Meanwhile, his cousin marries a schoolteacher who disgusts her. Finally, the two thwarted lovers marry, only to find themselves living in poverty and hopelessness. After this novel (said to be Hardy's favorite), he devoted the rest of his long life to poetry. On three cassettes. **262m/C VHS, DVD.** *GB* Robert Powell, Daphne Heard, Alex Marshall, John Franklyn-Robbins, Fiona Walker; ***D:*** Hugh David; ***W:*** Harry Green. **TV**

Judex 🦴🦴 *Justice* **1916** Feuillade's 12-episode serial finds the mysterious (and morally suspect hero) Judex torn between his quest for revenge against wealthy, greedy banker Favraux and his love for Favraux's daughter, Jacqueline. Musidora does some vamping as Favraux's wicked assistant. **300m/B DVD.** *FR* rene creste, Louis Leubas, Yvette Andreyor, Musidora, Marcel Levesque, Bout de-zan, Edouard Mathe; ***D:*** Louis Feuillade; ***W:*** Arthur Bernede; ***C:*** Andre Glatti, Leon Klausse.

Judex 🦴🦴 1/2 **1964** Judex, a sensitive cloaked hero-avenger, fights master criminal gangs. In French with English subtitles. Remake of the silent French serial. **103m/B VHS.** *FR IT* Channing Pollock, Francine Berge, Jacques Jouanneau; ***D:*** Georges Franju; ***M:*** Maurice Jarre.

The Judge 🦴 1/2 **1949** A courtroom crime-drama about the consequences of infidelity. A lawyer sends an acquitted hit man to kill his wife and her lover. Things go amiss and the lawyer winds up dead. **69m/B VHS.** Milburn Stone, Katherine DeMille, Paul Guilfoyle, Jonathan Hale; ***D:*** Elmer Clifton.

Judge & Jury 🦴 1/2 **1996 (R)** Convicted killer Joseph Miller (Keith) dies in the electric chair but then manages to return from the dead to get revenge. So how do you kill someone who's already dead? Well, Michael Silvano (Kove) will have to find a way to send Miller back where he belongs. **98m/C VHS, DVD.** David Keith, Martin Kove, Laura Johnson, Thomas Ian Nicholas, Paul Koslo; ***D:*** John Eyres; ***W:*** John Eyres, John Cianetti, Amanda I. Kirpaul; ***C:*** Bob Paone; ***M:*** Johnathon Flood. **VIDEO**

The Judge and the Assassin 🦴🦴🦴 1/2 *Le Juge et L'assassin* **1975** Intriguing courtroom drama. A prejudiced judge has his values challenged when he must decide if a child-killer is insane or not. The relationship that develops between the judge and the killer is the film's focus. Excellent direction by Tavernier. In French with English subtitles. **130m/C VHS.** *FR* Philippe Noiret, Michel Galabru, Isabelle Huppert, Jean-Claude Brialy, Yves Robert, Renee Faure; ***D:*** Bertrand Tavernier; ***W:*** Bertrand Tavernier, Jean Aurenche, Pierre Bost; ***C:*** Pierre William Glenn; ***M:*** Philippe Sarde. Cesar '77: Writing, Score.

Judge Dredd 🦴 1/2 **1995 (R)** Futuristic lawman Dredd (Stallone), who acts as cop, judge, jury, and executioner, is framed for murder by his "brother" Rico (Assante), a renegade misfit. With the help of a female Judge (Lane) and an ex-con (Schneider), Dredd fights to clear his name and save the people of Mega City One. Big names, big bangs, big budget—big disappointment. Dialogue makes "Rambo" sound like Shakespeare, and the choppy, convoluted plot doesn't help. Schneider provides a rare bright spot while acting circles around Sly, who hoped (in vain) that the project would provide him with another profitable action franchise. The source comic book has been a cult favorite in England for 20 years. **96m/C VHS, DVD.** Sylvester Stallone, Armand Assante, Diane Lane, Rob Schneider, Joan Chen, Jurgen Prochnow, Max von Sydow; ***D:*** Danny Cannon; ***W:*** Steven E. de Souza, Michael De Luca, William Wisher; ***C:*** Adrian Biddle; ***M:*** Alan Silvestri.

Judge Horton and the Scottsboro Boys 🦴🦴 1/2 **1976** A courtroom drama focusing on a famous 1931 trial. A courageous judge must battle the South in the case of nine black men charged with gang-raping two white women. **100m/C VHS.** Arthur Hill, Vera Miles, Ken Kercheval, Suzanne Lederer, Tom Ligon; ***D:*** Fielder Cook. **TV**

Judge Priest 🦴🦴🦴 **1934** Small-town judge in the old South stirs up the place with stinging humor and common-sense observances as he tangles with prejudices and civil injustices. Funny, warm slice-of-life is occasionally defeated by racist characterizations. Ford remade it later as "The Sun Shines Bright." Taken from the Irvin S. Cobb stories. **80m/B VHS, DVD.** Will Rogers, Stepin Fetchit, Anita Louise, Henry B. Walthall; ***D:*** John Ford.

The Judge Steps Out 🦴🦴 1/2 **1949** Pleasant, light comedy about a hen-pecked, Bostonian judge who decides he's had enough and heads for balmy California. There he finds a job in a restaurant and, more importantly, a sympathetic friend in its female owner. He soon finds himself falling for the woman, and realizes he faces an important decision. **91m/B VHS.** Alexander Knox, Ann Sothern, George Tobias, Sharyn Moffett, Florence Bates, Frieda Inescort, Myrna Dell, Ian Wolfe, H.B. Warner; ***D:*** Boris Ingster.

The Judgement 🦴🦴 *I Fak; Ai-Fak* **2004** Slow-moving, Thai Buddhist story from first-time director Thongsang is likely to appeal to cinephiles only. Novice monk Fak (Yaowananon) returns to his isolated village to care for his ailing father, whom he discovers has married young and beautiful Somson (Kongmalai). The villagers all think she's crazy and Somson doesn't help matters by promptly flirting with Fak, whose vows include chastity. Far from being the comedy it first seems, the flick turns down a dark road after dad dies and the self-righteous villagers get increasingly suspicious over the relationship between the two in-laws. Thai with subtitles. **110m/C** *TH* Bongkoj Khongmalai, Pitisak Yaowananon, Thedsak Yaemniyon; ***D:*** Pantham Thongsang; ***W:*** Somkiat Withuranich; ***C:*** Wisan Jiraaungkoonsakun; ***M:*** Hualampong Riddim.

Judgment 🦴🦴🦴 **1990 (PG-13)** A devout Catholic couple are shocked to learn that their young son has been molested by the popular priest of their small Louisiana parish. When they find out their son is not the first victim, and other families have been coerced into silence, they vow to fight back. Tasteful treatment of a real court case. **89m/C VHS, DVD.** Keith Carradine, Blythe Danner, Jack Warden, David Strathairn, Bob Gunton, Mitchell Ryan, Michael Faustino; ***D:*** Tom Topor; ***W:*** Tom Topor. **CABLE**

Judgment at Nuremberg 🦴🦴🦴🦴 **1961** It's 1948 and a group of high-level Nazis are on trial for war crimes. Chief Justice Tracy must resist political pressures as he presides over the trials. Excellent performances throughout, especially by Dietrich and Garland. Considers to what extent an individual may be held accountable for actions committed under orders of a superior officer. Consuming account of the Holocaust and WWII; deeply moving and powerful. Based on a "Playhouse 90" TV program. **178m/B VHS, DVD.** Spencer Tracy, Burt Lancaster, Richard Widmark, Montgomery Clift, Maximilian Schell, Judy Garland, Marlene Dietrich, William Shatner, Edward Binns, Werner Klemperer, Torben Meyer, Martin Brandt, Kenneth MacKenna, Alan Baxter, Ray Teal, Karl Swenson; ***D:*** Stanley Kramer; ***W:*** Abby Mann; ***C:*** Ernest Laszlo; ***M:*** Ernest Gold. Oscars '61: Actor (Schell), Adapt. Screenplay; Golden Globes '62: Actor—Drama (Schell), Director (Kramer); N.Y. Film Critics '61: Actor (Schell), Screenplay.

Judgment Day **1988 (PG-13)** Four college buddies pick the wrong New England town for their vacation. It seems that the town made a deal with the Devil in 1689 to save themselves from the plague, and now the Dark Master is here to collect. **93m/C VHS.** Kenneth McLeod, David Anthony Smith, Monte Markham, Gloria Hayes, Peter Mark Richman, Cesar Romero; ***D:*** Ferde Grofe Jr.

Judgment Day **1999 (R)** A meteor collides with an asteroid in deep space and if fragments from the mishap should hit Earth, it's goodbye planet. One scientist has an idea how to prevent disaster but he's kidnapped by a cult leader who thinks the planet's doom is foretold. Now the government has to get the scientist back before it's too late. **90m/C VHS, DVD.** Mario Van Peebles, Ice-T, Suzy Amis, Tommy (Tiny) Lister, Coolio; ***D:*** John Terlesky; ***W:*** William Carson; ***C:*** Maximo Munzi; ***M:*** Joseph Williams. **VIDEO**

Judgment in Berlin **1/2** *Escape to Freedom* **1988 (PG)** East German family hijacks a U.S. airliner into West Germany, and then must stand trial in Berlin before a troubled American judge. Based on a true 1978 incident and the book by Herbert J. Stern. **92m/C VHS, DVD.** Martin Sheen, Sam Wanamaker, Max Gail, Sean Penn, Heinz Hoenig, Carl Lumbly, Max Volkert Martens, Harris Yulin, Jutta Speidel, Juerger Hemrich; ***D:*** Leo Penn; ***W:*** Joshua Sinclair; ***M:*** Peter Goldfoot.

Judgment Night **1993 (R)** Four macho buddies on their way to a boxing match detour a highway traffic jam via surface streets and find themselves witnesses to a murder. The rest of their guys-night-out is spent trying to escape a gloomy ghetto and determined killer (played convincingly by Leary). All of the action takes place after dark on the streets and in the sewers and, subsequently, the scenes are extremely dark with only a burnt orange lighting. Lots of action and a little oomph. Based on a story by Lewis Colick and Jere Cunningham. **109m/C VHS, DVD.** Emilio Estevez, Cuba Gooding Jr., Stephen Dorff, Denis Leary, Jeremy Piven, Peter Greene; ***D:*** Stephen Hopkins; ***W:*** Lewis Colick; ***C:*** Peter Levy; ***M:*** Alan Silvestri.

Judicial Consent **1/2 1994** Gwen Warwick (Bedelia) is an accomplished criminal court judge with a bland husband (Patton) and a lot of unfulfilled desires. At least one desire is taken care of when Gwen succumbs to the charms of handsome law clerk Martin (Wirth). Then her colleague Charles (Coleman) is murdered and all the evidence points to Gwen. She knows she's been set up but can Gwen prove her innocence? Familiar plot, good performances although Patton gets stuck in an underwritten role. **101m/C VHS.** Bonnie Bedelia, Dabney Coleman, Billy Wirth, Will Patton, Lisa Blount; ***D:*** William Bindley; ***W:*** William Bindley; ***M:*** Christopher Young.

Judith of Bethulia **1914** A young widow uses her charm and wits to save her city from attack by the Assyrians. Based on the Apocrypha, this is the last film Griffith directed for Biograph. It was re-released as "Her Condoned Sin" in 1971, including two reels of Griffith's outtakes. **65m/B VHS.** Blanche Sweet, Henry B. Walthall, Mae Marsh, Robert "Bobbie" Harron, Lillian Gish, Dorothy Gish, Kate Bruce, Harry Carey Sr.; ***D:*** D.W. Griffith; ***W:*** D.W. Griffith.

Judy Berlin **1/2 1999** It's a school day in the placid suburb of Babylon, Long Island. Teacher Sue (Barrie) likes to flirt with weary principal Arthur (Dishy) who has a high-maintenance wife, Alice (Kahn), and a mopey grown son, David (Harnick), whose homecoming visit has gone on too long. Sue has her own offspring problems with sunnily ditsy, aspiring actress daughter Judy (Falco). Then Judy and David meet cute and a solar eclipse seems to inspire strange behavior. **97m/B VHS.** Barbara Barrie, Bob (Robert) Dishy, Edie Falco, Aaron Harnick, Madeline Kahn, Carlin Glynn, Julie Kavner, Anne Meara; ***D:*** Eric Mendelsohn; ***W:*** Eric Mendelsohn; ***C:*** Jeffrey Seckendorf; ***M:*** Michael Nicholas. Sundance '99: Director (Mendelsohn).

Juggernaut **1/2 1937** Not the classic disaster film of the '70s. A young woman hires a sinister doctor (Karloff) to murder her wealthy husband. The doctor, who happens to be insane, does away with the husband and then goes on a poisoning spree. Seems to drag on forever. **64m/B VHS, DVD.** Boris Karloff, Mona Goya, Arthur Margetson, Joan Wyndham, Anthony Ireland; ***D:*** Henry Edwards; ***W:*** Cyril Campion; ***C:*** Sydney Blythe, William Luff; ***M:*** W.L. Trytel.

Juggernaut **1974 (PG-13)** Well-done drama about a doomed luxury liner. A madman plants bombs aboard a cruise ship and mocks the crew about his plan over the wireless. The countdown ensues, while the bomb experts struggle to find the explosives. Suspenseful with good direction. **109m/C VHS, DVD.** *GB* Richard Harris, Omar Sharif, David Hemmings, Anthony Hopkins, Shirley Knight, Ian Holm, Roy Kinnear, Freddie Jones; ***D:*** Richard Lester; ***W:*** Richard DeKoker; ***C:*** Gerry Fisher; ***M:*** Ken Thorne.

Juice **1/2 1992 (R)** Day-to-day street life of four Harlem youths as they try to earn respect ("juice") in their neighborhood. Q, an aspiring deejay, is talked into a robbery by his friends but everything takes a turn for the worse when one of the others, Bishop, gets hold of a gun. The gritty look and feel of the drama comes naturally to Dickerson in his directorial debut. Prior to his first film, Dickerson served as cinematographer for Spike Lee's "Do the Right Thing" and "Jungle Fever." **95m/C VHS, DVD.** Omar Epps, Jermaine "Huggy" Hopkins, Tupac Shakur, Khalil Kain, Cindy Herron, Vincent Laresca, Samuel L. Jackson; ***D:*** Ernest R. Dickerson; ***W:*** Gerard Brown, Ernest R. Dickerson; ***C:*** Larry Banks.

Juke Girl **1/2 1942** Friends Steve (Reagan) and Danny (Whorf) are working the tomato fields of Cat Tail, Florida but wind up on opposite sides of a labor dispute when Steve sides with independent grower Nick (Tobias) and Danny takes a job with ruthless plant owner Henry (Lockhart). Sheridan comes into the picture as juke joint hostess Lola, who falls for Steve and loses her job for helping him. Nick gets murdered and the lovebirds wind up in more trouble. Reagan and Sheridan were previously paired in the much-better "Kings Row" (1942) but this is a good, if melodramatic, social issues pic, although it certainly seems oddly titled since Sheridan's character isn't the focus. **90m/B DVD.** Ronald Reagan, Ann Sheridan, Richard Whorf, Gene Lockhart, George Tobias, Alan Hale, Betty Brewer, Faye Emerson; ***D:*** Curtis Bernhardt; ***W:*** A(lbert) I(saac) Bezzerides, Kenneth Garmet; ***C:*** Bert Glennon; ***M:*** Adolph Deutsch.

Juke Joint **1/2 1947** "Amos 'n Andy" star Spencer Williams acted in and directed this tale of two men who arrive in Hollywood with only 25 cents between them. Features an all-black cast and musical numbers. **60m/B VHS, DVD.** Spencer Williams Jr., Judy Jones, Mantan Moreland; ***D:*** Spencer Williams Jr.

Jules and Jim *Jules et Jim* **1962** Beautiful film with perfect casting, particularly Moreau. Spanning from 1912 to 1932, it is the story of a friendship between two men and their 20-year love for the same woman. Werner is the shy German Jew and Serre the fun-loving Frenchman, who meet as students. The two men discover and woo the bohemian, destructive Moreau, although it is Werner she marries. After WWI, the friends are reunited but the marriage of Moreau and Werner is in trouble and she has an affair with Serre, which leads to tragedy for all three. Adapted from the novel by Henri-Pierre Roche. In French with English subtitles. **104m/B VHS, DVD.** *FR* Jeanne Moreau, Oskar Werner, Henri Serre, Marie DuBois, Vanna Urbino; ***D:*** Francois Truffaut; ***W:*** Jean Gruault, Francois Truffaut; ***C:*** Raoul Coutard; ***M:*** Georges Delerue.

Julia **1/2 1977 (PG)** The story recounted in Lillian Hellman's fictional memoir "Pentimento." Fonda plays Hellman as she risks her life smuggling money into Germany during WWII for the sake of Julia, her beloved childhood friend (Redgrave), who is working in the Resistance. All cast members shine in their performances; watch for Streep in her screen debut. **118m/C VHS, DVD.** Jane Fonda, Jason Robards Jr., Vanessa Redgrave, Maximilian Schell, Hal Holbrook, Rosemary Murphy, Meryl Streep, Lisa Pelikan, John Glover, Mark Metcalf, Lambert Wilson; ***D:*** Fred Zinnemann; ***W:*** Alvin Sargent; ***C:*** Douglas Slocombe; ***M:*** Georges Delerue. Oscars '77: Adapt. Screenplay, Support. Actor (Robards), Support. Actress (Redgrave); British Acad. '78: Actress (Fonda), Film, Screenplay, Support. Actress (Redgrave); Golden Globes '78: Actress—Drama (Fonda), Support. Actress (Redgrave); L.A. Film Critics '77: Cinematog., Support. Actor (Robards), Support. Actress (Redgrave); N.Y. Film Critics '77: Support. Actor (Schell); Writers Guild '77: Adapt. Screenplay.

Julia **2008 (R)** Self-absorbed, self-destructive alcoholic Julia (Swinton) has obviously lost a few too many brain cells to the booze when she agrees to a kidnapping plan proposed by a virtual stranger. Elena (Del Castillo), who Julia meets at an AA meeting, claims that she is forbidden to see her son who lives in Mexico with his wealthy grandfather. She proposes they kidnap the boy and split the ransom and Julia thinks this is a great idea. Watching Swinton in action makes the lengthy run time go by faster than it should. English and Spanish with subtitles. **144m/C DVD.** *FR* Tilda Swinton, Saul Rubinek, Kate del Castillo, Jude Ciccolella, Bruno Bichir, Kevin Kilner, Aidan Gould, Horacio Garcia Rojas; ***D:*** Erick Zonca; ***W:*** Erick Zonca, Aude Py; ***C:*** Yorick Le Saux; ***M:*** Pollard Berrier, Darius Keeter.

Julia and Julia **1/2 1987 (R)** A beautiful American woman in Trieste is tossed between two seemingly parallel dimensions, one in which her husband died six years earlier in a car crash, and the other in which he didn't. A purposefully obscure Italian-made psychological thriller, filmed in high-definition video and then transferred to film stock, it has a very different look and feel from other films of the genre. Intriguing and engaging most of the time, slow moving and confusing some of the time, it ultimately challenges but fails adequately to reward the viewer. **98m/C VHS.** Kathleen Turner, Sting, Gabriel Byrne, Gabriele Ferzetti, Angela Goodwin; ***D:*** Peter Del Monte; ***W:*** Joe Minion, Sandro Petraglia, Silvia Napolitano, Peter Del Monte; ***C:*** Giuseppe Rotunno; ***M:*** Maurice Jarre.

Julia Has Two Lovers **1991 (R)** Minimalist comedy-drama about a woman torn between two men—her dull fiance and a mysterious phone caller. Mostly a long phone conversation; don't expect blistering action. **87m/C VHS.** Daphna Kastner, David Duchovny, David Charles; ***D:*** Bashar Shbib.

Julia Misbehaves **1948** Charming comedy that has Garson returning to ex-husband Pidgeon and daughter Taylor after an 18-year absence. Taylor is about to be married at a chateau in France and wants Garson to be there. While traveling to France from England, Garson encounters a bunch of colorful circus characters who are taking their act to Paris. Wonderful slapstick scenes give the stars a chance to have some real fun. Based on the novel "The Nutmeg Tree" by Margery Sharp. **99m/B VHS.** Greer Garson, Walter Pidgeon, Peter Lawford, Cesar Romero, Elizabeth Taylor, Lucile Watson, Nigel Bruce, Mary Boland, Reginald Owen, Veda Ann Borg, Joi Lansing; ***D:*** Jack Conway.

Julian Po **1/2** *The Tears of Julian Po* **1997 (PG-13)** Nondescript bookkeeper Julian Po (Slater) has his car break down near an isolated mountain community and immediately comes under suspicion when he checks into the local boarding house, which never gets any guests. And the next day Julian's car has vanished, stranding him in nowherestown. The locals become convinced he's a hit man and demand explanations. Julian unexpectedly blurts out that the only person he's planning to kill is himself. Immediately the center of attention, Julian becomes confessor to everyone's darkest secrets and a recipient of their constant kindnesses but since he really doesn't intend to off himself, he's also got some unexpected problems. **82m/C VHS, DVD.** Christian Slater, Robin Tunney, Michael Parks, Frankie Faison, Harve Presnell, Allison Janney, Cherry Jones, LaTanya Richardson Jackson, Dina Spybey, Zeljko Ivanek; ***D:*** Alan Wade; ***W:*** Alan Wade; ***C:*** Bernd Heinl; ***M:*** Patrick Williams.

Julie & Julia **2009 (PG-13)** Yum. You may not find your inner chef but you'll definitely develop an appetite as foodie Ephron combines Julia Child's memoir "My Life in France" and Julie Powell's memoir "Julie & Julia" into a somewhat disjointed delight. Julie Powell (Adams) is tired of her boring job, her Queens apartment with its tiny kitchen, and her life in general. To break the monotony, Julie vows to use her mother's 1961 copy of Julia Child's "Mastering the Art of French Cooking" and make all 524 recipes in one year, while blogging about her experiences, encouraged by her usually-supportive husband Eric (Messina). The ever-enthusiastic Streep stars as the ever-enthusiastic Child, shown in flashbacks, as she lives and cooks in Paris in the late 1940s and 50s while her always-supportive husband Paul (an equally delightful Tucci) was stationed at the U.S. Embassy. Unfortunately for Adams, her New Yorker Julie is rather neurotic and dull, especially out of the kitchen. Bon appetit! **123m/C DVD.** *US* Amy Adams, Meryl Streep, Stanley Tucci, Jane Lynch, Chris Messina, Mary Lynn Rajskub, Vanessa Ferlito, Joan Juliet Buck, Linda Emond, Helen Carey, Frances Sternhagen; ***D:*** Nora Ephron; ***W:*** Nora Ephron; ***C:*** Stephen Goldblatt; ***M:*** Alexandre Desplat. Golden Globes '10: Actress—Mus./Comedy (Streep).

Julien Donkey-boy **1/2 1999 (R)** Harmony Korine's story of a schizophrenic young man and his disturbed family is the first American movie to be filmed using the principles of the restrictive Danish filmmaking method known as Dogma '95. Apparently, there must be some kind of restriction on the plot and narrative as well, because the audience is merely shown disturbing images of the mentally ill Julien (Bremner), his pregnant sister Pearl (Sevigny), his jock brother Chris (Neumann) and their abusive father (Herzog). Largely improvised and shot using hand-held digital video cameras, this unsettling project is for the cinematically adventurous only. **101m/C VHS, DVD.** Ewen Bremner, Chloe Sevigny, Werner Herzog, Evan Neumann, Joyce Korine, Chrissy Kobylak, Alvin Law; ***D:*** Harmony Korine; ***W:*** Harmony Korine; ***C:*** Anthony Dod Mantle.

Juliet of the Spirits *Giulietta Degli Spiriti* **1965** Fellini uses the sparse story of a woman (Fellini's real-life wife) deliberating over her husband's possible infidelity to create a wild, often senseless surrealistic film. With a highly symbolic internal logic and complex imagery, Fellini's fantasy ostensibly elucidates the inner life of a modern woman. In Italian with English subtitles. **142m/C VHS, DVD.** *IT* Giulietta Masina, Valentina Cortese, Sylva Koscina, Mario Pisu, Sandra Milo, Caterina Boratto, Valeska Gert; ***D:*** Federico Fellini; ***W:*** Federico Fellini, Tullio Pinelli, Ennio Flaiano, Brunello Rondi; ***C:*** Gianni Di Venanzo; ***M:*** Nino Rota. N.Y. Film Critics '65: Foreign Film.

Julius Caesar **1/2 1953** All-star version of the Shakespearean tragedy, heavily acclaimed and deservedly so. Working directly from the original Shakespeare, director Mankiewicz produced a lifelike, yet poetic production. **121m/B VHS, DVD.** James Mason, Marlon Brando, John Gielgud, Greer Garson, Deborah Kerr, Louis Calhern, Edmond O'Brien, George Macready, John Hoyt, Michael Pate; ***D:*** Joseph L. Mankiewicz; ***W:*** Joseph L. Mankiewicz; ***C:*** Joseph Ruttenberg; ***M:*** Miklos Rozsa. Oscars '53: Art Dir./Set Dec., B&W; British Acad. '53: Actor (Brando), Actor (Gielgud); Natl. Bd. of Review '53: Actor (Mason).

Julius Caesar **1970** Subpar adaptation of the Shakespeare play about political greed and corruption within the Roman Empire. **116m/C VHS, DVD.** *GB* Charlton Heston, John Gielgud, Jason Robards Jr., Richard Chamberlain, Robert Vaughn, Diana Rigg; ***D:*** Stuart Burge.

July Group **1/2 1981** A Quaker family's peaceful existence is threatened when kidnappers invade their home and hold them for ransom. **75m/C VHS.** *CA* Nicholas (Nick) Campbell, Maury Chaykin, Ken Pogue, Tom Butler; ***D:*** George McCowan; ***C:*** Brian R.R. Hebb; ***M:*** Samuel Matlovsky. **TV**

Jumanji 🦴🦴 1/2 **1995 (PG)** For the past 26 years Alan Parish (Williams) has been stuck in the netherworld of Jumanji, a jungle-themed board game that sucks players into its alternate universe. When unsuspecting youngsters Judy (Dunst) and Peter (Pierce) happen upon the game and begin to play, they release Williams and a jungle full of rampaging beasts from the game and into the present. Loosely based on Chris Van Allsburg's children's book, the film version relies too heavily on cutting-edge special effects to make up for a thin story. Many of the creatures and effects are utterly too bizarre and unsettling for younger audiences. With a $65 million pricetag, Jumanji is definitely a roll of the dice. **104m/C VHS, DVD, UMD.** Robin Williams, Kirsten Dunst, Bonnie Hunt, Bradley Michael Pierce, Bebe Neuwirth, Jonathan Hyde, David Alan Grier, Adam Hann-Byrd; ***D:*** Joe Johnston; ***W:*** Jonathan Hensleigh; ***C:*** Thomas Ackerman; ***M:*** James Horner.

Jump In! 🦴🦴 1/2 **2007** Relentlessly chipper Disney Channel movie finds Izzy (Bleu) taking up boxing to please his dad, a former Golden Gloves champ. When his sister takes Izzy to a double-dutch competition, he's surprised to see cutie girl-next-door Mary (Palmer) on a team. Mary convinces Izzy to take his moves to her sport when they need a replacement jumper, but the guy's worried about not appearing cool at school. But he soon learns, of course, that first you have to be true to yourself. **85m/C DVD.** Corbin Bleu, Keke Palmer, David Reivers, Shanica Knowles, Patrick Johnson Jr.; ***D:*** Paul Hoen; ***W:*** Doreen Spicer, Regina Hicks, Karin Gist; ***C:*** David Makin; ***M:*** Frank Fitzpatrick. **CABLE**

Jumper 🦴 1/2 **2008 (PG-13)** Picked-on kid David (Christensen) discovers that he has the ability to teleport at will, and he uses his gift to flit around the world, rob banks, and basically do what he pleases, including pursuing his childhood crush Millie (Bilson). Enter Roland (Jackson), a member of a mysterious group that hunts and kills "jumpers" like David. Heavy action fails to cover up the weak plot and David's brattiness. Loosely based on a series of young adult novels by Steven Gould. **88m/C DVD, Blu-ray Disc.** *US* Hayden Christensen, Jamie Bell, Samuel L. Jackson, Rachel Bilson, Diane Lane, Michael Rooker, AnnaSophia Robb, Max Thieriot; ***D:*** Doug Liman; ***W:*** David S. Goyer, Simon Kinberg, Jim Uhls; ***C:*** Barry Peterson; ***M:*** John Powell.

Jumpin' at the Boneyard 🦴🦴 **1992 (R)** Gritty family drama about the trials of two dispossessed brothers, set on the streets of New York. Deeply depressed, out-of-work, divorced Manny hates his recently deceased father, adores his mother, and is estranged from his younger brother, Danny. Danny is a scared crack addict who's supported by a hooker/girlfriend. The two brothers reunite for a trip into their scarred past when Danny tries to rob his brother's apartment to get dope money. Manny starts to believe that the only way to redeem his own life is to get his brother into a rehab program. Good acting helps to overcome some script weaknesses but this is one depressing movie. **107m/C VHS.** Tim Roth, Alexis Arquette, Danitra Vance, Samuel L. Jackson, Kathleen Chalfant, Luis Guzman; ***D:*** Jeff Stanzler; ***W:*** Jeff Stanzler.

Jumpin' Jack Flash 🦴🦴 1/2 **1986 (R)** A bank worker is humorously embroiled in international espionage when her computer terminal picks up distress signals from a British agent in Russia. Marshall's directing debut. Good performances from a fun cast and a particularly energetic effort by Goldberg are held back by an average and predictable script. **98m/C VHS, DVD.** Whoopi Goldberg, Stephen Collins, Carol Kane, Annie Potts, Jonathan Pryce, James Belushi, Jon Lovitz, John Wood; ***Cameos:*** Michael McKean, Tracey Ullman, Roscoe Lee Browne, Sara Botsford, Jeroen Krabbe, Phil Hartman, Tracy Reiner, Paxton Whitehead, Jamey Sheridan, Garry Marshall, Peter Michael Goetz; ***D:*** Penny Marshall; ***W:*** David Franzoni; ***C:*** Jan De Bont; ***M:*** Thomas Newman.

Jumping Jacks 🦴🦴 **1952** Martin and Lewis are a couple of nightclub performers who wind up in the paratroop corps instead of performing their act for the soldiers. Martin gets to sing and Lewis gets to parachute into enemy territory and capture a general. **96m/B VHS.** Dean Martin, Jerry Lewis, Mona Freeman, Don DeFore, Robert Strauss, Ray Teal; ***D:*** Norman Taurog; ***C:*** Daniel F. Fapp.

The Junction Boys 🦴🦴 **2002** A look at one phase in the career of legendary tough-guy college football coach Paul "Bear" Bryant (well-played by Berenger). Film starts in 1954 with Bryant's arrival at Texas A&M as he drives his players, eventually known as the Junction Boys, to make the team. (Drama sticks to football practice not competition.) The focus is on three key players (who, of course, have personal problems to overcome)—Skeet Keeler (Humphrys), Claude Gearheart (Kwanten), and Johnny Haynes (Curry). **93m/C VHS, DVD.** Tom Berenger, Bernard Curry, Fletcher Humphrys, Ryan Kwanten, Nick (Nicholas) Tate, Mark Lee, Andy Anderson; ***D:*** Mike Robe; ***W:*** Mike Robe; ***C:*** Stephen F. Andrich; ***M:*** Steve Dorff. **CABLE**

Junction 88 🦴 **1947** Early all-black musical chock full of great dancing and hot music. **60m/B VHS.** Noble Sissle, Bob Howard, Dewey "Pigmeat" Markham, J. Augustus Smith; ***D:*** George P. Quigley; ***C:*** John Visconti; ***M:*** J. Augustus Smith.

Juncture 🦴 1/2 **2007 (R)** Anna Carter (Blackport) is the director of a foundation that funds programs to help abused children. Learning she has terminal brain cancer and only three months to live, Anna takes a proactive approach and decides to get justice for those damaged kids by offing pedophile criminals who have slipped through the justice system. **106m/C DVD.** Andrew Porter, Kristine Blackport, John Hutton, Bill LeVasseur, Jeff Nicholson; ***D:*** James Seale; ***W:*** Robert Gosnell; ***C:*** Richard Lerner; ***M:*** Neal Acree. **VIDEO**

June Bride 🦴🦴🦴 **1948** Fast-paced and entertaining comedy in which Davis and Montgomery are teamed up as magazine writers. A hilarious battle of the sexes erupts as they're sent to Indiana to do a feature story on June brides. Look for Debbie Reynolds in her film debut. **97m/B VHS.** Bette Davis, Robert Montgomery, Fay Bainter, Betty Lynn, Tom Tully, Barbara Bates, Jerome Cowan, Mary Wickes; ***D:*** Bretaigne Windust; ***W:*** Ranald MacDougall.

June Night 🦴🦴 *Juninatten* **1940** A woman who was victimized by a shooting incident cannot escape the public eye due to her former promiscuous behavior. In Swedish with English subtitles. **90m/C VHS, DVD.** *SW* Ingrid Bergman, Marianne Lofgren, Gunnar Sjoberg, Olaf Widgren; ***D:*** Per Lindberg; ***W:*** Ragnar Hylten-Cavalius; ***C:*** Ake Dahlqvist; ***M:*** Jules Sylvain.

Junebug 🦴🦴🦴 **2005 (R)** Sophisticated Chicago art dealer Madeleine (Davidtz) has impulsively married enigmatic, ex-small town North Carolinian George (Nivola) and is finally about to meet her in-laws. George's homecoming is reluctant at best: his mom, Peg (Weston), is a busybody who immediately dislikes her new daughter-in-law; dad Eugene (Wilson) lives in his own quiet world; younger brother Johnny (McKenzie) is moody and resentful; and only his young and very pregnant bride Ashley (Adams) is happy and welcoming. It's a cultural and familial clash without being condescending. Pic is stolen by the delightful Adams as a sweetly wise chatterbox. **107m/C DVD.** *US* Embeth Davidtz, Alessandro Nivola, Amy Adams, Celia Weston, Ben(jamin) McKenzie, Scott Wilson, Frank Hoyt Taylor, Joanne Pankow; ***D:*** Phil Morrison; ***W:*** Angus MacLachlan; ***C:*** Peter Donahue; ***M:*** Yo LaTengo. Ind. Spirit '06: Support. Actress (Adams); Natl. Soc. Film Critics '05: Support. Actress (Adams); Broadcast Film Critics '05: Support. Actress (Adams).

Jungle 🦴 **1952** A princess and an American adventurer lead an expedition into the Indian wilds to discover the source of recent elephant attacks. **74m/B VHS.** Rod Cameron, Cesar Romero, Marie Windsor; ***D:*** William Berke; ***C:*** Clyde De Vinna.

Jungle Assault 🦴 **1989** Two Vietnam vets with nothing left to lose are called back into the bloodiest action of their lives. Their assignment is to locate and destroy a terrorist base and bring back an American general's brainwashed daughter. **86m/C VHS.** William (Bill) Smith, Ted Prior, William Zipp; ***D:*** David A. Prior.

The Jungle Book 🦴🦴 *Rudyard Kipling's Jungle Book* **1942** A lavish version of Rudyard Kipling's stories about Mowgli, the boy raised by wolves in the jungles of India. **109m/C VHS, DVD.** Sabu, Joseph Calleia, Rosemary DeCamp, Ralph Byrd, John Qualen; ***D:*** Zoltan Korda; ***W:*** Laurence Stallings; ***C:*** Lee Garmes; ***M:*** Miklos Rozsa.

The Jungle Book 🦴🦴🦴 **1967** Based on Kipling's classic, a young boy raised by wolves must choose between his jungle friends and human "civilization." Along the way he meets a variety of jungle characters including zany King Louie, kind-hearted Baloo, wise Bagherra and the evil Shere Khan. Great, classic songs including "Trust in Me," "I Wanna Be Like You," and Oscar-nominated "Bare Necessities." Last Disney feature overseen by Uncle Walt himself and a must for kids of all ages. **78m/C VHS, DVD.** ***D:*** Wolfgang Reitherman; ***M:*** George Bruns; ***V:*** Phil Harris, Sebastian Cabot, Louis Prima, George Sanders, Sterling Holloway, J. Pat O'Malley, Verna Felton, Darlene Carr.

The Jungle Book 2 🦴🦴 **2003 (G)** Sequel to the classic Disney version, it picks up where the original left off. Mowgli (voice by Osment) is now living in the village with a warmhearted human family. He misses the excitement of the jungle and sneaks back to his old pal, Baloo the Bear (a decent enough Goodman, but the original voice of Phil Harris is a tough act to follow). Two of the village children follow him and many adventures ensue. Although the animation is quite good, the plot merely recycles old material, even going so far as reprising the classic song "Bare Necessities" three times. Adults will find the movie tiresome, but the younger set won't be as picky. **72m/C VHS, DVD.** *US* ***D:*** Steve Trenbirth; ***W:*** Karl Guers; ***M:*** Joel McNeely; ***V:*** John Goodman, Haley Joel Osment, Mae Whitman, Tony Jay, Connor Funk, Bob Joles, John Rhys-Davies, Phil Collins.

Jungle Boy 🦴🦴 **1996 (PG)** After being lost in the jungles of India, Manling (Seth) is raised by a monkey and an elephant. Able to communicate with the animals, Manling uses his talents to defeat the evil poacher, Hook (Roberts), who's out to steal a sacred statue. **88m/C VHS, DVD.** Asif Mohammed Seth, Jeremy Roberts, Lea Moreno; ***D:*** Allan Goldstein; ***W:*** Allan Goldstein, John Lawson, Damian Lee; ***C:*** Nicholas Josef von Sternberg.

Jungle Bride 🦴🦴 1/2 **1933** Three people are shipwrecked and one of them is a suspected murderer. **66m/B VHS, DVD.** Anita Page, Charles Starrett, Kenneth Thomson, Clarence Geldart; ***D:*** Harry Hoyt, Albert Kelley; ***C:*** Harry Jackson.

Jungle Captive 🦴 1/2 **1945** Second campy sequel to "Captive Wild Woman" following "Jungle Woman." Mad scientist Dr. Stendahl (Kruger) has been experimenting on bringing dead animals back to life and then attempting to make them human. He steals the body of an female ape (Lane) to practice on and kidnaps his human assistant, Ann (Ward), so she can "donate" her blood. The ape becomes a woman but still has the brain of an animal. This leads to violence. **64m/B VHS.** Otto Kruger, Vicky Lane, Amelita Ward, Rondo Hatton, Phil Brown, Jerome Cowan; ***D:*** Harold Young; ***W:*** M. Coates Webster, Dwight V. Babcock; ***C:*** Maury Gertsman.

Jungle Drums of Africa *U-238 and the Witch Doctor* **1953** Jungle adventures abound as Moore and Coates encounter lions, wind tunnels, voodoo and enemy agents in deepest Africa. A 12-episode serial re-edited onto two cassettes. **167m/B VHS.** Clayton Moore, Phyllis Coates, Roy Glenn, John Cason; ***D:*** Fred Brannon.

Jungle Fever 🦴🦴🦴 **1991 (R)** Married black architect's affair with his white secretary provides the backdrop for a cold look at interracial love. Focuses more on the discomfort of friends and families than with the intense world created by the lovers for themselves. Provides the quota of humor and fresh insight we expect from Lee, but none of the joyous sexuality experienced by the lovers in "She's Gotta Have It." In fact, Lee tells viewers that interracial love is unnatural, never more than skin deep, never more than a blind obsession with the allure of the opposite race. Very fine cast but if you don't agree with Lee, a real disappointment as well. **131m/C VHS, DVD.** Michael Imperioli, Nicholas Turturro, Steven Randazzo, Joseph (Joe) D'Onofrio, Michael Badalucco, Debi Mazar, Gina Mastrogiacomo, Phyllis Stickney, Theresa Randle, Pamela Tyson, Rick Aiello, Miguel (Michael) Sandoval, Doug E. Doug, Queen Latifah, Wesley Snipes, Annabella Sciorra, John Turturro, Samuel L. Jackson, Ossie Davis, Ruby Dee, Lonette McKee, Anthony Quinn, Spike Lee, Halle Berry, Tyra Ferrell, Veronica Webb, Frank Vincent, Tim Robbins, Brad Dourif, Richard Edson; ***D:*** Spike Lee; ***W:*** Spike Lee; ***C:*** Ernest R. Dickerson; ***M:*** Terence Blanchard. N.Y. Film Critics '91: Support. Actor (Jackson).

Jungle Goddess 🦴 1/2 **1949** Two mercenaries set out for the reward offered for finding a wealthy heiress last seen in the jungles of Africa. **61m/B VHS, DVD.** George Reeves, Wanda McKay, Ralph Byrd, Armida; ***D:*** Lewis D. Collins.

Jungle Heat 🦴 1/2 *Dance of the Dwarfs* **1984 (PG)** While searching for a pygmy tribe, an anthropologist and her pilot run into a pack of anthropoid mutants. **93m/C VHS.** Peter Fonda, Deborah Raffin; ***D:*** Gus Trikonis.

Jungle Hell 🦴🦴 **1955** Sabu comes to the rescue of an Indian tribe being harassed by flying saucers, death rays and radioactive debris. **78m/B VHS.** Sabu, David Bruce, George E. Stone, K.T. Stevens; ***D:*** Norman A. Cerf.

Jungle Inferno 🦴 *Zambo, King of the Jungle* **1972** Nature boy, a fugitive from the government, fights lions, tigers and pursuing feds in this story of escape and survival. **90m/C VHS.** *IT* Gisela Hahn, Raf Baldassarre, Daniele Vargas, Attilio Dottesio, Brad Harris; ***D:*** Bitto Albertini; ***W:*** Bitto Albertini; ***M:*** Marcello Giombini.

Jungle Master 🦴 *Karzan, Jungle Lord; Karzan, il Favoloso Uomo della Jungla* **1972** Noble British types hunt for Karzan, the jungle's number one guy, with the aid of a tribal priestess and a lovely photo-journalist. Must see for trash movie fans. **90m/C VHS, DVD.** *IT* Johnny Kissmuller Jr., Ettore Manni, Roger Browne, Simonetta Vitelli; ***D:*** Demofilo Fidani; ***W:*** Demofilo Fidani; ***C:*** Franco Villa; ***M:*** Coriolano Gori.

Jungle Patrol 🦴 1/2 **1948** In 1943 New Guinea, a squadron of entrapped fliers are confronted with a beautiful USO entertainer. Romance and show tunes follow. **72m/B VHS.** Kristine Miller, Arthur Franz, Richard Jaeckel, Ross Ford, Tommy Noonan, Gene Reynolds; ***D:*** Joseph M. Newman.

Jungle Raiders 🦴 1/2 *Legenda Del Rudio Malese; Captain Yankee* **1985 (PG-13)** An Indiana Jones-esque mercenary searches the steamy jungles of Malaysia for a valuable jewel, the Ruby of Gloom. **102m/C VHS.** Lee Van Cleef, Christopher Connelly, Marina Costa; ***D:*** Anthony M. Dawson.

Jungle Siren 🦴🦴 **1942** Nazis in Africa try to foment rebellion amongst the black natives against the white residents. Crabbe and a white woman raised in the jungle set things right. **68m/B VHS, DVD.** Ann Corio, Buster Crabbe, Evelyn Wahl, Milton Kibbee; ***D:*** Sam Newfield.

Jungle 2 Jungle 🦴🦴 1/2 **1996 (PG)** Remake of French farce released as "Little Indian, Big City," changes little of the "wild child" premise. Workaholic Wall Streeter Michael Cromwell (Allen) decides to finalize the divorce from his long-estranged doctor wife, Patricia (Williams), who happens to have been ministering to a tribe in the Amazon rain forest for many years. He gets more than the divorce when he meets the 13-year-old son, Mimi-Siku (Huntington), he never knew he had. Although the boy speaks English, he's been raised as a tribal native, which causes quite a culture shock when he returns with Michael to the jungles of Manhattan. Of course the kid's more than a match for any situation. **105m/C VHS, DVD.** Tim Allen, Sam Huntington, Martin Short, JoBeth Williams, Lolita (David) Davidovich, David Ogden Stiers, Bob (Robert) Dishy, Valerie Mahaffey, Leelee Sobieski, Luis Avalos, Frankie J. Galasso; ***D:*** John Pasquin; ***W:*** Bruce A. Evans, Raynold Gideon; ***C:*** Tony Pierce-Roberts; ***M:*** Michael Convertino.

Jungle Warriors 🦴 1/2 **1984 (R)** Seven fashion models are abducted by a Peruvian cocaine dealer. To escape him, they must become Jungle Warriors. **96m/C VHS.** *GE MX* Sybil Danning, Marjoe Gortner, Nina Van Pallandt, Paul Smith, John Vernon, Alex Cord, Woody Strode, Kai Wulff; ***D:*** Ernst R. von Theumer.

Jungle Woman 1/2 **1944** Scientist Dr. Fletcher (Naish) is being tried for murder and relates his story in court. He does research on apes and has a female simian currently in his lab. The ape disappears and a young woman, Paula (Acquanetta), mysteriously appears. As you might guess, Paula and the ape are the same creature and a dangerous one at that. Follows "Captive Wild Woman" and is followed by "Jungle Captive." **61m/B VHS.** J. Carrol Naish, Acquanetta, Richard Davis, Evelyn Ankers, Samuel S. Hinds, Lois Collier, Milburn Stone, Douglass Dumbrille; ***D:*** Reginald LeBorg; ***W:*** Bernard Schubert, Henry Sucher, Edward Dein; ***C:*** Jack MacKenzie.

Jungleground 1/2 **1995 (R)** Jungleground is a urban wasteland controlled by rival gangs. Lt. Jake Cornel (Piper) gets caught in a shoot-out when a sting operation goes bad and winds up before psychotic gang leader Odin. Odin offers him one chance—Cornel's going to be hunted in Jungleground's abandoned streets and if he can escape before dawn, he gets to live. **90m/C VHS, DVD.** *CA* Roddy Piper, Torri Higginson, Peter Williams; ***D:*** Don Allan; ***W:*** Michael Stokes; ***C:*** Gilles Corbeil; ***M:*** Varouje.

Junior WOOF! **1986** A raving, drooling lunatic cuts up girls with a chainsaw. **80m/C VHS.** Suzanne DeLaurentis, Linda Singer, Jeremy Ruthford, Michael McKeever; ***D:*** Jim Hanley; ***W:*** Don Carmody, John Maxwell; ***C:*** Jean-Maurice de Ernsted; ***M:*** Allan Gerber.

Junior **1994 (PG-13)** Out of the way women! Schwarzenegger trades the war room for the delivery room to experience the miracle of birth. As scientists, he and DeVito take a dip in the gene pool once again to test an anti-miscarriage drug. Thompson provides the egg and some surprisingly good physical comedy as the klutzy cryogenics expert who moves into their university digs. Every pregnancy cliche is explored as Schwarzenegger and DeVito bring the concept to term. Sorry, action fans...nothing blows up except Arnold. **109m/C VHS, DVD.** Arnold Schwarzenegger, Danny DeVito, Emma Thompson, Frank Langella, Pamela Reed, Judy Collins, James Eckhouse, Aida Turturro; ***D:*** Ivan Reitman; ***W:*** Kevin Wade, Chris Conrad; ***C:*** Adam Greenberg; ***M:*** James Newton Howard.

Junior Army 1/2 **1942** English refugee Freddie Hewlett (Bartholomew) saves brash Jimmie Fletcher (Halop) from juvenile delinquent Bushy Thomas (Hall) and the two wind up at the same military academy. Jimmie wants to become a pilot but doesn't have the grades and gets kicked out. Bushy reappears, in the company of a Nazi saboteur, and Freddie and Jimmie save the day. **70m/B VHS.** Freddie Bartholomew, Billy Halop, Huntz Hall, Bobby Jordan, Joseph Crehan, Don Beddoe, Peter Lawford, Rudolph Anders; ***D:*** Lew Landers; ***W:*** Paul Gangelin; ***C:*** Charles E. Schoenbaum.

Junior Bonner **1972 (PG)** A rowdy modern-day western about a young drifting rodeo star who decides to raise money for his father's new ranch by challenging a formidable bull. **100m/C VHS, DVD.** Steve McQueen, Robert Preston, Ida Lupino, Ben Johnson, Joe Don Baker, Barbara Leigh; ***D:*** Sam Peckinpah; ***W:*** Jeb Rosebrook; ***C:*** Lucien Ballard; ***M:*** Jerry Fielding.

Junior G-Men **1940** The Dead End Kids fight Fifth Columnists who are trying to sabotage America's war effort. Twelve episodes. **237m/B VHS, DVD.** Billy Halop, Huntz Hall, Gabriel Dell, Bernard Punsley, Harris Berger, Hal E. Chester, Kenneth Howell, Kenneth Lundy; ***D:*** Ford Beebe, John Rawlins; ***W:*** Basil Dickey, George Plympton, Rex Taylor; ***C:*** Jerome Ash; ***M:*** Charles Previn.

Junior G-Men of the Air 1/2 **1942** The Dead End Kids become teenage flyboys in this 12-episode serial adventure. **215m/B VHS, DVD.** Billy Halop, Huntz Hall, Gene Reynolds, Lionel Atwill, Frank Albertson, Richard Lane, Gabriel Dell, Bernard Punsley, Frankie Darro, David Gorcey, Turhan Bey, Vinton (Hayworth) Haworth; ***D:*** Lewis D. Collins, Ray Taylor; ***W:*** George Plympton, Griffin Jay, Paul Huston; ***C:*** William Sickner.

Junior's Groove *The Planet of Junior Brown* **1997 (R)** Young piano prodigy grows up in a tough neighbor with a caring mom, eccentric piano teacher, and a group of street-smart friends. Based on the novel by Virginia Hamilton. **91m/C VHS, DVD.** Lynn Whitfield, Clark Johnson, Margot Kidder, Sarah Polley, Martin Villafana; ***D:*** Clement Virgo; ***W:*** Clement Virgo, Cameron Bailey; ***C:*** Jonathan Freeman; ***M:*** Christopher Dedrick. **VIDEO**

The Juniper Tree 1/2 **1987** Based on a tale by the Brothers Grimm, this Icelandic curio finds sisters Margit (Bjork) and Katla (Bragadottir) fleeing across the medieval countryside after their mother is burned at the stake for witchcraft. The sisters have their own special powers, which they turn on each other when they become romantic rivals over a young widower (Flygenring). **78m/B VHS, DVD.** *IC* Bjork, Bryndis Petra Bragadottir, Vladimar Orn Flygenring; ***D:*** Nietzchka Keene.

Junk Mail 1/2 *Budbringeren* **1997** Grimy Oslo postman Roy (Skjaerstad) enjoys reading other people's mail, stalking Line, a deaf girl (Saether) on his route, and not washing. One day the girl leaves her keys in the mailbox, so Roy decides to have a look around, later saving her from a suicide attempt. During another of his "visits," Roy learns that Line is involved in a violent crime, along with a thug named Georg (Aske). Through a series of mistaken identities and coicidences, he becomes deeply involved in the proceedings. Sletaune's promising debut is quirky and painstaking in its attention to detail. Skjaerstad does a fine job as the slovenly, slothful, though ultimately sympathetic, mailman. **83m/C VHS.** *NO* Robert Skjaerstad, Andrine Saether, Per Egil Aske, Eli Anne Linnestad; ***D:*** Pal Sletaune; ***W:*** Pal Sletaune, Jonny Halberg; ***C:*** Kjell Vassdal; ***M:*** Joachim Holbek.

The Junkman 1/2 **1982 (R)** Movie maker whose new film is about to be premiered is being chased by a mysterious killer. Promoted as "the ultimate car chase film" since the production used and destroyed over 150 automobiles. From the makers of "Gone in 60 Seconds." **97m/C VHS, DVD.** H.B. Halicki, Christopher Stone, Susan Shaw, Hoyt Axton, Lynda Day George; ***D:*** H.B. Halicki.

Juno 1/2 **2007 (PG-13)** Ultra-sassy Juno (Page) realizes she may not know it all after she finds herself facing teenage motherhood, with her goofy, lovable best friend Paulie (Cera) as the expectant dad. Her parents are concerned, but not angry, almost like they've been there before. Juno opts for adoption rather than abortion, but has trouble following through after she's met with the childless yuppie couple Venessa (Garner) and Mark (Bateman) who are first in line to snatch up her baby. Note-perfect performances all around, especially by Page as the girl unwillingly rocketing into womanhood. Director Jason Reitman retains expert balance for this very smart, funny, offbeat, and touching story, which easily could've come out as another lame teen comedy. **92m/C DVD.** *US* Ellen Page, Michael Cera, Jennifer Garner, Jason Bateman, Allison Janney, J.K. Simmons, Olivia Thirlby; ***D:*** Jason Reitman; ***W:*** Diablo Cody; ***C:*** Eric Steelberg; ***M:*** Mateo Messina. Oscars '07: Orig. Screenplay; British Acad. '07: Orig. Screenplay; Ind. Spirit '08: Actress, Film, First Screenplay; Writers Guild '07: Orig. Screenplay.

Juno and the Paycock 1/2 **1930** Perhaps if Hitchcock hadn't been so faithful to O'Casey this early effort would have been less stagey and more entertaining. In Dublin during the civil uprising, a poor family is torn apart when they receive news of an imminent fortune. Hitchcock's reported to have said that "drama is life with the dull bits left out," though here too many dull bits remain. **96m/B VHS, DVD.** Sara Allgood, Edward Chapman, John Longden, John Laurie, Maire O'Neill; ***D:*** Alfred Hitchcock; ***W:*** Alfred Hitchcock; ***Nar:*** Barry Fitzgerald.

Jupiter's Darling **1955** This spoof of Hannibal (Keel) and Amytis (Williams) gravely misses the mark in making funny the world of the Roman Empire. Amytis has the job of distracting Hannibal from attacking the Eternal City, and does so through musical interludes and unfunny jokes. ♫I Have A Dream; If This Be Slav'ry; I Never Trust A Woman; Hannibal's Victory March; Don't Let This Night Get Away; The Life Of An Elephant; Horatio's Narration. **96m/C** Esther Williams, Howard Keel, George Sanders, Gower Champion, Marge Champion, Norma Varden, Richard Haydn, William Demarest, Douglass Dumbrille, Michael Ansara, Martha Wentworth, Chris Alcaide, William Tannen; ***D:*** George Sidney; ***C:*** Charles Rosher.

Jupiter's Thigh 1/2 **1981** A madcap married pair of treasure-hunters honeymoon in Greece in search of an ancient statue's lost thigh. Available in French with English subtitles, or dubbed into English. **96m/C VHS.** *FR* Annie Girardot, Philippe Noiret, Francis Perrin, Catherine Alric, Marc Dudicourt, Paulette Dubost; ***D:*** Philippe de Broca; ***W:*** Philippe de Broca, Michel Audiard.

Jurassic Park 1/2 **1993 (PG-13)** Crichton's spine-tingling thriller translates well (but not faithfully) due to its main attraction: realistic, rampaging dinosaurs. Genetically cloned from prehistoric DNA, all is well until they escape from their pens—smarter and less predictable than expected. Contrived plot and thin characters (except Goldblum), but who cares? The true stars are the dinos, an incredible combination of models and computer animation. Violent, suspenseful, and realistic with gory attack scenes. Not for small kids, though much of the marketing was aimed at them. At the time, Spielberg knocked his own "E.T." out of the box office top spot, making "JP" the highest grossing movie ever. The T-Rex has since been bested by an iceberg and Celine Dion. **127m/C VHS, DVD.** Sam Neill, Laura Dern, Jeff Goldblum, Richard Attenborough, Bob Peck, Martin Ferrero, B.D. Wong, Joseph Mazzello, Ariana Richards, Samuel L. Jackson, Wayne Knight; ***D:*** Steven Spielberg; ***W:*** David Koepp, Michael Crichton; ***C:*** Dean Cundey; ***M:*** John Williams; ***V:*** Richard Kiley. Oscars '93: Sound, Sound FX Editing, Visual FX.

Jurassic Park 3 **2001 (PG-13)** Neill (who skipped JP2) is back as Dr. Alan Grant, reluctantly leading a seach-and-rescue mission when a plane crash-lands on an island populated by his old nemeses, the dinos. Another new dinosaur species, the Spinosaurus, shows up and to make some more humans into snack food. The talented, and probably over-qualified, group of writers mercifully makes this trip a short one, making sure that any dialogue is mostly expository or in-joke amusing while glossing over the dumb-as-a-box-of-fossils plot and characters. The dinosaurs are, once again, impressive, if you haven't gotten enough of the computer-generated ferocity in the first two outings. Warning: Just because this franchise is getting progressively worse doesn't mean they didn't set up JP4. **90m/C VHS, DVD.** *US* Sam Neill, William H. Macy, Tea Leoni, Alessandro Nivola, Michael Jeter, Trevor Morgan, John Diehl, Bruce A. Young, Taylor Nichols, Mark Harelik, Julio Oscar Mechoso, Laura Dern; ***D:*** Joe Johnston; ***W:*** Peter Buchman, Alexander Payne, Jim Taylor; ***C:*** Shelly Johnson; ***M:*** Don Davis.

The Juror 1/2 **1996 (R)** Plucky single mom (Moore) ends up on the jury in the trial of a powerful mobster and draws the attention of the smooth enforcer (Baldwin) who muscles her into providing a certain verdict. The usual good-vs.-evil, family-in-danger action ensues. Despite boasting a fine cast and impressive attention to detail, flick is guilty of ludicrous situations, a mechanical plot and a dopey ending. Based on the novel by George Dawes Green. **107m/C VHS, DVD.** Demi Moore, Alec Baldwin, Joseph Gordon-Levitt, Anne Heche, James Gandolfini, Lindsay Crouse, Tony LoBianco, Michael Constantine, Matt Craven, Polly Adams; ***D:*** Brian Gibson; ***W:*** Ted Tally; ***C:*** Jamie Anderson; ***M:*** James Newton Howard.

Jury Duty **1995 (PG-13)** Mama's boy loser Tommy Collins (Shore) gets jury duty on a serial-killer case and tries to keep what seems to be an open-and-shut case going so he can continue to get free room and board. He falls for babe juror Monica (Carrere) and really drags the trial (and the film) out in a pathetic attempt to woo her. Shore is even more annoying and unfunny than ever. Lowrent bastardization of "Twelve Angry Men" tries to pass off lame O.J. references and Shore falling out of chairs as humor. Creates reasonable doubt as to Shore's talent and movie execs' judgment. **88m/C VHS, DVD.** Pauly Shore, Tia Carrere, Shelley Winters, Brian Doyle-Murray, Abe Vigoda, Stanley Tucci, Charles Napier, Richard Edson; ***Cameos:*** Andrew (Dice Clay) Silverstein; ***D:*** John Fortenberry; ***W:*** Fax Bahr, Barbara Williams. Golden Raspberries '95: Worst Actor (Shore).

The Jury's Secret 1/2 **1938** Bill Sheldon (Blake) is tried for the murder of a newspaper publisher. The story is covered by reporter Linda Ware (Wray), who discovers that her old beau and fellow writer, Walter Russell (Taylor), is part of the jury and has something to hide. **65m/B VHS.** Kent Taylor, Fay Wray, Larry J. Blake, Jane Darwell, Nan Grey, Leonard Mudie, Samuel S. Hinds, Granville Bates; ***D:*** Edward Sloman; ***W:*** Lester Cole, Newman Levy; ***C:*** Milton Krasner.

Just a Gigolo 1/2 **1979 (R)** Bowie stars in this unusual melodrama about a Prussian war vet turned male prostitute. He spends most of his time working for the sexiest of women. Splendid cast, but a bit incoherent. **105m/C VHS.** *GE* David Bowie, Sydne Rome, Kim Novak, David Hemmings, Maria Schell, Curt Jurgens, Marlene Dietrich; ***D:*** David Hemmings.

Just a Kiss **2002 (R)** Actor Stevens' clever directorial debut shows the dark side of 30-something NYC hipsters whose infidelity and jealousy rival any low-brow talk show fodder. Chain of perilous events is set off by Dag (Eldard), who cheats on his live-in Halley (Sedgwick) with suicidal ballerina Rebecca (Shelton), the girlfriend of Dag's best friend Peter (Breen). When the secret is revealed, more cheating takes place with newcomers Diggs, Choudhury, and Tomei—who plays a hilarious bowling alley waitress. A quirky singles mixer/romantic comedy with a twist, characters are given the chance to go back in time and change their actions. Good performances and writing keep this a few notches above melodramatic send-up, even with somewhat gimmicky use of an animation technique called rotomation. **89m/C VHS, DVD.** *US* Ron Eldard, Kyra Sedgwick, Patrick Breen, Marisa Tomei, Marley Shelton, Taye Diggs, Sarita Choudhury, Zoe Caldwell; ***D:*** Fisher Stevens; ***W:*** Patrick Breen; ***C:*** Terry Stacey; ***M:*** Sean Dinsmore.

Just a Little Harmless Sex **1999 (R)** Alan (Mailhouse) has spent the evening with his buddies, Danny (Silverman) and Brent (Ragsdale), at a topless bar. Driving home, he offers help to a stranded motorist (who turns out to be a hooker) and winds up getting arrested. Alan's wife, Laura (Eastwood), is, naturally, not happy about the situation and discusses her plight with her gal pals while Alan and his buddies discuss his fractured marriage. Angsty but not particularly novel. **98m/C VHS, DVD.** Robert Mailhouse, Alison Eastwood, Jonathan Silverman, William Ragsdale, Lauren Hutton, Kimberly Williams, Jessica Lundy, Rachel Hunter, Michael Ontkean, Tito Larriva; ***D:*** Rick Rosenthal; ***W:*** Roger Miller, Marti Noxon; ***C:*** Bruce Surtees; ***M:*** Tito Larriva.

Just Add Water **2007 (R)** Mild-mannered, blue-collar Ray Tuckby (Walsh) lives in the dead-end desert community of Trona, California, in a lousy marriage and with a nothing job. The community has fallen prey to a slimy real estate speculator and a violent teenage meth dealer. But somewhere along the way, Ray decides it's time for a change—for himself and the town. **91m/C DVD.** Dylan Walsh, Tracy Middendorf, Danny DeVito, Justin Long, Jonah Hill, Anika Noni Rose, Brad Hunt; ***D:*** Hart Bochner; ***W:*** Hart Bochner; ***C:*** Aaron Barnes; ***M:*** John Swihart.

Just Another Girl on the I.R.T. 1/2 **1993 (R)** Double debut from two African American women, writer/director Harris, and actress Johnson, captures the sass and wit of a girl from the projects. Seventeen-year-old Chantal has a plan for her life and challenges authority with assurance, even after an unexpected pregnancy puts a twist into her plan. Strong initial statement tends to become weak and cloudy as Chantal loses her focus. This doesn't dismiss the remarkable realism and raw talent portrayed in a picture filmed in just seventeen days for $130,000. Winner of a special jury prize at the Sundance Film Festival.

96m/C VHS, DVD. Ariyan Johnson, Kevin Thigpen, Ebony Jerido, Jerard Washington, Chequita Jackson, William Badget; ***D:*** Leslie Harris; ***W:*** Leslie Harris; ***C:*** Richard Conners. Sundance '93: Special Jury Prize.

Just Another Love Story 🦴 ½ *Kaerlighed Pa Film* **2008** Danish potboiler is an overdone romantic thriller about identity. Despite his work as a crime-scene photographer, married Jonas' (Berthelsen) life is average and predictable. Until he and his family are involved in a serious car accident. They are fine but Julia (Hemse), the driver of the other car, is in a coma. Jonas lets her family believe that he is her mysterious boyfriend, wanting to help in her recovery, and when the troubled young woman regains consciousness, she allows the deception to continue. Of course the real boyfriend (Lie Kaas) will show up and trouble will escalate. Danish with subtitles. **104m/C DVD.** *DK* Anders W. Berthelsen, Nikolaj Lie Kaas, Bent Mejding, Rebecka Hemse, Charlotte Fich, Dejan Cukic, Karsten Jansfort, Ewa Frohling; ***D:*** Ole Bornedal; ***W:*** Ole Bornedal; ***C:*** Dan Laustsen; ***M:*** Joachim Holbek.

Just Another Pretty Face 🦴🦴 ½ *Be Beautiful but Shut Up* **1958** An aging detective catches a gang of jewel smugglers, and gets involved with their young moll. In French with English subtitles. **110m/B VHS.** *FR* Henri Vidal, Mylene Demongeot, Isa Miranda; ***D:*** Henri Verneuil.

Just Around the Corner 🦴 ½ **1938 (G)** Temple helps her Depression-poor father get a job after she befriends a cantankerous millionaire. Temple duets with Bill "Bojangles" Robinson with the fourth time. Also available colorized. ♫ This Is A Happy Little Ditty; I'm Not Myself Today; I'll Be Lucky With You; Just Around the Corner; I Love To Walk in the Rain; Brass Buttons and Epaulets. **71m/B VHS, DVD.** Shirley Temple, Charles Farrell, Bert Lahr, Joan Davis, Bill Robinson, Cora Witherspoon, Franklin Pangborn; ***D:*** Irving Cummings.

Just Before Dawn 🦴🦴 **1980 (R)** Another murderers stalk campers story; humans resort to their animal instincts in their struggle for survival. Not to be confused with the William Castle film (1946) from the "Crime Doctor" series. **90m/C VHS, DVD.** Chris Lemmon, Deborah Benson, Gregg Henry, George Kennedy; ***D:*** Jeff Lieberman; ***M:*** Brad Fiedel.

Just Before Nightfall 🦴🦴 ½ *Juste Avant la Nuit* **1971** Charles (Bouquet) is having an affair with Laura (Douking), the domineering wife of his best friend Francois (Tellier). Laura dies (apparently during a sex game) and Charles goes home to his wife Helene (Audran), pretending nothing has happened. Then the police investigation starts and Charles's guilt begins to gnaw at him. First he confesses to Helene—and then to Francois—but their bourgeois reactions are more shocking to Charles than Laura's death. French with subtitles. **100m/C DVD.** *FR* Stephane Audran, Michel Bouquet, Francois Perier, Jean Carmet, Anna Douking, Henri Attal; ***D:*** Claude Chabrol; ***W:*** Claude Chabrol; ***C:*** Jean Rabier; ***M:*** Pierre Jansen.

Just Between Friends 🦴🦴 **1986 (PG-13)** Two women become friends, not knowing that one is having an affair with the husband of the other. Allan Burns directorial debut. **110m/C VHS, DVD.** Mary Tyler Moore, Christine Lahti, Sam Waterston, Ted Danson, Jim MacKrell, Jane Greer; ***D:*** Allan Burns; ***W:*** Allan Burns; ***C:*** Jordan Cronenweth.

Just Buried 🦴 ½ **2007** Misanthropic would-be black comedy. N'er-do-well Oliver learns that he's inherited his dad's failing mortuary business, which he intends to sell until he gets interested in fixated embalmer Roberta. Accidentally killing a hiker in a car mishap, Oliver uses the funeral home to dispose of the body, which gives Roberta the idea that they should drum up clientele through murderous means. **94m/C DVD.** *CA* Jay Baruchel, Rose Byrne, Graham Greene, Nigel Bennett, Thomas Gibson, Reagan Pasternak, Sergio Di Zio; ***D:*** Chaz Thorne; ***W:*** Chaz Thorne; ***C:*** Christopher Porter; ***M:*** Darren Fung.

Just Business 🦴 ½ **2008** Elizar Perla (Pastko) can't resist coming out of cat burglar retirement to go after the art collection of David Gray (Watton). But when Perla disappears, his daughter Marty (Gershon) is forced to accept help from Gray to recover the art work, which may lead to her father's whereabouts. But it seems the rarest of the stolen pieces is beyond monetary value, so expect some complications. **85m/C DVD.** Gina Gershon, Jonathan Watton, John Robinson, Zachary Bennett, Earl Pastko; ***D:*** Jonathan Dueck; ***W:*** David Robinson; ***C:*** Mick Reynolds; ***M:*** Ryan Latham. **VIDEO**

Just Cause 🦴🦴 **1994 (R)** Incoherent mystery/thriller set in the Florida Everglades. Retired attorney, Paul Armstrong, now a Harvard law professor, decides to defend Bobby Earl (Underwood), on death row for the murder of a white girl. As Armstrong investigates the case, he discovers that the arresting officer Tanny Brown, (Fishburne) is corrupt and tortured the confession out of Bobby. Starts off promising with the electricity of Connery's and Fishburne's presence and a frigthening cameo by Ed Harris as an incarcerated serial killer, but once the barrage of plot twists start, creating gator size holes in the plot, the movie drifts into a murkey swamp of absurdity. Adapted from the legal thriller by John Katzenbach. **102m/C VHS, DVD.** Sean Connery, Laurence Fishburne, Kate Capshaw, Blair Underwood, Ruby Dee, Daniel J. Travanti, Ned Beatty, Lynne Thigpen, George Plimpton, Chris Sarandon, Kevin McCarthy, Ed Harris; ***D:*** Arne Glimcher; ***W:*** Jeb Stuart, Robert Stone; ***C:*** Lajos Koltai; ***M:*** James Newton Howard.

Just for the Hell of It **WOOF!** *Destruction, Inc* **1968** A quartet of teenage punks ruthlessly terrorize their suburban Miami 'hood while an innocent kid gets blamed. More exploitation from schlock king Lewis, who also wrote the theme song, "Destruction, Inc." (pic's alternate title). Essentially the same cast as the director's "She Devils on Wheels," filmed simultaneously. **85m/C VHS, DVD.** Rodney Bedell, Ray Sager, Nancy Lee Noble, Agi Gyenes, Steve White; ***D:*** Herschell Gordon Lewis; ***W:*** Allison Louise Downe; ***C:*** Roy Collodi; ***M:*** Larry Wellington.

Just for You 🦴🦴 ½ **1952** Entertaining musical about producer Crosby who doesn't have time for his kids until Wyman steps in and shows him the way. Based on Stephen Vincent Benet's novel "Famous." ♫ Zing A Little Zong; He's Just Crazy For Me; The Live Oak Tree; A Flight of Fancy; I'll Si-Si Ya In Bahia; On the 10:10; Just for You. **95m/C VHS, DVD.** Bing Crosby, Jane Wyman, Ethel Barrymore, Robert Arthur, Natalie Wood, Cora Witherspoon; ***D:*** Elliott Nugent; ***W:*** Robert Carson.

Just Friends 🦴 **2005 (PG-13)** No surprises in this romantic comedy, but it's sweet enough anyway. Chris (Reynolds), the chubby Jersey kid, is in love with his high school chick friend Jamie (Smart) but he's overweight, shy, and in the "friend zone." Chris moves to L.A., where he transforms into a super hot So-Cal babe collector before returning to his hometown 10 years later. **94m/C DVD.** *US* Ryan Reynolds, Amy Smart, Anna Faris, Julie Hagerty, Christopher Marquette, Stephen (Steve) Root, Chris Klein, Fred Ewanuick; ***D:*** Roger Kumble; ***W:*** Adam "Tex" Davis; ***C:*** Anthony B. Richmond; ***M:*** Jeff Cardoni.

Just Like a Woman 🦴🦴 **1995 (R)** Sweet-natured film about an unlikely romance with some decided quirks. Young American Gerald (Pasdar) is working for a London bank and renting a flat from lonely older divorcee Monica (Walters). Ideal tenant Gerald is also recently divorced and a mutual attraction develops, in fact Gerald trusts Monica enough to confess his darkest secret—seems his marriage broke up over women's lingerie—the ones Gerald likes to wear when he cross-dresses in his female persona of Geraldine. Does this put Monica off? Well, she turns out to be very understanding indeed. Based on the memoir "Geraldine" by Monica Jay. **102m/C VHS.** *GB* Adrian Pasdar, Julie Walters, Paul Freeman, Susan Wooldridge, Gordon Kennedy, Ian Redford, Shelley Thompson; ***D:*** Christopher Monger; ***W:*** Nick Evans; ***C:*** Alan Hume; ***M:*** Michael Storey.

Just Like Dad 🦴🦴 **1996 (PG)** Nerdy kid with an equally nerdy dad wants to actually win some of the Father/Son Picnic contests. Even if he has to hire a heroic dad substitute to do help him out. **102m/C VHS.** Wallace Shawn, Nick Cassavetes, Laura Innes, Ben Diskin; ***D:*** Blair Treu; ***W:*** Wayne Rice; ***C:*** Brian Sullivan; ***M:*** William Goldstein.

Just like Heaven 🦴🦴 **2005 (PG-13)** David Abbott (Ruffalo) tragically loses his wife, sending him into a tailspin of depression. Looking to start anew, Abbott moves into a new apartment, which just happens to be occupied—by a ghost, Elizabeth (Witherspoon), who doesn't know she's dead Actually she's only mostly dead—she's in limbo, in a coma after a car accident. Mindless romantic fluff worth it for fans of that sort of thing, or for those of you with a crash on one of the attractive leads. **101m/C VHS, DVD.** *US* Reese Witherspoon, Mark Ruffalo, Dina Spybey, Donal Logue, Ben Shenkman, Jon Heder, Ivana Milicevic, Rosalind Chao, Ron Canada; ***D:*** Mark S. Waters; ***W:*** Peter Tolan, Leslie Dixon; ***C:*** Daryn Okada; ***M:*** Rolfe Kent.

Just Like the Son 🦴🦴 **2006 (PG-13)** Petty criminal Daniel (Webber) is performing community service at a Brooklyn elementary school, which is where he meets eight-year-old Boone (Ortiz). When his mom is hospitalized, Boone is sent to a foster school upstate and Daniel decides he needs rescuing. So he steals a car, grabs the kid, and they embark on a cross-country road trip to find Boone's sister who's supposed to be living in Dallas. Has sentimental written all over the plot (and Ortiz is adorable) but Freeman doesn't overindulge in the schmaltz. **86m/C DVD.** Mark Webber, Antonio Ortiz, Rosie Perez, Brendan Sexton III, Bruce MacVittie, Adrian Martinez; ***D:*** Morgan Freeman; ***W:*** Morgan Freeman; ***C:*** Yaron Orbach; ***M:*** Dean Wareham, Britta Phillips.

Just Like Weather 🦴🦴🦴 **1986** Contemporary Hong Kong and the city's looming return to control by mainland China provide the backdrop for the troubled marriage of a young couple. Couple endure abortion, arrest, and veterinarian episodes before departing for on U.S. trip with high hopes. **98m/C VHS.** *HK* Christine Lee, Lee Chi-Keung, Allen Fong; ***D:*** Allen Fong.

Just Looking 🦴🦴 ½ *Cherry Pink* **1999 (R)** A comedy about teenaged voyeurism set in 1955. 14-year-old Lenny (Merriman) has only one thing on his mind for summer vacation in his Bronx neighborhood. He's determined to figure out what sex is all about by watching some adults "do it." Well, Lenny's mom decides to send him to stay in suburban Queens with her sister but that doesn't change his plans. Predictable coming of age comedy with Alexander making his directorial debut. **97m/C VHS, DVD.** *US* Ryan Merriman, Gretchen Mol, Patti LuPone, Peter Onorati, Ilana Levine, Richard V. Licata, John Bolger, Joey Franquinha; ***D:*** Jason Alexander; ***W:*** Marshall Karp; ***C:*** Fred Schuler; ***M:*** Michael Skloff.

Just Married 🦴 ½ **2003 (PG-13)** Mismatched newlyweds Tom (Kutcher) and Sarah (Murphy) find slapstick situations and jealousy instead of romantic bliss on their European honeymoon. Tom's a sports-lovin' regular guy, and Sarah's the well-educated daughter of a Beverly Hills tycoon. In Europe, they must deal with that, along with every ugly American and snooty European stereotype in the book, er, script. Kutcher plays his usual pretty-boy doofus, but Murphy is wasted in a stupid movie seemingly designed to give Kutcher pin-up status. **94m/C VHS, DVD.** *US* Ashton Kutcher, Brittany Murphy, Christian Kane, David Moscow, Monet Mazur, David Rasche, Veronica Cartwright, Raymond J. Barry, Thad Luckinbill, David Agranov, Taram Killam; ***D:*** Shawn Levy; ***W:*** Sam Harper; ***C:*** Jonathan Brown; ***M:*** Christophe Beck.

Just Me & You 🦴 ½ **1978** An "It Happened One Night" tale of an unlikely couple who fall in love with each other when chance brings them together on a cross-country drive. **100m/C VHS.** Louise Lasser, Charles Grodin; ***D:*** Charles Erman; ***W:*** Louise Lasser. **TV**

Just My Luck 🦴 ½ **2006 (PG-13)** Bland romantic fantasy finds Lohan growing up and trying to escape the teen queen ghetto. Ashley, a junior exec in Manhattan, is just the luckiest gal ever. Her opposite is cutie-pie Jake (Pine), whose life is one continuous calamity. They meet at a costume party, kiss, and their worlds turn—Jake can do no wrong and Ashley, well, life is just so not fair! Now she needs to kiss Jake again and do another switcheroo. Lohan's game for slapstick humiliation, but this one's just another rung up the acting ladder. **108m/C DVD.** *US* Lindsay Lohan, Chris Pine, Samaire Armstrong, Bree Turner, Faizon Love, Missi Pyle, Makenzie Vega, Tovah Feldshuh, Jaqueline Fleming, Carlos Ponce; ***D:*** Donald Petrie; ***W:*** I. Marlene King, Amy Harris; ***C:*** Dean Semler; ***M:*** Teddy Castellucci.

Just Off Broadway 🦴 ½ **1942** Private eye Michael Shayne (Nolan) is on the jury in the murder trial when a witness who could clear the accused is killed by a knife hurled from within the courtroom. Shayne hides the knife and, overnight, traces the knife to the thrower, but that's only the beginning of the trail. Shayne's back in the court the next morning and he's got the scoop, although he's in the hot seat for skipping out on jury duty. **65m/B DVD.** Lloyd Nolan, Marjorie Weaver, Phil Silvers, Janis Carter, Richard Derr; ***D:*** Herbert I. Leeds; ***W:*** Brett Halliday, Arnaud d'Usseau; ***C:*** Lucien N. Andriot; ***M:*** David Raksin.

Just One Night 🦴🦴 ½ **2000 (PG-13)** College professor Isaac Adler (Hutton) is spending the night before his wedding in San Francisco. His taxi collides with that of beautiful, married Aurora (Cucinotta) and maybe the collision shook them up more than they thought, since they decide to spend the evening getting to know each other better. **90m/C VHS, DVD.** Timothy Hutton, Maria Grazia Cucinotta, Udo Kier, Michael O'Keefe, Robert Easton, Don Novello, Seymour Cassel, Natalie Shaw; ***D:*** Alan Jacobs; ***W:*** Alan Jacobs; ***C:*** John Campbell; ***M:*** Anthony Marinelli.

Just One of the Girls 🦴 ½ **1993 (R)** Teen star Haim transfers to a new high school where he dresses in drag in order to avoid the itinerant leader of the school's toughest gang whom he has unwittingly enraged. Palling around with Eggert becomes one of his costume's unexpected perks. Sort of a cross between "Some Like It Hot" and "90210." **94m/C VHS, DVD.** Corey Haim, Nicole Eggert, Cameron Bancroft; ***D:*** Michael Keusch; ***M:*** Amin Bhatia.

Just One of the Guys 🦴🦴 **1985 (PG-13)** When the school newspaper refuses to accept the work of an attractive young girl, she goes undercover as a boy to prove that her work is good. She goes on to befriend the school's nerd, and even helps him grow out of his awkward stage, falling for him in the process. Very cute, but predictable. **100m/C VHS, DVD.** Joyce Hyser, Clayton Rohner, Billy Jacoby, Toni Hudson, Leigh McCloskey, Sherilyn Fenn, William Zabka; ***D:*** Lisa Gottlieb.

Just One Time 🦴🦴 **2000 (R)** New York-set romantic comedy about fulfilling fantasies. Fireman Anthony (Janger) is about to marry lawyer Amy (Carter) but can't resist telling her about his sexual dream to see her make out with another woman—just once—before the wedding. Distraught, Amy confides in their gay neighbor, Victor (Diaz), who admits to a crush on Anthony. So she offers a quid pro quo to her beau—she'll indulge him with sultry lesbian Michelle (Esposito) if Anthony will do the same for her with Victor, and he has to go first. **94m/C VHS, DVD.** *US* Lane Janger, Joelle Carter, Guillermo Diaz, Jennifer Esposito, Vincent Laresca, David Lee Russek, Domenick Lombardozzi; ***D:*** Lane Janger; ***W:*** Jennifer Vandever, Lane Janger; ***C:*** Michael St. Hilaire; ***M:*** Edward Bilous.

Just Suppose 🦴🦴 ½ **1926** Prince in waiting decides he'd prefer the simple life, travels to the land of the free in search of honest work and is felled by cupid's arrow. All's well 'til duty calls, and his princely presence is expected back in the royal fold. Features beautiful boy Barthelmess, whom Lillian Gish described as having "the most beautiful face of any man who ever went before a camera." Silent. **90m/B VHS.** Richard Barthelmess, Lois Moran, Geoffrey Kerr, Henry Vibart, George Spelvin; ***D:*** Kenneth Webb.

Just Tell Me What You Want 🦴🦴 ½ **1980 (R)** A wealthy, self-made married man finally drives his longtime mistress away when he refuses to let her take over the operation of a failing movie studio he has acquired. After she falls for another man, the tycoon does everything he can to win her back. The department store battle between MacGraw and King is priceless. **112m/C VHS, DVD.** Alan King, Ali MacGraw, Myrna Loy, Keenan Wynn, Tony Roberts; ***D:*** Sidney Lumet; ***W:*** Jay Presson Allen; ***C:*** Oswald Morris.

Just Tell Me You Love Me **1980 (PG)** Three budding con artists plot to make easy money in this Hawaiian romp. **90m/C VHS.** Robert Hegyes, Debralee Scott, Lisa Hartman Black, Ricci Martin, June Lockhart; ***D:*** Tony Mordente.

Just the Ticket *The Scalper* **1998 (R)** Romantic comedy set in the seedy world of ticket scalpers should have skipped the trite love story and centered on the ducat slingers. Gary (Garcia) is a fast talking huckster trying to win back ex-girlfriend Linda (MacDowell). He's also hoping for the ever-popular last big score before he goes legit. His opportunity arrives when the Pope announces a visit to Yankee Stadium, but he must out-hustle competitor Casino (Blake). Garcia wrote many of the Salsa-flavored songs used in the movie. **115m/C VHS, DVD.** Lenny Venito, Andy Garcia, Andie MacDowell, Richard Bradford, Laura Harris, Andre B. Blake, Elizabeth Ashley, Patrick Breen, Ron Leibman, Chris Lemmon, Don Novello, Abe Vigoda, Bill Irwin, Ronald Guttman, Donna Hanover, Irene Worth, Fred Asparagus, Louis Mustillo, Paunita Nichols, Joe Frazier; ***D:*** Richard Wenk; ***W:*** Richard Wenk; ***C:*** Ellen Kuras; ***M:*** Rick Marotta.

Just the Way You Are **1984 (PG)** An attractive musician struggles to overcome a physical handicap and winds up falling in love while on vacation in the French Alps. **96m/C VHS.** Kristy McNichol, Robert Carradine, Kaki Hunter, Michael Ontkean, Alexandra Paul, Lance Guest, Timothy Daly, Patrick Cassidy; ***D:*** Edouard Molinaro; ***W:*** Allan Burns; ***M:*** Vladimir Cosma.

Just Visiting **2001 (PG-13)** Remake of the 1993 French flick "Les Visiteurs" has Reno and Clavier reprising their roles as a medieval knight and his servant who find themselves in modern-day Chicago. Original was a huge hit in France, but bombed here. This one should do much better here, since there's much less reading of subtitles involved, and this one makes good use of the excellent leads and the transplanted Chicago locales. **88m/C VHS, DVD.** *US* Jean Reno, Christian Clavier, Christina Applegate, Tara Reid, Matt Ross, Bridgette Wilson-Sampras, John Aylward, George Plimpton, Malcolm McDowell, Sarah Badel, Richard Bremmer, Robert Glenister; ***D:*** Jean-Marie Poire; ***W:*** Christian Clavier, Jean-Marie Poire, John Hughes; ***C:*** Ueli Steiger; ***M:*** John Powell.

Just William's Luck **1947** A precocious English brat sneaks into an old mansion, which just happens to be the headquarters for a gang of thieves. Based on British series of children's books. **87m/B VHS.** *GB* William A. Graham, Garry Marsh; ***D:*** Val Guest.

Just Write **1/2 1997 (PG-13)** Sweet and slight romantic comedy about making your dreams come true. Harold (Piven) is a Hollywood tour bus driver who works for his well-meaning but overbearing father (Rocco). He meets cute with rising star Amanda (Fenn), who is mistakenly lead to believe Harold is a screenwriter. And Amanda just happens to have a script that needs some work. They begin to fall in love but sooner or later the truth is bound to come out. Leads play well together and the supporting cast is fine, especially Williams as a hard-charging agent. **95m/C VHS, DVD.** Jeremy Piven, Sherilyn Fenn, JoBeth Williams, Alex Rocco, Jeffrey D. Sams, Wallace Shawn, Costas Mandylor, Yeardley Smith, Holland Taylor; ***Cameos:*** Nancy McKeon, Ed McMahon; ***D:*** Andrew Gallerani; ***W:*** Stan Williamson; ***C:*** Michael Brown; ***M:*** Leland Bond.

Just Your Luck **1/2 1996 (R)** The New Sudka Cafe II, owned by the high strung Nick (Polito), is the setting for one wild night. An old man promptly keels over dead upon learning that his lottery ticket is a $6 million prize-winner. Customer Kim (Madsen) tries to convince Nick and her fellow diners that they should keep the ticket and split the winnings. **86m/C VHS.** Virginia Madsen, Sean Patrick Flanery, Ernie Hudson, Jon Polito, Alanna Ubach, Jon Favreau, Mike Starr, Carroll Baker; ***D:*** Gary Auerbach; ***W:*** Gary Auerbach.

Justice of the Range **1/2 1935** The McLean and Brennan ranches are losing cattle to rustlers but they blame each other instead. Cattle buyer Graves hires Tim Condon to sort things out but the situation isn't what it seems. **58m/B DVD.** Tim McCoy, Ward Bond, Guy Usher, George "Gabby" Hayes, Billie Seward, Ed LeSaint; ***D:*** David Selman; ***W:*** Ford Beebe; ***C:*** George Meehan Jr.

Justice of the West **1961** The Lone Ranger and his sidekick, Tonto, perform good deeds in the Old West, including helping to retrieve stolen gold, helping to build an Indian school, and giving a blind man a fresh perspective on life. **71m/C VHS.** Clayton Moore, Jay Silverheels; ***D:*** Earl Bellamy.

Justice Rides Again **1/2** *Destry Rides Again* **1932** Mix tries to uphold law and order, but he's up against some very tough outlaws. **55m/B VHS.** Tom Mix, Claudia Dell, Zasu Pitts, Stanley Fields, Edward Peil Sr., Francis Ford, George Ernest, Earle Foxe; ***D:*** Alan James, Ben Stoloff; ***W:*** Richard Schayer; ***C:*** Daniel B. Clark.

Justin Morgan Had a Horse **1981** The true story of a colonial school teacher in post-Revolutionary War Vermont who first bred the Morgan horse, the first and most versatile American breed. **91m/C VHS.** Don Murray, Lana Wood, Gary Crosby; ***D:*** Hollingsworth Morse.

Justine **1969** In the 1930s, a prostitute who marries an Egyptian banker becomes involved with a variety of men and a plot to arm Palestinian Jews in their revolt against English rule. A condensed film version of Lawrence Durrell's "The Alexandria Quartet." **115m/C VHS.** *IS* Anouk Aimee, Michael York, Dirk Bogarde, Philippe Noiret, Michael Constantine, John Vernon, Jack Albertson; ***D:*** George Cukor; ***W:*** Lawrence B. Marcus; ***C:*** Leon Shamroy; ***M:*** Jerry Goldsmith.

Juwanna Mann **2002 (PG-13)** Cross-dressing comedy plays like a "Tootsie" retread in sneakers. Jamal (Nunez) is an obnoxious pro basketball player booted out of the league after mooning a ref while protesting a call. Facing total bankruptcy and realizing his only skills are on the basketball court, Jamal dons make-up and falsies and joins a pro women's league as Juwanna Mann. Predictable situations occur, including Jamal falling for beautiful teammate Michelle (Fox) and being hit on by clueless suitor Puff Smokey Smoke (Davidson), but performances save what could have been a complete disaster. **91m/C VHS, DVD.** *US* Miguel A. Nunez Jr., Vivica A. Fox, Kevin Pollak, Tommy Davidson, Kim Wayans, Jenifer Lewis, Kimberly (Lil' Kim) Jones, Annie Corley, Ginuwine; ***D:*** Jesse Vaughan; ***W:*** Bradley Allenstein; ***C:*** Reynaldo Villalobos; ***M:*** Wendy Melvoin, Lisa Coleman.

K-9 **1/2 1989 (PG-13)** After having his car destroyed by a drug dealer, "I work alone" Belushi is forced to take on a partner—a German Shepherd. Together they work to round up the bad guys and maybe chew on their shoes a little. Sometimes amusing one-joke comedy done in by a paper-thin script. Both the dog and Belushi are good, however. **111m/C VHS, DVD.** James Belushi, Mel Harris, Kevin Tighe, Ed O'Neill, Cotter Smith, James Handy, Jerry Lee; ***D:*** Rod Daniel; ***W:*** Steven Siegel, Scott Myers; ***C:*** Dean Semler; ***M:*** Miles Goodman.

K-9 3: P.I. **1/2 2001 (PG-13)** Detective Dooley (Belushi) and Jerry Lee are heading for retirement and new careers as private eyes. But when they try stopping a crime in progress, they wind up as the prime suspects and now must try to find the real culprits. Oh, and Dooley thinks he can earn some extra cash by having Jerry Lee serve as a German Shepard stud for a dog breeder. Family friendly fun. **95m/C VHS, DVD.** James Belushi, Jason Schombing, Barbara Tyson, Gary Basaraba, Kymberley Huffman, Christopher Shyer; ***D:*** Richard J. Lewis; ***W:*** Gary Scott Thompson, Ed Horowitz. **VIDEO**

K-911 **1/2 1999 (PG-13)** Ten years after the original film, Belushi returns to his role of LAPD Detective Dooley, along with his German Sheperd partner, Jerry Lee. The aging duo are now reluctantly partnered with a younger K-9 unit—no-nonsense detective Welles (Tucci) and her partner, a Doberman named Zeus. But Dooley has some other things on his mind—some kook is trying to kill him. **91m/C VHS, DVD.** James Belushi, James Handy, Christine Tucci, Wade Andrew Williams, J.J. Johnston, Vincent Castellanos; ***D:*** Charles Kanganis; ***W:*** Gary Scott Thompson; ***C:*** George Mooradian; ***M:*** Stephen (Steve) Edwards. **VIDEO**

K-9000 **1989** The Hound salutes the idea behind this standard sci-fi crime-fighter; a cyberdog fights the forces of evil with the aid of a cop, a lady reporter, and the usual cliches. **96m/C VHS, DVD.** Chris Mulkey, Catherine Oxenberg; ***D:*** Kim Manners; ***M:*** Jan Hammer. **TV**

K-19: The Widowmaker **2002 (PG-13)** Cold War tensions abound in this aptly claustrophobic submarine suspenser involving the Soviet Union's first nuclear ballistic sub, which suffers a reactor malfunction during a test voyage in the North Atlantic. Ford plays the tough Russian captain, who takes command from the more-popular Neeson, and must deal with rebellion in the ranks in order to save his sub and crew, and prevent an all out World War. Sarsgaard is the panicky, inexperienced reactor officer who's every nuke sub captain's nightmare. Strong performances by the lead actors almost overshadows their flimsy Russian accents. Bigelow shot on a set built to scale, with parts salvaged from an old diesel sub. Loosely based on a military incident that happened in 1961 but wasn't publicly revealed until the 1990s. **138m/C VHS, DVD.** *US* Harrison Ford, Liam Neeson, Peter Sarsgaard, Joss Ackland, John Shrapnel, Donald (Don) Sumpter, Tim Woodward, Ravil Isyanov, Christian Camargo, Steve Nicholson; ***D:*** Kathryn Bigelow; ***W:*** Christopher Kyle; ***C:*** Jeff Cronenweth; ***M:*** Klaus Badelt.

K-PAX **1/2 2001 (PG-13)** Spacey plays his patented "smirky guy with a secret" again in this tale of aliens and the humans who love them. Prot (Spacey) is admitted to a psychiatric hospital when he claims to be from outer space. Dr. Powell (Bridges) is assigned his case and soon finds himself intrigued by Prot. It seems that he's going around helping the patients in the hospital to actually get better. His other quirks include an astounding knowledge of astrophysics and an amazing tolerance to Thorazine. After Powell hypnotizes Prot, a deeply hidden personality is unmasked, but the actual truth about his identity is left open to interpretation. Bridges and Spacey work well together, and they save this sentimental E.T. tale from turning to schmaltzy mush. **120m/C VHS, DVD.** *US* Kevin Spacey, Jeff Bridges, Mary McCormack, Alfre Woodard, David Patrick Kelly, Saul Williams, Peter Gerety, Celia Weston, Ajay Naidu, John Toles-Bey, Kimberly Scott, Mary Mara, Aaron Paul, William Lucking; ***D:*** Iain Softley; ***W:*** Charles Leavitt; ***C:*** John Mathieson; ***M:*** Ed Shearmur.

Kaaterskill Falls **2001** Indie horror flick suffers from its obvious low budget and stilted improvisations. Yuppie couple Mitchell (Riggs) and Ren (Howard) are driving to a cabin in upstate New York where they hope to rekindle their disintegrating marriage. Ren decides to offer monosyllabic hitchhiker Lyle (Leslie) a ride to a nearby motel. But Lyle soons makes an appearance at their cabin and they decide to extent their hospitality to inviting him in for dinner. This is the first of many mistakes. **87m/C VHS, DVD.** Mitchell Riggs, Hilary Howard, Anthony Leslie; ***D:*** Josh Apter, Peter Olsen; ***W:*** Mitchell Riggs, Hilary Howard, Anthony Leslie, Josh Apter, Peter Olsen; ***C:*** Peter Olsen.

Kabei: Our Mother **2008** Director Yamada's 80th film follows the vicissitudes of the Nogami family after professor Shigeru Nogami is thrown in prison in 1940 for protesting Japan's invasion of China. This leaves his delicate wife Kayo to support their two young daughters with the unexpected help of Shigeru's former student, clumsy, bumptious Toru. Narrow and soapy exploration about a paragon of motherhood. Japanese with subtitles. **133m/C DVD.** *JP* Sayuri Yoshinago, Mitsugoro Bando, Tsurube Shofukutei, Umenosuke Nakamura, Tadanobu Asano; ***D:*** Yoji Yamada; ***W:*** Emiko Hiramatsu, Yoji Yamada; ***C:*** Mutsuo Naganuma; ***M:*** Isao Tamita.

Kadosh **1999** Meir (Hattab) and his wife Rivka (Abecassis) are ultra-Orthodox Jews living in the Mea Shearim quarter of Jerusalem. They have been married for 10 years and are still childless, so Meir is being pressured by his rabbi father to divorce his wife (though they love each other) and remarry. Rivka learns the fertility problem is with her husband but can do nothing because of religious tenets and she leaves their home. Meanwhile, Rivka's younger sister, Malka (Barda), contemplates abandoning her unhappy arranged marriage to be with the man she loves. Hebrew with subtitles. **110m/C VHS, DVD.** *IS* Yael Abecassis, Yoram Hattab, Meital Barda, Sami Hori, Uri Klauzner, Yussef Abu-Warda; ***D:*** Amos Gitai; ***W:*** Amos Gitai, Eliette Abecassis; ***C:*** Renato Berta; ***M:*** Louis Sclavis.

Kaena: The Prophecy **1/2** *Kaena: La Prophetie* **2003 (PG-13)** Sci-fi fantasy epic about a brave young humanoid girl (Dunst) who resists her society's groveling submission to its tyrannical "gods." Once cast out, she discovers many hidden secrets about her world. She meets an old astronaut/scientist (Harris) who is the last survivor of the ancient spaceship-wreck that formed her world, and who may possess the power to revive or destroy it as well. Visually stunning movie is France's first entry into full-length CGI animation. Texture is so rich and intricate, it should hold up well to multiple viewings. Characters are a bit thin, and the dubbed dialogue is annoyingly flat and unnatural. It would be interesting to see the French version. One of Richard Harris' last performances. **91m/C DVD.** *FR CA FR* ***D:*** Chris Delaporte, Pascal Pinon; ***W:*** Chris Delaporte, Tarik Hamdine; ***M:*** Farid Russlan; ***V:*** Kirsten Dunst, Richard Harris, Anjelica Huston, Michael McShane, Greg Proops, Keith David.

Kafka **1/2 1991 (PG-13)** Disappointing and gloomy Soderbergh film that serves no purpose whatsoever. Irons plays Kafka, an insurance workers by day and a writer by night. The movie exists largely without interest until Kafka uncovers an office conspiracy and makes his way to the enemy's castle headquarters. From then on, "Kafka" is nothing but a conventional horror film. Irons is wasted in a role that requires nothing but an impeccable British accent. On the plus side, the film is exquisitely shot in black and white until the castle scenes, when the cinematography is switched to color. **100m/C VHS.** Jeremy Irons, Theresa Russell, Joel Grey, Ian Holm, Jeroen Krabbe, Armin Mueller-Stahl, Alec Guinness, Brian Glover, Robert Flemyng, Keith Allen, Simon McBurney; ***D:*** Steven Soderbergh; ***W:*** Lem Dobbs; ***C:*** Walt Lloyd; ***M:*** Cliff Martinez. Ind. Spirit '92: Cinematog.

Kagemusha **1/2** *The Shadow Warrior; The Double* **1980 (PG)** A thief is rescued from the gallows because of his striking resemblance to a warlord in 16th Century Japan. When the ambitious warlord is fatally wounded, the thief is required to pose as the warlord. In Japanese with English subtitles. **160m/C VHS, DVD.** *JP* Tatsuya Nakadai, Tsutomu Yamazaki, Kenichi Hagiwara, Hideji Otaki; ***D:*** Akira Kurosawa; ***W:*** Akira Kurosawa, Masato Ide; ***C:*** Kazuo Miyagawa, Masaharu Ueda; ***M:*** Shinichiro Ikebe. British Acad. '80: Director (Kurosawa); Cannes '80: Film; Cesar '81: Foreign Film.

The Kaiser's Lackey *Der Untertan* **1951** Cowardly but ambitious Diedrich Hessling has learned his lesson—in order to gain power, you must bow to those who have it and ignore those who don't. Diedrich thinks he's finally achieved his goal when he's chosen to give the keynote speech at the dedication of an Emperor's monument. Based on the novel by Heinrich Mann. German with subtitles. **105m/B VHS.** *GE* Werner Peters, Paul Esser; ***D:*** Wolfgang Staudte; ***W:*** Wolfgang Staudte.

Kaleidoscope **1/2 1966** Playboy Barney Lincoln (Beatty) likes to get into trouble for the thrill of it and his latest scheme is cheating the casinos at cards. This raises the suspicions of ex-flame Angel (York), who tells her Scotland Yard daddy (Revill). He offers Barney a chance at redemption if he'll help financially ruin illegal drug importer Dominion (Porter). Beatty is attractive but wooden and is constantly shown up by his Brit co-stars in this crime caper flop. **103m/C VHS.** *GB* Warren Beatty, Susannah York, Clive Revill, Eric Porter, Murray Melvin, George Sewell; ***D:*** Jack Smight; ***W:*** Robert B. Carrington, Jane-Howard Carrington; ***C:*** Christopher Challis; ***M:*** Howard Myers.

Kalifornia 𝒮𝒮 1/2 **1993 (R)** "Badlands" meets the '90s in a road trip with the hitchhikers from hell. Early Grayce (Pitt) is your average slimeball who murders his landlord and hops a ride with his waifish girlfriend Adele (Lewis) from Kentucky to California with Brian (Duchovny), a yuppie writer interested in mass murderers, and his sultry photographer girlfriend Carrie (Forbes). Pitt and Lewis were still an item when they made this. Pitt reportedly wanted to play against type, and as pretty boy gone homicidal, he succeeds. Extremely violent and disturbing. Also available in an unrated version. **117m/C VHS, DVD, UMD.** Brad Pitt, Juliette Lewis, David Duchovny, Michelle Forbes, Sierra Pecheur, Lois Hall, Gregory Mars Martin; ***D:*** Dominic Sena; ***W:*** Tim Metcalfe; ***C:*** Bojan Bazelli; ***M:*** Carter Burwell.

Kama Sutra: A Tale of Love 𝒮𝒮 **1996** Erotic but flawed fantasy covering the sexual and political wiles of palace life in 16th-century India. Princess Tara (Choudhury) and girlhood friend/servant Maya (Varma) are close until the Princess becomes jealous of the even-more beautiful Maya. In revenge for a public humiliation, Maya seduces Tara's dissolute fiance, Raj Singh (Andrews), and is banished from the palace after the wedding. She becomes involved with handsome royal sculptor Jai Kumar (Tikaram) and later learns the sexual arts of the Kama Sutra, becoming the chief courtesan to the Raj. Messy, somewhat overwrought plot, extremely attractive cast. Also available in an R-rated version. **117m/C VHS, DVD.** *IN* Indira Varma, Sarita Choudhury, Ramon Tikaram, Naveen Andrews, Devi Rekha; ***D:*** Mira Nair; ***W:*** Mira Nair, Helena Kriel; ***C:*** Declan Quinn; ***M:*** Mychael Danna. Ind. Spirit '98: Cinematog.

Kameradschaft 𝒮𝒮𝒮 1/2 *La Tragedie de la Mine; Comradeship* **1931** A great, early German sound film about Germans struggling to free themselves and French miners trapped underground on the countries' border. In German and French with English subtitles. **80m/B VHS.** *GE* Ernst Busch, Alexander Granach, Fritz Kampers, Gustav Puttjer, Daniel Mendaille, Elizabeth Wenst; ***D:*** G.W. Pabst; ***W:*** Laszlo Wajda, Karl Otten, Peter Martin Lampel; ***C:*** Fritz Arno Wagner, Robert Barberske.

Kamikaze '89 𝒮𝒮𝒮 **1983** German director Fassbinder has the lead acting role (his last) in this offbeat story of a police lieutenant in Berlin, circa 1989, who investigates a puzzling series of bombings. In German with English subtitles. **90m/C VHS.** *GE* Rainer Werner Fassbinder, Gunther Kaufman, Boy Gobert; ***D:*** Wolf Gremm; ***M:*** Tangerine Dream.

Kamikaze Girls 𝒮𝒮 1/2 *Shimotsuma monogatari* **2004** Momoko (Kyoko Fukada), is hit by a cabbage truck and her life is told in flashback. Her Yakuza father is abandoned by her mom for the doctor who delivered her, and instead of living in the fashion district they now live in a country backwater. Being devoted to Japanese Lolita fashion she is disgusted by the local rednecks who are proud of buying their clothes at the Japanese version of Walmart. Against all odds she befriends Ichigo (Anna Tsuchiya) a half Russian, half Japanese female biker. They go on a road trip to meet a legendary tailor for a special jacket for the retiring leader of Ichigo's gang. **103m/C DVD.** *JP* Kyoko Fukada, Sadao Abe, Anna Tsuchiya, Eiko Koike, Shin Yazawa; ***D:*** Tetsuya Nakashima; ***W:*** Tetsuya Nakashima, Nobara Takemoto; ***C:*** Masakazu Ato; ***M:*** Yoko Kanno.

Kamikaze Hearts 𝒮𝒮 **1991** A quasi-documentary set in the world of two lesbian-junkies (Sharon the actress and Tina the director/producer) making underground X-rated movies. **80m/C VHS.** Sharon Mitchell, Tina "Tigr" Mennett; ***D:*** Juliet Bashore; ***W:*** Tina "Tigr" Mennett.

Kanal 𝒮𝒮𝒮 1/2 *They Loved Life* **1956** Wajda's first major success, a grueling account of Warsaw patriots, upon the onset of the Nazis toward the end of the war, fleeing through the ruined city's sewers. Highly acclaimed. Part 2 of Wajda's "War Trilogy," preceded by "A Generation" and followed by "Ashes and Diamonds." In Polish with English subtitles or dubbed. **96m/B VHS, DVD.** *PL* Teresa Izewska, Tadeusz Janczar, Vladek Sheybal, Emil Kariewicz, Wienczylaw Glinski; ***D:*** Andrzej Wajda; ***W:*** Jerzy Stefan Stawinski; ***C:*** Jerzy Lipman; ***M:*** Jan Krenz. Cannes '57: Grand Jury Prize.

Kandahar 𝒮𝒮 **2001** Nafas (Pazira) and her family emigrated to Canada from Afghanistan, although they were forced to leave behind Nafas's crippled sister. Now, the sister has vowed to commit suicide rather than live any longer under Taliban rule and Nafas returns to try and save her. But journeying to Kandahar is a maze of obstacles and restrictions. Farsi and English. **85m/C VHS, DVD.** *IA* Nelofer Pazira, Hassan Tantai, Sadou Teymouri; ***D:*** Mohsen Makhmalbaf; ***W:*** Mohsen Makhmalbaf; ***C:*** Ebraheem Ghafouri; ***M:*** Mohammad Reza Darvishi.

Kandyland 𝒮 **1987 (R)** An over-the-hill stripper takes a young innocent stripper under her wing. **94m/C VHS.** Sandahl Bergman, Kimberly Evenson, Charles Laulette, Bruce Baum; ***D:*** Robert Allen Schnitzer; ***C:*** Robert Brinkmann.

Kangaroo 𝒮𝒮𝒮 **1986 (R)** An Australian adaptation of the semi-autobiographical D.H. Lawrence novel. A controversial English novelist and his wife move to the Outback in 1922, and are confronted with all manner of prejudice and temptation. **115m/C VHS.** *AU* Judy Davis, Colin Friels, John Walton, Hugh Keays-Byrne, Julie Nihill; ***D:*** Tim Burstall; ***W:*** Evan Jones; ***C:*** Dan Burstall; ***M:*** Nathan Waks. Australian Film Inst. '86: Actress (Davis).

Kangaroo Jack 𝒮 **2002 (PG)** Pals O'Connell and Anderson are forced to deliver mob money to Australia, but it's accidentally stolen from them by a kangaroo. If this sounds like a sad excuse for a movie, it is. Aside from some beautiful shots of the Australian landscape, there's little redeeming value. Jokes are lowbrow and (even worse) not funny, script is bland and mainly uninspired. Walken must've owed producer Jerry Bruckheimer a favor. The kangaroo was computer-generated, but still had more charisma than any of the leading actors. **88m/C VHS, DVD.** *US* Jerry O'Connell, Anthony Anderson, Estella Warren, Michael Shannon, Christopher Walken, Bill Hunter, Marton Csokas, David Ngoombujarra; ***D:*** David McNally; ***W:*** Steve Bing, Scott Rosenberg; ***C:*** Peter Menzies Jr.

The Kansan 𝒮𝒮 **1943** The marshall in a Kansas town won't rest until he's stamped out all traces of corruption. **79m/B VHS, DVD.** Richard Dix, Victor Jory, Albert Dekker, Jane Wyatt, Eugene Pallette, Robert Armstrong, Beryl Wallace, Clem Bevans, Hobart Cavanaugh, Francis McDonald, George Reeves, Willie Best; ***D:*** George Archainbaud; ***W:*** Harold Shumate; ***C:*** Russell Harlan; ***M:*** Gerard Carbonara.

Kansas 𝒮 **1988 (R)** Two young men, one a lawless rebel, the other a rational loner, stage a bank heist, and then go on the lam. Lame plot and very weak acting combine to make this film a dud. **111m/C VHS, DVD.** Matt Dillon, Andrew McCarthy, Leslie Hope, Kyra Sedgwick; ***D:*** David Stevens; ***W:*** Spencer Eastman; ***C:*** David Eggby; ***M:*** Pino Donaggio.

Kansas City 𝒮𝒮𝒮 **1995 (R)** Altman mixes music, politics, crime and the movies in this bittersweet homage to his hometown, set in the jazz-driven 1930s. Star-struck, tough-talking Blondie (Leigh) kidnaps Carolyn Stilton (Richardson), a self-sedating wife of a political shaker (Murphy), in a hairbrained scheme to save her husband from a local mobster (Belafonte). Styled to imitate the brilliant jazz scores played by the likes of Joshua Redman and James Carter, the action can become a bit confusing and Leigh is beyond irritating with her derivative dame routine. Belafonte, however, is brilliant, relishing the part of the legendary Seldom Seen, a real-life K.C. gangster. **110m/C VHS, DVD.** Jennifer Jason Leigh, Miranda Richardson, Harry Belafonte, Michael Murphy, Dermot Mulroney, Steve Buscemi, Brooke Smith, Jane Adams; ***D:*** Robert Altman; ***W:*** Frank Barhydt, Robert Altman; ***C:*** Oliver Stapleton; ***M:*** Hal Willner. N.Y. Film Critics '96: Support. Actor (Belafonte).

Kansas City Confidential 𝒮𝒮𝒮 **1952** An ex-cop on the wrong side of the law launches a sophisticated armored car heist. A disgruntled ex-con gets arrested for the crime on circumstantial evidence. When released, he scours the underworld for the real thieves. **98m/B VHS, DVD.** John Payne, Coleen Gray, Preston Foster, Neville Brand, Lee Van Cleef, Jack Elam, Carleton Young; ***D:*** Phil Karlson; ***W:*** Rowland Brown, George Bruce, Harry Essex, Harold Greene; ***C:*** George E. Diskant; ***M:*** Paul Sawtell.

Kansas Pacific 𝒮𝒮 **1953** A group of Confederate sympathizers try to stop the Kansas Pacific Railroad from reaching the West Coast in the 1860s. **73m/C VHS, DVD.** Sterling Hayden, Eve Miller, Barton MacLane, Reed Hadley, Douglas Hadley; ***D:*** Ray Nazarro.

The Kansas Terrors 𝒮𝒮 **1939** The "Three Mesquiteers" head for the Caribbean to deliver a herd of horses and wind up in a battle against local despot. **57m/B VHS.** Robert "Bob" Livingston, Raymond Hatton, Duncan Renaldo, Julie Bishop, Yakima Canutt, Richard Alexander, Merrill McCormick; ***D:*** George Sherman.

Kaos 𝒮𝒮𝒮 *Chaos* **1985 (R)** The Taviani brothers adaptation of four stories by Luigi Pirandello ("The Other Son," "Moonstruck," "The Jar," and "Requiem"), which look at peasant life in Sicily, ranging from the comic to the tragic. A fictional epilog, "Conversing with Mother," has Pirandello talking with the spirit of his dead mother. As with any anthology some stories are stronger than others but all possess the Taviani's great visual style and some fine acting. In Italian with English subtitles. **188m/C VHS.** *IT* Margarita Lozano, Claudio Bigagli, Massimo Bonetti, Omero Antonutti, Enrica Maria Modugno, Ciccio Ingrassia, Franco Franchi, Biagio Barone, Salvatore Rossi, Franco Scaldati, Pasquale Spadola, Regina Bianchi; ***D:*** Paolo Taviani, Vittorio Taviani; ***W:*** Paolo Taviani, Vittorio Taviani; ***C:*** Giuseppe Lanci; ***M:*** Nicola Piovani.

Kapo 𝒮𝒮𝒮 **1959** A 14-year-old Jewish girl and her family are imprisoned by the Nazis in a concentration camp. There, the girl changes identities with the help of the camp doctor, and rises to the position of camp guard. She proceeds to become taken with her power until a friend commits suicide and jolts the girl back into harsh reality. An Academy Award nominee for Best Foreign Film (lost to "The Virgin Spring"). Primarily English dialogue, with subtitles for foreign language. **116m/B VHS.** *IT FR YU* Susan Strasberg, Laurent Terzieff, Emmanuelle Riva, Gianni "John" Garko; ***D:*** Gillo Pontecorvo; ***W:*** Gillo Pontecorvo.

Karate Cop 𝒮 1/2 **1991 (R)** In a future without law or order John Travis (Marchini) is the last cop on earth. He saves Rachel, a beautiful scientist, from a band of scavengers and together they hunt for a hidden crystal with mysterious powers. Only first John has to defeat a gladiator in a martial arts fight to the death. **90m/C VHS.** Ron Marchini, Carrie Chambers, David Carradine, Michael Bristow, D.W. Landingham, Michael Foley, Dana Bentley; ***D:*** Alan Roberts.

Karate Dog WOOF! **2004 (PG)** Totally inept comedy finds wisecracking dog Cho-Cho (voiced by Chase) teaming up with a geeky detective (Rex) to investigate the murder of his Zen karate master (Morita). Presumably everyone involved had bills to pay. **?m/C DVD.** Simon Rex, Jon Voight, Jaime Pressly, Noriyuki "Pat" Morita, Thomas Kretschmann; ***D:*** Bob (Benjamin) Clark; ***W:*** Steven Paul; ***C:*** Brian Pearson; ***V:*** Chevy Chase, Lori Petty, Nicolette Sheridan. **VIDEO**

The Karate Kid 𝒮𝒮𝒮 1/2 **1984 (PG)** A teenage boy finds out that Karate involves using more than your fists when a handyman agrees to teach him martial arts. The friendship that they develop is deep and sincere; the Karate is only an afterthought. From the director of the original "Rocky," this movie is easy to like. **126m/C VHS, DVD.** Ralph Macchio, Noriyuki "Pat" Morita, Elisabeth Shue, Randee Heller, Martin Kove, Chad McQueen, William Zabka, Larry B. Scott, Robert Garrison, Tony O'Dell, Frances Bay, Peter Jason, Andrew Shue; ***D:*** John G. Avildsen; ***W:*** Robert Mark Kamen; ***M:*** Bill Conti.

The Karate Kid **2010** Will Smith's kid takes on Ralph Macchio's role of the bullied kid seeking to learn how to defend himself and Chan is his wise but eccentric mentor. Only there's probably no "wax on, wax off" since the flick is now set in Beijing, China. That's where 12-year-old Dre and his mom move for her work. But there's always a bully so Dre wants to learn kung fu and it turns out the school janitor is a master. **m/C DVD.** *US* Jaden Smith, Jackie Chan, Taraji P. Henson; ***D:*** Harald Zwart; ***W:*** Christopher Murphey.

The Karate Kid: Part 2 𝒮𝒮 1/2 **1986 (PG)** Sequel to the first film wherein our high-kicking hero tests his mettle in real-life karate exchanges in Okinawa, and settles a long-standing score. Followed by a second sequel. **95m/C VHS, DVD.** Ralph Macchio, Noriyuki "Pat" Morita, Danny Kamekona, Martin Kove, Tamlyn Tomita, Nobu McCarthy, Yuji Okumoto, William Zabka; ***D:*** John G. Avildsen; ***W:*** Robert Mark Kamen; ***C:*** James A. Crabe; ***M:*** Bill Conti.

The Karate Kid: Part 3 𝒮 1/2 **1989 (PG)** Second sequel takes a tired plot and doesn't do much to perk it up. Macchio again battles an evil nemesis and learns about himself, but this time Morita refuses to be a part of his training until, of course, Macchio desperately needs his help. Followed by "The Next Karate Kid," which introduces a new kid—a girl. **105m/C VHS, DVD.** Ralph Macchio, Noriyuki "Pat" Morita, Thomas Ian Griffith, Martin Kove, Sean Kanan, Robin (Robyn) Lively, Gabe Jarret, Frances Bay; ***D:*** John G. Avildsen; ***W:*** Robert Mark Kamen; ***C:*** Steve Yaconelli; ***M:*** Bill Conti.

Karate Warrior 𝒮 1/2 *The Boy in the Golden Kimono* **1988** Young martial artist is beaten and left for dead by Filipino crime syndicate. Bones mended, he prescribes a dose of their medicine. Plenty of rest and retaliation. **90m/C VHS.** *IT* Janet Agren, Enrico Torralba, Jared Martin, Ken(saku) Watanabe; ***D:*** Fabrizio de Angelis; ***W:*** Fabrizio de Angelis; ***C:*** Alberto Pinori; ***M:*** Simon Boswell.

Karla 𝒮 1/2 **2006 (R)** Routine true crime saga based on the story of Canadian serial killers Paul Bernardo and Karla Homolka, the girls they murdered through sexual torture, and the sensational trial that followed. Told in flashback as Karla talks to her shrink in an effort to mitigate her part in the crimes. **101m/C DVD.** Laura Prepon, Misha Collins, Tess Harper, Patrick Bauchau, Alexandra Boyd, Shawn Hoffman, Emilie Jacobs, Cherilyn Hayres, Adam Lieberman; ***D:*** Joel Bender; ***W:*** Joel Bender, Michael D. Sellers, Manette Beth Rosen; ***C:*** Charles Mills; ***M:*** Tim Jones.

Karma Police 𝒮 1/2 **2008** The karma police are a secret organization that believe in rewarding the good and punishing the bad. Newest recruit Charles West is happy with his job but finds that his own past may prove karma is not on his side. **90m/C DVD.** John Wesley Shipp, David Sullivan, Jessica Turner, Chamblee Ferguson, Nicole Leigh, Dan Forsythe; ***D:*** John Venable; ***W:*** John Venable; ***C:*** Red Sanders; ***M:*** Benjamin Stanton. **VIDEO**

Karmina 𝒮𝒮 **1996** Unusual French-Canadian vampire parody finds 140-year-old vamp Karmina (Cyr) fighting with her Transylvanian parents over their insistence that she marry nerdy Vlad (Pelletier). Karmina flees her home and heads to Montreal in search of her aunt, Esmeralda (Castel), who has managed to regain her humanity and now runs a dating service. A magic potion also makes Karmina human (it's a difficult transition) and she falls in love with Philippe (Brouillette) but Vlad's not out of the picture. He also turns up in Montreal, and begins adding to the vampire population. **109m/C VHS.** *CA* Isabelle Cyr, Yves Pelletier, Robert Brouillette, France Castel, Gildor Roy, Raymond Cloutier, Sylvie Potvin; ***D:*** Gabriel Pelletier; ***W:*** Gabriel Pelletier, Andree Pelletier, Ann Burke, Yves Pelletier; ***C:*** Eric Cayla; ***M:*** Patrick Bourgeois. Genie '97: Art Dir./Set Dec., Costume Des.

Kashmiri Run 𝒮𝒮 **1969 (R)** Action adventure about trio on the lam from Chinese communists chasing them through Tibet. **101m/C VHS.** *SP* Pernell Roberts, Alexandra Bastedo, Julian Mateos, Gloria Gamata; ***D:*** John Peyser.

Kaspar Hauser 𝒮𝒮 **1993** Historical epic based on the true story of Kaspar Hauser (Eisermann), a 16-year-old found abandoned in Nuremberg, Germany in 1828, who was unable to walk, write, or speak. Entrusted to the scientific concerns of Professor Daumer (Samel), rumors begin to circulate that the boy is actually the Crown Prince of Baden. Supposedly, Kaspar was abducted as a baby and substituted for a child who died so his Uncle Ludwig (Oscsenknecht) could become Grand Duke. Court intrigue and threats abound as Kaspar struggles to survive. German with subtitles. **137m/C VHS.** *GE* Andre Eisermann, Jeremy Clyde, Katharina Thalbach, Udo Samel, Uwe Ochsenknecht; *D:* Peter Sehr; *W:* Peter Sehr; *C:* Gernot Roll; *M:* Nikos Mamangakis.

Kate & Leopold 🦴🦴 1/2 **2001 (PG-13)** Cute but underwhelming romantic comedy involving time travel. Eccentric scientist Stuart (Schreiber) finds a portal that allows him to visit New York City in 1876. But his presence is noticed by dashing Leopold, the Duke of Albany (Jackman), who unwittingly follows Stuart to present-day Manhattan. The Duke manages the adjustment quite well, especially after meeting business exec Kay McKay (Ryan), Stuart's ex-girlfriend. Kate's more interested in a big promotion than romance, though she finds Leopold charming if strange. Too bad Leopold can't hang around, he has to go back to 1876 but can Kate be persuaded to go with him? This is familiar territory for Ryan (who's more brittle than perky) but Jackman does chivalry with the best of them. **121m/C VHS, DVD.** *US* Meg Ryan, Hugh Jackman, Liev Schreiber, Breckin Meyer, Natasha Lyonne, Bradley Whitford, Paxton Whitehead, Spalding Gray, Philip Bosco, David Aaron Baker; *D:* James Mangold; *W:* James Mangold, Steven Rogers; *C:* Stuart Dryburgh; *M:* Rolfe Kent. Golden Globes '02: Song ("Until").

Kate's Addiction 🦴🦴 **1999 (R)** Kate (Wuhrer) comes to L.A. in search of an old friend (Forke) but she's really interested in more than hanging around. And anyone who gets in her way may not live to regret it. **95m/C VHS, DVD.** Kari Wuhrer, Farrah Forke, Matt Borlenghi; *D:* Eric De La Barre. **VIDEO**

Katherine 🦴 *The Radical* **1975** A young heiress rejects her pampered lifestyle and becomes a violent revolutionary, rebelling against social injustices and the system that spawned them. **98m/C VHS, DVD.** Sissy Spacek, Art Carney, Jane Wyatt, Henry Winkler, Julie Kavner, Hector Elias, Jenny Sullivan; *D:* Jeremy Paul Kagan. **TV**

Katie Tippel 🦴🦴 *Katie's Passion; Cathy Tippel; Hot Sweat; Keetje Tippel* **1975 (R)** In 1881 Amsterdam, a young Dutch prostitute works her way out of poverty and enters a world of education and wealth. A Victorian tale of exploitation with a tough and intelligent Cinderella heroine. In Dutch with English subtitles. **104m/C VHS, DVD.** *NL* Monique Van De Ven, Rutger Hauer, Eddie Brugman, Hannah De Leeuwe, Andrea Domburg; *D:* Paul Verhoeven; *W:* Gerard Soeteman; *C:* Jan De Bont; *M:* Roger van Otterloo.

Katyn 🦴🦴 **2007** In 1939, Joseph Stalin and Adolf Hitler signed a nonaggression pact that allowed both countries to destroy Polish sovereignty. In 1940, Stalin ordered the massacre of 15,000 Polish officers, who were buried in the Katyn Forest, and then officially blamed the Nazis when the mass graves were discovered. Director Wajda dispenses with sentimentality, using restraint to tell the story from various viewpoints, including that of Anna (Ostaszewska), who's searching for her husband Andrzej (Zmijewski), who's in an internment camp and destined to be killed; Jerzy (Chyra), a guilt-ridden survivor; and two sisters (Cielecka, Glinska) who take opposite stances in the postwar Soviet regime. Polish, Russian, and German with subtitles. **121m/C DVD.** *PL* Jan Englert, Maja Ostaszewska, Artur Zmijewski, Andrzej Chyra, Magdalena Cielecka, Agnieszka Glinska; *D:* Andrzej Wajda; *W:* Andrzej Wajda, Wladyslaw Pasikowski, Przemyslaw Nowarkowski; *C:* Pawel Edelman; *M:* Krzysztof Penderecki.

Kavik the Wolf Dog 🦴 1/2 *The Courage of Kavik, the Wolf Dog* **1980** Heartwarming story of a courageous dog's love and suffering for the boy he loves. **99m/C VHS, DVD.** Ronny Cox, Linda Sorensen, Andrew Ian McMillian, Chris Wiggins, John Ireland; *D:* Peter Carter. **TV**

Kazaam 🦴 1/2 **1996 (PG)** Twelve-year-old Max (Capra) is having problems—bullies are chasing him and his single mom's just found a new boyfriend. But his luck seems ready to change when a battered boombox reveals a seven-foot rappin' genie named Kazaam (O'Neal). The kid's beyond obnoxious and Shaq shouldn't plan to give up b-ball anytime soon (at least for an acting career), even though director Glaser did think up the part for the tall guy just before he met him at an NBA All-Star Game. **93m/C VHS, DVD.** Francis Capra, Shaquille O'Neal, Ally Walker, John A. Costelloe, Marshall Manesh, James Acheson; *D:* Paul Michael Glaser; *W:* Christian Ford, Roger Soffer; *C:* Charles Minsky; *M:* Christopher Tyng.

Keane 🦴🦴🦴 **2004 (R)** Unflinching, unsettling, and intense portrait of grief, and one man's struggle to regain his sanity. William Keane (Lewis), a wanders an NYC bus terminal, searching for his daughter, who may or may not have disappeared from there a year earlier while in his care. He struggles to hold himself together to continue his search when he meets, and helps, a fellow lost soul, Lynn (Ryan), who trusts him enough to ask him to watch her seven year old daughter Kira. Lewis's performance more than stands up to the constant scrutiny director/writer keeps on his character, as the tension of his inner struggle with himself mounts. **100m/C DVD.** *US* Damian Lewis, Abigail Breslin, Amy Ryan; *D:* Lodge Kerrigan; *W:* Lodge Kerrigan; *C:* John Foster.

Keaton's Cop 🦴 **1990 (R)** Another cheap cop comedy involving the mistaken identity of an important mob witness. **95m/C VHS.** Lee Majors, Abe Vigoda, Don Rickles; *D:* Robert Burge.

The Keep 🦴🦴 **1983 (R)** At the height of the Nazi onslaught, several German soldiers unleash an unknown power from a medieval stone fortress. Technically impressive but lacking in all other aspects. From a novel by F. Paul Wilson. **96m/C VHS.** Scott Glenn, Alberta Watson, Jurgen Prochnow, Robert Prosky, Gabriel Byrne, Ian McKellen, William Morgan Sheppard; *D:* Michael Mann; *W:* Michael Mann, Dennis Lynton Clark; *C:* Alex Thomson; *M:* Tangerine Dream.

Keep 'Em Flying 🦴🦴 **1941** Bud and Lou star in the this wartime morale-booster that hasn't aged well. The duo follow their barnstorming friend into flight academy; a not-too-taxing plot includes five musical numbers and two Martha Rayes (she plays twins). ♫ Pig Foot Pete; Together; I'm Looking for the Boy with the Wistful Eyes; Let's Keep 'Em Flying; I'm Getting Sentimental Over You. **86m/B VHS, DVD.** Bud Abbott, Lou Costello, Martha Raye; *D:* Arthur Lubin.

Keep My Grave Open 🦴🦴 *The House Where Hell Froze Over* **1980 (R)** A woman lives in an isolated house where a series of strange murders take place. She attributes them to her brother, but does he really exist? Made cheaply, but not without style; filmed in Harrison County, Texas. **85m/C VHS, DVD.** Camilla Carr, Gene Ross, Stephen Tobolowsky, Ann Stafford, Sharon Bunn, Chelcie Ross; *D:* S.F. Brownrigg.

Keep Punching 🦴🦴 **1939** A gambler/boxer is almost destroyed by life in the fast lane, as well as by a seductive woman. **80m/C VHS.** Henry Armstrong, Mae Johnson; *Cameos:* Canada Lee; *D:* John Clein.

Keep Talking Baby 🦴🦴 *Cause Toujours, Mon Lapin* **1961** Action-packed thriller that finds Eddie in prison after being framed for murder. He escapes and is out for revenge on the organization that put him there. **90m/B VHS.** *FR* Eddie Constantine, Francois Chaumette, Renee Cosima; *D:* Guy Lefranc; *W:* Guy Lefranc, Roger Boussinot; *C:* Jean-Louis Picavet; *M:* Michel Legrand, Francis Lemarque.

Keep the Change 🦴🦴 **1992 (PG-13)** Joe Starling is an artist with painter's block, living in California with his girlfriend Astrid. He decides to revisit the family ranch in Deadrock, Montana, and his crackpot Uncle Smitty and saintly Aunt Lureen. The family ranch is coveted by the evil Overstreet (typecasting for Palance), whose daughter was once loved by Joe but is now married to his ex-best friend. Character more than plot rules this moody, low-key story based on a novel by Thomas McGuane. **95m/C VHS.** William L. Petersen, Lolita (David) Davidovich, Rachel Ticotin, Buck Henry, Jack Palance, Fred Dalton Thompson, Jeff Kober, Lois Smith; *D:* Andy Tennant. **CABLE**

Keeper 🦴🦴 **1976** Wealthy patients at Underwood Asylum suffer unspeakable horrors while under the care of Lee. Detective Dick Driver investigates. Obscure horror spoof. **96m/C VHS, DVD.** *CA* Christopher Lee, Tell Schreiber, Sally Gray; *D:* Tom Drake; *W:* Tom Drake.

The Keeper 🦴🦴 1/2 **1996** Disillusioned Paul Lamott (Esposito) is a corrections officer at the King's County House of Detention in Brooklyn. Nevertheless, Paul, who's earning a law degree, is moved by the pleas of Haitian prisoner Jean Baptiste (de Bankole), who swears he's been wrongly accused of rape. Paul, who's father was Haitian, manages to help Jean make bail and then invites him home—to the strong dismay of Paul's teacher wife Angela (Taylor). However, Angela begins warming to Jean's charm—but beware the stranger. **97m/C VHS, DVD.** Giancarlo Esposito, Regina Taylor, Isaach de Bankole; *D:* Joe Brewster; *W:* Joe Brewster; *C:* Igor Sunara; *M:* John Petersen.

The Keeper 🦴 1/2 **2009 (R)** Typical B-actioner from Seagal. Forcibly retired from the LAPD, Roland Sallinger gets a call from old friend Connor Wells (DuVall) asking him to become the bodyguard of Connor's trouble-attracting daughter Nikita (Carstens). So Roland heads to Texas where he learns Nikita has survived one kidnapping attempt and Connor hasn't exactly told him everything. **94m/C DVD.** Steven Seagal, Steph Duvall, Liezl Carstens, Aaron Shivers, Luce Rains, Brian Gamble; *D:* Keoni Waxman; *W:* Paul A. Birkett; *C:* Nathan Wilson; *M:* Philip White. **VIDEO**

Keeper of the City 🦴🦴 1/2 **1992 (R)** Gossett stars as a tough detective out to get a vigilante (LaPaglia) who is roaming the streets of Chicago. LaPaglia turns in a good performance as the son of a Mafia operative who wants to rid himself of the Mafia ties that have controlled him. As he pursues his deadly course of action, a newspaper journalist tags him "The Gangster Killer." Coyote plays the crusading journalist who is always interfering in Gossett's business. Good performances and an intriguing storyline combine to make this action-packed thriller worthwhile, although the script isn't as good as Di Pega's novel, which he adapted himself. **95m/C VHS.** Louis Gossett Jr., Peter Coyote, Anthony LaPaglia, Renee Soutendijk, Aeryk Egan, Tony Todd; *D:* Bobby Roth; *W:* Gerald Di Pego.

Keeper of the Flame 🦴🦴 1/2 **1942** Tracy and Hepburn manage to keep the murk of this story at bay as war correspondent Steven O'Malley (Tracy) is assigned to write about super patriot Robert V. Forrest, who's just died in an accident. Reclusive widow Christine Forrest (Hepburn) finally agrees to help O'Malley out but what our intrepid reporter discovers is that the hero was really a heel—something Christine still doesn't want known. Based on the novel by I.A.R. Wylie. **100m/B VHS.** Spencer Tracy, Katharine Hepburn, Richard Whorf, Margaret Wycherly, Donald Meek, Stephen McNally, Audrey Christie, Frank Craven, Forrest Tucker, Percy Kilbride, Howard da Silva, Darryl Hickman; *D:* George Cukor; *W:* Donald Ogden Stewart; *C:* William H. Daniels; *M:* Bronislau Kaper.

The Keeper: The Legend of Omar Khayyam 🦴🦴 **2005 (PG)** Account of 11th century poet-astronomer Omar Khayyam and his love triangle in 11th century Persia. First-time director Mashayekh intercuts an autobiographical tale of 12-year-old Kkayyam descendent Kamran (Echahly) in modern Houston. Respectable labor of love is an indie that looks quite epic. Unfortunately, the movie comes off more like an after-school special with a flair for bright costumes. Surprise cameo from Vanessa Redgrave sparks things only for as long as she's on the screen. **95m/C DVD.** *US* Bruno Lastra, Moritz Bleibtreu, Rade Serbedzija, Vanessa Redgrave, C. Thomas Howell, Diane Baker, Christopher Simpson, Adam Echahly, Marie Espinosa; *D:* Kayvan Mashayekh; *W:* Kayvan Mashayekh, Belle Avery; *C:* Dusan Joksimovic, Matt Cantrell; *M:* Elton Ahi.

Keeping Mum 🦴🦴 1/2 **2005 (R)** Smith steals the show in this black comedy as homicidal housekeeper Grace. She's just taken a job with harried, oblivious vicar Walter Goodfellow (Atkinson) and his neglected family. Bored wife Gloria (Scott Thomas) is flirting with her brash American golf pro Lance (Swayze); teen daughter Holly is a nympho; and younger son Petey (Parkes) is beset by bullies. But tart-tongued Grace will make everything all right since her lurid past (a stint in a prison for the criminally insane) has not made her squeamish about getting things done. **103m/C DVD.** *GB* Maggie Smith, Rowan Atkinson, Patrick Swayze, Kristin Scott Thomas, Emilia Fox, James Booth, Liz Smith, Tamsin Egerton, Toby Parkes; *D:* Niall Johnson; *W:* Niall Johnson, Richard Russo; *C:* Gavin Finney; *M:* Dickon Hinchliffe.

Keeping On 🦴🦴 1/2 **1981** TV movie with a pro-union stance. A preacher, who is also a millworker, teams up with an organizer to try to unionize the mill. Originally produced for the PBS "American Playhouse" series. **75m/C VHS.** Dick Anthony Williams, Carol Kane, James Broderick, Marcia Rodd, Rosalind Cash, Carl Lee, Danny Glover, Guy Boyd; *D:* Barbara Kopple. **TV**

Keeping the Faith 🦴🦴 1/2 **2000 (PG-13)** Norton's directorial debut sounds like a bad bar joke but turns out to be a slick, if meandering, romantic comedy. He's a priest, Brian, whose longtime best friend Jake (Stiller) is a rabbi with a congregation that wants him married to a nice Jewish girl. As kids, their mutual best pal was Anna, who returns to New York as a workaholic corporate exec (Elfman). The friendship is reestablished but so is something more—both men fall for the lady and, unbeknownst to Brian, Anna and Jake begin an affair. More than sparks fly. **127m/C VHS, DVD.** Edward Norton, Ben Stiller, Jenna Elfman, Anne Bancroft, Eli Wallach, Milos Forman, Ron Rifkin, Holland Taylor, Rena Sofer, Lisa Edelstein, Bodhi (Pine) Elfman; *D:* Edward Norton; *W:* Stuart Blumberg; *C:* Anastas Michos; *M:* Elmer Bernstein.

Keeping Track 🦴 **1986 (R)** Two tourists witness a murder and robbery and find the stolen $5 million on a New York-bound train. The two are relentlessly pursued by everyone, including the CIA and Russian spies. **102m/C VHS, DVD.** Michael Sarrazin, Margot Kidder, Alan Scarfe, Ken Pogue, Vlasta Vrana, Donald Pilon; *D:* Robin Spry.

Keeping Up with the Steins 🦴 **2006 (PG-13)** Benjamin Fiedler (Sabara) finds his bar mitzvah being turned into a chance for his Hollywood agent dad Adam (Piven) to one-up rival agent Arnie Stein (Miller) and the Steins' Titanic-themed event for their own son. But Ben sees it as the opportunity to reconcile his dad and his crazy, hippie grandfather, Irwin (Marshall). Director Scott Marshall, making his feature debut, is Garry's son. Flails wildly between sweet and cynical, with lessons learned in a "very special sitcom" way. Subtract at least a bone for the sight of Garry Marshall's naked backside. **99m/C DVD.** *US* Daryl Sabara, Jeremy Piven, Garry Marshall, Jami Gertz, Cheryl Hines, Daryl Hannah, Doris Roberts, Larry Miller, Carter Jenkins, Richard Benjamin, Miranda Cosgrove, Adam Goldberg, Sandra Taylor; *Cameos:* Neil Diamond; *D:* Scott Marshall; *W:* Mark Zakarin; *C:* Charles Minsky; *M:* John Debney.

Keillers Park 🦴🦴 **2005** A true hate crime story told in flashbacks. Peter sits in jail accused of a murder in Gothenburg's Keillers Park. Engaged and involved in the family business, Peter catches the eye of young street vendor Nassim and soon the two are lovers. Peter becomes obsessive and his life unravels with devastating consequences. Swedish with subtitles. **87m/C DVD.** *SW* Marten Klingberg, Piotr Giro, Karin Bergquist, Gosta Bredefeldt; *D:* Susanna Edwards; *W:* Pia Gradvall; *C:* Robert Nordstrom; *M:* Peter Adolfsson.

Keith 🦴 1/2 **2008** A weepie made for teenaged girls. High-school senior Natalie (Harnois) has set her path and thinks she knows exactly what she wants, which isn't free-spirited new student Keith (McCartney). Keith keeps trying to shake up her world and he tells Natalie stuff about his life that turns out to be untrue. Still, she's attracted to him and starts snooping, soon discovering that Keith is seriously ill. **95m/C DVD.** Elisabeth Harnois, Jesse McCartney, Jennifer Grey, Ignacio Serricchio, Tim Halligan, Zack Rockefeller; *D:* Todd A. Kessler; *W:* Todd A. Kessler, David Zabel; *C:* Darko Suvak; *M:* Tree Adams. **VIDEO**

Kelly of the Secret Service 🦴🦴 **1936** Agent tries to find out who stole the plans for a guided missile system. Fast-pace rides over the silliness of the plot. **69m/B VHS.** Lloyd Hughes, Sheila (Manors) Mannors, Fuzzy Knight, Syd Saylor, Jack Mulhall, Forrest Taylor; ***D:*** Robert F. "Bob" Hill; ***W:*** Al Martin.

Kelly the Second ½ **1936** Slow-moving boxing comedy about a punch-drunk fighter trying to win again with the encouragement of his trainer and manager. **70m/B VHS.** Guinn "Big Boy" Williams, Patsy Kelly, Charley Chase, Pert Kelton, Edward Brophy, Maxie "Slapsie" Rosenbloom, Harold Huber, DeWitt Jennings, Billy Gilbert, Syd Saylor; ***D:*** Gus Meins.

Kelly's Heroes ½ **1970 (PG)** A misfit band of crooks are led by Eastwood on a daring mission: to steal a fortune in gold from behind enemy lines. In the process, they almost win WWII. Sutherland is superb, as is McLeod, in his pre-Love Boat days. **145m/C VHS, DVD.** Clint Eastwood, Donald Sutherland, Telly Savalas, Gavin MacLeod, Don Rickles, Carroll O'Connor, Stuart Margolin, Harry Dean Stanton, Jeff Morris, Richard (Dick) Davalos, Perry Lopez, Tom Troupe, Len Lesser, David Hurst, George Savalas, Tom Signorelli; ***D:*** Brian G. Hutton; ***W:*** Troy Kennedy-Martin; ***C:*** Gabriel Figueroa; ***M:*** Lalo Schifrin.

Kemek **1970 (R)** An eccentric chemical company owner has his mistress push a new mind-control drug on an American writer, and has them killed after discovering their subsequent affair. Unfortunately, he didn't count on the woman's ex-husband seeking revenge. **82m/C VHS.** David Hedison, Helmut Snider, Mary Woronov, Alexandra Stewart, Cal Haynes; ***D:*** Theodore Gershuny; ***W:*** Theodore Gershuny; ***C:*** Enzo Barboni; ***M:*** John Lewis.

Kennedy **1983** NBC historical drama starring Martin Sheen as John F. Kennedy and focusing on events such as the abortive invasion of Cuba, national racial conflicts, America's growing involvment in Vietnam and the Cuban Missle Crisis. In addition to political aspirations, it also reveals parts of the man's private life, family tragedies, and chronic womanizing. **278m/C VHS, DVD.** Martin Sheen, Blair Brown, Vincent Gardenia, Geraldine Fitzgerald, E.G. Marshall, John Shea, Kevin Conroy, Nesbitt Blaisdell, John Glover, Kelsey Grammer, David Schramm, Trey Wilson, Jimmie Ray Weeks; ***D:*** Jim Goddard; ***W:*** Reg Gadney; ***C:*** Ernest Vincze; ***M:*** Richard Hartley. **TV**

The Kennedys of Massachusetts ½ **1995** Three cassette TV miniseries chronicles six decades of Kennedy life, from Joe Kennedy's (Petersen) courtship of Rose (O'Toole) to the presidential election of JFK and all the various scandals and tragedies. Adapted from the book "The Fitzgeralds and the Kennedys" by Doris Kearns Godwin. **278m/C VHS.** William L. Petersen, Annette O'Toole, Charles Durning, Steven Weber, Tracy Pollan, Campbell Scott; ***D:*** Lamont Johnson; ***W:*** William Hanley; ***M:*** David Shire. **TV**

The Kennel Murder Case **1933** Debonair detective Philo Vance suspects that a clear-cut case of suicide is actually murder. Fourth Vance mystery starring Powell. Remade as "Calling Philo Vance" in 1940. **73m/B VHS, DVD.** William Powell, Mary Astor, Jack La Rue, Ralph Morgan, Eugene Pallette; ***D:*** Michael Curtiz; ***W:*** Robert Presnell Sr., Robert N. Lee, Peter Milne; ***C:*** William Rees; ***M:*** Bernhard Kaun.

Kenny Rogers as the Gambler ½ **1980** Rogers stars as Brady Hawkes, debonair gambler searching for a son he never knew he had. Based on the Rogers song of the same name. One of the highest rated TV movies ever. Followed by several sequels. **94m/C VHS, DVD.** Kenny Rogers, Christine Belford, Bruce Boxleitner, Harold Gould, Clu Gulager, Lance LeGault, Lee Purcell, Noble Willingham; ***D:*** Dick Lowry. **TV**

Kenny Rogers as the Gambler, Part 2: The Adventure Continues ½ **1983** The surprise success of the made-for-TV western based on the popular Kenny Rogers' song spawned this equally popular sequel. Rogers returns as Brady Hawkes, this time searching for his kidnapped son. Followed by two more sequels. **195m/C VHS, DVD.** Kenny Rogers, Bruce Boxleitner, Linda Evans, Harold Gould, David Hedison, Clu Gulager, Johnny Crawford; ***D:*** Dick Lowry. **TV**

Kenny Rogers as the Gambler, Part 3: The Legend Continues **1987** Roger's third attempt at humanizing the gambler from his hit '70s song. This time, the Gambler gives a hand with the mediating between the warring U.S. government and the Sioux nation. Sitting Bull and Buffalo Bill add credibility to this average undertaking. Made for TV. **190m/C VHS.** Kenny Rogers, Bruce Boxleitner, Linda Gray, Melanie Chartoff, Matt Clark, George Kennedy, Dean Stockwell, Charles Durning, Jeffrey Jones, George American Horse; ***D:*** Dick Lowry. **TV**

Kent State **1981** Recounts the tragic events that took place at Kent State University in 1970, when student demonstrators faced National Guardsmen. Goldstone won an Emmy for Outstanding Direction. **120m/C VHS.** Talia Balsam, Ellen Barkin, Jane Fleiss, John Getz, Keith Gordon; ***D:*** James Goldstone. **TV**

The Kentuckian ½ **1955** Burt Lancaster stars as a rugged frontiersman who leaves with his son to go to Texas. On their journey the two are harassed by fighting mountaineers. **104m/C VHS, DVD.** Burt Lancaster, Walter Matthau, Diana Lynn, John McIntire, Dianne Foster, Una Merkel, John Carradine; ***D:*** Burt Lancaster; ***C:*** Ernest Laszlo.

Kentucky Blue Streak ½ **1935** Young jockey is framed for murder while riding at an "illegal" racetrack. Later, almost eligible for parole, he escapes from jail to ride "Blue Streak" in the Kentucky Derby. **61m/B VHS.** Eddie Nugent, Frank "Junior" Coghlan, Patricia Scott, Cornelius Keefe, Margaret Mann, Roy D'Arcy, Joseph Girard, Roy Watson; ***D:*** Bernard B. Ray; ***W:*** Rose Gordon.

Kentucky Fried Movie **1977 (R)** A zany potpourri of satire about movies, TV, commercials, and contemporary society. Written by Abrahams and the Zuckers, who later gave us "Airplane!" **85m/C VHS, DVD.** Bill Bixby, Jerry Zucker, Jim Abrahams, David Zucker, Donald Sutherland, Henry Gibson, George Lazenby, Tony Dow, Uschi Digart, Rick Baker, Marilyn Joi, Forrest J Ackerman; ***D:*** John Landis; ***W:*** Jerry Zucker, Jim Abrahams, David Zucker; ***C:*** Stephen M. Katz.

Kentucky Jubilee ½ **1951** At the jubilee, a movie director is kidnapped and the master of ceremonies, among others, decides to find him. **67m/B VHS.** Jerry Colonna, Jean Porter, James Ellison, Raymond Hatton, Fritz Feld, Vince Barnett, Michael Whalen, Archie Twitchell, Russell Hicks, Margia Dean, Si Jenks, Ralph Sanford, Jack Reitzen; ***D:*** Ron Ormond; ***W:*** Ron Ormond, Maurice Tombragel; ***C:*** Jack Greenhalgh.

Kentucky Kernels *Triple Trouble* **1934** A pair of down and out magicians ('30s comic duo Wheeler and Woolsey) happen upon a young boy (Little Rascal Spanky) who happens to be heir to a fortune. The three head for the rascal's Kentucky home, where they're welcomed with southern inhospitality. Much feuding and slapsticking. **75m/B VHS.** Bert Wheeler, Robert Woolsey, Mary Carlisle, George "Spanky" McFarland, Noah Beery Sr., Lucille LaVerne, Willie Best; ***D:*** George Stevens; ***M:*** Max Steiner.

Kentucky Rifle ½ **1955** A Comanche Indian tribe will let a group of stranded pioneers through their territory only if they agree to sell the Kentucky rifles aboard their wagon. **80m/C VHS, DVD.** Chill Wills, Lance Fuller, Cathy Downs, Jess Barker, Sterling Holloway, Jeanne Cagney; ***D:*** Carl K. Hittleman.

Kept **2001 (R)** Struggling architectural student Kyle Griffin thinks his worries are over when he lands a job at the firm owned by Barbara Weldon and her husband. But Barbara is a very hands-on employer and soon Kyle is involved in an affair and is a suspect in a murder. Now he has to save himself from being the fall guy. **98m/C VHS, DVD.** Ice-T, Yvette Nipar, Christian Oliver, Paul Michael Robinson, Michelle Von Flotow, Laura Rose, Art Hingle; ***D:*** Fred Olen Ray; ***W:*** Richard Uhug, Kimberly A. Ray; ***C:*** Theo Angell; ***M:*** Herman Jackson, Michael van Blum, Barry Taylor. **VIDEO**

Kept Husbands **1931** A factory worker saves two lives in an industrial accident, and the boss invites him home to dinner. When he meets the boss' daughter, romance blooms. But their different backgrounds cause difficulties. A bit dull, and dated by its chauvinism. **76m/B VHS, DVD.** Dorothy Mackaill, Joel McCrea, Robert McWade, Florence Roberts, Clara Kimball Young, Mary Carr, Ned Sparks, Bryant Washburn; ***D:*** Lloyd Bacon; ***M:*** Max Steiner.

Kettle of Fish **2006 (R)** Jazz sax man Mel (Modine) decides it's time to act like an adult and he moves in with his girlfriend—subletting his apartment to nerdy biologist Ginger (Gershon). But when Mel becomes obsessed with another woman, he gets tossed out on his ear, and is forced to beg Ginger to allow him to share the apartment. Romantic complications follow. Familiar story, rather engaging performances. **97m/C DVD.** Matthew Modine, Gina Gershon, Fisher Stevens, Isiah Whitlock Jr., Christy Scott Cashman, Kevin J. O'Connor; ***D:*** Claudia Myers; ***W:*** Claudia Myers; ***C:*** Neil Lisk; ***M:*** David Tobocman.

The Kettles in the Ozarks ½ **1956** Since Kilbride retired after the seventh comedy, Hunnicutt played a new male character, Uncle Sledge, in the eighth film. Ma (Main) takes the young'uns to visit their uncle in the Ozarks and finds she must help him and fiancee Bedelia (Merkel) save the failing farm from bootleggers. **81m/B VHS.** Marjorie Main, Arthur Hunnicutt, Una Merkel, Ted de Corsia, Richard Eyer, Joseph (Joe) Sawyer, Richard Deacon; ***D:*** Charles Lamont; ***W:*** Kay Lenard.

The Kettles on Old MacDonald's Farm ½ **1957** The ninth and last in the series finds Ma (Main in her final film) and Pa (Kennelly replacing the retired Kilbride) playing matchmakers for humble lumberman Brad (Smith). Seems he wants to marry the boss' spoiled daughter, Sally (Talbott), whom Ma decides needs a little backwoods seasoning before she'll make the proper wife. **82m/B VHS.** Marjorie Main, Parker Fennelly, John Smith, Gloria Talbott, Claude Akins, Roy Barcroft, Patricia Morrow, George Dunn; ***D:*** Virgil W. Vogel; ***W:*** Herbert Margolis, William Raynor.

Kevin & Perry Go Large ½ **2000 (R)** The Brits can make bad teen sex comedies adapted from TV shows just as easily as Americans can. Kevin (Enfield) and Perry (Burke in drag) are a couple of gormless teenage boys who have only one thing on their teeny brains. And since the Brits all seem to go to Spain to be naughty, the boys decide to take their summer holidays in party capital Ibiza and get some chicks. Only problem is Kevin's parents decide to accompany them. Bummer (or whatever the Brit equivalent would be). May make more sense if you've seen the characters on TV. **83m/C VHS, DVD.** *GB* Harry Enfield, Kathy Burke, Rhys Ifans, Laura Fraser, Tabitha Wady, James Fleet, Louisa Rix; ***D:*** Ed Bye; ***W:*** David Cummings, Harry Enfield; ***C:*** Alan Almond.

The Key ½ **1958** A long, slow WWII drama about the key to an Italian girl's apartment that gets passed from tugboat skipper to tugboat skipper before dangerous missions. Ultimately she finds true love, or does she? Based on the novel "Stella" by Jan de Hartog. **134m/B VHS.** *GB* William Holden, Sophia Loren, Trevor Howard, Oscar Homolka, Kieron Moore; ***D:*** Carol Reed; ***W:*** Carl Foreman; ***C:*** Oswald Morris; ***M:*** Malcolm Arnold. British Acad. '58: Actor (Howard).

Key Exchange ½ **1985 (R)** Kevin Scott and Paul Kurta based this contemporary look at love and commitments on Kevin Wade's popular play. Two New York City "yuppies" have reached a point in their relationship where an exchange of apartment keys commonly occurs—but they are hesitant. **96m/C VHS.** Brooke Adams, Ben Masters, Daniel Stern, Tony Roberts, Danny Aiello, Annie Golden, Nancy Mette; ***D:*** Barnet Kellman; ***W:*** Kevin Scott, Paul Kurta; ***M:*** Jonathan Elias.

Key Largo ½ **1948** WWII vet Bogart travels to the run-down Florida hotel owned by Barrymore and Bacall who are, respectively, the father and widow of a war buddy. Bogart notes the other guests are of a decidedly criminal bent, but as a hurricane threatens, no one can leave. One-time mob kingpin Robinson lords it over the others while Bogart keeps his usual cynical cool. Trevor, who plays Robinson's alcoholic ex-singer moll, deservedly won an Oscar for her role. Based on a play by Maxwell Anderson. **101m/B VHS, DVD.** Humphrey Bogart, Lauren Bacall, Claire Trevor, Edward G. Robinson, Lionel Barrymore, Thomas Gomez, Dan Seymour; ***D:*** John Huston; ***W:*** Richard Brooks, John Huston; ***C:*** Karl Freund; ***M:*** Max Steiner. Oscars '48: Support. Actress (Trevor).

The Key Man ½ *Life at Stake* **1957** A radio show host manages to get mixed up with gangsters after recreating a crime on the air. He uses his knowledge of crime to thwart the crooks. **63m/B VHS.** *GB* Lee Patterson, Hy Hazell, Colin Gordon, Philip Leaver, Paula Byrne; ***D:*** Montgomery Tully; ***M:*** Les Baxter.

The Key to Rebecca ½ **1985** The Nazis and the British go head-to-head in war torn North Africa. As the Germans push their way across Egypt, they find an unexpected ally in a half-German/half-Arab killer behind the British lines. Tense, well-made thriller; originally a miniseries. **190m/C VHS.** David Soul, Cliff Robertson, Robert Culp, Season Hubley, Lina Raymond, Anthony Quayle, David Hemmings; ***D:*** David Hemmings. **TV**

Key to the City ½ **1950** Light comedy featuring Gable and Young as two small town mayors who meet and fall in love at a convention in San Francisco. Throw in some sharp lines, a little slapstick, and a bit of satire for an amusing picture. Based on the story by Albert Beich. **99m/B VHS.** Clark Gable, Loretta Young, Frank Morgan, Marilyn Maxwell, Raymond Burr, James Gleason, Lewis Stone, Raymond Walburn; ***D:*** George Sidney; ***W:*** Robert Riley Crutcher.

The Keys of the Kingdom **1944** An earnest adaptation of A.J. Cronin's novel about a young Scottish missionary spreading God's word in 19th Century China. **137m/B VHS, DVD.** Gregory Peck, Thomas Mitchell, Edmund Gwenn, Vincent Price, Roddy McDowall, Cedric Hardwicke, Peggy Ann Garner, James Gleason, Anne Revere, Rose Stradner, Sara Allgood, Abner Biberman, Arthur Shields; ***D:*** John M. Stahl; ***W:*** Joseph L. Mankiewicz, Nunnally Johnson; ***C:*** Arthur C. Miller.

Keys to Tulsa ½ **1996 (R)** After losing his job as a lowly movie reviewer (gasp!), Richter Bourdreau (Stoltz), the black-sheep son of a wealthy Tulsa family, is lured into a blackmail scheme by his ex-flame Vicky (Unger) and her perpetually stoned husband Ronnie (Spader). When the tables are turned on him, Richter finally gets up off of his slacker butt for some revenge. Excellent cast includes Moore as his flinty mother and Coburn as a wealthy redneck patriarch. Stoltz's performance holds the spiraling story of class distinction, murder and deceit together, and Spader's Elvis-helmeted loser is fun to watch. Based on the novel by Brian Fair Berkey. **112m/C VHS, DVD.** Eric Stoltz, James Spader, Mary Tyler Moore, Joanna Going, Cameron Diaz, James Coburn, Michael Rooker, Peter Strauss, Deborah Kara Unger; ***D:*** Leslie Greif; ***W:*** Harley Peyton; ***C:*** Robert Fraisse; ***M:*** Stephen Endelman.

The KGB: The Secret War ½ *Lethal* **1986 (PG-13)** Reheated Cold War fare. **90m/C VHS.** Sally Kellerman, Michael Ansara, Michael Billington; ***W:*** Sandra K. Bailey; ***C:*** Peter Lyons Collister.

Khartoum ½ **1966** A sweeping but talky adventure epic detailing the last days of General "Chinese" Gordon as the title city is besieged by Arab tribes in 1884. **134m/C VHS, DVD.** Charlton Heston, Laurence Olivier, Ralph Richardson, Richard Johnson, Alexander Knox, Hugh Williams, Nigel Green, Michael Hordern, Johnny Sekka; ***D:*** Basil Dearden; ***W:*** Robert Ardrey; ***C:*** Edward Scaife; ***M:*** Frank Cordell.

Kibakichi *Kinakichi: Bokko-yokaiden; Werewolf Warrior* **2004 (R)** Part traditional samurai film, part spaghetti western, and part monster movie, the titular Kibakichi is a vagabond samurai werewolf—an unusual critter for an Asian horror movie. When the government decides to wipe out the Yokai (traditional Japanese spirit monsters), the

Yokai flee to the rural villages disguised as humans. In one village, a criminal boss proposes to the Yokai that if they will use their powers to help further his schemes, he will feed them people. Kibakichi agrees to be his bodyguard, unaware of what is truly going on. When the boss betrays the Yokai, Kibakichi defends the monsters against a human militia, while trying to bring the boss to justice. **95m/C DVD.** *JP* Ryuuji Harada, Nozomi Ando, Miki Tanaka; ***D:*** Tomoo Haraguchi; ***W:*** Mugi Kamio; ***C:*** Shoji Ebara; ***M:*** Kenji Kawai.

Kibakichi 2 1/2 *Kinakichi: Bokko-yo-kaiden 2* **2004 (R)** In this poor sequel, Kibakichi is helping a blind girl and her village gain revenge on a sadistic madman while being stalked by a female werewolf. Eventually all three of them team up to defeat a bad guy more evil than themselves. Notable for being a martial arts film wherein no one seems to be very accomplished at martial arts, and a horror film that seems confused as to actually how to scare an audience. The first film wasn't exactly great, but it had its uniqueness going for it. Even naked women dancing under the moon with polar bears doesn't save this thing. **80m/C DVD.** *JP* Ryuuji Harada, Miki Tanaka; ***D:*** Tomoo Haraguchi, Daiji Hattori; ***W:*** Baku Kamio; ***C:*** Shinji Watanabe; ***M:*** Kenji Kawai.

Kick-Ass **2010** Comic book fanboy teen Dave Lizewski wants to become a superhero. Of course he has no actual powers but that doesn't stop him from getting a costume and an alter ego. Dave then attracts the crazies, including 11-year-old vigilante Hit Girl and her father, Big Daddy, as well as bad guys with real weapons. Adapted from the Mark Millar comic book series. **m/C DVD.** Aaron Johnson, Nicolas Cage, Chloe Grace Moretz, Lyndsy Fonseca, Mark Strong, Christopher Mintz-Plasse, Xander Berkeley; ***D:*** Matthew Vaughn; ***W:*** Matthew Vaughn, Jane Goldman; ***C:*** Benjamin Davis; ***M:*** Marius De Vries.

The Kick Fighter **1991** Would you believe the hero has to kickbox to finance his kid sister's operation? Grungy, Bangkok-set chopsocky cheapie leaves no cliche untouched, but fights are well-staged. A strange end credit lauds real-life champ Urquidez, here a bad guy. **92m/C VHS.** Richard Norton, Benny "The Jet" Urquidez, Glen Ruehland, Franco Guerrero, Erica Van Wagener, Steve Rackman; ***D:*** Anthony Maharaj.

Kick of Death: The Prodigal Boxer *The Prodigal Boxer; Fang Shi Yu; Kung Fu: The Punch of Death* **1973 (R)** A young boxer is accused of a murder he didn't commit, and fights a battle to the death to prove it. **90m/C VHS, DVD.** Mang Sei, Suma Wah Lung, Pa Hung; ***D:*** Chai Yang Min.

Kickboxer 1/2 **1989 (R)** The brother of a permanently crippled kickboxing champ trains for a revenge match. **97m/C VHS, DVD.** Jean-Claude Van Damme, Rochelle Ashana, Dennis Chan, Dennis Alexio; ***D:*** Mark DiSalle; ***W:*** Jean-Claude Van Damme, Mark DiSalle, Glenn A. Bruce; ***C:*** Jon Kranhouse; ***M:*** Paul Hertzog.

Kickboxer 2: The Road Back 1/2 **1990 (R)** Mitchell takes over for Van Damme in this action sequel which finds our athletic hero seeking revenge on the kickboxer who murdered his brother. **90m/C VHS, DVD.** Sasha Mitchell, Peter Boyle, John Diehl; ***D:*** Albert Pyun.

Kickboxer 3: The Art of War 1/2 **1992 (R)** Mitchell returns in this second sequel. This time the American kickboxing champ flies to Rio for a big match which turns out to be fixed by a local mobster. For a little more fun our hero saves a kidnapped girl and fights a hired killer. **92m/C VHS, DVD.** Sasha Mitchell, Dennis Chan, Richard Comar, Noah Verduzco, Althea Miranda, Ian Jacklin; ***D:*** Rick King.

Kickboxer 4: The Aggressor 1/2 **1994 (R)** Martial arts expert David Sloan (Mitchell) was framed by sworn enemy Tong Po but now he's back and looking for revenge. **90m/C VHS, DVD.** Sasha Mitchell, Kamal Krifia, Nicholas Guest, Deborah Mansy, Brad Thornton; ***D:*** Albert Pyun.

Kickboxer the Champion **1991** The opium trade is in for a kick to the stomach when Archer challenges the big man in charge to a deathly duel. **?m/C VHS.** Don Murray, Wayne Archer; ***D:*** Alton Cheung.

Kicked in the Head **1997 (R)** Redmond, a loser who dreams of the Hindenburg disaster, is newly jobless, homeless and loveless. He decides to go on a "spiritual quest", which unfortunately consists of bad poetry and worse trouble, through Manhattan's Lower East Side. His Uncle Sam (Woods) wants him to deliver a package, his buddy Stretch (Rapaport) wants him to work for his shady (and sometimes violent) beer business and stewardess Megan (Fiorentino) wants him to leave her alone. It's all settled in a hail of gunfire and car chases, because that's how things are solved in the movies. Director Harrison did more with much less in debut "Rhythym Thief." **97m/C VHS, DVD.** Kevin Corrigan, Linda Fiorentino, James Woods, Lili Taylor, Michael Rapaport, Burt Young, Olek Krupa; ***D:*** Matthew Harrison; ***W:*** Matthew Harrison, Kevin Corrigan; ***C:*** John Thomas, Howard Krupa; ***M:*** Stephen Endelman.

Kickin' It Old Skool **2007 (PG-13)** Lame comedy has breakdancing Justin (Calvert) starring his 1986 school talent show until an accident puts him in a 20-year coma. Naturally, there's a big adjustment when Justin (an annoying Kennedy) wakes up, complicated by the fact that he thinks like a 13-year-old. Realizing his parents have gone broke paying for his care, Justin decides to get his old crew back together and enter a hip-hop dance contest, despite the fact that time has definitely marched on. **108m/C DVD.** *US* Jamie Kennedy, Miguel A. Nunez Jr., Maria Menounos, Michael Rosenbaum, Debra Jo Rupp, Christopher McDonald, Vivica A. Fox, Alan Ruck, Bobby Lee, Aris Alvarado, Alexander Calvert, Michelle Trachtenberg, Kira Clavell, Alexia Fast; ***Cameos:*** David Hasselhoff, Erik Estrada, Roddy Piper; ***D:*** Harvey Glazer; ***W:*** Trace Slobotkin, Josh Siegal, Dylan Morgan; ***C:*** Robert M. Stevens; ***M:*** Richard Glasser.

Kicking and Screaming **1995 (R)** Baumbach's deft, though slightly self-conscious directorial debut examines the post-college grad angst of Grover (Hamilton) and his three other slacker roomies. In denial of their recently achieved non-student status, the four bond together in pursuit of the inane and trivial, while their various girlfriends slip more easily into adulthood. Funny and tender flashback scenes of Grover and girlfriend Jane (D'Abo) add depth without all the dialogue, well-written though it is. Hilarious highlight occurs as roommate Otis interviews for that most popular of low-budget, Gen-X movie jobs—video store clerk. **96m/C VHS, DVD.** Josh Hamilton, Olivia D'Abo, Carlos Jacott, Christopher Eigeman, Eric Stoltz, Jason Wiles, Parker Posey, Cara Buono, Elliott Gould; ***D:*** Noah Baumbach; ***W:*** Oliver Berkman, Noah Baumbach; ***C:*** Steven Bernstein; ***M:*** Phil Marshall.

Kicking & Screaming 1/2 **2005 (PG)** Anemic family sports comedy that never would have been greenlit without a powerhouse like Ferrell in the lead. And it's to his sole credit that a movie this derivative works as well as it does. Mild-mannered Phil (Ferrell) is the anxiety-prone son of Buck (Duvall), a ridiculously competitive junior soccer coach who traded his own grandson, Phil's son Sam (McLaughlin), to another team. Determined to prove himself to Buck, Phil takes over coaching Sam's new soccer team, filled with losers and misfits, with the help of Buck's arch-rival Mike Ditka (yes, that Mike Ditka). Ferrell screaming at kids never stops being funny, but there's not an original moment in the entire film. **95m/C DVD.** *US* Will Ferrell, Robert Duvall, Steven Anthony Lawrence, Musetta Vander, Elliot Cho, Josh Hutcherson, Dylan McLaughlin, Eric Walker, Dallas McKinney, Jeremy Bergman, Kate Walsh, Francesco Liotti, Alessandro Ruggiero, Laura Kightlinger, Rachael Harris; ***Cameos:*** Mike Ditka; ***D:*** Jesse Dylan; ***W:*** Leo Benvenuti, Steve Rudnick; ***C:*** Lloyd Ahern II; ***M:*** Mark Isham.

Kicking It **2008** In 2006, four dozen soccer teams participated in the fourth annual World Homeless Cup, and this doc follows six of the players as they struggle with their personal demons while preparing for the tournament. The results are inspiring and depressing: the idea of staging a sporting event to bring attention to the homeless plight is interesting, as are the tales of participants who are said to have made their way off the streets, but the fates of most of the players remain iffy at best. **99m/C DVD.** ***D:*** Susan Koch, Jeff Warner; ***W:*** Susan Koch. **VIDEO**

Kicks 1/2 **1985** Two well-off San Francisco professionals play high-risk games with each other, culminating in a life-or-death hunt. **97m/C VHS.** Anthony Geary, Shelley Hack, Tom Mason, Ian Abercrombie, James Avery; ***D:*** William Wiard; ***M:*** Peter Bernstein. **TV**

The Kid **1921** Sensitive and sassy film about a tramp who takes home an orphan. Chaplin's first feature. Also launched Coogan as the first child superstar. **60m/B VHS, DVD.** Charlie Chaplin, Jackie Coogan, Edna Purviance; ***D:*** Charlie Chaplin; ***W:*** Charlie Chaplin.

Kid 1/2 **1990 (R)** Young guy carries grudge for the murder of his parents and seeks pound of flesh. Enter mysterious beautiful woman and copious complications. Good sound FX. **94m/C VHS.** C. Thomas Howell, R. Lee Ermey, Brian Austin Green, Sarah Trigger, Dale Dye; ***D:*** John Mark Robinson.

The Kid 1/2 **1997 (PG)** High schooler Jimmy Albright (Saumier) is secretly taking boxing lessons from trainer Harry Sloan (Steiger) since his parents don't approve. Jimmy is a natural and is ready to compete in the amateur championship match. Then Harry dies and fellow boxer Trey (Brochu) schemes to have Jimmy's parents find out about his secret life and forbid him to box. **89m/C VHS, DVD.** *CA* Jeff Saumier, Rod Steiger, Ray Aranha, Mark Camacho, Jane Wheeler, Tod Fennell, Daniel Brochu, Jason Tremblay; ***D:*** John Hamilton; ***W:*** Seymour Blicker; ***M:*** Normand Corbeil.

The Kid and I **2005 (PG-13)** A film about the making of a film, built around Aaron Roman (Gores) who, although born with cerebral palsy, dreams of starring in action movies like his favorite, "True Lies." Since his father (Mantegne) is a wealthy and powerful Los Angeles business mogul, Aaron gets his chance. Bill Williams (Arnold), whose acting career is floundering, is hired to write and co-star with Aaron. Actor Gores, who actually has cerebral palsy, is great as Aaron. Uplifting and fun, if you have a high schmaltz tolerance. **93m/C DVD.** *US* Tom Arnold, Linda Hamilton, Henry Winkler, Richard Edson, Joe Mantegna, Shannon Elizabeth, Arielle Kebbel, Brenda Strong, Eric Gores; ***Cameos:*** Penelope Spheeris; ***D:*** Penelope Spheeris; ***W:*** Tom Arnold; ***C:*** Robert E. Seaman.

Kid and the Killers **1974 (PG)** Young orphan and a hardened criminal band together to pursue a villain. **90m/C VHS.** Jon Cypher, John Garces, Ralph Bluemke; ***D:*** Ralph Bluemke; ***W:*** Ralph Bluemke.

The Kid Brother 1/2 **1927** The shy, weak son of a tough sheriff, Harold fantasizes about being a hero like his father and big brothers, falls in love with a carnival lady, and somehow saves the day. Classic silent comedy. **84m/B VHS, DVD.** Harold Lloyd, Walter James, Jobyna Ralston; ***D:*** Ted Wilde.

Kid Colter 1/2 **1985** Enjoyable family film about a city kid who goes to visit his dad in a remote wilderness area of the Pacific Northwest. While there he is abducted by two grizzly mountain men and left for dead, but survives and pursues his abductors relentlessly. Received the Film Advisory Board Award of Excellence and the Award of Merit from the Academy of Family Films. **101m/C VHS.** Jim Stafford, Jeremy Shamos, Hal Terrance, Greg Ward, Jim Turner; ***D:*** David O'Malley; ***W:*** David O'Malley.

Kid Courageous **1935** An athlete goes west, tracks ore mine thieves and prevents a hot-blooded spitfire from marrying the wrong man. **53m/B VHS.** Arthur Loft, Jack Cowell, Lafe (Lafayette) McKee, Rene Borden, Bob Steele; ***D:*** Robert North Bradbury; ***W:*** Robert North Bradbury; ***C:*** William (Bill) Hyer.

Kid Dynamite *Queen of Broadway* **1943** A Bowery Boys series episode. Gorcey is a boxer who is kidnapped to prevent his participation in a major fight. The real fighting occurs when his brother is substituted, and Gorcey is smitten. **73m/B VHS, DVD.** Leo Gorcey, Huntz Hall, Bobby Jordan, Gabriel Dell, Pamela Blake; ***D:*** Wallace Fox.

A Kid for Two Farthings 1/2 **1955** An episodic, sentimental portrait of the Jewish quarter in London's East End, centered on a boy with a malformed goat he thinks is a magic unicorn capable of granting wishes and bringing happiness to his impoverished 'hood. Acclaimed adaptation of a novel by screenwriter Wolf Mankowitz. **96m/C VHS, DVD.** *GB* Diana Dors, David Kossoff, Celia Johnson, Jonathan Ashmore, Joe Robinson, Brenda de Banzie, Primo Carnera, Lou Jacobi, Irene Handl; ***D:*** Carol Reed; ***W:*** Wolf Mankowitz; ***C:*** Edward Scaife; ***M:*** Benjamin Frankel.

Kid from Brooklyn **1946** A shy, musically inclined milkman becomes a middleweight boxer by knocking out the champ in a street brawl. Remake of "The Milky Way" by Harold Lloyd. Available with digitally remastered stereo and original movie trailer. ♫ Sunflower Song; Hey, What's Your Name; You're the Cause Of It All; Welcome, Burleigh; I Love An Old-Fashioned Song; Josie. **113m/C VHS.** Danny Kaye, Virginia Mayo, Eve Arden, Fay Bainter, Walter Abel; ***D:*** Norman Z. McLeod; ***C:*** Gregg Toland.

The Kid From Cleveland 1/2 **1949** Troubled teen Johnny (Tamblyn) is taken under the wing of sports announcer Mike Jackson (Brent) who introduces him to the owner and players of the Cleveland Indians. They do their best to set the kid on the straight and narrow as the baseball team enters the 1948 World Series. A real nostalgia piece. **89m/B DVD.** George Brent, Russ Tamblyn, Lynn Bari, Tommy Cook, Louis Jean Heydt, Ann Doran, Bill Veeck; ***D:*** Herbert Kline; ***W:*** John Bright; ***C:*** Jack Marta; ***M:*** Nathan Scott.

Kid from Gower Gulch **1950** A singing, non-horse-riding cowboy enters a rodeo through a clever ruse. **56m/B VHS, DVD.** Jack Baxley, Joe Hiser, Wanda Canton, Spade Cooley; ***D:*** Oliver Drake; ***W:*** Elmer Clifton; ***C:*** Harvey Hines.

The Kid from Left Field **1979** Bat boy for the San Diego Padres transforms the team from losers to champions when he passes on the advice of his father, a "has-been" ballplayer, to the team members. TV remake of the 1953 classic. **80m/C VHS.** Gary Coleman, Robert Guillaume, Ed McMahon, Tab Hunter; ***D:*** Adell Aldrich. **TV**

Kid from Not-So-Big **1978 (G)** A family film that tells the story of Jenny, a young girl left to carry on her grandfather's frontier-town newspaper. When two con-men come to town, Jenny sets out to expose them. **87m/C VHS.** Jennifer McAllister, Veronica Cartwright, Robert Viharo, Paul Tulley; ***D:*** William Crain.

Kid from Spain 1/2 **1932** Early Busby Berkeley choreography highlights this fun, if nonsensical, musical. Thanks to the usual mixups, college boy Eddie (Cantor) witnesses a bank robbery and flees to his friend Ricardo's (Young) home in Mexico, with the crooks on his trail. Then he gets mistaken for a famous bullfighter and is even forced into the ring. Oh, and there's some romantic complications as well. ♫ The College Song; Look What You've Done; In the Moonlight; What a Perfect Combination. **96m/B VHS.** Eddie Cantor, Robert Young, Lyda Roberti, Ruth Hall, John Miljan, Noah Beery Sr., J. Carrol Naish, Robert Emmett O'Connor; ***D:*** Leo McCarey; ***W:*** William Anthony McGuire, Bert Kalmar, Harry Ruby; ***C:*** Gregg Toland.

Kid Galahad *The Battling Bellhop* **1937** Well-acted boxing drama with Robinson playing an honest promoter who wants to make Morris into a prize fighter. Davis plays the girl they both want. Remade as "The Wagons Roll at Night" and then made again as an Elvis Presley vehicle. **101m/B VHS.** Edward G. Robinson, Bette Davis, Humphrey Bogart, Wayne Morris, Jane Bryan, Harry Carey Sr., Veda Ann Borg; ***D:*** Michael Curtiz; ***W:*** Seton I. Miller; ***C:*** Gaetano Antonio "Tony" Gaudio; ***M:*** Max Steiner.

Kid Galahad **1962** The King plays a young boxer who weathers the fight game, singing seven songs along the way. ♫ King of the Whole Wide World; This Is Living; I Got

Lucky; A Whistling Tune; Home Is Where The Heart Is; Riding the Rainbow; Love Is For Loves. **95m/C VHS, DVD.** Elvis Presley, Lola Albright, Charles Bronson, Ned Glass, Joan Blackman, Ed Asner, Gig Young; ***D:*** Phil Karlson; ***C:*** Burnett Guffey.

A Kid in Aladdin's Palace 1/2 **1997 (PG)** Burger flipper Calvin (Nicholas) time travels to anicent Arabia thanks to a mischief-making genie (Negron). He meets Princess Scheherazade (Mitra), who wants Calvin's help in fighting evil Luxor (Faulkner), who's overthrown her father, King Aladdin (Ipale). **89m/C VHS, DVD.** Thomas Ian Nicholas, Rhona Mitra, Taylor Negron, James Faulkner, Aharon Ipale; ***D:*** Robert L. Levy; ***W:*** Michael Part; ***C:*** Wally Pfister; ***M:*** David Michael Frank.

A Kid in King Arthur's Court 1/2 **1995 (PG)** Lame adaptation of Mark Twain's "A Connecticut Yankee in King Arthur's Court" finds insecure California teen Calvin Fuller (Nicholas), falling down a hole created by an earthquake and landing in Camelot. Arthur's (Ackland) a doddering old man with a cute teen daughter, Princess Katey (Baeza), who needs some help in defeating the evil Lord Belasco (Malik). Naturally, Calvin helps out and gains confidence in himself. Okay time-waster for the kids. **91m/C VHS, DVD.** Thomas Ian Nicholas, Joss Ackland, Art Malik, Paloma Baeza, Kate Winslet, Ron Moody, Daniel Craig; ***D:*** Michael Gottlieb; ***W:*** Michael Part, Robert L. Levy; ***C:*** Elemer Ragalyi; ***M:*** J.A.C. Redford.

Kid Millions 1/2 **1934** Vintage musical comedy in which a dull-witted Brooklyn boy must travel to exotic Egypt to collect an inherited fortune. The finale is filmed in early three-strip Technicolor. Lucille Ball appears as a Goldwyn Girl. ♫ Your Head on My Shoulder; Ice Cream Fantasy; An Earful of Music; When My Ship Comes In; Okay Toots; I Want to be a Minstrel Man; Mandy. **90m/B VHS.** Eddie Cantor, Ethel Merman, Ann Sothern, George Murphy; ***D:*** Roy Del Ruth.

Kid Monk Baroni 1/2 **1952** Street punk Baroni (Nimoy) leaves his gang behind when a good-guy priest (Rober) introduces him to boxing. The kid rises to success thanks to a cagey manager (Cabot) and despite the presence of organized crime. Typical B-movie melodrama. **80m/B VHS, DVD.** Leonard Nimoy, Bruce Cabot, Richard Rober, Kathleen Freeman; ***D:*** Harold Schuster.

Kid 'n' Hollywood and Polly Tix in Washington 1/2 *Polly Tix in Washington* **1933** These two "Baby Burlesks" shorts star a cast of toddlers, featuring the most famous moppet of all time, Shirley Temple, in her earliest screen appearances. **20m/B VHS, DVD.** Shirley Temple; ***D:*** Charles Lamont; ***C:*** Dwight Warren.

Kid Ranger **1936** A ranger shoots an innocent man, but later sets things straight by bringing the real culprit to justice. **57m/B VHS, DVD.** Bob Steele, William Farnum; ***D:*** Robert North Bradbury.

Kid Sister 1/2 **1945** A young girl is determined to grab her sister's boyfriend for herself, and enlists the aid of a burglar to do it. **56m/B VHS.** Roger Pryor, Judy Clark, Frank Jenks, Constance Worth, Tom Dugan, Minerva Urecal; ***D:*** Sam Newfield; ***W:*** Fred Myton; ***C:*** James S. Brown Jr.

The Kid Stays in the Picture **2002 (R)** Documentary covers the up-and-down career and life of one-time actor and '70s-super film producer Robert Evans. Evans narrates the film memoir that is taken from his 1994 autobiography—so don't expect objectivity (or, necessarily, accuracy). Evans discusses not only his career but his marriages, romances, drug problems, involvement in a murder investigation, and his rise-fall-rise life. **93m/C VHS, DVD.** *US* ***D:*** Brett Morgen, Nanette Burstein; ***W:*** Brett Morgen; ***C:*** John Bailey; ***M:*** Jeff Danna; ***Nar:*** Robert Evans.

Kid Vengeance 1/2 **1975 (R)** After witnessing the brutal slaying of his family, a boy carries out a personal vendetta against the outlaws. **90m/C VHS, DVD.** Leif Garrett, Jim Brown, Lee Van Cleef, John Marley, Glynnis O'Connor; ***D:*** Joseph Manduke.

The Kid Who Loved Christmas **1990** After his adoptive mother is killed in a car accident, a young boy is taken from his adoptive father. The boy, upset about being removed from his new family, writes to Santa Claus for help. A touching yuletide drama. This was Sammy Davis Jr.'s last film. **118m/C VHS.** Cicely Tyson, Michael Warren, Sammy Davis Jr., Gilbert Lewis, Ken Page, Della Reese, Esther Rolle, Ben Vereen, Vanessa L(ynne) Williams, John Beal, Trent Cameron; ***D:*** Arthur Allan Seidelman; ***C:*** Hanania Baer. **TV**

The Kid with the Broken Halo **1982** Coleman and Guillaume are paired again in this unsuccessful pilot for a TV series. A young angel, out to earn his wings, must try to help three desperate families, with the help of an experienced angel. **100m/C VHS.** Gary Coleman, Robert Guillaume, June Allyson, Mason Adams, Ray Walston, John Pleshette, Kim Fields, Georg Stanford Brown, Telma Hopkins; ***D:*** Leslie Martinson. **TV**

The Kid with the 200 I.Q. **1983** When an earnest boy genius enters college at age 13, predictable comic situations arise that involve his attempts at impressing his idolized astronomy professor (Guillaume), as well as an equally unrequited bout of first love. Harmless comedy, one of a series of squeaky-clean family fare starring Coleman. **96m/C VHS.** Gary Coleman, Robert Guillaume, Harriet Hilliard Nelson, Dean Butler, Karli Michaelson, Christina Murrull, Mel Stewart; ***D:*** Leslie Martinson. **TV**

The Kid with the X-Ray Eyes **1999 (PG)** Twelve-year-old Bobby wants to be a spy when he grows up. Then he finds a strange pair of glasses that allow him to see through anything. He attracts the attentions of the C.I.A., the police, and a pair of theives who all want his special specs. **84m/C VHS, DVD.** Justin Berfield, Robert Carradine, Mark Collie, Diane Salinger, Griffin (Griffen) Drew, Brinke Stevens; ***D:*** Fred Olen Ray; ***W:*** Sean O'Bannon; ***C:*** Theo Angell; ***M:*** Jay Bolton. **VIDEO**

Kidco **1983 (PG)** The true story of a money-making corporation headed and run by a group of children ranging in age from 9 to 16. **104m/C VHS.** Scott Schwartz, Elizabeth Gorcey, Cinnamon Idles, Tristen Skylar; ***D:*** Ronald F. Maxwell.

Kidnap Syndicate 1/2 **1976 (R)** Kidnappers swipe two boys, releasing one—the son of a wealthy industrialist who meets their ransom demands. When they kill the other boy, a mechanic's son, the father goes on a revengeful killing spree. **105m/C VHS.** *IT* James Mason, Valentina Cortese; ***D:*** Fernando Di Leo.

Kidnapped **1948** Low-budget version of the Robert Louis Stevenson classic from independent Monogram Studios. David (McDowall) comes to claim his inheritance only to be kidnapped and sold into slavery. He's rescued by adventurer Alan Breck (O'Herlihy) and the duo make their way across the Scottish Highlands to claim David's heritage from his greedy uncle. **81m/B DVD.** Roddy McDowall, Dan O'Herlihy, Sue England, Roland Winters, Jeff Corey, Houseley Stevenson; ***D:*** William Beaudine; ***W:*** W. Scott Darling; ***C:*** William Sickner; ***M:*** Edward Kay.

Kidnapped 1/2 **1960** A young boy is sold by his wicked uncle as a slave, and is helped by an outlaw. A Disney film based on the Robert Louis Stevenson classic. **94m/C VHS.** Peter Finch, James MacArthur, Peter O'Toole; ***D:*** Robert Stevenson.

Kidnapped WOOF! **1987 (R)** When a teenage girl is kidnapped by pornographers, her sister seeks help from a tough cop and together they go undercover to find her. Plot is flimsy cover for what is actually an exploitative piece. **100m/C VHS.** David Naughton, Barbara Crampton, Lance LeGault, Chick Vennera, Charles Napier; ***D:*** Howard (Hikmet) Avedis; ***W:*** Howard (Hikmet) Avedis.

Kidnapped 1/2 **1995** Cable adaptation of Robert Louis Stevenson's 1886 novel. In 1751 shanghaied young David Balfour (McCardie) and Highland patriot Aln Breck Stewart (Assante) escape from a slave ship and return to Scotland to battle the British. **142m/C VHS, DVD.** Armand Assante, Brian McCardie, Michael Kitchen, Brian Blessed, Patrick Malahide; ***D:*** Ivan Passer; ***W:*** John Goldsmith. **CABLE**

Kidnapped **2005** This BBC version of the Robert Louis Stevenson adventure tale finds orphaned Davie Balfour (Pearson) trying to claim his inheritance from his eccentric Uncle Ebeneezer (Dunbar). Instead, Davie gets kidnapped and imprisoned on a slave ship. Fortunately, he joins forces with exiled rebel Alan Breck (Glen) and the two wind up shipwrecked and running from evil English soldier Colonel McNabb (McGann) and his bounty hunters in the Scottish Highlands circa the 1750s. Exciting swashbuckling abounds. **150m/C VHS, DVD.** *GB* Iain Glen, Adrian Dunbar, Paul McGann, Gregor Fisher, John Bach, John Leigh, James Anthony Pearson, Kirstin Coulter Smith; ***D:*** Brendan Maher; ***W:*** Bev Doyle, Richard Kurti; ***C:*** Geoffrey Hall; ***M:*** David Hirschfelder. **TV**

Kidnapped in Paradise **1998 (PG-13)** Spoiled beauty Megan (Ross), her fiance Jack, and her practical sister, Beth (Fisher), are sailing in the Caribbean when their yacht is boarded by Renard, who's obsessed with Megan. He kills Jack, kidnaps Megan, and leaves Beth in the sinking vessel. She's rescued by Matt, who agrees to help her find her sister, which leads them to Renard's private island. **91m/C VHS.** Joely Fisher, Charlotte Ross, Robert Knepper, David Beecroft; ***D:*** Rob Hedden; ***W:*** David Chisholm. **CABLE**

Kidnapping of Baby John Doe **1988** Tragedy strikes a family's newborn, and they must make the terrifying decision between life and death. A doctor and nurse, however, take matters into their own hands to save the baby. **90m/C VHS.** Helen Hughes, Jayne (Jane) Eastwood, Janet-Laine Green, Geoffrey Boues, Peter Gerretsen; ***D:*** Peter Gerretsen; ***W:*** Peter Gerretsen; ***C:*** Douglas Koch; ***M:*** Heather Conkie.

The Kidnapping of the President 1/2 **1980 (R)** The U.S. president is taken hostage by Third World terrorists. The Secret Service is on the ball trying to recover the nation's leader. Well-integrated subplot involves the vice president in a scandal. Engrossing political thriller. Based on novel by Charles Templeton. **113m/C VHS, DVD.** *CA* William Shatner, Hal Holbrook, Van Johnson, Ava Gardner, Miguel Fernandes; ***D:*** George Mendeluk.

Kids **1995** Very controversial docudrama about 24 hours in the lives of some aimless New York teenagers. The sullen Telly (Fitzpatrick) enjoys bragging about his skill in deflowering virgins but his promiscuity has lead Jennie (Sevigny) to test H.I.V. positive—something Telly is as yet unaware of. Telly'd rather hang around with best friend Casper (Pierce) anyway, out on the streets, being generally profane and obnoxious. Can either be regarded as a brutally realistic look at teen life today or a lot of fuss about nothing. Korine was 19 when he wrote the screenplay. The MPAA rated the film NC-17, after a protest the distributors chose to release it unrated. **90m/C VHS, DVD.** Jon Abrahams, Leo Fitzpatrick, Justin Pierce, Chloe Sevigny, Rosario Dawson, Sarah Henderson, Harold Hunter, Yakira Peguero, Joseph Knafelmacher; ***D:*** Larry Clark; ***W:*** Harmony Korine; ***C:*** Eric Alan Edwards; ***M:*** Louis Barlow. Ind. Spirit '96: Debut Perf. (Pierce).

The Kids Are All Right **2010** L.A. lesbian couple Jules (Moore) and Nic (Bening) are thrown into a panic when they learn that their teenage children have secretly met with their biological dad, sperm donor Paul (Ruffalo). He starts coming to family dinners but uptight doctor Nic rightly has suspicions that he's getting a little too close to the family for comfort. **104m/C DVD.** *US* Julianne Moore, Annette Bening, Mark Ruffalo, Mia Wasikowska, Josh Hutcherson, Kunal Sharma, Yaya DaCosta, Joaquin Garrido, Eddie Hassell, Zosia Mamet; ***D:*** Lisa Cholodenko; ***W:*** Lisa Cholodenko, Stuart Blumberg; ***C:*** Igor Jadue-Lillo; ***M:*** Craig (Shudder to Think) Wedren, Nathan Larson.

The Kids Are Alright 1/2 **1979 (PG)** A feature-length compilation of performances and interviews spanning the first 15 years of the rock group, The Who. Includes rare footage from the "Rolling Stones Rock and Roll Circus" film. Songs include: "My Generation," "I Can't Explain," "Young Man's Blues," "Won't Get Fooled Again," "Baba O' Reilly," and excerpts from "Tommy." **106m/C VHS, DVD.** Roger Daltrey, Pete Townshend, Keith Moon, John Entwhistle, Ringo Starr, Keith Richards, Steve Martin, Tom Smothers, Rick Danko; ***D:*** Jeff Stein; ***W:*** Jeff Stein; ***C:*** Anthony B. Richmond, Norman Wexler; ***M:*** Roger Daltrey, Pete Townshend, Keith Moon, John Entwhistle.

Kids in America 1/2 **2005 (PG-13)** Self-satisfied satire finds ambitious, control-freak high school principal Donna Weller (Bowen) clamping down on various activities organized by her mildly-rebellious suburban students. They finally get fed up by her dictatorial policies and decide to fight back. Richie makes her film debut as a (what else?) bimbette cheerleader. **91m/C DVD.** *US* Andrew Shaifer, Gregory Edward Smith, Caitlin Wachs, Crystal Grant, Stephanie Sherrin, Chris Morris, Emy Coligado, Julie Bowen, Malik Yoba, George Wendt, Adam Arkin, Jeffrey Chase, Nicole Richie, Rosanna Arquette, Elizabeth Perkins, Charles Shaughnessy, Samantha Mathis, Rain Phoenix, Amy Hill, Michelle Phillips; ***D:*** Josh Stolberg; ***W:*** Josh Stolberg, Andrew Shaifer; ***C:*** Guy Livneh; ***M:*** B.C. Smith.

Kids in the Hall: Brain Candy *The Drug* **1996 (R)** The Canadian Kids bring their Monty Python-meets-SCTV humor to the big screen with moderate success. Dr. Cooper (McDonald), facing corporate downsizing, allows his new, untested anti-depressant to be released to the public after it shows promise. The drug, Gleemonex, sweeps the country by forcing the user's mind to focus on a favorite memory. As befits the troupe's twisted vision, these happy memories aren't always pleasant to the "Family Values" crowd. The easily offended should be warned—there's a character named "Cancer Boy." The story wanders a bit, giving everyone a chance to show their versatility (these Kids collectively play 32 different roles). Sophomore director Makin served the same duty on many of the TV episodes. **88m/C VHS, DVD.** Dave Foley, Bruce McCulloch, Kevin McDonald, Scott Thompson, Mark McKinney, Janeane Garofalo; ***D:*** Kelly Makin; ***W:*** Bruce McCulloch, Kevin McDonald, Scott Thompson, Mark McKinney, Norm Hiscock; ***C:*** David Makin; ***M:*** Craig Northey.

Kid's Last Ride **1941** Three tough guys come into town to settle a feud. **55m/B VHS, DVD.** Ray Corrigan, John "Dusty" King, Max Terhune, Luana Walters, Edwin Brian; ***D:*** S. Roy Luby.

Kids of the Round Table 1/2 **1996** Eleven-year-old Alex (Morina) and his buddies like to have mock sword battles, pretending to be King Arthur and his knights. When their games are broken up by the local bully, Alex takes off into the woods where he discovers a sword in a stone. It's the legendary Excalibur and when Alex removes it, Merlin (McDowell) appears, explaining the sword will give the boy special powers. Of course, Alex abuses his newfound strength until he comes to the rescue of his friends. **89m/C VHS, DVD.** *CA* Johnny Morina, Michael Ironside, Malcolm McDowell, Peter Aykroyd, Rene Simard; ***D:*** Robert Tinnell; ***W:*** David Sherman; ***C:*** Roxanne Di Santo; ***M:*** Normand Corbeil.

Kika **1994** Another flamboyant comedy from Almodovar finds irrepressible beautician Kika (Forque) involved with kinky photographer Ramon (Casanovas) and his stepfather Nicholas (Coyote), a sinister American pulp novelist. There's also Andrea Scarface (Jean-Paul Gaultier-costumed Abril), the host of a vile tabloid TV show called "Today's Worst," and Kika's lesbian maid Juana (de Palma) whose brother happens to be an escaped con/porn star, leading to an outlandish rape and...well, it's all pretty nonsensical, anyway. Spanish with subtitles. **115m/C VHS, DVD.** *SP* Veronica Forque, Peter Coyote, Victoria Abril, Alex Casanovas, Rossy de Palma; ***D:*** Pedro Almodovar; ***W:*** Pedro Almodovar; ***C:*** Alfredo Mayo; ***M:*** Enrique Granados.

Kiki's Delivery Service 1/2 **1998 (G)** Young witch Kiki, accompanied by her outspoken cat Jiji, tries to find her place in the world. She becomes the resident witch in a small town and uses her flying-broom to create a bakery delivery service, while making some new friends. Voice cast listed is for the American (dubbed) version. **104m/C VHS, DVD.** *JP* ***D:*** Hayao Miyazaki; ***W:*** Hayao Miyazaki; ***V:*** Kirsten Dunst, Phil Hartman, Debbie Reynolds, Janeane Garofalo, Matthew Lawrence, Jeff Glenn Bennett, Tress MacNeille, Debi Derryberry, Pamela Segall, Lewis Arquette. **VIDEO**

Kikujiro 1999 **(PG-13)** Eight-year-old Masao (Sekiguchi) lives with his grandmother. His father is dead and his mother lives in a distant town due to her job. Bored on his summer vacation, the boy decides to visit his mother—accompanied by the tough-guy husband, Kikujiro (Kitano), of a neighbor. Only this guy doesn't have much of an idea about kids and their travels lead to some unpredictable adventures. Clumsy and protracted; Japanese with subtitles. **116m/C VHS, DVD.** *JP* Takeshi "Beat" Kitano, Yusuke Sekiguchi; ***D:*** Takeshi "Beat" Kitano; ***W:*** Takeshi "Beat" Kitano; ***C:*** Katsumi Yanagishima; ***M:*** Joe Hisaishi.

The Kill 1/2 **1973** A rough, cynical, hard-boiled, womanizing detective tracks down stolen cash in downtown Macao. **81m/C VHS.** Richard Jaeckel, Henry Duval, Judy Washington; ***D:*** Rolf Bayer; ***W:*** Rolf Bayer; ***M:*** Noel Quinlan.

Kill Alex Kill WOOF! 1976 A Vietnam POW returns to find his family murdered, and uses the crime underworld to take revenge. **88m/C VHS.** Tony Zarindast, Tina Bowmann, Chris Ponti; ***D:*** Tony Zarindast; ***C:*** Nicholas Josef von Sternberg.

Kill and Kill Again 1/2 **1981 (PG)** A martial arts champion attempts to rescue a kidnapped Nobel Prize-winning chemist who has developed a high-yield synthetic fuel. Colorful, tongue-in-cheek, and fun even for those unfamiliar with the genre. **100m/C VHS, DVD.** James Ryan, Anneline Kriel, Stan Schmidt, Bill Flynn, Norman Robinson, Ken Gampu, John Ramsbottom; ***D:*** Ivan Hall; ***W:*** John Crowther; ***C:*** Tai Krige.

Kill, Baby, Kill *Curse of the Living Dead; Operacione Paura* **1966** A small Transylvania town is haunted by the ghost of a seven-year-old witchcraft victim, and the town's suicide victims all seem to have hearts of gold (coins, that is). Lots of style and atmosphere in this Transylvanian tale from horror tongue in cheekster Bava. Considered by many genre connoisseurs to be the B man's finest, except that it bears early symptoms of the director's late onset infatuation with the zoom shot. **83m/C VHS, DVD.** *IT* Erika Blanc, Giacomo "Jack" Rossi-Stuart, Fabienne Dali, Giana Vivaldi; ***D:*** Mario Bava; ***W:*** Mario Bava; ***C:*** Antonio Rinaldi; ***M:*** Carlo Rustichelli.

Kill Bill Vol. 1 1/2 **2003 (R)** Tarantino is back with a vengeance. In the first of two volumes of what originally was supposed to be a single film, Uma Thurman is spectacular as The Bride, a former assassin, betrayed and left for dead at her wedding by her associates and mysterious boss, Bill. When she awakens from a coma four years later she begins a mission of revenge that takes her from suburban L.A. to Okinawa, to Tokyo. Tarantino joyfully and masterfully immerses the audience in the different styles and ultra-violence of the Asian cinema he loves so much, even using anime for one backstory sequence, with some spaghetti western and '70s TV added for spice. His trademark sharp dialogue is not as plentiful as in the past, but what's here is layered, sometimes moving, and often humorous. Tarantino fave Chiba delivers as a master samurai swordmaker. **110m/C VHS, DVD, Blu-ray Disc, UMD.** *US* Uma Thurman, Lucy Liu, Vivica A. Fox, Michael Madsen, Daryl Hannah, Gordon (Chia Hui) Liu, Sonny Chiba, Michael Parks, Chiaki Kuriyama, Jun Kunimura, Julie Dreyfus, Larry Bishop, Michael Bowen; ***D:*** Quentin Tarantino; ***W:*** Quentin Tarantino; ***C:*** Robert Richardson; ***M:*** RZA; ***V:*** David Carradine.

Kill Bill Vol. 2 1/2 **2004 (R)** The Bride continues to work her way through her former associates on the way to the big showdown with Bill, where she discovers some unexpected developments. This volume has less action than the first, but it is just as intense. All that was hidden in Vol. 1 is revealed, and it's done with more of the character development and dialogue-driven scenes that some thought were lacking in the first installment. The two volumes are so vastly different in tone and style that it seems odd that they were intended as one (very) long movie, but the idea of seeing them united into one film is intriguing. Carradine gives what might be the finest performance of his career as the enigmatic Bill. Thurman proves that her work on set was more than just physical, and that she can carry a movie even when she isn't carrying a sword. **137m/C DVD, Blu-ray Disc, UMD.** *US* Uma Thurman, David Carradine, Lucy Liu, Michael Madsen, Vivica A. Fox, Daryl Hannah, Michael Parks, Julie Dreyfus, Chiaki Kuriyama, Sonny Chiba, Gordon (Chia Hui) Liu, LaTanya Richardson Jackson, Bo Svenson, Samuel L. Jackson, Jeannie Epper, Perla Haney-Jardine, Caitlin Keats, Christopher Allen Nelson, Stevo Polyi, Venessia Valentino; ***D:*** Quentin Tarantino; ***W:*** Uma Thurman, Quentin Tarantino; ***C:*** Robert Richardson; ***M:*** RZA, Robert Rodriguez.

Kill by Inches **1999** Strange and stylized story follows traumatized tailor Thomas Klamm (Salinger) who, as a child, was forced by his authortarian father (Powell) to literally eat a tape measure as punishment for a dispute with his sister. Since then, Tom finds a sexual thrill in the measurement of human bodies. Sister Vera (Cyr), also a tailor, suddenly shows up at Thomas' Brooklyn shop with her own special gifts and they play out their odd sibling rivalry. **85m/C VHS, DVD.** *FR* Emmanuel Salinger, Myriam Cyr, Marcus Powell, Peter McRobbie; ***D:*** Diane Doniol-Valcroze, Arthur Flam; ***W:*** Diane Doniol-Valcroze, Arthur Flam; ***C:*** Richard Rutkowski; ***M:*** Geir Jenssen.

Kill Castro **1980 (R)** Ever hear the one about the exploding cigar? Key West boat skipper is forced to carry a CIA agent to Cuba on a mission to assassinate Castro. Low-budget adventure that's deadly dull. **90m/C VHS, DVD.** Sybil Danning, Albert Salmi, Michael V. Gazzo, Raymond St. Jacques, Woody Strode, Stuart Whitman, Robert Vaughn, Caren Kaye; ***D:*** Chuck Workman.

Kill Cruise **1990 (R)** The depressed and alcoholic skipper of the yacht Bella Donna gives up sailing until he meets two beautiful young women who want to sail to Bermuda for a taste of the good life. The calm of the Atlantic is disturbed when they are plagued by bad weather and fierce storms, and tensions rise as the two women's jealousies erupt. Will it set the climate for murder? **99m/C VHS, DVD.** Jurgen Prochnow, Patsy Kensit, Elizabeth Hurley; ***D:*** Peter Keglevic; ***W:*** Peter Keglevic; ***C:*** Edward Klosinski; ***M:*** Brynmor Jones.

Kill Factor WOOF! *Death Dimension; Black Eliminator; The Freeze Bomb* **1978 (R)** Something stupid about a killer bomb tht could freeze the planet. So inept your brain cells will also be frozen if you watch it. **91m/C VHS, DVD.** Jim Kelly, George Lazenby, Aldo Ray, Harold Sakata, Terry Moore; ***D:*** Al Adamson.

Kill Line **1991 (R)** Kim stars as Joe, a street fighter who seeks to clear his name after serving a 10-year prison sentence for a crime he didn't commit. When he finds his brother's family has been murdered by criminals looking for the millions he supposedly stole, Joe wages a one-man martial arts war against a corrupt police force and the gang of thugs who are looking for the money. **93m/C VHS, DVD.** Bobby Kim, Michael Parker, Marlene Zimmerman, H. Wayne Lowery, C.R. Valdez, Mark Williams, Ben Pfeifer; ***D:*** Richard H. Kim; ***W:*** Richard H. Kim.

Kill Me Again 1/2 **1989 (R)** Director Dahl does the contemporary noir thing through the Nevada desert with Whalley as a beautiful femme fatale. She asks a detective (then husband Kilmer) to fake her death, which gets him targeted not only by the police, but also the mob and her psychoboyfriend (Madsen). Fun and full of plot twists that will satisfy fans of the noir persuasion. **93m/C VHS, DVD.** Val Kilmer, Joanne Whalley, Michael Madsen, Jon(athan) Gries, Bibi Besch; ***D:*** John Dahl; ***W:*** John Dahl, David Warfield; ***C:*** Jacques Steyn.

Kill Me Later **2001 (R)** Loan officer Shawn (Blair) has just broken up with her married lover/boss (Moffett) and decides to kill herself by jumping off the bank's roof. However, she's just in time to become the hostage of British thief Charlie (Beesley) whose robbery of the bank has gone wrong. Shawn agrees to help Charlie escape if he will agree to kill her later. An unlikely romance blossoms as the on the lam duo are tracked by a couple of FBI agents. **89m/C VHS, DVD.** *US* Selma Blair, Max Beesley, Lochlyn Munro, O'Neal Compton, Brendan Fehr, D.W. Moffett; ***D:*** Dana Lustig; ***W:*** Annette Goliti Gutierrez; ***C:*** David Ferrara; ***M:*** Tal Bergman, Renato Neto.

Kill Me Tomorrow **1957** Hard-drinking, widowed reporter Bart Crosbie loses his job just when he learns his son needs an expensive operation. He finds his ex-boss murdered and diamond smuggler Webber, who did the crime, makes a deal to pay Crosbie to take the fall. Only Scotland Yard doesn't believe Crosbie when he tries to confess and Webber starts thinking Crosbie reneged on their deal. **80m/B DVD.** *GB* Lois Maxwell, Wensley Pithey, George Coulouris, Pat O'Brien, Freddie Mills, Claude Kingston; ***D:*** Terence Fisher; ***W:*** Robert Falconer, Paddy Manning O'Brine; ***C:*** Geoffrey Faithfull; ***M:*** Temple Abady.

Kill Me Tomorrow 1/2 **1999** Teen-aged witch Holly (Vamshon) sets her sights on hunk Russell (Sheppard), which doesn't sit well with his present girlfriend Tricia (Shafia). So Holly decides to get even by stealing his soul. The inexperience of the cast shows up bigtime but they're very earnest. **80m/C VHS, DVD.** Louisa Shafia, Gregory Sheppard, Lyndee Yamshon; ***D:*** Patrick McGuinn; ***W:*** Patrick McGuinn. **VIDEO**

The Kill-Off **1990 (R)** Bedridden Luanne (Gross), married to janitor Ralph (Monroe), manages to cause dissension in her isolated New Jersey community with her vicious gossip. But when Luanne learns Ralph's involved with a stripper (Haase), it puts her own life in danger. Based on a story by Jim Thompson. **100m/C VHS.** Loretta Gross, Steve Monroe, Cathy Haase, Jackson Sims, Jorja Fox; ***D:*** Maggie Greenwald.

Kill or Be Killed **1980 (PG)** Martial arts champion is lured to a phony martial arts contest by a madman bent on revenge. **90m/C VHS.** James Ryan, Charlotte Michelle, Norman Coombes; ***D:*** Ivan Hall.

Kill or Be Killed 1/2 **1993** Michael Julian just spent eight years in jail for saving his brother Charlie's life. He must wonder why he bothered since Charlie has stolen his girl Beth and set up a drug empire. Michael ambushes Charlie's men and steals $1 million to use as leverage but Charlie thinks rival drug lords are out to get him and starts a street war. **97m/C VHS, DVD.** David Heavener, Joseph Nuzzolo, Paulo Tocha, Lynn Levand; ***D:*** Joe Straw; ***W:*** Joseph Nuzzolo.

The Kill Reflex **1989 (R)** A tough black cop and his beautiful rookie partner battle the mob and corruption. **90m/C VHS.** Maud Adams, Fred Williamson, Bo Svenson, Phyllis Hyman; ***D:*** Fred Williamson.

Kill Slade **1989 (PG-13)** When a United Nations food-aid diversion conspiracy is uncovered by a beautiful journalist, a plan to kidnap her is put into action. Romance follows. **90m/C VHS.** *SA* Patrick Dollaghan, Lisa Brady, Anthony Fridjhon, Danny Keogh, Alfred Nowke; ***D:*** Bruce McFarlane.

Kill Squad **1981 (R)** Squad of martial arts masters follow a trail of violence and bloodshed to a vengeful, deadly battle of skills. **85m/C VHS.** Jean Claude, Jeff Risk, Jerry Johnson, Bill Cambra, Cameron Mitchell; ***D:*** Patrick G. Donahue; ***W:*** Patrick G. Donahue; ***C:*** Christopher W. Strattan; ***M:*** Joseph Conlan.

Kill Switch *A Higher Form of Learning* **2008 (R)** Typically lumbering Seagal effort. Homicide detective Jacob King (Seagal) is so successful at apprehending serial killers that the FBI assigns naive agent Frankie Miller (Dignard) to study his methods. But King may have met his match in Lazereus (Filipowich), the current psycho terrorizing Memphis, who plants evidence that makes it look like King has finally gone over to the dark side. **96m/C DVD.** Steven Seagal, Chris Thomas King, Michael Filipowich, Mark Collie, Holly Dignard, Isaac Hayes; ***D:*** Jeff King; ***W:*** Steven Seagal; ***C:*** Thomas M. Harting; ***M:*** John Sereda. **VIDEO**

Kill the Golden Goose **1979 (R)** Two martial arts masters work on opposite sides of a government corruption and corporate influence peddling case. **91m/C VHS, DVD.** Brad von Beltz, Ed Parker, Master Bong Soo Han; ***D:*** Elliot Hong.

Kill the Poor **2006** When Joe's wife becomes pregnant, it's clear that their marriage of convenience will suddenly take emotional root and they'd better grow up, right now. Rather than moving out of their New York squatter building in the Lower East Side, Joe decides to become its co-op president, fighting off crackheads with a baseball bat and sleeping in the lobby as night security. Dark comedies normally only work if the comedy part is exercised. This one needs to lighten up. Labor of love for director Alan Taylor, who struggled to adapt Joel Rose's tragicomic novel for 15 years. **84m/C DVD.** *US* David Krumholtz, Clara Bellar, Paul Calderon, Larry (Lawrence) Gilliard Jr., Jon Budinoff, Cliff Gorman, Damian Young, Heather Burns, Otto Sanchez, Zak Orth; ***D:*** Alan Taylor; ***W:*** Daniel Handler; ***C:*** Harlan Bosmajian; ***M:*** Michel Delory, Anna Domino.

Kill the Umpire 1/2 **1950** Baseball comedy with much shtick and sight gags. Bill Johnson (Bendix) keeps losing jobs because he's always skipping work to go to baseball games. With his wife (Merkel) threatening to take the kids and leave, Bill's father-in-law Jonah (Collins), a retired ump, comes up with a solution and sends him to umpire school despite Bill's contempt for the guy the fans love to hate. After graduation, Bill is assigned to the Texas Interstate League where he discovers a couple of gamblers are trying to fix the pennant race. **78m/B DVD.** William Bendix, Una Merkel, Jeff Richards, Ray Collins, Gloria Henry, Connie Marshall, William Frawley, Tom D'Andrea, Jeff York, Robert J. Wilke; ***D:*** Lloyd Bacon; ***W:*** Frank Tashlin; ***C:*** Charles Lawton Jr.; ***M:*** Heinz Roemheld.

Kill Your Darlings **2006 (R)** Swede Erik (Wilson) is a failed Hollywood screenwriter. In an attempt to jump-start his life, Erik allows crazy free spirit Lola (Davidovich) to talk him into a road trip into the desert but she has ulterior motives. Meanwhile, celebrity shrink Dr. Bagley (Larroquette) has arranged for some of his suicidal patients to attend his book signing in Vegas. Think the two parallel plots will combine? **94m/C DVD.** *US SW* Andreas Wilson, Lolita (David) Davidovich, John Larroquette, Julie Benz, Alexander Skarsgard, Greg Germann, Skye McCole Bartusiak, Benito Martinez, Fares Fares, John Savage, Stellan Skarsgard, Terry Moore; ***D:*** Bjorne Larson; ***W:*** Bjorne Larson, Johan Sandstrom, Lisa Taube; ***C:*** Irek Hartowicz; ***M:*** Jon Rekdal.

Kill Zone 1/2 **2008** Fugitive Prescott Roeh has bounty hunters on his trail but he decides he must return to his hometown to make amends for his crimes. But not everyone is ready to forgive and forget. **110m/C DVD.** Brandon Chase, Troy Davidson, Ryan Michael Jones; ***D:*** Vitor Santos; ***W:*** Vitor Santos, Chris Carberg; ***C:*** Vitor Santos; ***M:*** Assaf Rinde. **VIDEO**

Killcrazy **1989 (R)** On the way to a weekend camping trip, five Vietnam vets released from a mental hospital are slowly massacred by a group of dangerous killers until one of the vets decides to fight back. **94m/C VHS.** David Heavener, Danielle Brisebois, Burt Ward, Lawrence-Hilton Jacobs, Bruce Glover, Gary Owens, Rachelle Carson; ***D:*** David Heavener; ***W:*** David Heavener.

Killer *The Insolent* **1973** An ex-convict sets up an ingenious bank robbery, and gets double-crossed himself. **87m/C VHS.** *FR* Andre Pousse, Georges Geret, Robert Dalban, Philippe Clay, Henry Silva; ***D:*** Jean-Claude Roy; ***W:*** Jean-Claude Roy; ***C:*** Claude Saunier; ***M:*** Bernard Gerard.

The Killer 1/2 *Die Xue Shuang Xiong* **1990 (R)** Jeffrey Chow is a gangster gunman who wants out. He's hired by his best friend to perform one last killing, but it doesn't go as smoothly as he wanted. He's almost caught by "Eagle" Lee, a detective who vows to hunt him down using Jennie, a singer blinded by Chow in crossfire. Lots of action and gunfights, but also pretty corny and sentimental. Very similar to American action movies, but using Chinese and Asian cultural conventions. A good introduction to the Chinese gangster-flick genre. Available with subtitles or dubbed in English. **110m/C VHS, DVD.** *HK* Chow Yun-Fat, Sally Yeh, Danny Lee, Kenneth Tsang, Chu Kong, Fui-On Shing; ***D:*** John Woo; ***W:*** John Woo; ***C:*** Wing-Hung Wong, Peter Pau; ***M:*** Lowell Lo.

Killer: A Journal of Murder **1995 (R)** Young, idealistic Jewish guard Henry Lesser (Leonard) befriends prisoner Carl Panzram (Woods) and encourages the man to write his life story. Then he must deal with the consequences of discovering the brutality behind Panzram's murderous crimes. The leads do fine but there's nothing new here. Inspired by true events and set in the 1920s. **91m/C VHS, DVD.** James Woods, Robert Sean Leonard, Ellen Greene, Cara Buono, Robert John Burke, Steve Forrest, John Bedford Lloyd, Harold Gould; ***D:*** Tim Metcalfe; ***W:*** Tim Metcalfe; ***C:*** Ken Kelsch; ***M:*** Graeme Revell.

Killer Bud 1/2 **2000 (R)** Best buds Waylon (Nemec) and Buzz (Faustino) get fired and decide to go on a road trip to score babes and marijuana. They're incredibly dumb—as is the movie—but it's funny in a stupid, I can't believe I'm watching this, kinda way. **92m/C VHS, DVD.** Corin "Corky" Nemec, David Faustino, Robert Stack, Danielle Harris, Caroline Keenan; ***D:*** Karl T. Hirsch; ***W:*** Greg DePaul, Hank Nelken; ***C:*** David Lewis; ***M:*** Russ Landau.

Killer Condom *Kondom des Grauens* **1995** Deadpan humor, gore, and severed flesh—all based on a Ralf Konig comic book that's definitely for adults. The killer condoms are jellyfish-like creatures with piranha-like teeth who have taken to feeding on the male sexual organs of the unfortunates who frequent Times Square's sleazy Hotel Quickie. Gay cop Luigi Macaroni (Semel) is determined to prevent any more emasculations. German with subtitles. **108m/C VHS, DVD.** *GE* Udo Samel, Peter Lohmeyer, Marc Richter, Leonard Lansink, Iris Berben, Hella Von Sinnen; ***D:*** Martin Walz; ***W:*** Martin Walz, Ralf Konig; ***C:*** Alexander Honisch; ***M:*** Emil Viklicky.

Killer Dill 1/2 **1947** Also killer dull. A meek salesman is misidentified as a death-dealing gangster, and the comic mixups begin. **71m/B VHS, DVD.** Stuart Erwin, Anne Gwynne, Frank Albertson, Mike Mazurki, Milburn Stone, Dorothy Granger; ***D:*** Lewis D. Collins.

Killer Diller 1/2 **1948** All-black musical revue featuring Nat King Cole and his Trio. **70m/B VHS, DVD.** Dusty Fletcher, Nat King Cole, Butterfly McQueen, Moms (Jackie) Mabley, George Wiltshire; ***D:*** Josh Binney.

Killer Diller **2004 (PG-13)** Trouble-making, guitar-playing Wesley (Scott) is sentenced to a halfway house located on a Baptist college campus where he's supposed to join in the gospel ensemble. But when he meets autistic Vernon (Black), a piano prodigy, he decides to form a blues group instead and convinces everyone to sneak away to play at the local honky-tonk. **95m/C DVD.** William Lee Scott, Lucas Black, Fred Willard, W. Earl Brown, Robert Wisdom, Mary Kay Place, Taj Mahal, Ashley Johnson, RonReaco Lee; ***D:*** Tricia Brock; ***W:*** Tricia Brock; ***C:*** Matthew Jensen; ***M:*** Tree Adama.

Killer Elephants **1976** A Thai man struggles to save his plantation, his wife, and his baby from the terrorists hired by a land baron to drive him away from his property. **83m/C VHS.** Sung Pa, Alan Yen, Nai Yen Ne, Yu Chien; ***D:*** Som Kit; ***C:*** Nu Ma.

The Killer Elite 1/2 **1975 (PG)** Straight-ahead Peckinpah fare examining friendship and betrayal. Two professional assassins begin as friends but end up stalking each other when they are double-crossed. This minor Peckinpah effort is murky and doesn't have a clear resolution, but is plenty bloody. Lots of Dobermans roam through this picture too. **120m/C VHS, DVD.** James Caan, Robert Duvall, Arthur Hill, Gig Young, Burt Young, Mako, Bo Hopkins, Helmut Dantine; ***D:*** Sam Peckinpah; ***W:*** Marc Norman, Stirling Silliphant; ***C:*** Peter Lathrop; ***M:*** Jerry Fielding.

Killer Fish *Deadly Treasure of the Piranha* **1979 (PG)** A scheme to steal and then hide a fortune in emeralds at the bottom of a tank full of piranhas backfires as the criminals find it impossible to retrieve them...as if that took a lot of foresight. Director Dawson is AKA Antonio Margheriti. Filmed in Brazil. **101m/C VHS.** *BR GB* Lee Majors, James Franciscus, Margaux Hemingway, Karen Black, Roy Brocksmith, Marisa Berenson; ***D:*** Anthony M. Dawson.

Killer Force 1/2 **1975 (R)** Predictable adventure involving international diamond smuggling. **100m/C VHS.** Telly Savalas, Peter Fonda, Maud Adams, Hugh O'Brian; ***D:*** Val Guest.

Killer Image **1992 (R)** A photographer unwittingly sees more than he should and becomes involved in a lethal political coverup. At the same time a wealthy senator targets him and he must fight for his life. Viewers might feel they have to fight their boredom. **97m/C VHS.** John Pyper-Ferguson, Michael Ironside, M. Emmet Walsh, Krista Errickson; ***D:*** David Winning.

A Killer in Every Corner **1974** Three psychology students visit a loony professor and succumb to his hair-raising shenanigans. **80m/C VHS.** Joanna Pettet, Patrick Magee, Max Wall, Eric Flynn; ***D:*** Malcolm Taylor; ***W:*** Brian Clemens.

The Killer Inside Me **1976 (R)** The inhabitants of a small Western town are unaware that their mild-mannered deputy sheriff is actually becoming a crazed psychotic murderer. From the novel by Jim Thompson. **99m/C VHS, DVD.** Stacy Keach, Susan Tyrrell, Tisha Sterling, Keenan Wynn, John Dehner, John Carradine, Don Stroud, Charles McGraw, Julie Adams, Royal Dano; ***D:*** Burt Kennedy; ***W:*** Robert Chandlee; ***C:*** William A. Fraker; ***M:*** Tim McIntire, John Rubinstein.

The Killer Inside Me **2010** West Texas deputy sheriff Lou Ford (Affleck) is a homicidal nutjob who thinks he's gotten away with murder. But he's got several people who are suspicious of his involvement with prostitute Joyce (Alba) and a very bloody crime scene. Adaptation of Jim Thompson's 1952 crime novel. **108m/C DVD.** *US* Casey Affleck, Kate Hudson, Jessica Alba, Simon Baker, Bill Pullman, Ned Beatty, Elias Koteas, Tom Bower, Jay R. Ferguson, Liam Aiken, Matthew Maher; ***D:*** Michael Winterbottom; ***W:*** John Curran; ***C:*** Marcel Zyskind; ***M:*** Mark Tildesley, Lynette Meyer, Melissa Parmenter, Joel Cadbury.

Killer Instinct **1992 (R)** Two brothers do bloody warfare with notorious mobster kingpins in prohibition-era New York City. **101m/C VHS.** Christopher Bradley, Bruce Nozick, Rachel York; ***D:*** Greydon Clark, Ken Stein.

Killer Instinct **2000 (R)** A bunch of teens attempt to spend the night in a creepy abandoned mental hospital, with predictably bloody results. Meanwhile, an outsider trying to broker the sale of a factory, the small town's main employer, finds out deadly secrets about the place. Somehow, the two stories are related and tied up nicely. **87m/C DVD.** Corbin Bernsen, Paige Moss, Jeannie Meyers, Brigitte Brooks, Dee Wallace; ***D:*** Ken Barbet; ***W:*** Christopher Stone, Bruce Cameron; ***C:*** Richard Ashbury; ***M:*** Timothy S. (Tim) Jones.

Killer Klowns from Outer Space 1/2 **1988 (PG-13)** Bozo-like aliens resembling demented clowns land on earth and set up circus tents to lure Earthlings in. Visually striking, campy but slick horror flick that'll make you think twice about your next visit to the big top. Mood is heightened by a cool title tune by the Dickies. Definitely has cult potential! **90m/C VHS, DVD.** Grant Cramer, Suzanne Snyder, John Allen Nelson, Royal Dano, John Vernon, Peter Licassi, Michael Siegel, Charles Chiodo; ***D:*** Stephen Chiodo; ***W:*** Stephen Chiodo, Charles Chiodo; ***C:*** Alfred Taylor; ***M:*** John Massari.

Killer Likes Candy **1978** An assassin stalks the King of Kafiristan, and a CIA operative tries to stop him. **86m/C VHS.** Kerwin Mathews, Marilu Tolo; ***D:*** Richard Owens.

Killer Looks 1/2 **1994 (R)** Phil likes to watch his wife Diane seduce strangers. Then they meet Mickey, a charmer with ideas of his own. Soon Diane and Phil find their kinky world threatened. Unrated version contains 13 minutes of additional footage. **87m/C VHS.** Michael Artura, Sara Suzanne Brown, Len Donato; ***D:*** Paul Thomas.

Killer McCoy **1947** Remake of 1938's "Crowded House" with Rooney in his first adult role. Hardworking Tommy McCoy does a boxing benefit with his drunken dad Brian (Dunn) and becomes intrigued by boxing champ Johnny Martin (Knox). Martin offers to mentor Tommy who turns out to be a natural. Eventually, Tommy must fight opposite Johnny and a horrible accident occurs, which earns Tommy his nickname. To makes matters worse, his dad is deeply in debt to gambler Jim Caighn (Donlevy) and has sold Tommy's contract to the ruthless man. Tommy's only bright spot is secretly dating Caighn's daughter Sheila (Blyth), who tries to keep Tommy honest. **104m/B DVD.** Mickey Rooney, Brian Donlevy, Ann Blyth, James Dunn, Mickey Knox, Samm Levine, Tom Tully; ***D:*** Roy Rowland; ***W:*** Frederick Hazlitt Brennan; ***C:*** Joseph Ruttenberg; ***M:*** David Snell.

Killer Me **2001** George (Foster) is a college student who takes criminology classes and works in the library—the kind of quiet kid nobody notices. Except for fellow loner Anna (Kew), who pratically stalks George in order to befriend him. Perhaps not the best of ideas since George had an abusive childhood and suffers from hallucinations in which he kills people with a straight-edged razor. Of course, they might not be just delusions at all. **80m/C VHS, DVD.** George Foster, Kirk B.R. Woller, Christina Kew; ***D:*** Zachary Hansen; ***W:*** Zachary Hansen; ***C:*** Neal Fredericks; ***M:*** Zachary Hansen.

Killer Movie **2008 (R)** Horror/showbiz comedy about the subjects and crew of a reality TV show who get stranded in a small North Dakota town. The town has an eerie history of deadly accidents and the outsiders soon become victims. Stereotypes deliberately abound, including the down-on-his-luck director, the diva, and the ruthless producer. **92m/C DVD.** Paul Wesley, Nestor Carbonell, Kaley Cuoco, Jason London, Cyia Batten, Leighton Meester, Robert Buckley, Andy Fischer-Price, J.C. Chasez; ***D:*** Jeff Fisher; ***W:*** Jeff Fisher; ***C:*** Dino Parks; ***M:*** Todd Haberman. **VIDEO**

The Killer Must Kill Again *Il Ragno; The Spider* **1975** After cheating hubby Giorgio Mainardi (Hilton) witnesses nameless killer (a very scary Antoine) dumping a body, he blackmails him into offing his rich wife while he sets up his alibi. The killer has the bad luck to have his car stolen—with the wife's body in the trunk. He goes after the joyriding teen thieves while Giorgio tries to convince the cops that his wife's been kidnapped. Italian with subtitles or dubbed. **90m/C DVD.** *IT FR* Teresa Velazquez, Eduardo Fajardo; ***D:*** Luigi Cozzi; ***W:*** Luigi Cozzi, Daniele Del Giudice; ***C:*** Riccardo (Pallton) Pallottini; ***M:*** Nand De Luca.

Killer of Sheep **1977** Age does nothing to date this seminal examination of urban poverty and race in 1970's Watts. Stan (Sanders) is a slaughterhouse worker plagued by insomnia who becomes increasingly disconnected from the rest of the world, including his wife (Moore). Nothing seems to help as a series of events just serves to compound Stan's sense of futility. Burnett wrote and directed as a student on a budget of $10,000. A popular part of the festival circuit that took 30 years to be released theatrically, in part because of the time and expense in licensing the music used in the soundtrack. **80m/B DVD.** *US* Henry Sanders, Kaycee Moore, Eugene Cherry, Charles Bracy; ***D:*** Charles Burnett; ***W:*** Charles Burnett; ***C:*** Charles Burnett. Natl. Film Reg. '90.

Killer on Board **1977** Folks spending their holiday on a cruise ship are afflicted by a fatal virus and subsequently quarantined. Typical made-for-TV disaster flick. **100m/C VHS.** Claude Akins, Beatrice Straight, George Hamilton, Patty Duke, Frank Converse, Jane Seymour, William Daniels; ***D:*** Philip Leacock.

Killer Pad 1/2 **2006 (R)** Silly horror comedy about three not-too-bright buddies who don't bother to question their luck when they get an exceptional deal on a Hollywood Hills mansion. But their dream pad is a nightmare since it's also a direct portal to Hell. **84m/C DVD.** Daniel Franzese, Eric Jungmann, Andy Milonakis, Hector Jimenez, Shane McRae, Joey Lawrence, Jennifer Lyons; ***D:*** Robert Englund; ***W:*** Dan Stoller; ***C:*** David G. Stump; ***M:*** Timothy Andrew Edwards. **VIDEO**

Killer Party **WOOF! 1986 (R)** Three coeds pledge a sorority and are subjected to a hazing that involves a haunted fraternity house. Standard horror plot; Paul Bartel ("Eating Raoul"; "Lust in the Dust") is the only significant element. **91m/C VHS.** Elaine Wilkes, Sherry Willis-Burch, Joanna Johnson, Paul Bartel, Martin Hewitt, Ralph Seymour, Woody Brown, Alicia Fleer; ***D:*** William Fruet; ***W:*** Barney Cohen; ***C:*** John Lindley; ***M:*** John Beal.

The Killer Shrews *Attack of the Killer Shrews* **1959** Lumet (Sidney's father) creates a serum that causes the humble shrew to take on killer proportions. The creatures are actually dogs in makeup. Goude was 1957's Miss Universe. **70m/B VHS, DVD.** James Best, Ingrid Goude, Baruch Lumet, Ken Curtis, Alfredo DeSoto, Gordon McLendon; ***D:*** Ray Kellogg; ***W:*** Jay Simms; ***C:*** Wilfrid M. Cline; ***M:*** Emil Cadkin, Harry Bluestone.

The Killer That Stalked New York 1/2 *Frightened City* **1947** Married couple Sheila (Keyes) and Matt (Korvin) arrive in New York City with $40,000 worth of smuggled diamonds. Sheila's not feeling so hot, and cheating Matt has his own plans for the diamonds, involving Sheila's sister. But Sheila's got bigger problems—she's brought home something far more sinister. Will the health department find the person who's spreading smallpox before the police catch the diamond thief? **79m/B DVD.** Evelyn Keyes, William Bishop, Charles Korvin, Dorothy Malone, Lola Albright, Carl Benton Reid, Barry Kelley, Ludwig Donath; ***D:*** Earl McEvoy; ***W:*** Milton Lehman, Harry Essex.

Killer Tomatoes Eat France 1/2 **1991** Professor Gangrene takes his tomato fetish to France, where the giant vegetables try to take over the streets. The fourth in the killer-vegetable series. **94m/C VHS, DVD.** John Astin, Marc Price, Steve Lundquist, John DeBello, Rick Rockwell, Angela Visser, Kevin West, Tom Ashworth, Suzanne Dean, Mary Egan, Debra Fares, Arnie Miller, J.R. Morley; ***D:*** John DeBello; ***W:*** John DeBello, Steve Peace, Constantine Dillon; ***C:*** Kevin Morrisey.

Killer Tomatoes Strike Back **1990** The third "Killer Tomatoes" movie isn't in the league of "The Naked Gun" satires, but it's still bright parody for the Mad Magazine crowd, as tomato-mad scientist Astin harnesses the powers of trash-TV in a planned vegetable invasion. Perhaps due to a 'Killer Tomatoes' cartoon series at the time, this isn't as saucy as its predecessors and is acceptable for family audiences. Followed by "Killer Tomatoes Eat France." **87m/C VHS, DVD.** John Astin, Rick Rockwell, Crystal Carson, Steve Lundquist, John Witherspoon, John DeBello, Tom Ashworth, Frank Davis, Debra Fares, Rock Peace, Constantine Dillon, Kevin West, Spike Sorrentino, D.J. Sullivan; ***D:*** John DeBello; ***W:*** Rick Rockwell, John DeBello, Constantine Dillon; ***C:*** Stephen F. Andrich; ***M:*** Neal Fox.

Killer Tongue *La Lengua Asesina* **1996 (R)** Okay, now here's a story (but not a good story, mind): Candy (Clarke) and Johnny (Durr) pull off a heist but Johnny winds up in jail while Candy hides out with the loot. She winds up in a desert hotel, near where a meteorite has landed. Somehow, Candy ingests a piece of the meteorite and an alien parasite (in the form of the titular killer tongue) takes over. The tongue is big on human sacrifices and Candy can't seem to do anything to stop it. Oh, and Candy's four poodles also get a meteorite taste and turn into drag queens. Just as gross as you may imagine it to be. **98m/C VHS, DVD.** *GB SP* Melinda (Mindy) Clarke, Jason Durr, Robert Englund, Mapi Golan, Doug Bradley, Jonathan Rhys Meyers; ***D:*** Alberto Sciamma; ***W:*** Alberto Sciamma; ***C:*** Denis Crossan.

Killer Wave 1/2 **2007** A series of tidal waves have left the major cities on the east coast of the U.S. in ruins. Maverick scientist John McAdams (Macfadyen) has his doubts that the waves are natural occurrences, believing that they are man-made disasters. The more McAdams investigates, the more dangerous his life becomes, especially when he learns who's behind all the destruction (it's not too hard to figure out). **175m/C DVD.**

Angus MacFadyen, Tom Skerritt, Stephen McHattie, John Robinson, Karine Vanesse, Louis-Philippe Dandenault; *D:* Bruce McDonald; *W:* William Gray; *C:* Pierre Jodoin; *M:* Normand Corbeil. **TV**

Killer with Two Faces ♂ **1974** A woman is terrorized by the evil twin of her boyfriend. **70m/C VHS.** Donna Mills, Ian Hendry, David Lodge, Roddy McMillan; *D:* John Scholz-Conway; *W:* Brian Clemens. **TV**

Killer Workout ♂ *Aerobicide* **1986 (R)** A murderer stalks the clients of a sweat/sex/muscle-filled gym. **89m/C VHS.** David James Campbell, Ted Prior; *D:* David A. Prior.

The Killers ♂♂♂♂ **1946** Classic film noir based on a Hemingway story. Lancaster's film debut comes as an ex-boxer, "The Swede," who's murdered in a contract hit. Insurance investigator Jim Reardon (O'Brien) reconstructs the young man's life, discovering his involvement with crime boss Big Jim Colfax (Dekker) and double-crossing femme fatale Kitty Collins (Gardner). So Reardon sets out to set up Colfax and Kitty. Rosza's musical score may sound familiar—it was later used on the TV series "Dragnet." **105m/B VHS, DVD.** Edmond O'Brien, Albert Dekker, Ava Gardner, Burt Lancaster, Sam Levene, William Conrad, Charles McGraw, Virginia Christine; *D:* Robert Siodmak; *W:* Anthony Veiller, John Huston; *C:* Elwood "Woody" Bredell; *M:* Miklos Rozsa. Natl. Film Reg. '08.

The Killers ♂♂ *Ernest Hemingway's the Killers* **1964** After two hired assassins kill a teacher, they look into his past and try to find leads to a $1,000,000 robbery. Reagan's last film. Remake of 1946 film of the same name, which was loosely based on a short story by Ernest Hemingway. Originally intended for TV, but released to theatres instead due to its violence. **95m/C VHS, DVD.** Lee Marvin, Angie Dickinson, John Cassavetes, Ronald Reagan, Clu Gulager, Claude Akins, Norman Fell, Don Haggerty, Seymour Cassel, Robert Phillips; *D:* Donald Siegel; *W:* Gene L. Coon; *C:* Richard L. Rawlings; *M:* John Williams.

Killers ♂ **1988** Remote jungles of southern Africa are the scene of a military coup. **83m/C VHS, DVD.** Cameron Mitchell, Alicia Hammond, Robert Dix; *D:* Ewing Miles Brown.

Killers 2010 After government-sanctioned hitman Spencer Aimes (Kutcher) falls in love with computer tech Jen (Heigl), he retires and they get married and move to the 'burbs. Three years into a happy life, Spencer learns there's a big money bounty placed on him. Who did it and why? Can Spencer and Jen survive long enough to figure it out? And how do you keep something like that from your nosy in-laws? **m/C DVD.** *US* Ashton Kutcher, Katherine Heigl, Katheryn Winnick, Rob Riggle, Kevin Sussman, Tom Selleck, Catherine O'Hara, Martin Mull, Alex Borstein; *D:* Robert Luketic; *W:* Ted Griffin, Bob DeRosa; *C:* Russell Carpenter.

The Killer's Edge ♂ ½ *Blood Money* **1990 (R)** Cop is caught between rock and hard place in L.A. when he's forced to confront criminal who once saved his life in 'Nam. Plenty of gut busting and soul wrenching. **90m/C VHS, DVD.** Wings Hauser, Robert Z'Dar, Karen Black.

Killers from Space WOOF! 1954 Cheap sci-fi flick in which big-eyed men from beyond Earth bring scientist Graves back to life to assist them with their evil plan for world domination. **80m/B VHS, DVD.** Peter Graves, Barbara Bestar, James Scay; *D:* W. Lee Wilder.

Killer's Kiss ♂♂ ½ **1955** A boxer and a dancer set out to start a new life together when he saves the woman from an attempted rape. Gritty, second feature from Kubrick was financed by friends and family and shows signs of his budding talent. **67m/C VHS, DVD.** Frank Silvera, Jamie Smith, Irene Kane, Jerry Jarrett; *D:* Stanley Kubrick; *W:* Stanley Kubrick; *C:* Stanley Kubrick; *M:* Gerald Fried.

The Killing ♂♂♂ **1956** The dirty, harsh, street-level big heist epic that established Kubrick and presented its genre with a new and vivid existentialist aura, as an ex-con engineers the rip-off of a racetrack with disastrous results. Displays characteristic nonsentimental sharp-edged Kubrick vision. Based on the novel "Clean Break" by Lionel White. **83m/B VHS, DVD.** Sterling Hayden, Marie Windsor, Elisha Cook Jr., Jay C. Flippen, Vince Edwards, Timothy Carey, Coleen Gray, Joseph (Joe) Sawyer, Ted de Corsia, James Edwards, Jay Adler, Kola Kwarian, Joe Turkel; *D:* Stanley Kubrick; *W:* Stanley Kubrick, Jim Thompson; *C:* Lucien Ballard; *M:* Gerald Fried.

A Killing Affair ♂ **1985 (R)** Set in West Virginia, 1943, this is the story of a widow who takes in a drifter who she believes is the man who killed her husband. She begins to fall for him, but cannot be sure if she should trust him. Vague and melodramatic. From the novel "Monday, Tuesday, Wednesday" by Robert Houston. Saperstein's directorial debut. **100m/C VHS, DVD.** Peter Weller, Kathy Baker, John Glover, Bill Smitrovich; *D:* David Saperstein; *M:* John Barry.

Killing at Hell's Gate ♂ ½ **1981** A group of white-water rafters are being picked off by snipers as they travel down river. **96m/C VHS.** Robert Urich, Deborah Raffin, Lee Purcell; *D:* Jerry Jameson; *M:* David Bell. **TV**

The Killing Beach ♂♂ *Turtle Beach* **1992 (R)** Australian photojournalist Judith Wilkes (Scacchi) travels to Malaysia in the late 1970s to report on the plight of the Vietnamese boat people seeking refuge there. She befriends the wife of the Australian ambassador, a former callgirl from Saigon, who hopes to find her own children among the refugees. But the native Malays resent the foreign intrusion and are determined to stop the boat people—no matter what the cost in blood. Based on the novel "Turtle Beach" by Blanche D'Alpuget. **105m/C VHS.** *AU* Greta Scacchi, Joan Chen, Jack Thompson, Art Malik, Norman Kaye; *D:* Stephen Wallace; *W:* Ann Turner; *C:* Russell Boyd.

The Killing Club ♂ ½ *You're Killing Me* **2001 (R)** When timid Jamie (Bowen) accidentally kills her controlling boyfriend, her tough best friend Laura (Lords) decides they should dispose of the body and give themselves an alibi. When this works, the ladies decide there's lots of losers who need disposing of—starting with the leering boss (McDonough) of another pal, Arlene (Maxey). There's neither enough black comedy nor suspense to make this anything but ordinary. **86m/C DVD.** Julie Bowen, Traci Lords, Dawn Maxey, Neal McDonough, David Packer; *D:* Antoni Stutz; *W:* Amy Kiehl; *C:* James Lawrence Spencer; *M:* Tom Hiel. **VIDEO**

The Killing Device ♂ ½ **1992** Two government scientists lose their funding on a covert political assassination project and decide to eliminate the government officials responsible. When two journalists attempt to solve the murders they become the next targets. **93m/C VHS, DVD.** Clu Gulager, Antony Alda, Gig Rauch; *D:* Paul MacFarlane; *W:* Kliff Keuhl; *C:* Paul MacFarlane.

The Killing Edge ♂ ½ **1986** In post-nuclear holocaust Earth, a lone warrior seeks justice, and his family, in a lawless land. **85m/C VHS.** Bill French, Marv Spencer; *D:* Lindsay Shonteff.

Killing 'Em Softly ♂ **1985** Segal portrays a down-on-his-luck musician who accidentally murders a music manager during an argument. Cara's boyfriend is accused and to clear his name, the singer moonlights as a detective. She and Segal end up falling in love. Disappointing. **90m/C VHS.** *CA* George Segal, Irene Cara; *D:* Max Fischer.

Killing Emmett Young ♂♂ *Emmett's Mark* **2002 (R)** Homicide detective Emmett Young (Wolf) has been told by his doctor that he has a terminal illness and only a short time to live. To avoid the disease's debilitating effects, Emmett takes up the offer of a mysterious stranger (Byrne) to arrange for a hit man (Roth) to do the job quickly. Of course, Emmett discovers he's not really dying (ALWAYS get a second opinion about a terminal disease) and tries to call the hit off. **104m/C VHS, DVD.** Scott Wolf, Tim Roth, Gabriel Byrne, Khandi Alexander, John Doman, Wayne Duvall; *D:* Keith Snyder; *W:* Keith Snyder; *C:* Lawrence Sher; *M:* Steve Porcaro.

The Killing Fields ♂♂♂ ½ **1984 (R)** Based on the New York Times' Sydney Schanberg's account of his friendship with Cambodian interpreter Dith Pran. They separated during the fall of Saigon, when Western journalists fled, leaving behind countless assistants who were later accused of collusion with the enemy by the Khmer Rouge and killed or sent to re-education camps during the bloodbath known as "Year Zero." Schanberg searched for Pran through the Red Cross and U.S. government, while Pran struggled to survive, finally escaping and walking miles to freedom. Ngor's own experiences echoed those of his character Pran. Malkovich's debut is intense. Joffe's directorial debut shows a generally sure hand, with only a bit of melodrama at the end. **142m/C VHS, DVD.** *GB* Sam Waterston, Haing S. Ngor, John Malkovich, Athol Fugard, Craig T. Nelson, Julian Sands, Spalding Gray, Bill Paterson; *D:* Roland Joffe; *W:* Bruce Robinson; *C:* Chris Menges. Oscars '84: Cinematog., Film Editing, Support. Actor (Ngor); British Acad. '84: Actor (Ngor), Adapt. Screenplay, Film; Golden Globes '85: Support. Actor (Ngor); L.A. Film Critics '84: Cinematog.; N.Y. Film Critics '84: Cinematog.; Natl. Soc. Film Critics '84: Cinematog.; Writers Guild '84: Adapt. Screenplay.

Killing Floor ♂♂ **1985 (PG)** During WWI, black sharecropper Frank Custer (Leake) travels to Chicago to get work in the stockyards and becomes a voice in the growing labor movement. The tensions in the factories lead to to bloody race riots of 1919. **118m/C VHS.** Damien Leake, Alfre Woodard, Moses Gunn, Clarence Felder, Mary Alice; *Cameos:* Peter J. D'Noto; *D:* Bill Duke; *W:* Leslie Lee; *M:* Elizabeth Swados. **TV**

The Killing Floor ♂ ½ **2006 (R)** David Lamont (Blucas), a literary agent who specializes in horror writers, has just moved into a lavish Manhattan penthouse, but weird things start happening. A young man turns up, claiming he inherited the place from his father. David is sent bloody crime scene photos that show his apartment, only the police have no record of any crimes, and he receives videotapes showing him sleeping. Obsessed, David will go to any length to find his stalker. **98m/C DVD.** Marc Blucas, Shiri Appleby, Reiko Aylesworth, John Bedford Lloyd, Joel Leffert, Andrew Weems, Jeff Carlson; *D:* Gideon Raff; *W:* Gideon Raff, Ryan Swanson; *C:* Martina Radwan; *M:* Michael Wandmacher. **VIDEO**

Killing for Love ♂ ½ **1995 (R)** Sleazy producer invites several couples for a weekend retreat at his mountain cabin. The unrated version is 90 minutes. **81m/C VHS.** Jay Richardson, Alex Demir, Lisa Haslehurst, Brandy (Jisel, Brandy Ledford) Sanders; *D:* Mike Kesey; *W:* H.M. Johnson.

The Killing Game ♂♂ ½ *All Weekend Lovers; Jeu de Massacre* **1967** A husband-wife cartoonist team link up with an unhinged playboy and act out a murder-mystery comic they produce together. In French with subtitles. **95m/C VHS.** *FR* Jean-Pierre Cassel, Claudine Auger, Michel Duchaussoy, Anna Gaylor; *D:* Alain Jessua.

The Killing Game ♂ **1987** A slew of Californians kill and betray each other for lustful reasons. **90m/C VHS.** Chard Hayward, Cynthia Killion, Geoffrey Sadwith; *D:* Joseph Merhi.

The Killing Gene ♂ ½ *WAZ* **2007 (R)** New York cop Eddie (Skarsgard) and his partner Helen (George) are called in for a couple of mutilated bodies that have the initials WAZ carved on them. Eddie thinks it's all gang-related (other pairs of victims with gang connections turn up) but the letters are actually W Delta Z, the beginning of something called the Price equation that's too convoluted to explain. Anyway, you find out the who and why about the killer early on so then you get to watch the cops play catch up. Lots of torture and gore but slightly more interesting than "Saw" and its spawn because it's got better actors. **104m/C DVD.** *GB* Stellan Skarsgard, Melissa George, Selma Blair, Ashley Walters, Thomas (Tom) Hardy, Paul Kaye; *D:* Tom Shankland; *W:* Clive Bradley; *C:* Morten Soborg; *M:* David Julyan.

Killing Grandpa ♂♂ *Matar al Abuelito* **1991** Wealthy family patriarch Don Mariano Aguero (Luppi) has lost the will to live and attempted suicide, which has left him comatose. His three greedy chldren are anxious for their inheritance but the Don's loyal handyman enlists the aid of his half-sister Rosita (Esteves), who possesses healing powers, to give his aged employer the strength to recover. Spanish with subtitles. **114m/C VHS.** *SP AR* Federico Luppi, Ines Estevez; *D:* Luis Cesar D'Angiolillo; *W:* Luis Cesar D'Angiolillo, Ariel Sienra; *C:* Miguel Abal.

The Killing Grounds ♂ ½ **1997 (R)** Killers Vince (Gains) and Art (Hall) are searching in the mountains for a missing plane that carried $3 million in gold. But it's already been found by a group of hikers, who think finders keepers. Boy, are they wrong. **93m/C VHS, DVD.** Anthony Michael Hall, Courtney Gains, Priscilla Barnes, Charles Rocket, Rodney A. Grant, Cynthia Geary; *D:* Kurt Anderson; *W:* Thomas Ritz. **VIDEO**

Killing Heat ♂ ½ *The Grass is Singing* **1984 (R)** An independent career woman living in South Africa decides to abandon her career to marry a struggling jungle farmer. Based on Doris Lessing's novel "The Grass is Singing." **104m/C VHS, DVD.** *GB SW* Karen Black, John Thaw, John Kani, John Moulder-Brown; *D:* Michael Raeburn.

Killing Hour ♂♂ *The Clairvoyant* **1984 (R)** A psychic painter finds that the visions she paints come true in a string of grisly murders. Her ability interests a TV reporter and a homicide detective. **97m/C VHS, DVD.** Elizabeth Kemp, Perry King, Norman Parker, Kenneth McMillan; *D:* Armand Mastroianni; *W:* Armand Mastroianni; *M:* Alexander Peskanov.

A Killing in a Small Town ♂♂♂ *Evidence of Love* **1990 (R)** Candy Morrison seems like the perfect member of her small Texas community—but appearances can be deceiving, particularly after she's charged with killing a fellow church-goer by striking her 41 times with an axe (shades of Lizzie Borden)! Dennehy is her skeptical lawyer who isn't sure if it was self-defense or a peculiar sort of revenge. Good performances by Hershey and Dennehy lift this above the usual tawdry made-for-TV level. Based on a true story. **95m/C VHS, DVD.** Barbara Hershey, Brian Dennehy, Hal Holbrook, Richard Gilliland, John Terry, Lee Garlington; *D:* Stephen Gyllenhaal; *C:* Robert Elswit; *M:* Richard Gibbs. **TV**

Killing in the Sun ♂ *The Men* **1973 (R)** Gripping struggle for prosperous smuggling in the Mediterranean consume mobsters from three countries. **90m/C VHS.** *FR IT* Henry Silva, Michael Constantine; *D:* Daniel Vigne; *W:* Leo Carrier; *C:* Jean Charvein; *M:* Francis Lai.

The Killing Jar ♂♂ ½ **1996 (R)** Michael Sanford (Cullen) has taken his pregnant wife Diane (Tomita) back to the California wine country to take over the failing family vineyard. A series of vicious murders occur in the area, one of which Michael may have witnessed. Hypnosis brings up a lot of Michael's repressed childhood memories, he begins to unravel, and becomes the prime suspect in the killings. **101m/C VHS, DVD.** Brett Cullen, Tamlyn Tomita, Wes Studi, Brion James, M. Emmet Walsh, Tom Bower, Xander Berkeley; *D:* Evan Crooke; *W:* Mark Mullin; *C:* Michael G. Wojciechowski; *M:* David Williams.

The Killing Kind ♂♂ ½ **1973** Man released from prison is obsessed with wreaking vengeance on his daft lawyer and his accuser. His vendetta eventually draws his mother into the fray as well. Fine performance by Savage. **95m/C VHS, DVD.** Ann Sothern, John Savage, Ruth Roman, Luana Anders, Cindy Williams; *D:* Curtis Harrington; *M:* Andrew Belling.

Killing Machine ♂ ½ *Daehakno-yeseo maechoon-hadaka tomaksalhae danghan yeogosang ajik Daehakno-ye Issda; Teenage Hooker Becomes a Killing Machine* **2002** A young girl who supports herself through school by prostitution tells one of the biology teachers she's pregnant with his child, and he gleefully hires three men to murder her and dispose of the body to protect his reputation. An anonymous voyeur then resurrects her as a cyborg killing machine, and she sets off for revenge. Part art film, part low budget exploitation, and part commentary on Korean society. **60m/C DVD.** *KN* So-yun Lee, Daetong Kim; *D:* Gee-Woong Nam, Ki-woong Nam;

W: Gee-Woong Nam, Ki-woong Nam; *C:* Ki-woong Nam.

The Killing Man 🦴🦴 **1994 (R)** Former mobster tries going legit by changing his identity and working for the government. **91m/C VHS, DVD.** Jeff Wincott, Terri Hawkes, Michael Ironside, David Bolt, Jeff Pustil; *D:* David Mitchell; *W:* David Mitchell, Damian Lee; *C:* David Pelletier.

Killing Me Softly 🦴 **2001 (R)** Chinese director Kaige's English-lanugage debut turned out to be an unfortunate choice—a turgid, sexual melodrama based on the novel by the pseudonymous Nicci French. American Alice (Graham) is living in London, seemingly content with boyfriend Jake (Hughes). Then she meets mysterious and intense mountaineer Adam (Fiennes) and she's soon agreeing to marry him despite evidence of his violent temper and how little she knows about him. Bouts of S&M sex follow but it's when Alice learns that her new hubby's previous lover disappeared that she decides maybe she's made a mistake. An unrated version is also available. **100m/C VHS, DVD.** Heather Graham, Joseph Fiennes, Jason Hughes, Natascha (Natasha) McElhone, Ulrich Thomsen, Ian Hart; *D:* Chen Kaige; *W:* Kara Lindstrom; *C:* Michael Coulter; *M:* Patrick Doyle.

The Killing Mind 1990 A young girl witnesses a grisly murder that is never solved. Twenty years later she (Zimbalist) becomes a cop who specializes in trapping psychos. Haunted by her memories, she and a reporter (Bill) team up to find the killer, never suspecting that she is his next victim. **96m/C VHS, DVD.** Stephanie Zimbalist, Tony Bill, Daniel Roebuck; *D:* Michael Rhodes. **CABLE**

Killing Mr. Griffin 🦴🦴 ½ **1997** If this sounds suspiciously akin to the plot for 1999's "Teaching Mrs. Tingle," it's not just your imagination. However, this TV movie is based on the novel by Lois Duncan. Evil high school teacher Mr. Griffin antagonizes all his students, who wind up kidnapping and humiliating him—leaving him tied up in the woods. But when Mr. G turns up dead, the students are all suspects unless they can point the cops in another direction. **108m/C VHS, DVD.** Scott Bairstow, Amy Jo Johnson, Mario Lopez, Chris Young, Michelle Williams, Jay Thomas, Scott Jaeck, Denise Dowse; *D:* Jack Bender; *W:* Michael Angeli, Kathleen Rowell; *C:* David Geddes; *M:* Christophe Beck. **TV**

Killing Moon WOOF! 2000 Abysmal air disaster flick features an airborne (on a plane!) virus that makes it's victims bleed from the eyes before dying and a mean G-man trying to weaponize the disease. On the ground, government doctor Miller is trying to stop the illness and get the passengers to stop oozing. Has all the elements of an "Airplane" spoof, but the comedy is purely unintentional. **95m/C DVD.** Penelope Ann Miller, Daniel Baldwin, Kim Coates, Daniel Kash, Denis Akayama, Tracy Cook, Christopher Bolton, Natalie Radford, Mark Camacho; *D:* John Bradshaw; *W:* Tony Johnston; *C:* Nicholas Josef von Sternberg. **TV**

Killing Obsession 🦴 ½ **1994** Albert (Savage) has been locked in the Parkview State Psychiatric Facility for 20 years, ever since he murdered 11-year-old Annie's mother. Annie is Albert's obsession and in his mind she's always remained a young girl. So when Albert is released, he goes looking for Annie—murdering along the way. Now that the real Annie is an adult will Albert finally accept the passage of time or will she be just another victim? **95m/C VHS, DVD.** Bobby DiCicco, John Savage, Kimberly Chase, John Saxon, Bernie (Bernard) White; *D:* Paul Leder; *W:* Paul Leder; *C:* Francis Grumman; *M:* Dana Walden.

The Killing of a Chinese Bookie 🦴🦴 **1976 (R)** Gazzara runs a Sunset Strip nightclub and is in hock to loan sharks. When he can't come up with the cash, he's offered a deal—get rid of a troublesome Chinese bookie and all debts will be forgiven. But it turns out the bookie is highly connected in the Asian mob and nothing goes as planned. Cassavette's improv technique makes for a self-indulgent and endless film. **109m/C VHS, DVD.** Ben Gazzara, Jean-Pierre Cassel, Zizi Johari, Soto Joe Hugh, Robert Phillips, Timothy Carey, Morgan Woodward; *D:* John Cassavetes; *W:* John Cassavetes; *C:* Frederick Elmes.

Killing of Angel Street 🦴🦴 **1981 (PG)** A courageous young woman unwittingly becomes the central character in an escalating nightmare about saving a community from corrupt politicians and organized crime. **101m/C VHS.** *AU* Elizabeth (Liz) Alexander, John Hargreaves; *D:* Donald Crombie; *W:* Evan Jones; *M:* Brian May.

The Killing of John Lennon 🦴🦴 **2007** Stylized pseudo-documentary examination of what led Mark David Chapman (Ball) to kill John Lennon. Using information from interviews and legal documents, movie charts Chapman's descent from married security guard in Hawaii to obsessed stalker who believed himself to be Holden Caulfield from "The Catcher in the Rye." Dark and disturbing, the movie never leaves Chapman's head as he loses touch with reality. Well made but too focused on Chapman's madness to give the viewer much perspective. **114m/C DVD.** *GB* Robert Kirk, Jonas Ball, Mie Omori, Krisha Fairchild; *D:* Andrew Piddington; *W:* Andrew Piddington; *C:* Roger Eaton; *M:* Makana.

Killing of Randy Webster 🦴 ½ **1981** A father attempts to prove that his son did not die as a criminal when Texas policemen shot him after transporting a stolen van across state lines. **90m/C VHS.** Hal Holbrook, Dixie Carter, Sean Penn, Jennifer Jason Leigh; *D:* Sam Wanamaker.

The Killing of Sister George 🦴🦴 **1969 (R)** Racy, sensationalized film based on the Frank Marcus black comedy/melodrama about a lesbian love triangle between a television executive, the soap opera star she's about to fire, and the soap star's girlfriend. **138m/C VHS, DVD.** Beryl Reid, Susannah York, Coral Browne, Ronald Fraser, Patricia Medina, Hugh Paddick, Cyril Delevanti, Brandan Dillon, Sivi Aberg, William Beckley, Elaine Church, Mike Freeman, Maggie Paige, Jack Raine, Dolly Taylor; *D:* Robert Aldrich; *W:* Lukas Heller, Frank Marcus; *C:* Joseph Biroc; *M:* Gerald Fried.

The Killing Room 🦴🦴 **2009 (R)** Four strangers sign up for a paid research study only to learn they've become part of a classified government program that's supposed to have been terminated. Confined to a white room, the quartet discover that the study is designed to find out what will break the human mind. The first step is a shocking violent act. **93m/C DVD.** Clea DuVall, Nick Cannon, Timothy Hutton, Peter Stormare, Chloe Sevigny, Shea Whigham; *D:* Jonathan Liebesman; *W:* Gus Krieger, Ann Peacock; *C:* Lukas Ettlin; *M:* Brian Tyler. **VIDEO**

A Killing Spring 🦴🦴 **2002 (R)** Former cop turned reporter, Joanne Kilbourn (Crewson), who once taught at Lanholme College, is pulled into the investigation of the suspicious death of the disliked dean of the School of Journalism. Ambition, jealousy, and corruption run rampant in academia. **85m/C VHS, DVD.** *CA* Wendy Crewson, Shawn Doyle, Michael Ontkean, Zachery Ty Bryan, Sherry Miller, John Furey, Bruce Gray; *D:* Stephen Williams; *W:* Joe Wiesenfeld, Jeremy Hole; *C:* David Herrington; *M:* Robert Carli. **TV**

Killing Stone 🦴🦴 **1978** A freelance writer uncovers a small town sheriff's plot to cover up a scandalous homicide. **120m/C VHS.** Gil Gerard, J.D. Cannon, Jim Davis, Nehemiah Persoff; *D:* Michael Landon; *W:* Michael Landon. **TV**

Killing Streets 🦴🦴 **1991** A commando learns that his twin brother is being held hostage in Lebanon and plans a rescue mission. A standard farfetched actioner; noteworthy for a real sense of despair over the endless carnage in the Mideast. Some dialogue in Arabic with subtitles. **109m/C VHS.** Michael Pare, Lorenzo Lamas; *D:* Stephen Cornwell; *W:* Stephen Cornwell.

The Killing Time 🦴🦴 **1987 (R)** A minor, effective murder thriller about a quiet small resort town suddenly beset by a web of murder, double-crossings, blackmail, and infidelity. They seem to coincide with the appearance of a mysterious stranger posing as the town's deputy sheriff just as the new sheriff is about to take up the badge. **94m/C VHS.** Kiefer Sutherland, Beau Bridges, Joe Don Baker, Wayne Rogers; *D:* Rick King; *W:* Don Bohlinger.

Killing Time 🦴🦴 **1997 (R)** Twisted little English thriller about a day in the life of Italian hitwoman Maria (Torgan), who's working in Northern England. Gangland boss Reilly (Leach) has killed a police officer and revenge is wanted by the cop's mate, fellow officer Bryant (Fairbass). Only Bryant can't really afford Maria so after she does the job, Bryant wants her killed by a cheaper hitman, Charlie (Thirkeld). But Reilly won't be back in town until the evening train—so Maria decides to take out a few of Reilly's henchmen to kill some time, leading to a police investigation (by Bryant), and leaving Charlie itching to carry out his part of the killing spree. **91m/C VHS.** *GB* Kendra Torgan, Craig Fairbrass, Nigel Leach, Stephen D. Thirkeld; *D:* Bharat Nalluri; *W:* Neil Marshall, Fleur Costello, Caspar Berry.

The Killing Yard 🦴🦴 **2001 (R)** Based on the true story of the 1971 Attica prison riots in New York State where nearly 50 people were killed and the state tried to avoid accountablility for its role in the massacre. Civil rights attorney Ernie Goodman (Alda) defends inmate Shango (Chestnut) who's been wrongly accused of a double homicide during the melee. **110m/C VHS.** Alan Alda, Morris Chestnut, Rose McGowan; *D:* Euzhan Palcy; *W:* Benita Garvin; *C:* Johnny (John W.) Simmons; *M:* Patrice Rushen. **CABLE**

Killing Zoe 🦴🦴 **1994 (R)** American safecracker travels to Paris for a little rest, recreation, and robbery. At the request of a childhood friend, he involves himself in an ill-conceived daytime bank heist, but not before enjoying a night with a local call girl and participating in some good ol' fashioned heroin-induced debauchery with the other bank robbers on the night before the job. Surprising no one (except maybe the still-stoned crooks), things don't go exactly as planned. Visually impressive debut for Tarantino collaborator Avary, who had his actors read "Beowulf" for its portrayal of Viking excess. **97m/C VHS, DVD.** Eric Stoltz, Julie Delpy, Jean-Hugues Anglade, Gary Kemp, Bruce Ramsay, Kario Salem, Carlo Scandiuzzi; *D:* Roger Avary; *W:* Roger Avary; *C:* Tom Richmond.

The Killing Zone 🦴 ½ **1990** Convict nephew of onetime Drug Enforcement agent rewrites zoning ordinances to hunt for Mexican drug lord south of the border. **90m/C VHS, DVD.** Daron McBee, James Dalesandro, Melissa Moore, Armando Silvestre, Augustine Beral, Sydne Squire, Debra (Deborah Dutch) Dare; *D:* Addison Randall.

Killings at Outpost Zeta 🦴 **1980** Earthmen investigate a barren planet where previous expeditions have disappeared, and find hordes of aliens. **92m/C VHS.** Gordon Devol, Jackie Ray, James A. Watson Jr.; *D:* Bob Emenegger, Allan Sandler; *W:* Peter Dawson; *M:* Bob Emenegger.

Killjoy 🦴🦴 ½ *Who Murdered Joy Morgan?* **1981** A sleazy surgeon's daughter is the prey in this TV thriller. The plot twists are led by the array of people who become involved. A clever suspense mystery. **100m/C VHS, DVD.** Kim Basinger, Robert Culp, Stephen Macht, Nancy Marchand, John Rubinstein, Ann Dusenberry, Ann Wedgeworth, Helene Winston; *D:* John Llewellyn Moxey; *M:* Bruce Broughton. **TV**

Killpoint 🦴 ½ **1984 (R)** Special task force is assembled to catch the criminals who robbed a National Guard armory for its weapons. **89m/C VHS.** Leo Fong, Richard Roundtree, Cameron Mitchell; *D:* Frank Harris.

Killshot 🦴 ½ **2009 (R)** Another unsuccessful adaptation of an Elmore Leonard novel that's primarily a routine crime thriller. Troubled contract killer Degas (Rourke) makes the mistake of hooking up with trigger-happy Richie Nix (Gordon-Levitt) and a botched job is witnessed by Carmen (Lane) and her estranged husband Wayne Colson (Jane). Degas is known for never leaving witnesses alive and the Colsons aren't going to be the exception. The film underwent numerous re-shoots and re-edits, which show in the uneven pacing and now-you-see-them, now-you-don't characters. **95m/C DVD.** Diane Lane, Mickey Rourke, Thomas Jane, Joseph Gordon-Levitt, Rosario Dawson, Hal Holbrook; *D:* John Madden; *W:* Hossein Amini; *C:* Caleb Deschanel; *M:* Klaus Badelt.

Killzone 🦴 **1985** A brainwashed Vietnam vet breaks down during a training exercise and embarks on a psychotic killing spree. **86m/C VHS.** Ted Prior, David James Campbell, Richard Massery; *D:* David A. Prior.

Kilma, Queen of the Amazons WOOF! 1975 A shipwrecked sailor finds himself on an island populated by man-hating Amazons. When a shipload of lusty sailors arrive to rescue him, carnage ensues. **90m/C VHS, DVD.** *SP* Francisco (Frank) Brana, Eva Miller, Claudia Gravy; *D:* Miguel Iglesias; *W:* Miguel Iglesias; *C:* Francisco Sanchez.

Kim 🦴🦴🦴 **1950** A colorful Hollywood adaptation of the Rudyard Kipling classic about an English boy disguised as a native in 19th Century India, and his various adventures. **113m/C VHS, DVD.** Errol Flynn, Dean Stockwell, Paul Lukas, Cecil Kellaway; *D:* Victor Saville; *M:* Andre Previn.

Kim 🦴🦴 ½ **1984** Kim (Sheth) is a 15-year-old boy living by his wits on the streets of 1890s India. Trying to discover his true identity, Kim's befriended by a Buddhist monk who wishes the boy to be his disciple and a British spy, who trains him for a daring mission against the Russians. Rousing TV adaptation of the Rudyard Kipling novel. **135m/C VHS, DVD.** Ravi Sheth, Peter O'Toole, Bryan Brown, John Rhys-Davies, Julian Glover; *D:* John Davies.

Kinatay *Slaughter* **2009** In the slums of Manila, police cadet Pepoy accepts a shady job offer to get some extra cash and it leads to the dismemberment death of a prostitute. Tagalog with subtitles. **109m/C DVD.** *PH FR* Rodel Nacianceno, Jhong Hilario, Mercedes Cabral, John Regala, Maria Isabel Lopez, Julio Diaz; *D:* Brillante Mendoza; *W:* Armando Lao; *C:* Odyssey Flores; *M:* Teresa Barrozo.

Kind Hearts and Coronets 🦴🦴🦴 ½ **1949** Black comedy, set in 1900, in which ambitious young Louis (Price) sets out to bump off eight relatives in an effort to claim a family title. Guinness is wonderful in his role as all eight (male and female) of the fated relations. There are a number of clever twists and turns and it proves that writing one's memoirs can be fatal. Very loosely based on Roy Horiman's novel "Israel Rank." **104m/B VHS, DVD.** *GB* Alec Guinness, Dennis Price, Valerie Hobson, Joan Greenwood, Audrey Fildes, Miles Malleson, Clive Morton, Cecil Ramage, John Penrose, Hugh Griffith, John Salew, Eric Messiter, Anne Valery, Arthur Lowe, Jeremy Spenser; *D:* Robert Hamer; *W:* Robert Hamer, John Dighton; *C:* Douglas Slocombe; *M:* Ernest Irving.

A Kind of Loving 🦴🦴🦴 **1962** Two North English young people marry rashly as a result of pregnancy, find they really didn't like each other all that much, but manage to adjust. **107m/B VHS.** *GB* Alan Bates, Thora Hird, June Ritchie, Pat Keen, James Bolam; *D:* John Schlesinger; *W:* Willis Hall, Keith Waterhouse; *C:* Denys Coop; *M:* Ron Grainer.

Kindergarten 🦴🦴🦴 **1984** Endearing tale based on a true story of a young Russian street violinist. During WWII, the boy meets a variety of interesting people as he travels throughout the Soviet Union. In Russian with English subtitles. **143m/C VHS.** *RU* Sergei Gusak, Sergei Bobrovsky, Galina Stakhanova, Klaus Maria Brandauer; *D:* Yevgeny Yevtushenko; *W:* Yevgeny Yevtushenko; *C:* Vladimir Papyan; *M:* Gleb Mai.

Kindergarten Cop 🦴🦴 ½ **1990 (PG-13)** Pectoral perfect cop Kimble (Schwarzenegger) stalks mama's boy/criminal Crisp (Tyson) by locating the drug lord's ex and his six-year-old son. When the pec man's female partner succumbs to a nasty bout of food poisoning, he's forced to take her place as an undercover kindergarten teacher in the drowsy Pacific northwest community where mother and son reside incognito. A cover all the bases Christmas release, it's got romance, action, comedy and cute. And boxoffice earnings to match

Arnie's chest measurements. A bit violent for the milk and cookie set. **111m/C VHS, DVD.** Arnold Schwarzenegger, Penelope Ann Miller, Pamela Reed, Linda Hunt, Richard Tyson, Carroll Baker, Cathy Moriarty, Park Overall, Richard Portnow, Jayne Brook; ***D:*** Ivan Reitman; ***W:*** Murray Salem, Herschel Weingrod, Timothy Harris; ***C:*** Michael Chapman; ***M:*** Randy Edelman.

Kindergarten Ninja 1/2 **1994** Football star is sentenced to community service after a drunk-driving arrest and is guided by a kung fu angel into helping a group of children. **80m/C VHS, DVD.** Dwight Clark; ***D:*** Anthony Chan.

The Kindred 1/2 **1987 (R)** A young student discovers that his mother the biologist has created a hybrid creature using his body tissue. Naturally, he is horrified and begins to search for his test-tube brother; the problem is, this brother likes eating people. Not too bad; boasts some good acting. **92m/C VHS.** Rod Steiger, Kim Hunter, David Allan Brooks, Timothy Gibbs, Amanda Pays, Talia Balsam, Jeffrey Obrow, Peter Frechette, Julia Montgomery; ***D:*** Stephen Carpenter, Jeffrey Obrow; ***W:*** Stephen Carpenter, Joseph Stefano, John Penney, Earl Ghaffari, Jeffrey Obrow; ***M:*** David Newman.

King **1978** Docudrama with terrific cast follows the life and career of one of the greatest non-violent civil rights leaders of all time, Martin Luther King. **272m/C VHS, DVD.** Paul Winfield, Cicely Tyson, Roscoe Lee Browne, Ossie Davis, Art Evans, Ernie Banks, Howard E. Rollins Jr., William Jordan, Cliff DeYoung; ***D:*** Abby Mann; ***W:*** Abby Mann; ***M:*** Billy Goldenberg. **TV**

The King 1/2 **2005 (R)** Illegitimate Elvis Valderez (Garcia Bernal) heads to Corpus Christi to meet his dad, David Sandow (Hurt), who's now a Baptist preacher. Elvis insinuates himself into the family (with no one else knowing who he really is) and seduces his sheltered 16-year-old half-sister, Malerie (James). When Sandow's son Paul (Dano) disappears, the preacher reaches out to Elvis. Only his wife, Twyla (Harring), suspects that the pleasant young man isn't what he seems at all. The sins of the father come back in a big way. **105m/C DVD.** *US* Gael Garcia Bernal, Pell James, Paul Franklin Dano, William Hurt, Laura Elena Harring, Milo Addica; ***D:*** James Marsh; ***W:*** Milo Addica, James Marsh; ***C:*** Eigil Bryld; ***M:*** Max Lichtenstein.

King and Country **1964** Aristocratic army officer, Capt. Hargreaves (Bogarde), serves as the defense lawyer for troubled Private Arthur Hamp (Courtenay), whose wartime experiences have caused him to desert. Hargreaves at first ignores the uneducated Hamp's obvious shell-shock but soon begins to feel sympathy for his confused client. Director Losey shows the effects of war rather than the war itself and provides a sincere and bitter condemnation of military mentality. Based on the play "Hamp" by John Wilson. **86m/B VHS, DVD.** *GB* Dirk Bogarde, Tom Courtenay, Leo McKern, Barry Foster, James Villiers, Peter Copley; ***D:*** Joseph Losey; ***W:*** Evan Jones; ***C:*** Denys Coop; ***M:*** Larry Adler. British Acad. '64: Film.

The King and Four Queens 1/2 **1956** Gable, on the run from the law, happens upon a deserted town, deserted, that is, except for a woman and her three daughters. Clark soon discovers that the women are looking for $100,000 in gold that one of their missing husbands had stolen. True to form, conniving Clark wastes no time putting the moves on each of them to find the whereabouts of the loot. **86m/C VHS.** Clark Gable, Eleanor Parker, Jo Van Fleet, Jean Wiles, Barbara Nichols, Sara Shane, Roy Roberts, Arthur Shields, Jay C. Flippen; ***D:*** Raoul Walsh; ***M:*** Alex North.

The King and I **1956** Wonderful adaptation of Rodgers and Hammerstein's Broadway play based on the novel "Anna and the King of Siam" by Margaret Landon. English governess Kerr is hired to teach the King of Siam's many children and bring them into the 20th century. She has more of a job than she realizes, for this is a king, a country, and a people who value tradition above all else. Features one of Rodgers and Hammerstein's best-loved scores. Brynner made this role his, playing it over 4,000 times on stage and screen before his death. Kerr's voice was dubbed when she sang; the voice you hear is Marni Nixon, who also dubbed the star's singing voices in "West Side Story" and "My Fair Lady." ♫ Shall We Dance?; Getting To Know You; Hello, Young Lovers; We Kiss in a Shadow; I Whistle a Happy Tune; March of the Siamese Children; I Have Dreamed; A Puzzlement; Something Wonderful. **133m/C VHS, DVD.** Deborah Kerr, Yul Brynner, Rita Moreno, Martin Benson, Terry Saunders, Rex Thompson, Alan Mowbray, Carlos Rivas, Patrick Adiate; ***D:*** Walter Lang; ***W:*** Ernest Lehman; ***C:*** Leon Shamroy; ***M:*** Richard Rodgers, Oscar Hammerstein. Oscars '56: Actor (Brynner), Art Dir./Set Dec., Color, Costume Des. (C), Sound, Scoring/Musical; Golden Globes '57: Actress—Mus./Comedy (Kerr), Film—Mus./Comedy.

The King and I **1999 (G)** Animated musical tries, but fails, to split the difference between faithfulness to the Broadway version and the action needed to entertain kids. Tells the story of Anna (Richardson), an English woman who travels to Siam in order to tutor the children of the King (Vidnovic). The evil Kralahome and stereotypical comic relief sidekick Master Little (Hammond) plan to use Anna to capture the throne. The ending is given a kid-friendly twist, but eight of the original 20 Broadway songs were slashed to keep it brief for the short attention span set. **87m/C VHS, DVD.** ***D:*** Richard Rich; ***W:*** Jacqueline Feather, David Seidler, Peter Bakalian; ***V:*** Miranda Richardson, Martin Vidnovic, Ian Richardson, Darrell Hammond, Allen D. Hong, Armi Arabe, Adam Wylie, Sean Smith.

King Arthur 1/2 **2004 (PG-13)** The noble knights are recast as centurions fighting for Rome in Britain circa 500 A.D. Arthur is Artorius, a mercenary from a backwater colony fighting to earn back his freedom by pacifying Celts. He and his men don't like this one bit, especially when sent to rescue a rich brat favored by the Pope from encroaching Saxon invaders. The filmmakers claim historical accuracy. Well...maybe, but it's still just an excuse to recycle a classic western/war story: corrupt command sends band of hardened roughnecks on suicide mission. Nothing feels very novel about this novel idea, but it is a fun ride. Owen is a terrific Arthur, all brooding and steely. Knightley is perhaps the sexiest (and most proactive) Guinevere ever. Skaargard hams it up as a nasty proto-fascist villain. **130m/C DVD, Blu-ray Disc, UMD.** *GB IR* Clive Owen, Stephen (Dillon) Dillane, Keira Knightley, Ioan Gruffudd, Stellan Skarsgard, Ray Winstone, Hugh Dancy, Ray Stevenson, Charlie Creed-Miles, Joel Edgerton, Ken Stott, Til Schweiger, Mads Mikkelsen, Sean Gilder, Ivano Marescotti, Lorenzo De Angelis; ***D:*** Antoine Fuqua; ***W:*** David Franzoni; ***C:*** Slawomir Idziak; ***M:*** Hans Zimmer.

King Arthur, the Young Warlord **1975 (PG)** The struggle that was the other side of Camelot—the campaign against the Saxon hordes. The early, somewhat violent years of King Art. **90m/C VHS, DVD.** Oliver Tobias, Michael Gothard, Jack Watson, Brian Blessed, Peter Firth; ***D:*** Sidney Hayers, Pat Jackson, Peter Sasdy.

King Boxer 1/2 *5 Fingers of Death; Tian xia di yi quan; Hand of Death; Shaolin Avenger* **1972 (R)** More commonly known in the U.S. as "Five Fingers of Death", this Shaw Brothers film's international success is said to be responsible for introducing kung fu films to the world at large and creating the martial arts craze of the 1970s. An old master sends his pupil Chao (Lo Lieh) to a martial arts school to learn the Iron Palm technique. Unfortunately a rival school has hired Japanese mercenaries to cripple Chao's teachers and has killed his master. He enters the All China Tournament in order to compete against them and get revenge with his new techniques. **98m/C DVD.** *HK* Lieh Lo, Feng Tien, James Nam, Bolo Yeung, Ping Wang, Hsiung Chiao, Chin-Feng Wang, Mien Fang, Shen Chan, Wen Chung Ku, Lung Yu, Yukio Sumeno, Chi Chu Chin, Bong-jin Jin; ***D:*** Chang-hwa Jeong; ***W:*** Yeung Kong; ***C:*** Yung-lung Wang; ***M:*** Yung-Yu Chen.

King Cobra 1/2 **1998 (PG-13)** If you like big snakes, this low-budgeter is for you! A mutant cobra/rattlesnake hybrid, having escaped its lab environment, threatens the populace of a small California town. **93m/C VHS, DVD.** Noriyuki "Pat" Morita, Hoyt Axton, Kasey Fallo, Scott Brandon, Joseph Ruskin, Courtney Gains; ***D:*** David Hillenbrand, Scott Hillenbrand; ***W:*** David Hillenbrand, Scott Hillenbrand; ***C:*** Philip D. Schwartz. **VIDEO**

King Creole 1/2 **1958 (PG)** The King goes film noir as a teenager with a criminal record who becomes a successful pop singer in New Orleans but is threatened by his ties to crime, represented by Walter Matthau. One of the better Elvis films, based on Harold Robbins' "A Stone for Danny Fisher." Features Elvis's last film appearance before his service in the Army. ♫ King Creole; Banana; New Orleans; Turtles, Berries and Gumbo; Crawfish; Don't Ask Me Why; As Long As I Have You; Trouble; Hard-Headed Woman. **115m/B VHS, DVD.** Elvis Presley, Carolyn Jones, Walter Matthau, Dean Jagger, Dolores Hart, Vic Morrow, Paul Stewart, Brian G. Hutton, Liliane Montevecchi, Jan Shepard, Jack Grinnage; ***D:*** Michael Curtiz; ***W:*** Herbert Baker, Michael V. Gazzo; ***C:*** Russell Harlan; ***M:*** Walter Scharf.

King David 1/2 **1985 (PG-13)** The story of David, the legendary Biblical hero whose acts of bravery paved the way for him to become king of Israel. **114m/C VHS, DVD.** Richard Gere, Alice Krige, Cherie Lunghi, Hurd Hatfield, Edward Woodward; ***D:*** Bruce Beresford; ***W:*** Andrew Birkin, James Costigan; ***M:*** Carl Davis.

King Dinosaur 1/2 **1955** A new planet arrives in the solar system, and a scientific team checks out its giant iguana-ridden terrain. **63m/B VHS, DVD.** Bill Bryant, Wanda Curtis, Patti Gallagher, Doug(las) Henderson; ***D:*** Bert I. Gordon; ***W:*** Bert I. Gordon, Tom Gries; ***C:*** Gordon Avil; ***M:*** Micha(el) Terr.

A King in New York **1957** Chaplin plays the deposed king of a European minimonarchy who comes to the United States in hope of making a new life. Looks critically at 1950s-era America, including Cold War paranoia and over reliance on technology. Containing Chaplin's last starring performance, this film wasn't released in the U.S. until 1973. Uneven but interesting. **105m/B VHS, DVD.** *GB* Charlie Chaplin, Dawn Addams, Michael Chaplin, Oliver Johnston, Maxine Audley, Harry Green; ***D:*** Charlie Chaplin; ***W:*** Charlie Chaplin; ***C:*** Georges Perinal; ***M:*** Charlie Chaplin.

The King Is Alive 1/2 **2000 (R)** A tourist bus traveling in Namibia strays off-course and runs out of gas. The passengers stumble into a deserted mining town with little food or water and only a small chance at survival. Retired actor Henry (Bradley) begins to think their situation resembles that of "King Lear" and he gradually begins to convince the others to rehearse the play as a way to pass the time. Much lunacy ensues. **118m/C VHS, DVD.** *DK* Miles Anderson, Romane Bohringer, David Bradley, David Calder, Bruce Davison, Brion James, Vusi Kunene, Peter Kubheka, Jennifer Jason Leigh, Janet McTeer, Lia Williams, Chris Walker; ***D:*** Kristian Levring; ***W:*** Anders Thomas Jensen, Kristian Levring; ***C:*** Jens Schlosser.

King Kelly of the U.S.A. **1934** Robertson carries on a forgettable romance with a princess aboard a trans-Atlantic line. **64m/B VHS, DVD.** Guy Robertson, Irene Ware, Edgar Kennedy, Franklin Pangborn, Joyce Compton, Ferdinand Gottschalk, Wilhelm von Brinken, Otis Harlan; ***D:*** Leonard Fields.

King Kong **1933** The original beauty and the beast film classic tells the story of Kong, a giant ape captured in Africa by filmmaker Carl Denham (Armstrong) and brought to New York as a sideshow attraction. Kong falls for starlet Ann (Wray), escapes from his captors, and rampages through the city, ending up on top of the newly built Empire State Building. Moody Steiner score adds color, and Willis O'Brien's stop-motion animation still holds up well. Scenes were cut during the 1938 re-release because of the Hays production code, including one where a curious Kong strips Wray of her clothes. Remade numerous times with various theme derivations. **105m/B VHS, DVD.** Fay Wray, Bruce Cabot, Robert Armstrong, Frank Reicher, Noble Johnson, Sam Hardy, James Flavin, Ernest B. Schoedsack, Merian C. Cooper; ***D:*** Ernest B. Schoedsack, Merian C. Cooper; ***W:*** James A. Creelman, Ruth Rose, Edgar Wallace; ***C:*** Edward Linden, J.O. Taylor, Vernon Walker; ***M:*** Max Steiner. AFI '98: Top 100, Natl. Film Reg. '91.

King Kong **1976 (PG)** Oil company official travels to a remote island to discover it inhabited by a huge gorilla. The transplanted beast suffers unrequited love in classic fashion: monkey meets girl, monkey gets girl and brandishes her while atop the World Trade Center. An updated remake of the 1933 movie classic that also marks the screen debut of Lange. Impressive sets and a believable King Kong romp around New York City in this film. Watch for Joe Piscopo, and quickly for Corbin Bernsen as a reporter. **135m/C VHS, DVD.** Jeff Bridges, Charles Grodin, Jessica Lange, Rene Auberjonois, John Randolph, Ed Lauter, Jack O'Halloran, Dennis Fimple, John Agar, Rick Baker, Joe Piscopo, Corbin Bernsen; ***D:*** John Guillermin; ***W:*** Lorenzo Semple Jr.; ***C:*** Richard H. Kline; ***M:*** John Barry. Oscars '76: Visual FX.

King Kong 1/2 **2005 (PG-13)** In this remake of the 1933 classic, Depression-era filmmaker Carl Denham (Black) lures starving ingenue Ann Darrow (Watts) and screenwriter Jack Driscoll (Brody) to the uncharted Skull Island to shoot his masterpiece. However, once they arrive, the crew meets angry natives, rampaging dinosaurs, and a massive, menacing monkey named Kong. We all know where the story goes from there, but Jackson enlivens the familiar with thrilling action sequences (Kong vs. T. Rexes equals awesome) and the most expressive simian ever put to film (WETA deserves an acting Oscar for Kong's face alone). Regrettably, the three-hour flick drags whenever Kong isn't on-screen, and Jackson spends way too much time with his so-so supporting cast. But, as always, Kong remains king. **187m/C DVD, Blu-ray Disc, HD DVD.** Naomi Watts, Jack Black, Adrien Brody, Thomas Kretschmann, Colin Hanks, Jamie Bell, Evan Dexter Parke, Kyle Chandler, Andy Serkis, Lobo Chan; ***D:*** Peter Jackson; ***W:*** Peter Jackson, Fran Walsh, Philippa Boyens; ***C:*** Andrew Lesnie; ***M:*** James Newton Howard. Oscars '05: Sound, Visual FX; British Acad. '05: Visual FX.

King Kong Escapes **WOOF!** *Kingu Kongu no gyakushu* **1967** After the success of "King Kong vs Godzilla" Rankin-Bass decided to have a cartoon series on Kong produced in Japan (for which this film was the lead-in). They got Toho to do a kid-friendly Kong film about a mad scientist who plans to kidnap the giant ape in order to mine a radioactive element in a plot to take over the world, because apparently radiation made his own giant robot ape shut off. So the robot ape is repaired and sent to hypnotize Kong as a replacement. How many films feature a giant robot gorilla hypnotist? At least it's unique. **96m/C DVD.** *JP* Rhodes Reason, Mie Hama, Linda Miller, Akira Takarada, Eisei Amamoto; ***D:*** Ishio Honda; ***W:*** Takeshi Kimura; ***C:*** Hajime Koizumi; ***M:*** Akira Ifukube.

King Kong Lives **1986 (PG-13)** Unnecessary sequel to the 1976 remake of "King Kong," in which two scientists get the big ape, now restored after his asphalt-upsetting fall, together with a lady ape his size and type. **105m/C VHS, DVD.** Brian Kerwin, Linda Hamilton, John Ashton, Peter Michael Goetz; ***D:*** John Guillermin; ***W:*** Steven Pressfield, Ronald Shusett.

King Kong vs. Godzilla 1/2 *King Kong tai Godzilla; KinguKongu tai Gojira* **1963** The planet issues a collective shudder as the two mightiest monsters slug it out for reasons known only to themselves. Humankind can only stand by and watch in impotent horror as the tide of the battle sways to and fro, until one monster stands alone and victorious. **105m/C VHS, DVD.** *JP* Michael Keith, Tadao Takashima, Mie Hama, Kenji Sahara, Yu Fujiki, Akihiko Hirata, Jun Tazaki, Akiko Wakabayashi, Ichiro Arishima, Haruo Nakajima, Katsumi Tezuka; ***D:*** Inoshiro Honda; ***W:*** Shinichi Sekizawa; ***C:*** Hajime Koizumi; ***M:*** Akira Ifukube, Robert Emmett Dolan, Henry Mancini, Herman Stein, Milton Rosen; ***Nar:*** Les Tremayne.

King Kung Fu **1987 (G)** A karate master raises a gorilla, and sends it from Asia to the U.S. There, two out-of-work reporters decide to release it from captivity and then recapture it so they can get the story and some needed recognition. The background they don't have on the gorilla is that its master taught it kung fu. **90m/C VHS, DVD.** John Balee, Tom Leahy, Maxine Gray, Bill Schwartz; ***D:*** Bill Hayes.

King Lear 🦴🦴🦴 1/2 **1971** Brook's version of Shakespeare tragedy. The king drives away the only decent daughter he has, and when he realizes this, it is too late. Powerful performances and interesting effort at updating the bard. **137m/B VHS.** *GB* Paul Scofield, Irene Worth, Jack MacGowran, Alan Webb, Cyril Cusack, Patrick Magee; ***D:*** Peter Brook.

King Lear 🦴 1/2 **1987** Loosely adapted from Shakespeare's tragedy of a king who loses everything. A fragmented French existential reading with gangster undercurrent. This updated version is dark, ominous, wandering, strange, and quite unlike the other 1984 remake. Or any other remake, for that matter. **91m/C VHS.** *SI* Peter Sellars, Burgess Meredith, Molly Ringwald, Jean-Luc Godard, Woody Allen; ***D:*** Jean-Luc Godard; ***W:*** Norman Mailer.

King Lear 🦴🦴🦴 **1998** Holm gives a powerful performance as the deluded monarch. The King comes to rue the day he banished faithful daughter Cordelia (Hamilton) in favor of dividing his kingdom between her manipulative siblings Goneril (Flynn) and Regan (Redman). As war engulfs his country, Lear descends into despair and madness. **150m/C VHS.** Ian Holm, Victoria Hamilton, Barbara Flynn, Amanda Redman, Michael Bryant, Paul Rhys, Timothy West, Finbar Lynch, David Burke; ***D:*** Richard Eyre; ***W:*** Richard Eyre; ***C:*** Roger Pratt; ***M:*** Dominic Muldowney. **TV**

The King Murder 🦴🦴 **1932** High-society sleuth Tearle tries to solve the mysterious death of a beautiful, yet dangerous extortionist. Looks a lot like murder, although no weapon can be found. **67m/B VHS, DVD.** Conway Tearle, Natalie Moorhead, Marceline Day, Dorothy Revier; ***D:*** Richard Thorpe; ***W:*** Charles Reed Jones.

King of Alcatraz 🦴 1/2 **1938** Alcatraz escapee takes over a passenger ship, but the ship's crew won't be going down without a fight. Two brave crewmates create a plan to overtake the convict and rescue the passengers. **68m/B VHS.** Gail Patrick, Lloyd Nolan, Harry Carey Jr., J. Carrol Naish, Robert Preston; ***D:*** Robert Florey; ***W:*** Irving Reis.

King of America 🦴 **1980** A Greek sailor and a local labor agent battle over who will become King of America. **90m/C VHS.** Larry Atlas, David Canary, Philip Casnoff, Michael Welden, Olympia Dukakis, Stephen Lang; ***D:*** Dezso Magyar; ***W:*** B.J. Merholz; ***C:*** Mike Fash; ***M:*** Elizabeth Swados.

King of California 🦴🦴 1/2 **2007 (PG-13)** Charlie (Douglas), a bipolar jazz musician, leaves his hospital in order to find the horde of Spanish treasure he's convinced is buried in his old neighborhood. His teenage daughter Miranda (Wood), abandoned by her mother, reluctantly joins him on his quest, and the two must seek clues as to the treasure's location amongst a sea of box stores and chain restaurants. Douglas is excellent as the erratic, Quixote-like Charlie in search of meaning in an alienated world, but the movie fails to dig much deeper than the superficial world it satirizes. **93m/C DVD, Blu-ray Disc, HD DVD.** *US* Michael Douglas, Evan Rachel Wood, Willis Burks II; ***D:*** Mike Cahill; ***W:*** Mike Cahill; ***C:*** James Whitaker; ***M:*** David Robbins.

King of Comedy 🦴🦴🦴 **1982 (PG)** An unhinged would-be comedian haunts and eventually kidnaps a massively popular Johnny Carson-type TV personality. A cold, cynical farce devised by Scorsese seemingly in reaction to John Hinckley's obsession with his film "Taxi Driver." Controlled, hard-hitting performances, especially by De Niro and Lewis. **101m/C VHS, DVD.** Robert De Niro, Jerry Lewis, Sandra Bernhard, Tony Randall, Diahnne Abbott, Shelley Hack, Liza Minnelli; ***D:*** Martin Scorsese; ***W:*** Paul Zimmerman; ***C:*** Fred Schuler; ***M:*** Robbie Robertson. British Acad. '83: Orig. Screenplay; Natl. Soc. Film Critics '83: Support. Actress (Bernhard).

The King of Hearts 🦴🦴🦴 *Le Roi de Coeur* **1966** In WWI, a Scottish soldier finds a battle-torn French town evacuated of all occupants except a colorful collection of escaped lunatics from a nearby asylum. The lunatics want to make him their king, which is not a bad alternative to the insanity of war. Bujold is cute as ballerina wanna-be; look for Serrault ("La Cage aux Folles") as, not surprisingly, a effeminate would-be hairdresser. Light-hearted comedy with a serious message; definitely worthwhile. **101m/C VHS, DVD.** *FR GB IT* Alan Bates, Genevieve Bujold, Adolfo Celi, Francoise Christophe, Micheline Presle, Michel Serrault, Julien Guiomar, Pierre Brasseur, Jean-Claude Brialy, Pier Paolo Capponi, Jacques Balutin, Marc Dudicourt, Daniel Boulanger; ***D:*** Philippe de Broca; ***W:*** Daniel Boulanger; ***C:*** Pierre Lhomme; ***M:*** Georges Delerue.

King of Jazz 🦴🦴 1/2 **1930** A lavish revue built around the Paul Whiteman Orchestra with comedy sketches and songs by the stars on Universal Pictures' talent roster. (Though billed as the King of Jazz, Whiteman was never as good as jazz's real royalty.) Filmed in two-color Technicolor with a cartoon segment by Walter Lantz. ♫ Rhapsody in Blue; So the Bluebirds and the Blackbirds Got Together; Mississippi Mud; It Happened in Monterey; Ragamuffin Romeo; Happy Feet; Song of the Dawn; A Bench in the Park. **93m/C VHS.** Paul Whiteman, John Boles, Jeanette Loff, Bing Crosby; ***D:*** John Murray Anderson.

King of Kings 🦴🦴 1/2 **1927** DeMille depicts the life of Jesus Christ in this highly regarded silent epic. The resurrection scene appears in color. Remade by Nicholas Ray in 1961. **115m/B VHS, DVD.** H.B. Warner, Dorothy (Dorothy G. Cummings) Cumming, Ernest Torrence, Joseph Schildkraut, Jacqueline Logan, Victor Varconi, William Boyd, James Neill, Robert Edeson, Charles Belcher, Montagu Love, Monte (Monty) Collins; ***D:*** Cecil B. DeMille; ***C:*** J. Peverell Marley.

The King of Kings 🦴🦴🦴 **1961** The life of Christ is intelligently told, with an attractive visual sense and a memorable score. Remake of Cecil B. DeMille's silent film, released in 1927. **170m/C VHS, DVD.** Jeffrey Hunter, Siobhan McKenna, Hurd Hatfield, Robert Ryan, Rita Gam, Viveca Lindfors, Rip Torn; ***D:*** Nicholas Ray; ***W:*** Philip Yordan; ***C:*** Milton Krasner; ***M:*** Miklos Rozsa; ***Nar:*** Orson Welles.

The King of Kong: A Fistful of Quarters 🦴🦴🦴 1/2 **2007 (PG-13)** Documentary follows the intense rivalry of two men battling to be declared the undisputed King of Donkey Kong, and you couldn't ask for two more intriguing characters. Hot-sauce tycoon and idly rich Billy Mitchell is at the top of the arcade champ heap, holding the high score in Donkey Kong for over 25 years until lowly, humble high school teacher Steve Wiebe appears on the scene with an even higher score. A battle on multiple fronts ensues as Mitchell challenges the validity of Weibe's score to respected video game authority Walter Day, but refuses a head-to-head battle with Weibe. Throughout, there's not a moment in which each man sees their dispute as anything but a conflict of epic proportions. Director Gordon skillfully takes us inside a competition few people (even video game enthusiasts) care about and turns it into an exploration of egoism, rivalry, and what it means to be a champion. The movie clearly roots for underdog Weibe, but the obvious slant is half the fun. **79m/C DVD.** *US* ***D:*** Seth Gordon; ***C:*** Seth Gordon; ***M:*** Craig Richey.

King of Kong Island WOOF! **1978** Intent on world domination, a group of mad scientists implant receptors in the brains of gorillas on Kong Island, and the monster apes run amok. **92m/C VHS, DVD.** *SP* Brad Harris, Marc Lawrence; ***D:*** Robert Morris.

The King of Marvin Gardens 🦴🦴 1/2 **1972 (R)** Nicholson stars as a radio personality who prefers to reminisce about his life and family back home rather than play records. When Nicholson returns for a visit he finds brother Dern, king of the get-rich-quick schemers, working for a black crime syndicate. Dern is involved in another scheme which means embezzling money from his boss—not a smart idea although Nicholson can't disuade him. Talky drama also features Burstyn as Dern's neglected girlfriend. **104m/C VHS, DVD.** Jack Nicholson, Bruce Dern, Ellen Burstyn, Scatman Crothers, Julia Anne Robinson, Charles Lavine, Arnold Williams, Josh Mostel; ***D:*** Bob Rafelson; ***W:*** Jacob Brackman.

The King of Masks 🦴🦴🦴 **1999** Wang (Xu) is an elderly street performer in 1930s China who practices the ancient art of face-changing with masks. Tradition has it that he pass his secrets to a male heir, which Wang doesn't have. So, he decides to purchase a boy child on the black market, only to later discover that his clever protege (Ren-ying) is actually a little girl. Chinese with subtitles. **101m/C VHS, DVD.** *CH* Zhu Xu, Zhou Renying; ***D:*** Wu Tianming; ***W:*** Wei Minglung; ***C:*** Mu Dayuan; ***M:*** Jiping Zhao.

King of New York 🦴🦴🦴 **1990 (R)** Drug czar Frank White (Walken), recently returned from a prison sabbatical, regains control of his New York drug empire with the aid of a loyal network of black dealers. How? Call it dangerous charisma, an inexplicable sympatico. Headquartered in Manhattan's chic Plaza hotel, he ruthlessly orchestrates the drug machine, while funneling the profits into a Bronx hospital for the poor. As inscrutable as White himself, Walken makes the drug czar's power tangible, believable, yet never fathomable. **106m/C VHS, DVD, Blu-ray Disc, UMD.** Christopher Walken, Laurence Fishburne, David Caruso, Victor Argo, Wesley Snipes, Janet (Johnson) Julian, Joey Chin, Giancarlo Esposito, Steve Buscemi; ***D:*** Abel Ferrara; ***W:*** Nicholas St. John; ***C:*** Bojan Bazelli; ***M:*** Joe Delia.

King of Texas 🦴🦴🦴 **2002** Shakespeare's "King Lear" set in 1840s Texas with Stewart as John Lear, the patriarch rancher who gives his property to greedy daughters Susannah (Harden) and Rebecca (Holly) instead of to sweet daughter Claudia (Cox). Then the bad girls kick him out into the wilderness. Powerful performance by Stewart does the Bard proud. **120m/C DVD.** Patrick Stewart, Marcia Gay Harden, Lauren Holly, Julie Cox, David Alan Grier, Roy Scheider, Colm Meaney, Matt Letscher, Steven Bauer, Patrick Bergin, Liam Waite; ***D:*** Uli Edel; ***W:*** Stephen Harrigan; ***C:*** Paul Elliott; ***M:*** John Altman. **CABLE**

King of the Airwaves 🦴🦴 1/2 *Louis 19, le Roi des Ondes* **1994** Louis (Drainville) is a dull salesman who spends his days working in an electronics store and his nights in front of the TV. This leads Louis to enter (and win) a contest sponsored by the local TV station, which promises to provide 24-hour-a-day coverage of the winner's every move. Now, ordinary Louis is a media celebrity who must deal with constant intrusion and the soap opera-ish changes wrought upon his life. **93m/C VHS.** *CA FR* Martin Drainville, Agathe de la Fontaine, Dominique Michel, Patricia Tulasne, Gilbert Lachance; ***D:*** Michel Poulette; ***W:*** Michael Michaud, Emile Gaudreault, Sylvie Bouchard; ***M:*** Jean-Marie Benoit.

King of the Ants 🦴🦴 1/2 **2003** Handyman Sean (McKenna) could stand a little excitement but he gets more than he bargained for when Duke (Wendt, convincing in quite the anti-"Norm" role) steers him to crooked businessman Ray (Baldwin) who wants Sean to clip a city accountant who's getting too close for comfort. He jumps at the chance but the feel-good ends there when Ray and Duke cut him loose and have his face rearranged. Whereupon, it becomes a standard revenge tale. Screenwriter Charlie Higson adapted from his 1992 novel of the same name. **103m/C VHS, DVD.** Kari Wuhrer, Daniel Baldwin, George Wendt, Ron Livingston, Chris(topher) McKenna, Timm Sharp, Vernon Wells, Lionel Mark Smith, Carlie Westerman; ***D:*** Stuart Gordon; ***W:*** Charles Higson; ***C:*** Mac Ahlberg. **VIDEO**

King of the Bullwhip 🦴 1/2 **1951** Two undercover U.S. Marshals are sent to Tioga City to stop the killing and looting of a masked bandit, whose whip is as dangerous as his gun. **59m/B VHS.** Lash LaRue, Al "Fuzzy" St. John, Anne Gwynne, Tom Neal, Jack Holt, Dennis Moore, Michael Whalen, George Lewis; ***D:*** Ron Ormond.

King of the Congo 🦴 1/2 **1952** Crabbe, in his last serial, as a pilot who is frantically searching for an important piece of film. In 15 parts. **?m/B VHS.** Buster Crabbe, Gloria Dee; ***D:*** Spencer Gordon Bennet, Wallace Grissell.

King of the Corner 🦴🦴🦴 **2004 (R)** Leo (Riegert) has hit the middle-age wall and can hardly hold back his angst. He abhors his lifelong VP status at a Manhattan marketing job, wife Rachel (Rossellini) appears mentally unstable, and teenage daughter Elena (Johnson) just started dating. Adding to the stress are every-other-weekend treks to Arizona to visit his dying father Sol, whose sage advice for Leo teaches him the real meaning about being a "good Jew." Adapted from the short-story collection "Bad Jews and Other Stories" by Gerald Shapiro, who co-wrote the screenplay along with actor/director Riegert. **93m/C VHS, DVD.** *US* Peter Riegert, Isabella Rossellini, Beverly D'Angelo, Eli Wallach, Ashley Johnson, Eric Bogosian, Dominic Chianese, Rita Moreno, Peter Friedman, Harris Yulin, Frank Wood; ***D:*** Peter Riegert; ***W:*** Peter Riegert; ***C:*** Mauricio Rubinstein.

King of the Cowboys 🦴🦴 **1943** Roy fights a gang of saboteurs and saves a defense installation. **54m/B VHS, DVD.** Roy Rogers, Smiley Burnette, James Bush, Bob Nolan, Peggy Moran, Gerald Mohr, Dorothea Kent, Lloyd Corrigan, Russell Hicks; ***D:*** Joseph Kane; ***W:*** J. Benton Cheney; ***C:*** Reggie Lanning.

King of the Damned 🦴 **1936** On an island prison Veidt leads a convict's revolt against the cruel administrator (Hallard), who gets killed. Before he dies, Hallard alerts a convenient warship, which begins shelling the island. Hallard's daughter, who has fallen for Veidt, pleads for the men and everyone is given a fair trial. Miscast and ineptly performed, although Veidt retains some dignity. **81m/B VHS.** *GB* Conrad Veidt, Helen Vinson, C.M. Hallard, Noah Beery Sr., Percy Walsh, Raymond Lovell, Cecil Ramage, Peter Croft; ***D:*** Walter Forde; ***W:*** Charles Bennett, Sidney Gilliat, Noel Langley.

King of the Forest Rangers **1946** Ranger Steve King must stop an evil archaeologist from finding a treasure whose secret lies within an ancient Indian rug pattern. Edited from an original, 12 episode serial on two cassettes. **167m/B VHS.** Larry Thompson, Helen Talbot, Stuart Hamblen, Anthony Warde, Scott Elliott; ***D:*** Spencer Gordon Bennet, Fred Brannon; ***W:*** Albert DeMond, Ronald Davidson, Basil Dickey, Jesse Duffy, Lynn Perkins; ***C:*** Bud Thackery.

King of the Grizzlies 🦴 1/2 **1969 (G)** The mystical relationship between a Cree Indian and a grizzly cub is put to the test when the full grown bear attacks a ranch at which the Indian is foreman. **93m/C VHS, DVD.** Chris Wiggins, John Yesno; ***D:*** Ron Kelly.

King of the Gypsies 🦴🦴 1/2 **1978 (R)** Interesting drama. A young man, scornful of his gypsy heritage, runs away from the tribe and tries to make a life of his own. He is summoned home to his grandfather's deathbed where he is proclaimed the new king of the gypsies, thus incurring the wrath of his scorned father. From Peter Maas's best-selling novel. **112m/C VHS, DVD.** Sterling Hayden, Eric Roberts, Susan Sarandon, Brooke Shields, Shelley Winters, Annie Potts, Annette O'Toole, Judd Hirsch, Michael V. Gazzo, Roy Brocksmith, Anthony Holland, Antonia Rey, Stephen Mendillo, Matthew Laborteaux, Patti LuPone, Rachel Ticotin; ***D:*** Frank Pierson; ***W:*** Frank Pierson; ***C:*** Sven Nykvist; ***M:*** David Grisman.

King of the Hill 🦴🦴🦴 1/2 **1993 (PG-13)** Quiet depression-era drama focuses on Aaron, a 12-year-old who lives in a seedy hotel in St. Louis. The family is barely scraping by: his mother is in a tuberculosis sanitarium, his younger brother has been sent away to live with relatives, and Aaron must fend for himself when his father gets work as a traveling salesman. Aaron excels at school and his efforts there, as well as his hotel friends, manage to provide him with some semblance of a regular life. Soderberg's third directorial effort is unsentimental but admiring of his character's resourcefulness and imagination during difficult times. Based on the book by A.E. Hochner describing his own childhood. **102m/C VHS.** Jesse Bradford, Jeroen Krabbe, Lisa Eichhorn, Karen Allen, Spalding Gray, Elizabeth McGovern, Joseph Chrest, Adrien Brody, Cameron Boyd, Chris Samples, Katherine Heigl, Amber Benson, John McConnell, Ron Vawter, John Durbin, Lauryn Hill, David Jensen; ***D:*** Steven Soderbergh; ***W:*** Steven Soderbergh; ***M:*** Cliff Martinez.

King of the Jungle 🦴🦴 **1933** Paramount's answer to Tarzan stars Crabbe as Kaspa the Lion Man. This jungle boy, raised by animals, is captured on safari and displayed (attired in a skimpy loincloth) as a circus attraction. Dee is the babe helping to soothe Kaspa's savage breast, or beast, or something. Big finale includes a circus fire and an elephant stampede. **73m/B VHS.** Buster Crabbe, Frances Dee, Sidney Toler, Nydia Westman, Douglass Dumbrille, Robert Barrat; ***D:*** H. Bruce Humberstone, Max Marcin; ***W:*** Max Marcin; ***C:*** Ernest Haller.

King of the Jungle **2001 (R)** Contrived story with an energized performance by Leguizamo. He's Seymour, a mentally challenged man with the intellectual and emotional capacity of a preadolescent. He lives with his long-divorced Puerto Rican mother Mona (Carmen) and her lover Joanne (Perez). His dad, Jack (Gorman), is a deadbeat poet who has never accepted his son's limitations. Seymour spends his time on the streets playing basketball until his mother is fatally shot and he wants revenge. **87m/C VHS, DVD.** John Leguizamo, Cliff Gorman, Julie Carmen, Rosie Perez, Michael Rapaport, Rosario Dawson, Marisa Tomei, Annabella Sciorra; ***D:*** Seth Zvi Rosenfeld; ***W:*** Seth Zvi Rosenfeld; ***C:*** Fortunato Procopio; ***M:*** Harry Gregson-Williams.

The King of the Kickboxers **WOOF! 1991 (R)** The villains make kung-fu snuff movies with unwitting actors killed on camera. Otherwise, same old junk about a karate cop back in Bangkok to get the dude who squashed his brother. Pretty racist at times. **90m/C VHS.** Loren Avedon, Richard Jaeckel, Billy Blanks, Don Stroud, Keith Cooke; ***D:*** Lucas Lowe.

King of the Kongo **1929** A handsome young man is sent by the government to Nuhalla, deep in the jungle, to break up a gang of ivory thieves. Serial was made in silent and sound versions. **213m/B VHS.** Jacqueline Logan, Boris Karloff, Richard Tucker; ***D:*** Richard Thorpe.

King of the Mountain ½ **1981 (PG)** The "Old King" and the "New King" must square off in this tale of daredevil road racers who zoom through the streets of Hollywood. Interesting cast trapped by tired script. **92m/C VHS.** Richard Cox, Harry Hamlin, Dennis Hopper, Joseph Bottoms, Deborah Van Valkenburgh, Dan Haggerty; ***D:*** Noel Nosseck; ***W:*** Roger Christian.

King of the Pecos ½ **1936** A young lawyer (who's also adept at the shootin' iron) exacts revenge on his parents' killers in the courtroom. Well made early Wayne outing, with good character development, taut pacing and beautiful photography. **54m/B VHS, DVD.** John Wayne, Muriel Evans, Cy Kendall, Jack Clifford, John (Jack) Beck, Yakima Canutt; ***D:*** Joseph Kane; ***W:*** Dorrell McGowan, Stuart E. McGowan, Bernard McConville; ***C:*** Jack Marta.

The King of the Roaring '20s: The Story of Arnold Rothstein ½ *The Big Bankroll* **1961** "True" story of infamous gangster, Arnold Rothstein, a brilliant and ruthless gambler who practically ran New York in the '20s. This version of his life focuses on his rise to power, the dealings with his enemies, and his crumbling personal life. Superficial due mostly to the weak screenplay. Adapted from the book "The Big Bankroll" by Leo Katcher. **106m/B VHS.** David Janssen, Dianne Foster, Mickey Rooney, Jack Carson, Diana Dors, Dan O'Herlihy, Mickey Shaughnessy, Keenan Wynn; ***D:*** Joseph M. Newman.

King of the Rocketmen *Lost Planet Airmen* **1949** Jeff King thwarts an attempt by traitors to steal government scientific secrets. Serial in 12 episodes. Later released as a feature titled "Lost Planet Airmen." **156m/B VHS, DVD.** Tristram Coffin, Mae Clarke, I. Stanford Jolley; ***D:*** Fred Brannon.

King of the Rodeo **1928** Cowpoke Hoot wins a rodeo and catches a thief in the Windy City. Hoot's final silent ride into the sunset. **54m/B VHS.** Hoot Gibson, Kathryn Crawford, Slim Summerville, Charles French, Monte Montague, Joseph Girard; ***D:*** Henry MacRae.

King of the Sierras ½ **1938** Bosworth tells his nephew the story of a white horse that protected his mares from a black stallion. The acting of the horses is better than that of the humans. **58m/B VHS.** Hobart Bosworth, Harry Harvey, Harry Harvey Jr., Jim Campeau; ***D:*** Samuel Diege; ***W:*** Scott Darling.

King of the Stallions ½ **1942** A dangerous stallion is a menacing threat to the herd and the cowboys and Indians and other scattered wildlife. Chief Thundercloud is the only one capable of tackling the matter. Largely Indian cast, including Iron Eyes Cody, famed for the anti-litter campaign. **63m/B VHS.** Chief Thundercloud, Princess Bluebird, Chief Yowlachie, Rick Vallin, Dave O'Brien, Barbara Felker, Iron Eyes Cody; ***D:*** Edward Finney.

King of the Texas Rangers **1941** Tom King, Texas Ranger, finds that his father's killers are a group of saboteurs who have destroyed American oil fields. This 12-episode serial comes on two tapes. **195m/B VHS.** Sammy Baugh, Neil Hamilton; ***D:*** William Witney, John English.

King of the Wild Horses **1924** Engaging children's story about a wild stallion that comes to the rescue. Terrific action photography of Rex going through his paces. Look for Chase in a rare dramatic role. Silent. **50m/B VHS.** Rex, Edna Murphy, Leon Bary, Pat Hartigan, Frank Butler, Charley Chase; ***D:*** Fred W. Jackman.

King of the Wild Stallions ½ **1959** Widowed rancher Martha (Brewster) needs $500 to pay off cattle baron Matt Maguire (Meyer), which happens to be the same amount he's put up for the capture of the wild black stallion roaming the hills. When Martha's son Bucky (Hartleben) captures the horse, he wants to keep him and it's up to ranch foreman Randy (Montgomery)—who's sweet on Martha—to settle the matter. **76m/C DVD.** George Montgomery, Diane Brewster, Emile Meyer, Edgar Buchanan, Denver Pyle, Jerry Hartleben; ***D:*** R.G. Springsteen, Ford Beebe; ***W:*** Ford Beebe; ***C:*** Carl Guthrie; ***M:*** Marlin Skiles.

King of the Wind ½ **1993 (PG)** An epic adventure featuring the true story of a legendary Arabian horse and a poor stable boy who gave the most precious gift of all: love. **101m/C VHS.** Richard Harris, Glenda Jackson.

King of the Zombies **WOOF! 1941** Mad scientist creates his own zombies without souls, to be used as the evil tools of a foreign government. Zombie nonsense. **67m/B VHS, DVD.** John Archer, Dick Purcell, Mantan Moreland, Henry Victor, Joan Woodbury; ***D:*** Jean Yarbrough; ***W:*** Edmond Kelso; ***C:*** Mack Stengler; ***M:*** Edward Kay.

King of Thieves *Konig der Diebe* **2004** Poor Ukrainian circus kids, 10-year-old Barbu and his 13-year-old sister Mimma, are sold to one-time circus performer Caruso who makes a lot of promises about a better life. After smuggling them into Berlin, the siblings are separated and Barbu learns to be a pickpocket. But when he discovers that Mimma is forced to work in a brothel, he tries to free her. German with subtitles. **101m/C DVD.** *GE* Lazar Ristovski, Paulus Manker, Katharina Thalbach, Iakov Kultiasov, Julia Khanverdieva; ***D:*** Ivan Fila; ***W:*** Ivan Fila; ***C:*** Vladimir Smutny; ***M:*** Michael Kocab.

The King on Main Street ½ **1925** King Serge of Molvania (Menjou) comes to America to get a loan for his country and falls for Gladys (Love), who returns his interest. But duty calls in the end. Based on the play "The King" by Leo Ditrichstein. **68m/B VHS.** Adolphe Menjou, Bessie Love, Greta Nissen, Joseph Kilgour, Oscar Shaw, Edgar Norton; ***D:*** Monta Bell; ***W:*** Monta Bell, Douglas Z. Doty; ***C:*** James Wong Howe.

King, Queen, Knave *Herzbube* **1972** Sexy black comedy about a shy, awkward 19-year-old boy, keenly aware that his interest in girls is not reciprocated. He has to go live with his prosperous uncle and his much younger wife when his parents are killed. Based on the Vladimir Nabokov novel. **94m/C VHS.** *GE* Gina Lollobrigida, David Niven, John Moulder-Brown; ***D:*** Jerzy Skolimowski; ***W:*** David Seltzer.

King Ralph **1991 (PG)** When the rest of the royal family passes away in a freak accident, lounge lizard Ralph finds himself the only heir to the throne. O'Toole is the long-suffering valet who tries to train him for the job. Funny in spots and Goodman is the quintessential good sport, making the whole outing pleasant. Sometimes too forced. **96m/C VHS, DVD.** John Goodman, Peter O'Toole, Camille Coduri, Joely Richardson, John Hurt; ***D:*** David S. Ward; ***W:*** David S. Ward; ***C:*** Kenneth Macmillan; ***M:*** James Newton Howard.

King Rat **1965** Drama set in a WWII Japanese prisoner-of-war camp. Focuses on the effect of captivity on the English, Australian, and American prisoners. An American officer bribes his Japanese captors to live more comfortably than the rest. Based on James Clavell's novel. **134m/B VHS, DVD.** George Segal, Tom Courtenay, James Fox, James Donald, Denholm Elliott, Patrick O'Neal, John Mills, Todd Armstrong, Gerald Sim, Leonard Rossiter, John Standing, Alan Webb, Sam Reese, Wright King, Joe Turkel, Geoffrey Bayldon, Reg Lye, Arthur Malet, Richard Dawson, William "Bill" Fawcett, John Warburton, John Ronane, Michael Lees, Hamilton Dyce, Hedley Mattingly, Dale Ishimoto; ***D:*** Bryan Forbes; ***W:*** Bryan Forbes, James Clavell; ***C:*** Burnett Guffey; ***M:*** John Barry.

King Richard and the Crusaders ½ **1954** Laughable costume epic with Sanders as Richard the Lionheart, who survives an assassination attempt during the Crusades. Harvey is a loyal knight sworn to find the traitors with Harrison as the noble leader of the Arab forces. Mayo plays Harvey's object of affection. Even the battle scenes are boring. Based on "The Talisman" by Sir Walter Scott. **113m/C VHS, DVD.** George Sanders, Rex Harrison, Laurence Harvey, Virginia Mayo, Robert Douglas, Michael Pate, Paula Raymond, Lester Matthews; ***D:*** David Butler; ***W:*** John Twist; ***M:*** Max Steiner.

King Solomon's Mines **1937** The search for King Solomon's Mines leads a safari through the treacherous terrain of the desert, fending off sandstorms, Zulus, and a volcanic eruption. Adapted from the novel by H. Rider Haggard and remade twice. **80m/B VHS, DVD.** Cedric Hardwicke, Paul Robeson, Roland Young, John Loder, Anna Lee; ***D:*** Robert Stevenson; ***W:*** Michael Hogan, Roland Pertwee; ***C:*** Cyril Knowles, Glen MacWilliams; ***M:*** Mischa Spoliansky.

King Solomon's Mines **1950** Hunter Allan Quartermain (Granger) is hired by Elizabeth Curtis (Kerr) and her brother John (Carlson) to find Elizabeth's missing husband who was searching for the legendary diamond mines of King Solomon. Naturally, there are numerous adventures during their expedition. Filmed on location in Nairobi, Tanganyika and the Belgian Congo. A lavish version of the classic H. Rider Haggard novel; remake of the 1937 classic and remade again in 1985. **102m/C VHS, DVD.** Stewart Granger, Deborah Kerr, Richard Carlson, Hugo Haas, Lowell Gilmore; ***D:*** Compton Bennett; ***W:*** Helen Deutsch; ***C:*** Robert L. Surtees. Oscars '50: Color Cinematog., Film Editing.

King Solomon's Mines ½ **1985 (PG-13)** The third remake of the classic H. Rider Haggard novel about a safari deep into Africa in search of an explorer who disappeared while searching for the legendary diamond mines of King Solomon. Updated but lacking the style of the previous two films. Somewhat imperialistic, racist point of view. **101m/C VHS, DVD.** Richard Chamberlain, John Rhys-Davies, Sharon Stone, Herbert Lom; ***D:*** J. Lee Thompson; ***W:*** Gene Quintano; ***M:*** Jerry Goldsmith.

King Solomon's Treasure **1976** The great white adventurer takes on the African jungle, hunting for hidden treasure in the Forbidden City. Ekland stars as a Phoenician Queen—need we say more?? **90m/C VHS.** *CA GB* David McCallum, Britt Ekland, Patrick Macnee, Wilfrid Hyde-White; ***D:*** Alvin Rakoff.

The Kingdom ½ *Riget* **1995** Danish director von Trier serves up what must be the first four-and-a- half-hour long hospital soap opera/ghost story/comedy/satire. Elderly Mrs. Drusse checks herself into a hospital known as the Kingdom, which is inhabited by the usual medical suspects: Pompous surgeons, incompetent buraucrats, and quirky residents. She hears the ghostly call of a child from an elevator shaft and sticks around to investigate. Made for Danish TV but released theatrically there and in the States, film owes a great deal to "Twin Peaks" and B-movie horror flicks. Doesn't take itself too seriously, but probably can't be watched all in one sitting. Danish and Swedish with subtitles. **279m/C VHS, DVD.** *DK* Kirsten Rolffes, Ghita Norby, Udo Kier, Ernst-Hugo Jaregard, Soren Pilmark, Holger Juul Hansen, Baard Owe, Birgitte Raaberg, Peter Mygind, Solbjorg Hojfeldt; ***D:*** Lars von Trier; ***W:*** Lars von Trier, Tomas Gislason, Niels Vorsel; ***C:*** Eric Kress; ***M:*** Joachim Holbek.

The Kingdom **2007 (R)** After a suicide bombing in Saudi Arabia kills over 100 Americans, FBI agent Ronald Fleury (Foxx) leads a hotshot team (Cooper, Garner, and a particularily obnoxious Bateman) to investigate, although officials from both governments aren't exactly happy about the situation. Fleury and company arrive on Saudi soil ready to open a can of American whoop-ass, but not everything is as simple as it seems for them or their Saudi handler Col. al Ghazi (Barhom). Culture clashes, personal agendas, and political intrigue prove complicated while they track the terrorist suspected of planning the bombing. Big-budget actioner strives for relevance with its true-life backdrop, but too often settles for exploitation, and director Berg never seems at ease with his subject until the movie's final explosion-fest. **110m/C DVD, HD DVD.** *US* Jamie Foxx, Chris Cooper, Jennifer Garner, Jason Bateman, Ashraf Barhoum, Ali Suliman, Jeremy Piven; ***D:*** Peter Berg; ***W:*** Matthew Carnahan; ***C:*** Mauro Fiore; ***M:*** Danny Elfman.

The Kingdom 2 ½ *Riget II* **1997** In the continuation of Von Trier's hospital soap/supernatural/satire, madness runs rampant through Copenhagen's Kingdom hospital. Spiritualist Mrs. Drosse comes back to life after dying during surgery. A baby, sired by a demon, grows at a monstrous rate. Pompous Swedish neurosurgeon Helmer returns from Haiti with voodoo potions and is beseiged by his unbalanced lover and on and on it goes in its quirky, bizarre way. Swedish and Danish with subtitles. **286m/C VHS, DVD.** *DK* Kirsten Rolffes, Ghita Norby, Udo Kier, Ernst-Hugo Jaregard, Soren Pilmark, Holger Juul Hansen, Baard Owe, Birgitte Raaberg, Peter Mygind, Solbjorg Hojfeldt; ***D:*** Lars von Trier; ***W:*** Lars von Trier, Niels Vorsel; ***C:*** Eric Kress; ***M:*** Joachim Holbek.

Kingdom Come **2001 (PG)** The death of an African-American family's patriarch brings archetypical relatives from near and far for the funeral. There's the wise, saintly widow (Goldberg), the stoic, hard-working son (LL Cool J) and his eager-to-please wife (Fox), the ne'er-do-well son (Anderson) and his shrewish wife (Pinkettt-Smith), the Bible-thumper (Devine), and the gold-digger (Braxton). Throw in an over-officious and unfortunately flatulent preacher (Cedric), let simmer, and bring to a boil. Most of the humor comes from the over-the-top renditions of the characters, as well as the aforementioned gastrointestinal distress, but it keeps getting in the way of the serious, and well-done drama between the at-odds family members. The swings in tone and mood are jarring, but the ride is made easier by the stellar performances, highlighted by LL Cool J's breakout as the eldest son. **89m/C VHS, DVD.** *US* LL Cool J, Jada Pinkett Smith, Vivica A. Fox, Loretta Devine, Anthony Anderson, Cedric the Entertainer, Darius McCrary, Whoopi Goldberg, Toni Braxton, Masasa, Clifton Davis, Richard Gant, Doug McHenry; ***D:*** Doug McHenry; ***W:*** Jessie Jones, David Bottrell; ***C:*** Francis Kenny; ***M:*** Tyler Bates.

Kingdom of Heaven **2005 (R)** Scott successfully moves from Roman epic "Gladiator" to the 12th century of the Crusades. Godfrey of Ibelin (Neeson) is a knight in the service of dying King Baldwin IV (Norton) of Jerusalem. He returns to France to recruit for a crusade and to seek out his illegitimate son, blacksmith Balian (Bloom). During his quest, Balian becomes a knight, falls in love with Baldwin's sister, Princess Sibylla (Green), and tries to protect Jerusalem from the conspirators within the city and the amassing forces of Saladin (Massoud) without. Of course, as the smart screenplay deftly points out, it's the self-interested extremists on both sides that cause most of the trouble. Despite the epic scale, Scott pays ample attention to the human aspect. **145m/C DVD, Blu-ray Disc, UMD.** *GB SP US GE* Orlando Bloom, Eva Green, Liam Neeson, Jeremy Irons, David Thewlis, Brendan Gleeson, Marton Csokas, Michael Sheen, Edward Norton, Alexander Siddig, Kevin McKidd, Jon Finch, Ghassan Massoud, Velibor Topi, Ulrich Thomsen, Nikolaj Coster-Waldau, Iain Glen; ***D:*** Ridley Scott; ***W:*** William Monahan; ***C:*** John Mathieson; ***M:*** Harry Gregson-Williams.

Kingdom of the Spiders 1/2 **1977 (PG)** A desert town is invaded by swarms of killer tarantulas, which begin to consume townspeople. **90m/C VHS, DVD.** William Shatner, Tiffany Bolling, Woody Strode; ***D:*** John Cardos; ***W:*** Alan Caillou, Richard Robinson; ***C:*** John Morrill.

Kingfish: A Story of Huey P. Long 1/2 **1995** Charismatic political kingpin of Louisiana, Huey P. Long is brought to vivid life with Goodman's swaggering portrayal. Story is told in flashback, beginning with Long's assassination in 1935. A champion of the working man, Long parlayed charm and corruption into a Depression-era political career as governor and U.S. Senator. But naturally, the hard-drinking, hard-loving Long makes a lot of enemies along the way. Long's life was also memorably recreated in Robert Penn Warren's "All the King's Men," as was that of his younger brother, Governor Earl Long, in the film "Blaze." **97m/C VHS.** John Goodman, Matt Craven, Anne Heche, Ann Dowd, Jeff(rey) Perry, Bob Gunton, Hoyt Axton, Kirk Baltz, Bill Cobbs; ***D:*** Thomas Schlamme; ***W:*** Paul Monash; ***M:*** Patrick Williams.

Kingfisher Caper **1976 (PG)** A power struggle between a businessman, his brother, and a divorced sister is threatening to rip a family-owned diamond empire apart. **90m/C VHS.** Hayley Mills, David McCallum; ***D:*** Dirk DeVilliers.

Kingfisher the Killer **1981** Charles, the Raging Titan of Ninja skill, stalks the bad gang that killed his mother and hits them with nunchakos. **90m/C VHS.** *HK* Sho Kosugi.

Kingpin 1/2 **1996 (PG-13)** Bowling epic serves up social satire while showcasing some of the worst hair ever seen at the cinema. Roy Munson (a very bald Harrelson, reasonably subdued in relation to rest of cast) is a former bowling champ who, thanks to his sleazy ways, lost a hand and is reduced to selling bowling equipment while wearing a crude rubber prosthetic (on his hand). That is until he meets innocent Amish phenom Ishmael (Quaid), resplendent in a dutch boy wig, whom he persuades to hit the road to a big money tournament in Reno, where Roy can confront an old nemesis (Murray) and compare shampoos, while Ish attempts to win enough money to save the family farm. Claudia (Angel) is around as the highly decorative love interest of Roy. Co-written by "Dumb & Dumber" writers the brothers Farrelly. Look for Amish sensations Blues Traveler at the credit roll. **107m/C VHS, DVD.** Woody Harrelson, Randy Quaid, Vanessa Angel, Bill Murray, Chris Elliott, Mike Cerrone, William Jordan, Richard Tyson, Lin Shaye, Zen Gesner, Prudence Wright Holmes, Rob Moran; ***D:*** Peter Farrelly, Bobby Farrelly; ***W:*** Bobby Farrelly, Mort Nathan; ***C:*** Mark Irwin; ***M:*** Freedy Johnston.

Kings **2007** In 1977, six friends leave Connemara, Ireland, for London to realize their dreams. Thirty years later, they reunite at the pub for the wake of Jackie, who's died under questionable circumstances. The years have left most of these middle-aged men bitter, drink-sodden, and resentful. Based on the play "The Kings of Kilburn High Road" by Jimmy Murphy. In English and Gaelic with subtitles. **89m/C DVD.** *IR* Colm Meaney, Donal O'Kelly, Barry Barnes, Donncha Crowley, Brendan Conroy, Sean O'Tarpaigh, Peadar O'Treasaigh; ***D:*** Tom Collins; ***W:*** Tom Collins; ***C:*** P.J. Collins; ***M:*** Pol O'Brennan.

Kings and Desperate Men 1/2 **1983** Apprentice terrorists plea their case at a public forum when they take a rakish talk show host hostage. **118m/C VHS.** *GB* Patrick McGoohan, Alexis Kanner, Andrea Marcovicci, Robin Spry, Frank Moore; ***D:*** Alexis Kanner.

Kings and Queen *Rois et reine* **2004** French portrait of seemingly ordinary life, steeped with hints at a dark reality that refuses to admit the truth. Nora is a dwice-divorced, hip, intelligent art gallery owner, and mother to an 11-year-old boy. She's now engaged to a very rich man, and has a father dying of stomach cancer. A standard set-up to any Hollywood melodrama, but Hollywood doesn't exist in France. Therefore, Nora may not care about any of them the way we think she should. Ismael is Nora's most recent lover, stuck in a mental institution only because of poor judgment. These characters talk for real, and walk right past the emotional traps that any Hollywood screenplay might fall into. Stunning conclusion leaves an almost dirty taste in the mouth. **150m/C DVD.** *FR* Emmanuelle Devos, Mathieu Amalric, Catherine Deneuve, Magali Woch, Olivier Rabourdin, Maurice Garrel, Nathalie Boutefeu, Hippolyte Girardot, Joachim Salinger; ***D:*** Arnaud Desplechin; ***W:*** Arnaud Desplechin, Roger Bohbot; ***C:*** Eric Gautier.

Kings Go Forth 1/2 **1958** Hormones and war rage in this love triangle set against the backdrop of WWII France. Sinatra loves Wood who loves Curtis. When Sinatra asks for her hand in marriage she refuses because she is mixed—half black, half white. He says it doesn't matter, but she still declines because she's in love with Curtis. When Sinatra tells Curtis that Wood is mixed, Curtis says that it doesn't matter to him either because he'd never planned on marrying her. Meanwhile, the war continues. Not particularly satisfying on either the war or race front. Based on a novel by Joe David Brown. **109m/B VHS, DVD.** Frank Sinatra, Tony Curtis, Natalie Wood, Leora Dana; ***D:*** Delmer Daves; ***W:*** Merle Miller; ***C:*** Daniel F. Fapp; ***M:*** Elmer Bernstein.

The King's Guard 1/2 **2001 (PG-13)** Captain Reynolds (St. John) and his men must accompany betrothed Princess Gwendolyn (Jones)—and her dowry of gold—to her intended's kingdom. But two traitors (Roberts, Perlman) seek both the princess and the treasure. Low-budget but the fast paced action helps keep things interesting. **94m/C VHS, DVD.** Ashley Jones, Eric Roberts, Ron Perlman, Trevor St. John, Lesley-Anne Down; ***D:*** Jonathan Tydor; ***W:*** Jonathan Tydor. **VIDEO**

Kings in Grass Castles 1/2 **1997** Aussie miniseries based on the memoirs of Dame Mary Durack and her immigrant family who leave famine-stricken Ireland in the 1850s for Australia. After dealing with an eight-year indenture, the family become Queensland cattle barons, lose everything, and struggle to rebuild, all the while dealing with more prejudice from the British colonials. **200m/C VHS.** *AU* Stephen (Dillon) Dillane, Essie Davis, Fionnula Flanagan, David Ngoombujarra, Susan Lynch, Ernie Dingo, James Fox, Max Cullen, Des McAleer; ***D:*** John Woods; ***W:*** Tony Morphett; ***C:*** Roger Lanser; ***M:*** Shaun Davey. **TV**

Kings of South Beach **2007** Remarkably dull and clichéd crime drama based on a true story. Chris Troiano (Gedrick) is a thuggish but popular Miami club owner in the 1990s, with Andy Burnett (Wahlberg) as his right-hand man. But Troiano's clubs are actually fronts for laundering mob money and the feds already have an op in motion to bring him down. **90m/C DVD.** Jason Gedrick, Donnie Wahlberg, Steven Bauer, Nadine Velazquez, Ricardo Chavira, Sean Poolman, Frank John Hughes, Maria Valentina Bove; ***D:*** Tim Hunter; ***W:*** Nicholas Pileggi; ***C:*** Patrick Cady; ***M:*** Rob Mounsey. **VIDEO**

Kings of the Road—In the Course of Time 1/2 *Im Lauf der Zeit* **1976** A writer and a film projectionist travel by truck across Germany. The film stands out for its simple and expressive direction, and truly captures the sense of physical and ideological freedom of being on the road. A landmark Wenders epic. In German with English subtitles. **176m/B VHS.** *GE* Ruediger Vogler, Hanns Zischler, Elisabeth (Lisa) Kreuzer; ***D:*** Wim Wenders; ***W:*** Wim Wenders; ***C:*** Robby Muller, Martin Schafer; ***M:*** Axel Linstadt.

Kings of the Sun 1/2 **1963** Balam (Chakiris), the newly crowned king of the Mayans, decides to resettle his people in another area of Mexico, thus angering the locals who are led by Black Eagle (Brynner). But the two make peace when a greater threat emerges. Brynner always has presence but Chakiris is solemn and lightweight and this story is more foolish than fact. **108m/C DVD.** Yul Brynner, George Chakiris, Shirley Anne Field, Richard Basehart, Brad Dexter, Barry Morse, Leo Gordon; ***D:*** J. Lee Thompson; ***W:*** Elliott Arnold, James R. Webb; ***C:*** Joe MacDonald; ***M:*** Elmer Bernstein.

King's Ransom WOOF! **1991** When the Japanese Emperor's Pearl is stolen, the underworld is abuzz with excitement. But only the wealthiest individuals are invited to bid for the jewel at Cameron King's secret casino. There, untold pleasures, and dangers, await them. **?m/C VHS.** Miles O'Keeffe, Dedee Pfeiffer, Christopher Atkins; ***D:*** Hugh Parks.

King's Ransom **2005 (PG-13)** Perennial comic sidekick Anderson proves that some actors are only funny in small doses with his first leading role as obnoxious self-obsessed billionaire Malcolm King. The deceitful mogul ignores his gold-digging wife (Smith), harasses his good-natured secretary (Devine), and makes life a living hell for the employees at his Chicago-based marketing firm. His enemies all get the same idea—kidnap King and teach him a lesson—and painfully unfunny hijinks ensue. Even King gets involved with faking his own kidnapping, which was amusing back when it was originally done in "Ruthless People." The cast features an ensemble of legitimately funny actors who are cast adrift in this pointless, humorless wreck. **97m/C DVD.** *US* Anthony Anderson, Jay Mohr, Kellita Smith, Nicole Ari Parker, Regina Hall, Loretta Devine, Donald Adeosun Faison, Charlie (Charles Q.) Murphy, Lisa Marcos, Brooke D'Orsay, Leila Arcieri, Jackie Burroughs; ***D:*** Jeff Byrd; ***W:*** Wayne Conley; ***C:*** Robert McLachlan.

The King's Rhapsody **1955** Flynn is an heir who abdicates his throne in order to be with the woman he loves. But when the king dies, Flynn sacrifices love for honor and goes back to marry a princess. Very dated and Flynn is long past his swashbuckling-romantic days. **93m/C VHS.** *GB* Errol Flynn, Anna Neagle, Patrice Wymore, Martita Hunt, Finlay Currie, Frank Wolff, Joan Benham, Reginald Tate, Miles Malleson; ***D:*** Herbert Wilcox.

Kings Row **1941** The Harry Bellamann best-selling Middle American potboiler comes to life. Childhood friends grow up with varying degrees of success, in a decidedly macabre town. All are continually dependent on and inspired by Parris (Cummings) a psychiatric doctor and genuine gentleman. Many cast members worked against type with unusual success. Warner held the film for a year after its completion, in concern for its dark subject matter, but it received wide acclaim. Shot completely within studio settings—excellent scenic design by William Cameron Menzies, and wonderful score. **127m/B VHS, DVD.** Ann Sheridan, Robert Cummings, Ronald Reagan, Betty Field, Charles Coburn, Claude Rains, Judith Anderson, Nancy Coleman, Karen Verne, Maria Ouspenskaya, Harry Davenport, Ernest Cossart, Pat Moriarity, Scotty Beckett; ***D:*** Sam Wood; ***C:*** James Wong Howe; ***M:*** Erich Wolfgang Korngold.

The King's Thief 1/2 **1955** Costume swashbuckler with Niven as the bad guy. He's a duke at the court of 17th-century English King Charles II and is involved in a plot to steal the crown jewels. **78m/C VHS.** David Niven, Edmund Purdom, George Sanders, Ann Blyth, Roger Moore, John Dehner, Sean McClory, Melville Cooper, Alan Mowbray; ***D:*** Robert Z. Leonard; ***W:*** Christopher Knopf; ***M:*** Miklos Rozsa.

The King's Whore **1990 (R)** Dalton stars as a 17th-century king who falls obsessively in love with the wife of one of his courtiers. His passions lead him to make a decision between the woman and the throne. Good-looking costume epic with obligatory sword fights. **111m/C VHS, DVD.** Timothy Dalton, Valeria Golino, Feodor Chaliapin Jr., Margaret Tyzack; ***W:*** Daniel Vigne, Frederic Raphael.

Kinjite: Forbidden Subjects **1989 (R)** A cop takes on a sleazy pimp whose specialty is recruiting teenage girls, including the daughter of a Japanese business man. Slimy, standard Bronson fare. **97m/C VHS, DVD.** Charles Bronson, Juan Fernandez, Peggy Lipton; ***D:*** J. Lee Thompson.

A Kink in the Picasso **1990** MTV personality Daddo joins a cast of criminals who chase after a Picasso artwork and a counterfeit. Artless Australian production. **84m/C VHS.** Peter O'Brien, Jon Finlayson, Jane Clifton, Andrew Daddo; ***D:*** Marc Gracie.

Kinky Boots 1/2 **2006 (PG-13)** Title says it all in this slight Brit comedy that's based on a true story. Charlie Price (Edgerton) reluctantly takes over the failing family shoe factory after his dad dies. They need a specialty product to save the day, and Charlie receives unexpected inspiration when he comes to the aid of big black drag queen Lola (a sweet Ejiofor), who bemoans that the average stiletto wasn't made to support someone of his size. With Lola offering expertise, Charlie and his workers find their new market in cross-dressers. A big fashion show finale adds to the feel-good fantasy. **106m/C DVD.** *GB* Joel Edgerton, Chiwetel Ejiofor, Sarah-Jane Potts, Jemima Rooper, Linda Bassett, Nick Frost, Ewan Hooper, Robert Pugh, Geoffrey Streatsfield; ***D:*** Julian Jarrold; ***W:*** Tim Firth, Geoff Deane; ***C:*** Eigil Bryld; ***M:*** Adrian Johnston.

Kinsey **2004 (R)** Well-written, well-acted, and provocative biopic on the life of still-controversial sex researcher Alfred Kinsey. Trained as a zoologist, Kinsey (Neeson) found his true calling when his own sexual ignorance and that of his equally inexperienced bride Clara (Linney) caused them marital problems. The Indiana U professor began by offering his students factual and explicit information on human sexuality and then embarked on a massive research project that involved interviewing thousands about their sexual histories. Rumpled but charismatic, Kinsey's own complicated sexual feelings, especially towards young associate Clyde Martin (Sarsgaard), offer emotional consequences Kinsey is unprepared for. Nor is he prepared for the increasingly shrill notoriety his published works bring him. Lynn Redgrave offers a striking cameo. **118m/C DVD.** *US* Liam Neeson, Laura Linney, Chris O'Donnell, Peter Sarsgaard, Timothy Hutton, John Lithgow, Tim Curry, Oliver Platt, Dylan Baker, Julianne Nicholson, William Sadler, Heather Goldenhersch, John McMartin, Veronica Cartwright, Kathleen Chalfant, Dagmara Dominczyk, Lynn Redgrave, John Krasinski; ***D:*** Bill Condon; ***W:*** Bill Condon; ***C:*** Joe Dunton; ***M:*** Carter Burwell.

Kipperbang *Ptang, Yang, Kipperbang* **1982 (PG)** During the summer of 1948, a 13-year-old boy wishes he could kiss the girl of his dreams. He finally gets the chance in a school play. Not unsatisfying, but falls short of being the bittersweet coming-of-age drama it could have been. **85m/C VHS.** *GB* John Albasiny, Abigail Cruttenden, Alison Steadman; ***D:*** Michael Apted.

Kipps *The Remarkable Mr. Kipps* **1941** Based on H.G. Wells's satirical novel. A young British shopkeeper inherits a fortune and tries to join high society while neglecting his working-class girlfriend. Set the stage for the musical "Half a Sixpence." **95m/B VHS.** *GB* Michael Redgrave, Phyllis Calvert, Michael Wilding; ***D:*** Carol Reed.

Kippur **2000** Set during Israel's 1973 Yom Kippur War—named after the Jewish holiday on which Egypt and Syria launched a surprise attack. Director Gitai's (a veteran himself) war drama concerns friends Weinraub (Levo) and Ruso (Ruso), who are in a rush to join their reserve unit. But their unit has already left, so they wind up in the company of Klauzner (Klauzner), a medic, and join a helicoptor rescue squad in evacuating the dead and wounded. It's a striking combination of commitment, tedium, frustration, fear, and disillusionment. Hebrew with subtitles. **117m/C VHS, DVD.** *IS* Liron Levo, Tomer Ruso, Uri Klauzner; ***D:*** Amos Gitai; ***W:*** Amos Gitai, Marie-Jose Sanselme; ***C:*** Renato Berta; ***M:*** Jan Garbarek.

Kira's Reason—A Love Story *En Kaerlighedshistorie* **2001** Uneven depiction of mental illness and a marriage in crisis. Thirtysomethings Kira (Stenegade) and Mads (Mikkelsen) have a seemingly comfortable life with a happy marriage and kids—until Kira has a breakdown and is committed to an institution. Even after returning to her family, Kira's behavior is erratic, disruptive, and sometimes publicly humiliating. Mads continues to stand by his troubled wife but though their love survives, can their lives together? Danish with subtitles. **94m/C VHS, DVD.** *DK* Stine Stengade, Lars Mikkelsen, Sven Wollter; ***D:*** Ole Christian Madsen; ***W:*** Ole Christian Madsen; ***C:*** Jorgen Johansson; ***M:*** Oyvind Ougaard, Cesar Berti.

The Kirlian Witness 🦴 *The Plants Are Watching* **1978 (PG)** A woman uses the power of telepathic communication with house plants to solve her sister's murder. **88m/C VHS.** Nancy Snyder, Joel Colodner, Ted Leplat; ***D:*** Jonathan Sarno.

Kismet 🦴🦴🦴 **1920** Original screen version of the much filmed lavish Arabian Nights saga (remade in '30, '44 and '55). A beggar is drawn into deception and intrigue among Bagdad upper-crusters. Glorious sets and costumes; silent with original organ score. **98m/B VHS.** Otis Skinner, Elinor Fair, Herschel Mayall; ***D:*** Louis Gasnier; ***C:*** Gaetano Antonio "Tony" Gaudio.

Kismet 🦴🦴 **1955** A big-budget Arabian Nights musical drama of a Baghdad street poet who manages to infiltrate himself into the Wazir's harem. The music was adapted from Borodin by Robert Wright and George Forrest. ♫ Fate; Not Since Ninevah; Baubles, Bangles, and Beads; Stranger in Paradise; Bored; Night of My Nights; The Olive Tree; And This Is My Beloved; Sands of Time. **113m/C VHS.** Howard Keel, Ann Blyth, Dolores Gray, Vic Damone; ***D:*** Vincente Minnelli; ***W:*** Charles Lederer, Luther Davis; ***C:*** Joseph Ruttenberg; ***M:*** Andre Previn.

The Kiss 🦴🦴🦴 **1929** Garbo, the married object of earnest young Ayres' lovelorn affection, innocently kisses him nighty night since a kiss is just a kiss. Or so she thought. Utterly misconstrued, the platonic peck sets the stage for disaster, and murder and courtroom anguish follow. French Feyder's direction is stylized and artsy. Garbo's last silent and Ayres' first film. **89m/B VHS.** Greta Garbo, Conrad Nagel, Holmes Herbert, Lew Ayres, Anders Randolf; ***D:*** Jacques Feyder; ***C:*** William H. Daniels.

The Kiss 🦴 **1988 (R)** A kind of "Auntie Mame from Hell" story in which a mysterious aunt visits her teenage niece in New York, and tries to apprentice her to the family business of sorcery, demon possession, and murder. Aunt Felicity's kiss will make you appreciate the harmless cheek-pinching of your own aunt; your evening would be better spent with her, rather than this movie. **98m/C VHS, DVD.** Pamela Collyer, Peter Dvorsky, Joanna Pacula, Meredith Salenger, Mimi Kuzyk, Nicholas Kilbertus, Jan Rubes; ***D:*** Pen Densham; ***W:*** Tom Ropelewski.

Kiss and Be Killed 🦴 1/2 **1991 (R)** Crazy guy with knife cuts short couple's wedding night. Shortchanged widow is mighty miffed. Will she have to return the wedding gifts? **89m/C VHS.** Caroline Ludvik, Crystal Carson, Tom Reilly, Chip Hall, Ken Norton, Jimmy Baio; ***D:*** Tom Milo.

Kiss and Kill 🦴🦴 *Blood of Fu Manchu; Against All Odds* **1968 (R)** Lee returns in his fourth outing as Fu Manchu. This time the evil one has injected beautiful girls with a deadly poison that reacts upon kissing. They are then sent out to seduce world leaders. Not on par with the previous movies, but still enjoyable. Sequel to "Castle of Fu Manchu." **91m/C VHS, DVD.** Christopher Lee, Richard Greene, Shirley Eaton, Tsai Chin, Maria Rohm, Howard Marion-Crawford; ***D:*** Jess (Jesus) Franco.

Kiss and Make Up 🦴🦴 1/2 **1934** Grants stars as suave Dr. Maurice Lamar—a purveyor of beauty creams, fad diets, and cosmetic surgery. He marries his best patient—Eve (Tobin)—without realizing that her beauty really is only skin deep since she's shallow and selfish. Meanwhile, Eve's sweet ex-husband Marcel (Horton) is charmed by the natural beauty of Lamar's loyal secretary Ann (Mack). Still a remarkably prescient, offbeat comedy where Grant winds up with "a" girl but not the "right" girl for a change. **78m/B DVD.** Cary Grant, Helen Mack, Genevieve Tobin, Edward Everett Horton, Lucien Littlefield, Mona Maris; ***D:*** Harlan Thompson; ***W:*** Harlan Thompson, Jane Hinton, George Marion Jr.; ***C:*** Leon Shamroy; ***M:*** Ralph Rainger.

Kiss and Tell 🦴🦴 **1996** Lonely undercover policewoman Jude (Rowell) tries to get a confession from a man suspected of murdering his wife. Becoming attracted to her quarry, Jude's previous relationship with her supervising officer (Craig) also clouds her judgment until Jude isn't sure what she believes. **110m/C DVD.** *GB* Rosie Rowell, Daniel Craig, Peter Howitt, David Bradley, Ralph Ines, Nicola Stephenson; ***D:*** David Richards; ***W:*** Heidi Thomas; ***C:*** Alan Almond; ***M:*** Hal Lindes. **TV**

Kiss & Tell 🦴🦴 **1999 (R)** Self-conscious black comedy about LAPD detective Arquette who's investigating the murder (by carrot) of performance artist Bateman. Naturally, the suspects are as weird as the crime. **90m/C VHS.** Richmond Arquette, Justine Bateman, Heather Graham, Pamela Gidley; ***D:*** Jordan Alan.

A Kiss Before Dying 🦴🦴 **1991 (R)** Botched adaptation of Ira Levin's cunning thriller novel (filmed before in 1956). This flick serves up an exploded head in the first few minutes. So much for subtlety. The highlight is Dillon's chilly role as a murderous opportunist bent on marrying into a wealthy family. Young plays two roles (not very well) as lookalike sisters on his agenda. The ending was hastily reshot and it shows. **93m/C VHS, DVD.** Matt Dillon, Sean Young, Max von Sydow, Diane Ladd, James Russo, Martha Gehman, Ben Browder, Joy Lee, Adam Horovitz; ***D:*** James Dearden; ***W:*** James Dearden. Golden Raspberries '91: Worst Actress (Young), Worst Support. Actress (Young).

Kiss Daddy Goodbye 🦴 1/2 *Revenge of the Zombie; The Vengeful Dead* **1981 (R)** A widower keeps his two children isolated in order to protect their secret telekinetic powers. When he is killed by bikers, the kids attempt to raise him from the dead. **81m/C VHS, DVD.** Fabian, Marilyn Burns, Jon Cedar, Marvin Miller; ***D:*** Patrick Regan.

Kiss Daddy Goodnight 🦴 **1987 (R)** A Danish-made thriller about a beautiful young girl who seduces men, drugs them and takes their money. One man turns the tables on her, however, and decides that she will only belong to him. **89m/C VHS, DVD.** *DK* Uma Thurman, Paul Dillon, Paul Richards, David Brisbin; ***D:*** P.I. Huemer; ***C:*** Bobby Bukowski.

A Kiss for Mary Pickford 🦴🦴 1/2 **1927** A rare, hilarious cinematic oddity, a film formulated from Kuleshov montage techniques from footage of the famous American couple's visit to Russia in 1926, wherein a regular guy tries to win a girl through friendship with the stars. Fairbanks and Pickford didn't know of their role in this film, being spliced in later according to montage theory. **70m/B VHS.** Mary Pickford, Douglas Fairbanks Sr., Igor Ilyinsky; ***D:*** Sergei Komarov.

A Kiss Goodnight 🦴🦴 1/2 **1994 (R)** Natalie (Trickey) has a romp in the sheets with ad exec Kurt (Corley) when regular beau Michael (Moses) ignores her for work. But when Natalie decides to break things off, Kurt won't take no for an answer. **88m/C VHS.** Paula Trickey, Al Corley, Mark Moses, Lawrence Tierney, Brett Cullen, James Karen, Robert Wuhl, Sydney Walsh; ***D:*** Daniel Raskov; ***W:*** Daniel Raskov; ***C:*** Glenn Kershaw.

Kiss Kiss Bang Bang 🦴🦴🦴 1/2 **2005 (R)** Making his directorial debut, Black—the screenwriter responsible for such awesome cinematic machismo as "Lethal Weapon" and "Last Boy Scout"—reinvents crime noir with this hilarious riff on hardboiled detective fiction and vapid LA culture. Harry Lockhart (Downey Jr.) is a two-bit thief who stumbles into an acting audition after a robbery gone wrong. The producers fly him to Hollywood where he takes private eye lessons from a gay PI named Perry (Kilmer) and gets embroiled in a complicated conspiracy involving a dead body and a femme fatale from his past (Monaghan). Kilmer and Downey have never been funnier, thanks to Black's sharp-as-a-laser dialogue, and Monaghan is insanely easy on the eyes. Sam Spade never had it this good. **103m/C DVD, Blu-ray Disc, HD DVD.** *US* Robert Downey Jr., Val Kilmer, Michelle Monaghan, Corbin Bernsen, Dash Mihok, Larry Miller, Shannyn Sossamon, Angela Lindvall, Rockmond Dunbar; ***D:*** Shane Black; ***W:*** Shane Black; ***C:*** Michael Barrett; ***M:*** John Ottman.

Kiss Me a Killer 🦴🦴 **1991 (R)** The ancient thriller plot about a young wife and her lover who scheme to kill her middle-aged husband. It's set in L.A.'s Latino community, but extensive shots of salsa music and ethnic cooking hardly raise this above the mediocre. **91m/C VHS.** Julie Carmen, Robert Beltran, Guy Boyd, Ramon Franco, Charles Boswell; ***D:*** Marcus De Leon; ***W:*** Marcus De Leon.

Kiss Me Deadly 🦴🦴🦴 1/2 **1955** Aldrich's adaptation of Mickey Spillane's private eye tale takes pulp literature high concept. Meeker, as Mike Hammer, is a self-interested rough-and-tumble all-American dick (detective, that is). When a woman to whom he happened to give a ride is found murdered, he follows the mystery straight into a nuclear conspiracy. Aldrich, with tongue deftly in cheek, styles a message through the medium; topsy-turvy camera work and rat-a-tat-tat pacing tell volumes about Hammer, the world he orbits, and that special '50s kind of paranoia. Now a cult fave, it's considered to be the American grandaddy to French New Wave. **105m/B VHS, DVD.** Ralph Meeker, Albert Dekker, Paul Stewart, Wesley Addy, Cloris Leachman, Strother Martin, Marjorie Bennett, Jack Elam, Maxine Cooper, Gaby Rodgers, Nick Dennis, Jack Lambert, Percy Helton; ***D:*** Robert Aldrich; ***W:*** A(lbert) I(saac) Bezzerides; ***C:*** Ernest Laszlo; ***M:*** Frank DeVol. Natl. Film Reg. '99.

Kiss Me Deadly 🦴🦴 **2008 (R)** Ex-spy Jacob Keane (Gant) is pulled away from his boyfriend and back into the espionage game when his former partner Marta (Doherty) suddenly reappears with her memory erased. They have to determine what classified info the villains want and avoid the pair of assassins who are hunting her. **91m/C DVD.** Robert Gant, Shannen Doherty, John Rhys-Davies, Fraser Brown; ***D:*** Ron Oliver; ***W:*** George Schenck, Frank Cardea; ***C:*** Neil Cervin; ***M:*** Claude Foisy. **CABLE**

Kiss Me Goodbye 🦴🦴 **1982 (PG)** Young widow Fields can't shake the memory of her first husband, a charismatic but philandering Broadway choreographer, who's the antithesis of her boring but devoted professor fiance. She struggles with the charming ghost of her first husband, as well as her domineering mother, attempting to understand her own true feelings. Harmless but two-dimensional remake of "Dona Flor and Her Two Husbands." **101m/C VHS, DVD.** Sally Field, James Caan, Jeff Bridges, Paul Dooley, Mildred Natwick, Claire Trevor; ***D:*** Robert Mulligan; ***W:*** Charlie Peters; ***M:*** Ralph Burns, Peter Allen.

Kiss Me, Guido 🦴🦴 1/2 **1997 (R)** Heterosexual and handsome Frankie (Scotti) is a Bronx-born and -raised pizza maker and De Niro wanna-be who's not too bright. Apartment hunting in Manhattan, he thinks an ad listing "GWM" stands for "guy with money" and mistakenly moves in with gay actor Warren (Barrile). Pokes fun at both Italian-American and gay stereotypes without offending or canonizing either group. Vitale and an excellent, if largely unknown, cast inject enough energy and humor to rise above the often predictable story. Low-budget independent sex farce that offers a promising start for first-time filmmaker Vitale. **90m/C VHS, DVD.** Nick Scotti, Anthony Barrile, Craig Chester, Anthony De Sando, Christopher Lawford, Molly Price; ***D:*** Tony Vitale; ***W:*** Tony Vitale; ***C:*** Claudia Raschke; ***M:*** Randall Poster.

Kiss Me Kate 🦴🦴🦴 **1953** A married couple can't separate their real lives from their stage roles in this musical-comedy screen adaptation of Shakespeare's "Taming of the Shrew," based on Cole Porter's Broadway show. Bob Fosse bursts from the screen—particularly if you see the 3-D version—when he does his dance number. ♫ Out of This World; From This Moment On; Wunderbar; So In Love; I Hate Men; Were Thine That Special Face; I've Come To Wive It Wealthily In Padua; Where Is The Life That Late I Led?; Always True To You Darling In My Fashion. **110m/C VHS, DVD.** Kathryn Grayson, Howard Keel, Ann Miller, Tommy (Thomas) Rall, Bob Fosse, Bobby Van, Keenan Wynn, James Whitmore; ***D:*** George Sidney; ***C:*** Charles Rosher; ***M:*** Andre Previn.

Kiss Me, Kill Me 🦴 1/2 *Devil's Witch; Baba Yaga; So Sweet, So Perverse; Cosi Dolce...Cosi Perversa; Baba Yaga—Devil Witch* **1973 (R)** Confused woman is on the run after she may have murdered someone. **91m/C VHS, DVD.** *IT* Carroll Baker, George Eastman, Isabelle DeFunes, Ely Gallo; ***D:*** Corrado Farina; ***W:*** Corrado Farina.

Kiss Me, Stupid! 🦴🦴 **1964 (PG-13)** Once condemned as smut, this lesser Billy Wilder effort now seems no worse than an average TV sitcom. Martin basically plays himself as a horny Vegas crooner stranded in the boondocks. A local songwriter wants Dino to hear his tunes but knows the cad will seduce his pretty wife, so he hires a floozy to pose as the tempting spouse. It gets better as it goes along, but the whole thing suffers from staginess, being an adaptation of an Italian play "L'Ora Della Fantasia" by Anna Bonacci. **126m/B VHS, DVD.** Dean Martin, Kim Novak, Ray Walston, Felicia Farr, Cliff Osmond, Barbara Pepper, Doro Merande, Howard McNear, Henry Gibson, John Fiedler, Mel Blanc; ***D:*** Billy Wilder; ***W:*** Billy Wilder, I.A.L. Diamond; ***C:*** Joseph LaShelle; ***M:*** Andre Previn.

KISS Meets the Phantom of the Park 🦴 1/2 *Attack of the Phantoms* **1978** The popular '70s rock band is featured in this Dr. Jekyll-esque Halloween horror tale, interspersed with musical numbers. **96m/C VHS.** Peter Criss, Ace Frehley, Gene Simmons, Paul Stanley, Anthony Zerbe, Carmine Caridi, Deborah Ryan, John Dennis Johnston, John Lisbon Wood, Lisa Jane Persky, Brion James, Bill Hudson; ***D:*** Gordon Hessler; ***W:*** J. Michael Sherman, Albert (Don) Buday; ***C:*** Robert Caramico; ***M:*** Hoyt Curtin, Fred Karlin.

Kiss My Grits 🦴 **1982 (PG)** A good ole boy hightails it to Mexico with his girlfriend and son, chased by mobsters and the law. **101m/C VHS.** Bruce Davison, Anthony (Tony) Franciosa, Susan George, Bruno Kirby; ***D:*** Jack Starrett.

Kiss of a Killer 🦴🦴 1/2 **1993** O'Toole is a mousy miss living a dead-end life with her nagging mother. But she has a secret—she spends weekends in a hotel, dressed to entice and picking up strangers. Involved in an auto mishap she's aided by a handsome mechanic, who turns out to be a rapist. When he accidentally kills his latest victim, he realizes our mystery woman can identify him and tries to find her. Based on the novel "The Point of Murder" by Margaret Yorke. **93m/C VHS.** Annette O'Toole, Brian Wimmer, Eva Marie Saint, Gregg Henry, Vic Polizos; ***D:*** Larry Elikann; ***W:*** David Warfield. **TV**

Kiss of Death 🦴🦴🦴 **1947** Paroled when he turns state's evidence, Mature must now watch his back constantly. Widmark, in his film debut, seeks to destroy him. Police chief Donlevy tries to help. Filmed on location in New York, this gripping and gritty film is a vision of the most terrifying sort of existence, one where nothing is certain, and everything is dangerous. Excellent. **98m/B VHS, DVD.** Victor Mature, Richard Widmark, Coleen Gray, Brian Donlevy, Karl Malden, Coleen Gray; ***D:*** Henry Hathaway.

Kiss of Death 🦴🦴 **1977** Weird comedy about a shy undertaker's assistant and his attempts at first romance. **80m/C VHS, DVD.** *GB* David Threlfall, John Wheatley, Kay Adshead, Angela Curran; ***D:*** Mike Leigh; ***W:*** Mike Leigh. **TV**

Kiss of Death 🦴🦴 1/2 **1994 (R)** Very loose contemporary remake of the 1947 film noir classic of the same name. Jimmy Kilmartin (Caruso) is a paroled car thief turned informant. He soon finds himself trapped in a web of deceit involving corrupt district attorneys and ruthless hoodlums like Little Junior (Cage, pumped up and playing against type), with no one to trust. Crime drama keeps the far-fetched genre conventions in check until the end. Caruso makes the transition from TV cop on "NYPD Blue" by not straying far from his small screen persona. Cage's standout performance may not be as chilling as Widmark's unforgettable debut in the original, but he's able to convey a level of mercilessness and depth that'll make you wince. **100m/C VHS, DVD.** David Caruso, Nicolas Cage, Samuel L. Jackson, Helen Hunt, Stanley Tucci, Michael Rapaport, Ving Rhames, Anthony Heald, Anne Meara, Hope Davis, Kathryn Erbe, Philip

Baker Hall, Kevin Corrigan, Michael Artura, Jay O. Sanders, Joe Lisi; ***D:*** Barbet Schroeder; ***W:*** Richard Price; ***M:*** Trevor Jones.

Kiss of Fire 🦴🦴 *Claudine's Return* **1998 (R)** Stefano (Dionisi) gets a job as the handyman at a Georgia motel and gets involved with laundress/stripper Claudine (Applegate) in what proves to be a dangerous relationship. And despite her role, Applegate does not get naked. **92m/C VHS, DVD.** Stefano Dionisi, Christina Applegate, Matt Clark, Gabriel Mann, Perry Anzilotti, Tom Nowicki; ***D:*** Antonio Tibaldi; ***W:*** Antonio Tibaldi, Heidi A. Hall; ***C:*** Luca Bigazzi; ***M:*** Michel Colombier. **VIDEO**

Kiss of the Dragon 🦴🦴 ½ **2001 (R)** Li is Chinese super-cop Liu who is sent to Paris to help stop a Chinese drug lord. Once there, he learns that the cop, Richard (Karyo), he was sent to help is actually running the drug ring, and has set Liu up for the dealer's murder. Fonda is the hooker/addict who helps Lui in order to free herself and her daughter from Richard. Spectacular action sequences, as well as Li's martial art skills and charisma more than make up for a pretty lame script which is little more than connective tissue anyway. Besson and Li co-produced the feature debut of director Nahon, who comes from the video/commercials world. **98m/C VHS, DVD, Blu-ray Disc, UMD.** *FR US* Jet Li, Bridget Fonda, Tcheky Karyo, Burt Kwouk; ***D:*** Chris Nahon; ***W:*** Luc Besson, Robert Mark Kamen; ***C:*** Thierry Arbogast; ***M:*** Craig Armstrong.

Kiss of the Spider Woman 🦴🦴🦴 *O Beijo da Mulher Aranha* **1985 (R)** From the novel by Manuel Puig, an acclaimed drama concerning two cell mates in a South American prison, one a revolutionary, the other a homosexual. Literate, haunting, powerful. **119m/C VHS, DVD, Blu-ray Disc.** *BR* William Hurt, Raul Julia, Sonia Braga, Jose Lewgoy, Milton Goncalves, Nuno Leal Maia, Denise Dumont, Antonio Petrim, Miriam Pires, Fernando Torres; ***D:*** Hector Babenco; ***W:*** Leonard Schrader; ***C:*** Rodolfo Sanchez; ***M:*** John Neschling, Wally Badarou. Oscars '85: Actor (Hurt); British Acad. '85: Actor (Hurt); Cannes '85: Actor (Hurt); Ind. Spirit '86: Foreign Film; L.A. Film Critics '85: Actor (Hurt); Natl. Bd. of Review '85: Actor (Hurt), Actor (Julia).

Kiss of the Tarantula 🦴 **1975 (PG)** Teen girl who lives with her family in a mortuary battles inner torment and vents anxiety by releasing her deadly pet spiders on those whom she despises. Eight-legged "Carrie" rip-off. **85m/C VHS, DVD.** Eric Mason; ***D:*** Chris Munger; ***W:*** Warren Hamilton.

Kiss of the Vampire 🦴🦴 ½ *Kiss of Evil* **1962** Newlywed couple is stranded in Bavaria near a villa of vampires and are invited in by its charmingly evil owner. Fortunately, hubby manages to escape and finds a knowledgeable professor who unleashes a horde of bats to rout the bloodsuckers. Properly creepy; producer Hinds used the pseudonym John Elder for his screenplay. **88m/C VHS, DVD.** *GB* Clifford Evans, Noel Willman, Edward De Souza, Jennifer Daniel, Barry Warren, Jacqueline Wallis, Peter Madden, Isobel Black, Vera Cook, Olga Dickie; ***D:*** Don Sharp; ***W:*** John (Anthony Hinds) Elder; ***C:*** Alan Hume; ***M:*** James Bernard.

Kiss or Kill 🦴🦴 **1997 (R)** Thieves/con artists and lovers Nikki (O'Connor) and Al (Day) head out across the Australian desert towards Perth when one of their schemes results in death. Since they've also got a videotape showing football player Zipper Doyle (Langrishe) engaged in pedophile activity, he's on their trail as are a couple of cops. But trouble also seems to follow them—everywhere the duo spend the night a dead body appears the next morning and soon the lovers begin wondering about each other. Quirky characters and fine performances from all concerned, even if the emotional core of the film is somewhat cold. **95m/C VHS.** *AU* Frances O'Connor, Matt(hew) Day, Chris Haywood, Barry Otto, Max Cullen, Andrew S. Gilbert, Barry Langrishe, Jennifer Cluff; ***D:*** Bill Bennett; ***W:*** Bill Bennett; ***C:*** Malcolm McCulloch. Australian Film Inst. '97: Director (Bennett), Film, Film Editing, Sound, Support. Actor (Gilbert); Montreal World Film Fest. '97: Actress (O'Connor).

Kiss Shot 🦴🦴 **1989** Goldberg is a struggling single mother who loses her job but still must make the mortgage payments. She takes a job as a waitress but realizes it isn't going to pay the bills so she tries her hand as a pool hustler. Frantz is the promoter who finances her bets and Harewood, the pool-shooting playboy whose romantic advances are destroying her concentration. **88m/C VHS, DVD.** Whoopi Goldberg, Dennis Franz, Dorian Harewood, David Marciano, Teddy Wilson; ***D:*** Jerry London; ***C:*** Chuy Elizondo; ***M:*** Steve Dorff.

Kiss the Bride 🦴 ½ **2007 (R)** Though Spelling is game, her co-stars don't have the light touch this featherweight gay comedy needs. Bride-to-be Alex runs into an unexpected complication when she meets Matt, her fiance Ryan's best friend from high school. Seems Matt and Ryan were very close indeed (wink, wink) and Matt has decided he should see if those youthful sparks can be rekindled before Ryan walks down the aisle. **100m/C DVD.** Tori Spelling, Philipp Karner, Robert Foxworth, Tess Harper, James O'Shea, Joanna Cassidy, Amber Benson, Steve Sandvoss; ***D:*** C. Jay Cox; ***W:*** Tyler Lieberman; ***C:*** Carl F. Bartels; ***M:*** Ben Holbrook.

Kiss the Girls 🦴🦴 **1997 (R)** After his niece is abducted, forensic psychologist Alex Cross (Freeman) joins the hunt for a lunatic who's kidnapping and collecting successful young women. After doctor Kate McTiernan (Judd), who also happens to be a kickboxer, escapes the sicko's love dungeon, she helps Cross track him down. Borrowing heavily from "Silence of the Lambs" and "Seven," this psycho-killer thriller falls far short of both. Adapted from the novel by James Patterson. **117m/C VHS, DVD.** Morgan Freeman, Ashley Judd, Cary Elwes, Tony Goldwyn, Jay O. Sanders, Bill Nunn, Brian Cox, Alex McArthur, Richard T. Jones, Jeremy Piven, William Converse-Roberts, Gina Ravera, Roma Maffia; ***D:*** Gary Fleder; ***W:*** David Klass; ***C:*** Aaron Schneider; ***M:*** Mark Isham.

Kiss the Night **1987 (R)** An unfortunate hooker falls head over heels for a man she had the pleasure of doing business with. To her chagrin, it is much harder to leave the street than she thought. A dramatic and timely presentation. **99m/C VHS.** Patsy Stephens, Warwick Moss, Gary Aron Cook; ***D:*** James Ricketson.

Kiss the Sky 🦴🦴 **1998 (R)** Suffering from midlife crises, Jeff (Petersen) and Marty (Cole) head off on a business trip to the Philippines. Once there, they decide to abandon their settled lives and families in order to experiment with recapturing their lost youth. In their case, it's by becoming a menage a trois with sexy Oxford grad, Andy (Lee). Provocative but hardly gratuitous. **105m/C VHS, DVD.** William L. Petersen, Gary Cole, Sheryl Lee, Terence Stamp, Patricia Charbonneau, Season Hubley; ***D:*** Roger Young; ***W:*** Eric Lerner; ***C:*** Donald M. Morgan; ***M:*** Patrick Williams.

Kiss Toledo Goodbye 🦴🦴 **2000 (R)** Young man finds out his biological dad is the local head mobster just before pops is rubbed out. The kid inherits the job (which he tries to keep a secret from his fiancee) as well as his father's enemies. **96m/C VHS, DVD.** Michael Rapaport, Christine Taylor, Christopher Walken, Robert Forster, Nancy Allen, Paul Ben-Victor, Bill Smitrovich; ***D:*** Lyndon Chubbuck; ***W:*** Robert Easter; ***C:*** Frank Byers; ***M:*** Phil Marshall. **VIDEO**

Kiss Tomorrow Goodbye 🦴🦴 **1950** A brutal, murderous escaped convict rises to crime-lord status before his inevitable downfall. Based on a novel by Horace McCoy. **102m/B VHS, DVD.** James Cagney, Barbara Payton, Ward Bond, Luther Adler, Helena Carter, Steve Brodie, Rhys Williams; ***D:*** Gordon Douglas.

Kiss Tomorrow Goodbye 🦴🦴 **2000 (R)** Based on 1942's "Moontide" this updated would-be modern noir suffers from unappealing characters. Dustin Yarma (Lea) is an arrogant, hard-partying Hollywood film exec who wakes up on the beach after a night of debauchery to find that his nameless female companion is dead. Suspicious drifter Minnow (McCallany) says he saw Dustin murder the girl in a drunken rage but will take care of the matter—for a price. The price turns out to be Dustin's life as Minnow moves in on his career and his girlfriend, D'Arcy (Wuhrer). Then Dustin discovers things aren't exactly as they seem. Director Priestley plays the small role of Dustin's buddy Jarred. **90m/C VHS, DVD.** Nicholas Lea, Holt McCallany, Kari Wuhrer, Jason Priestley, Philip Casnoff, Jennifer Blanc; ***D:*** Jason Priestley; ***W:*** Ozzie Cheek; ***C:*** Bruce Logan; ***M:*** Harald Kloser. **TV**

The Kiss You Gave Me 🦴🦴 *El Beso Que Me Diste* **2000** Set in 2006, Angela is the star reporter of Teledigital TV Network in Puerto Rico. When her marriage to Armando falls apart, he kidnaps their eight-year-old son Ivan and takes the boy to the U.S. Angela enlists lawyer (and old flame) Pedro to go to the States with her and get the boy back. Based on the novel by Stella Soto. Spanish with subtitles. **90m/C VHS, DVD.** Maricarmen Aviles, Jimmy Navarro, Rene Monclova, Carola Garcia, Ernesto Concepcion, Humberto Gonzales; ***D:*** Sonia Fritz; ***W:*** Sonia Fritz; ***C:*** Augustin Cubano; ***M:*** Miguel Cubano.

Kissed 🦴🦴 **1996 (R)** The subject matter (necrophilia) is sure to give one pause though debut director Stopkewich hardly dwells on the prurient. Sandra Larson (Parker) has been obsessed with death and its rituals since childhood. So as a young adult it seems natural when she gets a job in a funeral home, preparing the bodies for embalming. Only Sandra's obsession leads her to begin making love (shown through a gauzy white light) to the corpses. She does attract the attentions of a very alive medical student, Matt (Outerbridge), who becomes fascinated by Sandra's fetish and determined to make himself as appealing to her as the dead. Adapted from Barbara Gowdy's short story "We So Seldom Look on Love." **78m/C VHS, DVD.** *CA* Molly Parker, Peter Outerbridge, Jay Brazeau; ***D:*** Lynne Stopkewich; ***W:*** Lynne Stopkewich, Angus Fraser; ***C:*** Gregory Middleton; ***M:*** Don MacDonald. Genie '97: Actress (Parker).

Kisses for My President 🦴🦴 ½ **1964** Silly comedy about the first woman elected President and her trials and tribulations. MacMurray is the husband who has to adjust to the protocol of being "First Man." Bergen is miscast, but the other performances are just fine. **113m/C VHS.** Fred MacMurray, Polly Bergen, Arlene Dahl, Edward Andrews, Eli Wallach, Donald May; ***D:*** Curtis Bernhardt.

Kisses in the Dark 🦴🦴 **1997** Four short award-winning films. "Coriolis Effect" finds two daredevil tornado-chasers falling in love. "Solly's Diner" has a vagrant becoming a hero during a diner hold-up. "Looping" finds an egotistic Italian director deciding in the middle of shooting his big-budget Mafia musical that the material isn't worthy of him. "Joe" finds solace in his daily routine in a psych ward when an interloper disturbs his refuge. **75m/C VHS, DVD.** Jennifer Rubin, James Wilder, Dana Ashbrook, Corinne Bohrer, Katherine Wallach, Ronald Guttman, Quentin Tarantino; ***D:*** Larry Hankin, Louis Venosta, Roger Paradiso, Sasha Wolf; ***W:*** Louis Venosta, Roger Paradiso, Sasha Wolf.

Kissin' Cousins 🦴 ½ **1964** Air Force officer on a secluded base in the South discovers a local hillbilly is his double. Presley quickie that includes country tunes such as "Smokey Mountain Boy" and "Barefoot Ballad" as well as the title song. **96m/C VHS, DVD.** Elvis Presley, Arthur O'Connell, Jack Albertson, Glenda Farrell, Pam(ela) Austin, Yvonne Craig, Cynthia Pepper, Donald Woods, Tommy Farrell, Beverly (Hills) Powers; ***D:*** Gene Nelson.

Kissing a Fool 🦴 ½ **1998 (R)** Movie asks the titillating question: Who will smart, pretty Sam marry? The unctuous Schwimmer character, Max, or the sensitive writer guy Max sets up with Sam to test her fidelity? Who cares. Hunt sets up the utterly lame opening premise as Sam's boss, who is throwing her a wedding and explains to guests how Sam and her intended met while the rote triangle scenario plays out in flashback. Schwimmer, as a Chicago sportscaster with a roving eye, plays nicely (and wisely) against type while Lee's novelist Jay, a supposedly close friend of Max, occupies a less gratifying role. Avital has little to do but does is well. **93m/C VHS, DVD.** David Schwimmer, Jason Lee, Mili Avital, Bonnie Hunt, Vanessa Angel, Kari Wuhrer, Frank Medrano, Bitty Schram, Judy Greer; ***D:*** Doug Ellin; ***W:*** Doug Ellin, James Frey; ***C:*** Thomas Del Ruth; ***M:*** Joseph Vitarelli.

The Kissing Bandit 🦴 ½ **1948** A misbegotten MGM musical that's minor Sinatra. Mild-mannered, Boston-bred Ricardo inherits his father's inn in California. When he decides to take it over, he learns that dad was also a thief whose trademark was kissing his female victims. Dad's old gang wants Ricardo to carry on but he's more interested in Theresa (Grayson), the governor's daughter. Ricardo Montalban, Cyd Charisee, and Ann Miller are the dancers performing the number "Dance of Fury," which is the most exciting thing in the flick. **102m/B DVD.** Frank Sinatra, Kathryn Grayson, J. Carrol Naish, Mildred Natwick, Mikhail Rasumny, Billy Gilbert; ***D:*** Laszlo Benedek; ***W:*** Isobel Lennart, John Harding; ***C:*** Robert L. Surtees.

Kissing Jessica Stein 🦴🦴 ½ **2002 (R)** Neurotic, Jewish, and straight Jessica (Westfeldt) is tired of blind dates with loser guys so she decides to response to a personal ad that was placed by Helen (Jurgensen). Much to Jessica's surprise, the two have a lot in common and awkwardly begin a relationship, even though Jessica is skittish when it comes to sex. However, Jessica can't 'fess up to her family about Helen so they have some other issues to work out. Feldshuh, who plays Westfeldt's doting Jewish mama steals the film. **96m/C VHS, DVD.** *US* Jennifer Westfeldt, Heather Juergensen, Tovah Feldshuh, Scott Cohen, Jackie Hoffman, Michael Mastro, Carson Elrod, David Aaron Baker; ***D:*** Charles Herman-Wurmfeld; ***W:*** Jennifer Westfeldt, Heather Juergensen; ***C:*** Lawrence Sher; ***M:*** Marcelo Zarvos.

The Kissing Place 🦴🦴 **1990** A woman who abducted her "son" years ago tracks the boy to New York City to prevent him from finding his biological family. **90m/C VHS.** Meredith Baxter, David Ogden Stiers; ***D:*** Tony Wharmby; ***W:*** Richard Altabef, Cynthia A. Cherbak.

Kissinger and Nixon 🦴🦴 ½ **1996** Intrigue, ambition, and backbiting politics consume the 18 weeks leading up to the signing of the Vietnam peace accords in Paris in January, 1973. Egotistical Kissinger (Silver) is prepared to sacrifice South Vietnam for the sake of his own ambitions (and an end to the conflict) while a distrustful Nixon (Bridges) lurks uneasily in the background. TV docudrama offers little insight; based on Walter Isaacson's biography "Kissinger." **94m/C VHS.** Ron Silver, Beau Bridges, Matt Frewer, Ron White, George Takei, Kenneth Welsh; ***D:*** Daniel Petrie; ***W:*** Lionel Chetwynd; ***M:*** Jonathan Goldsmith.

Kit Carson 🦴🦴 **1940** Frontiersman Kit Carson leads a wagon train to California, fighting off marauding Indians all the way. **97m/B VHS.** Jon Hall, Dana Andrews, Ward Bond, Lynn Bari; ***D:*** George B. Seitz.

Kit Kittredge: An American Girl 🦴🦴🦴 ½ **2008 (G)** In Depression-era Cincinnati, young Kit Kittredge (Breslin) is an aspiring reporter with a penchant for bringing home strays (both animals and people). Tough times hit, and Dad (O'Donnell) is forced to seek work elsewhere while Mom (Ormond) and Kit grow vegetables and take in a colorful cast of boarders to help pay the bills. A crime spree hits town, and Kit and company set out defend a group of hobo suspects and find the real criminals, uncovering an even bigger plot than they imagined. Squeaky-clean minus any cloying sugar-sweet subtext adds up to worthwhile family viewing. First American Girl feature film, based on a doll in the product line. **100m/C DVD.** *US* Abigail Breslin, Julia Ormond, Chris O'Donnell, Joan Cusack, Madison Davenport, Jane Krakowski, Zach Mills, Max Thieriot, Stanley Tucci, Wallace Shawn, Willow Smith, Colin Mochrie, Glenne Headley; ***D:*** Patricia Rozema; ***W:*** Ann Peacock; ***C:*** David Boyd, Julie Rogers; ***M:*** Joseph Vitarelli.

Kitchen Privileges 🦴 ½ *Housebound* **2000 (R)** Rape victim Marie (Wressnig) now suffers from agoraphobia and hasn't left her house in a year. Still, she didn't take down her roommate-wanted sign and agrees to rent to chef Tom (Sarsgaard), who tempts her with gourmet meals. However, Tom's oddly secretive, and paranoid Marie becomes convinced he's the L.A. serial killer currently in the news. Must be all those sharp knives he's so good with. Not a horror or suspense flick despite the premise and not very interesting either. **89m/C DVD.** Peter Sarsgaard, Angeline Ball, Liz Stauber, Ann Magnuson, Katharina Wressnig, Geoffrey Lower; ***D:*** Mari Kornhauser; ***W:*** Mari Kornhauser; ***C:*** Garrett Fisher; ***M:*** Mark Binder.

Kitchen Stories 🦴🦴 *Salmer fra Kjokkenet* **2003** Subversive Scandinavian comedy set in the 1950s. A number of scientific observers from Sweden's Home Research Institute are sent to collect data from the homes of confirmed bachelors living in the rural community of Landstad, Norway. The idea is to track domestic habits and then standardize the average household kitchen for maximum efficiency. Folke (Norstrom) is sent to the tiny home of codger Isak (Calmeyer), who initially makes things as difficult as possible. The men slowly begin to bond even as the study begins to fall apart. Swedish and Norwegian with subtitles. **95m/C DVD.** *NO SW* Bjorn Floberg, Reine Brynolfsson, Joachim Calmeyer, Tomas Norstrom; ***D:*** Bent Hamer; ***W:*** Bent Hamer, Jorgen Bergmark; ***C:*** Philip Ogaard; ***M:*** Hans Mathisen.

The Kitchen Toto 🦴🦴🦴 **1987 (PG-13)** Set in 1950 Kenya as British rule was being threatened by Mau Mau terrorists. A young black boy is torn between the British for whom he works and the terrorists who want him to join them. Complex and powerful story of the Kenyan freedom crusade. **96m/C VHS.** *GB* Bob Peck, Phyllis Logan, Robert Urquhart, Edward Judd, Edwin Mahinda, Kirsten Hughes; ***D:*** Harry Hook; ***W:*** Harry Hook; ***C:*** Roger Deakins; ***M:*** John Keane.

The Kite Runner 🦴🦴🦴 ½ **2007 (PG-13)** Amir and Hassan spend their days flying kites in a safe and peaceful Afghanistan, before it descended into war and terror. But after secretly witnessing Hussan's brutal assault from neighborhood bullies, Amir turns to shame and eventual resentment. Hussan and his father leave the country, and the two friends never reconcile. Over the next twenty years Afghanistan is torn apart by war, and Amir, now living in the U.S., continues to struggle with his past, until an urgent phone call opens a window for his redemption. Majority of the story focuses on the boys, with each showing incredible range and emotion. A realistic and moving experience, based on the popular novel by Khaled Hosseini. **122m/C DVD.** *US* Khalid Abdalla, Homayon Ershadi, Shaun Toub, Zekiria Ebrahimi, Ahmad Khan Mahmoodzada; ***D:*** Marc Forster; ***W:*** David Benioff; ***C:*** Roberto Schaefer; ***M:*** Alberto Iglesias.

Kitten with a Whip 🦴🦴 ½ **1964** Whatever the film's original intentions, it's now become pure camp. Jody (Ann-Margaret) is a juvenile delinquent who's broken out of a girls' reformatory and breaks into the home of wannabe politician David Patton (Forsythe), who's separated from his wife. Jody works her considerable wiles and soon Patton's life is filled with wild parties, rampant teen lust, and violence. Too bad it wasn't filmed in the lurid color it deserved. Based on the book by Wade Miller. **84m/B VHS.** Ann-Margret, John Forsythe, Peter Brown, Patricia Barry, Richard Anderson, Diane Sayer, Ann Doran, Patrick Whyte, Audrey Dalton, Leo Gordon; ***D:*** Douglas Heyes; ***W:*** Douglas Heyes; ***C:*** Joseph Biroc.

Kitty and the Bagman 🦴🦴 **1982 (R)** A comedy about two rival madames who ruled Australia in the 1920s. **95m/C VHS.** *AU* Liddy Clark; ***D:*** Donald Crombie.

Kitty Foyle 🦴🦴🦴 **1940** From the novel by Christopher Morley, Rogers portrays the white-collar working girl whose involvement with a married man presents her with both romantic and social conflicts. **108m/B VHS, DVD.** Ginger Rogers, Dennis Morgan, James Craig, Gladys Cooper, Ernest Cossart, Eduardo Ciannelli; ***D:*** Sam Wood. Oscars '40: Actress (Rogers).

The Klansman 🦴 *Burning Cross; KKK* **1974 (R)** Race relations come out on the short end in this film about a sheriff trying to keep the lid on racial tensions in a southern town. Even the big-name cast can't save what comes off as a nighttime soaper rather than a serious drama. **112m/C VHS, DVD.** Lee Marvin, Richard Burton, Cameron Mitchell, Lola Falana, Luciana Paluzzi, Linda Evans, O.J. Simpson; ***D:*** Terence Young; ***W:*** Samuel Fuller.

Klepto 🦴🦴 **2003** Emily (Bishop) is a kleptomaniac. When ex-con/department store security guard Nick (Garcia) catches her stealing on camera, he decides to use Emily's talents to further a drug deal so that he can get enough money together to open his own private security business. Naturally, things don't go as planned. Okay crime thriller that's rough around the edges. **82m/C DVD.** *US* Jsu Garcia, Leigh Taylor-Young, Henry Czerny, Michael Nouri, Meredith Bishop; ***D:*** Thomas Trail; ***W:*** Thomas Trail, Ethan Gross; ***C:*** Peter Rieveschl; ***M:*** David DeLaski.

Kleptomania 🦴 ½ **1994 (R)** Socialite meets a runaway and discoers they're both kleptomaniacs. **90m/C VHS.** Amy Irving, Patsy Kensit, Victor Garber; ***D:*** Don Boyd; ***W:*** Don Boyd.

Klimt 🦴 ½ **2006** Unwieldy and unenlightening biopic of Austrian artist Gustav Klimt (Malkovich) that starts with him on his deathbed (in 1918), hallucinating as he's dying from syphilis. Jumps back to 1900 where Klimt scandalizes proper Viennese society with his fin-de-siecle style. Klimt also has a lot of mistresses, including Parisian muse Lea (Burrows), who highlight the eroticism of his work. English, German, and French with subtitles. **97m/C DVD.** *AT GB FR GE* John Malkovich, Saffron Burrows, Stephen (Dillon) Dillane, Nikolai Kinski, Veronica Ferres; ***D:*** Raul Ruiz; ***C:*** Ricardo Aronovich; ***M:*** Jorge Arriagada.

Klondike Annie 🦴🦴 ½ **1936** West stars as a woman on the lam for a murder (self-defense) who heads out for the Yukon aboard McLaglen's ship. He falls for her, finds out about her problems, and helps her with a scam to pass herself off as a missionary, only she begins to take her saving souls seriously (although in her own risque style). **77m/B VHS, DVD.** Mae West, Victor McLaglen, Philip Reed, Helen Jerome Eddy, Harry Beresford, Harold Huber, Conway Tearle, Esther Howard; ***D:*** Raoul Walsh; ***W:*** Mae West; ***C:*** George T. Clemens.

Klondike Fever 🦴 ½ *Jack London's Klondike Fever* **1979 (PG)** Join the young Jack London as he travels from San Francisco to the Klondike fields during the Great Gold Rush of 1898. **118m/C VHS, DVD.** Rod Steiger, Angie Dickinson, Lorne Greene; ***D:*** Peter Carter; ***M:*** Hagood Hardy.

Klute 🦴🦴🦴 ½ **1971 (R)** A small-town policeman (Sutherland) comes to New York in search of a missing friend and gets involved with a prostitute/would-be actress (Fonda) being stalked by a killer. Intelligent, gripping drama. **114m/C VHS, DVD.** Jane Fonda, Donald Sutherland, Charles Cioffi, Roy Scheider, Rita Gam, Jean Stapleton; ***D:*** Alan J. Pakula; ***W:*** Andy Lewis, Dave Lewis; ***C:*** Gordon Willis; ***M:*** Michael Small. Oscars '71: Actress (Fonda); Golden Globes '72: Actress—Drama (Fonda); N.Y. Film Critics '71: Actress (Fonda); Natl. Soc. Film Critics '71: Actress (Fonda).

The Klutz 🦴🦴 **1973** A bumbling fool, on the way to visit his girlfriend, becomes accidentally embroiled in a bank robbery and other ridiculous mishaps. Light French comedy; dubbed. **87m/C VHS.** *FR* Claude Michaud, Louise Portal, Guy Provost; ***D:*** Pierre Rose.

Km. 0 🦴🦴 ½ *Kilometer Zero* **2000 (R)** Good-natured romantic comedy takes its title from the marker in Madrid's Puerta del Sol plaza that designates the spot from which all road travel is measured. It's a popular meeting place as this mixed bag of stories show. Actress Silvia (Pons) forgets she's to meet her sister's friend, Pedro (Fuentes), and Pedro mistakes hooker Tatiana (Matilla) for Silvia. Tatiana thinks Pedro is her new client, but that's actually virginal Sergio (San Juan), who's comforted instead by kindly gay Maximo (del Rio). Lonely Benjamin (Garcia) is mistaken for the Internet date of hottie Bruno (Ullate) and neglected wife Marga (Velasco) finds her meeting with escort Miguel (Cabrero) doesn't go as planned. Amor in all its follies. Spanish with subtitles. **108m/C DVD.** *SP* Carlos Fuentes, Merce Pons, Georges Corraface, Elisa Matilla, Armando Del Rio, Jesus Cabrero, Tristan Ulloa, Alberto San Juan, Concha Velasco, Victor Ullate Jr., Miguel Garcia; ***D:*** Juan Luis Iborra, Yolanda Garcia Serrano; ***W:*** Juan Luis Iborra, Yolanda Garcia Serrano; ***C:*** Angel Luis Fernandez; ***M:*** Joan Bibiloni.

The Knack 🦴🦴🦴 *The Knack...and How to Get It* **1965** Amusing, fast-paced adaptation of the play by Ann Jellicoe. Schoolteacher Crawford is baffled by his tenant Brooks' extreme luck with the ladies so Brooks decides to teach him the "knack" of picking up women. Crawford promptly falls for the first woman (Tushingham) he meets. Swinging London at its most mod. **84m/B VHS, DVD.** *GB* Michael Crawford, Ray Brooks, Rita Tushingham, Donal Donnelly; ***D:*** Richard Lester; ***W:*** Charles Wood; ***C:*** David Watkin; ***M:*** John Barry.

Knife in the Head 🦴🦴 *Messer Im Kopf* **1978** Biogeneticist Berthold Hoffman (Ganz) is meeting his wife (Winkler) at the left-wing youth centre where she works when there's a police raid and Berthold is shot in the head. He awakens in the hospital having lost both his memory and all physical co-ordination. Determined to battle his disabilities, Berthold also becomes the pawn in a political game between the police and political dissidents. In German with English subtitles. **108m/C VHS.** *GE* Bruno Ganz, Angela Winkler, Hans Honig, Hans Brenner, Udo Samel, Carla Egerer; ***D:*** Reinhard Hauff; ***W:*** Peter Schneider.

Knife in the Water 🦴🦴🦴🦴 *Noz w Wodzie* **1962** A journalist, his wife and a hitchhiker spend a day aboard a sailboat. Sex and violence can't be far off. Tense psychological drama. Served as director Polanski's debut. In Polish with English subtitles. **94m/B VHS, DVD.** *PL* Leon Niemczyk, Jolanta Umecka, Zygmunt Malandowicz; ***D:*** Roman Polanski; ***W:*** Jakub Goldberg, Jerzy Skolimowski, Roman Polanski; ***C:*** Jerzy Lipman; ***M:*** Krzysztof Komeda.

Knight and Day **2010** A blind date leads unlucky-in-love June (Diaz) to super spy Milner (Cruise) and a worldwide adventure to protect a powerful new type of battery (eco-responsible, we assume). Also, June has to placate younger sister April (Grace), who's expecting her sibling to at least show up at her wedding. **m/C DVD.** *US* Cameron Diaz, Tom Cruise, Peter Sarsgaard, Maggie Grace, Jordi Molla, Viola Davis, Paul Franklin Dano, Marc Blucas; ***D:*** James Mangold; ***W:*** Scott Frank; ***C:*** Phedon Papamichael.

A Knight in Camelot 🦴🦴 ½ **1998** Oft told Mark Twain tale this time finds computer expert Vivien (Goldberg) conducting an experiment that transports her back to medieval England and the court of King Arthur (York). Lucky for Viv, she's travelling with her laptop, unluckily the kingly court think the tart-tongued woman is a witch. Bossy Vivien makes Merlin (Richardson) jealous and antagonizes everyone until lessons are learned by all. Engaging fluff. **88m/C VHS.** Whoopi Goldberg, Michael York, Amanda Donohoe, Ian Richardson, Robert Addie, Simon Fenton, Paloma Baeza, James Coombes; ***D:*** Roger Young; ***W:*** Joe Wiesenfeld; ***C:*** Elemer Ragalyi; ***M:*** Patrick Williams. **TV**

Knight Moves 🦴🦴 **1993 (R)** Suspenseful thriller about a series of murders which take place at an international resort where a championship chess match is underway. The prime suspect is a chess master who has an unlikely affair with a beautiful police psychologist called in to decipher the mind of the murderer. Filmed in the Pacific Northwest. **105m/C VHS, DVD.** Christopher Lambert, Diane Lane, Tom Skerritt, Daniel Baldwin; ***D:*** Carl Schenkel; ***W:*** Brad Mirman; ***C:*** Dietrich Lohmann; ***M:*** Anne Dudley.

Knight Without Armour 🦴🦴🦴 **1937** A journalist opposed to the Russian monarchy falls in love with the daughter of a czarist minister in this classic romantic drama. **107m/B VHS.** *GB* Marlene Dietrich, Robert Donat; ***D:*** Jacques Feyder; ***C:*** Harry Stradling Sr.; ***M:*** Miklos Rozsa.

Knightriders 🦴🦴 ½ **1981 (R)** The story of a troupe of motorcyclists who are members of a traveling Renaissance Fair and look and act like modern-day Knights of the Round Table. Their battles center around who is the bravest and strongest, and who deserves to be king. **145m/C VHS, DVD.** Ed Harris, Gary Lahti, Tom Savini, Amy Ingersoll; ***D:*** George A. Romero; ***W:*** George A. Romero; ***C:*** Michael Gornick; ***M:*** Donald Rubinstein.

Knights 🦴 ½ **1993 (R)** In a futuristic wasteland a young martial-arts warrior (Long) and a cyborg (Kristofferson) team up to battle rebel cyborgs that have discovered a new source of fuel—human blood. **89m/C VHS.** Kathy Long, Kris Kristofferson, Lance Henriksen, Scott Paulin, Gary Daniels; ***D:*** Albert Pyun; ***W:*** Albert Pyun.

Knights & Emeralds 🦴 ½ **1987 (PG)** Cross-cultural rivalries and romances develop between members of two high school marching bands in a British factory town as the national band championships draw near. **90m/C VHS.** *GB* Christopher Wild, Beverly (Hills) Powers, Warren Mitchell; ***D:*** Ian Emes; ***M:*** Colin Towns.

Knights of Bloodsteel 🦴 **2009** Muddled and dull fantasy flick with elves, goblins, and humans forced to work together when evil Dragon Eye (Gibbon) tries to grab all of Mirabilis' supply of the magical ore bloodsteel by gaining control of the Crucible. Sorcerer Tesselink (Lloyd) knows the only way to stop that from happening is through four warrior knights—Serragoth (Elliott), Perfidia (Malthe), Adric (Jacot), and Ber-Lak (Viergever). The makeup effects on the humans are decent enough but the CGI dragons look silly. **175m/C DVD. CABLE**

Knights of the City 🦴 **1985 (R)** Miami street gangs fight each other over their "turf." One leader decides to opt out, using music. ♫Let the Music Play; Cry of the City; Jailhouse Rap; T.K. and Jessie Rap; Kurtis Blow Rap; Bounce; My Part of Town; Can You Feel It; Love Goes Up and Down. **87m/C VHS.** Nicholas (Nick) Campbell, John Mengatti, Wendy Barry, Stoney Jackson, Janine Turner, Michael Ansara; ***D:*** Leon Isaac Kennedy, Dominic Orlando; ***W:*** Leon Isaac Kennedy.

Knights of the Range 🦴 ½ **1940** Vintage western. **66m/B VHS.** Russell Hayden, Victor Jory, Jean Parker, Britt Wood, J. Farrell MacDonald, Eddie Dean; ***D:*** Lesley Selander.

Knights of the Round Table 🦴🦴 ½ **1953** The story of the romantic triangle between King Arthur, Sir Lancelot, and Guinevere during the civil wars of 6th-century England. **106m/C VHS, DVD.** Robert Taylor, Ava Gardner, Mel Ferrer, Anne Crawford, Felix Aylmer, Stanley Baker; ***D:*** Richard Thorpe; ***C:*** Frederick A. (Freddie) Young; ***M:*** Miklos Rozsa.

Knights of the South Bronx 🦴🦴 ½ **2005 (PG)** Middle-aged and recently unemployed, Richard Mason (Danson) decides to return to teaching and works at an inner-city school with fourth-graders. He begins using chess to motivate his students and finds them responding—and becoming champions. Based on a true story and an ongoing project that uses chess as an educational tool. **90m/C DVD.** Ted Danson, Keke Palmer, Antonio Ortiz, Malcolm David Kelly, Yucini Diaz; ***D:*** Allen Hughes; ***W:*** Dianne Houston, Jamal Joseph; ***C:*** Derick Underschultz; ***M:*** Stephen Endelman. **CABLE**

A Knight's Tale 🦴🦴 ½ **2001 (PG-13)** Peasant squire William Thatcher (hunky Ledger) takes the identity of his recently deceased master in 14th-century France so that he may enter the jousting tournaments, which are only open to nobility. He also falls in love with Jocelyn (newcomer Sossamon), a noble lady who would be out of his league given his lowly birth. Count Adhemar (Sewell) is the bad guy rival and a young Geoffrey Chaucer (Bettany), pre-"Canterbury Tales," aids William. The soundtrack is strictly contemporary and filled with anthem rock—depending on your tolerance it's either weirdly complementary or a complete distraction. The movie's strictly popcorn entertainment for the teen set. **132m/C VHS, DVD.** *US* Heath Ledger, Mark Addy, Rufus Sewell, Shannyn Sossamon, Paul Bettany, Laura Fraser, Christopher Cazenove, Alan Tudyk, James Purefoy; ***D:*** Brian Helgeland; ***W:*** Brian Helgeland; ***C:*** Richard Greatrex; ***M:*** Carter Burwell.

Knives of the Avenger 🦴 ½ *Viking Massacre; I Coltelli Del Vendicatore* **1965** Brutal ax-bearing Vikings ruin the days of hundreds in this primitive story of courage and desperation. John Hold is the pseudonym for director Mario Bava. **85m/C VHS, DVD.** *IT* Cameron Mitchell, Elissa Pichelli, Luciano Pollentin, Fausto Tozzi, Giacomo "Jack" Rossi-Stuart; *D:* Mario Bava; *W:* Mario Bava, Alberto Liberati, Giorgio Simonelli; *M:* Marcello Giombini.

Knock Off ✓✓ **1998 (R)** As if anyone really cares whether the plot makes any sense (no) but a lot of booty is certainly kicked. Marcus Ray (Van Damme) and Tommy Hendricks (Schneider) are partners in a Hong Kong business that manufactures designer jeans. Marcus was once involved in the shady fashion "knock-off" business and still knows people in low places, where he hears about a Russian mob plot to sell bombs to terrorists. Oh yeah, seems Tommy has a little secret too—he's actually working undercover for the CIA. It's action schlock and you won't mind a bit. **91m/C VHS, DVD.** Jean-Claude Van Damme, Rob Schneider, Lela Rochon, Paul Sorvino, Michael Wong, Carman Lee, Wyman Wong; *D:* Tsui Hark; *W:* Steven E. de Souza; *C:* Arthur Wong Ngok Tai; *M:* Ron Mael, Russell Mael.

Knock on Any Door ✓✓ **1949** A young hoodlum from the slums is tried for murdering a cop. He is defended by a prominent attorney who has known him from childhood. **100m/B VHS.** Humphrey Bogart, John Derek, George Macready; *D:* Nicholas Ray; *W:* Daniel Taradash, John Monks Jr.; *C:* Burnett Guffey.

Knock Outs ✓ **1992** Samantha not only loses her shirt at a sorority strip poker marathon but she loses her tuition money to a gang of biker chicks. Then Samantha and a bevy of bikini-clad friends decide to pose for a swimsuit calendar to earn some cash but are secretly videotaped in the nude by some local sleaze promoters. Tired of being taken advantage of these lovelies take up martial arts and challenge their nefarious girl biker rivals to a winner-take-all wrestling match, not forgetting about the purveyors of the not-so-secret videotape. **90m/C VHS, DVD.** Chona Jason, Cindy Rome, Brad Zutaut; *D:* John Bowen.

Knockaround Guys ✓✓ ½ **2001 (R)** Matty (Pepper), the son of mobster Benny Chains (Hopper), finds it difficult to find normal work due to his notorious heritage. He pesters his dad to give him a chance, and with the backing of his uncle Teddy (Malkovich) is given an assignment to pick up a bag of cash in Spokane. His unreliable pal Johnny Marbles (Green) botches the job by losing the loot in a rural Wyoming town. Matty is forced to call in friends Chris (Davoli) and Taylor (Diesel) as muscle to deal with a couple of skate punks and a crooked sheriff (Noonan). Collected dust on the shelf for two years at New Line until executives noticed the cash that Diesel's "XXX" was making. **93m/C VHS, DVD.** *US* Barry Pepper, Seth Green, Dennis Hopper, Vin Diesel, Andrew Davoli, John Malkovich, Tom Noonan; *D:* Brian Koppelman, David Levien; *W:* Brian Koppelman, David Levien; *C:* Tom Richmond; *M:* Clint Mansell.

Knocked Up ✓✓ ½ **2007 (R)** Alison Scott (Heigl) is an ambitious blonde entertainment show producer who celebrates her promotion by getting drunk. This makes teddy-bearish chronic slacker Ben (Rogen) look appealing and they hook up—much to his amazement. And hers, when she winds up pregnant. Ben's initially horrified when she decides to have the baby and expects some type of commitment from him. They bond cute, although the situation remains uncertain, with Ben's equally clueless stoner buds and Alison's control-freak married sister Debbie (Mann) offering opinions and running commentary. Apatow has an ear for just the right line and pop-culture reference and knows how to cast his flicks to have quirky appeal. **132m/C DVD, HD DVD.** *US* Katherine Heigl, Seth Rogen, Leslie Mann, Paul Rudd, Tim Bagley, Jay Baruchel, Jonah Hill, Alan Tudyk, J.P. Manoux, B.J. Novak, Kristen Wiig, Harold Ramis, Martin Starr, Craig Robinson; *D:* Judd Apatow; *W:* Judd Apatow; *C:* Eric Alan Edwards; *M:* Loudon Wainwright III, Joe Henry.

Knocking on Death's Door ✓✓ **1999 (R)** Newlyweds Bloom and Rowe are students of the supernatural and head to a Maine town in order to document the ghosts haunting creepy Hillside House. Their investigation leads them to even more creepy doctor Carradine. Actually filmed in Ireland. **92m/C VHS, DVD.** David Carradine, Brian Bloom, Kimberly Rowe, John Doe; *D:* Mitch Marcus. **VIDEO**

Knocks at My Door ✓✓ *Golpes a Mi Puerta* **1993** A small Latin American town is in political turmoil, with military patrols making a brutal search for a rebel fugitive. The fugitive seeks refuge in the home of two Catholic nuns, Sister Ana (Oddo) and Sister Ursula (Escobar), who theoretically are protected by the Church. Ana knows the young man will be tortured and executed but when a neighbor betrays his presence, not only is he captured but Sister Ana is arrested. To save her own life Ana must sign a paper claiming the young man threatened her with a gun but will her religious faith transcend political expediencies? Adapted from a play by Gene; Spanish with subtitles. **105m/C VHS.** *VZ* Veronica Oddo, Elba Escobar; *D:* Alejandro Saderman; *W:* Juan Carlos Gene; *C:* Adriano Moreno; *M:* Julio D'Escrivan.

Knots ✓ **2005 (R)** Troubled married couple calls it quits when they turn to a seductive lawyer to sort things out. Meanwhile, one of the hubby's friends loses his girlfriend, while another can't even get anything going. A fizzling comedy that can't drive home the punchlines, so it turns to absurd "shocks" hoping to kickstart a reaction. **93m/C VHS, DVD.** Scott Cohen, John Stamos, Michael Leydon Campbell, Annabeth Gish, Tara Reid, KaDee Strickland, Paulina Porizkova; *D:* Guy Lombardo; *W:* Guy Lombardo; *C:* Michael Fimognari; *M:* Joseph Saba. **VIDEO**

Knowing ✓ **2009 (PG-13)** History professor Ted Myles (Cage) winds up with a mysterious page filled with seemingly random numbers. He soon discovers that the numbers represent every major disaster of the last 50 years with frightening accuracy. And, naturally, he also learns that he is part of the enigma, and the only one who can prevent further catastrophes, the last being the end of the world. Dark, dreary, sci-fi, quasi-religious, peri-apocalyptic pabulum is so bad, you will wish for the world to end rather than endure another painful minute. Various aspects make this flick laughable, including Cage, as usual, taking himself way too seriously and the movie opening with a flaming moose running in slow motion (seriously). **121m/C DVD.** *US* Nicolas Cage, Rose Byrne, Ben Mendelsohn, Chandler Canterbury, Lara Robinson, Nadia Townsend; *D:* Alex Proyas; *W:* Juliet Snowden, Stiles White, Ryne Pearson; *C:* Simon Duggan; *M:* Marco Beltrami.

Knute Rockne: All American ✓✓✓ *A Modern Hero* **1940** Life story of Notre Dame football coach Knute Rockne, who inspired many victories with his powerful speeches. Reagan, as the dying George Gipp, utters that now-famous line, "Tell the boys to win one for the Gipper." **96m/B VHS, DVD.** Ronald Reagan, Pat O'Brien, Gale Page, Donald Crisp, John Qualen; *D:* Lloyd Bacon. Natl. Film Reg. '97.

Kojak: The Belarus File ✓✓ **1985** The bald-headed detective of prime-time TV fame searches for a neo-Nazi who is killing Holocaust survivors in New York. **95m/C VHS.** Telly Savalas, Suzanne Pleshette, Max von Sydow, George Savalas; *D:* Robert Markowitz. **TV**

Kojiro ✓✓✓ **1967** A sprawling epic by prolific Japanese director Inagaki about a dashing rogue's bid for power in feudal times. With English subtitles. **152m/C VHS.** *JP* Kikunosuke Onoe, Tatsuya Nakadai; *D:* Hiroshi Inagaki.

Kolberg ✓✓ *Burning Hearts* **1945** The true story of a Prussian town heroically withstanding Napoleon. Produced by Joseph Goebbels in the last days of the Third Reich, it is best remembered as the film whose expensive production and momentous use of real German soldiers, supplies, and ammunition eventually helped to fell the Axis war machine. In German with English subtitles. **118m/C VHS.** *GE* Kristina Soderbaum, Heinrich George, Horst Caspar, Paul Wegener; *D:* Veit Harlan.

Kolobos ✓ **1999** Kyra and her fellow actors report to a remote filming location only to discover it's all a set-up. They've been lured into a fight for survival by a mutilated maniac—or have they? Low-budget hardcore gore. **87m/C VHS, DVD.** Amy Weber, Promise LeMarco, Linnea Quigley; *D:* Daniel Liatowitsch, David Todd Ocvirk. **VIDEO**

Kolya ✓✓✓ **1996 (PG-13)** Set in the late '80s, just before the Velvet Revolution ended Soviet domination of Czechoslovakia, womanizing Prague cellist Louka (Sverak) agrees to marry (for money) the Russian Klara (Safrankova) who wants Czech papers. She soon clears out to join her lover in Berlin and Louka finds himself saddled with her five-year-old son, Kolya (Chaliman). Grumpy Louka isn't obvious dad material and they don't even speak the same language but the kid (who's adorable without being cloying) manages to worm his way into his new life. Czech with subtitles or dubbed. **105m/C VHS, DVD.** *CZ* Zdenek Sverak, Andrej Chalimon, Libuse Safrankova; *D:* Jan Sverak; *W:* Zdenek Sverak; *C:* Vladimir Smutny; *M:* Ondrej Soukup. Oscars '96: Foreign Film; Golden Globes '97: Foreign Film.

Komodo ✓ ½ **1999 (PG-13)** Komodo dragons are pretty impressive in the wild but are they really scary? This low-budgeter tries to assure you that at least these animatronic/computer-generated versions are. The displaced lizards are breeding on an island off the North Carolina coast where teen Patrick (Zegers) and his aunt (Landis) have unwisely ventured. **85m/C VHS, DVD.** *AU* Kevin Zegers, Nina Landis, Jill(ian) Hennessey, Paul Gleeson, Billy Burke; *D:* Michael Lantieri; *W:* Hans Bauer, Craig Mitchell; *C:* David Burr; *M:* John Debney.

Konrad **1985** Konrad, an "instant" child made in a factory, is accidentally delivered to an eccentric woman. The factory wants him back when the mistake is discovered, but Konrad stands up against it. Includes a viewers' guide. Part of the "Wonderworks" series. **110m/C VHS.** Ned Beatty, Polly Holliday, Max Wright, Huckleberry Fox; *D:* Nell Cox; *W:* Malcolm Marmorstein.

Kontroll ✓✓✓ *Control* **2003 (R)** Hungary's claustrophobic, dimly fluorescent lit subways employ "kontrollers"—ticket inspectors roaming train to train without much inspiration, not many friends, and zero sunlight. Bulscu (Csanyi) is a kontroller stuck in endless catacomb searching for meaning and trying to fill his quota. Then one day a lovely young something happens to catch his eye. Just his luck, that same day he manages to catch the eye of a hooded killer stalking the trains. First time director Antal does a bang-up job on a limited budget. There's no digital effects, no bluescreens, no bungees, and that's precisely why it's so effective. Watching actors jump from train to train and narrowly avoid death looks much more real when it is real. **106m/C DVD.** *HU* Sandor Csanyi, Lajos Kovacs, Sandor Badar, Csaba Pindroch, Zsolt Nagy, Eszter Balla, Bence Matyasi, Szabo Gyozo, Balazs Mihalyfi; *D:* Nimrod Antal; *W:* Nimrod Antal; *C:* Gyula Pados; *M:* NEO.

Korczak ✓✓✓ **1990** Based on the life of Dr. Janusz Korczak, an outspoken critic of the Nazis, who ran the Jewish orphanage in Warsaw, Poland, and accompanied 200 children to to the Treblinka concentration camp. Harshly poetic film quietly details Polish resistance to the Nazi terror. Criticized for end scenes of the children romping in the countryside, implying that they were somehow freed—since the director did not want to show the children actually entering the gas chambers, he used this allegory to imply that their souls were freed. In Polish with English subtitles. **118m/C VHS.** *PL* Wojciech Pszoniak, Ewa Dalkowska, Piotr Kozlowski, Marzena Trybala, Wojciech Klata, Adam Siemion; *D:* Andrzej Wajda; *W:* Agnieszka Holland.

Korea Patrol ✓ ½ **1947** South Korean scout Kim (Fong) is charged with leading a group of UN soldiers through hostile territory in order to destroy a vital enemy bridge. The small troop is made smaller as they're killed off, and soon only three are left to carry out the orders. Stock newsreel footage makes for a documentary feel. **59m/B DVD.** Richard Emory, Al Eben, Benson Fong, Sung Li; *D:* Max Nosseck; *W:* Walter Shenson, Kenneth G. Brown; *M:* Alexander Gerens.

Koroshi ✓ ½ **1967** Secret Agent John Drake is dispatched to Hong Kong to disband a secret society who is killing off international political figures. **100m/C VHS.** Patrick McGoohan, Kenneth Griffith, Yoko Tani; *D:* Michael Truman, Peter Yates.

Kostas ✓✓ **1979 (R)** A migrant Greek taxi driver romantically pursues a wealthy Australian divorcee in England. **88m/C VHS.** Takis Emmanuel, Wendy Hughes; *D:* Paul Cox.

Kotch ✓✓✓ **1971 (PG)** An elderly man resists his children's attempts to retire him. Warm detailing of old age with a splendid performance by Matthau. Lemmon's directorial debut. **113m/C VHS, DVD.** Walter Matthau, Deborah Winters, Felicia Farr; *D:* Jack Lemmon; *M:* Marvin Hamlisch. Golden Globes '72: Song ("Life Is What You Make It"); Writers Guild '71: Adapt. Screenplay.

Kounterfeit ✓✓ **1996 (R)** Hopscotch (Hawkes) finds three million in counterfeit cash and tries to get some real cash for the fake stuff with his topless-bar owner buddy Frankie (Payne) serving as muscle. But things go bad. Bernsen has little more than a cameo role as Hopscotch's brother. **87m/C VHS, DVD.** Andrew Hawkes, Bruce Payne, Hilary Swank, Michael Gross, Mark Paul Gosselaar, Corbin Bernsen; *D:* John Mallory Asher; *W:* Jay Irwin, David Chase; *C:* Karl Herrmann. **VIDEO**

The Kovak Box ✓ **2006 (R)** Best-selling sci-fi author David Norton (Hutton) arrives on a Mediterranean island for a conference. His fiancee receives a mysterious phone call and inexplicably commits suicide. That's only the beginning as David's fictional world and his real world overlap, with a government conspiracy thrown in. Dull and confusing, with Hutton's acting consisting of a furrowed brow and grimaces. **102m/C DVD.** Timothy Hutton, Lucia Jimenez, David Kelly, Georgia Mackenzie, Gary Piquer, Annette Badland; *D:* Daniel Monzon; *W:* Daniel Monzon; *C:* Carlos Gusi; *M:* Roque Banos.

Koyaanisqatsi ✓✓✓✓ **1983** A mesmerizing film that takes an intense look at modern life (the movie's title is the Hopi word for "life out of balance"). Without dialogue or narration, it brings traditional background elements, landscapes and cityscapes, up front to produce a unique view of the structure and mechanics of our daily lives. Riveting and immensely powerful. A critically acclaimed score by Glass, and Reggio's cinematography prove to be the perfect match to this brilliant film. Followed by "Powaqqatsi." **87m/C VHS, DVD.** *D:* Godfrey Reggio; *W:* Godfrey Reggio, Ron Fricke, Michael Hoenig; *C:* Godfrey Reggio, Ron Fricke; *M:* Philip Glass, Michael Hoenig. L.A. Film Critics '83: Score, Natl. Film Reg. '00.

Krakatoa East of Java ✓✓ **1969 (G)** Oversized disaster pic was produced in Cinerama, an ultra-widescreen process that utilized three projectors. It immediately became the butt of jokes when people realized that the volcano Krakotoa had been west of Java. The plot is filled with potentially intriguing elements—sunken treasure, hot air balloons, erupting volcano, tidal wave—but they're never compelling. The film fared poorly in its initial theatrical run and was shortened for wider distribution in conventional theatres. (Even so, it can be seen as a precursor to the early '70s disaster pictures which which were built on the same combination of all-star casts and splashy special effects.) **131m/C DVD.** Maximilian Schell, Diane Baker, Brian Keith, Barbara Werle, John Leyton, Rossano Brazzi, Sal Mineo, J.D. Cannon, Jacqueline "Jackie" Chan, Marc Lawrence, Geoffrey Holder, Niall MacGinnis, Peter Graves; *D:* Bernard L. Kowalski; *W:* Bernard Gordon, Clifford Gould; *M:* Frank DeVol.

Kraken: Tentacles of the Deep ✓ **2006 (R)** Cheap CGI and an over-familiar story make this big beastie tale mostly a yawn. Ray (O'Connell) wants revenge on the multi-tentacled creature that killed his parents so he tracks it down with the help of underwater archeologist Nicole (Pratt, looking very—uh—fit in her scanty attire). But the creature is guarding a treasure that mobster Maxwell (Scalia) is determined to have. **87m/C DVD.** Charlie O'Connell, Victoria Pratt, Jack Scalia, Kristi Angus, Cory Monteith; *D:* Tibor Takacs; *W:* Sean Keller; *C:* George Campbell; *M:* Rich Walters. **CABLE**

Kramer vs. Kramer ✓✓✓ ½ **1979 (PG)** Highly acclaimed family drama about an advertising executive husband and child left behind when their wife and mother leaves on a quest to find herself, and the subsequent courtroom battle for custody when she returns. Hoffman and Streep give exacting performances as does young Henry. Successfully moves you from tears to laughter and back again. Based on the novel by Avery Corman. **105m/C VHS, DVD.** Dustin Hoffman, Meryl Streep, Jane Alexander, Justin Henry, Howard Duff, JoBeth Williams; ***D:*** Robert Benton; ***W:*** Robert Benton; ***C:*** Nestor Almendros. Oscars '79: Actor (Hoffman), Adapt. Screenplay, Director (Benton), Picture, Support. Actress (Streep); Directors Guild '79: Director (Benton); Golden Globes '80: Actor—Drama (Hoffman), Film—Drama, Screenplay, Support. Actress (Streep); L.A. Film Critics '79: Actor (Hoffman), Director (Benton), Film, Screenplay, Support. Actress (Streep); Natl. Bd. of Review '79: Support. Actress (Streep); N.Y. Film Critics '79: Actor (Hoffman), Film, Support. Actress (Streep); Natl. Soc. Film Critics '79: Actor (Hoffman), Director (Benton), Support. Actress (Streep); Writers Guild '79: Adapt. Screenplay.

The Krays 🦴🦴🦴 ½ **1990 (R)** An account of British gangsters Reggie and Ronnie Kray, the brothers who ruled London's East End with brutality and violence, making them bizarre celebrities of the '60s. The leads are portrayed by Gary and Martin Kemp, founders of the British pop group Spandau Ballet. **119m/C VHS.** *GB* Gary Kemp, Martin Kemp, Billie Whitelaw, Steven Berkoff, Susan Fleetwood, Charlotte Cornwell, Jimmy Jewel, Avis Bunnage, Kate Hardie, Alfred Lynch, Tom Bell, Victor Spinetti, Barbara Ferris, Julia Migenes, John McEnery, Sadie Frost, Norman Rossington, Murray Melvin; ***D:*** Peter Medak; ***W:*** Philip Ridley; ***C:*** Alex Thomson; ***M:*** Michael Kamen.

The Kreutzer Sonata 🦴 ½ **2008 (R)** Adaptation of Leo Tolstoy's 1889 novella was written as a morality tale about the dangers of too much carnal love but doesn't exactly play that way in Rose's version. Edgar (Huston) hooks up with classical pianist Abby (Rohm) the night they first meet and they keep it up until they are married with kids and a Beverly Hills mansion. Abby is bored, so Edgar urges her to do a charity gig with violinist Aiden (King) but gets fiercely jealous the more the duo rehearse. Since the pic begins with a bloody flashback you know things won't end well. **99m/C DVD.** Danny Huston, Elisabeth Rohm, Matthew Yang King, Anjelica Huston; ***D:*** Bernard Rose; ***W:*** Bernard Rose, Lisa Enos; ***C:*** Bernard Rose.

Kriemhilde's Revenge 🦴🦴🦴🦴 *Die Nibelungen* **1924** The second film, following "Siegfried," of Lang's "Die Nibelungen," a lavish silent version of the Teutonic legends Wagner's "Ring of the Nibelungen" was based upon. In this episode, Kriemhilde avenges Siegfried's death by her marriage to the Kings of the Huns, thus fulfilling a prophecy of destruction. **95m/B VHS, DVD.** *GE* Paul Richter, Margareta Schoen, Theodore Loos, Hanna Ralph, Rudolf Klein-Rogge; ***D:*** Fritz Lang.

Krippendorf's Tribe 🦴🦴 **1998 (PG-13)** James Krippendorf (Dreyfuss), a widowed anthropology professor, returns from an expedition to New Guinea after squandering all his grant money on his kids. Since he didn't find the rare tribe he was sent there for, he makes up tribal stories based on his own kids. When skeptic Tomlin demands proof of his amazing discoveries, the Krippendorf clan and an over-eager colleague (Elfman) go native in front of the camera. Works best when at its silliest, and in fact, could have been a fun family film. Unfortunately, most of the humor is of the smutty variety, involving mating rituals, tribal sex toys, circumcision jokes, and so on. **94m/C VHS, DVD.** Richard Dreyfuss, Jenna Elfman, Natasha Lyonne, Gregory Edward Smith, Stephen (Steve) Root, Elaine Stritch, Tom Poston, David Ogden Stiers, Lily Tomlin, Doris Belack, Julio Oscar Mechoso, Barbara Williams, Zakes Mokae, Carl Michael Lindner, Siobhan Fallon Hogan; ***D:*** Todd Holland; ***W:*** Charlie Peters; ***C:*** Dean Cundey; ***M:*** Bruce Broughton.

Kristin Lavransdatter 🦴 ½ **1995** Slow and tedious romance, set in 14th-century Norway, and based on the novel "Kransen" by Sigrid Undset. Teenaged Kristin causes much grief for her family when she rejects an arranged marriage to a decent man her father has chosen for the more exciting but morally dubious nobleman Erland. Norwegian with subtitles. **144m/C VHS.** *NO* Elisabeth Matheson, Bjorn Skagestad, Henry Moan, Rut Tellefsen, Sverre Anker Ousdal; ***W:*** Liv Ullmann; ***C:*** Sven Nykvist; ***M:*** Henryk Nikolai Gorecki.

Kronos 🦴🦴 ½ **1957** A giant robot from space drains the Earth of all its energy resources. A good example of this genre from the 50s. Includes previews of coming attractions from classic science fiction films. **78m/B VHS, DVD.** Jeff Morrow, Barbara Lawrence, John Emery; ***D:*** Kurt Neumann; ***W:*** Lawrence Louis Goldman; ***C:*** Karl Struss; ***M:*** Paul Sawtell, Bert Shefter.

Krull 🦴🦴 **1983 (PG)** Likeable fantasy adventure set in a world peopled by creatures of myth and magic. A prince embarks on a quest to find the Glaive (a magical weapon) and then rescues his young bride, taken by the Beast of the Black Fortress. **121m/C VHS, DVD.** *GB* Ken Marshall, Lysette Anthony, Freddie Jones, Francesca Annis, Liam Neeson; ***D:*** Peter Yates; ***W:*** Stafford Sherman; ***C:*** Peter Suschitzky; ***M:*** James Horner.

Krush Groove 🦴 **1985 (R)** The world of rap music is highlighted in this movie, the first all-rap musical. ♫ King of Rock; Don't You Dog Me; A Love Bizarre; Pick Up the Pace; If I Ruled the World; Holly Rock; It's Like That; Feel the Spin; I Can't Live Without My Radio. **95m/C VHS, DVD.** Blair Underwood, Lisa Gay Hamilton, Kurtis Blow, Sheila E, John MacKay, Richard Gant, LL Cool J; ***D:*** Michael A. Schultz.

K2: The Ultimate High 🦴🦴 **1992 (R)** Two men, one a skirt-chasing lawyer, the other a happily married physicist, tackle the world's second largest mountain—the K-2 in Kashmir, northern Pakistan. They encounter a number of dangers, including an ascent of sheer rock face, an avalanche, and a fall down perpendicular mountain ice, but even the exciting mountain-climbing scenes can't hold up this watered down movie. The film was actually shot on Canada's Mount Waddington. Based on the play by Patrick Meyers. **104m/C VHS.** Michael Biehn, Matt Craven, Raymond J. Barry, Luca Bercovici, Patricia Charbonneau, Julia Nickson-Soul, Hiroshi Fujioka, Jamal Shah; ***D:*** Franc Roddam; ***W:*** Patrick Meyers, Scott Roberts.

Kuffs 🦴🦴 **1992 (PG-13)** Slater stars as George Kuffs, a young guy who reluctantly joins his brother's highly respected private security team in this original action comedy. After his brother is gunned down in the line of duty, George finds himself the new owner of the business. Out to avenge his brother, George pursues a crooked art dealer as he battles crime on the streets of San Francisco. Worthwhile premise is hampered by a predictable plot and mediocre acting. **102m/C VHS, DVD.** Mary Ellen Trainor, Christian Slater, Tony Goldwyn, Milla Jovovich, Bruce Boxleitner, Troy Evans, George de la Pena, Leon Rippy; ***D:*** Bruce A. Evans; ***W:*** Bruce A. Evans, Raynold Gideon; ***M:*** Harold Faltermeyer.

Kuhle Wampe, Or Who Owns the World? 🦴🦴 *Kuhle Wampe, Oder Wen Gehort die Welt?* **1932** An avant-garde narrative about how hard times affect a working-class Berlin family. Anni's family is forced to move to a lakeside camp for the unemployed on the outskirts of the city. Anni eventually moves back to Berlin and gets involved in the workers' youth movement. German with subtitles. The film was banned by the Nazis in 1933 for its communist leanings. **69m/B DVD.** *GE* Hertha Thiele, Adolf Fischer, Martha Wolter, Lilli Schonborn; ***D:*** Slatan Dudow; ***W:*** Bertolt Brecht, Ernst Ottwalt; ***C:*** Gunther Krampf; ***M:*** Hanns Eisler.

Kull the Conqueror 🦴🦴 ½ **1997 (PG-13)** Sorbo goes from TV's heroic Hercules to action-fantasy hero Kull, a slave who becomes the warrior king of a mythic land. Overthrown by a corrupt nobility, Kull begins a perilous journey to find the one weapon that will destroy the she-demon Akivasha (Carrere) and save the land of Valusia. Lots of action, although the PG-13 rating keeps some of the mayhem less bloody than might be expected for this genre. Based on the '30s character created by pulp writer Robert E. Howard, who also originated "Conan the Barbarian." **96m/C VHS, DVD.** Kevin Sorbo, Tia Carrere, Thomas Ian Griffith, Karina Lombard, Litefoot, Harvey Fierstein, Roy Brocksmith, Douglas Henshall, Sven-Ole Thorsen, Terry O'Neill; ***D:*** John Nicolella; ***W:*** Charles Edward Pogue; ***C:*** Rodney Charters; ***M:*** Joel Goldsmith.

The Kumite 🦴 *Star Runner* **2003 (PG-13)** So it takes 40 minutes to get to any martial arts competition, as the first part of the flick is taken up by the romance between Hong Kong student Bond (Wu) and his young Korea-born teacher Mei (Kim). Bond wants to enter the Star Runner competition but has trouble finding the right mentor and then lets love get in the way of his training. Wu and Kim are both popular Asian pop stars but that doesn't mean they can act (not that it seems to be a requirement). Korean and Cantonese with subtitles. **104m/C DVD.** *HK KN* Hyung-koo Kim, David Chiang, Vanessa Wu, Andy On, Shawn Tam; ***D:*** Daniel Lee; ***W:*** Daniel Lee; ***M:*** Henry Lai.

Kundun 🦴🦴🦴 **1997 (PG-13)** Scorsese's cinematic portrait of the life of the young 14th Dalai Lama from 1937 through 1959, when he was forced to flee Chinese-occupied Tibet and live in exile in India. The incredibly detailed and sumptuous Tibetan journey begins with the discovery of the young boy as the Buddha reborn and uses different actors to portray him through young adulthood. Dramatic depiction of the Chairman Mao-ordered slaughter of Tibetan nuns and monks around the young Kundun illustrates theme of the dilemmas facing a nonviolent man in an increasingly violent world. The adult Dalai Lama's (Tsarong) meeting with cartoonishly evil incarnate Chairman Mao Zedong (Lin) mars an otherwise realistic and honest portrayal. Made with the cooperation of the 14th Dalai Lama, the story reflects the director's yen for accuracy and integrity. Scorsese's gamble on using a cast of non-professional Tibetan refugees pays off. Beautiful scenery and dreamy Philip Glass score set the proper mood. **134m/C VHS, DVD.** Tanzin Thuthob Tsarong, Robert Lin; ***D:*** Martin Scorsese; ***W:*** Melissa Mathison; ***C:*** Roger Deakins; ***M:*** Philip Glass. N.Y. Film Critics '97: Cinematog.; Natl. Soc. Film Critics '97: Cinematog.

Kung Fu 🦴🦴 ½ **1972** A fugitive Buddhist quasi-Asian martial arts master accused of murder in his native land, roams across the Old West fighting injustice. Pilot for the successful TV series; was reincarnated 14 years later in the sequel, "Kung Fu: The Movie." **75m/C VHS.** Keith Carradine, David Carradine, Barry Sullivan, Keye Luke; ***D:*** Jerry Thorpe; ***C:*** Richard L. Rawlings. **TV**

Kung Fu Hustle 🦴🦴 *Gong fu* **2004 (R)** Writer/director Chow casts himself as the lead in this goofy kung-fu comedy. Sing (Chow), a good-natured con man, desperately wants to join the evil Axe Gang. Posing as a gangster, Sing tries to shake down the poor residents of Pig Sty Alley, but a number of hapless martial arts masters have retired to the slum. Sing's scam starts an all-out war between the Axe Gang and Pig Sty Alley, resulting in a series of larger-than-life, CGI-enhanced battles that more closely resemble Looney Tunes than Bruce Lee. While the unrelenting action might cross cultural borders, Chow's sense of humor doesn't seem to. In Cantonese and Mandarin with English subtitles. **99m/C DVD, Blu-ray Disc, UMD.** Stephen (Chiau) Chow, Yuen Wah, Kwok-Kwan Chan, Feng Xiao Gang, Lam Suet, Leung Siu Lung, Dong Zhi Hua, Chiu Chi Ling, Yuen Qui, Xing Yu, Huang Sheng Yi, Lam Tze Chung; ***D:*** Stephen (Chiau) Chow; ***W:*** Stephen (Chiau) Chow, Kan-Cheung (Sammy) Tsang, Chan Man-keung, Lola Huo; ***C:*** Hang-Seng Poon; ***M:*** Raymond Wong.

Kung Fu Panda 🦴🦴🦴 **2008 (PG)** The title pretty much sums it up. Po (voiced by Black), a chubby panda working for his father's noodle shop, slowly learns of his secret kung fu prowess while bumbling through his daily routine. He comes across a contest held by the wise Shifu (voiced by Hoffman) that draws huge crowds to watch five chosen competitors battle it out for the title of Dragon Warrior. Somehow, Po is selected as the final competitor, and from there, he becomes a big furry Rocky. Kiddies and young teens will love it, while mom and dad may get sleepy. **90m/C DVD.** *US* ***D:*** John Stevenson, Mark Osborne; ***W:*** Jonathan Aibel, Glenn Berger; ***C:*** Yong Duk Jhun; ***M:*** Hans Zimmer, John Powell; ***V:*** Jack Black, Dustin Hoffman, Jackie Chan, Angelina Jolie, Lucy Liu, Ian McShane, Seth Rogen, David Cross, Michael Clarke Duncan, James Hong, Dan Fogler, Randall Duk Kim.

Kung Fu: The Movie 🦴🦴 ½ **1986** Carradine reprises his role as Kwai Chang Caine from the TV show of the '70s. Now, he's hunted by evil warlord Mako, who's involved in the California opium trade. Mako sends assassin Lee (son of martial-arts star Bruce) after Caine. Luke appears in flashbacks as the young Grasshopper's blind mentor, Master Po. **93m/C VHS.** David Carradine, Mako, Brandon Lee, Keye Luke, Kerrie Keane, Martin Landau, William Lucking, Luke Askew, Benson Fong; ***D:*** Richard Lang. **TV**

Kung Pow! Enter the Fist 🦴 ½ **2002 (PG-13)** Oedekerk, the "mind" behind such comedies as "Ace Ventura: When Nature Calls" and "Patch Adams," opts to put himself in front of the camera in this painfully boring kung-fu spoof. He splices new footage into a 1970s martial arts movie, making himself the lead character and adding in a liberal helping of scatological humor. It's "What's Up, Tiger Lily" meets "Dead Men Don't Wear Plaid," only without the comedic genius or even an elementary grasp of basic filmmaking. Leave this fist closed, grasshopper. **81m/C VHS, DVD.** Steve Oedekerk, Tad Horino, Simon Rhee, Lin Yan, Jennifer Tung, Lo Ming; ***D:*** Steve Oedekerk; ***W:*** Steve Oedekerk; ***C:*** John J. Connor; ***M:*** Robert Folk.

Kuni Lemel in Tel Aviv 🦴🦴 ½ **1977** The bungling folk-hero of the shtetl of 100 years ago is updated to the present. Grandpa Kuni is now 80 and living in Brooklyn. Anxious to see the family line continue, he offers $5 million to the first of his twin grandsons to marry a nice Jewish girl and settle in Israel. However, the grandsons have plans of their own which conflict with Grandpa's. In Hebrew with English subtitles. **90m/C VHS, DVD.** *IS* Mike Burstyn, Mandy Rice-Davies; ***D:*** Joel Silberg.

Kurt Vonnegut's Harrison Bergeron 🦴🦴 ½ *Harrison Bergeron* **1995 (R)** In the year 2053 the American government has gone to absurd lengths to ensure equality. Mediocrity is championed and everyone is forced to wear metallic headbands that stifle intellect through electronic impulses. Too bad for Harrison Bergeron (Astin), a smart young man being punished for his intelligence. But there's a secret undeground elite offering Harrison the chance to think freely, though this power comes with a price. Adapted from Vonnegut's 1961 short story. **99m/C VHS.** Sean Astin, Christopher Plummer, Miranda de Pencier, Nigel Bennett, Buck Henry, Eugene Levy, Howie Mandel, Andrea Martin; ***D:*** Bruce Pittman; ***W:*** Arthur Crimm. **CABLE**

Kurt Vonnegut's Monkey House 🦴🦴 **1991** Dramatization of four short stories from Vonnegut's "Welcome to the Monkey House" collection, including a twist on the familiar Frankenstein tale. **100m/C VHS.** Frank Langella, Madeline Kahn, Kaj-Erik Eriksen, Donnelly Rhodes, Len Cariou, Gordon Clapp; ***D:*** Allan King, Paul Shapiro; ***W:*** Jeff B. Cohen, Stan Daniels. **CABLE**

Kwaidan 🦴🦴🦴🦴 **1964** A haunting, stylized quartet of supernatural stories, each with a surprise ending. Adapted from the stories of Lafcadio Hearn, an American author who lived in Japan just before the turn of the century. The visual effects are splendid. In Japanese with English subtitles. **164m/C VHS, DVD.** *JP* Michiyo Aratama, Rentaro Mikuni, Katsuo Nakamura, Keiko Kishi, Tatsuya Nakadai, Takashi Shimura; ***D:*** Masaki Kobayashi; ***W:*** Yoko Mizuki; ***C:*** Yoshio Miyajima; ***M:*** Toru Takemitsu. Cannes '65: Grand Jury Prize.

The L-Shaped Room 🦴🦴🦴 **1962** Young Frenchwoman Jane (Caron) is living in London and has an affair that leaves her pregnant. She winds up moving to a tacky boarding house, into the small room of the title. Soon, Jane has fallen for fellow tenant, out-of-work writer Toby (Bell), without disclosing her situation. However, when Toby's jealous best friend, jazz musician Johnny (Peters), learns of Jane's pregnancy, he uses his knowledge to break the twosome up. In the kitchen-sink tradition of British films that doesn't expect a happy ending. Based on the novel by Lynne Reid Banks. **89m/B VHS.** *GB* Leslie Caron, Tom Bell, Brock Peters, Mark Eden, Cicely Courtneidge, Emlyn Williams, Bernard

Lee, Avis Bunnage; *D:* Bryan Forbes; *W:* Bryan Forbes; *C:* Douglas Slocombe; *M:* John Barry.

L.627 🦴🦴🦴 **1992** Melancholy police procedural about dedicated veteran narcotics cop Lulu (Bezace) who works with a small and ill-equipped Parisian drug squad prone to taking the law into their own hands. Lulu constantly finds himself thwarted by obtuse bureaucrats while his life is disturbed by an informant—a young, drug-addicted prostitute who has disappeared and whom Lulu desires to protect. Film title refers to the French anti-drug statute. French with subtitles. **145m/C VHS.** *FR* Didier Bezace, Jean-Paul Comart, Cecile Garcia-Fogel, Lara Guirao, Charlotte Kady, Jean-Roger Milo, Philippe Torreton, Nils (Niels) Tavernier; *D:* Bertrand Tavernier; *W:* Bertrand Tavernier, Michel Alexandre; *C:* Alain Choquart; *M:* Philippe Sarde.

L.A. Bad 🦴 **1985 (R)** A Puerto Rican street thug learns he has cancer, and must come to terms with his own impending death. **101m/C VHS.** Esai Morales, Janice Rule, John Phillip Law, Charles "Chuck" Bail, Carrie Snodgress; *D:* Gary Kent; *W:* Gary Kent; *M:* Jimmie Haskell.

La Balance 🦴🦴🦴 **1982 (R)** An underworld stool pigeon is recruited by the Parisian police to blow the whistle on a murderous mob. Baye, as a prostitute in love with the pimp-stoolie, is a standout. Critically acclaimed; French with subtitles. **103m/C VHS, DVD.** *FR* Philippe Leotard, Nathalie Baye, Bob Swaim; *D:* Reymond LePlont; *M:* Roland Bocquet. Cesar '83: Actor (Leotard), Actress (Baye), Film.

La Bamba 🦴🦴🦴 **1987 (PG-13)** A romantic biography of the late 1950s pop idol Ritchie Valens, concentrating on his stormy relationship with his half-brother Bob (Morales), his love for his WASP girlfriend Donna (Von Zerneck) for whom he wrote a hit song, and his tragic, sudden death in the famed plane crash that also took the lives of Buddy Holly and the Big Bopper. Soundtrack features Setzer, Huntsberry, Crenshaw, and Los Lobos as, respectively, Eddie Cochran, the Big Bopper, Buddy Holly, and a Mexican bordello band. **99m/C VHS, DVD.** Lou Diamond Phillips, Esai Morales, Danielle von Zerneck, Joe Pantoliano, Brian Setzer, Marshall Crenshaw, Howard Huntsberry, Rosanna Desoto, Elizabeth Pena, Rick Dees; *D:* Luis Valdez; *W:* Luis Valdez; *C:* Adam Greenberg; *M:* Miles Goodman, Carlos Santana.

La Belle Noiseuse 🦴🦴🦴 ½ *Divertimento; The Beautiful Troublemaker* **1990** The connections between art and life are explored in this beautiful (and long) drama. Creatively crippled, an aging painter has left unfinished a masterpiece work, entitled "La Belle Noiseuse," for ten years. When an admiring younger artist and his beautiful lover arrive for a visit, the painter is newly inspired by the young woman and makes her the model and muse for his masterwork. The film details every nuance of the work from the first to the last brushstroke and the battle of wills between artist and model over the symbiotic creative process. Based on a novella by Honore Balzac. French with subtitles. "Divertimento" is actually a recut and shortened version (126 minutes) of the original film. **240m/C VHS, DVD.** *FR* Michel Piccoli, Emmanuelle Beart, Jane Birkin, David Bursztein, Marianne (Cuau) Denicourt; *D:* Jacques Rivette; *W:* Jacques Rivette, Christine Laurent, Pascal Bonitzer; *C:* William Lubtchansky. Cannes '91: Grand Jury Prize; L.A. Film Critics '91: Foreign Film.

La Bete Humaine 🦴🦴🦴 ½ *The Human Beast* **1938** A dark, psychological melodrama about human passion and duplicity, as an unhinged trainman plots with a married woman to kill her husband. Wonderful performances and stunning photography. Based on the Emile Zola novel. In French with English subtitles. 1954 Hollywood remake, "Human Desire," was directed by Fritz Lang. **90m/B VHS, DVD.** *FR* Jean Gabin, Simone Simon, Julien Carette, Fernand Ledoux; *D:* Jean Renoir; *W:* Jean Renoir; *C:* Curt Courant; *M:* Joseph Cosma.

La Boca del Lobo 🦴🦴 *The Lion's Den* **1989** Peru's civil strife inspired this sluggish drama about government troops occupying a jungle village. Tormented by unseen communist guerillas, the stressed-out soldiers reach the breaking point. Spanish with subtitles. **111m/C VHS.** *AR* Gustavo Bueno, Tono Vega, Jose Tejada; *D:* Francisco J. Lombardi.

La Boum 🦴🦴 ½ **1981** A teenager's adjustment to the changes brought about by a move to Paris is compounded by her parents' marital problems. Followed by "La Boum 2." **90m/C VHS, DVD.** *FR* Sophie Marceau, Claude Brasseur, Brigitte Fossey, Denise Grey, Bernard Giraudeau; *D:* Claude Pinoteau; *M:* Vladimir Cosma.

L.A. Bounty 🦴 ½ **1989 (R)** A beautiful cop and a bounty hunter go after the same murderer. Hauser steals the show as a psychopath who has completely blown a gasket. **85m/C VHS.** Sybil Danning, Wings Hauser, Henry Darrow, Lenore Kasdorf, Robert Hanley; *D:* Worth Keeter.

La Buche 🦴🦴 **2000** The title refers to a special Christmas cake, fashioned in the shape of a yule log. The holiday season is proving to be particularly tiresome for three sisters: nightclub singer Louba (Azema) who's pregnant with her married lover's child; homemaker Sonia (Beart) whose husband is leaving her for a younger woman; and career-driven Milla (Gainsbourg) who becomes intrigued by melancholy Joseph (Thompson, the director's son). Family crises start with the funeral of the sisters' stepfather, leading to a reunion between their parents who haven't spoken in 25 years, and get more complicated from there. French with subtitles. **106m/C VHS, DVD.** *FR* Sabine Azema, Emmanuelle Beart, Charlotte Gainsbourg, Francoise Fabian, Claude Rich, Christopher Thompson, Jean-Pierre Darroussin; *D:* Daniele Thompson; *W:* Christopher Thompson, Daniele Thompson; *C:* Robert Fraisse; *M:* Michel Legrand.

La Cage aux Folles 🦴🦴🦴 ½ *Birds of a Feather* **1978 (R)** Adaption of the popular French play. Gay Saint-Tropez nightclub owner Renato (Tognazzi) and his drag queen lover Albin (Serrault) try to play it straight when Renato's son (Laurent) from a long-ago liaison brings his fiancee and her conservative parents home for dinner. Charming music and lots of fun. So successful, it was followed by two sequels in 1980 and 1985, a Broadway musical, and a 1995 American remake, "The Birdcage." French with subtitles. **91m/C VHS, DVD.** *FR* Ugo Tognazzi, Michel Serrault, Michel Galabru, Claire Maurier, Remy Laurent, Benny Luke, Carmen Scarpitta, Luisa Maneri; *D:* Edouard Molinaro; *W:* Edouard Molinaro, Francis Veber, Jean Poiret, Marcello Danon; *C:* Armando Nannuzzi; *M:* Ennio Morricone. Cesar '79: Actor (Serrault); Golden Globes '80: Foreign Film.

La Cage aux Folles 2 🦴🦴 ½ **1981 (R)** Albin sets out to prove to his companion that he still has sex appeal, and gets mixed up in some espionage antics. This sequel to the highly successful "La Cage aux Folles" loses some steam, but is still worth seeing. Followed by "La Cage Aux Folles 3: The Wedding." **101m/C VHS, DVD.** *FR* Ugo Tognazzi, Michel Serrault, Marcel Bozzuffi, Michel Galabru, Benny Luke; *D:* Edouard Molinaro; *W:* Francis Veber; *C:* Armando Nannuzzi; *M:* Ennio Morricone.

La Cage aux Folles 3: The Wedding 🦴 ½ **1986 (PG-13)** The flamboyant drag queen Albin must feign normalcy by marrying and fathering a child in order to collect a weighty inheritance. Final segment of the trilogy; inferior to the previous films. In French with English subtitles. **88m/C VHS.** *FR* Michel Serrault, Ugo Tognazzi, Michel Galabru, Benny Luke, Stephane Audran; *D:* Georges Lautner; *M:* Ennio Morricone.

La Ceremonie 🦴🦴🦴 *A Judgment in Stone* **1995** Sullen maid Sophie (Bonnaire) is hired by the rich Lelievre family to work at their country estate. She's befriended by independent postmistress Jeanne (Huppert), who's disliked by Sophie's employers, and who encourages Sophie into small defiant actions. Something's off about the entire situation and there's violence beneath the seemingly calm surface. Based on Ruth Rendell's chiller "Judgment in Stone." French with subtitles. **109m/C VHS, DVD.** *FR GE* Sandrine Bonnaire, Isabelle Huppert, Jacqueline Bisset, Jean-Pierre Cassel, Virginie Ledoyen, Valentine Merlet, Julien Rochefort, Dominique Frot, Jean-Francois Perrier; *D:* Claude Chabrol; *W:* Claude Chabrol, Caroline Eliacheff; *C:* Bernard Zitzermann; *M:* Matthieu Chabrol. Cesar '96: Actress (Huppert); L.A. Film Critics '96: Foreign Film; Natl. Soc. Film Critics '96: Foreign Film.

La Chartreuse de Parme 🦴🦴 ½ *Charterhouse at Parma* **1948** Nineteenth century period piece featuring an Archbishop willing to break his vows for the woman he loves, and the aunt who will make sure that if she can't have him only God will. French adaptation of the novel by Stendahl. Available dubbed. **170m/B VHS, DVD.** *FR* Gerard Philipe, Maria Casares, Renee Faure; *D:* Christian-Jaque; *W:* Christian-Jaque.

La Chevre 🦴🦴🦴 ½ *The Goat* **1981** A screwball French comedy about two policemen (Richard and Depardieu—picture Gene Wilder and Nick Nolte with accents) stumbling along the path of a missing heiress who suffers from chronic bad luck. Contains a hilarious scene with chairs used to test the luck of the investigative team; based on one partner's ability to sit on the only broken chair in a rather large collection, he is judged to be sufficiently jinxed to allow them to re-create the same outrageous misfortunes that befell the heiress in her plight. In French with English subtitles. **91m/C VHS, DVD.** *FR* Gerard Depardieu, Pierre Richard, Corynne Charbit, Michel Robin, Pedro Armendariz Jr.; *D:* Francis Veber; *M:* Vladimir Cosma.

La Chienne 🦴🦴🦴🦴 *Isn't Life A Bitch?; The Bitch* **1931** Dark, troubling tale of a bedraggled husband whose only excitement is his painting hobby until he becomes consumed by the ever-tempting prostitute Lulu. Director Renoir broke ground with his use of direct sound and Paris shooting locations, and the experiment was a hit. Portrays marriage with acidity; Renoir's own marriage broke up as a result of this film's casting. Mareze died shortly after the filming was complete in a car crash. Based on the novel by Georges de la Fouchardiere. Produced in 1931, but didn't reach American theatres until 1975. In French with English subtitles. Remade in 1945 as "Scarlet Street." **93m/B VHS.** *FR* Michel Simon, Janie Mareze, Georges Flament, Madeleine Berubet; *D:* Jean Renoir; *W:* Andre Girard, Jean Renoir.

La Chinoise 🦴🦴 *The Chinese* **1967** Godard's study in French intellectualism and the young left's discontent. Over a summer five students form a radical communist cell devoted to the teachings of Chairman Mao. The nominal leaders are uncompromising idealist Guillaume (Leaud) and his girlfriend Veronique (Wiazemsky), a daughter of the bourgeoisie. Henri (Semeniako) gets expelled for not being a true believer, but while the others stay in the apartment talking revolution, Henri is in the Paris streets taking action. French with subtitles. **93m/C DVD.** *FR* Jean-Pierre Leaud, Anna Wiazemsky, Juliet Berto, Michel Semeniako, Lex De Bruijn; *D:* Jean-Luc Godard; *W:* Jean-Luc Godard; *C:* Raoul Coutard.

La Chute de la Maison Usher 🦴🦴🦴 ½ *The Fall of the House of Usher* **1928** An expressionistic, abstracted adaptation of the Poe story "The Fall of the House of Usher" about an evil mansion and its ruined denizens. Epstein used slow motion, superimpressions, and weird camera angles to obtain the proper atmosphere. **48m/B VHS, DVD.** *FR* Marguerite Gance, Jean Debucourt, Charles Lamy; *D:* Jean Epstein; *W:* Jean Epstein; *C:* Georges Lucas, Jean Lucas. Natl. Film Reg. '00.

La Cicada 🦴 ½ *The Cricket* **1983** The sparks fly when a woman and her 17-year-old daughter become rivals for the affections of the same man. **90m/C VHS.** *IT* Clio Goldsmith, Virna Lisi, Anthony (Tony) Franciosa, Renato Salvatori; *D:* Alberto Lattuada.

La Collectionneuse 🦴🦴 *The Gentleman Tramp* **1967** The third of Rohmer's "Moral Tales" finds an artist (Bachau) and an antiques dealer (Pommereulle) vacationing in St. Tropez and sharing a villa with a young woman (Politoff) who picks a different man to sleep with each night. Both try to resist the sexual temptations of being added to her collection of lovers. French with subtitles. **88m/C VHS, DVD.** *FR* Patrick Bauchau, Daniel Pommereulle, Haydee Politoff, Alain Jouffroy; *D:* Eric Rohmer; *W:* Eric Rohmer; *C:* Nestor Almendros.

L.A. Confidential 🦴🦴🦴🦴 **1997 (R)** Hard-boiled, complicated crime drama based on James Ellroy's even more complex novel. Fifties Hollywood is ripe with corruption in many forms—politics, police, business, gangsters, racial tensions, and journalistic sleaze in the persona of Sid Hudgens (DeVito), editor of tabloid rag Hush-Hush. Sid's police contact is celebrity Sgt. Jack Vincennes (Spacey), who serves as an advisor to a TV cop show (think "Dragnet"). There's a bloodbath murder case that involves brutal-yet-tender cop Bud White (Crowe); the ruthlessly ambitious, college-educated neophyte Ed Exley (Pearce); and their veteran boss, Capt. Dudley Smith (Cromwell). There's also wealthy pimp/businessman Pierce Patchett (Strathairn) and his movie-star look-alike hookers, including world-weary Lynn (Basinger), who gets involved with Bud, who... Well, lets just say that Hanson does a masterful job tying up all the loose ends and still leaving you wanting more. **136m/C VHS, DVD, Blu-ray Disc.** Kevin Spacey, Russell Crowe, Guy Pearce, Danny DeVito, Kim Basinger, James Cromwell, David Strathairn, Ron Rifkin, Graham Beckel, Matt McCoy, Simon Baker, Paul Guilfoyle, Amber Smith, John Mahon, Paolo Seganti, Gwenda Deacon; *D:* Curtis Hanson; *W:* Curtis Hanson, Brian Helgeland; *C:* Dante Spinotti; *M:* Jerry Goldsmith. Oscars '97: Adapt. Screenplay, Support. Actress (Basinger); Australian Film Inst. '98: Foreign Film; British Acad. '97: Film Editing, Sound; Golden Globes '98: Support. Actress (Basinger); L.A. Film Critics '97: Cinematog., Director (Hanson), Film, Screenplay; Natl. Bd. of Review '97: Director (Hanson), Film; N.Y. Film Critics '97: Director (Hanson), Film, Screenplay; Natl. Soc. Film Critics '97: Director (Hanson), Film, Screenplay; Screen Actors Guild '97: Support. Actress (Basinger); Writers Guild '97: Adapt. Screenplay; Broadcast Film Critics '97: Adapt. Screenplay, Film.

L.A. Crackdown 🦴 **1987** A ruthless yet compassionate policewoman goes after crack dealers and pimps who are exploiting women. Pretty trashy fare; followed by "L.A. Crackdown 2." Made for video. **90m/C VHS.** Pamela Dixon, Tricia Parks, Kita Harrison, Jeffrey Olson, Michael Coon; *D:* Joseph Merhi. **VIDEO**

L.A. Crackdown 2 🦴 **1988** A woman cop goes undercover as a dancer in a dance hall to try to catch a psychotic killer who stalks hookers in this silly sequel to "L.A. Crackdown." **90m/C VHS.** Pamela Dixon, Anthony Gates, Joe Vance, Cynthia Miguel, Bo Sabato; *D:* Joseph Merhi.

La Cucaracha 🦴🦴 **1999 (R)** Ex-office worker Walter (Roberts) has hightailed it to Mexico to become a writer—or so he says. Instead, he's a drunk practically immobilized by night terrors. Then the local big shot (de Almeida) suddenly offers Walter money to kill someone. Things don't go as expected. **95m/C VHS, DVD.** Eric Roberts, Joaquim de Almeida, Tara Crespo, James McManus; *D:* Jack Perez; *W:* James McManus; *C:* Shawn Maurer; *M:* Martin Davich.

La Deroute 🦴🦴 **1998** Joe Aiello has made a successful life for himself and his family since emigrating from Sicily to Canada 30 years before. Since his son Nuccio is mentally handicapped, Joe rests his hopes on his 23-year-old daughter Bennie, who only wants freedom from her possessive father. And she takes it by impulsively marrying Diego, a South American refugee about to be deported. Feeling rejected and betrayed, Joe finds himself falling into despair. French with subtitles. **111m/C VHS.** *CA* Tony Nardi, Michelle-Barbara Pelletier, Hugolin Chevrette, John Dunn-Hill, Richard Lemire; *D:* Paul Tana; *W:* Tony Nardi, Paul Tana, Bruno Ramirez; *C:* Michel Caron; *M:* Pierre Desrochers.

L.A. Dicks 🦴 ½ **2005** Two private eyes fall victim to predictions about their own futures when their current job involves tracking a psychic while they also compete with some of L.A.'s finest to drum up Hollywood interest in their cases. **90m/C DVD.** Anthony Guidera, Michael Madsen, Sarah Wynter, Erik Palladino, Dean Alioto, Kym E. Whitley; *D:* Dean Alioto; *W:* Dean Alioto; *C:* Tim Gibbons; *M:* Ryan Beveridge. **VIDEO**

La Discrete 🦴🦴🦴 *The Discreet* **1990** Antoine (Luchini) is a cocky writer who is not the lothario he imagines himself to be—in fact his girlfriend has just dumped him. He and his publisher plan a sexist revenge with Antoine advertising for a young female typist whom he will seduce and abandon—all the while keeping a diary of the experience which will be published. The self-possessed Catherine (Henry) answers the ad and even though Antoine protests that she is not his type he finds himself falling in love. Then Catherine discovers Antoine's original scheme. Vincent's directorial debut. In French with English subtitles. **95m/C VHS.** *FR* Fabrice Luchini, Judith Henry, Maurice Garrel, Marie Bunel, Francois Toumarkine; ***D:*** Christian Vincent; ***W:*** Jean-Pierre Ronssin, Christian Vincent; ***M:*** Jay Gottlieb. Cesar '91: Writing.

La Dolce Vita 🦴🦴🦴🦴 **1960** In this influential and popular work a successful, sensationalistic Italian journalist covers the show-biz life in Rome, and alternately covets and disdains its glitzy shallowness. The film follows his dealings with the "sweet life" over a pivotal week. A surreal, comic tableaux with award-winning costuming; one of Fellini's most acclaimed films. In this film Fellini called his hungry celebrity photographers the Paparazzo—and it is as the paparazzi they have been ever since. In Italian with English subtitles. **174m/B VHS, DVD.** *IT* Marcello Mastroianni, Anita Ekberg, Anouk Aimee, Alain Cuny, Lex Barker, Yvonne Furneaux, Barbara Steele, Nadia Gray, Magali Noel, Walter Santesso, Jacques Sernas, Annibale Ninchi; ***D:*** Federico Fellini; ***W:*** Tullio Pinelli, Ennio Flaiano, Brunello Rondi, Federico Fellini; ***M:*** Nino Rota. Oscars '61: Costume Des. (B&W); Cannes '60: Film; N.Y. Film Critics '61: Foreign Film.

La Femme Infidele 🦴🦴🦴 1/2 *The Unfaithful Wife* **1969** When Charles (Bouquet) learns that his wife (Audran) has found the passion that their marriage now lacks in the arms of another man (Ronet), he confronts and kills him. This rekindles his wife's interest in him. Chabrol at his best. **98m/C VHS, DVD.** *FR* Stephane Audran, Michel Bouquet, Michel Duchaussoy, Henri Marteau, Maurice Ronet, Dominique Zardi; ***D:*** Claude Chabrol; ***W:*** Claude Chabrol; ***C:*** Jean Rabier; ***M:*** Pierre Jansen.

La Femme Nikita 🦴🦴🦴 **1991 (R)** Stylish French noir version of Pygmalion. Having killed a cop during a drugstore theft gone awry, young French sociopath Nikita (Parillaud) is reprieved from a death sentence in order to enroll in a government finishing school, of sorts. Trained in etiquette (by Moreau) and assasination (by Karyo), she's released after three years, and starts a new life with a new beau (Anglade), all the while carrying out agency-mandated assassinations. Parillaud is excellent as the once-amoral street urchin transformed into a woman of depth and sensitivity—a bitterly ironic moral evolution for a contract killer. Remade as "Point of No Return." **117m/C VHS, DVD.** *FR* Anne Parillaud, Jean-Hugues Anglade, Tcheky Karyo, Jeanne Moreau, Jean Reno, Jean Bouise; ***D:*** Luc Besson; ***W:*** Luc Besson; ***C:*** Thierry Arbogast; ***M:*** Eric Serra. Cesar '91: Actress (Parillaud).

L.A. Gangs Rising 🦴🦴 **1989** The streets of Los Angeles run red with blood as a gang war explodes into bloody fury. **87m/C VHS.** David Kyle, Steve Bond, John Ashton; ***D:*** John Bushelman.

L.A. Goddess 🦴 1/2 **1992 (R)** A hard-living, and drinking, movie star and her beautiful stunt double both fall for a studio head. Both of these women know what they want and the man in the middle hasn't got a clue. Also available in an unrated version. **92m/C VHS.** Kathy Shower, Jeff Conaway, David Heavener, Wendy McDonald, Joe Estevez, James Hong; ***D:*** Jag Mundhra; ***W:*** Jerry Davis.

La Grande Bouffe 🦴🦴🦴 *The Blow-Out* **1973** Four middle-aged men, bored with life, meet at a secluded mansion for one last excessive fling and to literally eat themselves to death. Four very fine actors in a vulgar feast. French with subtitles. **125m/C VHS, DVD.** *FR* Marcello Mastroianni, Philippe Noiret, Michel Piccoli, Ugo Tognazzi, Andrea Ferreol; ***D:*** Marco Ferreri; ***W:*** Marco Ferreri, Rafael Azcona; ***C:*** Mario Vulpiani; ***M:*** Philippe Sarde.

La Grande Bourgeoise 🦴🦴 1/2 *The Murri Affair* **1974** Historical romance about the clash of aristocratic society and the new bourgeoisie in 1897 Italy. Great cast tries to save the true tale of murder and political intrigue from film's slow pacing, but in the end it's the movie's visual polish that shines forth. In Italian with subtitles. **115m/C VHS.** *IT* Catherine Deneuve, Giancarlo Giannini, Fernando Rey, Tina Aumont; ***D:*** Mauro Bolognini; ***M:*** Ennio Morricone.

La Grande Vadrouille 🦴🦴🦴 *Don't Look Now, We've Been Shot At* **1966** In 1943 German-occupied France, three Allied parachutists drop in on a Paris Opera conductor and a house painter. If the pair wish to find some peace, they must help the trio get to the free zone. France's number one boxoffice hit for almost 30 years. Also available dubbed. **122m/C VHS.** *FR* Louis de Funes, Andre Bourvil, Terry-Thomas; ***D:*** Gerard Oury.

La Guerre Est Finie 🦴🦴🦴 1/2 *The War Is Over; Kriget ar Slut* **1966** Alain Resnais's understated suspense film makes a belated debut on home video. It's the story of Diego (Montand), a revolutionary who comes to wonder if he can still fight the good fight against the fascists who control Spain. Montand, one of the most deceptively effortless actors ever to appear on screen, is a commanding presence in this low-keyed exercise. **121m/C DVD.** *FR SW* Yves Montand, Michel Piccoli, Ingrid Thulin, Genevieve Bujold, Jean Daste, Dominique Rozan, Jean-Francois Remi; ***D:*** Alain Resnais; ***W:*** Jorge Semprun; ***C:*** Sacha Vierny; ***M:*** Giovanni Fusco; ***Nar:*** Jorge Semprun.

L.A. Heat 🦴 1/2 **1988** When a vice cop's partner is killed, he seeks revenge on the murderers, only to find that his own department may have been involved. Followed by "L.A. Vice." **90m/C VHS, DVD.** Jim Brown, Lawrence-Hilton Jacobs; ***D:*** Joseph Merhi.

L.A. Law 🦴🦴🦴 **1986** The pilot episode of the acclaimed dramatic series, in which the staff of a Los Angeles law firm tries a variety of cases. **97m/C VHS.** Michael Tucker, Jill Eikenberry, Harry Hamlin, Richard Dysart, Jimmy Smits, Alan Rachins, Susan Ruttan, Susan Dey, Corbin Bernsen; ***D:*** Gregory Hoblit. **TV**

La Lectrice 🦴🦴 1/2 *The Reader* **1988 (R)** Artesian landscapes, Beethoven sonatas, and a Raymond Jean novel titled "La Lectrice" provide the backdrop for Constance (Miou-Miou) to read aloud to her boyfriend in bed, and from there she imagines herself the novel's heroine, who hires out her services as a reader to various odd characters. She reads from "L'Amant," "Alice," "War and Peace," and "Les Fleurs du Mal." Richly textured and not overly intellectual. In French with English subtitles. **98m/C VHS.** *FR* Miou-Miou, Christian Ruche, Sylvie Laporte, Michael Raskine, Brigitte Catillon, Regis Royer, Maria Casares, Pierre Dux, Patrick Chesnais; ***D:*** Michel DeVille; ***W:*** Rosalinde DeVille, Michel DeVille. Cesar '89: Support. Actor (Chesnais); Montreal World Film Fest. '88: Film.

La Leon 🦴🦴 *The Lion* **2007** Beautifully photographed in black and white, this debut feature by Otheguy is a story of loneliness and isolation. Alvaro (Roman) works cutting reeds on a marshy Argentine island. The community's main contact with the outside world comes courtesy of Turu (Valenzuela), the captain of the Lion water taxi. Alvaro is even more isolated by the fact that he is gay and Turu is openly hostile although there's more than anger causing the tension between the two men. Spanish with subtitles. **85m/B DVD.** *AR* Daniel Valenzuela, Jorge Roman, Jose Munoz; ***D:*** Santiago Otheguy; ***W:*** Santiago Otheguy; ***C:*** Paula Grandio; ***M:*** Vincent Artaud.

La Marseillaise 🦴🦴🦴 1/2 **1937** Sweeping epic by Renoir made before he hit his stride with "Grand Illusion." It details the events of the French Revolution in the summer of 1789 using a cast of thousands. The opulent lifestyle of the French nobility is starkly contrasted with the peasant lifestyle of poverty and despair. The focus is on two new recruits who have joined the Marseilles division of the revolutionary army as they begin their long march to Paris, the heart of France. As they travel, they adopt a stirring and passionate song that embodies the spirit and ideals of the revolution known as "La Marseillaise," now France's national anthem. In French with English subtitles. **130m/B VHS.** *FR* Pierre Renoir, Lisa (Lise) Delamare, Louis Jouvet, Aime Clariond, Andrex Andrisson, Paul Dullac; ***D:*** Jean Renoir; ***W:*** Jean Renoir; ***C:*** Jean (Yves, Georges) Bourgoin.

La Merveilleuse Visite 🦴🦴 1/2 *The Marvelous Visit* **1974** Bittersweet fantasy about an angel that falls from the sky and is found unconcious by a priest. He's nursed back to health but causes problems for his host when he wanders into the nearby village and his curiosity is misunderstood. Adapted from a short story by H.G. Wells. In French with English subtitles. **102m/C VHS.** *FR* Gilles Kohler, Deborah Berger, Jean-Pierre Castaldi; ***D:*** Marcel Carne; ***W:*** Marcel Carne.

La Moustache 🦴🦴 *The Moustache* **2005** Carree adapts and directs his 1986 novel in which architect Marc (Lindon) decides to shave off the moustache he's had most of his life. He's taken aback when his wife Agnes (Devos) doesn't notice. Nor does anyone else. Marc first thinks it's an elaborate practical joke but then suspects everyone of more sinister motives. His marriage unravels as, perhaps, does Marc's sanity. French with subtitles. **86m/C DVD.** *FR* Vincent Lindon, Emmanuelle Devos, Mathieu Amalric, Hippolyte Girardot, Cylia Malki, Macha Polikarpova; ***D:*** Emmanuel Carrere; ***W:*** Jerome Beaujour, Emmanuel Carrere; ***C:*** Patrick Blossier.

La Mujer de Mi Hermano 🦴🦴 *My Brother's Wife* **2006 (R)** Glossy, romantic melodrama set in Mexico City. Beautiful Zoe (Mori) is bored as well as childless in her marriage to rich, uptight Ignacio (Meier). Is it any wonder she's so very attracted to Ignacio's hot-blooded younger brother Gonzalo (Cardona)? Soon they're tearing up the sheets with Gonzalo making insinuations about his brother's manhood and revealing some family secrets while Zoe feels guilty. Screenwriter Bayly adapted his own novel. Spanish with subtitles. **93m/C DVD.** *MX* Christian Meier, Bruno Bichir, Angelica Aragon, Barbara Mori, Manolo Cardona, Beto Cuevas; ***D:*** Ricardo de Montreuil; ***W:*** Jamie Bayly; ***C:*** Andres E. Sanchez; ***M:*** Angelo Milli.

La Notte 🦴🦴🦴🦴 *The Night; La Nuit* **1960** 4Milan, a middle-class writer (Mastroianni) and his wife (Moreau) appear to have come to the end of their road together; without passion or a conviction that they need to stay together, they spend one long and lonely night observing the city around them, trying to make sense of what appears to be a chaotic and uncaring world. Without specific references to post-war/cold war angst, Antonioni nevertheless evokes that world vividly. By dawn, the couple have indeed come to an understanding, but it's not the simple Hollywood solution of simply staying or leaving. Antonioni's concern is with coping with the modern world while not living in denial. Won the Grand Prize (Golden Bear) at the Berlin Film Festival. **122m/B VHS, DVD.** *IT* Jeanne Moreau, Marcello Mastroianni, Monica Vitti, Bernhard Wicki, Maria Pia Luzi, Rosy Mazzacurati, Grigor Taylor; ***D:*** Michelangelo Antonioni; ***W:*** Michelangelo Antonioni, Ennio Flaiano, Tonino Guerra; ***C:*** Gianni Di Venanzo; ***M:*** Giorgio Gaslini.

La Nuit de Varennes 🦴🦴🦴 **1982 (R)** This semi-historical romp is based on an actual chapter in French history when King Louis XVI and Marie Antoinette fled from revolutionary Paris to Varennes in 1791. On the way they meet an unlikely group of characters, including Cassanova and Thomas Paine. At times witty and charming, the melange of history and fiction is full of talk, sometimes profane, punctuated by sex and nudity. Director Scola's imagination stretches to light up this night. In French with English subtitles. **133m/C VHS.** *FR IT* Marcello Mastroianni, Harvey Keitel, Jean-Louis Barrault, Hanna Schygulla, Jean-Claude Brialy, Michel Piccoli, Jean-Louis Trintignant; ***D:*** Ettore Scola; ***W:*** Ettore Scola.

La Passante 🦴🦴🦴 *La Passante du Sans Souci; The Passerby* **1983** An otherwise peace-loving man murders the Paraguayan ambassador to France. In somewhat clumsy flashback style the murderer's orphaned childhood and other memories provide motives for the murder. Though posed more slowly than typical intrigue plots, the movie blends love and the legacy of Nazism, passion and politics in an engaging way, spiced with nudity and some violence. In her last screen appearance Schneider movingly portrays dual roles. In French with English subtitles. **106m/C VHS.** *FR GE* Romy Schneider, Michel Piccoli, Helmut Griem, Gerard Klein, Matthieu Carriere, Maria Schell; ***D:*** Jacques Rouffio; ***M:*** Georges Delerue. Cesar '83: Sound.

La Petite Jerusalem 🦴🦴 *Little Jerusalem* **2005** Two sisters live in a drab housing project in Sarcelles, a Paris suburb that is home to such a number of Orthodox Jewish immigrants that it is known as "Little Jerusalem." Laura (Valette) is a philosophy student and skeptic who finds herself interested in Algerian Muslim Djamel (Tillette de Clermont-Tonnerre). Her religious married sister Mathilde (Zylberstein) figures out that her devotions to God are causing her frustrated husband, Ariel (Todeschini), to stray. The sisters have trouble reconciling intimacy with their cultural upbringing but debut writer/director Albou really doesn't go anywhere with her story. French and Hebrew with subtitles. **96m/C DVD.** *FR* Fanny Valette, Elsa Zylberstein, Bruno Todeschini, Michael Cohen, Aurore Clement, Francois Marthouret, Hedi Tillette de Clermont-Tonerre, Sonia Tahar, Saida Bekkouche, Salah Teskouk, Marlon Altiparmakian, Michel Hadjadj; ***D:*** Karin Albou; ***W:*** Karin Albou; ***C:*** Laurent Brunet; ***M:*** Cyril Morin.

La Petite Lili 🦴 1/2 *Little Lili* **2003** Miller develops a freeform adaptation of Chekhov's 1895 "The Seagull," moving it from 19th-century Russia to 21st-century rural France and shifting the literature/theater emphasis to filmmaking. What transpires is much unrequited love, geriatric loathing, and opinions about making art. In French with subtitles. **104m/C DVD.** *FR CA* Nicole Garcia, Bernard Giraudeau, Jean-Pierre Marielle, Ludivine Sagnier, Robinson Stevenin, Julie Depardieu, Yves Jacques, Anne LeNy, Marc Betton; ***D:*** Claude Miller; ***C:*** Gerard de Battista.

La Petite Sirene 🦴🦴 *The Little Mermaid* **1980** Isabelle is a 14-year-old schoolgirl, obssessed with the story of the Little Mermaid, who tries to ingratiate herself to Georges, a 40-year-old garage mechanic. Seeing him as her prince charming, she persists in trying to make him a part of her life, in spite of his resistance. In French with English subtitles. **104m/C VHS.** *FR* Laura Alexis, Philippe Leotard, Evelyne Dress, Marie DuBois; ***D:*** Roger Andrieux; ***W:*** Roger Andrieux.

La Piscine 🦴🦴 *The Swimming Pool; The Sinners* **1969** Jean-Paul (Delon) and his wife Marianne (Schneider) are on vacation at a villa near St. Tropez. Marianne invites her ex-lover Harry (Ronet) and his teenaged daughter Penelope (Birkin) to join them and the foursome spend most of their time lounging around the pool. But tensions develop and the consequences are dramatic when Jean-Paul decides to seduce the nubile Penelope. French with subtitles. **120m/C DVD.** *FR* Alain Delon, Romy Schneider, Maurice Ronet, Jane Birkin; ***D:*** Jacques Deray; ***W:*** Jacques Deray, Jean-Claude Carriere; ***C:*** Jean-Jacques Tarbes; ***M:*** Michel Legrand.

La Promesse 🦴🦴 *The Promise* **1996** Fifteen-year-old Igor (Renier) helps his disreputable father Roger (Gourmet) run an illegal immigrant operation in the Beligan town of Liege. African immigrant Amidou (Ouedraogo) has just been joined by his wife Assita (Ouedraogo) and their baby. When Amidou dies in an accident, Roger forces Igor to help him bury the body secretly and tells the bewildered wife that her husband has left her. But Igor is caught in the middle—he'd promised the dying Amidou to look after Assita and he still has enough conscience to want to help—but it also puts Igor into a dangerous conflict with his father. French with subtitles. **93m/C VHS, DVD.** *FR BE* Jeremie Renier, Olivier Gourmet, Assita Ouedraogo, Rasmane Ouedraogo; ***D:*** Jean-Pierre Dardenne, Luc Dardenne; ***W:*** Jean-Pierre Dardenne, Luc Dardenne; ***C:*** Alain Marcoen; ***M:*** Jean-Marie Billy. L.A. Film Critics '97: Foreign Film; Natl. Soc. Film Critics '97: Foreign Film.

La Puritaine 🦴🦴 1/2 **1986** Before his planned reconciliation with his daughter, the artistic manager of a theatre has young actresses portray different sides of the daughter's personality. In French with English subtitles. **90m/C VHS.** Michel Piccoli, Sandrine Bonnaire; ***D:*** Lou Doillon.

La Ronde 🦴🦴🦴 1/2 **1951** A classic comedy of manners and sharply witty tour-de-farce in which a group of people in 1900

Vienna keep changing romantic partners until things wind up where they started. Ophuls' swirling direction creates a fast-paced farce of desire and regret with wicked yet subtle style. Based on Arthur Schnitzler's play and remade as "Circle of Love." In French with English subtitles. **97m/B VHS, DVD.** *FR* Simone Signoret, Anton Walbrook, Simone Simon, Serge Reggiani, Daniel Gelin, Danielle Darrieux, Jean-Louis Barrault, Fernand Gravey, Odette Joyeux, Isa Miranda, Gerard Philipe; ***D:*** Max Ophuls. British Acad. '51: Film.

La Roue 🦴🦴🦴 *The Wheel* **1923** Locomotive engineer Sisif saves the infant Norma from a train wreck and raises her as his daughter. When she becomes a beautiful young woman, Sisif realizes he has romantic feelings for her as does his son Elie so a horrified Norma (who finally learns she was adopted) goes off to marry Jacques. Tragedy strikes, leaving Sisif embittered and blind but a widowed Norma secretly cares for him. Gance's epic was primarily filmed on location and his experimental techniques, including rapid montage, were taken up by numerous other filmmakers. **270m/B DVD.** *FR* Severin Mars, Ivy Close, Gabriel de Gravone, Pierre Magnier; ***D:*** Abel Gance; ***W:*** Abel Gance; ***C:*** Leonce-Henri burel, Gaston Burn.

L.A. Rules: The Pros and Cons of Breathing 🦴 1/2 **1994** Four friends meet regularly at the same trendy L.A. bar, discussing their travails as they try to make it in Hollywood. **92m/C VHS.** Joey Lauren Adams, Phil Brock, Noelle Parker, Barry Sobel, Joey Dedeo, Ira Heiden, Philip Tanzini; ***D:*** Robert Munic; ***W:*** Robert Munic; ***C:*** Steve Adcock.

La Rupture 🦴🦴 1/2 *The Breakup* **1970** Thriller about a wife trying to protect her child from her husband's unsavory family. Audran and her son are attacked by her husband (Drouot), who's high on drugs. She fights back and he winds up in the hospital. Her father-in-law (Bouquet), who wants his grandson to live with him, then hires a seedy investigator (Cassel) to spy on Audran. Based on the Charlotte Armstrong novel. In French with English subtitles. **124m/C VHS, DVD.** *FR* Stephane Audran, Jean-Claude Drouot, Michel Bouquet, Jean-Pierre Cassel, Catherine Rouvel, Jean Carmet, Annie Cordy; ***D:*** Claude Chabrol; ***W:*** Claude Chabrol; ***M:*** Pierre Jansen.

La Salamandre 🦴🦴 *The Salamander* **1971** Non-conformist Rosemonde, suspected of shooting her guardian, is being interviewed by a novelist and a journalist trying to write a television script about the incident. The more they supposedly learn, the more they are both intimately drawn towards her. French with subtitles. **119m/B VHS.** *SI* Bulle Ogier, Jean-Luc Bideau, Jacques Denis; ***D:*** Alain Tanner; ***W:*** Alain Tanner, John Berger; ***M:*** Patrick Moraz.

La Scorta 🦴🦴🦴 1/2 *The Bodyguards; The Escorts* **1994** Slick, fact-based political thriller focuses on four carabinieri (state police officers) who struggle to maintain some semblance of their normal lives after they are assigned to protect a judge investigating government corruption and a related murder in a Sicilian town. A crackling alternative to Americanized mobster melodrama, marked by taut direction, meaty characters, and coolly understated performances that seamlessly portray brotherhood, heroism, suspicion, and betrayal amid the battle for power between the Italian state and the Mafia. In Italian with English subtitles. **92m/C VHS, DVD.** *IT* Claudio Amendola, Enrico Lo Verso, Tony Sperandeo, Ricky Memphis, Carlo Cecchi, Leo Gullotta, Angelo Infanti; ***D:*** Ricky Tognazzi; ***W:*** Graziano Diana, Simona Izzo; ***M:*** Ennio Morricone.

La Scoumoune 🦴🦴 1/2 *The Pariah; Hit Man* **1972** The local "fixer" and heavy gets into trouble and no one comes to help. A movie that searches for honesty. Dubbed in English. **87m/C VHS.** *FR* Jean-Paul Belmondo, Claudia Cardinale, Luciano Catenacci, Michel Constantin; ***D:*** Jose Giovanni; ***W:*** Jose Giovanni; ***C:*** Andreas Winding; ***M:*** Francois de Roubaix.

La Sentinelle 🦴🦴 *The Sentinel* **1992** Morose Mathias (Salinger)is traveling by train from Germany to France to attend medical school. The sinister Bleicher (Richard), who seems to be a customs official, grills Mathias but lets him go. In his hotel, Mathias finds a strange package in his luggage and discovers it contains the shrunken head of a man. He keeps his discovery a secret but tests samples of the head in the school laboratory on a quest to figure out who the man was. May sound like a thriller but it's too talky and paced too slowly to hold complete interest. French with subtitles. **139m/C VHS, DVD.** *FR* Emmanuel Salinger, Jean-Louis Richard, Thibault de Montalembert, Valerie Dreville, Marianne (Cuau) Denicourt, Bruno Todeschini, Jean-Luc Boutte; ***D:*** Arnaud Desplechin; ***W:*** Arnaud Desplechin; ***C:*** Caroline Champetier; ***M:*** Marc Oliver Sommer.

La Separation 🦴🦴🦴 **1998** Pierre (Auteuil) and Anne (Huppert) share a long-term relationship and a 15-month-old son. What they no longer seem to have is any passion for each other as they go through their daily routine. Anne decides to have an affair—but doesn't see any reason it should break up her household. However, the increasingly miserable Pierre doesn't share her belief. Based on the 1991 novel "Separation" by Franck. French with subtitles. **85m/C VHS, DVD.** *FR* Daniel Auteuil, Isabelle Huppert, Karin Viard, Jerome Deschamps; ***D:*** Christian Vincent; ***W:*** Christian Vincent, Dan Franck; ***C:*** Denis Lenoir.

La Signora di Tutti 🦴🦴🦴 **1934** An early Italian biography of Gaby Doriot, a movie star whose professional success is paired by personal misery. Prestigious director Ophuls, working in exile from his native Germany, was unable to complete many projects in the years leading up to and during WWII. This is one of the few. Watch for innovative camera work intended to underscore the film's mood. In Italian with English subtitles. **92m/B VHS.** *IT* Isa Miranda; ***D:*** Max Ophuls.

La Silence de la Mer 🦴🦴🦴 *The Silence of the Sea* **1947** An old French farmer (Robian) and his niece (Stephane) are forced to billet a German officer (Vernon) in their home during the Occupation. They've vowed never to speak to him but the German continues to pour out his thoughts on music, war, and his love of France into their silence. Melville's first feature; French with subtitles. **86m/B VHS.** *FR* Howard Vernon, Jean-Marie Robian, Nicole Stephane; ***D:*** Jean-Pierre Melville; ***W:*** Jean-Pierre Melville; ***C:*** Henri Decae; ***M:*** Edgar Bischoff.

L.A. Story 🦴🦴🦴 **1991 (PG-13)** Livin' ain't easy in the city of angels. Harris K. Telemacher (Martin), a weatherman in a city where the weather never changes, wrestles with the meaning of life and love while consorting with beautiful people, distancing from significant other Henner, cavorting with valley girl Parker, and falling for newswoman Tennant (Martin's real life wife). Written by the comedian, the story's full of keen insights into the everyday problems and ironies of living in the Big Tangerine. It's no wonder the script's full of so much thoughtful detail: Martin is said to have worked on it intermittently for seven years. Charming, fault forgiving but not fault ignoring portrait. **98m/C VHS, DVD.** Steve Martin, Victoria Tennant, Richard E. Grant, Marilu Henner, Sarah Jessica Parker, Sam McMurray, Patrick Stewart, Iman, Kevin Pollak; ***D:*** Mick Jackson; ***W:*** Steve Martin; ***C:*** Andrew Dunn; ***M:*** Peter Melnick.

La Strada 🦴🦴🦴🦴 *The Road* **1954** Simple-minded girl, played by Fellini's wife, Masina, is sold to a brutal, coarse circus strongman and she falls in love with him despite his abuse. They tour the countryside and eventually meet up with a gentle acrobat, played by Basehart, who alters their fate. Fellini masterwork was the director's first internationally acclaimed film, and is, by turns, somber and amusing as it demonstrates the filmmaker's sensitivity to the underprivileged of the world and his belief in spiritual redemption. Subtitled in English. **107m/B VHS, DVD.** *IT* Giulietta Masina, Anthony Quinn, Richard Basehart, Aldo Silvani; ***D:*** Federico Fellini; ***W:*** Ennio Flaiano, Brunello Rondi, Tullio Pinelli, Federico Fellini; ***M:*** Nino Rota. Oscars '56: Foreign Film; N.Y. Film Critics '56: Foreign Film.

La Symphonie Pastorale 🦴🦴🦴 1/2 **1946** A Swiss pastor takes in an orphan blind girl who grows up to be beautiful. The pastor then competes for her affections with his son. Quiet drama based on the Andre Gide novel, with breathtaking mountain scenery as the backdrop for this tragedy rife with symbolism. **105m/B VHS.** *FR* Pierre Blanchar, Michele Morgan, Jean Desailly, Line Noro, Andree Clement; ***D:*** Jean Delannoy. Cannes '46: Actress (Morgan).

La Terra Trema 🦴🦴🦴 1/2 *Episoda Del Mare; The Earth Will Tremble* **1948** The classic example of Italian neo-realism, about a poor Sicilian fisherman, his family and their village. A spare, slow-moving, profound and ultimately lyrical tragedy, this semi-documentary explores the economic exploitation of Sicily's fishermen. Filmed on location with the villagers playing themselves; highly acclaimed though not commercially successful. In Sicilian with English subtitles. Some radically cut versions may be available, but are to be avoided. Franco Zefferelli was one of the assistant directors. **161m/B VHS, DVD.** *IT* Antonio Pietrangeli; ***D:*** Luchino Visconti.

La Truite 🦴🦴🦴 *The Trout* **1983 (R)** A young woman leaves her family's rural trout farm and a loveless marriage to seek her fortune in high finance and corporate mayhem. The complicated plot, full of intrigue and sexual encounters, sometimes lacks focus. Slickly filmed. **80m/C VHS, DVD.** *FR* Isabelle Huppert, Jean-Pierre Cassel, Daniel Olbrychski, Jeanne Moreau, Jacques Spiesser, Ruggero Raimondi, Alexis Smith, Craig Stevens; ***D:*** Joseph Losey. Cesar '83: Cinematog.

L.A. Twister 🦴 **2004** Sloppy buddy comedy has unemployed actor Lenny (Ward) convincing his best friend Ethan (Daly) to produce a movie about their misadventures in Hollywood. It's showbiz cliches all the way with a couple of disagreeable leads. **92m/C DVD.** Zack (Zach) Ward, Jennifer Aspen, Susan Blakely, Tony Daly, Wendy Worthington; ***D:*** Sven Pape; ***W:*** Geoffrey Saville-Reed; ***C:*** Patrice Lucien Cochet; ***M:*** Ben Moody. **VIDEO**

La Vengeance d'une Femme 🦴🦴 *A Woman's Revenge* **1989** Refined Cecile and sultry Suzy are two sides of a love triangle whose third member, Cecile's husband, has just died. Cecile decides to get to know his mistress better, which naturally has Suzy worried. Is Cecile out for revenge or does she sincerely want to befriend the "other woman." Based on Dostoyevski's "The Eternal Husband." In French with English subtitles. **133m/C VHS.** *FR* Isabelle Huppert, Beatrice Dalle; ***D:*** Jacques Doillon; ***W:*** Jean-Francois Goyet, Jacques Doillon.

L.A. Vice 🦴 1/2 **1989** A detective is transferred to the vice squad, where he must investigate a series of murders. Sequel to "L.A. Heat." **90m/C VHS, DVD.** Jim Brown, Lawrence-Hilton Jacobs, William (Bill) Smith; ***D:*** Joseph Merhi.

La Vie Continue 🦴🦴 1/2 **1982** A middle-aged woman suddenly finds herself widowed after 20 years of marriage and tries to build a new life for herself and her children. Girardot's performance can't quite dispel melodramatic suds. Loosely and more effectively remade as "Men Don't Leave." In French with English subtitles or dubbed. **93m/C VHS.** *IT* Annie Girardot, Jean-Pierre Cassel, Michel Aumont, Pierre Dux, Guilia Salvatori, Emmanuel Goyet, Rivera Andres; ***D:*** Moshe Mizrahi; ***W:*** Moshe Mizrahi; ***M:*** Georges Delerue.

La Vie de Boheme 🦴🦴🦴 *Bohemian Life* **1993** Comedy takes a mocking look at art and romantic love. A trio of hapless but dedicated comrades, Rodolfo (Pellonpaa) the painter, Marcel (Wilms) the poet, and Schaunard (Vaananen), must scrounge around the mealy edges of modern Paris because their art isn't filling their stomachs. Meanwhile, they experience the pangs of love like everyone else, although each is devoutly committed to his art as well. Starkly different from the lush, operatic version by Puccini, but based on the same source, a 19th century novel by Henri Mullet. French with subtitles. **100m/C VHS.** Matti Pellonpaa, Andre Wilms, Kari Vaananen, Jean-Pierre Leaud, Samuel Fuller, Louis Malle, Evelyne Didi, Christine Murillo, Laika, Carlos Salgado, Alexis Nitzer, Sylvie van den Elsen, Gilles Charmant, Dominique Marcas; ***D:*** Aki Kaurismaki; ***W:*** Aki Kaurismaki.

La Vie en Rose 🦴🦴 *La Mome; The Kid* **2007 (PG-13)** Think Judy Garland—only French. Somewhat old-fashioned, non-chronological biopic follows the triumphs and tragedies of Edith Piaf (Cotillard), France's famous "little sparrow." Dirt-poor little Edith grows up in a brothel, sings on street corners, gets discovered (by Depardieu's oily impresario), and finds success in cabaret with her astonishing voice. She also finds alcohol and drug addiction, ill health, and a tragic love with married boxer Marcel Cerdan (Martins). Cotillard is amazing in the lead, getting both Piaf's gestures and attitude just right (she lip-synchs her vocals). French with subtitles. **140m/C DVD.** *FR GB CZ* Marion Cotillard, Gerard Depardieu, Emmanuelle Seigner, Pascal Greggory, Sylvie Testud, Clotilde Courau, Jean-Paul Rouve, Catherine Allegret, Jean-Pierre Martins; ***D:*** Olivier Dahan; ***W:*** Olivier Dahan, Isabelle Sobelman; ***C:*** Tetsuo Nagata; ***M:*** Christopher Gunning. Oscars '07: Actress (Cotillard), Makeup; British Acad. '07: Actress (Cotillard), Costume Des., Makeup, Orig. Score; Golden Globes '08: Actress—Mus./Comedy (Cotillard).

La Vie Est Belle 🦴🦴 *Life Is Rosy* **1987** The rags to riches story of a poor rural musician from Zaire who goes to the city to break into radio and TV. He uses his wit and talent to foil a greedy boss, win a beautiful wife, and make himself a singing sensation. French with subtitles. **85m/C VHS.** ***D:*** Nagangura Mweze, Bernard Lamy.

La Vie Promise 🦴🦴 1/2 *The Promised Life* **2002** Cold, aging French prostitute reevaluates her life after meeting the daughter she abandoned years ago. Pic turns into a road movie as the decidedly unmaternal Sylvia (Huppert) and her stubborn 14-year-old Laurence (Forget) go on the lam after Laurence rashly murders Sylvia's abusive pimp. They separately meet up with the mysterious Joshua (Gerggory) who joins them on their journey which has now become Sylvia's quest to reunite with her former husband (Marcon) and 8-year-old son she abandoned shortly after giving birth—an experience which drove her into a mental asylum. In an otherwise mediocre film, Huppert turns in a stunning performance as the streetwalker who must face a past she's trying to forget. Haunting soundtrack and lush French scenery are highlights. **94m/C DVD.** *FR* Isabelle Huppert, Pascal Greggory, Maud Forget, Fabienne Babe, Andre Marcon; ***D:*** Olivier Dahan; ***W:*** Agnes Fustier-Dahan; ***C:*** Alex Lamarque.

L.A. Wars 🦴 1/2 **1994 (R)** A Latin American drug dealer moves into the territory of an Italian mobster, causing a turf war. When a cop rescues the mobster's daughter from the scuzzball, his boss forces him to infiltrate the mobster's organization. Abundant body count, lots of T&A. **94m/C VHS.** Vince Murdocco, Mary Zilba, A.J. Stevens, Rodrigo Obregon; ***D:*** Martin Morris, Tony Kandah.

Labor Pains 🦴🦴 1/2 **1999 (R)** Sedgwick gets preggers by artist Morrow who disappears for eight months. When he returns, she's in labor and both her parents (Klein and Moore) and her best friend (Rochon) are trying to convince Sedgwick not to give the baby up for adoption. Meanwhile, the new parents decide to get re-acquainted. **89m/C VHS.** Kyra Sedgwick, Rob Morrow, Lela Rochon, Mary Tyler Moore, Robert Klein, Dann Fink; ***D:*** Tracy Alexson; ***W:*** Tracy Alexson.

Labor Pains 🦴🦴 **2009 (PG-13)** ABC Family wound up with this comedy when Lohan's career imploded and it wasn't deemed worthy of a theatrical release. Still, the flick and Lindsay are amusing if you can completely suspend all common sense since the plot is ridiculous. Mouthy publishing assistant Thea needs to keep her job since she's raising her younger sister. About to be fired, she plays the pregnancy card and suddenly everyone in the office is falling for her lie and getting all gooey over her impending single motherhood. Thea even gets the chance to work on a pregnancy book with cutie Nick (Kirby). **89m/C DVD.** Lindsay Lohan, Luke Kirby, Cheryl Hines, Chris Parnell, Janeane Garofalo, Bridgit Mendler, Tracee Ellis Ross; ***D:*** Lara Shapiro; ***W:*** Lara Shapiro; ***C:*** Stacy Kramer, Dan Stoloff; ***M:*** Andrew Hollander. **CABLE**

Laboratory 🦴 **1980** Things go awry when the earthling subjects of an alien experiment revolt against their captors. **93m/C VHS.** Camille Mitchell, Martin Kove, Ken Washington, Corinne Michel; ***D:*** Allan Sandler, Bob Emenegger; ***W:*** Steve Marshall, Allan Sandler.

Labyrinth **1986 (PG)** While babysitting her baby brother Froud, Connelly is so frustrated she asks the goblins to take him away. When the Goblin King, played by Bowie, comes to answer her idle wish, she must try to rescue Froud by solving the fantastic labyrinth. If she does not find him in time, Froud will become one of the goblins forever. During her journey, Connelly is befriended by all sorts of odd creatures created by Henson, and she grows up a little along the way. A fascinating adventure movie for the whole family. **90m/C VHS, DVD.** David Bowie, Jennifer Connelly, Toby Froud, Shelley Thompson, Dave Goetz, Karen Prell, Steve Whitmire; ***D:*** Jim Henson; ***W:*** Jim Henson, Terry Jones; ***C:*** Alex Thomson; ***M:*** Trevor Jones, David Bowie.

Labyrinth of Passion 1/2 *Laberinto de Pasiones* **1982** A screwball farce, directed by Almodovar, featuring a host of strange characters running around Madrid in search of sex and laughter. They find plenty of both. An early film by an influential director. In Spanish with English subtitles. **100m/C VHS.** *SP* Antonio Banderas, Imanol Arias, Cecilia (Celia) Roth; ***D:*** Pedro Almodovar; ***W:*** Pedro Almodovar.

The Lacemaker 1/2 *La Dentielliere* **1977** Huppert's first shot at stardom, on videodisc with digital sound and a letterboxed print. A young beautician and a university student fall in love on vacation but soon begin to realize the differences in their lives. Adapted from the novel by Pascal Laine. In French with English subtitles. **107m/C** *FR SI GE* Isabelle Huppert, Yves Beneyton, Florence Giorgetti, Anna Marie Duringer; ***D:*** Claude Goretta.

Ladder 49 1/2 **2004 (PG-13)** An old-fashioned homage to firefighters begins when Jack Morrison (Phoenix) is injured and trapped in a burning warehouse. While his chief and mentor, Mike Kennedy (Travolta), coordinates a rescue effort, Jack remembers his first day as a rookie. The movie will continue alternating between Jack's career as a firefighter and his current predicament as well as his personal life, which includes his supportive, loving wife Linda (Barrett). That's pretty much it; you watch pros doing a job that can be very dangerous and how firehouse camaraderie helps them cope. The actors are earnest and the action convincing; it's not ground-breaking but it's not boring either. **115m/C VHS, DVD, Blu-ray Disc.** *US* Joaquin Rafael (Leaf) Phoenix, John Travolta, Jacinda Barrett, Robert Patrick, Morris Chestnut, Billy Burke, Balthazar Getty, Tim Guinee; ***D:*** Jay Russell; ***W:*** Lewis Colick, Scott B. Smith; ***C:*** James L. Carter; ***M:*** William Ross.

L'Addition 1/2 *The Patsy; Caged Heart* **1985 (R)** According to some cinematic code, the male lead always gets in lots of trouble whenever he tries to help a beautiful stranger. This time, Berry, as Bruno Windler, winds up arrested for shoplifting when he attempts to help Abril. Jailed and on the verge of parole, Windler unwittingly becomes involved in a prison break and is accused of helping a crime don mastermind the escape and of shooting a guard. That's where that gallic flair for capturing the sado-masochistic underbelly of humanity comes in, as Windler is viciously pursued by the malevolent guard. **85m/C VHS.** Richard Berry, Victoria Abril, Richard Bohringer, Farid Chopel, Fabrice Eberhard; ***D:*** Denis Amar; ***W:*** Jean Curtelin; ***C:*** Robert Fraisse; ***M:*** Jean-Claude Petit.

Ladies and Gentlemen, the Fabulous Stains 1/2 **1982** Minor price-of-fame drama mainly notable for the beautiful presence of 15-year-old Lane as lead Stain, troubled teen Corinne Burns. She forms an all-girl punk rock band that lacks talent but has a look that can be marketed by their unscrupulous agent Dave (Clennon). They go on the road with a Brit punk quartet and ambitious Corinne steals their songs, leading to public humiliation and a little soul searching. **87m/C DVD.** Diane Lane, Laura Dern, David Clennon, Ray Winstone, Marin Kanter, Peter Donat, Cynthia Sikes, John Lehne; ***D:*** Lou Adler; ***W:*** Nancy Dowd; ***C:*** Bruce Surtees.

The Ladies Club 1/2 **1986 (R)** A group of rape victims get together and begin to victimize rapists. **86m/C VHS.** Bruce Davison, Karen Austin, Diana Scarwid, Shera Danese, Beverly Todd; ***D:*** A.K. Allen.

Ladies in Lavender **2004 (PG-13)** Sisters Janet (Smith) and Ursula (Dench) Widdington have their routine Cornwall cottage life turned about when a handsome, half-drowned young man (Bruhl), who happens to be a Polish violin virtuoso, washes up on their pebbled beach. How, we never find out. Passions and jealousies ignite in the sisters as they nurse him back to health and intercept the advances of a pretty young artist who is attracted to their patient's musical talents. The dames' performances do not disappoint, but the same cannot be said for Bruhl, who lacks depth in comparison. Gallant effort by Dance in reworking William J. Locke's short story, although a bit overreaching. **103m/C DVD.** *GB* Judi Dench, Maggie Smith, Daniel Bruhl, Miriam Margolyes, David Warner, Natascha (Natasha) McElhone, Freddie Jones, Clive Russell; ***D:*** Charles Dance; ***W:*** Charles Dance; ***C:*** Peter Biziou; ***M:*** Nigel Hess.

The Ladies' Man **1961** Piecemeal Lewis farce, with Jerry playing a clutzy handyman working at a girls' boarding house. Some riotous routines balanced by slow pacing. **106m/C VHS, DVD.** Jerry Lewis, Helen Traubel, Jack Kruschen, Doodles Weaver, Gloria Jean; ***D:*** Jerry Lewis; ***W:*** Jerry Lewis.

Ladies' Man *Lemmy Pour les Dames* **1962** Super agent Lemmy Caution (Constantine) is relaxing on the French Riviera when a woman is murdered. He learns that a Communist government has been blackmailing some married gals whose husbands work for western intelligence agencies and Lemmy comes to their rescue. The sixth time Constantine played the character. Dubbed. **97m/B DVD.** *FR* Eddie Constantine, Francoise Brion, Yvonne Monlaur, Jacques Berthier, Robert Berri, Claudine Coster, Elaine D'Almeida, Guy Delorme; ***D:*** Bernard Borderie; ***W:*** Bernard Borderie; ***C:*** Armand Thirard; ***M:*** Paul Misraki.

The Ladies Man 1/2 **2000 (R)** Producer Lorne Michaels was allegedly the model for Mike Myers' Dr. Evil. It's becoming clear that his repeated abduction of SNL skits in order to stretch them out on the rack and loose them on the public is part of some nefarious plan. The victim this time is Leon Phelps (Meadows), a stuck-in-the-'70s late-night talk show host who dispenses inappropriate romantic advice. Raised by Hugh Hefner but banished for sleeping with the wrong bunny, Leon soon becomes banished from his radio gig, too. He eases the pain by seducing other men's wives, leading to the formation of an anti-Leon posse. Meanwhile, his faithful ex-producer Julie (Parsons) inexplicably sticks by his side hoping to tame Leon's wild ways. In the end, Leon is converted to a one-lady man, and the comic possibilities of this lame flick are squandered. **84m/C VHS, DVD.** Tim Meadows, Will Ferrell, Tiffani(-Amber) Thiessen, Billy Dee Williams, Karyn Parsons, Lee Evans, John Witherspoon, Eugene Levy, Tamala Jones, Julianne Moore, Sean Thibodeau; ***D:*** Reginald (Reggie) Hudlin; ***W:*** Tim Meadows, Dennis McNicholas, Andrew Steele; ***C:*** Johnny E. Jensen; ***M:*** Marcus Miller.

The Ladies of the Bois de Bologne *Les Dames du Bois de Bologne; Ladies of the Park* **1944** Beware the woman scorned—as Jean (Bernard) learns. He ends his longtime relationship with Helene (Casares), although they vow to stay friends, but she secretly plots revenge and finds it in the person of Agnes (Labourdette), a former prostitute. Helene introduces Agnes to Jean, hoping they'll be attracted to one another. They are but after the wedding ceremony Helene reveals the truth about Agnes' sordid past. Updated adaptation of a story in Diderot's "Jacques Le Fatalist." French with subtitles. **83m/B VHS, DVD.** *FR* Maria Casares, Paul Bernard, Elina Labourdette; ***D:*** Robert Bresson; ***W:*** Robert Bresson, Jean Cocteau.

Ladies of the Chorus **1949** Monroe stars as a burlesque chorus girl who shares the stage with her mom (Jergens) and a handful of other beauties. She meets and falls in love with a wealthy socialite (Brooks), but her mother completely disapproves of the relationship. Monroe later learns that her mother was in the same circumstances several years before. Although only her second film appearance, Monroe's talents are already quite apparent in this low-budget musical romance. ♫ Every Baby Nees a Da Da Daddy; Anyone Can Tell I Love You; Crazy For You; You're Never Too Old; Ladies of the Chorus. **61m/B VHS.** Adele Jergens, Marilyn Monroe, Rand Brooks, Nana Bryant, Steven Geray, Bill Edwards; ***D:*** Phil Karlson.

Ladies of the Lotus **1987** Bloodthirsty Vancouver gangsters raid Lotus, Inc., a modeling agency, and sell beautiful young women into slavery. As bad as it sounds. **120m/C VHS.** *CA* Richard Dale, Angela Read, Patrick Bermel, Darcia Carnie; ***D:*** Lloyd A. Simandl, Douglas C. Nicolle.

Ladies on the Rocks 1/2 *Koks I Kulissen* **1983** Aspiring comediennes Micha and Laura pack up their van and take their bizarre cabaret act on the road through rural Denmark. They find their private lives disintegrating but turn each disaster into new material for their act. In Danish with English subtitles. **100m/C VHS.** *DK* Helle Ryslinge, Anne Marie Helger, Flemming Quist Moller; ***D:*** Christian Braad Thomsen.

Ladies They Talk About 1/2 *Women in Prison* **1933** Stanwyck stars as a tough-talking gun moll who belongs to a gang of bank robbers. They get caught and Stanwyck is sent to the female division of San Quentin. The acting is great in this pre-Code prison movie, but the film gets a bit punchy at times. Based on the true-life experiences of actress Dorothy Mackaye, who went to jail after her husband was killed in a fight with actor Paul Kelley, who was also sent to prison. Adapted from the play "Women in Prison" by Dorothy Mackaye and Carlton Miles. **69m/B VHS.** Barbara Stanwyck, Preston Foster, Lyle Talbot, Dorothy Burgess, Lillian Roth, Maude Eburne, Harold Huber, Ruth Donnelly; ***D:*** Howard Bretherton, William Keighley.

Ladies Who Do 1/2 **1963** A group of cleaning ladies band together against the unscrupulous businessman who wants to tear down their homes in order to build an office tower. Along with a retired colonel, they use the stock market secrets gleaned from the rubbish they toss away to make a killing in the market and save the day. **90m/B VHS.** *GB* Peggy Mount, Robert Morley, Harry H. Corbett, Miriam Karlin, Avril Elgar, Dandy Nichols, Jon Pertwee, Nigel Davenport; ***D:*** C.M. Pennington-Richards; ***W:*** Michael Pertwee.

The Lady and the Duke 1/2 *L'Anglaise et le Duc* **2001 (PG-13)** Based on the memoirs of Englishwoman Grace Elliott (Russell), who lived in Paris during the French Revolution and remained a loyal supporter of King Louis XVI. The Duke in question is her former lover, Philippe, Duc d'Orleans (Dreyfus), with whom Grace has remained friends. A cousin to the King, Philippe himself is a moderate revolutionary and encourages Grace to return to England for her own safety, which she refuses to do. 81-year-old Rohmer commissioned a series of painted backdrops depicting 18th-century France rather than build sets and then superimposed his actors upon the backdrops, offering remarkably effective visuals. French with subtitles. **129m/C VHS, DVD.** *FR* Lucy Russell, Jean-Claude Dreyfus, Francois Marthouret, Leonard Cobiant, Caroline Morin, Alain Libolt, Marie Riviere, Helena Dubeil; ***D:*** Eric Rohmer; ***W:*** Eric Rohmer; ***C:*** Diane Baratier.

The Lady and the Highwayman 1/2 **1989** TV adaptation of the Barbara Cartland historical romance finds a rogue falling for the lady he's sworn to protect. Naturally, there's a happy ending. **100m/C VHS, DVD.** *GB* Hugh Grant, Emma Samms, Oliver Reed, Michael York, Robert Morley, John Mills, Lysette Anthony; ***D:*** John Hough; ***W:*** Terence Feely; ***M:*** Laurie Johnson.

Lady and the Tramp **1955 (G)** The animated Disney classic about two dogs who fall in love. Tramp is wild and carefree; Lady is a spoiled pedigree who runs away from home after her owners have a baby. They just don't make dog romances like this anymore. ♫ He's a Tramp; La La Lu; Siamese Cat Song; Peace on Earth; Bella Notte. **76m/C VHS, DVD.** ***D:*** Hamilton Luske, Clyde Geronimi, Wilfred Jackson; ***W:*** Erdman Penner, Ralph Wright, Don DaGradi; ***M:*** Sonny Burke, Peggy Lee; ***V:*** Larry Roberts, Peggy Lee, Barbara Luddy, Stan Freberg, Alan Reed, Bill Thompson, Bill Baucon, Verna Felton, George Givot, Dallas McKennon, Lee Millar.

Lady Audley's Secret **2000** Old-fashioned and rather dull potboiler based on the 1862 novel by Mary Elizabeth Braddon. Governess Lucy (McIntosh) marries her employer, Sir Michael Audley (Cranham). But Lucy has a shady past, including a previous husband, George (Bamber), who turns out to be a friend of Sir Michael's nephew, Robert (Mackintosh). Then George disappears and Robert wonders just how dangerous the new Lady Audley is. **120m/C VHS, DVD.** *GB* Neve McIntosh, Steven Mackintosh, Kenneth Cranham, Jamie Bamber, Juliette Caton, Melanie Clark Pullen; ***D:*** Betsan Morris-Evans; ***W:*** Donal Hounam; ***C:*** Julian Court; ***M:*** Paul Carr. **TV**

Lady Avenger **1989 (R)** A woman is bent on getting revenge on her brother's killers. **90m/C VHS.** Peggie Sanders, Michelle (McClellan) Bauer, Daniel Hirsch; ***D:*** David DeCoteau; ***C:*** Thomas Callaway.

Lady Be Good 1/2 **1941** Adapted from the 1924 Gershwin Broadway hit, the plot's been revamped, much to the critics' distaste ("Variety" called it "molasses paced"). Sothern and Young play a tunesmith duo who excel at musical harmony and marital strife. Applauded for its music (the critics loved Hammerstein's and the Gershwins' tunes), the show's Academy Award-winning song was, ironically, written by Jerome Kern. And if that's not enough, levity man Skelton and hoofer Powell are thrown in for good measure. ♫ The Last Time I Saw Paris; So Am I; Oh Lady Be Good; Fascinating Rhythm; Hang On To Me; You'll Never Know; You're Words, My Music; Saudades. **111m/B VHS.** Eleanor Powell, Ann Sothern, Robert Young, Lionel Barrymore, John Carroll, Red Skelton, Dan Dailey, Virginia O'Brien, Tom Conway, Phil Silvers, Doris Day; ***D:*** Norman Z. McLeod; ***C:*** George J. Folsey; ***M:*** Oscar Hammerstein, Ira Gershwin, Jerome Kern, George Bassman. Oscars '41: Song ("The Last Time I Saw Paris").

Lady Beware **1987 (R)** A psychotic doctor becomes obsessed with a beautiful store-window dresser who specializes in steamy, erotic fantasies. When he wages a campaign of terror against her, she realizes that she must stop him before he kills her. **108m/C VHS.** Diane Lane, Michael Woods, Cotter Smith, Viveca Lindfors, Tyra Ferrell, Peter Nevargic, Edward Penn; ***D:*** Karen Arthur; ***W:*** Charles Zev Cohen.

Lady by Choice 1/2 **1934** Lombard stars as a beautiful young fan dancer who is arrested for a lewd public performance. Taking the advice of her press agent, she hires an old bag lady to pose as her mother on Mother's Day. Robson portrays her "mother" and comes to think of Lombard as her own daughter. Robson encourages Lombard to give up fan dancing and to strive for greater things in life. She also pushes her into romance with a wealthy young man (Pryor). Robson is excellent in her role as "mother" and Lombard shows great comic talent in this charming film. **78m/C VHS.** Carole Lombard, May Robson, Roger Pryor, Walter Connolly, Raymond Walburn, James Burke; ***D:*** David Burton; ***W:*** Jo Swerling.

Lady Caroline Lamb **1973** Lady Caroline is a passionate young lady in 19th-century England, who, although the wife of a member of Parliament, has an affair with Lord Byron and brings about her own downfall. Costume drama that never quite goes anywhere. **123m/C** *GB IT* Sarah Miles, Richard Chamberlain, Jon Finch, Laurence Olivier, John Mills, Ralph Richardson; ***D:*** Robert Bolt; ***W:*** Robert Bolt; ***C:*** Oswald Morris; ***M:*** Richard Rodney Bennett.

Lady Chatterley **1992** Oh my, Russell takes his provocative ways to D.H. Lawrence's scandalous novel about the adulterous affair between aristocratic Lady Connie Chatterley (Richardson) and her husband's gamekeeper, Oliver Mellors (Bean). Also includes material taken from two early drafts of the book "The First Lady Chatterley" and "John Thomas and Lady Jane." **210m/C VHS, DVD.** *GB* Joely Richardson, Sean Bean, James Wilby, Shirley Anne Field, Roger Hammond; ***D:*** Ken Russell; ***W:*** Ken Russell; ***C:*** Robin Vidgeon; ***M:*** Jean-Claude Petit. **TV**

Lady Chatterley 2006 Lady Chatterley (Hinds) spends her days collecting flowers after her husband (Giradot) is paralyzed in World War I. She encounters gamekeeper Parkin (Coullo'ch) and the two begin an affair that brings about her sexual awakening. Stunningly shot, and director Ferran manages to maintain a high level of eroticism and character development. French adaptation of the second version of the D.H. Lawrence novel. **168m/C DVD.** *BE FR* Marina Hands, Hippolyte Girardot, Jean-Louis Coulloc'h, Helene Alexandridis; ***D:*** Pascal Ferran; ***W:*** Roger Bohbot, Pierre Trividic, Pascal Ferran; ***C:*** Julien Hirsch; ***M:*** Beatrice Thiriet.

Lady Chatterley's Lover ½ *L'Amant de Lady Chatterley* **1955** English-woman has bad luck to have husband shot up during WWI and sent home paralyzed. In her quest for sexual fulfillment, she takes a new lover, the estate's earthy gamekeeper. Limp adaptation of D.H. Lawrence's novel. In French with English subtitles. **102m/B VHS.** *FR* Danielle Darrieux, Erno Crisa, Leo Genn; ***D:*** Marc Allegret.

Lady Chatterley's Lover ½ **1981 (R)** Remake of the 1955 film version of D.H. Lawrence's classic novel of an English lady who has an affair with the gamekeeper of her husband's estate. Basically soft-focus soft porn. **107m/C VHS, DVD.** *GB FR* Sylvia Kristel, Nicholas Clay, Shane Briant; ***D:*** Just Jaeckin; ***C:*** Robert Fraisse.

Lady Cocoa ½ **1975 (R)** Routine story of a young woman who gets released from jail for 24 hours and sets out for Las Vegas to find the man who framed her. **93m/C VHS, DVD.** Lola Falana, Joe "Mean Joe" Greene, Gene Washington, Alex Dreier; ***D:*** Matt Cimber.

The Lady Confesses **1945** Average mystery that involves Hughes trying to clear her boyfriend of murder. Independently produced. "Leave it to Beaver" fans will want to watch for "Ward Cleaver" Beaumont. **66m/B VHS, DVD.** Mary Beth Hughes, Hugh Beaumont, Edmund MacDonald, Claudia Drake, Emmett Vogan, Barbara Slater, Edward Howard, Dewey Robinson, Carol Andrews; ***D:*** Sam Newfield; ***W:*** Helen Martin, Irwin H. Franklyn; ***C:*** Jack Greenhalgh; ***M:*** Lee Zahler.

Lady Dragon **1992 (R)** A woman and her husband are viciously attacked and only she survives. Found by an old man, she learns a number of martial arts tricks and goes out to get her revenge. **89m/C VHS, DVD.** Cynthia Rothrock, Richard Norton, Robert Ginty, Bella Esperance, Hengko Tornando; ***D:*** David Worth; ***W:*** David Worth; ***C:*** David Worth; ***M:*** Jim West.

Lady Dragon 2 **1993 (R)** Martial arts queen Rothrock returns in another saga of kickboxing vengeance. Susan Morgan seeks revenge on the three killers who terrorized her family. When she unleashes the power of the dragon they don't stand a chance. **92m/C VHS.** Cynthia Rothrock, Billy Drago, Sam Jones, Greg Stuart, Bella Esperance, George Rudy, Adisoerya Abdi; ***D:*** David Worth; ***W:*** Clifford Mohr; ***C:*** David Worth; ***M:*** Jim West.

The Lady Eve **1941** Father/daughter (Coburn, Stanwyck) con artists, out to trip up wealthy beer tycoon Charles Pike (Fonda), instead find themselves tripped up when Jean falls in love with the mark. Ridiculous situations, but Sturges manages to keep them believable and funny. With a train scene that's every man's nightmare. Perhaps the best Sturges ever. Based on the story "The Faithful Heart" by Monckton Hoffe. Later remade as "The Birds and the Bees." **93m/B VHS, DVD.** Barbara Stanwyck, Henry Fonda, Charles Coburn, Eugene Pallette, William Demarest, Eric Blore, Melville Cooper; ***D:*** Preston Sturges; ***W:*** Preston Sturges; ***C:*** Victor Milner. Natl. Film Reg. '94.

Lady for a Day ½ **1933** Delightful telling of the Damon Runyon story, "Madame La Gimp," about an apple peddler (Robson) down on her luck, who is transformed into a lady by a criminal with a heart. "Lady By Choice" is the sequel. **96m/B VHS, DVD.** May Robson, Warren William, Guy Kibbee, Glenda Farrell, Ned Sparks, Jean Parker, Walter Connolly; ***D:*** Frank Capra; ***W:*** Robert Riskin; ***C:*** Joseph Walker.

Lady for a Night **1942** The female owner of a gambling riverboat does her best to break into high society, when murder threatens to spoil her plans. Cast and costumes burdened by pacing. **88m/B VHS.** John Wayne, Joan Blondell, Ray Middleton, Philip Merivale, Blanche Yurka, Edith Barrett, Leonid Kinskey, Montagu Love; ***D:*** Leigh Jason.

Lady Frankenstein ½ *La Figlia di Frankenstein; The Daughter of Frankenstein; Madame Frankenstein* **1972 (R)** Frankenstein's lovely daughter graduates from medical school and returns home. When she sees what her father's been up to, she gets some ideas of her own. Good fun for fans of the genre. **84m/C VHS, DVD.** *IT* Joseph Cotten, Rosalba Neri, Mickey Hargitay, Paul Muller, Herbert (Fuchs) Fux, Renate Kasche, Ada Pometti, Lorenzo Terzon, Paul Whiteman; ***D:*** Mel Welles; ***W:*** Edward Di Lorenzo; ***C:*** Riccardo (Pallton) Pallottini.

Lady from Louisiana **1942** A lawyer in old New Orleans out to rid the city of corruption falls in love with the daughter of a big-time gambler. Great storm scene. **84m/B VHS.** John Wayne, Ona Munson, Dorothy Dandridge, Ray Middleton, Henry Stephenson, Helen Westley, Jack Pennick; ***D:*** Bernard Vorhaus.

Lady from Nowhere **1936** A woman is the only witness to a gangland rub-out and is subsequently pursued by both the mob and the police. Unfortunately for her, the gangsters catch up with her first. **60m/B VHS.** Mary Astor, Charles Quigley, Thurston Hall, Victor Kilian, Spencer Charters; ***D:*** Gordon Wiles.

The Lady from Shanghai ½ **1948** An unsuspecting seaman becomes involved in a web of intrigue when a woman hires him to work on her husband's yacht. Hayworth (a one-time Mrs. Orson Welles), in her only role as a villainess, plays a manipulative, sensual schemer. Wonderful and innovative cinematic techniques from Welles, as usual, including a tense scene in a hall of mirrors. Filmed on a yacht belonging to Errol Flynn. **87m/B VHS, DVD.** Orson Welles, Rita Hayworth, Everett Sloane, Glenn Anders, Ted de Corsia, Erskine Sanford, Gus Schilling; ***D:*** Orson Welles; ***W:*** Orson Welles; ***C:*** Charles Lawton Jr.; ***M:*** Heinz Roemheld.

Lady from Yesterday **1985** An American couple's life is shattered by the appearance of the husband's Vietnamese mistress and her 10-year-old son. **87m/C VHS.** Wayne Rogers, Bonnie Bedelia, Pat Hingle, Barrie Youngfellow, Blue Dedeort, Tina Chen; ***D:*** Robert Day. **TV**

Lady Godiva ½ **1955** The lovely O'Hara is wasted in the title role as a Saxon noblewoman married to Leofric (Nader). They're trying to stem Norman influence and Godiva vows to ride naked through the streets of Canterbury to prove the Saxon people's loyalty to King Edward (Franz). Cardboard costumer. Clint Eastwood has a bit as a Saxon soldier. **89m/C VHS.** Maureen O'Hara, George Nader, Eduard Franz, Leslie Bradley, Victor McLaglen, Torin Thatcher, Rex Reason; ***D:*** Arthur Lubin; ***W:*** Oscar Brodney, Harry Ruskin; ***C:*** Carl Guthrie.

Lady Godiva Rides ½ *Lady Godiva Meets Tom Jones* **1968** A bad, campy version of the story of Lady Godiva. Godiva comes to the United States with a bevy of scantily clad maidens and winds up in the Old West. When the town villain threatens to compromise her, Tom Jones comes to the rescue. The film (of course) features Godiva's naked ride on horseback through the town. **88m/C VHS, DVD.** Marsha Jordan, Forman Shane, Deborah Downey, Elizabeth Knowles, James E. Myers, Jennie Jackson, Liz Renay, Vincent Barbi; ***D:*** A.C. (Stephen Apostoloff) Stephen; ***W:*** A.C. (Stephen Apostoloff) Stephen; ***C:*** R.C. Ruben; ***M:*** Jay Colonna, Robert E. Lee.

Lady Grey **1982** A poor farmer's daughter rises to the top of the country music charts, but at a price. **111m/C VHS.** Ginger Alden, David Allan Coe; ***D:*** Worth Keeter.

Lady Ice **1973 (PG)** Sutherland, as an insurance investigator on the trail of jewel thieves, follows them to Miami Beach and the Bahamas. After stealing a diamond he enters into partnership with a crook's daughter. Worth seeing for the cast. **93m/C VHS, DVD.** Donald Sutherland, Jennifer O'Neill, Robert Duvall, Eric (Hans Gudegast) Braeden; ***D:*** Tom Gries; ***W:*** Alan R. Trustman; ***M:*** Perry Botkin.

Lady in a Cage **1964** A wealthy widow is trapped in her home elevator during a power failure and becomes desperate when hoodlums break in. Shocking violence ahead of its time probably plays better than when first released. Young Caan is a standout among the star-studded cast. **95m/B VHS, DVD.** Olivia de Havilland, Ann Sothern, James Caan, Jennifer Billingsley, Jeff Corey, Scatman Crothers, Rafael Campos; ***D:*** Walter Grauman; ***W:*** Luther Davis.

Lady in Cement ½ **1968 (R)** The second Tony Rome mystery, in which the seedy Miami dick finds a corpse with cement shoes while swimming. **93m/C VHS, DVD.** Frank Sinatra, Raquel Welch, Richard Conte, Martin Gabel, Lainie Kazan, Pat Henry, Steve Peck, Joe E. Lewis, Dan Blocker; ***D:*** Gordon Douglas; ***C:*** Joseph Biroc.

Lady in Distress ½ *A Window in London* **1939** A British drama about an unhappily married man who witnesses an apparent murder. He discovers, however, it was actually the prank of an illusionist and his flirtatious wife. He soon finds himself becoming increasingly involved with their lives. **59m/B VHS.** *GB* Michael Redgrave, Paul Lukas, Sally Gray; ***D:*** Herbert Mason.

The Lady in Question ½ *It Happened in Paris* **1940** A Parisian shopkeeper, played by Aherne, sits on a jury that acquits Hayworth of murder. His interest doesn't end with the trial, however, and matters heat up when his son also becomes involved. Remake of a melodramatic French release. **81m/B VHS.** Rita Hayworth, Glenn Ford, Brian Aherne, Irene Rich, Lloyd Corrigan, George Coulouris, Evelyn Keyes, Curt Bois, Edward Norris; ***D:*** Charles Vidor; ***W:*** Ben Barzman.

The Lady in Question ½ **1999** Sequel to "Murder in a Small Town" finds Broadway director Larry "Cash" Carter (Wilder) pursuing his amateur gumshoe sideline once again. This time it's the poisoning death of his wealthy friend, Emma Sachs (Bloom). And there are lots of suspects. Everyone seems to be enjoying themselves in this stylish period mystery, especially Wilder. **100m/C VHS.** Gene Wilder, Mike Starr, Cherry Jones, Claire Bloom, Barbara Sukowa, John Benjamin Hickey, Michael Cumpsty, Dixie Seatle, Kerry McPherson; ***D:*** Joyce Chopra; ***W:*** Gilbert Pearlman; ***C:*** Bruce Surtees; ***M:*** John Morris. **CABLE**

Lady in Red *Guns, Sin and Bathtub Gin* **1979** A story of America in the '30s, and the progress through the underworld of the woman who was Dillinger's last lover. **90m/C VHS, DVD.** Pamela Sue Martin, Louise Fletcher, Robert Conrad, Christopher Lloyd, Dick Miller, Laurie Heineman, Robert Hogan, Glenn Withrow, Rod Gist, Mary Woronov; ***D:*** Lewis Teague; ***W:*** John Sayles; ***C:*** Daniel Lacambre; ***M:*** James Horner.

Lady in the Death House **1944** A framed woman is set to walk the last mile, as a scientist struggles to find the real killer in time. **57m/B VHS.** Jean Parker, Lionel Atwill, Marcia Mae Jones; ***D:*** Steve Sekely; ***W:*** Harry Hoyt; ***C:*** Gus Peterson; ***M:*** Jan Gray.

Lady in the Lake ½ **1946** Why is it everyone wants to get artsy with pulp fiction? Actor Montgomery directs himself in this Philip Marlowe go-round, using a subjective camera style to imitate Chandler's first person narrative (that means the only time we get to see Marlowe/Montgomery's mug is in a mirror. That pretty well says it all). Having decided to give up eyeing privately, Marlowe turns to the pen to tell the tangled tale of the lady in the lake: once upon a time, a detective was hired to find the wicked wife of a paying client...Some find the direction clever. Others consider MGM chief Louis B. Mayer, who made sure this was Montgomery's last project with MGM, to be a wise man. **103m/B VHS.** Robert Montgomery, Lloyd Nolan, Audrey Totter, Tom Tully, Leon Ames, Jayne Meadows; ***D:*** Robert Montgomery; ***C:*** Paul Vogel.

Lady in the Water **2006 (PG-13)** Another Shyamalan vehicle full of darkness, mysterious creatures that go bump in the night, and himself (literally and figuratively). This attempt at a modern-day Brothers Grimm fable follows Cleveland Heep (Giamatti), the gloomy superintendent of a gloomy Philadelphia apartment complex, who discovers a translucent creature (Howard) skinny-dipping in the apartment pool after hours. He tries to rescue the nymph (or "narf" in Shymalan's unoriginal world), the apartment's residents, and himself from a variety of evil forces, only some of which are actually shown. More of the same heavy-handed symbolism and convoluted storyline that passed for plot twists in his earlier work. Shyamalan wrote, directed, and, as always, gave himself a role in this fairy tale, which he states is based on a bedtime story he made up for his daughters. **108m/C DVD, Blu-ray Disc, HD DVD.** *US* Bryce Dallas Howard, Paul Giamatti, Jeffrey Wright, Bob Balaban, Freddy Rodriguez, Sarita Choudhury, Jared Harris, Bill Irwin, Mary Beth Hurt, Tovah Feldshuh, M. Night Shyamalan, Cindy Cheung, Noah Gray-Cabey; ***D:*** M. Night Shyamalan; ***W:*** M. Night Shyamalan; ***C:*** Christopher Doyle; ***M:*** James Newton Howard; ***Nar:*** David Ogden Stiers. Golden Raspberries '06: Worst Actor (Shyamalan), Worst Director (Shyamalan).

Lady in Waiting **1994 (R)** Detective Jimmy Scavetti (Nouri) is hunting down a serial kill preying on call girls when he meets the seductive Lori (Whirry). Then he discovers his ex-wife's new hubby was the lawyer for each of the victims—only the lawyer turns up dead and Jimmy becomes a suspect. Also available in an unrated version. **85m/C VHS.** Michael Nouri, Shannon Whirry, William Devane, Karen Kopins, Crystal Chappell, Robert Costanzo, Meg Foster, Charles Grant; ***D:*** Fred Gallo.

The Lady in White **1988 (PG-13)** Small-town ghost story about murder and revenge. When young Haas is locked in school one night, he's visited by the ghost of a little girl who wants his help in discovering who murdered her. Well-developed characters, interesting style, and suspenseful plot make for a sometimes slow but overall exceptional film. **92m/C VHS, DVD.** Lukas Haas, Len Cariou, Alex Rocco, Katherine Helmond, Jason Presson, Renata Vanni, Angelo Bertolini, Jared Rushton, Joelle Jacob; ***D:*** Frank Laloggia; ***W:*** Frank Laloggia; ***C:*** Russell Carpenter; ***M:*** Frank Laloggia.

The Lady Is Willing ½ **1942** Dietrich is a stage star who longs for a baby and when an abandoned infant comes her way she decides to keep the child. Only she hasn't a clue about any of the practical aspects. Lucky for her MacMurray is a friendly pediatrician who gives her some advice. Dietrich finds out she can't adopt as a single parent and persuades MacMurray to marry her, in name only, but since this is a romantic comedy the two eventually fall in love. **91m/B VHS.** Marlene Dietrich, Fred MacMurray, Aline MacMahon, Stanley Ridges, Arline Judge, Roger Clark, Ruth Ford, Sterling Holloway, Harvey Stephens, Harry Shannon, Elisabeth Risdon, Charles Halton; ***D:*** Mitchell Leisen; ***W:*** James Edward Grant, Albert McCleery.

Lady Jane ½ **1985 (PG-13)** An accurate account of the life of 15-year-old Lady Jane Grey, who secured the throne of England for nine days in 1553 as a result of political maneuvering by noblemen and the Church of England. A wonderful film even for non-history buffs. Carter's first film. **140m/C VHS, DVD.** *GB* Helena Bonham Carter, Cary Elwes, Sara Kestelman, Michael Hordern, Joss Ackland, Richard Johnson, Patrick Stewart; ***D:*** Trevor Nunn.

Lady Jayne Killer *Betrayal* **2003 (R)** Jayne Ferre (Du Page) is an L.A. hit-woman for mobster Frank Bianchi (Mandylor) from whom she has just stolen a million bucks. So she needs to get quietly out of town fast. Emily (Eleniak) and her 16-year-old son Kerry (Lelliott) need money to get to Texas. When Jayne and Emily meet, she offers to foot the bill if she can hitch a ride. Then Kerry discovers the cash, steals it from Jayne, and heads back to L.A. Naturally, Jayne and Emily are soon behind him. And then FBI agent Alex Tyler (Remar) comes into the picture. **90m/C VHS, DVD.** Julie Du Page, Erika Eleniak, Jeremy Lelliott, James Remar, Louis Mandylor, Adam Baldwin, Damian Chapa, Don Swayze, Peter Dobson; *D:* Mark L. Lester; *W:* C. Courtney Joyner; *C:* Joao Fernandes. **VIDEO**

Lady Killer **1933** Racy, pre-Code comedy with mobster Cagney hiding out in Hollywood. He gets discovered and becomes a big star, but his old gang turns up to blackmail him. Lots of movie "in" jokes and Clarke (of "Public Enemy" fame) is great as a wisecracking moll. Based on the story "The Finger Man" by Rosalind Keating Shaffer. **74m/B VHS.** James Cagney, Mae Clarke, Leslie Fenton, Margaret Lindsay, Henry O'Neill, Raymond Hatton, George Chandler; *D:* Roy Del Ruth; *W:* Ben Markson, Lillie Hayward.

Lady Killer *Ladykiller* **1997 (R)** A serial killer called the Piggyback Murderer is terrorizing a college campus. Police Lt. Jack Lasky (Gazzara) is particularly anxious since his daughter Jennifer (Allman) is a student at the school. When her new boyfriend, aspiring actor Richard Darling (McArthur), keeps turning up at the murder scenes, guess who becomes dad's prime suspect. **80m/C VHS, DVD.** Ben Gazzara, Alex McArthur, Terri Treas, Renee Allman; *D:* Terence H. Winkless; *W:* Craig J. Nevius; *C:* Christopher Baffa.

Lady L 1/2 **1965** Silly turn-of-the-century farce about a sexy laundress (Loren), married to a French anarchist (Newman!), who also marries the aristocratic Niven (in name only). Elaborate sets and Paris and London backgrounds couldn't overcome the odd casting and weak script. Adapted from the novel by Romain Gary. **107m/C VHS.** *FR IT* Sophia Loren, Paul Newman, David Niven, Cecil Parker, Claude Dauphin, Marcel Dalio, Philippe Noiret, Michel Piccoli, Daniel Emilfork, Eugene Deckers; ***Cameos:*** Peter Ustinov; *D:* Peter Ustinov; *W:* Peter Ustinov.

Lady Mobster **1988 (PG-13)** When her parents are murdered a young girl is taken in by a Mafia family. She grows up to be a shrewd lawyer but winds up working in her adoptive family's crime syndicate in order to take revenge on her parents' murderers. Exaggerated and silly but watchable for its so-bad-it's-good qualities. **94m/C VHS.** Susan Lucci, Michael Nader, Roscoe Born, Joseph Wiseman; *D:* John Llewellyn Moxey. **TV**

Lady of Burlesque 1/2 *Striptease Lady* **1943** Burlesque dancer is found dead, strangled with her own G-string. Clever and amusing film based on "The G-String Murders" by Gypsy Rose Lee. **91m/B VHS, DVD.** Barbara Stanwyck, Michael O'Shea, Janis Carter, Pinky Lee; *D:* William A. Wellman.

A Lady of Chance **1928** Tough as nails babe redeemed by true love. Con woman Dolly (Shearer) is forced back into blackmailing wealthy marks when she's recognized by her ex-partners Bradley (Sherman) and Gwen (Lee). Doublecrossing them, Dolly picks up Steve Crandall (Brown), thinking he's a wealthy southern businessman. When she's really fallen for him, Dolly learns Steve's got lots of charm but not much dough. Although when Bradley and Gwen track Dolly down again, they don't believe her. **79m/B DVD.** Norma Shearer, Johnny Mack Brown, Lowell Sherman, Gwen Lee, Eugenie Besserer, Gwen Lee, Norma Shearer, Johnny Mack Brown, Lowell Sherman, Gwen Lee, Eugenie Besserer, Buddy Messinger; *D:* Robert Z. Leonard, Lowell Sherman, Robert Z. Leonard, Cedric Gibbons; *W:* Ralph Spence, Ralph Spence; *C:* J. Peverell Marley, William H. Daniels, J. Peverell Marley, William H. Daniels, Margaret Booth.

Lady of the Evening *Gun Moll; Get Rita; Oopsie Poopsie; La Gangster del Pupa* **1975 (R)** A prostitute and a crook team up to seek revenge against the mob. **110m/C VHS.** *IT* Sophia Loren, Marcello Mastroianni, Pierre Brice, Dalia di Lazzaro, Aldo Maccione; *D:* Giorgio Capitani; *W:* Ernesto Gastaldi; *C:* Alberto Spagnoli; *M:* Pierro Umiliani.

Lady of the House **1978** A true story about a madame who rose from operator of a brothel to become a political force in San Francisco. **100m/C VHS.** Dyan Cannon, Susan Tyrrell, Colleen Camp, Armand Assante; *D:* Ralph Nelson.

Lady of the Lake **1928** Rare silent adventure film in which an exiled girl saves the king from outlaws in Scotland. Orchestra score. **47m/B VHS, DVD.** *GB* Percy Marmont, Benita Hume, Huddon Mason, Lawson Butt; *D:* James A. Fitzpatrick.

Lady on a Train **1945** Travelling at Christmas, wealthy young Nicky Collins (Durbin) thinks she sees a murder from her train window but when she arrives in New York she can't get anyone to believe her. But not willing to give up, Nicky turns to Wayne Morgan (Bruce), a mystery writer for help. Recognizing the victim from a newspaper photo, Nicky checks out his family and gets mistaken for a nightclub singer (so Durbin can vamp a torch song). Lots of comedy amidst the mystery and romance, and some surprizes as well. Based on a story by Leslie Charteris. ♫Gimme a Little Kiss, Will You, Huh?; Night and Day; Silent Night. **95m/B VHS, DVD.** Deanna Durbin, David Bruce, Ralph Bellamy, Dan Duryea, Edward Everett Horton, Allen Jenkins, Elizabeth Patterson, William Frawley, Jacqueline DeWit, George Coulouris; *D:* Charles David; *W:* Robert O'Brien, Edmund Beloin; *C:* Elwood "Woody" Bredell; *M:* Miklos Rozsa.

Lady on the Bus **1978 (R)** Sexually frustrated newlywed bride rides the city buses looking for men to satisfy her. This bothers her husband. Shot in Rio de Janeiro. In Portuguese with English subtitles. **102m/C VHS.** *BR* Sonia Braga; *D:* Neville D'Almedia.

The Lady Refuses **1931** A stuffy Victorian father is disappointed in his wastrel son and decides a poor but honest young woman could be the making of him. Problems arise when the girl falls for the father instead. **70m/B VHS, DVD.** Betty Compson, John Darrow, Margaret Livingston, Gilbert Emery, Ivan Lebedeff, Edgar Norton, Daphne Pollard, Halliwell Hobbes; *D:* George Archainbaud; *W:* Wallace Smith; *C:* Leo Tover.

The Lady Says No **1951** A photographer must photograph an attractive author who has written a book uncomplimentary toward the male sex. **80m/B VHS, DVD.** Joan Caulfield, David Niven, James Robertson Justice, Frances Bavier, Henry Jones, Jeff York; *D:* Frank Ross.

Lady Scarface **1941** Murderous mobster queen breaks the law, bats men around, and takes the cops on a merry chase. Cheap, fast-paced action. **66m/B VHS.** Mildred Coles, Dennis O'Keefe, Frances Neal, Judith Anderson, Eric Blore, Charles Halton; *D:* Frank Woodruff.

Lady Sings the Blues 1/2 **1972 (R)** Jazz artist Billie Holiday's life becomes a musical drama depicting her struggle against racism and drug addiction in her pursuit of fame and romance. What could be a typical price-of-fame story is saved by Ross' inspired performance as the tragic singer. ♫My Man; Strange Fruit; God Bless the Child; Don't Explain; T'Ain't Nobody's Business If I Do; Lady Sings the Blues; All Of Me; The Man I Love; Our Love Is Here to Stay. **144m/C VHS, DVD.** Diana Ross, Billy Dee Williams, Richard Pryor, James Callahan, Paul Hampton, Sid Melton; *D:* Sidney J. Furie; *C:* John A. Alonzo.

Lady Snowblood *Shurayukihime; Lady Snowblood: Blizzard from the Nether World; Blood Snow* **1973** A group of thieves break into the house of a rural couple, murder the husband, and rape the wife, who later dies in childbirth after becoming pregnant. A priest raises her daughter to be a skilled swordswoman and sends her out to murder the men who wronged her family when she becomes an adult. Adapted from the comic by Kazuo Koike, who is famous for the Lone Wolf and Cub series, it is the inspiration for much of the film "Kill Bill" by Quentin Tarantino. **67m/C DVD.** *JP* Meiko Kaji, Toshio Kurosawa, Masaki Daimon, Sanae Nakahara, Eiji Okada, Ko Nishimura, Miyoko Akaza, Shinichi Uchida, Takeo Chii, Noboru Nakaya, Yoshiko Nakada, Akemi Negisha, Kaoru Kusuda, Hosei Kimatsu, Makoto Matsuzaki, Hiroshi Hasegawa, Hitoshi Takagi; *D:* Toshiya Fujita; *W:* Kazuo Koike, Kazuo Kamimura; *C:* Masaki Tamura; *M:* Masaaki Hirao.

Lady Street Fighter **1986** A well-armed female combat fighter battles an organization of assassins to avenge her sister's murder. **73m/C VHS.** Renee Harmon, Joel McCrea Jr.; *D:* James Bryan; *C:* Max Reed.

Lady Takes a Chance **1943** A romantic comedy about a New York working girl with matrimonial ideas and a rope-shy rodeo rider who yearns for the wide open spaces. Fine fun on the range. **86m/B VHS, DVD.** John Wayne, Jean Arthur, Phil Silvers, Charles Winninger; *D:* William A. Seiter.

Lady Terminator 1/2 **1989 (R)** A student on an anthropology expedition digs up more than she bargained for when she is possessed by an evil spirit and goes on a rampage. **83m/C VHS, DVD.** Barbara Constable, Christopher J. Hart, Joseph McGlynn, Claudia Rademaker; *D:* Jalil Jackson.

The Lady Vanishes **1938** Kindly old lady, Miss Froy (Witty) seemingly disappears from a fast-moving train bound for England. But when her young friend Iris (Lockwood) investigates, she finds no one appears to believe her and she has a spiraling mystery to solve. Of course, Irish has music scholar Gilbert (Redgrave) eager to help her out. Hitchcock's first real winner, a smarmy, wit-drenched British mystery that precipitated his move to Hollywood. Along with "39 Steps," considered an early Hitchcock classic. From the novel "The Wheel Spins," by Ethel Lina White. Remade in 1979. **99m/B VHS, DVD.** *GB* Margaret Lockwood, Paul Lukas, Michael Redgrave, May Whitty, Googie Withers, Basil Radford, Naunton Wayne, Cecil Parker, Linden Travers, Catherine Lacey, Alfred Hitchcock; *D:* Alfred Hitchcock; *W:* Sidney Gilliat, Frank Launder; *C:* Jack Cox; *M:* Louis Levy. N.Y. Film Critics '38: Director (Hitchcock).

The Lady Vanishes 1/2 **1979** In this reworking of the '38 Alfred Hitchcock film, a woman on a Swiss bound train awakens from a nap to find that the elderly woman seated next to her was kidnapped. Falls short of the original movie due to the "screwball" nature of the main characters, Gould and Shepherd. Based on Ethel Lina White's novel "The Wheel Spins." **95m/C VHS, DVD.** *GB* Elliott Gould, Cybill Shepherd, Angela Lansbury, Herbert Lom; *D:* Anthony Page; *W:* George Axelrod.

Lady Vengeance 1/2 **2005 (R)** Violent and bloody revenge saga. Geum-ja (Lee) spent 13 years in prison after being forced to help her former teacher, Mr Baek (Choi), abduct and murder a young boy and was then being betrayed by him. (Baek kidnapped her own baby as leverage.) Now out of prison, Geun-ja is also out for a grisly payback. Korean with subtitles. **112m/C DVD.** *KN* Min-Sik Choi, Yeong-ae Lee; *D:* Chanwook Park; *W:* Chan-wook Park, Seo-gyeong Jeong; *C:* Jeong-hun Jeong; *M:* Seung-hyun Choi.

Lady Windermere's Fan 1/2 **1925** The silent, Lubitsch adaptation of the Oscar Wilde tale concerning an upper-class couple's marriage being almost destroyed by suspected adultery. **66m/B VHS, DVD.** Ronald Colman, May McAvoy, Bert Lytell; *D:* Ernst Lubitsch. Natl. Film Reg. '02.

The Lady with the Dog **1959** A bittersweet love story based on the Anton Chekhov story, about two married Russians who meet by chance in a park, fall in love, and realize they are fated to a haphazard, clandestine affair. In Russian with English titles. **86m/B VHS, DVD.** *RU* Iya Savvina, Alexei Batalov, Ala Chostakova, N. Alisova; *D:* Yosif Heifitz.

The Lady Without Camelias 1/2 *La Signora Senza Camelie* **1953** A young woman is discovered by a film producer who casts her in a successful movie and eventually marries her. Convinced that she can sustain a career as a serious actress, the producer is dismayed by the job offers that come her way, usually of a sexually exploitive nature. What follows is a tragic decline for both. **106m/B VHS.** *IT* Lucia Bose, Gino Cervi, Andrea Checchi, Ivan Desny, Alain Cuny; *D:* Michelangelo Antonioni; *W:* Michelangelo Antonioni, Suso Cecchi D'Amico; *C:* Enzo Serafin; *M:* Giovanni Fusco.

Ladybird, Ladybird **1993 (R)** Loach's emotionally bruising look at working-class life and family in the '90s. Maggie (Rock) is a tough unmarried mother of four who's been battered by her lovers and has come under the over-watchful eye of Britain's social services. She meets Jorge (Vega), a gentle Paraguayan, and just when things are looking up, Jorge gets immigration heat, Maggie's insecurities surface, and her baby daughter is taken into care by child welfare. Rock has a no-nonsense manner and acerbic wit that precludes any hand-wringing for her character, even as you hope she'll win out over circumstance. Based on a true story. **102m/C VHS.** *GB* Crissy Rock, Vladimir Vega, Ray Winstone, Sandie Lavelle, Mauricio Venegas, Clare Perkins, Jason Stracey, Luke Brown, Lily Farrell; *D:* Ken Loach; *W:* Rona Munro; *C:* Barry Ackroyd; *M:* George Fenton. Berlin Intl. Film Fest. '94: Actress (Rock).

Ladybugs 1/2 **1992 (PG-13)** Hangdog salesman Dangerfield would like to move up the corporate ladder, but must first turn the company-sponsored girl's soccer team into winners. Routine Dangerfield vehicle exploits nearly everything for laughs, including dressing an athletic boy as a girl so he can play on the team. Obvious fluff. **91m/C VHS, DVD.** Rodney Dangerfield, Jackee, Jonathan Brandis, Ilene Graff, Vinessa Shaw, Tom Parks, Jeanetta Arnette, Nancy Parsons, Blake Clark, Tommy Lasorda; *D:* Sidney J. Furie; *W:* Curtis Burch; *C:* Dan Burstall; *M:* Richard Gibbs.

Ladyhawke 1/2 **1985 (PG-13)** In medieval times, a youthful pickpocket befriends a strange knight who is on a mysterious quest. This unlikely duo, accompanied by a watchful hawk, are enveloped in a magical adventure. **121m/C VHS, DVD.** Matthew Broderick, Rutger Hauer, Michelle Pfeiffer, John Wood, Leo McKern, Alfred Molina, Ken Hutchison; *D:* Richard Donner; *W:* Edward Khmara, Michael Thomas, Tom Mankiewicz; *C:* Vittorio Storaro; *M:* Andrew Powell.

Ladykiller **1992 (R)** Rogers stars as a burned-out cop who goes to a dating service to find a man who'll give her the attention she craves. When she meets wealthy professional Shea she thinks he's the one but her cop's curiosity about her lover's past may cost her her life. **92m/C VHS.** Mimi Rogers, John Shea, Alice Krige, Tom Irwin; *D:* Michael Scott; *W:* Shelley Evans.

The Ladykillers 1/2 *The Lady Killers* **1955** A gang of bumbling bank robbers is foiled by a little old lady. Hilarious antics follow, especially on the part of Guinness, who plays the slightly demented-looking leader of the gang. **87m/C VHS, DVD.** *GB* Alec Guinness, Cecil Parker, Katie Johnson, Herbert Lom, Peter Sellers, Danny Green, Jack Warner, Kenneth Connor, Edie Martin, Jack Melford; *D:* Alexander MacKendrick; *W:* William Rose; *C:* Otto Heller; *M:* Tristram Cary. British Acad. '55: Actress (Johnson), Screenplay.

Ladykillers **1988** At the glitzy L.A. club Ladykillers, men strip as the women cheer. At the climax of the performance, one of the dancers is brutally murdered, live on stage. In this decadent world of glitter and sex, the women are the hunters and the men are the reward. **97m/C VHS.** Marilu Henner, Susan Blakely, Lesley-Anne Down, Thomas Calabro; *D:* Robert Lewis; *W:* Greg Dinallo.

The Ladykillers 1/2 **2004 (R)** It takes an actor with a lot of gumption to take on a classic role that was played by the classiest of thespians, Alec Guinness, but Hanks (as G.H. Dorr, Ph.D.) takes to the task with gusto and mostly positive results. In this quirky remake of the 1955 British offering, the setting shifts to Mississippi, where the robbers attempt to burrow from little old lady Mrs. Munson's (Hall) basement to the nearby casino's money room. While Hall is superb and Hanks is often dynamic as he plows through ornate speeches with a wicked laugh, it will depend on your tolerance for flowery language and a mannered Southern drawl whether you think it's melodious or annoying. Overall enjoyable, if uneven effort by the Coen brothers falls a bit short of the original. **104m/C DVD.** *US* Tom Hanks, Irma P. Hall, Marlon Wayans, J.K. Simmons, Tzi Ma, Ryan Hurst, Diane Delano, George Wallace, John McConnell, Stephen (Steve) Root, Jason Weaver, Greg Grunberg, Blake Clark, Jeremy Suarez; *D:* Ethan Coen, Joel Coen; *W:* Ethan Coen, Joel Coen; *C:* Roger Deakins; *M:* Carter Burwell.

The Lady's Not for Burning 1/2 **1987** Romantic comedy, set in a medieval English village, finds ex-soldier Thomas Mendip (Branagh) invading the home of querulous Mayor Hebble Tyson (Hepton), demanding to be hanged. He says he's murdered the local rag and bone merchant but the townspeople insist Jennet Jourdemayne (Lunghi), who's seeking refuge at the mayor's, has turned him into a dog. They demand she be burned as a witch (hence the title, since Thomas, unwillingly but strongly, objects to this action). Adapted by Fry from his play; made for TV. **90m/C VHS.** Kenneth Branagh, Cherie Lunghi, Bernard Hepton, Tim Watson, Susannah Harker, Angela Thorne, Shaun Scott; ***D:*** Julian Amyes; ***W:*** Christopher Fry. **TV**

Lafayette Escadrille 1/2 *Hell Bent for Glory* **1958** Action and romance in WWI via the famed flying unit manned by American volunteers. Hunter is banal in the lead role as is his romance with a reformed prostitute (Choreau). Director Wellman actually was a member of the squadron and his son plays him in the film but the director regarded the film as a failure because of studio interference. **92m/B VHS.** Tab Hunter, Etchika Choureau, William Wellman Jr., Joel McCrea, Dennis Devine, Marcel Dalio, David Janssen, Paul Fix, Will Hutchins, Clint Eastwood, Tom Watson; ***D:*** William A. Wellman; ***W:*** A.S. Fleischman; ***C:*** William Clothier; ***M:*** Leonard Rosenman.

Lagaan: Once upon a Time in India **2001 (PG)** Bollywood musical set in 1893, in the drought-striken village of Champaner. The lagaan is a tax levied by the occupying British on the local rajahs, which the village can't pay. The region's nasty British commander, Captain Russell (Blackthorne), states that if the villagers can beat his soldiers at cricket, the lagaan will be cancelled for three years; if they lose, the lagaan will be tripled. Heroic Bhuvan (Khan) persuades the locals that even if they don't understand the game, they can certainly show those arrogant Brits a thing or two! English, Hindi and Bhojpuri with subtitles. **225m/C DVD.** *IN* Aamir Khan, Gracy Singh, Rachel Shelley, Paul Blackthorne, Suhasini Mulay, Kulbashan Kharbanda, Raghuvir Yadav; ***D:*** Ashutosh Gowariker; ***W:*** Ashutosh Gowariker, Kumar Dave, Sanjay Dayma, K.P. Saxena; ***C:*** Anil Mehta; ***M:*** A.R. Rahman.

L'Age D'Or *Age of Gold; The Golden Age* **1930** Bunuel's first full-length film and his masterpiece of sex, repression, and of course, death. A hapless man is prevented from reaching his beloved by middle-class morality, forces of the establishment, the Church, government and every bastion of modern values. Banned for years because of its anti-religious stance. Coscripted by Dali. A mercilessly savage, surreal satire, the purest expression of Bunuel's wry misanthropy. In French with English subtitles. **62m/B VHS, DVD.** *FR* Gaston Modot, Lya Lys, Max Ernst, Pierre Prevert, Marie Berthe Ernst, Paul Eluard; ***D:*** Luis Bunuel; ***W:*** Salvador Dali, Luis Bunuel; ***C:*** Albert Duverger.

Laguna Heat 1/2 **1987** A tired LA cop investigates a series of murders that are related to an old friend of his father's. Based on a novel by T. Jefferson Parker. **110m/C VHS.** Harry Hamlin, Jason Robards Jr., Catherine Hicks, Rip Torn, Anne Francis; ***D:*** Simon Langton. **TV**

The Lair of the White Worm **1988 (R)** Scottish archaeologist uncovers a strange skull, and then a bizarre religion to go with it, and then a very big worm. An unusual look at the effects of Christianity and paganism on each other, colored with sexual innuendo and, of course, giant worms. A cross between a morality play and a horror film. Adapted from Bram Stoker's last writings, done while he was going mad from Bright's disease. Everything you'd expect from Russell. **93m/C VHS, DVD.** *GB* Amanda Donohoe, Sammi Davis, Catherine Oxenberg, Hugh Grant, Peter Capaldi, Stratford Johns, Paul Brooke, Christopher Gable; ***D:*** Ken Russell; ***W:*** Ken Russell; ***C:*** Dick Bush; ***M:*** Stanislas Syrewicz.

Lake City 1/2 **2008 (R)** City boy Billy is on the run from drug dealers after a deal goes bad, and he heads for his mother's farm in Virginia. Mom and son have some emotional baggage to sort out as a long-past family tragedy has kept them apart, but it's all quite uninteresting, convoluted, and remarkably impersonal. A family drama that combines forced, unmatched characters and manufactured, contrived drama with not one but two rookie directors. Spacek is the only positive aspect and script doesn't give her much to work with. **92m/C DVD.** *US* Troy Garity, Sissy Spacek, Rebecca Romijn, Dave Matthews, Drea De Matteo, Keith Carradine, Barry Corbin, Colin Ford; ***D:*** Hunter Hill, Perry Moore; ***W:*** Hunter Hill, Perry Moore; ***C:*** Robert Gantz; ***M:*** Aaron Zigman.

Lake Consequence **1992 (R)** Severance plays a suburban housewife who accidentally gets locked in the camper of the tree-trimmer stud (Zane) she's been eyeing while he's been working in her neighborhood. Next thing she knows they wind up at a distant lake where the bored housewife is more than willing to give into her growing sexual fantasies. An unrated version at 90 minutes is also available. **85m/C VHS, DVD.** Joan Severance, Billy Zane, May Karasun; ***D:*** Rafael Eisenman; ***W:*** Zalman King, Melanie Finn, Henry Cobbold; ***M:*** George S. Clinton.

Lake Dead **2007** Not dead enough. Three sisters learn that the grandfather they never knew has died and left them a motel in the mountains. They promptly get some friends together and decide to check things out. What they find is your basic murderous, inbred family of hillbilly lunatics already occupying the real estate and they're determined that no one is going to leave. At least not alive. **91m/C DVD.** Kelsey Crane, Tara Gerard, Kelsey Wedeen, James C. Burns, Dan Woods, Jim Devoti, Alex A. Quinn, Malea Richardson, Vanessa Viola, Pat McNeely, Christian Stokes, Trevor Torseth; ***D:*** George Bessudo; ***W:*** Daniel P. Coughlin; ***C:*** Curtis Petersen; ***M:*** Mark Petrie.

The Lake House 1/2 **2006 (PG)** Confusing time-travel romance that appeals because of its leads, who haven't worked together since 1994's "Speed." Chicago doctor Kate (Bullock) leaves a note for the next renter of her glass box lakeside house. Only architect Alex (Reeves) insists that no one has lived in the rundown property for years before him. Hmmm, somehow the attractive twosome communicates with each other despite a two-year time gap. They fall in love, but trying to meet face-to-face is a complicated business. A remake of the 2000 South Korean film "Siworae." **108m/C DVD, Blu-ray Disc, HD DVD.** *US* Keanu Reeves, Sandra Bullock, Shohreh Aghdashloo, Dylan Walsh, Christopher Plummer, Ebon Moss-Bachrach, Willeke Van Ammelrooy, Lynn Collins; ***D:*** Alejandro Agresti; ***W:*** David Auburn; ***C:*** Alar Kivilo; ***M:*** Rachel Portman.

Lake Placid 1/2 **1999 (R)** Hotshot TV producer David E. Kelley lures some acting careers into deadly peril in this lame comedy/horror ripoff of "Jaws." Paleontologist Fonda is sent to examine a tooth after a grisly death occurs in rural Maine. She discovers that the tooth is prehistoric, but she decides to stick around with game warden Pullman, sheriff Gleeson and eccentric professor Platt anyway. You know, just in case the crocodile that escaped through a hole in the plot is still hungry after eating the fatter (and therefore more buttery) cast members. Betty White is the lone bright spot as a foul-mouthed old woman who is rooting for the crocodile. You'll be rooting for it too, but you'll be rooting for it to devour the movie exec who green-lighted this crock. **82m/C VHS, DVD.** Bridget Fonda, Bill Pullman, Oliver Platt, Brendan Gleeson, Mariska Hargitay, Meredith Salenger, Betty White, David Lewis; ***D:*** Steve Miner; ***W:*** David E. Kelley; ***C:*** Daryn Okada; ***M:*** John Ottman.

Lake Placid 2 **WOOF! 2007 (R)** A sheriff, a wildlife agent, and a big game hunter track three hungry 30-foot prehistoric crocodiles munching on the local populace. Sci-Fi Channel sequel-in-name-only with really bad CGI and possibly worse acting and script. **84m/C DVD.** John Schneider, Sam McMurray, Cloris Leachman, Sarah Lafleur, Chad Collins, Alicia Ziegler; ***D:*** David Flores; ***W:*** Todd Hurvitz, Howie Miller; ***C:*** Lorenzo Senatore; ***M:*** Nathan Furst. **CABLE**

Lakeboat 1/2 **2000 (R)** Longtime Mamet collaborator Mantegna makes his directorial debut adapting one of Mamet's earliest (and most autobiographical) plays. Grad student Dale (Mamet's younger brother Tony) signs on a Great Lakes ore freighter as the cook. Plot consists of Canturbury Tales-esque storytelling by the crew, along with differing opinions on what happened to the previous cook, ala "Roshamon." The thrust of the film is Dale's observations and gleanings from the crew, especially Joe (Forster), who once had artistic and educational ambitions which he gave up for a regular paycheck. Excellent, understated performances by all help mask the film's inability to escape its stage limitations and Mantegna's uneven first-time direction. Dialogue shows the promise, as well as the themes, realized in Mamet's later work. **98m/C VHS, DVD.** Charles Durning, Peter Falk, Robert Forster, J.J. Johnston, Denis Leary, Jack Wallace, George Wendt, Saul Rubinek, Tony Mamet, Andy Garcia; ***Cameos:*** Joe Mantegna; ***D:*** Joe Mantegna; ***W:*** David Mamet; ***C:*** Paul Sarossy; ***M:*** Bob Mamet.

Lakeview Terrace **2008 (PG-13)** Newlyweds Chris and Lisa (Wilson and Washington) move into the posh LA suburb of Lakeview Terrace, and unbeknownst to the interracial couple, they're now next door to a nightmare. Hard-headed neighbor Abel Turner (Jackson) starts off a nosey pest but his hatred and brutal racism soon come to a head, trying to pit husband and wife against each other. They turn to the law, but problem is, Abel's a cop. It's almost disturbing to see Jackson as such a cold-blooded sociopath, with razor-sharp writing letting him go off like a wild dog. An intense study of role-reversed racism with all involved confused about who's to blame. **110m/C DVD, Blu-ray Disc.** *US* Samuel L. Jackson, Patrick Wilson, Kerry Washington, Regine Nehy, Jay Hernandez, Keith Loneker, Eva LaRue, Mel Rodriguez, Jaishon Fisher, Ron Glass; ***D:*** Neil LaBute; ***W:*** David Loughery, Howard Korder; ***C:*** Rogier Stoffers; ***M:*** Jeff Danna, Mychael Danna.

Lakota Woman: Siege at Wounded Knee 1/2 **1994** Autobiography of Mary Crow Dog (Bedard) and her coming of age during the American Indian Movement's 1973 occupation of Wounded Knee. Tangled loyalties and the battle between Native Americans and U.S. troops make for strong drama. Bedard is remarkable in her film debut. Based on the book by Mary Crow Dog and Richard Erdoes. Filmed on location in South Dakota. **113m/C VHS.** Irene Bedard, August Schellenberg, Joseph Runningfox, Floyd "Red Crow" Westerman, Tantoo Cardinal, Michael Horse, Lawrence Bayne, Nancy Parsons; ***D:*** Frank Pierson; ***W:*** Bill Kerby; ***C:*** Toyomichi Kurita; ***M:*** Richard Horowitz.

The Lamb 1/2 **1915** Intent on proving to his sweetheart that he's not the coward people say he is, a guy heads west to engage in various manly activities, including fisticuffs, karate and Indian kidnapping. Fairbanks' debut on film (he was already an established Broadway star) set the mold for the American leading man: moral, cheerful, physical, and not hard to look at. A popular guy with the public, Fairbanks formed his own film company the following year. Story's based on D.W. Griffith's book, "The Man and the Test." **60m/B VHS.** Douglas Fairbanks Sr., Seena Owen, Lillian Langdon, Monroe Salisbury, Kate Toncray, Alfred Paget, William E. (W.E., William A., W.A.) Lowery; ***D:*** Christy Cabanne.

Lamb **1985** Troubled 10-year-old epileptic Owen Kane (Kane) has been dumped by his abusive mother at a Catholic-run institution for wayward boys in Ireland, run by self-righteous headmaster Brother Benedict (Bannen). Owen becomes Benedict's scapegoat—much to the dismay of Brother Michael Lamb (Neeson). When Lamb claims a small family inheritance, he decides to take Owen and head to London, posing as father and son, where they live in increasingly depressed surroundings while Michael tries painfully to make them into a real family. Based on the novel by MacLaverty, who also wrote the screenplay. **110m/C VHS, DVD.** *IR* Liam Neeson, Hugh O'Conor, Ian Bannen, Frances Tomelty; ***D:*** Colin Gregg; ***W:*** Bernard MacLaverty; ***C:*** Mike Garfath; ***M:*** Van Morrison.

Lambada **1989 (PG)** By day, he's a high school teacher in Beverly Hills; by night, a Latin dirty dancer cum tutor of ghetto teens. The very first of several films based on the short-lived dance craze. **92m/C VHS, DVD.** J. Eddie Peck, Melora Hardin, Adolfo "Shabba Doo" Quinones, Ricky Paull Goldin, Basil Hoffman, Dennis Burkley; ***D:*** Joel Silberg.

Lamerica **1995** Two Italian hustlers, Fiore (Placido) and his younger partner Gino (Lo Verso), head for poverty-stricken Albania in 1991, the first year after the collapse of the Communist dictatorship. They intend to set up a phony corporation and scam money from government grants but they need an Albanian figurehead. The duo find simple-minded, elderly Spiro (Di Mazzarelli), who's spent most of his life in prison camps, and stash him in an orphanage for safe keeping. Only when Spiro gets away, Gino heads for the countryside to find him and discovers some secrets about Spiro's past and just how the wily Albanians have been surviving. Italian with subtitles. **116m/C VHS, DVD.** *IT* Enrico Lo Verso, Michele Placido, Carmelo Di Mazzarelli, Piro Milkani; ***D:*** Gianni Amelio; ***W:*** Gianni Amelio, Andrea Porporati, Alessandro Sermoneta; ***C:*** Luca Bigazzi; ***M:*** Franco Piersanti.

L'Amour en Herbe *Budding Love; Tender Love* **1977** His parents realize Pascal has something on his mind when he fails school. It turns out to be lovely Martine, whom he is then forbidden to see. But Pascal remains true—until betrayed. In French with subtitles. **100m/C VHS.** *FR* Pascal Meynier, Guilhaine Dubos, Bruno Raffaeli, Michel Galabru, Francoise Prevost, Alix Mahieux; ***D:*** Roger Andrieux; ***W:*** Roger Andrieux, Jean-Marie Benard; ***C:*** Ramon Suarez; ***M:*** Maxime Le Forestier.

Lamp at Midnight 1/2 **1966** Presentation from "George Schaefer's Showcase Theatre" deals with three critical periods in the life of Italian astronomer Galileo Galilei, from his invention of the telescope, through his appearance at the Holy Office of the Inquisition, to the publication of his "Dialogue on the Two Systems of the World." For those in a planetary state of mind. **76m/C VHS.** Melvyn Douglas, David Wayne, Michael Hordern, Hurd Hatfield, Kim Hunter; ***D:*** George Schaefer. **TV**

Lan Yu **2001** Lan Yu (Ye) is a young architecture student, newly arrived in Beijing in 1988. He's introduced to older businessman Hangdong (Jun) and the two become lovers, though Hangdong is chronically unfaithful and they become estranged. When Lan Yu participates in the demonstrations at Tiananmen Square, Hangdong goes looking for him and the two resume their affair, which continues to be rocky. Based on the anonymous novel "Beijing Story," published only on the Internet in 1997 in order to avoid Chinese censorship. Chinese with subtitles. **86m/C VHS, DVD.** *HK* Hu Jun, Liu Ye; ***D:*** Stanley Kwan; ***W:*** Jimmy Ngai; ***C:*** Yang Tao; ***M:*** Zhang Yadong.

Lana in Love **1992** A lonely woman places an ad in the personal section in hopes of finding her Mr. Right. **90m/C VHS.** Daphna Kastner, Clark Gregg; ***D:*** Bashar Shbib; ***W:*** Bashar Shbib; ***C:*** Stephen Reizes; ***M:*** Harry Mayronne Jr.

Lancelot of the Lake *Lancelot du Lac; The Grail; Le Graal* **1974** The Knights of the Round Table return to the court of King Arthur after a long, bloody, and fruitless search for the Holy Grail. Rivalries and jealousies debase the heroes as Lancelot struggles with his feelings for Arthur's Queen Guinevere. Austere acting but the film's rich visuals provide a sensuous air. French with subtitles. **85m/C VHS, DVD.** *FR* Luc Simon, Laura Duke Condominas, Vladimir Antolek-Oresek, Humbert Balsan, Patrick Bernard, Arthur De Montalembert; ***D:*** Robert Bresson; ***W:*** Robert Bresson; ***C:*** Pasqualino De Santis; ***M:*** Philippe Sarde.

Land and Freedom **1995** Earnestly talky drama focusing on idealist Liverpudlian communist David Carr (Hart), who heads to Spain in 1937 to fight against Franco's fascists. What David learns is that the Republican forces, made up of independent militia, are bitterly divided, with much infighting and betrayal from the Stalinist forces within David's own party. He falls for socialist Blanca (Pastor) and learns how terrifying and haphazard war can be (with timeout for ideological discussions). Sympathetic characters and sweeping action help to compensate for the political polemics. **109m/C VHS.** *GB SP GE* Ian Hart, Rosana Pastor, Iciar Bollain, Tom Gilroy, Frederic Pierrot, Marc Martinez, Angela Clarke, Dave Allen; ***D:*** Ken Loach; ***W:*** Jim Allen; ***C:*** Barry Ackroyd; ***M:*** George Fenton. Cesar '96: Foreign Film.

The Land Before Time 1988 **(G)** Lushly animated children's film about five orphaned baby dinosaurs who band together and try to find the Great Valley, a paradise where they might live safely. Works same parental separation theme as Bluth's "American Tail." Charming, coy, and shamelessly tearjerking; producers included Steven Spielberg and George Lucas. **67m/C VHS, DVD.** ***D:*** Don Bluth; ***W:*** Stu Krieger; ***M:*** James Horner; ***V:*** Pat Hingle, Helen Shaver, Gabriel Damon, Candice Houston, Burke Barnes, Judith Barsi, Will Ryan.

The Land Before Time 2: The Great Valley Adventure 1/2 **1994 (G)** Sequel to 1988's animated adventure finds dinosaur pals Littlefoot, Cera, Ducky, Petrie, and Spike happily settled in the Great Valley. But their adventures don't stop as they chase two egg-stealing Struthiomimuses and retrieve an egg of unknown origin from the Mysterious Beyond. **75m/C VHS, DVD.** ***D:*** John Loy, Roy Allen Smith; ***W:*** John Ludin, Dev Ross; ***M:*** Michael Tavera; ***V:*** Candy Hutson, Jeff Glenn Bennett, Kenneth Mars, Rob Paulsen, Scott McAfee, Heather Hogan, John Ingle, Linda Gary.

The Land Before Time 3: The Time of the Great Giving 1/2 **1995 (G)** Littlefoot and his pals try to find a new source of water when the Great Valley experiences a severe water shortage. **71m/C VHS, DVD.** ***D:*** Roy Allen Smith; ***W:*** John Loy, Dev Ross, John Ludin; ***M:*** Michael Tavera; ***V:*** Scott McAfee, Candy Hutson, Heather Hogan, Jeff Glenn Bennett, Kenneth Mars, John Ingle, Rob Paulsen, Linda Gary.

The Land Before Time 4: Journey Through the Mists 1/2 **1996** The little dinosaurs travel through the land of the mists in search of a rejuvenation flower that can save the life of Litefoot's sick grandpa. **74m/C VHS, DVD.** ***D:*** Roy Allen Smith; ***W:*** Dev Ross; ***M:*** Michael Tavera; ***V:*** Scott McAfee, Candy Hutson, Heather Hogan, Jeff Glenn Bennett, Kenneth Mars, John Ingle, Rob Paulsen, Linda Gary.

The Land Before Time 5: The Mysterious Island 1/2 **1997 (G)** When a swarm of insects devour all the plants in the Great Valley, the herds are forced to move. But with the adults fighting, Littlefoot and his pals go off on their own. They cross the Big Water to a mysterious island, which just happens to be the home of their old friend, the baby T-Rex, Chomper. And it's up to Chomper to protect his plant-eating friends from the island's meat-eaters, who look on the little band as dinner. **74m/C VHS, DVD.** ***D:*** Charles Grosvenor; ***W:*** John Loy; ***M:*** Michael Tavera; ***V:*** Jeff Glenn Bennett, Kenneth Mars, John Ingle, Rob Paulsen, Thomas Dekker, Aria Noelle Curzon, Miriam Flynn, Andi McAfee, Brandon Lacroix.

The Land Before Time 6: The Secret of Saurus Rock 1/2 **1998 (G)** Children's animated tale takes place in the age of the dinosaurs. In this sequel, Littlefoot and the rest of his dinosaur pals explore the myth of a mysterious lone dinosaur and accidentally set off a series of mishaps in the Great Valley. **77m/C VHS, DVD.** ***D:*** Charles Grosvenor; ***W:*** John Loy, Libby Hinson; ***M:*** Michael Tavera; ***V:*** Jeff Glenn Bennett, Nancy Cartwright, Aria Noelle Curzon, Thomas Dekker, Kris Kristofferson, Miriam Flynn, Kenneth Mars, Andi McAfee.

Land Before Time 7: The Stone of Cold Fire **2000 (G)** In the seventh installment of the popular kid's series, the young dinosaurs Littlefoot, Cera, Spike, Ducky, and Petrie go off in search of a meteor that only Littlefoot saw. Petrie's disreputable uncle Pterano eggs them on. The moral lessons are simple; the animation is bright; the story moves quickly. In short, the movie delivers exactly what its young fans want to see. The pidgin English dialog will be hard for adults to take. **75m/C DVD.** ***D:*** Charles Grosvenor; ***W:*** Len Uhley; ***V:*** Jeff Glenn Bennett, Anndi McAfee, Rob Paulsen, Thomas Dekker, Aria Noelle Curzon.

The Land Girls 1/2 **1998 (R)** Based on the real life Women's Land Army in England, which consisted of female volunteers who helped take over the duties of farmers who were fighting WWII. Stella (McCormack), Ag (Weisz) and Prue (Friel) are three city girls who come to Dorset in rural Britain to work on the farm of crusty Mr. Lawrence (Georgeson). Since the war started he has had only his submissive wife (O'Brien) and headstrong son Joe (Mackintosh) to help him. Joe, who dreams of being a fighter pilot, ends up in bed with each of the women; but on their terms, not his own. The movie is more concerned with the hard work these women did and the historical context than with the individual characters, however. The shared sacrifice and camaraderie overshadow the romantic subplots. Shot on location in western England. **110m/C VHS.** *GB* Catherine McCormack, Rachel Weisz, Anna Friel, Steven Mackintosh, Tom Georgeson, Maureen O'Brien, Paul Bettany, Lucy Akhurst; ***D:*** David Leland; ***W:*** David Leland, Keith Dewhurst; ***C:*** Henry Braham; ***M:*** Brian Lock.

Land of Doom **1984** An amazon and a warrior struggle for survival in a post-holocaust fantasy setting. **87m/C VHS.** Deborah Rennard, Garrick Dowhen; ***D:*** Peter Maris.

The Land of Faraway *Mio in the Land of Faraway* **1987 (G)** A Swedish boy is whisked off to a magical land where he does battle with evil knights and flies on winged horses. Dubbed; based on a novel by Astrid Lindgren. **95m/C VHS, DVD.** Timothy Bottoms, Christian Bale, Susannah York, Christopher Lee, Nicholas Pickard; ***D:*** Vladimir Grammatikov.

Land of Fury *The Seekers* **1955** British naval officer Hawkins steps on New Zealand's shore and into trouble when he accidently walks on sacred Maori burial ground. Very British, very dated colonial saga, based on the novel "The Seekers" by John Guthrie. **90m/C VHS.** *GB* Jack Hawkins, Glynis Johns, Noel Purcell, Ian Fleming; ***D:*** Ken Annakin.

Land of Hunted Men **1943** The Range Busters are on the case as they track down the hideout of terrorizing gunmen. **58m/B VHS.** Ray Corrigan, Dennis Moore, Max Terhune, Phyllis Adair, Charles "Blackie" King, John Merton, Forrest Taylor, Steve Clark; ***D:*** S. Roy Luby; ***W:*** Elizabeth Beecher; ***C:*** James S. Brown Jr.

Land of Plenty **2004** Director Wenders takes on some post-9/11 angst in this well-meaning digital video feature. Lana (Williams), the daughter of missionaries, arrives in LA after living in the Middle East. She takes a job at a homeless shelter while she searches for her long-estranged Uncle Paul (Diehl). Paul is a troubled Vietnam vet who has become a self-appointed homeland security expert—traveling the streets in a van filled with surveillance equipment. The two finally meet, and bond, over their mutual sense of helplessness and confusion. **119m/C DVD.** *US* Michelle Williams, John Diehl, Shaun Toub, Wendell Pierce, Richard Edson, Burt Young, Gloria Stuart, Bernie (Bernard) White; ***D:*** Wim Wenders; ***W:*** Wim Wenders, Michael Meredith; ***C:*** Franz Lustig; ***M:*** Thomas Hanreich.

Land of Promise 1/2 *Ziemia Obiecana* **1974** At the turn of the century three men build a textile factory in Lodz, Poland. They each represent a particular ethnic group: a Pole (Olbrychski), a German (Seweryn), and a Jew (Pszoniak). Class conflicts threaten to overwhelm as their overworked and underpaid workers plan a revolt. Based on the novel by Wladyslav Reymont. In Polish with English subtitles. **178m/C VHS, DVD.** *PL* Daniel Olbrychski, Wojciech Pszoniak, Andrzej Seweryn, Anna Nehrebecka; ***D:*** Andrzej Wajda; ***W:*** Andrzej Wajda; ***M:*** Wojciech Kilar.

Land of the Blind **2006 (R)** Failed political satire about a revolution set in an unknown time and a nameless country. Thorne (Sutherland) is a leftist rebel leader who's imprisoned and tortured for his beliefs. But once the dictatorship is overthrown and Thorne assumes power, he becomes just as repressive as the old regime. Former jailer turned second-in-command Joe (Fiennes) realizes what a mistake he's made. Edwards' first feature is also an all-around mistake that even professionals like Fiennes and Sutherland can't salvage. **101m/C DVD.** *GB* Ralph Fiennes, Donald Sutherland, Tom Hollander, Lara Flynn Boyle, Mark Warren, Camilla Rutherford, Mackenzie Crook, Jodhi May; ***D:*** Robert Edwards; ***W:*** Robert Edwards; ***C:*** Barbara Parkins; ***M:*** Guy Farley, Simon White, Doug Edwards.

Land of the Free **1998 (R)** Frank Jennings (Speakman) is the campaign manager for super-patriot Senate hopeful Aidan Carvell (a deliberately hammy Shatner). Then Jennings discovers his boss has big ambitions—he wants to take over the government as the head of a terrorist organization. **96m/C VHS, DVD.** Jeff Speakman, William Shatner, Chris Lemmon, Charles Robinson; ***D:*** Jerry Jameson; ***W:*** Terry Cunningham; ***C:*** Ken Blakey. **VIDEO**

Land of the Lawless **1947** A group of outlaws rule over a barren wasteland. What's the point? **54m/B VHS.** Rachel Brown, Raymond Hatton, Christine McIntyre, Tristram Coffin; ***D:*** Lambert Hillyer.

Land of the Lost 1/2 **2009 (PG-13)** The humor certainly got lost somewhere in this loud, irritating rather than funny reimaging of the 1970s Sid and Marty Krofft children's TV series. Rick Marshall (Ferrell) is a disgraced paleontologist whose research involved parallel universes. He manages to find himself in a primeval world, accompanied by winsome Holly (Friel) and goofy tour guide Will (McBride). They encounter the ape-like Chaka (Taccone) as well as the lizard Sleestaks, a very thirsty (and large) mosquito, and a T-Rex that constantly torments Rick. Ferrell is game as usual but his shtick is tired. **93m/C DVD.** *US* Will Ferrell, Anna Friel, Danny McBride, Jorma Taccone, John Boylan, Matt Laurer; ***D:*** Brad Silberling; ***W:*** Dennis McNicholas, Chris Henchy; ***C:*** Dion Beebe; ***M:*** Michael Giacchino. Golden Raspberries '09: Worst Remake.

Land of the Minotaur *The Devil's Men* **1977 (PG)** Small village is the setting for horrifying ritual murders, demons, and disappearances of young terrorists. Fans of Pleasence and Cushing won't want to miss this. **88m/C VHS, DVD.** *GB* Donald Pleasence, Peter Cushing, Luan Peters; ***D:*** Costa Carayiannis; ***M:*** Brian Eno.

Land of the Pharaohs 1/2 **1955** Epic about the building of Egypt's Great Pyramid. Hawkins is the extremely talkative pharoah and Collins plays his sugary-sweet yet villainous wife. Sort of campy, but worth watching for the great surprise ending. **106m/C VHS, DVD.** Jack Hawkins, Joan Collins, James Robertson Justice, Dewey Martin, Alexis Minotis, Sydney Chaplin; ***D:*** Howard Hawks; ***W:*** Harold Jack Bloom; ***C:*** Lee Garmes.

Land Raiders **1969** Savalas plays a man who hates Apaches and wants their land, but is distracted when his brother arrives on the scene, igniting an old feud. **101m/C VHS, DVD.** Telly Savalas, George Maharis, Arlene Dahl, Janet Landgard; ***D:*** Nathan "Jerry" Juran.

The Land That Time Forgot **1975 (PG)** A WWI veteran, a beautiful woman, and their German enemies are stranded in a land outside time filled with prehistoric creatures. Based on the 1918 novel by Edgar Rice Burroughs. Followed in 1977 by "The People that Time Forgot." **90m/C VHS, DVD.** *GB* Doug McClure, John McEnery, Susan Penhaligon, Keith Barren, Anthony Ainley, Godfrey James, Bobby Parr, Declan Mulholland, Colin Farrell, Ben Howard, Roy Holder, Andrew McCulloch, Ron Pember, Steve James; ***D:*** Kevin Connor; ***W:*** James Cawthorn, Michael Moorcock; ***C:*** Alan Hume; ***M:*** Douglas Gamley.

The Land That Time Forgot **2009** Two newlywed couples are enjoying a charter boat cruise through the Caribbean when they are caught in a bizarre storm. The boat emerges offshore of the island of Caprona, which apparently exists in its own time zone inside the Bermuda Triangle. The charter boat captain and the newlyweds discover they aren't the only ones who have been pulled through time: there's also the crew of a WWII German U-Boat and the island is filled with dinosaurs and other prehistoric creatures. Based on the Edgar Rice Burroughs adventure fantasy. **90m/C DVD.** C. Thomas Howell, Timothy Bottoms, Lindsey McKeon, Darren Dalton, Anya Benton, Stephen Blackehart, Chris Showerman, Patrick Gorman, Scott Subiono; ***D:*** C. Thomas Howell; ***W:*** Darren Dalton; ***C:*** Mark Atkins; ***M:*** Chris Ridenhour. **VIDEO**

The Land Unknown 1/2 **1957** A Naval helicopter is forced down in a tropical land of prehistoric terror, complete with ferocious creatures from the Mesozoic Era. While trying to make repairs, the crew discovers the sole survivor of a previous expedition who was driven to madness by life in the primordial jungle. Good performances from cast, although monsters aren't that believable. Based on a story by Charles Palmer. **78m/B VHS.** Jock Mahoney, Shawn Smith, William Reynolds, Henry (Kleinbach) Brandon, Douglas Kennedy; ***D:*** Virgil W. Vogel; ***W:*** Laszlo Gorog; ***M:*** Henry Mancini.

The Landlady **1998 (R)** Melanie Leroy (Shire) kills her hubby after discovering him cheating on her. When she becomes the landlady of an apartment house, she decides one of her tenants, nice-guy Patrick (Coleman), would be ideal husband material. And Melanie intends to get rid of any obstacles in her way. **98m/C VHS, DVD.** Talia Shire, Jack Coleman, Bruce Weitz, Melissa Behr, Susie Singer, Bette Ford; ***D:*** Rob Malenfant; ***W:*** Frank Rehwaldt, George Saunders; ***C:*** Darko Suvak; ***M:*** Eric Lundmark.

Landlord Blues 1/2 **1987** A trashy slumlord without morals or a conscience goes one step too far, and a tenant retaliates with munitions. **96m/C VHS.** Mark Boone Jr., Raye Dowell, Richard Litt, Bill Rice, Mary Schultz, Gigi Williams; ***D:*** Jacob Burckhardt.

Landscape After Battle *Krajobraz Po Bitwie* **1970** A group of concentration camp survivors are awaiting repatriation in a disused barracks in a German stalag in 1945. Among them are young Poles, Nina and Tadeusz, who fall in love. But tragedy continues when Nina is accidentally killed by an American guard. Based on the stories of Tadeusz Borowski, an Auschwitz survivor who later committed suicide. Polish with subtitles. **101m/C DVD.** *PL* Daniel Olbrychski, Stanislawa Celinska, Tadeusz Janczar; ***D:*** Andrzej Wajda; ***W:*** Andrzej Wajda, Andrzej Brzozowski; ***C:*** Zygmunt Samosiuk; ***M:*** Zygmunt Konieczny.

Landscape in the Mist *Topio Stin Omichli* **1988** A stark Greek landscape in a rainy winter sets the scene for a tragic search by two children for their unknown father. Relies heavily on symbolism to make its point about unfulfilled desire (including the film's imaginary German-Greek border). In Greek with English subtitles. **126m/C VHS, DVD.** *GR FR IT* Tania Palaiologou, Michalis Zeke, Stratos Tzortzoglou, Eva Kotamanidou, Aliki Georgouli; ***D:*** Theo Angelopoulos; ***W:*** Thanassis Valtinos, Tonino Guerra, Theo Angelopoulos; ***C:*** Yorgos Arvanitis; ***M:*** Eleni Karaindrou.

Landslide 1/2 **1992 (PG-13)** As a geologist, suffering from memory loss, comes closer to discovering his identity his life is endangered by a sinister plot. **95m/C VHS.** Anthony Edwards, Tom Burlinson, Joanna Cassidy, Melody Anderson, Ronald Lacey, Ken James, Lloyd Bochner; ***D:*** Jean-Claude Lord.

L'Annee des Meduses 1/2 *The Year of the Jellyfish* **1986 (R)** An 18-year-old girl tries to seduce the local Monsieur Beefcake she meets on her vacation. When he doesn't return her interest, she decides to teach him a lesson. In French with English subtitles, or dubbed. **110m/C VHS.** *FR* Valerie Kaprisky, Barnard Giradeau; ***D:*** Christopher Frank; ***C:*** Renato Berta.

L'Annee Sainte 1/2 *Pilgrimage to Rome; Holy Year* **1976** In his last film, Gabin is an escaped convict returning to his hidden loot in Rome when his plane is hijacked by international terrorists. Available dubbed. **85m/C VHS, DVD.** *FR* Jean Gabin, Jean-Claude Brialy, Paul(o) Giusti, Danielle Darrieux; ***D:*** Jean Girault; ***W:*** Louis-Emile Galey, Jacques Vilfrid; ***C:*** Guy Suzuki; ***M:*** Claude Bolling.

Lansdown 1/2 **2001** Flat attempt at a neo-noir/crime comedy. Jake (Sheilds) is a bland criminal defense attorney in the fictitious New jersey title town. His wife Lexi (Carlson) is bored and has been fooling around with roofer Pat (Stewart). When Jake finds out, he decides he wants the lover dead but can't get his former client Gustav (Warren)—who provided the info on the infidelity—to do the hit himself. Instead, Gustav subcontracts to a couple of doofus hit men, who botch it. So Jake is forced to get more personally involved. **80m/C VHS, DVD.** Adam Fidusiewicz, Jennifer Carlson, Chris Stewart, D.W. Warren, Patrick Louis, Chris Baran, Marc Krinsky; ***D:*** Tom Zuber; ***W:*** Tom Zuber; ***C:*** Ty Bolia; ***M:*** Atli Ovarsson.

Lansky 1/2 **1999 (R)** Traces some 70 years in the life of Jewish mobster Meyer Lansky (Dreyfuss), which, surprisingly, doesn't make for exciting drama. Lansky grew up on New York's Lower East Side with Benjamin "Bugsy" Siegel (Roberts) and Charlie "Lucky" Luciano (LaPaglia). Th trio would mastermind a crime syndicate, with Lansky basically serving as the Mob accountant. Story is told in flashbacks as the aged Lansky awaits federal trial in Miami. **120m/C VHS, DVD.** Richard Dreyfuss, Eric Roberts, Anthony LaPaglia, Illeana Douglas, Beverly D'Angelo, Ryan Merriman, Francis Guinan, Stanley DeSantis, Nick(y) Corello; ***D:*** John McNaughton; ***W:*** David Mamet; ***C:*** John A. Alonzo; ***M:*** George S. Clinton. **CABLE**

Lantana **2001 (R)** This impressive Aussie thriller starts off as a seemingly straightforward murder mystery, but that's only the jumping-off point. The burned-out cop, Leon (LaPaglia) investigating the murder, is cheating on his wife with a woman, Jane (Blke), who may know something about the case. His wife is consulting a psychiatrist, Valerie (Hershey), whose marriage to John (Rush) has been damaged by the murder of their 11-year-old daughter. John may also be having a homosexual affair with one of his wife's patients. Jane's neighbors, Nik (Colosimo) and Paula (Farinacci) seem like the only happy ones in the mix, but they, too, are touched by the mystery. LaPaglia stands out in a brilliant cast, and the deep character studies and attention to detail add dimension to what could have been a standard whodunit. **120m/C VHS, DVD.** *AU* Anthony LaPaglia, Kerry Armstrong, Geoffrey Rush, Barbara Hershey, Rachael Blake, Vince Colosimo, Peter Phelps, Daniela Farinacci, Leah Purcell, Glenn Robbins; ***D:*** Ray Lawrence; ***W:*** Andrew Bovell; ***C:*** Mandy Walker; ***M:*** Paul Kelly. Australian Film Inst. '01: Actor (LaPaglia), Actress (Armstrong), Adapt. Screenplay, Director (Lawrence), Film, Support. Actor (Colosimo), Support. Actress (Blake).

Lantern Hill 1/2 **1990 (G)** During the Depression, a 12-year-old girl attempts to fan the embers between her estranged parents. A Wonderworks production, filmed partly on Canada's Prince Edward Island. Based on a story by Lucy Maud Montgomery, whose "Anne of Green Gables" is also part of the Wonderworks series. **112m/C VHS.** *CA* Sam Waterston, Colleen Dewhurst, Sarah Polley, Marion Bennett, Zoe Caldwell; ***D:*** Kevin Sullivan. **CABLE**

Lap Dancing WOOF! **1995 (R)** What hath "Showgirls" wrought? Small town gal Angie Parker moves to Hollywood to become an actress and, when the money runs out, winds up as an exotic dancer. Also available unrated. **90m/C VHS, DVD.** Lorissa McComas, Tane McClure, C.T. Miller; ***D:*** Mike Sedan; ***W:*** K.C. Martin; ***C:*** Carlos Montaner; ***M:*** Ron Allen, Todd Schroeder. **VIDEO**

L.A.P.D.: To Protect and Serve **2001** Hey, Hopper is actually a good guy in this police corruption drama! He's a captain determined to weed out a group of bad apples in the department. **98m/C VHS, DVD.** Dennis Hopper, Michael Madsen, Charles Durning, Marc Singer; ***D:*** Ed Anders; ***W:*** Rob Neighbors; ***C:*** Michael Balery. **VIDEO**

L'Appat *Fresh Bait; Live Bait; The Bait* **1994** Deglamourizing, if familiar, look at amoral teens and violence. 18-year-old salesgirl Nathalie (Gillain) supports her unemployed boyfriend Eric (Sitruk) and his dimbulb buddy Bruno (Putzulu). The guys hang out, watch too many gangster videos, and try to be tough, deciding to get rich by dangling Nathalie as bait. She goes to a man's home (presumably for sex) but Eric and Bruno will break in and rob the mark instead. Plan goes awry when their first victim is killed. What's truly disturbing is the trio's blase attitude that crime is a viable way to obtain money or that anything would happen to them should they be caught. Based on the book by Morgan Sportes, which recounted the 1984 crime. French with subtitles. **117m/C VHS.** *FR* Marie Gillain, Olivier Sitruk, Bruno Putzulu, Philippe Duclos, Richard Berry; ***D:*** Bertrand Tavernier; ***W:*** Bertrand Tavernier, Colo Tavernier O'Hagan; ***M:*** Philippe Haim. Berlin Intl. Film Fest. '94: Film.

Lara Croft: Tomb Raider *Tomb Raider* **2001 (PG-13)** Laura Croft (Jolie), the daughter of a British aristocrat/adventurer (Jolie's real-life dad Voight), gives up her upper-crusty life to hunt down ancient treasures that hold the key to controlling time before they fall into the wrong hands. Sounds straightforward enough, right? Maybe it once was but too much tinkering results in a muddled story and foggy details that do, however, divert your attention away from the cheesy dialogue and flimsy characters. Stunning sets and visuals, along with Jolie's "let's have some fun" attitude go a long way toward making this disappointment more entertaining than it probably should be. **96m/C VHS, DVD, Blu-ray Disc, UMD.** *US* Angelina Jolie, Iain Glen, Daniel Craig, Leslie Phillips, Jon Voight, Noah Taylor, Richard Johnson, Julian Rhind-Tutt, Chris (Christopher) Barrie; ***D:*** Simon West; ***W:*** Patrick Massett, John Zinman; ***C:*** Peter Menzies Jr.; ***M:*** Graeme Revell.

Lara Croft Tomb Raider: The Cradle of Life 1/2 **2003 (PG-13)** Arguably better than its predecessor, sequel has Croft (Jolie) searching for Pandora's box: a mythical container which is supposed to contain unfathomable evils. Our intrepid hero must outsmart the diabolical Dr. Reiss (Hinds) who wants to use it to wipe out all humanity save a lucky few over which he would, naturally, rule. With her hunky Scottish ex (Butler) in tow, the quest takes the pillow-lipped raider of the lost box on an undersea adventure in Greece and other exotic locales, including Shanghai and Mt. Kilimanjaro. Jolie injects Lara with more character, while the plethora of action scenes and special effects are deftly directed by De Bont, MIA since 1999's "The Haunting." Less noisy scenes, however, lack luster. **116m/C VHS, DVD, UMD.** *US* Angelina Jolie, Gerard Butler, Ciaran Hinds, Til Schweiger, Djimon Hounsou, Noah Taylor, Chris (Christopher) Barrie, Simon Yam; ***D:*** Jan De Bont; ***W:*** Dean Georgaris; ***C:*** David Tattersall; ***M:*** Alan Silvestri.

Laramie Kid **1935** A vintage Tyler sagebrush saga. **60m/B VHS.** Tom Tyler, Alberta Vaughn, Al Ferguson, Murdock MacQuarrie, George Chesebro; ***D:*** Harry S. Webb.

The Laramie Project **2002 (R)** A docudrama that explores the 1998 gay-bashing death of Matthew Shepard in Laramie, Wyoming. Shortly after the crime, Moises Kaufman (here played by Carbonell) and members of his New York Tectonic Theater Project arrived in Laramie to interview residents and others associated with the crime. Kaufman then adapted the transcripts into a stage piece, which debuted in Denver. Kaufman himself directs the film adaptation, which includes actual news footage interspersed with actor re-creations. **87m/C VHS, DVD.** Nestor Carbonell, Peter Fonda, Amy Madigan, Janeane Garofalo, Jeremy Davies, Steve Buscemi, Christina Ricci, Mark Webber, Laura Linney, Terry Kinney; ***D:*** Moises Kaufman; ***W:*** Moises Kaufman; ***C:*** Terry Stacey; ***M:*** Peter Golub. **CABLE**

Larceny in her Heart 1/2 **1946** Private eye Michael Shayne (Beaumont) is asked to track down the missing stepdaughter of a local bigwig. Shayne figures out that the stepdaughter has been committed to an asylum, presumably by the bigwig who purports to be searching for her. Then Shayne's client shows up dead and the mystery deepens. **68m/B DVD.** Hugh Beaumont, Cheryl Walker, Ralph Dunn, Charles C. Wilson, Douglas Fowley; ***D:*** Sam Newfield; ***W:*** Brett Halliday, Raymond L. Schrock; ***C:*** Jack Greenhalgh; ***M:*** Leo Erdody.

Larceny, Inc. 1/2 **1942** Maxwell (Robinson) and pal Martin (Crawford) are being released from Sing Sing and plan to open a dog track but their outside partner Davis (Brophy) has lost their bankroll. Maxwell reluctantly agrees to a bank job planned by fellow prisoner Dexter (Quinn) that involves buying the luggage shop next door to the bank and digging a tunnel, but Maxwell is dumbfounded when the store is a success. Thinking his partners are getting cold feet, Dexter escapes to oversee the operation himself. Robinson's last contract film for Warner Bros. **95m/B DVD.** Edward G. Robinson, Broderick Crawford, Anthony Quinn, Edward Brophy, Jane Wyman, Jack Carson, Harry Davenport, John Qualen; ***D:*** Lloyd Bacon; ***W:*** Everett Freeman, Edwin Gilbert; ***C:*** Gaetano Antonio "Tony" Gaudio; ***M:*** Adolph Deutsch.

Larceny On the Air 1/2 **1937** Righteous Dr. Lawrence Baxter (Livingston) is appalled by quacks selling their patent cures on the radio and is determined to force them out of business, even when he falls for the daughter (Bradley) of one scammer. **67m/B VHS.** Robert "Bob" Livingston, Grace Bradley, Willard Robertson, Pierre Watkin, Smiley Burnette, Granville Bates; ***D:*** Irving Pichel; ***W:*** Richard English; ***C:*** Jack Marta.

L'Argent *Money* **1983** When a young man's parents refuse to lend him any money a friend helps out by giving him a counterfeit 500-franc note. This sets off a chain of events, with every passing of the money leading to another lie, betrayal, and increasingly violent crime. Austere and stylized vision is not for all tastes. In French with English subtitles. **82m/C VHS, DVD.** *FR* Christian Patey, Sylvie van den Elsen, Michel Briguet, Caroline Lang; ***D:*** Robert Bresson; ***W:*** Robert Bresson; ***C:*** Pasqualino De Santis. Cannes '83: Director (Bresson); Natl. Soc. Film Critics '84: Director (Bresson).

Larger Than Life 1/2 *Nickel and Dime; Large as Life* **1996 (PG)** The pitch for this movie (Murray takes an elephant on a cross-country trip) must have sounded terrific. Unfortunately, the pitch was fouled off. Murray is his usual smarmy self as cut-rate motivational speaker Jack Corcoran, who inherits the pachyderm and a pile of bills after his circus clown father dies. Following the "road movie" formula, he encounters wacky characters along the way, including a speed-freak trucker (McConaughey), a sexy animal trainer (Fiorentino) and a strait-laced zookeeper (Garofalo). In a piece of brilliant casting, Tai, the star of "Operation Dumbo Drop" appears as...the elephant. **93m/C VHS, DVD.** Bill Murray, Janeane Garofalo, Linda Fiorentino, Matthew McConaughey, Keith David, Pat Hingle, Jeremy Piven, Lois Smith, Anita Gillette, Maureen Mueller, Harve Presnell, Tracey Walter; ***D:*** Howard Franklin; ***W:*** Roy Blount Jr.; ***C:*** Elliot Davis; ***M:*** Miles Goodman.

Larks on a String 1/2 **1968** Banned for 23 years, this wonderful film is Menzel's masterpiece, even better than his Oscar winning "Closely Watched Trains." Portrays the story of life in labor camps where men and women are re-educated at the whim of the government. No matter what the hardships, these people find humor, hope and love. Their individuality will not be lost, nor their humanity dissolved. Excellent performances, tellingly directed with a beautiful sense of composition and tone. Screenplay written by Menzel and Bohumil Hrabil, author of the short story on which it is based. In Czech with English subtitles. **96m/C VHS.** *CZ* Vaclav Neckar, Jitka Zelenohorska, Jaroslav Satoransky, Rudolf Hrusinsky; ***D:*** Jiri Menzel; ***W:*** Jiri Menzel.

Larry **1974** Based on the Nevada State Hospital case history of a 26-year-old man, institutionalized since infancy, who is discovered to be of normal intelligence and must learn to live the life he has always been capable of living. **80m/C VHS.** Frederic Forrest, Tyne Daly, Katherine Helmond, Michael McGuire, Robert Walden; ***D:*** William A. Graham. **TV**

Larry McMurtry's Dead Man's Walk 1/2 *Dead Man's Walk* **1996 (PG-13)** McMurtry's prequel to "Lonesome Dove" focuses on the teenaged Gus McCrae (Arquette) and Woodrow Call (Miller) and their first adventures as Texas Rangers in the 1840s. They're involved in the ill-fated Texas-Santa Fe Expedition, led by parrot-owning former seafarer Caleb Cobb (Abraham), to take Santa Fe and make New Mexico part of the Texas Republic. Instead, a Mexican Army detachment led by Capt. Salazar (Olmos), captures the rag-tag group, which is then forced to march across a deadly stretch of desert that few survive. Likeable leads but the supporting actors, including Carradine and Stanton as scouts, steal the show. **271m/C VHS, DVD.** Jonny Lee Miller, David Arquette, Keith Carradine, Harry Dean Stanton, F. Murray Abraham, Edward James Olmos, Eric Schweig, Patricia Childress, Jennifer Garner, Haviland (Haylie) Morris, Brian Dennehy, Joaquim de Almeida, Ray McKinnon, Akosua Busia; ***D:*** Yves Simoneau; ***W:*** Larry McMurtry, Diana Ossana; ***C:*** Edward Pei; ***M:*** David Bell. **TV**

Larry McMurtry's Streets of Laredo *Lonesome Dove: Streets of Laredo* **1995** Texas Ranger-turned-bounty hunter Woodrow F. Call (a splendid Garner) is hired by the railroad to track down ruthless Mexican bandit Joey Garza (Cruz), pitting an old man's skills against a young man's daring, and driving both men across Texas, deep into Mexican territory. Call's old friend Pea Eye Parker (Shepard) reluctantly comes along, with ex-prostitute Lorena (Spacek), who's Parker's wife, and Maria (Braga), Joey's tough-but-deluded mom, providing strong support. Casual cruelty and violence are the norm in the sunset days of both Call's life and that of the west itself. Third in the TV sagas, following "Return to Lonesome Dove." **227m/C VHS, DVD.** James Garner, Alexis Cruz, Sam Shepard, Sissy Spacek, Sonia Braga, Wes Studi, Randy Quaid, Charles Martin Smith, Kevin Conway, George Carlin, Ned Beatty, James Gammon, Tristan Tait, Anjanette Comer; ***D:*** Joseph Sargent; ***W:*** Larry McMurtry, Diana Ossana; ***C:*** Edward Pei; ***M:*** David Shire. **TV**

Larry the Cable Guy: Health Inspector WOOF! **2006 (PG-13)** Gross-out comedy appealing to those who like flatulence, vomiting, and other sorts of intestinal distress. Blue-collar comedian Larry the Cable Guy is Larry the Florida health inspector guy, who suspects someone is deliberately causing the food poisoning epidemic that's hitting a number of upscale restaurants. So he goes undercover, along with his uptight partner Amy (Bahr), to find the culprit. Hilarity doesn't ensue. Who let the guys who greenlit "Chairman of the Board" back on the lot? **89m/C DVD.** *US* Larry the Cable Guy, Joanna Cassidy, David Koechner, Thomas F. Wilson, Joe Pantoliano, Iris Bahr, Bruce Bruce, Brooke Dillman, Tony Hale, Lisa Lampanelli, Megyn Price; ***Cameos:*** Jerry Mathers, Kid Rock; ***D:*** Trent Cooper; ***W:*** Jon Bernstein, James Greer; ***C:*** Kim Marks; ***M:*** Steven R. Phillips, Tim P.

Lars and the Real Girl 1/2 **2007 (PG-13)** Lars (Gosling) is one of those sweetly awkward small-town loonies that movies are so fond of. He's a damaged soul who tries to avoid too much human contact, including that of his well-meaning brother Gus (Schneider) and sister-in-law Karin (Mortimer). Then Lars buys a customized life-size sex doll (no, he's not a perv) online and begins introducing her as his girlfriend, Bianca. Family doctor Dagmar (Clarkson) persuades everyone to go along with Lars' delusion for the time being and Bianca is quickly integrated into the community. Fortunately, Gosling et al manage to sell this story without too much ick or schmaltz. **106m/C DVD.** *US* Ryan Gosling, Paul Schneider, Emily Mortimer, Patricia Clarkson, Kelli Garner, Nancy Beatty, Karen Robinson; ***D:*** Nancy Oliver; ***W:*** Gerri Gillan; ***C:*** Adam Kimmel; ***M:*** David Torn.

Las Vegas Hillbillys *Country Music* **1966** A pair of country-singing hillbillies inherit a saloon in Las Vegas and enjoy wine, moonshine, and song. These two make the Clampetts look like high society. Followed, believe it or not, by "Hillbillys in a Haunted House." ♫Money Greases the Wheel. **85m/C VHS, DVD.** Mamie Van Doren, Jayne Mansfield, Ferlin Husky, Sonny James; ***D:*** Arthur C. Pierce.

Las Vegas Lady **1976 (PG)** Three shrewd casino hostesses plot a multi-million dollar heist in the nation's gambling capital. Non-captivating caper. **90m/C VHS, DVD.** Stella Stevens, Stuart Whitman, George DiCenzo, Andrew Stevens, Lynne Moody, Linda Scruggs; ***D:*** Noel Nosseck; ***W:*** Walter Dallenbach; ***C:*** Stephen M. Katz; ***M:*** Alan Silvestri.

Las Vegas Serial Killer WOOF! **1986** A serial killer, let out of prison on a technicality, starts killing again. **90m/C VHS, DVD.** Pierre Agostino, Ron Jason, Tara MacGowran, Kathryn Downey; ***D:*** Ray Dennis Steckler; ***W:*** Ray Dennis Steckler. **VIDEO**

The Las Vegas Story WOOF! 1952 Gambling, colorful sights, and a murder provide the framework for this non-compelling fictional guided-tour of the city. Save your money for the slots. **88m/B VHS.** Victor Mature, Jane Russell, Vincent Price, Hoagy Carmichael, Brad Dexter; ***D:*** Robert Stevenson; ***W:*** Paul Jarrico.

Las Vegas Weekend 1985 A computer nerd goes to Las Vegas and discovers fun. **83m/C VHS.** Barry Hickey, Macka Foley, Ray Dennis Steckler; ***D:*** Dale Trevillion; ***W:*** Dale Trevillion.

Laser Mission 1/2 **1990** When it is discovered that the Soviets have laser weapon capabilities, an agent is given the task of destroying the weapon and kidnapping the scientist who developed it. **83m/C VHS, DVD.** Brandon Lee, Debi Monahan, Ernest Borgnine, Werner Pochath, Graham Clarke, Maureen Lahoud, Pierre Knoessen; ***D:*** Beau Davis; ***M:*** David Knopfler.

Laser Moon 1992 A serial killer uses a surgical laser beam to kill his beautiful victims, and he strikes at every full moon. When he announces his next attack on a late-night radio talk show the police call in a beautiful rookie cop (Lords) to use as bait. **90m/C VHS, DVD.** Traci Lords, Crystal Shaw, Harrison Leduke, Bruce Carter; ***D:*** Douglas K. Grimm.

Laserblast WOOF! 1978 (PG) Standard wimp-gets-revenge story in which a frustrated young man finds a powerful and deadly laser which was left near his home by aliens; upon learning of its devastating capabilities, his personality changes and he seeks revenge against all who have taken advantage of him. **87m/C VHS, DVD.** Kim Milford, Cheryl "Rainbeaux" Smith, Keenan Wynn, Roddy McDowall; ***D:*** Michael Raeburn; ***W:*** Frank Ray Perilli, Franne Schacht; ***C:*** Terry Bowen; ***M:*** Richard Band, Joel Goldsmith.

Laserhawk 1/2 **1999 (PG-13)** Now here's an interesting take on the origin of species—millions of years ago carnivorous aliens planted humans as a crop on earth. Now they've returned to harvest their goods and only a band of misfits may have a chance to save humanity if they can find one of the aliens' crashed spacecraft/weapons called a Laserhawk to use against them. **102m/C VHS, DVD.** Mark Hamill, Jason James Richter, Gordon Currie, Melissa Galianos; ***D:*** Jean Pellerin; ***W:*** John A. Curtis. **VIDEO**

The Laserman 1990 (R) Exotic black comedy about a Chinese-American scientist who, when not fending off his overbearing Jewish mother or having telepathic orgasms, is contending with a band of political terrorists. **92m/C VHS.** Marc Hayashi, Peter Wang, Tony Leung Ka-Fai, Sally Yeh, Maryann Urbano, Joan Copeland; ***D:*** Peter Wang; ***W:*** Peter Wang; ***M:*** Mason Daring.

Lassie 1/2 **1994 (PG)** Everyone's favorite collie returns as the Turner family moves to Virginia's Shenandoah Valley to take up sheep ranching. However, because this is the '90s, Dad meets financial disaster, and junior can't stand his stepmom. Can Lassie meet the challenges of dysfunctional family living? "What is it girl? Call a therapist?" This Lassie is a direct descendant of Pal, the original 1943 star. **92m/C VHS, DVD.** Helen Slater, Jon Tenney, Tom Guiry, Brittany Boyd, Richard Farnsworth, Frederic Forrest, Michelle Williams; ***D:*** Daniel Petrie; ***W:*** Matthew Jacobs, Gary Ross, Elizabeth Anderson; ***C:*** Kenneth Macmillan; ***M:*** Basil Poledouris.

Lassie 1/2 **2005 (PG)** Lassie goes back to her British roots (based on Eric Knight's 1938 novel) in this sentimental adventure. Young Joe (Mason) is heartbroken when Lassie must be sold because his miner father has lost his job. Lassie's new owner, the Duke of Rudling (O'Toole), has bought the photogenic collie for his granddaughter Cilla (Odgers), and both dog and girl are soon sent up to Scotland. Lassie's having none of it and escapes to start a 500-mile trek back to Yorkshire, surviving a number of trials along the way. Sweet yet realistic, with great performances throughout. **100m/C DVD.** *US GB IR FR* Peter O'Toole, Samantha Morton, John Lynch, Peter Dinklage, Jonathan Mason, Steve Pemberton, Jemma Redgrave, Edward Fox, John Standing, Kelly Macdonald, Robert Hardy, Hester Odgers; ***D:*** Charles Sturridge; ***W:*** Charles Sturridge; ***C:*** Howard Atherton; ***M:*** Adrian Johnston.

Lassie: Adventures of Neeka 1968 America's best friend joins her Native American buddy, Neeka, for a journey through a forest in the Pacific Northwest. They camp out in a deserted settlement, pull an elderly gentleman out of a frigid pond, and risk their lives to release horses from a stable during a raging wildfire. **75m/B VHS.** Jed Allan, Mark Miranda, Robert Rockwell; ***D:*** Richard (Dick) Moder, Jack B. Hively.

Lassie, Come Home 1/2 **1943 (G)** In first of the Lassie series, the famed collie is reluctantly sold and makes a treacherous cross-country journey back to her original family. **90m/C VHS, DVD.** Roddy McDowall, Elizabeth Taylor, Donald Crisp, Edmund Gwenn, May Whitty, Nigel Bruce, Elsa Lanchester, J. Pat O'Malley; ***D:*** Fred M. Wilcox. Natl. Film Reg. '93.

Lassie from Lancashire 1938 Not the famous Collie—but here, a Colleen. A pair of struggling lovebirds try to make it in show biz against all odds, including the girl's lunatic aunt, who locks her away before an audition. **67m/B VHS.** Marjorie Brown, Hal Thompson, Marjorie Sandford, Mark Daly; ***D:*** Jack Paddy Carstairs; ***W:*** Doreen Montgomery, Ernest Dudley; ***C:*** Bryan Langley.

Lassie: Well of Love 1970 Various installments of the classic TV series featuring the heroic collie are combined to create a movie-length presentation for home video. Lassie takes two young pups under her paw and, in the process, loses her way. As she tries to get home, she brings joy back into the lives of two despondent children. Finally, the old girl faces death when she tumbles into an abandoned well and must depend on humans for rescue. **76m/C VHS.** Mary Gregory, Robert Donner, Robert Sampson, Bruce Bennett, Sean Kelly; ***D:*** James B. Clark, Jack B. Hively; ***W:*** Eric Freiwald, Robert Schaefer; ***C:*** Robert Sparks; ***M:*** Nathan Scott. **TV**

Lassie's Great Adventure 1/2 **1962** Lassie and her master Timmy are swept away from home by a runaway balloon. After they land in the Canadian wilderness, they learn to rely on each other through peril and adventure. **104m/C VHS, DVD.** June Lockhart, Jon(athan) Provost, Hugh Reilly; ***D:*** William Beaudine; ***W:*** Charles "Blackie" O'Neal. **TV**

Lassiter 1/2 **1984 (R)** Selleck plays a jewel thief who is asked to steal diamonds from the Nazis for the FBI. Supporting cast adds value to what is otherwise a fairly ordinary adventure drama. **100m/C VHS.** Tom Selleck, Jane Seymour, Lauren Hutton, Bob Hoskins, Joe Regalbuto, Ed Lauter, Warren Clarke, William Morgan Sheppard; ***D:*** Roger Young.

Last Action Hero 1993 (PG-13) Newcomer O'Brien finds himself in a movie starring his idol Jack Slater, the kind of guy who never loses a fight and is impervious to gunfire and explosions (and he has a really cool car and a really big gun). Disappointing action/spoof of movies within a movie (rumored to have cost $80 million) was critically maimed and never recovered. The concept isn't new and has been done better before, though Ah-nold possesses his usual self-mocking charm, which is more than can be said for the movie. Look for lots of big stars in small roles and cameos. Cluttered with inside Hollywood gags, the script was given uncredited assistance from William Goldman. **131m/C VHS, DVD.** Arnold Schwarzenegger, Austin O'Brien, Mercedes Ruehl, F. Murray Abraham, Charles Dance, Anthony Quinn, Robert Prosky, Tom Noonan, Frank McRae, Art Carney, Bridgette Wilson-Sampras; ***Cameos:*** Sharon Stone, Hammer, Chevy Chase, Jean-Claude Van Damme, Tori Spelling, Joan Plowright, Adam Ant, James Belushi, James Cameron, Tony Curtis, Timothy Dalton, Tony Danza, Edward Furlong, Little Richard, Damon Wayans, Robert Patrick; ***D:*** John McTiernan; ***W:*** David Arnott, Shane Black; ***C:*** Dean Semler; ***M:*** Michael Kamen.

The Last Adventure 1/2 *Les Aventuriers* **1967** Two friends find themselves swindled in an insurance scam and set out after the perpetrator who sent them off to Africa in search of a treasure. Available dubbed. **112m/C VHS.** *FR* Alain Delon, Lino Ventura, Joanna Shimkus; ***D:*** Robert Enrico; ***W:*** Robert Enrico; ***C:*** Jean Boffety; ***M:*** Francois de Roubaix.

The Last Airbender 2010 The harmony of the Air Nomads, Water Tribes, and Earth Kingdoms are torn apart when the Fire Nation launches a war that lasts more than 100 years. Twelve-year-old Aang discovers he's the last of the avatars who can manipulate all four elements and he teams up with waterbender Katara and her brother to restore balance to the land. Based on the Nickelodeon animated TV series. **m/C DVD.** *US* Noah Ringer, Nicola Peltz, Jackson Rathbone, Dev Patel, Aasif Mandvi, Clifford Curtis, Shaun Toub, Randall Duk Kim, Jessica Andres, Seychelle Gabriel; ***D:*** M. Night Shyamalan; ***W:*** M. Night Shyamalan; ***C:*** Andrew Lesnie; ***M:*** James Newton Howard.

The Last American Hero *Hard Driver* **1973 (PG)** The true story of how former moonshine runner Junior Johnson became one of the fastest race car drivers in the history of the sport. Entertaining slice of life chronicling whiskey running and stock car racing, with Bridges superb in the lead. Based on a series of articles written by Tom Wolfe. **95m/C VHS, DVD.** Jeff Bridges, Valerie Perrine, Gary Busey, Art Lund, Geraldine Fitzgerald, Ned Beatty, Ed Lauter, Lane Smith, Gregory Walcott; ***D:*** Lamont Johnson; ***W:*** William Roberts; ***M:*** Charles Fox.

Last American Virgin 1982 (R) Usual brainless teen sex comedy about three school buddies who must deal with a plethora of problems in their search for girls who are willing. Music by Blondie, The Cars, The Police, The Waitresses, Devo, U2, Human League, and Quincy Jones. **92m/C VHS, DVD.** Lawrence Monoson, Diane Franklin, Steve Antin, Louisa Moritz; ***D:*** Boaz Davidson; ***W:*** Boaz Davidson.

The Last Angry Man 1/2 **1959** An old, idealistic Brooklyn doctor attracts a TV producer wanting to make a documentary about his life and career, and the two conflict. Muni was Oscar-nominated for this, his last film. **100m/B VHS.** Paul Muni, David Wayne, Betsy Palmer, Luther Adler, Dan Tobin; ***D:*** Daniel Mann; ***C:*** James Wong Howe.

The Last Assassins *Dusting Cliff Seven* **1996 (R)** Ex-CIA agent Anne Bishop (Allen) is persuaded to reunite with former commander McBride (Henriksen) for another mission. Then she discovers he has his own agenda, but when Anne tries to get out, McBride kidnaps her daughter to ensure her cooperation. **90m/C VHS, DVD.** Lance Henriksen, Nancy Allen, Floyd "Red Crow" Westerman, Dean Scofield; ***D:*** William H. Molina; ***W:*** William H. Molina, Jim Menza, Charles Philip Moore, Justin Stanley; ***C:*** William H. Molina; ***M:*** David Wurst, Eric Wurst. **VIDEO**

The Last Bastion 1984 A WWII drama emphasizing the political struggle between Churchill, MacArthur, Roosevelt, and Australia's John Curtin. **160m/C VHS.** *AU* Michael Blakemore, John Wood, Warren Mitchell, Ray Barrett, Robert Vaughn, Timothy West; ***D:*** Chris Thomson; ***W:*** Denis Whitburn, David Williamson; ***C:*** Louis Irving; ***M:*** Colin Stead.

The Last Best Sunday 1998 Mexican-American Joseph (Spain) kills the two racist thugs who beat him and hides out in the isolated home of religiously brought up classmate Lolly (Bettis), whose parents are away for the weekend. Naturally, the teens bond and then they fall in love. Not quite as obvious as it all sounds. **101m/C VHS, DVD.** Douglas Spain, Angela Bettis, Kim Darby, William Lucking, Marion Ross, Craig Wasson, Daniel Beer; ***D:*** Donny Most; ***W:*** Karen Kelly; ***C:*** Zoran Hochstatter; ***M:*** Tim Westergren.

The Last Best Year 1/2 **1990 (PG)** Basic TV tearjerker has lonely psychologist Wendy (Moore) befriending patient Jane (Peters), who has a terminal illness. **88m/C VHS, DVD.** Mary Tyler Moore, Bernadette Peters, Brian Bedford, Dorothy McGuire, Kate Reid, Kenneth Welsh; ***D:*** John Erman; ***W:*** David W. Rintels.

The Last Boy Scout 1991 (R) Are you ready for some gunplay? Formula thriller stars Willis as a private eye and Wayans as an ex-quarterback teaming up against a football team owner who will stop at nothing to get political backing for a bill promoting legalized gambling on sports. Another variation of the violent buddy-picture by "Lethal Weapon" screenwriter Black. **105m/C VHS, DVD.** Bruce Willis, Damon Wayans, Halle Berry, Chelsea Field, Noble Willingham, Taylor Negron, Danielle Harris, Chelcie Ross, Bruce McGill, Morris Chestnut, Eddie Griffin, Kim Coates, Joe Santos, Tony Longo, Billy Blanks, Jack Kehler, Michael (Mike) Papajohn; ***D:*** Tony Scott; ***W:*** Shane Black; ***C:*** Ward Russell; ***M:*** Michael Kamen.

Last Breath *Lifebreath* **1996 (R)** Martin (Perry) is obsessively devoted to his dying wife, Chrystie (Swift), who needs a double lung transplant to survive. So Martin decides to romance lovely Gail (Carides)—with murder on his mind. Twisted ending. **90m/C VHS, DVD.** Luke Perry, Gia Carides, Francie Swift, David Margulies, Lisa Gay Hamilton, Jack Gilpin, Matt McGrath, Hillary Bailey Smith; ***D:*** P.J. Posner; ***W:*** P.J. Posner, Joel Posner; ***C:*** Oliver Bokelberg; ***M:*** Michael Kessler. **VIDEO**

The Last Bridge *Die Letzte Brucke* **1954** German doctor Schell is captured by Yugoslavian partisans during WWII and forced to tend to their wounded, gradually realizing that suffering is universal. German with subtitles. **104m/B VHS.** *AT* Maria Schell, Bernhard Wicki, Barbara Rutting, Carl Mohner; ***D:*** Helmut Kautner; ***W:*** Helmut Kautner, Norbert Kunze; ***C:*** Fred Kollhanek; ***M:*** Carol De Groof. Cannes '54: Special Jury Prize, Actress (Schell).

The Last Broadcast 1998 Festival hit—and the first film to be digitally distributed to theatres—predates "The Blair Witch Project" in telling the story of a group of young people who go into the woods with video cameras and meet a grisly fate. But this one is much more complicated and ambitious. Directors Steven Avalos and Lance Weiler play public access cable TV show hosts who take a sound man (Clabbers) and a psychic (Seward) into the Pine Barrens for a live broadcast of their search for the legendary Jersey Devil. Only one comes out. A year later, a documentary filmmaker (Beard) and a video editor (Pulaski) try to find the truth of the matter. **87m/C DVD.** Stefan Avalos, Lance Weiler, David Beard, Rein Clabbers, Michele Pulaski; ***D:*** Stefan Avalos, Lance Weiler; ***W:*** Stefan Avalos, Lance Weiler; ***C:*** Lance Weiler; ***M:*** Stefan Avalos.

Last Bullet *Crooked River* **1950** A young westerner chases after a band of outlaws to avenge the cold-blooded murder of his parents. **55m/B VHS.** James Ellison, Russell Hayden, John Cason, Raymond Hatton, Fuzzy Knight, Julie Adams, Tom Tyler; ***D:*** Thomas Carr; ***W:*** Ron Ormond, Maurice Tombragel; ***C:*** Ernest Miller; ***M:*** Walter Greene.

The Last Butterfly 1992 Quiet Holocaust movie set in Theresienstadt, the Czechoslovak ghetto city used by the Nazis to persuade the outside world of their humane treatment of the Jews. Noted French mime Antoine Moreau (Courtenay) has fallen under suspicion by the Gestapo. He's "persuaded" to give a performance in Theresienstadt for the benefit of the visiting Red Cross but decides to subvert Nazi propaganda with his own version of "Hansel and Gretel." This time the witch feeds the children into her oven. Muted performances and screenplay (adapted from the Michael Jacot novel) heightened the film's surreal calmness. **106m/C VHS, DVD.** *CZ* Tom Courtenay, Brigitte Fossey, Freddie Jones, Ingrid Held, Linda Jablonska; ***D:*** Karel Kachyna; ***W:*** Karel Kachyna, Ota Hofman; ***M:*** Alex North.

Last Call 1990 (R) Clearly, Joe Six-pack won't rent this bimbo fest for its subtle plot. Katt, a mafiosi-cheated real estate guy, decides to even the score with the assistance of gal pal/playmate of the year Tweed, who's more than willing to compromise her position. Also features the talents of playboy emerita Stevens. Available in rated and unrated versions. **90m/C VHS, DVD.** William Katt, Shannon Tweed, Joseph Campanella, Stella Stevens, Matt Roe; *D:* Jag Mundhra. **VIDEO**

Last Call: The Final Chapter of F. Scott Fitzgerald 🦴🦴 1/2 **2002** In 1939, aspiring writer Frances Kroll (Campbell) interviews for a secretarial position with F. Scott Fitzgerald (Irons). Alcoholic, in declining health, and haunted by images of his institutionalized wife Zelda (Spacek), Fitzgerald hasn't published in years. She becomes his confidante and Fitzgerald is inspired to stop drinking and begin work on his new novel—a scathing indictment of Hollywood (which will become the unfinished "The Last Tycoon"). Based on the memoir by Kroll Ring. **108m/C VHS, DVD.** Jeremy Irons, Neve Campbell, Sissy Spacek, Natalie Radford, Shannon Lawson, Paul Hecht; *D:* Henry Bromell; *W:* Henry Bromell; *C:* Jeffrey Jur; *M:* Brian Tyler. **CABLE**

The Last Castle 🦴🦴 1/2 **2001 (R)** Redford is Gen. Irwin, a legendary army officer sent to prison on a charge that isn't clear until well into the film. The warden of the prison, Col. Winter (Gandolfini), is a dictatorial collector of military memorabilia who clearly admires his new inmate. After overhearing a remark by Irwin disparaging his collection, Winter begins to resent him. Irwin witnesses the cruelty administered by the warden and begins to win over his fellow inmates' loyalty by restoring their pride. As Winter notices control of the men slipping away, his punishments grow worse, until finally Irwin leads the inmates in an insurrection. Although driven by powerhouse performances by Redford and Gandolfini, the plot spends too much time on the battle of wills and not enough on the background of the other inmates, while a storyline about Irwin's daughter is dropped altogether. **133m/C VHS, DVD.** *US* Robert Redford, James Gandolfini, Mark Ruffalo, Delroy Lindo, Steve (Stephen) Burton, Paul Calderon, Samuel Ball, Clifton (Gonzalez) Collins Jr., Frank Military, George W. Scott, Brian Goodman, Michael Irby, Maurice Bullard, Jeremy Childs, Robin Wright Penn; *D:* Rod Lurie; *W:* Graham Yost, David Scarpa; *C:* Shelly Johnson; *M:* Jerry Goldsmith.

The Last Chance 🦴🦴🦴 **1945** A realistic look at the efforts of three WWII Allied officers to help a group of refugees escape across the Alps from Italy to Switzerland. The officers are played by former pilots who were shot down over Switzerland. In spite of this—or perhaps because of it—the acting is superb. Watch for inspirational scene of refugees singing. **105m/B VHS, DVD.** E.G. Morrison, John Hoy, Ray Reagan, Odeardo Mosini, Sigfrit Steiner, Emil Gerber; *D:* Leopold Lindtberg.

Last Chance 🦴 1/2 **2007** Hitman Rob gets involved with a beautiful woman who turns out to have close ties to his latest target. Does Rob blow the hit or betray the woman he loves when his own life is on the line? **92m/C DVD.** Kristof Robinson, Kate Potter, Bob Ferguson, Brandon Michaels, Ben Lawton; *D:* Benjamin Todd; *W:* Benjamin Todd. **VIDEO**

Last Chance Harvey 🦴🦴 1/2 **2008 (PG-13)** Just before flying to London for his daughter's wedding, Harvey (Hoffman) is canned from his jingle-writing job in NYC, officially making him a washed-up jazz musician. Adding insult, the ex-wife (Baker) breaks the news that stepdad (Brolin) will be giving away the bride. Meanwhile, Kate (Thompson), an interviewer for a government agency in London, is having a decidedly poor time in the dating world. Of course fate brings the two together in the airport where Harvey is a complete jerk and then later as they end up the only two patrons in a local pub. Harvey attempts an apology and poof, the magic begins. An endearing romance ensues as the two pros lift an otherwise forgettable story. **92m/C DVD.** *US* Dustin Hoffman, Emma Thompson, Kathy Baker, James Brolin, Eileen Atkins, Richard Schiff, Liane Balaban, Michael Landes; *D:* Joel Hopkins; *W:* Joel Hopkins; *C:* John de Borman; *M:* Dickon Hinchliffe.

Last Chase 🦴 1/2 **1981 (PG)** Famed race car driver becomes a vocal dissenter against the sterile society that has emerged, in this drama set in the near future. Screenplay written by Christopher Crowe under the pseudonym C.R. O'Cristopher. **106m/C VHS.** *CA* Lee Majors, Burgess Meredith, Chris Makepeace, Alexandra Stewart; *D:* Martyn Burke; *W:* Martyn Burke, Christopher Crowe. **TV**

Last Command 🦴🦴🦴🦴 **1928** Famous powerful silent film by Sternberg about an expatriate Czarist general forging out a pitiful living as a silent Hollywood extra, where he is hired by his former adversary to reenact the revolution he just left. Next to "The Last Laugh," this is considered Jannings' most acclaimed performance. Deeply ironic, visually compelling film with a new score by Gaylord Carter. **88m/B VHS.** Emil Jannings, William Powell, Evelyn Brent, Nicholas Soussanin, Michael Visaroff, Jack Raymond, Fritz Feld; *D:* Josef von Sternberg; *W:* Warren Duff; *M:* Max Steiner, Gaylord Carter. Oscars '28: Actor (Jannings), Natl. Film Reg. '06.

The Last Command 🦴🦴 1/2 **1955** Jim Bowie and his followers sacrifice their lives in defending the Alamo. A good cast holds its own against a mediocre script; battle scenes are terrific. **110m/C VHS.** Sterling Hayden, Richard Carlson, Ernest Borgnine, J. Carrol Naish, Virginia Grey, Anna Maria Alberghetti; *D:* Frank Lloyd.

The Last Confederate: The Story of Robert Adams 🦴🦴 *Strike the Tent* **2005 (R)** Adams portrays his own great-great grandfather Robert, a South Carolina native who becomes a captain in the Confederacy. He falls in love with northern belle Evilyn McCord (Edwards), the sister of best friend Nelson (Lindsey), who also joins the southern cause. When both men are captured and sent to a Union prison camp, Robert plans an escape that will eventually bring him back to Evilyn. **96m/C DVD.** Amy Redford, Tippi Hedren, Mickey Rooney, Julian Adams, Gwendolyn Edwards, Joshua Lindsey, Eric Holloway, Timmy Sherrill; *D:* Julian Adams, A. Blaine Miller; *W:* Julian Adams, Gwendolyn Edwards, Joshua Lindsey; *C:* Shawn Lewallen; *M:* Atli Orvarsson.

The Last Contract 🦴🦴 *Portrait of a Hitman* **1977 (R)** An artist who pays his bills by working as a hitman, kills the wrong man. As a result, he must fear for his life since a counterhit is inevitable. **85m/C VHS.** Jack Palance, Rod Steiger, Bo Svenson, Richard Roundtree, Ann Turkel; *D:* Allan A. Buckhantz; *W:* Lothrop Jordan, Yabo Yablonsky; *C:* Charles Correll; *M:* Robert Farrar, Laurence Rosenthal.

Last Cry for Help 🦴 1/2 **1979** A psychiatrist helps a 17-year-old high school coed who, fearing she has disappointed her parents, attempts suicide. Typical melodrama that attempts to make a statement, but falls short. Definitely not the "Partridge Family." **98m/C VHS.** Linda Purl, Shirley Jones, Tony LoBianco, Murray Hamilton, Grant Goodeve; *D:* Hal Sitowitz; *M:* Miles Goodman. **TV**

Last Dance 🦴 1/2 **1991** Five scantily clad exotic dancers are ready to compete for the title of Miss Dance-TV, but trouble ensues when the dancers start turning up dead. **86m/C VHS, DVD.** Cynthia Bassinet, Elaine Hendrix, Kurt T. Williams, Allison Rhea, Erica Ringston; *D:* Anthony Markes.

The Last Dance 🦴🦴 *Sista Dansen* **1993** Two couples, Claus and Tove (Brynolfsson, Bergstrom) and best friends Lennart and Liselott (Andersson, Froling), have a shared obsession with ballroom dance competitions and some secret desires. Seems Claus and Tove have a rocky marriage and think their friends have the perfect union. Instead, Lennart is tired of his overbearing wife and longs for Tove, to whom he was once engaged. Then Liselott's body is found beneath the pier after a competition. Swedish with subtitles. **109m/C VHS.** *SW* Helena Bergstrom, Reine Brynolfsson, Ewa Froling, Peter Andersson; *D:* Colin Nutley; *W:* Colin Nutley; *C:* Jens Fischer.

Last Dance 🦴🦴 **1996 (R)** Following closely on the heels of "Dead Man Walking," this death-row drama suffered from bad timing and was dubbed by some as "Bad Hair Walking." Stone plays a convicted murderess condemned to die in an unnamed Southern state. Morrow's the rookie attorney for the state's clemency office assigned to her case. As a bond grows between the two, he uncovers errors in her trial that his bosses would rather have him ignore. The movie makes its big mistake by centering on Morrow's callow lawyer instead of Stone's embittered con. The clock-ticking countdown to the execution (which will amuse fans of "The Player") even fails to hold attention. **103m/C VHS.** Sharon Stone, Rob Morrow, Randy Quaid, Peter Gallagher, Jack Thompson, Jayne Brook, Pamela Tyson, Skeet Ulrich, Don Harvey, Diane Sellers; *D:* Bruce Beresford; *W:* Ron Koslow; *C:* Peter James; *M:* Mark Isham.

Last Day of the War 🦴 1/2 **1969 (PG)** A German scientist is chased by Americans and Germans as WWII winds to its conclusion. Filmed in Spain. **96m/C VHS.** *SP* George Maharis, Maria Perschy, James Philbrook, Gerard Herter; *D:* Juan Antonio Bardem.

Last Days 🦴🦴 1/2 **2005 (R)** A recluse rock star (Pitt) lives an increasingly bizarre existence, barely interacting with the trail of hangers-on and band members that frequent his stone mansion until he finally takes his own life. Loosely based on the Kurt Cobain tragedy but emphatically denied as any type of biography. **97m/C DVD.** *US* Michael Pitt, Lukas Haas, Asia Argento, Ricky Jay, Harmony Korine, Scott Green, Nicole Vicius, Ryan Orion, Kim Gordon, Adam Friberg, Andy Friberg, Thadeus A. Thomas, Chip Marks; *D:* Gus Van Sant; *W:* Gus Van Sant; *C:* Harris Savides.

The Last Days of Chez Nous 🦴🦴 1/2 **1992 (R)** Armstrong's dramatic comedy about a family falling apart has Ganz as a homesick Frenchman married to controlling, successful Australian writer Harrow. Trouble starts when his wayward sister-in-law Fox returns home to live with them and his wife decides to take an extended holiday with her father. Ganz suddenly finds himself only too involved in Fox's complicated life. Self-involved characters with messy emotional lives leave viewers feeling rather distant, though cast, and particularly Ganz, strive for intimacy. **96m/C VHS.** *AU* Bruno Ganz, Lisa Harrow, Kerry Fox, Kiri Paramore, Bill Hunter, Miranda Otto; *D:* Gillian Armstrong; *W:* Helen Garner; *M:* Paul Grabowsky. Australian Film Inst. '92: Actress (Harrow).

The Last Days of Disco 🦴🦴🦴 **1998 (R)** It's the early 80s and the disco scene is still alive, although it's beginning to develop a wet, hacking cough. Oblivious to this fact are brash Charlotte (Beckinsale) and reserved Alice (Sevigny), recent college grads who work as low-level corporate drones by day and party at an exclusive Studio 54-like club by night. The girls mingle with a group of Harvard educated proto-yuppie clones that include hot shot assistant D.A. Josh (Keeslar), environmental lawyer Tom (Leonard) and ad man Jimmy (Astin). Also populating the club are assistant club manager Des (Eigeman) and shady club owner Bernie (Thornton). Sharp, funny dialogue (and plenty of it) help ease the fact that the characters are merely poor little rich kids who need to shut up and dance. **113m/C VHS, DVD.** Chloe Sevigny, Kate Beckinsale, Christopher Eigeman, MacKenzie Astin, Robert Sean Leonard, Matt Keeslar, Tara Subkoff, Jennifer Beals, David Thornton, Michael Weatherly, Burr Steers; *D:* Whit Stillman; *W:* Whit Stillman; *C:* John Thomas; *M:* Mark Suozzo.

The Last Days of Dolwyn 🦴🦴 1/2 *Woman of Dolwyn; Dolwyn* **1949** A man banned for thievery from his Welsh village returns bent upon revenge. He plans to buy the entire district when it is designated part of a water reservoir project, but finds plans thwarted by a dowager and her stepson. Burton's first film was based on a true story. **95m/B VHS.** *GB* Edith Evans, Emlyn Williams, Richard Burton, Anthony James, Barbara Couper, Alan Aynesworth, Hugh Griffith, Roddy Hughes, Tom Jones; *D:* Emlyn Williams; *W:* Emlyn Williams.

Last Days of Frank & Jesse James 🦴 1/2 **1986** A tired TV rehash of the well-known western legend in which the famous brothers try to be like others after their personal war against society ends. **100m/C VHS, DVD.** Johnny Cash, Kris Kristofferson, June Carter Cash, Willie Nelson, Margaret Gibson, Gail Youngs; *D:* William A. Graham. **TV**

The Last Days of Frankie the Fly 🦴🦴 **1996 (R)** It's gonna seem familiar because it's yet another criminal low-life story set in L.A. but at least Hopper's presence makes this slightly more than routine. He's Frankie, a semi-pathetic petty thief with big dreams and not much talent. He works for vicious gangster Sal (Madsen) and becomes smitten with ex-junkie Margaret (Hannah), who would like to be a legit actress but is instead working in porn. When Frankie decides to impress Margaret, he naturally gets into trouble. **96m/C VHS, DVD.** Dennis Hopper, Daryl Hannah, Michael Madsen, Kiefer Sutherland, Dayton Callie, Jack McGee; *D:* Peter Markle; *W:* Dayton Callie; *C:* Phil Parmet; *M:* George S. Clinton.

The Last Days of Patton 🦴 1/2 **1986** Depicts the aging general's autumn years as a controversial ex-Nazi defender and deskbound WWII historian. Scott reprises his feature-film role. **146m/C VHS, DVD.** George C. Scott, Ed Lauter, Eva Marie Saint, Richard Dysart, Murray Hamilton, Kathryn Leigh Scott; *D:* Delbert Mann. **TV**

Last Days of Planet Earth WOOF! *Prophecies of Nostradamus; Catastrophe 1999; Nostradamus No Daiyogen* **1974** Really stinky Japanese doomsday movie about a scientist who charges that a build-up of pollution is responsible for giant mutant sea slugs and other environmental disasters. Dubbed. **88m/C VHS.** *JP* Tetsuro Tamba, So Yamamura, Takashi Shimura; *D:* Toshio Masuda.

Last Days of Pompeii 🦴🦴 1/2 **1935** Vintage DeMille-style epic based on Lord Lytton's book, where the eruption of Vesuvius threatens noblemen and slaves alike. State-of-the-art special effects still look fantastic today. Remade in 1960; available colorized. **96m/B VHS, DVD.** Preston Foster, Alan Hale, Basil Rathbone, George L. Baxt, Louis Calhern, David Holt, Dorothy Wilson, Wryley Birch, Gloria Shea; *D:* Ernest B. Schoedsack; *C:* Jack Cardiff.

The Last Days of Pompeii 🦴🦴 *Ultimi Giorni di Pompeii* **1960** Superman Reeves plays a gladiator trying to clean up the doomed town of Pompeii in this remake of the 1935 classic. Some spectacular scenes, including the explosive climax when the mountain blows its top. **105m/C VHS.** *IT* Steve Reeves, Christine Kaufmann, Barbara Carroll, Anne Marie Baumann, Mimmo Palmara; *D:* Mario Bonnard; *W:* Sergio Leone.

The Last Days of Summer 🦴 1/2 **2007** Bland and predictable kiddie comedy. Fifth-grader Luke (Panettiere) doesn't want his summer vacation to be over, especially with the threat of middle school looming. When he has a perfect day at the town's Labor Day carnival, he wishes it would never end and, as fast as you can say "Groundhog Day," it doesn't. But even Luke eventually gets tired of the endless repetition and tries to figure out how to move forward. **88m/C DVD.** Jessica Tuck, Jackee Harry, Jansen Panettiere, Eli Vargas, Jon Kent Ethridge, Alexandra Krosney, Daniel Samonas, Denyse Tontz, Brendan Miller, Vince Grant; *D:* Blair Treu; *W:* Kent Pierce; *C:* Brian Sullivan; *M:* James L. Venable. **CABLE**

The Last Debate 🦴🦴 1/2 **2000** Presidential candidates Richard Meredith (Young) and Paul Greene (Gray) are having only one televised debate in their tight race, which is being moderated by political columnist Mike Howley (Garner) and three fellow journalists (McDonald, Murphy, Sanchez). Just before the debate, Howley is given damaging info about Meredith, which he and the other panelists use without verification. Then investigative journalist Tom Chapman (Gallagher) comes in with a lot of questions about the leak and its source. Based on the novel by Jim Lehrer. **90m/C VHS, DVD.** James Garner, Peter Gallagher, Audra McDonald, Donna Murphy, Marco Sanchez, Stephen Young, Bruce Gray, Dorian Harewood; *D:* John Badham; *W:* John Maass; *C:* Norayr Kasper. **CABLE**

The Last Detail 🦴🦴🦴🦴 **1973 (R)** Two hard-boiled career petty officers (Nicholson and Young) are commissioned to transfer a young sailor facing an eight-year sentence for petty theft from one brig to another. In an act of compassion, they attempt to show the prisoner a final good time. Nicholson shines in both the complexity and completeness of his character. Adapted from a Daryl Ponicsan novel. **104m/C VHS, DVD.** Jack Nicholson, Otis Young, Randy Quaid, Clifton James, Michael Moriarty, Carol Kane, Nancy Allen, Gilda Radner; *D:* Hal Ashby; *W:* Robert Towne; *C:* Michael

Chapman; *M:* Johnny Mandel. British Acad. '74: Actor (Nicholson), Screenplay; Cannes '74: Actor (Nicholson); N.Y. Film Critics '74: Actor (Nicholson); Natl. Soc. Film Critics '74: Actor (Nicholson).

The Last Don ½ *Mario Puzo's The Last Don* **1997 (R)** Re-edited version of the TV miniseries finds author Puzo, of "Godfather" fame, sticking to what he knows best. The Don in question is Domenico Clericuzo (Aiello), a ruthless patriarch who wipes out the rival family his pregnant daughter Rose Marie marries into (and doesn't spare her hubby). Carrying out the Don's orders is nephew Pippi (Mantegna), an enforcer who weds Vegas showgirl Nalene (Miller) and who gets involved in the casino business. The years pass with the Don manipulating the next generation, as bloodthirsty grandchild Dante (Cochrane) fights for control with Pippi's cool-headed son Cross (Gedrick). Divided loyalties abound. A complete five-hour version of the saga is also available. **150m/C VHS, DVD.** Nick(y) Corello, Danny Aiello, Joe Mantegna, Jason Gedrick, Rory Cochrane, Penelope Ann Miller, Daryl Hannah, Kirstie Alley, Michelle Rene Thomas, David Marciano, Robert Wuhl, k.d. lang, John Colicos, Cliff DeYoung, Michael Massee; *D:* Graeme Clifford; *W:* Joyce Eliason; *C:* Gordon C. Lonsdale; *M:* Angelo Badalamenti, Roger Bellon.

The Last Don 2 ½ *Mario Puzo's The Last Don 2* **1998 (R)** Since Don Clericuzio (Aiello) has died there's a power vacuum that forces widower Cross De Lena (Gedrick) back into the family business. The family is besieged by traitors, even as Cross gets involved in a tentative romance with his autistic stepdaughter's teacher, Josie (Kensit). Then there's crazy, vindictive Aunt Rose Marie (Alley) who falls in love with her conflicted priest (Isaacs), problems with the Hollywood studio headed by Cross's sister Claudia (Thomas), and ambitious mobster Billy D'Angelo (Wilder) for Cross to deal with. Unwittingly campy but slower moving than the first installment. **127m/C VHS, DVD.** Jason Gedrick, Kirstie Alley, Patsy Kensit, James Wilder, David Marciano, Jason Isaacs, Michelle Rene Thomas, Conrad Dunn, Robert Wuhl, Andrew Jackson, Joe Mantegna; ***Cameos:*** Danny Aiello; *D:* Graeme Clifford; *W:* Joyce Eliason; *C:* David Franco; *M:* Roger Bellon. **TV**

The Last Dragon ½ *Berry Gordy's The Last Dragon* **1985 (PG-13)** It's time for a Motown kung fu showdown on the streets of Harlem, for there is scarcely enough room for even one dragon. **108m/C VHS, DVD.** Taimak, Vanity, Christopher Murney, Julius J. Carry III, Faith Prince; *D:* Michael A. Schultz; *W:* Louis Venosta; *C:* James A. Contner; *M:* Misha Segal.

The Last Drop **2005 (R)** Overstuffed WWII adventure that takes place during Operation Market Drop, a failed mission that parachuted British troops into German-occupied Holland. One unit has a separate agenda—they are to rendezvous with Dutch resistance to prevent the Nazis from sending some looted national treasures to Berlin. Only a trio of Nazi deserters are after the same goods. Zane is supposed to be a Canadian pilot and Madsen briefly wanders through as a crusty American officer. **110m/C DVD.** *GB* Billy Zane, Karel Roden, Michael Madsen, Tommy Flanagan, Alexander Skarsgard, Sean Pertwee, Laurence Fox, Neil Newbon; *D:* Colin Teague; *W:* Colin Teague, Gary Young; *C:* Maxime Alexandre; *M:* David Julyan.

Last Embrace **1979 (R)** A feverish thriller in the Hitchcock style dealing with an ex-secret serviceman who is convinced someone is trying to kill him. **102m/C VHS.** Roy Scheider, Janet Margolin, Christopher Walken, John Glover, Charles Napier, Mandy Patinkin; *D:* Jonathan Demme; *M:* Miklos Rozsa.

The Last Emperor **1987 (PG-13)** Deeply ironic epic detailing life of Pu Yi, crowned at the age of three as the last emperor of China before the onset of communism. Follows Pu Yi from childhood to manhood (sequestered away in the Forbidden City) to fugitive to puppet-ruler to party proletariat. O'Toole portrays the sympathetic Scot tutor who educates the adult Pu Yi (Lone) in the ways of the western world after Pu Yi abdicates power in 1912. Shot on location inside the People's Republic of China with a cast of thousands; authentic costumes. Rich, visually stunning movie. The Talking Heads' David Byrne contributed to the score. **140m/C VHS, DVD, Blu-ray Disc.** *IT* John Lone, Peter O'Toole, Joan Chen, Victor Wong, Ryuichi Sakamoto, Dennis Dun, Maggie Han, Ying Ruocheng, Ric Young; *D:* Bernardo Bertolucci; *W:* Mark Peploe, Bernardo Bertolucci; *C:* Vittorio Storaro; *M:* Ryuichi Sakamoto, David Byrne. Oscars '87: Adapt. Screenplay, Art Dir./Set Dec., Cinematog., Costume Des., Director (Bertolucci), Film Editing, Picture, Sound, Orig. Score; British Acad. '88: Film; Cesar '88: Foreign Film; Directors Guild '87: Director (Bertolucci); Golden Globes '88: Director (Bertolucci), Film—Drama, Screenplay, Score; L.A. Film Critics '87: Cinematog.; N.Y. Film Critics '87: Cinematog.

The Last Enemy **2008** Big brother is watching in this overly-complicated but still fascinating Brit thriller. Introverted mathematician Stephen Ezard (Cumberbatch) returns to London for the first time in years for the funeral of his estranged doctor brother Michael (Beesley). Michael was supposedly killed in the Middle East while treating refugees who came down with a deadly virus despite being inoculated. Stephen is then recruited into helping introduce a controversial national ID program (using his math/computer skills) while getting involved with his brother's widow Yasim (Marinca). Then Michael turns up alive, wanting to learn what the government knows about the dead refugees. **310m/C DVD.** *GB* Benedict Cumberbatch, Max Beesley, Anamaria Marinca, Robert Carlyle, Eva Birthistle, Geraldine James, David Harewood; *D:* Iain B. MacDonald; *W:* Peter Berry; *C:* Nigel Willoughby; *M:* Magnus Fiennes. **TV**

Last Exit to Brooklyn ½ **1990 (R)** Hubert Selby Jr.'s shocking book comes to the screen in a vivid film. Leigh gives a stunning performance as a young Brooklyn girl caught between the Mafia, union men, and friends struggling for something better. Set in the 1950s. Fine supporting cast; excellent pacing. **102m/C VHS.** Jennifer Jason Leigh, Burt Young, Stephen Lang, Ricki Lake, Jerry Orbach, Maia Danziger, Stephen Baldwin; *D:* Uli Edel; *C:* Stefan Czapsky. N.Y. Film Critics '89: Support. Actress (Leigh).

Last Exit to Earth *Roger Corman Presents Last Exit to Earth* **1996 (R)** Your basic male fantasy. Lusty alien babes from dying world need to find some fertile males, since the men of their home planet shoot blanks. They plan to hijack a male-inhabited spaceship that's stuck in a timewarp and has (unbeknownst to the femmes) already been taken over by hijackers. Anyway, the guys get to the planet and being aggressive male pigs decide they want to run things. **80m/C VHS.** Costas Mandylor, Kim Greist, David Groh, Hilary Shepard, Michael Cudlitz, Lisa Banes, Zoe Trilling; *D:* Katt Shea; *W:* Katt Shea. **CABLE**

The Last Fight ½ **1982 (R)** Boxer risks his life and his girlfriend for a shot at the championship title. Watch and see if he could've been a contender. **85m/C VHS.** Fred Williamson, Willie Colon, Ruben Blades, Joe Spinell, Darlanne Fluegel; *D:* Fred Williamson.

The Last Five Days **1982** Based on the true story of a girl and her brother who, in 1943 Munich, were arrested for distributing anti-Nazi propaganda. The film covers the five days between their capture and execution. In German with English subtitles. **112m/C VHS.** *GE* Lena Stolze, Irm Hermann; *D:* Percy Adlon.

The Last Flight of Noah's Ark ½ **1980 (G)** Disney adventure concerns a high-living pilot, a prim missionary, and two stowaway orphans who must plot their way off a deserted island following the crash landing of their broken-down plane. **97m/C VHS, DVD.** Elliott Gould, Genevieve Bujold, Rick Schroder, Vincent Gardenia, Tammy Lauren; *D:* Charles Jarrott; *W:* Steven W. Carabatsos, George Arthur Bloom; *C:* Charles F. Wheeler; *M:* Maurice Jarre.

Last Flight Out: A True Story **1990** Hours before Saigon fell to the Vietcong in 1975, Vietnamese and Americans rushed to board the last commercial flight out of Vietnam. Lukewarm account of a true story. **99m/C VHS.** James Earl Jones, Richard Crenna, Haing S. Ngor, Eric Bogosian; *D:* Larry Elikann; *W:* Walter Halsey Davis; *C:* Laszlo George; *M:* Christopher Young.

Last Flight to Hell **1991** When a drug lord is kidnapped, Brown is sent to South America to rescue the slimeball. His interest in the job picks up when the drug lord's 11-on-a-scale-of-ten daughter joins him for the chase. **94m/C VHS.** Reb Brown, Chuck Connors; *D:* Paul D. Robinson.

The Last Fling ½ **1986** When Sellecca has her mind set on a romantic fling, Ritter is headed for trouble. She wants love for one night, he wants it forever. Will they solve this difference of opinion? Will true love prevail? Will Ritter consent to being used as a one-night stand? Weakly plotted and poorly acted comedy. **95m/C VHS.** John Ritter, Connie Sellecca, Scott Bakula, Shannon Tweed, Paul Sand, John Bennett Perry; *D:* Corey Allen; *M:* Charles Bernstein. **TV**

Last Four Days **1977 (PG)** A chronicle of the final days of Benito Mussolini. **91m/C VHS, DVD.** Rod Steiger, Henry Fonda, Franco Nero; *D:* Carlo Lizzani.

Last Frontier ½ **1932** Serial of 12 chapters contains shades of spectacular figures in Western history: Custer, Hickok, and others in a background of grazing buffalo, boom towns, and covered wagon trails. **216m/B VHS, DVD.** Lon Chaney Jr., Yakima Canutt, Francis X. Bushman; *D:* Spencer Gordon Bennet, Thomas L. Story.

Last Game **1980** A college student is torn between his devotion to his blind father and going out for the college's football team. **107m/C VHS, DVD.** Howard Segal, Ed L. Grady, Terry Alden; *D:* Martin Beck.

The Last Gangster **1937** Robinson snarls his way through another gangster role as crime boss Joe Krozac. Joe returns from Europe with young bride Talya (Stradner) but soon winds up in Alcatraz, thanks to a tax evasion conviction. The newspapers hound his wife and young son until nice guy reporter Paul North (Stewart in a cheesy mustache) steps in. With Talya learning what a brute Joe really is, she divorces him and marries Paul. After 10 years, Joe gets out of the slammer vowing to get to know his son (who doesn't know anything about him) but his old gang has other plans for Joe. **81m/B DVD.** Edward G. Robinson, James Stewart, Rose Stradner, Lionel Stander, Edward Brophy, John Carradine, Douglas Scott, Alan Baxter, Grant Mitchell; *D:* Edward Ludwig; *W:* John Lee Mahin; *C:* William H. Daniels; *M:* Edward Ward.

The Last Gasp ½ **1994 (R)** Contractor Patrick murders the Mexican Indian who's interfering with his project and is cursed. He turns into a wild killer who must satisfy his blood lust every 20 days. Only Pacula tries to save him. Gory and predictable. **90m/C VHS.** Robert Patrick, Joanna Pacula, Vyto Ruginis, Mimi (Meyer) Craven; *D:* Scott McGinnis.

The Last Good Time ½ **1994 (R)** Old-world violinist Joseph Kopple (Mueller-Stahl), retired and living in a small Brooklyn apartment, has his world turned upside down when his street-smart neighbor Charlotte (d'Abo) seeks refuge from her abusive boyfriend Eddie (Pasdar). An unsentimental friendship develops between the two in spite of the differences in their ages, educations, and lifestyles. Terrific performance from Mueller-Stahl as the lonely but dignified old man. Based on the novel by Richard Bausch. **90m/C VHS.** Armin Mueller-Stahl, Olivia D'Abo, Maureen Stapleton, Lionel Stander, Adrian Pasdar; *D:* Bob Balaban; *W:* Bob Balaban, John McLaughlin; *C:* Claudia Raschke.

Last Gun **1964** A legendary gunman on the verge of retirement has to save his town from a reign of terror before turning his gun in. **98m/C VHS.** *IT* Carl Mohner, Livio Lorenzon, Celina Cely, Kitty Carver, Cameron Mitchell; *D:* Sergio Bergonzelli; *W:* Ambrogio Molteni; *C:* Romolo Garroni; *M:* Marcello Gigante.

The Last Hard Men ½ **1976** Retired sheriff Sam Burgade (Heston) must save his daughter (Hershey) from escaped convict Provo (Coburn) who kidnapped her as revenge for jailing him and accidently killing his wife. Provo and his gang force a showdown with the reluctant former lawman by threatening bodily harm and worse to the daughter if he doesn't show. Solid work by the leads raises this one above the usual genre fare. **103m/C VHS.** Charlton Heston, James Coburn, Barbara Hershey, Michael Parks, Jorge (George) Rivero, Larry Wilcox, Thalmus Rasulala, Chris Mitchum, Morgan Paull, John Quade, Robert Donner; *D:* Andrew V. McLaglen; *W:* Guerdon (Gordon) Trueblood; *C:* Duke Callaghan; *M:* Jerry Goldsmith.

The Last Hit ½ **1993 (R)** Michael Grant (Brown) is a professional assassin, working for the CIA, who's very good at his job. But now he's burned out and ready to retire to New Mexico for some peace and quiet. He buys a house from the widowed Anna (Adams), naturally falling in love with her. Then one last assignment comes along and, wouldn't you know, his target turns out to be Anna's father (Yulin). Based on the novel "The Large Kill" by Patrick Ruell. **93m/C VHS.** Bryan Brown, Brooke Adams, Harris Yulin; *D:* Jan Egleson; *W:* Walter Klenhard, Alan Sharp; *M:* Gary Chang.

The Last Hit Man **2008** Aging hitman Harry (Mantegna) botches his latest job (probably because he's dying), but keeps the info from his daughter Racquel (Whitmere) who's been serving as his getaway driver. When younger killer Billy (Orzari) is sent in to fix things, daddy's little girl decides she should take a more active role in the business to protect their interests. **87m/C DVD.** Joe Mantegna, Romano Orzari, Elizabeth Whitmere, Michael Majeski; *D:* Christopher Warre Smets; *W:* Christopher Warre Smets; *C:* Joe Turner; *M:* Alphonse Lanza. **VIDEO**

Last Holiday **1950** A man who is told he has a few weeks to live decides to spend them in a posh resort where people assume he is important. **89m/B VHS.** *GB* Alec Guinness, Kay Walsh, Beatrice Campbell, Wilfrid Hyde-White, Bernard Lee; *D:* Henry Cass; *W:* J.B. Priestley.

Last Holiday ½ **2006 (PG-13)** Georgia Byrd (Queen Latifah) is a shy New Orleans salesclerk with a passion for gourmet cooking and a habit of setting her dreams aside. This changes when Georgia is (mis)diagnosed with a fatal disease that gives her only weeks to live. She decides to make the most of her time by giving herself a makeover and a holiday at the ritzy Czech Grandhotel Pupp so she can enjoy the gastronomical delights of her favorite chef, Didier (the charming Depardieu). The Queen is as appealing as ever, even in this warmed-over comedy, which is a remake of the 1950 Alec Guinness comedy. **112m/C DVD.** *US* Queen Latifah, LL Cool J, Timothy Hutton, Giancarlo Esposito, Alicia Witt, Gerard Depardieu, Jane Adams, Susan Kellerman, Jascha Washington, Matt Ross, Ranjit (Chaudry) Chowdhry, Mike Estime, Michael Nouri, Julia Lashae, Richmond Werner, Emeril Lagasse, Shirl Cieutat; *D:* Wayne Wang; *W:* Jeffrey Price, Peter S. Seaman; *C:* Geoffrey Simpson; *M:* George Fenton.

The Last Hour **1991 (R)** A Wall Street crook crosses a Mafia punk, so the latter holds the former's wife hostage in an unfinished skyscraper. Fortunately the lady's first husband is a gung-ho cop eager to commence the DIE HARD-esque action. Undistinguished fare that gives away the climax in an opening flash-forward. **85m/C VHS.** Michael Pare, Shannon Tweed, Bobby DiCicco, Robert Pucci; *D:* William Sachs.

Last Hour **WOOF! 2008** Confusing, dumb, dull, and amateurish crime drama. Five criminals (Madsen, D'Amario, DMX, Wong, Caubet) each receive a letter summoning them to a house in Beijing. The guys show up and are trapped in the house (with an assassin no less), which is surrounded by cops who give them an hour to surrender. Remember that mug shot of a drunken, disheveled Nick Nolte? Well, that's what Madsen looks like, and D'Amario died in 2005, so this stinker was moldering somewhere where it should have been left. **95m/C DVD.** *FR HK* DMX, Michael Madsen, David Carradine, Paul Sorvino, Pascal Caubet, Tony D'Amario, Kwong Leung Wong, Bettina Antoni, Monica Cruz; *D:* Pascal Caubet; *W:* Pascal Caubet, Maxime Lemaitre; *C:* Ting Wo Kwong; *M:* DMX, Alain Mouysset. **VIDEO**

Last House on Dead End Street **WOOF!** *The Fun House* **1977 (R)** Gore galore as actors die for their art in this splatter flick about snuff films. **90m/C VHS, DVD.** Steven Morrison, Dennis Crawford, Lawrence Bornman, Janet Sorley; ***D:*** Victor Janos.

Last House on the Left *Krug and Company; Sex Crime of the Century* **1972 (R)** Two girls are kidnapped from a rock concert by a gang of escaped convicts; the girls' parents exact bloody revenge when the guilty parties pay an intended housecall. Controversial and grim low-budget shocker; loosely based on Bergman's "The Virgin Spring." **83m/C VHS, DVD.** David A(lexander) Hess, Lucy Grantham, Sandra Cassel, Mark Sheffler, Fred J. Lincoln, Jeramie Rain, Gaylord St. James, Cynthia Carr, Ada Washington, Martin Kove; ***D:*** Wes Craven; ***W:*** Wes Craven; ***C:*** Victor Hurwitz; ***M:*** David A(lexander) Hess.

The Last House on the Left **2009 (R)** Grisly, graphic remake of Wes Craven's 1972 original. John (Goldwyn), Emma (Potter), and teenaged Mari (Paxton) Collingwood are vacationing in their country home. Mari joins friends Paige (MacIssac) and Justin (Clark) in some pot-induced motel room antics when they are interrupted by Justin's sadistic escaped con daddy Krug (Dillahunt) and a couple of sleazoids. Bad things happen and continue when the creep trio inadvertently seek shelter with the Collingwoods, who only have revenge on their minds. **109m/C DVD.** *US* Garret Dillahunt, Michael Bowen, Riki Lindhome, Sara Paxton, Monica Potter, Tony Goldwyn, Aaron Paul, Martha MacIsaac, Spencer (Treat) Clark, Joshua Cox; ***D:*** Dennis Iliadis; ***W:*** Carl Ellsworth, Adam Alleca; ***C:*** Sharon Meir; ***M:*** John Murphy.

The Last Hunt 1/2 **1956** Well-performed western starring Taylor as a seedy buffalo hunter who gains his identity from senseless acts of murder. When personalities clash, he seeks revenge on fellow buffalo hunter Granger. Shot in Custer National Park, the buffalo scenes were real-life attempts at keeping the animals controlled. Based on the novel by Milton Lott. **108m/C VHS.** Robert Taylor, Stewart Granger, Lloyd Nolan, Debra Paget, Russ Tamblyn, Constance Ford, Ainslie Pryor, Ralph Moody, Fred Graham, Dan(iel) White, Bill Phillips, Roy Barcroft; ***D:*** Richard Brooks; ***W:*** Richard Brooks; ***M:*** Daniele Amfitheatrof.

The Last Hunter *Hunter of the Apocalypse* **1980 (R)** A soldier fights for his life behind enemy lines during the Vietnam War. **97m/C VHS.** *IT* Tisa Farrow, David Warbeck, Tony King, Bobby Rhodes, Margit Evelyn Newton, John Steiner, Alan Collins; ***D:*** Anthony M. Dawson.

Last Hurrah 1/2 **1958** An aging Irish-American mayor battles corruption and political backbiting in his effort to get reelected for the last time. Semi-acclaimed heart warmer, based on the novel by Edwin O'Connor. **121m/B VHS, DVD.** Spencer Tracy, Basil Rathbone, John Carradine, Jeffrey Hunter, Dianne Foster, Pat O'Brien, Edward Brophy, James Gleason, Donald Crisp, Ricardo Cortez, Wallace Ford, Frank McHugh, Jane Darwell, Arthur Walsh; ***D:*** John Ford; ***W:*** Frank Nugent; ***C:*** Charles Lawton Jr. Natl. Bd. of Review '58: Actor (Tracy), Director (Ford).

Last Hurrah for Chivalry *Hao xia* **1978** An honorable man cannot defend his family from a ruthless enemy and turns to two swordsmen-for-hire for help. Chinese with subtitles or dubbed. **108m/C VHS, DVD.** *HK* Damian Lau, Wei Pei, San Lee Hoi; ***D:*** John Woo; ***W:*** John Woo; ***C:*** Ching Yu, Yao Chu Chang.

The Last Innocent Man 1/2 **1987** An attorney who quit law due to a guilty conscience is lured into defending a suspected murderer. Things become even more complicated when he begins having an affair with his client's seductive wife. A well-acted and suspense-filled flick. **113m/C VHS.** Ed Harris, Roxanne Hart, Bruce McGill, Clarence Williams III, Rose Gregorio, David Suchet, Darrell Larson; ***D:*** Roger Spottiswoode; ***W:*** Dan Bronson; ***M:*** Brad Fiedel. **CABLE**

The Last King of Scotland **2006 (R)** Raging biopic recounts the Ugandan dictatorship of Idi Amin, which lasted from 1971-1979 and devastated the country. Whitaker's performance captures the leader's charisma and savagery without flinching. A fictionalized composite character, Scotsman Nicholas Garrigan (McAvoy), enters Amin's camp in 1971 as a doctor determined to help, but slowly finds himself in the unenviable position of being Amin's right-hand man. Title refers to Amin's obsession with British imperialism and his belief that the Scots, whom he admired as fierce fighters, were equally ill-treated. Based on Giles Foden's 1998 novel. **121m/C DVD.** *GB GE* Forest Whitaker, James McAvoy, Kerry Washington, Gillian Anderson, Simon McBurney; ***D:*** Kevin MacDonald; ***W:*** Peter Morgan, Jeremy Brock; ***C:*** Anthony Dod Mantle; ***M:*** Alex Heffes. Oscars '06: Actor (Whitaker); British Acad. '06: Actor (Whitaker), Adapt. Screenplay; Golden Globes '07: Actor—Drama (Whitaker); Screen Actors Guild '06: Actor (Whitaker).

The Last Kiss 1/2 *L'Ultimo Bacio* **2001 (R)** Responsibility and midlife crisis and romantic complications. Carlo (Accorsi) is living with his longtime girlfriend Guilia (Mezzogiorno), who tells him she's pregnant. This throws him into a tizzy since he doesn't really want to be a grown-up. Carlo's fading beauty mother, Anna (Sandrelli), also reacts badly to the news since she doesn't want to be a grandma; she abruptly decides to leave her boring hubby for some new romantic possibilities. Both mother and son use their angst to justify affairs as they try to figure out what they really want from their lives. A generally sophisticated melodrama that doesn't take itself too seriously. Italian with subtitles. **115m/C DVD.** *IT* Stefano Accorsi, Stefania Sandrelli, Giovanna Mezzogiorno, Martina Stella, Claudio Santamaria, Marco Cocci, Pierfrancesco Favino, Regina Orioli, Giorgio Pasotti; ***D:*** Gabriele Muccino; ***W:*** Gabriele Muccino; ***C:*** Marcello Montarsi; ***M:*** Paolo Buonino.

The Last Kiss 1/2 **2006 (R)** Botched remake of the Italian hit "L'Ultimo Bacio," now taking place in Madison, WI. About to hit 30, Michael (Braff, with a constant hangdog expression) finds his life spinning out of control after meeting sexy undergrad Kim (Bilson), while trying to balance the revelation that his live-in girlfriend Jenna (Barrett) is pregnant. Self-conscious dramedy about men unwilling to accept adult responsibility (yawn) and the exasperated women around them. How did Ed Burns not make this? **105m/C DVD.** *US* Zach Braff, Jacinda Barrett, Casey Affleck, Michael Weston, Blythe Danner, Tom Wilkinson, Lauren Lee Smith, Marley Shelton, Rachel Bilson, Eric Christian, Harold Ramis; ***D:*** Tony Goldwyn; ***W:*** Paul Haggis; ***C:*** Tom Stern; ***M:*** Michael Penn.

The Last Laugh 1/2 *Der Letzte Mann* **1924** An elderly man, who as the doorman of a great hotel was looked upon as a symbol of "upper class," is demoted to washroom attendant due to his age. Important due to camera technique and consuming performance by Jannings. Silent with music score. A 91-minute version is also available. **88m/B VHS, DVD.** *GE* Emil Jannings, Maly Delshaft, Max Hiller; ***D:*** F.W. Murnau; ***W:*** Carl Mayer; ***C:*** Karl Freund; ***M:*** Giuseppe Becce.

The Last Legion **2007 (PG-13)** Barbarians have taken Rome, and Britain's heroes haven't even been born in this revision of the Arthurian legend. Romulus (Sangster), last of the Caesars, flees to Britain under the protection of General Aurelius (Firth), wiseman Ambrosinius (Kingsley), and a rag-tag group of cohorts. Seeking the Roman 9th Legion for protection, they find a group of men who have become farmers and avoid conflict with evil warlord Vortigern. Bloody battles for control of Britain ensue, although they're reduced to cheap CGI sequences worthy only as a distraction from the unlikeable characters and weak plot. Sangster is adequate as the boy emperor, Firth is desperately miscast as an action hero and cannot muster any chemistry with token female warrior Mira (Rai), while Kingsley chews scenery throughout in what's best described as an imitation of Obi-Wan Kenobi. **110m/C DVD.** *FR GB IT* Colin Firth, Ben Kingsley, Thomas Sangster, Kevin McKidd, John Hannah, Iain Glen, Aishwarya Rai, Rupert Friend, Peter Mullan, Alexander Siddig, Robert Pugh, James Cosmo, Owen Teale; ***D:*** Doug Lefler; ***W:*** Jez Butterworth, Tom Butterworth; ***C:*** Marco Pontecorvo; ***M:*** Patrick Doyle.

The Last Letter 1/2 **2004 (R)** A twist ending somewhat redeems the slow pace of this courtroom thriller. Forceful jury foreman Griffith (Forsythe) leads the other jurors in deciding the verdict for a serial killer (writer/director Gannon) accused of 14 gory murders (shown in flashbacks). But their deliberations aren't as clear-cut as you might imagine since the foreman seems determined to raise more than a reasonable doubt that the right man is on trial. **80m/C DVD.** William Forsythe, Yancy Butler, Grace Zabriskie, Leo Rossi, Russell Gannon; ***D:*** Russell Gannon; ***W:*** Russell Gannon; ***C:*** Sean Dinwoodie; ***M:*** Terry Plumeri. **VIDEO**

The Last Lieutenant 1/2 *The Second Lieutenant; Secondloitnanten* **1994** Aging Thor Espedal (Skjonberg) is a one-time second lieutenant who has just retired from the Merchant Marines and returned home to his beloved wife, Anna (Tellefsen). But since the year is 1940, his retirement is interrupted by the German Army invading his country. Espedal enlists in the resistance effort but finds the army in complete disarray. Still the old man and a group of volunteers become determined to hold a key mountain pass. Norwegian with subtitles. **102m/C VHS, DVD.** *NO* Espen Skjonberg, Bjorn Sundquist, Rut Tellefsen, Gard B. Eidsvold, Lars Andreas Larssen; ***D:*** Hans Petter Moland; ***W:*** Hans Petter Moland, Axel Hellstenius; ***C:*** Harald Gunnar Paalgard; ***M:*** Randall Meyers.

Last Life in the Universe 1/2 *Ruang rak noi nid mahasan* **2003** Kenji (Tadanobu) is a suicidal ex-yakuza living in exile in Bangkok where he works as a librarian at the Japan Cultural Center. He meets Noi (Boonyasak), an equally suicidal hooker and is soon living with her at her family's derelict beach house. The opposites (he has OCD, she lives in filth) attract and various magical realism sequences take place until the past comes to haunt them both. English, Thai, and Japanese with subtitles. **112m/C DVD.** Tadanobu Asano, Sinitta Boonyasak, Laila Boonyasak, Yutaka Matsushige, Takeuchi Riki, Takashi Miike, Yohji Tanaka, Sakichi Sato, Thiti Phum-Orn; ***D:*** Pen-ek Ratanaruang; ***C:*** Christopher Doyle; ***M:*** Hualampong Riddim.

Last Light **1993 (R)** A prison guard (Whitaker) on death row forms a tenuous bond with an incorrigible inmate (Sutherland) who's about to be executed. Disturbing, especially the execution scene. Filmed on location at California's Soledad Prison. Sutherland's directorial debut. **95m/C VHS, DVD.** Kiefer Sutherland, Forest Whitaker, Clancy Brown, Lynne Moody, Kathleen Quinlan, Amanda Plummer; ***D:*** Kiefer Sutherland. **CABLE**

Last Lives **1998 (R)** Confusing parallel universe story has Malakai (Wirth) traveling to an alternate world to search for his lost wife. He discovers Adrienne (Rubin) about to marry Aaron (Howell) and Malakai kidnaps her to take her back to his world. **99m/C VHS.** C. Thomas Howell, Jennifer Rubin, Billy Wirth, Judge Reinhold; ***D:*** Worth Keeter; ***W:*** Dan Duling; ***C:*** Kent Wakeford; ***M:*** Greg Edmonson. **VIDEO**

The Last Man **2000 (R)** Overweight, balding, neurotic graduate student Alan (Arnott), who believes he's the last man alive on earth, is thrilled to discover Sarah (Ryan), a babe who would never have even looked at him pre-apocalypse. But a snake appears in Alan's paradise in the form of hitchhiker Raphael (Montgomery), who's as dumb as he is good-looking (and he's very good looking). Naturally, Sarah is attracted to him—much to Alan's jealous dismay. So if you were the last three people alive, just how would you handle the situation? **93m/C VHS, DVD.** David Arnott, Jeri Ryan, Dan Montgomery Jr.; ***D:*** Harry Ralston; ***W:*** Harry Ralston; ***C:*** Michael Grady; ***M:*** Woody Jackson, Ivan Knight.

The Last Man on Earth *L'Ultimo Uomo Della Terra* **1964** Price is the sole survivor of a plague which has turned the rest of the world into vampires, who constantly harass him. Uneven U.S./Italian production manages to convey a creepy atmosphere of dismay. **86m/B VHS, DVD.** *IT* Vincent Price, Franca Bettoya, Giacomo "Jack" Rossi-Stuart, Emma Danieli; ***D:*** Ubaldo Ragona, Sidney Salkow; ***W:*** Richard Matheson, William P. Leicester, Furio M. Menotti; ***C:*** Franco Delli Colli; ***M:*** Paul Sawtell, Bert Shefter.

Last Man Standing **1987 (R)** A cheap, gritty drama about bare-knuckle fist fighting. Wells stars as a down-on-his-luck prizefighter trying to find work that doesn't involve pugilism. **89m/C VHS.** William Sanderson, Vernon Wells, Franco (Columbo) Columbu; ***D:*** Damian Lee.

Last Man Standing **1995 (R)** L.A. police officer Wincott discovers corruption after his partner Banks is murdered. **96m/C VHS, DVD.** Jeff Wincott, Jillian McWhirter, Jonathan Banks, Steve Eastin, Jonathan Fuller, Michael Greene, Ava Fabian; ***D:*** Joseph Merhi; ***W:*** Joseph Merhi; ***M:*** Louis Febre.

Last Man Standing 1/2 *Welcome to Jericho* **1996 (R)** Engaging, but not terribly original gangster/western features a plot taken from Clint Eastwood's career-making "Fistful of Dollars" (in turn, an adaptation of Akira Kurosawa's "Yojimbo"). The producers and credits claim lineage directly from the Kurosawa film, but this story's been around for a while, folks. In the small 1930s border town of Jericho Texas, Willis, under the pseudonym John Smith, hires himself out to both sides of a bootlegging war in an effort to make some quick cash. Bigger roles for Walken, the flinty trigger man for Irish boss Doyle (Kelly), and Dern, the town sheriff on the mob payroll, could have perked things up a little. Willis nicely injects his smirking brand of wit into a film that may have benefitted from more of the dark "Yojimbo" humor. Hill provides his trademark visually exciting action sequences. **101m/C VHS, DVD.** Bruce Willis, Bruce Dern, Christopher Walken, Karina Lombard, William Sanderson, David Patrick Kelly, Alexandra Powers, Leslie Mann, Michael Imperioli, R.D. Call, Ken Jenkins, Ned Eisenberg; ***D:*** Walter Hill; ***W:*** Walter Hill; ***C:*** Lloyd Ahern II; ***M:*** Ry Cooder.

The Last Married Couple in America **1980 (R)** A couple fight to stay happily married amidst the rampant divorce epidemic engulfing their friends. **103m/C VHS.** George Segal, Natalie Wood, Richard Benjamin, Valerie Harper, Dom DeLuise, Priscilla Barnes; ***D:*** Gilbert Cates; ***M:*** Charles Fox.

The Last Marshal **1999 (R)** Tough Texas lawman Glenn is mighty riled when some no-account prisoners manage to escape from his jail. So he trails them to Miami to get them back. **102m/C VHS, DVD.** Scott Glenn, Constance Marie, Randall Batinkoff, Vincent Castellanos, John Ortiz, Raymond Cruz, William Forsythe, Lisa Boyle; ***D:*** Mike Kirton. **VIDEO**

Last Mercenary **WOOF!** *Rolf* **1984** An angry ex-soldier kills everyone who makes him mad. **90m/C VHS.** *IT* Tony Marsina, Malcolm Duff, Kitty Nichols, Louis Walser; ***D:*** Mario Siciliano; ***W:*** Mario Siciliano; ***C:*** Louis Smith; ***M:*** Fabio Frizzi.

The Last Metro *Le Dernier Metro* **1980 (PG)** Truffaut's alternately gripping and touching drama about a theatre company in Nazi-occupied Paris. In 1942, Lucas Steiner (Bennent) is a successful Jewish theatre director who is forced into hiding. He turns the running of the theatre over to his wife, Marion (the always exquisite Deneuve), who must contend with a pro-Nazi theatre critic (Richard) and her growing attraction to the company's leading man (Depardieu), who is secretly working with the Resistance. In French with English subtitles. **135m/C VHS, DVD.** *FR* Catherine Deneuve, Gerard Depardieu, Heinz Bennent, Jean-Louis Richard, Jean Poiret, Andrea Ferreol, Paulette Dubost, Sabine Haudepin, Maurice Risch, Jean-Pierre Klein, Martine Simonet, Franck Pasquier, Jean-Jose Richer, Laszlo Szabo, Jessica Zucman; ***D:*** Francois Truffaut; ***W:*** Francois Truffaut, Suzanne Schiffman, Jean-Claude Grumberg; ***C:*** Nestor Almendros; ***M:*** Georges Delerue. Cesar '81: Actor (Depardieu), Actress (Deneuve), Art Dir./Set Dec., Cinematog., Director (Truffaut), Film, Sound, Writing, Score.

The Last Mile **1932** The staff of a prison prepares for the execution of a celebrated murderer. **70m/B VHS.** Preston Foster, Howard Phillips, George E. Stone; ***D:*** Sam Bischoff.

The Last Mimzy **2007 (PG)** Loose adaptation of Lewis Padgett's short story "All Mimzy Were the Borogroves" (yeah, it's from Lewis Carroll's "Jabberwocky"). Noah (O'Neil) and his sister Emma (Wynn) find a box that's filled with odd objects, including a cute stuffed rabbit named Mimzy, who is actually a spokes—uh—rabbit from the future, where things are bad because of pollution and disease. The objects give the kids extraordinary powers that they are expected to use to solve these eco problems. Noah's spiritually-minded science teacher Larry (Wilson) thinks this is very cool, while the kids' parents seem to be fairly oblivious. Overstuffed with ideas but not condescending, which is a plus. **90m/C DVD.** *US* Joely Richardson, Timothy Hutton, Rainn Wilson, Kathryn Hahn, Noah Wilder, Rhiannon Leigh Wyn, Michael Clarke Duncan; ***D:*** Robert Shaye; ***W:*** Bruce Joel Rubin, Toby Emmerich; ***C:*** J.(James) Michael Muro; ***M:*** Howard Shore.

The Last Minute **2001 (R)** Billy Byrne (Beesley) is the "next big thing" and subjected to an incredible amount of media hype. But when his latest project is considered a dud, he falls just as fast. Jobless, friendless, and hopeless, Billy is taken in by Anna (Corrie), a young ruffian living with a group of adolescents under the thrall of Fagin-like drug dealer Grimshanks (Bell). Billy gets sucked into this new world as easily as he was manipulated in the old one. **104m/C VHS, DVD.** *GB* Max Beesley, Tom Bell, Emily Corrie, Ciaran McMenamin, Jason Isaacs, Kate Ashfield, Anthony (Corlan) Higgins, Udo Kier, Stephen Dorff; ***D:*** Stephen Norrington; ***W:*** Stephen Norrington; ***C:*** James Welland; ***M:*** Paul Rabjohns.

The Last Movie **1/2** *Chinchero* **1971 (R)** A movie stunt man stays in a small Peruvian town after his filming stint is over. Hopper's confused, pretentious follow-up to "Easy Rider," has a multitude of cameos but little else. Given an award by the Italians; nobody else understood it. Kristofferson's film debut; he also wrote the music. Based on a story by Hopper and Stern. **108m/C VHS.** Dennis Hopper, Julie Adams, Peter Fonda, Kris Kristofferson, Sylvia Miles, John Phillip Law, Russ Tamblyn, Rod Cameron; ***D:*** Dennis Hopper; ***W:*** Stewart Stern; ***M:*** Kris Kristofferson.

The Last Musketeer **1/2 2000** Gifted fencer Steve McTeer (Green) wants to get away from his past and his family's criminal activities. So when he's falsely accused of a crime, he decides to hide out in the Scottish Highlands, taking an instructor position at a girls' boarding school. But he can't really escape. **85m/C DVD.** *GB* Robson Green, Arkie Whiteley, Maureen Beattie, John McGlynn; ***D:*** Bill Britten; ***W:*** Sebastian Secker Walker; ***C:*** Tony Miller; ***M:*** John Rea. **TV**

Last Night **1998 (R)** It's 6 p.m. in the city of Toronto and the world will come to an end in six hours. And no one's going to save the day. So all the characters are deciding how they'd like to spend their last few hours. Patrick (McKellar) is attending a family dinner and then wants to spend his last hours alone—instead he's drawn into Sandra's (Oh) drama. She's stuck in traffic across town from her husband and Patrick tries to help her get to her rendezvous. Meanwhile, his best friend Craig (Rennie) has a few sexual conquests he still wants to make, including one with their high school French teacher, Mrs. Carlton (Bujold). Mordant humor; appealing performances. **94m/C VHS, DVD.** *CA* Don McKellar, Sandra Oh, Callum Keith Rennie, Sarah Polley, David Cronenberg, Genevieve Bujold, Tracy Wright, Roberta Maxwell, Robin Gammell, Karen Glave, Jackie Burroughs; ***D:*** Don McKellar; ***W:*** Don McKellar; ***C:*** Douglas Koch; ***M:*** Alexina Louie, Alex Pauk. Genie '98: Actress (Oh), Support. Actor (Rennie).

Last Night **2010** Joanna and Michael Reed are separated for a night by Michael's business trip. Michael finds himself attracted to colleague Laura while Joanna encounters her former flame Alex and their marriage is suddenly imperiled. **m/C DVD.** Keira Knightley, Sam Worthington, Eva Mendes, Guillaume Canet, Griffin Dunne; ***D:*** Massy Tadjedin; ***W:*** Massy Tadjedin; ***C:*** Peter Deming; ***M:*** Clint Mansell.

Last Night at the Alamo **1983** Patrons fight to stop the destruction of their Houston bar, the Alamo, which is about to be razed to make room for a modern skyscraper. Insightful comedy written by the author of "The Texas Chainsaw Massacre." **80m/B VHS.** Sonny Carl Davis, Lou Perry, Steve Matilla, Tina Hubbard, Doris Hargrave; ***D:*** Eagle Pennell; ***W:*** Ken Henkel; ***M:*** Wayne Bell.

The Last of England **1/2 1987** A furious non-narrative film by avant-garde filmmaker Jarman, depicting the modern British landscape as a funereal, waste-filled rubble-heap—as depleted morally as it is environmentally. **87m/C VHS, DVD.** *GB* Tilda Swinton, Spencer Leigh, Spring, Gerrard McArthur; ***D:*** Derek Jarman; ***W:*** Derek Jarman; ***C:*** Derek Jarman, Richard Helsop, Christopher Hughes; ***M:*** Simon Fisher Turner.

The Last of His Tribe **1992 (PG-13)** In 1911 an anthropologist befriends an Indian and discovers that Ishi is the last surviving member of California's Yahi tribe. Ishi then becomes a media and scientific society darling, spending the remainder of his remaining life in captivity to academia. A good portrayal of the Native American plight. Based on a true story. **90m/C VHS, DVD.** Jon Voight, Graham Greene, David Ogden Stiers, Jack Blessing, Anne Archer, Daniel Benzali; ***D:*** Harry Hook. **CABLE**

The Last of Mrs. Cheyney **1937** Remake of Norma Shearer's 1929 hit, based on the play by Frederick Lonsdale, about a sophisticated jewel thief in England. Crawford stars as the jewel thief who poses as a wealthy woman to get into parties hosted by London bluebloods. Dripping with charm, she works her way into Lord Drilling's mansion where she plans a huge heist. The film is handled well, and the cast gives solid performances throughout. This chic comedy of high society proved to be one of Crawford's most popular films of the '30s. **98m/B VHS.** Joan Crawford, Robert Montgomery, William Powell, Frank Morgan, Nigel Bruce, Jessie Ralph; ***D:*** Richard Boleslawski, George Fitzmaurice; ***C:*** George J. Folsey.

The Last of Mrs. Lincoln **1/2** **1976** Intimate made for TV portrayal of the famous first lady. Film focuses on Mary Todd Lincoln's life from the assassination of her husband, through her autumn years, and her untimely downfall. **118m/C VHS, DVD.** Julie Harris, Robby Benson, Patrick Duffy; ***D:*** George Schaefer; ***M:*** Lyn Murray. **TV**

The Last of Philip Banter **1/2 1987 (R)** An alcoholic writer is terrified to learn events in his life exactly match a mysterious manuscript. **105m/C VHS.** Tony Curtis, Gregg Henry, Irene Miracle, Scott Paulin, Kate Vernon; ***D:*** Herve Hachuel.

The Last of Sheila **1/2 1973 (PG)** A movie producer invites six big-star friends for a cruise aboard his yacht, the "Sheila." He then stages an elaborate "Whodunnit" parlor game to discover which one of them murdered his wife. **119m/C VHS, DVD.** Yvonne Romain, Pierre Rosso, Serge Citon, Roberto Rossi, Richard Benjamin, James Coburn, James Mason, Dyan Cannon, Joan Hackett, Raquel Welch, Ian McShane; ***D:*** Herbert Ross; ***W:*** Anthony Perkins, Stephen Sondheim; ***C:*** Gerry Turpin; ***M:*** Billy Goldenberg.

The Last of the Blonde Bombshells **1/2 2000 (PG-13)** Elizabeth (Dench) played sax with the all-girl swing band, The Blonde Bombshells, during WWII. With the urgings of granddaughter Joan (Findlay) and drummer Patrick (Holm)—who played in drag—Elizabeth is encouraged to reunite the band members. If they can find them and get them to agree. Good cast but the charm is on the low-burner and rather than swinging, it's more a sedate fox-trot. **80m/C VHS, DVD.** Judi Dench, Ian Holm, Olympia Dukakis, Leslie Caron, Cleo Laine, Joan Sims, Billie Whitelaw, June Whitfield, Felicity Dean, Valentine Pelka, Millie Findlay; ***D:*** Gilles Mackinnon; ***W:*** Alan Plater; ***C:*** Richard Greatrex; ***M:*** John Keane. **CABLE**

Last of the Clintons **1/2 1935** A range detective tracks an outlaw gang amid spur jinglin', sharp shootin' and cow punchin'. **64m/B VHS.** Betty Mack, Del Gordon, Victor Potel, Harry Fraser, Harry Carey Sr.; ***D:*** Slim Whitaker; ***W:*** Slim Whitaker; ***C:*** Robert E. Cline.

Last of the Comanches *The Sabre and the Arrow* **1952** Cavalry and Indians fight for water when both are dying of thirst in the desert. **85m/C VHS.** Broderick Crawford, Barbara Hale, John Stewart, Lloyd Bridges, Mickey Shaughnessy, George Mathews; ***D:*** Andre de Toth.

The Last of the Dogmen **1/2** **1995 (PG)** Cliched modern western with an intriguing premise and good actors. Montana bounty hunter Lewis Gates (Berenger) is recruited to nab three escaped cons but finds them dead and a Cheyenne arrow nearby. Gates does some investigating (in a library no less!) and discovers that maybe some descendants of the 1864 Sand Creek massacre are existing in the woods. He gets anthropologist Lillian Sloan (Hershey) involved, discovers a tribe of modern-day dog soldiers, and finds a very angry sheriff (Smith) on their trail. Alberta, Canada passes for Big Sky country. **117m/C VHS, DVD.** Tom Berenger, Barbara Hershey, Kurtwood Smith, Steve Reevis, Andrew Miller, Gregory Scott Cummins; ***D:*** Tab Murphy; ***W:*** Tab Murphy; ***C:*** Karl Walter Lindenlaub; ***M:*** David Arnold; ***Nar:*** Wilford Brimley.

The Last of the Finest **1/2** *Street Legal; Blue Heat* **1990 (R)** Overzealous anti-drug task force cops break the rules in trying to put dealer-drug lords in prison; ostensibly a parallel on the Iran-Contra affair. **106m/C VHS.** Brian Dennehy, Joe Pantoliano, Jeff Fahey, Bill Paxton, Deborra-Lee Furness, Guy Boyd, Henry Darrow, Lisa Jane Persky, Michael C. Gwynne; ***D:*** John MacKenzie; ***W:*** George Armitage, Jere P. Cunningham; ***M:*** Jack Nitzsche.

The Last of the High Kings **1/2** *Summer Fling* **1996 (R)** Underachieving Irish Frankie (Leto) decides to forget about his university entrance exams and enjoy his summer (it's 1977) by cutting loose and fantasizing about various girls he knows. What he doesn't realize is that young American Erin (Ricci), who's staying with his crazy family, has fallen for him. Pleasant romance with a talented cast. Based on the novel "The Last of the High Kings" by Ferdia Mac Anna. **103m/C VHS, DVD.** *IR GB DK* Catherine O'Hara, Jared Leto, Christina Ricci, Gabriel Byrne, Stephen Rea, Colm Meaney, Lorraine Pilkington, Jason Barry, Emily Mortimer, Karl Hayden, Ciaran Fitzgerald, Darren Monks, Peter Keating, Alexandra Haughey, Renee Weldon, Amanda Shun; ***D:*** David Keating; ***W:*** David Keating, Gabriel Byrne; ***C:*** Bernd Heinl; ***M:*** Michael Convertino.

The Last of the Mohicans **1920** Color tints enhance this silent version of the James Fenimore Cooper rouser. Beery is the villainous Magua, with Bedford memorable as the lovely Cora and Roscoe as the brave Uncas. Fine action sequences, including the Huron massacre at Fort Henry. Director credit was shared when Tourneur suffered an on-set injury and was off for three months. **75m/B VHS, DVD.** Wallace Beery, Barbara Bedford, Albert Roscoe, Lillian Hall-Davis, Henry Woodward, James Gordon, George Hackathorne, Harry Lorraine, Nelson McDowell, Theodore Lorch, Boris Karloff; ***D:*** Maurice Tourneur, Clarence Brown; ***W:*** Robert A.(R.A.) Dillon; ***C:*** Charles Van Enger. Natl. Film Reg. '95.

The Last of the Mohicans **1932** Serial based on James Fenimore Cooper's novel of the life-and-death struggle of the Mohican Indians during the French and Indian War. Twelve chapters, 13 minutes each. Remade as a movie in 1936 and 1992 and as a TV movie in 1977. **230m/B VHS, DVD.** Edwina Booth, Harry Carey Sr., Hobart Bosworth, Frank "Junior" Coghlan; ***D:*** Ford Beebe, B. Reeves Eason.

The Last of the Mohicans **1/2** **1936** James Fenimore Cooper's classic about the French and Indian War in colonial America is brought to the screen. Remake of the 1932 serial. **91m/B VHS.** Randolph Scott, Binnie Barnes, Bruce Cabot, Henry Wilcoxon, Heather Angel, Hugh Buckler; ***D:*** George B. Seitz.

The Last of the Mohicans **1985** The classic novel by James Fenimore Cooper about the scout Hawkeye and his Mohican companions, Chingachgook and Uncas, during the French and Indian War, comes to life in this TV film. **97m/C VHS.** Steve Forrest, Ned Romero, Andrew Prine, Don Shanks, Robert Tessier, Jane Actman; ***D:*** James L. Conway. **TV**

The Last of the Mohicans **1992 (R)** It's 1757, at the height of the French and English war in the American colonies, with various Native American tribes allied to each side. Hawkeye (Day-Lewis), a white frontiersman raised by the Mohicans, wants nothing to do with either "civilized" side, until he rescues the beautiful Cora (Stowe) from the revenge-minded Huron Magua (Studi in a powerful performance). Graphically violent battle scenes are realistic, but not gratuitous. The real pleasure in this adaptation, which draws from both the James Fenimore Cooper novel and the 1936 film, is in its lush look and attractive stars. Means is terrific in his film debut as Hawkeye's foster-father. Released in a letterbox format to preserve the original integrity of the film. **114m/C VHS, DVD.** Daniel Day-Lewis, Madeleine Stowe, Wes Studi, Russell Means, Eric Schweig, Jodhi May, Steven Waddington, Maurice Roeves, Colm Meaney, Patrice Chereau, Pete Postlethwaite, Terry Kinney, Tracey Ellis, Dennis Banks, Dylan Baker; ***D:*** Michael Mann; ***W:*** Christopher Crowe, Michael Mann; ***C:*** Dante Spinotti; ***M:*** Trevor Jones, Randy Edelman. Oscars '92: Sound.

Last of the Pony Riders **1/2 1953** When the telegraph lines linking the East and West Coasts are completed, Gene and the other Pony Express riders find themselves out of a job. Autry's final feature film. **59m/B VHS.** Gene Autry, Smiley Burnette, Kathleen Case; ***D:*** George Archainbaud.

Last of the Red Hot Lovers **1/2** **1972 (PG)** Not so funny adaptation of Neil Simon's Broadway hit. Middle-aged man decides to have a fling and uses his mother's apartment to seduce three very strange women. **98m/C VHS, DVD.** Alan Arkin, Paula Prentiss, Sally Kellerman, Renee Taylor; ***D:*** Gene Saks; ***W:*** Neil Simon.

The Last of the Redmen **1/2 1947** An adaptation of James Fenimore Cooper's "The Last of the Mohicans" geared toward youngsters. Hall must lead three children of a British general through dangerous Indian territory. They have a number of adventures including meeting up with Uncas, the last of the Mohicans, who's a villain in this mangled version. **79m/B VHS.** Jon Hall, Michael O'Shea, Evelyn Ankers, Julie Bishop, Buster Crabbe, Rick Vallin, Frederick Worlock, Guy Hedlund; ***D:*** George Sherman; ***W:*** Herbert Dalmas.

Last of the Warrens **1936** A cowboy returns home after WWI to discover that an unscrupulous storekeeper has stolen his property. **56m/C VHS.** Bob Steele, Charles "Blackie" King, Lafe (Lafayette) McKee, Margaret Marquis, Horace Murphy; ***D:*** Robert North Bradbury.

Last of the Wild Horses **1/2 1949** Range war almost starts when ranch owner is accused of trying to force the small ranchers out of business. **86m/B VHS.** Mary Beth Hughes, James Ellison, Jane Frazee, Douglass Dumbrille, James Millican, Reed Hadley, Olin Howlin, Grady Sutton; ***D:*** Robert L. Lippert; ***W:*** Jack Harvey; ***C:*** Benjamin (Ben H.) Kline.

Last Orders **2001 (R)** Based on Graham Swift's award-winning 1996 novel, which covers some 50 years in the lives of four London friends. Vic (Courtenay), Ray (Hoskins), and Lenny (Hemmings) all meet in their favorite East London pub to toast their recently deceased friend Jack (Caine), along with Jack's son, Vince (Winstone). Jack's last request was to have his ashes scattered in the sea at Margate, where he spent his honeymoon with wife Amy (Mirren) in 1939. Amy, however, will not make the trip as she has is going to visit their severely handicapped daughter June (Morelli), whom Jack could never accept, at the institution where June lives. Flashbacks fill out the storylines and the cast is stellar. **109m/C VHS, DVD.** *GB* Michael Caine, Bob Hoskins, Tom Courtenay, David Hemmings, Ray Winstone, Helen Mirren, J.J. Feild, Cameron Fitch, Nolan Hemmings, Anatol Yusef, Kelly Reilly, Laura Morelli; ***D:*** Fred Schepisi; ***W:*** Fred Schepisi; ***C:*** Brian Tufano; ***M:*** Paul Grabowsky.

The Last Outlaw **1927** Action-packed western with Cooper following his success of "Wings" with Paramount. Most excellent equine stunts. **61m/B VHS.** Gary Cooper, Jack Luden, Betty Jewel; ***D:*** Arthur Rosson.

Last Outlaw ☙☙ **1936** The last of the famous badmen of the old West is released from jail and returns home to find that times have changed. The action climaxes in an old-time blazing shoot-out. **79m/B VHS.** Harry Carey Sr., Hoot Gibson, Henry B. Walthall, Tom Tyler, Russell Hopton, Alan Curtis, Harry Woods, Barbara Pepper; ***D:*** Christy Cabanne.

The Last Outlaw ☙☙ ½ **1993 (R)** Rourke stars as an ex-Confederate officer who leads a gang of outlaws until his violent excesses leave even them disgusted. The gang shoots Rourke but of course he doesn't die and then he sets out for revenge. **90m/C VHS, DVD.** Mickey Rourke, Dermot Mulroney, Ted Levine, John C. McGinley, Steve Buscemi, Keith David; ***D:*** Geoff Murphy; ***W:*** Eric Red. **CABLE**

The Last Outpost ☙☙ **1935** During WWI, intelligence agent Stevenson (Rains) rescues British officer Andrews (Grant) from a hostile Kurdish tribe. After being wounded, Andrews is hospitalized in Cairo where he falls for his nurse Rosemary (Michael), who's actually Stevenson's wife. There's a climactic battle at a remote outpost in the Sudan and the two men meet once again. **72m/B DVD.** Claude Rains, Cary Grant, Gertrude Michael, Akim Tamiroff, Kathleen Burke, Billy Bevan, Colin Tapley; ***D:*** Louis Gasnier, Charles T. Barton; ***W:*** Charles Brackett, Frank Partos, Philip MacDonald; ***C:*** Theodor Sparkuhl.

The Last Picture Show ☙☙☙☙ **1971 (R)** Slice of life/nostalgic farewell to an innocent age, based on Larry McMurtry's novel. Set in Archer City, a backwater Texas town, most of the story plays out at the local hangout run by ex-cowboy Sam the Lion (Johnson). Duane (Bridges) is hooked up with spoiled pretty girl Jacy (Shepherd), while Sonny (Bottoms), a sensitive guy, is having an affair with the coach's neglected wife, Ruth (Leachman). Loss of innocence, disillusionment and confusion are played out against the backdrop of a town about to close its cinema. Shepherd's and Bottoms' film debut. Stunningly photographed in black and white (Bogdanovich claimed he didn't want to "prettify" the picture by shooting in color) by Robert Surtees. Followed by a weak sequel, "Texasville." **118m/B VHS, DVD.** Jeff Bridges, Timothy Bottoms, Ben Johnson, Cloris Leachman, Cybill Shepherd, Ellen Burstyn, Eileen Brennan, Clu Gulager, Sharon Taggart, Randy Quaid, Sam Bottoms, Bill (Billy) Thurman, John Hillerman; ***D:*** Peter Bogdanovich; ***W:*** Peter Bogdanovich, Larry McMurtry; ***C:*** Robert L. Surtees. Oscars '71: Support. Actor (Johnson), Support. Actress (Leachman); British Acad. '72: Screenplay, Support. Actor (Johnson), Support. Actress (Leachman); Golden Globes '72: Support. Actor (Johnson); Natl. Bd. of Review '71: Support. Actor (Johnson), Support. Actress (Leachman), Natl. Film Reg. '98;; N.Y. Film Critics '71: Screenplay, Support. Actor (Johnson), Support. Actress (Burstyn); Natl. Soc. Film Critics '71: Support. Actress (Burstyn).

The Last Place on Earth ☙☙ ½ **1985** Saga of bitter hardship and ambition depicting the 1911 race between the British Antarctic Expedition, led by Captain Robert Falcon (Shaw), and his Norwegian rival Roald Amundsen (Ousdal) to conquer the South Pole. On seven cassettes. **385m/C VHS, DVD.** *CA* Martin Shaw, Sverre Anker Ousdal, Max von Sydow, Susan Wooldridge; ***D:*** Ferdinand Fairfax; ***W:*** Trevor Griffiths; ***C:*** John Coquillon; ***M:*** Trevor Jones. **TV**

Last Plane Out ☙ ½ **1983 (R)** A Texas journalist sent out on assignment to Nicaragua falls in love with a Sandanista rebel. Based on producer Jack Cox's real-life experiences as a journalist during the last days of the Samosa regime. Low-budget propaganda. **90m/C VHS.** Jan-Michael Vincent, Lloyd Battista, Julie Carmen, Mary Crosby, David Huffman, William Windom; ***D:*** David Nelson.

The Last Polka ☙☙☙ **1984** SCTV vets Candy and Levy are Yosh and Stan Schmenge, polka kings interviewed for a "documentary" on their years in the spotlight and on the road. Hilarious spoof on Martin Scorsese's "The Last Waltz," about The Band's last concert. Several fellow Second City-ers keep the laughs coming. If you liked SCTV or "This Is Spinal Tap," you'll like this. **54m/C VHS.** John Candy, Eugene Levy, Rick Moranis, Robin Duke, Catherine O'Hara; ***D:*** John Blanchard. **CABLE**

The Last Porno Flick ☙ **1974 (PG)** A pornographic movie script winds up in the hands of a couple of goofy cab drivers. The twosome sneak the movie's genre past the producers, families, and police. **90m/C VHS, DVD.** Michael Pataki, Marianna Hill, Carmen Zapata, Mike Kellin, Colleen Camp, Tom Signorelli, Antony Carbone; ***D:*** Ray Marsh.

The Last Prostitute ☙☙ **1991 (PG-13)** Two teenage boys search for a legendary prostitute to initiate them into manhood, only to discover that she has retired. They hire on as laborers on her horse farm, and one of them discovers the meaning of love. **93m/C VHS.** Sonia Braga, Wil Wheaton, David Kaufman, Woody Watson, Dennis Letts, Cotter Smith; ***D:*** Lou Antonio; ***W:*** Carmen Culver. **CABLE**

The Last Remake of Beau Geste ☙☙ **1977 (PG)** A slapstick parody of the familiar Foreign Legion story from the Mel Brooks-ish school of loud genre farce. Gary Cooper makes an appearance by way of inserted footage from the 1939 straight version. **85m/C VHS.** Marty Feldman, Ann-Margret, Michael York, Peter Ustinov, James Earl Jones; ***D:*** Marty Feldman; ***W:*** Marty Feldman, Chris Allen.

The Last Request ☙☙ **2006 (R)** Borscht Belt one-liners find their place in this dark family comedy as dying comedian Pop (Aiello) wants one of his two sons to get married and provide an heir to the family name. Womanizing Tom (Scotti) actually dies trying, which leads to shy seminarian Jeff (Knight) embarking on a disastrous sexual quest. He meets a lot of lunatic prospects while the perfect girl (Lloyd) is right in front of him. **91m/C DVD.** Danny Aiello, T.R. Knight, Sabrina Lloyd, Nick Scotti, Barbara Feldon, Mario Cantone, Joe Piscopo, Frank Vincent, Vincent Pastore, Tony Lo Bianco; ***D:*** John DeBellis; ***W:*** John DeBellis; ***C:*** Dan Karlok; ***M:*** Waddy Wachtel. **VIDEO**

Last Resort ☙☙ *She Knew No Other Way* **1986 (R)** A married furniture executive unknowingly takes his family on vacation to a sex-saturated, Club Med-type holiday spot, and gets more than he anticipated. **80m/C VHS, DVD.** Charles Grodin, Robin Pearson Rose, John Aston, Ellen Blake, Megan Mullally, Christopher Ames, Jon Lovitz, Scott Nemes, Gerrit Graham, Mario Van Peebles, Phil Hartman, Mimi Lieber, Steve Levitt; ***D:*** Zane Buzby; ***W:*** Jeff Buhai; ***C:*** Stephen M. Katz, Alex Nepomniaschy; ***M:*** Steven Nelson, Thom Sharp.

Last Resort ☙ *Kill Theory* **2009 (R)** Predictable plot, annoying and stupid characters. A group of friends are celebrating their college graduation at a secluded lakeside house. A man just released from a hospital for the criminally insane traps them inside and forces them into a game where they have to kill each other to survive (until only one is left) or they all die. **82m/C DVD.** Agnes Bruckner, Taryn Manning, Patrick Flueger, Teddy Dunn, Theo Rossi, Daniel Franzee, Kevin Gage, Steffi Wickens; ***D:*** Chris Moore; ***W:*** Kelly Palmer; ***C:*** David Armstrong; ***M:*** Michael Suby. **VIDEO**

The Last Reunion ☙ ½ **1980** The only witness to a brutal killing of a Japanese official and his wife during WWII seeks revenge on the guilty American platoon, 33 years later. Violent. **98m/C VHS.** Cameron Mitchell, Leo Fong, Chanda Romero, Vic Silayan, Hal Bokar, Philip Baker Hall; ***D:*** Jay Wertz.

The Last Ride ☙ **1991** Another movie probing the dark side of hitchhiking. This time our hero thumbs a ride with a truck driver who plans to bypass the next city...for hell. **84m/C VHS.** Dan Ranger, Michael Hilow; ***D:*** Karl Krogstad, Karl Krogstad; ***W:*** Ted Prior; ***C:*** David Crowther; ***M:*** Tony Capelli, Charles Shepard.

The Last Ride ☙☙ *F.T.W* **1994 (R)** Frank T. Wells (Rourke) is out of prison after 10 years and free to try to recapture his former rodeo glory. Hellcat Scarlett Stuart's on the run from a botched bank job/murder perpetrated by her vicious brother Clem (Berg). Scarlett manages to hook up with Frank and decides to help him out financially by robbing convenience stores. Frank's not too happy when he finds out. Rourke is surprisingly subdued and Singer's properly unsympathetic but they don't seem to be working in the same movie. Nice Montana scenery though. **102m/C VHS, DVD.** Mickey Rourke, Lori Singer, Brion James, Peter Berg, Rodney A. Grant, Aaron Neville; ***D:*** Michael Karbelnikoff; ***W:*** Mari Kornhauser; ***C:*** James L. Carter; ***M:*** Gary Chang.

The Last Ride of the Dalton Gang ☙☙ **1979** A long-winded retelling of the wild adventures that made the Dalton gang legendary among outlaws. **146m/C VHS, DVD.** Larry Wilcox, Jack Palance, Randy Quaid, Cliff (Potter) Potts, Dale Robertson, Don Collier; ***D:*** Dan Curtis.

The Last Riders ☙ **1990 (R)** Motorcycle centaur Estrada revs a few motors fleeing from cycle club cronies and crooked cops. Full throttle foolishness. **90m/C VHS, DVD.** Erik Estrada, William (Bill) Smith, Armando Silvestre, Kathrin Lautner; ***D:*** Joseph Merhi.

Last Rites ☙☙ **1988 (R)** A priest at St. Patrick's Cathedral in New York allows a young Mexican woman to seek sanctuary from the Mob, who soon come after both of them. **103m/C VHS, DVD.** Tom Berenger, Daphne Zuniga, Chick Vennera, Dane Clark, Carlo Pacchi, Anne Twomey, Paul Dooley, Vassili Lambrinos; ***D:*** Donald P. Bellisario; ***W:*** Donald P. Bellisario; ***C:*** David Watkin; ***M:*** Bruce Broughton.

Last Rites ☙☙ **1998 (R)** Dillon (Quaid) is a Florida Death Row serial killer, whose execution goes awry when the electric chair blows the generator and Dillon is left with amnesia. Oh, and he's suddenly gained psychic powers that allow him to solve crimes. A shrink (Davidtz) is brought in to see if he's faking, while the warden just wants to try fying Dillon again. **88m/C VHS.** Randy Quaid, Embeth Davidtz, A. Martinez; ***D:*** Kevin Dowling; ***W:*** Richard Outten, Tim Frost. **CABLE**

Last Run ☙ ½ **2001 (R)** Frank (Assante) is a former top-secret op who specialized in rescuing Russian defectors. His last assignment got his lover killed and now Frank is after the assassin who caused his life to go wrong. **98m/C VHS, DVD.** Armand Assante, Jurgen Prochnow, Ornella Muti, David Lipper, Corey Johnson; ***D:*** Anthony Hickox; ***W:*** Anthony Hickox. **VIDEO**

The Last Safari ☙☙ ½ **1967** A young man on safari in Africa befriends a bitter professional guide in a drama hampered by a poor script. Granger and Garas set out to hunt the rampaging elephant which killed Granger's friend. Granger thinks killing the beast will restore his courage and help him overcome the guilt he feels. Based on the novel "Gilligan's Last Elephant" by Gerald Hanley. **111m/C VHS.** Stewart Granger, Kaz Garas, Gabriella Licudi, Johnny Sekka, Liam Redmond; ***D:*** Henry Hathaway; ***W:*** John Gay; ***C:*** Ted Moore.

The Last Samurai ☙ **1990 (R)** Arab arms dealer Saxon arranges a fake kidnapping by rebel military leader Cele in order to keep their weapons deal a secret. But among the other hostages is mercenary Hendricksen, who escapes and wrecks havoc on their plotting. **94m/C VHS.** Lance Henriksen, John Saxon, Henry Cele, Arabella Holzbog, John Fujioka, James Ryan, Duncan Regehr, Lisa Eilbacher; ***D:*** Paul Mayersberg.

The Last Samurai ☙☙☙ ½ **2003 (R)** Embittered ex-Army Captain Nathan Algren (Cruise) is hired to train Japanese soldiers in modern warfare in order to quell a rebellion led by samurai Katsumoto (Watanabe). The inexperienced soldiers are forced to go into battle too early and, despite the superior firepower of their American rifles, are quickly defeated. Algren is taken prisoner and brought to a remote mountain village, where he learns the Japanese, swordplay, and the samurai's ancient code of honor(all in one winter). While Cruise is certainly the big name of the film, Watanabe is the one to watch as the magnetic and charismatic samurai leader. A bit over-romanticized, but the intricate battle sequences and spectacular cinematography make up for it. **150m/C VHS, DVD, Blu-ray Disc, HD DVD.** *US* Tom Cruise, Ken(saku) Watanabe, Timothy Spall, Billy Connolly, Tony Goldwyn, Masato Harada, Hiroyuki (Henry) Sanada, Koyuki, William Atherton, Scott Wilson, Togo Igawa, Shun Sugata, Shin Koyamada, Shichinosuke Nakamura; ***D:*** Edward Zwick; ***W:*** Edward Zwick, John Logan, Marshall Herskovitz; ***C:*** John Toll; ***M:*** Hans Zimmer.

The Last Season **WOOF!** **1987** Shoot 'em up involving a bunch of hunters. Their aimless destruction provokes the good guy to save the forest they are demolishing. A battle ensues. **90m/C VHS.** Christopher Gosch, Louise Dorsey, David A. Cox; ***D:*** Raja Zahr.

The Last Seduction ☙☙☙☙ **1994 (R)** Dahl, the master of modern noir, delivers another stylish hit exploring the darker side of urban life. Fiorentino gives the performance of her life as the most evil, rotten femme fatale to ever hit the big screen. Bridget (Fiorentino) rips off the money her husband Clay (Pullman) made in a pharmaceutical drug deal and leaves Manhattan for a small town in Upstate New York. Once there, she takes nice, naive Mike (Berg) as her lover, while Clay tries to ferret her out and get his money back. Lots of dry humor and a wickedly amusing heroine make for a devilishly entertaining film. **110m/C VHS, DVD.** Linda Fiorentino, Peter Berg, J.T. Walsh, Bill Nunn, Bill Pullman; ***D:*** John Dahl; ***W:*** Steve Barancik; ***C:*** Jeffrey Jur; ***M:*** Joseph Vitarelli. Ind. Spirit '95: Actress (Fiorentino); N.Y. Film Critics '94: Actress (Fiorentino).

The Last Seduction 2 ☙ **1998 (R)** Low-rent sequel finds Bridget Gregory (Severance) enjoying her spoils in Barcelona where she runs a scam on a phone sex service to get even more cash. But a detective, Murphy (Goddard), has been hired to track Bridget down—only the femme fatale has no intention of getting caught. Severance looks sexy but can't match predecessor Fiorentino's cold-blooded wiles. **96m/C VHS.** Joan Severance, Beth Goddard, Con O'Neill, Rocky Taylor, Dave Atkins; ***D:*** Terry Marcel; ***W:*** David Cummings; ***C:*** Geza Sinkovics; ***M:*** Jon Mellor. **VIDEO**

The Last Sentinel ☙ **2007 (R)** Loner Tallis (Wilson) is a scarred, part bionic super soldier battling cloned drones that have exceeded their protective purpose and are now exterminating humans. Together with an unnamed freedom fighter (Sackhoff), Tallis is out to destroy the drone police command center. If you like either of the leads, you may be able to sit through this crappy Sci-Fi Channel original. **94m/C DVD.** Don Wilson, Katee Sackhoff, Bokeem Woodbine, Keith David; ***D:*** Jesse Johnson; ***W:*** Jesse Johnson; ***C:*** Robert Hayes; ***M:*** Marcello De Francisci. **CABLE**

The Last September ☙☙ **1999 (R)** Danielstown is an Anglo-Irish estate located in County Cork in 1920—just four years after the Irish rebellion of 1916. Sir Richard (Gambon) and his wife, Lady Myra (Smith), have a houseful of guests, including Richard's overly romantic young niece Lois (Hawes), who's flirting with British officer, Gerald Colthurst (Tennant). But Lois has also taken to frequently visiting an old mill—where Irish guerilla fighter Peter (Lydon) is hiding out. Based on the novel by Elizabeth Bowen; first-time film director Warner is best known for her long career in the theatre. **103m/C VHS, DVD.** *IR GB FR* Maggie Smith, Michael Gambon, Keeley Hawes, David Tennant, Gary Lydon, Fiona Shaw, Lambert Wilson, Jane Birkin, Jonathan Slinger, Richard Roxburgh; ***D:*** Deborah Warner; ***W:*** John Banville; ***C:*** Slawomir Idziak; ***M:*** Zbigniew Preisner.

The Last Shot ☙☙ **2004 (R)** Negligible comedy is an exaggeration of a true story about the FBI, mobsters, and an eager beaver filmmaker. Set in 1985, undercover agent Joe Devine (Baldwin) is bent on ensnaring minor mobster Tommy Sanz (Shalhoub) who's taking bribes to keep teamsters in line on film shoots. So Joe poses as a producer and gets a script and director in one package with nebbish Steven Schats (Broderick), who doesn't know the whole thing is a hoax. The fantasy begins to take over as the production rolls along. Joan Cusack has an unbilled cameo as a movie exec. Too-crowded story collapses under the weight after a promising set-up. **93m/C DVD.** *US* Matthew Broderick, Alec Baldwin, Toni Collette, Tony Shalhoub, Calista Flockhart, Tim Blake Nelson, Ray Liotta, James Rebhorn, Buck Henry, Ian Gomez, Troy Winbush, Evan Jones, Glenn Morshower, Michael (Mike) Papajohn, Jon Polito, Joan Cusack, Sean M. Whalen; ***D:*** Jeff Nathanson; ***W:***

Jeff Nathanson; *C:* John Lindley; *M:* Rolfe Kent.

The Last Slumber Party WOOF!
1987 A slumber party is beset by a homicidal maniac. Heavy metal soundtrack. **89m/C VHS, DVD.** Jan Jensen, Nancy Meyer; *D:* Stephen Tyler; *W:* Stephen Tyler; *C:* Georges Cardona; *M:* John Brennan.

Last Song 🦴 1/2 **1980 (PG)** A singer's husband discovers a plot to cover up a fatal toxic-waste accident, and is killed because of it. It's up to her to warn the authorities before becoming the next victim. **96m/C VHS, DVD.** Lynda Carter, Ronny Cox, Nicholas Pryor, Paul Rudd, Jenny O'Hara; *D:* Alan J. Levi.

The Last Song 2010 Rebellious teen Veronica Miller is sent by her mother to Tybee Island, Georgia to stay with her divorced dad Steve, a former concert pianist, for the summer. The two have been estranged but they find common ground because of their mutual love of music. Based on the novel by Nicholas Sparks, who co-wrote the script. **m/C DVD.** Miley Cyrus, Greg Kinnear, Liam Hemsworth, Nick Searcy, Kelly Preston, Bobby Coleman, Hallock Beals; *D:* Julie Anne Robinson; *W:* Nicholas Sparks, Jeff Van Wie; *C:* John Lindley; *M:* Joseph Magee.

Last Stand at Saber River 🦴🦴 1/2
1996 Adaptation of Elmore Leonard's 1959 western novel finds Confederate Civil War vet Paul Cable (Selleck) coming home to his wife Martha's (Amis) family in Texas, having been wounded in the fighting. However, Martha was informed he was dead, so imagine her surprise. What Cable wants to do now is return to his pre-war life—a horse ranch in Arizona—but after making the journey the family discovers their ranch has been taken over by Union sympathizer Duane Kidston (Carradine) and he's not intending to let it go. Selleck was born to ride tall in the saddle. **95m/C VHS, DVD.** Tom Selleck, Suzy Amis, David Carradine, Keith Carradine, David Dukes, Tracey Needham, Rachel Duncan, Haley Joel Osment, Harry Carey Jr., Lumi Cavazos, Patrick Kilpatrick; *D:* Dick Lowry; *W:* Ronald M. Cohen; *C:* Ric Waite; *M:* David Shire. **CABLE**

The Last Starfighter 🦴🦴 **1984 (PG)** A young man who becomes an expert at a video game is recruited to fight in an intergalactic war. Listless adventure which explains where all those video games come from. Watch for O'Herlihy disguised as a lizard. **100m/C VHS, DVD, HD DVD.** Lance Guest, Robert Preston, Barbara Bosson, Dan O'Herlihy, Catherine Mary Stewart, Cameron Dye, Kimberly Ross, Wil Wheaton; *D:* Nick Castle; *W:* Jonathan Betuel; *C:* King Baggot; *M:* Craig Safan.

The Last Station 🦴🦴 1/2 **2009 (R)** In 1910, revered Russian author Leo Tolstoy (Plummer) is 82 but he still leads an energetic life on his country estate while trying (unsuccessfully) to hold to his utopian philosophy of celibacy, vegetarianism, pacifism, and social equality. His wife, the Countess Sofya (Mirren), is equally passionate, mercurial, and demanding, especially since—after being married for 48 years—she feels entitled to the inheritance of Tolstoy's literary estate. This legacy comes into dispute with the writer's pompous, zealous disciple Chertkov (Giamatti) who believes it to be the property of the Russian people and wants it in the public domain. To this purpose, Chertkov inserts a new assistant, the naive and worshipful Valentin (McAvoy), into the household as his spy. The film, however, belongs to Mirren and Plummer who offer seductive, intelligent performances. Adapted from the 1990 novel by Jay Parini. **112m/C DVD.** *GB GE RU* Christopher Plummer, Helen Mirren, Paul Giamatti, James McAvoy, Anne-Marie Duff, Kerry Condon, John Sessions, Patrick Kennedy; *D:* Michael Hoffman; *W:* Michael Hoffman; *C:* Sebastian Edscmid; *M:* Sergey Yevtushenko.

The Last Stop 🦴🦴 1/2 **1999 (R)** Colorado State Trooper Jason (Beach) gets stranded because of a snowstorm at the remote "The Last Stop Cafe and Motel." He greets the other stranded souls who include his ex-girlfriend Nancy (McGowan) and soon finds out that owner Fritz (Prochnow) has stumbled on a murder and a bag of cash that's probably the loot from a recent bank robbery. So just who's guilty? **94m/C VHS, DVD.** *CA* Adam Beach, Jurgen Prochnow, Rose McGowan, Callum Keith Rennie, Winston Rekert; *D:* Mark Malone; *W:* Bart Sumner; *C:* Tony Westman; *M:* Terry Frewer.

Last Stop for Paul 🦴🦴 **2008 (PG-13)** Writer/director Mandt and cinematographer Carter serve as both cast and crew in this genial road trip/travelogue. Charlie (Mandt) and Cliff (Carter) are L.A. salesmen and cubicle mates. Charlie has been pestering Cliff to join him on one of his international holidays and he finally agrees with a proviso: his best friend Paul has suddenly died and Cliff wants to scatter his ashes along their global trek. So they load the ashes into a thermos and are off on some mild misadventures with an ultimate destination of Thailand. **82m/C DVD.** Neil Mandt, Marc Carter, Heather Petrone, Eric Wing; *D:* Neil Mandt; *W:* Neil Mandt; *C:* Marc Carter; *M:* Doug Spicka.

Last Summer 🦴🦴 1/2 **1969 (R)** Three teenagers discover love, sex, and friendship on the white sands of Fire Island, N.Y. The summer vacation fantasy world they create shatters when a sweet but homely female teenager joins their group. Based on a novel by Evan Hunter. **97m/C VHS.** Barbara Hershey, Richard Thomas, Bruce Davison, Cathy Burns; *D:* Frank Perry.

Last Summer in the Hamptons 🦴🦴🦴 **1996 (R)** In her last film, Lindfors stars as Helena Mora, the matriarch of a charming three generation theatrical clan that gets together one weekend a year at her spacious, slightly run-down estate to participate in drama workshops and perform plays. When Helena is forced to sell the estate, the family reunites for one last weekend of bickering and performing. Featuring fine performances from the entire ensemble (including Lindfors' son and Jaglom's wife), Jaglom's touching and engaging tribute to his family gives nepotism a good name. **105m/C VHS, DVD.** Victoria Foyt, Viveca Lindfors, Jon Robin Baitz, Andre Gregory, Melissa Leo, Martha Plimpton, Roddy McDowall, Nick Gregory, Savannah Smith Boucher, Roscoe Lee Browne, Ron Rifkin, Diane Salinger, Brooke Smith, Kristopher Tabori, Holland Taylor, Henry Jaglom; *D:* Henry Jaglom; *W:* Victoria Foyt, Henry Jaglom; *C:* Hanania Baer.

The Last Supper 🦴🦴🦴 **1976** A repentant Cuban slave-owner in the 18th-century decides to cleanse his soul and convert his slaves to Christianity by having 12 of them reenact the Last Supper. Based on a true story. In Spanish with English subtitles. **110m/C VHS.** *CU* Nelson Villagra, Silvano Rey, Lamberto Garcia, Jose Antonio Rodriguez, Samuel Claxton, Mario Balmasada; *D:* Tomas Gutierrez Alea.

The Last Supper 🦴🦴 1/2 **1996 (R)** First-time feature director Title dishes out an extremely black comedy about a group of liberal roommates who accidentally kill a racist marine they've invited to dinner. This leads to the devious plan of inviting more right wingers over, baiting them into arguments about controversial topics, then killing and burying them in a vegetable garden. Somehow manages to avoid excessive preachiness despite taking on all political comers. Not exactly a great feast, but there's enough tasty snacks to be satisfying. Performances are good and the victims (led by Perlman's Limbaugh turn) really shine. Too bad their characters aren't on screen very long before they become tomato fertilizer. **91m/C VHS, DVD.** Cameron Diaz, Annabeth Gish, Ron Eldard, Jonathan Penner, Courtney B. Vance, Nora Dunn, Ron Perlman, Jason Alexander, Charles Durning, Mark Harmon, Bill Paxton; *D:* Stacy Title; *W:* Dan Rosen; *C:* Paul Cameron; *M:* Mark Mothersbaugh.

Last Tango in Paris 🦴🦴🦴 1/2 *L'Ultimo Tango a Parigi; Le Dernier Tango a Paris* **1973 (R)** Brando plays a middle-aged American who meets a French girl and tries to forget his wife's suicide with a short, extremely steamy affair. Bertolucci proves to be a master; Brando gives one of his best performances. Very controversial when made, still quite explicit. Visually stunning. The X-rated version, at 130 minutes, is also available. **126m/C VHS, DVD.** *FR IT* Marlon Brando, Maria Schneider, Jean-Pierre Leaud, Maria Michi, Massimo Girotti, Catherine Allegret; *D:* Bernardo Bertolucci; *W:* Bernardo Bertolucci; *C:* Vittorio Storaro; *M:* Gato Barbieri. N.Y. Film Critics '73: Actor (Brando); Natl. Soc. Film Critics '73: Actor (Brando).

The Last Templar 🦴🦴 **2009** Overextended quasi-historical adventure based on a novel by Raymond Khoury. Resourceful archeologist Tess Chaykin (Sorvino) is on the trail of a stolen artifact, originally possessed by the titular religious order that disappeared 700 years ago. The theft brings in FBI agent Sean Daley (Foley) and a sinister Vatican representative, Monsignor De Angelis (Garber), as well as a lot of international travel, conspiracy theories, shipwrecks, and a romantic interlude on an idyllic island. **170m/C DVD.** Mira Sorvino, Scott Foley, Victor Garber, Omar Sharif; *D:* Tessa la; *W:* Suzette Couture; *C:* Thomas Burstyn; *M:* Normand Corbeil. **TV**

The Last Temptation of Christ 🦴🦴🦴 1/2 **1988 (R)** Scorsese's controversial adaptation of the Nikos Kazantzakis novel, portraying Christ in his last year as an ordinary Israelite tormented by divine doubt, human desires and the voice of God. The controversy engulfing the film, as it was heavily protested and widely banned, tended to divert attention from what is an exceptional statement of religious and artistic vision. Excellent score by Peter Gabriel. **164m/C VHS, DVD.** *CA* Willem Dafoe, Harvey Keitel, Barbara Hershey, Harry Dean Stanton, Andre Gregory, David Bowie, Verna Bloom, Juliette Caton, John Lurie, Roberts Blossom, Irvin Kershner, Barry Miller, Tomas Arana, Nehemiah Persoff, Paul Herman, Illeana Douglas; *D:* Martin Scorsese; *W:* Paul Schrader; *C:* Michael Ballhaus; *M:* Peter Gabriel.

The Last Time 🦴🦴 **2006 (R)** Ted's (Keaton) a cynical middle-aged salesman in New York who decides to go after new partner Jamie's (Fraser) beautiful fiancee Belisa (Valletta). Belisa is bored with her boyish Midwesterner and ready to move on but the two guys' mental stability seems to short-circuit as they battle in boardroom and bedroom. Keaton's good but Fraser overplays the idiot role; Valletta slinks and pouts convincingly. **97m/C DVD.** Michael Keaton, Brendan Fraser, Amber Valletta, Daniel Stern, Neal McDonough, Michael Lerner; *D:* Michael Caleo; *W:* Michael Caleo; *C:* Tim Suhrstedt; *M:* Randy Edelman.

The Last Time I Committed Suicide 🦴🦴 **1996 (R)** Based on a Beat-era letter from Neal Cassady to Jack Kerouac and set in the late '40s, this insubstantial pic follows a 20-year-old Cassady (Jane) as he drifts into Denver's bars, and a friendship with poolhall regular Harry (Reeves), in order to escape dealing with girlfriend Joan's (Forlani) attempted suicide. Joan's eventual recovery leads Neal to consider settling down but he blows a job interview thanks to a drunken Harry and decides to take off instead. No background is provided on the characters so their actions are inexplicable although Jane offers some appeal. **93m/C VHS, DVD.** Thomas Jane, Keanu Reeves, Tom Bower, Adrien Brody, Claire Forlani, Marg Helgenberger, Gretchen Mol; *D:* Stephen Kay; *W:* Stephen Kay; *C:* Bobby Bukowski.

The Last Time I Saw Paris 🦴🦴 1/2
1954 A successful writer reminisces about his love affair with a wealthy American girl in post-WWII Paris. **116m/C VHS, DVD, Blu-ray Disc.** Elizabeth Taylor, Van Johnson, Walter Pidgeon, Roger Moore, Donna Reed, Eva Gabor; *D:* Richard Brooks; *W:* Richard Brooks, Julius J. Epstein, Philip G. Epstein; *C:* Joseph Ruttenberg; *M:* Conrad Salinger.

Last Time Out 🦴🦴 1/2 **1994 (PG-13)** Danny Dolan (Conrad) is a hard-partying college wide receiver who gets a shock when the father who abandoned him enrolls at his school to finish a college degree. Seems Joe (Beck) had his pro quarterback career cut short by a drinking problem and he's worried his son will follow in his unsteady footsteps. **92m/C VHS.** John Beck, Christian Conrad, Lori Werner, Gail Strickland, Betty Buckley; *D:* Don Fox Greene.

The Last Tomahawk 🦴🦴 **1965** Colorful and action packed reworking of Cooper's "Last of the Mohicans." **92m/C VHS.** *GE IT* Anthony Steffen, Karin Dor, Dan (Daniel, Danny) Martin, Joachim Fuchsberger; *D:* Harald Reinl.

The Last Train 🦴🦴 **1974** Romance most hopeless in the heart of France during zee beeg war. During the 1940 invasion of Paris a man and woman turn to each other for comfort when separated from their families while trying to escape the city. French, very French. **101m/C VHS, DVD.** *FR* Romy Schneider, Jean-Louis Trintignant, Maurice Biraud; *D:* Pierre Granier-Deferre; *W:* Pierre Granier-Deferre; *C:* Walter Wottitz; *M:* Philippe Sarde.

Last Train from Gun Hill 🦴🦴🦴
1959 An all-star cast highlights this suspenseful story of a U.S. marshall determined to catch the man who raped and murdered his wife. Excellent action packed western. **94m/C VHS, DVD.** Kirk Douglas, Anthony Quinn, Carolyn Jones, Earl Holliman, Brad Dexter, Brian Hutton, Ziva Rodann; *D:* John Sturges; *C:* Charles B(ryant) Lang Jr.

The Last Tycoon 🦴🦴🦴 **1976 (PG)** An adaptation of the unfinished F. Scott Fitzgerald novel about the life and times of a Hollywood movie executive of the 1920s. Confusing and slow moving despite a blockbuster conglomeration of talent. Joan Collins introduces the film. **123m/C VHS, DVD.** Robert De Niro, Tony Curtis, Ingrid Boulting, Jack Nicholson, Jeanne Moreau, Peter Strauss, Robert Mitchum, Theresa Russell, Donald Pleasence, Ray Milland, Dana Andrews, John Carradine, Anjelica Huston; *D:* Elia Kazan; *W:* Harold Pinter; *M:* Maurice Jarre.

The Last Unicorn 🦴🦴 1/2 **1982 (G)** Peter Beagle's popular tale of a beautiful unicorn who goes in search of her lost, mythical "family." **95m/C VHS, DVD.** *D:* Jules Bass; *W:* Peter S. Beagle; *M:* Jim Webb; *V:* Alan Arkin, Jeff Bridges, Tammy Grimes, Angela Lansbury, Mia Farrow, Robert Klein, Christopher Lee, Keenan Wynn.

The Last Valley 🦴🦴 **1971 (PG)** A scholar tries to protect a pristine 17th century Swiss valley, untouched by the Thirty Years War, from marauding soldiers. Historical action with an intellectual twist. **128m/C VHS, DVD.** Michael Caine, Omar Sharif, Florinda Bolkan, Nigel Davenport, Per Oscarsson, Arthur O'Connell; *D:* James Clavell; *W:* James Clavell; *C:* John Wilcox; *M:* John Barry.

The Last Voyage 🦴🦴 1/2 **1960** Suspenseful disaster film in which Stack and Malone play a married couple in jeopardy while on an ocean cruise. To make the film more realistic, the French liner Ile de France was actually used in the sinking scenes. Although a bit farfetched, film is made watchable because of fine performances and excellent camera work. **91m/C VHS, DVD.** Robert Stack, Dorothy Malone, George Sanders, Edmond O'Brien, Woody Strode, Jack Kruschen; *D:* Andrew L. Stone; *W:* Andrew L. Stone; *C:* Hal Mohr; *M:* Rudolph (Rudy) Schrager.

The Last Waltz 🦴🦴🦴 1/2 **1978 (PG)** Martin Scorsese filmed this rock documentary featuring the farewell performance of The Band, joined by a host of musical guests that they have been associated with over the years. Songs include: "Up On Cripple Creek," "Don't Do It," "The Night They Drove Old Dixie Down," "Stage Fright" (The Band), "Helpless" (Neil Young), "Coyote" (Joni Mitchell), "Caravan" (Van Morrison), "Further On Up the Road" (Eric Clapton), "Who Do You Love" (Ronnie Hawkins), "Mannish Boy" (Muddy Waters), "Evangeline" (Emmylou Harris), "Baby, Let Me Follow You Down" (Bob Dylan). **117m/C VHS, DVD, Blu-ray Disc.** *D:* Martin Scorsese; *C:* Michael Chapman.

Last War 🦴 **1968** A nuclear war between the United States and Russia triggers Armageddon. **79m/C VHS.** Frankie Sakai, Nobuko Otowa, Akira Takarada, Yuriko Hoshi; *D:* Shue Matsubayashi.

The Last Warrior 🦴 1/2 *Coastwatcher* **1989 (R)** A good-looking but exploitive "Hell in the Pacific" rip-off, as an American and a Japanese soldier battle it out alone on a remote island during WWII. **94m/C VHS, DVD.** Gary (Rand) Graham, Cary-Hiroyuki Tagawa, Maria Holvoe; *D:* Martin Wragge.

The Last Warrior 🦴🦴 **1999 (PG-13)** A devastating earthquake has turned Southern California into an island and Green Beret Nick Preston (Lundgren) takes it upon himself to help a group of survivors finds civilization. Of course there's a villain—a murderer (Mer) who has taken over a maximum security prison and has his own ideas.

95m/C VHS, DVD. Dolph Lundgren, Rebecca Cross, Julino Mer, Sherrie Alexander, Joe Michael Burke; *D:* Sheldon Lettich; *W:* Stephen J. Brackely, Pamela K. Long; *C:* David Garfinkel; *M:* David Michael Frank. **VIDEO**

The Last Wave ♪♪♪ **1977 (PG)** An Australian attorney takes on a murder case involving an aborigine and he finds himself becoming distracted by apocalyptic visions concerning tidal waves and drownings that seem to foretell the future. Weir's masterful creation and communication of time and place are marred by a somewhat pat ending. **109m/C VHS, DVD.** *AU* Richard Chamberlain, Olivia Hamnett, David Gulpilil, Frederick Parslow, Vivean Gray, Nadjiwarra Amagula, Roy Bara, Walter Amagula, Cedric Lalara, Morris Lalara, Peter Carroll; *D:* Peter Weir; *W:* Peter Weir, Tony Morphett, Petru Popescu; *C:* Russell Boyd.

The Last Winter ♪♪ **1984 (R)** An American woman fights to find her Israeli husband who has disappeared in the 1973 Yom Kippur War. Trouble is, an Israeli woman thinks the man she's looking for is really her husband too. **92m/C VHS.** *IS* Kathleen Quinlan, Yona Elian, Zipora Peled, Michael Schneider; *D:* Riki Shelach.

The Last Winter ♪♪ 1/2 **1989 (PG)** Ten-year-old Will (Murray) has always lived in the country and finds it hard to accept his parents' decision to move to the city. But with the help of his grandfather (Parkes), Will begins to understand about change and growing up. **103m/C VHS.** *CA* Joshua Murray, Gerard Parkes, David Ferry, Wanda Cannon, Marsha Moreau, Nathaniel Moreau, Katie Murray; *D:* Aaron Kim Johnston; *W:* Aaron Kim Johnston; *C:* Ian Elkin; *M:* Victor Davies.

The Last Winter ♪♪ **2006** Atmospheric eco-disaster pic that uses its locations (in Alaska and Iceland) to tell a disturbing tale. Eco-author James Hoffman (LeGros) and his assistant Elliot (Harrold) have been hired as PR props by North Industries. The company wants to begin oil drilling in the previously protected Arctic National Wildlife Refuge and they are to accompany the first team and say everything is hunky-dory. Team leader Pollack (Perlman) scoffs at Hoffman's global-warming scenarios but the permafrost is melting and releasing who knows what into the air and maybe that's why everyone starts acting hinky. **101m/C DVD.** *IC US* James LeGros, Ron Perlman, Connie Britton, Jamie Harrold, Pato Hoffmann, Kevin Corrigan, Zachary Gifford, Joanne Shenandoah; *D:* Larry Fessenden; *W:* Larry Fessenden, Robert Leaver; *C:* G. Magni Agustsson; *M:* Jeff Grace.

The Last Winters ♪♪ 1/2 **1971** From Jean Charles Tacchella, writer-producer-director of "Cousin Cousine," comes his first short film about an old couple's bittersweet romance. In French with English subtitles. **23m/C VHS.** *FR* *D:* Jean-Charles Tacchella.

Last Witness ♪ **1988** A man on the run from the government claims that he is innocent and was unjustly persecuted, but the government sees him as a dangerous threat. Nothing will stop the hunt for the escaped man, no matter what it costs. **85m/C VHS.** Mike Schuster, Jeff Henderson; *D:* E. Bruce Weiss.

The Last Woman on Earth WOOF! **1961** Two men vie for the affections of the sole surviving woman after a vague and unexplained disaster of vast proportions. Robert Towne, who appears herein under the pseudonym Edward Wain, wrote the script (his first screenwriting effort). You might want to watch this if it were the last movie on earth, although Corman fans will probably love it. **71m/C VHS, DVD.** Antony Carbone, Edward (Robert Towne) Wain, Betsy Jones-Moreland; *D:* Roger Corman; *W:* Robert Towne.

The Last Word ♪♪ *Danny Travis* **1980 (PG)** Comedy drama about struggling inventor Harris fighting to protect his home, family, and neighbors from a corrupt real estate deal involving shady politicians, angry policemen, and a beautiful TV reporter. **103m/C VHS.** Richard Harris, Karen Black, Martin Landau, Dennis Christopher, Bill McGuire, Christopher Guest, Penelope Milford, Michael Pataki; *W:* Michael Varhol, L.M. Kit Carson.

The Last Word ♪♪ **1995 (R)** Journalist Martin (Hutton) writes a newspaper column, often featuring characters based on hometown Detroit mob figures, with info supplied to him by his friend, Doc (Pantoliano), who owes the gangsters some big bucks. Doc also introduces Martin to his latest column subject—stripper Caprice (Burke)—and, thanks again to Doc, a Hollywood studio gets interested in filming her story but wants more sex and violence, which means Martin will be betraying her deepest secrets. Now, he must choose between love, success, or friendship. **95m/C VHS, DVD.** Timothy Hutton, Joe Pantoliano, Michelle Rene Thomas, Chazz Palminteri, Tony Goldwyn, Richard Dreyfuss, Cybill Shepherd, Jimmy Smits; *D:* Tony Spiridakis; *W:* Tony Spiridakis; *C:* Zoltan David; *M:* Paul Buckmaster.

The Last Word ♪♪ **2008 (R)** Evan (Bentley) composes epitaphs for people planning suicides. Paying his respects to a late client, Evan meets the man's sister, Charlotte (Ryder), and lies that they were friends in college. Extroverted Charlotte insists upon befriending morose Evan, which has him neglecting his work to placate her. There's a surprise to tidy up the ending. **95m/C DVD.** Wes Bentley, Winona Ryder, Ray Romano, Allan Rich, Gina Hecht; *D:* Geoffrey Haley; *W:* Geoffrey Haley; *C:* Kees Van Oostrum; *M:* John Swihart.

Last Year at Marienbad ♪♪♪ *L'Anee Derniere a Marienbad* **1961** A young man tries to lure a mysterious woman to run away with him from a hotel in France. Once a hit on the artsy circuit, it's most interesting for its beautiful photography. In French with English subtitles. **93m/B VHS, DVD.** *FR IT* Delphine Seyrig, Giorgio Albertazzi, Sacha (Sascha) Pitoeff, Luce Garcia-Ville; *D:* Alain Resnais; *W:* Alain Resnais, Alain Robbe-Grillet; *C:* Sacha Vierny; *M:* Francis Seyrig.

L'Atalante ♪♪♪ 1/2 *Le Chaland qui Passe* **1934** Vigo's great masterpiece, a slight story about a husband and wife quarreling, splitting, and reuniting around which has been fashioned one of the cinema's greatest poetic films. In French with English subtitles. **82m/B VHS, DVD.** *FR* Dita Parlo, Jean Daste, Michel Simon; *D:* Jean Vigo; *W:* Jean Vigo, Jean Guinee, Albert Riera; *C:* Boris Kaufman, Louis Berger; *M:* Maurice Jaubert.

Late August, Early September ♪♪ 1/2 *Fin Aout Debut Septembre* **1998** Self-absorbed group of friends and lovers find their relationships in flux and their mortality in question over the course of a year (from August of one year to the September of the next). Adrien (Cluzet) is a serious writer whose work elicits critical but not commercial acclaim. His indecisive friend Gabriel (Amalric) is an editor at a publishing house who has split with long-time love, Jenny (Balibar), for the young Anne (Ledoyen). Meanwhile, Adrien, who's learned he has a terminal illness, plunges into a reckless affair with the teenaged Vera (Hansen-Love). French with subtitles. **112m/C VHS, DVD.** *FR* Mathieu Amalric, Virginie Ledoyen, Francois Cluzet, Jeanne Balibar, Alex Descas, Arsinee Khanjian, Mia Hansen-Love; *D:* Olivier Assayas; *W:* Olivier Assayas; *C:* Denis Lenoir; *M:* Ali Sarka Toure.

Late Bloomers ♪♪ **1995** Romantic comedy focuses on what happens when two Midwestern women fall in love. Math teacher/basketball coach Dinah (Nelson) is friendly with fellow teacher Rom (Carter) and his wife, Carly (Hennigan), the high school secretary. A misinterpreted note, an impulsive kiss, and Carly's soon out of door and living with Dinah, which leads to a community uproar. The two leads are likeable but the other characters and the situation are heavily cliched. **105m/C VHS, DVD.** Connie Nelson, Dee Hennigan, Gary Carter, Lisa Peterson; *D:* Julia Dyer; *W:* Gretchen Dyer; *C:* Bill Schwarz; *M:* Ted Pine.

Late Chrysanthemums ♪♪ *Bangiku* **1954** A middle-aged geisha has settled into comfortable retirement as a money lender. When she hears a former lover wants to visit her, she tries to recapture her old glamour only to be disillusioned. Based on a short story by Fumiko Hayashi. In Japanese with English subtitles. **101m/B VHS.** *JP* Haruko Sugimura, Chikako Hosokawa, Sadako Sawahura; *D:* Mikio Naruse.

Late Extra ♪♪ **1935** A novice reporter attempts to track down a notorious bank robber and gets some help from a savvy female journalist. Mason's first role of substance. **69m/B VHS.** *GB* Virginia Cherrill, James Mason, Alastair Sim, Ian Colin, Clifford McLaglen, Cyril Cusack, David Horne, Antoinette Cellier, Donald Wolfit, Michael Wilding; *D:* Albert Parker.

Late for Dinner ♪♪ **1991 (PG)** In 1962 Willie, a young, married man, and his best friend Frank are framed by a sleazy land developer. On the run, the two decide to become guinea pigs in a cryonics experiment and wind up frozen for 29 years. It's now 1991 and Willie wants to find his family—only his wife is middle-aged and his daughter is all grown-up. Can he make a life with them again or has time indeed passed him by? **93m/C VHS, DVD.** Brian Wimmer, Peter Berg, Marcia Gay Harden, Peter Gallagher, Ross Malinger; *D:* W.D. Richter; *W:* Mark Andrus.

Late Last Night ♪♪ **1999 (R)** After a big fight with his wife, Dan (Estevez) hooks up with best pal, Jeff (Weber), who proposes they cut loose for the evening. So they pick up a couple of women and proceed to party, which eventually lands them in the slammer. **90m/C VHS, DVD.** Emilio Estevez, Steven Weber, Catherine O'Hara, Leah Lail, Lisa Robin Kelly; *D:* Steven Brill.

Late Marriage ♪♪ 1/2 *Hatouna Mehuheret* **2001** Thirty-one-year-old Zaza (Ashkenazi) is an Israeli of Georgian descent who lives in a very close-knit and traditional community. His parents are appalled that he's still single and keep setting him up with virginal likely prospects. They don't know that he's devoted to Judith (Elkabetz), who's not only slightly older (she's 34) but a divorced single mom and Moroccan! When they do find out, they barge into her apartment—humiliating both. But is Zaza strong enough to defy conventions and stay with his true love? In Georgian and Hebrew with subtitles. **100m/C VHS, DVD.** *IS FR* Lior Loui Ashkenazi, Ronit Elkabetz, Moni Moshonov, Lili Kosashvili, Sapir Kugman, Aya Steinovits Laor; *D:* Dover Kosashvili; *W:* Dover Kosashvili; *C:* Dani Schneor; *M:* Joseph Bardanashvili.

The Late Shift ♪♪ 1/2 **1996 (R)** Cable adaptation of Bill Carter's book chronicling the follies surrounding NBC's "The Tonight Show" succession battle between Jay Leno (Roebuck) and Dave Letterman (Higgins). It's the behind-the-scenes dealmakers that really steal the show, however, including Jay's profane manager Helen Kushnick (Bates) and superagent Michael Ovitz (Williams), who ultimately orchestrated Dave's move to rival CBS. Both Letterman and Leno made the movie/book fodder for their opening monologues. **96m/C VHS, DVD.** Daniel Roebuck, John Michael Higgins, Kathy Bates, Treat Williams, Bob Balaban, Ed Begley Jr., Rich Little, Sandra Bernhard, Peter Jurasik, Reni Santoni, John Kapelos, John Getz, Lawrence Pressman; *D:* Betty Thomas; *W:* Bill Carter, George Armitage; *C:* Mac Ahlberg; *M:* Ira Newborn. **CABLE**

The Late Show ♪♪♪ **1977 (PG)** A veteran private detective finds his world turned upside down when his ex-partner comes to visit and winds up dead, and a flaky woman whose cat is missing decides to become his sidekick. Carney and Tomlin are fun to watch in this sleeper, a tribute to the classic detective film noirs. **93m/C VHS, DVD.** Art Carney, Lily Tomlin, Bill Macy, Eugene Roche, Joanna Cassidy, John Considine; *D:* Robert Benton; *W:* Robert Benton. Natl. Soc. Film Critics '77: Actor (Carney).

Late Spring ♪♪♪♪ **1949** An exquisite Ozu masterpiece. A young woman lives with her widowed father for years. He decides to remarry so that she can begin life for herself. Highly acclaimed, in Japanese with English subtitles. Reworked in 1960 as "Late Autumn." **107m/B VHS, DVD.** *JP* Setsuko Hara, Chishu Ryu, Jun Usami, Haruko Sugimura; *D:* Yasujiro Ozu.

Late Summer Blues ♪♪ *Blues La-Chofesh Ha-Godol* **1987** Experience the life and death decisions of seven teenagers who have finished their finals and face now a more difficult test: serving in the Israeli Armed Forces in the Suez Canal. In Hebrew with English subtitles. **101m/C VHS.** *IS* Dor Zweigenbom, Shahar Segal, Yoav Zafir; *D:* Renen Schorr.

The Lathe of Heaven ♪♪ 1/2 **1980** In a late 20th century world suffocating from pollution, George Orr (Davison) visits a dream specialist because he can dream things into being. The specialist wants George to dream of a world free from war, pestilence, and overpopulation, but these dreams have disastrous side effects. Based on the futuristic novel by Ursula K. LeGuin. **100m/C VHS, DVD.** Bruce Davison, Kevin Conway, Margaret Avery, Peyton E. Park; *D:* David Loxton, Fred Barzyk; *W:* Roger E. Swaybill, Diane English; *C:* Robbie Greenberg; *M:* Michael Small. **TV**

The Lathe of Heaven ♪♪ **2002** Remake of the 1980 PBS pic based on the 1971 novel by Ursula LeGuin. George Orr (Haas) refuses to sleep because when he does, his dreams alter reality. Or at least George thinks so, which is why he's forced to see a court-appointed shrink, Dr. William Haber (Caan), after a drug overdose. But when Haber discovers George's ability is real, he uses it for his own purpose. **100m/C VHS, DVD.** Lukas Haas, James Caan, Lisa Bonet, David Strathairn, Sheila McCarthy, Serge Houde; *D:* Philip Haas; *W:* Alan Sharp; *C:* Pierre Mignot; *M:* Angelo Badalamenti. **CABLE**

The Lather Effect ♪♪ **2006** High school friends from the '80s reunite for a wild weekend and find they're older but no wiser. They face the morning after cleaning up after their shindig, reminiscing, and revealing various issues and disappointments. Situations are predictable, but if you lived through the era they'll be familiar (as will the music). **95m/C DVD.** Connie Britton, Sarah Clarke, Tate Donovan, David Herman, Peter Facinelli, Caitlin Keats, William Mapother, Ione Skye, Eric Stoltz, Kevin Heffernan, Monica Keena; *D:* Sarah Kelly; *W:* Sarah Kelly, Tim Talbott; *C:* Eric Haase; *M:* Dominic Kelly.

Latin Dragon ♪ 1/2 **2003 (R)** Home sweet home is in ruins when Danny Silva returns from war duty to find gangs in charge of his L.A. 'hood. Disgusted, he takes it upon himself to hunt down the rotten head honchos behind the chaos. Typical war-hero-turned-vigilante fare. **101m/C VHS, DVD.** Gary Busey, Lorenzo Lamas, Robert LaSardo, Pepe Serna, Fabian Carrillo, Joyce Giraud, Luis Antonio Ramos, James Hong; *D:* Scott Thomas; *W:* Fabian Carrillo, James Becket; *C:* Mark Eberle; *M:* H. Scott Salinas. **VIDEO**

Latin Lovers ♪♪ 1/2 **1953** Turner plays a wealthy heiress who can't decide if men love her for herself or her money in this festive Brazilian romp. Lund and Montalban portray the suitors vying for her affection. Although not one of MGM's best musicals, the music is good because of the Brodszky-Robin tunes. ♫ Night and You; Carlotta, You Gotta Be Mine; A Little More of Your Armor; Come To My Arms; I Had To Kiss You. **104m/C VHS.** Lana Turner, Ricardo Montalban, John Lund, Louis Calhern, Jean Hagen, Eduard Franz, Beulah Bondi; *D:* Mervyn LeRoy; *W:* Isobel Lennart.

Latino ♪♪ 1/2 **1985** The self-tortured adventures of a Chicano Green Beret who, while fighting a covert U.S. military action in war-torn Nicaragua, begins to rebel against the senselessness of the war. **108m/C VHS.** Robert Beltran, Annette Cardona, Tony Plana, James Karen, Ricardo Lopez, Luis Torrentes, Juan Carlos Ortiz, Julio Medina; *D:* Haskell Wexler; *W:* Haskell Wexler; *M:* Diane Louie.

Latitude Zero ♪♪ *Ido Zero Daisakusen; Atragon II; Latitude Zero Military Tactics; Latitude Zero: Big Military Operation* **1969** A quake traps three men in a bathyscaphe, but they're rescued by a 200-year-old man in a high tech submarine built in the 1800s and taken to an underground paradise called Latitude Zero, where an evil scientist attempts to destroy them with monsters, James Bond gadgets, and his own super submarine. He even transplants his partner's brain into the body of a lion onto which he's grafted wings. A Japanese and American co-production from the writer of "Them!" and the director of "Godzilla." The effects haven't aged well, but it is considered a classic by many vintage scifi fans. **99m/C DVD.** *JP* Cesar Romero, Akira Takarada, Masumi Okada, Richard Jaeckel, Joseph Cotton, Patricia Medina, Tetsu Nakamura, Linda Haynes, Mari Nakayama, Akihiko Kurata, Hikaru Kuroki, Susumu Kurobe, Haruo Nakajima; *D:* Ishio Honda; *W:* Warren

Lewis, Shinichi Sekizawa, Ted Sherdeman; ***C:*** Taiichi Kankura; ***M:*** Akira Ifukube.

Latter Days 🦴🦴 1/2 **2004** Melodramatic gay romance finds wide-eyed young Aaron Davis (Sandvoss), an earnest Mormon missionary from Idaho, sent to bring the good word to the heathens of West Hollywood. This would include his new neighbor, handsome, heedless gay waiter Christian (Ramsey), who sets out to seduce the virgin on a bet. Seeing as how this is a really big religious no-no for Aaron, you know there's trouble ahead, even as the hot twosome find themselves falling in love. Bisset adds some class as sardonic restaurant owner and surrogate mother figure Lila. Writer-director Cox (directing his first film) is a former Mormon and has some definite issues to air but he manages to offer a certain sweetness along with all the overwrought angst. **108m/C DVD.** *US* Steve Sandross, Wes Ramsey, Rebekah Jordan, Khary Payton, Amber Benson, Jacqueline Bisset, Joseph Gordon-Levitt, Erik Palladino, Mary Kay Place, Rob McElhenney, David Poser, Jim Ortlieb; ***D:*** C. Jay Cox; ***W:*** C. Jay Cox; ***C:*** Carl F. Bartels; ***M:*** Eric Allaman.

L'Auberge Espagnole 🦴🦴🦴 *The Spanish Apartment; Euro Pudding* **2002 (R)** Exuberant comedy that follows a French student during an eventful year in Barcelona. Xavier (Duris) is advised to study Spanish and Spanish economics in order to secure a government job. So he signs up for a European exchange program, bids goodbye to girlfriend Martine (Tantou), and heads to Spain where he eventually moves into a lively rooming house filled with fellow students. Xavier is al ittle bit of a rogue and is soon squiring around (at her husband's request), the shy wife (Godreche) of an obnoxious countryman and developing a crush on a Belgian exchange student (de France), who is interested in Xavier only as a friend. Barcelona's baroque charms are also another character in Klapisch's light-hearted production. English, French, and Spanish with subtitles. **117m/C VHS, DVD.** *FR SP* Romain Duris, Audrey Tautou, Judith Godreche, Cecile de France, Kelly Reilly, Kevin Bishop, Xavier De Guillebon; ***D:*** Cedric Klapisch; ***W:*** Cedric Klapisch; ***C:*** Dominique Colin.

Lauderdale WOOF! *Spring Fever USA; Spring Break USA* **1989 (R)** Two college schmoes hit the beach looking for beer and babes. Few laughs for the sober and mature. Surf's down in this woofer. **91m/C VHS, DVD.** Darrel Guilbeau, Michelle Kemp, Jeff Greenman, Lara Belmonte; ***D:*** Bill Milling; ***W:*** Bill Milling.

Laughing at Danger 🦴🦴 1/2 **1924** Talmadge is the supposedly playboy son of a Washington politician. In reality, he's the dashing "Mr. Pep" who comes to the rescue of a scientist who has invented a death ray and is being stalked by agents of a sinister foreign power. Talmadge was a fine silent-screen action star, though his heavy German action proved a barrier with sound films. **45m/B VHS.** Richard Talmadge, Joseph Girard, Eva Novak, Joe Harrington, Stanhope Wheatcroft; ***D:*** James W. Horne.

Laughing at Life 🦴 1/2 **1933** A mercenary leaves his family to fight in South America. Years later, when he is the leader of said country, he meets a man who turns out to be his son. Rehashed plot has been done better. **72m/B VHS, DVD.** Victor McLaglen, William "Stage" Boyd, Lois Wilson, Henry B. Walthall, Regis Toomey; ***D:*** Ford Beebe.

The Laughing Policeman 🦴🦴 1/2 *An Investigation of Murder* **1974 (R)** Two antagonistic cops embark on a vengeful hunt for a mass murderer through the seamy underbelly of San Francisco. Adapted from the Swedish novel by Per Wahloo and Maj Sjowallo. **111m/C VHS, DVD.** Walter Matthau, Bruce Dern, Louis Gossett Jr.; ***D:*** Stuart Rosenberg; ***M:*** Charles Fox.

Laughing Sinners 🦴🦴 **1931** Society girl Crawford attempts suicide after Hamilton dumps her and is rescued by Gable—a Salvation Army worker! Predictable drama with some unintentionally funny moments. Gable and Crawford were having an off-screen romance at the time which accounts for the sparks generated on-screen. Based on the play "Torch Song" by Kenyon Nicholson. **71m/B VHS.** Joan Crawford, Neil Hamilton, Clark Gable, Marjorie Rambeau, Guy Kibbee, Cliff Edwards, Roscoe Karns; ***D:*** Harry Beaumont; ***C:*** Charles Rosher.

Laura 🦴🦴🦴🦴 **1944** Detective Mark McPherson (Andrews) assigned to the murder investigation of the late Laura Hunt (Tierney) finds himself falling in love with her painted portrait and discovering some surprising facts. Superb collaboration by excellent cast and fine director. Superior suspense yarn, enhanced by a love story. Based on the novel by Vera Caspary. Rouben Mamoulian was the original director, then Preminger finished the film. **85m/B VHS, DVD.** Gene Tierney, Dana Andrews, Clifton Webb, Lane Chandler, Vincent Price, Judith Anderson, Grant Mitchell, Dorothy Adams, Ron Dunn, Clyde Fillmore, James Flavin; ***D:*** Otto Preminger; ***W:*** Elizabeth Reinhardt, Jay Dratler, Samuel Hoffenstein, Ring Lardner Jr.; ***C:*** Joseph LaShelle; ***M:*** David Raksin. Oscars '44: B&W Cinematog., Natl. Film Reg. '99.

Laurel & Hardy and the Family 1933 Four zany comedies seeing the boys in all kinds of trouble involving homelife. Includes "Brats," "Perfect Day," "Their First Mistake" and "Twice Two." **85m/B VHS.** Stan Laurel, Oliver Hardy.

Laurel & Hardy: Another Fine Mess 🦴🦴 1/2 **1930** The boys find themselves the owners of a magnificent Beverly Hills mansion. Yeah right. Lots of physical comedy and hilarious dialogue with a "special appearance" by Laurel in drag as a maid. Based on a sketch written by Laurel's father. Colorized. **25m/C VHS, DVD.** Stan Laurel, Oliver Hardy; ***D:*** James Parrott; ***W:*** H.M. Walker; ***C:*** Jack Stevens; ***M:*** Leroy Shield.

Laurel & Hardy: At Work 1932 Three short films collected here. Includes "Towed in a Hole," "Busy Bodies," and "The Music Box." **70m/B VHS.** Oliver Hardy, Stan Laurel.

Laurel & Hardy: Be Big 🦴🦴 1/2 **1931** Stan and Ollie ditch their wives to go to a swinging stag party at their club. Of course everything goes wrong in their quest for lascivious fun. Filled with tons of sight gags. Colorized. **25m/C VHS, DVD.** Stan Laurel, Oliver Hardy; ***D:*** James Parrott; ***W:*** H.M. Walker; ***C:*** Art Lloyd; ***M:*** Leroy Shield.

Laurel & Hardy: Below Zero 🦴🦴 1/2 **1930** It's the Great Depression of 1929, and Laurel and Hardy are about as depressed as you can get, working for pennies as street musicians. Their luck changes when they find a full wallet lying in the snow. But, as the saying goes, a fool and his money are soon parted. Colorized. **25m/C VHS.** Stan Laurel, Oliver Hardy; ***D:*** James Parrott; ***W:*** H.M. Walker; ***C:*** George Stevens.

Laurel & Hardy: Berth Marks 1929 Laurel & Hardy take a hilarious train trip to Pottsville for a vaudeville performance. Colorized. **25m/C VHS.** Stan Laurel, Oliver Hardy; ***D:*** Lewis R. Foster; ***W:*** H.M. Walker, Leo McCarey; ***C:*** Len Powers.

Laurel & Hardy: Blotto 1930 Laurel and Hardy want to get drunk, but they can't get any alcohol and their wives won't let them get away. When they finally do escape, they wind up at the swanky Rainbow Club, where they're drastically out of their element. Colorized. **25m/C VHS.** Stan Laurel, Oliver Hardy; ***D:*** Lewis R. Foster; ***W:*** H.M. Walker, Leo McCarey; ***C:*** George Stevens; ***M:*** Nathaniel Shilkert.

Laurel & Hardy: Brats 🦴🦴 1/2 **1930** Stan and Ollie play not only themselves but also their children when their wives go away and they have to babysit. The children, of course, wreak havoc wherever they go, playing on the hilariously oversized props and sets. One of the few films in which only Laurel and Hardy appear. Colorized. **25m/C VHS.** Stan Laurel, Oliver Hardy; ***D:*** James W. Horne; ***W:*** H.M. Walker, Leo McCarey; ***C:*** George Stevens.

Laurel & Hardy: Chickens Come Home 🦴🦴 1/2 **1931** Ollie is running for mayor, but things go crazy when an ex-girlfriend shows up and blackmails him with a compromising photo. Stan, acting as Ollie's campaign manager, tries to help, but things just get worse. A remake of their own film "Love 'Em and Weep." Colorized. **25m/C VHS, DVD.** Stan Laurel, Oliver Hardy, James Finlayson; ***D:*** James W. Horne; ***W:*** H.M. Walker; ***C:*** Jack Stevens.

Laurel & Hardy: Hog Wild 🦴🦴 1/2 **1930** Hilarity ensues when Laurel and Hardy try to fix the radio antenna on Hardy's roof. It may sound easy, but come on, this is Laurel and Hardy. Colorized. **25m/C VHS.** Stan Laurel, Oliver Hardy; ***D:*** James Parrott; ***W:*** H.M. Walker; ***C:*** Jack Stevens; ***M:*** William Axt.

Laurel & Hardy: Laughing Gravy 🦴🦴 1/2 **1931** The boys' pet dog, oddly named Laughing Gravy, gets them into trouble with their landlord who keeps trying to evict them. So funny even the mashed potatos will laugh. Colorized. **25m/C VHS.** Stan Laurel, Oliver Hardy.

Laurel & Hardy: Men O'War 1929 Laurel & Hardy star as two sailors on shore leave trying to impress the ladies. Things go from bad to worse when they take two ladies out on a date. Features the memorable soda fountain and canoe scenes. Colorized. **25m/C VHS.** Stan Laurel, Oliver Hardy, Gloria Greer, Anne Cornwall; ***D:*** Lewis R. Foster; ***W:*** H.M. Walker, Leo McCarey; ***C:*** George Stevens.

Laurel & Hardy: Night Owls 1930 When a cop needs to capture some crooks to save his job, he sets up a fake break-in and catches two bungling burglars—Laurel and Hardy. Lots of sight gags and slapstick. Colorized. **25m/C VHS.** Stan Laurel, Oliver Hardy, Edgar Kennedy; ***D:*** James Parrott; ***W:*** H.M. Walker; ***C:*** George Stevens; ***M:*** Marvin Hatley, Harry von Tilzer.

Laurel & Hardy On the Lam 1930 Four Laurel & Hardy classics are collected, including "Scram," "Another Fine Mess," "One Good Turn," and "Going Bye-Bye." **90m/B VHS.** Oliver Hardy, Stan Laurel.

Laurel & Hardy: Perfect Day 1929 Laurel & Hardy plan a quiet picnic with their wives, but car trouble turns their day into a disaster. Colorized. **25m/C VHS.** Stan Laurel, Oliver Hardy, Edgar Kennedy; ***D:*** James Parrott; ***W:*** H.M. Walker; ***M:*** Nathaniel Shilkert.

Laurel & Hardy Spooktacular 1934 Stan and Ollie scream through four spooky comedies, including "The Live Ghost," "The Laurel-Hardy Murder Case," "Oliver the Eighth" and "Dirty Work." **95m/B VHS.** Stan Laurel, Oliver Hardy.

Laurel & Hardy: Stan "Helps" Ollie 1933 Four Stan and Ollie classics including "County Hospital," "Me and My Pal," "Hog Wild" and "Helpmates." **85m/B VHS.** Stan Laurel, Oliver Hardy.

Laurel & Hardy: The Hoose-Gow 1929 Laurel and Hardy are mistakenly picked up by the police and sent to prison to do hard labor. Hilarity ensues when they try to convince the warden that they're innocent. Colorized. **25m/C VHS.** Stan Laurel, Oliver Hardy; ***D:*** James Parrott; ***W:*** H.M. Walker; ***C:*** George Stevens; ***M:*** William Axt.

Laurel Avenue 🦴🦴 1/2 **1993** Looks at the life of an extended working-class black family in St. Paul, Minnesota, over a busy weekend. Large cast includes family heads Jake and Maggie who live with their basketball coach son, teenage daughter, and elderly uncle. Other children include fraternal twin Yolanda, a cop married to a white man, who knows sister Rolanda's (a recovering drug addict) son is a dealer. Their brother Marcus manages a Mafia-controlled clothing store and is involved in some shady deals while brother Woody is an aspiring musician. The four households are all united at a disasterous Sunday afternoon party. **156m/C VHS.** Mary Alice, Mel Winkler, Scott Lawrence, Malinda Williams, Jay Brooks, Juanita Jennings, Rhonda Stubbins White, Monte Russell, Vonte Sweet; ***D:*** Carl Franklin; ***W:*** Michael Henry Brown, Paul Aaron. **CABLE**

Laurel Canyon 🦴🦴 **2002 (R)** Aspiring shrink Sam (Bale) brings fiance and fellow doctor Alex (Beckinsale) home to meet mom Jane (McDormand), a bohemian record producer with a very non-maternal view of sex and drugs—she likes 'em, a lot. Sam still resents her for the way he was brought up, and she hasn't changed much, as she's currently sleeping with the young musician (Nivola) whose album she's producing. Alex is soon drawn into the care-free world around her as Sam is tempted by a collegue at work. Cholodenko tries to recreate the insight and verve of her debut, "High Art," but falls short by making the story predictable and the characters flat. The only one who comes alive is Jane, and that's due more to McDormand's performance than anything she's given to work with. Nivola has a nice turn as her beau of the month. **101m/C VHS, DVD.** *US* Frances McDormand, Christian Bale, Kate Beckinsale, Alessandro Nivola, Natascha (Natasha) McElhone; ***D:*** Lisa Cholodenko; ***W:*** Lisa Cholodenko; ***C:*** Wally Pfister; ***M:*** Craig (Shudder to Think) Wedren.

The Lavender Hill Mob 🦴🦴🦴 1/2 **1951** A prim and prissy bank clerk schemes to melt the bank's gold down and re-mold it into miniature Eiffel Tower paper-weights for later resale. The foolproof plan appears to succeed, but then develops a snag. An excellent comedy that is still a delight to watch. **78m/B VHS, DVD.** *GB* Alec Guinness, Stanley Holloway, Sidney James, Alfie Bass, Marjorie Fielding, John Gregson; ***Cameos:*** Audrey Hepburn; ***D:*** Charles Crichton; ***W:*** T.E.B. Clarke. Oscars '52: Story & Screenplay; British Acad. '51: Film.

L'Avventura 🦴🦴🦴 1/2 *The Adventure* **1960** A stark, dry and minimalist exercise in narrative by Antonioni, dealing with the search for a girl on an Italian island by her lethargic socialite friends who eventually forget her in favor of their own preoccupations. A highly acclaimed, innovative film; somewhat less effective now, in the wake of many film treatments of angst and amorality. Subtitled in English. Laser edition features the original trailer, commentary and a collection of still photographs from Antonioni's work. **145m/C VHS, DVD.** *IT* Monica Vitti, Gabriele Ferzetti, Lea Massari, Dominique Blanchar, James Addams; ***D:*** Michelangelo Antonioni; ***W:*** Tonino Guerra, Michelangelo Antonioni; ***C:*** Aldo Scavarda; ***M:*** Giovanni Fusco. Cannes '60: Special Jury Prize.

Law Abiding Citizen 🦴🦴 **2009 (R)** After 10 years, Clyde Shelton (Butler) returns to Philadelphia to get his own justice against Assistant District Attorney Nick Rice (Foxx) the prosecutor who made an expedient deal with one of the suspects. Brutally dispatching the perps is only the beginning for Clyde. Starts out as an effective revenge thriller, but the plot holes and increasing absurdity take the whole thing down. **109m/C DVD.** *US* Gerard Butler, Jamie Foxx, Leslie Bibb, Colm Meaney, Viola Davis, Bruce McGill, Regina Hall, Josh Stewart, Michael Irby; ***D:*** F. Gary Gray; ***W:*** Kurt Wimmer; ***C:*** Jonathan Sela; ***M:*** Brian Tyler.

Law and Disorder 🦴🦴🦴 **1974 (R)** Two average Joes, fed up with the rate of rising crime, start their own auxiliary police group. Alternately funny and serious with good performances from the leads. **103m/C VHS, DVD.** Carroll O'Connor, Ernest Borgnine, Ann Wedgeworth, Anita Dangler, Leslie Ackerman, Karen Black, Jack Kehoe; ***D:*** Ivan Passer; ***W:*** Ivan Passer, William Richert, Kenneth Harris Fishman; ***C:*** Arthur Ornitz; ***M:*** Angelo Badalamenti.

The Law and Jake Wade 🦴🦴 1/2 **1958** Gripping western starring Taylor as a former bank robber turned marshal. His old partner (Widmark) turns up and forces Taylor to lead him to buried loot. **86m/C VHS.** Robert Taylor, Richard Widmark, Patricia Owens, Robert Middleton, Henry Silva, DeForest Kelley, Burt Douglas, Eddie Firestone; ***D:*** John Sturges.

Law and Lawless 🦴 **1933** A roving cowboy brings justice to a gang of cattle thieves in this film. **58m/B VHS.** Julian Rivero, Yakima Canutt, Jack Mower, Wally Wales, Hilda Moreno, Jack Hoxie; ***D:*** Armand Schaefer; ***W:*** Oliver Drake; ***C:*** William Nobles.

Law and Order 🦴 1/2 **1940** Retired U.S. marshal Bill Ralston and his pals Deadwood and Brant get caught up in the fight between the townsfolk of Rhyolite and Poe Daggett and his gang. When death comes to those on both sides, Ralston must put on his badge again in order to settle matters. **57m/B DVD.** Johnny Mack Brown, Fuzzy Knight, Nell O'Day,

James Craig, Harry Cording, Earle Hodgins, Robert (Fisk) Fiske, Jimmie Dodd, Ted Adams; *D:* Ray Taylor; *W:* Sherman Lowe, Victor McLeod; *C:* Jerome Ash.

Law and Order ♂♂ *Billy the Kid's Law and Order* **1942** Billy the Kid impersonates a Cavalry lieutenant in order to swindle his aunt out of her money. **58m/B VHS.** Dave O'Brien, Sarah Padden, Wanda McKay, Charles King, Buster Crabbe, Al "Fuzzy" St. John; *D:* Sam Newfield; *W:* Sam Robins; *C:* Jack Greenhalgh.

Law and Order ♂♂ ½ **1953** Remake of 1932 and 1940 films is a solid B-movie oater with Reagan a competent, if stiff, lead. Frame Johnson (Reagan) is the former marshal of Tombstone, having decided to retire to marry saloon owner Jeannie (Malone) and become a rancher in nearby Cottonwood. Only his new town is under the sway of old nemesis Durling (Foster) and his gang. The townsfolk want Johnson to strap his gunbelt back on and take care of the varmints so they can have a peaceful community and, of course, he does. **80m/C DVD.** Ronald Reagan, Dorothy Malone, Preston Foster, Alex Nicol, Russell Johnson, Barry Kelley, Chubby Johnson, Dennis Weaver, Wally Cassell, Ruth Hampton; *D:* Nathan "Jerry" Juran; *W:* D.D. Beauchamp; *C:* Clifford Stine; *M:* Henry Mancini, Milton Rosen, Herman Stein.

Law for Tombstone ♂♂ **1935** Alamo Bowie (Jones) must protect the Wells Fargo stagecoach from outlaw Twin Gun Jack. Includes chapter 1 of the serial "Gordon of Ghost City," which features Jones as retired ranch hand Buck Gordon who's on the trail of rustlers and meets a mysterious girl. **81m/B VHS.** Buck Jones, Muriel Evans, Harvey Clark, Carl Stockdale, Earle Hodgins, Madge Bellamy, Walter Miller; *D:* Ray Taylor, Buck Jones.

Law of Desire ♂♂♂ ½ *La Ley del Deseo* **1986** A wicked, Almodovarian attack-on-decency farce about a promiscuous gay filmmaker, Pablo (Pancela), who becomes the object of desire for obsessive Antonio (Banderas), whom Pablo treats too casually for his own safety. Also in the mix is Pablo's sister, the transsexual Tina (Maura), and his current lover Juan (Molina). Romantic complications and violence abound. Unlike the work of any other director; Spanish with subtitles. **100m/C VHS, DVD.** *SP* Carmen Maura, Eusebio Poncela, Antonio Banderas, Bibi Andersson, Miguel Molina, Manuela Valasco, Nacho Martinez; *D:* Pedro Almodovar; *W:* Pedro Almodovar; *C:* Angel Luis Fernandez.

Law of the Jungle ♂ ½ **1942** A lady scientist and a fugitive team up to uncover a secret Nazi radio base in the jungle. **61m/B VHS, DVD.** Arline Judge, John "Dusty" King, Mantan Moreland, Martin Wilkins, Arthur O'Connell; *D:* Jean Yarbrough.

Law of the Land ♂ **1976** Sagebrush epic with the author/artist of "Garfield" portraying an accused but innocent man searching for a murderer. **100m/C VHS.** Jim Davis, Don Johnson, Barbara Parkins, Charles Martin Smith; *D:* Virgil W. Vogel; *W:* Sam Rolfe, John Wilder; *C:* William Spencer Jr.; *M:* John Parker. **TV**

Law of the Lash ♂ **1947** Cowboys and rustlers battle it out. **54m/B VHS, DVD.** Lee Roberts, Charles "Blackie" King, Lash LaRue, Al "Fuzzy" St. John; *D:* Ray Taylor; *C:* Robert E. Cline; *M:* Albert Glasser.

Law of the Pampas ♂♂ **1939** Boyd and Hayden ride off to South America to deliver some cattle, but the bad guys intervene. This is Toler's first outing as Hoppy's sidekick, briefly replacing "Gabby" Hayes. **72m/B VHS.** William Boyd, Russell Hayden, Steffi Duna, Sidney Toler, Sidney Blackmer, Pedro de Cordoba, Eddie Dean, Glenn Strange; *D:* Nate Watt.

Law of the Saddle ♂ ½ **1943** The Lone Rider pits himself against a gang of outlaws. **60m/B VHS.** Robert "Bob" Livingston, Al "Fuzzy" St. John, Betty Miles, Lane Chandler, John Elliott, Reed Howes, Curley Dresden, Al Ferguson; *D:* Melville De Lay; *W:* Fred Myton; *C:* Robert E. Cline.

Law of the Sea ♂ **1932** A family on a sinking ship is rescued by a lecherous sea captain who makes advances on the wife and blinds the husband in a fight. Twenty years later, the husband meets him again, recognizes his laugh, and exacts revenge. **63m/B VHS.** Priscilla Dean, Sally Blane, Ralph Ince, Rex Bell, William Farnum, Wally Albright, Jack Clifford, Frank LaRue, Syd Saylor, Eve Southern; *D:* Otto Brower; *C:* Archie Stout.

Law of the Texan ♂ ½ **1938** Jones goes undercover to stop Harlan and his gang from stealing a town's store of silver bullion. **54m/B VHS.** Buck Jones, Dorothy Fay, Kenneth Harlan, Donald "Don" Douglas, Matty Kemp, Robert F. (Bob) Kortman, Dave O'Brien; *D:* Elmer Clifton.

Law of the Underworld ♂ ½ **1938** An innocent couple is framed for the robbery of a jewelry store which resulted in the death of a clerk. When they are arrested, their fate lies in the hands of the gangster responsible for the crime. Will he let them fry in the electric chair, or will his conscience get the better of him? **58m/B VHS.** Chester Morris, Anne Shirley, Eduardo Ciannelli, Walter Abel, Richard Bond, Lee Patrick, Paul Guilfoyle, Frank M. Thomas Sr., Eddie Acuff, Vinton (Hayworth) Haworth; *D:* Lew Landers.

Law of the Wild ♂♂ **1934** The search for a magnificent stallion that was hijacked by race racketeers before a big sweepstakes race is shown in this 12 chapter serial. **230m/B VHS, DVD.** Bob Custer, Ben Turpin, Lucille Browne, Lafe (Lafayette) McKee; *D:* B. Reeves Eason, Armand Schaefer.

The Law Rides ♂ **1936** Rush of gold claims causes an outbreak of murder and robbery. **57m/B VHS.** Bob Steele, Charles "Blackie" King, Buck Connors, Harlene Wood, Margaret Mann, Jack Rockwell; *D:* Robert North Bradbury; *W:* Al Martin; *C:* Bert Longenecker.

The Law Rides Again ♂ **1943** Prairie lawmen bring a cheating Indian agent to justice. **56m/B VHS, DVD.** Ken Maynard, Hoot Gibson, Betty Miles, Jack La Rue; *D:* William Castle.

Law West of Tombstone ♂♂ ½ **1938** A former outlaw moves to a dangerous frontier town in order to restore the peace. **73m/B VHS.** Tim Holt, Harry Carey Sr., Evelyn Brent; *D:* Glenn Tryon.

The Lawless Breed ♂♂♂ **1952** Episodic saga based on the autobiography of outlaw John Wesley Hardin, published after his release from prison in 1896. Hardin's (Hudson) life of crime begins with a killing in self-defense that escalates into further bloodshed and flights from the law. Along the way Hardin marries (Adams) and has a son, whom he fears will follow in his violent footsteps. Walsh directs with plenty of brio. **83m/C VHS, DVD.** Rock Hudson, Julie Adams, John McIntire, Hugh O'Brian, Lee Van Cleef, Dennis Weaver, Glenn Strange, Michael Ansara; *D:* Raoul Walsh; *W:* Bernard Gordon; *C:* Irving Glassberg; *M:* Joseph Gershenson.

Lawless Frontier ♂ ½ **1935** In the early West, the Duke fights for law and order. **53m/B VHS, DVD.** John Wayne, George "Gabby" Hayes, Sheila Terry, Earl Dwire; *D:* Robert North Bradbury.

Lawless Heart ♂♂ ½ **2001 (R)** Divided into three sections, with the characters seen from different perspectives. We start out with the funeral of Stuart, a local restauranteur with his partner, Nick (Hollander). Stuart died without a will so his sister (Haddington) becomes his unexpected heir and has to decide whether to share with Nick or not. Meanwhile, her husband, Dan (Nighy), thinking life has passed him by, is having a flirtation with florist, Corinne (Celarie). Nick is also having some unexpected feelings towards Charlie (Smith), a fun-loving party girl who helps with the loneliness (and more). Finally, there's Tim (Henshall) a feckless boyhood chum of Stuart's who's just returned home and who suddenly falls in love with shop owner Leah (Butler). **99m/C VHS, DVD.** *GB* Tom Hollander, Douglas Henshall, Bill Nighy, Clementine Celarie, Josephine Butler, Ellie Haddington, Stuart Laing, Sukie Smith, David Coffey, Dominic Hall, June Barrie, Peter Symonds; *D:* Neil Hunter, Tom Hunsinger; *W:* Neil Hunter, Tom Hunsinger; *C:* Sean Bobbitt; *M:* Adrian Johnston. L.A. Film Critics '03: Support. Actor (Nighy).

The Lawless Land ♂♂ **1988 (R)** Post-holocaust America is ruled by a tyrant. Two young lovers who can't take it anymore go on the lam to escape the despotic rule. **81m/C VHS.** Leon Berkeley, Xander Berkeley, Jsu Garcia, Amanda Peterson; *D:* Jon Hess; *W:* Tony Cinciripini, Larry Leahy.

The Lawless Nineties ♂♂ **1936** Wayne plays a government agent sent to guarantee honest elections in the Wyoming territory. Hayes is exceptional as the newspaper editor who backs him up. Re-made in 1940 as "The Dark Command." **55m/B VHS.** John Wayne, Ann Rutherford, Lane Chandler, Harry Woods, George "Gabby" Hayes, Charles "Blackie" King, Sam Flint; *D:* Joseph Kane.

Lawless Plainsmen ♂ ½ **1942** Ranch foreman Steve Rideen (Starrett) and his sidekick Lucky (Hayden) get caught up in a brawl at Baltimore Bonnie's (Walters) saloon. It's a ruse set-up by her ex-husband Seth McBride (Bennett) so he can clean out her safe. Ruined, Bonnie, along with Steve and a wounded Lucky, take refuge in a wagon train. Unfortunately for them, McBride is close by with a wagonload of guns he intends to sell to the Indians, which results in a lot of trouble. **59m/B DVD.** Charles Starrett, Russell Hayden, Luana Walters, Ray Bennett, Cliff Edwards, Stanley Brown, Eva LaRue, Gwen Kenyon, Nick Thompson; *D:* William Berke; *W:* Lucille Ward; *C:* Benjamin (Ben H.) Kline.

Lawless Range ♂ ½ **1935** Wayne and the marshal's posse save the ranchers from trouble. **56m/B VHS, DVD.** John Wayne, Sheila (Manors) Mannors, Jack Curtis, Earl Dwire; *D:* Robert North Bradbury.

A Lawless Street ♂♂ ½ **1955** Scott portrays a sheriff who rides the Colorado Territory cleaning up lawless towns. His dedication to duty has caused his wife to leave him and she won't come back until he lays downs his guns forever, which may come sooner than they think after he rides into the corrupt town of Medicine Bend. Based on the novel "Marshal of Medicine Bend" by Brad Ward. **78m/B VHS, DVD.** Randolph Scott, Angela Lansbury, Warner Anderson, Jean Parker, Wallace Ford, John Emery, James Bell, Ruth Donnelly, Michael Pate, Don Megowan, Jeannette Nolan; *D:* Joseph H. Lewis; *W:* Kenneth Gamet; *C:* Ray Rennahan.

Lawman ♂♂♂ **1971 (PG)** Brutal western about a fanatical U.S. marshall (Lancaster) who rides into town after Cobb and his six ranch hands. The cowboys have accidentally killed a man and Lancaster is determined to bring them to justice no matter what the cost. Though the entire town is against him that doesn't stop his mission. Brooding and relentless with fine performances, particularly by Ryan as the local marshall living on past glories. **95m/C VHS, DVD.** Burt Lancaster, Robert Ryan, Lee J. Cobb, Sheree North, Joseph Wiseman, Robert Duvall, Albert Salmi, J.D. Cannon, John McGiver, Richard Jordan, John Beck, Ralph Waite, John Hillerman, Richard Bull; *D:* Michael Winner; *W:* Gerald Wilson; *C:* Robert Paynter; *M:* Jerry Fielding.

A Lawman Is Born ♂♂♂ **1937** A tough-as-nails marshal goes gunning for a pack of no-good, land-stealing varmits in this installment of the Johnny Mack Brown movie serials. Be sure to count the number of bullets each cowboy can fire from a six-shooter before being forced to reload; you may be surprised. **58m/B VHS.** Johnny Mack Brown, Iris Meredith, Warner Richmond, Mary MacLaren, Dick Curtis, Earle Hodgins, Charles "Blackie" King, Frank LaRue; *D:* Sam Newfield.

Lawmen ♂ ½ **1944** Government agents fight to enforce the law in the badlands. **55m/B VHS, DVD.** Johnny Mack Brown, Raymond Hatton, Jan Wiley, Kirby Grant, Robert Frazer, Edmund Cobb, Hal Price, Marshall Reed; *D:* Lambert Hillyer; *W:* Glenn Tryon; *C:* Harry Neumann.

Lawn Dogs ♂♂ ½ **1996** After moving into an overly manicured suburban complex for the financially secure but morally bankrupt, Morton (McDonald) and Clare (Quinlan) want their daughter to mix with the social elite. Instead, the imaginative Devon (Barton) strikes up a friendship with Trent (Rockwell), an outsider who cuts lawns in the sterile burb. At first Trent, fearing the repercussions of such a friendship, pushes Devon away. The two eventually bond over their mutual dislike for the lifeless complex. After a conflict with a couple of dim college boys, events take a turn for the worse; and Trent is forced to escape from the community with Devon's help. Interweaved with the Russian fairy tale of Baba Yaga, the climax is visually stunning. Excellent performances from both Rockwell and Barton as the unlikely friends. **101m/C VHS, DVD.** *GB* Sam Rockwell, Mischa Barton, Kathleen Quinlan, Christopher McDonald, Bruce McGill, David Barry Gray, Eric Mabius, Tom Aldredge, Beth Grant; *D:* John Duigan; *W:* Naomi Wallace; *C:* Elliot Davis; *M:* Trevor Jones.

The Lawnmower Man ♂♂ **1992 (R)** Brosnan is a scientist who uses Fahey, a dim-witted gardener, as a guinea pig to test his experiments in "virtual reality," an artificial computer environment. With the use of drugs and high-tech equipment, Brosnan is able to increase Fahey's mental powers—but not necessarily for the better. Fantastic special effects and a memorable "virtual reality" sex scene. Available in an unrated version which contains 32 more minutes of footage. So minimally based on a short story by Stephen King that the author sued (and won) to have his name removed from the film. **108m/C VHS, DVD.** Jeff Fahey, Pierce Brosnan, Jenny Wright, Mark Bringleson, Geoffrey Lewis, Jeremy Slate, Dean Norris, Troy Evans, John Laughlin; *D:* Brett Leonard; *W:* Brett Leonard, Gimel Everett; *C:* Russell Carpenter; *M:* Danny Wyman.

Lawnmower Man 2: Beyond Cyberspace ♂♂ *Lawnmower Man 2: Jobe's War* **1995 (PG-13)** Resurrecting Jobe (the title character from number one) was easy. So was blowing off his face to explain the new actor (Frewer in for Fahey) playing him. The hard part was tring to make an original movie with a decent script and believable characters. Better luck next time. Corporate baddie Walker (Conway) enlists Jobe to (what else?) take over the world using Virtual Reality. To the rescue comes one burned-out computer expert (Bergin) and a group of VR-addicted kids living in an abandoned subway. Techno-babble abounds but nothing interesting ever happens. Mann and Frewer must've raided their old "Max Headroom" set for the dreary near-future L.A. landscape scenes. **93m/C VHS, DVD.** Patrick Bergin, Matt Frewer, Austin O'Brien, Kevin Conway, Ely Pouget, Camille (Cami) Cooper; *D:* Farhad Mann; *W:* Farhad Mann; *C:* Ward Russell; *M:* Robert Folk.

Lawrence of Arabia ♂♂♂♂ **1962 (PG)** Exceptional biography of T.E. Lawrence, a British military "observer" who strategically aids the Bedouins battle the Turks during WWI. Lawrence, played masterfully by O'Toole in his first major film, is a hero consumed more by a need to reject British tradition than to save the Arab population. He takes on Arab costume and a larger-than-life persona. Stunning photography of the desert in all its harsh reality. Blacklisted co-writer Wilson had his screen credit restored by the Writers Guild of America in 1995. Laser edition contains 20 minutes of restored footage and a short documentary about the making of the film. Available in letterboxed format. **221m/C VHS, DVD.** *GB* Peter O'Toole, Omar Sharif, Anthony Quinn, Alec Guinness, Jack Hawkins, Claude Rains, Anthony Quayle, Arthur Kennedy, Jose Ferrer, Michel Ray, Norman Rossington, John Ruddock, Donald Wolfit; *D:* David Lean; *W:* Robert Bolt, Michael Wilson; *C:* Frederick A. (Freddie) Young; *M:* Maurice Jarre. Oscars '62: Art Dir./Set Dec., Color, Color Cinematog., Director (Lean), Film Editing, Picture, Sound, Orig. Score; AFI '98: Top 100; British Acad. '62: Actor (O'Toole), Film, Screenplay; Directors Guild '62: Director (Lean); Golden Globes '63: Director (Lean), Film—Drama, Support. Actor (Sharif); Natl. Bd. of Review '62: Director (Lean), Natl. Film Reg. '91.

The Lawrenceville Stories ♂♂ ½ *The Prodigious Hickey* **1988** Chronicles the life and times of a group of young men at the prestigious Lawrenceville prep school in 1905. Galligan plays William Hicks, alias "The Prodigious Hickey," the ringleader of their obnoxious stunts. Based on the stories of Owen Johnson, which originally ran in the Saturday Evening Post. Shown on "American Playhouse" and The Disney Channel. Tapes are available separately or as a set. **180m/C VHS.** Zach Galligan, Edward Herrmann, Nicholas (Nick) Rowe, Allan Goldstein, Robert Joy, Stephen Baldwin; *D:* Robert Iscove.

Laws of Attraction ♂♂ **2004 (PG-13)** Powerhouse New York divorce lawyers Daniel (Brosnan) and Audrey (Moore) fight for their opposing clients and against their growing attraction to each other in this formulaic romantic comedy that attempts to recall classic Hollywood screwballs. The case between fashion designer Posey and rock star Sheen allows them to engage in the kind of witty banter, bickering, and heated sparring that everyone knows will eventually lead to the bedroom. The brief, drunken romp leaves them both in emotional denial until one of the disputed assets in the case, an Irish castle, forces the two to travel to the quaint country where they proceed to get drunk (again) and married. The two leads provide plenty of chemistry and charm despite a wafer thin premise, stale scripting and characterization, and weak direction. **89m/C DVD.** Pierce Brosnan, Julianne Moore, Michael Sheen, Parker Posey, Frances Fisher, Nora Dunn, Allan Houston, Vincent Marzello, Mina (Badiyi) Badie; ***D:*** Peter Howitt; ***W:*** Aline Brosh McKenna, Robert Harling; ***C:*** Adrian Biddle; ***M:*** Ed Shearmur.

Laws of Deception 1/2 **1997** As a child, Evan Marino (Howell) witnessed the murder of his parents by mobster Gino Carlucci (Russo). After becoming a ruthlessly successful criminal attorney in Miami, Evan gets drawn back into the life of former flame Elise (Smith), who happens to be Mrs. Carlucci and is accused of murdering her scummy husband. She says she didn't do it. You'll figure out all the would-be twists in this wanna-be thriller without any problem. **98m/C VHS.** C. Thomas Howell, Amber Smith, Brian Austin Green, James Russo, Nick Mancuso, Robert Miano; ***Cameos:*** John Landis; ***D:*** Joey Travolta; ***W:*** Rollin Jarrett; ***C:*** Dan Heigh; ***M:*** Jeff Lass. **VIDEO**

Laws of Gravity **1992 (R)** Critically acclaimed debut film from 29-year-old writer/director Gomez is a three day slice of life set in Brooklyn. Hotheaded Jon (Trese) and married friend Jimmy (Greene) channel violent energy into their relationships and illegal activities. Camera follows "cinema verite" style and captures urban tension as it trails them through a gun heist and subsequent arrest. **100m/C VHS.** Peter Greene, Edie Falco, Adam Trese, Arabella Field, Paul Schulze; ***D:*** Nick Gomez; ***W:*** Nick Gomez; ***C:*** Jean De Segonzac.

Layer Cake **2005 (R)** The unnamed protagonist (Craig), referred to only as "XXXX" in the closing credits, is a too-cool-for-you cocaine dealer trying to leave the business. But, just as we all could've guessed, somehow he's convinced to pull "one last job," searching out the daughter of a fellow crime-boss and, oh yeah, coordinate the sale of a million stolen tablets of Ecstasy along the way. And, of course, a few things go wrong. Guy Ritchie's producer Matthew Vaughn's directorial debut. Vaughn successfully negotiates the cockney-chocked, bass-thumping, and humorously violent British crime genre his colleague defined so well with just as much pizzazz and twists. **105m/C DVD, Blu-ray Disc, UMD, HD DVD.** *GB* Daniel Craig, Colm Meaney, Kenneth Cranham, George Harris, Jamie Foreman, Michael Gambon, Tamer Hassan, Ben Whishaw, Burn Gorman, Sally Hawkins, Sienna Miller, Stephen Walters, Jason Flemyng, Dragan Micanovic, Dexter Fletcher, Steve John Shepherd, Marvin Benoit, Marcel Iures; ***D:*** Matthew Vaughn; ***W:*** J.J. Connolly; ***C:*** Benjamin Davis; ***M:*** Lisa Gerrard, Ilan Eshkeri.

Lazarillo *El Lazarillo de Tormes* **1959** In 17th-century Castille, a fatherless boy, abandoned by his mother, finds work with a strange succession of employers, including a blind beggar, fake nobleman, and traveling band of performers. They all teach him lessons in survival as well as cunning and deception. Spanish with subtitles. **109m/B VHS.** *SP* Marco Paoletti, Juan Jose Menendez, Carlos Casaravilla, Margarita Lozano; ***D:*** Cesar Ardavin; ***W:*** Cesar Ardavin; ***M:*** Ruiz De Luna. Berlin Intl. Film Fest. '60: Film.

The Lazarus Man 1/2 **1996** Pilot episode of the TV series finds the amnesiac Urich discovering he's linked to the assassination of President Lincoln. In 1865 Texas he literally claws his way out of the grave and is taken in by a farming family. This back from the dead Lazarus may not remember who he is but a trip to town demonstrates his gunslinger skills and images from his dreams may provide clues to his past. Now, he has to stay alive long enough to figure them out. **90m/C VHS.** Robert Urich, Elizabeth Dennehy, David Marshall Grant, John Diehl, Wayne Grace, Brion James; ***D:*** Johnny E. Jensen; ***W:*** Dick Beebe; ***C:*** Gary Holt; ***M:*** John Debney. **TV**

The Lazarus Project 1/2 **2008 (PG-13)** Muddled psycho-drama with an unsatisfying ending. Ex-con Ben Garvey's (Walker) new life is going so well something bad has to happen. First he gets fired and then he makes a really terrible decision to participate in a heist that goes verywrong, and Ben gets the death penalty. He's given a lethal injection and then wakes up a patient in a mental hospital with his previous life just a part of his delusions. Or was it? **99m/C DVD.** Paul Walker, Piper Perabo, Malcolm Goodwin, Bob Gunton, Tony Curran, Linda Cardellini, Lambert Wilson, Shawn Hatosy; ***D:*** John Glenn; ***W:*** John Glenn; ***C:*** Jerzy Zielinski; ***M:*** Brian Tyler. **VIDEO**

The Lazarus Syndrome **1979** Astute doctor teams up with an ex-patient of the chief of surgery in an effort to expose the chief's unethical surgical procedures. **90m/C VHS.** Ronald Hunter, Sheila Frazier, Lara Parker, Louis Gossett Jr., E.G. Marshall; ***D:*** Michael Firth; ***W:*** William Blinn; ***C:*** Chuck (Charles G.) Arnold; ***M:*** John Rubenstein.

Lazybones **1925** Steve (Jones), the lazybones of the title, likes nothing better than to nap, but he steps up when desperate Ruth (Pitts) is forced to give up her daughter Kit (Marsall), and he raises the girl despite small town scandal. After returning from WWI, Steve figures out he's in love with the now-adult Kit (Bellamy) but his mother (Chapman) helps him realize it's not meant to be. **78m/B DVD.** Buck Jones, Zasu Pitts, Madge Bellamy, Edythe Chapman, Leslie Fenton, Virginia Marsall; ***D:*** Frank Borzage; ***W:*** Frances Marion; ***C:*** Glen MacWilliams, George Schneiderman.

LBJ: A Biography **1991** Produced for the PBS series "The American Experience," this four-hour revisionist look at LBJ is one of the most critically acclaimed political documentaries of our time. Divided into four segments. "Beautiful Texas" chronicles Johnson's rise to power. "My Fellow Americans" focuses on his years as an unelected president. The Great Society and and the escalation of war in Vietnam are covered in "We Shall Overcome." "The Last Believer" highlights events leading to Johnson's withdrawal from politics. **240m/C VHS, DVD.** ***D:*** David Grubin; ***W:*** David Grubin.

LBJ: The Early Years **1988** The early years of President Lyndon Baines Johnson's political career are dramatized. Winning performances hoist this above other biographies. **144m/C VHS.** Randy Quaid, Patti LuPone, Morgan Brittany, Pat Hingle, Kevin McCarthy, Barry Corbin, Charles Frank; ***D:*** Peter Werner. **TV**

Le Bal **1982** You won't find many films with the music of Paul McCartney and Chopin in the credits, and even fewer without dialogue. With only music and dancing the film uses a French dance hall to illustrate the changes in French society over a 50-year period. Based on a French play. ♫ La Vie en Rose; In the Mood; Michelle; Top Hat White Tie and Tails; Let's Face the Music and Dance; Harlem Nocturne; Shuffle Blues; Tutti Frutti; Only You. **112m/C VHS.** *IT FR* ***D:*** Ettore Scola; ***M:*** Irving Berlin, Paul McCartney, John Lennon, Vladimir Cosma. Cesar '84: Director (Scola), Film, Score.

Le Beau Mariage *A Good Marriage; The Well-Made Marriage* **1982 (R)** An award-winning comedy from the great French director about a zealous woman trying to find a husband and the unsuspecting man she chooses to marry. The second in Rohmer's Comedies and Proverbs series. French with subtitles. **97m/C VHS, DVD.** *FR* Beatrice Romand, Arielle Dombasle, Andre Dussollier, Feodor Atkine, Pascal Greggory, Sophie Renoir; ***D:*** Eric Rohmer; ***W:*** Eric Rohmer; ***C:*** Bernard Lutic; ***M:*** Ronan Girre, Simon des Innocents. Venice Film Fest. '82: Actress (Romand).

Le Beau Serge *Handsome Serge* **1958** Young theology student Francois returns to his home village and discovers his friend Serge, in despair of ever changing his life, has become a hopeless drunk. So Francois meddles in his life (with the best of intentions) and only causes Serge further disaster. Chabrol's first film, and a major forerunner of the nouvelle vague. In French with English subtitles. **97m/B VHS.** *FR* Gerard Blain, Jean-Claude Brialy, Michele Meritz, Bernadette LaFont; ***D:*** Claude Chabrol; ***W:*** Claude Chabrol.

Le Bonheur 1/2 *Happiness* **1965** A seemingly happily married carpenter (Drouot) takes a vacation with his wife and children where he meets the local postal clerk and the two begin a passionate affair. Unwilling to leave his family, Drouot believes the two women can share him but when his wife discovers his infidelity she kills herself. His grief does not cause Drouot to stop the affair, instead he moves in with his mistress. An uninvolving, unbelievable tale with a lovely Mozart score. In French with English subtitles. **87m/C VHS.** *FR* Jean-Claude Drouot, Claire Drouot, Marie-France Boyer; ***D:*** Agnes Varda; ***W:*** Agnes Varda; ***C:*** Jean Rabier, Claude Beausoleil.

Le Bonheur Est Dans le Pre *Happiness Is In the Fields; Happiness* **1995** Francis (Serrault) is the harried owner of a toilet brush-making business that is about to undergo a tax audit and is threatened by a workers strike. His wife and daughter are never happy and Francis' one relief is to have lunch with his macho, easy-going friend, Gerard (Mitchell). One day, he watches a TV show about missing persons and sees that a woman is looking for her husband who disappeared 28 years before—a man who looks suspiciously like Francis. The plot's convoluted and the comedy's flat. French with subtitles. **105m/C VHS.** *FR* Michel Serrault, Sabine Azema, Eddy Mitchell, Carmen Maura, Alexandra London; ***D:*** Etienne Chatiliez; ***W:*** Florence Quentin; ***C:*** Philippe Welt; ***M:*** Pascal Andreacchio. Cesar '95: Support. Actor (Mitchell).

Le Boucher *The Butcher; Il Tagliagole* **1969** In a provincial French town a sophisticated schoolmistress is courted by the shy local butcher—who turns out to be a sex murderer. A well-played thriller that looks at sexual frustration. French with subtitles. **94m/C VHS, DVD.** *FR* Stephane Audran, Jean Yanne, Antonio Passallia; ***D:*** Claude Chabrol; ***W:*** Claude Chabrol.

Le Cas du Dr. Laurent **1957** A country doctor in a small French town tries to introduce methods of natural childbirth to the native women, but meets opposition from the superstitious villagers. Fine performance by Gabin. **88m/B VHS.** *FR* Jean Gabin, Nicole Courcel; ***D:*** Jean-Paul LeChanois.

Le Cavaleur *Practice Makes Perfect* **1978** A light hearted comedy about a philandering concert pianist. **90m/C VHS.** *FR* Jean Rochefort, Lila Kedrova, Nicole Garcia, Annie Girardot, Danielle Darrieux; ***D:*** Philippe de Broca; ***M:*** Georges Delerue.

Le Cercle Rouge *The Red Circle* **1970** An ex-con, an escaped prisoner, a diamond heist, a police manhunt, and mob vengeance—all set during a wet Paris winter. Ex-con Corey (Delon) is planning to rob a jewelry store; Vogel (Volonte) escapes from his police guard, Mattei (Bourvil), during a train trip; fate brings the two together. Corey is in trouble for stealing from the mob and Vogel helps him out. They seek the help of ex-con Jansen (Montand) for their heist (which isn't even the most important part of the movie), while Mattei is out to re-capture Vogel to salvage his reputation. It's trench coats and fedoras and the ever-present smoldering cigarette—and it's all very, very cool. French with subtitles. **140m/C DVD.** *FR* Alain Delon, Gian Marie Volonte, Yves Montand, Andre Bourvil, Francois Perier; ***D:*** Jean-Pierre Melville; ***W:*** Jean-Pierre Melville; ***C:*** Henri Decae; ***M:*** Eric Demarsen.

Le Chat 1/2 *The Cat* **1975** A middle-aged couple's marriage dissolves into a hate-filled battle of wits, centering around the husband's love for their cat. In French with English subtitles. **88m/C VHS.** *FR* Jean Gabin, Simone Signoret, Annie Cordy, Jacques Rispal; ***D:*** Pierre Granier-Deferre. Berlin Intl. Film Fest. '71: Actor (Gabin).

Le Choc *Shock; Contract in Blood* **1982** Martin (Delon) is a hitman whose boss, Cox (Perrot), refuses to let him retire. His banker Jeanne (Audran) has invested part of Martin's money in a farm managed by Claire (Deneuve) and her alcoholic husband. When Martin goes to check things out, the farm is attacked by some of his enemies and Claire's husband is killed, but she and Martin escape. Martin then finds Jeanne dead and his money gone, but Cox offers him a lot of francs for one last job and the chance to take Claire away to an island paradise. French with subtitles. **100m/C DVD.** *FR* Alain Delon, Catherine Deneuve, Stephane Audran, Francois Perrot, Philippe Leotard, Etienne Chicot, Jean-Louis Richard, Feodor Atkine, Feodor Atkine; ***D:*** Jean-Louis Richard; ***W:*** Alain Delon, Jean-Louis Richard, Robin Davis; ***C:*** Pierre William Glenn; ***M:*** Philippe Sarde.

Le Complot *The Conspiracy* **1973** When de Gaulle announces his intention to abandon Algeria, several army officers, feeling that their service has been in vain, stage a coup. There's suspense aplenty as the Gaulists, the leftists, and the police spy and are spied upon. In French with English subtitles. **120m/C VHS.** *FR* Michel Bouquet, Jean Rochefort; ***D:*** Rene Gainville.

Le Corbeau *The Raven* **1943** A great, notorious drama about a small French village whose everyday serenity is ruptured by a series of poison pen letters that lead to suicide and despair. The film was made within Nazi-occupied France, sponsored by the Nazis, and has been subjected to much misdirected malice because of it. In French with English subtitles. **92m/B VHS, DVD.** *FR* Pierre Fresnay, Noel Roquevert, Ginette LeClerc, Pierre Larquey, Antoine Belpetre; ***D:*** Henri-Georges Clouzot.

Le Crabe Tambour **1977** Rochefort plays a dying naval captain remembering his relationship with his first officer. Revealed via flashbacks, the recollections concern the adventures which transpired on a North Atlantic supply ship. Great performances from all and award-winning cinematography by Raoul Coutard. Winner of several French Cesars. A French script booklet is available. **120m/C VHS.** *FR* Jean Rochefort, Claude Rich, Jacques Dufilho, Jacques Perrin, Odile Versois, Aurore Clement; ***D:*** Pierre Schoendoerffer; ***C:*** Raoul Coutard. Cesar '78: Actor (Rochefort), Cinematog., Support. Actor (Dufilho).

Le Dernier Combat *The Last Battle* **1984 (R)** A stark film about life after a devastating nuclear war marks the directorial debut of Besson. The characters fight to survive in a now speechless world by staking territorial claims and forming new relationships with other survivors. An original and expressive film made without dialogue. **93m/B VHS, DVD.** *FR* Pierre Jolivet, Fritz Wepper, Jean Reno, Jean Bouise, Christiane Kruger; ***D:*** Luc Besson; ***W:*** Luc Besson; ***C:*** Carlo Varini; ***M:*** Eric Serra.

Le Deuxieme Souffle *Second Breath* **1966** An overly-long crime saga that still intrigues. Aging gangster Gustave (Ventura) escapes from prison but doesn't have the money to leave France. He agrees to join in an armored car heist in Paris despite the fact that the job is run by Paul Ricci (Pellegrin), whose brother Jo (Bozzuffi) framed Gustave and sent him to the slammer. The gangster is pursued by the ruthless Commissaire Blot (Meurisse), who isn't afraid of using violence or branding Gustave a stoolie when things don't go as planned. French with subtitles. **144m/B DVD.** *FR* Lino Ventura, Paul Meurisse, Raymond Pellegrin, Marcel Bozzuffi, Michel Constantin, Paul Frankeur, Christine Fabrega, Pierre Zimmer, Pierre Grasset; ***D:*** Jean-Pierre Melville; ***W:*** Jose Giovanni; ***C:*** Jose Giovanni; ***M:*** Bernard Gerard.

Le Divorce **2003 (PG-13)** Cutie blonde American Isabel Walker (Hudson) heads to Paris to support her equally blonde but depressed pregnant sister Roxeanne (Watts) whose French husband Charles-Henri (Poupard) has walked out because of an obsessive affair. Hubby insists on a quick divorce but Roxy is refusing. Meanwhile, Isabel becomes involved with Charles-Henri's worldly uncle, Edgar (Lhermitte), who knows how to begin and end an affair with aplomb (and gifts). A culture clash comedy of manners that's brittle with artifice. Based on the 1997 novel by Diane Johnson. **115m/C VHS, DVD.** *US* Kate Hudson, Naomi Watts,

Thierry Lhermitte, Melvil Poupaud, Leslie Caron, Glenn Close, Stockard Channing, Sam Waterston, Thomas Lennon, Matthew Modine, Rona Hartner, Jean-Marc Barr, Stephen Fry, Bebe Neuwirth, Samuel Labarthe, Nathalie Richard, Romain Duris, Daniel Mesguich; ***D:*** James Ivory; ***W:*** Ruth Prawer Jhabvala; ***C:*** Pierre Lhomme; ***M:*** Richard Robbins.

Le Doulos *Doulos—The Finger Man* **1961** Compelling story of an ex-convict and his buddy, a man who may be a police informant. Chronicles the efforts of the snitch (the "doulos" of the title) to bring the criminal element before the law. Melville blends in several plot twists and breathes a new-French life into the cliche-ridden genre. **108m/B VHS.** *FR* Serge Reggiani, Jean-Paul Belmondo, Michel Piccoli; ***D:*** Jean-Pierre Melville.

Le Gentleman D'Epsom **1962** A French comedy about a breezy con man who scams everyone around him in order to keep up his upwardly mobile appearance and to put his bets down at the racetrack. Subtitled in English. **83m/B VHS.** *FR* Jean Gabin, Paul Frankeur.

Le Gitan *The Gypsy* **1975** Gypsy Hugo (Delon) steals from the rich to provide for his fellows, who are poverty-stricken outcasts in French society. But no good deed goes unpunished. French with subtitles. **102m/C DVD.** *FR* Alain Delon, Paul Meurisse, Annie Girardot, Marcel Bozzuffi, Bernard Giraudeau; ***D:*** Jose Giovanni; ***W:*** Jose Giovanni; ***C:*** Jean-Jacques Tarbes; ***M:*** Claude Bolling.

Le Grand Chemin *The Grand Highway* **1987** A sweet, slice-of-life French film about a young boy's idyllic summer on a family friend's farm while his mother is having a baby. Hubert's son plays the boy Louis in this retelling of the director's own childhood. In French with English subtitles. Remade with an American setting in 1991 as "Paradise." **107m/C VHS.** *FR* Anemone, Richard Bohringer, Antoine Hubert, Vanessa Guedj, Christine Pascal, Raoul Billerey, Pascale Roberts; ***D:*** Jean-Loup Hubert; ***W:*** Jean-Loup Hubert; ***C:*** Claude Lecomte; ***M:*** Georges Granier. Cesar '88: Actor (Bohringer), Actress (Anemone).

Le Joli Mai **1962** A famous documentary that established Marker, depicting the everyday life of Paris denizens on the occasion of the end of the Algerian War, May 1962, when France was at peace for the first time since 1939. In French with English subtitles. **180m/B VHS.** *FR* ***D:*** Chris Marker; ***Nar:*** Yves Montand, Simone Signoret.

Le Jour Se Leve ½ *Daybreak* **1939** The dark, expressionist film about a sordid and destined murder/love triangle that starts with a police stand-off and evolves into a series of flashbacks. The film that put Carne and Gabin on the cinematic map. Highly acclaimed. French with English subtitles. Remade in 1947 as "The Long Night." **89m/B VHS.** *FR* Jean Gabin, Jules Berry, Arletty, Jacqueline Laurent; ***D:*** Marcel Carne.

Le Jupon Rouge *Manuela's Loves* **1987** Bacha (Valli) is a human rights activist and concentration camp survivor who is involved with younger fashion designer Manuela (Barrault). But when Manuela becomes drawn to the even younger Claude (Grobon), Bracha's overwhelmed with jealousy and Manuela is torn by her feelings for both women. French with subtitles. **90m/C VHS.** *FR* Alida Valli, Marie-Christine Barrault, Guillemette Grobon; ***D:*** Genevieve Lefebvre.

Le Magnifique *The Magnificent One* **1976** Belmondo is a master spy and novelist who mixes fantasy with reality when he chases women and solves cases. **84m/C VHS, DVD.** *FR* Jean-Paul Belmondo, Jacqueline Bisset, Hans Meyer, Vittorio Caprioli; ***D:*** Philippe de Broca; ***W:*** Francis Veber, Philippe de Broca; ***C:*** Rene Mathelin; ***M:*** Claude Bolling.

Le Mans **1971 (G)** The famous 24-hour sports car race sets the stage for this tale of love and speed. McQueen (who did his own driving) is the leading race driver, a man who battles competition, fear of death by accident, and emotional involvement. Excellent documentary-style race footage almost makes up for weak plot and minimal acting. **106m/C VHS, DVD.** Steve McQueen, Elga Andersen, Ronald Leigh-Hunt, Luc Merenda, Angelo Infanti; ***D:*** Lee H. Katzin; ***W:*** Harry Kleiner; ***C:*** Robert B. Hauser.

Le Million ½ **1931** A comedy/musical masterpiece of the early sound era which centers on an artist's adventures in searching for a winning lottery ticket throughout Paris. Highly acclaimed member of the Clair school of subtle French farce. In French with English subtitles. **89m/B VHS, DVD.** *FR* Annabella, Rene Lefevre, Paul Olivier, Louis Allibert; ***D:*** Rene Clair.

Le Petit Amour *Kung Fu Master* **1987 (R)** Popular French comedy about the fateful romance between a 40-year-old divorced woman and a 15-year-old boy obsessed with a kung fu video game. In French with English subtitles. **80m/C VHS.** *FR* Jane Birkin, Mathieu Demy, Charlotte Gainsbourg, Lou Doillon, David Birkin; ***D:*** Agnes Varda.

Le Petit Lieutenant *The Young Lieutenant* **2005** Rookie detective Antoine (Lespert) leaves his wife in Normandy so he can find some action in Paris by working in homicide. His commander is Catherine (Baye), a recovering alcoholic who has just returned to the job, and she takes the new guy under her professional wing. A homeless man is the latest victim of a robbery and murder crew that Antoine investigates with unexpectedly devastating consequences to all. French with subtitles. **110m/C DVD.** *FR* Nathalie Baye, Jalil Lespert, Roschdy Zem, Antoine Chappey, Jacques Perrin, Berangere Allaux; ***D:*** Xavier Beauvois; ***W:*** Xavier Beauvois, Guillaume Breaud, Jean-Eric Troubat; ***C:*** Caroline Champetier.

Le Petit Soldat **1960** The passage of time has softened the controversy that swirled about Godard's second film (after "Breathless") in the initial release. It's the story of photographer Bruno Forestier (Subor), who joins the French nationalist movement against Algeria. While he tries to decide whether to follow orders to kill one of the opposition, he falls in love with a model (the lovely Karina, in her debut), unaware of her political beliefs. Godard's once-revolutionary on-the-fly filmmaking techniques seem completely contemporary and natural now. For serious students of film, this one makes a long-overdue debut on home video. **88m/B VHS, DVD.** *FR* Michel Subor, Anna Karina, Henri-Jacques Huet, Paul Beauvais, Georges De Beauregard, Jean-Luc Godard, Laszlo Szabo; ***D:*** Jean-Luc Godard; ***W:*** Jean-Luc Godard; ***C:*** Raoul Coutard; ***M:*** Maurice Leroux.

Le Plaisir ½ *House of Pleasure* **1952** An anthology of three Guy de Maupassant stories, "Le Masque," "Le Modele," and "La Maison Teillier," about the search for pleasure. In French with English subtitles. **97m/B VHS, DVD.** *FR* Claude Dauphin, Simone Simon, Jean Gabin, Danielle Darrieux, Madeleine Renaud, Gaby Morlay, Jean Galland, Ginette LeClerc, Mila Parely, Pierre Brasseur, Daniel Gelin; ***D:*** Max Ophuls; ***W:*** Max Ophuls, Jacques Matras; ***C:*** Christian Matras, Philippe Agostini; ***M:*** Joe Hajos; ***Nar:*** Peter Ustinov, Jean Servais.

Le Polygraphe *The Lie Detector* **1996** Francois (Goyette) is still a suspect in the murder of his girlfriend, Marie-Claire, two years after her death. The murder has so affected her friend Judith (Descenes) that she's written a screenplay about the unsolved crime (blaming the crime on a rogue cop). Meanwhile, actress Lucie (Brassard), who auditions for the role of Marie-Claire, gets involved with mystery man Christof (Stormare). English and French with subtitles. **97m/C VHS.** *CA* Patrick Goyette, Jose Descenes, Marie Brassard, Peter Stormare, Maria De Medeiros; ***D:*** Robert Lepage; ***W:*** Marie Brassard, Robert Lepage; ***C:*** Georges Dufaux.

Le Professionnel ½ *The Professional* **1981** French assassin Joss Beaumont (Belmondo) returns from the African republic of Malagasy, where he's been imprisoned for two years because his own superiors turned him in to the authorities when they decided to abort his mission. Instantly his old department is mobilized to eliminate him, but Beaumont is faster and smarter than all of them put together. Fast, clever, and beholden to nothing done before, the film is a slick package, a spy thriller that relies on brains instead of guns. There's a constant flow of fistfights and combat encounters in the picture, none of which are hyped with cutting or music. Belmondo makes them all credible. A surprise picture for people who like intelligent thrillers. **109m/C DVD.** *FR* Jean-Paul Belmondo, Jean Desailly, Robert Hossein, Michel Beaune, Cyrielle Claire, Jean-Louis Richard, Sidiki Bakaba; ***D:*** Georges Lautner; ***W:*** Georges Lautner, Michel Audiard; ***C:*** Henri Decae; ***M:*** Ennio Morricone.

Le Repos du Guerrier *Warrior's Rest* **1962** Star vehicle for Bardot in which she plays a respectable woman who abandons societal norms to pursue an unbalanced lover. In French with English subtitles. **100m/C VHS, DVD.** *FR* Brigitte Bardot, Robert Hossein, James Robertson Justice, Jean-Mark Bory; ***D:*** Roger Vadim.

Le Samourai ½ *The Samurai; Godson* **1967** Cold, precise professional killer Jef Costello (Delon) lives by his version of the code of the Japanese samurai. Hired to kill a nightclub owner, he establishes an alibi with the help of his lover Jane (Nathalie Delon, Alain's then-wife) and, unexpectedly, by Valerie (Rosier), the club's black pianoplayer. Jef finds Valerie's aid suspicious and begins to dig deeper, finding himself betrayed by his employers, and the subject of a police chase throughout Paris. The icy Delon was perfect for the anti-hero role and Melville's stylized filming heightens the tension and inevitable tragedy. A film much-admired, and copied, by contemporary filmmakers. French with subtitles. **95m/C VHS, DVD.** *FR* Alain Delon, Francois Perier, Cathy Rosier, Nathalie Delon, Jacques Leroy, Jean-Pierre Posier; ***D:*** Jean-Pierre Melville; ***W:*** Jean-Pierre Melville; ***C:*** Henri Decae; ***M:*** Francois de Roubaix.

Le Schpountz *Heartbeat* **1938** Satire on filmmaking and film-loving fans finds a small town grocer (Fernandel) in southern France becoming the victim of a practical joke when a visiting film crew promises to make him a star (signing him to a phony contract) if he'll come to Paris. Naturally, the joke's on them when the naive grocer arrives in the City of Light and becomes a successful movie comic. French with subtitles. **135m/B VHS.** *FR* Fernandel, Charpin, Orane Demazis, Odette Roger, Jean Castan, Leon Belieres; ***D:*** Marcel Pagnol; ***W:*** Marcel Pagnol; ***C:*** Willy; ***M:*** Casimir Oberfeld.

Le Secret **1974** This classic French thriller with a shocking ending finds an escaped convict seeking shelter with a reclusive couple in the mountains. His tales of abuse and torture create tension for the pair as one believes the woeful story and the other doesn't. Dubbed in English. **103m/C VHS.** *FR* Jean-Louis Trintignant, Philippe Noiret, Jean-Francois Adam; ***D:*** Robert Enrico; ***M:*** Ennio Morricone.

Le Sex Shop **1973 (R)** A man turns his little book store into a porn equipment palace, to make ends meet. When his relationship with his wife gets boring, they begin to use their erotic merchandise and adopt a swinging lifestyle. **92m/C VHS.** *FR* Claude Berri, Juliet Berto, Daniel Auteuil, Nathalie Delon; ***D:*** Claude Berri; ***M:*** Serge Gainsbourg.

Le Sexe des Etoiles *The Sex of the Stars* **1993** Curiously uninvolving film about 12-year-old Camille who discovers that the father who abandoned her is now a transsexual. Pierre walked out years before and Camille has always dreamed of his return but though they reach a tentative relationship, it's not what Camille hoped for. Title refers to Camille's obsession with astronomy because stars have no sex. Based on the novel by Proulx (who also wrote the screenplay). In French with English subtitles. **100m/C VHS.** *CA* Marianne-Coquelicot Mercier, Denis Mercier, Tobie Pelletier, Sylvie Drapeau; ***D:*** Paule Baillargeon; ***W:*** Monique Proulx; ***C:*** Eric Cayla. Genie '93: Sound.

Le Trou *The Hole; The Night Watch; Il Buco* **1959** Four long-term convicts in a Paris prison cell are planning to escape by tunneling to freedom. Then, a fifth prisoner joins them—is he going to betray them? Or is there already a Judas amongst the men? Based on a true story, the film has no musical score in order to heighten the tension and the actors were all nonprofessionals. Becker died in 1960; this is his final film. French with subtitles. **123m/B VHS, DVD.** *FR* Philippe LeRoy, Marc Michel, Catherine Spaak, Andre Bervil, Michel Constantin, Jean-Paul Coquelin, Jean Keraudy, Raymond Meunier, Eddy Rasimi, Dominique Zardi; ***D:*** Jacques Becker; ***W:*** Jacques Becker, Jose Giovanni, Jean Aurel; ***C:*** Ghislan Cloquet.

Lea **1996** Lea (Vlasakova) becomes mute after witnessing her abusive father kill her mother but writes the dead woman poems and letters to express her motions. However, Lea becomes even more withdrawn from the world when she's given in an arranged marriage to the much-older Herbert (Redl). Herbert marries Lea because she resembles his dead wife but Lea finds he has disturbing similarities to her father. German with subtitles. **100m/C VHS, DVD.** *GE* Lenka Vlasakov, Christian Redl, Hanna Schygulla; ***D:*** Ivan Fila; ***W:*** Ivan Fila.

Leader of the Band **1987 (PG)** An out-of-work musician tries to train the world's worst high school band. Landesberg helps this attempted comedy along. **90m/C VHS.** Steve Landesberg, Gailard Sartain, Mercedes Ruehl, James Martinez, Calvert Deforest; ***D:*** Nessa Hyams; ***M:*** Dick Hyman.

The Leading Man ½ **1996 (R)** Bon Jovi's charming in the title role as American movie star Robin Grange. Grange has come to London to work in the prestige stage production by playwright Felix Webb (Wilson) and he's also become aware of Webb's complex romantic situation. Although married to Elena (Galiena), Felix is having an affair with young leading lady, Hilary Rule (Newton). So the studly Robin proposes that he seduce Elena, thus leaving Felix free to carry on with his own affair. Except Felix gets jealous when Robin succeeds and soon realizes that the actor has his own agenda. **96m/C VHS, DVD.** *GB* Lambert Wilson, Jon Bon Jovi, Anna Galiena, Thandie Newton, David Warner, Barry Humphries, Patricia Hodge, Diana Quick, Nicole Kidman; ***D:*** John Duigan; ***W:*** John Duigan; ***C:*** Jean-Francois Robin; ***M:*** Ed Shearmur.

The League of Extraordinary Gentlemen **2003 (PG-13)** There's little left of the "League" featured in the 1999 comic book by Alan Moore and Kevin O'Neill. Instead, there's overblown action and a lack of heart. Aging adventurer Allan Quartermain (Connery) is but one of the literary characters called to defeat a madman bent on starting a world war for profit in 1899. He's somewhat reluctantly teamed with Captain Nemo (Shah) and his Nautilus submarine, vampiric scientist Mina Harker (Wilson), the ageless Dorian Gray (Townsend), the invisible man Rodney Skinner (Curran), Dr. Jekyll and his hulkish alter ego Mr. Hyde (Flemyng), and Tom Sawyer (West), who's grown up to be a member of the American secret service. Clumsily telegraphs many plot twists, but the well-read should get a kick out of the many literary references. **110m/C VHS, DVD, Blu-ray Disc, UMD.** *US* Sean Connery, Stuart Townsend, Peta Wilson, Shane West, Tony Curran, Richard Roxburgh, Jason Flemyng, Naseeruddin Shah, David Hemmings, Terry O'Neill, Max Ryan, Tom Goodman-Hill; ***D:*** Stephen Norrington; ***W:*** James Robinson; ***C:*** Dan Laustsen; ***M:*** Trevor Jones.

The League of Gentlemen ½ **1960** An ex-Army officer plots a daring bank robbery using specially skilled military personnel and irreproachable panache. Hilarious British humor fills the screen. **115m/B VHS, DVD.** *GB* Jack Hawkins, Nigel Patrick, Richard Attenborough, Roger Livesey, Bryan Forbes; ***D:*** Basil Dearden.

League of Ordinary Gentlemen **2004** Three former Microsoft execs purchased the Pro Bowlers Association for $5 million and hired Steve Miller from Nike to help revive and make it more exciting and media friendly. Film documents the 2003 nationwide tour, which culminated in a tense world championship in Detroit. We witness the tour through the fortunes of four pros, Pete Weber, a flamboyant player, Walter Ray Williams Jr., a low-key guy who can be a bit imposing, Chris Barnes, a clean-cut but moody fellow, and Wayne

Webb, who knows after his past broken marriages and bankruptcies this tour will make or break his bowling career. An endearing film touching on American life and the eccentricities and hardships of competition. **100m/C DVD.** *US* ***D:*** Christopher Browne; ***C:*** Ken Seng.

A League of Their Own **1992 (PG)** Charming look at sports history and the Rockford Peaches, one of the teams in the real-life All American Girls Professional Baseball League, formed in the 40s when the men were off at war. Main focus is on sibling rivalry between Dottie Hinson (Davis), the beautiful, crackerjack catcher, and Kit Keller (Petty), her younger, insecure sister and team pitcher. Boozy coach Jimmy Dugan (Hanks) is wonderful as he reluctantly leads the team; he also gets credit for the classic "There's no crying in baseball" scene. Great cast of supporting characters, including sarcastic talent scout Ernie (Lovitz), opinionated, sleazy taxi dancer Mae (Madonna), loud-mouthed Doris (O'Donnell), and shy, homely Marla (Cavanagh). Lots of baseball for the sports fan. **127m/C VHS, DVD.** Geena Davis, Tom Hanks, Lori Petty, Madonna, Rosie O'Donnell, Megan Cavanagh, Tracy Reiner, Bitty Schram, Jon Lovitz, David Strathairn, Garry Marshall, Bill Pullman, Ann Cusack, Anne Elizabeth Ramsay, Freddie Simpson, Renee Coleman, Tea Leoni, Joey Slotnick, Mark Holton, Gregory Sporleder, David Lander; ***D:*** Penny Marshall; ***W:*** Lowell Ganz, Babaloo Mandel; ***C:*** Miroslav Ondricek; ***M:*** Hans Zimmer; ***V:*** Harry Shearer.

Lean on Me **1989 (PG-13)** The romanticized version of the career of Joe Clark, a tough New Jersey teacher who became the principal of the state's toughest, worst school and, through controversial hardline tactics, turned it around. **109m/C VHS, DVD.** Morgan Freeman, Robert Guillaume, Beverly Todd, Alan North, Lynne Thigpen, Robin Bartlett, Michael Beach, Ethan Phillips, Regina Taylor; ***D:*** John G. Avildsen; ***W:*** Michael Schiffer; ***C:*** Victor Hammer; ***M:*** Bill Conti.

Leap of Faith **½ 1992 (PG-13)** Jonas Nightengale (Martin) is a traveling evangelist/scam artist whose tour bus is stranded in an impoverished farm town. Nevertheless he sets up his show and goes to work, aided by the technology utilized by accomplice Winger. Both Martin and Winger begin to have a change of heart after experiencing love—Winger with local sheriff Neeson and Martin after befriending a waitress (Davidovich) and her crippled brother (Haas). Martin is in his element as the slick revivalist with the hidden heart but the film is soft-headed as well as soft-hearted. **110m/C VHS, DVD.** Steve Martin, Debra Winger, Lolita (David) Davidovich, Liam Neeson, Lukas Haas, Meat Loaf Aday, Philip Seymour Hoffman, M.C. Gainey, La Chanze, Delores Hall, John Toles-Bey, Albertina Walker, Ricky Dillard; ***D:*** Richard Pearce; ***W:*** Janus Cercone; ***M:*** Cliff Eidelman.

Leap Year **½ 1921** Made at the apex of the 300-pound comedian's career, "Leap Year" wasn't released in the States until the '60s. Tried for manslaughter in 1921 (with two hung juries), Fatty was forced off camera and his films were taken out of circulation (although he did return to cinema behind the camera using the pseudonym William Goodrich). **60m/B VHS, DVD.** Mary Thurman, Lucien Littlefield, Clarence Geldart, Harriet Hammond, Fatty Arbuckle; ***D:*** James Cruze; ***W:*** Walter Woods; ***C:*** Karl Brown.

Leap Year **½ 2010 (PG)** Uptight bride wanna-be Anna (Adams) decides to follow her boyfriend Jeremy (Scott) to Dublin after being told of an Irish tradition that says that men must say yes to a proposal made on Leap Year Day. Stranded on the other side of the country, Anna must depend on surly (but handsome) innkeeper Declan (Goode) to help her out in this all-too-familiar "opposites attract" romantic comedy. Little wit or charm, but plenty of stock characters and gags you've seen a million times before, set against a scenic Irish backdrop in hopes that the uneven story and unappealing characters isn't noticeable. **100m/C DVD.** *US* Amy Adams, Matthew Goode, Adam Scott, John Lithgow, Kaitlin Olson; ***D:*** Anand Tucker; ***W:*** Harry Elfont, Deborah Kaplan; ***C:*** Newton Thomas (Tom) Sigel; ***M:*** Randy Edelman.

Leapin' Leprechauns **½ 1995 (PG)** John Dennehy's dad Michael has arrived from Ireland for a visit, accompanied by some "wee folk" who are invisible to all non-believers. Seems the little leprechauns are just in time to rescue their ancestral home from a plot by John to turn their Irish land into a theme park and make believers out of a family of skeptics. **84m/C VHS.** Grant Cramer, John Bluthal, Sharon Lee Jones, Gregory Edward Smith, Sylvester McCoy, James Ellis, Godfrey James, Tina Martin, Erica Nicole Hess; ***D:*** Ted Nicolaou; ***W:*** Ted Nicolaou, Michael McGann.

The Learning Curve **2001 (R)** Hospital orderly Paul (Giovinazzo) comes to the rescue of Georgia (Mazur) and gets involved in a shady sex scam. These small-timers are in for trouble when they target Marshal (Ventresca) who turns out to be a ruthless L.A. record producer with a lot of clout. Marshal's amused by their chutzpah and decides to bring them into his own shady deals where they are in over their heads. **97m/C VHS, DVD.** Carmine D. Giovinazzo, Monet Mazur, Vincent Ventresca, Steven Bauer, Majandra Delfino, Richard Erdman, Jack Laufer; ***D:*** Eric Schwab; ***W:*** Eric Schwab; ***C:*** Michael Hofstein; ***M:*** Zoran Boris.

The Learning Tree **1969 (PG)** A beautifully photographed adaptation of Parks' biographical novel about a 14-year-old black boy in the 1920s South, living on the verge of manhood, maturity, love, and wisdom. **107m/C VHS.** Kyle Johnson, Alex Clarke, Estelle Evans, Dana Elcar; ***D:*** Gordon Parks; ***C:*** Burnett Guffey. Natl. Film Reg. '89.

The Leather Boys *The Leatherboys* **1963** Teenaged Dot (Tushingham) marries mechanic Reggie (Campbell) and soon both begin to look beyond the boundaries of marriage. Dot enjoys her freedom from parental supervision by staying out and coming home drunk while Reggie takes up his friendship with biker pal, Pete (Sutton). Then Dot begins wondering just how close her husband and his best pal really are. Considered very controversial in the '60s, but looks staid now. **110m/B VHS, DVD.** *GB* Rita Tushingham, Colin Campbell, Dudley Sutton, Gladys Henson, Avice Landon, Betty Marsden, Dandy Nichols, Johnny Briggs, Geoffrey Dunn, Lockwood West, Denholm Elliott; ***D:*** Sidney J. Furie; ***W:*** Gillian Freeman; ***C:*** Gerald Gibbs.

Leather Burners **1943** Hoppy goes under cover to get the goods on a suspected rustler. When his cover is blown, the bad guys frame him for murder. Look for Robert Mitchum in his third bit part in this series. **66m/B VHS, DVD.** William Boyd, Andy Clyde, Jay Kirby, Victor Jory, George Givot, Bobby Larson, George Reeves, Hal Taliaferro, Forbes Murray, Robert Mitchum; ***D:*** Joseph Henabery.

Leather Jacket Love Story **1998** Remarkably sweet, campy, and raunchy romance finds 18-year-old Valley boy Kyle (Tataryn) taking a summer rental in bohemian Silver Lake in order to get the proper inspiration for his poetry. The local coffee shop is the preferred hangout and that's where Kyle spots leather-jacketed motorcycle man Mike (Bradley). Some 12 years older than Kyle, easygoing carpenter Mike is not adverse to some sexual fun, but both men are suprised when their feelings for each other start turning serious. **85m/B VHS.** Sean Tataryn, Christopher Bradley, Hector Mercado, Geoffrey Moody; ***Cameos:*** Mink Stole; ***D:*** David DeCoteau; ***W:*** Rondo Mieczkowski; ***C:*** Howard Wexler; ***M:*** Jeremy Jordan.

Leather Jackets **1990 (R)** Sweeney plays a nice guy who lets involvement with a childhood pal destroy his life. Elwes is the friend, now gang member, in trouble with both the cops and members of a rival gang, who needs Sweeney's help to escape. Fonda plays Sweeney's girlfriend caught between the two men. Essentially a routine fugitive pic with an attractive cast. **90m/C VHS.** D.B. Sweeney, Bridget Fonda, Cary Elwes, Christopher Penn, Marshall Bell, James LeGros, Jon Polito, Craig Ng, Ginger Lynn Allen; ***D:*** Lee Drysdale; ***W:*** Lee Drysdale.

Leatherface: The Texas Chainsaw Massacre 3 *Texas Chainsaw Massacre 3: Leatherface* **1989 (R)** The human-skin-wearing cannibal is at it again in this, the second sequel to the Tobe Hooper protomess. This one sports a bit more humor and is worth seeing for that reason. **81m/C VHS, DVD.** Kate Hodge, William Butler, Ken Foree, Tom Hudson, R.A. Mihailoff, Miriam Byrd-Nethery, Tom Everett, Joe Unger, Viggo Mortensen, David Cloud, Beth de Patie; ***D:*** Jeff Burr; ***W:*** David J. Schow; ***C:*** James L. Carter; ***M:*** Jim Manzie.

Leatherheads **½ 2008 (PG-13)** The 1925 Duluth Bulldogs, led by star player and all-around charmer Dodge Connelly (Clooney), are an upstart professional football team during a time when the pros lack the polish and respect of the college game. In a top-notch marketing move, Connelly adds well-known war hero Carter "The Bullet" Rutherford (Krasinski) to the roster in an effort to turn the tide of popular opinion. Unfortunately for the Bulldogs, Rutherford's war-hero credentials may have a few holes in them, which draw the attention of cute and sassy newspaper reporter Lexie Littleton (Zellweger). A kooky romantic triangle ensues as Connelly, the reporter and "The Bullet" ride the train between games and speakeasies through the season. Handsome threesome never quite pulls us in and the script's a clunker, but the chuckles are good and the period details are spot on. **113m/C DVD, Blu-ray Disc.** *US* George Clooney, Renee Zellweger, John Krasinski, Jonathan Pryce, Peter Gerety, Jack Thompson, Stephen (Steve) Root, Wayne Duvall, Keith Loneker; ***W:*** Duncan Brantley, Rick Reilly; ***C:*** Newton Thomas (Tom) Sigel; ***M:*** Randy Newman.

The Leatherneck **1928** Love unrequited in a faraway place starring soon to be cowboy (Hopalong Cassidy) matinee idol Boyd and Hale, the real life dad of Gilligan Island's skipper. **65m/B VHS.** William Boyd, Alan Hale, Diane Ellis; ***D:*** Howard Higgin; ***W:*** Elliot J. Clawson; ***C:*** John Mescall.

Leave 'Em Laughing **1981** Rooney plays Chicago clown Jack Thum in this based-on-real-life TV movie. Thum takes in orphans even though he cannot find steady work, and then discovers he has cancer. **103m/C VHS.** Mickey Rooney, Anne Jackson, Allen (Goorwitz) Garfield, Elisha Cook Jr., William Windom, Red Buttons, Michael LeClair; ***D:*** Jackie Cooper.

Leave Her to Heaven **1945** Beautiful neurotic Tierney takes drastic measures to keep hubby all to herself and will do anything to get what she wants. Tierney, in a departure from her usual roles, is excellent as this pathologically possessive creature. Oscar-winner Leon Shamroy's photography (in Technicolor) is breathtaking. Based on the novel by Ben Ames Williams. **110m/C VHS, DVD.** Gene Tierney, Cornel Wilde, Jeanne Crain, Vincent Price, Mary (Phillips) Philips, Ray Collins, Darryl Hickman, Gene Lockhart; ***D:*** John M. Stahl; ***W:*** Jo Swerling; ***C:*** Leon Shamroy; ***M:*** Alfred Newman. Oscars '45: Color Cinematog.

Leave It to Beaver **1997 (PG)** Gee, Mrs. Cleaver, that's an awful nice updating of an old TV favorite you have there. Cut the crap, Eddie. The "let's plop a lovable sitcom family into the dysfunctional 90s" bit has had its run. This time the victims are the Cleavers: wise dad Ward (McDonald), perfect mom June (Turner), popular older brother Wally (von Detten)...and newcomer Cameron Finley as the Beaver. Unlike the Bradys, the modern world has made some impact here. Beav has an African American friend while Mom wears jeans and owns a business. Gosh Wally, do you really think America was anxiously awaiting the return of the impossible-to-live-up-to clan? Don't be such a little dope. **88m/C VHS, DVD.** Christopher McDonald, Janine Turner, Erik von Detten, Cameron Finley, Barbara Billingsley, Ken Osmond, Adam Zolotin, Alan Rachins; ***D:*** Andy Cadiff; ***W:*** Brian Levant; ***C:*** Thomas Del Ruth; ***M:*** Randy Edelman.

Leave It to the Marines **½ 1951** A jerky guy wanders into a recruiting office instead of a marriage license bureau and unwittingly signs on for military service. **66m/B VHS.** Sid Melton, Mara Lynn, Gregg Martell, Ida Moore, Sam Flint, Douglas Evans, Margia Dean; ***D:*** Sam Newfield; ***W:*** Orville H. Hampton; ***C:*** Jack Greenhalgh.

Leaves from Satan's Book **½ 1919** Impressionistic episodes of Satan's fiddling with man through the ages, from Christ to the Russian Revolution. An early cinematic film by Dreyer, with ample indications of his later brilliance. Silent. **165m/B VHS, DVD.** *DK* Helge Milsen, Halvart Hoft, Jacob Texiere; ***D:*** Carl Theodor Dreyer.

Leaving Barstow **2008** Andrew wants to leave Barstow, CA but his devotion to his single mom Sandra and his interest in newcomer Jenny hold him back. Eventually Andrew realizes he has to choose whether to put his own dreams first or stay tied to the people he loves. **89m/C DVD.** Michelle Clunie, Steven Culp, Kevin Sheridan, Ryan Michelle Bathe, Ryan Carnes; ***D:*** Peter Paige; ***W:*** Kevin Sheridan, Jayson Crothers; ***M:*** Kurt Swinghammer.

Leaving Las Vegas **½ 1995 (R)** Ben Sanderson (Cage) is a hopeless alcoholic who goes to Vegas to drink himself to death, which is where he meets Sera (Shue), a lonely hooker who loves him enough not to stop him. Definitely as depressing as it sounds, but still manages to have both a subtle sense of humor and compassion. Cage tops his best work and Shue proves she deserves better than the lightweight roles she's had in the past. Not for everyone, but worth the effort for people who like to see honest emotion and hate Hollywood's insistence on happy endings. Based on the semi-autobiographical novel by John O'Brien, who committed suicide shortly before pre-production on the film began. **120m/C VHS, DVD.** Nicolas Cage, Elisabeth Shue, Julian Sands, Laurie Metcalf, David Brisbin, Richard Lewis, Valeria Golino, Steven Weber, Mariska Hargitay, Julian Lennon, Carey Lowell, Lucinda Jenney, Ed Lauter, R. Lee Ermey; ***D:*** Mike Figgis; ***W:*** Mike Figgis; ***C:*** Declan Quinn; ***M:*** Mike Figgis. Oscars '95: Actor (Cage); Golden Globes '96: Actor—Drama (Cage); Ind. Spirit '96: Actress (Shue), Cinematog., Director (Figgis), Film; L.A. Film Critics '95: Actor (Cage), Actress (Shue), Director (Figgis), Film; Natl. Bd. of Review '95: Actor (Cage); N.Y. Film Critics '95: Actor (Cage), Film; Natl. Soc. Film Critics '95: Actor (Cage), Actress (Shue), Director (Figgis); Screen Actors Guild '95: Actor (Cage).

Leaving Metropolis **2002** Successful Winnipeg artist David (Ruptash) is creatively blocked so he decides to get some inspiration by rejoining the real world as a waiter for married diner owners Violet (Taylor) and Matt (Corrazza). David's keeping his past quiet but finds himself attracted to Matt, who's confused by his own feelings. The two eventually have an affair, with Violet increasingly suspicious of her hubby and David's volatile best gal pal Kryla (Boyd) increasingly acting like a jealous spouse herself. The aftermath when the secrets are revealed is messy indeed. Well-played drama that Fraser adapted from his play "Poor Super Man." **89m/C VHS, DVD.** *CA* Troy Ruptash, Vincent Corazza, Lynda Boyd, Cherilee Taylor, Thom Allison; ***D:*** Brad Fraser; ***W:*** Brad Fraser; ***C:*** Daniel Vincelette; ***M:*** Dennis Burke.

Leaving Normal **½ 1992 (R)** Darly, a fed-up waitress, and Marianne, an abused housewife, meet at a bus stop in Normal, Wyoming and decide to blow town. They travel across the American West, through Canada, and up to Alaska, where Lahti's ex-boyfriend has left her a house. Because both women have made bad choices all their lives, they decide to leave their futures to chance, and end up finding their nirvana. Plot is similar to "Thelma & Louise," but "Leaving Normal" doesn't come close to the innovativeness of the former. Sappy and sentimental to the point of annoyance at times. **110m/C VHS.** Christine Lahti, Meg Tilly, Lenny Von Dohlen, Maury Chaykin, James Gammon, Patrika Darbo; Eve Gordon, James Eckhouse, Brett Cullen, Rutanya Alda; ***D:*** Edward Zwick; ***W:*** Edward Solomon; ***C:*** Ralf Bode.

Lebanon **2009** Set on the first day of the 1982 invasion of Lebanon by Israel. The majority of the film is set inside an Israeli tank as it moves across the border and is told from the viewpoint of the four 20-something soldiers who occupy the vehicle—commander Assi (Tiran), loader Hertzel (Cohen), driver Yigal (Moshonov), and gunner Shmulik (Donat). English, Hebrew, and Arabic with subtitles. **93m/C DVD.** *IS FR GE* Itay Tiran, Oshri Cohen, Michael Moshonov, Zohar Strauss, Yoav Donat; ***D:*** Samuel Maoz; ***W:*** Samuel Maoz; ***C:*** Gloria Bejach.

The Leech Woman 1959 While in Africa, an older woman (Gray) discovers how to restore her youth through a tribal ritual. The only problem is it requires the pineal gland of males, which causes her to go on a killing spree to keep that youthful look. Based on a story by Ben Pivar and Francis Rosenwald. **77m/B VHS.** Coleen Gray, Grant Williams, Gloria Talbott, Phillip Terry; ***D:*** Edward Dein; ***W:*** David Duncan.

Left Bank *Linkeroever* **2008** Until it descends into predictability in its last half, van Hees' feature debut is a solid Belgian chiller. To get away from her mother, Marie (Kuppens) decides to move in with new boyfriend Bobby (Schoenaerts) and discovers that the previous female tenant of his apartment disappeared. When Marie investigates, she learns that the complex was built on the site of a village that practiced sinister, possibly satanic rituals, and the building's blocked-up cellar may provide answers that Marie doesn't really want to know. English, Flemish, and French with subtitles. **102m/C DVD.** *BE* Eline Kuppens, Matthias Schoenaerts, Sien Eggers, Tom de Wispelaere, Marilou Mermans; ***D:*** Pieter vanHees; ***W:*** Pieter vanHees, Dimitri Karaktsanis; ***C:*** Nicols Karakatsanis; ***M:*** Simon Lenski.

Left Behind: The Movie **2000** Ace TV newsman Buck Williams (Cameron) is on hand for a sneak attack on Israel. Right after it, devout Christians and innocent children mysteriously vanish. The film is a dramatization of the novels based on a conservative Christian interpretation of the Book of Revelation. As entertainment, it's heavy handed at every level—plotting, acting, writing, directing. **95m/C VHS, DVD.** Kirk Cameron, Brad Johnson, Chelsea Noble, Clarence Gilyard Jr., Colin Fox, Gordon Currie, Daniel Pilon, Jack Langedijk; ***D:*** Vic Savin; ***W:*** Alan B. McElroy, Joe Goodman; ***C:*** Jiri (George) Tirl.

Left for Dead ½ **1978** A millionaire is accused of brutally killing his wife, and discovers in his search for an alibi that he is the victim of a conspiracy. **82m/C VHS.** Elke Sommer, Donald Pilon; ***D:*** Murray Markowitz.

The Left Hand of God **1955** After an American pilot escapes from a Chinese warlord in post-WWII, he disguises himself as a Catholic priest and takes refuge in a missionary hospital. Bogie is great as the flyboy/cleric. **87m/C VHS.** Humphrey Bogart, E.G. Marshall, Lee J. Cobb, Agnes Moorehead, Gene Tierney; ***D:*** Edward Dmytryk.

The Left-Handed Gun **1958** An offbeat version of the exploits of Billy the Kid, which portrays him as a 19th-century Wild West juvenile delinquent. Newman's role, which he method-acted, was originally intended for James Dean. Based on a 1955 Philco teleplay by Gore Vidal. **102m/B VHS, DVD.** Paul Newman, Lita Milan, John Dehner; ***D:*** Arthur Penn.

Left in Darkness ½ **2006** Well-done creepfest. Celia (Keena) goes to a frat party on her 21st birthday and dies after being given a date rape drug. She winds up in an otherworld, battling soul eaters, while her guardian/guide Donovan (Anders) tries to help Celia complete her journey to heaven. **88m/C DVD.** Monica Keena, Tim Thomerson, David Anders, Chris Engen; ***D:*** Steve Monroe; ***W:*** Philip Daay; ***C:*** Matthew Heckerling; ***M:*** Corey A. Jackson. **VIDEO**

Left Luggage ½ **1998** Sticky family saga set in Antwerp, Belgium in 1972. Non-religious college student Chaja (Fraser) is the daughter of Holocaust survivors (Sagebrecht and Schell), but has never sought to understand their ordeal or her religion. But that doesn't prevent her from taking a job as a nanny to a strict Hasidic family, the Kalmans. Carefree Chaja even manages to coax her mute four-year-old charge into speaking. She learns some lessons, the families learn some lessons (there's the prerequisite tragedy), and it's all so much unfortunate overkill. **100m/C VHS, DVD.** Laura Fraser, Isabella Rossellini, Jeroen Krabbe, Maximilian Schell, Marianne Saegebrecht, Chaim Topol; ***D:*** Jeroen Krabbe; ***W:*** Edwin de Vries; ***C:*** Walther Vanden Ende; ***M:*** Henny Vrienten.

The Legacy ½ *The Legacy of Maggie Walsh* **1979 (R)** An American couple become privy to the dark secrets of an English family gathering in a creepy mansion to inherit an eccentric millionaire's fortune. Death and demons abound. **100m/C VHS, DVD.** *GB* Katharine Ross, Sam Elliott, John Standing, Roger Daltrey, Ian Hogg; ***D:*** Richard Marquand; ***C:*** Dick Bush.

A Legacy for Leonette **WOOF! 1985** A girl is led into a web of murder and love in this torrid romance novel brought to video. **90m/C** Loyita Chapel, Michael Anderson Jr., Dinah Anne Rogers; ***D:*** Jim Drake.

Legacy of Horror **WOOF! 1978 (R)** A weekend at the family's island mansion with two unfriendly siblings sounds bad enough, but when terror, death, and a few family skeletons pop out of the closets, things go from bad to weird. All-round poor effort with substantial gore. A remake of the director's own "The Ghastly Ones." **83m/C VHS.** Elaine Boies, Chris Broderick, Marilee Troncone, Jeannie Cusik; ***D:*** Andy Milligan.

Legacy of Lies ½ **1992 (R)** Zack Resnick is a serious, honest Chicago cop assigned to a murder investigation. He first discovers the killers got the wrong man and then finds out a lot of family secrets he wishes he didn't know. His cop-father is on the take to the Mob, which is really no surprise since Zack's grandfather turns out to be a retired gangland boss, all of which leaves Zack wondering where his loyalties lie. Too intricate plot hampers the story's flow but the cast performances are well worth watching. **94m/C VHS.** Michael Ontkean, Martin Landau, Eli Wallach, Joe Morton, Patricia Clarkson, Gerry Becker, Chelcie Ross, Ron Dean; ***D:*** Jason Meshover-Iorg; ***W:*** David Black. **CABLE**

Legacy of Rage **1986** Brandon (Lee), a waiter, befriends young mobster Michael (Wong), who turns out to be in love with Brandon's fiancee, May (Kent). In fact, Michael frames Brandon on a murder charge and gets him thrown in prison in order to get the girl. And what's Brandon's first thought when he gets out of the slammer? Revenge. Lee's first feature film. Chinese with subtitles or dubbed. **86m/C VHS, DVD.** *HK* Brandon Lee, Michael Wong, Bolo Yeung, Regina Kent; ***D:*** Ronny Yu.

Legal Deceit ½ *The Promised Land* **1995 (R)** Ambitious new lawyer Sydney Banks (Rochone) is taken under the wing of corporate hotshot Todd Hunter (Morgan). Then she learns his success is based on blackmail and murder, so she and boyfriend Derek (Morris) work to save her life as well as her career. **93m/C VHS.** Lela Rochon, Jeffrey Dean Morgan, Phil Morris, John Stockwell, Cheryl Francis Harrington, Jeff Marcus; ***D:*** Monika Harris; ***W:*** Monika Harris; ***C:*** Stan McClain; ***M:*** Michael Giacchino.

Legal Eagles ½ **1986 (PG)** An assistant D.A. faces murder, mayhem, and romance while prosecuting a girl accused of stealing a portrait painted by her father. Redford sparkles in this otherwise convoluted tale from Reitman, while Hannah lacks depth as the daffy thief. **116m/C VHS, DVD.** Robert Redford, Debra Winger, Daryl Hannah, Brian Dennehy, Terence Stamp, Steven Hill, David Clennon, Roscoe Lee Browne, John McMartin, Jennifer (Jennie) Dundas Lowe, Ivan Reitman; ***D:*** Ivan Reitman; ***W:*** Jack Epps Jr., Jim Cash; ***C:*** Laszlo Kovacs; ***M:*** Elmer Bernstein.

Legal Tender ½ **1990 (R)** Rude talk-show host Downey as a corrupt S & L chief? Big, menacing Davi as a romantic hero? Give this often-inept thriller credit for creative casting, if little else. Roberts adds steamy sex appeal as a lovely saloon-keeper imperiled by deadly bank fraud. **93m/C VHS.** Robert Davi, Tanya Roberts, Morton Downey Jr.; ***D:*** Jag Mundhra.

Legalese ½ **1998 (R)** Solid cast provides solid enjoyment in this skewering of tabloid journalists and the legal system. Celeb lawyer Norman Keane (Garner) doesn't take the case of actress Angela Beale (Gershon), who's accused of killing her brother-in-law. But he does recommend new kid attorney, Roy Guyton (Kerr), to take the heat while Keane works behind the scenes. This raises the antennae of tabloid TV anchorwoman Brenda Whitlass (Turner) who winds up with a video of Guyton getting up close and personal with fellow lawyer Rica Martin (Parker). Needless to say, ethics have very little to do with anything. **105m/C VHS.** James Garner, Edward Kerr, Kathleen Turner, Mary-Louise Parker, Gina Gershon; ***D:*** Glenn Jordan; ***W:*** Billy Ray; ***C:*** Tobias Schliessler; ***M:*** Stewart Copeland. **CABLE**

Legally Blonde ½ **2001 (PG-13)** Beverly Hills blonde Elle Woods (Witherspoon) is a sorority babe who dresses in pink and has her Chihuahua Bruiser as a constant companion. After getting dumped by frat boyfriend Warner (Davis), who's on his way to Harvard Law School, Elle wallows in chocolate-fueled misery. But determined to show him that's she more than the sum of her pretty parts, Elle also gets accepted and shows all those pasty-faced easterners, including Warner's new fiancee, brunette Vivian (Blair), that she has brains as well as blonde roots when she gets involved in a big murder case. Witherspoon is a delight in a very lightweight comedy. **95m/C VHS, DVD.** *US* Reese Witherspoon, Matthew Davis, Selma Blair, Luke Wilson, Ali Larter, Holland Taylor, Victor Garber, Jessica Cauffiel, Jennifer Coolidge, Oz (Osgood) Perkins II, Alanna Ubach, Raquel Welch, Linda Cardellini, Meredith Scott Lynn; ***D:*** Robert Luketic; ***W:*** Karen McCullah Lutz, Kirsten Smith; ***C:*** Anthony B. Richmond; ***M:*** Rolfe Kent.

Legally Blonde 2: Red White & Blonde **2003 (PG-13)** In the sequel to the 2001 surprise hit, Boston lawyer Elle Woods (Witherspoon) heads to D.C. and becomes the aide to congresswoman Rudd (Field) and takes up the cause of animal rights. Witherspoon's zest and charm are the only things to recommend about this mostly unfunny cliche-fest that traps some real talent in ridiculously cardboard roles. Other than Witherspoon, the only bright spots are Coolidge as Elle's manicurist friend, and the dog whose family provides the main plot push-start. **95m/C VHS, DVD.** *US* Reese Witherspoon, Sally Field, Bob Newhart, Luke Wilson, Jennifer Coolidge, Regina King, Bruce McGill, Dana Ivey, Mary Lynn Rajskub, Jessica Cauffiel, Alanna Ubach, J Barton; ***D:*** Charles Herman-Wurmfeld; ***W:*** Kate Kondell; ***C:*** Elliot Davis; ***M:*** Rolfe Kent.

Legend **1986 (PG)** A colorful, unabashedly Tolkien-esque fantasy about the struggle to save an innocent waif from the Prince of Darkness. Set in a land packed with unicorns, magic swamps, bumbling dwarves and rainbows. Produced in Great Britain. **89m/C VHS, DVD.** *GB* Tom Cruise, Mia Sara, Tim Curry, David Bennent, Billy Barty, Alice Playten; ***D:*** Ridley Scott; ***M:*** Jerry Goldsmith.

Legend of Alfred Packer ½ **1980** The true story of how a guide taking five men searching for gold in Colorado managed to be the sole survivor of a blizzard. **87m/C VHS, DVD.** Patrick Dray, Ron Haines, Bob Damon, Dave Ellingson; ***D:*** Jim Roberson.

The Legend of Bagger Vance ½ **2000 (PG-13)** Director Redford misses the cut by presenting golf as a mystical experience instead of a bunch of guys in funny pants torturing a lawn. Rannulph Junuh (Damon) returns from WWI a vastly changed man. The former golf golden boy seems content to squander the rest of his life drinking at the 19th hole. His former girlfriend Adele (Theron), facing a pile of debts, convinces him to participate in an exhibition against golf giants Bobby Jones (Gretsch) and Walter Hagen (McGill) to showcase her new course. As he's shanking practice shots in every direction, the mysterious Bagger (Smith) appears, offering him guidance about golf and life in Eastern philosophy sound bites. Junuh finds his "Authentic Swing" with the help of Bagger, but it may be too late to catch his competition. Beautiful scenery, but the pace is a little too slow (just like golf!). Fits in well with the flawed American hero theme that has run through Redford's work since his turn as Jay Gatsby. Based on the novel by Steven Pressfield. Once upon a time director Redford wanted to star himself before deciding he was too mature for the part. **127m/C VHS, DVD.** Matt Damon, Will Smith, Charlize Theron, Jack Lemmon, Bruce McGill, Lane Smith, Harve Presnell, Peter Gerety, Michael O'Neill, Thomas Jay Ryan, Joel Gretsch, J. Michael Moncrief; ***D:*** Robert Redford; ***W:*** Jeremy Leven; ***C:*** Michael Ballhaus; ***M:*** Rachel Portman.

Legend of Billie Jean **1985 (PG-13)** Billie Jean believed in justice for all. When the law and its bureaucracy landed hard on her, she took her cause to the masses and inspired a generation. **92m/C VHS.** Helen Slater, Peter Coyote, Keith Gordon, Christian Slater, Richard Bradford, Yeardley Smith, Dean Stockwell; ***D:*** Matthew Robbins; ***W:*** Mark Rosenthal.

The Legend of Black Thunder Mountain ½ **1979 (G)** A children's adventure in the mold of "Grizzly Adams" and "The Wilderness Family." **90m/C VHS, DVD.** Holly Beeman, Steve Beeman, Ron Brown, F.A. Milovich; ***D:*** Tom Beeman.

The Legend of Blood Castle *The Female Butcher; Blood Ceremony; Ceremonia Sangrienta* **1972 (R)** Another version of the Countess of Bathory legend, in which an evil woman bathes in the blood of virgins in an attempt to keep the wrinkles away. Released hot on the heels of Hammer's "Countess Dracula." **87m/C VHS.** *IT SP* Lucia Bose, Ewa Aulin; ***D:*** Jorge Grau.

The Legend of Bloody Mary **2008** Long ago some lady named Mary Worth was impregnated by a priest and refused to fess up who the father was. Apparently the standard punishment for Puritan women who get pregnant out of wedlock was to have their face carved off in front of a mirror. Centuries later, partygoers make a game of Mary's plight: write your friends' names on a mirror while chanting her name and she pops out and kills you, all because she's "vengeful." Apparently charades isn't the crowd-pleaser it once was. **93m/C DVD.** Robert Locke, Caitlin Wachs, Rachael Taylor, Dean O'Gorman, Nicole Aiken, Brittany Miller, Inna Costa, Cooper Campbell, Joseph Domingo, Elissa Dowling, Kristen Dalto, Lauren Phillips; ***D:*** John Stecenko; ***W:*** John Stecenko, Dominic R. Domingo; ***C:*** John Stecenko, Joe Hendrick; ***M:*** Steven Keifer. **VIDEO**

Legend of Boggy Creek ½ **1975 (G)** A dramatized version of various Arkansas Bigfoot sightings. **87m/C VHS, DVD.** Willie E. Smith, John P. Nixon, John W. Gates, Jeff Crabtree, Buddy Crabtree; ***D:*** Charles B. Pierce; ***W:*** Earl E. Smith; ***C:*** Charles B. Pierce; ***Nar:*** Vern Stierman.

The Legend of Butch & Sundance ½ **2004 (PG-13)** This unsold NBC TV pilot is a generally lively western that finds Butch Parker (Rogers) going from easy-going cowboy to bank robber alongside his best friend, gunslinger Harry "Sundance Kid" Longabaugh (Browning). Both become part of Mike Cassidy's (Biehn) "Wild Bunch" gang, targeting banks that are controlled by greedy railroad barons. The two men are also equally attached to schoolteacher Etta Place (Lefevre). When Pinkerton agent Durango (Gibbons) kills Cassidy, Butch takes his last name out of respect and vows vengeance. **120m/C DVD.** Ryan Browning, Rachelle Lefevre, Michael Biehn, Susan Ruttan, David Clayton Rogers, Blake Gibbons; ***D:*** Sergio Mimica-Gezzan; ***W:*** John Fasano; ***C:*** Igor Maglic; ***M:*** Basil Poledouris. **TV**

The Legend of Cryin' Ryan **1998 (PG)** After leveling the tombstone of a long-dead school bully, teenager Kris freaks out when his ghost is set loose. But when the boy, who died at age 13 of unknown causes, tells her about his abusive father she's bent on setting the record straight so that his soul can move along. **90m/C VHS, DVD.** Harrison Myers, Ernie Lively, Harold Jacob Smith, Dean Tschetter, Rhelda Mortensen, Rob Lunn, Christian LeBrun, Charlie Foster Fulkerson, Anne Marie Fulkerson; ***D:*** Julie St. Claire; ***C:*** Mark Foggetti; ***M:*** Sean Murray. **VIDEO**

The Legend of Drunken Master *Drunken Master 2; Jui Kun 2* **1994 (R)** Jackie Chan shows the moves that made him the Charlie Chaplin of chopsocky in this sequel to the original "Drunken Master," the movie that made him a star in Hong Kong. Chan plays legendary Chinese folk hero Wong Fei-hong as a rowdy young man (although Chan was nearly 40 when it was filmed) whose martial arts moves get better as he gets drunker. While traveling by train with his father Wong Kei-ying (Lung), he mistakenly takes a package that contains a priceless imperial Chinese artifact that is in the process of being smuggled out of the country by a corrupt British official. Evil henchmen are then sent to be pummeled by Fei-hong's inebriated fists. Director Lau Kar-leung performs double duty by playing Fu Min-chi, a grizzled old man also on the trail of the stolen artifact. If you're a fan of the kung-fu genre, the finale between Chan and Low Houi-kang (also known as Ken Lo, Chan's bodyguard) is not to be missed. Re-released in America six years after its original Asian release complete with classic "bad Chinese accent" dubbing. **102m/C VHS, DVD.** *HK* Jackie Chan, Lau Kar Leung, Anita (Yim-Fong) Mui, Ti Lung, Andy Lau; ***D:*** Lau Kar Leung; ***W:*** Edward Tang; ***C:*** Yiu-tsou Cheung, Tong-Leung Cheung, Jingle Ma, Man-Wan Wong; ***M:*** Michael Wandmacher.

Legend of Earl Durand 1/2 **1974** In Wyoming 1939, a man spends his life searching for freedom and justice. His Robin Hood actions cause a manhunt of massive proportions. **90m/C VHS.** Martin Sheen, Peter Haskell, Keenan Wynn, Slim Pickens, Anthony Caruso; ***D:*** John D. Patterson.

The Legend of Frank Woods **1977** Gunslinger returns to the land of the free after an extended holiday south of the border. Mistaken for an expected preacher in a small town, he poses as the padre and signs on the dotted line to take out a new lease on life. **88m/C VHS, DVD.** Troy Donahue, Brad Steward, Kitty Vallacher, Michael Christian; ***D:*** Deno Paoli.

Legend of Frenchie King 1/2 *Petroleum Girls* **1971** When prospectors discover oil on disputed land, two families feud over their conflicting claims to the property. Adult western still working out the kinks has Bardot heading a band of female outlaws. **96m/C VHS.** Brigitte Bardot, Claudia Cardinale, Michael J. Pollard, Micheline Presle; ***D:*** Christian-Jaque.

The Legend of Gator Face 1/2 **1996 (PG)** Hermit Winfield fills three youngsters in on their small community's legend of Gator Face—half-man, half-alligator. Kids being kids, they decide to wade through the swamps in search of the creature, which they find and also realize is harmless. Too bad the local folk don't believe the same thing and call out the national guard to destroy it. **100m/C VHS, DVD.** Paul Winfield, John White, Dan Warry-Smith, C. David Johnson, Gordon Michael Woolvett; ***D:*** Vic Sarin.

The Legend of Hell House **1973 (PG)** A multi-millionaire hires a team of scientists and mediums to investigate his newly acquired haunted mansion. It seems that the creepy house has been the site of a number of deaths and may hold clues to the afterlife. A suspenseful, scary screamfest. Matheson wrote the screenplay from his novel "Hell House." **94m/C VHS, DVD.** Roddy McDowall, Pamela Franklin, Clive Revill, Gayle Hunnicutt, Peter Bowles, Roland Culver, Michael Gough; ***D:*** John Hough; ***W:*** Richard Matheson; ***C:*** Alan Hume; ***M:*** Brian Hodgson, Delia Derbyshire.

The Legend of Hillbilly John *Who Fears the Devil; My Name is John* **1973 (G)** Hillbilly John holds off the devil with a strum of his six-string. While demons plague the residents of rural America, the hayseed messiah wanders about saving the day. **86m/C VHS.** Severn Darden, Denver Pyle, Susan Strasberg, Hedge Capers; ***D:*** John Newland.

The Legend of Jedediah Carver **1976** A rancher battles desert elements and hostile Indians in a desperate bid for survival. **90m/C VHS.** DeWitt Lee, Joshua Hoffman, Val Chapman, Richard Montgomery, David Terril; ***D:*** DeWitt Lee.

The Legend of Johnny Lingo **2003 (G)** Orphaned as an infant, Tama winds up on a remote South Pacific island where he is initially revered as a god but ultimately is cast aside. He befriends Mahana, and when he decides to sail away in search of a better life he assures her that he'll come back for her. Washing up on another island, he meets a well-to-do trader, Johnny Lingo, who becomes his life mentor and aides him in fulfilling his promise. Drawing from Patricia McGerr's "Johnny Lingo's Eight-Cow Wife" and the 1969 film short "Johnny Lingo" by Wezel O. Whitaker, rookie director Ramirez holds to the tale's feel-good essence but drifts astray in the execution. **95m/C VHS, DVD.** George Henare, Joe Folau, Rawiri Paratene, Kayte Ferguson; ***D:*** Steve Ramirez; ***W:*** Riwia Brown; ***C:*** Allen Guilford; ***M:*** Kevin Kiner. **VIDEO**

Legend of Lobo 1/2 **1962** The story of Lobo, a crafty wolf who seeks to free his mate from the clutches of greedy hunters. A Disney wildlife adventure. **67m/C VHS, DVD.** ***D:*** James Nelson Algar; ***W:*** James Nelson Algar; ***Nar:*** Rex Allen.

The Legend of Lucy Keyes **2006 (R)** The Cooley family moves into the old Keyes house in Massachusetts, which is reputed to be haunted. In 1755, young Lucy Keyes disappeared while in the nearby woods and her mother Martha went mad searching for her daughter. Now, mom Jeanne (Delpy) begins to have nightmares and fears for her own daughter Lucy (Hinkle), especially when ghostly visions seem to want Jeanne to solve the mystery and let Lucy Keyes finally rest. **93m/C DVD.** Julie Delpy, Justin Theroux, Brooke Adams, Mark Boone Jr., Cassidy Hinkle, Anna Friedman; ***D:*** John Stimpson; ***W:*** John Stimpson; ***C:*** Gary Henoch; ***M:*** Ed Grenga.

The Legend of 1900 *The Legend of the Pianist on the Ocean; La Leggenda del Pianista Sull'Oceano* **1998 (R)** Originally released under a different title and at 170 minutes, this re-cut English-language debut feature for Italian director Tornatore still has its problems. An abandoned infant is discovered aboard the luxury liner Virginian in 1900 and reared by the engine crew. As an adult, the nicknamed 1900 (Roth), has become a virtuoso pianist in the ship's orchestra and has superstitiously never set foot off the boat. His best friend is trumpet player Max (Vince), who tells the story in flashback after learning the ship has been condemned. But since 1900 remains an enigma, you won't really care what happens to him. **116m/C VHS, DVD.** Tim Roth, Pruitt Taylor Vince, Clarence Williams III, Bill Nunn, Melanie Thierry; ***D:*** Giuseppe Tornatore; ***W:*** Giuseppe Tornatore; ***C:*** Lajos Koltai; ***M:*** Ennio Morricone. Golden Globes '00: Score.

The Legend of Paul and Paula *Die Legende von Paul und Paula* **1973** East German censors tried to ban Carow's film, which focuses on personal freedoms, but it proved to be so popular with audiences that the ban never worked. Paula (Domrose) is a free-spirited unmarried salesclerk with two children while Paul (Glatzeder) is a conservative bureaucrat in a loveless marriage. They met by accident and fall in love while Paula tries to liberate Paul from his dull existence. But Paul finds it difficult to let go—until tragedy beset them. German with subtitles. **106m/C VHS, DVD.** *GE* Angelica Domrose, Winfried Glatzeder; ***D:*** Heiner Carow; ***W:*** Heiner Carow, Ulrich Plenzdorf; ***C:*** Jurgen Brauer; ***M:*** Peter Gotthardt.

The Legend of Rita *Die Stille Nach Dem Schuss; The Silence After the Shot* **1999** Rita (Beglau) is part of a West German left-wing terrorist group in the 1970s. She's caught attempting to enter East Germany by Stasi officer Erwin Hull (Wuttke), who lets her go but slyly offers to come to her aid when needed. After some trouble, Rita agrees to Hull's offer to assume a new identity and live a worker's life in East Germany. Then Rita discovers that her political ideals are at odds with ordinary, everyday life and people disenchanted by socialism. But she faces a greater change when the Berlin Wall comes down and Rita's terrorist past is exposed. German with subtitles. **101m/C VHS, DVD.** *GE* Bibiana Beglau, Martin Wuttke, Nadja Uhl, Harald Schrott, Alexander Beyer, Jenny Schily; ***D:*** Volker Schlondorff; ***W:*** Volker Schlondorff, Wolfgang Kohlhaase; ***C:*** Andreas Hofer.

The Legend of Sea Wolf *Wolf Larsen* **1975 (PG)** A sadistic sea captain forcefully rules his crew in this weak version of Jack London's novel. **90m/C VHS, DVD.** *IT* Chuck Connors, Barbara Bach, Joseph Palmer; ***D:*** Giuseppe Vari; ***W:*** Marcello Ciorciolini; ***C:*** Sergio Rubini; ***M:*** Guido de Angelis, Maurizio de Angelis.

The Legend of Sleepy Hollow 1/2 **1949** The story of Ichabod Crane and the legendary ride of the headless horseman by Washington Irving; narrated by Crosby. Also includes two classic short cartoons, "Lonesome Ghosts" (1932) with Mickey Mouse and "Trick or Treat" (1952) with Donald Duck. **45m/C VHS.** ***D:*** Jack Kinney, Clyde Geronimi, James Nelson Algar; ***Nar:*** Bing Crosby.

The Legend of Sleepy Hollow 1/2 **1979 (G)** Washington Irving's classic tale of the Headless Horseman of Sleepy Hollow is brought to life on the screen. **100m/C VHS.** Jeff Goldblum, Dick Butkus, Paul Sand, Meg Foster, James J. Griffith, John S. White; ***D:*** Henning Schellerup; ***W:*** Malvin Wald. **TV**

The Legend of Sleepy Hollow **1986** Classic Washington Irving tale is given the Shelly Duvall treatment in her "Tall Tales and Legends" series. When a snooty teacher goes too far, the town blacksmith decides to play the ultimate Halloween trick on him. **51m/C VHS.** Ed Begley Jr., Beverly D'Angelo, Charles Durning, Tim Thomerson. **CABLE**

The Legend of Suram Fortress *Legenda Suramskoi Kreposti* **1985** Based on a Georgian folktale about a medieval fortress that collapses as soon as it is built. The village soothsayer tells a young man he must sacrifice himself, by bricking himself up alive within the fortress walls, if the building is every to stand. In Russian with English subtitles. **89m/C VHS, DVD.** *RU* Levani Outchanechvili, Zourab Kipchidze; ***D:*** Sergei Paradjanov; ***W:*** Vaja Gigashvili; ***C:*** Yuri Klimenko.

The Legend of Suriyothai 1/2 *Francis Ford Coppola Presents: The Legend of Suriyothai; Suriyothai* **2002 (R)** In Siam (now Thailand) in 1528, the north and south each elected their own kings, and a young girl named Suriyothai (Bhirombhakdi) is forced to leave her true love to marry the man who will become the future king. In 1548 he dies in battle with rival nation Burma, and she must lead her people's army to confront the invaders. Originally 185 minutes long, it has been trimmed to 142 minutes for international release with the help of Francis Ford Coppola. The film was directed and made by Thai royalty. **142m/C DVD.** *TH* M. L. Piyapas Bhirombakdi, Sarunyu Wongkrachang, Chatchai Plengpanich, Johnny Anfone, Mai Charoenpura, Sinjai Plengpanit, Sorapong Chatree, Ampol Lamppon, Supakorn Kitsuwon, Penpak Sirikul, Wannasa Thongviset, Ronrittichai Khanket, Saharath Sangkapreecha, Varuth Waratham, Suphakit Tangthatswasd, Sombat Metanee, Akekaphan Bunluerit, Saad Peampongsanta, Manop Aswathep, Krung Srivilai; ***D:*** Chatrichalerm Yukol; ***W:*** Chatrichalerm Yukol, Sunait Chutintaranond; ***C:*** Igor Luther, Anupap Buachand, Stanislav Dorsic; ***M:*** Richard Harvey.

Legend of the Bog 1/2 *Bog Bodies* **2008 (R)** A 2000-year-old mummified murder victim is disturbed from its Irish bog resting place and causes havoc for a group of strangers who turn out to share a disturbing secret. **92m/C DVD.** Vinnie Jones, Jason Barry, Nora-Jane Noone, Adam Fogerty, Gavin Kelly; ***D:*** Brendan Foley; ***W:*** Brendan Foley; ***C:*** Stephen Murphy; ***M:*** Graham Slack. **VIDEO**

Legend of the Dinosaurs and Monster Birds **WOOF!** *Legend of the Dinosaurs; Legend of Dinosaurs and Ominous Birds; Kyoryuu: Kaicho no densetsu* **1977** Generally recognized by monster movie fans as one of the worst films of all time. Severe weather changes in the Mount Fuji area awaken a plesiosaur, which immediately begins to perform a bad "Jaws" parody. Meanwhile a gigantic pterodactyl hatches in a nearby cave and adds to the chaos. Eventually they meet in an epic battle. Oddly bloody for an early Japanese monster movie. **92m/C DVD.** *JP* Mineko Maruhira, Satoru Nabe; ***D:*** Junji Kurata; ***W:*** Masaru Igami, Takeshi Matsumoto, Ichiro Otsu; ***C:*** Shigeru Akatsuka; ***M:*** Masao Yagi.

Legend of the Liquid Sword **WOOF!** *Siu hap Cho Lau Heung; The Liquid Sword; Xiao xia Chu Liu Xiang* **1993** A twisting mess of intrigue where people fight, make friends, fight again, and end up who knows where as well as a weird vampire bad guy named Batman. Even weirder martial arts comedy inspired by a popular Chinese story, and the usual poorly-translated dialogue. Despite Gordon Liu being on the cover, he's only in the film for a scene or two. **82m/C DVD.** *HK* Julian Cheung, Norman Chu, Aaron Kwok, Chingmy Yau, Anita Yuen, Sharla Cheung, Winnie Lau, Kei Mai, Siu-Lun Wan, Wan-Si Wong, Gloria Yip, Fennie Yuen; ***D:*** Jing Wong; ***W:*** Jing Wong.

Legend of the Lone Ranger 1/2 **1981 (PG)** The fabled Lone Ranger (whose voice is dubbed throughout the entire movie) and the story of his first meeting with his Indian companion, Tonto, are brought to life in this weak and vapid version of the famous legend. The narration by Merle Haggard leaves something to be desired as do most of the performances. **98m/C VHS.** Klinton Spilsbury, Michael Horse, Jason Robards Jr., Richard Farnsworth, Christopher Lloyd, Matt Clark; ***D:*** William A. Fraker; ***W:*** William Roberts, Ivan Goff, Michael Kane; ***M:*** John Barry. Golden Raspberries '81: Worst Actor (Spilsbury), Worst New Star (Spilsbury).

Legend of the Lost **1957** Two men vie for desert treasure and desert women. Interesting only because of Wayne, but certainly not one of his more memorable films. **109m/C VHS, DVD.** John Wayne, Sophia Loren, Rossano Brazzi, Kurt Kasznar, Sonia Moser; ***D:*** Henry Hathaway; ***C:*** Jack Cardiff.

Legend of the Lost Tomb 1/2 **1997 (PG)** Adventure finds Egyptologist Dr. Leonhardt (Rossovich) discovering half of an ancient papyrus that could lead to the riches of the desert tomb of pharaoh Ramses II. But Leonhardt is ambused by his rival Dr. Bent (Keach), who demands the rest of the document, which just happens to be in the hands of Leonhardt's son (Pierce) and his archaeologist associate Karen (Peterson). **90m/C VHS.** Rick Rossovich, Stacy Keach, Kimberlee Peterson, Brock Pierce; ***D:*** Jonathan Winfrey. **CABLE**

The Legend of the Sea Wolf 1/2 *Wolf Larsen; Larsen, Wolf of the Seven Seas* **1958** Adaptation of Jack London's dramatic adventure novel, "The Sea Wolf." A slave driving ship captain rescues a shipwreck victim and sets to abusing him along with the rest of his crew. A rebellion ensues. Superb musical score benefits the strong acting and good pace. **83m/B VHS.** Barry Sullivan, Peter Graves, Gita Hall, Thayer David; ***D:*** Harmon Jones; ***W:*** Jack DeWitt.

The Legend of the 7 Golden Vampires *The Seven Brothers Meet Dracula; Dracula and the Seven Golden Vampires* **1973** It's kung-fu meets horror as Van Helsing pursues Dracula to 19th-century China and is assisted by martial artists. One of the last Hammer coproductions. The Anchor Bay release also contains the 75-minute "Seven Brothers Meet Dracula," which was the U.S. version of the movie. **89m/C VHS, DVD.** *GB* Peter Cushing, David Chang, Robin Stewart, Julie Ege, John Forbes-Robertson; ***D:*** Roy Ward Baker; ***W:*** Don Houghton; ***C:*** Roy Ford, John Wilcox; ***M:*** James Bernard.

Legend of the Werewolf **1975 (R)** A child who once ran with the wolves has forgotten his past, except when the moon is full. **90m/C VHS.** *GB* Peter Cushing, Hugh Griffith, Ron Moody, David Rintoul, Lynn Dalby, Stefan Gryff, Renee Houston, Norman Mitchell, Marjorie Yates, Roy Castle; ***D:*** Freddie Francis; ***W:*** Renee Houston.

The Legend of the Wolf Woman 1/2 *Daughter of the Werewolf; Werewolf Woman; She-Wolf* **1977 (R)** The beautiful Daniella assumes the personality of the legendary wolfwoman, leaving a trail of gruesome killings across the countryside. Genre fans will find this one surprisingly entertaining. Also on video as "Werewolf Woman." **84m/C VHS, DVD.** *IT* Anne Borel, Frederick Stafford, Tino Carey, Elliot Zamuto, Ollie Reynolds, Andrea Scotti, Karen Carter, Howard (Red) Ross; ***D:*** Rino Di Silvestro; ***W:*** Rino Di Silvestro, Howard (Red) Ross.

Legend of Tom Dooley **1959** Somber western about three Confederate soldiers who rob a Union stagecoach and kill two soldiers, not knowing that the Civil War has ended. Landon turns in a good performance as the Rebel soldier turned outlaw. Based on the hit song by the Kingston trio. **79m/B VHS.** Michael Landon, Jo Morrow, Jack Hogan, Richard Rust, Dee Pollock, Ken Lynch; ***D:*** Ted Post; ***M:*** Ronald Stein.

Legend of Valentino 🦴🦴 **1975** Docudrama traces the legendary exploits of one of the silver screen's greatest lovers, Rudolph Valentino. Typical TV-movie fare that lacks the power of the legend's life. **96m/C VHS, DVD.** Franco Nero, Suzanne Pleshette, Lesley Ann Warren, Yvette Mimieux, Judd Hirsch, Milton Berle, Harold J. Stone; ***D:*** Melville Shavelson. **TV**

Legend of Walks Far Woman 🦴 **1982** A proud Sioux woman fights for survival and her tribe during the American-Indian Wars. Welch is miscast. From Colin Stuart's novel. **120m/C VHS.** Raquel Welch, Nick Mancuso, Bradford Dillman; ***D:*** Mel Damski. **TV**

The Legend of Wolf Mountain 🦴🦴 ½ **1992 (PG)** Three children are held hostage by two prison escapees in the Utah mountains. They are aided in their escape by a Native American "wolf spirit." With the criminals on their trail will the three be able to survive in the wilderness until a search party can find them? **91m/C VHS.** Mickey Rooney, Bo Hopkins, Don Shanks, Vivian Schilling, Robert Z'Dar, David "Shark" Fralick, Nicole Lund, Natalie Lund, Matthew Lewis, Jonathan Best; ***D:*** Craig Clyde; ***W:*** Craig Clyde.

The Legend of Zorro 🦴🦴 ½ **2005 (PG)** Noisy sequel to "The Mask of Zorro" finds Banderas returning as our swashbuckling masked hero, along with Zeta-Jones as his equally hot-blooded spouse, Elena. They are now the parents of impetuous 10-year-old Joaquin (Alonso), but the marriage has enough cracks that Elena kicks Zorro out on his cape. There's also a couple of bad guys—sneering aristocrat Armand (Sewell) and scurvy McGivens (Chinlund)—and a plot that has to do with California becoming part of the United States. The leads are having a lot of fun and there's enough ridiculous action to make the pic speed by. **129m/C DVD, Blu-ray Disc, UMD.** *US* Antonio Banderas, Catherine Zeta-Jones, Rufus Sewell, Nicholas Chinlund, Julio Oscar Mechoso, Shuler Hensley, Michael Emerson, Adrian Alonso; ***D:*** Martin Campbell; ***W:*** Roberto Orci, Alex Kurtzman; ***C:*** Phil Meheux; ***M:*** James Horner.

Legends of the Fall 🦴🦴 **1994 (R)** Sweeping, meandering, melodramatic family saga set in Montana (though filmed in Alberta, Canada). Patriarch William Ludlow (Hopkins), a retired Army colonel, is raising three sons: reserved Alfred (Quinn), idealistic Samuel (Thomas), and wild middle son Tristan (Pitt). In 1913, Samuel returns from Boston with a fiancee, the lovely and refined Susannah (Ormond). Only problem is Alfred and Tristan take one look and also desire her—a passion that will carry them through some 20 years of heartbreak. Film loses the spare toughness of the Jim Harrison novella but is a visual feast (and not just because the camera seems to drool every time Pitt appears on screen.) **134m/C VHS, DVD, Blu-ray Disc.** Brad Pitt, Aidan Quinn, Julia Ormond, Anthony Hopkins, Henry Thomas, Gordon Tootoosis, Tantoo Cardinal, Karina Lombard, Paul Desmond, Kenneth Welsh; ***D:*** Edward Zwick; ***W:*** Susan Shilliday, William D. Wittliff; ***C:*** John Toll; ***M:*** James Horner. Oscars '94: Cinematog.

Legends of the North 🦴🦴 ½ *Adventures of the Great North* **1995 (PG)** Crusty prospector Whip Gorman (Quaid) and partner Paul Bel Air are searching for a mythical lake of gold when Paul takes a fall off a mountain. Whip sends for Paul's son Charles so that he can translate his father's diary (it's in French) and get the clues to the gold's whereabouts. Naturally, some rival prospectors, some Indians, and even a feisty gal or two help or hinder our treasure seekers. Based on a story by Jack London. **95m/C VHS.** *CA FR* Georges Corraface, Sandrine Holt, Serge Houde, Macha Grenon, Randy Quaid; ***D:*** Rene Manzor; ***W:*** Rene Manzor; ***C:*** Pal Gyulay; ***M:*** Milan Kymlicka.

Legends of the Poisonous Seductress 1: Female Demon Ohyaku 🦴🦴 ½ *Ohyaku: The Female Demon; Yoen dokufuden hannya no ohyaku* **1968** First of a trilogy starring Junko Miyazono that are considered prototypes of the successful Pinky Violence films introduced into Japan in the 1970s (later inspiring "Kill Bill"). Ohyaku (Junko) is a female acrobat/prostitute who is sold to the highest bidder after each performance. Rescued by a thief, they settle down to a married life but she is framed and sentenced to years of hell on an island prison. She vows to escape and cut down her tormentors one by one. **90m/B DVD.** *JP* Tomisaburo Wakayama, Kunio Murai, Junko Miyazono; ***D:*** Yoshihiro Ishikawa; ***W:*** Koji Takada; ***C:*** Nagaki Yamagishi; ***M:*** Toshiaki Tsushima.

Legends of the Poisonous Seductress 2: Quick Draw Okatsu 🦴🦴 ½ *Yoen dokufuden: Hitokiri okatsu* **1969** The second film of the series, and the first one in color. Okatsu (Junko Miyazono) is the adopted daughter of a master swordsman who is killed when his son gets too far in debt gambling. It seems the corrupt local magistrate is enamored with Okatsu, and orchestrated the events to make her his concubine. Joined by wild swordswoman Rui (Reiko Oshida, who became a Pinky exploitation film star in the 1970s), Okatsu carves a bloodstained path of retribution through the local gamblers. **90m/C DVD.** *JP* Junko Miyazono, Ko Nishimura, Kenji Imai; ***D:*** Nobuo Nakagawa; ***W:*** Koji Takada; ***C:*** Masahiko Iimura; ***M:*** Koichi Kawabe.

Legends of the Poisonous Seductress 3: Okatsu the Fugitive 🦴🦴 *Yoen dokufuden: Okatsu kyojo tabi* **1969** The only thing the third film in this series has to connect to the others is that the female lead is the same woman (with the same theme of a female swordswoman wanting revenge). This time Okatsu is a tomboy, who is good with a sword, chasing down a group of corrupt tobacco smugglers who have murdered her parents. There's also many little subplots involving an arranged marriage, a betraying fiance, etc., but they don't detract from the pretty women whacking people with swords. **84m/C DVD.** *JP* Junko Miyazono; ***D:*** Nobuo Nakagawa; ***W:*** Koji Takada, Hideaki Yamamoto; ***C:*** Yoshikazu Yamisawa; ***M:*** Koichi Kawabe.

Legion 🦴🦴 **1998 (R)** Major Agatha Doyle (Farrell) is given a group of convicts to lead on a mission to destroy The Legion, a genetically engineered killing machine. But first she has to keep them from killing each other—or her. **97m/C VHS, DVD.** Terry Farrell, Corey Feldman, Rick Springfield, Parker Stevenson, Audie England; ***D:*** Jon Hess. **CABLE**

Legion 🦴 **2010 (R)** God loses faith in mankind and sends his angels to begin the apocalypse. A pregnant waitress (Palicki) and the Archangel Michael (Bettany) are humanity's only hope for survival. Unfortunately, they're trapped in a diner with a host of underdeveloped stock characters prone to long, boring speeches, wasting the time and talent of everyone involved. Director Stewart is well-versed in horror movie cliches and not afraid to use them to bludgeon the audience, but doesn't seem to realize that a thriller about the end of the entire world shouldn't be exclusively set in a truck stop. If humanity in this film is as stupid as the characters depicted, there's no wonder God gave up on them. **100m/C DVD.** Paul Bettany, Kevin Durand, Dennis Quaid, Tyrese Gibson, Charles S. Dutton, Lucas Black, Kate Walsh, Adrianne Palicki; ***D:*** Scott Stewart; ***W:*** Scott Stewart, Peter Schink; ***C:*** John Lindley; ***M:*** John (Gianni) Frizzell.

Legion of Iron 🦴 **1990 (R)** Adventures in a computer-run, neo-Roman civilization where men and women battle for supremacy. **85m/C VHS.** Kevin T. Walsh, Erica Nann, Regie De Morton, Camille Carrigan; ***D:*** Yakov Bentsvi.

Legion of Missing Men 🦴 ½ **1937** Professional soldiers of fortune, the French Foreign Legion, fight the evil sheik Ahmed in the Sahara. **62m/B VHS, DVD.** Ralph Forbes, Ben Alexander, Hala Linda, Roy D'Arcy, Paul Hurst, Jimmy Aubrey; ***D:*** Hamilton MacFadden.

Legion of the Lawless 🦴 ½ **1940** Group of outlaws band together in order to spread terror and confusion among the populace. **59m/B VHS.** George O'Brien, Virginia Vale, Norman Willis, Herbert Heywood, Hugh Sothern, William Benedict, Eddy (Eddie, Ed) Waller; ***D:*** David Howard; ***W:*** Doris Schroeder; ***C:*** Harry Wild.

Legionnaire 🦴🦴 **1998 (R)** In the 1920s, Alain Lefevre (Van Damme) enlists in the French Foreign Legion and is stationed in Morocco with other new recruits. After rigorous training, the men find themselves being sent into battle at a remote outpost, where they'll learn about war and survival. **99m/C VHS, DVD.** Jean-Claude Van Damme, Nicholas Farrell, Steven Berkoff, Jim Carter, Adewale Akinnuoye-Agbaje; ***D:*** Peter Macdonald; ***W:*** Sheldon Lettich, Rebecca Morrison; ***C:*** Doug Milsome; ***M:*** John Altman.

Legs 🦴🦴 **1983** Backstage story of three girls who are competing for a job with Radio City Music Hall's Rockettes. **91m/C VHS.** Gwen Verdon, John Heard, Sheree North, Shanna Reed, Maureen Teefy; ***D:*** Jerrold Freedman; ***C:*** Allen Daviau. **TV**

Leila 🦴🦴 **1997** Leila, an Iranian woman, finds that she cannot have children shortly after she is married. Although her husband does not mind, Leila's mother-in-law convinces her to let her son take another wife in order to produce an heir. Farsi with subtitles. **129m/C VHS, DVD.** *IA* Leila Hatami, Ali Mosaffa, Jamileh Sheikhi; ***D:*** Dariush Mehrjui.

L'Eleve 🦴🦴 *The Pupil* **1995** In 1897 Europe, an aristocratic family hires inexperienced 25-year-old Julien (Cassel) to tutor their precocious teenaged son, Morgan (Salmon). After a tentative battle for control, the two establish a strong emotional rapport and Julien learns that the family is not only in financial difficulty but is part of an empty, amoral social class only concerned with appearance. Based on a story by Henry James; French with subtitles. **92m/C VHS.** *FR* Vincent Cassel, Caspar Solmon, Caroline Cellier, Jean-Pierre Marielle, Sabine Destailleur, Sandrine Le Berre; ***D:*** Olivier Schatzky; ***W:*** Eve Deboise, Olivier Schatzky; ***C:*** Carlo Varini; ***M:*** Romano Musumarra. Montreal World Film Fest. '95: Director (Schatzky).

Lemming 🦴🦴 **2005** Moll's French puzzler involves the creature of the title—a Scandinavian lemming that somehow finds itself clogging up the French plumbing of computer gadget designer Alain (Lucas) and his wife Benedicte (Gainsbourg). Naturally this happens during a dinner party for Alain's boss, Richard (Dussollier), and his very difficult wife, Alice (Rampling). Alain's life goes from ordinary and pleasant to sinister and unsettled but the flick offers more questions than solutions. French with subtitles. **129m/C DVD.** *FR FR* Laurent Lucas, Charlotte Gainsbourg, Charlotte Rampling, Andre Dussollier, Jacques Bonnaffe, Veronique Affholder; ***D:*** Dominik Moll; ***W:*** Dominik Moll, Gilles Marchand; ***C:*** Jean-Marc Fabre; ***M:*** David Whitaker.

The Lemon Drop Kid 🦴🦴 ½ **1951** Second version of the Damon Runyon chestnut about a racetrack bookie who must recover the gangster's money he lost on a bet. As the fast-talking bookie, Hope sparkles. ♫ Silver Bells; It Doesn't Cost a Dime to Dream; They Obviously Want Me to Sing. **91m/B VHS, DVD.** Bob Hope, Lloyd Nolan, Fred Clark, Marilyn Maxwell, Jane Darwell, Andrea King, William Frawley, Jay C. Flippen, Harry Bellaver; ***D:*** Sidney Lanfield; ***W:*** Frank Tashlin, Edmund Hartmann, Robert O'Brien; ***C:*** Daniel F. Fapp; ***M:*** Ray Evans, Jay Livingston, Victor Young.

The Lemon Sisters 🦴🦴 **1990 (PG-13)** Three women, friends and performance partners since childhood, struggle to buy their own club. They juggle the men in their lives with less success. Great actresses like these should have done more with this interesting premise, and the excellent male cast has much more potential. **93m/C VHS, DVD.** Diane Keaton, Carol Kane, Kathryn Grody, Elliott Gould, Ruben Blades, Aidan Quinn; ***D:*** Joyce Chopra; ***W:*** Jeremy Pikser; ***C:*** Bobby Byrne; ***M:*** Dick Hyman.

Lemon Tree 🦴🦴 *Etz Limon* **2008** Widowed Palestinian Salma (Abbass) has inherited a lemon grove that's right on the Israeli-West Bank border. When Israeli Defense Minister Navon (Tavory) decides to build a new house on the Israeli side, the lemon grove is deemed a security risk and the military fences it off, prior to cutting the trees down. Incensed, Salma hires a young Palestinian lawyer (Suliman) to take on her seemingly hopeless case, which is soon making international headlines. English, Arabic, and Hebrew with subtitles. **106m/C DVD.** *IS FR GE* Hiam Abbass, Ali Suliman, Rona Lipaz-Michael, Doron Tavory, Tarik Kopty, Amos Lavi, Amnon Wolf; ***D:*** Eran Riklis; ***W:*** Eran Riklis, Suha Arraf; ***C:*** Rainer Klausmann; ***M:*** Habib Shehadeh Hanna.

Lemonade Joe 🦴🦴 *Limonadovy Joe aneb Konska Opera* **1964** The Czech New Wave does a broad spoof of the American western complete with good guys in white hats, bad guys in black hats, and a saloon gal with a heart of gold. Doug Badman (Kopecky) runs the Trigger Whiskey Saloon, along with his hotsie singer Tornado Lou (Fialova). The hard-drinking bar flies harass sweet temperance worker Winifred (Schoberova) until clean-living soft drink salesman Lemonade Joe (Fiala) shows up to save the day. Czech with subtitles. **87m/B VHS, DVD.** *CZ* Milos Kopecky, Karel Fiala, Kveta Fialova, Olga Schoberova; ***D:*** Oldrich Lipsky; ***W:*** Oldrich Lipsky, Jiri Brdecka; ***C:*** Vladimir Novotny; ***M:*** Vlastimil Hala, Jan Rychlik.

Lemony Snicket's A Series of Unfortunate Events 🦴🦴 ½ **2004 (PG)** Visually splendid Burtonesque Victorian Gothic adaptation of three books from the series by Snicket (aka Daniel Handler) is playfully gruesome yet not quite subversive enough. Violet (Browning), Klaus (Aiken), and Sunny Baudelaire are wealthy orphans shuttled from one peculiar, distant relative to another. These include sinister Count Olaf (Carrey), who is determined to obtain the family fortune, snake-loving Uncle Monty (Connolly), and phobic Aunt Josephine (Streep). The siblings survive every calamity through pluck, brains, and the fact that toddler Sunny is a ferocious biter. Much hammy villainy and episodic adventure abounds, to enjoyable effect. a silhouetted Law (as Snicket himself) supplies ominous narration. **107m/C VHS, DVD, UMD.** *US* Jim Carrey, Liam Aiken, Emily Browning, Kara Hoffman, Shelby Hoffman, Jude Law, Timothy Spall, Catherine O'Hara, Billy Connolly, Meryl Streep; ***D:*** Brad Silberling; ***W:*** Robert Gordon; ***C:*** Emmanuel Lubezki; ***M:*** Thomas Newman. Oscars '04: Makeup.

Lemora, Lady Dracula 🦴 *The Lady Dracula; The Legendary Curse of Lemora; Lemora: A Child's Tale of the Supernatural* **1973 (PG)** A pretty young church singer is drawn into the lair of the evil Lady Dracula, whose desires include her body as well as her blood. Horror fans will enjoy some excellent atmosphere, particularly in a scene where the girl's church bus is attacked by zombie-like creatures; Smith remains a '70s "B" movie favorite. Perhaps a double feature with "Lady Frankenstein"...? **80m/C VHS, DVD.** Leslie Gilb, Cheryl "Rainbeaux" Smith, William Whitton, Steve Johnson, Hy Pyke, Maxine Ballantyne, Parker West, Richard Blackburn; ***D:*** Richard Blackburn; ***W:*** Robert Fern, Richard Blackburn; ***C:*** Robert Caramico.

Lena's Holiday 🦴🦴 **1990 (PG-13)** Fluffy comedy about a winsome East German girl visiting L.A. for the first time, and the culture-shock that ensues. Sharp script and performances. **97m/C VHS, DVD.** Felicity Waterman, Chris Lemmon, Noriyuki "Pat" Morita, Susan Anton, Michael Sarrazin, Nick Mancuso, Bill Dana, Liz Torres; ***D:*** Michael Keusch; ***W:*** Michael Keusch, Deborah Tilton; ***C:*** Louis DiCesare.

L'Enfant d'Eau 🦴🦴 *Water Child; Behind the Blue* **1995** Mentally handicapped twentysomething Emile (La Haye) and precocious 12-year-old Cedrine (Monette) must learn to work together to survive after a plane crash strands them on an island in the Bahamas. Familiar story offers no surprises and the script shies away from any sexual implications, negating two excellent performances. French with subtitles. **103m/C VHS.** *CA* David La Haye, Marie-France Monette; ***D:*** Robert Menard; ***W:*** Claire Wojas. Genie '95: Actor (La Haye).

L'Enfer 🦴🦴🦴 *Jealousy; Torment* **1993** Claustrophobic thriller chronicles the descent into madness of an unstable hotel owner (Cluzet) convinced that his beautiful wife

(Beart) is having an affair. Intriguing plot points that blur appearances and reality lead to ambiguous and unsatisfying ending. Clouzot himself began filming his screenplay in 1964, but a heart attack forced him to abandon the project. So this version uses the same script. In French with English subtitles. **103m/C VHS, DVD.** *FR* Emmanuelle Beart, Francois Cluzet, Nathalie Cardone, Andre Wilms, Marc Lavoine; ***D:*** Claude Chabrol; ***W:*** Claude Chabrol, Henri-Georges Clouzot, Jose-Andre Lacour; ***C:*** Bernard Zitzermann; ***M:*** Matthieu Chabrol.

Leningrad Cowboys Go America 1/2 **1989 (PG-13)** An outlandish Finnish band, the Leningrad Cowboys, pack up their electric accordians and their one dead member and go on tour in America. With matching front-swept pompadours and pointy shoes, the group's appearance is the picture's best joke—and one of its only jokes, as the road trip plods in deadpan fashion that may bore viewers. It's best appreciated by fans of comic minimalist Jim Jarmusch (who has a guest role). In Finnish with English subtitles. **78m/C VHS.** *FI* Matti Pellonpaa, Kari Vaananen, Sakke Jarvenpaa, Silu Seppala, Mauri Sumen, Mato Valtonen, Nicky Tesco, Jim Jarmusch; ***D:*** Aki Kaurismaki; ***W:*** Aki Kaurismaki; ***C:*** Timo Salminen; ***M:*** Mauri Sumen.

L'Ennui **1998** Detached rather than titillating look at sexual obsession. Middle-aged, middle-class philosophy prof Martin (Berling) has recently separated from his wife and is dealing (or rather not dealing) with his midlife crisis. Until he meets teenaged artist's model Cecilia (Guillemin) and the two begin a very carnal affair, though Martin thinks his paramour is shallow and stupid. Then he discovers Cecilia also has a lover her own age and she wants to keep them both. In response, Martin turns obsessively jealous. Based on the novel "La Noia" by Alberto Moravia. French with subtitles. **120m/C VHS, DVD.** *FR* Charles Berling, Sophie Guillemin, Arielle Dombasle, Robert Kramer, Tom Ouedraoge; ***D:*** Cedric Kahn; ***W:*** Cedric Kahn, Laurence Ferreira Barbosa; ***C:*** Pascal Marti.

Lenny **1974 (R)** Smoky nightclubs, drug abuse, and obscenities abound in Hoffman's portrayal of the controversial comedian Lenny Bruce, whose use of street language led to his eventual blacklisting. Perrine is a gem as his stripper wife. Adapted from the Julian Barry play, this is a visually compelling piece that sharply divided critics upon release. **111m/B VHS, DVD.** Dustin Hoffman, Valerie Perrine, Jan Miner, Stanley Beck; ***D:*** Bob Fosse; ***W:*** Julian Barry; ***C:*** Bruce Surtees; ***M:*** Ralph Burns. Cannes '75: Actress (Perrine); Natl. Bd. of Review '74: Support. Actress (Perrine); N.Y. Film Critics '74: Support. Actress (Perrine).

Lensman **1984** In the 25th century space pirates known as the Boskande are threatening the civilized universe. Young Kimall Kenison is chosen by a higher power to become a lensman—and live or die for freedom. Based on the E.E. "Doc" Smith novels, this production is a combination of animation and computer graphics. Dubbed in English. **107m/C VHS.** *JP* ***D:*** Kazuyuki Hirokawa, Yoshiaki Kawajiri; ***W:*** Soji Yoshikawa; ***M:*** Akira Inoue; ***V:*** Robert Axelrod, Richard Barnes, Michael Forest, Michael Kenworthy.

Leo **2002 (R)** Craving love from his dispirited mom who sees him as all that went wrong in her past, Leo connects with incarcerated Stephen during a class writing project. Through their letters they become each other's lifeline and upon his release Stephen is determined to find him. Wants to give an twisty ending and boasts lots of acting talent but payoff doesn't deliver. **103m/C VHS, DVD.** Mary Stuart Masterson, Joseph Fiennes, Sam Shepard, Elisabeth Shue, Davis Sweat, Dennis Hopper, Deborah Kara Unger, Jake Weber, Justin Chambers; ***D:*** Mehdi Norowzian; ***W:*** Massy Tadjedin, Amir Tadjedin; ***C:*** Zubin Mistry; ***M:*** Mark Adler. **VIDEO**

Leo Tolstoy's Anna Karenina 1/2 *Leo Tolstoy's Anna Karenina* **1996 (PG-13)** Well, the third film version of Tolstoy's tempestuous, tragic romance certainly looks good, even if the performances don't engender the passion the story demands. Beautiful married Anna (Marceau) leaves stuffy husband Karenin (Fox) and their son to travel to 1880 Moscow and mend the marriage of her philandering brother Stiva (Huston). But she meets dashing soldier, Count Alexei Vronsky (Bean), who immediately decides to pursue the beauty and the two begin an all-encompassing affair that leads to tragedy. This version also includes the secondary, contrasting romance between young Kitty (Kirshner) and Tolstoy's alter ego, questioning aristo Levin (Molina). Filmed on location in St. Petersburg, Russia. The classical score includes selections from Tschaikovsky, Rachmaninoff and Prokofiev, under the direction of Georg Solti. **120m/C VHS, DVD.** Sophie Marceau, Sean Bean, Alfred Molina, Mia Kirshner, James Fox, Danny Huston, Fiona Shaw, Phyllida Law, David Schofield, Saskia Wickham; ***D:*** Bernard Rose; ***W:*** Bernard Rose; ***C:*** Daryn Okada.

Leolo **1992** Deeply disturbing black comedy about one of the screen's most dysfunctional families. Leo is a 12-year-old French Canadian from Montreal who is determined to remake himself. He's decided to be a Sicilian lad named Leolo, escaping from his horrific family into his fantasies (and potential madness). "I dream, therefore I am not," he thinks. His parents are obsessed with toilet training, his cowardly brother with body-building, his sisters are demented, and his grandfather is a sadistic, dirty old man. Striking cinematography and great soundtrack, but not for the faint of heart (or stomach). In French with English subtitles. **107m/C VHS, DVD.** *CA* Maxime Collin, Julien Guiomar, Ginette Reno, Pierre Bourgault, Yves Montmarquette, Roland Blouin, Giuditta del Vecchio; ***D:*** Jean-Claude Lauzon; ***W:*** Jean-Claude Lauzon. Genie '92: Costume Des., Film Editing, Orig. Screenplay.

Leon Morin, Priest 1/2 **1961** A young priest and a widow, who happens to be a Communist, fall in love during the WWII German occupation of France. Based on the novel by Beatrix Beck. In French with English subtitles. **118m/B VHS.** *IT FR* Jean-Paul Belmondo, Emmanuelle Riva; ***D:*** Jean-Pierre Melville.

Leon the Pig Farmer 1/2 **1993** Dry comedic satire about identity. Leon Geller has never quite fitted into his parents' comfortable Jewish society and no wonder—Leon accidentally discovers he is the product of artificial insemination. And what's more, the lab made a mistake and Leon isn't a true Geller after all. His father is actually a genial (and Gentile) Yorkshire pig farmer named Brian Chadwick, who cheerfully welcomes Leon as his long-lost son. All four parents try to cope while Leon moves bewilderedly amongst them. Film tends to be too timid in its satire but still has its witty moments. **98m/C VHS.** *GB* Mark Frankel, Janet Suzman, Brian Glover, Connie Booth, David de Keyser, Maryam D'Abo, Gina Bellman; ***D:*** Vadim Jean, Gary Sinyor; ***W:*** Gary Sinyor, Michael Normand.

Leonard Part 6 **1987 (PG)** A former secret agent comes out of retirement to save the world from a crime queen using animals to kill agents. In the meantime, he tries to patch up his collapsing personal life. Wooden and disappointing; produced and co-written by Cosby, who himself panned the film. **83m/C VHS, DVD.** Bill Cosby, Gloria Foster, Tom Courtenay, Joe Don Baker; ***D:*** Paul Weiland; ***W:*** Bill Cosby, Jonathan Reynolds; ***C:*** Jan De Bont; ***M:*** Elmer Bernstein. Golden Raspberries '87: Worst Picture, Worst Actor (Cosby), Worst Screenplay.

Leonor **1975** Idiotic medieval drivel with Ullmann rising from the dead after husband Piccoli seals her in a tomb. Directed by the son of Luis Bunuel. **90m/C VHS.** *FR SP IT* Liv Ullmann, Michel Piccoli, Ornella Muti; ***D:*** Juan Bunuel; ***M:*** Ennio Morricone.

The Leopard 1/2 *Il Gattopardo* **1963** American Lancaster (allegedly foisted on the movie by the studio to help bring in box office cash for the sumptuous production) holds his own in meeting the style of master director Visconti in this adaptation of Guiseppe di Lampedusa's 1958 bestseller. Sicilian nobility, Prince Don Fabrizio Salina realizes his privileged way of life is doomed as revolution overthrows the old order in the 1860s. Ever practical, he looks for ways for his family to survive, including marrying his ambitious nephew Tancredi (Delon) to Angelica (Cardinale), the daughter of a buffoonish local bureaucrat (Stoppa) who's suddenly gained power with the new regime. The beautiful ending ballroom sequence, with Salina contemplating life, lasts some 45 minutes. Italian with subtitles or dubbed. There are many butchered versions of this film but the Criterion release was meticulously restored and is the closest available to Visconti's original (now lost), which was 205 minutes. **185m/C DVD.** *IT* Burt Lancaster, Alain Delon, Claudia Cardinale, Paolo Stoppa, Rina Morelli, Romolo Valli, Terence Hill, Pierre Clementi; ***D:*** Luchino Visconti; ***W:*** Luchino Visconti, Enrico Medioli, Suso Cecchi D'Amico, Pasquale Festa Companile; ***C:*** Giuseppe Rotunno; ***M:*** Nino Rota.

Leopard in the Snow **1978 (PG)** The romance between a race car driver allegedly killed in a crash and a young woman is the premise of this film. **89m/C VHS, DVD.** Keir Dullea, Susan Penhaligon, Kenneth More, Billie Whitelaw; ***D:*** Gerry O'Hara.

The Leopard Man 1/2 **1943** An escaped leopard terrorizes a small town in New Mexico. After a search, the big cat is found dead, but the killings continue. Minor but effective Jacques Tourneur creepie. Based on Cornell Woolrich's novel "Black Alibi." Another Val Lewton Horror production. **66m/B VHS, DVD.** Jean Brooks, Isabel Jewell, James Bell, Margaret Landry, Dennis O'Keefe, Margo, Rita (Paula) Corday, Abner Biberman; ***D:*** Jacques Tourneur; ***W:*** Ardel Wray; ***C:*** Robert De Grasse; ***M:*** Roy Webb.

The Leopard Son **1996 (G)** Beautiful documentary follows the birth and first two years of life for a leopard cub born on Africa's Serengeti plain. Mom leopard shows him how to survive and then he's out into the harsh world on his own. Parents should be forewarned that the hunt-and-kill scenes may upset the little ones. **87m/C VHS.** ***D:*** Hugo Van Lawick; ***W:*** Michael Olmert; ***C:*** Hugo Van Lawick, Matthew Aeberhard; ***M:*** Stewart Copeland; ***Nar:*** John Gielgud.

The Leopard Woman **1920** Long before the cat lady cut her first claws, there was the leopard woman. Vamp Glaum finds much trouble to meow about on the Equator. **66m/B VHS.** House Peters Sr., Noble Johnson, Louise Glaum; ***D:*** Wesley Ruggles.

Leper *Tredowata* **1976** A melodrama of forbidden love between a wealthy nobleman and a beautiful high school teacher. The townspeople try to destroy the love between the two because of their different social classes. In Polish with English subtitles. **100m/C VHS, DVD.** *PL* Elzbieta Starostecka, Leszek Teleszynski; ***D:*** Jerzy Hoffman.

Lepke 1/2 **1975 (R)** The life and fast times of Louis "Lepke" Buchalter from his days in reform school to his days as head of Murder, Inc. and his execution in 1944. **110m/C VHS.** Tony Curtis, Milton Berle, Gianni Russo, Vic Tayback, Michael Callan; ***D:*** Menahem Golan.

Leprechaun WOOF! **1993 (R)** A sadistic 600-year-old leprechaun winds up wreaking havoc in North Dakota. If this makes no particular sense, neither does the film which is basic horror story excess. A man goes to Ireland for his mother's funeral, steals the gold belonging to the leprechaun, locks the creature up, and winds up accidentally taking the evil imp back to the States with him. When the leprechaun gets free, he wants a bloodthirsty revenge—and shoes. One of the so-called humorous bits is the leprechaun's shoe fetish. Irish eyes will not be smiling watching this mess. **92m/C VHS, DVD.** Warwick Davis, Jennifer Aniston, Ken Olandt, Mark Holton, John Sanderford, Robert Gorman, Shay Duffin, John Voldstad; ***D:*** Mark Jones; ***W:*** Mark Jones; ***C:*** Levie Isaacks. **VIDEO**

Leprechaun 2 **1994 (R)** Sequel to the horror flick about a malevolent Irish gnome. It seems one of his fairy entitlements is that he can possess any woman he wants if she sneezes three times. Thwarted in his attempt to snare a comely lass one thousand years earlier, he returns to present-day California to exact revenge on her descendant Durkin. Contrary to the popular legend that leprechauns are benign kind-hearted sprites, this nasty combines the treachery of a Gestapo officer with the firepower of Rambo in his attempt to harass the unimpressed Durkin into his clutches. **85m/C VHS, DVD.** Warwick Davis, Sandy Baron, Adam Biesk, James Lancaster, Clint Howard, Kimmy Robertson, Charlie Heath, Shevonne Durkin; ***D:*** Rodman Flender; ***W:*** Turi Meyer, Al Septien; ***C:*** Jane Castle; ***M:*** Jonathan Elias.

Leprechaun 3 **1995 (R)** A student steals the nasty little beastie's gold and he's off to Las Vegas to get it back and to kill the gamblers, also after his magic money, in decidedly disgusting ways. **93m/C VHS, DVD.** Warwick Davis, John Gatins, Michael Callan, Caroline Williams, Lee Armstrong; ***D:*** Brian Trenchard-Smith; ***W:*** Brian Dubos; ***C:*** David Lewis; ***M:*** Dennis Michael Tenney.

Leprechaun 4: In Space WOOF! **1996 (R)** Who knows how the little imp got there but now our old friend the Leprechaun (Davis) is busy terrorizing an alien princess (Carlton) on a distant planet. He wants to marry the babe and rule the universe but its the Marines to the rescue! Yes, an Earth platoon arrives to foil his plans. **98m/C VHS, DVD.** Warwick Davis, Rebekah Carlton, Brent Jasmer, Debbe Dunning, Rebecca Cross, Tim Colceri; ***D:*** Brian Trenchard-Smith; ***W:*** Dennis Pratt; ***C:*** David Lewis; ***M:*** Dennis Michael Tenney.

Leprechaun 5: In the Hood WOOF! **1999 (R)** This time around the bloodthirsty leprechaun wants revenge on a group of wannabe rap artists who use his magic (and steal his gold) in order to become successful. If you've seen any of the others in this series, you know what to expect. **91m/C VHS, DVD.** Warwick Davis, Ice-T, Coolio; ***D:*** Robert Spera. **VIDEO**

Leprechaun 6: Back 2 Tha Hood WOOF! **2003 (R)** This series becomes campier horror with each new installment. Beautician Emily and her friends find the Leprechaun's gold and foolishly spend it, which earns the little imp's wrath. **87m/C VHS, DVD.** Warwick Davis, Tangi Miller, Kirk "Sticky Fingaz" Jones, Shiek Mahmud-Bey; ***D:*** Steven Ayromlooi; ***W:*** Steven Ayromlooi; ***C:*** David Daniel. **VIDEO**

Les Apprentis *The Apprentices* **1995** Womanizing deadbeat Fred (Depardieu) winds up sharing an apartment with antisocial journalist Antoine (Cluzet) and the mismatched duo eventually form an uneasy (though comic) bond. In need of cash, they decide to rob Antoine's office, but bungle the job, which leads to disturbing consequences. Watchable leads, intelligent script. French with subtitles. **95m/C VHS.** *FR* Guillaume Depardieu, Francois Cluzet; ***D:*** Pierre Salvadori; ***W:*** Pierre Salvadori, Philippe Harel.

Les Assassins de L'Ordre *Law Breakers* **1971** A righteous French judge faces the case of an innocent man killed by police brutality. Subtitled in English. **100m/C VHS.** *FR* Jacques Brel, Catherine Rouvel, Michael (Michel) Lonsdale, Charles Denner; ***D:*** Marcel Carne; ***M:*** Michel Colombier.

Les Biches 1/2 *The Does; Girlfriends; Bad Girls* **1968 (R)** An exquisite film that became a landmark in film history with its theme of bisexuality and upper class decadence. A rich socialite picks up a young artist drawing on the streets of Paris, seduces her, and then takes her to St. Tropez. Conflict arises when a suave architect shows up and threatens to come between the two lovers. In French with English subtitles. **95m/C VHS, DVD.** *FR* Stephane Audran, Jean-Louis Trintignant, Jacqueline Sassard; ***D:*** Claude Chabrol; ***W:*** Claude Chabrol.

Les Bonnes Femmes *The Good Girls; The Girls; The Good Time Girls; Donne facili* **1960** Four Paris shopgirls dream of escaping the monotony of their lives and finding romance but instead discover broken dreams and danger. Chabrol's New Wave thriller focuses more on character and irony than suspense. French with subtitles. **105m/B VHS, DVD.** *FR* Bernadette LaFont, Stephane Audran, Clothilde Joano, Lucile Saint-Simon; ***D:*** Claude Chabrol; ***W:*** Paul Geoauff; ***C:*** Henri Decae; ***M:*** Pierre Jansen, Paul Misraki.

Les Bons Debarras 1/2 **1981** In French with English subtitles, this Canadian film follows a lonely 13-year-old's effort to win her mother's exclusive love. **114m/C VHS.** *CA* Marie Tifo, Charlotte Laurier, Germain

Houde; *D:* Francis Mankiewicz. Genie '81: Actress (Tifo), Director (Mankiewicz), Film, Support. Actor (Houde).

Les Carabiniers *The Soldiers* **1963** A cynical, grim anti-war tract, detailing the pathetic adventures of two young bums lured into enlisting with promises of rape, looting, torture and battle without justification. Controversial in its day, and typically elliptical and non-narrative. In French with English subtitles. **80m/B VHS, DVD.** *GB IT FR* Albert Juross, Marino (Martin) Mase, Catherine Ribeiro, Genevieva Galea, Anna Karina; *D:* Jean-Luc Godard; *W:* Jean-Luc Godard; *C:* Raoul Coutard; *M:* Philippe Arthuys.

Les Comperes **1983** A woman suckers two former lovers into finding her wayward son by secretly telling each ex he is the natural father of the punk. Depardieu is a streetwise journalist who teams up with a suicidal hypochondriac/wimp (Richard) to find the little brat. Humorous story full of bumbling misadventures. In French with English subtitles. **92m/C VHS, DVD.** *FR* Pierre Richard, Gerard Depardieu, Anny (Annie Legras) Duperey, Michel Aumont; *D:* Francis Veber; *W:* Francis Veber; *M:* Vladimir Cosma.

Les Destinees 1/2 *Les Destinees Sentimentales; Sentimental Destinies* **2000** Lavish, sprawling, but emotionally flat costume drama follows forty years in the life of Jean Barnery. Jean, a Protestant minister, finds that his wife, Nathalie, has been unfaithful and sends her, along with their daughter Aline away. After he meets, and falls in love with the independent Pauline, his estranged wife, World War I, the call to return to his family's porcelain business, and the Wall Street crash impose themselves into Jean and Pauline's life. Film is technically and visually impressive, but a lack of any real spark (except when Huppert is onscreen) and the film's length combine to blunt its impact. Based on the novel by Jacques Chardonne. **174m/C VHS, DVD.** *FR SI* Charles Berling, Emmanuelle Beart, Isabelle Huppert, Olivier Perrier, Dominique Reymond, Andre Marcon, Alexandra London, Julie Depardieu; *D:* Olivier Assayas; *W:* Olivier Assayas, Jacques Fieschi; *C:* Eric Gautier; *M:* Guillaume Lekeu.

Les Enfants Terrible *The Strange Ones* **1950** The classic, lyrical treatment of adolescent deviance adapted by Cocteau from his own play, wherein a brother and sister born into extreme wealth eventually enter into casual crime, self-destruction, and incest. In French with English subtitles. **105m/B VHS.** *FR* Edouard Dermithe, Nicole Stephane; *D:* Jean-Pierre Melville; *W:* Jean Cocteau, Jean-Pierre Melville.

Les Girls 1/2 **1957** When one member of a performing troupe writes her memoirs, the other girls sue for libel. Told through a series of flashbacks, this story traces the girls' recollections of their relationships to American dancer Kelly. Cole Porter wrote the score for this enjoyable "Rashomon"-styled musical. ♫Les Girls; Flower Song; You're Just Too, Too; Ca C'est L'Amour; Ladies In Waiting; La Habanera; Why Am I So Gone (About That Gal?). **114m/C VHS, DVD.** Gene Kelly, Mitzi Gaynor, Kay Kendall, Taina Elg, Henry Daniell, Patrick Macnee; *D:* George Cukor; *C:* Robert L. Surtees. Oscars '57: Costume Des.; Golden Globes '58: Actress—Mus./Comedy (Kendall), Film—Mus./Comedy.

Les Grandes Manoeuvres *Summer Manoeuvres; The Grand Maneuvers* **1955** Clair's first film in color depicts the romance between a seductive soldier (Philipe) and a divorcee (Morgan) in a pre-WWI garrison town. Gentle comedy has Philipe falling in love but his reputation as a Don Juan comes between them. French with subtitles. **106m/C VHS.** *FR* Gerard Philipe, Michele Morgan, Yves Robert, Brigitte Bardot, Jean Desailly, Pierre Dux; *D:* Rene Clair; *W:* Rene Clair; *M:* Georges Van Parys.

Les Miserables **1935** Victor Hugo's classic novel about small-time criminal Jean Valjean and 18th-century France. After facing poverty and prison, escape and torture, Valjean is redeemed by the kindness of a bishop. As he tries to mend his ways, he is continually hounded by the policeman Javert, who is determined to lock him away. The final act is set during a student uprising in the 1730s. This version is the best of many, finely detailed and well-paced with excellent cinematography by Gregg Toland. **108m/B VHS.** Fredric March, Charles Laughton, Cedric Hardwicke, Rochelle Hudson, John Beal, Frances Drake, Florence Eldridge, John Carradine, Jessie Ralph, Leonid Kinskey; *D:* Richard Boleslawski; *W:* W.P. Lipscomb; *C:* Gregg Toland; *M:* Alfred Newman.

Les Miserables 1/2 **1952** Hugo's classic novel done up Italian style with lavish sets and spectacle. Dubbed in English. **119m/B VHS.** *IT* Charlotte Austin, Gino Cervi, Valentina Cortese; *D:* Riccardo Freda; *C:* Joseph LaShelle; *M:* Alex North.

Les Miserables **1957** An epic French adaptation of the Victor Hugo standard about Valjean, Javert, and injustice. Although this doesn't reach the level of the 1935 classic, it is still worth watching. Dubbed in English. **210m/C VHS.** *FR GE* Jean Gabin, Daniele Delorme, Bernard Blier, Andre Bourvil, Gianni Esposito, Serge Reggiani; *D:* Jean-Paul LeChanois.

Les Miserables 1/2 **1978** An excellent made-for-TV version of the Victor Hugo classic about the criminal Valjean and the policeman Javert playing cat-and-mouse in 18th-century France. Dauphin's last film role. **150m/C VHS.** Richard Jordan, Anthony Perkins, John Gielgud, Cyril Cusack, Flora Robson, Celia Johnson, Claude Dauphin; *D:* Glenn Jordan. **TV**

Les Miserables 1/2 **1995 (R)** Clever, modern rendering of the famous Victor Hugo novel, set in WWII. Humble furniture mover Fortin (Belmondo), nicknamed Valjean for displaying the same brutish strength as his Hugo counterpart, helps a Jewish family escape German occupation. The family becomes separated in the attempt, with lawyer Monsieur Ziman (Boujenah) being hidden by farmers in the country, Madame Ziman (Martines) relegated to a Polish concentration camp, and their daughter Salome (Lelouch, daughter of the director) protected by a nun at a Catholic school. Gump-like, the unusually strong but illiterate Fortin becomes involved with the French resistance and joins in D-Day. Events, though obviously updated, mirror experiences of Hugo's characters. In one sequence, the Ziman's even teach Fortin to read Hugo's "Les Miserables," with actors playing their counterparts in dramatizations. Reportedly France's most expensive film ever. **174m/C VHS.** Jean-Paul Belmondo, Michel Boujenah, Annie Girardot, Philippe Leotard, Clementine Celarie, Rufus, Alessandra Martines, Salome, Philippe Khorsand; *D:* Claude Lelouch; *W:* Claude Lelouch; *C:* Claude Lelouch; *M:* Francis Lai. Cesar '96: Support. Actress (Girardot); Golden Globes '96: Foreign Film.

Les Miserables **1997 (PG-13)** Yet another adaptation of the Victor Hugo novel. Paroled convict Jean Valjean (Neeson) gets chased by police inspector Javert (Rush) while factory worker Fantine (Thurman) turns to prostitution to survive. August chose to begin this tale after Valjean's trial and imprisonment for petty theft, and until the final third of the film, doesn't really deal with the political upheaval of the time. Not as sweeping or grand as other versions, but what this adaptation lacks in scope, it makes up for with top-notch performances (especially by Neeson and Rush) and more careful study of the characters themselves. **134m/C DVD.** Liam Neeson, Geoffrey Rush, Uma Thurman, Claire Danes, Paris Vaughan, Reine Brynolfsson, Hans Matheson, Mimi Newman; *D:* Bille August; *W:* Rafael Yglesias; *C:* Jorgen Persson; *M:* Basil Poledouris.

Les Mistons *The Mischief-Makers; The Kids* **1957** This study of male adolescence finds five teenage boys worshiping a beautiful girl from afar, following her everywhere, spoiling her dates, and finally reaching maturity in light of their mistakes. **18m/C VHS, DVD.** *FR* Gerard Blain, Bernadette LaFont, Michel Francois; *D:* Francois Truffaut; *W:* Francois Truffaut; *C:* Jean Malige; *M:* Maurice Leroux.

Les Nuits Fauves *Savage Nights* **1992** Collard's semi-autobiographical film about the emotional and physical havoc an H.I.V.-positive filmmaker visits on the two objects of his violent affections—an innocent 18-year-old girl and a sadomasochistic 20-year-old boy. As Jean displays increasing desperation with his situation, the life around him shows an equally arbitrary violence and humor. In French with English subtitles. Collard died of AIDS shortly before his film won both best first film and best French film at the 1993 Cesars—a first in the ceremony's history. **129m/C VHS.** *FR* Cyril Collard, Romane Bohringer, Carlos Lopez, Maria Schneider; *D:* Cyril Collard; *W:* Cyril Collard. Cesar '93: Film.

Les Patterson Saves the World 1/2 **1990 (R)** An obnoxious ambassador to an anonymous Middle Eastern country teams up with the singularly distastefully named Dr. Herpes to stop a new killer disease about to engulf the world. **105m/C VHS.** Barry Humphries, Pamela Stephenson, Thaao Penghlis, Andrew Clarke, Joan Rivers; *D:* George Miller; *C:* David Connell.

Les Rendez-vous D'Anna *The Meetings of Anna* **1978** An independent woman travels through Europe and comes face to face with its post-war modernism. In French with English subtitles. **120m/C VHS.** *FR BE GE* Aurore Clement, Helmut Griem, Magali Noel, Hanns Zischler, Lea Massari, Jean-Pierre Cassel; *D:* Chantal Akerman; *W:* Chantal Akerman.

Les Vampires **1915** Irma Vep (an anagram for vampire) leads a bloodthirsty gang of thieves in Paris. She and her cohorts will use kidnapping, gas, sexual domination, and murder to gain power over the city's elite. Fueillade's 10-part serial has been restored with color-tinting and title cards in English. **420m/B VHS, DVD.** *FR* Musidora, Jean Ayme, Marcel Levesque, Edouard Mathe; *D:* Louis Feuillade; *W:* Louis Feuillade.

Les Violons du Bal **1974** Follows the story of a young Jewish boy and his family's attempted escape from Nazi-occupied France during WWII. The boy grows up to be a filmmaker obsessed with making a movie about his childhood experiences. In French with English subtitles. **110m/C VHS.** *FR* Marie-Jose Nat, Jean-Louis Trintignant; *D:* Michael Drach. Cannes '74: Actress (Nat).

Les Visiteurs du Soir 1/2 *The Devil's Envoys* **1942** A beautiful, charming fairy tale about the devil's intrepid interference with a particular love affair in 15th-century France, which he cannot squelch. Purportedly a parable about Hitler's invasion of France. Interestingly, this was released after the Nazi occupation of France, so one assumes that the Germans didn't make the connection. In French with English subtitles. **120m/B VHS.** *FR* Arletty, Jules Berry, Marie Dea, Alain Cuny, Fernand Ledoux, Marcel Herrand; *D:* Marcel Carne; *W:* Jacques Prevert, Pierre Laroche.

Les Voleurs *Thieves* **1996 (R)** Unexpected romantic triangle among desperate, lonely people, set against a crime backdrop and told from a variety of viewpoints. Edgy cop Alex (Auteuil) is from a family of thieves, including his older brother Ivan (Bezace) who's been murdered. Alex gets involved with sullen Juliette (Cote) without realizing, at first, that her brother Jimmy (Magimel) is a member of Ivan's gang or that she has another lover, her philosophy teacher, Marie (Deneuve). Events finally force a meeting between Marie and Alex over the unstable Juliette (the scenes between Auteuil and Deneuve being the most interesting in the film). French with subtitles. **116m/C VHS.** *FR* Catherine Deneuve, Daniel Auteuil, Laurence Cote, Benoit Magimel, Didier Bezace, Fabienne Babe, Ivan Desny, Julien Riviere; *D:* Andre Techine; *W:* Andre Techine, Gilles Taurand; *C:* Jeanne Lapoirie; *M:* Philippe Sarde.

L'Escorte *The Escort* **1996** Thirty-years-old and long-term lovers, Jean-Marc and Philippe find their relationship in crisis thanks to both the stress caused by their failing Montreal restaurant and the intrusion of a third party. Free-spirited Steve works as an escort and soon becomes an object of desire for both men as well as a catalyst for the revelation of long-held secrets. French with subtitles. **91m/C VHS.** *CA* Eric Cabana, Paul-Antoine Taillefer, Robin Aubert, Marie Lefebvre; *D:* Denis Langlois; *W:* Denis Langlois, Bertrand Lachance; *C:* Yves Beaudoin; *M:* Bertrand Chenier.

Less Than Zero **1987 (R)** An adaptation of Bret Easton Ellis' popular, controversial novel about a group of affluent, drug-abusing youth in Los Angeles. McCarthy and Gertz play friends of Downey who try to get him off his self-destructive path—to no avail. Although it tries, the film fails to inspire any sort of sympathy for this self-absorbed and hedonistic group. Mirrors the shallowness of the characters although Downey manages to rise above this somewhat. Music by the Bangles, David Lee Roth, Poison, Roy Orbison, Aerosmith and more. **98m/C VHS, DVD.** Andrew McCarthy, Jami Gertz, Robert Downey Jr., James Spader; *D:* Marek Kanievska; *W:* Harley Peyton; *C:* Edward Lachman; *M:* Thomas Newman.

The Lesser Evil 1/2 **1997 (R)** Derek (Feore), the struggling owner of a lumber business, has invited three former high school buddies to his cabin in the Missouri woods. Ivan (Howard) is now a priest, Frank (Goldwyn) is a police officer, and George (Paymer) is a big-shot attorney. As teens they got mixed up with two deaths and a coverup that has now come back to haunt them. Now, just what kind of justice will prevail? Good cast, nice mix of flashbacks, and a satisfying final twist. **97m/C VHS.** Colm Feore, Tony Goldwyn, Arliss Howard, David Paymer, Jonathan Scarfe, Steven Petrarca, Adam Scott, Marc Worden, Jack Kehler, Richard Riehle, Mason Adams, Anne Haney; *D:* David Mackay; *W:* David Mackay, Jeremy Levine; *C:* Stephan Schultze; *M:* Don Davis.

A Lesson Before Dying **1999 (PG-13)** Cheadle's impressive as idealistic teacher Grant Wiggins, who has a one-room school for black children in 1948 Louisiana. He's reluctantly pressed into service by his formidable Aunt Lou (Tyson) and her friend Miss Emma (Hall), who want him to bring some dignity to the life of Jefferson (Phifer). This is no easy task since the young man is awaiting execution for a crime he didn't commit. Based on the 1993 novel by Ernest J. Gaines. **100m/C VHS, DVD.** Don Cheadle, Cicely Tyson, Mekhi Phifer, Irma P. Hall, Brent Jennings, Lisa Arrindell Anderson, Frank Hoyt Taylor; *D:* Joseph Sargent; *W:* Ann Peacock; *C:* Donald M. Morgan; *M:* Ernest Troost. **CABLE**

Lesson in Love 1/2 *En Lektion i Karlek* **1954** A gynecologist's philandering is discovered by his wife, who then starts an affair of her own. Change of pace for Bergman as he does this modest comedy. In Swedish with English subtitles. **95m/B VHS.** *SW* Gunnar Bjornstrand, Eva Dahlbeck, Harriet Andersson; *D:* Ingmar Bergman; *W:* Ingmar Bergman.

Let 'Em Have It 1/2 *False Faces* **1935** Exciting action saga loosely based on the newly formed FBI and its bouts with John Dillinger. Car chases and tommy guns abound in this fairly ordinary film. **90m/B VHS, DVD.** Richard Arlen, Virginia Bruce, Bruce Cabot, Harvey Stephens, Eric Linden, Joyce Compton, Gordon Jones; *D:* Sam Wood.

Let 'er Go Gallegher **1928** A youngster sees a murder, tells his newspaper buddy about it, and the guy writes an article about the crime. It's a big hit, the guy's ego starts to overinflate, and his life starts to head downwind until he decides its time for him and the little guy to rope themselves a miscreant. **57m/B VHS.** Frank "Junior" Coghlan, Elinor Fair, Wade Boteler; *D:* Elmer Clifton.

Let Freedom Ring 1/2 **1939** Sappy, yet enjoyable patriotism that has lawyer Eddy returning to small hometown and fighting corruption. Hokey, but it works largely due to Hecht's fine script. ♫Dusty Road; Love Serenade; Home Sweet Home; When Irish Eyes Are Smiling; America; Pat Sez He; Where Else But Here; Funiculi Funicula; Ten Thousand Cattle Straying. **100m/B VHS.** Nelson Eddy, Virginia Bruce, Victor McLaglen, Lionel Barrymore, Edward Arnold, Guy Kibbee, Charles Butterworth, H.B. Warner, Raymond Walburn; *D:* Jack Conway; *W:* Ben Hecht.

Let Him Have It 1/2 **1991 (R)** Compelling, controversial film about a miscarriage of British justice. In 1952 Christopher Craig, 16, and Derek Bentley, 19, climbed onto the roof of a warehouse in an apparent burglary attempt. The police arrived and captured Bentley; Craig shot and wounded one policeman and killed another.

According to testimony Bentley shouted "Let him have it" but did he mean shoot or give the officer the gun? Bentley, whose IQ was 66, was sentenced to death by the British courts—though he didn't commit the murder. The uproar over the sentence was reignited by this release, leading to a request for a reexamination of evidence and sentencing by the British Home Office. **115m/C VHS, DVD.** *GB* Christopher Eccleston, Paul Reynolds, Tom Bell, Eileen Atkins, Clare Holman, Michael Elphick, Mark McGann, Tom Courtenay, Ronald Fraser, Michael Gough, Murray Melvin, Clive Revill, Norman Rossington, James Villiers; ***D:*** Peter Medak; ***W:*** Oliver Stapleton, Neal Purvis, Robert Wade.

Let It Be 1970 Documentary look at a Beatles recording session, giving glimpses of the conflicts which led to their breakup. Features appearances by Yoko Ono and Billy Preston. **80m/C VHS, DVD.** John Lennon, Paul McCartney, George Harrison, Ringo Starr, Billy Preston, Yoko Ono; ***D:*** Michael Lindsay-Hogg; ***M:*** John Lennon, Paul McCartney, George Harrison, Ringo Starr. Oscars '70: Orig. Song Score and/or Adapt.

Let It Ride 1989 **(PG-13)** Dreyfuss is a small-time gambler who finally hits it big at the track. Some funny moments but generally a lame script cripples the cast, although the horses seem unaffected. Garr is okay as his wife who slips further into alcoholism with each race. **91m/C VHS, DVD.** Richard Dreyfuss, Teri Garr, David Johansen, Jennifer Tilly, Allen (Goorwitz) Garfield, Ed Walsh, Michelle Phillips, Mary Woronov, Robbie Coltrane, Richard Edson, Cynthia Nixon; ***D:*** Joe Pytka; ***W:*** Nancy Dowd; ***C:*** Curtis J. Wehr; ***M:*** Giorgio Moroder.

Let It Rock 1986 A maniacal promoter makes superstars out of his new band by staging publicity stunts. Not one of Hopper's better efforts. Filmed in Germany, but Roger Corman bought the U.S. rights and added clips from other movies before it was released here. **75m/C VHS.** *GE* Dennis Hopper, David A(lexander) Hess; ***D:*** Roland Klick.

Let It Snow ½ *Snow Days* 1999 **(R)** Appealing romantic comedy centers on the emotional insecurity of James Ellis (scripter Marcus, whose brother, Adam, directs), who witnessed his mother Elise's (Peters) post-divorce series of loser boyfriends. His best friend is Sarah (Dylan) and the two dance around the romantic possibilities until a sudden kiss throws their relationship into turmoil. Some mis-communication has Sarah leaving to study in England and James becoming determined to win her love. **90m/C VHS, DVD.** Kipp Marcus, Alice Dylan, Bernadette Peters, Judith Malina, Henry Simmons, Miriam Shor, Larry Pine, Debra Sullivan; ***D:*** Adam Marcus; ***W:*** Kipp Marcus; ***C:*** Ben Weinstein; ***M:*** Sean McCourt.

Let No Man Write My Epitaph 1960 Winters emotes theatrically as Nellie, a southside Chicago junkie mom who is trying to raise her son, Nick (Darren), to live a better life. Based on the novel by Willard Motley. **105m/B VHS.** Shelley Winters, James Darren, Burl Ives, Ricardo Montalban, Jean Seberg, Ella Fitzgerald, Rodolfo Acosta, Jeanne Cooper, Michael Davis; ***D:*** Philip Leacock; ***W:*** Robert Presnell Jr.; ***C:*** Burnett Guffey; ***M:*** George Duning.

Let Sleeping Corpses Lie ½ *The Living Dead at Manchester Morgue* 1974 England's answer to "Night of the Living Dead" is more polished and has a more pronounced environmental edge. George (Lovelock) and Edna (Galbo) are the heroes who must confront the cannibalistic animated corpses. If the film lacks the single-mindedness and originality of Romero's work, it's an accurate snapshot of the early 1970s with appropriately gruesome special effects. **93m/C VHS, DVD, Blu-ray Disc.** *GB* Ray Lovelock, Christine Galbo, Arthur Kennedy; ***D:*** Jorge Grau; ***W:*** Alessandro Continenza, Marcello Coscia; ***C:*** Francisco Sempere; ***M:*** Giuliano Sorgini.

Let the Devil Wear Black ½ 1999 **(R)** A "Hamlet" update gets the noir treatment. Jack (Penner) is suspicious about his dad's murder, especially when his mom (Bisset) suddenly marries his uncle (Sheridan). Jack becomes obsessed with linking his uncle to some shady business dealings also involving dear old dad, while his girlfriend, Julia (Parker), goes a little crazy from Jack's neglect. Cleverly done. **89m/C VHS, DVD.** Jonathan Penner, Jacqueline Bisset, Jamey Sheridan, Mary-Louise Parker, Philip Baker Hall, Jonathan Banks, Maury Chaykin, Chris Sarandon, Randall Batinkoff, Norman Reedus; ***D:*** Stacy Title; ***W:*** Jonathan Penner, Stacy Title; ***C:*** James Whitaker.

Let the Right One In *Lat den Ratte Komma In* 2008 **(R)** Freakishly compelling variation of the vampire story. Lonely, neglected 12-year-old Oskar (Hedebrant) is constantly bullied at school and dreams of violent revenge. His new apartment neighbor is seemingly young Eli (Leandersson), whom he sees only at night, and who is cared for by the shifty Hakan (Ragnar). Oskar is unfazed when he realizes that Eli needs fresh blood to live and they become friendly. A vampire is good to know when you are targeted by bullies. Swedish with subtitles. **114m/C DVD.** *SW* Kare Hedebrant, Lina Leandersson, Per Ragnar, Henrik Dahl, Karen Berquist, Peter Carlberg; ***D:*** Thomas Alfredson; ***W:*** John Ajvide Lindqvist; ***C:*** Hoyte van Hoytema; ***M:*** Johan Soderqvist.

Let Us Be Gay 1930 Plain housewife Kitty (Shearer) discovers husband Bob (La Rocque) has been cheating and divorces him. She moves to Paris and, three years later, has become a glamorous flirt. Kitty is befriended by wealthy Mrs. Boucicault (Dressler) who invites Kitty to her Long Island estate. However, Mrs. Boucicault has an ulterior motive: her granddaughter is involved with Bob and she wants Kitty to break up their romance. **82m/B DVD.** Norma Shearer, Rod La Rocque, Marie Dressler, Sally Eilers, Hedda Hopper, Gilbert Emery, Raymond Hackett; ***D:*** Robert Z. Leonard; ***W:*** Frances Marion; ***C:*** Norbert Brodine.

L'Etat Sauvage ½ *The Savage State* 1978 This French political thriller finds its heart in the middle of racism. The story unfolds around a newly independent African republic and a love affair between a black cabinet minister and a white Frenchwoman. Corruption abounds in this film based on George Conchon's award-winning novel. In French with English subtitles. **111m/C VHS.** *FR* Marie-Christine Barrault, Claude Brasseur, Jacques Dutronc, Doura Mane, Michel Piccoli; ***D:*** Francis Girod. Cesar '79: Sound.

Lethal WOOF! 2004 (R) Bounty hunter Sara (Marsden) teams up with an FBI agent (Zagarino) to bring down Russian mobster/weapons smuggler Federov (Lamas, he of the wandering accent). Lethally inept. **90m/C DVD.** Lorenzo Lamas, Frank Zagarino, Heather Marie Marsden, Mark Mortimer, John Colton; ***D:*** Dustin Rikert; ***W:*** Jeff Wright, Robert Yap; ***C:*** John Muscatine. **VIDEO**

Lethal Charm *Her Wicked Ways* **1990** Two power-hungry journalists go head-to-head in the high stakes arena of Washington D.C. **92m/C VHS.** Stuart Wilson, David James Elliott, Julie Fulton, Jed Allan, Barbara Eden, Heather Locklear; ***D:*** Richard Michaels; ***W:*** Janice Hickey, Michael Pardridge; ***C:*** Steve (Steven) Shaw; ***M:*** Fred Karlin.

Lethal Dose ½ *LD 50 Lethal Dose* **2003 (R)** Extremist animal activist group ditches team member Gary during a botched rescue mission and wants to make it up to him a year later by springing him from the slammer. Instead, a freaky e-mail directs them to a long-deserted lab where grisly torture awaits. **97m/C VHS, DVD.** Katharine Towne, Melanie (Scary Spice) Brown, Thomas (Tom) Hardy, Ross McCall, Philip Winchester, Stephen Lord, Toby Fisher, Leo Bill, Tania Emery, Alan Talbot, Antony Zaki, Xanthe Elbrick; ***D:*** Simon DeSelva; ***W:*** Matthew McGuchan; ***C:*** Robin Vidgeon; ***M:*** Michael Price. **VIDEO**

Lethal Force ½ *Cottonmouth* **2000** Houston cop Carruth (Tyson) turns vigilante on criminals with the backing of a judge (Vaughn) and some powerful businessmen. Unfortunately, there are innocent victims, including the family of former D.A. Thornton (Owsley), who is persuaded by noisy lawyer Rene (Stafford) to investigate and bring the rogue cop to justice. **95m/C VHS, DVD.** Richard Tyson, Robert Vaughn, Michelle Stafford, Steven Owsley; ***D:*** James Dalthorp; ***W:*** Steven Owsley. **VIDEO**

Lethal Games 1990 Stallone and Vaccaro lead a small community against a blood-thirsty band of criminals. **83m/C VHS.** Frank Stallone, Brenda Vaccaro, Dave Adams, Christopher Whalley, Heidi Paine, Karen Russell; ***D:*** John Bowen.

Lethal Lolita—Amy Fisher: My Story *Amy Fisher: My Story* **1992** The only made-for-TV Amy Fisher story out of three whose cast members even remotely resemble the real people—except of course actress Parker is actually pretty. Minor details aside, this account is Amy's story, purchased by NBC for an undisclosed amount, portraying her as an incest victim who gets involved with an opportunistic married jerk who drags her into prostitution, leading her to take out her frustration on his wife. If this is true, the obvious question is "why?"...to which she answers, "He loves me. We have great sex. And he fixes my car." Oh. See also: "The Amy Fisher Story" and "Casualties of Love: The 'Long Island Lolita' Story." **93m/C VHS, DVD.** Noelle Parker, Ed Marinaro, Kathleen Lasky, Boyd Kestner, Mary Ann Pascal, Lawrence Dane, Kate Lynch; ***D:*** Bradford May. **TV**

Lethal Ninja 1993 **(R)** Kickboxers Joe and Pete set out to rescue Joe's wife from some third-world country overrun by ninjas. Hackneyed but lots of action for martial arts fans. **97m/C VHS, DVD.** Ross Kettle, David Webb, Karyn Hill, Frank Notaro; ***D:*** Yossi Wein; ***W:*** Chris Dresser; ***C:*** Yossi Wein.

Lethal Obsession ½ *Der Joker* **1987 (R)** Two cops battle street crime and a powerful drug ring. Filmed in Germany. **100m/C VHS, DVD.** *GE* Michael York, Elliott Gould, Tahnee Welch, Peter Maffay, Armin Mueller-Stahl; ***D:*** Peter Patzak; ***M:*** Tony Carey.

Lethal Panther 1990 A film where the female is indeed deadlier than the male. Japanese hit woman Ling (Miyamoto) gets involved with drug-smuggling gangsters operating out of the Philippines and is opposed by CIA agent Betty Lee (Hu). Dubbed. **120m/C VHS, DVD.** *HK* Yoko Miyamoto, Sibelle Hu, Lawrence Ng; ***D:*** Godfrey Ho.

Lethal Pursuit 1988 A popular singer who returns to the town where she grew up is tormented by her ex-boyfriend, a criminal. **90m/C VHS.** Mitzi Donahue, Blake Gahner, John Wildman; ***D:*** Donald M. Jones.

Lethal Seduction ½ 1997 Local crime boss Gus Gruman (Estevez) is rapidly losing friends and associates to a sexually oriented serial killer. And there's obsessed cop Trent Jacobson (Mitchum) who's determined to solve the crimes. The one clue is a mystery brunette seen leaving a crime scene. **110m/C VHS, DVD.** Julie Strain, Chris Mitchum, Joe Estevez; ***D:*** Frederick P. Watkins; ***C:*** Robert Dracup.

Lethal Tender 1996 **(R)** A tour group is held hostage by a gang of terrorists as part of a plot to steal $400 million and it's up to a lone Chicago cop to save the day. Fahey does equally well in both bad and good guy roles and here he's in hero mode. **93m/C VHS.** Jeff Fahey, Kim Coates, Gary Busey, Carrie-Anne Moss; ***D:*** John Bradshaw.

Lethal Weapon 1987 **(R)** In Los Angeles, a cop nearing retirement (Glover) unwillingly begins work with a new partner (Gibson), a suicidal, semi-crazed risk-taker who seems determined to get the duo killed. Both Vietnam vets, the pair uncover a vicious heroin smuggling ring run by ruthless ex-Special Forces personnel. Packed with plenty of action, violence, and humorous undertones. Clapton's contributions to the musical score are an added bonus. Gibson and Glover work well together and give this movie extra punch. Followed by three sequels. **110m/C VHS, DVD, Blu-ray Disc, HD DVD.** Mel Gibson, Danny Glover, Gary Busey, Mitchell Ryan, Tom Atkins, Darlene Love, Traci Wolfe, Steve Kahan, Jackie Swanson, Damon Hines, Lycia Naff, Mary Ellen Trainor, Jack Thibeau, Ed O'Ross, Gustav Vintas, Al Leong, Joan Severance; ***D:*** Richard Donner; ***W:*** Shane Black; ***C:*** Stephen Goldblatt; ***M:*** Michael Kamen, Eric Clapton.

Lethal Weapon 2 1989 **(R)** This sequel to the popular cop adventure finds Gibson and Glover taking on a variety of blond South African "diplomats" who try to use their diplomatic immunity status to thwart the duo's efforts to crack their smuggling ring. Gibson finally finds romance, and viewers learn the truth about his late wife's accident. Also features the introduction of obnoxious, fast-talking con artist Leo ("OK, OK") Getz, adeptly played by Pesci, who becomes a third wheel to the crime-fighting team. **114m/C VHS, DVD, Blu-ray Disc, HD DVD.** Mel Gibson, Danny Glover, Joe Pesci, Joss Ackland, Derrick O'Connor, Patsy Kensit, Darlene Love, Traci Wolfe, Steve Kahan, Mary Ellen Trainor, Damon Hines, Jenette Goldstein, Mark Rolston, Dean Norris, Nestor Serrano, Grand L. Bush; ***D:*** Richard Donner; ***W:*** Jeffrey Boam; ***C:*** Stephen Goldblatt; ***M:*** Michael Kamen, Eric Clapton, David Sanborn.

Lethal Weapon 3 ½ 1992 **(R)** Murtaugh and Riggs return for more action in another slam-bang adventure. Murtaugh hopes his last week before retirement will be a peaceful one, but partner Riggs isn't about to let him go quietly. Not many changes from the successful formula with bickering buddies, lots of adventure, exploding buildings, a little comic relief from Pesci, and the addition of Russo as an Internal Affairs cop who proves to be more than a match for Riggs. **118m/C VHS, DVD.** Mel Gibson, Danny Glover, Joe Pesci, Rene Russo, Stuart Wilson, Steve Kahan, Darlene Love, Traci Wolfe, Gregory Millar, Jason Meshover-Iorg, Delores Hall, Mary Ellen Trainor, Nicholas Chinlund, Damon Hines, Miguel A. Nunez Jr.; ***D:*** Richard Donner; ***W:*** Jeffrey Boam, Robert Mark Kamen; ***C:*** Jan De Bont; ***M:*** Eric Clapton, David Sanborn, Michael Kamen. MTV Movie Awards '93: On-Screen Duo (Mel Gibson/Danny Glover), Action Seq.

Lethal Weapon 4 ½ 1998 **(R)** It's old home week as Gibson, Glover, Pesci, and Russo all reunite for one more escapade, six years after 1992's "Lethal Weapon 3." Rock joins the veterans as junior detective Lee Butters, who has some unexpected ties to Murtaugh. They're investigating Asian crimelord Wah Sing Ku (Chinese action star Li) who's involved in smuggling and counterfeiting and has no problem with violence, including kicking the bejeezus out of Riggs on more than one occasion. Russo had to do her action sequences with a prosthetic belly since her character, Lorna Cole, and Riggs are about to become parents. It's the same old-same old but it's still a good time. **125m/C VHS, DVD.** Mel Gibson, Danny Glover, Joe Pesci, Rene Russo, Chris Rock, Jet Li, Steve Kahan, Darlene Love, Mary Ellen Trainor, Jack Kehler, Damon Hines, Traci Wolfe, Richard Libertini, Richard Riehle; ***D:*** Richard Donner; ***W:*** Channing Gibson; ***C:*** Andrzej Bartkowiak; ***M:*** Michael Kamen, Eric Clapton, David Sanborn.

Lethal Woman ½ 1988 A group of beautiful women, all once victimized by rapes, is recruited to an island by the "Lethal Woman," who plots revenge on any man who dares to vacation on the island. **96m/C VHS.** Robert Lipton, James Luisi, Shannon Tweed, Merete Van Kamp; ***D:*** Christian Marnham; ***W:*** Gabe Ellis; ***C:*** Vincent Cox; ***M:*** Meir Eshel.

Let's Dance ½ 1950 A young widow tries to protect her son from his wealthy, paternal grandmother, while Fred dances his way into her heart. More obscure Astaire vehicle, but as charming as the rest. Needless to say, great dancing. ♫ Tunnel of Love; The Hyacinth; Piano Dance; Jack and the Beanstalk; Can't Stop Talking; Oh, Them Dudes; Why Fight the Feeling?. **112m/C VHS.** Betty Hutton, Fred Astaire, Roland Young, Ruth Warrick, Shepperd Strudwick, Lucile Watson, Barton MacLane, Gregory Moffett, Melville Cooper; ***D:*** Norman Z. McLeod.

Let's Do It Again ½ 1975 **(PG)** Atlanta milkman and his pal, a factory worker, milk two big-time gamblers out of a large sum of money in order to build a meeting hall for their fraternal lodge. Lesser sequel to "Uptown Saturday Night." **113m/C VHS, DVD.** Sidney Poitier, Bill Cosby, John Amos, Jimmie Walker, Ossie Davis, Denise Nicholas, Calvin Lockhart; ***D:*** Sidney Poitier; ***W:*** Richard Wesley.

Let's Get Harry ½ *The Rescue* 1987 **(R)** Americans led by mercenaries mix it up with a Columbian cocaine franchise in an attempt to rescue their friend, Harry. Never released theatrically, for good reason. **107m/C VHS.** Robert Duvall, Gary Busey, Michael Schoeffling, Thomas F. Wilson, Glenn

Frey, Rick Rossovich, Ben Johnson, Matt Clark, Mark Harmon, Gregory Sierra, Elpidia Carrillo; ***D:*** Alan Smithee; ***W:*** Samuel Fuller, Charles Robert Carner; ***M:*** Brad Fiedel.

Let's Get Lost **1988** Absorbing documentary of Chet Baker, the prominent '50s "cool" jazz trumpeter (and occasional vocalist) who succumbed, like many of his peers, to drug addiction. Weber's black-and-white, fashion photography style well suits his subject. Downbeat, but rarely less than worthy. **125m/B VHS.** Chet Baker; ***D:*** Bruce Weber.

Let's Get Married 🦴 **1960** A young doctor's weakness under pressure brings him to the brink of babbling idiocy when his wife goes into early labor. **90m/B VHS.** Hermione Baddeley, Jason Booth, Jack (Gwyllam) Gwillim, Bernie Winters, Anthony Newley, Ann Aubrey; ***D:*** Peter Graham Scott; ***W:*** Kent Taylor; ***C:*** Ted Moore; ***M:*** Edwin Astley.

Let's Get Tough 🦴 **1942** The East Side Kids, unable to enlist because of their age, harass local Oriental shopkeepers and eventually get involved with a murder. **52m/B VHS, DVD.** Leo Gorcey, Bobby Jordan, Huntz Hall, Gabriel Dell, Sammy (Earnest) Morrison; ***D:*** Wallace Fox.

Let's Go! 🦴 **1/2** **1923** The son of a cement company president sets out to prove his worth to the firm by landing a contract with the town of Hillsboro. For some unknown reason, he sets off on an amazing set of stunts. Silent with original organ music. **79m/B VHS.** Richard Talmadge, Hal Clements, Eileen (Elaine Persey) Percy, Tully Marshall; ***D:*** William K. Howard.

Let's Go Collegiate 🦴 **1/2** **1941** Two college rowers promise their girlfriends that they'll win the big race, but their plans are almost frustrated when their best oarsman is drafted. Their only hope lies in replacing him with a truck driver. ♫ Look What You've Done To Me; Sweet 16; Let's Do A Little Dreaming. **62m/B VHS, DVD.** Frankie Darro, Marcia Mae Jones, Jackie Moran, Keye Luke, Mantan Moreland, Gale Storm; ***D:*** Jean Yarbrough.

Let's Go to Prison 🦴 **1/2** **2006 (R)** What we have here is a failure to entertain. John Lyshitski (Shepard) is a bitter ex-con who plots revenge on the judge who sent him up the river three times. John sets up the judge's preppy son Nelson (Arnett), then gets himself thrown back in the pokey so he can give Nelson terrible advice on prison survival. Standard jokes about bad food, soap-dropping and license plates ensue. Eventually, situations involving a psycho white supremacist (Shannon) and an amorous black prisoner (McBride) turn the tables on John. It's not very funny considering the comedy pedigree of director Odenkirk and the majority of the cast. **84m/C DVD.** *US* Dax Shepard, Will Arnett, Chi McBride, David Koechner, Dylan Baker, Michael Shannon; ***D:*** Bob Odenkirk; ***W:*** Robert Ben Garant, Thomas Lennon, Michael Patrick Jann; ***C:*** Ramsay Nickell; ***M:*** Alan Elliott.

Let's Kill All the Lawyers 🦴🦴 **1/2** **1993 (R)** Low-budget satire about one man's angst over whether to become a lawyer is witty, entertaining, and not just for legal eagles. Law-firm intern Foster Merkul (Frederick) is apprenticed to a sleazeball (Vezina) who teaches him that money—not justice—is the name of the game in the law biz. Growing increasingly disillusioned, Foster sets out to reform the system with the help of Satori, a beautiful and mysterious creature of his imagination. Shot at sites in and around Detroit, this independent production features lots of cameos by local media celebrities. **103m/C VHS.** Rick Frederick, James Vezina, Michelle De Vuono, Maggie Patton, Marty Smith; ***D:*** Ron Senkowski; ***W:*** Ron Senkowski.

Let's Make It Legal 🦴🦴 **1/2** **1951** Amusing comedy of a married couple who decide to get a divorce after 20 years of marriage. Colbert stars as the woman who decides to leave her husband, Carey, because he's a chronic gambler. They part as friends, but soon Colbert's old flame, Scott, is back in town and things get rather complicated. A solid cast serves as the main strength in this film. **77m/B VHS, DVD.** Claudette Colbert, MacDonald Carey, Zachary Scott, Barbara Bates, Robert Wagner, Marilyn Monroe, Frank Cady, Kathleen Freeman; ***D:*** Richard Sale; ***W:*** F. Hugh Herbert, I.A.L. Diamond; ***C:*** Lucien Ballard; ***M:*** Cyril Mockridge.

Let's Make Love 🦴🦴 **1/2** **1960** An urbane millionaire discovers he is to be parodied in an off-Broadway play, and vows to stop it—until he falls in love with the star of the show. He then ends up acting in the play. ♫ My Heart Belongs to Daddy; Let's Make Love; Specialization; Incurably Romantic; Sing Me a Song That Sells; You With the Crazy Eyes; Give Me the Simple Life. **118m/C VHS, DVD.** Yves Montand, Marilyn Monroe, Tony Randall, Frankie Vaughan, Bing Crosby, Gene Kelly, Milton Berle; ***D:*** George Cukor; ***W:*** Norman Krasna; ***C:*** Daniel F. Fapp; ***M:*** Lionel Newman.

Let's Make Up 🦴🦴 *Lilacs in the Spring* **1955** When it comes to giving her heart, Neagle can't decide between two dashing men. **94m/C VHS.** *GB* Errol Flynn, Anna Neagle, David Farrar, Kathleen Harrison, Peter Graves; ***D:*** Herbert Wilcox.

Let's Scare Jessica to Death 🦴🦴 **1971 (PG)** A young woman who was recently released from a mental hospital is subjected to unspeakable happenings at a country home with her friends. She encounters murder, vampires, and corpses coming out of nowhere. A supernatural thriller with quite a few genuine scares. **89m/C VHS, DVD.** Zohra Lampert, Barton Heyman, Kevin J. O'Connor, Gretchen Corbett, Alan Manson; ***D:*** John Hancock.

Let's Sing Again 🦴🦴 **1936** Eight-year-old singing sensation Bobby Breen made his debut in this dusty musical vehicle, as a runaway orphan who becomes the pal of a washed-up opera star in a traveling show. ♫ Let's Sing Again; Lullaby; Farmer in the Dell; La Donna e Mobile. **70m/B VHS.** Bobby Breen, Henry Armetta, George Houston, Vivienne Osborne, Grant Withers, Inez Courtney, Lucien Littlefield; ***D:*** Kurt Neumann.

Let's Talk About Sex 🦴 **1/2** **1998 (R)** Miami magazine columnist Jazz (Beyer) pitches her idea for a TV show about women who candidly discuss sex (more accurately, their complaints about men), but is told she has the weekend to create a sample video. Jazz enlists the help of her equally frustrated and unhappy friends, Michelle and Lena (Brewster and Ingerman), and armed with a video camera, the three comb the steamy streets of Miami asking random women personal questions about their sex lives and baiting them into complaining about men. Tries to be a hip sorta-documentary blending hand-held shots with staged scenes, but comes across as a soft-core sex farce/soap opera. Beyer also wrote and directed. **82m/C VHS.** Troy Beyer, Randi Ingerman, Joseph C. Phillips, Paget Brewster, Michaline Babich, Tina Nguyen; ***D:*** Troy Beyer; ***W:*** Troy Beyer; ***C:*** Kelly Evans; ***M:*** Michael Carpenter.

The Letter 🦴🦴🦴🦴 **1940** When a man is shot and killed on a Malaysian plantation, the woman who committed the murder pleads self-defense. Her husband and his lawyer attempt to free her, but find more than they expected in this tightly paced film noir. Based on the novel by W. Somerset Maugham. Davis emulated the originator of her role, Jeanne Eagels, in her mannerisms and line readings, although Eagels later went mad from drug abuse and overwork. **96m/B VHS, DVD.** Bette Davis, Herbert Marshall, James Stephenson, Gale Sondergaard, Bruce Lester, Cecil Kellaway, Victor Sen Yung, Frieda Inescort; ***D:*** William Wyler; ***W:*** Howard Koch; ***C:*** Gaetano Antonio "Tony" Gaudio; ***M:*** Max Steiner.

Letter from an Unknown Woman 🦴🦴🦴 **1948** A woman falls in love with a concert pianist on the eve of his departure. He promises to return but never does. The story is told in flashbacks as the pianist reads a letter from the woman. A great romantic melodrama. **90m/B VHS, DVD.** Joan Fontaine, Louis Jourdan, Mady Christians, Marcel Journet, Art Smith; ***D:*** Max Ophuls. Natl. Film Reg. '92.

Letter of Introduction 🦴🦴 **1/2** **1938** A struggling young actress learns that her father is really a well known screen star and agrees not to reveal the news to the public. **104m/B VHS, DVD.** Adolphe Menjou, Edgar Bergen, George Murphy, Eve Arden, Ann Sheridan, Andrea Leeds; ***D:*** John M. Stahl; ***C:*** Karl Freund.

Letter to Brezhnev 🦴🦴🦴 **1986 (R)** Acclaimed independent film about two working-class Liverpool girls who fall in love with two furloughed Russian sailors. When the men eventually return to the USSR, one of the girls contacts the Russian Secretary General in an effort to rejoin her lover. Amusing tale of different relationships. **94m/C VHS.** *GB* Margi Clarke, Alexandra Pigg, Peter Firth, Ken Campbell, Tracy Lea, Alfred Molina, Angela Clarke; ***D:*** Chris Bernard; ***W:*** Frank Clarke; ***M:*** Alan Gill.

Letter to My Killer 🦴🦴 **1/2** **1995 (PG-13)** Construction worker Nick Parma (Chinlund) finds an unmailed letter in a demolished building, which he and wife Judy (Winningham) discover is 30 years old. The woman letter writer is describing major fraud and when Judy learns that she was murdered, she and Nick decide to blackmail the probable suspects—a powerful business cartel. But if they killed once.... **92m/C VHS.** Mare Winningham, Nicholas Chinlund, Rip Torn, Josef Sommer, Eddie Jones, Dey Young; ***D:*** Janet Meyers; ***W:*** Norman Strum; ***C:*** Stephen M. Katz; ***M:*** Mason Daring. **CABLE**

A Letter to Three Wives 🦴🦴🦴🦴 **1949** Crain, Darnell, and Sothern star as three friends who, shortly before embarking on a Hudson River boat trip, each receive a letter from Holm (who's never shown), the fourth member in their set. The letter tells them that she has run off with one of their husbands but does not specify his identity. The women spend the rest of the trip reviewing their sometimes shaky unions which provides some of the funniest and most caustic scenes, including Douglas (as Sothern's husband) ranting against the advertising business which supports his wife's radio soap opera. Sharp dialogue, moving performances. Based on the novel by John Klempner. Remade for TV in 1985. **103m/B VHS, DVD.** Jeanne Crain, Linda Darnell, Ann Sothern, Kirk Douglas, Paul Douglas, Jeffrey Lynn, Thelma Ritter, Barbara Lawrence, Connie Gilchrist, Florence Bates; ***D:*** Joseph L. Mankiewicz; ***W:*** Joseph L. Mankiewicz; ***C:*** Arthur C. Miller; ***M:*** Alfred Newman; ***V:*** Celeste Holm. Oscars '49: Director (Mankiewicz), Screenplay; Directors Guild '48: Director (Mankiewicz).

Letters from a Killer 🦴🦴 **1998 (R)** Death-row con Race Darnell (Swayze) has been corresponding with four women every since writing a best-seller about his life in prison. After a new trial overturns his conviction and sets him free, Race discovers that one of his correspondents—who believed she was his only love—is framing him for murder in revenge for his "betrayal" of her. **103m/C VHS, DVD.** Patrick Swayze, Gia Carides, Kim Myers, Olivia Birkelund, Tina Lifford, Elizabeth Ruscio, Roger E. Mosley, Bruce McGill, Mark Rolston; ***D:*** David Carson; ***W:*** Nicholas Hicks-Beach; ***C:*** John A. Alonzo; ***M:*** Dennis McCarthy.

Letters from Alou 🦴🦴 *Las Cartas de Alou* **1990** African immigrant Alou is trying to get to Barcelona to meet up with a friend but faces much exploitation and discrimination along the way. Spanish with subtitles. **100m/C VHS.** *SP* Mulie Jarju, Eulalia Ramon; ***D:*** Montxo Armendariz; ***W:*** Montxo Armendariz.

Letters from Iwo Jima 🦴🦴🦴🦴 **2006 (R)** Recounts the dramatic 36 days of battle on Iwo Jima that began in February 1945, as told from the Japanese viewpoint. Serves as a companion to director Eastwood's "Flags of Our Fathers." Facing a completely lopsided confrontation, the 22,000 Japanese military men kept about 110,000 American troops in combat far longer than anticipated under the guidance of the gifted Lt. Gen. Tadamichi Kuribayashi (Watanabe), whose letters to his wife provide the story's narrative. Setting a somber tone for the horrific losses incurred by both sides—nearly 21,000 Japanese and 7,000 Americans—are the muted colors used by Eastwood, who admirably captures the humanity of the Japanese men as they confront the impossible mission ahead. In direct comparison to "Flags," the ending has the Japanese viewing the raising of the American flag in the distance rather than close-up. First screenplay by Yamashita after being a research assistant on "Flags." In Japanese with subtitles. **145m/C DVD, Blu-ray Disc, HD DVD.** *US* Ken(saku) Watanabe, Tsuyoski Ihara, Shido Nakamura, Kazunari Ninomiya, Ryo Kase; ***D:*** Clint Eastwood; ***W:*** Iris Yamashita, Paul Haggis; ***C:*** Tom Stern; ***M:*** Kyle Eastwood, Michael Stevens. Oscars '06: Sound FX Editing; Golden Globes '07: Foreign Film.

Letters from My Windmill 🦴🦴🦴 **1/2** **1954** A series of three short stories: "The Three Low Masses," "The Elixir of Father Gaucher," and "The Secret of Master Cornille" from respected director Pagnol. The unique format only enhances this film. In French with English subtitles. **116m/B VHS.** *FR* Henri Velbert, Yvonne Gamy, Robert Vattier, Roger Crouzet; ***D:*** Marcel Pagnol.

Letters from the Park 🦴🦴🦴 *Cartas del Parque* **1988** In Cuba, 1913, two taciturn would-be lovers hire a poet, Victor La Place, to write love letters to each other. Normal proboscis aside, the poet follows the fate of Cyrano, and finds himself the unhappy hypotenuse in a triangular romance. Based on an original story by Marquez; made for Spanish TV. Subtitled. **85m/C VHS.** *CU* Victor Laplace, Ivonne Lopez, Miguel Paneque; ***D:*** Tomas Gutierrez Alea; ***W:*** Tomas Gutierrez Alea, Gabriel Garcia Marquez; ***C:*** Mario Garcia Joya. **TV**

Letters to an Unknown Lover 🦴🦴 **1/2** *Les Louves* **1984** During WWII, a man and woman engage in sexual and emotional combat. **101m/C VHS.** *GB FR* Cherie Lunghi, Mathilda May, Yves Beneyton, Ralph Bates; ***D:*** Peter Duffell.

Letters to Juliet **2010 (PG)** Young American Sophie (Seyfried) travels to Verona, Italy, the setting for Shakespeare's tragic play "Romeo and Juliet." She joins a group of volunteers who reply to letters found in the fictional lovers' courtyard. When Sophie finds a letter from 1951, her response inspires Juliet (Redgrave) to travel to Italy in search of her long-lost love and also gets Sophie involved in an unexpected romance. **m/C DVD.** *US* Amanda Seyfried, Vanessa Redgrave, Christopher Egan, Franco Nero, Gael Garcia Bernal; ***D:*** Gary Winick; ***W:*** Jose Rivera, Tim Sullivan; ***C:*** Marco Pontecorvo; ***M:*** Andrea Guerra.

Letting Go 🦴🦴 **1985 (PG)** Comedy-drama about a broken-hearted career woman and a young widower who fall in love. **94m/C VHS, DVD.** John Ritter, Sharon Gless, Joe Cortese; ***D:*** Jack Bender. **TV**

Letting the Birds Go Free **1986** When a stranger is caught stealing from a farmer's barn, the farmer and his son decide to let the villain work off his crime. Some very interesting relationships develop from this arrangement. **60m/C VHS.** Lionel Jeffries.

Leviathan 🦴🦴 **1989 (R)** A motley crew of ocean-floor miners are trapped when they are accidentally exposed to a failed Soviet experiment that turns humans into insatiable, regenerating fish-creatures. **98m/C VHS, DVD.** Peter Weller, Ernie Hudson, Hector Elizondo, Amanda Pays, Richard Crenna, Daniel Stern, Lisa Eilbacher, Michael Carmine, Meg Foster; ***D:*** George P. Cosmatos; ***W:*** David Peoples, Jeb Stuart; ***C:*** Alex Thomson; ***M:*** Jerry Goldsmith.

Levitation 🦴 **1/2** **1997** Pregnant teenager, Acey (Paulson), decides to leave her unhappy adoptive parents and search for her birth mother. She has an imaginary friend (possibly her guardian angel) she calls Bob (London) and a real friend, DJ Downtime (Hudson), to help her out but her quest doesn't end in happiness. Title refers to Acey's weird uncontrollable ability to levitate, unfortunately the film doesn't—it's a muddled mess. **99m/C VHS, DVD.** Sarah Paulson, Ernie Hudson, Jeremy London, Ann Magnuson, Brett Cullen, Christopher Boyer; ***D:*** Scott Goldstein; ***W:*** Scott Goldstein; ***C:*** Michael G. Wojciechowski; ***M:*** Leonard Rosenman.

Levity 🦴🦴 **2003 (R)** Manuel Jordan (Thornton) has just been released from prison after serving 22 years of a life sentence for killing a clerk during a botched robbery. He returns to his neighborhood, looking for, but not expecting to find redemption. What he finds is a job working at a community center run by a fire-and-brimstone preacher, possible romance with the sister (Hunter) of his victim, her troubled son, and a self-destructive club kid, along with the wish to protect them all from contrived coincidences and overwrought sentimentality. Soloman was going for mood and atmospheric, and while it is moody (and crushingly boring), it's not very atmospheric. What it is is a complete waste of a talented cast. **100m/C VHS, DVD.** *US* Billy Bob Thornton, Morgan Freeman, Holly Hunter, Kirsten Dunst, Dorian Harewood, Geoff Wigdor, Catherine Colvey, Manuel Aranguiz, Luke Robertson, Billoah Greene; ***D:*** Edward Solomon; ***W:*** Edward Solomon; ***C:*** Roger Deakins; ***M:*** Mark Oliver Everett.

Lewis and Clark and George 🦴🦴 **1997 (R)** Lewis (Xuereb) is a dim-witted killer and Clark (Gunther) is a computer nerd. Both are prison escapees in possession of what is supposed to be a map to a gold mine. Lewis happens to be illiterate and needs Clark, who's afraid of Lewis's trigger-happy ways. George (McGowan) is a sexy mute thief who takes both men for quite a wild ride. Filmed in rural New Mexico. **84m/C VHS, DVD.** Salvator Xuereb, Dan Gunther, Rose McGowan, Art LaFleur, Aki Aleong, James Brolin, Paul Bartel; ***D:*** Rod McCall; ***W:*** Rod McCall; ***C:*** Mike Mayers; ***M:*** Ben Vaughn.

L'Homme Blesse 🦴🦴🦴 *The Wounded Man* **1983** A serious erotic film about 18-year-old Henri (Anglade), cloistered by an overbearing family, and his sudden awakening to his own homosexuality. Anglade's film debut. In French with English subtitles. **90m/C VHS, DVD.** *FR* Jean-Hugues Anglade, Roland Bertin, Vittorio Mezzogiorno; ***D:*** Patrice Chereau; ***C:*** Renato Berta. Cesar '84: Writing.

Liam 🦴🦴 **2000 (R)** Stuttering, 7-year-old Liam (Borrows) is an Irish Catholic living in Liverpool in the 1930s. His hardworking mother is determined that Liam will look presentable for his first Communion no matter what the sacrifice but his family's struggles worsen when his father (Hart) loses his job and becomes increasingly bitter, blaming his woes on others and turning to violence as a solution. **90m/C VHS, DVD.** *GE GB* Ian Hart, Claire Hackett, David Hart, Anthony Borrows, Megan Burns, Anne Reid, Russell Dixon, Julia Deakin, Andrew Schofield, Bernadette Shortt, David Corey; ***D:*** Stephen Frears; ***W:*** Jimmy McGovern; ***C:*** Andrew Dunn; ***M:*** John Murphy.

Liane, Jungle Goddess 🦴🦴 **1956** A variation on the Greystoke legend featuring a beautiful (and topless) jungle goddess who is discovered living in the wilds of Africa. Thinking that she may be the lost granddaughter of a wealthy English nobleman, she's brought back to London for a reunion. Will civilization prove to be as dangerous as the jungle? **88m/C VHS, DVD.** *GE* Marion Michael, Hardy Kruger, Irene Galter, Peter Mosbacher; ***D:*** Eduard von Borsody; ***W:*** Ernst von Salomon; ***C:*** Bruno Timm; ***M:*** Erwin Halletz.

Lianna 🦴🦴🦴 **1983 (R)** Acclaimed screenwriter/director John Sayles wrote and directed this story of a woman's romantic involvement with another woman. Chronicles an unhappy homemaker's awakening to the feelings of love that she develops for a female professor. Sayles makes an appearance as a family friend. **110m/C VHS, DVD.** Jon (John) DeVries, Linda Griffiths, Jane Hallaren, Jo Henderson, Jessica Wright MacDonald; ***Cameos:*** John Sayles; ***D:*** John Sayles; ***W:*** John Sayles; ***M:*** Mason Daring.

Liar Liar 🦴🦴 ½ **1997 (PG-13)** Carrey takes on one of his less manic but still appealing personas as compulsive liar and attorney Fletcher Reid. A constant disappointment to his ex-wife Audrey (Tierney) and young son Max (Cooper), Fletcher is forced to tell nothing but the truth for 24 hours, thanks to his son's supernatural birthday wish. This puts a crimp in his legal practice, especially as he tries to defend brazen would-be divorcee Samantha Cole (Tilly). Gets kinda sappy but Carrey can carry almost any situation. **87m/C VHS, DVD, HD DVD.** Jim Carrey, Jennifer Tilly, Maura Tierney, Amanda Donohoe, Swoosie Kurtz, Justin Cooper, Jason Bernard, Mitchell Ryan, Anne Haney, Chip (Christopher) Mayer, Randall "Tex" Cobb, Cary Elwes, Eric Pierpoint, Cheri Oteri; ***D:*** Tom Shadyac; ***W:*** Paul Guay, Stephen Mazur; ***C:*** Russell Boyd; ***M:*** John Debney. MTV Movie Awards '98: Comedic Perf. (Carrey).

The Liars 🦴🦴 **1964** Mystery in which a Frenchman strikes it rich in Africa, then returns home to Paris in search of a wife. He advertisies for a mate, but is set up by con artists instead. In French with English subtitles. **92m/C VHS.** Dawn Addams, Jean Servais; ***D:*** Edmond T. Greville.

The Liar's Club 🦴 ½ **1993 (R)** High-school football teammates try to cover up a rape and wind up involved in murder. **100m/C VHS.** Wil Wheaton, Brian Krause, Soleil Moon Frye, Jennifer Burns, Michael Cudlitz, Bruce Weitz; ***D:*** Jeffrey Porter.

Liar's Edge 🦴🦴 **1992 (R)** Tweed portrays a single mother whose teenaged son, Mark, is plagued by violent fantasies. When she remarries and her new husband and sleazy brother-in-law move in, Mark's hallucinations become stronger until he believes he's witnessed a murder. The murder turns out to be a fact and his new stepfather is involved but can Mark prove it. Filmed on location in Niagra Falls. **97m/C VHS.** Shannon Tweed, Nicholas Shields, David Keith, Joseph Bottoms, Christopher Plummer; ***D:*** Ron Oliver; ***W:*** Ron Oliver.

Liar's Moon 🦴🦴 **1982 (PG)** A local boy woos and weds the town's wealthiest young lady, only to be trapped in family intrigue. **106m/C VHS, DVD.** Cindy Fisher, Matt Dillon, Christopher Connelly, Susan Tyrrell; ***D:*** David Fisher.

Liar's Poker 🦴 ½ **1999** Car salesman Jack (Tyson) has invested a quarter-million bucks in friend Vic's (Blondell) club and Vic is beginning to resent Jack's not-to-silent partnership. Married Jack is also competing with bud, Niko (Luisi), for the affections of young babe, Rebecca (Heinle) while his own wife, Linda (Gridley), plays around. And fourth buddy Freddie (Flea) enjoys knowing too much about everybody else's business. It finally comes down to a deadly confrontation between the male foursome. Unfortunately, bland acting and a lack of plot details detract from this macho crime drama's twisty ending. **93m/C VHS, DVD.** Richard Tyson, Flea, Jimmy Blondell, Caesar Luisi, Pamela Gidley, Amelia Heinle, Neith Adriana, Colin Patrick Lynch; ***D:*** Jeff Santo; ***W:*** Jeff Santo; ***C:*** Giles M.I. Dunning; ***M:*** Peter Himmelman.

Libeled Lady 🦴🦴🦴 ½ **1936** A fast, complicated screwball masterwork. Newspaper editor Warren Haggerty (Tracy) prints an erroneous story that heiress Connie Allenbury (Loy) is after a married man. Connie sues and in order to defuse the lawsuit, Warren comes up with an elaborate scheme (certain to backfire) that involves his own fiancee Galdys (Harlow) and recently fired reporter Bill (Powell). Remade in 1946 as "Easy to Wed." **98m/B VHS, DVD.** Myrna Loy, Spencer Tracy, Jean Harlow, William Powell, Walter Connolly, Charley Grapewin, Cora Witherspoon, E.E. Clive, Charles Trowbridge, Dennis O'Keefe, Hattie McDaniel; ***D:*** Jack Conway; ***W:*** George Oppenheimer, Howard Emmett Rogers, Maurine Watkins; ***C:*** Norbert Brodine; ***M:*** William Axt.

The Liberation of L.B. Jones 🦴🦴 **1970 (R)** A wealthy black undertaker wants a divorce from his wife, who is having an affair with a white policeman. Wyler's final film. **101m/C VHS.** Lee J. Cobb, Lola Falana, Barbara Hershey, Anthony Zerbe, Roscoe Lee Browne; ***D:*** William Wyler; ***W:*** Stirling Silliphant; ***M:*** Elmer Bernstein.

Liberators 🦴 **1969** Kinski stars as a criminal soldier battling with the American authorities, German troops, and his fugitive partner. **91m/C VHS, DVD.** *IT* George Hilton, Ray Saunders, Betsy Bell, Klaus Kinski; ***D:*** Tonino Ricci; ***W:*** Tonino Ricci; ***C:*** Sandro Mancori; ***M:*** Riz Ortolani.

The Libertine 🦴🦴 *La Matriarca* **1969** Mimi (Spaak) is a young widow who's just discovered her late husband kept a separate apartment equipped to satisfy his more unusual sexual desires. Intrigued, Mimi decides to keep the apartment and do her own sexual exploring. Dubbed. **90m/C VHS, DVD.** *IT* Catherine Spaak, Jean-Louis Trintignant, Luigi Pistilli, Luigi Proietti, Renzo Montagnani; ***D:*** Pasquale Festa Campanile; ***C:*** Alfio Contini; ***M:*** Armando Trovajoli.

The Libertine 🦴 ½ **2005 (R)** Covering a portion of the life of the 17th century's famous degenerate the 2nd Earl of Rochester, John Wilmot (Depp). Depp's portrayal is well done, but the story eventually collapses under its own weight. A little taste of Wilmot's naughtiness might be interesting, even fun, but watching him destroy himself with dreadful behavior over and over begins to feel tiresome. Like watching a heavyweight prize fight, eventually you hope the fallen fighter just stays down, relieving everyone's pain. **130m/C DVD.** Johnny Depp, Samantha Morton, John Malkovich, Rosamund Pike, Tom Hollander, Kelly Reilly, Jack Davenport, Richard Coyle, Francesca Annis, Rupert Friend, Clare Higgins, Johnny Vegas; ***D:*** Laurence Dunmore; ***W:*** Stephen Jeffreys; ***C:*** Alexander Melman; ***M:*** Michael Nyman.

Liberty & Bash 🦴 **1990 (R)** Two boyhood friends who served together in Vietnam reunite to rid their neighborhood of drug pushers and save the life of a friend. **92m/C VHS.** Miles O'Keeffe, Lou Ferrigno, Mitzi Kapture, Richard Eden, Cheryl Paris, Gary Conway; ***D:*** Myrl A. Schreibman.

Liberty Heights 🦴🦴 ½ **1999 (R)** Levinson heads back to Baltimore (for the fourth time) for his 1954 coming of age/family drama with his focus on the city's Jewish community and the Kurtzman family in particular. Nate (Mantegna) has a two-bit numbers racket and a failing burlesque house, college son Van (Brody) falls for a shiksa (Murphy), while high schooler Ben (Foster) is captivated by Sylvia (Johnson), the first black student in his class. It may be too early for Bob Dylan but the times were a-changin' indeed and Levinson takes an unsentimental, if heartfelt, look at his past. **127m/C VHS, DVD.** Adrien Brody, Joe Mantegna, Ben Foster, Bebe Neuwirth, Rebekah Johnson, Orlando Jones, Frania Rubinek, David Krumholtz, Richard Kline, Vincent Guastaferro, Carolyn Murphy, Justin Chambers, James Pickens Jr., Anthony Anderson, Kiersten Warren; ***D:*** Barry Levinson; ***W:*** Barry Levinson; ***C:*** Christopher Doyle; ***M:*** Andrea Morricone.

Liberty Stands Still 🦴🦴 **2002 (R)** Title lends itself to several interpretations, one of which is literal. If Liberty Wallace (Fiorentino) doesn't stand still, she's a dead woman. Liberty is the wife of gun manufacturer Victor (Platt). She takes a cell call while walking in downtown L.A. and is informed if she doesn't handcuff herself to a nearby hotdog cart and keep talking that she will immediately be shot. Joe (Snipes), the sniper/caller, then informs Liberty that he has placed a bomb in the cart itself. His daughter was murdered by a gun and this is his way to bring attention to the situation. Good cast but the points are belabored—guns bad, we get it. **96m/C VHS, DVD.** Wesley Snipes, Linda Fiorentino, Oliver Platt, Martin Cummins, Hart Bochner, Jonathan Scarfe, Ian Tracey; ***D:*** Keri Skogland; ***W:*** Keri Skogland; ***C:*** Denis Maloney; ***M:*** Michael Convertino.

The Librarian: Curse of the Judas Chalice 🦴🦴 ½ **2008** Flynn Carsen (Wyle) is a little tired as this third adventure begins but he's soon ready to save the world again when he must find the chalice made from Judas' 30 pieces of silver. This time Flynn has a very unusual assistant, New Orleans nightclub singer Simone (Katic) who's also a vampire babe. Seems the chalice is the key to resurrecting a nasty bloodsucker with a desire for world domination. **90m/C DVD.** Noah Wyle, Bob Newhart, Jane Curtin, Stana Katic, Bruce Davidson, Dirkan Tulane; ***D:*** Jonathan Frakes; ***W:*** Marco Schnabel; ***C:*** David Connell. **CABLE**

The Librarian: Quest for the Spear 🦴🦴 ½ **2004** Cable comic adventure is Indiana Jones-lite. Flynn Carsen (Wyle) is a perpetual student (22 degrees) who finally lands a job as a librarian at the mysterious Metropolitan Public Library, which contains such top-secret and mythic treasures as Excalibur and the Ark of the Covenant. When the Serpent Brotherhood steals the Spear of Destiny, intrepid geek Flynn is paired up with butt-kicking bodyguard Nicole (Walger) to retrieve the spear before it can be used for evil purposes. **92m/C DVD.** Noah Wyle, Sonya Walger, Bob Newhart, Jane Curtin, Olympia Dukakis, Kyle MacLachlan, Kelly Hu; ***D:*** Peter Winther; ***W:*** David Titcher; ***C:*** Alan Caso; ***M:*** Joseph LoDuca. **CABLE**

The Librarian: Return to King Solomon's Mines 🦴🦴 ½ **2006** In this second adventure, it's up to brainy-not-brawny librarian Flynn (Wyle) to retrieve the stolen map to the legendary King Solomon's Mines. Aided by attractive archeologist Emily Davenport (Anwar), Flynn learns that some miscreants are counting on using the map to gain possession of the Key of Solomon, a powerful book of magic. **92m/C DVD.** Noah Wyle, Gabrielle Anwar, Bob Newhart, Jane Curtin, Olympia Dukakis, Erik Avari, Hakeem Kae-Kazim, Robert Foxworth; ***D:*** Jonathan Frakes; ***W:*** Marco Schnabel; ***C:*** Walt Lloyd; ***M:*** Joseph LoDuca. **CABLE**

License to Drive 🦴🦴 **1988 (PG-13)** When teen Haim fails the road test for his all-important driver's license, he steals the family car for a hot date with the girl of his dreams. The evening starts out quietly enough, but things soon go awry. If Haim survives the weekend, he'll definitely be able to pass his driving test on Monday morning. Semi-funny in a demolition derby sort of way. **90m/C VHS, DVD.** Corey Feldman, Corey Haim, Carol Kane, Richard Masur, Michael Manasseri; ***D:*** Greg Beeman; ***C:*** Bruce Surtees; ***M:*** Jay Ferguson.

License to Kill 🦴🦴 **1964** Constantine stars as Agent Nick Carter involved with Oriental spies and a new secret weapon. **100m/C VHS.** *FR* Eddie Constantine, Yvonne Monlaur, Paul Frankeur; ***D:*** Henri Decoin.

License to Kill 🦴🦴 **1984** A young girl is killed by a drunk driver, devastating both families. Offers a strong message against drinking and driving. **96m/C VHS, DVD.** James Farentino, Don Murray, Penny Fuller, Millie Perkins, Donald Moffat, Denzel Washington, Ari Meyers; ***D:*** Jud Taylor. **TV**

License to Kill 🦴🦴🦴 **1989 (PG-13)** Dalton's second Bond effort, in which drug lords try to kill 007's best friend and former CIA agent. Disobeying orders for the first time and operating without his infamous "license to kill," Bond goes after the fiends. Fine outing for Dalton (and Bond, too). **133m/C VHS, DVD.** *GB* Timothy Dalton, Carey Lowell, Robert Davi, Frank McRae, Talisa Soto, David Hedison, Anthony Zerbe, Everett McGill, Wayne Newton, Benicio Del Toro, Desmond Llewelyn, Priscilla Barnes, Robert Brown, Tom Adams; ***D:*** John Glen; ***W:*** Michael G. Wilson, Richard Maibaum; ***C:*** Alec Mills; ***M:*** Michael Kamen.

License to Wed 🦴 **2007 (PG-13)** Nothing redeems this dull, obnoxious comedy that mostly serves as a vehicle for Williams to do the same ad-libbed characters he's been doing for years. Newly engaged couple Ben and Sadie (Krasinski and Moore) must undergo Rev. Frank's (Williams) premarital counseling, but what they get is an endless series of laugh-free, sadism-lite tests of endurance. Nothing, from Ben and Sadie's cliche personality mismatch, to Frank's junior sadist sidekick Choir Boy (Flitter), saves this movie from being a big "I don't" for all involved. **91m/C DVD, Blu-ray Disc, HD DVD.** *US* Robin Williams, Mandy Moore, John Krasinski, Eric Christian Olsen, Christine Taylor, Peter Strauss, Rachael Harris, DeRay Davis, Angela Kinsey, Mindy Kaling, Brian Baumgartner, Josh Flitter; ***D:*** Ken Kwapis; ***W:*** Kim Barker, Tim Rasmussen, Vince DeMeglio; ***C:*** John Bailey; ***M:*** Christophe Beck.

The Lickerish Quartet 🦴🦴 **1970 (R)** A bored, aristocratic couple live with their teenaged son in a secluded castle in Italy's Abruzzi mountains. Traveling to a nearby carnival, they think they recognize the female daredevil as the same actress they've just seen in a home-viewed porno film. So they invite her back to the castle for a little family fun—only she may not be the same woman at all. **90m/C VHS, DVD.** Silvana Venturelli, Frank Wolff, Erika Remberg, Paolo Turco; ***D:*** Radley Metzger; ***W:*** Michael DeForrest; ***C:*** Hans Jura.

L'Idiot 🦴🦴 *The Idiot* **1946** Smooth adaptation of Dostoevsky's novel about noble Prince Mishkin's (Philipe) attempts to bring peace to the life of tormented Nastasia Filipovna (Feuillere). First feature for Lampin; French with subtitles. **98m/B VHS.** *FR* Gerard Philipe, Edwige Feuillere, Lucien Coedel, Nathalie Nattier, Marguerite Moreno; ***D:*** Georges Lampin; ***W:*** Charles Spaak; ***C:*** Christian Matras; ***M:*** Maurice Thiriet.

L.I.E. 🦴🦴 **2001 (NC-17)** Can you say "controversial"? 15-year-old Howie's (Dano) mother has recently died in a car accident on the Long Island Expressway (hence the title) and his world is falling apart. His dad, Marty (Blitzer), brings his bimbo girlfriend to stay and has some very shady business dealings. Meanwhile, Howie is hanging out with teen troublemaker Gary (Kay), who is both a thief and a hustler. Gary and Howie break into the home of ex-Marine, Big John Harrigan (Cox), who as it turns out, is a pedophile who discovers and confronts the boys and takes a purient interest in Howie's charms. At least at first, since the complex Harrigan realizes Howie really needs some friendly guidance and not a sex partner. Cuesta offers no apologies or explanations for the behavior he depicts and Cox is both commanding and subtle. **97m/C VHS, DVD.** *US* Brian Cox, Paul Franklin Dano, Billy Kay, Bruce Altman, James Costa, Tony Donnelly, Walter Masterson, Marcia DeBonis, Adam LeFevre; ***D:*** Michael Cuesta; ***W:*** Michael Cuesta, Stephen M. Ryder, Gerald Cuesta; ***C:*** Romeo Tirone; ***M:*** Pierre Foldes. Ind. Spirit '02: Debut Perf. (Dano).

Lie Down with Dogs **1995 (R)** You will wake up with fleas if you watch this dull, very low-budget comedy about young Tommie (White), who heads out of New York for some summer fun in the gay-friendly resort of Provincetown, Massachusetts. There's lots of temporary (discreetly filmed) encounters but no lasting romance and Tommie heads back to the Big Apple at season's end satisfied but no wiser. White's debut film. **85m/C VHS, DVD.** Wally White, Randy Becker, Darren Dryden; ***D:*** Wally White; ***W:*** Wally White; ***C:*** George Mitas.

Lie Down with Lions **1/2 1994** Long and dull TV adaptation of the Ken Follett spy novel. American nurse Kate Neeson (Helgenberger) is aghast when she discovers her lover, Jack Carver (Dalton), is a CIA agent. She marries Czech doctor Peter Husak (Havers) on the rebound and the newleyweds travel to Azerbijan to run a clinic, where Kate has a baby. But Jack's not out of the picture since his current assignment takes him into the war-torn region—and back into Kate's life, especially when he discovers Peter is not what he seems. On three cassettes. **136m/C VHS.** Timothy Dalton, Marg Helgenberger, Nigel Havers, Omar Sharif, Kabir Bedi, Jurgen Prochnow; ***D:*** Jim Goddard; ***W:*** Guy Andrews, Julian Bond; ***C:*** Eddy van der Enden.

Liebelei **1932** Fritz (Liebeneiner), a handsome lieutenant, has broken off his romance with a married baroness and fallen for young opera singer Christine (Schneider) in turn-of-the-century Vienna. However, when the jealous baron (Grundgens) learns of his wife's infidelity, he challenges Fritz to a duel. Remade as "Christine" in 1967, with Romy Schneider in her mother's role. In German with English subtitles. **82m/B VHS.** *GE* Magda Schneider, Wolfgang Liebeneiner, Gustav Grundgens; ***D:*** Max Ophuls.

Liebestraum **1991 (R)** An architectural expert, his old college friend, and the friend's wife form a dangerous triangle of passion and lust that strangely duplicates a situation that led to a double murder 40 years earlier. The unrated version clocks in at 116 minutes. **109m/C VHS, DVD.** Kevin Anderson, Bill Pullman, Pamela Gidley, Kim Novak; ***D:*** Mike Figgis; ***W:*** Mike Figgis; ***C:*** Juan Ruiz-Anchia; ***M:*** Mike Figgis.

Lies **1/2 1983 (PG)** Complicated mystery about a murder/thriller movie plot becoming reality as it is being filmed, revolving around a scam to collect an inheritance from a rich guy in a mental hospital. **93m/C VHS.** *GB* Ann Dusenberry, Gail Strickland, Bruce Davison, Clu Gulager, Bert Remsen, Dick Miller; ***D:*** Ken Wheat, Jim Wheat; ***C:*** Robert Ebinger; ***M:*** Marc Donahue.

Lies & Alibis **1/2** *The Alibi* **2006 (R)** Ray Elliot (Coogan) runs a successful L.A. service that offers alibis to cheating spouses. But he doesn't expect Wendell (Marsden), the screw-up son of Ray's best client, tycoon Robert Hatch (Brolin), to accidentally kill his fling Heather (King) during some kinky sex play. So Ray and his new assistant Lola (Romijn), she of the cool head and hot bod, have to really come up with a good alibi, especially when a police detective (Mazar) comes around. Clever crime comedy with Coogan a capable leading man and old pros Brolin and Elliott (as an unhappy Mormon with a cheating wife) obviously enjoying their roles. **90m/C DVD.** Steve Coogan, Rebecca Romijn, James Brolin, John Leguizamo, James Marsden, Sam Elliott, Debi Mazar, Selma Blair, Deborah Kara Unger, Henry Rollins, Sharon Lawrence, Jaime (James) King; ***D:*** Matt Checkowksi, Kurt Mattila; ***W:*** Noah Hawley; ***C:*** Enrique Chediak; ***M:*** Alexandre Desplat.

Lies and Illusions **2009 (R)** When his fiancee Samantha (Schultz) disappears, successful self-help author Wes Wilson (Slater) finds himself targeted by her ruthless boss Isaac (Gooding Jr.), who says Samantha stole from him. Suddenly, Wes learns that the woman he was planning to marry is involved in an international smuggling ring but he's clueless as to what's going on. So's the movie, which is implausible and dull. **93m/C DVD.** Christian Slater, Cuba Gooding Jr., Christa Campbell, Sarah Ann Schultz, Robert Giardina, Al Madrigal, Sarah Ann Schultz; ***D:*** Tibor Takacs; ***C:*** Zoran Popovic; ***M:*** Stephen (Steve) Edwards. **VIDEO**

Lies and Whispers *Prague Duet* **1998 (R)** American child psychologist Dr. Lauren Graham (Gershon) is attending a medical convention in Prague, meets dissident Czech writer Jiri Kolmar (Serbedzija), falls instantly in love, and becomes engaged. Lauren decides to explore her own family's ties to the country and discovers grandad was a Nazi war criminal—a very embarassing revelation for Jiri, who's about to be appointed to a government post. **99m/C VHS, DVD.** Gina Gershon, Rade Serbedzija, Patricia Hodge, Otakar Brousek, Gordon Lovitt, Stuart Milligan; ***D:*** Roger L. Simon; ***W:*** Roger L. Simon, Sheryl Longin; ***C:*** Ivan Slapeta; ***M:*** Boris Zelkin.

Lies Before Kisses **1992 (PG-13)** A woman finds out her loving husband has been spending time with a beautiful call girl. When the call girl is murdered the husband is accused. His wife decides to help him clear his name but she just may have her own type of revenge in mind. **93m/C VHS.** Jaclyn Smith, Ben Gazzara, Nick Mancuso, Greg Evigan, Penny Fuller, James Karen; ***D:*** Lou Antonio; ***W:*** Ellen Weston.

Lies My Father Told Me **1975 (PG)** Simple drama about growing up in the 1920s in a Jewish ghetto. The story revolves around a young boy's relationship with his immigrant grandfather. Quiet and moving. **102m/C VHS.** *CA* Yossi Yadin, Len Birman, Marilyn Lightstone, Jeffery Lynas; ***D:*** Jan Kadar; ***W:*** Ted Allan. Golden Globes '76: Foreign Film.

Lies of the Twins **1991** A beautiful model becomes involved with her therapist and his identical, and irresponsible, twin brother. **93m/C VHS.** Isabella Rossellini, Aidan Quinn, Iman, John Pleshette; ***D:*** Tim Hunter.

Lt. Robin Crusoe, U.S.N. **1966 (G)** A lighthearted navy pilot crash lands amusingly on a tropical island, falls hard for an island babe and schemes intensely against the local evil ruler. Lackluster Disney debacle. **113m/C VHS, DVD.** Dick Van Dyke, Nancy Kwan, Akim Tamiroff; ***D:*** Byron Paul; ***M:*** Robert F. Brunner.

Life **1995** Explores the relationships between a group of prisoners doing time in a prison unit for HIV-positive inmates and what it means to be a man. Stylized production was developed from Brumpton's 1991 play "Containment." Feature film debut for director Johnston. **85m/C VHS.** *AU* John Brumpton, David Tredinnick, Robert Morgan, Noel Jordan, Luke Elliot, Jeff Kovski; ***D:*** Lawrence Johnston; ***W:*** John Brumpton, Lawrence Johnston.

Life **1/2 1999 (R)** New Yorkers Ray (Murphy) and Claude (Lawrence) head south on a moonshine run to pay off a debt to a bootlegger (James). Along the way, ther're framed for murder and sentenced to life on a Mississippi prison farm. Through the years, the two develop a deep, but insult-filled friendship while adjusting to prison life and harboring dreams of freedom. Murphy and Lawrence click well as a comic team, and the movie is best when it stays out of their way. The institutionalized racism of the setting is treated superficially, with the prison appearing to be, despite the slave-like work and gun-toting guards, not an entirely horrible place to live. **108m/C VHS, DVD.** Eddie Murphy, Martin Lawrence, Ned Beatty, Cicely Tyson, Clarence Williams III, Obba Babatunde, Bernie Mac, Michael "Bear" Taliferro, Miguel A. Nunez Jr., Bokeem Woodbine, Barry (Shabaka) Henley, Brent Jennings, Guy Torry, Lisa Nicole Carson, O'Neal Compton, Poppy Montgomery, Ned Vaughn, R. Lee Ermey, Nick Cassavetes, Noah Emmerich, Anthony Anderson, Rick James; ***D:*** Ted (Edward) Demme; ***W:*** Robert Ramsey, Matthew Stone; ***C:*** Geoffrey Simpson; ***M:*** Nelust Wyclef Jean.

Life According to Muriel *La Vida Segun Muriel* **1997** After her husband abandons her, Laura takes 9-year-old daughter Muriel and leaves Buenos Aires for the peace of the countryside. Only they lose all their stuff in an accident and are forced to rely on Mirta—another single mom who owns a rundown hotel. The women bond and start to fix up the place when Muriel's dad shows up wanting a second chance. Spanish with subtitles. **97m/C VHS, DVD.** *AR* Ines Estevez, Jorge Perugorria, Florencia Camiletti, Federico Olivera, Soledad Villamil; ***D:*** Eduardo Milewicz; ***W:*** Eduardo Milewicz, Susana Silvestre; ***C:*** Estaban Sapir; ***M:*** Bob Telson.

The Life and Adventures of Nicholas Nickleby **1/2** *Nicholas Nickleby* **1981** Nine-hour performance of the 1838 Dickens' tale by the Royal Shakespeare Company, featuring the work of 39 actors portraying 150 characters. Wonderful performances are characterized by frantic action and smoothly meshing intertwining plots, focusing on the trials and tribulations of the Nickleby family, amidst wealth, poverty, and injustice in Victorian England. Nine cassettes. **540m/C VHS, DVD.** *GB* Roger Rees, David Thewlis, Emily Richard, John Woodvine; ***D:*** Jim Goddard; ***W:*** David Edgar; ***M:*** Stephen Oliver.

The Life and Assassination of the Kingfish **1976** Recommended by the NEA, this story of Louisiana politician Huey Long is riveting. Asner gives a profound performance. **96m/C VHS.** Ed Asner, Nicholas Pryor, Diane Kagan; ***D:*** Robert E. Collins.

The Life and Death of Colonel Blimp *Colonel Blimp* **1943** Chronicles the life of a British soldier who survives three wars (Boer, WWI, and WWII), falls in love with three women (all portrayed by Kerr), and dances a fine waltz. Fine direction and performance abound. **115m/C VHS, DVD.** *GB* Roger Livesey, Deborah Kerr, Anton Walbrook, Ursula Jeans, Albert Lieven, John Varley; ***D:*** Michael Powell, Emeric Pressburger; ***C:*** Georges Perinal.

The Life and Loves of Mozart **1/2 1959** Despite the title, this is really about the great composer's later life at the time of the premiere of "Die Zauberfloete" ("The Magic Flute"). This is only partly saved by a stellar performance from Werner, as well as the music. Other than that, it gets bogged down in titillation about W.A.M.'s romantic life. In German with English subtitles. **87m/C VHS, DVD.** Oskar Werner, Johanna (Hannerl) Matz, Angelika Hauff; ***D:*** Karl Hartl; ***V:*** Anton Dermota.

Life and Nothing But **1/2** *La Vie est Rien d'Autre* **1989 (PG)** Two young women search for their lovers at the end of WWI. They're helped by a French officer brutalized by the war and driven to find all of France's casualties. Romantic, evocative, and saddening. In French with English subtitles. **135m/C VHS, DVD.** *FR* Philippe Noiret, Sabine Azema, Francois Perrot; ***D:*** Bertrand Tavernier; ***W:*** Bertrand Tavernier; ***C:*** Bruno de Keyzer. British Acad. '89: Foreign Film; Cesar '90: Actor (Noiret), Score; L.A. Film Critics '90: Foreign Film.

Life and Nothing More ... *And Life Goes On ...; Zendegi Va Digar Hich ...* **1992** Following Iran's devastating 1990 earthquake, a filmmaker and his son search for the young actors who previously worked with him to see if they've survived, meeting various villagers trying to rebuild their lives. Sequel to Kiarostami's film "Where Is My Friend's House?" and followed by "Through the Olive Trees." Farsi with subtitles. **91m/C VHS, DVD.** *IA* Farhad Kheradmand, Pooya Payvar; ***D:*** Abbas Kiarostami; ***W:*** Abbas Kiarostami; ***C:*** Homayun Payvar.

Life & Times of Grizzly Adams **1974 (G)** Lightweight family adventure film based on the rugged life of legendary frontiersman, Grizzly Adams, that served as the launching pad for the TV series. Grizzly is mistakenly chased for a crime he didn't commit and along the way befriends a big bear. **93m/C VHS.** Dan Haggerty, Denver Pyle, Lisa Jones, Marjorie Harper, Don Shanks; ***D:*** Richard Friedenberg.

The Life and Times of Hank Greenberg **1999 (PG)** Excellent documentary tells the story of Detroit Tiger Hall of Fame first baseman Hank Greenberg though interviews with sportswriters, teammates, other players of the era, and fans (many of which were young Jewish boys who later became famous themselves), and archival footage from on and off the field. Details Greenberg's struggles as a high-profile Jew in a very anti-Semitic era and as a hero and source of inspiration to the Jewish community. Also does a fine job of exploring the settings (New York and Detroit during the '20s and '30s) in which Greenberg grew up and rose to stardom. **95m/C VHS, DVD.** ***D:*** Aviva Kempner; ***W:*** Aviva Kempner.

Life & Times of Judge Roy Bean **1/2 1972 (PG)** Based on the life of the famed Texas "hanging judge," the film features Newman as the legendary Bean who dispenses frontier justice in the days of the Wild West. Filled with gallows humor. Gardner sparkles as actress Lily Langtry. **124m/C VHS, DVD.** Paul Newman, Stacy Keach, Ava Gardner, Jacqueline Bisset, Anthony Perkins, Roddy McDowall, Victoria Principal; ***D:*** John Huston; ***W:*** John Milius; ***M:*** Maurice Jarre.

The Life & Times of the Chocolate Killer **1/2 1988** Police turn against the hand that's helped them save property and lives, by framing a good samaritan with deeds done by the "Chocolate Killer." **75m/C VHS.** Michael Adrian, Rod Browning, Tabi Cooper.

The Life Aquatic with Steve Zissou **2004 (R)** Director Anderson's muddled comedy follows the career of oceanographer Steve Zissou (Murray), famed for his series of pop-culture documentaries (think Jacques Cousteau). Zissou's latest mission is to take revenge on the shark that ate his longtime partner (Cassel). Besides his motley crew (including Dafoe and Gambon), there is Zissou's business partner/wife Eleanor (Huston), nosy reporter Jane (Blanchett), and amiable newcomer Ned (Wilson), who may be Steve's illegitimate son, as well as his archrival, slick Alistair Hennessey (Goldblum). The detached and melancholy Murray had much better luck with Anderson in "The Royal Tenenbaums" and "Rushmore." Here, he appears to be going through the motions as the rest of cast follows along in his wake. **118m/C VHS, DVD.** *US* Bill Murray, Owen Wilson, Cate Blanchett, Anjelica Huston, Willem Dafoe, Jeff Goldblum, Michael Gambon, Bud Cort, Seymour Cassel; ***D:*** Wes Anderson; ***W:*** Wes Anderson, Noah Baumbach; ***C:*** Robert Yeoman; ***M:*** Mark Mothersbaugh, Randall Poster.

Life as a House **1/2 2001 (R)** George (Kline) is an architect who lives in a broken down shack surrounded by ritzy homes on California's Pacific shore. His ex-wife Robin (Thomas) is raising their drugged-out Goth son Sam (Christensen) with her emotionally unavailable husband Peter (Sheridan). In quick succession, George is fired from his job and learns he has a fatal disease. He examines his life and decides to use his remaining time to tear down the old house and build a new one. He forces Sam to help him, intending to use the project as a means to repair his relationship with his son. Robin's feelings for George also rekindle, and they become more than friends once again. The performances of the excellent ensemble cast, especially Kline and Thomas, save this from being called "Sappy Symbolism as a Movie." **124m/C VHS, DVD.** Kevin Kline, Hayden Christensen, Kristin Scott Thomas, Jena Malone, Mary Steenburgen, Jamey Sheridan, Scott Bakula, Sam Robards, Mike Weinberg, Scotty Leavenworth, Ian Somerhalder, Sandra Nelson; ***D:*** Irwin Winkler; ***W:*** Mark Andrus; ***C:*** Vilmos Zsigmond; ***M:*** Mark Isham. Natl. Bd. of Review '01: Breakthrough Perf. (Christensen).

The Life Before Her Eyes **1/2** *In Bloom* **2007 (R)** Diana (played as a teen by Wood and as an adult by Thurman) attempts to engage in her current life as an art professor, wife and mother while wrestling with the devastating memories of a Columbine-like tragedy she survived some 15 years earlier. The story shifts between present and past memories in which the younger Diana, a loose and wild teen dissatisfied with small-town life, is inseparable from best friend Maureen (Amurri), a straight-laced church-goer whose life is mapped out in that same little town. As the tragedy's anniversary approaches, Diana's grip on reality, the present day, and her own sanity becomes increasingly strained. Director Vadim Perelman uses images from the past filled with life and energy to illustrate the incredible toll of surviving such trauma. The melodrama may be too much for some, but Wood's performance as young Diana is worthwhile. **90m/C DVD.** *US* Uma Thurman, Evan Rachel Wood, Eva Amurri, Jack Gilpin, Oscar Marcus, Gabrielle Brennan, Brett Gilpin; ***D:*** Vadim Perelman; ***W:*** Emil Stern; ***C:*** Pawel Edelman; ***M:*** James Horner.

The Life Before This **1999** Complicated tale has six overlapping stories and 44 characters that follow the lives of a group of Torontonians for 12 hours and ends in a casino heist and a related cafe shootout. Film begins and ends with the shooting and takes place in flashbacks that show how each person came to be in the wrong place at the wrong time. Very loosely based on a true incident. **92m/C VHS, DVD.** *CA* Leslie Hope, David Hewlett, Joel S. Keller, Jacob Tierney, Alberta Watson, Jennifer Dale, Dan Lett, Catherine O'Hara, Martha Burns, Joe Pantoliano, Sarah Polley, Stephen Rea, Callum Keith Rennie; ***D:*** Gerard Ciccoritti; ***W:*** Semi Chellas; ***C:*** Norayr Kasper; ***M:*** Ron Sures. Genie '99: Support. Actress (O'Hara).

Life Begins at Forty 1/2 **1935** Small-town newspaper owner Kenesaw Clark (Rogers) befriends young Lee Austin (Cromwell), who was framed for bank robbery. In retaliation, banker Abercrombie (Barbier) forecloses on the paper, but that doesn't stop Clark's investigation. Meanwhile, he decides to humiliate Abercrombie by cleaning up town bum Meriwether (Summerville) and making him Abercrombie's opposing candidate in a political race. **85m/B DVD.** Will Rogers, Richard Cromwell, George Barbier, Rochelle Hudson, Jane Darwell, Slim Summerville, Sterling Holloway, Thomas Beck, Roger Imhof, Charles Sellon; ***D:*** George Marshall; ***W:*** Lamar Trotti; ***C:*** Harry Jackson.

Life Begins for Andy Hardy **1941** Andy gets a job in New York before entering college and finds the working world to be a sobering experience. Surprisingly downbeat and hard-hitting for an Andy Hardy film. Garland's last appearance in the series. **100m/B VHS.** Mickey Rooney, Judy Garland, Lewis Stone, Ann Rutherford, Fay Holden, Gene Reynolds, Ralph Byrd; ***D:*** George B. Seitz.

Life During Wartime **2009** Setting his story in Miami's Jewish community, Solondz updates (using different actors) the characters and stories from his 1998 film "Happiness." Child molester William (Hinds) wants to reconnect with his sons after being released from prison. Meanwhile, his ex-wife Trish (Janney) has fallen in love while her sister Joy's (Henderson) latest marriage has broken up, although Joy is still being haunted by the ghost of her dead ex Andy (Reubens). **96m/C DVD.** *US* Shirley Henderson, Allison Janney, Ciaran Hinds, Dylan Riley Snyder, Christopher Marquette, Paul (Pee-wee Herman) Reubens, Michael Lerner, Rich Pecci, Ally Sheedy, Michael K. Williams, Charlotte Rampling, Gaby Hoffman, Renee Taylor; ***D:*** Todd Solondz; ***W:*** Ally Sheedy, Todd Solondz; ***C:*** Edward Lachman; ***M:*** Doug Bernheim.

Life Gamble *Sheng si dou; Sang sei dau; Life Combat* **2004** A group of four bandits steal a priceless piece of Jade they can't split up, and decide to hold a gambling contest to see which of them gets it. They ask the famous gambler Golden Lion (Mao Kai Yuan) to act as an impartial judge, but he has plans on stealing the jade for himself, as does every other martial artist within the city. Caught up in this mess are the local constable and a blacksmith who forged most of the weapons used by all the fighters (as well as his young daughter). **109m/C DVD, Blu-ray Disc.** *HK* Philip Kwok, Meng Lo, Sheng Fu, Feng Lu, Lung Wei Wang; ***D:*** Cheh Chang; ***W:*** Cheh Chang, Kuang Ni.

Life in the Fast Lane **2000 (R)** Mona has accidentally killed her boyfriend. And when his ghost starts to follow her everywhere, Mona realizes how much she still loves him. So just how do you make a romance between a live girl and a dead guy work? **92m/C VHS, DVD.** Fairuza Balk, Patrick Dempsey, Tea Leoni, Debi Mazar, Noah Taylor, Udo Kier.

A Life in the Theater 1/2 **1993** Life in the theatre as a hammy stage veteran (Lemmon) shares his experiences (and his dressing room) with a callow newcomer (Broderick). Petty squabbles, missed cues, and rare candor are displayed as the two stage scenes from their various repertory. Gentle, slight Mamet play, written when he was 25. **78m/C VHS.** Jack Lemmon, Matthew Broderick; ***D:*** Gregory Mosher; ***W:*** David Mamet. **TV**

Life Is a Bed of Roses *La Vie est un Roman; Life Is a Fairy Tale* **1983** Three intertwined stories from Resnais. Count Forbeck is building a castle in Ardennes, planning to start a utopian society before WWI interferes. After the war, Forbeck tries again, offering his friends a drug that will make them forget the past, although his former love Livia refuses the offer. By the 1980s, the castle has been transformed into a progressive school that allows children's imaginations to roam free, although not all the educators are comfortable with the idea. While the adults fuss over their methods, the children play a fairytale game of knights and dragons. French with subtitles. **110m/C DVD.** *FR* Ruggero Raimondi, Fanny Ardant, Andre Dussollier, Veronique Silver, Robert Manuel, Vittorio Gassman, Sabine Azema, Geraldine Chaplin, Pierre Arditti; ***D:*** Alain Resnais; ***W:*** Jean Gruault; ***C:*** Bruno Nuytten; ***M:*** Michel Philipe-Gerard.

Life Is a Long Quiet River *La Vie Est Une Longue Fleuve Tranquille* **1988** Social comedy about a nurse who, infuriated with her married doctor employer/lover, switches two babies at birth. Twelve years later, after her lover's wife has died and he still refuses to marry her, she reveals the swap. The children are returned to their rightful families causing a multitude of confusion and adjustment. Directorial debut of Chatiliez. In French with English subtitles. **89m/C VHS.** *FR* Benoit Magimel, Helene Vincent, Andre Wilms, Daniel Gelin, Catherine Hiegel, Christine Pignet, Patrick Bouchitey, Valerie Lalande, Tara Romer, Jerome Floch, Sylvie Cubertafon; ***D:*** Etienne Chatiliez; ***W:*** Florence Quentin, Etienne Chatiliez; ***M:*** Gerard Kawczynski. Cesar '89: Support. Actress (Vincent), Writing.

Life Is Beautiful 1/2 **1979** A politically neutral man is arrested and tortured in pre-revolutionary Lisbon, and forced to make, and act on, a political commitment. Dubbed. **102m/C VHS.** *PT* Giancarlo Giannini, Ornella Muti; ***D:*** Grigori Chukhraj.

Life Is Beautiful *La Vita E Bella* **1998 (PG-13)** The notion of a "feel-good Holocaust comedy" shouldn't work. But Benigni's stunning epic is not, at its core, a Holocaust movie, but rather a story of endurance of family love. Benigni's Guido is so intent on *believing* that life is—and should be—beautiful, he goes to great lengths to ensure that vision for his wife and, particularly, his son. The first half is an amusing boy-meets-girl Italian comedy, with Benigni chasing his real-life wife (Braschi). The second half shifts to the concentration camp where Guido, his son, and—because she would not be parted from him—his wife are imprisoned. Guido invents an elaborate game to convince his son that the whole ordeal—the "trip"—is an endurance test to be won, with prizes forthcoming. If Benigni depicts the concentration camps as less than horrifying, he should be forgiven; his focus is on the love between father, son, and wife. Italian with subtitles. **122m/C VHS, DVD.** *IT* Roberto Benigni, Nicoletta Braschi, Giustino Durano, Sergio Bustric, Horst Buchholz, Giorgio Cantarini, Marisa Paredes, Lidia Alfonsi, Giuliana Lojodice; ***D:*** Roberto Benigni; ***W:*** Vincenzo Cerami, Roberto Benigni; ***C:*** Tonino Delli Colli; ***M:*** Nicola Piovani. Oscars '98: Actor (Benigni), Foreign Film, Orig. Dramatic Score; Australian Film Inst. '99: Foreign Film; British Acad. '98: Actor (Benigni); Cannes '98: Grand Jury Prize; Cesar '99: Foreign Film; Screen Actors Guild '98: Actor (Benigni); Broadcast Film Critics '98: Foreign Film.

Life is Hot in Cracktown 1/2 **2008 (R)** Ruthlessly downbeat look at crack cocaine addiction based on Giovinazzo's own 1993 short story collection. Unfortunately it also pushes all the usual buttons about being a poor druggie in a big city complete with crime, gangs, prostitution, homelessness, violence, indifference, and child abuse. **99m/C DVD.** Victor Razuk, Kerry Washington, Desmond Harrington, Evan Ross, Brandon Routh, Shannyn Sossamon, Vondie Curtis-Hall, RZA, Lara Flynn Boyle, Thomas Ian Nicholas; ***D:*** Buddy Giovinazzo; ***W:*** Buddy Giovinazzo; ***C:*** Kat Westergaard, Russell Jaeger; ***M:*** RZA.

Life Is Sweet 1/2 **1990 (R)** The consuming passions of food and drink focus the lives of an oddball English working-class family beset by hopeless dreams and passions. Mother is always fixing family meals—in between helping her friend open a gourmet restaurant which features such revolting dishes as pork cyst and prune quiche. Dad is a chef who buys a snack truck and dreams of life on the road. Natalie and Nicola, the grown twins, eat their meals in front of the television but Nicola is also a bulimic who binges and purges on chocolate bars behind her bedroom door. (Note the chocolate scene between Nicola and her boyfriend). An affectionate, if sometimes unattractive, look at a chaotic family. **103m/C VHS.** *GB* Alison Steadman, Jane Horrocks, Jim Broadbent, Claire Skinner, Timothy Spall, Stephen Rea, David Thewlis; ***D:*** Mike Leigh; ***W:*** Mike Leigh. L.A. Film Critics '91: Support. Actress (Horrocks); Natl. Soc. Film Critics '91: Actress (Steadman), Film, Support. Actress (Horrocks).

A Life Less Ordinary 1/2 **1997 (R)** Third outing from U.K. team of Boyle/Hodge/Macdonald, who made "Shallow Grave" and "Trainspotting," has hapless janitor Robert (MacGrgor) lose his job, girlfriend, and home. He reacts by kidnapping the boss's daughter Celine (Diaz), who's more upset at Robert's ineptness than anything else. Meanwhile two angels (Hunter and Lindo) are sent to make these two kids fall in love. Confused? You should be. Hodge's script looks like someone threw "It Happened One Night," "Stairway to Heaven," outtakes from a Tarantino movie, and a Road Runner cartoon into a blender and hit frappe. Some of the surreal set pieces work, and the MacGregor/Diaz chemistry clicks sporadically, but the overall effect is overkill. Producer MacDonald is the grandson of Emeric Pressberger, co-director of "Stairway to Heaven." **103m/C VHS, DVD.** Ewan McGregor, Cameron Diaz, Holly Hunter, Delroy Lindo, Ian Holm, Ian McNeice, Stanley Tucci, Dan Hedaya, Tony Shalhoub, Maury Chaykin, Judith Ivey, K.K. Dodds; ***D:*** Danny Boyle; ***W:*** John Hodge; ***C:*** Brian Tufano; ***M:*** David Arnold.

The Life of David Gale **2003 (R)** David Gale (Spacey) is an anti-death penalty activist awaiting his execution after being convicted for the rape and murder of his collegue Constance (Linney, in the film's only worthy performance). Told in flashback to hard-boiled reporter Bitsey (Winslet), his story plays out from his fall from respected philosophy professor to boorish drunk after an ill-advised dalliance with a student turns into a rape accusation. Pick your poison with this one. If you want social commentary, the heavy-handed diatribes and speechifying will assault you while you wait for the murder mystery-thriller elements to insult your intelligence with their telegraphed clues and convoluted, implausible plots and red herrings. Even more of a spectacular failure at blending the two genres than "Mississippi Burning." **130m/C VHS, DVD.** *US* Kevin Spacey, Kate Winslet, Laura Linney, Gabriel Mann, Matt Craven, Rhona Mitra, Leon Rippy, Jim Beaver; ***D:*** Alan Parker; ***W:*** Charles Randolph; ***C:*** Michael Seresin; ***M:*** Alex Parker, Jake Parker.

The Life of Emile Zola 1/2 **1937** Writer Emile Zola intervenes in the case of Alfred Dreyfus who was sent to Devil's Island for a crime he did not commit. Well-crafted production featuring a handsome performance from Muni. **117m/B VHS, DVD.** Paul Muni, Gale Sondergaard, Gloria Holden, Joseph Schildkraut; ***D:*** William Dieterle; ***W:*** Norman Reilly Raine; ***C:*** Gaetano Antonio "Tony" Gaudio; ***M:*** Max Steiner. Oscars '37: Picture, Screenplay, Support. Actor (Schildkraut), Natl. Film Reg. '00;; N.Y. Film Critics '37: Actor (Muni), Film.

A Life of Her Own 1/2 **1950** Turner stars as a farm girl who takes her dream of becoming a top model to the Big Apple. She signs with an agency and is befriended by Dvorak, an aging model, who acts as her mentor. Turner finds success and is soon the toast of the town until she gets involved with a married man (Milland) and her life starts to crumble. Average soap opera with flimsy script. Turner is good, but Dvorak steals the show in her role as an over-the-hill fashion plate. **108m/B VHS.** Lana Turner, Ray Milland, Tom Ewell, Louis Calhern, Ann Dvorak, Barry Sullivan, Jean Hagen, Phyllis Kirk, Sara Haden; ***D:*** George Cukor; ***W:*** Isobel Lennart; ***C:*** George J. Folsey.

The Life of Jesus *La Vie de Jesus* **1996** Small town boredom and despair—French style. Twenty-year-old Freddy (Douche) is an unemployed epileptic, who lives with his mother. He spends his time with girlfriend Marie (Cottreel) or riding his moped with his equally disenfranchised buddies. When a young Arab, Kader (Chaatouf), shows an interest in Marie (that's reciprocated), Freddy and his friends beat him up. Apparently the title is a reference to the spiritual suffering Freddy feels, even if he doesn't know exactly how to articulate his emotions. French with subtitles. **96m/C VHS, DVD.** *FR* David Douche, Marjorie Cottreel, Kader Chaatouf, Samuel Boidin, Genevieve Cottreel; ***D:*** Bruno Dumont; ***W:*** Bruno Dumont; ***C:*** Philippe Van Leeuw; ***M:*** Richard Cuvillier.

The Life of Lucky Cucumber **WOOF!** **2008** Amateur night drivel. A couple of aspiring filmmakers get a government grant to make a film about local Missouri weirdo Lucky, who's had more than 100 jobs and lives in a cave. **82m/C DVD.** Dian Bachar, Preston Lacy, Stella Keitel, Sam Maccarone, Patrick O'Hagan; ***D:*** Sam Maccarone; ***W:*** Preston Lacy, Sam Maccarone; ***C:*** Edward Gutentag; ***M:*** Tim Montijo. **VIDEO**

Life of Oharu 1/2 *Diary of Oharu; Saikaku Ichidai Onna* **1952** A near masterpiece rivaled only by "Ugetsu" in the Mizoguchi canon, this film details the slow and agonizing moral decline of a woman in feudal Japan, from wife to concubine to prostitute. A scathing portrait of social pre-destination based on a novel by Ibara Saikaku. In Japanese with English subtitles. **136m/B VHS.** *JP* Kinuyo Tanaka, Toshiro Mifune; ***D:*** Kenji Mizoguchi.

A Life of Sin **1992 (R)** Scandalous drama about an impoverished Caribbean girl who rises to wealth and power as a world-famous madame. Colon stars as the beautiful Isabel, who is betrayed by her childhood friend Paulo (Julia) and rejected by the Catholic bishop (Ferrer) in this tragic story of passion and greed. **112m/C VHS.** Raul Julia, Miriam Colon, Jose Ferrer; ***D:*** Efrain Lopez Neris; ***W:*** Emilio Diaz Valcarcel.

Life of the Party **2005 (R)** Michael (Bailey), an ex-golden boy turned alcoholic, goes into a panic when his wife Phoebe (Pompeo) finally leaves him. With Michael in the hospital after a car crash, everyone close to him decides its past time to hold an intervention, which turns into chaos. Refrains from pomposity while showing the consequences alcoholic behavior has on not just the drinker but those around him. **87m/C DVD.** Eion Bailey, Ellen Pompeo, John Ales, Clifton (Gonzalez) Collins Jr., Gabriel Olds, David Clennon, Pamela Reed, Rosalind Chao, Larry Miller; ***D:*** Barra Grant; ***W:*** Barra Grant; ***C:*** Lawrence Sher; ***M:*** Mark Adler.

Life of Verdi *Verdi* **1982** Epic miniseries biography of the famous composer, with many excerpts of his music sung by Luciano Pavarotti, Renata Telbaldi, and Maria Callas. **600m/B VHS, DVD.** *IT* Ronald Pickup, Carla Fracci, Daria Nicolodi, Omero Antonutti, Giampiero Albertini; ***D:*** Renato Castellani; ***W:*** Renato Castellani; ***C:*** Giuseppe Ruzzolini. **TV**

Life on a String **1990** Set in the distant past, this is a lyrical story of a young boy searching for a cure for his blindness. His possible cure involves a myth which requires him to devote his life to music and the breaking of 1000 strings on a banjo. Adapted from a story by Shi Tiesheng. In Chinese with English subtitles. **110m/C VHS, DVD.** *CH* Xu Qing; ***D:*** Chen Kaige; ***W:*** Chen

Kaige; *C:* Gu Changwei; *M:* Xiao-Song Qu.

Life 101 ✌✌ 1/2 **1995** Innocent freshman Haim tries to adjust to college life in the '60s, aided by his hippie roommate Coogan, who introduces Haim to the pleasures of life. Innocuous coming-of-age comedy. **95m/C VHS.** Corey Haim, Keith Coogan, Ami Dolenz; *D:* Redge Mahaffey; *W:* Redge Mahaffey.

Life or Something Like It ✌ 1/2 **2002 (PG-13)** Disappointing fluff bunny blonde role for Jolie, who's best when she's edgy. Instead, she plays shallow Seattle newscaster Lanie Kerigan who has a fab life and a fab famous boyfriend in Seattle Mariners player Cal (Kane). Then she interviews street prophet Jack (Shalhoub), who tells Lanie that she's going to die next week—and since all his other predictions have come true, Lanie gets stressed and decides she needs to get in touch with her regular-gal roots again. Of course it doesn't hurt that her cameraman, sexy Pete (Burns), is willing to do all he can to make things better. **104m/C VHS, DVD.** *US* Angelina Jolie, Edward Burns, Tony Shalhoub, Christian Kane, Melissa Errico, Stockard Channing, James Gammon, Gregory Itzin; *D:* Stephen Herek; *W:* John Scott Shepherd, Dana Stevens; *C:* Stephen Burum; *M:* David Newman.

Life-Size ✌✌ 1/2 **2000** Twelve-year-old tomboy, Casey (Lohan), desperately misses her recently deceased mother but her dad, Ben (Burns), is dealing with his own grief by becoming a workaholic. Casey tries out a magic spell to resurrect her mom and instead makes her beauty pageant doll, Eve (Banks), come to life. Casey's horrified and wants to send Eve back to her doll world but Eve loves becoming a human and wants to stay. **89m/C VHS, DVD.** Lindsay Lohan, Tyra Banks, Jere Burns, Anne Marie Loder, Garwin Sanford, Tom Butler; *D:* Mark Rosman; *W:* Mark Rosman, Stephanie Moore; *C:* Philip Linzey; *M:* Eric Colvin. **TV**

Life Stinks ✌ **1991 (PG-13)** So does the film. A grasping tycoon bets he can spend a month living on the street without money, resulting in cheap laughs, heavy-handed sentiment and one musical number. Those expecting the innovative, hilarious Brooks of "Young Frankenstein" or "Blazing Saddles" will be very disappointed—these jokes are stale and the timing is tedious. Those looking for a Chaplinesque tale for modern times should stick with Chaplin. **93m/C VHS, DVD.** Mel Brooks, Jeffrey Tambor, Lesley Ann Warren, Stuart Pankin, Howard Morris, Teddy Wilson, Michael Ensign, Billy Barty, Carmine Caridi, Rudy DeLuca; *D:* Mel Brooks; *W:* Mel Brooks, Rudy DeLuca; *C:* Steven Poster.

Life Support ✌✌✌ **2007** Ana Williams (Queen Latifah) is an HIV-positive, recovering junkie, trying to win back the affections of her estranged daughter Kelly (Nicks), who elects to live with her grandmother (Smith). The story begins to unravel when Kelly ask her mother to help her find her best friend Omari (Ross—as in Diana's son), who is gay and very sick from AIDS. As the two search the city talking with Omari's friends and lovers, Ana's heartfelt activism for the community is seen and her daughter's guard begins to let down. Nelson George's portrayal of his sister's real life battle could have come off as sap, but instead it is a solid effort with equally substantial performances. **88m/C DVD.** Queen Latifah, Anna Deavere Smith, Wendell Pierce, Evan Ross, Rachel Nicks, Gloria Reuben, Tracee Ellis Ross, Darrin Dewitt Henson, Tony Rock; *D:* Nelson George; *W:* Nelson George, Jim McKay, Hannah Weyer; *C:* Uta Briesewitz; *M:* Stuart Matthewman. **CABLE**

Life Tastes Good ✌✌ **1999** San Franciscan Harry has been laundering money for the mob and skimming some off the top. He wants to leave a suitcase of cash to his abandoned kids but the wiseguys he stole from want their money back and send a hitman after Harry. Told in beyond-the-grave flashbacks. Gotanda adapted his own play. **88m/C DVD.** Sab Shimono, Tamlyn Tomita, Julia Nickson-Soul, Kelvin Han Yee, Bob Todd, Tim Lounibos; *D:* Sue Upton; *W:* Sue Upton; *C:* Michael G. Chin; *M:* Dan Kuramato.

Life Upside Down ✌✌ *La Vie a L'Envers* **1964** Ordinary Paris worker (Denner) decides to withdraw from his seemingly perfect life, including his wife and friends. He ends staring at a blank wall in a mental institution. French with subtitles. **115m/B VHS.** *FR* Charles Denner, Anna Gaylor, Jean Yanne; *D:* Alain Jessua; *W:* Alain Jessua; *C:* Jacques Robin; *M:* Jacques Loussier.

Life with Father ✌✌✌ 1/2 **1947** Based on the writings of the late Clarence Day Jr., this is the story of his childhood in NYC during the 1880s. A delightful saga about a stern but loving father and his relationship with his knowing wife and four red-headed sons. **118m/C VHS, DVD.** William Powell, Irene Dunne, Elizabeth Taylor, Edmund Gwenn, Zasu Pitts, Jimmy Lydon, Martin Milner; *D:* Michael Curtiz; *W:* Donald Ogden Stewart; *C:* William V. Skall, J. Peverell Marley; *M:* Max Steiner. Golden Globes '48: Score; N.Y. Film Critics '47: Actor (Powell).

Life with Judy Garland—Me and My Shadows ✌✌✌ 1/2 **2001 (PG)** Sharp direction, a solid script that goes beyond the cliches, plus excellent performances (especially by Davis and Blanchard) prevent this telling of the tortured life of Judy Garland from slipping into made-for-TV docudrama hell. Garland's life is followed, from her insecure early teens, through the movie success and the many marriages and the drug addiction that brought her downfall. Based on the book "Me and My Shadows: A Family Memoir" by daughter Lorna Luft, who participated in the production. **107m/C VHS, DVD.** Judy Davis, Victor Garber, Hugh Laurie, Tammy Blanchard, Stewart Bick, John Benjamin Hickey, Sonja Smits, Dwayne Adams, Al Waxman, Jayne (Jane) Eastwood, Marsha Mason, Daniel Kash, Aidan Devine; ***Cameos:*** Lorna Luft; *D:* Robert Allan Ackerman; *W:* Robert Freedman; *C:* James Chressanthis; *M:* William Ross; ***Nar:*** Cynthia Gibb. **TV**

Life with Mikey ✌✌ 1/2 **1993 (PG-13)** Michael "Mikey" Chapman (Fox) is a washed-up former child star who now half-heartedly runs a minor talent agency for other pint-sized would-be thespians. Ever mindful of his previous glory, he believes he is doomed to obscurity when a 10-year-old Brooklyn pickpocket reanimates his taste for life. Light, sweet comedy is generally predictable, a typical Fox effort. Unbilled cameo from Reuben Blades as Vidal's father. **92m/C VHS, DVD.** Michael J. Fox, Christina Vidal, Cyndi Lauper, Nathan Lane, David Huddleston, Victor Garber, David Krumholtz, Tony Hendra; ***Cameos:*** Ruben Blades; *D:* James Lapine; *W:* Marc Lawrence; *M:* Alan Menken.

Life Without Dick ✌ 1/2 **2001 (PG-13)** Would-be romantic comedy that does passably on the romance and fails completely at the comedy. Ditzy Colleen (Parker) is devastated when she discovers sleazy boyfriend Dick (Knoxville) is cheating on her. She threatens him with a gun and accidentally kills him. Then Daniel (Connick Jr.) shows up. He works for the Irish mob as a hitman only he can't actually kill anyone. (He really wants to be a professional singer.) Dick was his assignment and he's pleased that everything is already taken care of. Colleen thinks Daniel is just grand and decides she will help him out by taking on his hitman duties herself. **96m/C VHS, DVD.** Sarah Jessica Parker, Harry Connick Jr., Teri Garr, Johnny Knoxville, Craig Ferguson, Geoffrey Blake, Brigid Brannah, Ever Carradine, Erik Palladino, Claudia Schiffer; *D:* Bix Skahill; *W:* Bix Skahill; *C:* James Glennon; *M:* David Lawrence.

Lifeboat ✌✌✌ 1/2 **1944** When a German U-boat sinks a freighter during WWII, the eight survivors seek refuge in a tiny lifeboat. Tension peaks after the drifting passengers take in a stranded Nazi. Hitchcock saw a great challenge in having the entire story take place in a lifeboat and pulled it off with his usual flourish. In 1989, the film "Dead Calm" replicated the technique. From a story by John Steinbeck. Bankhead shines. **96m/B VHS, DVD.** Tallulah Bankhead, John Hodiak, William Bendix, Canada Lee, Walter Slezak, Hume Cronyn, Henry Hull, Mary Anderson, Heather Angel, William Yetter Jr.; *D:* Alfred Hitchcock; *W:* Jo Swerling; *C:* Glen MacWilliams; *M:* Hugo Friedhofer. N.Y. Film Critics '44: Actress (Bankhead).

Lifeforce ✌✌ 1/2 **1985 (R)** A beautiful female vampire from outer space drains Londoners and before long the city is filled with disintegrating zombies in this hi-tech thriller. Sex was never stranger. Screenwriters O'Bannon and Jakoby adapted the story from Colin Wilson's novel, "The Space Vampires." **100m/C VHS, DVD.** Steve Railsback, Peter Firth, Frank Finlay, Patrick Stewart, Michael Gothard, Nicholas Ball, Aubrey Morris, Nancy Paul, Mathilda May, John Hallam; *D:* Tobe Hooper; *W:* Dan O'Bannon, Don Jakoby; *C:* Alan Hume; *M:* Henry Mancini, Michael Kamen.

Lifeform ✌ 1/2 **1996 (R)** Human beings may believe they're tops in the universe but when a Viking spaceship suddenly returns to Earth from a mission to Mars, NASA scientists discover a lifeform that thinks differently. **90m/C VHS.** Cotter Smith, Deirdre O'Connell, Ryan Phillippe, Raoul O'Connell, Leland Orser; *D:* Mark H. Baker; *W:* Mark H. Baker; *C:* James Glennon; *M:* Kevin Kiner.

Lifeguard ✌✌ **1976 (PG)** The lifeguard lives by the credo that work is for people who cannot surf. But 30ish Rick (Elliott) is wondering if it's time to give up beach life and get a "real" job, especially after his 15th year high school reunion where he hooks up with old flame Cathy (Archer), who's now a divorcee with a young child, and a buddy offers him a job selling Porsches. **96m/C VHS, DVD.** Sam Elliott, Anne Archer, Stephen Young, Parker Stevenson, Kathleen Quinlan; *D:* Daniel Petrie; *W:* Ron Koslow.

Lifepod ✌ **1980** A group of intergalactic travelers is forced to evacuate a luxury space liner when a mad computer sabotages the ship. **94m/C VHS.** Joe Penny, Jordan Michaels, Kristine DeBell; *D:* Bruce Bryant; *W:* Bruce Bryant, Carol Johnson.

Lifepod ✌✌ 1/2 **1993** Trapped on a ship with a killer—only this time it's a space ship. In the year 2169 an interplanetary liner is sabotaged. Nine people escape in a damaged lifepod emergency craft. The survivors are perilously short of food and water and cannot contact Earth. They also face frightening evidence that the terrorist is among their group and is determined to kill the remaining survivors. Very loose adaptation of Alfred Hitchcock's 1944 film "Lifeboat." **120m/C VHS, DVD.** Ron Silver, Robert Loggia, CCH Pounder, Stan Shaw, Adam Storke, Jessica Tuck, Kelli Williams, Ed Gate; *D:* Ron Silver; *W:* M. Jay Roach, Pen Densham. **TV**

Lifespan ✌ **1975** A young American scientist visiting Amsterdam discovers experiments involving a drug that halts aging. **85m/C VHS, DVD.** *GB* Klaus Kinski, Hiram Keller, Tina Aumont; *D:* Alexander Whitelaw.

The Lifetaker WOOF! **1989** A woman lures an unsuspecting young man into her home where she seduces him. Violence and sex ensue. **97m/C VHS.** Lea Dregorn, Peter Duncan, Terence Morgan; *D:* Michael Papas.

The Lift ✌✌ **1985 (R)** Unsuspecting passengers meet an unfortunate fate when they take a ride in a demonic elevator in a highrise. In this film the last stop isn't ladies' lingerie, but death. In Dutch with English subtitles. **95m/C VHS.** *NL* Huub Stapel, Willeke Van Ammelrooy; *D:* Dick Maas.

Lift ✌✌ 1/2 **2001** Niecy (Washington) is a fashionable designer at a tony Boston store whose second job is as a "booster." She steals jewelry and couture clothes and adds to her own wardrobe while selling some of the merchandise. Her boyfriend Angelo (Byrd) urges Niecy to quit but she's seeking the approval of her embittered mother Elaine (McKee) and decides to boost an expensive necklace her mother has admired. Naturally, this job is the one that goes very wrong. **85m/C VHS, DVD.** *US* Kerry Washington, Lonette McKee, Eugene Byrd, Todd Williams, Samantha Brown, Kirk "Sticky Fingaz" Jones, Braun Philip, Barbara Montgomery, Annette Miller, Jacqui Parker, Naheem Allah, Susan Alger; *D:* DeMane Davis, Khari Streeter; *W:* DeMane Davis; *C:* David Phillips; *M:* Ryan Shore.

The Light Ahead ✌✌ 1/2 **1939** Lovers Fishke and Hodel dream of escaping the poverty and prejudices of their shtetl for the possibilities of big city life in Odessa. They're aided in their quest by enlightened bookseller Mendele who turns the town's superstitions to their advantage. Based on the stories of social satirist Mendele Mokher Seforim. In Yiddish with English subtitles. **94m/B VHS.** David Opatoshu, Isadore Cashier, Helen Beverly; *D:* Edgar G. Ulmer.

Light at the Edge of the World ✌✌ **1971 (PG)** A band of pirates torments a lighthouse keeper near Cape Horn after he sees a shipwreck they caused. **126m/C VHS, DVD.** Kirk Douglas, Yul Brynner, Samantha Eggar; *D:* Kevin Billington; *W:* Tom Rowe; *C:* Henri Decae; *M:* Piero Piccioni.

A Light in the Darkness ✌ 1/2 **2002 (R)** Familiar and not very creepy story that finds Taylor (Terzian) released from a mental hospital after many years. Unfortunately, he's still tormented by hallucinations of his dead shrew of a mom (Black). Given his fragile grip on sanity, Taylor doesn't need the added pressure of his scheming Uncle Stanley (Lewis) or drunken housekeeper Kira (Keyer). **99m/C DVD.** Karen Black, Geoffrey Lewis, Troy Beyer, Troy Winbush, Matt Terzian; *D:* Marshall E. Uzzle; *W:* Matt Terzian, Marshall E. Uzzle; *C:* Carl F. Bartels; *M:* Steve Yeaman.

The Light in the Forest ✌✌ 1/2 **1958** Disney adaptation of the classic Conrad Richter novel about a young man, kidnapped by Indians when he was young, who is forcibly returned to his white family. **92m/C VHS.** James MacArthur, Fess Parker, Carol Lynley, Wendell Corey, Joanne Dru, Jessica Tandy, Joseph Calleia, John McIntire; *D:* Herschel Daugherty; *C:* Ellsworth Fredericks.

The Light in the Jungle ✌✌ 1/2 **1991 (PG)** The biography of Nobel Peace Prize winner Dr. Albert Schweitzer. He established a hospital in Africa and had to overcome many obstacles, including tribal superstitions and European bureaucracy to make it successful and bring health care to the area. **91m/C VHS.** Malcolm McDowell, Susan Strasberg, Andrew Davis; *D:* Gray Hofmeyr.

Light It Up ✌ 1/2 **1999 (R)** Tedious hostage flick plays like a humorless "Breakfast Club" with guns. When their favorite high school teacher (Nelson) gets unfairly suspended, a group of fed-up students led by jock Lester (Raymond) stage a sit-in. After a confrontational security guard (Whitaker) is shot, the students take him and the crumbling school building hostage. The usual hostage situation mind games are played until the arrival of a police negotiator (Williams). The youngsters then appeal to the public through the use of the Internet, giving their side of the story and asking for public school reform. The young cast does a good job, but they can't make us believe the wildly inane chain of events. **99m/C VHS, DVD.** Forest Whitaker, Judd Nelson, Sara Gilbert, Rosario Dawson, Usher Raymond, Robert Ri'chard, Fredro Starr, Glynn Turman, Clifton (Gonzalez) Collins Jr., Vic Polizos, Vanessa L(ynne) Williams; *D:* Craig Bolotin; *W:* Craig Bolotin; *C:* Elliot Davis; *M:* Harry Gregson-Williams.

Light of Day ✌✌ **1987 (PG-13)** A rock 'n' roll semi-musical about a working-class brother and sister who escape from their parents and aimless lives through their bar band. Script tends to fall flat, although both Fox and Jett are believable. Title song written by Bruce Springsteen. **107m/C VHS.** Michael J. Fox, Joan Jett, Gena Rowlands, Jason Miller, Michael McKean, Michael Rooker, Michael Dolan; *D:* Paul Schrader; *W:* Paul Schrader; *C:* John Bailey; *M:* Thomas Newman.

The Light of Faith ✌ 1/2 **1922** A sick young woman is cured when she touches the Holy Grail, which a man stole from her former lover in order to help her. Silent. **33m/C VHS.** Lon Chaney Sr., Hope Hampton; *D:* Clarence Brown.

Light of My Eyes ✌✌ *Luce Dei Miei Occhi* **2001** Chauffeur Antonio (Lo Cascio) is heading home when he nearly hits a young girl who's wandered into the street. When her mother, Maria (Ceccarelli), comes to rescue the child, Antonio is immediately attracted. He begins to hang around and worms his way into Maria's life but, frankly, it doesn't seem worth the effort. The characters talk a lot (without saying anything worth noting) and, besides Lo Cascio, they're not particularly interesting. Italian with subtitles. **114m/C DVD.** *IT* Luigi Lo Cascio, Sandra Ceccarelli, Silvio Orlando; *D:* Giuseppe Piccioni; *W:* Giuseppe Piccioni, Umberto Contarello, Linda Ferri; *C:* Arnaldo Catinari; *M:* Ludovico Einaudi.

The Light of Western Stars ✌✌ 1/2 **1930** Brian plays a young woman from the east who comes to claim her late brother's ranch. She meets her murdered brother's best friend (Arlen) who is a drunken cowboy, and he falls madly in love with her. Wanting to impress her, he quickly sobers up and prevents a gang from taking over the ranch. This was Paramount's first talking adaptation of a Grey novel and the third version of this particular Grey novel; silent versions were made in 1918 and 1925. **70m/B VHS, DVD.** Richard Arlen, Mary Brian, Regis Toomey, Harry Green, Syd Saylor, George Chandler; ***D:*** Otto Brower, Edwin H. Knopf.

The Light of Western Stars **1940** A proper Eastern woman goes West and falls in love with a drunken lout. **67m/B VHS, DVD.** Victor Jory, Jo Ann Sayers, Russell Hayden, Morris Ankrum; ***D:*** Lesley Selander.

Light Sleeper **1992 (R)** Schrader's moody look at upscale drug dealers in New York. Dafoe is John LaTour, a 40 year-old drug courier to the club scene. Since his boss (Sarandon) is giving up the drug business for the safer world of natural cosmetics, John must look to his own future. His life becomes even more complicated when he runs into a bitter ex-flame (Delany) and finds the attraction is still overpowering. Cynical, contemplative, and menacing. **103m/C VHS, DVD.** Willem Dafoe, Susan Sarandon, Dana Delany, David Clennon, Mary Beth Hurt; ***D:*** Paul Schrader; ***W:*** Paul Schrader; ***C:*** Edward Lachman; ***M:*** Michael Been.

Light Years 1/2 **1988 (PG)** Garish animated fantasy epic about an idyllic land suddenly beset by evil mutations and death rays. Based on the novel "Robots Against Gondohar" by Jean-Pierre Andrevan. **83m/C VHS.** ***D:*** Harvey Weinstein; ***W:*** Isaac Asimov, Raphael Cluzel; ***M:*** Gabriel Yared; ***V:*** Glenn Close, Jennifer Grey, Christopher Plummer, Penn Jillette, John Shea, David Johansen, Bridget Fonda, Paul Shaffer, Terrence Mann, Teller.

Lightblast **1985** A San Francisco policeman tries to stop a deadly explosive-wielding mad scientist from blowing the city to kingdom come. **89m/C VHS.** Erik Estrada, Michael Pritchard; ***D:*** Enzo G. Castellari.

The Lighthorsemen **1987 (PG-13)** Compelling WWI drama follows several battle-hardened men of the Australian Light-Horse mounted infantry stationed in the Middle Eastern desert and the new recruit who joins their ranks and craves acceptance. Superbly filmed, particularly the final battle scene which pits the Aussies against the Turks for control of the wells at Beersheba. Fine performance by Andrews in this epic which contains the essential elements of a good war movie—horses, guns, and more horses. Originally filmed at 140 minutes. Good companion film for another Aussie WWI saga: "Gallipoli." **110m/C VHS.** *AU* Jon Blake, Peter Phelps, Tony Bonner, Bill Kerr, Nick Waters, John Walton, Tim McKenzie, Sigrid Thornton, Anthony Andrews, Shane Briant, Gary Sweet, Gerard Kennedy; ***D:*** Simon Wincer; ***W:*** Ian Jones; ***C:*** Dean Semler; ***M:*** Mario Millo.

Lighthouse Hill **2004** When his best friend and business partner Peter dies, Charlie suddenly decides to hit the road and winds up in the mysterious hamlet of Lighthouse Hill, which features a landlocked lighthouse and very welcoming residents. Charlie eventually decides to settle in, especially after getting romantically involved with villager Grace. **94m/C DVD.** *GB* Jason Flemyng, Kirsty Mitchell, Frank Finlay, Maureen Lipman, John Sessions; ***D:*** David Fairman; ***W:*** Sharon Y. Cobb; ***C:*** Tony Imi; ***M:*** Christopher Gunning.

Lighting in a Bottle 1/2 **2004 (PG-13)** Smokin' hot concert film documenting the roots and progression of the blues, structured around a 2003 show at New York's Radio City Music Hall. Director Antoine Fuqua and producer Martin Scorsese call on just about every face in the biz, over 50 musicians, to do what they do best—plug in and howl at the moon. The requisite blues legends abound, but it's the more contemporary artists paired with legendary blues songs that really bring down the house. Will undoubtedly generate a new fan base for the genre. **103m/C DVD.** *US* ***D:*** Antoine Fuqua; ***C:*** Lisa Rinzler; ***M:*** Steve Jordan.

Lightnin' Bill Carson **1936** Marshal Bill Carson chased outlaws Breed Hawkins and the Pecos Kid out of the town of Blue Gap. The Kid witnesses Hawkins kill a deputy during a stage holdup and hides out at his brother Tom's, where Carson arrests him. When the Pecos Kid is lynched, Tom vows revenge on all those involved, including Bill, who learned too late that the Kid wasn't the killer. **75m/B DVD.** Tim McCoy, Rex Lease, Lois January, Harry Worth, Karl Hackett, John Merton, Jack Rockwell, Edmund Cobb, Lafe (Lafayette) McKee; ***D:*** Sam Newfield; ***W:*** Joseph O'Donnell; ***C:*** Jack Greenhalgh.

Lightnin' Carson Rides Again 1/2 **1938** A tough frontier lawman tracks down his payroll-carrying nephew who's been accused of murder and thievery. **58m/B VHS, DVD.** Tim McCoy, Joan Barclay, Ted Adams, Forrest Taylor; ***D:*** Sam Newfield.

Lightning Bill **1935** A ranchhand helps his boss fend off a gang of outlaws in this inept outing. **46m/B VHS.** Buffalo Bill Jr., Nelson McDowell, Bud Osborne, William (Bill, Billy) McCall, Allen Holbrook, Lafe (Lafayette) McKee; ***D:*** Victor Adamson; ***W:*** L.V. Jefferson; ***C:*** Frank Bender.

Lightning Bill Crandall 1/2 **1937** Gunman heads south for the quiet life. Unfortunately, Arizona proves the scene of a fierce battle between various factions of cattlemen. The gunman aids the good guys, and tries to win the daughter's heart. **60m/B VHS.** Bob Steele, Lois January, Charles "Blackie" King, Frank LaRue, Ernie Adams, Earl Dwire, Dave O'Brien; ***D:*** Sam Newfield.

Lightning Bolt *Operazione Goldman* **1967** Someone is stealing moon rockets from Cape Kennedy, and secret agent Harry Sennet must find out who is doing this devilish deed. It leads him to an evil madman who plots to destroy the world from his underwater hideout. Cheap and unintentionally funny. **96m/C VHS.** *IT SP* Anthony Eisley, Wandisa Leigh, Folco Lulli, Diana Lorys, Ursula Parker; ***D:*** Anthony M. Dawson.

Lightning Hutch **1926** This is a rare example of the chapter serial genre from the late silent film era. Charles Hutchison battles the bad guys who want to steal the formula for a deadly poisonous gas, while also defending himself from an attempted framing for the theft of valuable bonds. Hutchinson produces an impressive athletic performance including swimming and rock climbing, all in the pursuit of good over evil. **230m/B DVD.** Charles (Hutchison) Hutchinson, Edith Thornton, Sheldon Lewis, Eddie (Edward) Phillips, Violet Schram, Ben Walker, Virginia Pearson, Gordon Sackville, Leroy Mason; ***D:*** Charles (Hutchison) Hutchinson; ***W:*** Jack Natteford.

The Lightning Incident **1991 (R)** McKeon plays a young Santa Fe sculptor whose worst nightmares come true when her baby is kidnapped by a devil-worshipping cult. Discovering she has a powerful psychic gift, she pursues the kidnappers across the country in a race to save her baby. Almost as bad as it sounds. **90m/C VHS.** Nancy McKeon, Polly Bergen, Tantoo Cardinal, Elpidia Carrillo, Tim Ryan; ***D:*** Michael Switzer; ***W:*** Michael J. Murray.

Lightning Jack 1/2 **1994 (PG-13)** Western comedy about Lightning Jack Kane (Hogan), an aging second-rate outlaw who desperately wants to become a western legend. Mute store clerk Ben (Gooding) winds up as his partner in crime, while barely eluding criticisms of Stepin Fetchitism. Cliches galore, the running gags (including Kane's surreptitious use of his eyeglasses so he can see his shooting targets) fall flat. **93m/C VHS, DVD.** Paul Hogan, Cuba Gooding Jr., Beverly D'Angelo, Kamala Dawson, Pat Hingle, Richard Riehle, Frank McRae, Roger Daltrey, L.Q. Jones, Max Cullen; ***D:*** Simon Wincer; ***W:*** Paul Hogan; ***C:*** David Eggby; ***M:*** Bruce Rowland.

Lightning Raiders **1945** When a stage coach filled with mail gets robbed, Billy Carson (Crabbe) and Fuzzy (St. John) set off to avenge the postal system. One of the last Crabbe/St. John efforts; perhaps they should have called it quits a few films earlier. **61m/C VHS.** Buster Crabbe, Al "Fuzzy" St. John, Mady Lawrence, Henry Hall, Steve Darrell, I. Stanford Jolley, Karl Hackett, Roy Brent, Marin Sais, Al Ferguson; ***D:*** Sam Newfield; ***W:*** Elmer Clifton.

Lightning Range **1933** Roosevelt stars as a U.S. Deputy Marshal who continually foils the nefarious plots of a gang of outlaws. **50m/B VHS.** Buddy Roosevelt, Lafe (Lafayette) McKee, Patsy Bellamy, Olin Francis; ***D:*** Victor Adamson; ***W:*** L.V. Jefferson; ***C:*** Brydon Baker.

Lightning Strikes West 1/2 **1940** U.S. Marshal trails an escaped convict, eventually catches him, and brings him in to finish paying his debt to society. **57m/B VHS, DVD.** Ken Maynard, Claire Rochelle, Bob Terry, Charles "Blackie" King, Michael Vallon, Reed Howes, George Chesebro, William (Bill) Gould; ***D:*** Harry Fraser; ***W:*** Martha Chapin, Monro Talbot; ***C:*** Elmer Dyer; ***M:*** Lew Porter.

Lightning: The White Stallion 1/2 **1986 (PG)** An old gambler and his two young friends enter a horse race in order to win their beloved white stallion back from thieves. **93m/C VHS, DVD.** Mickey Rooney, Susan George, Isabel Lorca; ***D:*** William A. Levey.

Lightning Warrior **1931** Western suspense about pioneer life and the unraveling of a baffling mystery. Twelve chapters, 13 minutes each. **156m/B VHS, DVD.** George Brent, Frankie Darro; ***D:*** Armand Schaefer, Benjamin (Ben H.) Kline.

Lights! Camera! Murder! *Death Force* **1989** When a 12-year-old boy witnesses a filmed murder, he becomes the next target. **89m/C VHS.** Graham Clarke, Robin Smith, John Barrett; ***D:*** Frans Nel; ***W:*** Emil Kolbe; ***C:*** Paul Morkel.

Lights in the Dusk 1/2 *Laitakaupungin Valot* **2006** Limp noir finds lonely shopping mall security guard Koiskinen (Hyytiainen) falling for the charms of bombshell Mirja (Jarvenhelmi), who works for sleazy businessman Lindholm (Koviula). Koiskinen becomes the patsy in a jewel robbery and goes to prison, not even ratting out Mirja. Things don't improve from there. Finnish with subtitles. **80m/C DVD.** *FI* Janne Hyytiainen, Maria Jarvenhelmi, Ilkka Koivula, Maria Heiskanen; ***D:*** Aki Kaurismaki; ***W:*** Aki Kaurismaki; ***C:*** Timo Salminen.

Lights of Old Santa Fe 1/2 **1947** A cowboy rescues a beautiful rodeo owner from bankruptcy. The original, unedited version of the film. **78m/B VHS, DVD.** Roy Rogers, Dale Evans, George "Gabby" Hayes, Lloyd Corrigan, Tom Keene, Arthur Loft, Roy Barcroft, Lucien Littlefield, Sam Flint, Bob Nolan; ***D:*** Frank McDonald; ***W:*** Gordon Kahn; ***C:*** Reggie Lanning.

The Lightship **1986 (PG-13)** On a stationary lightship off the Carolina coast, the crew rescues three men from a disabled boat, only to find they are murderous criminals. Duvall as a flamboyant homosexual psychopath is memorable, but the tale is pretentious, overdone, and hackneyed. Based on Siegfried Lenz's story. **87m/C VHS, DVD.** Robert Duvall, Klaus Maria Brandauer, Tom Bower, William Forsythe, Arliss Howard; ***D:*** Jerzy Skolimowski.

Like A Bride *Novia Que Te Vea* **1994** Two teenage Jewish girls grapple with their families' expectations and cultural norms during the 1960s in Mexico City when one resists marriage to be an artist while the other falls in love with a Gentile. In Spanish, with subtitles. **115m/C VHS, DVD.** *MX* Caludette Maille, Maya Michalska, Angelica Aragon, Ernesto Laguardia, Pedro Armendariz Jr.; ***D:*** Guita Schyfter, John Gorrie, Christopher Hodson, Tony Wharmby; ***W:*** Guita Schyfter, Hugo Hiriart, John Gorrie, David Butler; ***C:*** Toni Kuhn; ***M:*** Joaquin Gutierrez Heras, Joseph Horovitz. **VIDEO**

Like a Brother 1/2 *Comme un Frere* **2005** Eighteen-year-old Sebastian moves to Paris to get away from his unrequited crush on Romain. He decides a new life deserves a new name—Zack—as he explores the gay clubs. But he can't get away from his feelings, especially when Romain says he's coming for a visit. Short run time and abrupt ending makes you wonder if this indie ran out of money before completion. French with subtitles. **55m/C DVD.** *FR* Bill Hays, Don Shaw, Rebecca Hall; ***D:*** Guy Henry, Cyril Legann; ***W:*** Guy Henry, Cyril Legann; ***C:*** Joachim Villain.

Like a Fish Out of Water *Comme un Poisson Hors de'Eau* **1999** Muller is an average loveless, middle-aged nobody with a tropical fish hobby. This is how he's set up by a trio of con artists who need his help in stealing a very rare and valuable tropical fish, which they will hold for ransom until the eccentric owner pays up. Belucci's the femme who entices Muller while Karyo is the alleged brains of the operation and Pinon the crazy muscle. French with subtitles. **90m/C VHS, DVD.** *FR* Michel Muller, Monica Bellucci, Tcheky Karyo, Dominique Pinon; ***D:*** Herve Hadmar; ***W:*** Michel Muller, Herve Hadmar, Christopher Bergeronneau; ***C:*** Jacques Boumendil.

Like a Puppet Out of Strings 1/2 **2005** Brothers Tom and Felipe watch out for each other as they gain more power in the local gangs. Cop Luis, a former gangbanger whose life was turned around by police officer Angelica, goes after the brothers when she's murdered. Tom gets accused although Felipe did the crime, and Felipe does a deal with Luis to save his brother. Eventually, the siblings wind up confronting each other in a situation that calls their loyalty into question. **83m/C DVD.** *CA* Tom Rodriguez, Ed Casagrande, Leslie Hibberd, Catherine Braund, Felipe Rodriguez; ***D:*** Felipe Rodriguez; ***W:*** Felipe Rodriguez; ***C:*** Felipe Rodriguez, Dylan Harrison; ***M:*** Louis Marc Vautour.

Like Father, Like Son **1987 (PG-13)** First and worst of a barrage of interchangeable switcheroo movies that came out in '87-'88. Moore is in top form, but the plot is contrived. **101m/C VHS, DVD.** Dudley Moore, Kirk Cameron, Catherine Hicks, Margaret Colin, Sean Astin; ***D:*** Rod Daniel; ***W:*** Steven L. Bloom, Lorne Cameron; ***M:*** Miles Goodman.

Like Father Like Son 1/2 **2005** When teacher Dominic Milne gets engaged to Dee Stanton, she finally admits that she isn't a widow but that her ex-husband, Paul, is imprisoned as a serial killer. Her 15-year-old son Jamie overhears Dee's confession and demands to see the father he was told was dead and Dee is frightened that Jamie will become fascinated by the manipulative monster. Then Morag, a pupil whom Jamie was accused of stalking, is strangled and he falls under suspicion. Is Jamie following in his father's footsteps or is someone else close to Dee actually the killer? **137m/C DVD.** *GB* Robson Green, Jemma Redgrave, Somerset Prew, Philip Davis, Tara Fitzgerald, Francesca Fowler, Georgia Moffett, Florence Bell; ***D:*** Nicholas Laughland; ***W:*** Shaun McKenna; ***C:*** Dominic Clemence; ***M:*** John Lunn. **TV**

Like It Is **1998** Young Craig (Bell) makes his living in illegal bare-knuckles fighting matches in the old British beach resort town of Blackpool. After one win, he heads for a local disco where he meets ambitious London record producer, Matt (Rose), who's accompanying his roommate, singer Paula (Behr), to a gig. Uncertain of his sexual feelings, Craig can't follow through on his attraction to the willing Matt but does soon turn up on his London doorstep. However, not only is jealous Paula a problem for their budding romance but so is Kelvin (Daltry), Matt's manipulative gay boss. Appealing lead performances but vet Daltry steals scenes with smarmy charm. Accents and slang will be a challenge to American ears. **95m/C VHS, DVD.** *GB* Steve Bell, Ian Rose, Dani Behr, Roger Daltrey; ***D:*** Paul Oremland; ***W:*** Robert Cray; ***C:*** Alistair Cameron; ***M:*** Don McGlashan.

Like It Never Was Before *Pensionat Oskar* **1995** Conventional, middleaged marrieds Rune (Falkman) and Gunnel (Ekblad) Runeberg travel to a seaside hotel for their annual vacation with their three children. Ordinary family man Rune, though dissatisfied, is expecting little until he meets, and falls in love with, young handyman Petrus (Norrthon), and suddenly decides to break free. Swedish with subtitles. **108m/B VHS.** *SW* Loa Falkman, Stina Ekblad, Simon Norrthon, Philip Zanden, Sif Ruud, Ghita Norby; ***D:*** Suzanne (Susanne) Bier; ***W:*** Jonas Gardell; ***C:*** Kjell Lagerros; ***M:*** Johan Soderqvist.

Like Mike 1/2 **2002 (PG)** That's "Mike" as in basketball legend Michael Jordan—or at least his basketball shoes. A pair of old shoes, supposedly once belonging to Jordan, is donated to an orphanage and ending up the property of teen Calvin (Bow Wow). The shoes give him super skills on the basketball court, and he wins a chance to play spoiled star Tracey (Chestnutt) during halftime of a game. Impressed, the coach (Forster) signs Calvin to the fictional L.A. Knights. The hoops story is merely window dressing, however, because most of the story revolves around the efforts of Calvin and fellow orphans Murph (Lipnicki) and Reg (Song) to get adopted. NBA players Gary Payton, Alonzo Mourning, Rasheed Wallace, and Jason Kidd make appearances. **100m/C VHS, DVD, UMD.** *US* Bow Wow, Jonathan Lipnicki, Morris Chestnut, Eugene Levy, Crispin Glover, Robert Forster, Brenda Song, Jesse Plemons, Julius Charles Ritter, Anne Meara, Vanessa Williams; *D:* John Schultz; *W:* Jordan Moffet, Mike Elliot; *C:* Shawn Maurer; *M:* Richard Gibbs.

Like Water for Chocolate ♪♪♪ 1/2 *Como Agua para Chocolate* **1993 (R)** Magical Mexican fairytale set in the early 1900s about family, love, and the power of food. Formidable Mama Elena is left a widow with three daughters. The youngest, Tita, grows up in the kitchen surrounded by all the magic. Nacha, the housekeeper, can impart to her about food. Doomed by tradition to spend her days caring for her mother, Tita escapes by cooking, releasing her sorrows and longings into the food, infecting all who eat it. Wonderfully sensuous and slyly exaggerated. Based on the novel by Esquival, who also wrote the screenplay and whose husband, Arau, directed. In Spanish with English subtitles; also available dubbed. **105m/C VHS, DVD.** *MX* Lumi Cavazos, Marco Leonardi, Regina Torne, Mario Ivan Martinez, Ada Carrasco, Yareli Arizmendi, Claudette Maille, Pilar Aranda; *D:* Alfonso Arau; *W:* Laura Esquivel; *C:* Steven Bernstein; *M:* Leo Brouwer.

Li'l Abner ♪ 1/2 *Trouble Chaser* **1940** Al Capp's famed comic strip comes somewhat to life in this low-budget comedy featuring all of the Dogpatch favorites. **78m/C VHS.** Cranville Owen, Martha Driscoll, Buster Keaton; *D:* Albert Rogell.

Li'l Abner ♪♪ 1/2 **1959** High color Dogpatch drama adapted from the Broadway play (with most of the original cast) based on the Al Capp comic strip. When Abner's berg is considered as a site for atomic bomb testing, the natives have to come up with a reason why they should be allowed to exist. Choreography by Michael Kidd and Dee Dee Wood. ♫ Jubilation T. Cornpone; Don't Take That Rag Off'n the Bush; A Typical Day; If I Had My Druthers; Room Enuff for Us; Namely You; The Country's in the Very Best of Hands; Unnecessary Town; I'm Past My Prime. **114m/C VHS, DVD.** Peter Palmer, Leslie Parrish, Stubby Kaye, Julie Newmar, Howard St. John, Stella Stevens, Billie Hayes, Joe E. Marks; *D:* Melvin Frank; *W:* Norman Panama; *C:* Daniel F. Fapp; *M:* Johnny Mercer, Jean De Paul.

Lila Says ♪♪ *Lila Dit Ca* **2004** Chimo (Khouas) is a handsome 19-year-old Arab boy in Marseilles who, rather than further his writing talent, hangs out with his layabout friends and dabbles in petty crime. Along comes Lila (Giocante), a beautiful blond 16-year-old, who ensnares Chimo with her teasing talk. His friends blatantly disapprove of her and as he clings to his chivalrous demeanor, her antics become more annoying. **89m/C DVD.** *FR GB* Vahina Giocante, Mohammed Khouas, Karim Ben Haddou, Carmen Lebbos, Hamid Dkhissi, Lotfi Chakri, Edmonde Franchi, Stephanie Fatout; *D:* Ziad Doueiri; *W:* Ziad Doueiri, Joelle Touma; *C:* John Daly.

Lili ♪♪♪ **1953** Delightful musical romance about a 16-year-old orphan who joins a traveling carnival and falls in love with a crippled, embittered puppeteer. Heartwarming and charming, if occasionally cloying. Leslie Caron sings the films's song hit, "Hi-Lili, Hi-Lo." **81m/C VHS.** Leslie Caron, Jean-Pierre Aumont, Mel Ferrer, Kurt Kasznar, Zsa Zsa Gabor; *D:* Charles Walters; *M:* Bronislau Kaper. Oscars '53: Orig. Dramatic Score; British Acad. '53: Actress (Caron); Golden Globes '54: Screenplay.

Lilian's Story ♪♪ 1/2 **1995** Aging Lilian (Cracknell) has just been released after spending 40 years in a mental institution, placed there as an adolescent by her controlling, possessive father. The haunted Lilian is given a room at a residential hotel in Sydney's red-light district where the local prostitutes look out for her and she spends her days wandering the streets. Flashbacks reveal what lead the high-strung young Lilian (Collette) to her incarceration. Based on Kate Greville's 1984 novel, which was a fictional account of real-life Sydney eccentric Bea Miles. **94m/C VHS, DVD.** *AU* Ruth Cracknell, Barry Otto, Toni Collette, John Flaus, Essie Davis, Susie Lindemann, Anne Louise Lambert, Iris Shand; *D:* Jerzy Domaradzki; *W:* Steve Wright; *C:* Slawomir Idziak; *M:* Cezary Skubiszewski. Australian Film Inst. '95: Support. Actress (Collette).

Lilies ♪♪ *Les Feluettes* **1996 (R)** Strange revenge fantasy set in a northern Quebec men's prison in 1952. A bishop (Sabourin) goes to the prison to hear the confession of a dying convict and is taken hostage in the chapel by the prison's homosexual population. There, he's forced to watch a play that recreates a 40-year-old incident in his own life. As the prison walls fade away, the actor/prisoners turn into students Simon (Cadieux) and Vallier (Gilmore), who take the lovers' roles in a pageant about the martyrdom of St. Sebastien too seriously for comfort. The female roles in the flashbacks (which include Vallier's crazy mother and Simon's would-be fiance) are played by men. Adapted from Bouchard's play "Les Feluettes out La Repetition d'un Drame Romantique." **95m/C VHS, DVD.** *CA* Marcel Sabourin, Jason Cadieux, Danny Gilmore, Brent Carver, Matthew Ferguson, Alexander Chapman, Aubert Pallascio; *D:* John Greyson; *W:* Michel Marc Bouchard; *C:* Daniel Jobin; *M:* Mychael Danna. Genie '96: Art Dir./Set Dec., Costume Des., Film, Sound.

Lilies of the Field ♪♪♪ **1963** Five former East German nuns, living on a small farm in the Southwest U.S., enlist the aid of a free-spirited Army veteran Homer Smith (Poitier) to build a chapel for them and teach them English. Poitier is excellent as the itinerant laborer, holding the saccharine to an acceptable level, bringing honesty and strength to his role. Actress Skala, as Mother Maria, had been struggling to make ends meet in a variety of day jobs until this opportunity. Poitier was the first African American man to win an Oscar, and the first African American nominated since Hattie MacDaniel in 1939. Followed by "Christmas Lilies of the Field" (1979). **94m/B VHS, DVD.** Sidney Poitier, Lilia Skala, Lisa Mann, Isa Crino, Stanley Adams, Francesca Jarvis, Pamela Branch, Dan Frazer, Ralph Nelson; *D:* Ralph Nelson; *W:* James Poe; *C:* Ernest Haller; *M:* Jerry Goldsmith. Oscars '63: Actor (Poitier); Berlin Intl. Film Fest. '63: Actor (Poitier); Golden Globes '64: Actor—Drama (Poitier).

Liliom ♪♪♪ **1935** Boyer goes to heaven and is put on trial to see if he is deserving of his wings. Lang's first film after leaving Nazi Germany is filled with wonderful ethereal imagery, surprising coming from the man responsible for such grim visions as "Metropolis." In French only. **85m/B VHS, DVD.** *FR* Charles Boyer, Madeleine Ozeray, Florelle, Roland Toutain; *D:* Fritz Lang.

Lilith ♪♪♪ **1964** Therapist-in-training Beatty falls in love with beautiful mental patient Seberg and approaches madness himself. A look at the doctor-patient relationship among the mentally ill and at the nature of madness and love. Doesn't always satisfy, but intrigues. Rossen's swan song. **114m/B VHS, DVD.** Warren Beatty, Jean Seberg, Peter Fonda, Gene Hackman, Kim Hunter, Anne Meacham, Jessica Walter, Robert Reilly, Rene Auberjonois, Olympia Dukakis, James Patterson; *D:* Robert Rossen; *W:* Robert Rossen; *C:* Eugen Shufftan; *M:* Kenyon Hopkins.

Lillian Russell ♪♪ **1940** Often draggy biopic of the theatrical legend. In the 1890s, Helen Leonard (Faye) is taking singing lessons when she's heard by impresario Tony Pastor (Carrillo). He changes her name and hires her to sing in his theater, where Lillian becomes the toast of New York and has numerous suitors. She decides to marry musician Edward Solomon (Ameche) and is aided in her continued success by the flattering articles written by old friend Alexander Moore (Fonda). But it wouldn't be showbiz if there wasn't some sorrow to dim the bright lights. **127m/B DVD.** Alice Faye, Don Ameche, Henry Fonda, Edward Arnold, Leo Carrillo, Warren William, Lynn Bari, Nigel Bruce, Claud Allister, Helen Westley; *D:* Irving Cummings Jr.; *W:* William Anthony McGuire; *C:* Leon Shamroy; *M:* Alfred Newman.

Lillie ♪♪♪ **1979** The life of Edwardian beauty Lillie Langtry, known as "The Jersey Lily," is portrayed in this British drama. Defying the morals of the times, Lillie was the first publicly acknowledged mistress of the Prince of Wales, only one of her numerous lovers. Shown on "Masterpiece Theatre" on PBS. **690m/C VHS, DVD.** *GB* Francesca Annis, Cheryl Campbell, John Castle, Dennis (Denis) Lill, Peter Egan, Anton Rodgers, Ann(e) Firbank. **TV**

Lilo & Stitch ♪♪♪ **2002 (PG)** Modern and entertaining animated tale of problem child Lilo, a Hawaiian orphan being raised by her sister, who finds an unlikely soulmate when she adopts Stitch, a strange little alien banished from his home planet, who hides out in an animal shelter. Stitch is rife with socially unacceptable behavior (including naughty words, drooling, and spitting food) and creates chaos everywhere they go, which worsens Lilo's situation with a concerned social worker investigating her upbringing. Kiddies will love the sassy humor and gross-out behavior while parents will love the Elvis references (and songs), and the message of ohana—the Hawaiian word for family. Disney resurrected the appealing hand drawn and watercolored animation, unused since 1942's "Bambi." **85m/C VHS, DVD.** *US D:* Dean DeBlois, Christopher Sanders; *W:* Dean DeBlois, Christopher Sanders; *M:* Alan Silvestri; *V:* Daveigh Chase, Tia Carrere, Jason Scott Lee, David Ogden Stiers, Christopher Sanders, Kevin McDonald, Ving Rhames, Zoe Caldwell, Kevin M. Richardson, Amy Hill, Susan Hegarty.

Lilo & Stitch 2: Stitch Has a Glitch ♪♪ 1/2 **2005 (PG)** Lilo enters a hula contest and Stitch has a personality shift to evil and even more destructive in this well-done sequel, which will still please the intended audience while amusing teens and adults as well. **68m/C VHS, DVD.** *D:* Michael LaBash, Anthony Leondis; *W:* Michael LaBash, Anthony Leondis, Alexa Junge, Eddie Guzelian; *V:* Tia Carrere, Dakota Fanning, Jason Scott Lee, Christopher Sanders, Kevin McDonald, David Ogden Stiers, Liliana Mumy, Holliston Coleman, Jillian Henry. **VIDEO**

Lily Dale ♪♪ 1/2 **1996 (PG)** Nineteen-year-old Horace Robedaux (Guinee) is in Houston to visit his estranged mother Corella (Channing) and sister Lily Dale (Masterson) while his taciturn stepfather Pete Davenport (Shepard) is supposed to be away. Pete dislikes Horace and left the boy behind with relatives when he married Corella and they moved away. Self-centered Lily Dale resents Horace taking away attention from herself and matters only get worse when Pete comes home early and Horace becomes so ill that he can't leave. Set in 1910; Foote wrote the play as a memoir to his father, Horace. Made for TV. **95m/C VHS, DVD.** Tim Guinee, Stockard Channing, Mary Stuart Masterson, Sam Shepard, John Slattery, Jean Stapleton; *D:* Peter Masterson; *W:* Horton Foote; *C:* Don E. Fauntleroy; *M:* Peter Melnick.

Lily in Love ♪♪ 1/2 *Playing for Keeps; Jatszani Kell* **1985 (PG-13)** An aging stage star disguises himself as a suave Italian to star in his playwright wife's new play, and woos her to test her fidelity. Charming, warm, and sophisticated. Loosely based on Molnar's "The Guardsman." **100m/C VHS.** *HU* Maggie Smith, Christopher Plummer, Elke Sommer, Adolph Green; *D:* Karoly Makk; *W:* Frank Cucci. **TV**

Lily in Winter ♪♪ 1/2 **1994 (PG)** Christmas story about families and the ties that bind, set in 1957. Black nanny Lily (Cole in her film debut) works for busy showbiz New Yorkers, the Towlers (Hoffmann and Brown), looking after their neglected 10-year-old son Michael (Bonsall). But Lily thinks she's in trouble, thanks to her no-account brother Booker (Russell), and takes off to her rural Alabama roots without realizing Michael has followed her. His parents, however, think Lily has kidnapped him. **120m/C VHS.** Natalie Cole, Brian Bonsall, Dwier Brown, Cecil Hoffmann, Marla Gibbs, Monte Russell, Rae'ven (Alyia Larrymore) Kelly, Salli Richardson, James Pickens Jr., Matthew Faison; *D:* Delbert Mann; *W:* Robert Eisele; *C:* Charles Mills; *M:* David Shire. **CABLE**

Lily of Killarney ♪♪ *The Bride of the Lake* **1934** A musical comedy romance about a British lord who arranges to pay his debts via horse-races, arranged marriages and inheritances. **82m/B VHS.** *GB* Gina Malo, John Garrick, Stanley Holloway; *D:* Maurice Elvey.

Lily Was Here ♪ 1/2 **1989 (R)** After her fiancee is senselessly murdered, a young woman named Lily is forced to turn to a life of crime in order to survive. A series of petty thefts evolves into a huge crime wave and Lily soon finds herself the object of a massive manhunt. Lily must make the ultimate choice between freedom and motherhood in this shocking thriller. Soundtrack by Dave Stewart features hit instrumental theme "Lily was Here" by saxophonist Candy Dulfur. **110m/C VHS.** Marion Van Thijn, Thom Hoffman, Adrian Brine, Dennis Rudge; *D:* Ben Verbong; *W:* Ben Verbong, Sytze Van Der Laan, Willem Jan Otten.

The Limbic Region ♪♪ **1996** Terminally ill police detective Jon Lucca (Olmos) has spent 20 years tracking a serial killer known as "The Scorekeeper," who likes to shotgun the young inhabitants of small-town lovers' lanes. His most likely suspect is Lloyd Warden (Dzundza) and the duo engage in a deadly cat-and-mouse battle that may destroy them both. **96m/C VHS.** Edward James Olmos, George Dzundza, Gwynyth Walsh; *D:* Michael Pattinson; *W:* Patrick Ranahan, Todd Johnson; *C:* Tobias Schliessler. **CABLE**

Limbo ♪♪ **1999 (R)** Ambivalent family saga that leaves the viewers deliberately in limbo for good or ill. Alaskan Joe Gastineau (Strathairn) is a former fisherman traumatized by an accident at sea years before. Into his life comes smalltime singer Donna de Angelo (Mastrantonio) and her depressed teen daughter Noelle (Martinez). Joe and Donna start a tentative romance and Joe even goes back to fishing. Then Joe's fast-talking half-brother Bobby (Siemaszko) shows up, precipitating a crisis that leaves Bobby dead and Joe, Donna, and Noelle stranded on a deserted island. **126m/C VHS, DVD.** David Strathairn, Mary Elizabeth Mastrantonio, Vanessa Martinez, Casey Siemaszko, Kris Kristofferson, Kathryn Grody, Rita Taggart, Leo Burmester, Michael Laskin; *D:* John Sayles; *W:* John Sayles; *C:* Haskell Wexler; *M:* Mason Daring.

Lime Salted Love ♪ 1/2 **2006** Set in L.A. and told in flashbacks. David Treibel has been released from a mental hospital though he's obviously still got a lot of problems. As does his younger brother Chase, an emotional basket case who can only live in the present. Their guilt from a family tragedy (a third brother's accidental death) consumes them and brings them into contact with fellow lost souls, including Chase's encounter with Ellie, a victim of child abuse. **92m/C DVD.** David O'Donnell, Kate del Castillo, Kristanna Loken, Billy Drago, Joe Hall, Danielle Agnello, George Castaneda; *D:* Joe Hall, Danielle Agnello; *W:* Joe Hall, Danielle Agnello; *C:* Matthew Rudenberg; *M:* John Langdon. **VIDEO**

Limelight ♪♪♪ **1952** A nearly washed-up music hall comedian is stimulated by a young ballerina to a final hour of glory. A subtle if self-indulgent portrait of Chaplin's own life, featuring an historic pairing of Chaplin and Keaton. **120m/B VHS, DVD.** Charlie Chaplin, Claire Bloom, Buster Keaton, Nigel Bruce, Sydney Chaplin; *D:* Charlie Chaplin; *W:* Charlie Chaplin; *C:* Karl Struss; *M:* Charlie Chaplin.

The Limey ♪♪♪ **1999 (R)** Sixties icons Stamp and Fonda show that age has not withered their acting chops in Soderbergh's revenge thriller. Wilson (Stamp) is a Cockney career criminal who gets out of a Brit prison and immediately flies to L.A. to investigate the death of his daughter Jenny. She was involved with self-important record producer Valentine (Fonda), who has an obvious fondness for young women. Wilson may be out-of-touch with California culture but he's definitely in control of any situation. Soderbergh's flashback sequences make use of footage from Ken Loach's 1967 film "Poor Cow," which featured Stamp as a young thief named Wilson. **90m/C VHS, DVD.** Terence Stamp, Peter Fonda, Lesley Ann Warren, Luis Guzman, Barry Newman, Joe Dallesandro, Nicky Katt, Amelia Heinle, Melissa George, Bill Duke; *D:* Steven Soderbergh; *W:* Lem Dobbs; *C:* Edward Lachman; *M:* Cliff Martinez.

Limit Up **1989 (PG-13)** An ambitious Chicago Trade Exchange employee makes a deal with the devil to corner the market in soybeans. Turgid attempt at supernatural comedy, featuring Charles as God. Catch Sally Kellerman in a cameo as a nightclub singer. **88m/C VHS, DVD.** Nancy Allen, Dean Stockwell, Brad Hall, Danitra Vance, Ray Charles, Luana Anders; ***Cameos:*** Sally Kellerman; *D:* Richard Martini; *C:* Peter Lyons Collister.

The Limits of Control **2009 (R)** Jarmusch's self-indulgent travelogue features a nameless, emotionless man who is given a series of cryptic instructions as he makes his way across Spain. **116m/C DVD.** *US* Isaach de Bankole, Paz de la Huerta, Alex Descas, Luis Tosar, John Hurt, Tilda Swinton, Jean-Francois Stevenin, Gael Garcia Bernal, Bill Murray; *D:* Jim Jarmusch; *W:* Jim Jarmusch; *C:* Christopher Doyle; *M:* Boris.

The Limping Man **1953** Bridges returns to post-WWII London to renew a wartime romance. On the way, he gets caught up in solving a murder. Unexceptional of-its-era thriller. **76m/B VHS, DVD.** *GB* Lloyd Bridges, Moira Lister, Leslie Phillips, Helene Cordet, Alan Wheatley; *D:* Charles De Latour.

Linda 1/2 **1929** Linda, a young mountain girl, is forced to marry a much older man though her heart belongs to a young doctor. Her kind husband tries to make the best of the situation. **75m/B VHS.** Helen Foster, Warner Baxter, Noah Beery Sr., Mitchell Lewis, Kate Price, Alan Connor; *D:* Dorothy Davenport Reid.

Linda **1993 (PG-13)** Madsen in her femme fatale mode as treacherous wife Linda who wants to frame her schlump husband (Thomas) for murder. Whose murder? Why the inconvenient wife (Harrington) of her boyfriend (McGinley). The two homicidal lovebirds want to take the insurance money and run—leaving hubby to face the consequences. Based on the novella "Linda" by John D. MacDonald. **88m/C VHS.** Virginia Madsen, Richard Thomas, Ted McGinley, Laura Harrington; *D:* Nathaniel Gutman; *W:* Nevin Schreiner; *M:* David Michael Frank.

Linda Linda Linda **2005** It's their last annual high school festival, and classmates Nozumi (Shiori Sekine) and Kyoto (Aki Maeda) decide to put together a rock band to play "Linda Linda Linda," a hit punk song in Japan. But their singer and guitarist quit, so they get a Korean girl (who can barely speak Japanese) to sing and a guitarist who usually plays keyboards. They have two days to learn to play together and win the school festival before graduation comes and they must enter the real world. **114m/C DVD.** *JP* Du-na Bae, Kahori Fujii, Pierre Taki, Aki Maeda, Yu Kashii, Shiori Sekine, Takayo Mimura, Shione Yukawa, Yuko Yamazaki, Masahiro Komoto, Ken'ichi Matsuyama, Katsuya Kobayashi, Keisuke Koide, Masaki Miura; *D:* Nobuhiro Yamashita; *W:* Nobuhiro Yamashita, Wakako Miyashita, Kosuke Mukai; *C:* Yoshihiro Ikeuchi; *M:* James Iha.

The Lindbergh Kidnapping Case **1976** The famous Lindbergh baby kidnapping in 1932 and the trial and execution of Bruno Hauptmann, convincingly portrayed by Hopkins. DeYoung as Lindbergh is brilliant, but the script is quite good. Made for TV. **150m/C VHS.** Anthony Hopkins, Joseph Cotten, Cliff DeYoung, Walter Pidgeon, Dean Jagger, Martin Balsam, Laurence Luckinbill, Tony Roberts; *D:* Buzz Kulik; *W:* J(ames) P(inckney) Miller; *M:* Billy Goldenberg. **TV**

The Line 1/2 **1980 (R)** Not-so-hot anti-war drama about a sit-down strike at a military installation by Vietnam veteran prison inmates. Leans heavily on recycled footage from director Siegel's own "Parade" (1971). **94m/C VHS.** Russ Thacker, David Doyle, Erik Estrada; *D:* Robert Siegel.

The Line *La Linea* **2008 (R)** A bilingual crime drama with some action, a lot of character study, and some twists to keep things interesting. Salazar (Garcia), the head of a Tijuana cartel, is dying and has already passed on his power to unstable second-in-command Pelon (Morales). Against Salazar's wishes, Pelon makes a deal with Afghani terrorists to trade heroin for U.S. smuggling routes. Shady U.S. authorities secretly hire hitman Shields (Liotta) to off Pelon, but Shields is sidetracked by a guilt complex. English and Spanish with subtitles. **95m/C DVD.** Andy Garcia, Esai Morales, Ray Liotta, Valerie Cruz, Armand Assante, Danny Trejo, Bruce Davison, Joe Morton; *D:* James Cotten; *W:* R. Ellis Frazier; *C:* Miguel Bunster; *M:* David Torn.

The Line of Beauty 1/2 **2006** Middle-class Nick Guest (Stevens) is befriended at Oxford by wealthy Toby Fedden (Coleman), whose father Gerald (McInnerney) is a rising Tory politician in Thatcher's Britain of the 1980s. Guest moves into the family's London home—in part to keep an eye on Toby's trouble-prone sister Catherine (Atwell). The gay Nick also starts exploring his sexuality: first with working-class Leo (Gilet) and then with Wani (Wyndham), the closeted druggie son of a Lebanese tycoon. Scandals eventually catch up with both Nick and the Feddens. Based on the novel by Alan Hollinghurst. **180m/C DVD.** Tim (McInnerny) McInnery, Alice Krige, Dan Stevens, Oliver Coleman, Hayley Atwell, Alex Wyndham, Don Gilet; *D:* Saul Dibb; *W:* Andrew Davies; *C:* David Odd; *M:* Martin Phipps. **TV**

The Lineup **1958** Volatile mob killer Dancer (Wallach) and his mentor Julian (Keith) have to retrieve three packages of heroin that have been planted on unsuspecting travelers to San Francisco. Dancer easily bumps off the first two carriers but the third package was hidden inside a child's doll and the girl mistook the drugs for face powder. Dancer is enraged when his boss accuses him of stealing the drugs and gets more violent even as the cops close in. **85m/B DVD.** Eli Wallach, Robert Keith, Warner Anderson, Richard Jaeckel, William Leslie, Mary Laroche, Emile Meyer, Marshall Reed, Vaughn Taylor; *D:* Donald Siegel; *W:* Stirling Silliphant; *C:* Hal Mohr; *M:* Mischa Bakaleinikoff.

Linewatch 1/2 **2008 (R)** Dull story finds Michael Dixon's (Gooding Jr.) past coming back to haunt him. Michael works for the border patrol along the U.S./Mexico divide. Now a family man, he was once part of a violent L.A. gang, and a chance encounter with leader Drake (Hardwick) finds Michael being pressured to help the gang smuggle drugs. **90m/C DVD.** Cuba Gooding Jr., Omari Hardwick, Sharon Leal, Evan Ross, Dean Norris, Chris Browning; *D:* Kevin Bray; *W:* David Warfield; *C:* Paul M. Sommers. **VIDEO**

The Linguini Incident **1992 (R)** An inept escape artist, a pathological liar, a lingerie designer, a deaf restaurant hostess who throws out one-liners in sign language, and two sinister, yet chic, restaurant owners get together in this marginal comedy about magic and adventure. **99m/C VHS.** Rosanna Arquette, David Bowie, Eszter Balint, Andre Gregory, Buck Henry, Viveca Lindfors, Marlee Matlin, Lewis Arquette, Andrea King; ***Cameos:*** Julian Lennon, Iman; *D:* Richard Shepard; *W:* Tamar Brott, Richard Shepard; *C:* Robert Yeoman; *M:* Thomas Newman.

Link **WOOF!** **1986 (R)** A primatologist and his nubile assistant find their experiment has gone—you guessed it—awry, and their hairy charges are running—yep, that's right—amok. Run for your life! **103m/C VHS, DVD.** *GB* Elisabeth Shue, Terence Stamp, Steven Pinner, Richard Garnett; *D:* Richard Franklin; *W:* Everett DeRoche; *C:* Mike Molloy; *M:* Jerry Goldsmith.

The Lion Has Wings 1/2 **1940** The story of how Britain's Air Defense was set up to meet the challenge of Hitler's Luftwaffe during their "finest hour." Dated, now-quaint but stirring wartime period piece. "Docudrama" style was original at the time. **75m/B VHS.** Merle Oberon, Ralph Richardson, Flora Robson, June Duprez, John Robinson; *D:* Brian Desmond Hurst, Michael Powell; *C:* Harry Stradling Sr.

The Lion Hunters 1/2 **1947** Greedy lion-hunters Forbes (Ankrum) and Martin (Kennedy) have set up camp in the land of the Masai—where lions are sacred—but they've no interest in local customs. Bomba the Jungle Boy (Sheffield) is tasked with setting them straight, saving the lions, and saving kidnapped Jean as well. **75m/B DVD.** John(ny) Sheffield, Morris Ankrum, Ann E. Todd, Douglas Kennedy, Smoki Whitfield, Davis Roberts, Woody Strode; *D:* Ford Beebe; *W:* Ford Beebe, Roy Rockwood.

A Lion in the Streets *A Lion Is in the Streets* **1953** Southern peddler Hank (Cagney) plays on how corrupt politicians exploit the local sharecroppers and launches a grassroots campaign for the governorship. But he betrays his followers when his ambition gets the best of him. A pale comparison to 1949's "All the King's Men" since the script was rewritten to prevent a lawsuit by the family of governor Huey Long. Jeanne Cagney, who plays Jennie, is the star's sister. **88m/C DVD.** James Cagney, Barbara Hale, Anne Francis, Warner Anderson, John McIntire, Jeanne Cagney, Lon Chaney Jr., Frank McHugh, Larry Keating, Onslow Stevens, James Millican; *D:* Raoul Walsh; *W:* Luther Davis; *C:* Harry Stradling Sr.; *M:* Franz Waxman.

The Lion in Winter **1968 (PG)** Medieval monarch Henry II and his wife, Eleanor of Aquitaine, match wits over the succession to the English throne and much else in this fast-paced film version of James Goldman's play. The family, including three grown sons, and visiting royalty are united for the Christmas holidays fraught with tension, rapidly shifting allegiances, and layers of psychological manipulation. Superb dialogue and perfectly realized characterizations. O'Toole and Hepburn are triumphant. Screen debuts for Hopkins and Dalton. Shot on location, this literate costume drama surprised the experts with its boxoffice success. **134m/C VHS, DVD.** Peter O'Toole, Katharine Hepburn, Jane Merrow, Nigel Terry, Timothy Dalton, Anthony Hopkins, John Castle, Nigel Stock; *D:* Anthony Harvey; *W:* James Goldman; *M:* John Barry. Oscars '68: Actress (Hepburn), Adapt. Screenplay, Orig. Score; Directors Guild '68: Director (Harvey); Golden Globes '69: Actor—Drama (O'Toole), Film—Drama; N.Y. Film Critics '68: Film.

The Lion in Winter **2003** In this Showtime miniseries remake of the 1968 masterpiece, Close and Stewart gracefully, if not quite as joyously, inhabit the lead roles made classic by Hepburn and O'Toole. Using Goldman's screenplay, Konchalovsky's presentation is admirably true to its source, and the scenery in Hungary and Slovakia splendidly suits the subject. Certainly an excellent effort by a talented cast and crew, but it won't dethrone its predecessor. **167m/C VHS, DVD.** Patrick Stewart, Glenn Close, John Light, Jonathan Rhys Meyers, Ralph Spall, Yuliya Vysotskaya, Andrew Howard, Clive Wood; *D:* Andrei Konchalovsky; *W:* James Goldman; *C:* Sergei Kozlov; *M:* Richard Hartley. **CABLE**

A Lion Is in the Streets **1953** Cagney stars as a backwoods politician in a southern state who fights on the side of the sharecroppers and wins their support when he exposes the corrupt practices of a powerful businessman. On his way up the political ladder, however, Cagney betrays and exploits the very people who support him. Although this is a familiar storyline, Cagney is riveting as the corrupt politician, and Hale is wonderful as his patient wife. **88m/C VHS.** James Cagney, Barbara Hale, Anne Francis, Warner Anderson, John McIntire, Jeanne Cagney, Lon Chaney Jr., Frank McHugh, Larry Keating, Onslow Stevens; *D:* Raoul Walsh.

The Lion King **1994 (G)** A winner for kids and their folks. Like his dad Mufasa (Jones), lion cub Simba (Taylor) is destined to be king of the beasts, until evil uncle Scar (Irons) goes all "Hamlet" and makes him an outcast. Growing up in the jungles of Africa, Simba (now Broderick) learns about life and responsibility, before facing his uncle once again. Supporting characters frequently steal the show, with Sabella's Pumba the warthog and Lane's Timon the meerkat heading the procession. Disney epic features heartwarming combo of crowd-pleasing songs, a story with depth, emotion, and politically correct multiculturalism, and stunning animation. Thirty-second Disney animated feature is the first without human characters, and the first to use the voices of a well known, ethnically diverse cast. Scenes of violence in the animal kingdom may be too much for younger viewers. ♫Can You Feel the Love Tonight; The Circle of Life; I Just Can't Wait to Be King; Be Prepared; Hakuna Matata. **88m/C VHS, DVD.** *D:* Rob Minkoff, Roger Allers; *W:* Jonathan Roberts, Irene Mecchi; *M:* Elton John, Hans Zimmer, Tim Rice; *V:* Matthew Broderick, Jeremy Irons, James Earl Jones, Madge Sinclair, Robert Guillaume, Jonathan Taylor Thomas, Richard "Cheech" Marin, Whoopi Goldberg, Rowan Atkinson, Nathan Lane, Ernie Sabella, Niketa Calame, Moira Kelly, Jim (Jonah) Cummings. Oscars '94: Song ("Can You Feel the Love Tonight"), Orig. Score; Golden Globes '95: Film—Mus./Comedy, Song ("Can You Feel the Love Tonight?"), Score; Blockbuster '95: Family Movie, T., Soundtrack.

The Lion King 1 1/2 **2004 (G)** Timon and Pumbaa tell the story of the original from their point of view, so we get to see what happened to Simba and how he grew up between the time he ran away and when he returned. Sort of a "Rosencrantz and Guildenstern are Dead" for the pre-teen set. Offers up the original cast (with some new additions), and a new song. Doesn't disappoint fans of the franchise, with plenty of enjoyment for every age group. **77m/C VHS, DVD.** *W:* Tom Rogers; *M:* Don Harper; *V:* Nathan Lane, Ernie Sabella, Matthew Broderick, Robert Guillaume, Moira Kelly, Whoopi Goldberg, Richard "Cheech" Marin, Julie Kavner, Jerry Stiller, Jim (Jonah) Cummings, Edward Hibbert, Bradley Raymond, Matt Weinberg, Jason Rudofsky. **VIDEO**

The Lion King: Simba's Pride **1998** Simba's heir comes of age and must be prepared to assume the responsibility of leadership. **75m/C VHS, DVD.** *D:* Darrell Rooney, Rob LaDuca; *W:* Flip Kobler, Cindy Marcus; *V:* Matthew Broderick, James Earl Jones, Nathan Lane, Ernie Sabella, Robert Guillaume, Andy Dick, Neve Campbell, Suzanne Pleshette, Jason Marsden. **VIDEO**

The Lion Man **1936** Arabian tale of a boy raised by lions. **67m/B VHS, DVD.** Jon Hall, Ted Adams, Kathleen Burke, Richard Carlyle; *D:* John P. McCarthy; *W:* Richard Gordon; *C:* Robert E. Cline.

Lion Man *Aslan Adam* **1975** Raised by wild animals, the son of King Solomon returns to his father's kingdom and roars his way to the throne. **91m/C VHS.** *TU* Barbara Lake, Charles Garrett, Alison Soames, Steve Arkin; *D:* Natuk Baytan.

The Lion of Africa **1987** A down-to-earth woman doctor and an abrasive diamond dealer share a truck ride across Kenya. Filmed on location in East Africa. Fine lead performances in otherwise nothing-special adventure. **115m/C VHS.** Brian Dennehy, Brooke Adams, Joseph Shiloah; *D:* Kevin Connor; *M:* George S. Clinton. **CABLE**

Lion of the Desert *Omar Mukhtar* **1981 (PG)** Bedouin horse militias face-off against Mussolini's armored terror in this epic historical drama. Omar Muktar (Quinn as the "Desert Lion") and his Libyan guerrilla patriots kept the Italian troops of Mussolini (Steiger) at bay for 20 years. Outstanding performances enhanced by the desert backdrop. A British-Libyan co-production. **162m/C VHS, DVD.** *GB* Anthony Quinn, Oliver Reed, Irene Papas, Rod Steiger, Raf Vallone, John Gielgud; *D:* Moustapha Akkad; *W:* H.A.L. Craig; *C:* Jack Hildyard; *M:* Maurice Jarre.

The Lion of Thebes **1964** A muscleman unhesitatingly jumps into the thick of things when Helen of Troy is kidnapped. A superior sword and sandal entry. **87m/C VHS, DVD.** *IT* Massimo Serato, Pierre Cressoy, Alberto Lupo, Rosalba Neri, Mark Forest, Yvonne Furneaux; *D:* Giorgio Ferroni; *W:* Giorgio Ferroni, Andrei De Coligny; *C:* Angelo Lotti; *M:* Francesco De Masi.

Lionheart 1/2 **1987 (PG)** A romantic portrayal of the famous English King Richard the Lionheart's early years. Meant for kids, but no Ninja turtles herein—and this is just as silly, and slow to boot. **105m/C VHS.** Eric Stoltz, Talia Shire, Nicola Cowper, Dexter Fletcher, Nicholas Clay, Deborah Maria Moore, Gabriel Byrne; *D:* Franklin J. Schaffner; *W:* Richard Outten; *M:* Jerry Goldsmith.

Lionheart 1/2 *A.W.O.L.; Wrong Bet* **1990 (R)** Van Damme deserts the foreign legion and hits the streets when he learns his brother has been hassled. Many fights ensue, until you fall asleep. **105m/C VHS, DVD.** Jean-Claude Van Damme, Harrison Page, Deborah Rennard, Lisa Pelikan, Brian Thompson, Ashley Johnson; ***D:*** Sheldon Lettich; ***W:*** Sheldon Lettich, Jean-Claude Van Damme; ***C:*** Robert New; ***M:*** John Scott.

Lion's Den 1/2 **1936** A night club performer and a detective head west to fight crime in this film. **59m/B VHS.** Joan Woodbury, Don Barclay, J. Frank Glendon, John Merton, Tim McCoy, Dave O'Brien; ***D:*** Sam Newfield; ***W:*** John Thomas "Jack" Neville; ***C:*** Jack Greenhalgh.

Lion's Den 1/2 *Leonera* **2008** Pregnant Julia is accused of murdering her lover and sent to an Argentine prison where she's assigned to a ward for women with kids. Julia gives birth and raises her son in prison as she goes from overwhelmed to confident about her maternal abilities with the help of her fellow inmates. Spanish with subtitles. **113m/C DVD.** *AR* Martina Gusman, Laura Garcia, Elli Medeiros, Rodrigo Santoro, Leonardo Sauma, Tomas Plotinsky; ***D:*** Pablo Trapero; ***W:*** Pablo Trapero, Alejandro Fadel, Marin Mauregui, Santiago Mitre; ***C:*** Guillermo Nieto.

Lions for Lambs **2007 (R)** Three interrelated stories of those affected by the Iraq war, including a hawkish politician, an anti-war professor, and the soldiers stuck in between. Senator Irving (Cruise) pushes a war strategy destined for failure in Iraq and Afghanistan while Professor Malley (Redford) debates the validity of the war with his students and worries about two in particular (Pena and Luke) who, as soldiers, are part of Irving's strategy. Director Redford boldly strives to say something meaningful about the war on terror but fails to give his characters any depth. Instead, they all function as flat representations of different viewpoints, spouting talking points rather than actually interacting. Co-stars Cruise and Streep (as the skeptical journalist Roth) do their best, but a bunch of A-list actors making speeches is less a drama than a series of lectures. **92m/C DVD.** *US* Robert Redford, Meryl Streep, Tom Cruise, Michael Pena, Peter Berg, Kevin Dunn, Derek Luke, Andrew Garfield; ***D:*** Robert Redford; ***W:*** Matthew Carnahan; ***C:*** Philippe Rousselot; ***M:*** Mark Isham.

The Lion's Share **1979** A gang of bank robbers have their loot stolen and go after the guy who ripped them off. **105m/C VHS.** *SP* Julio de Grazia, Luisina Brando, Fernanda Mistral, Ulises Dumont, Julio Chavez; ***D:*** Adolfo Aristarain; ***W:*** Adolfo Aristarain; ***C:*** Horacio Maira; ***M:*** Annibal Gruart, Jorge Navarro.

Lip Service **1988** Satirical comedy-drama about the TV news industry. An ambitious young newscaster befriends a veteran reporter. He then manipulates his way to replace him on the reporter's morning program. Dooley as the veteran and Dunne as the upstart are fun to watch in this well-done cable rip-off of "Broadcast News." **67m/C VHS.** Griffin Dunne, Paul Dooley; ***D:*** William H. Macy. **CABLE**

Lip Service 1/2 *Kat and Allison* **2000 (R)** Allison (Temchen) is a conservative, successful, furniture designer with a successful lawyer boyfriend, Stuart (Camargo). She reunites with her old college roommate, Kat (Gertz), a high-strung free spirit who moves into Allison's home. Then Kat discovers that Allison's success is predicated on selling copies of a chair that Kat herself designed and gave to Allison as a gift. So Kat decides to get revenge. **95m/C VHS, DVD.** Jami Gertz, Sybil Temchen, Jonathan Silverman, Christian Camargo, Adewale Akinnuoye-Agbaje, Jenna Byrne; ***D:*** Shawn Schepps; ***W:*** Shawn Schepps; ***C:*** Feliks Parnell.

Lip Service 1/2 *Out of Synch* **2000** Down-and-out record producer Roger Deacon (Outerbridge) is charged with making a singing star out of Sunni (Wuhrer), an industry bigwig's talentless girlfriend. Roger discovers shy housewife Maggie (O'Grady) has a terrific voice and persuades her to record the vocals while Sunni lip synchs. A VH1 original movie. **91m/C VHS, DVD.** Gail O'Grady, Kari Wuhrer, Peter Outerbridge, Stewart Bick; ***D:*** Graeme Campbell; ***W:*** Eric Williams; ***C:*** Nikos Evdemon; ***M:*** Jonathan Goldsmith. **CABLE**

Lips of Blood 1/2 *Levres de Sang* **1975** Rollin whips up a typically festive mix of sex, horror, and hallucination in what some have dubbed his best film. A young man (Philippe) has visions of a woman (Briand, AKA Annie Belle) he met as a child in an abandoned castle. When he sees her again, she persuades him to unleash a couple of female vampires. Do not expect anything more in the way of narrative, but it is a well-made low-budget French horror movie. French with subtitles. **88m/C DVD.** *FR* Jean-Loup Philippe, Annie Belle; ***D:*** Jean Rollin.

Lipstick **WOOF! 1976 (R)** Fashion model Margaux seeks revenge on the man who brutally attacked and raped her, after he preys on her kid sister (real-life sis Mariel, in her debut). Exquisitely exploitative excuse for entertainment. **90m/C VHS, DVD.** Margaux Hemingway, Anne Bancroft, Perry King, Chris Sarandon, Mariel Hemingway; ***D:*** Lamont Johnson; ***W:*** David Rayfiel; ***C:*** Bill Butler, William A. Fraker.

Lipstick Camera **1993 (R)** Keats wants a career in TV news and seeks out a successful freelance cameraman (Wimmer) to help her out. She also asks to borrow her techno-friend Feldman's mini-camera and then goes after a story on an ex-spy and his sexy companion. Only no one expects what the camera captures. Weak plot but strong cast and high-end production. **93m/C VHS, DVD.** Ele Keats, Brian Wimmer, Corey Feldman, Sandahl Bergman, Terry O'Quinn; ***D:*** Mike Bonifer; ***W:*** Mike Bonifer; ***C:*** M. David Mullen; ***M:*** Jeff Rona.

Lipstick on Your Collar 1/2 **1994** British TV fantasy/drama set in the stuffy confines of the British War Offices during the Suez Crisis of 1956. Two army clerks fantasize about the world outside through daydreams set to original tunes. Last series for the innovative Potter; on three cassettes. **360m/C VHS.** *GB* Ewan McGregor, Giles Thomas, Louise Germaine, Bernard Hill; ***D:*** Renny Rye; ***W:*** Dennis Potter. **TV**

Liquid Dreams **1992 (R)** In this fast-paced, futuristic thriller, Daly goes undercover as an erotic dancer in a glitzy strip joint to try and solve her sister's murder. She finds that the owner and clientele deal not only in sexual thrills, but also in a strange brain-sucking ritual that provides the ultimate rush. Also available in an unrated version. **92m/C VHS, DVD.** Richard Steinmetz, Candice Daly, Barry Dennen, Juan Fernandez, Tracey Walter, Frankie Thorn, Paul Bartel, Mink Stole, John Doe, Mark Manos; ***D:*** Mark Manos; ***W:*** Zach Davis, Mark Manos; ***C:*** Ed Tomney, Alexandre Magno.

Liquid Sky **1983 (R)** An androgynous bisexual model living in Manhattan is the primary attraction for a UFO, which lands atop her penthouse in search of the chemical nourishment that her sexual encounters provide. Low-budget, highly creative film may not be for everyone, but the audience for which it was made will love it. Look for Carlisle also playing a gay male. **112m/C VHS, DVD.** Anne Carlisle, Paula Sheppard, Bob Brady, Susan Doukas, Otto von Wernherr, Elaine C. Grove, Stanley Knap, Jack Adalist, Lloyd Ziff; ***D:*** Slava Tsukerman; ***W:*** Slava Tsukerman, Anne Carlisle; ***C:*** Yuri Neyman; ***M:*** Slava Tsukerman, Brenda Hutchinson.

Lisa **1990 (PG-13)** A young girl develops a crush on the new guy in town and arranges a meeting with him in which she pretends to be her mother. Little does she realize he's a psychotic serial killer. Lock your doors! Don't let anyone in if they have this video! **95m/C VHS.** Staci Keanan, Cheryl Ladd, D.W. Moffett, Tanya Fenmore, Jeffrey Tambor, Julie Cobb; ***D:*** Gary Sherman; ***W:*** Karen Clark; ***C:*** Alex Nepomniaschy.

Lisa and the Devil **WOOF!** *The House of Exorcism; La Casa Dell'Exorcismo; The Devil and the Dead; The Devil in the House of Exorcism; El Diablo se Lleva a los Muertos; Il Diavolo e i Morti; Lisa e il Diavolo* **1975 (R)** An unfortunate outing for Savalas and Sommer, about devil worship. Poor quality leaves little room for redemption. Just like on the telly, Telly's sucking on a sucker. A shortened version of the director's original 1972 release, re-edited and with additional footage added by producer Alfred Leone. **93m/C VHS, DVD.** *IT SP* Telly Savalas, Elke Sommer, Sylva Koscina, Robert Alda, Alessio Orano, Gabriele Tinti, Eduardo Fajardo, Espartaco (Spartaco) Santoni, Alida Valli; ***D:*** Mario Bava; ***W:*** Mario Bava, Alfred Leone; ***C:*** Cecilio Paniagua; ***M:*** Carlo Savina.

Lisa Picard Is Famous 1/2 **2001** Well, New Yorker Lisa (Wolf) would like to be famous but right now, she's best known for a cereal commercial. Neurotic, self-absorbed Lisa just can't catch that one big break—unlike her gay pal Tate (DeWolf) whose one-man confessional show becomes a hit. So Lisa agrees to let a filmmaker (Dunne) document her struggling career in the hopes it will help her would-be career. **87m/C VHS, DVD.** Laura Kirk, Nat DeWolf, Griffin Dunne; ***Cameos:*** Sandra Bullock, Charlie Sheen, Spike Lee; ***D:*** Griffin Dunne; ***W:*** Laura Kirk, Nat DeWolf; ***C:*** William Rexer; ***M:*** Evan Lurie.

Lisboa *Lisbon* **1999** Joao (Lopez) is a salesman who travels between Portugal and Spain. One day he picks up Berta (Maura) who is on her way to Lisbon and who refuses to tell him anything about herself. If he knew what was good for him, Joao would have made Berta get out of the car since her nasty husband Jose Luis (Luppi) and psychotic family are soon after them. Spanish with subtitles. **100m/C VHS, DVD.** *SP* Sergi Lopez, Carmen Maura, Federico Luppi; ***D:*** Antonio Hernandez; ***W:*** Antonio Hernandez, Enrique Braso; ***C:*** Aiter Mantxola; ***M:*** Victor Reyes.

Lisbon **1956** First film directed by Milland, shot in Portugal, details the adventures of a sea captain entangled in international espionage and crime while attempting to rescue damsel O'Hara's husband from communist doings. A familiar plot told with less-than-average panache. **90m/C VHS.** Ray Milland, Claude Rains, Maureen O'Hara, Francis Lederer, Percy Marmont; ***D:*** Ray Milland.

Lisbon Story **1994** Director Friedrich Monroe (Bauchau) calls his friend, sound engineer Phillip Winter (Vogler), to come to Lisbon to help him finish his film on the city. By the time Winter arrives in Portugal, Monroe has vanished, leaving the unfinished silent film behind. While waiting for his friend to return, Winter starts work, wandering through the city streets in search of inspiring sounds. English, German, and Portuguese with subtitles. **100m/C VHS.** *GE* Ruediger Vogler, Patrick Bauchau; ***D:*** Wim Wenders; ***W:*** Wim Wenders; ***C:*** Lisa Renzler.

The List **1999 (R)** When prostitute Gabrielle (Amick) gets herself arrested and tried for solicitation, she attempts to use her client book to barter for her freedom. Judge Miller (O'Neal) has to decide whether to make the list public and embarass many of his wealthy and powerful friends, but when Gabrielle's clients start turning up dead, the judge is forced to take action. **93m/C VHS, DVD.** Madchen Amick, Ryan O'Neal, Roc Lafortune, Ben Gazzara; ***D:*** Sylvain Guy; ***W:*** Sylvain Guy; ***C:*** Yves Belanger; ***M:*** Louis Babin. **VIDEO**

The List **2007 (PG)** Good vs. evil, but it can't get very intense with that rating. After Renny's (Jacobsen) father suddenly dies, the only son is surprised that the majority of his father's wealth has been left to a mysterious trust called the Covenant List of South Carolina, Ltd. When Renny investigates, he meets Jo Johnston (Burton), whose deceased father was also a member. The current head is the somewhat malevolent Desmond Larochette (McDowell), who tells them that the List dates back to the end of the Civil War and only male heirs are allowed to assume their father's place. But the more Renny and Jo learn, the less they like what's going on. Based on the novel by Robert Whitlow. **105m/C DVD.** Hilarie Burton, Malcolm McDowell, Will Patton, Pat Hingle, Chuck Carrington, Mary Beth Peil; ***D:*** Gary Wheeler; ***W:*** Gary Wheeler; ***C:*** Tom Priestley; ***M:*** James Covell. **VIDEO**

The List of Adrian Messenger **1963** A crafty murderer resorts to a variety of disguises to eliminate potential heirs to a family fortune. Solid Huston-directed thriller with a twist: you won't recognize any of the name stars. **98m/B VHS.** Kirk Douglas, George C. Scott, Robert Mitchum, Dana Wynter, Burt Lancaster, Frank Sinatra; ***D:*** John Huston; ***M:*** Jerry Goldsmith.

Listen 1/2 **1996 (R)** Sex and violence and a faulty cordless telephone. Krista's (Buxton) suffered a nervous breakdown after her breakup with Sarah (Langton). But now they're friends again and Krista's even encouraging Sarah's new romance with weirdo boyfriend Jake (Currie) who likes phone sex. Then there's the obscene phone caller who seems to live in Sarah's apartment building and a serial killer who preys on women. Lots of nastiness and it's easy to figure out who the real killer is. **104m/C VHS.** Brooke Langton, Sarah Buxton, Gordon Currie, Andy Romano, Joel Wyner; ***D:*** Gavin Wilding; ***W:*** Jonas Quastel, Michael Bafaro; ***C:*** Brian Pearson; ***M:*** David Davidson.

Listen, Darling 1/2 **1938** Garland is appealing in her first big screen role as Pinky Wingate, who decides to find the perfect husband for her widowed mother (Astor). Pinky and her friend Buzz (Bartholomew) manage to find Pidgeon and have him become the engaging objection of everyone's affections. ♫Zing! Went the Strings of My Heart; Ten Pins in the Sky; On the Bumpy Road to Love. **70m/C VHS.** Judy Garland, Freddie Bartholomew, Mary Astor, Walter Pidgeon, Alan Hale, Scotty Beckett; ***D:*** Edwin L. Marin.

Listen to Me 1/2 **1989 (PG-13)** A small-town college debate team heads for the big time when they go to a national debate tournament. The usual mutual-distaste-turns-to-romance thing. Cheesy-as-all-get-out climactic abortion debate, in front of supposed real-life Supreme Court justices—yeah, right. And Kirk Cameron: get an accent, will ya? **109m/C VHS.** Kirk Cameron, Jami Gertz, Roy Scheider, Amanda Peterson, Tim Quill, Christopher Atkins; ***D:*** Douglas Day Stewart; ***C:*** Fred W. Koenekamp; ***M:*** David Foster. Golden Raspberries '89: Worst Support. Actor (Atkins).

Listen to Your Heart 1/2 **1983** Office romance in the '80s! Sounds like a mediocre, forgettable made-for-TV comedy-drama—which is exactly what it is. If Jackson was the brainy one on "Charlie's Angels," why wasn't she smart enough to avoid this one? **90m/C VHS.** Tim Matheson, Kate Jackson; ***D:*** Don Taylor.

The Listening 1/2 **2006 (R)** Confusing thriller, set in 1999 in Rome, about global audio surveillance and corporate shenanigans. NSA official James (Parks) is after the perps who stole sensitive software. The trail leads to an unwitting Francesca (Sansa), who may become collateral damage if James can't prevent it. **103m/C DVD.** *GB IT* Michael Parks, Maya Sansa, Andrea Tidona, James Parks; ***D:*** Giacomo Martelli; ***W:*** Giacomo Martelli, Inigo Dominguez, Ricardo Brun; ***C:*** Eric Maddison; ***M:*** Christian Kusche-Tomasini.

Lisztomania **WOOF! 1975 (R)** Russell's excessive vision of what it must have been like to be classical composer/musician Franz Liszt, who is depicted as the first pop star. Rock opera in the tradition of "Tommy" with none of the sense or music. **106m/C VHS.** *GB* Roger Daltrey, Sara Kestelman, Paul Nicholas, Fiona Lewis, Ringo Starr, Veronica Quilligan, Nell Campbell, John Justin, Andrew Reilly, Anulka Dziubinska, Rick Wakeman, Rikki Howard, Felicity Devonshire, Aubrey Morris, Kenneth Colley, Ken Parry, Otto Diamont, Murray Melvin, Andrew Faulds, Oliver Reed; ***D:*** Ken Russell; ***W:*** Ken Russell; ***C:*** Peter Suschitzky; ***M:*** Rick Wakeman.

The Little American 1/2 **1917** German-American Karl Von Austreim leaves behind sweetheart Angela Moore, returning to Germany to fight in WWI. Angela travels to France to care for her dying aunt and discovers her aunt's chateau has been turned into a hospital. She remains in the face of a German advance and is naturally reunited with her much-changed beau. **80m/B VHS.** Mary Pickford, Jack Holt, Raymond Hatton, Walter Long, Hobart Bosworth, Ben Alexander, DeWitt Jennings; ***D:*** Cecil B. DeMille; ***W:*** Jeanie Macpherson; ***C:*** Alvin Wyckoff.

Little Annie Rooney **1925** A policeman's tomboy daughter spends her time mothering her father and brother while getting into mischief with street punks. Minor melodrama. Silent. **60m/B VHS, DVD.** Mary Pickford, William Haines, Walter James, Gordon Griffith, Vola Vale; ***D:*** William Beaudine; ***C:*** Charles Rosher.

Little Athens **2005 (R)** A day in the life of a multitude of annoying characters who live in Little Athens, Arizona. Drug dealer

Jimmy is in hock to a bookie; Heather's paranoid that her boyfriend is cheating on her; self-involved Jessica is worried that her boyfriend will come after her for allegedly giving him an STD; and loopy buds Pedro and Corey are scrambling to pay their overdue rent before they're evicted. All come together at the same party where they'll continue to make bad choices and you won't care. **105m/C DVD.** John Patrick Amedori, Erica Leerhsen, Eric Szmanda, Rachel Miner, Jill Ritchie, Kenny Morrison, Jorge Garcia, DJ Qualls, Michael Pena, Michelle Horn; ***D:*** Tom Zuber; ***W:*** Tom Zuber, Jeff Zuber; ***C:*** Lisa Wiegand; ***M:*** Barak Moffitt.

Little Ballerina **1947** A young dancer struggles against misfortune and jealousy to succeed in the world of ballet, under the auspices of Fonteyn. **62m/B VHS.** Margot Fonteyn, Anthony Newley, Martita Hunt, Yvonne Marsh; ***D:*** Lewis Gilbert; ***W:*** Lewis Gilbert; ***C:*** Frank North.

Little Big Horn 1/2 *The Fighting Seventh* **1951** Low-budget depiction of Custer et al. at Little Big Horn actually has its gripping moments; solid acting all around helps. **88m/B VHS, DVD.** Marie Windsor, John Ireland, Lloyd Bridges, Reed Hadley, Hugh O'Brian, Jim Davis; ***D:*** Charles Marquis Warren.

Little Big League 1/2 **1994 (PG)** 12-year-old inherits the Minnesota Twins baseball team from his grandfather, appoints himself manager when everyone else declines, and becomes the youngest owner-manager in history. Nothing new about the premise, but kids and America's favorite pastime add up to good clean family fun. Features real-life baseball players, including the Ken Griffey, Jr. and Paul O'Neill. Good cast features TV's Busfield at first base. Screenwriting debut from Pincus, and directorial debut from the executive producer of "Seinfeld," Scheinman. **120m/C VHS, DVD.** Michael (Mike) Papajohn, Luke Edwards, Jason Robards Jr., Kevin Dunn, Dennis Farina, John Ashton, Jonathan Silverman, Wolfgang Bodison, Timothy Busfield, Ashley Crow, Scott Patterson, Billy L. Sullivan, Miles Feulner, Kevin Elster, Leon "Bull" Durham, Brad "The Animal" Lesley; ***Cameos:*** Don Mattingly, Ken Griffey Jr., Paul O'Neill; ***D:*** Andrew Scheinman; ***W:*** Gregory Pincus, Adam Scheinman.

Little Big Man 1/2 **1970 (PG)** Based on Thomas Berger's picaresque novel, this is the story of 121-year-old Jack Crabb and his quixotic life as gunslinger, charlatan, Indian, ally to George Custer, and the only white survivor of Little Big Horn. Told mainly through flashbacks. Hoffman provides a classic portrayal of Crabb, as fact and myth are jumbled and reshaped. **135m/C VHS, DVD.** Dustin Hoffman, Faye Dunaway, Chief Dan George, Richard Mulligan, Martin Balsam, Jeff Corey, Aimee (Amy) Eccles; ***D:*** Arthur Penn; ***W:*** Calder Willingham; ***C:*** Harry Stradling Jr. N.Y. Film Critics '70: Support. Actor (George); Natl. Soc. Film Critics '70: Support. Actor (George).

Little Bigfoot 1/2 **1996 (PG)** The Shoemaker family are taking a camping vacation when the kids discover a baby bigfoot in the wilderness. They find out the hairy little guy and his mom are threatened by the owner of a logging company, who's hired a group of hunters to get rid of the critters. **99m/C VHS, DVD.** Ross Malinger, P.J. Soles, Ken Tigar, Kelly Packard, Don Stroud, Matt McCoy; ***D:*** Art Camacho; ***W:*** Richard Preston Jr.; ***C:*** Ken Blakey; ***M:*** Louis Febre. **VIDEO**

Little Bigfoot 2: The Journey Home **1997 (PG)** Dull and saccharine sequel has an unlikeable family on a camping trip finding and protecting the titular critter from hunters and an evil industrialist. **93m/C VHS, DVD.** Stephen Furst, Steve Eastin, Tom Bosley, Taran Noah Smith, Michael Fishman, Art Camacho; ***D:*** Art Camacho; ***W:*** Art Camacho; ***M:*** Jim Halfpenny.

A Little Bit of Soul 1/2 **1997 (R)** Godfrey Usher (Rush) is an ambitious politician whose present position is that of federal treasurer, a job he has no clue about. Usher is married to Grace Michael (Mitchell) the head of a philanthropic foundation. Scientist Richard Shorkinghorm (Wenham) and rival, ex-lover Kate Haslett (O'Connor), have both applied for funding from the foundation and are invited to the Usher/Michael home for a weekend. Surprises abound for Richard and Kate when they discover their kinky hosts are Satanists. Amusing comedy does falter but its not the fault of the performers. **83m/C VHS, DVD.** *AU* Geoffrey Rush, David Wenham, Frances O'Connor, Heather Mitchell, John Gaden, Kerry Walker; ***D:*** Peter Duncan; ***W:*** Peter Duncan; ***C:*** Martin McGrath; ***M:*** Nigel Westlake.

Little Black Book **2004 (PG-13)** You know times are tough for actresses of a certain age (in this case Hunter) when they are reduced to playing eccentric mentors to the pouty blonde flavor of the moment. That would be Murphy as Stacy, who wants to be a broadcast journalist but is slaving away at a lousy daytime talk show hosted by Kippie Kann (a slumming Bates). Maybe things will go better in her romance with sports agent Derek (Livingston). Oops, shouldn't have peeked at his Palm Pilot, which lists his glamorous, maybe-not-so-ex-girlfriends. Since Derek doesn't talk about his past relationships, Stacy sets up "interviews" with three of the gals (Maran, Jones, Nicholson) to check out her possible rivals. Eventually, her snooping and her job converge into one big mess—a fitting description of the movie. **95m/C DVD.** *US* Brittany Murphy, Holly Hunter, Kathy Bates, Ron Livingston, Julianne Nicholson, Stephen Tobolowsky, Kevin Sussman, Josie Maran, Rashida Jones, Jason Antoon; ***D:*** Nick Hurran; ***W:*** Elisa Bell, Melissa Carter; ***C:*** Theo van de Sande; ***M:*** Christophe Beck.

Little Boy Blue **1997** You want dysfunction? This movie has got it. Controlling husbands, impotence, uncontrollable rage, incest, family secrets, alcoholics... Southern Gothic family drama focuses on Jimmy (Phillippe), the son of paranoid and impotent Vietnam vet Ray West (Savage). He decides not to go to college because he's afraid to leave his younger brothers with dear ol' abusive alcoholic Dad. Ray runs a bar with his timid wife Kate (Kinski), who he also forces to sleep with son Jimmy to satisfy his own twisted sexual kicks. After a man comes snooping around and ends up dead in the bathroom of the bar, secrets from the past are dredged up. A mysterious woman (Knight) arrives bringing revenge on Ray for ruining her life and the possibility of freedom for the tormented family. Excellent performances (especially Kinski and Phillippe) save the twisted ball of loose strings that make up the farfetched plot. **107m/C VHS.** Ryan Phillippe, John Savage, Nastassja Kinski, Shirley Knight, Jenny Lewis, Tyrin Turner; ***D:*** Antonio Tibaldi; ***W:*** Michael Boston; ***C:*** Ron Hagen; ***M:*** Stewart Copeland.

Little Boy Lost **1978 (G)** The true story of the disappearance of a young boy in Australia. **92m/C VHS.** *AU* John Hargreaves, Tony Barry, Lorna Lesley; ***D:*** Alan Spires.

Little Buddha **1993 (PG)** Tibetan Lama Norbu informs the Seattle Konrad family that their 10-year-old son Jesse may be the reincarnation of a respected monk. He wants to take the boy back to Tibet to find out and, with some apparently minor doubts, the family head off on their spiritual quest. In an effort to instruct Jesse in Buddhism, this journey is interspersed with the story of Prince Siddhartha, who will leave behind his worldly ways to follow the path towards enlightenment and become the Buddha. The two stories are an ill-fit, the acting awkward (with the exception of Ruocheng as the wise Norbu), but boy, does the film look good (from cinematographer Vittorio Storaro). Filmed on location in Nepal and Bhutan. **123m/C VHS, DVD.** Keanu Reeves, Alex Wiesendanger, Ying Ruocheng, Chris Isaak, Bridget Fonda; ***D:*** Bernardo Bertolucci; ***W:*** Mark Peploe, Rudy Wurlitzer; ***C:*** Vittorio Storaro; ***M:*** Ryuichi Sakamoto.

Little Caesar **1930** A small-time hood rises to become a gangland czar, but his downfall is as rapid as his rise. Still thrilling. The role of Rico made Robinson a star and typecast him as a crook for all time. **80m/B VHS, DVD.** Edward G. Robinson, Glenda Farrell, Sidney Blackmer, Douglas Fairbanks Jr.; ***D:*** Mervyn LeRoy; ***C:*** Gaetano Antonio "Tony" Gaudio. Natl. Film Reg. '00.

Little Chenier: A Cajun Story **2006 (R)** Beaux Dupuis (Schaech) looks out for his mentally retarded brother Pemon (Koehler) while scratching out a living on the titular Louisiana bayou. Beaux's reckless enough to have taken up again with Mary-Louise (Braun), an ex-girlfriend who married deputy sheriff Carl Lebauve (Davidson). When Pemon is accused of a crime, jealous Carl works to turn the community against the brothers. The area where the film was shot was destroyed by Hurricane Rita only weeks after shooting was completed. **100m/C DVD.** Johnathon Schaech, Frederick Koehler, Clifton (Gonzalez) Collins Jr., Chris Mulkey, Tamara Braun, Jeremy Davidson; ***D:*** Bethany Wolf; ***W:*** Tamara Braun, Bethany Wolf, Jace Johnson; ***C:*** Tanya Koop; ***M:*** Michael Picton.

Little Children **2006 (R)** Adultery in the 'burbs and a vulnerable sex offender on parole collide in Perrotta's adaptation of his 2004 novel. Bored outsider Sarah (Winslet) is with the other moms at the playground where handsome house husband Brad (Wilson) also plays with his son. A brief first meeting slowly leads to an affair, eventually discovered by Brad's successful wife Kathy (Connelly). Meanwhile, Brad's tightly wound, ex-cop buddy Larry (Emmerich) is on a mission to rid the neighborhood of ex-con Ronald (Haley), who's living with his doting mom (Somerville). Field drags things out too long but the performances are strong. **130m/C DVD.** *US* Kate Winslet, Patrick Wilson, Jennifer Connelly, Jackie Earle Haley, Noah Emmerich, Gregg Edelman, Phyllis Somerville, Sadie Goldstein; ***D:*** Todd Field; ***W:*** Todd Field, Tom Perrotta; ***C:*** Antonio Calvache; ***M:*** Thomas Newman; ***Nar:*** Will Lyman.

Little Church Around the Corner 1/2 **1923** Silent small town melodrama about a preacher who falls in love with a mine owner's daughter, but finds he isn't dad's favorite fella when he confronts him about poor mining conditions. When the mine caves in, the preacher man's caught between a rock and hard place when his sweetie's family needs protection from an angry mob. **70m/B VHS.** Kenneth Harlan, Hobart Bosworth, Walter Long, Pauline Starke, Alec B. Francis, Margaret Seddon, George Cooper; ***D:*** William A. Seiter.

Little City 1/2 **1997 (R)** Best friends Kevin (Bon Jovi) and Adam (Charles) discover sex can screw up the best relationship. Adam's current girlfriend Nina (Sciorra) is having an affair with Kevin, while his ex-girlfriend Kate (Going) is having problems with her girlfriend Ann (Williams), who broke up Adam and Kate. Now Kate is having a fling with Rebecca (Miller), who's just flirting with lesbianism, and Rebecca then gets involved with Adam. Meanwhile, Kevin decides he's in love with Nina (she's not reciprocating that emotion) and Kate begins thinking about going back to Adam. San Francisco turns out to be a very small town. **90m/C VHS, DVD.** Jon Bon Jovi, Penelope Ann Miller, Annabella Sciorra, Josh Charles, Joanna Going, JoBeth Williams; ***D:*** Roberto Benabib; ***W:*** Roberto Benabib; ***C:*** Randall Love.

The Little Colonel **1935 (PG)** After the Civil War, an embittered Southern patriarch turns his back on his family, until his dimple-cheeked granddaughter softens his heart. Hokey and heartwarming. Shirley's first teaming with Bill "Bojangles" Robinson features the famous dance scene. Adapted by William Conselman from the Annie Fellows Johnston best-seller. **80m/B VHS, DVD.** Shirley Temple, Lionel Barrymore, Evelyn Venable, John Lodge, Hattie McDaniel, Bill Robinson, Sidney Blackmer; ***D:*** David Butler; ***C:*** Arthur C. Miller.

Little Darlings **WOOF!** **1980 (R)** Distasteful premise has summer campers Kristy and Tatum in a race to lose their virginity. Kristy is better (at acting, that is); but who cares? And just who is meant to be the market for this movie, anyway? **95m/C VHS.** Tatum O'Neal, Kristy McNichol, Matt Dillon, Armand Assante, Margaret Blye; ***D:*** Ronald F. Maxwell; ***M:*** Charles Fox.

The Little Death **1995** Struggling musician Nick Hannon (Fraser) is forced to work for wealthy dad Ted (Walsh), who's married to young trophy wife Kelly (Gidley). She's being stalked by weirdo Bobby (Yoakam), who kills Ted but manages to get off by claiming self-defense. Kelly's no lonely widow since she's now bedding Nick but he soon has suspicions about his former stepmom's involvement in her hubby's death. **91m/C VHS.** Brent Fraser, Pamela Gidley, Dwight Yoakam, J.T. Walsh, Troy Beyer, D.W. Moffett, Richard Beymer; ***D:*** Jan Verheyen; ***W:*** Nicholas Bogner, Michael Holden; ***C:*** David Phillips; ***M:*** Christopher Tyng.

Little Devil **2007** Ten-year-old Oliver knows his parents' marriage is failing. Though they try to keep it from him, they can't stop drinking, fighting, and walking out. Upset that they may get divorced, Ollie first tries to be very, very good but when that doesn't work, he decides to be very, very bad instead. **131m/C DVD.** *GB* Robson Green, Maggie O'Neill, James Wilby, Emily Joyce, Joseph Friend; ***D:*** David Richards; ***W:*** Tim Loane; ***C:*** Andrew Speller; ***M:*** Hal Lindes. **TV**

Little Dorrit 1/2 **2008** Sprawling BBC miniseries based on the sprawling novel by Charles Dickens exposing the 19th-century's harsh class distinctions. Seamstress Amy Dorrit (Foy) has grown up in debtor's prison where her addled father William (Courtenay) has been held for more than 20 years. Employed by Mrs. Clennam (Parfit), Dorrit's plight comes to the attention of Arthur Clennam (Macfadyen), who fears his family is responsible for the Dorrits' misfortune. Romantic impediments keep them apart and there's blackmail, bureaucracy, and shady financial doings besides. **452m/C DVD.** Matthew Macfayden, Tom Courtenay, Judy Parfitt, Alun Armstrong, Claire Foy, Andy Serkis, Emma Pierson, Eddie Marsan, Bill Paterson, Sue Johnston, Russell Tovey, Georgia King, James Fleet; ***D:*** Diarmuid Lawrence, Dearbhla Walsh, Adam Smith; ***W:*** Andrew Davies; ***C:*** Owen McPolin, Lukas Strebel, Alan Almond; ***M:*** John Lunn. **TV**

Little Dorrit, Film 1: Nobody's Fault **1988** The mammoth version of the Dickens tome, about a father and daughter trapped interminably in the dreaded Marshalsea debtors' prison, and the good samaritan who works to free them. Told in two parts (on four tapes), "Nobody's Fault," and "Little Dorrit's Story." **180m/C VHS.** *GB* Alec Guinness, Derek Jacobi, Cyril Cusack, Sarah Pickering, Joan Greenwood, Max Wall, Amelda Brown, Daniel Chatto, Miriam Margolyes, Bill Fraser, Roshan Seth, Michael Elphick, Eleanor Bron, Patricia Hayes, Robert Morley, Sophie Ward; ***D:*** Christine Edzard; ***W:*** Christine Edzard; ***C:*** Bruno de Keyzer. L.A. Film Critics '88: Film, Support. Actor (Guinness). **TV**

Little Dorrit, Film 2: Little Dorrit's Story **1988** The second half of the monumental adaptation of Dickens' most popular novel during his lifetime tells of Amy Dorrit's rise from debtor's prison to happiness. **189m/C VHS.** *GB* Alec Guinness, Derek Jacobi, Cyril Cusack, Sarah Pickering, Joan Greenwood, Max Wall, Amelda Brown, Daniel Chatto, Miriam Margolyes, Bill Fraser, Roshan Seth, Michael Elphick, Patricia Hayes, Robert Morley, Sophie Ward, Eleanor Bron; ***D:*** Christine Edzard; ***W:*** Christine Edzard; ***C:*** Bruno de Keyzer. L.A. Film Critics '88: Film, Support. Actor (Guinness). **TV**

Little Dragons **1980** A grandfather and two young karate students rescue a family held captive by a backwoods gang. **90m/C VHS.** Ann Sothern, Joe Spinell, Charles Lane, Chris Petersen, Pat Petersen, Sally Boyden, Rick Lenz, Sharon Weber, Tony Bill; ***D:*** Curtis Hanson; ***W:*** Alan Ormsby.

The Little Drummer Girl **1984 (R)** An Israeli counterintelligence agent recruits an actress sympathetic to the Palestinian cause to trap a fanatical terrorist leader. Solid performances from Keaton as the actress and Kinski as the Israeli counter-intelligence office sustain interest through a puzzling, sometimes boring and frustrating, cinematic maze of espionage. Keaton is at or near her very best. Based on the bestselling novel by John Le Carre. **130m/C VHS.** Diane Keaton, Klaus Kinski, Yorgo Voyagis, Sami Frey, Michael Cristofer, Anna Massey, Thorley Walters; ***D:*** George Roy Hill; ***M:*** Dave Grusin.

Little Fish **2005 (R)** As an Asian video store manager in the tough "Little Saigon" suburb of Sydney, Australia, Tracy Heart (Blanchett) has bigger dreams of starting her own business, although the recovering junkie is having trouble securing the funds—a fact she often fibs about in conversation. Her protective mother Janelle (Hazlehurst) labors to keep her daughter away from the bad influences that surround her, including the return of her old boyfriend and her estranged stepfather Lionel (Weaving), a user who Janelle accuses of influencing Tracy's addiction. Vivid storyline focuses on living life as a post-addict. Blanchett deftly delivers (as usual). **114m/C DVD.** Cate Blanchett, Sam Neill, Hugo Weaving, Martin Henderson, Noni Hazlehurst, Dustin Nguyen, Joel Tobeck; ***D:*** Rowan Woods; ***W:*** Jacquelin Perske; ***C:*** Danny Ruhlmann; ***M:*** Nathan Larson.

The Little Foxes ½ **1941** A vicious southern woman will destroy everyone around her to satisfy her desire for wealth and power. Filled with corrupt characters who commit numerous revolting deeds. The vicious matriarch is a part made to fit for Davis, and she makes the most of it. Script by Lillian Hellman from her own play. **116m/B VHS, DVD.** Bette Davis, Herbert Marshall, Dan Duryea, Teresa Wright, Charles Dingle, Richard Carlson, Carl Benton Reid, Patricia Collinge; ***D:*** William Wyler; ***W:*** Lillian Hellman; ***C:*** Gregg Toland; ***M:*** Meredith Willson.

Little Fugitive **1953** Seven-year-old Joey (Andrusco) is convinced by his Brooklyn pals that he's murdered his brother. So the tyke takes off and winds up wandering lost around Coney Island. Independent feature made on a miniscule budget features endearing performances from non-pros. **80m/C VHS, DVD.** Richie Andrusco, Ricky Brewster, Winnifred Cushing, Jay Williams; ***D:*** Morris Engel, Ruth Orkin, Ray Ashley; ***W:*** Ray Ashley; ***C:*** Morris Engel; ***M:*** Eddy Manson. Natl. Film Reg. '97.

Little Fugitive **2006** His dad's in prison and his mom's neglectful, so Lenny must look after his 7-year-old brother Joey. On his 12th birthday, Lenny and his friends intend to go to Coney Island and he tells Joey he must stay behind. When Joey disobeys, Lenny plays a prank that backfires and Joey runs away. A more downbeat remake of the 1953 film. **87m/C DVD.** Justina Machado, Peter Dinklage, Lois Smith, Brendan Sexton III, David Castro, Nicolas Marti-Salgado, Austin Talynn Carpenter; ***D:*** Joanna Lipper; ***W:*** Joanna Lipper; ***C:*** Richard Sands; ***M:*** Barrington Pheloung.

The Little Giant ½ **1933** Gangster spoof finds successful Chicago bootlegger Bugs Ahearn (Robinson) deciding to move to California and live the society life. He falls for Polly (Vinson), a cold-hearted dame with a larcenous family who get Bugs involved in a stock swindle. When it looks like Bugs is going to take the fall, he contacts his Chicago cohorts and uses them as muscle to clear himself. Meanwhile, sweet Ruth (Astor), who's been working as Bugs' social secretary, waits for the lug to realize she's the perfect doll for him. **70m/B DVD.** Edward G. Robinson, Helen Vinson, Mary Astor, Kenneth Thomson, Russell Hopton, Berton Churchill, Shirley Grey, Donald Dillaway, Louise Mackintosh; ***D:*** Roy Del Ruth; ***W:*** Robert Lord, Wilson Mizner; ***C:*** Sid Hickox.

Little Giant ½ **1946** The duo fly separately in this entry, which highlights Costello's comic talents and leaves Abbott in the supporting role. Costello is a country bumpkin come to the big city to get enough money to marry his sweetheart. He's hired to sell vacuum cleaners by Abbott and becomes the butt of everyone's jokes but the joke's on them when Lou becomes the company's top-selling salesman. **92m/B VHS, DVD.** Bud Abbott, Lou Costello, Brenda Joyce, Jacqueline DeWit, George Cleveland, Elena Verdugo, Mary Gordon, Pierre Watkin; ***D:*** William A. Seiter; ***W:*** Walter DeLeon.

Little Giants ½ **1994 (PG)** Familiar kids/sport movie about the klutzy coach (Moranis) of an equally woeful pee-wee football team. Coach Danny is up against his overbearing big brother Kevin (O'Neill), former local football hero and the coach of the best team in town. Naturally, there's the big game between the misfit underdogs and the stars. Predictable, of course, but not without some amusing moments. **106m/C VHS, DVD.** Rick Moranis, Ed O'Neill, Shawna Waldron, Mary Ellen Trainor, Devon Sawa, Susanna Thompson, Todd Bosley, Alexa Vega, Joey Simmrin, Sam Horrigan, Brian Haley, Mathew McCurley, Harry Shearer, Dabbs Greer; ***Cameos:*** John Madden; ***D:*** Duwayne Dunham; ***W:*** Tommy Swerdlow, Michael Goldberg, James Ferguson, Robert Shallcross; ***C:*** Janusz Kaminski; ***M:*** John Debney.

Little Girl... Big Tease **1975 (R)** Teen society girl is kidnapped and exploited (along with the viewer) by a group which includes her teacher. **86m/C VHS.** Jody Ray, Rebecca Brooke; ***D:*** Roberto Mitrotti.

The Little Girl Who Lives down the Lane ½ **1976 (PG)** Engrossing, offbeat thriller about a strange 13-year-old girl whose father is never home, and who hides something—we won't say what—in her basement. Very young Foster is excellent, as are her supporters, including Sheen as the child molester who knows what she's hiding. Based on the novel by Koenig, who also penned the script. **90m/C VHS, DVD.** *CA FR* Jodie Foster, Martin Sheen, Alexis Smith, Scott Jacoby, Mort Shuman, Dorothy Davis, Hubert Noel, Jacques Famery, Mary Morter, Judie Wildman; ***D:*** Nicolas Gessner; ***W:*** Laird Koenig; ***C:*** Rene Verzier; ***M:*** Christian Gaubert.

Little Gloria... Happy at Last ½ **1984** Miniseries based on the best-selling book about the custody battle over child heiress Gloria Vanderbilt, and her tumultuous youth. Lansbury leads a fine cast as the poor little rich girl's aunt Gertrude, the matriarchal family power broker. **180m/C VHS.** Bette Davis, Angela Lansbury, Christopher Plummer, Maureen Stapleton, Martin Balsam, Barnard Hughes, John Hillerman; ***D:*** Waris Hussein. **TV**

Little Heroes ½ **1991 (G)** An impoverished little girl gets through hard times with the aid of her loyal dog (the Hound can relate). A low-budget family tearjerker that nonetheless works, it claims to be based on a true story. **78m/C VHS, DVD.** Raeanin Simpson, Katherine Willis, Keith Christensen; ***D:*** Craig Clyde; ***W:*** Craig Clyde; ***M:*** Jon McCallum.

Little House on the Prairie **1974** Pilot for the TV series based on the life of Laura Ingalls Wilder and her family's struggles on the American plains in the 1860s. Other episodes are also available on tape, including one in which Patricia Neal guest stars as a terminally ill widow seeking a home for her children. Neal's performance earned her a best actress Emmy in 1975. **98m/C VHS, DVD.** Michael Landon, Karen Grassle, Victor French, Melissa Gilbert, Melissa Sue Anderson; ***D:*** Michael Landon. **TV**

Little Indian, Big City ½ *An Indian in the City; Un Indien dans la Ville* **1995 (PG)** French blockbuster dubbed over with "Americanized" English to give U.S. audiences an appetite for upcoming Disney remake. Lhermitte travels to the Amazon to finalize the divorce of a long-dead marriage, only to find he has a 12-year-old son, Mimi-Siku (Briand). Father and son bond and Dad decides to bring the jungle-bred boy to his home in Paris. Dubbing process unfortunately tomahawks this charming story as loin cloth meets Eiffel Tower, but Lhermitte, Briand and Miou-Miou (as estranged wife Patricia) shine through. Subplot of Russian mobsters who cut the fingers off their victims gives an indication of the French definition of "family fare." **90m/C VHS.** *FR* Thierry Lhermitte, Miou-Miou, Patrick Timsit, Arielle Dombasle, Ludwig Briand; ***D:*** Herve Palud; ***W:*** Thierry Lhermitte, Herve Palud, Philippe Bruneau, Igor Aptekman; ***C:*** Pierre Lorraine; ***M:*** Manu Katche.

A Little Inside ½ **2001 (PG)** Ed Mills (King) is a promising minor-league baseball player who quits the game when his wife dies so he can care for their daughter. Five years later, Ed is still struggling with this parenting gig, especially since Abby (Eisenberg) is growing up and getting into girlier things than Ed can cope with. So, since Abby does like baseball, Ed decides to take a second shot at rejoining his old team and regaining Abby's attention. The pint-sized Eisenberg is a scene-stealer par excellence. **95m/C VHS, DVD.** Benjamin King, Hallie Kate Eisenberg, Kathy Baker, Frankie Faison, Amanda Detmer, Jay Harrington, Sean Michael Arthur, Jared Padalecki; ***D:*** Kara Harshbarger; ***W:*** Kara Harshbarger; ***M:*** James Levine. **VIDEO**

Little John ½ **2002** Natalie Britain (Reuben) is a Family Court judge with a secret of her own. Twelve years ago, she gave birth to a baby boy that she thought was put up for adoption. Instead, Little John (Bailey Jr.), known as L.J., was raised on a Texas farm by Natalie's estranged father John (Rhames). When John's health begins to fail, it's time for his daughter to learn the truth and for L.J. to get to know his mom. **98m/C VHS, DVD.** Gloria Reuben, Ving Rhames, Robert Bailey Jr., Patty Duke; ***D:*** Dick Lowry. **TV**

The Little Kidnappers ½ **1990 (G)** Embittered man (Heston) is forced to take in his Scottish grandsons when the two boys are orphaned. They settle in with gramps in Nova Scotia but when the duo decide to adopt the abandoned baby they've found, they are accused of being kidnappers. Cable remake of 1953 British film. **100m/C VHS.** *CA* Charlton Heston, Bruce Greenwood, Leah K. Pinsent, Charles Miller, Leo Wheatley, Patricia Gage; ***D:*** Donald Shebib. **CABLE**

Little Ladies of the Night *Diamond Alley* **1977** Former pimp tries to save Purl and other teenagers from the world of prostitution. Exploitation posing as "significant drama." **96m/C VHS, DVD.** Linda Purl, David Soul, Clifton Davis, Carolyn Jones, Louis Gossett Jr.; ***D:*** Marvin J. Chomsky.

Little Laura & Big John **1973** The true-life exploits of the small-time Ashley Gang in the Florida everglades around the turn of the century. Fabian's comeback vehicle, for what it's worth. **82m/C VHS, DVD.** Fabian, Karen Black; ***D:*** Luke Moberly.

Little Lord Fauntleroy ½ **1936** The vintage Hollywood version of the Frances Hodgson Burnett story of a fatherless American boy who discovers he's heir to a British dukedom. Also available in computer-colorized version. Well cast, charming, remade for TV in 1980. Smith is loveable as the noble tyke's crusty old guardian. **102m/B VHS, DVD.** Freddie Bartholomew, Sir C. Aubrey Smith, Mickey Rooney, Dolores Costello, Jessie Ralph, Guy Kibbee; ***D:*** John Cromwell; ***W:*** Hugh Walpole; ***C:*** Charles Rosher; ***M:*** Max Steiner.

Little Lord Fauntleroy ½ **1980** A poor boy in New York suddenly finds himself the heir to his grandfather's estate in England. Lavish remake of the 1936 classic, adapted from Frances Hodgson Burnett's novel. Well-deserved Emmy winner for photography; Guinness is his usual old-pro self. **98m/C VHS.** Rick Schroder, Alec Guinness, Victoria Tennant, Eric Porter, Colin Blakely, Connie Booth, Rachel Kempson; ***D:*** Jack Gold. **TV**

Little Lord Fauntleroy ½ **1995 (G)** British TV adaptation of the Frances Hodgson Burnett classic finds Cedric Erroll's life changing forever when he's discovered to be the only heir to the Earl of Dorincourt. But the Earl turns out to be a bitter miser and it's up to the innocent child to get grandpa to enjoy life. **100m/C VHS, DVD.** *GB* Michael Benz, Betsy Brantley, George Baker, Bernice Stegers; ***D:*** Andrew Morgan.

Little Man **2006 (PG-13)** Another Wayans family vehicle, probably the worst yet, attempts to make a film about a dwarf jewel thief who poses as a baby in order to retrieve a stolen diamond he stashed with an unsuspecting couple. CGI-manipulation puts Wayans' face on a pint-sized body, while the "humor" seems to have been lifted directly from old Bugs Bunny cartoons and the crotch-shots of "America's Funniest Home Videos," either of which are better than this clunker. Directed by elder Wayans sib, Keenen Ivory. **97m/C DVD, Blu-ray Disc.** *US* Marlon Wayans, Shawn Wayans, Kerry Washington, Tracy Morgan, John Witherspoon, Lochlyn Munro, Chazz Palminteri, Linden Porco, Molly Shannon, Gabe Pimental, Paul DeMielche, Alex Borstein, Brittany Daniel; ***D:*** Keenen Ivory Wayans; ***W:*** Marlon Wayans, Shawn Wayans, Keenen Ivory Wayans; ***C:*** Steven Bernstein; ***M:*** Teddy Castellucci. Golden Raspberries '06: Worst Actor (Wayans), Worst Actor (Wayans), Worst Remake.

Little Man Tate **1991 (PG)** A seven-year-old genius is the prize in a tug of war between his mother, who wants him to lead a normal life, and a domineering school director who loves him for his intellect. An acclaimed directorial debut for Foster, with overtones of her own extraordinary life as a child prodigy. **99m/C VHS, DVD.** Jodie Foster, Dianne Wiest, Harry Connick Jr., Adam Hann-Byrd, George Plimpton, Debi Mazar, Celia Weston, David Hyde Pierce, Danitra Vance, Josh Mostel, P.J. Ochlan; ***D:*** Jodie Foster; ***W:*** Scott Frank; ***C:*** Mike Southon; ***M:*** Mark Isham.

Little Manhattan **2005 (PG)** Puppy love. Average 11-year-old Gabe (Hutcherson) likes to hang out with his pals and play hoops. Then, in karate class, he meets Rosemary (Ray) and Gabe is instantly smitten. But handling all these new emotions makes for some awkward moments. The overly-adult narration by Gabe is jarring but the outlook is sunny. **90m/C DVD.** Bradley Whitford, Cynthia Nixon, Josh Hutcherson, Willie Garson, Charlie Ray; ***D:*** Marc Levin; ***W:*** Jennifer Flacket; ***C:*** Tim Orr; ***M:*** Chad Fischer.

Little Marines **1990** Three young boys journey into the wilderness for three days of fun and instead embark on an incredible adventure. **90m/C VHS, DVD.** Stephen Baker, Steve Landers Jr., Noah Williams; ***D:*** A.J. Hixon.

The Little Match Girl **1984** A musical version of the Hans Christian Andersen classic about a girl whose dying grandmother tells her of the magic in the matches she sells. **54m/C VHS.** Monica McSwain, Nancy Duncan, Matt McKim, Don Hays; ***D:*** Mark Hoeger.

The Little Match Girl **1987** The Hans Christian Andersen Yuletide classic about an orphan selling magical matches, this time set in the 1920s, with the littlest "Cosby" kid in the title role. Ain't she cute? **96m/C VHS.** *GB* Keisha Knight Pulliam, Maryedith Burrell, William Daniels, Hallie Foote, Bill Davis, Rue McClanahan, John Rhys-Davies, Jim Metzler; ***D:*** Michael Lindsay-Hogg; ***W:*** Maryedith Burrell.

Little Men ½ **1940** A modern version of the classic juvenile story by Louisa May Alcott is too cute for words. **86m/B VHS, DVD.** Jack Oakie, Jimmy Lydon, Kay Francis, George Bancroft, Anne Howard; ***D:*** Norman Z. McLeod.

Little Men ½ **1998 (PG)** Louisa May Alcott's sequel to "Little Women" hits the screen with a lot less hoopla than its 1994 predecessor. Jo March (Hemingway) has grown up, married Fritz Bhaer (Sarandon), and opened an idyllic, wholesome school for troubled boys. The house is immaculate, the grounds are beautiful, and the boys are little angels. That is, until streetwise 14-year-old Dan (Cook) shows up. He soon has the boys smoking, drinking, and stealing, until they almost burn the place down. Since this is a family movie, with moral lessons to be learned, all's well by the end. Adults may find the syrupy sweetness too much to take, and the characters are barely two-dimensional, but young kids should enjoy it. **98m/C VHS.** Mariel Hemingway, Chris Sarandon, Michael Caloz, Ben Cook, Michael Yarmush, Gabrielle Boni, Ricky Mabe, Julia Garland, B.J. McLellan, Tyler Hines, Kathleen Fee; ***D:*** Rodney Gibbons; ***W:*** Mark Evan Schwartz; ***C:*** Arch Archambault; ***M:*** Milan Kymlicka.

The Little Mermaid ½ **1975 (G)** An animated version of Hans Christian Andersen's tale about a little mermaid who rescues a prince whose boat has capsized. She immediately falls in love and wishes that she could become a human girl. Not to be confused with the 1989 Disney version. **71m/C VHS.** *JP* ***D:*** Tim Reid; ***M:*** Ronald Goodwin; ***V:*** Kirsten Bishop, Ian Finley, Thor Bishopric.

The Little Mermaid ½ **1989 (G)** Headstrong teenage mermaid falls in love with a human prince and longs to be human too. She makes a pact with the evil Sea Witch to trade her voice for a pair of legs; based on the famous Hans Christian Andersen tale. Charming family musical, which harks back to the days of classic Disney animation, and hails a new era of superb Disney animated musicals. Sebastian the Crab nearly steals the show with his wit and showstopping number "Under the Sea." ♫Under the Sea; Kiss the Girl; Daughters of Triton; Part of Your World; Poor Unfortunate Souls; Les Poissons. **82m/C VHS, DVD.** ***D:*** John Musker, Ron Clements; ***W:*** John Musker, Ron Clements; ***M:*** Alan Menken, Howard Ashman; ***V:*** Jodi Benson, Christopher Daniel Barnes, Pat Carroll, Rene Auberjonois, Samuel E. Wright,

Buddy Hackett, Jason Marin, Edie McClurg, Kenneth Mars, Nancy Cartwright. Oscars '89: Song ("Under the Sea"), Orig. Score; Golden Globes '90: Song ("Under the Sea"), Score.

Little Minister 1934 An adaptation of the James Barrie novel about a prissy Scottish pastor who falls in love with a free-spirited gypsy...he thinks she is, in fact, the local earl's daughter, played to perfection by the young Hepburn. **101m/B VHS.** Katharine Hepburn, John Beal, Alan Hale, Donald Crisp; ***D:*** Richard Wallace; ***W:*** Victor Heerman; ***M:*** Max Steiner.

Little Miss Broadway 1938 Orphan Temple brings the residents of a theatrical boarding house together in hopes of getting them into show business. She and Durante give worthwhile performances. Also available in computer-colorized version. ♫ Be Optimistic; How Can I Thank You; I'll Build a Broadway For You; If All the World Were Paper; Thank You For the Use of the Hall; We Should Be Together; Swing Me an Old-Fashioned Song; When You Were Sweet Sixteen; Happy Birthday to You. **70m/B VHS, DVD.** Shirley Temple, George Murphy, Jimmy Durante, Phyllis Brooks, Edna May Oliver, George Barbier, Donald Meek, Jane Darwell; ***D:*** Irving Cummings; ***C:*** Arthur C. Miller.

Little Miss Innocence 1973 Recording executive tries to survive the amorous advances of the two attractive female hitchhikers that he drove home. **79m/C VHS.** John Alderman, Sandy Dempsey, Judy Medford; ***D:*** Chris Warfield.

Little Miss Marker *Girl in Pawn* **1934** Heartwarming story starring Temple as the title character, who is left with bookie Sorrowful Jones (Menjou) as the IOU for a gambling debt. But when her father doesn't return, it's up to Jones and his racetrack friends to make little Marky a home. Naturally, Temple steals her way into everyone's heart. Based on a story by Damon Runyon; remade three times as "Sorrowful Jones," as "40 Pounds of Trouble," and in 1980 with the original title. **88m/B VHS, DVD.** Adolphe Menjou, Shirley Temple, Dorothy Dell, Charles Bickford, Lynne Overman; ***D:*** Alexander Hall; ***W:*** Sam Hellman, Gladys Lehman, William R. Lipman; ***M:*** Ralph Rainger. Natl. Film Reg. '98.

Little Miss Marker ½ **1980 (PG)** Mediocre remake of the often retold story of a bookie who accepts a little girl as a security marker for a $10 bet. Disappointing performance from Curtis adds to an already dull film. **103m/C VHS, DVD.** Walter Matthau, Julie Andrews, Tony Curtis, Bob Newhart, Lee Grant, Sara Stimson, Brian Dennehy; ***D:*** Walter Bernstein; ***W:*** Walter Bernstein; ***M:*** Henry Mancini.

Little Miss Sunshine **2006 (R)** A quirky, dysfunctional family piles into their VW bus and road trips to California so little sis, Olive (Breslin), can compete (as an alternate from the Albuquerque region) in the titular pre-teen pageant, her young life's ambition. Along for the ride are her hugely unsuccessful motivational speaker dad (Kinnear), ready-to-snap mom (Collette), crass drug-snorting grandpa (Arkin), mute-by-choice Nietzschean brother (Dano), and suicidal despondent uncle (Carrell). Smart script in the hands of top-notch cast results in memorable, off-beat characters and an original, enjoyable movie. **101m/C DVD, Blu-ray Disc.** *US* Greg Kinnear, Toni Collette, Abigail Breslin, Steve Carell, Alan Arkin, Paul Franklin Dano, Bryan Cranston, Wallace (Wally) Langham, Mary Lynn Rajskub, Beth Grant; ***D:*** Jonathan Dayton, Valerie Faris; ***W:*** Michael Arndt; ***C:*** Tim Suhrstedt; ***M:*** Mychael Danna. Oscars '06: Orig. Screenplay, Support. Actor (Arkin); British Acad. '06: Orig. Screenplay, Support. Actor (Arkin); Ind. Spirit '07: Director (Dayton), Director (Faris), Film, Support. Actor (Arkin), First Screenplay; Screen Actors Guild '06: Cast; Writers Guild '06: Orig. Screenplay.

Little Monsters **1989 (PG)** A young boy (Savage) discovers a monster (Mandel) under his bed and eventually befriends it. The pair embark on adventures that land them in trouble. Hardworking, talented cast hurdles the weak script, but can't save the film. **100m/C VHS, DVD.** Fred Savage, Howie Mandel, Margaret Whitton, Ben Savage, Daniel Stern, Ric(k) Ducommun, Frank Whaley; ***D:*** Richard Alan Greenberg; ***W:*** Ted Elliott, Terry Rossio; ***C:*** Dick Bush; ***M:*** David Newman.

Little Moon & Jud McGraw ½ **1978** A wronged Indian woman and a framed cowpoke take their revenge on a small, corrupt town, razing it overnight. Already-weak plot is disabled by too many flashbacks. **92m/C VHS, DVD.** James Caan, Sammy Davis Jr., Stefanie Powers, Aldo Ray; ***D:*** Bernard Girard.

Little Mother 1971 Metzger's take on Argentina's Eva Peron highlights her sexual powers (of course) as it tells of Eva's climb out of poverty and into the heights of political power. Filmed in Yugoslavia. **95m/C VHS, DVD.** Christiane Kruger, Ivan Desny, Anton Diffring; ***D:*** Radley Metzger; ***W:*** Brian Phelan; ***C:*** Hans Jura.

Little Murders **1971 (PG)** Black comedy set in NYC. A woman convinces a passive photographer to marry her. Gardenia gives an excellent performance as the woman's father. A shadow of crime, depression, and strife seem to hangs over the funny parts of this film; more often depressing than anything else. Adapted by Jules Feiffer from his own play. **108m/C VHS, DVD.** Elliott Gould, Marcia Rodd, Vincent Gardenia, Elizabeth Wilson, Jon Korkes, Donald Sutherland, Alan Arkin, Lou Jacobi; ***D:*** Alan Arkin; ***W:*** Jules Feiffer; ***C:*** Gordon Willis.

Little Nellie Kelly ½ **1940** Garland plays both mother and daughter in a film based on a musical comedy by George M. Cohan. Garland is married to Irish cop Murphy but dies in childbirth. The film then advances 20 years to daughter Garland who is trying to make good on the stage and have a romance with a young man her father disapproves of. ♫ Nellie Kelly I Love You; Nellie is a Darling; It's a Great Day For the Irish; A Pretty Girl Milking Her Cow; Danny Boy; Singing in the Rain. **100m/B VHS.** Judy Garland, George Murphy, Charles Winninger, Douglas McPhail; ***D:*** Norman Taurog.

Little Nemo: Adventures in Slumberland ½ **1992 (G)** A bland animated tale of a young boy whose dreams take him to Slumberland. There, Nemo unwittingly unleashes a monster from Nightmare Land who kidnaps Slumberland's king. Nemo must then rescue the king—aided by the king's daughter, a comic squirrel sidekick, and a mischievous con-frog. Based on Winsor McCay's 1900 comic strip. Has some cute comic moments for the kiddies and, while the animation is better than Saturday-morning cartoon quality, it's not Disney. **85m/C VHS, DVD.** ***D:*** William T. Hurtz, Masami Hata; ***W:*** Chris Columbus, Richard Outten; ***M:*** Tom Chase, Steve Rucker; ***V:*** Gabriel Damon, Mickey Rooney, Rene Auberjonois, Daniel Mann, Laura Mooney, Bernard Erhard, William E. Martin.

Little Nicky **2000 (PG-13)** All hail Adam Sandler, King of the Idiot Boys! Notoriously bashed by critics, Sandler doesn't seem too worried about their opinions as he rolls around on the giant pile of money his crude but funny movies make. This time his underdog hero is Nicky (Sandler), the son of Satan (Keitel) and an angel (Witherspoon), who hangs out in a very cartoony hell. When Satan calls his sons together to name his heir, he instead declares that he will rule for another 10,000 years, causing brothers Adrian and Cassius to stage a rebellion by bringing hell to New York City. Nicky and his talking dog sidekick Mr. Beefy (voice of Smigel) are then sent to capture them. Along the way, he gains the standard Hollywood-issued love interest (Arquette). Broader and more satirical than most of Sandler's work, it's also the first that has him surrounded by top-line talent (not that it helps any). **93m/C VHS, DVD.** Adam Sandler, Rhys Ifans, Tommy (Tiny) Lister, Harvey Keitel, Patricia Arquette, Allen Covert, Blake Clark, Rodney Dangerfield, Kevin Nealon, Reese Witherspoon, Lewis Arquette, Dana Carvey, Jon Lovitz, Michael McKean, Quentin Tarantino, Carl Weathers, Rob Schneider, Clint Howard, Ellen Cleghorne, Fred Wolf; ***Cameos:*** Dan Marino, Henry Winkler, Regis Philbin, Ozzy Osbourne, Bill Walton; ***D:*** Steven Brill; ***W:*** Adam Sandler, Steven Brill, Tim Herlihy; ***C:*** Theo van de Sande; ***M:*** Teddy Castellucci; ***V:*** Robert Smigel.

A Little Night Music ½ **1977 (PG)** Features four interwoven, contemporary love stories adapted from the Broadway play, and based loosely on Bergman's "Smiles of a Summer Night." Taylor's pathetic rendition of "Send in the Clowns" should be banned. Filmed on location in Austria. **110m/C VHS, DVD.** Elizabeth Taylor, Diana Rigg, Hermione Gingold, Len Cariou, Lesley-Anne Down; ***D:*** Harold Prince. Oscars '77: Orig. Song Score and/or Adapt.

Little Nikita **1988 (PG)** A California boy (Phoenix) discovers that his parents are actually Soviet spies planted as American citizens for eventual call to duty. Poitier's performance as the FBI agent tracking the spies is about the only spark in this somewhat incoherent thriller. **98m/C VHS, DVD.** River Phoenix, Sidney Poitier, Richard Bradford, Richard Lynch, Caroline Kava, Lucy Deakins; ***D:*** Richard Benjamin; ***W:*** Bo Goldman, John Hill; ***M:*** Marvin Hamlisch.

Little Ninjas ½ **1992** Three top-notch ninja kids go up against the Sarak to rescue their friend who is being held hostage. **85m/C VHS.** Steven Nelson, Jon Anzaldo, Alan Godshaw; ***D:*** Emmett Alston.

Little Noises **1991** Glover stars as an artist who seeks not only fame and fortune, but also the love of his best friend (O'Neal). He finally creates a piece that his agent loves, but problems arise. **91m/C VHS.** Crispin Glover, Tatum O'Neal, Rik Mayall, Tate Donovan, John C. McGinley; ***D:*** Jane Spencer; ***W:*** Jane Spencer.

Little Odessa ½ **1994 (R)** Working for the stateside Russian mafia, hitman Joshua Shapira (Roth) returns to his childhood neighborhood to carry out his next assignment. Set in the Russian-Jewish emigre community of Brooklyn's Brighton Beach, Gray's directorial debut explores Joshua's relationship with his family—especially kid brother Reuben (Furlong). Not your typical mob opera, this one focuses more on characters than killing. Relationships between family members are explored to the hilt, but the audience is left with too many unanswered questions. Dimly lit and entirely too ambiguous, this family tragedy could spawn a serious case of depression. **98m/C VHS, DVD.** Tim Roth, Edward Furlong, Moira Kelly, Vanessa Redgrave, Maximilian Schell, Paul Guilfoyle, Natasha Andreichenko, David Vadim, Mina Bern, Boris McGiver, Mohammed Ghaffari, Michael Khumrov, Dmitry Preyers, David Ross, Ron Brice, Jace Kent, Marianna Lead, Gene Ruffini; ***D:*** James Gray; ***W:*** James Gray; ***C:*** Tom Richmond; ***M:*** Dana Sano.

Little Old New York ½ **1923** Set in 1806 New York, with Davies starring as a feisty Irish lass who, at her father's (Kerrigan) urging, disguises herself as her late brother so the family can claim an inheritance left to him. Cousin Larry (Ford) would have inherited had the O'Days not shown up but he still befriends young Pat, whom the confused guy eventually realizes is a girl. **106m/B DVD.** Marion Davies, Harrison Ford, J.M. Kerrigan, Stephen Carr, Sam Hardy, Riley Hatch, Mahlon Hamilton, Louis Wolheim, George Barraud, Courtenay Foote, Andrew Dillon, Harry Watson; ***D:*** Sidney Olcott; ***W:*** Luther Reed; ***C:*** Ira Morgan, Gilbert Warrenton.

Little Orphan Annie **1918** Surrounded by a group of children, poet James Whitcomb Riley narrates the story of Little Orphant Annie, who loses her mother at an early age and is sent to an orphanage where she charms the other children with her stories of ghosts and elves. **57m/B VHS.** Thomas Santschi, Eugenie Besserer, Ben Alexander, Lillie Hayward, Lafe (Lafayette) McKee, Colleen Moore, Harry Lonsdale, Doris Baker, Lillian Wade, Billy Jacobs, James Whitcomb Riley; ***D:*** Colin Campbell.

Little Orphan Annie ½ **1932** The unjustly forgotten first sound adaptation of the comic strip. Fun score adds a lot, as does the good cast. **60m/B VHS.** May Robson, Buster Phelps, Mitzie Green, Edgar Kennedy; ***D:*** John S. Robertson; ***M:*** Max Steiner.

The Little Prince **1974 (G)** Disappointing adaptation of the classic children's story by Antoine de Saint-Exupery, about a little boy from asteroid B-612. Lousy Lerner and Loewe score underscores a general lack of magic or spontaneity. ♫ It's a Hat; I Need Air; I'm On Your Side; Be Happy; You're a Child; I Never Met a Rose; Why Is the Desert (Lovely to See)?; Closer and Closer and Closer; Little Prince (From Who Knows Where). **88m/C VHS, DVD.** *GB* Richard Kiley, Bob Fosse, Steven Warner, Gene Wilder, Joss Ackland, Clive Revill, Victor Spinetti, Graham Crowden, Donna McKechnie; ***D:*** Stanley Donen; ***W:*** Alan Jay Lerner; ***C:*** Christopher Challis; ***M:*** Frederick Loewe, Alan Jay Lerner. Golden Globes '75: Score.

The Little Princess ½ **1939 (G)** Based on the Frances Hodgson Burnett children's classic; perhaps the best of the moppet's films. Shirley is a young schoolgirl in Victorian London sent to a harsh boarding school when her Army officer father is posted abroad. When her father is declared missing, the penniless girl must work as a servant at the school to pay her keep, all the while haunting the hospitals, never believing her father has died. A classic tearjerker. **91m/B VHS, DVD.** Shirley Temple, Richard Greene, Anita Louise, Ian Hunter, Cesar Romero, Arthur Treacher, Sybil Jason, Miles Mander, Marcia Mae Jones, E.E. Clive; ***D:*** Walter Lang; ***W:*** Ethel Hill, Walter Ferris; ***C:*** Arthur C. Miller; ***M:*** Walter Bullock.

The Little Princess **1987** A three-cassette adaptation of Frances Hodgson Burnett's book. In Victorian England, kindhearted Sara is forced into poverty when her father suddenly dies. Can his longtime friend find her and restore her happiness? Originally aired on PBS as part of the "Wonderworks" family movie series. **180m/C VHS.** *GB* Amelia Shankley, Nigel Havers, Maureen Lipman; ***D:*** Carol Wiseman. **TV**

A Little Princess ½ **1995 (G)** Compelling fantasy, based on the children's book by Frances Hodgson Burnett, and previously best known for the 1939 Shirley Temple incarnation. Sara (Matthews) has been raised in India by her widowed father (Cunningham). When he's called up to fight in WWI, Sara is taken to New York to be educated at stern Miss Michin's (Bron) school, where her money makes her a favored boarder. However, the irrepressible Sara suffers a severe reversal of fortune when her father is reported killed and Miss Michin promptly makes her a servant to pay her way. But Sara's charm has made her some true friends who become her allies under trying circumstances. Lively script, dazzling visuals, and a welcome lack of sappiness create a classic-in-the-making. **97m/C VHS, DVD.** Liesl Matthews, Eleanor Bron, Liam Cunningham, Rusty Schwimmer, Arthur Malet, Vanessa Lee Chester, Errol Sitahal, Heather DeLoach, Taylor Fry; ***D:*** Alfonso Cuaron; ***W:*** Richard LaGravenese, Elizabeth Chandler; ***C:*** Emmanuel Lubezki; ***M:*** Patrick Doyle.

The Little Rascals ½ **1994 (PG)** Alfalfa runs afoul of the membership requirements for the "He-Man Womun Haters Club" when he starts to fall for Darla. Charming remake of the short film series, now set in suburban L.A., from Spheeris, who also redid another TV favorite, "The Beverly Hillbillies." **83m/C VHS, DVD.** Daryl Hannah, Courtland Mead, Travis Tedford, Brittany Ashton Holmes, Bug Hall, Zachary Mabry, Kevin Jamal Woods, Ross Bagley, Sam Saletta, Blake Collins, Jordan Warkol, Blake Ewing, Juliette Brewer, Heather Karasek; ***Cameos:*** Whoopi Goldberg; ***D:*** Penelope Spheeris; ***W:*** Penelope Spheeris, Paul Guay, Stephen Mazur; ***C:*** Richard Bowen; ***M:*** David Foster, Linda Thompson.

Little Red Riding Hood **1983** From "Faerie Tale Theatre" comes the retelling of the story about a girl (Mary Steenburgen) off to give her grandmother a picnic basket, only to get stopped by a wicked wolf McDowell. Not particularly faithful, but fun and scary. **60m/C VHS, DVD.** Mary Steenburgen, Malcolm McDowell; ***D:*** Graeme Clifford. **CABLE**

Little Red Schoolhouse **1936** A hard-nosed schoolteacher hunts for a truant lad and both of them land in jail. **64m/C VHS.** Frank "Junior" Coghlan, Dickie Moore, Ann Doran, Lloyd Hughes, Richard Carle, Ralf Harolde, Matthew Betz, Kenneth Howell, Sidney Miller, Lafe (Lafayette) McKee; ***D:*** Charles Lamont; ***W:*** Paul Perez; ***C:*** M.A. Anderson.

Little Richard ½ **2000** The struggle between rock 'n' roll and religion is the story behind this biography of the legendary

Little Richard Penniman (well-played by Leon). Born in Georgia in 1943, the boy is too much of a sissy for his stern father (Lumbly) although his mother (Lewis) and local minister Preacher Rainey (Morris) encourage his singing in the choir. But soon Little Richard has succumbed to the secular and found success, although he comes to realize the inequities of the music business for a black man. But he also sees signs from God to leave show business for life in the ministry and continues to struggle between the two. **120m/C VHS, DVD.** Leon, Jenifer Lewis, Carl Lumbly, Tamala Jones, Mel Jackson, Garrett Morris; ***D:*** Robert Kevin Townsend; ***W:*** Daniel Taplitz; ***C:*** Edward Pei. **TV**

A Little Romance **1979 (PG)** An American girl living in Paris falls in love with a French boy; eventually they run away, to seal their love with a kiss beneath a bridge. Olivier gives a wonderful, if not hammy, performance as the old pickpocket who encourages her. Gentle, agile comedy based on the novel by Patrick Cauvin. **110m/C VHS, DVD.** Laurence Olivier, Diane Lane, Thelonious Bernard, Sally Kellerman, Broderick Crawford; ***D:*** George Roy Hill; ***W:*** Allan Burns; ***M:*** Georges Delerue. Oscars '79: Orig. Score.

Little Secrets ½ **2002 (PG)** Fourteen-year-old Emily (Wood) is spending the summer practicing her violin in hopes of auditioning for a place in the local orchestra. As a sideline, she runs a service in her backyard for the neighbor kids, where they can reveal their secrets, which Emily writes down and locks away for safekeeping. The film reassures that it's better to tell the truth than keep secrets and that even big problems are able to be solved if you talk about them. It may not be the real world but it's a nice one to visit. **107m/C VHS, DVD.** *US* Evan Rachel Wood, David Gallagher, Vivica A. Fox, Michael Angarano, Jan Gardner; ***D:*** Blair Treu; ***W:*** Jessica Barondes; ***C:*** Brian Sullivan; ***M:*** Sam Cardon.

A Little Sex **1982 (R)** Capshaw, in her screen debut, finds herself the wife of womanizer Matheson. Harmless, but pointless, with a TV-style plot. **94m/C VHS, DVD.** Tim Matheson, Kate Capshaw, Edward Herrmann, Wallace Shawn, John Glover; ***D:*** Bruce Paltrow; ***W:*** Robert De Laurentis; ***C:*** Ralf Bode; ***M:*** Georges Delerue.

Little Shop of Horrors ½ **1960** The landmark cheapie classic, which Roger Corman reputedly filmed in three days, about a nebbish working in a city florist shop who unknowingly cultivates an intelligent plant that demands human meat for sustenance. Notable for then-unknown Nicholson's appearance as a masochistic dental patient. Hilarious, unpretentious farce—if you liked this one, check out Corman's "Bucket of Blood" for more of the same. Inspired a musical of the same name; remade as a movie again in 1986. Available colorized. **70m/B VHS, DVD.** Jonathan Haze, Jackie Joseph, Mel Welles, Jack Nicholson, Dick Miller, Myrtle Vail; ***D:*** Roger Corman; ***W:*** Charles B. Griffith; ***C:*** Arch R. Dalzell.

Little Shop of Horrors **1986 (PG-13)** During a solar eclipse, Seymour buys an unusual plant and takes it back to the flower shop where he works. The plant, Audrey 2, becomes a town attraction as it grows at an unusual rate, but Seymour learns that he must feed Audrey fresh human blood to keep her growing. Soon, Audrey is giving the orders ("Feed me") and timid Seymour must find "deserving" victims. Martin's performance as the masochistic dentist is alone worth the price. Song, dance, gore, and more prevail in this outrageous musical comedy. Four Tops Levi Stubbs is the commanding voice of Audrey 2. Based on the Off-Broadway play, which was based on Roger Corman's 1960 horror spoof. ♫ Mean Green Mother From Outer Space; Some Fun Now; Your Day Begins Tonight. **94m/C VHS, DVD.** Rick Moranis, Ellen Greene, Vincent Gardenia, Steve Martin, James Belushi, Christopher Guest, Bill Murray, John Candy, Tisha Campbell, Tichina Arnold, Michelle Weeks; ***D:*** Frank Oz; ***W:*** Howard Ashman; ***C:*** Robert Paynter; ***M:*** Miles Goodman, Alan Menken, Howard Ashman; ***V:*** Levi Stubbs Jr.

Little Shots of Happiness **1997 (R)** Prim Frances leaves her unstable husband and, unbeknownst to her co-workers, is living out of her office. In the evenings, she creates a wild new identity for herself and hits the Boston nightclubs where she picks up a different man each night. Of course, Frances discovers there's a price to pay for her new liberation. **85m/C VHS, DVD.** Bonnie Dickenson, Todd Verow, Linda Ekoian, Rita Gavelis, P.J. Marino, Castalia Jason, Leanne Whitney, Bill Dwyer, Eric Sapp, Maureen Picard, Eric Romley; ***D:*** Todd Verow; ***W:*** Jim Dwyer, Todd Verow; ***C:*** Todd Verow.

Little Sister ½ **1992 (PG-13)** Prankster Silverman, on a dare, dresses up as a girl and joins a sorority. Problems arise when he falls in love with his "big sister" (Milano) in the sorority. What will happen when she finds out the truth? Will we care? **94m/C VHS.** Jonathan Silverman, Alyssa Milano; ***W:*** Sergio D. Altieri.

A Little Stiff **1991** Slacker romantic comedy about the unrequited romance between filmmaker Caveh and fellow UCLA student McKim from first meeting, through angst, and grand final gestures. **85m/C VHS.** Erin McKim, Caveh Zahedi; ***D:*** Caveh Zahedi, Greg Watkins; ***M:*** Kath Bloom.

Little Sweetheart ½ **1990 (R)** A reworking of "The Bad Seed," with a nine-year-old girl engaging in murder, burglary, and blackmail, ruining the adults around her. Based on "The Naughty Girls" by Arthur Wise. **93m/C VHS.** John Hurt, Karen Young, Barbara Bosson, John McMartin, Cassie Barasch; ***D:*** Anthony Simmons.

The Little Theatre of Jean Renoir **1971** A farewell by director Jean Renoir featuring three short films. In the first, Renoir's humanist beliefs are apparent in "The Last Christmas Dinner," a Hans Christian Andersen-inspired story. Next, "The Electric Floor Waxer" is a comic opera. The third piece is called "A Tribute to Tolerance." Slight but important late statement by a great director. In French with English subtitles. **100m/C VHS.** Jean Renoir, Fernand Sardou, Jean Carmet, Francoise Arnoul, Jeanne Moreau; ***D:*** Jean Renoir; ***W:*** Jean Renoir.

The Little Thief **1989 (PG-13)** Touted as Francois Truffaut's final legacy, this trite minidrama is actually based on a story he co-wrote with Claude de Givray about a post-WWII adolescent girl who reacts to the world around her by stealing and petty crime. Truffaut's hand is markedly absent, but this film is a testament to his abruptly and sadly truncated career. Director Miller was Truffaut's longtime assistant. French with subtitles. **108m/C VHS.** *FR* Charlotte Gainsbourg, Simon de la Brosse, Didier Bezace, Raoul Billerey, Nathalie Cardone; ***D:*** Claude Miller; ***W:*** Annie Miller, Claude Miller; ***C:*** Dominique Chapuis; ***M:*** Alain Jomy.

Little Tough Guys **1938** The Little Tough Guys (a.k.a. Dead End Kids) come to the rescue of Halop, a young tough guy gone bad to avenge his father's unjust imprisonment. First of the "Little Tough Guys" series for the former Dead End Kids, who later became the East Side Kids before eventually evolving into the Bowery Boys. **84m/B VHS.** Helen Parrish, Billy Halop, Leo Gorcey, Marjorie Main, Gabriel Dell, Huntz Hall; ***D:*** Harold Young.

Little Treasure ½ **1985 (R)** A stripper heads for Mexico to search for her long-lost father, but ends up looking for treasure with an American guy. Disappointing effort of director Sharp. **95m/C VHS.** Burt Lancaster, Margot Kidder, Ted Danson, Joseph Hacker, Malena Doria; ***D:*** Alan Sharp; ***W:*** Alan Sharp.

A Little Trip to Heaven ½ **2005 (R)** Muddled noir wannabe is the first English-language film for Icelandic director Kormakur and something got lost in translation. Insurance agent Abe Holt (Whitaker using a strange accent) is sent to rural Minnesota to investigate the death of a driver in a burned-out car. The alleged corpse was a heavily-insured scam artist and his beneficiary is his hard-luck sister Isold (Stiles) and her drunken husband Fred (Renner), which puts Abe's instincts on red alert. **86m/C DVD.** *US IC* Forest Whitaker, Julia Stiles, Jeremy Renner, Peter Coyote, Philip Jackson, Anne Reid, Phyllida Law; ***D:*** Baltasar Kormakur; ***W:*** Baltasar Kormakur, Edward Martin Weinman; ***C:*** Ottar Gudnason; ***M:*** Mugison.

The Little Valentino **1979** One day in the aimless life of a young punk who gets by on his wits and petty theft. Jeles' directorial debut. In Hungarian with English subtitles. **102m/B VHS.** *HU* Janos Opoczki, Denes Ladanyi, Sandorne Arpa, Phyllis Fraser; ***D:*** Andras Jeles; ***W:*** Andras Jeles; ***C:*** Sandor Kavdos; ***M:*** Kamillo Lendvay.

The Little Vampire **2000 (PG)** A cluttered storyline and wandering direction help put a stake in the heart of this tale of a lonely boy and a family of vegetarian vampires. Tony (Lipnicki) is forced to move from sunny California to gloomy Scotland when his father gets a job building a golf course for crusty Lord Ashton (Wood). After being bullied by the local kids at school, Tony starts daydreaming about vampires to take his mind off his loneliness. As if summoned by magic, soon a young vampire named Rudolph (Weeks) appears at his window, befriending Tony and taking him on a flight through the countryside. After he introduces Rudolph to American slang and Nintendo, Tony is introduced to Rudolph's family. Rudolph's father Frederick (Grant) and mother Freda (Krige) explain to Tony that they are trying to become human once again, but need the other half of a magic amulet held by Lord Ashton to complete the spell. Meanwhile, crazed vampire hunter Rookery (Carter) stalks the family. Some scenes are visually stunning (especially those vampire cows) but the convoluted plot puts this one six feet under. **91m/C VHS, DVD.** Jonathan Lipnicki, Richard E. Grant, Alice Krige, Jim Carter, John Wood, Pamela Gidley, Tommy Hinkley, Rollo Weeks, Anna Popplewell, Dean Cook; ***D:*** Uli Edel; ***W:*** Karey Kirkpatrick, Larry Wilson; ***C:*** Bernd Heinl; ***M:*** Nigel Clarke, Michael Csanyi-Wills.

Little Vegas ½ **1990 (R)** Looks like easy street for a young man who inherits a bundle from his girlfriend, but he's forced to wake up and smell the cappucino when her family and the other residents of the tiny desert berg think there's a gigolo in the woodpile. Much strife with siblings as he wages a battle for the bucks with the son while wooing the woman's daughter, with a measure of mob inflicted plot twists. Mildly amusing, cut from vein of you can't get rich quick and get away with it. **90m/C VHS.** Michael Nouri, Jerry Stiller, John Sayles, Anthony John (Tony) Denison, Catherine O'Hara, Bruce McGill, Anne Francis, Bob(cat) Goldthwait, Jay Thomas, Perry Lang; ***D:*** Perry Lang; ***W:*** Perry Lang; ***M:*** Mason Daring.

Little Vera *Malenkaya Vera* **1988** Extremely well-done Soviet film chronicles the life of a young working-class woman who loves rock music and who has been profoundly affected by Western civilization. Post-glasnost Soviet production gives Westerners a glimpse into the Russian way of life. A boxoffice bonanza back home. Russian with subtitles. **130m/C VHS, DVD.** *RU* Natalia (Natalya) Negoda, Andrei Sokolov, Yuri Nazarov, Ludmila Zaisova, Alexander Niegreva; ***D:*** Vassili Pitchul.

Little Voice **1998 (R)** Little Voice (Horrocks) misses her dead father so much that she withdraws from the world, communicating only by singing along with the records Dad loved. Whether it's Judy Garland, Shirley Bassey, or Edith Piaf, "LV" can match the voice exactly. When her mom's (Blethyn) sleazy talent-agent boyfriend (Caine) heart her, he knows she's the ticket to fame and fortune. Little Voice has no desire to be a star, so she clams up whenever there's an audience. Club owner and weasel Mr. Boo (Broadbent) books her for several shows, including one with a London talent scout on hand, and everyone wonders if she'll sing. Caine and Broadbent do their best to out-slime each other and deliver most of the comedy. Horrocks gives a showcase performance, re-creating her role from the stage play "The Rise and Fall of Little Voice." The play was written specifically to take advantage of her spectacular impersonation talents. **97m/C VHS, DVD.** *GB* Jane Horrocks, Michael Caine, Ewan McGregor, Brenda Blethyn, Jim Broadbent, Annette Badland, Philip Jackson; ***D:*** Mark Herman; ***W:*** Mark Herman; ***C:*** Andy Collins; ***M:*** John Altman. Golden Globes '99: Actor—Mus./Comedy (Caine).

Little White Lies **1989** Jillian and Matheson meet and fall in love during an exotic vacation. But both are traveling under assumed identities—she's a policewoman tracking a jewel thief and he's an incognito doctor. When they reunite stateside they try to stick to their ruses in humdrum comedic fashion. Made for network TV. **88m/C VHS.** Ann Jillian, Tim Matheson; ***D:*** Anson Williams. **TV**

Little Witches **1996 (R)** Rejected group of seniors at Catholic girls' high school are transformed into a witches coven, thanks to a book of spells. A rip-off of "The Craft." **91m/C VHS, DVD.** Mimi Reichmeister, Jack Nance, Jennifer Rubin, Sheeri Rappaport, Melissa Taub, Zoe Alexander, Zelda Rubinstein, Eric Pierpoint; ***D:*** Jane Simpson; ***W:*** Brian DiMuccio, Dino Vindeni; ***C:*** Ron Turowski; ***M:*** Nicholas Rivera.

Little Women **1933** Louisa May Alcott's Civil War story of the four March sisters—Jo, Beth, Amy, and Meg—who share their loves, their joys, and their sorrows. Everything about this classic film is wonderful, from the lavish period costumes to the excellent script, and particularly the captivating performances by the cast. A must-see for fans of Alcott and Hepburn, and others will find it enjoyable. **107m/B VHS, DVD.** Katharine Hepburn, Joan Bennett, Paul Lukas, Edna May Oliver, Frances Dee, Spring Byington, Jean Parker, Douglass Montgomery; ***D:*** George Cukor; ***W:*** Victor Heerman, Sarah Y. Mason; ***C:*** Henry W. Gerrard; ***M:*** Max Steiner. Oscars '33: Adapt. Screenplay; Venice Film Fest. '34: Actress (Hepburn).

Little Women **1949** Stylized color remake of the George Cukor 1933 classic. Top-notch if too obvious cast portrays Louisa May Alcott's story of teenage girls growing up against the backdrop of the Civil War. **121m/C VHS, DVD.** June Allyson, Peter Lawford, Margaret O'Brien, Elizabeth Taylor, Janet Leigh, Mary Astor; ***D:*** Mervyn LeRoy; ***W:*** Andrew Solt; ***M:*** Adolph Deutsch. Oscars '49: Art Dir./Set Dec., Color.

Little Women **1978** The third screen version of Louisa May Alcott's classic story. Lackluster compared to the previous attempts, particularly the sterling 1933 film, but still worthwhile. During the Civil War, four sisters share their lives as they grow up and find romance. Garson's TV debut. Followed by a TV series. **200m/C VHS, DVD.** Meredith Baxter, Susan Dey, Ann Dusenberry, Eve Plumb, Dorothy McGuire, Robert Young, Greer Garson, Cliff (Potter) Potts, William Shatner; ***D:*** David Lowell Rich; ***M:*** Elmer Bernstein. **TV**

Little Women **1994 (PG)** Beloved story of the March women is beautifully portrayed in a solid production that blends a seamless screenplay with an excellent cast, authentic period costumes, and lovely cinematography and music. Ryder, perfectly cast as the unconventional Jo, is also the strongest of the sisters: domestically inclined Meg (Alvarado), the fragile Beth (Danes), and the youngest, mischevious Amy (the delightful Dunst) who grows up into a sedate young lady (Mathis). Charming adaptation remains faithful to the spirit of the Alcott classic while adding contemporary touches. Fittingly brought to the big screen by producer Denise Di Novi, writer/co-producer Swicord, and director Armstrong. **118m/C VHS, DVD.** Winona Ryder, Gabriel Byrne, Trini Alvarado, Samantha Mathis, Kirsten Dunst, Claire Danes, Christian Bale, Eric Stoltz, John Neville, Mary Wickes, Susan Sarandon; ***D:*** Gillian Armstrong; ***W:*** Robin Swicord; ***C:*** Geoffrey Simpson; ***M:*** Thomas Newman.

Little World of Don Camillo *Le Petit Monde de Don Camillo* **1951** A French-made farce based on the beloved novels of Giovanni Guareschi. Earthy priest Don Camillo clashes repeatedly with his friendly enemy, the communist mayor of a tiny Italian village. The hero talks directly to God, whose voice is provided by Orson Welles, also narrator of the English version. Charming, good-natured approach. **106m/B VHS.** *FR IT* Fernandel, Gino Cervi, Sylvia, Vera Talchi; ***D:*** Julien Duvivier; ***Nar:*** Orson Welles.

The Littlest Angel **1969** Musical about a shepherd boy who dies falling off a cliff and wants to become an angel. He learns a valuable lesson in the spirit of giving. Made for TV. **77m/C VHS, DVD.** Johnny Whitaker, Fred Gwynne, E.G. Marshall, Cab Calloway, Connie Stevens, Tony Randall; ***D:*** Joe Layton; ***W:***

Patricia Gray, Lan O'Kun; *M:* Joseph Howard. **TV**

The Littlest Horse Thieves 1/2 *Escape from the Dark* **1976 (G)** Good Disney film about three children and their efforts to save some ponies who work in mines. The children take it upon themselves to see that the animals escape the abuse and neglect they are put through. Filmed on location in England with excellent photography. **109m/C VHS, DVD.** Maurice Colbourne, Susan Tebbs, Andrew Harrison, Chloe Franks, Alastair Sim, Peter Barkworth; *D:* Charles Jarrott; *W:* Rosemary Anne Sisson; *C:* Paul Beeson; *M:* Ronald Goodwin.

The Littlest Outlaw 1/2 **1954** A Mexican peasant boy steals a beautiful stallion to save it from being destroyed. Together, they ride off on a series of adventures. Disney movie filmed on location in Mexico. **73m/C VHS.** Pedro Armendariz Sr., Joseph Calleia, Andres Velasquez; *D:* Roberto Gavaldon.

The Littlest Rebel 1/2 **1935 (PG)** Temple stars in this well-done piece set during the Civil War in the Old South. She befriends a Union officer while protecting her father at the same time. She even goes to Washington to talk with President Lincoln. Nice dance sequences by Temple and Robinson. Available in computer-colored version. **70m/B VHS, DVD.** Shirley Temple, John Boles, Jack Holt, Bill Robinson, Karen Morley, Willie Best; *D:* David Butler.

The Littlest Viking 1/2 **1994 (PG)** Twelve-year-old Sigurd finds archery practice and mock battles an exciting way to learn to be a Viking. But when his older brother is killed in battle, Sigurd's father expects him to avenge the death, and Sigurd must decide just what being a Viking prince means. Scenic Scandinavian settings; obvious dubbing. **85m/C VHS.** Kristian Tonby, Per Jansen, Terje Stromdahl; *D:* Knut W. Jorfald, Lars Rasmussen, Paul Trevor Bale.

Live a Little, Love a Little **1968 (PG)** Itinerant photographer Elvis juggles two different jobs by running around a lot. Sexually more frank than earlier King vehicles. ♫ Almost in Love; A Little Less Conversation; Edge of Reality; Wonderful World. **90m/C VHS, DVD.** Elvis Presley, Michele Carey, Rudy Vallee, Don Porter, Dick Sargent, Sterling Holloway, Eddie Hodges; *D:* Norman Taurog.

Live and Let Die **1973 (PG)** Agent 007 (Moore) is out to thwart the villainous Dr. Kananga (Kotto), a black mastermind who plans to control western powers with voodoo and hard drugs. He's aided by psychic tarot-reading virgin Solitaire (Seymour), who falls prey to Bond's charms. Moore's first appearance as Bond in the 8th film in the series. Can't we have the real Bond back? Title song by Paul McCartney and Wings. **131m/C VHS, DVD, Blu-ray Disc.** *GB* Roger Moore, Jane Seymour, Yaphet Kotto, Clifton James, Julius W. Harris, Geoffrey Holder, David Hedison, Gloria Hendry, Bernard Lee, Lois Maxwell, Madeleine Smith; *D:* Guy Hamilton; *W:* Tom Mankiewicz; *C:* Ted Moore; *M:* George Martin.

Live Bait 1/2 **1995** Canadian-flavored Gen-X comedy features suburban 23-year-old virgin Trevor MacIntosh (Scholte) trying for a little romance (or at least sex) but seemingly doomed to failure. At least until he meets much older artist Charlotte (Maunsell). Sweeney handles his debut writing, directing, and producing skills with equal aplomb. **84m/B VHS.** *CA* Tom Scholte, Micki Maunsell, Kevin McNulty, Babz Chula, David Lovgren, Laara Sadiq, Michelle Beaudoin, Kelly Aisenstat; *D:* Bruce Sweeney; *W:* Bruce Sweeney; *C:* David Pelletier. Toronto-City '95: Canadian Feature Film.

Live Flesh 1/2 *Carne Tremula* **1997 (R)** The courses of five lives in Madrid are forever altered when naive, young Victor (Rabal) accidentally shoots cop David (Bardem) and is sent to prison after an argument with Elena (Neri), a one-night stand he falls for. When he gets out he discovers Elena has transformed from junkie to model wife who runs a home for children and has married David, now a paraplegic. Still, Victor both wants and resents Elena, who he blames for the accident. While apparently stalking Elena, Victor enters into a relationship with Clara, the wife of David's former partner, Sancho (Sancho) which dramatically draws all five back together. Complex, noirish drama shows a new, more serious side for director Almadovar, who still manages some of his patented brand of humor. Highly original plot and unexpected twists delivered by a talented and attractive cast. Adapted from a British novel by Ruth Rendell. **100m/C VHS, DVD.** *FR SP* Javier Bardem, Francesca Neri, Angela Molina, Liberto Rabal, Jose Sancho, Penelope Cruz, Pilar Bardem, Alex Angulo; *D:* Pedro Almodovar; *W:* Pedro Almodovar, Ray Loriga, Jorge Guerricaechevarria; *C:* Alfonso Beato; *M:* Alberto Iglesias.

Live Free or Die Hard 1/2 **2007 (PG-13)** The last "Die Hard" was released in 1995 and director Wiseman plays to the fact that times have changed, even if John McClane (Willis) has not. His analog cop in a digital world first thinks he's going to be stuck babysitting smart-mouthed twenty-something computer hacker Matt (Long), who's wanted for questioning when the government's computers go wonky. Ah, but it's really supercilious disaffected techie Thomas Gabriel (Olyphant) showing off what happens when you ignore his warnings. Well, you really shouldn't ignore McClane either. Willis acknowledges his years while still kicking bad-guy butt in some ludicrous but amazing action sequences. **129m/C DVD, Blu-ray Disc.** *US* Bruce Willis, Justin Long, Mary Elizabeth Winstead, Timothy Olyphant, Maggie Q, Jeffrey Wright, Kevin Smith, Yancey Arias, Tim Russ, Cyril Raffaelli, Clifford Curtis, Yorgo Constantine, Andrew Friedman; *D:* Len Wiseman; *W:* Mark Bomback; *C:* Simon Duggan; *M:* Marco Beltrami.

Live from Baghdad **2003** In 1991, veteran CNN producer Robert Wiener (Keaton) and his longtime producing partner Ingrid Formanek (Bonham Carter) find themselves in Baghdad at the start of the first Gulf War. The other networks have pulled out for safety reasons and CNN is the only game around with Wiener and Formanek risking their lives to get the story. Adapted from the book by Wiener. **108m/C VHS, DVD.** Michael Keaton, Helena Bonham Carter, Lili Taylor, Bruce McGill, David Suchet, Joshua Leonard, Michael Cudlitz, Matt Keeslar, Robert Wisdom, Michael Murphy, Paul Guilfoyle, John Carroll Lynch, Tom Amandes, Murphy Dunne; *D:* Mick Jackson; *W:* Richard Chapman, John Patrick Shanley, Timothy J. Sexton; *C:* Ivan Strasburg. **CABLE**

Live! From Death Row **1992** Cassidy plays a tabloid TV host who'll do anything to get ratings. She's set to do a live interview with a condemned serial killer (Davison) shortly before his execution. But Davison and his fellow death-row inmates take Cassidy and her crew hostage as he decides to use the show for his own media message. **94m/C VHS.** Joanna Cassidy, Bruce Davison, Art LaFleur, Calvin Levels, Michael D. Roberts; *D:* Patrick Sheane Duncan; *W:* Patrick Sheane Duncan.

Live-In Maid *Cama Adentro* **2004** With Argentina in the midst of an economic meltdown, once-privileged divorcee Beba can't afford to pay her longtime maid Dora and she eventually quits. But after spending nearly 30 years together, despite class and other differences, the women find it tough to let go. Spanish with subtitles. **87m/C DVD.** *AR SP* Norma Aleandro, Norma Argentina, Marcus Mundstock, Raul Panguinao; *D:* Jorge Gaggero; *W:* Jorge Gaggero; *C:* Javier Julia.

Live Nude Girls **1995 (R)** Group of 30-something girlfriends get together to throw a bachelorette party for one of their number and sit around gossiping about sex, relationships, family, and friends. Not much plot but nice ensemble work. **92m/C VHS, DVD.** Dana Delany, Kim Cattrall, Cynthia Stevenson, Laila Robins, Olivia D'Abo, Lora Zane, Glenn Quinn, Tim Choate; *D:* Julianna Lavin; *W:* Julianna Lavin; *C:* Christopher Taylor; *M:* Anton Sanko.

The Live Wire **1934** Stunt-ridden action fare featuring Talmadge at his most daring. This adventure is complete with desert island, lost treasure, stowaways, evildoers, and a race against the clock. **57m/B VHS, DVD.** Richard Talmadge, George Walsh, Charles French, Alberta Vaughn; *D:* Harry S. Webb.

Live Wire 1/2 **1992 (R)** Brosnan is an FBI bomb expert who needs a new line of work. He's up against a terrorist psychopath who has his greedy hands on a new type of explosive. It's liquid, undetectable, looks as innocent as a glass of water, and is capable of blowing up Washington, D.C. Also available in an unrated version. **85m/C VHS, DVD.** Pierce Brosnan, Ben Cross, Ron Silver, Lisa Eilbacher; *D:* Christian Duguay; *W:* Bart Baker. **CABLE**

Live Wire: Human Timebomb 1/2 **1995 (R)** FBI agent Jim Parker is captured by a Cuban general who implants a computer chip into his neck—turning Parker into a human timebomb. **98m/C VHS, DVD.** Bryan Genesse, Joe Lara, Frantz Dobrowsky, J. Cynthia Brooks; *D:* Mark Roper; *W:* Jeff Albert; *C:* Rod Stewart; *M:* Itai Haber.

The Lives of a Bengal Lancer **1935** One of Hollywood's greatest rousing adventures. Based in northwest India, Lt. McGregor (Cooper) is a seasoned frontier fighter in the Bengals Lancers who befriends new officer Lt. Forsythe (Tone). Also new to the regiment is Donald Stone (Cromwell), the son of the current commanding officer (Standing). All three will soon test their courage when the Brits encounter a vicious local revolution against colonial rule. Swell plot, lotsa action, great comradery. Based on the novel by Major Francis Yeats-Brown, and remade in 1939 as "Geronimo." **110m/B VHS, DVD.** Gary Cooper, Franchot Tone, Richard Cromwell, Guy Standing, Sir C. Aubrey Smith, Douglass Dumbrille, Kathleen Burke, Noble Johnson, Lumsden Hare, Akim Tamiroff, J. Carrol Naish, Monte Blue, Ray Cooper, Leonid Kinskey, George Regas, Reginald (Reggie, Reggy) Sheffield, Mischa Auer, Charles Stevens, James Warwick, Clive Morgan, Colin Tapley, Rollo Lloyd, Maj. Sam Harris; *D:* Henry Hathaway; *W:* Waldemar Young, John Lloyd Balderston, Grover Jones, William Slavens McNutt; *C:* Charles B(ryant) Lang Jr.; *M:* Milan Roder.

The Lives of Others *Das Leben der Anderen* **2006 (R)** Oscar-winning drama is set in East Berlin in 1984. The population is controlled by the Stasi (the secret police) and its informers. Strict bureaucrat Wiesler (Muehe) doesn't believe that successful playwright Dreyman (Koch) is a true socialist so he wires the man's apartment and becomes intrigued with his life and lover, actress Christa-Maria (Gedeck). Wiesler's loyalty (and belief in the system) is shaken when a superior orders him to pin something on Dreyman; instead, he decides to protect him. Impressive debut for writer/director von Donnersmarck. German with subtitles. **137m/C DVD, Blu-ray Disc.** *GE* Martina Gedeck, Ulrich Tukur, Ulrich Muehe, Sebastian Kock, Volkmar Kleinert; *D:* Florian Henskel von Donnersmarck; *W:* Florian Henskel von Donnersmarck; *C:* Hagen Bogdanski; *M:* Gabriel Yared, Stephane Moucha. Oscars '06: Foreign Film; British Acad. '07: Foreign Film.

Livin' for Love: The Natalie Cole Story **2000** Singer Natalie Cole plays herself (at least in her adult years), telling the harrowing story of her slide into drug addiction after growing up the adored daughter of the legendary Nat King Cole. Based on her autobiography. **120m/C VHS.** Natalie Cole, Theresa Randle, James McDaniel, Diahann Carroll; *D:* Robert Kevin Townsend. **TV**

Livin' Large **1991 (R)** An African-American delivery boy gets the break of his life when a nearby newscaster is shot dead. Grabbing the microphone and continuing the story, he soon finds himself hired by an Atlanta news station as an anchorman, fulfilling a life-long dream. But problems arise when he finds himself losing touch with his friends, his old neighborhood and his roots. Comedy "deals" with the compelling issue of blacks finding success in a white world by trivializing the issue at every turn and resorting to racial stereotypes. **96m/C VHS, DVD.** Terrence "T.C." Carson, Lisa Arrindell Anderson, Blanche Baker, Nathaniel "Afrika" Hall, Julia Campbell; *D:* Michael A. Schultz; *C:* Peter Lyons Collister; *M:* Herbie Hancock.

Living & Dying **2007 (R)** Supremely stupid crime-doesn't-pay pic. A team of bank robbers become involved in a hostage situation when their job is botched. Unfortunately, among the hostages are a couple of gun-happy killers and outside are a lot of equally trigger-happy cops. **90m/C DVD.** Edward Furlong, Bai Ling, Jordana Spiro, Michael Madsen, Tom Zembrod, Maurice Ripke, Arnold Vosloo; *D:* Jon Keeyes; *W:* Jon Keeyes; *C:* Sammy Inayeh q; *M:* David Rosenblad, John Dufilho.

The Living Coffin 1/2 *El Grito de la Muerte* **1958** Woman has alarm rigged on her coffin in case she's buried alive. And they called her paranoid. Loosely based on Poe's "Premature Burial." **72m/C VHS, DVD.** *MX* Gaston Santos, Maria Duval, Pedro de Aguillon; *D:* Fernando Mendez.

The Living Daylights **1987 (PG)** After being used as a pawn in a fake Russian defector plot, our intrepid spy tracks down an international arms and opium smuggling ring. Fine debut by Dalton, who takes his role as 007 in a more serious vein, in a rousing, refreshing cosmopolitan shoot-em-up. Let's be frank: we were all getting a little fatigued by Roger Moore. The 15th film in the series. **130m/C VHS, DVD.** Timothy Dalton, Maryam D'Abo, Jeroen Krabbe, John Rhys-Davies, Robert Brown, Joe Don Baker, Desmond Llewelyn, Art Malik, Geoffrey Keen, Walter Gotell, Andreas Wisniewski; *D:* John Glen; *W:* Richard Maibaum, Michael G. Wilson; *C:* Alec Mills; *M:* John Barry.

The Living Dead *The Scotland Yard Mystery* **1933** An English film about a mad, re-animating scientist. **76m/B VHS.** *GB* Grete Natzler, Belle Chrystall, Leslie Perrins, Gerald du Maurier, George Curzon; *D:* Thomas Bentley; *W:* Frank Miller; *C:* James Wilson.

The Living Dead Girl 1/2 *La Morte Vivante* **1982** Workers illegally trying to dispose of hazardous chemical wastes in a cellar make the mistake of indulging in a bit of grave robbing at the next-door crypt. A 55-gallon drum cracks open; the stuff hits an open coffin and a blonde (Blanchard) with long sharp fingernails and a taste for blood is reanimated. It's another sex-and-gore fest from the prolific Rollin, though this is one of his more polished productions. French with subtitles. **91m/C DVD.** *FR* Marina Pierro, Francoise Blanchard, Mike Marshall, Carina Barone, Fanny Magier; *D:* Jean Rollin; *W:* Jean Rollin.

Living Doll 1/2 **1990 (R)** A mentally unbalanced med student abducts a cadaver and brings it to his apartment. The beautiful female corpse takes to telling him to seek revenge on those that killed her. **95m/C DVD.** *GB* Mark Jax, Eartha Kitt, Katie Orgill; *D:* George Dugdale, Peter MacKenzie Litten; *W:* George Dugdale, Peter MacKenzie Litten, Mark Ezra. **VIDEO**

The Living End **1992** Director Araki's radical lovers-on-the-lam story concerns freelance L.A. writer Jon (Gilmore) who has just learned he is H.I.V.-positive. He meets a handsome, violent, hustler named Luke (Dytri) and the two begin a desperate road trip along the California coast which can only end in tragedy. Araki not only wrote and directed the film but also served as cinematographer and editor—all on a $23,000 budget. Stylish, tragic, and filled with black humor and frank homoeroticism. **92m/C VHS, DVD.** Craig Gilmore, Mike Dytri, Darcy Marta; *D:* Gregg Araki; *W:* Gregg Araki; *C:* Gregg Araki.

Living Free 1/2 **1972 (G)** Sequel to "Born Free," based on the nonfictional books by Joy Adamson. After Elsa's death, Joy and George Adamson are called in to take charge of her three cubs, who are causing havoc on nearby villages. Nice and pleasant, but could you pick up the pace? **91m/C VHS, DVD.** Susan Hampshire, Nigel Davenport; *D:* Jack Couffer; *W:* Millard Kaufman; *C:* Jack Couffer.

The Living Head 1/2 *La Cabeza Viviente* **1959** Archaeologists discover the ancient sepulcher of the great Aztec warrior, Acatl. Ignoring a curse, they steal his severed head and incur the fury of Xitsliapoli. They should have known better. Dubbed in English. **75m/B VHS, DVD.** *MX* Mauricio Garces, Ana Luisa Peluffo, German Robles, Abel Salazar; *D:* Chano Urueto.

Living Hell: A Japanese Chainsaw Massacre *Iki-jigoku* **2000 (R)** A young wheelchair bound boy named Yasu spends his days being ignored or smothered in his family home. One night a freakish young mute girl and her grandmother appear and move in. Distant relatives of Yasu, they are the sole survivors of a horrifying crime that wiped out their entire family. They spend their nights physically and mentally torturing Yasu, who tries to warn his unloving kin about them. Wanna take bets on how successful he is? **104m/C DVD.** *JP* Naoki Mori, Hirohito Honda, Yoshiko Shiraishi, Rumi, Kazuo Yashiro, Shugo Fujii, Hitoashi Suwabe; *D:* Shugo Fujii; *W:* Shugo Fujii; *M:* Koji Tabuchi.

Living in Oblivion **1994 (R)** Humorous tri-part story is an insiders joke on the problems of low-budget filmmaking, including talent, libido, ego, and pervasive chaos. First, director Nick Reve (Buscemi) tries to film an emotional scene with leading lady Nicole (Keener) only to have everything go wrong; then star Chad (LeGros), a dimwit but a "name," arrives to throw his weight around (and seduce Nicole); and finally the leading lady must deal with an overly sensitive dwarf and Nick's mother. A sleeper. **92m/C VHS, DVD.** Steve Buscemi, Catherine Keener, James LeGros, Dermot Mulroney, Danielle von Zerneck, Robert Wightman, Rica Martens, Hilary Gilford, Peter Dinklage, Kevin Corrigan, Matthew Grace, Michael Griffiths, Ryna Bowker, Francesca DiMauro; *D:* Tom DiCillo; *W:* Tom DiCillo; *C:* Frank Prinzi; *M:* Jim Farmer. Sundance '95: Screenplay.

Living in Peril **1997 (R)** Ambitious architect Walter Woods (Lowe) is in L.A. to design a mansion for an eccentric client (Belushi). But a series of accidents threaten to ruin his reputation, if not provoke something more deadly. **95m/C VHS.** Rob Lowe, James Belushi, Dean Stockwell, Dana Wheeler-Nicholson, Richard Moll, Alex Meneses, Patrick Ersgard; *D:* Joakim (Jack) Ersgard; *W:* Joakim (Jack) Ersgard, Patrick Ersgard; *C:* Ross Berryman; *M:* Randy Miller. **VIDEO**

Living on Love **1937** Remake of 1934's "Rafter Romance" is shorter, with a lesser-known cast, and because the Hays Code was in effect the material is less risque. Otherwise it's the same story about two roommates (this time it's in a shared basement apartment) who fall in love. **60m/B DVD.** James Dunn, Whitney Bourne, Joan Woodbury, Franklin Pangborn, Tom Kennedy, Solly Ward; *D:* Lew Landers; *W:* Franklin Coen; *C:* Nicholas Musuraca.

Living on Tokyo Time **1/2 1987** Interesting but often dull, low budget independent comedy about a young Japanese woman who hitches up with a boorish Japanese-American man in order to stay in the United States. An Asian view of Asian-America, filmed on location in San Francisco. **83m/C VHS.** Minako Ohashi, Ken Nakagawa, Kate Connell, Mitzi Abe, Bill Bonham, Brenda Aoki; *D:* Steven Okazaki; *W:* Steven Okazaki, John McCormick.

Living Out Loud **1998 (R)** Judith (Hunter) is dumped by her cardiologist husband for a younger women and spirals downward into depression. Of course, this leads to dramatic self-discovery, and Judith opens her eyes to the world around her, including the nice-guy elevator operator (DeVito) in her building. The two wallow in their respective personal loss and form an unlikely friendship, which teeters on becoming something more. Screenwriter LaGravanese tries his hand at directing but delivers a choppy, hard-to-believe tale of female independence and self-fulfillment. The reliable Hunter seems miscast; she's just too intense and jittery to appear sullen and reflective. DeVito gives his usual excellent performance, but also appears miscast as the debt-ridden gambler who catches Judith's refined eye. Significant events take place off-screen and the audience is left to fill in the blanks. **102m/C VHS, DVD.** Holly Hunter, Danny DeVito, Queen Latifah, Martin Donovan, Elias Koteas, Richard Schiff; *D:* Richard LaGravenese; *W:* Richard LaGravenese; *C:* John Bailey; *M:* George Fenton.

Living Proof **1/2 2008** Sentimental fact-based drama from Lifetime about the work of Dr. Dennis Slamon (Connick Jr.), an oncologist looking to use Herceptin as an experimental drug for breast cancer. Frustrated by his lack of funding, Slamon's work eventually comes to the notice of Lily Tartikoff (Harmon) whose (then-)husband Brandon was the president of NBC Entertainment and had been treated by Slamon. Lily makes fundraising her personal crusade (along with financier Ron Perelman) and raises enough money to have Slamon launch clinical trials. Story is told from multiple viewpoints, including Slamon's patients. **89m/C DVD.** Harry Connick Jr., Angie Harmon, Tammy Blanchard, Amanda Bynes, John Benjamin Hickey, Regina King, Jennifer Coolidge, Swoosie Kurtz, Amy Madigan, Bernadette Peters, Trudie Styler; *D:* Dan Ireland; *W:* Vivienne Radkoff; *C:* James Chressanthis; *M:* Halli Cauthery. **CABLE**

Living Proof: The Hank Williams Jr. Story **1/2 1983** TV biopic focusing on the country singer's hell-raising ways as he seeks to get out from under the shadow of his famous father and into the spotlight on his own right. Based on Williams Jr.'s autobiography; includes 10 songs by Sr. and Jr. **97m/C VHS.** Richard Thomas, Clu Gulager, Allyn Ann McLerie, Naomi Judd, Christian Slater; *D:* Dick Lowry; *W:* I.C. Rapoport, Stephen Kandel. **TV**

Living to Die **1/2 1991 (R)** Vegas gumshoe is assigned to investigate a blackmailed official, and discovers a woman believed to be dead is alive and beautiful and living incognito. This mystifies him. **84m/C VHS, DVD.** Wings Hauser, Darcy Demoss, Asher Brauner, Arnold Vosloo, Jim Williams; *D:* Wings Hauser.

A Lizard in a Woman's Skin *Una Lucertola con la Pelle di Donna* **1971** Carol (Bolkan) tells her shrink about dreams in which she kills her party girl neighbor Julia (Strindberg, in her film debut). Of course, Julia winds up dead in exactly the manner Carol has described. Cop Corvin (Baker) thinks Carol is being set up by her two-timing husband Frank (Sorel). Then other people from Carol's dreams begin to die as well. There's some freaky-deaky druggie hippie stuff included, too. Italian with subtitles. **98m/C DVD.** *IT* Florinda Bolkan, Stanley Baker, Jean Sorel, Alberto De Mendoza, Leo Genn, Silvia Monti, Anita Strindberg; *D:* Lucio Fulci; *W:* Lucio Fulci, Robert Gianviti, Andre Tranche; *C:* Luigi Kuveiller; *M:* Ennio Morricone.

The Lizzie McGuire Movie **1/2 2003 (PG)** Let's just call this "Lizzie Goes to Rome." Tweenie heroine Lizzie (an endearingly klutzy Duff) celebrates her graduation from junior high with a two-week trip to Italy with some classmates. On an outing, Lizzie meets the slightly older teen Europop star Paolo (Gelman), whose singing partner Isabella has just left him. Lizzie looks like her (Duff plays both roles), and agrees to put on a dark wig and impersonate the Italian diva for an awards show. Some sightseeing and a little romance follow. An adaptation of the Disney Channel series. **90m/C VHS, DVD.** *US* Hilary Duff, Robert Carradine, Hallie Todd, Jake Thomas, Yani Gellman, Adam Lamberg, Brendan Kelly, Ashlie Brillault, Clayton Snyder, Alex Borstein, Carly Schroeder; *D:* Jim Fall; *W:* Edward Decter, John J. Strauss, Susan Estelle Jansen; *C:* Jerzy Zielinski; *M:* Cliff Eidelman.

Lloyd **2000 (PG)** Goofy 11-year-old Lloyd is the class clown always getting in trouble in school. In fact, he gets demoted to a class of losers where Lloyd gets a crush on pretty Tracy. But how can he compare with junior high rebel Storm for her affections? **72m/C VHS, DVD.** Todd Bosley, Brendon Ryan Barrett, Mary Mara, Taylor Negron, Tom Arnold, Kristen Parker; *D:* Hector Barron; *W:* Hector Barron; *C:* Michael Orefice; *M:* Conrad Pope. **VIDEO**

Lloyds of London **1936** If you wonder how the story of a British insurance company can be exciting, just watch this lavish spectacular (which, of course, lacks historical accuracy). Jonathan Blake (Power) has risen in the ranks of the firm, thanks in part to his lifelong friendship with Lord Horatio Nelson (Burton), much to the disgust of haughty Lord Everett Stacy (an ever-supercilious Sanders). As Bonaparte comes to power, Blake travels to France to rescue some friends and saves Elizabeth (Carroll), who turns out to be Stacy's wife. Stacy is also spreading rumors about Lloyds' solvency and Nelson's heroics at Trafalgar and his machinations lead to further trouble with Blake. **115m/B VHS.** Tyrone Power, George Sanders, Madeleine Carroll, John Burton, Guy Standing, Sir C. Aubrey Smith, Freddie Bartholomew, Virginia Field, Montagu Love, Una O'Connor, Anne Howard; *D:* Henry King; *W:* Ernest Pascal, Walter Ferris; *C:* Bert Glennon.

Loaded *Bloody Weekend* **1994 (R)** Writer-director Campion (sister of director Jane) follows a group of teens to an abandoned English mansion as they try to film an amateur horror movie. While there, the group decides to have some fun, with the help of LSD. This leads to some therapeutic and angst-ridden discussions about each of their problems, as well as a tragic accident, which changes the lives of all involved. There's some nice character sketches, unfortunately they're more interesting than the loose plot, which leaves too many questions unanswered. Retitled and recut since its original '94 release. **95m/C VHS, DVD.** *NZ GB* Thandie Newton, Catherine McCormack, Oliver Milburn, Nick Patrick, Danny Cunningham, Mathew Eggleton, Biddy Hodson; *D:* Anna Campion; *W:* Anna Campion; *C:* Alan Almond; *M:* Simon Fisher Turner.

Loaded **1/2 2008 (R)** Tristan Price (Metcalfe) is a handsome young law student from a wealthy family who goes looking for some extra excitement. Then he meets upscale coke dealer Sebastian Cole (Large) and gets more than he bargained for. As Tristan descends deeper into addiction, he's pulled into Sebastian's drug deals, which lead to murder and even more plot twists. **100m/C DVD.** Jesse Metcalfe, Corey Large, Monica Keena, Nathalie Kelley, Johnny Messner, Jimmy Jean-Louis, Chace Crawford, Vinnie Jones, Erin Gray, John Bennett Perry; *D:* Alan Pao; *W:* Corey Large, Alan Pao; *C:* Roger Chingirian; *M:* Ralph Rieckermann. **VIDEO**

Loaded Guns **WOOF!** **1975** Airline stewardess-cum-double agent must totally immobilize a top drug trafficking ring. Pathetic spy tale with plenty of unintended laughs. **90m/C VHS.** Ursula Andress, Woody Strode; *D:* Fernando Di Leo.

Loaded Pistols **1948** Story set in the old West starring Gene Autry. **80m/B VHS, DVD.** Gene Autry, Jack Holt, Barbara Britton; *D:* John English.

Loan Shark **1952** An ex-convict gets a job at a tire company, working undercover to expose a loan shark ring. Hackneyed plot moves quickly. **79m/B VHS, DVD.** George Raft, John Hoyt, Dorothy Hart, Paul Stewart, Robert Bice, Russell Johnson, Benny Baker, Lawrence (Larry) Dobkin, Harlan Warde, Margia Dean, William Phipps; *D:* Seymour Friedman; *W:* Martin Rackin, Eugene Ling; *C:* Joseph Biroc; *M:* Heinz Roemheld.

Lobster for Breakfast **1/2 1982 (R)** An Italian gag-fest about a toilet salesman infiltrating his friend's confused marital existence just to make a sale. With English subtitles; also available in a dubbed version. **96m/C VHS.** *IT* Enrico Montesano, Claude Brasseur, Claudine Auger; *D:* Giorgio Capitani.

Lobster Man from Mars **1989 (PG)** When rich movie producer (Curtis) learns from his accountant that he must produce a flop or be taken to the cleaners by the IRS, he buys a homemade horror movie from a young filmmaker. The film is an ultra-low budget production featuring a kooky lobster man and a screaming damsel. The premise peters out about halfway through, but there are enough yuks to keep you going. **84m/C VHS, DVD.** Tony Curtis, Deborah Foreman, Patrick Macnee, Tommy Sledge, Billy Barty, Phil(ip) Proctor, Anthony Hickox, Bobby "Boris" Pickett, Stanley Sheff; *D:* Stanley Sheff; *W:* Bob Greenberg; *C:* Gerry Lively; *M:* Sasha Matson.

A Lobster Tale **1/2 2006** Guess "A Moss Tale" wouldn't have been as good a title. Cody Brewer (Meaney) is a Maine lobsterman suffering hard times, which are also affecting his family. While checking his traps, he discovers an odd green moss that has magical properties. As soon as word gets out, Cody is everyone's best friend so they can get their own piece of the special vegetation. Quirky family fare. **95m/C DVD.** Colm Meaney, Alberta Watson, Jack Knight, Graham Greene; *D:* Adam Massey; *W:* Court Crandall; *C:* Patrick Mcgowan; *M:* Eric Cadesky, Nick Dyer. **VIDEO**

Local Badman **1932** A dim-witted cowhand saves the day in this rip-roaring tale of the old west. **60m/B VHS.** Sally Blane, Hooper Atchley, Edward Hearn, Edward Peil Sr., Hoot Gibson; *D:* Otto Brower; *W:* Philip Graham White; *C:* Tom Galligan, Harry Neumann.

Local Boys **1/2 2002 (PG-13)** California surf dude Randy (Olsen) buys his brother Skeet (Sumpter) his first board for his 12th birthday. But Randy gets jealous when Skeet turns to surfing legend Jim Wesley (Harmon) to be his mentor. Things get even more complicated when Wesley begins romancing the boys' widowed mom (Edwards). **103m/C VHS, DVD.** Mark Harmon, Eric Christian Olsen, Jeremy Sumpter, Stacy Edwards, Giuseppe Andrews, Travis Aaron, Shelby Fenner, Lukas Behnken; *D:* Ron Moler; *C:* James Glennon. **VIDEO**

Local Color **2006 (R)** Sentimental drama turns soft-headed rather than soft-hearted. In 1974, John (Morgan) is a teenager living in Port Chester, New York. He's an admirer of reclusive landscape artist Nicolai Seroff (Mueller Stahl) and pesters the old man until he agrees to tutor John at his Pennsylvania summer home. At first, John is merely household help but Seroff eventually works with him on his paintings amidst various artistic discussions that tend to stop the story cold. **107m/C DVD.** Trevor Morgan, Samantha Mathis, Ray Liotta, Ron Perlman, Diana Scarwid, Charles Durning, Armin Mueller-Stahl, Julie Lott; *D:* George Gallo; *C:* Michael Negrin; *M:* Chris Boardman.

Local Hero **1983 (PG)** Riegert is a yuppie representative of a huge oil company who endeavors to buy a sleepy Scottish fishing village for excavation, and finds himself hypnotized by the place and its crusty denizens. Back in Texas at company headquarters, tycoon Lancaster deals with a psycho therapist and gazes at the stars looking for clues. A low-key, charmingly offbeat Scottish comedy with its own sense of logic and quiet humor, poetic landscapes, and unique characters, epitomizing Forsyth's original style. **112m/C VHS, DVD.** *GB* Peter Riegert, Denis Lawson, Burt Lancaster, Fulton Mackay, Jenny Seagrove, Peter Capaldi, Norman Chancer; *D:* Bill Forsyth; *W:* Bill Forsyth; *C:* Chris Menges; *M:* Mark Knopfler. British Acad. '83: Director (Forsyth); N.Y. Film Critics '83: Screenplay; Natl. Soc. Film Critics '83: Screenplay.

Loch Ness **1/2 1995 (PG)** American zoologist Jonathan Dempsey (Danson) specializes in hunting legendary animals and his latest assignment is to head for the Scottish highlands and take on the Nessie legend. He gets an assistant (Frain), a potential romance with single mom Laura (Richardson), and a lot of grief from some hostile locals before Laura's young daughter Isabel (Graham) decides to help him out. Jim Henson's Creature Shop takes care of the monster's animatronics. **101m/C VHS, DVD.** *GB* Ted Danson, Ian Holm, Joely Richardson, Kirsty Graham, James Frain, Harris Yulin, Keith Allen, Nick Brimble; *D:* John Henderson; *W:* John Fusco; *C:* Clive Tickner; *M:* Trevor Jones.

The Loch Ness Horror **WOOF!** **1982** The famed monster surfaces and chomps on the local poachers—and with good reason. Would that it had munched this movie's producer in, say, 1981. **93m/C VHS.** Barry Buchanan, Miki McKenzie, Sandy Kenyon; *D:* Larry Buchanan.

Loch Ness Terror *Beyond Loch Ness* **2007 (R)** Yeah it's cheap and cheesy and the story is silly but it's surprising B-movie monster fun as well. A Nessie relation has somehow made her way to Lake Superior and she and her bloodthirsty offspring are stomping and chomping locals and vacationers alike. James Murphy (Krause) is the only person to survive an attack and now he's ready to fry some beastie behind. A Sci-Fi Channel original. **91m/C DVD.** Brian Krause, Don S. Davis, Paul McGillion, Carrie Genzel, Donnelly Rhodes, Niall Matter, Paul Ziller, Jason Bourque; *W:* Pinar Toprak; *C:* Anthony C. Metchie; *M:* Amber Boryicki. **CABLE**

Lock 'n' Load **1990 (R)** Why are all the soldiers in the 82nd Airborne stealing vast sums, then committing suicide? One of the guys involved wants to know. **89m/C VHS.** Renee Cline, Jeffrey Smith, Greg E. Russell, Jack Vogel; *D:* David A. Prior, David A. Prior;

W: David A. Prior; *C:* Brian Veatch; *M:* Tony Cappelli.

Lock, Stock and 2 Smoking Barrels 1998 **(R)** Plot twist-laden British caper comedy plays like Tarantino and crumpets. Four dim hoods, Bacon (Statham), Soap (Fletcher), Eddy (Moran) and Tom (Flemyng), pool their ill-gotten gains so that Eddy can play in a high stakes card game. They don't know that the game is fixed, however, and they end up owing gambler Hatchet Harry (Moriarity) 500,000 pounds. The bumbling band plan to rob their drug dealing neighbor Dog (Harper), who's planning on robbing an upper class rival of his own. Throw in a wandering pair of antique shotguns and you have the recipe for a cap-poppin' good time. Rock star Sting appears as the pub-owning father of one of the lads. **105m/C VHS, DVD.** *GB* Jason Flemyng, Dexter Fletcher, Nick Moran, Jason Statham, Steven Mackintosh, Vinnie Jones, Sting, Lenny McLean, P. H. Moriarty, Steve Sweeney, Frank Harper, Stephen Marcus; *D:* Guy Ritchie; *W:* Guy Ritchie; *C:* Tim Maurice-Jones; *M:* David A. Hughes, John Murphy. MTV Movie Awards '99: New Filmmaker (Ritchie).

Lock Up ½ **1989 (R)** Peaceful con Stallone, with only six months to go, is harassed and tortured by vicious prison warden Sutherland in retribution for an unexplained past conflict. Lackluster and moronic; semi-color; surely Sutherland can find better roles. **115m/C VHS, DVD.** Sylvester Stallone, Donald Sutherland, Sonny Landham, John Amos, Darlanne Fluegel, Frank McRae; *D:* John Flynn; *W:* Jeb Stuart; *C:* Donald E. Thorin; *M:* Bill Conti.

Lockdown ½ **1990** Charged with his partner's murder, a detective is forced to ponder the perennial puzzle of life. Not a pretty sight. **90m/C VHS, DVD.** Joe Estevez, Mike Farrell, Richard Lynch; *D:* Frank Harris. **VIDEO**

Lockdown ½ **2000 (R)** Brutal men in the big house pic follows the fortunes of three friends who wind up doing time in New Mexico. Violent drug dealer Cashmere (Casseus) is framed by another player and manages to take two right-living buddies—Avery (Jones) and Dre (Bonds)—down with him. Cashmere joins the in-house crew of black boss Clean Up (Master P) while Avery is lucky enough to be taken under the wing of a self-educated cellmate who passes on wise advice for doing time. Dre is the one who winds up in situations familiar to viewers of the cable series "Oz." Grim watching. **105m/C VHS, DVD.** Richard T. Jones, De'Aundre Bonds, Gabriel Casseus, Master P, Bill Nunn, Clifton Powell, Joe Torry, Anna Maria Horsford, Melissa De Sousa, Kirk "Sticky Fingaz" Jones; *D:* John Luessenhop; *W:* Preston A. Whitmore II; *C:* Chris Chomyn; *M:* John (Gianni) Frizzell.

Locked in Silence **1999** Young boy becomes electively mute after believing he saw his older brother kill another boy. His farm family nearly goes bankrupt trying to find a cure until a psychologist is able to help the child deal with reality. Based on a true story. **94m/C VHS.** Bonnie Bedelia, Bruce Davison, Dan Hedaya, Marc Donato, Ron White, Steven McCarthy; *D:* Bruce Pittman; *W:* Dalene Young; *C:* Michael Storey; *M:* Gary Chang. **CABLE**

The Locket ½ **2002** After his mother dies, Michael Keddington (Willett) takes a job at a health-care facility to pay off debts. There he meets Esther Huish (Redgrave), a lonely widow who encourages Michael not to give up his dreams. But when his supportive girlfriend Faye (Moreau) goes off to college and a jealous co-worker (Heuring) accuses Michael of a crime, he needs Esther's strength to see him through. Based on the novel by Richard Paul Evans. **100m/C VHS, DVD.** Chad Willet, Vanessa Redgrave, Marguerite Moreau, Lori Heuring, Mary (Elizabeth) McDonough, Brock Peters, Terry O'Quinn; *D:* Karen Arthur; *W:* Ron Raley; *C:* Thomas Neuwirth; *M:* Bruce Broughton. **TV**

Loco Love ½ *Mi Casa, Su Casa* **2003 (PG)** Flat and hopelessly dumb romantic comedy. Gardener Miguel (Mejia) wins big in the lottery and makes a deal with former client Donald (Werner): if Donald will make a green card marriage with his sister Catalina (Harring) so she can come to the U.S., Miguel will give Donald a big chunk of change. Donald wants to open a restaurant so he agrees, not realizing that this means Catalina's entire family will be joining them. And (for no apparent reason) Donald's ex-wife Barbara (Scarborough) gets suddenly jealous and decides she wants Donald back. **94m/C VHS, DVD.** Laura Elena Harring, Gerardo Mejia, Roy Werner, Margaret Scarborough, Barbara Eden; *D:* Bryan Lewis; *W:* Steven Baer; *C:* Thaddeus Wadleigh; *M:* Jon McCallum.

The Locusts ½ **1997 (R)** Backwater beefcake Clay Hewitt (Vaughn) swaggers into a small Kansas town where everyone has a lit cigarette and a secret and no one is safe from hopeless cliches and corny dialogue. Clay's sweaty, sleeveless t-shirts and choir-boy face soon have the women swarming, but he's only interested in helping a mentally and emotionally challenged kid named Flyboy (Davies) get out from under his emasculating and abusive mother Delilah (Capshaw), also Clay's boss and overly ardent admirer. Judd is barely used as Clay's spunky squeeze in this slow-paced, small-town drama by first-time director Kelley. Any high school freshman with an English lit class under his belt won't miss the not-so-subtle metaphors at play—Delilah has workers castrating bulls a lot. **123m/C VHS, DVD.** Kate Capshaw, Jeremy Davies, Vince Vaughn, Ashley Judd, Paul Rudd, Daniel Meyer, Jessica Capshaw; *D:* John Patrick Kelley; *W:* John Patrick Kelley; *C:* Phedon Papamichael; *M:* Carter Burwell.

Locusts: The 8th Plague **2005** Too bad a plague of locusts couldn't have attacked this movie and saved the unwary viewer a lot of suffering. Top-secret experiments at an Idaho government lab result in genetically-modified locusts, which escape. The insects turn out to be have a taste for human flesh (because we taste just like chicken). A Sci-Fi Channel original. **88m/C DVD.** Dan Cortese, Julie Benz, David Keith, Jeff Fahey, Kirk B.R. Woller; *D:* Ian Gilmour; *W:* D.R. Rosen; *C:* Lorenzo Senatore; *M:* Pierpaolo Tiano. **CABLE**

L'Odeur des Fauves **1966** One of a cynical reporter's scandalous stories gets an innocent man killed, compelling the reporter somehow to make restitution. Subtitled in English. **86m/C VHS.** *FR* Maurice Ronet, Josephine Chaplin, Vittorio De Sica; *D:* Richard Balducci.

The Lodger *The Case of Jonathan Drew; The Lodger: A Case of London Fog* **1926** A mysterious lodger is thought to be a rampaging mass murderer of young women. First Hitchcock film to explore the themes and ideas that would become his trademarks. Silent. Climactic chase is memorable. Remade three times. Look closely for the Master in his first cameo. **91m/B VHS, DVD.** *GB* Ivor Novello, Marie Ault, Arthur Chesney, Malcolm Keen, June; ***Cameos:*** Alfred Hitchcock; *D:* Alfred Hitchcock; *W:* Alfred Hitchcock, Eliot Stannard.

The Lodger **2009 (R)** Artificial and melodramatic psycho-thriller. Detective Chandler Manning (Molina) is hunting a serial killer who murders prostitutes along Sunset Boulevard. The killer's M.O. is the same as someone Manning previously put away who was also fixated on Jack the Ripper's crimes in Victorian London. Meanwhile, Ellen Burling (Davis) has suspicions about Malcolm (Baker), the mysterious man that has become the Burlings' new lodger. **95m/C DVD.** Alfred Molina, Simon Baker, Hope Davis, Donal Logue, Shane West, Rachael Leigh Cook, Philip Baker Hall; *D:* David Ondaatje; *W:* David Ondaatje; *C:* David Armstrong; *M:* John (Gianni) Frizzell.

Logan's Run ½ **1976** In the 23rd century, a hedonistic society exists in a huge bubble and people are only allowed to live to the age of 30. Intriguing concepts and great futuristic sets prevail here. Based on the novel by William Nolan and George Clayton Johnson. **120m/C VHS, DVD.** Michael York, Jenny Agutter, Richard Jordan, Roscoe Lee Browne, Farrah Fawcett, Peter Ustinov, Camilla Carr, Ann Ford; *D:* Michael Anderson Sr.; *W:* David Zelag Goodman; *C:* Ernest Laszlo; *M:* Jerry Goldsmith. Oscars '76: Visual FX.

Loggerheads **2005** Families and the ties that bind. Drifter Mark (Pardue) heads to Kure Beach, North Carolina to help rescue the endangered loggerhead turtle. Mark ran away from his adoptive parents, well-meaning religious conservatives Robert (Sarandon) and Elizabeth (Harper), when they learned he was gay. Also living in NC is Mark's birth mother, Grace (Hunt), who's recovering from a breakdown and has decided to find the baby she gave up as a teenager. Meanwhile, Mark is bonding with gentle George (Kelly), whose male lover has died. More enjoyable for fans of the sincere and sentimental, it's well worth a look, especially for the strong performances of Harper and Hunt. **93m/C DVD.** *US* Bonnie Hunt, Kip Pardue, Tess Harper, Chris Sarandon, Michael Learned, Michael Kelly, Robin Weigert; *D:* Tim Kirkman; *W:* Tim Kirkman; *C:* Oliver Bokelberg; *M:* Mark Geary.

Lois Gibbs and the Love Canal **1982** Mason's TV movie debut as Lois Gibbs, a housewife turned activist, fighting the authorities over chemical-dumping in the Love Canal area of Niagara Falls, New York. The script doesn't convey the seriousness of developments in that region. **100m/C VHS.** Marsha Mason, Bob Gunton, Penny Fuller, Roberta Maxwell, Jeremy Licht, Louise Latham; *D:* Glenn Jordan. **TV**

Lola **1961** A wonderful tale of a nightclub dancer and her amorous adventures. Innovative film that marked the beginning of French New Wave. In French with English subtitles. **90m/B VHS, DVD.** *FR* Anouk Aimee, Marc Michel, Elina Labourdette, Jacques Harden; *D:* Jacques Demy.

Lola ½ *The Statutory Affair; Twinky* **1969 (PG)** A teenaged girl links up romantically with a considerably older writer of pornographic books. One would expect more from such a good cast, but the film never follows through. British release was originally 98 minutes. **88m/C VHS, DVD.** *GB IT* Charles Bronson, Susan George, Trevor Howard, Michael Craig, Honor Blackman, Lionel Jeffries, Robert Morley, Jack Hawkins, Orson Bean, Kay Medford, Paul Ford; *D:* Richard Donner.

Lola and Billy the Kid *Lola + Bilikid* **1998** Murat (Davrak) is a closeted gay Turkish teenager living in Berlin with his widowed mother and homophobic brother Osman (Mete). Lola (Mukli) is a travestite dancer at a nightclub who lives with hustler Bili (Yildiz). When Lola tries to contact Murat's family, the boy discovers that Lola is his brother, who was thrown out by Osman. Murat meets Lola, who is later killed—apparently by neo-Nazi thugs. Bili vows revenge but Murat learns that the situation isn't as clear as it seems. German and Turkish with subtitles. **95m/C VHS, DVD.** *GE* Baki Darrak, Gandi Mukli, Erdal Yildiz, Hasan Ali Mete, Michael Gerber, Murat Yilmaz, Inge Keller; *D:* Kutlug Ataman; *W:* Kutlug Ataman; *C:* Chris Squires; *M:* Arpad Bondy.

Lola Montes **1955** Ophuls' final masterpiece (and his only film in color) recounts the life and sins of the famous courtesan, mistress of Franz Liszt and the King of Bavaria. Ignored upon release, but hailed later by the French as a cinematic landmark. Adapted from an unpublished novel by Cecil Saint-Laurent. French with subtitles. The original widescreen release clocked in at 140 minutes. **110m/C DVD.** *FR* Martine Carol, Peter Ustinov, Anton Walbrook, Ivan Desny, Oskar Werner; *D:* Max Ophuls; *W:* Max Ophuls; *C:* Christian Matras; *M:* Georges Auric.

Lolida 2000 ½ *Lolita 2000* **1997** In the future all sexual activity is prohibited (bummer). Lolita's working for an organization that destroys sexual material but three particular stories arouse feelings in her that she just has to act on. **90m/C VHS, DVD.** Jacqueline Lovell, Gabriella Hall, Eric Acsell; *D:* Cybil (Sybil) Richards.

Lolita **1962** A middle-aged professor is consumed by his lust for a teenage nymphet in this strange film considered daring in its time. Based on Vladimir Nabokov's novel. Watch for Winters' terrific portrayal as Lolita's sex-starved mother. **152m/B VHS, DVD.** *GB* James Mason, Shelley Winters, Peter Sellers, Sue Lyon, Gary Cockrell, Jerry Stovin, Diana Decker, Lois Maxwell, Cec Linder, Bill Greene, Shirley Douglas, Marianne Stone, Marion Mathie, James Dyrenforth, C. Denier Warren, Terence (Terry) Kilburn, John Harrison; *D:* Stanley Kubrick; *W:* Vladimir Nabokov; *C:* Oswald Morris; *M:* Nelson Riddle.

Lolita **1997 (R)** Middle-aged college professor Humbert Humbert (Irons) becomes obsessed with nymphet Lolita (Swain), even to the point of marrying her mother Charlotte (Griffith) so he can always be close by. Then Charlotte dies, and the unlikely duo begin an aimless road trip that eventually leads Lolita to a fateful meeting with yet another older man, Quilty (Langella). Director Lyne's no stranger to controversy but his reverential take on the Vladimir Nabokov novel turns out to be much ado about nothing. Then 14-year-old Swain (in a fetchingly flirty performance) debuts as Lolita (along with a body-double). **137m/C VHS, DVD.** Jeremy Irons, Melanie Griffith, Frank Langella, Dominique Swain, Suzanne Shepherd, Keith Reddin, Erin J. Dean, Ben Silverstone; *D:* Adrian Lyne; *W:* Stephen Schiff; *C:* Howard Atherton; *M:* Ennio Morricone.

Lolo **1992** Outcast Lolo loses his job in Mexico City and then accidentally kills the local moneylender. The only one who will help him is his girlfriend Sonia, who gets the money for them to flee the city by prostituting herself. Spanish with subtitles. **88m/C VHS, DVD.** *MX* Roberto Sosa, Lucha Villa; *D:* Francisco Athie; *W:* Francisco Athie; *C:* Jorge Medina; *M:* Juan Cristobal Perez Grobert.

London **2005 (R)** Syd (Evans) is a pathetic drunk and druggie whose girlfriend London (Biel) has unsurprisingly left him for a new guy. She is also leaving New York, and Syd decides to crash her going-away party, accompanied by dealer Bateman (Stratham) from whom Syd has just scored a lot of coke. The two guys spend most of their time in the bathroom doing blow and yapping. They are tiresome and misogynistic and so is the entire enterprise. **92m/C DVD.** *US* Chris Evans, Jessica Biel, Jason Statham, Isla Fisher, Joy Bryant, Kelli Garner, Dane Cook; *D:* Hunter Richards; *W:* Hunter Richards; *C:* Jo Willems.

London Kills Me **1991 (R)** A slice-of-life story London-style. Set at the end of the Thatcher era, Clint is a homeless drifter dealing drugs to get by. He's trying to get enough money for a new pair of shoes which will enable him to get a job in a fancy restaurant and away from his aimless life. His friend Muffdiver leads the group of drug pushers and is obsessed with money and power. Sylvie is the sultry junkie who drifts between Clint, Muffdiver, and her drug needs. The directorial debut of Kureishi is more a collection of characters and situations than a complete film but there are moments of disturbing intensity and odd sweetness. **105m/C VHS.** *GB* Justin Chadwick, Steven Mackintosh, Emer McCourt, Roshan Seth, Fiona Shaw, Brad Dourif, Gordon Warnecke, Dave Atkins; *D:* Hanif Kureishi; *W:* Hanif Kureishi; *C:* Edward Lachman.

London Melody ½ *Girl in the Street* **1937** Neagle is a spirited Cockney busker who meets a kindly Italian diplomat who decides to finance her musical education. He promptly also falls in love with her. **71m/B VHS.** *GB* Anna Neagle, Tullio Carminati, Robert Douglas, Horace Hodgers; *D:* Herbert Wilcox.

London Voodoo ½ **2004** Workaholic Lincoln (Cockle) and wife Sarah (Stewart) are Yanks in London who, while renovating their new digs, discover a grave in their cellar. It's that of a voodoo priestess who then possesses Sarah. Sex and exorcism are involved. **90m/C DVD.** *GB* Sara Stewart, Trisha Mortimer, Sven-Bertil Taube, Doug Cockle, Vonda Barnes, Michael Nyquist; *D:* Robert Pratten; *W:* Robert Pratten; *C:* Patrick Jackson; *M:* Steven Severin.

The Lone Avenger **1933** Average oater centers around a bank panic, with two-gun Maynard clearing up the trouble. **60m/B VHS.** Ken Maynard, Muriel Gordon, James A. Marcus, Charles "Blackie" King, Jack Rockwell, Alan Bridge, Niles Welch, William Bailey; *D:* Alan James; *W:* Alan James, Betty Burbridge, Forrest Sheldon; *C:* William Nobles.

Lone Bandit ½ **1933** Vintage western starring Chandler. **57m/B VHS.** Lane Chandler, Doris Brook, Wally Wales; *D:* J(ohn) P(aterson) McGowan.

The Lone Defender **1932** A dozen episodes of the western serial starring the canine crusader, Rin Tin Tin. **235m/B VHS.** Walter Miller, June Marlowe, Buzz Barton, Josef Swickard, Frank Lanning, Robert F. (Bob) Kortman; ***D:*** Richard Thorpe.

Lone Hero ✓✓ **2002 (R)** You can tell by the video box that Phillips is not the titular hero—in fact, he's Bart (Phillips), a psycho biker gang leader who terrorizes a small town. Flanery is the somewhat goofball hero, John, who plays a gunfighter in the local Wild West show and who is the only one willing to stand up to the violent menace. **91m/C VHS, DVD.** Lou Diamond Phillips, Sean Patrick Flanery, Robert Forster, Tanya Allen, Garry Chalk; ***D:*** Ken Sanzel; ***W:*** Ken Sanzel; ***C:*** David Pelletier; ***M:*** Anthony Marinelli.

Lone Justice ✓✓ ½ **1993 (R)** Cowboy Ned Blessing has seen and done it all (from outlaw to sheriff) but his wild ways have caught up with him. Now, he's relating his exploits from a jail cell as he awaits his fate at the end of a rope. Beware—this looks like the first chapter of a series and there's no real ending. **94m/C VHS.** Daniel Baldwin, Luis Avalos, Chris Cooper, Sean Baca, Taylor Fry, Julia Campbell, Rene Auberjonois, Timothy Scott, Bob Gunton, Miguel (Michael) Sandoval, Jeff Kober; ***D:*** Peter Werner; ***W:*** William D. Wittliff; ***M:*** Basil Poledouris.

Lone Justice 2 ✓✓ ½ *Ned Blessing: The Story of My Life and Times* **1993 (PG-13)** Laconic hero Ned Blessing (Johnson), along with Mexican sidekick Crecencio (Avalos), return to Blessing's hometown after a six-year absence and find it ruled by six-shooters and fists. The despicable Borgers clan has murdered the local sheriff (who happens to be Blessing's daddy) and rules by intimidation—until Ned gets involved. Cliched but amusing. **93m/C VHS, DVD.** Brad Johnson, Luis Avalos, Wes Studi, Bill McKinney, Brenda Bakke, Julius Tennon, Richard Riehle, Gregory Scott Cummins, Rob Campbell, Rusty Schwimmer; ***D:*** Jack Bender; ***W:*** William D. Wittliff; ***C:*** Neil Roach; ***M:*** David Bell. **TV**

Lone Justice 3: Showdown at Plum Creek ✓✓ ½ **1996 (PG)** Ex-outlaw-turned-sheriff Ned Blessing (Johnson) discovers the body of the previous sheriff has disappeared from its grave, Big Emma has taken over the saloon and wants Blessing out of the way, and Oscar Wilde comes to town. Three re-edited stories from the TV miniseries. **94m/C VHS, DVD.** Brad Johnson, Wes Studi, Brenda Bakke, William Sanderson, Luis Avalos, Rusty Schwimmer, Stephen Fry; ***D:*** Jack Bender, Dan Lerner, David Hemmings; ***W:*** Stephen Harrigan; ***C:*** Neil Roach. **TV**

The Lone Ranger ✓ ½ **1938** Western serial about the masked man and his faithful Indian sidekick. From a long-sought print found in Mexico, this program is burdened by a noisy sound track, two completely missing chapters, an abridged episode 15, and Spanish subtitles. **234m/B VHS.** Lee Powell; ***D:*** William Witney, John English.

Lone Ranger ✓✓ ½ **1956** Tonto and that strange masked man must prevent a war between ranchers and Indians in the first of the "Lone Ranger" series. "Hi-ho Silver!" **87m/C VHS, DVD.** Clayton Moore, Jay Silverheels, Lyle Bettger, Bonita Granville; ***D:*** Stuart Heisler; ***W:*** Herb Meadow; ***C:*** Edwin DuPar; ***M:*** David Buttolph.

Lone Rider ✓ ½ **2008** Honored Civil War soldier Bobby Hattaway (Phillips) returns to his hometown to find ruthless Stu Croaker (Spano) trying to gain a business monopoly for when the railroad arrives. Bobby discovers his father (Keach) has taken out a mortgage on the family ranch in order to prevent their mercantile business from going under and Croaker is determined to foreclose. The title character is not related to the western movie series. **80m/C DVD.** Lou Diamond Phillips, Vincent Spano, Stacy Keach, Cynthia (Cyndy, Cindy) Preston, Angela Alvarado, Tom Schanley, Timothy Bottoms, Mike Starr; ***D:*** David S. Cass Sr.; ***W:*** Frank Sharp; ***C:*** James W. Wrenn; ***M:*** Joe Kraemer. **TV**

The Lone Rider Crosses the Rio ✓ ½ **1941** The Lone Rider (Houston) and his sidekick Fuzzy (St. John) are accused of kidnapping while searching for bad guy "El Puma" (King) in Mexico. The second film in the series. **63m/B DVD.** George Houston, Charles King, Al "Fuzzy" St. John, Julian Rivero, Roquell Verria, Thornton Edwards, Howard Masters; ***D:*** Sam Newfield; ***W:*** William Lively; ***C:*** Jack Greenhalgh.

The Lone Rider in Cheyenne ✓ ½ **1942** One of the last in the "Lone Rider" series. The Lone Rider is out to clear the name of an innocent man accused of murder. **59m/B VHS.** George Houston, Al "Fuzzy" St. John; ***D:*** Sam Newfield.

The Lone Rider in Frontier Fury ✓ ½ **1941** The Lone Rider (Houston) has been wrongly accused of murdering a rancher and must clear his name. **60m/B VHS.** George Houston, Hillary Brooke, Al "Fuzzy" St. John, Karl Hackett, Ted Adams, Arch (Archie) Hall Sr., Budd Buster, Edward Peil Sr., Tom London; ***D:*** Sam Newfield; ***W:*** Fred Myton.

The Lone Rider in Ghost Town ✓ ½ **1941** Outlaws "haunt" a ghost town to protect their hidden mine and the Lone Rider and his pal, Fuzzy, are out to solve the mystery. Installment in the short-lived "Lone Rider" series. **64m/B VHS, DVD.** George Houston, Al "Fuzzy" St. John, Budd Buster; ***D:*** Sam Newfield.

The Lone Runner WOOF! **1988 (PG)** An adventurer rescues a beautiful heiress from Arab kidnappers in this dud. **90m/C VHS.** Miles O'Keeffe, Ronald Lacey, Michael J. Aronin, John Steiner, Hal Yamanouchi; ***D:*** Ruggero Deodato.

Lone Star ✓✓ ½ **1952** Big stars, big budget western in which Texas fights for independence as good guy Gable and badman Crawford fight each other. Gardner plays a fiery newspaper editor as well as Gable's love interest. Script is chock full of holes, but great action scenes make up for it. Based on the story by Borden Chase. **94m/B VHS.** Clark Gable, Ava Gardner, Broderick Crawford, Lionel Barrymore, Beulah Bondi, Ed Begley Sr., William Farnum, Lowell Gilmore; ***D:*** Vincent Sherman; ***W:*** Howard Estabrook, Borden Chase.

Lone Star ✓✓✓ ½ **1995 (R)** Terrific contemporary western set in the border town Frontera, Texas. Sheriff Sam Deeds (Cooper) is still dealing with the legacy of his father, legendary lawman Buddy Deeds (McConaughey) who, 40 years before, wrestled control of the town from his racist, corrupt predecessor Charlie Wade (Kristofferson) and supposedly sent him packing. But when skeletal remains and a sheriff's badge turn up on an abandoned Army rifle range, guess whose bones they turn out to be. Buddy's friends would like Sam to just leave the past lie but he can't, and learns some hard home truths. This is only one of the town's stories that Sayles gracefully tells and, as always, his ensemble cast all offer outstanding performances. **137m/C VHS, DVD.** Gabriel Casseus, Chris Cooper, Matthew McConaughey, Kris Kristofferson, Elizabeth Pena, Joe Morton, Ron Canada, Clifton James, Miriam Colon, Frances McDormand, Richard Jones; ***D:*** John Sayles; ***W:*** John Sayles; ***C:*** Stuart Dryburgh; ***M:*** Mason Daring. Ind. Spirit '97: Support. Actress (Pena).

Lone Star Kid **1988** 11-year-old Brian Zimmerman lives in Crabb, Texas—population 400. After he witnesses a car accident death because there's no adequate emergency service, he decides to run for mayor and help modernize the town. Based on a true story. Includes a viewers' guide. Presented as part of the "Wonderworks" series. **55m/C VHS.** James Earl Jones, Chad Sheets; ***M:*** Charlie Daniels.

Lone Star Law Men ✓ **1942** A U.S. marshal has his hands full in a border town overrun with bandits. Keene stars as the deputy marshall who goes undercover and joins the gang in an attempt to foil their crooked plans. **58m/B VHS.** Tom Keene, Frank Yaconelli, Sugar Dawn, Betty Miles; ***D:*** Robert Emmett Tansey.

The Lone Star Ranger ✓ ½ **1930** Former outlaw O'Brien is trying to go straight by helping to bring a gang of rustlers to justice. Interesting plot twist in the link between his girlfriend and the head of the gang. **64m/B VHS.** George O'Brien, Sue Carol, Walter McGrail, Warren Hymer, Russell Simpson; ***D:*** A.F. Erickson.

Lone Star State of Mind ✓ ½ **2002 (PG-13)** That state seems to be perplexed if not downright idiotic. Good-hearted Earl (Jackson) has promised his ditsy girlfriend Baby (King) that he will take her to L.A. so that she can fulfill her dream of becoming a soap opera actress. Only before they can leave their redneck community, Baby's doofus cousin Junior (Qualls) lands in a whole heap 'o trouble and Earl promises to set things right. **88m/C VHS, DVD.** Joshua Jackson, Jaime (James) King, DJ Qualls, Matthew Davis, Ryan Hurst, John Cougar Mellencamp, Thomas Haden Church, Sam McMurray; ***D:*** David Semel; ***W:*** Trevor Munson; ***C:*** Michael Barrett; ***M:*** Tyler Bates.

The Lone Star Trail ✓ ½ **1943** Blaze Barker is paroled after being framed for robbery and serving two years. Returning to his home in Dead Falls, Barker learns that landgrabbers are after all the valley's property before a new dam is constructed. He teams up with pal Angus and Marshal Steele to clear his name and find justice. Robert (credited as Bob) Mitchum has a small role as Ben Slocum. **57m/B DVD.** Johnny Mack Brown, Fuzzy Knight, Tex Ritter, Jennifer Holt, George Eldredge, Harry Strang, Jimmy Wakely, Earle Hodgins, Jack Ingram, Robert Mitchum; ***D:*** Ray Taylor; ***W:*** Oliver Drake; ***C:*** William Sickner.

Lone Wolf ✓ **1988** A werewolf terrorizes a high school, and a few computerniks track it down. **97m/C VHS.** Dyann Brown, Kevin Hart, Jamie Newcomb, Ann Douglas; ***D:*** John Callas.

Lone Wolf and Cub ✓ *Baby Cart 1: Lend a Child...Lend an Arm* **1972** First in a series of six from the sword-wielding samurai genre. Chronicles the events leading up to a samurai warrior's (Wakayama) expulsion from his native village along with his infant son (Tomikawa). Father's intense rivalry with the evil Shogun whom he was ousted by becomes an epic struggle of good vs. evil. The adorable little "Lone Cub" provides an effective counterpoint for Dad's sideline excursion into a local brothel. In Japanese with English subtitles in a letterbox format. **83m/C VHS.** *JP* Tomisaburo Wakayama, Akihiro Tomikawa; ***D:*** Kenji Misumi.

Lone Wolf and Cub 4 ✓ **1972** Fourth in a series of six. A man (Wakayama) pushes his son (Tomikawa) across Japan in a baby cart loaded with deadly accessories including built-in guns and switchblades. Copious amounts of bloodshed. In Japanese with English subtitles in a letterbox format. **80m/C VHS.** *JP* Tomisaburo Wakayama, Akihiro Tomikawa; ***D:*** Buichi Sato.

Lone Wolf and Cub: Baby Cart at the River Styx ✓ *Baby Cart at the River Styx; Baby Cart 2* **1972** Second of six parts in the "Kozure Ohkami" ("Sword of Vengeance") series about a man who wheels his motherless infant through the Chinese countryside in a baby cart armed with secret weapons, plotting his revenge on the warlord who expelled him. This one features the intro of Sayka and her fellow female assassins. Subtitled in English. **80m/C VHS, DVD.** *JP* Tomisaburo Wakayama, Akihiro Tomikawa; ***D:*** Kenji Misumi.

Lone Wolf and Cub: Baby Cart to Hades ✓ *Baby Cart to Hades* **1972** The third "Kozure Ohkami" ("Sword of Vengeance") film once again finds samurai Itto Ogami and his son Diagoro embroiled in a power struggle between a regional landlord and a governor in feudal Japan. Subtitled in English. **88m/C VHS, DVD.** *JP* Tomisaburo Wakayama, Akihiro Tomikawa; ***D:*** Kenji Misumi.

Lone Wolf McQuade ✓✓ ½ **1983** Martial arts action abounds in this modern-day Western which pits unorthodox Texas Ranger Norris against a band of gun-running mercenaries led by Carradine. Oh, and there's a conflict-ridden love interest as well. Violent (and not particularly literary) but worthy entry in chop-socky genre. **107m/C VHS, DVD.** Chuck Norris, Leon Isaac Kennedy, David Carradine, L.Q. Jones, Barbara Carrera; ***D:*** Steve Carver; ***W:*** H. Kaye Dyal; ***C:*** Roger Shearman; ***M:*** Francesco De Masi.

The Loneliest Runner ✓✓ **1976** Based on the true story of an Olympic track star who, as a teenager, suffered humiliation as a bed-wetter. The real-life experiences of producer-director Landon are presented in a touching and sensitive manner. **74m/C VHS.** Michael Landon, Lance Kerwin, DeAnn Mears, Brian Keith, Melissa Sue Anderson; ***D:*** Michael Landon. **TV**

The Loneliness of the Long Distance Runner ✓✓✓ *Rebel with a Cause* **1962** Courtenay, in his film debut, turns in a powerful performance as an angry young man infected by the poverty and hopelessness of the British slums. His first attempt at crime is a bust and lands him in a boys reformatory where he is recruited for the running team. While training for the big event with a rival school, Redgrave's obsession with winning the race and Courtenay's continued indifference to the outcome lock the two in an intriguing, seemingly one-sided power struggle. Though widely overlooked when first released, it has since been praised as one of the finest teenage angst films of the '60s. Riveting depiction on a boy's rite of passage into manhood. **104m/B VHS, DVD.** *GB* Tom Courtenay, Michael Redgrave, Avis Bunnage, Peter Madden, James Bolam, Julia Foster, Topsy Jane, Frank Finlay, Christopher Parker; ***D:*** Tony Richardson; ***C:*** Walter Lassally; ***M:*** John Addison.

Lonely Are the Brave ✓✓✓ **1962** A free-spirited cowboy out of sync with the modern age tries to rescue a buddy from a local jail, and in his eventual escape is tracked relentlessly by modern law enforcement. A compelling, sorrowful essay on civilized progress and exploitation of nature. Adapted from the novel "Brave Cowboy" by Edward Abbey. **107m/B VHS.** Kirk Douglas, Walter Matthau, Gena Rowlands, Carroll O'Connor, George Kennedy, Michael Kane, Karl Swenson, William Schallert, Bill Bixby; ***D:*** David Miller; ***W:*** Dalton Trumbo; ***C:*** Philip Lathrop; ***M:*** Jerry Goldsmith.

The Lonely Guy ✓✓ ½ **1984 (R)** Romantic comedy with Martin as a jilted writer who writes a best-selling book about being a lonely guy and finds stardom does have its rewards. Based on "The Lonely Guy's Book of Life" by Bruce Jay Friedman. **91m/C VHS, DVD.** Steve Martin, Charles Grodin, Judith Ivey, Steve Lawrence, Robyn Douglass, Merv Griffin, Dr. Joyce Brothers, Tony Giorgio; ***D:*** Arthur Hiller; ***W:*** Stan Daniels; ***C:*** Victor Kemper; ***M:*** Jerry Goldsmith.

Lonely Hearts ✓✓✓ **1982 (R)** An endearing Australian romantic comedy about a piano tuner, who at 50 finds himself alone after years of caring for his mother, and a sexually insecure spinster, whom he meets through a dating service. Wonderful performances and a good script make this a delightful film that touches the human heart. **95m/C VHS, DVD.** *AU* Wendy Hughes, Norman Kaye, Jon Finlayson, Julia Blake, Jonathan Hardy; ***D:*** Paul Cox; ***W:*** Paul Cox, John Clarke; ***C:*** Yuri Sokol; ***M:*** Norman Kaye. Australian Film Inst. '82: Film.

Lonely Hearts ✓ ½ **1991 (R)** A handsome con man works his wiles on a lonely woman in this erotic thriller. Standard plot wastes a good cast. **109m/C VHS.** Eric Roberts, Beverly D'Angelo, Joanna Cassidy; ***W:*** R.E. Daniels.

Lonely Hearts ✓✓ **2006 (R)** True crime thriller based on the 1940s Lonely Hearts Killers, previously filmed as "The Honeymoon Killers" (1970). Raymond (Leto) is a smalltime con artist who's overwhelmed by possessive—and homicidal— partner Martha (Hayek), who decides it's best to off their female marks. Morose New York detective Elmer Robinson (Travolta) and partner Hildebrandt (Gandolfini) are assigned to the case. Director Robinson (the grandson of the real-life detective) is matter-of-fact about the violence, which makes it more shocking, and Hayek is the ultimate fatal beauty. **107m/C DVD.** *US* John Travolta, James Gandolfini, Salma Hayek, Jared Leto, Laura Dern, Scott Caan, Alice Krige; ***D:*** Todd Robinson; ***W:*** Todd Robinson; ***C:*** Peter Levy; ***M:*** Mychael Danna.

Lonely in America ✓✓ ½ **1990** Charming romantic comedy of a newcomer in New York City. Arun (Chowdhry) has just arrived from India and has quite a few things to learn about life in the Big Apple. **96m/C VHS.** Ranjit (Chaudry) Chowdhry, Adelaide Miller, Robert Kessler, Melissa Christopher, David Toney, Tirlok Malik; ***D:*** Barry Alexander Brown; ***W:*** Barry Alexander Brown, Satyajit Joy Palit.

The Lonely Lady WOOF! 1983 (R) Young writer comes to Hollywood with dreams of success, gets involved with the seamy side of movie-making, and is driven to a nervous breakdown. Pia needs acting lessons, yet it probably wouldn't have helped this trash. Adapted from the novel by Harold Robbins. **92m/C VHS.** Pia Zadora, Lloyd Bochner, Bibi Besch, Joseph Cali, Ray Liotta, Jared Martin, Anthony Holland, Carla Romanelli, Olivier Pierre, Craig G. Kelly; ***D:*** Peter Sasdy; ***W:*** John Kershaw, Shawn Randall; ***C:*** Brian West; ***M:*** Charlie Calello. Golden Raspberries '83: Worst Picture, Worst Actress (Zadora), Worst Director (Sasdy), Worst Screenplay, Worst Song ("The Way You Do It").

Lonely Man 1/2 1957 A gunfighter tries to end his career, but is urged into one last battle. Strong performances and tight direction make up for weak plot. **87m/B VHS, DVD.** Jack Palance, Anthony Perkins, Neville Brand, Elaine Aiken; ***D:*** Henry Levin; ***C:*** Lionel Lindon.

The Lonely Passion of Judith Hearne 1987 (R) A self-effacing Dublin spinster meets a man who gives her his attention, but she must overcome her own self-doubt and crisis of faith. Adapted from Brian Moore's 1955 novel. Excellent performances from both Hoskins and Smith. **116m/C VHS.** *GB* Maggie Smith, Bob Hoskins, Wendy Hiller, Marie Kean, Ian McNeice, Alan Devlin, Rudi Davies, Prunella Scales; ***D:*** Jack Clayton; ***W:*** Peter Nelson; ***C:*** Peter Hannan; ***M:*** Georges Delerue. British Acad. '88: Actress (Smith).

The Lonely Sex 1/2 1959 Creepy and bizarre film in which a maniac kidnaps a young girl and is then harassed by her psychotic housemate. **?m/C VHS, DVD.** Jean Evans, Karl Light, Mary Gonzales; ***D:*** Richard Hilliard; ***W:*** Richard Hilliard; ***C:*** Richard Hilliard.

Lonely Wives 1931 A lawyer hires an entertainer to serve as his double because of his marital problems. **86m/B VHS, DVD.** Edward Everett Horton, Patsy Ruth Miller, Laura La Plante, Esther Ralston; ***D:*** Russell Mack; ***W:*** Walter DeLeon; ***C:*** Edward Snyder.

Lonelyhearts 1/2 1958 Clift plays a reporter who is assigned the lovelorn column of his paper and gets too immersed in the problems of his readers. Given the superior cast and excellent material, this is a somewhat disappointing adaptation of the brilliant Nathanael West novel "Miss Lonelyhearts." Film debuts of both Stapleton and director Donehue. **101m/B VHS.** Montgomery Clift, Robert Ryan, Myrna Loy, Dolores Hart, Maureen Stapleton, Frank Maxwell, Jackie Coogan, Mike Kellin; ***D:*** Vincent J. Donehue.

Loners 1972 (R) Three teenagers run from the Southwest police after they are accused of murdering a highway patrolman. **80m/C VHS.** Dean Stockwell, Gloria Grahame, Scott Brady, Alex Dreier, Pat Stich; ***D:*** Sutton Roley; ***W:*** Barry Sandler.

Lonesome Dove 1/2 1989 Classic western saga with Duvall and Jones in outstanding roles as two aging ex-Texas Rangers who decide to leave their quiet lives for a last adventure—a cattle drive from Texas to Montana. Along the way they encounter a new love (Lane), a lost love (Huston), and a savage renegade Indian (well-played by Forrest). Based on Pulitzer prize-winner Larry McMurtry's novel, this handsome TV miniseries is a finely detailed evocation of the Old West, with a wonderful cast and an equally fine production. Followed by "Return to Lonesome Dove." **480m/C VHS, DVD.** Robert Duvall, Tommy Lee Jones, Anjelica Huston, Danny Glover, Diane Lane, Rick Schroder, Robert Urich, D.B. Sweeney, Frederic Forrest; ***D:*** Simon Wincer; ***W:*** William D. Wittliff; ***M:*** Basil Poledouris. **TV**

Lonesome Jim 2006 (R) Jim (Affleck) is an aimless, melancholic 27-year-old returning to his dull hometown in Indiana after a spirit-crushing stint in New York. Low-key, with mildly eccentric characters, it paints a nice little picture of Midwestern alienation, soaked with dry humor. Buscemi is subtle and meticulous with his direction, working in familiar territory. **91m/C DVD.** *US* Casey Affleck, Liv Tyler, Mary Kay Place, Seymour Cassel, Kevin Corrigan, Jack Rovello, Mark Boone Jr.; ***D:*** Steve Buscemi; ***W:*** James C. Strouse; ***C:*** Phil Parmet.

Lonesome Trail 1/2 1955 Routine Western that differs from the average oater by having the good guys use bows and arrows to fight their battles. **73m/B VHS, DVD.** John Agar, Margia Dean, Edgar Buchanan, Wayne Morris, Adele Jergens, Douglas Fowley, Earle Lyon, Richard Bartlett; ***D:*** Richard Bartlett; ***W:*** Richard Bartlett; ***M:*** Leo Klatzkin.

Long Ago Tomorrow *The Raging Moon* **1971 (PG)** A paralyzed athlete enters a church-run home for the disabled rather than return to his family as the object of their pity. A love affair with a woman, who shares the same disability, helps the athlete to adapt. **90m/C VHS.** *GB* Malcolm McDowell, Nanette Newman, Bernard Lee, Georgia Brown, Gerald Sim; ***D:*** Bryan Forbes.

The Long Dark Hall 1/2 1951 Courtroom drama in which an innocent man is brought to trial when his showgirl mistress is found dead. **86m/B VHS.** *GB* Rex Harrison, Lilli Palmer, Denis O'Dea, Raymond Huntley, Patricia Wayne, Anthony Dawson; ***D:*** Anthony Bushell, Reginald Beck.

The Long Day Closes 1992 (PG) It's 1956 Liverpool and 11-year-old Bud (McCormack) is part of a working-class Catholic family who longs to escape from his humdrum life. And how? By going to the movies of course and filling his head with pop songs. Nostalgic view of family life filled with sweet, small everyday moments set in a dreary postwar England. Sequel to Davies's also autobiographical film "Distant Voices, Still Lives." **84m/C VHS.** *GB* Leigh McCormack, Marjorie Yates, Anthony Watson, Ayse Owens; ***D:*** Terence Davies; ***W:*** Terence Davies; ***C:*** Michael Coulter.

Long Day's Journey into Night 1962 A brooding, devastating film based on Eugene O'Neill's most powerful and autobiographical play. Depicts a day in the life of a family deteriorating under drug addiction, alcoholism, and imminent death. Hepburn's performance is outstanding. In 1988, the Broadway version was taped and released on video. **174m/B VHS, DVD.** Ralph Richardson, Katharine Hepburn, Dean Stockwell, Jeanne Barr, Jason Robards Jr.; ***D:*** Sidney Lumet; ***C:*** Boris Kaufman; ***M:*** Andre Previn. Cannes '62: Actress (Hepburn); Natl. Bd. of Review '62: Support. Actor (Robards).

Long Day's Journey into Night 1988 A taped version of the Broadway production of the epic Eugene O'Neill play about a Southern family deteriorating under the weight of terminal illness, alcoholism and drug abuse. In 1962 a movie adaptation of the play was released with outstanding performances from its cast. **169m/C VHS, DVD.** Jack Lemmon, Bethel Leslie, Peter Gallagher, Kevin Spacey, Jodie Lynne McLintock; ***D:*** Jonathan Miller.

Long Day's Journey Into Night 1996 Eugene O'Neill's autobiographical play about his family is adapted from Canada's Stratford Festival production. The Tyrones are a troubled Irish-American family: bullying James (Hutt) was a once-great Shakespearean actor who has been typecast in a popular stage potboiler; wife Mary (Henry) is a morphine addict; elder son James Jr. (Donaldson) is an alcoholic; and O'Neill's alter-ego is Edmund (McCamus), an overly sensitive, consumptive writer. Fine performances, excellent production. **174m/C VHS.** *CA* William Hutt, Martha Henry, Tom McCamus, Peter Donaldson, Martha Burns; ***D:*** David Wellington; ***C:*** David Franco; ***M:*** Ron Sures. Genie '96: Actor (Hutt), Actress (Henry), Support. Actor (Donaldson), Support. Actress (Burns); Toronto-City '96: Canadian Feature Film.

The Long Days of Summer 1980 Set in pre-WWII America, this film portrays a Jewish attorney's struggle against the prejudices of the New England town where he lives. Sequel to "When Every Day Is the Fourth of July." **105m/C VHS.** Dean Jones, Joan Hackett, Louanne, Donald Moffat, Andrew Duggan, Michael McGuire; ***D:*** Dan Curtis. **TV**

Long Gone 1/2 1987 In the '50s, an over-the-hill minor-league player/manager is given a last lease on life and the pennant with two talented rookies and a sexy baseball groupie. **113m/C VHS.** William L. Petersen, Henry Gibson, Katy Boyer, Virginia Madsen, Dermot Mulroney, Larry Riley, Teller; ***D:*** Martin Davidson. **CABLE**

The Long Good Friday 1/2 1980 Set in London's dockland, this is a violent story of a crime boss who meets his match. Hoskin's world crumbles over an Easter weekend when his buildings are bombed and his men murdered. He thinks its the work of rival gangsters only to discover an even deadlier threat is behind his troubles. One of the best of the crime genre, with an exquisitely charismatic performance by Hoskins. **109m/C VHS, DVD.** *GB* Bob Hoskins, Helen Mirren, Dave King, Bryan Marshall, George Coulouris, Pierce Brosnan, Derek Thompson, Eddie Constantine, Brian Hall, Stephen Davies, P. H. Moriarty, Paul Freeman, Charles Cork, Paul Barber, Patti Love, Ruby Head, Dexter Fletcher, Roy Alon; ***D:*** John MacKenzie; ***W:*** Barrie Keefe; ***C:*** Phil Meheux; ***M:*** Francis Monkman.

The Long Goodbye 1973 (R) Raymond Chandler's penultimate novel with the unmistakable Altman touch—which is to say that some of the changes to the story have pushed purist noses out of joint. Gould is cast as an insouciant anti-Marlowe, the film noir atmosphere has been transmuted into a Hollywood film neon, genre jibing abounds, and the ending has been rewritten. But the revamping serves a purpose, which is to make Marlowe a viable character in a contemporary world. Handsomely photographed by Vilmos Zsigmond. Don't miss bulky boy Arnold's cameo (his second film appearance). **112m/C VHS, DVD.** Elliott Gould, Nina Van Pallandt, Sterling Hayden, Henry Gibson, Mark Rydell, David Arkin, Warren Berlinger; ***Cameos:*** Arnold Schwarzenegger, David Carradine; ***D:*** Robert Altman; ***W:*** Leigh Brackett; ***C:*** Vilmos Zsigmond; ***M:*** John Williams. Natl. Soc. Film Critics '73: Cinematog.

The Long Gray Line 1955 Power gives an outstanding performance as Marty Maher, a humble Irish immigrant who became an institution at West Point. This is the inspiring story of his rise from an unruly cadet to one of the academy's most beloved instructors. O'Hara does a fine job of playing his wife, who like her husband, adopts the young cadets as her own. Director Ford gracefully captures the spirit and honor associated with West Point in this affectionate drama. **138m/C VHS, DVD.** Tyrone Power, Maureen O'Hara, Robert Francis, Donald Crisp, Ward Bond, Betsy Palmer, Phil Carey; ***D:*** John Ford; ***W:*** Edward Hope; ***C:*** Charles Lawton Jr.

The Long Haul 1957 A truck driver becomes involved with crooks as his marriage sours. **88m/C VHS.** Victor Mature, Diana Dors, Patrick Allen, Gene Anderson; ***D:*** Ken Hughes.

The Long, Hot Summer 1/2 1958 A tense, well-played adaptation of the William Faulkner story about drifter Ben Quick (Newman), who latches himself onto a tyrannical Mississippi family, the Varners, led by larger-than-life Will Varner (Welles). The first on-screen pairing of Newman and Woodward (who plays spinster daughter Clara), and one of the best. Remade for TV in 1986. **117m/C VHS, DVD.** Paul Newman, Orson Welles, Joanne Woodward, Lee Remick, Anthony (Tony) Franciosa, Angela Lansbury, Richard Anderson; ***D:*** Martin Ritt; ***W:*** Harriet Frank Jr., Irving Ravetch; ***C:*** Joseph LaShelle; ***M:*** Alex North. Cannes '58: Actor (Newman).

The Long, Hot Summer 1/2 1986 TV version of the William Faulkner story, "The Hamlet," about a drifter taken under a Southern patriarch's wing. He's bribed into courting the man's unmarried daughter. Wonderful performances from the entire cast, especially Ivey and surprisingly, Johnson. Remake of the 1958 film with Paul Newman and Joanne Woodward that is on par with the original. **172m/C VHS.** Don Johnson, Cybill Shepherd, Judith Ivey, Jason Robards Jr., Ava Gardner, William Russ, Wings Hauser, William Forsythe, Albert Hall; ***D:*** Stuart Cooper; ***M:*** Charles Bernstein. **TV**

Long John Silver 1/2 *Long John Silver Returns to Treasure Island* **1954** Famed pirate John Silver plans a return trip to Treasure Island to search for the elusive treasure; unofficial sequel to "Treasure Island" by Disney. **103m/C VHS, DVD.** *AU* Robert Newton, Connie Gilchrist, Kit Taylor, Grant Taylor, Rod Taylor; ***D:*** Byron Haskin; ***W:*** Martin Rackin; ***C:*** Carl Guthrie; ***M:*** David Buttolph.

Long Journey Back 1978 The biographical story of a young woman's rehabilitation after her injury in a school bus accident. **100m/C VHS.** Mike Connors, Cloris Leachman, Stephanie Zimbalist, Katy Kurtzman; ***D:*** Mel Damski. **TV**

The Long Kiss Goodnight 1/2 1996 (R) Audience-pleasing, blood-soaked, foul-mouthed, and action-packed. Davis obviously has a career as a '90s action star (female division), displaying the proper bravado, and muscles, necessary for her dual role. As mild-mannered, brown-haired Samantha Caine, she's a schoolteacher with an eight-year-old daughter, Caitlin (Zima), a nice boyfriend, Hal (Amandes), and amnesia. Sam begins having flashbacks to her past—and what a past it turns out to be. With the help of seedy PI Mitch Henessey (Jackson), she discovers her name is Charly Baltimore and she's a highly trained and very deadly CIA assassin. And the now bleached-blonde, beyond-tough Charly must match her quickly regained lethal abilities with ruthless former nemesis Timothy (Bierko). The body count's high, the blood flows freely, and there's some spectacular stunts. If you're not squeamish it's a guaranteed wild ride. Black got $4 million for his script. **120m/C VHS, DVD.** Geena Davis, Samuel L. Jackson, Craig Bierko, Patrick Malahide, Brian Cox, David Morse, Yvonne Zima, Tom Amandes, Melina Kanakaredes, G.D. Spradlin; ***D:*** Renny Harlin; ***W:*** Shane Black; ***C:*** Guillermo Navarro; ***M:*** Alan Silvestri.

Long Life, Happiness and Prosperity 2002 Set in Vancouver's Chinatown. Twelve-year-old Mindy Lum turns to Taoist magic to fix her overworked single mother Kin's financial and romantic problems. But Mindy's magic charms seem to go astray when the local butcher Bing Lai wins the lottery, elderly security guard Shuck Wong loses his job, and her mother's admirer Alvin becomes interested in someone else. **91m/C DVD.** *CA* Sandra Oh, Valerie Tian, Russell Yuen, Ric Young, Chang Tseng, Tsai Chin; ***D:*** Mina Shum; ***W:*** Mina Shum, Dennis Foon; ***C:*** Peter Wunstorf; ***M:*** Andrew Lockington.

The Long, Long Trailer 1/2 1954 A couple on their honeymoon find that trailer life is more than they bargained for. Lots of fun with charming direction from Minelli, and Ball's incredible slapstick style. **97m/C VHS, DVD.** Desi Arnaz Sr., Lucille Ball, Marjorie Main, Keenan Wynn, Gladys Hurlbut, Moroni Olsen, Bert Freed, Madge Blake, Walter Baldwin; ***D:*** Vincente Minnelli; ***W:*** Albert Hackett, Frances Goodrich; ***C:*** Robert L. Surtees; ***M:*** Adolph Deutsch.

The Long Night 1/2 1947 Remake of Marcel Carne's "Le Journe Se Leve/Daybreak" (1939). WWII vet Joe Adams (Fonda) is having a hard time with civilian life. In fact, he's just killed con man/magician Maximilian (Price) and has barricaded himself from the cops in his apartment. Flashbacks serve to show how Joe got into his present situation (women are involved, naturally). Not too involving. **101m/B VHS, DVD.** Henry Fonda, Vincent Price, Barbara Bel Geddes, Ann Dvorak, Howard Freeman, Moroni Olsen, Elisha Cook Jr.; ***D:*** Anatole Litvak; ***W:*** John Wexley; ***C:*** Sol Polito; ***M:*** Dimitri Tiomkin.

Long Pants 1927 Langdon, in a typical man/child role, plays a naive young man who gets his first pair of long pants, which officially ushers him into adulthood. He immediately falls for the wrong gal (Bonner), a drug runner who winds up in jail. So he breaks her out and they go on the lam. **58m/B VHS, DVD.** Harry Langdon, Priscilla Bonner, Alma Bennett; ***D:*** Frank Capra.

A Long Ride From Hell *Vivo per la Tua Morte; I Live for Your Death* **1968 (R)** Reeves stars in (and co-wrote) this spaghetti western that was his last film before his retirement. Rancher Mike Sturges (Reeves) and his brother Roy (Fantasia) are falsely imprisoned for rustling. When his brother dies in the pen, Mike escapes to get revenge on the actual bad guys. Italian with subtitles or dubbed. **104m/C DVD.** *IT* Steve Reeves, Wayde Preston, Mimmo Palmara, Silvana Venturelli, Nello Pazzafini, Franco Fatasia, Guido Lollobrigida; *D:* Camillo Bazzoni; *W:* Steve Reeves, Roberto Natale; *C:* Enzo Barboni; *M:* Carlo Savina.

The Long Ride Home ✂✂ **2001 (PG-13)** After being accused of being a gunslinger, Jack Cole (Travis) has spent eight years running from the law and various vigilantes. He finally decides it's time to clear his name and be reunited with his family so he heads home for the final showdown. Plot's more convoluted that it may seem and it's a cliched story to begin with. **?m/C VHS, DVD.** Randy Travis, Eric Roberts, Ernest Borgnine, Stella Stevens; *D:* Robert Marcarelli; *C:* Gary Graver.

The Long Riders ✂✂✂ **1980 (R)** Excellent mythic western in which the Jesse James and Cole Younger gangs raid banks, trains, and stagecoaches in post-Civil War Missouri. Stylish, meticulous and a violent look back, with one of the better slow-motion shootouts in Hollywood history. Notable for the portrayal of four sets of outlaw brothers (James, Younger, Miller, Ford) by four Hollywood brother (Keach, Carradine, Quaid, Guest) sets. Complimented by excellent Cooder score. **100m/C VHS, DVD.** Stacy Keach, James Keach, Randy Quaid, Dennis Quaid, David Carradine, Keith Carradine, Robert Carradine, Christopher Guest, Nicholas Guest, Pamela Reed, Savannah Smith, James Whitmore Jr., Harry Carey Jr.; *D:* Walter Hill; *W:* Stacy Keach, James Keach, Bill Bryden; *C:* Ric Waite; *M:* Ry Cooder.

Long Road Home ✂✂ ½ **1991 (PG)** Migrant family must decide between working under inhumane conditions or risk losing everything by joining the labor movement during the depression. TV movie. **88m/C VHS.** Mark Harmon, John Evans, Adam Horovitz, Lee Purcell, Leon Russom, Donald Sutherland, Morgan Weisser; *D:* John Korty; *C:* Kees Van Oostrum.

Long Shadows ✂ ½ **1986** An analysis of how the resonating effects of the Civil War can still be felt on society, via interviews with a number of noted writers, historians, civil rights activists and politicians. **88m/C VHS, DVD.** Robert Penn Warren, Studs Terkel, Jimmy Carter, Robert Coles, Tom Wicker; *D:* Ross Spears.

The Long Ships ✂ **1964** Silly Viking saga finds brothers Rolfe (Widmark) and Orm (Tamblyn) stealing a ship and heading off in search of a solid-gold bell. Among their trials are a mutinous crew and battling Moorish Prince El Mansuh (Poitier). Something to be left off the resume. **125m/C VHS, DVD.** Richard Widmark, Russ Tamblyn, Sidney Poitier, Oscar Homolka, Rosanna Schiaffino, Beba Loncar, Lionel Jeffries, Edward Judd; *D:* Jack Cardiff; *W:* Beverley Cross, Berkely Mather; *C:* Christopher Challis; *M:* Dusan Radic.

Long Shot Kids ✂ *Longshot* **1981** Two foosball enthusiasts work their way through local tournaments to make enough money to make it to the World Championships in Tahoe. **100m/C VHS, UMD.** Ian Giatti, Leif Garrett, Arlene Golonka, Linda Manz; *D:* E.W. Swackhamer; *W:* Russell V. Manzatt; *C:* Jacques Haitkin.

Long-Term Relationship ✂✂ **2006** Glenn's (Montgomery) been a longtime player on L.A.'s gay single scene when he finds his would-be soulmate in the personals—traditional southern charmer Adam (Beach). Only their differences may make a long-term relationship an impossibility. Low-budget romantic comedy (the debut for writer-director Williams) offers a compelling performance from Montgomery but shoves conflicts out of the way to get to a forced happy ending. **97m/C DVD.** Matthew Montgomery, Windham Beach, Artie O'Daly, Jeremy Lucas; *D:* Rob Williams; *W:* Rob Williams; *C:* Shawn Grice; *M:* Ben Holbrook.

Long Time Gone ✂ **1986** An over-the-hill detective tries to solve a murder while dealing with his bratty, alienated 11-year-old son. **97m/C VHS.** Paul LeMat, Wil Wheaton, Ann Dusenberry, Barbara Stock; *D:* Robert Butler. **TV**

Long Time Since ✂ ½ **1997** A bit too remote and artsy to be involving. On New Year's Eve in 1971, Diane (Porizkova) hit something (or someone) with her car while driving on a remote country road. The repressed Diane has blocked all memories for some 24 years—until she hears "Auld Lang Syne" on the radio and fragments begin to come by. Putting these bits together leads her to the solitary Michael (Sands) whose wife and baby daughter when missing around the same time as Diane's accident. **89m/C VHS, DVD.** Paulina Porizkova, Julian Sands, Julianne Nicholson, Jeff Webster; *D:* Jay Anania; *W:* Jay Anania; *C:* Oliver Bokelberg; *M:* Judy Kuhn.

The Long Voyage Home ✂✂✂ ½ **1940** A talented cast performs this must-see screen adaptation of Eugene O'Neill's play about crew members aboard a merchant steamer in 1939. Wayne plays a young lad from Sweden who is trying to get home and stay out of trouble as he and the other seaman get shore leave. **105m/B VHS, DVD.** John Wayne, Thomas Mitchell, Ian Hunter, Barry Fitzgerald, Mildred Natwick, John Qualen; *D:* John Ford; *C:* Gregg Toland. N.Y. Film Critics '40: Director (Ford).

The Long Walk Home ✂✂✂ **1989 (PG)** In Montgomery Alabama, in the mid 1950s, sometime after Rosa Parks refused to sit in the black-designated back of the bus, Martin Luther King Jr. led a bus boycott. Spacek is the affluent wife of a narrow-minded businessman while Goldberg is their struggling maid. When Spacek discovers that Goldberg is supporting the boycott by walking the nine-mile trek to work, she sympathizes and tries to help, antagonizing her husband. The plot marches inevitably toward a white-on-white showdown on racism while quietly exploring gender equality between the women. Outstanding performances by Spacek and Goldberg, and a great 50s feel. **95m/C VHS, DVD.** Dan E. Butler, Sissy Spacek, Whoopi Goldberg, Dwight Schultz, Ving Rhames, Dylan Baker; *D:* Richard Pearce; *W:* John Cork; *C:* Roger Deakins; *M:* George Fenton; *Nar:* Mary Steenburgen.

A Long Way Home ✂✂ **1981** A grown man searches for his long-lost siblings, after the three of them were given up for adoption after birth. **97m/C VHS.** Timothy Hutton, Brenda Vaccaro, Rosanna Arquette, Paul Regina, George Dzundza, John Lehne, Bonnie Bartlett; *D:* Robert Markowitz; *C:* Ralf Bode; *M:* William Goldstein. **TV**

The Long Weekend WOOF! **2005 (R)** Dismal, crude sex comedy. Ad exec Ed (Fehr) needs to come up with a new campaign to save his job but his sleazy horndog older brother Cooper (Klein) is just interested in getting them laid. Ed is a porn watcher and the (deemed too raunchy for TV) clips actually come from "America's Funniest Home Videos." **85m/C DVD.** *GB CA* Chris Klein, Brendan Fehr, Chandra West, Craig Fairbrass, Cobie Smulders, Paul Campbell; *D:* Pat Holden; *W:* Tad Safran; *C:* Brian Pearson; *M:* David A. Hughes. **VIDEO**

The Longest Day ✂✂✂ ½ **1962** The complete story of the D-Day landings at Normandy on June 6, 1944, as seen through the eyes of American, French, British, and German participants. Exhaustively accurate details and extremely talented cast make this one of the all-time great Hollywood epic productions. The first of the big budget, all-star war productions; based on the book by Cornelius Ryan. Three directors share credit. Also available in a colorized version. **179m/C VHS, DVD, Blu-ray Disc.** John Wayne, Richard Burton, Red Buttons, Robert Mitchum, Henry Fonda, Robert Ryan, Paul Anka, Mel Ferrer, Edmond O'Brien, Fabian, Sean Connery, Roddy McDowall, Arletty, Curt Jurgens, Rod Steiger, Jean-Louis Barrault, Peter Lawford, Robert Wagner, Sal Mineo, Leo Genn, Richard Beymer, Jeffrey Hunter, Stuart Whitman, Eddie Albert, Tom Tryon, Alexander Knox, Ray Danton, Kenneth More, Richard Todd, Gert Frobe, Christopher Lee, John Robinson; *D:* Bernhard Wicki, Ken Annakin, Andrew Marton; *W:* James Jones, David Pursall, Jack Seddon, Romain Gary; *C:* Jean (Yves, Georges) Bourgoin, Pierre Levent, Henri Persin, Walter Wottitz; *M:* Maurice Jarre. Oscars '62: B&W Cinematog.

The Longest Drive ✂✂ *The Quest* **1976** Two brothers comb the wildest parts of the West for their sister, whom they believe is living with Indians. TV movie originally titled "The Quest," which became a brief television series. Highlights include colorful performances from the veteran actors and a unique horse/camel race. A continuation of the series is available on video as "The Captive: The Longest Drive 2." **92m/C VHS, DVD.** Kurt Russell, Tim Matheson, Brian Keith, Keenan Wynn, Neville Brand, Cameron Mitchell, Morgan Woodward, Iron Eyes Cody, Luke Askew; *D:* Lee H. Katzin. **TV**

The Longest Yard ✂✂✂ **1974 (R)** A one-time pro football quarterback, now an inmate, organizes his fellow convicts into a football team to play against the prison guards. Of course, he's being pressured by the evil warden to throw the game. One of the all-time classic football movies. Filmed on location at Georgia State Prison. **121m/C VHS, DVD.** Sonny Shroyer, Michael Conrad, James Hampton, Harry Caesar, Charles Tyner, Mike Henry, Anitra Ford, Michael Fox, Joe Kapp, Pepper Martin, Robert Tessier, Burt Reynolds, Eddie Albert, Bernadette Peters, Ed Lauter, Richard Kiel; *D:* Robert Aldrich; *W:* Tracy Keenan Wynn; *C:* Joseph Biroc; *M:* Frank DeVol. Golden Globes '75: Film—Mus./Comedy.

The Longest Yard ✂✂ **2005 (PG-13)** Does anyone really believe Sandler as a QB? Well, in this remake of the more brutal 1974 original, Sandler is ex-pro Paul 'Wrecking' Crewe, who's stuck in a Texas federal pen that also houses one-time college football legend Nate Scarborough (Reynolds, who formerly played the QB). The football-obsessed warden (Cromwell) okays a televised game that pits Paul and his woeful cons against the bone-crunching guards (many cameos by ex-jocks). Motor-mouthed Rock makes a relatively brief appearance as a prison fixer and game day takes up a big part of the movie's running time. The comedy's been amped up, the pace is brisk, and Sandler is actually tolerable, but none of that makes up for doing it in the first place. **113m/C DVD, UMD.** *US* Adam Sandler, Burt Reynolds, Chris Rock, James Cromwell, Nelly, David Patrick Kelly, Nicholas Turturro, William Fichtner, Tracy Morgan, Brian Bosworth, Ed Lauter, Cloris Leachman, Steve Austin, Bob Sapp, Dalip Singh, Lobo Sebastian, Rob Schneider, Courteney Cox, Edward (Eddie) Bunker, Terry Crews; *D:* Peter Segal; *W:* Sheldon Turner; *C:* Dean Semler; *M:* Teddy Castellucci.

Longford ✂✂ **2006** In 1967, Lord Frank Aungier Pakenham (Broadbent), 7th Earl of Longford, is the respected leader of the House of Lords and a tireless worker for prison rehabilitation. He stakes his name and career when he befriends notorious convicted child murderess, Myra Hindley (Morton), and campaigns for her parole (over a 30-year period), believing his fellow Catholic convert is truly redemptive. But few share his belief. **90m/C DVD.** *GB* Jim Broadbent, Samantha Morton, Tam Dean Burn, Lindsay Duncan, Lee Boardman, Andy Serkis, Robert Pugh, Anton Rodgers, Kate Miles, Kika Markham; *D:* Tom Hooper; *W:* Peter Morgan; *C:* Danny Cohen; *M:* Robert (Rob) Lane. **TV**

Longitude ✂✂✂ **2000** In 1714, England's Parliament offered a large reward to anyone who could discover a way to accurately measure longitude at sea to prevent nautical disasters. Carpenter John Harrison (Gambon) decided on a mechanical solution in the form of a clock (now known as the marine chronometer) and strove to have his ideas excepted (for 40 years). His story is paralleled with that of shellshocked ex-WWI soldier Rupert Gould (Irons), who discovered Harrison's neglected originals and became equally obsessed with restoring them to working order. The performances carry the somewhat diffuse plot. Based on the book by Dava Sobel. **200m/C VHS, DVD.** *GB* Jeremy Irons, Michael Gambon, Anna Chancellor, Ian Hart, Peter Vaughan, Gemma Jones, John Wood, Stephen Fry, Alec McCowen, Frank Finlay, John Standing, Samuel West, Bill Nighy, Brian Cox, Barbara Leigh-Hunt, Clive Francis, Daragh O'Malley, Tim (McInnerny) McInnery, Nicholas (Nick) Rowe; *D:* Charles Sturridge; *W:* Charles Sturridge; *C:* Peter Hannan; *M:* Geoffrey Burgon. **TV**

The Longshot WOOF! **1986 (PG-13)** Four bumblers try to raise cash to put on a sure-bet racetrack tip in this sorry comedy. Mike Nichols is the executive producer. **89m/C VHS, DVD.** Tim Conway, Harvey Korman, Jack Weston, Ted Wass, Jonathan Winters, Stella Stevens, Anne Meara; *D:* Paul Bartel; *W:* Tim Conway, John Myhers; *M:* Charles Fox.

The Longshots ✂✂ ½ **2008 (PG)** Another based-on-a-true story about a team of misfit athletes has enough trick plays to rise above the typical formula. Director Durst, Limp Bizkit's apparently multi-talented frontman, sticks to a genuine and authentic aesthetic for the story's hard-luck backdrop of Minton, Illinois, where eleven-year-old honor roll student Jasmine (Palmer) is stuck with her unemployed Uncle Curtis (Ice Cube), a broken down ex-jock who discovers that she has a surprisingly strong throwing arm and persuades her to try out for the local football team. Jasmine ends up becoming the first girl to play quarterback in Pop Warner. Palmer's performance is honest and compelling and is a highlight in a film that skips cliche and hyperbole in favor of a nice warm vibe. **94m/C DVD, Blu-ray Disc.** *US* Ice Cube, Tasha Smith, Keke Palmer, Matt Craven, Jill Marie Jones, Glenn Plummer, Malcolm Goodwin, Dash Mihok, Miles Chandler; *D:* Fred Durst; *W:* Doug Atchison, Nick Santora; *C:* Conrad W. Hall; *M:* John Swihart, Teddy Castellucci.

Longtime Companion ✂✂✂ ½ **1990 (R)** Critically acclaimed film follows a group of gay men and their friends during the 1980s. The closely knit group monitors the progression of the AIDS virus from early news reports until it finally hits home and begins to take the lives of their loved ones. One of the first films to look at the situation in an intelligent and touching manner. Produced by the PBS "American Playhouse" company. **100m/C VHS, DVD.** Dan E. Butler, Stephen Caffrey, Patrick Cassidy, Brian Cousins, Bruce Davison, John Dossett, Mark Lamos, Dermot Mulroney, Mary-Louise Parker, Michael Schoeffling, Campbell Scott, Robert Joy, Brad O'Hara; *D:* Norman Rene; *W:* Craig Lucas; *C:* Tony Jennelli. Golden Globes '91: Support. Actor (Davison); Ind. Spirit '91: Support. Actor (Davison); N.Y. Film Critics '90: Support. Actor (Davison); Natl. Soc. Film Critics '90: Support. Actor (Davison); Sundance '90: Aud. Award.

Look at Me ✂✂✂ ½ *Comme une image* **2004 (PG-13)** Unhappy Parisian tale of gigantically egotistical father (Bacri) jetsetting his way around town and his plump daughter (Berry) unsuccessfully vying for his attention. She is a gifted singer, constantly tuning her voice. He is an acclaimed novelist, constantly tuning her out. He's also got a young trophy wife (Desarnauts) who gets nothing from her husband but ridicule and indifference. He wants his wife to look perfect, he wants his daughter to look like her voice sounds. French co-writers and co-stars Agnes Jaoui and Jean-Pierre Bacri craft a poignant, unpredictable film defying stereotype. Awarded best screenplay at Cannes. **110m/C DVD.** *FR* Agnes Jaoui, Jean-Pierre Bacri, Laurent Grevill, Marilou Berry, Virginie Desarnauts, Keine Bouhiza, Gregoire Oestermann; *D:* Agnes Jaoui; *W:* Agnes Jaoui, Jean-Pierre Bacri; *C:* Stephane Fontaine; *M:* Philippe Rombi.

Look Back in Anger ✂✂✂ ½ **1958** Based on John Osbourne's famous play, the first British "angry young man" film, in which a squalor-living lad takes out his anger on the world by seducing his friend's wife. **99m/B VHS, DVD.** *GB* Richard Burton, Claire Bloom, Mary Ure, Edith Evans, Gary Raymond, Glen Byam Shaw, George Devine, Donald Pleasence, Phyllis Neilson-Terry; *D:* Tony Richardson; *W:* John Osborne, Nigel Kneale; *C:* Oswald Morris; *M:* John Addison.

Look Back in Anger ✂✂ **1980** A working class man angered by society's hypocrisy lashes out at his upper class wife, his mistress, and the world. Inferior remake of 1958 film version starring Richard Burton, based on '50s stage hit. **100m/C VHS.** *GB* Malcolm McDowell, Lisa Banes, Fran Brill, Raymond Hardie, Robert Burr; *D:* Lindsay Anderson; *W:* John Osborne.

Look Back in Anger ✂✂✂ **1989** There's something about John Osborne's play that brings out the angry young man in British leads. Richard Burton played Osborne's irascible guy in 1958, Malcom McDowell looked back angrily in '80, and now Branagh convincingly vents his spleen on wife and mistress in this made for British TV production. Director Jones earlier filmed "84 Charing Cross Road" and "Jacknife." **114m/C VHS, DVD.** *GB* Kenneth Branagh, Emma Thompson, Gerard Horan, Siobhan Redmond; ***D:*** David Hugh Jones. **TV**

Look Both Ways **2005 (PG-13)** In Watt's first feature-length film, she examines our fears of dying and death. Artist Meryl (Clarke) is constantly imagining disasters (depicted in animated sequences), but then she witnesses a real tragedy—a man getting killed by a train. Local photographer Nick (McInnes), who's just been told he has cancer, takes a picture of the man's anguished widow, which is printed on the newspaper's front page along with reporter Andy's (Hayes) somewhat brutal story. Nick and Meryl make a tentative connection while struggling with fear, loneliness, hope, and forgiveness. The secondary characters and their problems (including an unplanned pregnancy) are a distraction but the film's overall quirkiness tends to work well. **100m/C DVD.** *AU* Justine Clarke, Anthony Hayes, Andrew S. Gilbert, Daniela Farinacci, William McInnes, Lisa Flanagan, Maggie Dence, Sacha Horler, Edwin Hodgeman; ***D:*** Sarah Watt; ***W:*** Sarah Watt; ***C:*** Ray Argall; ***M:*** Amanda Brown.

Look for the Silver Lining **1/2** **1949** Insipid musical biography of Broadway star Marilyn Miller (Haver). Bolger is the highlight as Miller's mentor from vaudeville to the Great White Way. ♫ Look for the Silver Lining; Whip-Poor-Will; A Kiss in the Dark; Pirouette; Just a Memory; Time On My Hands; Wild Rose; Shine On Harvest Moon; Back, Back, Back to Baltimore. **100m/C VHS.** June Haver, Ray Bolger, Gordon MacRae, Charlie Ruggles, Rosemary DeCamp, S.Z. Sakall; ***D:*** David Butler; ***W:*** Phoebe Ephron, Henry Ephron, Marian Spitzer.

Look Out Sister **1948** Jordan and an all-black cast star in this musical satire of westerns. "Two Gun" Jordan saves a dude ranch from foreclosure and wins the girl. Lots of black culture, slang and music from the '40s. Broad but enjoyable humor. ♫ Caldonia; Don't Burn the Candle at Both Ends. **64m/B VHS, DVD.** Louis Jordan, Suzette Harbin, Monte Hawley, Maceo B. Sheffield; ***D:*** Bud Pollard.

Look Who's Laughing **1941** Bergen's plane lands in a town conveniently populated by radio stars. Not much plot here, but it might be worth a look to fans of the stars including Jim and Marion Jordan, better known as Fibber McGee and Molly. **79m/B VHS.** Edgar Bergen, Jim Jordan, Marian Jordan, Lucille Ball, Harold (Hal) Peary, Lee Bonnell, Charles Halton; ***D:*** Allan Dwan.

Look Who's Talking **1989 (PG-13)** When Alley bears the child of a married, and quite fickle man, she sets her sights elsewhere in search of the perfect father; Travolta is the cabbie with more on his mind than driving Alley around and babysitting. All the while, the baby gives us his views via the voice of Bruce Willis. A very light comedy with laughs for the whole family. **90m/C VHS, DVD.** John Travolta, Kirstie Alley, Olympia Dukakis, George Segal, Abe Vigoda; ***D:*** Amy Heckerling; ***W:*** Amy Heckerling; ***M:*** David Kitay; ***V:*** Bruce Willis.

Look Who's Talking Now **1/2** **1993 (PG-13)** Continuing to wring revenue from a tired premise, the family dogs throw in their two cents in the second sequel to "Look Who's Talking." For anyone who thinks Diane Keaton's hair makes her look a little like a hound dog, here's a chance to visualize her as a similarly long-eared poodle with an attitude. DeVito is also cast in character as the voice of a rough street-smart mutt, who happens to get thrown into the same household as the bosses' pure-bred poodle. Sparks, Alpo, and butt jokes fly as the dogs mark their territory. Meanwhile, dimwit wife Alley is worried that husband Travolta is having an affair, and is determined to get him back. **95m/C VHS, DVD.** John Travolta, Kirstie Alley, Olympia Dukakis, George Segal, Lysette Anthony; ***D:*** Tom Ropelewski; ***W:*** Leslie Dixon, Tom Ropelewski; ***C:*** Oliver Stapleton; ***M:*** William Ross; ***V:*** Diane Keaton, Danny DeVito.

Look Who's Talking, Too **1990 (PG-13)** If Academy Awards for Stupidest Sequel and Lamest Dialogue existed, this diaper drama would have cleaned up. The second go-round throws the now married accountant-cabbie duo into a marital tailspin when Alley's babysitting brother moves in and the Saturday Night dancer moves out. Meanwhile, Willis cum baby smartasses incessantly. A once-clever gimmick now unencumbered by plot; not advised for linear thinkers. The voice of Arnold, though, is a guarantee you'll get one laugh for your rental. **81m/C VHS, DVD.** Kirstie Alley, John Travolta, Olympia Dukakis, Elias Koteas; ***D:*** Amy Heckerling; ***W:*** Amy Heckerling, Neal Israel; ***C:*** Thomas Del Ruth; ***M:*** David Kitay; ***V:*** Bruce Willis, Mel Brooks, Damon Wayans, Roseanne.

The Lookalike **1990 (PG-13)** Cable adaptation of Kate Wilhelm's novel. Bereaved mother Gilbert questions her sanity when she thinks she sees her daughter after she was killed in an automobile accident. Could this girl provide answers to questions about her past? **88m/C VHS.** Melissa Gilbert, Diane Ladd, Frances Lee McCain, Jason Scott Lee, Thaao Penghlis; ***D:*** Gary Nelson; ***W:*** Linda J. Bergman. **CABLE**

Looker **1/2** **1981 (PG)** Stunning models are made even more beautiful by a plastic surgeon, but one by one they begin to die. Finney plays the Beverly Hills surgeon who decides to investigate when he starts losing all his clients. **94m/C VHS, DVD.** Albert Finney, James Coburn, Susan Dey, Leigh Taylor-Young; ***D:*** Michael Crichton; ***W:*** Michael Crichton.

Lookin' to Get Out **1/2** **1982 (R)** Comedy about two gamblers running from their debts. They wind up at the MGM Grand in Las Vegas trying to get out of a mess. **70m/C VHS.** Ann-Margret, Jon Voight, Burt Young; ***D:*** Hal Ashby; ***M:*** John Beal, Miles Goodman.

Looking for an Echo **1/2** **1999 (R)** Vince (Assante) is a widower pushing 50 who had some teen success in a do-wop group and then put his singing aside to marry and raise his kids. His middle son, Anthony (Balerini), is now bringing up dad's old dreams (and some regrets) by being in his own rock band. But Vince's main concerns are for youngest child, Tina (Romano), who's in the hospital battling leukemia. This puts Vince in the flirty orbit of brassy nurse Joanne (Venora), who would like to offer the guy some personal care. Assante supplies lots of charm in a glossy, sentimental tearjerker. **97m/C VHS, DVD.** Armand Assante, Diane Venora, Joe Grifasi, Tom Mason, Anthony John (Tony) Denison, Edoardo Ballerini, David Margulies, Christy Carlson Romano; ***D:*** Martin Davidson; ***W:*** Martin Davidson, Jeffrey Goldenberg, Robert Held; ***C:*** Charles Minsky.

Looking for Comedy in the Muslim World **1/2** **2006 (PG-13)** Lame conceit has comedian Brooks play himself, more or less. He's asked by the State Department to spend a month traveling in India and Pakistan in order to figure out what Muslims find funny and write a government-sized (500 pages) report. Why this would matter is best left to the bureaucrats. There are some funny moments but not enough to carry the film, and Brooks' mild-mannered neurotic is something of an acquired taste. **98m/C DVD.** *US* Albert Brooks, Sheetal Sheth, John Carroll Lynch, Jon Tenney, Fred Dalton Thompson, Amy Ryan, Homie Doroodian, Penny Marshall, Duncan Bravo, Emma Lockhart; ***D:*** Albert Brooks; ***W:*** Albert Brooks; ***C:*** Thomas Ackerman; ***M:*** Michael Giacchino.

Looking for Eric **2009** Fortysomething Manchester postal worker Eric Bishop (Evets) returns from a hospital stay to find his home life in chaos per usual. A Manchester United fan, Eric begins seeing visions of retired French-born player Eric Cantona, who gives the English Eric advice on how to win back his long-estranged wife Lily (Bishop). English and French with subtitles. **116m/C DVD.** *GB FR IT BE SP* Eric Cantona, Gerard Kearns, Steve Evets, Stephanie Bishop, Lucy-Jo Hudson, Stefan Gumbs, John Henshae; ***D:*** Ken Loach; ***W:*** Paul Laverty; ***C:*** Barry Ackroyd; ***M:*** George Fenton.

Looking for Kitty **2004 (R)** Upstate New York high school baseball coach Abe (Krumholtz in a bad mustache) comes to Manhattan to look for his missing wife Kitty, who supposedly ran off and is now shacked up with a rock star. Abe hires widowed PI Jack (Burns) and decides to tag along as the two lonely guys begin to bond while looking for Abe's missus. Low-key, low-budget. **95m/C DVD.** David Krumholtz, Edward Burns, Max Baker, Connie Britton; ***D:*** Edward Burns; ***W:*** Edward Burns; ***C:*** William Rexer; ***M:*** Robert Gary, P.T. Walkley.

Looking for Miracles **1/2** **1990 (G)** Two brothers, separated during the Depression because of poverty, get a chance to cultivate brotherly love when they're reunited in 1935. A Wonderworks production based on the A.E. Hochner novel. **104m/C VHS.** *CA* Zachary Bennett, Greg Spottiswood, Joe Flaherty; ***D:*** Kevin Sullivan; ***W:*** Kevin Sullivan, Stuart McLean; ***C:*** Brian Thomson; ***M:*** John Welsman.

Looking for Mr. Goodbar **1977 (R)** Young teacher Keaton seeks companionship and love by frequenting single's bars and furthers her self-destruction by her aimless intake of drugs and alcohol. In need of a father figure, she makes herself available to numerous men and eventually regrets her hedonistic behavior. Unpleasant, aimless characters do little for this dreary film, whose sexual theme sparked a bit of public conversation when first released. Based on the bestselling novel by Judith Rossner. Oscar nominations for supporting actress Weld, and cinematography. **136m/C VHS.** Diane Keaton, Tuesday Weld, Richard Gere, Tom Berenger, William Atherton, Richard Kiley; ***D:*** Richard Brooks; ***W:*** Richard Brooks; ***C:*** William A. Fraker.

Looking for Richard **1996 (PG-13)** A Shakespearean "Vanya on 42nd Street," "Richard" is the first semi-documentary addition to the barrage of Bard adaptations. Pacino's protracted pic dwells on a filmmaker's struggles to understand the play. Punctuated with comic relief, Pacino makes a pilgrimage to the Globe Theatre, taps Brit theatre heavyweights Gielgud and Redgrave for thoughts on interpreting Shakespeare, and combs New York for candid "man in the street" impressions in a quest to bring his subject to a wider public. Over the course of four years, Pacino, in various stages of facial hair growth, plays the deformed usurper with a cast of worthy Americans (Spacey, Kline, Ryder, Baldwin, and Quinn), illustrating key scenes of the play. **108m/C VHS, DVD.** Dominic Chianese, Paul Guilfoyle, Alec Baldwin, Winona Ryder, Kevin Spacey, Aidan Quinn, F. Murray Abraham, Kenneth Branagh, Kevin Conway, John Gielgud, James Earl Jones, Kevin Kline, Estelle Parsons, Vanessa Redgrave, Harris Yulin, Penelope Allen, Al Pacino; ***D:*** Al Pacino; ***C:*** Robert Leacock; ***M:*** Howard Shore. Directors Guild '96: Feature Doc. (Pacino).

Looking for Trouble **1996 (PG)** Lame kid-friendly movie finds young Jaime (Butler) befriending a baby circus elephant she names Trouble, who has an abusive owner. When the circus leaves town, worried Jaime follows along. **73m/C VHS, DVD.** Holly Butler, Shawn McAllister, Art Turk; ***D:*** Peter Tors, Jay Aubrey; ***W:*** Peter Tors, Jay Aubrey.

The Looking Glass War **1969 (PG)** Polish defector is sent behind the Iron Curtain on a final mission to photograph a rocket in East Berlin. He's guided by frustrated British security officers Rogers and Richardson, who both offer sly turns. An otherwise slow-moving adaptation of John Le Carre's bestselling spy novel. **108m/C VHS.** *GB* Christopher Jones, Ralph Richardson, Pia Degermark, Anthony Hopkins, Susan George, Paul Rogers; ***D:*** Frank Pierson; ***W:*** Frank Pierson.

The Lookout **2007 (R)** Crime thriller with a stellar performance by Gordon-Levitt as former golden boy jock Chris. After a car accident that left him with severe brain trauma, Chris struggles with emotional outbursts, memory gaps, and everyday tasks. He lives with sardonic blind roommate Lewis (Daniels, offering superb support) in a small Kansas town and works as a janitor at the bank, giving Chris the perfect in when con man/criminal Gary (Goode) shows up to entice him into a heist to restore some self-esteem. Gary dangles luscious Luvlee (Fisher) as a prize but Chris isn't as dumb as everyone supposes. Screenwriter Frank uses his knowledge of neo-noir territory in his directorial debut. **99m/C DVD, Blu-ray Disc.** *US* Joseph Gordon-Levitt, Jeff Daniels, Matthew Goode, Isla Fisher, Carla Gugino, Bruce McGill, Alberta Watson, Alex Borstein, Sergio Di Zio, Greg Dunham; ***D:*** Scott Frank; ***W:*** Scott Frank; ***C:*** Alar Kivilo; ***M:*** James Newton Howard. Ind. Spirit '08: First Feature.

Looney Looney Looney Bugs Bunny Movie *Friz Freleng's Looney Looney Looney Bugs Bunny Movie* **1981 (G)** A feature-length compilation of classic Warner Bros. cartoons tied together with new animation. Cartoon stars featured include Bugs Bunny, Elmer Fudd, Porky Pig, Yosemite Sam, Duffy Duck, and Foghorn Leghorn. **80m/C VHS.** ***D:*** Isadore "Friz" Freleng, Chuck Jones, Bob Clampett; ***V:*** Mel Blanc, June Foray.

Looney Tunes: Back in Action **2003 (PG)** Mixing live action with animation, the familiar cast of Looney Toon characters participate in a series of hi-jinx with a selection of normally funny human actors. Sure there's a plot somewhere, as Daffy Duck teams up with human buddy D.J. (Fraser) to find a Blue Monkey Diamond before the bad guys, but that's secondary to pushing out as many pop culture references and corny jokes as possible in a 90 minute span. Since the people who actually knew how to do that best did it right 50 (or so) years ago, your time and money are better spent on seeking out and viewing the original cartoons. **91m/C VHS, DVD.** *US* Brendan Fraser, Jenna Elfman, Steve Martin, Timothy Dalton, Heather Locklear, Joan Cusack, Bill Goldberg; ***D:*** Joe Dante; ***W:*** Larry Doyle; ***C:*** Dean Cundey; ***M:*** Jerry Goldsmith; ***V:*** Joe Alaskey, Billy West, Jeff Glenn Bennett, Eric Goldberg.

Loophole **1954** Bank teller Mike Donovan (Sullivan) is robbed—not by the usual masked gunmen, but by a pair of phony bank examiners who've managed to lift $49,900 right from under Donovan's nose. Donovan finds the shortage but doesn't report it right away, and when he does—days later—he's accused of theft and fired, starting a string of lousy luck for him and his wife Ruthie (Malone). Donovan tries to clear his name, but thanks to nasty insurance investigator Gus Slavin (McGraw), he can't get hired anywhere else. **80m/B DVD.** Barry Sullivan, Dorothy Malone, Charles McGraw, Don Haggerty, Mary Beth Hughes, Don Beddoe, Dayton Lummis, Joanne Jordan, John Eldredge, Richard Reeves; ***D:*** Harold Schuster; ***W:*** Dwight V. Babcock, George Bricker.

Loophole *Break In* **1983** An out-of-work architect, hard pressed for money, joins forces with an elite team of expert criminals, in a scheme to make off with millions from the most established holding bank's vault. **105m/C VHS, DVD.** *GB* Albert Finney, Martin Sheen, Susannah York, Robert Morley, Colin Blakely, Jonathan Pryce; ***D:*** John Quested.

Loose Cannons **1990 (R)** Yet another mismatched-cop-partner comedy, wherein a mystery is ostensibly solved by a veteran cop and a schizophrenic detective. **95m/C VHS, DVD.** Gene Hackman, Dan Aykroyd, Dom DeLuise, Ronny Cox, Nancy Travis, David Alan Grier; ***D:*** Bob (Benjamin) Clark; ***W:*** Bob (Benjamin) Clark, Richard Christian Matheson.

Loose Connections **1987** A feminist driving to a convention in Europe advertises for a travelmate, and gets a hopeless chauvinist who is masquerading as a gay man in this offbeat cult comedy. **90m/C VHS.** *GB* Lindsay Duncan, Stephen Rea, Robbie Coltrane; ***D:*** Richard Eyre.

Loose in New York *Fischia il sesso* **1974** Much to her surprise, a cynical socialite begins to fall for her computer-arranged mate. **91m/C VHS.** *IT* Rita Tushingham, Aldo Maccione, George Dzundza, Leopoldo Trieste; ***D:*** Gian Luigi Polidoro.

Loose Screws **1985 (R)** Four perverted teenagers are sent to a restrictive academy where they continue their lewd ways in this stupid sequel to "Screwballs." **75m/C VHS, DVD.** *CA* Bryan Genesse, Karen Wood, Alan Deveau, Jason Warren; ***D:*** Rafal Zielinski; ***W:*** Michael Cory.

Loot... Give Me Money, Honey! **1/2** **1970** Black comedy about a motley crew of greed-driven golddiggers who chase after a heisted fortune in jewels, which is hidden in a coffin belonging to one of the thieves' mother. From Joe Orton's play. **101m/C VHS.** *GB* Richard Attenborough, Lee Remick, Hywel Bennett, Milo O'Shea, Roy Holder; ***D:*** Silvio Narizzano.

Lord Jim **1965** A ship officer (O'Toole) commits an act of cowardice that results in his dismissal and disgrace, which leads him to the Far East in search of self-respect. Excellent supporting cast. Based on Joseph Conrad's novel. **154m/C VHS, DVD.** Peter O'Toole, James Mason, Curt Jurgens, Eli Wallach, Jack Hawkins, Paul Lukas, Akim Tamiroff, Daliah Lavi, Andrew Keir, Jack MacGowran, Walter Gotell; ***D:*** Richard Brooks; ***W:*** Richard Brooks; ***C:*** Frederick A. (Freddie) Young; ***M:*** Bronislau Kaper.

Lord Love a Duck 1/2 **1966** McDowall plays a high school nerd who grants the wishes of classmate Weld, even as they get increasingly complicated. Excellent '60s satire of society in and around high school. **105m/C VHS, DVD.** Roddy McDowall, Tuesday Weld, Lola Albright, Martin West, Ruth Gordon, Harvey Korman, Sarah Marshall, Max (Casey Adams) Showalter, Donald Murphy, Joseph Mell, Dan Frazer, Martine Bartlett; ***D:*** George Axelrod; ***W:*** George Axelrod; ***C:*** Daniel F. Fapp; ***M:*** Neal Hefti.

Lord of Illusions 1/2 *Clive Barker's Lord of Illusions* **1995 (R)** New York P.I. Harry D'Amour (Bakula), who has an affinity for the occult, becomes involved with Dorothea (Janssen), the supposed widow of magician Philip Swann (O'Connor). As Harry investigates he discovers some terrifying secrets, including resurrected cult leader Nix (Von Bargen). Gruesome effects rather than excessive gore but you'll feel like you've been dropped in the middle of a plot without a clear idea what's happening. Bakula's Harry obviously has more stories to tell but Janssen's Dorothea, while attractive, is just around to cower. Barker directs from his own short story "The Last Illusion." The unrated director's cut clocks in at 120 minutes. **109m/C VHS, DVD.** Scott Bakula, Famke Janssen, Kevin J. O'Connor, Daniel von Bargen, Joel Swetow, Barry Sherman, Jordan Marder, Joseph Latimore, Vincent Schiavelli; ***D:*** Clive Barker; ***W:*** Clive Barker; ***C:*** Ronn Schmidt; ***M:*** Simon Boswell.

Lord of the Flies 1/2 **1963** Proper English schoolboys stranded on a desert island during a nuclear war are transformed into savages. A study in greed, power, and the innate animalistic/survivalistic instincts of human nature. Based on William Golding's novel, which he described as a "journey to the darkness of the human heart." **91m/B VHS, DVD.** *GB* James Aubrey, Tom Chapin, Hugh Edwards, Roger Elwin, Tom Gamen; ***D:*** Peter Brook; ***W:*** Peter Brook; ***C:*** Tom Hollyman; ***M:*** Raymond Leppard.

Lord of the Flies **1990 (R)** Inferior second filming of the famed William Golding novel about schoolboys marooned on a desert island who gradually degenerate into savages. Lushly photographed, yet redundant and poorly acted. **90m/C VHS, DVD.** Balthazar Getty, Danuel Pipoly, Chris Furrh, Badgett Dale, Edward Taft, Andrew Taft; ***D:*** Harry Hook; ***W:*** Sara Schiff; ***C:*** Martin Fuhrer; ***M:*** Philippe Sarde.

The Lord of the Rings **1978 (PG)** An animated interpretation of Tolkien's classic tale of the hobbits, wizards, elves, and dwarfs who inhabit Middle Earth. Animator Ralph Bakshi used live motion animation (roto-scoping) to give his characters more life-like and human motion. Well done in spite of the difficulty of adapting from Tolkien's highly detailed and lengthy works. **128m/C VHS, DVD.** ***D:*** Ralph Bakshi; ***W:*** J.C. (Chris) Conkling, Peter S. Beagle; ***V:*** Christopher Guard, John Hurt.

Lord of the Rings: The Fellowship of the Ring 1/2 **2001 (PG-13)** The first in Jackson's trilogy of films based on the books by J.R.R. Tolkein. Young hobbit Frodo Baggins, after inheriting a mysterious ring from his uncle Bilbo, must leave his home in order to keep it from falling into the hands of its evil creator. Along the way, a fellowship is formed to protect the ringbearer and make sure that the ring arrives at its final destination: Mt. Doom, the only place where it can be destroyed. Jackson's amazing visuals bring the imaginary world and mythology of Tolkein to life. The three and a half hour pic stays closer to the original novel than any of the previous efforts (all animated), while still managing to keep a quick enough pace for those unfamiliar with the lengthy literary work. Should get repeated viewing in parents' basements for years to come. **178m/C VHS, DVD.** Elijah Wood, Ian McKellen, Liv Tyler, Viggo Mortensen, Sean Astin, Cate Blanchett, John Rhys-Davies, Dominic Monaghan, Billy Boyd, Orlando Bloom, Christopher Lee, Hugo Weaving, Sean Bean, Ian Holm, Andy Serkis, Marton Csokas; ***D:*** Peter Jackson; ***W:*** Peter Jackson, Fran Walsh, Philippa Boyens; ***C:*** Andrew Lesnie; ***M:*** Howard Shore. Oscars '01: Cinematog.; British Acad. '01: Director (Jackson), Film, Visual FX; L.A. Film Critics '01: Score; Natl. Bd. of Review '01: Support. Actress (Blanchett); Screen Actors Guild '01: Support. Actor (McKellen); Broadcast Film Critics '01: Song ("May It Be"), Score.

Lord of the Rings: The Two Towers **2002 (PG-13)** The second installment of the "Rings" trilogy does not disappoint. Picking up shortly after the first one left off, Frodo and Samwise are still heading toward Mordor, with Gollum following/abetting their progress. Aragorn, Legolas, and Gimli join together with the denizens of Rohan to fight Saruman's army of Orcs. Gandalf is back to make with the white magic heroics as well. Plenty of action (the battle scenes are incredible) and plot twists (Frodo's battle of wills with himself and Gollum add yet more depth to both characters), provide enough entertainment to keep the chat rooms humming until the last chapter comes out. Speaking of final chapters, George Lucas must be sweating bullets right about now. **179m/C VHS, DVD.** *US* Elijah Wood, Sean Astin, Viggo Mortensen, Orlando Bloom, John Rhys-Davies, Ian McKellen, Christopher Lee, Billy Boyd, Dominic Monaghan, Liv Tyler, Bernard Hill, Miranda Otto, David Wenham, Karl Urban, Brad Dourif, Cate Blanchett, Hugo Weaving; ***D:*** Peter Jackson; ***W:*** Peter Jackson, Fran Walsh, Philippa Boyens, Stephen Sinclair; ***C:*** Andrew Lesnie; ***M:*** Howard Shore; ***V:*** John Rhys-Davies, Andy Serkis. Oscars '02: Visual FX; British Acad. '02: Costume Des., Visual FX.

Lord of the Rings: The Return of the King **2003 (PG-13)** Jackson's triumphant last chapter of the superb Tolkien trilogy brings the story to a satisfying close. After the climactic battle for Helm's Deep in "The Two Towers," Rohan's forces, along with most of the original members of the Fellowship, must come to the aid of Minas Tirith, the capital city of Gondor, and Sauron's next target. They also attempt to distract Sauron from Frodo and Sam, who encounter even worse hardships, including misplaced trust, deceit, and giant spiders, on their way to Mt. Doom to destroy the ring. Although the two main plots are very different in scope and dynamics, each is equally adept at maintaining depth and character development, while keeping the plot moving along. As with the first two installments, the photography is breathtaking. **200m/C VHS, DVD.** *US* Elijah Wood, Sean Astin, Viggo Mortensen, Orlando Bloom, John Rhys-Davies, Ian McKellen, Billy Boyd, Dominic Monaghan, Liv Tyler, Bernard Hill, Miranda Otto, David Wenham, Karl Urban, Hugo Weaving, Andy Serkis, Cate Blanchett, John Noble, Ian Holm, Sean Bean, Lawrence Makoare, Marton Csokas; ***D:*** Peter Jackson; ***W:*** Peter Jackson, Fran Walsh, Philippa Boyens; ***C:*** Andrew Lesnie; ***M:*** Howard Shore. Oscars '03: Adapt. Screenplay, Art Dir./Set Dec., Costume Des., Director (Jackson), Film, Film Editing, Makeup, Song ("Into the West"), Sound, Visual FX, Orig. Score; British Acad. '03: Adapt. Screenplay, Cinematog., Film, Visual FX; Directors Guild '03: Director (Jackson); Golden Globes '04: Director (Jackson), Film—Drama, Song ("Into the West"), Orig. Score; L.A. Film Critics '03: Director (Jackson); N.Y. Film Critics '03: Film; Screen Actors Guild '03: Cast.

Lord of War **2005 (R)** Niccol's look into the dark world of international weapons trade says guns are evil but its vivid imagery suggests something very different. Yuri Orlov (Cage), a Ukrainian immigrant living in Manhattan, would like to put a gun in the hand of every person on the planet. Aided in business by his brother Vitally (Leto) and pursued by Interpol agent Valentine (Hawke), Yuri slickly operates in his frightening underworld of bloody regional conflict. His fabulous life is fueled by profits extracted from the ever-growing stack of dead bodies. Cage's performance is at the center of a satisfying movie experience. **122m/C DVD, Blu-ray Disc, UMD.** *US* Nicolas Cage, Jared Leto, Bridget Moynahan, Ian Holm, Ethan Hawke, Eamonn Walker, Sammi Rotibi, Eugene (Yevgeny) Lazarev; ***D:*** Andrew Niccol; ***W:*** Andrew Niccol; ***C:*** Amir M. Mokri; ***M:*** Antonio Pinto.

The Lords of Discipline 1/2 **1983 (R)** A military academy cadet is given the unenviable task of protecting a black freshman from racist factions at a southern school circa 1964. Based on Pat Conroy's autobiographical novel. **103m/C VHS, DVD.** David Keith, Robert Prosky, Barbara Babcock, Judge Reinhold, G.D. Spradlin, Rick Rossovich, Michael Biehn, Bill Paxton, Matt Frewer; ***D:*** Franc Roddam; ***C:*** Brian Tufano; ***M:*** Howard Blake.

Lords of Dogtown **2005 (PG-13)** Another ego-trip down memory lane for writer and original Z-Boy Stacy Peralta, serving as a dramatic reenactment to his documentary "Dogtown and Z-Boys." A motley crew of surfer-turned-skater kids in 1975's Venice, CA, turn skateboarding into a pop-culture revolution. The movie version of their story, however, is a bit of a wipe out. The skating looks great, but some botched acting and poor pacing confuses everything. Ledger does his best with the clumsy role of Zephyr founder Skip Englom, but others, mostly real life skater kids, aren't as convincing. Starts to click in the second-half, but still riddled with bad dialogue and rushed storytelling. Loaded with cameos, mostly by pro skate veterans, and one by the late, great, cult stand-up comic Mitch Hedberg. **107m/C DVD, UMD.** *US* Heath Ledger, Emile Hirsch, Victor Rasuk, John Robinson, Nikki Reed, Michael Angarano, Rebecca De Mornay, Johnny Knoxville; ***D:*** Catherine Hardwicke; ***W:*** Stacy Peralta; ***C:*** Elliot Davis; ***M:*** Mark Mothersbaugh.

The Lords of Flatbush 1/2 **1974 (PG)** Four street toughs battle against their own maturation and responsibilities in 1950s Brooklyn. Winkler introduces the leather-clad hood he's made a career of and Stallone introduces a character not unlike Rocky. Interesting slice of life. **88m/C VHS, DVD.** Sylvester Stallone, Perry King, Henry Winkler, Susan Blakely, Armand Assante, Paul Mace; ***D:*** Stephen Verona, Martin Davidson; ***W:*** Sylvester Stallone, Stephen Verona, Martin Davidson; ***M:*** Joseph Brooks.

Lords of Magick **1988 (PG-13)** Two warriors chase an evil sorcerer and the princess he's kidnapped across time to the 20th century. **98m/C VHS.** Jarrett Parker, Matt Gauthier, Brendan Dillon Jr.; ***D:*** David Marsh.

Lords of the Deep WOOF! **1989 (PG-13)** A Roger Corman cheapie about underwater technicians trapped on the ocean floor with a race of aliens. A film rushed out to capitalize on the undersea sci-fi subgenre highlighted by "The Abyss." **95m/C VHS.** Bradford Dillman, Priscilla Barnes, Melody Ryane, Eb Lottimer, Daryl Haney; ***Cameos:*** Roger Corman; ***D:*** Mary Ann Fisher; ***W:*** Howard R. Cohen, Daryl Haney.

Lords of the Street *Jump Out Boys* **2008 (R)** Mexican drug lord Santiago Rodriguez (Leduc) has escaped from jail with the help of his uncle, who expects compensation. Santiago's girlfriend (Berry) stashed millions away before he was arrested but in a post-Hurricane Katrina New Orleans it won't be easy getting to the money, especially when a determined (and way past retirement-aged) cop (Kritofferson) and his hot-headed partner (DMX) have other ideas. **82m/C DVD.** DMX, Kris Kristofferson, Veronica Berry, Armando Leduc, Sheldon Robins; ***D:*** Amir Valinia; ***W:*** Sheldon Robins, Dan Garcia; ***C:*** Tom Baks; ***M:*** Mary Alice Corton. **VIDEO**

Lorenzo's Oil **1992 (PG-13)** Based on the true story of Augusto and Michaela Odone's efforts to find a cure for their five-year-old, Lorenzo, diagnosed with the rare and incurable disease ALD (Adrenoleukodystrophy). Confronted by a slow-moving and clinically cold medical community, the Odones embark on their own quest for a cure. Sarandon delivers an outstanding and emotionally charged performance as Lorenzo's determined mother. Nolte is his equally devoted Italian father, complete with black hair and hand gestures. They are a powerful presence in a film which could have easily degenerated into a made-for-TV movie, but is instead a tribute to what love and hope can accomplish. **135m/C VHS, DVD.** Nick Nolte, Susan Sarandon, Zach O'Malley-Greenberg, Peter Ustinov, Kathleen Wilhoite, Gerry Bamman, Margo Martindale, James Rebhorn, Ann Hearn, Elizabeth (E.G. Dailey) Daily; ***D:*** George Miller; ***W:*** George Miller, Nick Enright; ***C:*** John Seale.

The Loretta Claiborne Story 1/2 **2000** Your basic inspirational TV movie based on a true story. Loretta (Elise) is black, poor, partially blind, and mildly retarded. She's mercilessly teased until a grade-school teacher (Palk) interests the young Loretta in running. But it's not until she's a teenager that Loretta finds her own cheerleader—social worker Janet McFarland (Manheim) who signs the girl up to participate in the Special Olympics. **90m/C VHS.** Kimberly Elise, Camryn Manheim, Tina Lifford, Nancy Palk, Damon Gupton, Nicole Ari Parker; ***D:*** Lee Grant; ***W:*** Grace McKeaney; ***C:*** Laszlo George; ***M:*** Stanley Clarke. **TV**

Lorna Doone 1/2 **1922** A young girl of royal descent is kidnapped and raised by the bandit Doone family in the highlands of Scotland. Adapted from the novel by R.D. Blackmore. **79m/B VHS, DVD.** Madge Bellamy, John Bowers; ***D:*** Maurice Tourneur.

Lorna Doone 1/2 **1934** Early version of the R.D. Blackmore novel about an English farmer who falls in love with the daughter of an outlaw family. Set in rural England in the 1600s; remade in 1951 and 1990. **90m/B VHS.** *GB* Victoria Hopper, John Loder, Margaret Lockwood, Roy Emerton, Mary Clare, Edward Rigby, Roger Livesey; ***D:*** Basil Dean; ***W:*** Miles Malleson.

Lorna Doone 1/2 **1990 (PG)** Classic romance set in 17th-century England and based on the novel by R.D. Blackmore. John Ridd (Bean) vows to destroy the land-grabbing Doone family, whom he blames for the death of his parents. Then he meets, and immediately falls in love with, the beautiful and innocent Lorna Doone (Walker). **90m/C VHS.** *GB* Sean Bean, Polly Walker, Clive Owen, Billie Whitelaw; ***D:*** Andrew Grieve; ***W:*** Matthew Jacobs. **TV**

Lorna Doone **2001** Based on R.D. Blackmore's novel, which is set in the west country of 17th-century Britain, this swashbuckler is a star-crossed romance with an ultimately happy ending. John Ridd (Coyle) is a common farmer who discovers that Lorna (Warner), the young beauty he loves, is a member of the infamous Doone clan—a once aristocratic family that has turned outlaw. To make things worse for John, Lorna is already betrothed to the violent Carver Doone (Gillen) who will do anything to keep her. **150m/C VHS, DVD.** *GB* Richard Coyle, Amelia Warner, Aidan Gillen, Martin Clunes, Michael Kitchen, Martin Jarvis, Barbara Flynn, Peter Vaughan, Anton Lesser, Jack Shepherd; ***D:*** Mike Barker; ***W:*** Adrian Hodges; ***C:*** Chris Seager; ***M:*** John Lunn. **TV**

Lorna's Silence *Le Silence de Lorna* **2008 (R)** Albanian immigrant Lorna (Dobroshi) hopes to get her Belgian citizenship papers by agreeing to a green card marriage to junkie Claudy (Renier), which was arranged by lowlife Fabio (Rongione). But Fabio wants Lorna to do something for him in return that will probably result in Claudy's death. Lorna may be desperate but she also turns out to have a (very inconvenient) conscience. Albanian, French, and Russian with subtitles. **95m/C DVD.** *BE FR GE IT* Jeremie Renier, Fabrizio Rongione, Morgan Marinne, Olivier Gourmet, Arta Dobroshi, Alban Ukaj; ***D:*** Jean-Pierre Dardenne, Luc Dardenne; ***W:*** Jean-Pierre Dardenne, Luc Dardenne; ***C:*** Alain Marcoen.

Los Locos Posse **1997 (R)** Uneven would-be sequel to 1993's "Posse." Chance (Van Peebles) is a black military scout who is found, injured, by one of the unhinged denizens of a nearby mission. The Mother Superior enlists Chance to lead the nuns and their "Los Locos" charges to another mission some hundred miles away. The trip doesn't go smoothly and their arrival only leads to more problems. First English-language feature for Montreal director Vallee. **100m/C VHS.** Mario Van Peebles, Rene Auberjonois, Kathryn Witt, Danny Trejo, Melora Walters, Rusty Schwimmer; ***D:*** Jean-Marc Vallee; ***W:*** Mario Van Peebles; ***C:*** Pierre Gill; ***M:*** Lesley Barber.

Los Olvidados 1/2 *The Young and the Damned* **1950** From surrealist Bunuel, a powerful story of the poverty and violence of young people's lives in Mexico's slums. In Spanish with English subtitles. **88m/B VHS, DVD.** *MX* Alfonso Mejias, Roberto Cobo; ***D:*** Luis Bunuel. Cannes '51: Director (Bunuel), Film.

Loser 1/2 **1997 (R)** Very low-budget street drama concerns young small-time drug dealer James Dean Ray (Harris) and his self-destruction slide towards oblivion. **90m/C VHS, DVD.** Kirk Harris, Jonathon Chaus, Peta Wilson, Norman Salect, Jack Rubio; ***D:*** Kirk Harris; ***W:*** Kirk Harris; ***C:*** Kent Wakeford.

Loser **2000 (PG-13)** College comedy finds nerdy midwesterner Biggs branded a loser by his dorm mates at New York University. He's also pining over beauty Suvari, who's having an affair with heartless prof Kinnear. Writer-director Heckerling's trademark sympathy for the adolescent outcast is intact, but this outing is missing the insight, subtlety, and (most importantly) the fun of her earlier efforts. Biggs and Suvari give passable performances, but Kinnear is the bright spot. **95m/C VHS, DVD.** Jason Biggs, Mena Suvari, Greg Kinnear, Zak Orth, Dan Aykroyd, Tom Sadoski, Jimmi Simpson, Colleen Camp, Robert Miano, Andy Dick, David Spade, Steven Wright, Taylor Negron, Andrea Martin, Scott Thompson; ***D:*** Amy Heckerling; ***W:*** Amy Heckerling; ***C:*** Rob Hahn; ***M:*** David Kitay.

The Losers 1/2 *Nam's Angels* **1970 (R)** Four motorcyclists are hired by the U.S. Army to rescue a presidential advisor who is being held captive by Asian bad guys. **96m/C VHS, DVD.** William (Bill) Smith, Bernie Hamilton, Adam Roarke, Houston Savage, Paul Koslo, John Garwood, Jack Starrett, Alan Caillou; ***D:*** Jack Starrett; ***W:*** Alan Caillou; ***C:*** Nonong Rasca; ***M:*** Stu Phillips.

The Losers **2010** A U.S. black ops unit in Bolivia is betrayed and left for dead by Max, who is bent on starting a high-tech global war. The unit remains undercover while planning their revenge. **m/C DVD.** Jeffrey Dean Morgan, Idris Elba, Zoe Saldana, Columbus Short, Chris Evans, Oscar Jaenada, Jason Patric, Holt McCallany; ***D:*** Sylvain White; ***W:*** Peter Berg, James Vanderbilt; ***C:*** Scott Kevan.

Losin' It **1982 (R)** Four teens travel across the Mexican border to Tijuana on a journey to lose their virginity. Cruise meets a married woman who says she is in town for a divorce, while the others become caught up in frenzied undertakings of their own. **104m/C VHS, DVD.** Tom Cruise, John Stockwell, Shelley Long, Jackie Earle Haley, John P. Navin Jr., Timothy Brown, Rick Rossovich; ***D:*** Curtis Hanson; ***W:*** Bill W.L. Norton; ***C:*** Gilbert Taylor; ***M:*** Kenneth Wannberg.

Losing Chase 1/2 **1996 (R)** Bacon makes his directorial debut in this drama that features wife Sedgwick as Elizabeth, mother's helper to Chase (Mirren) and Richard Philips (Bridges) at their summer home on Martha's Vineyard. Chase is still recovering from a mental breakdown, having spent several months in an institution, and she resents Elizabeth's presence, constantly criticizing her. But when the two women are alone together a confusing and emotional bond gradually begins to form between them. **95m/C VHS, DVD.** Helen Mirren, Kyra Sedgwick, Beau Bridges; ***D:*** Kevin Bacon; ***W:*** Anne Meredith; ***C:*** Dick Quinlan; ***M:*** Michael Bacon. **CABLE**

Losing Isaiah **1994 (R)** "Kramer vs. Kramer" meets the movie-of-the-week in this controversial and emotionally moving story of a social worker (Lange) who adopts the title character, an African American baby abandoned by his drug-addicted mother (Berry). Courtroom battle ensues when four years later mom, now clean and sober, discovers Isaiah is alive. She enlists the aid of a lawyer (Jackson) known for his high-profile, racially charged cases. Lange and Berry lead the parade of fine performances. Taking on some volatile issues, director Gyllenhaal manages (for the most part) to refrain from melodrama. Based on the novel by Seth Margolis. **108m/C VHS, DVD.** Jessica Lange, Halle Berry, David Strathairn, Samuel L. Jackson, Cuba Gooding Jr., LaTanya Richardson Jackson; ***D:*** Stephen Gyllenhaal; ***W:*** Naomi Foner; ***C:*** Andrzej Bartkowiak; ***M:*** Mark Isham.

The Loss of a Teardrop Diamond 1/2 **2008 (PG-13)** Musty attempt at resurrecting an unproduced Tennessee Williams scenario from the 1950s. In 1920s Memphis, heiress Fisher Willow (Howard) behaves too outrageously to be willingly accepted at high-society gatherings. Needing an escort, she hires Jimmy Dobyne (Evans), an impoverished employee of her father's. He's indifferent to her charms and Fisher gets jealous when Jimmy reunites with an ex-flame, so she accuses him of stealing a diamond earring (that she's lost at a party). **102m/C DVD.** *US* Bryce Dallas Howard, Chris Evans, Ellen Burstyn, Mamie Gummer, Ann-Margret, Will Patton, Peter Gerety, Jessica Collins; ***D:*** Jodie Markell; ***W:*** Tennessee Williams; ***C:*** Giles Nuttgens; ***M:*** Mark Orton.

The Loss of Sexual Innocence 1/2 **1998 (R)** Figgis' ambitious film follows the fall from grace (literally of Adam and Eve), and the nature of sex, love, jealousy, and violence. Unfortunately, this turns out to be less than scintillating material. Interspersed with scenes from the Garden of Eden story is that of dissatisfied filmmaker Nic (Sands), as he relives his past and ponders his unhappy present. **101m/C VHS, DVD.** Julian Sands, Saffron Burrows, Stefano Dionisi, Jonathan Rhys Meyers, Kelly Macdonald, Femi Ogumbanjo, Hanne Klintoe, Johanna Torrel, George Moktar, John Cowey; ***D:*** Mike Figgis; ***W:*** Mike Figgis; ***C:*** Benoit Delhomme; ***M:*** Mike Figgis.

Lost 1/2 **1983** A young girl runs away into the wilderness because of the resentment she feels toward her new stepfather. **92m/C VHS.** Sandra Dee, Don Stewart, Ken Curtis, Jack Elam, Sheila Newhouse; ***D:*** Al Adamson; ***W:*** Don Buday; ***C:*** Gary Graver.

Lost **1986** When their boat capsizes in the Pacific, three sailors desperately cling to life, drifting aimlessly for 74 days. Based on a true story, this film is adult-fare. **93m/C VHS.** *CA* Michael Hogan, Helen Shaver, Kenneth Welsh; ***D:*** Peter Rowe.

Lost 1/2 **2005** Former L.A. resident Jeremy Stanton (Cain) gets lost on a Mojave highway while driving to meet his family at their new Nevada home. His nightmare journey turns into a maze of detours on flood-closed roads, while he gets bad directions from clueless road-service operator Judy (voiced by Scott). A bank VP, the increasingly panicked Jeremy also has to worry about being tracked by sadistic thug Archer (Trejo) for reasons that are only gradually revealed. A tight thriller in the best B-movie tradition and the debut feature for Lemke. **86m/C DVD.** *US* Dean Cain, Ashley Scott, Danny Trejo, Irina Bjorklund, Justin Henry, Griffin Armstorff; ***D:*** Darren Lemke; ***W:*** Darren Lemke; ***C:*** Paul Emami; ***M:*** Russ Landau.

Lost and Delirious **2001** Teen angst, romance, and sexuality taken to extremes. Shy Mouse (Barton) is trying to settle in at her exclusive girls' boarding school with new roomies, wealthy Tory (Pare) and wild Paulie (Perabo). When Mouse realizes that the girls are lovers she takes it in stride but Tory gets anxious and denies the relationship. Mouse watches helplessly as Paulie gets increasingly desperate to win Tory back and matters take a turn for the baroque. Based on the novel "The Wives of Bath" by Susan Swan. **100m/C VHS, DVD.** *CA* Mischa Barton, Piper Perabo, Jessica Pare, Jackie Burroughs, Graham Greene, Mimi Kuzyk, Luke Kirby; ***D:*** Lea Pool; ***W:*** Judith Thompson; ***C:*** Pierre Gill; ***M:*** Yves Chamberland. Genie '01: Cinematog.

Lost and Found 1/2 **1979 (PG)** An American professor of English and an English film production secretary fall in love on a skiing vacation. Good cast but Segal and Jackson did romance better in "A Touch of Class." **104m/C VHS.** George Segal, Glenda Jackson, Maureen Stapleton, Hollis McLaren, John Cunningham, Paul Sorvino, John Candy, Martin Short; ***D:*** Melvin Frank; ***W:*** Jack Rose.

Lost and Found **1999 (PG-13)** The only, repeat ONLY, reason to see this movie is Sophie Marceau. Spade, in a bold bit of casting, plays Dylan, a sniveling pipsqueak taken with his French neighbor Lila (the aforementioned Marceau). In a sick attempt to win her love, he kidnaps her dog in order to "find" him a few days later. When the dog swallows an anniversary ring Dylan's holding for a friend, many tasteless dog poo jokes ensue. Wants to be "There's Something About Mary," but doesn't have its winking sense of absurdity. Spade should stick to the snarky sidekick roles and Marceau should fire whoever told her that this would be a good career move. **97m/C VHS, DVD.** David Spade, Sophie Marceau, Artie Lange, Martin Sheen, Patrick Bruel, Jon Lovitz, Mitchell Whitfield, Carole Cook, Estelle Harris, Marla Gibbs, Natalie Barish, Phil Leeds, Christian Clemenson, Daphne Lynn Duplaix; ***D:*** Jeff Pollack; ***W:*** J.B. Cook, Marc Meeks, David Spade; ***C:*** Paul Elliott; ***M:*** John Debney.

The Lost Angel **2004** Plagued by the memory of her mother's death and facing an internal investigation, a police inspector (Eastwood) must overcome her own demons along with intense media scrutiny to track down a serial killer. **99m/C VHS, DVD.** Alison Eastwood, Nicholas Celozzi, Judd Nelson, John Rhys-Davies, C. Thomas Howell, Eugene Lipinski, Neville Edwards; ***D:*** Dimitri Logothetis; ***W:*** Dimitri Logothetis; ***C:*** Paul Mitchnick; ***M:*** Trevor Morris. **VIDEO**

Lost Angels 1/2 **1989 (R)** A glossy "Rebel Without a Cause" '80s reprise providing a no-holds-barred portrait of life in the fast lane. A wealthy, disaffected San Fernando Valley youth immerses himself in sex, drugs and rock 'n' roll. Ultimately he is arrested and sent by his parents to a youth home, where a dedicated therapist assists his tortuous road back to reality. **116m/C VHS.** Donald Sutherland, Adam Horovitz, Amy Locane, Kevin Tighe, John C. McGinley, Graham Beckel, Park Overall, Don Bloomfield, Celia Weston; ***D:*** Hugh Hudson; ***W:*** Michael Weller; ***M:*** Philippe Sarde.

Lost Battalion 1/2 **2001** True story based on the heroism of U.S. Major Charles Whittlesey (Schroder), who won the Congressional Medal of Honor during the closing days of WWI. Part of the Army's 77th Division, Whittlesey and his troops find themselves separated from their allies and surrounded by German forces in the Argonne Forest. Whittlesey led his men on a five-day defensive back to Allied lines despite limited supplies and constant battle. **100m/C VHS, DVD.** Rick Schroder, Jamie Harris, Phil McKee, Jay Rodan, Adam James; ***D:*** Russell Mulcahy; ***W:*** James (Jim) Carabatsos; ***C:*** Jonathan Freeman; ***M:*** Richard (Rick) Marvin. **CABLE**

Lost Boundaries 1/2 **1949** Respected physician Scott Carter (debut role for Ferrer) and his family live and work in a small New Hampshire town, hiding the fact that they are black, passing for white, in their segregated society. But then the truth becomes known. Strong, if slow-moving, and based on a true story; the use of white leads for black roles was common casting. **99m/B VHS.** Mel Ferrer, Beatrice Pearson, Richard Hylton, Susan Douglas, Canada Lee, Carleton Carpenter, Seth Arnold, Wendell Holmes; ***D:*** Alfred Werker; ***W:*** Virginia Shaler, Eugene Ling, Charles A. Palmer, Furland de Kay; ***C:*** William J. Miller; ***M:*** Louis Applebaum.

The Lost Boys **1978** Holm gives a brilliant performance as writer J.M. Barrie, whose friendship with young George Llewelyn-Davies and his four brothers will lead to the story of Peter Pan. But as the depressed Barrie's marriage falls apart and tragedy strikes the Llewelyn-Davies family, the relationship grows ever more complex. **270m/C DVD.** *GB* Ian Holm, Tim Pigott-Smith, Anna Cropper, Maureen O'Brien, Ann Bell; ***D:*** Rodney Bennett; ***W:*** Andrew Birkin; ***M:*** Dudley Simpson. **TV**

The Lost Boys **1987 (R)** Santa Cruz seems like a dull town when Michael, his younger brother, and their divorced mom move into their eccentric grandfather's home. But when Michael falls for a pretty girl with some hard-living friends he takes on more than he imagines—these partying teens are actually a group of vampires. Some humor, some bloodletting violence, and an attractive cast help out this updated vampire tale. Rock-filled soundtrack. **97m/C VHS, DVD.** Jason Patric, Kiefer Sutherland, Corey Haim, Jami Gertz, Dianne Wiest, Corey Feldman, Barnard Hughes, Edward Herrmann, Billy Wirth, Jamison Newlander, Brooke McCarter, Alex Winter; ***D:*** Joel Schumacher; ***W:*** Jeffrey Boam, Janice Fischer, James Jeremias; ***C:*** Michael Chapman; ***M:*** Thomas Newman.

Lost Boys: The Tribe **WOOF!** **2008 (R)** Why bother with this inept mess? Exsurfer Chris (Hilgenbrink) and his teen sister Nicole (Resser) move to seaside Luna Bay, California, to start over after their parents die. The town happens to be populated by bloodsuckers and vamp Shane (Sutherland) goes after Nicole, leaving Chris to wonder why she's acting weird. (Dude, she's a teenaged chick!) Anyway, Frog brother Edgar (Feldman, using the same old shtick) offers his vampire-disposing assistance. Angus Sutherland is the half-brother of Keifer, who starred in the 1987 original; unfortunately, the charisma and acting genes seemed to have passed him by. **94m/C DVD.** Tad Hilgenbrink, Corey Feldman, Gabrielle Rose, Autumn Reeser, Angus Sutherland; ***D:*** P.J. Pesce; ***W:*** Hans Rodionoff; ***C:*** Barry Donlevy; ***M:*** Nathan Barr. **VIDEO**

Lost Canyon **1943** Hoppy tries to help a fugitive who's been framed for bank robbery. This is the second installment distributed by United Artists. The song "Jingle, Jangle, Jingle" is sung by the Sportsman Quartet. **61m/B VHS, DVD.** William Boyd, Jay Kirby, Andy Clyde, Lola Lane, Douglas Fowley, Herbert Rawlinson; ***D:*** Lesley Selander.

The Lost Capone **1990 (PG-13)** Cable TV version of the story of Al Capone's youngest brother, a clean living small town sheriff who struggles with his sibling's reputation at every turn. **93m/C VHS.** Dominic Chianese, Ally Sheedy, Eric Roberts, Adrian Pasdar, Titus Welliver, Jimmie F. Skaggs, Maria Pitillo, Anthony Crivello; ***D:*** John Gray; ***W:*** John Gray; ***C:*** Paul Elliott. **CABLE**

The Lost Child 1/2 **2000** Remarkable true story about a search for identity. Rebecca (Ruehl) always knew she was adopted, being raised Jewish in Pennsylvania. After her adoptive parents are both dead, Rebecca decides to search for her birth parents and discovers that she is a full-blooded Navaho who was taken from her family on the reservation. She immediately decides to take her children to meet her relatives in Arizona, where they are welcomed into the community. But it isn't so simple for Rebecca's husband, Jack (Sheridan), to deal with his outsider status. Based on the autobiography "Looking for Lost Bird" by Yvette Melanson and Claire Safran. **100m/C VHS, DVD.** Mercedes Ruehl, Jamey Sheridan, Irene Bedard, Dinah Manoff, Ned Romero, Tantoo Cardinal, Michael Greyeyes, Julia McIlvaine; ***D:*** Karen Arthur; ***W:*** Sally Robinson; ***C:*** Thomas Neuwirth; ***M:*** Mark McKenzie. **TV**

The Lost City **1934** A feature version of the rollicking vintage movie serial about a lost jungle city, adventurers and mad scientists. **74m/B VHS, DVD.** William "Stage" Boyd, Kane Richmond, George "Gabby" Hayes, Claudia Dell; ***D:*** Harry Revier.

The Lost City **2005 (R)** Garcia's directorial debut is a 20-year, overextended labor of love. Set in 1958 Havana, the old-fashioned saga focuses on the three Fellove brothers and their reactions to the Batista dictatorship and Castro's revolution. Fico (Garcia), the eldest, is an apolitical nightclub owner who wants life to go on as it always has, while his two younger brothers, Luis (Carbonell) and Rico (Murciano), believe in violent change. Politics not only divides the family but soon shatters their comfortable existence, leading Fico into exile from his beloved home (as it did for Garcia's own family). The numerous musical interludes are only in Spanish. **143m/C DVD, HD DVD.** *US* Andy Garcia, Nestor Carbonell, Enrique Murciano, Richard Bradford, Steven Bauer, Dustin Hoffman, Julio Oscar Mechoso, Tomas Milian, William Marquez, Bill Murray, Elizabeth Pena, Millie Perkins, Tony Plana, Ines Sastre, Juan Fernandez, Gonzalo Menendez, Jsu Garcia, Ruben Rabasa; ***D:*** Andy Garcia; ***W:*** G. Cabrera

Infante; *C:* Emmanuel (Manu) Kadosh; *M:* Andy Garcia.

Lost City of the Jungle ✌✌ 1/2 **1945** 13-chapter serial focusing on a crazed Atwill, in his last screen role, believing that he can rule the world from the heart of a deep, dark jungle by utilizing a special mineral. The final Universal serial. **169m/B VHS, DVD.** Russell Hayden, Lionel Atwill, Jane Adams; *D:* Ray Taylor, Lewis D. Collins.

Lost Colony: The Legend of Roanoke ✌ 1/2 *The Wraiths of Roanoke* **2007 (R)** Low-budget, not terribly scary supernatural horror based on the true story of the first English colony in the U.S. that disappeared without a trace in 1587. Ananias Dare (Paul) is in charge of the colony on Roanoke Island, Virginia. When the colonists start dying in terrible ways, Dare learns from the local tribe that the malevolent Norse spirits of early explorers haunt the island (and apparently want it all to themselves). A Sci-Fi Channel original. **95m/C DVD.** Adrian Paul, Rhett Giles, Alex McArthur, Frida Show, Michael The, Mari Mascaro, George Calil; *D:* Matt Codd; *W:* Rafael Jordan; *C:* Anton Bakarski; *M:* John Dickson. **CABLE**

The Lost Command ✌✌ 1/2 **1966** A French colonel, relieved of his command, endeavors to regain power by battling a powerful Arab terrorist with his own specially trained platoon of soldiers. Crisp adventure set in post-WWII North Africa. Based on "The Centurions" by Jean Larteguy. **129m/C DVD.** Anthony Quinn, Michele Morgan, George Segal, Alain Delon, Maurice Ronet, Claudia Cardinale; *D:* Mark Robson; *C:* Robert L. Surtees.

The Lost Continent ✌ 1/2 **1951** An expedition searching for a lost rocket on a jungle island discovers dinosaurs and other extinct creatures. **82m/B VHS, DVD.** Cesar Romero, Hillary Brooke, Chick Chandler, John Hoyt, Acquanetta, Sid Melton, Whit Bissell, Hugh Beaumont; *D:* Sam Newfield; *W:* Richard H. Landau; *C:* Jack Greenhalgh; *M:* Paul Dunlap.

Lost Diamond ✌ *En Busca del Brillante Perdido* **1986** Bumbling spies search for a smuggled gem. **83m/C VHS.** *AR* Juan Ramon, Sonia Rivas, Ricardo Bauleo; *D:* Sergio Mottola; *W:* Gustavo Ghirardi; *C:* Jorge Pizzi; *M:* Emilio Kauderer.

Lost Embrace ✌✌ *El Abrazo Partido* **2004** Aimless Ariel (Hendler), the son of Jewish immigrants, lives in Buenos Aires and helps his mother (Aizenberg) at her lingerie store in a downscale shopping mall. Ariel asks his Polish emigrant grandma (Londner) to help him claim Polish citizenship in order to get a Polish passport so he can move to Europe and start over (he wants to feel "European"). Since grams fled Poland during WWII, she's naturally reluctant and is wise enough to realize that Ariel needs to change his inner self and not merely his outer surroundings. Spanish with subtitles. **99m/C DVD.** *AR IT SP* Daniel Hendler, Jorge d'Elia, Sergio Boris, Adriana Aizenberg, Rosita Londner; *D:* Daniel Burman; *W:* Daniel Burman, Marcelo Biromajer; *C:* Ramiro Civita; *M:* Cesar Lerner.

The Lost Empire ✌ **1983 (R)** Three bountiful and powerful women team up to battle the evil Dr. Syn Do. **86m/C VHS.** Melanie Vincz, Raven De La Croix, Angela Aames, Paul Coufos, Robert Tessier, Angus Scrimm, Angelique Pettyjohn, Kenneth Tobey; *D:* Jim Wynorski; *W:* Jim Wynorski.

The Lost Empire ✌ 1/2 **2001** Lavish but muddled (and ultimately dull) story originally broadcast as a four-hour miniseries. American businessman Nicholas Orton (Gibson), who once studied Chinese literature and history, meets cute with a mystery woman who turns out to be Kwan Ying (Ling), the Goddess of Mercy. She tells Nick he has 3 days to save the human world from slavery by saving the classic Chinese manuscript "The Journey to the West" from falling into the wrong hands. Helping Nick are characters from the story, including the anarchic Monkey King (Wong). **134m/C VHS, DVD.** Thomas Gibson, Bai Ling, Russell Wong, Ric Young, Kabir Bedi, Henry O; *D:* Peter Macdonald; *W:* David Henry Hwang; *C:* David Connell; *M:* John Altman. **TV**

Lost for Words ✌✌✌ **1999** Aging and the parent/child bond has never been more bittersweet and amusing as in this British production, which is based on the memoirs of Deric Longden (he also wrote the teleplay). Elderly Annie (88-year-old Hird in a touchingly tart performance) lives alone, with her middleaged son Deric (Postlethwaite) and his blind wife Aileen (Downie) popping in to offer support and company. But then a series of strokes rob Annie of her ability to speak coherently and of her cherished independence. **90m/C VHS.** *GB* Thora Hird, Pete Postlethwaite, Penny Downie, Tom Higgins; *D:* Alan J.W. Bell; *W:* Deric Longden. **TV**

Lost Highway ✌✌ **1996 (R)** Welcome once again to Lynch-world—that parallel universe understood only by master David. Jazz musician Fred Madison (Pullman) is on Death Row—supposedly for the murder of his wife Renee (Arquette). Only why does young mechanic Pete Dayton (Getty) wind up in Fred's cell (with Fred missing)? Oh, and why does gangster Mr. Eddy (Loggia) have a girlfriend named Alice (Arquette again) who looks just like Renee? And is she real—or did Fred conjure her up? Who's the Mystery Man (Blake), who literally looks like death warmed over. And.....well, you get the idea. Or maybe you're not supposed to. **135m/C VHS, DVD.** Bill Pullman, Patricia Arquette, Balthazar Getty, Robert Loggia, Robert (Bobby) Blake, Gary Busey, Jack Nance, Richard Pryor, Natasha Gregson Wagner, Lisa Boyle, Michael Massee, Jack Kehler, Henry Rollins, Gene Ross, Scott Coffey; *D:* David Lynch; *W:* David Lynch, Barry Gifford; *C:* Peter Deming; *M:* Angelo Badalamenti.

Lost Honeymoon ✌✌ **1947** Monkeyshines abound as a soldier marries a girl while in a state of amnesia, and then wakes up to find twin daughters. **70m/B VHS, DVD.** Franchot Tone, Ann Richards; *D:* Leigh Jason.

The Lost Honor of Katharina Blum ✌✌✌ *Die Verlorene Ehre Der Katharina Blum* **1975 (R)** A woman becomes involved with a man who's under police surveillance and finds her life open to public scrutiny and abuse from the media and the government. Based on Heinrich Boll's prize-winning novel. In German with English subtitles. Remade for TV as "The Lost Honor of Kathryn Beck." **97m/C VHS, DVD.** *GE* Angela Winkler, Mario Adorf, Dieter Laser, Jurgen Prochnow; *D:* Volker Schlondorff, Margarethe von Trotta.

Lost Horizon ✌✌✌✌ **1937** A group of strangers fleeing revolution in China are lost in the Tibetan Himalayas and stumble across the valley of Shangri La. The inhabitants of this Utopian community have lived for hundreds of years in kindness and peace—but what will the intrusion of these strangers bring? The classic romantic role for Colman. Capra's directorial style meshed perfectly with the pacifist theme of James Hilton's classic novel, resulting in one of the most memorable films of the 1930s. This version restores more than 20 minutes of footage which had been cut from the movie through the years. **132m/B VHS, DVD.** Ronald Colman, Jane Wyatt, H.B. Warner, Sam Jaffe, Thomas Mitchell, Edward Everett Horton, Isabel Jewell, John Howard, Margo; *D:* Frank Capra; *W:* Robert Riskin; *C:* Joseph Walker; *M:* Dimitri Tiomkin. Oscars '37: Film Editing.

Lost in a Harem ✌✌ 1/2 **1944** Abbott & Costello play magicians in a theatrical troupe stranded in a desert kingdom ruled by an evil sheik. The sheik's nephew (and rightful heir) hires the two to steal some magic rings and the pretty Maxwell to play footsie with his susceptible uncle in an attempt to regain his kingdom. Average comedy with musical numbers by Jimmy Dorsey and His Orchestra. **89m/B VHS, DVD.** Bud Abbott, Lou Costello, Marilyn Maxwell, John Conte, Douglass Dumbrille, Lottie Harrison; *D:* Charles Reisner.

Lost in Alaska ✌✌ 1/2 **1952** Up in the Alaskan wilderness, Abbott & Costello save Ewell from a greedy saloon owner and his cohorts who are trying to get their hands on Ewell's fortune. **87m/B VHS, DVD.** Bud Abbott, Lou Costello, Tom Ewell, Mitzie Green, Bruce Cabot, Emory Parnell, Jack Ingram, Rex Lease; *D:* Jean Yarbrough; *W:* Martin Ragaway, Leonard Stern; *M:* Henry Mancini.

Lost in America ✌✌✌ **1985 (R)** After deciding that he can't "find himself" at his current job, ad exec David Howard and his wife sell everything they own and buy a Winnebago to travel across the country. This Albert Brooks comedy is a must-see for everyone who thinks that there is more in life than pushing papers at your desk and sitting on "Mercedes leather." **91m/C VHS, DVD.** Albert Brooks, Julie Hagerty, Michael Greene, Tom Tarpey, Garry Marshall, Art Frankel; *D:* Albert Brooks; *W:* Albert Brooks, Monica Johnson; *M:* Arthur B. Rubinstein. Natl. Soc. Film Critics '85: Screenplay.

Lost in Austen ✌✌ 1/2 **2008** This sweetly fun and literary romp finds average Londoner Amanda Price (Rooper) yearning for the world depicted by her favorite author. She gets her wish when one of those inexplicable time travel portals suddenly opens up in her bathroom. Amanda's transported to the world of "Pride and Prejudice" while Elizabeth Bennet (Arterton) exchanges places with her. Amanda's strangeness is rather easily accepted but she finds herself unwittingly changing Austen's story and must try to re-establish the proper plot. **177m/C DVD.** *GB* Jemima Rooper, Gemma Arterton, Elliot Cowan, Alex Kingston, Hugh Bonneville, Daniel Percival; *D:* Dan Zeff; *W:* Guy Andrews; *C:* David Higgs; *M:* Christian Henson. **TV**

Lost in Beijing ✌ *Ping Guo* **2007** Tawdry drama of sex and betrayal. Massage parlor worker Ping-guo (Fan) gets drunk at an office party and is raped by her boss Lin (Leung Ka Fai). Her attack just happens to be witnessed by her window cleaner husband An-kun (Tong). When Ping-guo discovers she's pregnant, An-kun thinks it's a great idea to blackmail the married Lin. Only the childless Lin persuades his betrayed wife (Jin) they should adopt the baby, and then An-Kun decides to have a payback affair with Mrs. Lin. Chinese with subtitles. **112m/C DVD.** *CH* Elaine Jin, Bingbing Fan, Dawei Tong, Tony Leung Ka Fai; *D:* Yu Li; *W:* Yu Li, Fang Li; *C:* Yu Wang; *M:* Peyman Yazdanian.

Lost in La Mancha ✌✌✌ 1/2 **2003 (R)** Once upon a time, director Terry Gilliam set out to make a film about Don Quixote, called "The Man Who Killed Don Quixote," starring Jean Rochefort and Johnny Depp. In August, 2000, Gilliam arrived in Spain to start filming and watched one disaster (illness, weather, budget problems) after another unfold until the project had to be abandoned (and has yet to be resurrected). Gilliam provided the filmmakers with complete access, even after the misfortunes piled up enough to make the cancellation inevitable. The result is a fascinating inside look at the derailment of the creative process. **93m/C VHS, DVD.** *GB* *D:* Keith Fulton, Louis Pepe; *W:* Keith Fulton, Louis Pepe; *C:* Louis Pepe; *M:* Miriam Cutler; *Nar:* Jeff Bridges.

Lost in Space ✌✌ 1/2 **1998 (PG-13)** Big-screen remake of the cheesy '60s sci-fi TV show retains the basic plot and premise, but jettisons the camp. In 2058, the Robinsons and pilot Don West (LeBlanc) are chosen to pioneer the colonization of a far-off world because Earth has become nearly uninhabitable. The evil Dr. Smith (Oldman) sabotages the mission but gets stuck on board. Once the family is appropriately lost, the story veers into familiar sci-fi territory of apparently deserted spaceships, marauding aliens, and time warps. It's visually impressive, but writer Goldsman can't resist turning the Robinsons into an annoying collection of 1990s dysfunction. The plot pretty much hinges on Dad's lousy parenting skills, and the kids are disaffected and resentful. Eye-candy effects, the occasionally witty inside joke for fans of the show, and Oldman's deliciously oily Smith provide plenty of fun, but where's the giant carrot? **131m/C VHS, DVD.** William Hurt, Mimi Rogers, Gary Oldman, Heather Graham, Matt LeBlanc, Lacey Chabert, Jack Johnson, Lennie James, Jared Harris, Mark Goddard, Edward Fox, Adam Sims; *Cameos:* June Lockhart, Marta Kristen, Angela Cartwright; *D:* Stephen Hopkins; *W:* Akiva Goldsman; *C:* Peter Levy; *M:* Bruce Broughton; *V:* Dick Tufeld.

Lost in the Barrens ✌✌ **1991** Two young boys, one a Canadian Indian and the other a rich white boy, get lost in the wilderness of the Canadian north. Out of necessity and common need they become close and form a lifelong friendship. Based on the book by Farley Mowat. **95m/C VHS, DVD.** *CA* Evan Adams, Lee J. Campbell, Graham Greene, Nicholas Shields; *D:* Michael Scott; *W:* Keith Ross Leckie; *C:* Ina Elkin; *M:* Randolph Peters.

Lost in the Bermuda Triangle ✌ 1/2 **1998 (PG)** Brian (Verica) searches for his wife Mary (Haag), who was lost at sea, and gets sucked into the same parallel universe she was transported to after they entered the Bermuda Triangle. Dumb and dull. **88m/C VHS.** Tom Verica, Graham Beckel, Ron Canada, Charlotte d'Amboise, Christina Haag; *D:* Norberto Barba; *M:* Christopher Franke. **TV**

Lost in Translation ✌✌✌ 1/2 **2003 (R)** Coppola's pitch-perfect moody dramedy of mannerisms and loneliness stars Murray as Bob, a washed-up action star in Japan to shoot a lucrative liquor commercial. Homesick, displaced and jet-lagged, Bob heads to the hotel bar and meets fellow Yank Charlotte (Johansson). Also married and lonely, Charlotte is accompanying her photographer husband (Ribisi), whose glamorous job takes him away to far-flung locations and beautiful people that she can't understand. Despite their age difference, the two bond over cocktails and karaoke (a memorable scene), discussing the difficulties of marriage and life while steering clear of the formulaic May/December romance trappings. Murray's restrained performance speaks volumes, conveying a weary acceptance of his life. Johansson deftly displays a suitably discontented air. **105m/C VHS, DVD, HD DVD.** *US* Bill Murray, Scarlett Johansson, Giovanni Ribisi, Anna Faris, Yutaka Tadokoro, Catherine Lambert, Fumihiro Hayashi; *D:* Sofia Coppola; *W:* Sofia Coppola; *C:* Lance Acord. Oscars '03: Orig. Screenplay; British Acad. '03: Actor (Murray), Actress (Johansson), Film Editing; Golden Globes '04: Actor—Mus./Comedy (Murray), Film—Mus./Comedy, Screenplay; Ind. Spirit '04: Actor (Murray), Director (Coppola), Film, Screenplay; L.A. Film Critics '03: Actor (Murray); N.Y. Film Critics '03: Actor (Murray), Director (Coppola); Natl. Soc. Film Critics '03: Actor (Murray); Writers Guild '03: Orig. Screenplay.

Lost in Yonkers ✌✌ 1/2 *Neil Simon's Lost in Yonkers* **1993 (PG)** Arty and Jay are two teenage brothers who, while their widowed father looks for work, are sent to live with their stern grandmother, small-time gangster uncle, and childlike aunt in 1942 New York. Ruehl reprises her Tony award-winning performance as Aunt Bella, who loses herself in the movies while trying to find a love of her own, out from under the oppressive thumb of her domineering mother (Worth). Performances by the adults are more theatrical than necessary but the teenagers do well in their observer roles. Based on the play by Neil Simon, which again chronicles his boyhood. **114m/C VHS, DVD.** Mercedes Ruehl, Irene Worth, Richard Dreyfuss, Brad Stoll, Mike Damus, David Strathairn, Robert Miranda, Jack Laufer, Susan Merson; *D:* Martha Coolidge; *W:* Neil Simon; *M:* Elmer Bernstein.

Lost Junction ✌✌ **2003 (R)** Jimmy bums a ride from Missy not knowing she's got extra cargo in the trunk—her murdered husband. Unsure of her guilt but totally smitten, Jimmy is game to dumping the body for her but the plan gets mucked up when her crazy boyfriend shows up on their tail. **95m/C VHS, DVD.** Neve Campbell, Billy Burke, Jake Busey, Charles Powell, Michel Perron, David Gow, Norman Mikeal Berketa, Mariah Inger, Dawn Ford, Matt O'Toole; *D:* Peter Masterson; *W:* Jeff Cole; *C:* Thomas Burstyn; *M:* Normand Corbeil. **VIDEO**

The Lost Jungle ✌✌ **1934** Circus legend Beatty searches for his girl and her dad in the jungle. Animal stunts keep it interesting. Serial in 12 chapters, 13 minutes each. **156m/B VHS, DVD.** Clyde Beatty, Cecilia Parker, Syd Saylor, Warner Richmond, Wheeler Oakman; *D:* Armand Schaefer, David Howard.

The Lost Language of Cranes ✌✌✌ **1992** David Leavitt's novel is transported from New York to present-day London but the wrenching emotional drama remains the same. A family is in crisis as long-hidden secrets concerning homosexuality and infidelity are finally revealed. The title refers to one character's social worker's thesis on a young boy from a dysfunctional family who imitates the movements of the building cranes he sees. Fine performances by all. Adult sexual situations. **90m/C VHS, DVD.** *GB* Brian Cox, Eileen Atkins, Angus MacFadyen, Corey Parker, Cathy Tyson; *Cameos:* John Schlesinger, Rene Auberjonois; *D:* Nigel Finch; *C:* Remi Adefarasin.

Lost Legacy: A Girl Called Hatter Fox ½ **1977** Tradition and technology are at odds in the life of a young Indian girl. Strong cast makes this work. **100m/C VHS.** Ronny Cox, Joanelle Romero, Conchata Ferrell; *D:* George Schaefer. **TV**

Lost, Lonely, and Vicious **1959** Clayton is a suicidal Hollywood actor who spends much of his time indulging his penchant for women, figuring he may as well enjoy what little time he has left. Then he meets Wilson, a drugstore clerk who moves him to reconsider his self-destructive ways. **73m/B VHS, DVD.** Ken Clayton, Barbara Wilson, Lilyan Chauvin, Richard Gilden, Carole Nugent, Sandra Giles, Allen Fife, Frank Stallworth, Johnny Erben, Clint Quigley, T. Earl Johnson; *D:* Frank Myers; *W:* Norman Graham; *C:* Ted Saizis, Vincent Saizis; *M:* Frederick David.

The Lost Man ½ **1969 (PG-13)** Odd, updated remake of 1947's "Odd Man Out," which was based on the novel by F.L. Green. Jason (Poitier) leads a group of black militants in robbing a factory in order to provide money for some civil rights organizations. Two are killed during the crime, which leads to various police shootouts. Meanwhile, Jason enlists the help of white social worker Cathy (Shimkus) to help him escape the country. **122m/C VHS.** Sidney Poitier, Joanna Shimkus, Al Freeman Jr., Michael (Lawrence) Tolan, Richard Dysart, Paul Winfield, Bernie Hamilton, Dolph Sweet, David Steinberg; *D:* Robert Arthur; *W:* Robert Arthur; *C:* Gerald Perry Finnerman; *M:* Quincy Jones.

The Lost Missile **1958** A lost, alien missile circles the Earth, causing overheating and destruction on the planet's surface. A scientist works to find a way to save the planet before it explodes into a gigantic fireball. Director Burke's last film. **70m/B VHS.** Robert Loggia, Ellen Parker, Larry Kerr, Phillip Pine, Marilee Earle; *D:* William Berke.

Lost Moment **1947** A publisher travels to Italy to search for a valuable collection of a celebrated author's love letters, but finds a neurotic woman in his way. Based on Henry James' "Aspern Papers." **89m/B VHS.** Robert Cummings, Agnes Moorehead, Susan Hayward; *D:* Martin Gabel; *C:* Hal Mohr.

The Lost One *Der Verlone* **1951** A German scientist's lover is suspected of selling his findings to England during WWII. Based on a true story; Lorre's only directorial outing. **97m/B VHS.** *GE* Peter Lorre, Karl John, Renate Mannhardt; *D:* Peter Lorre.

The Lost Patrol ½ **1934** WWI British soldiers lost in the desert are shot down one by one by Arab marauders as Karloff portrays a religious soldier convinced he's going to die. The usual spiffy Ford exteriors peopled by great characters with a stirring score. Based on the story, "Patrol" by Philip MacDonald. **66m/B VHS, DVD.** Victor McLaglen, Boris Karloff, Reginald Denny, Wallace Ford, Alan Hale, J.M. Kerrigan, Billy Bevan, Brandon Hurst, Douglas Walton; *D:* John Ford; *W:* Dudley Nichols, Garrett Fort; *C:* Harold Wenstrom; *M:* Max Steiner.

Lost Planet Airmen ½ **1949** A feature-length condensation of the 12-part sci-fi serial "King of the Rocket Men." Rocket Man is pitted against the sinister Dr. Vulcan in this intergalactic battle of good and evil. **65m/B VHS.** Tristram Coffin, Mae Clarke, Dale Van Sickel; *D:* Fred Brannon.

The Lost Platoon ½ **1989 (R)** A troop of soldiers are transformed into vampires. **120m/C VHS.** David Parry, William Knight, Sean Heyman; *D:* David A. Prior.

The Lost Samaritan **2008** Dumb story, bad acting. Accountant William Archer (Somerhalder) stops to assist an injured motorist and finds himself the target of government assassins. **88m/C DVD.** Ian Somerhalder, Ruta Gedmintas, David Scheller, Anna Fin, Oliver Debuschewitz; *D:* Thomas Jahn; *W:* Chris Artiga-Oliver. **VIDEO**

The Lost Son **1998 (R)** Former French narcotics cop Xavier Lombard (Auteuil) has relocated to London where he works as a P.I. An ex-colleague, Carlos (Hinds), asks Lombard to locate his wife Deborah's (Kinski) missing brother Leon, a photographer who has somehow gotten involved with a pedophile ring. Lombard eventually tracks the supposed leader of the ring to Mexico but finds his ultimate answer lies closer to home. A serious topic undone by a one-dimensional script. **102m/C VHS.** *GB FR* Daniel Auteuil, Katrin Cartlidge, Ciaran Hinds, Nastassja Kinski, Bruce Greenwood, Marianne (Cuau) Denicourt, Billie Whitelaw; *D:* Chris Menges; *W:* Eric Leclere, Margaret Leclere, Mark Mills; *C:* Barry Ackroyd; *M:* Goran Bregovic.

Lost Souls ½ **2000 (R)** If the devil keeps showing up in second-rate horror flicks like this, he should get himself an agent. Although in all likelihood he probably is an agent. At any rate, he's back and trying to take over the world again by possessing the body of atheistic New York crime journalist Peter Kelson (Chaplin). Maya (Ryder), a former possession victim herself, is one of a group of New York exorcists who become aware of the conspiracy. She tries to convince the cynical Peter, but he scoffs at the idea until he begins to experience creepy hallucinations. Rent "The Exorcist" instead. Directorial debut of "Saving Private Ryan" and "Schindler's List" cinematographer Kaminski, who offers up some beautiful scenes in the midst of an ugly movie. **98m/C VHS, DVD.** Winona Ryder, Ben Chaplin, John Hurt, Elias Koteas, John Diehl, W. Earl Brown, Sarah Wynter, Philip Baker Hall, Brian Reddy, John Beasley, Victor Slezak, Brad Greenquist; *D:* Janusz Kaminski; *W:* Pierce Gardner, Betsy Stahl; *C:* Mauro Fiore; *M:* Jan A.P. Kaczmarek.

Lost Squadron ½ **1932** World War I vet pilots chafe under an autocratic director as they act as stuntmen for a war picture. Pre-Code actioner depicts vets' adjustment upon returning home. **79m/B VHS.** Richard Dix, Erich von Stroheim, Mary Astor, Robert Armstrong, Joel McCrea, Dorothy Jordan, Hugh Herbert, Ralph Ince; *D:* George Archainbaud; *W:* Herman J. Mankiewicz, Wallace Smith, Humphrey Pearson; *C:* Leo Tover, Edward Cronjager; *M:* Max Steiner.

The Lost Stooges ½ **1933** From the trio's one year at MGM, rare clips of them performing their famous slaptick gags. In black and white and color. **68m/B VHS.** Moe Howard, Curly Howard, Larry Fine, Clark Gable, Joan Crawford, Jimmy Durante, Robert Montgomery; *Nar:* Leonard Maltin.

The Lost Treasure of the Grand Canyon ½ **2008** Archeologist Susan Jordan (Doherty) leads an expedition to rescue her father (Fraser) who disappeared while searching for a lost city somewhere in the Grand Canyon. A hidden valley reveals evidence of human sacrifice by Aztec warriors, a winged serpent, and lots of treasure. Your generic SciFi Channel feature with mediocre special effects to go along with a mediocre script and acting. **90m/C DVD.** Shannen Doherty, Michael Shanks, J.R. Bourne, Duncan Fraser, Toby Berner, Heather Doerksen; *D:* Farhad Mann; *W:* Clay Carmouche; *C:* Adam Sliwinski; *M:* Michael Neilson. **CABLE**

Lost Treasure of the Maya ½ *No Bad Days* **2008 (PG-13)** Generic action flick with an Indiana Jones-wannabe. Tomb raiders working in the Yucatan discover a trove of Mayan artifacts but run afoul of ex-military man Nico (Protasio, also co-writer and producer) who has been hired to find a missing archeologist by her sister Alexis (Storm). **90m/C DVD.** Michael Madsen, Keith David, Richard Tyson, Declan Joyce, Heather Storm, Protasio; *D:* David Murphy; *W:* David Murphy; *C:* Eric Felland; *M:* Marcello DeFrancisici. **VIDEO**

The Lost Tribe **1989** A man takes his wife on a trek through the jungle to find his lost brother. **96m/C VHS.** John Bach, Darien Teakle; *D:* John Laing.

Lost Voyage **2001 (R)** The cruise ship Corona Queen disappears in the Bermuda Triangle in the early seventies. Aaron Roberts (Nelson) grew up obsessed by the event since his father and stepmother were aboard. Then the ship mysteriously reappears. Roberts, TV reporter Dana Elway (Gunn) and salvager David Shaw (Henriksen) helicopter aboard and unsettling things begin to happen. **95m/C VHS, DVD.** Judd Nelson, Lance Henriksen, Janet Gunn, Jeff Kober, Mark Sheppard, Robert Pine, Scarlet Chorvat; *D:* Christian McIntire; *W:* Christian McIntire; *C:* Todd Baron; *M:* Rich McHugh. **CABLE**

The Lost Weekend **1945** The heartrending Hollywood masterpiece about alcoholism, depicting a single weekend in the life of struggling writer Don Birnam (Milland), who cannot believe he's addicted until he finally hits bottom. Except for its pat ending, it is an uncompromising, startlingly harsh treatment, with Milland giving one of the industry's bravest lead performances ever. Acclaimed then and now. **100m/B VHS, DVD.** Ray Milland, Jane Wyman, Phillip Terry, Howard da Silva, Doris Dowling, Frank Faylen, Mary (Marsden) Young; *D:* Billy Wilder; *W:* Charles Brackett, Billy Wilder; *C:* John Seitz; *M:* Miklos Rozsa. Oscars '45: Actor (Milland), Director (Wilder), Picture, Screenplay; Cannes '46: Actor (Milland), Film; Golden Globes '46: Actor—Drama (Milland), Director (Wilder), Film—Drama; Natl. Bd. of Review '45: Actor (Milland); N.Y. Film Critics '45: Actor (Milland), Director (Wilder), Film.

The Lost World ½ **1925** A zoology professor leads a group on a South American expedition in search of the "lost world," where dinosaurs roam in this silent film. Based on a story by Sir Arthur Conan Doyle. A 90-minute version includes the film's original trailer and a re-creation of some of the missing footage (the film was released at 108 minutes). **93m/B VHS, DVD.** Wallace Beery, Lewis Stone, Bessie Love, Lloyd Hughes; *D:* Harry Hoyt; *W:* Marion Fairfax; *C:* Arthur Edeson. Natl. Film Reg. '98.

The Lost World ½ **1992** "Land of the Lost"/"Jurassic Park" themes, based on the story by Sir Arthur Conan Doyle. A scientific team ventures deep into uncharted African jungles where they find themselves confronted by dinosaurs and other dangers. **99m/C VHS, DVD.** John Rhys-Davies, David Warner; *D:* Timothy Bond.

The Lost World ½ **2002** Another version of the Arthur Conan Doyle story about a British expedition to the Amazon in 1912. Eccentric Professor George Challenger (Hoskins) leads a mixed group of characters in search of a remote plateau where he believes dinosaurs still exist. And he turns out to be right. **200m/C VHS, DVD.** Bob Hoskins, Peter Falk, James Fox, Tom Ward, Matthew Rhys, Elaine Cassidy; *D:* Stuart Orme; *W:* Adrian Hodges, Tony Mulholland; *C:* David Odd; *M:* Robert (Rob) Lane. **CABLE**

The Lost World: Jurassic Park 2 ½ *Jurassic Park 2* **1997 (PG-13)** Sequel to "Jurassic Park," proves only that Spielberg has tapped this well one too many times. It's four years after the first adventure and the surviving dinos have peacefully set up house on a deserted island near Costa Rica. Mathematician Ian Malcolm (Goldblum, reprising his role) reluctantly becomes part of an expedition to monitor the beasts, only because his paleontologist girlfriend (Moore) is so gung-ho. Other characters exist, but are reduced to the role of entrees. More dinos (two T-Rexs, a clan of Raptors, and bite-sized newcomers Compsognathus), thrilling special effects, and more gore make up for thin subplots involving a rich businessman who wants to use the dinosaurs for a new zoo and another who hunts them for sport. Ironically, Spielberg's predictablity owes much to better films such as "King Kong," "Aliens" and "Godzilla." Still, T-Rex and buddies, the true stars, rise to the occasion to entertain in an otherwise lackluster sequel. Based on Michael Crichton's book. **129m/C VHS, DVD.** Jeff Goldblum, Julianne Moore, Vince Vaughn, Richard Attenborough, Arliss Howard, Pete Postlethwaite, Peter Stormare, Vanessa Lee Chester, Richard Schiff, Harvey Jason, Thomas F. Duffy, Ariana Richards, Joseph Mazzello; *D:* Steven Spielberg; *W:* David Koepp; *C:* Janusz Kaminski; *M:* John Williams.

A Lost Year *Un Ano Perdido* **1993** It's 1976 and Matilde and Yolanda are best friends struggling to follow their own dreams against parental authority, difficult boyfriends, and their coming-of-age from girls to women. Spanish with subtitles. **91m/C VHS, DVD.** *MX* Vanessa Bauche, Bruno Bichir, Tiare Scanda; *D:* Gerardo Lara; *W:* Gerardo Lara; *C:* Luis Manuel Serrano.

Lost Zeppelin **1929** A dirigible becomes lost in the wastes of Antarctica, forcing its passengers to combat the elements. Impressive special effects and miniatures for its time. **73m/B VHS, DVD.** Conway Tearle, Virginia Valli, Ricardo Cortez, Duke Martin, Kathryn McGuire; *D:* Edward Sloman.

Lotna ½ **1964** Wadja's first color film serves as a tribute to the Polish calvary who fought against the Germans in WWII. The story is told through the trials of a horse that passes to various military officials until it breaks a leg and must be shot. Wadja himself is the son of a cavalryman killed in the war. Polish with subtitles. **89m/C VHS, DVD.** *PL* Bozena Kurowska, Jerzy Pichelski, Jerzy Moes, Adam Pawlikowski; *D:* Andrzej Wajda; *W:* Andrzej Wajda, Wojciech Zukrowski; *C:* Jerzy Lipman; *M:* Tadeusz Baird.

Lots of Luck **1985** A knee-slapping comedy about a family that wins the million-dollar lottery and sees that money doesn't solve all problems. **88m/C VHS.** Martin Mull, Annette Funicello, Fred Willard, Polly Holliday, Hamilton Camp, Vincent Schiavelli; *D:* Peter Baldwin; *M:* William Goldstein. **CABLE**

Lottery Bride ½ **1930** In this charming musical, Jeanette MacDonald is the lottery bride who is won by the brother of the man she really loves. A fine outing for all involved, particularly the supporting cast. ♫You're an Angel; My Northern Lights; Come Drink to the Girl That You Love; Yubla; Round She Whirls; Shoulder to Shoulder; High and Low; Napoli; Two Strong Men. **85m/B VHS, DVD.** Jeanette MacDonald, Joe E. Brown, Zasu Pitts, John Garrick, Carroll Nye; *D:* Paul Stein.

The Lottery Ticket **2010** Kevin Carson (Bow Wow) is living in the projects when he wins a $370 million lottery jackpot. But he has to keep his good fortune from his greedy and threatening neighbors over a three-day holiday weekend before he can claim the winning ticket. **m/C DVD.** *US* Bow Wow, Brandon T. Jackson, Keith David, Terry Crews, Naturi Naughton, Ice Cube, Bill Bellamy; *D:* Erik White; *W:* Erik White, Abdul Williams; *C:* Patrick Cady.

Lotto Land ½ **1995** Looks at the lives of black and Hispanic characters from the same Brooklyn neighborhood. Ambitious high school grad Hank (Gilliard, Jr.) works stocking shelves at the local liquor store for manager Flo (Costallos), who's raised Hank's girlfriend, the college-bound Joy (Gonzalez). The neighborhood's abuzz when someone in their area holds the winning ticket for a $27 million lottery, which was sold from Flo's store, but just who it is and what happens when the money is claimed leads to a dramatic twist. Debut for Rubino, who shows real affection for his characters. **90m/C VHS, DVD.** Larry (Lawrence) Gilliard Jr., Barbara Gonzalez, Suzanne Costallos, Wendell Holmes, Jamie Tirelli, Luis Guzman, Paul Calderon; *D:* John Rubino; *W:* John Rubino; *C:* Rufus Standefer; *M:* Sherman Holmes, Wendell Holmes.

The Lotus Eaters **1993 (PG-13)** Sensitive family drama set in British Columbia in the 1960s about a wife who discovers her husband has fallen in love with their childrens' new teacher. Domestic angst done with naturalism and not without humor. **100m/C VHS.** *CA* Sheila McCarthy, R.H. Thomson, Michelle-Barbara Pelletier, Frances Hyland, Paul Soles; *D:* Paul Shapiro; *W:* Peggy Thompson. Genie '93: Actress (McCarthy), Orig. Screenplay, Sound.

Louder than Bombs **2001** Twenty-one-year-old Marcin is making his father's funeral arrangements, which means he must also deal with his out-of-town relatives who disparage his life as a small-town mechanic. If this wasn't enough stress, Marcin learns his girlfriend Kaska is going to America to attend college. Can he convince her to change her mind by asking him to marry her or should he give her the chance to lead a better life than their small town can offer? Polish with subtitles. **92m/C VHS, DVD.** *PL* Rafal Mackowiak, Sylwia Juszczak, Magdalena Schejbal; *D:* Przemyslaw Wojcieszek; *W:* Przemyslaw Wojcieszek; *C:* Jolanta Dylewska; *M:* Bartek Straburzynski.

Louisiana **1987** A belle of the Old South tries to get back the family plantation by romancing the new owner, even though she loves someone else. Oh, and then the Civil War breaks out. **130m/C VHS.** Ian Charleson, Margot Kidder, Victor Lanoux, Len Cariou, Lloyd Bochner; ***D:*** Philippe de Broca. **TV**

Louisiana Hayride 🦴🦴 **1944** A couple of con men dupe a country girl into forking over all her money with the promise of Hollywood stardom in her future. But the crooks disappear with the cash, and the would-be starlet and her family (still clueless that they've been taken) track them down in Hollywood, where the villains enlist others to keep the farce going. **67m/B VHS.** Judy Canova, Ross Hunter, Richard Lane, Lloyd Bridges; ***D:*** Charles T. Barton; ***W:*** Manuel Seff.

Louisiana Purchase 🦴🦴 1/2 **1941** Successful screen adaptation of the Broadway musical features several performers from the original cast, lavish costumes, and great musical numbers. As usual, Hope's comedy is extremely funny, especially his famous filibuster scene in Congress. Based on the stage musical by Morrie Ryskind and B. G. DeSylva. **95m/C VHS, DVD.** Bob Hope, Vera Zorina, Victor Moore, Dona Drake, Irene Bordoni, Raymond Walburn, Maxie "Slapsie" Rosenbloom, Frank Albertson, Barbara Britton; ***D:*** Irving Cummings; ***W:*** Jerome Chodorov, Joseph Fields; ***C:*** Harry Hallenberger, Ray Rennahan.

Louisiana Story 🦴🦴🦴 **1948** The final effort by the master filmmaker, depicting the effects of oil industrialization on the southern Bayou country as seen through the eyes of a young boy. One of Flaherty's greatest, widely considered a premiere achievement. **77m/B VHS, DVD.** ***D:*** Robert Flaherty; ***M:*** Virgil Thomson. Natl. Film Reg. '94.

Loulou 🦴🦴🦴 1/2 **1980 (R)** A woman leaves her middle-class husband for a leather-clad, uneducated jock who is more attentive. Romantic and erotic. In French with English subtitles. **110m/C VHS, DVD.** *FR* Isabelle Huppert, Gerard Depardieu, Guy Marchand; ***D:*** Maurice Pialat; ***W:*** Maurice Pialat, Arlette Langmann; ***C:*** Pierre William Glenn; ***M:*** Philippe Sarde.

The Lovable Cheat 🦴🦴 **1949** Pretty lame adapatation of Balzac's play "Mercadet Le Falseur," about a father who cons money from his friends in order to line up a marriage suitable for his daughter. **75m/B VHS.** Charlie Ruggles, Peggy Ann Garner, Richard Ney, Alan Mowbray, Iris Adrian, Ludwig Donath, Fritz Feld; ***D:*** Richard Oswald.

Love 🦴🦴🦴 1/2 *Szerelem* **1971** Torocsik, touted as Hungary's leading actress in the '70s, plays a young woman whose husband has been imprisoned for political crimes. Living in a cramped apartment with her mother-in-law, she keeps the news from the aged and dying woman (Darvas) by reading letters she's fabricated to keep alive the woman's belief that her son is a successful movie director in America. The story is punctuated by the older woman's dreamy remembrances of things past. Exceptional performances by both women, it was Darvas' final film. Based on two novellas by Tibor Dery. Hungarian with subtitles. **92m/B VHS, DVD.** *HU* Lili Darvas, Mari Torocsik, Ivan Darvas; ***D:*** Karoly Makk.

Love 🦴🦴 **2005** Dreary thriller set in New York City about Yugoslav hitman Vanya (Trifunovic) who runs into his ex-wife Anna (Lechner) while performing one last job for his old crime boss as repayment for his escape to the United States. Caught in a drug deal gone fatally wrong, Vanya takes Anna as his hostage while her new boyfriend—a police officer—scours the city in search of the pair. Things get mucked up a bit when Anna and Vanya find out that they still have feelings for one another. **90m/C DVD.** Geno Lechner, Sergej Trifunovic, Didier Flamand, Peter Gevisser, Mario Padula, Al Naz, Eric Frandsen, Liat Glick, Kerry Rossi, Vija Vetra, Mariano Mederos; ***D:*** Vladan Nikolic; ***W:*** Vladan Nikolic; ***C:*** Vladimir Subotic.

Love Actually 🦴🦴 1/2 **2003 (R)** One movie, ten love stories, and like any episodic multi-character, intertwining storyline romance, some work and some don't. The most engaging are those involving the bachelor Prime Minister (Grant), his sister (Thompson) with the wandering husband, and the aging rocker Billy Mack (Nighy). Richard Curtis, already established as a worthy romantic comedy writer, crams in absolutely every possible love situation as if he may never direct again. The good is sweet enough to mostly offset the bad, but a less-crowded story would help. **129m/C VHS, DVD.** *GB* Hugh Grant, Martine McCutcheon, Bill Nighy, Emma Thompson, Alan Rickman, Heike Makatsch, Keira Knightley, Chiwetel Ejiofor, Andrew Lincoln, Laura Linney, Rodrigo Santoro, Thomas Sangster, Liam Neeson, Kris Marshall, Colin Firth, Lucia Moniz, Joanna Page, Martin Freeman, Billy Bob Thornton, Rowan Atkinson, Claudia Schiffer, Shannon Elizabeth, Denise Richards, Sienna Guillory, Gregor Fisher; ***D:*** Richard Curtis; ***W:*** Richard Curtis; ***C:*** Michael Coulter; ***M:*** Craig Armstrong. British Acad. '03: Support. Actor (Nighy); L.A. Film Critics '03: Support. Actor (Nighy).

Love Affair 🦴🦴🦴 1/2 **1939** Multi-kleenex weepie inspired countless romantic dreams of true love atop the Empire State Building. Dunn and Boyer fall in love on a ship bound for NYC, but they're both involved. They agree to meet later at, guess where, to see if their feelings hold true, but tragedy intevenes. Excellent comedy-drama is witty at first, more subdued later, with plenty of romance and melodrama. Remade in 1957 (by McCarey) as "An Affair to Remember," a lesser version whose popularity overshadows the original. Look for fleeting glimpses of Leslie, Beckett, and Mohr. Ignore the public domain video, which replaces the original music. Remade again in 1994 as "Love Affair." **87m/B VHS, DVD.** Irene Dunne, Charles Boyer, Maria Ouspenskaya, Lee Bowman, Astrid Allwyn, Maurice (Moscovitch) Moscovich, Scotty Beckett, Joan Leslie, Gerald Mohr, Dell Henderson, Carol Hughes; ***D:*** Leo McCarey; ***W:*** Leo McCarey, Delmer Daves, Donald Ogden Stewart; ***C:*** Rudolph Mate; ***M:*** Roy Webb.

Love Affair 🦴🦴 **1994 (PG-13)** Second remake of the timeless classic has a contemporary look and feel but doesn't justify a new version. The photogenic leads may meet on a plane, but never fear, the Empire State Building and a tragedy are still the main plot devices. The problem is viewers never feel drawn into their lives. Hepburn has a small but moving role as Beatty's aunt. Superb cinematography makes it easy on the eyes and Morricone's lush romantic score makes it easy on the ears, but ultimately, it's all gloss with little substance. Watch this one, but then set aside time to see the superior original (made in 1939) or the better known 1957 attempt "An Affair to Remember." **108m/C VHS, DVD.** Warren Beatty, Annette Bening, Katharine Hepburn, Garry Shandling, Chloe Webb, Pierce Brosnan, Kate Capshaw, Paul Mazursky, Brenda Vaccaro, Glenn Shadix, Barry Miller, Harold Ramis; ***D:*** Glenn Gordon Caron; ***W:*** Warren Beatty, Robert Towne; ***M:*** Ennio Morricone.

The Love Affair, or The Case of the Missing Switchboard Operator 🦴🦴🦴 *Switchboard Operator; Case of the Missing Switchboard Operator; Ljubarni Slucaj; An Affair of the Heart* **1967** Makavejev's second film, a dissertation on the relationship between sex and politics, involving an affair between a switchboard operator and a middle-aged ex-revolutionary, is told in the director's unique, farcically disjointed manner. In Serbian with English subtitles. **73m/B VHS.** *YU* Eva Ras, Slobodan Aligrudic, Ruzica Sokic; ***D:*** Dusan Makavejev; ***W:*** Dusan Makavejev.

Love Affair: The Eleanor & Lou Gehrig Story 🦴🦴🦴 **1977** The true story, told from Mrs. Gehrig's point of view, of the love affair between baseball great Lou Gehrig and his wife Eleanor from his glory days as a New York Yankee, to his battle with an incurable disease. Drama supported by Herrmann and Danner's convincing portrayals. **96m/C VHS.** Blythe Danner, Edward Herrmann, Patricia Neal, Ramon Bieri, Lainie Kazan; ***D:*** Fielder Cook. **TV**

Love After Love 🦴🦴 *Apres l'Amour* **1994** A look at sex and relationships among 30-something professionals in Paris. Lola (Huppert), a successful romance novelist, is suffering a crisis in both her career and, ironically, her love life. She is involved with two men who, in turn, are involved with different women who happen to have borne them children. The movie starts off with so much mate switching and secret sexual rendezvous, that by the second half, you really don't care who Lola ends up with. French with English subtitles. **104m/C VHS, DVD.** *FR* Isabelle Huppert, Hippolyte Girardot, Lio; ***D:*** Diane Kurys; ***W:*** Diane Kurys, Antoine Lacomblez; ***C:*** Fabio Conversi; ***M:*** Yves Simon, Serge Perathone, Jannick Top.

Love Among the Ruins 🦴🦴🦴 **1975** Romance about an aging, wealthy widow who, after being scandalously sued for breach of promise by her very young lover, turns for aid to an old lawyer friend who has loved her silently for more than 40 years. **100m/C VHS.** Laurence Olivier, Katharine Hepburn, Leigh Lawson, Colin Blakely; ***D:*** George Cukor; ***M:*** John Barry. **TV**

Love Among Thieves 🦴🦴 1/2 **1986** A rare acting outing for the mature Hepburn turns out to be a routine TV crime caper although she is charmingly paired up with the shady character played by Wagner. Renowned pianist Caroline DuLac is forced to steal three Faberge eggs from a San Francisco museum as ransom for her kidnapped fiance. She's pursued by some questionable characters, including Mike who travels with Caroline to Mexico where they are captured by bandits who may be in on the plot. **94m/C DVD.** Audrey Hepburn, Robert Wagner, Patrick Bauchau, Jerry Orbach, Brion James, Samantha Eggar, Christopher Neame; ***D:*** Roger Young; ***W:*** Stephen Black, Henry Stern; ***C:*** Gayne Rescher; ***M:*** Arthur B. Rubinstein. **TV**

Love and a.45 🦴🦴 **1994 (R)** Satirical and violent road movie finds petty career criminal Watty Watts (Bellows) living in a Texas trailer park with gal Starlene (Zellweger), for whom he's just purchased an expensive engagement ring. But he's borrowed the money from some crazed gangster types who want the loan repaid in a timely fashion. Soon, the dippy duo are on the run to Mexico with a trail of dead bodies behind them and the media just delighted to make them the next tabloid darlings. **101m/C VHS, DVD.** Renee Zellweger, Rory Cochrane, Ann Wedgeworth, Peter Fonda, Gil Bellows, Jeffrey Combs, Jace Alexander, Charlotte Ross, Michael Bowen; ***D:*** C.M. Talkington; ***W:*** C.M. Talkington; ***C:*** Tom Richmond; ***M:*** Tom Verlaine.

Love and Action in Chicago 🦴🦴 **1999 (R)** Eddie Jones (Vance) works for the State Department's Eliminator Corps, getting rid of anyone the government doesn't want around. Eddie wants to leave and make a new life with girlfriend Lois (King) but his bosses are pressing him to take one more job. And if he doesn't, he could become number one on the Corps hit parade. Although there's action, this one is of the black comedy variety with Vance particularly good as the reluctant hitman. **97m/C VHS, DVD.** Courtney B. Vance, Regina King, Jason Alexander, Kathleen Turner, Ed Asner; ***D:*** Dwayne Johnson-Cochran; ***W:*** Dwayne Johnson-Cochran; ***C:*** Phil Parmet; ***M:*** Russ Landau.

Love and Anarchy 🦴🦴🦴 *Film d'Amore et d'Anarchia* **1973** An oppressed peasant vows to assassinate Mussolini after a close friend is murdered. Powerful drama about the rise of Italian facism. In Italian with English subtitles. **108m/C VHS, DVD.** *IT* Giancarlo Giannini, Mariangela Melato; ***D:*** Lina Wertmuller; ***W:*** Lina Wertmuller; ***C:*** Giuseppe Rotunno; ***M:*** Nino Rota. Cannes '73: Actor (Giannini).

Love and Basketball 🦴🦴🦴 **2000 (R)** Childhood friends and high school sweethearts Monica (Lathan) and Quincy (Epps) pursue their dreams of pro basketball careers and try to sort out their feelings for each other over a 12-year period. First-time director Prince-Bythewood avoids the cliches of most sports movies by removing the Big Game climax and replacing it with thoughtful character study and the understanding of the sacrifices athletes make to excel at their chosen profession. Leads Lathan and Epps are impressive. **124m/C VHS, DVD.** Omar Epps, Sanaa Lathan, Alfre Woodard, Dennis Haysbert, Debbi (Deborah) Morgan, Harry J. Lennix, Kyla Pratt, Glenndon Chatman; ***D:*** Gina Prince-Bythewood; ***W:*** Gina Prince-Bythewood; ***C:*** Reynaldo Villalobos; ***M:*** Terence Blanchard.

Love and Bullets 🦴 1/2 **1979 (PG)** An Arizona homicide detective is sent on a special assignment to Switzerland to bring a mobster's girlfriend back to the United States to testify against him in court. **95m/C VHS.** *GB* Charles Bronson, Jill Ireland, Rod Steiger, Strother Martin, Bradford Dillman, Henry Silva, Michael V. Gazzo; ***D:*** Stuart Rosenberg; ***W:*** Wendell Mayes; ***C:*** Fred W. Koenekamp; ***M:*** Lalo Schifrin.

Love and Death 🦴🦴🦴 **1975 (PG)** In 1812 Russia, a condemned man reviews the follies of his life. Woody Allen's satire on "War and Peace," and every other major Russian novel. **89m/C VHS, DVD.** Woody Allen, Diane Keaton, Georges Adel, Despo Diamantidou, Frank Adu, Harold Gould; ***D:*** Woody Allen; ***W:*** Woody Allen; ***C:*** Ghislan Cloquet.

Love and Death on Long Island 🦴🦴 1/2 **1997 (PG-13)** Stuffy English author Giles De'Ath (Hurt), barely on speaking terms with the 20th century, wanders into the wrong theatre, encounters a teen exploitation flick and becomes obsessed with Ronnie Bostock (Priestley), one of the movie's "stars." De'Ath's obsession leads to his discovery of fan magazines, TV, and video, which provide some moments of amusement as he comes to grips with the technology. It also leads Giles to seek out Bostock at his home on Long Island, where Hurt shines as Giles tries to reconcile his dignity and increasingly irrational behavior. Priestley does a fine job lampooning his own image (while not exactly dispelling it), and the supporting characters (especially Chaykin's diner owner) are appropriately quirky. Subtle reworking of "Death in Venice," based on a novel by Gilbert Adair, has its moments, but is probably best enjoyed by the same type of people who would like De'Ath's books. **93m/C VHS, DVD.** *GB CA* John Hurt, Jason Priestley, Fiona Loewi, Sheila Hancock, Maury Chaykin, Gawn Grainger, Elizabeth Quinn, Danny (Daniel) Webb; ***D:*** Richard Kwietniowski; ***W:*** Richard Kwietniowski; ***C:*** Oliver Curtis; ***M:*** Richard Grassby-Lewis.

Love and Debate 🦴🦴 *Thanks to Gravity* **2006** Miami-born Jordan (Philips) is a Jewish-Latina who wins a scholarship to Harvard thanks to her debating skills. She's pursued by a couple of cute guys but, after being raped by a debate opponent at a party, Jordan quits the team. Eventually deciding to pursue her oratory skills again, Jordan makes it to the national finals—only to be confronted by her rapist, who is her debate opponent. **95m/C DVD.** Gina Philips, Adam Rodriguez, Bryan Greenberg, Austin Nichols, Sean Astin, Shirley Knight, Joaquim de Almeida, Rachel Miner, Chris Mulkey, Azura Skye, Sendhil Ramamurthy; ***D:*** Jessica Kavana; ***W:*** Jessica Kavana; ***C:*** Bryan Greenberg, Mauricio Rubinstein; ***M:*** Jeff Cardoni.

Love and Faith 🦴🦴🦴 **1978** Two lovers are torn between their love for each other and their faiths during 16th-century Japan. English subtitles. **154m/C VHS.** *JP* Toshiro Mifune, Takashi Shimura, Yoshiko Nakana; ***D:*** Kei Kumai.

Love and Hate: A Marriage Made in Hell 🦴🦴 1/2 *Love and Hate: The Story of Colin and Joanne Thatcher* **1990** Marital murder mystery based on a true Canadian case. Joanne (Nelligan), the wife of wealthy rancher-politico Colin (Walsh), leaves her publicly charismatic and privately abusive husband with two thirds of their brood. A bitter battle for custody is waged, and Joanne is soon found savagely slain. The number one suspect: philandering ex-spouse Colin. Based on Maggie Siggins' "A Canadian Tragedy," the faux biography originally aired in two parts on Canadian TV. **156m/C VHS.** Kate Nelligan, Kenneth Welsh, Leon Pownall, John Colicos, Noam Zylberman, Victoria Snow, Cedric Smith, R.H. Thomson, Victoria Wauchope, Doris Petrie, Duncan Ollenenshaw; ***D:*** Francis Mankiewicz; ***W:*** Suzette Couture.

Love and Human Remains 🦴🦴🦴 **1993 (R)** Director Arcand's first English-language film features a group of late 20ish urbanites trying to come to grips with their place in the world (and their sexuality). David (Gibson) is an ammoral Lothario who doesn't believe in love and can only manage casual gay relationships. He hangs out with a variety of friends, all of whom are trying to cope with their varying sexual natures. Melodramatic framing story about a serial murderer who may, or may not, be one of the principal characters proves somewhat of a distraction. Lots of caustically witty dialogue and some fine performances (particularly Gibson's); filmed in Montreal. Adaptation of the play "Unidentified Human Remains and the True Nature of Love" by Fraser, who also did the screenplay. **100m/C VHS, DVD.** *CA* Thomas Gibson, Ruth Marshall, Cameron Bancroft, Mia Kirshner, Joanne Vannicola, Matthew Ferguson, Rick Roberts; ***D:*** Denys Arcand; ***W:*** Brad Fraser; ***C:*** Paul Sarossy. Genie '94: Adapt. Screenplay.

Love and Mary 2007 **(PG-13)** Pastry chef Mary (German) is facing eviction from her struggling bakery so she decides to collect on a sizeable engagement gift by hauling her fiance Brent (Mann) home to Houston to meet her eccentric family. When Brent is unable to travel, resourceful Mary bails his n'er-do-well twin brother Jake out of jail to pass him off as her intended. Of course, she just may realize that she's engaged to the wrong brother. **104m/C DVD.** Lauren German, Gabriel Mann, Whitney Able, Tommy Townsend, Mary Bonner Baker, Bonnie Gallup, Brian Thornton; ***D:*** Elizabeth Harrison; ***W:*** Elizabeth Harrison; ***C:*** Brad Rushing; ***M:*** Tony Tisdale.

Love & Murder 1/2 **1991 (R)** Poorly developed tale of a photographer and his bevy of with beautiful models involved with murder and love, not necessarily in that order. **87m/C VHS.** Todd Waring, Kathleen Lasky, Ron White, Wayne Robson; ***D:*** Steven Hilliard Stern.

Love and Other Catastrophes **1995 (R)** Short, low-budget first feature from 23-year-old Croghan engagingly focuses on 24 hours in the lives of five confused college students. Film students Alice (Garner) and Mia (O'Connor) need a third roommate for their new apartment. Danni (Mitchell), Mia's girlfriend, is upset that Mia doesn't want them living together, while Alice is eyeing potential boyfriends, including shy med student Michael (Day) and womanizing Ari (Dyktynski). Meanwhile, both Alice and Mia try to cope with various academic frustrations. **76m/C VHS.** *AU* Frances O'Connor, Alice Garner, Matt(hew) Day, Radha Mitchell, Matthew Dyktynski, Suzi Dougherty, Kim Gyngell; ***D:*** Emma-Kate Croghan; ***W:*** Emma-Kate Croghan, Yael Bergman, Helen Bandis; ***C:*** Justin Brickle; ***M:*** Oleh Witer.

Love and Other Disasters 1/2 **2006 (R)** Romantic comedy that will remind you of many other such flicks. Free-spirited Emily "Jacks" Jackson (Murphy, trying a little too hard to be winsome and kooky) lives in London and works for a British fashion mag. She shares a flat with gay best friend Peter (Rhys), a struggling screenwriter, whom she's always trying to set up with Mr. Right. When Jacks meets hot Argentine photo assistant Paolo (Cabrera), she's convinced he's the man for Peter. But that's not who Paolo is actually interested in. Gwyneth Paltrow and Orlando Bloom have last act cameos. **90m/C DVD.** *GB* Brittany Murphy, Matthew Rhys, Santiago Cabrera, Catherine Tate, Elliot Cowan, Stephanie Beacham, Jamie Sives, Michael Lerner; ***D:*** Alek Keshishian; ***W:*** Alek Keshishian; ***C:*** Pierre Morel; ***M:*** Alexandre Azaria.

Love and Other Four Letter Words 1/2 **2007 (R)** Attractive cast, good romance vibes. Stormy LaRue (Miller) sounds like she should be an exotic dancer but she's actually a TV talk show host. She would do anything to please her dying Nana (Wright), including lying about getting married. Soon, Stormy's lie is spinning out of control as she plans for her fake wedding, even auditioning grooms. But when Nana sends her childhood friend Arnold (Alexander), now a pastor, to perform the ceremony, Stormy finds herself truly falling in love and wondering how she can turn her lie into the truth. **87m/C DVD.** Tangi Miller, Flex Alexander, Marcus Patrick, Aloma Wright, Essence Atkins, Tasha Smith; ***D:*** Steven Ayromlooi; ***W:*** Mandel Holland; ***C:*** Jose Estrada Aguirre, David Daniel; ***M:*** Todd Cochran. **VIDEO**

Love and Pain and the Whole Damn Thing **1973** Clumsy middle-aged British spinster Lila (Smith) is on a bus tour in Spain when she is suddenly wooed by insecure young American misfit Walter (Bottom), who's bicycling through the countryside. But their oddball happiness can't last since Lila has a terminal illness. Not quite "Harold and Maude" but eccentrically charming. **110m/C DVD.** Maggie Smith, Timothy Bottoms, Charles Baxter, Margaret Modlin, Elmer Modling; ***D:*** Alan J. Pakula; ***W:*** Alvin Sargent; ***C:*** Geoffrey Unsworth; ***M:*** Michael Small.

Love and Rage **1999 (R)** James Lynchehaun (Craig) turns up on the remote island of Achill in 1896 and soon gets a job looking after the estate of wealthy widow Agnes MacDonnell (Scacchi). He also becomes her lover and the two engage in some unnerving psycho-sexual games that lead to Agnes' being brutalized by James. Based on a true story; adapted from the novel "The Playboy and the Yellow Lady" by James Carney. **100m/C VHS, DVD.** *IR GE GB* Daniel Craig, Greta Scacchi, Stephen (Dillon) Dillane, Donal Donnelly, Valerie Edmond; ***D:*** Cathal Black; ***W:*** Brian Lynch; ***C:*** Slawomir Idziak; ***M:*** Ralf Wienrich.

Love & Sex 1/2 **2000** Famke Janssen shines in her role as Kate, a manic L.A. magazine writer who nearly gets fired due to her inability to write about good relationships because she hasn't had many. She begins to remember fondly her relationship with Adam (Favreau), a doughy artist whose fast talk made up for his slow looks. Their relationship is traced from its initial spark to its last gasp, when Adam breaks up with Kate due to a feeling of complacency. Kate then attempts to make Adam jealous by dating a string of pretty-boy losers, including his favorite actor. Kate becomes increasingly depressed and Adam becomes increasingly obsessed, setting the stage for the inevitable happy ending. Good performances and chemistry between the lead actors saves this indie effort from feeling like a really long sitcom episode. **82m/C VHS, DVD.** Famke Janssen, Jon Favreau, Noah Emmerich, Ann Magnuson, Cheri Oteri, Josh Hopkins, Robert Knepper, Vincent Ventresca; ***D:*** Valerie Breiman; ***W:*** Valerie Breiman; ***C:*** Adam Kane.

Love and the Frenchwoman *La Francaise et L'Amour* **1960** A French tale tracing the nature of love through stages. Deals with a story about where babies come from, puppy love, saving sex for marriage, and the way some men treat women. **135m/B VHS, DVD.** *FR* Jean-Paul Belmondo, Pierre-Jean Vaillard, Marie-Jose Nat, Annie Girardot; ***D:*** Jean Delannoy; ***M:*** Georges Delerue.

Love at First Bite 1/2 **1979 (PG)** Intentionally campy spoof of the vampire film. Dracula is forced to leave his Transylvanian home as the Rumanian government has designated his castle a training center for young gymnasts. Once in New York, the Count takes in the night life and falls in love with a woman whose boyfriend embarks on a campaign to warn the city of Dracula's presence. Hamilton of the never-fading tan is appropriately tongue-in-cheek in a role which resurrected his career. **93m/C VHS, DVD.** George Hamilton, Susan St. James, Richard Benjamin, Dick Shawn, Arte Johnson, Sherman Hemsley, Isabel Sanford, Barry J. Gordon, Michael Pataki, Basil Hoffman, Eric Laneuville; ***D:*** Stan Dragoti; ***W:*** Robert Kaufman; ***M:*** Charles Bernstein.

Love at First Sight *Love is Blind; At First Sight* **1976** A pre-"Saturday Night Live" hack job for Aykroyd, playing a blind man who falls in love with a girl he bumps into. ♫Love at First Sight. **86m/C VHS.** Dan Aykroyd, Mary Ann McDonald, George Murray, Barry Morse; ***D:*** Rex Bromfield.

Love at Large **1989 (R)** Hired by a beautiful woman, a private detective accidentally follows the wrong man and winds up being followed himself. He vies with a female detective in solving this case of mistaken identity. **90m/C VHS, DVD.** Tom Berenger, Elizabeth Perkins, Anne Archer, Ann Magnuson, Annette O'Toole, Kate Capshaw, Ted Levine, Kevin J. O'Connor, Ruby Dee, Neil Young, Barry Miller; ***D:*** Alan Rudolph; ***W:*** Alan Rudolph; ***C:*** Elliot Davis.

Love at Stake 1/2 **1987 (R)** It's condo owners versus the witches in this charming parody that features a hilarious cameo by Dr. Joyce Brothers and a very sexy performance from Carrera. **83m/C VHS, DVD.** Patrick Cassidy, Kelly Preston, Bud Cort, Barbara Carrera, Stuart Pankin, Dave Thomas, Georgia Brown, Annie Golden; ***Cameos:*** Dr. Joyce Brothers; ***D:*** John Moffitt; ***M:*** Charles Fox.

Love at the Top 1/2 **1986** Ladies' foundation designer falls in love with her boss's son-in-law, jeopardizing her career. **90m/C VHS.** Janis Paige, Richard Young, Jim MacKrell; ***D:*** John Bowab.

Love Beat the Hell Outta Me **2000 (R)** Four friends get together for what's supposed to be a friendly game of dominos, only to find some serious rivalries surfacing. **89m/C VHS, DVD.** Glenn Plummer, Terrence Howard, Clyde Jones, Charles R. Penland; ***D:*** Kennedy Goldsby; ***W:*** Kennedy Goldsby.

The Love Bug 1/2 **1968 (G)** A race car driver (Jones) is followed home by Herbie, a white Volkswagen with a mind of its own. Eventually, Jones follows the "Love Bug" to a life of madcap fun. Followed by several sequels. **110m/C VHS, DVD.** Dean Jones, Michele Lee, Hope Lange, Robert Reed, Bert Convy; ***D:*** Robert Stevenson; ***C:*** Edward Colman; ***M:*** George Bruns.

The Love Bug 1/2 **1997** Herbie, the magical Volkswagen Beetle, is now owned by egotistical English nobleman Simon Moore III (Hannah), who junks him after he loses a race. Then Herbie gets a new owner, down-on-his-luck mechanic Hank (Campbell), who decides the little guy can make a comeback. And when Herbie sees Hank and his ex-girlfriend Alex (Wentworth) together, the car decides he should live up to his nickname and get the two back together. **88m/C VHS.** Bruce Campbell, John Hannah, Alexandra Wentworth, Kevin J. O'Connor, Mickey Dolenz, Dean Jones, Clarence Williams III, Harold Gould; ***D:*** Peyton Reed. **TV**

Love Butcher 1/2 **1982 (R)** A crippled old gardener kills his female employers with his garden tools and cleans up neatly afterward. **84m/C VHS, DVD.** Erik Stern, Kay Neer, Robin Sherwood; ***D:*** Mikel Angel, Donald M. Jones.

Love by Appointment **1976** An unlikely romantic comedy with a very unlikely cast has two businessmen meeting up with European prostitutes. **96m/C VHS, DVD.** *IT* Ernest Borgnine, Robert Alda, Francoise Fabian, Corinne Clery; ***D:*** Armando Nannuzzi; ***M:*** Riz Ortolani. **TV**

Love Camp *Divine Emmanuelle* **1981** A woman is invited to a swinger's holiday camp, frolics for a while, then is told she can never leave. Suspenseful hijinks ensue. **100m/C VHS, DVD.** *GE* Laura Gemser, Christian Anders, Gabriele Tinti; ***D:*** Christian Anders; ***W:*** Christian Anders; ***C:*** Vassilis Christomoglou; ***M:*** Christian Anders.

Love Can Seriously Damage Your Health 1/2 *Amor Perjudica Seriamente la Salud* **1996** At a gala dinner Santi (Puigcorbe) and Diana (Belen) are reunited. Thirty years before, young Beatles fan Diana (Cruz) hides out in John Lennon's room when the group comes to Madrid, reluctantly aided by young hotel bellman Santi (Diego). It's love at first sight and they spend the intervening years falling in and out of a crazy romance. Spanish with subtitles. **118m/C VHS, DVD.** *SP* Ana Belen, Penelope Cruz, Gabino Diego, Janjo Puigcorbe, Carles Sans, Lola Herrera; ***D:*** Manuel Gomez Pereira; ***W:*** Manuel Gomez Pereira; ***C:*** Juan Amoros.

Love, Cheat & Steal **1993 (R)** Convicted murderer Reno Adams (Roberts) breaks out of prison when he hears that his luscious ex (Amick) has just married another man (Lithgow). He turns up on her door, threatening to destroy her new life, but things aren't exactly what they seem. Faux noir. **95m/C VHS.** Eric Roberts, Madchen Amick, John Lithgow, Richard Edson, Donald Moffat, David Ackroyd, Dan O'Herlihy; ***D:*** William Curran; ***W:*** William Curran.

Love Child **1982 (R)** The story of a young woman in prison who becomes pregnant by a guard and fights to have and keep her baby. **97m/C VHS.** Amy Madigan, Beau Bridges, MacKenzie Phillips, Albert Salmi; ***D:*** Larry Peerce; ***M:*** Charles Fox.

Love Come Down **2000 (R)** Matthew (Cummins) is white; his half-brother Neville (Tate) is black. Their mother is in prison for killing Neville's abusive father but there's a definite question about her guilt. Both boys have been hugely affected by their pasts—Matthew puts his anger into his boxing career while Neville has become a drug addicted stand-up comic. Neville tries to stay clean when he falls for a singer (Cox) with her own family issues but the brothers also have to lay their traumatic past to rest. **102m/C VHS, DVD.** *CA* Larenz Tate, Martin Cummins, Sarah Polley, Deborah Cox, Travis Davis, Jake LeDoux, Rainbow Sun Francks, Barbara Williams, Peter Williams, Clark Johnson, Kenneth Welsh, Jennifer Dale, Naomi Gaskin; ***D:*** Clement Virgo; ***W:*** Clement Virgo; ***C:*** Dylan Mcleod; ***M:*** Aaron Davis, John Lang. Genie '01: Sound, Support. Actor (Cummins).

Love Comes Lately **2007** Elderly Austrian emigre Max (Tausig) continues to write stories, deliver college lectures, and romance the ladies though his reality is now getting confused with his fictional world. Various mishaps while traveling have Max writing a new story, which he reads at a lecture, which then segues into another of his fictional worlds. This blurring isn't as confusing as it seems because of the sly charm of octogenarian actor Tausig. Based on the stories of Isaac Bashevis Singer. **86m/C DVD.** Barbara Hershey, Tovah Feldshuh, Rhea Perlman, Elizabeth Pena, Otto Tausig, Caroline Aaron; ***D:*** Jan Schuette; ***W:*** Jan Schuette; ***C:*** Edward Klosinski, Chris Squires; ***M:*** Henning Lohner.

Love Comes Softly 1/2 **2003** Marty Claridge (Heigl) has just moved west with her husband when he suddenly dies. Alone and afraid, she accepts the offer of widowed neighbor Clark Davis (Midkiff) to becomes his housekeeper and look after his tomboy daughter Missie (Bartusiak). Naturally as Marty and Missie slowly bond, Clark and the pretty widow gradually find themselves growing closer. Adapted from the first book in inspirational author Janette Oke's series. **88m/C DVD.** Katherine Heigl, Dale Midkiff, Skye McCole Bartusiak, Corbin Bernsen, Theresa Russell; ***D:*** Michael Landon Jr.; ***W:*** Michael Landon Jr., Cindy Kelley; ***C:*** James W. Wrenn; ***M:*** Ken Thorne, William Ashford. **CABLE**

Love Crazy 1/2 **1941** Powell and Loy team once again for a non-"Thin Man" romp through a married-people farce. Via a nosy mother-in-law and a series of misunderstandings, Powell and Loy squabble almost to the point of divorce. Not the wry wit the team was known for, but zany, high-action comedy at its best. **99m/B VHS, DVD.** William Powell, Myrna Loy, Gail Patrick, Jack Carson, Florence Bates, Sidney Blackmer, Sig Rumann; ***D:*** Jack Conway.

Love Crimes **1992 (R)** A con man (Bergin) poses as a photographer who sexually intimidates women while playing on their erotic fantasies. Young is the Atlanta district attorney who sets out to nail him when none of his victims will testify against him, only she may be enjoying her undercover work more than she realizes. Implausible and sleazy. Also available in an unrated version. **84m/C VHS.** Sonny Shroyer, Sean Young, Patrick Bergin, Arnetia Walker, James Read; ***D:*** Lizzie Borden; ***W:*** Laurie Frank, Allan Moyle; ***C:*** Phedon Papamichael; ***M:*** Graeme Revell.

Love Desperados *The Hot Spur* **1968** Cowboys and ranchers' wives mix it up in a lot of softcore hay. **99m/C VHS.** James Arena, Virginia Gordon, John Alderman, Joseph Mascolo, Wes Bishop; ***D:*** Lee Frost; ***W:*** Lee Frost.

A Love Divided **2001** In 1950s Ireland, Protestant Sheila Kelly (Brady) marries Catholic Sean Cloney (Cunningham) and signs an agreement to raise their children Catholic to appease the mostly Catholic farming community, County Wexford. When it comes time for their daughter Eileen (Bolger) to attend school, however, a battle emerges over religion between headstrong Sheila and Milquetoast Sean. When things begin escalating into an all-out war that divides the villagers, Sheila flees with her two daughters to Scotland. Heavy-handed, melodramatic script displays a movie-of-the-week lack of subtlety, while one-dimensional characters offer little in the way of sympathy for anyone involved. Based on a true story. **98m/C VHS, DVD.** Orla Brady, Liam Cunningham, Brian

McGrath, Sarah Bolger, Nicole Bohan, Peter Caffrey, Tony Doyle, Ali White; ***D:*** Syd Macartney; ***W:*** Deirdre Dowling, Gerry Gregg, Stuart Hepburn; ***C:*** Cedric Culliton; ***M:*** Fiachra Trench.

Love Don't Cost a Thing 1/2 **2003 (PG-13)** Amusing remake of the 1987 movie "Can't Buy Me Love." Alvin Johnson (Cannon) pays the most popular girl in high school, Paris Morgan (Milian), to pretend to be his girlfriend for two weeks in order to be popular. Charming leads make this one a touch better than the original. **101m/C VHS, DVD.** *US* Nick Cannon, Christina Milian, Kenan Thompson, Kal Penn, Steve Harvey, Vanessa Bell Calloway, Al Thompson; ***D:*** Troy Beyer; ***W:*** Troy Beyer, Michael Swerdlick; ***C:*** Chuck Cohen; ***M:*** Richard Gibbs.

Love 'Em and Leave 'Em **1926** Two sisters, with opposite personalities, are department store sales clerks. Brent is the "good" girl and Brooks the "bad" flirt who, under the influence of Perkins, bets the store's welfare benefit money on the horses and loses it all. Brent manages to make things right, while keeping boyfriend Gray from her sister's clutches. Brooks' baby vamp (the actress was 19) stole the picture. Introduced the "Black Bottom" shimmy dance to the screen. Remade in 1929 as "The Saturday Night Kid" with Clara Bow and Jean Arthur. **70m/B VHS.** Louise Brooks, Evelyn Brent, Lawrence Gray, Osgood Perkins; ***D:*** Frank Tuttle.

Love, etc. **1996** Another messy romantic triangle played for both comedy and tragedy. Shy, thirtysomething bank employee Benoit (Attal) takes out a personal ad, but supplies a picture of his egocentric best friend Pierre (Berling) instead of his own. He meets twentysomething art restorer Marie (Gainsbourg) and, despite the deception and the fact that she's not swept away by romantic passion, Marie marries him. Then Benoit discovers that Pierre thinks he's in love with Marie and has decided to win her away—and she's torn by the attention. Based on the novel "Taking It Over" by Julian Barnes. French with subtitles. **105m/C VHS, DVD.** *FR* Charlotte Gainsbourg, Yvan Attal, Charles Berling; ***D:*** Marion Vernoux; ***W:*** Marion Vernoux, Dodine Herry; ***C:*** Eric Gautier; ***M:*** Leonard Cohen, Alexandre Desplat.

Love Field 1/2 **1991 (PG-13)** Pfeiffer is a Jackie Kennedy-obsessed hairdresser who decides to travel by bus to D.C. when she hears about President Kennedy's assassination. Along the way she gets involved in an interracial friendship with the secretive Haysbert, who's traveling with his young daughter. Pfieffer's Lurene is basically a sweet dim bulb and Haysbert has an unfortunately written one-note character (mainly exasperation). The six-year-old McFadden (in her debut) makes the most impact. **104m/C VHS, DVD.** Michelle Pfeiffer, Dennis Haysbert, Stephanie McFadden, Brian Kerwin, Louise Latham, Peggy Rea, Beth Grant, Cooper Huckabee, Mark Miller, Johnny Rae McGhee; ***D:*** Jonathan Kaplan; ***W:*** Don Roos; ***C:*** Ralf Bode; ***M:*** Jerry Goldsmith.

Love Film *Szerelmesfilm; A Film about Love* **1970** A train trip from Budapest, Hungary to Lyon, France leads a young man to recall his past as he journeys to visit a childhood sweetheart. Jancsi and Kata's friendship has been disrupted by the 1956 uprising and Jancsi wonders if the love once developing between them has been broken by distance and time. In Hungarian with English subtitles. **123m/C VHS, DVD.** *HU* Andras Balint, Judit Halasz, Edit Kelemen, Andras Szamosfalvi; ***D:*** Istvan Szabo; ***W:*** Istvan Szabo; ***C:*** Josef Lorinc.

Love Finds a Home 1/2 **2009** A Hallmark Channel movie, the sequel to "Love Finds a Wing," that's based on the novels by Janette Oke. Dr. Belinda Simpson Owens (Jones) is now married to blacksmith Lee (Bridges) and they have adopted the orphaned Lillian (Halverson). However, Belinda is dismayed that she seemingly cannot have children of her own and her feelings are heightened when her pregnant friend Annie (Duff) comes to visit. Belinda suspects there's a health problem but she continually clashes with Annie's mother-in-law Mary (Duke), a midwife who seems set in her ways. **88m/C DVD.** Sarah Jones, Jordan Bridges, Haylie Duff, Patty Duke, Courtney Halverson, Dahlia Salem, Thomas Kopache; ***D:*** David S. Cass Sr.; ***W:*** Donald Davenport; ***C:*** Dane Peterson; ***M:*** Stephen Graziano. **CABLE**

Love Finds Andy Hardy **1938** Young Andy Hardy finds himself torn between three girls before returning to the girl next door. Garland's first appearance in the acclaimed Andy Hardy series features her singing "In Between" and "Meet the Best of my Heart." **90m/B VHS, DVD.** Mickey Rooney, Judy Garland, Lana Turner, Ann Rutherford, Fay Holden, Lewis Stone, Marie Blake, Cecilia Parker, Gene Reynolds; ***D:*** George B. Seitz. Natl. Film Reg. '00.

The Love Flower 1/2 **1920** A man kills his second wife's lover and escapes with his daughter to a tropical island, pursued by a detective and a young adventurer. Interesting ending wraps things up nicely. Silent. **70m/B VHS.** Carol Dempster, Richard Barthelmess, George MacQuarrie, Anders Randolf, Florence Short; ***D:*** D.W. Griffith; ***W:*** D.W. Griffith.

Love for Lydia **1979** British TV miniseries following wayward beauty Lydia, orphaned heiress to a manufacturing fortune, through the high-spirited 1920s. Set in the industrial Midlands and farming communities of England, Lydia dazzles every man she meets, often to an unhappy end. Based on the novel by H.E. Bates. Available as a boxed set. **657m/C VHS, DVD.** *GB* Mel Martin, Christopher Blake, Peter Davison, Jeremy Irons, Michael Aldridge, Rachel Kempson, Beatrix Lehmann; ***D:*** John Glenister, David Brenner, Simon Langton, Tony Wharmby; ***W:*** Julian Bond; ***C:*** Tony Maynard, Jeff Shepherd. **TV**

Love for Rent 1/2 **2005 (R)** Slight romantic comedy finds Colombian immigrant Sofia's (Cepeda) life falling apart when her green card hubby (Rowe) steals their money. Sofia has big dreams, so rather than return home she becomes a surrogate mother for a wealthy, eccentric couple (Piddock, Dunn). But how will Sofia explain the situation to her new doctor boyfriend Neil (Marino)? **90m/C DVD.** *US* Ken Marino, Nora Dunn, Jim Piddock, Brad Rowe, Angie Cepeda, Richard Speight Jr., Martita Roca, Max Burkholder; ***D:*** Shane Edelman; ***W:*** Andrew Miles; ***C:*** David Rush Morrison; ***M:*** Jeff Cardoni.

Love from a Stranger **1937** Thriller about a working woman who wins a lottery. Soon she is charmed by and marries a man whom she later suspects may be trying to kill her. Remade in 1947. **90m/B VHS, DVD.** *GB* Ann Harding, Basil Rathbone, Binnie Hale, Bruce Seton, Bryan Powley, Jean Cadell; ***D:*** Rowland V. Lee.

Love from a Stranger 1/2 *A Stranger Walked In* **1947** In this remake of the 1937 film, a young newlywed bride fears that the honeymoon is over when she suspects that her husband is a notorious killer and that she will be his next victim. **81m/B VHS.** Sylvia Sidney, John Hodiak, John Howard, Ann Richards, Isobel Elsom, Ernest Cossart, Philip Tonge, Frederick Worlock; ***D:*** Richard Whorf; ***W:*** Philip MacDonald; ***C:*** Gaetano Antonio "Tony" Gaudio; ***M:*** Hans J. Salter.

The Love God? 1/2 **1970 (PG-13)** Very silly comedy finds mild-mannered Abner Peacock (Knotts) trying on Hugh Hefner's mantle. With his bird-watcher's magazine in financial trouble, Abner takes on a couple of shifty partners who change it into a different kind of bird watching magazine (the nude female kind) that gets Abner charged with pornography and finds him becoming a (very) unlikely sex symbol. **103m/C VHS, DVD.** Don Knotts, Edmond O'Brien, Anne Francis, Maureen Arthur, James Gregory, Margaret (Maggie) Peterson, Marjorie Bennett; ***D:*** Nat Hiken; ***W:*** Nat Hiken; ***C:*** William Margulies; ***M:*** Vic Mizzy.

The Love Goddesses **1965** A 60-year examination of some of the most beautiful women on the silver screen, reflecting with extraordinary accuracy the customs, manners and mores of the times. Released theatrically in 1972. **83m/B VHS, DVD.** Marlene Dietrich, Greta Garbo, Jean Harlow, Gloria Swanson, Mae West, Betty Grable, Rita Hayworth, Elizabeth Taylor, Marilyn Monroe, Theda Bara, Claudette Colbert, Dorothy Lamour, Lillian Gish, Sophia Loren; ***D:*** Saul J. Turell; ***W:*** Saul J. Turell, Graeme Ferguson; ***Nar:*** Carl King.

Love Goggles **1999** A low-budget indie that tries to do some interesting things with titles, narration, and monologues to break up the familiar plot before it turns preachy. Nightclub owner and ladies man Topcat (David) is afraid of losing his best friend and fellow player Ollie (Jacoby) to potential new girlfriend Mona (Campbell). However, if he follows Topcat's misogynistic views, Ollie isn't going to have to worry about Mona sticking around. But then those 'love goggles' on his heart are focusing all Ollie's thoughts on romance. **106m/C DVD.** Trevor David, Ruby Campbell, Steven Peacock Jacoby, Q-Tip, Kirk "Sticky Fingaz" Jones; ***D:*** Anthony Travis.

The Love Guru **2008 (PG-13)** Guru Pitka (Myers), an American raised in an Indian ashram, becomes the world's number two guru, second only to real-life romantic mystic and on-screen buddy Deepak Chopra. Things get nutty after the owner of the Toronto Maple Leafs (Alba) hires Pitka to reignite the flame between a hockey star and his estranged wife. Pitka has to deal with the team's dwarf coach (Troyer back for more Mini-Me jabs), fight off enemies using urine-soaked mops (his specialty, kid you not), and ham it up in lame music video spoofs. Myers spends the entire movie cackling at his own dopey wisecracks, thinking it'll somehow make them funny. It doesn't. **88m/C DVD, Blu-ray Disc.** *US* Mike Myers, Jessica Alba, Romany Malco, Justin Timberlake, Meagan Good, Verne Troyer, Ben Kingsley, Telma Hopkins, Omid Djalili, Stephen Colbert, Jim Gaffigan, Manu Narayan, John Oliver; ***Cameos:*** Deepak Chopra; ***D:*** Marco Schnabel; ***W:*** Mike Myers, Graham Gordy; ***C:*** Peter Deming; ***M:*** George S. Clinton. Golden Raspberries '08: Worst Picture, Worst Actor (Myers), Worst Screenplay.

Love Happens *Brand New Day* **2009 (PG-13)** Clunky, tear-filled (it's wetter than the Seattle setting) romantic comedy that's not very funny and has a cookie-cutter romance with attractive but mismatched leads. Motivational speaker Burke Ryan (Eckhart) is still devastated after the death of his wife and having a hard time following his own advice. On a speaking trip to Seattle, Burke meets movie cute with goofy, unlucky-in-love florist Eloise (Aniston) when she attends his seminar and decides he might have a second chance at love after all. A parrot is involved—but not in any sort of kinky way that might have been humorous. **109m/C DVD.** *US* Jennifer Aniston, Aaron Eckhart, Martin Sheen, Judy Greer, Sasha Alexander, Gina Holden, John Carroll Lynch; ***D:*** Brandon Camp; ***W:*** Brandon Camp, Mike Thompson; ***C:*** Eric Alan Edwards; ***M:*** Christopher Young.

Love Happy 1/2 **1950** A group of impoverished actors accidentally gain possession of valuable diamonds. Unfortunately for them, detective Groucho is assigned to recover them! **85m/B VHS, DVD.** Groucho Marx, Harpo Marx, Chico Marx, Vera-Ellen, Ilona Massey, Marion Hutton, Raymond Burr, Marilyn Monroe, Eric Blore; ***D:*** David Miller; ***W:*** Frank Tashlin, Mac Benoff; ***C:*** William Mellor; ***M:*** Ann Ronell.

Love Has Many Faces 1/2 **1965** Judith Crist was too kind when she said this was for connoisseurs of truly awful movies. Playgal Turner marries beachboy Robertson and many faces come between them. Much melodrama. Filmed on location. **104m/C VHS.** Lana Turner, Cliff Robertson, Hugh O'Brian, Ruth Roman, Stefanie Powers, Virginia Grey, Ron Husmann; ***D:*** Alexander Singer.

Love, Honour & Obey **2000** Lowlife London bad boys and a karaoke bar. Jonny (Miller) wants his best bud Jude (Law) to get him a job with Jude's gangster uncle, Ray (Winstone), who loves to croon a tune at the local karaoke club. But Jonny loves his new life too much and can't resist stirring up local gangland rivalries—to the grief of everyone. Low-budget, sometime puerile comedy. **95m/C VHS, DVD.** *GB* Jonny Lee Miller, Jude Law, Ray Winstone, Sadie Frost, Sean Pertwee, Kathy Burke, Rhys Ifans, Laila Morse, Dominic Anciano, Ray Burdis; ***D:*** Dominic Anciano, Ray Burdis; ***W:*** Dominic Anciano, Ray Burdis; ***C:*** John Ward.

Love Hurts **1991 (R)** A guy looking for romance finds his hands full with a number of beautiful women. Will he find the love he craves, or will the pain be too much to bear? **110m/C VHS, DVD.** Jeff Daniels, Judith Ivey, John Mahoney, Cynthia Sikes, Amy Wright; ***D:*** Bud Yorkin; ***W:*** Ron Nyswaner.

Love in Bloom **1935** Predictable romance, with Burns and Allen providing some much-needed comic relief. Carnival gal Violet Downey (Lee) falls for struggling songwriter Larry Deane (Morrison) but thinks her tawdry background will ruin his chances and takes off. After Larry becomes successful he searches for Violet, still determined to marry her. **75m/B VHS, DVD.** George Burns, Gracie Allen, Joe Morrison, Dixie Lee, Lee Kohlmar, Richard Carle; ***D:*** Elliott Nugent; ***W:*** J.P. McEvoy, Keene Thompson; ***C:*** Leo Tover.

A Love in Germany 1/2 *Un Amour En Allemagne; Eine Liebe in Deutschland* **1984 (R)** A tragic love affair develops between a German shopkeeper's wife and a Polish prisoner-of-war in a small German village during WWII. In German with English subtitles. **110m/C VHS.** *FR GE* Hanna Schygulla, Piotr Lysak, Elisabeth Trissenaar, Armin Mueller-Stahl; ***D:*** Andrzej Wajda; ***W:*** Andrzej Wajda, Agnieszka Holland, Boleslaw Michalek.

Love in Pawn 1/2 **1953** A very silly plot will cause eye-rolling for this cheap Britcom. Struggling artist Roger Fox (Braden) is offered money by an uncle if his work becomes more commercial. The uncle decides to send his attorney to evaluate the worth of Roger and his wife Jean (Kelly) and, to make a good showing, Jean actually pawns Roger to get money to make some improvements. Then she is forced to leave Roger in the pawnshop when she can't meet her payments and becomes a cause celebre. **81m/B DVD.** *GB* Bernard Braden, Barbara Kelly, Laurence Naismith, John Laurie, Reg Dixon, Jeannie Carson, Walter Crisham; ***D:*** Charles Saunders; ***W:*** Denis Norden, Frank Muir, Guy Morgan; ***C:*** Monty Berman; ***M:*** Temple Abady.

Love in the Afternoon 1/2 **1957** A Parisian private eye's daughter (Hepburn) decides to investigate a philandering American millionaire (Cooper) and winds up falling in love with him. Cooper's a little old for the Casanova role but Hepburn is always enchanting. **126m/B VHS, DVD.** Gary Cooper, Audrey Hepburn, John McGiver, Maurice Chevalier; ***D:*** Billy Wilder; ***W:*** Billy Wilder, I.A.L. Diamond; ***C:*** William Mellor.

Love in the City *Amore in Citta* **1953** Five stories of life, love and tears in Rome. In Italian with English subtitles and narration. **90m/B VHS.** *IT* Ugo Tognazzi, Maresa Gallo, Caterina Rigoglioso, Silvia Lillo; ***D:*** Michelangelo Antonioni, Federico Fellini, Dino Risi, Carlo Lizzani, Alberto Lattuada, Francesco Maselli, Cesare Zavattini; ***W:*** Aldo Buzzi, Luigi Malerba, Luigi Chiarini, Tullio Pinelli, Vittorio Vettreni; ***C:*** Gianni Di Venanzo; ***M:*** Mario Nascimbene.

Love in the Time of Cholera **2007 (R)** In 19th century Columbia, Florentino (Bardem) is a low-born young man who falls madly in love with neighbor Fermina (Mezzogiorno), but cannot have her. Constrained by social and class rules, Fermina marries a doctor (Bratt) and Florentino throws himself into a lifetime of meaningless sexual relationships, but his love for Fermina never truly wanes, even over decades. Based on the novel by Nobel Prize winner G.G. Marquez, the movie loses much of its magic and philosophical quality and ends up being a straightforward, somewhat dull romantic tragicomedy, a soap opera disguised under layers of age-enhancing makeup. **138m/C DVD.** *US* Javier Bardem, Giovanna Mezzogiorno, Benjamin Bratt, Catalina Sandino Moreno, Hector Elizondo, Liev Schreiber, Ana Claudia Talancon, John Leguizamo, Laura Elena Harring; ***D:*** Mike Newell; ***W:*** Ronald Harwood; ***C:*** Alfonso Beato; ***M:*** Antonio Pinto.

Love in the Time of Money 1/2 **2002 (R)** Overly-familiar story about a group of lonely and/or opportunistic New Yorkers and their various encounters, beginning with hooker Greta (Farmiga), whose client, Eddie (Lombardozzi) won't pay up. From there we go to the dissatisfied drunken wife (Hennessey) of a sexually confused businessman (Gets) who makes a pass at an artist (Buscemi) who's more interest in a gallery assistant (Dawson) who has a boyfriend (Grenier). With a couple of more people on the daisy chain, the bored viewer eventually finds themselves back with Greta. **90m/C DVD.** *US* Vera Farmiga, Domenick Lombardozzi, Jil-l(ian) Hennessey, Malcolm Gets, Steve Buscemi, Rosario Dawson, Adrian Grenier, Carol Kane, Michael Imperioli; ***D:*** Peter Mattei; ***W:*** Peter Mattei; ***C:*** Stephen Kazmierski; ***M:*** Theodore Shapiro.

Love Is a Gun 🦴 1/2 **1994 (R)** A police photographer (Roberts) begins having violent and erotic hallucinations that begin to affect his fiancee (Garrett). Things get even weirder when a femme fatale model (Preston) enters the picture. **92m/C VHS.** Jack Kehler, Eric Roberts, Kelly Preston, Eliza (Simons) Garrett, R. Lee Ermey; ***D:*** David Hartwell.

Love Is a Many-Splendored Thing 🦴🦴 1/2 **1955** A married American war correspondent and a beautiful Eurasian doctor fall in love in post-WWII Hong Kong. They struggle with racism and unhappiness, until he's sent to Korea to observe the Army's activities there. Based on the novel by Han Suyin. The extensive L.A. Asian acting community got some work out of this film, although the leads are played by Caucasians. Oscar-winning song was a very big popular hit. ♫ Love is a Many-Splendored Thing. **102m/C VHS, DVD.** William Holden, Jennifer Jones, Torin Thatcher, Isobel Elsom, Jorja Curtright, Virginia Gregg, Richard Loo; ***D:*** Henry King; ***W:*** John Patrick; ***C:*** Leon Shamroy; ***M:*** Alfred Newman. Oscars '55: Costume Des. (C), Song ("Love Is a Many-Splendored Thing"), Orig. Dramatic Score.

Love Is All There Is 🦴🦴 1/2 **1996 (R)** It's a kind of comedic (happy-ending) version of "Romeo and Juliet," set in the Bronx, about rival restaurant families. Beautiful Gina's (Jolie) a finishing-school grad and Rosario's (Marston) the local boy too handsome for his own good. Both sets of parents are crazy. Oddly enough, Sorvino also plays the heroine's dad in the '96 "William Shakespeare's Romeo & Juliet." **98m/C VHS, DVD.** Dominic Chianese, Angelina Jolie, Nathaniel Marston, Paul Sorvino, Renee Taylor, Joseph Bologna, Lainie Kazan, Barbara Carrera, William Hickey, Abe Vigoda, Dick Van Patten, Connie Stevens; ***D:*** Renee Taylor, Joseph Bologna; ***W:*** Renee Taylor, Joseph Bologna; ***C:*** Alan Jones; ***M:*** Jeff Beal.

Love Is Better Than Ever 🦴🦴 1/2 *The Light Fantastic* **1952** Lightweight romantic-comedy casts Taylor as a dancing instructor who travels to the Big Apple for a convention. Once there, she meets and falls for talent agent Parks. Carefree, bachelor Parks is too busy to be bothered by small town Taylor, but Liz is determined to land her man. Release of this picture was held back because of Parks' blacklisting by the McCarthy committee. **81m/B VHS.** Larry Parks, Elizabeth Taylor, Josephine Hutchinson, Tom Tully, Ann Doran, Elinor Donahue, Kathleen Freeman; ***Cameos:*** Gene Kelly; ***D:*** Stanley Donen; ***W:*** Ruth Brooks Flippen.

Love Is Colder Than Death 🦴🦴 *Liebe Ist Kalter Als Der Tod* **1969** Fassbinder's first feature film has a smalltime pimp hooking up with another low-life to go on a crime spree that ends in a botched bank robbery. German with subtitles. **85m/B VHS, DVD.** *GE* Ulli Lommel, Hanna Schygulla, Katrin Schaake, Liz Scellner; ***D:*** Rainer Werner Fassbinder; ***W:*** Rainer Werner Fassbinder; ***C:*** Dietrich Lohmann; ***M:*** Peer Raben, Holger Munzer.

Love Is News 🦴🦴🦴 **1937** Snappy screwball comedy finds madcap heiress Toni Gateson (Young) sick of being hounded by the press. Newsman Steve Layton (Power) tricks Toni into an interview and she's so steamed she tells all the other papers that she and Steve are engaged. Steve protests in vain but of course they do fall in love. Since neither will admit it, many more complications follow until the final clinch. Remade as "Sweet Rosie O'Grady" (1943) and "That Wonderful Urge" (1948). **78m/B DVD.** Tyrone Power, Loretta Young, Don Ameche, Dudley Digges, George Sanders, Pauline Moore, Slim Summerville, Walter Catlett, Jane Darwell, Stepin Fetchit, Elisha Cook Jr.; ***D:*** Tay Garnett; ***W:*** Jack Yellen, Harry Tugend; ***C:*** Ernest Palmer; ***M:*** David Buttolph.

Love Is the Devil 🦴🦴🦴 1/2 **1998** British painter Francis Bacon (Jacobi), at the height of his career, takes on petty thief George Dyer (Craig) as his model, lover, and whipping-post. Bacon exposes his dim lover to a world of high-brow drunks and addicts who entertain themselves by humiliating others, with Bacon viciously leading the verbal and emotional attacks. Although the estate refused director/writer Maybury permission to use Bacon's actual paintings, he captures the painful emotions expressed in the art in different ways. The incredible lead performances by Jacobi and Craig are as brilliant but ferocious as the artist himself. While at times tender and moving, their destructive relationship is difficult to watch, but worth it you do. Appeal is definitely art-house niche, but those who see it will be rewarded. **90m/C VHS, DVD.** *GB* Derek Jacobi, Daniel Craig, Tilda Swinton, Karl Johnson, Anne Lambton; ***D:*** John Maybury; ***W:*** John Maybury; ***C:*** John Mathieson; ***M:*** Ryuichi Sakamoto.

Love Jones 🦴🦴🦴 **1996 (R)** A contemporary Chicago nightclub, the Sanctuary, is the gathering spot for middle-class black urbanites looking for romance. Would-be writer/poet Darius (Tate) spouts provocative verse to beautiful photographer Nina (Long), who's not too happy with men at the moment (she's just been dumped). But they make a connection, with both protesting a little too much that's it just a "sex thing." Funny what happens when love clearly enters the picture. Witcher's directorial debut features fine lead performances. **105m/C VHS, DVD.** Larenz Tate, Nia Long, Isaiah Washington IV, Lisa Nicole Carson, Khalil Kain, Bill Bellamy, Leonard Roberts, Bernadette L. Clarke; ***D:*** Theodore Witcher; ***W:*** Theodore Witcher; ***C:*** Ernest Holzman; ***M:*** Darryl Jones. Sundance '97: Aud. Award.

Love Kills 🦴🦴 **1991 (PG-13)** Is the man a beautiful heiress falls in love with actually an assassin hired by her husband to kill her? Find out in this steamy suspenser. **92m/C VHS.** Virginia Madsen, Lenny Von Dohlen, Erich Anderson, Kate Hodge, Jim Metzler; ***D:*** Brian Grant.

Love Kills 🦴 1/2 **1998 (R)** Good cast can't hold this messy film together. New Age masseur Poe Finklestein (Van Peebles) arrives at the Beverly Hills estate of wealthy widow Evelyn Heiss (Warren). Also living with Evelyn are her no-account, gay stepson Dominique (Leitch) and her voyeurish sister-in-law Alena (Fletcher). There's shots fired, and drugs, and a cop (Baldwin) and various other hijinks but not much of it makes sense. **97m/C VHS, DVD.** Mario Van Peebles, Lesley Ann Warren, Daniel Baldwin, Donovan Leitch, Louise Fletcher, Loretta Devine, Melvin Van Peebles, Susan Ruttan, Alexis Arquette; ***D:*** Mario Van Peebles; ***W:*** Mario Van Peebles; ***C:*** George Mooradian.

Love Laughs at Andy Hardy 🦴🦴 **1946** Andy Hardy, college boy, is in love and in trouble. Financial and romantic problems come to a head when Andy is paired with a six-foot tall blind date. One in the series. **93m/B VHS, DVD.** Mickey Rooney, Lewis Stone, Sara Haden, Lina Romay, Bonita Granville, Fay Holden; ***D:*** Willis Goldbeck.

Love Leads the Way 🦴🦴 **1984** The true story of how Morris Frank established the seeing-eye dog system in the 1930s. **99m/C VHS.** Richard Speight Jr., Timothy Bottoms, Eva Marie Saint, Arthur Hill, Susan Dey, Ralph Bellamy, Ernest Borgnine, Patricia Neal; ***D:*** Delbert Mann.

The Love Letter 🦴🦴 1/2 **1998** Scotty Corrigan (Scott) discovers a love letter in the antique desk he's purchased, written by Lizzie Whitcomb (Leigh) who lived during the Civil War. Haunted, Scotty decides to reply to the missive and, magically, Lizzie receives his letter. Soon, they not only have a regular correspondence but a romance that transcends time. Based on a story by Jack Finney. **99m/C VHS, DVD.** Campbell Scott, Jennifer Jason Leigh, David Dukes, Estelle Parsons, Daphne Ashbrook, Gerrit Graham, Irma P. Hall; ***D:*** Dan Curtis; ***W:*** James Henerson; ***M:*** Robert Cobert. **TV**

The Love Letter 🦴 1/2 **1999 (PG-13)** Disappointingly loose adaptation of the novel by Cathleen Schine feels the need to take the focus off the unexpected love story developing between fortysomething bookstore owner Helen MacFarquhar (Capshaw) and college student Johnny (Scott), with too many peripheral characters. (Yeah, Tom Selleck's charming but his character's a goofy distraction.) Anyway, the love letter in question is an anonymous missive Helen receives at her bookstore. She's not certain it's meant for her, and if it is, just who the secret admirer might be. Then Johnny finds the letter and thinks it's meant for him—or maybe it was for Helen's cynical partner, Janet (DeGeneres). The biggest mystery is why the lovely Danner is playing Capshaw's MOTHER (under a ton of rubber makeup) for heaven's sake! **88m/C VHS, DVD.** Kate Capshaw, Tom Everett Scott, Tom Selleck, Ellen DeGeneres, Blythe Danner, Gloria Stuart, Geraldine McEwan, Alice Drummond, Jack Black; ***D:*** Peter Chan; ***W:*** Maria Maggenti; ***C:*** Tami Reiker; ***M:*** Luis Bacalov.

Love Letters 🦴🦴 1/2 **1945** Typical '40s weepie finds Victoria (Jones) marrying soldier Roger Morland (Sully) because of the beautiful letters he wrote her. Only he didn't write them, his best bud Alan Quinton (Cotten) did. Roger's actually a wife-beater and winds up dead. Victoria becomes an amnesiac from the shock but when Alan comes to check out the situation he falls immediately in love with her anyway. Based on the novel "Pity My Simplicity" by Chris Massie. **101m/B VHS.** Jennifer Jones, Joseph Cotten, Robert Sully, Ann Richards, Anita Louise, Cecil Kellaway, Gladys Cooper, Byron Barr, Reginald Denny; ***D:*** William Dieterle; ***W:*** Ayn Rand; ***C:*** Lee Garmes; ***M:*** Victor Young.

Love Letters 🦴🦴🦴 *Passion Play; My Love Letters* **1983 (R)** A young disc jockey falls under the spell of a box of love letters that her mother left behind which detailed her double life. She, in turn, begins an affair with a married man. Thoughtful treatment of the psychology of infidelity. **102m/C VHS, DVD.** Jamie Lee Curtis, Amy Madigan, Bud Cort, Matt Clark, Bonnie Bartlett, Sally Kirkland, James Keach; ***D:*** Amy Holden Jones; ***W:*** Amy Holden Jones; ***C:*** Alec Hirschfeld; ***M:*** Ralph Jones.

Love Letters 🦴🦴🦴 **1999 (PG-13)** Andy (Weber) and Melissa's (Linney) tender friendship began as children and their attraction continued throughout their lives, as Andy recounts after Melissa's death via many years worth of letters between them. Despite the intense feelings, their careers took them in opposite directions as Andy flourished as a lawyer-turned-senator and Melissa toiled as an artist. Directed by the legendary Dohen and based on A.R. Guerney's smash play. **90m/C VHS, DVD.** Steven Weber, Laura Linney, Emily Hampshire, Chas Lawther, Marcia Diamond; ***D:*** Stanley Donen; ***W:*** A.R. Gurney; ***C:*** Mike Fash; ***M:*** Lee Holdridge. **TV**

Love, Lies and Murder 🦴🦴 1/2 **1991 (PG-13)** Shocking psychological thriller in which a businessman convinces his daughter and sister-in-law to murder his wife and then sends his daughter to prison for the crime. The "perfect murder" is not so perfect, however, when the daughter learns that her father has remarried and is now living an insurance-rich lifestyle. She decides to fight back in this true story of bizarre murder and deception. **190m/C VHS.** Clancy Brown, John Ashton, Sheryl Lee, Moira Kelly, Ramon Bieri, Kenneth Welsh, Tom Bower, John M. Jackson, Kate McGregor-Stewart; ***D:*** Robert Markowitz. **TV**

Love Lies Bleeding 🦴 1/2 **2007 (R)** Hapless Duke (Geraghty) stumbles across a duffel bag full of money from a drug deal gone bad, grabs it and wife Amber (Dewan), and they head out on the road to start a new life. But they are soon pursued by very ticked-off (and corrupt) DEA agent Pollen (Slater), who wants that money for himself. **91m/C DVD.** Christian Slater, Jenna Dewan, Brian Geraghty, Craig Sheffer, Jacob Vargas, Tara Summers; ***D:*** Keith Samples; ***W:*** Brian Strasmann. **VIDEO**

The Love Light 🦴🦴 1/2 **1921** Angela (Pickford) is a lighthouse keeper in Italy who's awaiting her soldier brother's return from war. Instead, she learns of his death. When a wounded soldier is washed ashore, Angela rescues him and nurses him back to health, thinking he's an American sailor. They fall in love and marry before she learns that he's really a German spy and may have killed her brother. There's a lot more tragedy before Angela finds happiness. One of Pickford's rare adult roles. **75m/B VHS, DVD.** Mary Pickford, Raymond Bloomer, Jean De Briac, Evelyn Dumo, Eddie (Edward) Phillips, Albert Priscoe, George Regas, Fred Thomson; ***D:*** Frances Marion; ***W:*** Frances Marion; ***C:*** Henry Cronjager, Charles Rosher.

Love Liza 🦴🦴 **2002 (R)** An acquired taste of a film that rests firmly on the slumped shoulders of Hoffman. He's Wilson Joel, whose wife Liza has just committed suicide (by carbon-monoxide poisoning in her car). He can't read the note she left him, can't deal with her sympathetic mother Mary Ann (Bates), can't—in fact—do much of anything except mope. Oh, and huff. Yes, Wilson decides to cope with his trauma by inhaling gasoline fumes (the fuel used in his model airplane hobby). Soon, his addiction is all there is to his sad sack existence. **90m/C VHS, DVD.** Philip Seymour Hoffman, Kathy Bates, Jack Kehler, Stephen Tobolowsky, Sarah Koskoff, Erika Alexander; ***D:*** Todd Louiso; ***W:*** Gordy Hoffman; ***C:*** Lisa Rinzler; ***M:*** Jim O'Rourke. Sundance '02: Screenplay.

Love, Ludlow 🦴🦴 **2005 (R)** Bipolar painter Ludlow (Sexton) has been cared for by his tough older sister Myra (Goranson) since their mother's death. So he feels especially threatened when Myra agrees to date shy co-worker Reggie (Eigenberg) and it turns into something more than casual. Modest romantic comedy that Paterson adapted from his play "Finger Painting in a Murphy Bed." **86m/C DVD.** Alicia (Lecy) Goranson, Brendan Sexton III, David Eigenberg; ***D:*** Adrienne J. Weiss; ***W:*** David Paterson; ***C:*** Ruben O'Malley; ***M:*** Tomandandy, James Kole.

The Love Machine 🦴 1/2 **1971 (R)** A power-hungry newscaster climbs the corporate ladder by sleeping with many, including the president's wife. An adaptation of Jacqueline Susann's novel. **108m/C VHS.** John Phillip Law, Dyan Cannon, Robert Ryan, Jackie Cooper, David Hemmings, Jodi Wexler, William Roerick, Maureen Arthur, Shecky Greene, Clinton Greyn, Sharon Farrell, Alexandra Hay, Eve Bruce, Greg Mullavey, Edith Atwater, Gene Baylos, Claudia Jennings, Mary Collinson, Madeleine Collinson, Ann Ford, Gayle Hunnicutt; ***D:*** Jack Haley Jr.; ***W:*** Samuel A. Taylor; ***C:*** Charles B(ryant) Lang Jr.; ***M:*** Artie Butler.

Love Matters 🦴🦴 **1993 (R)** Tom and Julie's fast-track marriage is hovering on the brink when Tom's best friend Geoff, who's also married, shows up on their doorstep with his sexy mistress and announces he's getting a divorce. Reluctantly, Tom and Julie allow the X-rated lovebirds to stay the night but all that heat only shows up the flaws in their own marriage even more. An unrated version at 103 minutes is also available. **97m/C VHS.** Griffin Dunne, Tony Goldwyn, Annette O'Toole, Gina Gershon, Kate Burton; ***D:*** Eb Lottimer; ***W:*** Eb Lottimer; ***M:*** Simon Boswell.

Love Me Deadly 🦴 **1973 (R)** A young woman tries to get her husband interested in her new hobby—necrophilia. **95m/C VHS, DVD.** Mary Wilcox, Lyle Waggoner, Christopher Stone, Timothy Scott; ***D:*** Jacques Lacerte; ***W:*** Jacques Lacerte; ***C:*** David Aaron; ***M:*** Phil Moody.

Love Me if You Dare 🦴 *Jeux D'Enfants; Child's Play* **2003 (R)** Overwrought romance-French style. Julien (Canet) and Sophie (Cotillard) have played a game of dare since childhood-no matter how embarrassing or dangerous the challenge. Obsessed with each other, they are unable to admit their devotion in any conventional way and perpetuate their play for the excitement it brings them even as they risk self-destruction. Unfortunately for the viewer, the duo are mainly exasperating. French with subtitles. **95m/C DVD.** *FR BE* Guillaume Canet, Marion Cotillard, Thibault Verhaeghe, Josephine Lebas Joly, Emmanuelle Gronvold, Gerard Watkins; ***D:*** Yann Samuell; ***W:*** Yann Samuell, Jacky Cuckier; ***C:*** Antoine Roch; ***M:*** Philippe Rombi.

Love Me or Leave Me 🦴🦴🦴 **1955** A hard-hitting biography of '20s torch singer Ruth Etting and her rise and fall at the hand of her abusive, gangster husband, a part just made for Cagney. Day emotes and sings expressively in one of the best performances of her career. ♫ I'll Never Stop Loving You; Never Look Back; Shaking the Blues Away; Mean to Me; Love Me or Leave Me; Sam, the Old Accordian Man; At Sundown; Everybody Loves My Baby; Five Foot Two. **122m/C VHS, DVD.** Doris Day, James Cagney, Cameron Mitchell, Robert Keith, Tom Tully, Veda Ann Borg; ***D:*** Charles Vidor. Oscars '55: Story.

Love Me Tender 1956 A Civil War-torn family is divided by in-fighting between two brothers who both seek the affections of the same woman. Presley's first film. Songs include "Poor Boy," "We're Gonna Move," and the title tune. **89m/B VHS, DVD.** Richard Egan, Debra Paget, Elvis Presley, Neville Brand, Mildred Dunnock, James Drury, Barry Coe, Robert Middleton, William Campbell, Russ Conway, L.Q. Jones; ***D:*** Robert D. Webb; ***W:*** Robert Buckner; ***C:*** Leo Tover; ***M:*** Lionel Newman.

Love Meetings *Comizi d'Amore* **1964** Pasolini acts as director and interviewer to query a wide-range of individuals on their experiences at love, including homosexuality, prostitution, marital and non-marital interludes. In Italian with English subtitles. **90m/B VHS, DVD.** *IT* ***D:*** Pier Paolo Pasolini; ***W:*** Pier Paolo Pasolini; ***C:*** Tonino Delli Colli, Mario Bernardo.

Love Nest 1951 Lundigan stars as Jim Scott, the landlord of an apartment building brimming with wacky tenants, including Monroe, Paar, and Fay. He dreams of becoming a famous writer, but his time is always filled with fixing up the building and trying to pay the mortgage. When one of the tenants ends up in jail because he was living off wealthy widows, Scott's luck changes. This moderately funny film is a good look at the early careers of Monroe and Paar. **84m/B VHS, DVD.** William Lundigan, June Haver, Frank Fay, Marilyn Monroe, Jack Paar; ***D:*** Joseph M. Newman; ***W:*** I.A.L. Diamond; ***M:*** Cyril Mockridge.

Love Notes **1988** Three short vignettes of soft core fantasy, in the life of an ordinary guy. **60m/C VHS.** Jeff Daniels, Christine Veronica.

The Love of Jeanne Ney 1/2 **1927** Wildly convoluted silent film begins in Russia where Jeanne's (Jehanne) Bolshevik lover (Henning) kills her father for betraying the cause, and then shifts to Paris where the pair face even more daunting obstacles. The new score by Timothy Brock is engaging and effective. **113m/B VHS, DVD.** *GE* Edith Jehanne, Brigitte Helm, Uno Henning, Eugen Jenson, Fritz Rasp; ***D:*** G.W. Pabst; ***W:*** Ilya Ehrenburg, Ladislaus Vayda.

The Love of Three Queens 1/2 **1954** The loves, on and off stage, of a beautiful actress in a European traveling theatre group. **80m/C VHS.** Gerard Oury, Massimo Serato, Robert Beatty, Cathy O'Donnell, Terence Morgan, Hedy Lamarr; ***D:*** Marc Allegret.

Love on a Pillow 1/2 *Les Repos du Guerrier; The Rest of the Warrior* **1962** Beautiful Genevieve (Bardot) accidentally prevents the suicide of alcoholic Renaud (Hossein) and decides she must redeem him. They fall in love but Genevieve finally tires of his cynical abuse and leaves, which serves as a wake-up call to Renaud. Bardot's a looker but the film is very slooooow and her character is a masochist for sticking with such a loser. French with subtitles. **102m/C DVD.** *FR IT* Brigitte Bardot, Robert Hossein, Jean-Mark Bory, Michel Serrault; ***D:*** Roger Vadim; ***W:*** Roger Vadim, Claude Choublier; ***C:*** Armand Thirard, Edmond Sechan; ***M:*** Michel Magne.

Love on the Dole 1941 In a gloomy industrial section of England during the early '30s a family struggles to survive and maintain dignity. Grim Depression drama salvaged by great acting. **89m/B VHS.** *GB* Deborah Kerr, Clifford Evans, George Carney; ***D:*** John Baxter.

Love on the Run 1/2 **1936** Enjoyable romantic comedy starring Crawford as a rich American heiress and Gable and Tone (Crawford's real husband at the time) as journalists stationed in Europe. Gable and Tone are assigned to cover an international aviator, who turns out to be an evil spy, as well as the upcoming wedding of flighty Crawford. When Crawford asks for help in getting out of her marriage, Gable and Tone steal a plane and the trio is chased across Europe by spies. Wild and farfetched plot, but the stars make it worthwhile. Based on the story "Beauty and the Beast" by Alan Green and Julian Brodie. **80m/B VHS.** Joan Crawford, Clark Gable, Franchot Tone, Reginald Owen, Mona Maris, Ivan Lebedeff, Charles (Judel, Judells) Judels, William Demarest; ***D:*** Woodbridge S. Van Dyke; ***W:*** John Lee Mahin, Manuel Seff, Gladys Hurlbut.

Love on the Run *L'Amour en Fuite* **1978 (PG)** The further amorous adventures of Antoine Doinel, hero of "The 400 Blows," "Stolen Kisses," and "Bed and Board." Doinel is now in his 30s and newly divorced. He renews affairs with several women from his past but, after his mother's death, must contend with his emotional immaturity and his inability to sustain a relationship. In French with English subtitles. **95m/C VHS, DVD.** *FR* Jean-Pierre Leaud, Marie-France Pisier, Claude Jade; ***D:*** Francois Truffaut; ***C:*** Nestor Almendros; ***M:*** Georges Delerue. Cesar '80: Score.

Love on the Run 1/2 **1985** A beautiful lawyer helps a wrongly accused convict escape from prison, then they both evade the law. **102m/C VHS.** Stephanie Zimbalist, Alec Baldwin, Constance McCashin, Howard Duff; ***D:*** Gus Trikonis; ***M:*** Billy Goldenberg. **TV**

Love on the Side *Deluxe Combo Platter* **2004 (R)** Quirky small town comedy. When tall, blonde, gorgeous Linda (Schnarre) suddenly turns up in Squamish, British Columbia, she brings trouble to the would-be romance of waitress Eve (Sokoloff), who has big self-esteem issues, and local dumb hunk Jeff (Watson). But Linda is keeping secrets—such as the fact that she's romantically attracted to Eve and has some interest in the local real estate too. **102m/C DVD.** *CA* Monica Schnarre, Marla Sokoloff, Barry Watson, Dave Thomas, Jennifer Tilly; ***D:*** Vic Sarin; ***W:*** Brigitte Talevski; ***C:*** Vic Sarin; ***M:*** Daryl Bennett.

Love or Money **2001** Daniel (Duffy) and Samantha (Cunniffe) are strangers to each other when they become contestants on a reality TV show where they are chosen by the audience to get married. If they can form a relationship and stay together for six months, they win $1 million. But between media scrutiny, family interference, and personal difficulties, the pressure may be too much. **90m/C DVD.** *GB* Emma Cunniffe, George Costigan, Sheila Hancock, David Calder, Steven Duffy, Nicky Henson, Pippa Heywood, Toby Jones; ***D:*** Martyn Friend; ***W:*** Elizabeth (Lizzie) Mickery; ***C:*** Sean Van Hales; ***M:*** Nigel Hess. **TV**

The Love Parade 1/2 **1929** Lubitsch's first sound film takes place in Sylvania, one of those mythic, musical, mitt-European countries with a royal ruler. In this case, it's unmarried and lonely Queen Louise (MacDonald in her film debut). Recalling her randy ambassador, Count Alfred Renard (Chevalier), from Paris for his indiscretions, Louise is nonetheless entranced by his charms and they quickly marry. But Count Alfred soon discovers that being a royal consort is not to his liking. **107m/B DVD.** Jeanette MacDonald, Maurice Chevalier, Lupino Lane, Lillian Roth, Edgar Norton, Lionel Belmore, Eugene Pallette, E.H. Calvert; ***D:*** Ernst Lubitsch; ***W:*** Ernest Vajda, Guy Bolton; ***C:*** Victor Milner; ***M:*** Victor Schertzinger.

Love Play *Playtime; La Recreation* **1960** Debut film for Moreuil, who was married to leading lady Seberg at the time, is a bland drama based on a story by Francoise Sagan (who also wrote the much better "Bonjour Tristesse" that Seberg starred in). Young American Kate Hudson (Seberg), enrolled in a Paris school, becomes obsessed with her next-door neighbors—sculptor Philippe (Marquand) and his wealthy older mistress and patron (Prevost). Soon Kate's involved in a triangle that's even more complicated than it first appears. **87m/B VHS.** *FR* Jean Seberg, Christian Marquand, Francoise Prevost, Evelyne Ker; ***D:*** Francois Moreuil; ***W:*** Francois Moreuil, Daniel Boulanger; ***C:*** Jean Penzer; ***M:*** Georges Delerue.

Love Potion #9 1/2 **1992 (PG-13)** Two nerdy biochemists procure a love potion that they test on animals. Meeting with success they agree to test it on themselves. Predictably, the scientists are transformed and fall in love with each other. Features a talented young cast, with an amusing cameo by Bancroft, but the script is a real disappointment because of its shallow characters and lame gags. Inspired by the song by Jerry Leiber and Mike Stoller. **96m/C VHS, DVD.** Tate Donovan, Sandra Bullock, Mary Mara, Dale Midkiff, Hillary Bailey Smith, Dylan Baker, Anne Bancroft, Rebecca Staab; ***D:*** Dale Launer; ***W:*** Dale Launer; ***C:*** William Wages; ***M:*** Jed Leiber.

Love Serenade **1996 (R)** Former big-time Brisbane DJ and 70s refugee Ken Sherry (Shevtsov) arrives in a sleepy Australian backwater town, setting off a rivalry between two bored sisters, Dimity (Otto) and Vicki-Ann (Frith). Fishing is one of their hobbies and metaphorically, Ken is the big fish in a very little pond. To them, his pretentious disco-era schmooze comes off as sophistication, mostly because he uses Barry White lyrics and his pillow-talk DJ voice to sell it. Critically speaking, director/writer Barrett's debut demonstrates a keen ear for dialogue and comic timing. To the average viewer though, this one's a dog, boring and very strange. If you're looking for a good Aussie comedy rent "Strictly Ballroom" or "Muriel's Wedding" instead. **101m/C VHS, DVD.** *AU* Miranda Otto, Rebecca Frith, George Shevtsov, John Alansu, Jessica Napier; ***D:*** Shirley Barrett; ***W:*** Shirley Barrett; ***C:*** Mandy Walker.

Love Song 1/2 **2000** Camille (Arnold) is a college student from an upper-crust African-American family whose surgeon father expects her to follow him into the medical field. She's also expected to marry earnest but dull Calvin (Francks). Then Camille meets white blues musician/singer Billy Ryan (Kane) and begins to question just whose dreams she's following as she discovers unexpected romance. Appealing story with sexy leads. **120m/C VHS.** Monica Arnold, Christian Kane, Rainbow Sun Francks, Peter Francis James, Vanessa Bell Calloway, Rachel True, Essence Atkins, Teck Holmes, Tyrese Gibson; ***D:*** Julie Dash; ***W:*** Josslyn Luckett; ***C:*** David Claessen; ***M:*** Frank Fitzpatrick. **CABLE**

A Love Song for Bobby Long **2004 (R)** Bobby Long (Travolta) and protege Lawson Pines (Macht) are alcoholic literary has-beens who escape a shady past by relocating to a notorious singer's house in New Orleans. When the singer dies, her 18-year-old daughter (Johansson) shows up to claim the house, but must share it with the shabby twosome. Heartwarming misunderstandings and bonding moments ensue. Very over-the-top story actually manages to charm, saved by the relaxed performances of talented cast. Neither Travolta nor Johansson ever master a believable southern accent, yet for some odd reason it doesn't seem to matter. And Travolta gets to sing again. **119m/C VHS, DVD.** *US* John Travolta, Scarlett Johansson, Gabriel Macht, Deborah Kara Unger, Sonny Shroyer, Dane Rhodes; ***D:*** Shainee Gabel; ***W:*** Shainee Gabel; ***C:*** Elliot Davis; ***M:*** Nathan Larson.

Love Songs *Paroles et Musique* **1984** Margaux's (Deneuve) husband is on an extended trip to New York to write a book, leaving her with their two kids and a demanding job as a recording company exec. She's being pressured to find and sign new talent and discovers the duo of Michel (Anconina) and Jeremy (Lambert). Complications arise when Jeremy becomes more interested in Margaux than his music, but he needs to makes a decision when Michel goes alone to an ultimately successful audition. French with subtitles. **107m/C DVD.** *FR* Catherine Deneuve, Christopher Lambert, Richard Anconina, Jacques Perrin, Nick Mancuso, Charlotte Gainsbourg; ***D:*** Elie Chouraqui; ***W:*** Elie Chouraqui; ***C:*** Robert Alazraki; ***M:*** Michel Legrand.

Love Songs **1985 (R)** A mother of two is confronted with her husband's abandonment and a subsequent romance with a younger man. In French with English subtitles or dubbed. ♫Leave It to Me; Psychic Flash; I Am With You Now; Human Race; We Can Dance; One More Moment; From the Heart; This Must Be Heaven. **107m/C VHS, DVD.** *FR CA* Catherine Deneuve, Christopher Lambert; ***D:*** Elie Chouraqui; ***C:*** Robert Alazraki.

Love Songs 1/2 **1999** Trilogy of stories all set in the same black neighborhood. "A Love Song for a Champ" concerns boxer Townsend who agrees to throw a fight. "A Love Song for Jean and Ellis" concerns the would-be romance between grocer Braugher and the haughty Whitfield. "A Love Song for Dad" follows bartender Grossett who comes to the aid of his abused sister-in-law. **101m/C VHS, DVD.** Robert Kevin Townsend, Andre Braugher, Louis Gossett Jr., Rachael Crawford, Carl Gordon, Lynn Whitfield, Brent Jennings, Dule Hill, Sandra Caldwell; ***D:*** Robert Kevin Townsend, Andre Braugher, Louis Gossett Jr.; ***W:*** Charles Fuller; ***C:*** James R. Bagdonas; ***M:*** Pete Anthony, Ronnie Laws. **CABLE**

Love Songs *Les Chansons d'Amour* **2007** Ismael (Garel) lives with longtime girlfriend Julie (Sagnier) and has just persuaded her (reluctantly) into a three-way with his co-worker Alice (Hesme). Julie's sudden death plunges the immature Ismael into a series of complicated emotional situations that involve Julie's sister Jeanne (Mastroiani), Alice taking up with new beau Gwendal (Renier), and Gwendal's teenaged brother Erwann (Leprince-Riguet) developing a serious crush on Ismael. And every so often the cast bursts out singing pop songs, which sometimes works (and sometimes doesn't) but at least writer/director Honore is trying for something out of the ordinary. French with subtitles. **95m/C DVD.** *FR* Ludivine Sagnier, Chiara Mastroianni, Gregoire Leprince-Ringuet, Yannick Renier, Louis Garrel, Brigitte Rouan; ***D:*** Christophe Honore; ***W:*** Christophe Honore; ***C:*** Remy Chevrin; ***M:*** Alexandre Beaupain.

Love Stinks 1/2 **1999 (R)** Apparently designed as an antidote to the date movie, this joyless "unromantic" comedy gives off a few rank fumes of its own. Writer Seth Winnick (Stewart) meets Chelsea (Wilson) at the wedding of his pals Larry (Bellamy) and Holly (Banks). After he's lured into Chelsea's clutches, she begins to take over his life while dropping hints that he should pop the big question. After he promises to marry her in a year but doesn't follow through, Chelsea decides to sue him for palimony. The non-couple then inexplicably live together until the trial so that further "funny comedy jokes" can be inflicted on the audience. Stewart attempts to rise above the material with his excellent comedic timing, but he's unable to escape this misogynistic mess. **94m/C VHS, DVD.** French Stewart, Bridgette Wilson-Sampras, Tyra Banks, Bill Bellamy, Steve Hytner, Jason Bateman, Tiffani(-Amber) Thiessen; ***D:*** Jeff Franklin; ***W:*** Jeff Franklin; ***C:*** Uta Briesewitz; ***M:*** Bennett Salvay.

Love Story **1970 (PG)** Melodrama had enormous popular appeal. O'Neal is the son of Boston's upper crust at Harvard; McGraw's the daughter of a poor Italian on scholarship to study music at Radcliffe. They find happiness, but only for a brief period. Timeless story, simply told, with artful direction from Hiller pulling exceptional performances from the young duo (who have never done as well since). The end result is perhaps better than Segal's simplistic novel, which was produced after he sold the screenplay and became a best-seller before the picture's release—great publicity for any film. Remember: "Love means never having to say you're sorry." **100m/C VHS, DVD.** Ryan O'Neal, Ali MacGraw, Ray Milland, John Marley, Tommy Lee Jones; ***D:*** Arthur Hiller; ***W:*** Erich Segal; ***C:*** Richard Kratina; ***M:*** Francis Lai. Oscars '70: Orig. Score; Golden Globes '71: Actress—Drama (MacGraw), Director (Hiller), Film—Drama, Screenplay, Score.

Love Strange Love 1/2 *Amor Estranho Amor* **1982 (R)** A young boy develops a bizarre relationship with his mother who works in a luxurious bordello. Also available in an unedited 120-minute version. **97m/C VHS.** *BR* Vera Fischer, Mauro Mendonca, Tarcisio Meira; ***D:*** Walter Hugo Khouri; ***W:*** Walter Hugo Khouri; ***C:*** Antonio Meliande; ***M:*** Rogerio Duprat.

Love Streams 1/2 **1984 (PG-13)** A quirky character drama about a writer and his sister who struggle to find love despite their personal problems. **122m/C VHS.** Gena Rowlands, John Cassavetes, Diahnne Abbott, Seymour Cassel; ***D:*** John Cassavetes; ***W:*** Ted Allan. Berlin Intl. Film Fest. '84: Golden Berlin Bear.

Love Takes Wing 1/2 **2009** Usual sentimental story is the seventh film based on Janette Oke's novels. After her husband dies, grieving Dr. Belinda Simpson (Jones) accepts a job in rural Sikeston, Missouri. A cholera epidemic, which apparently started at the orphanage run by Hattie Clarence (Leachman), has the townspeople fearful and determined to shut the place down. Belinda must win everyone's trust, relying on her faith and the friendships of Annie (Duff) and blacksmith Lee (Bridges) to help her. **88m/C DVD.** Sarah Jones, Haylie Duff, Cloris Leachman, Jordan Bridges, Patrick Duffy, John Bishop, Erin Cottrell, Lou Diamond Phillips, Analise Basso; ***D:*** Lou Diamond Phillips; ***W:*** Rachel Stuhler; ***C:*** Dane Peterson; ***M:*** Terry Plumeri. **CABLE**

Love the Hard Way **2001** Would-be hipster writer Jack Grace (Brody) runs smalltime scams with his friend Charlie (Seda). Grad student Claire (Ayanna) falls for the romeo, even though she can see he's a loser. Though Jack cheats on her, Claire hangs around, even deciding that the best way to keep him is to join in Jack's con games. The characters are tedious as is the story; Grier shows up to give the film some spark in the small role of a cop out to bust Jack. "Inspired" by the Chinese novel "Fire and Ice" by Wang Shuo. **104m/C VHS, DVD.** *US* Adrien Brody, Charlotte Ayanna, Jon Seda, Pam Grier, August Diehl, David W. Ross; ***D:*** Peter Sehr; ***W:*** Peter Sehr, Marie Noelle; ***C:*** Guy Dufaux; ***M:*** Darien Dahoud.

Love Thrill Murders WOOF! *Sweet Savior* **1971 (R)** A film about a Mansonesque lunatic who is worshipped and obeyed by a mob of runaways and dropouts. **89m/C VHS.** Fran Middleton, Talie Cochrane, Matt Greene, Tobi Marsh, Troy Donahue; ***D:*** Robert L. Roberts; ***W:*** Matt Cavanagh; ***C:*** Victor Petrashevich; ***M:*** Jeff Barry.

Love Thy Neighbor 1/2 **2002** Two married neighbors, Jack (Gwaltney) and Molly (Overbey), decide to hook up, and the simple affair leads to potentially disastrous fallout when Molly's husband admits to Jack that he might have AIDS. The resulting juxtaposition of emotions—marital boredom, betrayal among friends, and threat of disease—is awkward at best and ultimately forgettable. **87m/C VHS, DVD.** Jack Gwaltney, Kellie Overbey, John Enos, Jennifer Bransford, Roy Scheider, Wallace Shawn, Jake Weber; ***D:*** Nick Gregory; ***W:*** Nick Gregory, Kirk Aanes; ***C:*** Dejan Georgevich; ***M:*** Stephen Coleman. **VIDEO**

A Love to Keep *Electroshock* **2007** Teachers Pilar and Elvira fall in love during the waning days of the Franco dictatorship in the 1970s. Pilar's domineering mother is so appalled that she has her daughter committed to an asylum, where Pilar undergoes brutal electroshock and other therapy. Eventually she's released to her parents' house where the ever-faithful Elvira tries to contact her. Pilar makes her escape but the women's reunion is overshadowed by the physical and mental effects of Pilar's ordeal. Spanish with subtitles. **98m/C DVD.** *SP* Carmen Elias, Julieta Serrano, Juan Fernandez, Susi Sanchez, Juli Mira, Sergio Caballero; ***D:*** Juan Carlos Claver; ***W:*** Juan Carlos Claver, Agustin Madariaga; ***C:*** Javier Quintanilla; ***M:*** Alejandro Roman.

Love to Kill *The Girl Gets Moe* **1997 (R)** Moe (Danza) is a low-level arms dealer who falls for Elizabeth (Barondes), a gal who happens to like guns. But things go wrong thanks to dead bodies, double-crosses, and dirty cops. **102m/C VHS, DVD.** Tony Danza, Michael Madsen, James Russo, Elizabeth Barondes, Louise Fletcher, Amy Locane, Richmond Arquette, Rustam Branaman; ***D:*** James Bruce; ***W:*** Monica Clemens, Rustam Branaman; ***C:*** Keith L. Smith; ***M:*** Barry Coffing. **CABLE**

The Love Trap 1/2 **1929** Early partial talkie (the film starts off as a silent with captions) is your basic Cinderella story. Chorus girl Laura Todd (La Plante) loses her job and gets booted out of her apartment. Cabbie Peter Cadwallader (Hamilton) offers his taxi as shelter and the two fall in love and marry—much to the displeasure of his snooty (and wealthy) family. The DVD includes the documentary "Directed by William Wyler." **71m/B VHS, DVD.** Laura La Plante, Neil Hamilton, Robert Ellis, Rita La Roy, Jocelyn Lee, Norman Trevor, Clarissa Selwynne; ***D:*** William Wyler; ***W:*** Clarence Marks, John B. Clymer, Albert DeMond, Clarence Thompson; ***C:*** Gilbert Warrenton.

Love Under Pressure *Because He's My Friend* **1978** Man and woman's marriage starts to evaporate when they realize their son is seriously disturbed. **92m/C VHS.** *AU* Jack Thompson, Tom Oliver, Barbara Stephens, Don Reid, Karen Black, Keir Dullea; ***D:*** Ralph Nelson; ***W:*** Peter Schreck; ***C:*** Peter Hendry; ***M:*** Pete Jones.

Love Unto Death *L'Amour a Mort* **1984** Simon (Arditi) and Elisabeth (Azema) are still working out their romantic relationship when he suddenly dies—and is quickly revived. His near-death experience has Simon becoming obsessed with mortality and he starts to withdraw from daily life. Friends Judith (Ardant) and Jerome (Dussollier), who are also Protestant ministers, offer their guidance but the idea of a love beyond death is all Simon can think about. French with subtitles. **92m/C DVD.** *FR* Jean Daste, Pierre Arditti, Sabine Azema, Fanny Ardant, Andre Dussollier, Alain Resnais; ***W:*** Jean Gruault; ***C:*** Sacha Vierny; ***M:*** Hans Werner Henze.

Love! Valour! Compassion! 1/2 **1996 (R)** Follows eight gay men, longtime friends, who spend summer holiday weekends together at a beach house. Excellent cast features Alexander as Buzz, who has a severe show tune fixation, and Glover playing a pair of twins with very different personalities (and they're actually named Jeckyll). Together they wander through the turmoil of AIDS, infidelity, rage and impromptu ballet practice. Excellent cast only occasionally swerves from humor and genuine pathos into maudlin. Intermittent periods of stagy claustrophobia betray pic's Broadway origin. Based on the play by Terrence McNally. **120m/C VHS, DVD.** Jason Alexander, John Glover, Randy Becker, John Benjamin Hickey, Stephen Bogardus, Stephen Spinella, Justin Kirk; ***D:*** Joe Mantello; ***W:*** Terrance McNally; ***C:*** Alik Sakharov; ***M:*** Harold Wheeler.

Love Walked In *The Bitter End* **1997 (R)** Hardly an original story but this B-movie has a standout performance from the edgy Leary. He's Jack Hanaway, a lounge piano player with a sultry singer/wife, Vicky (Sanchez-Gijon). Jack's old P.I. friend Eddie (Badalucco) shows up with a scheme to make them all rich. He's been hired by a wealthy woman (Dusay) who suspects her husband Fred (Stamp) of infidelity. Fred's faithful (he likes his wife's money) but he's a patron of Jack's and is naturally appreciative of Vicky's charms. So they try to set Fred up. Scenes of would-be writer Jack's pulp novel intrude into the action and provide an unneeded distraction. Adapted from the novel by Jose Pable Feinmann. **90m/C VHS.** J.K. Simmons, Denis Leary, Aitana Sanchez-Gijon, Terence Stamp, Michael Badalucco, Marj Dusay, Danny Nucci, Moira Kelly, Neal Huff; ***D:*** Juan J. Campanella; ***W:*** Larry Golin, Juan J. Campanella; ***C:*** Daniel Shulman; ***M:*** Wendy Blackstone.

Love with a Perfect Stranger **1986** This Harlequin Romance takes place in Italy where a young widow meets a dashing Englishman. He changes her life forever. **102m/C VHS.** Marilu Henner, Daniel Massey; ***M:*** John Du Prez.

Love with the Proper Stranger **1963** A quiet, gritty romance about an itinerant musician and a young working girl in Manhattan awkwardly living through the consequences of their one-night stand. Moved Wood well into the realm of adult roles, after years playing teenagers and innocents. Although the story is about an Italian neighborhood and family, an exceptional number of the cast members were Jewish, as was the screenwriter. Story does not conclude strongly, although this did not hamper the boxoffice returns. **102m/B VHS.** Natalie Wood, Steve McQueen, Edie Adams, Herschel Bernardi, Tom Bosley, Harvey Lembeck, Penny Santon, Virginia Vincent, Nick Alexander, Augusta Ciolli; ***D:*** Robert Mulligan; ***W:*** Arnold Schulman; ***C:*** Milton Krasner; ***M:*** Elmer Bernstein.

Love Without Pity 1/2 **1991** Rochant's theatrical debut is a modern romance, with more distance and alienation than joy. A lovely, successful grad student loses her heart to a jobless, unambitious layabout who wants total commitment from her. Untypical, sardonic love story may be too cynical for sentimental types. In French with English subtitles. **95m/C VHS.** *FR* Hippolyte Girardot, Mireille Perrier, Jean Marie Rollin; ***D:*** Eric Rochant; ***W:*** Eric Rochant; ***M:*** Gerard Torikian.

Love Your Mama 1/2 **1989 (PG-13)** An urban black drama about the strong Dorothy whose faith helps her cope with her many family complications, including her drunken husband, car thief son, and pregnant teenage daughter. Believable role models and good performances help out this amatuer filmmaking effort. **93m/C VHS.** Audrey Morgan, Carol E. Hall, Andre Robinson, Ernest Rayford, Kearo Johnson, Jacqueline Williams; ***D:*** Ruby L. Oliver; ***W:*** Ruby L. Oliver.

Loved **1997 (PG-13)** Hedda's (Wright Penn) obsessively and destructively in love with the nameless ex-boyfriend (Lucero) who left her scarred after a suspicious fall out a window. The loser's being arraigned for the murder of his latest girlfriend and prosecutor Dietrickson (Hurt) wants Hedda to testify. But what no one counts on, and what no one can understand, is Hedda's justification of her ex's abuse. Pic and performances are vague. **109m/C VHS.** Robin Wright Penn, William Hurt, Amy Madigan, Anthony Lucero, Lucinda Jenney, Joanna Cassidy, Paul Dooley, Jennifer Rubin; ***Cameos:*** Sean Penn; ***D:*** Erin Dignam; ***W:*** Erin Dignam; ***C:*** Reynaldo Villalobos; ***M:*** David Baerwald.

The Loved One 1/2 **1965** A famously outlandish, death-mocking farce based on Evelyn Waugh's satire about a particularly horrendous California funeral parlor/cemetery and how its denizens do business. A shrill, protracted spearing of American capitalism. **118m/B VHS, DVD.** Robert Morse, John Gielgud, Rod Steiger, Liberace, Anjanette Comer, Jonathan Winters, James Coburn, Dana Andrews, Milton Berle, Tab Hunter, Robert Morley, Lionel Stander, Margaret Leighton, Roddy McDowall, Bernie Kopell, Alan Napier, Paul Williams, Barbara Nichols, Jamie Farr; ***D:*** Tony Richardson; ***W:*** Terry Southern, Christopher Isherwood; ***C:*** Haskell Wexler; ***M:*** John Addison.

Loveless **1983 (R)** A menacing glance into the exploits of an outcast motorcycle gang. In the 50s, a group of bikers on their way to the Florida Cycle Races stop for lunch in a small-town diner. While repairs are being made on their motorcycles, they decide to take full advantage of their situation. **85m/C VHS, DVD.** Robert Gordon, Willem Dafoe, J. Don Ferguson; ***D:*** Kathryn Bigelow; ***W:*** Kathryn Bigelow.

Loveless in Los Angeles **2007 (R)** Dave (Mihok) has a good job producing a reality TV dating show but he strenuously avoids commitment. That is until he bumps into now-divorced Kelly (Daniel), the girl he crushed on in college. But Dave's sleazy womanizing drives Kelly up the wall and he needs her to find his inner nice guy once again. Standard romance isn't really worth the effort. **95m/C DVD.** Dash Mihok, Brittany Daniel, James Lesure, Navi Rawat, Christopher Coppola, Stephen Tobolowsky, Geoffrey Arend; ***D:*** Archie Gip; ***W:*** Archie Gip; ***C:*** Michael Marius Passah; ***M:*** Gregg Lehrman. **VIDEO**

Lovelife 1/2 **1997 (R)** Yet another romantic saga about a group of disenchanted boomer friends who can't seem to make that love connection work. Maybe they should stop serial dating within their same small circle and take advantage of the outside world. **97m/C VHS, DVD.** Sherilyn Fenn, Bruce Davison, Saffron Burrows, Jon Tenney, Carla Gugino, Matt Letscher, Tushka Bergen, Peter Krause; ***D:*** John Harmon Feldman; ***W:*** John Harmon Feldman; ***C:*** Anthony C. "Tony" Jannelli; ***M:*** Adam Fields. **VIDEO**

Lovelines **1984 (R)** Two rock singers from rival high schools meet and fall in love during a panty raid. Laughs uncounted ensue. **93m/C VHS.** Greg Bradford, Michael Winslow, Mary Beth Evans, Don Michael Paul, Tammy Taylor, Stacey Toten, Miguel Ferrer, Shecky Greene, Aimee (Amy) Eccles, Sherri Stoner; ***D:*** Rod Amateau.

Lovely & Amazing **2002 (R)** Mom Blethyn watches over her three dysfunctional daughters: Michelle (Keener), who's bored by her marriage; insecure wannabe actress Elizabeth (Mortimer) and adopted eight-year-old African-American Annie (Goodwin), who's preoccupied with her looks. Unstable Michelle begins a hopeless affair with a teenager (Gyllenhaal), while a post-coital scene between Elizabeth and lover Mulroney shows the extent of the neurotic actresses' body image problem. Annie is the least disturbed of the three sisters, who just wants to look like everyone else in the family. Led by Blethyn, the cast expertly embody their complicated, quirky characters. Skillfully written and directed study in character flaws and family by Holofcener. **91m/C VHS, DVD.** *US* Brenda Blethyn, Catherine Keener, Emily Mortimer, Raven Goodwin, Dermot Mulroney, Jake Gyllenhaal, Aunjanue Ellis, Clark Gregg, James LeGros, Michael Nouri; ***D:*** Nicole Holofcener; ***W:*** Nicole Holofcener; ***C:*** Harlan Bosmajian; ***M:*** Craig Richey. Ind. Spirit '03: Support. Actress (Mortimer).

The Lovely Bones **2009 (PG-13)** Just before Christmas 1973, 14-year-old Susie Salmon (Ronan) encounters neighbor George Harvey (Tucci) and is never seen alive again. Susie narrates from beyond the grave as she watches her mother (Weisz) and father (Wahlberg), her killer, and the police investigation. Eventually, Susie must decide whether to move on or continue observing what she can't change. Director Jackson chooses to give the Alice Sebold novel a fantasized, effects-heavy approach but in doing so drowns much of the quiet intimacy and nuance of the book. The end result is a movie that's shallow with too much style despite fine performances by the leads. **139m/C DVD.** *US* Saoirse Ronan, Mark Wahlberg, Rachel Weisz, Stanley Tucci, Susan Sarandon, Michael Imperioli, Rose McIver, Carolyn Dando; ***D:*** Peter Jackson; ***W:*** Peter Jackson, Fran Walsh, Philippa Boyens; ***C:*** Andrew Lesnie.

Lovely... But Deadly 1/2 **1982 (R)** Young girl wages a war against the drug dealers in her school after her brother dies of an overdose. **95m/C VHS.** Lucinda Dooling, John Randolph, Richard Herd, Susan Mechsner, Mel Novak; ***D:*** David Sheldon.

Lovely by Surprise **2007** Quirky, low-budget indie. Novelist Marian (Preston) has severe writer's block and can't figure out what to do with the two brothers—Humkin (Chernus) and Mopekey (Roberts)—in her latest work. She decides to take the advice of mentor (and ex-lover) Jackson (Pendleton) and kill off one brother to add some drama. Marian decides on Humpkin, only he actually survives the threat and takes off—into the real world. When Marian realizes what's happened, her own grip on reality begins to loosen. **99m/C DVD.** Carrie Preston, Michael Chernus, Dallas Roberts, Austin Pendleton, Reg Rogers, Kate Burton, Richard Masur; ***D:*** Kirt Gunn; ***W:*** Kirt Gunn; ***C:*** Steve Yedlin; ***M:*** Shelby Bryant.

Lovely to Look At **1952** Three wanna-be Broadway producers (Skelton, Keel, Champion) go to gay Paree to peddle Skelton's half interest in Madame Roberta's, a chi chi dress shop. There, they meet the shop's other half interest, two sisters (Champion and Miller), and together they stage a fashion show to finance the floundering hospice of haute couture. Lavish production, light plot. Filmed in Technicolor based on Kern's 1933 Broadway hit (inspired by Alice Duer Miller's "Gowns by Roberta"). Vincent Minelli staged the fashion show, with gowns by Adrian (watch for cop-beater Zsa Zsa as a model). ♫Opening Night; Smoke Gets in Your Eyes; Lovely to Look At; The Touch of Your Hand; Yesterdays; I Won't Dance; You're Devastating; The Most Exciting Night; I'll Be Hard to Handle. **105m/C VHS.** Kathryn Grayson, Red Skelton, Howard Keel, Gower Champion, Marge Champion, Ann Miller, Zsa Zsa Gabor, Kurt Kasznar, Marcel Dalio, Diane Cassidy; ***D:*** Mervyn LeRoy; ***C:*** George J. Folsey.

The Lover *L'Amant* **1992 (R)** Portrays the sexual awakening of a French teenager and her older Chinese lover in Indochina in 1929. The characters, who remain nameless, meet on a ferry where the man is smitten by the girl's beauty. Detached, determined, and unromantic (the opposite of her indolent lover), she allows herself to be seduced for the experience, and money, he offers. The film is equally detached, including the beautifully photographed but uninvolving sex scenes. Moreau narrates as an adult looking back on her life. March's debut; filmed on location in Vietnam. Based on the semi-autobiographical novel by Marguerite Duras who repudiated director Annaud's film when it was released in France. Also available in an unrated, letterbox version at 115 minutes. **103m/C VHS, DVD.** *FR* Jeanne March, Tony Leung Ka-Fai, Frederique Meininger, Arnaud Giovanietti, Melvil Poupaud, Lisa Faulkner, Xiem Mang; ***D:*** Jean-Jacques Annaud; ***W:*** Gerard Brach, Jean-Jacques Annaud; ***C:*** Robert Fraisse; ***M:*** Gabriel Yared; ***Nar:*** Jeanne Moreau. Cesar '93: Score.

Lover Come Back 1/2 **1961** More Day-Hudson antics in which an advertising executive falls in love with his competitor but that doesn't stop him from stealing her clients. Is there no shame? **107m/C VHS, DVD.** Rock Hudson, Doris Day, Tony Randall, Edie Adams, Joe Flynn, Ann B. Davis, Jack Oakie, Jack Albertson, Jack Kruschen, Howard St. John; ***D:*** Delbert Mann.

Lover Girl **1997 (R)** When teenager Jake Ferrari (Subkoff) is abandoned by her mother, she decides to track down long-gone sister, Darlene (Swanson). But when Darlene doesn't want her either, Jake is at a loss until she's reluctantly befriended by Marci (Bernhard), manager of a massage parlor. Underage Jake even badgers tough Marci into giving her a job, although the film is skittish about just how far Jake goes with her clients. Still, given the sleazy and potentially exploitative premise, the film is surprizing cheerful and light. **87m/C VHS.** Tara Subkoff, Sandra Bernhard, Kristy Swanson, Loretta Devine, Renee Humphrey, Susan Barnes, Sahara Lotti, Tim Griffin; ***D:*** Lisa Addario, Joe Syracuse; ***W:*** Lisa Addario, Joe Syracuse; ***C:*** Dean Lent; ***M:*** Mark Killian.

Loverboy **1989 (PG-13)** A college schnook takes a summer job as a Beverly Hills pizza delivery boy and is preyed upon by many rich and sex-hungry housewives. **105m/C VHS, DVD.** Patrick Dempsey, Kate Jackson, Barbara Carrera, Kirstie Alley, Carrie Fisher, Robert Ginty, Elizabeth (E.G. Dailey) Daily; ***D:*** Joan Micklin Silver; ***W:*** Tom Ropelewski, Leslie Dixon; ***M:*** Michel Colombier.

Loverboy **2005 (R)** Obsessive mom love. Bacon directs wife Sedgwick in this adaptation of Victoria Redel's novel. Young Emily (played by daughter Sosie Bacon) always felt like an outsider because her parents (Tomei, Bacon) were so wrapped up in each other. So when she's an adult, Emily ruthlessly decides to become a single mom and give son Paul all the love she missed out on. But Emily freaks out at the slightest hint of independence from the growing Paul (Kay), who she still insists on calling "Loverboy." Really creepy pic is spent waiting for Emily to go completely off the rails. **86m/C DVD.** *US* Kyra Sedgwick, Kevin Bacon, Blair Brown, Matt Dillon, Oliver Platt, Campbell Scott, Marisa Tomei, John Lafayette, Dominic Scott, Sosie Bacon, Jessica Stone, Melissa Errico, Nancy Giles, Sandra Bullock; ***D:*** Kevin Bacon; ***W:*** Hannah Shakespeare; ***C:*** Nancy Schreiber; ***M:*** Michael Bacon.

The Lovers **1959** Chic tale of French adultery with Moreau starring as a provincial wife whose shallow life changes overnight when she meets a young man. Had a controversial American debut because of the film's tender eroticism and innocent view of adultery. In French with English subtitles. **90m/B VHS.** *FR* Jeanne Moreau, Alain Cuny, Jose-Luis De Villalonga, Jean-Mark Bory; ***D:*** Louis Malle; ***W:*** Louis Malle. Venice Film Fest. '59: Special Jury Prize.

Lovers: A True Story *Amantes* **1990 (R)** Erotic love triangle in 1950s Madrid, while Spain is under the suffocating dictatorship of Franco. Naive, young Paco has a virginal, hardworking fiancee named Trini. Things would seem to be headed for an average life until Paco rents a room from young widow Luisa and they embark on a sexual affair bordering on obsession. When Trini discovers what's going on she turns out to have a more passionate, and violent, nature than even Paco could imagine. Steamy and highly dramatic with excellent performances. Based on a true story. In Spanish with English subtitles. An unrated version is also available. **105m/C VHS.** *SP* Victoria Abril, Jorge Sanz, Maribel Verdu; ***D:*** Vicente Aranda; ***W:*** Vicente Aranda, Alvaro del Amo; ***C:*** Jose Luis Alcaine; ***M:*** Jose Nieto. Berlin Intl. Film Fest. '91: Actress (Abril).

Lovers and Liars *Travels with Anita; A Trip with Anita* **1981 (R)** A romantic adventure in Rome turns into a symphony of zany mishaps when the man forgets to tell the woman that he is married!! **93m/C VHS, DVD.** *IT* Goldie Hawn, Giancarlo Giannini, Laura Betti; ***D:*** Mario Monicelli; ***W:*** Mario Monicelli, Paul Zimmerman; ***C:*** Tonino Delli Colli; ***M:*** Ennio Morricone.

Lovers and Other Strangers **1970 (R)** Two young people decide to marry after living together for a year and a half. Various tensions surface between them and among their families as the wedding day approaches. Good comedy features some charming performances. Keaton's first film. ♫ For All We Know. **106m/C VHS, DVD.** Gig Young, Bea Arthur, Bonnie Bedelia, Anne Jackson, Harry Guardino, Michael Brandon, Richard S. Castellano, Bob (Robert) Dishy, Marian Hailey, Cloris Leachman, Anne Meara, Diane Keaton; ***D:*** Cy Howard; ***W:*** Renee Taylor, Joseph Bologna, David Zelag Goodman. Oscars '70: Song ("For All We Know").

Lover's Knot 1/2 **1996 (R)** Cutesy romantic comedy has Curry as an angel whose heavenly mission is to get the proper romantic couples together. His current pair are poetic college English prof Steve (Campbell) and practical pediatrician Megan (Grey). Steve's imaginative courtship wins Megan but day-to-day living takes its toll and the duo separate, leaving their angelic guide to get them back together. **82m/C VHS.** Billy Campbell, Jennifer Grey, Tim Curry, Adam Baldwin; ***Cameos:*** Adam Ant, Anne Francis; ***D:*** Peter Shaner; ***W:*** Peter Shaner; ***C:*** Garett Griffin; ***M:*** Laura Karpman.

Lovers Like Us 1/2 *Le Sauvage; The Savage* **1975** Two people each leave their spouses, meet one another, and fall in love. **103m/C VHS.** *FR* Catherine Deneuve, Yves Montand, Luigi Vannucchi, Tony Roberts, Dana Wynter; ***D:*** Jean-Paul Rappeneau; ***W:*** Jean-Paul Rappeneau.

Lovers' Lovers 1/2 **1994** All sorts of bizarre and erotic adventures ensue when Blaire the jilted narcissist meets Michael, who doesn't want to commit to girlfriend Teri. Michael plans an affair with Blaire without realizing that Teri is already having a fling with Ray, Blaire's ex. Some funny situations but too many talky scenes stop the film cold. **90m/C VHS.** Serge Rodnunsky, Jennifer Ciesar, Cindy Parker, Ray Bennett; ***D:*** Serge Rodnunsky; ***W:*** Serge Rodnunsky; ***M:*** Pierre Rodnunsky.

Lovers of the Arctic Circle *Los Amantes del Circulo Polar* **1998 (R)** Complex romantic drama set in Spain and Finland. Otto and Ana meet as children and instantly recognized each other as soul mates—their first kiss occuring over a geography book describing the Arctic Circle. When Otto's divorced father takes up with Ana's widowed mother, the now-adolescent pair wind up sharing the same house, and secretly become lovers. When Otto's mother dies, he blames himself for abandoning her and leaves Ana to become a pilot. She, in turn, becomes obsessed with being where the Arctic sun never sets, and fate, eventually, brings the adult duo together in Finland. Spanish with subtitles. **112m/C VHS.** *SP* Fele Martinez, Najwa Nimri, Nancho Novo, Maru Valdivielso, Beate Jensen; ***D:*** Julio Medem; ***W:*** Julio Medem; ***C:*** Gonzalo F. Berridi; ***M:*** Alberto Iglesias.

Lovers of Their Time **1985** A romantic novel on tape, about forbidden love and other problems. **60m/C** Edward Petherbridge, Cheryl Prime, Lynn Farleigh; ***D:*** Robert Knights.

The Lovers on the Bridge *Les Amants du Pont-Neuf* **1991 (R)** Overblown, extravagent romantic drama about two homeless lovers who live on Paris' Pont-Neuf bridge, which is closed for repairs. Michele (Binoche) is a disoriented artist losing her eyesight to a degenerative eye disease. She has left her home and stumbles upon the bridge squatters who include Alex (Lavant), a disturbed and alcoholic street performer. Alex rescues her and becomes Michele's protector and lover. He also becomes obsessive—fearing Michele will leave him and desperate to stop her. Set in 1989, the bicentennial of the French Revolution. The Alex character also appears in the Carax films "Boy Meets Girl" (1984) and "Bad Blood" (1986). French with subtitles. **125m/C VHS, DVD.** *FR* Juliette Binoche, Denis Lavant, Klaus-Michael Gruber, Marion Stalens; ***D:*** Leos Carax; ***W:*** Leos Carax; ***C:*** Jean-Yves Escoffier.

Lover's Prayer 1/2 *All Forgotten* **1999 (PG-13)** Wealthy, innocent young man (Stahl) becomes infatuated with a mysterious young woman (Dunst) who has moved next door for the summer. Then he learns that romance isn't what he had fantasized it to be. **106m/C VHS, DVD.** Nick Stahl, Kirsten Dunst, Julie Walters, Geraldine James, Nathaniel Parker, James Fox; ***D:*** Reverge Anselmo; ***W:*** Reverge Anselmo; ***C:*** David Watkin; ***M:*** Joel McNeely.

Love's Abiding Joy 1/2 **2006 (PG)** The fourth in the series, following "Love's Long Journey." Missie (Cottrell) and Willie (Bartholomew) are struck by tragedy when their baby daughter dies and a lingering drought devastates their cattle ranch. Willie reluctantly agrees to an offer from Mayor Doros (Laughlin) to become the new sheriff to earn some extra money but finds his job involves evicting neighbors who have fallen behind on loans made by Doros, who wants to control the community. Based on the novel by Janette Oke. **87m/C DVD.** Erin Cottrell, Logan Bartholomew, John Laughlin, Dale Midkiff, Drew Tyler Bell, Mae Whitman, William Morgan Sheppard, James Tupper; ***D:*** Michael Landon Jr.; ***W:*** Michael Landon Jr., Douglas Lloyd McIntosh, Bridget Terry; ***C:*** Brian Shanley; ***M:*** Kevin Kiner.

Loves & Times of Scaramouche 1/2 *Scaramouche* **1976** Eighteenth-century rogue becomes involved in a plot to assassinate Napoleon and winds up seducing Josephine in the process. Dubbed. **92m/C VHS.** *IT* Michael Sarrazin, Ursula Andress, Aldo Maccione; ***D:*** Enzo G. Castellari.

Love's Enduring Promise 1/2 **2004** In this follow-up to "Love Comes Softly," it's 10 years later and Marty and Clark are happily married and raising their young children while the now-grown Missie (Jones) has become a teacher. She is also being courted by both the wealthy Grant (Astin) and poor but hard-working Willie (Bartholomew). But romance will have to wait when Clark has an accident and Missie must help out on the farm. From the novel by Janette Oke. **88m/C DVD.** Katherine Heigl, Dale Midkiff, January Jones, MacKenzie Astin, Logan Bartholomew, Cliff De Young; ***D:*** Michael Landon Jr.; ***W:*** Michael Landon Jr., Cindy Kelley; ***C:*** Maximo Munzi; ***M:*** Kevin Kiner. **CABLE**

Love's Labour's Lost **2000 (PG)** Branagh's latest dip into the Bard is moved into the 1930s and accompanied by the music of Cole Porter, the Gershwins, and Jerome Kern. Just as four men vow to swear off women and concentrate on their studies along comes a French princess and her three companions. Guess what happens. As with the 1996 Woody Allen film, "Everyone Says I Love You," the actors try their best to be singing/dancing fools but most just end up looking foolish. As for Shakespeare, well about two-thirds of the text is actually gone and even lesser Will shouldn't be treated like that. **93m/C VHS, DVD.** *GB* Kenneth Branagh, Alicia Silverstone, Natascha (Natasha) McElhone, Alessandro Nivola, Matthew Lillard, Nathan Lane, Timothy Spall, Geraldine McEwan, Carmen Ejogo, Adrian Lester, Emily Mortimer, Richard Briers, Stefania Rocca, Jimmy Yuill; ***D:*** Kenneth Branagh; ***W:*** Kenneth Branagh; ***C:*** Alex Thomson; ***M:*** Patrick Doyle.

Love's Long Journey 1/2 **2005** The third in the series, following "Love's Enduring Promise." Missie (Cottrell) has married Willie LaHaye (Bartholomew) and the two have left their families and community to begin a new life together on a cattle ranch. A pregnant Missie befriends their Native American neighbor Miriam (Bedard) but there's trouble when three strangers show up, looking for money that's supposedly hidden on the property. From the novel by Janette Oke. **88m/C DVD.** Irene Bedard, William Morgan Sheppard, Richard Lee Jackson, Erin Cottrell, Logan Bartholomew, James Tupper, Cindy Kelley; ***D:*** Michael Landon Jr.; ***W:*** Michael Landon Jr., Douglas Lloyd McIntosh; ***C:*** Brian Shanley; ***M:*** Kevin Kiner. **CABLE**

Loves of a Blonde 1/2 *A Blonde in Love; Lasky Jedne Plavovlasky* **1965** A shy teenage factory girl falls in love with a visiting piano player when the reservist army comes to her small town. But when she goes to visit his family, she discovers things aren't as she imagined. Touching look at the complications of love and our expectations. Czech with subtitles. **88m/B VHS, DVD.** *CZ* Hana Brejchova, Josef Sebanek, Vladimir Pucholt, Milada Jezkova; ***D:*** Milos Forman; ***W:*** Milos Forman, Vaclav Sasek, Ivan Passer, Jaroslav Papousek; ***C:*** Miroslav Ondricek; ***M:*** Evsen Illin.

The Loves of Carmen 1/2 **1948** Film version of the classic Prosper Merrimee novel about a tempestuous Spanish gypsy and the soldier who loves her. Hayworth is great to look at and the film's main selling point. **98m/C VHS, DVD.** Rita Hayworth, Glenn Ford, Ron Randell, Victor Jory, Arnold Moss, Luther Adler, Joseph Buloff; ***D:*** Charles Vidor; ***W:*** Helen Deutsch; ***C:*** William E. Snyder; ***M:*** Mario Castelnuovo-Tedesco.

The Loves of Edgar Allen Poe **1942** A bland biographical drama about young Poe's adoption, his treatment at the hands of his foster father, his rejection by a woman for a more well-off man, his marriage to his first cousin, and his early death from alcoholism. **67m/B VHS.** Linda Darnell, Shepperd Strudwick, Virginia Gilmore, Jane Darwell, Mary Howard; ***D:*** Harry Lachman.

The Loves of Hercules WOOF! *Hercules and the Hydra; Hercules vs. the Hydra; Gli Amori di Ercole* **1960** The mythic mesomorph finds a mate with equiponderant chest measurements, and must save her from an evil queen. Somehow it eludes him that both queen and maiden are Miss Jayne in red and black wigs. Kudos for worst dubbing and special effects; a must see for connoisseurs of kitsch. **94m/C VHS, DVD.** *IT FR* Jayne Mansfield, Mickey Hargitay; ***D:*** Carlo L. Bragaglia; ***W:*** Alessandro Continenza.

Love's Savage Fury WOOF! **1979** Two escapees from a Union prison camp seek out a hidden treasure that could determine the outcome of the Civil War. Bad ripoff of "Gone with the Wind." **100m/C VHS.** Jennifer O'Neill, Perry King, Robert Reed, Raymond Burr, Connie Stevens, Ed Lauter; ***D:*** Joseph Hardy; ***M:*** John Addison. **TV**

Love's Unending Legacy 1/2 **2007** The fifth film in author Janette Oke's bestselling series. After Willie LeHaye's death, Missie (Cottrell) returns to her father's (Midkiff) ranch and eventually adopts a troubled teenaged girl. As Missie becomes romantically interested in town sheriff Zach Tyler (Browne), she discovers that her new daughter's brother is being mistreated by the family who adopted him. **84m/C DVD.** Erin Cottrell, Dale Midkiff, Victor Browne, Samantha Smith, Holliston Coleman, Brett Coker, Hank Stratton, Braeden Lemasters; ***D:*** Mark Griffiths; ***W:*** Pamela Wallace; ***C:*** Brian Stanley; ***M:*** Kevin Kiner. **CABLE**

Love's Unfolding Dream 1/2 **2007** Belinda Tyler (Taylor-Compton), Missie's (Cottrell) adopted daughter, is determined to become a doctor—not something done by a woman in the 19th-century. But she proves her worth to Dr. Jackson (Pine) and he grudgingly agrees to help her. Then young lawyer Drew Simpson (Levis) comes to town to sell the farm he's inherited. As soon as that's done, he intends to return to New York—until he meets Belinda, that is. But she has her dream and Drew expects a traditional marriage. Based on the sixth novel in the series by Janette Oke. **88m/C DVD.** Scout Taylor-Compton, Patrick Levis, Erin Cottrell, Victor Browne, Dale Midkiff, Robert Pine, Samantha Smith; ***D:*** Harry Frost; ***W:*** Michael Landon Jr., Cindy Kelley; ***C:*** Brian Shanley; ***M:*** Stephen Graziano. **CABLE**

Lovesick **1983 (PG)** A very-married New York psychiatrist goes against his own best judgment when he falls in love with one of his patients. **98m/C VHS, DVD.** Dudley Moore, Elizabeth McGovern, Alec Guinness, John Huston, Ron Silver; ***D:*** Marshall Brickman; ***W:*** Marshall Brickman; ***C:*** Gerry Fisher; ***M:*** Philippe Sarde.

Lovespell *Tristan and Isolde* **1979** A retelling of the legend of Isolde and Tristan. Stilted direction and writing, but another chance to reminisce on Richard Burton.

91m/C VHS, DVD. Richard Burton, Kate Mulgrew, Nicholas Clay, Cyril Cusack, Geraldine Fitzgerald, Niall Toibin, Diana Van Der Vlis, Niall O'Brien; *D:* Tom Donovan.

Lovey: A Circle of Children 2 **1982** Teacher for special children takes in a terrified girl diagnosed as brain damaged or schizophrenic, and discovers love and intelligence in the girl as well as finding some important insights into her own life. **120m/C VHS.** Jane Alexander, Kris McKeon, Karen Allen; *D:* Jud Taylor.

Loving **1970 (R)** Nondescript dramedy has Segal as a commercial artist whose midlife crisis comes to a head when his wife, mistress, and neighborhood witness his drunken tryst with a neighbor's wife via closed-circuit TV. Saint is very good as the wronged wife, but the whole thing is much duller than it should be. **89m/C DVD.** George Segal, Eva Marie Saint, Sterling Hayden, Keenan Wynn, David Doyle, Paul Sparer, Andrew Duncan, Roland Winters, Edgar Stehli, Diana Douglas, Roy Scheider, Sab Shimono, Janis Young, Nancie Phillips, Sherry Lansing; *D:* Irvin Kershner; *W:* Don Devlin; *C:* Gordon Willis; *M:* Bernardo Segall.

Loving 1/2 **1984** The full-length, shot-on-video pilot for the daytime TV soap opera, with various guest stars. Exteriors shot at C.W. Post Center on Long Island. **120m/C VHS.** Lloyd Bridges, Geraldine Page. **TV**

Loving Annabelle **2006** Senator's daughter Annabelle (Kelly) attends St. Theresa's, a strict Catholic boarding school where her rebelliousness gives the Mother Superior (Graff) fits. So she instructs Annabelle's favorite teacher, Simone Bradley (Gaidry), to help the girl cope. But what teacher and student soon realize is that there's a romantic attraction between them, which Annabelle is determined to pursue. A modern update of the 1931 German film "Maedchen in Uniform." **79m/C DVD.** Ilene Graff, Kevin McCarthy, Michelle Horn, Marla Maples, Diane Gaidry, Erin Kelly, Wendy Schaal; *D:* Katherine Brooks; *W:* Katherine Brooks; *C:* Cynthia Pusheck.

Loving Couples **1980 (PG)** Two happily married couples meet at a weekend resort...and switch partners. Tired and predictable but it has its moments. **120m/C VHS, DVD.** Shirley MacLaine, James Coburn, Susan Sarandon, Stephen Collins, Sally Kellerman; *D:* Jack Smight.

Loving Evangeline 1/2 **1998** Robert (Mancuso) is convinced that the boating mishap that killed his brother was no accident. And his suspicions are echoed by marina owner Evie Shaw (Rowan). From the Harlequin Romance Series; adapted from the Lisa Howard novel. **95m/C DVD.** *CA* Nick Mancuso, Kelly Rowan, Shari Belafonte, Winston Rekert, Eugene Robert Glazer; *D:* Timothy Bond; *W:* Charles Lazar; *C:* Peter Benison; *M:* Ian Thomas. **TV**

A Loving Father 1/2 *Aime Ton Pere; Honor They Father* **2002** After famed French writer Leo Shepherd wins the Nobel Prize for Literature, he decides to ride his motorcycle to the Stockholm ceremony. His estranged son Paul has been trying to contact him and decides to follow, causing a freak accident that has the police thinking Leo is dead. Instead, Paul has kidnapped Leo and is forcing him to confront the problems of their past. Writer/director Berger used his own relationship with his father, writer John Berger, as the basis for this odd concoction, but pere and fils Depardieu, renowned for their own familial battles, must have found circumstances hitting very close to home. French with subtitles. **100m/C DVD.** *FR* Gerard Depardieu, Guillaume Depardieu, Sylvie Testud, Julien Boisselier; *D:* Jacob Berger; *W:* Jacob Berger, Edward A. Radtke, Pascal Bavollier; *C:* Pascal Martin; *M:* Jean-Claude Petit.

Loving Jezebel **1999 (R)** If anything, writer/director Kwyn Bader's "Loving Jezebel" proves that Hill Harper ("The Skulls," "In Too Deep," etc.) is a terrific talent. The problem is, even at a mere 88 minutes, Bader's film seems long and even Harper can't act his way out of a weak and contrived script. The gist of the story is that he, Hill Harper, has a track record for falling in love with his friends' and other men's girlfriends—the theme of many a sit-com—with consistently bad results. Of course you have to give Harper credit for one thing, he has excellent taste in women as all of his "girlfriends" are "eye-candy" super models. **88m/C DVD.** Hill Harper, Laurel Holloman, Nicole Ari Parker, Sandrine Holt, David Moscow, Elisa Donovan, Phylicia Rashad; *D:* Kwyn Bader; *W:* Kwyn Bader; *C:* Horacio Marquinez; *M:* Tony Prendatt.

Loving Leah 1/2 **2009** A gently sentimental and romantic Hallmark Hall of Fame production. According to a tenet of Orthodox Judaism, a man should marry his brother's childless widow to carry on the brother's name. Secular cardiologist Jake Lever (Kaufman) was estranged from his rabbi brother but he still feels obligated to his pretty widow Leah (Ambrose). He impulsively agrees to a marriage of convenience and invites Leah to move to his home in D.C., which allows her to pursue her college dreams. But the changes from Brooklyn nearly overwhelm Leah and Jake is having trouble coping with his new situation as well. Goldstein adapted from her play. **90m/C DVD.** Lauren Ambrose, Adam Kaufman, Susie Essman, Mercedes Ruehl, Harris Yulin, Natasha Lyonne, Ricki Lake; *D:* Jeff Bleckner; *W:* P'nenah Goldstein; *C:* Charles Minsky; *M:* Jeff Beal. **TV**

Loving You **1957** A small town boy with a musical style all his own becomes a big success thanks to the help of a female press agent. Features many early Elvis hits. ♫ Loving You; Teddy Bear; Lonesome Cowboy; Got a Lot of Livin' To Do; Party; Mean Woman Blues; Hot Dog. **101m/C VHS, DVD.** Elvis Presley, Wendell Corey, Lizabeth Scott, Dolores Hart, James Gleason, Paul Smith, Jana Lund, Grace Hayle; *D:* Hal Kanter; *W:* Hal Kanter; *C:* Charles B(ryant) Lang Jr.; *M:* Walter Scharf.

The Low Down **2000** Not much happens in this sketchy tale of London gameshow worker Frank (Gillen), who dreams of maybe becoming a sculptor while running the prop business with his less-than-eager roommates. Tiring of their layabout ways, he moves out, facilitating his hook-up with Ruby (Ashfield), the real estate agent. Film then follows, but not too closely or attentively, their budding romance and his passive-agressiveness and growing dissatisfaction with his own life. Thraves's directorial debut is laid-back to the point of being comatose, but some interesting scenes do occur between Gillen and Ashfield. **96m/C VHS.** *GB* Aidan Gillen, Kate Ashfield, Dean Lennox Kelly, Tobias Menzies, Rupert Proctor, Samantha Powers; *D:* Jamie Thraves; *W:* Jamie Thraves; *C:* Igor Jadue-Lillo; *M:* Nick Currie, Fred Thomas.

A Low Down Dirty Shame **1994 (R)** Shame (Wayans) is a down-on-his-luck private eye, with the obligatory wisecracking secretary, Peaches (Pinkett), who's hired by an old friend to find a vicious drug lord, a sultry ex-girlfriend, and $20 million. Lots of fun stunts and one liners can't make up for major plot holes. **100m/C VHS, DVD.** Keenen Ivory Wayans, Jada Pinkett Smith, Salli Richardson, Charles S. Dutton, Andrew Divoff, Corwin Hawkins; *D:* Keenen Ivory Wayans; *W:* Keenen Ivory Wayans.

The Low Life 1/2 **1995 (R)** A "day in the life" sort of story about aspiring writer John (Cochrane) who comes to L.A. with high hopes but instead gets stuck in the low life of awful temp jobs, a lousy landlord (LeGros), and now, his newly arrived loser cousin Andrew (Astin). He tries to cozy up to looker Sedgwick but she doesn't seem too interested—so what's a would-be cool guy to do? **96m/C VHS, DVD.** Rory Cochrane, Kyra Sedgwick, Sean Astin, James LeGros, Christian Meoli, Shawnee Smith, J.T. Walsh, Renee Zellweger; *D:* George Hickenlooper; *W:* George Hickenlooper, John Enbom; *C:* Richard Crudo; *M:* Bill Boll.

The Lower Depths 1/2 *Les Bas Fonds; Underground* **1936** Renoir's adaptation of the Maxim Gorky play about a thief and a financially ruined baron learning about life from one another. In French with English subtitles. **92m/B VHS, DVD.** *FR* Jean Gabin, Louis Jouvet, Vladimir Sokoloff, Robert Le Vigan, Suzy Prim; *D:* Jean Renoir; *W:* Jean Renoir, Charles Spaak; *C:* Jean Bachelet; *M:* Jean Wiener.

The Lower Depths 1/2 *Donzoko* **1957** Kurosawa sets the Maxim Gorky play in Edo during the final Tokugawa period, using Noh theatre elements in depicting the lowly denizens of a low-rent hovel. In Japanese with English subtitles. **125m/B VHS, DVD.** *JP* Toshiro Mifune, Isuzu Yamada, Ganjiro Nakamura, Kyoko Kagawa, Bokuzen Hidari; *D:* Akira Kurosawa; *W:* Akira Kurosawa, Hideo Oguni; *C:* Kazuo Yamazaki; *M:* Masaru Sato.

Lower Learning 1/2 **2008 (R)** The Geraldine Ferraro Elementary School will be closed unless hapless vice-principal Tom (Biggs) can convince district inspector Rebecca (Longoria Parker) to help him rally the lazy teachers, expose Principal Billings' (Corddry) corruption, and get those test scores up! **97m/C DVD.** Jason Biggs, Eva Longoria, Rob Corddry, Ryan Newman, Monica Potter, Will Sasso; *D:* Mark Lafferty; *W:* Mark Lafferty; *C:* David Robert Jones; *M:* Ryan Shore. **VIDEO**

Lower Level **1991 (R)** While working late, an attractive business woman becomes trapped in an office building by her psychotic secret admirer. **88m/C VHS, DVD.** David Bradley, Elizabeth (Ward) Gracen, Jeff Yagher; *D:* Kristine Peterson; *W:* Joel Soisson; *C:* Wally Pfister; *M:* Terry Plumeri.

Loyalties 1/2 **1986 (R)** A strong treatment of the issue of sexual abuse of girls by men, and of an upper-class woman's willingness to establish a true friendship with a woman of a so-called lower economic class. **98m/C VHS.** *CA* Kenneth Welsh, Tantoo Cardinal, Susan Wooldridge, Vera Martin, Christopher Barrington-Leigh; *D:* Anne Wheeler; *W:* Sharon Riis; *M:* Michael Conway Baker.

Loyola, the Soldier Saint **1952** A biography of the founder of the Jesuits from his years as a page in the Spanish court to his daring exploits on the battle field and, finally, his spiritual awakening at the University of Paris. Narrated by Father Alfred J. Barrett. **93m/B VHS.** Rafael Duran, Maria Rosa Jiminez; *D:* Jose Diaz Morales.

Lucas **1986 (PG-13)** A high school brain falls in love with the new girl in town, and tries to win her by trying out for the football team. Genuine film about the perils of coming of age. Thoughtful, non-condescending, and humorous. **100m/C VHS, DVD.** Corey Haim, Kerri Green, Charlie Sheen, Winona Ryder, Courtney Thorne-Smith, Tom (Thomas E.) Hodges; *D:* David Seltzer; *W:* David Seltzer; *M:* Dave Grusin.

Lucia, Lucia *La Hija del Canibal; The Cannibal's Daughter* **2003 (R)** Middle-aged Lucia (Roth) is the unreliable narrator of this Mexican fable. Lucia's husband, Ramon (Moreno), dispppears in the Mexico City airport. Since their marriage was unhappy, maybe he decided to abandon her, or maybe Ramon was kidnapped. Since the police are no help, Lucia turns to two neighbors for assistance—Felix (Alvarez-Novoa), an elderly Spanish Civil War veteran, and young and handsome Adrian (Becker). There's a botched ransom drop and Ramon's exposure as an embezzler and Lucia's tryst with Adrian and many, many red herrings. Maybe Lucia is just spinning one big tale (she turns out to be a writer). And maybe it just doesn't matter. Adapted from the novel "La Hija del Canibal" by Rosa Montero. Spanish with subtitles. **113m/C VHS, DVD.** *MX SP* Cecilia (Celia) Roth, Carlos Alvarez-Novoa, Kuno Becker, Jose Elias Moreno Jr., Margarita Isabel, Javier Diaz Duenas, Hector Ortega; *D:* Antonio Serrano; *W:* Antonio Serrano; *C:* Xavier Perez Grobet; *M:* Nacho Mastretta.

Lucie Aubrac **1998 (R)** In 1943, having freed her Resistance fighter husband, Raymond Samuel (Auteuil), from the Vichy police, Lucie Aubrac (Bouquet), is not about to let the Germans execute him. Even if it means using her pregnancy and tricking Gestapo commander Klaus Barbie (Ferch). Noble but rather emotionless. Based on a true story and Aubrac's novel "Ils Partiront Dans l'Ivresse." French with subtitles. **116m/C VHS.** *FR* Daniel Auteuil, Carole Bouquet, Patrice Chereau, Heino Ferch, Jean-Roger Milo, Jean Martin, Bernard Verley, Andrzej Seweryn, Hubert Saint Macary, Eric Boucher, Gregoire Oestermann; *D:* Claude Berri; *W:* Claude Berri; *C:* Vincenzo Marano; *M:* Philippe Sarde.

The Lucifer Complex **1978** Nazi doctors are cloning exact duplicates of such world leaders as the Pope and the President of the United States on a remote South American island in the year 1996. **91m/C VHS, DVD.** Robert Vaughn, Merrie Lynn Ross, Keenan Wynn, Aldo Ray; *D:* David L. Hewitt, Kenneth Hartford.

Luck of the Draw **2000 (R)** Ex-con Marshall, who finds going straight to be very dull, finds some unexpected excitement when a couple of counterfeit printing plates come into his possession. He soon realizes that a lot of unsavory types are after the plates, including mob boss Hopper. Run-of-the-mill. **108m/C VHS, DVD.** James Marshall, Michael Madsen, Ice-T, Frank Gorshin, Eric Roberts, Dennis Hopper, Wendy Benson, William Forsythe, Sasha Mitchell, Richard Ruccolo; *D:* Luca Bercovici; *W:* Namon Ami, Rick Bloggs, Kandice King; *C:* Keith L. Smith; *M:* Stephen (Steve) Edwards. **VIDEO**

The Luck of the Irish 1/2 **1948** A comedy that forgoes being twee and twinkly despite the presence of a leprechaun. Hard-boiled reporter Stephen Fitzgerald (Power) takes a trip to Ireland and gets stuck at a rural inn when his car breaks down. Owner Nora (Baxter) tells him local legends about leprechauns and their pot o' gold and when he spots a strange man (Kellaway), he follows him and jokingly demands his treasure. Stephen's so surprised when the gold actually appears that he refuses it, so the leprechaun then owes Stephen a favor. When he returns to New York, Stephen takes a speech writing job with right-wing publisher Auger (Cobb) who's going into politics. An apartment and a valet come with the deal and Stephen's shocked when Horace the valet looks exactly like his leprechaun. **99m/B DVD.** Tyrone Power, Anne Baxter, Cecil Kellaway, Lee J. Cobb, Jayne Meadows, James Todd; *D:* Henry Koster; *W:* Philip Dunne; *C:* Joseph LaShelle; *M:* Cyril Mockridge.

Lucky Break **2001 (PG-13)** Small-time crooks Jimmy (Nesbitt) and Rudy (James) wind up in the same prison after a bank job gone wrong. Eccentric prison governor Mortimer (Plummer) loves musicals and has written one of his own. Jimmy encourages Mortimer to let the prisoners stage his opus and plans an escape attempt during the performance. Film gets schzoid with comic rehearsals, a tentative romance between Jimmy and support worker Annabel (Williams), a suicide, and the confusing prison break. **109m/C VHS, DVD.** *GB* James Nesbitt, Lennie James, Christopher Plummer, Olivia Williams, Timothy Spall, Bill Nighy, Ron Cook, Frank Harper, Peter Wight, Celia Imrie, Raymond Waring, Julian Barratt; *D:* Peter Cattaneo; *W:* Ronan Bennett; *C:* Alwin Kuchler; *M:* Anne Dudley.

Lucky Cisco Kid 1/2 **1940** Romero takes over from Warner Baxter in the fourth entry in the series, with Martin as his loyal sidekick. This time a rustler and his gang are stealing cattle and using the Kid's name to place the blame. Fast-paced with Romero appropriately debonair. Andrews screen debut. **67m/B VHS.** Cesar Romero, Chris-Pin (Ethier Crispin Martini) Martin, Mary Beth Hughes, Dana Andrews, Evelyn Venable, Joseph (Joe) Sawyer, Francis Ford; *D:* H. Bruce Humberstone; *W:* Robert Ellis, Helen Logan; *C:* Lucien N. Andriot; *M:* Cyril Mockridge.

Lucky Devil 1/2 **1925** Lucky devil wins car and motors around the country to the tune of organ music. **63m/B VHS.** Richard Dix, Esther Ralston, Edna May Oliver, Tom Findley; *D:* Frank Tuttle.

Lucky Devils 1/2 **1933** A group of Hollywood stuntmen call themselves the "Lucky Devils" and live by the motto "a stuntman makes a bad husband and a husband makes a bad stuntman." This proves to be true when Slugger Jones (Bakewell) dies on a stunt shortly after his marriage. When Skipper (Boyd) marries an extra he quickly loses his edge but tries again to pull off one last stunt when he needs the money to cover his wife's hospital bill. **64m/B VHS.** William Boyd, Dorothy Wilson, William Gargan, Roscoe Ates, William "Billy" Bakewell; *D:* Ralph Ince; *W:* Agnes Christine Johnston, Ben Markson. **VIDEO**

Lucky Jim 1/2 **1958** A junior lecturer in history at a small university tries to get himself in good graces with the head of his department, but is doomed from the start by doing the wrong things at the worst possible times. Minus the social satire of the Kingsley Amis novel on which it was based; what's left is a cheerful comedy. **91m/B VHS.** *GB* Ian Carmichael, Terry-Thomas, Hugh Griffith, Sharon Acker, Jean Anderson, Maureen Connell, Clive Morton, John Welsh, Reginald Beckwith, Kenneth Griffith, Jeremy Hawk, Harry Fowler; ***D:*** John Boulting, Roy Boulting; ***W:*** Jeffrey Dell, Patrick Campbell; ***C:*** Mutz Greenbaum; ***M:*** John Addison.

Lucky Luciano *A Proposito Luciano; RE: Lucky Luciano* **1974 (R)** A violent depiction of the final years of Lucky Luciano, gangster kingpin. **108m/C VHS, DVD.** *IT FR* Edmond O'Brien, Rod Steiger, Vincent Gardenia, Gian Marie Volonte; ***D:*** Francesco Rosi; ***C:*** Pasqualino De Santis.

Lucky Luke 1/2 **1994 (PG)** Fastest gun in the west brings the law to Daisy Town, aided by his horse, Jolly Jumper—who can talk. Not exactly John Wayne material but amusing. **91m/C VHS, DVD.** Terence Hill, Nancy Morgan, Ron Carey; ***D:*** Terence Hill; ***W:*** Rene Goscinny; ***C:*** Carlo Tafani, Gianfranco Transunto; ***M:*** David Grover, Aaron Schroeder; ***V:*** Roger Miller.

Lucky Me **1954** A group of theatre entertainers are stranded in Miami and are forced to work in a hotel kitchen. They soon acquire the support of a wealthy oilman (Goodwin) who invests in their show, but not before his spoiled daughter tries to thwart all plans. ♫Lucky Me; Superstition Song; I Speak to the Stars; Take a Memo to the Moon; Love You Dearly; Bluebells of Broadway; Parisian Pretties; Wanna Sing Like an Angel; High Hopes. **100m/C VHS, DVD.** Doris Day, Robert Cummings, Phil Silvers, Eddie Foy Jr., Nancy Walker, Martha Hyer, Bill Goodwin, Marcel Dalio, James Burke, Jack Shea, William "Billy" Bakewell, Charles Cane, Ray Teal, Tom Powers, Angie Dickinson, Dolores Dorn; ***D:*** Jack Donohue.

Lucky Number Slevin **2006 (R)** This too-twisty thriller owes a lot to "Pulp Fiction" and "The Usual Suspects," although it doesn't come close to their league. What it does have is the wicked gravitas of Freeman and Kingsley as rival New York mobsters (known respectively as "The Boss" and "The Rabbi") who both mistake sweet-faced Slevin (Hartnett) for his missing friend Nick, who owes big money to both men. The Boss will forgive the debt if Slevin will kill someone for him, while the Rabbi just wants the cash. Meanwhile, sexy neighbor Lindsey (Liu), who's a coroner, is romancing the hunk and trying to help him avoid certain death—maybe at the hands of hitman Mr. Goodkat (Willis). Except, nothing is really as it appears to be. **110m/C DVD, HD DVD.** *US* Josh Hartnett, Morgan Freeman, Ben Kingsley, Lucy Liu, Stanley Tucci, Bruce Willis, Peter Outerbridge, Mykelti Williamson, Danny Aiello, Robert Forster, Dorian Missick, Jennifer Miller, Kevin Chamberlin, Oliver Davis, Michael Rubenfeld; ***D:*** Paul McGuigan; ***W:*** Jason Smilovic; ***C:*** Peter Sova; ***M:*** J. Ralph.

Lucky Numbers 1/2 **2000 (R)** Here's a lucky number for you: Zero. That's the amount of time you should spend on this unfortunate comedy. TV weatherman Russ (Travolta) is caught up in a lavish lifestyle he can't afford because unseasonably warm weather is ruining his on-the-side snowmobile business. He schemes with the station's morally lax lotto ball girl Crystal (Kudrow) to fix a jackpot lottery, with her oafish cousin Walter (Moore) as the front man with the ticket. Their plan slips out, so they're hounded by a host of greedy dimwits hoping to get in on the action. Resnick, who hails from Harrisburg PA, where the movie is set, apparently has no qualms painting his fellow townspeople as amoral losers. Loosely based on a 1980 attempt to fix the Pennsylvania State Lottery. **105m/C VHS, DVD.** John Travolta, Lisa Kudrow, Tim Roth, Ed O'Neill, Michael Rapaport, Daryl (Chill) Mitchell, Bill Pullman, Richard Schiff, Michael Moore, Michael Weston, Sam McMurray; ***D:*** Nora Ephron; ***W:*** Adam Resnick; ***C:*** John Lindley; ***M:*** George Fenton.

The Lucky Ones **2008 (R)** Collee (McAdams), T.K. (Pena), and Cheever (Robbins) are three Iraq War vets who find their homecomings delayed when their flights out of a NYC airport are cancelled. So they road-trip it across the country, meeting a bevy of fellow-citizen stereotypes along the way, all with strong opinions, good and bad, about the war and vets. Stacked with too many trite coincidences and too much melodrama, but the performances of the three leads salvage an otherwise sappy road trip. Tries to be too many things and ends up being nothing special. **115m/C DVD.** *US* Rachel McAdams, Tim Robbins, Michael Pena, Molly Hagan, Mark L. Young, Annie Corley, John Diehl, John Heard; ***D:*** Neil Burger; ***W:*** Neil Burger, Dirk Wittenborn; ***C:*** Declan Quinn; ***M:*** Rolfe Kent.

Lucky Partners **1940** When an artist and an errand girl share a winning lottery ticket, funny complications arise as they embark on a fantasy honeymoon. Although Rogers' innocence and Coleman's savoir faire provide an interesting contrast, the script isn't equal to the status of its stars. **101m/B VHS.** Ronald Colman, Ginger Rogers, Jack Carson, Spring Byington, Harry Davenport, Cecilia Loftus; ***D:*** Lewis Milestone; ***W:*** Lewis Milestone, Allan Scott, John Van Druten; ***C:*** Robert De Grasse; ***M:*** Dimitri Tiomkin.

Lucky Seven 1/2 **2003 (PG-13)** Amy's dying mother (O'Grady) informs her seven-year-old daughter that she has drawn a timeline for her life, including the fact that Amy will marry her seventh boyfriend. Amy (Williams) has always followed her mother's advice, but the successful lawyer now has a problem—she's fallen for boyfriend #6, Peter (Dempsey). So should she follow her heart or wait for #7, who's the equally handsome and charming Daniel (Rowe). Amusing romantic comedy with a very attractive cast. **90m/C VHS, DVD.** Kimberly Williams, Patrick Dempsey, Brad Rowe, Gail O'Grady; ***D:*** Harry Winer; ***W:*** Jessica Barondes; ***C:*** Jon Joffin; ***M:*** Danny Lux. **CABLE**

Lucky Star **1929** Poverty-stricken Mary (Gaynor) lives in a shack with her widowed mother (Reicher), who wants her daughter to marry Martin (Williams), an ex-soldier with good prospects. However, Mary's already in love with Timothy (Farrell), who's been looking out for her, but he's crippled from war wounds and is doing menial work so he doesn't fit in with her mother's plans. Miraculously, Timothy regains his strength before the wedding and fights his rival for the girl. **85m/B DVD.** Janet Gaynor, Charles Farrell, Guinn "Big Boy" Williams, Paul Fix, Hedwig Reicher; ***D:*** Frank Borzage; ***W:*** Sonya Levien, John Hunter Booth; ***C:*** Chester Lyons, William Cooper Smith.

Lucky Stiff **1988 (PG)** A fat, unpopular dweeb has the shock of his life when a radiant woman falls in love with him, the strangeness of which becomes evident when he meets her very weird family. **93m/C VHS, DVD.** Donna Dixon, Joe Alaskey, Jeff Kober, Elizabeth Arlen, Charles Frank, Barbara Howard; ***D:*** Anthony Perkins; ***W:*** Pat Proft.

Lucky Terror **1936** Routine Hoot cowboy drama. **60m/B VHS.** Hoot Gibson, Lona Andre, Charles "Blackie" King; ***D:*** Alan James.

Lucky Texan 1/2 **1934** Wayne plays a tough easterner who goes West and finds himself involved with miners and claim jumpers. **61m/B VHS, DVD.** John Wayne, George "Gabby" Hayes, Yakima Canutt, Lloyd Whitlock, Eddie (Ed, Eddy, Edwin) Parker, Gordon DeMain; ***D:*** Robert North Bradbury; ***W:*** Robert North Bradbury; ***C:*** Archie Stout.

Lucky You **2007 (PG-13)** Huck Cheever (Bana) is a talented poker player who makes his living fleecing tourists in Las Vegas but dreams of making it big in the World Championship (Series) of Poker. Unfortunately, his emotions usually get in the way, especially when it comes to dealing with his deadbeat father, L.C. (Duvall), who becomes his poker arch-nemesis. On his way to a showdown with Dad, Huck alternately romances and rips off struggling lounge singer Billie (Barrymore). Hansen obviously loves his characters, poker, and the eccentrics that make up Las Vegas's underbelly, but it's not enough to help this movie's desperate identity crisis. Had it not sat on the shelf through the boom of the poker craze this would have been a better-than-standard poker movie; instead, it's a weak romantic drama with a cast and director who should have created something much better. **123m/C DVD.** *US* Eric Bana, Robert Duvall, Drew Barrymore, Debra Messing, Horatio Sanz, Jean Smart, Charles Martin Smith, Robert Downey Jr., Kelvin Han Yee, Evan Jones, Michael Shannon; ***D:*** Curtis Hanson; ***W:*** Curtis Hanson, Eric Roth; ***C:*** Peter Deming; ***M:*** Christopher Young.

Luckytown 1/2 **2000 (R)** Part road movie, part Vegas movie, part family ties, and none of the parts turn out to fit together. Oklahoman Lidda (Dusnt) gets a check on her 18th birthday from her long-gone dad, gambler Charlie (Caan), so she decides to track him down in Vegas. Along for the ride is store clerk and potential beau Colonel (Kartheiser), who happens to know his way around the cards himself. Only it turns out dad is in big trouble with club owner Tony (Miano) and the kids are soon caught in the middle. **101m/C VHS, DVD.** Kirsten Dunst, Vincent Kartheiser, James Caan, Robert Miano, Luis Guzman, Jennifer Gareis, Theresa Russell; ***D:*** Paul Nicholas; ***W:*** Brendon Beseth; ***C:*** Denis Maloney; ***M:*** Greg Edmonson.

Lucy and Desi: Before the Laughter 1/2 **1991 (PG-13)** The meeting and early married life of actress/comedian Lucille Ball and Cuban bandleader Desi Arnaz is depicted in this routine biopic. Film depicts Desi's womanizing, their struggles with fame, and their efforts to get their show on the air. Fisher does well as TV's favorite redhead but this effort is melodramatic. Daughter Lucy Arnaz vehemently opposed this depiction of her parents life. **95m/C VHS.** Frances Fisher, Maurice Benard, John Wheeler, Robin Pearson Rose; ***D:*** Charles Jarrott; ***W:*** William Luce. **TV**

L'Udienza 1/2 **1971** A bizarre black comedy about a guy who does anything he can, at any criminal cost, to obtain an audience with the Pope. In Italian with subtitles. **111m/C VHS.** *IT* Claudia Cardinale, Ugo Tognazzi; ***D:*** Marco Ferreri.

Ludwig **1972 (PG)** Lavish-but-slow epic bio of Bavaria's mad monarch, Ludwig II (Berger), who built extravagant fantasy castles and sponsored composer Richard Wagner (Howard), whom the king became obsessed with. Italian with subtitles. **231m/C VHS.** *IT GE* Helmut Berger, Trevor Howard, Romy Schneider, Silvana Mangano, Helmut Griem, Gert Frobe; ***D:*** Luchino Visconti; ***W:*** Luchino Visconti; ***C:*** Armando Nannuzzi.

Luggage of the Gods **1987 (G)** A lost tribe of cave people are confronted with civilization when suitcases fall from an airplane. Low-budget comedy reminiscent of "The Gods Must Be Crazy." **78m/C VHS.** Mark Stolzenberg, Gabriel Barre, Gwen Ellison; ***D:*** David Kendall.

Lullaby 1/2 **2008** American Stephanie travels to Johannesburg after being notified that her drug addict son has been kidnapped and is being held for ransom. When the ransom meet doesn't go as planned, Stephanie's only chance is to work with her son's pregnant girlfriend Tina against the drug lord holding Kyle hostage. **96m/C DVD.** Melissa Leo, Russel Savadier, Joey Dedio, Lisa-Marie Schneider, Kyle Siebert; ***D:*** Darrell Roodt; ***W:*** Michael D. Sellers, Donald A. Barton; ***M:*** Alun Richards. **VIDEO**

Lullaby of Broadway 1/2 **1951** Many songs highlight this flimsy musical about a girl (Day) who ventures from England to the Big Apple in search of an acting career. She soon discovers that her mom has become a has-been actress now performing in a Greenwich Village dive. Day struggles to gain her own success while coping with her mother's downfall. ♫Lullaby of Broadway; You're Getting to Be a Habit With Me; Just One of Those Things; Somebody Loves Me; I Love the Way You Say Goodnight; Fine and Dandy; Please Don't Talk About Me When I'm Gone; A Shanty in Old Shanty Town; We'd Like to Go On A Trip. **93m/C VHS, DVD.** Doris Day, Gene Nelson, S.Z. Sakall, Billy DeWolfe, Gladys George, Florence Bates; ***D:*** David Butler.

Lulu on the Bridge 1/2 **1998 (PG-13)** Jazz saxman Izzy Maurer (Keitel) sinks into depression when he can no longer perform. Walking one night, Izzy stumbles across a dead body and finds no ID—only a phone number and a mysterious stone that emits a blue light. Izzy calls the number, which belongs to actress/waitress Celia (Sorvino), and their first meeting finds them instantly in love (or some variation). Meanwhile, the mysterious Dr. Van Horn (Dafoe) questions Iggy about finding the stone. And things don't get much clearer. First solo directorial effort for Auster, who co-directed Keitel in "Blue in the Face," the spinoff to his screenplay "Smoke." **104m/C VHS, DVD.** Harvey Keitel, Mira Sorvino, Willem Dafoe, Gina Gershon, Mandy Patinkin, Vanessa Redgrave, Victor Argo, Kevin Corrigan, Richard Edson; ***D:*** Paul Auster; ***W:*** Paul Auster; ***C:*** Alik Sakharov; ***M:*** Graeme Revell.

Lumiere 1/2 **1976 (R)** An acclaimed drama about four actresses who, during the course of one night together, make pivotal decisions about their lives and relationships. Moreau's first directorial effort; dubbed. **101m/C VHS.** *FR* Jeanne Moreau, Lucia Bose, Francine Racette, Caroline Cartier, Keith Carradine, Francois Simon, Francis Huster, Bruno Ganz, Rene Feret, Niels Arestrup, Jerome Lapperrousaz; ***D:*** Jeanne Moreau; ***W:*** Jeanne Moreau; ***C:*** Ricardo Aronovich; ***M:*** Astor Piazzolla.

Luminarias **1999 (R)** Romantic comedy about four Hispanic friends looking for love in East L.A. and meeting to console each other at the Luminarias restaurant. Lawyer Andrea (Fernandez), who's divorcing her philandering husband (Beltran), finds herself attracted to anglo Joseph (Bakula). Therapist Sofia (DuBois) has always tried to distance herself from her roots but gets is surprised by her feelings for cute Mexican waiter Pablo (Lopez). Artist Lilly (Moya) is hoping to change her luck in love with Korean Lu (Lim) only to run into prejudice from his parents and sexy designer Irene (Ortelli) has sworn off sex for Lent and is trying to accept her cross-dressing gay brother (Rivas). The friendships are believable even if there's too much going on with the plot. **101m/C VHS, DVD.** Evelina Fernandez, Marta DuBois, Dyana Ortelli, Angela Moya, Scott Bakula, Robert Beltran, Sal Lopez, Andrew C. Lim, Geoffrey Rivas, Richard "Cheech" Marin; ***D:*** Jose Luis Valenzuela; ***W:*** Evelina Fernandez; ***C:*** Alex Phillips Jr.; ***M:*** Eric Allaman.

Luminous Motion **2000** Phillip (Lloyd) is an introspective 10-year-old who spends his life on the road travelling in a red Impala with his mother (Unger), a beautiful, depressed lush who drifts from man to man. But the only male she's really close to is her son—until Phillip's father (Sheridan) finds them and wants to reclaim his family. Except the boundaries between Phillip's reality and his imagination aren't very clear at all. Based on Bradfield's novel "The History of Luminous Motion." **94m/C VHS, DVD.** Eric Lloyd, Deborah Kara Unger, Jamey Sheridan, Terry Kinney, Paz de la Huerta, James Berland; ***D:*** Bette Gordon; ***W:*** Scott Bradfield, Robert Roth; ***C:*** Teodoro Maniaci; ***M:*** Lesley Barber.

Lumumba 1/2 **2001** Powerful biopic of Patrice Lumumba, the first elected Prime Minister of the Congo, who was assassinated mere months after the country gained its independence from Belgium. Director-writer Peck, who also filmed the documentary "Lumumba—Death of a Prophet" uses flashbacks to show Lumumba's ascent from beer salesman to prominence in the independence movement and his eventual rise to, and violent removal from power. Peck neccesarily omits some details of Lumumba's early life, but in the process glosses over his ealy work in the Congolese National Movement. French actor Ebouanay gives a masterful performance, finding the humanity behind the icon. Filmed in Zimbabwe and Mozambique because the Congo was suffering through yet another civil war. **115m/C VHS, DVD.** *FR BE GE* Eriq Ebouaney, Alex Descas, Theophile Moussa Sowie, Maka Kotto, Dieudonne Kabongo, Pascal Nzonzi, Mariam Kaba; ***D:*** Raoul Peck; ***W:*** Raoul Peck, Pascal Bonitzer; ***C:*** Bernard Lutic; ***M:*** Jean-Claude Petit.

Luna e L'Altra **1996** Dizzy schoolteacher Luna (Forte) is the butt of practical jokes by her students and ignored by the other faculty. Dutiful and self-effacing, she's also the secret crush of school custodian Angelo (Nichetti). But Luna has a hidden side that comes to the surface thanks to magician

Igor's magic latern and it turns out to be a sexy one. Italian with subtitles. **92m/C VHS.** *IT* Iaia Forte, Maurizio Nichetti, Aurelio Fierro, Luigi Burruano; *D:* Maurizio Nichetti; *W:* Maurizio Nichetti; *C:* Luca Bigazzi; *M:* Carlo Siliotto.

Luna Park **1991** In contemporary Russia, Andrei (Goutine) is the leader of a gang of body-builder, right-wing skinheads who beat up Jews, foreigners, and anyone else they dislike. Then the anti-Semitic Andrei learns his father is Jewish and he frantically searches through Moscow to find him and discover his past. In Russian with subtitles. **105m/C VHS.** *RU* Oleg Borisov, Andrei Goutine, Natalya Yegorova; *D:* Pavel (Lungin) Lounguine; *W:* Pavel (Lungin) Lounguine.

Luna: Spirit of the Whale 1/2 **2007 (PG)** A young orphaned killer whale has taken up residence in a small Canadian coastal town bay and government official Priestley has been hired to capture the whale and try to return it to its pod. Only the local native peoples would rather that the whale was left alone. Based on a true story. **93m/C DVD.** *CA* Jason Priestley, Adam Beach, Graham Greene, Tantoo Cardinal, Michelle Harrison, Aaron Miko; *D:* Don McBrearty; *W:* Elizabeth Stewart; *C:* Jan Kiesser. **TV**

Lunatic **1991** "Some minds should be wasted" according to the film promo and if you're in the mood for an amateur mind (and time) waster, this is for you. High schoolers in the woods encounter mayhem in the best horror tradition as the innocents are slaughtered by an escapee from the local lunatic asylum. **90m/C VHS.** Rocky Tucker, Ondrea Tucker, Brian D'Lawrence, Keith Vallot, Bronwyn St. John, Cameron Derrick, Ernest Jackson, Rookie Macpherson, Susan Spain; *D:* James Tucker; *W:* James Tucker.

The Lunatic **1992 (R)** A robust, oversexed, and scheming German tourist travels to Jamaica where she meets the village idiot, a man who regularly holds conversations with the local plants. The two hook up with a butcher, and the three live happily in the hills, that is until the money is gone. The Jamaican scenery, a few bawdy laughs, and a great reggae soundtrack make this one worthwhile. **93m/C VHS.** *GB* Julie Wallace, Paul Campbell, Reggie Carter, Carl Bradshaw; *D:* Lol Creme; *M:* Wally Badarou.

Lunatics: A Love Story **1992 (PG-13)** Hank (Raimi) is an ex-mental patient poet suffering from hallucinations and afraid to leave his Los Angeles apartment. For companionship he dials a party-line until, one day, he misdials and insteads gets the number of a local pay telephone, which is answered by a naive woman dumped by her boyfriend. When Nancy (Foreman) decides to visit Hank you learn she's as crazy as he is—so it only makes sense they would fall in love. A well-acted fable of how love fragilely connects even the most unlikely of people. **87m/C VHS.** Theodore (Ted) Raimi, Deborah Foreman, Bruce Campbell, Brian McCree, Eddie Rosmaya, Michele Stacey, George Aguilar; *D:* Josh Becker; *W:* Josh Becker; *C:* Jeffrey Dougherty; *M:* Joseph LoDuca.

Lunatics & Lovers 1/2 **1976 (PG)** Musician meets a bizarre nobleman who is in love with an imaginary woman. **92m/C VHS.** *IT* Marcello Mastroianni, Lino Toffalo; *D:* Flavio Mogherini.

Lunch Wagon *Come 'n' Get It; Lunch Wagon Girls* **1981 (R)** Two co-eds are given a restaurant to manage during summer vacation and wind up involved in a hilarious diamond chase and sex romp. **88m/C VHS.** Rick Podell, Candy Moore, Pamela Bryant, Rosanne Katon; *D:* Ernest Pintoff.

Lupo **1970 (G)** When threatened with the loss of his home and the separation of his family, an exuberant Greek man challenges the modern world. **99m/C VHS.** Yehuda Barkan, Gabi Armoni, Esther Greenberg; *D:* Menahem Golan.

Lure of the Islands **1942** Federal agents track wanted criminals to an island retreat in this highly predictable low-budget thriller. **61m/B VHS.** Margie Hart, Robert Lowery, Guinn "Big Boy" Williams, Warren Hymer, Gale Storm; *D:* Jean Yarbrough.

Lure of the Sila 1/2 **1949** Italian melodrama about a young peasant girl infiltrating a landowner's home in order to avenge the death of her brother and mother. Dubbed and more interesting than it sounds. **72m/B VHS.** *IT* Silvana Mangano, Amedeo Nazzari, Vittorio Gassman; *D:* Duilio Coletti.

Lured 1/2 **1947** Ball gives a fine dramatic performance in Sirk's glossy thriller. Sandra (Ball) is an American dancer in London whose friend falls victim to a lonelyhearts killer. She agrees to act as a decoy for Scotland Yard even while getting involved with nightclub owner Robert Fleming (Sanders), who turns out to be one of the suspects. **103m/B VHS, DVD.** Lucille Ball, George Sanders, Charles Coburn, Cedric Hardwicke, Boris Karloff, Alan Mowbray, George Zucco, Joseph Calleia, Tanis Chandler, Alan Napier, Robert Coote; *D:* Douglas Sirk; *W:* Leo Rosten; *C:* William H. Daniels; *M:* Michel Michelet.

Lured Innocence **1997 (R)** Steamy romance in a small town leads to murderous impulses. Elsie (Shelton) is having an affair with older, married Rick (Hopper). Then his ailing wife (Shire) finds out and threatens the twosome. The lovers aren't pleased and there's an eventual murder trial where one of the key witnesses is a newspaper reporter (Gummersall), who was also Elsie's lover. **97m/C VHS, DVD.** Dennis Hopper, Marley Shelton, Devon Gummersall, Talia Shire; *D:* Kikuo Kawasaki; *W:* Kikuo Kawasaki; *C:* Irek Hartowicz.

Lurkers **WOOF!** **1988 (R)** An unappealing metaphysical morass about a woman who has been haunted throughout her life by...something. **90m/C VHS, DVD.** Christine Moore, Gary Warner, Marina Taylor, Carissa Channing, Tom Billett; *D:* Roberta Findlay; *W:* Ed Kelleher, Hariette Vidal; *C:* Roberta Findlay.

Lurking Fear **1994 (R)** The town of Lefferts Corner has suffered from generations of horror thanks to man-eating ghouls that dwell beneath the local graveyard and arise whenever a storm breaks out. The inhabitants prepare to fight back but their plan is hindered by the arrival of a group of criminals who are after a fortune supposedly hidden in one of the graves. Based on a story by H.P. Lovecraft. **78m/C VHS.** Jon Finch, Blake Bailey, Ashley Laurence, Jeffrey Combs, Paul Mantee, Allison Mackie, Joe Leavengood, Vincent Schiavelli; *D:* C. Courtney Joyner; *W:* C. Courtney Joyner; *M:* Jim Manzie.

Luscious 1/2 *Vivid* **1997 (R)** It's about sex. Cole (Shellan) is a painter having inspiration problems. Then he splashes girlfriend Billie (Wuhrer) with paint and they have sex on the canvas. Suddenly his art is selling like hotcakes but Billie gets a little tired being a literal paint brush. An unrated version has three more minutes of sex and nudity. **83m/C VHS, DVD.** Stephen Shellen, Kari Wuhrer; *D:* Evan Georgiades. **VIDEO**

Lush **2001 (R)** The New Orleans setting is the best thing about this limp drama. Alcoholic golf pro Lionel Exley (Scott) is friends with alcoholic lawyer Carter (Harris), who names his buddy his beneficiary in an insurance policy. The lawyer promptly gets murdered and Exley decides to go on the lam from the suspicious cops, winding up taking refuge with two upper-crusty sisters Ahley (Holloman) and Rachel (Linney). **94m/C VHS, DVD.** Campbell Scott, Laura Linney, Jared Harris, Laurel Holloman; *D:* Mark Gibson; *W:* Mark Gibson; *C:* Caroline Champetier; *M:* Barrett Martin.

Lush Life **1994 (R)** New York jazz session musicians Al (Goldblum) and Buddy (Whitaker) roam the city's musical scene until dawn, on the prowl for food, women, and ever more music. When trumpeter Buddy is diagnosed with an inoperable brain tumor, saxophonist Al decides on a grand final gesture—a Park Avenue farewell bash, though no one is to know just how final the farewell is to be. Great jazz soundtrack, fine acting, and atmospheric use of the Big Apple. And it avoids overt tearjerking. **96m/C VHS.** Jeff Goldblum, Forest Whitaker, Kathy Baker, Lois Chiles, Don Cheadle; *D:* Michael Elias; *W:* Michael Elias. **CABLE**

Lust and Revenge **1995** When wealthy George Oliphant (Haywood) needs a tax break, he commissions a statue (to be donated to the National Gallery) and gets daughter Georgina (Karvan) to choose the subject and artist. Flirty Georgina hires lesbian sculptress Lily (Eagger) and decides on the depiction of a male nude, for which Karl-Heniz Applebaum (Hope) is hired to pose. Applebaum's religious wife Cecilia (Dobrowolska) is not pleased, especially when hubby begins an affair. But she's also not above plotting a suitable revenge. Last role for Hargreaves (a cameo as a gallery habitue) while Hughes, who also worked for director Cox in "My First Wife," plays a male financial adviser. **95m/C VHS.** *AU* Claudia Karvan, Chris Haywood, Nicholas Hope, Gosia Dobrowolska, Victoria Eagger, Norman Kaye; ***Cameos:*** Wendy Hughes, John Hargreaves; *D:* Paul Cox; *W:* Paul Cox, John Clarke; *C:* Nino Martinetti; *M:* Paul Grabowsky.

Lust, Caution *Se, Jie* **2007 (NC-17)** Director Lee extensively expanded Eileen Chang's short story to create this broad epic of intrigue and lust in Japanese-occupied China during World War II. Wong (Wei) is a Chinese patriot involved in a plot to assassinate Mr. Yee (Leung), a collaborator with the Japanese. Once she seduces him, however, she begins to realize that she's in way over her head. Wei and Leung are both excellent, but Lee's adaptation goes beyond the original short story, and much of the early portion of the film seems unfocused, with lots of filler; the heart of the story is in the second half. Earned an NC-17 rating and a great deal of attention because of its extremely erotic and explicit sex scenes. **158m/C DVD.** *US HK CH* Tony Leung Chiu-Wai, Tang Wei, Joan Chen, Wang Leehom, Chu Tsz-ying; *D:* Ang Lee; *W:* James Schamus, Wang Hui-ling; *C:* Rodrigo Prieto; *M:* Alexandre Desplat.

Lust for a Vampire *To Love a Vampire* **1971 (R)** The sanguine tale of a deadly vampire who indiscriminately preys on pupils and teachers when she enrolls at a British finishing school. Moody and erotically charged, with an impressive ending. Quasi-sequel to "The Vampire Lovers." **95m/C VHS, DVD.** *GB* Ralph Bates, Barbara Jefford, Suzanna Leigh, Michael Johnson, Yutte Stensgaard, Pippa Steele, Helen Christie, David Healy, Mike Raven; *D:* Jimmy Sangster; *W:* Tudor Gates; *C:* David Muir.

Lust for Dracula **WOOF!** **2004 (R)** Softcore Dracula story has Mina Harker (Mundae) kept in a drugged stupor by husband Jonathan (Wells)—so drugged that she apparently doesn't realize her husband is a woman. But then, so is Dracula (Caine) and all the vamp minions. Mina's sister Abigail (Shelly Jones) wants to destroy Dracula and get Jonathan for herself. Let's face it, no one's watching this for the plot but for skin and girl-on-girl action. **90m/C DVD.** Darian Caine, Misty Mundae, Shelly Jones, Julian Wells, Andrea Davis; *D:* Anthony Marsiglia; *W:* Anthony Marsiglia; *C:* Dang Lenawea; *M:* Don Mike. **VIDEO**

Lust for Freedom **1987** An undercover cop decides to hit the road after she sees her partner gunned down. She winds up near the California-Mexico border, where she is wrongly imprisoned with a number of other young women in a white slavery business. This low-budget film includes lots of steamy women-behind-bars sex scenes. **92m/C VHS, DVD.** Melanie Coll, William J. Kulzer; *D:* Eric Louzil.

Lust for Gold **1949** Ford battles against greedy former lover Lupino and her husband for control of the Lost Dutchman gold mine. **90m/B VHS, DVD.** Ida Lupino, Glenn Ford, Gig Young, William Prince, Edgar Buchanan, Will Geer, Paul Ford, Jay Silverheels; *D:* S. Sylvan Simon; *M:* George Duning.

Lust for Life 1/2 **1956** Absorbing, serious biography of Vincent Van Gogh, from his first paintings to his death. Remarkable for Douglas' furiously convincing portrayal. Featuring dozens of actual Van Gogh works from private collections. Based on an Irving Stone novel, produced by John Houseman. **122m/C VHS, DVD.** Kirk Douglas, Anthony Quinn, James Donald, Pamela Brown, Everett Sloane, Henry Daniell, Niall MacGinnis, Noel Purcell, Lionel Jeffries, Jill Bennett; *D:* Vincente Minnelli; *M:* Miklos Rozsa. Oscars '56: Support. Actor (Quinn); Golden Globes '57: Actor—Drama (Douglas); N.Y. Film Critics '56: Actor (Douglas).

Lust in the Dust **1985 (R)** When part of a treasure map is found on the derriere of none other than Divine, the hunt is on for the other half. This comedy western travels to a sleepy town called Chile Verde (green chili for those who don't speak Spanish) and the utterly ridiculous turns comically corrupt. Deliciously distasteful fun. Features Divine singing a bawdy love song in his/her break from John Waters. **85m/C VHS, DVD.** Tab Hunter, Divine, Lainie Kazan, Geoffrey Lewis, Henry Silva, Cesar Romero, Gina Gallego, Courtney Gains, Woody Strode, Pedro Gonzalez-Gonzalez; *D:* Paul Bartel; *W:* Philip John Taylor; *C:* Paul Lohmann; *M:* Peter Matz.

Luster 1/2 **2002** A look at the L.A. gay/punk scene that coasts by on its own oddball charms. Skateboarding, blue-haired Jackson (Herwick) works at a record store while aspiring to be a poet. After too many drunken, druggy sexual encounters, he decides he needs a real romance—maybe with crush Billy (Blechman) who'd rather just be friends. Meanwhile, preppie customer Derek (Thibodeau) thinks Jackson is swell. Then add to the mix naive newcomer Jed (Wyatt), willing to try anything, and closeted rock star Sonny Spike (Garson), who has an unsavory past with Billy, as well as Jackson's chic lesbian pals, Alyssa (Gidley) and Sandra (Melvoin). **90m/C DVD.** Justin Herwick, Shane Powers, B. Wyatt, Jonah Blechman, Pamela Gidley, Sean Thibodeau, Willie Garson, Susanna Melvoin; *D:* Everet Lewis; *W:* Everet Lewis; *C:* Humberto DeLuna; *M:* Michael Leon.

The Lusty Men **1952** Two rival rodeo champions, both in love with the same woman, work the rodeo circuit until a tragic accident occurs. Mitchum turns in a fine performance as the has-been rodeo star trying to make it big again. **113m/B VHS.** Robert Mitchum, Susan Hayward, Arthur Kennedy, Arthur Hunnicutt; *D:* Nicholas Ray; *C:* Lee Garmes.

Luther 1/2 **1974 (G)** A well-acted characterization of Martin Luther's development from a young seminarian to his leadership of the Reformation Movement. **112m/C VHS, DVD.** Stacy Keach, Patrick Magee, Hugh Griffith, Robert Stephens, Alan Badel, Julian Glover, Judi Dench, Leonard Rossiter, Maurice Denham, Peter Cellier, Thomas Heathcote, Malcolm Stoddard, Bruce Carstairs; *D:* Guy Green; *W:* Edward Anhalt, John Osborne; *C:* Frederick A. (Freddie) Young; *M:* John Addison.

Luther 1/2 **2003 (PG-13)** Tame religious biopic follows the 16th century law student turned young monk who started the Protestant religious movement. Despite depicting a plethora of the remarkable moments that made up Luther's life, pic lacks focus that might have illuminated this important historical figure. Refusing to recant his beliefs, including the famous 95 Theses questioning Catholic Church practices, Luther was excommunicated, which sparked the Reformation and Protestantism. Fiennes gives an able but diluted performance in the title role while Ustinov as Prince Frederick is at his scene-stealing best. **112m/C VHS, DVD.** *GE* Joseph Fiennes, Alfred Molina, Jonathan Firth, Claire Cox, Peter Ustinov, Bruno Ganz, Uwe Ochsenknecht, Matthieu Carriere, Jochen Horst; *D:* Eric Till; *W:* Camille Thomasson, Bart Gavigan; *C:* Robert Fraisse; *M:* Richard Harvey.

Luther the Geek **WOOF!** **1990** Little Luther's visit to the circus is dramatically changed when he sees the geek, a sideshow freak. Since then Luther has taken to biting off chicken's heads and drinking their blood in his small Illinois town; the town will never be the same. (And neither will you if you watch this stupid film.) **90m/C VHS, DVD.** Edward Terry, Joan Roth, J. Jerome Clarke, Tom Mills, Stacy Haiduk; *D:* Carlton J. Albright; *W:* Whitey Styles; *C:* David Knox.

Luv 1/2 **1967 (PG)** Although good cast tries hard, they can't do much with this comic farce. Three intellectuals, including one that's suicidal, discuss the trials and tribulations of their middle-class New York existence. **95m/C VHS.** Jack Lemmon, Peter Falk, Elaine May; *D:* Clive Donner; *W:* Murray Schisgal; *C:* Ernest Laszlo.

Luxury Liner 1/2 **1948** Typical MGM musical fare although Brent also played the same role in the 1933 non-musical version. Polly (Powell), the daughter of widowed captain Jeremy Bradford (Brent), wants to go on his next cruise to Rio but he insists she stay at boarding school. So Polly stows away and then decides the best thing would be for her dad to remarry so she picks a likely passenger in the bewildered Laura (Gifford). **98m/C DVD.** George Brent, Jane Powell, Frances Gifford, Lauritz Melchior, Thomas E. Breen, Xavier Cugat; ***D:*** Richard Whorf; ***W:*** Karl Kamb, Gladys Lehman, Richard Connell; ***C:*** Robert Planck; ***M:*** Georgie Stoll.

The Luzhin Defence **2000 (PG-13)** Luzhin (Turturro) is an eccentric Russian chess genius who is staying at an Italian lakeside resort in 1929 preparing for an important match. Also preparing for a match—the marital kind—is Russian emigre Natalia (Watson) and her aristocratic mother Vera (James). And Luzhin is not the man Vera has in mind for her daughter, no matter what Natalia thinks. But as the stress of the match takes its toll on Luzhin, he believes he cannot have both love and the game. Based on the 1930 novel by Vladimir Nabokov. **106m/C VHS, DVD.** *FR GB* John Turturro, Emily Watson, Geraldine James, Stuart Wilson, Christopher Thompson, Peter Blythe, Orla Brady, Fabio Sartor; ***D:*** Marleen Gorris; ***W:*** Peter Berry; ***C:*** Bernard Lutic; ***M:*** Alexandre Desplat.

Luzia ½ **1988** Ohana stars as a tough and sexy Brazilian cowgirl who is caught in the middle of a class struggle where the personal is definitely political. Her horseriding skills and beauty give her options in both lifestyles. Will she choose to side with the squatters or the wealthy landowners? In Portuguese with English subtitles. **112m/C VHS.** *BR* Claudia Ohana, Thales Pan Chacon, Jose de Abreu, Luiza Falcao; ***D:*** Fabio Barreto.

Lydia **1941** Sentimental drama in which an elderly lady (Oberon) gets to relive her romantic past when she has a reunion with four of her lost loves. Well acted and directed, Oberon gives one of her best performances ever. Adapted from the highly regarded French film "Un Carnet de Bal." **98m/B VHS.** Merle Oberon, Joseph Cotten, Alan Marshal, George Reeves; ***D:*** Julien Duvivier; ***C:*** Lee Garmes; ***M:*** Miklos Rozsa.

Lying Lips ½ **1939** All-black detective mystery about a young nightclub singer framed for murder. Her boyfriend then turns detective to clear her name. **60m/B VHS.** Edna Mae Harris, Carmen Newsome, Earl Jones, Amanda Randolph; ***D:*** Oscar Micheaux.

Lymelife **2008 (R)** Wood-tick fearing Long Islanders give the film its odd title in this vividly-acted black comedy. Timid teen Scott (Rory Culkin) exists to be bullied although things get better when his longtime crush Adrianna (Roberts) finally starts taking an interest. His brother Jim (Kieran Culkin) is off to serve in the military, their mother Brenda (Hennessy) is over-anxious about Lyme disease while their workaholic dad Mickey (Baldwin) is having an affair with Adrianna mom's Melissa (Nixon). Her dad Charlie (Hutton) is a pill-popper who likes to randomly shoot into the woods with his rifle. There's an awkward first time sex scene between the teens and a lot of marital squabbling. **95m/C DVD.** Rory Culkin, Alec Baldwin, Jill Hennessy, Kieran Culkin, Emma Roberts, Timothy Hutton, Cynthia Nixon; ***W:*** Derick Martini, Steven Martini; ***C:*** Frank Goodwin; ***M:*** Derick Martini, Steven Martini.

M **1931** The great Lang dissection of criminal deviance, following the tortured last days of a child murderer, and the efforts of both the police and the underground to bring him to justice. Poetic, compassionate, and chilling. Inspired by real-life serial killer Peter Kurten, known as "Vampire of Dusseldorf," Lang also borrowed story elements from Jack the Ripper's killing spree. Lorre's screen debut. Lang's personal favorite among his own films. In German with English subtitles. Remade in 1951. **111m/B VHS, DVD.** *GE* Peter Lorre, Ellen Widmann, Inge Landgut, Gustav Grundgens, Otto Wernicke, Ernest Stahl-Nachbaur, Franz Stein, Theodore Loos, Fritz Gnass, Fritz Odemar, Paul Kemp, Theo Lingen, Georg John, Karl Platen, Rosa Valetti, Hertha von Walther, Rudolf Blumner; ***D:*** Fritz Lang; ***W:*** Fritz Lang, Thea von Harbou; ***C:*** Fritz Arno Wagner, Gustav Rathje; ***M:*** Edvard Grieg.

M. Butterfly **1993 (R)** Disappointing adaptation of Hwang's award-winning play, which was based on a true story. Irons is Rene Gallimard, a minor French diplomat sent to China in 1964. Taken in by the exoticism of the mysterious east, he falls for a Chinese opera performer, Song Liling (Lone). Only she's no lady and the oblivious diplomat turns out to be a patsy as Song Liling uses him to gather information. The story only works if the passion, however deceptive, between Gallimard and Song Liling is believable, passion which is noticeably lacking between Irons and Lone. Irons comes across as too intelligent to be gullibile and the usually excellent Lone does not make his role believable. **101m/C VHS.** Jeremy Irons, John Lone, Ian Richardson, Barbara Sukowa, Vernon Dobtcheff, Annabel Leventon, Shizuko Hoshi, Richard McMillan; ***D:*** David Cronenberg; ***W:*** David Henry Hwang; ***M:*** Howard Shore.

Ma and Pa Kettle ½ *The Further Adventures of Ma and Pa Kettle* **1949** The hillbilly couple were supporting characters in "The Egg and I" but their popularity found them spun off into their own cornpone series. This first feature finds the couple and their 15 children about to be evicted only to have Pa win a tobacco slogan contest. The prize is a brand-new fully automated house whose futuristic contraptions get the better of Pa. **76m/B VHS.** Marjorie Main, Percy Kilbride, Richard Long, Meg Randall, Esther Dale, Barry Kelley, Patricia Alphin; ***D:*** Charles Lamont; ***W:*** Al Lewis, Herbert Margolis, Louis Morheim.

Ma and Pa Kettle at Home ½ **1954** Elwin, one of the Kettle's 15 children, is a finalist in an essay contest that could win him a college scholarship. Then Pa Kettle hears the two judges plan to visit each of the finalists' homes so he tries to spruce-up the family's tumbled-down farm. **80m/B VHS, DVD.** Marjorie Main, Percy Kilbride, Alan Mowbray, Ross Elliott, Brett Halsey, Mary Wickes, Irving Bacon, Emory Parnell; ***D:*** Charles Lamont; ***W:*** Kay Lenard.

Ma and Pa Kettle at the Fair ½ **1952** The Kettle's eldest daughter Rosie wants to go to college so Ma enters the county fair baking contest to win some money and Pa buys a decrepit old nag to enter in the fair's horse race. Somehow things just have a way of working out for the Kettles. **79m/B VHS, DVD.** Marjorie Main, Percy Kilbride, Lori Nelson, James Best, Esther Dale, Russell Simpson, Emory Parnell; ***D:*** Charles T. Barton; ***W:*** John Grant, Richard Morris.

Ma and Pa Kettle at Waikiki ½ **1955** Ma (Main) and Pa (Kilbride), as well as oldest daughter Rosie (Nelson), head for Hawaii to help out cousin Rodney's (Smith) pineapple factory. Seems he's ill and about to go bankrupt and he thinks Pa is some kind of financial whiz who can bail him out. Pa accidentally does help the business and then gets kidnapped by some sleazy competitors. But it's Ma to the rescue (and the bad guys don't stand a chance). Kilbride retired after his seventh take as Pa in the comedy series. **79m/B VHS, DVD.** Marjorie Main, Percy Kilbride, Lori Nelson, Loring Smith, Russell Johnson, Byron Palmer, Mabel Albertson, Hilo Hattie, Fay Roope, Oliver Blake, Lowell Gilmore, Teddy Hart; ***D:*** Lee Sholem; ***W:*** Jack Henley, Harry Clork, Elwood Ullman.

Ma and Pa Kettle Back On the Farm ½ **1951** First-time grandparents, the Kettles have to deal with their daughter-in-law's snobby Bostonian parents and their parenting ideas. The family's also moved back to their ramshackle farm where Pa thinks he's found uranium, leading to all sorts of problems. **81m/B VHS, DVD.** Marjorie Main, Percy Kilbride, Richard Long, Meg Randall, Ray Collins, Barbara Brown, Emory Parnell; ***D:*** Edward Sedgwick; ***W:*** Jack Henley.

Ma and Pa Kettle Go to Town ½ **1950** Ma and Pa head off for New York City when Pa wins a jingle-writing contest, unknowingly leaving their brood in the care of on the lam mobster Mike, who asks the Kettles to deliver a package to his brother. This gets both the crooks and the cops trailing the hillbilly couple, whose backwoods ways are more than a match for any city slicker. **80m/B VHS, DVD.** Marjorie Main, Percy Kilbride, Richard Long, Meg Randall, Charles McGraw, Ray Collins, Esther Dale, Ellen Corby, Barbara Brown; ***D:*** Charles Lamont; ***W:*** Martin Ragaway, Leonard Stern.

Ma and Pa Kettle on Vacation ½ *Ma and Pa Kettle Go to Paris* **1953** Ma and Pa visit Paris as guests of their son's wealthy in-laws and Pa unwittingly gets involved with spies and shady ladies. **79m/B VHS, DVD.** Marjorie Main, Percy Kilbride, Ray Collins, Sig Rumann, Bodil Miller, Barbara Brown, Peter Brocco, Jay Novello; ***D:*** Charles Lamont; ***W:*** Jack Henley.

Ma Barker's Killer Brood **1960** Biography of the infamous American criminal and her four sons, edited together from a TV serial. The shoot-'em-up scenes and Tuttle's performance keep the pace from slackening. **82m/B VHS, DVD.** Lurene Tuttle, Tristram Coffin, Paul Dubov, Nelson Leigh, Myrna Dell, Vic Lundin, Donald Spruance; ***D:*** Bill Karn.

Ma Saison Preferee *My Favorite Season* **1993** Focuses on the intense relationship between a middleaged brother (Auteuil) and sister (Deneuve). When the elderly Berthe (Villalonga) collapses, she goes to stay with daughter Emilie and her family, which provides Emilie with an excuse to invite her estranged brother Antoine for Christmas. It's a disaster with numerous family fights, that leads Emilie to declare her marriage over and to an eventual reapproachment with Antoine. Film is divided into four parts, to coincide with the four seasons, beginning with autumn and ending with summer. French with subtitles. Deneuve and Auteuil reteamed for Techine's "Les Voleurs." **124m/C VHS, DVD.** *FR* Daniel Auteuil, Catherine Deneuve, Marthe Villalonga, Jean-Pierre Bouvier, Chiara Mastroianni, Anthony Prada, Carmen Chaplin; ***D:*** Andre Techine; ***W:*** Andre Techine; ***C:*** Thierry Arbogast; ***M:*** Philippe Sarde.

Ma Saison Super 8 ½ **2005** A radical leftist student rebellion briefly unites disparate groups in May, 1968 Paris. Marc is thrown out of the house when his father finds out he's gay and he moves in with best friend Julie, who is experimenting with being a lesbian. Meanwhile, Marc picks up working-class Andre, who doesn't admit he's gay, and gets involved in an early gay rights movement. French with subtitles. **74m/C DVD.** *FR* Axel Philippon, Roman Girelli, Celia Pilastre, Antoine Mory, Magali Domec, Thierry Bareges; ***D:*** Alessandro Avellis; ***W:*** Alessandro Avellis; ***C:*** Nicolas Lefievre.

Ma Vie en Rose *My Life in Pink* **1997 (R)** Berliner's debut portrays seven-year-old misfit Ludovic (du Fresne), who is convinced he's really a girl and likes to dress in girls' clothes. His close-knit family merely regards this as a childhood eccentricity Ludovic will grow out of. But when the child decides he's going to marry Jerome (Rivere), the boy next door, and stages a mock wedding ceremony, things get a bit dicey. Jerome's father is the straitlaced Albert (Hanssens), who happens to be the boss of Ludovic's father, Pierre (Ecoffey), and he's not nearly so understanding (neither are the other neighbors in the conservative Parisian suburb). Poignant and funny look at a child's search for identity. Convincing turn by prepubescent performer du Fresne. **90m/C VHS, DVD.** *BE FR GB* Georges DuFresne, Jean-Philippe Ecoffey, Michele Laroque, Daniel Hanssens, Julien Riviere, Helene Vincent, Laurence Bibot, Jean-Francois Galotte, Caroline Baehr, Marie Bunel; ***D:*** Alain Berliner; ***W:*** Alain Berliner, Chris Vander Stappen; ***C:*** Yves Cape; ***M:*** Dominique Dalcan. Golden Globes '98: Foreign Film.

Mabel & Fatty **1916** Three silent shorts featuring the two stars, made with Mack Sennett: "He Did and He Didn't," "Mabel and Fatty Viewing The World's Fair at San Francisco" (with scenes of the actual 1914 World's Fair) and "Mabel's Blunder." **61m/B VHS.** Mabel Normand, Fatty Arbuckle, Al "Fuzzy" St. John.

Maborosi *Mirage; Maboroshi no Hikari* **1995** Yumiko (Esumi) has a contented life in Osaka with her husband Ikuo (Asano) and their newborn son. Yet, inexplicably, her husband commits suicide one night. Later, a neighbor of Yumiko's helps her with an arranged marriage to prosperous widower Tamio (Naitoh), who lives in a remote fishing village, and once again things seem to be happy. But her first husband's death still haunts her and Yumiko seeks an explanation that will allow her to have some peace in her life. Adapted from a story by Teru Miyamoto. Japanese with subtitles. **110m/C VHS, DVD.** *JP* Makiko Esumi, Takashi Naito, Tadanobu Asano, Gohki Kashiyama; ***D:*** Hirokazu Kore-eda; ***W:*** Yoshihisa Ogita; ***C:*** Masao Nakabori; ***M:*** Chen Ming-Chang.

Mac **1993 (R)** It's a family affair. Immigrant carpenter's funeral is the starting point for the story of his three sons, construction workers who live in Queens, New York in the 1950s. The passionate bros battle, bitch, and build, with Turturro as the eldest summing up the prevailing philosophy: "It's the doing, that's the thing." Turturro's directorial debut is a labor of love and a tribute to his own dad. Filmed on location in New York City. Fine performances from newcomers Badalucco and Capotorto are complemented by smaller roles from Amos, Barkin, and Turturro's real-life wife Borowitz and brother Nick. **118m/C VHS, DVD.** John Turturro, Carl Capotorto, Michael Badalucco, Katherine Borowitz, John Amos, Olek Krupa, Ellen Barkin, Joe Paparone, Nicholas Turturro, Dennis Farina, Steven Randazzo; ***D:*** John Turturro; ***W:*** Brandon Cole, John Turturro; ***C:*** Ron Fortunato; ***M:*** Richard Termini, Vin Tese.

Mac and Me **1988 (PG)** Lost E.T.-like alien stranded on Earth befriends a wheelchair-bound boy. Aimed at young kids, it's full of continual product plugs, most notably for McDonald's. Make the kids happy and stick to the real thing. **94m/C VHS, DVD.** Christine Ebersole, Jonathan Ward, Katrina Caspary, Lauren Stanley, Jade Calegory; ***D:*** Stewart Raffill; ***W:*** Stewart Raffill; ***M:*** Alan Silvestri. Golden Raspberries '88: Worst Director (Raffill).

Macabre **1969** A beautiful woman, lustful and precocious, kills her husband and his twin brother. **89m/C VHS.** *IT SP* Larry Ward, Teresa Gimpera, Giacomo "Jack" Rossi-Stuart; ***D:*** Javier Seto; ***W:*** Javier Seto; ***C:*** Antonio Piazza; ***M:*** Franco Micalizzi.

Macabre *Frozen Terror* **1980** A madman resembling both Jack Frost and Jack the Ripper claims victims at random. **90m/C VHS, DVD.** Bernice Stegers, Stanko Molnar, Veronica Zinny, Roberto Posse; ***D:*** Lamberto Bava; ***W:*** Lamberto Bava, Antonio Avati; ***C:*** Franco Delli Colli.

Macao **1952** On the lam for a crime he didn't commit, an adventurer sails to the exotic Far East, meets a buxom cafe singer, and helps Interpol catch a notorious crime boss. A strong film noir entry. Russell sneers, Mitchum wise cracks. Director von Sternberg's last film for RKO. **81m/B VHS, DVD.** Robert Mitchum, Jane Russell, William Bendix, Gloria Grahame; ***D:*** Josef von Sternberg.

Macaroni ½ *Maccheroni* **1985 (PG)** An uptight American businessman returns to Naples 40 years after being stationed there in WWII. Comedic situations abound when he is reunited with his Italian war buddy, brother of his lover. Pleasant acting can't save irritating script. **104m/C VHS.** *IT* Jack Lemmon, Marcello Mastroianni, Daria Nicolodi, Isa Danieli; ***D:*** Ettore Scola; ***W:*** Ettore Scola.

MacArthur **1977 (PG)** General Douglas MacArthur's life from Corregidor in 1942 to his dismissal a decade later in the midst of the Korean conflict. Episodic sage with forceful Peck but weak supporting characters. Fourteen minutes were cut from the original version; intended to be Peck's "Patton," it falls short of the mark. **130m/C VHS, DVD.** Gregory Peck, Ivan Bonar, Ward (Edward) Costello, Nicolas Coster, Dan O'Herlihy; ***D:*** Joseph Sargent; ***W:*** Hal Barwood, Matthew Robbins; ***C:*** Mario Tosi; ***M:*** Jerry Goldsmith.

MacArthur Park ½ **2001 (R)** A group of L.A. crack addicts try to escape the despair of their lives by duping a celebrity junkie. Cody (Byrd), a middle-aged former musician, is the de facto leader of the group, whose estranged son brings news that his ex-wife has died. Actor-turned-director Wirth turns in a fine film which includes excellent performances and a rare insight into the inner lives of the "crackheads" that are often just part of the periphery of most urban dramas. **86m/C DVD.** Thomas Jefferson Byrd, Louis Freese, Ellen Cleghorne, Brandon Adams, Lori Petty, Julie Delpy, Balthazar Getty, David Faustino, Rachel Hunter, Glenn Plummer, Miguel A. Nunez Jr., Sydney Tamiia Poitier, Sydney Walsh, Cynda Williams, Kirk "Sticky Fingaz" Jones, Bad Azz; ***D:*** Billy Wirth; ***W:*** Billy Wirth, Tyrone Atkins, Aaron Courseault, Sheri Sussman; ***C:*** Kristian Bernier; ***M:*** Stephen Perkins. **VIDEO**

MacArthur's Children 1985 A poignant evocation of life in a Japanese fishing village as it faces the end of WWII and American occupation. Not as good as some of the other Japanese films, but it is an interesting look at the changes in culture caused by their defeat in the war. In Japanese with English subtitles. **115m/C VHS.** *JP* Masako Natsume, Shima Iwashita, Hiromi Go, Takaya Yamamauchi, Shiori Sakura, Ken(saku) Watanabe, Juzo Itami, Yoshiyuka Omori; ***D:*** Masahiro Shinoda; ***W:*** Takeski Tamura.

Macbeth 1/2 **1948** Shakespeare's classic tragedy is performed with a celebrated lead performance by Welles, who plays the tragic king as a demonic leader of a barbaric society. A low budget adaptation with cheap sets, a three-week shooting schedule, lots of mood, and an attempt at Scottish accents. After making this film, Welles took a 10-year break from Hollywood. **111m/B VHS.** Orson Welles, Jeannette Nolan, Dan O'Herlihy, Roddy McDowall, Robert Coote; ***D:*** Orson Welles.

Macbeth *Play of the Month: MacBeth* **1970** An extraordinary version of Shakespeare's "Macbeth" in which all the fire, ambition and doom of his text come brilliantly to life. **137m/C DVD.** Eric Porter, Janet Suzman, John Alderton, Michael Goodliffe, John Thaw, Daphne Heard, Hilary Mason; ***D:*** John Gorrie. **TV**

Macbeth **1971 (R)** Polanski's notorious adaptation of the Shakespearean classic, marked by realistic design, unflinching violence, and fatalistic atmosphere. Finch and Annis star as Macbeth and his equally murderous lady (who appears nude in the sleepwalking scene). Polanski's first film following the grisly murder of his pregnant wife, actress Sharon Tate, was torn apart by critics but it contains stunning fight scenes and fine acting. It is in fact a worthy continuation of his work in the horror genre. Very well made. First film made by Playboy Enterprises. Originally rated X. **139m/C VHS, DVD.** Jon Finch, Nicholas Selby, Martin Shaw, Francesca Annis, Terence Baylor, John Stride, Stephan Chase, Noelle Rimmington, Maisie Farquhar, Elsie Taylor; ***D:*** Roman Polanski; ***W:*** Roman Polanski, Kenneth Tynan; ***C:*** Gilbert Taylor.

Macbeth **1988** Another production of the classic tragedy by Shakespeare. Produced as part of HBO's Thames Collection. **110m/C VHS.** Michael Jayston, Leigh Hunt; ***D:*** Charles Marquis Warren.

Macbeth 1/2 **2006** MacBeth as gangster tale? Interesting idea but it loses much in translation. Director Wright moves the action to modern day Melbourne, where MacBeth (Worthington) whacks his boss Duncan (Sweet), as well as anyone he thinks is a threat. Lacking in subtlety, too dark, too gloomy, too stylish, and occasionally too campy for its own good. But other than that, it's fine. Weak rip-off of better gangster movies with a slightly more ambitious pedigree. **109m/C DVD.** *AU* Sam Worthington, Victoria Hill, Lachy Hulme, Gary Sweet, Steve Bastoni; ***D:*** Geoffrey Wright; ***W:*** Victoria Hill, Geoffrey Wright; ***C:*** William Gibson; ***M:*** John Clifford White.

MacGruber **2010** Will SNL never learn that you can't make a movie from a one-joke skit? Here they attempt to sustain their MacGyver TV parody into a full-length feature. Clueless MacGruber searches for enemy Dieter Von Cunth after he steals a nuclear warhead. **m/C DVD.** Will Forte, Kristen Wiig, Val Kilmer, Ryan Phillippe; ***D:*** Jorma Taccone; ***W:*** Will Forte, Jorma Taccone, John Solomon; ***C:*** Brandon Trost.

Mach 2 1/2 **2000 (R)** A senator, who's running for president, has gotten hold of a computer disk that reveals treachery by the current vice president. White House Secret Service agents are sent to retrieve the disk from the Senator (who's boarded the Concorde) and set it up so that the plane will be destroyed. Bosworth is the Air Force hero who won't let that happen. **94m/C VHS, DVD.** Brian Bosworth, Michael Dorn, Shannon Whirry, Cliff Robertson, Lance Guest, Bruce Weitz; ***D:*** Fred Olen Ray; ***W:*** Steve Latshaw; ***C:*** Thomas Callaway; ***M:*** Eric Wurst, David Wurst. **VIDEO**

The Machine **1996** Psychiatrist and inventor Marc Lacroix (Depardieu) is obsessed with the brain. He develops a brain transfer machine and decides to test it on himself (naturally) by fusing his psyche with that of his patient, cold-blooded killer Michael Zyto (does this sound like a good idea to you?). Naturally, the experiment causes terrifying consequences for Lacroix and his family. **96m/C VHS.** Gerard Depardieu, Nathalie Baye, Didier Boundon, Natalia Woerner, Erwan Baynaud; ***D:*** Francois Dupeyron; ***W:*** Francois Dupeyron; ***C:*** Dietrich Lohmann; ***M:*** Michel Portal.

The Machine Girl *Kataude mashin garu* **2007** If played as pure comedy, or as pure horror, this pic might have worked. As it stands, with the deliberately bad (and over-the-top gory) effects, campy acting, and just plain weirdness (the lead female baddie sports a pair of lethal drills on her, um, chest), it amounts to little more than dumb fun. Includes a bloody, knife-wielding schoolgirl, ninjas, vengeful parents in football uniforms, chainsaws, yakuza, and throwing stars in cgi (how hard is it to find actors who can throw the real thing?). **96m/C DVD.** *JP* Kentaro Shimizu, Taro Suwa, Minase Yoshiro, Asami, Honoka, Nobuhiro Nishihara, Yuya Ishikawa, Ryosuke Kawamura, Demo Tanaka, Nahana; ***D:*** Noboru Iguchi; ***W:*** Noboru Iguchi; ***C:*** Yasatako Nagano; ***M:*** Takashi Nakagawa.

Machine Gun Blues *Black Rose of Harlem; Pistol Blues* **1995 (R)** 1930s jazz singer Georgia (Williams) sings at a black-owned club that mobster Constanza (Viterelli) wants to take over. Right-hand man Johnny Verona (Cassavettes) is sent to help things along and makes the mistake of falling for the chanteuse amidst a scene of moonshine, gunrunning and racketeering. **80m/C VHS.** Cynda Williams, Nick Cassavetes, Joe (Johnny) Viterelli, Maria Ford, Lawrence Monoson, Garrett Morris, Richard Brooks; ***D:*** Fred Gallo; ***W:*** Charles Philip Moore; ***C:*** John Aronson; ***M:*** David Wurst, Eric Wurst.

Machine Gun Kelly 1/2 **1958** Corman found Euro-appeal with this '30s style gangster bio. Bronson, who was just gaining a reputation as an action lead, stars as criminal Kelly, who's convinced by his moll to give up bank robbery for kidnapping. Amsterdam, the wisecracking writer from "The Dick Van Dyke Show," is the fink who turns him in. **80m/B VHS.** Charles Bronson, Susan Cabot, Morey Amsterdam, Barboura Morris, Frank De Kova, Jack Lambert, Wally Campo, Richard Devon, Bob Griffin; ***D:*** Roger Corman; ***W:*** Mike Werb, Robert W(right) Campbell; ***C:*** Floyd Crosby; ***M:*** Gerald Fried.

Machine to Kill Bad People *La Macchina Ammazzacattivi* **1948** In a small Italian village, a photographer receives a magical camera that has the power to terrify and kill anyone it photographs. The photographer decides to get rid of all the village's evil people but soon learns the difficulty of distinguishing between the grey areas of good and bad. Italian with subtitles. **80m/B VHS.** *IT* Gennaro Pisano, Giovanni Amato, Marilyn Buferd; ***D:*** Roberto Rossellini; ***W:*** Roberto Rossellini.

Machined **WOOF!** **2006 (R)** Sicko Motor Man Dan accidentally runs over Ryan, so he takes him back to his shack to "fix" him. Which means Dan robocops him into a half-man/half-machine, all serial killer freak. Then the two go on a murder spree. As nasty as it sounds. **92m/C DVD.** *US* David C. Hayes, Jose Rosette, Patti Tindall; ***D:*** Craig McMahon; ***W:*** Craig McMahon; ***M:*** Craig McMahon. **VIDEO**

The Machinist *El Maquinista* **2004 (R)** Best-known as the film in which Bale dropped more than 60 pounds to portray the cadaverous title role. Trevor (Bale) is a lonely, disturbed insomniac whose inattention causes a co-worker (Ironside) to lose an arm. Trevor comes to believe that his fellow workers want revenge, including the sinister Ivan (Sharian) who may actually be a figment of Trevor's paranoid imagination; that his hooker girlfriend Stevie (Leigh) may be playing him false; that he is the victim of a conspiracy and bedeviled by unseen tormentors; and that his only solace is kindly waitress Marie (Sanchez-Gijon). It's creepy and stylistic (there's a kind of cold blue tinge to the photography) and Anderson provides a quasi-believable conclusion as a payoff for all the misery endured. **102m/C DVD.** *US* Christian Bale, Jennifer Jason Leigh, Michael Ironside, Reg E. Cathey, Anna Massey, Aitana Sanchez-Gijon, John Sharian, Larry (Lawrence) Gilliard Jr., Matthew Romero Moore; ***D:*** Brad Anderson; ***W:*** Scott Kosar; ***C:*** Xavi Gimenez; ***M:*** Roque Banos.

Macho Callahan **1970 (R)** A Civil War convict escapes from a frontier jail bent on tracking down the man who imprisoned him. (The escaped prisoner bit is a recurring theme in Janssen's oeuvre.) Confused script even has a one-armed Carradine! **99m/C VHS.** David Janssen, Jean Seberg, David Carradine, Lee J. Cobb; ***D:*** Bernard L. Kowalski.

Maciste in Hell 1/2 *Witch's Curse* **1960** Inexplicably living in 17th century Scotland, Italian hero Maciste pursues a witch into the depths of Hell. She's placed a curse on the world and he wants her to remove it. **78m/C VHS, DVD.** *IT* Kirk Morris, Helene Chanel, Vira (Vera) Silenti, Andrea Bosic, Angelo Zanolli, John Karlsen; ***D:*** Riccardo Freda.

The Mack 1/2 **1973 (R)** The Mack is a pimp who comes out of retirement to reclaim a piece of the action in Oakland, California. Violent blaxploitation flick was boxoffice dynamite at time of release. Early Pryor appearance. **110m/C VHS, DVD.** Max Julien, Richard Pryor, Don Gordon, Roger E. Mosley, Carol Speed; ***D:*** Michael Campus.

Mack & Carole 1/2 **1928** Lombard began her screen career, in earnest, as a Mack Sennett comedienne. These three shorts represent her earliest screen work. **60m/B VHS.** Carole Lombard.

Mack the Knife **WOOF!** *The Threepenny Opera* **1989 (PG-13)** Terrible adaptation of Brecht and Weill's "Threepenny Opera," detailing the adventures of a master thief in love with an innocent girl. Too much music, too much dancing, too much emoting. **121m/C VHS.** Raul Julia, Roger Daltrey, Richard Harris, Julie Walters, Clive Revill, Erin Donovan, Rachel Robertson, Julia Migenes; ***D:*** Menahem Golan.

MacKenna's Gold 1/2 **1969 (PG)** Grim desperados trek through Apache territory to uncover legendary cache of gold in this somewhat inflated epic. Subdued stars Peck and Shariff vie for attention here with such overactors as Cobb, Meredith, and Wallach. Meanwhile, Newmar (Catwoman of TV's Batman) swims nude. A must for all earthquake buffs. **128m/C VHS, DVD.** Gregory Peck, Omar Sharif, Telly Savalas, Julie Newmar, Edward G. Robinson, Keenan Wynn, Ted Cassidy, Eduardo Ciannelli, Eli Wallach, Raymond Massey, Lee J. Cobb, Burgess Meredith, Anthony Quayle, John David Garfield, Robert Phillips; ***D:*** J. Lee Thompson; ***W:*** Carl Foreman; ***C:*** Joe MacDonald; ***M:*** Quincy Jones.

Mackintosh Man 1/2 **1973 (PG)** An intelligence agent must undo a communist who has infiltrated the free world's network in this solid but somewhat subdued thriller. Good cast keeps narrative rolling, but don't look here for nudity-profanity-violence fix. **100m/C VHS, DVD.** Paul Newman, Dominique Sanda, James Mason, Ian Bannen, Nigel Patrick, Harry Andrews, Leo Genn, Peter Vaughan, Michael Hordern; ***D:*** John Huston; ***W:*** Walter Hill; ***M:*** Maurice Jarre.

Macon County Line 1/2 **1974 (R)** A series of deadly mistakes and misfortunes lead to a sudden turn-around in the lives of three young people when they enter a small Georgia town and find themselves accused of brutally slaying the sheriff's wife. Sequelled by "Return to Macon County" in 1975, starring Don Johnson and Nick Nolte. **89m/C VHS, DVD.** Alan Vint, Jesse Vint, Cheryl Waters, Geoffrey Lewis, Joan Blackman, Max Baer Jr.; ***D:*** Richard Compton.

Macumba Love **1960** An author journeys to Brazil to prove a connection between mysterious murders and voodoo. A tedious suspense exploitation travelogue with generous servings of cheesecake and calypso music. **86m/C VHS.** Walter Reed, Ziva Rodann, William Wellman Jr., June Wilkinson, Ruth de Souza; ***D:*** Douglas Fowley.

Mad About Mambo 1/2 **2000 (PG-13)** Lucy McLoughlin (Russell) is an upper-class student in Belfast who's determined to prove herself as a Latin dancer. So she teams up with a working-class athlete, Danny Mitchell (Ash), who wants to play pro soccer and who needs to improve his timing, and the duo polish their moves on the dance floor. Appealing wrong-side-of-the-tracks dance/romance that doesn't ignore its setting but doesn't dwell on religious differences and soldiers either. **92m/C VHS.** Keri Russell, William Ash, Brian Cox, Rosaleen Linehan, Theo Fraser Steele; ***D:*** John Forte; ***W:*** John Forte; ***C:*** Ashley Rowe; ***M:*** Richard Hartley.

Mad About Money *He Loved an Actress; Stardust* **1937** Comedy about a bespectacled mild-mannered fellow who runs up against a Mexican spitfire. ♫Oh So Beautiful; Perpetual Motion; Little Lost Tune; Dustin' The Stars. **80m/B VHS.** *GB* Lupe Velez, Wallace Ford, Ben Lyon, Harry Langdon, Jean Colin; ***D:*** Melville Brown.

Mad About Music **1938** On the advice of her publicist, film star Gwen Taylor (Patrick) sends her teenaged daughter Gloria (Durbin) off to a Swiss boarding school and keeps her identity a secret. So Gloria invents an exciting world-traveler father that envious schoolmate Felice (Parrish) insists upon meeting. Gloria manages to persuade a complete stranger, composer Richard Todd (Marshall), into playing the role (he's charmed by her singing). Naturally, there's lots of confusion, especially when mother and "father" finally meet. ♫I Love to Whistle; Chapel Bells; Serenade to the Stars; There Isn't a Day Goes By. **92m/B VHS.** Deanna Durbin, Herbert Marshall, Gail Patrick, Arthur Treacher, Helen Parrish, William Frawley, Marcia Mae Jones, Jackie Moran; ***D:*** Norman Taurog; ***W:*** Bruce Manning, Felix Jackson; ***C:*** Joseph Valentine.

Mad About You **WOOF!** **1990 (PG)** Millionaire helps his daughter measure prospective suitors. Adam West is not the fourth man in the Montgomery Clift-James Dean-Marlon Brando chain of American acting greats. **92m/C VHS.** Claudia Christian, Joseph Gian, Adam West, Shari Shattuck; ***D:*** Lorenzo Doumani.

The Mad Adventures of Rabbi Jacob *Les Adventures de Rabbi Jacob* **1973 (G)** In order to hide out from Arab revolutionaries and the police, bigoted businessman Victor Pivert borrows the identity of a beloved Rabbi returning to France after 30 years. Much French slapstick hilarity and some musings on racism and tolerance ensues. One of the most popular comedies of all time in France (even though Jerry Lewis is nowhere to be seen!), it's also one of the most-requested video releases here in the States. Suitable for children, it might serve as a good way to introduce them to foreign films. **100m/C VHS, DVD.** *FR* Louis de Funes, Suzy Delair, Marcel Dalio, Claude Giraud, Renzo Montagnani, Andre Falcon, Henri Guybet, Miou-Miou; ***W:*** Josy Eisenberg; ***M:*** Vladimir Cosma.

Mad at the Moon **1992 (R)** Western thriller in which a young bride (Masterson) discovers that the man she married is less than human with the rising of the full moon. The only one who can protect her is her husband's half-brother played by Bochner. Masterson gives a great performance as a woman torn apart by a terrifying family secret out on the American plains. **98m/C VHS.** Mary Stuart Masterson, Hart Bochner, Fionnula Flanagan, Cec Verrell, Stephen Blake; ***D:*** Martin Donovan; ***W:*** Martin Donovan, Richard Pelusi.

Mad Bad 1/2 **2007 (R)** Justin DeMeer (Everett) just got out of prison after 10 years and is trying to reconnect with his angry younger sister Haydon (Dunning). She's got a promising music career but no money for recording sessions so Justin teams up with buddy Ethan (Gamble) to boost cars to sell to chop shops. He then puts his ill-gotten gains into Haydon's music. Justin steals a car filled with heroin and dealer Gino (Riverside) will do anything to get his merchandise back.

93m/C DVD. Maurice Ripke, Denton Blane Everett, Landon Dunning, Vince Riverside, Anna Zelinski, Terry Gamble, Russell Fuentes; *D:* Jon Keeyes; *W:* Jason Kabolati, Chip Joslin; *C:* Jason Todd Hampton; *M:* David Rosenblad. **VIDEO**

The Mad Bomber WOOF! *Police Connection; Detective Geronimo* **1972** Grim lawman Edwards tracks deranged bomber Connors, who is determined to blow up anyone who ever offended him. A must for all connoisseurs of acting that is simultaneously overblown and flat. **80m/C VHS, DVD.** Vince Edwards, Chuck Connors, Neville Brand; *D:* Bert I. Gordon.

Mad Bull 🦴 **1977** Sensitive wrestler finds meaning in life when he falls in love. If you ever cared about Karras, then you probably already saw this. If you never cared about Karras, then you probably never heard of this. If you ever cared about Anspach, rent "Five Easy Pieces" instead. **96m/C VHS.** Alex Karras, Susan Anspach, Nicholas Colasanto, Tracey Walter; *D:* Walter Doniger.

The Mad Butcher 🦴 *The Mad Butcher of Vienna; The Strangler of Vienna; The Vienna Strangler; Der Wurger kommt auf leisen Socken; Lo Strangolatore di Vienna; Meat Is Meat* **1972 (R)** Typically unhinged mental patient seeks teenage flesh for his various instruments of torture and death. Buono has never been more imposing. **82m/C VHS, DVD.** *IT* Victor Buono, Karin (Karen) Field, Brad Harris; *D:* Guido Zurli.

Mad City 🦴🦴 ½ **1997 (PG-13)** Out-of-work security guard Sam Baily (Travolta) goes postal, taking hostages in a museum while has-been journalist Max Brackett (Hoffman) manages to exploit Baily and hype the situation into a massive broadcast news event. The media circus that ensues provides social commentary on the questionable state of journalism. Drawing from famously explored material in numerous older films ("Network" and "All the President's Men") the subject is also enjoying a revival in current films ("Primary Colors" and "Wag the Dog"). Relationship between Max and Sam carries most interest in Costa-Gravas' intense drama, while uneven tone and script inadequacies hold back satisfying story development. Talented supporting cast (Alda, Danner, Kirshner, Prosky) have little to do. **114m/C VHS, DVD.** John Travolta, Dustin Hoffman, Mia Kirshner, Alan Alda, Blythe Danner, Robert Prosky, William Atherton, Ted Levine, Bill Nunn; *D:* Constantin Costa-Gavras; *W:* Tom Matthews; *C:* Patrick Blossier; *M:* Thomas Newman.

Mad Cowgirl 🦴🦴 **2006** Probably the first mad cow disease movie. Meat inspector Therese (Lassez) goes off the rails when she's diagnosed with brain cancer, possibly caused by tainted beef. She revels in various surreal sex and splatter scenarios, including assuming the identity of her favorite kung-fu TV heroine and having a torrid liaison with her brother (Duval). Designed to turn watchers into vegetarians, if not vegans. **89m/C DVD.** Sarah Lassez, James Duval, Devon Odessa, Walter Koenig, Vic Chao, Chris Dimassis; *D:* Gregory Hatanka; *W:* Gregory Hatanka, Norith Soth; *C:* Gregory Hatanka.

Mad Death 🦴🦴 **1983** The British Isles take extreme steps to quarantine themselves against rabies from the European continent. This condensed TV miniseries preys on fears of the worst, as an outbreak of the virus spreads from dogs and other pets to humans, and special commandoes are mobilized. **120m/C VHS.** *GB* Richard Heffer, Barbara Kellerman, Richard Morant, Brenda Bruce, Debbi Blythe; *D:* Robert Young; *W:* Sean Hignett.

Mad Doctor of Blood Island WOOF! *Tomb of the Living Dead; Blood Doctor* **1968** Dull band of travelers arrive on mysterious tropical island and encounter bloodthirsty creature. Warning: This film is not recognized for outstanding achievements in acting, dialogue, or cinematography. **110m/C VHS, DVD.** *PH* John Ashley, Angelique Pettyjohn, Ronald Remy, Alicia Alonzo, Alfonso Carvajal, Johnny Long, Nadja, Bruno Punzalan; *D:* Gerardo (Gerry) De Leon, Eddie Romero; *W:* Reuben Candy; *C:* Justo Paulino; *M:* Tito Arevalo.

Mad Dog WOOF! 1984 An escaped convict seeks revenge on the cop responsible for his imprisonment. **90m/C VHS, DVD.** Helmut Berger, Marisa Mell; *D:* Sergio Grieco.

Mad Dog and Glory 🦴🦴🦴 **1993 (R)** Cast against type, Murray and De Niro play each other's straight man in this dark romantic comedy. Meek "Mad Dog" (De Niro) is an off-duty police photographer who happens upon a convenience store robbery and manages to save the life of Frank (Murray), obnoxious gangster by day, obnoxious stand-up comic by night. To settle up, Frank offers him Glory (Thurman), for a week. Eventually, Frank wants Glory back, forcing wimpy Mad Dog to either confront or surrender. Directed by McNaughton, who established himself with "Henry: Portrait of a Serial Killer." Uneven and not of the knee-slapper ilk, but the performances are tight, including Caruso as a cop buddy of De Niro's. **97m/C VHS, DVD.** Robert De Niro, Uma Thurman, Bill Murray, David Caruso, Mike Starr, Tom Towler, Kathy Baker, Derek Anunciation, J.J. Johnston, Richard Belzer; *D:* John McNaughton; *W:* Richard Price; *C:* Robby Muller; *M:* Elmer Bernstein.

Mad Dog Killer 🦴🦴 *La Belva Col Mitra; Beast with a Gun* **1977** Sleazy Eurotrash of the type that seems especially suited to the 1970s. Rabidly violent Nanni Vitali (Berger) busts out of the slammer with several cohorts and proceeds to go on a revenge and crime spree, starting with the gruesome execution of the snitch who put him behind bars. The snitch's girlfriend Giuliana (Mell) is an unfortunate witness so Nanni kidnaps and brutalizes her, even forcing her to help plan his next heist. She eventually escapes and exposes Nanni's plan to cop Santini (Harrison). So the heist is botched and the psycho is royally ticked off. Last film for director/writer Grieco. Italian with subtitles. **91m/C DVD.** *IT* Helmut Berger, Marisa Mell, Richard Harrison, Maria Angela Giordano, Vittorio Duse, Luigi Bonos; *D:* Sergio Grieco; *W:* Sergio Grieco; *C:* Vittorio Bernini; *M:* Umberto Smaila.

Mad Dog Morgan 🦴🦴 ½ *Mad Dog* **1976 (R)** Hopper delivers as engaging outlaw roaming outlands of 19th-century Australia. Quirky and violent G'day man. Based on a true story. **93m/C VHS, DVD.** *AU* Dennis Hopper, David Gulpilil; *D:* Philippe Mora.

The Mad Executioners 🦴🦴 *Der Henker Von London* **1965** Scotland Yard inspector searches for a sex maniac who decapitates women. In the meantime, a group of vigilantes capture criminals and sentence them without a trial. Confusing film with a predictable ending. Based on the book "White Carpet" by Bryan Edgar Wallace. **92m/B VHS.** *GE* Hansjorg Felmy, Maria Perschy, Dieter Borsche, Rudolph Forster, Chris Howland, Wolfgang Preiss; *D:* Edwin Zbonek.

The Mad Ghoul 🦴🦴 **1943** Creepy, if minor, Universal horror. Mad scientist Morris (Zucco) experiments with an ancient gas that turns those who inhale into zombies who go after hearts instead of brains. Lab assistant Ted (Bruce) is victimized because Morris wants Ted's girlfriend Isabel (Ankers) for himself. **64m/B DVD.** George Zucco, David Bruce, Evelyn Ankers, Turhan Bey, Robert Armstrong, Milburn Stone, Andrew Tombes; *D:* James Hogan; *W:* Paul Gangelin, Brenda Weisberg; *C:* Milton Krasner.

Mad Hot Ballroom 🦴🦴🦴 **2005 (PG)** Sweet documentary about ballroom dancing. Only the participants are New York City fifth graders participating in a 10-week program organized by the American Ballroom Theater. The doc follows students from Bensonhurst, Tribeca, and Washington Heights (a mixture of races, ethnicities, and incomes) as they learn the fox trot, meringue, rumba, swing, and tango (and how to deal with the opposite sex) in order to take part in an annual city-wide competition. **105m/C DVD.** *US D:* Marilyn Agrelo; *W:* Amy Sewell; *C:* Claudia Raschke; *M:* Steven Lutvak, Joseph Baker.

Mad Love 🦴🦴🦴 *The Hands of Orlac* **1935** Brilliant surgeon Gogol (Lorre) falls madly in love with actress Yvonne Orlac (Drake), but she rebuffs him. When her pianist husband Stephen's (Clive) hands are cut off in a train accident, Gogol agrees to attach new hands, using those of a recently executed knife-wielding murderer, Reagan (Brophy). Gogol then kills Stephen's stepfather and uses psychological terror to make the pianist think he killed him. There's also an appearance by the supposedly dead murderer who shows up to reclaim his hands. A real chiller about obsessive love and psychological fear. The only downfall to this one is the unnecessary comic relief by Healy. Lorre's first American film. **70m/B VHS.** Peter Lorre, Colin Clive, Frances Drake, Ted Healy, Edward Brophy, Sara Haden, Henry Kolker, Keye Luke, May (Mae) Beatty; *D:* Karl Freund; *W:* P.J. Wolfson, John Lloyd Balderston, Guy Endore; *C:* Gregg Toland, Chester Lyons; *M:* Dimitri Tiomkin.

Mad Love 🦴 ½ **1995 (PG-13)** Teen love has rarely been so insipid. Impulsive, fragile, and annoyingly melodramatic Casey (Barrymore) bewitches responsible, straightlaced Matt (O'Donnell) with her kewpie-doll charm and penchant for mischief. When Casey's bipolar ways land her in a mental hospital, Matt breaks her out and the unconvincing duo hit the road, where their supposedly free-spirited, passion-filled escapades grow increasingly inconsistent and silly, eventually halted by Casey's clinical crash. Slightly redeemed by a cool soundtrack and decent acting, but otherwise dull and insignificant, with an ending that may induce involuntary eyerolling. You've been warned. **95m/C VHS, DVD.** Chris O'Donnell, Drew Barrymore, Joan Allen, Kevin Dunn, Jude Ciccolella, Amy Sakasitz, T.J. Lowther; *D:* Antonia Bird; *W:* Paula Milne; *C:* Fred Tammes.

Mad Love 🦴🦴 ½ *Madness of Love; Juana la Loca; Joan the Mad* **2001 (R)** Peculiar costume drama is base on the life of Spanish queen Joan (known as "Joan the Mad" or "Juana La Loca"), daughter of King Ferdinand and Queen Isabella. In 1496, she is sent to marry Prince Philip of Flanders (known as "Philip the Handsome"). Although the marriage is arranged, the two are instantly smitten, Joan exceedingly so. As the passion wears thin for Philip and he begins fooling around, her intense love is enhanced by jealousy, which Philip uses to ascend to the throne by having Joan declared insane after Isabella dies. Considered tame in comparison to Aranda's previous work (especially considering the passionate subject matter), pic does well on his attention to subtle detail and the standout performance of Lopez de Ayala as the lusty queen. **117m/C VHS, DVD.** *SP IT PT* Pilar Lopez de Ayala, Daniele Liotti, Manuela Arcuri, Eloy Azorin, Rosana Pastor, Giuliano Gemma; *D:* Vicente Aranda; *W:* Vicente Aranda; *C:* Paco Femenia; *M:* Jose Nieto.

Mad Max 🦴🦴🦴 ½ **1980 (R)** Set on the stark highways of the post-nuclear future, an ex-cop seeks personal revenge against a rovin' band of vicious outlaw bikers who killed his wife and child. Futuristic scenery and excellent stunt work make for an exceptionally entertaining action-packed adventure. Followed by "The Road Warrior" (also known as "Mad Max 2") in 1981 and "Mad Max Beyond Thunderdome" in 1985. **93m/C VHS, DVD, UMD.** *AU* Mel Gibson, Joanne Samuel, Hugh Keays-Byrne, Steve Bisley, Tim Burns, Roger Ward, Vincent (Vince Gill) Gil; *D:* George Miller; *W:* George Miller; *C:* David Eggby; *M:* Brian May.

Mad Max: Beyond Thunderdome 🦴🦴 ½ **1985 (PG-13)** Max drifts into evil town ruled by Turner and becomes gladiator, then gets dumped in desert and is rescued by band of feral orphans. Third in a bleak, extremely violent, often exhilirating series. **107m/C VHS, DVD.** *AU* Mel Gibson, Tina Turner, Helen Buday, Frank Thring Jr., Bruce Spence, Robert Grubb, Angelo Rossitto, Angry Anderson, George Spartels, Rod Zuanic; *D:* George Miller, George Ogilvie; *W:* Terry Hayes, George Miller; *C:* Dean Semler; *M:* Maurice Jarre.

Mad Miss Manton 🦴🦴 **1938** A socialite turns detective to solve murder. Pleasant comedy-mystery provides occasional laughs and suspense. **80m/B VHS.** Barbara Stanwyck, Henry Fonda, Hattie McDaniel, Sam Levene, Miles Mander, Charles Halton; *D:* Leigh Jason.

Mad Mission 3 🦴 ½ *Aces Go Places 3: Our Man From Bond Street* **1984** Chinese man vacationing in Paris becomes involved in plot to recover precious jewels stolen from England's royal crown. Has there already been "Mad Mission" and "Mad Mission 2"? **81m/C VHS, DVD.** *HK* Richard Kiel, Sam Hui, Peter Graves, Sylvia Chang; *Cameos:* Tsui Hark; *D:* Tsui Hark; *W:* Raymond Wong; *C:* Henry Chan; *M:* Lynsey De Paul, Terry Britten.

Mad Money 🦴 ½ **2008 (PG-13)** Bridget (Keaton), a middle-class wife and mother, is in trouble when her husband (Danson) is downsized and her comfortable home and lifestyle are threatened. The only job she can find is as a janitor at the Federal Reserve Bank, where she forges unlikely friendships with single mom Nina (Queen Latifah) and young dreamer Jackie (Holmes). Of course, the women aren't content in their menial positions and find, ahem, an opportunity to even the score. Reluctant at first, Nina and Jackie end up following Bridget's lead, and the gals hatch a scheme to "recycle" (i.e., steal) old, out-of-circulation bills that are about to be destroyed anyway. What can it hurt? Bridget gets greedy and the plan starts to fall apart, but no matter, the fizzling silliness continues in this madcap caper that's just a little too mad. **104m/C DVD, Blu-ray Disc.** *US GB* Diane Keaton, Queen Latifah, Katie Holmes, Ted Danson, Stephen (Steve) Root, Christopher McDonald, Adam Rothenberg, Barry; *D:* Callie Khouri; *W:* Glen Gers; *C:* John Bailey; *M:* Martin Davich, James Newton Howard.

The Mad Monster 🦴 ½ **1942** This "Wolf Man"-inspired cheapie looks like a misty relic today. A mad scientist furthers the war effort by injecting wolf's blood into a handyman, who becomes hairy and anti-social. **77m/B VHS, DVD.** Johnny Downs, George Zucco, Anne Nagel, Sarah Padden, Glenn Strange, Gordon DeMain, Mae Busch; *D:* Sam Newfield.

Mad Monster Party 🦴🦴 ½ **1968** Frankenstein is getting older and wants to retire from the responsibilities of being senior monster, so he calls a convention of creepy creatures to decide who should take his place—The Wolfman, Dracula, the Mummy, the Creature, It, the Invisible Man, or Dr. Jekyll and Mr. Hyde. Animated feature using the process of "Animagic." **94m/C VHS, DVD.** *D:* Jules Bass; *V:* Boris Karloff, Ethel Ennis, Phyllis Diller.

Mad Wax: The Surf Movie 🦴 **1990** A flimsy plot about a window-cleaner who discovers a magical surfing wax serves as a framework for lots and lots of scenes of surfin' dudes. **45m/C VHS.** Richard Cram, Marvin Foster, Aaron Napolean, Tom Carroll, Bryce Andrews, Ross Clarke-Jones; *D:* Michael Hohensee.

The Mad Whirl 🦴 ½ **1925** The Roarin' '20s are a mad mad whirl in this silent silent period piece. **80m/B VHS.** Myrtle Stedman, Barbara Bedford, Alec B. Francis, George Fawcett, Joseph Singleton; *D:* William A. Seiter; *W:* Harvey Thew; *C:* Merritt B. Gerstad.

Mad Youth WOOF! 1940 A teenage girl falls in love with a man whom her slutty, alcoholic mother had been chasing. Bottom of the barrel production provides many unintentional laughs. Extraneous South American dance sequences included as character development. **61m/B VHS, DVD.** Mary Ainslee, Betty Atkinson, Willy Castello, Betty Compson, Tommy Wonder; *D:* Melville Shyer; *W:* Willis Kent.

Madagascar 🦴🦴 ½ **2005 (PG)** Marty the Zebra (Rock) just turned 10 and he wants to escape the comfortable confines of New York's Central Park Zoo and head off into "the wild" (okay, Connecticut). Aided by a group of sassy penguins, he makes his break, but his zoo buddies—Alex the Lion (Stiller), Gloria the Hippo (Pinkett Smith), and Melman the Giraffe (Schwimmer)—escape to stop him. Things go awry and the authorities ship them off to a Kenyan animal reserve. Things go more awry and the group ends up on the shores of Madagascar. A romp for the kids with lots of pizzazz but not much substance. Adults will find some "Shrek"-type jokes to enjoy, but this one's mainly for the kiddies. **80m/C DVD, Blu-ray Disc.** *US D:* Eric Darnell, Tom McGrath; *W:* Eric Darnell, Tom McGrath, Billy Frolick, Mark Burton; *M:* Hans Zimmer; *V:* Ben Stiller, Chris Rock, Jada Pinkett Smith, David Schwimmer, Cedric the Entertainer, Andy Richter, Sacha Baron Cohen.

Madagascar: Escape 2 Africa 🦴🦴 ½ **2008 (PG)** For an animated sequel it's about as good as you could ask for. The strong cast is all back from the original "Madagascar" and the top-notch computer animation is super sharp. The former Central Park Zoo inhabitants Alex, Marty, Melman, and Gloria—along with King Julien, Maurice, and the penguins—have been stranded in Madagascar and attempt to escape to Africa. The penguins have been enlisted to repair a questionable aircraft for the journey. They end up in an African preserve were Alex (Stiller) is reunited with his father (Mac) and mother (Shepherd). Other plots involve a romantic triangle between a giraffe (Schwimmer) and a couple of hippos (Smith and will.i.am). Baron Cohens's King Julien the Lemur serves up some of the best laughs and may make the whole thing worth sitting through with the kids who will fully appreciate the sophomoric gag fest. **89m/C DVD.** *US* ***D:*** Eric Darnell, Tom McGrath; ***W:*** Eric Darnell, Tom McGrath; ***M:*** Hans Zimmer, will-.i.am; ***V:*** Ben Stiller, David Schwimmer, Chris Rock, Jada Pinkett Smith, Sacha Baron Cohen, Cedric the Entertainer, Bernie Mac, Andy Richter, Alec Baldwin, Sherri Shepherd, Tom McGrath, Christopher Knight, Conrad Vernon, will.i.am, Chris Miller, Elisa Gabrielli.

Madagascar Skin **1995 (R)** Harry (Hannah) is a young gay man who's disfigured by a large port-wine birthmark on one side of his face (in the shape of Madagascar). Suicidally depressed he drives to a deserted beach on the Welsh coast but before making any final decisions, he picks up an overturned bucket lying on the sand. To his shock, it's covering the head of the very much alive middle-aged Flint (Hill), who's been buried up to his neck in sand and left to drown by some fellow crooks. Flint knows of a deserted beach shack, the oddly matched duo move in, and Harry falls in love. Deliberately dreamlike in some respects, the leads provide a bittersweet, adult romance. **95m/C VHS.** *GB* John Hannah, Bernard Hill; ***D:*** Chris Newby; ***W:*** Chris Newby; ***C:*** Oliver Curtis.

Madam Satan 1/2 **1930** Extremely bizarre DeMille film highlighted by lavish musical numbers and outrageous costumes. Wealthy socialite realizes she's losing her husband to a young showgirl, so she disguises herself as a sultry French tramp and entices her husband at a masquerade party aboard a zeppelin—surely one of the wildest party scenes ever captured on film. Chorus girls perform several exotic dance numbers inside the airship that are nothing short of fantastic. A storm breaks out and the floating dirigible is struck by lightning—leading viewers to wonder if the mad party-goers will make it to safety or crash and burn like this pic did at the boxoffice. **115m/B VHS.** Kay Johnson, Reginald Denny, Lillian Roth, Roland Young, Boyd Irwin, Elsa Peterson; ***D:*** Cecil B. DeMille.

Madame Bovary **1934** A young adultress with delusions of romantic love finds only despair in this offbeat adaptation of Flaubert's masterpiece. In French with English subtitles. **102m/B VHS.** *FR* Pierre Renoir, Valentine Tessier, Max Dearly; ***D:*** Jean Renoir.

Madame Bovary **1949** Young adultress with delusions of romantic love finds only despair, even in this Hollywood version of Flaubert's classic. Mason/Flaubert is put on trial for indecency following publication of the novel, with the story told from the witness stand. While this device occasionally slows the narrative, astute direction helps the plot along. Minnelli's handling of the celebrated ball sequence is superb. **115m/B VHS, DVD.** Jennifer Jones, Van Heflin, Louis Jourdan, James Mason, Gene Lockhart, Gladys Cooper, George Zucco; ***D:*** Vincente Minnelli; ***M:*** Miklos Rozsa.

Madame Bovary 1/2 **1991 (PG-13)** Provincial 19th century France is the setting for the tragedy of a romantic woman. Emma Bovary is bored by her marriage to an unsuccessful country doctor and longs for passion and excitement. She allows herself to be seduced (and abandoned) by a local aristocrat and herself seduces a young banker. She also struggles with an increasing burden of debt as she continues her quest for luxury. Realizing she will never find the passion she desires, Emma takes drastic, and tragic, measures. Sumptuous-looking film, with an extraordinary performance by Huppert. In French with English subtitles. Based on the novel by Gustave Flaubert. **130m/C VHS, DVD.** *FR* Isabelle Huppert, Jean-Francois Balmer, Christophe MaLavoy, Jean Yanne; ***D:*** Claude Chabrol; ***W:*** Claude Chabrol; ***M:*** Matthieu Chabrol.

Madame Bovary 1/2 **2000** British adaptation of Gustave Flaubert's scandalous novel, which is set in rural Normandy in the 1830s and '40s. Emma (O'Connor) is the convent-educated daughter of a farmer, who makes an unwise marriage to country doctor Charles Bovary (Bonneville), whom she doesn't love. Indeed, Emma has some overly romantic notions about love that lead to infidelity and despair. But it's Emma's extravagence and her borrowing from the usurious Lheureux (Barron) that bring her to disaster. None of the characters are particularly bright (or likeable) so your sympathy is at a minimum. **140m/C VHS.** *GB* Frances O'Connor, Hugh Bonneville, Greg Wise, Hugh Dancy, Keith Barron, Trevor Peacock; ***D:*** Tim Fywell; ***W:*** Heidi Thomas. **TV**

Madame Butterfly **1995** A French production, filmed in Tunisia, with a Chinese soprano, and Italian subtitles. Mitterrand takes on Puccini's opera, setting it in 1904 Nagasaki, but playing most of the story straight (he adds some documentary footage of old Japan between the acts). 15-year-old Butterfly (Huang) is a geisha who makes the mistake of falling in love and marrying deceitful American naval officer Pinkerton (Troxell). She's disowned by her family, he eventually sails away, and when he does return, it's with an American bride. Tragedy ensues. Newcomer Huang's fine but the handsome Troxell's a little stiff. **129m/C VHS, DVD.** *FR* Ying Huang, Richard Troxell, Ning Liang, Richard Cowan; ***D:*** Frederic Mitterrand; ***W:*** Frederic Mitterrand; ***C:*** Philippe Welt.

Madame Curie **1943** The film biography of Madame Marie Curie, the woman who discovered Radium. A deft portrayal by Garson, who is reteamed with her "Mrs. Miniver" co-star, Pidgeon. Certainly better than most biographies from this time period and more truthful as well. **124m/B VHS, DVD.** Greer Garson, Walter Pidgeon, Robert Walker, May Whitty, Henry Travers, Sir C. Aubrey Smith, Albert Bassermann, Victor Francen, Reginald Owen, Van Johnson; ***D:*** Mervyn LeRoy; ***C:*** Joseph Ruttenberg.

Madame O 1/2 *Zoku akutokui: Joi-hen* **1967** Sequel to a film unreleased in the States, provides generous flashbacks telling the story of its main character. Seiko (Michiko Aoyama) is raped at 16 and suffers not only impregnation and syphilis, but also an uncontrollable sexual desire and hatred of men whom she believes are all evil. Now one of the country's most successful doctors by day, she prowls the street at night looking for evil men to infect. Falling in love with another doctor she decides to call it quits until she starts getting blackmailed by a former victim. **81m/B DVD.** *JP* Michiko Sakyo, Naomi Tani; ***D:*** Seiichi Fukuda; ***W:*** Tomomi Tsukasa; ***C:*** Jiro Ooyama.

Madame Rosa *La Vie Devant Soi* **1977 (PG)** An aging Jewish prostitute tends prostitutes' offspring in this warmhearted work. A survivor of the Holocaust, the old woman finds her spirit revived by one of her charges—an abandoned Arab boy. In French with English subtitles. **105m/C VHS.** *FR IS* Simone Signoret, Claude Dauphin, Samy Ben Youb, Michal Bat-Adam; ***D:*** Moshe Mizrahi; ***W:*** Moshe Mizrahi; ***C:*** Nestor Almendros; ***M:*** Philippe Sarde. Oscars '77: Foreign Film; Cesar '78: Actress (Signoret); L.A. Film Critics '78: Foreign Film.

Madame Sans-Gene *Madame* **1962** Bawdy laundress Catherine (Loren) falls for Lefevre (Hossein), a soldier in Napoleon's (Berthea) army. While the French battle the Austrians, Catherine seeks her new husband on the battlefield and they both become accidental heroes. When Napoleon becomes emperor, he rewards them with a title but his sisters think Catherine is too uncouth and try to force the couple apart. But they don't know who they're dealing with. French and Italian with subtitles. **104m/C DVD.** *FR IT* Sophia Loren, Robert Hossein, Julien Bertheau, Marina Berti, Analia Gade, Laura Valenzuela, Mary Renaud; ***D:*** Christian-Jaque; ***W:*** Christian-Jaque; ***C:*** Roberto Gerardi; ***M:*** Angelo Francesco Lavagnino.

Madame Sata **2002** Frist feature for director Karim Ainouz is a stylized portrait of Joao Francisco dos Santos, who became a legend in the slums and prisons of Brazil as both a criminal and the cabaret performer Madame Sata. The film covers a period in 1930s Rio showcasing Joao's (Ramos) life at the Blue Danube club where he performs and the boarding-house where he lives with his ready-made family—hooker Laurita (Cartaxo) and her baby daughter and flamboyant hustler Taboo (Bauraqui). Ramos gives a compelling performance of a sometimes violent character who lives his life without apologies. Portuguese with subtitles. **105m/C VHS, DVD.** *BR FR* Lazaro Ramos, Marcella Cartaxo, Flavio Bauraqui, Felippe Marques; ***D:*** Karim Ainouz; ***W:*** Karim Ainouz; ***C:*** Walter Carvalho; ***M:*** Marcos Suzano, Sacha Ambak.

Madame Sin 1/2 **1971** Aspiring world dominator enlists former CIA agent in scheme to obtain nuclear submarine. Davis is appealing as evil personified, in her first TV movie. **91m/C VHS.** Bette Davis, Robert Wagner; ***D:*** David Greene; ***M:*** Michael Gibbs. **TV**

Madame Sousatzka **1988 (PG-13)** Eccentric, extroverted piano teacher helps students develop spiritually as well as musically. When she engages a teenage Indian student, however, she finds herself considerably challenged. MacLaine is perfectly cast in this powerful, winning film. **113m/C VHS, DVD.** Shirley MacLaine, Peggy Ashcroft, Shabana Azmi, Twiggy, Leigh Lawson, Geoffrey Bayldon, Navin Chowdhry, Lee Montague; ***D:*** John Schlesinger; ***W:*** Ruth Prawer Jhabvala, John Schlesinger; ***M:*** Gerald Gouriet. Golden Globes '89: Actress—Drama (MacLaine); Venice Film Fest. '88: Actress (MacLaine).

Madame X 1/2 **1937** Fourth version of this classic tearjerker finds diplomat's wife George having a fling with a playboy. There's a murder and she turns to her nasty mother-in-law for aid. She arranges for daughter-in-law-dearest's "death" in order to prevent a scandal. Then George is on the slippery path to alcoholism and prostitution. Adapted from the play by Alexandre Bisson. Run-of-the-mill; Lana Turner's 1966 version is still the one to watch. **96m/B VHS.** Gladys George, John Beal, Warren William, Reginald Owen, William Henry, Henry Daniell, Philip Reed, Lynne Carver, Emma Dunn, Ruth Hussey; ***D:*** Sam Wood; ***W:*** John Meehan.

Madame X 1/2 *Absinthe* **1966** Lonely diplomat's wife Holly (Turner) has a fling with playboy Phil (Montalban) who dies in her presence. Her nasty mother-in-law (Bennett in her last role) advises her to skedaddle or ruin hubby Clay's (Forsythe) career. She leaves her young son and eventually winds up a prostitute in Mexico where she falls in with slimy crook Sullivan (Meredith). Holly winds up killing him and goes on trial as Madame X. Oft-filmed melodrama works because of Turner's heartfelt and affecting performance. **100m/C VHS.** Lana Turner, John Forsythe, Ricardo Montalban, Burgess Meredith, Virginia Grey, Constance Bennett, Keir Dullea; ***D:*** David Lowell Rich; ***W:*** Jean Holloway; ***C:*** Russell Metty; ***M:*** Frank Skinner.

M.A.D.D.: Mothers Against Drunk Driving 1/2 **1983** Emotionally gripping movie recounts the story of Candy Lightner, who, after her daughter was killed in a drunk driving accident, founded M.A.D.D. and built it into a nationwide organization. Similar to "License to Kill," which dramatized the effect that a drunk driving accident can have on the families of those involved. **97m/C VHS.** Mariette Hartley, Paula Prentiss, Bert Remsen; ***D:*** William A. Graham; ***C:*** Dean Cundey; ***M:*** Bruce Broughton. **TV**

The Maddening 1/2 **1995 (R)** When their car breaks down in a remote area, Cassie (Sara) and daughter Samantha find refuge at the home of Roy Scudder (Reynolds) and his wife Georgina (Dickinson). At least Cassie thought it was a refuge—until she realizes the Scudders are crazy killers. **97m/C VHS.** Burt Reynolds, Angie Dickinson, Mia Sara, Brian Wimmer, Josh Mostel, William Hickey; ***D:*** Danny Huston; ***W:*** Leslie Greif.

Made 1/2 **2001 (R)** Favreau, who also wrote and directed, teams up again with "Swingers" buddy Vaughn in this tale of two-bit losers trying to weasel their way into the mob. Bobby (Favreau), a past-his-prime boxer and construction worker, chauffeurs his stripper girlfriend Jessica (Janssen) to her gigs at night. Ricky (Vaughn), his irritating, motor-mouthed friend, wants to get mobbed up with crime boss Max (Falk). Hoping to earn enough money to "save" Jessica, Bobby reluctantly agrees. Max sends them to New York with cryptic instructions to follow the orders of slick gangsta Ruiz (Puff Da...um...P. Did...er...Sean Combs). While Bobby tries to follow orders, Ricky's rash behavior lands them in constant trouble. Vaughn's comic riffing occasionally crosses the line into excess, but the chemistry between the two leads is excellent and the laughs are plentiful. **94m/C VHS, DVD, UMD.** *US* Jon Favreau, Vince Vaughn, Famke Janssen, Faizon Love, David O'Hara, Vincent Pastore, Peter Falk, Sean (Puffy, Puff Daddy, P. Diddy) Combs, Drea De Matteo; ***D:*** Jon Favreau; ***W:*** Jon Favreau; ***C:*** Christopher Doyle; ***M:*** John O'Brien, Lyle Workman.

Made for Each Other **1939** Newlyweds John (Stewart) and Jane (Lombard) Mason must overcome meddlesome in-laws, poverty, and even the arrival of a baby in this classic melodrama. Things become so serious, they decide to separate but their child's serious illness brings them together for a second chance. Dated but appealing. **94m/B VHS, DVD.** James Stewart, Carole Lombard, Charles Coburn, Lucile Watson; ***D:*** John Cromwell; ***W:*** Jo Swerling; ***C:*** Leon Shamroy; ***M:*** Louis Forbes.

Made for Love 1/2 **1926** Couple journeys romantically in Egypt until disaster strikes: they fall into a tomb and can't get out. **65m/B VHS.** Leatrice Joy, Edmund Burns, Ethel Wales, Brandon Hurst, Frank Butler; ***D:*** Paul Sloane.

Made in America **1993 (PG-13)** High-energy, lightweight comedy stars Whoopi as a single mom whose daughter Long discovers her birth was the result of artifical insemination. More surprising is her biological dad: white, obnoxious, country-western car dealer Danson. Overwrought with obvious gags, basically a one-joke movie. Nonetheless, Goldberg and Danson chemically connect onscreen (and for a short time offscreen as well) while supporting actor Smith grabs comedic attention as Teacake, Long's best friend. Both Goldberg and Danson deserve better material. **111m/C VHS, DVD.** Whoopi Goldberg, Ted Danson, Will Smith, Nia Long, Paul Rodriguez, Jennifer Tilly, Peggy Rea, Clyde Kusatsu; ***D:*** Richard Benjamin; ***W:*** Holly Goldberg Sloan; ***C:*** Ralf Bode; ***M:*** Mark Isham.

Made in Argentina **1986** An Argentinean couple living in New York decide to return for a visit. Having left for political reasons, they still harbor bitterness. **90m/C VHS.** *AR* Luis Brandoni, Marta Bianchi, Leonor Manso; ***D:*** Juan Jose Jusid.

Made in Heaven **1952** Arid comedy in which British newlyweds try to sustain honeymoon for entire year. The bride, however, eventually suspects her husband of shenanigans with the maid. If this sounds good, then you may like it. **90m/C VHS.** *GB* Petula Clark, David Tomlinson, Sonja Ziemann, A.E. Matthews, Charles Victor, Sophie Stewart, John Stainton, Ferdinand "Ferdy" Mayne, Richard Wattis, Alfie Bass, Dora Bryan; ***D:*** Jack Paddy Carstairs; ***W:*** George H. Brown, William Douglas-Home; ***C:*** Geoffrey Unsworth.

Made in Heaven 1/2 **1987 (PG)** Two souls in heaven fall in love and must find each other after being reborn on Earth if they are to remain eternal lovers. Contains ethereal interpretations of heaven and several cameo appearances by famous actors and musicians. **105m/C VHS.** Timothy Hutton, Kelly McGillis, Maureen Stapleton, Mare Winningham, Ann Wedgeworth, Don Murray, Amanda Plummer, Timothy Daly, Marj Dusay; ***Cameos:*** Ellen Barkin, Neil Young, Tom Petty, Ric Ocasek, Tom Robbins, Debra Winger, Gary Larsen, David Rasche; ***D:*** Alan Rudolph; ***W:*** Raynold Gideon, Bruce A. Evans; ***M:*** Mark Isham.

Made in Paris 1/2 **1965** Maggie (Ann-Margaret), Barclay Department Store's assistant fashion buyer, is sent to Paris when her boss Irene (Adams) decides to get married. Maggie is wooed by ladies' man designer Marc Fontaine (Jourdan) and newspaperman Herb Stone (Crenna), who is actually supposed to keep an eye on her for Ted Barclay (Everett), the store owner's son who is in love with her. When it looks like Maggie has cost the store the Fontaine account, Ted comes to Paris on the pretext of straightening things out. Ann-Margaret has little to do beyond exploiting her sex-kitten persona. **103m/C DVD.** Ann-Margret, Louis Jourdan, Richard Crenna, Chad Everett, John McGiver, Edie Adams; ***D:*** Boris Sagal; ***W:*** Stanley Roberts; ***C:*** Milton Krasner; ***M:*** Georgie Stoll.

Made in USA 🦴 1/2 **1988 (R)** Wayward dudes engage vixen while cruising Midwest. Trouble, however, awaits. Note: This is not Godard's mid-'60s classic. **82m/C VHS.** Adrian Pasdar, Lori Singer, Christopher Penn; ***D:*** Ken Friedman; ***W:*** Ken Friedman.

Made Men 🦴🦴 **1999 (R)** Former hitman, now in the witness protection program, gets caught stealing 12 million from the mob. If he wants to save his life, he's got to outwit four mobsters sent to get the money. **90m/C VHS, DVD.** James Belushi, Michael Beach, Timothy Dalton, Vanessa Angel, Steve Railsback; ***D:*** Louis Morneau; ***C:*** George Mooradian; ***M:*** Stewart Copeland. **VIDEO**

Made of Honor 🦴 1/2 **2008 (PG-13)** Swinging single Tom (Dempsey) brags to his buddies that he lives a perfect life: he bags a new babe almost every night and still has the companionship of his lovely long-time best friend Hannah (Monaghan) for balance. But when Hannah returns from a Scotland vacation with the ultimate souvenir—a fiance—Tom quickly realizes he's missed his chance at true love. He accepts her offer to be the "maid" of honor (thus the ultra-clever title), hoping to sabotage the wedding from the inside. Little more than a bland gender-reversed version of "My Best Friend's Wedding" with paper-thin characters that bomb the chemistry test. **101m/C DVD, Blu-ray Disc.** *US* Patrick Dempsey, Michelle Monaghan, Kevin McKidd, Kathleen Quinlan, Sydney Pollack, Kadeem Hardison, Chris Messina, Busy Philipps, Kelly Carlson, James B. Sikking, Richmond Arquette, Beau Garrett, Whitney Cummings, Emily Nelson, Kevin Sussman, Selma Stern; ***D:*** Paul Weiland; ***W:*** Deborah Kaplan, Adam Sztykiel, Harry Elfont; ***C:*** Tony Pierce-Roberts; ***M:*** Rupert Gregson-Williams.

Madea Goes to Jail 🦴🦴 *Tyler Perry's Madea Goes to Jail* **2009 (PG-13)** Formulaic dramedy that makes outlaw grandma Medea (Perry) even more obnoxious than usual. This time Medea's law-breaking antics takes second place to the story of up-from-the-ghetto assistant DA Joshua Hardaway (Luke) who's shocked by the arrest of childhood friend Candace (Knight Pulliam), now a druggie hooker. Joshua's upscale fiancee Linda (Overman) is naturally upset by Joshua's persistence in trying to help Candace (which isn't selfless). Medea comes in when she winds up in the joint with Candace as a fellow inmate, thus allowing Medea to offer her own brand of trash-talking inspiration. **103m/C DVD.** *US* Keisha Knight Pulliam, Tyler Perry, Derek Luke, Vanessa Ferlito, RonReaco Lee, Ion Overman, Viola Davis, David Mann, Tamela Mann; ***D:*** Tyler Perry; ***W:*** Tyler Perry; ***C:*** Alexander Grusynski; ***M:*** Aaron Zigman.

Madea's Family Reunion 🦴 1/2 **2006 (PG-13)** Director/writer/actor Perry dresses in drag again to fill grandmamma's shoes in this sequel to his popular "Diary of a Mad Black Woman." Madea now must use her sassy tongue to help her nieces deal with their messed-up love lives while keeping her new foster child on the right track. The witty banter stumbles when mixed with serious social issues. **107m/C DVD.** *US* Tyler Perry, Blair Underwood, Lynn Whitfield, Boris Kodjoe, Henry Simmons, Lisa Arrindell Anderson, Maya Angelou, Rochelle Aytes, Jenifer Lewis, Cicely Tyson, Keke Palmer; ***D:*** Tyler Perry; ***W:*** Tyler Perry; ***C:*** Toyomichi Kurita; ***M:*** Tyler Perry, Elvin D. Ross.

Madeleine 🦴🦴 1/2 *The Strange Case of Madeleine* **1950** Courtroom drama of woman charged with poisoning her French lover in 1850s Scotland. Directed by the same David Lean who made "Bridge on the River Kwai" and "Lawrence of Arabia." Here, though, he was merely trying to provide a vehicle for his wife, actress Todd. Intrigued? **114m/B VHS, DVD.** Ann Todd, Leslie Banks, Ivan Desny, Norman Wooland, Barbara Everest, Susan Stranks, Patricia Raine, Elizabeth Sellars, Edward Chapman, Jean Cadell, Eugene Deckers, Amy Veness, John Laurie, Henry Edwards, Ivor Barnard, Barry Jones, David Morne, Andre Morell; ***D:*** David Lean; ***W:*** Nicholas Phipps, Stanley Haynes; ***C:*** Guy Green; ***M:*** William Alwyn.

Madeline 🦴🦴 **1998 (PG)** Adaptation of Ludwig Bemelmans' classic 1939 children's book about the trouble-finding orphan Madeline (Jones), her schoolmates, and their patient teacher Miss Clavel (McDormand). As the credits open, Bemelmans' familiar paintings are animated. After the live action starts, you'll wish that the producers had animated the entire film. Travelling through the plots of four of the six Madeline books, the acting seems a little flat, even for kids. McDormand and Hawthorne as Lord "Cucuface" Covington are unable to act to their fullest, and the child actors are mostly forgettable. If you liked the books as a kid, you may be disappointed; but it's a good way to introduce your own children to the series. **90m/C VHS, DVD.** Hatty Jones, Frances McDormand, Nigel Hawthorne, Ben Daniels, Arturo Venegas, Stephane Audran, Katia Caballero; ***D:*** Daisy von Scherler Mayer; ***W:*** Marc Levin, Jennifer Flacket, Chris Weitz, Paul Weitz; ***C:*** Pierre Aim; ***M:*** Michel Legrand.

Mademoiselle 🦴🦴 **1966** Moreau is a psychotic, sexually repressed schoolteacher in a small village who manages to keep herself under control until studly woodcutter Manni and his son take up residence. The locals distrust the stranger but Moreau can't wait to get her hands on him. Suddenly, the village is battered by a rash of poisonings, fires, and floods, all of which are blamed on Manni, leading the locals to exact a terrible vengeance. In French with English subtitles. **105m/B VHS, DVD.** *FR GB* Jeanne Moreau, Ettore Manni, Umberto Orsini, Keith Skinner, Jane Berretta, Mony Rey; ***D:*** Tony Richardson; ***W:*** Jean Genet; ***C:*** David Watkin.

Mademoiselle Fifi 🦴 1/2 **1944** Simon stars as a French laundress in 1870 France who refuses to give in to her small town's Prussian oppressors. The film title is the nickname of the most brutal of the Prussian officers, played by Kreuger. An unsucessful attempt at political allegory for the devastation of WWII. **69m/B VHS.** Simone Simon, John Emery, Kurt Kreuger, Alan Napier, Jason Robards Sr.; ***D:*** Robert Wise.

Madeo 🦴🦴 *Mother* **2009 (R)** Tough widow Hye-ja (Kim) runs a shop in a rural Korean town and tries to watch out for her mentally-challenged 27-year-old son Do-joon (Bin) who lives with her. Unfortunately, his best friend is local troublemaker Jin-tae (Jin). Do-joon becomes an easy target for the lazy local cops when a teenaged girl is the victim of a brutal sexual murder and they get a confession from the confused man. His mother knows better and she is on a one-woman crusade, determined to prove his innocence. Bong tends to throw in plot curves and he likes his small towns to have dark secrets but Kim gives an engrossing performance about maternal love. Korean with subtitles. **128m/C DVD.** *KN* Hye-ja Kim, Bin Won, Ku Jin; ***D:*** Joon-ho Bong; ***W:*** Joon-ho Bong, Eun-kyo Park; ***C:*** Kyung-Pyo Hong; ***M:*** Byeong-woo Lee.

Madhouse 🦴🦴 **1974** A troubled horror film star tries to bring his "Dr. Death" character to TV, but during production people begin dying in ways remarkably similar to the script. A strong genre cast should hold the fans' attention during this mild adaptation of Angus Hall's novel "Devilday." **92m/C VHS, DVD.** *GB* Vincent Price, Peter Cushing, Robert Quarry, Adrienne Corri, Natasha Pyne, Linda Hayden, Michael Parkinson; ***D:*** Jim Clark.

Madhouse 🦴🦴 **1987** A woman has bizarre recollections of her twin sister whom she finally meets when she escapes from a mental hospital. Lots of violence and gore, has definite cult potential. **90m/C VHS.** Trish Everly, Michael MacRae, Dennis Robertson, Morgan Hart; ***D:*** Ovidio G. Assonitis.

Madhouse 🦴🦴 **1990 (PG-13)** New homeowners find themselves unable to expel loathsome, boorish guests. Presumably, a comedy cashing in on two of sitcom's brightest lights. **90m/C VHS.** John Larroquette, Kirstie Alley, Alison La Placa, John Diehl, Jessica Lundy, Bradley Gregg, Dennis Miller, Robert Ginty; ***D:*** Tom Ropelewski; ***W:*** Tom Ropelewski; ***M:*** David Newman.

Madhouse 🦴🦴 **2004 (R)** Clark Stevens (Leonard) accepts a psychiatric internship at a dilapidated asylum where murders begin to occur, and he's haunted by the figure of a young boy. He teams up with sympathetic nurse Sara (Ladd) to find out what's going on. **91m/C DVD.** Joshua Leonard, Jordan Ladd, Natasha Lyonne, Lance Henriksen, Leslie Jordan, Patrika Darbo, Christian Leffler, Dendrie Taylor, Aaron Strongoni; ***D:*** William Butler; ***W:*** William Butler, Aaron Strongoni; ***C:*** Viorel Sergovici Jr.; ***M:*** Alberto Caruso.

Madhouse Mansion 🦴🦴 1/2 *Ghost Story* **1974 (PG)** A horror actor revives his career and becomes embroiled in murder. Plenty of in-jokes and clips from older movies. **86m/C VHS.** *GB* Marianne Faithfull, Leigh Lawson, Anthony Bate, Larry Dann, Sally Grace, Penelope Keith, Vivian Mackerell, Murray Melvin, Barbara Shelley; ***D:*** Stephen Weeks; ***C:*** Peter Hurst.

Madigan 🦴🦴🦴 **1968** Realistic and exciting and among the best of the behind-the-scenes urban police thrillers. Hardened NYC detectives (Widmark and Guardino) lose their guns to a sadistic killer and are given 72 hours to track him down. Fonda is the police chief none too pleased with their performance. Adapted by Howard Rodman, Abraham Polonsky, and Harry Kleiner from Richard Dougherty's "The Commissioner." **101m/C VHS, DVD.** Richard Widmark, Henry Fonda, Inger Stevens, Harry Guardino, James Whitmore, Susan Clark, Michael Dunn, Don Stroud; ***D:*** Donald Siegel; ***W:*** Abraham Polonsky; ***C:*** Russell Metty; ***M:*** Don Costa.

Madigan's Millions **WOOF!** **1967 (G)** Incompetent Treasury agent treks to Italy to recover funds swiped from deceased gangster. This is Hoffman's first film, and is to his career what "The Last Chalice" was to Paul Newman's and "Studs and Kitty" was Sylvester Stallone. Recommended only to the terminally foolhardy. **89m/C VHS, DVD.** Dustin Hoffman, Elsa Martinelli, Cesar Romero; ***D:*** Stanley Prager.

Madison 🦴🦴 1/2 **2001 (PG)** Predictably cliched sports drama based on a true story. Title refers to Madison, Indiana, a hard-luck community that, by 1971, has little going for it but a tradition of hydroplane racing and a chance to host the Gold Cup tournament. It also has all-around great guy Jim McCormick (Caviezel), a former pilot of the community-owned race boat, the Miss Madison. Both McCormick and Miss Madison have seen better days but golly, Jim just has to make his son Mike (Lloyd) proud. There's nothing actually wrong with the film (which sat on the shelf since 2001) but, boy, have you seen this story before. **94m/C DVD.** *US* James (Jim) Caviezel, Jake Lloyd, Mary McCormack, Bruce Dern, Brent Briscoe, Paul Dooley, Reed Edward Diamond, Chelcie Ross, Frank Knapp, Byrne Piven, William Shockley, Matt Letscher, Richard Lee Jackson, Kristina Anapau, Vincent Ventresca, Cody McMains; ***D:*** William Bindley; ***W:*** William Bindley, Scott Bindley; ***C:*** James Glennon; ***M:*** Kevin Kiner.

Madman 🦴 **1979 (R)** Deranged Soviet Jew joins Israeli army to more effectively fulfill his desire to kill loathsome Soviets. Good date movie for those nights when you're home alone. Weaver's first starring role. **95m/C VHS, DVD.** *IS* Sigourney Weaver, Michael Beck, F. Murray Abraham; ***D:*** Dan Cohen.

Madman 🦴 **1982 (R)** Camp leader prompts terror when he revives legend regarding ax murderer. Seems that when you call his name, he appears. Buffoon does not believe story and calls out madman's name. Madman hears the call and emerges from forest, says hi, and hacks everyone to death. Lesson learned, case closed. Filmed on Long Island. **89m/C VHS, DVD.** Carl Fredericks, Alexis Dubin, Tony Fish, Paul Ehlers; ***D:*** Joe Giannone; ***W:*** Joe Giannone, Gary Sales; ***C:*** James (Momel) Lemmo; ***M:*** Gary Sales, Stephen Horelick.

The Madness of King George 🦴🦴🦴 1/2 **1994 (R)** Poor King George is a monarch with problems—his 30 years of royal authority are being usurped by Parliament, his American colonies have been lost, and, in 1788, he's begun to periodically lose his mind. So what do you do when a ruler becomes irrational? The royal physicians are baffled, his loving Queen Charlotte (Mirren) is in despair, but the noxious Prince of Wales (Everett) can barely contain his glee at finally having a chance at the throne. A last resort is offered by Dr. Willis (Holm), a former clergyman with some unusual and sadistic ideas about treating the mentally ill (even if they do have royal blood). Brilliant performance by Hawthorne (who originated the stage role in Bennett's 1991 play "The Madness of George III"). Screen note explains that King George suffered from the metabolic disorder known as porphyria. A Tony Award-winner for his Broadway productions of "Miss Saigon" and "Carousel," Hytner makes his feature-film directing debut. **110m/C VHS, DVD.** *GB* Nigel Hawthorne, Helen Mirren, Ian Holm, Rupert Everett, Amanda Donohoe, Rupert Graves, Julian Wadham, John Wood, Julian Rhind-Tutt, Jim Carter; ***D:*** Nicholas Hytner; ***W:*** Alan Bennett; ***C:*** Andrew Dunn; ***M:*** George Fenton. Oscars '94: Art Dir./Set Dec.; British Acad. '95: Actor (Hawthorne); Cannes '95: Actress (Mirren).

Mado 🦴🦴🦴 **1976** A middle-aged businessman's life is undone when he falls for a mysterious woman. Piccoli and Schneider are, as usual, convincing. Another of underrated director Sautet's effective, low-key works. In French with subtitles. **130m/C VHS.** Romy Schneider, Michel Piccoli, Charles Denner; ***D:*** Claude Sautet. Cesar '77: Sound.

Madonna: Innocence Lost 🦴 1/2 **1995** Tacky TV movie focusing on the ambitious singer and would-be actress who made wearing underwear as outerwear almost acceptable. Tawdry gossip highlights this laughfest as the trash talker hustles her way to the top of the heap, uncaring of whom she steps on along the way. Toronto substitutes for New York City grit. **90m/C VHS.** Terumi Matthews, Wendie Malick, Jeff Yagher, Dean Stockwell, Nigel Bennett, Don Francks, Rod Wilson, Tom Melissis; ***D:*** Bradford May; ***W:*** Michael J. Murray.

Madron 🦴 1/2 **1970 (PG)** Road western filmed in the Israel desert, complete with menacing Apaches, wagon train massacre, a nun and a gunslinger. **93m/C VHS, DVD.** Richard Boone, Leslie Caron, Paul Smith; ***D:*** Jerry Hopper; ***W:*** Edward Chappell, Lee McMahon; ***C:*** Marcel Grignon, Adam Greenberg; ***M:*** Riz Ortolani.

The Madwoman of Chaillot 🦴 1/2 **1969 (G)** Four men conspire to drill for oil which they believe lurks under Paris. Hepburn finds out about their plot and tells each man that oil is bubbling up through her basement. Before the men can arrive at her house to confirm this, she and her three cronies hold a mock trial and sentence the men to death. Features a stellar cast, but this modern-day adaptation of Jean Giraudoux's play "La Folle de Chaillot" falls flat. **142m/C VHS.** Katharine Hepburn, Charles Boyer, Claude Dauphin, Edith Evans, John Gavin, Paul Henreid, Oscar Homolka, Margaret Leighton, Giulietta Masina, Nanette Newman, Richard Chamberlain, Yul Brynner, Donald Pleasence, Danny Kaye, Fernand Gravey; ***D:*** Bryan Forbes; ***W:*** Edward Anhalt.

Mae West 🦴🦴 1/2 **1984** Details West's life from her humble beginnings to her racy film stardom. Jillian does a good job bringing the buxom legend back to life. **97m/C VHS.** Ann Jillian, James Brolin, Piper Laurie, Roddy McDowall; ***D:*** Lee Philips; ***M:*** Brad Fiedel. **TV**

Maedchen in Uniform 🦴🦴🦴 1/2 *Girls in Uniform* **1931** A scandalous early German talkie about a rebellious schoolgirl who falls in love with a female teacher and attempts suicide when the teacher is punished for the relationship. A controversial criticism of lesbianism and militarism that impelled the Nazis, rising to power two years later, to exile its director. It was also banned in the United States. In German with English subtitles; edited versions are also in circulation. Remade in 1965. **90m/B VHS.** *GE* Dorothea Wieck, Ellen Schwannecke, Hertha Thiele; ***D:*** Leontine Sagan.

Maelstrom 🦴🦴 **2000** Offbeat mixture of the surreal, the whimsical, and the melodramatic. A drunken Bibliane (Croze) commits a hit-and-run and reads in the next day's newspaper that the man, a fishmonger, has died. Guilt-stricken, she meets the man's son, a deep sea diver named Evian (Verrault), at the funeral home and he mistakes her for a concerned neighbor. Bibliane's friendship with Evian leads to an affair but she becomes compelled to tell him the truth and accept whatever punishment he decrees. There's lots of water and fish imagery. French with subtitles. **86m/C VHS, DVD.** *CA* Marie Josee Croze, Jean-Nicholas Verreault, Stephanie Morgenstern, Bobby Beshro; ***D:*** Denis Villenueve; ***W:*** Denis Villenueve; ***C:*** Andre Turpin; ***M:*** Pierre Desrochers. Genie '00: Actress (Croze), Cinematog., Director (Villenueve), Film, Screenplay.

Mafia! *Jane Austen's Mafia!* **1998 (PG-13)** Director Abrahams returns to the "Airplane" well once again as he takes aim at the Mafia movies of Coppola and Scorsese. As usual, the results are hit and miss, with the joke machine gun set on full automatic. Plot follows that of the Godfather trilogy most closely, with Bridges (in his last film) as klutzy patriarch Vincenzo Cortino. His sons, sensitive war hero Anthony (Mohr) and hot tempered Joey (Burke), wrestle for control of the keystone kriminal empire after pop takes the dirt nap. Basically, the actors' jobs are to remain deadpan while all manner of shenanigans and hijinks take place and hilarity allegedly ensues. This genre is quickly running out of ammo. It's time for someone to administer the kiss of death. **87m/C VHS, DVD.** Lloyd Bridges, Jay Mohr, Billy Burke, Olympia Dukakis, Christina Applegate, Pamela Gidley, Tony LoBianco, Joe (Johnny) Viterelli, Vincent Pastore, Jason Fuchs, Gregory Sierra, Louis Mandylor; ***D:*** Jim Abrahams; ***W:*** Jim Abrahams, Michael McManus, Greg Norberg; ***C:*** Pierre Letarte; ***M:*** John (Gianni) Frizzell.

Mafia Princess **1986** The daughter of a Mafia boss tries to discover her own identity despite her father's involvement in crime. Based on a best-selling autobiography by a real-life member of a Mob family, Antoinette Giancana. **100m/C VHS.** Tony Curtis, Susan Lucci, Kathleen Widdoes, Chuck Shamata, Louie Dibianco; ***D:*** Robert E. Collins. **TV**

Mafia vs. Ninja ½ **1984** The mob wants to control the city, but the Ninja has other ideas. **90m/C VHS, DVD.** Alexander Lou, Wang Hsia, Charlema Hsu, Eugene Trammel; ***D:*** Robert Tai.

Mafioso ½ **1962** Black comedy from Lattuada that was revolutionary for its depiction of everyday Mafia life in Sicily. Nino (Sordi) is a longtime foreman at the Fiat plant in Milan. He decides to use his vacation time and take his wife (Conti) and daughters to visit his small hometown of Calamo. It's Nino's first visit home in years (and quite a culture shock for his wife) but that doesn't mean he's forgotten where to pay his respects. But town boss Don Vincenzo (Attanasio) is quick to remind Nino that he still owes him a favor and the Don now wants to collect. Italian with subtitles. **108m/B DVD.** *IT* Alberto Sordi, Norma Bengell, Cinzia Bruno, Ugo Attanasio, Gabriella Conti, Armando Tine, Francesco Lo Briglio, Katiusca Piretti; ***D:*** Alberto Lattuada; ***W:*** Rafael Azcona, Marco Ferreri, Agenore Incrocci, Furio Scarpelli; ***C:*** Armando Nannuzzi; ***M:*** Piero Piccioni.

Magdalene ½ **1988 (PG)** Somewhere in medieval Europe, a violent Baron seeks revenge on a beautiful whore that spurned him. Small-budget costumer. **89m/C VHS.** Steve Bond, Nastassja Kinski, David Warner, Gunter Meisner, Ferdinand "Ferdy" Mayne, Anthony Quayle, Franco Nero, Janet Agren; ***D:*** Monica Teuber.

The Magdalene Sisters ½ **2002 (R)** Semi-fictionalized stories of four young Irish women sentenced to life in a religious labor camp run by the Sisters of the Magdalene Order from 1964 to 1969. Their "crimes" include overt flirtatiousness, having been raped, bearing a child out of wedlock, and other perceived sexual offenses. They're treated cruelly by the ogre in authority, Sister Bridget (McEwan) and any attempt at escape is met with more brutality. Grim, powerful film captures the atrocities of 1960s-era Irish Catholicism with frightful clarity. **119m/C VHS, DVD.** *GB IR* Geraldine McEwan, Anne-Marie Duff, Nora-Jane Noone, Dorothy Duffy, Eileen Walsh, Mary Murray, Britta Smith, Frances Healy, Eithne McGuinness, Daniel Costello; ***D:*** Peter Mullan; ***W:*** Peter Mullan; ***C:*** Nigel Willoughby; ***M:*** Craig Armstrong. Venice Film Fest. '02: Film.

Magee and the Lady *She'll Be Sweet* **1978 (PG)** The crusty captain of a rusty ship must warm up to a spoiled debutante or lose his ship to a foreclosure firm. Could be better. Made for TV. **92m/C VHS.** *AU* Tony LoBianco, Sally Kellerman; ***D:*** Gene Levitt. **TV**

Magenta **1996 (R)** Don't mess around with your teenaged sister-in-law! You'd think guys would've learned that lesson by now. Handsome Dr. Michael Walsh (McMahon) and his lovely wife, Helen (Storry), have a seemingly happy life with their daughter Brittany. Then Helen's sister Magenta (Atkins) comes to stay and she and Michael are soon exchanging more than eye contact. Naturally, all this leads to betrayal, lies, and even more problems. **94m/C VHS.** Julian McMahon, Crystal Atkins, Alison Storry, Marklen Kennedy; ***D:*** Gregory C. Haynes; ***W:*** Gregory C. Haynes; ***C:*** Mark Anthony Galluzzo; ***M:*** Harald Kloser. **VIDEO**

Magic ½ **1978 (R)** Ventriloquist Hopkins and his dummy, an all-too-human counterpart, get involved with a beautiful but impressionable woman lost between reality and the irresistible world of illusion. Spine-chilling psycho-drama with a less-than-believable premise. Screenplay by Goldman from his novel. **106m/C VHS, DVD.** Anthony Hopkins, Ann-Margret, Burgess Meredith, Ed Lauter, Jerry Houser, David Ogden Stiers, Lillian Randolph; ***D:*** Richard Attenborough; ***W:*** William Goldman; ***C:*** Victor Kemper; ***M:*** Jerry Goldsmith.

The Magic Bow ½ **1947** Typically ridiculous musical bio—this time of violinist Nicolo Paganini (Granger). He's the talented poor boy who falls for the wealthy Jeanne (Calvert) but his one true love is for his Stradivarius. Yehudi Menuhim plays the solos. Based on the novel by Manuel Komroff. **105m/B VHS.** *GB* Stewart Granger, Phyllis Calvert, Jean Kent, Dennis Price, Cecil Parker, Felix Aylmer, Frank Cellier, Marie Lohr; ***D:*** Bernard Knowles; ***W:*** Roland Pertwee, Norman Ginsburg; ***C:*** Jack Asher, Jack Cox.

The Magic Bubble ½ **1993 (PG-13)** On her 40th birthday, Julia Cole finds the fountain of youth...inside a bottle of enchanted bubbles. Ageless and timeless, she begins to know the meaning of true happiness. **90m/C VHS, DVD.** Diane Salinger, John Calvin, Priscilla Pointer, Colleen Camp, Tony Peck, Wallace Shawn, George Clooney; ***D:*** Alfredo Ringel, Deborah Taper Ringel; ***W:*** Meridith Baer, Geof Pryssir.

The Magic Christian **1969 (PG)** A series of related skits about a rich man (Sellers) and his son (Starr) who try to prove that anyone can be bought. Raucous, now somewhat dated comedy; music by Badfinger, including Paul McCartney's "Come and Get It." **101m/C VHS, DVD.** *GB* Peter Sellers, Ringo Starr, Isabel Jeans, Wilfrid Hyde-White, Graham Chapman, John Cleese, Peter Graves, John Lennon, Yoko Ono, Richard Attenborough, Leonard Frey, Laurence Harvey, Christopher Lee, Spike Milligan, Yul Brynner, Roman Polanski, Raquel Welch, Caroline Blakiston, Ferdinand "Ferdy" Mayne; ***D:*** Joseph McGrath; ***W:*** Terry Southern, Peter Sellers, Graham Chapman, John Cleese; ***C:*** Geoffrey Unsworth; ***M:*** Ken Thorne.

The Magic Flute ½ **1973 (G)** Bergman's acclaimed version of Mozart's famous comic opera, universally considered one of the greatest adaptations of opera to film ever made. Staged before a live audience for Swedish TV. Subtitled. **134m/C VHS, DVD.** *SW* Josef Kostlinger, Irma Urrila, Hakan Hagegard, Elisabeth Erikson; ***D:*** Ingmar Bergman.

The Magic Fountain **1961** Three princes search for a magic fountain whose waters will cure their ailing father. Two of them, however, take the evil course and are turned into ravens by a wicked dwarf. Based on the fairy tale "Das Wasser des Lebens" by the Brothers Grimm. **82m/C VHS.** Peter Nestler, Helmo Kinderman, Josef Marz, Catherine Hansen, Cedric Hardwicke; ***D:*** Allan David.

Magic Hunter **1996** Max (Kemp) is supposed to be the best sharpshooter on the Budapest police force, but his skill deserts him and he accidentally shoots the woman he was assigned to protect. A sinister colleague gives him seven magic bullets guaranteed to hit their target but what Max doesn't realize is that he's made a bargain with the Devil, and the Devil gets to choose the seventh target. Hungarian with subtitles. **106m/C VHS.** *HU* Gary Kemp, Alexander Kaidanovsky, Sadie Frost; ***D:*** Ildiko Enyedi.

Magic in the Mirror: Fowl Play ½ **1996 (G)** Young Mary Margaret (Smith) does an "Alice Through the Looking Glass" when she steps through an antique mirror bequeathed to her by her grandmother and discovers an enchanted kingdom run by giant ducks. But just how will MM find her way back? **86m/C VHS.** Jamie Renee Smith, Kevin Wixted, Saxon Trainor, David Brooks, Godfrey James; ***D:*** Ted Nicolaou; ***W:*** Frank Dietz, Ken Carter Jr.; ***C:*** Adolfo Bartoli; ***M:*** Richard Kosinski.

Magic in the Water ½ **1995 (PG)** Divorced, obnoxious radio shrink and neglectful dad Dr. Jack Black (Harmon) takes the kiddies on a summer jaunt to a Canadian lake, where they begin to explore the legend of Orky, Canada's answer to the Loch Ness monster. Dad becomes a believer when Orky possesses his body and (New Age Alert!) releases his inner child. Harmless fun for the kids, but parents will gag at the attempt to provide a meaningful and symbolic message, which arrives with all the subtlety of an Oliver Stone history lesson. Sort of an "E.T." meets "Free Willy" with Orky shilling for the EPA. Beautiful cinematography showcasing the British Columbia landscape helps, but not enough. **100m/C VHS, DVD.** Mark Harmon, Joshua Jackson, Harley Jane Kozak, Sarah Wayne, Willie Nark-Orn, Frank S. Salsedo; ***D:*** Rick Stevenson; ***W:*** Icel Dobell Massey, Rick Stevenson; ***C:*** Thomas Burstyn; ***M:*** David Schwartz. Genie '95: Cinematog., Sound.

Magic Island ½ **1995 (PG)** Thirteen-year-old Jack (Bryan) gets sucked into the pages of a pirate book and finds himself with Blackbeard and his scurvy crew. They're on a treasure hunt and figure Jack's book contains some missing clues. Naturally, Jack finds himself in lots of trouble. **88m/C VHS.** Zachery Ty Bryan, Edward Kerr, Lee Armstrong, French Stewart, Abraham Benrubi, Jessie-Ann Friend, Oscar Dillon, Sean O'Kane, Schae Harrison, Ja'net DuBois, Andrew Divoff; ***D:*** Sam Irvin; ***W:*** Neil Ruttenberg, Brent Friedman; ***C:*** James Lawrence Spencer; ***M:*** Richard Band.

Magic Kid ½ *Ninja Dragons* **1992 (PG)** Thirteen-year-old martial-arts champ Kevin and his older sister vacation in L.A., staying with their shady Uncle Bob, a second-rate talent agent. Kevin wants to meet his martial arts movie idol and his sister her favorite soap opera hunk. But they wind up being chased by the mobsters Uncle Bob owes money to. **91m/C VHS, DVD.** Ted Jan Roberts, Shonda Whipple, Stephen Furst, Joseph Campanella, Billy Hufsey, Sondra Kerns, Pamela Dixon, Lauren Tewes, Don "The Dragon" Wilson; ***D:*** Joseph Merhi; ***W:*** Stephen Smoke; ***M:*** Jim Halfpenny.

Magic Kid 2 ½ **1994 (PG)** The young star of a popular martial arts program wants to quit and go to high school like a normal teenager. But the studio execs have other ideas. **90m/C VHS, DVD.** Ted Jan Roberts, Stephen Furst, Donald Gibb, Jennifer Savidge; ***D:*** Stephen Furst.

Magic Moments ½ **1989** Ambitious British TV exec Melanie James (Seagrove) is about to score the coup of her career. She's persuaded charismatic American illusionist Troy Gardner (Shea) to recreate his death-defying act on TV—but only if Melanie will produce the show herself. Too bad her power-hungry boss is out to cause trouble. Made for British TV. **103m/C VHS.** *GB* Jenny Seagrove, John Shea; ***D:*** Lawrence Gordon-Clark; ***W:*** Charlotte Bingham, Terence Brady; ***C:*** Ken Westbury; ***M:*** Alan Hawkshaw. **TV**

Magic of Lassie **1978 (G)** Stewart is engaging as the nice grandpa who refuses to sell his land to mean rich guy Roberts. Innocuous, pleasant remake of "Lassie Come Home." Stewart sings, as do Pat Boone and daughter Debby. **100m/C VHS.** James Stewart, Mickey Rooney, Stephanie Zimbalist, Alice Faye, Pernell Roberts; ***D:*** Don Chaffey.

Magic on Love Island **1980** Romantic misadventures ensue when eight ladies go on vacation to Love Island, a tropical paradise. **96m/C VHS.** Adrienne Barbeau, Bill Daily, Howard Duff, Dody Goodman, Dominique Dunne, Lisa Hartman Black, Janis Paige; ***D:*** Earl Bellamy.

Magic Serpent **1966** Fantasy set in medieval Japan features a grand duel in magic between a good hero and evil sorcerer who transform into a giant dragon and a giant frog to do battle. **86m/C VHS, DVD.** Hiroki Matsukata, Tomoko Ogawa, Ryutaro Otomo, Bin Amatsu; ***D:*** Tetsuya Yamauchi.

The Magic Stone ½ *Kilian's Chronicle* **1995** Kilian is the 10th-century Irish slave of brutish Viking Ivar, who decides to sacrifice him to the Norse god Thor when the Vikings become lost while sailing off the North American coast. Kilian manages to escape and make it to shore where he's rescued by a Native American tribe and falls in love with local beauty, Turtle. But Ivar goes after Kilian to steal his magic stone, which can navigate a ship through the worst weather, and begins a Viking war with the tribe. **95m/C VHS.** Christopher Johnson, Robert McDonough, Eva Kim, Jonah Ming Lee; ***D:*** Pamela Berger; ***W:*** Pamela Berger; ***C:*** John Hoover; ***M:*** R. Carlos Nakai, Bevan Manson.

The Magic Sword *St. George and the Seven Curses; St. George and the Dragon* **1962** A family-oriented adventure film about a young knight who sets out to rescue a beautiful princess who is being held captive by an evil sorcerer and his dragon. **80m/C VHS, DVD.** Basil Rathbone, Estelle Winwood, Gary Lockwood; ***D:*** Bert I. Gordon.

Magic Town ½ **1947** An opinion pollster investigates a small town which exactly reflects the views of the entire nation, making his job a cinch. The publicity causes much ado in the town with ensuing laughs. Uneven but entertaining. **103m/B VHS.** Jane Wyman, James Stewart, Kent Smith, Regis Toomey, Donald Meek; ***D:*** William A. Wellman; ***C:*** Joseph Biroc.

The Magic Voyage ½ **1993 (G)** Animated tale of a friendly woodworm named Pico who voyages with Columbus to the new world and convinces him that the world is indeed round. He then comes to the aid of a magical firefly named Marilyn who helps Columbus find gold to bring back to Spain. **82m/C VHS, DVD.** ***D:*** Michael Schoemann; ***V:*** Dom DeLuise, Mickey Rooney, Corey Feldman, Irene Cara, Dan Haggerty, Samantha Eggar.

The Magic Voyage of Sinbad *Sadko* **1952** Sinbad embarks on a fantastic journey after promising the people of his Covasian home that he will find the elusive Phoenix, the bird of happiness. Unreleased in the U.S. until 1962; rewritten for the American screen by a young Coppola. **79m/C VHS, DVD.** *RU* Sergey Stolyarov, Alla Larionova, Mark Troyanovsky; ***D:*** Alexander Ptushko; ***W:*** Francis Ford Coppola.

The Magical Legend of the Leprechauns ½ **1999** Goofy fantasy finds American businessman Jack Woods (Quaid) sent to a remote part of Ireland where he happens to save the life of leprechaun, Seamus Muldoon (Meaney), which puts the "little person" in his debt. While Jack tries to romance neighbor Kathleen (Brady), the leprechauns are getting into a fracas with their enemies, the Trooping Fairies, leading to a battle and Jack's involvement. **139m/C VHS, DVD.** Randy Quaid, Colm Meaney, Orla Brady, Whoopi Goldberg, Roger Daltrey, Daniel Betts, Zoe Wanamaker, Caroline Carver, Kieran Culkin, Frank Finlay, Phyllida Law; ***D:*** John Henderson; ***W:*** Peter Barnes; ***C:*** Clive Tickner; ***M:*** Richard Harvey. **TV**

Magical Mystery Tour ½ **1967** On the road with an oddball assortment of people, the Beatles experience a number of strange incidents around the English countryside. ♫Magical Mystery Tour; Blue Jay Way; Your Mother Should Know; The Fool on the Hill. **55m/C VHS, DVD.** *GB* John Lennon, George Harrison, Ringo Starr, Paul McCartney, Victor Spinetti, Neil Innes, Jessie Robins; *D:* John Lennon, George Harrison, Ringo Starr, Paul McCartney; *C:* Daniel Lacambre; *M:* John Lennon, George Harrison, Ringo Starr, Paul McCartney. **TV**

The Magician **1958** A master magician in 19th century Sweden (von Sydow) wreaks ill in this darkly comical, supernatural parable. Dark, well photographed early Bergman effort. In Swedish with English subtitles. **101m/B VHS.** *SW* Max von Sydow, Ingrid Thulin, Gunnar Bjornstrand, Bibi Andersson, Naima Wifstrand; *D:* Ingmar Bergman; *W:* Ingmar Bergman. Venice Film Fest. '59: Special Jury Prize.

The Magician 1/2 **1993** In the early 1980s, Scotland Yard detective George Byrne (Owen) partners with shady American businessman David Katz (Acovone) to bring down a counterfeiting ring. Katz goes undercover to try and meet the mysterious head of the ring (the title character) but risks his family by getting too involved. Meanwhile, the IRA also wants the counterfeiter so they can destabilize the British economy by flooding the country with fake currency. Based on a true story. **99m/C DVD.** *GB* Jay Acovone, Clive Owen, Jeremy Kemp, Peter Howitt, Jennifer Calvert; *D:* Terry Winsor; *W:* Jeff Pope. **TV**

The Magician of Lublin 1/2 **1979 (R)** Based on an unusual story by Issac Bashevis Singer. Follows the exploits of a magician/con man in turn-of-the century Poland whose personal flaws kill his career, until a chance emerges for one last trick. A good example of movie not as good as book; this rendering is superficial, badly acted and unsatisfying. Made soon after Singer won the Nobel Prize for literature in 1978. **105m/C VHS.** Alan Arkin, Valerie Perrine, Louise Fletcher, Lou Jacobi, Shelley Winters, Elspeth March, Lisa Whelchel; *D:* Menahem Golan; *M:* Maurice Jarre.

Magma: Volcanic Disaster **2006 (PG-13)** Silly cable disaster flick with cheesy CGI. Dr. Peter Shepard (Berkley) believes that volcanic eruptions in Iceland are the precursor to global catastrophe. Naturally, the bureaucrats don't believe him until there's more explosions. Now it's up to Peter to test out his theory that deep sea ventilation will relieve the pressure build-up and save the planet! **87m/C DVD.** Xander Berkeley, Amy Jo Johnson, Michael Durrell, Reiko Aylesworth, Doug Dearth, David O'Donnell; *D:* Ian Gilmore; *W:* Rebecca Rian; *M:* Nathan Furst. **CABLE**

The Magnet 1/2 **1950** Young Johnny Brent (Fox) finds a horseshoe-shaped magnet he believes will bring him good luck but the possession becomes a coveted object in the schoolyard, causing all sorts of problems. **79m/B DVD.** *GB* James Fox, Stephen Murray, Kay Walsh, Meredith Edwards, Gladys Henson, Wylie Watson; *D:* Charles Friend; *W:* T.E.B. Clarke; *C:* Lionel Banes; *M:* William Alwyn.

Magnificent Adventurer **1963** Ostensibly a biography of Benvenuto Cellini, the Florentine sculptor, with a concentration on his love life and swordplay. **94m/C VHS.** *IT* Claudia Mori, Francoise Fabian, Jose Nieto, Felix Defauce, Brett Halsey; *D:* Riccardo Fredo; *W:* Filippo Sanjust; *C:* Raffaele Masciocchi; *M:* Francesco De Masi.

The Magnificent Ambersons **1942** Welles's second film. A fascinating, inventive translation of the Booth Tarkington novel about a wealthy turn of the century family collapsing under the changing currents of progress. Pure Welles, except the glaringly bad tacked-on ending that the studio shot (under the direction of the great Robert Wise and Fred Fleck), after taking the film from him. It seems they wanted the proverbial happy ending. **88m/B VHS.** Joseph Cotten, Anne Baxter, Tim Holt, Richard Bennett, Dolores Costello, Erskine Sanford, Ray Collins, Agnes Moorehead; *D:* Freddie Fleck, Robert Wise, Orson Welles; *W:* Orson Welles; *M:* Bernard Herrmann, Roy Webb. Natl. Film Reg. '91;; N.Y. Film Critics '42: Actress (Moorehead).

The Magnificent Ambersons 1/2 **2002** George Amberson (Rhys Meyers) is the spoiled son of an upper-class, turn-of-the-century Midwestern family. When his widowed mother Isabel (Stowe) is reunited with old flame Eugene Morgan (Greenwood), George becomes obsessively jealous and schemes to break up the match even as he romances Eugene's daughter, Lucy (Mol). Stowe looks beautiful but Rhys Meyers over-emphasizes George's less-than-filial response to his mother. Adaptation of Booth Tarkington's novel that reportedly used Orson Welles original script for his 1942 film. **139m/C VHS, DVD.** Madeleine Stowe, Bruce Greenwood, Jonathan Rhys Meyers, Jennifer Tilly, Gretchen Mol, James Cromwell, William Hootkins; *D:* Alfonso Arau. **CABLE**

Magnificent Doll **1946** Boring Hollywood bio of first lady Dolly Madison (Rogers) who is wooed by dynamic Aaron Burr (Niven) before she decides on marrying quiet James Madison (Meredith) and pushing his political career to the office of the presidency. **93m/B VHS.** Ginger Rogers, David Niven, Burgess Meredith, Stephen McNally, Peggy Wood, Grandon Rhodes, Arthur Space, Robert Barrat; *D:* Frank Borzage; *W:* Irving Stone; *C:* Joseph Valentine; *M:* Hans J. Salter.

The Magnificent Dope 1/2 **1942** Fonda is likeable, as usual, as the hapless yokel in the big city. A trip to New York to take a course on being successful is his prize for winning a "laziest man" contest. He falls for his teacher; she uses his crush to motivate him. Funny and entertaining. **83m/B VHS.** Henry Fonda, Lynn Bari, Don Ameche, Edward Everett Horton, Hobart Cavanaugh, Pierre Watkin; *D:* Walter Lang.

The Magnificent Matador 1/2 *The Brave and the Beautiful* **1955** The story of an aging matador who faces death in the bullring to win the love of a woman. Quinn is the bullfighter on the horns of a dilemma. Lots of bull in script carried by harried bull in ring. **94m/C VHS.** Anthony Quinn, Maureen O'Hara, Thomas Gomez; *D:* Budd Boetticher.

Magnificent Obsession 1/2 **1935** Drunken playboy Bob Merrick (Taylor) indirectly causes the death of Helen Hudson's (Dunne) beloved and dedicated doctor husband. Then Bob's later apology causes Helen to flee, get hit by a car, and blinded. This double whammy to Bob's conscience leads him to resume his medical studies in an effort to become a brain surgeon. He also secretly befriends Helen and falls in love with her until she finds out about their past connection. But you know his medical skills will later come in handy. Shameless but well-done weepy based on the 1929 novel by Lloyd C. Douglas. Remade in Technicolor in 1954. **112m/B DVD.** Irene Dunne, Robert Taylor, Charles Butterworth, Ralph Morgan, Betty Furness, Sara Haden, Arthur Treacher; *D:* John M. Stahl; *W:* Sarah Y. Mason, Victor Heerman, George O'Neil; *C:* John Mescall.

Magnificent Obsession 1/2 **1954** A drunken playboy (Hudson) kills a man and blinds his wife in an automobile accident. Plagued by guilt, he devotes his life to studying medicine in order to restore the widow's sight. Well-acted melodrama lifted Hudson to stardom. Faithful to the 1935 original, based on a novel by Lloyd C. Douglas. **108m/C VHS.** Jane Wyman, Rock Hudson, Barbara Rush, Agnes Moorehead; *D:* Douglas Sirk; *W:* Robert Blees; *C:* Russell Metty.

The Magnificent Seven **1960** Western remake of Akira Kurosawa's classic "The Seven Samurai." Mexican villagers hire gunmen to protect them from the bandits who are destroying their town. Most of the actors were relative unknowns, though not for long. Sequelled by "Return of the Seven" in 1966, "Guns of the Magnificent Seven" in 1969, and "The Magnificent Seven Ride" in 1972. Excellent score. Uncredited writing by Walter Newman and Walter Bernstein. **126m/C VHS, DVD.** Yul Brynner, Steve McQueen, Robert Vaughn, James Coburn, Charles Bronson, Horst Buchholz, Eli Wallach, Brad Dexter; *D:* John Sturges; *W:* William Roberts; *C:* Charles B(ryant) Lang Jr.; *M:* Elmer Bernstein.

The Magnificent Seven 1/2 **1998** Pilot movie for the brief TV series that was loosely based on the 1960 film. An indian chief hires seven gunslingers to help defend tribal land from a gang of greedy outlaws who want the tribe's gold mine. **90m/C VHS.** Michael Biehn, Ron Perlman, Dale Midkiff, Eric Close, Anthony Starke, Laurie Holden, Andrew Kavovit, Rick Worthy, Kurtwood Smith, Ned Romero, Daragh O'Malley, Michael Greyeyes, Tony Burton; *D:* Geoff Murphy; *W:* Frank Q. Dobbs, Chris Black; *C:* Jack Conroy; *M:* Don Harper. **TV**

The Magnificent Two 1/2 **1967** The comedy team of Morecambe and Wise did better on the telly than in their movie appearances, particularly this lame foreign adventure comedy. Eric and Ernie are traveling toy salesman who arrive in Parazuelia, South America, in the midst of a revolution. Since Eric looks like the son of a dead revolutionary hero, he's forced to pose as the man at official events. A lingerie-clad female army finally solves the crisis. **92m/C DVD.** *GB* Margit Saad, Virgilio Teixeira, Eric Morecambe, Ernie Wise; *D:* Cliff Owen; *W:* Peter Blackmore, S.C. Green, R.M. Hills; *C:* Ernest Steward; *M:* Ronald Goodwin.

The Magnificent Yankee *The Man with Thirty Sons* **1950** Adaptation of Emmet Lavery's Broadway play on the life of Supreme Court Justice Oliver Wendell Holmes, starring Calhern (who also did the stage version). America's foremost legal mind was well-served by Calhern, with Harding as his ever-patient wife. **80m/B VHS.** Louis Calhern, Ann Harding, Eduard Franz, Philip Ober, Ian Wolfe, Edith Evanson, Richard Anderson, Jimmy Lydon, Robert Sherwood, Hugh Sanders; *D:* John Sturges; *W:* Emmet Lavery.

Magnolia **1999 (R)** It's a really long, frantic, and surreal look into a 24-hour series of interlocking stories, with a fine ensemble cast. Bad dads Jimmy Gator (Hall) and Earl Partridge (Robards) are both dying and estranged from their children—Jimmy's coke-addicted daughter, Claudia (Walters), and Earl's flashy motivational speaker son, Frank (Cruise). Earl's trophy wife Linda (Moore) is having a breakdown but he's being cared for by kind-hearted nurse Phil (Hoffman). And then there's a popular game show (of which Jimmy is the host) and its current and past quiz kids, and a rain of frogs, and everyone suddenly breaks into song, and, well, just watch it. **188m/C VHS, DVD.** Jason Robards Jr., Julianne Moore, Tom Cruise, Philip Seymour Hoffman, Philip Baker Hall, Melora Walters, John C. Reilly, Melinda Dillon, William H. Macy, Michael Bowen, Jeremy Blackman, Emmanuel Johnson; *D:* Paul Thomas Anderson; *W:* Paul Thomas Anderson; *C:* Robert Elswit; *M:* Jon Brion, Aimee Mann. Golden Globes '00: Support. Actor (Cruise); Natl. Bd. of Review '99: Support. Actor (Hoffman), Support. Actress (Moore).

Magnum Force 1/2 **1973 (R)** Eastwood's second "Dirty Harry" movie. Harry finds a trail leading from a series of gangland killings straight back to the P.D. Less gripping than "Dirty Harry" (1971), but still effective. Holbrook is cast intriguingly against type. **124m/C VHS, DVD, Blu-ray Disc.** Clint Eastwood, Hal Holbrook, Mitchell Ryan, David Soul, Robert Urich, Tim Matheson, Kip Niven, Albert "Poppy" Popwell, John Mitchum, Christine White, Richard Devon, Felton Perry, Margaret Avery, Will Hutchins, Suzanne Somers, Tony Giorgio; *D:* Ted Post; *W:* Michael Cimino, John Milius; *C:* Frank Stanley; *M:* Lalo Schifrin.

Magnum Killers **1976** A young man becomes involved in a web of deadly intrigue when he sets out to find who cheated him out of a small fortune during a card game. **92m/C VHS.** Sombat Methance, Prichela Lee.

Magnum P.I.: Don't Eat the Snow in Hawaii 1/2 **1980** Series pilot finds Vietnam-vet-turned-private-eye Thomas Sullivan Magnum (Selleck) living in Hawaii (in the guest house of never-seen mystery writer Robin Masters) and investigating the death of a wartime buddy. Hillerman excels as autocratic major domo Higgins. **99m/C VHS, DVD.** Tom Selleck, John Hillerman, Roger E. Mosley, Larry Manetti; *D:* Roger Young; *W:* Donald P. Bellisario, Glen Larson. **TV**

The Mahabharata **1989** Adapted from the myths and folklore of ancient India, the screen version of the original nine-hour stage play is the story of a devastating war between two powerful clans. Initially broadcast on public TV, the six-hour movie is divided into three two-hour segments: "The Game of Dice," "Exile in the Forest," and "The War." **318m/C VHS, DVD.** *GB FR* Robert Langton-Lloyd, Antonin Stahly-Vishwanadan, Bruce Myers; *D:* Peter Brook; *W:* Jean-Claude Carriere; *M:* Toshi Tsuchitori. **TV**

Mahler **1974 (PG)** Strange Russell effort on the life of the great composer Gustav Mahler. Imperfect script is rescued by fine acting. **110m/C VHS, DVD.** Robert Powell, Georgina Hale, Richard Morant, Lee Montague, Terry O'Quinn; *D:* Ken Russell; *W:* Ken Russell; *C:* Dick Bush.

Mahogany 1/2 **1975 (PG)** Poor girl becomes world-famous high fashion model and designer, ditches boyfriend in the old neighborhood, gets a career boost when she daringly appears in a dress of her own creation at a Roman fashion show, and still yearns for the boy back home. Motown attempt to make mainstream hit that's glossy and predictable. **109m/C VHS, DVD.** Diana Ross, Billy Dee Williams, Jean-Pierre Aumont, Anthony Perkins, Nina Foch; *D:* Berry Gordy; *W:* John Byrum; *C:* David Watkin.

The Maid 1/2 **1990 (PG)** An offbeat comedy romance with Sheen as the house husband to Bisset's female executive character. Nice acting; charming, if unoriginal, premise. **91m/C VHS.** Martin Sheen, Jacqueline Bisset, Jean-Pierre Cassel, James Faulkner, Victoria Shalet; *D:* Ian Toynton.

The Maid 1/2 *Kimyo na sakasu* **2005** Rosa has traveled from the Philippines to Singapore seeking work as a maid to provide money for her ill brother back home. But she has arrived during the seventh month of the Chinese Lunar Calendar, known as the Hungry Ghost Festival. For 30 days the gates of hell are opened, and the dead are allowed to walk among the living. To avoid repercussions one must follow several rules, among them: don't swim, never turn your head at night when someone calls your name, and don't speak to strangers on a deserted road. But Rosa doesn't know the rules. And her employers don't seem especially sympathetic to her plight. **93m/C DVD.** Allesandra de Rossi, Huifang Hong, Benny Soh, Zhenwei Guan, Mohd Haizad Bin Imram, Griffin Chan, Shucheng Chen, Celine Chia, Tan Ooh Chye, Christina Goh, Cecilia Heng, Li Rong Heng, Chua Swee Hwang, Nur Awal'liyah Ja'afar, Zen Law; *D:* Kelvin Tong; *W:* Kelvin Tong; *C:* Lucas Jodogne; *M:* Joe Ng, Alex Oh.

The Maid 1/2 *La Nana* **2009** After 23 years of unappreciated live-in maid service, Raquel hears her Chilean family employer may hire another maid to pick up her slack. Infuriated with the insulting decision, she sets out to run off all applicants with fierce passive aggression until her cheerful polar opposite, Lucy, plays against her every move. An incredible performance from Catalina Saavedra carries the emotional arch, with almost haunting results. A Sundance favorite, honoring first time director Sebastian Silva. Spanish with subtitles. **96m/C DVD.** *CL* Catalina Saavedra, Cladia Celedon, Mariana Loyola, Alejandro Goic, Delfina Guzman, Andrea Garcia-Huidobro, Augustin Silva; *D:* Sebastian Silva; *W:* Sebastian Silva, Pedro Peirano; *C:* Sergio Armstrong.

Maid in Manhattan 1/2 **2002 (PG-13)** Ralph Fiennes smiles! Okay, so it's not Greta Garbo laughs but the serious-minded Brit is not known for romantic comedies—in fact, this bit of fluff is his first. He's wealthy political scion Christopher Marshall, who's running for a New York Senate seat when he meets cute with Marisa (Lopez). She's the ambitious Latina single mom who's working as a maid in a posh NYC hotel but he mistakes her for a guest. Much angst (and tabloid gossip) when the truth is revealed until the prerequisite happy ending. Lopez is tenacious but her best scenes are with cutie newcomer Posey, who plays her 10-year-old son, and loud-mouthed best friend Matrone. **105m/C VHS, DVD.** *US* Jennifer Lopez, Ralph Fiennes, Natasha Richardson, Stanley Tucci, Tyler Garcia Posey, Marissa Matrone, Bob Hoskins, Frances Conroy, Christopher Eigeman, Priscilla Lopez, Amy Sedaris; *D:* Wayne Wang; *W:* Kevin Wade; *C:* Karl Walter Lindenlaub; *M:* Alan Silvestri.

Maid to Order 1/2 **1987 (PG)** Rich girl Sheedy's fairy godmother puts her in her place by turning her into a maid for a snooty Malibu couple. Good-natured and well-acted if rather mindless Cinderella story. **92m/C**

VHS, DVD. Ally Sheedy, Beverly D'Angelo, Michael Ontkean, Dick Shawn, Tom Skerritt, Valerie Perrine, Rigg Kennedy; *D:* Amy Holden Jones; *W:* Perry Howze; *M:* Georges Delerue.

The Maiden Heist *The Lonely Maiden* **2008 (PG-13)** Best seen for the three leads because the heist story is rather a letdown. Three longtime museum security guards (Walken, Freeman, Macy) plot to steal their three favorite artworks rather than let them be sold and taken out of the country when the museum is undergoing renovations. Despite meticulous planning, their heist (naturally) faces complications. **89m/C DVD.** Morgan Freeman, Christopher Walken, William H. Macy, Marcia Gay Harden; *D:* Peter Hewitt; *W:* Michael LeSieur; *C:* Ueli Steiger; *M:* Rupert Gregson-Williams. **VIDEO**

Maiden Voyage: Ocean Hijack ½ **2004** Former Special Forces officer Kyle Considine (square-jawed Van Dien) brings his son Zach along when he gets a job evaluating security on a cruise ship. Too bad Kyle didn't start sooner because the ship is hijacked shortly out of port, with the terrorists threatening to blow up the liner unless the ransom is paid. Zach and ship's officer Lynn Fabrizio (Cormack) team up to distract the terrorists so Kyle can diffuse the bombs. **90m/C DVD.** Casper Van Dien, Danielle Cormack, Angela Dotchin, Peter Anthony Elliott, Christopher Stollery, Anton Tennet, John Sumner; *D:* Colin Budds; *W:* James Makichuk, Ron McGee; *C:* Renaud Maire; *M:* Peter Blake, Tom McLeod. **CABLE**

Maid's Night Out **1938** Pleasant, simple-minded mistaken-identity comedy. Fontaine is an heiress; rich-guy posing-as-milkman Lane thinks she is a maid. They fall in love, of course. **64m/B VHS.** Joan Fontaine, Allan "Rocky" Lane, Hedda Hopper, George Irving, William Brisbane, Billy Gilbert, Cecil Kellaway; *D:* Ben Holmes.

Maids of Wilko *The Young Ladies of Wilko; Panny z Wilka; The Young Girls of Wilko* **1979** Wajda's adaptation of Jaroslav Iwaszkiewicz's memoirs set in the late '20s. Viktor Ruben (Olbrychski) reexamines his life following the death of a friend. He returns to the home of his aunt and uncle in Wilko where he renews friendships with five sisters on a neighboring estate in an attempt to resurrect a happier past. Lots of fruitless romantic yearning. In French and Polish with English subtitles. **118m/C VHS, DVD.** *PL FR* Daniel Olbrychski, Christine Pascal, Maja Komorowska, Anna Seniuk, Krystyna Zachwatowicz, Stanislawa Celinska, Zofia Jaroszewska, Tadeusz Bialoszczynski; *D:* Andrzej Wajda; *W:* Zbigniew Kaminski.

Mail Order Bride ½ **1963** Silly western comedy. Aging cowpoke Will (Ebsen) inherits the ranch of a friend and the duty of shaping up the man's troublesome son Lee (Dullea). Will thinks Lee will settle down if he marries so he finds him a mail order bride in Annie (Nettleton), a widow with a young son. Lee agrees to the marriage to get the ranch back but it's not smooth going. **83m/C DVD.** Buddy Ebsen, Keir Dullea, Lois Nettleton, Warren Oates, Barbara Luna, Paul Fix, Marie Windsor, William (Bill) Smith, Denver Pyle; *D:* Burt Kennedy; *W:* Burt Kennedy; *C:* Paul Vogel; *M:* George Bassman.

Mail Order Bride ½ **2008** Hallmark Channel movie set in the 1880s. Con woman Diana McQueen (Zuniga) is working for Tom Rourke (Evigan) in Boston but wants out from under his control. She appears to get her chance when a dying friend, who was about to become the mail order bride of Wyoming rancher Beau (Bancroft), asks Diana to take her place. But can Diana really change her ways? A sassy woman, a handsome cowboy, and a shoot-out—what more could you ask for? **88m/C DVD.** Daphne Zuniga, Cameron Bancroft, Greg Evigan, Tom Heaton, Vincent Gale, Ted Whittall, Katharine Isabelle, William Macdonald; *D:* Anne Wheeler; *W:* Tippi Dobrofsky, Neal Dobrofsky; *C:* David Pelletier. **CABLE**

Mail Order Wife **2004 (R)** Making a documentary parody really only works if the subject is funny and the characters are caricatures (see "This is Spinal Tap"). Abusive men who order wives through the mail doesn't quite have the same wink-wink-nudge-nudge appeal. Director Andrew Gurland, playing himself, is a documentary filmmaker getting wrapped up in a mail-order marriage gone bad, who then offers the overseas newlywed a place to stay (i.e. his bed) and helps her find a job. The camera bobs and weaves, trying to focus the entire time. It's almost like it doesn't want to watch, either. An unlikable cast of fictional characters is trumped by a cameo from unlikable non-fictional caricature Jose Canseco. **92m/C DVD.** *US* Andrew Gurland, Eugenia Yuan, Adrian Martinez, Deborah Teng; *D:* Huck Botko, Andrew Gurland; *W:* Huck Botko, Andrew Gurland; *C:* Luke Geissbuhler.

Mail to the Chief **2000** Junior high schooler Kenny has a school assignment on the upcoming presidential election. So he goes to a chat room and starts dissing the incumbent's gaffes, only to discover his online chat buddy is actually the President himself. The eighth-grader gives the prez some advice and when he starts to follow it, the President's popularity starts to rise in the polls. **89m/C VHS.** Randy Quaid, Holland Taylor, Bill Switzer, Ashley Gorrell, Martin Doyle; *D:* Eric Champnella; *W:* Eric Champnella; *C:* Albert J. Dunk; *M:* Peter Bernstein. **VIDEO**

The Main Event **1979 (PG)** Streisand plays a wacky—and bankrupt—cosmetic executive who must depend on the career of washed-up boxer O'Neal to rebuild her fortune. Desperate (and more than a little smitten), she badgers and bullies him back into the ring. Lame, derivative screwball comedy desperate to suggest chemistry of Streisand and O'Neal's "What's Up, Doc?" (1972). Streisand sings the title song. **109m/C VHS, DVD.** Barbra Streisand, Ryan O'Neal; *D:* Howard Zieff.

Main Street to Broadway **1953** Superficial story of a struggling playwright. Interesting mainly for abundant big-name cameos. Based on a story by Robert E. Sherwood. **102m/B VHS.** Tom Morton, Mary Murphy, Agnes Moorehead, Herb Shriner, Rosemary DeCamp, Clinton Sundberg; ***Cameos:*** Lionel Barrymore, Ethel Barrymore, Tallulah Bankhead, Shirley Booth, Cornel Wilde, Rex Harrison, Joshua Logan, Helen Hayes, Mary Martin; *D:* Tay Garnett.

Mainline Run ½ **1998** Smalltime drug runner Taro (Speer) gets out of prison and immediately goes back to work for crime boss Mr. Fletcher (Ward). Taro sets up a deal, which goes bad, the drugs are lost, and one of his men is killed. Now Taro and his buddy Sean (Joseph) are looking to get out, but Mr. Fletcher has something else in mind. **96m/C VHS, DVD.** Hugo Speer, Andrew Joseph, Nelson E. Ward, Kelly Marcel; *D:* Howard Ford; *C:* Jonathan Ford.

Maitresse ½ **1976** An examination of the sexual underworld in the same vein as "Blue Velvet" and "Crimes of Passion" as a man falls for a high-priced dominatrix. Director Scroeder also created "Reversal of Fortune." In French with English subtitles. **112m/C VHS, DVD.** *FR* Gerard Depardieu, Bulle Ogier; *D:* Barbet Schroeder; *C:* Nestor Almendros.

The Majestic ½ **2001 (PG)** Carrey is a blacklisted writer who suffers from amnesia after a car crash. He winds up in a small town where he's mistaken for a presumed MIA soldier, who was the son of Landau, the local movie theatre owner. Darabont's self-admitted ode to Frank Capra evokes the All-American innocence and decency that Capra's films revelled in, but doesn't quite match the charm. Cynics will think it's too sentimental and tries too hard, romantics and others not quick to sneer at nostalgia should enjoy themselves. Carrey does a fine job with the lead role. **152m/C VHS, DVD.** *US* Jim Carrey, Martin Landau, Laurie Holden, David Ogden Stiers, James Whitmore, Jeffrey DeMunn, Ron Rifkin, Hal Holbrook, Bob Balaban, Brent Briscoe, Gerry Black, Susan Willis, Catherine Dent, Chelcie Ross, Amanda Detmer, Allen (Goorwitz) Garfield, Daniel von Bargen, Shawn Doyle, Bruce Campbell, Clifford Curtis; *D:* Frank Darabont; *W:* Michael Sloane; *C:* David Tattersall; *M:* Mark Isham.

The Major and the Minor ½ **1942** Very funny comedy that marked Wilder's directorial debut. Susan Applegate (Rogers) decides she's had it with New York and wants to head home to Iowa, but she only has enough money for a child's half-price train ticket. So she passes herself off as a 12-year-old (!) and then runs into problems when Army major Kirby (Milland), who's traveling to a boys military school, decides to take the child under his protective wing. Soon he's insisting Susan stay at the school until her mother (played by Rogers' mother Lela) can collect her. Potentially risque situations never cross the line into sleaze but remain bright and breezy. **101m/B VHS.** Ginger Rogers, Ray Milland, Rita Johnson, Robert Benchley, Diana Lynn, Frankie Thomas Jr.; *D:* Billy Wilder; *W:* Billy Wilder, Charles Brackett; *C:* Leo Tover; *M:* Robert Emmett Dolan.

Major Barbara ½ **1941** A wealthy, idealistic girl joins the Salvation Army against her father's wishes. Based on the play by George Bernard Shaw. The excellent adaptation of the original and the cast make this film a winner. Deborah Kerr's film debut. **90m/B VHS.** *GB* Wendy Hiller, Rex Harrison, Robert Morley, Sybil Thorndike, Deborah Kerr; *D:* Gabriel Pascal.

Major Dundee ½ **1965** A Union army officer (Heston) chases Apaches into Mexico with a motley collection of prisoner volunteers. Too long and flawed; would have been better had Peckinpah been allowed to finish the project. Excellent cast. **124m/C VHS, DVD.** Charlton Heston, Richard Harris, James Coburn, Jim Hutton, Ben Johnson, Slim Pickens; *D:* Sam Peckinpah; *C:* Sam Leavitt.

Major League ½ **1989 (R)** Comedy about the Cleveland Indians, a pathetic major league baseball team whose new owner, ex-showgirl Rachel (Wilton) who inherited from her late hubby, schemes to lose the season and relocate the team to Miami. Sheen is okay as pitcher Ricky "Wild Thing" Vaughan, who suffers with control problems (both on and off the field), while Bernsen (as third baseman Roger Dorn) seems to be gazing affectionately at "L.A. Law" from a distance. Predictable sports spoof is good for a few laughs, particularly those scenes involving Haysbert as slugger Pedro Cerrano with voodoo on his mind (and in his locker) and Snipes as base stealer Willie Mays Hayes, whose only problem is getting on base. Followed by two sequels. **107m/C VHS, DVD.** Tom Berenger, Charlie Sheen, Corbin Bernsen, James Gammon, Margaret Whitton, Bob Uecker, Rene Russo, Wesley Snipes, Dennis Haysbert, Charles Cyphers, Chelcie Ross; *D:* David S. Ward; *W:* David S. Ward; *C:* Reynaldo Villalobos; *M:* James Newton Howard.

Major League 2 ½ **1994 (PG)** It's been five years since they won the series, and this plodding sequel finds the wacky championship Cleveland Indians ruined by success and once again struggling in last place. Limited charm of original is lost; dull and filled with so many lame jokes that you won't care if they manage to make it to the top again. Cast returns, with the exception of Wesley Snipes as Willie Mays Hays (now played by Epps). **105m/C VHS, DVD.** Charlie Sheen, Tom Berenger, Corbin Bernsen, James Gammon, Dennis Haysbert, Omar Epps, David Keith, Bob Uecker, Alison Doody, Michelle Rene Thomas, Margaret Whitton, Eric Bruskotter, Takaaki Ishibashi, Randy Quaid; *D:* David S. Ward; *W:* R.J. Stewart; *C:* Victor Hammer; *M:* Michel Colombier.

Major League 3: Back to the Minors ½ **1998 (PG-13)** Three strikes and this franchise is out. Gus Cantrell (Bakula) is a burned-out pitcher who's offered the chance to manage the Minnesota Twins' Triple A team and finds a bunch of central casting misfits. Just when you thought they'd run out of baseball cliches, in comes a young prospect who won't take advice (Goggins), an arrogant manager (McGinley), and the "big game" showdown (twice!). We've seen this stuff done (not much better) in the first two "Major Leagues" and (very much better) elsewhere. Bakula's always solid, but it's not enough to get the save. Take an intentional pass on this one. **90m/C VHS, DVD.** Scott Bakula, Corbin Bernsen, Dennis Haysbert, Takaaki Ishibashi, Jensen (Jennifer) Daggett, Eric Bruskotter, Walton Goggins, Ted McGinley, Kenneth Johnson, Peter M. MacKenzie, Bob Uecker, Steve Yeager, Larry Brandenburg, Judson Mills, Lobo Sebastian, Thom Barry, Tim DiFilippo, Tom DiFilippo, Ted DiFilippo; *D:* John Warren; *W:* John Warren; *C:* Tim Suhrstedt; *M:* Robert Folk.

Major Payne **1995 (PG-13)** When the marines have no more use for killing-machine Major Payne (Wayans), he reluctantly agrees to train the inept junior ROTC cadets at academically challenged Madison Academy. The misfit brigade contains the usual assortment of stock loser-types who follow the predictable "outcasts get even" plot to the letter. Wayans shows flashes of comic genius, but not nearly enough to make up for the one-dimensional characters and indifferent writing. Most of the showcase jokes involve the humiliation and degradation of the kids, always a laugh-riot. Sub-moronic remake of 1955's "The Private War of Major Benson." **97m/C VHS, DVD.** Damon Wayans, Karyn Parsons, William Hickey, Albert Hall, Steven Martini, Andrew Harrison Leeds, Scott "Bam Bam" Bigelow; *D:* Nick Castle; *W:* Dean Lorey, Gary Rosen, Damon Wayans; *C:* Richard Bowen; *M:* Craig Safan.

The Majorettes **1987 (R)** Eek! Someone is lurking around a high school murdering the majorettes with their own batons. A bare-bones plot lurks within this otherwise worthless pic. **93m/C VHS, DVD.** Kevin Kindlin, Terrie Godfrey, Mark V. Jevicky, Sueanne Seamans, John A. Russo, Bill (William Heinzman) Hinzman, Russell Streiner; *D:* Bill (William Heinzman) Hinzman; *W:* John A. Russo.

A Majority of One ½ **1956** Dated comedy about late-in-life romance and prejudice. Russell stars as Jewish Brooklyn widow Mrs. Jacoby, who tags along with her daughter and diplomat son-in-law on their shipboard trip to Japan. She meets the charming Koichi Asano (a surprisingly effective Guinness), who's with the Japanese diplomatic corp, runs into problems with her family, and decides she must give up her chance at romance. Adapted from the play by Leonard Spigelgass. **149m/C VHS.** Rosalind Russell, Alec Guinness, Ray Danton, Madlyn Rhue, Mae Questel, Frank Wilcox, Alan Mowbray; *D:* Mervyn LeRoy; *W:* Leonard Spigelgass.

Make a Million **1935** The Depression is played (successfully) for yuks in this tale of an economics professor fired from his post for advocating radical income redistribution. He doesn't get mad, he gets even: he makes a million by advertising for money. **66m/B VHS, DVD.** Charles Starrett, Pauline Brooks, George E. Stone, James Burke, Guy Usher, Norman Houston; *D:* Lewis D. Collins; *W:* Charles Logue; *C:* Milton Krasner.

Make a Wish **1937** A noted composer goes stale in this colorful musical about backstage life. The comic relief provides the films best moments. ♫ Music In My Heart; My Campfire Dreams; Make a Wish; Old Man Rip. **80m/B VHS.** Basil Rathbone, Leon Errol, Bobby Breen, Ralph Forbes; *D:* Kurt Neumann; *M:* Oscar Straus.

Make Haste to Live ½ **1954** Good, scary thriller. A woman survives attempted murder by her husband; moves far away to raise their infant daughter. He does time, then returns for revenge. McGuire is good as the terrorized wife. **90m/B VHS.** Dorothy McGuire, Stephen McNally, Edgar Buchanan, John Howard; *D:* William A. Seiter; *M:* Elmer Bernstein.

Make It Happen ½ **2008 (PG-13)** Harmless, cliched dance flick. Smalltown Lauryn heads to Chicago to audition for dance school but is rejected. Not wanting to go back home, Lauryn accepts help from fellow dancer Dana in landing a bookkeeping job at a dance club. Soon Lauryn is moving from the office to the stage in order to regain her confidence. **90m/C DVD.** Mary Elizabeth Winstead, Tessa Thompson, John Reardon, Riley Smith, Julissa Bermudez; *D:* Darren Grant; *W:* Duane Adler, Nicole Avril; *C:* David Claessen; *M:* Paul Haslinger. **VIDEO**

Make Me an Offer **1955** Somewhat slow-moving comedy centering on an antique dealer who attempts to buy an expensive vase from an old man. From the novel by Wolf Mankowitz. **88m/C VHS.** *GB* Peter Finch, Adrienne Corri, Rosalie Crutchley, Finlay Currie; *D:* Cyril Frankel.

Make Me an Offer ½ **1980** Made-for-TV movie about selling real estate in

Hollywood. Better than similar efforts. **97m/C VHS.** Susan Blakely, Stella Stevens, Patrick O'Neal; *D:* Jerry Paris; *M:* Ralph Burns.

Make Mine Mink **1960** Oft-hilarious British comedy about guests at an elegant but run-down mansion who become unlikely thieves, stealing furs for charity. Good cast headed by Terry-Thomas. **100m/C VHS, DVD.** *GB* Terry-Thomas, Billie Whitelaw, Hattie Jacques; *D:* Robert Asher.

Make Room for Tomorrow **1981 (R)** Subtle, somewhat funny French comedy about generations in a family. A man in mid-life crisis has to cope with his father, son, and grandfather on the grandfather's 90th birthday. **106m/C VHS.** *FR* Victor Lanoux, Jane Birkin, Georges Wilson; *D:* Peter Kassovitz.

Make the Yuletide Gay ½ **2009** Out at college, Gunn lives with his sweetie Nathan. The boys go their separate ways at Christmas break but when Nathan's parents desert him for a trip to Israel, he decides to surprise Gunn by showing up at his parental home in Wisconsin. Nathan's surprised too since Gunn is in the closet at home, his dad's a stoner, and his mom is a holiday freak who wants to fix up her boy with his ex-girlfriend. Now Gunn needs to decide whether to tell the truth before Nathan decides to leave. **89m/C DVD.** Keith Jordan, Adamo Ruggiero, Hallee Hirsh, Kelly Keaton, Derek Long, Alison Arngrim, Gates (Cheryl) McFadden, Ian Buchanan; *D:* Rob Williams; *W:* Rob Williams; *C:* Ian Mcglocklin; *M:* Austin Wintory. **VIDEO**

Make-Up **1937** A doctor turned circus clown uses his medical skills when an elephant renders a society girl unconscious. After she awakens the two become involved. The clown's daughter objects, but is soon caught up in an accusation that she murdered the lion tamer. Her father the clown tries to save the day. Predictable doctor/clown relationship. **72m/B VHS.** Nils Asther, June Clyde, Judy Kelly, Kenne Duncan, John Turnbull; *D:* Alfred Zeisler.

Make Way for Tomorrow ½ **1937** Multi-hankie family drama about loving elderly couple Barkley and Lucy Cooper. They lose their home to foreclosure during the Depression and the couple must separate since none of their children are willing to care for both parents. Eventually, feeling unwanted and realizing they will probably be apart the rest of their lives, Barkley and Lucy spend one last day together revisiting their honeymoon spot. **91m/B DVD.** Victor Moore, Beulah Bondi, Thomas Mitchell, Fay Bainter, Barbara Read, Elisabeth Risdon, Porter Hall, Minna Gombell, Ralph Remley; *W:* Vina Delmar; *C:* William Mellor; *M:* Victor Young, George Antheil.

Make Your Bets Ladies ½ *Faites Vous Jeux, Mesdames* **1965** Secret agent Mike Warner (Constantine) is searching for a missing NATO scientist, which leads him to a Russian agent and a female gang. They are lead by gypsy Soledad (Benedetti) and their ransom demands for said scientist are diamonds and fur coats! Dubbed. **90m/B DVD.** *FR SP* Eddie Constantine, Nelly Benedetti, Daniel Ceccaldi, Laura Valenzuela, Luis Davila, Dieter Kollesch; *D:* Marcel Ophuls; *W:* Jacques Robert; *C:* Alain Boisnard; *M:* Ward Swingle.

The Maker ½ **1998 (R)** Restless SoCal high-schooler Josh (Rhys Myers) indulges in petty crime with lesbian friend Bella (Balk) but isn't really in trouble until his long-missing older brother Walter (Modine) hits town. Walter soon pulls Josh into his shady schemes that turn into some very dangerous games. **98m/C VHS, DVD.** Jonathan Rhys Meyers, Matthew Modine, Mary-Louise Parker, Fairuza Balk, Michael Madsen, Jesse Borrego, Kate McGregor-Stewart, Lawrence Pressman, Jeff Kober; *D:* Tim Hunter; *W:* Rand Ravich; *C:* Hubert Taczanowski; *M:* Paul Buckmaster.

Maker of Men ½ **1931** Melodrama finds tough college football coach Dudley pushing son Bob to play. Only the kid's inexperience causes the team's defeat in the big game. Humiliated, Bob transfers to a rival school and gives football another try, going up against his old man. **71m/B VHS.** Jack Holt, Richard Cromwell, Joan Marsh, John Wayne, Walter Catlett; *D:* Edward Sedgwick; *W:* Howard J. Green; *C:* L.W. O'Connell.

Makin' Baby **2002 (R)** Newlyweds Michael and Alicia are having a tough time coping with the married life itself, when Alicia suddenly raises the stakes, deciding she wants a baby. If that isn't enough to push hip-hop-hopeful Michael over the edge, the temptation of a slimy music exec (Mystikal, in his feature debut) offering to take him under his wing and transform him into a full-time rhymin' thug puts the sweethearts in danger. Mean-spirited jokes fall flat and come at the worst times. Fans of Mystikal will be severely dissed by his limited screen time. And, nope, he doesn't even rap. **94m/C VHS, DVD.** Portia Realer, Aaron Spears, Mystikal, Sheila Lussier, Kim Hill; *D:* Paul Wynne; *W:* Brennon Jones. **VIDEO**

Making Contact ½ **1986 (PG)** A small boy's telekinetic powers enable him to bring to life his favorite toys. The ridicule he endures because of this leads him to set off on terrifying adventures with only his toys and a friend for company. **83m/C VHS, DVD.** Joshua Morrell, Eve Kryll; *D:* Roland Emmerich.

Making Love **1982 (R)** A closet homosexual risks his eight-year marriage by getting involved with a carefree writer. What could be a powerful subject gets only bland treatment. **112m/C VHS, DVD.** Kate Jackson, Harry Hamlin, Michael Ontkean, Wendy Hiller, Arthur Hill, Nancy Olson, Terry Kiser, Camilla Carr, Michael Dudikoff; *D:* Arthur Hiller; *W:* Barry Sandler.

Making Mr. Right ½ **1986 (PG-13)** Under-rated satire about a high-powered marketing and image consultant who falls in love with the android that she's supposed to be promoting. Unbelievable comedy is shaky at times, but Magnuson and Malkovich create some magic. **95m/C VHS, DVD.** John Malkovich, Ann Magnuson, Glenne Headly, Ben Masters, Laurie Metcalf, Polly Bergen, Hart Bochner, Polly Draper, Susan Anton; *D:* Susan Seidelman; *W:* Laurie Frank, Floyd Byars.

Making the Grade *Preppies* **1984 (PG)** Jersey tough kid owes the mob; attends prep school in place of a rich kid who can't be bothered. Better than similar '80s teen flicks, but not by much. **105m/C VHS, DVD.** Judd Nelson, Joanna Lee, Dana Olsen, Ronald Lacey, Scott McGinnis, Gordon Jump, Carey Scott, Andrew (Dice Clay) Silverstein; *D:* Dorian Walker; *W:* Gene Quintano; *C:* Jacques Haitkin; *M:* Basil Poledouris.

The Makioka Sisters **1983** Much praised drama centering around the lives of four Japanese sisters who are heiresses to the family fortune and, hence, must be found proper husbands. The efforts of the older sisters to "match" their younger siblings are entwined with a gradual realization on the part of the elders that the quiet way of life representative of their own formative years is passing away with the advent of WWII. The movie is as visually stunning as it is poignant. In Japanese with English subtitles. **140m/C VHS.** *JP* Keiko Kishi, Yoshiko Sakuma, Sayuri Yoshinaga; *D:* Kon Ichikawa.

Malarek **1989 (R)** Tough Montreal journalist Victor Malarek exposed abuse in that city's teen detention center in his book "Hey, Malarek." Compelling lead performance from Koteas in decent though not great screen adaptation. **95m/C VHS.** Michael Sarrazin, Elias Koteas, Al Waxman, Kerrie Keane; *D:* Roger Cardinal.

Malaya ½ *East of the Rising Sun* **1949** Hokey adventure tale set in WWII that's based on a true story. Stewart and Tracy are hired to smuggle a huge shipment of rubber out of Malaya to waiting U.S. ships without the Japanese finding out. Greenstreet does his usual shifty role. **98m/B VHS.** Spencer Tracy, James Stewart, Sydney Greenstreet, Valentina Cortese, John Hodiak, Lionel Barrymore, Gilbert Roland, Richard Loo, Roland Winters; *D:* Richard Thorpe; *W:* Frank Fenton; *C:* George J. Folsey; *M:* Bronislau Kaper.

Malcolm ½ **1986 (PG-13)** An offbeat comedy about a slightly retarded young man who is mechanically inclined and his unusual entry into a life of crime. Directorial debut for actress Tass, whose husband Parker wrote the screenplay (and designed the Tinkertoys). Music score performed by The Penguin Cafe Orchestra. **86m/C VHS.** *AU* Colin Friels, John Hargreaves, Lindy Davies, Chris Haywood, Charles "Bud" Tingwell, Beverly Phillips, Judith Stratford; *D:* Nadia Tass; *W:* David Parker; *C:* David Parker; *M:* Simon Jeffes. Australian Film Inst. '86: Actor (Friels), Film.

Malcolm X **1992 (PG-13)** Stirring tribute to the controversial black activist, a leader in the struggle for black liberation. Hitting bottom during his imprisonment in the '50s, he became a Black Muslim and then a leader in the Nation of Islam. His assassination in 1965 left a legacy of black nationalism, self-determination, and racial pride. Marked by strong direction from Lee and good performances (notably Freeman Jr. as Elijah Muhammad), it is Washington's convincing performance in the title role that truly brings the film alive. Based on "The Autobiography of Malcolm X" by Malcolm X and Alex Haley. **201m/C VHS, DVD.** Denzel Washington, Angela Bassett, Albert Hall, Al Freeman Jr., Delroy Lindo, Spike Lee, Theresa Randle, Kate Vernon, Lonette McKee, Tommy Hollis, James McDaniel, Ernest Thompson, Jean LaMarre, Giancarlo Esposito, Craig Wasson, John Ottavino, David Patrick Kelly, Shirley Stoler; *Cameos:* Christopher Plummer, Karen Allen, Peter Boyle, William Kunstler, Bobby Seale, Al Sharpton; *D:* Spike Lee; *W:* Spike Lee, Arnold Perl, James Baldwin; *M:* Terence Blanchard. MTV Movie Awards '93: Male Perf. (Washington); N.Y. Film Critics '92: Actor (Washington).

Malcolm X: Make It Plain **1995** In-depth portrait of the life of Malcolm X as told through the memories of many of Malcolm's close personal friends and individuals who had worked closely with him. Contains footage of Malcolm X speaking at rallies, meetings, and interviews with Maya Angelou, Ossie Davis, Alex Haley, Mike Wallace, and his family. **136m/C VHS.** *Nar:* Alfre Woodard.

The Maldonado Miracle ½ **2003 (PG)** The small desert border town of San Ramos is slowly dying until the church's Jesus statue is found to be crying tears of blood. This development brings pilgrims, media, and curiosity seekers at the same time a Mexican boy arrives looking for his father and on the run from Immigration. Hayek's directorial debut is uplifting and earnest, if a bit predictable, and she gets solid performances from an excellent cast. **100m/C DVD.** Peter Fonda, Mare Winningham, Ruben Blades, Bill Sage, Eddy Martin, Soledad St. Hilaire, Scott Michael Campbell, Jesse Borrego, Christina Cabot; *D:* Salma Hayek; *W:* Paul Cooper; *C:* Claudio Rocha; *M:* Leonardo Heiblum, Jacobo Lieberman. **CABLE**

Male and Female **1919** A group of British aristocrats is shipwrecked on an island and must allow their efficient butler (Meighan) to take command for their survival. Swanson is the spoiled rich girl who falls for her social inferior. Their rescue provides a return to the rigid British class system. Based on the play "The Admirable Crichton" by James M. Barrie. **110m/B VHS, DVD.** Gloria Swanson, Thomas Meighan, Lila Lee, Raymond Hatton, Bebe Daniels; *D:* Cecil B. DeMille; *W:* Jeanie Macpherson; *C:* Alvin Wyckoff.

The Male Animal ½ **1942** Fonda uses his penchant for playing principled men to uneven comedic effect as stuffy English professor Tommy Turner. He gets into trouble with university trustees over his views about free speech and it threatens his job, which worries wife Ellen (de Havilland). Tommy gets jealous when Ellen's college beau, ex-football star Joe Ferguson (Carson), suddenly shows up on campus and seems to want to rekindle the flame. The men behave like idiots while Ellen deals with their male posturing. Based on the play by James Thurber and director Nugent. Fonda later played the same role in a Broadway revival. **101m/B VHS.** Henry Fonda, Olivia de Havilland, Jack Carson, Joan Leslie, Eugene Pallette, Herbert Anderson, Hattie McDaniel, Don DeFore; *D:* Elliott Nugent; *W:* Julius J. Epstein, Philip G. Epstein, Stephen Morehouse Avery; *C:* Arthur Edeson; *M:* Heinz Roemheld.

Malena **2000** Nostalgic coming of age story centered on a fantasy woman. The beautiful Malena (Bellucci) inspires lust in the men and jealousy in the women of her Sicilian village in 1940. Her husband is away fighting and, because of unjustified gossip, Malena loses her teaching job and eventually turns to prostitution to support herself. Only puberty-struck 13-year-old Renato (Sulfaro) shows any interest in her plight, which becomes worse as the war drags on. Italian with subtitles. **106m/C VHS, DVD.** *IT* Monica Bellucci, Giuseppe Sulfaro, Luciano Federico, Matilde Piana, Pietro Notarianni, Gaetano Aronica; *D:* Giuseppe Tornatore; *W:* Giuseppe Tornatore; *C:* Lajos Koltai; *M:* Ennio Morricone.

Malevolence **1995 (R)** Billy Bob Jones (Cortese) was unjustly imprisoned as a boy and has now spent half his life in jail. Shortly after his release, he drifts into petty crime and is suddenly the prime suspect in the murder of a black politician. The only thing is, Billy Bob is being framed. **95m/C VHS.** Joe Cortese, Michael McGrady, Tom Bower, Lou Rawls; *D:* Belle Avery; *W:* Belle Avery; *C:* Joe C. Maxwell.

Malevolence **2004 (R)** Debut for writer/director Mena is a basic slasher film. There's something about a serial killer, an abducted single mom, a bank heist gone wrong, and lots of blood. Mena had to start somewhere but this effort is unmemorable at best. **90m/C DVD.** *US* Samantha Dark, Brandon Johnson, Heather Magee, Richard Glover, Courtney Bertolone, John Richard Ingram; *D:* Stevan Mena; *W:* Stevan Mena; *C:* Tsuyashi Kimoto; *M:* Stevan Mena.

Malibu Beach ½ **1978 (R)** The California beach scene is the setting for this movie filled with bikini clad girls, tanned young men, and instant romances. For connoisseurs of the empty-headed teen beach movie. **93m/C VHS, DVD.** Kim Lankford, James Daughton; *D:* Robert J. Rosenthal; *C:* Jamie Anderson.

The Malibu Beach Vampires **1991 (R)** Three unscrupulous yuppies, Congressman Teri Upstart, Col. Ollie West and Rev. Timmy Fakker, keep beautiful mistresses in their Malibu beach house. What they don't know is, the girls are all really vampires who have injected them with a serum that compels them to tell the truth! Will our "heroes" continue to dupe the American Public, or will the sexy blood suckers cause their downfall? **90m/C VHS, DVD.** Angelyne, Becky LeBeau, Joan Rudelstein, Marcus A. Frishman, Rod Sweitzer, Francis Creighton, Anet Anatelle, Yvette Buchanan, Cherie Romaors, Kelly Galindo; *D:* Francis Creighton.

Malibu Bikini Shop **1986 (R)** Two brothers manage a beachfront bikini shop in Malibu, and spend their time ogling the customers and arguing about running the "business." Just another excuse for parading babes in bathing suits across the naked screen. **90m/C VHS.** Michael David Wright, Bruce Greenwood, Barbara Horan, Debra Blee, Jay Robinson, Galyn Gorg, Ami Julius, Frank Nelson, Kathleen Freeman, Rita Jenrette; *D:* David Wechter; *W:* David Wechter.

Malibu Express **1985 (R)** Mystery/adventure plot about a P.I. is the excuse; babes in swimsuits is the reason for this waste of time. **101m/C VHS, DVD.** Darby Hinton, Sybil Danning, Art Metrano, Shelley Taylor Morgan, Niki Dantine, Barbara (Lee) Edwards; *D:* Andy Sidaris.

Malibu High **1979 (R)** The accidental death of a young prostitute's client leads her to a new series of illegal activities of the "sex and hit" variety. Dark, sleazy, and antisocial; belies Beach Boys-esque title. **92m/C VHS, DVD.** Jill Lansing, Stuart Taylor; *D:* Irvin Berwick.

Malibu's Most Wanted **2003 (PG-13)** Kennedy brings his TV character Brad "B-Rad" Gluckman to the big screen with minimal success. "B-Rad" is a rich white wannabe rapper from Malibu, whose dad (O'Neal) is running for governor. When he embarrasses pop at a campaign stop, dad takes drastic action. He hires classically trained black actors Sean and PJ to kidnap Brad to South Central for a little "Scared White" therapy. Since the middle class actors have no idea how to be "gangsta" they enlist the help of Sean's cousin Shondra, who promptly falls for Brad, angering her ex boyfriend Tec (yet another Wayans), who lives the thug life. Shows flashes of the clever, biting satire it could've been, but fades in the end by backing off on some of the wry observations it makes early on. Diggs and Anderson click, and O'Neal is amusingly smarmy. **86m/C VHS, DVD.** *US* Jamie Kennedy, Taye Diggs, Anthony Anderson, Blair Underwood, Regina Hall, Ryan O'Neal, Bo Derek, Damien Dante Wayans, Jeffrey Tambor, Kal Penn; ***D:*** John Whitesell; ***W:*** Jamie Kennedy, Fax Bahr, Adam Small, Nick Swardson; ***C:*** Mark Irwin; ***M:*** John Van Tongeren, Damon Elliott; ***V:*** Snoop Dogg.

Malice ½ **1993 (R)** In a sleepy little college town, strange things sure do happen. Too bad rumpled college dean Andy Safian (Pullman) didn't see "Pacific Heights." If he did, he would know that sometimes roommates are more trouble than they're worth, even if renovation on that old Victorian is getting expensive. Routine thriller throws out an inventive twist to keep things moving, but manages to be fairly predictable anyway. **107m/C VHS, DVD.** Alec Baldwin, Nicole Kidman, Bill Pullman, Bebe Neuwirth, Anne Bancroft, George C. Scott, Peter Gallagher, Josef Sommer, Gwyneth Paltrow; ***D:*** Harold Becker; ***W:*** Aaron Sorkin, Scott Frank; ***C:*** Gordon Willis; ***M:*** Jerry Goldsmith.

Malicious *Malizia* **1974 (R)** A housekeeper hired for a widower and his three sons becomes the object of lusty affection of all four men. As Papa makes plans to court and marry her, his 14-year-old son plots to have her as a companion on his road to sensual maturity. Dubbed in English. **98m/C VHS.** *IT* Laura Antonelli, Turi Ferro, Alessandro Momo, Tina Aumont; ***D:*** Salvatore Samperi.

Malicious **1995 (R)** College athlete Doug Gordon (McGaw) impulsively has what he thinks is a one-nighter with mystery lady, Melissa (Ringwald). Only she's not willing to give him up and his rejection sends her on the road to revenge. **92m/C VHS.** Molly Ringwald, Patrick McGaw, Sarah Lassez, John Vernon, Mimi Kuzyk, Rick Henrickson; ***D:*** Ian Corson; ***W:*** George Saunders; ***C:*** Michael Slovis; ***M:*** Graeme Coleman.

Malicious Intent ½ *Civility* **1999** Young man returns home for his father's funeral and learns that he was murdered. So he gets together with some of his father's buddies on a plan for revenge—and money. **86m/C VHS, DVD.** Zack (Zach) Ward, Tom Arnold, William Forsythe, Rachel Ticotin, Clarence Williams III, Ed Lauter, Liam Waite, Christopher Atkins; ***D:*** Caesar Cavaricci; ***W:*** Caesar Cavaricci. **VIDEO**

Mallrats ½ **1995 (R)** Smith's better-financed follow-up to the legendary "Clerks" follows Jersey slackers T.S. (London) and Brodie (Lee) to the mall, where they intend to wallow in food-court cookies and reclaim their girlfriends, who recently dumped them. While wandering the mall in low-key and confused pursuit of their women and self respect, they encounter the usual band of bizarre inhabitants, including Ivannah, the topless psychic, Silent Bob (Smith) and stoner Jay (Mewes). Dialogue and sightgags are director/writer Smith's strong point; moving the plot forward is not high on the priority list. The ensemble cast, featuring Doherty as the bored babe who spurns Brodie, is up to the often funny sidebits and gen-x references. **95m/C VHS, DVD, HD DVD.** Jeremy London, Jason Lee, Shannen Doherty, Claire Forlani, Kevin Smith, Michael Rooker, Priscilla Barnes, Renee Humphrey, Ben Affleck, Joey Lauren Adams, Jason Mewes, Brian O'Halloran, David Brinkley, Art James, Ethan Suplee, Sven-Ole Thorsen; ***Cameos:*** Stan Lee; ***D:*** Kevin Smith; ***W:*** Kevin Smith; ***C:*** David Klein; ***M:*** Ira Newborn.

Malone ½ **1987 (R)** A burnt-out secret agent stumbles into a real-estate swindle/murder plot in Oregon and sets out to stop it. Film tries hard but doesn't succeed in being believable. **92m/C VHS.** Burt Reynolds, Lauren Hutton, Cliff Robertson, Kenneth McMillan, Scott Wilson, Cynthia Gibb; ***D:*** Harley Cokliss; ***M:*** David Newman.

Malou **1983 (R)** A young French woman tries to uncover the truth about her late mother's life, sifting through wildly contradictory evidence in the desire to discover her own identity and avoid her mother's mistakes. A feminist story. In German with English subtitles. **95m/C VHS.** *GE* Grischa Huber, Ingrid Caven, Helmut Griem; ***D:*** Jeanine Meerapfel; ***C:*** Michael Ballhaus.

Malta Story ½ **1953** A British WWII flier becomes involved with the defense of Malta. **103m/B VHS.** Alec Guinness, Jack Hawkins, Anthony Steel, Flora Robson, Muriel Pavlow; ***D:*** Brian Desmond Hurst.

The Maltese Falcon *Dangerous Female* **1931** A good first screen version of the Dashiell Hammett story about private detective Sam Spade's search for the elusive Black Bird. Remade five years later as "Satan Met a Lady" with Bette Davis. Its most famous remake, however, occurred in 1941 with Humphrey Bogart in the lead. **80m/B VHS.** Bebe Daniels, Ricardo Cortez, Dudley Digges, Thelma Todd, Una Merkel, Dwight Frye, Robert Elliott; ***D:*** Roy Del Ruth.

The Maltese Falcon **1941** After the death of his partner, detective Sam Spade (Bogart) finds himself enmeshed in a complicated, intriguing search for a priceless statuette. "It's the stuff dreams are made of," says Bogart of the Falcon. Excellent, fast-paced film noir with outstanding performances, great dialogue, and concentrated attention to details. Director Huston's first film and Greenstreet's talky debut. First of several films starring Bogart and Astor. Based on the novel by Dashiell Hammett. Also available colorized. **101m/B VHS, DVD.** Humphrey Bogart, Mary Astor, Peter Lorre, Sydney Greenstreet, Ward Bond, Barton MacLane, Gladys George, Lee Patrick, Elisha Cook Jr., Jerome Cowan, Walter Huston; ***D:*** John Huston; ***W:*** John Huston; ***C:*** Arthur Edeson; ***M:*** Adolph Deutsch. AFI '98: Top 100, Natl. Film Reg. '89.

Mama Africa ½ **2002** Three segments, directed by three different African filmmakers are tied together by the authoritative introductions of Queen Latifah. Stylistically plain but emotionally charged, all three tales involve young, poverty-stricken but promising Africans facing difficult moral choices for a better life. In two of the stories young, single mothers Raya (Abrahams) and Uno (David) take up with questionable men for love or money and find themselves tempted to enter their world of crime. Director Onwurah's modern-day fable, the best of the three, focuses on young Nigerian Kwame, who desperately needs $100 to buy a pair of basketball sneakers for a tryout with an American scout. As the day approaches, Kwame is enticed by a slimy gangster to join up with his crew as a way to get what he desperately needs. Fine performances and a refreshing lack of melodrama or moralizing. **89m/C VHS, DVD.** Rehane Abrahams, Damien Chamley, Ivan Lucas, Oscar Petersen, Denise Newman, Hyppolite Ouangrawa, Alima Salouka, Cindy Sampson, Graham Weir; ***D:*** Fanta Regina Nacro, Zulfar Otto-Sallies, Ingrid Sinclair.

Mama Dracula **WOOF!** **1980** Fletcher stars in this poor satire of the horror genre. She's a vampire who needs the blood of virgins to stay young. Her son helps out—what good son wouldn't? **90m/C VHS, DVD.** *FR* Louise Fletcher, Bonnie Schneider, Maria Schneider, Marc-Henri Wajnberg, Alexander Wajnberg, Jess Hahn; ***D:*** Boris Szulzinger.

Mama Flora's Family ½ **1998** Based on the novel by Alex Haley, which was finished by co-author Stevens after Haley's 1992 death. Loosely based on Haley's mother, Mama Flora (Tyson) endures one tragedy after another while raising her family. First, as a teenaged servant, Flora gets pregnant and is forced to give the child up. Then when she does marry, her husband is killed and their property burned. Meanwhile, her other children and grandchildren struggle with discrimination and grow up angry and resentful. Holds together because of the force of Tyson's portrayal. **175m/C VHS, DVD.** Cicely Tyson, Mario Van Peebles, Blair Underwood, Queen Latifah, Hill Harper, Shemar Moore, Della Reese; ***D:*** Peter Werner; ***W:*** David Stevens, Carol Schreder; ***C:*** Neil Roach. **TV**

Mama, There's a Man in Your Bed *Romauld et Juliet* **1989 (PG)** When a powerful executive is framed for insider trading, the only witness to the crime and his only hope is an earthy cleaning woman named Juliette. Together they plot revenge and takeovers in her tiny apartment, filled with children. Soon, he regains his former position of power but realizes his life isn't complete without his co-conspirator. In French with English subtitles. **111m/C VHS.** *FR* Daniel Auteuil, Firmine Richard, Pierre Vernier, Maxime LeRoux, Gilles Privat, Muriel Combeau, Catherine Salviat, Sambou Tati; ***D:*** Coline Serreau; ***W:*** Coline Serreau.

Mama Turns a Hundred **1979 (R)** A baronial family (a bizarre set of characters) is celebrating their mother's 100th birthday at her estate. One of the daughter's seduces her brother-in-law, another has a uniform fetish, a religious zealot is desperate to hang-glide, and several of them are trying to kill poor Mama. But of course she prevails, although sick and ailing. Slow-paced yet uproarious film full of inept characters who bumble along. In Spanish with English subtitles. **100m/C VHS.** *SP* Geraldine Chaplin, Fernando Fernan-Gomez, Amparo Munoz; ***D:*** Carlos Saura.

Mama's Boy **WOOF!** **2007 (PG-13)** Jeffrey (Heder) is a 29-year-old slacker who's happy living with his mom Jan (Keaton). But his free ride is threatened when mom announces she's marrying her boyfriend Mert (Daniels). So Jeffrey enlists aspiring singer Nora (Faris) to help him dislodge Mert from his mom's life and—horrors!—grows up in the process. Heder's indifferent portrayal of his irredeemably shelfish character is only the most obvious of many problems with this unfunny mess. Watch it with "Step Brothers" and weep for the future—and the present. **93m/C DVD.** *US* Jon Heder, Diane Keaton, Jeff Daniels, Anna Faris, Dorian Missick, Sarah Chalke, Eli Wallach, Mary Kay Place, Laura Kightlinger, Simon Helberg; ***D:*** Tim Hamilton; ***W:*** Hank Nelken; ***C:*** Jonathan Brown; ***M:*** Mark Mothersbaugh.

Mama's Dirty Girls **1974 (R)** A gangster mom's daughters take over where their mother left off and have the time of their lives. **82m/C VHS.** Gloria Grahame, Paul Lambert, Sondra Currie, Candice Rialson, Mary Stoddard; ***D:*** John Hayes; ***M:*** Don Bagley.

Mambo ½ **1955** A poor young dancer inspires patronage and lust by dancing the Mambo. Although attracted to Gassman, she marries Rennie for his money. Technically weak but artistically interesting, though Rennie and Mangano have done their roles somewhat better elsewhere. **94m/B VHS.** Silvana Mangano, Michael Rennie, Vittorio Gassman, Shelley Winters, Katherine Dunham, Mary Clare, Eduardo Ciannelli; ***D:*** Robert Rossen; ***M:*** Nino Rota.

Mambo Cafe **2000 (PG-13)** Low-budget mob comedy with a quirky premise. The Mambo Cafe is a Spanish Harlem restaurant in dire need of some business. So the owners invite a local mobster to dine at their establishment in hopes he'll be murdered and they'll get a boost from the publicity. He is, business improves, but the restaurant and the family also draw unwelcome Mob scrutiny. **98m/C VHS, DVD.** Paul Rodriguez, Rosanna Desoto, Danny Aiello, Thalia, Kamar De Los Reyes; ***D:*** Reuben Gonzalez; ***W:*** Reuben Gonzalez. **VIDEO**

Mambo Italiano **2003 (R)** Broad, ethnic romantic comedy that could be titled "My Big Gay Italian/Canadian Wedding." Kirby plays Angelo Barberini, a 30-year-old nice Italian boy still living with his parents in Montreal's version of Little Italy when he falls for childhood bully Nino (Miller), now a cop and secretly also gay. The two begin a clandestine relationship and move in together while both families unsuccessfully begin a whirlwind of last-ditch matchmaking activities. A pleasant turn by lead Kirby highlights this good-natured yet technically simple comedy where most of the performances, and accents, are uneven. **99m/C VHS, DVD.** *CA* Luke Kirby, Ginette Reno, Paul Sorvino, Claudia Ferri, Peter Miller, Mary Walsh, Sophie Lorain, Tim Post, Lisa Bronwyn Moore; ***D:*** Emile Gaudreault; ***W:*** Emile Gaudreault, Steve Galluccio; ***C:*** Serge Ladouceur.

The Mambo Kings **1992 (R)** Armand and Banderas (in his first English speaking role) are Cesar and Nestor Castillo, two brothers who flee Cuba for New York City with dreams of hitting it big with their mambo music. Desi Arnaz Jr. gets to play his own dad in a funny and technical scene that leads to a climactic confrontation between the brothers. Good cast and great music make this one worthwhile. Based on the Pulitzer prizewinning novel "The Mambo Kings Play Songs of Love" by Oscar Hijuelos. **100m/C VHS, DVD.** Armand Assante, Antonio Banderas, Cathy Moriarty, Maruschka Detmers, Desi Arnaz Jr., Celia Cruz, Roscoe Lee Browne, Vondie Curtis-Hall, Tito Puente, Talisa Soto; ***D:*** Arne Glimcher; ***W:*** Cynthia Cidre; ***C:*** Michael Ballhaus; ***M:*** Robert Kraft, Carlos Franzetti.

Mame **1974 (PG)** In an adaptation of the Broadway musical "Auntie Mame" by Jerry Herman, Ball plays a dynamic woman who takes it upon herself to teach a group of eccentrics how to live life to the fullest. Arthur plays Mame's friend just as splendidly as she did in the Broadway version, but Ball in her last feature film is a lame Mame. Overly ambitious production avoids reaching goal. ♫Mame; We Need a Little Christmas; If He Walked Into My Life; Bosom Buddies; It's Today; Loving You; My Best Girl; What Do I Do Now? (Gooch's Sont); Open a New Window. **132m/C VHS, DVD.** Lucille Ball, Bea Arthur, Robert Preston, Joyce Van Patten, Bruce Davison, Jane Connell, Doria Cook, Don Porter, Audrey Christie, John McGiver, Patrick Labyorteaux, Lucille Benson, Burt Mustin, Barbara Bosson; ***D:*** Gene Saks; ***W:*** Paul Zindel; ***C:*** Philip Lathrop; ***M:*** Jerry Herman.

Mamele ½ *Little Mother* **1938** Picon prematurely becomes the "mother" of her seven siblings when their mother dies. Quintessential Yiddish musical with the usual shimmering performance from Picon. In Yiddish with English subtitles. **95m/B VHS.** *PL* Molly Picon, Max Bozyk, Edmund Zayenda; ***D:*** Joseph Green.

Mamma Mia! ½ **2008 (PG-13)** Tunes from the Swedish '70s popsters ABBA provide the backdrop for this 2001 Broadway-musical-turned-film. Sophie (Seyfried) and mom Donna (Streep), who run an inn on a gorgeous Greek island, are preparing for Sophie's wedding. Sophie wants her dad, whom she's never known, to show, so she finds mom's diary and invites the three of Donna's long-ago summer flings (Firth, Brosnan, and Skarsgard) to attend, which throws mom for a loop and makes for all sorts of romance, hijinks, and lavish musical numbers over the wedding weekend. Yes, even Brosnan sings, and it's not pretty. Skip if you're not longing to relive your youthful love of ABBA or if anachronism bugs you, but otherwise it's a harmless romp. **108m/C DVD, Blu-ray Disc.** *US GB* Meryl Streep, Pierce Brosnan, Colin Firth, Amanda Seyfried, Stellan Skarsgard, Julie Walters, Christine Baranski, Dominic Cooper; ***D:*** Phyllida Lloyd; ***W:*** Catherine Johnson; ***C:*** Haris Zambarloukos; ***M:*** Benny Andersson, Bjorn Ulvaes, Stig Anderson. Golden Raspberries '08: Worst Support. Actor (Brosnan).

Mamma Roma ½ **1962** Pasolini's second film is a heartbreaking story of family ties, escaping the past, and dreams of the future. The title character (Magnani) is a former prostitute who attempts respectability for herself and her teenaged son (Garofolo). But her ex-pimp (Citti) threatens her new life and Rome's big-city temptations prove to be a pathway to crime and tragedy for the boy. Magnani gives one of her finest performances. Italian with subtitles. **110m/B VHS, DVD.** *IT* Anna Magnani, Ettore Garofolo, Franco Citti, Silvana Corsini, Luisa Loiano; ***D:*** Pier Paolo Pasolini; ***W:*** Pier Paolo Pasolini; ***C:*** Tonino Delli Colli.

Mammoth **2006** Frank Abernathy (Ventresca) is the curator of a natural history museum in Blackwood, Louisiana. When a meteor hits the building, it thaws the ice-encased star attraction. That would be a mammoth that can suck the life out of people with its trunk when it's not stomping on 'em. Unfortunately, the pic's tone varies from goofy to banal to gross, which diminishes it's cheese factor. A Sci-Fi Channel original. **90m/C DVD.** Vincent Ventresca, Summer Glau, Leila Arcieri, Tom Skerritt, Cole Williams, Marcus Lyle Brown, Charles Carroll; ***D:*** Tim Cox; ***W:*** Sean Keller, Tim Cox, Brooke Durham; ***C:*** Bing Sokolsky; ***M:*** John Dickson. **CABLE**

Mammoth ½ **2009** First English-language film from Moodysson is a repetitive narrative about three sets of working parents that takes place in the United States, the Philippines, and Thailand. Naturally the Americans, Ellen (Williams) and Leo (Garcia Bernal), are wealthy and shallow (yawn) absentee parents whose daughter is cared for by their live-in Filipino nanny, Gloria (Necesito). Gloria's own young sons (who live in Manila) lay a guilt trip on mom for being away. Then, when Leo travels to Thailand for business, he meets bargirl Cookie (Srinikornchot), who's another working mom using the sex industry to support her own baby. Title refers to a very expensive pen made from woolly mammoth ivory. **125m/C DVD.** *DK GE SW* Gael Garcia Bernal, Michelle Williams, Thomas (Tom) McCarthy, Maria del Carmen, Marife Necesito, Sophie Nyweide, Run Srinikornchot, Jan Nicdao, Martin Delos Santos; ***D:*** Lukas Moodysson; ***W:*** Lukas Moodysson; ***C:*** Marcel Zyskind; ***M:*** Jesper Kurlandsky, Linus Gierta, Erik Holmquist.

Mam'zelle Pigalle 🦴 1/2 *Naughty Girl* **1958** Bardot portrays a songstress involved with criminals. French with subtitles. **77m/C VHS, DVD.** *FR* Brigitte Bardot, Jean Bretonniere, Francoise Fabian, Bernard Lancret; ***D:*** Michel Boisrond.

The Man 🦴 **2005 (PG-13)** Andy Fiddler (Levy) an eccentrically nerdy dental-supply salesman from Milwaukee, travels to Detroit for a convention where some illegal arms-dealing crooks mistake him for hard-boiled ATF agent, Derrick Vann (Jackson). Andy gets drawn into the crime-busting plot. Jackson and Levy deliver exactly what you expect in this old school kooky crime buster, but nothing more in this seen-it-done-better-elsewhere attempt at mismatched buddy comedy. **79m/C DVD.** *US* Samuel L. Jackson, Eugene Levy, Luke Goss, Miguel Ferrer, Anthony Mackie, Horatio Sanz, Rachael Crawford, Susie Essman, Tomorrow Baldwin; ***D:*** Les Mayfield; ***W:*** Jim Piddock, Margaret Grieco Oberman, Stephen Carpenter; ***C:*** Adam Kane; ***M:*** John Murphy, Dana Sano.

A Man, a Woman, and a Bank 🦴🦴 1/2 *A Very Big Weekend* **1979 (PG)** Two con-men plan to rob a bank by posing as workers during the bank's construction. An advertising agency woman snaps their picture for a billboard to show how nice the builders have been, then becomes romantically involved with one of the would-be thieves. Nice performances, but wacky touches aren't plentiful enough or well timed to sustain comedy. **100m/C VHS, DVD.** *CA* Donald Sutherland, Brooke Adams, Paul Mazursky; ***D:*** Noel Black; ***W:*** Bruce A. Evans, Raynold Gideon; ***C:*** Jack Cardiff; ***M:*** Bill Conti.

A Man About the House 🦴🦴 1/2 **1947** Two unmarried English sisters move into the Italian villa they have inherited. There, one marries the caretaker, who secretly plans to regain the property that once belonged to his family. When the newly married sister is found dead, her sibling sets out to solve the murder. **83m/B VHS.** *GB* Kieron Moore, Margaret Johnston, Dulcie Gray, Guy Middleton, Felix Aylmer; ***D:*** Leslie Arliss.

Man About Town 🦴🦴 1/2 **1939** Bob Templeton (Benny), an American producing a play in London, falls for a beautiful actress who won't give him the time of day. As a ploy to make her jealous and gain her affections, he woos Lady Arlington who is all for making her inattentive husband jealous as well. Music and dance enchant as our playboy barely escapes alive. **85m/B VHS.** Zion Myers, Jack Benny, Dorothy Lamour, Edward Arnold, Binnie Barnes, Monty Woolley, Phil Harris, Betty Grable; ***D:*** Mark Sandrich.

A Man Alone 🦴🦴 **1955** Man falsely accused of robbing a stagecoach hides not alone but with comely sheriff's daughter. Milland's debut behind the camera. **96m/C VHS.** Ray Milland, Ward Bond, Mary Murphy, Raymond Burr, Lee Van Cleef; ***D:*** Ray Milland; ***C:*** Lionel Lindon.

A Man and a Woman 🦴🦴🦴 *Un Homme et Un Femme* **1966** When a man and a woman, both widowed, meet and become interested in one another but experience difficulties in putting their past loves behind them. Intelligently handled emotional conflicts within a well-acted romantic drama, acclaimed for excellent visual detail. Remade in 1977 as "Another Man, Another Chance." Followed in 1986 with "A Man and A Woman: 20 Years Later." Dubbed. **102m/C VHS, DVD.** *FR* Anouk Aimee, Jean-Louis Trintignant, Pierre Barouh, Valerie Lagrange; ***D:*** Claude Lelouch; ***W:*** Claude Lelouch, Pierre Uytterhoeven; ***C:*** Claude Lelouch; ***M:*** Francis Lai. Oscars '66: Foreign Film, Story & Screenplay; British Acad. '67: Actress (Aimee); Cannes '66: Film; Golden Globes '67: Actress—Drama (Aimee), Foreign Film.

A Man and a Woman: 20 Years Later 🦴 1/2 *Un Homme Et Une Femme: Vingt Ans Deja* **1986 (PG)** Slouchy sequel to the highly praised "A Man and a Woman" that catches up with a couple after a long separation. The sad romantic complications of the original are more mundane in this sequel, which is burdened by a film-within-a-film script as well as shots from the original. In French with English subtitles. **112m/C VHS.** *FR* Jean-Louis Trintignant, Anouk Aimee, Richard Berry; ***D:*** Claude Lelouch; ***W:*** Claude Lelouch.

Man & Boy 🦴🦴 *Ride a Dark Horse* **1971 (G)** A black Civil War veteran, played by Bill Cosby, encounters bigotry and prejudice when he tries to set up a homestead in Arizona. An acceptable family film, some might be disappointed that Cosby is not playing this one for laughs. **98m/C VHS, DVD.** Bill Cosby, Gloria Foster, George Spell, Henry Silva, Yaphet Kotto; ***D:*** E.W. Swackhamer; ***M:*** Quincy Jones.

The Man and the Monster 🦴 1/2 **1965** When a concert pianist sells his soul to the devil, he fails to realize that part of the deal has him turning into a hideous beast every time he hears a certain piece of music. Maybe it was "Stairway to Heaven." **78m/B VHS, DVD.** *MX* Enrique Rambal, Abel Salazar, Martha Roth; ***D:*** Rafael Baledon Sr.

A Man Apart 🦴🦴 **2003 (R)** As action buddy cop movies go, this is one. Sean Vetter (Diesel) is a DEA agent, who, along with partner and childhood pal Hicks (Tate), has just closed a seven-year case by busting cartel head Lucero (Silva). Before the ink is dry on Lucero's fingerprints, Vetter's plot device wife is killed on the orders of the supposedly-defunct cartel's new ruler, El Diablo. Vetter goes into full revenge mode, and all semblence of restraint is eliminated, from Sean and the movie. No cop revenge flick cliche (or pyrotechic equipment) goes unused as Vetter and Diablo careen toward the inevitable showdown, with Hicks and many other cannon-fodder secondary characters hanging on for the wild ride. As you might expect, it all looks really cool, and stuff continues to get blowed up real good. **114m/C VHS, DVD.** *US* Vin Diesel, Larenz Tate, Timothy Olyphant, Geno Silva, Jacqueline Obradors, Steve Eastin, Juan Fernandez, Jeff Kober, George Shaperson; ***D:*** F. Gary Gray; ***W:*** Christian Gudegast, Paul Scheuring; ***C:*** Jack N. Green; ***M:*** Anne Dudley.

Man Bait 🦴🦴 1/2 *The Last Page* **1952** A complex web of intrigue and mystery surrounds a blackmailed book dealer when he allows a blonde woman to catch his eye. A competently made film. **78m/B VHS, DVD.** *GB* George Brent, Marguerite Chapman, Diana Dors; ***D:*** Terence Fisher.

Man Beast 🦴 **1955** The abominable snowman is sought and found in this grade-Z '50s monster movie. **65m/B VHS, DVD.** Virginia Maynor, George Skaff, Lloyd Nelson, Tom Maruzzi; ***D:*** Jerry Warren.

Man Bites Dog 🦴🦴 *C'est Arrive pres de Chez Vous* **1991 (NC-17)** A pseudo-documentary about a serial killer, filled with ever-mounting violence. Ben is the killer being followed by a two-man camera/sound crew (which he's hired), who record his casual carnage without lifting a finger to stop him. Indeed his continued killing and robbing is to pay for financing the documentary about himself. This satire on film violence, as well as reality-based TV shows, is both appalling and humorous in a sick way. French with English subtitles. Also available in an unrated edited version. **95m/B VHS, DVD.** *BE* Benoit Poelvoorde, Remy Belvaux, Andre Bonzel, Vincent Tavier, Jean-Marc Chenut; ***D:*** Benoit Poelvoorde, Remy Belvaux, Andre Bonzel; ***W:*** Benoit Poelvoorde, Remy Belvaux, Andre Bonzel, Vincent Tavier; ***C:*** Andre Bonzel; ***M:*** Laurence Dufrene, Jean-Marc Chenut.

A Man Called Adam 🦴 1/2 **1966** A jazz musician is tortured by prejudice and the guilt created by his having accidentally killed his wife and baby years before. Davis is appropriately haunted, but the film is poorly produced. **103m/B VHS.** Sammy Davis Jr., Louis Armstrong, Ossie Davis, Cicely Tyson, Frank Sinatra Jr., Lola Falana, Mel Torme, Peter Lawford; ***D:*** Leo Penn; ***C:*** Jack Priestley.

A Man Called Horse 🦴🦴🦴 **1970 (PG)** After a wealthy Britisher is captured and tortured by the Sioux Indians in the Dakotas, he abandons his formal ways and discovers his own strength. As he passes their torture tests, he is embraced by the tribe. In this very realistic and gripping portrayal of American Indian life, Harris provides a strong performance. Sequelled by "Return of a Man Called Horse" (1976) and "Triumphs of a Man Called Horse" (1983). **114m/C VHS, DVD.** Richard Harris, Judith Anderson, Jean Gascon, Stanford Howard, Manu Tupou, Dub Taylor; ***D:*** Elliot Silverstein; ***W:*** Jack DeWitt; ***C:*** Robert B. Hauser.

A Man Called Peter 🦴🦴🦴 **1955** A biographical epic about Peter Marshall, a Scottish chaplain who served the U.S. Senate. Todd does his subject justice by sensitively showing all that was human in Marshall, and a talented supporting cast makes for a thoroughly watchable film. **119m/C VHS, DVD.** Richard Todd, Jean Peters, Marjorie Rambeau, Jill Esmond, Les Tremayne, Robert Burton; ***D:*** Henry Koster.

A Man Called Rage WOOF! **1984** Rage is the only man capable of safely escorting a group of pioneers through a nuclear wasteland infested with mutants and cannibals. **90m/C VHS.** *IT* Stelio Candelli, Conrad Nichols; ***D:*** Anthony Richmond.

A Man Called Sarge 🦴 1/2 **1990 (PG-13)** Sophomoric comedy about a daffy WWII sergeant leading his squad against the Germans at Tobruk. **88m/C VHS.** Bobby DiCicco, Gary Kroeger, Marc Singer, Gretchen German, Jennifer Runyon; ***D:*** Stuart Gillard.

A Man Called Sledge 🦴🦴 **1971** Garner fans might be surprised to see the star play a villain in this violent story of a gang of outlaws who wind up fighting each over a cache of gold. This is mainstream Western entertainment. **93m/C VHS, DVD.** James Garner, Dennis Weaver, Claude Akins, John Marley, Laura Antonelli, Angelo Infanti; ***D:*** Vic Morrow.

A Man Escaped 🦴🦴🦴 1/2 *Un Condamne a Mort s'est Echappe, Ou le Vent Souffle ou il Vent; A Man Escaped, or the Wind Bloweth Where It Listeth; A Condemned Man Has Escaped* **1957** There's an excruciating realism about Bresson's account of a WWII Resistance fighter's escape from a Nazi prison just before he was to be executed by the Gestapo. It's the sounds and lingering camera shots, not the wham bam variety of action, that create and sustain the film's suspense. Bresson, who had been a Nazi prisoner, solicited the supervision of Andre Devigny, whose true story the film tells. Contributing to the realistic feel was the use of non professional actors. An award-wiining film that fellow director Truffaut lauded as the most crucial French film of the previous ten years. In French with English subtitles. **102m/B VHS, DVD.** Francois Leterrier, Charles Le Clainche, Roland Monod, Maurice Beerblock, Jacques Ertaud, Jean-Paul Delhumeau, Roger Treherne, Jean-Philippe Delamarre, Cesar Gattegno, Jacques Oerlemans, Klaus Detlef Grevenhorst, Leonard Schmidt; ***D:*** Robert Bresson; ***W:*** Robert Bresson; ***C:*** Leonce-Henri Burel. Cannes '57: Director (Bresson).

Man Facing Southeast 🦴🦴🦴 1/2 *Hombre Mirando Al Sudeste; Man Looking Southeast* **1986 (R)** The acclaimed Argentinean film about the sudden appearance of a strange man in an asylum who claims to be an extraterrestrial, and a psychologist's attempts to discover his true identity. The sense of mystery intensifies when the new patient indeed seems to have some remarkable powers. Although the pace at times lags, the story intriguingly keeps one guessing about the stranger right to the end. In Spanish, with English subtitles. **105m/C VHS.** *AR* Lorenzo Quinteros, Hugo Soto, Ines Vernengo; ***D:*** Eliseo Subiela; ***C:*** Ricardo De Angelis; ***M:*** Pedro Aznar.

A Man for All Seasons 🦴🦴🦴🦴 **1966 (G)** Sterling, heavily Oscar-honored biographical drama concerning the life and subsequent martyrdom of 16th-century Chancellor of England, Sir Thomas More (Scofield). Story revolves around his personal conflict when King Henry VIII (Shaw) seeks a divorce from his wife, Catherine of Aragon, so he can wed his mistress, Anne Boleyn—events that ultimately lead the King to bolt from the Pope and declare himself head of the Church of England. Remade for TV in 1988 with Charlton Heston in the lead role. **120m/C VHS, DVD.** *GB* Paul Scofield, Robert Shaw, Orson Welles, Wendy Hiller, Susannah York, John Hurt, Nigel Davenport, Vanessa Redgrave; ***D:*** Fred Zinnemann; ***W:*** Constance Willis, Robert Bolt; ***C:*** Ted Moore; ***M:*** Georges Delerue. Oscars '66: Actor (Scofield), Adapt. Screenplay, Color Cinematog., Costume Des. (C), Director (Zinnemann), Picture; British Acad. '67: Actor (Scofield), Film, Screenplay; Directors Guild '66: Director (Zinnemann); Golden Globes '67: Actor—Drama (Scofield), Director (Zinnemann), Film—Drama, Screenplay; Natl. Bd. of Review '66: Actor (Scofield), Director (Zinnemann), Support. Actor (Shaw); N.Y. Film Critics '66: Actor (Scofield), Director (Zinnemann), Film, Screenplay.

A Man for All Seasons 🦴🦴🦴 **1988** Fresh from the London stage, Heston directs and stars in this version of Robert Bolt's play depicting the conflict between Henry VIII and his chief advisor, Sir Thomas More. Strong supporting cast. **150m/C VHS.** Charlton Heston, Vanessa Redgrave, John Gielgud, Richard Johnson, Roy Kinnear, Martin Chamberlain; ***D:*** Charlton Heston. **CABLE**

Man Friday 🦴🦴 **1975 (PG)** Stranded on a deserted island, a man forces a native from a neighboring island to be his slave. Based on the classic story "Robinson Crusoe" by Daniel Defoe, this adaptation charts the often-brutal treatment the native receives as his captor tries to civilize him. Through his intelligence, the enslaved man regains his freedom and returns home with his former captor, who then seeks acceptance from the native's tribe. A sometimes confusing storyline and excessive blood and guts detract from this message-laden effort. **115m/C VHS, DVD.** *GB* Peter O'Toole, Richard Roundtree, Peter Cellier, Christopher Cabot, Joel Fluellen; ***D:*** Jack Gold; ***M:*** Carl Davis.

The Man from Atlantis 🦴🦴 **1977** Patrick Duffy stars as the water-breathing alien who emerges from his undersea home, the Lost City of Atlantis. Led to a brief TV series. **60m/C VHS.** Patrick Duffy, Belinda J. Montgomery, Victor Buono; ***D:*** Lee H. Katzin. **TV**

The Man from Beyond 🦴🦴 1/2 **1922** Frozen alive, a man returns 100 years later to try and find his lost love. Silent. **50m/B VHS, DVD.** Harry Houdini, Arthur Maude, Nita Naldi; ***D:*** Burton King.

Man from Button Willow 🦴🦴 **1965 (G)** Classic animated adventure is the story of Justin Eagle, a man who leads a double life. He is a respected rancher and a shrewd secret agent for the government, but in 1869 he suddenly finds himself the guardian of a four-year-old Oriental girl, leading him into a whole new series of adventures. Strictly for younger audiences. **79m/C VHS, DVD.** ***M:*** George Bruns; ***V:*** Dale Robertson, Edgar Buchanan, Barbara Jean Wong, Howard Keel.

Man from Cairo 🦴🦴 **1954** An American in Algiers is mistaken for a detective in search of gold lost during WWII and decides to play along. **82m/B VHS, DVD.** *IT* George Raft, Gianna Maria Canale; ***D:*** Ray Enright.

Man from Cheyenne 🦴 **1942** Cowboy comes home to find his town under a siege of terror from a lawless gang of cattle rustlers. He gets mad and seeks some frontier justice. **54m/B VHS.** Roy Rogers, Gale Storm, George "Gabby" Hayes, Sally Payne, Lynne Carver; ***D:*** Joseph Kane; ***W:*** Winston Miller; ***C:*** Reggie Lanning.

Man from Colorado 🦴🦴 1/2 **1949** An odd Technicolor western about two Civil War vets at odds, one an honest marshall, the other a sadistic judge. Solid Western fare with a quirky performance by Ford. **99m/C VHS, DVD.** William Holden, Glenn Ford, Ellen Drew, Ray Collins, Edgar Buchanan, Jerome Courtland, James Millican, Jim Bannon; ***D:*** Henry Levin; ***M:*** George Duning.

Man from Deep River WOOF! 1977 (R) A photographer is captured by a savage tribe in Thailand and forced to undergo a series of grueling initiation rites. Full of very violent and sickening tortures inflicted on both human and animal victims. **90m/C VHS, DVD.** *IT* Ivan Rassimov; ***D:*** Umberto Lenzi.

The Man from Earth ½ *Jerome Bixby's Man from Earth* **2007** College professor John Oldman (Smith) gathers his most trusted colleagues at a remote cabin to inform them that he's actual an immortal who has been evolving since the Cro-Magnon age. So is he telling the truth or just nuts? Low-key, speculative fiction from classic sci-fi writer Bixby. Falls apart at the end but until then it's an interesting look at belief. **90m/C DVD.** David Lee Smith, John Billingsley, Richard Riehle, Tony Todd, William Katt, Ellen Crawford, Annika Peterson, Alexis Thorpe; ***D:*** Richard Schenkman; ***W:*** Jerome Bixby; ***C:*** Afshin Shahidi. **VIDEO**

The Man from Elysian Fields **2001 (R)** Byron (Garcia) is a failing novelist who's having trouble supporting his wife (Margulies) and family. At his lowest point Byron meets dapper escort service operator Luther (Jagger), who offers him a job as a highly paid gigolo. Hiding his new job from his wife, Byron begins seeing Andrea (Williams), who happens to be the wife of his literary hero Tobias Alcott (Coburn). Tobias, who is agreeable to the arrangement, soon begins to ask Byron for help on his novel, which he believes will be his swan song. Meanwhile, Luther is having his own complications with a client (Huston) with whom he has fallen in love. An offbeat, satisfying look at seduction, betrayal and forgiveness of all kinds. **106m/C VHS, DVD.** *US* Andy Garcia, Mick Jagger, Julianna Margulies, Olivia Williams, James Coburn, Anjelica Huston, Michael Des Barres, Richard Bradford; ***D:*** George Hickenlooper; ***W:*** Jayson Philip Lasker; ***C:*** Kramer Morgenthau; ***M:*** Anthony Marinelli.

Man From Galveston ½ **1963** Intended as the TV pilot for the 1963 "Temple Houston" series although Warner Bros. chose to release it as a (short) feature to drum up publicity. Higgins (Hunter) is a Texas frontier lawyer defending his former girlfriend Rita (Moore) from a murder charge. **54m/B DVD.** Jeffrey Hunter, Preston Foster, Joanna Moore, James Coburn, Edward Andrews, Ed Nelson, Kevin Hagen; ***D:*** William Conrad; ***W:*** Dean Riesner, Michael Zagor; ***C:*** Bert Glennon; ***M:*** David Buttolph.

Man From God's Country ½ **1958** Uninvolving western. Gunslinging ex-sheriff Dan Beattie (Montgomery) heads to lawless Sundown to join his friend Curt (Peters) but is mistaken for a railroad agent after he arrives. Businessman Beau Santee (Wilcox) wants to keep the railroad out and has his thugs try to get rid of Beattie. **72m/C DVD.** George Montgomery, Randy Stuart, House Peters Jr., Frank Wilcox, Gregg Barton, Kim Charney, Susan Cummings, James J. Griffith; ***D:*** Paul Landres; ***W:*** George Waggner; ***C:*** Harry Neumann; ***M:*** Marlin Skiles.

The Man from Gun Town ½ **1936** McCoy comes to the rescue of a woman who has been framed by an evil gang for the murder of her brother. **58m/B VHS.** Tim McCoy, Billie Seward, Rex Lease, Jack Clifford, Wheeler Oakman, Bob McKenzie; ***D:*** Ford Beebe.

Man from Headquarters **1928** Good silent mystery in which a U.S. agent takes on a gang of foreign operatives. **?m/B VHS.** Cornelius Keefe, Edith Roberts, Charles West, Lloyd Whitlock; ***D:*** Duke Worne; ***W:*** Arthur Hoerl; ***C:*** Hap Depew.

The Man from Hell **1934** Sheriff Russell goes undercover to expose the head of a gang of outlaws. Low-budget fare. **55m/B VHS.** Reb Russell, Fred Kohler Jr., Ann Darcy, George "Gabby" Hayes, Jack Rockwell, Charles French, Charles "Slim" Whitaker, Yakima Canutt; ***D:*** Lewis D. Collins.

Man from Hell's Edges ½ **1932** An innocent cowpoke escapes from jail and brings the real baddy to justice. **63m/B VHS, DVD.** Bob Steele, Nancy Drexel, Julian Rivero, Robert E. Homans, George "Gabby" Hayes; ***D:*** Robert North Bradbury.

The Man from Laramie ½ **1955** Aging ranch baron Alec Waggoman (Crisp), who is going blind, worries about which of his two sons he will leave the ranch to. Into this tension-filled familial atmosphere rides Lockhart (Stewart), a cow-herder obsessed with hunting down the men who sold guns to the Indians that killed his brother. Needless to say, the tension increases. Tough, surprisingly brutal western, the best of the classic Stewart-Mann films. **104m/B VHS, DVD.** James Stewart, Arthur Kennedy, Donald Crisp, Alex Nicol, Cathy O'Donnell, Aline MacMahon, Wallace Ford, Jack Elam; ***D:*** Anthony Mann; ***W:*** Philip Yordan; ***C:*** Charles B(ryant) Lang Jr.; ***M:*** George Duning.

The Man from Left Field ½ **1993** Homeless man winds up coaching a little league baseball team, inspiring the kids, and turning his life around. Made for TV. **96m/C VHS, DVD.** Burt Reynolds, Reba McEntire; ***D:*** Burt Reynolds; ***M:*** Bobby Goldsboro. **TV**

Man from Mallorca *Mannen fran Mallorca* **1984** Sgts. Jarnebring (Wollter) and Johansson (von Bromssen) are in pursuit of a gunman who robbed a Stockholm post office. The robber gets away and the investigation stalls until two witnesses are murdered. The detectives begin to suspect an official cover-up and think that senior police officer Hedberg (Hellberg) has something to hide. When they're taken off the case, the duo forge ahead on their own time with some disturbing results. Swedish with subtitles. **104m/C VHS.** *SW* Sven Wollter, Tomas von Bromssen, Thomas Hellberg; ***D:*** Bo Widerberg; ***W:*** Bo Widerberg; ***C:*** Thomas Wahlberg.

Man from Montana ½ *Montana Justice* **1941** Brown is a sheriff who battles outlaws trying to stir up trouble between ranchers and homesteaders. **56m/B VHS.** Johnny Mack Brown, Fuzzy Knight, William (Bill) Gould, Kermit Maynard, Nell O'Day, Billy Lenhart, Murdock MacQuarrie; ***D:*** Ray Taylor; ***W:*** Bennett Cohen; ***C:*** Charles Van Enger.

Man from Monterey **1933** South-of-the-border Western has U.S. Army captain Wayne trying to get Mexican landowners to register their property under Spanish land grants or lose them to public domain. Wayne's last series western for Warner Bros. **59m/B VHS, DVD.** John Wayne, Ruth Hall, Luis Alberni, Francis Ford, Lafe (Lafayette) McKee, Lillian (Lillianne, Lyllian) Leighton, Charles "Slim" Whitaker; ***D:*** Mack V. Wright; ***W:*** Lesley Mason.

The Man from Music Mountain **1938** Worthless mining stock is sold in a desert mining town, but Gene and Smiley clear that up, with a little singing as well. **54m/B VHS.** Gene Autry, Smiley Burnette, Carol Hughes, Polly Jenkins.

Man from Nowhere ½ **1937** A henpecked man gets the break of his life when his domineering wife and mother-in-law believe he's dead. Based on the novel by Luigi Pirandello. In French with English subtitles. **98m/B VHS.** *FR* Pierre Blanchar, Ginette LeClerc; ***D:*** Pierre Chenal.

The Man From Oklahoma ½ **1926** The heroic title character (Perrin) arrives in town with his trusty (and heroic) dog Rex and is pitted against a crooked, murderous ranch foreman (Meehan). **55m/B DVD.** Jack Perrin, Lew Meehan, Josephine Hill, Lafe (Lafayette) McKee, Edmund Cobb, Martin Turner; ***D:*** Harry S. Webb.

The Man from Painted Post **1917** Fairbanks plays a Cattlemen's Association detective who comes to the range to stop the cattle rustlers as well as to find the man who murdered his sister. **?m/B VHS.** Douglas Fairbanks Sr., Eileen (Elaine Persey) Percy, Frank Campeau, Monte Blue; ***D:*** Joseph Henabery.

The Man from Planet X **1951** Making a belated arrival on home video is this prototypical low-budget first-contact tale. All the elements are there—reporter, aging scientist, his nubile daughter, crafty associate—but the setting is Scotland. Not that it matters, because virtually all of the action takes place on sets. **71m/B DVD.** Robert Clarke, Margaret Field, William Schallert; ***D:*** Edgar G. Ulmer; ***W:*** Aubrey Wisberg, Jack Pollexfen; ***C:*** John L. "Jack" Russell; ***M:*** Charles Koff.

The Man from Snowy River ½ **1982 (PG)** Stunning cinematography highlights this otherwise fairly ordinary adventure story set in 1880s Australia. Jim Craig (Burlinson) is an orphaned young man coming of age in the mountains while seeking a life of his own and falling in love with the well-brought up Jessica (Thornton). In a dual role, Douglas portrays battling brothers, one a rich landowner and the other a one-legged prospector. A wild horse roundup is a stunning highlight. Based on the epic poem by A.B. "Banjo" Paterson and followed by "Return to Snowy River." A big hit in Australia and not directed by "Mad Max's" Miller, but another Miller named George. **104m/C VHS, DVD.** *AU* Kirk Douglas, Tom Burlinson, Sigrid Thornton, Terence Donovan, Tommy Dysart, Jack Thompson, Bruce Kerr; ***D:*** George Miller; ***W:*** Fred Cullen, John Dixon; ***C:*** Keith Wagstaff; ***M:*** Bruce Rowland.

Man from Texas **1939** Singing and gun-slinging Tex defends a kid accused of horse thieving until the kid turns bad and Tex must bring him in. **55m/B VHS, DVD.** Tex Ritter, Hal Price, Charles B. Wood, Vic Demourelle Sr.; ***D:*** Al(bert) Herman.

Man from the Alamo **1953** A soldier sent from the Alamo during its last hours to get help is branded as a deserter, and struggles to clear his name. Well acted, this film will satisfy those with a taste for action. **79m/C VHS, DVD.** Glenn Ford, Julie Adams, Chill Wills, Victor Jory, Hugh O'Brian; ***D:*** Budd Boetticher.

The Man from the Pru ½ **1989** Shocking 1931 murder case follows insurance agent William Wallace (Pryce) who was sentenced to hang for the murder of his wife, Julia. Wallace insisted he was called from home on a possible insurance sale and returned home to find his wife dead. His case made British legal history when the appeals court overturned the verdict. Made for TV. **90m/C VHS.** *GB* Jonathan Pryce, Anna Massey, Susannah York; ***D:*** Rob Rohrer. **TV**

Man from Thunder River **1943** A group of cowboys uncover a plot to steal gold ore and wind up saving a young girl's life in the process. Standard western with lots of action. **55m/B VHS.** William (Wild Bill) Elliott, George "Gabby" Hayes, Anne Jeffreys, Ian Keith, John James; ***D:*** John English.

Man from Utah ½ **1934** The Duke tangles with the crooked sponsor of some rodeo events who has killed several of the participants. **55m/B VHS, DVD.** John Wayne, George "Gabby" Hayes, Polly Ann Young, Yakima Canutt, Lafe (Lafayette) McKee; ***D:*** Robert North Bradbury; ***W:*** Lindsley Parsons; ***C:*** Archie Stout.

Man Hunt **1941** Atmospheric wartime thriller from Lang finds English big-game hunter Thorndike (Pidgeon) making his way to Bavaria with a chance to assassinate Hitler. He's captured and tortured by the Gestapo (Sanders), escapes, and is pursued while returning to England aboard a Danish steamer. Aboard the ship Thorndike discovers his identity has been usurped by the mysterious Mr. Jones (Carradine). Befriended by a cockney prostitute (Bennett), Thorndike's plight comes down to a confrontation in a London subway tunnel. **105m/B DVD.** Walter Pidgeon, Joan Bennett, George Sanders, John Carradine, Roddy McDowall; ***D:*** Fritz Lang; ***W:*** Dudley Nichols; ***C:*** Arthur C. Miller; ***M:*** Alfred Newman.

The Man I Love **1946** Slick drama about nightclub singer Lupino falling for no-good mobster Alda. Enjoyable and well-acted, although script doesn't make sense. Great selection of tunes. This film inspired Scorsese's "New York, New York." Based on the novel "Night Shift" by Maritta Wolff. ♫ Body and Soul; Why Was I Born; Bill; The Man I Love; Liza; If I Could Be With You. **96m/B VHS.** Ida Lupino, Robert Alda, Andrea King, Martha Vickers, Bruce Bennett, Alan Hale, Dolores Moran, John Ridgely, Don McGuire, Warren Douglas, Craig Stevens; ***D:*** Raoul Walsh, John Maxwell; ***W:*** W.R. Burnett, Catherine Turney, Jo Pagano; ***M:*** Max Steiner.

The Man I Love *L'Homme Qui J'aime* **1997** Heart-on-its-sleeve romance originally made for French TV. Martin (Di Fonzo Bo) is hired to work at a Marseilles municipal swimming pool and falls immediately for golden boy lifeguard Lucas (Portal), who has a live-in girlfriend, Lise (Seigner). Lise thinks Lucas's new buddy is lots of fun—never suspecting that exuberant Martin is after the hunk. Of course, Lucas isn't as straight as he seems and eventually switches partners. But there's another problem, Martin, who's HIV-positive, decides to take a break from his onerous treatment, despite the consequences. French with subtitles. **87m/C VHS, DVD.** *FR* Marcial Di Fonzo Bo, Jean-Michel Portal, Mathilde Seigner, Vittoria Scognamiglio, Jacques Hansen; ***D:*** Stephane Giusti; ***W:*** Stephane Giusti; ***C:*** Jacques Bouquin; ***M:*** Lazare Boghossian. **TV**

The Man in Grey **1945** In a story of romantic intrigue set in 19th-century England, a Marquis's wife is betrayed by her vile husband and the schoolmate she once befriended who has an affair with him. Stunning costumes and fine performances compensate for the overly extravagant production values in a work that helped bring stardom to Mason. **116m/B VHS.** *GB* James Mason, Margaret Lockwood, Stewart Granger, Phyllis Calvert; ***D:*** Leslie Arliss.

A Man in Love *Un Homme Amoureux* **1987 (R)** An international romantic melodrama set during the Italian filming of a biography of suicidal author Cesar Pavese. The self-important lead actor and a beautiful supporting actress (Coyote and Scacchi) become immersed in the roles and fall madly in love, oblivious to the fact that Coyote is married and Scacchi's engaged. The two make a steamy pair, to the detriment of friends, family, and the movie they're making. Kurys' first English-language film is visually appealing with a lush, romantic score, seamlessly weaving the storylines among vivid characters. **110m/C VHS.** *FR* Peter Coyote, Greta Scacchi, Jamie Lee Curtis, Peter Riegert, Jean Pigozzi, John Berry, Claudia Cardinale, Vincent Lindon; ***D:*** Diane Kurys; ***W:*** Diane Kurys, Olivier Schatzky, Israel Horovitz; ***M:*** Georges Delerue.

Man in the Attic ½ **1953** Mild but creepy pathologist Slade (Palance) rents an attic room from Mrs. Harley and moons over her actress daughter Lily (Smith) in late 1880s London. About the same time Lily starts finding Slade attractive and interesting, Mrs. Harvey starts suspecting him of being Jack the Ripper. Satisfying suspenser keeps the audience guessing thanks largely to Palance's ambiguous performance. **82m/B VHS, DVD.** Jack Palance, Constance Smith, Byron Palmer, Frances Bavier, Rhys Williams, Sean McClory, Leslie Bradley, Lester Matthews, Harry Cording, Lillian Bond, Isabel Jewell; ***D:*** Hugo Fregonese; ***W:*** Barre Lyndon, Robert Presnell Jr.; ***C:*** Leo Tover; ***M:*** Hugo Friedhofer.

The Man in the Attic ½ **1994 (R)** Harris certainly leaves his "Doogie Howser" past behind as he takes a grownup turn in an erotic thriller based on a true case history from the early 20th century, gathered from the book "Sex and the Criminal Mind." Teenaged Edward (Harris) has a blazing affair with married, mature Krista (Archer), who does indeed hide her young lover in the family attic when her clueless husband (Cariou) returns home at night. But such consuming passion can hardly be kept a secret for long—and takes a decidedly deadly turn. **97m/C VHS.** Anne Archer, Neil Patrick Harris, Len Cariou, Alex Carter; ***D:*** Graeme Campbell; ***W:*** Duane Poole, Tom Swale; ***C:*** Dick Bush; ***M:*** Lou Natale. **CABLE**

The Man in the Glass Booth **1975 (PG)** In this adaptation of a play written by actor Robert Shaw, a successful Jewish businessman is suspected of being a Nazi war criminal. Loosely based on the life of death camp commandant Otto Adolf Eichmann, the film depicts the arrest and subsequent trial of the former Nazi by the Israelis. The film's title is derived from the fact that Eichmann sat in a glass booth during his trial. Schell's performance is outstanding. **117m/C VHS, DVD.** Maximilian Schell, Lois Nettleton, Luther Adler, Lawrence Pressman, Henry Brown,

Richard Rasof; *D:* Arthur Hiller; *W:* Edward Anhalt; *C:* Sam Leavitt.

The Man in the Gray Flannel Suit ✗✗ 1/2 **1956** A very long and serious adaptation of the Sloan Wilson novel about a Madison Avenue advertising exec trying to balance his life between work and family. The Hollywood treatment falls short of the adaptation potential of the original story. **152m/C VHS, DVD.** Gregory Peck, Fredric March, Jennifer Jones, Ann Harding, Arthur O'Connell, Henry Daniell, Lee J. Cobb, Marisa Pavan, Gene Lockhart, Keenan Wynn, Gigi Perreau, Joseph Sweeney, Kenneth Tobey, DeForest Kelley; *D:* Nunnally Johnson.

The Man in the Iron Mask ✗✗✗ **1939** Swashbuckling tale about twin brothers (played by Hayward) separated at birth. One turns out to be King Louis XIV of France, and the other is imprisoned and forced to wear an iron mask that hides his identity. Philippe is eventually rescued by musketeer D'Artagnan (William) and the musketeers join forces for action-packed adventure and royal revenge. Remake of the "The Iron Mask" (1929) with Douglas Fairbanks and subsequently remade several times for both TV and the big screen. **110m/B VHS, DVD.** Louis Hayward, Alan Hale, Joan Bennett, Warren William, Joseph Schildkraut, Walter Kingsford, Marion Martin; *D:* James Whale; *W:* George Bruce; *C:* Robert Planck; *M:* Lucien Moraweck.

The Man in the Iron Mask ✗✗✗ **1977** A tyrannical French king kidnaps his twin brother and imprisons him on a remote island. Chamberlain, the king of the miniseries, is excellent in a dual role in this big production swashbuckler. Adapted from the Dumas classic. **105m/C VHS.** Richard Chamberlain, Patrick McGoohan, Louis Jourdan, Jenny Agutter, Ian Holm, Ralph Richardson; *D:* Mike Newell. **TV**

The Man in the Iron Mask ✗ 1/2 **1997** Low-budget, personalized version of the Dumas swashbuckler from director Richert, which he filmed at the historic Mission Inn in Riverside, CA. Prologue establishes the birth of twin royals to the French Queen (Foster) and the fate of Philippe (Richert's son Nick) as the man in the iron mask. A deathbed confession to Count Aramis (the director himself) alerts the Musketeers, who decide to set things right. Well-intentioned but not a lot of fun. **85m/C VHS, DVD.** William Richert, Edward Albert, Rex Ryon, Timothy Bottoms, Dennis Hayden, Nick Richert, Meg Foster, James Gammon, Dana Barron, Brigid Brannah, Fannie Brett; *D:* William Richert; *W:* William Richert; *C:* William Barber; *M:* Jim Ervin.

The Man in the Iron Mask ✗✗✗ **1998 (PG-13)** Lavish retelling of Alexandre Dumas's classic story boasts a stellar cast with teen heartthrob DiCaprio in a dual role. Snotty tyrant King Louis XIV's (DiCaprio) lust for women inadvertently leads to the reunion of the retired Musketeers, bent on replacing cold Louis with his more sensitive twin brother Phillippe (DiCaprio, again), an inmate of the Bastille and hidden behind a ghastly mask. Irons, Malkovich, Depardieu, and Byrne bring a welcome seriousness and style to the often-told story as the older, jaded Musketeers, while DiCaprio holds his own in the presence of such formidable company. Although first-time director Wallace doesn't balance the star power with enough swordplay, the high gloss production provides old-fashioned escapist entertainment. **132m/C VHS, DVD.** Leonardo DiCaprio, Gabriel Byrne, Jeremy Irons, John Malkovich, Gerard Depardieu, Anne Parillaud, Judith Godreche, Edward Atterton, Peter Sarsgaard, Hugh Laurie; *D:* Randall Wallace; *W:* Randall Wallace; *C:* Peter Suschitzky; *M:* Nick Glennie-Smith.

Man in the Mirror: The Michael Jackson Story ✗ **2004 (PG-13)** Like rubber-necking at a car wreck. Poorly-dramatized showbiz bio of the pop star (Alexander) in all his legendary weirdness. It takes us from Jackson's musical success to his career slide, unnerving marriages, and the scandals that plagued him. Listen to the music instead. **87m/C DVD.** Flex Alexander, Eugene Clark, Jason Griffith, April Telek, Krista Rae; *D:* Allan Moyle; *W:* Claudia Salter; *C:* David (Robert) A. Greene; *M:* Bruce Leitl. **CABLE**

The Man in the Moon ✗✗✗ 1/2 **1991 (PG-13)** Beautifully rendered coming-of-age tale. On a farm outside a small Louisiana town in the 1950s, 14-year-old Dani wonders if she will ever be as pretty and popular as her 17-year-old sister Maureen. This becomes especially important as Dani is beginning to notice boys, particularly Court, the 17-year-old young man she meets when swimming. Although Dani and Maureen have always been especially close, a rift develops between the sisters after Court meets Maureen. Intelligently written, excellent direction, lovely cinematography, and exceptional acting make this a particularly worthwhile and entertaining film. **100m/C VHS, DVD.** Reese Witherspoon, Emily Warfield, Jason London, Tess Harper, Sam Waterston, Gail Strickland; *D:* Robert Mulligan.

The Man in the Raincoat ✗✗ **1957** French film about a bumbling clarinet player who is erroneously tracked down as a murderer. Strenuous efforts to evoke laughter usually fail. Dubbed. **97m/B VHS.** *FR* Fernandel, John McGiver, Bernard Blier; *D:* Julien Duvivier.

Man in the Saddle ✗✗ 1/2 *The Outcast* **1951** Western star Scott gets roped in a romantic triangle out on the range, leading to some exciting gunplay. As usual, justice triumphs in this above average oater. Based on the novel by Ernest Haycox. **87m/C VHS, DVD.** Randolph Scott, Joan Leslie, Ellen Drew, Alexander Knox, Richard Rober, John Russell; *D:* Andre de Toth; *W:* Kenneth Gamet.

The Man in the Santa Claus Suit ✗✗ **1979** A costume shop owner has an effect on three people who rent Santa Claus costumes from him. Astaire plays seven different roles in this average holiday feel-good movie. **96m/C VHS.** Fred Astaire, Gary Burghoff, John Byner, Nanette Fabray, Bert Convy; *D:* Corey Allen. **TV**

Man in the Shadow ✗✗ 1/2 *Pay the Devil; Seeds of Wrath* **1957** Sheriff Ben Sadler (Chandler) is the only man in the county willing to stand up to wealthy Texas rancher Virgil Renchler (Welles). Sadler suspects Renchler is behind the brutal death of a Mexican laborer but gets no support when he tries to find justice. **80m/C VHS.** Jeff Chandler, Orson Welles, Ben Alexander, Colleen Miller, John Larch, James Gleason, Barbara Lawrence, Royal Dano, Paul Fix, William Schallert; *D:* Jack Arnold; *W:* Gene L. Coon; *C:* Arthur E. Arling; *M:* Joseph Gershenson.

Man in the Silk Hat ✗✗ **1915** A collection of the nearly forgotten French comic's early silent comedy shorts, made in France before his resettlement in America. **96m/B VHS.** *FR* Max Linder; *D:* Maud Linder.

Man in the Silk Hat ✗✗✗ **1983** Gabriel-Maximilien Leuvielle, known in films as Max Linder, is now credited with developing the style of silent-movie slapstick comedy that Mack Sennett, Charlie Chaplin, and others became more famous for in their time. Here, Linder's daughter has done a fine job writing and directing a film full of historic footage of her father's work. **99m/B VHS.** Mack Sennett, Buster Keaton, Charlie Chaplin, Max Linder; *D:* Maud Linder; *W:* Maud Linder; *M:* Jean-Marie Senia; *Nar:* Maud Linder.

Man in the Vault ✗✗ **1956** Low-budget crime noir from John Wayne's Batjac production company. Locksmith Tommy Dancer (Campbell) is hired by hood Willis Trent (Kroeger) for a simple job and then is invited to a party at Trent's where he meets wealthy Betty (Sharpe). She's on the rebound from her cheating lawyer beau Farraday (Keys), but is out of Tommy's pay scale. At least until Trent offers Tommy a lot of dough to make keys to open a safety deposit box that happens to belong to crime boss DeCamp (Seay), which is just asking for trouble. **72m/C DVD.** William Campbell, Berry Kroeger, Anita Ekberg, James Seay, Paul Fix, Mike Mazurki, Karen Sharpe, Robert Keys; *D:* Andrew V. McLaglen; *W:* Burt Kennedy; *C:* William Clothier; *M:* Henry Vars.

The Man in the White Suit ✗✗✗ 1/2 **1951** A humble laboratory assistant in a textile mill invents a white cloth that won't stain, tear, or wear out, and can't be dyed. The panicked garment industry sets out to destroy him and the fabric, resulting in some sublimely comic situations and a variety of inventive chases. **82m/B VHS, DVD.** *GB* Alec Guinness, Joan Greenwood; *D:* Alexander MacKendrick.

Man in the Wilderness ✗✗ 1/2 **1971 (PG)** Harris is part of an expedition traveling through the Northwest Territory. He's mauled by a grizzly and left for dead by leader Huston. While Harris fights for survival, he also plots revenge. Blood and violence is somewhat offset by good lead performances. **108m/C VHS.** Richard Harris, John Huston, Henry Wilcoxon, Percy Herbert, Dennis Waterman, Prunella Ransome, Norman Rossington, James Doohan; *D:* Richard Sarafian; *W:* Jack DeWitt; *M:* Johnny Harris.

A Man in Uniform ✗✗ *I Love a Man in Uniform* **1993 (R)** A look at the making of a sociopath. Henry (McCamus) is a quiet bank employee who moonlights as an actor. Then he gets his big break in the role of a self-righteous cop in a TV series. Only the lines between his make-believe cop and the real world begin to blur and Henry's intensity turns to violence. Fine performances lead to an unsatisfying film conclusion. **99m/C VHS, DVD.** *CA* Tom McCamus, Brigitte Bako, Kevin Tighe, David Hemblen, Alex Karzis, Graham McPherson, Richard Blackburn; *D:* David Wellington; *W:* David Wellington; *C:* David Franco; *M:* Ron Sures. Genie '93: Actor (McCamus), Support. Actor (Tighe).

The Man Inside ✗ 1/2 **1976** Undercover agent infiltrates a powerful underworld narcotics ring and finds his honesty tested when $2 million is at stake. **96m/C VHS.** *CA* James Franciscus, Stefanie Powers, Jacques Godin; *D:* Gerald Mayer.

The Man Inside ✗✗ **1990 (PG)** Lukewarm Cold War saga based on the true story of Gunther Wallraff, a West German journalist who risked all to expose the corruption behind a large European newspaper. **93m/C VHS.** *NL GE* Jurgen Prochnow, Peter Coyote, Nathalie Baye, Dieter Laser, Monique Van De Ven, Sylvie Granotier; *D:* Bobby Roth; *W:* Bobby Roth.

Man Is Not a Bird ✗✗ 1/2 *Covek Nije Tica* **1965** Follows the destructive love of a factory engineer and a hairdresser in a small Yugoslavian mining town. In Serbian with English subtitles. **80m/B VHS.** *YU* Eva Ras, Milena Dravic, Janez Urhovec; *D:* Dusan Makavejev; *W:* Dusan Makavejev; *C:* Aleksandar Petkovic; *M:* Petar Bergamo.

A Man Like Eva ✗✗✗ *Ein Mann wie Eva* **1983** A weird, morbid homage to and portrait of Rainer Werner Fassbinder after his inevitable death, detailing his work-obsessed self-destruction. Mattes, one of Fassbinder's favorite actresses, plays him in drag, in an eerie gender-crossing transformation. In German with English subtitles. **92m/C VHS.** *GE* Eva Mattes, Elisabeth (Lisa) Kreuzer, Charles Regnier, Werner Stocker; *D:* Radu Gabrea.

Man Made Monster ✗✗ 1/2 *Atomic Monster; The Electric Man* **1941** Chaney stars as carnival performer "Dynamo" Dan McCormick, whose act has caused Dan to build up an immunity to electrical charges. Dan falls prey to the mad Dr. Rigas (Atwill) who seeks to create a race of electro-men who'll do his bidding. Experiments on the hapless Dan turn him into a glowing monster whose very touch can kill. Chaney's first role in the horror genre led to Universal's casting him in "The Wolf Man" and "The Ghost of Frankenstein." **61m/B VHS.** Lon Chaney Jr., Lionel Atwill, Anne Nagel, Frank Albertson, Samuel S. Hinds; *D:* George Waggner; *W:* Joseph West; *C:* Elwood "Woody" Bredell.

Man of a Thousand Faces ✗✗✗ 1/2 **1957** A tasteful and touching portrayal of Lon Chaney, from his childhood with his deaf and mute parents to his success as a screen star. Recreates some of Chaney's most famous roles, including the Phantom of the Opera and Quasimodo in "Notre Dame." Cagney is magnificent as the long-suffering film star who was a genius with makeup and mime. **122m/B VHS, DVD.** James Cagney, Dorothy Malone, Jane Greer, Marjorie Rambeau, Jim Backus, Roger Smith, Robert Evans; *D:* Joseph Pevney; *W:* Ivan Goff; *C:* Russell Metty; *M:* Frank Skinner.

Man of Action ✗ 1/2 **1933** Texas Ranger McCoy is out to solve the mystery of what happened to money, recovered from a robbery, which has vanished once again. **56m/B VHS.** Tim McCoy, Wheeler Oakman, Walter Brennan, Stanley Blystone, Charles French; *D:* George Melford.

Man of Aran ✗✗✗ **1934** Celebrated account of a fisherman's struggle for survival on a barren island near the west coast of Ireland, featuring amateur actors. Three years in the making, it's the last word in man against nature cinema, and a visual marvel. A former explorer, Flaherty became an influential documentarian. Having first gained fame with "Nanook of the North," he compiled an opus of documentaries made for commercial release. **132m/B VHS, DVD.** *D:* Robert Flaherty. **TV**

Man of Ashes ✗✗ *Rih Essed* **1986** Hachemi is terrified of women though he is a bridegroom-to-be. He and his friend Farfat have kept hidden the fact that they were molested by their male employer. They try to overcome their insecurities by visiting a prostitute but this experience is only successful for one of the men, leading the other to more torment. Arabic with subtitles. **109m/C VHS, DVD.** Imad Maalal, Khalid Ksouri; *D:* Nouri Bouzid; *W:* Nouri Bouzid; *C:* Youssef Ben Youssef; *M:* Salah Mahdi.

Man of Destiny ✗✗ 1/2 **1973** Bonaparte (Keach) and a mysterious woman battle good-humoredly over a collection of love letters. From a Bernard Shaw story. Charming and well-acted. **60m/C VHS.** Stacy Keach, Samantha Eggar; *D:* Joseph Hardy; *M:* Robert Prince.

Man of Evil ✗✗ *Fanny by Gaslight* **1948** The hard times of the illegitimate daughter of a member of the British Parliament in the early 1900s, told with an astonishing number of plot twists and a plodding melodramtic style. Based on the novel "Fanny by Gaslight." **108m/B VHS.** *GB* Phyllis Calvert, James Mason, Wilfred Lawson, Stewart Granger, Margaretta Scott, Jean Kent, John Laurie, Stuart Lindsell, Nora Swinburne, Amy Veness, Ann Wilton, Helen Haye, Cathleen Nesbitt, Guy Le Feuvre, John Turnbull, Peter Jones; *D:* Anthony Asquith.

Man of Flowers ✗✗ 1/2 **1984** Because of his puritan upbringing, a reclusive art collector has trouble coping with his feelings of sexuality. He pays a woman to disrobe in front of him, but is never able to bring himself to see her naked. A moody piece with overtones of black humor, this work has limited audience appeal. **91m/C VHS, DVD.** *AU* Norman Kaye, Alyson Best, Chris Haywood, Sarah Walker, Julia Blake, Bob Ellis, Werner Herzog; *D:* Paul Cox; *W:* Bob Ellis, Paul Cox; *C:* Yuri Sokol; *M:* Gaetano Donizetti. Australian Film Inst. '83: Actor (Kaye).

Man of Iron ✗✗✗ *Wajda: Czlowiek Z Zelaza* **1981 (PG)** Director Wajda's follow-up to "Man of Marble" deals with a reporter (Odania) who is expected to tow the government line when writing about the Gdansk shipyard strike of 1980. He meets the harassed laborer son (Radziwilowicz) of worker-hero Birkut, against whom Odania is expected to conduct a smear campaign, and finds his loyalties tested. In Polish with English subtitles. **116m/C VHS, DVD.** *PL* Jerzy Radziwilowicz, Marian Opania, Krystyna Janda; *D:* Andrzej Wajda; *W:* Aleksander Scibor-Rylski; *C:* Edward Klosinski; *M:* Andrzej Korzynski. Cannes '81: Film.

Man of La Mancha ✗ 1/2 **1972 (PG)** Arrested by the Inquisition and thrown into prison, Miguel de Cervantes relates the story of Don Quixote. Not nearly as good as the Broadway musical it is based on. ♫ It's All the Same; The Impossible Dream; Barber's Song; Man of La Mancha; Dulcinea; I'm Only Thinking of Him; Little Bird, Little Bird; Life as It Really Is; The Dubbing. **129m/C VHS, DVD.** Peter O'Toole, Sophia Loren, James Coco, Harry Andrews, John Castle, Brian Blessed; *D:* Arthur Hiller. Natl. Bd. of Review '72: Actor (O'Toole).

Man of Legend ✗✗ **1971 (PG)** An adventure-romance filmed in Morocco; a WWI German soldier flees to the Foreign Legion and fights with nomadic rebels, ultimately falling in love with their chief's beautiful daughter. An unoriginal desert saga. **95m/C VHS.** *IT SP* Peter Strauss, Tina Aumont, Pier Paolo Capponi; *D:* Sergio Grieco.

Man of Marble **1976** A satire on life in post-WWII Poland. A young filmmaker sets out to tell the story of a bricklayer who, because of his exceptional skill, once gained popularity with other workers. He became a champion for worker rights, only to then find himself being persecuted by the government. The conclusion was censored by the Polish government. Highly acclaimed and followed by "Man of Iron" in 1981. In Polish with English subtitles. **160m/C VHS, DVD.** *PL* Krystyna Janda, Jerzy Radziwilowicz, Tadeusz Lomnicki, Jacek Lomnicki, Krystyna Zachwatowicz; ***D:*** Andrzej Wajda; ***W:*** Aleksander Scibor-Rylski; ***M:*** Andrzej Korzynski.

The Man of My Life *L'Homme de Sa Vie* **2006** Frederic (Campan) is on holiday with his wife (Drucker) at his family's home in the Provencale countryside. They invite their new neighbor, cynical gay Hugo (Berling), to a party and he and Frederic wind up talking for hours. An unexpected bond develops between the two middle-aged men and starts disrupting Frederic's marriage. French with subtitles. **111m/C DVD.** *FR IT* Bernard Campan, Charles Berling, Lea Drucker; ***D:*** Zabou Breitman; ***W:*** Zabou Breitman, Agnes de Sacy; ***C:*** Michel Amathieu; ***M:*** Liviu Badiu, Laurent Korcia.

A Man of No Importance **1994 (R)** Touching and entertaining saga of lovable Alfie Byrne (Finney), a 1960s Dublin bus conductor with a passion for the work of Oscar Wilde, who successfully represses his own homosexuality. He also moonlights as director of a community theatre, where he sets out to produce Wilde's controversial play "Salome" starring fetching new bus passenger Adele (Fitzgerald), who further confuses Alfie's take on his identity. Finney is both delightful and heartbreaking in this character study of an innocent soul whose life is tested by the social code of his day. Equally affecting and charming supporting performances round out this witty but sad tale. **98m/C VHS.** *GB* Albert Finney, Brenda Fricker, Michael Gambon, Tara Fitzgerald, Rufus Sewell, Patrick Malahide, David Kelly, Mick (Michael) Lally; ***D:*** Suri Krishnamma; ***W:*** Barry Devlin; ***M:*** Julian Nott.

A Man of Passion **1988 (R)** Quinn plays an aging artist living pleasurably on a Mediterranean isle. His summer guest is his uptight grandson, a classical pianist. Naturally, Gramps is about to teach the kid to loosen up, including appreciating one of his lovely artist's models. Another variation for Quinn on his "Zorba" personality but it works. **90m/C VHS.** Anthony Quinn, Ramon Sheen, Maud Adams, Elizabeth Ashley, R.J. Williams, Ray Walston, Victoria Vera; ***D:*** Jose Antonio De La Loma; ***W:*** Jose Antonio De La Loma.

Man of the Century 1/2 **1999 (R)** Journalist Johnny Twennies (Frazier) is an anachronism living in 1990s Manhattan. He dresses, talks, and acts as if it were the 1920s. But Johnny doesn't seem to find anything strange in this, nor does anyone else. **77m/C VHS, DVD.** Gibson Frazier, Susan Egan, Anthony Rapp, Cara Buono, Dwight Ewell, Brian Davies, Frank Gorshin; ***D:*** Adam Abramham; ***W:*** Adam Abramham, Gibson Frazier; ***C:*** Matthew Jensen; ***M:*** Michael Weiner.

Man of the Forest **1933** A cowboy goes to the aid of a damsel in distress and he winds up being framed for murder for his efforts. Based on Zane Grey's novel. **59m/B VHS, DVD.** Randolph Scott, Verna Hillie, Harry Carey Sr., Noah Beery Sr., Barton MacLane; ***D:*** Henry Hathaway.

Man of the House **1995 (PG)** Kids' comedy about a boy's scheme to sabotage his mother's new love interest. Ben (Thomas) concocts a plan to join the YMCA Indian Guides to discourage daddy wanna-be Jack (Chase), while mom (Fawcett) stands idly by tolerating her son's bratty behavior. Subplot involves a screwy gangster theme that deteriorates into a "Home Alone-ish" ending. Film attempts to play off of Chase's knack for physical comedy, but falls short. And what's with the mime? Wendt is amusing as the Indian Guide leader. Will probably appeal more to younger crowds as Thomas's scheming teen upstages Chase's deadpan dad-to-be. **97m/C VHS, DVD.** Chevy Chase, Farrah Fawcett, Jonathan Taylor Thomas, George Wendt, David Shiner, Art LaFleur, Richard Portnow, Richard Foronjy, Spencer Vrooman, John Disanti, Chief Leonard George, Peter Appel, George Greif, Chris Miranda, Ron Canada, Zachary Browne, Nicholas Garrett; ***D:*** James Orr; ***W:*** James Orr, Jim Cruickshank; ***C:*** Jamie Anderson; ***M:*** Mark Mancina.

Man of the House **2005 (PG-13)** Jones, with his weathered face and deadpan grumpiness, goes slumming in this silly comedy about cheerleaders who witness a murder. Roland Sharp is a stoic Texas Ranger assigned to protect five giggly (and jiggly) members (Milian, Keena, Garces, Ferlito, Garner) of the University of Texas Longhorns' cheerleading squad. He moves into their sorority house and offers fatherly advice while trying to awkwardly woo an age-appropriate professor (Archer) and find the bad guy. For some reason Cedric the Entertainer turns up briefly as an ex-con preacher with his own pep squad moves. **99m/C VHS, DVD, UMD.** *US* Tommy Lee Jones, Cedric the Entertainer, Christina Milian, Paula Garces, Monica Keena, Vanessa Ferlito, Kelli Garner, Anne Archer, Brian Van Holt, Shea Whigham, R. Lee Ermey, Paget Brewster, Liz Vassey, Curtis Armstrong, Terry Parks, Marie Woodward; ***Cameos:*** James Richard Perry; ***D:*** Stephen Herek; ***W:*** Robert Ramsey, Matthew Stone, John McLaughlin; ***C:*** Peter Menzies Jr.; ***M:*** David Newman.

Man of the West 1/2 **1958** Reformed bad guy Cooper is asked to deliver a tidy hunk of cash to another city to recruit a school marm. Ambushed en route by his former partners in crime (who are led by his wacko uncle) he's forced to revert to his wanton ways in order to survive and save innocent hostages. There's a raging debate among Cooper fans whether this late effort has been unduly overlooked or duly ignored. A number of things conspire to give it a bad rap: Cooper does little but look mournful until the very end; there's no hiding the fact that he's older than Cobb, who plays his uncle; and the acting is in general more befitting of a B-grade slice and dicer. You be the judge. **100m/C VHS.** Gary Cooper, Julie London, Lee J. Cobb, Arthur O'Connell, Jack Lord, John Dehner, Royal Dano, Guy Wilkerson, Emory Parnell; ***D:*** Anthony Mann; ***W:*** Reginald Rose.

Man of the World **1931** Outcast journalist Michael Trevor (Powell) lives in Paris and blackmails wealthy Americans, aided by girlfriend Irene (Gibson). He wants to go straight when he falls for debutante Mary Kendall (Lombard) but tables are turned when Irene threatens to expose Michael's schemes. Pre-Production Code flick says crime may not pay but you still can get away. **74m/B VHS, DVD.** William Powell, Carole Lombard, Wynne Gibson, Guy Kibbee, Lawrence Gray; ***D:*** Richard Wallace, Edward Goodman; ***W:*** Herbert J. Mankiewicz; ***C:*** Victor Milner.

Man of the Year **2006 (PG-13)** Schizoid blend of comedy and political thriller that features a subdued Williams as Tom Dobbs, a late-night talk show host whose joke about running for president turns into the real thing. But when he wins, it's thanks to a voting machine glitch that computer nerd Eleanor (Linney) warned her company about. When Eleanor tries to turn whistleblower, things really turn ridiculous, with the lady on the run from corporate hit men. Levinson should have stuck with a political satire about a well-intentioned guy taking on the biggest job in the land, which he is totally unequipped to handle. **108m/C DVD.** *US* Robin Williams, Laura Linney, Christopher Walken, Lewis Black, Jeff Goldblum, Rick Roberts; ***D:*** Barry Levinson; ***W:*** Barry Levinson; ***C:*** Dick Pope; ***M:*** Graeme Revell.

Man of Violence *The Sex Racketeers* **1971** A vulgar, tasteless man spends the worthless hours of his wasted life lurking about the more wretched entrance-ways of his native land. **107m/C VHS.** Michael Latimer, Luan Peters; ***D:*** Pete Walker.

Man on a String 1/2 **1971 (PG)** In order to bring down a Mob boss the feds first frame cop Peter King and send him to the pen. When he gets out, King uses his prison contacts to get in with the Mob and winds up pitting two rival gangs against each other in order to destroy them both. **73m/C VHS.** Christopher George, Jack Warden, Keith Carradine, Joel Grey, William Schallert, Kitty Winn; ***D:*** Joseph Sargent. **TV**

Man on Fire **1987 (R)** Told via flashback, a cynical ex-CIA man is hired as a bodyguard for the daughter of a wealthy Italian couple, who is soon thereafter kidnapped by terrorists. He goes to her rescue with all the subtlety of a wrecking ball. Decent cast goes down the tubes in this botched thriller. **92m/C VHS.** *FR* Scott Glenn, Brooke Adams, Danny Aiello, Joe Pesci, Paul Shenar, Jonathan Pryce, Jade Malle; ***D:*** Elie Chouraqui.

Man on Fire 1/2 **2004 (R)** Slick actioner deploys the effective Washington as a world-weary anti-hero whose mission is to find a kidnapped young girl in Mexico City. Problem is, Creasy (Washington), a former government assassin who admittedly drinks too much, was hired as the bodyguard for nine-year-old Pita (Fanning) and her Mexican businessman father Samuel Ramos (Anthony) and American mother Lisa (Mitchell). The plot thickens as Creasy's investigation into the kidnapping reveals Mexican police involvement (surprise) and government ties. A botched ransom drop sets Creasy off on a rage-fueled rampage through the city. Vet Walken shows up to help goose the plot along as an old military buddy of Creasy's. Though plot comes up lacking, pic is full of non-stop action and gritty style highlighted by an excellent Washington. **145m/C DVD, Blu-ray Disc, UMD.** *US* Denzel Washington, Christopher Walken, Dakota Fanning, Radha Mitchell, Marc Anthony, Giancarlo Giannini, Rachel Ticotin, Mickey Rourke, Jesus Ochoa; ***D:*** Tony Scott; ***W:*** Brian Helgeland; ***C:*** Paul Cameron; ***M:*** Harry Gregson-Williams.

The Man on the Box 1/2 **1925** Chaplin is a wealthy bachelor who takes a job as a gardener to be near his girl. He overhears a plot by the butler, who's an enemy agent, to steal the secret plans for a helicopter from his sweetie's father. In order to thwart the dastardedly scheme Chaplin dresses as a maid to infiltrate the household. **58m/B VHS.** Sydney Chaplin, David Butler, Alice Calhoun, Kathleen Calhoun, Helene Costello, Theodore Lorch; ***D:*** Charles Reisner.

Man on the Eiffel Tower **1948** Laughton plays Inspector Maigret, the detective created by novelist Georges Simenon, in a highly suspenseful and cerebral mystery about a crazed killer who defies the police to discover his identity. This is the first film Meredith directed. **82m/C VHS, DVD.** Charles Laughton, Burgess Meredith, Franchot Tone, Patricia Roc; ***D:*** Burgess Meredith.

Man on the Moon **1999 (R)** Clunky bio of bizarro comedian Andy Kaufman (Carrey) who died of cancer at age 35 in 1984. The problem is that Kaufman is opaque—he doesn't seem to have a true personality but assumes bizarre alter-egos, including obnoxious lounge singer Tony Clifton. Kaufman turned out to be most appealing as innocent Latka on the sitcom "Taxi," which he professes to despise. For all Carrey's expertise, you won't care too much about what's onscreen. Title comes from R.E.M.'s song about Kaufman; they also supplied the film's music. **118m/C VHS, DVD.** Jim Carrey, Courtney Love, Danny DeVito, Paul Giamatti, Vincent Schiavelli, Peter Bonerz, Marilu Henner, Judd Hirsch; ***D:*** Milos Forman; ***W:*** Scott M. Alexander, Larry Karaszewski; ***C:*** Terry Michos. Golden Globes '00: Actor—Mus./Comedy (Carrey).

The Man on the Roof *Manen Pa Taket* **1976** A police officer, who's been accused of brutality, is murdered and Martin Beck (Lindstedt) and his colleagues are called in to investigate. Then someone climbs a roof in central Stockholm and begins killing policemen with a rifle. Turns out the cases are related and involve an ex-cop named Eriksson (Hirdwall). Based on the novel "The Abominable Man" by Maj Sjowall and Per Wahloo. Swedish with subtitles. **110m/C VHS.** *SW* Carl Gustav Lindstedt, Ingvar Hirdwall, Sven Wollter, Thomas Heelberg; ***D:*** Bo Widerberg; ***W:*** Bo Widerberg; ***C:*** Odd Geir Saether, Per Kallberg.

Man on the Run **1949** A robbery takes place in the store where an Army deserter is trying to sell his gun, and he ends up taking the rap. It's up to a lovely lady lawyer to prove his innocence. Efficiently told "B" crime drama. **82m/B VHS.** *GB* Derek Farr, Joan Hopkins, Edward Chapman, Laurence Harvey, Howard Marion-Crawford, Alfie Bass, John Bailey, John Stuart, Edward Underdown, Leslie Perrins, Kenneth More, Martin Miller, Eleanor Summerfield; ***D:*** Lawrence Huntington; ***W:*** Lawrence Huntington.

Man on the Run 1/2 **1974 (R)** After an unwitting involvement with a small robbery, a teenager finds himself the object of a police manhunt for a murder suspect. **90m/C VHS.** Kyle Johnson, James B. Sikking, Terry Carter; ***D:*** Herbert L. Strock.

The Man on the Train *L'Homme du Train* **2002 (R)** A chance encounter between two very different men offers viewers subtle pleasures. Elderly retired teacher Manesquier (Rochefort) is intrigued when weary, leather-jacketed stranger Milan (Hallyday) turns up in his small provincial town. Since the only hotel is closed, the bored Manesquier offers Milan hospitality. He shows little concern after realizing that Milan is a thief, who is waiting for his dim partner to turn up so that they can rob the local bank. Manesquier has always led a proper dull life while Milan has done just the opposite and they begin to envy each other as an odd friendship develops. Old-pro Rochefort, in his seventh film with Leconte, is engaging while French pop icon Hallyday offers a surprisingly strong performance that is a mixture of machismo and sensitivity. French with subtitles. **90m/C VHS, DVD.** *FR* Jean Rochefort, Johnny Hallyday, Jean-Francois Stevenin, Charlie Nelson, Isabelle Petit-Jacques, Edith Scob, Pascal Parmentier; ***D:*** Patrice Leconte; ***W:*** Claude Klotz; ***C:*** Jean-Marie Dreujou; ***M:*** Pascal Esteve. L.A. Film Critics '03: Foreign Film.

Man on Wire 1/2 **2008 (PG-13)** On August 7, 1974, French aerialist Philippe Petit and his team entered the not-yet-completed World Trade Center and strung a high-wire between the two towers, which Petit proceeded to illegally cross. A documentary hybrid of actual and restaged footage shows Petit training for his walk (across the towers of Notre Dame and the Sydney Bridge) as well as the extensive preparations for the New York walk. Petit is a charming raconteur and his feat still astonishes; based on his memoir "To Reach the Clouds." (Director Marsh does not mention the 9/11 destruction of the World Trade Center.) **94m/C DVD.** *GB* ***C:*** Igor Martinovic. Oscars '08: Feature Doc.

Man or Gun 1/2 **1958** Standard western yarn involving a drifter who rides into a town operated by a powerful family and liberates the cowardly townsfolk. **79m/B VHS.** MacDonald Carey, Audrey Totter, James Craig, James Gleason, Warren Stevens, Harry Shannon; ***D:*** Albert C. Gannaway; ***W:*** Vance Skarstedt, James C. Cassity.

The Man Outside **1968 (R)** After a CIA agent is fired for allegedly assisting another agent in defecting to the East, he becomes involved in further intrigue. A Russian spy is looking to defect. In the process, the ex-agent is framed for murder. Straightforward espionage tale taken from Gene Stackleborg's novel "Double Agent." **98m/C VHS, DVD.** *GB* Van Heflin, Heidelinde Weis, Pinkas Braun, Peter Vaughan, Charles Gray, Ronnie Barker; ***D:*** Samuel Gallu.

Man Outside **1988 (PG-13)** Logan is an ex-lawyer who takes to the Arkansas outback after his wife dies. Anthropologist/teacher Quinlan takes a shine to him. He seems like an okay guy, but bad guy Dillman has made it look like he's a child snatcher. Slick on the outside but empty inside independent effort. Look for former members of The Band in supporting roles. **109m/C VHS, DVD.** Robert F. Logan, Kathleen Quinlan, Bradford Dillman, Rick Danko, Levon Helm; ***D:*** Mark Stouffer.

The Man They Could Not Hang 1/2 **1939** A good doctor tinkering with artificial hearts is caught by police while experimenting on a willing student. When the doctor is convicted and hanged for a murder, his assistant uses the heart to bring him back to life. No longer a nice guy, he vows revenge against the jurors that sentenced him. Karloff repeated the same story line in several films, and this one is representative of the type. **70m/B VHS, DVD.** Boris Karloff, Adrian Booth, Roger Pryor, Robert Wilcox; ***D:*** Nick Grinde.

A Man to Remember 🦴🦴 1/2 **1939** Remake of 1933's "One Man's Journey" begins with Dr. Abbott's (Ellis) funeral and then uses a series of flashbacks to show the life of the kindly country doc. Again his selflessness precludes wealth and professional notice although a polio epidemic figures in. Kanin's directorial debut. **79m/B DVD.** Edward Ellis, Anne Shirley, Lee Bowman, John Wray, William Henry, Granville Bates, Frank M. Thomas Sr., Harlan Briggs; ***D:*** Garson Kanin; ***W:*** Dalton Trumbo; ***C:*** J. Roy Hunt; ***M:*** Roy Webb.

Man Trouble 🦴🦴 **1992 (PG-13)** A divorcing opera singer (Barkin) seeks the help of a sleazy attack-dog trainer (Nicholson) when she becomes the victim of a stalker. Nicholson hits on her, first because that's one of his habits, and then because he is being paid to by a billionaire who wants him to steal the manuscript of a tell-all book about him written by Barkin's sister. Although both Nicholson and Barkin are excellent actors, they lack the electricity to make the romance credible, and the jokes are weak. Supporting cast, including D'Angelo, Stanton, and McKean, provide the funny parts in this otherwise dull film. **100m/C VHS, DVD.** Jack Nicholson, Ellen Barkin, Harry Dean Stanton, Beverly D'Angelo, Michael McKean, Saul Rubinek, Viveka Davis, Veronica Cartwright, David Clennon, John Kapelos, Paul Mazursky; ***D:*** Bob Rafelson; ***W:*** Adrien (Carole Eastman) Joyce; ***C:*** Stephen Burum; ***M:*** Georges Delerue.

The Man Upstairs 🦴🦴 1/2 **1993** Escaped con Moony Polaski (O'Neal) hides out in the home of crotchety spinster Victoria Brown (Hepburn). When she finds the crook in her attic, instead of turning him in, Victoria befriends the slob and soon the two are sharing dinner and secrets. Meanwhile, the manhunt for Moony is intensifying and, oh yes, Christmas is coming as well. TV cornpone barely saved by some professional performances. Executive producer Burt Reynolds was hoping for a part until scheduling made it impossible. **95m/C VHS.** Katharine Hepburn, Ryan O'Neal, Henry Beckman, Helen Carroll, Brenda Forbes; ***D:*** George Schaefer; ***W:*** James Prideaux. **TV**

The Man Who Broke 1,000 Chains 🦴🦴 **1987** Tells the story of a man who is committed to a chain gang after WWII for a petty crime, and his efforts, after escaping, in making a new life for himself. An unimaginative plot is occasionally highlighted by a good scene or two. **113m/C VHS.** Val Kilmer, Charles Durning, Sonia Braga; ***D:*** Daniel Mann; ***M:*** Charles Bernstein. **TV**

The Man Who Came Back 🦴 1/2 **2008 (R)** When a former Confederate army officer defends black plantation workers in 1876, he's framed for murder and his family is killed. So he comes back for revenge. **112m/C DVD.** Eric (Hans Gudegast) Braeden, Billy Zane, George Kennedy, Armand Assante, Carol Alt, Sean Young, James Patrick Stuart, Peter Jason, Ken Norton; ***D:*** Glen Pitre; ***W:*** Glen Pitre, Chuck Walker; ***C:*** Stops Langensteiner; ***M:*** Phil Marsell. **VIDEO**

The Man Who Came to Dinner 🦴🦴🦴 1/2 **1941** Based on the Moss Hart-George S. Kaufman play, this comedy is about a bitter radio celebrity (Woolley) on a lecture tour (a character based on Alexander Woolcott). He breaks his hip and must stay in a quiet suburban home for the winter. While there, he occupies his time by barking orders, being obnoxious and generally just driving the other residents nuts. Woolley reprises his Broadway role in this film that succeeds at every turn, loaded with plenty of satiric jabs at the Algonquin Hotel Roundtable regulars. **112m/B VHS, DVD.** Monty Woolley, Bette Davis, Ann Sheridan, Jimmy Durante, Reginald Gardiner, Richard Travis, Billie Burke, Grant Mitchell, Mary Wickes, George Barbier, Ruth Vivian, Elisabeth Fraser; ***D:*** William Keighley; ***W:*** Julius J. Epstein, Philip G. Epstein; ***C:*** Gaetano Antonio "Tony" Gaudio.

The Man Who Captured Eichmann 🦴🦴 1/2 **1996** In 1960 Israeli Mossad agents prepare to capture Adolf Eichmann (Duvall), who organized the transport of millions of Jews to the concentration camps, from his home in Argentina. Peter Malkin (Howard), the agent responsible for the kidnapping, holds Eichmann in a Buenos Aires safe house before smuggling him into Israel as Eichmann tries to ingratiate himself with Malkin, refusing to accept responsiblity and constantly maintaining his innocence. Based on the book "Eichmann In My Hands" by Peter Z. Malkin and Harry Stein. **96m/C VHS.** Robert Duvall, Arliss Howard, Jeffrey Tambor, Jack Laufer, Nicolas Surovy, Joel Brooks, Sam Robards, Michael Tucci; ***D:*** William A. Graham; ***W:*** Lionel Chetwynd; ***C:*** Robert Steadman; ***M:*** Laurence Rosenthal. **CABLE**

The Man Who Could Work Miracles 🦴🦴🦴 1/2 **1937** A mild-mannered draper's assistant becomes suddenly endowed with supernatural powers to perform any feat he wishes. Great special effects (for an early film) and fine performances result in a classic piece of science fiction. **82m/B VHS.** Ralph Richardson, Joan Gardner, Roland Young; ***D:*** Lothar Mendes.

The Man Who Cried 🦴🦴 **2000 (R)** In 1927 Russia, young Jewish Fegele is separated from her father (who manages to emigrate to America) and instead winds up in England, where she's adopted and renamed Suzie. An adult Suzie (Ricci) heads to Paris in the late '30s and finds bit work in an opera company, sharing a garret with gold-digging Russian Lola (a lively Blanchett) and a romance with gypsy Cesar (Depp). Lola has set her sights on hammy opera singer, Dante (Turturro). Then the Nazis invade Paris. The film's surprisingly plodding and the characters either stereotypical and/or underwritten. **97m/C VHS, DVD.** *GB FR* Christina Ricci, Johnny Depp, Cate Blanchett, John Turturro, Harry Dean Stanton, Oleg Yankovsky; ***D:*** Sally Potter; ***W:*** Sally Potter; ***C:*** Sacha Vierny; ***M:*** Osvaldo Golijoy. Natl. Bd. of Review '01: Support. Actress (Blanchett).

The Man Who Envied Women 🦴 1/2 **1985** The non-narrative feminist story of a smug womanizer: the man "who knows almost too much about women." **125m/C VHS.** Bill Raymond, Larry Loonin, Trisha Brown; ***D:*** Yvonne Rainer; ***W:*** Yvonne Rainer.

The Man Who Fell to Earth 🦴🦴🦴 1/2 **1976 (R)** Entertaining and technically adept cult classic about a man from another planet (Bowie, in a bit of typecasting) who ventures to earth in hopes of finding water to save his family and drought-stricken planet. Instead he becomes a successful inventor and businessman, along the way discovering the human vices of booze, sex, and television. Also available in a restored version at 138 minutes. Remade for TV in 1987 and based on Walter Tevis's novel. **118m/C VHS, DVD, Blu-ray Disc.** *GB* David Bowie, Candy Clark, Rip Torn, Buck Henry, Bernie Casey, Jackson D. Kane, Rick Riccardo, Tony Mascia; ***D:*** Nicolas Roeg; ***W:*** Paul Mayersberg; ***C:*** Anthony B. Richmond; ***M:*** John Phillips.

The Man Who Guards the Greenhouse **1988** Tracy must come to terms with her attraction for Jeff as well as once again trying to write a meaningful novel. **150m/C VHS.** *CA* Christopher Cazenove, Rebecca Dewey; ***D:*** Marc Boizard; ***W:*** George Arthur Bloom; ***C:*** Karol Ike.

Man Who Had Power Over Women 🦴🦴 **1970 (R)** Disappointing sex farce about the exploits of a carnally insatiable (and married) talent executive (Taylor) who has an affair with every woman he meets and creates problems aplenty. Adapted from a novel by Gordon Williams. **89m/C VHS.** *GB* Rod Taylor, James Booth, Carol White, Penelope Horner, Clive Francis; ***D:*** John Krish; ***W:*** Chris Bryant, Allan Scott.

The Man Who Haunted Himself 🦴🦴 **1970** While a man lies in critical condition on the operating table after a car accident, his alter-ego emerges and turns his ideal life into a nightmare until the man recovers and moves toward a fateful encounter. An expanded version of an episode of the TV series "Alfred Hitchcock Presents," this was Moore's first movie after having starred in the TV series "The Saint," and it was Dearden's last film; he died in a car accident the following year. Appeals primarily to those fascinated by "Hitchcock" or "The Twilight Zone"—where mystery matters most. Filmed in London. **94m/C VHS, DVD.** *GB* Roger Moore, Hildegard(e) Neil, Olga Georges-Picot; ***D:*** Basil Dearden; ***W:*** Bryan Forbes; ***C:*** Tony Spratling; ***M:*** Michael Lewis.

The Man Who Knew Too Little 🦴🦴 1/2 *Watch That Man* **1997 (PG)** Wallace (Murray), a video store clerk from Iowa, travels to London in order to surprise his yuppie brother James (Gallagher) on his birthday. James is hosting an important dinner party, however, so he sends his less than upper-crusty brother to the Theater of Life, where the patrons take part in scenes with actors in real-life settings. Unbeknownst to Wallace, the designated call to start the play is intended for a real hit man, and he is thrown into a plot to rekindle the Cold War. Totally oblivious to the danger he is in, he treats every threat and tense situation with a sly smile and a smart-aleck remark. Joanne Whalley is the call girl/spy who turns into the sidekick/love interest. Although it's mainly a stretched out one-joke premise, that joke is delivered by comedy maestro Bill Murray. If you like his previous work, you'll love him as he messes with snooty Europeans. If you don't, seek professional help immediately. **94m/C VHS, DVD.** Bill Murray, Peter Gallagher, Joanne Whalley, Alfred Molina, Richard Wilson, Geraldine James, John Standing, Anna Chancellor, Nicholas Woodeson, Simon Chandler; ***D:*** Jon Amiel; ***W:*** Howard Franklin, Robert Harrar; ***C:*** Robert M. Stevens; ***M:*** Chris Young.

The Man Who Knew Too Much 🦴🦴🦴 **1934** Hitchcock's first international success. A British family man on vacation in Switzerland is told of an assassination plot by a dying agent. His daughter is kidnapped to force his silence. In typical Hitchcock fashion, the innocent person becomes caught in a web of intrigue; the sticky situation culminates with surprising events during the famous shootout in the final scenes. Remade by Hitchcock in 1956. **75m/B VHS, DVD.** *GB* Leslie Banks, Edna Best, Peter Lorre, Nova Pilbeam, Pierre Fresnay, Frank Vosper, Hugh Wakefield, Cicely Oates, D. A. Clarke-Smith, George Curzon, Henry Oscar, Wilfrid Hyde-White; ***D:*** Alfred Hitchcock; ***W:*** Emlyn Williams, Charles Bennett, A.R. Rawlinson, Edwin Greenwood, D. B. Wyndham-Lewis; ***C:*** Curt Courant.

The Man Who Knew Too Much 🦴🦴 1/2 **1956 (PG)** Hitchcock's remake of his 1934 film, this time about an American doctor and his family vacationing in Marrakech. They become involved in a complicated international plot involving kidnapping and murder. While Doris tries to save the day by singing "Que Sera, Sera," Stewart tries to locate his abducted son. More lavish settings and forms of intrigue make this a less focused and, to some, inferior version. ♫Que Sera, Sera. **120m/C VHS, DVD.** James Stewart, Doris Day, Brenda de Banzie, Bernard Miles, Ralph Truman, Daniel Gelin, Alan Mowbray, Carolyn Jones, Hillary Brooke; ***D:*** Alfred Hitchcock; ***W:*** John Michael Hayes; ***C:*** Robert Burks; ***M:*** Bernard Herrmann. Oscars '56: Song ("Que Sera, Sera").

The Man Who Laughs 🦴🦴🦴 1/2 **1927** Veidt's sensitive performance highlights this silent classic. He plays a young man whose features are surgically altered into a permanent smile because his family are political enemies of the current ruler. The man is befriended by the owner of a sideshow who first exhibits him as a freak but later finds Veidt gaining fame as a clown. A beautiful blind girl in the show loves Veidt for who he is and the two find happiness. **110m/B VHS, DVD.** Conrad Veidt, Mary Philbin, Olga Baclanova, Josephine Crowell, George Siegmann, Brandon Hurst; ***D:*** Paul Leni.

The Man Who Lived Again 🦴🦴 1/2 *The Man Who Changed His Mind; The Brainsnatchers; Dr. Maniac* **1936** Boris strives to be a brain-switcher, and suspense builds around the question of whether or not he will change his mind. Shot in England with fine sets and a definite Anglo feel to the proceedings, with Karloff doing one of his better mad scientist routines. **61m/B VHS, DVD.** *GB* Boris Karloff, Anna Lee, John Loder, Frank Cellier, Lyn Harding, Cecil Parker; ***D:*** Robert Stevenson.

Man Who Loved Cat Dancing 🦴🦴 **1973 (PG)** Reynolds is an outlaw on the run after avenging his wife's murder and robbing a safe with pals Hopkins and Warden, and Miles has recently escaped from her abusive husband. It's love on the run as Burt and Sarah are pursued by bounty hunters and their tragic pasts—coming close to making us care, but close doesn't mean as much in movies as it does in dancing. Based on Marilyn Durham's novel. **114m/C VHS.** Burt Reynolds, Sarah Miles, Jack Warden, Lee J. Cobb, Jay Silverheels, Robert Donner, Bo Hopkins, Nancy Malone; ***D:*** Richard Sarafian; ***W:*** Eleanor Perry; ***C:*** Harry Stradling Jr.; ***M:*** John Williams.

The Man Who Loved Women 🦴🦴🦴 *L'Homme Qui Aimait les Femmes* **1977** An intelligent, sensitive bachelor writes his memoirs and recalls the many, many, many women he has loved. Truffaut couples sophistication and lightheartedness, the thrill of the chase and, when it leads to an accidental death, the wondering what-it's-all-about in the mourning after. In French with English subtitles. Remade in 1983. **119m/C VHS, DVD.** *FR* Charles Denner, Brigitte Fossey, Leslie Caron, Nelly Borgeaud, Genevieve Fontanel, Nathalie Baye, Sabine Glaser; ***D:*** Francois Truffaut; ***W:*** Francois Truffaut, Suzanne Schiffman, Michel Fermaud; ***C:*** Nestor Almendros; ***M:*** Maurice Jaubert.

The Man Who Loved Women 🦴🦴 **1983 (R)** A remake of the 1977 French film, this is slower, tries to be funnier, and is less subtle than the original. Reynolds is a Los Angeles sculptor whose reputation as a playboy leads him to a psychoanalyst's couch, where a lot of talk slows the action—though Burt & Julie (the shrink) do share the couch. **110m/C VHS, DVD.** Burt Reynolds, Julie Andrews, Kim Basinger, Marilu Henner, Cynthia Sikes, Jennifer Edwards; ***D:*** Blake Edwards; ***W:*** Blake Edwards; ***C:*** Haskell Wexler; ***M:*** Henry Mancini.

The Man Who Made Husbands Jealous 🦴🦴 1/2 *Jilly Cooper's The Man Who Made Husbands Jealous* **1998** Young, handsome ne'er-do-well Lysander Hawkley (Billington) is broke. He has few prospects but one undeniable talent—women love him. So his friend Ferdie (Bonneville) looks around at the unhappily married women he knows (and their cheating spouses) and comes up with a plan. The wives will hire Lysander to make their neglectful husbands jealous. And the plan is very enjoyable for both Lysander and the ladies, until he falls in love. Based on the naughty novel by Jilly Cooper. **150m/C VHS.** *GB* Stephen Billington, Hugh Bonneville, Kate Byers, Gilly Coman, Kim Criswell, Derek de Lint; ***D:*** Robert Knights; ***W:*** Andrew Maclear, Harvey Bamburg. **TV**

The Man Who Never Was 🦴🦴🦴 **1955** Tense true story (with melodramatic embroidery) from WWII shows in step-by-step detail how Britain duped the Axis by letting them find an Allied corpse bearing phony invasion plans. Based on the book by the scheme's mastermind Ewen Montagu, played by Webb; Peter Sellers provides the voice of an offscreen Winston Churchill. **102m/C VHS, DVD.** *GB* Clifton Webb, Gloria Grahame, Robert Flemyng, Josephine Griffin, Stephen Boyd, Andre Morell, Laurence Naismith, Geoffrey Keen, Michael Hordern; ***D:*** Ronald Neame; ***C:*** Oswald Morris. British Acad. '56: Screenplay.

The Man Who Shot Liberty Valance 🦴🦴🦴 1/2 **1962** Tough cowboy Wayne and idealistic lawyer Stewart join forces against dreaded gunfighter Liberty Valance, played leatherly by Marvin. While Stewart rides to Senatorial success on his reputation as the man who shot the villain, he suffers moral crises about the act, but is toughened up by Wayne. Wayne's use of the word "pilgrim" became a standard for his impersonators. Strong character acting, great Western scenes, and value judgments to ponder over make this last of Ford's black-and-white westerns among his best. **123m/B VHS, DVD.** James Stewart, John Wayne, Vera Miles, Lee Marvin, Edmond O'Brien, Andy Devine, Woody Strode, Ken Murray, Jeannette Nolan, John Qualen, Strother Martin, Lee Van Cleef, John Carradine, Carleton Young, Willis Bouchey, Denver Pyle, Robert F. Simon, O.Z. Whitehead, Paul Birch, Joseph Hoover, Earle Hodgins, Jack Pennick; ***D:*** John Ford; ***W:*** James Warner Bellah,

Willis Goldbeck; **C:** William Clothier; **M:** Cyril Mockridge, Alfred Newman. Natl. Film Reg. '07.

The Man Who Wagged His Tail ½ *An Angel Passed Over Brooklyn; Un Angelo e Sceso a Brooklyn* **1957** A mean slumlord is turned into a dog as the result of a curse cast upon him. In order to return to his human form, he must be loved by someone. Despite his attempts to be loved, the dog alienates his only friend and must try to redeem himself. Played for fun, this is a mildly amusing fantasy filmed in Spain and Brooklyn. Not released in the U. S. until 1961. **91m/B VHS.** *IT SP* Peter Ustinov, Pablito Calvo, Aroldo Tieri, Silvia Marco; **D:** Ladislao Vajda.

The Man Who Wasn't There **1983 (R)** A member of the State department receives a formula from a dying spy that can render him invisible, see? He has to use the formula to protect himself from the police and other spies, becoming a comic "Invisible Man," see? Generally chaotic tale that's bad, but not so bad that it's worth seeing, though you might want to see what invisibility looks like in 3-D. **111m/C VHS.** Steve Guttenberg, Jeffrey Tambor, Art Hindle, Lisa Langlois, Victor Rendina; **D:** Bruce Malmuth; **M:** Miles Goodman.

The Man Who Wasn't There **2001 (R)** Ed Crane (Thornton, in a masterfully underplayed performance) is a small-town barber who goes unnoticed by many. He suspects that his wife Doris (McDormand) is cheating on him with Dave (Gandolfini), who owns the store where she works. When Ed decides that he wants to invest in the new "dry cleaning" process that a stranger tells him about, he decides to try blackmail. What follows is a series of stately paced twists and complications. **116m/B VHS, DVD.** *US* Billy Bob Thornton, Frances McDormand, Michael Badalucco, James Gandolfini, Katherine Borowitz, Jon Polito, Scarlett Johansson, Richard Jenkins, Tony Shalhoub; **D:** Joel Coen; **W:** Joel Coen, Ethan Coen; **C:** Roger Deakins; **M:** Carter Burwell. L.A. Film Critics '01: Cinematog.; Natl. Bd. of Review '01: Actor (Thornton).

The Man Who Would Be King **1975 (PG)** A grand, old-fashioned adventure based on the classic story by Rudyard Kipling about two mercenary soldiers who travel from India to Kafiristan in order to conquer it and set themselves up as kings. Splendid characterizations by Connery and Caine, and Huston's royal directorial treatment provides it with adventure, majestic sweep, and well-developed characters. **129m/C VHS, DVD.** Sean Connery, Michael Caine, Christopher Plummer, Saeed Jaffrey, Shakira Caine; **D:** John Huston; **W:** Gladys Hill, John Huston; **C:** Oswald Morris; **M:** Maurice Jarre.

The Man Who Would Not Die *Target in the Sun* **1975 (PG)** During his investigation of several deaths, a man discovers that all of the deceased were actually the same man. It seems the deaths were part of a intricate scheme to cover up a $1 million heist. Two of the top three actors are killed early on; it's not very suspenseful. It's more like the mystery that would not die. From Charles Williams's novel "The Sailcloth Shroud." **83m/C VHS.** Dorothy Malone, Keenan Wynn, Aldo Ray; **D:** Robert Arkless.

The Man Who Wouldn't Die **1942 65m/B DVD.** Lloyd Nolan, Marjorie Weaver, Helene Reynolds, Henry Wilcoxon, Richard Derr, Olin Howland, Leroy Mason, Jeff Corey, Robert Emmett Keane, Billy Bevan; **D:** Herbert I. Leeds; **C:** Joe MacDonald; **M:** David Raksin.

Man with a Cross **1943** Archaeologists of the cinema may want to unearth this early Rossellini, made by the future father of neo-realist cinema as a propaganda piece for the fascist war effort. A heroic Italian chaplain on the Russian front ministers to foe and friend alike, and even converts a few commies to Christ. Not as awful as it sounds—but never forget where this came from. **88m/B VHS.** *IT* Alberto Tavazzi, Roswita Schmidt, Attilio Dottesio; **D:** Roberto Rossellini; **W:** Roberto Rossellini; **C:** Guglielmo Lombardi; **M:** Renzo Rossellini.

Man with a Gun ½ **1995 (R)** Hitman John Hardin (Madsen) is asked by mobster employer Jack Rushton (Busey) to kill his ex-girlfriend Rena (Tilly) and get a CD-ROM filled with info he doesn't want to get out. Rena now happens to be John's gal pal but isn't too upset since she figures they'll substitute Rena's goody two-shoes twin sister Kathy for the needed corpse. Too bad John starts to fall for the intended victim, leaving the plan to unravel. It's a connect-the-dots plot with a creditable cast. Based on the novel "The Shroud Society" by Hugh C. Rae. **100m/C VHS, DVD.** Michael Madsen, Jennifer Tilly, Gary Busey, Robert Loggia, Ian Tracey, Bill Cobbs; **D:** David Wyles; **W:** Laurie Finstad-Knizhik; **C:** Jan Kiesser; **M:** George Blondheim.

A Man with a Maid *The Groove Room; What the Swedish Butler Saw; Swedish Wildcats* **1973** A bizarre British exploitation pic mixes spookhouse cliches and sex, as a young man finds his new bachelor pad haunted by Jack the Ripper. Originally shot in 3-D. **83m/C VHS, DVD.** Sue Longhurst, Martin Long, Diana Dors; **D:** Vernon Becker.

The Man with Bogart's Face *Sam Marlowe, Private Eye* **1980 (PG)** Sacchi is no Bogart, but he does imitate him well. Bogart fans will enjoy this fond tribute to the late great actor, but the story uncertainly wavers between genuine detective story and detective spoof. **106m/C VHS, DVD.** Robert Sacchi, Misty Rowe, Sybil Danning, Franco Nero, Herbert Lom, Victor Buono, Olivia Hussey; **D:** Robert Day; **W:** Andrew J. Fenady; **M:** John Beal, George Duning. Golden Raspberries '80: Worst Song ("The Man with Bogart's Face").

The Man with One Red Shoe **1985 (PG)** Hanks is a lovable clod of a violinist who ensnares himself in a web of intrigue when CIA agents, both good and evil, mistake him for a contact by his wearing one red shoe. Sporadically funny remake of the French "The Tall Blond Man with One Black Shoe." **92m/C VHS, DVD.** Tom Hanks, Dabney Coleman, Lori Singer, Carrie Fisher, James Belushi, Charles Durning, Edward Herrmann, Tom Noonan, Gerrit Graham, David Lander, David Ogden Stiers; **D:** Stan Dragoti; **M:** Thomas Newman.

The Man with the Golden Arm **1955** A gripping film version of the Nelson Algren junkie melodrama, about an ex-addict who returns to town only to get mixed up with drugs again. Crooked card dealer Frankie Machine (Sinatra in a standout performance) returns after a stint in rehab, hoping to pursue new dreams. But his crippled wife Zosch (Parker) wants him to stick with what he knows while drug dealer Louie (McGavin) makes Frankie offers he finds harder and harder to refuse, even with blonde beauty Molly (Novak) to offer Frankie comfort. Considered controversial in its depiction of addiction when released. **119m/B VHS, DVD.** Frank Sinatra, Kim Novak, Eleanor Parker, Arnold Stang, Darren McGavin, Robert Strauss, George Mathews, John Conte, Doro Merande; **D:** Otto Preminger; **W:** Lewis Meltzer, Walter Newman; **C:** Sam Leavitt; **M:** Elmer Bernstein.

The Man with the Golden Gun ½ **1974 (PG)** Roger Moore is the debonair secret agent 007 in this ninth James Bond flick. Assigned to recover a small piece of equipment which can be utilized to harness the sun's energy, Bond engages the usual bevy of villains and beauties. **134m/C VHS, DVD.** *GB* Roger Moore, Christopher Lee, Britt Ekland, Maud Adams, Herve Villechaize, Clifton James, Soon-Teck Oh, Richard Loo, Marc Lawrence, Bernard Lee, Lois Maxwell, Desmond Llewelyn; **D:** Guy Hamilton; **W:** Tom Mankiewicz; **C:** Ted Moore; **M:** John Barry.

The Man with the Movie Camera ½ *Chelovek s Kinoapparatom* **1929** A plotless, experimental view of Moscow through the creative eye of the cameraman Dziga Vertov, founder of the Kino Eye. The editing methods and camera techniques used in this silent film were very influential and still stand up to scrutiny today. **69m/B VHS, DVD.** *RU* **D:** Dziga Vertov; **W:** Dziga Vertov; **C:** Mikhail Kaufman; **M:** Pierre Henry.

The Man with the Perfect Swing ½ **1995** Middle-aged ex-baseball player-turned-business entrepreneur Anthony "Babe" Lombardo (Black) is deep in debt and having trouble with the IRS even as he schemes to find success with his latest endeavor—designing specialty golf equipment. But Babe's latest design is a radically new golf swing (combining putting with his baseball expertise) featured in a how-to video with a budding PGA star. Naturally, given Babe's woeful record, the money just doesn't seem to be coming his way. **94m/C VHS.** James Black, Suzanne Savoy, Marco Perella, James Belcher, Richard Bradshaw; **D:** Michael Hovis; **W:** Michael Hovis; **C:** Jim Barham; **M:** Paul English.

The Man with Two Brains **1983 (R)** Did you hear the one about the brilliant neurosurgeon who falls in love with a woman's diembodied brain in his laboratory? Dr. Michael Hfuhruhurr (Martin) only has two problems: dealing with his frigid, covetous wife (Turner) and finding a body for his cerebral lover. Isn't it nice that a serial murderer, known as the Elevator Killer, is on the loose. Plenty of laughs in this spoof of mad scientist movies that is redeemed from potential idiocy by the cast's titillating performances. Listen closely and you'll recognize the voice of Spacek as the brain-in-the-jar of Martin's dreams. **91m/C VHS, DVD.** Steve Martin, Kathleen Turner, David Warner, Paul Benedict, James Cromwell, Francis X. (Frank) McCarthy, George Furth, Randi Brooks, Bernard Behrens, Stephanie Kramer; **Cameos:** Merv Griffin; **D:** Carl Reiner; **W:** Carl Reiner, George Gipe, Steve Martin; **C:** Michael Chapman; **M:** Joel Goldsmith; **V:** Sissy Spacek.

The Man with Two Faces **1934** Flamboyant stage actor-manager Dawson Wells (Robinson) plots revenge on his evil brother-in-law Stanley Vance (Calhern) for ruining the life of his actress sister Jessica (Astor). Vance is visited by European producer Jules Chautard (you might guess from the title who that really is) and a murder occurs. Based on the comic-mystery play "The Dark Tower" by Alexander Woollcott and George S. Kaufman. Filmed with two endings: one that adhered to the stage version and one more ambiguous. **72m/B DVD.** Edward G. Robinson, Louis Calhern, Mary Astor, Ricardo Cortez, Mae Clarke, David Landau, Margaret Dale; **D:** Archie Mayo; **W:** Niven Busch, Tom Reed; **C:** Gaetano Antonio "Tony" Gaudio.

Man with Two Heads **1972 (R)** Doctor Jekyll gets in touch with his innermost feelings when his muffed experiments turn him into, gasp, Mr. Blood. Another forlorn addition to the Dr. Jekyll retread collection. **80m/C VHS.** Denis DeMarne, Gay Feld, Julia Stratton, Jaqueline Lawrence; **D:** Andy Milligan; **W:** Andy Milligan; **C:** Andy Milligan.

The Man with Two Lives ½ **1942** Well done horror thriller about a wealthy young man who's killed in a car accident, then brought back to life by a mad scientist. At precisely the moment his life is restored, a murderous gangster is executed and his soul enters the young man's body. **65m/B VHS, DVD.** Edward Norris, Addison Richards, Marlo Dwyer, Eleanor Lawson; **D:** Phil Rosen; **W:** Joseph Hoffman; **C:** Harry Neumann.

The Man Without a Country **1973** Faithful adaptation of Everett Edward Hale's short story features a sparkling performance by Robertson as Lt. Philip Nolan, who is court-martialed for treason and denounces his country, proclaiming that he never wishes to see or hear of the United States again. He gets his wish when his sentence is to spend the rest of his life aboard a ship sailing the U.S. coast but never docking. The crew of the ship is forbidden from giving him news of America. Beautifully illustates the old warning "Be careful what you wish for." **90m/C VHS.** Cliff Robertson, Beau Bridges, Peter Strauss, Robert Ryan, Walter Abel, Geoffrey Holder, Shepperd Strudwick, John Cullum, Peter Coffield, Addison Powell, Peter Weller; **D:** Delbert Mann; **W:** Sidney Carroll; **C:** Andrew Laszlo; **M:** Jack Elliott, Allyn Ferguson. **TV**

The Man Without a Face ½ **1993 (PG-13)** Gibson plays a badly scarred recluse in Maine who develops a mentor relationship with a lonely, fatherless boy. Chuck (Stahl) wants to go away to military school, but flunks the extrance exam, and enlists former teacher McLeod as a tutor. First foray for Gibson into the director's chair tends to be overly melodramatic. Adapted from a novel by Isabelle Holland. **115m/C VHS, DVD.** Mel Gibson, Nick Stahl, Margaret Whitton, Fay Masterson, Richard Masur, Gaby Hoffman, Geoffrey Lewis, Jack DeMave; **D:** Mel Gibson; **W:** Malcolm MacRury; **M:** James Horner.

The Man Without a Past *Mies Vailla Menneisyytta* **2002** Deadpan comedy/drama takes place on the outskirts of Helsinki and the fringes of society. A man (Peltola) is robbed and left for dead; he stumbles out of the hospital with amnesia and is found by two young brothers who take him home to their parents and a shantytown existence in a shipping container. He gets housing in his own container, does odd jobs to make some money, and finds romance with Salvation Army worker Irma (Outinen). When his identity is finally discovered, it doesn't matter, he has made a new life and decides to let go of his past. Finnish with subtitles. **97m/C VHS, DVD.** *FI GE FR* Markku Peltola, Kati Outinen, Juhani Nielmela, Kaija Pakarinen, Sakari Kuosmanen; **D:** Aki Kaurismaki; **W:** Aki Kaurismaki; **C:** Timo Salminen. Natl. Soc. Film Critics '03: Foreign Film.

Man Without a Star **1955** A cowboy helps ranchers stop a ruthless cattle owner from taking over their land. The conflict between freedom in the wild west and the need for order and settlements is powerfully internalized in Douglas, whose fight for justice will tame the cowboy code he lives by. You'll shed a tear for the fading frontier. **89m/B VHS, DVD.** Kirk Douglas, Jeanne Crain, Claire Trevor, William Campbell; **D:** King Vidor.

Man, Woman & Child **1983 (PG)** A close, upscale California family is shocked when a child from the husband's long-ago affair with a Frenchwoman appears at their door. Pure sentimentalism, as the family confronts this unexpected development. Two hankies—one each for fine performances by Sheen and Danner. Based on a sentimental novel by Erich Segal of "Love Story" fame, who co-wrote the script. **99m/C VHS.** Martin Sheen, Blythe Danner, Craig T. Nelson, David Hemmings; **D:** Dick Richards; **W:** Erich Segal; **M:** Georges Delerue.

Management **2009 (R)** Upwardly-mobile sales rep Sue (Aniston) spends lots of time on the road in no-name motels, such as the one in Arizona that is owned by night manager Mike's (Zahn) folks. Mike is a nice, aimless guy and, after he admires her butt, he and Sue have an afternoon quickie resulting in the smitten stoner following Sue back to Baltimore. Rather than think him a freaky stalker, Sue lets him hang around. Mike is still determined to win Sue's love even when her ex-boyfriend, yogurt mogul Jango (Harrelson), gets back into the picture. Harmless rom-com that offers nothing much new, especially for Aniston. **93m/C DVD.** *US* Jennifer Aniston, Steve Zahn, Woody Harrelson, Fred Ward, Margo Martindale, James Hiroyuki Liao; **D:** Stephen Belber; **W:** Stephen Belber; **C:** Eric Alan Edwards; **M:** Mychael Danna, Rob Simonsen.

Managua **1997 (R)** Paul Gleason (Gossett Jr.) goes to Nicaragua to claim the body of old friend Dennis Rice (Savage) but gets stonewalled by the authorities. Rice was working undercover, going after drug cartels and supposedly crossed over to the bad guys. Gleason decides to find out the truth and, of course, discovers Rice is alive. **108m/C VHS.** Louis Gossett Jr., Assumpta Serna, John Savage, Robert Beltran, Michael Moriarty, John Diehl; **D:** Michele Taverna.

Manchurian Avenger **1984 (R)** Desperados have wrested control of a Colorado gold rush town from Joe Kim's family, but he'll put an end to that, chop chop. **87m/C VHS.** Bobby Kim, Bill Wallace; **D:** Ed Warnick.

The Manchurian Candidate **1962** Political thriller about an American Korean War vet who suspects that he and his platoon may have been brainwashed during the war, with his highly decorated, heroic friend programmed by commies to be an operational assassin. Loaded with shocks, conspiracy, inventive visual imagery, and bitter political satire of naivete and machinations of the left and right. Excellent performances by an all-star cast, with Lansbury and Gregory particularly frightening. Based on the Richard Condon novel. Featuring a special interview with Sinatra and Frankenheimer in which Sinatra is deified. **126m/B VHS, DVD.** Frank Sinatra, Laurence Harvey, Angela Lansbury, Janet Leigh, James Gregory, Leslie Parrish, John McGiver, Henry Silva, Khigh (Kaie Deei) Deigh, James Edwards, Doug(las) Henderson, Albert Paulsen, Barry Kelley, Lloyd Corrigan, Whit Bissell, Joe Adams, Madame Spivy, Mimi Dillard, John Lawrence, Tom Lowell; ***D:*** John Frankenheimer; ***W:*** John Frankenheimer, George Axelrod; ***C:*** Lionel Lindon; ***M:*** David Amram. AFI '98: Top 100; Golden Globes '63: Support. Actress (Lansbury); Natl. Bd. of Review '62: Support. Actress (Lansbury), Natl. Film Reg. '94.

The Manchurian Candidate **2004 (R)** Political cynicism is at its most sinister in this updated take on the 1962 John Frankenheimer classic. Remake changes Ben Marco (Washington) and Raymond Shaw (Schreiber) from Korean War to Gulf War I vets. Shaw is now a New York congressman, with mom, Sen. Eleanor Shaw (Streep) pulling his strings. Marco comes to believe that his men were brainwashed by mega-corporation Manchurian Global who, with Eleanor's aid, are positioning Shaw to be a vice-presidential candidate who they can control via microchip. Washington is properly heroic and tormented while Schreiber is tormented and forlorn. Streep has fun with her power-hungry, mother-knows-best viper. Based on the novel by Richard Condon. **130m/C DVD, Blu-ray Disc, UMD, HD DVD.** *US* Denzel Washington, Liev Schreiber, Meryl Streep, Kimberly Elise, Vera Farmiga, Jon Voight, Jeffrey Wright, Sakina Jaffrey, Simon McBurney, Pablo Schreiber, Ted Levine, Bruno Ganz, Dean Stockwell, Miguel Ferrer, Jude Ciccolella, Zeljko Ivanek, Obba Babatunde, Charles Napier, Roger Corman, Robert Castle, John Bedford Lloyd, Anthony Mackie, Paul Lazar, Tom Stechschulte, Be Be Winans, Robyn Hitchcock, David Keeley, Dan Olmstead, Walter Mosley; ***D:*** Jonathan Demme; ***W:*** Dean Georgaris, Daniel Pyne; ***C:*** Tak Fujimoto; ***M:*** Rachel Portman, Nelust Wyclef Jean.

Mandabi 1/2 *The Money Order; Le Mandat* **1968** Unlocking, perhaps for the first time onscreen, the complex daily world of modern Africa, Senegalese filmmaker Ousmane Sembene's second feature is a deceptively simple story of a man who receives a money order and runs straight into a barrage of bureaucracy—Third World bureaucracy, but bureaucracy nevertheless—when he attempts to cash it. Gradually but unmistakably gaining deeper and more far-reaching meaning as it progresses, Sembene's moving, witty, masterful storytelling is also a sharply etched portrait of a civilization in the throes of change. Thirty years after its initial release, it remains fresh, exciting, warm, subtle, and heartbreaking. **90m/C DVD.** *SE* Christoph Colomb, Makhouredia Gueye, Isseu Niang, Mustapha Ture; ***D:*** Ousmane Sembene.

The Mandarin Mystery 1/2 **1937** In the process of trying to retrieve a stolen Mandarin stamp, detective Ellery Queen uncovers a counterfeiting ring. Some fine performances, but a muddled script creates a mystery as to whether or not the action is played for laughs. **65m/B VHS, DVD.** Eddie Quillan, Charlotte Henry, Rita La Roy, Wade Boteler, Franklin Pangborn, George Irving, Kay Hughes, William "Billy" Newell; ***D:*** Ralph Staub.

Mandela **1987** A gripping, powerful drama about human rights and dignity, tracing the real-life trials of Nelson and Winnie Mandela. The story focuses on the couple's early opposition to South African apartheid, as well as the events leading up to Nelson's life-imprisonment sentencing in 1964. Excellent, restrained performances from Glover and Woodard. **135m/C VHS, DVD.** Danny Glover, Alfre Woodard, John Matshikiza, Warren Clarke, Allan Corduner, Julian Glover; ***D:*** Philip Saville. **CABLE**

Mandela and de Klerk 1/2 **1997 (PG)** Docudrama about the two men who changed South Africa. White Afrikaaner president F.W. de Klerk (Caine) declared an end to apartheid in 1992 and two years later was succeeded as the country's president by Nelson Mandela (Poitier), a black activist imprisoned on treason charges for 27 years before his release. Both men shared the Nobel Peace Prize for their efforts to unite South Africa. **114m/C VHS, DVD.** Sidney Poitier, Michael Caine, Tina Lifford, Ian Roberts, Gerry Maritz, Jerry Mofokeng; ***D:*** Joseph Sargent; ***W:*** Richard Wesley; ***C:*** Tobias Schliessler; ***M:*** Cedric Gradus-Samson. **CABLE**

Manderlay **2005** Yet another tiresome screed from Danish director Von Trier, following 2003's "Dogville." In 1933, Grace (now played by Howard instead of Nicole Kidman) comes across the titular Alabama plantation where slavery still exists. Grace self-righteously decides to meddle, against her gangster father's (Dafoe) warnings, and finds out that, despite appearances, everyone else is okay with the status quo and it's Grace who must change. Deliberately artificial and of interest only to the director's devotees. **139m/C DVD.** Bryce Dallas Howard, Isaach de Bankole, Danny Glover, Willem Dafoe, Lauren Bacall, Jean-Marc Barr, Geoffrey Bateman, Jeremy Davies, Michael Abiteboul, Virgile Bramly, Ruben Brinkman, Dona Croll, John Hurt, Zeljko Ivanek, Udo Kier, Rik Launspach, Llewella Gideon, Mona Hammond, Ginny Holder, Emmanuel Idowu, Teddy Kempner, Suzette Llewellyn, Chloe Sevigny, Charles Maquignon, Joseph Mydell, Javone Pierce, Clive Rowe, Nina Sosanya; ***D:*** Lars von Trier; ***W:*** Lars von Trier; ***C:*** Anthony Dod Mantle.

Mandinga **1977** A plantation owner develops an obsession for one of his female slaves. Made to cash in on the already exploitive "Mandingo"; two wrongs don't make a right. **100m/C VHS.** *IT* Paul D'Egidio, Serafino Profumo, Anthony Gismond; ***D:*** Mario Pinzauti; ***W:*** Tecla Romanelli; ***C:*** Maurizio Centini; ***M:*** Marcello Giombini.

Mandingo **1975 (R)** Overheated Southern-fried tale of slavery in the Deep South, circa 1840, dealing with the tangled loves and hates of a family and their slaves. Heavyweight boxer Norton made his screen debut in the title role as the slave who makes his master money with his boxing prowess. King is the wastrel son who makes Norton's wife, another slave, his mistress. Followed by 1975's "Drum." Based on the novel by Kyle Onstott. **127m/C VHS, DVD.** James Mason, Susan George, Perry King, Richard Ward, Ken Norton, Ben Masters, Brenda Sykes, Paul Benedict, Ji-Tu Cumbuka, Debbi (Deborah) Morgan; ***D:*** Richard Fleischer; ***W:*** Richard H. Kline, Norman Wexler; ***M:*** Maurice Jarre.

Mandragora **1997** Marek (Caslavka) is a 16-year-old small town boy who takes off for the bright lights of post-Communist Prague. He's soon selling his body on the streets and makes friends with fellow hustler, David (Svec), but the duo sink into the usual morass of drugs and self-destruction. Czech with subtitles. **133m/C VHS, DVD.** *CZ* Miroslav Caslavka, David Svec, Miroslav Breu, Pavel Skripaz; ***D:*** Wiktor Grodecki; ***W:*** Wiktor Grodecki, David Svec; ***C:*** Vladimir Holomek; ***M:*** Wolfgang Hammerschmid.

Mandroid 1/2 **1993 (R)** Two scientists design a high-tech robot, Mandroid, to handle a powerful new element they've discovered. Dr. Zimmer and daughter Zanna want to use their creation to help mankind while mad scientist Dr. Drago wants the power Mandroid can give him. When a laboratory accident leaves Drago horribly disfigured it also gives him the chance to steal Mandroid and put his evil plan into action. Filmed on location in Romania. **81m/C VHS.** Brian Cousins, Jane Caldwell, Michael DellaFemina, Curt Lowens, Patrick Ersgard, Robert Symonds; ***D:*** Joakim (Jack) Ersgard; ***W:*** Jackson Barr, Earl Kenton.

Mandy *Crash of Silence* **1953** Poignant drama of a deaf child and the family who must come to terms with her deafness. Well-developed plot and well performed; an intelligent treatment in all. **93m/B VHS.** *GB* Phyllis Calvert, Jack Hawkins, Mandy Miller; ***D:*** Alexander MacKendrick.

Maneater 1/2 **2007** Here, big stripey puddy-cat! A dismembered body turns up on the Appalachian Trail near Mount Raven, Georgia. A print proves the predator is a Bengal tiger that's escaped from a traveling carnival. Big-game hunter Graham (Clark) arrives to track the cat but the story has hit the national headlines, bringing TV reporters, the National Guard, and thrill-seekers into the area, making things a lot more difficult. **88m/C DVD.** Gary Busey, Ian D. Clark, Ty Wood, Marina Stephenson Kerr, Sarah Constible, Diana Reis, Blake Taylor; ***D:*** Gary Yates; ***W:*** Phil Morton; ***C:*** Peter Benison; ***M:*** Glenn Burr. **TV**

Maneater **2009** In this Lifetime two-parter, based on the novel by Gigi Levangie Grazer, 32-year-old party girl Clarissa (Chalke) is horrified at the thought of having to support herself when her dad Teddy (Harrison) pushes her off the gravy train. Naturally she decides to marry rich and weds hot producer Aaron Mason (Winchester) but they don't live happily ever after. Probably because, even in Hollywood, Clarissa stands out for her snarky shallowness. **176m/C DVD.** Sarah Chalke, Philip Winchester, Gregory Harrison, Judy Greer, Paul Leyden, Maria Conchita Alonso, Marla Sokoloff, Garcelle Beauvais; ***D:*** Timothy Busfield; ***W:*** Suzanne Martin; ***C:*** Kenneth Zunder; ***M:*** Daniel Licht. **CABLE**

Manfish 1/2 **1956** Two men venture out in a boat, the Manfish, to hunt for sunken treasure in the Caribbean. Only one survives the trip, as his greed destroys the other. The scenes off the Jamaican coast are lovely, but the story fails to take hold. Though there is a star aboard in Chaney, you'll look astern and bow out with a sinking feeling. Derived from two Edgar Allan Poe stories, "The Gold Bug" and "The Tell-Tale Heart." **76m/C VHS.** John Bromfield, Lon Chaney Jr., Victor Jory, Barbara Nichols; ***D:*** W. Lee Wilder.

The Mangler **1994 (R)** Laundry machine munches workers in a small-town Maine industrial plant. Bossman Englund's only concern (besides huge workman's comp premiums) is keeping the machine well-fed. Weak attempt at horror by veteran Tobe "If it's worth doing, it's worth overdoing" Hooper that tries to capitalize on the popularity of story originator Stephen King. Offers little in plot or scare, but fans of the gore genre will enjoy the overuse of chunky-style blood and guts spewed from the monstrous steam ironer and folder that is apparently possesed by the devil. About 45 minutes too long for anybody to suspend their disbelief. **106m/C VHS, DVD.** Robert Englund, Ted Levine, Daniel Matmor, Vanessa Pike, Demetre Phillips, Lisa Morris, Ashley Hayden, Vera Blacker; ***D:*** Tobe Hooper; ***W:*** Tobe Hooper, Harry Alan Towers, Stephen Brooks; ***C:*** Amnon Salomon; ***M:*** Barrington Pheloung.

The Mango Tree 1/2 **1977** A young man comes of age in a small Australian town during the 1920s. Everything is well done, if not dramatic or fascinating. **93m/C VHS.** *AU* Geraldine Fitzgerald, Robert Helpmann, Diane Craig, Gerald Kennedy, Christopher Pate; ***D:*** Kevin James Dobson.

Mango Yellow *Amarelo Manga* **2002** A volatile brew of conniving characters in the seedy underbelly of a sweltering, poor Brazilian neighborhood. A slaughterhouse butcher is having an affair behind the back of his devout church-going wife. He delivers meat to a rickety hotel with a kitchen run by a flamboyantly gay cook, who is plotting to win over the heart of the butcher. Somewhere around the corner a sultry barkeep pours her sleazy sexuality into the glass of every customer while still fighting off their dirtbag advances. As expected, paths cross and things get sticky in this steambath of a Brazilian dramedy. Dirty hodgepodge character piece is at best an entertaining glimpse into a very deranged subculture, but too often feels cheap and easy. **100m/C DVD.** Chico Diaz, Dira Paes, Matheus Nachtergaele, Leona Cavalli; ***D:*** Claudio Assis.

Manhandled 1/2 **1924** Department store clerk Swanson is the hit of an artist's party with her impersonations and is asked by Morgan to impersonate a Russian countess to lend some class to his store. She winds up with lots of suitors. **67m/B VHS.** Gloria Swanson, Frank Morgan, Tom Moore, Lilyan Tashman, Ian Keith, Arthur Houseman; ***D:*** Allan Dwan.

The Manhandlers **1973 (R)** After the uncle of a young woman is killed by the mob, she goes after them for revenge. For your entertainment pleasure, best stick with the soup commercial of the same name. **87m/C VHS.** Cara Burgess, Judy (Judith) Brown, Vince Cannon, Rosalind Miles; ***D:*** Lee Madden.

Manhattan **1979 (R)** Successful TV writer Isaac Davis (Allen) yearns to be a serious writer. He struggles through a series of ill-fated romances, including one with high school senior Tracy (Hemingway) and another with Mary (Keaton), who's also having an on-again, off-again affair with Yale (Murphy), Isaac's best friend. Streep does very well with her role of Jill, Isaac's ex-wife who's come out as a lesbian and written a withering (and successful) account of their marriage. Scathingly serious and comic view of modern relationships in urban America and of the modern intellectual neuroses. Shot in black-and-white to capture the mood of Manhattan and mated with an excellent Gershwin soundtrack. **96m/B VHS, DVD.** Woody Allen, Diane Keaton, Meryl Streep, Mariel Hemingway, Michael Murphy, Wallace Shawn, Anne Byrne, Tisa Farrow, Mark Linn-Baker, David Rasche, Karen Allen; ***D:*** Woody Allen; ***W:*** Woody Allen, Marshall Brickman; ***C:*** Gordon Willis. British Acad. '79: Film, Screenplay; Cesar '80: Foreign Film; L.A. Film Critics '79: Support. Actress (Streep), Natl. Film Reg. '01;; N.Y. Film Critics '79: Director (Allen), Support. Actress (Streep); Natl. Soc. Film Critics '79: Director (Allen), Support. Actress (Streep).

Manhattan Baby **1982** Unscary horror film about an archaeologist who digs up a relic that draws evil into the world and infects an American girl with powers that lead to many deaths. Advice to you that might have saved the archaeologist: don't dig this. **90m/C VHS, DVD.** *IT* Christopher Connelly, Martha Taylor, Brigitta Boccoli, Giovanni Frezza, Lucio Fulci; ***D:*** Lucio Fulci; ***W:*** Elisa Briganti, Dardano Sacchetti; ***C:*** Guglielmo Mancori; ***M:*** Fabio Frizzi.

Manhattan Melodrama 1/2 **1934** Powell and Gable are best friends from childhood, growing up together in an orphanage. Their adult lives take different paths, however, as Powell becomes a respected prosecuting attorney while Gable becomes a notorious gambler/racketeer. Lovely Loy is Gable's girl who comes between the two. Eventually, Powell must prosecute his lifelong friend for murder in order to win the governorship. One of Gable's toughest roles; Powell's character, however, is a bit unbelievable as his ethics seem to extend beyond love and friendship. This is the first film to team Powell and Loy, who would go on to make 13 more films together, including the "Thin Man" series. **93m/B VHS, DVD.** Clark Gable, William Powell, Myrna Loy, Leo Carrillo, Nat Pendleton, George Sidney, Isabel Jewell, Muriel Evans, Claudelle Kaye, Frank Conroy, Jimmy Butler, Mickey Rooney, Edward Van Sloan; ***D:*** Woodbridge S. Van Dyke; ***W:*** Joseph L. Mankiewicz, Oliver H.P. Garrett; ***C:*** James Wong Howe. Oscars '34: Story.

Manhattan Merenque! 1/2 *Rice, Beans and Ketchup* **1995 (R)** Young mambo dancer Miguel (Perez) has been unable to get a visa to come to the U.S. from the Dominican Republic so he stows away and eventually makes it to New York with new friend Carmello (Leonardi), who's searching for an old girlfriend and their son. While Miguel tries for dance work on Broadway, he makes a friend in dance instructor Susan (Reed) and locates long-lost girlfriend Rosita (Cavazos). Too bad Carmello's luck isn't as good. Sweetly cornball and romantic. **100m/C VHS, DVD.** George Perez, Lumi Cavazos, Marco Leonardi, Alyson Reed; ***D:*** Joseph B. Vasquez; ***W:*** Joseph B. Vasquez, Rue Kent Wildman; ***C:*** David Castillo; ***M:*** Lalo Schifrin.

Manhattan Merry-Go-Round **1937** One of the movies where a corrupt boss—in this case a record producer—threatens a bunch of good people as a pretense for a plot when the movie simply serves as a showcase for stars. Features many singing stars of the '30s ("where have you gone Cab Calloway?") plus Joltin' Joe, who ended up having a hit-streak in another genre. ♫ Mama I Wanna Make Rhythm; Manhattan Merry-Go-Round; Heaven?; I Owe You; It's Round Up Time in Reno. **89m/B VHS, DVD.** Cab Calloway, Louis Prima, Ted Lewis, Ann Dvorak, Phil Regan, Kay Thompson, Gene Autry, Joe DiMaggio; ***D:*** Charles Reisner.

Manhattan Murder Mystery **1993 (PG)** Keaton and Allen team up again as two New Yorkers who get involved in a mystery when their neighbor dies under strange circumstances. Light, entertaining comedy steers clear of some of Allen's heavier themes and should keep audiences laughing till the end. Allen, writing with Brickman for the first time since "Annie Hall" and "Manhattan," makes viewers fall in love with the magic of NYC all over again. **105m/C VHS, DVD.** Woody Allen, Diane Keaton, Anjelica Huston, Alan Alda, Jerry Adler, Ron Rifkin, Joy Behar, Lynn Cohen, Melanie Norris, Zach Braff; ***D:*** Woody Allen; ***W:*** Marshall Brickman, Woody Allen; ***C:*** Carlo Di Palma.

The Manhattan Project 🦴🦴 *Manhattan Project: The Deadly Game* **1986 (PG-13)** An exceptionally bright teenager decides to build a nuclear bomb for his project at the New York City science fair. He's out to prove how dangerously easy it is to build big bombs. When he steals plutonium from a local government installation, the feds attempt to nab the precocious youngster. Light moral overtones abound. Director Brickman co-wrote similarly titled "Manhattan." **112m/C VHS, DVD.** Dan E. Butler, Robert Sean Leonard, John David (J.D.) Cullum, Richard Jenkins, Timothy Carhart, Sully Boyar, Jimmie Ray Weeks, John Lithgow, Christopher Collet, Cynthia Nixon, Jill Eikenberry, John Mahoney, Richard Council, Robert Schenkkan, Paul Austin; ***D:*** Marshall Brickman; ***W:*** Marshall Brickman, Thomas Baum; ***C:*** Billy Williams.

Manhunt 🦴🦴 *The Italian Connection; La Mala Ordina* **1973 (R)** A man marked for execution by the mob launches his own assault on the organization's headquarters. Action and Italian food, but not much else. Dubbed. **93m/C VHS, DVD.** *IT* Henry Silva, Mario Adorf, Woody Strode, Luciana Paluzzi; ***D:*** Fernando Di Leo.

The Manhunt 🦴🦴 **1986** A framed cowhand escapes from prison to prove his innocence. De Angelis used the pseudonym Larry Ludman. **89m/C VHS, DVD.** Ernest Borgnine, Bo Svenson, John Ethan Wayne; ***D:*** Fabrizio de Angelis. **TV**

Manhunt 🦴🦴 *Caceria* **2001** Daniel used to work for a gangster named Lucas but he betrayed him and now Lucas wants revenge. Daniel has returned to his hometown of Redemption and re-establishes his friendship with boyhood chum Miguel and long-lost love Elisa, even though he knows his chance of happiness is fleeting. And soon enough Lucas and his men show up to hunt Daniel down. Spanish with subtitles. **90m/C VHS, DVD.** *AR* Luis Luque, Claribel Medina, Juan Palomino, Matias Sansone, Carlos Leyes; ***D:*** Ezio Massa; ***W:*** Ezio Massa, Jorge Bechara; ***C:*** Mariano Cuneo, Ada Frontini; ***M:*** Mariano Nunez West.

Manhunt for Claude Dallas 🦴🦴 **1986** Mountain man uses game wardens for firing practice, ticks off local sheriff Torn, is tossed behind bars, checks out ahead of schedule and becomes a legend in his own time. Mediocre made-for-TV macho man melodrama. From the novel "Outlaw" by Jeff Long. **93m/C VHS.** Matt Salinger, Rip Torn, Claude Akins, Pat Hingle, Lois Nettleton, Beau Starr, Frederick Coffin; ***D:*** Jerry London; ***W:*** John Gay; ***M:*** Steve Dorff.

Manhunt in the African Jungles 🦴🦴 *Secret Service in Darkest Africa* **1943** An American undercover agent battles Nazi forces in Africa. A serial in 15 episodes. **240m/B VHS.** Rod Cameron, Joan Marsh, Duncan Renaldo, Lionel Royce, Kurt Kreuger, Georges Renavent, Ralf Harolde; ***D:*** Spencer Gordon Bennet; ***W:*** Ronald Davidson, Basil Dickey, Jesse Duffy, Joseph O'Donnell, Joseph Poland; ***C:*** William Bradford; ***M:*** Paul Sawtell, Marlin Skiles.

Manhunt of Mystery Island *Captain Mephisto and the Transformation Machine* **1945** Serial about the super-powered Captain Mephisto. **100m/C VHS.** Linda Stirling, Roy Barcroft, Richard Bailey, Kenne Duncan; ***D:*** Spencer Gordon Bennet, Yakima Canutt, Wallace Grissell; ***W:*** Albert DeMond, Basil Dickey, Jesse Duffy, Joseph Poland; ***C:*** Bud Thackery.

Manhunter 🦴 **1974** A WWI Marine returns home from China in 1933 to track down a bunch of gangsters headed by his sister. **78m/C VHS.** Ken Howard, Stefanie Powers, Gary Lockwood, Tim O'Connor, L.Q. Jones; ***D:*** Walter Grauman. **TV**

Manhunter 🦴🦴 ½ **1983** A mercenary sets out to disengage organized crime from high-level politics. Produced by Owensby. **92m/C VHS.** Earl Owensby, Johnny Popwell, Doug Hale, Elizabeth Upton; ***D:*** Earl Owensby.

Manhunter 🦴🦴🦴 *Red Dragon* **1986 (R)** Will Graham (Petersen) was the FBI's top guy in their Behavioral Science Unit who retired after a harrowing pursuit of a serial killer. Now, he's called back to duty to find a psychotic family killer. Will's technique: to match the thought processes of serial killers and thus anticipate their moves. Intense thriller, based on the Thomas Harris novel "Red Dragon." Harris also wrote "The Silence of the Lambs," whose most notorious character Hannibal ("The Cannibal") Lecter, appears in this movie as well (spelled Lektor and played by Cox). Graham visits the prisoner to get fresh insights into his new case and Lektor plays his usual nasty mind games. Director Mann applies the slick techniques he introduced in the popular TV series "Miami Vice," creating a quiet, moody intensity broken by sudden onslaughts of violence. **100m/C VHS, DVD.** William L. Petersen, Kim Greist, Joan Allen, Brian Cox, Dennis Farina, Stephen Lang, Tom Noonan, Benjamin Hendrickson, David Seaman, Dan E. Butler, Michael Talbott, Michele Shay, Paul Perri, Patricia Charbonneau, Norman Snow, Frankie Faison, Garcelle Beauvais, Joanne Camp, David Allan Brooks, Chris Elliott, Kin Shriner, Bill Smitrovich, Kristin Holby; ***D:*** Michael Mann; ***W:*** Michael Mann; ***C:*** Dante Spinotti; ***M:*** Michel Rubini.

Maniac WOOF! **1934** A scientist has designs on raising the dead and searches for victims on which to experiment. Bizarre "adults only" exploitation feature was considered very risque for its time, and includes eaten eyeballs, a cat fight with syringes, and a rapist who thinks he's an orangutan. A must for genre aficionados. **67m/B VHS, DVD.** Bill Woods, Horace Carpenter, Ted Edwards, Thea Ramsey, Jennie Dark, Marcel Andre, Celia McGann; ***D:*** Dwain Esper; ***W:*** Hildegarde Stadie; ***C:*** William C. Thompson.

Maniac 🦴🦴 **1963** An American artist living in France becomes involved with the daughter of a cafe owner, not suspecting that murder will follow. Seems that her old man is locked up in an insane asylum for torching the daughter's rapist several years earlier. **86m/B VHS.** *GB* Kerwin Mathews, Nadia Gray, Donald Houston, Liliane Brousse; ***D:*** Michael Carreras; ***W:*** Jimmy Sangster; ***C:*** Wilkie Cooper; ***M:*** Stanley Black.

Maniac 🦴 *Ransom; Assault on Paradise; The Town That Cried Terror* **1977 (PG)** A New York cop hunts down an arrow-shooting and obviously crazed Vietnam veteran who endeavors to hold an entire Arizona town for ransom. Which is entirely appropriate, since the cast is in it only for the money. **87m/C VHS.** Bill Allen, Oliver Reed, Deborah Raffin, Stuart Whitman, Jim Mitchum, Edward Brett, John Ireland, Paul Koslo; ***D:*** Richard Compton.

Maniac WOOF! **1980** A psycho murderer slaughters and scalps his victims, adding the "trophies" to his collection. Carries a self-imposed equivalent "X" rating due to its highly graphic gore quotient. For extremely strong stomachs only. **91m/C VHS, DVD.** Joe Spinell, Caroline Munro, Gail Lawrence, Kelly Piper, Tom Savini, Rita Montone, Hyla Marrow, William Lustig, Sharon Mitchell; ***D:*** William Lustig; ***W:*** C.A. Rosenberg, Joe Spinell; ***C:*** Robert Lindsay; ***M:*** Jay Chattaway.

Maniac Cop 🦴 **1988 (R)** In New York city, a cop goes beyond the realm of sanity and turns vigilante. Low-budget slasher/thriller that too often sags. **92m/C VHS, DVD.** Tom Atkins, Bruce Campbell, Laurene Landon, Richard Roundtree, William (Bill) Smith, Robert Z'Dar, Sheree North, Sam Raimi; ***D:*** William Lustig; ***W:*** Larry Cohen; ***C:*** Vincent Rabe, James (Momel) Lemmo; ***M:*** Jay Chattaway.

Maniac Cop 2 🦴 **1990 (R)** Everyone thought he was dead but you can't keep a bad guy down so this grossly disfigured policeman forms a one-man vigilante squad, seeking revenge (why never matters—just the body count). Blood and guts fly as any plot shortcomings are cleverly disguised by an array of violent video deaths. Sequel to "Maniac Cop." **90m/C VHS.** Robert Davi, Claudia Christian, Michael Lerner, Bruce Campbell, Laurene Landon, Robert Z'Dar, Clarence Williams III, Leo Rossi, James Dixon, Robert Earl Jones; ***D:*** William Lustig; ***W:*** Larry Cohen; ***C:*** James (Momel) Lemmo.

Maniac Cop 3: Badge of Silence 🦴 **1993 (R)** The grossly disfigured policeman returns yet again to exact gory vengeance as the good guys try to get rid of him once and for all. **85m/C VHS, DVD.** Bobby DiCicco, Robert Z'Dar, Robert Davi, Gretchen Becker, Paul Gleason, Doug Savant, Caitlin Dulany, Jackie Earle Haley, Robert Forster; ***D:*** William Lustig, Joel Soisson; ***W:*** Larry Cohen; ***M:*** Jerry Goldsmith.

Maniac Nurses Find Ecstasy WOOF! **1994** Even by Troma standards, this one's scraping the bottom of the barrel. The nearly non-existent plot is an excuse to present several young women dressed in nurse uniforms and underwear while holding various weapons. The sense of energy that's needed for good exploitation is lacking. **80m/C VHS, DVD.** Susanna Makay, Hajni Brown, Nicole A. Gyony, Csilia Farago; ***D:*** Harry M. (Leon P. Howard) Love; ***W:*** Harry M. (Leon P. Howard) Love.

Maniac Warriors 🦴 *Empire of Ash* **1988** A nuclear apocalypse has caused some strange changes in the population—and not for the better. Blood-crazed mutants attack the heavily armed inhabitants of New State Idaho and there's lots of mayhem in store. **91m/C VHS.** *CA* Tom Schioler, John Wood, Melanie Kilgour; ***D:*** Michael Mazo, Lloyd A. Simandl; ***W:*** John Ogis; ***C:*** Danny Nowak; ***M:*** Andrew Menzies.

Manic 🦴🦴 ½ **2001 (R)** Lyle (Gordon-Levitt), prone to fits of violent rage, is sent to a juvenile psychiatric hospital to control his temper. There he meets, but doesn't exactly warm up to, a variety of other mentally and emotionally troubled teens. Led by patient counselor David (Cheadle), they endure group sessions that do little but introduce the audience to the varied, if stereotypical problems of the other patients. These scenes do point out the reality that there are rarely any quick fixes in this area. Lyle eventually is drawn to shy Tracy, who suffers from crushingly low self-esteem. Excellent performances and script keep the situations and emotions realistic, mostly avoiding cliche, but the affected Dogme-style jittery hand-held digital camera work is a distraction that's not needed. **100m/C VHS, DVD.** *US* Joseph Gordon-Levitt, Don Cheadle, Zooey Deschanel, Cody Lightning, Sara Rivas, Michael Bacall, William Richert, Elden (Ratliff) Henson, Blayne Weaver; ***D:*** Jordan Melamed; ***W:*** Michael Bacall, Blayne Weaver; ***C:*** Nick Hay.

The Manions of America 🦴🦴 ½ **1981** The long and sometimes interesting rags-to-riches tale of Rory O'Manion, a feisty Irish patriot who leaves his native land during the potato famine of 1845 to settle in America. Originally a TV miniseries. **290m/C VHS.** Pierce Brosnan, Kate Mulgrew, Linda Purl, David Soul, Kathleen Beller, Simon MacCorkindale; ***D:*** Joseph Sargent, Charles S. Dubin. **TV**

Manipulator 🦴 **1971 (R)** A deranged ex-movie makeup man (Rooney, playing to type) kidnaps a young actress and holds her prisoner in a deserted Hollywood sound stage. **91m/C VHS.** Mickey Rooney, Luana Anders, Keenan Wynn; ***D:*** Yabo Yablonsky.

Manito 🦴🦴🦴 **2003** Slice of life family drama set in New York City's largely Hispanic Washington Heights neighborhood. Manny Moreno (Minaya) is about to graduate from high school and has been accepted to college on a full scholarship. His older brother, Junior (Franky G), is an ex-con who was busted for working with their drug-dealer dad (Cabral). Junior is trying to go straight and keep Manny away from trouble as well by refusing to allow their father any contact with the family. But it's just not that simple. Debut film for Eason is somewhat limited by being shot on digital video, but the performances are powerful. **77m/C DVD.** *US* Franky G., Leo Minaya, Manuel Cabral, Hector Gonzalez, Julissa Lopez, Jessica Morales; ***D:*** Eric Eason; ***W:*** Eric Eason; ***C:*** Didier Gertsch; ***M:*** Saundi Wilson.

The Manitou 🦴🦴 **1978 (PG)** A San Francisco woman suffers from a rapidly growing neck tumor which eventually grows into a 400-year-old Indian witch doctor. (I hate when that happens.) Redeemed only by good special effects, especially those that kept Curtis, Strasberg, and Meredith from laughing. **104m/C VHS, DVD.** Susan Strasberg, Tony Curtis, Stella Stevens, Ann Sothern, Burgess Meredith, Michael Ansara, Jon Cedar, Paul Mantee, Lurene Tuttle, Jeannette Nolan; ***D:*** William Girdler; ***W:*** William Girdler, Tom Pope, Jon Cedar; ***C:*** Michael Hugo; ***M:*** Lalo Schifrin.

Mankillers 🦴 **1987** A group of tough female convicts are enlisted to hunt down and rub out a psycho drug dealer, all the while displaying their feminine charms. **90m/C VHS.** Edd Byrnes, Gail Fisher, Edy Williams, Lynda Aldon, William Zipp, Christopher Lunde, Susanne Tegman, Marilyn Stafford, Paul Bruno, Byron Clark; ***D:*** David A. Prior.

Manna from Heaven 🦴🦴 **2002 (PG)** A cash-strapped extended family, living in a working-class Buffalo neighborhood, receive an unexpected windfall when a passing truck with a faulty door dumps a load of $20 bills. A pious young girl thinks the money is a gift from God but, 30 years later, Sister Teresa (Burton) has now decided the money was just a loan and God must be repaid. However, the money's long spent and the rest of those involved are reluctant (at first) to go along with the nun's fund-raising efforts. **119m/C DVD.** Shirley Jones, Cloris Leachman, Harry Groener, Jill Eikenberry, Ursula Burton, Faye Grant, Wendie Malick, Seymour Cassel; ***D:*** Gabrielle C. Burton, Maria Burton; ***W:*** Gabrielle B. Burton; ***C:*** Ed Slattery.

Mannequin 🦴🦴 ½ **1937** Tracy and Crawford star in this romantic story of a poor girl who finds temporary happiness by marrying a wealthy man after ditching her con-artist husband. Somewhat predictable, the movie reads like a "People" magazine story on The Donald and Ivana. Tracy and Crawford keep the story afloat (in their only film together), with an able assist from Curtis. **95m/B VHS.** Joan Crawford, Spencer Tracy, Alan Curtis, Ralph Morgan, Leo Gorcey, Elisabeth Risdon, Paul Fix; ***D:*** Frank Borzage; ***W:*** Lawrence Hazard; ***C:*** George J. Folsey.

Mannequin 🦴🦴 **1987 (PG)** A young artist creates a store window display using various mannequins, one of which contains the spirit of an ancient Egyptian woman. She comes to life when he is around, and naturally none of his co-workers believe him. Very light comedy, featuring two pretty stars and music by Jefferson Starship. **90m/C VHS, DVD.** Andrew McCarthy, Kim Cattrall, Estelle Getty, James Spader, Meshach Taylor, Carole (Raphaelle) Davis, G.W. Bailey; ***D:*** Michael Gottlieb; ***W:*** Ed Rugoff; ***C:*** Tim Suhrstedt; ***M:*** Sylvester Levay.

Mannequin 2: On the Move WOOF! **1991 (PG)** Less of a sequel, more of a lame rehash proving that the first "Mannequin" could have been even dumber. At this rate part three will be off the scale. Now it's a lovesick Teutonic princess frozen for 1,000 years who revives in a department store. Taylor reprises his grotesque gay role. **95m/C VHS.** Kristy Swanson, William Ragsdale, Meshach Taylor, Terry Kiser, Stuart Pankin; ***D:*** Stewart Raffill; ***W:*** Ed Rugoff.

Manny & Lo 🦴🦴🦴 **1996 (R)** Krueger's directorial debut features fine performances in a story about three misfits forming a unique family bond. Surly 16-year-old Lo (Palladino) and her serious 11-year-old sister Manny (Johansson) have run away from their foster homes and hit the road together. Living hand-to-mouth, it's Manny who persuades her irresponsible pregnant sister that they need a home and they settle into an isolated cabin. When the sisters visit a baby store, eccentric clerk Elaine (Place) seems such a font of wisdom that the girls kidnap her and hold her as a hostage to help with the pregnancy. But Elaine's not trying to escape and has an agenda of her own. **90m/C VHS, DVD.** Mary Kay Place, Scarlett Johansson, Aleksa Palladino, Paul Guilfoyle, Glenn Fitzgerald, Cameron Boyd, Novella Nelson, Angie Phillips; ***D:*** Lisa Krueger; ***W:*** Lisa Krueger; ***C:*** Tom Krueger; ***M:*** John Lurie.

Manny's Orphans 🦴 *Here Come the Tigers* **1978 (PG)** An out-of-work teacher takes on a lovable home for orphaned boys. Dull remake of "Bad News Bears." **92m/C VHS.** Richard Lincoln, Malachy McCourt, Sel Skolnick; ***D:*** Sean S. Cunningham.

Manon 🦴🦴 **1950** Tragic tale of a French woman condemned for her affair with a Resistance fighter. They flee to Paris, where her brother forces her into prostitution. Based on the novel "Manon Lescaut" by Abbe Antoine-Francois Prevost. In French with English subtitles. **91m/B VHS.** Cecile Aubry, Michel Auclair, Serge Reggiani, Henri Vilbert, Daniel Ivernel; ***D:*** Henri-Georges Clouzot.

Manon ♂♂ *Manon 70* **1968** Updated version of the 18th-century novel "Manon Lescaut." Prostitute Manon (Deneuve) caters to a rich clientele but falls for poor reporter Des Grieux (Frey). Since she has expensive tastes, Manon keeps her job and sees her lover on the side although he's unhappy about the situation. French with subtitles. **105m/C DVD.** *FR* Catherine Deneuve, Sami Frey, Jean-Claude Brialy, Elsa Martinelli, Robert Webber, Paul (Christian) Hubschmid; ***D:*** Jean-Claude Brialy, Jean Aurel, Cecil Saint-Laurent; ***W:*** Jean-Claude Brialy, Jean Aurel, Cecil Saint-Laurent; ***C:*** Edmond Richard; ***M:*** Serge Gainsbourg.

Manon of the Spring ♂♂♂ 1/2 *Manon des Sources; Jean de Florette 2* **1987 (PG)** In this excellent sequel to "Jean de Florette," the adult daughter of the dead hunchback, Jean, discovers who blocked up the spring on her father's land. She plots her revenge, which proves greater than she could ever imagine. Montand is astonishing. Based on a Marcel Pagnol novel. In French with English subtitles. **113m/C VHS, DVD.** *FR* Yves Montand, Daniel Auteuil, Emmanuelle Beart, Hippolyte Girardot, Margarita Lozano, Elisabeth Depardieu, Yvonne Gamy, Armand Meffre, Gabriel Bacquier; ***D:*** Claude Berri; ***W:*** Claude Berri, Gerard Brach; ***C:*** Bruno Nuytten; ***M:*** Jean-Claude Petit, Roger Legrand.

Manos, the Hands of Fate WOOF! **1966** Horrible acting and laughable special effects elevate this story of a family ensnared by a satanic cult a notch above your average bad horror film. Highlights include a Satan-like character who can't stop laughing; the dreaded "hounds of hell" (or are those mangy dogs with big ears glued on?); and Torgo the monstrous henchman, who you know is evil because he has giant kneecaps (a sure sign of the devil's work). Notable as the one of the most often requested movies on Comedy Central's satiric "Mystery Science Theatre 3000," this one is good for a laugh. **74m/C VHS, DVD.** Tom Nayman, Diane Mahree, Hal P. Warren, John Reynolds; ***D:*** Hal P. Warren; ***W:*** Hal P. Warren.

Manpower ♂♂ **1941** A dame comes between pals and it doesn't end well. Linemen Hank (Robinson) and Johnny (Marshall) compete for the attention of L.A. nightclub floozy Fay (Dietrich) but Fay accepts Hank's marriage proposal since he's the more stable guy. Still, Fay tells Johnny she loves him but he rejects her out of loyalty to Hank, who finds out his new missus doesn't plan to hang around—and why. **105m/B DVD.** Edward G. Robinson, George Raft, Marlene Dietrich, Alan Hale, Frank McHugh, Eve Arden, Barton MacLane, Ward Bond, Walter Catlett, Joyce Compton; ***D:*** Raoul Walsh; ***W:*** Jerry Wald, Richard Macaulay; ***C:*** Ernest Haller; ***M:*** Adolph Deutsch.

Man's Best Friend ♂ 1/2 **1993 (R)** A guard dog is the object of a genetic experiment that has given him the agressiveness of other creatures, including a cobra and a leopard. Since Max is an enormous Tibetan mastiff this means big trouble for everyone but the reporter (Sheedy) who rescued him—and even she better watch out. **87m/C VHS, DVD.** Ally Sheedy, Lance Henriksen, Frederic Lehne, Robert Costanzo, John Cassini, J.D. Daniels; ***D:*** John Lafia; ***W:*** John Lafia; ***M:*** Joel Goldsmith.

Man's Country ♂♂ **1938** A rip-roarin' western saga filled with the usual action and danger, as ranger Randall leads the fight against a band of nasties headed by Long, in a dual role as twin brothers. **55m/B VHS.** Addison "Jack" Randall, Ralph Peters, Marjorie Reynolds, Walter Long; ***D:*** Robert F. "Bob" Hill.

Man's Favorite Sport? ♂♂ 1/2 **1963** A slapstick comedy about a renowned fishing expert author who actually hates fishing, but is forced to compete in a major tournament by a romantically inclined publicity agent. Very funny in spots. **121m/C VHS, DVD.** Rock Hudson, Paula Prentiss, Charlene Holt, Maria Perschy, John McGiver; ***D:*** Howard Hawks; ***M:*** Henry Mancini.

Man's Land ♂ 1/2 **1932** A ranch needs savin', and Hoot's the guy to do it in this formulaic Gibson epic. **65m/B VHS.** Hoot Gibson, Marion Shilling, Skeeter Bill Robbins, Alan Bridge; ***D:*** Phil Rosen.

Mansfield Park ♂♂ 1/2 **1985** Fanny is an impoverished young woman, snubbed by society, who earns the respect and love of her cousin in a BBC miniseries adaptation of the Jane Austen classic set in 19th-century England. **261m/C VHS, DVD.** *GB* Sylvestria Le Touzel, Bernard Hepton, Anna Massey, Donald Pleasence; ***D:*** David Giles. **TV**

Mansfield Park ♂♂ 1/2 **1999 (PG-13)** Fanny Price (O'Connor) is a poor relation, who has grown up with her wealthy cousins at their elegant home, Mansfield Park. While some of the Bertrams have been civil, others have treated Fanny as little better than a servant. However, cousin Edmund (Miller) has been very kind indeed and Fanny develops very warm feelings towards him. Then the entire family is thrown into chaos by the arrival of Henry Crawford (Nivola) and his sister Mary (Davidtz) and scandal seems about to break. Jane Austen's 3rd novel has been given a feminist slant and some belabored relevancy by Rozema. **110m/C VHS, DVD.** Frances O'Connor, Jonny Lee Miller, Alessandro Nivola, Embeth Davidtz, Harold Pinter, Lindsay Duncan, Sheila Gish, Justine Waddell, Victoria Hamilton, James Purefoy, Hugh Bonneville; ***D:*** Patricia Rozema; ***W:*** Patricia Rozema; ***C:*** Michael Coulter; ***M:*** Lesley Barber.

Mansfield Park ♂♂ 1/2 **2007** As a child, Fanny Price (Piper) was sent to grow up with her rich relatives, the Bertrams, at Mansfield Park. As the poor relation, plucky Fanny is subjected to much belittling by everyone except handsome cousin Edmund (Ritson). But their new and flirtatious neighbors the Crawfords cause trouble: Mary (Atwell) sets her eyes on Edmund while her brother Henry (Beattie) flirts with both Fanny and her cousin Maria (Ryan). Only Fanny seems to realize their insincerity and her insight does her no good (at first). Based on the novel by Jane Austen. **90m/C DVD.** *GB* Billie Piper, Blake Ritson, Hayley Atwell, James D'Arcy, Joseph Beattie, Michelle Ryan, Jemma Redgrave, Douglas Hodge, Rory Kinnear, Catherine Steadman, Maggie O'Neill; ***D:*** Iain B. MacDonald; ***W:*** Maggie Wadey; ***C:*** Nick Dance; ***M:*** John Keane. **TV**

The Manson Family ♂ 1/2 **2004** A graphic depiction of Charlie (Games), his followers, and their crimes, which took director Van Bebber something like 15 years to finance and complete. You can admire his dedication without admiring the results, which intentionally look like exploitation schlock. A framing device has a TV reporter (Day) working on a documentary of the Family that leads to flashbacks of the sex, drugs, and violence that consume them. **95m/C DVD.** *US* ***D:*** Jim Van Bebber; ***C:*** Mike King.

The Manster ♂ *The Manster—Half Man, Half Monster; The Split; The Two-Headed Monster* **1959** Another masterpiece from the director who brought us "Monster from Green Hell." Womanizing, whiskey swilling American journalist receives mysterious injection from crazed scientist and sprouts unsightly hair and extra head. Although shot in the land of the rising sun, lips move in sync with dialogue. **72m/B VHS, DVD.** *JP* Peter Dyneley, Jane Hylton, Satoshi Nakamura, Terri Zimmern, Tetsu Nakamura, Jerry Ito, Toyoko Takechi; ***D:*** Kenneth Crane, George Breakston; ***W:*** William J. Sheldon; ***C:*** David Mason; ***M:*** Hirooki Ogawa.

Manticore ♂ **2005** Usual low-budget cheesefest from the Sci-Fi Channel. American soldiers patrolling an Iraqi town check a bombed-out museum and are attacked by insurgents. An ancient medallion was stolen from the museum and megalomaniac Umari wants to use it to unleash the power of the manticore, only to figure out too late that he can't control it. **88m/C DVD.** Robert Beltran, Jeff Fahey, Chase Masterson, Faran Tahir, Heather Donahue, A.J. Buckley; ***D:*** Tripp Reed; ***W:*** John Werner; ***C:*** Lorenzo Senatore; ***M:*** David Williams. **CABLE**

Mantis in Lace ♂ 1/2 *Lila* **1968 (R)** A go-go dancer slaughters men while tripping on LSD. Watch it for the "hep" dialogue. **68m/C VHS, DVD.** Susan Stewart, Steve Vincent, M.K. Evans, Vic Lance, Pat (Barringer) Barrington, Janu Wine, Stuart Lancaster, John Carrol, Judith Crane, Cheryl Trepton; ***D:*** William Rotsler; ***W:*** Sanford White; ***C:*** Laszlo Kovacs; ***M:*** Frank A. Coe.

Mantrap ♂♂ 1/2 **1926** Early silent success by Fleming, who later directed "Gone with the Wind" and "The Wizard of Oz." Fabled flapper Bow tempts a lawyer on retreat in the woods. **66m/B VHS.** Clara Bow, Ernest Torrence, Percy Marmont, Eugene Pallette, Tom Kennedy; ***D:*** Victor Fleming.

The Manxman ♂♂ 1/2 **1929** Hitchcock's last silent film, a romantic melodrama about ambition and infidelity on the Isle of Man. **129m/B VHS, DVD.** *GB* Carl Brisson, Anny Ondra, Malcolm Keen, Randle Ayrton; ***D:*** Alfred Hitchcock; ***W:*** Hall Caine, Eliot Stannard; ***C:*** Jack Cox.

The Many Adventures of Winnie the Pooh **1977 (G)** Disney's 22nd animated feature offers A.A. Milne's beloved characters and their adventures in the Hundred Acre Wood. Includes a behind-the-scenes featurette with the original creators, animators, and voices. **83m/C VHS, DVD.** ***D:*** John Lounsbery, Wolfgang Reitherman; ***V:*** Sterling Holloway, Paul Winchell, John Fiedler, Junius Matthews, Howard Morris; ***Nar:*** Sebastian Cabot.

Many Faces of Sherlock Holmes **1986** A documentary look at the various incarnations of the famous sleuth from A. Conan Doyle's stories to various film portrayals. **58m/C VHS, DVD.** Christopher Plummer, Basil Rathbone, Christopher Lee.

Many Rivers to Cross ♂♂ **1955** Western comedy finds Kentucky frontiersman Bushrod Gentry (Taylor) setting his traps for furs, not a wife. But this doesn't stop feisty spinster Mary (Parker) from setting her sights on becoming Mrs. Gentry. And her pappy's (McLaglen) shotgun is mighty persuasive. **92m/C DVD.** Robert Taylor, Eleanor Parker, Russ Tamblyn, James Arness, Alan Hale, Rosemary DeCamp, Russell Johnson, Victor McLaglen; ***D:*** Roy Rowland; ***W:*** Harry Brown, Guy Trosper; ***C:*** John Seitz; ***M:*** Cyril Mockridge.

Map of the Human Heart ♂♂ **1993 (R)** Thirty-year saga told in flashback. Young Eskimo Avik (Lee) and his Metis love interest Albertine (Parillaud) struggle with racism in a white world. They meet and become friends as children and years later meet again in Dresden during WWII, but now Albertine is married to Avik's once close friend, denying her heritage and living in the white world that he has been fighting for so long. Mediocre movie with extraordinary Arctic scenery. Cusack has a small role as a mapmaker. **109m/C VHS, DVD.** Jason Scott Lee, Anne Parillaud, Patrick Bergin, Robert Joamie, Annie Galipeau, John Cusack, Jeanne Moreau; ***D:*** Vincent Ward; ***W:*** Vincent Ward, Louis Nowra.

A Map of the World ♂♂ **1999 (R)** Excellent cast; tough story, based on the novel by Jane Hamilton. Flinty would-be farm wife/mom Alice Goodwin (Weaver) hasn't endeared herself to her Wisconsin community. But she's a good deal more vulnerable than anyone suspects as Alice finds her life falling apart. Her neighbor Theresa's (Moore) daughter accidentally drowns while in Alice's care and soon after Alice is shockingly accused of sexual abuse in her role as school nurse, which lands her jail. Uneven script is part family drama, part prison drama, part courtroom drama, part melodrama, and all the drama doesn't necessarily make for a coherent movie. **125m/C VHS, DVD.** Sigourney Weaver, David Strathairn, Julianne Moore, Ron Lea, Arliss Howard, Chloe Sevigny, Louise Fletcher; ***D:*** Scott Elliott; ***W:*** Peter Hedges, Polly Platt; ***C:*** Seamus McGarvey; ***M:*** Pat Metheny. Natl. Bd. of Review '99: Support. Actress (Moore).

The Mapmaker ♂♂ 1/2 **2001** Engineer Richard Markey is hired to map out some land in a rural border town in Northern Ireland. Only he uncovers the body of an alleged informer tied to the IRA and puts his own life in danger when old hostilities surface. **89m/C DVD.** *GB IR* Brian F. O'Byrne, Susan Lynch, Brendan Coyle, Ian McElhinney, Oisin Kearney; ***D:*** Johnny Gogan; ***W:*** Johnny Gogan; ***C:*** Owen McPolin; ***M:*** Cathal Coughlan. **TV**

Mapp & Lucia ♂♂ 1/2 **1985** British TV adaptation of H.E. Benson's stories of provincial English society in the fictional village of Tilling-on-Sea in the 1920s. Miss Mapp (Scales) holds local court but finds a potential usurper when elegant widow Lucia (McEwan) comes to town. Battle lines are formed between the two women in this sharp-tongued satire. On five cassettes; followed by a second series of five episodes. **270m/C VHS, DVD.** *GB* Prunella Scales, Geraldine McEwan, Nigel Hawthorne; ***D:*** Donald McWhinnie; ***W:*** Gerald Savory; ***C:*** Lisle Middleditch; ***M:*** Jim Parker.

Mararia ♂♂ **1998** Romantic triangle set amidst the heat and beauty of 1940s island life on Lanzarote in the Canary Islands. The newly arrived Dr. Fermin (Gomez) falls under the spell of enticing local beauty Mararia (Toledo), who returns his affections. At least until British surveyor Bertrand (Glen) comes to the island and she changes her mind. This might be a woman's perogative but in Mararia's case, it leads to tragedy for all. Spanish with subtitles. **109m/C VHS, DVD.** *SP* Goya Toledo, Carmelo Gomez, Iain Glen, Mirta Ibarra; ***D:*** Antonio J. Betancor; ***W:*** Antonio J. Betancor, Carlos Alvarez; ***C:*** Juan Ruiz-Anchia; ***M:*** Pedro Guerra.

Marathon ♂♂ **1980** When a middle-aged jogger's ego gets a boost through the attention of a beautiful young woman, he takes up marathon running. Light comedy. **100m/C VHS, DVD.** Bob Newhart, Leigh Taylor-Young, Herb Edelman, Dick Gautier, Anita Gillette, John Hillerman; ***D:*** Jackie Cooper. **TV**

Marathon Man ♂♂♂ **1976 (R)** Nightmarish chase-thriller in which a graduate student becomes entangled in a plot involving a murderous Nazi fugitive. As student Hoffman is preparing for the Olympic marathon, he is reunited with his secret-agent brother, setting the intricate plot in motion. Courtesy of his brother, Hoffman becomes involved with Olivier, an old crazed Nazi seeking jewels taken from concentration camp victims. Non-stop action throughout, including a torture scene sure to set your teeth on edge. Goldman adapted the screenplay from his novel. **125m/C VHS, DVD.** Dustin Hoffman, Laurence Olivier, Marthe Keller, Roy Scheider, William Devane, Fritz Weaver, Richard Bright, Marc Lawrence; ***D:*** John Schlesinger; ***W:*** William Goldman; ***C:*** Conrad L. Hall; ***M:*** Michael Small. Golden Globes '77: Support. Actor (Olivier).

Marauder ♂♂ **1965** The prince of Venice leads a sea-faring onslaught against ransacking pirates and enemy fleets. **90m/C VHS.** *IT* Gordon Scott, Gianna Maria Canale, Franca Bettoya; ***D:*** Luigi Capuano.

Marbella ♂ 1/2 **1985** A luxury resort in Spain is the setting for a big caper heist of $3 million from a monarchical tycoon. **96m/C VHS.** Rod Taylor, Britt Ekland; ***D:*** Miguel Hermoso.

The Marc Pease Experience ♂ 1/2 **2009 (PG-13)** Stale showbiz comedy. Marc Pease (Schwartzman) is a limo-driving wannabe singer who can't get over a high-school debacle in which he humiliated himself and infuriated his arrogant director Gribble (Stiller) during a production of "The Wiz." Still, Marc naively believes that Gribble will actually produce his a cappella group's demo album if he can find the financing. **84m/C DVD.** Jason Schwartzman, Ben Stiller, Anna Kendrick, Ebon Moss-Bachrach, Gabrielle Dennis, Jay Paulson; ***D:*** Todd Louiso; ***W:*** Todd Louiso, Jacob Koskoff; ***C:*** Tim Suhrstedt; ***M:*** Christophe Beck. **VIDEO**

March of the Penguins ♂♂♂ **2005 (G)** Oscar winner for Best Documentary proves that animals can be movie stars even if they aren't animated by Pixar or Dreamworks. Director Jacquet traveled to Antarctica to film the mating rituals of the Emperor penguin and walked away with pure Animal Planet gold. You'll marvel at how ridiculously far the penguins will go to propagate their species—endless marching over frozen wastelands, working daily to escape predators, cutely ignoring the French camera crew. It's "Booty Call" meets National Geographic, all brought together by the smooth vocal stylings of narrator Morgan Freeman. Tries a bit too hard to imbue the birds with human personalities, but the astounding footage wins in the end. **80m/C DVD, Blu-ray Disc, HD DVD.** *US* ***D:*** Luc Jacquet; ***W:*** Jordan Roberts; ***C:*** Laurent Chalet, Jerome Maison; ***Nar:*** Morgan Freeman. Oscars '05: Feature Doc.; Natl. Bd. of Review '05: Feature Doc.; Broadcast Film Critics '05: Feature Doc.

March of the Wooden Soldiers 🦴🦴🦴 *Babes in Toyland* **1934** The classic Mother Goose tale about the secret life of Christmas toys, with Laurel and Hardy as Santa's helpers who must save Toyland from the wicked Barnaby. A Yuletide "must see." Also available in a colorized version. **73m/B VHS, DVD.** Stan Laurel, Oliver Hardy, Charlotte Henry, Henry (Kleinbach) Brandon, Felix Knight, Jean Darling, Johnny Downs, Marie Wilson; ***D:*** Charles R. Rogers, Gus Meins; ***W:*** Frank Butler, Nick Grinde; ***C:*** Art Lloyd, Francis Corby.

March or Die 🦴🦴 1/2 **1977 (PG)** Great potential, unrealized. An American joins the French Foreign Legion during WWI after his dismissal from West Point. Following the brutality of training, he is assigned to guard an archeological expedition in Morocco, where he pulls together a rag-tag outfit for the mission. Hackman proves once again the wide range of his acting abilities, surmounting the cliched and fairly sadistic plot. Shot on location in the Sahara Desert. **104m/C VHS, DVD.** *GB* Gene Hackman, Terence Hill, Max von Sydow, Catherine Deneuve, Ian Holm; ***D:*** Dick Richards; ***W:*** David Zelag Goodman; ***M:*** Maurice Jarre.

Marci X 🦴 **2003 (R)** Ill-begotten social satire stars Kudrow as the title character, who takes over for dad Ben (director Benjamin) at his record company after he suffers a heart attack. When the the lyrics of Dr. S (Wayans), the label's top rapper, provoke conservative U.S. Senator Spinkle (Baranski) to attempt to ban the rapper's songs, the uptown, Jewish Marci tries to smooth things over and ends up falling for the Dr.'s downtown charms. Culture clash comedy has its moments, but is ultimately too predictable and the characters too one-dimensional to care about. Rap soundtrack is similarly uninspired, except a hilarious number by the fictitious boy band, Boyz 'R' Us. **97m/C VHS, DVD.** *US* Lisa Kudrow, Damon Wayans, Richard Benjamin, Christine Baranski, Paula Garces, Jane Krakowski, Veanne Cox; ***D:*** Richard Benjamin; ***W:*** Paul Rudnick; ***C:*** Robbie Greenberg; ***M:*** Mervyn Warren.

Marciano 🦴🦴 **1979** Average fight movie chronicling the great boxer's life. **97m/C VHS.** Tony LoBianco, Vincent Gardenia; ***D:*** Bernard L. Kowalski; ***M:*** Ernest Gold. **TV**

Marco 🦴🦴 **1973** Entertaining musical adventure of Marco Polo's life casts Arnaz as Marco Polo and Mostel as Kublai Khan. A couple of cut-ups, right? One of the first films to combine animation with live action. Shot partially on location in the Orient. ♫By Damn; Walls; A Family Man; Spaghetti. **109m/C VHS, DVD.** Desi Arnaz Jr., Zero Mostel, Jack Weston, Cie Cie Win; ***D:*** Seymour Robbie.

Marco Polo 🦴 1/2 **2007** Thirteenth-century explorer Marco Polo (Somerhalder) reminisces about his travels from his home in Venice, recalling his time in China and his meeting with leader Kublai Khan (uh, Dennehy? Who cast this thing?). Cheesy, but the scenery's pretty. **176m/C DVD.** Ian Somerhalder, Brian Dennehy, B.D. Wong, Desiree Slahaan; ***D:*** Kevin Connor; ***W:*** Ron Hutchinson; ***C:*** Thomas Burstyn. **CABLE**

Marco Polo, Jr. 🦴 *Marco Polo Junior Versus the Red Dragon* **1972** Marco Polo Jr., the daring descendant of the legendary explorer, travels the world in search of his destiny in this song-filled, feature-length, but poorly animated, fantasy. **82m/C VHS.** *AU* ***D:*** Eric Porter; ***W:*** Sheldon Moldoff; ***V:*** Arnold Stang, Kevin Golsby, Corie Sims, Bobby Rydell.

Mardi Gras for the Devil 🦴🦴 *Night Trap* **1993 (R)** Black magic and the occult combine as a New Orleans cop tries to catch a killer who strikes only at Mardi Gras. The cop's got his work cut out for him since the killer is no mere mortal but a demon who believes in human sacrifice. **95m/C VHS.** Robert Davi, Michael Ironside, Lesley-Anne Down, Lydie Denier, Mike Starr, Margaret Avery, John Amos; ***D:*** David A. Prior; ***W:*** David A. Prior.

Mardi Gras Massacre **WOOF!** *Crypt of Dark Secrets* **1978** Aztec priest arrives in New Orleans during Mardi Gras to revive the blood ritual of human sacrifice to an Aztec god. A police detective relentlessly pursues him. Much gore and gut-slicing, with no redeeming social value. **92m/C VHS, DVD.** Curt Dawson, Gwen Arment, Wayne Mack, Laura Misch; ***D:*** Jack Weis.

Marebito 🦴🦴 *The Stranger from Afar* **2004 (R)** In his quest to capture the ultimate moment of fear, Masuoka (Tsukamoto), a freelance cameraman, becomes engrossed by video he films of a seemingly-possessed man as he violently commits suicide in a Tokyo subway. While searching for more clues in the macabre underground, he happens upon a naked, mute girl who he calls "F" (Miyashita) and decides taking her home would be a good idea. He soon find her behavior distressing and her means of survival alarming. Very dark, though much of the scary stuff isn't shown. In Japanese with subtitles. **92m/C DVD.** *JP* Shinya Tsukamoto, Shun Sugata, Tomomi Miyashita, Kazuhiro Nakahara, Miho Ninagawa; ***D:*** Takashi Shimizu; ***W:*** Chiaki Konaka. **VIDEO**

Margaret's Museum 🦴🦴🦴 1/2 **1995 (R)** The museum of the title is the bizarre shrine Margaret (Bonham Carter) dedicates to the family members who have been killed in the coal mines that dominate her small (1940s) Cape Breton, Nova Scotia town. Both Margaret and her mother, Catherine (Nelligan), are embittered by their tragedies and when Margaret finds romance with eccentric bagpiper Neil (Russell), she makes him promise he'll never return to mine work. But with a bad economy, Neil is forced back to the pits and inevitable disaster. It's Bonham Carter's picture all the way and she shows a wide (and welcome) range of emotions and strength. Adapted from a story by Sheldon Currie. **114m/C VHS.** *CA GB* Helena Bonham Carter, Clive Russell, Kate Nelligan, Kenneth Welsh, Craig Olejnik; ***D:*** Mort Ransen; ***W:*** Mort Ransen, Gerald Wexler; ***C:*** Vic Sarin; ***M:*** Milan Kymlicka. Genie '95: Actress (Bonham Carter), Adapt. Screenplay, Costume Des., Support. Actor (Welsh), Support. Actress (Nelligan), Score.

Margarita Happy Hour 🦴🦴 **2001** Zelda (Hutchins) is a hard-partying New York single mom who makes a living (barely) as an illustrator and lives with her toddler daughter's unemployed, passive father Max (Fessenden), who has a drinking problem. Zelda's support group are her single mom friends whom she regularly meets at a local bar for happy hour. Zelda's life gets more complicated when her recovering junkie friend Natali (Ramos) moves in, needing to get her act together although she hasn't a clue how to do it. She's in good company. **98m/C DVD.** *US* Eleanor Hutchins, Larry Fessenden, Holly Ramos, Barbara Sicuranza, Amanda Vogel, Macha Ross, Kristen Dispaltro, Will Keenan; ***D:*** Ilya Chaiken; ***W:*** Ilya Chaiken; ***C:*** Gordon Chou; ***M:*** Max Lichtenstein.

Margin for Murder 🦴🦴 *Mickey Spillane's Margin for Murder* **1981** Mike Hammer investigates a mysterious accident that killed his best friend. **98m/C VHS.** Kevin Dobson, Cindy Pickett, Donna Dixon, Charles Hallahan; ***D:*** Daniel Haller. **TV**

Margot at the Wedding 🦴🦴 **2007 (R)** Writer Margot (Kidman) returns to her family's home for her sister Pauline's (Leigh) wedding to "artist" Malcolm (Black), but years of contempt, ego, and neuroses boil over among the sisters, their children, and anyone else who happens to be around. Writer/director Baumbach specializes in finding biting humor and poignancy in the struggles of flawed, overly educated East Coasters, but the nasty, petty characters he's created here are so hard to relate to that anything funny or moving is buried under an avalanche of meanness. **92m/C DVD.** *US* Nicole Kidman, Jennifer Jason Leigh, Jack Black, John Turturro, Ciaran Hinds, Flora Cross, Halley Feiffer, Zane Pais; ***D:*** Noah Baumbach; ***W:*** Noah Baumbach; ***C:*** Harris Savides.

Maria Candelaria 🦴🦴 *Portrait of Maria; Xochimilco* **1946** Society rejects a woman because people don't like her mother. (She posed nude for an artist, and the town responds by stoning her to death, proving that going against small-town morals can be lethal). Eventually, time and circumstance push daughter onto mother's path in this tragic soaper. Del Rio portrays the scorned young woman, although she was 40 years old. **96m/B VHS.** *MX* Dolores Del Rio, Pedro Armendariz Sr., Margarita Cortes; ***D:*** Emilio Fernandez.

Maria Chapdelaine 🦴🦴🦴 **1934** An early film from the renowned French director, in which a brutish trapper and a sophisticate battle for the love of a girl in the Canadian wilderness. English subtitles. Remade in 1984. **75m/B VHS.** *FR* Jean Gabin, Jean-Pierre Aumont, Madeleine Renaud; ***D:*** Julien Duvivier.

Maria Chapdelaine 🦴🦴 1/2 **1984** Around the turn of the century, a young girl in the Northern Canadian wilderness endures a year of passion, doomed love, and tragedy. In French with subtitles. Remake of a 1935 French film. **108m/C VHS.** *FR CA* Nick Mancuso, Carole Laure, Claude Rich, Pierre Curzi; ***D:*** Gilles Carle.

Maria Full of Grace 🦴🦴🦴 *Maria, llena eres de gracia* **2004 (R)** Moreno (in her film debut) gives a graceful performance in the title role of also-debuting director Marston's all-too-human look at desperation and heroin trafficking in Colombia. Maria is a 17-year-old working for a pittance at a flower factory in her rural hometown. She realizes she's pregnant just as she impulsively quits her job and is ripe for the sweet talk of Franklin (Toro), who tells Maria about all the money to be made if she'll only become a drug mule. After swallowing heroin-filled pellets, Maria boards a plane for New York along with her best friend Blanca (Vega) and fellow courier Lucy (Lopez). Problems arise when Lucy becomes ill, thugs threaten the girls if any of the drugs come up missing, and Maria flees into the city's Colombian immigrant community for safety. Spanish with subtitles. **101m/C VHS, DVD.** *US* Catalina Sandino Moreno, Yenny Paola Vega, Giulied Lopez, John Alex Toro, Patricia Rae, Wilson Guerrero, Jaime Osorio Gomez, Johanna Andrea Mora, Orlando Tobon, Fernando Velasquez; ***D:*** Joshua Marston; ***W:*** Joshua Marston; ***C:*** Jim Denault; ***M:*** Jacobo Lieberman, Leonardo Heiblum. Ind. Spirit '05: Actress (Moreno), First Screenplay.

Marianne and Juliane 🦴🦴🦴 1/2 *The German Sisters; Die Bleierne Zeit* **1982** Powerful combination of relationships and politics in West Germany as experienced through the lives of two sisters—Juliane, a feminist editor, and Marianne, a political terrorist. Based on the lives of Gudrun and Christiane Ensslin. German with subtitles. **106m/C VHS.** *GE* Jutta Lampe, Barbara Sukowa, Ruediger Vogler, Doris Schade, Franz Rudnick; ***D:*** Margarethe von Trotta; ***W:*** Margarethe von Trotta; ***C:*** Franz Rath; ***M:*** Nicolas Economou.

Maria's Child 🦴🦴 1/2 **1993** Light comedy about a dancer who becomes pregnant and must decide whether or not to keep the baby. When her live-in boyfriend (not the father) admits he cheated on her, she kicks him out. Unable to make up her mind, she imagines a dialogue with the fetus. Second of a trilogy by British TV screenwriter Malcolm McKay on the subject of forgiveness. **97m/C VHS.** *GB* Yolanda Vasquez, David O'Hara, Fiona Shaw, Alec McCowen, Sophie Okonedo, Linda Davidson, Rudi Davies, Nicholas Woodeson, Anita Zagaria; ***D:*** Malcolm McKay; ***W:*** Malcolm McKay; ***M:*** Philip Appleby.

Maria's Day 🦴🦴🦴 *Maria-nap* **1984** Chronicles the plague-riddled downfall of a formerly aristocratic and wealthy Hungarian family in the years following the failed 1849 Revolution. In Hungarian with English subtitles. **113m/C VHS.** Sandor Szabo, Lajos Kovacs, Edit Handel, Eva Igo, Imre Csiszar, Tamas Fodor; ***D:*** Judit Elek; ***W:*** Luca Karall, Gyorgy Petho; ***C:*** Emil Novak; ***M:*** Gabor Csalog.

Maria's Lovers 🦴🦴 1/2 **1984 (R)** The wife (Kinski) of an impotent WWII veteran (Savage) succumbs to the charms of a rakish lady-killer (Spano). Savage turns to the charms of an older woman, finds love again with Kinski, but is still impotent; she gets pregnant by a wandering minstrel (Carradine) and on we go to film climax. Offbeat and uneven, representing Russian director Konchalovsky's first American film and one of Kinski's better roles. **103m/C VHS, DVD.** Nastassja Kinski, John Savage, Robert Mitchum, Keith Carradine, Anita Morris, Bud Cort, Karen Young, Tracy Nelson, John Goodman, Vincent Spano; ***D:*** Andrei Konchalovsky; ***W:*** Andrei Konchalovsky, Marjorie David, Gerard Brach, Paul Zindel; ***C:*** Juan Ruiz-Anchia; ***M:*** Gary S. Remal.

Maricela **1988** Young Maricela Flores and her mother have come to the U.S. from El Salvador to escape the fighting. Living with a Southern Californian family, Maricela has a hard time adjusting to American life and, in particular, dealing with prejudice. An entry in the PBS "Wonderworks" series. **55m/C VHS, DVD.** Linda Lavin, Carlina Cruz.

Marie 🦴🦴🦴 **1985 (PG-13)** In this true story, a divorced (and battered) mother works her way through school and the system to become the first woman to head the Parole Board in Tennessee. Finding rampant corruption, she blows the whistle on her bosses, who put her life in jeopardy. Spacek gives a powerful performance, as does first-time actor Thompson, portraying himself as the abused woman's attorney. Based on the book by Peter Maas. **113m/C VHS, DVD.** Sissy Spacek, Jeff Daniels, Keith Szarabajka, John Cullum, Morgan Freeman, Fred Dalton Thompson, Don Hood, Lisa Banes, Vincent Irizarry; ***D:*** Roger Donaldson; ***W:*** John Briley; ***C:*** Chris Menges; ***M:*** Francis Lai.

Marie and Bruce 🦴 1/2 **2004 (R)** It doesn't make for a very interesting evening, watching a dysfunctional marriage disintegrate. Shrill Marie is determined to leave her plodding husband Bruce. Marie has several surreal experiences before meeting Bruce at a party, where she's irked by the chatter and Bruce's sociability. They finally have a disastrous dinner where Marie springs her news and Bruce gets drunk. Adaptation of Wallace Shawn's 1979 play. **90m/C DVD.** Julianne Moore, Matthew Broderick, Bob Balaban; ***D:*** Tom Cairns; ***W:*** Tom Cairns, Wallace Shawn; ***C:*** Patrick Cady; ***M:*** Mar Degli Antoni.

Marie Antoinette 🦴🦴 1/2 **1938** An elephantine costume drama chronicling the French queen's life from princesshood to her final days before the Revolution. A Shearer festival all the way, and a late example of MGM's overstuffed period style and star-power. Overlong, but engrossing for the wrong reasons. Morley, in his first film, plays Louis XVI. Power's only MGM loan-out casts him as a Swedish count and Marie's romantic dalliance. Based on a book by Stephan Zweig, with script assistance from (among others) F. Scott Fitzgerald. **160m/B VHS, DVD.** Norma Shearer, Tyrone Power, John Barrymore, Robert Morley, Gladys George, Anita Louise, Joseph Schildkraut, Henry Stephenson, Reginald Gardiner, Peter Bull, Albert Dekker, Joseph Calleia, George Zucco, Cora Witherspoon, Barry Fitzgerald, Mae Busch, Harry Davenport, Scotty Beckett; ***D:*** Woodbridge S. Van Dyke; ***W:*** F. Scott Fitzgerald; ***C:*** William H. Daniels.

Marie Antoinette 🦴🦴 **2006 (PG-13)** Coppola goes her own anachronistic way in this revisionist biopic. Pink-and-white Dunst dimples her way through as the teenaged Marie Antoinette, an Austrian princess who is married off at 14 to bumptious French prince (and eventual king) Louis (Schwartzman), who can't even bed her properly. So what's a bored and lonely young woman, stuck in a hostile royal court, to do? Why, party, party, party (extravagantly) of course. It's all pop tunes and lavish costumes and splendid isolation at Versailles while the rabble rouses. Fortunately, Coppola ends her confection before tragedy befalls the delectable Marie. **123m/C DVD.** *US* Kirsten Dunst, Jason Schwartzman, Judy Davis, Rip Torn, Rose Byrne, Asia Argento, Molly Shannon, Shirley Henderson, Danny Huston, Marianne Faithfull, Jamie Dornan, Mary Nighy, Steve Coogan, Lauriane Mascaro, Florrie Betts; ***D:*** Sofia Coppola; ***W:*** Sofia Coppola; ***C:*** Lance Acord. Oscars '06: Costume Des.

Marie Baie des Anges 🦴🦴 *Angel Sharks; Marie Bay of Angels* **1997 (R)** Although Nice's harbor is known as "The Bay of Angels," Pradal sets his film in a sort of mythic French port, filled with French teens, gang members, American sailors, and tourists. Pretty gypsy Marie (Giocante) likes to flirt with the Americans but after getting dumped goes back to the local toughs, including petty criminal Orso (Malgras). They manage a brief idyll, then Orso begins pressuring Marie to steal a gun for him. She does, and you can imagine how things turn out. French with subtitles. **90m/C VHS.** *FR* Vahina Giocante, Frederic Malgras; ***D:*** Manuel Pradal; ***W:*** Manuel Pradal; ***C:*** Christophe Pollock; ***M:*** Carlo Crivelli.

Marie Galante 1934 Fine spy drama has Tracy running into Gallian in Panama (years earlier she had been left there after a kidnapping). He finds her most helpful in his attempt to thwart the bombing of the Panama Canal. It's the performances that raise this otherwise standard thriller up a few notches. **88m/B VHS, DVD.** Spencer Tracy, Ketti Gallian, Ned Sparks, Helen Morgan, Sig Rumann, Leslie Fenton, Jay C. Flippen; ***D:*** Henry King.

Marigold **2007 (PG-13)** Cultural clash romance that's Westernized Bollywood. Marigold Lexton (Larter) is a first-class diva and a third-rate actress. She heads to Goa, India, for a low-budget film and then is stranded when it falls through. Stumbling across a local movie production, she convinces the director she knows how to dance (she doesn't) and falls for handsome choreographer Prem (Khan). Getting interested in him means Marigold also gets interested in the culture before Prem reveals he's betrothed in an arranged marriage. **107m/C DVD.** *US IN* Ali Larter, Salman Khan, Ian Bohen, Nandana Sen, Helen Khan; ***D:*** Willard Carroll; ***W:*** Willard Carroll; ***C:*** Anil Mehta; ***M:*** Graeme Revell.

Marihuana 1/2 *Marijuana: The Devil's Weed; Marijuana, Weed with Roots in Hell* **1936** An unintentionally hilarious, "Reefer Madness"-type cautionary film about the exaggerated evils of pot smoking. A real dopey film favored by right-winger zealots. **57m/B VHS, DVD.** Harley Wood, Hugh McArthur, Pat Carlyle, Dorothy Dehn, Paul Ellis, Richard Erskine; ***D:*** Dwain Esper; ***W:*** Rex Elgin, Hildegarde Stadie; ***C:*** Roland Price.

Marilyn & Bobby: Her Final Affair 1/2 **1994** Sordid account of the alleged romance between movie star Monroe (Anderson) and Attorney General Robert Kennedy (Kelly). Culminates in a silly scene at Marilyn's home, on the night of her death, where various men all try to find her tell-all diary while keeping out of sight of each other. **95m/C VHS.** Melody Anderson, James F. Kelly, Richard Dysart, Thomas Wagner, Raymond Serra, Kristopher Tabori, Jonathan Banks, Geoffrey Blake, Ian Buchanan; ***D:*** Bradford May. **CABLE**

Marilyn Hotchkiss' Ballroom Dancing & Charm School 1/2 **2006 (PG-13)** When he was only 8 years old, Steve (Goodman) promised his sweetheart Lisa that in forty years they would meet again at their dance school's class reunion. Now here we are, forty years later, trying to believe that this is all going down and that Steve is still passionately fixated on this historic moment. Not buying it. Everything goes wrong and Steve wonders if he'll ever get to see his long-lost love again. Silly side-tracking story that takes itself too seriously, gushing its own bittersweet sentiment all over the place. Somehow snagged an incredible cast. Based on the director's own short film made 15 years earlier. **103m/C DVD.** Robert Carlyle, Marisa Tomei, Mary Steenburgen, John Goodman, Donnie Wahlberg, Sonia Braga, Sean Astin, Danny DeVito, David Paymer, Camryn Manheim, Adam Arkin, Elden (Ratliff) Henson, Ernie Hudson, Miguel (Michael) Sandoval, Ian Abercrombie, Mary Pat Gleason; ***D:*** Randall Miller; ***W:*** Randall Miller, Jody Savin; ***C:*** Jonathan Sela; ***M:*** Mark Adler.

Marilyn: The Untold Story **1980** Nominated for an Emmy, Hicks elevates what could easily have been a dull made-for-TV movie with her remarkable performance as Marilyn Monroe. Based on the book by Norman Mailer. **156m/C VHS.** Catherine Hicks, Richard Basehart, Frank Converse, John Ireland, Sheree North, Anne Ramsey, Viveca Lindfors, Jason Miller, Bill Vint; ***D:*** Jack Arnold, John Flynn, Lawrence Schiller; ***M:*** William Goldstein.

The Marine 1/2 **2006 (PG-13)** A frozen slab of grade-A beef, wrestler Cena makes his movie debut (as does director Bonito) in this slam-bang actioner. When John Triton is shipped back to South Carolina from Iraq, he decides to take his hottie wife Kate (Carlson) on vacation. But they wind up in the wrong place just when a violent gang of jewel thieves need a hostage and take Kate. This pisses off John and you don't want anybody that big angry at you. Cartoonish mayhem follows (it's PG-13, remember). Patrick has fun with his villainous ringleader role but you know he's slumming. **93m/C DVD, Blu-ray Disc.** *US* Robert Patrick, Kelly Carlson, Anthony Ray Parker, Jerome Ehlers, John Cena, Abigail Bianca; ***D:*** John Bonito; ***W:*** Alan B. McElroy, Michell Gallagher; ***C:*** David Eggby; ***M:*** Don Davis.

The Marine 2 1/2 **2009 (R)** A competent in-name-only action sequel has recon sniper Joe Linwood and his wife vacationing at a Thailand resort that's suddenly besieged by a separatist group. With the terrorists taking hostages, it's up to Joe to come up with a plan to save the day. **95m/C DVD.** Ted DiBiase Jr., Michael Rooker, Temuera Morrison, Lara Cox; ***D:*** Roel Reine; ***W:*** Christopher Borrelli, John Chapin Morgan; ***M:*** Trevor Morris. **VIDEO**

Marine Raiders **1943** Marines train and then fight at Guadalcanal. A typical flag-waver, watchable but not particularly engaging. **90m/B VHS.** Pat O'Brien, Robert Ryan, Ruth Hussey, Frank McHugh, Barton MacLane; ***D:*** Harold Schuster.

Marion Bridge **2002** Chain-smoking alcoholic Rose (McNeil) is dying, which brings her three daughters back together with all their past family traumas unresolved. Former wild child Agnes (Parker) was sexually abused by their father, which resulted in the birth of a child whom she gave up. Now that child is a sullen teen living nearby with her adoptive mother and Agnes would like to befriend her. Eldest sister Theresa (Jenkins) is a bitter divorcee who can't let go of her ex and middle sister Louise (Smith) is a couch potato who is slowly working up the courage to admit she's a lesbian. Much angst ensues for all. Screenwriter McIvor adapted from his play. **90m/C DVD.** *CA* Molly Parker, Rebecca Jenkins, Stacy Smith, Marguerite McNeill; ***D:*** Wiebke von Carolsfeld; ***W:*** Daniel McIvor; ***C:*** Stefan Ivanov; ***M:*** Lesley Barber.

Marius **1931** This is the first of Marcel Pagnol's trilogy ("Fanny" and "Cesar" followed), about the lives and adventures of the people of Provence, France. Marius is a young man who dreams of going away to sea. When he acts on those dreams, he leaves behind his girlfriend, Fanny. Realistic dialogue and vivid characterizations. Adapted by Pagnol from his play. The musical play and film "Fanny" (1961) were adapted from this trilogy. **125m/B VHS, DVD.** *FR* Raimu, Pierre Fresnay, Charpin, Orane Demazis; ***D:*** Alexander Korda; ***W:*** Marcel Pagnol; ***M:*** Francis Gromon.

Marius and Jeannette 1/2 *Marius et Jeannette: Un Conte de L'Estaque* **1997** Single mother of two, Jeannette (Ascaride), works as a checkout clerk in a poor Marseilles neighborhood. Marius (Meylan) works as a security guard at a closed cement factory and meets Jeannette when he catches her stealing paint cans from the property. He offers to help her paint her apartment and the two begin a tentative romance. But something spooks Marius and he begins to drink heavily, abandoning Jeannette. Two of Jeannette's male neighbors decide to find out what Marius' problem is and get the twosome back together. Very sweet and sentimental. **101m/C VHS, DVD.** *FR* Ariane Ascaride, Gerard Meylan, Pascale Roberts, Jacques Boudet, Jean-Pierre Darroussin, Frederique Bonnal; ***D:*** Robert Guediguian; ***W:*** Robert Guediguian, Jean-Louis Milesi; ***C:*** Bernard Cavile. Cesar '98: Actress (Ascaride).

Marjoe **1972 (PG)** Documentary follows the career of rock-style evangelist Marjoe Gortner, who spent 25 years of his life touring the country as a professional preacher. Marjoe later went on to become an actor and professional fundraiser. **88m/C VHS, DVD.** Marjoe Gortner; ***D:*** Howard Smith, Sarah Kernochan. Oscars '72: Feature Doc.

Marjorie Morningstar **1958** A temperate Hollywood adaptation of the Herman Wouk story of a young actress who fails to achieve stardom and settles on being a housewife. Wood slipped a bit in this story. **123m/C VHS, DVD.** Natalie Wood, Gene Kelly, Martin Balsam, Claire Trevor, Ed Wynn, Everett Sloane, Carolyn Jones; ***D:*** Irving Rapper; ***C:*** Harry Stradling Sr.; ***M:*** Max Steiner.

The Mark 1/2 **1961** Story of a convicted child molester who cannot escape his past upon his release from prison. Whitman gives a riveting performance as the convict. **127m/B VHS, DVD.** *GB* Stuart Whitman, Maria Schell, Rod Steiger, Brenda de Banzie, Maurice Denham, Donald Wolfit, Paul Rogers, Donald Houston, Amanda Black, Russell Napier, Marie Devereux; ***D:*** Guy Green; ***W:*** Sidney Buchman, Raymond Stross; ***C:*** Dudley Lovell; ***M:*** Richard Rodney Bennett.

Mark of Cain 1/2 **1984** Twin brothers, one normal, the other a raving lunatic with murderous tendencies, confuse the authorities who imprison the nice guy, allowing the nutcase to chase after his beautiful sister-in-law. **90m/C VHS.** Robin Ward, Wendy Crewson, August Schellenberg; ***D:*** Bruce Pittman; ***W:*** Peter Colley.

Mark of the Beast **1987** Two students inadvertently videotape an assassination, and are then relentlessly pursued by the killer. **90m/C VHS.** Carolyn Guillet, David Smulker; ***D:*** Robert Stewart.

Mark of the Devil *Burn, Witch, Burn; Brenn, Hexe, Brenn; Austria 1700; Satan; Hexen bis aufs Blut Gequaelt* **1969 (R)** Witchcraft and romance don't mix, as a Medieval witch hunter and a sexy girl accused of witchery discover. Notoriously graphic torture scenes add to the mayhem but the weird part is that this is based on true stories. **96m/C VHS, DVD.** *GB GE* Herbert Lom, Olivera Vuco, Udo Kier, Reggie Nalder, Herbert (Fuchs) Fux, Michael Maien, Ingeborg (Inge) Schoener, Johannes Buzalski, Gaby Fuchs, Adrian Hoven; ***D:*** Michael Armstrong; ***W:*** Sergio Casstner, Adrian Hoven; ***C:*** Ernst W. Kalinke; ***M:*** Michael Holm.

Mark of the Devil 2 **1972 (R)** Sadistic witchhunters torture satan's servants and torch sisters of mercy, whilst trying to horn in on a nobleman's fortune. It's just not as gross without the vomit bags. **90m/C VHS, DVD.** *GB GE* Erika Blanc, Anton Diffring, Reggie Nalder; ***D:*** Adrian Hoven.

The Mark of the Hawk *The Accused* **1957** A uniquely told story of African nations struggling to achieve racial equality after gaining independence. Songs include "This Man Is Mine," sung by Kitt. **83m/C VHS.** *GB* Sidney Poitier, Eartha Kitt, Juano Hernandez, John McIntire; ***D:*** Michael Audley.

Mark of the Spur 1/2 **1932** The mark on an injured man's face is used to track down his attacker. **60m/B VHS.** Bob Custer, Lillian Rich, Franklyn Farnum, Bud Osborne; ***D:*** J(ohn) P(aterson) McGowan.

Mark of the Vampire *Vampires of Prague* **1935** A murder in a small town is solved through the use of vaudeville actors who pose as vampires. Great cast, surprise ending. **61m/B VHS, DVD.** Lionel Barrymore, Bela Lugosi, Elizabeth Allan, Lionel Atwill, Jean Hersholt, Donald Meek, Carroll Borland; ***D:*** Tod Browning; ***W:*** Tod Browning, Guy Endore, Bernard Schubert; ***C:*** James Wong Howe.

Mark of Zorro **1920** Fairbanks plays a dual role as the hapless Don Diego and his dashing counterpart, Zorro, the hero of the oppressed. Silent film. **80m/B VHS, DVD.** Douglas Fairbanks Sr., Marguerite de la Motte, Noah Beery Sr., Mary Astor, Noah Beery Jr., Milton Berle, Charles Stevens; ***D:*** Fred Niblo; ***W:*** Douglas Fairbanks Sr.; ***C:*** William McGann, Harris (Harry) Thorpe.

The Mark of Zorro 1/2 **1940** The dashing Power swashbuckles his way through this wonderfully acted and directed romp. He plays the foppish son of a 19th-century California aristocrat who is secretly the masked avenger of the oppressed peons. Bromberg plays the wicked governor, with the beautiful niece (Darnell) beloved by Power, and Rathbone is supremely evil as his cruel minion. Lots of swordplay with a particularly exciting duel to the death between Rathbone and Power. Based on the novel "The Curse of Capistrano" by Johnston McCulley. Remake of the 1921 silent film and followed by a number of other Zorro incarnations. **93m/B VHS, DVD.** Tyrone Power, Linda Darnell, Basil Rathbone, Gale Sondergaard, Eugene Pallette, J. Edward Bromberg, Montagu Love, Janet Beecher; ***D:*** Rouben Mamoulian; ***W:*** John Taintor Foote; ***C:*** Arthur C. Miller; ***M:*** Alfred Newman. Natl. Film Reg. '09.

Mark Twain and Me 1/2 **1991** Robards portrays the aging and irascible Mark Twain, attended by a neglected but devoted daughter, and befriended by 11-year-old Dorothy Quick, as they travel on the same ship. Based on a true story. **93m/C VHS.** Jason Robards Jr., Talia Shire, Amy Stewart, Chris Wiggins, R.H. Thomson, Fiona Reid; ***D:*** Daniel Petrie. **TV**

Marked for Death 1/2 *Screwface* **1990 (R)** Having killed a prostitute, DEA agent Seagal decides it's time to roll out the white picket fence in the 'burbs with the little woman and brood. Trouble is, a bunch of guys with dreadlocks don't approve of his early retirement, and the Jamaican gangsters plan to send him and his family to the great Rasta playground in the sky. Whereupon the Stevester kicks and punches and wags his ponytail. Much blood flows, mon. Tunes by Jimmy Cliff. **93m/C VHS, DVD.** Steven Seagal, Joanna Pacula, Basil Wallace, Keith David, Danielle Harris, Arlen Dean Snyder, Teri Weigel; ***D:*** Dwight Little; ***W:*** Mark Victor, Michael Grais; ***C:*** Ric Waite; ***M:*** James Newton Howard.

Marked for Murder 1/2 **1945** Another in the Texas Ranger series. In this entry, the Rangers come to the rescue when a rancher war appears inevitable. **58m/B VHS.** Tex Ritter, Dave O'Brien, Guy Wilkerson; ***D:*** Elmer Clifton; ***W:*** Elmer Clifton.

Marked for Murder 1/2 **1989 (R)** Two TV station employees are framed for murder after being sent out to find a missing videocassette. Renee Estevez is part of the Sheen/Estevez dynasty. **88m/C VHS.** Renee Estevez, Wings Hauser, Jim Mitchum, Ross Hagen, Ken Abraham; ***D:*** Rick Sloane.

Marked Man **1996 (R)** After auto mechanic Frank Stanton (Piper) witnesses a murder he finds himself accused of the crime and on the run, trying to prove his innocence. **94m/C VHS.** Roddy Piper, Jane Wheeler, Alina Thompson, Miles O'Keeffe; ***D:*** Marc Voizard; ***W:*** Thomas Ritz; ***C:*** Stephen Reizes; ***M:*** Marty Simon. **VIDEO**

Marked Money **1928** Amiable captain takes in boy who'll soon roll in the dough and swindlers show up on the scene. The captain's courageous girl and her pilot beau step in to right the rookery. **61m/B VHS.** Frank "Junior" Coghlan, Tom Keene, Tom Kennedy, Bert Woodruff, Virginia Bradford, Maurice Black, Jack (H.) Richardson; ***D:*** Spencer Gordon Bennet.

Marked Trails **1944** One clue stamps out the guilty parties in this wild west saga. **59m/B VHS, DVD.** Hoot Gibson, Bob Steele, Veda Ann Borg; ***D:*** John P. McCarthy; ***W:*** John P. McCarthy, Victor Hammond; ***C:*** Harry Neumann.

Marked Woman **1937** Gangster drama about crusading District Attorney who persuades a group of clipjoint hostesses to testify against their gangster boss. A gritty studio melodrama loosely based on a true story. **97m/B VHS, DVD.** Bette Davis, Humphrey Bogart, Eduardo Ciannelli, Isabel Jewell, Jane Bryan, Mayo Methot, Allen Jenkins, Lola Lane; ***D:*** Lloyd Bacon; ***C:*** George Barnes. Venice Film Fest. '37: Actress (Davis).

Marking Time **2003** Coming-of-age first romance that starts off with hope and ends in disillusionment. In 2000, the small Australian town of Brackley is excited by the Sydney Olympics and the fact that former Olympian Geoff Fleming (Morrell) is part of their community. Meanwhile, his teenaged son Hal (Forsythe) is falling in love with Afghani refugee Randa (Novakovic) despite the disapproval of his no-account friends. Then a new election brings in an anti-immigration government and, after 9/11, Hal has to find a way to protect Randa from racist insults and violence as well as the threat of deportation. **206m/C DVD.** *AU* Geoff Morrell, Abbie Cornish, Katie Wall, Graeme Blundell, Abe Forsythe, Bojana Novakovic, Elena Carapetis,

Lech Mackiewicz, Matt LeNevez; *D:* Cherie Nowlan; *W:* John (Roy Slaven) Doyle; *C:* Anna Howard; *M:* Martin Armiger, John Butler. **TV**

Marley & Me 🦴🦴 ½ **2008 (PG)** Based on John Grogan's own 2005 memoir, follows his (Wilson) and wife Jenny's (Aniston) lives as reporters in Florida. John is unhappy when the local paper editor (Arkin, with great comedic effect) gives him a column-writing assignment while also tentative about Jenny's desire to start their family. Enter Marley, a loveable but highly energetic and destructive yellow lab John dubs "the world's worst dog," who manages to win their hearts as he eats their furniture and becomes their constant companion as they journey into parenthood. Undoubtedly appealing to the younger set but parents need to beware a major tearjerker at the end. Wilson and Aniston are easy on the eyes and get along well enough, but it plays more as a sitcom then a major film. **116m/C DVD.** *US* Owen Wilson, Jennifer Aniston, Haley Bennett, Eric Dane, Alan Arkin, Kathleen Turner, Nathan Gamble, Ann Dowd; *D:* David Frankel; *W:* Scott Frank, Don Roos; *C:* Florian Ballhaus; *M:* Theodore Shapiro.

Marlowe 🦴🦴 ½ **1969 (PG)** Updated telling by Stirling Silliphant of Chandler's "The Little Sister" sports retro guy Garner as Philip Marlowe, gumshoe. Hired by a mystery blonde to find her misplaced brother, rumpled sleuth Marlowe encounters kicking Bruce Lee in his first film. Slick looking, but the story's a bit slippery. **95m/C VHS.** James Garner, Gayle Hunnicutt, Carroll O'Connor, Rita Moreno, Sharon Farrell, William Daniels, Bruce Lee; *D:* Paul Bogart; *W:* Stirling Silliphant; *C:* William H. Daniels.

Marmaduke 2010 (PG) Yep, now it's the big screen version of Brad Anderson's comic strip, which began in 1954. The Winslows, and their trouble-prone Great Dane (who talks as do his new pals), move from Kansas to Orange County, California and get to upset a whole new neighborhood. **m/C DVD.** *US* Judy Greer, Lee Pace, William H. Macy, Finley Jacobsen, Caroline Sunshine; *D:* Tom Dey; *W:* Vince Di Meglio, Tim Rasmussen; *C:* Greg Gardiner; *M:* Christopher Lennertz; *V:* Owen Wilson, Emma Stone, Christopher Mintz-Plasse, Ron Perlman, Steve Coogan, George Lopez, Damon Wayans Jr., Jeremy Piven, Stacy "Fergie" Ferguson.

Marnie 🦴🦴🦴 ½ **1964** A lovely blonde with a mysterious past robs her employers and then changes her identity. When her current boss catches her in the act and forces her to marry him, he soon learns the puzzling aspects of Marnie's background. Criticized at the time of its release, the movie has since been accepted as a Hitchcock classic. **130m/C VHS, DVD.** Tippi Hedren, Sean Connery, Diane Baker, Bruce Dern, Louise Latham, Martin Gabel, Henry Beckman, Mariette Hartley, Alan Napier; *D:* Alfred Hitchcock; *W:* Jay Presson Allen; *C:* Robert Burks; *M:* Bernard Herrmann.

Maroc 7 🦴 **1967** Slow story of a secret agent after a thief suffering from a split personality. **92m/C VHS.** Gene Barry, Elsa Martinelli, Cyd Charisse, Leslie Phillips; *D:* Gerry O'Hara.

Marooned 🦴 ½ *Space Travellers* **1969 (G)** Tense thriller casts Crenna, Hackman, and Franciscus as astronauts stranded in space after a retro-rocket misfires and their craft is unable to return to earth. Amazingly inept despite an Academy Award for effects and an excellent cast. Story bears a striking resemblance to 1995's "Apollo 13." **134m/C VHS, DVD.** Gregory Peck, David Janssen, Richard Crenna, James Franciscus, Gene Hackman, Lee Grant; *D:* John Sturges; *C:* Daniel F. Fapp. Oscars '69: Visual FX.

Marooned in Iraq 🦴🦴 *The Songs of My Homeland; Avazhaye Sarzamine Madariyam* **2002** Set between 1989 and 1991, this is a road movie about family and survival. Victimized by Suddam Hussein, Iraqi Kurds fled towards the Iranian border and an uncertain future in refugee camps. One such family is led by the aged Mirza (Ebrahimi), a locally famous singer who has summoned his two sons, Barat (Mohammadi) and Audeh (Rashtiani), to accompany him back to Iraq in order to find his ex-wife, Hanareh (Ghobadi), whom he has learned is in trouble and needs him. Armed robbers steal all their possessions on their journey and they are forced to walk, eventually coming to other camps of displaced people (one has orphaned children, other contains only women). Folk music and comic bits help break up the admittedly bleak story. Kurdish with subtitles. **97m/C VHS, DVD.** *IA* Shahab Ebrahimi, Fa-eq Mohammadi, Alahmorad Rashtiani, Iran Ghobadi; *D:* Bahman Ghobadi; *W:* Bahman Ghobadi; *C:* Saed Nikzat, Shahriar Asadi; *M:* Arsalan Komkar.

Marquis 🦴🦴 **1990** A bizarre satire combining sex, lust, and the French Revolution, based on the writings of the Marquis de Sade. Amusing, decadent, and not for the prudish. In French with English subtitles. **88m/C VHS.** *FR D:* Henri Xhonneux; *W:* Henri Xhonneux, Roland Topor; *C:* Etienne Fauduet; *M:* Reinhardt Wagner; *V:* Francois Marthouret, Michel Robin, Valerie King, Isabelle Wolfe.

Marquis de Sade 🦴 ½ *Dark Prince: Intimate Tales of Marquis de Sade* **1996 (R)** Justine searches for her sister Juliette in 17th-century Paris and is drawn into the sexually deviant world of the Marquis de Sade. Also available unrated. **88m/C VHS, DVD.** Nick Mancuso, Janet Gunn, John Rhys-Davies; *D:* Gwyneth Gibby; *W:* Craig J. Nevius; *C:* Eugeny Guslinsky. **CABLE**

The Marquise of O 🦴🦴 *Die Marquise Von O* **1976 (PG)** In the early 18th century, the Russian army is invading Lombardy. The widowed Marquise (Clever) is drugged and raped by Count F (Ganz), an officer with the Russians. When the Marquise discovers she's pregnant, she forces the Count to marry her, although they separate immediately after the ceremony. Adaptation of Heinrich Von Kleist's novella. German with subtitles. **102m/C VHS, DVD.** *FR GE* Edith Clever, Bruno Ganz, Peter Luhr, Edda Seipel, Otto Sander, Ruth Drexel; *D:* Eric Rohmer; *W:* Eric Rohmer; *C:* Nestor Almendros.

The Marriage Circle 🦴🦴🦴 **1924** A pivotal silent comedy depicting the infidelity of several married couples in Vienna. Director Lubitsch's first American comedy. Remade as a musical, "One Hour With You," in 1932. Silent. **90m/B VHS, DVD.** Florence Vidor, Monte Blue, Marie Prevost, Creighton Hale, Adolphe Menjou, Harry C. (Henry) Myers, Dale Fuller; *D:* Ernst Lubitsch; *W:* Paul Bern; *C:* Charles Van Enger.

Marriage Is Alive and Well 🦴 **1980** A wedding photographer reflects on the institution of marriage from his unique perspective. **100m/C VHS.** Joe Namath, Jack Albertson, Melinda Dillon, Judd Hirsch, Susan Sullivan, Fred McCarren, Swoosie Kurtz; *D:* Russ Mayberry. **TV**

Marriage Italian Style 🦴🦴🦴 **1964** When an engaged man hears that his mistress is on her death bed, he goes to her side and, in an emotional gesture, promises to marry her if she survives. She does, and holds him to his promise. After they're married, however, she gives him a big surprise—three grown sons. A silly film, but DeSica's direction keeps it from being too fluffy. Lots of fun. Based on the play "Filumena Marturano" by Eduardo De Filippo. **102m/C VHS, DVD.** *IT* Sophia Loren, Marcello Mastroianni, Aldo Puglisi, Tecla Scarano, Marilu Tolo; *D:* Vittorio De Sica. Golden Globes '65: Foreign Film.

The Marriage of Figaro 🦴🦴 *Figaros Hochzeit* **1949** DEFA studio's lavish adaptation of Mozart's opera. Count Almaviva's valet, Figaro, plans to marry the Countess's chambermaid, Susanna. But since the Count also fancies Susanna, he keeps coming up with plans to postpone the wedding and the lovestuck duo must use their own trickery to forge ahead. German with subtitles. **109m/B VHS.** *GE* Angelika Hauff, Willi Domgraf-Fassbaender, Sabine Peters, Mathieu Ahlersmeyer; *D:* Georg Wildhagen; *W:* Georg Wildhagen; *C:* Eugen Klagemann, Karl Plintzner.

The Marriage of Maria Braun 🦴🦴🦴🦴 *Die Ehe Der Maria Braun* **1979 (R)** In post-WWII Germany, a young woman uses guile and sexuality to survive as the nation rebuilds itself into an industrial power. The first movie in Fassbinder's trilogy about German women in Germany during the post war years, it is considered one of the director's finest films, and an indispensable example of the New German Cinema. In German with English subtitles. **120m/C VHS, DVD.** *GE* Hanna Schygulla, Klaus Lowitsch, Ivan Desny, Gottfried John, Gisela Uhlen; *D:* Rainer Werner Fassbinder; *W:* Rainer Werner Fassbinder, Peter Marthesheimer, Pea Frolich; *C:* Michael Ballhaus; *M:* Peer Raben. Berlin Intl. Film Fest. '79: Actress (Schygulla).

Marriage on the Rocks 🦴🦴 **1965** Mildly amusing marital comedy finds Valerie (Kerr) bored by her 20-year marriage to Dan (Sinatra) so she decides to divorce him. The family lawyer (McGiver) persuades them to take a would-be second honeymoon to Mexico instead, which is cut short for Dan by business. Meanwhile, a mix-up with Mexican lawyer Santos (Romero) actually has the couple divorced. Then, when Dan's womanizing best buddy Ernie (Martin) shows up, he accidentally marries Valerie. More complications ensue but not much comes of all the havoc. **109m/C VHS.** Frank Sinatra, Deborah Kerr, Dean Martin, Cesar Romero, John McGiver, Hermione Baddeley, Tony Bill, Nancy Sinatra; *D:* Jack Donohue; *W:* Cy Howard; *C:* William H. Daniels; *M:* Nelson Riddle.

Married? 🦴 ½ **1926** Couple endures 365 days of marital bliss in order to inherit big bucks. Some do it for less. **65m/B VHS.** Owen Moore, Constance Bennett; *D:* George Terwilliger.

Married Life 🦴🦴🦴 **2007 (PG-13)** Set in 1949 and steeped in the style, mood, and sensibilities of the time, this is the story of Harry Allen (Cooper), a buttoned-down married man who falls in love with young and gorgeous widow Kay (McAdams). Burdened with guilt and hoping for understanding, Harry confides in his womanizing pal Richard (Brosnan), who then becomes fascinated with Kay, too. Harry's marriage to Pat (Clarkson) is functional if not entirely satisfying and Pat appears to know nothing of the affair. Harry decides to end his marriage but is so duty bound to Pat that he plans to murder her rather than subject her to the pain of a divorce (hmm, wonder if that's the option she'd pick). Several big surprises hold together this intriguing, smart drama. **90m/C DVD, Blu-ray Disc.** *US* Chris Cooper, Patricia Clarkson, Rachel McAdams, Pierce Brosnan, David Wenham; *D:* Ira Sachs; *W:* Ira Sachs, Oren Moverman; *C:* Peter Deming; *M:* Dickon Hinchliffe.

A Married Man 🦴🦴 **1984** Story focusing on a bored British lawyer who begins cheating on his wife. Amid the affair, someone gets murdered. **200m/C VHS, DVD.** *GB* Anthony Hopkins, Ciaran Madden, Lise Hilboldt, Yvonne Coulette, John Le Mesurier, Sophie Ashton; *D:* John Davies. **TV**

Married People, Single Sex 🦴🦴 ½ **1993 (R)** Three couples decide to spread their sexual wings. Shelly takes a new lover; Artie makes obscene phone calls; and Beth and Mike, who end their relationship, still can't keep out of bed. An unrated version is also available. **110m/C VHS, DVD.** Chase Masterson, Joe Pilato, Darla Haun, Shelley Michelle, Wendi Westbrook, Robert Zachar, Samuel Mongiello, Teri Thompson; *D:* Mike Sedan; *W:* Catherine Tavel.

Married People, Single Sex 2: For Better or Worse 🦴 ½ **1994 (R)** Three women are faced with sexual unhappiness: Carol's hubby had an affair, Valerie wants a baby but her spouse doesn't, and Karen's husband is just too darn nice (she wants some spice in her life). So, there's lots of sexual encounters to solve their problems. Also available unrated. **93m/C VHS.** Kathy Shower, Monique Parent, Liza Smith, Craig Stepp, Doug Jeffery; *D:* Mike Sedan.

Married to It 🦴🦴 **1993 (R)** Three vastly different couples work together to plan a pageant at a private school. The oil and water group includes struggling hippie leftovers Bridges and Channing, '80s-era corporate cutthroats Shepherd and Silver, and starry-eyed newlyweds Masterson and Leonard. Contrived plot offers few humourous moments, with the main focus revolving around coping rather than comedy. And the coping is slow business, done by characters you don't really care about with problems that don't really matter. **112m/C VHS, DVD.** Beau Bridges, Stockard Channing, Robert Sean Leonard, Mary Stuart Masterson, Cybill Shepherd, Ron Silver; *D:* Arthur Hiller; *W:* Janet Kovalcik; *M:* Henry Mancini.

Married to the Mob 🦴🦴🦴 **1988 (R)** After the murder of her husband, an attractive Mafia widow tries to escape "mob" life, but ends up fighting off amorous advances from the current mob boss while being wooed by an undercover cop. A snappy script and a spry performance by Pfeiffer pepper this easy-to-watch film. **102m/C VHS, DVD.** Michelle Pfeiffer, Dean Stockwell, Alec Baldwin, Matthew Modine, Mercedes Ruehl, Anthony J. Nici, Joan Cusack, Ellen Foley, Chris Isaak, Trey Wilson, Charles Napier, Tracey Walter, Al Lewis, Nancy Travis, David Johansen, Jonathan Demme; *D:* Jonathan Demme; *W:* Mark Burns, Barry Strugatz; *C:* Tak Fujimoto; *M:* David Byrne. N.Y. Film Critics '88: Support. Actor (Stockwell); Natl. Soc. Film Critics '88: Support. Actor (Stockwell), Support. Actress (Ruehl).

Married Too Young 🦴🦴 *I Married Too Young* **1962** High school honeys elope, despite disapproval from the parental units. When the boy groom trades his med school plans for a monkey wrench in order to support the little missus, he finds much trouble with the hot rod heavies. **76m/B VHS.** Harold Lloyd Jr., Jana Lund, Anthony Dexter, Marianna Hill, Trudy Marshall, Brian O'Hara, Nita Loveless; *D:* George Moskov; *W:* Nat Tanchuck; *C:* Ernest Haller.

The Married Virgin 🦴🦴 **1918** One of the earliest films in which Valentino appeared in a featured role prior to "The Four Horsemen of the Apocalypse" and "The Sheik." Count Roberto di Fraccini (Valentino) is a fortune hunter having an affair with Ethel Spencer McMillan (Kirkham), wife of wealthy older businessman Fiske McMillan (Jobson). After the couple unsuccessfully plot to blackmail McMillan, the Count tells his lover's daughter, Mary (Sisson), that in return for her hand in marriage (and her dowry), he will save her father from a life in prison. **71m/B DVD.** Rudolph Valentino, Kathleen Kirkham, Edward Jobson, Vera Sisson, Frank Newburg; *D:* Joe Maxwell; *W:* Hayden Talbott.

A Married Woman 🦴🦴🦴 *La Femme Mariee* **1965** Dramatizes a day in the life of a woman who has both a husband and a lover. One of Godard's more mainstream efforts. **94m/B VHS.** *FR* Macha Meril, Phillippe LeRoy, Bernard Noel; *D:* Jean-Luc Godard; *W:* Jean-Luc Godard; *C:* Raoul Coutard.

Marrionnier 🦴 *Marrionnier: Doll Horror Movie* **2005 (R)** Wigged-out Japanese horror film with a confused, convoluted plot involving a psycho stalker, his sadistically violent method of turning girls into wax dolls, and the kidnapping of his obsession so she can meet the demonic creations. Subtitled. **79m/C DVD.** *JP* Mayu, Hime, Yuriko Anjho, Masakazu Yoshida, Haruna Hoshino, Miyako Cojima, Takanori Kagami, Hideyuki Kobayashi, Hiroto Nakayama, Tetsuya Shibata, Miki Yoshida; *D:* Akira Kobayashi.

Marry Me, Marry Me 🦴🦴🦴 *Mazel Tov Ou le Mariage* **1969 (R)** While in Paris, a Jewish encyclopedia salesman falls in love with a pregnant Belgian woman. A sensitive story about European Jewish families. Berri wrote, produced, directed, and starred in this romantic comedy. **87m/C VHS.** *FR* Elisabeth Wiener, Regine, Claude Berri, Louisa Colpeyn; *D:* Claude Berri; *C:* Ghislan Cloquet.

The Marrying Kind 🦴🦴 ½ **1952** Marrieds Florence (Holliday) and Chet (Ray) Keefer are in the chambers of Judge Carroll (Kennedy) talking about why they want a divorce. They flashback to their courtship and marriage and the bumps they've endured along the way, and then realize they still love each other. Holliday reunited with Cukor and scriptwriters Gordon and Kanin after their triumph with "Born Yesterday." **92m/B VHS, DVD.** Judy Holliday, Aldo Ray, Madge Kennedy, Sheila Bond, John Alexander, Peggy Cass, Rex Williams; *D:* George Cukor; *W:* Ruth Gordon, Garson Kanin; *C:* Joseph Walker; *M:* Hugo Friedhofer.

The Marrying Man 🦴 ½ **1991 (R)** Young man meets his match when his buddies take him to Las Vegas for his bachelor party. He falls like a ton of bricks for the singer, not knowing she belongs to the local crime lord, who catches them together and forces them to marry. They immediately divorce, can't forget each other and eventually re-marry, again and again and again. Silly story supposedly based on the story of Harry Karl (eventual husband of Debbie Reynolds) and Marie MacDonald. Basinger and Baldwin's off-stage romance created quite a stir but their chemistry onscreen is zilch. Ineffective, not funny, poorly paced and acted: a good example of what happens when egotistical stars get their way. **116m/C VHS, DVD.** Alec Baldwin, Kim Basinger, Robert Loggia, Armand Assante, Elisabeth Shue, Paul Reiser, Fisher Stevens, Peter Dobson, Gretchen Wyler; ***D:*** Jerry Rees; ***W:*** Neil Simon; ***M:*** David Newman.

Mars 1/2 **1996** Fast-paced space western finds independent lawman Caution Templar (Gruner) receiving a frantic message from his brother to return to the wild mining town of Alpha City, Mars. Only by the time he arrives his brother is dead and Templar is determined to find out what happened. **92m/C VHS, DVD.** Olivier Gruner, Shari Belafonte, Scott Valentine, Amber Smith, Alex Hyde-White, Lee DeBroux, Gabriel Dell; ***D:*** Jon Hess; ***W:*** Patrick Highsmith, Steven Hartov. **VIDEO**

Mars Attacks! 1/2 **1996 (PG-13)** Only director Burton could make a movie based on a series of 1960s trading cards. Intentionally tacky, this huge scale epic spoof of monster, sci-fi, and disaster flicks finds moronic President Dale (Nicholson), his frigid wife (Close) and a cast of thousands battling the green-skinned invaders. Jack's back for a second role as Vegas hotel developer Art Land, who tries to cash in on the opportunities the invasion brings. Plot is relatively nonexistent and zig-zags wildly throughout, but the gist is that the aliens are bent on destroying the population, and have little trouble battling the bumbling humans. Brosnan is the hilariously deluded alien-hugger, Professor Kessler. A semi-lampoon of fellow alien flick competitor "Independence Day," this film goes all out for the camp laugh, but its big budget effects, way over-the-top style and all-star cast can't conquer the audience. **106m/C VHS, DVD.** Jack Black, Jack Nicholson, Glenn Close, Martin Short, Pierce Brosnan, Lukas Haas, Sarah Jessica Parker, Michael J. Fox, Natalie Portman, Rod Steiger, Paul Winfield, Annette Bening, Sylvia Sidney, Danny DeVito, Joe Don Baker, Pam Grier, Jim Brown, Lisa Marie; ***Cameos:*** Tom Jones; ***D:*** Tim Burton; ***W:*** Jonathan Gems; ***C:*** Peter Suschitzky; ***M:*** Danny Elfman.

Mars Needs Women **1966** When the Martian singles scene starts to drag, Mars boys cross the galaxy in search of fertile earth babes to help them repopulate the planet. Seems Batgirl Craig, the go-go dancing lady scientist, is at the top of their dance cards. **80m/C VHS, DVD.** Tommy Kirk, Yvonne Craig, Warren Hammack, Tony Houston, Larry Tanner, Cal Duggan; ***D:*** Larry Buchanan; ***W:*** Larry Buchanan; ***C:*** Robert C. Jessup.

Marshal Law **1996 (R)** Highland Glen is a gated community in L.A. that seems very secure, especially to ex-Texas Marshal Jack Coleman (Smits) and his family. But an earthquake leaves the neighborhood prey to a vicious gang unless Coleman can find a way to outwit them. **96m/C VHS.** Jimmy Smits, James LeGros, Vonte Sweet, Scott Plank, Kristy Swanson, Channon Roe, Michael Cavalieri, Rodriey Rowland, Tai Thai; ***D:*** Stephen Cornwell; ***W:*** Stephen Cornwell, Nick Gregory; ***C:*** Levie Isaacks; ***M:*** Tim Truman.

Marshal of Cedar Rock **1953** Marshal Rocky Lane sets a prisoner free, thinking the guy will lead him to a stash of stolen bank funds. Seems he miscalculates, but by way of consolation, he routs a rotten railroad agent who's rooking innocent people. Features the equine talent of Black Jack. **54m/B VHS, DVD.** Allan "Rocky" Lane, Phyllis Coates, Roy Barcroft, William Henry, Robert Shayne, Eddy (Eddie, Ed) Waller; ***D:*** Harry Keller; ***W:*** Albert DeMond.

Marshal of Heldorado **1950** An outlaw-infested town needs an injection of law and order. **53m/B VHS.** James Ellison, Russell Hayden, Raymond Hatton, Fuzzy Knight; ***D:*** Thomas Carr.

The Marshal's Daughter 1/2 **1953** A father and daughter team up to outwit an outlaw. Features many cowboy songs, including the title track by Tex Ritter. **71m/B VHS.** Tex Ritter, Ken Murray, Laurie Anders, Preston Foster, Hoot Gibson; ***D:*** William Berke.

Martha and I **1991** In 1934 Czechoslovakia, distinguished Jewish doctor Ernest Paul Fuchs (Piccoli), having divorced his unfaithful wife, impulsively marries his lower-class gentile German maid Martha (Sagebrecht). What turns out to be a true love match is witnessed through the adolescent eyes of nephew Emil (Chalupa), who comes to live with the couple. With the rise of Nazism and increased Jewish persecution the devoted Martha begins to fear for her husband and makes a futile attempt to find a safe haven. Stirring drama based on the director's childhood (he's the semi-fictionalized Emil). German with subtitles. **107m/C VHS.** *GE* Marianne Saegebrecht, Michel Piccoli, Vaclov Chalupa, Ondrej Vetchy; ***D:*** Jiri Weiss; ***W:*** Jiri Weiss; ***C:*** Viktor Ruzicka; ***M:*** Jiri Stivin.

Martial Law 1/2 **1990 (R)** A film solely for martial arts fans. Two cops use their hands, feet, and other body parts to fight crime. **90m/C VHS.** Chad McQueen, Cynthia Rothrock, David Carradine, Andy McCutcheon; ***D:*** S.E. Cohen; ***W:*** Richard Brandes.

Martial Law 2: Undercover 1/2 **1991 (R)** Two cops, martial arts experts and part of an elite police force called Martial Law, go undercover to investigate the murder of a colleague. They uncover a fast-growing crime ring headed by a bad cop and a nightclub owner. The nightclub is host to the city's rich and powerful, who are treated to a bevy of beautiful women, protected by martial arts experts, and entertained by martial arts fights to the death. Lots of high-kicking action. **92m/C VHS.** Jeff Wincott, Cynthia Rothrock, Paul Johansson, Evan Lurie, L. Charles Taylor, Sherrie Rose, Billy Drago; ***D:*** Kurt Anderson; ***W:*** Richard Brandes, Jiles Fitzgerald.

Martial Outlaw **1993 (R)** DEA man Kevin White (Wincott) has been following a drug-dealing ex-KGB kingpin from Moscow to San Francisco. The Russian's latest move takes him to Los Angeles where Kevin meets up with his older brother Jack (Hudson), a maverick LA cop. Jack persuades Kevin to let him in on the action but Kevin begins to suspect Jack is playing both sides and their sibling rivalry could lead to death. **89m/C VHS.** Jeff Wincott, Gary Hudson, Richard Jaeckel, Krista Errickson, Vladimir Skomarovsky, Liliana Komorowska, Gary Wood; ***D:*** Kurt Anderson; ***W:*** Thomas Ritz, John Bryant.

Martian Child 1/2 **2007 (PG)** Who better to adopt orphan Dennis (Coleman), who believes he is from Mars, than a successful science fiction writer? A two-year widower, David (Cusack) lives a relatively lonely life with his dog, a frenetic agent who's on his back to write the sequel to his successful novel, the cute friend (Peet) of his dead wife, and his harried sister (real-life sibling Joan Cusack). David and his wife were about to adopt a child when she died; although David's now certain that the timing is wrong, he's drawn to Dennis, the kid at the orphanage who lives in a cardboard box. The mild tale of love and patience and identity never packs much of a punch, but this suitable-for-the-entire-family film is relatively charming and generally unoffending. **106m/C DVD.** *US* John Cusack, Bobby Coleman, Amanda Peet, Sophie Okonedo, Oliver Platt, Joan Cusack, Anjelica Huston; ***D:*** Menno Meyjes; ***W:*** Seth Bass, Jonathan Tolins; ***C:*** Robert Yeoman; ***M:*** Aaron Zigman.

The Martian Chronicles: Part 1 **1979** Series episode "The Explorers." Adapted from Ray Bradbury's critically acclaimed novel. Futuristic explorations of the planet Mars. Strange fates of the discovery teams make everything more curious. **120m/C VHS, DVD.** Rock Hudson, Bernie Casey, Nicholas Hammond, Darren McGavin; ***D:*** Michael Anderson Sr. **TV**

The Martian Chronicles: Part 2 1/2 **1979** Episode following the television movie. This part is called "The Settlers." The planet Mars meets with its first colonization and the settlers watch the Earth explode. **97m/C VHS, DVD.** Rock Hudson, Fritz Weaver, Roddy McDowall, Bernie Casey, Darren McGavin, Gayle Hunnicutt, Barry Morse, Bernadette Peters; ***D:*** Michael Anderson Sr. **TV**

The Martian Chronicles: Part 3 1/2 **1979** In the final chapter of this space saga, the Martian's secrets become known and will forever change man's destiny. Adapted from Ray Bradbury's classic novel. **97m/C VHS, DVD.** Rock Hudson, Bernadette Peters, Christopher Connelly, Fritz Weaver, Roddy McDowall, Bernie Casey, Nicholas Hammond, Darren McGavin, Gayle Hunnicutt, Barry Morse; ***D:*** Michael Anderson Sr. **TV**

Martians Go Home! 1/2 **1990 (PG-13)** Joke-loving Martians come to earth and pester a nerdy composer. **89m/C VHS.** Randy Quaid, Margaret Colin, Anita Morris, John Philbin, Ronny Cox, Gerrit Graham, Barry Sobel, Vic Dunlop; ***D:*** David Odell.

Martin **1977 (R)** Martin is a charming young man, though slightly mad. He freely admits the need to drink blood. Contemporary vampire has found a new abhorrent means of killing his victims. **96m/C VHS, DVD.** John Amplas, Lincoln Maazel, Christine Forrest, Elayne Nadeau, Tom Savini, Sarah Venable, George A. Romero, Fran Middleton; ***D:*** George A. Romero; ***W:*** George A. Romero; ***C:*** Michael Gornick; ***M:*** Donald Rubinstein.

Martin Chuzzlewit 1/2 **1994** Martin Chuzzlewit (Scofield) is a rich and elderly man with a lot of greedy relatives just waiting for him to die so they can get their hands on his money. The only exceptions being his already disinherited namesake grandson and his young orphaned nurse, Mary Graham. Adapted from the Charles Dickens novel. On three cassettes. **288m/C VHS, DVD.** Paul Scofield, John Mills, Pete Postlethwaite, Tom Wilkinson, Julia Sawalha, David Bradley; ***D:*** Pedr James. **TV**

Martin (Hache) **1997** "Hache" means Junior, and 19-year-old Martin is named after his estranged film director father. When the teenager accidentally overdoses after a bad break-up, his remarried mother insists her ex finally take responsibility and sends Martin to live with his dad in Madrid. Alicia, his dad's lover, and flamboyant best friend Dante try to make the boy feel welcome, but Martin Sr. is not doing his part. Spanish with subtitles. **123m/C DVD.** *AR SP* Federico Luppi, Juan Diego Botto, Cecilia (Celia) Roth, Eusebio Poncela; ***D:*** Adolfo Aristarain; ***W:*** Adolfo Aristarain, Kathy Saavedra; ***C:*** Porfirio Enriquez; ***M:*** Fito Paez.

Martin Luther 1/2 **1953** French-made biography of the 16th century reformer who began the Protestant Reformation. **105m/B VHS, DVD.** *FR* Niall MacGinnis, John Ruddock, Pierre Leeavre, Guy Verney; ***D:*** Irving Pichel; ***W:*** Allan Sloane, Lothar Wolff; ***C:*** Joseph Brun; ***M:*** Mark Lothar.

Martin's Day **1985 (PG)** An unusual friendship develops between an escaped convict and the young boy he kidnaps. **99m/C VHS.** *CA* Richard Harris, Lindsay Wagner, James Coburn, Justin Henry, Karen Black, John Ireland; ***D:*** Alan Gibson; ***W:*** Chris Bryant, Allan Scott.

Marty 1/2 **1955** Marty is a painfully shy bachelor who feels trapped in a pointless life of family squabbles. When he finds love, he also finds the strength to break out of what he feels is a meaningless existence. A sensitive and poignant film from the writer of "Altered States." Remake of a TV version that originally aired in 1953. Notable for Borgnine's sensitive portrayal, one of his last quality jobs before sinking into the B-movie sludge pit. **91m/B VHS, DVD.** Ernest Borgnine, Betsy Blair, Joe Mantell, Esther Minciotti, Jerry Paris, Karen Steele, Augusta Ciolli, Frank Sutton, Walter Kelley, Robin Morse; ***D:*** Delbert Mann; ***W:*** Paddy Chayefsky; ***C:*** Joseph LaShelle; ***M:*** Roy Webb, Harry Warren. Oscars '55: Actor (Borgnine), Director (Mann), Picture, Screenplay; British Acad. '55: Actor (Borgnine), Actress (Blair); Directors Guild '55: Director (Mann); Golden Globes '56: Actor—Drama (Borgnine); Natl. Bd. of Review '55: Actor (Borgnine), Natl. Film Reg. '94;; N.Y. Film Critics '55: Actor (Borgnine), Film.

Marvin & Tige 1/2 **1984 (PG)** A deep friendship develops between an aging alcoholic and a street-wise 11-year-old boy after they meet one night in an Atlanta park. **104m/C VHS.** John Cassavetes, Gibran Brown, Billy Dee Williams, Fay Hauser, Denise Nicholas-Hill; ***D:*** Eric Weston; ***W:*** Eric Weston, Wanda Dell.

Marvin's Room 1/2 **1996 (PG-13)** Guaranteed sobfest with a gifted set of performers. Sensitive spinster Bessie (Keaton) is living in Orlando where she's been caring for her bedridden father, Marvin (Cronyn), who's been dying for the last 20 years, and her eccentric aunt Ruth (Verdon). When she's stricken with leukemia and needs a bone marrow donor, Bessie must rely on tough, estranged sister Lee (Streep) to help out. But divorcee Lee's got her hands full with rebellious teenaged son Hank (DiCaprio) and his geeky younger bro Charlie (Scardino) and is none too eager to renew the family ties. Based on Scott McPherson's 1991 Off-Broadway play. **98m/C VHS, DVD.** Diane Keaton, Meryl Streep, Leonardo DiCaprio, Hume Cronyn, Gwen Verdon, Hal Scardino, Robert De Niro, Dan Hedaya, Margo Martindale, Cynthia Nixon; ***D:*** Jerry Zaks; ***W:*** Scott McPherson; ***C:*** Piotr Sobocinski; ***M:*** Rachel Portman.

The Marx Brothers in a Nutshell 1/2 **1990** A tribute to the Marx Brothers, narrated by Gene Kelly. Contains clips from "Duck Soup," "Horse Feathers," "Animal Crackers," "Cocoanuts," and "Room Service." Also contains rare outtakes and interviews with the brothers, plus guest appearances by Dick Cavett, Robert Klein, David Steinberg, and others. Indispensable. **100m/B VHS.** Groucho Marx, Chico Marx, Harpo Marx, Zeppo Marx, Robert Klein, David Steinberg, George Fenneman, Dick Cavett; ***D:*** Richard Patterson; ***W:*** Joseph Adamson; ***Nar:*** Gene Kelly.

Mary and Joseph: A Story of Faith 1/2 **1979** A speculative look at the experiences and courtship of Mary and Joseph before the birth of Jesus. **100m/C VHS.** Blanche Baker, Jeff East, Colleen Dewhurst, Stephen McHattie, Lloyd Bochner, Paul Hecht; ***D:*** Eric Till. **TV**

Mary and Max 1/2 **2009** Claymation feature from Australia about a couple of pen pals. Mary (Collette) lives in Melbourne; an unloved, lonely child, she randomly picks a name from a New York phone book, writes a letter, and receives a reply from elderly Jewish Max (Hoffman). They bond over their mutual love of candy and their dismal social status (and way too many scatological references). The two remain friends as Max eventually reveals his emotional problems while Mary outgrows her awkwardness. The story becomes repetitive although the detailed visuals hold the eye. **92m/C DVD.** *AU* Toni Collette, Philip Seymour Hoffman, Eric Bana, Barry Humphries; ***C:*** Gerald Thompson; ***Nar:*** Barry Humphries.

Mary, Mary **1963** Overlong comedy (with quippy dialogue) based on the play by Jean Kerr. Separated and finalizing divorce details, New York publisher Bob (Reynolds) is in trouble with the IRS and has to ask his nearly-ex wife Mary (Reynolds) to help him explain some expenses. Bob is already seeing Tiffany (McBain) and when the two go out of town, Mary winds up staying at Bob's apartment where his actor friend Dirk (Rennie) makes a play for her. Bob's unexpected return leads to surprising results. **126m/C DVD.** Debbie Reynolds, Barry Nelson, Diane McBain, Michael Rennie, Hiram Sherman; ***D:*** Mervyn LeRoy; ***W:*** Richard L. Breen; ***C:*** Harry Stradling Sr.; ***M:*** Frank Perkins.

Mary, Mary, Bloody Mary **1976 (R)** Young beautiful artist ravages Mexico with her penchant for drinking blood. Turns out she's a bisexual vampire. When even her friends become victims, her father steps in to end the bloodbath. **85m/C VHS, DVD.** Christina Ferrare, David Young, Helena Rojo, John Carradine; ***D:*** Juan Lopez Moctezuma; ***W:*** Malcolm Marmorstein; ***M:*** Tom Bahler.

Mary, Mother of Jesus 1/2 **1999** The life of Jesus (Bale) is retold through the eyes of his mother (August), as her faith is tested by her son's ultimate sacrifice. The production stays close to the Biblical scripts of Matthew, Mark, Luke, and John and the characters are pretty much reverential cardboard. **94m/C VHS, DVD.** Christian Bale, Pernilla August, Geraldine Chaplin, David Threlfall,

Hywel Bennett, Christopher Lawford; *D:* Kevin Connor; *W:* Albert Ross; *C:* Elemer Ragalyi; *M:* Mario Klemens. **TV**

Mary, My Dearest *Maria di Mi Corazon* **1983** Maria (Rojo) persuades her smalltime crook boyfriend Hector (Bonilla) to join her in a traveling magic show. When the van breaks down while they're touring, Maria goes in search of a telephone and winds up in a mental institution. Mixture of styles—from an everyday look at the bourgeoise to magic realism and terror—may confuse. Spanish with subtitles. **100m/C VHS.** *MX* Maria Rojo, Hector Bonilla, Salvador Sanchez; *D:* Jaime Humberto Hermosillo; *W:* Gabriel Garcia Marquez, Jaime Humberto Hermosillo; *C:* Angel Goded; *M:* Joaquin Gutierrez Heras.

Mary of Scotland **1936** The historical tragedy of Mary, Queen of Scots and her cousin, Queen Elizabeth I of England is enacted in this classic film. Traces Mary's claims to the throne of England which ultimately led to her execution. Based on the Maxwell Anderson play. **123m/B VHS, DVD.** Katharine Hepburn, Fredric March, Florence Eldridge, Douglas Walton, John Carradine, Robert Barrat, Gavin Muir, Ian Keith, Moroni Olsen, William Stack, Alan Mowbray; *D:* John Ford.

Mary Poppins ½ **1964** Magical English nanny arrives one day on the East Wind and takes over the household of a very proper London banker. She introduces her two charges to her friends and family, including Bert, the chimney sweep (Van Dyke), and eccentric Uncle Albert (Wynn). She also changes the lives of everyone in the family. From her they learn that life can always be happy and joyous if you take the proper perspective. Film debut of Andrews. Based on the books by P.L. Travers. A Disney classic that hasn't lost any of its magic. Look for the wonderful sequence where Van Dyke dances with animated penguins. ♫ Chim Chim Cheree; A Spoonful of Sugar; The Perfect Nanny; Sister Suffragette; The Life I Lead; Stay Awake; Feed the Birds; Fidelity Feduciary Bank; Let's Go Fly a Kite. **139m/C VHS, DVD.** Julie Andrews, Dick Van Dyke, Ed Wynn, Hermione Baddeley, David Tomlinson, Glynis Johns, Karen Dotrice, Matthew Garber; *D:* Robert Stevenson; *W:* Bill Walsh, Whip Wilson; *C:* Edward Colman; *M:* Richard M. Sherman, Robert B. Sherman. Oscars '64: Actress (Andrews), Film Editing, Song ("Chim Chim Cher-ee"), Visual FX, Orig. Score; Golden Globes '65: Actress—Mus./Comedy (Andrews).

Mary, Queen of Scots ½ **1971 (PG-13)** Redgrave does a spirited job in the title role as the headstrong and romantic queen who came to an unfortunate end. Mary is raised in France by her mother's Catholic family, from whom she inherits the Scottish title after her mother's death. She claims the throne much to the dismay of her Protestant half-brother James Stuart (McGoohan) and England's equally Protestant Queen Elizabeth (Jackson), who does not want her own Catholic subjects to get any ideas. Mary makes two unfortunate marriages and winds up being betrayed, eventually forcing Elizabeth to eliminate her dangerous cousin. **128m/C VHS.** Vanessa Redgrave, Glenda Jackson, Patrick McGoohan, Timothy Dalton, Nigel Davenport, Trevor Howard, Daniel Massey, Ian Holm; *D:* Charles Jarrott; *W:* John Hale; *C:* Christopher Challis; *M:* John Barry.

Mary Reilly **1995 (R)** Mary (Roberts) is an innocent maid whose employer happens to be the infamous Dr. Jekyll (Malkovich). They both seem to be employed by Dr. Freud in this dank, dreary psychosexual thriller. Mary is torn between the repressed affection of the doctor and the oily sexuality of his alter ego, who conjures up images of her abusive father. Reuniting the crew and some of the cast of "Dangerous Liaisons" (Glenn Close also appears as a bawdy brothel owner), they fail to reach their previous heights. Most of the gloomy sets will make you wish you were wearing galoshes. Release date was bumped several times as the ending of the film was reshot (more than once). Based on the novel by Valerie Martin. **108m/C VHS, DVD.** Julia Roberts, John Malkovich, George Cole, Michael Gambon, Kathy Staff, Glenn Close, Michael Sheen, Bronagh Gallagher, Linda Bassett, Henry Goodman, Ciaran Hinds, Sasha Hanav, David Ross; *D:* Stephen Frears; *W:* Christopher Hampton; *C:* Philippe Rousselot; *M:* George Fenton.

Mary Shelley's Frankenstein ½ *Frankenstein* **1994 (R)** Branagh turns from Shakespeare to another form of literary classic with his operatic (and loose) adaptation of the Shelley novel. He also plays Victor, the overwrought medical student who decides that death can be vanquished and sets out to prove his theories by making a man. De Niro is sufficiently grisly (though lacking in pathos) as the reanimated corpse with Bonham Carter alternately suffering and excitable as Victor's fiancee Elizabeth. Visually arresting—particularly the Creature's birth scene—pic doesn't engender audience sympathy for the characters' trials and final fates. **123m/C VHS, DVD.** Kenneth Branagh, Robert De Niro, Helena Bonham Carter, Tom Hulce, Aidan Quinn, John Cleese, Ian Holm, Richard Briers, Robert Hardy, Cherie Lunghi, Celia Imrie, Trevyn McDowell; *D:* Kenneth Branagh; *W:* Frank Darabont, Steph Lady; *C:* Roger Pratt; *M:* Patrick Doyle.

Mary White **1977** The true story of Mary White, the 16-year-old daughter of a newspaper editor who rejects her life of wealth and sets out to find her own identity. **102m/C VHS, DVD.** Ed Flanders, Kathleen Beller, Tim Matheson, Donald Moffat, Fionnula Flanagan; *D:* Jud Taylor; *C:* Bill Butler.

Maryam ½ **2000** High school senior Maryam (Parris) considers herself a typical New Jersey teen, circa 1979. She doesn't think much about her Iranian or Muslim heritage and works her way around some of her father's cultural strictures. But then the Iran hostage crisis provokes knee-jerk hostility from her classmates and Maryam's fundamentalist cousin Ali (Ackert) arrives from Tehran to pursue his college studies. Maryam's father feels compelled to take in the orphaned Ali for unhappy family reasons Maryam is only learning. Ali causes tensions to rise within while Maryam and her family also try to cope with the tensions they experience in their community as the hostage crisis continues. **90m/C VHS, DVD.** Mariam Parris, David Ackert, Shaun Toub, Shohreh Aghdashloo; *D:* Ramin Serry; *W:* Ramin Serry; *C:* Harlan Bosmajian; *M:* Ahrin Mishram.

Masada **1981** Based on Ernest K. Gann's novel "The Antagonists," this dramatization re-creates the 1st-century A.D. Roman siege of the fortress Masada, headquarters for a group of Jewish freedom fighters. Abridged from the original TV presentation. **131m/C VHS.** Peter O'Toole, Peter Strauss, Barbara Carrera, Anthony Quayle, Giulia Pagano, David Warner; *D:* Boris Sagal; *M:* Jerry Goldsmith.

Masala **1991** An experiment in a variety of genres, including glitzy musical-comedy numbers, erotic fantasy sequences, and all manner of kitsch. Krishna (who both stars and directs in his feature film debut) is a violence-prone, ex-junkie still trying to recover from the deaths of his family in a plane crash as they travelled from their home in Toronto to a vacation in India. Jaffrey has multi-roles as Krishna's unscrupulous uncle and cousin as well as the blue-skinned Indian deity, Lord Krishna, who appears to an Indian grandmother on her TV set. Multicultural confusion. **105m/C VHS, DVD.** *CA* Srinivas Krishna, Saeed Jaffrey, Zohra Sehgal, Sakina Jaffrey; *D:* Srinivas Krishna; *W:* Srinivas Krishna.

Mascara **1987 (R)** A group inspecting a transvestite's death are led into the seedy underground world of Belgian nightlife. **99m/C VHS.** *BE* Derek de Lint, Charlotte Rampling, Michael Sarrazin; *D:* Patrick Conrad.

Masculine Feminine ½ *Masculin Feminin* **1966** A young Parisian just out of the Army engages in some anarchistic activities when he has an affair with a radical woman singer. Hailed as one of the best French New Wave films. In French with English subtitles. **103m/B VHS, DVD.** *FR* Jean-Pierre Leaud, Chantal Goya, Marlene Jobert; *D:* Jean-Luc Godard. Berlin Intl. Film Fest. '66: Actor (Leaud).

M*A*S*H **1970 (R)** Hilarious, irreverent, and well-cast black comedy about a group of surgeons and nurses at a Mobile Army Surgical Hospital in Korea. The horror of war is set in counterpoint to their need to create havoc with episodic late-night parties, practical jokes, and sexual antics. An all-out anti-war festival, highlighted by scenes that starkly uncover the chaos and irony of war, and establish Altman's influential style. Watch for real-life football players Fran Tarkenton, Ben Davidson, and Buck Buchanan in the game. Loosely adapted from the novel by the pseudonymous Richard Hooker (Dr. H. Richard Hornberger and William Heinz). Subsequent hit TV series moved even further from the source novel. **116m/C VHS, DVD.** Carl Gottlieb, Donald Sutherland, Elliott Gould, Tom Skerritt, Sally Kellerman, JoAnn Pflug, Robert Duvall, Rene Auberjonois, Roger Bowen, Gary Burghoff, Fred Williamson, John Schuck, Bud Cort, G(eorge) Wood, David Arkin, Michael Murphy, Indus Arthur, Ken Prymus, Bobby Troup, Kim Atwood, Timothy Brown; *D:* Robert Altman; *W:* Ring Lardner Jr.; *C:* Harold E. Stine; *M:* Johnny Mandel; *V:* Sal Viscuso. Oscars '70: Adapt. Screenplay; AFI '98: Top 100; Cannes '70: Film; Golden Globes '71: Film—Mus./Comedy, Natl. Film Reg. '96;; Natl. Soc. Film Critics '70: Film; Writers Guild '70: Adapt. Screenplay.

M*A*S*H: Goodbye, Farewell & Amen ½ **1983** The final two-hour special episode of the TV series "M*A*S*H" follows Hawkeye, B.J., Colonel Potter, Charles, Margaret, Klinger, Father Mulcahy, and the rest of the men and women of the 4077th through the last days of the Korean War, the declaration of peace, the dismantling of the camp, and the fond and tearful farewells. **120m/C VHS.** Alan Alda, Mike Farrell, Harry (Henry) Morgan, David Ogden Stiers, Loretta Swit, Jamie Farr, William (Bill) Christopher, Allan Arbus, G.W. Bailey, Rosalind Chao; *D:* Alan Alda; *W:* Alan Alda. **TV**

The Mask *Eyes of Hell; The Spooky Movie Show* **1961** A deservedly obscure gory horror film about a masked killer, filmed mostly in 3-D. With special 3-D packaging and limited edition 3-D glasses. **85m/B VHS.** *CA* Paul Stevens, Claudette Nevins, Bill Walker, Anne Collings, Martin Lavut, Leo Leyden, Bill Bryden, Eleanor Beecroft, Steven Appleby; *D:* Julian Roffman; *W:* Slavko Vorkapich, Franklin Delessert, Sandy Haver, Frank Taubes; *C:* Herbert S. Alpert; *M:* Louis Applebaum.

Mask **1985 (PG-13)** A dramatization of the true story of a young boy afflicted with craniodiaphyseal dysplasia (elephantiasis). The boy overcomes his appearance and revels in the joys of life in the California bikers' community. Well acted, particularly the performances of Stoltz and Cher. A touching film, well-directed by Bogdanovich, that only occasionally slips into maudlin territory. **120m/C VHS, DVD.** Cher, Sam Elliott, Eric Stoltz, Estelle Getty, Richard Dysart, Laura Dern, Harry Carey Jr., Lawrence Monoson, Marsha Warfield, Barry Tubb, Andrew (Andy) Robinson, Alexandra Powers; *D:* Peter Bogdanovich; *W:* Anna Hamilton Phelan; *C:* Laszlo Kovacs. Oscars '85: Makeup; Cannes '85: Actress (Cher).

The Mask **1994 (PG-13)** Adolescent supernatural comedy with lollapalooza special effects is Carrey's follow-up to "Ace Ventura." Mild-mannered bank clerk Carrey discovers an ancient mask that has supernatural powers. Upon putting on the mask, he turns into one truly animated guy. He falls for a dame mixed up with gangsters and from there on, our hero deals not only with the incredible powers of the mask, but with hormones and bad guys as well. Based on the Dark Horse comic book series and originally conceived as a horror flick, director Russell, who gave Freddy Krueger a sense of humor, recast this one as a hellzapoppin' cartoon-action black comedy. Carrey's rubber face is an asset magnified by the breakthrough special effects courtesy of Industrial Light and Magic. **100m/C VHS, DVD.** Jim Carrey, Cameron Diaz, Peter Greene, Peter Riegert, Amy Yasbeck, Orestes Matacena, Richard Jeni, Ben Stein; *D:* Chuck Russell; *W:* Mike Werb; *C:* John R. Leonetti; *M:* Randy Edelman. Blockbuster '95: Comedy Actor, T. (Carrey), Female Newcomer, T. (Diaz); Blockbuster '96: Comedy Actor, V. (Carrey).

Mask of Death **1997 (R)** Detective Dan McKenna's (Lamas) wife is killed by Frank Dallio (Dunn) during the criminal's escape from the FBI and he's shot in the face by Dallio's buddy Mason, who happens to be a ringer for McKenna and conveniently dies in a car crash. Since the FBI want Dallio, Agent Jeffries (Williams) persuades McKenna to pose as Mason, which he does in order to get revenge. **125m/C VHS, DVD.** Lorenzo Lamas, Billy Dee Williams, Rae Dawn Chong, Conrad Dunn; *D:* David Mitchell; *C:* David Pelletier; *M:* Norman Orenstein.

The Mask of Diijon ½ **1946** A mad magician suspects that his wife is cheating on him and tries to hypnotize her into killing her supposed paramour. Von Stroheim's performance makes it worthwhile. **73m/B VHS, DVD.** Erich von Stroheim, Jeanne Bates, William Wright, Edward Van Sloan, Denise Vernac; *D:* Lew Landers; *W:* Griffin Jay, Arthur St. Claire; *C:* Jack Greenhalgh; *M:* Lee Zahler.

The Mask of Dimitrios **1944** Dutch mystery writer Leyden (Lorre) is vacationing in Instanbul, where he meets a fan, Col. Haki (Katch), at a party. Haki, the head of the secret police, informs Leyden that the body of arch criminal Dimitrios Makropoulous (Scott) has washed ashore and the man was stabbed to death. Leyden decides to write a novel about the criminal and delves into a dark world of intrigue and danger. Adapted from Eric Ambler's novel "A Coffin for Dimitrios." **96m/B VHS.** Peter Lorre, Kurt Katch, Zachary Scott, Sydney Greenstreet, Faye Emerson, George Tobias, Victor Francen, Steven Geray, Florence Bates, Eduardo Ciannelli, George Metaxa, Monte Blue; *D:* Jean Negulesco; *W:* Frank Gruber; *C:* Arthur Edeson; *M:* Adolph Deutsch.

The Mask of Fu Manchu ½ **1932** The evil Dr. Fu Manchu and his equally evil daughter set out to capture the scimitar and golden mask of Genghis Khan. With them, they will be able to destroy all white men and rule the world. Although a detective from Scotland Yard tries to stop them, the pair obtain the treasures and begin sadistically torturing their victims to death. Can they be stopped before they destroy the earth? One of the creepiest entries in the Fu Manchu series, and Loy's last oriental role. Based on the novel by Sam Rohmer. **72m/B VHS.** Boris Karloff, Lewis Stone, Karen Morley, Charles Starrett, Myrna Loy, Jean Hersholt, Lawrence Grant, David Torrence; *D:* Charles Brabin; *C:* Gaetano Antonio "Tony" Gaudio.

Mask of the Dragon **1951** A soldier's friend and girlfriend track down his killer after he delivers a golden curio to a shop in Los Angeles. **54m/B VHS, DVD.** Richard Travis, Sheila Ryan, Richard Emory, Jack Reitzen, Sid Melton, Michael Whalen, Lyle Talbot; *W:* Orville H. Hampton; *C:* Jack Greenhalgh.

The Mask of Zorro *Zorro* **1998 (PG-13)** The dashing masked swordsman, who first made an appearance in a 1919 newspaper comic, returns to the big screen. Aging Zorro (Hopkins) escapes from 20 years in prison when he discovers his mortal enemy Montero (Wilson) is looking to establish an independent republic of California. But he needs some help and picks bandit Alejandro (Banderas), who needs a lot of training. Caught in the middle is Elena (Zeta Jones), a spirited beauty who was raised by Montero (Wilson) and doesn't know she's really Zorro's daughter. She wields quite a mean sword herself as Alejandro learns before any romancing can begin. A little long but offering swashbuckling fun. **136m/C VHS, DVD, UMD.** Antonio Banderas, Anthony Hopkins, Catherine Zeta-Jones, Stuart Wilson, Matt Letscher, Maury Chaykin, Tony Amendola, Pedro Armendariz Jr., L.Q. Jones; *D:* Martin Campbell; *W:* Ted Elliott, Terry Rossio, John Eskow; *C:* Phil Meheux; *M:* James Horner.

Masked and Anonymous **2003 (PG-13)** For hard-core Dylan fans only. He may be the only reason to see this one. The abundant, muddled meanderings about fame, life, politics and the like sure aren't. Co-written and starring the enigmatic folk legend, the tenuous threads of a plot have Dylan as a has-been musical legend who's been sprung from jail by rock promoter Uncle Sweetheart (Goodman) and partner Nina Veronica (Lange) for a dubious benefit concert in a post-revolutionary, America-like country. Dylan is then given a chance to croon, and his "Dixie" alone may be enough to satisfy fans. A host of big-names drop in for walk-ons and seeming improv performances. **113m/C VHS, DVD.** *US GB* Bob Dylan, Jeff Bridges, Penelope Cruz, John Goodman, Jessica

Lange, Luke Wilson, Angela Bassett, Bruce Dern, Ed Harris; *D:* Larry Charles; *W:* Rene Fontaine, Sergei Perov; *C:* Rogier Stoffers; *M:* Bob Dylan.

The Masked Marvel 🦴🦴 *Sakima and the Masked Marvel* **1943** The Masked Marvel saves America's war industries from sabotage. Serial in 12 episodes. **195m/B VHS.** William Forrest, Louise Currie, Johnny Arthur; *D:* Spencer Gordon Bennet.

The Masked Rider 🦴🦴 ½ **1941** Drifters Brown and Knight head south of the border and find themselves trying to solve crimes committed by a mysterious masked rider. Latin American dancers and singers provide a nice change of pace from the usual cowpoke musical relief. Based on a story by Sam Robins. **57m/B VHS.** Johnny Mack Brown, Fuzzy Knight, Nell O'Day, Grant Withers; *D:* Ford Beebe; *W:* Sherman Lowe, Victor McLeod.

Masked Rider—The First 🦴🦴 *Kamen Rider First; Kamen Raida: The First* **2005** Next to Godzilla, Ultraman, and possibly Astro Boy, few old school Japanese fantasy series are as immediately recognizable to longtime fans as Kamen Rider. It started as a manga, then became several television live action series, and even had a movie or two. This attempted reboot falls a little flat, and keeps only some of the original story. Takeshi Hongo (Kikawada) is turned into a monstrous bug-eyed cyborg by the terrorist organization Shocker, but escapes before his brainwashing can commence and uses his newfound powers to hunt them down. **90m/C DVD.** *JP* Masaya Kikawada, Hassei Takano, Rena Komine, Hiroshi Miyauchi, Eisei Amamoto; *D:* Takao Ngaishi; *W:* Toshiki Inoue, Shotaro Ishinomori; *C:* Kazunari Tanaka; *M:* Goro Yasukawa.

Masks of Death 🦴🦴 **1986** New adventure for Sherlock Holmes, as he is pulled from retirement to find the murderer of three unidentified corpses found in London's East End. **80m/C VHS.** Peter Cushing, John Mills, Anne Baxter, Ray Milland; *D:* Roy Ward Baker.

Maslin Beach **WOOF!** **1997** Hmmm, if this flick was intended as some sort of romantic comedy, it failed. Of course, probably having a coherent script and a cast who could do more than appear comfortable nude (or in minimal beach attire) would have helped too. Yep, the titular beach is a real nudist beach in South Australia where these characters bare their bodies as they look for love or sex or friendship or something. The Hound hopes they used lots of sunscreen. **80m/C VHS, DVD.** *AU* Garry Waddell, Bonnie-Jaye Lawrence, Michael Allen, Eliza Lovell; *D:* Wayne Groom; *W:* Wayne Groom; *C:* Rodney Bolton; *M:* Robert Kral.

Mason of the Mounted 🦴🦴 **1932** Harmless enough western in which a Canadian Mountie tracks down a murderer in the U.S. **58m/B VHS.** Bill Cody, Nancy Drexel, Art Mix, Nelson McDowell; *D:* Harry Fraser.

Masque of the Red Death 🦴🦴🦴 **1965** An integral selection in the famous Edgar Allan Poe/Roger Corman canon, it deals with an evil prince who traffics with the devil and playfully murders any of his subjects not already dead of the plague. Remade in 1989 with Corman as producer. **88m/C VHS, DVD.** *GB* Vincent Price, Hazel Court, Jane Asher, Patrick Magee, David Weston, Nigel Green, Julian Burton, Skip Martin, Gaye Brown, John Westbrook; *D:* Roger Corman; *W:* Charles Beaumont, Robert W(right) Campbell; *C:* Nicolas Roeg; *M:* David Lee.

Masque of the Red Death 🦴🦴 **1989 (R)** Roger Corman's second attempt at Edgar Allan Poe's horror tale pales compared to his Vincent Price version made 25 years earlier. Under-aged cast adds youth appeal but subtracts credibility from the fable of a sadistic prince and his sycophants trying to ignore the plague outside castle walls. Only late in the plot does veteran actor Macnee add proper note of doom. **90m/C VHS.** Patrick Macnee, Jeffery Osterhage, Adrian Paul, Tracy Reiner, Maria Ford, Clare Hoak; *D:* Larry Brand; *W:* Larry Brand, Daryl Haney; *C:* Edward Pei; *M:* Mark Governor.

Masque of the Red Death 🦴 ½ **1990 (R)** Unrecognizable Poe mutation has guests invited to the mansion of a dying millionaire, only to be murdered by an unknown stalker. One scene features a pendulum, and that's it for literary faithfulness. **94m/C VHS.** Frank Stallone, Brenda Vaccaro, Herbert Lom, Michelle McBride, Christine Lunde; *D:* Alan Birkinshaw.

Masquerade 🦴🦴🦴 **1988 (R)** A lonely young heiress meets a handsome "nobody" with a mysterious background and it is love at first sight. The romance distresses everyone in the circle of the elite because they assume that he is after her money and not her love. At first it seems decidedly so, then definitely not, and then nothing is certain. A real romantic thriller, with wonderful scenes of the Hamptons. **91m/C VHS, DVD.** Rob Lowe, Meg Tilly, John Glover, Kim Cattrall, Doug Savant, Dana Delany, Eric Holland; *D:* Bob Swaim; *W:* Dick Wolf; *C:* David Watkin; *M:* John Barry.

Mass Appeal 🦴🦴 **1984 (PG)** An adaptation of the Bill C. Davis play about the ideological debate between a young seminarian and a complacent but successful parish pastor. Lemmon has had better roles and done better acting. **99m/C VHS.** Jack Lemmon, Zeljko Ivanek, Charles Durning, Louise Latham, James Ray, Sharee Gregory, Talia Balsam; *D:* Glenn Jordan; *W:* Bill Davis; *M:* Bill Conti.

Massacre 🦴 ½ **1934** That would be what the cavalry frequently did to the Indians. Joe Thunder Horse (miscast Barthelmess) is a Sioux who has been appearing in a Wild West show. He learns his father is dying and returns to the reservation, only to see how his people have been mistreated by the corrupt agents of the Bureau of Indian Affairs. So he goes to Washington to protest. **70m/B VHS.** Richard Barthelmess, Ann Dvorak, Dudley Digges, Sidney Toler, Claire Dodd, Henry O'Neill, Robert Barrat, Arthur Hohl; *D:* Alan Crosland; *W:* Ralph Block, Sheridan Gibney; *C:* George Barnes.

Massacre 🦴🦴 **1956** Mexican Federales Ramon (Clark) and Ezparza (Craig) suspect trading post owner Miguel Chavez (Torruco) and his wife Angelica (Roth) of selling guns to the Yaqui Indians. Chavez gets away but the two arrest Angelica hoping she will decide to lead them to her husband. Instead, Angelica uses her feminine wiles to pit the two partners against each other. Lives up to its title but not in the way you might expect. **76m/C DVD.** Dane Clark, James Craig, Martha Roth, Jaime Fernandez, Miguel Torruco; *D:* Louis King; *W:* D.D. Beauchamp; *C:* Gilbert Warrenton; *M:* Gonzalo Curiel.

Massacre at Central High 🦴🦴 ½ *Blackboard Massacre* **1976 (R)** A new student takes matters into his own hands when gang members harass other students at a local high school. Other than some silly dialogue, this low-budget production is above average. **85m/C VHS, DVD.** Derrel Maury, Andrew Stevens, Kimberly Beck, Robert Carradine, Roy Underwood, Steve Bond, Steve Sikes, Lani O'Grady, Damon Douglas, Cheryl "Rainbeaux" Smith; *D:* Renee Daalder; *W:* Renee Daalder; *C:* Bert Van Munster.

Massacre in Dinosaur Valley 🦴 ½ **1985** A dashing young paleontologist and his fellow explorers go on a perilous journey down the Amazon in search of the Valley of the Dinosaur. **98m/C VHS, DVD.** *IT* Milton Morris, Marta Anderson, Michael Sopkiw, Suzanne Carvall; *D:* Michael Tarantini; *W:* Michael Tarantini; *C:* Edson Batista.

Massacre in Rome 🦴🦴 ½ **1973 (PG)** A priest opposes a Nazi colonel's plan to execute Italian civilians in retaliation for the deaths of 33 German soldiers. Strong drama based on a real event. **110m/C VHS, DVD.** Richard Burton, Marcello Mastroianni, Leo McKern, John Steiner, Anthony Steel; *D:* George P. Cosmatos; *W:* George P. Cosmatos; *M:* Ennio Morricone.

Masseuse 🦴 **1995 (R)** Kristy (Drew) decides to get back at cheating fiance Jack (Abell), who's out of town on a business trip, by turning their house into a massage parlor. **90m/C VHS, DVD.** Griffin (Griffen) Drew, Monique Parent, Tim Abell, Brinke Stevens; *D:* Daniel Peters; *W:* Steve Armogida; *C:* Gary Graver; *M:* Paul Di Franco.

Massive Retaliation 🦴 **1985** Hordes of pesky villagers seek refuge within the secluded safety of a family's country house as WWIII approaches. **90m/C VHS.** Tom Bower, Peter Donat, Karlene Crockett, Jason Gedrick, Michael Pritchard; *D:* Thomas A. Cohen.

The Master 🦴🦴 *Three Evil Masters; Bui bun si mun* **1980** An aging kung fu master is attacked and gravely injured by three evil rivals called (appropriately enough) the Three Devils. He is returned to health by a young orphan boy named Gao Jian (Tak Yuan) who wants to be a kung fu master himself, but his skills are pitiful. Eventually the master agrees to teach Gao all his secrets, and he must return the favor and defend his teacher when the Three Devils return. A bit cheesy but the fight scenes make up for it. **92m/C DVD.** *HK* Kuan Tai Chen, Tak Yuen, Hsueh-erh Wen, Lung Wei Wang; *D:* Chin-Ku Lu; *W:* Kuang Ni; *C:* Lu Ying Ho; *M:* Eddie Wang.

Master and Commander: The Far Side of the World 🦴🦴🦴🦴 **2003 (PG-13)** Captain Jack Aubrey (Crowe) is the relentless commander of the HMS Surprise of the British navy, whose mission is to capture and destroy the Acheron, a much superior and larger French ship. Among the crew is best friend Maturin (Bettany), the ship's surgeon who serves as a quiet balance to Aubrey's fiery man of action. Epic contains some of the most spectacular naval battles ever filmed, but pays close attention to the relationships and respect that are forged in such extreme living conditions. Crowe does a brilliant job showcasing Aubrey's leadership and poise in battle, while Bettany takes a back seat to no one. Based on the first and tenth book of the nautical series by Patrick O'Brien. **139m/C VHS, DVD, Blu-ray Disc.** *US* Russell Crowe, Paul Bettany, Billy Boyd, Max Pirkis, James D'Arcy, Mark Lewis Jones, Chris Larkin, Richard McCabe, Robert Pugh, Lee Ingleby, George Innes, David Threlfall, Edward Woodall, Ian Mercer, Max Benitz; *D:* Peter Weir; *W:* Peter Weir, John Collee; *C:* Russell Boyd; *M:* Christopher Gordon, Iva Davies, Richard Tognetti. Oscars '03: Cinematog., Sound FX Editing; British Acad. '03: Costume Des., Director (Weir), Sound; Natl. Soc. Film Critics '03: Cinematog.

Master Blaster 🦴 ½ **1985 (R)** Friendly game of survival with paintball guns goes awry when one of the contestants exchanges the play guns for deadly weapons. **94m/C VHS.** Jeff Moldovan, Donna Rosae, Joe Hess, Peter Lunblad, Robert Goodman, Richard St. George, George Gill, Jim Reynolds; *D:* Glenn Wilder; *W:* Glenn Wilder, Randy Grinter Jr., Jeff Moldovan; *C:* F. Pershing Flynn; *M:* Alain Salvati.

Master Harold and the Boys 🦴🦴🦴 **1984** Stagey cable presentation of South African Athol Fugard's play about relationship between white man and two black servants. Occasionally provocative. **90m/C VHS.** John Kani, Zakes Mokae, Matthew Broderick; *D:* Michael Lindsay-Hogg; *W:* Athol Fugard. **CABLE**

Master Key 🦴 ½ **1944** Federal agents battle Nazis in this action-packed 12-chapter serial. **169m/B VHS, DVD.** Jan Wiley, Milburn Stone, Lash LaRue, Dennis Moore; *D:* Ray Taylor, Lewis D. Collins.

Master Mind 🦴🦴 **1973** A renowned Japanese super sleuth attempts to solve the theft of a sophisticated midget android. **86m/C VHS.** Zero Mostel, Keiko Kishi, Bradford Dillman, Herbert Berghof, Frankie Sakai; *D:* Alex March.

Master Minds 🦴 ½ **1949** The Bowery Boys run into trouble when Hall gets a toothache and can suddenly predict the future. He takes a job at a carnival where a mad scientist wants to transplant his brain into that of a monster ape man. **64m/B VHS.** Leo Gorcey, Huntz Hall, Glenn Strange, Gabriel Dell, Alan Napier, William Benedict, Bennie Bartlett, David Gorcey; *D:* Jean Yarbrough.

The Master of Ballantrae 🦴🦴 **1953** Flynn plays James Durrisdear, the heir to a Scottish title, who gets involved in a rebellion with Bonnie Prince Charlie against the English crown. When the rebellion fails, Flynn heads for the West Indies where he and his partner amass quite a fortune through piracy. Flynn eventually returns to Scotland where he finds that his brother has taken over his title as well as his longtime love. Based on the novel by Robert Louis Stevenson. Flynn's riotous life had put him long past his peak swashbuckling days, as this film unfortunately demonstrates. **89m/C VHS, DVD.** Errol Flynn, Roger Livesey, Anthony Steel, Beatrice Campbell, Yvonne Furneaux, Jacques Berthier, Felix Aylmer, Mervyn Johns; *D:* William Keighley; *C:* Jack Cardiff.

Master of Disguise 🦴 ½ **2002 (PG)** This disjointed patchwork of lame comedy routines tries to masquerade as "family friendly" entertainment, but is revealed to be a mess that kids may tolerate and parents will hate. Pistachio Disguisey (Carvey) is a waiter at his father Fabbrizio's (Brolin) restaurant, where he displays a talent for mimicking all the customers. Turns out this is a family legacy, coveted by flatulent criminal Devlin Bowman (Spiner) who kidnaps Fabbrizio. So Pistachio has to get his act together, rescue dad, and defeat Devlin. There is no saving the movie, however. Running time is actually padded with 15 minutes of credits and outtakes. **80m/C VHS, DVD.** *US* Dana Carvey, Jennifer Esposito, Brent Spiner, James Brolin, Edie McClurg, Harold Gould, Maria Canals, Austin Wolff; *D:* Perry Andelin Blake; *W:* Dana Carvey, Harris Goldberg; *C:* Peter Lyons Collister; *M:* Marc Ellis.

Master of Dragonard Hill 🦴 ½ **1989** A low-rent swashbuckling romance-novel pastiche. **92m/C VHS.** Oliver Reed, Eartha Kitt; *W:* R.J. Marx.

Master of the Flying Guillotine 🦴🦴 ½ *Du bi quan wang da po xue di zi; One Armed Boxer II; One Armed Boxer vs. the Flying Guillotine; Duk bei kuen wong daai poh huet dik ji* **1975** One of the most famously over-the-top Kung-Fu films, this is actually a sequel to "The One-Armed Boxer." The Manchu Dynasty wishes to quell rebellion in the recently acquired Han province, and sends the Master of the Flying Guillotine (Kang Chin) to murder as many people as are necessary to get the job done. A local fighting tournament is announced not long after he arrives, and the One-Armed Boxer is said to be participating. Since he killed several of the Master's disciples, the Master decides to participate, beginning a series of ever-more bizarre fights between ever-more bizarre martial artists. **83m/C DVD.** *HK* Yu Wang, Kang Chin, Chung-erh Lung, Chia Yung Liu, Lung-Wai Wang, Tsim Po Sham, Fei Lung, Pai Cheng Hau; *D:* Yu Wang; *W:* Yu Wang; *C:* Yao Hu Chiu; *M:* Hsun Chi Chen.

Master of the House 🦴🦴🦴 *Thou Shalt Honour Thy Wife* **1925** Story of a spoiled husband, a type extinct in this country but still in existence abroad. Silent with titles in English. **118m/B VHS.** *CZ* Johannes Meyer, Astrid Holm, Mathilde Nielsen, Karin Nellemose; *D:* Carl Theodor Dreyer; *W:* Carl Theodor Dreyer; *C:* George Schneevoigt.

Master of the World 🦴🦴 ½ **1961** Visionary tale of a fanatical 19th century inventor who uses his wonderous flying fortress as an antiwar weapon. Adapted from "Robur, the Conqueror" and "Master of the World," both by Jules Verne. **95m/C VHS, DVD.** Vincent Price, Charles Bronson, Henry Hull; *D:* William Witney; *W:* Richard Matheson; *M:* Les Baxter.

The Master Race 🦴🦴 **1944** Propaganda film, released in September of 1944, meant as a warning that the Nazi threat still remained. Zealous Nazi officer Von Beck (Coulouris) poses as a guerilla fighter to infiltrate a small bombed-out Belgian village that has been liberated by the Allies. He's there to sow dissent amongst the war-weary townspeople and intimates that the 'master race' will rise again although his own identity is threatened by the presence of German POWs. **96m/B DVD.** George Coulouris, Stanley Ridges, Carl Esmond, Osa Massen, Nancy Gates, Lloyd Bridges, Helen Beverly; *D:* Herbert Biberman; *W:* Herbert Biberman, Rowland Leigh, Anne Froelich; *C:* Russell Metty; *M:* Roy Webb.

Master Spy: The Robert Hanssen Story 🦴🦴 **2002 (R)** Drawn-out drama that finds FBI agent Robert Hanssen (Hurt), deeply in debt and frustrated by his lack of career advancement, selling documents to the KGB. Hanssen's so low-key he would be completely uninteresting if not for a couple of personal quirks: he likes to take naughty photos of his deeply devoted wife Bonnie (Parker) and pass them along to best buddy Jack (Strathairn) and he has a platonic relationship with stripper Priscilla (Pace), who becomes Hanssen's confidante. **122m/C VHS, DVD.** William Hurt, Mary-Louise Parker, David Strathairn, Hilit Pace, Ron Silver, Wayne Knight, Peter Boyle; ***D:*** Lawrence Schiller; ***W:*** Norman Mailer; ***C:*** Alan Caso; ***M:*** Laurence Rosenthal. **TV**

Master Touch 1/2 *Hearts and Minds; Un Uomo da Rispettare* **1974 (PG)** When a legendary safecracker is released from prison, he attempts one last heist at a Hamburg insurance company. **96m/C VHS, DVD.** *GE IT* Kirk Douglas, Florinda Bolkan, Giuliano Gemma; ***D:*** Michele Lupo; ***M:*** Ennio Morricone.

Master with Cracked Fingers *Snake Fist Fighter* **1971 (R)** In one of the highest-grossing martial arts movies of all time, Jackie Chan uses the deadly "snake fist" technique against the bad guys. Chan's first feature is an abominable low-budget flick which, reportedly, sat on a shelf until he became a star. Then it was re-edited and footage of a double was inserted. **83m/C VHS, DVD.** *HK* Jackie Chan; ***D:*** Chin Hsin.

Mastergate 1/2 **1992** Satire on mass media and the government features the Totally News Network's coverage of a Senate investigation of a CIA not-so-secret arms deal with Central American revolutionaries. Masterful dialogue fuels this thinly-veiled spoof of the Iran-Contra hearings. **90m/C VHS.** Richard Kiley, David Ogden Stiers, Ed Begley Jr., Bruno Kirby, Tim Reid, Marcia Strassman, Ken Howard, Darren McGavin, James Coburn, Burgess Meredith, Dennis Weaver, Noriyuki "Pat" Morita, Jerry Orbach, Buck Henry, Ben Stein, Robert Guillaume, Ron Vawter, Louis Giambalvo; ***D:*** Michael Engler; ***W:*** Larry Gelbart. **TV**

Masterminds 1/2 **1996 (PG-13)** Mildly diverting actioner has teen troublemaker Ozzie (Kartheiser) once again on the outs with his workaholic father Jake (Craven) and stepmom Helen (Hurwitch). Forced to take bratty stepsister Melissa (Stuart) to the private school he's been expelled from, Ozzie plans one more prank on officious principal Claire Maloney (Fricker). But the joke's on everyone when security analyst Ralph Bentley (Stewart) puts his plan in motion, taking control of the school and asking a ransom for a group of the wealthiest children. But the ingenious Ozzie's lurking about to get the best of the adults. **105m/C VHS.** Vincent Kartheiser, Patrick Stewart, Brenda Fricker, Matt Craven, Bradley Whitford, Annabelle Gurwitch, Katie Stuart, Callum Keith Rennie, Michael MacRae, Earl Pastko, Michael Simms, Jon Abrahams; ***D:*** Roger Christian; ***W:*** Floyd Byars; ***C:*** Nic Morris; ***M:*** Anthony Marinelli.

Masters of Horror: Cigarette Burns 2005 Repertory theater owner Kirby Sweetman searches for "Le Fin Absolue du Monde," at the request of an eccentric millionaire rare film collector. The film is believed to be destroyed after its only showing caused viewers to become homicidal, cannibalistic maniacs. As Reedus researches interviews with the director and closes in on the mysterious print he begins to fall prey to its supernatural effects. **59m/C DVD.** Norman Reedus, Udo Kier; ***D:*** John Carpenter.

Masters of Horror: Deer Woman 2005 Detective Dwight Faraday is seduced into a case involving the murder of several men killed while at the height of sexual arousal and found trampled into hamburger by what appear to be hoof marks. Each of the men was last seen in the company of a mysteriously sexy Native American woman. **59m/C DVD.** Anthony Griffith, Brian Benden, Cinthia Moura; ***D:*** John Landis.

Masters of Horror: Dream Cruise 2007 An American businessman working in Japan is having an affair with Yuri, the lovely wife of one of his clients, Eiji Saito. When the three embark on a cruise together it turns into terror on the high seas. **87m/C DVD.** Daniel Gillies, Ryo Ishibashi, Yoshino Kimura; ***D:*** Norio Tsurata.

Masters of Horror: Dreams in the Witch House 2005 A stressed-out graduate student rents a room in an old boarding house and starts to experience nightmares about a rapacious rat with a human face, suspects his wall contains a gateway to another dimension, and thinks he's being seduced by a she-demon thirsty for innocent souls. Based on a short story by H.P. Lovecraft. **59m/C DVD.** Jay Brazeau, Ezra Godden, Chelah Horsdal; ***D:*** Stuart Gordon.

Masters of Horror: Fair Haired Child 2006 A psychotic couple kidnaps the virgin Tara and hold her in their locked basement for a sacrifice to the Devil, who has promised to bring their drowned son back from the dead. Child zombie Johnny is mute and communicates through scribbling in the dirt his guilt over living at the expense of others. **59m/C DVD.** Lori Petty, Lindsay Pulsipher, Jesse Haddock; ***D:*** William Malone; ***W:*** Matt Greenburg.

Masters of Horror: Family 2005 George Wendt plays a groomed-lawn, sweater-vest-wearing suburbanite who is by true nature a bloodthirsty serial killer, kidnapping and mutilating strangers in order to put together his own perfect nuclear family. **58m/C DVD.** George Wendt, Meredith Monroe, Matt Keeslar, Haley Guiel, Kerry Sandomirsky; ***D:*** John Landis; ***W:*** Brent Hanley.

Masters of Horror: Homecoming 2005 In an attempt to finally bring the Iraq war to an end, veteran zombie soldiers rise up to vote the president out of office. Unable to slay the already dead, political officials realize the zombies die on their own after casting their ballots in this satire of the war on terrorism. **59m/C DVD.** Jon Tenney, Thea Gill, Wanda Cannon, Terry David Mulligan, Robert Picardo; ***D:*** Joe Dante.

Masters of Horror: Imprint 2005 An American returns to an eerie Japanese island bordello in search of a girl he lost long ago. The prostitute he meets there has many stories to share, laced with incest, abortion, murder, and torture in one of the most grisly "Masters of Horror" productions. **63m/C DVD.** Billy Drago, Youki Kudoh, Toshie Negishi, Michie Ito, Shiho Marumi; ***D:*** Takashi Miike.

Masters of Horror: Jenifer 2005 One of the most eerily stomach-flipping installments of "Masters of Horror" centers on a police detective who saves a young girl with a luscious body but face that has been horribly disfigured by homicidal lunatic. He takes responsibility for the mentally challenged orphan and begins to realize she is a creature of secret carnal pleasures and violent depravities. Star and writer Stephen Weber adapted the script from a short story by Bruce Jones. **59m/C DVD.** Steven Weber, Brenda James, Harris Allan, Beau Starr, Carrie Fleming; ***D:*** Dario Argento; ***W:*** Steven Weber; ***M:*** Claudio Simonetti.

Masters of Horror: Pelts 2006 A sleazy furrier obsessed with a lesbian stripper sets out to make her a coat from the finest furs he can obtain. His trapper comes through with some beautiful raccoon skins that unbeknownst to him are magical guardians of a lost raccoon city whereby all associated with their deaths are cursed with the desire to commit gory suicides. **55m/C DVD.** John Saxon, Meat Loaf Aday, Ellen Ewusie, Link Baker, Brenda McDonald; ***D:*** Dario Argento.

Masters of Horror: Pro-Life 2005 After being raped by the Devil, 15-year old Angelique seeks an abortion at a local clinic. Believing his daughter is about to birth God's child, the right wing Christian father guns his way into the operating room as doctors discover they are unable to exterminate the evil spawn. **57m/C DVD.** Caitlin Wachs, Ron Perlman, Emmanuelle Vaugier, Mark Feuerstein, John Carpenter.

Masters of Horror: Right to Die 2007 A couple is involved in a fiery car wreck late one night, leaving her hideously burned and comatose, while he remains unscathed. The family enters into great debate about whether to pull the plug while her spirit goes on a vengeful rampage against her philandering husband, the heartless money-grubbing lawyer, and others looking to profit from her plight. **58m/C DVD.** Martin Donovan, Anna Galvin, Corbin Bernsen, Julie Anderson, Robin Sydney; ***D:*** Rob Schmidt.

Masters of Horror: Sick Girl 2006 The life of a shy entomologist changes dramatically after the arrival of a large, mysterious bug and the beginning of a steamy affair with a sexy lesbian. As the women enter into their relationship one of them is bitten by the bug and begins to undergo a metamorphosis that is emotional at first but then escalates to horrific mutation and eventually murder. **60m/C DVD.** Angela Bettis, Jesse Hlubik, Misty Mundae, Marcia Bennett, Mike McKee; ***D:*** Lucky McKee.

Masters of Horror: Sounds Like 2006 Office drone Larry Pearce is suffering after the loss of his young son. This excruciating grief triggers his acute sense of hearing allowing him to hear whispered conversations from hundreds of feet away, leading to the slow and tragic decline of his sanity. **58m/C DVD.** Chris Bauer, Laura Margolis, David Pearson, Richard Kahan, Michael Daingerfield; ***D:*** Brad Anderson.

Masters of Horror: The Screwfly Solution 2006 Adaptation of the 1977 short story written by James Tiptree wherein men are suddenly brutally attacking women when they become sexually aroused. As scientists Jason Priestley and Elliott Gould work to remedy the situation it quickly escalates into a global epidemic, leaving women and children to fend for their lives in a world that wants to eliminate them. **60m/C DVD.** Jason Priestley, Elliott Gould, Kerry Norton, Linda Darlow, Brenna O'Brien, Steve Lawlor; ***D:*** Joe Dante; ***W:*** Sam Hamm.

Masters of Horror: The V Word 2005 Two college students enter a mortuary in the middle of the night to view the body of a dead bully. The bully awakens and attacks one boy, turning him into a semi-vampire who then goes after his friend. The friends then band together against their collective foe. **59m/C DVD.** Michael Ironside, Jodelle Ferland, Arjay Smith, Branden Nadon; ***D:*** Ernest R. Dickerson.

Masters of Horror: The Washingtonians 2007 Based on Bentley Little's short story, this black humorish tale presents the exploits of a group of cannibals that have existed since the beginning of America. **58m/C DVD.** Johnathon Schaech, Venus Terzo, Myron Natwick, Duncan Fraser, Julia Tortolano; ***D:*** Peter Medak.

Masters of Horror: Valerie on the Stairs 2006 A haunted writer moves into a community that houses a crazed creature who is holding a beautiful young woman as his sexual prisoner in this tale based on a Clive Barker story. **60m/C DVD.** Tyron Leitso, Christopher Lloyd, Nicola Lipman, Jonathan Watton, Christine Barrie; ***D:*** Mick Garris.

Masters of Horror: We All Scream for Ice Cream 2007 A group of ill-reputed youths play a prank on a mentally-challenged ice cream truck driver that results in his accidental death. Years later the maniac zombie clown returns to take revenge on the now grown-up pranksters. **57m/C DVD.** William Forsythe, Colin Cunningham, Tim Henry, Ingrid Tesch, Spencer Achtymichuk; ***D:*** Tom Holland.

The Masters of Menace 1/2 **1990 (PG-13)** The men in blue are mighty miffed when a bunch of bikers break parole to pay their last respects to a comrade in leather. Comic bits by Candy, Belushi, Aykroyd and Wendt provide little relief. **97m/C VHS.** David Rasche, Catherine Bach, Dan Aykroyd, James Belushi, John Candy, George Wendt, Tino Insana; ***D:*** Daniel Raskov; ***W:*** Tino Insana.

Masters of the Universe **1987 (PG)** A big-budget live-action version of the cartoon character's adventures, with He-Man battling Skeletor for the sake of the universe. **109m/C VHS, DVD.** Dolph Lundgren, Frank Langella, Billy Barty, Courteney Cox, Meg Foster; ***D:*** Gary Goddard; ***W:*** David Odell; ***C:*** Hanania Baer; ***M:*** Bill Conti.

Masters of Venus 1/2 **1962** Eight-part serial about spaceships, space maidens and the like. **121m/B VHS.** *GB* Norman Wooland, Robin Stewart, Mandy Harper, Ferdinand "Ferdy" Mayne; ***D:*** Ernest Morris; ***W:*** Michael Burns; ***C:*** Reg Wyer; ***M:*** Eric Rogers.

Master's Revenge 1/2 *Devil Rider* **1971** When a girl is kidnapped by a violent motorcycle gang, martial artists are called in to rescue her. Originally released as "Devil Rider." **78m/C VHS.** Sharon Mahon, Ridgely Abele, Johnny Pachivas; ***D:*** Brad Grinter; ***W:*** Brad Grinter; ***C:*** Barry Mahon; ***M:*** Gil Wood.

Mata Hari **1932** During WWI, a lovely German spy steals secrets from the French through her involvement with two military officers. Lavish production and exquisite direction truly make this one of Garbo's best. Watch for her exotic pseudo-strip tease. **90m/B VHS, DVD.** Greta Garbo, Ramon Novarro, Lionel Barrymore, Lewis Stone, C. Henry Gordon, Karen Morley, Alec B. Francis; ***D:*** George Fitzmaurice; ***C:*** William H. Daniels.

Mata Hari **1985 (R)** Racy, adventure-prone story of WWI's most notorious spy, Mata Hari, who uses her seductive beauty to seduce the leaders of Europe. Stars "Emmanuelle" Kristel. **105m/C VHS, DVD.** Sylvia Kristel, Christopher Cazenove, Oliver Tobias, Gaye Brown, Gottfried John; ***D:*** Curtis Cunningham.

Matador 1/2 **1986** Bizarre, entertaining black comedy about a retired matador who finds a new way to satiate his desire to kill. He meets his match in an equally deadly woman and the two are drawn closer together by a young bullfighting student who confesses to a series of murders. Not for all tastes, but fine for those who like the outrageous. In Spanish with English subtitles. **90m/C VHS.** *SP* Assumpta Serna, Antonio Banderas, Nacho Martinez, Eva Cobo, Carmen Maura, Julieta Serrano, Chus (Maria Jesus) Lampreave, Eusebio Poncela; ***D:*** Pedro Almodovar; ***W:*** Pedro Almodovar, Jesus Ferrere; ***C:*** Angel Luis Fernandez; ***M:*** Bernardo Bonezzi.

The Matador **2006 (R)** Quirky black comedy stars Brosnan as a veteran hitman with a case of the yips. Boorish, drunken Julian Noble meets desperate businessman Danny Wright (Kinnear) in a Mexico City bar and the unlikely duo become increasingly simpatico. After botching two assignments, Julian needs his only friend Danny's help in fulfilling his last-chance contract. The men are complemented by Davis' portrayal of Danny's devoted wife, Carolyn, who's titillated by Julian's fatal attractions. **96m/C DVD, HD DVD.** *US* Pierce Brosnan, Greg Kinnear, Hope Davis, Philip Baker Hall, Dylan Baker, Adam Scott; ***D:*** Richard Shepard; ***W:*** Richard Shepard; ***C:*** David Tattersall; ***M:*** Rolfe Kent.

Matango 1/2 *Attack of the Mushroom People; Matango the Fungus of Terror; Curse of the Mushroom People* **1963 (PG)** If you took some really good drugs, watched a "Gilligan's Island" marathon, and decided to write a horror movie back in the day, "Matango" would be that film. Directed by Ishiro Honda (director of most of the classic "Godzilla" films), this is the story of an asylum inmate being interviewed by doctors. He, along with six other men and two women get lost on a yacht in foggy waters, and stop on an uncharted isle because of the damage their boat has taken in a night storm. While searching for food and water they notice that large mushrooms seem to be everywhere, and eventually they find a wrecked research ship. And then something finds them. **70m/C DVD.** *JP* Akira Kubo, Kumi Mizuno, Hiroshi Koizumi, Yoshio Tsuchiya, Kenji Sahara, Hiroshi Tachikawa, Miki Yashiro, Haruo Nakajima, Eisei Yamamoto, Jiro Kumagai, Akio Kusama, Yutaka Oka, Kazuo Higata, Keisuke Yamada, Toku Okawa, Mitsuko Hayashi, Kakue Ishibanji, Katsumi Tezuka, Masashi Shinohara, Koji Irugi, Toku Ihara; ***D:*** Ishio Honda; ***W:*** Masami Fukushima, William Hope Hodgson, Shinichi Hoshi, Takeshi Kimura, Sakyo Kimatsu; ***M:*** Sadao Bekku.

The Match 1/2 **1999 (PG-13)** The small Scottish Highland village of Inverdoune has a very important soccer match on its collective minds. It's the annual grudge match with Le Bistro against rival pub Benny's Bar. Benny's has lost all previous 99 matches and, according to an ancient wager, if they lose the 100th match, Le Bisto can shut them down for good. So it's up to eccentric milkman Wullie (Beesley) to save the day. Predictable but filled with eccentric characters and a lot of heart. **96m/C VHS.** *GB* Max Beesley, James Cosmo, Laura Fraser, Isla Blair, Richard E. Grant, Ian Holm, Neil Morrissey, David Hayman, Bill Paterson, David O'Hara, Iain Robertson, Tom Sizemore; ***Cameos:*** Pierce Brosnan; ***D:*** Mick Davis; ***W:*** Mick Davis; ***C:*** Witold Stok; ***M:*** Harry Gregson-Williams.

The Match Factory Girl *Tulitikkutehtaan Tytto* **1990** Kaurismak's final segment of his "working class" trilogy. Iris, a plain, shy outsider shares a drab dwelling with her one-dimensional mother and stepfather, works in a match factory, and hopes desperately for romantic love. Her world is transformed when the extraordinary occurs—she spots a brightly colored party dress in a shop window, buys it, wears it to a bar, and meets the Scandinavian creep who will soon get her pregnant and dump her. Angry at the world, Iris seeks revenge, and in so doing the audience learns that she has become very real and human. Kaurismaki makes his point that beauty can exist in ugly places. In Finnish with English subtitles. **70m/C VHS.** *SW FI* Kati Outinen, Elina Salo, Esko Nikkari, Vesa Vierikko; ***D:*** Aki Kaurismaki; ***W:*** Aki Kaurismaki.

Match Point 1/2 **2005 (R)** Brilliantly Allen-esque—full of layers and complexities—but with a new setting, new scenery, and some new players too. Allen ventures far from his usual cinematic haunts, all the way to London, where gorgeous, tortured social-climbers find themselves torn apart by lust, morality, and class divisions. Chris Wilton (Rhys-Meyers), a former tennis pro of modest means, is introduced to high society through the wealthy family of his pal Tom Hewett (Goode). He soon hooks up with Tom's sister Chloe (Mortimer), but Chris' tryst with Tom's smoldering American girlfriend (Johannson) sets the scene for good old-fashioned murder. Light on the laughs, but Allen hasn't been this thrilling in years. **124m/C DVD.** Scarlett Johansson, Jonathan Rhys Meyers, Emily Mortimer, Matthew Goode, Brian Cox, Penelope Wilton, Ewen Bremner, James Nesbitt, Rupert Penry-Jones, Margaret Tyzack; ***D:*** Woody Allen; ***W:*** Woody Allen; ***C:*** Remi Adefarasin.

The Matchmaker **1958** An adaptation of the Thornton Wilder play concerning two young men in search of romance in 1884 New York. Later adapted as "Hello Dolly." An amusing diversion. **101m/B VHS, DVD.** Shirley Booth, Anthony Perkins, Shirley MacLaine, Paul Ford, Robert Morse, Perry Wilson, Wallace Ford, Russell Collins, Rex Evans, Gavin Gordon, Torben Meyer; ***D:*** Joseph Anthony; ***W:*** John Michael Hayes; ***C:*** Charles B(ryant) Lang Jr.

The Matchmaker 1/2 **1997 (R)** Big city girl Marcy (Garofalo) heads to a wee quaint Ireland burgh where she finds love and humanity amid the beer-guzzling, blarney-slinging locals. Jaded aide to a politico spin doctor (Leary), Marcy is there to track down some McGlory's, the Irish relatives of an American senator, in order to help his re-election campaign but hits town during the annual matchmaking festival and becomes the target of Irish marriage broker O'Shea. O'Hara is Sean, Marcy's laconic and appealing local suitor. Entertaining enough, with Garofalo and O'Hara more than filling the bill in a romantic comedy that heavily flirts with cliche. Sweeping vistas and a soundtrack appropriately filled with Irish favorites, old and new. Filmed in the village of Roundstone, Ireland. **97m/C VHS, DVD.** Janeane Garofalo, Milo O'Shea, David O'Hara, Denis Leary, Jay O. Sanders, Rosaleen Linehan, Maria Doyle Kennedy, Saffron Burrows, Paul Hickey, Jimmy Keogh; ***D:*** Mark Joffe; ***W:*** Louis Nowra, Karen Janszen, Graham Linehan, Greg Dinner; ***C:*** Ellery Ryan; ***M:*** John Altman.

Matchstick Men 1/2 **2003 (PG-13)** Roy (Cage) is a small time con man suffering from a host of psychological tics, including obsessive-compulsive disorder, who's urged by his longtime partner (Rockwell) into a "really big score." Enter a teenage daughter, Angela (Lohman), he never knew. While Roy occasionally displays a kind of smug pride in his work as a con "artist," being with the ever-more-present Angela causes Roy to admit that he actually has little to be truly proud of. Cage is at the top of his game, and he and Rockwell play off each other perfectly, while Lohman proves a worthy co-star as well. Director Scott mixes just the right amounts of comedy, drama, and suspense. Adapted from the novel by Eric Garcia. **120m/C VHS, DVD.** *US* Nicolas Cage, Alison Lohman, Sam Rockwell, Bruce Altman, Bruce McGill, Sheila Kelley, Beth Grant, Steve Eastin; ***D:*** Ridley Scott; ***W:*** Ted Griffin, Nicholas Griffin; ***C:*** John Mathieson; ***M:*** Hans Zimmer.

Material Girls WOOF! 2006 (PG) And we are living in a material world, which explains why movies like this get made. Two snotty, vapid cosmetic-heir sisters (Hilary and Haylie Duff) find themselves suddenly penniless when their company faces scandal. They spend much of the running time yelling at each other as they primp and mug and fuss over the indignities of being poor (or at least at the same economic level as the wanna-be teen queens to whom the flick might possibly appeal). By the time they make their obligatory transformation to girls with hearts of gold, they're so unlikable it's impossible to give a darn. Huston's appearance as the menacing Fabiella is hardly a consolation. And the Duffs' limp cover of the title song sounds like it was performed by automatons on karaoke night. **100m/C DVD.** *US* Haylie Duff, Hilary Duff, Anjelica Huston, Brent Spiner, Lukas Haas, Judy Tenuta, Maria Conchita Alonso, Obba Babatunde, Marcus Coloma; ***D:*** Martha Coolidge; ***W:*** Amy Rardin, John Quaintance, Jessica O'Toole; ***C:*** Johnny E. Jensen; ***M:*** Jennie Muskett.

Maternal Instincts 1/2 **1996 (PG-13)** Tracy (Burke) is a childless woman who undergoes an emergency hysterectomy without her consent. But she badly wants a baby and decides to get revenge on anyone thwarting her plans. **92m/C VHS.** Delta Burke, Beth Broderick, Garwin Sanford, Sandra Nelson, Gillian Barber, Kevin McNulty, Tom Butler, Tom Mason; ***D:*** George Kaczender. **CABLE**

Matewan 1/2 **1987 (PG-13)** An acclaimed dramatization of the famous Matewan massacre in the 1920s, in which coal miners in West Virginia, reluctantly influenced by union organizer Joe Kenehan (Cooper), rebelled against terrible working conditions. Complex and imbued with myth, the film is a gritty, moving, and powerful drama with typically superb Sayles dialogue and Haskell Wexler's beautiful and poetic cinematography. Jones delivers an economical yet intense portrayal of the black leader of the miners. Sayles makes his usual on-screen appearance, this time as an establishment-backed reactionary minister. Partially based on the Sayles novel "Union Dues." **130m/C VHS, DVD.** John Sayles, Chris Cooper, James Earl Jones, Mary McDonnell, William Oldham, Kevin Tighe, David Strathairn, Jace Alexander, Gordon Clapp, Mason Daring, Joe Grifasi, Bob Gunton, Jo Henderson, Jason Jenkins, Ken Jenkins, Nancy Mette, Josh Mostel, Michael B. Preston, Maggie Renzi, Frank Hoyt Taylor; ***D:*** John Sayles; ***W:*** John Sayles; ***C:*** Haskell Wexler; ***M:*** Mason Daring. Ind. Spirit '88: Cinematog.

Matilda **1978 (PG)** Family fare about a entrepreneur who decides to manage a boxing kangaroo, which nearly succeeds in defeating the world heavyweight champion. Uneven and occasionally engaging. Based on Paul Gallico's novel. **103m/C VHS.** Elliott Gould, Robert Mitchum, Harry Guardino, Clive Revill; ***D:*** Daniel Mann.

Matilda **1996 (PG)** Intelligent child Matilda Wormwood (Wilson) is oppressed by both her monstrous parents (DeVito and Perlman) and awful school principal, Trunchbull (Ferris). However, her first grade teacher, appropriately named Miss Honey (Davidtz), believes in her, which is enough to make Matilda plot an appropriate fate for the miserable people in her life. Excellent adaptation of a typically subversive book by Roald Dahl. Director DeVito, who wanted to create the illusion of a live-action cartoon, built among other things a "Carrot-cam" to capture the flying food of a food fight. **93m/C VHS, DVD.** Mara Wilson, Danny DeVito, Rhea Perlman, Embeth Davidtz, Pam Ferris, Paul (Pee-wee Herman) Reubens, Tracey Walter; ***D:*** Danny DeVito; ***W:*** Robin Swicord, Nicholas Kazan; ***C:*** Stefan Czapsky; ***M:*** David Newman.

Matinee 1/2 **1992 (PG)** "MANT: Half-man, Half-ant, All Terror!" screams from the movie marquee after Lawrence Woolsey, promoter extraordinare, and Ruth Corday, his leading lady, roll into Key West circa 1962. Meanwhile, teen Gene Loomis listens to his health teacher push the benefits of red meat and his girlfriend question life, while worrying about his dad, stationed in Cuba. Builds sly parallels between real life and movie horror by juxtaposing Woolsey (modeled after B-movie king William Castle) hyping his schlock, shown in "Atomo-Vision," against JFK solemnly announcing the Russian's approach. Fun, nostalgic look at days gone by—and the matinees that died with them. **98m/C VHS, DVD.** John Goodman, Cathy Moriarty, Omri Katz, Lisa Jakub, Lucinda Jenney, James Villemaire, Robert Picardo, Dick Miller, John Sayles, Charles S. Haas, Mark McCracken, Simon Fenton, Kellie Martin, Jesse Lee, Jesse White, David Clennon, Luke Halpin, Robert Cornthwaite, Kevin McCarthy, William Schallert; ***D:*** Joe Dante; ***W:*** Charles S. Haas, Jerico Stone; ***C:*** John Hora; ***M:*** Jerry Goldsmith.

Matinee Idol 1/2 **1933** When a famous actor is murdered, actress Sonia (Horn) turns amateur sleuth because her sister Christine (Allan) has been accused of the crime. **75m/B DVD.** *GB* Camilla Horn, Miles Mander, Anthony Hankey, Marguerite Allan, Viola Keats; ***D:*** George King; ***W:*** Charles Bennett; ***C:*** Eric Cross; ***M:*** Arthur Dulay.

Mating Dance **2008** Pam keeps setting up her cop husband's best friend on blind dates. Then one of her coworkers seems to be the perfect match but she's got a furry supernatural secret. **102m/C DVD.** Shawn Christian, Lauren German, Susan Blakely, Lisa Rotondi, Roberto Sanchez, Eric Lange; ***D:*** Cate Caplin; ***W:*** Cate Caplin; ***C:*** Eric MacIver. **VIDEO**

The Mating Game **1959** A fast-paced comedy about a tax collector, a beautiful girl, and a wily farm couple. Randall is the straitlaced IRS agent who finds out that the farming Larkins have never paid taxes and use a complicated barter system to get along. Randall falls for farm daughter Reynolds, gets drunk with her Pa, and decides to help the family out of their government dilemma—to the dismay of his superiors. Randall has a terrific drunk scene among his many comedic capers and Reynolds is a highlight. **96m/C VHS.** Tony Randall, Debbie Reynolds, Paul Douglas, Una Merkel, Fred Clark, Philip Ober, Charles Lane; ***D:*** George Marshall; ***W:*** William Roberts.

The Mating Habits of the Earthbound Human 1/2 **1999 (R)** One-joke premise has an alien narrator (Pierce) making a nature doumentary about humans, focusing on the mating habits of nebbishy accountant Bill (Astin) and babe Jenny (Electra). The actors do what they can but the humor and situations are predictable. **90m/C VHS.** MacKenzie Astin, Carmen Electra, Markus Redmond, Lucy Liu, Jack Kehler; ***D:*** Jeff Abugov; ***W:*** Jeff Abugov; ***C:*** Michael Bucher; ***M:*** Michel McCarty; ***Nar:*** David Hyde Pierce.

Mating Season 1/2 **1981** Successful female attorney Arnaz meets good-natured laundromat owner Luckinbill at a bird-watching retreat. Romance ensues. **96m/C VHS.** Lucie Arnaz, Laurence Luckinbill; ***D:*** John Llewellyn Moxey. **TV**

Matrimaniac **1916** A man goes to great lengths to marry a woman against her father's wishes. Silent with music score. **48m/B VHS.** Douglas Fairbanks Sr., Constance Talmadge, Wilbur Higby, Fred Warren; ***D:*** Paul Powell; ***W:*** Anita Loos.

The Matrix 1/2 **1999 (R)** Visually wild ride (and rather complicated plot), courtesy of the brothers Wachowski. Mild-mannered computer programmer Thomas Anderson (Reeves) turns into hacker Neo by night. Neo thinks something is off about his world and he's right. Seems everything around him is just a computer-generated illusion, fostered by machines who use human beings as an electrical energy source. Neo is shown the truth by the mysterious Morpheus (Fishburne) and his renegade team, including capable and beautiful Trinity (Moss). Is Neo the chosen one, who'll make the world safe for humanity once again? Spectacular action sequences, a hissably evil villain (Weaving), a magisterial mentor, and a reluctant hero. What more could you ask for? **136m/C VHS, DVD, Blu-ray Disc, UMD.** Keanu Reeves, Carrie-Anne Moss, Laurence Fishburne, Joe Pantoliano, Hugo Weaving, Gloria Foster, Marcus Chong, Paul Goddard, Robert Taylor, Julian (Sonny) Arahanga, Matt Doran, Belinda McClory, Anthony Ray Parker; ***D:*** Andy Wachowski, Larry Wachowski; ***W:*** Andy Wachowski, Larry Wachowski; ***C:*** Bill Pope; ***M:*** Don Davis. Oscars '99: Film Editing, Sound, Visual FX; British Acad. '99: Sound, Visual FX; MTV Movie Awards '00: Film, Male Perf. (Reeves), Fight (Keanu Reeves/Laurence Fishburne).

The Matrix Reloaded 1/2 **2003 (R)** Neo, Morpheus, Trinity, and the denizens of Zion brace for the machines' attempt to find and destroy the last human stronghold. Neo also discovers more about his destiny as he deals with the ubiquitous and even more powerful Agent Smith. The Wachowski brothers have gone all-out to top the original, and at least visually, they have succeeded. But this one suffers from the attempt to mix navel-gazing ponderings on such topics as choice, destiny, and fate with the visceral thrills, all while trying to move the story forward. A daunting task, which "Reloaded" almost fulfills, providing a complicated twist on the story created in the original, but not mixing it as smoothly with the action set-pieces that, out of necessity, had to be (and definitely are) show-stopping. By no means a failure, it's just not the overwhelming success many hoped it would be. **138m/C VHS, DVD, Blu-ray Disc.** *US* Keanu Reeves, Carrie-Anne Moss, Laurence Fishburne, Hugo Weaving, Jada Pinkett Smith, Monica Bellucci, Gloria Foster, Nona Gaye, Randall Duk Kim, Lambert Wilson, Harold Perrineau Jr., Harry J. Lennix, Helmut Bakaitis, Anthony Zerbe, Neil Rayment, Adrian Rayment, Matt McColm, Daniel Bernhardt, Gina Torres, Collin Chou, Ian Bliss, Robyn Nevin, Essie Davis; ***D:*** Andy Wachowski, Larry Wachowski; ***W:*** Andy Wachowski, Larry Wachowski; ***C:*** Bill Pope; ***M:*** Don Davis.

The Matrix Revolutions **2003 (R)** The battle for the last human stronghold continues, as Zion itself comes under attack. Meanwhile Neo continues his battle with Agent Smith and the machines in his own way, in and out of the Matrix. Better blending of action (there's plenty), philosophy, and narrative helps this one surpass the somewhat disappointing previous installment. It also helps that the effects are more smoothly integrated and less obvious. Add a half-bone if you think the Wachhowski boys can do no wrong, subtract one if you thought the whole thing was ridiculous to begin with. You must choose. **130m/C VHS, DVD.** *US* Keanu Reeves, Laurence Fishburne, Carrie-Anne Moss, Hugo Weaving, Mary Alice, Monica Bellucci, Jada Pinkett Smith, Harold Perrineau Jr., Nona Gaye, Anthony Zerbe, Lambert Wilson, Harry J. Lennix, Collin Chou, Ian Bliss, Bruce Spence, Gina Torres, Helmut Bakaitis, Lachy Hulme, Robyn Nevin, Essie Davis, Anthony Wong, Kevin M. Richardson; ***D:*** Andy Wachowski, Larry Wachowski; ***W:*** Andy Wachowski, Larry Wachowski; ***C:*** Bill Pope; ***M:*** Don Davis.

A Matter of Degrees **1990 (R)** Weeks before his graduation, a beatnik-type college senior finally acquires a goal: romancing a mystery girl...or maybe saving the student radio station...or not. The hero's aimlessness permeates the script, which never goes anywhere in its exploration of campus ennui. Good photography and a great stratum of alternative music groups on the soundtrack: Dream Syndicate, Pere Ubu, Schooly D, Pixies, Poi Dog Pondering, Minutemen, and Throwing Muses. **89m/C VHS.** Arye Gross, Judith Hoag, Tom Sizemore, John Doe; ***Cameos:*** John F. Kennedy Jr., Fred Schneider, Kate Pierson; ***D:*** W.T. Morgan.

A Matter of Dignity *To Telefteo Psemma* **1957** Chloe (Lambetti), whose family is on the brink of financial ruin, agrees to marriage with an incredibly boring millionaire to try and save them. She has to make a painful journey of self-discovery in order to escape the shallowness of how she was raised and the life she doesn't want to lead. Greek with subtitles. **104m/B VHS, DVD.** *GR* Georges Pappas, Ellie Lambetti, Athena Michaelidou, Eleni Zafirou; ***D:*** Michael Cacoyannis; ***W:*** Michael Cacoyannis; ***C:*** Walter Lassally; ***M:*** Manos Hadjidakis.

A Matter of Honor **1995 (PG)** Rugby player is killed during match and his coach gets blamed. So, to clear his name, said coach takes up an unusual challenge with the captain of the opposing team. **95m/C VHS.** Jackson Bostwick, Allen Arkus, Rebecca Gray, David Michie; ***D:*** Frederick P. Watkins.

A Matter of Life and Death **1981** True story follows the real-life experiences of nurse Joy Ufema who has devoted her life to helping terminally ill patients. Exceptional work from Lavin. **98m/C VHS.** Linda Lavin, Salome Jens, Gail Strickland, Gerald S. O'Loughlin, Ramon Bieri, Tyne Daly, Lara Breeding, John Bennett Perry; ***D:*** Russ Mayberry. **TV**

A Matter of Love **1978 (R)** Two couples indulge in spouse swapping while vacationing at the beach. **89m/C VHS.** Michelle Harris, Mark Anderson, Christy Neal, Jeff Allin; ***D:*** Chuck Vincent.

A Matter of Principle **1983** The perennial Christmas special about a Scrooge-like character's yuletide change of heart. He decides it's time to shape up when he realizes he may lose his family permanently. **60m/C VHS, DVD.** Alan Arkin, Barbara Dana, Tony Arkin; ***D:*** Gwen Arner.

A Matter of Time **WOOF! 1976 (PG)** Maid is taught to enjoy life by an eccentric, flamboyant contessa, then finds the determination to become an aspiring actress. Often depressing and uneven, arguably Minnelli's worst directing job and his last film. Also Boyer's last appearance and first bit for Bergman's daughter Rosellini, in a small part as a nun. **97m/C VHS.** Liza Minnelli, Ingrid Bergman, Charles Boyer, Tina Aumont, Spiros Andros, Anna Proclemer, Isabella Rossellini; ***D:*** Vincente Minnelli; ***C:*** Geoffrey Unsworth.

Matter of Trust **1998 (R)** Mike D'Angelo (Howell) is an alcoholic L.A. cop barely hanging onto his job. The woman he loves, Theresa (Severance), is not only an Assistant D.A. but is married to a prominent doctor, Peter (Mancuso). But their paths aren't as separate as Mike might believe. **90m/C VHS, DVD.** C. Thomas Howell, Joan Severance, Nick Mancuso, Robert Miano, Jennifer Leigh Warren, Randee Heller; ***D:*** Joey Travolta; ***W:*** John Penney; ***C:*** Dan Heigh; ***M:*** Jeff Lass. **VIDEO**

A Matter of WHO **1962** A detective for the World Health Organization, or WHO, investigates the disease related deaths of several oil men. Travelling to the Middle East, he uncovers a plot by an unscrupulous businessman to control the oil industry by killing off its most powerful members. Although intended as a comedy, the subject matter is too grim to be taken lightly. **92m/B VHS.** *GB* Terry-Thomas, Alex Nicol, Sonja Ziemann, Richard Briers, Clive Morton, Vincent Ball, Honor Blackman, Carol White, Martin Benson, Geoffrey Keen; ***D:*** Don Chaffey; ***M:*** Edwin Astley.

Matters of the Heart **1990** Young pianist searches for an opportunity to display his talents, much to the disapproval of his veteran father. He meets a successful but embittered musician who takes him under her wing and passion between the two soon flares. Based on "The Country of the Heart" by Barbara Wershba. **94m/C VHS.** Jane Seymour, Christopher Gartin, James Stacy, Geoffrey Lewis, Nan Martin, Allan Rich, Clifford David, Katherine (Kathy) Cannon; ***D:*** Michael Rhodes; ***W:*** Linda J. Bergman. **CABLE**

Maurice **1987 (R)** Based on E.M. Forster's novel about a pair of Edwardian-era Cambridge undergraduates who fall in love, but must deny their attraction and abide by British society's strict norms regarding homosexuality. Maurice finds, however, that he cannot deny his nature, and must come to a decision regarding family, friends, and social structures. A beautiful and stately film of struggle and courage. **139m/C VHS, DVD.** *GB* James Wilby, Hugh Grant, Rupert Graves, Mark Tandy, Ben Kingsley, Denholm Elliott, Simon Callow, Judy Parfitt, Helena Bonham Carter, Billie Whitelaw, Phoebe Nicholls, Barry Foster; ***D:*** James Ivory; ***W:*** James Ivory, Kit Hesketh-Harvey; ***C:*** Pierre Lhomme; ***M:*** Richard Robbins.

Mausoleum **1983 (R)** Only one man can save a woman from eternal damnation. **96m/C VHS, DVD.** Marjoe Gortner, Bobbie Bresee, Norman Burton, LaWanda Page, Shari Mann, Julie Christy Murray, Laura Hippe, Maurice Sherbanee; ***D:*** Michael Dugan; ***W:*** Robert Madero, Robert Barich; ***C:*** Robert Barich.

Mauvais Sang *Bad Blood* **1986** Carax's second film tells the story of rival gangsters who are searching for a serum that cures a devastating disease. Streetwise Alex (Lavant) from "Boy Meets Girl" (1984) also returns as the thief who is supposed to steal the serum (his character is again seen in 1991's "The Lovers on the Bridge."). French with subtitles. **125m/C VHS, DVD.** *FR* Michel Piccoli, Denis Lavant, Juliette Binoche, Hans Meyer, Julie Delpy, Carroll Brooks, Serge Reggiani, Hugo Pratt, Mireille Perrier; ***D:*** Leos Carax; ***W:*** Leos Carax; ***C:*** Jean-Yves Escoffier; ***M:*** Serge Reggiani, Charles Aznavour.

Mauvaise Graine *Bad Seed* **1933** Wilder (in his debut) filmed this comedy-drama (along with Esway) before heading off to Hollywood. Parisian wastrel Henri Pasquier (Mingand) impulsively steals a car when his disgusted wealthy father cuts him off. This lands Henri in with a professional gang of thieves, headed by Jean (Galle), who uses his pretty teenaged sister Jeannette (Darrieux) as a decoy. Henri enjoys his new career (and Jeannette) until jealousy gets in the way. French with subtitles. **76m/B VHS, DVD.** *FR* Pierre Mingand, Danielle Darrieux, Raymond Galle, Jean Wall; ***D:*** Billy Wilder, Alexander Esway; ***W:*** Billy Wilder, Alexander Esway; ***C:*** Paul Cotteret, Maurice Delattre; ***M:*** Franz Waxman, Walter Gray.

Maverick **½ 1994 (PG)** Entertaining remake of the popular ABC series is fresh and funny, with sharp dialogue and a good cast. Everybody looks like they're having a great time, not difficult for the charming Gibson, but a refreshing change of pace for the usually serious Foster and Greene. In a fun bit of casting, Garner, the original Maverick, shows up as Marshal Zane Cooper. Lightweight, fast-paced comedy was reportedly highly improvised, though Donner retained enough control to keep it coherent. The end is left wide open so a sequel seems likely. Keep your eyes peeled for cameos from country stars, old time Western actors, and an unbilled appearance from Glover. **127m/C VHS, DVD.** Mel Gibson, Jodie Foster, James Garner, Graham Greene, James Coburn, Alfred Molina, Paul Smith, Geoffrey Lewis, Max Perlich; ***Cameos:*** Dub Taylor, Dan Hedaya, Robert Fuller, Doug McClure, Bert Remsen, Denver Pyle, Will Hutchins, Waylon Jennings, Kathy Mattea, Danny Glover, Clint Black; ***D:*** Richard Donner; ***W:*** William Goldman; ***C:*** Vilmos Zsigmond; ***M:*** Randy Newman. Blockbuster '95: Comedy Actress, T. (Foster).

The Maverick Queen **½ 1955** Barbara Stanwyck, owner of a gambling casino and a member of the "Wild Bunch" outlaw gang, is torn between going straight for the love of a lawman or sticking with the criminals. Stanwyck is perfectly cast in this interesting Western. **90m/C VHS.** Barbara Stanwyck, Barry Sullivan, Wallace Ford, Scott Brady, Jim Davis, Mary Murphy; ***D:*** Joseph Kane.

Max **2002 (R)** Historical fantasy has an interesting premise: what would have happened if Adolf Hitler had been successful as an artist? In 1919, Hitler (Taylor) is a starving, embittered (but ambitious) war veteran in Munich who is befriended by Max Rothman (Cusack), a Jewish art dealer and fellow veteran who has just opened his own avant-garde gallery. Hitler's art is kitsch but Max encourages him anyway and shrugs off his rantings, which draw more attention from fellow Army officer Mayr (Thomsen). Mayr thinks Adolf would make a good political spokesman. Guess who was proved right? Rothman is a fictional character, Mayr is not, and the film drew a lot of protest for "humanizing" Hitler. The movie is flawed but not for that reason. **106m/C VHS, DVD.** *HU CA GB* John Cusack, Noah Taylor, Leelee Sobieski, Molly Parker, David Horovitch, Janet Suzman, Peter Capaldi, Kevin McKidd, John Grillo, Ulrich Thomsen; ***D:*** Menno Meyjes; ***W:*** Menno Meyjes; ***C:*** Lajos Koltai; ***M:*** Dan (Daniel) Jones.

Max and Helen **½ 1990** Uneven, but sensitive and at times highly moving made for TV story of two lovers who are victims of the holocaust. Max (Williams) survives both Nazi and Stalinist camps out of both love for his fiancee and guilt for having lived while she did not. **94m/C VHS.** *GB* Treat Williams, Alice Krige, Martin Landau, Jodhi May, John Phillips, Adam Kotz; ***D:*** Philip Saville; ***W:*** Corey Blechman. **TV**

Max Dugan Returns **1983 (PG)** A Simon comedy about an ex-con trying to make up with his daughter by showering her with presents bought with stolen money. Sweet and light, with a good cast. **98m/C VHS, DVD.** Jason Robards Jr., Marsha Mason, Donald Sutherland, Matthew Broderick, Kiefer Sutherland; ***D:*** Herbert Ross; ***W:*** Neil Simon; ***M:*** David Shire.

Max Is Missing **½ 1995 (PG)** Twelve-year-old Max (Caudell) gets separated from his father, is given a priceless Incan artifact by a dying man, and joins with a local lad to guard it from fortune hunters. Set in the ruins of Machu Picchu in the Peruvian Andes. **95m/C VHS.** Toran Caudell, Victor Rojas, Matthew Sullivan, Rick Dean, Charles Napier; ***D:*** Mark Griffiths. **CABLE**

Max Keeble's Big Move **2001 (PG)** Max (Linz), a kid on the verge of entering seventh grade, decides that he must change his image to be a little cooler, much to the dismay of his pals Megan (Grey) and Robe (Peck). On the first day of school, however, he is confronted with two bullies, a fussy principal (Miller) who wants to tear down an animal shelter that Max loves, and a renegade ice cream man. Max's dad comes home and announces that the family is moving to Chicago. Thinking that he can avoid the consequences by moving out of town, Max hatches numerous messy plots to get back at everyone who's tormenting him. After Max has taken revenge, dad reveals that the family is staying put after all, leaving Max to face the music. Not very original, but the kids will get a kick out of the food fight scene. **101m/C VHS, DVD.** *US* Alex D. Linz, Larry Miller, Jamie Kennedy, Zena Grey, Josh Peck, Orlando Brown, Noel Fisher, Nora Dunn, Robert Carradine, Clifton Davis, Amy Hill, Amber Valletta, Justin Berfield; ***D:*** Timothy Hill; ***W:*** Jon Bernstein, Mark Blackwell, James Greer; ***C:*** Arthur Albert; ***M:*** Michael Wandmacher.

Max, Mon Amour *Max, My Love* **1986** A very refined British diplomat in Paris discovers his bored wife has become involved with Max, who happens to be a chimpanzee. Instead of being upset, the husband decides Max should live with them. Very strange menage a trois manages to avoid the obvious vulgarities. In French with English subtitles. **97m/C VHS.** *FR* Anthony (Corlan) Higgins, Charlotte Rampling, Victoria Abril, Christopher Hovik, Anne-Marie Besse, Pierre Etaix; ***D:*** Nagisa Oshima; ***W:*** Jean-Claude Carriere, Nagisa Oshima; ***C:*** Raoul Coutard; ***M:*** Michel Portal.

Max Payne **½ 2008 (PG-13)** Another cold, dreary, emotionless videogame unnecessarily brought to the big screen. DEA agent Max Payne (Wahlberg), and assassin Mona Sax (Kunis), come together to solve a series of murders sweeping New York City. These vigilantes, fighting to avenge the deaths of family members, are being hunted not only by the mob, but also by the police and a major corporation as well. A step back for Wahlberg, feeling more like a movie he would've made ten years earlier. Aimless plot stays true to its roots, with stilted dialogue and stone-faced performances lifted straight from the game. Little more than an excuse for slow-mo gun firing and mindless action—neither of which is much fun without a joystick. **99m/C DVD, Blu-ray Disc.** *US* Mark Wahlberg, Mila Kunis, Beau Bridges, Chris Bridges, Donal Logue, Chris O'Donnell, Kate Burton, Ted Atherton, Joel Gordon, Rico Simonini, Amaury Nolasco, Olga Kurylenko, Jamie Hector; ***D:*** John Moore; ***W:*** Beau Thorne; ***C:*** Jonathan Sela; ***M:*** Marco Beltrami, Buck Sanders.

Max Rules **½ 2005** Young Max and his friends Jessica and Scott like to play spy games and stage elaborate pranks. Thanks to Max's scientist uncle, who works for the government, the kid has access to some high-tech gizmos. But when the trio discovers the whereabouts of a stolen microchip, the junior spies put all their know-how to work. Amusing kid fare. **80m/C DVD.** William B. Davis, Jason Dittmer, Andrew C. Maier, Jennifer Lancheros, Spencer Esau, Paul Eenhoorn; ***D:*** Robert Burke; ***W:*** Robert Burke; ***C:*** John Jeffcoat; ***M:*** Matthew Bennett. **VIDEO**

Maxed Out: Hard Times, Easy Credit and the Era of Predatory Lenders **½ 2006** Scurlock tries to explain the wheeling and dealing of the financial community by focusing on the worst case scenarios of the consumer-lending industry, involving massive consumer debt, too easy credit, ill-advised loans, and bankruptcy and foreclosures. Basically most people are dumb about money and even dumber when it comes to borrowing and getting into (and less likely out of) debt. **86m/C DVD.** *US* ***D:*** James D. Scurlock; ***W:*** James D. Scurlock; ***C:*** Jon Aaron Aaseng; ***M:*** Benoit Vharest.

Maxie **1985 (PG)** Highly predictable, and forgettable, comedy where a ghost of a flamboyant flapper inhabits the body of a modern-day secretary, and her husband is both delighted and befuddled with the transformations in his spouse. Close is okay, but the film is pretty flaky. **98m/C VHS, DVD.** Glenn Close, Ruth Gordon, Mandy Patinkin, Barnard Hughes, Valerie Curtin, Harry Hamlin; ***D:*** Paul Aaron; ***W:*** Patricia Resnick; ***M:*** Georges Delerue.

Maxim Xul **WOOF! 1991** A professor of the occult is forced to tangle with a beast from Hell that possesses enormous strength and an insatiable appetite for human blood. **90m/C VHS.** Adam West, Jefferson Leinberger, Hal Strieb, Mary Schaeffer; ***D:*** Arthur Egeli.

Maximum Breakout **½ 1991** A beautiful and wealthy girl is kidnapped, her boyfriend left for dead. But he recovers and leads a posse of mercenaries to the rescue. **93m/C VHS.** Sydney Coale Phillips; ***D:*** Tracy Lynch Britton.

Maximum Force **½ 1992 (R)** Three renegade cops join together to infiltrate the underworld and bring to justice both the city's leading crime king and their own corrupt chief of police. **90m/C VHS.** Sam Jones, Sherrie Rose, Jason Lively, John Saxon, Richard Lynch, Mickey Rooney, Jeff Langton; ***D:*** Joseph Merhi.

Maximum Overdrive **1986 (R)** Based upon King's story "Trucks," recounts what happens when a meteor hits Earth and machines run by themselves, wanting only to kill people. Score by AC/DC. King shows that as a director, he's an excellent horror writer. **97m/C VHS, DVD.** Emilio Estevez, Pat Hingle, Laura Harrington, Christopher Murney, Yeardley Smith, Stephen King; ***D:*** Stephen King; ***W:*** Stephen King; ***C:*** Armando Nannuzzi; ***M:*** AC/DC.

Maximum Risk **½ 1996 (R)** Like we need two of them? Van Damme, in a deja vu storyline (see "Double Impact") plays identical twins—a good French guy and a bad Russian guy—and when the bad guy gets killed, his brother takes over his life to find out whodunit. Risk and danger aside, the ruse is not all that bad, what with Henstridge as his sib's squeeze, unaware that the man she has in a lip lock is not her beloved. Has all the action you'd expect from a pic with "The Muscles from Brussels" and more guns, fists, and car chases is, of course, the major reason to invest your entertainment dollars here. Hong Kong action auteur Lam's stateside debut ensures that fast-paced chases and full-throttle combat is well done and visually appealing. **100m/C VHS, DVD.** Jean-Claude Van Damme, Natasha Henstridge, Jean-Hugues Anglade, Stephane Audran, Paul Ben-Victor, Zach Grenier, Frank Senger; ***D:*** Ringo Lam; ***W:*** Larry Ferguson; ***C:*** Alexander Grusynski; ***M:*** Robert Folk.

Maximum Security **1987** A small-budget prison film detailing the tribulations of a model prisoner struggling to resist mental collapse. **113m/C VHS, DVD.** Geoffrey Lewis, Jean Smart, Robert Desiderio; ***D:*** Bill Duke.

Maximum Thrust **WOOF!** *Waldo Warren: Private Dick Without a Brain* **1988** A few white men confront a deadly Caribbean voodoo tribe. **80m/C VHS, DVD.** Rick Gianasi, Joe Derrig, Jennifer Kanter, Mizan Nunes; ***D:*** Tim Kincaid.

May **2002 (R)** May's (Bettis) motto is "If you can't find a friend, make one." Thanks to a disturbed childhood (where her only companion was a doll), May is one messed-up chick. She works at an animal hospital with lesbian Polly (Faris), sews as a hobby, and falls for Adam (Sisto), who thinks he likes weird girls. He doesn't know from weird. When Adam finally rejects May, she looks around and decides to make her own best friend—using only the choicest body parts. **95m/C VHS, DVD.** Angela Bettis, Jeremy Sisto, Anna Faris, James Duval, Nichole Hiltz, Kevin Gage, Merle Kennedy; ***D:*** Lucky McKee; ***W:*** Lucky McKee; ***C:*** Steve Yedlin; ***M:*** Jaye Barnes-Luckett.

May Fools *Milou en Mai; Milou in May* **1990 (R)** Malle portrays individuals collectively experiencing personal upheaval against the backdrop of unrelated social upheaval. An upper-crust family gathers at a country estate for the funeral of the clan's matriarch, while the May of '68 Parisian riots unfold. Few among the family members mourn the woman's passing, save her son Milou (Piccoli) who leads a pastoral existence tending grapes on the estate. Milou's daughter (Miou-Miou), like the others, is more concerned with her personal gain, suggesting, to her father's horror, that they divide the estate in three. Touching, slow, keenly observed. In French with English subtitles. **105m/C VHS.** *FR* Michel Piccoli, Miou-Miou, Michel Duchaussoy, Dominique Blanc, Harriet Walter, Francois Berleand, Paulette Dubost, Bruno Carette, Martine Gautier; ***D:*** Louis Malle; ***W:*** Jean-Claude Carriere, Louis Malle; ***C:*** Renato Berta; ***M:*** Stephane Grappelli. Cesar '91: Support. Actress (Blanc).

May Wine **1990 (R)** A sexy, romantic comedy starring "Twin Peaks" alumna, Boyle. **85m/C VHS.** Paul Freeman, Guy Marchand, Lara Flynn Boyle, Joanna Cassidy; ***D:*** Carol Wiseman; ***W:*** Peter Lefcourt; ***C:*** Yves Dahan; ***M:*** Andre Georget.

Maya **1/2 1966** After the death of his mother, young Terry (North) goes to join his big-game hunting father in India. After a quarrel Terry runs off and meets an Indian boy who has promised his dying father he will deliver a sacred white elephant to a jungle temple. The two lads join forces for the trek and have all sorts of adventures along the way. Basis for a short-lived TV series. **91m/C VHS.** Jay North, Clint Walker, Sajid Khan, I.S. Johar; ***D:*** John Berry; ***W:*** John Fante.

Maya **WOOF! 1982** A teacher of fashion in a high school becomes the object of a student's devotion and another teacher's insane jealousy. **114m/C VHS.** Berta Dominguez, Joseph D. Rosevich; ***D:*** Agust Agustsson.

Mayalunta*Bad Company* **1986** A young artist is emotionally tortured by a dying older couple. **90m/C VHS.** *SP* Federico Luppi, Miguel Angel Sola, Barbara Mujica; ***D:*** Jose Santiso; ***W:*** Jose Santiso; ***C:*** Eduardo Legaria; ***M:*** Litto Nebbia.

Maybe Baby **1/2 1999 (R)** Sam (Laurie) and Lucy (Richardson) Bell are a happily married couple trying to have a baby. She's a talent agent and he works for the BBC. Dissatisfied at work, Sam tries his hand at scriptwriting and decides his subject will be a comic look at the couple's infertility problems. Naturally, he keeps this a secret from Lucy, although she finds out when his script is accepted and walks out on Sam. Tends towards the smug and the leads don't particularly click as a couple, which makes the supporting players the most interesting to watch onscreen. **93m/C VHS, DVD.** *GB FR* Hugh Laurie, Joely Richardson, Adrian Lester, James Purefoy, Tom Hollander, Joanna Lumley, Rowan Atkinson, Dawn French, Emma Thompson, Rachael Stirling; ***D:*** Ben Elton; ***W:*** Ben Elton; ***C:*** Roger Lanser; ***M:*** Colin Towns.

Maybe I'll Be Home in the Spring **1/2** *Deadly Desire* **1970 (PG)** Denise (Field) is estranged from her family and decides to leave home for life on a commune where she becomes involved with drugs. When she decides to return home everyone finds it hard to adjust. **90m/C VHS, DVD.** Sally Field, Jackie Cooper, Eleanor Parker, David Carradine, Lane Bradbury; ***D:*** Joseph Sargent. **TV**

Maybe I'll Come Home in the Spring **1971** Originally shown as an ABC movie of the week. Teenager Denise (Field) runs away from her middle-class suburban life to live on a hippie commune with boyfriend Flack (Carradine). When she comes home you see how dysfunctional her family is and although she's changed, nothing else has. Denise tries to warn younger sister Susie (Bradbury) away from drugs and following in her footsteps, but she won't listen. **75m/C DVD.** Sally Field, Eleanor Parker, Jackie Cooper, David Carradine, Lane Bradbury; ***D:*** Joseph Sargent; ***W:*** Bruce Feldman; ***C:*** Russell Metty; ***M:*** Earl Robinson. **TV**

Maybe... Maybe Not *Der Bewegte Mann; The Most Desired Man* **1994 (R)** The German title refers to a man who moves between both sexual preferences although the film takes a straighter line. Hunky-but-dumb Axel (Schweiger) has cheated on girlfriend Dorothy (Riemann) once too often and she kicks him out. Axel winds up staying with gay pal Norbert (Krol), who would like to go from friendship to lovers, which Axel doesn't pick up on. Dorothy does, however, and wonders if Axel is really gay, but when she discovers she's pregnant, Dorothy decides to marry him anyway. Warm-hearted and campy, with some blatantly sexual dialogue. Based on two gay comic books by Ralf Koenig. German with subtitles or dubbed. **93m/C VHS.** *GE* Til Schweiger, Katja Riemann, Joachim Krol, Rufus Beck; ***D:*** Soenke Wortmann; ***W:*** Soenke Wortmann; ***C:*** Gernot Roll; ***M:*** Torsten Breuer.

Mayday at 40,000 Feet **1/2 1976** Typically ridiculous '70s TV disaster flick finds the pilot of a 747 dealing with engine trouble, a violent snowstorm, and a madman with a gun. **97m/C DVD.** David Janssen, Jane Powell, Ray Milland, Don Meredith, Christopher George, Lynda Day George, Marjoe Gortner, Broderick Croawford, Hari Rhodes; ***D:*** Robert Butler; ***W:*** Dick Nelson, Andrew J. Fenady; ***C:*** William B. Jurgensen; ***M:*** Richard Markowitz. **TV**

Mayerling **1/2 1936** Considered one of the greatest films about doomed love. Story of the tragic and hopeless affair between Crown Prince Rudolf of Hapsburg and young Baroness Marie Vetsera. Heart wrenching and beautiful, with stupendous acting. Remade in 1968. In French with English subtitles. **95m/B VHS.** Charles Boyer, Danielle Darrieux; ***D:*** Anatole Litvak. N.Y. Film Critics '37: Foreign Film.

Mayerling **1/2 1968 (PG-13)** Based on the tragic romance between Crown Prince Rudolf of Hapsburg (Sharif) and the teenaged Baroness Maria Vetsera (Deneuve). Set in 1888, the royal Rudolf defies his father, the Emperor Franz Josef (Mason), to take part in a student revolt for the liberation of Hungary and to fall for the common-born Maria (despite his political marriage). No doubt meant to be a sweeping combo of politics and love ala "Doctor Zhivago," it's mostly tedious; see the 1936 version instead. **140m/C VHS, DVD.** *GB FR* Omar Sharif, Catherine Deneuve, James Mason, Ava Gardner, James Robertson Justice, Genevieve Page, Ivan Desny, Fabienne Dali; ***D:*** Terence Young; ***W:*** Terence Young; ***C:*** Henri Alekan; ***M:*** Francis Lai.

Mayflower Madam **1987 (R)** Fairly unsexy and uninteresting TV movie recounting the business dealings and court battles of the real-life Sydney Biddle Barrows. Barrows/Bergen is a prominent New York socialite and madam of an exclusive escort service whose clientele includes businessmen and dignitaries. **93m/C VHS, DVD.** Candice Bergen, Chris Sarandon, Chita Rivera; ***D:*** Lou Antonio; ***M:*** David Shire. **TV**

Mayflower: The Pilgrims' Adventure **1/2 1979** The Pilgrims flee religious persecution in England in 1620 and sail to America on the Mayflower, which is captained by Hopkins. Crenna plays the leader of the Puritans, the Rev. William Brewster. **96m/C VHS.** Anthony Hopkins, Richard Crenna, Jenny Agutter, Michael Beck, David Dukes, Trish Van Devere, Guy Sorel, Paul Sparer; ***D:*** George Schaefer; ***W:*** James Lee Barrett. **TV**

Mayhem **1987** Two loners in Hollywood confront all types of urban low-life murderers, drug pushers, and child molesters. **90m/C VHS.** Raymond Martino, Pamela Dixon, Robert Gallo, Wendy MacDonald; ***D:*** Joseph Merhi; ***W:*** Joseph Merhi; ***C:*** Richard Pepin; ***M:*** John Gonzalez.

The Mayor of Casterbridge **1/2 2003** Appropriately brooding adaptation of Thomas Hardy's dark novel of regret. Farm worker Michael Henchard (Hinds) gets drunk and sells his wife Susan (Aubrey) and their baby daughter at a country fair. Since her husband is an abusive drunk and the buyer (Russell) is a good-natured sailor, Susan decides to take her chances. Suffering from a drunkard's remorse, Henchard searches fruitlessly for his family. He eventually settles in Casterbridge where, through sobriety and hard work, Henchard becomes the town's mayor. Then his past returns to haunt him when Susan and his now-grown daughter, Elizabeth-Jane (May), seek him out. But when young rival Farfrae (Purefoy) romances his daughter, Henchard's darker nature resurfaces. **200m/C DVD.** *GB* Ciaran Hinds, James Purefoy, Jodhi May, Juliet Aubrey, Polly Walker, Clive Russell; ***D:*** David Thacker; ***W:*** Ted Whitehead; ***C:*** Ivan Strasburg; ***M:*** Adrian Johnston. **CABLE**

The Mayor of Hell **1/2 1933** Gangster Patsy Gargan (Cagney) has his political cronies appoint him the titular head of a state reformatory. But when he sees the brutal conditions, Gargan makes improvements and tries to get the teenaged criminal inmates to see the error of their ways. However, when Gargan is forced into hiding after killing a rival, things get bad again until he finally decides to step up. Remade as 1938's "Crime School." **85m/B DVD.** James Cagney, Madge Evans, Allen Jenkins, Dudley Digges, Frankie Darro, Carolyn Farina; ***D:*** Archie Mayo; ***W:*** Edward Chodorov; ***C:*** Barney McGill.

Mayor of the Sunset Strip **2003 (R)** As a popular Los Angeles disc jockey, Rodney Bingenheimer pushed new musical acts into the limelight—including the Sex Pistols, Blondie, and Nirvana—meanwhile living as the greatest groupie, befriending The Beatles, Elton John, Elvis, and the Doors. But in his documentary, director-writer Hickenlooper poignantly reveals how this man rose up from a lonely childhood to unexpectedly become the "get to know me" guy on the music scene, only to learn that life inside all of the glittering lights can be just as harsh and emotionally isolating as was his youth. Music industry cameos and interviews abound. **94m/C VHS, DVD.** ***D:*** George Hickenlooper; ***W:*** George Hickenlooper; ***C:*** Kramer Morgenthau, Igor Meglic; ***M:*** Anthony Marinelli.

Maytime **1937** Lovely story of an opera star (MacDonald) and penniless singer (Eddy) who fall in love in Paris, but her husband/teacher (Barrymore) interferes. One of the best films the singing duo ever made. ♫ Maytime Finale; Virginia Ham and Eggs; Vive l'Opera; Student Drinking Song; Carry Me Back to Old Virginny; Reverie; Jump Jim Crow; Road to Paradise; Page's Aria. **132m/B VHS.** Jeanette MacDonald, Nelson Eddy, John Barrymore, Herman Bing, Tom Brown, Lynne Carver; ***D:*** Robert Z. Leonard; ***W:*** Noel Langley.

Maytime in Mayfair **1949** A dress shop owner's rival is getting all the goodies first, for which he takes the heat from his partner. When he finds out how the rival is doing it, the partners up and head for a vacation in the south of France. Overly simplistic but charming kitsch, helped along by Technicolor shots of the fashions and sets. **94m/C VHS.** Anna Neagle, Michael Wilding, Peter Graves, Nicholas Phipps, Tom Walls, Tom Walls Jr.; ***D:*** Herbert Wilcox.

The Maze **1985** Mystery about a young girl who meets the ghost of her mother's first love in her garden estate. **60m/C VHS.** *GB* Francesca Annis, James Bolam, Sky McCatskill; ***D:*** Peter Hammond; ***W:*** Kenneth Taylor; ***C:*** Ken Morgan; ***M:*** Paul Lewis. **TV**

Maze **1/2 2001 (R)** Introverted New York artist Lyle Maze (Morrow) is a sculptor afflicted with Tourette's syndrome, which makes him romantically hesitant. Lyle's best friend is a doctor named Mike (Sheffer), whose devotion is to his career rather than his girlfriend Callie (Linney). Mike leaves Callie for a months-long tour with Doctors Without Borders in Africa and when Callie discovers she is pregnant, she turns to Lyle for emotional support. Unsurprisingly, the needy duo fall in love before they have to explain what's happened on Mike's return. **98m/C VHS, DVD.** Rob Morrow, Laura Linney, Craig Sheffer, Gia Carides, Rose Gregorio, Robert Hogan; ***D:*** Rob Morrow; ***W:*** Rob Morrow, Bradley White; ***C:*** Wolfgang Held; ***M:*** Bobby Previte.

Mazes and Monsters **1/2** *Rona Jaffe's Mazes and Monsters; Dungeons and Dragons* **1982** A group of university students becomes obsessed with playing a real life version of the fantasy role-playing game, Dungeons and Dragons (known in the film as Mazes & Monsters since D&D is trademarked). Early Hanks appearance is among the film's assets. Adapted from the book by Rona Jaffe. **100m/C VHS, DVD.** *CA* Tom Hanks, Wendy Crewson, David Wallace, Chris Makepeace, Lloyd Bochner, Peter Donat, Murray Hamilton, Vera Miles, Louise Sorel, Susan Strasberg, Anne Francis; ***D:*** Steven Hilliard Stern; ***M:*** Hagood Hardy. **TV**

McBain **1991 (R)** In this exciting fast-paced action-thriller, POW Robert McBain (Walken) leads a group of veterans into battle against the Columbian drug cartel. Stunning cinematography and superb performances combine to make this a riveting action film you won't soon forget. **104m/C VHS.** Christopher Walken, Maria Conchita Alonso, Michael Ironside, Steve James, Jay Patterson, Thomas G. Waites; ***D:*** James Glickenhaus; ***W:*** James Glickenhaus.

McCabe & Mrs. Miller **1971 (R)** Altman's characteristically quirky take on the Western casts Beatty as a self-inflated entrepreneur who opens a brothel in the Great North. Christie is the madame who helps stabilize the haphazard operation. Unfortunately, success comes at a high price, and when gunmen arrive to enforce a business proposition, Beatty must become the man he has, presumably, merely pretended to be. A poetic, moving work, and a likely classic of the genre. Based on the novel by Edmund Naughton. **121m/C VHS, DVD.** Warren Beatty, Julie Christie, William Devane, Keith Carradine, John Schuck, Rene Auberjonois, Shelley Duvall, Bert Remsen, Michael Murphy, Hugh Millais, Jack Riley; ***D:*** Robert Altman; ***W:*** Robert Altman; ***C:*** Vilmos Zsigmond; ***M:*** Leonard Cohen.

The McConnell Story **1/2** *Tiger in the Sky* **1955** True story of ace flyer McConnell, his heroism during WWII and the Korean conflict, and his postwar aviation pioneer efforts. Fine acting from Allyson and Ladd, with good support from Whitmore and Faylen. **107m/C VHS.** Alan Ladd, June Allyson, James Whitmore, Frank Faylen; ***D:*** Gordon Douglas; ***M:*** Max Steiner.

The McCullochs **1/2** *The Wild McCullochs* **1975 (PG)** Texas millionaire J.J. McCulloch (Tucker) is the kind of domineering patriarch whose kids wind up hating him and destroying their own lives. Stereotypical family saga set in 1949. **93m/C VHS, DVD.** Forrest Tucker, Julie Adams, Janice Heiden, Max Baer Jr., Don Grady, Chip Hand, Dennis Redfield, William Demarest, Harold J. Stone, Vito Scotti, James Gammon, Mike Mazurki; ***D:*** Max Baer Jr.; ***W:*** Max Baer Jr.; ***C:*** Fred W. Koenekamp; ***M:*** Ernest Gold.

The McGuffin **1985** A film critic's inquisitiveness about the activities of his neighbors gets him caught up in murder and a host of other problems. A takeoff of Alfred Hitchcock's 1954 classic "Rear Window." **95m/C VHS.** *GB* Charles Dance, Ritza Brown, Francis Matthews, Brian Glover, Phyllis Logan, Jerry Stiller, Anna Massey; ***D:*** Colin Bucksey.

McHale's Navy **1/2 1964** The TV sitcom came to the big screen with its silly humor intact as Lt. Commander Quinton McHale (Borgnine) and the reprobate crew of PT-73 get into debt gambling with a bunch of marines, which they try to get out of in a variety of unorthodox ways. **93m/C VHS.** Ernest Borgnine, Tim Conway, Joe Flynn, Bob Hastings, Billy (Billie) Sands, Gavin MacLeod, George Kennedy; ***D:*** Edward Montagne; ***W:*** Frank Gill Jr., George Carleton Brown; ***C:*** William Margulies.

McHale's Navy **1/2 1997 (PG)** Yet another (unsuccessful) attempt to take a TV series and let it loose on the big screen. Retired Navy skipper McHale (Arnold) has set up his scheming ways on the Caribbean island of San Ysidro, where he can be a thorn in the side of Capt. Binghampton (Stockwell), the newly transferred commanding officer of the island's sleepy naval base. McHale's former cronies aid their leader when he's reluctantly reunited with the Navy in order to prevent the terrorist threats of his former Soviet nemesis Vladakov (Curry). A shining example of "why bother?" moviemaking. TV's original McHale, Borgnine, has a cameo (and gets a promotion to admiral). **108m/C VHS, DVD.** Tom Arnold, Tim Curry, Dean Stockwell, David Alan Grier, Debra Messing, Thomas Chong, Bruce Campbell, French Stewart, Brian Haley, Danton Stone; ***Cameos:*** Ernest Borgnine; ***D:*** Bryan Spicer; ***W:*** Peter Crabbe; ***C:*** Buzz

Feitshans IV; *M:* Dennis McCarthy.

McHale's Navy Joins the Air Force ♪♪ 1/2 **1965** McHale is conspicuously missing from this sequel (Borgnine had a contract dispute) so second banana Conway, as Ensign Charles Parker, gets to shine in slapstick gags. A drunken Parker winds up in an Air Force uniform and is mistaken for a hot-shot flier, gets involved with some Russians, and is even cited for bravery by President Franklin D. Roosevelt. **91m/C VHS.** Tim Conway, Joe Flynn, Tom Tully, Ted Bessell, Bob Hastings, Gavin MacLeod, Billy (Billie) Sands; *D:* Edward Montagne; *W:* John Fenton Murray; *C:* Lionel Lindon.

McKenzie Break ♪♪♪ **1970** Irish intelligence agent John Connor (Keith) is sent to Scotland to Camp McKenzie, a prison for German POWs during WWII. Captured U-boat commander Schluetter (Griem) is suspected of planning a mass escape and Connor is supposed to stop the action. The battle of wills between the hard-headed Connor and wily Schluetter provides taut, suspenseful drama. Adapted from "The Bowmanville Break" by Sidney Shelley. **106m/C VHS, DVD.** Brian Keith, Helmut Griem, Ian Hendry, Jack Watson, Horst Janson, Patrick O'Connell; *D:* Lamont Johnson; *W:* William W. Norton Sr.; *C:* Michael Reed; *M:* Riz Ortolani.

McLintock! ♪♪♪ **1963** Rowdy western starring Wayne as a tough cattle baron whose refined wife (O'Hara) returns from the east after a two-year separation. She wants a divorce and custody of their 17-year-old daughter (Powers), who's been away at school. In the meantime, he's hired a housekeeper (De Carlo), whose teenage son (real-life son Patrick) promptly falls for Powers. It's a battle royal between the feisty wife and cantankerous husband but no one out-dukes the Duke. Other Wayne family members involved in the production include daughter Aissa (as the housekeeper's daughter) and son Michael who produced the film. **127m/C VHS, DVD.** John Wayne, Maureen O'Hara, Yvonne De Carlo, Patrick Wayne, Stefanie Powers, Jack Kruschen, Chill Wills, Jerry Van Dyke, Edgar Buchanan, Bruce Cabot, Perry Lopez, Michael Pate, Strother Martin, Gordon Jones; *D:* Andrew V. McLaglen; *W:* James Edward Grant; *C:* William Clothier.

The McMasters ♪♪ *The Blood Crowd; The McMasters...Tougher Than the West Itself* **1970 (PG)** Set shortly after the Civil War, the film tells the story of the prejudice faced by a black soldier who returns to the southern ranch on which he was raised. Once there, the rancher gives him half of the property, but the ex-soldier has difficulty finding men who will work for him. When a group of Native Americans assist him, a band of bigoted men do their best to stop it. The movie was released in two versions with different endings: in one, prejudice prevails; in the other, bigotry is defeated. **89m/C VHS, DVD.** Burl Ives, Brock Peters, David Carradine, Nancy Kwan, Jack Palance, Dane Clark, L.Q. Jones, Alan Vint, John Carradine; *D:* Alf Kjellin.

McQ ♪♪ 1/2 **1974 (PG)** After several big dope dealers kill two police officers, a lieutenant resigns to track them down. Dirty Harry done with an aging Big Duke. **116m/C VHS, DVD.** John Wayne, Eddie Albert, Diana Muldaur, Clu Gulager, Colleen Dewhurst, Al Lettieri, Julie Adams, David Huddleston; *D:* John Sturges; *C:* Harry Stradling Jr.; *M:* Elmer Bernstein.

McVicar ♪♪ 1/2 **1980 (R)** A brutish and realistic depiction of crime and punishment based on the life of John McVicar, who plotted to escape from prison. From the book by McVicar. **90m/C VHS.** *GB* Roger Daltrey, Adam Faith, Cheryl Campbell; *D:* Tom Clegg; *W:* Tom Clegg.

Me and Him ♪ 1/2 *Ich und Er* **1989 (R)** An unsuspecting New Yorker finds himself jockeying for position with his own instincts when his libido decides it wants a life of its own. **94m/C VHS.** *GE* Griffin Dunne, Carey Lowell, Ellen Greene, Craig T. Nelson; *D:* Doris Dorrie; *M:* Klaus Doldinger; *V:* Mark Linn-Baker.

Me & Mrs. Jones ♪♪ 1/2 **2002** Unhappy divorced tabloid reporter Liam Marple (Green) writes a gossip column under the nom de plume "Mrs. Jones." He knows nothing about politics but his ex-wife Jane (Hawes), who's also his boss, wants dirt on female prime minister Laura Bowden (Goodall), who is in the middle of an election campaign. Liam manages to worm his way into Laura's confidence (naturally, she doesn't know who he really is) but he finds himself with unwanted pangs of conscience when they unexpectedly fall in love. **100m/C VHS, DVD.** *GB* Robson Green, Caroline Goodall, Philip Quast, Keeley Hawes, Michael Maloney, Peter Firth, Aisling O'Sullivan; *D:* Catherine Morshead; *W:* Caleb Ranson; *C:* John Daly; *M:* Simon Lacey. **TV**

Me and Orson Welles ♪♪ 1/2 **2009 (PG-13)** In 1937, 17-year-old theater lover Richard Samuels (Efron) has a chance encounter with 22-year-old Orson Welles (McKay), who offers the teen a small role in his upcoming Mercury Theater production of "Julius Caesar" (with Welles playing Brutus). This gives Richard the chance for a behind-the-scenes look at the genius' charm, confidence, abrasiveness, and manipulations as well as the egos, insecurities, and squabbles that envelop the company. The experience for the cocky Richard is exhilarating and disillusioning with Efron rather overshadowed by the larger-than-life performance of McKay. Adapted from the 2003 novel by Robert Kaplow. **114m/C DVD.** *GB* Christian McKay, Zac Efron, Claire Danes, Zoe Kazan, James Tupper, Leo Bill, Eddie Marsan, Ben Chaplin, Kelly Reilly, Patrick Kennedy; *D:* Richard Linklater; *W:* Holly Gent Palmo, Vince Palmo; *C:* Richard Pope; *M:* Michael J. McEvoy.

Me and the Colonel ♪♪ 1/2 **1958** Average satire finds Jewish refugee S.L. Jacobowsky (Kaye) trying to get out of Paris to Spain before the Nazis occupy the city. He gets stuck travelling with anti-Semitic Polish colonel Prokoszny (Jurgens), who's also not eager to fall into German hands. If the trip went smoothly, there wouldn't be a story, so naturally the men are forced to put aside their differences to survive. Adapted from Franz Werfel's play "Jacobowsky and the Colonel." **110m/B VHS.** Danny Kaye, Curt Jurgens, Akim Tamiroff, Nicole Maurey, Francoise Rosay, Martita Hunt, Alexander Scourby, Liliane Montevecchi; *D:* Peter Glenville; *W:* S.N. Behrman, George Froeschel; *C:* Burnett Guffey; *M:* George Duning.

Me and the Kid ♪♪ 1/2 **1993 (PG)** Minor career criminals Aiello and Pantoliano try a robbery on a ruthless financier's (Dukes) home and wind up kidnapping his 10-year-old son instead. But dad doesn't want to pay the ransom and Aiello dumps his partner (who wants to kill the kid) and heads out on the road with the boy. **97m/C VHS, DVD.** Danny Aiello, Joe Pantoliano, Alex Zuckerman, Cathy Moriarty, David Dukes, Anita Morris; *D:* Dan Curtis.

Me and the Mob ♪ 1/2 *Wo Do I Gotta Kill?* **1994 (R)** Writer Jimmy Corona (Lorinz) thinks the way to get some colorful stories is to join up with his mobster uncle (Darrow). But Jimmy's no tough guy and the feds coerce him into wearing a wire to bust the local godfather. Low-budget comedy is a lesson in tedium. **85m/C VHS, DVD.** James Lorinz, Tony Darrow, John A. Costelloe, Sandra Bullock, Anthony Michael Hall, Stephen Lee, Ted (Theodore) Sorel; *Cameos:* Steve Buscemi; *D:* Frank Rainone; *W:* James Lorinz, Frank Rainone.

Me & Veronica ♪♪ **1993 (R)** Two estranged sisters try to come to terms with each other and their dead end lives. Good sister Fanny (McGovern) is a divorced waitress living in a run-down seaside town in New Jersey. One day bad sister Veronica (Wettig) shows up, announcing she's about to be sent to jail for welfare fraud. Veronica asks Fanny to look after her two kids while she's in jail and it is while visiting Veronica in prison that Fanny comes to realize her seemingly flamboyant sister is actually mentally ill and possibly suicidal. Grim little film with good lead performances. **97m/C VHS.** Elizabeth McGovern, Patricia Wettig, Michael O'Keefe, John Heard; *D:* Don Scardino; *W:* Leslie Lyles; *M:* David Mansfield.

Me & Will ♪ 1/2 **1999 (R)** Babes on bikes take to the road. Aspiring writer Jane (Rose) and artist Will (Behr) both have bad luck with men and drug problems, as well as a liking for chopper-riding. They meet in rehab and decide a road trip in search of the cycle ridden by Peter Fonda in "Easy Rider" is just the kind of quest they need. Uneven quality but a lot of recognizable faces in supporting roles. **93m/C VHS, DVD.** Sherrie Rose, Melissa Behr, Patrick Dempsey, Seymour Cassel, Grace Zabriskie, M. Emmet Walsh, Steve Railsback, Traci Lords, Billy Wirth; *D:* Sherrie Rose, Melissa Behr; *W:* Sherrie Rose, Melissa Behr; *C:* Joey Forsyte. **VIDEO**

Me and You and Everyone We Know ♪♪♪ **2005 (R)** Debut feature from conceptual artist July finds her playing wistful, struggling video artist Christine, who supports herself by chauffeuring senior citizens. She becomes unexpectedly involved with Richard (Hawkes), a shoe salesmen with a raw heart from his recent divorce and two precocious sons with their own problems. Seven-year-old Robby (Ratcliff) unwittingly visits an online sex chat room, where he's mistaken for an adult with kinky sexual ideas. Meanwhile, his older brother Peter (Thompson) is tormented by two classmates who want to practice their oral sex techniques on him while he is more interested in a domestically-inclined neighbor. Saves itself from just being quirky and precious with winning performances. **95m/C DVD.** *US GB US* John Hawkes, Carlie Westerman, Miranda July, Miles Thompson, Brandon Ratcliff, Natasha Slayton, Najarra Townsend; *D:* Miranda July; *W:* Miranda July; *C:* Chuy Chavez; *M:* Michael Andrews.

Me, Myself & I ♪♪ 1/2 **1992 (R)** Segal is a successful New York writer who falls in love with next-door neighbor Williams. But the road to romance is never smooth—particularly when your paranoid gal suffers from multiple personality disorder. Fun leads, dumb movie. **97m/C VHS.** George Segal, JoBeth Williams, Shelley Hack, Don Calfa, Bill Macy, Betsey Lynn George, Sharon McNight, Ruth Gilbert; *D:* Pablo Fero; *W:* Julian Barry.

Me, Myself, and Irene ♪♪♪ **2000 (R)** Carrey is Charlie, a Rhode Island state trooper whose split personality (one meek and mild-mannered, the other an out-of-control sociopath) is controlled by medication, which he loses when transporting crime suspect Irene (Zellweger). Both sides fall for the girl and declare war on each other. Carrey's verbal and physical acrobatics, along with the Farrellys' patented gross-out scenes are as hilarious, and joyfully disgusting, as you'd imagine. And if you're into that kind of thing, you'll not be disappointed, but the movie shares the lead character's ailment: it has another side. The romance between Charlie and Irene can't keep up with the energy of the comedic scenes, especially the ones involving Charlie's three Mensa-candidate, African-American sons, who almost steal the movie right out from under him (who'd a thunk it?) **117m/C VHS, DVD, Blu-ray Disc.** Jim Carrey, Renee Zellweger, Robert Forster, Chris Cooper, Richard Jenkins, Traylor Howard, Daniel Greene, Zen Gesner, Tony Cox, Anthony Anderson, Lenny Clarke, Shannon Whirry, Rob Moran, Mongo Brownlee, Jerod Mixon, Michael Bowman, Mike Cerrone; *Cameos:* Anna Kournikova, Cam Neely, Brendan Shanahan; *D:* Bobby Farrelly, Peter Farrelly; *W:* Bobby Farrelly, Peter Farrelly, Mike Cerrone; *C:* Mark Irwin; *M:* Peter Yorn, Lee Scott; *V:* Rex Allen.

Me Myself I ♪♪ **1999 (R)** Pamela Drury (Griffiths) is a successful Sydney journalist who's also single, in her late 30s, and depressed by both situations. She moans about not marrying her long-ago beau Robert Dickson (Roberts) and, lo and behold, Pam's whisked into the life she could have had—marriage and mother of three in the suburbs. Of course, this Pam doesn't have a clue as to how her new life runs, which makes for some comic mileage. But it's the appealing Griffiths that holds all the unlikely yet cliched situations together. **104m/C VHS, DVD.** *AU* Rachel Griffiths, David Roberts, Sandy Winton; *D:* Pip Karmel; *W:* Pip Karmel; *C:* Graeme Lind; *M:* Charlie Chan.

Me Without You ♪♪ **2001 (R)** Marina (Friel) and Holly (Williams) are adolescent friends in London in 1974, whose changing relationship is seen over a 20-year period. Holly fancies Marina's brother Nat (Milburn) but Marina's jealousy prevents anything serious from developing. In college, Holly studies, Marina parties, and both become rivals for American lecturer Daniel (MacLachlan). Holly becomes increasingly dissatisfied with Marina's selfishness and eventually decides to pursue a relationship with Nat after all. Friel plays a brat whose vulnerability is occasionally revealed, while Williams works on her English accent as the idealistic nice girl. **107m/C VHS, DVD.** *GB* Anna Friel, Michelle Williams, Oliver Milburn, Kyle MacLachlan, Trudie Styler, Nicky Henson, Allan Corduner, Deborah Findlay, Marianne (Cuau) Denicourt, Steve John Shepherd; *D:* Sandra Goldbacher; *W:* Sandra Goldbacher, Laurence Coriat; *C:* Denis Crossan; *M:* Adrian Johnston.

Me You Them ♪♪ *Eu Tu Eles* **2000 (PG-13)** Hard-working Darlene (Case) returns to her dusty Brazilian village with a young son (and no husband) upon the death of her mother. She marries elderly Osias (Duarte) basically because he has a new house and has another son, whose father is probably not Osias. Then Osias's younger cousin Zezinho (Garcia) moves in and takes over household management while Darlene works in the fields. Yep, there's another baby. Finally, Darlene meets younger Ciro (Vasconcelos), a migrant worker, and invites him to stay around. You can guess what happens next. There's a little squabbling but soon everyone settles into a big, contented family. Portuguese with subtitles. **107m/C VHS, DVD.** *BR PT* Regina Case, Lima Duarte, Stenio Garcia, Luiz Carlos Vasconcelos, Nilda Spencer; *D:* Andrucha Waddington; *W:* Elena Soarez; *C:* Breno Silveira; *M:* Gilberto Gil.

The Meal ♪♪ *Deadly Encounter* **1975 (R)** During a dinner party held by a wealthy woman, the rich and powerful guests divulge each others' secrets with reckless disregard for the consequences. **90m/C VHS.** Dina Merrill, Carl Betz, Leon Ames, Susan Logan, Vicki Powers, Steve Potter; *D:* R. John Hugh.

Mean Creek ♪♪♪ **2004 (R)** The feature debut of Estes goes beyond teen coming-of-age cliches to tell a hard tale of moral choices. Shy, slight 13-year-old Sam (Culkin) is the favorite target of school bully George (Peck). Tough older bro Rocky (Morgan) decides to get even by inviting George on a boat trip and then humiliating and stranding him. Along for the ride are Rocky's friends, Marty (Mechlowicz) and Clyde (Kelley), and Sam's potential girlfriend Millie (Schroeder). Of course, the plan goes awry as the characters prove to be multi-dimensional: the bully is lonely and vulnerable; the macho kid hides deep insecurities. Unexpected consequences reveal that the taste of revenge isn't sweet at all. The rating is primarily for language but isn't likely to shock the film's peer group. **89m/C DVD.** *US* Rory Culkin, Ryan Kelley, Scott Mechlowicz, Trevor Morgan, Josh Peck, Carly Schroeder; *D:* Jacob Aaron Estes; *W:* Jacob Aaron Estes; *C:* Sharon Meir; *M:* Tomandandy.

Mean Dog Blues ♪♪ 1/2 **1978 (PG)** A musician is convicted of hit-and-run driving after hitching a ride with an inebriated politician. **108m/C VHS.** George Kennedy, Kay Lenz, Scatman Crothers, Gregg Henry, Gregory Sierra, Tina Louise, William Windom; *D:* Mel Stuart; *C:* Robert B. Hauser.

Mean Frank and Crazy Tony ♪♪ **1975 (R)** A mobster and the man who idolizes him attempt a prison breakout in this fun, action-packed production. **92m/C VHS, DVD.** *IT* Lee Van Cleef, Tony LoBianco, Jean Rochefort, Jess Hahn; *D:* Michele Lupo.

Mean Girls ♪♪♪ **2004 (PG-13)** "SNL" head writer/performer Fey successfully takes her sassy wit to the big screen with this clever teen comedy. Cady (Lohan) is a home-schooled kid raised in Africa attending school for the first time at 16 who uses jungle animals as her frame of reference. The popular girls are The Plastics, Barbie-esque divas led by Regina (McAdams), who take in the brainy Cady for sport. When Cady stupidly reveals her crush on Regina's ex, she quickly becomes a target. Familiar but updated, edgy portrayal of the high school social caste system is probably the smartest teen comedy since the heyday of John Hughes. Based on the non-fiction book "Queen Bees and Wannabees" by Rosalind Wiseman. **97m/C DVD.** *US* Lindsay Lohan, Rachel McAdams, Lacey Chabert, Amanda Seyfried, Tina Fey, Lizzy Caplan, Tim Meadows, Amy Poehler, Ana Gasteyer, Daniel Franzese, Courtney Chase, Neil Flynn, Jonathan Bennett; *D:*

Mark S. Waters; ***W:*** Tina Fey; ***C:*** Daryn Okada; ***M:*** Rolfe Kent.

Mean Guns 🦴 1/2 **1997 (R)** Lots of mayhem will redeem this silly plot for the action fan. Moon (Ice-T) lures 100 assassins to an abandoned prison with the promise of $10 million for the last three men standing. Lou (Lambert) and Marcus (Halsey) are Moon's rivals. **90m/C VHS, DVD.** Ice-T, Christopher Lambert, Michael Halsey, Deborah Van Valkenburgh, Tina Cote, Yuji Okumoto; ***D:*** Albert Pyun; ***W:*** Andrew Witham, Nat Whitcomb; ***C:*** George Mooradian; ***M:*** Tony Riparetti. **VIDEO**

Mean Johnny Barrows 🦴 1/2 **1975** When Johnny Barrows returns to his home town after being dishonorably discharged from the Army he is offered a job as a gang hitman. **83m/C VHS, DVD.** Fred Williamson, Roddy McDowall, Stuart Whitman, Luther Adler, Jenny Sherman, Elliott Gould; ***D:*** Fred Williamson.

Mean Machine 🦴🦴 *Un Tipo con Una Faccia Strana ti Cerca per Ucciderti; Cauldron of Death; Gangland; The Dirty Mob; Ricco* **1973 (R)** A man and his beautiful cohort plot revenge on organized crime for the murder of his father. **89m/C VHS, DVD.** *IT SP* Chris Mitchum, Barbara Bouchet, Arthur Kennedy, Eduardo Fajardo, Paola Senatore; ***D:*** Tulio Demicheli; ***W:*** Mario di Nardo, Santiago Moncada; ***C:*** Francisco Fraile; ***M:*** Nando De Luca.

Mean Machine 🦴🦴 **2001 (R)** British remake of Robert Aldrich's 1974 film, "The Longest Yard," that stresses comedy and crazies. Danny Meechan (former soccer star Jones) is a disgraced pro player who winds up in prison on assault charges. The warden (Hemmings) wants Danny to coach the guards' soccer team instead of chief guard Burton (Brown), who will make Danny's life very difficult if he accepts. So Danny proposes a compromise—he'll train and coach an inmate team in a match against the guards. You can guess where this one is going but Jones and Statham (who plays a violent con) are worth watching. **98m/C VHS, DVD.** *US GB* Vinnie Jones, Jason Statham, David Hemmings, Ralph Brown, David Kelly, Jason Flemyng, Danny Dyer, Vas Blackwood, John Forgeham, Robbie Gee; ***D:*** Barry Skolnick; ***W:*** Charlie Fletcher, Chris Baker, Andrew Day; ***C:*** John Murphy; ***M:*** Alex Barber.

Mean Season 🦴🦴 **1985 (R)** A vicious mass murderer makes a Miami crime reporter his confidante in his quest for publicity during his killing spree. In time, the madman's intentions become clear as the tensions and headlines grow with each gruesome slaying. Then the reporter must come to terms with the idea that he is letting himself be used due to the success that the association is bringing him. Suspenseful story with a tense ending. Good performance from Russell as the reporter. Screenplay written by Christopher Crowe under the pseudonym Leon Piedmont. **106m/C VHS, DVD.** Kurt Russell, Mariel Hemingway, Richard Jordan, Richard Masur, Andy Garcia, Joe Pantoliano, Richard Bradford, William (Bill) Smith; ***D:*** Phillip Borsos; ***W:*** Christopher Crowe; ***M:*** Lalo Schifrin.

Mean Streak 🦴🦴 **1999 (R)** White supremacist serial killer goes after black baseball player Cash Manley (Dell), who's about to break Joe DiMaggio's hitting streak record of 56 baseball games. White cop Lou Mattoni (Bakula) and black FBI agent Altman Rogers (Leon) are out to stop him if their own prejudices don't derail the investigation. **97m/C VHS.** Scott Bakula, Leon, Howard G.H. Dell, Wayne Best, Ron McLarty, Beau Starr, Brigid Coulter, Michael Filipowich; ***D:*** Tim Hunter; ***W:*** David Ryan, John Fasano; ***C:*** Denis Lenoir; ***M:*** Paul Buckmaster. **CABLE**

Mean Streets 🦴🦴🦴🦴 **1973 (R)** A grimy slice of street life in Little Italy among lower echelon Mafiosos, unbalanced punks, and petty criminals. Charlie (Keitel), the nephew of mob boss Giovanni (Danova), struggles to keep his crazy friend Johnny Boy (De Niro) out of serious trouble. A riveting, free-form feature film, marking the formal debut by Scorsese (five years earlier he had completed a student film, "Who's That Knocking At My Door?"). Unorthodox camera movement and gritty performances by De Niro and Keitel, with underlying Catholic guilt providing the moral conflict. Excellent early '60s soundtrack. **112m/C VHS, DVD.** Harvey Keitel, Robert De Niro, David Proval, Amy Robinson, Richard Romanus, David Carradine, Robert Carradine, Cesare Danova, George Memmoli, Victor Argo; ***D:*** Martin Scorsese; ***W:*** Martin Scorsese, Mardik Martin; ***C:*** Kent Wakeford. Natl. Film Reg. '97;; Natl. Soc. Film Critics '73: Support. Actor (De Niro).

The Meanest Men in the West 🦴 **1967 (PG)** Two criminal half-brothers battle frontier law and each other. **92m/C VHS, DVD.** Charles Bronson, Lee Marvin, Lee J. Cobb, James Drury, Albert Salmi, Charles Grodin; ***D:*** Samuel Fuller; ***W:*** Charles S. Dubin; ***C:*** Lionel Lindon, Alric Edens; ***M:*** Hal Mooney. **TV**

Meantime 🦴🦴 **1981** British TV comedy/drama about the working class finds brothers Mark (Daniels) and Colin (Roth) living with their unemployed dad in a depressing East London flat. Colin, who's looking to escape his dreary life, befriends skinhead Coxy (Oldman) to the dismay of the rest of the family. **90m/C VHS, DVD.** *GB* Tim Roth, Gary Oldman, Phil Daniels, Alfred Molina, Pam Ferris; ***D:*** Mike Leigh; ***C:*** Roger Pratt; ***M:*** Andrew Dickson.

Meat Loaf: To Hell and Back 🦴🦴 **2000 (PG-13)** Saga of rock singer Meat Loaf (Brown), born Marvin Lee Aday, from his dsyfunctional family life to his early musical start and his first success in the '70s with the Top 10 hits from "Bat Out of Hell." Of course, there's also the inevitable decline and resurrection. Brown's a Meat Loaf lookalike and Pfeiffer is good as his loyal wife, Leslie, but this is a very familiar story. **90m/C VHS.** W. Earl Brown, Dedee Pfeiffer, Zachary Throne, Jesse Lenat, Lisa Jane Persky; ***D:*** Jim McBride; ***W:*** Ron McGee; ***C:*** Denis Lenoir; ***M:*** Hummie Mann. **CABLE**

Meatballs 🦴🦴 **1979 (PG)** The Activities Director at a summer camp who is supposed to organize fun for everyone prefers his own style of "fun." If you enjoy watching Murray blow through a movie, you'll like this one even as it lapses into boxoffice sentimentality. **92m/C VHS, DVD.** *CA* Bill Murray, Harvey Atkin, Kate Lynch; ***D:*** Ivan Reitman; ***W:*** Len Blum, Harold Ramis, Janis Allen; ***C:*** Donald Wilder; ***M:*** Elmer Bernstein. Genie '80: Actress (Lynch).

Meatballs 2 🦴 1/2 **1984 (PG)** The future of Camp Sasquatch is in danger unless the camp's best fighter can beat Camp Patton's champ in a boxing match. The saving grace of Bill Murray is absent in this one. **87m/C VHS.** Archie Hahn, John Mengatti, Tammy Taylor, Kim Richards, Ralph Seymour, Richard Mulligan, Hamilton Camp, John Larroquette, Paul (Pee-wee Herman) Reubens, Misty Rowe, Elayne Boosler; ***D:*** Ken Wiederhorn.

Meatballs 3 **WOOF!** **1987 (R)** Second sequel to the teenage sex/summer camp comedy. Enough is enough! **95m/C VHS.** Sally Kellerman, Shannon Tweed, George Buza, Isabelle Mejias, Al Waxman, Patrick Dempsey; ***D:*** George Mendeluk.

Meatballs 4 🦴 1/2 **1992 (R)** Feldman stars as a water skier hired to serve as recreation director of Lakeside Water Ski Camp. His enemy is Monica (Douglas) of a nearby rival camp who wants to buy out Lakeside's owner and use the land for real estate development. Lame plot only serves to showcase some good water skiing stunts. **87m/C VHS, DVD.** Corey Feldman, Jack Nance, Sarah Douglas, Bojesse Christopher; ***D:*** Bob Logan.

The Meateater **WOOF!** **1979** Disgusting horror flick of a disfigured hermit who inhabits a closed-up movie house. When it is reopened he turns into a stereotypical slasher. Vegetarians beware: references throughout about eating meat. **84m/C VHS.** Arch Joboulian, Diane Davis, Emily Spendler; ***D:*** Derek Savage.

The Mechanic 🦴🦴 1/2 *Killer of Killers* **1972 (R)** Bronson stars as Arthur Bishop, a wealthy professional killer for a powerful organization. When old friend "Big Harry" comes to him for help against the organization, he becomes Bishop's next job. Harry's son then shows up, wanting Bishop to mentor him in the ways of a hit man. A little slow but well done. One of Bronson's better action outings. **100m/C VHS, DVD.** Charles Bronson, Jan-Michael Vincent, Keenan Wynn, Jill Ireland, Linda Ridgeway; ***D:*** Michael Winner; ***W:*** Lewis John Carlino; ***C:*** Richard H. Kline; ***M:*** Jerry Fielding.

The Medallion 🦴🦴 *Highbinders* **2003 (PG-13)** So-so actioner has Hong Kong cop Eddie (Chan) transformed into an immortal warrior with superhuman powers thanks to a mysterious medallion. Eddie teams up with British Interpol agents Watson (Evans) and the beautiful Nicole (Forlani) and travels to Dublin to learn the medallion's secrets, rescue a kidnapped holy child, and fight the evil Snakehead (Sands), who wants the medallion for his own nefarious purposes (no doubt, world domination is involved). Nothing special in the way of plot but pic is watchable due to Chan's usual skills and considerable charm. Though still impressively doing much of his own stunt work, Chan's signature brand of gymnastic-style martial-arts is slightly undercut here by digital enhancement and an unnecessary array of special effect, fast-motion sequences. **90m/C VHS, DVD.** *US HK* Jackie Chan, Claire Forlani, Julian Sands, Lee Evans, John Rhys-Davies, Anthony Wong, Christy Chung, Johann Myers; ***D:*** Gordon Chan; ***W:*** Gordon Chan, Bey Logan; ***C:*** Arthur Wong Ngok Tai; ***M:*** Adrian Lee.

Medea 🦴🦴 1/2 **1970** Cinema poet Pasolini directs opera diva Callas in this straightforward adaptation of Euripides's classic about a sorceress whose escapades range from assisting in the theft of the Golden Fleece to murdering her own children. Not Pasolini at his best, but still better than most if what you're looking for is something arty. In Italian with English subtitles. **118m/C VHS, DVD.** *IT* Maria Callas, Guiseppi Gentile, Laurent Terzieff; ***D:*** Pier Paolo Pasolini.

Medea 🦴🦴 **1988** Director von Trier's adaptation of the classic Greek play by Euripides was filmed for Danish TV from a script originally co-written by Carl-Theodor Dreyer. Jason (Kier) betrays his lover Medea (Olesen) and their two sons when he agrees to a marriage with the daughter (Glinska) of King Creon (Jensen). Medea enacts a very bloody revenge. Danish with subtitles. **76m/C VHS, DVD.** *DK* Udo Kier, Kirsten Olesen, Henning Jensen, Ludmilla Glinska, Baard Owe; ***D:*** Lars von Trier; ***W:*** Lars von Trier, Carl Theodor Dreyer, Preben Thomsen; ***C:*** Sejr Brockmann; ***M:*** Joachim Holbek. **TV**

Medicine for Melancholy 🦴🦴 **2008** Jenkins' feature debut offers stylish if momentary pleasures. After a drunken-party sexual encounter, upscale San Franciscan Joanne (Heggins) and downscale Micah (Cenac) share a cab, with Joanne making it clear that she's not interested in continuing their acquaintance. But when Micah returns her forgotten wallet, Joanne agrees to hang out although not much more happens than a contemplation of the city's housing woes and small African-American population. **88m/C DVD.** Wyatt Cenac, Tracey Heggins; ***D:*** Barry Jenkins; ***W:*** Barry Jenkins; ***C:*** James Laxton.

Medicine Man 🦴 1/2 **1930** Benny stars as a con-man who fronts a medicine show in this early talkie comedy. **57m/B VHS, DVD.** Jack Benny, Betty Bronson, E. Alyn (Fred) Warren, George E. Stone, Tom Dugan; ***D:*** Scott Pembroke.

Medicine Man 🦴🦴 **1992 (PG-13)** Connery's usual commanding presence and the beautiful scenery are the only things to recommend in this lame effort. Dr. Robert Campbell (Connery) is a biochemist working in the Amazon rain forest on a cancer cure. Bracco is Dr. Rae Crane, a fellow researcher sent by the institute sponsoring Campbell to see how things are going. Although Crane is uptight and Campbell is gruff, they fall in love (supposedly), but they're sorely lacking in chemistry. Oh, Campbell's cancer cure is made from a rare flower being eradicated by the destruction of the rain forest. This politically correct cause meets romance falls short of ever being truly entertaining. **105m/C VHS, DVD.** Sean Connery, Lorraine Bracco, Jose Wilker, Rodolfo de Alexandra, Francisco Tsirene Tsere Rereme, Elias Monteiro da Silva; ***D:*** John McTiernan; ***W:*** Tom Schulman; ***C:*** Donald McAlpine; ***M:*** Jerry Goldsmith.

Medicine River 🦴🦴 1/2 **1994 (PG)** A Native American photojournalist returns to his hometown after a 20-year absence and winds up in hot water with newfound friend Harlen Bigbear. **96m/C VHS.** *CA* Graham Greene, Tom Jackson, Sheila Tousey, Jimmy Herman, Raoul Trujillo, Byron Chief-Moon, Janet-Laine Green; ***D:*** Stuart Margolin.

The Medicine Show 🦴🦴 1/2 **2001 (R)** Dark comedy in which sarcastic cartoon writer Taylor (Silverman) is diagnosed with colon cancer. As the disease, and treatment, progresses, he views the reactions of coworkers and family, the absurdity of the hospital experience, and impending surgery with sardonic wit. This is a welcome departure from the treacly, disease-of-the week approach most filmmakers take to the subject. The proceedings begin to lose their edge, however, when Taylor meets, and begins a romance with cute, quirky leukemia patient Lynn. Silverman does an excellent job in the lead role. Based on the experiences of writer-director Morris. **100m/C DVD.** Jonathan Silverman, Natasha Gregson Wagner, Greg Grunberg, Kari Wuhrer, Annabelle Gurwitch, Maz Jobrani, Dennis Libscomb; ***D:*** Wendell Morris; ***W:*** Wendell Morris; ***C:*** Ramsay Nickell. **CABLE**

The Mediterranean in Flames 🦴 1/2 **1972** In Nazi-occupied Greece, a small but brave resistance is formed to fight its captors. One of the women within the group is forced to seduce a Nazi officer in an attempt to learn enemy secrets. **85m/C VHS, DVD.** *GR* Costas Karras, Costas Precas; ***D:*** Dimis Dadiras.

Mediterraneo 🦴🦴🦴 **1991 (R)** Languid, charming comedy based on the premise that love does make the world go 'round—especially in wartime. In 1941, eight misfit Italian soldiers are stranded on a tiny Greek island and are absorbed into the life of the island, finding love and liberty in the idyllic setting. Lighthearted fun. In Italian with English subtitles. **90m/C VHS.** *IT* Diego Abatantuono, Giuseppe Cederna, Claudio Bigagli, Vanna Barba, Claudio Bisio, Luigi Alberti, Ugo Conti, Memo Dini, Vasco Mirandola, Luigi Montini, Irene Grazioli, Antonio Catania; ***D:*** Gabriele Salvatores. Oscars '91: Foreign Film.

The Medium 🦴🦴 **1951** A phony medium is done in by her own trickery in this filmed version of the Menotti opera. **80m/B VHS, DVD.** Marie Powers, Anna Maria Alberghetti, Leo Coleman; ***D:*** Gian-Carlo Menotti; ***W:*** Gian-Carlo Menotti.

Medium Cool 🦴🦴🦴 1/2 **1969** Commentary on life in the '60s focuses on a TV news cameraman and his growing apathy with the events around him. His involvement with a Appalachian woman and her young son reawakens his conscience, leading to the three getting caught up in the turbulence of the 1968 Chicago Democratic convention. A frightening depiction of detachment in modern society. **111m/C VHS, DVD.** Robert Forster, Verna Bloom, Peter Bonerz, Marianna Hill, Peter Boyle, Harold Blankenship, Charles Geary, Sid McCoy, Christine Bergstrom, William Sickingen; ***D:*** Haskell Wexler; ***W:*** Haskell Wexler; ***C:*** Haskell Wexler; ***M:*** Michael Bloomfield. Natl. Film Reg. '03.

Medusa 🦴 *Twisted* **1974** A bizarre series of events occur when an abandoned yacht containing two lifeless bodies is found on the Aegean Sea. **103m/C VHS.** George Hamilton, Cameron Mitchell, Luciana Paluzzi, Theodore Roubanis; ***D:*** Gordon Hessler.

Medusa Against the Son of Hercules 🦴 *Perseus the Invincible; Perseo l'Invincibile; Medusa vs. the Son of Hercules* **1962** This time the strongman takes on the evil Medusa and her deadly army of rock men. **90m/C VHS, DVD.** *IT* Richard Harrison, Elisa Cegani, Anna Panalli, Angel Jordan; ***D:*** Alberto De Martino; ***W:*** Mario Caiano; ***C:*** Eloy Mella; ***M:*** Carlo Franci.

The Medusa Touch 🦴 **1978 (R)** A man is struck over the head and is admitted to a hospital. Meanwhile, strange disasters befall the surrounding city. It seems that despite his unconscious state, the man is using his telekinetic powers to will things to happen.... **110m/C VHS.** *GB* Richard Burton, Lino Ventura, Lee Remick, Harry Andrews, Alan Badel, Marie-Christine Barrault, Michael Hordern, Derek Jacobi, Jeremy Brett; ***D:*** Jack Gold; ***W:*** Jack Gold, John Briley.

Meet Bill 🦴🦴 *Bill* **2007 (R)** Bill (Eckhart) is a pudgy, nice guy doormat. He works a dead-end job for his father-in-law, and his indifferent wife Jess (Banks) is having an affair with a sleazy local TV anchorman (Olyphant). Then he becomes a reluctant mentor to a self-assured prep student (Lerman) who encourages Bill to confront his mid-life crisis and go after what he wants—which happens to be a donut franchise. Alba pops up in the relatively thankless role of a lingerie saleswoman who gives Bill fashion advice. About as memorable as its title, pic just never engages the viewer enough to care if Bill becomes his own man or not. **97m/C DVD.** Aaron Eckhart, Jessica Alba, Elizabeth Banks, Logan Lerman, Timothy Olyphant, Holmes Osborne, Kristen Wiig, Jason Sudeikis; ***D:*** Bernie Goldman, Melisa Wallack; ***W:*** Melisa Wallack; ***C:*** Peter Lyons Collister; ***M:*** Ed Shearmur.

Meet Danny Wilson 🦴🦴 1/2 **1952** Talented New York singer Wilson (Siantra) and his pianist buddy Mike Ryan (Nicol) head out to Hollywood to try their luck. Danny meets club singer Joy Carroll (Winters) who introduces him to gangster owner Nick Driscoll (Burr). Nick manages Danny for a hefty percentage and makes him a star at his club but Danny's lovelife goes south when Joy picks Mike over him. Then Driscoll demands his money. Sinatra gets to croon some great tunes. ♫ I've Got a Crush on You; How Deep Is the Ocean; When You're Smiling; All of Me; She's Funny That Way; That Old Black Magic; You're a Sweetheart; Lonesome Man Blues; A Good Man Is Hard to Find. **88m/B VHS.** Frank Sinatra, Alex Nicol, Shelley Winters, Raymond Burr, Tommy Farrell, Vaughn Taylor, Jack Kruschen, Donald MacBride; ***D:*** Joseph Pevney; ***W:*** Don McGuire.

Meet Dave 🦴 **2008 (PG)** Teeny-tiny alien Commander Dave (Murphy) and his teeny-tiny alien crew land on Earth in their human-form spaceship, which happens to look just like Commander Dave. The crew is tasked with making Spaceship Dave move and act just like a human while Commander Dave and the crew (are you keeping all of this straight?) search for an orb that went off-course, landing in Manhattan. At first the aliens are snobs, but they eventually warm to the humans and make a few friends that help in their quest. Reminiscent of Will Ferrell in "Elf," the real laughs happen as Spaceship Dave wanders the city with the crew desperately pulling levers and pressing buttons, trying to figure out how to make Dave walk and smile and talk. The physical comedy is funny, but the rest of it falls predictably flat. **90m/C DVD.** *US* Eddie Murphy, Elizabeth Banks, Gabrielle Union, Ed Helms, Judah Friedlander, Shawn Christian, Scott Caan, Marc Blucas, Pat Kilbane, Michael O'Malley, Kevin Hart, Austin Lind Myers; ***D:*** Brian Robbins; ***W:*** Bill Corbett, Rob Greenberg; ***C:*** Clark Mathis; ***M:*** John Debney.

Meet Dr. Christian 🦴 1/2 **1939** The good old doctor settles some problems. Part of a series. **72m/B VHS, DVD.** Jean Hersholt, Robert Baldwin, Paul Harvey; ***D:*** Bernard Vorhaus.

Meet Joe Black 🦴🦴 **1998 (PG-13)** It's too long. And it's unremittingly hokey. But, it does have the savvy Hopkins and Pitt in full desirable object mode. In this reworking of 1934's "Death Takes a Holiday," Pitt plays a not-so-Grim Reaper who decides to see what living is all about by inhabiting the body of a recently deceased man. He grants some extra time to wealthy businessman William Parrish (Hopkins), if he'll serve as Death's guide. Now named Joe Black, Death takes to his new life but causes problems in Parrish's household, especially when he falls in love with Parrish's doctor daughter, Susan (a weak Forlani). **180m/C VHS, DVD, HD DVD.** Brad Pitt, Anthony Hopkins, Claire Forlani, Marcia Gay Harden, Jeffrey Tambor, Jake Weber; ***D:*** Martin Brest; ***W:*** Ron Osborn, Jeff Reno, Kevin Wade, Bo Goldman; ***C:*** Emmanuel Lubezki; ***M:*** Thomas Newman.

Meet John Doe 🦴🦴🦴 **1941** A social commentary about an unemployed, down-and-out man selected to be the face of a political goodwill campaign. Honest and trusting, he eventually realizes that he is being used to further the careers of corrupt politicians. Available in colorized version. **123m/B VHS, DVD.** Gary Cooper, Barbara Stanwyck, Edward Arnold, James Gleason, Walter Brennan, Spring Byington, Gene Lockhart, Regis Toomey, Ann Doran, Rod La Rocque; ***D:*** Frank Capra; ***W:*** Robert Riskin, Robert Presnell Sr.; ***C:*** George Barnes; ***M:*** Dimitri Tiomkin.

Meet Market 🦴 1/2 **2008 (R)** Obvious comedy about the dating scene. L.A. singles hang out at the local grocery store on Saturday nights hoping to meet like-minded shoppers. Oblivious soap star Hutch (McMahon), dweeby screenwriter Danny (Tudyk), kooky Jane (Tyler) and her best friend, cynic Lucinda (Allen), and would-be actress Linda (Berkley) are among the selections. Squeeze at your own risk. **80m/C DVD.** Julian McMahon, Alan Tudyk, Krista Allen, Aisha Tyler, Elizabeth Berkley, Missi Pyle, Laurie Holden, Susan Egan, Jennifer Sky; ***D:*** Charles Loventhal; ***W:*** Charles Loventhal; ***C:*** David Robbins, Steven Fierberg. **VIDEO**

Meet Me in Las Vegas 🦴🦴 **1956** Compulsive gambler/cowboy Dailey betters his luck when he hooks up with hoofer girlfriend Charisse. Much frolicking and dancing and cameo appearances by a truckload of stars. A little more entertaining than a game of solitaire. ♫ The Girl With the Yaller Shoes; If You Can Dream; Hell Hath No Fury; Lucky Charm; I Refuse to Rock 'n Roll; Rehearsal Ballet; Sleeping Beauty Ballet; Frankie and Johnny. **112m/C VHS.** Dan Dailey, Cyd Charisse, Agnes Moorehead, Lili Darvas, Jim Backus, Cara Williams, Betty Lynn, Oscar Karlweis, Liliane Montevecchi, Jerry Colonna, Frankie Laine; ***Cameos:*** Debbie Reynolds, Frank Sinatra, Peter Lorre, Vic Damone, Tony Martin, Elaine Stewart; ***D:*** Roy Rowland; ***W:*** Isobel Lennart.

Meet Me in St. Louis 🦴🦴🦴 1/2 **1944** Wonderful music in this charming tale of a St. Louis family during the 1903 World's Fair. One of Garland's better musical performances. ♫ You and I; Skip to My Lou; Over the Bannister; Meet Me In St. Louis; Brighten the Corner; Summer In St. Louis; All Hallow's Eve; Ah, Love; The Horrible One. **113m/C VHS, DVD.** Judy Garland, Margaret O'Brien, Mary Astor, Lucille Bremer, Tom Drake, June Lockhart, Harry Davenport; ***D:*** Vincente Minnelli; ***C:*** George J. Folsey. Natl. Film Reg. '94.

Meet Mr. Callaghan 🦴 1/2 **1954** Cynthia (Johns) gets suspicious when she learns that her wealthy, elderly uncle suddenly changed his will in her favor so she hires hard-boiled PI Slim Callaghan (de Marney) to investigate. He discovers that the uncle is already dead, so who rewrote the will? Based on the novel by Peter Cheyney. **88m/B DVD.** *GB* Derrick DeMarney, Harriette Johns, Peter Neil, Adrienne Corri, Trevor Reid; ***D:*** Charles Saunders; ***W:*** Brock Williams; ***C:*** Harry Waxman; ***M:*** Eric Spear.

Meet Sexton Blake 🦴🦴 **1944** A detective is hired to find a ring and some secret papers that were stolen from the corpse of a man killed in an air raid. He discovers that the papers contained the plans for a new metal alloy to be used in planes. Entertaining for its melodramatic elements. **80m/B VHS.** *GB* David Farrar, John Varley, Magda Kun, Gordon McLeod, Manning Whiley, Charles Farrell; ***D:*** John Harlow; ***W:*** John Harlow.

Meet the Deedles 🦴 1/2 **1998 (PG)** The answer to the question, "What would happen if Bill and Ted or Wayne and Garth were even dumber?" Hard to believe? No, just hard to watch. Phil and Stew Deedle (Walker and Van Wormer) are two rich surfer airheads who just wanna have fun, dude. Facing expulsion from school, the twins are forced to attend the bogus Camp Broken Spirit by their father. The boys slip and fall on a plot device and wake up in the hospital, mistaken for rookie Yellowstone park rangers there to fight a mounting prarie dog problem. It seems that bitter ex-ranger Slater (Hopper, phoning in his patented mondo-weirdo) has enslaved the rodents and is trying to redirect the geyser Old Faithful. Features heinous dialogue and stunts lifted from Mountain Dew commercials. **94m/C VHS.** Steve Van Wormer, Paul Walker, A.J. (Allison Joy) Langer, John Ashton, Dennis Hopper, Eric (Hans Gudegast) Braeden, Richard Lineback, Robert Englund, Ana Gasteyer, Megan Cavanagh; ***D:*** Steve Boyum; ***W:*** Jim Herzfeld, Dale Pollock; ***C:*** David Hennings; ***M:*** Steve Bartek.

Meet the Feebles 🦴🦴 **1989** Sex and violence gorefest perpetuated by puppets—and the dementia of director Jackson. A TV variety show, populated by animal puppets and humans in costume, is the setting for backstage mayhem, including sex, drugs, and a shooting spree. Among the characters are a sleazy walrus producer, his slinky Siamese cat mistress, a junkie frog, and a manic-depressive elephant. There's also several musical production numbers, if things aren't strange enough for you already. **94m/C VHS, DVD.** *NZ* ***D:*** Peter Jackson; ***W:*** Peter Jackson, Danny Mulheron, Fran Walsh, Stephen Sinclair; ***C:*** Murray Milne; ***M:*** Peter Dasent; ***V:*** Peter Vere-Jones, Mark Hadlow, Stuart Devine, Donna Atkinson, Mark Wright, Brian Sergent.

Meet the Fockers 🦴🦴 1/2 **2004 (PG-13)** Free-spirited Jews meet uptight WASPs in this long-awaited sequel to 2000's "Meet the Parents." Nervous Greg Focker (Stiller) and fiancee Pam (Polo) take Dina and Jack (De Niro) to finally meet his folks: lawyer turned house hubby Bernie (Hoffman) and senior citizen sex therapist Roz (Streisand). The duo extravagantly adores each other, much to Greg's embarrassment, and of course, there's more cat issues and a baby to create more problems for poor Greg. Culture clashes follow predictably and everyone seems to be coasting comfortably on their talent. **116m/C VHS, DVD, HD DVD.** *US* Robert De Niro, Ben Stiller, Dustin Hoffman, Barbra Streisand, Blythe Danner, Teri Polo, Tim Blake Nelson, Alanna Ubach, Ray Santiago, Kail Rocha, Shelley Berman, Owen Wilson, Spencer Pickren, Bradley Pickren; ***D:*** Jay Roach; ***W:*** Jim Herzfeld, John Hamburg; ***C:*** John Schwartzman; ***M:*** Randy Newman.

Meet the Hollowheads 🦴 1/2 **1989 (PG-13)** Family situation comedy set in a futuristic society. **89m/C VHS, DVD.** John Glover, Nancy Mette, Richard Portnow, Matt Shakman, Juliette Lewis, Anne Ramsey; ***D:*** Tom Burman; ***W:*** Tom Burman.

Meet the Mob 🦴🦴 *So's Your Aunt Emma* **1942** A country spinster visits her son in the big city and is mistaken for a notorious murderess. Complications arise when she tries to keep the boy honest. Could have worked better. **62m/B VHS, DVD.** Zasu Pitts, Roger Pryor, Warren Hymer, Gwen Kenyon, Douglas Fowley, Elizabeth Russell, Tristram Coffin, Lester Dorr, Wheeler Oakman, Malcolm "Bud" McTaggart; ***D:*** Jean Yarbrough.

Meet the Navy 🦴🦴 **1946** Post-war musical revue about a pianist and a dancer. **81m/B VHS.** Lionel Murton, Margaret Hurst, John Pratt, Robert Goodier; ***D:*** Alfred Travers; ***W:*** Lester Cooper; ***C:*** Ernest Palmer, Geoffrey Unsworth; ***M:*** Louis Silvers.

Meet the Parents 🦴🦴 **1991** A young man visits his fiance's parents and every nightmare, every tragedy that can possibly happen, does. From the minds of "National Lampoon," with an appearance by beyond-bizarre comedian Emo Phillips. **72m/C VHS.** Greg Glienna, Jacqueline Cahill, Dick Galloway, Carol Wheeler, Mary Ruth Clarke, Emo Philips; ***D:*** Greg Glienna; ***W:*** Mary Ruth Clarke.

Meet the Parents 🦴🦴🦴 **2000 (PG-13)** If you have any sense of empathy at all, you'll be squirming uncomfortably for Greg (Stiller), a nice Jewish boy who suffers an extended brainlock when he meets his girlfriend Pam's (Polo) WASPy parents during her sister's wedding weekend. It doesn't help that one of those parents is Jack (De Niro), an ex-CIA psychological profiler who takes an immediate dislike to his prospective son-in-law. Greg starts off on the wrong foot by accidentally smashing the urn holding the ashes of Jack's mother with a champagne cork, and his luck goes down from there. The rest of the cast performs well, especially Danner as Pam's mother, and De Niro plays off of his tough guy image for a brilliant comedic performance. **108m/C VHS, DVD, HD DVD.** Ben Stiller, Robert De Niro, Teri Polo, Blythe Danner, James Rebhorn, Jon Abrahams, Owen Wilson, Phyllis George, Kail Rocha, Thomas (Tom) McCarthy, Nicole DeHuff; ***D:*** Jay Roach; ***W:*** Jim Herzfeld, John Hamburg; ***C:*** Peter James; ***M:*** Randy Newman.

Meet the People 🦴🦴 **1944** Patriotic propaganda in a musical setting. Shipyard welder William Swanson (Powell) writes a patriotic play and it's optioned by Broadway star Julie Hampton (Ball) who wants to make it into a musical. Hearing this, Swanson withdraws his consent and she is left to prove to him that she's just folks and can make his play work. **100m/B DVD.** Lucille Ball, Dick Powell, Virginia O'Brien, Bert Lahr, Rags Ragland, June Allyson, Steven Geray; ***D:*** Charles Riesner; ***W:*** Sid Herzig, Fred Saidy; ***C:*** Robert L. Surtees.

Meet the Robinsons 🦴🦴 1/2 **2007 (G)** Based on William Joyce's book "A Day With Wilbur Robinson," which finds young science geek Lewis despairing of ever being adopted. But his luck changes thanks to teenager Wilbur Robinson and his time machine. Wilbur takes Lewis into the future to meet his eccentric family, but everyone's dreams are threatened by the sinister man in the bowler hat, who's got it out for Lewis. The jovial T-Rex, who's meant to aid the bad guy, is a scene-stealer. Hyperactive animated comedy is the first release by Disney in its Digital 3-D process. **102m/C DVD, Blu-ray Disc.** *US* ***D:*** Stephen John Anderson; ***W:*** Jon Bernstein, Donald Hall, Stephen John Anderson, Michelle Spitz, Nathan Greno, Aurian Redson, Joe Mateo; ***M:*** Danny Elfman; ***V:*** Jordan Fry, Angela Bassett, Tom Selleck, Harland Williams, Daniel Hansen, Wesley Singerman, Laurie Metcalf, Adam West, Nicole Sullivan, Stephen John Anderson.

Meet the Spartans WOOF! **2008 (PG-13)** Brain-dead spoof of the hardly cerebral but ripe for parody "300" swords-and-sandals epic hangs on the story of Leonidas (Maguire) leading his fierce army of 13 into battle against the invading hordes of Xerxes (Davitian), supported by his Queen Margo (Electra). But plot hardly matters as Seltzer and Friedberg once again scrape the bottom of the pop-culture barrel for a make-it-stop string of lazy swipes at movies and celebs buoyed by body-function gags and gay jokes that barely bother to be funny, let alone subversive. Way too long and way too dumb. **83m/C DVD, Blu-ray Disc.** *US* Carmen Electra, Ken Davitian, Kevin Sorbo, Diedrich Bader, Sean Maguire, Method Man, Phil Morris, Travis Van Winkle, Jareb Dauplaise; ***D:*** Aaron Seltzer, Jason Friedberg; ***W:*** Aaron Seltzer, Jason Friedberg.

Meet Wally Sparks 🦴🦴 **1997 (R)** No-brow "Man Who Came to Dinner." Smutty TV shock-talk host Sparks (Dangerfield) is given one week to save his failing show when producer Reynolds (with a noticeably bad rug) puts him on notice. Opportunity knocks when he is invited to a party at the governor's mansion to interview the conservative head honcho (Stiers). Once there, a freak accident with a drunken horse prevents Sparks from leaving, and the new guest makes himself right at home by turning the fancy digs into a broadcast studio. Dangerfield's machine gun spray of one liners occasionally hits, as do his sometimes lengthy and elaborately set up jokes that do little to propel the plot along but are pure Dangerfield. Not much beyond Rodney makes lackluster "Sparks" fly. **107m/C VHS, DVD.** Rodney Dangerfield, David Ogden Stiers, Burt Reynolds, Debi Mazar, Cindy Williams, Alan Rachins; ***D:*** Peter Baldwin; ***W:*** Rodney Dangerfield, Harry Basil; ***C:*** Richard H. Kline; ***M:*** Michel Colombier.

Meeting at Midnight 🦴🦴 **1944** Charlie Chan is invited to a seance to solve a perplexing mystery. Chan discovers that they use mechanical figures and from there on solving the murder is easy. **67m/B VHS, DVD.** Sidney Toler, Joseph Crehan, Mantan Moreland, Frances Chan, Ralph Peters, Helen Beverly; ***D:*** Phil Rosen.

Meeting Daddy 🦴🦴 1/2 **1998 (R)** Neurotic New Yorker Peter (Charles) falls in love with Georgia peach Melanie (Wentworth) and then he travels to Savannah to meet her southern-fried family, including her eccentric, irascible father, The Colonel (Bridges). **91m/C VHS, DVD.** Lloyd Bridges, Josh Charles, Alexandra Wentworth, Beau Bridges, Walter Olkewicz, Kristy Swanson; ***D:*** Peter Gould; ***W:*** Peter Gould; ***C:*** Mike Mayers; ***M:*** Adam Fields. **VIDEO**

Meeting Venus 🦴🦴 1/2 **1991 (PG-13)** Backstage drama featuring Close as Karin Anderson, a world-famous Swedish opera diva. An international cast of characters adds to this sophisticated film of romance, rivalry and political confrontation set amidst a newly unified Europe. **121m/C VHS.** Glenn Close, Niels Arestrup, Erland Josephson, Johanna Ter

Steege, Maria De Medeiros, Ildiko Bansagi, Macha Meril, Dorottya Udvaros, Jay O. Sanders, Victor Poletti; ***D:*** Istvan Szabo; ***W:*** Istvan Szabo, Michael Hirst; ***C:*** Lajos Koltai; ***V:*** Kiri Te Kanawa.

Meetings with Remarkable Men 1/2 **1979** An acclaimed, visually awesome film version of the memoir by Gurdjieff, about his wanderings through Asia and the Middle East searching for answers and developing his own spiritual code. Mildly entertaining but only of true interest to those familiar with the subject. **108m/C VHS.** Terence Stamp, Dragan Maksimovic, Mikica Dmitrijevic; ***D:*** Peter Brook.

Mega Shark Vs. Giant Octopus 1/2 **2009 (R)** Well, doesn't the title just say it all. Two Ice Age sea critters get thawed out and the octopus attacks Tokyo while the shark goes after San Francisco. It takes international cooperation (via submarine) to end the madness by getting the two together for a mega-confrontation. Sushi and calamari for everyone! **90m/C DVD.** Lorenzo Lamas, Deborah Gibson, Vic Chao, Sean Lawlor, Jonathan Nation; ***D:*** Jack Perez; ***W:*** Jack Perez; ***C:*** Alexander Yellen; ***M:*** Chris Ridenhour. **VIDEO**

Megaforce WOOF! 1982 (PG) Futuristic thriller directed by stuntman Needham follows the adventures of the military task force, Megaforce, on its mission to save a small democratic nation from attack. Bostwick leads the attack. 'Nuff said. **99m/C VHS.** Barry Bostwick, Persis Khambatta, Edward Mulhare, Henry Silva, Michael Beck, Ralph Wilcox; ***D:*** Hal Needham.

Megalodon **2003 (PG-13)** Prehistoric 11-ton shark, Carchardodon Megalodon, is rudely awakened by unsuspecting deep-sea oil diggers and he's not in the mood to make nice with the trespassers. **91m/C VHS, DVD.** Robin Sachs, Al Sapienza, Leighanne Littrell, Mark Sheppard, Jennifer Sommerfield, Evan Mirand, Steve Scionti, Gary J. Tunnicliffe, Fred Belford, Yasmine Delawari, Stanley Isaacs, Will Boroers, John Michael Mauer; ***D:*** Pat Corbitt; ***W:*** Gary J. Tunnicliffe, Stanley Isaacs; ***C:*** Timothy Housel; ***M:*** Tony Fennell, Billy T. James, Brian Randazzo. **VIDEO**

Megasnake 1/2 *Mega Snake* **2007 (R)** Ah yes, another Sci-Fi Channel original (with some decent CGI). In a backwater town filled with snakes and snake handlers, dimwit Duff steals a very rare snake to add to his collection. It must be super-snake because, given the chance, it grows and grows and grows until it can swallow a man in a single gulp. Having escaped Duff, Megasnake heads off to have some fun at the county fair (and we don't mean elephant ears and ring toss). **90m/C DVD.** Michael Shanks, Siri Baruc, Mick Harvey, Ben Cardinal, John T. Woods, Matthew Atherton; ***D:*** Tibor Takacs; ***W:*** Rob Robinson, Alexander Volz; ***C:*** Emil Topuzov; ***M:*** Guy Zerafa, Dave Klotz. **CABLE**

Megaville **1991 (R)** Set in the not too distant future, corrupt politician Travanti struggles to corner the market on the evil technology "Dream-a-Life," which aims to control the rebellious "riff-raff" of Megaville. He does all of his dealings while up against a hitman who has a defective memory chip in his brain. **96m/C VHS.** Billy Zane, Daniel J. Travanti, J.C. Quinn, Grace Zabriskie; ***D:*** Peter Lehner; ***W:*** Peter Lehner.

Melanie 1/2 **1982 (PG)** Drama tells the tale of one poor woman's courage, determination, and optimism, as she tries to regain her child from her ex-husband. She befriends musician Cummings (a founding member of "Guess Who" rock band) who helps. Usual cliches balanced by good performances. **109m/C VHS.** *CA* Glynnis O'Connor, Paul Sorvino, Don Johnson, Burton Cummings; ***D:*** Rex Bromfield.

Melanie Darrow 1/2 **1997 (PG-13)** Routine drama finds relentless attorney Melanie Darrow (Burke) defending the younger husband of a socialite friend for the woman's murder, much to the dismay of Melanie's homicide cop brother (Bloom). **88m/C VHS.** Delta Burke, Brian Bloom, Daniel Birt, Jonathan Banks, Bruce Abbott, Shawn Ashmore, Wendel Meldrum; ***D:*** Gary Nelson. **CABLE**

Melinda and Melinda **2005 (PG-13)** Allen sticks to the familiar in a talky tale of Manhattanites debating the tragic and comic. Over dinner, playwright Sy (Shawn), who writes comedies, and tragedienne Max (Pine) entertain themselves with an urban anecdote about an unhappy, neurotic woman named Melinda (Mitchell). In both stories she crashes the dinner party of friends with her tale of disaster, causing marital misunderstandings and emotional dramas. The leading males in the story are both ineffectual, unemployed actors (Miller, Ferrell) while their wives (Sevigny, Peet) are successful. And what does that say, we wonder. Or maybe we don't because, despite the talent involved, it all seems rather too precious and rarefied an atmosphere to take much interest. **99m/C DVD.** *US* Radha Mitchell, Chloe Sevigny, Jonny Lee Miller, Will Ferrell, Amanda Peet, Chiwetel Ejiofor, Wallace Shawn; ***D:*** Woody Allen; ***W:*** Woody Allen; ***C:*** Vilmos Zsigmond.

Melissa **1997** Unemployed reporter Guy Foster (Dutton) is trying to make a new career as a novelist. But when his wife Melissa (Ehle) is murdered, all the evidence points to Guy and he has to find the real killer to prove his innocence. Based on the novel by Francis Durbridge. **150m/C DVD.** *GB* Tim Dutton, Jennifer Ehle, Adrian Dunbar, Julie Walters, Faith Edwards, Hugh Quarshie, Diana Weston; ***D:*** Bill Anderson; ***W:*** Alan Bleasdale; ***C:*** Dick Dodd; ***M:*** Richard Harvey. **TV**

Melo **1986** The title is short for "melodrama" so you know exactly when sort of story you're in for. Discontented Romaine begins an affair with womanizing concert violinist Marcel, an old friend of her boring husband Pierre's. While Marcel is away on tour, Pierre becomes seriously (and suspiciously) ill. When Romaine's perfidy is discovered, she commits suicide. However, years later, Pierre demands the truth from Marcel. French with subtitles. **112m/C DVD.** *FR* Sabine Azema, Pierre Arditti, Andre Dussollier, Fanny Ardant, Jacques Dacqmine; ***D:*** Alain Resnais; ***W:*** Alain Resnais; ***C:*** Charlie Van Damme, Michel Philippe-Gerard.

Melody **1971 (G)** Sensitive but slow study of a special friendship which enables two pre-teens to survive in a regimented and impersonal world. Features music by the Bee Gees. **106m/C VHS.** *GB* Tracy Hyde, Jack Wild, Mark Lester, Colin Barrie, Roy Kinnear; ***D:*** Waris Hussein; ***W:*** Alan Parker.

Melody Cruise **1932** Boring musical romantic comedy that can't stay with any one of those three things for more than a minute without careening into one of the other two. ♫I Met Her at a Party; He's Not the Marrying Kind; Isn't This a Night For Love; This is the Hour. **75m/B VHS.** Phil Harris, Charlie Ruggles, Greta Nissen, Helen Mack, Chick Chandler; ***D:*** Mark Sandrich; ***M:*** Max Steiner.

Melody for Three **1941** In the tradition of matchmaker, Doctor Christian aids in the reuniting of music-teacher mother and great-conductor father, who have been divorced for years, in order to help the couple's son, a violin prodigy. **69m/B VHS, DVD.** Jean Hersholt, Fay Wray; ***D:*** Erle C. Kenton.

Melody in Love **1978** A young girl visits her cousin and her swinging friends on a tropical island. Dubbed. **90m/C VHS.** Melody O'Bryan, Sasha Hehn; ***D:*** Hubert Frank.

Melody Master *New Wine* **1941** Romanticized biography of composer Franz Schubert, chronicling his personal life and loves, along with performances of his compositions. If you just have to know what drove the composer of "Ave Maria" it may hold your interest, but otherwise not very compelling. **80m/B VHS.** Alan Curtis, Ilona Massey, Binnie Barnes, Albert Bassermann, Billy Gilbert, Sterling Holloway; ***M:*** Miklos Rozsa.

Melody of the Plains **1937** Singing cowpoke teams up with a young girl for some cattle-rustlin' adventure. Substandard horse opry due to poor direction and haphazard lensing. **53m/B VHS.** Fred Scott, Louise Small, Al "Fuzzy" St. John, David Sharpe, Lafe (Lafayette) McKee, Charles "Slim" Whitaker, Hal Price, Lew Meehan; ***D:*** Sam Newfield; ***W:*** Bennett Cohen.

Melody Ranch 1/2 **1940** Gene returns to his home town as an honored guest and appointed sheriff. But gangster MacLane is determined to drive him out of town. ♫Melody Ranch; Call of the Canyon; We Never Dream the Same Dream Twice; Vote for Autry; My Gal Sal; Torpedo Joe; What Are Cowboys Made Of?; Rodeo Rose; Back in the Saddle Again. **84m/C VHS, DVD.** Gene Autry, Jimmy Durante, George "Gabby" Hayes, Ann Miller, Barton MacLane, Joseph (Joe) Sawyer, Horace McMahon, Veda Ann Borg; ***D:*** Joseph Santley. Natl. Film Reg. '02.

Melody Time **1948** Seven animated/musical tales from the Disney studios, including "Blame It On the Samba" with Donald Duck; "Once Upon a Wintertime;" "Bumble Boogie;" "Johnny Appleseed;" "Little Toot" with musical narration provided by the Andrews Sisters; Fred Waring and the Pennsylvanians singing "Trees," the Joyce Kilmer poem; and Roy Rogers narrating the story of "Pecos Bill." **75m/C VHS, DVD.** Roy Rogers; ***D:*** Clyde Geronimi, Wilfred Jackson, Jack Kinney, Hamilton Luske; ***C:*** Winton C. Hoch; ***V:*** Dennis Day, Ethel Smith, Buddy Clark, Bob Nolan, The Andrews Sisters, Frances Langford.

Melody Trail **1935** Autry wins $1000 in a rodeo, loses the money to a gypsy, gets a job, falls for his employer's daughter...and in the end captures a kidnapper and cattle rustlers. ♫Hold On, Little Doggie, Hold On; On the Prairie; Lookin for the Lost Chord; The Hurdy Gurdy Man; My Prayer For Tonight; End of the Trail; I'd Love a Home in the Mountains. **60m/B VHS.** Gene Autry, Smiley Burnette, Ann Rutherford; ***D:*** Joseph Kane.

Meltdown *High Risk; Shu Dan Long Wei* **1995** Apparently producer/director Wong Jing has a score to settle with Jackie Chan. This action/comedy revolves around a drunken action star called Frankie (Cheung) who claims to do all of his own stunts but uses a team of stuntmen, including former cop Kit Li (Li), whose wife and son were killed (in a particularly ridiculous opening sequence) by an evil criminal mastermind (Wong). Who, with his gang, turns up to steal the Russian crown jewels that are being exhibited in a Hong Kong hotel. Think slapstick "Die Hard," although it's virtually impossible for western audiences to figure out where the action ends and the comedy begins. **100m/C VHS, DVD.** *HK* Jet Li, Jacky Cheung, Chingmy Yau, Valerie Chow, Charlie Yoeh, Kelvin Wong; ***D:*** Wong Jing; ***W:*** Wong Jing.

Meltdown WOOF! 2006 Which is what you'll want to do to the DVD after you've wasted your time on this lame "Armageddon-is-a-comin'" flick. Scientist blows up an asteroid endangering earth, but the fragments push our planet's orbit closer to the sun, causing intense global warming and evacuations to the Arctic. Uh, isn't all that ice supposed to melt? What do these people have—an ark? Maybe the hungry polar bears will get to them first. **93m/C DVD.** Casper Van Dien, Stefanie von Pfetten, Venus Terzo, Amanda Crew, Vincent Gale, Ryan McDonell; ***D:*** J.P. Howell; ***W:*** Rick Drew; ***C:*** Adam Sliwinski; ***M:*** Ron Ramin. **CABLE**

Melvin and Howard 1/2 **1980 (R)** Story of Melvin Dummar, who once gave Howard Hughes a ride. Dummar later claimed a share of Hughes's will. Significant for Demme's direction and fine acting from Steenburgen/LeMat, and Robards in a small role as Hughes. Offbeat and very funny. **95m/C VHS, DVD.** Paul LeMat, Jason Robards Jr., Mary Steenburgen, Michael J. Pollard, Dabney Coleman, Elizabeth Cheshire, Pamela Reed, Cheryl "Rainbeaux" Smith; ***D:*** Jonathan Demme; ***W:*** Bo Goldman; ***C:*** Tak Fujimoto; ***M:*** Bruce Langhorne. Oscars '80: Orig. Screenplay, Support. Actress (Steenburgen); Golden Globes '81: Support. Actress (Steenburgen); L.A. Film Critics '80: Support. Actress (Steenburgen); N.Y. Film Critics '80: Director (Demme), Screenplay, Support. Actress (Steenburgen); Natl. Soc. Film Critics '80: Film, Screenplay, Support. Actress (Steenburgen); Writers Guild '80: Orig. Screenplay.

Melvin Goes to Dinner **2003 (R)** Joey (Price) invites Melvin (Blieden) and Alex (Courtney) to dinner as a way of catching up; they are also unexpectedly joined by Alex's friend Sarah (Gurwitch). Since each person is a stranger to at least one other person at the table, there's a certain awkwardness at first, but then the conversation (often confessional) starts to flow. Oh, and despite the title, the characters are not actually shown dining, so at least you won't get hungry, although all the talking may make you sleepy. **83m/C VHS, DVD.** Michael Blieden, Stephanie Courtney, Matt Price, Annabelle Gurwitch, Maura Tierney; ***D:*** Bob Odenkirk; ***W:*** Michael Blieden; ***C:*** Alex Vendler; ***M:*** Michael Penn.

Melvin Purvis: G-Man *The Legend of Machine Gun Kelly; Kansas City Massacre* **1974** Mediocre action film has dedicated federal agent tracking killer Machine Gun Kelly across American Midwest during Depression. **78m/C VHS.** Dale Robertson, Harris Yulin, Margaret Blye, Matt Clark, Elliot Street, Dick Sargent, John Karlen, David Canary; ***D:*** Dan Curtis. **TV**

The Member of the Wedding **1952** While struggling through her adolescence, 12-year-old tomboy Frankie (played by 26-year-old Harris) is growing up in 1945 Georgia and seeking solace from her family's cook, Berenice (Waters) and her cousin, John Henry (de Wilde). Based on Carson McCullers's play, this story of family, belonging, and growth is well acted and touching. **90m/C VHS, DVD.** Ethel Waters, Julie Harris, Brandon de Wilde, Arthur Franz, William Hansen, Nancy Gates, James Edwards, Harry Bolden; ***D:*** Fred Zinnemann; ***W:*** Edward Anhalt; ***C:*** Hal Mohr; ***M:*** Alex North.

The Member of the Wedding **1983** TV rehash of Carson McCuller's play about a young girl who finds she's got some growing up to do when big brother marries. No match for Zinnemann's '52 version, or for Mann's earlier "All Quiet on the Western Front" and "Marty." **90m/C VHS.** Dana Hill, Pearl Bailey, Howard E. Rollins Jr.; ***D:*** Delbert Mann.

The Member of the Wedding 1/2 **1997 (PG)** The second TV remake of Carson's McCuller's 1946 novel follows the adolescent struggles of 12-year-old Frankie Adams (Paquin). It's the summer of 1944 in Georgia and desperate for a change, Frankie decides the wedding of her brother Jarvis (McGrath) will give her the opportunity to leave her troubles behind. Woodard is the family's gentle but no-nonsense housekeeper Berenice. **93m/C VHS.** Anna Paquin, Alfre Woodard, Matt McGrath, Corey Dunn, Anne Tremko, Enrico Colantoni; ***D:*** Fielder Cook; ***W:*** David W. Rintels; ***C:*** Paul LaMastra; ***M:*** Laurence Rosenthal.

Memento 1/2 **2000 (R)** Twisty and engaging noir thriller of a man searching for his wife's killer in Los Angeles. Only problem is, Leonard Shelby (Pearce) lost his short-term memory after the attack and forgets all current events every 15 minutes, or so. Problem solved as Shelby tattoos the most vital info all over his body and leaves less permanent "clues" for himself on Post-Its and Polaroids of the usual suspects. Shelby meets Natalie (Moss) and Teddy (Pantoliano) who may want to help him, but like his own memory, definitely can't be trusted. Ingeniously constructed story is told backwards, from Pearce's shooting of the killer to his puzzle-like construction of events and renders the audience as clueless as the impaired hero. Clever use of flashbacks and black-and-white segs help define events in time. More than normally required mental exercise is more than worth the effort. Director Nolan adapted the film from short story by brother Jonathan. **116m/C VHS, DVD, Blu-ray Disc.** *US* Guy Pearce, Carrie-Anne Moss, Joe Pantoliano, Mark Boone Jr., Stephen Tobolowsky, Callum Keith Rennie, Harriet Sansom Harris, Jorja Fox; ***D:*** Christopher Nolan; ***W:*** Christopher Nolan; ***C:*** Wally Pfister; ***M:*** David Julyan. Ind. Spirit '01: Director (Nolan), Screenplay; Ind. Spirit '02: Film, Support. Actress (Moss); L.A. Film Critics '01: Screenplay; Broadcast Film Critics '01: Screenplay.

Memento Mori *Yeogo Goedam 2* **2000 (R)** The second film in the Ghost School trilogy has many subplots, and one viewing generally won't pick them all up. At the center of it all is Min-Ah, who discovers a strange diary detailing a torrid lesbian affair between two of her classmates, Shi-eun and Hyo-Shin. The diary is very unusual, with many hidden passages, and eventually Min-Ah starts calling off sick to go through it all. When Hyo-Shin appears to commit suicide, Min-Ah shows the diary to friends and they try to find out what really happened. It's then that the hallucinations and unusual occurrences start, and Min-Ah suddenly realizes the diary is more than what it seems. **94m/C DVD.** *KN* Ji-yeon Park, Min-sun Kim, Yeh-jin Park, Young-jin Lee, Jong-hak Baek, Jae-in Kim, Hyo-jin Kong, Min Han, Seung-Yeon Han, Hye-mi Lee, Seong-Eon Lim; *D:* Tae-Yong Kim, Kyu-Dong Min; *W:* Tae-Yong Kim, Kyu-Dong Min; *C:* Yoon-soo Kim; *M:* Sun-woo Jo.

Memoirs of a Geisha **2005 (PG-13)** This look into the world of Japan's "Geisha" escorts in the 1930s flounders thanks to Marshall's bizarre decision to cast the film with Chinese actors and shoot it in the U.S., but cultural insensitivity isn't this melodrama's only sin. Sayuri (Zhang) is sold into a geisha household, where her companionship skills are refined by Mameha (Yeoh), the chief rival of the household's "Mother" (Momoi). Sayuri is ambivalent about being a geisha until she realizes that it can get her closer to The Chairman (Watanabe), a kindly businessman. Sayuri begins relishing her role as a renowned geisha, and the predictable plot grows in both heft and velocity, straining audience patience with its two and a half hour running time. **137m/C DVD, Blu-ray Disc, UMD.** *US* Ken(saku) Watanabe, Michelle Yeoh, Koji Yakusho, Youki Kudoh, Tsai Chin, Cary-Hiroyuki Tagawa, Gong Li, Randall Duk Kim, Mako, Kenneth Tsang, Shizuko Hoshi, Zhang Ziyi, Kaori Momoi, Suzuka Ohgo, Thomas Ikeda, Zoe Weizenbaum; *D:* Rob Marshall; *W:* Robin Swicord; *C:* Dion Beebe; *M:* John Williams. Oscars '05: Art Dir./Set Dec., Cinematog., Costume Des.; British Acad. '05: Cinematog., Costume Des., Orig. Score; Golden Globes '06: Orig. Score; Natl. Bd. of Review '05: Support. Actress (Li); Broadcast Film Critics '05: Orig. Score.

Memoirs of an Invisible Man ½ **1992 (PG-13)** Nick Halloway, a slick and shallow stock analyst, is rendered invisible by a freak accident. When he is pursued by a CIA agent-hit man who wants to exploit him, Nick turns for help to Alice, a documentary filmmaker he has just met. Naturally, they fall in love along the way. Effective sight gags, hardworking cast can't overcome pitfalls in script, which indecisively meanders between comedy and thrills. **99m/C VHS, DVD.** Chevy Chase, Daryl Hannah, Sam Neill, Michael McKean, Stephen Tobolowsky, Jim Norton, Patricia Heaton, Rosalind Chao; *D:* John Carpenter; *W:* Robert Collector.

Memorial Day **1983** Good cast highlights this TV outing covering a Vietnam veterans reunion. With the old memories come new problems for the men and their families. **120m/C VHS.** Mike Farrell, Shelley Fabares, Keith Michell, Bonnie Bedelia, Robert Walden, Edward Herrmann, Danny Glover; *D:* Joseph Sargent; *M:* Billy Goldenberg. **TV**

Memorial Day ½ **1998 (R)** Routine to the point of boredom. Downey (Speakman) is an ex-Marine/government operative who's just been released from a mental ward. He's needed to stop a terrorist group that's stolen a Russian satellite. **95m/C VHS.** Jeff Speakman, Bruce Weitz, Paul Mantee, Stephanie Niznik; *D:* Worth Keeter. **VIDEO**

Memorial Valley Massacre **1988 (R)** When campers settle for a weekend in a new, unfinished campground, they're slaughtered in turn by a nutty hermit. **93m/C VHS, DVD.** Cameron Mitchell, William (Bill) Smith, John Kerry, Mark Mears, Lesa Lee, John Caso; *D:* Robert C. Hughes.

Memories of a Marriage **1990** A nostalgic look at a couple's many years of marriage, from the husband's point of view, as they face their most trying times. Touchingly reminiscent as it spans the youthful years of new love and marriage to the more quiet, solid years of matured love. In Danish with English subtitles. **90m/C VHS.** *DK* Ghita Norby, Frits Helmuth, Rikke Bendsen, Henning Moritzen; *D:* Kaspar Rostrup.

Memories of Me **1988 (PG-13)** A distraught doctor travels to L.A. to see his ailing father and make up for lost time. Both the doctor and his father learn about themselves and each other. Story of child/parent relationships attempts to pull at the heartstrings but only gets as far as the liver. Co-written and co-produced by Crystal, this film never quite reaches the potential of its cast. **103m/C VHS, DVD.** Angela Clarke, Billy Crystal, Alan King, JoBeth Williams, David Ackroyd, Sean Connery, Janet Carroll; *D:* Henry Winkler; *W:* Billy Crystal, Eric Roth; *M:* Georges Delerue.

Memories of Murder ½ **1990** A woman suffering from amnesia is stalked by a merciless killer, apparently seeking revenge. Can she regain her memory and understand why she is being hunted, before it's too late? **104m/C VHS.** Vanity, Nancy Allen, Robin Thomas, Olivia Brown; *D:* Robert Lewis; *W:* John Kent Harrison, Nevin Schreiner.

Memories of Murder *Salinui chueok* **2003** Effective South Korean thriller based on a true incident. In 1986, the body of a young woman is found raped and murdered in a backwater town near Seoul. The two local detectives, Park (Song) and Jo (Rwe-ha Kim), are ill-equipped to deal with what turns into bizarre serial killings in a country where multiple homicides are a rarity. An experienced big city cop, Seo (Sang-kyung Kim), shows up and clashes with the others. Frustration mounts as bodies continue to be found (until 1991, in fact) and the investigation drags on. A coda is set in 2003. Korean with subtitles. **132m/C DVD.** *KN* Song Kang-ho, Kim Sang-gyeong, Kim Roi-ha, Song Jae-ho, Byeon Heui-bong, Ryu Tae-ho, Park Noh-shik, Park Hae-il; *D:* Bong Joon-ho; *W:* Bong Joon-ho, Shim Seong-bo; *C:* Kim Hyeong-gu; *M:* Taro Iwashiro.

Memories of Underdevelopment ½ *Memorias del Subdesarrollo* **1968** Set in the early 1960s. An anti-revolutionary, Europeanized intellectual takes a stand against the new government in Cuba. In Spanish with English subtitles. **97m/B VHS.** *CU* Sergio Corrieri, Daisy Granados, Eslinda Nunez, Beatriz Ponchora; *D:* Tomas Gutierrez Alea; *W:* Tomas Gutierrez Alea, Edmundo Desnoes; *C:* Ramon Suarez; *M:* Leo Bower.

Memory **2006 (R)** Nonsensical story with Zane chewing scenery. While in Brazil, Dr. Taylor Briggs (Zane) accidentally ingests a hallucinogen that a local tribe uses in rituals that bestow memories of the user's ancestors. But Taylor has visions of little girls being kidnapped and killed and hopes to discover who's behind the crimes. Hmmmm, could it be someone close to him? **98m/C DVD.** Billy Zane, Tricia Helfer, Ann-Margret, Dennis Hopper, Terry Chen; *D:* Bennett Davlin; *W:* Bennett Davlin, Anthony Badalucco; *C:* Peter Benison; *M:* Anthony Marinelli, Clint Bennett.

The Memory Keeper's Daughter **2008** Lifetime cable drama based on the best-selling novel by Kim Edwards. Dr. David Henry (Mulroney) is horrified when he sees that one of the twins his wife Norah (Mol) has just delivered has Down's Syndrome. Afraid of the toll the care of a special needs child will take, David tells his wife their daughter was stillborn and arranges for attending nurse Caroline (Watson) to take the baby to an institution. Horrified by the conditions she finds, Caroline decides to keep the child and immediately moves away to begin a new life. But the circumstances will haunt everyone for more than 20 years. **90m/C DVD.** Dermot Mulroney, Gretchen Mol, Emily Watson, Hugh Thompson, Hope Nausbaum, Paul Henry; *D:* Mick Jackson; *W:* John Pielmeier; *M:* Daniel Licht. **CABLE**

The Memory of a Killer *The Alzheimer Affair; De Zaak Alzheimer* **2003 (R)** Kinky crime thriller takes places in 1995 when tough, aging hitman Angelo (Declair) travels to Antwerp for a job. But when he won't fulfill his contract, his employers turn on him. Angelo may be in the early stages of Alzheimer's (which he realizes) but he's still not a guy you mess with. There's a nasty tie-in to a child prostitution ring and blackmail that has local cop Vincke (De Bouw) working the case and he and Angelo soon cross paths. In Flemish and French with English subtitles. **120m/C DVD.** Jan Decleir, Werner De Smedt, Gene Bervoets, Koen de Bouw, Jo de Meyere, Koen de Bouw, Jo de Meyere, Tom Van Dyck; *D:* Erik van Looy; *W:* Erik van Looy; *C:* Danny Elsen, Carl Joos; *M:* Stephen Warbeck.

Memory of Us **1974 (PG)** Still-relevant story of a married, middle-aged woman who starts to question her happiness as a wife and mother. Written by its star Geer, whose father, Will, plays a bit part. **93m/C VHS.** Ellen Geer, Jon Cypher, Barbara Colby, Peter Brown, Robert Hogan, Rose Marie, Will Geer; *D:* H. Kaye Dyal.

Memphis ½ **1991 (PG-13)** In 1957 three white drifters (two men and a woman) decide to secure some easy money by kidnapping the young grandson of the richest black businessman in Memphis. They think it's an easy job since, given the prejudice of the times, the police will do little or nothing but they reckon without the resources of the black community itself. Based on the novel "September, September" by Shelby Foote. **92m/C VHS.** Cybill Shepherd, John Laughlin, J.E. Freeman, Richard Brooks, Moses Gunn, Vanessa Bell Calloway, Martin C. Gardner; *D:* Yves Simoneau; *W:* Cybill Shepherd, Larry McMurtry; *M:* David Bell. **CABLE**

Memphis Belle **1990 (PG-13)** Satisfying Hollywood version of the documentary of the same name captures the true story of the final mission of a WWII bomber crew stationed in England. The boys of the Memphis Belle were the first group of B-17 crewmen to complete a 25 mission tour—no small feat in an air war that claimed many lives. Good ensemble cast of up and coming young actors; Lithgow has a nice turn as an army PR guy determined to exploit their boyish good looks on the homefront. Caton-Jones effectively uses 1940s film techniques and some original footage, making up for a rather hokey script. Film debut of singer Connick. Produced by Catherine Wyler, whose father made the original. **107m/C VHS, DVD.** Matthew Modine, John Lithgow, Eric Stoltz, Sean Astin, Harry Connick Jr., Reed Edward Diamond, Tate Donovan, D.B. Sweeney, Billy Zane, David Strathairn, Jane Horrocks, Courtney Gains, Neil Giuntoli; *D:* Michael Caton-Jones; *W:* Monte Merrick; *C:* David Watkin; *M:* George Fenton.

Memron WOOF! **2004** Thoroughly unfunny attempt at a mockumentary of the Enron scandal. The bankrupt company's CEO (McShane) is locked away at a country club prison where he spends his time practicing his golf swing. Meanwhile, his greedy wife (Forlani) spends what cash is left, and the company's former employees (all of whom seem to be mentally challenged) scramble to find new jobs. **79m/C DVD.** Michael McShane, Claire Forlani, Mary Pat Gleason, Tim Bagley, John Lehr, David Wiater, Joey Slotnik; *D:* Nancy Hower; *W:* Nancy Hower, Robert Stark Hickey; *C:* Nancy Hower; *M:* Steven Argila. **CABLE**

The Men ½ *Battle Stripe* **1950** A paraplegic WWII veteran sinks into depression until his former girlfriend manages to bring him out of it. Marlon Brando's first film. A thoughtful story that relies on subtle acting and direction. **85m/B VHS, DVD.** Marlon Brando, Teresa Wright, Everett Sloane, Jack Webb; *D:* Fred Zinnemann.

Men... ½ **1985** A funny and insightful satire about a man who discovers his loving wife has been having an affair with a young artist. In a unique course of revenge, the husband ingratiates himself with the artist and gradually turns him into a carbon copy of himself. In German with English subtitles or dubbed. **96m/C VHS.** *GE* Heiner Lauterbach, Uwe Ochsenknecht, Ulrike Kriener, Janna Marangosoff; *D:* Doris Dorrie.

Men **1997 (R)** Aspiring chef Stella James (Young) is encouraged by best friend Teo (Dylan Walsh) to move from New York to L.A. in search of romance. Stella promptly lands a job and gets involved with George (Heard), the restaurant's owner. However, a new man, photographer Frank (Hillman), comes onto the scene and Stella decides she likes him too. But what she thinks will be another casual encounter becomes unexpectedly serious. Based on the novel by Margaret Diehl. **93m/C VHS, DVD.** Sean Young, John Heard, Dylan Walsh, Richard Hillman, Karen Black; *D:* Zoe Clarke-Williams; *W:* Zoe Clarke-Williams, Karen Black; *C:* Susan Emerson; *M:* Mark Mothersbaugh.

Men Are Not Gods ½ **1937** Verbose film (precursor to "A Double Life") about an actor playing Othello who nearly kills his wife during Desdemona's death scene. **90m/B VHS.** *GB* Rex Harrison, Miriam Hopkins, Gertrude Lawrence; *D:* Walter Reisch.

Men at Work **1990 (PG-13)** Garbage collectors Sheen and Estevez may not love their work, but at least it's consistent from day to day. That is, until they get wrapped up in a very dirty politically motivated murder. And who will clean up the mess when the politicians are through trashing each other? A semi-thrilling semi-comedy that may leave you semi-satisfied. **98m/C VHS, DVD.** Charlie Sheen, Emilio Estevez, Leslie Hope, Keith David; *D:* Emilio Estevez; *W:* Emilio Estevez; *C:* Tim Suhrstedt; *M:* Stewart Copeland.

Men Cry Bullets **2000** Low-budget weird comedy has midnight movie potential. Billy (Nelson) is a naive performance artist who falls for hard-drinking writer Gloria (Lauren), who introduces him to the world of rough sex. And Gloria's unhappy when her debutante cousin Lydia (Ryan) comes to pay a visit and Billy starts looking her way. **106m/C VHS.** Steven Nelson, Jeri Ryan, Honey Lauren; *D:* Tamara Hernandez; *W:* Tamara Hernandez.

Men Don't Leave ½ **1989 (PG-13)** A recent widow tries to raise her kids single-handedly, suffers big city life, and takes a chance at a second love. Good performances by all, especially Cusack as the sweet seducer of teenaged O'Donnell. By the director of "Risky Business." **115m/C VHS.** Jessica Lange, Arliss Howard, Joan Cusack, Kathy Bates, Charlie Korsmo, Corey Carrier, Chris O'Donnell, Tom Mason, Jim Haynie; *D:* Paul Brickman; *W:* Barbara Benedek, Paul Brickman; *C:* Bruce Surtees; *M:* Thomas Newman.

Men in Black *MIB* **1997 (PG-13)** Charm, wit and some outrageous insect-type aliens make a winning cosmic combination. K (Jones) and J (Smith) are top-secret government operatives, investigating alien visitations on Earth, who must stop terrorist extraterrestrial D'Onofrio from causing a galactic disaster. Excellent chemistry between deadpan Jones and hip-hop Smith is strengthened by a very funny script. Director Sonnenfeld tops it off with just enough detail and human element to keep the special effects from stealing the show, and with Rick Baker around, that's not easy to do. Boxoffice hit that should spawn a sequel or two. Adapted from the Marvel comic book. **98m/C VHS, DVD, Blu-ray Disc, UMD.** Tommy Lee Jones, Will Smith, Linda Fiorentino, Rip Torn, Vincent D'Onofrio, Tony Shalhoub, Carel Struycken, Sergio Calderon, Siobhan Fallon Hogan; *D:* Barry Sonnenfeld; *W:* Edward Solomon; *C:* Don Peterman; *M:* Danny Elfman. Oscars '97: Makeup; MTV Movie Awards '98: Song ("Men in Black"), Fight (Will Smith/alien).

Men in Black 2 **2002 (PG-13)** Kay (Jones) had returned to civilian life at the end of the first film (with no memory of his past life), while Jay (Smith) went on with the men in black. When evil alien Serleena (Boyle) takes the entire MiB hostage, lone escapee Jay must convince Kay to help him save the galaxy. So-so effort suffers from lackluster script and doesn't have the spark of the original, but is helped along by solid performances all around. There are plenty of amusing scenes, mostly provided by the supporting players. Warburton is funny as an early MiB washout, Shalhoub provides some instant energy, and the talking dog does yeoman's work. Should hold up better on the small screen. **88m/C VHS, DVD.** *US* Tommy Lee Jones, Will Smith, Lara Flynn Boyle, Johnny Knoxville, Rosario Dawson, Rip Torn, Tony Shalhoub, Patrick Warburton, Jack Kehler, David Cross, Colombe Jacobsen, Peter Spellos, Lenny Venito; *Cameos:* Michael Jackson, Martha Stewart, Peter Graves; *D:* Barry Sonnenfeld; *W:* Robert Gordon, Barry Fanaro; *C:* Greg Gardiner; *M:* Danny Elfman; *V:* Tim Blaney.

Men in Love **1990** A young San Franciscan travels to Hawaii with the cremated remains of his lover, who has succumbed to AIDS. There he encounters a supportive group of men who nurse him back to sexual and spiritual wholeness. **93m/C VHS.** Doug Self, Joe Tolbe, Emerald Starr, Kutira Decosterd, Scott Catamas; *D:* Marc Huestis; *W:* Emerald Starr, Scott Catamas; *C:* Fawn Yacker.

Men in War ½ **1957** Korean War drama about a small platoon trying to take an enemy hill by themselves. A worthwhile effort with some good action sequences. **100m/B VHS, DVD.** Robert Ryan, Robert Keith, Aldo

Ray, Vic Morrow, Phillip Pine, Nehemiah Persoff, James Edwards, L.Q. Jones, Scott Marlowe, Adam Kennedy, Race Gentry, Walter Kelley, Anthony Ray, Robert Normand, Michael Miller, Victor Sen Yung; ***D:*** Anthony Mann; ***W:*** Philip Yordan, Ben Maddow; ***C:*** Ernest Haller; ***M:*** Elmer Bernstein.

Men in White **1934** Dedicated physician George Ferguson (Gable) is engaged to wealthy Laura Hudson (Loy) who wants him to spend more time with her by taking up a society practice. While on the outs with Laura, George has a fling with nurse Barbara (Allan), who gets pregnant. She has a backalley abortion and dies, which makes George and Laura both realize that he needs to do more serious work. Adapted from the Sidney Kingsley play. The first of several pairings for Gable and Loy. **73m/B DVD.** Clark Gable, Myrna Loy, Jean Hersholt, Elizabeth Allan, Otto Kruger, C. Henry Gordon, Henry B. Walthall; ***D:*** Richard Boleslawski; ***W:*** Waldemar Young; ***C:*** George J. Folsey; ***M:*** William Axt.

Men Men Men *Uomini Uomini Uomini* **1995** Quartet of gay friends are permanent Peter Pans. Never having grown up, they extend their adolescence in a series of increasingly vicious pranks at the expense of both strangers and friends. But eventually they're forced to re-examine their behavior. Very funny, if certainly non-pc, comedy. Italian with subtitles. **84m/C VHS, DVD.** *IT* Christian de Sica, Massimo Ghini, Leo Gullotta, Alessandro Haber, Monica Scattini, Paco Reconti; ***D:*** Christian de Sica; ***W:*** Christian de Sica; ***C:*** Gianlorenzo Battaglia; ***M:*** Manuel De Sica.

Men of America *The Great Decision* **1932** A group of not-so-bright criminals is hiding out after robbing a bank of $50,000 in $1000 bills they cannot spend. When they murder a farmhand who's on to them, an innocent townsman is suspected but sets out to set the record straight and capture the true villains. **58m/B VHS.** William Boyd, Charles "Chic" Sale, Dorothy Wilson, Ralph Ince; ***D:*** Ralph Ince; ***W:*** Humphrey Pearson, Jack Jungmeyer, Henry McCarty, Samuel Ornitz. **VIDEO**

Men of Boys Town 1/2 **1941** Sequel to 1938's "Boys Town" has the same sentimentality, even more if that's possible. Father Flanagan's reformatory faces closure, while the kids reach out to an embittered new inmate. Worth seeing for the ace cast reprising their roles. **106m/B VHS.** Spencer Tracy, Mickey Rooney, Darryl Hickman, Henry O'Neill, Lee J. Cobb, Sidney Miller; ***D:*** Norman Taurog.

Men of Honor 1/2 *Navy Diver* **2000 (R)** Based on the true story of Carl Brashear, the first African-American to break the color barrier in the U.S. Navy's diving program, this biography is a straightforward no-frills tribute. Played by Gooding, Brashear comes across as the very embodiment of perseverence, as shown in his rise from sharecropper's son to military man. De Niro plays Billy Sunday, a racist training officer whose discrimination nearly kills Brashear on several occasions before Brashear earns Sunday's respect. As Brashear's career advances, Sunday's declines due to drunkenness and insubordination. When Brashear loses his leg in the line of duty, the now-recovered Sunday helps him retrain using a prosthetic leg. The character of Billy Sunday is actually a composite drawn from many men in Carl Brashear's military career. **129m/C VHS, DVD, Blu-ray Disc.** Cuba Gooding Jr., Robert De Niro, Charlize Theron, David Keith, Michael Rapaport, Hal Holbrook, Powers Boothe, Aunjanue Ellis, Joshua Leonard, David Conrad, Glynn Turman, Holt McCallany, Lonette McKee, Carl Lumbly; ***D:*** George Tillman Jr.; ***W:*** Scott Marshall Smith; ***C:*** Anthony B. Richmond; ***M:*** Mark Isham.

Men of Ireland **1938** A Dublin medical student cavorts with islanders off the Irish coast. Uninspired programmer with authentic native folk of the Blasket Islands, plus their songs and dances. **62m/B VHS.** *IR* Cecil Ford, Eileen Curran, Brian O'Sullivan, Gabriel Fallon; ***D:*** Richard Bird.

Men of Means **1999 (R)** Mob goon Rico Burke (Pare) decides it's time to get out when he sees his boss (Serra) becoming increasingly psychotic. Only he gets double-crossed. Lots of action and avoids most mob movie cliches. **80m/C VHS.** Michael Pare, Raymond Serra, Austin Pendleton, Kaela Dobkin; ***D:*** George Mendeluk. **VIDEO**

Men of Respect **1991 (R)** Shakespeare meets the mafia in this misbegotten gangster yarn. Turturro, a gangster MacBeth, is prodded by wife and psychic to butcher his way to the top o' the mob. Well acted but ill conceived, causing Bard's partial roll over in grave. **113m/C VHS, DVD.** John Turturro, Katherine Borowitz, Peter Boyle, Dennis Farina, Chris Stein, Steven Wright, Stanley Tucci; ***D:*** William Reilly; ***W:*** William Reilly; ***C:*** Bobby Bukowski.

Men of Sherwood Forest 1/2 **1957** Robin Hood and his band take it to the sheriff et al in this colorful Hammer version of the timeless legend. **77m/C VHS.** *GB* Don Taylor, Reginald Beckwith, Eileen Moore, David King-Wood, Patrick Holt, John Van Eyssen, Douglas Wilmer; ***D:*** Val Guest.

Men of Steel *The Fighting Men* **1977 (PG)** Two Canadian military officers, one French and one English, must struggle to survive when their plane crashes in the wilderness. Besides contending with the surroundings, they must deal with one another's instilled bitterness and underlying prejudices. **91m/C VHS.** Allan Royal, Robert Lalonde, David Ferry, Mavor Moore, Yvan Ponton; ***D:*** Donald Shebib; ***W:*** Tony Sheer; ***C:*** Vic Sarin; ***M:*** Samuel Matlovsky.

Men of the Fighting Lady 1/2 *Panther Squadron* **1954** Action-adventure offers plenty of exciting battle footage. Features the stories of selected pilots stationed on a U.S. aircraft carrier in the Pacific during the Korean War. The stories, told to Calhern as writer James A. Michener, center around the lead pilot Johnson. Dramatic airflights include a scene in which Johnson helps a blinded Martin land his plane safely on the carrier deck. Gene Ruggerio's editing of the war footage was so expertly done that he was questioned by the Pentagon when they had a hard time believing the scenes were achieved by skillful editing and painted backdrops. Look for "Beaver" Mathers as one of Wynn's sons. **81m/C VHS.** Van Johnson, Walter Pidgeon, Louis Calhern, Dewey Martin, Keenan Wynn, Frank Lovejoy, Robert Horton, Bert Freed, Lewis Martin, Dick Simmons, Paul Smith, George Cooper, Ann Baker, Jonathan Hale, Dorothy Patrick, Jerry Mathers, Sarah Selby; ***D:*** Andrew Marton; ***W:*** Art Cohn; ***C:*** George J. Folsey; ***M:*** Miklos Rozsa.

Men of Two Worlds *Witch Doctor; Kisenga, Man of Africa* **1946** Classical musician raised in Africa is the toast of Europe until he finds out he's got a voodoo curse, and suddenly he's got the heebie jeebies too bad to play chopsticks. **90m/C VHS.** *GB* Robert Adams, Eric Portman, Orlando Martins, Phyllis Calvert, Arnold Marle, Cathleen Nesbitt, David Horne, Cyril Raymond; ***D:*** Thorold Dickinson.

Men of War 1/2 **1994 (R)** Ex-Special Forces mercenaries decide to defend, rather than destroy, the inhabitants of an exotic island, whose land is wanted by a suspicious company interested in mining rights. **102m/C VHS, DVD.** Dolph Lundgren, Charlotte Lewis, B.D. Wong, Anthony John (Tony) Denison, Tim Guinee, Don Harvey, Tommy (Tiny) Lister, Trevor Goddard, Kevin Tighe; ***D:*** Perry Lang; ***W:*** John Sayles, Ethan Reiff, Cyrus Voris; ***C:*** Ronn Schmidt; ***M:*** Gerald Gouriet.

The Men Who Stare at Goats **2009 (R)** The sort of film that proves 'military intelligence' is an oxymoron. After his marriage falls apart, journalist Bob Wilton (McGregor) is looking for a good war story when he goes to Kuwait City in 2003. He's already been told about a secret government op to utilize psychic abilities and that the lead loon is a guy named Cassady (Clooney)—who does stare at goats. Wilton persuades Cassady to take him along on his secret mission to Iraq to find the founder (Bridges) of the New Age psychic soldiers, who has gone missing. A strong cast, led by a scruffy, wild-eyed Clooney ditching his suave persona in favor of his mischievous side, seems to have a great time—almost spoofing—while making this otherwise meandering film watchable. You'll feel most sorry for the goats. Based on events of journalist Jon Ronson's 2004 nonfiction work of the same name—or, as it says in the opening, "more of this is true than you would believe." **94m/C DVD.** *US* George Clooney, Ewan McGregor, Jeff Bridges, Kevin Spacey, Rebecca Mader, Robert Patrick, Stephen Lang, Stephen (Steve) Root, Glenn Morshower; ***D:*** Grant Heslov; ***W:*** Peter Straughan; ***C:*** Robert Elswit; ***M:*** Rolfe Kent.

The Men Who Tread on the Tiger's Tail 1/2 *Tora No O Wo Fumu Otokotachi; They Who Step on the Tiger's Tail; Walkers on the Tiger's Tail* **1945** Twelfth-century Japan is the setting for this struggle of power between two brothers, one a reigning shogun, the other on the run. English subtitles. **60m/B VHS.** *JP* Denjiro Okochi, Susumu Fujita, Masayuki Mori, Takashi Shimura, Yoshio Kosugi; ***D:*** Akira Kurosawa; ***W:*** Akira Kurosawa; ***C:*** Takeo Ito; ***M:*** Tadashi Hattori.

Men with Brooms 1/2 **2002** Goofy Canadian comedy about curling. In the small mining town of Long Bay, curling player/coach Donald Foley (Douglas) has just died (although his narration continues throughout the pic). At his funeral, members of his last team reunite and decide to reform the team and compete for the Golden Broom curling championship trophy in Foley's honor. Among them are oil roughneck Chris (Gross), who convinces his eccentric dad Gordon (Nielsen) to coach the team. **102m/C VHS, DVD.** *CA* Paul Gross, Molly Parker, Peter Outerbridge, Leslie Nielsen, James Allodi, James B. Douglas, Polly Shannon, Jed Rees, Michelle Nolden, Barbara Gordon, Kari Matchett, Jane Spidell; ***D:*** Paul Gross; ***W:*** Paul Gross, John Krizanc; ***C:*** Thom Best; ***M:*** Paul Gross, Jack Lenz.

Menace on the Mountain **1970 (G)** Family-oriented drama about a father and son who battle carpetbagging Confederate deserters during the Civil War. **89m/C VHS.** Pat(ricia) Crowley, Albert Salmi, Charles Aidman; ***D:*** Vincent McEveety.

Menace II Society 1/2 **1993 (R)** Portrayal of black teens lost in inner-city hell is realistically captured by 21-year-old twin directors, in their big-screen debut. Caine (Turner) lives with his grandparents and peddles drugs for spending money, from the eve of his high school graduation to his decision to escape south-central Los Angeles for Atlanta. Bleak and haunting, with some of the most unsettling, bloodiest violence ever shown in a commercial film. Disturbing to watch, but critcally acclaimed. The Hughes' make their mark on contemporary black cinema with intensity, enhanced by an action-comics visual flair. Based on a story by the Hughes' and Tyger Williams. **104m/C VHS, DVD.** Tyrin Turner, Larenz Tate, Samuel L. Jackson, Glenn Plummer, Julian Roy Doster, Bill Duke, Charles S. Dutton, Jada Pinkett Smith, Vonte Sweet, Ryan Williams; ***D:*** Allen Hughes, Albert Hughes; ***W:*** Tyger Williams; ***C:*** Lisa Rinzler. Ind. Spirit '94: Cinematog.; MTV Movie Awards '94: Film.

Menage *Tenue de Soiree* **1986** Depardieu is the homosexual crook who breaks into the home of an impoverished couple—the dominating Miou-Miou and her submissive husband, Blanc. An unrepentant thief, he begins to take over their lives, introducing them to the wonderful world of crime, among other, more kinky, pastimes. Gender-bending farce that doesn't hold up to the end but is worth watching for sheer outrageousness. In French with English subtitles. **84m/C VHS.** *FR* Gerard Depardieu, Michel Blanc, Miou-Miou, Bruno Cremer, Jean-Pierre Marielle; ***D:*** Bertrand Blier; ***W:*** Bertrand Blier; ***M:*** Serge Gainsbourg. Cannes '86: Actor (Blanc).

Mendel **1998** Mendel (Sorenson) is the nine-year-old son of German-Jewish concentration camp survivors and displaced persons, who are relocated to Norway in 1954. Mendal is too young to know about the horrors that befell his family and that still cause them all nightmares. His parents are determined to shield him from their past while Mendel is equally determined to discover the family secrets. German and Norwegian with subtitles. **98m/C VHS.** *NO* Thomas Jungling Sorensen, Teresa Harder, Hans Kremer, Martin Meingast; ***D:*** Alexander Rosler; ***W:*** Alexander Rosler; ***C:*** Helge Sembe; ***M:*** Geir Bohren, Bent Aserud.

Menno's Mind 1/2 **1996** Rebel leader Bruce Campbell downloads his brain into a computer before being killed. Now his associates force computer techie Menno (Bill Campbell) to upload the material into his own mind in order to thwart presidential candidate Bernsen, who wants to use his online skills to influence the outcome of the election. **95m/C VHS, DVD.** Billy Campbell, Corbin Bernsen, Bruce Campbell, Michael Dorn, Robert Picardo, Robert Vaughn, Richard Speight Jr.; ***D:*** Jon Kroll; ***W:*** Mark Valenti; ***C:*** Gary Tieche; ***M:*** Christopher Franke. **CABLE**

The Men's Club 1/2 **1986 (R)** Seven middle-aged buddies get together for a single night, and bare their respective souls and personal traumas, talking about women and eating and drinking. Banal. Based on novel by Leonard Michael. **100m/C VHS.** Harvey Keitel, Roy Scheider, Craig Wasson, Frank Langella, David Dukes, Richard Jordan, Treat Williams, Stockard Channing, Jennifer Jason Leigh, Ann Dusenberry, Cindy Pickett, Gwen Welles; ***D:*** Peter Medak.

Mephisto 1/2 **1981** Egomaniacal stage actor Hendrik Hofgren (compellingly played by Brandauer) sides with the Nazis to further his career, with disastrous results. An updated version of the Faust legend and the first of three brilliant films by Szabo and Brandauer exploring the price of power and personal sublimation in German history. Klaus Mann based his 1936 novel on the career of German stage actor Gustaf Grundgens who became the director and star of Berlin's Prussian State Theater during WWII. German with subtitles. Followed by "Colonel Redl" and "Hanussen." **144m/C VHS, DVD.** *HU* Klaus Maria Brandauer, Krystyna Janda, Ildiko Bansagi, Karin Boyd, Rolf Hoppe, Christine Harbort, Gyorgy Cserhalmi, Christiane Graskoff, Peter Andorai, Ildiko Kishonti; ***D:*** Istvan Szabo; ***W:*** Istvan Szabo, Peter Dobai; ***C:*** Lajos Koltai; ***M:*** Zdenko Tamassy. Oscars '81: Foreign Film.

The Mephisto Waltz **1971 (R)** Journalist gets more than a story when he is granted an interview with a dying pianist. It turns out that he is a satanist and the cult he is a part of wants the journalist. Chilling adaptation of the Fred Mustard Stewart novel features a haunting musical score. **108m/C VHS.** Alan Alda, Jacqueline Bisset, Barbara Parkins, Curt Jurgens, Bradford Dillman, William Windom, Kathleen Widdoes; ***D:*** Paul Wendkos; ***M:*** Jerry Goldsmith.

The Mercenaries 1/2 *I Masnadieri* **1962** Romantic warrior fights to save the lives and honor of his people who are under attack from mercenaries murdering and raping their way across Europe. **98m/C VHS, DVD.** *IT* Daniela Rocca, Antonio Cifariello, Folco Lulli, Debra Paget, Salvo Randone; ***D:*** Mario Bonnard; ***W:*** Mario Bonnard, Nino Minuto; ***C:*** Marco Scarpelli; ***M:*** Giulio Bonnard.

The Mercenaries *Cuba Crossing; Kill Castro; Assignment: Kill Castro; Key West Crossing; Sweet Dirty Tony* **1980** A tough guy, given the assignment to kill Fidel Castro, encounters all sorts of adversity along the way. Key West scenery is the only thing of interest. **92m/C VHS, DVD.** Stuart Whitman, Robert Vaughn, Caren Kaye, Raymond St. Jacques, Woody Strode, Sybil Danning, Albert Salmi, Michael V. Gazzo; ***D:*** Chuck Workman.

Mercenary **1996** Ex-Commando-turned-mercenary Alex Hawks (Gruner) is hired by wealthy businessman Jonas Ambler (Ritter) to avenge his wife's death at the hands of terrorists. Only Ambler's desk jockey doesn't want to stay on the sidelines and watch—he wants to do. So, Hawks is forced to take him along to Iraq when he goes after the bad guys. **97m/C VHS.** Olivier Gruner, John Ritter, Robert Culp, Ed Lauter, Martin Kove; ***D:*** Avi Nesher; ***W:*** Avi Nesher, Steven Hartov; ***C:*** Irek Hartowicz; ***M:*** Roger Neill.

Mercenary 2: Thick and Thin 1/2 **1997 (R)** Mercenaries Hawk (Gruner) and Ray (Turturro) are hired to rescue a businessman (Townsend) who's apparently been kidnapped by a druglord and who's being held in a Central America jungle. Turns out it's all a set-up. **100m/C VHS.** Robert Kevin Townsend, Olivier Gruner, Nicholas Turturro, Claudia Christian, John Dennis Johnston, Tom Towler, Sam Bottoms; ***D:*** Philippe Mora. **VIDEO**

Mercenary Fighters 1/2 **1988 (R)** An American soldier-of-fortune fights for both sides of an African revolution. Shot in South

Africa. **90m/C VHS.** Peter Fonda, Reb Brown, Ron O'Neal, Jim Mitchum; ***D:*** Riki Shelach.

The Merchant of Four Seasons 🦴🦴🦴 **1971** Story focuses on the depression and unfulfilled dreams of an average street merchant. Direction from Fassbinder is slow, deliberate, and mesmerizing. In German with English subtitles. **88m/C VHS, DVD.** Hans Hirschmuller, Irm Hermann, Hanna Schygulla, Andrea Schober, Gusti Kreissl; ***D:*** Rainer Werner Fassbinder; ***W:*** Rainer Werner Fassbinder.

The Merchant of Venice 🦴🦴🦴 **1973** Shakespeare's tragedy of prejudice, vengeance, and sacrifice stars Olivier as the persecuted money lender Shylock, who demands his payment of a pound of flesh for a defaulted loan. **131m/C VHS.** *GB* Michael Jayston, Anthony Nicholls, Laurence Olivier, Joan Plowright, Jeremy Brett; ***D:*** John Sichel.

The Merchant of Venice 🦴🦴🦴 *William Shakespeare's The Merchant of Venice* **2004 (R)** Antonio (Irons) makes a deal with calculating moneylender Shylock (Pacino) to help his friend Bassanio (Fiennes) gain the hand of fair Portia (Collins). When the deal goes south, Shylock demands a pound of flesh from Antonio's breast and it's up to Portia, disguised as a young lawyer, to save him. Lavish, but subtle, take on Shakespeare's classic comedy. Pacino takes care to make Shylock as sympathetic as possible; and director Radford places the play's overt racism in historical context, making the play feel less viciously anti-semitic than usual. **138m/C DVD.** *US* Al Pacino, Jeremy Irons, Joseph Fiennes, Zuleikha Robinson, Kris Marshall, Heather Goldenhersch, John Sessions, Mackenzie Crook, Gregor Fisher, Ron Cook, Allan Corduner, Anton Rodgers, Lynn Collins, Charlie Cox; ***D:*** Michael Radford; ***W:*** Michael Radford; ***C:*** Benoit Delhomme; ***M:*** Jocelyn Pook.

Merchants of Death 🦴 **1999** Fairly perverse schlock about an aspiring actress lured into an audition at a mysterious mansion. Soon enough she's bound and gagged by some raw dog dudes who toss her in a room with another woman, also tied up, who came to avenge her sister's death. With the audition still underway and the cameras set to roll, they realize they're about to become reluctant (to say the least) stars in a snuff film. A maniacal priest is thrown into the mix for some reason, too. Only the slight campy smirk saves it from complete disaster. **81m/C VHS.** Christine Lydon, Jason Robert Stephens, Raquel Maldonado, Raymond Sorti; ***D:*** Jason Robert Stephens, Dennis Devine; ***W:*** Jason Robert Stephens, Dennis Devine; ***C:*** Dennis Devine; ***M:*** Jonathan Price. **VIDEO**

Merchants of War 🦴 **1990 (R)** Sent out by the CIA on a mission, two best friends are soon the target of one of the most dangerous terrorists in the world. The fanatical Islamic terrorist soon casts his wrath upon the two men. **100m/C VHS, DVD.** Asher Brauner, Jesse Vint, Bonnie Beck; ***D:*** Peter M. MacKenzie.

Merci Docteur Rey 🦴🦴🦴 **2004 (R)** Odd choice for a Merchant-Ivory production. Enjoyable French farce mixes questionable sexual orientation, mistaken identity, murder, and an estranged father for a rousing ride. Wiest's opera diva visits her closeted gay son, who witnesses a murder on a blind date with a chat room hook-up. Complimented by an eclectic soundtrack ranging from pop to opera. **91m/C DVD.** *FR* Dianne Wiest, Jane Birkin, Stanislas Merhar, Bulle Ogier, Jerry Hall, Simon Callow; ***Cameos:*** Vanessa Redgrave; ***D:*** Andrew Litvack; ***W:*** Andrew Litvack; ***C:*** Laurent Machuel; ***M:*** Geoff(rey) Alexander. **VIDEO**

Merci pour le Chocolat 🦴🦴🦴 *Nightcap* **2000** This is Huppert's movie all the way. She's Mika Muller, a chocolate company manager in Switzerland who has just re-married widowed concert pianist Andre (Dutronc) after 18 years. In the meantime, Andre married and had son Guillaume (Pauly), who was nearly switched at birth for Jeanne (Mouglalis), an 18-year-old with musical talent (unlike Guillaume). Jeanne impulsively decides to meet Andre and they bond over music, which causes the polite but pathologically jealous Mika to pour hot chocolate and plot. Based on the novel "The Chocolate Cobweb" by Charlotte Armstrong. French with subtitles. **99m/C VHS, DVD.** *FR SI* Isabelle Huppert, Jacques Dutronc, Anna Mouglalis, Rodolphe Pauly, Michel Robin, Brigitte Catillon, Mathieu Simonet; ***D:*** Claude Chabrol; ***W:*** Claude Chabrol, Caroline Eliacheff; ***C:*** Renato Berta; ***M:*** Matthieu Chabrol.

Mercury Rising 🦴🦴 ½ **1998 (R)** Renegade FBI agent Art Jeffries (Willis) must protect an autistic child who has inadvertently cracked a secret government code. Together, they dodge bullets from evil government forces headed by Nicholas Kudrow (Baldwin), who insist on having the innocent boy killed rather than change the code. That glaring logic aside, Willis does more than grunt here, showing moments of tenderness as he bonds with the oprhaned boy in between nailing bad guys and amassing an assortment of cuts and bruises. Baldwin is effective as the snake who truly believes killing a child will benefit national security. When action time isn't being sacrificed for Jeffries' paternal aspirations, film rises slightly above tepid to provide substantial thrills. **112m/C VHS, DVD.** Bruce Willis, Alec Baldwin, Miko Hughes, Kim Dickens, Chi McBride, Robert Stanton, Peter Stormare, Kevin Conway; ***D:*** Harold Becker; ***W:*** Larry Konner, Mark Rosenthal; ***C:*** Michael Seresin; ***M:*** John Barry. Golden Raspberries '98: Worst Actor (Willis).

Mercy 🦴🦴 **1996 (R)** When New York lawyer Frank Kramer's (Rubenstein) daughter is kidnapped he comes to realize it wasn't for ransom but for revenge. **82m/C VHS, DVD.** John Rubinstein, Sam Rockwell, Phil Brock, Novella Nelson, Amber Kain, Jane Lanier; ***D:*** Richard Shepard; ***W:*** Richard Shepard; ***C:*** Sarah Cawley.

Mercy 🦴🦴 **2000 (R)** Glossy sleaze based on the book by David L. Lindsey. Catherine Barker (Barkin) is a hard-drinking homicide detective investigating a serial killer with sexual kinks. Bombshell Vickie Kittrie (Wilson) reveals that each female victim belonged to an exclusive club that liked to experiment with the wilder side of life. All the victims also turn out to be patients of psychotherapist Dominick Broussard (Sands), who may be more psycho than anyone knows. **94m/C VHS, DVD.** Ellen Barkin, Peta Wilson, Julian Sands, Wendy Crewson, Karen Young, Marshall Bell, Stephen Baldwin, Beau Starr, Bill MacDonald, Stewart Bick; ***D:*** Damian Harris; ***W:*** Damian Harris; ***C:*** Manuel Teran; ***M:*** B.C. Smith.

Mercy Mission 🦴🦴 ½ **1993** Young pilot Bakula runs into trouble over the Pacific with his small plane and it's upto Air New Zealand airline pilot Loggia, who risks the lives of his passengers and crew, to come to his rescue. **92m/C VHS.** Scott Bakula, Robert Loggia; ***D:*** Roger Young.

Mercy Streets 🦴 ½ **2000 (PG-13)** Neo-noir, spiritually-themed crime drama about brotherly redemption. Con man John plans to go straight after getting out of prison but falls right back into a counterfeiting scheme with mentor Rome. This soon involves John's estranged twin brother Jeremiah, an Episcopal priest, after John tries double-crossing Rome and Jeremiah is mistaken for John and held hostage. **106m/C DVD.** Eric Roberts, Cynthia Watros, Shiek Mahmud-Bey, Robert LaSardo, Stacy Keach, Lawrence Taylor, David A.R. White; ***D:*** Jon Gunn; ***W:*** Jon Gunn, John Mann; ***C:*** Chris Magee; ***M:*** Staffan Fantini. **VIDEO**

Meridian: Kiss of the Beast 🦴 ½ **1990 (R)** A beautiful heiress is courted, kidnapped and loved by a demonic man-beast. **90m/C VHS.** Sherilyn Fenn, Malcom Jamieson, Hilary Mason, Alex Daniels, Phil Fondacaro, Charlie Spradling; ***D:*** Charles Band; ***W:*** Dennis Paoli; ***M:*** Pino Donaggio.

Merlin 🦴🦴 ½ **1992 (PG-13)** In a remote California town reporter Christy Lake is stunned to discover her ancient heritage. Turns out she's the reincarnated daughter of legendary Merlin the magician and it is her duty to protect the Sword of Power from the evil sorcerer Pendragon. And aided by a handsome warrior and an ancient sage, that's just what she intends to do. **112m/C VHS.** Nadia Cameron, Peter Phelps, Richard Lynch, James Hong, Ted Markland, Desmond Llewelyn; ***D:*** Paul Hunt; ***W:*** Nick McCarty.

Merlin 🦴🦴🦴 **1998** Legend of Camelot and Arthur's mentor is brought to the small screen with fine performances and equally impressive special effects. Merlin is conceived through the magic of evil Queen Mab (Richardson) to bring Britain back to its pagan roots. But Merlin doesn't really like magic and grows up to be (in the commanding persona of Neill) a most reluctant sorcerer. Still, he mentors Arthur (Curran) and continues to battle Mab, who works with Arthur's half sister Morgan Le Fey (Bonham Carter) to destroy Camelot. Merlin also pursues a long-time romance with Nimue (Rossellini), who falls victim to Mab's treachery. **140m/C VHS, DVD.** Sam Neill, Miranda Richardson, Isabella Rossellini, Martin Short, Helena Bonham Carter, Rutger Hauer, Paul Curran, Billie Whitelaw, Lena Headey, Jason Done, Mark Jax, John McEnery, Nicholas Clay, Sebastien Roche, Jeremy Sheffield; ***Cameos:*** John Gielgud; ***D:*** Steven Barron; ***W:*** David Stevens, Edward Khmara; ***C:*** Sergei Kozlov; ***M:*** Trevor Jones; ***V:*** James Earl Jones. **TV**

Merlin and the Book of Beasts 🦴 *Book of Beasts* **2009** Bad CGI and a dull narrative doom this SciFi saga about the dark side of Camelot. Arthur is gone and the Round Table has been destroyed. Terror reigns from evil sorcerer Arkadian (Thorburn) and his equally evil creatures so Camelot's remaining knights must look to a bitter Merlin (Callis) to save them. **92m/C DVD.** James Callis, Laura Harris, Jim Thorburn, Patrick Sabongui, Donald Adams, Jesse Moss, Megan Vincent, Maja Stace-Smith; ***D:*** Warren Sonoda; ***W:*** Brooke Durham; ***C:*** Mathias Herndl, Adam Sliwinski; ***M:*** Craig McConnell. **CABLE**

Merlin and the Sword 🦴 *Arthur the King* **1985** Poor use of a good cast in this treatment of the legend of Merlin, Arthur and Excalibur. **94m/C VHS.** Malcolm McDowell, Edward Woodward, Candice Bergen, Dyan Cannon; ***D:*** Clive Donner.

Merlin's Apprentice 🦴 ½ **2006** Disappointingly cheesy sort of sequel to the 1998 miniseries "Merlin." Merlin (Neill again) takes a 50-year nap and awakens to find Arthur dead, the Holy Grail missing, and Camelot under siege. When a young thief, Jack (Reardon), tries to steal his wand, Merlin discovers he has magical abilities and takes Jack on as his apprentice to help save Camelot. Richardson is back too, but this time she plays the Lady of the Lake. **185m/C DVD.** *US CA* Sam Neill, John Reardon, Miranda Richardson, Duncan Fraser, Christopher Jacot, Andrew Jackson, Garwin Sanford, Meaghan Ory, Alexander Kalugin; ***D:*** David Wu; ***W:*** Christian Ford, Roger Soffer; ***C:*** John Spooner; ***M:*** Lawrence Shragge. **CABLE**

Mermaid 🦴🦴 ½ **2000** Young Desi is mourning her father's death. She writes a letter to him and ties it to a balloon, hoping that it will fly to heaven so he can read it. Instead, the winds blow the balloon to Canada's St. Edward's Island and the small town of Mermaid. When the letter is found, the islanders decide to respond to Desi's message. **94m/C VHS, DVD.** Samantha Mathis, Ellen Burstyn, David Kaye, Jodelle Ferland, Blu Mankuma, Tom Heaton; ***D:*** Peter Masterson; ***W:*** Todd Robinson; ***C:*** Jon Joffin; ***M:*** Peter Melnick. **CABLE**

Mermaids 🦴🦴🦴 **1990 (PG-13)** Mrs. Flax (Cher) is the flamboyant mother of two who hightails out of town every time a relationship threatens to turn serious. Having moved some 18 times, her daughters, Charlotte (Ryder), 15, and Kate (Ricci), 8, are a little worse for the wear, psychologically speaking. One aspires to be a nun though not Catholic, and the other holds her breath under water. Now living in Massachusetts, Mrs. Flax starts having those "I got you, babe" feelings for Hoskins, a shoestore owner. Amusing, well-acted multi-generational coming of ager based on a novel by Patty Dann. **110m/C VHS, DVD.** Cher, Winona Ryder, Bob Hoskins, Christina Ricci, Michael Schoeffling, Caroline McWilliams, Jan Miner; ***D:*** Richard Benjamin; ***W:*** June Roberts; ***C:*** Howard Atherton; ***M:*** Jack Nitzsche. Natl. Bd. of Review '90: Support. Actress (Ryder).

The Mermaids of Tiburon 🦴 *The Aqua Sex* **1962** A marine biologist and a criminal travel to a remote island off Mexico in search of elusive, expensive "fire pearls." There they encounter a kingdom of lovely mermaids who promptly liven things up. Filmed in "Aquascope" for your viewing pleasure. **77m/C VHS.** Diane Webber, George Rowe, Timothy Carey, Jose Gonzalez-Gonzalez, John (Jack) Mylong, Gil Baretto, Vicki Kantenwine, Nani Morrissey, Judy Edwards, Jean Carroll, Diana Cook, Karen Goodman, Nancy Burns; ***D:*** John Lamb; ***W:*** John Lamb.

Merrill's Marauders 🦴🦴 ½ **1962** Chandler is the commander of a battle-hardened regiment fighting in the jungles of Burma in 1944. The exhausted unit gains their latest objective and expects to be relieved, only to be continuously pushed into more fighting down the line. Director Fuller excels at showing the confusion of battle; Chandler's last film role (he died before the film was released). **98m/C VHS.** Jeff Chandler, Ty Hardin, Peter Brown, Andrew Duggan, Will Hutchins, Claude Akins, John Hoyt, Chuck Hicks, Charles Briggs, Vaughan Wilson, Pancho Magalona; ***D:*** Samuel Fuller; ***W:*** Samuel Fuller, Milton Sperling, Charlton Ogburn Jr.; ***C:*** William Clothier; ***M:*** Howard Jackson.

Merrily We Go to Hell 🦴🦴 **1932** Jerry Corbett (March) is a frequently drunk reporter and an aspiring playwright. He misses his engagement party to status-conscious heiress Joan (Sidney) by going on a bender and continues drinking even after they marry. When Joan finds out Jerry has been flirting with an old flame (Allen) as well, she goes back home to dad (Irving) only to discover she's pregnant. Complications arise and Jerry eventually finds out his missus is in the hospital and he begs for a second chance. **78m/B DVD.** Fredric March, Sylvia Sidney, George Irving, Richard "Skeets" Gallagher, Cary Grant, Adrienne Allen; ***D:*** Dorothy Arzner; ***W:*** Edwin Justus Mayer; ***C:*** David Abel.

Merry Christmas, Mr. Lawrence 🦴🦴🦴 **1983 (R)** An often overlooked drama about a WWII Japanese POW camp. Taut psychological drama about clashing cultures and physical and emotional survival focusing on the tensions between Bowie as a British POW and camp commander Sakamato, who also composed the outstanding score. A haunting and intense film about the horrors of war. Based on the novel by Laurens van der Post. **124m/C VHS, DVD.** *JP GB* David Bowie, Tom Conti, Ryuichi Sakamoto, Takeshi "Beat" Kitano, Jack Thompson, Takashi Naito, Alistair Browning, Johnny Okura, Yuya Uchida, Ryunosuke Kaneda, Kan Mikami, Yuji Honma, Diasuke Iijima; ***D:*** Nagisa Oshima; ***W:*** Nagisa Oshima, Paul Mayersberg; ***C:*** Toichiro Narushima. Natl. Bd. of Review '83: Actor (Conti).

The Merry Gentleman 🦴🦴 ½ **2008 (R)** Frank Logan (Keaton) is a gentlemanly Chicago hitman who is apparently depressed by his job since he tries to commit suicide after his latest killing. Kate (Macdonald, a particularly lovely presence) spots Frank as he is about to jump, screams, and inadvertently saves his life. But Frank also realizes she may be able to identify him so he has to make her acquaintance. Since Kate is a fellow bruised and lonely soul (having fled an abusive marriage) the two seem made for each other as long as Frank doesn't decide to kill her. Keaton, in his directorial debut, refrains from most cliches. **110m/C DVD.** *US* Michael Keaton, Kelly Macdonald, Tom Bastounes, Bobby Cannavale, Darlene Hunt, Guy Van Swearingen, William Dick; ***D:*** Michael Keaton; ***W:*** Ron Lazzeretti; ***C:*** Chris Seager; ***M:*** Jonathan Sadoff, Sean Douglas.

Merry-Go-Round 🦴🦴🦴 **1923** A handsome Austrian count is engaged to a woman of his class when he meets the beautiful Agnes, who works as an organ grinder for the local merry-go-round. He disguises himself to woo her but finally decides to marry his fiance, although Agnes continues to love him. But the story doesn't end for the two lovers who are destined to be together. Producer Thalberg and director von Stroheim battled over the expense and length of the film until Thalberg had the director replaced. However, much of the film still shows the von Stroheim brillance and attention to lavish detail. **110m/B VHS, DVD.** Norman Kerry, Mary Philbin, Cesare Gravina, Edith Yorke, George Hackathorne; ***D:*** Rupert Julian, Erich von Stroheim.

A Merry War 🦴🦴🦴 *Keep the Aspidistra Flying* **1997** Gordon Comstock (Grant) is a frustrated ad-man in London, circa 1935. He believes that his comfortable middle-class lifestyle is stifling his creativity (he is mistakenly lead to believe that he is a poet when he gets published). Convinced that slumming is the only way to tap into his supposed talent, he quits his advertising job and moves into a shabby little apartment to augment his misery, despite the doubts of girlfriend Rosemary (Bonham Carter). Based on George Orwell's only comedy, which fictionalizes his own experiences in London and Paris. In spite of being a comedy (and a funny one at that), story has that Orwellian feel of political commentary and, naturally, makes a statement on social classes. Performances are solid, with the beautiful Bonham Carter showing her comedic chops. Very British pic will appeal to fans of '30s era dialogue. **101m/C VHS, DVD.** Richard E. Grant, Helena Bonham Carter, Julian Wadham, Jim Carter, Harriet Walter, Liz Smith, Barbara Leigh-Hunt; ***D:*** Robert Bierman; ***W:*** Alan Plater; ***C:*** Giles Nuttgens; ***M:*** Mike Batt.

The Merry Widow 1/2 *The Lady Dances* **1934** The first sound version of the famous Franz Lehar operetta, dealing with a playboy from a bankrupt kingdom who must woo and marry the land's wealthy widow or be tried for treason. A delightful musical comedy, with a sterling cast and patented Lubitschian gaiety. Made as a silent in 1912 and 1925; remade in color in 1952. ♫ Girls, Girls, Girls; Vilia; Tonight Will Teach Me to Forget; Melody of Laughter; Maxim's; The Girls at Maxim's; The Merry Widow Waltz; If Widows are Rich; Russian Dance. **99m/B VHS.** Maurice Chevalier, Jeanette MacDonald, Edward Everett Horton, Una Merkel, George Barbier, Minna Gombell, Ruth Channing, Sterling Holloway, Henry Armetta, Barbara Leanard, Donald Meek, Akim Tamiroff, Herman Bing; ***D:*** Ernst Lubitsch; ***M:*** Franz Lehar, Lorenz Hart.

The Merry Widow 1/2 **1952** Rich widow Turner travels to her husband's homeland of Marshovia to dedicate a statue to his memory. The country is deeply in debt and the king would like the widow to marry a local count and remain (along with her fortune). Lamas is charming as the intended bridegroom but Turner, though lovely looking, is miscast; her singing was dubbed by Erwin. Uninspired remake of the 1934 film only benefits from being shot in color and the lavish production values. Based on the operetta by Lehar. ♫ The Merry Widow Waltz; Can-Can; Girls, Girls, Girls; I'm Going to Maxim's. **105m/C VHS.** Lana Turner, Fernando Lamas, Una Merkel, Richard Haydn, Thomas Gomez, John Abbott, Marcel Dalio, King Donovan, Robert Coote, Joi Lansing; ***Cameos:*** Gwen Verdon; ***D:*** Curtis Bernhardt; ***W:*** Sonya Levien, William Ludwig; ***C:*** Robert L. Surtees; ***M:*** Franz Lehar; ***V:*** Trudy Erwin.

The Merry Wives of Windsor *Die Lustigen Weiber von Windsor* **1950** Fat, ribald, and boastful Sir John Falstaff indulges in excess at his favorite Windsor tavern. He also likes the ladies and has taken to flattering both Mistress Reich and Fluth. The ladies and the townspeople eventually decide that Falstaff needs to be taught a lesson. German with subtitles. **96m/B VHS.** *GE* Paul Esser, Sonja Ziemann, Camilla Spira; ***D:*** Georg Wildhagen; ***W:*** Georg Wildhagen, Wolff von Gordon; ***C:*** Karl Plintzner, Eugen Klagemann; ***M:*** Otto Nikolai.

Merton of the Movies 1/2 **1947** Skelton stars as star-struck, small town theatre usher Merton Gill who wins a trip to Hollywood. He's befriended by stunt double Phyllis (O'Brien) who recognizes his comedic talents and works to get him that big break. Based on the play by George S. Kaufman and Marc Connelly and previously filmed in 1924 and 1932 (as "Make Me a Star"). **82m/B VHS.** Red Skelton, Virginia O'Brien, Gloria Grahame, Leon Ames, Alan Mowbray, Charles D. Brown, Hugo Haas, Harry Hayden; ***D:*** Robert Alton; ***W:*** George Wells, Lou Breslow.

Mesa of Lost Women WOOF! *Lost Women; Lost Women of Zarpa* **1952** Mad scientist creates brave new race of vicious women with long fingernails. So bad it's a wanna-B. Addams Family buffs will spot the Fester in Coogan. **70m/B VHS, DVD.** Jackie Coogan, Richard Travis, Allan Nixon, Mary Hill, Robert Knapp, Tandra Quinn, Lyle Talbot, Katherine Victor, Angelo Rossitto, Dolores Fuller, John Martin; ***D:*** Ron Ormond, Herbert Tevos; ***W:*** Herbert Tevos; ***C:*** Gilbert Warrenton, Karl Struss; ***M:*** Hoyt Curtin.

Mesmer **1994** Rickman gives a bravura performance in the title role of controversial 18th-century Austrian doctor Franz Anton Mesmer, who put the term "mesmerize" in the dictionary. This court (in Vienna and Paris) physician's unorthodox healing practices were concerned with filtering out negative magnetism through hypnotism and positive thinking. Was he a charlatan or merely a man ahead of his time? **107m/C VHS, DVD.** *GB* Alan Rickman, Donal Donnelly, Peter Dvorsky, David Hemblen, Simon McBurney, Gillian Barge, Jan Rubes; ***D:*** Roger Spottiswoode; ***W:*** Dennis Potter; ***C:*** Elemer Ragalyi; ***M:*** Michael Nyman.

Mesmerized *Shocked* **1984** Based on the work by Jerzy Skolimowski, the film is a dramatization of the Victoria Thompson murder case in 1880s New Zealand. A teenaged orphaned girl marries an older man and decides after years of abuse to kill him through hypnosis. An unengaging drama, though the lovely New Zealand landscape serves as a fitting contrast to the film's ominous tone. **90m/C VHS, DVD.** *GB NZ AU* John Lithgow, Jodie Foster, Michael Murphy, Dan Shor, Harry Andrews; ***D:*** Michael Laughlin; ***W:*** Michael Laughlin; ***C:*** Louis Horvath; ***M:*** Georges Delerue.

Mesquite Buckaroo **1939** Two cowboys bet over who is the better bronco buster, but one of them gets kidnapped. **59m/B VHS.** Bob Steele, Carolyn Curtis, Frank LaRue, Juanita Fletcher, Charles "Blackie" King; ***D:*** Harry S. Webb.

The Message *Mohammad: Messenger of God; Al-Ris-Alah* **1977 (PG)** Sprawling saga of the genesis of the religion of Islam, with Quinn portraying Mohammad's uncle, Hamza, an honored warrior. The story behind the movie might prove much more successful as a sequel than did the movie itself. The filming itself created a religious controversy. **220m/C VHS, DVD.** *GB* Damien Thomas, Anthony Quinn, Irene Papas, Michael Ansara, Johnny Sekka, Michael Forest, Neville Jason; ***D:*** Moustapha Akkad; ***W:*** H.A.L. Craig; ***C:*** Jack Hildyard; ***M:*** Maurice Jarre.

Message in a Bottle **1998 (PG-13)** Romantic drama that's paced slower than the method of mail delivery in the title. Wright Penn is a divorced mother who finds a love note written to a mystery man's lost love floating in the Atlantic. She tracks the note to strong silent guy Costner, still grieving for his dead wife. She tries to get him to open up and move on with his life (with her preferably), but this takes a mind-numbingly long time. The two are destined to be together, but half of those watching are destined to be asleep by the time it happens. The sole reason to watch this movie is to see old pro Paul Newman steal every scene he's in as Costner's father. **132m/C VHS, DVD.** Kevin Costner, Robin Wright Penn, Paul Newman, John Savage, Illeana Douglas, Robbie Coltrane, Jesse James, Bethel Leslie, Tom Aldredge, Viveka Davis, Raphael Sbarge, Richard Hamilton, Rosemary Murphy, Stephen Eckholdt; ***D:*** Luis Mandoki; ***W:*** Gerald Di Pego; ***C:*** Caleb Deschanel; ***M:*** Gabriel Yared.

Messalina vs. the Son of Hercules **1964** A Roman slave leads a rebellion against the emperor Messalina. Italian; dubbed into English. **105m/C VHS.** *IT* Richard Harrison, Marilu Tolo, Lisa Gastoni; ***D:*** Umberto Lenzi.

The Messenger **1987 (R)** A man right out of prison sets out to avenge his wife's murder by an Italian drug syndicate. **95m/C VHS.** Fred Williamson, Sandy Cummings, Christopher Connelly, Cameron Mitchell; ***D:*** Fred Williamson; ***W:*** Brian Johnson, Conchita Lee, Anthony Wisdom; ***C:*** Giancarlo Ferrando, Craig Greene; ***M:*** William Stuckley.

The Messenger **2009 (R)** Realistic but not melodramatic look at a soldier's difficulties readjusting to life back home. Iraq War vet Will Montgomery (Foster) is assigned to the Casualty Notification Office, which informs next of kin of a soldier's death. His own wounds cause post-traumatic stress and his job only intensifies his problems even as Will falls for widowed Olivia (Morton) and struggles with his recovering alcoholic commanding officer Anthony Stone (Harrelson). First-time director Moverman takes on one of the darkest and most unseen aspects of war and treats it with skillful respect and dignity, thanks largely to outstanding performances by the leads. **112m/C DVD.** *US* Ben Foster, Woody Harrelson, Samantha Morton, Eamonn Walker, Jena Malone, Steve Buscemi; ***D:*** Oren Moverman; ***W:*** Oren Moverman, Alessandro Camon; ***C:*** Bobby Bukowski; ***M:*** Nathan Larson. Ind. Spirit '10: Support. Actor (Harrelson).

Messenger of Death 1/2 **1988 (R)** A tough detective investigates the slaughter of a Mormon family, and uncovers a conspiracy centering around oil-rich real estate. **90m/C VHS, DVD.** Charles Bronson, Trish Van Devere, Laurence Luckinbill, Daniel Benzali, Marilyn Hassett, Jeff Corey, John Ireland, Penny Peyser, Gene Davis; ***D:*** J. Lee Thompson; ***W:*** Paul Jarrico; ***M:*** Robert O. Ragland.

The Messenger: The Story of Joan of Arc **1999 (R)** Besson's take on the legendary 15th-century French teen martyr Joan of Arc (Jovovich) leans heavily on gory battle scenes, stilted dialogue, and spectacle to tell her story. After seeing her sister murdered and raped (actually in that order) by English soldiers, Joan begins to hear heavenly voices that tell her that she must free her country and king from the invaders. After a visit with the Dauphin, several bloody battles ensue, and Joan is eventually captured and put on trial for sorcery and heresy. Awaiting her fate, she has conversations with a character that is actually billed as her Conscience (Hoffman), which brings up questions in her mind whether she was really divinely inspired or merely a cake du fruit. Jovovich's pop-eyed, semi-intelligible performance helps this poor effort go up in flames. **148m/C VHS, DVD.** Milla Jovovich, John Malkovich, Faye Dunaway, Dustin Hoffman, Pascal Greggory, Vincent Cassel, Tcheky Karyo, Richard Ridings, Desmond Harrington; ***D:*** Luc Besson; ***W:*** Luc Besson, Andrew Birkin; ***C:*** Thierry Arbogast; ***M:*** Eric Serra.

The Messengers 1/2 **2007 (PG-13)** Hong Kong filmmakers, the Pang brothers, go Americana with a derivative haunted farmhouse tale. The Solomon family moves onto a dilapidated North Dakota farm (the previous owners were slaughtered) in a last-ditch effort to forestall personal and economic ruin. No one believes sullen teenager Jess (Stewart), who thinks the place has some bad juju, and only toddler Ben (the Turner twins) can see the ghosts skittering around. Dull rather than ominous. **84m/C DVD, Blu-ray Disc, HD DVD.** *US* Kristen Stewart, Dylan McDermott, Penelope Ann Miller, John Corbett, Evan Turner, Theodore Turner, Dustin Milligan; ***D:*** Danny Pang, Oxide Pang; ***W:*** Mark Wheaton; ***C:*** David Geddes; ***M:*** Joseph LoDuca.

Messengers 2: The Scarecrow **2009 (R)** In a prequel to the first flick, farmer John Rollins (Reedus) places a mysterious scarecrow in his fields and finds his bad luck changing for the better. Of course it doesn't last. **94m/C DVD.** Norman Reedus, Claire Holt, Richard Riehle, Darcy Fowers, Matthew McNulty, Heather Stephens; ***D:*** Martin Barnewitz; ***W:*** Todd Farmer; ***C:*** Lorenzo Senatore; ***M:*** Joseph LoDuca. **VIDEO**

The Messiah 1/2 *Il Messia* **1975** Rossellini's final film, a rarely seen version of the life of Christ, completely passed over any notions of divinity to portray him as a morally perfect man. In Italian with subtitles. **145m/C VHS.** *IT* Tina Aumont, Flora Carabella, Vernon Dobtcheff, Jean Martin; ***D:*** Roberto Rossellini; ***W:*** Roberto Rossellini; ***C:*** Mario Montuori; ***M:*** Mario Nascimbene.

Messiah of Evil *Dead People; Return of the Living Dead; Revenge of the Screaming Dead; The Second Coming* **1974 (R)** California coastal town is invaded by zombies. Confusing low-rent production from the writers of "American Graffiti." **90m/C VHS, DVD.** Marianna Hill, Joy Bang, Royal Dano, Elisha Cook Jr., Michael Greer; ***D:*** Gloria Katz, Willard Huyck; ***W:*** Gloria Katz, Willard Huyck.

Messidor **1977** Bored university student Jeanne (Amouroux) and shop assistant Marie (Retore) meet while hitchhiking and decide to travel together through Europe—committing robberies when they run out of money. French with subtitles. **118m/C VHS.** *SI* Clementine Amouroux, Catherine Retore, Franziskus Abgottspon, Gerald Battiaz, Hansjorg Bedschard; ***D:*** Alain Tanner; ***W:*** Alain Tanner; ***C:*** Renato Berta; ***M:*** Arie Dzierlatka.

Metal Skin 1/2 **1994** Nihilistic nightmare, set in Melbourne, plays like an unintentional parody of '50s "B" juvenile delinquent movies. Aimless Joe (Young) has been taken under the wing of local Romeo Dazey (Mendelsohn), who's been romancing Roslyn (Garner) and Savina (Morice), two girls Joe is also interested in. Dazey also has Joe involved in illegal drag racing, leading, after much interim angst, to a racing battle between the two. Director Wright has shown his way with violent characters living on the fringes of society (see "Romper Stomper") but this is too much of a bad thing. **115m/C DVD.** *AU* Aden Young, Ben Mendelsohn, Tara Morice, Nadine Garner; ***D:*** Geoffrey Wright; ***W:*** Geoffrey Wright.

Metallica *Space Odyssey; Captive Planet; Star Odyssey; Sette Uomini d'Oro Nello Spazio* **1985** Alien warmongers endeavor to conquer Earth and scientists try to stop them. **90m/C VHS.** *IT* Chris Avran, Malisa Longo, Robert Dell' Acqua, Yanti Somer, Gianni "John" Garko; ***D:*** Al (Alfonso Brescia) Bradley; ***W:*** Al (Alfonso Brescia) Bradley; ***C:*** Silvio Fraschetti; ***M:*** Marcello Giombini.

Metallica: Some Kind of Monster **2004** Headbangers' "Let It Be" is a story of celebrity confession and, possibly, redemption. No Metallica career overview, concert showcases, or archival clips included. What you'll see is the psychoanalytically-assisted recording misadventure of St. Anger, a warts and all portrait exposing artist insecurity. Originally Elektra Records commissioned Bruce Sinofsy and Joe Belinger to create a film promoting the making of an album, but when talk of turning the footage into a half-hour reality series ensued, Metallica quickly reimbursed the $2 million to the label and added another $2.3 to have it completed. **140m/C DVD.** James Hetfield, Lars Ulrich, Kirk Hammett, Robert Trujillo, Jason Newsted, Dave Mustaine, Bob Rock, Phil Towle; ***D:*** Joe Berlinger, Bruce Sinofsky; ***C:*** Robert Richman. Ind. Spirit '05: Feature Doc.

Metalstorm: The Destruction of Jared Syn **1983 (PG)** It's the science fiction battle of the ages with giant cyclopes and intergalactic magicians on the desert planet of Lemuria. **84m/C VHS.** Jeffrey Byron, Mike (Michael) Preston, Tim Thomerson, Kelly Preston, Richard Moll; ***D:*** Charles Band; ***W:*** Alan J. Adler; ***C:*** Mac Ahlberg; ***M:*** Richard Band.

Metamorphosis **1990 (R)** Novice scientist foolishly uses himself as the guinea pig for his anti-aging experiments. He quickly loses control of the project. **90m/C VHS.** Gene Le Brock, Catherine Baranov, Stephen Brown, Harry Cason, Jason Arnold; ***D:*** G.L. Eastman.

Metamorphosis: The Alien Factor 1/2 **1993 (R)** Gerard is a genetic engineer who is bitten by a frog injected with a mutation sample from outer space. He turns into a slimy virus that infects everything he touches. **92m/C VHS, DVD.** George Gerard, Tony Gigante, Katharine Romaine; ***D:*** Glen Takakjian.

Meteor WOOF! 1979 (PG) American and Soviet scientists attempt to save the Earth from a fast-approaching barrage of meteors from space in this disaster dud. Destruction ravages parts of Hong Kong and the Big Apple. **107m/C VHS, DVD.** Sean Connery, Natalie Wood, Karl Malden, Brian Keith, Martin Landau, Trevor Howard, Henry Fonda, Joseph Campanella, Richard Dysart; ***D:*** Ronald Neame; ***W:*** Stanley Mann; ***C:*** Paul Lohmann; ***M:*** Laurence Rosenthal.

Meteor **2009** Unintentionally campy TV miniseries about a chunk of space rock destined to annihilate the planet. Unless, of course, a couple of unlikely scientists can save the day. There are various side plots but it's all so silly that they don't matter. **180m/C DVD.** Jason Alexander, Marla Sokoloff, Billy Campbell, Michael Rooker, Stacy Keach, Ernie Hudson, Christopher Lloyd, Mimi Michaels; ***D:*** Ernie Barbarash; ***W:*** Alexander Greenfield; ***C:*** Maximo Munzi; ***M:*** Jonathan Snipes. **TV**

Meteor & Shadow *Meteoro Kai Skia* **1985** Based on the life of esteemed Greek poet Napoleon Lapathiotis (1888-

1944), whose openly gay lifestyle shocked conservative Athenian society. A leftist charmer, Lapathiotis indulged in the bohemian life until it finally destroyed him. Greek with subtitles. **101m/C VHS, DVD.** *GR* Takis Moschos; *D:* Takis Spetsiotis; *W:* Takis Spetsiotis.

The Meteor Man 1/2 **1993 (PG)** Townsend is a school teacher who reluctantly becomes a hero when he acquires semi-super powers after being hit by a meteor. Meteor Man flies only four feet off the ground (because he's afraid of heights) and wears costumes fashioned by his mother. Funny premise satires "superhero" movies, but is inconsistent with some hilarious gags and others that fall flat. Includes interesting cameos by Cosby, Sinbad, Vandross, and Page. **100m/C VHS, DVD.** Robert Kevin Townsend, Robert Guillaume, Marla Gibbs, James Earl Jones, Frank Gorshin, Bill Cosby, Sinbad, Luther Vandross, LaWanda Page, Louis Freese; *D:* Robert Kevin Townsend; *W:* Robert Kevin Townsend; *C:* John A. Alonzo.

The Method *El Metodo* **2005** Seven job applicants for a high-end position at a corporation in Madrid participate in the Gronholm method of selection. Individuals play games using the monitor and keyboard provided them, setting out to destroy the competition while proving their own credibility. After each round the monitor shuts down on the candidate being eliminated and an electronic voice announces "It's over." Humorous, dark, and engaging view of business culture. English and Spanish with subtitles. **115m/C DVD.** *AR IT SP* Eduardo Noriega, Najwa Nimri, Eduardo Fernandez, Pablo Echarvi, Ernesto Alterio, Natalia Verbeke, Adriana Ozores, Carmelo Gomez; *D:* Marcelo Pineyro; *W:* Marcelo Pineyro; *C:* Alfredo Mayo; *M:* Frederic Begin.

Metro 1/2 **1996 (R)** Murphy has now officially made this exact movie one kajillion times. He plays fast-talking, fast-shooting cop Axel Fo... er... Scott Roper, who's forced to accept a partner that he doesn't want, played by Nick... um... Judge... uh... Michael Rapaport! When a villain kills his best friend, he vows revenge. He and his sidekick are involved in car chases, shoot-outs and a tense situation where his girlfriend is taken hostage. Any of this ring a bell? Maybe it was in that "Another 48 Beverly Hills Cop Movies." **117m/C VHS, DVD.** Eddie Murphy, Michael Rapaport, Michael Wincott, Carmen Ejogo, Denis Arndt, Art Evans, Donal Logue, Paul Ben-Victor, Kim Miyori, David Michael Silverman; *D:* Thomas Carter; *W:* Randy Feldman; *C:* Fred Murphy; *M:* Steve Porcaro.

Metroland **1997 (R)** Marital ennui and male friendship is explored in this adaptation of Julian Barnes' 1980 novel. In 1977, advertising exec Chris Lloyd (Bale) is settled in a London suburb with his wife, Marion (Watson), and their baby. His predictable existence is blasted when old chum, Toni (Ross), arrives. The duo once shared a dream of living a bohemian life and Chris is reminded of a time he spent in Paris in the late-'60s and his wild French lover. Toni increasingly tries to undermine Chris' marriage as he struggles to decide what he expects from life. **105m/C VHS, DVD.** *GB FR* Christian Bale, Emily Watson, Lee Ross, Elsa Zylberstein, Ifan Meredith, Rufus, Amanda Ryan; *D:* Philip Saville; *W:* Adrian Hodges; *C:* Jean-Francois Robin; *M:* Mark Knopfler.

Metropolis **1926** Now a classic meditation on futurist technology and mass mentality, this fantasy concerns mechanized society. Original set design and special effects made this an innovative and influential film in its day. Is now considered one of the hippest films of the sci-fi genre. Silent, with musical score. The 1984 re-release features some color tinting, reconstruction, and a digital score with songs by Pat Benatar, Bonnie Tyler, Giorgio Moroder, and Queen. **115m/B VHS, DVD.** *GE* Brigitte Helm, Alfred Abel, Gustav Froehlich, Rudolf Klein-Rogge, Fritz Rasp, Heinrich George, Theodore Loos, Erwin Biswanger, Olaf Storm, Hans Leo Reich, Heinrich Gotho, Fritz Alberti, Max Dietze; *D:* Fritz Lang; *W:* Fritz Lang, Thea von Harbou; *C:* Karl Freund, Gunther Rittau, Eugen Shufftan; *M:* Gottfried Huppertz.

Metropolitan **1990 (PG-13)** The Izod set comes of age on Park Avenue during Christmas break. Tom Townsend (Clements), a member of the middle class, finds himself drawn into a circle of self-proclaimed urban haute bourgeoisie types. They're embarrassingly short on male escorts for the holiday season's parties so he stands in and gets an inside look at life with the brat pack. Intelligently written and carefully made, it transcends the flirting-with-adulthood genre. **98m/C VHS, DVD.** Carolyn Farina, Edward Clements, Taylor Nichols, Christopher Eigeman, Allison Rutledge-Parisi, Dylan Hundley, Isabel Gillies, Bryan Leder, Will Kempe, Elizabeth Thompson; *D:* Whit Stillman; *W:* Whit Stillman; *C:* John Thomas; *M:* Mark Suozzo. Ind. Spirit '91: First Feature; N.Y. Film Critics '90: Director (Stillman).

The Mexican **2001 (R)** South-of-the-border snorer has Jerry (Pitt), an inept go-fer for mobster Margolese (Hackman), on a mission for a priceless antique gun with a name which gives the movie its title. Jerry's quirky girlfriend Samantha (Roberts) wants him to go straight and, when he refuses, heads to Vegas to pursue her dreams of becoming a croupier. Sam's dreams are temporarily sidetracked when she's kidnapped as leverage for the supposedly cursed gun by homosexual hitman Leroy (Gandolfini). Gandolfini is far-and-away the standout as the sensitive hood with whom Samantha bonds during her captivity. Screwball romantic comedy is neither, as the few but much-anticipated scenes with Pitt and Roberts are easily outshone by Roberts' chemistry with Gandolfini. Pitt does his part, providing some comic moments in Mexico but can't save cliched tale. **123m/C VHS, DVD.** *US* Brad Pitt, Julia Roberts, James Gandolfini, Bob Balaban, Gene Hackman, J.K. Simmons, David Krumholtz, Michael Ceveris; *D:* Gore Verbinski; *W:* J.H. Wyman; *C:* Darius Wolski; *M:* Alan Silvestri.

Mexican Blow *Warrior* **2002 (R)** Dangerous drug lords invade the deepest jungles of South America to build their drug manufacturing and distribution headquarters. Dreadmon (Klyn) watches the marauders kill his adopted father and then scares them away with his supernatural powers, but they're not happy to go. Dreadmon must fight inner battles and overcome both his own demons and the drug lords. Shot in the jungles of Costa Azul and the urban setting of Puerto Vallarta, it's a truly bizarre and pointless mix of action, adventure and fantasy. **97m/C VHS, DVD.** Vincent Klyn, Ron Joseph, Yukmouth; *D:* Will Harper; *W:* William Lawlor; *C:* Rick Lamb; *M:* Peter Meisner. **VIDEO**

Mexican Bus Ride 1/2 *Ascent to Heaven; Subida Al Cielo* **1951** A good-natured Bunuel effort about a newlywed peasant who travels to the big city to attend to his mother's will. While en route, he encounters a diversity of people on the bus and some temptation. In Spanish with English subtitles. **85m/B VHS.** *MX* Lilia Prado, Esteban Marquez, Carmelita Gonzalez; *D:* Luis Bunuel.

Mexican Gangster **2008** Orphaned Johnny Sunshine has always lived the life of a barrio thug but he wants something better for his younger brother than a life of smuggling and drug dealing. But his protectiveness is seen as a weakness by other gangsters who want Johnny's business. **96m/C DVD.** Damian Chapa, Joe Loretto, Christine Manoukian, Stanley Griego, Augustine Torres, Tom Druilhet; *D:* Damian Chapa; *W:* Damian Chapa; *C:* Pierre Chemaly; *M:* Don Bodin. **VIDEO**

Mexican Hayride **1948** Bud heads a gang of swindlers and Lou is the fall guy. When things up north get too hot, the boys head south of the border to cool off and start a mining scam. Watch for the hilarious bullfighting scene. Believe it or not, this is based on a Cole Porter musical—minus the music. **77m/B VHS, DVD.** Bud Abbott, Lou Costello, Virginia Grey, Luba Malina, John Hubbard, Pedro de Cordoba, Fritz Feld, Tom Powers, Pat Costello, Frank Fenton; *D:* Charles T. Barton; *W:* Oscar Brodney.

Mexican Spitfire **1940** Velez is typecast as the title character—newlywed Carmelita who has some problems to deal with in her brand-new marriage to Dennis (Woods). There's her fiery temper, a meddling aunt, and an ex-fiancee who's determined to wreck the twosome. First in the series. **67m/B VHS, DVD.** Lupe Velez, Leon Errol, Donald Woods, Linda Hayes, Elisabeth Risdon, Cecil Kellaway; *D:* Leslie Goodwins; *W:* Joseph Fields, Charles E. Roberts; *C:* Jack MacKenzie.

Mexican Spitfire at Sea 1/2 **1942** The feisty wife from South of the Border heads for Hawaii to close a deal for her husband. He goes along to help her, impersonating nobility. The thin storyline keeps it from being quite as good as the first "Mexican Spitfire" film. Most of the action takes place aboard ship. **73m/B VHS.** Lupe Velez, Leon Errol, Charles "Buddy" Rogers, Zasu Pitts, Elisabeth Risdon, Florence Bates, Marion Martin, Eddie Dunn, Harry Holman; *D:* Leslie Goodwins.

Mexico City 1/2 **2000 (R)** This one gets points for having a strong heroine in Edwards. She plays Mitch who takes a holiday in Mexico with photographer brother Sam (Zander). Only Sam disappears and Mitch enlists the help of a local taxi driver (Robles) to help her find him. Shows the seedy underworld side of Mexico City—not exactly a tourist mecca. **88m/C VHS, DVD.** Stacy Edwards, Jorge Robles, Johnny Zander, Robert Patrick, Alexander Gould; *D:* Richard Shepard; *W:* Richard Shepard, Jonathan Stern. **VIDEO**

Mi Vida Loca *My Crazy Life* **1994 (R)** Looks at the lives of Latina gang members from L.A.'s Echo Park. The women talk about their romantic dreams, friendships, families, and raising children amidst the pervasive violence and despair of their tough neighborhood. Small budget and some unpolished performances don't lessen film's impact—about the stupidity of violence and how "average" the hopes and dreams of these women are. **92m/C VHS, DVD.** Angel Aviles, Jacob Vargas, Jesse Borrego, Seidy Lopez, Marlo Marron, Neilida Lopez, Bertila Damas, Art Esquer, Christina Solis, Salma Hayek, Magali Alvarado, Julian Reyes, Panchito Gomez; *D:* Allison Anders; *W:* Allison Anders; *M:* John Taylor.

Miami Beach Cops 1/2 **1993** Two vets return home expecting life to be routine when they become sheriff's deputies. But when bad guys murder a local merchant things heat up fast. **97m/C VHS, DVD.** Frank Maldonatti, Salvatore Rendino, William Childers, Joyce Geier, Raff Baker, Dan Preston, Deborah Daniels; *D:* James R. Winburn.

Miami Blues 1/2 **1990 (R)** Cold-blooded killer plays cat-and-mouse with bleary cop while diddling with an unflappable prostitute. Violent and cynical, with appropriate performances from three leads. Based on the novel by Charles Willeford. **97m/C VHS, DVD.** Fred Ward, Alec Baldwin, Jennifer Jason Leigh, Nora Dunn, Charles Napier, Jose Perez, Paul Gleason, Obba Babatunde, Martine Beswick, Shirley Stoler; *D:* George Armitage; *W:* George Armitage; *C:* Tak Fujimoto; *M:* Gary Chang. N.Y. Film Critics '90: Support. Actress (Leigh).

Miami Cops **1989** When a cop's father is killed by a drug smuggler, he and his partner pursue the murderer over two continents. Italian-made adventure is a bit drawn-out. **103m/C VHS.** *IT* Richard Roundtree, Harrison Muller, Dawn Baker, Michael J. Aronin; *D:* Al (Alfonso Brescia) Bradley.

Miami Horror **1987** A Florida scientist is experimenting with bacteria from space, trying to recreate a human only to have his efforts stolen by a crook. His intentions for the use of the experiment are not exactly for the furtherance of science. De martino used the pseudonym Martin Herbert. **85m/C VHS.** *IT* David Warbeck, Laura Trotter, Lawrence Loddi, John Ireland; *D:* Alberto De Martino.

Miami Hustle 1/2 **1995 (R)** Con artist Marsha (Ireland) is forced by a sleazy lawyer to impersonate a bar waitress (England) who's about to inherit a fortune. But when things turn sour, she gets a computer mogul (Enos) to figure out who's setting her up. **81m/C VHS, DVD.** Kathy Ireland, John Enos, Audie England, Richard Sarafian; *D:* Lawrence Lanoff. **CABLE**

Miami Rhapsody **1995 (PG-13)** Woody Allen-ish romantic comedy about a young, neurotic copywriter who becomes disillusioned with the idea of marriage as she discovers every member of her family is having an affair. Parker plays the newly engaged Gwyn who is not entirely sure if she wants to marry her cute, zoologist boyfriend. Most of the characters come across as annoying, self-absorbed whiners, except for Banderas, who charms as a sexy Cuban nurse. Film moves along with its light-hearted narrative, but never reaches the comic or emotional depth of Allen's work. Director/writer Frankel shows promise, but should come out from behind the Woodman's shadow. Filmed on location in Miami. **95m/C VHS, DVD.** Sarah Jessica Parker, Gil Bellows, Antonio Banderas, Mia Farrow, Paul Mazursky, Kevin Pollak, Barbara Garrick, Carla Gugino, Bo Eason, Naomi Campbell, Jeremy Piven, Kelly Bishop, Ben Stein; *D:* David Frankel; *W:* David Frankel; *C:* Jack Wallner; *M:* Mark Isham.

Miami Supercops 1/2 **1985** Two goofy policemen strike out against such threats as a gang that hassles buses, the attempted kidnapping of an Orange Bowl quarterback, and a multi-million-dollar robbery. **97m/C VHS.** Terence Hill, Bud Spencer, Jackie Castellano, C.V. Wood Jr.; *D:* Bruno Corbucci.

Miami Vendetta **1987** L.A. vice cop risks it all to avenge his friend's death at the hands of Cuban drug smugglers. **90m/C VHS.** Sandy Brooke, Frank Gargani, Maarten Goslins, Barbara Pilavin; *D:* Steven Seemayer.

Miami Vice 1/2 **1984** Pilot for the popular TV series paired Crockett and Tubbs for the first time on the trail of a killer in Miami's sleazy underground. Music by Jan Hammer and other pop notables. **99m/C VHS, DVD.** Don Johnson, Philip Michael Thomas, Saundra Santiago, Michael Talbott, John Diehl, Gregory Sierra; *D:* Thomas Carter. **TV**

Miami Vice 1/2 **2006 (R)** Writer/director Michael Mann gives his Miami cop story the big-screen treatment in this update of his popular '80s TV series. Today's Crockett (Colin Farrell) and Tubbs (Jamie Foxx) find themselves dangerously deep undercover with the same curious access to super-fast, super-expensive cars and boats as their small-screen predecessors, essential, no-doubt, to catching the multicultural, drug-dealing bad guys and attracting their multicultural, multitalented girlfriends. The actors' pursuit of "cool" comes across as stiff and void of expression, while the story is overly complicated and ultimately secondary to film's style, which really is everything in this case. But then, did you really expect that to change? **132m/C DVD, HD DVD.** *US* Colin Farrell, Jamie Foxx, Gong Li, Naomie Harris, Luis Tosar, John Ortiz, Barry (Shabaka) Henley, Ciaran Hinds, Justin Theroux, Elizabeth Rodriguez, John Hawkes; *D:* Michael Mann; *W:* Michael Mann; *C:* Dion Beebe; *M:* John Murphy.

Michael 1/2 **1996 (PG)** Following up "Phenomenon" with another celestial storyline, Travolta tries on the giant, molting wings of Michael, an atypical archangel with an amazing joie de vive and an appetite for alcohol, women, and sugar. Residing in Iowa with the elderly Pansy (Stapleton), Michael is being tracked by a cynical tabloid reporter (Hurt) and an angel expert (MacDowell), so he figures he might as well play cupid. The now standard dance sequence in Travolta movies takes place in a bar to the tune of "Chain of Fools" and is one of the movie's stand-outs. While Travolta gives another stellar performance, Hurt and MacDowell have little to do but play out their tired romantic subplot in a script that could've used some inspiration from its lead character. **105m/C VHS, DVD.** John Travolta, William Hurt, Andie MacDowell, Bob Hoskins, Robert Pastorelli, Jean Stapleton, Teri Garr; *D:* Nora Ephron; *W:* Nora Ephron, Delia Ephron, Pete Dexter; *C:* John Lindley; *M:* Randy Newman.

Michael Clayton 1/2 **2007 (R)** The titular Clayton (Clooney) is a ruthless, conflicted "fixer" for a giant law firm—the guy you bring in to do whatever it takes, no matter how unethical, to secure a win for the firm. When Clayton's friend and top-notch litigator Arthur (Wilkinson) suffers a breakdown over a pollution case where their client is clearly in the wrong, Clayton's boss (Pollack) tells him to fix the problem, but Clayton can't help but see just how in the wrong his firm truly is. Unfortunately, he's too good, and in too deep, to give it all up. The ending is in doubt right up until the final, powerful scene. A heady, fascinating exploration of a world where people spend so much time inhabiting grey areas, they've forgotten what black and white look like. **119m/C DVD.** *US* George Clooney, Tom Wilkinson, Tilda Swinton, Sydney Pollack, Michael O'Keefe, Jennifer Van Dyck, Ken Howard, Robert Prescott; ***D:*** Tony Gilroy; ***W:*** Tony Gilroy; ***C:*** Robert Elswit; ***M:*** James Newton Howard. Oscars '07: Support. Actress (Swinton); British Acad. '07: Support. Actress (Swinton).

Michael Collins 𝒷𝒷𝒷 **1996 (R)** Collins (Neeson) was a revolutionary leader with the Irish Volunteers, a guerilla force (an early version of the IRA) dedicated to freeing Ireland from British rule by any means necessary. After a number of successful moves against British intelligence, Collins is unwillingly drawn into a statesman's role as negotiations for an Anglo-Irish Treaty begin in 1921, ultimately dividing the country in two and leading to Collins' own assassination. Controversy surrounded the film as historians, politicians, and the media took potshots at director Jordan's admittedly personal look at the complexities of Irish life and one of its equally complicated heroes. **117m/C VHS, DVD.** Liam Neeson, Aidan Quinn, Alan Rickman, Stephen Rea, Julia Roberts, Ian Hart, Sean McGinley, Gerard McSorley, Stuart Graham, Brendan Gleeson, Charles Dance, Jonathan Rhys Meyers; ***D:*** Neil Jordan; ***W:*** Neil Jordan; ***C:*** Chris Menges; ***M:*** Elliot Goldenthal. L.A. Film Critics '96: Cinematog.; Venice Film Fest. '96: Golden Lion, Actor (Neeson).

Michael Jackson's This Is It 𝒷𝒷 ½ *This Is It* **2009 (PG)** In more ways than one. Hastily compiled homage taken from some 120 hours of rehearsal footage recorded between March and June at L.A.'s Staples Center for Jackson's comeback London concerts before his death on June 25, 2009. Jackson is very much in work mode—generally holding back as he tries out dance moves, arrangements, etc. Interest will probably vary between those who are true fans and those who are morbidly curious to see how the singer/dancer looked and acted given the mass media hysteria surrounding his sudden demise. Includes numerous dance numbers as well as conversations between Jackson, director Ortega, the dancers and musicians, and others. **112m/C DVD.** *US* Michael Jackson; ***D:*** Kenny Ortega; ***C:*** Sandrine Orabona; ***M:*** Michael Bearden.

Michael Shayne: Private Detective 𝒷𝒷 ½ **1940** Brett Halliday's shamus made it to the big screen in a seven-film series starring Nolan. Shayne is a wisecracking, usually broke PI with ethics, which is why he first refuses the suspicious job offer made by wealthy Hiram Brighton (Kolb). Hiram wants him to keep an eye on Phyllis (Weaver), his gambling-addicted daughter, who's been betting on the ponies. When a shady money lender is murdered, Shayne is set up to take the fall but he learns the suspect list is long. First in the series. **77m/B DVD.** Lloyd Nolan, Clarence (C. William) Kolb, Marjorie Weaver, Douglass Dumbrille, George Meeker, Walter Abel, Joan Valerie, Donald MacBride, Elizabeth Patterson, Charles Coleman; ***D:*** Eugene Forde; ***W:*** Stanley Rauh, Manning O'Connor; ***C:*** George Schneiderman; ***M:*** Cyril Mockridge.

The Michigan Kid 𝒷𝒷 **1928** Two boys fight for the same girl in this silent love triangle set in Alaska. Film's most notable scene is of a raging forest fire, considered a classic even today. **62m/B VHS.** Conrad Nagel, Renee Adoree, Fred Esmelton, Virginia Grey, Adolph Milar, Lloyd Whitlock; ***D:*** Irvin Willat.

Mickey 𝒷𝒷 **1917** Spoof on high society as a penniless young woman moves in with relatives and works as the family's maid. Silent film. **105m/B VHS.** Mabel Normand, Lew Cody, Minta Durfee; ***D:*** Mack Sennett.

Mickey 𝒷 **1948** A tomboy becomes a woman even as she plays matchmaker for her own father and sings a few songs. Not too exciting; you may fall alseep if you're slipped this "Mickey." Based on the novel "Clementine," by Peggy Goodin. **87m/C VHS, DVD.** Lois Butler, Bill Goodwin, Irene Hervey, John Sutton, Hattie McDaniel; ***D:*** Ralph Murphy.

Mickey Blue Eyes 𝒷𝒷 ½ **1999 (PG-13)** Grant reprises his role as the maddeningly polite, apologetic British guy for about the bazillionth time. This time he plays Michael Felgate, an art auctioneer who proposes to schoolteacher Gina (Tripplehorn). Her father Frank (Caan) turns out to be a mobster, whose boss wants to use his auction house as a front for money laundering. After Michael tells a string of lies to hide his involvement from Gina, a series of wild events and misunderstandings leads to Michael posing as mobster Little Big Mickey Blue Eyes from Kansas City. Listening to tea-and-crumpety Grant trying to pronounce "fuhgeddaboudit" briefly brings the movie to life, but the premise is quickly abandoned and he sinks back into his droopy British bit again. All is wrapped up in your standard issue romantic comedy ending. **103m/C VHS, DVD.** Hugh Grant, Jeanne Tripplehorn, James Caan, Burt Young, Gerry Becker, James Fox, Joe (Johnny) Viterelli, Maddie Corman, Tony Darrow, Kathryn Witt, Vincent Pastore, Frank Pellegrino, Scott Thompson, John Ventimiglia; ***D:*** Kelly Makin; ***W:*** Robert Kuhn, Adam Scheinman; ***C:*** Donald E. Thorin; ***M:*** Wolfgang Hammerschmid.

Mickey One 𝒷𝒷 ½ **1965** Nightclub comic Mickey (Beatty) gets into trouble when he can't pay his gambling debts. So he hides out in Chicago under an assumed name, working as a janitor, but can't live without the applause. His agent finds him a club job but Mickey panics, thinking the place is under mob control, and spends a lot of time running around, trying to clear his debts. Finally, returning to the club, Mickey resigns himself to a bleak fate. Beatty's jumpy character is an acquired taste—as is the film. **93m/B** Warren Beatty, Hurd Hatfield, Alexandra Stewart, Franchot Tone, Teddy Hart, Jeff Corey; ***D:*** Arthur Penn; ***W:*** Alan M. Surgal; ***C:*** Ghislan Cloquet; ***M:*** Jack Shaindlin, Eddie Sauter.

Mickey the Great **1939** Stitched together from several late '20s Mickey McGuire shorts, starring 10-year-old Rooney. **70m/B VHS.** Billy Barty, Mickey Rooney.

Micki & Maude 𝒷𝒷 **1984 (PG-13)** When a man longs for a baby, he finds that his wife, Micki, is too busy for motherhood. Out of frustration, he has an affair with Maude that leads to her pregnancy. Still shocked by the news of his upcoming fatherhood, the man learns that his wife is also expecting. **117m/C VHS, DVD.** Dudley Moore, Amy Irving, Ann Reinking, Richard Mulligan, Wallace Shawn, George Gaynes, Andre the Giant; ***D:*** Blake Edwards; ***W:*** Jonathan Reynolds; ***C:*** Harry Stradling Jr. Golden Globes '85: Actor—Mus./Comedy (Moore).

Micmacs *Micmac a Tire-Larigot* **2009 (R)** Bazil's (Boon) dad was killed by a roadside bomb while serving in the military and later Bazil is hit by a stray bullet during a drive-by shooting. It's lodged in his brain and the doctors don't want to remove it, so he leaves the hospital with various physical and behavioral issues. Bazil hooks up with some other misfits and persuades them to assist him in a revenge plot against two armament manufacturers he blames for his troubles. French with subtitles. **105m/C DVD.** *FR* Dany Boon, Andre Dussollier, Jean-Pierre Marielle, Yolande Moreau, Nicolas Marie, Dominique Pinon, Julie Ferrier, Marie-Julie Baup; ***D:*** Jean-Pierre Jeunet; ***W:*** Jean-Pierre Jeunet, Guillaume Laurant; ***C:*** Tetsuo Nagata; ***M:*** Raphael Beau.

Microcosmos 𝒷𝒷𝒷 **1996 (G)** Warning: Do not attempt to smash the bugs on the screen with your shoe. They're supposed to be there. This French documentary uses special cameras and sound recording devices to explore the world of insects like never before. The editing and score also add a human dimension to the creepy-crawly world under the lawn, making amorous snails and workaholic beetles seem like people you know (well, if they had an extra set of legs and a shell-like carapace). Of course, if you don't like bugs, then this is just a 77-minute gross out. Cameo appearances by some birds and frogs. **77m/C VHS, DVD.** *FR* ***D:*** Claude Nuridsany, Marie Perennou; ***C:*** Claude Nuridsany, Marie Perennou, Hughes Ryffel, Thierry Machado; ***M:*** Bruno Coulais. Cesar '97: Art Dir./Set Dec., Cinematog., Film Editing, Sound, Score.

Microwave Massacre 𝒷 **1983 (R)** Killer kitchen appliances strike again as late lounge comic Vernon murders nagging wife and 'waves her. Overcome by that Betty Crocker feeling, he goes on a microwave murdering/feeding spree of the local ladies. Lots of Roger Corman copying. **80m/C VHS, DVD.** Jackie Vernon, Loren Schein, Al Troupe, Claire Ginsberg, Lou Ann Webber, Sarah Alt; ***D:*** Wayne Berwick; ***W:*** Thomas Singer; ***C:*** Karen Grossman; ***M:*** Leif Horvath.

Mid-Channel 𝒷𝒷 ½ **1920** A married couple become bored with each other and the wife seeks diversion with other men. Surprise ending. **70m/B VHS.** Clara Kimball Young, J. Frank Glendon, Edward M. Kimball, Bertram Grassby, Eileen Robinson, Helen Sullivan, Katherine Griffith, Jack Livingston; ***D:*** Harry Garson.

Mid Knight Rider 𝒷 *Hard Knocks; Hollywood Knight* **1979** Penniless actor becomes a male prostitute at the service of bored, rich women. At an all-night orgy, he suddenly goes on a rampage, nearly killing one of his customers. **76m/C VHS.** Michael Christian, Keenan Wynn, Donna Wilkes, Henry (Kleinbach) Brandon; ***D:*** David Worth.

Midaq Alley 𝒷𝒷𝒷 *The Alley of Miracles; El Callejon de los Milagros* **1995** Amusing melodrama based on the 1947 novel by Egyptian Naguib Mahfouz and transported from Cairo's backstreets to those of a rundown, modern-day Mexico City neighborhood known as "The Alley of Miracles." Four segments all begin on the same Sunday afternoon and follow a variety of the Alley's inhabitants, including a married man who becomes attracted to a young male clerk, a beauty who falls prey to a suave pimp, and a homely woman looking for love and finding Mr. Wrong. Spanish with subtitles. **140m/C VHS, DVD.** *MX* Ernesto Cruz, Maria Rojo, Salma Hayek, Bruno Bichir, Claudio Obregon, Delia Casanova, Margarita Sanz, Juan Manuel Bernal, Luis Felipe Tovar, Daniel Gimenez Cacho; ***D:*** Jorge Fons; ***W:*** Vicente Lenero; ***C:*** Carlos Marcovich; ***M:*** Lucia Alvarez.

The Midas Touch 𝒷𝒷 *Eldorado* **1989** A flea market merchant in 1956 Budapest has the ability to turn items into gold. In Hungarian with English subtitles. **100m/C VHS.** *HU* Karoly Eperies, Judith Pogany, Eniko Eszenyi, Barnabas Toth; ***D:*** Geza Beremenyi; ***W:*** Geza Beremenyi; ***C:*** Sandor Kardos; ***M:*** Ferenc Darvas.

Middle Age Crazy 𝒷 ½ **1980 (R)** Story of a Texas building contractor who takes life pretty lightly until his own father dies. Then he becomes immersed in a mid-life crisis and has an affair with a Dallas Cowboys' cheerleader. Ann-Margaret plays the victim wife of the middle aged swingin' guy. **95m/C VHS.** *CA* Bruce Dern, Ann-Margret, Graham Jarvis, Eric Christmas, Deborah Wakeham; ***D:*** John Trent.

The Middleman 𝒷𝒷 *Jana Aranya* **1976** Recent college graduate Somnath has struggled to find a job and eventually enters the business world as a middleman, where he soons discovers that success will depend on his willingness to break the rules. Bengali with subtitles. **131m/B VHS.** *IN* Pradip Mukherjee; ***D:*** Satyajit Ray; ***W:*** Satyajit Ray; ***C:*** Soumendu Roy.

Middlemarch 𝒷𝒷𝒷 **1993** Stylish British TV costume drama, adapted from George Eliot's 1872 novel, finds idealistic Dorothea Brooke (Aubrey) determined to be a helpmate to the older scholar, the Rev. Edward Casaubon (Malahide), whom she marries. Too bad that he takes so little interest in her ability (or in Dorothea herself). This leads Casaubon's distant cousin, young and handsome Will Ladislaw (Sewell), to discreetly make his interest clear. Naturally, Eliot has a number of other plots (some dealing with the impact of the Industrial Revolution on 19th-century life) and romances worked into the mix. Filmed in Stamford, England. On three cassettes. **360m/C VHS, DVD.** *GB* Juliet Aubrey, Patrick Malahide, Rufus Sewell, Douglas Hodge, Trevyn McDowell, Michael Hordern, Robert Hardy, John Savident, Jonathan Firth, Peter Jeffrey, Simon Chandler, Julian Wadham; ***D:*** Anthony Page; ***W:*** Andrew Davies, Stanley Myers; ***C:*** Brian Tufano.

Middletown 𝒷 **2006** Story goes off the rails as does its lead character. After serving as a missionary in Africa, Reverend Gabriel Hunter (Macfayden) returns to his small Irish hometown to take up his new pastoral duties. He's shocked to find various vices are prevalent and that his black sheep brother Jim (Mays) and Jim's pregnant wife Caroline (Birthistle) are no exceptions. The fanatical Gabriel becomes even more zealous, determined to save the souls of the town's inhabitants whether they want him to or not. **89m/C DVD.** *GB IR* Matthew Macfayden, Daniel Mays, Eva Birthistle, Gerard McSorley, Richard Dormer, Sorcha Cusack, David Wilmot; ***D:*** Brian Kirk; ***W:*** Daragh Carville; ***C:*** Adam Suschitzky; ***M:*** Debbie Wiseman.

Midnight 𝒷𝒷 ½ *Call It Murder* **1934** A jury foreman's daughter is romantically involved with a gangster who is interested in a particular case before it appears in court. The foreman, who sentenced a girl to death, faces a dilemma when his own daughter is arrested for the same crime. An early Bogart appearance in a supporting role led to a re-release of the film as "Call it Murder" after Bogart made it big. Weak melodrama. **74m/B VHS, DVD.** Humphrey Bogart, Sidney (Sydney) Fox, O.P. Heggie, Henry Hull, Richard Whorf, Margaret Wycherly, Lynne Overman; ***D:*** Chester Erskine; ***W:*** Chester Erskine.

Midnight 𝒷𝒷𝒷 ½ **1939** Struggling showgirl Colbert masquerades as Hungarian countess in sophisticated comedy of marital conflicts. Near-classic film scripted by Wilder and Brackett. Based on a story by Edwin Justus Mayer and Franz Schulz. Remade as "Masquerade in Mexico." **94m/B VHS, DVD.** Claudette Colbert, Don Ameche, John Barrymore, Francis Lederer, Mary Astor, Hedda Hopper, Rex O'Malley; ***D:*** Mitchell Leisen; ***W:*** Billy Wilder, Charles Brackett; ***C:*** Charles B(ryant) Lang Jr.

Midnight 𝒷 *Backwoods Massacre* **1981 (R)** Russo, who cowrote the original "Night of the Living Dead," wrote and directed this film about a runaway girl who is driven out of her home by a lecherous stepfather and meets two young thieves and then a family of cultists. Russo adapted his own novel. He also attains some of "Night of the Living Dead's" low-budget ambience. **88m/C VHS, DVD.** Lawrence Tierney, Melanie Verliin, John Hall, John Amplas; ***D:*** John A. Russo.

Midnight 𝒷 **1989 (R)** Murder-thriller involving the vampirish hostess of a TV horror movie showcase and a fanatical fan. **90m/C VHS.** Lynn Redgrave, Tony Curtis, Steve Parrish, Rita Gam, Gustav Vintas, Karen Witter, Frank Gorshin, Wolfman Jack; ***D:*** Norman Thaddeus Vane.

Midnight 2: Sex, Death, and Videotape 𝒷 **1993** Sequel to "Midnight" finds the sole surviving member of the crazed family stalking a beautiful unsuspecting teller with a video camera. Only she's teamed up with a detective to solve the murder of her best friend—even if it means she's bait for a psycho. **70m/C VHS.** Matthew Jason Walsh, Jo Norcia; ***D:*** John A. Russo.

Midnight at the Wax Museum 𝒷 *Midnight at Madame Tussaud's* **1936** A man attempts to spend an evening in a wax museum's chamber of horrors, only to find that he is the target of a murder plot. **66m/B VHS.** Lucille Lisle, James Carew, Charles Oliver, Kim Peacock; ***D:*** George Pearson.

Midnight Auto Supply 𝒷 ½ *Love and the Midnight Auto Supply* **1978** Dealers in hot car parts, working out of the garage behind the local brothel, become persuaded to donate some of their profits to the cause of Mexican farm workers. **91m/C VHS.** Michael Parks, Rory Calhoun, Scott Jacoby, Rod Cameron, Colleen Camp, Linda Cristal, John Ireland; ***D:*** James Polakof.

Midnight Bayou 𝒷𝒷 **2009** Lawyer Declan Fitzpatrick (O'Connell) impulsively buys Manet Hall, a newly-restored plantation house near New Orleans that's reputed to be haunted. Declan begins having visions of life in the house more than 100 years ago that are linked to present-day Cajun beauty Lena (Stamile) and murder. Romantic suspense from Lifetime that's based on the book by Nora Roberts. **90m/C DVD.** Jerry O'Connell, Lauren Stamile, Faye Dunaway, Isabella Hofmann, Isabella Hofmann; ***D:*** Ralph Hemecker; ***W:*** Stephen Tolkin, Stephen Tolkin; ***C:*** Anghel

Decca; *M:* Chris P. Bacon, Stuart M. Thomas. **CABLE**

Midnight Blue ✐✐ **1996 (R)** Martin Blake (Chapa) is a lonely banker on a trip to Atlanta where he meets prostitute Martine (Schofield). They have a one-nighter and Martin later decides he loves her and hires a detective (Stockwell) to find her—only Martine has disappeared. After Martin has moved to L.A., he discovers his new boss' wife, Georgine, just happens to be a double for Martine. Naturally, Martin becomes obsessed and this leads to big trouble. **95m/C VHS.** Damian Chapa, Annabel Schofield, Steve Kanaly, Dean Stockwell, Harry Dean Stanton, Jennifer Jostyn; *D:* Skott Snider; *W:* Douglas Brode; *C:* Mark Vicente; *M:* Eric Allaman.

Midnight Cabaret WOOF! **1990 (R)** A New York nightclub-based Satanic cult selects a child actress to bear Satan's child. **94m/C VHS.** Michael Des Barres, Thom Mathews, Carolyn Seymour, Leonard Termo, Norbert Weisser, Lydie Denier, Wilhelm von Homburg; *D:* Pece Dingo; *W:* Pece Dingo; *M:* Michel Colombier.

A Midnight Clear ✐✐✐ **1992 (PG)** Sensitive war drama that takes place in the Ardennes Forest, near the French-German border in December 1944. It's Christmastime and six of the remaining members of a 12-member squad are sent on a dangerous mission to an abandoned house to locate the enemy. Filmed in a dreamy surreal style, the setting is somewhat reminiscent of a fairytale, although a sense of anguish filtrates throughout the picture. A solid script, excellent direction, and a good cast make this a worthwhile film that pits the message of peace against the stupidity of war. Adapted from the novel by William Wharton. **107m/C VHS, DVD.** Peter Berg, Kevin Dillon, Arye Gross, Ethan Hawke, Gary Sinise, Frank Whaley, John C. McGinley, Larry Joshua, Curt Lowens, David Jensen, Rachel Griffin, Tim Shoemaker; *D:* Keith Gordon; *W:* Keith Gordon; *C:* Tom Richmond; *M:* Mark Isham.

Midnight Clear ✐✐ **2006 (PG-13)** Five strangers, battling misfortune and loneliness, cross paths on Christmas Eve and find their lives changed by acts of kindness. Keeps its Christian themes low-key. Jenkins directs from an adaptation of his father Jerry's short story. **102m/C DVD.** Stephen Baldwin, K. Callan, Kirk B.R. Woller, Victoria Jackson, Richard Riehle, Richard Fancy, Mary Thornton, Mitchell Jarvis; *D:* Dallas Jenkins; *W:* Wes Halula; *C:* Randall Walker Gregg; *M:* Jeehun Hwang.

Midnight Confessions ✐ **1995 (R)** Provocative night-time DJ Vannesse (Hoyt) lures her listeners into revealing their sexual fantasies. But when an obsessed fan begins killing women just how deeply is she involved? **98m/C VHS, DVD.** Carol Hoyt, Julie Strain, Monique Parent, Richard Lynch; *D:* Allan Shustak; *W:* Jake Jacobs, Allan Shustak, Marc Cushman, Timothy O'Rawe; *C:* Tom Frazier; *M:* Scott Singer.

Midnight Cop ✐ **1988 (R)** A young woman gets tangled up in a web of murder, intrigue, prostitution and drugs, and she enlists the aid of a cop to help get her out of it. **100m/C VHS, DVD.** Michael York, Morgan Fairchild, Frank Stallone, Armin Mueller-Stahl; *D:* Peter Patzak.

Midnight Cowboy ✐✐✐ 1/2 **1969 (R)** Drama about the relationship between a naive Texan hustler and a seedy derelict, set in the underbelly of NYC. Graphic and emotional character study is brilliantly acted and engaging. Shocking and considered quite risque at the time of its release, this film now carries an "R" rating. It was the only "X"-rated film ever ever to win the Best Picture Oscar. From James Leo Herlihy's novel. **113m/C VHS, DVD.** Dustin Hoffman, Jon Voight, Sylvia Miles, Brenda Vaccaro, John McGiver, Bob Balaban, Barnard Hughes; *D:* John Schlesinger; *W:* Waldo Salt; *C:* Adam Holender; *M:* John Barry. Oscars '69: Adapt. Screenplay, Director (Schlesinger), Picture; AFI '98: Top 100; British Acad. '69: Actor (Hoffman), Director (Schlesinger), Film, Screenplay; Directors Guild '69: Director (Schlesinger), Natl. Film Reg. '94;; N.Y. Film Critics '69: Actor (Voight); Natl. Soc. Film Critics '69: Actor (Voight); Writers Guild '69: Adapt. Screenplay.

Midnight Crossing ✐✐ **1987 (R)** Two married couples are subjected to jealousy, betrayal and uncloseted-skeletons as their pleasure cruise on a yacht turns into a ruthless search for sunken treasure. **96m/C VHS, DVD.** Faye Dunaway, Daniel J. Travanti, Kim Cattrall, John Laughlin, Ned Beatty; *D:* Roger Holzberg.

Midnight Dancer ✐✐ **1987** A young ballerina is forced to work as an erotic dancer. **97m/C VHS.** *AU* Deanne Jeffs, Mary Regan; *D:* Pamela Gibbons.

Midnight Dancers ✐✐ **1994** Seamy look at Manila's gay subculture and male prostitution. Sonny and his older brothers Dennis and Joel work as dancers at a sleazy club whose upstairs apartments are used for prostitution. The boys need the money to help their impoverished family survive in the slums but the emotional wear and tear (not to mention police raids and assorted brutalities) provide lots of melodrama. Filipino with subtitles. **115m/C VHS, DVD.** *PH* Alex Del Rosario, Gandong Cervantes, Laurence David, Perla Bautista, Soxy Topacio; *D:* Mel Chionglo; *W:* Ricardo Lee; *C:* George Tutanes; *M:* Nonong Buenoamino.

Midnight Edition ✐✐ **1993 (R)** Investigative reporter Jack Travers (Patton) returns to his Georgia hometown newspaper just in time to write the story of his life. Nineteen-year-old Darryl Weston (DeLuise) massacres a local family for no apparent reason, is tried, convicted, and sentenced to die. Jack's death row interviews with Darryl become hot news but his reporter's objectivity is lost and he becomes a pawn in an escape plan. Good interplay between the charming sociopath and the self-deluded reporter in a sometimes confusing thriller. Based on the autobiography "Escape of My Dead Men" by Charles Postell. **98m/C VHS.** Will Patton, Michael DeLuise, Clare Wren, Nancy Moore Atchison, Sarabeth Tucek, Judson Vaughn, Ji-Tu Cumbuka, Jay Bernard; *D:* Howard Libov; *W:* Howard Libov, Yuri Zeltser, Michael Stewart; *M:* Murray Attaway.

Midnight Express ✐✐✐ **1978 (R)** Gripping and powerful film based on the true story of Billy Hayes (Davis), a young American busted in Turkey wfor trying to smuggle hashish. He is sentenced to a brutal and nightmarish prison for life as an example to other potential smugglers. After enduring tremendous mental and physical torture, Billy seeks the "Midnight Express," his chance at escape. Not always easy to watch, but the overall effect is riveting and unforgettable. Adapted from the book by Hayes and William Hoffer. **120m/C VHS, DVD.** John Hurt, Randy Quaid, Brad Davis, Paul Smith, Bo Hopkins, Oliver Stone; *D:* Alan Parker; *W:* Oliver Stone; *C:* Michael Seresin; *M:* Giorgio Moroder. Oscars '78: Adapt. Screenplay, Orig. Score; British Acad. '78: Director (Parker), Support. Actor (Hurt); Golden Globes '79: Film—Drama, Screenplay, Support. Actor (Hurt), Score; Writers Guild '78: Adapt. Screenplay.

Midnight Faces ✐✐ **1926** Mysterious doings abound in a house in the Florida bayous, recently inherited by Bushman. Silent, with original organ music. **72m/B VHS, DVD.** Francis X. Bushman, Jack Perrin, Kathryn McGuire; *D:* Bennett Cohen; *W:* Bennett Cohen; *C:* King Gray.

Midnight Fear ✐ 1/2 **1990** When a sexually demented killer skins a woman alive, Sheriff Hanley sets out to find whodunit. He suspects two weird brothers, who turn out to be holding a woman hostage, but the situation may not be so simple. Carradine plays the good-guy sheriff in this creeper. **90m/C VHS.** David Carradine, Craig Wasson; *D:* William Crain.

Midnight Girl ✐ 1/2 **1925** A fading opera impresario plots to steal a family's fortune. Lugosi before he became Dracula. Silent. **84m/B VHS.** Charlotte Walker, Gareth Hughes, Dolores Cassinelli, Bela Lugosi, Lila Lee; *D:* Wilfred Noy; *W:* Jean Conover, Wilfred Noy; *C:* Frank Zucker, G.W. Blitzer.

Midnight Heat ✐✐ 1/2 *Black Out* **1995 (R)** Football player is the prime suspect when his lover's husband (who happens to be the team owner) is murdered. **97m/C VHS, DVD.** Tim Matheson, Stephen Mendel, Mimi (Meyer) Craven; *D:* Harvey Frost.

The Midnight Hour ✐ 1/2 **1986** A group of high schoolers stumbles upon a vintage curse that wakes up the dead. More humor than horror. **97m/C VHS, DVD.** Shari Belafonte, LeVar Burton, Lee Montgomery, Dick Van Patten, Kevin McCarthy, Jonelle Allen, Peter DeLuise, Dedee Pfeiffer, Mark Blankfield; *D:* Jack Bender; *C:* Rexford Metz; *M:* Brad Fiedel. **TV**

Midnight in Saint Petersburg ✐✐ 1/2 **1997 (R)** Caine once again returns to his role of super spy Harry Palmer, who's after terrorists buying stolen plutonium to use in nuclear weapons. Harry's aided by Nikolai (Connery), whose girlfriend Tatiana is kidnapped, leading the men to a link between the kidnapping, the terrorists, and recent art thefts from the Hermitage Museum. Adapted from stories by Len Deighton. **90m/C VHS.** Michael Caine, Jason Connery, Michael Gambon, Michael Sarrazin, Michelle Rene Thomas. **CABLE**

Midnight in the Garden of Good and Evil ✐✐ **1997 (R)** An all-star cast can't save Eastwood's grossly mishandled adaptation of John Berendt's best-selling novel on the eccentric citizens and lush scenery of Savannah. New York journalist John Kelso (Cusack) is sent on assignment to report on the glamourous Christmas parties of famed citizen and ham Jim Williams (Spacey, oozing his usual silky charm), only to be detoured by Williams shooting his male, live-in companion. Was it cold-blooded murder or self defense? With Eastwood's clumsy direction, a dragging running time, an overabundance of characters taken verbatim from the book (including drag queen Lady Chablis playing herself, unfortunately), and a dull romance between Kelso and local flower Mandy (Eastwood's daughter), the rich subject which made the book a top-seller for four years is all but lost and the answer to the above question moot. "Midnight" has the star power for greatness, but looks certainly are deceiving. **155m/C VHS, DVD.** Kevin Spacey, John Cusack, Jack Thompson, Alison Eastwood, The Lady Chablis, Irma P. Hall, Paul Hipp, Jude Law, Dorothy Loudon, Anne Haney, Kim Hunter, Geoffrey Lewis; *D:* Clint Eastwood; *W:* John Lee Hancock; *C:* Jack N. Green; *M:* Lennie Niehaus.

Midnight Kiss ✐✐ 1/2 **1993 (R)** When a woman police detective investigates a mysterious series of deaths—women whose blood has been drained—she gets more than she bargains for. She's attacked by a vampire and is herself turned into a reluctant bloodsucker. Quick moving and some gross special effects. Also available in an unrated version. **85m/C VHS, DVD.** Michelle Owens, Gregory A. Greer, Celeste Yarnall; *D:* Joel Bender; *W:* John Weidner, Ken Lamplugh.

Midnight Lace ✐✐ 1/2 **1960** Acceptable thriller about a woman in London who is being harassed by a telephone creep. Day is at her frantic best, and Harrrison is suitably charming. Handsome Gavin later became American ambassador to Mexico. Adapted from the play "Matilda Shouted Fire." **108m/C VHS.** Doris Day, Rex Harrison, John Gavin, Myrna Loy, Roddy McDowall, Elspeth March; *D:* David Miller; *W:* Ivan Goff; *C:* Russell Metty.

The Midnight Lady ✐ 1/2 **1932** Speakeasy owner Nita St. George (Padden) decides to take the rap when her long-lost daughter Jean (Dell) is accused of murdering her louse of a boyfriend. But Jean actually didn't do the crime so Nita's going to the slammer for nothing unless someone finds out the truth. A low-rent "Madame X." **65m/B DVD.** Sarah Padden, Claudia Dell, John Darrow, Montagu Love, Theodore von Eltz, Lena Basquette, Brandon Hurst; *D:* Richard Thorpe; *W:* Edward T. Lowe; *C:* M.A. Anderson.

Midnight Limited ✐✐ **1940** A detective sets out to thwart the criminals who would rob the "Midnight Limited" train on its route from New York to Montreal. **61m/B VHS, DVD.** John "Dusty" King, Marjorie Reynolds, George Cleveland, Edward (Ed Kean, Keene) Keane, Pat Flaherty, Monte (Monty) Collins Jr., I. Stanford Jolley; *D:* Howard Bretherton.

Midnight Madness ✐ **1980 (PG)** Five teams of college stereotypes search the city of Los Angeles for clues as part of a wacky scavenger hunt designed by a fellow student. Features the big-screen debut of Michael J. Fox as the little brother of David "I'm a Pepper" Naughton (look closely to see the former Pepper pitchman drinking a bottle of the stuff; it's the only near-witty moment). Also casts Stephen "Flounder" Dorf, making this flick somewhat of an "It's a Mad, Mad, Mad, Mad Animal House," but to say that is an insult to both of those films. Even the presence of arch-geek Eddie Deezen can't save the outing. **110m/C VHS, DVD.** David Naughton, Stephen Furst, Debra Clinger, Eddie Deezen, Michael J. Fox, Maggie Roswell; *D:* David Wechter; *W:* David Wechter; *C:* Frank Phillips; *M:* Julius Wechter.

Midnight Mary ✐✐ **1933** Orphaned Mary (Young) gets involved with a gang of thieves and becomes gangster Leo's (Cortez) moll. She falls for wealthy playboy Tom (Tone) and tries to go straight but her past catches up with her. We see Mary's life in flashbacks as she awaits trial for murder. It may be a pre-Hays Code film but that doesn't mean there can't be a (somewhat unlikely) happy ending. **71m/B DVD.** Loretta Young, Ricardo Cortez, Andy Devine, Una Merkel, Warren Hymer, Frank Conroy, Franchot Tone; *D:* William A. Wellman; *W:* Kathryn Scola, Gene Markey; *C:* James Van Trees; *M:* William Axt.

The Midnight Meat Train ✐ **2008 (R)** Photographer Leon Kaufman (Cooper) is encouraged by gallery owner Susan Hoff (Shields) to dig more deeply into the darkest, most disturbing aspects of grim human potential, which draws him into the frightening world of a serial killer/mutilator known only as Mahogany (Jones), who searches the subway for victims. Kaufman falls further and further into the inhuman world of Mahogany, pulling his innocent, vegan girlfriend Maya (Bibb) along with him, and the two slip into a world of ghastly executions. Based on a short story by Clive Barker, this Ryuhei Kitamura directed film is an artful slasher in the J-Horror tradition but offers nothing particularly original. **100m/C DVD.** *US* Bradley Cooper, Leslie Bibb, Vinnie Jones, Brooke Shields, Roger Bart, Tony Curran, Barbara Harris, Theodore (Ted) Raimi; *D:* Ryuhei Kitamura; *W:* Jeff Buhler; *C:* Jonathan Sela; *M:* Robert Williamson, Johannes Kobilke.

Midnight Murders ✐✐ 1/2 *Manhunt in the Dakotas; In the Line of Duty: Manhunt in the Dakotas* **1991 (R)** Steiger stars as a farmer and Posse Commitatus member whose paramilitary pretensions lead to a bloody confrontation with federal marshals. Gross is the FBI agent sent to hunt him down. Made for TV. **95m/C VHS.** Rod Steiger, Michael Gross, Gary Basaraba, Christopher Rich, Henderson Forsythe; *D:* Dick Lowry. **TV**

The Midnight Phantom ✐✐ **1935** Incredibly rare horror film featuring a bizarre murder at a midnight lecture. **63m/B VHS, DVD.** Reginald Denny, Lloyd Hughes, Claudia Dell, Jim Farley, John Elliott, Barbara Bedford; *D:* Bernard B. Ray; *W:* John Thomas "Jack" Neville; *C:* Pliny Goodfriend.

Midnight Ride ✐ 1/2 **1992** Lots of silly action fails to save this slight tale of a cop (Dudikoff) chasing after his runaway wife (Gersak), who has made the mistake of picking up a psycho hitchhiker (Hamill, gleefully overacting). **95m/C VHS.** Michael Dudikoff, Mark Hamill, Savina Gersak; *Cameos:* Robert Mitchum; *D:* Robert Bralver.

Midnight Run ✐✐✐ **1988 (R)** An ex-cop, bounty hunter must bring in an ex-mob accountant who has embezzled big bucks from his former boss. After he catches up with the thief, the hunter finds that bringing his prisoner from New York to Los Angeles will be very trying, especially when it is apparent that the Mafia and FBI are out to stop them. The friction between the two leads—De Niro and Grodin—is fun to watch, while the action and comic moments are enjoyable. **125m/C VHS, DVD, HD DVD.** Robert De Niro, Charles Grodin, Yaphet Kotto, John Ashton, Dennis Farina, Joe Pantoliano, Richard Foronjy, Wendy Phillips; *D:* Martin Brest; *W:* George Gallo; *C:* Donald E. Thorin; *M:* Danny Elfman.

Midnight Tease ✐ 1/2 **1994** Strip bar, the Club Fugazi, is having trouble with its help—the dancers keep getting murdered. Dancer Samantha (Leigh) actually dreams about the murders before they occur, so naturally she becomes the prime suspect. Leigh can actually do more than look fetching but plot is barely apparent. **87m/C VHS, DVD.** Cassandra Leigh, Rachel Reed, Edmund Halley, Ashlie Rhey, Todd Joseph; *D:* Scott Levy;

W: Daniella Purcell; *C:* Dan E. Toback; *M:* Christopher Lennertz.

Midnight Tease 2 1995 (R) Jen Brennan (Kelly) goes undercover at an L.A. strip club to find out who's been murdering the dancers, including her sister. **93m/C VHS, DVD.** Kimberly Kelley, Tane McClure, Ross Hagen; *D:* Richard Styles; *W:* Richard Styles; *C:* Gary Graver.

Midnight Warning 1/2 1932 A woman thinks she's going off the deep-end when her brother and all records of his existence disappear. Based on an urban legend that appeared somewhere around the time of the 1893 World's Fair. Remade in 1952 as "So Long at the Fair." **63m/B VHS, DVD.** William Boyd, Claudia Dell, Henry Hall, John Harron, Hooper Atchley; *D:* Spencer Gordon Bennet.

Midnight Warrior 1989 A reporter strikes it big when he investigates the underside of L.A. nightlife, but things go terribly wrong when he becomes wrapped up in the sleaze. **90m/C VHS, DVD.** Bernie Angel, Michelle Berger, Kevin Bernhardt, Lilly Melgar; *D:* Joseph Merhi.

Midnight Witness 1/2 1993 (R) Guy finds himself on the run when after he videotapes the beating of a young drug dealer by corrupt cops. Plot bears more than a little resemblance to the Rodney King incident, but according to writer Foldy it was written before it took place. Low-budget thriller went direct to video. **90m/C VHS, DVD.** Maxwell Caulfield, Jan-Michael Vincent, Paul Johansson, Karen Moncrieff, Mark Pellegrino, Virginia Mayo; *D:* Peter Foldy; *W:* Peter Foldy; *M:* Graydon Hillock. **VIDEO**

Midnight's Child 1/2 1993 Another Nanny-from-Hell story, only this time it's literal. D'Abo is the Nanny in question, who belongs to a Satanic cult. Her mission is to select the young daughter in her care as a bride for the devil, even if the girl's parents don't approve of the match. **89m/C VHS, DVD.** Olivia D'Abo, Marcy Walker, Cotter Smith, Elisabeth (Elissabeth, Elizabeth, Liz) Moss, Jim Norton, Judy Parfitt, Roxann Biggs-Dawson, Mary Larkin; *D:* Colin Bucksey; *W:* David Chaskin.

Midnite Spares 1985 A young man's search for the men who kidnapped his father leads him into the world of car thieves and chop-shops. **90m/C VHS.** Bruce Spence, Gia Carides, James Laurie; *C:* Geoff Burton; *M:* Cameron Allan.

A Midsummer Night's Dream 1935 Famed Reinhardt version of the Shakespeare classic, featuring nearly every star on the Warner Bros. lot. The plot revolves around the amorous battle between the king (Jory) and queen (Louise) of a fairy kingdom, and the humans who are drawn into their sport. Features de Haviland's first film role (as Hermia), althogh Rooney, as the fairy Puck, seems to be having the most fun. Classic credit line: Dialogue by William Shakespeare. **117m/B VHS.** James Cagney, Dick Powell, Joe E. Brown, Hugh Herbert, Olivia de Havilland, Ian Hunter, Mickey Rooney, Victor Jory, Arthur Treacher, Billy Barty, Ross Alexander; *D:* Max Reinhardt, William Dieterle; *W:* Mary C. McCall, Charles Kenyon; *C:* Hal Mohr. Oscars '35: Cinematog., Film Editing.

A Midsummer Night's Dream 1/2 1968 Fine acting from the Royal Shakespeare Company cast in this filmed version of the play. Makes very little use of the Athens, Greece scenery. **124m/C VHS, DVD.** *GB* David Warner, Diana Rigg, Ian Richardson, Judi Dench, Ian Holm, Barbara Jefford, Nicholas Selby, Helen Mirren, Michael Jayston, Derek Godfrey, Hugh Sullivan, Paul Rogers, Sebastian Shaw, Bill Travers; *D:* Peter Hall.

A Midsummer Night's Dream 1/2 1996 (PG-13) The Royal Shakespeare Company offers their version of the Shakespeare classic in which a spat between Oberon and Titania, the king and queen of the fairies, leads to a romantic and comedic woodland fantasy for a quartet of would-be lovers who get caught up in their spells, as well as a group of rustics rehearsing their own play. **103m/C VHS, DVD.** *GB* Lindsay Duncan, Alex Jennings, Desmond Barrit, Barry Lynch, Monica Dolan, Emily Raymond; *D:* Adrian Noble; *C:* Ian Wilson; *M:* Howard Blake.

A Midsummer Night's Sex Comedy 1/2 1982 (PG) Allen's homage to Shakespeare, Renoir, Chekhov, Bergman, and who knows who else is an engaging ensemble piece about hijinks among friends and acquaintances gathered at a country house at the turn of the century. Standouts include Ferrer as pompous professor and Steenburgen as Allen's sexually repressed wife. Mia's first for the Woodman. **88m/C VHS, DVD.** Woody Allen, Mia Farrow, Mary Steenburgen, Tony Roberts, Julie Hagerty, Jose Ferrer, Kate McGregor-Stewart; *D:* Woody Allen; *W:* Woody Allen; *C:* Gordon Willis.

Midway 1976 (PG) The epic WWII battle of Midway, the turning point in the war, is retold through Allied and Japanese viewpoints by a big all-star cast saddled with dumpy dialogue and enough weaponry to seize Hollywood on any given Wednesday. **132m/C VHS, DVD.** Sab Shimono, Robert Webber, Ed Nelson, James Shigeta, Monte Markham, Biff McGuire, Glenn Corbett, Gregory Walcott, Noriyuki "Pat" Morita, John Fujioka, Dale Ishimoto, Dabney Coleman, Erik Estrada, Clyde Kusatsu, Robert Ito, Steve Kanaly, Kip Niven, Mitchell Ryan, Susan Sullivan, Charlton Heston, Henry Fonda, James Coburn, Glenn Ford, Hal Holbrook, Robert Mitchum, Cliff Robertson, Robert Wagner, Kevin Dobson, Christopher George, Toshiro Mifune, Tom Selleck; *D:* Jack Smight; *W:* Donald S. Sanford; *C:* Harry Stradling Jr.; *M:* John Williams.

A Midwinter's Tale 1/2 *In the Bleak Midwinter* 1995 (R) Branagh assembles a largely unknown cast in this low-budget backstage saga about an out-of-work thesp, Joe Harper (Maloney), who assembles a shaggy crew of actors to stage an alternative "Hamlet" in a small English country church. The diverse cast squabble, stumble, and emote their way through rehearsals, finally pulling together for the big show. Funny and interesting performances manage to show through the dense and somewhat cliched script. Maloney's Joe, who exhibits the proper frustration of being forced to deal with amateurs and Sessions as a camp queen playing the Queen (Gertrude, that is) stand out. **98m/B VHS.** *GB* Michael Maloney, Richard Briers, Mark Hadfield, Nicholas Farrell, Gerard Horan, John Sessions, Celia Imrie, Hetta Charnley, Julia Sawalha, Joan Collins, Jennifer Saunders; *D:* Kenneth Branagh; *W:* Kenneth Branagh; *C:* Roger Lanser; *M:* Jimmy Yuill.

Mifune *Mifunes Sidste Sang; Mifune's Last Song* 1999 (R) Third release for the Danish film collective Dogma 95 (following "The Idiots" and "The Celebration") is a comedy/romance with a couple of twists. Yuppie Kresten (Berthelsen) travels to the family's run-down farm to check on his mentally handicapped brother, Rud (Asholt), after their father's death. Kresten needs a housekeeper and winds up with attractive Livia (Hjeljle), who neglects to tell him she is a hooker on the lam from her threatening pimp and also shows up with her younger brother (Tarding). Kresten and Livia soon share a mutual attraction and lots of obstacles. Title refers to Rud's hero worship of actor Toshiro Mifune. Danish with subtitles. **102m/C VHS, DVD.** *DK* Iben Hjejle, Anders W. Berthelsen, Jesper Asholt, Emil Tarding, Anders (Tofting) Hove, Sofie Grabol, Paprika Steen, Mette Bratlann; *D:* Soeren Kragh-Jacobsen; *W:* Soeren Kragh-Jacobsen, Anders Thomas Jensen; *C:* Anthony Dod Mantle; *M:* Karl Bille, Christian Sievert.

The Mighty 1998 (PG-13) Like "Simon Birch," this one also features a central character, Kevin (Culkin), who's smart and brave despite suffering from Morquio's syndrome. His new neighbor, Max (Henson), is just the opposite: large in size, not too bright, and afraid of everything. The two quickly find they're much stronger as a team than individually. When Kevin becomes Max's reading tutor, he brings along a book on the legend of King Arthur. Kevin rides Max's shoulders and, dubbing themselves "Freak the Mighty" (the title of Rodman Philbrick's novel, on which the film is based), the inspired boys embark on knightly neighborhood quests, even facing the evil Black Knight—in the form of Max's ex-con father. Henson is amazing as the at-first introverted Max, and Culkin does a good job as Kevin. Stone's understated performance as Kevin's mom shows she's more than a sexpot. **100m/C VHS, DVD.** Kieran Culkin, Elden (Ratliff) Henson, Sharon Stone, Gillian Anderson, Harry Dean Stanton, Gena Rowlands, James Gandolfini, Joe Perrino, Meat Loaf Aday, Jenifer Lewis; *D:* Peter Chelsom; *W:* Charles Leavitt; *C:* John de Borman; *M:* Trevor Jones.

Mighty Aphrodite 1/2 1995 (R) Neurotic (Surprise!) New York sportswriter Lenny Weinrib (Allen) is trapped in an unhappy marriage to art dealer Amanda (Bonham Carter), who talks him into adopting a child. Film comes alive when Lenny tracks down his son's biological mother, consummate dumb blond and hooker/porno actress Linda, played with over-the-top (in a good way) gusto by Sorvino. Lenny attempts to reform his son's real mother while a Greek chorus (including Abraham and Dukakis) provide a running commentary on the tragedy/comedy of Lenny's predicaments. Allen's 31st film treads into familiar Woodman waters but falls short of his past comic genius. **95m/C VHS, DVD.** Woody Allen, Helena Bonham Carter, Mira Sorvino, F. Murray Abraham, Michael Rapaport, Jack Warden, Olympia Dukakis, Peter Weller, Claire Bloom, David Ogden Stiers; *D:* Woody Allen; *W:* Woody Allen; *C:* Carlo Di Palma; *M:* Dick Hyman. Oscars '95: Support. Actress (Sorvino); Golden Globes '96: Support. Actress (Sorvino); Natl. Bd. of Review '95: Support. Actress (Sorvino); N.Y. Film Critics '95: Support. Actress (Sorvino); Broadcast Film Critics '95: Support. Actress (Sorvino).

The Mighty Celt 1/2 2005 Donal (McKenna) is 14 and lives in Belfast with his hard-pressed single mum Kate (Anderson). Donal is crazy about greyhound racing and he works for trainer Good Joe (Stott), who's far from good since he drowns the greyhounds who lose a race. The teen has been training an unlikely dog he's named the Mighty Celt, and Joe promises him ownership if the dog wins three races in a row. Of course, Joe's a liar and a problem for ex-IRA man O (Carlyle), who returns from exile and has ties with Joe he'd sooner forget. What he hasn't forgotten is Kate. **82m/C DVD.** *GB IR* Gillian Anderson, Robert Carlyle, Ken Stott, Tyrone McKenna; *D:* Pearse Elliott; *W:* Pearse Elliott; *C:* Seamus Deasy; *M:* Adrian Johnston.

The Mighty Ducks 1/2 1992 (PG) Bad News Bears on skates. Selfish yuppie lawyer is arrested for drunk driving and as part of his community service sentence, he is forced to coach an inner-city hockey team full of the usual misfits and underachievers. Although sarcastic and skeptical, Coach Gordon Bombay (Estevez) eventually bonds with the Ducks and learns to treat them with respect. Dual themes of teamwork and redemption are repeated constantly, and it gets a bit hokey at times, but the kids won't mind with this fun Disney film, while adults will appreciate the sarcasm. Followed by "D2: The Mighty Ducks." **114m/C VHS, DVD.** Emilio Estevez, Joss Ackland, Lane Smith, Heidi Kling, Josef Sommer, Matt Doherty, Steven Brill, Joshua Jackson, Elden (Ratliff) Henson, Shaun Weiss; *D:* Stephen Herek; *W:* Brian Hohlfield, Steven Brill; *C:* Thomas Del Ruth; *M:* David Newman.

A Mighty Heart 2007 (R) Based on Mariane Pearl's memoir about the kidnapping and execution of her husband, Wall Street Journal reporter Daniel, when he was on assignment in Karachi, Pakistan in 2002. His beheading by Islamic extremists was videotaped for broadcast on the Internet while the pregnant Mariane (a journalist herself) worked her way through bureaucrats and false leads to get answers. Brit director Winterbottom has done films on the complexities of the Mideast before, and he treats his harrowing story matter-of-factly. Jolie (a somewhat controversial choice for the role) does a fine, low-key job with Futterman, as Daniel, in flashbacks during happier times. **103m/C DVD, HD DVD.** *US* Angelina Jolie, Dan Futterman, Will Patton, Archie Panjabi, Irfan Khan, Denis O'Hare, Sajid Hasan, Gary Wilmes; *D:* Michael Winterbottom; *W:* Michael Winterbottom, Laurence Coriat, John Orloff; *C:* Marcel Zyskind; *M:* Molly Nyman, Harry Escott.

Mighty Joe Young 1/2 1949 Tongue-in-cheek King Kong variation features giant ape brought to civilization and exploited in a nightclub act, whereupon things get darned ugly. Bullied and given the key to the liquor cabinet, mild-mannered Joe goes on a drunken rampage, but eventually redeems himself by rescuing orphans from a fire. Special effects (courtesy of Willis O'Brien and the great Ray Harryhausen) are probably the film's greatest asset. Also available colorized. **94m/B VHS, DVD.** Terry Moore, Ben Johnson, Robert Armstrong, Frank McHugh; *D:* Ernest B. Schoedsack.

Mighty Joe Young 1998 (PG) Loose adaptation of the 1949 film has special effects wizard Rick Baker creating a very life-like model of the 15-foot, 2,000-lb. gorilla. With his elaborate features, including a pair of huge brown eyes, this Joe has more personality than his human allies Jill (Theron) and O'Hara (Paxton) who, in between saving Joe from evil South African poachers, spend most of the film giving each other the googoo eyes. Wholesome, harmless, lightweight (the movie, not the gorilla) family entertainment. **114m/C VHS, DVD.** Bill Paxton, Charlize Theron, David Paymer, Regina King, Rade Serbedzija, Peter Firth, Lawrence Pressman, Linda Purl, Ray Harryhausen; *D:* Ron Underwood; *W:* Mark Rosenthal, Larry Konner; *C:* Don Peterman, Oliver Wood; *M:* James Horner.

Mighty Jungle 1964 Lost in the Amazon jungle, a hunter must fight off killer iguanas, man-eating crocodiles and bloodthirsty natives who perform human sacrifices. **90m/C VHS.** Marshall Thompson, David DaLie, Antonio Gutierrez, Rosenda Monteros; *D:* David DaLie, Arnold Belgard; *W:* Arnold Belgard; *C:* J. Carlos Carbajal; *M:* Les Baxter.

Mighty Morphin Power Rangers: The Movie 1995 (PG) From the living room onto the big screen, these six surburban teenagers with super powers battle the evil Ivan Ooze to save Earth. Offers more special effects, new Zord animals, more ooze and more growth to the retail toy industry than the small screen could provide. A child's dream come true, but a parent's nightmare. **93m/C VHS, DVD.** Paul Freeman, Jason Harold Yost, Amy Jo Johnson, Jason David Frank, John Yong Bosch, Stephen Antonio Cardenas; *D:* Bryan Spicer; *W:* Arne Olsen, John Kamps; *C:* Paul Murphy; *M:* Graeme Revell.

The Mighty Pawns 1987 Inner-city kids turn to chess when their teacher inspires them to stay off the streets. Originally aired on PBS as part of the "Wonderworks" family movie series. **58m/C VHS.** Paul Winfield, Alfonso Ribeiro, Terence Knox, Rosalind Cash, Teddy Wilson; *D:* Eric Laneuville.

The Mighty Peking Man **WOOF!** *Goliathon* 1977 (PG-13) A ten-story-tall gorilla resides in the jungle and is sought by a group of Hong Kong businessmen who want to display the creature. Johnny, the hunter hired to find the beast, discovers both the gorilla and a beautiful jungle goddess. Incredibly campy, with badly dubbed and hilariously awful dialogue. **91m/C VHS, DVD.** *HK* Evelyn Kraft, Danny Lee, Chen Cheng-Fen; *D:* Meng Hua Ho; *W:* Yi Kuang; *C:* Tsao Hui-Chi, Wu Cho-Hua; *M:* Chuen Yung-Yu, Chuen Yung-Yu.

The Mighty Quinn 1/2 1989 (R) While investigating the local murder of a rich white guy, the black Jamaican head of police becomes convinced that the prime suspect, a childhood friend, is innocent. As the police chief, Denzel is good in this off-beat comedy mystery. **98m/C VHS, DVD.** Denzel Washington, Robert Kevin Townsend, James Fox, Mimi Rogers, M. Emmet Walsh, Sheryl Lee Ralph, Esther Rolle, Art Evans, Norman Beaton, Keye Luke; *D:* Carl Schenkel; *W:* Hampton Fancher; *C:* Jacques Steyn; *M:* Anne Dudley.

A Mighty Wind 2003 (PG-13) Folk music and its aging practitioners are the targets for Guest and company's observant eye and sharp wit. When legendary folk music producer/promoter Irving Sheinbloom dies, his neurotic son Jonathan organizes a tribute concert of his father's favorite acts. They include the earnest, WASPy trio The Folksmen; nine-member, terminally perky cult/troupe New Main Street Singers; and former marrieds Mitch and Mickey. While the dead-on satire is still present, it's muted and more subtle than in Guest's previous outings, maybe because the characters are more fully-realized and engaging, maybe because Guest knows this particular genre may be running out of air. Virtually all of the excellent ensemble from "Best in Show" returns, with co-writer Levy standing out as the depressed Mitch. Too Young to remember folk? Dont worry Good satire done right is worth a look, no matter the subject. **92m/C VHS, DVD.** *US* Bob Balaban, Christopher Guest, John Michael Higgins, Jane Lynch, Eugene Levy, Catherine O'Hara, Michael McKean, Parker Posey, Harry Shearer, Fred Willard, Ed Begley Jr., Larry Miller, Jennifer Coolidge, Michael Hitchcock; ***D:*** Christopher Guest; ***W:*** Christopher Guest, Eugene Levy; ***C:*** Arlene Donnelly Nelson; ***M:*** John Michael Higgins, Eugene Levy, Catherine O'Hara, Michael McKean, Harry Shearer, Annette O'Toole, C.J. Vanston. N.Y. Film Critics '03: Support. Actor (Levy).

The Migrants **1974** Adaptation of the Tennessee Williams play about the hard-scrabble world of a migrant family yearning for a better life. Made for TV. **83m/C VHS.** Cloris Leachman, Ron Howard, Sissy Spacek, Cindy Williams, Ed Lauter, Lisa Lucas, Mills Watson, Claudia McNeil, Dolph Sweet; ***D:*** Tom Gries; ***W:*** Lanford Wilson. **TV**

Mike's Murder 1/2 **1984 (R)** Disjointed drama about a shy bank teller who falls for a slick tennis player. When he is murdered, she investigates the circumstances, placing herself in dangerously close contact with his seedy, drug-involved buddies. The twists and confused plot leave the viewer bewildered. **109m/C VHS.** Debra Winger, Mark Keyloun, Paul Winfield, Darrell Larson, Dan Shor, William Ostrander; ***D:*** James Bridges; ***W:*** James Bridges; ***M:*** John Barry.

Mikey 1/2 **1992 (R)** Mikey seems like such a sweet little boy—but these awful things keep happening all around him. At every foster home and every school people have such dreadful, and deadly, accidents. But innocent Mikey couldn't be to blame—or could he. **92m/C VHS, DVD.** Brian Bonsall, John Diehl, Lyman Ward, Josie Bissett, Ashley Laurence, Mimi (Meyer) Craven, Whitby Hertford; ***D:*** Dennis Dimster-Denk; ***W:*** Jonathan Glassner; ***C:*** Thomas Jewett; ***M:*** Tim Truman.

Mikey & Nicky 1/2 **1976 (R)** Quirky, uneven film about longtime friends dodging a hit man during one long night. Bears little evidence of time and money invested. Cassavetes and Falk, however, provide some salvation. **105m/C VHS, DVD.** John Cassavetes, Peter Falk, Ned Beatty, Oliver Clark, William Hickey; ***D:*** Elaine May; ***W:*** Elaine May.

The Milagro Beanfield War 1/2 **1988 (R)** Redford's endearing adaptation of John Nichols's novel about New Mexican townfolk opposing development. Seemingly simple tale provides plenty of insight into human spirit. Fine cast, with especially stellar turns from Blades, Braga, and Vennera. **118m/C VHS, DVD.** Chick Vennera, John Heard, Ruben Blades, Sonia Braga, Daniel Stern, Julie Carmen, Christopher Walken, Richard Bradford, Carlos Riqueline, James Gammon, Melanie Griffith, Freddy Fender, M. Emmet Walsh; ***D:*** Robert Redford; ***W:*** David S. Ward; ***C:*** Robbie Greenberg; ***M:*** Dave Grusin. Oscars '88: Orig. Score.

Mildred Pierce 1/2 **1945** Gripping melodrama features Crawford as hard-working divorcee rivaling daughter for man's love. Things, one might say, eventually get ugly. Adaptation of James M. Cain novel is classic of its kind. **113m/B VHS, DVD.** Joan Crawford, Jack Carson, Zachary Scott, Eve Arden, Ann Blyth, Bruce Bennett; ***D:*** Michael Curtiz; ***W:*** Ranald MacDougall; ***M:*** Max Steiner. Oscars '45: Actress (Crawford), Natl. Film Reg. '96.

Miles from Home *Farm of the Year* **1988 (R)** Times are tough for farmers Frank and Terry Roberts. The brothers are about to have another bad harvest and the bank is threatening to foreclose. In a symbolic last ditch effort to save their pride, they decide to burn the farm and leave. On their journey, they meet strangers who recognize the pair and help them escape the police. A melodrama with many members of Chicago's Steppenwolf Theater. **113m/C VHS.** Richard Gere, Kevin Anderson, John Malkovich, Brian Dennehy, Judith Ivey, Penelope Ann Miller, Laurie Metcalf, Laura San Giacomo, Daniel Roebuck, Helen Hunt; ***D:*** Gary Sinise; ***W:*** Chris Gerolmo; ***C:*** Elliot Davis; ***M:*** Robert Folk.

Miles to Go 1/2 **1986** A successful businesswoman tries to enjoy her last days after learning she has terminal cancer. **88m/C VHS, DVD.** Mimi Kuzyk, Tom Skerritt, Jill Clayburgh; ***D:*** David Greene.

Miles to Go Before I Sleep 1/2 **1974** A retired, lonely man and a delinquent girl distrust each other but eventually reach out in mutual need. **78m/C VHS.** Martin Balsam, MacKenzie Phillips, Kitty Winn, Elizabeth Wilson; ***D:*** Fielder Cook. **TV**

Military Intelligence and You! **2006** At times this spoof of WWII newsreels, propaganda, and training films is a fairly heavy-handed allegory on 9/11 and the invasion of Iraq but it's also generally funny. Military analyst Major Nick Reed (Muldoon) is the subject of a training film that has him working with former flame Lt. Monica Tasty (Bennett). Reed's efforts to locate a hidden German airbase are stymied by the lack of accurate intelligence and those darn foreigners (who aren't necessarily enemy agents but should be looked upon with suspicion anyway). **78m/B DVD.** Patrick Muldoon, Elizabeth Bennett, MacKenzie Astin, John Moore, Eric Jungmann; ***D:*** Dale Kutzera; ***W:*** Dale Kutzera; ***C:*** Mark Parry.

Militia **1999 (R)** ATF agents Ethan Carter (Cain) and Julie Sanders (Beals) must enlist the help of William Fain (Forrest), an imprisoned member of a radical militia group, in order to stop the deployment of three stolen missiles and an assassination attempt on the President. **97m/C VHS, DVD.** Dean Cain, Jennifer Beals, Frederic Forrest, Stacy Keach, John Beck, Jeff Kober, Brett Butler; ***D:*** Jim Wynorski; ***W:*** Steve Latshaw, William Carson; ***C:*** Mario D'Ayala; ***M:*** Neal Acree. **VIDEO**

Milk 1/2 **2008 (R)** After moving to San Francisco with lover Scott Smith (Franco), businessman and political activist Harvey Milk (Penn) becomes the first openly gay man to be elected to public office. But Milk is soon clashing with fellow city supervisor Dan White, who eventually assassinates Milk and Mayor George Mascone after losing his job. Penn delivers another top-notch turn as he immerses himself into the role with enough skill and talent to honor Milk without portraying merely a characterization. Both Penn's performance and the film as a whole seem rooted in genuine passion and admiration for the man and his legacy. **127m/C DVD.** *US* Sean Penn, Josh Brolin, Emile Hirsch, James Franco, Diego Luna, Brandon Boyce, Lucas Grabeel, Victor Garber, Alison Pill, Denis O'Hare, Stephen Spinella, Kelvin Yu, Joseph Cross, Zvi Howard Rosenman, Jeff Koons; ***D:*** Gus Van Sant; ***W:*** Dustin Lance Black; ***C:*** Harris Savides; ***M:*** Danny Elfman. Oscars '08: Actor (Penn), Orig. Screenplay; Ind. Spirit '09: Support. Actor (Franco), First Screenplay; Screen Actors Guild '08: Actor (Penn); Writers Guild '08: Orig. Screenplay.

Milk and Honey **2003** Manhattan stockbroker Rick Johnson (Jordan) goes on a midlife freak-out touched off by his suspicion that his wife Joyce (Russell) is cheating on him. What ensues is a string of events that spirals downward, ensnaring people along the way in the most incredibly absurd ways. The digital video filming suits the frenzied nature of this off the wall romp, but the characters are utterly unsympathetic and the string of events falls just outside of the realm of believability. **91m/C DVD.** *US* Clint Jordan, Kirsten Russell, Eleanor Hutchins, Dudley Findlay Jr., Anthony Howard, Greg Amici; ***D:*** Joe Maggio; ***W:*** Joe Maggio; ***C:*** Gordon Chou; ***M:*** Hal Hartley, Yo La Tengo.

Milk Money 1/2 **1994 (PG-13)** Twelve year-old Frank (Carter) talks his pals into pooling their milk money and heading to the big city so they can get a look at a naked woman. They find a prostitute (Griffith) for the job, whom Frank decides would be perfect to bring home to his widower dad (Harris). Although Griffith is generally adorable and the movie is actually less salacious than the premise might suggest, overall, it's sappy and another in the long line of cute-hooker/Cinderella fairytales. **110m/C VHS, DVD.** Michael Patrick Carter, Melanie Griffith, Ed Harris, Malcolm McDowell, Casey Siemaszko, Anne Heche, Philip Bosco; ***D:*** Richard Benjamin; ***W:*** John Mattson; ***M:*** Michael Convertino.

The Milk of Sorrow *La Teta Asustada* **2009** Title refers to the trauma (including rape and torture) suffered by women during the violent Peruvian regime change, which they are alleged to have passed onto their daughters through breastfeeding. (The literal translation of the title is "the frightened breast.") Young Lima maidservant Fausta suffers from paralyzing fear and her only solace is in her improvised songs, which are heard and appreciated by pianist Aida. Spanish and Quechua with subtitles. **95m/C DVD.** *PV* Susi Sanchez, Magaly Solier, Marino Ballon, Efrain Solis, Barbara Lazon; ***D:*** Claudia Llosa; ***W:*** Claudia Llosa; ***C:*** Natasha Braier; ***M:*** Selma Mutal.

Milky Way 1/2 **1936** Loopy comedy about milkman who finds unhappiness after accidentally knocking out champion boxer. Adequate, but not equal to Lloyd's fine silent productions. **89m/B VHS, DVD.** Harold Lloyd, Adolphe Menjou, Verree Teasdale, Helen Mack, William Gargan; ***D:*** Leo McCarey.

The Milky Way **1968** Wicked anti-clerical farce. Two bums team on religious pilgrimage and encounter seemingly all manner of strangeness and sacrilege in this typically peculiar Bunuel work. Perhaps the only film in which Jesus is encouraged to shave. In French with English subtitles. **102m/C VHS.** *FR* Laurent Terzieff, Paul Frankeur, Delphine Seyrig, Alain Cuny, Bernard Verley, Michel Piccoli, Edith Scob; ***D:*** Luis Bunuel; ***W:*** Jean-Claude Carriere.

The Milky Way *Shvil Hahalav* **1997** The Palestinian occupants of a small village in the Galilee try to balance their traditions against the Israeli military occupation in 1964. Many of the villagers were traumatized as children by the 1948 war and old fears and resentments linger as the village's mukhtar (Khoury) tries to placate the occupiers. Meanwhile, the Israelis are investigating forged work passes and a village murder leads to trouble for everyone. Arabic and Hebrew with subtitles. **104m/C VHS.** *IS* Muhamad Bakri, Suheil Haddad, Makram Khoury, Yussef Abu-Warda; ***D:*** Ali Nassar; ***W:*** Ali Nassar, Ghalib Shaath; ***C:*** Amnon Salomon; ***M:*** Nachum Heiman.

Mill of the Stone Women 1/2 *Il Mulino delle Donne di Pietra; Horror of the Stone Women; The Horrible Mill Women; Drops of Blood* **1960** Sculpture-studying art student encounters strange carousel with beautiful babes rather than horsies, and soon finds out that the statues contain shocking secrets. Filmed in Holland, it's offbeat and creepy. **94m/C VHS, DVD.** *FR IT* Pierre Brice, Scilla Gabel, Dany Carrel, Wolfgang Preiss, Herbert Boenne, Liana Orfei, Marco Guglielmi, Olga Solbelli; ***D:*** Giorgio Ferroni; ***W:*** Giorgio Ferroni, Giorgio Stegani, Remigio del Grosso, Ugo Liberatore; ***C:*** Pier Ludovico Pavoni; ***M:*** Carlo Innocenzi.

The Mill on the Floss **1937** Based on George Eliot's classic novel, this film follows the course of an ill-fated romance and family hatred in rural England. Underwhelming, considering the source. **77m/B VHS.** *GB* James Mason, Geraldine Fitzgerald, Frank Lawton, Victoria Hopper, Fay Compton, Griffith Jones, Mary Clare; ***D:*** Tim Whelan.

The Mill on the Floss 1/2 **1997** Maggie Tulliver (Watson) is a smart, emotional young woman painfully at odds with her conventional times. She adores her intolerant older brother Tom (Meredith) but when Maggie becomes involved with Philip Wakeum (Frain), the son of their father Edward's (Hill) greatest enemy, she reluctantly acquieses when Tom forbids the romance. When Stephen Guest (Weber-Brown), the fiance of Maggie's cousin Lucy (Whybrow), falls in love with her, his attentions bring scandal and tragedy to both Maggie and Tom. Watson is fine as the harried heroine but Meredith seems too young for his role, upsetting the sibling balance between the two. Based on the novel by George Eliot. **90m/C VHS.** *GB* Emily Watson, Ifan Meredith, James Frain, Bernard Hill, James Weber-Brown, Lucy Whybrow, Nicholas Gecks, Cheryl Campbell; ***D:*** Graham Theakston; ***W:*** Hugh Stoddart; ***C:*** David C(lark) Johnson; ***M:*** John Scott.

Mille Bolle Blu **1993** Follows the lives of the inhabitants of a single block in 1961 Rome, on the eve of a solar eclipse. The neighborhood children take the opportunity to spy on their elders, including the engaged Elvira, whose old boyfriend Antonio wants her back, escaped convict Caligiuri who returns to his loving wife, and blind Guido, who's undergone an operation to restore his sight. Italian with subtitles. **83m/C VHS.** *IT* Stefano Dionisi, Claudio Bigagli, Paolo Bonacelli, Nicoletta Boris; ***D:*** Leone Pompucci; ***W:*** Leone Pompucci; ***M:*** Franco Piersanti.

Millennium 1/2 **1989 (PG-13)** The Earth of the future is running out of time. The people are sterile and the air is terrible. To keep the planet viable, Ladd and company must go back in time and yank people off planes that are doomed to crash. Great special effects and well-thought out script make this a ball of fun. **108m/C VHS, DVD.** Kris Kristofferson, Cheryl Ladd, Daniel J. Travanti, Lloyd Bochner, Robert Joy, Brent Carver, Maury Chaykin, David McIlwraith, Al Waxman; ***D:*** Michael Anderson Sr.; ***W:*** John Varley; ***C:*** Rene Ohashi; ***M:*** Eric N. Robertson.

Miller's Crossing 1/2 **1990 (R)** From the Coen brothers comes this extremely dark entry in the gangster movie sweepstakes of 1990. Jewish, Italian, and Irish mobsters spin webs of deceit, protection, and revenge over themselves and their families. Byrne is the protagonist, but no hero, being as deeply flawed as the men he battles. Harden stuns as the woman who sleeps with Byrne and his boss, Finney, in hopes of a better life and protection for her small-time crook brother. Visually exhilarating, excellently acted and perfectly paced. **115m/C VHS, DVD.** Albert Finney, Gabriel Byrne, Marcia Gay Harden, John Turturro, Jon Polito, J.E. Freeman; ***D:*** Joel Coen; ***W:*** Ethan Coen, Joel Coen; ***M:*** Carter Burwell.

The Millerson Case 1/2 *The Crime Doctor's Vacation* **1947** Dr. Ordway (Baxter) takes a much-needed vacation in the Blue Ridge Mountains. Instead of hunting, fishing and relaxing, he's pressed into service by the county health department to help with a typhoid breakout. But during an autopsy of one of the victims, the doc finds no trace of typhoid—this guy was poisoned. Now Ordway has to help solve a murder mystery and rid the town of infection. **72m/B DVD.** Warner Baxter, Nancy Saunders, Clem Bevans, Griff Barnett, Paul Guilfoyle, James Bell, Addison Richards, Mark Dennis, Robert Kellard; ***D:*** George Archainbaud; ***C:*** Philip Tannura; ***M:*** Mischa Bakaleinikoff.

Millie 1/2 **1931** Creaky melodrama about a divorcee who wants every man but one. He pursues her teenage daughter instead, leading to tragedy and courtroom hand-wringing. Twelvetrees still stands out in this hokum, based on a Donald Henderson novel considered daring in its day. **85m/B VHS.** Helen Twelvetrees, Robert Ames, Lilyan Tashman, Joan Blondell, John Halliday, James Hall, Anita Louise, Frank McHugh; ***D:*** John Francis Dillon.

Million Dollar Baby 1/2 **2004 (PG-13)** Multi-Oscar winning flick left conservative pundits frothing and hurling baseless allegations at the ever-gracious Eastwood (directing his 25th film). As always, you should make up your own minds. Old school boxing trainer Frankie Dunn (Eastwood) manages a rundown LA gym, aided by his best friend, former boxer Scrap (Freeman, who also narrates). Abrasive Frankie, long estranged from his own daughter, is very reluctant to have anything to do with 30-ish, uneducated waitress Maggie (Swank), whom he deems too old to train. But Maggie fiercely bets that boxing can change her life—and it does, although not in a way anyone could have expected. Downer ending doesn't negate the heart-tugging vulnerability of its characters or its emotional power. A knockout. Based upon "Rope Burns: Stories From the Corner" by Jerry Boyd, under the pen name F.X. Toole. **133m/C VHS, DVD, Blu-ray Disc, HD DVD.** *US* Clint Eastwood, Hilary Swank, Morgan Freeman, Anthony Mackie, Jay Baruchel, Mike Colter, Lucia Rijker, Brian F. O'Byrne, Margo Martindale, Riki Lindhome; ***D:*** Clint Eastwood; ***W:*** Paul Haggis; ***C:*** Tom Stern; ***M:*** Clint Eastwood. Oscars '04: Actress (Swank), Director (Eastwood), Film, Support. Actor (Freeman); Directors Guild '04: Director (Eastwood); Golden Globes '05: Actress—Drama (Swank), Director (Eastwood); Screen Actors Guild '04: Actress (Swank), Support. Actor (Freeman).

Million Dollar Duck 1/2 **1971 (G)** A family duck is doused with radiation and begins to lay gold eggs. Okay Disney family fare, especially for youngsters. **92m/C VHS, DVD.** Dean Jones, Sandy Duncan, Joe Flynn, Tony Roberts; ***D:*** Vincent McEveety; ***M:*** Buddy (Norman Dale) Baker.

The Million Dollar Hotel **1999 (R)** Director Wenders displays his obsession with disposable Americana in this tale of the murder of an entertainment mogul's son in a sleazy, run-down hotel. FBI special agent Skinner (Gibson) is sent to investigate and discovers a group of oddballs and losers inhabit the hotel, including mildly retarded narrator Tom Tom (Davies), intellectual hooker Eloise (Jovovich), creepy artist Geronimo (Smits), and self-proclaimed "fifth Beatle" Dixie (Stormare). Skinner carries on the investigation by spying on the tenants and making life even more miserable for them. The scattered storyline is countered somewhat by Wenders always brilliant visual style, but the performances are mixed, with Gibson giving the only notable performance. Bono, lead singer for the rock group U2, allegedly came up with the original idea for the film, as the hotel used in the movie was the one on which U2 performed in the video for "Where the Streets Have No Name." **122m/C VHS, DVD.** *US* Conrad Roberts, Mel Gibson, Jeremy Davies, Milla Jovovich, Jimmy Smits, Peter Stormare, Amanda Plummer, Gloria Stuart, Tom Bower, Donal Logue, Bud Cort, Julian Sands, Tim Roth, Richard Edson, Harris Yulin, Charlaine Woodard; ***D:*** Wim Wenders; ***W:*** Nicholas Klein; ***C:*** Phedon Papamichael; ***M:*** Brian Eno, Bono, Daniel Lanois, John Hassell.

Million Dollar Kid **1944** When a group of thugs wreak havoc in the neighborhood, the East Side Kids try to help a wealthy man put a stop to it. They face an even greater dilemma when they discover that the man's son is part of the gang. Part of the "Bowery Boys" series. **65m/B VHS, DVD.** Leo Gorcey, Huntz Hall, Gabriel Dell, Louise Currie, Noah Beery Jr., Iris Adrian, Mary Gordon; ***D:*** Wallace Fox.

The Million Dollar Kid **1/2 1999 (PG)** A $50 million lottery jackpot is up for grabs when the winning ticket goes missing. Now Shane and his family must find their lost prize before someone else does. **92m/C VHS, DVD.** Richard Thomas, Maureen McCormick, John Ritter, C. Thomas Howell, Corey Feldman, Clint Howard, Randy Travis, Andrew Sandler; ***D:*** Neil Mandt. **VIDEO**

Million Dollar Mermaid **1952** The prototypical Williams aquashow, with the requisite awesome Berkeley dance numbers. As a biography of swimmer Annette Kellerman it isn't much, but as an MGM extravaganza, it fits the bill. **115m/C VHS.** Esther Williams, Victor Mature, Walter Pidgeon, Jesse White, David Brian, Maria Tallchief, Howard Freeman, Busby Berkeley; ***D:*** Mervyn LeRoy; ***C:*** George J. Folsey.

Million Dollar Mystery **1/2 1987 (PG)** A dying man's last words indicate that several million dollars have been stashed near a diner. Chaos breaks out as nearly everyone in town tries to dig up the loot. **95m/C VHS, DVD.** Eddie Deezen, Penny Baker, Tom Bosley, Rich Hall, Wendy Sherman, Rick Overton, Mona Lyden; ***D:*** Richard Fleischer; ***W:*** Rudy DeLuca, Tim Metcalfe; ***C:*** Jack Cardiff.

A Million to Juan **1/2 1994 (PG)** Familiar rags-to-riches tale, this time set in a L.A. barrio, centers on Juan Lopez (Rodriguez), an uneducated good guy struggling to raise his son. Juan gets his lucky break when a stranger hands him a check for $1 million, explains it's a loan, and if Juan can use the money properly for a month, he'll get a reward. Juan remains incredibly noble; the movie remains mushy. Loose adaptation of the Mark Twain story "The Million Pound Bank Note." Directorial debut for Rodriguez. **97m/C VHS, DVD.** Paul Rodriguez, Polly Draper, Pepe Serna, Bert Rosario, Jonathan Hernandez, Gerardo Mejia, Victor Rivers, Edward James Olmos, Paul Williams; ***Cameos:*** Tony Plana, Ruben Blades, Richard "Cheech" Marin, David Rasche, Liz Torres; ***D:*** Paul Rodriguez; ***W:*** Francisca Matos, Robert Grasmere.

A Million to One **1/2 1937** An athlete trains for the Olympic decathlon, and catches the eye of an upper-class woman in the process. The lead Bennett was actually a shot-putter in the 1932 Olympic Games. **60m/B VHS.** Bruce Bennett, Joan Fontaine, Monte Blue, Kenneth Harlan, Reed Howes; ***D:*** Lynn Shores.

The Millionaire's Express *Shanghai Express; Fu Gui Lie Che* **1986** Hung returns to his village with a plan to derail the local train, which carries a number of wealthy passengers, in hopes of saving his poor hometown. Chinese with subtitles or dubbed. **107m/C VHS, DVD.** *HK* Sammo Hung, Yuen Biao, Cynthia Rothrock, Richard Norton, Yukari Oshima; ***D:*** Sammo Hung; ***W:*** Sammo Hung.

The Millionairess **1/2 1960** Loren is an incredibly rich woman who has ended a bad marriage, and feels that the only thing she still needs to fulfill her life is a good husband. She meets a humble doctor from India, in the person of Sellers, and finds he evades her every effort to snare him. In the process she learns that money can't buy everything. From a play by George Bernard Shaw. **90m/C VHS, DVD.** *GB* Sophia Loren, Peter Sellers, Alastair Sim, Vittorio De Sica, Dennis Price; ***D:*** Anthony Asquith; ***C:*** Jack Hildyard.

Millions **1/2 1990 (R)** To a family of millionaires, money is everything, and the heir to the family fortune is willing to do anything to get his hands on all that money. Even if it means sleeping with his sister-in-law and cousin! Lucky for him they happen to be beautiful models. **118m/C VHS, DVD.** *IT* Billy Zane, Lauren Hutton, Carol Alt, Alexandra Paul, Catherine Hickland, Donald Pleasence; ***D:*** Carlo Vanzina.

Millions **2005 (PG)** Boyle shows he can do sweet family entertainment with the same ease he does violent and creepy (a la "Trainspotting" and "28 Days Later"). Set just before Christmas, practical 9-year-old Anthony (McGibbon) and his dreamer 7-year-old brother Damian (Etel) have just moved with their recently widowed father Ronnie (Nesbitt) into a new neighborhood outside Liverpool. Damian is hanging out near the rail line when a bag filled with (stolen) English pound notes literally comes flying through the air. Damian, who sees and talks to a variety of saints, wants to use the money to help the poor while Anthony would prefer to keep it for themselves. In any case, the boys have only a few days to use the loot since the currency will become scrap paper as Britain makes an (imagined) switch to the euro. Child-centered story may be whimsical but stays firmly away from the sappy. **97m/C DVD.** James Nesbitt, Christopher Fulford, Alun Armstrong, Kathryn Pogson, Alex(ander Nathan) Etel, Lewis Owen McGibbon, Daisy Donovan, Pearce Quigley, Jane Hogarth, Enzo Cilenti, Nasser Memarzia, Harry Kirkham, Cornelius Macarthy, Kolade Agboke; ***Cameos:*** Leslie Phillips; ***D:*** Danny Boyle; ***W:*** Frank Cottrell Boyce; ***C:*** Anthony Dod Mantle; ***M:*** John Murphy.

Milo **1998 (R)** Four young girls are lured to the home of creepy kid Milo where they witness the murder of one of their friends. Sixteen years later, the girls are reunited for a wedding and Milo returns as well. **94m/C VHS, DVD.** Jennifer Jostyn, Maya McLaughlin, Asher Metchik, Paula Cale, Vincent Schiavelli, Antonio Fargas, Rae'ven (Alyia Larrymore) Kelly, Walter Olkewicz; ***D:*** Pascal Franchot; ***W:*** Craig Mitchell; ***C:*** Yuri Neyman; ***M:*** Kevin Manthei. **VIDEO**

Milo & Otis **1/2 1989 (G)** Charming tale of a kitten named Milo and his best friend, a puppy named Otis. The two live on a farm and, when exploring the countryside, Milo is swept down a rushing river. Otis goes after to rescue his friend and the two begin a series of adventures as they try to return home. **76m/C VHS, DVD.** ***D:*** Masanori Hata; ***W:*** Mark Saltzman; ***C:*** Hideo Fujii, Shinji Tomita; ***M:*** Michael Boddicker; ***Nar:*** Dudley Moore.

Milo Milo **1979** Comedy about some very silly French people who propose to steal the Venus de Milo from the Louvre. **110m/C VHS.** *GR GE GR* Mario Adorf, Andrea Ferreol, Andreas Katsulas, Christopher Doherty, Antonio Fargas, Joe Higgins; ***D:*** Nicos Perakis; ***W:*** Christopher Doherty, Nicos Perakis, Vassilis Alexakis; ***C:*** Dietrich Lohmann; ***M:*** Nikos Mamangakis.

The Milpitas Monster **1975 (PG)** Creature spawned in a Milpitas, California, waste dump terrorizes the town residents. **80m/C VHS, DVD.** Doug Hagdahl, Scott A. Henderson, Scott Parker; ***D:*** Robert L. Burrill; ***Nar:*** Paul Frees.

Milwaukee, Minnesota **2003 (R)** Chaotic comedy features a number of oddballs who inhabit a weird Midwestern world. Albert (Garity in a strong performance) is a champion ice fisherman looked after by his overprotective mother Edna (Monks) since he's a bit slow and overly eager-to-please. When mom dies suddenly, Albert is left at the mercy of various con artists who want a piece of his inheritance and fishing prize money. Dern plays a kindly protector to Albert, who has more on the ball than people suspect. Mindel's feature debut. **95m/C DVD.** *US* Troy Garity, Alison Folland, Randy Quaid, Bruce Dern, Hank Harris, Debra Monk, Josh Brolin, Holly Woodlawn; ***D:*** Allan Mindel; ***W:*** Richard D. (R.D.) Murphy; ***C:*** Bernd Heinl.

Mimi **1935** Melodrama with a down-on-his-luck playwright falling for a poor lass who provides him with the needed inspiration to be a winner. The question is, will she die before he hits the big time? Loosely based on "La Vie de Boheme" by Henri Murger. **98m/B VHS.** *GB* Douglas Fairbanks Jr., Gertrude Lawrence, Diana Napier, Harold Warrender, Carol Goodner, Richard Bird, Austin Trevor, Lawrence Hanray, Paul Graetz, Martin Walker; ***D:*** Paul Stein.

Mimic **1/2 1997 (R)** Married biotech scientists Sorvino and Northam upset the balance of nature when they cure a plague only to have their insectoid concoction unleashed in the New York subways. This causes giant cockroaches to mimic—and kill—humans. Far-fetched story is forgiven with a unique script (both John Sayles and Steven Soderbergh made additions) and original kills and thrills. Plenty of gore also makes it a worthy addition to the horror genre. **105m/C VHS, DVD.** Jeremy Northam, Mira Sorvino, Josh Brolin, Charles S. Dutton, Giancarlo Giannini, F. Murray Abraham, Alexander Goodwin; ***D:*** Guillermo del Toro; ***W:*** John Sayles, Steven Soderbergh, Matthew Robbins; ***C:*** Dan Laustsen; ***M:*** Marco Beltrami.

Mimic 2 **1/2 2001 (R)** If you like squishy giant bug movies, this direct-to-video sequel is for you. New York detective Campos and entomologist Koromzay discover that a mutant six-foot cockroach is responsible for three murders where the victims' face has been ripped off. And now it wants to mate. **82m/C VHS, DVD.** Alix Koromzay, Bruno Campos, Will Estes, Edward Albert, Jon Polito, Gaven Eugene Lucas; ***D:*** Jean De Segonzac; ***W:*** Joel Soisson; ***C:*** Nathan Hope. **VIDEO**

Mimic 3: Sentinel **2003 (R)** Those gigantic humanoid cockroaches are back and badder than ever in this second sequel. Severely asthmatic Marvin (Geary), who's confined to his apartment, thinks he and his sister Rosy (Dziena) are witnesses to a murder. Then they realize that it's just giant bugs invading the neighborhood and they must put up a defense or become victims. **76m/C VHS, DVD.** Karl Geary, Lance Henriksen, Alexis Dziena, Rebecca Mader, John Kapelos, Amanda Plummer; ***D:*** J.T. Petty; ***W:*** J.T. Petty; ***C:*** Alexandru Sterian; ***M:*** Henning Lohner. **VIDEO**

Min & Bill **1930** Patchy early talkie about two houseboat dwellers fighting to preserve their waterfront lifestyle and keep their daughter from being taken to a "proper" home. **66m/B VHS.** Marie Dressler, Wallace Beery, Marjorie Rambeau, Dorothy Jordan; ***D:*** George Hill. Oscars '31: Actress (Dressler).

Mina Tannenbaum **1993** Touching but unsentimental look at the 25-year friendship between two Jewish women in Paris. Mina (Bohringer) and Ethel (Zylberstein) meet as seven-year-olds and go through various childhood and teenage tramas together, including the desperate pangs of first love. Mina becomes an intense artist while flirty Ethel works as a freelance journalist. And, naturally, their friendship undergoes its own relentless changes. Pacing problems cause something of a letdown. Directorial debut for cinematographer Dugowson. French with subtitles. **128m/C VHS.** *FR* Romane Bohringer, Elsa Zylberstein, Nils (Niels) Tavernier, Florence Thomassin, Jean-Philippe Ecoffey, Stephane Slima; ***D:*** Martine Dugowson; ***W:*** Martine Dugowson; ***C:*** Dominique Chapuis; ***M:*** Peter Chase.

Minbo—Or the Gentle Art of Japanese Extortion *Minbo No Onna; The Gangster's Moll; The Anti-Extortion Woman* **1992** Satire on Japanese mobsters, known as the Yakuza, focusing on the blackmail and intimidation that gives these criminals a great deal of their power. The ill-mannered group like to congregate at a local hotel—much to the detriment of business—and hotel management finally hire a hardball-playing female lawyer to solve their problems with the thugs. Japanese with subtitles. **123m/C VHS.** *JP* Nobuko Miyamoto, Akira Takarada, Takehiro Murata, Yasuo Daichi, Hideji Otaki; ***D:*** Juzo Itami; ***W:*** Juzo Itami; ***C:*** Yonezo Maeda; ***M:*** Toshiyuki Honda.

The Mind Benders **1/2 1963** Bogarde is a scientist who volunteers to undergo an experimental sensory deprivation/brainwashing technique after the suicide of a colleague. Why would he do something that may have caused one death already? He's trying to convince an agent that there was no traitorous activity going on, but the price of clearing his name may be the love of his family. Sharp execution of an interesting idea. **99m/C DVD.** Dirk Bogarde, Mary Ure, John Clements, Michael Bryant, Wendy Craig, Harold Goldblatt, Geoffrey Keen, Norman Bird, Roger Delgado, Edward Fox, Terence Alexander; ***D:*** Basil Dearden; ***W:*** James Kennaway; ***C:*** Denys Coop; ***M:*** Georges Auric.

Mind, Body & Soul **1992 (R)** When a woman witnesses a human sacrifice performed by her boyfriend's satanic cult, she goes to the police. The cops, however, believe she is part of the cult, so she is forced to rely on the public defender to protect her from angry cult members. Pretty dull, but Hauser and Allen add some spice to this hokey thriller. **93m/C VHS, DVD.** Wings Hauser, Ginger Lynn Allen, Jay Richardson, Ken Hill, Jesse Kaye, Tami Bakke; ***D:*** Rick Sloane; ***W:*** Rick Sloane; ***C:*** Robert Hayes; ***M:*** Alan Der Marderosian.

Mind Games **1/2 1989 (R)** A young couple and their ten-year-old son pick up a hitcher in their mobile home, never suspecting that he's a deranged psychology student ready to pit the family against each other as an experiment. **93m/C VHS.** Edward Albert, Shawn Weatherly, Matt Norero, Maxwell Caulfield; ***D:*** Bob Yari.

Mind Lies *Mind Rage* **2000** Middle-aged detective Jack Stillman is investigating a series of stabbings, where the killer has left messages implicating Jack's estranged brother, Michael. So Jack decides he and Michael have to work together to find out who's setting Michael up. The problem is all the likely suspects keep turning up dead. **m/C VHS.** Charles Hallahan, Dennis Christopher, Tippi Hedren, Max Gail; ***D:*** Mark Allen Michaels. **VIDEO**

Mind Snatchers **1/2 1972 (PG)** An American G.I. becomes involved in U.S. Army experimental psychological brain operations when he is brought into a western European hospital for treatment. Also know as "The Happiness Cage." **94m/C VHS, DVD.** Christopher Walken, Ronny Cox, Ralph Meeker, Joss Ackland; ***D:*** Bernard Girard.

Mind the Gap **2004 (R)** Fate brings five lonely people together in New York City to deal with past guilt and unhappiness in an effort to make a fresh start. Cranky senior citizen Herb (King in his last role) plans to fulfill a promise to his late wife; single dad Sam (Schaeffer) suspects he's terminally ill; introverted folkie busker Jody (singer-songwriter Sobule) has heart trouble; John's (Parnell) a suicidal yuppie; and Malissa's (Reaser) an eccentric country gal saddled with a nasty dying mom. Film is less indulgent than Schaeffer's usual oeuvre but it's also less than noteworthy. **130m/C DVD.** Eric Schaeffer, Alan King, John Heard, Mina (Badiyi) Badie, Elizabeth Reaser, Jill Sobule, Charles Parnell, Christopher Kovaleski, Kim Raver, Todd Weeks, Deirdre Kingsbury; ***D:*** Eric Schaeffer; ***W:*** Eric Schaeffer; ***C:*** Marc Blandori; ***M:*** Veigar Margeirsson.

A Mind to Kill **1995** When a murdered girl is found in a small English seaside town, the crime is linked to a previous death.

Police call on a university professor for help but then a new victim, with ties to the professor, is discovered and the police detective in charge finds that his own loved ones are now in danger. **95m/C VHS.** *GB* Hywel Bennett, Philip Madoc, Sue Jones-Davies, Nicola Beddoe; ***D:*** Peter Edwards.

A Mind to Murder ✗✗ 1/2 *P.D. James: A Mind to Murder* **1996** Scotland Yard Commander Adam Dalgliesh (Marsden) is still depressed over the murder of a colleague some months earlier when he's discreetly called in to investigate the stabbing death of the administrator of the Steen Clinic, located in East Anglia. The exclusive psychiatric facility is home to some politically sensitive patients and Dalgleish is under pressure to solve the crime quickly and quietly. His work would go a lot easier if people cooperated, but naturally the investigation doesn't go smoothly at all. Based on the 1963 novel by P.D. James and updated for the TV movie. **100m/C VHS, DVD.** *GB* Roy Marsden, Sean Scanlan, Robert Pugh, Mairead Carty, Frank Finlay, Cal Macaninch, Ann-Gisel Glass, Sian Thomas, Jerome Flynn, Suzanne Burden, Donald Douglas, Christopher Ravenscroft; ***Cameos:*** David Hemmings; ***D:*** Gareth Davies; ***C:*** Bill Broomfield. **TV**

Mind Trap ✗ 1/2 **1991** A beautiful movie star's family is killed due to her father's involvement with naval research. The government wants no part of her troubles so she is forced to take the law into her own hands. **90m/C VHS.** Dan Haggerty, Lyle Waggoner, Martha Kincare, Thomas Elliot, Samuel Steven; ***D:*** Eames Demetrios.

Mind Twister ✗ 1/2 **1993 (R)** Erotic thriller finds a tough police detective on the trail of a sadistic killer with a twist. An unrated version is available at 94 minutes. **87m/C VHS.** Telly Savalas, Gary Hudson, Richard Roundtree, Erica Nann, Suzanne Slater; ***D:*** Fred Olen Ray.

Mind Warp ✗ 1/2 *Grey Matter; The Brain Machine* **1972 (R)** A future society exercises mental control and torture over its citizens. **92m/C VHS, DVD.** James Best, Barbara Burgess, Gil Peterson, Gerald McRaney, Marcus J. Grapes, Doug Collins, Anne Latham; ***D:*** Joy Houck Jr.

Mindfield ✗ 1/2 **1989 (R)** An innocent man gets trapped by the CIA and is used by them in mind control experiments. **91m/C VHS.** *CA* Michael Ironside, Lisa Langlois, Christopher Plummer, Stefan Wodoslowsky, Sean McCann; ***D:*** Jean-Claude Lord.

Mindhunters WOOF! 2005 (R) A group of FBI profilers-in-training are sent to a deserted island for their final test but end up victims of a real serial killer through a gamut of enormously complicated, special-effect-laden murders. Disappointing execution of an interesting premise. **106m/C DVD.** *US GB NL FI* Val Kilmer, Christian Slater, LL Cool J, Eion Bailey, Clifton (Gonzalez) Collins Jr., Will(iam) Kemp, Jonny Lee Miller, Kathryn Morris, Patricia Velasquez; ***D:*** Renny Harlin; ***W:*** Wayne Kramer, Kevin Brodbin; ***C:*** Robert Gantz; ***M:*** Tuomas Kantelinen.

Mindkiller ✗ 1/2 **1987** A tongue-in-cheek gore-fest about a shy young guy who develops his brain in an effort to be socially accepted. Unfortunately, he overdoes it and his brain mutates, bursts from his head, and runs around on its own. **84m/C VHS.** Joe McDonald, Christopher Wade, Shirley Ross, Kevin Hart; ***D:*** Michael Krueger.

Mindstorm ✗✗ 1/2 **2001 (R)** The plot has holes big enough to fly a helicopter through but the action keeps things from being boring. Psychic private eye Tracy Wellman (Vaugier) is hired to free Senator Armitage's (Ironside) daughter from the clutches of cult leader David Mendez (a prototypically evil Roberts) and is aided by FBI hunk Dan Oliver (Sabato). Turns out that Mendez and Wellman have a past together—they're both telepaths as the result of a government mind control experiment when they were children—a project headed by Armitage. **106m/C VHS, DVD.** *CA* Emmanuelle Vaugier, Antonio Sabato Jr., Eric Roberts, Michael Ironside, Clarence Williams III, Michael Moriarty, Ed O'Ross, William B. Davis, James Kirk; ***D:*** Richard Pepin; ***W:*** Paul A. Berkitt; ***C:*** Adam Sliwinski; ***M:*** John Sereda. **CABLE**

Mindwalk: A Film for Passionate Thinkers ✗✗✗ **1991 (PG)** A feature-length intellectual workout; a physicist, poet and politician stroll the ancient grounds of Mont St. Michel monastery in France and discuss the need to change mankind's view of the universe. Uncinematic? Perhaps, but it entertainingly conveys the epochal ideas of scientist/author Fritjof Capra (whose book was adapted for the screen by younger brother Bernt). **111m/C VHS.** Liv Ullmann, Sam Waterston, John Heard, Ione Skye; ***D:*** Bernt Capra; ***W:*** Fritjof Capra, Floyd Byars; ***M:*** Philip Glass.

Mindwarp ✗✗ **1991 (R)** After an ecological disaster, residents of Earth move to a sterile haven known as "Inworld." When survivor Judy (Alicia) seeks answers about her missing father (accidentally killing her mother in the process), she is cast from "Inworld" into Earth's wasteland, where she and human compatriot Stover (Campbell) are left to fight the elements and learn the awful truth about Judy's father. **91m/C VHS.** Marta Alicia, Bruce Campbell, Angus Scrimm, Elizabeth Kent, Mary Becker; ***D:*** Steve Barnett; ***W:*** John Brancato, Michael Ferris.

Mine Own Executioner ✗✗✗ **1947** Determined but unstable psychologist in postwar London struggles to treat schizophrenic who suffered torture by Japanese while wartime prisoner. Strong, visually engrossing fare. **102m/B VHS.** *GB* Burgess Meredith, Kieron Moore, Dulcie Gray, Christine Norden, Barbara White, John Laurie, Michael Shepley; ***D:*** Anthony Kimmins.

Mines of Kilimanjaro ✗ 1/2 **1987 (PG-13)** An archaeology student heads for Africa to investigate his professor's murder and comes up with a heap of trouble. **88m/C VHS.** Christopher Connelly, Tobias Hoesl, Gordon Mitchell, Elena Pompei; ***D:*** Mino Guerrini.

The Minion ✗✗ *Fallen Knight* **1998 (R)** Lucas (Lundgren) is a modern-day Knights Templar, the emissary of an ancient religious order that guards a temple door, which is the gateway to the antichrist. When the key to the door is discovered, Lucas must battle an ancient demon who has risen from hell to claim possession. But since the demon can inhabit anyone, how's Lucas going to know who to fight? **97m/C VHS, DVD.** *CA* Dolph Lundgren, Francoise Robertson, Roc Lafortune, Michael Greyeyes, David Nerman, Karen Goodleaf; ***D:*** Jean-Marc Piche; ***W:*** Matt Roe, Ripley Highsmith; ***C:*** Barry Parrell.

Ministry of Fear ✗✗✗ **1944** Creepy noir based on the novel by Graham Greene. Stephen Neale (Milland) has just been released from two years in an insane asylum. As he waits for a train, he decides to visit a nearby carnival that turns out to be fronted by a Nazi organization, where Neale's mistaken for an agent. After finally reaching London, he's later accused of murder, escapes the police, and is aided by the sympathetic Carla (Reynolds). No one and nothing is as it seems, however, and soon the unwitting Neale is deeply involved in espionage. Since the viewer sees only what Neale does, it's just as puzzling for the audience as it is for the character. **85m/B VHS.** Ray Milland, Marjorie Reynolds, Percy Waram, Dan Duryea, Carl Esmond, Hillary Brooke, Alan Napier, Erskine Sanford; ***D:*** Fritz Lang; ***W:*** Seton I. Miller; ***C:*** Henry Sharp; ***M:*** Victor Young.

Ministry of Vengeance ✗ **1989 (R)** A psychotic murderer who hates grapes of any kind finds the woman of his dreams—she's a psychotic murderer who hates grapes! Together they find bliss—until the plumber discovers their secret! **90m/C VHS, DVD.** John Schneider, Ned Beatty, George Kennedy, Yaphet Kotto, James Tolkan, Apollonia; ***D:*** Peter Maris; ***W:*** Mervyn Emeryys; ***C:*** Mark Harris; ***M:*** Scott Roewe.

The Miniver Story ✗✗ **1950** Weepy sequel to "Mrs. Miniver" reunites the family in post-WWII England, but clearly lacks the inspiration of the original. Garson is again Mrs. Miniver and she's secretly suffering from a never-named fatal disease. She decides to straighten out the family troubles before her time is up, including her daughter's love life and her husband's plan to move to Brazil. Depressing and glum. **104m/B VHS.** *GB* Greer Garson, Walter Pidgeon, John Hodiak, Leo Genn, Cathy O'Donnell, Reginald Owen, Anthony Bushell; ***D:*** H.C. Potter; ***W:*** Ronald Millar, George Froeschel; ***C:*** Joseph Ruttenberg; ***M:*** Miklos Rozsa.

Minna von Barnhelm or The Soldier's Fortune ✗✗ *Minna von Barnhelm oder das Soldatengluck* **1962** Prussian nobleman Major von Tellheim becomes engaged to noblewoman Minna von Barnhelm during the Seven Year's War. But after the war has ended, the King inexplicably deprives von Tellheim of his title, leaving him humiliated and impoverished, and causing him to break his engagement. But Minna loves her man and refuses to let him go. Based on the drama by Gotthold Ephraim Lessing. German with subtitles. **103m/C VHS.** *GE* Marita Bohme, Otto Mellies, Manfred Krug; ***D:*** Martin Hellberg.

Minnesota Clay ✗ 1/2 *L'Homme du Minnesota* **1965** A blind gunman, who aims by sound and smell, is marked by two rival gangs and a tempestuous tramp. **89m/C VHS, DVD.** *FR IT* Cameron Mitchell, Diana Martin; ***D:*** Sergio Corbucci.

Minnie and Moskowitz ✗✗ 1/2 **1971** Minnie's (Rowlands) about to turn 40 and wants out of her affair with married man, Jim (Cassavetes). She accepts a blind date with Zelmo (Avery) and when he turns out to be a nut, Minnie's rescued by parking attendant Moskowitz (Cassel). Through the opposites attract ploy, Minnie and Moskowitz start dating and soon decide to get married. It's basically a Cassavetes home movie, featuring a number of family and friends who probably had a better time making it than you'll have watching it. **114m/C VHS, DVD.** Gena Rowlands, Seymour Cassel, Val Avery, Timothy Carey, Holly Near, Katherine Cassavetes, Mary Allen "Lady" Rowlands, David Rowlands, Elizabeth Deering, Elsie Adams, John Cassavetes; ***D:*** John Cassavetes; ***W:*** John Cassavetes; ***C:*** Arthur Ornitz.

A Minor Miracle ✗✗ **1983 (G)** Tender family fare about a group of orphaned children who band together under the loving guidance of their guardian (Huston) to save St. Francis School for boys from the town planners. Warms the cockles. **100m/C VHS.** John Huston, Pele, Peter Fox; ***D:*** Terrell Tannen.

Minority Report ✗✗✗ 1/2 **2002 (PG-13)** In 2054 Washington, D.C., a law enforcement agency employs seers called Pre-Cogs to anticipate homicides. Cruise plays John Anderton, chief of the Pre-Crime unit, created to go after potential perps before they can commit the crime. When one of the Pre-Cogs names Anderton as a suspect, however, he's forced to go on the run. Realistic mix of 19th century tradition (classic architecture) and cool, new innovations (retinal scanning robotic spiders), blend into a detailed and believable future world. Engaging story and interesting characters help pic race along, figuratively and literally, with visual sophistication and technical wizardry that Spielberg does so well. Based on a 1956 short story by Philip K. Dick. **145m/C VHS, DVD.** *US* Tom Cruise, Samantha Morton, Colin Farrell, Max von Sydow, Neal McDonough, Lois Smith, Peter Stormare, Tim Blake Nelson, Steve Harris, Kathryn Morris, Mike Binder, Daniel London, Spencer (Treat) Clark, Jessica Capshaw, Patrick Kilpatrick, Jessica Harper, Ashley Crow, Arye Gross; ***D:*** Steven Spielberg; ***W:*** Scott Frank, Jon Cohen; ***C:*** Janusz Kaminski; ***M:*** John Williams.

The Minus Man ✗✗ **1999 (R)** Vann Siegert (Wilson) is the blandest, nicest serial killer you are ever likely to meet. A drifter, Vann has settled into a small California town where he boards with a troubled married couple, Doug (Cox) and Jane (Ruehl), who come to think of ever-smiling Vann as a surrogate son. Vann gets a job at the post office (!), befriends lonely co-worker Ferrin (Garofalo), and calmly proceeds to off the locals. Eerie thriller offers no explanations for Vann's behavior, which makes it all the creepier. Adapted from the 1990 novel by Lew McCreary, who has a cameo as a victim. **112m/C VHS, DVD.** Owen Wilson, Brian Cox, Mercedes Ruehl, Janeane Garofalo, Dwight Yoakam, Dennis Haysbert, Eric Mabius, Sheryl Crow, Larry Miller; ***D:*** Hampton Fancher; ***W:*** Hampton Fancher; ***C:*** Bobby Bukowski; ***M:*** Marco Beltrami.

A Minute to Pray, a Second to Die ✗✗ *Un Minuto Per Pregare, Un Istante Per Morire; Dead or Alive; Outlaw Gun* **1967** A notorious, wanted-dead-or-alive gunman retreats to the amnesty of the New Mexico Territory, but finds he cannot shake his past. **100m/C VHS, DVD.** *IT* Robert Ryan, Arthur Kennedy, Alex Cord; ***D:*** Franco Giraldi.

Minutemen ✗✗ 1/2 **2008 (G)** Social outcasts Virgil (Dolley) and genius Charlie (Benward) are high school seniors who team up with metal-shop loner Zeke (Braun) to build a time machine so they can right various high-school injustices. But when the trio's adventures are noticed by the FBI, they learn that fooling with the timeline has made the whole space-time continuum shaky, leading to a wormhole forming that could swallow the planet! A Disney Channel original. **92m/C DVD.** Jason Dolley, Luke Benward, Nicholas Braun, Chelsea Staub, Steve McQueen, J.P. Manoux; ***D:*** Lev L. Spiro; ***W:*** John Killoran; ***C:*** Bruce Douglas Johnson; ***M:*** Nathan Wang. **CABLE**

The Miracle ✗✗✗ *Ways of Love* **1948** An innocent peasant woman is seduced by a shepherd and becomes convinced that her pregnancy will produce a second Christ. Controversial, compelling film derived from a story by Federico Fellini. In Italian with English subtitles. **43m/B VHS.** *IT* Anna Magnani, Federico Fellini; ***D:*** Roberto Rossellini; ***W:*** Federico Fellini; ***C:*** Aldo Tonti.

The Miracle ✗✗ 1/2 **1991 (PG)** Irish teens, whose strong friendship is based upon their equally unhappy home lives, find both tested when a secretive American woman turns up in town. Excellent debuts from Byrne and Pilkington but tedious pacing in a dreamy script that tells too much too soon. Worth watching just for D'Angelo's smouldering rendition of "Stardust." **97m/C VHS.** *GB* Beverly D'Angelo, Donal McCann, Niall Byrne, Lorraine Pilkington, J.G. Devlin; ***D:*** Neil Jordan; ***W:*** Neil Jordan; ***C:*** Philippe Rousselot; ***M:*** Anne Dudley.

Miracle ✗✗✗ **2004 (PG)** Russell stars as coach Herb Brooks, who led the upstart 1980 U.S. Olympic hockey team to victory against the Russians and a gold medal. Brooks, driven by his own failure to capture a medal as an Olympic player, uses aggressive mind-games and innovative strategy to take a squad of college hotshots and turn them into a single unit capable of defeating the Russian powerhouse. Russell is excellent as Minnesotan Brooks, down to his clipped accent and bad pants. O'Connor, directing newcomer Guggenheim's script, manages to push all the right buttons while mostly avoiding heavy-handed cliches. The end result is a solid sports movie. Most of the actors had hockey experience, adding to the realism of the on-ice scenes. Brooks served as an advisor but died during post-production. **135m/C VHS, DVD.** *US* Kurt Russell, Patricia Clarkson, Noah Emmerich, Sean McCann, Kenneth Welsh, Nathan West, Kenneth Mitchell, Eddie Cahill, Patrick O'Brien Demsey, Michael Mantenuto, Eric Peter-Kaiser, Bobby Hanson, Joseph Cure, Billy Schneider, Nate Miller; ***D:*** Gavin O'Connor; ***W:*** Eric Guggenheim; ***C:*** Dan Stoloff; ***M:*** Mark Isham.

Miracle at Midnight ✗✗ 1/2 **1998** Having occupied Denmark for several years, the Nazis decide to round up all Danish Jews on October 1, 1943. Word is leaked and a number of citizens risk their lives to warn and hide the Jews, spiriting more than 7,000 to safety in Sweden. This Disney version focuses on the non-Jewish Kloster family and how each of them become involved in the rescue. **89m/C VHS, DVD.** Sam Waterston, Mia Farrow, Justin Whalin, Nicola Mycroft, Barry McGovern, Patrick Malahide; ***D:*** Ken Cameron; ***W:*** Chris Bryant, Monte Merrick. **TV**

Miracle at Moreaux 1986 Three Jewish children fleeing from Nazis find sanctuary with a nun and her wards. Based on Clare Huchet Bishop's book "Twenty and Ten." Originally aired on PBS as part of the "Wonderworks" family movie series. **58m/C VHS, DVD.** Loretta Swit, Marsha Moreau, Robert Joy, Ken Pogue, Robert Kosoy, Talya Rubin; ***D:*** Paul Shapiro; ***M:*** Jonathan Goldsmith.

Miracle at Sage Creek ✗✗ 1/2 **2005 (PG)** Uplifting drama begins in 1888 Wyoming. Crusty rancher Ike (Carradine) is still enraged by the murder of his wife by a Sioux war party 10 years earlier. This turns him against his neighbor John (Abell), whose wife Sunny (Bedard) is Sioux, although she and Ike's married daughter Mary (Aldrich) are close friends. Ike tries to take their ranch until a tragedy and a Christmas miracle occur. **85m/C DVD.** David Carradine, Tim Abell, Irene Bedard, Wes Studi, Sarah Aldrich, Daniel Quinn, Fred Griffith; *D:* James Intveld; *W:* Thadd Turner; *C:* Virgil Harper; *M:* James Intveld. **VIDEO**

Miracle at St. Anna ✓✓ 1/2 **2008 (R)** After complaining about the lack of African-American representation in previous WWII dramas, Lee steps up and directs his own. His version focuses on four American soldiers from the all-black 92nd Buffalo Solider Division who get separated from their unit while trying to save a young Italian boy and become trapped behind enemy lines in a small Tuscan village in 1944. Lee goes for epic with a 160- minute runtime, but it backfires on him, resulting in a scattered, tedious, meandering patchwork of takes on history, war, race, religion, and sentimentality, all under the guise of a mystery/crime story. Pic has its moments, but a heavy dose of editing and focus would have resulted in a much stronger finished product. McBride adapted his own 2002 novel. **160m/C DVD, Blu-ray Disc.** *US IT* Derek Luke, Michael Ealy, Laz Alonso, Omar Benson Miller, Pierfrancesco Favino, Valentina Cervi, John Turturro, Joseph Gordon-Levitt, Matteo Sciabordi, John Leguizamo, Kerry Washington, D.B. Sweeney, Robert John Burke, Malcolm Goodwin, James Gandolfini, Walton Goggins, Omari Hardwick; *D:* Spike Lee; *W:* James McBride; *C:* Matthew Libatique; *M:* Terence Blanchard.

Miracle Beach ✓ 1/2 **1992 (PG-13)** Scotty McKay has lost his job, his apartment, and his girl. Then he gets rejected by Dana, the super model he's secretly adored. Can things get any worse? Scotty decides to take a walk along the beach and sort things out when he stumbles across a girl genie, named Jeanie, who has been sent to Earth on a good will mission. Scotty gets Jeanie to grant his every material wish in order to dazzle model Dana. But when Jeanie falls in love with Scotty can she get him to recognize the difference between true love and fantasy? **88m/C VHS.** Dean Cameron, Felicity Waterman, Ami Dolenz, Alexis Arquette, Martin Mull, Noriyuki "Pat" Morita, Vincent Schiavelli; *D:* Skott Snider.

Miracle Dogs ✓✓ 1/2 **2003** After accidentally running over a stray springer spaniel, the Logans (Jackson, Shackelford) discover that the dog has cancer and must have a foreleg amputated. Son Charlie (Hutcherson) cares for the dog in the basement of the hospital where his folks work. When dog Annie recovers, she takes to visiting patients and miraculously starts making them feel better too. **105m/C DVD.** *US* Josh Hutcherson, Kate Jackson, Ted Shackleford, Rue McClanahan, Stacy Keach, Alana Austin, Wayne Rogers; *D:* Craig Clyde; *W:* Craig Clyde; *C:* Neal Brown; *M:* Joseph Conlan. **CABLE**

Miracle Dogs Too ✓✓ 1/2 **2006** When 10-year-old Zack (Evans) discovers two stolen cocker spaniels caged and abandoned in the woods, he frees the dogs and takes them home. Turns out Sissy and Buddy have healing powers that change those around them. When the crooks discover that, they want the dogs back. **90m/C DVD.** *US* Dustin Hunter Evans, Casey Evans, Patrick Muldoon, Janine Turner, Lesley Ann Warren, Jaleel White, Alana Austin, Charles Durning, David Keith; *D:* Richard Gabai; *W:* Leland Douglas; *C:* Hank Baumert Jr.; *M:* Boris Zelkin, Deeji Mincey. **CABLE**

Miracle Down Under ✓✓ **1987** A family endures arduous times in 1890s Australia before a Christmas miracle changes their fortunes. Inoffensive Disney-produced drama. Australia has two directors named George Miller—one directs Mad Max movies; the other directs family fare such as "The Man from Snowy River." This Miller is the latter. **101m/C VHS.** *AU* Dee Wallace, John Waters, Charles "Bud" Tingwell, Bill Kerr, Andrew Ferguson; *D:* George Miller.

Miracle in Harlem ✓✓ **1948** A gang tries to take over a candy shop and when the gang leader is killed, the evidence points to the foster daughter of the shop owner. The script suffers from cliched dialog and less-than-believable situations, but the all-black cast turns in good performances. **69m/B VHS.** Sheila Guyse, Stepin Fetchit, Hilda Offley, Lawrence Criner, Monte Hawley; *D:* Jack Kemp.

Miracle in Lane Two ✓✓ **2000** Based on the true story of 12-year-old Justin Yoder (Muniz) who's confined to a wheelchair but still wins a national soap box derby championship. **89m/C VHS, DVD.** Frankie Muniz, Roger Aaron Brown, Molly Hagan, Rick Rossovich, Tuc Watkins; *D:* Greg Beeman. **CABLE**

Miracle in Milan ✓✓✓ *Miracolo a Milano* **1951** An innocent, child-like fantasy about heavenly intervention driving capitalists out of a Milanese ghetto and helping the poor to fly to a new Utopia. Happy mixture of whimsy and neo-realism. In Italian with English subtitles. **95m/B VHS, DVD.** *IT* Francesco Golisano, Brunella Bovo, Emma Gramatica, Paolo Stoppa; *D:* Vittorio De Sica; *W:* Cesare Zavattini. Cannes '51: Film; N.Y. Film Critics '51: Foreign Film.

Miracle in Rome ✓✓ 1/2 *Milagro en Roma* **1988** Margarito Duarte digs up his dead daughter and finds her body in perfect condition despite 12-year internment. Attempting to convince the local clergy that she's miracle material, he finds them less than eager to elect her to sainthood. Based on a story by Gabriel Garcia Marquez; made for Spanish TV. In Spanish with English subtitles. **76m/C VHS.** *SP* Frank Ramirez, Gerardo Arellano, Amalia Duque Garcia, Lisandro Duque, Daniel Priolett; *D:* Lisandro Duque Naranjo; *W:* Lisandro Duque Naranjo, Gabriel Garcia Marquez. **TV**

Miracle in the Wilderness ✓✓ 1/2 **1991** A Christmas western based on Paul Gallico's novella, "The Snow Goose." Kristofferson stars as Jericho Adams, a former Indian fighter, who turns to farming to support his wife and child. When they are captured by a raiding party of Blackfeet, Adams discovers they have never heard the story of the Nativity. **88m/C VHS.** Kris Kristofferson, Kim Cattrall, John Dennis Johnston, Joanelle Romero, Dennis Olvers, Sheldon Peters Wolfchild, David Oliver; *D:* Kevin James Dobson; *W:* Jim Byrnes.

Miracle Kid ✓✓ **1942** Standard story of a young boxer who'd rather be something else. His romance is interrupted when he becomes successful in the ring. **66m/B VHS.** Tom Neal, Carol Hughes, Betty Blythe, Minta Durfee, Gertrude Messinger; *D:* William Beaudine.

The Miracle Maker: The Story of Jesus ✓✓ 1/2 **2000** Elaborate 3-D claymation is surprisingly effective in telling the story of Jesus, based on the Gospel of St. Luke. Christ's ministry is seen through the eyes of sickly child, Tamar, who is healed by one of his miracles. **87m/C VHS, DVD.** *D:* Derek Hayes, Stanislav Sokolov; *W:* Murray Watts; *M:* Anne Dudley; *V:* Ralph Fiennes, Rebecca Callard, Michael Bryant, Julie Christie, James Frain, Richard E. Grant, Ian Holm, William Hurt, Daniel Massey, Alfred Molina, Bob Peck, Miranda Richardson, Anthony Sher, Ken Stott, David Thewlis. **TV**

Miracle Mile ✓✓✓ **1989 (R)** A riveting, apocalyptic thriller about a mild-mannered misfit who, while inadvertently standing on a street corner at 2 a.m., answers a ringing pay phone. The caller is a panicked missile-silo worker who announces that the bombs have been launched for an all-out nuclear war. With about an hour left before the end, he decides to head into the city and rendezvous with his new girlfriend. A surreal, wicked farce sadly overlooked in theatrical release. Music by Tangerine Dream. **87m/C VHS, DVD.** Edward (Eddie) Bunker, Anthony Edwards, Mare Winningham, John Agar, Denise Crosby, Lou Hancock, Mykelti Williamson, Kelly Jo Minter, Kurt Fuller, Robert DoQui, Danny De La Paz, O-lan Jones, Alan Rosenberg, Claude Earl Jones; *D:* Steve DeJarnatt; *W:* Steve DeJarnatt; *C:* Theo van de Sande; *M:* Tangerine Dream.

The Miracle of Marcelino ✓✓ 1/2 *Marcelino, Pan y Vino; Marcelino* **1955** Marcelino (Calvo) was left at birth on a monastery doorstep and raised by the Franciscan friars. The high-spirited young boy finds a life-sized crucifix in the church attic and, believing the figure of Christ to be real, befriends the image, bringing it food and wine. Then, one day, the image of Jesus comes to life. Spanish with subtitles. **88m/B VHS, DVD.** *SP* Pablito Calvo, Fernando Rey, Rafael Rivelles; *D:* Ladislao Vajda; *W:* Ladislao Vajda; *C:* Enrique Guerner; *M:* Pablo Sarosabal.

Miracle of Morgan's Creek ✓✓✓✓ **1944** Sturges's breakneck comedy details the misadventures of wartime floozy Trudy Kockenlocker (Hutton) who gets drunk at a party, thinks she marries a soldier on leave, gets pregnant, forgets the whole thing, and then tries to evade scandal by getting local schnook and sometimes boyfriend Norval (Bracken) to take responsibility. Oh yeah, and it turns out Trudy's expecting sextuplets. Hilarious, out-to-make-trouble farce that shouldn't have, by all rights, made it past the censors of the time. The director's most scathing assault on American values. Loosely remade as 1958's "Rock-A-Bye Baby" starring Jerry Lewis. **98m/B VHS, DVD.** Eddie Bracken, Betty Hutton, Diana Lynn, Brian Donlevy, Akim Tamiroff, Porter Hall, Emory Parnell, Alan Bridge, Julius Tannen, Victor Potel, Almira Sessions, Chester Conklin, William Demarest, Jimmy Conlin; *D:* Preston Sturges; *W:* Preston Sturges; *M:* Leo Shuken, Charles Bradshaw. Natl. Film Reg. '01.

Miracle of Our Lady of Fatima ✓✓ *The Miracle of Fatima* **1952** Slick cold-war version of the supposedly true events surrounding the sighting of a holy vision by three children in Portugal during WWI. **102m/C VHS, DVD.** Gilbert Roland, Susan Whitney, Sherry Jackson, Sammy Ogg, Angela (Clark) Clarke, Frank Silvera, Jay Novello; *D:* John Brahm; *M:* Max Steiner.

The Miracle of the Bells ✓✓ **1948** A miracle occurs after a dead movie star is buried in the cemetary of her modest hometown. Given the premise, the casting is all the more peculiar. Adapted by Ben Hecht from Russell Janney's novel. **120m/B VHS.** Fred MacMurray, Alida Valli, Frank Sinatra, Lee J. Cobb; *D:* Irving Pichel.

Miracle of the Heart: A Boys Town Story ✓✓ **1986** Based on the story of Boys Town, and an old priest who sticks up for Boys Town's principles in the face of a younger priest with rigid ideas. **100m/C VHS.** Art Carney, Casey Siemaszko, Jack Bannon; *D:* Georg Stanford Brown. **TV**

The Miracle of the White Stallions ✓ 1/2 *The Flight of the White Stallions* **1963** A disappointing Disney adventure about the director of a Viennese riding academy who guides his prized Lipizzan stallions to safety when the Nazis occupy Austria in WWII. **92m/C VHS, DVD.** Robert Taylor, Lilli Palmer, Eddie Albert, Curt Jurgens; *D:* Arthur Hiller; *W:* A.J. Carothers.

Miracle on Ice ✓✓ 1/2 **1981** Occasionally stirring TV film recounts the surprise triumph of the American hockey team over the touted Soviet squad during the 1980 Winter Olympics at Lake Placid. **150m/C VHS.** Karl Malden, Steve Guttenberg, Andrew Stevens, Lucinda Dooling, Jessica Walter; *D:* Steven Hilliard Stern. **TV**

Miracle on 34th Street ✓✓✓✓ *The Big Heart* **1947** The actual Kris Kringle is hired as Santa Claus for the Macy's Thanksgiving parade but finds difficulty in proving himself to the cynical parade sponsor. When the boss's daughter also refuses to acknowledge Kringle, he goes to extraordinary lengths to convince her. Holiday classic equal to "It's a Wonderful Life," with Gwenn and Wood particularly engaging. Also available colorized. **97m/B VHS, DVD.** Maureen O'Hara, John Payne, Edmund Gwenn, Natalie Wood, William Frawley, Porter Hall, Gene Lockhart, Thelma Ritter, Jack Albertson; *D:* George Seaton; *W:* George Seaton; *C:* Lloyd Ahern, Charles G. Clarke; *M:* Cyril Mockridge. Oscars '47: Screenplay, Story, Support. Actor (Gwenn); Golden Globes '48: Screenplay, Support. Actor (Gwenn), Natl. Film Reg. '05.

Miracle on 34th Street ✓✓ 1/2 **1994 (PG)** Updated remake of the 1947 Christmas classic in which a jolly, bearded gent (Attenborough) claiming to be Santa Claus brings happiness to a doubting girl (Wilson) and her jaded mother (Perkins). Before he can prove himself to the precocious child, he must prove himself in a court of law with the help of Perkins's impossibly perfect neighbor (McDermott), a lawyer with a heart of gold (talk about your Christmas miracles!). This version can't compete with the original's "classic" status, but Attenborough and Wilson bring soul and substance to this otherwise average adaptation. **114m/C VHS, DVD.** Richard Attenborough, Elizabeth Perkins, Dylan McDermott, J.T. Walsh, Mara Wilson, Joss Ackland, James Remar, Jane Leeves, Simon Jones, Robert Prosky, William Windom; *D:* Les Mayfield; *W:* John Hughes, George Seaton; *M:* Bruce Broughton.

The Miracle Rider ✓✓ **1935** A 15-chapter serial finds the bad guys trying to run the Indians off their lands in this saga of the old west. **295m/B VHS.** Tom Mix, Joan Gale, Charles Middleton, Jason Robards Sr., Pat O'Malley, Robert Frazer, Wally Wales, Tom London, George Chesebro, Lafe (Lafayette) McKee; *D:* B. Reeves Eason, Armand Schaefer.

The Miracle Woman ✓✓ 1/2 **1931** Stanwyck's particularly fine as evangelist Florence "Faith" Fallon, who becomes very successful thanks to her way with words, some fake miracles, and the talents of shady promoter Hornsby (Hardy). After blind ex-pilot John Carson (Manners) hears her on the radio, he decides Faith might be able to cure him. Florence winds up falling in love with John but Hornsby starts to worry she's going soft and will end their scam. Even Capra apparently thought this film was corny but it still works. Based on the play "Bless You Sister" by John Meehan and Robert Riskin. **90m/B VHS.** Barbara Stanwyck, David Manners, Sam Hardy, Beryl Mercer, Russell Hopton, Charles Middleton, Eddie Boland; *D:* Frank Capra; *W:* Dorothy Howell, Jo Swerling; *C:* Joseph Walker.

The Miracle Worker ✓✓✓ 1/2 **1962** Depicts the unconventional methods that teacher Anne Sullivan used to help the deaf and blind Helen Keller adjust to the world around her and shows the relationship that built between the two courageous women. An intense, moving experience. William Gibson adapted his own play for the screen. **107m/B VHS, DVD.** Anne Bancroft, Patty Duke, Victor Jory, Inga Swenson, Andrew Prine, Beah Richards; *D:* Arthur Penn; *W:* William Gibson; *C:* Ernesto Caparros; *M:* Laurence Rosenthal. Oscars '62: Actress (Bancroft), Support. Actress (Duke); British Acad. '62: Actress (Bancroft); Natl. Bd. of Review '62: Actress (Bancroft).

The Miracle Worker ✓✓✓ **1979** Remade for TV story of blind, deaf and mute Helen Keller and her teacher, Annie Sullivan, whose patience and perseverance finally enable Helen to learn to communicate with the world. Duke was Keller in the 1962 original, but plays the teacher in this version. **98m/C VHS.** Patty Duke, Melissa Gilbert; *D:* Paul Aaron; *M:* Billy Goldenberg. **TV**

The Miracle Worker ✓✓ 1/2 **2000** Yet another remake of William Gibson's Tony award-winning play, following the 1962 movie and the 1979 TV version. This time around precocious Eisenberg is young Helen Keller and Elliott (particularly good) is her dedicated teacher Annie Sullivan. Rather a genteel retelling although Annie's breakthrough with Helen still carries a strong emotional power. **90m/C VHS, DVD.** Hallie Kate Eisenberg, Alison Elliott, David Strathairn, Lucas Black, Kate Greenhouse; *D:* Nadia Tass; *W:* Monte Merrick; *C:* David Parker; *M:* William Goldstein. **TV**

Miracles ✓ 1/2 **1986 (PG)** Comedic misfire pairs a recently divorced couple as reluctant adventurers dodging jewel thieves and peculiar tribes in South America. In a desperate move to create a plot, Mexican jewel thieves, strange tribal rites, and some outrageously unlikely coincidences reunite the family. If this sounds good, see "Romancing the Stone" instead. **90m/C VHS.** Tom Conti, Teri Garr, Paul Rodriguez, Christopher Lloyd, Jorge Russek, Charles Rocket, Bob Nelson; *D:* Jim Kouf; *M:* Peter Bernstein.

Miracles ✓✓ 1/2 *Qiji; Black Dragon* **1989 (PG-13)** Chan stars (and writes and directs) as a bumpkin who saves the life of a mob boss and is thrust into the world of crime in 1930s Hong Kong. He gets some social help from a mysterious woman that gives him the confidence to romance nightclub singer Mui. But when his mob patron is murdered,

Chan decides he has to show his loyalty by seeking justice. Humor and action turn out to be a winning combo. **106m/C VHS, DVD.** *HK* Jackie Chan, Anita (Yim-Fong) Mui, Richard Ng, Yuen Biao; ***D:*** Jackie Chan; ***W:*** Jackie Chan.

Mirage 🦴🦴🦴 **1966** An amnesiac finds himself the target of a dangerous manhunt in New York City in this offbeat thriller. Peck is particularly sympathetic in the lead, and McCarthy, Matthau, and Kennedy all shine in supporting roles. Worth it just to hear thug Kennedy grunt, "I owe this man some pain!" **108m/B VHS.** Gregory Peck, Diane Baker, Walter Matthau, Jack Weston, Kevin McCarthy, Walter Abel, George Kennedy; ***D:*** Edward Dmytryk; ***M:*** Quincy Jones.

Mirage 🦴 1/2 **1994 (R)** Neo-noir with plot problems has former Palm Springs cop Matteo Juarez (Olmos) hired to protect Jennifer (Young), the wife of wealthy environmentalist Donald Gale (Williams). But Jennifer just happens to suffer from multiple personality disorder, leading a not-so-secret second life as a stripper and having trouble always on her heels. **106m/C VHS.** Edward James Olmos, Sean Young, James Andronica, Paul W. Williams; ***D:*** Paul W. Williams; ***W:*** James Andronica.

Miranda 🦴 1/2 **2001 (R)** A romantic fantasy that takes too many complicated turns for its own good. Naive librarian Frank (Simm) is instantly smitten by the oh-so-experienced Miranda (Ricci), who is working on a real estate scam. She heads to London after one night with Frank for a new target, twisted tycoon Nailor (MacLachlan), with her foolish lover trailing behind. Miranda tries to get Frank to leave and instead he gets overly involved in her business. Ricci gets to play dress-up as Miranda goes through a lot of disguises and she's intriguing—the movie's not. **92m/C VHS, DVD.** *GB* Christina Ricci, John Simm, Kyle MacLachlan, John Hurt, Julian Rhind-Tutt, Matthew Marsh; ***D:*** Marc Munden; ***W:*** Rob Young; ***C:*** Benjamin Davis; ***M:*** Murray Gold.

Mirele Efros 🦴🦴 1/2 **1938** A widowed but successful businesswoman finds herself at odds with her daughter-in-law in this film set in the turn of the century. In Yiddish with English subtitles. **80m/B VHS.** Berta Gersten, Michael Rosenberg, Ruth Elbaum, Albert Lipton, Sarah Krohner, Moishe Feder; ***D:*** Joseph Berne.

The Mirror 🦴🦴🦴 *Zerkalo; A White White Boy* **1975** Wonderful child's view of life in Russia during WWII. Black and white flashbacks of important events in the country's history are interspersed with scenes of day-to-day family life. In Russian with English subtitles. **106m/C VHS, DVD.** *RU* Margarita Terekhova, Philip Yankovsky, Ignat Daniltsev, Oleg (Yankovsky) Jankovsky; ***D:*** Andrei Tarkovsky; ***W:*** Andrei Tarkovsky; ***C:*** Georgy Rerberg; ***M:*** Eduard Artemyev.

The Mirror Crack'd 🦴🦴 **1980 (PG)** While filming a movie in the English countryside, an American actress is murdered and Miss Marple must discover who the killer is. Based on the substantially better Agatha Christie novel. **105m/C VHS, DVD.** *GB* Angela Lansbury, Wendy Morgan, Margaret Courtenay, Charles Gray, Maureen Bennett, Carolyn Pickles, Elizabeth Taylor, Rock Hudson, Kim Novak, Tony Curtis, Edward Fox, Geraldine Chaplin, Pierce Brosnan; ***D:*** Guy Hamilton; ***W:*** Barry Sandler; ***C:*** Christopher Challis; ***M:*** John Cameron.

The Mirror Has Two Faces 🦴🦴 **1996 (PG-13)** Gregory (Bridges) is a hunky, but flustered, professor (hunky professor?) looking for romance without all that complicated sex, which shortly leads him to plain but soulful Rose (Streisand), the ugly duckling of her family. Rose's mother (Bacall) seems more happy with her much married sister (Rogers), who is headed down the aisle again with gorgeous Alex (Brosnan). Rose decides it's her turn, despite Gregory's protests, and she weds the bow-tied (and perhaps hog-tied?) educator anyway. When Gregory leaves her on a promotional book tour, frumpy Babs decides a big makeover is in order. Her newfound outer beauty, however, becomes the beast on the inside. Premise is marred by Streisand's unwillingness to look bad, and there's a too-subtle transformation between the "ugly" Rose and the updated version. Bacall gives a memorable, Oscar-nominated performance. Remake of 1959 French film. La Streisand added to her reputation for being a "difficult" perfectionist with her constant reshoots and personnel firings that extended the film's schedule. **127m/C VHS, DVD.** Barbra Streisand, Jeff Bridges, Pierce Brosnan, Mimi Rogers, Lauren Bacall, Brenda Vaccaro, Austin Pendleton, George Segal, Elle Macpherson; ***D:*** Barbra Streisand; ***W:*** Richard LaGravenese; ***C:*** Dante Spinotti, Andrzej Bartkowiak; ***M:*** Barbra Streisand, Marvin Hamlisch. Golden Globes '97: Support. Actress (Bacall); Screen Actors Guild '96: Support. Actress (Bacall).

Mirror Images 🦴 1/2 **1991 (R)** Although sexy twins Kaitlin and Shauna may look alike, they couldn't have more diverse personalities. Yet the gorgeous twins find their lives thrown together in a mad tornado of passion and danger when they each encounter a handsome, mysterious stranger. Could it be that this guy has something more on his mind than love, something like... murder? Also available in an even steamier unrated version. **94m/C VHS.** Delia Sheppard, Jeff Conaway, Richard Arbolino, John O'Hurley, Korey Mall, Julie Strain, Nels Van Patten; ***D:*** Alexander Gregory (Gregory Dark) Hippolyte.

Mirror Images 2 🦴🦴 **1993** Direct-to-video erotic thriller features identical twins Carrie and Terrie (Whirry in a dual role). Carrie's Miss Goody Two-Shoes and Terrie's a murderous nympho who likes Carrie's guys. Terrie dies in a mysterious fire and Carrie sets out to investigate. Sex and nudity sells. **92m/C VHS.** Shannon Whirry, Luca Bercovici, Tom Reilly; ***D:*** Alexander Gregory (Gregory Dark) Hippolyte.

Mirror, Mirror 🦴🦴 **1990 (R)** The prolific Ms. Black turns on the ol' black magic when her daughter's classmates decide it's open season for taunting shrinking violets. Thanks to a magical mirror on the wall, the cheerleading classmates are willed to the great pep rally in the sky. **105m/C VHS, DVD.** Karen Black, Rainbow Harvest, Kristin Dattilo-Hayward, Ricky Paull Goldin, Yvonne De Carlo, William Sanderson, Charlie Spradling, Ann Hearn, Stephen Tobolowsky; ***D:*** Marina Sargenti; ***W:*** Marina Sargenti; ***C:*** Robert Brinkmann; ***M:*** Jimmy Lifton.

Mirror, Mirror 2: Raven Dance 🦴 1/2 **1994 (R)** Teenaged Marlee (Wells) and her brother are temporarily housed in a convent after the death of their parents. The mystery mirror is discovered and looking into it causes Marlee to become partially blind. Meanwhile, her inheritance is threatened and a mysterious stranger, living in the convent's basement, may be Marlee's only hope. **91m/C VHS, DVD.** Tracy Wells, Roddy McDowall, Sally Kellerman, Veronica Cartwright, William Sanderson, Lois Nettleton; ***D:*** Jimmy Lifton; ***W:*** Jimmy Lifton, Virginia Perfili; ***C:*** Troy Cook; ***M:*** Jimmy Lifton.

Mirror, Mirror 3: The Voyeur 🦴 1/2 **1996** Artist discovers a mirror in an abandoned mansion and sees that it reflects the presence of his lost lover, who is now able to manipulate his dreams. **91m/C VHS, DVD.** Billy Drago, Monique Parent, David Naughton, Mark Ruffalo, Elizabeth Baldwin, Richard Cansino; ***D:*** Rachel Gordon, Virginia Perfili; ***W:*** Steve Tymon; ***C:*** Nils Erickson.

Mirror of Death 🦴 *Dead of Night* **1987** A woman subject to physical abuse gets more than she bargains for when she seeks revenge by unleashing the gruesome Queen of Hell. Watch this if you dare! **85m/C VHS, DVD.** Julie Merrill, Kuri Browne, John Reno, Deryn Warren; ***D:*** Deryn Warren; ***W:*** Jerry Daly; ***M:*** David Michael Frank.

Mirror Wars: Reflection One WOOF! **2005** Something obviously got lost in translation with the Russian portion of the cast and crew since this minor actioner is a muddled mess. A terrorist wants to steal a new Russian stealth-fighter prototype and provoke a war between Russia and the USA, but the plane's young pilot proves uncooperative. The "names" in the cast apparently were just picking up a paycheck. **109m/C DVD.** Malcolm McDowell, Armand Assante, Rutger Hauer, Alexander Efimov, Olga Yakovtseva; ***D:*** Vasili Chiginsky; ***W:*** Alex Kustanovich; ***M:*** David Robbins.

MirrorMask 🦴🦴 **2005 (PG)** McKean teams with "Sandman" author Neil Gaiman in this otherworldly escapade from the Jim Henson Company. Helena (Leonidas) is the teenaged daughter of circus performers who longs for a "normal" life. But when her mom (McKee) lapses into a coma, Helena has to travel into a fantasy world to recover the MirrorMask from the Queen of Shadows. McKean's trippy CGI landscapes (rendered on a bare-bones budget) produce some of the most exciting film visuals in years, but you'll be so bored waiting for the story to kick in that the sugar rush from the eye candy wears off way too fast. **101m/C DVD, UMD.** Jason Barry, Stephanie Leonidas, Gina McKee, Rob Brydon, Dora Bryan, Stephen Fry; ***D:*** David McKean; ***W:*** Neil Gaiman, David McKean; ***C:*** Antony Shearn; ***M:*** Ian Ballamy.

Mirrors 🦴 **1978** Woman finds that her dreams lead to death and destruction in New Orleans. **83m/C VHS.** Kitty Winn, Peter Donat, William Swetland, Mary-Robin Redd, William Burns; ***D:*** Noel Black.

Mirrors 🦴🦴 1/2 **1985** A Detroit-born ballerina goes to the Big Apple in search of fame and glory, leaving behind her journalist boyfriend. This upbeat love story features some spectacular dance routines and a behind-the-scenes look at a Broadway dancer's lifestyle. **99m/C VHS.** Timothy Daly, Marguerite Hickey, Antony (Tony) Hamilton; ***D:*** Harry Winer. **TV**

Mirrors 🦴 **2008 (R)** Ben Carson (Sutherland), embattled on nearly every personal front, takes a job as night watchman at a burned out department store while suspended from the NYPD, estranged from his wife (Patton) and children (Gluck and Boyce), and struggling to defeat alcoholism. So is it any surprise that no one wants to believe his story of haunted mirrors? The malevolent spirits go after Carson's wife and kids, rendering some of the most disturbing scenes. Director Aja manages to mix in a little psychological thriller with the ample gore in this K-Horror remake. Tracks along the expected path, except perhaps the false endings, which are more annoying than shocking. Genre fans only here. **110m/C DVD, Blu-ray Disc.** *US* Kiefer Sutherland, Paula Patton, Amy Smart, Cameron Boyce, Mary Beth Peil, Julian Glover, John Shrapnel, Erica Gluck; ***D:*** Alexandre Aja; ***W:*** Alexandre Aja, Gregory Levasseur; ***C:*** Maxime Alexandre; ***M:*** Javier Navarrete.

The Misadventures of Merlin Jones 🦴 1/2 **1963 (G)** A pair of college sweethearts become embroiled in a rollicking chimp-napping scandal. Disney pap done appropriately. A sequel, "The Monkey's Uncle," followed. **90m/C VHS, DVD.** Tommy Kirk, Annette Funicello, Leon Ames, Stuart Erwin, Connie Gilchrist, Kelly Thordsen; ***D:*** Robert Stevenson; ***W:*** Alfred Lewis Levitt, Helen Levitt; ***C:*** Edward Colman; ***M:*** Buddy (Norman Dale) Baker.

The Misadventures of Mr. Wilt 🦴🦴 *Wilt* **1990 (R)** Bumbling college lecturer has to convince inept inspector that he murdered a blowup doll, not his mean missing wife. Based on Tom Sharpe's best-seller. **84m/C VHS.** *GB* Griff Rhys Jones, Mel Smith, Alison Steadman, Diana Quick; ***D:*** Michael Tuchner; ***M:*** Anne Dudley.

Misbegotten 🦴🦴 **1998 (R)** Infertile couple Paul (Mancuso) and Caitlin (Anthony) are able to have their bundle of joy thanks to artifical insemination. Only psycho donor daddy Billy Crapshoot (Dillon) finds out who they are and decides to come for his soon-to-be-born offspring. **97m/C VHS.** Kevin Dillon, Nick Mancuso, Lysette Anthony, Robert Lewis, Matthew (Matt) Walker, Stefan Arngrim; ***D:*** Mark L. Lester; ***W:*** Larry Cohen; ***C:*** Mark Irwin. **CABLE**

Misbehaving Husbands 🦴 1/2 **1941** Weak story finds store-owner Langton suspected of being untrue by wife Blythe—thanks to rumors spread by a shyster lawyer only too happy to console the lady after the divorce. **65m/B VHS, DVD.** Harry Langdon, Betty Blythe, Ralph Byrd, Esther Muir, Luana Walters; ***D:*** William Beaudine.

Mischief 🦴🦴 **1985 (R)** Alienated youths form a friendship during James Dean's heyday. Warning: this film offers a fairly convincing recreation of the 1950s. **97m/C VHS, DVD.** Doug McKeon, Catherine Mary Stewart, Kelly Preston, Chris Nash, D.W. Brown, Jami Gertz, Margaret Blye, Graham Jarvis, Terry O'Quinn; ***D:*** Mel Damski; ***W:*** Noel Black.

Misery 🦴🦴🦴 **1990 (R)** Author Caan decides to chuck his lucrative but unfulfilling pulp novels and write seriously by finishing off his most popular character, Misery Chastain. However, fate intervenes when he crashes his car near the home of Bates, his "biggest fan ever," who saves his life, but then tortures him into resurrecting her favorite character. Bates is chillingly glib and calmly brutal—watch your ankles. Based on the novel by Stephen King. **107m/C VHS, DVD.** James Caan, Kathy Bates, Lauren Bacall, Richard Farnsworth, Frances Sternhagen, Graham Jarvis; ***D:*** Rob Reiner; ***W:*** William Goldman; ***C:*** Barry Sonnenfeld; ***M:*** Marc Shaiman. Oscars '90: Actress (Bates); Golden Globes '91: Actress—Drama (Bates).

The Misfit Brigade 🦴🦴 *Wheels of Terror* **1987 (R)** Variation on the "Dirty Dozen" finds German misfits recruited for warfare by desperate Nazis during WWII. **99m/C VHS.** Bruce Davison, Oliver Reed, David Carradine, David Patrick Kelly, D.W. Moffett, Keith Szarabajka; ***D:*** Gordon Hessler.

The Misfits 🦴🦴🦴 **1961** A cynical floozy befriends grim cowboys in this downbeat drama. Compelling performances from leads Clift, Monroe (screenwriter Miller's wife), and Gable. Last film for the latter two performers, and nearly the end for Clift. **124m/B VHS, DVD.** Clark Gable, Marilyn Monroe, Montgomery Clift, Thelma Ritter, Eli Wallach, James Barton, Estelle Winwood; ***D:*** John Huston; ***W:*** Arthur Miller; ***C:*** Russell Metty; ***M:*** Alex North.

Misfits of Science 🦴 **1985** Pilot for a failed TV series about a group of teens with special powers who fight to save the world. **96m/C VHS.** Dean Paul (Dino Martin Jr.) Martin, Kevin Peter Hall, Mark Thomas Miller, Kenneth Mars, Courteney Cox; ***D:*** Philip DeGuere. **TV**

Mishima: A Life in Four Chapters 🦴🦴🦴 **1985 (R)** Somewhat detached account and indulgent portrayal of the narcissistic Japanese author (and actor, filmmaker, and militarist) alternates between stylized interpretations of his books and a straightforward account of his life. Culminates in a pseudo-military operation that, in turn, resulted in Mishima's ritualistic suicide. A U.S./Japanese production. Innovative design by Eiko Ishioka. In Japanese with English subtitles. **121m/C VHS, DVD.** Ken Ogata, Kenji Sawada, Yasosuke Bando; ***D:*** Paul Schrader; ***W:*** Leonard Schrader, Paul Schrader; ***C:*** John Bailey; ***M:*** Philip Glass; ***Nar:*** Roy Scheider.

Misleading Lady 🦴 1/2 **1932** A dingy well-to-do socialite tries to bribe herself a part as a seductress in an upcoming film, proving her worthiness on an unsavvy bachelor. **70m/B VHS.** Claudette Colbert, Edmund Lowe, Stuart Erwin, Robert Strange, Edmund Lowe, Stuart Erwin, Robert Strange; ***D:*** Stuart Walker; ***W:*** Paul Dickey, Adelaide Heilbron, Charles W. Goddard, Caroline Francke. **VIDEO**

Miss A & Miss M **1986** A young girl is shocked when she realizes that two teachers she has befriended also live together. **60m/C VHS.** Kika Markham, Jennifer Hilary; ***D:*** Robert Knights; ***W:*** Deborah Wakeham.

Miss All-American Beauty 🦴 1/2 **1982** A behind-the-scenes look at a small-time Texas beauty pageant. Lane stars as a contestant who comes to realize her self-respect is more important than winning an award. Meadows's mean pageant director adds an ironic edge that the movie as a whole lacks. **96m/C VHS, DVD.** Diane Lane, Cloris Leachman, David Dukes, Jayne Meadows, Alice Hirson, Brian Kerwin; ***D:*** Gus Trikonis. **TV**

Miss Annie Rooney 🦴🦴 **1942 (G)** Intended to bill the child star in a more mature role, Temple receives her first screen kiss in this story about a poor Irish girl who falls in love with a wealthy young man. The well-worn plot is weighed down by lifeless dialogue. **86m/B VHS.** Shirley Temple, Dickie Moore, William Gargan, Guy Kibbee, Peggy Ryan, June Lockhart; ***D:*** Edwin L. Marin.

Miss Austen Regrets 🦴🦴 1/2 **2007** A "what-if" biography of the writer. Jane Austen (Williams) receives a proposal from a wealthy suitor but changes her mind when she realizes that a wife's duties will prevent her from writing. So she and her unmarried older sister Cassandra (Scacchi) live with their waspish mother (Law) under strained financial circumstances. Her favorite niece Fanny (Poots) insists on asking Jane's opinion on her own potential suitors, though she doesn't like the advice she's given. This causes Jane to wonder if she's made the right choices even as she gains success as an author. Is included with the DVD of the 2008 BBC production of "Sense and Sensibility." **90m/C DVD.** *GB* Olivia Williams, Greta Scacchi, Phyllida Law, Pip Torrens, Adrian Edmondson, Hugh Bonneville, Imogen Poots, Jack Huston, Tom Hiddleston; ***D:*** Jeremy Lovering; ***W:*** Gwyneth Hughes; ***C:*** Michas Kotz; ***M:*** Luke Dunkley. **TV**

Ms. Bear 1/2 **1997 (G)** Logging operations in a Canadian forest have disturbed the local bear population and down-on-his-luck Barney decides to make some money by tranquilizing the animals and selling them to a zoo importer. A cub escapes and wanders into the yard of lonely, seven-year-old Emily, who befriends the cute critter. Then, with Emily's help, Barney learns the importer is actually killing the bears and only selling their paws to the overseas market. So a rescue is in order. **95m/C VHS.** Ed Begley Jr., Kaitlyn Burke, Shawn Johnston; ***D:*** Paul Ziller.

Miss Cast Away *Miss Castaway and the Island Girls* **2004** Absurd antics abound in this wide-ranging parody of big-budget flicks such as "The Perfect Storm" and "The Lord of the Rings." An airplane filled with beauty-pageant contestants crash-lands on a deserted island on its way to Japan and its two pilots (Roberts and Schlatter) must protect the ladies by fending off all manner of strange inhabitants including ape people. Features cameo by the former King of Pop himself, Michael Jackson, as Special Agent M. Surely you can't be serious if you think this ranks anywhere near the Zucker/Abrahams/Zucker ouvre. **91m/C DVD.** Eric Roberts, Charlie Schlatter, Joyce Giraud, Stuart Pankin, Evan Marriott; ***D:*** Bryan Michael Stoller; ***W:*** Bryan Michael Stoller. **VIDEO**

Miss Conception 1/2 **2008 (R)** A misconceived comedy for sure. Thirty-something Londoner Georgina (Graham) has just waved bye-bye to boyfriend Zak (Ellis), who's off to Ireland on business. Desperately wanting a baby (despite Zak's protests), Georgina checks in with a fertility doctor and is horrified to learn that she's on the verge of early menopause and her next ovulation cycle is her last chance. With Zak a chancy possibility, Georgina goes on a misguided search for a shag who'll get her pregnant. Although she's blonde and beautiful, this isn't as easy as you might think. **94m/C DVD.** Heather Graham, Mia Kirshner, Nicholas Le Prevost, Vivienne Moore, Orlando Seale, Will Mellor; ***D:*** Eric Styles; ***W:*** Camilla Leslie; ***C:*** Tom Ellis, Ed Mash; ***M:*** Christian Henson, Ruta Gedmintas.

Miss Congeniality **2000 (PG-13)** Tough FBI agent Gracie Hart (Bullock) must go undercover at the Miss USA Pageant after the event is threatened by terrorists. Eric (Bratt) is a helpful fellow agent (and potential beau) while down-on-his-luck consultant Victor Melling (Caine) is hired to girly-up Gracie and make her pageant material. Predictable comedy shows flashes of witty satire but lives up to its name by easing up on intended targets at the moment of truth. Bullock, as always, is game and both Bergen as a former beauty queen turned pageant manager and Shatner as unctuous pageant host add a spark to the proceedings. **111m/C VHS, DVD.** Sandra Bullock, Benjamin Bratt, Michael Caine, William Shatner, Ernie Hudson, Candice Bergen, Heather Burns, Melissa De Sousa, Steve Monroe, John DiResta, Jennifer Gareis, Wendy Raquel Robinson; ***D:*** Donald Petrie; ***W:*** Donald Petrie, Marc Lawrence; ***C:*** Laszlo Kovacs; ***M:*** Ed Shearmur.

Miss Congeniality 2: Armed and Fabulous 1/2 **2005 (PG-13)** It took five years for Bullock to make this contrived sequel and you have to wonder why she bothered. Set a few weeks after the first flick, Gracie Hart has become such a celebrity that she can no longer work undercover and has been reassigned as the public face of the FBI. Gracie, accompanied by her flamboyant personal stylist Joel (Bader), even has her own FBI bodyguard, Sam Fuller (King), who has anger management issues. When the current Miss United States (Burns), and pageant director Stan (Shatner) are kidnapped, Gracie and her entourage head for Vegas where the agent is expected to be the bureau spokesperson. But by golly, Gracie wants to rescue Heather since she's her only friend. Many slapstick shenanigans follow in this trifling female buddy comedy. **115m/C DVD.** *US* Sandra Bullock, Regina King, Enrique Murciano, William Shatner, Ernie Hudson, Heather Burns, Diedrich Bader, Treat Williams, Abraham Benrubi, Nick Offerman, Elisabeth Rohm; ***D:*** John Pasquin; ***W:*** Marc Lawrence; ***C:*** Peter Menzies Jr.

Miss Evers' Boys 1/2 **1997 (PG)** Wrenching docudrama covers a 40-year U.S. Public Health Service study in which black men suffering from syphillis were monitored but not treated for the disease. Eunice Evers (Woodard) is a nurse at Alabama's Tuskegee Hospital in 1932, assisting Dr. Brodus (Morton) in the care of the afflicted men. White Dr. Douglas (Sheffer) first has a funded government program for treatment but when the program is cut, he's offered funding only for the study of syphilitic black men and establishing whether the disease affects blacks and whites differently. Brodus and Evers both lie to their patients as each comes to realize that treatment will never be re-established and only the deaths of their patients will provide the final information for the study. Based on the play by David Feldshuh. **120m/C VHS, DVD.** Alfre Woodard, Laurence Fishburne, Joe Morton, Craig Sheffer, Obba Babatunde, Ossie Davis, E.G. Marshall; ***D:*** Joseph Sargent; ***W:*** Walter Bernstein; ***C:*** Donald M. Morgan; ***M:*** Charles Bernstein. **CABLE**

Miss Firecracker **1989 (PG)** Hunter, longing for love and self-respect, decides to change her promiscuous image by entering the local beauty pageant in her conservative southern hometown. The somewhat drippy premise is transformed by a super script and cast into an engaging and upbeat film. Henley's script was adapted from her own Off-Broadway play where Hunter created the role. Actress Lahti, wife of director Schlamme, makes a brief appearance. **102m/C VHS, DVD.** Holly Hunter, Scott Glenn, Mary Steenburgen, Tim Robbins, Alfre Woodard, Trey Wilson, Bert Remsen, Ann Wedgeworth, Christine Lahti, Amy Wright; ***D:*** Thomas Schlamme; ***W:*** Beth Henley; ***C:*** Arthur Albert; ***M:*** David Mansfield.

Ms. 45 *Angel of Vengeance* **1981 (R)** Rough, bristling cult favorite about a mute girl who, in response to being raped and beaten twice in one night, goes on a man-killing murder spree. Wild ending. **84m/C VHS, DVD.** Abel Ferrara, Zoe Tamerlis, Steve Singer, Jack Thibeau, Peter Yellen, Darlene Stuto, Editta Sherman, Albert Sinkys; ***D:*** Abel Ferrara; ***W:*** Nicholas St. John; ***C:*** James (Momel) Lemmo; ***M:*** Joe Delia.

Miss Grant Takes Richmond *Innocence is Bliss* **1949** Zipperhead secretary finds herself in hot water a la Lucy when she finds out the company she's been working for is really the front for a gambling getup. Only Lucy fans need apply. **87m/B VHS.** Lucille Ball, William Holden, Janis Carter, James Gleason, Gloria Henry, Frank McHugh, George Cleveland, Arthur Space, Will Wright, Jimmy Lloyd; ***D:*** Lloyd Bacon.

Miss Julie *Froken Julie* **1950** Melodramatic stew adapted from from the August Strindberg play about a confused noblewoman who disgraces herself when she allows a servant to seduce her. In Swedish with English subtitles. **90m/B VHS.** *SW* Anita Bjork, Ulf Palme, Anders Henrikson, Max von Sydow; ***D:*** Alf Sjoberg; ***W:*** Alf Sjoberg; ***C:*** Goran Strindberg; ***M:*** Dag Wiren. Cannes '51: Film.

Miss Julie **1999 (R)** Dry adaptation of August Strindberg's 1889 banned-in-Sweden play about the turbulent relationship between an imperious young noblewoman and an ambitious servant. Neurotic Miss Julie (Burrows), restless and bored, strides into the servants' kitchen and begin ordering about her father's footman, Jean (Mullan). Their upstairs/downstairs division deteriorates into a series of psycho/sexual clashes over an evening where mutual loathing, humiliation, and self-destruction are the only means of communication. **101m/C VHS, DVD.** *GB* Saffron Burrows, Peter Mullan, Maria Doyle Kennedy; ***D:*** Mike Figgis; ***W:*** Helen Cooper; ***C:*** Benoit Delhomme; ***M:*** Mike Figgis.

Miss March WOOF! **2009 (R)** You don't expect much from your typical raunchy sex comedy, but it should at least attempt to be funny—this is just ragged and moronic. Goody two-shoes virgin Eugene (Cregger) is pressed by girlfriend Cindi (Alessi) to have sex after their prom. Instead, Eugene has an accident and goes into a coma for four years. When he wakes up, his horn-dog best bud Tucker (Moore) informs Eugene that Cindi has become a Playboy Playmate, so they take off for the Chicago Playboy Mansion so Eugene and Cindi can be reunited. Hugh Hefner (who looks like a wax effigy) cameos. **89m/C DVD.** *US* ZACH CREGGER, TREVOR MOORE, Raquel Alessi, Craig Robinson, Molly Stanton, Geoff Meed; ***Cameos:*** Hugh Hefner; ***D:*** ZACH CREGGER, TREVOR MOORE; ***W:*** ZACH CREGGER, TREVOR MOORE; ***C:*** Anthony B. Richmond; ***M:*** Jeff Cardoni.

Miss Mary 1/2 **1986 (R)** A compassionate English governess in Buenos Aires conflicts with the honor-obsessed family she works for and Argentina's tumultuous history. Christie gives a wonderful performance. **100m/C VHS.** *AR* Julie Christie, Donald McIntire, Sofia Viruboff, Luisina Brando; ***D:*** Maria-Luisa Bemberg; ***W:*** Jorge Goldenberg, Maria-Luisa Bemberg.

Miss Melody Jones **1973** A beautiful young black woman's dreams of stardom unravel as she is forced to pander to prurient men by disrobing publicly for financial recompense. **86m/C VHS.** Philomena Nowlin, Ronald Warren, Jacqueline Dalya, Peter Jacob; ***D:*** Bill Brame; ***W:*** Bill Brame.

Miss Monday **1998 (R)** A blocked writer turns voyeur and begins watching a young woman in order to get material for his work. **90m/C DVD.** Andrea Hart, James Hicks, Nick Moran, Michael Coles, Alex Giannini, John Woolvett; ***D:*** Benson Lee; ***W:*** Benson Lee, Richard Morel; ***M:*** Woody Pak.

Miss Pettigrew Lives for a Day **2008 (PG-13)** As a middle-aged governess, and a lousy one at that, Miss Guinevere Pettigrew (McDormand) finds herself yet again out of a job in 1939 London. Flat broke, she comes to the realization that she must RIGHT NOW seize the day, so she pushes her way into employment as a social secretary for American actress/singer Delysia Lafosse (Adams) and thus into glamorous high society. Delysia's love interests are as dizzying as her busy career. But Miss Pettigrew might just find love of her own in dashing and kind fashion designer Joe (Hinds), although he's engaged to snob Edythe (Henderson). It doesn't matter one bit that we know from nearly the beginning exactly where this film is going—the journey is so fun and the characters so charming, we happily jaunt right along. **92m/C DVD.** *GB US* Frances McDormand, Amy Adams, Lee Pace, Ciaran Hinds, Mark Strong, Shirley Henderson, Christina Cole, Tom Payne; ***D:*** Bharat Nalluri; ***W:*** David Magee, Simon Beaufoy; ***C:*** John de Borman; ***M:*** Paul Englishby.

Miss Potter 1/2 **2006 (PG)** Charming, though staid, bio of the creator of Peter Rabbit. Beatrix Potter (Zellweger) was a genteel spinster from a nouveau riche family (the film covers 1902-06). Her talents were generally dismissed until the elder editors at the Warne family publishing firm decide the project will keep youngest brother Norman (McGregor) busy. He turns out to be enthusiastic for not only the book but for Beatrix herself, and she is soon friendly with both Norman and his unmarried sister, Millie (Watson). Noonan has Potter's drawings come to life when she talks to them, otherwise this is standard fare. Watson and McGregor make a lively, charming duo while Zellweger seems rather too restrained. **92m/C DVD.** *GB US* Renee Zellweger, Ewan McGregor, Emily Watson, Barbara Flynn, Bill Paterson, Matyclock Gibbs, Anton Lesser, David Bamber, Phyllida Law, Lloyd Owen; ***D:*** Chris Noonan; ***W:*** Richard Maltby Jr.; ***C:*** Andrew Dunn; ***M:*** Nigel Westlake.

Miss Right **1981 (R)** A young man determines to find the ideal woman for himself and casts aside his other romantic interests. Sputtering lightweight comedy. **98m/C VHS, DVD.** William Tepper, Karen Black, Virna Lisi, Margot Kidder, Marie-France Pisier; ***D:*** Paul Williams.

Miss Rose White **1992 (PG)** Sedgwick is Rose, a modern young career woman in post-WWII New York, as American as apple pie, who lives two very separate lives. Born Rayzel Weiss, a Polish Jew, she immigrated to the U.S. with her father as a very young girl, before the holocaust devastated her remaining family in Poland. After the war her older sister, thought dead, comes to America. The haunted Luisa causes Rose to question whether she can ever leave her past behind. Above average Hallmark Hall of Fame presentation has a good cast, particularly Plummer as Luisa. Based on the play "A Shayna Maidel" by Barbara Lebow. **95m/C VHS.** Kyra Sedgwick, Amanda Plummer, Maximilian Schell, D.B. Sweeney, Penny Fuller, Milton Selzer, Maureen Stapleton; ***D:*** Joseph Sargent; ***W:*** Anna Sandor. **TV**

Miss Sadie Thompson **1953** Based on the novel "Rain" by W. Somerset Maugham. Promiscuous tart Hayworth arrives on a Pacific island occupied by a unit of Marines and a sanctimonious preacher played by Ferrer While Hayworth parties with the Marines and becomes involved with Ray's Sgt. O'Hara, Ferrer moralizes and insists she return to the mainland to face moral charges. Quasi-musical with a scattering of dubbed songs by Hayworth includes a memorable erotic dance scene complete with tight dress and dripping sweat. Hayworth's strong performance carries the picture with Ferrer and Ray turning in cardboard versions of their Maugham characters. Originally filmed in 3-D. **91m/C VHS.** Rita Hayworth, Jose Ferrer, Aldo Ray, Charles Bronson; ***D:*** Curtis Bernhardt.

Miss Tatlock's Millions 1/2 **1948** In this amusing screwball comedy, caretaker Denno (Fitzgerald) doesn't want to admit that crazy Schuyler Tatlock is missing just when he's needed to attend the reading of a family will. So he hires Hollywood stuntman Burke (Lund) to impersonate the man (who's lived for years in Hawaii, estranged from his family) so his sister Nan (Hendrix) can get her inheritance. Too bad that Burke is soon having inappropriate feelings for his 'sister.' **101m/B DVD.** John Lund, Wanda Hendrix, Barry Fitzgerald, Monty Woolley, Ilka Chase, Robert Stack, Dorothy Stickney, Leif Erickson; ***D:*** Richard Haydn; ***W:*** Charles Brackett, Richard L. Breen; ***C:*** Charles B(ryant) Lang Jr.; ***M:*** Victor Young.

Missile to the Moon 1/2 **1959** First expedition to the moon encounters not acres of dead rock but a race of gorgeous women in lingerie and high heels. A bad but entertaining remake of "Cat Women of the Moon," featuring a bevy of beauty contest winners from New Hampshire to Yugoslavia. Who says truth is stranger than fiction. **78m/B VHS, DVD.** Gary Clarke, Cathy Downs, K.T. Stevens, Laurie Mitchell, Michael Whalen, Nina Bara, Richard Travis, Tommy Cook, Marjorie Hellen; ***D:*** Richard Cunha; ***W:*** Vincent Fotre, H.E. Barrie; ***C:*** Meredith Nicholson; ***M:*** Nicholas Carras.

Missiles from Hell 1/2 *Battle of the V-1* **1958** Very stiff-upper-lip WWII drama. In 1943, Stefan (Rennie) and his friend Tadek (Knight) are members of the Polish resistance. They allow themselves to be captured and taken to a labor camp in order to find out about the Nazis' V-1 rocket program. They manage to get word to the allies, who destroy the camp, but the Nazis regroup and the next move is to get a completed V-1 rocket, smuggle it out of the country, and send it to Britain. Utilizes footage of actual air raids. **80m/B DVD.** *GB* Michael Rennie, David Knight, Peter Madden, Christopher Lee, Patricia Medina, Milly Vitale, Esmond Knight; ***D:*** Vernon Sewell; ***W:*** Jack Hanley, Eryk Wlodek; ***C:*** Basil Emmott; ***M:*** Robert Sharples.

Missiles of October **1974** Telling the story of the October 1962 Cuban Missile crisis, this TV drama keeps you on the edge of your seat while unfolding the sequence of events within the U.S. government. Well written, with a strong cast including Devane, who turns in a convincing performance as—guess who—J.F.K. **155m/C VHS, DVD.** James Hong, James Callahan,

Keene Curtis, John Dehner, Peter Donat, Andrew Duggan, Charles Cyphers, Dana Elcar, Arthur Franz, Larry Gates, Richard Karlan, Michael Lerner, Stacy Keach Sr., Wright King, Will Kuluva, Paul Lambert, Doreen Lang, Byron Morrow, Stewart Moss, James Olson, Dennis Patrick, Albert Paulsen, Nehemiah Persoff, William Prince, John Randolph, Kenneth Tobey, Harris Yulin, George Wyner, William Devane, Ralph Bellamy, Martin Sheen, Howard da Silva; ***D:*** Anthony Page; ***M:*** Laurence Rosenthal. **TV**

Missing 🦴🦴🦴 1/2 **1982 (PG)** At the height of a military coup in Chile (never named in the movie), a young American writer (Shea) disappears. His right-wing father Lemmon tries to get to the bottom of his disappearance while bickering with Shea's wife, played by Spacek, a bohemian who is the political opposite of her father-in-law. Outstanding performances by Spacek and Lemmon along with excellent writing and direction result in a gripping and thought-provoking thriller. Based on the book by Thomas Hauser from the true story of Charles Horman. **122m/C VHS, DVD.** Jack Lemmon, Sissy Spacek, John Shea, Melanie Mayron, David Clennon, Charles Cioffi, Joe Regalbuto, Richard Venture, Janice Rule; ***D:*** Constantin Costa-Gavras; ***W:*** Constantin Costa-Gavras, Donald Stewart; ***M:*** Vangelis. Oscars '82: Adapt. Screenplay; British Acad. '82: Screenplay; Cannes '82: Actor (Lemmon), Film; Writers Guild '82: Adapt. Screenplay.

The Missing 🦴🦴🦴 **2003 (R)** Director Ron Howard successfully tries his hand at a gritty western. Blanchett plays Maggie Gilkeson, a mother of two daughters, who supports her family by working the ranch and serving as a healer to the community. Maggie is estranged from her father Samuel Jones (the perfectly craggy-faced Jones) who left her and her mother years ago to live with the Apache tribe. But she soon seeks her father's help after her oldest daughter Lilly (Wood) is kidnapped by an evil Native American shaman (Schweig). Blanchett and Jones both have the acting chops to keep this story interesting and well worth watching. Based on the Thomas Eidson novel "The Last Ride." **135m/C VHS, DVD.** *US* Tommy Lee Jones, Cate Blanchett, Eric Schweig, Jenna Boyd, Evan Rachel Wood, Steve Reevis, Ray McKinnon, Val Kilmer, Aaron Eckhart, Simon Baker, Jay Tavare, Sergio Calderon, Clint Howard, Elisabeth (Elissabeth, Elizabeth, Liz) Moss, Max Perlich; ***D:*** Ron Howard; ***W:*** Ken Kaufman; ***C:*** Salvatore Totino; ***M:*** James Horner.

Missing Brendan 🦴🦴 1/2 **2003** After three painful decades, George Calden (Asner) goes to Vietnam with his two sons and grandson upon learning that his MIA-son Brendan's crashed plane has been found. Desperate to fulfill his wife's dying wish to bring his remains home, the family grapples with many more challenges including lack of cooperation by the Vietnamese government, a father-son clash when his grandson dates a local girl, and George's hidden terminal illness. **100m/C VHS, DVD.** Ed Asner, Robin Thomas, Illeana Douglas, Richard Cox, Adam Brody, Harold Sylvester, Kathleen Luong, Aki Aleong, Dale Dye, Brenda Strong; ***D:*** Eugene Brady; ***W:*** Christopher White; ***C:*** Jeffrey Smith. **VIDEO**

The Missing Corpse 🦴🦴 **1945** When a newspaper publisher's worst rival is murdered, he fears that he will be implicated. He decides the only thing to do is hide the body to prevent its being discovered. Enjoyable, light comedy/mystery. **62m/B VHS.** J. Edward Bromberg, Eric Sinclair, Frank Jenks, Isabelle Randolph, Paul Guilfoyle, John Shay, Lorell Sheldon; ***D:*** Al(bert) Herman.

The Missing Gun 🦴🦴 1/2 *Xun qiang* **2002 (PG-13)** Detective Ma Shen (Wen Jiang) loses his gun after getting stone drunk at his sister's wedding reception. This is bad for him because the gun is government issued, and its loss means the possible end of his job, especially if it ends up involved in a crime. Obligingly, his old girlfriend soon ends up dead in her new lover's residence, and tests confirm the bullets are from Ma's gun. Now not only must he find the gun, he has to clear himself of any possible charges in his old flame's death. **90m/C DVD.** *CH* Wen Jiang, Nina Huang, Shi Liang, Jing Ning; ***D:*** Chuan Lu; ***W:*** Chuan Lu; ***C:*** Zhengyu Xie.

Missing in Action 🦴 1/2 **1984 (R)** An army colonel returns to the Vietnam jungle to settle some old scores and rescue some POWs while on an MIA fact-finding mission. Box office smash. **101m/C VHS, DVD.** Chuck Norris, M. Emmet Walsh; ***D:*** Joseph Zito; ***W:*** James Bruner; ***C:*** Joao Fernandes; ***M:*** Jay Chattaway.

Missing in Action 2: The Beginning 🦴 **1985 (R)** Set in Vietnam, this prequel to the original "Missing in Action" provides some interesting background on Norris's rocky relationship with communism. Packed with violence, bloodshed and torture. **96m/C VHS, DVD.** Chuck Norris, Soon-Teck Oh, Cosie Costa, Steven Williams; ***D:*** Lance Hool; ***W:*** Steve Bing.

Missing Link 🦴🦴 1/2 **1988 (PG)** A strange, meditative quasi-documentary depicting the singular adventures of a humanoid silently transversing the African wilderness and confronting various natural phenomena. Beautifully photographed. Make-up by Rick Baker. **92m/C VHS.** Peter Elliott, Michael Gambon; ***D:*** David Hughes.

Missing Pieces 🦴🦴 1/2 **1983** A woman takes a job as a private investigator in order to find her journalist husband's killer. Effective mystery taken from the novel "A Private Investigation" by Karl Alexander. **96m/C VHS.** Elizabeth Montgomery, Louanne, John C. Reilly, Ron Karabatsos, Robin Gammell, Julius W. Harris; ***D:*** Mike Hodges. **TV**

Missing Pieces 🦴🦴 1/2 **1991 (PG)** Goof-ups Wuhl and Idle find out about a potential inheritance thanks to a fortune cookie. Now if they can jut figure out what the riddle means. **93m/C VHS.** Eric Idle, Robert Wuhl, Lauren Hutton; ***D:*** Leonard Stern; ***W:*** Leonard Stern.

Missing Pieces 🦴🦴 **2000** Rancher Atticus Cody (Coburn) leaves his home in Colorado to investigate his estranged artist son Scott's (Kersey) supposed suicide in a remote part of Mexico. And what he finds are more questions and lots of lies. Unfortunately lame script filled with cliches. Based on the Ron Hansen novel "Atticus." **90m/C VHS.** James Coburn, Lisa Zane, Paul Kersey, Finn Carter, William R. Moses, Julio Oscar Mechoso, Maxwell Caulfield; ***D:*** Carl Schenkel; ***W:*** Philip Rosenberg, Richard Kletter, D.W. Owen, Peachy Markowitz; ***C:*** Karl Herrmann; ***M:*** Lawrence Shragge. **TV**

The Mission 🦴🦴🦴 **1986 (PG)** Sweeping, cinematically beautiful historical drama about an 18th-century Jesuit mission in the Brazilian jungle. The missionaries struggle against the legalized slave trade of Portugal and political factions within the church. Written by Bolt (of "A Man for All Seasons" fame), its visual intensity is marred by length and so much overt symbolism that an emotional coolness surfaces when the action slows. Nonetheless, epic in ambition and nearly in quality. Magnificent musical score. **125m/C VHS, DVD.** Robert De Niro, Jeremy Irons, Ray McAnally, Aidan Quinn, Liam Neeson, Cherie Lunghi, Rev. Daniel Berrigan, Ronald Pickup; ***D:*** Roland Joffe; ***W:*** Robert Bolt; ***C:*** Chris Menges; ***M:*** Ennio Morricone. Oscars '86: Cinematog.; British Acad. '86: Support. Actor (McAnally); Cannes '86: Film; Golden Globes '87: Screenplay, Score; L.A. Film Critics '86: Cinematog.

The Mission 🦴🦴 1/2 *Cheung Fo* **1999** A Hong Kong mobster hires five gunmen to be his bodyguards. Everything's cool until one of them has an affair with the boss's wife. Director To revisits Tarantino-Woo territory. Most of the guys have bad haircuts and all of them have big pistols. **84m/C DVD.** *HK* Anthony Wong, Frances Ng, Roy Cheung, Simon Yam, Jackie Lui, Lam Suet; ***D:*** Johnny To; ***W:*** Nai-Hoi Yau.

Mission 🦴🦴 **2000** New York native Marvin (Coburn) moves to the Mission District of San Francisco to write a novel. He rooms with wannabe musician Jay (Leonard) and falls for beauty Ima (Holt), who tells him that he's too uptight to be a good writer. Well, if the Mission District can't loosen Marvin up, he's doomed. **87m/C VHS, DVD.** Chris Coburn, Joshua Leonard, Sandrine Holt, Bellamy Young, Adam Arkin; ***D:*** Loren Marsh; ***W:*** Loren Marsh; ***C:*** Matthew Uhry.

Mission Batangas 🦴 1/2 **1969** Unremarkable adventure-war-heist movie tells the story of a shallow American WWII pilot (Weaver) and a missionary nurse (Miles), who team up to steal the Philippine government's entire stock of gold bullion from the Japanese who captured it. Beautiful scenery, shot in the Philippines, adds something to an otherwise vacant effort. **100m/C VHS.** Dennis Weaver, Vera Miles, Keith Larsen; ***D:*** Keith Larsen.

Mission Galactica: The Cylon Attack 🦴🦴 **1978** Spaceship Battlestar Galactica is stranded in space without fuel and open to attack from the chrome-plated Cylons. Adama (Greene) is forced to stop Commander Cain's (Bridges) efforts to launch an attack against the Cylons, while countering the attacks of the Cylon leader. Warmed over TV sci-fi. **108m/C VHS.** Lorne Greene, Lloyd Bridges, Richard Hatch, Dirk Benedict, Herbert Jefferson Jr., John Colicos, Maren Jensen, Laurette Spang, Anne Lockhart, Terry Carter, George Murdock; ***D:*** Vince Edwards, Christian Nyby; ***W:*** Jim Carlson, Glen Larson; ***C:*** H. John Penner, Frank Thackery. **TV**

Mission: Impossible 🦴🦴🦴 **1996 (PG-13)** Cruise and director DePalma did not completely succeed or fail in their mission to create a blockbuster hit based on the popular '60s TV series. Cruise (one of the film's producers) is Ethan Hunt, pointman extraordinaire of the IMF team headed by Jim Phelps (Jon Voight). Their team is sent to recover a computer disk with devastating information from a mercenary Russian spy. Smelling a double cross, Hunt confronts his conniving agency boss Kitteridge (the perfectly cast Czerny) and creates his own team of crack agents to get to the truth, mind-boggling plot twists and crazy train rides be damned. The plotline may have self-destructed two-thirds into the movie and the absence of a truly sinister villain causes some damage, but with solid acting talent, tight pacing, alluring European locales, and tension-inducing special effects, who has time to notice? $100 million gross in the first two weeks would seem to indicate a sequel is in order. **110m/C VHS, DVD, Blu-ray Disc, HD DVD.** Tom Cruise, Jon Voight, Emmanuelle Beart, Ving Rhames, Henry Czerny, Emilio Estevez, Vanessa Redgrave, Jean Reno, Dale Dye; ***D:*** Brian De Palma; ***W:*** Robert Towne, David Koepp; ***C:*** Stephen Burum; ***M:*** Danny Elfman.

Mission: Impossible 2 🦴🦴🦴 *M:I 2* **2000 (PG-13)** In this visually stunning sequel to the 1996 film, Ethan Hunt tracks a rogue IMF agent Ambrose (Scott), who threatens to release deadly virus on Sydney, Australia and corner the market on the cure. Ambrose's ex-girlfriend Nyah (Newton), a jewel theif, is recruited by Hunt to spy on Ambrose from inside. Of course Nyah and Hunt fall in love (the weakest element of the movie, by the way). Director Woo brings his trademark balletic style to the action, although it seems to take a while to actually get to it. The stunts and fights, while completely preposterous, are beautifully done. The plot is a lot less convoluted than the first 'Mission,' which is either good or bad, depending on how you feel about the original. **125m/C VHS, DVD, Blu-ray Disc, HD DVD.** Tom Cruise, Anthony Hopkins, Dougray Scott, Thandie Newton, Ving Rhames, Brendan Gleeson, John Polson, Richard Roxburgh, Rade Serbedzija; ***D:*** John Woo; ***W:*** Robert Towne; ***C:*** Jeffrey L. Kimball; ***M:*** Hans Zimmer.

Mission: Impossible 3 🦴🦴🦴 **2006 (PG-13)** Tom Cruise may have transformed into Hollywood's most bizarre leading man (take that, Mel Gibson!), but you can't deny that this third MI chapter is a cracking good yarn. Abrams, in his feature debut, grounds the film by bringing back the cool gadgets and teamwork that everyone loved about the original TV show. Ethan Hunt (Cruise) is ready to retire from the IMF, when evil arms dealer Davian (a scene-stealing Hoffman) kills Hunt's protege and kidnaps his wife (Monaghan). Hunt goes into rescue/revenge mode and the non-stop action... well... never stops. Great example of a summer blockbuster that works. **126m/C DVD, Blu-ray Disc, HD DVD.** Tom Cruise, Ving Rhames, Keri Russell, Philip Seymour Hoffman, Michelle Monaghan, Laurence Fishburne, Billy Crudup, Simon Pegg, Jonathan Rhys Meyers, Sasha Alexander, Greg Grunberg, Carla Gallo, Eddie Marsan, Jose Zuniga, Maggie Q; ***D:*** J.J. (Jeffrey) Abrams; ***W:*** J.J. (Jeffrey) Abrams, Alex Kurtzman, Roberto Orci; ***C:*** Dan Mindel; ***M:*** Michael Giacchino.

Mission in Morocco 🦴 **1959** When an oilman scouting for oil fields in the Sahara is killed, his partner, Barker, hops a jet to Morocco to find the whereabouts of a microfilm that gives the location of a valuable oil deposit. The search for the secret microfilm is complicated by competing parties also interested in the black gold. Ho-hum action adventure. **79m/C VHS.** Fernando Rey, Alfredo Mayo, Silvia Morgan, Lex Barker, Juli Reding; ***D:*** Anthony Squire, Carlos Arevalo; ***W:*** Carlos Arevalo; ***C:*** Cecilio Paniagua.

Mission Kashmir 🦴🦴 **2000 (R)** Altaff (Roshan) is a young Kashmiri whose family is killed by state police hunting a rebel leader. He's adopted by Inayat Khan (Dutt), whom Altaff eventually learns was the man who lead the raid. Fleeing, Altaff seeks the tutelage of Hila Kohistani (Shroff), a militant whose only aim is the independence of Kashmir and Altaff is his weapon. But when Altaff returns to Kashmir, he unexpectedly meets his childhood girlfriend, Sufi (Zinta), and is torn between love and revenge. Hindi with subtitles or English dubbed. **157m/C VHS, DVD.** *IN* Hrithik Roshan, Sanjay Dutt, Jackie Shroff, Preity Zinta, Sonali Kulkarni; ***D:*** Vidhu Vinod Chopra; ***W:*** Vidhu Vinod Chopra, Vikram Chandra; ***C:*** Vinod Pradhan.

Mission... Kill 🦴 1/2 **1985 (R)** An American demolitions expert (Ginty) joins a Latin American guerrilla force in battling tyrannical junta force. Fast-paced thriller is big on revenge and violence but not much else. **97m/C VHS, DVD.** Robert Ginty, Olivia D'Abo, Cameron Mitchell; ***D:*** David Winters.

Mission Manila 🦴 **1987 (R)** An ex-CIA operative and Manila-based drug addict is called by his ex-lover to return to Manila to help his brother, who has gotten in much the same trouble he had. **98m/C VHS, DVD.** Larry Wilcox, Tetchie Agbayani, Sam Hennings, Al Mancini, James Wainwright, Robin Eisenman; ***D:*** Peter M. MacKenzie; ***W:*** Peter M. MacKenzie; ***C:*** Les Parrott; ***M:*** Nicholas Pike.

Mission Mars 🦴 **1967** American astronauts McGavin and Adams, on a mission to the red planet, discover the bodies of two cosmonauts floating in space. After landing on the planet's surface, they find a third cosmonaut, this one in a state of suspended animation. While putting the viewer to sleep, they proceed to revive the third cosmonaut and have at it with the sinister alien force responsible for all the trouble. **87m/C VHS.** Darren McGavin, Nick Adams, George DeVries; ***D:*** Nicholas Webster.

Mission of Death 🦴🦴 *Merchant of Death* **1997 (R)** Cop Jim Randall (Pare) has been accused of murder and suspended from the force. Something in his past offers the clue to proving his innocence but Randall doesn't want to remember. **96m/C VHS.** Michael Pare, Linda Hoffman, John Simon Jones, Anthony Fridjhon, Justin Illusion; ***D:*** Yossi Wein; ***W:*** Dan Lerner, David Sparling; ***C:*** Peter Belcher; ***M:*** Serge Colbert. **VIDEO**

Mission of Justice 🦴🦴 **1992 (R)** Revel in non-stop martial arts action with this tale of a cop who goes undercover to get the goods on a corrupt female politico, who also happens to run her own ruthless private army. **95m/C VHS.** Jeff Wincott, Brigitte Nielsen, Matthias Hues, Luca Bercovici, Cyndi Pass, Billy "Sly" Williams, Tony Burton; ***D:*** Steve Barnett.

Mission of the Shark 🦴🦴🦴 **1991** A top secret naval mission leads to a scandal-ridden court martial in this true WWII saga, based on the worst sea disaster in naval history. The USS Indianapolis has just completed a secret mission when it is torpedoed by enemy subs. The survivors spend five days in shark-infested waters awaiting rescue and, when the Navy points fingers, the ship's highly decorated and well-respected Captain McVay accepts responsibility for the good of the service. Contains some harrowing scenes of sailors versus sharks. **92m/C VHS.** Stacy Keach, Richard Thomas, Steve Landesberg, Carrie Snodgress, Bob Gunton, Andrew Prine, Stacy Keach Sr., Don Harvey; ***D:*** Robert Iscove. **TV**

Mission Phantom 🦴 **1979** A group of spies on a mission in Russia plans to steal some diamonds and help a woman get to the

United States. **90m/C VHS.** Andrew Ray, Ingrid Sholder, Peter Martellanza; ***D:*** James Reed.

Mission Stardust ½ *4...3...2...1...Morte* **1968** An internationally produced but thoroughly unambitious adaptation of the once-popular Perry Rhodan sci-fi serial, in which Rhodan and his team bring ill aliens back to Earth and defend them against evil spies. Dubbed. **90m/C VHS.** *GE IT SP* Essy Persson, Gianni Rizzo, Lang Jeffries, Pinkas Braun; ***D:*** Primo Zeglio.

Mission to Death **1966** Small American patrol during WWII is beset by numerous attacks on their way to their final destination and each time more members of the unit are wounded or killed. **71m/C VHS, DVD.** Jim Brewer, James E. McLarty, Jim Westerbrook, Robert Stolper, Dudley Hafner, Jerry Lasater; ***D:*** Kenneth W. Richardson; ***C:*** Ronald Perryman; ***M:*** Emil Cadkin, William Loose.

Mission to Glory *The Father Kino Story* **1980 (PG)** This dozer tells the story of Father Francisco "Kino" Kin, a tough, 17th-century priest in California who took on the Apaches and murderous Conquistadors in defense of his people. **100m/C VHS, DVD.** Richard Egan, John Ireland, Cesar Romero, Ricardo Montalban, Rory Calhoun, Michael Ansara, Keenan Wynn, Aldo Ray; ***D:*** Ken Kennedy.

Mission to Mars ½ **2000 (PG)** When the first manned flight to Mars ends in disaster, leaving Commander Luke Graham (Cheadle) as the only survivor, NASA sends a rescue mission consisting of Graham's best friend Jim (Sinise), married astronauts Woody (Robbins) and Terri (Nielsen), and generic tech guy Phil (O'Connell). On the way to Mars they encounter problems you've seen in other, better-done sci-fi flicks. Once on Mars, they find the New Age-y, touchy-feely secrets of creation. DePalma is known for his visual wizardry, and on that element he doesn't disappoint, but the horrible script and indifferent performances undermine whatever it was he was trying to accomplish. **112m/C VHS, DVD.** Tim Robbins, Gary Sinise, Don Cheadle, Connie Nielsen, Jerry O'Connell, Kim Delaney, Elise Neal, Peter Outerbridge, Jill Teed, Kavan Smith; ***D:*** Brian De Palma; ***W:*** Jim Thomas, John Thomas, Graham Yost; ***C:*** Stephen Burum; ***M:*** Ennio Morricone.

Mission to Moscow ½ **1943** Blatant propaganda piece made at the time the Soviet Union was allied with the U.S. against Hitler (whose troops had invaded the USSR). Based on the book by U.S. Ambassador Joseph E. Davies (Huston) who comes across as remarkably naive and accommodating as he arrives in Moscow. (Gee, that Stalin—what a great guy!) **123m/B DVD.** Walter Huston, Ann Harding, Oscar Homolka, Gene Lockhart, George Tobias, Eleanor Parker, Helmut Dantine, Henry Daniell, Dudley Field Malone, Manart Kippen; ***D:*** Michael Curtiz; ***W:*** Howard Koch; ***C:*** Bert Glennon; ***M:*** Max Steiner.

Mission to Venice **1963** Flynn plays a sleuth attempting to find a missing husband when he accidentally stumbles upon a ring of spies. **88m/C VHS.** Sean Flynn, Madeleine Robinson.

The Missionary ½ **1982 (R)** A mild-mannered English missionary returns to London from his work in Africa and is recruited into saving the souls of a group of prostitutes. Aspiring to gentle comedy status, it's often formulaic and flat, with Palin and Smith fighting gamely to stay above script level. Still, good for some laughs, particularly during the near classic walking butler sequence. **86m/C VHS, DVD.** *GB* Michael Palin, Maggie Smith, Trevor Howard, Denholm Elliott, Michael Hordern; ***D:*** Richard Loncraine; ***W:*** Michael Palin.

Missionary Man **2007 (R)** Ryder comes into town on his hog and learns that a friend was murdered because he got in the way of John Reno's plans to build a casino on an Indian reservation. So Ryder decides to bring some of that old-time, eye-for-an-eye religion and a case of whup-ass on those evildoers. **92m/C DVD.** Dolph Lundgren, Matthew Tompkins, John Enos, August Schellenberg, James Chalke, Morgana Shaw; ***D:*** Dolph Lundgren; ***W:*** Dolph Lundgren, Frank Valdez; ***C:*** Xiaobing Rao; ***M:*** Elia Cmiral. **VIDEO**

Mississippi **1935** In this uneven musical comedy, Philadelphia Yankee Tom Grayson (Crosby) is engaged to southern belle Elvira Rumford (Patrick). But when he refuses to duel one of her other suitors, the engagement is off and he's branded a coward. Tom gets a job singing aboard a riverboat piloted by Commodore Orlando Jackson (Fields) and eventually realizes that his true love is actually Elvira's younger and more sympathetic sister Lucy (Bennett). Fields steals everything that's not nailed down, leaving ostensible star Bing in the dust. Based on the play "Magnolia" by Booth Tarkington. **80m/B DVD.** Bing Crosby, W.C. Fields, Joan Bennett, Gail Patrick, Fred Kohler Sr., Claude Gillingwater, Queenie Smith, John Miljan; ***D:*** Edward Sutherland; ***W:*** Francis Martin, Jack Cunningham, Herbert Fields, Claude Binyon; ***C:*** Charles Lang.

Mississippi Burning **1988 (R)** Hard-edged social drama centers around the civil rights movement in Mississippi in 1964. When three activists turn up missing, FBI agents Anderson (Hackman) and Ward (Dafoe) are sent to head up the investigation. Unfortunately, this is another example of a "serious" film about racial conflict in which white characters predominate and blacks provide background. **127m/C VHS, DVD.** Gene Hackman, Willem Dafoe, Frances McDormand, Brad Dourif, R. Lee Ermey, Gailard Sartain, Stephen Tobolowsky, Michael Rooker, Pruitt Taylor Vince, Badja (Medu) Djola, Kevin Dunn, Frankie Faison, Tom Mason, Park Overall; ***D:*** Alan Parker; ***W:*** Chris Gerolmo; ***C:*** Peter Biziou; ***M:*** Trevor Jones. Oscars '88: Cinematog.; Berlin Intl. Film Fest. '88: Actor (Hackman); Natl. Bd. of Review '88: Actor (Hackman), Director (Parker), Support. Actress (McDormand).

Mississippi Masala **1992 (R)** "Masala" is an Indian seasoning blending different-colored spices, as this film is a blend of romance, comedy, and social conscience. An interracial romance sets off a cultural collision and escalates racial tensions in a small Southern town when Mina, a sheltered young Indian woman, falls in love with Demetrius, an ambitious black man with his own carpet-cleaning business. Washington and Choudhury are engaging as the lovers with Seth, as Mina's unhappy father, especially watchable. **118m/C VHS, DVD.** Denzel Washington, Sarita Choudhury, Roshan Seth, Sharmila Tagore, Charles S. Dutton, Joe Seneca, Ranjit (Chaudry) Chowdhry; ***Cameos:*** Mira Nair; ***D:*** Mira Nair; ***W:*** Sooni Taraporevala; ***M:*** L. Subramaniam.

Mississippi Mermaid *Le Sirene du Mississippi* **1969 (PG)** Truffaut generally succeeds in merging his own directorial style with Hitchcockian suspense, but the U.S. release was cut by some 13 minutes and the restored version deserves a re-appraisal. Millionaire tobacco planter Louis (Belmondo) looks for a bride in the personals and finds Julie (Deneuve). Louis feels lucky landing this beauty until she leaves him and takes his money with her. After a breakdown, he finds his wife working in a dance-hall under another name. Louis agrees to a reconciliation, which proves to be a mistake. Look for numerous references to the movies, including Bogart, Balzac and Cocteau. Based on the Cornell Woolrich novel "Waltz into Darkness." French with subtitles. **110m/C VHS, DVD.** *FR IT* Jean-Paul Belmondo, Catherine Deneuve, Michel Bouquet, Nelly Borgeaud, Marcel Berbert, Martine Ferriere; ***D:*** Francois Truffaut; ***W:*** Francois Truffaut; ***C:*** Denys Clerval; ***M:*** Antoine Duhamel.

Missouri Breaks **1976 (PG)** Thomas McGuane wrote the screenplay for this offbeat tale of Montana ranchers and rustlers fighting over land and livestock in the 1880s. Promising combination of script, cast and director unfortunately yields rather disappointing results, though both Brando and Nicholson chew up scenery to their hearts' content. **126m/C VHS, DVD.** Jack Nicholson, Marlon Brando, Randy Quaid, Kathleen Lloyd, Frederic Forrest, Harry Dean Stanton; ***D:*** Arthur Penn; ***W:*** Thomas McGuane; ***M:*** John Williams.

Missouri Traveler **1958** An orphan boy struggles to get his own farm in Missouri. Family fare based on John Buress' novel. **103m/C VHS, DVD.** Lee Marvin, Gary Merrill, Brandon de Wilde, Paul Ford; ***D:*** Jerry Hopper; ***W:*** Norman S. Hall; ***C:*** Winton C. Hoch; ***M:*** Jack Marshall.

Missourians ½ **1950** Small-town sheriff Hale helps a Polish rancher overcome ethnic prejudice among the townspeople. The situation worsens with the arrival in town of the rancher's outlaw brother. Strong direction and engaging story line. **60m/B VHS.** Roy Barcroft, Lyn Thomas, Lane Bradford, Scott Elliott, Monte Hale, Paul Hurst; ***D:*** George Blair; ***W:*** Arthur Orloff; ***C:*** John MacBurnie; ***M:*** Stanley Wilson.

Mrs. 'Arris Goes to Paris ½ **1992** Ada Harris (Lansbury) is a widowed charwoman, living in '50s London, whose one dream is to visit Paris and buy a Christian Dior gown at the designer's own salon. Naturally, her dream comes true—and she even finds a little romance too. Adapted from the Paul Gallico novel; made for TV. **90m/C VHS.** Angela Lansbury, Omar Sharif, Diana Rigg, Lothaire Bluteau, Lila Kaye, John Savident. **TV**

Mrs. Brown *Her Majesty Mrs. Brown* **1997 (PG)** Unusual drama finds Queen Victoria (Dench), bereft by the death of Prince Albert, withdrawing from public life to her Scottish retreat at Balmoral. There she's looked after by coarse highlander John Brown (Connolly), who encourages her to take an interest in life. As he rises in the Queen's esteem, the brash commoner begins to become overly protective of her; leading to whispers of an affair. The powers-that-be, including the Prince of Wales (Westhead) and the oily Prime Minister Disraeli (Sher), then must persuade Brown to withdraw from her company in order to preserve her reputation. Merely hints at what may or may not have been a sexual relationship between the two, but isn't that the Victorian way? **103m/C VHS, DVD.** *GB* Judi Dench, Billy Connolly, Geoffrey Palmer, Anthony Sher, Richard Pasco, Gerard Butler, David Westhead; ***D:*** John Madden; ***W:*** Jeremy Brock; ***C:*** Richard Greatrex; ***M:*** Stephen Warbeck. British Acad. '97: Actress (Dench), Costume Des.; Golden Globes '98: Actress—Drama (Dench).

Mrs. Brown, You've Got a Lovely Daughter ½ **1968 (G)** The Herman's Hermits gang inherits a greyhound and attempts to make a racer out of him while singing their songs. For the Brit group's die-hard fans only. ♫It's Nice To Be Out in the Morning; Ooh, She's Done It Again; Lemon and Lime; The World is for the Young; Holiday Inn; The Most Beautiful Thing in My Life; Daisy Chain; Mrs. Brown, You've Got a Lovely Daughter; There's a King of Hush. **95m/C VHS.** Peter Noone, Stanley Holloway, Mona Washbourne; ***D:*** Saul Swimmer.

Mrs. Dalloway ½ **1997 (PG-13)** Mannered retelling of the Virginia Woolf novel has a radiant performance by Redgrave in the title role. Wealthy, middle-aged, and long-married to boring politician Richard (Standing), Clarissa Dalloway is making preparations for her latest soiree in 1923 London. But the past rudely intrudes when old flame Peter Walsh (Kitchen) suddenly re-enters, causing Clarissa to reflect on her youth and the choices she's made. She's also shaken out of her social ennui by the unexpected sight of a shell-shocked WWI veteran (Graves) whose tragic plight disturbs her placid life. Director Gorris' English-language debut. **97m/C VHS, DVD.** *GB* Vanessa Redgrave, Michael Kitchen, John Standing, Rupert Graves, Natascha (Natasha) McElhone, Alan Cox, Sarah Badel, Lena Headey, Robert Portal, Amelia Bullmore, Margaret Tyzack, Robert Hardy; ***D:*** Marleen Gorris; ***W:*** Eileen Atkins; ***C:*** Sue Gibson; ***M:*** Ilona Sekacz.

Mrs. Doubtfire ½ **1993 (PG-13)** Williams is an unemployed voiceover actor going through a messy divorce. When his wife gets custody, the distraught father decides to dress up as a woman and become a nanny to his own children. He also has to deal with the old flame who re-enters his ex-wife's life. Williams schtick extraordinaire with more than a little sugary sentimentality. Based on the British children's book "Madame Doubtfire" by Anne Fine. **120m/C VHS, DVD.** Robin Williams, Sally Field, Pierce Brosnan, Harvey Fierstein, Robert Prosky, Mara Wilson, Paul Guilfoyle, Lisa Jakub, Joey Lawrence, Martin Mull, Polly Holliday; ***D:*** Chris Columbus; ***W:*** Randi Mayem Singer, Leslie Dixon; ***C:*** Donald McAlpine; ***M:*** Howard Shore. Oscars '93: Makeup; Golden Globes '94: Actor—Mus./Comedy (Williams), Film—Mus./Comedy; MTV Movie Awards '94: Comedic Perf. (Williams).

Mrs. Harris **2005** Jean Harris (Bening) is the head of a posh girls' school and the longtime mistress of Scarsdale diet doctor Herman Tarnower (Kingsley), a chronic womanizer. The depressed, pill-popping Jean gets fed up and kills her lover and then endures a sensational trial, which Nagy revisits from both Jean's point of view (a suicide attempt gone wrong) or that she committed cold-blooded murder. The cast is fine but the goings-on get tedious. True crime from the 1980s. **94m/C DVD.** Annette Bening, Ben Kingsley, Frances Fisher, Frank Whaley, Cloris Leachman, Chloe Sevigny, Bill Smitrovich, Michael Gross; ***Cameos:*** Ellen Burstyn; ***D:*** Phyllis Nagy; ***W:*** Phyllis Nagy; ***C:*** Steven Poster; ***M:*** John (Gianni) Frizzell. **CABLE**

Mrs. Henderson Presents **2005 (R)** The recently widowed Mrs. Henderson (Dench), in an attempt to relieve her own boredom, purchases the rundown and struggling Windmill Theatre in 1930s-40s London. Working her way through the theatre's revitalization, she hires Vivian Van Damm (Hoskins) as the theatre's manager. The two come up with the idea of staging all-nude revues, which are suitably tasteful but still a bit racy for the time. Once World War II breaks out, the story becomes one of British determination to cling to fragile everyday life in the face of the difficulties of war. All told, an interesting look at homefront England. **102m/C DVD.** Judi Dench, Bob Hoskins, Christopher Guest, Kelly Reilly, Will Young, Thelma Barlow; ***D:*** Stephen Frears; ***W:*** Martin Sherman; ***C:*** Andrew Dunn; ***M:*** George Fenton. Natl. Bd. of Review '05: Cast.

Mrs. Mike ½ **1949** Boston-bred Kathy O'Fallon (Keyes) falls in love with Canadian Mountie Mike Flannigan (Powell) and then finds it hard to adjust to a rural life in Northwest woods. Based on the novel by Benedict and Nancy Freedman. **98m/B VHS.** Evelyn Keyes, Dick Powell, J.M. Kerrigan, Angela (Clark) Clarke, John Miljan; ***D:*** Louis King; ***W:*** Alfred Lewis Levitt, DeWitt Bodeen; ***C:*** Joseph Biroc.

Mrs. Miniver **1942** A moving tale of a courageous, gentle middle-class British family and its struggle to survive during WWII. A classic that garnered six Academy Awards, it's recognized for contributions to the Allied effort. Contains one of the most powerful orations in the film history, delivered by Wilcoxon, who portrayed the vicar. Followed by "The Miniver Story." Adapted from Jan Struther's book. **134m/B VHS, DVD.** Greer Garson, Walter Pidgeon, Teresa Wright, May Whitty, Richard Ney, Henry Travers, Reginald Owen, Henry Wilcoxon, Helmut Dantine, Aubrey Mather, Rhys Williams, Tom Conway, Peter Lawford, Christopher Severn, Clare Sandars, Marie De Becker, Connie Leon, Brenda Forbes, John Abbott, Billy Bevan, John Burton, Mary Field, Forrester Harvey, Arthur Wimperis, Ian Wolfe; ***D:*** William Wyler; ***W:*** George Froeschel, James Hilton, Claudine West, Arthur Wimperis; ***C:*** Joseph Ruttenberg; ***M:*** Herbert Stothart. Oscars '42: Actress (Garson), B&W Cinematog., Director (Wyler), Picture, Screenplay, Support. Actress (Wright), Natl. Film Reg. '09.

Mrs. Munck **1995 (R)** Creepy cable thriller finds widowed Rose Munck (Ladd) agreeing to care for bitter father-in-law Patrick Leary (Dern, Ladd's real-life ex-hubby), who's suffered a debilitating stroke. But they share a nasty past—seems he seduced a teenaged Rose (played by Preston), she had a child, Patrick refused any responsibility, and the child died. So whacked-out Rose is really out for revenge. Based on a novel by Ella Leffland. Ladd's debut as writer/director. **99m/C VHS.** Diane Ladd, Bruce Dern, Kelly Preston, Shelley Winters; ***D:*** Diane Ladd; ***W:*** Diane Ladd; ***C:*** James Glennon; ***M:*** Leonard Rosenman. **CABLE**

Mrs. Palfrey at the Claremont ½ **2005** Charming, gentle and somewhat melancholy comedy about the unlikely friendship between a 70-something widow and a 20-something writer. Mrs. Palfrey (Plowright) lives as independently as possible at a London residential hotel for the elderly. She's hoping to become closer to her grandson Desmond (O'Toole), but he doesn't visit. Instead, she literally stumbles into young Ludovic Meyer (Friend), an equally lonely soul. A bond begins that extends to Ludovic passing himself off as the absent grandson to maintain Mrs. Palfrey's pride (which will cause later confusion). An adaptation of the Elizabeth Taylor novel, which was set in the 1950s. This film's budget couldn't stretch to such a re-creation so it was updated to the present, with some awkwardness. **108m/C DVD.** *GB* Joan Plowright, Rupert Friend, Zoe Tapper, Anna Massey, Robert Lang, Marcia Warren, Millicent Martin, Lorcan O'Toole, Anna Carteret; ***D:*** Dan Ireland; ***W:*** Ruth Sacks; ***C:*** Claudio Rocha; ***M:*** Stephen Barton.

Mrs. Parker and the Vicious Circle 1/2 *Mrs. Parker and the Round Table* **1994 (R)** Bio of witty, suicidal writer Dorothy Parker and her equally witty friends, including theatre critics, playwrights, and novelists, who lunched together at New York's Algonquin Hotel for most of the 1920s. An irreverant band known as the Algonquin Round Table, their numerous bon mots were regularly reported in the papers. Their private lives were often less than happy with alcohol, drug addiction and depression prominent factors. Parker's downward spiral is depressing though compelling to watch, thanks to Leigh's performance (in spite of much criticism for her lockjawed accent) but many of the characters come and go so quickly they make little impression. **124m/C VHS, DVD.** Mina (Badiyi) Badie, Natalie Strong, Jennifer Jason Leigh, Matthew Broderick, Andrew McCarthy, Campbell Scott, Jennifer Beals, Tom McGowan, Nick Cassavetes, Sam Robards, Rebecca Miller, Wallace Shawn, Martha Plimpton, Gwyneth Paltrow, Peter Gallagher, Lili Taylor; ***D:*** Alan Rudolph; ***W:*** Rudolph Coburn, Randy Sue Coburn; ***C:*** Jan Kiesser; ***M:*** Mark Isham. Natl. Soc. Film Critics '94: Actress (Leigh).

Mrs. Parkington 1/2 **1944** Overblown epic drama spanning six decades tells the story of the rise and fall of an American dynasty made on easy money. Garson plays the woman who goes from working as a maid in a boarding house to living a life of luxury when she marries a multimillionaire. This was the fifth pairing of Garson and Pidgeon and although it's not one of their best, it proved to be a big hit with audiences. Lavish costumes and good performances by Garson and Moorehead. Based on the novel by Louis Bromfield. **124m/B VHS.** Greer Garson, Walter Pidgeon, Edward Arnold, Frances Rafferty, Agnes Moorehead, Selena Royle, Gladys Cooper, Lee Patrick; ***D:*** Tay Garnett; ***W:*** Robert Thoeren, Polly James; ***C:*** Joseph Ruttenberg. Golden Globes '45: Support. Actress (Moorehead).

Mrs. R's Daughter **1979** An outraged mother fights the judicial systems in order to bring her daughter's rapist to trial. Based on a true story. **97m/C VHS.** Cloris Leachman, Season Hubley, Donald Moffat, John McIntire, Stephen Elliott, Ron Rifkin; ***D:*** Dan Curtis. **TV**

Mrs. Santa Claus 1/2 **1996 (G)** Who better than Lansbury to star as the title character in this sweet TV musical set in 1910. Vivacious Mrs. C is tired of being left home during Santa's (Durning) annual trip and decides to borrow the sleigh for a test drive just before the big day. But bad weather and an injured reindeer force an emergency landing in New York City where she befriends the young sweatshop workers at villainous toy-maker A.P. Tavish's (Mann) factory and does a little matchmaking too. But Mrs. Claus still must make it back to the North Pole by Christmas Eve. ♫Avenue A; Almost Jolly; We Don't Go Together; Suffragette March; He Needs Me. **90m/C VHS, DVD.** Angela Lansbury, Charles Durning, Terrence Mann, David Norona, Debra Wiseman, Rosalind Harris, Bryan Murray, Lynsey Bartilson, Michael Jeter; ***D:*** Terry Hughes; ***W:*** Mark Saltzman; ***C:*** Stephen M. Katz; ***M:*** Jerry Herman.

Ms. Scrooge 1/2 **1997 (G)** Modern-day distaff version of the Dickens Christmas saga. Ebenita Scrooge (Tyson) is a miserly banker but you get the same familiar characters with the Crachits and Tiny Tim as well as the various ghosts to show Ebenita the errors of her ways. **87m/C VHS.** Cicely Tyson, Katherine Helmond, Michael Beach, John Bourgeois, Arsinee Khanjian, William Greenblatt, Rae'ven (Alyia Larrymore) Kelly, Michael J. Reynolds; ***D:*** John Korty; ***W:*** John McGreevey; ***C:*** Elemer Ragalyi; ***M:*** David Shire. **CABLE**

Mrs. Silly **1985** Romance novel on tape, following the exploits of an aging woman who in losing material wealth, gains contentment. **60m/C** Maggie Smith, James Villiers, Cyril Luckham.

Mrs. Soffel 1/2 **1984 (PG-13)** Falling in love with a convicted murderer and helping him flee confinement occupies the time of the prison warden's wife. Effectively captures the 1901 setting, yet a dark pall fairly strangles any emotion. Based on a true story. **110m/C VHS, DVD.** Diane Keaton, Mel Gibson, Matthew Modine, Edward Herrmann, Trini Alvarado, Terry O'Quinn, Jennifer (Jennie) Dundas Lowe, Danny Corkill, Maury Chaykin, Dana Wheeler-Nicholson; ***D:*** Gillian Armstrong; ***W:*** Ron Nyswaner; ***C:*** Russell Boyd; ***M:*** Mark Isham.

Mrs. Wiggs of the Cabbage Patch 1/2 **1934** A warm, funny, and altogether overdone story of a mother whose husband abandons her, leaving the woman to raise their four children alone. It's Thanksgiving, so the rich visit the poor household to deliver a turkey dinner, and in the end all live happily ever after. Not one of Fields' larger roles; he doesn't even make an appearance until midway through the schmaltz. **80m/B VHS.** Pauline Lord, Zasu Pitts, W.C. Fields, Evelyn Venable, Donald Meek, Kent Taylor, Charles Middleton; ***D:*** Norman Taurog; ***M:*** Val Burton.

Mrs. Winterbourne **1996 (PG-13)** Pregnant loser Connie Doyle (Lake) is whisked into the lap of luxury when she's assumed to be the widowed Patricia Winterbourne after a train wreck. The grieving family (who had never met the bride) take her in and accept her and her baby as part of the household. Since her life is now going well, Connie decides to keep her true identity a secret while she falls for faux-brother-in-law Bill (Fraser). MacLaine is brilliant as the spirited matriarch of the family. Retooled as a comedy, the story is actually based on the noirish novel "I Married a Dead Man" by Cornell Woolrich and a remake of the equally dark "No Man of Her Own" from 1950. **106m/C VHS, DVD.** Ricki Lake, Brendan Fraser, Shirley MacLaine, Miguel (Michael) Sandoval, Loren Dean, Susan Haskell, Paula Prentiss; ***D:*** Richard Benjamin; ***W:*** Phoef Sutton, Lisa-Marie Rodano; ***C:*** Alex Nepomniaschy; ***M:*** Patrick Doyle.

The Mist **2007 (R)** Writer director Frank Derabant adapts Stephen King's short story into what on the surface appears to be a typical horror film, replete with fantastic creatures hell-bent on annihilating anyone or anything in their path. There's also tense drama, which unfolds in the grocery store of a typical Maine town, where locals and tourists are trapped by a thick, malevolent fog that follows after a freak storm. Local commercial artist David Drayton (Jane) and Mrs. Carmody (Harden), a bible-thumping kook, both try to lead the others through the crisis as people begin to crack under the pressure and turn on each other. Andre Braugher is a big-city lawyer, a thoroughly rational outsider who refuses to accept the small town mentality of the citizenry. Ultimately the inhumanity they direct at each other proves to be as great a threat as whatever is in the mist. The ending may be mildly disappointing but the movie is otherwise well done. **125m/C DVD, Blu-ray Disc.** *US* Thomas Jane, Marcia Gay Harden, Laurie Holden, Andre Braugher, Nathan Gamble, Toby Jones, William Sadler, Jeffrey DeMunn, Alexa Davalos; ***D:*** Frank Darabont; ***W:*** Frank Darabont; ***C:*** Ronn Schmidt; ***M:*** Mark Isham.

The Mistake *Die Verfehlung* **1991** In 1988, Jacob (who's from Hamburg in West Germany) falls in love with Elisabeth, who lives in an East German village. They secretly meet in East Berlin, but the Stasi are informed of the affair by someone in Elisabeth's village and Jacob is deported. Elisabeth knows who done her wrong and plans her revenge. German with subtitles. **100m/C DVD.** *GE* Angelica Domrose, Gottfried John, Jorg Gudzuhn, Dagmar Manzel, Katja Paryla; ***D:*** Heiner Carow; ***W:*** Wolfram Witt; ***C:*** Martin Schlesinger; ***M:*** Stefan Carow.

Mistaken Identity 1/2 **1936** A swank hotel is the setting for this so-so comedy about three con men who wind up conning each other as much as their supposed victims. A couple of light romances are also thrown in for good measure. **75m/B VHS.** Chick Chandler, Evalyn Knapp, Berton Churchill, Patricia Farr, Richard Carle, Bradley Page, Lew Kelly; ***D:*** Phil Rosen.

Mistaken Identity 1/2 *Murder with Music* **1941** All-black mystery set against the background of a nightclub, and featuring a production number, "I'm a Bangi from Ubangi." **60m/B VHS.** Nellie Hill, George Oliver, Noble Sissle; ***D:*** George P. Quigley; ***W:*** Victor Vicas; ***C:*** John Visconti, George Webster.

Mr. Accident 1/2 **1999 (PG-13)** Australian comedian Serious returns as star/writer/director/producer. Accident-prone Roger Crumpkin (Serious) finds out his egg-processing factory boss (Fiels) is planning to produce eggs that are filled with nicotine so that people will become addicted. No, not to eggs!—to cigarettes! A lame attempt at comedy. **89m/C VHS, DVD.** *AU* Yahoo Serious, David Field, Helen Dallimore, Grant Piro, Jeanette Cronin; ***D:*** Yahoo Serious; ***W:*** Yahoo Serious; ***C:*** Steve Arnold; ***M:*** Nerida Tyson-Chew.

Mr. Ace 1/2 **1946** A congresswoman decides to run for governor without the approval of the loyal political kingpin, Mr. Ace. **85m/B VHS, DVD.** George Raft, Sylvia Sidney, Sara Haden, Stanley Ridges; ***D:*** Edwin L. Marin; ***W:*** Fred Finklehoffe; ***C:*** Karl Struss; ***M:*** Heinz Roemheld.

Mr. & Mrs. Bridge **1990 (PG-13)** Set in the '30s and '40s in Kansas City, Ivory's adaptation of Evan S. Connell's novels painstakingly portrays an upper middle-class family struggling to survive within an emotional vacuum. Newman and Woodward, together for the first time in many years as Walter and Ivory Bridge, bring a wealth of experience and insight to their characterizations. Many consider this to be Newman's best, most subtle and nuanced performance. **127m/C VHS, DVD.** Joanne Woodward, Paul Newman, Kyra Sedgwick, Blythe Danner, Simon Callow, Diane Kagan, Robert Sean Leonard, Saundra McClain, Margaret Welsh, Austin Pendleton, Gale Garnett, Remak Ramsay; ***D:*** James Ivory; ***W:*** Ruth Prawer Jhabvala; ***C:*** Tony Pierce-Roberts; ***M:*** Richard Robbins. N.Y. Film Critics '90: Actress (Woodward), Screenplay.

Mr. & Mrs. Loving **1996 (PG-13)** Fact-based movie, set in the 1960s, follows the romance, marriage, and struggle of Richard Loving (Hutton) and Mildred "Bean" Jeter (Rochon). Growing up in rural Virginia, their interracial relationship isn't considered uncommon. But when Bean gets pregnant, they aren't allowed to marry and live together because of Virginia's racial laws. Instead, the Lovings start a life in Washington, D.C., but desperately homesick and increasingly aware of the civil rights movement, Bean writes a letter to the Attorney General's office. What results is young ACLU lawyer Bernie Cohen (Parker) taking on their case—which eventually leads to a landmark Supreme Court decision about miscegenation laws. **95m/C VHS, DVD.** Timothy Hutton, Lela Rochon, Corey Parker, Ruby Dee, Isaiah Washington IV, Bill Nunn, Charles Gray; ***D:*** Richard Friedenberg; ***W:*** Richard Friedenberg; ***C:*** Kenneth Macmillan; ***M:*** Branford Marsalis. **CABLE**

Mr. & Mrs. Smith 1/2 **1941** Hitchcock's only screwball comedy, an underrated, endearing farce about a bickering but happy modern couple who discover their marriage isn't legitimate and go through courtship all over again. Vintage of its kind, with inspired performances and crackling dialogue. **95m/B VHS, DVD.** Carole Lombard, Robert Montgomery, Gene Raymond, Jack Carson, Lucile Watson, Charles Halton; ***D:*** Alfred Hitchcock; ***W:*** Norman Krasna.

Mr. & Mrs. Smith **2005 (PG-13)** Who knew that pretty people shooting at each other could be so much fun? Director Liman fuses "The War of the Roses" with "The Killer" in this stylish tale of hitman love-gone-wrong. Suburban couple John (Pitt) and Jane (Jolie) are getting bored with their marriage, but they're both hiding a big secret—they're the world's top assassins who unwittingly fell in love and got hitched. When they're assigned to kill each other, every ounce of their simmering martial tensions finds expression through shotguns and drop-kicks. The plot wanes and bad guys are ridiculously disposable, but the leads have such palpable on-screen chemistry that you'll find yourself wondering how to discreetly introduce a rocket launcher into your own bedroom. **119m/C DVD, Blu-ray Disc, UMD.** *US* Brad Pitt, Angelina Jolie, Adam Brody, Vince Vaughn, Kerry Washington, Chris Weitz, Keith David, Rachael Huntley, Michelle Monaghan, Stephanie March, Jenny (Jennifer) Morrison; ***D:*** Doug Liman; ***W:*** Simon Kinberg; ***C:*** Bojan Bazelli; ***M:*** John Powell; ***V:*** Angela Bassett, William Fichtner.

Mr. Arkadin *Confidential Report* **1955** Screenwriter, director, star Welles, adapting from his own novel, gave this plot a dry run on radio during early 1950s. Welles examines the life of yet another ruthless millionaire, but this one can't seem to remember the sordid source of all that cash. Investigator Arden follows the intriguing and descending trail to a surprise ending. As in "Citizen Kane," oblique camera angles and layered dialogue prevail, but this time only serve to confuse the story. Shot over two years around Europe, required seven years of post production before finding distribution in 1962. **99m/B VHS, DVD.** *GB* Orson Welles, Akim Tamiroff, Michael Redgrave, Patricia Medina, Robert Arden, Mischa Auer; ***D:*** Orson Welles; ***W:*** Orson Welles; ***C:*** Jean (Yves, Georges) Bourgoin.

Mr. Art Critic 1/2 **2007 (PG-13)** Caustic Chicago art critic M.J. Clayton (Pinchot) gets a reaming from his boss over his brutal reviews and goes to lick his wounds at his Mackinac Island cottage. He runs into one of the artists he's criticized and makes a drunken bet that anyone can make art. So he decides to enter the local art festival. **90m/C DVD.** Toni Trucks, John Lepard; ***D:*** Richard Brauer; ***W:*** Richard Brauer. **VIDEO**

Mr. Average *Comme Tout le Monde* **2006** Jalil (Maadour) wins big on a game show that's a front for a market research company looking for test subjects. Jalil is so adept at agreeing with survey questions that the firm secretly tracks his every move and even hires a would-be girlfriend, actress Claire (Dhavernas), to move in and funnel products to Jalil that they want tested. But then Claire develops a conscience. French with subtitles. **90m/C DVD.** *FR* Caroline Dhavernas, Thierry Lhermitte, Amina Annabi, Gilbert Melki, Delphine Rich, Khalid Maadour, Chantal Lauby; ***D:*** Pierre-Paul Renderss, Pierre-Paul Renders; ***W:*** Pierre-Paul Renderss, Pierre-Paul Renders, Denis Lapiere; ***C:*** Virginie Saint-Martin.

Mr. Barrington 1/2 **2003** Agoraphobic poet Lila (Porter) is at first charmed and then menaced by mysterious neighbor, Mr. Barrington (McArdie). Is this some reflection of her tragic past at St. Agatha's orphanage? Mr. Barrington certain wants to settle some old score and Samuel (Schweig), Lila's supportive husband, decides to investigate so they can overcome the danger. Filmed in Maine. **100m/C DVD.** Eric Schweig, Jonelle Allen, Jennifer Nicole Porter, Brian McArdie; ***D:*** Dana Packard; ***C:*** Eric Goldstein.

Mr. Baseball **1992 (PG-13)** Washed-up American baseball player tries to revive his career by playing in Japan and experiences cultures clashing under the ballpark lights. Semi-charmer swings and misses often enough to warrant return to minors. Film drew controversy during production when Universal was bought by the Japanese Matsushita organization and claims of both Japan- and America-bashing were thrown about. **109m/C VHS, DVD.** Tom Selleck, Ken Takakura, Toshi Shioya, Dennis Haysbert, Aya Takanashi; ***D:*** Fred Schepisi; ***W:*** Gary Ross, Kevin Wade, Monte Merrick; ***C:*** Ian Baker; ***M:*** Jerry Goldsmith.

Mr. Bean's Holiday **2007 (PG)** Love him or hate him, Mr. Bean (Atkinson) has returned for yet another round of low-brow slapstick. On his way to France for vacation, Mr. Bean manages to lose his wallet and gain a lost child (Baldry), and spends much of the rest of the movie in awkward situations trying to reunite the boy and his father. Plenty of Atkinson's physical gags and base jokes, but there's not much here for non-Bean fans. Title is an homage to Jacques Tati's 1953 comedy "M Hulot's Holiday." **90m/C DVD, HD DVD.** *GB US* Rowan Atkinson, Emma de Caunes, Willem Dafoe, Jean Rochefort, Max Baldry, Karel Roden, Steve Pemberton; ***D:*** Steve Bendelack; ***W:*** Robin Driscoll, Hamish McColl; ***C:*** Baz Irvine; ***M:*** Howard Goodall.

Mr. Billion 🦴🦴 **1977 (PG)** Engaging chase adventure comedy about an Italian mechanic who stands to inherit a billion dollar fortune if he can travel from Italy to San Francisco in 20 days. Of course, things get in his way. Hill made his American debut in this film. **89m/C VHS, DVD.** Jackie Gleason, Terence Hill, Valerie Perrine, Slim Pickens, Chill Wills; ***D:*** Jonathan Kaplan; ***W:*** Jonathan Kaplan, Ken Friedman; ***M:*** Dave Grusin.

Mr. Blandings Builds His Dream House 🦴🦴🦴 ½ **1948** Jim Blandings (Grant), wife Muriel (Loy), and their two daughters must give up their Manhattan apartment for new digs. City boy Jim wants to become a suburbanite and the Blandings decide to build their dream house—with many complications. Timely at its release because of the post-WWII housing shortage and building boom, this classic comedy is still a humorous treat with Grant at his funniest. Loy and Douglas provide strong backup. A must for all homeowners. Based on the novel by Eric Hodgins. **93m/B VHS, DVD.** Cary Grant, Myrna Loy, Melvyn Douglas, Lex Barker, Reginald Denny, Louise Beavers, Jason Robards Sr.; ***D:*** H.C. Potter; ***W:*** Norman Panama, Melvin Frank; ***C:*** James Wong Howe; ***M:*** Leigh Harline.

Mr. Boggs Steps Out 🦴 ½ **1938** A pencil-pusher wins a bundle and invests it in a barrel factory. Trouble arises when a slickster tries to close it down. Even with the usual romantic entanglements, the film has trouble staying interesting. **68m/B VHS, DVD.** Stuart Erwin, Helen Chandler, Toby Wing, Tully Marshall, Spencer Charters, Otis Harlan, Walter Byron, Milburn Stone; ***D:*** Gordon Wiles.

Mr. Brooks 🦴🦴 **2007 (R)** Costner goes the bad guy route in this suspense thriller about a serial killer who's the family man next door (if more tightly wound). Earl Brooks is a loving father and husband, a successful businessman, and a philanthropist. If he just didn't have that pesky alter-ego, Marshall (Hurt), constantly telling him it's time to kill again. But Brooks makes an uncharacteristic mistake and is seen by Mr. Smith (Cook), who blackmails him into coming along on his next bloody excursion. Detective Tracy Atwood (Moore) is burdened by too many personal issues to be very effective. It's really the Brooks/Marshall show and if you're interested in either/both Costner and Hurt, you'll enjoy yourself. **120m/C DVD, Blu-ray Disc.** *US* Kevin Costner, William Hurt, Marg Helgenberger, Demi Moore, Dane Cook, Danielle Panabaker, Ruben Santiago-Hudson, Lindsay Crouse, Jason Lewis, Reiko Aylesworth, Aisha Hinds, Matt Schulze, Michael Cole; ***D:*** Bruce A. Evans; ***W:*** Bruce A. Evans, Raynold Gideon; ***C:*** John Lindley; ***M:*** Ramin Djawadi.

Mr. Corbett's Ghost 🦴🦴 **1990** A young man, displeased with his boss's managerial finesse, cuts a deal with a soul collector who pink slips the guy to the great unemployment line in the sky. Once a boss always a boss, and the guy's ghost stops in to say boo, while the soul collector is hot to get his hands on his part of the bargain. Huston's final film appearance. **60m/C VHS.** John Huston, Paul Scofield, Burgess Meredith; ***D:*** Danny Huston; ***C:*** Robin Vidgeon; ***M:*** John Cameron. **TV**

Mr. Deeds 🦴 ½ **2002 (PG-13)** With more chutzpah than money (and he's got $40 billion), Sandler plays the must miss Deeds of this joyless remake's title. Longfellow Deeds is an owner of a New Hampshire pizza joint and aspiring greeting card poet (gag) before learning of a multi-billion dollar inheritance that gives him control of a mammoth media company. Gallagher is the slimy CEO who secretly wants hayseed Deeds to disappear back to the boonies, while Ryder is tabloid reporter/love interest Babe Bennett, out to dupe man-child Deeds for a sensational story. Turturro, as Deeds' sneaky butler is the sole comic relief, while Buscemi does his best Marty Feldman to no avail. Paired with the much-better-by-comparison "Little Nicky," Sandler's schtick is wearing thin. **97m/C VHS, DVD.** *US* Adam Sandler, Winona Ryder, John Turturro, Peter Gallagher, Steve Buscemi, Jared Harris, Allen Covert, Erik Avari, Peter Dante, Conchata Ferrell, Harve Presnell, Blake Clark, JB Smoove, Rob Schneider; ***Cameos:*** John McEnroe; ***D:*** Steven Brill; ***W:*** Tim Herlihy; ***C:*** Peter Lyons Collister; ***M:*** Teddy Castellucci.

Mr. Deeds Goes to Town 🦴🦴🦴 ½ **1936** Typical Capra fare offers Cooper as small town Vermonter and philanthropic fellow Longfellow Deeds, who inherits $20 million and promptly donates it to the needy, which leads to a courtroom hearing on his sanity. He also manages to find time to fall in love with beautiful reporter and tough cookie, Babe Bennett (Arthur), who's determined to fathom the good guy's motivation. Superior entertainment. Based on Clarence Budington Kelland's story "Opera Hat." **118m/B VHS, DVD.** Gary Cooper, Jean Arthur, Raymond Walburn, Walter Catlett, Lionel Stander, George Bancroft, H.B. Warner, Ruth Donnelly, Douglass Dumbrille, Margaret Seddon, Margaret McWade; ***D:*** Frank Capra; ***W:*** Robert Riskin; ***C:*** Joseph Walker. Oscars '36: Director (Capra); N.Y. Film Critics '36: Film.

Mr. Destiny 🦴🦴 **1990 (PG-13)** Mid-level businessman Belushi has a mid-life crisis of sorts when his car dies. Wandering into an empty bar, he encounters bartender Caine who serves cocktails and acts omniscient before taking him on the ten-cent tour of life as it would've been if he hadn't struck out in a high school baseball game. Less than wonderful rehash of "It's a Wonderful Life." **110m/C VHS, DVD.** James Belushi, Michael Caine, Linda Hamilton, Jon Lovitz, Bill McCutcheon, Hart Bochner, Rene Russo, Jay O. Sanders, Maury Chaykin, Pat Corley, Douglas Seale, Courteney Cox, Kathy Ireland; ***D:*** James Orr; ***W:*** James Orr, Jim Cruickshank.

Mr. District Attorney 🦴 **1941** Minor low-budget noir adapted from the radio series. Fresh out of law school, Jones (O'Keefe) botches a case so he's shuffled off into investigating the whereabouts of politician Hyde (Lorre), who disappeared after a big payoff. Newspaper dame Terry (Rice) helps Jones out. **69m/B DVD.** Dennis O'Keefe, Florence Rice, Peter Lorre, Minor Watson, Stanley Ridges, Joan Blair; ***D:*** William M. Morgan; ***W:*** Malcolm Stuart Boylan, Karl Brown; ***C:*** Reggie Lanning; ***M:*** Cy Feuer.

Mister Drake's Duck 🦴🦴 ½ **1950** American newlyweds Don (Fairbanks Jr.) and Penny (Donlan) Drake settle down on the English farm that Don has inherited. At a auction, Penny mistakenly buys five dozen ducks, one of which turns out to lay radioactive eggs. Soon the British Army has quarantined the farm and then other branches of the military turn up—all claiming the duck and turning the Drakes' life into chaos. Rather dated, but still amusing, satire on nuclear arms and the military. Based on a play by Ian Messiter. **80m/B VHS.** *GB* Douglas Fairbanks Jr., Yolande Donlan, Reginald Beckwith, Howard Marion-Crawford, Wilfrid Hyde-White, Jon Pertwee, John Boxer, A.E. Matthews; ***D:*** Val Guest; ***W:*** Val Guest; ***C:*** Jack Cox, Harry Gillam; ***M:*** Bruce Campbell.

Mr. Emmanuel 🦴🦴 ½ **1944** An elderly Jewish widower leaves his English home in 1935 in quest of the mother of a German refugee boy, and is subjected to shocking treatment in Germany. **97m/B VHS.** Felix Aylmer, Greta Gynt, Walter Rilla, Peter Mullins, Ursula Jeans, Elspeth March, Irene Handl; ***D:*** Harold French; ***W:*** Gordon Wellesley; ***C:*** Otto Heller; ***M:*** Mischa Spoliansky.

Mr. Fix It 🦴🦴 ½ **2006 (R)** Charming romantic comedy. Lance Valenteen (Boreanaz) is a relationship fixer. Lovelorn guys who want to get back the gal who dumped them come to Lance and he makes like Casanova with said ex. But he breaks their heart and, suddenly, that former boyfriend is the greatest guy in the world. Then Lance gets hired by Bob (Healy), who got dumped for lying to beautiful Sophia (de la Garza). Too bad Lance actually falls for Sophia and then has to figure out how to come clean without her dumping him too. **93m/C DVD.** David Boreanaz, Patricia Healy, Paul Sorvino, Terrence Evans, Alana de la Garza, Herschel Bleefeld; ***D:*** Darin Ferriola; ***W:*** Darin Ferriola; ***C:*** Irek Hartowicz; ***M:*** Kevin Saunders Hayes.

Mister Foe 🦴🦴 *Hallam Foe* **2007** A surprisingly sweet tale about voyeurism. Troubled teen Hallam Foe (Bell) blames his new stepmother (Forlani) for his mother's death and retreats into a semi-fantasy world where he spies on people from his treehouse. Moving to Edinburgh for a fresh start, Hallam is instantly smitten by attractive Kate (Myles), a ringer for his late mom, and gets a job at the hotel where she works. He also takes to the roofs to spy on her and when he gets caught peeping, she's titillated instead of outraged. Especially good performances by Bell and Myles. **95m/C DVD.** *GB* Jamie Bell, Sophia Myles, Ciaran Hinds, Jamie Sives, Claire Forlani, Maurice Roeves, Ewen Bremner; ***D:*** David Mackenzie; ***W:*** David Mackenzie, Ed Whitmore; ***C:*** Giles Nuttgens.

Mr. Frost 🦴 **1989 (R)** Goldblum feigns fascination in this lackluster tale of the devil incarnate, who is imprisoned after owning up to a series of grisly murders, and who hides his true identity until approached by a woman psychiatrist. **92m/C VHS.** Jeff Goldblum, Kathy Baker, Alan Bates, Roland Giraud, Jean-Pierre Cassel; ***D:*** Philippe Setbon; ***W:*** Philippe Setbon, Brad Lynch.

Mr. Headmistress 🦴🦴 ½ **1998** Small-time con man Tucker (Williams) is trying to avoid a couple of thugs out to collect a bad debt when he assumes the identity of the headmistress of the Rawlings Academy for Girls. Seems the school is about to receive a big donation if grades improve and Tucker wants the money. But of course, he learns more than how to walk like a lady along the way. **89m/C VHS.** Harland Williams, Katey Sagal, Shawna Waldron; ***D:*** James Frawley. **TV**

Mr. Hobbs Takes a Vacation 🦴🦴🦴 **1962** Good-natured comedy in which beleagured parents try to resolve family squabbles while the entire brood is on a seaside vacation. Stewart and O'Hara are especially fine and funny as the well-meaning parents. **116m/C VHS, DVD.** James Stewart, Maureen O'Hara, Fabian, John Saxon, Marie Wilson, John McGiver, Reginald Gardiner; ***D:*** Henry Koster; ***W:*** Nunnally Johnson; ***M:*** Henry Mancini. Berlin Intl. Film Fest. '62: Actor (Stewart).

Mr. Holland's Opus 🦴🦴🦴 **1995 (PG)** Well-done Disney tearjerker begins in 1965 as musician Glenn Holland (Dreyfuss) takes a teaching job to get himself off the wedding reception circuit and help support his wife, Iris (Headly), and their deaf son. Spanning three decades, with actual newsreel footage thrown in to highlight time passing, Holland sets aside his dream of composing a great symphony and finds his true calling—mentoring and inspiring young minds. Holland's son being deaf might have proved corny, but their rocky relationship is deeply rooted to the storyline. Dreyfuss turns in his most vibrant performance in years and, while sentimental buttons are definitely pushed, director Herek avoids falling into sappiness. **142m/C VHS, DVD.** Richard Dreyfuss, Glenne Headly, Jay Thomas, Olympia Dukakis, William H. Macy, Alicia Witt, Jean (Louisa) Kelly, Anthony Natale, Mark Daniels; ***D:*** Stephen Herek; ***W:*** Patrick Sheane Duncan; ***C:*** Oliver Wood; ***M:*** Michael Kamen.

Mr. Horn 🦴🦴 **1979** Slow-paced film about folk-hero Scott Tom Horn capturing the famous Apache warrior, Geronimo, is average at best. **200m/C VHS.** David Carradine, Richard Widmark, Karen Black, Jeremy Slate, Enrique Lucero, Jack Starrett; ***D:*** Jack Starrett; ***W:*** William Goldman.

Mr. Hulot's Holiday 🦴🦴🦴 ½ *Les Vacances de Monsieur Hulot; Monsieur Hulot's Holiday* **1953** Superior slapstick details the misadventures of an oblivious bachelor's seaside holiday, where disaster follows his every move. Inventive French comedian Tati at his best. Light-hearted and natural, with magical mime sequences. Followed by "Mon Oncle." French with subtitles. **86m/B VHS, DVD.** *FR* Jacques Tati, Natalie Pascaud, Michelle Rolia; ***D:*** Jacques Tati; ***W:*** Jacques Tati, Henri Marquet, Jacques Lagrange, Pierre Aubert; ***C:*** Jacques Mercanton; ***M:*** Alain Romans.

Mr. Imperium 🦴 ½ **1951** Lousy title, trite story, and there's no romantic chemistry between the leads although Turner looks great and Pinza sings. A playboy prince falls for a nightclub singer but must leave her when he becomes king. Years later, when she's a Hollywood star, they briefly resume their romance until duty calls him home again. **87m/C DVD.** Ezio Pinza, Lana Turner, Marjorie Main, Debbie Reynolds, Cedric Hardwicke, Barry Sullivan; ***D:*** Don Hartman; ***W:*** Don Hartman, Edwin H. Knopf; ***C:*** George J. Folsey; ***M:*** Bronislau Kaper.

Mr. Inside, Mr. Outside 🦴 ½ **1974** Two N.Y.C. cops, one undercover, one not, try to infiltrate a tough diamond-smuggling ring. **74m/C VHS.** Tony LoBianco, Hal Linden; ***D:*** William A. Graham. **TV**

Mr. Jealousy 🦴🦴 ½ **1998 (R)** When Lester Grimm (Stoltz) was 15, he chickened out on a good night kiss with his girl, and later spied her necking with another boy. Ever since then, he's had this thing about infidelity and he trashes every relationship because of his suspicions. It's no different when he meets the vivacious Ramona (Sciorra), who has recently broken up with arrogant author Dashiell (Eigemann). Lester joins Dashiell's therapy group to spy on his possible competition. Writer-director Baumbach stretches this thin material by making the characters interesting and the dialogue funny. Fonda's role is a cameo as Dashiell's stuttering girlfriend. **105m/C VHS, DVD.** Eric Stoltz, Annabella Sciorra, Christopher Eigeman, Carlos Jacott, Marianne Jean-Baptiste, Brian Kerwin, Peter Bogdanovich; ***Cameos:*** Bridget Fonda; ***D:*** Noah Baumbach; ***W:*** Noah Baumbach; ***C:*** Steven Bernstein; ***M:*** Robert Een, Luna.

Mr. Jingles WOOF! *2 S.I.C.K. (Serial Insane Clown Killer)* **2006 (R)** Angie has been in a psych ward for years, ever since the murder of her parents by Mr. Jingles. Finally released into the care of her aunt and cousins, Angie's nightmare comes back when the clown also returns to finish off his only witness. No wonder clowns have such bad reps, with flicks like these. **80m/C DVD.** *US* Kelli Jensen, Jessica Hall, John Anton, Nathaniel Ketcham, Heather Doba, Nicole Majdali; ***D:*** Tommy Brunswick; ***W:*** Todd Brunswick; ***C:*** Todd Brunswick; ***M:*** James Souva.

Mister Johnson 🦴🦴🦴 **1991 (PG-13)** In 1923 Africa, an educated black man working for the British magistrate constantly finds himself in trouble, thanks to backfiring schemes. This highly enjoyable film from the director of "Driving Miss Daisy" suffers only from the underdevelopment of the intriguing lead character. Based on the novel by Joyce Cary. **105m/C VHS, DVD.** Pierce Brosnan, Edward Woodward, Maynard Eziashi, Beatie Edney, Denis Quilley, Nick Reding; ***D:*** Bruce Beresford; ***W:*** Bruce Beresford, William Boyd; ***C:*** Peter James; ***M:*** Georges Delerue.

Mr. Jones 🦴 ½ **1993 (R)** Psychiatrist (Olin) falls in love with her manic-depressive patient (Gere). Head case Mr. Jones (Gere) is a charmer who gets a rush from tightrope walking a high beam on a construction site, yet is prone to bad moods when he fails to remember his own name. He can't resist flirting with the seductive Dr. Bowen, who eagerly leaps past professional boundaries while trying to coax him out of his illness. Wastes the talents of its stars with Gere showy, Olin brittle, and the whole story as contrived as their prefunctory love affair. Psychiatrists are getting as bad a rep professionally as lawyers in their recent film appearances. **110m/C VHS, DVD.** Richard Gere, Lena Olin, Anne Bancroft, Tom Irwin, Delroy Lindo, Bruce Altman, Lauren Tom; ***D:*** Mike Figgis; ***W:*** Michael Cristofer, Eric Roth; ***C:*** Juan Ruiz-Anchia; ***M:*** Maurice Jarre.

Mr. Kingstreet's War 🦴🦴 ½ *Heroes Die Hard* **1971** An idealistic game warden and his wife defend the wildlife of Africa against the fighting Italian and British armies at the dawn of WWII. **92m/C VHS.** John Saxon, Tippi Hedren, Rossano Brazzi, Brian O'Shaughnessy; ***D:*** Percival Rubens.

Mr. Klein 🦴🦴🦴 **1976 (PG)** Cleverly plotted script and fine direction in this dark and intense film about French-Catholic art dealer Robert Klein (Delon), who buys valuables from Jews trying to escape Nazi occupied France in 1942, paying far less than what the treasures are worth. Ironically, he is mistaken for another Robert Klein, a Jew who's wanted for anti-Nazi activities. French with subtitles. **122m/C VHS, DVD.** *FR* Alain Delon, Jeanne Moreau, Suzanne Flon, Michael (Michel) Lonsdale, Juliet Berto, Louis Seigner, Francine Racette, Massimo Girotti; ***D:*** Joseph Losey; ***W:*** Franco Solinas; ***C:*** Gerry Fisher; ***M:*** Egisto Macchi. Cesar '77: Film.

Mister Lonely 🦴 ½ **2007** Former enfant terrible Korine foists this self-conscious cult item about celebrity impersonators on an uncaring public. It begins with a Michael Jackson impersonator (Luna) meeting a Marilyn Monroe impersonator (Morton) who lives with a bunch of other oddballs in a commune in the Scottish Highlands. Michael joins them but there's trouble a-brewing. There's also a bunch of weird scenes involving Herzog as a priest who's running a jungle mission with some nuns. Nah, we didn't get it either. **112m/C DVD.** Diego Luna, Samantha Morton, Denis Lavant, James Fox, Esme Creed-Miles, Anita Pallenberg, Werner Herzog, Melita Morgan, Jason Pennycooke, Richard Strange; ***D:*** Harmony Korine; ***W:*** Harmony Korine, Avi Korine; ***C:*** Marcel Zyskind; ***M:*** Jason Spaceman.

Mr. Love 🦴🦴 ½ **1986 (PG-13)** A meek gardener is perceived by neighbors as a fool until he dies and numerous women arrive for his funeral. Is it his cologne? The radishes? **91m/C VHS.** *GB* Barry Jackson, Maurice Denham, Margaret Tyzack, Linda Marlowe; ***D:*** Roy Battersby; ***M:*** Willy Russell.

Mr. Lucky 🦴🦴🦴 **1943** Likeable wartime drama about a gambler who hopes to swindle a philanthropic organization, but then falls in love and determines to help the group in a fundraising effort. Grant is, no surprise, excellent as the seemingly cynical con artist who actually has a heart of gold. Cliched, but nonetheless worthwhile. Later developed into a TV series. **99m/B VHS, DVD.** Cary Grant, Laraine Day, Charles Bickford, Gladys Cooper, Paul Stewart, Henry Stephenson, Florence Bates; ***D:*** H.C. Potter; ***C:*** George Barnes.

Mr. Magoo 🦴 **1997 (PG)** Ah Magoo, we wish you wouldn't have done it again! Live-action version of the cartoon character popular in the '50s and '60s. Elderly myopic millionaire Quincy Magoo (Nielsen) unwittingly comes into possession of a stolen gem that he gives to his bulldog Angus as a toy. Bumbling government agents and evil arch-criminals are after the gem and Magoo, but he avoids them through luck and bad plot devices. Meanwhile, Magoo is mistaking a mummy's sarcophagus for a phone booth, a riverboat paddle wheel for an escalator and-...well, you get the idea. Nielsen puts a "Naked Gun" spin on Magoo, and that routine is getting a bit stale. Although criticized by some blind groups as an inaccurate portrayal of the visually challenged, after a very brief run in the theatres, no one was able to see it. Opening and closing sequences include animated Magoo bits. **87m/C VHS, DVD.** Leslie Nielsen, Kelly Lynch, Matt Keeslar, Nicholas Chinlund, Ernie Hudson, Malcolm McDowell, Stephen Tobolowsky, Jennifer Garner, Miguel Ferrer; ***D:*** Stanley Tong; ***W:*** Pat Proft, Tom Sherohman; ***C:*** Jingle Ma; ***M:*** Michael Tavera.

Mr. Magorium's Wonder Emporium 🦴🦴 **2007 (G)** Mr. Magorium (Hoffman) is the ageless owner of a magic toy store who's gearing up to retire and wants to turn the store over to his manager Mahoney (Portman), who dreams of being a classical pianist. In the meantime, he hires uptight accountant Henry (Bateman) to assess the value of the store (and perhaps find a little magic in himself). An unapologetically whimsical family movie, it has occasional charming moments but mostly leans on its far superior influences ("Pee-Wee's Big Adventure" and "Willie Wonka and the Chocolate Factory," to name a few) for inspiration, and much of the fairy-tale feel seems forced and unoriginal. **94m/C DVD.** *US* Dustin Hoffman, Natalie Portman, Jason Bateman, Zach Mills; ***D:*** Zach Helm; ***W:*** Zach Helm; ***C:*** Roman Osin; ***M:*** Aaron Zigman, Alexandre Desplat.

Mr. Majestyk 🦴🦴 ½ **1974 (PG)** When a Vietnam veteran's attempt to start an honest business is thwarted by Mafia hitmen and the police, he goes after them with a vengeance. Based on Leonard's novel (he also did the screenplay). **103m/C VHS, DVD.** Charles Bronson, Al Lettieri, Linda Cristal, Lee Purcell; ***D:*** Richard Fleischer; ***W:*** Elmore Leonard; ***M:*** Charles Bernstein.

Mister Mean 🦴 **1977** A man who once worked for a mafia don is now given the task of rubbing him out. For Cosa Nostra diehards and gluttons for Roman scenery. **98m/C VHS.** *IT* Fred Williamson; ***D:*** Fred Williamson.

Mr. Mike's Mondo Video 🦴🦴 **1979 (R)** A bizarre, outrageous comedy special declared too wild for TV and conceived by the "Saturday Night Live" alumnus Mr. Mike. **75m/C VHS.** Michael O'Donoghue, Dan Aykroyd, Jane Curtin, Carrie Fisher, Teri Garr, Joan Haskett, Deborah Harry, Margot Kidder, Bill Murray, Laraine Newman, Gilda Radner, Julius La-Rosa, Paul Shaffer, Sid Vicious; ***W:*** Mitch Glazer.

Mr. Mom 🦴🦴🦴 **1983 (PG)** Tireless auto exec Jack (Keaton) loses his job and stays home with the kids while his wife Caroline (Garr) becomes the breadwinner. He's forced to cope with the rigors of housework and child care, resorting to drugs, alcohol and soap operas. Keaton's hilarious as the home-bound dad chased by killer appliances and poker buddy to the ladies in the neighborhood. **92m/C VHS, DVD.** Jeffrey Tambor, Michael Keaton, Teri Garr, Christopher Lloyd, Martin Mull, Ann Jillian, Edie McClurg, Valri Bromfield; ***D:*** Stan Dragoti; ***W:*** John Hughes; ***C:*** Victor Kemper; ***M:*** Lee Holdridge.

Mr. Moto in Danger Island 🦴🦴 **1939** Mr. Moto (Lorre) is after diamond smugglers (this sounds familiar) in Puerto Rico and is aided by wrestler Twister McGurk (Hymer). 7th in the series. **80m/B DVD.** Peter Lorre, Warren Hymer, Jean Hersholt, Richard Lane, Amanda Duff, Leon Ames, Douglass Dumbrille, Charles D. Brown; ***D:*** Peter Milne; ***W:*** Herbert I. Leeds; ***C:*** Lucien N. Andriot; ***M:*** Samuel Kaylin.

Mr. Moto Takes a Chance 🦴🦴 **1938** Mr. Moto (Lorre), who also works for an international police agency, is told to destroy an armory hidden by a fanatical priest (Regas) in the jungles of Cambodia while also foiling anti-government plots against the French. He's helped by aviatrix (and fellow agent) Vicki Mason (Hudson) as well as a couple of fumbling newsreel photographers, Marty (Kent) and Chick (Chandler). 4th in the series. **63m/B DVD.** Peter Lorre, Rochelle Hudson, Robert Kent, Chick Chandler, George Regas, J. Edward Bromberg, Frederick Vogeding; ***D:*** Norman Foster; ***W:*** Lou Breslow, John Patrick; ***C:*** Virgil Miller; ***M:*** Samuel Kaylin.

Mr. Moto Takes a Vacation 🦴 ½ **1939** Mr. Moto (Lorre) is overseeing security for the priceless crown of the Queen of Sheba, which was discovered in Egypt and is now going on display in a San Francisco museum. Moto postpones his vacation when he believes that master criminal Metaxa is one of many interested in stealing the crown. The last in the Lorre series. **65m/B DVD.** Peter Lorre, Joseph Schildkraut, Lionel Atwill, Virginia Field, Victor Varconi, G.B. Huntley; ***D:*** Norman Foster; ***W:*** Norman Foster, Philip MacDonald; ***C:*** Charles G. Clarke.

Mr. Moto's Gamble 🦴🦴 **1938** Mr. Moto (Lorre) is teaching a class for would-be sleuths and one of his students is Charlie Chan's son, Lee (Luke), who helps out when Moto investigates the murder of a boxer during a fight. Originally intended as a Charlie Chan film that was already in production, the script was rewritten because of Warner Oland's health problems and doesn't quite fit the other Moto adventures. 3rd in the series. **72m/B DVD.** Peter Lorre, Keye Luke, Maxie "Slapsie" Rosenbloom, Lynn Bari, Dick Baldwin, Douglas Fowley, Jayne Regan, Harold Huber, Ward Bond, Lon Chaney Jr.; ***D:*** James Tinling; ***W:*** Charles Belden, Jerome Cady; ***C:*** Lucien N. Andriot; ***M:*** Samuel Kaylin.

Mr. Moto's Last Warning 🦴🦴🦴 **1939** One of the better in the series of Mr. Moto, the wily detective! Lorre is convincing in the title role and gets good support from character villains Carradine and Sanders in this story of saboteurs converging on the Suez Canal plotting to blow up the French Fleet. **71m/B VHS, DVD.** Peter Lorre, George Sanders, Ricardo Cortez, John Carradine, Virginia Field, Robert Coote; ***D:*** Norman Foster.

Mr. Muggs Rides Again 🦴 ½ **1945** The East Side Kids (think Dead End Kids, the Bowery Boys and the rest of their ilk) are featured in a horseracing adventure. Honest jockey Muggs (Gorcey) is framed by gamblers and barred from the track but must still find a way to save the horse farm of Ma Brown (Urecal) from foreclosure. **63m/B VHS.** Leo Gorcey, Minerva Urecal, Huntz Hall, William Benedict, John Duncan, Buddy Gorman, Nancy Brinckman, Mende Koenig; ***D:*** Wallace Fox; ***W:*** Harvey Gates; ***C:*** Ira Morgan.

Mr. Music 🦴🦴 ½ **1950** Crosby is a successful songwriter who would rather enjoy life on the golf course than pen any more tunes. He's persuaded by his secretary to help out an old-time producer who's fallen on hard times by writing a new Broadway show. Light-hearted fluff. Based on the play "Accent on Youth" by Samson Raphaelson which had been filmed in 1935. ♫ Life is So Precious; Accidents Will Happen; High on the List; Wouldn't It Be Funny; Wasn't I There?; Mr. Music; Once More the Blue and White; Milady; Then You'll Be Home. **113m/B VHS.** Bing Crosby, Nancy Olson, Charles Coburn, Robert Stack, Tom Ewell, Ruth Hussey, Charles Kemper, Donald Woods, Gower Champion, Marge Champion; ***Cameos:*** Groucho Marx, Peggy Lee; ***D:*** Richard Haydn.

Mr. Nanny 🦴🦴 **1993 (PG)** For those who fear change, this predictable plot should serve as comforting assurance that Hollywood will still sacrifice substance for the quick buck. Basic storyline has the child-hating Hulkster playing nanny/bodyguard to a couple of bratty kids. Meanwhile, his arch rival (Johansen) hatches a scheme to gain world dominance by kidnapping the kids for the ransom of their father's top secret computer chip. Never fear—in this world, the good guys kick butt, naturally, and everyone learns a lesson. **85m/C VHS, DVD.** Hulk Hogan, Sherman Hemsley, Austin Pendleton, Robert Gorman, Madeline Zima, Mother Love, David Johansen; ***D:*** Michael Gottlieb; ***W:*** Ed Rugoff, Michael Gottlieb; ***M:*** David Johansen, Brian Koonin.

Mr. Nice Guy 🦴 **1986 (PG-13)** In the near future, a hired gun strives for national recognition as the best of his now legitimate profession. Comedy with few laughs. **92m/C VHS.** Jan Smithers, Joe Silver; ***D:*** Henry Wolfond; ***W:*** Michael MacDonald, Henry Wolfond; ***C:*** Leonard Smofsky; ***M:*** Paul Hoffert.

Mr. Nice Guy 🦴🦴 ½ *Yatgo Ho Yan* **1998 (PG-13)** Jackie Chan brings another installment of his Bruce Lee-meets-Charlie Chaplin action adventure shenanigans to the screen. This time he plays a TV cooking show host who gets into boiling water when he saves a female reporter (Fitzpatrick) who has videotaped a drug deal. He ends up with the videotape, so reptilian bad guy Giancarlo (Norton) sends his lackeys out to chop-suey Jackie, though they turn out to be boneless chickens. The high action/low talk meter is cranked up in this outing, due to the fact that it's Chan's first movie filmed primarily in English (although it was still produced in Hong Kong). The plot seems to have been chopped up a bit while travelling over the Pacific, but Chan fans are well aware that the whirling dervish stunts are more important than a silly old story anyway. **90m/C VHS, DVD.** *HK* Jackie Chan, Richard Norton, Gabrielle Fitzpatrick, Miki Lee, Karen McLymont, Vince Poletto, Barry Otto, Sammo Hung; ***D:*** Sammo Hung; ***W:*** Edward Tang, Fibe Ma; ***C:*** Raymond Lam; ***M:*** J. Peter Robinson.

Mr. North 🦴🦴 ½ **1988 (PG)** Capra-corn fable about a charming, bright Yale graduate who encounters admiration and disdain from upper-crust Rhode Island residents when news of his miraculous "cures" spreads. Marks the directorial debut of Danny Huston, son of John Huston, who co-wrote the script and served as executive producer before dying several weeks into shooting. Set in the 1920s and adapted from Thornton Wilder's "Theophilus North." **90m/C VHS, DVD.** Anthony Edwards, Robert Mitchum, Lauren Bacall, Harry Dean Stanton, Anjelica Huston, Mary Stuart Masterson, Virginia Madsen, Tammy Grimes, David Warner, Hunter Carson, Christopher Durang, Mark Metcalf, Katharine Houghton, Christopher Lawford; ***D:*** Danny Huston; ***W:*** John Huston, Janet Roach, James Costigan; ***C:*** Robin Vidgeon; ***M:*** David McHugh.

Mr. Peabody & the Mermaid 🦴🦴 ½ **1948** Lightweight fish story about a middle-aged married man who hooks a beautiful mermaid while fishing in the Caribbean and eventually falls in love with her. Powell is smooth as always, though hampered by the unrestrained absurdity of it all. Based on the novel by Guy and Constance Jones. Also available colorized. **89m/B VHS.** William Powell, Ann Blyth, Irene Hervey, Andrea King, Clinton Sundberg, Art Smith; ***D:*** Irving Pichel; ***W:*** Nunnally Johnson.

Mr. Peek-A-Boo 🦴🦴 ½ *Garou Garou le Passe Muraille* **1950** A French clerk discovers he has the ability to walk through walls. Although friends try to coax him into a life of crime, he instead comes to the aid of an English girl who is being blackmailed. Good-natured French comedy was shot with English dialogue for the American market. **74m/B VHS.** *FR* Joan Greenwood, Andre Bourvil, Marcel Arnold, Roger Treville; ***D:*** Jean Boyer.

Mr. Reeder in Room 13 🦴🦴 **1938** Based on the mystery stories created by Edgar Wallace, Mr. Reeder (a cultured English gentleman who fights crime) enlists the aid of a young man to get evidence on a gang of counterfeiters. **66m/B VHS.** *GB* Gibb McLaughlin, Sally Gray, Malcolm Keen, Peter Murray-Hill, Leslie Perrins, D.J. Williams, Robert Cochran; ***D:*** Norman Lee; ***W:*** Victor Kendall, Doreen Montgomery; ***C:*** Eric Cross.

Mr. Reliable: A True Story 🦴🦴 **1995 (R)** A "truth is stranger than fiction" comedy about Australia's first hostage situation. During the summer of 1968, recently released car thief Wally Mellish (Friels) rents a run-down cottage in a Sydney suburb. He finds a girlfriend in Beryl Muddle (McKenzie), who moves in with her two-year-old daughter. When Wally steals some trifles to brighten up the place, the cops come 'round and Wally, who's still on probation, pulls a gun. The authorities think Beryl and the baby are hostages and are afraid to storm the cottage while the standoff becomes hot media news. Wally and Beryl are thrilled with the attention but there's increasing political pressure to put an end to the farcical situation. **112m/C VHS.** *AU* Colin Friels, Jacqueline McKenzie, Paul Sonkkila, Frank Gallacher, Barry Otto, Lisa Hensley, Ken Radley, Neil Fitzpatrick; ***D:*** Nadia Tass; ***W:*** Terry Hayes, Don Catchlove; ***C:*** David Parker; ***M:*** Phil Judd.

Mr. Rice's Secret 🦴🦴 **2000 (PG)** Mysterious Englishman Mr. Rice (Bowie) lives next door to 13-year-old Owen (Switzer), who has cancer. He's struggling but Mr. Rice offers words of wisdom (that come from the fact he's lived hundreds of years). When Mr. Rice suddenly does die, it's not before letting Owen in on some posthumous life-saving secrets. **113m/C VHS, DVD.** *CA* David Bowie, Garwin Sanford, Bill Switzer, Teryl Rothery; ***D:*** Nicholas (Nick) Kendall; ***W:*** J.H. Wyman; ***C:*** Gregory Middleton; ***M:*** Simon Kendall, Al Rodger.

Mr. Right 🦴🦴 **2006** Gay rom com that finds Louise (Zaris) narrating the love problems of three London couples. Her best friend Alex (de Woolfson) is a working-class actor/caterer who has found security with upper-class reality TV producer Harry (Lance). Art dealer William (Marshall) is falling for soap actor Lawrence (Ockenden) while professionally queer artist Tom (screenwriter Morris) is trying to hold on to hustler Lars (Hart). A disaster of a dinner party forces the couples out of their usual habitues to which they can either comfortably return or break free. **94m/C DVD.** *GB* Luke De Woolfson, James Lance, Rocky Marshall, Leon Ockenden, Benjamin Hart, Georgia Zaris, Maddie Planer, David Morris; ***D:*** David Morris, Jacqui Morris; ***W:*** David Morris, Jacqui Morris; ***C:*** Michael Wood; ***M:*** Jacqueline Kroft.

Mister Roberts 🦴🦴🦴🦴 **1955** Crew of a Navy cargo freighter in the South Pacific during WWII relieves the boredom of duty with a series of elaborate practical jokes, mostly at the expense of their long-suffering and slightly crazy captain, who then determines that he will get even. The ship's cargo officer, Mr. Roberts, longs to be transferred to a fighting vessel and see some action. Originally a hit Broadway play (based on the novel by Thomas Heggen) which also featured Fonda in the title role. Great performance from Lemmon as Ensign Pulver. Powell's last film. Sequelled in 1964 by "Ensign Pulver," and later a short-lived TV series as well as a live TV special. Newly transferred in 1988 from a pristine stereo print. **120m/C VHS, DVD.** Henry Fonda, James Cagney, Jack Lemmon, William Powell, Betsy Palmer, Ward Bond, Harry Carey Jr., Nick Adams, Phil Carey, Ken Curtis, Martin Milner, Jack Pennick, Perry Lopez, Patrick Wayne, Tige Andrews, William Henry; ***D:*** John Ford, Mervyn LeRoy; ***W:*** Frank Nugent, Joshua Logan, Thomas Heggen; ***C:*** Winton C. Hoch; ***M:*** Franz Waxman. Oscars '55: Support. Actor (Lemmon).

Mr. Robinson Crusoe 🦴🦴 ½ **1932** Rollicking adventure in the South Seas as Fairbanks makes a bet that he can live on a desert island for a year without being left any refinements of civilization. Lucky for him, a woman arrives. Also written by Fairbanks. **76m/B VHS, DVD.** Douglas Fairbanks Sr., William Farnum, Maria Alba, Earle Brown; ***D:*** Edward Sutherland; ***W:*** Douglas Fairbanks Sr.; ***M:*** Alfred Newman.

Mr. Rock 'n' Roll: The Alan Freed Story 1/2 **1999** In the early 1950s, Cleveland disc jockey Alan Freed (Nelson) decides to play the newfangled rock 'n' roll on his station, where it becomes an immediate hit and an immediate controversy. Freed's success takes him to New York and further celebrity but career missteps lead to the payola scandal and his eventual disgrace. Original recordings are used and they turn out to be the most exciting thing about this TV movie. Based on the book by John A. Jackson. **91m/C VHS.** Judd Nelson, Madchen Amick, Leon, Paula Abdul; ***Cameos:*** Bobby Rydell, Fabian; ***D:*** Andy Wolk; ***W:*** Matt Dorff; ***C:*** Derick Underschultz. **TV**

Mr. St. Nick 1/2 **2002** Agreeable Christmas comedy with a little twist. It seems that being Santa is a family business—each St. Nick gets 100 years on the job. The current Santa (Durning) should be settling into retirement and leaving things to Santa Jr. (Grammer) soon, but Junior's been waiting so long that he's more bah-humbug than ho-ho-ho. So, it's about time that he learned the true meaning of the holiday. **100m/C DVD.** Kelsey Grammer, Charles Durning, Katherine Helmond, Brian Bedford, Elaine Hendrix, Lupe Ontiveros, Wallace Shawn, Ana Ortiz; ***D:*** Craig Zisk; ***W:*** Maryedith Burrell, Steve Hayes, Debra Frank; ***C:*** David Franco; ***M:*** John Altman. **TV**

Mr. Sardonicus *Sardonicus* **1961** Tidy little horror film finds the title character's (Rolfe) face frozen in a hideous grin after being cursed for stealing a winning lottery ticket from his father's corpse. Sardonicus has been experimenting with solutions to his problem (each more disgusting than the last) and finally forces neurosurgeon, Sir Robert Cargrave (Lewis), to assist him with his dilemma. **89m/B VHS, DVD.** Guy Rolfe, Ronald Lewis, Oscar Homolka, Audrey Dalton, Vladimir Sokoloff; ***D:*** William Castle; ***W:*** Ray Russell; ***C:*** Burnett Guffey; ***M:*** Von Dexter.

Mr. Saturday Night 1/2 **1992 (R)** Crystal, in his directorial debut, stars as Buddy Young Jr., a self-destructive comedian whose career spans five decades. His nasty one-liners and witty jokes combine with poignancy in this satisfying comedy/drama. Paymer is excellent as Young's long-suffering, faithful brother and manager. Watch for Lewis in a cameo role. Expectations were very high and the boxoffice results were disappointing, but fans of Crystal shouldn't miss this one. **118m/C VHS, DVD.** Billy Crystal, David Paymer, Julie Warner, Helen Hunt, Mary Mara, Jerry Orbach, Ron Silver, Sage Allen, Jackie Gayle, Carl Ballantine, Slappy (Melvin) White, Conrad Janis, Jerry Lewis; ***D:*** Billy Crystal; ***W:*** Babaloo Mandel, Lowell Ganz, Billy Crystal; ***C:*** Don Peterman; ***M:*** Marc Shaiman.

Mr. Scarface 1/2 **1977 (R)** A young man searches for the man who murdered his father years earlier in a dark alley. **85m/C VHS, DVD.** Jack Palance, Edmund Purdom, Al Cliver, Harry Baer, Gisela Hahn; ***D:*** Fernando Di Leo.

Mr. Skeffington **1944** A supergrade soap opera spanning 26 years in the life of a ravishing, spoiled New York socialite. The beauty with a fondness for bedrooms marries for convenience, abuses her husband, then enjoys a highly equitable divorce settlement. Years later when diphtheria leaves her totally deformed and no man will have her, she is saved by her former husband. Based on the novel by "Elizabeth" (Mary Annette Beauchamp Russell) and adapted by "Casablanca's" Julius and Philip Epstein. **147m/B VHS, DVD.** Bette Davis, Claude Rains, Walter Abel, Richard Waring, George Coulouris, John Alexander; ***D:*** Vincent Sherman.

Mr. Skitch **1933** Weak Rogers offering. Couple loses their farm and begins cross country jaunt with mishaps at every turn. All ends well when their daughter meets an Army cadet, but few laughs and lots of loose ends. **70m/B VHS.** Will Rogers, Zasu Pitts, Rochelle Hudson, Charles Starrett; ***D:*** James Cruze.

Mr. Smith Goes to Washington **1939** Another classic from Hollywood's golden year of 1939. Jimmy Stewart is an idealistic and naive young man selected to fill in for an ailing Senator. Upon his arrival in the Capitol, he is inundated by a multitude of corrupt politicians. He takes a stand for his beliefs and tries to denounce many of those he feels are unfit for their positions, meeting with opposition from all sides. Great cast is highlighted by Stewart in one of his most endearing performances. Quintessential Capra tale sharply adapted from Lewis Foster's story. Outstanding in every regard. **130m/B VHS, DVD.** James Stewart, Jean Arthur, Edward Arnold, Claude Rains, Thomas Mitchell, Beulah Bondi, Eugene Pallette, Guy Kibbee, Harry Carey Sr., H.B. Warner, Porter Hall, Jack Carson, Charles Lane; ***D:*** Frank Capra; ***W:*** Sidney Buchman; ***M:*** Dimitri Tiomkin. Oscars '39: Story; AFI '98: Top 100, Natl. Film Reg. '89;; N.Y. Film Critics '39: Actor (Stewart).

Mr. Stitch **1995 (R)** Demented scientist (Hauer) plays Frankenstein and makes a creature, named Lazarus (Wheaton), from the body parts of more than 80 men and women. Unfortunately, the sensitive Lazarus has retained the collective memories of all these people and becomes obsessed with finding the reason for his existence. He receives compassion from a shrink (Peeples) but his maker has less-than-honorable plans for Lazarus. **98m/C VHS.** Rutger Hauer, Wil Wheaton, Nia Peeples, Taylor Negron, Ron Perlman, Michael (M.K.) Harris; ***Cameos:*** Tom Savini; ***D:*** Roger Avary; ***W:*** Roger Avary.

Mr. Superinvisible *Mr. Invisible; L'Inafferrabile Invincible* **1973 (G)** Searching to cure the common cold, a bumbling scientist invents a bizarre virus, then strives with his loyal (of course) sheepdog to keep it from falling into the wrong hands. The Disney-like plot, featuring enemy agents and invisibility, may appeal to youngsters. **90m/C VHS.** *IT GE SP* Dean Jones, Ingeborg (Inge) Schoener, Gastone Moschin; ***D:*** Anthony M. Dawson.

Mr. Sycamore 1/2 **1974** A sappy mail carrier escapes his badgering wife by sprouting into a tree. A potentially whimsical piece that wilts. **90m/C VHS.** Jason Robards Jr., Jean Simmons, Sandy Dennis; ***D:*** Pancho Kohner; ***M:*** Maurice Jarre.

Mr. 3000 1/2 **2004 (PG-13)** Lackluster sports comedy follows egotistical Milwaukee Brewers star Stan Ross (Mac), who abruptly quit the team as soon as he got his 3,000 hit. His comfy retirement of 10 years is interrupted when an old record-keeping error is corrected, revealing that Stan only has 2,997 career hits. So, the 47-year-old decides to come back long enough to get those missing hits. He must contend with resentful younger teammates, numerous strikeouts, the accompanying ridicule, and Mo, his beautiful former flame who's now a reporter for ESPN covering his comeback. Mac and Bassett have a lot of charm together but much of the film is predictable, and the on-field action lacks any urgency. **104m/C VHS, DVD.** *US* Bernie Mac, Angela Bassett, Michael Rispoli, Evan Jones, Dondre T. Whitfield, Paul Sorvino, Earl Billings, Christopher Noth, Brian White, Ian Anthony Dale, Amaury Nolasco; ***Cameos:*** Tom Arnold, John Salley; ***D:*** Charles Stone III; ***W:*** Eric Champnella, Keith Mitchell; ***C:*** Shane Hurlbut; ***M:*** John Powell.

Mr. Toad's Wild Ride *The Wind in the Willows* **1996 (PG)** Kenneth Grahame's 1908 children's book gets the Monty Python treatment. Set in Edwardian England, but with a definitely modern slant, Jones' adaptation removes much of the gentle whimsy and replaces it with Pythonesque skits. Mole (Coogan) wakes up one day to find his home being bulldozed by the industrialist weasels who have purchased the property from the motorcar-infatuated Mr. Toad (Jones). Toad keeps selling more land to buy more cars as the weasels take over the area and Toad is sent to jail for reckless driving. Mole, along with friends Rat (Idle) and Badger (Williamson) must help him escape and reclaim his land. Grahame's early 20th century fable railing against modern industrialism's encroachment on the countryside becomes a satire on '90s consumerism and corporate greed. Mighty heady stuff for a kid's movie. **88m/C VHS, DVD.** *GB* Terry Jones, Steve Coogan, Eric Idle, Anthony Sher, Nicol Williamson, John Cleese, Stephen Fry, Bernard Hill, Michael Palin, Nigel Planer, Julia Sawalha, Victoria Wood, Richard James; ***D:*** Terry Jones; ***W:*** Terry Jones; ***C:*** David Tattersall; ***M:*** John Du Prez, Terry Jones.

Mr. Troop Mom 1/2 **2009 (G)** In this Nickelodeon family comedy, widowed lawyer Eddie wants to spend more time with his nine-year-old daughter Naomi so they can bond. When a mom drops out of chaperone duty, Eddie agrees to step in at the Go Girls Jamboree at Running Pines Camp without realizing just what he's letting himself in for. **84m/C DVD.** George Lopez, Daniela Bobadilla, Jane Lynch, Julia Anderson, Elizabeth Thai; ***D:*** William Dear; ***W:*** Thomas Ian Griffith; ***C:*** Ron Stannett; ***M:*** David Kitay. **CABLE**

Mr. Vampire **1986** Undertaker Uncle Kau (Ying) is also a master vampire hunter—necessary when your town is under siege from a vampire army who can make new converts with a single bite. Vampire movie with a Chinese twist combines elements of both comedy and horror, presenting a vampire who comes closer to resembling a corpse, who, when not levitating, hops like a bunny. Chinese with subtitles or dubbed. **99m/C VHS, DVD.** *CH* Moon Lee, Ching-Ying Lam, Ricky Hui, Pauline Wong; ***D:*** Ricky Lau; ***W:*** Roy Szeto; ***C:*** Peter Ngor.

Mr. Walkie Talkie **1952** Tired of a sargeant's jabber-jaws, a soldier requests to be relocated to the front lines, only to find his catty comrade has followed. Set during the Korean War and featuring some truly amusing escapades set between the lulls in the war. **65m/B VHS.** William Tracy, Joseph (Joe) Sawyer, Margia Dean, Robert Shayne, Alan Hale Jr., Russell Hicks; ***D:*** Fred Guiol; ***W:*** George Carleton Brown, Edward E. Seabrook; ***C:*** Walter Strenge; ***M:*** Leo Klatzkin.

Mr. Winkle Goes to War *Arms and the Woman* **1944** A weak, nerdy former banker is drafted for service during WWII and proves himself a hero by bulldozing a Japanese foxhole. Bits of genuine war footage add a measure of realism to an otherwise banal flag-waving comedy that is based on a novel by Theodore Pratt. **80m/B VHS.** Edward G. Robinson, Ruth Warrick, Richard Lane, Robert Armstrong, Ted Donaldson, Richard Gaines, Bob Haymes, Hugh Beaumont, Walter Baldwin, Howard Freeman; ***D:*** Alfred E. Green; ***W:*** Waldo Salt, Louis Solomon; ***C:*** Joseph Walker; ***M:*** Paul Sawtell, Carmen Dragon.

Mr. Wise Guy **1942** The East Side Kids break out of reform school to clear one of the Kids' brother of a murder charge. Typical pre-Bowery Boys vehicle. **70m/B VHS, DVD.** Leo Gorcey, Huntz Hall, Billy Gilbert, Guinn "Big Boy" Williams, Benny Rubin, Douglas Fowley, Ann Doran, Jack Mulhall, Warren Hymer, David Gorcey; ***D:*** William Nigh.

Mr. Wonderful 1/2 **1993 (PG-13)** Bittersweet (rather than purely romantic) look at love and romance. Divorced Con Ed worker Gus (Dillon) is hard up for cash and tries to marry off ex-wife Lee (Sciorra) so he can use her alimony to invest in a bowling alley with his buddies. Routine flick's saved by the cast, who manage to bring a small measure of believability to a transparent plot. This was director Minghella's sophomore effort, between "Truly, Madly, Deeply" and "The English Patient." **99m/C VHS, DVD.** James Gandolfini, Bruce Kirby, Jessica Harper, Bruce Altman, Paul Bates, Matt Dillon, Annabella Sciorra, William Hurt, Mary-Louise Parker, Luis Guzman, Dan Hedaya, Vincent D'Onofrio; ***D:*** Anthony Minghella; ***W:*** Amy Schor, Vicki Polon; ***C:*** Geoffrey Simpson; ***M:*** Michael Gore.

Mr. Wong, Detective **1938** The first in the Mr. Wong series, the cunning detective traps a killer who feigns guilt to throw suspicion away from himself. The plot is loaded with the usual twists and villains. However, Karloff is a standout. **69m/B VHS, DVD.** Boris Karloff, Grant Withers; ***D:*** William Nigh; ***W:*** Houston Branch; ***C:*** Harry Neumann.

Mr. Wong in Chinatown 1/2 **1939** Third of the Mr. Wong series finds James Lee Wong investigating the murder of a wealthy Chinese woman. She had been helping to fund the purchase of airplanes to equip China in its 1930s' struggle with Japan. **70m/B VHS, DVD.** Boris Karloff, Grant Withers, William Royle, Marjorie Reynolds, Peter George Lynn, Lotus Long, Richard Loo; ***D:*** William Nigh.

Mr. Woodcock 1/2 **2007 (PG-13)** Thornton plays yet another misanthropic, nasty tormenter of kids, this time as the world's nastiest (and most unfortunately named) gym teacher Mr. Woodcock. Former student John (Scott) has turned his childhood trauma at Woodcock's hands into a self-help book, and he returns home to discover that his nemesis is now dating his mother Beverly (Sarandon). Vulgar jokes, slapstick, and cruel antics ensue. Thornton phones in a character he's played a million times before, while Scott serves up a meltdown of epic proportions, all leading up to a contrived happy ending that makes any legitimate bite the movie had ring false. Everyone involved should take a lap, and hopefully not come back. **87m/C DVD, Blu-ray Disc.** *US* Billy Bob Thornton, Seann William Scott, Susan Sarandon, Kyley Baldridge, Melissa Sagemiller, Amy Poehler, Melissa Leo, Bill Macy, Ethan Suplett; ***D:*** Craig Gillespie; ***W:*** Michael Carnes, Josh Gilbert; ***C:*** Tami Reiker; ***M:*** Theodore Shapiro.

Mr. Write **1992 (PG-13)** Modest advertising satire mixed with romance. Aspiring writer Charlie (Reiser) decides to make some money by acting in commercials. He falls for ad exec Nicole (Tuck) but there are some complications to be overcome first, including her dim bulb boyfriend and obnoxious father. Adapted from the play by Howard J. Morris. **89m/C VHS.** Paul Reiser, Jessica Tuck, Doug Davidson, Martin Mull, Wendie Jo Sperber, Eddie Barth, Darryl M. Bell, Thomas F. Wilson, Jane Leeves, Calvert Deforest, Ben Stein; ***D:*** Charles Loventhal; ***W:*** Howard J. Morris; ***C:*** Elliot Davis.

Mr. Wrong **1995 (PG-13)** In her feature film debut, DeGeneres plays Martha, a 30-something single woman with wacky friends who's being pressured by parents toward marriage while having little luck in the dating scene. Hmm...sounds familiar. Pullman plays Whitman, her dreamboat who quickly turns into the Titanic. Along the relationship road to ruin she is forced to deal with bad poetry, charades and...gum in her hair!! The usually entertaining DeGeneres is given little to do but react lamely to the wild events going on around her. Those that have had an experience with "the ex that would not go away" might want to rent something more calming, such as "Psycho." **97m/C VHS, DVD.** Ellen DeGeneres, Bill Pullman, Joan Cusack, Dean Stockwell, Joan Plowright, John Livingston, Robert Goulet, Ellen Cleghorne, Brad William Henke, Polly Holliday, Briant Wells; ***D:*** Nick Castle; ***W:*** Chris Matheson, Kerry Ehrin, Craig Munson; ***C:*** John Schwartzman; ***M:*** Craig Safan.

Mistral's Daughter 1/2 **1984** Frothy miniseries, based on the Judith Krantz novel, about a French artist and his relationship with three beautiful women. Formulaic TV melodrama offers sexual scenes and revealing glimpses. Produced, like other Krantz miniseries, by author's hubby, Steve. **390m/C VHS.** Stefanie Powers, Lee Remick, Stacy Keach, Robert Urich, Timothy Dalton; ***D:*** Douglas Hickox; ***M:*** Vladimir Cosma. **TV**

Mistress *Wild Geese* **1953** A classic Japanese period piece about an innocent woman who believes she's married to a ruthless industrialist, only to find he is already married and she is but his mistress. Her love for a medical student unleashes tragedy. Subtly moving in a low-key way; starkly beautiful in black and white. In Japanese, with English subtitles. **106m/B VHS.** *JP* Hideko Takamine, Hiroshi Akutagawa; ***D:*** Shiro Toyoda.

Mistress 1/2 **1987** Weepy melodrama about a woman who makes a living as a mistress. When her lover dies, she must learn to stand on her own two feet. **96m/C VHS.** Victoria Principal, Alan Rachins, Don Murray; ***D:*** Michael Tuchner; ***M:*** Michael Convertino. **TV**

Mistress **1991 (R)** A weak script does in a formidable cast in a behind-the-scenes look at movie making. Wuhl plays Marvin Landisman, a failed director/screenwriter, who's approached by has-been producer Jack Roth (Landau) who says he's found a backer to finance a movie from one of Marvin's old scripts. It turns out Roth has three men (De Niro, Aiello, and Wallach) ready to finance the film as long as each of their mistresses, who all have acting ambitions, gets the starring role. Double-dealing at a bargain basement level sets up the rest of this lifeless comedy. **100m/C VHS, DVD.** Robert Wuhl, Martin Landau, Robert De Niro, Eli Wallach, Danny Aiello, Sheryl Lee Ralph, Jean Smart, Tuesday Weld, Jace Alexander, Laurie Metcalf, Christopher Walken, Ernest Borgnine; *D:* Barry Primus; *W:* J.F. Lawton, Barry Primus; *C:* Sven Kirsten; *M:* Galt MacDermot.

The Mistress of Spices ½ **2005** Beautiful but remarkably inert attempt at magical realism. Tilo (Rai) has second sight and has been taught to use the magic of various spices to help others. She emigrates from India and opens a spice shop in Oakland, but there are three severe restrictions she must follow: she can't use the spices for personal gain; she can't touch the skin of another human being; and she can't ever leave the shop. Tilo seems okay with all this until studly Doug (McDermott) has an accident right outside. She helps him, he helps her, and the spices turn on Tilo (and her clients). Although it hardly seems fair that anyone as luscious as Rai should be held hostage by saffron (which attracts love by the way). **96m/C DVD.** *US GB* Aishwarya Rai, Dylan McDermott, Ayesha Dharker, Nitin Ganatra, Anupam Kher, Adewale Akinnuoye-Agbaje, Sonny Gill Dulay, Padma Lakshmi; *D:* Paul Mayeda Berges; *W:* Paul Mayeda Berges, Gurinder Chadha; *C:* Santosh Sivan; *M:* Craig Pruess.

Mistress of the Apes WOOF! **1979 (R)** A woman searches for her missing husband in Africa with a group of scientists and discovers a tribe of near-men, who may be the missing link in evolution (or perhaps, a professional football team). Into their little group she is accepted, becoming their queen. Buchanan earned his reputation as a maker of horrible films honestly. Includes the songs "Mistress of the Apes" and "Ape Lady." **88m/C VHS.** Jenny Neumann, Barbara Leigh, Garth Pillsbury, Walt Robin, Stuart Lancaster, Suzy Mandel; *D:* Larry Buchanan; *W:* Larry Buchanan.

Mistress of the World **1959** A scientist, aided by Swedish Intelligence agent Ventura, works to protect his gravity-altering invention from Chinese agents. Partly based on a German serial from the silent film era, but not up to director Dieterle's usual fare. A must-see for Ventura fans and Mabuse mavens. **107m/C VHS.** Martha Hyer, Micheline Presle, Gino Cervi, Lino Ventura, Sabu, Wolfgang Preiss; *D:* William Dieterle.

Mistress Pamela ½ **1974 (R)** When young Pamela goes to work in the household of handsome Lord Devonish, he sets about in wild pursuit of her virginity. Loosely based on the 1740 work "Pamela" by Samuel Richardson, considered the first modern English novel. Read the book unless you only have 95 minutes to spend finding out who gets what. **95m/C VHS.** Anne Michelle, Julian Barnes, Anna Quayle, Rosemary Dunham; *D:* Jim O'Connor.

Mistrial **1996 (R)** NYC cop Steve Donohue (Pullman) is incensed when accused cop killer Eddie Rios (Seda) is acquited and Donohue himself is about to be charged in the wrongful deaths of the suspect's wife and brother, which occurred during his pursuit. So he takes the entire courtroom hostage. **90m/C VHS, DVD.** Bill Pullman, Robert Loggia, Jon Seda, Blair Underwood, Casey Siemaszko, Josef Sommer, Roberta Maxwell, James Rebhorn, Leo Burmester, Roma Maffia, Kate Burton; *D:* Heywood Gould; *W:* Heywood Gould; *C:* Paul Sarossy; *M:* Brad Fiedel. **CABLE**

Mists of Avalon **2001** A woman-centric version of the story of Camelot based on Marion Zimmer Bradley's 1982 bestseller. Morgaine (Margulies) is the niece of the Lady of the Lake, Viviane (Huston), who raises her in the mother/goddess religion even as Christianity takes hold of the land. Morgaine is reunited with her half-brother Arthur (Atterton), who is betrothed to the Christian Gwenhwyfer (Mathis), who falls for Arthur's best friend and knight, Lancelot (Vartan). But as the years pass, Viking invasions and familial circumstances threaten to tear Arthur's kingdom apart and Morgaine can only watch as the vision of Avalon disappears as well. **180m/C VHS, DVD.** Julianna Margulies, Anjelica Huston, Samantha Mathis, Edward Atterton, Joan Allen, Michael Vartan, Hans Matheson, Caroline Goodall, Michael Byrne, Clive Russell, Mark Lewis Jones; *D:* Uli Edel; *W:* Gavin Scott; *C:* Vilmos Zsigmond; *M:* Lee Holdridge. **CABLE**

Misty ½ **1961** Based on the Marguerite Henry novel "Misty of Chincoteague." Every year some of the wild ponies who live on the islands off the Virginia coast are rounded up and auctioned off to thin out the herd. Young Paul and Maureen Beebe want to help capture the elusive Phantom so they can buy her, but they discover the mare has had a foal and they name her Misty. Only when the duo comes up for sale, they are bought by someone else. **91m/C DVD.** David Ladd, Pam Smith, Arthur O'Connell, Anne Seymour, Duke Farley; *D:* James B. Clark; *W:* Ted Sherdeman; *C:* Lee Garmes, Leo Tover; *M:* Paul Sawtell, Bert Shefter.

Misunderstood ½ **1984 (PG)** A former black market merchant has to learn how to relate to his sons after his wife dies. The father, now a legitimate businessman, is more concerned with running his shipping business than growing closer to his boys. Fine acting can't overcome a transparent plot. **92m/C VHS.** Gene Hackman, Susan Anspach, Henry Thomas, Rip Torn, Huckleberry Fox; *D:* Jerry Schatzberg; *C:* Pasqualino De Santis.

Misunderstood **1987** A father learns his lonely son is full of love and sensitivity when a tragedy reveals that it is this son who takes the blame for all the wrongs his brother commits. **101m/C VHS.** Anthony Quayle, Stefano Colagrande, Simone Gianozzi, John Sharp; *D:* Luigi Comencini.

Mitchell **1975 (R)** Tough cop battles drug traffic and insipid script. Big screen release with that certain TV look. **90m/C VHS, DVD.** Joe Don Baker, Linda Evans, Martin Balsam, John Saxon, Merlin Olsen, Harold J. Stone, Robert Phillips; *D:* Andrew V. McLaglen; *W:* Ian Kennedy Martin; *C:* Harry Stradling Jr.; *M:* Jerry Styner.

Mixed Blood ½ **1984 (R)** From the renowned underground film-maker, a dark comedy that examines the seedy drug subculture in New York. Violent, fast, and funny. **98m/C VHS, DVD.** Marilia Pera, Richard Ulacia, Linda Kerridge, Geraldine Smith, Angel David; *D:* Paul Morrissey; *W:* Paul Morrissey.

Mixed Nuts *Lifesavers* **1994 (PG-13)** Misfits man a suicide hotline on Christmas Eve in this unfunny, pathetic comedy that's a real downer. Director/writer Ephron (along with her co-writer sister Delia) try way too hard to fashion a hip, racy, madcap farce reminiscent of the screwball comedies that Hollywood churned out in the 1930s and '40s. Film never finds its style and the storyline is very weak. Most of the performances are over the top, although Martin, Shandling, and Kahn are good for a few amusing scenes. Ephron and the cast are capable of doing so much better, it's a shame their talents are virtually wasted here. Adapted from the French film "Le Pere Noel Est une Ordure." **97m/C VHS, DVD.** Steve Martin, Madeline Kahn, Robert Klein, Anthony LaPaglia, Juliette Lewis, Rob Reiner, Adam Sandler, Rita Wilson, Garry Shandling, Liev Schreiber; *D:* Nora Ephron; *W:* Nora Ephron, Delia Ephron; *M:* George Fenton.

Mixing Nia ½ **1998 (R)** Biracial ad exec Nia (Parsons) becomes upset when she is asked to head a new beer campaign aimed at black youth. She quits, and decides to write a novel about the black experience and then realizes that she's lost touch with that part of her heritage. So, Nia decides to regain her roots and finds a real culture clash. **93m/C VHS, DVD.** Karyn Parsons, Isaiah Washington IV, Eric Thal, Diego Serrano, Heidi Schanz, Rosalyn Coleman; *D:* Alison Swan.

M'Lady's Court **1973** A lawyer searching for an heiress in a convent of lusty maidens has loads of fun. None too captivating. **92m/C VHS.** *GE* Gabriele Tinti, Femi Benussi, Sonia Jeanine, Maja Hoppe; *D:* Franz Antel; *W:* Kurt Nachmann; *C:* Siegfried Hold; *M:* Stelvio Cipriani.

Mo' Better Blues ½ **1990 (R)** Not one of his more cohesive or compelling works, Lee's fourth feature is on the surface a backstage jazz biopic. But all Lee features are vitally concerned with complicated racial issues, and though subtle, this is no exception. Bleek Gilliam is a handsome, accomplished jazz trumpeter who divides his limited extra-curricular time between Clarke (newcomer Williams) and Indigo (junior Lee sibling Joie). What's interesting is not so much the story of self-interested musician and ladies' man Gilliam, but the subtle racial issues his life draws into focus. The Branford Marsalis Quartet provides the music for Bleek's group, scored by Lee's dad Bill (on whose life the script is loosely based). **129m/C VHS, DVD.** Denzel Washington, Spike Lee, Joie Lee, Wesley Snipes, Cynda Williams, Giancarlo Esposito, Robin Harris, Bill Nunn, John Turturro, Dick Anthony Williams, Ruben Blades, Nicholas Turturro, Samuel L. Jackson, Abbey Lincoln, Tracy C. Johns, Joe Seneca; *D:* Spike Lee; *W:* Spike Lee; *C:* Ernest R. Dickerson; *M:* Bill Lee, Branford Marsalis.

Mo' Money ½ **1992 (R)** Damon Wayans is a small-time con-artist who is inspired to go straight by a beautiful woman (Dash). He lands a job at the credit card company she works for, but temptation overcomes him, he swipes some plastic, and the scamming begins anew. With the help of his younger brother (played by real-life younger brother Marlon), they get involved in an even bigger, more dangerous scam being operated by the credit card company's head of security. Crude formula comedy driven by energetic, inventive performances by the brothers Wayans. Needless to say, will be especially enjoyed by fans of TV's "In Living Color." **97m/C VHS, DVD.** Damon Wayans, Marlon Wayans, Stacey Dash, Joe Santos, John Diehl, Harry J. Lennix, Mark Beltzman, Quincy Wong, Larry Brandenburg, Almayvonne; *D:* Peter Macdonald; *W:* Damon Wayans; *C:* Don Burgess; *M:* Jay Gruska.

Moana, a Romance of the Golden Age ½ **1926** An early look through American eyes at the society of the people of Samoa, in the Pacific Islands. Picturesque successor to Flaherty's "Nanook of the North." **76m/B VHS.** Ta'avale, Fa'amgase, Moana; *D:* Robert Flaherty.

Mob Boss **1990 (R)** Gangster films spoof starring Hickey as the head of a successful California crime ring. When his beautiful wife conspires to have him killed, he is left just breaths away from his demise. He calls his nerdy son to his bedside to ask him to take over the family business. But this kid thinks that money laundering requires detergent! Take this one down for a walk by the river in its new cement shoes. **93m/C VHS.** Eddie Deezen, Morgan Fairchild, William Hickey, Stuart Whitman; *D:* Fred Olen Ray.

Mob Queen ½ **1998** Dim low-level Brooklyn mobsters George (Proval) and Dip (Moran) want to impress their boss, Joey "The Heart" Aorta (Sirico), by giving him a memorable birthday present. So George sets up a "date" with sexy new prostitute on the docks, Glorice (Cayne). And it works—Joey's smitten by the tough babe and George and Dip figure they're in clover. Until they find out that Glorice is actually a he—and they decide the safest thing would be to end the budding romance before Joey finds out too. Set in 1957. **87m/C VHS.** David Proval, Dan Moran, G. Anthony "Tony" Sirico, Candis Cayne, Marlene Forte, Jerry Grayson, Gerry Cooney; *D:* Jon Carnoy; *W:* Mike Horelick; *C:* Nils Kenaston; *M:* Jonathan Cossu.

Mob Story ½ **1990 (R)** Vernon stars as a big-wig mob boss on the run from the government and a few of his "closest" friends. He plans to disappear into Canada, but if his girl (Kidder) and best friend (Waxman) find him first he'll be traveling in a body-bag. Very silly, but fun. **98m/C VHS, DVD.** John Vernon, Margot Kidder, Al Waxman, Kate Vernon; *D:* Gabriel Markiw, Jancarlo Markiw.

Mob War ½ **1988 (R)** A war breaks out between the head of New York's underworld and a media genius. After deciding to become partners, the "family" tries to take over. For fun, count how many times the word "respect" pops up in the script. Tries hard but fails. **96m/C VHS, DVD.** John Christian, David Henry Keller, Jake LaMotta, Johnny Stumper; *D:* J. Christian Ingvordsen; *W:* J. Christian Ingvordsen, John Weiner; *C:* Steven Kaman.

Mobsters ½ **1991 (R)** It sounded like a great idea, casting the hottest young actors of the '90s as youthful racketeers "Lucky" Luciano, Meyer Lansky, Bugsy Siegel, and Frank Costello. But it would take an FBI probe to straighten out the blood-choked plot, as the pals' loyalties get tested the hard way in a dismembered narrative. Sicker than the violence is a seeming endorsement of the glamorous hoods. **104m/C VHS, DVD, HD DVD.** Joe (Johnny) Viterelli, Christian Slater, Patrick Dempsey, Richard Grieco, Costas Mandylor, Anthony Quinn, F. Murray Abraham, Lara Flynn Boyle, Michael Gambon, Christopher Penn; *D:* Michael Karbelnikoff; *W:* Nicholas Kazan; *C:* Lajos Koltai.

Moby Dick **1956** This adaptation of Herman Melville's high seas saga features Peck as Captain Ahab. His obsession with revenge upon the great white whale, Moby Dick, isn't always believable, but the moments that click make the film more than worthwhile. **116m/C VHS, DVD.** Gregory Peck, Richard Basehart, Orson Welles, Leo Genn, Harry Andrews, Friedrich Ledebur; *D:* John Huston; *W:* Ray Bradbury, John Huston; *C:* Oswald Morris. Natl. Bd. of Review '56: Director (Huston); N.Y. Film Critics '56: Director (Huston).

Moby Dick ½ **1998 (PG)** TV adaptation of Herman Melville's 1851 novel, starring a mesmerizing Stewart as the obsessive peg-legged Captain Ahab. Novice seaman Ishmael (Thomas) signs aboard the whaling ship Pequod, making friends with Polynesian native, harpooner Queequeg (Waretini). Soon enough Ishmael learns about the great white whale who claimed the captain's leg and Ahab's determination to seek revenge on the beast, no matter what the cost to himself, his crew, or the ship. Peck, who starred as Ahab in the 1956 movie version, takes on the role of Jonah-and-the-whale sermonizing Father Mapple. **145m/C VHS, DVD.** Patrick Stewart, Henry Thomas, Ted Levine, Piripi Waretini, Gregory Peck, Bill Hunter, Hugh Keays-Byrne, Norman D. Golden II, Bruce Spence; *D:* Franc Roddam; *W:* Franc Roddam, Anton Diether; *C:* David Connell; *M:* Christopher Gordon. **TV**

Mockery ½ **1927** Chaney plays a peasant working for a Russian countess. He becomes involved in a peasant revolution against the rich and threatens the countess but eventually saves her from the mob. **75m/B VHS, DVD.** Lon Chaney Sr., Barbara Bedford, Ricardo Cortez, Emily Fitzroy; *D:* Benjamin Christiansen.

Mockingbird Don't Sing **2001** Based on the true story of Katie, which came to light in 1970. She is rescued from some 12 years of abuse and isolation imposed by her mentally unbalanced parents. Unable to speak and with no social skills, Katie is little more than a lab rat to a variety of psychologists and doctors who see her more as a case study than a person. Even her caring social worker Sandra (Errico) is unable to beat a system that just offers a different type of abuse to the young girl. **98m/C VHS, DVD.** Tarra Steele, Melissa Errico, Sean Young, Joe Regalbuto, Michael Lerner; *D:* Harry Bromley-Davenport; *W:* Daryl Haney; *C:* Jeff Baustert; *M:* Mark Hart.

The Mod Squad **1999 (R)** Tangled rehash of the '60s series tries very hard to be cool, but ends up as hip as a $2 haircut. Attempts to update the premise, but teen criminals-turned-cops Pete (Ribisi), Linc (Epps), and Julie (Danes) merely look like they're guilty of shoplifting from The Gap and making unwise acting career decisions. They all glower sullenly as they try to crack a convoluted case involving drugs, prostitution and their dead boss Capt. Greer (Farina). Director Silver manages to crush what little dramatic tension was left in the stale script into a bland pulp. This shameless attempt to hijack youth culture in order to sell jeans is just another case of the man trying to keep you down. **94m/C VHS, DVD.** Claire Danes, Giovanni Ribisi, Omar Epps, Dennis Farina, Josh Brolin, Richard Jenkins, Larry Brandenburg, Steve Harris, Sam McMurray, Michael Lerner, Bodhi (Pine) Elfman, Holmes Osborne, Dey

Young, Eddie Griffin, Carmen (Lee) Llywelyn; *D:* Scott Silver; *W:* Scott Silver, Stephen Kay, Kate Lanier; *C:* Ellen Kuras; *M:* B.C. Smith.

Model Behavior ½ **1982** Fresh from college, an aspiring photographer pines for a glamorous model. **86m/C VHS.** Richard Bekins, Bruce Lyons, Cindy Harrel, Anne Marie Howard; *D:* Bud Gardner.

Model Behavior **2000** Shy, boy-friendless, 16-year-old Alex (Lawson) is your typically anguished teen. She wishes she had the life of teen supermodel Janine and gets her chance when the girls accidentally meet and realize they are lookalikes. So they decide to trade places for a week—Alex gets to do fashion shoots, go to parties, and hang-out with fellow model Jason (played by 'N Sync's Timberlake) and Janine gets to go to high school, eat stuff that's bad for her, and laze around. It's kind of a "The Prince and the Pauper" for girls with no one threatening their lives. Based on the book by Michael Levin. **90m/C VHS.** Maggie Lawson, Justin Timberlake, Kathie Lee Gifford, Cody Gifford, Jim Abele, Daniel Clark, Karen Hines, Jesse Nilsson; ***Cameos:*** Vendela Thommessen; *D:* Mark Rosman; *W:* David Kukoff, Matt Roshkow; *C:* Laszlo George; *M:* Eric Colvin. **TV**

Model by Day ½ **1994 (R)** When New York model Janssen's father is murdered, she takes up martial arts training and becomes the vengeful "Lady X." Then she becomes the prime suspect in a murder and finds herself falling for a plainsclothes cop. Fair amount of action, somewhat less exploitive than usual for the genre. **89m/C VHS.** Famke Janssen, Stephen Shellen, Shannon Tweed, Sean Young; *D:* Christian Duguay.

A Model Employee **2002** A modest thriller. Francois Maurey is the owner of a small software company who refuses to sell his latest products to a large American firm. Then Florence is hired and becomes a model employee and the middle-aged Francois is smitten, but Florence is a femme who's definitely fatale. French with subtitles. **88m/C DVD.** *FR* Francois Berleand, Bruno Todeschini, Nicole Calfan, Francois Morel, Delphine Rollin; *D:* Jacques Otmezguine; *W:* Jacques Otmezguine; *C:* Alain Marcoen; *M:* Philippe Rombi.

Model Shop ½ **1969** American film from French director Demy is filled with talky angst and ennui. L.A. architect George (a dull Lockwood), who's about to be drafted, spots beautiful Lola (Aimee) and becomes very interested. The world-weary Frenchwoman is working as a nude pin-up model after being stranded when her husband ran out. **90m/C DVD.** Gary Lockwood, Anouk Aimee, Alexandra Hay, Tom Holland, Carol Cole, Neil Elliot; *D:* Jacques Demy; *W:* Jacques Demy, Adrien (Carole Eastman) Joyce; *C:* Michael Hugo.

The Modern Adventures of Tom Sawyer **1999 (PG)** Title sums it up. Mark Twain's mischevious hero is still getting into trouble only this time in the present-day. Harmless, but insubstantial time-waster tries to capitalize on the enduring popularity of the character. **92m/C VHS, DVD.** Laraine Newman, Erik Estrada, David Lander, Phillip Van Dyke, Bethany Richards, Adam Dior; *D:* Adam Weissman; *W:* Adam Weissman; *C:* Howard Wexler; *M:* Kristopher Carter. **VIDEO**

A Modern Affair ½ *Mr. 247* **1994 (R)** Single executive Grace Rhodes' (Eichorn) biological clock is ringing and without Mr. Right in sight, she decides to visit a sperm bank. Grace gets pregnant and also very curious about her anonymous donor—who of course doesn't stay anonymous. Grace even manages to fall for photographer Peter Kessler (Tucci) but how does she tell him she's carrying his baby when they haven't even had sex yet? **91m/C VHS.** Lisa Eichhorn, Stanley Tucci, Caroline Aaron, Tammy Grimes, Robert Joy, Wesley Addy, Cynthia Martells, Mary Jo Salerno; *D:* Vern Oakley; *W:* Paul Zimmerman; *C:* Rex Nicholson; *M:* Jan Hammer.

Modern Girls ½ **1986 (PG-13)** Teen comedy about three bubble-headed LA rock groupies and their various wild adventures during a single night on the town. Surprising in that the three lead actresses waste their talents in this lesson in exploitation. Bruce Springsteen's younger sister portrays a drug user. **82m/C VHS.** Cynthia Gibb, Daphne Zuniga, Virginia Madsen; *D:* Jerry Kramer; *W:* Laurie Craig; *M:* Eddie Arkin.

Modern Love **1990 (R)** An average slob realizes that marriage, fatherhood and in-law-ship isn't quite what he expected. Benson stars, directs and produces as well as co-starring with real-life wife DeVito. A plotless hodgepodge of bits that were more successful in "Look Who's Talking" and "Parenthood." **89m/C VHS, DVD.** Robby Benson, Karla DeVito, Rue McClanahan, Kaye Ballard, Frankie Valli, Cliff Bemis, Louise Lasser, Burt Reynolds, Lyric Benson; *D:* Robby Benson; *W:* Robby Benson.

Modern Problems **1981 (PG)** A man involved in a nuclear accident discovers he has acquired telekinetic powers, which he uses to turn the tables on his professional and romantic rivals. A fine cast but an unsuccessful fission trip. **93m/C VHS, DVD.** Chevy Chase, Patti D'Arbanville, Mary Kay Place, Brian Doyle-Murray, Nell Carter, Dabney Coleman; *D:* Ken Shapiro.

Modern Romance **1981 (R)** The romantic misadventures of a neurotic film editor who is hopelessly in love with his girlfriend but can't seem to maintain a normal relationship with her. Smart and hilarious at times and always simmering with anxiety. Offers an honest look at relationships as well as an accurate portrait of filmmaking. **102m/C VHS, DVD.** Albert Brooks, Kathryn Harrold, Bruno Kirby, George Kennedy, James L. Brooks, Bob Einstein; *D:* Albert Brooks; *W:* Albert Brooks, Monica Johnson.

Modern Times **1936** This "mostly" silent film finds Chaplin playing a factory worker who goes crazy from his repetitious job on an assembly line and his boss's demands for greater speed and efficiency. Ultimately encompassing the tyranny of machine over man, this cinematic masterpiece has more relevance today than ever. Chaplin wrote the musical score which incorporates the tune "Smile." Look for a young Gloria De Haven as one of Goddard's sisters; she's the real-life daughter of Chaplin's assistant director. **87m/B VHS, DVD.** Charlie Chaplin, Paulette Goddard, Henry Bergman, Stanley Sandford, Gloria De Haven, Chester Conklin; *D:* Charlie Chaplin; *W:* Charlie Chaplin; *C:* Ira Morgan, Roland H. Totheroh; *M:* Charlie Chaplin. AFI '98: Top 100, Natl. Film Reg. '89.

Modern Vampires ½ *Revenant* **1998 (R)** Think vampire-lite. A community of European vamps have moved to L.A., where the beautiful Nico (Wagner) is threatening their anonymity by her bloody kills. Dallas (Van Dien), Nico's vampire boyfriend, tries to protect her from Dracula (Pastorelli), who wants her destroyed. Meanwhile, vampire hunter Van Helsing (Steiger) seeks to get rid of the entire community. **95m/C VHS, DVD.** Casper Van Dien, Natasha Gregson Wagner, Rod Steiger, Robert Pastorelli, Kim Cattrall, Natasha Andreichenko, Gabriel Casseus, Udo Kier, Natasha Lyonne; *D:* Richard Elfman; *W:* Matthew Bright; *M:* Danny Elfman, Michael Wandmacher.

The Moderns **1988 (R)** One of the quirkier directors around, this time Rudolph tries a comedic period piece about the avant-garde art society of 1920s Paris. Fleshed out with some familiar characters (Ernest Hemingway, Gertrude Stein) and some strange art-world types. The tone is not consistently funny but, instead, romantic as the main characters clash over art and love. **126m/C VHS, DVD.** Keith Carradine, Linda Fiorentino, John Lone, Genevieve Bujold, Geraldine Chaplin, Wallace Shawn, Kevin J. O'Connor; *D:* Alan Rudolph; *W:* Alan Rudolph; *M:* Mark Isham. L.A. Film Critics '88: Support. Actress (Bujold).

Modesty Blaise ½ **1966** Adaptation of Peter O'Donnell's comic strip finds his tough British babe spy embodied by Italian beauty Vitti, aided by her right-hand man Willie Garvin (Stamp). The secret agent is watching out for a diamond shipment, which is the target of her archrival Gabriel (Bogarde). Very campy and '60s pop-arty, with everyone having fun and not taking any situation seriously. O'Donnell retired himself and Modesty in 2001. **118m/C VHS, DVD.** *GB* Monica Vitti, Terence Stamp, Dirk Bogarde, Harry Andrews, Michael Craig, Clive Revill, Alexander Knox, Rossella Falk; *D:* Joseph Losey; *W:* Evan Jones; *C:* Jack Hildyard; *M:* John Dankworth.

Modigliani ½ *Montparnasse 19; The Lovers of Montparnasse; Modigliani of Montparnasse* **1958** Life of dissolute 19th-century painter Modigliani (Philipe), which tracks his affairs with British poet Beatrice Hastings (Palmer) and later mistress Jeanne (Aimee), who commits suicide shortly before his death. Female performances make up for the lackluster lead. Becker inherited the film from director Max Ophuls, who co-wrote the screenplay but who died before the start of production. In French with English subtitles. **110m/B VHS.** *FR* Gerard Philipe, Lilli Palmer, Anouk Aimee, Gerard Sety, Lino Ventura, Lila Kedrova, Lea Padovani; *D:* Jacques Becker; *W:* Max Ophuls, Henri Jeanson, Jacques Becker.

Modigliani **2004 (R)** Garcia is miscast as debauched Italian Jewish artist Amedeo Modgliani, who's living it up in Paris, circa 1919, and having a tragic love affair with his beautiful Catholic mistress, Jeanne (Zylberstein), who leaves her family for him. Writer/director Davis invents a feud between Modigliani and a glowering Picasso (Djalili) to further liven up the action. It doesn't work and neither does the film, which is almost a melodramatic parody of screen bios about the art world. **128m/C DVD.** *FR IT RO GE GB US* Andy Garcia, Elsa Zylberstein, Omid Djalili, Hippolyte Girardot, Udo Kier, Peter Capaldi, Miriam Margolyes, Eva Herzigova, Susie Amy, Louis Hilyer, Stevan Rimkus, Dan Astileanu, George Ivascu, Michelle Newell, Frederico Ambrosino, Irina Dinescu, Theodor Danetti, Ion Siminie, Lance Henriksen, Beatrice Chiriac; *D:* Mick Davis; *W:* Mick Davis; *C:* Emmanuel (Manu) Kadosh; *M:* Guy Farley.

Mogambo **1953** Remake of "Red Dust," this is the steamy story of a love triangle between an African game hunter, a proper British lady, and an American showgirl in the jungles of Kenya. **115m/C VHS, DVD.** Clark Gable, Ava Gardner, Grace Kelly, Donald Sinden, Philip Stainton, Eric Pohlmann, Denis O'Dea; *D:* John Ford; *W:* John Lee Mahin; *C:* Robert L. Surtees. Golden Globes '54: Support. Actress (Kelly).

The Moguls *The Amateurs* **2005 (R)** Good cast is wasted in a lame comedy about middle-aged small-town guys who decide to make their own porn flick. Genial loser Andy (Bridges) comes up with the initial idea and gets local video store clerk Emmett (Fugit) to operate the camera while closeted Moose (Danson) offers to be the on-camera stud, and the appropriately nicknamed Some Idiot (Pantoliano) is writer-director. Other pals fill in as needed. One-note joke with equally one-note roles for the women involved. **100m/C DVD, HD DVD.** *GB US* Jeff Bridges, Ted Danson, William Fichtner, Patrick Fugit, Tim Blake Nelson, Joe Pantoliano, Glenne Headly, Lauren Graham, Jeanne Tripplehorn, Valerie Perrine, Isaiah Washington IV; *D:* Michael Traeger; *W:* Michael Traeger; *C:* Denis Maloney; *M:* Nicolas Tenbroek.

Mohawk ½ **1956** A cowboy and his Indian maiden try to stop a war between Indian tribes and fanatical landowners. **80m/C VHS, DVD.** Rita Gam, Neville Brand, Scott Brady, Lori Nelson; *D:* Kurt Neumann; *W:* Maurice Geraghty, Milton Krims; *C:* Karl Struss; *M:* Edward L. Alperson Jr.

Mojave Moon ½ **1996 (R)** Middle-aged car dealer Al (Aiello) is asked by nymphet Ellie (Jolie) to drive her home—a trailer in the desert where Al meets her perky-yet-kinky mom Julie (Archer) and Julie's violent boyfriend Boyd (Biehn). A series of strange happenings finds Al tied to the trio and discovering both adventure and romance. **95m/C VHS, DVD.** Danny Aiello, Anne Archer, Angelina Jolie, Michael Biehn, Alfred Molina; *D:* Kevin Dowling; *W:* Leonard Glasser; *C:* James Glennon.

Mole Men Against the Son of Hercules **1961** Italian muscleman Maciste battles the pale-skinned denizens of an underground city. **99m/C VHS.** *IT* Moira Orfei, Raffaella Carra, Paul Wynter, Enrico Glori, Roberto Miali, Mark Forest; *D:* Antonio Leonviola; *W:* Marcello Baldi, Giuseppe Mangione; *C:* Alvaro Mancori; *M:* Armando Trovajoli.

The Mole People **1956** A really bad '50s creature feature which finds two archeologists accidentally discovering an underground civilization of albinos who shun all forms of light. They've also enslaved the local populace of half-human, half-mole creatures who decide to help the good guys escape by rising up in a revolt against their evil masters. When the weapon of choice is a flashlight you know not to expect much. **78m/B VHS, DVD.** John Agar, Cynthia Patrick, Hugh Beaumont, Alan Napier, Nestor Paiva, Phil Chambers; *D:* Virgil W. Vogel; *W:* Laszlo Gorog.

Moliere **2007** Bittersweet costume farce that explores the lost months in 1644 between the French satirist's release from prison and his return to Paris. In order to avoid his creditors, Moliere (Duris) agrees to board at the home of wealthy bourgeois Jourdain (Luchini) who wants acting lessons so he can perform in a play he has written to impress the marquise Celimere (Sagnier). Meanwhile, Moliere flirts with Jourdain's wife Elmire (Morante) and she returns his interest, although she thinks his name is Tartuffe. French with subtitles. **120m/C DVD.** *FR* Romain Duris, Laura Morante, Fabrice Luchini, Ludivine Sagnier, Edouard Baer, Fanny Valette, Gilian Petrovsky, Gonzague Requillart; *D:* Laurent Tirard; *W:* Gregoire Vigneron; *C:* Gilles Henry; *M:* Frederic Talgorn.

Moll Flanders ½ **1996 (PG-13)** Writer/director Densham takes only the title character and the 18th-century London setting from Daniel Defoe's 1722 novel in telling of spirited heroine Moll Flanders' (Wright) life. Orphaned Moll eventually finds herself working at the brothel of greedy, scheming Mrs. Allworthy (Channing). Her life as a prostitute leads her to drink and near suicide—despite the unwavering friendship of Hibble (Freeman), Allworthy's dignified servant—until she falls for an impoverished artist (Lynch) and briefly finds happiness. Wright's heartfelt performance holds everything together (with help from a talented supporting cast) but things get dreary. **120m/C VHS, DVD.** Robin Wright Penn, Morgan Freeman, Stockard Channing, John Lynch, Brenda Fricker, Aisling Corcoran, Geraldine James, Jim Sheridan, Jeremy Brett, Britta Smith, Ger Ryan; *D:* Pen Densham; *W:* Pen Densham; *C:* David Tattersall; *M:* Mark Mancina.

Moll Flanders ½ *The Fortunes and Misfortunes of Moll Flanders* **1996** Rousing, bawdy retelling of Daniel Defoe's 1722 novel about the wickedly seductive Moll (Kingston). Born in London's Newgate prison, Moll becomes a house servant, embarks on her first marriage, is soon widowed, and decides to make her own way (and fortune). She becomes a thief, a whore, marries several more times, and eventually winds up back in prison and a likely candidate for the gallows. But the ever-enterprising Moll always finds her way. TV miniseries on two cassettes. **210m/C VHS, DVD.** *GB* Alex Kingston, Daniel Craig, Diana Rigg, Colin Buchanan, Christopher Fulford, James Fleet, Ian Driver, Tom Ward; *D:* David Attwood; *W:* Andrew Davies; *C:* Ivan Strasburg; *M:* Jim Parker. **TV**

Molly **1999 (PG-13)** Sounds like a ripoff of 1968's "Charly," which was more successful and sensitive. Molly (Shue) is a mentally challenged woman who undergoes experimental surgery which leaves her functionally normal—temporarily. She begins to gain overly powerful senses and sex drive, leading her to have an affair with fellow patient Sam (Jane). As her brain rejects the cells from the operation, she sinks back into the fog of her previous illness. Her brother Buck (Eckhart) goes from apathetic to overprotective seemingly overnight. He also begins a relationship with Molly's surgeon Susan (Hennessy) without any initial romantic foundations being shown. While Shue's performance is fairly good, the horrible editing and ill-conceived storyline doom this would-be drama. **87m/C VHS, DVD.** Elisabeth Shue, Aaron Eckhart, Jill(ian) Hennessey, Thomas Jane, D.W. Moffett, Elizabeth Mitchell, Robert Harper, Elaine Hendrix, Michael Paul Chan, Lucy Liu; *D:* John Duigan; *W:* Dick Christie; *C:* Gabriel Beristain; *M:* Trevor Jones.

Molly and Gina **1994 (R)** The very different lives of Molly and Gina intersect suddenly when their boyfriends are killed in the street by gunfire. They are drawn into the underworld of gun-runners and violence, as they seek justice for the men they loved. **90m/C VHS.** Frances Fisher, Natasha Gregson Wagner, Bruce Weitz, Stella Stevens, Peter

Fonda; *D:* Paul Leder; *W:* Reuben Leder; *M:* Dana Walden.

Molly & Lawless John 🦴🦴 **1972** Average western, with Miles the wife of a sadistic sheriff who helps a prisoner escape the gallows so they can run away together. Enough cliches for the whole family to enjoy. **90m/C VHS, DVD.** Sam Elliott, Vera Miles; *D:* Gary Nelson.

Molly Maguires 🦴🦴 ½ **1970 (PG)** Dramatization based on a true story, concerns a group of miners called the Molly Maguires who resort to using terrorist tactics in their fight for better working conditions during the Pennsylvania Irish coal mining rebellion in the 1870s. During their reign of terror, the Mollies are infiltrated by a Pinkerton detective who they mistakenly believe is a new recruit. It has its moments but never fully succeeds. Returned less than 15% of its initial $11 million investment. **123m/C VHS, DVD.** Sean Connery, Richard Harris, Samantha Eggar, Frank Finlay; *D:* Martin Ritt; *W:* Walter Bernstein; *C:* James Wong Howe; *M:* Henry Mancini.

The Mollycoddle 🦴🦴 **1920** Fairbanks is a British-educated American whom everyone thinks is less-than-manly until he brings a smuggler to justice. **86m/B VHS.** Douglas Fairbanks Sr., Wallace Beery, Ruth Renick; *D:* Victor Fleming; *W:* Douglas Fairbanks Sr.

Molokai: The Story of Father Damien 🦴🦴 ½ **1999** In the 19th century, the government sent suspected lepers to the island of Molokai in an effort to stop the spread of infection. The inhabitants were dependant on the efforts of the church to ease their suffering. Father Damien (Wenham) volunteers to go to the island to provide spiritual and physical comfort and care, even at the risk of contracting the disease himself. Based on a true story. **112m/C VHS, DVD.** Jan Decleir, David Wenham, Derek Jacobi, Alice Krige, Kris Kristofferson, Peter O'Toole, Sam Neill, Leo McKern, Tom Wilkinson; *D:* Paul Cox; *W:* John Briley; *M:* Wim Mertens. **VIDEO**

Mom WOOF! **1989 (R)** When his mother is bitten by a flesh-eater, Clay Dwyer is at a loss as to what to do. How do you tell your own mother that she must be destroyed, lest she continue to devour human flesh? A campy horror/comedy. **95m/C VHS.** Mark Thomas Miller, Art Evans, Mary (Elizabeth) McDonough, Jeanne Bates, Brion James, Stella Stevens, Claudia Christian; *D:* Patrick Rand.

Mom & Dad 🦴🦴 **1947** An innocent young girl's one night of passion leads to an unwanted pregnancy. Stock footage of childbirth and a lecture on the evils of syphilis concludes this campy schlock that features the national anthem. Banned or denied release for years, this movie is now a cult favorite for its time-capsule glimpse at conventional 1940s sexual attitudes. **97m/B VHS.** Hardie Albright, Sarah Blake, George Eldredge, June Carlson, Jimmy Clark, Bob Lowell; *D:* William Beaudine; *W:* Mildred Horn; *C:* Barney A. Sarecky.

Mom and Dad Save the World 🦴 ½ **1992 (PG)** A suburban housewife (Garr) is transported along with her husband in the family station wagon to the planet Spengo, ruled by King Tod Spengo (Lovitz), who has fallen in love with her and wants to save her from his plans to blow up Earth. While trying to prevent the king from marrying her and killing him, Garr and Jones wind up in many goofy situations and wind up saving the Earth from its imminent doom. Uninspired comedy just isn't funny, and the excellent cast is misused, especially Idle and Shawn. Save this one for the kiddies. **87m/C VHS, DVD.** Teri Garr, Jeffrey Jones, Jon Lovitz, Eric Idle, Wallace Shawn, Dwier Brown, Kathy Ireland, Thalmus Rasulala; *D:* Greg Beeman; *M:* Jerry Goldsmith.

Mom, Can I Keep Her? 🦴 ½ **1998 (PG)** Goofy family film features 12-year-old Timmy who's having problems at school and at home with a too-busy father and a new stepmom. But that's nothing compared to the new friend that follows Timmy home—a 500 lb. gorilla. **90m/C VHS, DVD.** Gil Gerard, Kevin Dobson, Terry Funk, Justin Berfield, Alana Stewart, Henry Darrow, Don Mcleod; *D:* Fred Olen Ray; *W:* Sean O'Bannon; *C:* Jesse Weathington. **VIDEO**

Mom, the Wolfman and Me 🦴🦴 ½ **1980** An 11-year-old girl arranges and manages the love affair of her mother, an ultra-liberated photographer, and an unemployed teacher, who is also the owner of an Irish wolfhound. Charming adaptation of a novel by Norma Klein. **100m/C VHS.** Patty Duke, David Birney, Danielle Brisebois, Keenan Wynn, Viveca Lindfors, John Lithgow; *D:* Edmond Levy. **TV**

Moment to Moment 🦴🦴 ½ **1966** Standard romantic suspenser set on the French Riviera. Kay Stanton (Seberg) is being neglected by her shrink hubby Neil (Hill). So she decides to fool around with young Navy stud Mark (Garrison). Only she accidentally shoots him during a quarrel and then asks her best pal, Daphne (Blackman), to help her get rid of the body. Only Mark isn't so dead after all. **108m/C VHS.** Jean Seberg, Arthur Hill, Honor Blackman, Sean Garrison, Gregoire Aslan; *D:* Mervyn LeRoy; *W:* John Lee Mahin, Alec Coppel; *C:* Harry Stradling Sr.; *M:* Henry Mancini.

Momentum 🦴🦴 **2003** Although reluctant to use his unwanted telekinetic powers, physics professor Zach Shefford (McCouch) agrees to help FBI agent Raymond Addison (Gossett Jr.) by going undercover in a gang of telekinetic troublemakers. But things get a little blurry when he learns that the group's leader Adrian Greer (Massee) was once part of a government project that went fatally awry at the hands of Addison. Meanwhile another agent (a wickedly fun Hatcher) tails both Shefford and Addison. Created for cable's Sci-Fi Channel. **97m/C VHS, DVD.** Louis Gossett Jr., Teri Hatcher, Grayson McCouch, Michael Massee, Nicki Aycox, Daniel Dae Kim; *D:* James Seale; *W:* Deverin Karol; *C:* Maximo Munzi; *M:* Joseph Williams. **CABLE**

Mommie Dearest 🦴🦴 **1981 (PG)** Film based on Christina Crawford's memoirs of her incredibly abusive and violent childhood at the hands of her adoptive mother, actress Joan Crawford. The story is controversial and sometimes trashy, but fairly well done nevertheless. However, it is also so campy and the immortal Crawford/Dunaway screech "No wire hangers—ever!" became so associated with Dunaway's over-the-top performance that it was thought by some to have damaged the actress's career. **129m/C VHS, DVD.** Faye Dunaway, Diana Scarwid, Steve Forrest, Mara Hobel, Rutanya Alda, Harry Goz, Howard da Silva; *D:* Frank Perry; *W:* Frank Perry, Robert Getchell, Frank Yablans; *C:* Paul Lohmann; *M:* Henry Mancini. Golden Raspberries '81: Worst Picture, Worst Actress (Dunaway), Worst Support. Actor (Forrest), Worst Support. Actress (Scarwid), Worst Screenplay.

Mommy 🦴🦴 ½ **1995** Schoolteacher is stalked by murderous mom who'll do anything for her daughter. Mommy McCormack was the original "Bad Seed" child. Filmed in Muscatine, Iowa. **89m/C VHS, DVD.** Patty McCormack, Majel Barrett, Jason Miller, Brinke Stevens, Rachel Lemieux, Mickey Spillane, Michael Cornelison, Sarah Jane Miller; *D:* Max Allan Collins; *W:* Max Allan Collins; *C:* Phillip W. Dingeldein; *M:* Richard Lowry.

Mommy 2: Mommy's Day 🦴🦴 ½ **1996** Murderous Mommy (McCormack) returns as does her beloved daughter (now rebellious teenager), Jessica Ann (Lemieux). Mommy's on Death Row, awaiting execution after her murder spree but the Mommy-style killings continue. Shot on location in Iowa. **89m/C VHS, DVD.** Patty McCormack, Rachel Lemieux, Brinke Stevens, Michael Cornelison, Sarah Jane Miller, Mickey Spillane, Gary Sandy, Paul Petersen, Arlen Dean Snyder, Todd Eastland, Del Close; *D:* Max Allan Collins; *W:* Max Allan Collins; *C:* Phillip W. Dingeldein; *M:* Richard Lowry.

Mom's Outta Sight 🦴 **2001 (PG)** Substandard kiddie SF comedy exudes cheapness. Special effects and props are bargain-basement material. The story has something to do with a matter transmission machine that turns a sexy woman into a mincing man and makes another (Williamson) invisible. The only redeeming feature is an all-too-brief cameo by Brinke Stevens. **89m/C VHS, DVD.** Hannes Jaenicke, Melissa Williamson, Steve Scionti, Ariauna Albright, Brinke Stevens; *D:* Stewart Peter; *W:* Sean O'Bannon; *C:* Theo Angell; *M:* Jay Bolton. **VIDEO**

Mon Amie Max 🦴🦴 **1994** Marie-Alexandrine (Max) Babant (Bujold) is a middle-aged former pianist who returns to her native Quebec City after 25 years of self-imposed exile. Pregnant at 15, Max was forced to give her son up for adoption and ran away from friends and family. Now, she's meet former best friend Catherine (Keller), who's had the concert career Max never did, who's also agreed to help Max find her son. Slow-going melodrama with little emotional impact. **107m/C VHS.** *CA FR* Genevieve Bujold, Marthe Keller, Michel Rivard, Johanne McKay; *D:* Michel Brault; *W:* Jefferson Lewis.

Mon Homme 🦴🦴 *My Man* **1996** Marie's (Grinberg) a very happy hooker (think male fantasy) whose kindly impulses wind up getting her into difficulty. She picks up the homeless Jeannot (Lanvin), invites him in for a meal, offers him sex, and is enthralled by his unexpected prowess. Marie decides Jeannot should become her pimp but, unfortunately for her, he takes to his new job with great zeal, seducing manicurist Sanguine (Bruni-Tedeschi) as another lover/prostitute. But when Jeannot gets arrested, his two women decide to abandon him and turn respectable. Nothing exactly works out. French with subtitles. **95m/C VHS.** *FR* Anouk Grinberg, Gerard Lanvin, Valeria Bruni-Tedeschi, Olivier Martinez; ***Cameos:*** Mathieu Kassovitz, Jean-Pierre Leaud; *D:* Bertrand Blier; *W:* Bertrand Blier; *C:* Pierre Lhomme.

Mon Oncle 🦴🦴🦴🦴 *My Uncle; My Uncle, Mr. Hulot* **1958** Tati's celebrated comedy contrasts the simple life of Monsieur Hulot with the technologically complicated life of his family when he aids his nephew in war against his parents' ultramodern, push-button home. An easygoing, delightful comedy, this is the director's first piece in color. Sequel to "Mr. Hulot's Holiday," followed by "Playtime." In French with English subtitles. **110m/C VHS, DVD.** *FR* Jacques Tati, Jean-Pierre Zola, Adrienne Serrantie, Alain Bacourt; *D:* Jacques Tati; *W:* Jacques Lagrange, Jacques Tati; *C:* Jean (Yves, Georges) Bourgoin; *M:* Alain Romans, AMG. Oscars '58: Foreign Film; Cannes '58: Grand Jury Prize; N.Y. Film Critics '58: Foreign Film.

Mon Oncle Antoine 🦴🦴🦴 ½ **1971** A splendid tale of young Benoit, who learns about life from a surprisingly compassionate uncle, who works as everything from undertaker to grocer in the depressed area where they live. **104m/C VHS, DVD.** *CA* Jean Duceppe, Olivette Thibault; *D:* Claude Jutra.

Mon Oncle d'Amerique 🦴🦴🦴 ½ *Les Somnambules* **1980 (PG)** Three French characters are followed as they try to find success of varying kinds in Paris, interspersed with ironic lectures by Prof. Henri Laborit about the biology that impels human behavior. Their disappointments lead them to dream of a legendary American uncle, who could make their desires come true. An acclaimed, witty comedy by former Nouvelle Vague filmmaker, dubbed into English. **123m/C VHS, DVD.** *FR* Gerard Depardieu, Nicole Garcia, Roger-Pierre, Marie DuBois; *D:* Alain Resnais; *W:* Jean Gruault; *C:* Sacha Vierny; *M:* Arie Dzierlatka. Cannes '80: Grand Jury Prize; N.Y. Film Critics '80: Foreign Film.

Mona Lisa 🦴🦴🦴 ½ **1986 (R)** Jordan's wonderful, sad, sensitive story of a romantic, small-time hood who gets personally involved with the welfare and bad company of the high-priced whore he's been hired to chauffeur. Hoskins is especially touching and Caine is chilling as a suave gangster. Fine film debut for Tyson. Brilliantly filmed and critically lauded. **104m/C VHS, DVD.** *GB* Bob Hoskins, Cathy Tyson, Michael Caine, Clarke Peters, Kate Hardie, Robbie Coltrane, Zoe Nathenson, Sammi Davis, Rod Bedall, Joe Brown, Pauline Melville; *D:* Neil Jordan; *W:* David Leland, Neil Jordan; *C:* Roger Pratt; *M:* Michael Kamen. British Acad. '86: Actor (Hoskins); Cannes '86: Actor (Hoskins); Golden Globes '87: Actor—Drama (Hoskins); L.A. Film Critics '86: Actor (Hoskins), Support. Actress (Tyson); N.Y. Film Critics '86: Actor (Hoskins); Natl. Soc. Film Critics '86: Actor (Hoskins).

Mona Lisa Smile 🦴🦴 ½ **2003 (PG-13)** Julia Roberts is Katherine Watson, an art history professor from California who takes a position at Wellesley College, an all girl college of impeccable standing. Watson, of course, wants to enlighten her students to the possibilities that lay outside of their safe, WASPish upbringing and expectations. You've seen the "Maverick-teacher-tries-to-inspire-the-complacent" plot before (think "Dead Poet's Society" on estrogen), and really there's nothing new here but the gender. Strong ensemble cast doesn't have much to work with. **117m/C DVD.** *US* Julia Roberts, Kirsten Dunst, Julia Stiles, Maggie Gyllenhaal, Ginnifer Goodwin, Juliet Stevenson, Dominic West, Topher Grace, John Slattery, Marcia Gay Harden, Jordan Bridges, Marian Seldes, Donna Mitchell, Terence Rigby; *D:* Mike Newell; *W:* Larry Konner, Mark Rosenthal; *C:* Anastas Michos; *M:* Rachel Portman.

Monaco Forever 🦴🦴 **1983** An enigmatic American meets a mysterious Frenchwoman and they set off on a string of unusual romantic adventures. Set around the 1956 marriage of Grace Kelly to Prince Rainier of Monaco. Film debut of Van Damme. **79m/C VHS.** Charles Pitt, Martha Farris, Sydney Lassick, Jean-Claude Van Damme; *D:* William A. Levey; *W:* C. William Pitt, William A. Levey.

Monday Night Mayhem 🦴🦴 ½ **2002** Behind-the-scenes look at "Monday Night Football," the unexpectedly sucessful televised game sanctioned by the NFL in 1969 and produced for ABC by Roone Arledge (Heard). TV broadcaster Howard Cosell (John Turturro) makes his mark but comes to resent players-turned-commentators Frank Gifford (Anderson) and Don Meredith (Beyer) who join him. **98m/C VHS, DVD.** John Turturro, John Heard, Kevin Anderson, Nicholas Turturro, Brad Beyer, Patti LuPone, Eli Wallach; *D:* Ernest R. Dickerson; *W:* Bill Carter; *C:* Jonathan Freeman; *M:* Van Dyke Parks. **CABLE**

Mondays in the Sun 🦴🦴 *Los Lunes al Sol* **2002 (R)** Hard times and no easy answers in this biting drama—often filled with corrosive humor—about unemployment and its consequences. The shipyard where Santa (Bardem) and his friends work has been shut down after being sold to a Korean company. Rico (Climent), the only one to accept a management severance package, opens a waterfront bar where the others hang out: hot-headed activits Santa is deeply in debt and dreams of emigrating, Jose (Tosar) drinks too much and is resentful his working wife is supporting the family, and Lino (Egido) finds himself unqualified and competing against much younger men in a tight job market. Spanish with subtitles. **113m/C VHS, DVD.** *SP* Javier Bardem, Luis Tosar, Jose Angel Egido, Joaquin Climent, Nieve De Medina, Enrique Villen, Celso Bugallo; *D:* Fernando Leon de Aranoa; *W:* Fernando Leon de Aranoa, Ignacio del Moral; *C:* Alfredo Mayo; *M:* Lucio Godoy.

Mondo 🦴🦴 **1996** Orphaned gypsy boy Mondo (Balan) winds up living on the streets of Nice looking for a new family. He's befriended and sheltered by various street people as he hides from the police who want to place him in care. Based on the novel "Ed. Gallinard" by J.M.G. Le Clezio. French with subtitles. **80m/C VHS.** *FR* Ovidiu Balan, Philippe Petit, Pierrette Fesch, Jerry Smith; *D:* Tony Gatlif; *W:* Tony Gatlif; *C:* Eric Guichard.

Mondo Balordo 🦴 **1964** Translated as "Crazy World," this is crude sensationalism masked as a horror story. Karloff guides the viewer through a curious mixture of society's fringe elements. A loosely connected series of sketches includes portraits of a reincarnated Rudolph Valentino, practitioners of transvestism, Roman coke whores, and an Italian-Japanese rock 'n roll midget (Drago) in director Montero's unusual vision of an anti-paradise. Includes standard lesbian club scene. Volume 11 of Frank Henenlotter's Sexy Shockers. **86m/C VHS, DVD.** Franz Drago; *D:* Robert Bianchi Montero; *W:* Albert T. Viola; ***Nar:*** Boris Karloff.

Mondo Cane 🦴🦴 *A Dog's Life* **1963 (R)** A documentary showcasing the eccentricities of human behavior around the world, including cannibalism, pig killing and more. Dubbed in English. Inspired a rash of "shockumentaries" over the next several years. The song "More" made its debut in this film. **105m/C VHS, DVD.** *IT* *D:* Gualtiero Jacopetti; *W:* Gualtiero Jacopetti; *C:* Antonio Climati, Benito

Frattari; *M:* Riz Ortolani, Nino Oliviero; *Nar:* Stefano Sibaldi.

Mondo Cane 2 🦴 *Mondo Pazzo; Mondo Insanity; Crazy World; Insane World* **1964 (R)** More documentary-like views of the oddities of mankind and ethnic rituals around the world. Enough, already. **94m/C VHS, DVD.** *IT D:* Gualtiero Jacopetti, Franco Prosperi.

Mondo Trasho WOOF! 1969 A major trasho film of the last day in the life of a most unfortunate woman, complete with sex and violence. First full length effort from cult filmmaker Waters, who was also writer, producer, and editor. **95m/B VHS.** Mary Vivian Pearce, Divine, John Leisenring, Mink Stole, David Lochary, Chris Atkinson, Mark Isherwood; *D:* John Waters; *W:* John Waters; *C:* John Waters.

Mondovino 🦴🦴 1/2 **2004 (PG-13)** French/American documentary looks at the wine industry in the context of the rise of globalization, marketing, and corporate groupthink vs. craftsmanship, independent thought, and tradition. Thought-provoking, if somewhat meandering and bloated piece also explores issues such as relations between the U.S and France, and America's perceived economic imperialism. **131m/C DVD.** *US D:* Jonathan Nossiter; *C:* Jonathan Nossiter, Stephanie Pommez.

The Money 🦴🦴 **1975 (R)** The quest for money drives a young man to kidnap the child that his girlfriend is baby-sitting. Average but Workman's direction is right on the money. **88m/C VHS, DVD.** Laurence Luckinbill, Elizabeth Richards, Danny DeVito, Graham Beckel; *D:* Chuck Workman.

Money Buys Happiness 🦴🦴 1/2 **1999** Money (Weatherford) and Georgia (Murphy) are on the verge of divorce when a friend commits suicide and leaves them an upright piano. Their problems crystallize as they attempt to transport the instrument 50 blocks across town. That's a curious premise for a comedy but this one manages to generate some genuine wit. **104m/C DVD.** Megan Murphy, Jeff Weatherford, Michael Chick, Cynthia Whalen, Caveh Zahedi; *D:* Gregg Lachow; *W:* Gregg Lachow; *C:* Jamie Hook; *M:* Jim Ragland.

Money for Nothing 🦴🦴 **1993 (R)** $1.2 million falls off a truck in the warehouse district of Philadelphia where a simple-minded unemployed longshoreman (Cusack) finds the chance of a lifetime. Indiscreetly leaving behind a trail of spending, he soon has a detective (Madsen) snooping around dangerously close. But he only digs himself deeper by enlisting the assistance of the mob to help him launder the money. At this point the film disintegrates into a limp diatribe on the injustice of capitalism on society's downtrodden. Mazar plays Joey's ex-girlfriend who double-times it back to the fold after his find. Based on a true story. **100m/C VHS, DVD.** John Cusack, Michael Madsen, Benicio Del Toro, Michael Rapaport, Debi Mazar, Fionnula Flanagan, Maury Chaykin, James Gandolfini, Elizabeth Bracco, Ashleigh Dejon, Lenny Venito; *D:* Ramon Menendez; *W:* Ramon Menendez, Carol Sobieski, Tom Musca; *M:* Craig Safan.

Money from Home 🦴🦴 1/2 **1953** Typical Martin-Lewis musical comedy, their first to be filmed in color. Gambler Herman "Honey Talk" Nelson (Martin) is being pressured by tough guy Jumbo (Leonard) to pay up. So he promises to fix a horse race by using his cousin Virgil (Lewis), a vet's apprentice. But Herman falls for the horse's owner (Millar), while Virgil gets mixed up with a horse-owning sheik (Vincent) and ends up impersonating a famous jockey. Based on a story by Damon Runyon. **100m/C DVD.** Dean Martin, Jerry Lewis, Sheldon Leonard, Marjie Millar, Dean Martin, Jerry Lewis, Sheldon Leonard, Marjie Millar, Pat Crowley, Richard Haydn, Robert Strauss, Gerald Mohr, Jack Kruschen, Romo Vincent; *D:* George Marshall; *W:* James Allardice, Hal Kanter; *C:* Daniel F. Fapp; *M:* Leigh Harline.

Money Kings 🦴🦴 1/2 *Vig* **1998 (R)** Slow-starter is worth the time it takes to get the story moving. Soft-hearted Vinnie Glenn (Falk) runs a Boston bar and serves as a small-time bookie for some backroom gambling. Then the local mob decide Vinnie needs an assistant to help him collect on the bad debts and send in a young hothead, Anthony (Prinze). Vinnie would like to restore the status quo before he heads to a Florida vacation with loyal wife Ellen (Daly), if only Anthony will listen. **96m/C VHS, DVD.** Peter Falk, Freddie Prinze Jr., Lauren Holly, Timothy Hutton, Tyne Daly; *D:* Graham Theakston.

Money Madness 🦴🦴 **1947** Beaumont (Ward Cleaver) plays a taxi driver turned thief in this curiosity. **73m/C VHS.** Hugh Beaumont, Frances Rafferty, Harlan Warde, Cecil Weston, Ida Moore, Danny Morton, Joel Friedkin, Lane Chandler; *D:* Sam Newfield; *W:* Al Martin; *C:* Jack Greenhalgh.

Money Movers 🦴🦴 **1978** Aussie thieves plan megabuck bank robbery but heist and plot go sour. An oft told tale based on a true story. Features early appearance from burly boy Brown. **94m/C VHS.** *AU* Terence Donovan, Ed Devereaux, Tony Bonner, Lucky Grills, Charles "Bud" Tingwell, Candy (Candida) Raymond, Bryan Brown, Alan Cassell; *D:* Bruce Beresford; *W:* Bruce Beresford.

The Money Pit 🦴🦴 **1986 (PG)** A young yuppie couple encounter sundry problems when they attempt to renovate their newly purchased, seemingly self-destructive, Long Island home. However, the collapse of their home leads directly to the collapse of their relationship as well. Somewhat modeled after "Mr. Blandings Builds His Dream House." Hanks and Long fail to jell as partners and the many sight gags are on the predictable side. A Spielberg production. **91m/C VHS, DVD.** Tom Hanks, Shelley Long, Alexander Godunov, Maureen Stapleton, Philip Bosco, Joe Mantegna, Josh Mostel, Yakov Smirnoff, Carmine Caridi, Brian Backer, Wendell Pierce, Mike Starr, Frankie Faison, Nestor Serrano, Michael Jeter; *D:* Richard Benjamin; *W:* David Giler; *C:* Gordon Willis; *M:* Michel Colombier.

Money Talks 🦴🦴 **1997 (R)** Hustler Franklin Hatchett (Tucker) is falsely accused of orchestrating a violent jail break. Ratings-hungry TV reporter James Russell (Sheen) agrees to help Franklin clear his name in return for exclusive rights to his story. The mismatched pair search for stolen jewels, dodge bullets and endure explosive escapes, but this being an action-comedy, there needs to be some laughs. These are provided (intermittently) by the frenzied comic style of Tucker, who easily eclipses Sheen's straight man demeanor (which could be mistaken for acting if you've never seen any of Sheen's previous films). Tucker shows flashes of deserving better material than he has to work with here. **92m/C VHS, DVD.** Chris Tucker, Charlie Sheen, Heather Locklear, Paul Sorvino, Veronica Cartwright, Elise Neal, Paul Gleason, Larry Hankin, Daniel Roebuck, David Warner, Michael Wright, Gerard Ismael; *D:* Brett Ratner; *W:* Joel Cohen, Alec Sokolow; *C:* Russell Carpenter, Robert Primes; *M:* Lalo Schifrin.

Money to Burn 🦴🦴 **1983** Aging high school counselor and two senior citizens develop a plan to steal $50 million from the Federal Reserve Bank. Harmless bit of fun. **90m/C VHS.** Jack Kruschen, Meegan King, David Wallace, Phillip Pine; *D:* Virginia Lively Stone.

Money to Burn 🦴 1/2 **1994 (R)** Two buddies go off on a wild spending spree when $2 million in cash falls into their laps. Only one problem—a crazy cop who's determined to stop them squandering the money. **96m/C VHS.** Chad McQueen, Don Swayze, Joe Estevez, Julie Strain, Sydney Lassick; *D:* John Sjogren; *W:* John Sjogren, Scott Ziehl.

Money Train 🦴 1/2 **1995 (R)** Snipes and Harrelson team up again, this time as New York City transit cops (and foster brothers) who decide to rob the money train—a subway car that collects all the cash accrued from the transit system each day. To complicate matters, they're both in love with their new Latina partner (Lopez). Lame attempt to cash in on the Snipes and Harrelson chemistry leaves out one important ingredient—a competent script. The movie is almost over before the train actually becomes part of the plotline. Film came under criticism when it was blamed for a series of "copycat" arsons in which a New York City subway clerk was killed. **110m/C VHS, DVD.** Skipp (Robert L.) Sudduth, Vincent Laresca, Aida Turturro, Vincent Pastore, Enrico Colantoni, Jose Zuniga, Bill Nunn, Larry (Lawrence) Gilliard Jr., Michael Artura, Woody Harrelson, Wesley Snipes, Jennifer Lopez, Robert (Bobby) Blake, Chris Cooper, Joe Grifasi; *D:* Joseph Ruben; *W:* Doug Richardson, David Loughery; *C:* John Lindley; *M:* Mark Mancina.

The Money Trap 🦴🦴 1/2 **1965** New York police detective Joe Baron (Ford) lives large because wife Lisa (Sommer) inherited a stock portfolio. When the dividends stop, the Barons are in deep financial trouble just as Joe discovers wealthy physician Van Tilden (Cotten) is a pusher to the Park Avenue crowd. He also learns the doc keeps dough and heroin in his safe so he and partner Peter (Montalban) decide on a rip-off and things go from bad to worse. **92m/B DVD.** Glenn Ford, Elke Sommer, Joseph Cotten, Ricardo Montalban, Rita Hayworth, Tom Reese, James Mitchum; *D:* Burt Kennedy; *W:* Walter Bernstein; *C:* Pavel Vogel; *M:* Hal Schaefer.

The Moneytree 🦴 1/2 **1993** A carefree would-be actor decides to make some money by harvesting a huge marijuana crop in the California hills, all the while fending off his girlfriend, the cops, and some wild boars. **92m/C VHS.** Christopher Dienstag; *D:* Alan Dienstag.

Mongol 🦴🦴🦴 **2007 (R)** Russian director Bodrov brings a beautiful, sweeping, and internationally-appealing historical epic, intended as the first installment in a trilogy of films covering the life of the infamous Genghis Khan. The story begins in 1192 as nine-year-old Temudgin (Odsuren), not yet known as Genghis Khan, is traveling with his father (Ba Sen) to meet with a rival clan to select his future bride. En route they visit a lesser clan and encounter Borte (Erdenabat), who Temudgin selects as his future bride instead. What follows are the brutal and tragedy-laden years that see the mature Temudgin (Asano) develop into the powerful leader capable of uniting the Mongol clans framed by the enduring romance and partnership between he and his wife and advisor, Borte (Chuluun). The Mongol leader is treated as a complicated, conflicted and ultimately sympathetic character in spite of the relentless bloody scenes of warring factions. **120m/C DVD.** *KZ* Tadanobu Asano, Honglei Sun, Khulan Chuluun, Odnyam Odsuren, Amarbold Tuvinbayar, Bayartsetseg Erdenasbat, Ba Sen; *D:* Sergei Bodrov; *W:* Sergei Bodrov, Arif Aliyev; *C:* Sergei Trofimov, Rogier Stoffers; *M:* Tuomas Kantelinen.

A Mongolian Tale 🦴🦴 *Hei Ma* **1994** Nai Nai has raised her granddaughter Somiya and the abandoned Bayingbulag among the Mongolian steppes. Eventually, Bayingbulag leaves to get an education but promises to return and marry Somiya. Away three years, he comes back only to discover Somiya pregnant, so he takes off, finds success as a folk singer, and doesn't return for 12 years. Somiya now has a drunken husband, four sons, and an illegitimate 12-year-old daughter who is desperate for a father. Mongolian dialogue. Adapted by Chengzhi from his story "A Song of the Grassland." **105m/C VHS.** *CH HK* Narenhua, Tengger; *D:* Xie Fei; *W:* Zhang Chengzhi; *C:* Jing Sheng Fu; *M:* Tengger. Montreal World Film Fest. '95: Director (Fei).

The Mongols 🦴🦴 1/2 *Les Mongols* **1960** Splashy Italian production has Genghis Khan's son repelling invading hordes while courting buxom princess. Pairing of Palance and Ekberg makes this one worthy of consideration. **105m/C VHS.** *IT FR* Jack Palance, Anita Ekberg, Antonella Lualdi, Franco Silva, Gianni "John" Garko, Roldano Lupi, Gabriella Pallotta; *D:* Andre de Toth, Leopoldo Savona, Riccardo Freda.

Mongrel WOOF! 1983 El-cheapo kennel horror about a man who dreams he's a wild murderous mutt. His relief upon waking up is short-lived, however, when he discovers the people he killed in his dreams are actually dead. Flick will make you want to gnaw on a bone. **90m/C VHS.** Aldo Ray, Terry Evans; *D:* Robert Burns.

Monika 🦴🦴 1/2 *Summer with Monika* **1952** Two teenagers who run away together for the summer find the winter brings more responsibility than they can handle when the girl becomes pregnant and gives birth. Lesser, early Bergman, sensitively directed, but dull. Adapted by Bergman from a Per Anders Fogelstrom novel. In Swedish with English subtitles. **96m/B VHS.** *SW* Harriet Andersson, Lars Ekborg, John Harryson, Georg Skarstedt, Dagmar Ebbesen, Ake Gronberg; *D:* Ingmar Bergman; *W:* Ingmar Bergman; *M:* Les Baxter.

Monique 🦴 **1976** A sophisticated career woman is about to unleash a terrifying secret on her new husband. **96m/C VHS.** Florence Giorgetti, John Ferris; *D:* Jacques Scandelari; *W:* Louisa Rose.

Monkey Boy 🦴🦴 1/2 **1990** Decent sci-fi horror from Britain, about a cunning human-ape hybrid that escapes from a genetics lab after massacring the staff. Not excessively gruesome or vulgar, and some sympathy is aroused for the killer mutant. Based on the novel "Chimera." **104m/C VHS.** John Lynch, Christine Kavanagh, Kenneth Cranham; *D:* Lawrence Gordon-Clark.

Monkey Business 🦴🦴🦴 1/2 **1931** Marx Brothers run amok as stowaways on ocean liner. Fast-paced comedy provides seemingly endless amount of gags, quips, and pratfalls, including the fab four imitating Maurice Chevalier at Immigration. This film, incidentally, was the group's first to be written—by noted humorist Perelman—directly for the screen. **77m/B VHS, DVD.** Groucho Marx, Harpo Marx, Chico Marx, Zeppo Marx, Thelma Todd, Ruth Hall, Harry Woods, Tom Kennedy, Rockliffe Fellowes, Maxine Castle; *D:* Norman Z. McLeod; *W:* S.J. Perelman, Arthur Sheekman; *C:* Arthur L. Todd.

Monkey Business 🦴🦴🦴 **1952** A scientist invents a fountain-of-youth potion, a lab chimpanzee mistakenly dumps it into a water cooler, and then grown-ups start turning into adolescents. Top-flight crew occasionally labors in this screwball comedy, though comic moments shine. Monroe is the secretary sans skills, while absent-minded Grant and sexy wife Rogers race hormonally as teens. **97m/B VHS, DVD.** Charlotte Austin, Cary Grant, Ginger Rogers, Charles Coburn, Marilyn Monroe, Hugh Marlowe, Larry Keating, George Winslow; *D:* Howard Hawks; *W:* Ben Hecht, Charles Lederer, I.A.L. Diamond; *C:* Milton Krasner; *M:* Leigh Harline.

Monkey Grip 🦴🦴🦴 **1982** An unmarried woman copes with parenthood and a drug-addicted boyfriend while working on the fringe of Australia's music business. Grim but provocative, based on Helen Graham's novel. **101m/C VHS.** *AU* Noni Hazlehurst, Colin Friels, Alice Garner, Harold Hopkins, Candy (Candida) Raymond; *D:* Ken Cameron; *W:* Ken Cameron. Australian Film Inst. '82: Actress (Hazlehurst).

Monkey Hustle 🦴 **1977 (PG)** Vintage blaxploitation has trouble hustling laffs. The Man plans a super freeway through the ghetto, and law abiding do gooders join forces with territorial lords of vice to fight the project. Shot in the Windy City. **90m/C VHS, DVD.** Yaphet Kotto, Rudy Ray Moore, Rosalind Cash, Debbi (Deborah) Morgan, Thomas Carter; *D:* Arthur Marks.

Monkey Shines 🦴🦴 *Monkey Shines: An Experiment in Fear; Ella* **1988 (R)** Based on the novel by Michael Stuart, this is a sick, scary yarn about a quadriplegic who is given a specially trained capuchin monkey as a helpmate. However, he soon finds that the beast is assuming and acting on his subconscious rages. **108m/C VHS, DVD.** Jason Beghe, John Pankow, Kate McNeil, Christine Forrest, Stephen (Steve) Root, Joyce Van Patten, Stanley Tucci, Janine Turner; *D:* George A. Romero; *W:* George A. Romero; *C:* James A. Contner; *M:* David Shire.

Monkey Trouble 🦴🦴 1/2 **1994 (PG)** Lonely schoolgirl Birch is feeling abandoned when mom and stepdad shower attention on her new baby brother. Then a monkey trained as a pickpocket enters her life. Keitel is the organ grinder turned bad who must answer to the mob when the monkey scampers off to suburbia. Stakes a lot of its entertainment wallop on the considerable talents of the slippery-fingered monkey, who steals the show. Birch is amusing as the youngster caught in all sorts of uncomfortable situations. Formula abounds, but the milk and cookies set won't notice; fine family fare. **95m/C VHS, DVD.** Thora Birch, Harvey Keitel, Mimi Rogers, Christopher McDonald; *D:* Franco Amurri; *W:* Franco Amurri, Stu Krieger; *M:* Mark Mancina.

Monkeybone 🦴🦴 **2001 (PG-13)** Weird comedy about comatose cartoonist Stu Miley (Fraser), who must escape from his own comic fantasy world in order to return to consciousness after an accident. Monkeybone, a chimp embodiment of a teenager's libido from his "Show Me the Monkey" animated pilot is the focus of the rest of the film as he escapes from the underworld and "steals" Stu's body to romance his awaiting girlfriend (Fonda). Kattan is funny as the organ donor and Turturro, who puts his considerable talent to voicing a monkey, is successful, but one-note libidinous simian humor makes flimsy material for a film. Based on the graphic novel "Dark Town" by Kaja Blackley. **92m/C VHS, DVD.** *US* Brendan Fraser, Bridget Fonda, Whoopi Goldberg, Chris Kattan, Dave Foley, Giancarlo Esposito, Rose McGowan, Megan Mullally, Lisa Zane; ***D:*** Henry Selick; ***W:*** Sam Hamm; ***C:*** Andrew Dunn; ***M:*** Anne Dudley; ***V:*** John Turturro.

Monkeys, Go Home! 🦴 ½ **1966** Dumb Disney yarn about young American who inherits a badly neglected French olive farm. When he brings in four chimpanzees to pick the olives, the local townspeople go on strike. People can be so sensitive. Based on "The Monkeys" by G. K. Wilkinson. Chevalier's last film appearance. **89m/C VHS, DVD.** Dean Jones, Yvette Mimieux, Maurice Chevalier, Clement Harari, Yvonne Constant; ***D:*** Andrew V. McLaglen; ***M:*** Robert F. Brunner.

The Monkey's Mask 🦴🦴 **2000** Lesbian private detective Jill Fitzpatrick (Porter) is hired by the parents of missing student Mickey Norris (Cornish). Jill meets Mickey's married poetry professor Diana (McGillis) and the two soon embark on a torrid affair. Then Mickey is found strangled and Jill searches (rather ineptyly) for the killer and nearly becomes a victim herself. Who knew poetry could be so dangerous? Based on the 1994 nonrhyming verse thriller by Dorothy Porter. **94m/C VHS, DVD.** *AU* Susie Porter, Kelly McGillis, Marton Csokas, Francoise Verley, Caroline Gillmer, Jean-Pierre Mignon, Jim Holt, John Noble, Linden Wilkinson; ***D:*** Samantha Lang; ***W:*** Anne Kennedy; ***C:*** Garry Phillips.

Monkey's Uncle 🦴 ½ **1965** A sequel to Disney's "The Misadventures of Merlin Jones" and featuring more bizarre antics and scientific hoopla, including chimps and a flying machine. **90m/C VHS.** Tommy Kirk, Annette Funicello, Leon Ames, Arthur O'Connell; ***D:*** Robert Stevenson; ***W:*** Alfred Lewis Levitt, Helen Levitt; ***C:*** Edward Colman; ***M:*** Buddy (Norman Dale) Baker.

The Monocle 🦴🦴 **1964** Steele plays a seductive villainess in this rare, spy/comedy thriller. **100m/C VHS.** *FR* Paul Meurisse, Barbara Steele, Marcel Dalio; ***D:*** Georges Lautner; ***W:*** Jacques Robert; ***C:*** Maurice Fellous; ***M:*** Michel Magne.

Monolith 🦴🦴 ½ **1993 (R)** Tucker (Paxton) and Flynn (Frost) are unlikely partners on the LAPD. But they're teamed up on an unlikely case: a Russian scientist commits a seemingly senseless murder and is taken away by a mystery man (Hurt) before she can be interrogated. What the curious duo discover is a lethal alien force capable of posessing any living creature and whose objective is the destruction of the planet. **96m/C VHS.** Bill Paxton, Lindsay Frost, John Hurt, Louis Gossett Jr.; ***D:*** John Eyres; ***W:*** Stephen Lister.

The Monolith Monsters 🦴🦴 **1957** A geologist investigates a meteor shower in Arizona and discovers strange crystals. The crystals attack humans and absorb their silicone, causing them to grow into monsters. Good "B" movie fun. **76m/B VHS.** Grant Williams, Lola Albright, Les Tremayne, Trevor Bardette; ***D:*** John Sherwood; ***W:*** Jack Arnold, Norman Jolley, Robert M. Fresco; ***M:*** Joseph Gershenson.

Monsieur Beaucaire 🦴 ½ **1924** The Duke of Chartres ditches France posing as a barber, and once in Britain, becomes a lawman. Not a classic Valentino vehicle. **100m/B VHS.** Rudolph Valentino, Bebe Daniels, Lois Wilson, Doris Kenyon, Lowell Sherman, John Davidson; ***D:*** Sidney Olcott.

Monsieur Beaucaire 🦴🦴🦴 **1946** Entertaining Hope vehicle that casts him as a barber impersonating a French nobleman in the court of Louis XV. He's set to wed a Spanish princess in order to prevent a full-scale war from taking place. However, he really wants to marry social-climber chambermaid Caulfield. Director Marshall was at his best here. Based on the novel by Booth Tarkington. **93m/B VHS, DVD.** Bob Hope, Joan Caulfield, Patric Knowles, Marjorie Reynolds, Cecil Kellaway, Joseph Schildkraut, Reginald Owen, Constance Collier; ***D:*** George Marshall; ***W:*** Melvin Frank, Norman Panama; ***C:*** Lionel Lindon.

Monsieur Hire 🦴🦴🦴 ½ *M. Hire* **1989 (PG-13)** The usual tale of sexual obsesssion and suspense. Mr. Hire spends much of his time trying to spy on his beautiful young neighbor woman, alternately alienated and engaged by her love affairs. The voyeur soon finds his secret desires have entangled him in a vicious intrigue. Political rally set-piece is brilliant. Excellent acting, intense pace, elegant photography. Based on "Les Fiancailles de M. Hire" by Georges Simenone and adapted by Leconte and Patrick Dewolf. In French with English subtitles. **81m/C VHS.** *FR* Michel Blanc, Sandrine Bonnaire, Luc Thuillier, Eric Berenger, Andre Wilms; ***D:*** Patrice Leconte; ***W:*** Patrice Leconte. Cesar '90: Sound.

Monsieur Ibrahim 🦴🦴🦴 *Monsieur Ibrahim and the Flowers of the Koran; Monsieur Ibrahim et les Fleurs du Coran* **2003 (R)** Coming-of-age story set in the low-rent district of 1960s Paris. Momo (Boulanger) is a Jewish street youth burdened with a chronically depressed father (Melki) and a mother who deserted him. Sharif excels as Ibrahim, a philosophy-spouting Turkish Muslim shopkeeper who befriends and adopts Momo after his father kills himself. Ibrahim tends to Momo's spiritual development while the local prostitutes and the girl next door teach him about sex and romance. Duperyon creates a lighthearted, sentimental fairytale about tolerance and spirituality. Adapted from writer Schmitt's semi-autobiographical book and play. **94m/C DVD.** *FR* Omar Sharif, Pierre Boulanger, Gilbert Melki, Lola Naymark, Anne Suarez, Isabelle Renauld, Isabelle Adjani; ***D:*** Francois Dupeyron; ***W:*** Francois Dupeyron; ***C:*** Remy Chevrin.

Monsieur N. 🦴🦴🦴 **2003** A charming work of historical speculation that wonders if the body believed to belong to Napoleon Bonaparte truly is the corpse of the legendary French emperor. Opening in 1840, when Napoleon's remains were returned to Paris, the narrative shifts back in time to the emperor's exile on the island of St. Helena after 1815. The narrator, Basil Heathcoate (Rodan), is the liaison between Napoleon's (Torreton) staff and Sir Hudson Lowe (Grant), the British governor of the island. Plots against Bonaparte abound as Lowe fumes at the expense of the exile and the emperor's retinue lusts after their promised inheritance. Caunes deftly keeps the mystery brisk and engaging, while Torreton delivers a hypnotic portrayal of the tactical genius. **127m/C DVD.** Philippe Torreton, Richard E. Grant, Jay Rodan, Elsa Zylberstein, Bruno Putzulu, Stephane Freiss, Frederic Pierrot, Roschdy Zem, Siobhan Hewlett; ***D:*** Antoine de Caunes; ***W:*** Rene Manzor; ***C:*** Pierre Aim; ***M:*** Stephan Eicher.

Monsieur Verdoux 🦴🦴🦴 **1947** A thorough Chaplin effort, as he produced, directed, wrote, scored and starred. A prim and proper bank cashier in Paris marries and murders rich women in order to support his real wife and family. A mild scandal in its day, though second-thought pacifism and stale humor date it. A bomb upon release (leading Chaplin to shelve it for 17 years) and a cult item today, admired for both its flaws and complexity. Raye fearlessly chews scenery and croissants. Initially based upon a suggestion from Orson Welles. **123m/B VHS, DVD.** Charlie Chaplin, Martha Raye, Isobel Elsom, Mady Correll, Marilyn Nash, Irving Bacon, William Frawley, Allison Roddan, Robert Lewis; ***D:*** Charlie Chaplin; ***W:*** Charlie Chaplin; ***C:*** Curt Courant, Roland H. Totheroh; ***M:*** Charlie Chaplin.

Monsieur Vincent 🦴🦴🦴 **1947** True story of 17th century French priest who became St. Vincent de Paul (Fresnay). He forsakes worldly possessions and convinces members of the aristocracy to finance his charities for the less fortunate. Inspirational. French with subtitles. **112m/B VHS.** *FR* Pierre Fresnay, Lisa (Lise) Delamare, Aime Clariond, Jean Debucourt, Pierre Dux, Gabrielle Dorziat, Jean Carmet, Michel Bouquet; ***D:*** Maurice Cloche; ***W:*** Jean Anouilh, Jean-Bernard Luc; ***C:*** Claude Renoir; ***M:*** Jean Jacques Grunenwald. Oscars '48: Foreign Film.

Monsignor WOOF! **1982 (R)** Callow, ambitious priest befriends mobsters and even seduces a nun while managing Vatican's business affairs. No sparks generated by Reeve and Bujold (who appears nude in one scene), and no real conviction related by most other performers. Absurd, ludicrous melodrama best enjoyed as unintentional comedy. Based on Jack Alain Leger's book. **121m/C VHS.** Christopher Reeve, Fernando Rey, Genevieve Bujold, Jason Miller; ***D:*** Frank Perry; ***W:*** Abraham Polonsky, Wendell Mayes; ***C:*** Billy Williams; ***M:*** John Williams.

Monsignor Quixote 🦴🦴 ½ **1991** A small town priest takes on the persona of his ancestor, Don Quixote, and prepares to battle the evil he sees around him. Based on the novel by Graham Greene. **118m/C VHS.** Alec Guinness, Ian Richardson, Graham Crowden, Maurice Denham, Philip Stone, Rosalie Crutchley, Valentine Pelka, Don Fellows, Leo McKern; ***D:*** Rodney Bennett.

Monsoon 🦴🦴 **1997** Ambitious project from director Mundhra (known best for his erotic thrillers) is set in Goa, India. That's where Kenneth Blake (Tyson) and his fiancee Sally Stephens (McShane) go to visit his friend (McCoy). But in a previous incarnation Kenneth was a lover of Leela (Brodie), who's now married to the local drug lord Miranda (Grover). Their centuries-spanning affair causes the usual complications. Local color is actually much more interesting and the film looks very sharp. **96m/C DVD.** Richard Tyson, Matt McCoy, Gulshan Grover, Jenny (Jennifer) McShane, Doug Jeffery, Helen Brodie; ***D:*** Jag Mundhra; ***C:*** Blain Brown; ***M:*** Alan Dermot Derosian.

Monsoon Wedding 🦴🦴🦴 **2001 (R)** Outlines the clash of India's traditional culture with the growing modern sensibilities of the new Delhi. Aditi Vermas (Das) is promised in marriage to Hemant (Dabas) an Indian computer programmer living in Houston, whom she has yet to meet. The problem is, Aditi has a life of her own, including a married TV host for a boyfriend. When the couple eventually meet, tensions and attraction arises as a bevy of romantic subplots swirl like the title's monsoon around them. Film's large, Altman-esque cast of characters include both sides of the intendeds' family. Nair's engaging storylines, fresh premise and lush cinematography succeed in depicting the turbulent modern life in Delhi. In English, and Hindi and Punjabi (with English subtitles). **113m/C VHS, DVD.** *IN US* Naseeruddin Shah, Lillete Dubey, Shefali Shetty, Vasundhara Das, Parvin Dabas, Vijay Raaz, Tilotama Shome, Rajat Kapoor; ***D:*** Mira Nair; ***W:*** Sabrina Dhawan; ***C:*** Declan Quinn; ***M:*** Mychael Danna.

The Monster 🦴🦴🦴 **1925** This silent horror film has all the elements that would become genre standards. Mad scientist Dr. Ziska (Chaney), working in an asylum filled with lunatics, abducts strangers to use in his fiendish experiments to bring the dead back to life. There's the obligatory dungeon and even a lovely heroine (Olmsted) that needs rescuing. Great atmosphere and Chaney's usual spine-tingling performance. Based on the play by Crane Wilbur. **86m/B VHS.** Lon Chaney Sr., Gertrude (Olmstead) Olmsted, Johnny Arthur, Charles Sellon, Walter James, Hallam Cooley; ***D:*** Roland West; ***W:*** Albert Kenyon, Willard Mack; ***C:*** Hal Mohr.

Monster 🦴 **1978 (R)** Bloodthirsty alien indiscriminately preys on gaggle of teens in wilds of civilization. Performers struggle with dialogue and their own self-esteem. **98m/C VHS.** Jim Mitchum, Diane McBain, Roger Clark, John Carradine, Phil Carey, Anthony Eisley, Keenan Wynn; ***D:*** Herbert L. Strock.

The Monster 🦴🦴 ½ *Il Monstro; Le Monstre* **1996 (R)** Italian impresario of comedy Benigni co-wrote, directed and starred in this film that has become the highest grossing film in Italian history to date. Jaded American audiences, however, may find the broad comedy of errors all too familiar territory with Loris (Benigni) as a criminal Clouseau, an incompetent petty thief whom police mistake for a serial murderer on the loose. Cops install an attractive female detective (Braschi, Benigni's wife) in the sexually strained shyster's apartment to tempt him into striking again. Sight gags aplenty populate Benigni's highly physical performance, including: being pulled wildly around a garage attached to an out-of-control chainsaw; contending with a lit cigarette down his pants; and scores of pratfalls, all of which garner comparisons to comedy phenom, Jim Carrey. French director and actor Blanc ("Dead Tired") is great as the loony police psychiatrist. **110m/C VHS, DVD.** *IT* Roberto Benigni, Nicoletta Braschi, Michel Blanc, Dominque Lavanant, Jean-Claude Brialy, Ivano Marescotti, Laurent Spielvogel, Massimo Girotti, Franco Mescolini; ***D:*** Roberto Benigni; ***W:*** Roberto Benigni, Vincenzo Cerami; ***C:*** Carlo Di Palma; ***M:*** Evan Lurie.

Monster 🦴🦴🦴 **2003 (R)** Charlize Theron plays Aileen Wuornos, the first woman serial killer executed in the U.S., who murdered seven men on the highways of Florida in the 1980s. Focuses on the love affair between Selby Wall (Ricci) and Wuornos. While the film itself has some flaws, not the least of which is portraying Wournos as a victim whose motive was self-defense, Theron's complete transformation for and commitment to the role is fascinating to watch. Her performance alone is worth the rental. **111m/C DVD.** *US* Charlize Theron, Christina Ricci, Bruce Dern, Scott Wilson, Pruitt Taylor Vince, Lee Tergesen, Annie Corley; ***D:*** Patty Jenkins; ***W:*** Patty Jenkins; ***C:*** Steven Bernstein; ***M:*** BT (Brian Transeau). Oscars '03: Actress (Theron); Golden Globes '04: Actress—Drama (Theron); Ind. Spirit '04: Actress (Theron), First Feature; Natl. Soc. Film Critics '03: Actress (Theron); Screen Actors Guild '03: Actress (Theron).

Monster a Go-Go! WOOF! **1965** Team of go-go dancers battle a ten-foot monster from outerspace whose mass is due to a radiation mishap. He can't dance, either. **70m/B VHS, DVD.** Phil Morton, June Travis, Bill Rebane, Herschell Gordon Lewis, Lois Brooks, George Perry; ***D:*** Bill Rebane, Herschell Gordon Lewis; ***W:*** Herschell Gordon Lewis.

The Monster and the Girl 🦴🦴 ½ **1941** It's the mob vs. the ape in this tale of revenge. Scott (Terry) discovers innocent sister Susan (Drew) is being lead down the path to prostitution by suave mobster Reed (Paige). But Reed manages to frame Scott for murder and he's executed, although not before donating his brain to science. Then scientist Parry (Zucco) decides to transplant the brain into the body of an ape who goes on a rampage aimed at the mobster. **65m/B VHS.** Ellen Drew, Robert Paige, Phillip Terry, Paul Lukas, Joseph Calleia, Onslow Stevens, Rod Cameron, George Zucco, Marc Lawrence, Gerald Mohr; ***D:*** Stuart Heisler; ***W:*** Stuart Anthony; ***C:*** Victor Milner.

The Monster Club 🦴🦴 **1985** Price and Carradine star in this music-horror compilation, featuring songs by Night, B.A. Robertson, The Pretty Things and The Viewers. Soundtrack music by John Williams, UB 40 and The Expressos. **104m/C VHS, DVD.** *GB* Vincent Price, Donald Pleasence, John Carradine, Stuart Whitman, Britt Ekland, Simon Ward, Patrick Magee; ***D:*** Roy Ward Baker.

The Monster Demolisher 🦴🦴 **1960** Nostradamus' descendent shares the family penchant for sanguine cocktails, and threatens a professor who protects himself with an electronic wonder of modern technology. Edited from a sombrero serial; if you make it through this one, look up its Mexican siblings, "Curse of Nostradamus" and "Genie of Darkness." **74m/B VHS.** *MX* Domingo Soler, Julio Aleman, Aurora Alvarado, German Robles; ***D:*** Frederick Curiel; ***W:*** Alfredo Ruanova; ***C:*** Fernando Colin; ***M:*** Jorge Perez.

Monster Dog WOOF! **1982** A rock band is mauled, threatened, and drooled upon by an untrainable mutant canine. Rock star Cooper plays the leader of the band. No plot, but the German shepherd is worth watching. **88m/C VHS, DVD.** Alice Cooper, Victoria Vera; ***D:*** Clyde (Claudio Fragasso) Anderson.

Monster from Green Hell 🦴 **1958** An experimental rocket containing radiation-contaminated wasps crashes in Africa, making giant killer wasps that run amok. Stinging big bug horror. **71m/B VHS, DVD.** Jim Davis, Robert E. (Bob) Griffin, Barbara Turner, Eduardo Ciannelli; ***D:*** Kenneth Crane; ***W:*** Endre Bohem,

Louis Vittes; *C:* Ray Flin; *M:* Albert Glasser.

Monster from the Ocean Floor ✐ *It Stalked the Ocean Floor; Monster Maker* **1954** An oceanographer in a deep-sea diving bell is threatened by a multi-tentacled creature. Roger Corman's first production. **66m/C VHS, DVD.** Anne Kimball, Stuart Wade, Jonathan Haze, Wyott Ordung, David Garcia, Dick Pinner; *D:* Wyott Ordung; *W:* William Danch; *C:* Floyd Crosby; *M:* Andre Brummer.

Monster High ✐ **1989 (R)** Bloodthirsty alien indiscriminately preys on gaggle of teens in wilds of civilization. Even the people who made this one may not have seen it all the way through. **89m/C VHS, DVD.** David Marriott, Dean Iandoli, Diana Frank, D.J. Kerzner; *D:* Rudiger Poe.

Monster House ✐✐✐ **2006 (PG)** Artistically and effectively creepy outing from executive producers Zemeckis and Spielberg is just the second film to utilize stop-motion animation (their "Polar Express" was the first). Halloween-worthy story follows a trio of kids who investigate the neighborhood haunted house, which devours anything or anyone who gets too close. State-of-the-art technique allows animated characters, including the house, to show emotion and expression while excellent voice work from the likes of Buscemi and Gyllenhaal lend real human talent to the eye-popping visual technology. **91m/C DVD, Blu-ray Disc.** *US D:* Gil Kenan; *W:* Pamela Pettler, Dan Harmon, Rob Schrab; *C:* Xavier Perez Grobet; *M:* Douglas Pipes; *V:* Sam Lerner, Steve Buscemi, Maggie Gyllenhaal, Jon Heder, Mitchel Musso, Spencer Locke, Nick Cannon, Kevin James, Jason Lee, Catherine O'Hara, Kathleen Turner, Fred Willard.

Monster in a Box ✐✐✐ **1992 (PG-13)** Master storyteller Gray spins a wonderful tale about his life, including stories about his adventures at a Moscow film festival, a trip to Nicaragua, and his first experience with California earthquakes. Filled with wit, satire, and hilarity. Filmed before an audience, this is based on Gray's Broadway show of the same title. By the way, the monster in the box is a 1,900-page manuscript of his autobiography and the box in which he lugs it around. **88m/C VHS, DVD.** Spalding Gray; *D:* Nick Broomfield; *W:* Spalding Gray; *C:* Michael Coulter; *M:* Laurie Anderson.

Monster-in-Law ✐ **2005 (PG-13)** Awfully nice girl from Venice Beach (Lopez) has a whirlwind courtship and romance with an Adonis-like surgeon (Vartan) but meets with great resistance from his has-been television reporter mother (Fonda) upon the announcement of their engagement. A bevy of battles to put-down or one-up one another ensues. Lopez's character is nothing new, Vartan shows no personality, and although Fonda makes the atrocious behavior of her character palatable, one still wonders why she choose this one-dimensional and craven comedy for a comeback. **100m/C VHS, DVD.** *US* Jane Fonda, Jennifer Lopez, Michael Vartan, Wanda Sykes, Will Arnett, Adam Scott, Annie Parisse, Monet Mazur, Elaine Stritch, Stephen Dunham; *D:* Robert Luketic; *W:* Anya Kochoff, Scott Hill; *C:* Russell Carpenter; *M:* David Newman, Dana Sano.

Monster in the Closet ✐✐ **1986 (PG)** A gory horror spoof about a rash of San Francisco murders that all take place inside closets. A news reporter and his scientist friend decide they will be the ones to protect California from the evil but shy creatures. From the producers of "The Toxic Avenger." **87m/C VHS, DVD.** Paul Dooley, Donald Grant, Claude Akins, Denise DuBarry, Stella Stevens, Howard Duff, Henry Gibson, Jesse White, John Carradine; *D:* Bob Dahlin; *W:* Bob Dahlin; *C:* Ronald W. McLeish; *M:* Barrie Guard.

The Monster Maker ✐✐ **1944** Low-budget gland fest in which deranged scientist develops serum that inflates heads, feet, and hands. He recklessly inflicts others with this potion, then must contend with deformed victims while courting a comely gal. **65m/B VHS, DVD.** J. Carrol Naish, Ralph Morgan, Wanda McKay, Terry Frost; *D:* Sam Newfield; *W:* Martin Mooney, Pierre Gendron; *C:* Robert E. Cline; *M:* Albert Glasser.

Monster Man ✐✐ **2003 (R)** Horror flick rule number one: don't be the idiots who rile up the disfigured, ill-tempered guy with the big truck. College buddies Adam and Harley, road tripping to reach the girl they both love to prevent her impending nuptials, are just such idiots. Could be enjoyable genre fun if you're in the mood. **95m/C VHS, DVD.** Eric Jungmann, Justin Urich, Aimee Brooks, Michael Bailey Smith, Robert (Bobby Ray) Shafer, Joe Goodrich; *D:* Michael Davis; *W:* Michael Davis; *C:* Matthew Irving; *M:* John Coda. **VIDEO**

The Monster of London City ✐ 1/2 *Das Ungeheuer von London City* **1964** During a stage play about Jack the Ripper, murders occur paralleling those in the production. The lead actor finds himself to be the prime suspect. Lightweight horror from Germany. **87m/B VHS, DVD.** *GE* Hansjorg Felmy, Marianne Koch, Dietmar Schoenherr, Hans Nielsen; *D:* Edwin Zbonek.

The Monster of Piedras Blancas WOOF! **1957** During a seaside festival, two fisherman are killed by a bloodthirsty oceanic critter with no respect for holidays. The fishing village is determined to find it and kill it. Low-budget, with amateurish effects and poor acting. **72m/B VHS.** Les Tremayne, Jeanne Carmen, Forrest Lewis, John Harmon, Don Sullivan; *D:* Irvin Berwick; *W:* H. Haile Chace; *C:* Philip Lathrop.

Monster on the Campus ✐✐ 1/2 *Monster in the Night; Stranger on the Campus* **1959** Science-fiction thriller about the blood of a prehistoric fish turning college professor into murderous beast. Will the halls of Dunsfield University ever be safe again? **76m/B VHS, DVD.** Arthur Franz, Joanna Moore, Judson Pratt, Nancy Walters, Troy Donahue; *D:* Jack Arnold; *W:* David Duncan.

The Monster Squad ✐ 1/2 **1987 (PG-13)** Youthful monster enthusiasts find their community inundated by Dracula, Frankenstein creature, Wolf Man, Mummy, and Gill Man(!?!), who are all searching for a life-sustaining amulet. Somewhat different, but still somewhat mediocre. **82m/C VHS, DVD.** Mary Ellen Trainor, Andre Gower, Stephen Macht, Tom Noonan, Duncan Regehr; *D:* Fred Dekker; *W:* Fred Dekker, Shane Black; *M:* Bruce Broughton.

The Monster That Challenged the World ✐✐ 1/2 **1957** Huge, ancient eggs are discovered in the Salton Sea and eventually hatch into killer, crustaceous caterpillars. Superior monster action. **83m/B VHS, DVD.** Tim Holt, Audrey Dalton, Hans Conried, Harlen Ward, Max (Casey Adams) Showalter, Mimi Gibson, Gordon Jones; *D:* Arnold Laven; *W:* Pat Fielder; *C:* Lester White; *M:* Heinz Roemheld.

The Monster Walks ✐✐ *The Monster Walked* **1932** A whodunit thriller, complete with stormy nights, suspicious cripples, weird servants, a screaming gorilla, and a spooky house. Not unique but entertaining. **60m/B VHS, DVD.** Rex Lease, Vera Reynolds, Mischa Auer, Willie Best; *D:* Frank Strayer.

Monster's Ball ✐✐✐✐ **2001 (R)** Georgia death-row prison guard Hank (Thornton) is following in his father Buck's (Boyle) footsteps as a guard, and as a bigot. His son (Ledger) also has joined the family business, but doesn't seem to have the heart or stomach for it. When his son throws up during the execution of Lawrence Musgrove (Combs), Hank flies into a rage that makes him reexamine his life. Soon after, he helps the waitress, Leticia (Berry) from the diner he frequents after an auto accident. Leticia is Musgrove's widow, unbeknownst to Hank, who begins what at first is a desperate, sexual relationship with her that changes both of them. Director Forster and scripters Addica and Rokos provide a well-done, raw, and unflinching story that the excellent cast, especially Berry (who won the Best Actress Oscar) and Thornton inhabit perfectly. Boyle is also powerful as the malevolent patriarch. Everything comes together to announce Forster's arrival as a directorial force. **111m/C VHS, DVD.** *US* Billy Bob Thornton, Halle Berry, Heath Ledger, Peter Boyle, Sean (Puffy, Puff Daddy, P. Diddy) Combs, Coronji Calhoun, Mos Def, Will Rokos, Milo Addica; *D:* Marc Forster; *W:* Will Rokos, Milo Addica; *C:* Roberto Schaefer. Oscars '01: Actress (Berry); Natl. Bd. of Review '01: Actor (Thornton), Actress (Berry); Screen Actors Guild '01: Actress (Berry).

Monsters Crash the Pajama Party ✐✐ **1965** Mad scientist is discovered conducting weird experiments by a group of teens who enter a supposedly haunted house. This one was much better in the theatre, because "monsters" would run through the audience and select a victim. Then the monsters and the victim would magically appear on the screen. Weird. **31m/C VHS, DVD.** Peter J. D'Noto, Vic McGee, James Reason, Pauline Hilcurt, Charles Egan, Joseph Ormond; *D:* David L. Hewitt; *W:* David L. Hewitt, Jay Lister; *C:* David L. Hewitt, Austin McKay.

Monsters, Inc. ✐✐✐ 1/2 **2001 (G)** Sweet-natured animated film from Pixar that's geared more towards the younger end of the family spectrum than films like "Toy Story." Monstropolis is a town that is powered by the screams of human children, which are captured in tanks thanks to "scarers" who invade the kids' bedrooms via their closet doors. Sully (Goodman) is the best there is, with the help of buddy Mike (Crystal), but he has a problem when human toddler Boo (Gibbs) accidentally gets loose in monster town, which is a big no-no, and Sully has to get her safely home. There's also some sinister goings-on at a company level causing problems for our boys. Very colorful and more silly than scary (what's scary is the familiar toddler behavior). **92m/C VHS, DVD.** *US D:* Pete Docter; *W:* Andrew Stanton, Daniel Gerson; *M:* Randy Newman; *V:* John Goodman, Billy Crystal, Steve Buscemi, Mary Gibbs, James Coburn, Jennifer Tilly, John Ratzenberger, Frank Oz, Bob Peterson, Bonnie Hunt. Oscars '01: Song ("If I Didn't Have You").

Monsters vs. Aliens ✐✐ 1/2 **2009 (PG)** Bride-to-be, Susan (Witherspoon) is struck by a meteorite on her wedding day, causing her to suddenly grow to nearly 50-feet tall. The army immediately drops in to sweep the giant bride off to a top-secret military silo. While inside, Susan, renamed Ginormica, meets four other misfit monsters confined to the prison-like conditions—a dim-witted blob (Rogan), a cockroach humanoid mad scientist (Laurie), a courageous fishman creature (Arnett), and a giant snot-shooting caterpillar. They are soon released into society with the intention of stopping the impending assault on planet Earth from evil alien mastermind, Gallaxhar (Wilson). Smart animated Dreamworks feature disguised as a '50s B-movie, loaded with quick sci-fi references and outrageous sight gags for both kiddies and their parents. Initially released as an IMAX 3-D extravaganza. **94m/C DVD.** *US D:* Rob Letterman, Conrad Vernon; *W:* Rob Letterman, Maya Forbes, Wally Wolodarsky, Jonathan Aibel, Glenn Berger; *M:* Henry Jackman; *V:* Reese Witherspoon, Seth Rogen, Kiefer Sutherland, Paul Rudd, Hugh Laurie, Rainn Wilson, Will Arnett, Stephen Colbert, John Krasinski, Renee Zellweger, Jeffrey Tambor, Ed Helms, Amy Poehler, Julie White.

Montana ✐✐ **1950** Miniscule-budgeted western filmed at Warner's studio-owned Calabasas Ranch in the San Fernando Valley. Australian sheep man Morgan Lane (Flynn) comes to Montana cattle country looking for government-owned grazing space for his woolies. He hides his profession from cattle owner Maria Singleton (Smith) because he's smitten but a range war nearly breaks out when she discovers the truth. Cuddly Sakall provides his usual comic relief. **76m/C DVD.** Errol Flynn, Alexis Smith, S.Z. Sakall, Douglas Kennedy, James Brown, Ian MacDonald, Charles Irwin; *D:* Ray Enright; *W:* Ian MacDonald, Charles "Blackie" O'Neal, Borden Chase, James R. Webb; *C:* Karl Freund; *M:* David Buttolph.

Montana ✐✐ 1/2 **1990 (PG)** Hoyce and Bess Guthrie are long-married and strong-willed ranchers who are at odds over the family ranch in Montana. He wants to sell the land to a power company for oil drilling but she wants to keep the land in the family. **91m/C VHS.** Gena Rowlands, Richard Crenna, Lea Thompson, Justin Deas, Elizabeth Berridge, Scott Coffey, Darren Dalton; *D:* William A. Graham; *W:* Larry McMurtry. **CABLE**

Montana ✐✐ **1997 (R)** Claire (Sedgwick) is a professional killer, who works with partner Nick (Tucci) for the eccentric Boss (Coltrane). When Boss' drug addict mistress Kitty (Tunney) runs away, Claire and Nick are given the thankless task of retrieving her and have to also endure the presence of the man's imbecilic son, Jimmy (Embry). Then Kitty kills Jimmy and Claire and Nick are also accused of embezzling from the organization—so the lethal trio are now being hunted by their own syndicate. Good cast is hampered by a not particularly memorable story. **96m/C VHS.** Kyra Sedgwick, Stanley Tucci, Robbie Coltrane, Robin Tunney, Philip Seymour Hoffman, John Ritter, Ethan (Randall) Embry; *D:* Jennifer Leitzes; *W:* Erich Hoeber, Jon Hoeber; *C:* Ken Kelsch; *M:* Cliff Eidelman.

Montana Belle ✐✐ **1952** A buxom bandit teams with the notorious Dalton Brothers before embarking on a life of reform. In the cardgame of life, Russell is always holding a pair. **81m/C VHS.** Jane Russell, George Brent, Scott Brady, Forrest Tucker, Andy Devine, Jack Lambert, John Litel, Ray Teal; *D:* Allan Dwan.

Montana Sky ✐✐ 1/2 **2007** Jack Mercy's will is very clear—his three daughters must live on his Montana ranch for one year in order to claim their inheritance. But the women, who are half-sisters, are strangers to each other and they anticipate trouble with their forced family reunion. What they get is a saboteur who is determined to drive them from the ranch before they can claim dad's fortune. A Lifetime original movie based on the novel by Nora Roberts. **95m/C DVD.** Charlotte Ross, John Corbett, Diane Ladd, Nathaniel Arcand, Ashley Williams, Laura Mennell, Aaron Pearl; *D:* Mike Robe; *W:* April Smith; *C:* Eric Van Haren Noman; *M:* Steve Porcaro. **CABLE**

Monte Carlo ✐✐ 1/2 **1930** Poor Countess Vera (MacDonald) dumps her boring rich fiance, Prince Otto (Allister), and heads to Monte Carlo, hoping to win big. Shy Count Rudolph (Buchanan) thinks Vera will bring him good luck and asks to stroke her blonde curls. When Vera wins instead, she decides to hire Rudolph, whom she mistakenly believes is a hairdresser. When her fortunes reverse, Vera contemplates marrying the boring prince again without realizing that Rudolph is in love with her (and that he has loads of cash). **90m/B DVD.** Jeanette MacDonald, Jack Buchanan, Zasu Pitts, Claud Allister, Lionel Belmore, Tyler Brooke, John Roche; *D:* Ernst Lubitsch; *W:* Ernest Vajda; *C:* Victor Milner; *M:* W. Franke Harling.

Monte Carlo ✐✐ **1986** A sexy Russian woman aids the Allies by relaying important messages during WWII. Fun TV production featuring Collins at her seductive best. **200m/C VHS.** Joan Collins, George Hamilton, Lisa Eilbacher, Lauren Hutton, Robert Carradine, Malcolm McDowell; *D:* Anthony Page. **TV**

Monte Carlo Nights ✐ 1/2 **1934** Wrongly convicted murderer determines to prove his innocence even as he is tracked by police. **60m/B VHS, DVD.** Mary Brian, John Darrow, Kate Campbell, Robert Frazer, Astrid Allwyn, George "Gabby" Hayes, George Cleveland; *D:* William Nigh.

Monte Cristo ✐✐ **1922** Adaptation of the Alexandre Dumas novel with Gilbert starring as the unjustly imprisoned Edmond Dantes. Escaping after 20 years, Edmond finds the vast treasure promised to him by crazy fellow prisoner, the Abbe Faria, and sets out to wreak revenge on those who wronged him. **100m/B DVD.** John Gilbert, Estelle Taylor, Robert McKim, Spottiswoode Aitken, Virginia Brown Faire, Ralph Cloninger; *D:* Emmett j. Flynn; *W:* Bernard McConville; *C:* Lucien N. Andriot.

Monte Walsh ✐✐✐ **1970 (PG)** Aging cowboy sees declining of Old West, embarks on mission to avenge best friend's death. Subdued, moving western worthy of genre greats Marvin and Palance. Cinematographer Fraker proves himself a proficient director in this, his first venture. Based on Jack Schaefer's novel. **100m/C VHS.** Lee Marvin, Jack Palance, Jeanne Moreau, Jim Davis, Mitchell Ryan; *D:* William A. Fraker; *W:* David Zelag Goodman; *M:* John Barry.

Monte Walsh ✐✐ 1/2 **2003** Tried-and-true horse opera adapted from the novel by Jack Schaefer and a remake of the 1970 film. Aging cowpoke Monte Walsh (Selleck) realizes that life in 1892 Wyoming's Antelope Junction is changing. An eastern company is taking over the western free-range society and fewer cowboys are making a living. Monte has his loyal love Martine (Rossellini) to sustain him, but pal Chet (Carradine) needs a way to support his family and hot-headed Shorty (Eads) has turned to crime. Selleck has become a comfortable old hand at these roles; the pleasures may be undemanding but they're still present. **120m/C DVD.** Tom Selleck, Isabella Rossellini, Keith Carradine, George Eads, William Devane, Barry Corbin, James Gammon, William Sanderson, Wallace Shawn, Joanna Miles; ***D:*** Simon Wincer; ***W:*** Robert B. Parker, Michael Brandman, David Zelag Goodman, Lukas Heller; ***C:*** David Eggby; ***M:*** Eric Colvin. **CABLE**

Montenegro 1/2 *Montenegro—Or Pigs and Pearls* **1981** Offbeat, bawdy comedy details experiences of bored, possibly mad housewife who lands in a coarse, uninhibited ethnic community. To its credit, this film remains unpredictable to the end. And Anspach, an intriguing, resourceful—and attractive—actress, delivers what is perhaps her greatest performance. **97m/C VHS, DVD.** *SW* Susan Anspach, Erland Josephson; ***D:*** Dusan Makavejev; ***W:*** Dusan Makavejev; ***C:*** Tomislav Pinter; ***M:*** Kornell Kovac.

Monterey Pop 1/2 **1968** This pre-Woodstock rock 'n' roll festival in Monterey, California, features landmark performances by some of the most popular '60s rockers. Compelling for the performances, and historically important as the first significant rock concert film. Appearances by Jefferson Airplane, Janis Joplin, Jimi Hendrix, Simon and Garfunkel, The Who, and Otis Redding. **72m/C VHS, DVD.** ***D:*** James Desmond, Richard Leacock, D.A. Pennebaker.

A Month by the Lake 1/2 **1995 (PG)** Redgrave takes the plunge into highly familiar romantic comedy of the Proper English sort and glides effortlessly through this slow-moving but often charming adaptation of an H. E. Bates short story. Set in pre-WWII northern Italy, Miss Bentley (Redgrave) sets her spinster's eye on the somewhat wooden, but gradually warming, English Major Wilshaw (Fox). Petulant American nanny Thurman arrives to provide an arresting diversion for Wilshaw, while Gassman proves an unwitting pawn for Miss Bentley's game of "get the major." Touching and lighthearted performances, especially by heavyweight Redgrave, are complemented by glorious cinematography. **92m/C VHS, DVD.** Vanessa Redgrave, Edward Fox, Uma Thurman, Alida Valli, Alessandro Gassman, Carlo Cartier; ***D:*** John Irvin; ***W:*** Trevor Bentham; ***C:*** Pasqualino De Santis; ***M:*** Nicola Piovani.

A Month in the Country **1987** The reverently quiet story of two British WWI veterans, one an archaeologist and the other a church painting restorer, who are working in a tiny village while trying to heal their emotional wounds. Based on the novel by J.L. Carr. **92m/C VHS.** *GB* Colin Firth, Natasha Richardson, Kenneth Branagh, Patrick Malahide, Tony Haygarth, Jim Carter; ***D:*** Pat O'Connor; ***W:*** Simon Gray; ***C:*** Kenneth Macmillan; ***M:*** Howard Blake.

Monty Python and the Holy Grail 1/2 **1975 (PG)** Britain's famed comedy band assaults the Arthurian legend in a cult classic replete with a Trojan rabbit and an utterly dismembered, but inevitably pugnacious, knight. Fans of manic comedy—and graphic violence—should get more than their fill here. **90m/C VHS, DVD, UMD.** *GB* Graham Chapman, John Cleese, Terry Gilliam, Eric Idle, Terry Jones, Michael Palin, Carol Cleveland, Connie Booth, Neil Innes, Patsy Kensit; ***D:*** Terry Gilliam, Terry Jones; ***W:*** Graham Chapman, John Cleese, Terry Gilliam, Eric Idle, Terry Jones, Michael Palin; ***C:*** Terry Bedford; ***M:*** De Wolfe, Neil Innes.

Monty Python's Life of Brian 1/2 *Life of Brian* **1979 (R)** Often riotous spoof of Christianity tracks hapless peasant mistaken for the messiah in A.D. 32. Film reels from routine to routine, and only the most pious will remain unmoved by a chorus of crucifixion victims. Probably the group's most daring, controversial venture. **94m/C VHS, DVD.** *GB* Graham Chapman, John Cleese, Terry Gilliam, Eric Idle, Michael Palin, George Harrison, Terry Jones, Kenneth Colley, Spike Milligan, Carol Cleveland, Neil Innes, Andrew MacLachlan; ***D:*** Terry Jones; ***W:*** Graham Chapman, John Cleese, Terry Gilliam, Eric Idle, Michael Palin, Terry Jones; ***C:*** Peter Biziou; ***M:*** Geoffrey Burgon.

Monty Python's The Meaning of Life **1983 (R)** Funny, technically impressive film conducts various inquiries into the most profound questions confronting humanity. Notable among the sketches here are a live sex enactment performed before bored schoolboys, a student-faculty rugby game that turns quite violent, and an encounter between a physician and a reluctant, untimely organ donor. Another sketch provides a memorable portrait of a glutton prone to nausea. And at film's end, the meaning of life is actually revealed. **107m/C VHS, DVD, HD DVD.** *GB* Graham Chapman, John Cleese, Terry Gilliam, Eric Idle, Terry Jones, Michael Palin, Carol Cleveland, Matt Frewer, Simon Jones, Patricia Quinn, Andrew MacLachlan; ***D:*** Terry Gilliam, Terry Jones; ***W:*** Graham Chapman, John Cleese, Terry Gilliam, Eric Idle, Terry Jones, Michael Palin; ***C:*** Peter Hannan; ***M:*** John Du Prez, Graham Chapman, John Cleese, Eric Idle, Terry Jones, Michael Palin. Cannes '83: Grand Jury Prize.

Monument Ave. 1/2 *Snitch* **1998** Updated, Irish-American version of Martin Scorsese's "Mean Streets" focuses on a group of petty thieves from Boston's mostly Irish Charleston neighborhood. The hoods, lead by Bobby O'Grady (Leary), pass time stealing cars, snorting cocaine, and waxing poetic about their dead-end lives. But when a recently paroled member of their gang is murdered by the neighborhood kingpin Jackie O' (Meaney), Bobby must decide between upholding the gang's code of silence and avenging his pal's death. Excellent performances all around, especially from Leary, who grew up in this neighborhood. Originality, however, is not the film's strong suit. In addition to borrowing from Scorsese, script is full of Tarantinoesque banter. Worthy effort, just don't expect anything you haven't seen before. **90m/C VHS, DVD.** Denis Leary, Billy Crudup, Famke Janssen, Colm Meaney, Martin Sheen, Jeanne Tripplehorn, Ian Hart, Jason Barry, John Diehl, Noah Emmerich, Greg Dulli; ***D:*** Ted (Edward) Demme; ***W:*** Mike Armstrong; ***C:*** Adam Kimmel; ***M:*** Amanda Scheer-Demme.

Moola 1/2 **2007 (PG-13)** A truth-is-stranger-than-fiction comedy that's nothing special but amusing enough for a look-see. Best pals and business partners Steve (Mapother) and Harry (Baldwin) both have crumbling marriages and a business making chemical light sticks that's about to go under. Then they learn that dairy farmers are using their glow-sticks to determine a cow's fertility cycle. Soon slimy businessman Montgomery (Hutchison) is offering to buy them out and the guys start spending money they don't actually have, which gets them into further trouble. **110m/C DVD.** William Mapother, Daniel Baldwin, Doug Hutchison, Curtis Armstrong, Treat Williams, Efren Ramirez, Charlotte Ross, Annabelle Gurwitch; ***D:*** Donny Most; ***W:*** Jeffrey Allen Arbaugh; ***M:*** Rick Marotta, Roberto Blasini. **VIDEO**

Moolaade *Protection* **2004** Eighty-one-year-old Senegalese filmmaker/activist Sembene focuses on the practice of female genital mutilation that still occurs in a number of African countries. In a small village, Colle (Coulibaly), the fearless second wife of a village elder, refuses to allow her daughter Amasatou (Traore) to undergo the purification ceremony that has caused her own lifelong pain. She then becomes the protector of four young girls, also fleeing the ceremony, who seek sanctuary. To defend the girls, Colle invokes the traditional protective spirit of the title so the girls cannot be removed from her care and discovers her resistance is considered a threat to the social order of village life. Bambara and French with subtitles. **124m/C** Fatoumata Coulibaly, Maimouna Helene Diarra, Salimata Traore, Dominique T. Zeida, Mah Compaore, Aminata Dao; ***D:*** Ousmane Sembene; ***W:*** Ousmane Sembene; ***C:*** Dominique Gentil; ***M:*** Boncana Maiga.

Moon **2009 (R)** First feature for director Duncan Jones, son of David Bowie, was filmed on the soundstages of England's Shepperton Studios. Sam Bell (Rockwell) is a lonely corporate astronaut completing a solo three-year stint on the Moon for a mining company. His only companion is the snarky voice of his robot Gerty (Spacey) and long-distance contact with his wife and daughter. Then Sam suddenly becomes ill and starts having hallucinations (or are they?) of a cloned Sam. Space Oddity indeed. **97m/C DVD.** *US GB* Sam Rockwell, Kaya Scodelario, Matt Berry, Robin Chalk, Benedict Wong, Dominique McElligott; ***D:*** Duncan Jones; ***W:*** Nathan Parker; ***C:*** Gary Shaw; ***M:*** Clint Mansell; ***V:*** Kevin Spacey.

The Moon and Sixpence **1943** Stockbroker turns ambitious painter in this adaptation of W. Somerset Maugham's novel that was, in turn, inspired by the life of artist Paul Gauguin. Fine performance from Sanders. Filmed mainly in black and white, but uses color sparingly to great advantage. Compare this one to "Wolf at the Door," in which Gauguin is played by Donald Sutherland. **89m/B VHS, DVD.** George Sanders, Herbert Marshall, Steven Geray, Doris Dudley, Eric Blore, Elena Verdugo, Florence Bates, Albert Bassermann, Heather Thatcher; ***D:*** Albert Lewin.

The Moon & the Stars **2007** Davide (Molina) is a gay, Jewish film producer trying to get a non-operatic version of "Tosca" made in 1939 as the fascists come power in Italy. Money problems plague the production being filmed at Rome's Cinecitta Studio where Davide needs a fascist patron to make things legit and there are tensions on and off the set. **90m/C DVD.** *GB HU IT* Alfred Molina, Jonathan Pryce, Catherine McCormack, Andras Balint, Rupert Friend, Roberto Purvis, Ivano Marescotti, Surama DeCastro, Niccolo Senni; ***D:*** John Irvin; ***W:*** Peter Barnes; ***C:*** Elemer Ragalyi; ***M:*** Adriano Maria Vitali.

Moon 44 1/2 **1990 (R)** A space prison is overrun by thugs who terrorize their fellow inmates. Fine cast, taut pacing. Filmed in Germany. **102m/C VHS, DVD.** *GE* Malcolm McDowell, Lisa Eichhorn, Michael Pare, Stephen Geoffreys, Roscoe Lee Browne, Brian Thompson, Dean Devlin, Mechmed Yilmaz, Leon Rippy; ***D:*** Roland Emmerich.

Moon in Scorpio 1/2 **1986** Three Vietnam-vet buddies go sailing and are attacked by the back-from-the-dead victims of a bloody war crime. **90m/C VHS.** John Phillip Law, Britt Ekland, William (Bill) Smith; ***D:*** Gary Graver.

Moon in the Gutter 1/2 *La Lune Dans le Caniveau* **1983 (R)** In a ramshackle harbor town, a man searches despondently for the person who killed his sister years before. Various sexual liaisons and stevedore fights intermittently spice up the action. Nasty story that doesn't make much sense on film; adapted from a book by American pulp writer David Goodis. In French with English subtitles. **109m/C VHS.** *IT FR* Gerard Depardieu, Nastassja Kinski, Victoria Abril, Vittorio Mezzogiorno, Dominique Pinon; ***D:*** Jean-Jacques Beineix; ***W:*** Jean-Jacques Beineix; ***C:*** Philippe Rousselot; ***M:*** Gabriel Yared. Cesar '84: Art Dir./Set Dec.

The Moon Is Blue 1/2 **1953** A young woman flaunts her virginity in this stilted adaptation of F. Hugh Herbert's play. Hard to believe that this film was once considered risque. Good performances, though, from Holden and Niven. **100m/B** William Holden, David Niven, Maggie McNamara, Tom Tully; ***D:*** Otto Preminger; ***C:*** Ernest Laszlo. Golden Globes '54: Actor—Mus./Comedy (Niven).

Moon of the Wolf **1972** A small town in bayou country is terrorized by a modern-day werewolf that rips its victims to shreds. **74m/C VHS, DVD.** David Janssen, Barbara Rush, Bradford Dillman, John Beradino, Geoffrey Lewis, Royal Dano; ***D:*** Daniel Petrie; ***W:*** Alvin Sapinsley; ***C:*** Richard C. Glouner; ***M:*** Bernardo Segall. **TV**

Moon over Broadway **1998** Filmmakers (and spouses) Pennebaker and Hegedus follow the Broadway-bound comedy "Moon over Buffalo" in its evolution from pen to premiere—a lot like "Waiting for Guffman," but for real. Along the way we see how a bunch of professionals try to fine-tune a very average script into a funny comedy, and all the rewrites, conflicts, and jealousies that entails. As the celebrity of the cast, Burnett is at first resented (this isn't TV and she hasn't been on Broadway in 30 years), but winds up the life of the party, injecting most of the humor, and shows herself to be the real trouper among them. All in all an interestingly tense, and sometimes funny, behind-the-scenes look—with the biggest disappointment being the play itself, which did manage to run for nine months, probably thanks to Burnett. **92m/C VHS, DVD.** Carol Burnett, Philip Bosco; ***D:*** D.A. Pennebaker, Chris Hegedus; ***C:*** D.A. Pennebaker, James Desmond.

Moon over Harlem 1/2 **1939** A musical melodrama about a widow who unwittingly marries a fast-talking gangster involved in the numbers racket. The film features 20 chorus girls, a choir, and a 60-piece orchestra. **67m/B VHS, DVD.** Bud Harris, Cora Green, Alec Lovejoy, Sidney Bechet; ***D:*** Edgar G. Ulmer.

Moon over Miami **1941** Man-hunting trio meet their match in this engaging musical. A remake of 1938's "Three Blind Mice," this was later remade in 1946 as "Three Little Girls in Blue." ♫ Moon Over Miami; I've Got You All To Myself; What Can I Do For You?; Kindergarten Congo; You Started Something; Oh Me Oh Mi-Am-Mi; Solitary Seminole; Is That Good?; Loveliness and Love. **91m/C VHS, DVD.** Don Ameche, Betty Grable, Robert Cummings, Carole Landis, Charlotte Greenwood, Jack Haley; ***D:*** Walter Lang; ***W:*** Mitch Glazer; ***C:*** Leon Shamroy.

Moon over Parador 1/2 **1988 (PG-13)** An uneven comedy about a reluctant American actor who gets the role of his life when he gets the chance to pass himself off as the recently deceased dictator of a Latin American country. A political strongman wants to continue the charade until he can take over, but the actor begins to enjoy the benefits of dictatorship. Look for a cameo by director/writer Mazursky in drag. **103m/C VHS, DVD.** Richard Dreyfuss, Sonia Braga, Raul Julia, Jonathan Winters, Fernando Rey, Ed Asner, Dick Cavett, Michael Greene, Sammy Davis Jr., Polly Holliday, Charo, Marianne Saegebrecht, Dana Delany, Ike Pappas, Paul Mazursky; ***D:*** Paul Mazursky; ***W:*** Leon Capetanos, Paul Mazursky; ***M:*** Maurice Jarre.

Moon over Tao **1997** In 16th-century Japan, a Samurai (Abe) and a sorcerer (Nagashima) are dispatched to discover the origins of a strange sword which can cut through solid stone. Once on their quest, they learn that the sword was forged from a meteorite, which also housed a strange orb. This orb contains the power to destroy the world. Meanwhile, three mysterious alien females are dispatched to Earth to retrieve the orb. Unfortunately, it has fallen into the hands of an evil tyrant (Enoki) who wants to use its powers to rule the planet. Successfully mixes sword & sorcery action with a science fiction slant. Director Amemiya is best known for making films featuring futuristic creatures, but he tones that down here, evoking an interesting narrative and impressive fight scenes. American viewers familiar with similar films will find the pacing here a bit different, but the film is engrossing all the same. **96m/C DVD.** *JP* Toshiyuki Nagashima, Hiroshi Abe, Takaaki Enoki; ***D:*** Keito Amamiya.

Moon Pilot **1962** An astronaut on his way to the moon encounters a mysterious alien woman who claims to know his future. **98m/C VHS.** Tom Tryon, Brian Keith, Edmond O'Brien, Dany Saval, Tommy Kirk; ***D:*** James Neilson.

The Moon-Spinners 1/2 **1964 (PG)** Lightweight Disney drama featuring Mills as a young tourist traveling through Crete who meets up with a young man, accused of being a jewel thief, and the two work together to find the real jewel thieves. Watch for silent film star Pola Negri. **118m/C VHS, DVD.** Hayley Mills, Peter McEnery, Eli Wallach, Pola Negri, Joan Greenwood, Irene Papas, Sheila Hancock; ***D:*** James Neilson; ***W:*** Michael Dyne; ***M:*** Ron Grainer.

The Moon Stallion 1/2 **1985** A charming tale of mystery and fantasy for children and adults. Professor Purwell is researching King Arthur. His blind daughter soon becomes involved with supernatural events and a white horse that appears to lead her into adventures not of this age. **95m/C VHS.** *GB* Sarah Sutton, David Haig, James Greene, John Abineri, Caroline Goodall; ***D:*** Dorothea Brooking.

Moonbase ♪♪ **1997 (R)** In the year 2045, John Russell, manager of the Moonbase Waste Disposal Plant, has his hands full with more than garbage when a group of prison escapees take over the facility. **89m/C VHS.** Scott Plank, Jocelyn Seagrave, Kurt Fuller, Robert O'Reilly; ***D:*** Paolo Mazzucato; ***W:*** Brian DiMuccio, Dino Vindeni; ***M:*** Michael Sherwood. **VIDEO**

Mooncussers ♪ ½ **1962** A children's film detailing the exploits of a precocious 12-year-old determined to exact revenge upon a band of ruthless pirates. **85m/C VHS.** Kevin Corcoran, Rian Garrick, Oscar Homolka; ***D:*** James Neilson.

Moondance ♪♪ **1995 (R)** When lovely young German tourist Anya (Brendler) comes to an Irish fishing village on a summer holiday, two young brothers, Patrick (Shaw) and Dominic (Conroy), vie for her affections causing a family rift. Adapted from the novel "The White Hare" by Francis Stuart. **96m/C VHS, DVD.** *GB* Ruaidhri Conroy, Ian Shaw, Julia Brendler, Marianne Faithfull, Gerard McSorley, Kate Flynn, Brendan Grace; ***D:*** Dagmar Hirtz; ***W:*** Burt Weinshanker, Matt Watters; ***C:*** Steven Bernstein; ***M:*** Van Morrison, Fiachra Trench.

Moondance Alexander ♪♪ ½ **2007 (G)** Appealing family film. Awkward 15-year-old Moondance (Panabaker) lives with her eccentric mom Gelsey (Loughlin) and expects to have an uneventful summer. Then she finds pinto pony Checkers has jumped his paddock fence, so she returns him to ranch owner Dante Longpre (Johnson). Convinced that Checkers is a champion jumper just waiting for his chance, Moondance then convinces Dante to train her and Checkers for an upcoming competition. **94m/C DVD.** Kay Panabaker, Don Johnson, Lori Loughlin, James Best, Sasha Cohen, Whitney Sloan, Joe Norman Shaw; ***D:*** Michael Damian; ***W:*** Michael Damian, Janeen Damian; ***C:*** Julien Eudes; ***M:*** Mark Thomas. **VIDEO**

Moonfleet ♪♪ ½ **1955** Follows the adventures of an 18th century buccaneer who tries to swindle a young lad in his charge of a valuable diamond. From J. Meade Falkner's novel. **89m/C VHS.** Stewart Granger, Jon Whiteley, George Sanders, Viveca Lindfors, Joan Greenwood, Ian Wolfe; ***D:*** Fritz Lang; ***M:*** Miklos Rozsa.

Moonlight & Mistletoe ♪♪ **2008** Passable holiday fare from the Hallmark Channel finds Nick's (Arnold) business about to go bankrupt. He runs a year-round Christmas attraction called Santaville and his troubling news brings daughter Holly (Cameron-Bure) back to try and help her dad save not only his livelihood but the holiday spirit. Arnold is a little grating but Cameron-Bure is sweet. **90m/C DVD.** ***W:*** Duane Poole. **CABLE**

Moonlight and Valentino ♪♪ **1995 (R)** To help her recover from the death of her husband, Rebecca turns to the comfort of flaky neighbor Sylvie (Goldberg), self-destructive sis Lucy (Paltrow), and overbearing ex-stepmother Alberta (Turner). Together they sit around and talk some of the more contrived and cliched "women talk" ("Chicken soup is the most womanly thing on the face of the planet") in recent film history. The finale, a hokey ritual in a cemetery, will have you pulling out hair rather than hankies. Rock star Bon Jovi makes his screen debut as the beefcake (discussion of his butt takes up about two-thirds of the dialogue) who puts the fire back into Rebecca's life. Not for the estrogen impaired. **104m/C VHS, DVD.** Elizabeth Perkins, Whoopi Goldberg, Gwyneth Paltrow, Kathleen Turner, Jon Bon Jovi, Jeremy Sisto, Josef Sommer, Peter Coyote; ***D:*** David Anspaugh; ***W:*** Ellen Simon; ***C:*** Julio Macat; ***M:*** Howard Shore.

Moonlight Mile ♪♪♪ **2002 (PG-13)** Quirky look at dealing with grief in the aftermath of tragedy. Circa 1973, Joe Nast (Gyllenhaal) has attended the funeral of his fiancee Diana Floss at the home of her parents Ben (Hoffman) and JoJo (Sarandon). Literally at a loss, Joe moves in to the Floss home and forms an unusual bond with these virtual strangers. To fill his void, Ben tries to get Joe to go into the real estate development business with him. The strident JoJo guesses there's more to Joe's loss than meets the eye. Joe is aided in his grief when he meets attractive postal worker Bertie (Pompeo) who has experienced similar loss. Coleman gives an animated performance as the local rich guy who shatters Ben's dreams. Great performances all around, especially by newcomer Pompeo. Loosely based on director Silberling's experience as the boyfriend of murdered actress Rebecca Schaffer. **112m/C VHS, DVD.** *US* Jake Gyllenhaal, Dustin Hoffman, Susan Sarandon, Holly Hunter, Ellen Pompeo, Richard T. Jones, Allan Corduner, Dabney Coleman, Akelsia Landeau, Roxanne Hart; ***D:*** Brad Silberling; ***W:*** Brad Silberling; ***C:*** Phedon Papamichael; ***M:*** Mark Isham.

Moonlight Serenade ♪♪ **2009 (PG-13)** Successful financial manager Nate (Newman) is a closet piano player who hears an exceptional voice singing outside his apartment window. The tuneful sparrow is coat check girl Chloe (Adams) who works at a jazz club. Soon the two decide to perform together and their beautiful music extends offstage as well. **91m/C DVD.** Alec Newman, Amy Adams, Harriet Sansom Harris, Moon Bloodgood, Scott Cohen; ***D:*** Giacarlo Tallarico; ***W:*** Jonathan Abrahams; ***C:*** Eric William Larson; ***M:*** Joey DeFrancesco. **VIDEO**

Moonlight Sonata ♪♪ ½ **1938** Professional concert pianist Paderewski performs his way through a confusing soap-opera of a film. Includes performances of Franz Liszt's "Second Hungarian Rhapsody" and Frederic Chopin's "Polonaise." **80m/B VHS, DVD.** *GB* Ignace Jan Paderewski, Charles Farrell, Marie Tempest, Barbara Greene, Eric Portman; ***D:*** Lothar Mendes.

Moonlight Whispers ♪♪ ½ *Gekko no sasayaki; Sasayaki* **1999 (R)** An unusual teen romance, to say the least. A young woman discovers her boyfriend has been collecting her used socks and undies, and he breaks down and admits he wants to be her dog. She freaks out and dumps him, but he continues to vie for her affections anyway, and she soon realizes she actually enjoys tormenting him and that they both share a common fetish. So she must either choose a conventional but boring relationship with her new boyfriend, or return to a decidedly unusual one with her former lover who won't give her up. Despite what could be disturbing subject matter the film is a romantic drama as opposed to an exploitation film. **100m/C DVD.** *JP* Kenji Mizuhashi, Tsugumi, Kouta Kisano, Harumi Inoue; ***D:*** Akihiko Shiota; ***W:*** Masahiko Kikuni, Yoichi Nishiyama, Skihiko Shiota; ***C:*** Shigeru Kumatsubara; ***M:*** Shinsuke Honda.

The Moonlighter ♪♪ **1953** Title refers to MacMurray's jailed character Wes Anderson who herds cows by day and rustles 'em by night. When a lynch mob attacks the jail, Wes escapes but an innocent man is hanged in his place. Wes vows revenge and turns bank robber and his ex-gal Rela (Stanwyck), obviously a match for any man, is deputized to bring him in. Disjointed western story; watch the film noir pairing of MacMurray and Stanwyck in 1944's "Double Indemnity" instead. **77m/B DVD.** Barbara Stanwyck, Fred MacMurray, Ward Bond, William Ching, John Dierkes, Jack Elam; ***D:*** Roy Rowland; ***W:*** Niven Busch; ***C:*** Heinz Roemheld; ***M:*** Bert Glennon.

Moonlighting ♪♪♪ ½ **1982 (PG)** Compelling drama about Polish laborers illegally hired to renovate London flat. When their country falls under martial law, the foreman conceals the event and pushes workers to complete project. Unlikely casting of Irons as foreman is utterly successful. **97m/C VHS, DVD.** *PL GB* Jeremy Irons, Eugene Lipinski, Jiri Stanislay, Eugeniusz Haczkiewicz; ***D:*** Jerzy Skolimowski; ***C:*** Tony Pierce-Roberts; ***M:*** Hans Zimmer.

Moonlighting ♪♪ ½ **1985** Pilot for the popular detective show, where Maddie and David, the daffy pair of impetuous private eyes, meet for the first time and solve an irrationally complex case. **93m/C VHS, DVD.** Cybill Shepherd, Bruce Willis, Allyce Beasley; ***D:*** Robert Butler; ***W:*** Glenn Gordon Caron; ***C:*** Michael D. Margulies; ***M:*** Lee Holdridge. **TV**

The Moonraker ♪♪ ½ **1958** Compelling action scenes highlight this tale set at the end of the English Civil War, as the Royalists attempt to sneak the king out of England and into France. **82m/C VHS.** *GB* George Baker, Sylvia Syms, Peter Arne, Marius Goring, Clive Morton, Gary Raymond, Richard Leech, Patrick Troughton; ***D:*** David MacDonald.

Moonraker ♪♪ **1979 (PG)** Uninspired Bond fare has 007 unraveling intergalactic hijinks. Bond is aided by a female CIA agent, assaulted by a giant with jaws of steel, and captured by Amazons when he sets out to protect the human race. Moore, Chiles, and Lonsdale all seem to be going through the motions only. **136m/C VHS, DVD.** *GB* Roger Moore, Lois Chiles, Richard Kiel, Michael (Michel) Lonsdale, Corinne Clery, Geoffrey Keen, Emily Bolton, Walter Gotell, Bernard Lee, Lois Maxwell, Desmond Llewelyn; ***D:*** Lewis Gilbert; ***W:*** Christopher Wood; ***C:*** Jean Tournier; ***M:*** John Barry.

The Moon's Our Home ♪♪ ½ **1936** A fast-paced, breezy, screwball comedy about an actress and adventurer impulsively marrying and then bickering through the honeymoon. Silliness at its height. Fonda and Sullavan were both married and then divorced before filming this movie. **80m/B VHS.** Margaret Sullavan, Henry Fonda, Beulah Bondi, Charles Butterworth, Margaret Hamilton, Walter Brennan, Grace Hayle, Lucien Littlefield, Spencer Charters, Henrietta Crosman, Margaret Fielding; ***D:*** William A. Seiter; ***W:*** Alan Campbell, Isabel Dawn, Dorothy Parker; ***C:*** Joseph Valentine.

Moonshine County Express ♪ ½ **1977 (PG)** Three sexy daughters of a hillbilly moonshiner set out to run the still and avenge their father's murder. **97m/C VHS.** John Saxon, Susan Howard, William Conrad, Morgan Woodward, Claudia Jennings, Jeff Corey, Dub Taylor, Maureen McCormick, Albert Salmi, Candice Rialson; ***D:*** Gus Trikonis.

Moonshine Highway ♪♪ **1996 (PG-13)** Redneck alert! '50s Tennessee moonshiner Jed Muldoon (MacLachlan) clashes with Sheriff Miller (Quaid), who's not only aggrieved about Jed's illegal liquor running but is not happy that his estranged wife Ethel (Del Mar) has taken up with the miscreant. Lots of backwoods car chases. **96m/C VHS.** Kyle MacLachlan, Randy Quaid, Maria Del Mar, Gary Farmer, Jeremy Ratchford; ***D:*** Andy Armstrong; ***W:*** Andy Armstrong; ***C:*** Dick Quinlan. **CABLE**

Moonshine Mountain WOOF! *White Trash on Moonshine Mountain* **1964** A country-western star travels with his girlfriend to the singer's home in backwoods Carolina. When the girl is killed by a lusting resident, all hell breaks loose. One of gore-meister Lewis' excursions into the dramatic. **90m/C VHS.** Chuck Scott, Adam Sorg, Jeffrey Allen, Bonnie Hinson, Carmen Sotir, Ben Moore, Pat Patterson, Mark Douglas; ***D:*** Herschell Gordon Lewis; ***W:*** Herschell Gordon Lewis; ***C:*** Herschell Gordon Lewis; ***M:*** Herschell Gordon Lewis.

The Moonstone ♪ ½ **1934** A low-budget Monogram mystery based on the novel by Wilkie Collins. A British soldier steals the title gem from an Indian idol and it eventually winds up as a birthday present for heiress Anne Verinder (Barry). Then the cursed jewel is stolen from Anne and havoc ensues as Scotland Yard is called in to investigate. **62m/B DVD.** David Manners, Phyllis Barry, Herbert Bunston, Charles Irwin, Claude King, Jameson Thomas, Gustav von Seyffertitz; ***D:*** Reginald Barker; ***W:*** Adele Buffington; ***C:*** Robert Planck; ***M:*** Abe Meyer.

The Moonstone ♪♪ ½ **1972** The moonstone is a fabulous jewel from India that lovely Rachel Verinder (Heilbron) receives on her birthday. However, the gem is stolen property and is now stolen from Rachel, which brings Sgt. Cuff (Welsh) of Scotland Yard in to solve the crime. Adaptation of the 1868 Wilkie Collins novel. **221m/C DVD.** *GB* Vivien Heilbron, John Welsh, Robin Ellis, Martin Jarvis, Basil Dignam, Colin Baker, Anna Cropper, Kathleen Byron; ***D:*** Paddy Russell; ***W:*** Hugh Leonard. **TV**

The Moonstone ♪♪♪ **1997** In the mid-19th century, the Moonstone, a sacred Hindu diamond, is stolen from a shrine in India. The jewel, which carries a curse, winds up in the hands of heiress Rachel Verinder (Hawes), thanks to her suitor Franklin Blake (Wise). But when the diamond is stolen from Rachel, police Sergeant Cuff (Sher) investigates and uncovers deception and a variety of villains. Based on the novel by Wilkie Collins and considered the first detective story, some 20 years before Conan Doyle's Sherlock Holmes. **120m/C VHS, DVD.** Greg Wise, Anthony Sher, Keeley Hawes, Patricia Hodge; ***D:*** Robert Bierman. **TV**

Moonstruck ♪♪♪ ½ **1987 (PG-13)** Winning romantic comedy about widow engaged to one man but falling in love with his younger brother in Little Italy. Excellent performances all around, with Cher particularly fetching as attractive, hapless widow. Unlikely casting of usually dominating Aiello, as unassuming mama's boy also works well, and Cage is at his best as a tormented one-handed opera lover/baker. **103m/C VHS, DVD.** Cher, Nicolas Cage, Olympia Dukakis, Danny Aiello, Vincent Gardenia, Julie Bovasso, Louis Guss, Anita Gillette, Feodor Chaliapin Jr., John Mahoney; ***D:*** Norman Jewison; ***W:*** John Patrick Shanley; ***C:*** David Watkin; ***M:*** Dick Hyman. Oscars '87: Actress (Cher), Orig. Screenplay, Support. Actress (Dukakis); Berlin Intl. Film Fest. '87: Director (Jewison); Golden Globes '88: Actress—Mus./Comedy (Cher), Support. Actress (Dukakis); L.A. Film Critics '87: Support. Actress (Dukakis); Natl. Bd. of Review '87: Support. Actress (Dukakis); Writers Guild '87: Orig. Screenplay.

Moontide ♪♪ **1942** French star Gabin made his American debut in a routine melodrama about a drunken longshoreman accused of murder. Awakening from his latest drunken spree, Bobo can't remember committing any crime but he decides to lay low on a bait boat with his derelict friend Tiny (Mitchell) who promises to keep quiet. Then Bobo saves waitress Anna (Lupino) from a suicide attempt, invites her onboard, and three's a crowd. Especially when Anna is able to figure out who really committed the crime. **94m/B DVD.** Jean Gabin, Thomas Mitchell, Ida Lupino, Claude Rains, Jerome Cowan, Ralph Byrd, Victor Sen Yung; ***D:*** Archie Mayo; ***W:*** John O'Hara; ***C:*** Charles G. Clarke.

Moontrap ♪♪ **1989** An astronaut discovers an alien frozen in space and returns to Earth with it. Once thawed, the creature reveals its horrible secret. **92m/C VHS.** Walter Koenig, Bruce Campbell, Leigh Lombardi; ***D:*** Robert Dyke.

Morals for Women ♪ ½ **1931** This soap-opera's so old it almost predates soap. A secretary becomes the Kept Woman of her boss in the Big Bad City. She escapes, but not for long. **65m/B VHS.** Bessie Love, Conway Tearle, John Holland, Natalie Moorhead, Emma Dunn, June Clyde; ***D:*** Mort Blumenstock.

Moran of the Lady Letty ♪♪ ½ **1922** Seaweed saga of Ramon Laredo (Valentino), a high society guy who's kidnapped aboard a pirate barge. When the salty dogs rescue/capture Moran (a theme ahead of its time?) from a ship fuming with burning coal, Ramon is smitten in a big way with the boyish girl and battles contagiously to prevent the pirates from selling her as a slave. Excellent fight scenes with much hotstepping over gangplanks and swinging from masts, with a 60-foot death dive from above. Little known Dalton was a celluloid fave in the 'teens and twenties, and Valentino is atypically cast as a man's man. The sheik himself is said not to have like this one because it undermined his image as a ladies' man. **71m/B VHS.** Dorothy Dalton, Rudolph Valentino, Charles Brinley, Walter Long, Emil Jorgenson; ***D:*** George Melford.

More ♪♪ ½ **1969** Smells like teen angst in the '60s when a German college grad falls for an American in Paris, to the tune of sex, drugs, and Pink Floyd. Schroeder's first effort as director, it's definitely a '60s pic. In French with English subtitles. **110m/C VHS, DVD.** Mimsy Farmer, Klaus Grunberg, Heinz Engelmann, Michel Chanderli; ***D:*** Barbet Schroeder; ***C:*** Nestor Almendros.

More about the Children of Noisy Village ♪♪ ½ *More About the Children of Bullerby Village; Mem om oss barn i Bullerby* **1987** The six adventurous children, who live in an idyllic Swedish village before WWII, return. This time they're ready to start a new school year, including playing pranks on the teacher, getting stranded during a blizzard, and enjoying a memorable New

Year's Eve. Based on stories by Astrid Lindgren. Dubbed. **85m/C VHS.** *SW* Linda Bergstrom, Ellem Demerus, Crispin Wendenius, Henrik Larsson; ***D:*** Lasse Hallstrom; ***C:*** Jens Fischer; ***M:*** George Riedel.

More American Graffiti 1/2 **1979 (PG)** Sequel to 1973's acclaimed '50s homage "American Graffiti" charts various characters' experiences in the more radical '60s. George Lucas didn't direct, Richard Dreyfuss didn't reprise. Ron Howard doesn't direct, he acts. B.W.L. Norton doesn't direct either, though he's credited. Pass on this one and have that root canal done instead. **111m/C VHS, DVD.** Delroy Lindo, James Houghton, John Lansing, Mary Kay Place, Rosanna Arquette, Jon(athan) Gries, Naomi Judd, Harrison Ford, Candy Clark, Bo Hopkins, Ron Howard, Paul LeMat, MacKenzie Phillips, Charles Martin Smith, Anna Bjorn, Richard Bradford, Cindy Williams, Scott Glenn; ***D:*** Bill W.L. Norton; ***W:*** Gloria Katz, Willard Huyck; ***C:*** Caleb Deschanel.

More Dead Than Alive 1/2 **1968** Gunslinger Cain (Walker) is released from an 18-year prison stint and is soon taking his sharpshooter credentials to a cheap wild west show run by Ruffalo (Price). But Cain's presence upsets former headliner, hot-headed young shooter Billy (Hampton). Surprise ending. **101m/C DVD.** Clint Walker, Vincent Price, Anne Francis, Paul Hampton, Mike Henry, Craig Littler; ***D:*** Robert Sparr; ***W:*** George Schenck; ***C:*** Jacques "Jack" Marquette; ***M:*** Philip Springer.

More Dogs Than Bones **2000 (R)** Crook Victoria (Ruehl) is on the lam, so she decides to hide $1 million in the luggage of Indian tourist Raj (Girafi), who's on his way to L.A. When she sends her boys (Mantegna, Hipp) to retrieve the loot, they discover Raj is staying at his nephew Andy's (Naidu) apartment and Andy's dog has buried the bag—only no one knows where. Too bad the pooch couldn't have buried this movie as well. **92m/C VHS, DVD.** Mercedes Ruehl, Joe Mantegna, Paul Hipp, Peter Coyote, Chaim Girafi, Ajay Naidu, Debi Mazar, Louise Fletcher, DB Woodside, Whoopi Goldberg, Kevin Weisman, Eddie Kaye Thomas; ***D:*** Michael Browning; ***W:*** Michael Browning.

More Than a Game 1/2 **2008 (PG)** Would anyone really be interested in Belman's familiar basketball documentary (no matter how well-done) if LeBron James wasn't an NBA superstar? The true story focuses on five basketball players at St. Vincent-St. Mary High School in Akron, Ohio, who played for coach Dru Joyce II since grade school. Over a six-year period LeBron James becomes a teen superstar with solid NBA prospects who, along with his teammates Romeo Travis, Sian Cotton, Dru Joyce III, and Willie McGee, bulldozed their competition to the 2003 High School National Championship amidst various personal and professional dramas. **105m/C DVD.** *US* LeBron James, Dru Joyce, Romeo Travis, Sian Cotton, Willie McGee; ***D:*** Kristopher Belman; ***W:*** Kristopher Belman, Brad Hogan; ***C:*** Kristopher Belman; ***M:*** Harvey W. Mason.

The More the Merrier **1943** Likeable romantic comedy in which working girl must share apartment with two bachelors in Washington, D.C., during WWII. Arthur is especially endearing as a young woman in male company. **104m/B VHS, DVD.** Joel McCrea, Jean Arthur, Charles Coburn, Richard Gaines, Bruce Bennett, Ann Savage, Ann Doran, Frank Tully, Grady Sutton; ***D:*** George Stevens. Oscars '43: Support. Actor (Coburn); N.Y. Film Critics '43: Director (Stevens).

More Wild, Wild West **1980** Another feature-length continuation of the satirical TV western series, with Winters taking on Conrad and Martin. **94m/C VHS.** Robert Conrad, Ross Martin, Jonathan Winters, Victor Buono; ***D:*** Burt Kennedy. **TV**

Morgan: A Suitable Case for Treatment 1/2 *Morgan!; A Suitable Case for Treatment* **1966** Offbeat comedy in which deranged artist copes with divorce by donning ape suit. Some laughs ensue. Based on David Mercer's play. **93m/B VHS, DVD.** *GB* Vanessa Redgrave, David Warner, Robert Stephens, Irene Handl, Bernard Bresslaw, Arthur Mullard, Newton Blick, Nan Munro, Graham Crowden, John Rae, Peter Collingwood, Edward Fox; ***D:*** Karel Reisz; ***W:*** David Mercer; ***C:*** Larry Pizer; ***M:*** John Dankworth. British Acad. '66: Screenplay; Cannes '66: Actress (Redgrave).

Morgan Stewart's Coming Home *Home Front* **1987 (PG-13)** When Dad needs a good family image in his political race, he brings Morgan home from boarding school. Fortunately, Morgan can see how his parents are using him and he doesn't approve at all. He decides to turn his family's life upside down while pursuing the love of his life. **96m/C VHS.** Jon Cryer, Lynn Redgrave, Nicholas Pryor, Viveka Davis, Paul Gleason, Andrew Duncan, Savely Kramorov, John David (J.D.) Cullum, Robert Sedgwick, Waweru Njenga, Sudhir Rad; ***D:*** Alan Smithee; ***M:*** Peter Bernstein.

Morgan the Pirate *Capitaine Morgan; Morgan il Pirata* **1960** Steve Reeves is at his finest as Morgan, an escaped slave who becomes a notorious pirate in the Caribbean and is wrongly condemned to death in this brisk, sea-going adventure. **93m/C VHS.** *FR IT* Steve Reeves, Valerie Lagrange; ***D:*** Andre de Toth.

Morgan's Ferry **1999 (PG-13)** Kinder, gentler "Desperate Hours" has three escaped cons, Sam (Zane), Monroe (Rollins), and Darcy (Galecki) happen upon the modest cottage of spinster Vonee (McGillis) and hold her hostage. Not only is she not afraid of the trio, but she falls in love with charming, sensitive Sam and hides him when his buddies decide to split. Interesting cast and nice twist on the escaped-cons-take-hostage story make this one better than it should be. **91m/C VHS, DVD.** Billy Zane, Kelly McGillis, Henry Rollins, Johnny Galecki, Roscoe Lee Browne, Muse Watson; ***D:*** Sam Pillsbury; ***C:*** Johnny E. Jensen; ***M:*** Mader.

The Morgue 1/2 **2007 (R)** Margo's job involves vacuuming the local morgue and handing the night watchman his nightly whiskey ration. A family stops by and asks to use the bathroom (yes, morgues have bathrooms), and following close behind is a group of heavily injured men. Then the power goes out as they all get stalked and killed by a shadowy figure. For poor Margo, it's all in a day's work. **84m/C DVD.** Bill Cobbs, Heather Donahue, Googy Gress, Michael Raye, Lisa Crilley, Chris Devlin, Taylor Lipman, Brady Matthews, Fred Ochs, Brandon Quinn, Sammy Sheik, Chris Torres; ***D:*** Halder Gomes, Gerson Sanginitte; ***W:*** Najla Ann Al-Doori, Andrew Pletcher; ***C:*** Jack Anderson; ***M:*** Perry La Marca. **VIDEO**

Morituri *Saboteur: Code Name Morituri; The Saboteur* **1965** Gripping wartime drama in which an Allied spy tries to persuade German gunboat captain to surrender his vessel. Brando is—no surprise—excellent. **123m/C VHS, DVD.** Marlon Brando, Yul Brynner, Trevor Howard, Janet Margolin, Wally Cox, William Redfield; ***D:*** Bernhard Wicki; ***W:*** Daniel Taradash; ***C:*** Conrad L. Hall; ***M:*** Jerry Goldsmith.

A Mormon Maid 1/2 **1917** Young woman and her family, after being saved from an Indian attack by a Mormon group, come to live among them without converting to their beliefs. Considered a shocking expose of controversial Mormon practices, including polygamy. **78m/B VHS.** Mae Murray, Frank Borzage, Hobart Bosworth, Noah Beery Sr.; ***D:*** Robert Z. Leonard.

The Morning After **1986 (R)** A predictable suspense-thriller about an alcoholic actress who wakes up one morning with a corpse in bed next to her, but cannot remember anything about the night before. She evades the police, accidentally meets up with an ex-cop, and works with him to unravel an increasingly complicated mystery. **103m/C VHS, DVD.** Jane Fonda, Jeff Bridges, Raul Julia, Diane Salinger, Richard Foronjy, Geoffrey Scott, Kathleen Wilhoite, Frances Bergen, Rick Rossovich, Kathy Bates; ***D:*** Sidney Lumet; ***W:*** James Cresson; ***C:*** Andrzej Bartkowiak.

Morning Departure 1/2 **1950** Suspenseful disaster story. During a postwar mission a British submarine hits a forgotten electric mine and sinks to the sea-bed with 12 survivors. Eight men use the only working snorkel equipment to get to safety while the sub's captain, Armstrong (Mills), tries to keep a stiff upper lip and keep the remaining three sailors calm while they await rescue. **102m/B DVD.** *GB* John Mills, Richard Attenborough, James Hayter, Nigel Patrick, Bernard Lee, Kenneth More; ***D:*** Roy Ward Baker; ***W:*** William Fairchild; ***C:*** Desmond Dickinson.

Morning Glory 1/2 **1933** Small-town girl finds love and fame in the big city. Predictable fare nonetheless boasts fine performances from Hepburn and Fairbanks. Adapted from Zoe Atkins' stage play. **74m/B VHS, DVD.** Katharine Hepburn, Douglas Fairbanks Jr., Adolphe Menjou, Mary Duncan; ***D:*** Lowell Sherman; ***M:*** Max Steiner. Oscars '33: Actress (Hepburn).

Morning Glory 1/2 **1993 (PG-13)** Sappy romance, set during the Depression, about a pregnant widow (Raffin) trying to survive on her hardscrabble farm in Georgia. Elly Dinsmore advertises for a husband, not for romance but to help with the work, and is answered by Will Parker (Reeve), an ex-con trying to live down his past. When a local floozy who's been eyeing Will is killed, the sheriff (Walsh) is only too happy to go after the stranger in town. Light-weight with some unbelievable plot twists. Based on the novel "Morning Glory" by LaVyrle Spencer. **90m/C VHS.** Deborah Raffin, Christopher Reeve, Lloyd Bochner, Nina Foch, Helen Shaver, J.T. Walsh; ***D:*** Steven Hilliard Stern; ***W:*** Charles Jarrott, Deborah Raffin; ***M:*** Jonathan Elias.

Morning Glory **2010** Young TV producer Becky Fuller (McAdams) has the unenviable job of trying to save a failing morning show by controlling its veteran feuding anchors Mike Pomeroy (Ford) and Colleen Peck (Keaton). **m/C DVD.** *US* Harrison Ford, Diane Keaton, Rachel McAdams, Jeff Goldblum, Patrick Wilson; ***D:*** Roger Mitchell; ***W:*** Aline Brosh McKenna; ***C:*** Alwin Kuchler; ***M:*** David Arnold.

Morning Light 1/2 **2008 (PG)** Squeaky-clean Disney-made documentary following fifteen young sailors as they embark on the 2500 mile TransPac race from Los Angeles to Hawaii. The ships' crews are obviously aware that they're on camera, which leads to very few spontaneous moments, as well as a few seemingly rigged scenes. Aware of the small audience that actually follows this kind of elite sailing competition, Disney sets it up like a lame reality show, complete with a climactic elimination. Too bad Fox wasn't involved. They could've at least brought in some bikini babes and a keg. **98m/C DVD.** *US* ***D:*** Paul Crowder, Mark Monroe; ***C:*** Josef Nalevansky, Richard Deppe.

Morocco 1/2 **1930** A foreign legion soldier falls for a world-weary chanteuse along the desert sands. Cooper has never been more earnest, and Dietrich has never been more blase and exotic. In her American film debut, Dietrich sings "What Am I Bid?" A must for anyone drawn to improbable, gloriously well-done kitsch. Based on Benno Vigny's novel, "Amy Jolly." **92m/B VHS, DVD.** Marlene Dietrich, Gary Cooper, Adolphe Menjou, Ullrich Haupt, Francis McDonald, Eve Southern, Paul Porcasi; ***D:*** Josef von Sternberg; ***C:*** Lee Garmes. Natl. Film Reg. '92.

Morons from Outer Space **1985 (PG)** Slow-witted aliens from elsewhere in the universe crash onto Earth, but unlike other sci-fis, these morons become internationally famous, despite them acting like intergalactic stooges. Plenty of sight gags. **87m/C VHS, DVD.** *GB* Griff Rhys Jones, Mel Smith, James B. Sikking, Dinsdale Landen, Jimmy Nail, Joanne Pearce, Paul Bown; ***D:*** Mike Hodges; ***W:*** Griff Rhys Jones, Mel Smith; ***C:*** Phil Meheux; ***M:*** Peter Brewis.

Mortal Challenge 1/2 **1997 (R)** A corrupt police force, known as the Centurions, guard a futuristic L.A., which is divided into rich and poor sectors. When wealthy Tori is captured visiting her wrong-side-of-the-sectors boyfriend, the Centurions decide to have some fun by matching her with a cyborg in a death game. **77m/C VHS, DVD.** Timothy Bottoms, David McCallum, Evan Lurie, Nick (Nicholas, Niko) Hill; ***D:*** Randolph Cheveldare. **VIDEO**

Mortal Danger 1/2 *Turn Your Pony Around* **1994 (PG-13)** Kathy and Phil are suicidal teens finding different solutions to their difficulties over the same weekend. Comes across like a TV movie but does maintain an honest message with affecting performances. **86m/C VHS.** Ami Dolenz, Noah Hathaway, Paul Coufos, Larry Gatlin, Charles Napier; ***D:*** Brianne Murphy.

Mortal Kombat 1: The Movie **1995 (PG-13)** Inevitable film version of mega popular arcade game intended to cash in fast on the game's popularity. Shameless nirvana for youngin's with permanent joystick scars on their hands. Grown-ups forced to sit through it may get into some of the eye-popping special effects and nifty martial arts sequences if they can block out the contrived plot, lame acting, and Lambert's presence as Thunder God. **101m/C VHS, DVD.** Christopher Lambert, Talisa Soto, Cary-Hiroyuki Tagawa, Bridgette Wilson-Sampras; ***D:*** Paul W.S. Anderson; ***W:*** Kevin Droney; ***C:*** John R. Leonetti; ***M:*** George S. Clinton.

Mortal Kombat 2: Annihilation 1/2 **1997 (PG-13)** The treacherous Shao-Khan brings his evil horde of video-game villians through a portal ripped in the universe and threatens to destroy the Earth in this highly unneccesary sequel. Liu Kang and his buds are on the scene to once again do battle to save humanity. Moves from one badly staged fight scene to another with little story or acting (except for Remar in the role of Rayden, replacing Christopher Lambert in the first "Kombat"), and adults should quickly tire of the non-stop back flips and somersaulting that combine with computer graphics to give each character their own special abilities. Kids and gamers, however, should enjoy the new characters, the same-sounding pulse-pounding techno music, and the non-stop, but fairly bloodless, violence. **98m/C VHS, DVD.** James Remar, Robin Shou, Talisa Soto, Daron McBee, Sandra Hess, Brian Thompson, Reiner Schone, Musetta Vander, Marjean Holden, Litefoot, Lynn Red Williams, Irina Pantaeva; ***D:*** John R. Leonetti; ***W:*** Brent Friedman, Bruce Zabel; ***C:*** Matthew F. Leonetti; ***M:*** George S. Clinton.

Mortal Passions 1/2 **1990 (R)** Another "Double Indemnity" rip-off, with a scheming tramp manipulating everyone around her with betrayal, sex, and murder. Her dead husband's brother eventually ignites old flames to steer her away from his money. **96m/C VHS.** Zach Galligan, Krista Errickson, Michael Bowen, Luca Bercovici, Sheila Kelley, David Warner; ***D:*** Andrew Lane.

Mortal Sins **1990 (R)** A TV evangelist finds more than salvation at the altar, when bodies begin to turn up. The detective he hires is close-mouthed, but more than a little interested in the preacher's daughter. A tense psycho-sexual thriller. **85m/C VHS.** Brian Benben, Anthony LaPaglia, Debrah Farentino; ***D:*** Yuri Sivo.

Mortal Sins **1992 (PG-13)** Reeve stars as parish priest Thomas Cusack, who hears the confession of a serial killer. What's worse is that the killer is preying on the women of Cusack's parish. Since he can't break the seal of the confessional, the good Father tries to stop the killer himself before another murder takes place. **93m/C VHS.** Roxann Biggs-Dawson, Francis Duinan, Weston McMillan, Phillip R. Allen, Lisa Vultaggio, Christopher Reeve; ***D:*** Bradford May; ***W:*** Dennis Paoli, Greg Martinelli; ***C:*** Peter Woeste; ***M:*** Joseph Conlan.

The Mortal Storm 1/2 **1940** Phyllis Bottome's famous novel comes to life in this extremely well acted film about the rise of the Nazi regime. Stewart and Sullavan are young lovers who risk everything to escape the country after their families are torn apart by the Nazi takeover. Although Germany is never identified as the country, it is obvious in this story about the early days of WWII. Hitler took one look at this and promptly banned all MGM movies in Nazi Germany. **100m/B VHS.** Margaret Sullavan, James Stewart, Robert Young, Frank Morgan, Robert Stack, Bonita Granville, Irene Rich; ***D:*** Frank Borzage; ***W:*** Claudine West, George Froeschel, Anderson Ellis; ***C:*** William H. Daniels.

Mortal Thoughts 1/2 **1991 (R)** Best friends find their relationship tested when the brutal husband of one of them is murdered. Moore and Headly are exceptional, capturing the perfect inflections and attitudes of the hard-working New Jersey beauticians sure of their friendship. Excellent pacing, fine supporting cast, with Keitel and Willis stand-outs. **104m/C VHS, DVD.** Demi Moore, Bruce Willis, Glenne Headly, Harvey Keitel, John Pankow, Billie Neal; ***D:*** Alan Rudolph; ***W:*** William Reilly, Claude Kerven; ***C:*** Elliot Davis; ***M:*** Mark Isham. Natl. Soc. Film Critics '91: Support. Actor (Keitel).

Mortal Transfer **2001** Comic mystery finds Paris shrink Michel Durand (Anglade) in trouble after getting a call from police inspector Chapireau (Podalydes). Klepto Olga (De Fougerolles) claims she was in Durand's office after she's accused of shoplifting and he covers for her because he falls asleep during her sessions. Only the next time it happens, Durand wakes up to find a tragedy has occurred. Rather than fessing up, Durand opts for a cover-up. French with subtitles. **122m/C DVD.** *FR GE* Jean-Hugues Anglade, Helene de Fougerolles, Denis Podalydes, Miki (Predrag) Manojlovic, Yves Renier, Robert Hirsch, Valentina Sauca; ***D:*** Jean-Jacques Beineix; ***C:*** Benoit Delhomme; ***M:*** Reinhardt Wagner.

Mortuary **1981 (R)** Young woman's nightmares come startlingly close to reality. **91m/C VHS.** Christopher George, Lynda Day George, Paul Smith; ***D:*** Howard (Hikmet) Avedis; ***W:*** Howard (Hikmet) Avedis.

Mortuary WOOF! 2005 (R) The Doyle family (widowed mom and two kids) move to a small California town where mom (Crosby) thinks it's a great idea to reopen the long-abandoned funeral home that has a cemetery in the yard. According to townspeople, the mortuary is built on haunted property and soon some sort of toxic killer fungus that's oozing around is raising the corpses. Ick in more ways than one. **94m/C DVD.** Denise Crosby, Dan Byrd, Courtney Peldon, Bug Hall, Stephanie Patton; ***D:*** Tobe Hooper; ***W:*** Jace Anderson, Adam Grerasch; ***C:*** Jaron Presant; ***M:*** Joseph Conlan. **VIDEO**

Mortuary Academy **1991 (R)** To win an inheritance two brothers must attend the family mortician school, a situation paving the way for aggressively tasteless jokes on necrophilia. An attempt to recapture the successful black humor of the earlier Bartel/Woronov teaming "Eating Raoul," this one's dead on arrival. **86m/C VHS, DVD.** Christopher Atkins, Perry Lang, Paul Bartel, Mary Woronov, Tracey Walter, Lynn Danielson-Rosenthal, Cesar Romero, Wolfman Jack; ***D:*** Michael Schroeder; ***W:*** William Kelman; ***C:*** Roy Wagner, Ronald Vidor; ***M:*** David Spear.

Morvern Callar **1/2 2002** A young woman (Morton) wakes on Christmas morning to find her boyfriend's body, wrists slashed, beside her bed. His legacy is a personalized compilation tape, his cash card, and a novel he's written for her, complete with publishers to send it to. After she dismembers and disposes of his body, replaces his name on the manuscript with her own and sends it off to a publisher (who buys it), she goes off on a holiday to Spain with her sex and drug crazed girlfriend (McDermott). Morvern's emotions are revealed through the lyrics of the compilation tape constantly pounding through her headphones. Morton, known for other speech-challenged roles in "Sweet and Low Down" (mute girlfriend) and "Minority Report" (precognitive psychic) has become adept at making passivity riveting. Ramsey's second film, based on a novel by Alan Warner, is a moody beauty that's not altogether gratifying. **97m/C VHS, DVD.** *GB CA* Samantha Morton, Kathleen McDermott; ***D:*** Lynne Ramsay; ***W:*** Lynne Ramsay, Liana Dognini; ***C:*** Alwin Kuchler.

The Mosaic Project **1/2 1995 (R)** Action junkies should be happy with the chases, explosions, and other mayhem engendered by this story of two buddies who find themselves the victims of a mad scientist. Now they have experimental computer chips implanted in their brains that make them skilled in 25 martial arts forms (and some other stuff that doesn't matter much). **89m/C VHS.** Jon Tabler, Ben Marley, Joe Estevez, Julie Strain, Colleen T. Coffey, Robert Z'Dar; ***D:*** John Sjogren; ***W:*** John Sjogren.

Mosby's Marauders **1966** A young boy joins a Confederate raiding company during the Civil War and learns about bravery, war, and love. **79m/C VHS.** Kurt Russell, James MacArthur, Jack Ging, Peggy Lipton, Nick Adams; ***D:*** Michael O'Herlihy.

Moscow, Belgium *Aanrijding in Moscou* **2008** Working-class comedy-drama with a compellingly world-weary performance by Sarafian. Tough 40-something postal worker Matty (Sarafian) has three kids with art teacher hubby Werner (Hildenbergh) whose midlife crisis results in his leaving his family for a student. Matty gets into a fender-bender with younger truck driver Johnny (Delnaet) and decides to indulge her sexual curiosity. And then Werner decides to return. As if Matty didn't have enough to deal with. Flemish with subtitles. **106m/C DVD.** *BE* Barbara Sarafian, Jurgen Delnaet, Johan Hildenbergh, Anemone Valcke, Sofia Ferri, Julian Borsani; ***D:*** Christophe van Rompaey; ***W:*** Jean-Claude van Rijkeghem, Pat van Biers; ***C:*** Ruben Impens.

Moscow Does Not Believe in Tears *Moscow Distrusts Tears; Moskwa Sljesam Nje Jerit* **1980** Three provincial girls—Lyuda (Muravyova), Tonya (Ryazanova), and Katya (Alentova)—realize very different fates when they pursue their dreams in 1958 Moscow. The film picks up 20 years later to see what became of the women. Bittersweet, moving fare that seems a somewhat surprising production from pre-Glasnost USSR. In Russian with English subtitles. A 150-minute version has also been released. **115m/C VHS, DVD.** *RU* Vera Alentova, Irina Muravyova, Raisa Ryazanova, Natalie Vavilova, Alexei Batalov, Alexander Fatyushin, Yuri Vasilyev; ***D:*** Vladimir Menshov; ***W:*** Valentin Chernykh; ***C:*** Igor Slabnevich; ***M:*** Sergei Nikitin. Oscars '80: Foreign Film.

Moscow on the Hudson **1984 (R)** Good-natured comedy has Williams as Soviet defector trying to cope with new life of freedom in fast-paced, freewheeling melting pot of New York City. Williams is particularly winning as naive jazzman, though Alonso also scores as his Hispanic love interest. Be warned though, it's not just played for laughs. **115m/C VHS, DVD.** Robin Williams, Maria Conchita Alonso, Cleavant Derricks, Alejandro Rey, Elya Baskin; ***D:*** Paul Mazursky; ***W:*** Paul Mazursky, Leon Capetanos; ***C:*** Donald McAlpine; ***M:*** David McHugh.

Moscow Parade *Prorva* **1992** Sexy cabaret singer gets caught up in the shifting alliances caused by war. Set in Russia before the Nazi invasion. Russian with subtitles. **103m/C VHS.** *RU* Ute Lemper, Vladimir Simonov; ***D:*** Ivan Dykhovichny.

Moscow Zero WOOF! 2006 (R) Incoherent and laughably bad. After an anthropologist vanishes in the catacombs beneath the streets of Moscow, a rescue team is sent searching for him and discovers a strange occult society that believes in demons and a gateway to Hell. **82m/C DVD.** *SP* Vincent Gallo, Rade Serbedzija, Joss Ackland, Val Kilmer, Joaquim de Almeida, Sage Stallone; ***D:*** Maria Lidon; ***W:*** Adela Ibanez; ***C:*** Ricardo Aronovich; ***M:*** Javier Navarrete.

Moses WOOF! 1976 (PG) Lancaster goes biblical as Moses, the man with the tablets. Edited from the 360-minute British TV series, with no improvement obvious from the economy, except that the bad parts are shorter. Poor chatter and scattered bouts of acting are surpassed in inadequacy only by special effects. **141m/C VHS, DVD.** Burt Lancaster, Anthony Quayle, Ingrid Thulin, Irene Papas, William Lancaster; ***D:*** Gianfranco DeBosio; ***W:*** Anthony Burgess, Vittorio Bonicelli; ***M:*** Ennio Morricone.

Moses **1/2 1996** Another entry in TNT's series of Bible stories finds a humble Moses (Kingsley), raised in the Egyptian court, finding his way to his own people, the Israelites. Chosen by God to be his messenger and lead his people out of bondage, Moses must unleash a series of plagues upon Egypt before pharaoh Mernefta (Langella) will let them go. If you want action, look to "The Ten Commandments," since this is a faithful but tedious retelling. Filmed on location in Morocco; on two cassettes. **185m/C VHS, DVD.** Ben Kingsley, Frank Langella, David Suchet, Christopher Lee, Anna Galiena, Enrico Lo Verso, Geraldine McEwan, Maurice Roeves, Anthony (Corlan) Higgins, Anton Lesser; ***D:*** Roger Young; ***W:*** Lionel Chetwynd; ***C:*** Raffaele Mertes; ***M:*** Marco Frisina.

Mosley **1998** Looks at the life and political career of Oswald "Tom" Mosley (Cake), the leader of the British Fascist Movement from the end of WWI to his rise to prominence and eventual imprisonment during WWII. **240m/C VHS.** *GB* Jonathan Cake, Hugh Bonneville, Jeremy Child, Eric Allan, Caroline Langrishe, Jemma Redgrave, Windsor Davies; ***D:*** Robert Knights. **TV**

Mosquito **1995 (R)** Alien forces transform the annoying insects into monstrous mutants. Schlocky special effects are good for laughs. **92m/C VHS, DVD.** Gunnar Hansen, Ron Asheton, Steve Dixon, Rachel Loiselle, Tim Loveface; ***D:*** Gary Jones; ***W:*** Gary Jones, Steve Hodge, Tom Chaney; ***C:*** Tom Chaney; ***M:*** Allen Lynch, Randall Lynch.

The Mosquito Coast **1/2 1986 (PG)** Ambitious adaptation of Paul Theroux's novel about an asocial inventor who transplants his family to a rainforest to realize his utopian dream. A nightmare ensues. Ford tries hard, but supporters Mirren and Phoenix are main appeal of only intermittently successful drama. **119m/C VHS, DVD.** Harrison Ford, Helen Mirren, River Phoenix, Andre Gregory, Martha Plimpton, Conrad Roberts, Butterfly McQueen, Jadrien Steele, Hilary Gordon, Rebecca Gordon, Dick O'Neill, Jason Alexander; ***D:*** Peter Weir; ***W:*** Paul Schrader; ***C:*** John Seale; ***M:*** Maurice Jarre.

Mosquitoman **1/2** *Mansquito* **2005** Break out the giant can of mosquito repellent for this genre cheese of '50s big bug flicks. A death row convict (Jordan) is used for scientific experiments and exposed to a DNA-altering concoction that turns him into the blood-slurping creature of the title. Cop Tom Randall (Nemec) tracks the blood trail while scientist babe Jennifer Allen (Vander) tries to prevent the change from happening again—to her. Originally shown on the Sci-Fi Channel. **m/C DVD.** Corin "Corky" Nemec, Musetta Vander, Jay Benedict, Patrick Dreikauss, Austin Jordan; ***D:*** Tibor Takas; ***W:*** Michael Hurst; ***C:*** Emil Topuzov; ***M:*** Joseph Conlan, Sophia Morizet. **CABLE**

The Most Dangerous Game *The Hounds of Zaroff* **1932** Shipwrecked McRae washed ashore on the island of Banks's Count Zaroff, a deranged sportsman with a flair for tracking humans. Guess who becomes the mad count's next target. Oft-told tale is compellingly related in this, the first of many using Richard Connell's famous short story. If deja vu sets in, don't worry. This production uses most of the scenery, staff, and cast from its studio cousin, "King Kong." Remade in 1945 as "A Game of Death" and in 1956 as "Run for the Sun." **78m/B VHS, DVD.** Joel McCrea, Fay Wray, Leslie Banks, Robert Armstrong, Noble Johnson; ***D:*** Ernest B. Schoedsack, Irving Pichel; ***W:*** James A. Creelman; ***C:*** Henry W. Gerrard; ***M:*** Max Steiner.

Most Wanted **1/2 1976** A psychopath with a penchant for raping nuns and collecting crucifixes is tracked down by a special police unit in this successful TV pilot. **78m/C VHS.** Robert Stack, Shelly Novack, Leslie Charleson, Tom Selleck, Sheree North; ***D:*** Walter Grauman. **TV**

Most Wanted **1/2 1997 (R)** Marine Sgt. James Dunn (Wayans), framed for the assassination of the first lady, is on the run from the CIA, FBI, LAPD, and the covert team he was working with, which is led by Voight, the gung-ho general who set up the whole scam. Wayans, who wrote and produced, seems convinced that an action hero must be of the strong-silent-superhero mold, and appears at a loss without a joke to crack. Voight, however, is right at home in the bad-guy role, employing an overdone but effective southern drawl. Plenty of elaborate stunts, oversized fireballs, shootings, and chases provide the expected wild ride, including the film's funniest sequence as thousands of L.A. natives spontaneously become wild-in-the-street bounty hunters. **99m/C VHS, DVD.** Keenen Ivory Wayans, Jon Voight, Jill(ian) Hennessey, Eric Roberts, Paul Sorvino, Robert Culp, Wolfgang Bodison, Simon Baker; ***D:*** David Hogan; ***W:*** Keenen Ivory Wayans; ***C:*** Marc Reshovsky; ***M:*** Paul Bruckmaster.

The Most Wonderful Time of the Year **1/2 2008** Optimistic Uncle Ralph (Winkler), a retired cop, thinks his bah-humbug niece Jen (Burns) needs some Christmas spirit. And what better way than to introduce her to a great guy named Morgan (Christie) that even her six-year-old son Brian (Levins) likes. It's meddling for such a good reason. **87m/C DVD.** Henry Winkler, Brooke Burns, Connor Christopher Levins, Warren Christie, Rosalind Ivan, Paul Cavanagh, Morton Lowry; ***D:*** Henry Winkler, Don Siegel; ***W:*** Peter Milne; ***C:*** Ernest Haller, Frederick "Friedrich" Hollander; ***M:*** Frederick "Friedrich" Hollander. **CABLE**

Mostly Martha *Drei Sterne; Bella Martha* **2001 (PG)** Martha, a top chef at a fancy French restaurant in Hamburg, is so obsessed with her job that she really only connects with life through food. Things get stirred up when two new ingredients are added. First, a new sous-chef (Castellitto), scruffy and care-free as opposed to Martha's icy professionalism, enters her kitchen. Then, she takes in her 8-year-old neice (Foerste) after the death of the child's mother (Martha's sister). Appealing romantic comedy benefits form excellent performances by the leads, as well director Nettlebeck's assured style. German with subtitles. **107m/C VHS, DVD.** *GE AT SI IT* Martina Gedeck, Sergio Castellitto, Ulrich Thomsen, Maxime Foerste, Sibylle Canonica, August Zirner; ***D:*** Sandra Nettelbeck; ***W:*** Sandra Nettelbeck; ***C:*** Michael Bertl.

Motel Blue **1/2 1998 (R)** Kyle Rivers (Frye) is an agent with the Department of Defense, who's doing a security clearance check on scientist Lana Hawking (Young). Lana maintains an expensive lifestyle that suggests she may be selling government secrets. But when Lana finds out about Kyle's suspicions, she frames her and Kyle gets suspended. But she decides to continue the investigation on her own terms. No particular surprises but there are a number of sleazy sex scenes. **96m/C VHS, DVD.** Sean Young, Soleil Moon Frye, Seymour Cassel, Robert Vaughn, Robert Stewart, Lou Rawls, Spencer Rochfort; ***D:*** Sam Firstenberg; ***W:*** Marianne S. Wibberley, Cormac Wibberley; ***C:*** Moshe Levin. **VIDEO**

Motel Hell **1/2 1980 (R)** A completely tongue-in-cheek gore-fest about a farmer who kidnaps tourists, buries them in his garden, and reaps a human harvest to grind into his distinctive brand of smoked, preservative-free sausage. **102m/C VHS, DVD.** Rory Calhoun, Nancy Parsons, Paul (Link) Linke, Nina Axelrod, Wolfman Jack, Elaine Joyce, Dick Curtis, Rosanne Katon, Monique St. Pierre, John Ratzenberger; ***D:*** Kevin Connor; ***W:*** Robert Jaffe, Steven-Charles Jaffe; ***C:*** Thomas Del Ruth; ***M:*** Lance Rubin.

Mother **1/2 1926** Pudovkin's innovative classic about a Russian family shattered by the uprising in 1905. A masterpiece of Russian cinema that established Pudovkin, and rivaled only Eisenstein for supremacy in montage, poetic imagery, and propagandistic ideals. Based on Maxim Gorky's great novel, it's one of cinematic history's seminal works. Striking cinematography, stunning use of montage make this one important. Silent with English subtitles. **70m/B VHS, DVD.** *RU* Vera Baranovskaya, Nikolai Batalov; ***D:*** Vsevolod Pudovkin.

Mother **1/2** *Okasan* **1952** A Japanese family is undone after the devastation of WWII. An uncharacteristically dramatic, and thus more accessible, film from one of the Japanese cinema's greatest masters. In Japanese with English subtitles. **98m/B VHS.** *JP* Kinuyo Tanaka, Kyoko Kagawa, Eiji Okada, Akihiko Katayama; ***D:*** Mikio Naruse.

Mother **1/2 1994 (R)** Olivia Hendrix (Ladd) is a very over-protective mom—even though son Tom (Weisser) is nineteen and anxious to untie the apron strings. But Mom thinks she knows best and she's willing to kill to make certain Tom stays home where he belongs. **90m/C VHS, DVD.** Diane Ladd, Olympia Dukakis, Morgan Weisser, Ele Keats; ***D:*** Frank Laloggia.

Mother **1/2 1996 (PG-13)** Yes, you will shake your head in recognition of that parent-child bond. Twice-divorced writer John Henderson (Brooks) decides it's all Mom's fault he has problems with women, so he decides to move back home and figure out what went wrong. Mom Beatrice (Reynolds) is exasperated and married younger brother Jeff (Morrow) winds up jealous of mom's attentions to his sibling. Reynolds' first feature film in 25 years. **104m/C VHS, DVD.** Albert Brooks, Debbie Reynolds, Rob Morrow, Lisa Kudrow, John C. McGinley, Isabel Glasser, Peter White, Vanessa Williams; ***D:*** Albert Brooks; ***W:*** Monica Johnson, Albert Brooks; ***C:*** Lajos Koltai; ***M:*** Marc Shaiman. N.Y. Film Critics '96: Screenplay; Natl. Soc. Film Critics '96: Screenplay.

The Mother **2003 (R)** Reid gives a ferociously honest performance as the 60-ish May, a lifelong suburban wife and mother left bereft of purpose when her husband (Vaughn) suddenly dies. She moves to London to live temporarily with her preoccupied son Bobby (Mackintosh) and his indifferent wife Helen (Wilson Jones) and tries to straighten out the life of her self-pitying divorcee daughter, Paula (Bradshaw). Paula is involved in a messy relationship with rugged married builder, Darren (Craig). May finds herself attracted to the younger man's unexpected kindness and, unresigned to going quietly into old age, also begins an affair with the weak-willed Darren—the revelation of which causes no end of drama. The only false note comes in a late scene when May allows Paula to take her rage out on her mother by hitting her. The newly liberated May should have instead knocked her whiny child on her ass. **111m/C VHS, DVD.** *GB* Anne Reid, Daniel Craig, Steven Mackintosh, Cathryn Bradshaw, Oliver Ford Davies, Peter Vaughan, Anna Wilson Jones; ***D:*** Roger Michell; ***W:*** Hanif Kureishi; ***C:*** Alwin Kuchler; ***M:*** Jeremy Sams.

Mother and Child **2009 (R)** Karen (Bening) is 50 and living in L.A. when she decides to look for the daughter she gave up 35 years before after a teen pregnancy. That would be Elizabeth (Watts). Meanwhile, married Lucy (Washington) discovers she's infertile and she wants to adopt the child of an unmarried young woman (Epps). **125m/C DVD.** *US* Annette Bening, Naomi Watts, Kerry Washington, Samuel L. Jackson, Jimmy Smits, Shareeka Epps, Amy Brenneman, David Morse, David Ramsey, Cherry Jones, Marc Blucas, Ahmed Best, S. Epatha Merkerson, Lisa Gay Hamilton; ***D:*** Rodrigo Garcia; ***W:*** Rodrigo Garcia; ***C:*** Xavier Perez Grobet; ***M:*** Ed Shearmur.

Mother & Daughter: A Loving War 1/2 **1980** Three women experience motherhood. Special appearance by Harry Chapin as himself. **96m/C VHS.** Tuesday Weld, Frances Sternhagen, Kathleen Beller, Jeanne Lang, Edward Winter; ***D:*** Burt Brinckerhoff. **TV**

Mother and Son **1931** Melodrama finds the wayward Young shielding her son from the fact that she runs a gambling hall. He grows up to be a society lad before discovering the devastating truth. **67m/B VHS.** Clara Kimball Young, Bruce Warren, Mildred Golden, John Elliott, Gordon Wood, Ernest Hilliard; ***D:*** John P. McCarthy.

Mother and Son *Mat i Syn; Mutter und Sohn* **1997** Slow-paced, dreamlike story about a dedicated son's (Ananishnov) caring for his dying mother (Geyer) in their old house in the country. She wishes to go outside—he carries her along a path in the woods and they recall his childhood. She eventually goes back to her bed where they discuss death and she falls asleep, never to waken. Russian with subtitles. **73m/C VHS, DVD.** *RU GE* Gudrun Geyer, Alexi Ananishnov; ***D:*** Alexander Sokurov; ***W:*** Yuri Arabov; ***C:*** Aleksei Federov; ***M:*** Otmar Nussio.

The Mother and the Whore *La Maman et la Putain* **1973** Alexander (Leaud) lives with slightly older Marie (Lafont) but still can't resist picking up sexy Veronika (Lebrun). Their menage works for a while but then tensions between the sexual threesome force them to discuss their situation. Talky, witty, provocative example of French New Wave, which Eustache shot in his own apartment and local bistros. French with subtitles. **210m/B VHS.** *FR* Jean-Pierre Leaud, Bernadette LaFont, Francoise Lebrun, Isabelle Weingarten, Jean-Noel Picq, Jessa Darrieux, Genevieve Mnich, Marinka Matuszewski; ***D:*** Jean Eustache; ***W:*** Jean Eustache; ***C:*** Pierre Lhomme.

Mother Goose Rock 'n' Rhyme **1990** Duvall follows the success of her "Faerie Tale Theatre" series with a new comedic fable, starring some of Hollywood's top names. Great fun for the whole family. **96m/C VHS.** Shelley Duvall, Teri Garr, Howie Mandel, Jean Stapleton, Ben Vereen, Bobby Brown, Art Garfunkel, Dan Gilroy, Deborah Harry, Cyndi Lauper, Little Richard, Paul Simon, Harry Anderson, Elayne Boosler, Woody Harrelson, Richard "Cheech" Marin, Garry Shandling.

Mother Joan of the Angels *The Devil and the Nun; Matka Joanna Od Aniolow* **1960** A priest investigating demonic possession among nuns in a 17th-century Polish convent becomes involved in a mutual attraction with the Mother Superior. A powerful allegory complemented by the stylized narrative and performances. Polish with subtitles. Based on actual events at Loudun and also the subject of a play by John Whiting, an opera by Krzysztof Penderecki, "The Devils of Loudon" novel by Aldous Huxley, and Ken Russell's movie "The Devils." **108m/B VHS, DVD.** *PL* Lucyna Winnicka, Mieczyslaw Voit, Anna Ciepielewska, Maria Chwalibog; ***D:*** Jerzy Kawalerowicz; ***W:*** Jerzy Kawalerowicz, Tadeusz Konwicki; ***M:*** Adam Walacinski. Cannes '61: Grand Jury Prize.

Mother, Jugs and Speed 1/2 **1976 (PG)** Black comedy about the day-to-day tragedies encountered by a group of ambulance drivers. Interesting mix of stars. **95m/C VHS, DVD.** Bill Cosby, Raquel Welch, Harvey Keitel, Allen (Goorwitz) Garfield, Larry Hagman, Bruce Davison, Dick Butkus, L.Q. Jones, Toni Basil; ***D:*** Peter Yates; ***W:*** Tom Mankiewicz.

Mother Kusters Goes to Heaven *Mutter Kusters Fahrt Zum Himmel* **1976** Mrs. Kusters's husband is a frustrated factory worker who goes over the edge and kills the factory owner's son and himself. Left alone, she learns that everyone is using her husband's death to further their own needs, including her daughter, who uses the publicity to enhance her singing career. A statement that you should trust no one, not even your family and friends. This film was banned from the Berlin Film Festival because of its political overtones. In German with English subtitles. **108m/C VHS, DVD.** *GE* Brigitte Mira, Ingrid Caven, Armin Meier, Irm Hermann, Gottfried John, Margit Carstensen, Karl-Heinz Boehm; ***D:*** Rainer Werner Fassbinder; ***W:*** Rainer Werner Fassbinder; ***C:*** Michael Ballhaus.

Mother Lode 1/2 *Search for the Mother Lode; The Last Great Treasure* **1982 (PG)** The violent conflict between twin brothers (played by Heston) is intensified by greed, near madness, and the all-consuming lust for gold in this action-adventure. Heston's son, Fraser Clarke Heston, wrote as well as produced the film. **101m/C VHS.** Charlton Heston, Nick Mancuso, Kim Basinger; ***D:*** Charlton Heston.

Mother Night **1996 (R)** American writer Howard Campbell (Nolte) is recruited as a spy in pre-WWII Germany in this adaptation of Kurt Vonnegut's 1962 novel. He poses as a Nazi sympathizer in broadcasts to American troops, but his anti-semitic diatribes are actually coded information crucial to the Allies. After the war, Campbell's life unravels as he loses his young wife (Lee) and the U.S. government refuses to acknowledge his efforts. He is smuggled back to the U.S., where both Israeli Nazi-hunters and twisted neo-Nazis search for him. After being captured, imprisoned in Israel, and conversing with fellow prisoner Adolf Eichmann (Gibson), Campbell realizes the moral of this dark comedy: "We are what we pretend to be." Arkin is excellent as his Greenwich Village neighbor who also has some secrets. If you look closely, you can see author Vonnegut in a cameo. **113m/C VHS, DVD.** Nick Nolte, Sheryl Lee, Alan Arkin, John Goodman, Kirsten Dunst, David Strathairn, Arye Gross, Frankie Faison, Bernard Behrens, Henry Gibson; ***D:*** Keith Gordon; ***W:*** Robert B. Weide; ***C:*** Tom Richmond; ***M:*** Michael Convertino.

Mother of Kings **1982** Livin' ain't easy for a widowed charwoman thanks to WWII and Stalinism. Innovative use of newsreel scenes. In Polish with English subtitles. **126m/C VHS.** *PL* Zbigniew Zapasiewicz, Franciszek Pieczka, Boguslaw Linda, Adam Ferency, Magda Teresa Wojcik; ***D:*** Janusz Zaorski; ***W:*** Janusz Zaorski; ***C:*** Edward Klosinski; ***M:*** Przemyslaw Gintrowski.

Mother of Mine *Aideista Parhain* **2005** During World War II, when conflict breaks out between Finland and Russia, 9-year-old Eero (Majaniemi) is sent to live with a neutral family in Sweden by his Finnish mother (Maijala) after his solider father is killed. She believes he will be safer there. The lad adapts well to the new language and although his foster father (Nygvist) takes a shine to him immediately, his harsh new mother (Lundqvist) takes some time to warm up to him. When he finally returns home, all parties have much trauma to endure, the final repair coming when Eero attends his surrogate mother's funeral and then visits his elderly Finnish mum, finally understanding the motive behind her difficult choice long ago. Visually pleasing, emotionally engaging, with a fabulous score to boot. Finnish and Swedish with subtitles. **111m/C DVD.** *FI* Michael Nyquist, Topi Majaniemi, Maria Lundqvist, Kari-Pekka Toivonen; ***D:*** Klaus Haro; ***W:*** Jimmy Karlsson, Kirsi Vikman; ***C:*** Jarkko T. Laine; ***M:*** Tuomas Kantelinen.

Mother of Tears *La Terza Madre; The Third Mother* **2008** The third and final installment in Argento's loosely formed "mother witches" trilogy is a hallucinogenic tale of a horde of lesbian witches rampaging through Rome, encountering psychic girls, zombies, deranged priests, and a resurrected witch who may signal the end of the world. Completely bonkers, yet visually compelling. **102m/C DVD.** Asia Argento, Cristian Solimeno, Adam James, Valeria Cavalli, Moran Atias, Phillippe LeRoy, Daria Nicolodi, Coralina Cataldi-Tassoni, Udo Kier, Jun Ichikawa, Clive Riche, Robert Madison, Tommaso Banfi, Paolo Stella, Barbara Mautino, Franco Leo, Silvia Rubino, Luca Pescatore, Alessandro Zeme, Simonetta Solder; ***D:*** Dario Argento; ***W:*** Dario Argento, Jace Anderson, Adam Gierasch, Walter Fasano, Simona Simonetti; ***C:*** Frederic Fasano; ***M:*** Claudio Simonetti. **VIDEO**

Mother Teresa: In the Name of God's Poor **1997** Bio of the missionary begins when the 36-year-old cloistered nun (Chaplin) starts her work in the Calcutta slums and founds the Missionaries of Charity, and culminates with her 1979 Nobel Peace Prize acceptance speech. This drama was unauthorized and reportedly did not receive the approval of Mother Teresa when she learned of the project. **93m/C VHS, DVD.** Geraldine Chaplin, Keene Curtis, William Katt, Alan Shearman, Cornelia Hayes O'Herlihy; ***D:*** Kevin Connor; ***W:*** Dominique Lapierre, Carol Kaplan. **CABLE**

Mother Wore Tights **1947** Colorful nostalgic musical stars Grable as married turn-of-the-century vaudevillian Myrtle McKinley Burt, who leaves the stage to raise her two daughters. Once they're grown, Myrtle decides to rejoin husband Frank (Dailey) in the theatre again, thus embarassing daughter Iris (Freeman) who's at a snotty finishing school. Of course, Iris learns what's really important in life. **107m/C VHS.** Betty Grable, Dan Dailey, Mona Freeman, Connie Marshall, Vanessa Brown, Robert Arthur, Sara Allgood, William Frawley; ***D:*** Walter Lang; ***W:*** Lamar Trotti; ***C:*** Harry Jackson; ***M:*** Josef Myrow, Alfred Newman, Mack Gordon. Oscars '47: Scoring/Musical.

Motherhood 1/2 **2009 (PG-13)** Messy and self-conscious comedy, taking place over a single day, about harried (and annoying) Manhattan mom and children's blog writer Eliza Welch (Thurman with dark brown hair and nerd glasses). Nothing much happens as Eliza checks her to-do list and schleps through her domestic and childcare routines, including gossiping on the playground with other moms and preparing for her 6-year-old daughter's birthday party. **90m/C DVD.** *US* Uma Thurman, Minnie Driver, Anthony Edwards, Stephanie Szostak; ***Cameos:*** Jodie Foster; ***D:*** Katherine Dieckmann; ***W:*** Katherine Dieckmann; ***C:*** Nancy Schreiber; ***M:*** Joe Henry.

Mother's Boys **1994 (R)** Estranged mother Curtis attempts to reunite with the family she abandoned only to be snubbed, inspiring in her a ruthless effort to win back the children and oust father Gallagher's new live-in girlfriend Whalley-Kilmer. With an almost psychotic devotion, she terrorizes everyone in the family, including enticing her 12-year-old son Edwards into a nude bathtub game of peek-a-boo. Film lacks the tension necessary to carry suspense. Based on the novel by Bernard Taylor. **96m/C VHS, DVD.** Jamie Lee Curtis, Peter Gallagher, Joanne Whalley, Luke Edwards, Vanessa Redgrave, Colin Ward, Joss Ackland, Paul Guilfoyle, John C. McGinley, J.E. Freeman, Ken Lerner, Lorraine Toussaint, Joey Zimmerman, Jill Freedman; ***D:*** Yves Simoneau; ***W:*** Richard Hawley, Barry Schneider; ***C:*** Elliot Davis; ***M:*** George S. Clinton.

Mother's Day 1/2 **1980** Three women who were former college roommates plan a reunion together in the wilderness. All goes well until they are dragged into an isolated house by two insane boys who constantly watch TV, ardently consume the products advertised, and then terrorize and torture people to please their mom. Sanitized gore with black satiric intentions. **98m/C VHS, DVD.** Tiana Pierce, Nancy Hendrickson, Deborah Luce, Holden McGuire, Billy Ray McQuade, Rose Ross; ***D:*** Charles Kaufman; ***W:*** Charles Kaufman, Warren Leight; ***C:*** Joseph Mangine; ***M:*** Phil Gallo, Clem Vicari Jr.

A Mother's Prayer 1/2 **1995 (PG-13)** Fact-based story about young mom Rosemary Holmstrom (Hamilton), who has AIDS, and is determined to find a home for her eight-year-old son T.J. (Fleiss) before she dies. Guaranteed to make the tear ducts flow, with a determined performance from Hamilton that lessens the sentimentality. Holmstrom died at the age of 36 in 1994. **94m/C VHS.** Linda Hamilton, Noah Fleiss, Bruce Dern, Kate Nelligan, S. Epatha Merkerson, Corey Parker, Jenny O'Hara, RuPaul Charles; ***D:*** Larry Elikann; ***W:*** Lee Rose; ***C:*** Eric Van Haren Noman; ***M:*** Tom Scott. **CABLE**

The Mothman Prophecies **2002 (PG-13)** Supernatural thriller based on true events occurring in Point Pleasant, WV, in the mid-1960s. John and Mary Klein (Gere and Messing) are happily married, until a car crash with a moth-like creature only seen by Mary, who later dies, but not before making some preliminary sketches of the insect-like beast. John, a "Washington Post" reporter, mysteriously ends up in the town of Point Pleasant, where things get weird. The town, which is actually far from pleasant, boasts cop Connie (Linney) the sole voice of reason in the superstitious bunch of locals, some of whom have seen the same creature Mary did, and John and Connie team to solve the Mothman mystery. Gere and Linney are fine actors wasted in this ho-hum story. Movie does have an aptly creepy tone, however, and Bates is good as the hermit-ish psychic phenomena expert. **119m/C VHS, DVD.** *US* Richard Gere, Laura Linney, Will Patton, Debra Messing, Lucinda Jenney, Alan Bates, David Eigenberg, Nesbitt Blaisdell; ***D:*** Mark Pellington; ***W:*** Richard Hatem; ***C:*** Fred Murphy; ***M:*** Tomandandy.

Mothra *Mosura; Daikaiju Masura* **1962** Classic Japanese monster shenanigans about an enraged giant caterpillar that invades Tokyo while searching for the Alilenas, a set of very tiny, twin princesses who've been kidnapped by an evil nightclub owner in the pursuit of big profits. After tiring of crushing buildings and wreaking incidental havoc, the enormous crawly thing zips up into a cocoon and emerges as Mothra, a moth distinguished by both its size and bad attitude. Mothra and the wee babes make appearances in later Godzilla epics. **101m/C VHS.** *JP* Frankie Sakai, Hiroshi Koizumi, Kyoko Kagawa, Yumi Ito, Emi Ito, Lee Kresel, Ken Uehara, Akihiko Hirata, Kenji Sahara, Takashi Shimura; ***D:*** Inoshiro Honda; ***W:*** Shinichi Sekizawa; ***C:*** Hajime Koizumi; ***M:*** Yuji Koseki.

Motive for Revenge **1935** Bank teller Barry (Cook) starts stealing after his nagging mother-in-law (Lloyd) complains he's not a good enough provider to Muriel (Hervey). Barry gets caught and sent to the slammer so Mom forces Muriel to divorce him and marry a wealthy industrialist. When Barry is released, the new hubby gets himself murdered and both Barry and Muriel become suspects. **59m/B DVD.** Donald Cook, Irene Hervey, Doris Lloyd, Edwin Maxwell, Russell Simpson, LeStrange Millman; ***D:*** Burt Lynwood; ***W:*** Stuart Anthony; ***C:*** Herbert Kirkpatrick.

Motives **2003 (R)** Handsome, successful, and married businessman Emery Simms (Moore) indulges in a dangerous fling with free-spirited Allanah (Brooks) and winds up involved in murder. **87m/C VHS, DVD.** Shemar Moore, Vivica A. Fox, Keisha Knight Pulliam, Golden Brooks, Victoria Rowell, Mel Jackson, Joe Torry, Sean Blakemore; ***D:*** Craig Ross Jr.; ***W:*** Kelsey Scott; ***C:*** Ken Stipe. **VIDEO**

Mr. Takes a Vacation 1/2 **1939** Lorre was bored with his character and afraid of being typecast and it shows in this 8th and final entry in the series. Mr. Moto must cut his holiday short to protect the priceless crown of the Queen of Sheba, which is on display at a New York museum. But he's up against international jewel thief Metaxa as well as gangsters who want the prize. **63m/B DVD.** Joseph Schildkraut, Lionel Atwill, Virginia Field, Peter Lorre, John "Dusty" King, G.P. (Tim) Huntley Jr., Victor Varconi, Iva Stewart; ***D:*** Norman Foster; ***W:*** Norman Foster, Philip MacDonald; ***C:*** Charles G. Clarke; ***M:*** Samuel Kaylin.

Motor Home Massacre **2005 (R)** Typical low-budget slasher that has the good sense not to take itself seriously. Seven friends set out for a woodland adventure in a vintage RV and come under attack from a power-tool wielding psycho. **91m/C DVD.** *US* Shan Holleman, Nelson Bonilla, Justin Geer, Tanya Fraser, Breanne Ashley, Greg Corbett; ***D:*** Allen Wilbanks; ***W:*** Allen Wilbanks; ***C:*** Allen Wilbanks. **CABLE**

Motor Patrol 1/2 **1950** A cop poses as a racketeer to infiltrate a car-stealing ring. **66m/B VHS.** Don Castle, Jane Nigh, Charles Victor, Reed Hadley, William Henry, Sid Melton, Richard Travis, Frank Jenks, Onslow Stevens; ***D:*** Sam Newfield; ***W:*** Orville H. Hampton, Maurice Tombragel; ***C:*** Ernest Miller.

Motor Psycho **WOOF!** *Motor Rods and Rockers; Rio Vengeance* **1965** When a motorcycle gang rapes a woman, she and her husband pursue them into the desert to seek their brutal revenge. **73m/B VHS, DVD.** Haji, Alex Rocco, Stephen Oliver, Holle K. Winters, Joseph Cellini, Thomas Scott, Coleman Francis, Sharon Lee, Russ Meyer; ***D:*** Russ Meyer; ***W:*** William E. Sprague, Russ Meyer; ***C:*** Russ Meyer.

Motorama **1991 (R)** A 10-year-old juvenile delinquent becomes obsessed with winning a gas station contest which involves collecting game cards. So he steals a car and hits the road where he gets his first tattoo and encounters a beautiful "older" woman (Barrymore) and lots of trouble. **89m/C VHS, DVD.** Jordan Christopher Michael, Martha Quinn, Flea, Michael J. Pollard, Meat Loaf Aday, Drew Barrymore, Garrett Morris, Robin Duke, Sandy Baron, Mary Woronov, Susan Tyrrell, John Laughlin, John Diehl, Robert Picardo, Jack Nance, Vince Edwards, Dick Miller, Allyce Beasley, Shelley Berman; ***D:*** Barry Shils; ***W:*** Joe Minion; ***C:*** Joseph Yacoe; ***M:*** Andy Summers.

The Motorcycle Diaries *Diarios de motocicleta* **2004 (R)** Unadorned narrative about the life of a pre-revolutionary Che Guevara, based on his diaries and a memoir from his best friend. In 1952, naive, asthmatic 23-year-old middle-class medical student Ernesto Guevara (Garcia Bernal) and his rowdy, older compadre, Alberto Granado (de la Serna) decide to take what will be a life-changing adventure. They spend a few months on Ernesto's motorcycle traveling from Buenos Aires to Venezuela. By the time they reach Chile, and then Peru, Ernesto is dismayed by the poverty and injustice he sees around him; an extended stay caring for the sick in the San Pablo leper colony provides an emotional turning point. The film avoids being either a travelogue or a political polemic, thanks to the skill of both director Salles and his two leads. Spanish with subtitles. **128m/C DVD.** *CL US AR PV* Gael Garcia Bernal, Rodrigo de la Serna, Mia Maestro, Gustavo Bueno, Jorge Chiarella; ***D:*** Walter Salles; ***W:*** Jose Rivera; ***C:*** Eric Gautier; ***M:*** Gustavo Santaolalla. Oscars '04: Song ("Al Otro Lado Del Rio"); British Acad. '04: Foreign Film; British Acad. '05: Orig. Score; Ind. Spirit '05: Cinematog., Debut Perf. (de la Serna).

Motorcycle Gang **1957** It's the summer of '57, and Randy plans to bring home the title at the Pacific Motorcycle Championships for his club, the "Skyriders." But first his old rival Nick, who's just out of jail, turns up and challenges Randy to an illegal street race. Will Randy succumb to peer pressure and race? Lame plot + lame acting = lame movie. **78m/B VHS.** Paul Blaisdell, Steven Terrell, John Ashley, Anne Neyland, Carl "Alfalfa" Switzer, Raymond Hatton; ***D:*** Edward L. Cahn; ***W:*** Lou Rusoff.

Motorcycle Squad 1/2 *Double Cross* **1941** A policeman is dishonorably discharged so he can get the "inside" dope on a gang of crooks in this 'B' thriller. **61m/B VHS.** Kane Richmond, Wynne Gibson, Pauline Moore, John Miljan, Mary Gordon, Frank Moran; ***D:*** Albert Kelley; ***W:*** Milton Raison; ***C:*** Arthur Martinelli.

Mouchette 1/2 **1967** A lonely 14-year-old French girl, daughter of a drunk father and dying mother, eventually finds spiritual release by committing suicide. Typically somber, spiritual fare from unique master filmmaker Bresson. Perhaps the most complete expression of Bresson's austere, Catholic vision. In French with English subtitles. **80m/B VHS, DVD.** *FR* Nadine Nortier, Maria Cardinal, Paul Hebert; ***D:*** Robert Bresson; ***C:*** Ghislan Cloquet.

Moulin Rouge 1/2 **1952** Colorful, entertaining portrait of acclaimed Impressionist painter Toulouse-Lautrec, more famous for its production stories than onscreen drama, Ferrer delivers one of his most impressive performances as the physically stunted, cynical artist who basked in the seamy Montmartre nightlife. **119m/C VHS, DVD.** Jose Ferrer, Zsa Zsa Gabor, Christopher Lee, Peter Cushing, Colette Marchand, Katherine Kath, Michael Balfour, Eric Pohlmann, Suzanne Flon, Claude Nollier, Muriel Smith, Mary Clare, Walter Crisham, Harold Kasket, Jim Gerald, George Lannes, Lee Montague, Maureen Swanson, Tutte Lemkow, Jill Bennett, Theodore Bikel; ***D:*** John Huston; ***W:*** John Huston, Anthony Veiller; ***C:*** Oswald Morris. Oscars '52: Art Dir./Set Dec., Color, Costume Des. (C).

Moulin Rouge **2001 (PG-13)** Luhrmann resurrects the famed Parisian/Montmartre nightclub decadence in his surreal quasi 1899-set movie musical that stars Kidman as the club's star singer/dancer/courtesan Satine, who entrances McGregor's naive poet, Christian. Naturally, their love is doomed—in part because she has this nasty cough. Leguizamo shows up as artist Toulouse Lautrec. Luhrmann likes to shake up staid genres (witness "Strictly Ballroom" and "Romeo + Juliet") and in this case he married pop music (uneasily) with extraordinary elaborate visuals. This doesn't always work but the director deserves points for sheer chutzpah and Kidman has never looked more stunning. **126m/C VHS, DVD.** *AU US* Nicole Kidman, Ewan McGregor, John Leguizamo, Jim Broadbent, Garry McDonald, Kylie Minogue, Richard Roxburgh, David Wenham, Natalie Mendoza; ***D:*** Baz Luhrmann; ***W:*** Baz Luhrmann, Craig Pearce; ***C:*** Donald McAlpine; ***M:*** Craig Armstrong. Oscars '01: Art Dir./Set Dec., Costume Des.; Australian Film Inst. '01: Cinematog., Costume Des., Film Editing, Sound; British Acad. '01: Sound, Support. Actor (Broadbent), Score; Golden Globes '02: Actor—Mus./Comedy, Actress—Mus./Comedy (Kidman), Film—Mus./Comedy, Score; L.A. Film Critics '01: Support. Actor (Broadbent); Natl. Bd. of Review '01: Film, Support. Actor (Broadbent).

The Mountain **1956** A man and his shady younger brother set out to inspect a Paris-routed plane that crashed in the French Alps. After some harrowing experiences in climbing the peak, it becomes evident that one brother has designs to save whatever he can, while the other intends to loot it. Many real, as well as staged, climbing scenes. Based on Henri Troyat's novel. **105m/C VHS.** Spencer Tracy, Robert Wagner, Claire Trevor, William Demarest, Richard Arlen, E.G. Marshall; ***D:*** Edward Dmytryk.

Mountain Charlie 1/2 **1980** Mountain girl's life is destroyed by three drifters. **96m/C VHS.** Denise Neilson, Dick Robinson, Rick Guinn, Lynn Seus; ***D:*** George Stapleford.

Mountain Family Robinson **1979 (G)** An urban family, seeking escape from the hassles of city life, moves to the Rockies, determined to get back to nature. They soon find that nature may be more harsh than rush-hour traffic and nasty bosses when a bear comes calling. More "Wilderness Family"-type adventures. **102m/C VHS, DVD.** Robert F. Logan, Susan Damante-Shaw, Heather Rattray, Ham Larsen, William (Bill) Bryant, George "Buck" Flower; ***D:*** John Cotter.

Mountain Justice 1/2 *Kettle Creek* **1930** Maynard's first all-talkie western finds our hero in search of his father's murderer. Good action sequences (with stunts performed by Maynard), including those aboard a moving train and a buckboard. **73m/B VHS.** Ken Maynard, Otis Harlan, Kathryn Crawford, Paul Hurst; ***D:*** Harry Joe Brown.

Mountain Man 1/2 *Guardian of the Wilderness* **1977** Historically accurate drama about Galen Clark's successful fight in the 1860s to save the magnificent wilderness area that is now Yosemite National Park. Together with naturalist John Muir, he fought a battle against the lumber companies who wanted the timber and won President Lincoln's support for his cause. **96m/C VHS.** Denver Pyle, John Dehner, Ken Berry, Cheryl Miller, Don Shanks, Cliff Osmond, Jack Kruschen, Ford Rainey; ***D:*** David O'Malley; ***W:*** David O'Malley.

The Mountain Men 1/2 **1980 (R)** Dull adventure drama set in the American West of the 1880s. Two trappers argue about life and have trouble with Indians. **102m/C VHS, DVD.** Charlton Heston, Brian Keith, John Glover, Seymour Cassel, Victor Jory; ***D:*** Richard Lang; ***W:*** Fraser Heston; ***C:*** Michael Hugo; ***M:*** Michel Legrand.

Mountain of the Cannibal God **WOOF!** *Il Montagna di Dio Cannibale; Slave of the Cannibal God* **1979** Beautiful Andress is captured by "native" cannibals; Keach must save her. **103m/C VHS, DVD.** *IT* Stacy Keach, Ursula Andress, Claudio Cassinelli, Franco Fantasia; ***D:*** Sergio Martino; ***M:*** Guido de Angelis, Maurizio de Angelis.

Mountain Patrol: Kekexili *Kekexili* **2004** Kekexili is a brutally dangerous, remote, and beautiful part of Tibet that is home to the endangered chiru antelopes, which are prized by poachers for the price that their wool coats bring. The slaughter is so bad that the mountain people have formed their own patrol to hunt the poachers. In 1996, young Beijing journalist Ga Yu (Zhang) shows up to shadow the patrol and bring attention to the animals' plight. Based on a true story. Mandarin and Tibetan with subtitles. **92m/C DVD.** *CH HK* Duo Bujie, Zhang Lei, Qi Lang, Zhao Xueying; ***D:*** Lu Chuan; ***W:*** Lu Chuan; ***C:*** Cao Yu; ***M:*** Lao Zai.

The Mountain Road 1/2 **1960** Listless drama of an American squadron stationed in China during the last days of WWII. Only Stewart makes this drab film worthwile. **102m/B VHS.** James Stewart, Harry (Henry) Morgan, Glenn Corbett, Mike Kellin; ***D:*** Daniel Mann.

Mountains of the Moon 1/2 **1990 (R)** Sprawling adventure detailing the obsessive search for the source of the Nile conducted by famed Victorian rogue/explorer Sir Richard Burton and cohort John Hanning Speke in the late 1800s. Spectacular scenery and images. Director Rafelson, better known for overtly personal films such as "Five Easy Pieces" and "The King of Marvin Gardens," shows considerable skill with this epic. From William Harrison's novel "Burton and Speke." **140m/C VHS, DVD.** Patrick Bergin, Iain Glen, Fiona Shaw, Richard E. Grant, Peter Vaughan, Roger Rees, Bernard Hill, Anna Massey, Leslie Phillips, John Savident, James Villiers, Delroy Lindo, Roshan Seth; ***D:*** Bob Rafelson; ***W:*** Bob Rafelson; ***C:*** Roger Deakins; ***M:*** Michael Small.

Mountaintop Motel Massacre **WOOF!** **1986 (R)** A resort motel's hostess is a raving lunatic who regularly slaughters her guests. **95m/C VHS, DVD.** Bill (Billy) Thurman, Anna Chappell, Will Mitchell; ***D:*** Jim McCullough Sr.; ***W:*** Jim McCullough Jr.; ***C:*** Joseph M. Wilcots; ***M:*** Ron Di Lulio.

Mountbatten: The Last Viceroy 1/2 *Lord Mountbatten: The Last Viceroy* **1986** Originally a British TV miniseries detailing English viceroy Lord Mountbatten's (Williamson) turning over ruling power from Great Britain to India in 1947 and the birth of Pakistan. **107m/C VHS, DVD.** *GB* Nicol Williamson, Janet Suzman, Sam Dastor, Nigel Davenport, Wendy Hiller, Ian Richardson, Julian Wadham; ***D:*** Tom Clegg; ***W:*** David Butler; ***C:*** Peter Jessop; ***M:*** John Scott.

Mouse and His Child **1977** A gentle animated fantasy adventure about a toy wind-up mouse and his child who fall into the clutches of a villainous rat when they venture into the outside world. **83m/C VHS.** ***D:*** Fred Wolf; ***V:*** Peter Ustinov, Cloris Leachman, Andy Devine.

Mouse Hunt **1997 (PG)** The Smuntz brothers (Lane and Evans) inherit a run-down mansion from their wealthy string magnate father (Hickey, in his last role). Since the boys are involved in a bitter long-standing argument over cord versus twine, they're happy to learn about an offer from a preservation society for a small fortune. The boys try to fix up the house, only to be foiled by the mouse who had been the sole occupant. There are plenty of new mouse traps and tricks thanks to the 65 trained mice (along with 3-D animation) who play the hero. The plucky rodent must also battle a psychotic cat and an obsessed exterminator (Walken, or Lord High King Psycho). If you've ever laughed at a cartoon character taking an anvil to the head, you'll like this. The cartoon-like action livens up the otherwise dismal setting of the mansion and its surroundings. Directorial debut by Verbinski, the man who brought you the Bud frogs. **97m/C VHS, DVD.** Nathan Lane, Lee Evans, Christopher Walken, William Hickey, Vicki Lewis, Maury Chaykin, Eric Christmas, Michael Jeter, Debra Christofferson, Camilla Soeberg; ***D:*** Gore Verbinski; ***W:*** Adam Rifkin; ***C:*** Phedon Papamichael; ***M:*** Alan Silvestri.

The Mouse on the Moon **1962** Sort-of sequel to "The Mouse That Roared" lacks the presence of Peter Sellers but maintains the whimsical tone of the original. The prime minister (Moody) of the Duchy of Grand Fenwick asks for American aid in setting up a space program. (Actually, he wants the money for indoor plumbing.) When it turns out that the local wine is actually rocket fuel, his amiable goof of a son (Cribbins) fulfills his lifelong dream of becoming an astronaut. The mild spoof of cold war politics lacks the anarchic spirit that director Lester has brought to "Help!" and his "Musketeer" films. **85m/C DVD.** *GB* Margaret Rutherford, Ron Moody, Bernard Cribbins, Terry-Thomas, June Ritchie, David Kossoff; ***D:*** Richard Lester; ***W:*** Michael Pertwee; ***C:*** Wilkie Cooper; ***M:*** Ron Grainer.

The Mouse That Roared **1959** With its wine export business going down the drain, a tiny, desperate country decides to declare war on the United States in hopes that the U.S., after its inevitable triumph, will revive the conquered nation. So off to New York go 20 chain-mail clad warriors armed with bow and arrow. Featured in three roles, Sellers is great as the duchess, less effective (though still funny) as the prime minister, and a military leader. A must for Sellers' fans; maintains a sharp satiric edge throughout. Based on the novel by Leonard Wibberley. **83m/C VHS, DVD.** *GB* Peter Sellers, Jean Seberg, Leo McKern, David Kossoff, William Hartnell, Timothy Bateson, MacDonald Parke, Monte Landis; ***D:*** Jack Arnold; ***W:*** Roger MacDougall, Stanley Mann; ***M:*** Edwin Astley.

Mouth to Mouth *Boca a Boca* **1995 (R)** Budding actor Victor (Bardem) is working in Madrid as a phone sex operator while waiting to hear about his big break on an American picture. Victor's regularly called by repressed gay surgeon Ricardo (Flotats) and Amanda (Sanchez-Gijon), who says she's Ricardo's wife. Naive Victor falls for Amanda—who of course isn't Ricardo's wife but seems to be involved in a plot to kill Ricardo masterminded by his real wife Angela (Barranco) and her lover David (Gutierrez Caba). The plot's a little tangled but there's lots of visual gags and bedroom farce and the virile Bardem turns out to be a gifted comedian. Spanish with subtitles. **97m/C VHS, DVD.** *SP* Javier Bardem, Aitana Sanchez-Gijon, Josep Maria Flotats, Maria Barranco, Emilio Gutierrez-Caba, Fernando Guillen, Myriam Meziere; ***D:*** Manuel Gomez Pereira; ***W:*** Manuel Gomez Pereira, Joaquin Oristrell, Naomi Wise, Juan Luis Iborra; ***C:*** Juan Amoros; ***M:*** Bernardo Bonezzi.

Mouvements du Desir *Desire in Motion* **1994** Sex-on-a-train sequences add more than a little steam to this romantic drama. Catherine (Kaprisky) is travelling with her young daughter on the Montreal to Vancouver train in order to forget a failed relationship. She meets shy Vincent (Pichette), who is supposed to be on his way to meet his lover, but somewhere on the journey the sexual sparks start igniting. There are some eccentric fellow passengers to contend with (and director Pool drops in some surreal dream sequences as well) but the heat generated by the leads is genuine enough. **94m/C VHS.** *CA SI* Valerie Kaprisky, Jean-Francois Pichette, Jolianne L'Allier-Matteau, Matthew Mackay, William Jacques; ***D:*** Lea Pool; ***W:*** Lea Pool; ***C:*** Pierre Mignot; ***M:*** Zbigniew Preisner.

Move Over, Darling ½ *Something's Gotta Give* **1963** Remake of 1938's "My Favorite Wife" has widower Garner having his wife Ellen (Day) declared legally dead five years after a plane crash. He remarries, only to have Ellen turn up on his mother's doorstep. Turns out she was stranded on a desert island for those years, and she wasn't alone. Fluffy but enjoyable Day vehicle is the second attempt to remake "Wife," after the ill-fated "Something's Gotta Give," the film Marilyn Monroe was working on when she died. Garner and Day are fine, but are often upstaged by the excellent supporting cast. **103m/C VHS, DVD.** Doris Day, James Garner, Polly Bergen, Thelma Ritter, Chuck Connors, Fred Clark, Don Knotts, Edgar Buchanan, Elliott Reid, John Astin, Pat Harrington, Eddie Quillan, Max (Casey Adams) Showalter, Alvy Moore; ***D:*** Michael Gordon; ***W:*** Hal Kanter, Leo McCarey, Jack Sher; ***C:*** Daniel F. Fapp; ***M:*** Lionel Newman. Golden Globes '63: Actress—Mus./Comedy (Day).

Movers and Shakers ½ **1985 (PG)** An irreverent spoof of Hollywood depicting a filmmaker's attempt to render a best-selling sex manual into a blockbuster film. Fails to live up to its potential and wastes a star-studded cast. **100m/C VHS.** Walter Matthau, Charles Grodin, Gilda Radner, Vincent Gardenia, Bill Macy, Tyne Daly, Steve Martin, Penny Marshall, Luana Anders; ***D:*** William Asher; ***W:*** Charles Grodin.

The Movie House Massacre **1978** A psychopath runs rampant in a theatre killing and maiming moviegoers. No refunds are given. **80m/C VHS.** Jenny Cunningham, Jonathan Blakely, Andrew Cofrin, Mary Woronov; ***D:*** Rick Sloane; ***W:*** Rick Sloane; ***C:*** Bill Fishman; ***M:*** Rick Sloane.

Movie... In Your Face **1990** Japanese mobsters want to take over a movie studio. This supposed comedy comes with a "PU-13" rating—"Stinks to anyone with an I.Q. over 13," make of that what you will and be forewarned that it's also sophomoric and tasteless. **85m/C VHS.** Tommy Sledge.

Movie Maker *Smart Alec* **1986** A young filmmaker ineptly raises money for his next film. **87m/C VHS.** Zsa Zsa Gabor, Antony Alda, Orson Bean, Bill Henderson; ***D:*** Jim Wilson.

Movie, Movie ½ **1978 (PG)** Acceptable spoof of 1930s films features Scott in twin-bill of black and white "Dynamite Hands," which lampoons boxing dramas, and "Baxter's Beauties," a color send-up of Busby Berkeley musicals. There's even a parody of coming attractions. Wholesome, mildly entertaining. **107m/B VHS.** Stanley Donen, George C. Scott, Trish Van Devere, Eli Wallach, Red Buttons, Barbara Harris, Barry Bostwick, Harry Hamlin, Art Carney; ***D:*** Stanley Donen; ***W:*** Larry Gelbart; ***M:*** Ralph Burns. Writers Guild '78: Orig. Screenplay.

Movie Stuntmen *Hollywood Thrillmakers; Hollywood Stunt Man* **1953** A retired Hollywood stunt man takes a job for a dead friend so that the friend's widow can receive the fee. Good stunt work taken mostly from old Richard Taldmadge movies almost makes up for poor production. **56m/B VHS.** James Gleason, William Henry; ***D:*** Bernard B. Ray.

Movies Money Murder **1996** Ruthless actress Lee McNight (Purcell) seduces Dr. Jim (Mull) into helping her produce a movie and then invites the moviemakers, including the writer (Black), to his beach house. Too bad the doc's wife (Kazan) shows up unexpectedly and the doc kills her. And when Dr. Jim hears the plot of the movie (about a murder in a doctor's house), he figures he's being blackmailed and decides to get rid of the suspects. **?m/C VHS.** Martin Mull, Lee Purcell, Karen Black, Lainie Kazan; ***D:*** Arthur Webb.

Moving **1988 (R)** An engineer must relocate his family from New Jersey to Idaho in order to get his dream job. Predictable calamities ensue. Not apt to move you. **89m/C VHS.** Richard Pryor, Randy Quaid, Dana Carvey, Dave Thomas, Rodney Dangerfield, Stacey Dash; ***D:*** Alan Metter; ***W:*** Andy Breckman; ***M:*** Howard Shore.

Moving Malcolm **2003** Feature directorial debut of screenwriter and star Ratner. Gene Maxwell was dumped at the altar by B-movie actress Liz Woodward (Berkley). He's surprised when Liz suddenly shows up at his door, but all she wants is a favor: help move her eccentric elderly father Malcolm (Neville) into a new apartment. Still smitten, Gene agrees, hoping it will rekindle their romance. Instead, Liz heads off to Prague for a movie shoot and he and Malcolm become kindred spirits. **83m/C DVD.** *CA* Benjamin Ratner, Elizabeth Berkley, John Neville, Jay Brazeau, Babz Chula, Nicholas Lea, Rebecca Harker; ***C:*** Gregory Middleton; ***M:*** Chris Ainscough.

Moving McAllister ½ **2007 (PG-13)** Rick Robinson (Gourley) is a lowly intern at a Miami law firm. Desperate to score points with his boss, Maxwell McAllister (Hauer), he agrees to move McAllister's seductive niece Michelle (Kunis), her pet pig Dorothy, and various possessions cross-country. They pick up quirky hitchhiker Orlick Prescott Hope (Heder), and Rick finds his adventures just beginning. Unfortunately, they're boring and predictable and so's the movie. **90m/C DVD.** Mila Kunis, Jon Heder, Rutger Hauer, Ben Gourley; ***D:*** Andrew Black; ***W:*** Ben Gourley; ***C:*** Douglas Chamberlain; ***M:*** Didier Rachou.

Moving Out **1983** Adolescent migrant Italian boy finds it difficult to adjust to his new surroundings in Melbourne, Australia. **91m/C VHS, DVD.** Vince Colosimo, Sally Cooper, Maurice Devincentis, Tibor Gyapjas; ***D:*** Michael Pattinson.

Moving Target ½ **1989 (R)** A young woman witnesses the brutal murder of her boyfriend by mobsters and flees to Florida. Unbeknownst to her, the thugs are still after her. Although top-billed, Blair's role is actually a supporting one. **85m/C VHS, DVD.** *IT* Linda Blair, Ernest Borgnine, Stuart Whitman, Charles Pitt, Jainine Linde, Kurt Woodruff; ***D:*** Marius Mattei.

Moving Target **1996 (R)** Sonny McClean (Dudikoff) is a bounty hunter. But his latest job has him framed for murder and caught up in the middle of mob rivalries. So in order to clear his name, Sonny has to avoid getting killed by violent gangs and quick-draw cops. **106m/C VHS, DVD.** *CA* Michael Dudikoff, Billy Dee Williams, Michelle Johnson, Ardon Bess, Tom Harvey, Len Doncheff, Noam Jenkins; ***D:*** Damian Lee; ***W:*** Mark Sevi, Kevin McCarthy; ***C:*** David Pelletier; ***M:*** David Lawrence.

Moving Target **2000 (R)** Martial arts expert Wilson is framed for murder and must battle the mob to clear his name. **86m/C VHS, DVD.** Don "The Dragon" Wilson, Bill Murphy, Hilary Kavanagh, Terry McMahon, Eileen McCloskey, Lisa Duane; ***D:*** Paul Ziller; ***W:*** Paul Ziller; ***C:*** Yoram Astrakhan; ***M:*** Derek Gleason. **VIDEO**

Moving Targets **1987** A young girl and her mother find themselves tracked by a homicidal maniac. **95m/C VHS, DVD.** *AU* Michael Aitkens, Carmen Duncan, Annie Jones, Shane Briant; ***D:*** Chris Langman.

Moving Violation **1976 (PG)** Crooked cops chase two young drifters who have witnessed the local sheriff commit a murder. Corman car chase epic. **91m/C VHS, DVD.** Eddie Albert, Kay Lenz, Stephen McHattie, Will Geer, Lonny (Lonnie) Chapman; ***D:*** Charles S. Dubin; ***W:*** William W. Norton Sr.

Moving Violations **1985 (PG-13)** This could be entitled "Adventures in Traffic Violations School." A wise-cracking tree planter is sent to traffic school after accumulating several moving violations issued to him by a morose traffic cop. Bill Murray's little brother in feature role. **90m/C VHS, DVD.** John Murray, Jennifer Tilly, James Keach, Brian Backer, Sally Kellerman, Fred Willard, Clara Peller, Wendie Jo Sperber; ***D:*** Neal Israel; ***W:*** Pat Proft; ***C:*** Robert Elswit; ***M:*** Ralph Burns.

Mozart: A Childhood Chronicle **1976** An experimental, semi-narrative portrait of the immortal composer, from the ages of seven to twenty, filmed on authentic locations and with the original instruments of the era. Entire soundtrack is composed of Mozart's music. In German with English subtitles. **224m/B VHS.** *GE* Pavlos Bekiaris, Diego Crovetti, Santiago Ziesmer, Marianne Lowitz, Karl Maria Schley; ***D:*** Klaus Kirschner; ***W:*** Klaus Kirschner; ***C:*** Philip Koch.

Mozart and the Whale ½ **2005 (PG-13)** Based on a true story. Donald (Hartnett) and Isabelle (Mitchell) both have Asperger's Syndrome (a form of autism), which results in problems dealing with the outside world or other people. Donald has assembled a support group, which Isabelle decides to join. Since Donald is so shy, she makes the first romantic move at a Halloween party where she's dressed as Mozart and Donald hides inside a whale costume. The relationship grows stronger but has a lot of pitfalls as Donald gains self-confidence while Isabelle grows more uncertain. Filmed on location in Spokane, Washington. **93m/C DVD.** Josh Hartnett, Radha Mitchell, Gary Cole, Sheila Kelley, John Carroll Lynch, Rusty Schwimmer, Robert Wisdom; ***D:*** Petter Naess; ***W:*** Ronald Bass; ***C:*** Svein Krovel; ***M:*** Deborah Lurie.

The Mozart Brothers **1986** An angst-ridden Swedish opera director decides to break all the rules while doing an innovative production of Mozart's "Don Giovanni." At first he horrifies his conservative opera company but as his vision is gradually realized their resistance breaks down. A wonderful look at behind-the-scenes chaos and not just for opera aficionados. In Swedish with English subtitles. **111m/C VHS.** *SW* Etienne Glaser, Philip Zanden, Henry Bronett; ***D:*** Suzanne Osten.

The Mozart Story **1948** After Mozart's death, music minister to the Emperor, Antonio Salieri, reflects on how his jealousy and hatred of the musical genius held the great composer back and contributed to his death. Originally filmed in Austria in 1937, scenes were added for the U.S. release in 1948. **91m/B VHS.** Hans Holt, Winnie Markus, Irene von Meyendorf, Rene Deltgen, Edward Vedder, Wilton Graff, Walther Jansson, Curt Jurgens, Paul Hoerbiger; ***D:*** Karl Hartl.

MTV's Wuthering Heights ½ *Wuthering Heights* **2003 (PG-13)** MTV pop-rock version, set in California, of Emily Bronte's classic romantic tragedy. The star-crossed lovers are blonde beauty Cate (Christensen) and a motorcyle-riding, up-and-coming rocker named Heath (Vogel). Cate's brother Hendrix (Whitworth) is suspicious and jealous and Cate, who's scared of her feelings, impulsively decides to marry nice guy Edward (Masterton). Certainly not for purists—or anyone out of their teen years. **88m/C VHS, DVD.** Erika Christensen, Mike Vogel, Christopher K. Masterson, Katherine Heigl, Johnny Whitworth, John Doe; ***D:*** Suri Krishnamma; ***W:*** Max Enscoe, Annie de Young; ***C:*** Claudio Chea; ***M:*** Stephen Trask. **CABLE**

Much Ado about Nothing ½ **1993 (PG-13)** Shakespeare for the masses details romance between two sets of would-be lovers—the battling Beatrice and Benedick (Thompson and Branagh) and the ingenuous Hero and Claudio (Beckinsale and Leonard). Washington is the noble warrior leader, Reeves his evil half-dressed half-brother, and Keaton serves comic relief as the officious, bumbling Dogberry. Sunlit, lusty, and revealing about all the vagaries of love, Branagh brings passion to his quest of making Shakespeare more approachable. His second attempt after "Henry V" after breaking the stuffy Shakespearean tradition. Filmed on location in Tuscany, Italy. **110m/C VHS, DVD.** *GB* Kenneth Branagh, Emma Thompson, Robert Sean Leonard, Kate Beckinsale, Denzel Washington, Keanu Reeves, Michael Keaton, Brian Blessed, Phyllida Law, Imelda Staunton, Gerard Horan, Jimmy Yuill, Richard Clifford, Ben Elton, Richard Briers; ***D:*** Kenneth Branagh; ***W:*** Kenneth Branagh; ***C:*** Roger Lanser; ***M:*** Patrick Doyle.

The Mudge Boy ½ **2003 (R)** Duncan Mudge (Hirsch) is not your average teenage boy. Wearing his dead mother's clothing, he bikes around town with his pet chicken in tow. Not surprisingly, he's picked on by the other boys and scorned by his own father (Jenkins). But one boy is drawn to Duncan, a tough kid named Perry (Guiry). Perry's confused sexuality leads him to abuse and then reject Duncan, with gruesome results. Explores the pain of loss and youth well. Cast is uniformly good, particularly Hirsch and Jenkins. And hey, who knew you could calm a chicken by sticking its head in your mouth? **94m/C DVD.** Emile Hirsch, Tom Guiry, Richard Jenkins, Pablo Schreiber, Zachery Knighton, Ryan Donowho, Meredith Handerhan, Beckie King; ***D:*** Michael Burke; ***W:*** Michael Burke; ***C:*** Vanja Cernjul; ***M:*** Marcelo Zarvos.

Mugsy's Girls *Delta Pi* **1985 (R)** A messy comedy about six sorority women, educated in the refined skills of bar mud wrestling, who wallow in a Las Vegas championship tournament. Features pop singer Laura Branigan. **87m/C VHS.** Ruth Gordon, Laura Branigan, Eddie Deezen; ***D:*** Kevin Brodie.

Mulan ½ **1998 (G)** Disney's 36th animated tale is taken from a Chinese fable. The Emperor (Morita) sends out an order that one man from every family must become a soldier in order to repel the advances of Shan-Yu (Ferrer) and his army of Huns. But Mulan's (Wen) father (Oh) is ill and she's afraid he won't return, so she decides to take his place and disguises herself as a warrior. The family's ancestral spirits enlist a guardian—the pint-sized dragon, Mushu (Murphy)—as Mulan goes off to war. The two mainstays of Disney's previous animated features—the songs and the comedy-relief sidekicks—turn out to be the weak links in this story. While Murphy's Mushu does have the funniest lines, he doesn't quite fit the more serious tone. Impressive visuals, and careful characterization by the voice actors make up for any formulaic missteps so that adults, as well as kids, should enjoy the show. **87m/C VHS, DVD.** ***D:*** Barry Cook, Tony Bancroft; ***W:*** Philip LaZebnik, Raymond Singer, Rita Hsiao, Christopher Sanders, Eugenia Bostwick-Singer; ***M:*** Matthew Wilder, Jerry Goldsmith, David Zippel; ***V:*** Matthew Wilder, Ming Na, Eddie Murphy, B.D. Wong, Miguel Ferrer, Soon-Teck Oh, Noriyuki "Pat" Morita, Harvey Fierstein, Gedde Watanabe, James Hong, Freda Foh Shen, June Foray, Marni Nixon, George Takei, Miriam Margolyes, James Shigeta, Frank Welker, Lea Salonga, Donny Osmond, Jerry S. Tondo.

Mulberry Street **2006 (R)** Everyone knows that there's lots of rats in New York City. Only this time the rodents are infected with a virus that has them attacking humans. The humans are then transformed into rat/human, flesh-eating zombies. Former boxer Clutch (Damici) looks out for his Mulberry Street neighbors but he really has him work cut out for him now. Low-budget but surprisingly scary. **84m/C DVD.** Nick Damici, Kimberly Blair, Ron Brice, Larry Fleishman, Bo Corre, Larry Medich, Javier Picyo; ***D:*** Jim Mickle; ***W:*** Nick Damici, Jim Mickle; ***C:*** Ryan Samul; ***M:*** Andreas Kapsalis.

Mulholland Drive **2001 (R)** David Lynch is back to his old trippy surrealistic tricks again, folks. Lush visuals and atmospheric Badalamenti music are once again the key ingredients in this hypnotic look at Hollywood through a kaleidoscope. Betty (Watts), an aspiring actress staying at her aunt's vacant apartment, comes home to find mystery girl Rita (Harring) taking a shower there. Rita, who has taken her name from a movie poster, has amnesia, and Betty tries to help her piece her life together. Meanwhile, successful young director Adam (Theroux) is threatened with death unless he casts a certain actress favored by a wheelchair-bound dwarf who issues orders over a cell phone. Then (if you can believe it) things get even weirder. Originally conceived as a pilot for ABC television, but reshot as a feature. Execs must have guessed the public wasn't ready for "Laverne and Shirley Drop Acid." **146m/C VHS, DVD.** *US* Naomi Watts, Laura

Elena Harring, Justin Theroux, Ann Miller, Dan Hedaya, Lafayette Montgomery, Michael J. Anderson, Scott Coffey, Chad Everett, Melissa George, James Karen, Katharine Towne, Billy Ray Cyrus, Angelo Badalamenti, Mark Pellegrino, Lee Grant, Kathrine (Kate) Forster, Missy (Melissa) Crider, Brent Briscoe, Marcus Graham, Vincent Castellanos, Michael Des Barres, Robert Forster; ***D:*** David Lynch; ***W:*** David Lynch; ***C:*** Peter Deming; ***M:*** Angelo Badalamenti. Cesar '01: Foreign Film; Ind. Spirit '02: Cinematog.; L.A. Film Critics '01: Director (Lynch); Natl. Bd. of Review '01: Breakthrough Perf. (Watts); N.Y. Film Critics '01: Film; Natl. Soc. Film Critics '01: Actress (Watts), Film.

Mulholland Falls 1/2 **1995 (R)** Noir meets the nuclear age in this stylish period piece from New Zealand director Tamahori. Nolte plays the leader of the Hat Squad, a vicious group of fedora-sporting detectives assigned to bust organized crime in '50s L.A. at all costs. While investigating the murder of his ex-mistress, Nolte and cohorts Madsen, Palminteri and Penn discover evidence linking the murder to a general (Malkovich) in charge of the top secret nuclear program. Although the cast is dripping with big name stars, the best performance is put in by the glossy set design of Richard Sylbert, who probably had a strong case of deja vu, having previously done "Chinatown." **107m/C VHS, DVD.** Nick Nolte, Melanie Griffith, Chazz Palminteri, Michael Madsen, Christopher Penn, Treat Williams, Jennifer Connelly, Andrew McCarthy, John Malkovich, Daniel Baldwin, Bruce Dern, Ed Lauter; ***Cameos:*** William L. Petersen, Rob Lowe; ***D:*** Lee Tamahori; ***W:*** Pete Dexter; ***C:*** Haskell Wexler; ***M:*** Dave Grusin. Golden Raspberries '96: Worst Support. Actress (Griffith).

Mulligan 1/2 **2000** Amateurish indie buddy comedy. Jordan hates his job and his girlfriend has left him so he plays golf with his three equally messed-up buddies. They all need a do-over (and not just in their golf game). **86m/C DVD.** Cedric Yarbrough, Steve Lattery, Joshua Will, Trei Michaels, Bill Borea; ***D:*** Tim Vandesteeg; ***W:*** Kevin Ross, Joshua Will, Bill Borea, Tim Vandesteeg; ***C:*** Afshin Shahidi; ***M:*** Michael Whalen.

Mulligans 1/2 **2008** Tyler Davidson brings gay college buddy Chase home to quaint Prospect Lake and they both get summer jobs at the golf course. Tyler's parents got married right after high school and his dad Nathan has been repressing some long-held feelings. The situation gets worse when Chase realizes he's attracted to Nathan. Well-told family drama that never descends into bathos. **90m/C DVD.** *CA* Dan Payne, Thea Gill, Charlie David, Derek Baynham, Grace Vukovic; ***D:*** Chip Hale; ***W:*** Charlie David; ***C:*** Alice Brooks; ***M:*** Robert Buckley.

Multiple Maniacs **1970** Waters at his most perverse. Divine's travelling freak show, filled with disgusting side-show sex acts, is the vehicle used for robbing and killing hapless spectators. One of the best scenes of a sordid lot is Divine being raped by Lobstora, a 15-foot broiled lobster. **90m/B VHS.** Divine, David Lochary, Mary Vivian Pearce, Edith Massey, Mink Stole, Susan Lowe, Cookie Mueller, Pat Moran, Paul Swift, Jack Walsh, Susan Walsh, Ed Peranio, George Figgs; ***D:*** John Waters; ***W:*** John Waters; ***C:*** John Waters.

Multiplicity 1/2 **1996 (PG-13)** With too many business and personal responsibilities, construction supervisor Doug Kinney (Keaton) is a prime candidate for the cloning experiments of Dr. Leeds (Yulin). Since the cloning process isn't exactly perfect, each clone (Doug winds up with three) has a different dominant personality trait—a hard-charger, a "Mister Mom," and a dopey slacker. Confusion reigns as wife Laura (MacDowell) deals with separation anxiety on a grand scale. Pleasant comedy shows Keaton can still be funny given the chance. Keaton had his choice of cloning comedies and chose this one over Chris Columbus's "More." **117m/C VHS, DVD.** Michael Keaton, Andie MacDowell, Harris Yulin, Richard Masur, Eugene Levy, Obba Babatunde, Ann Cusack, Brian Doyle-Murray, Julie Bowen; ***D:*** Harold Ramis; ***W:*** Harold Ramis, Chris Miller, Lowell Ganz, Babaloo Mandel, Mary Hale; ***C:*** Laszlo Kovacs; ***M:*** George Fenton.

Mumford **1999 (R)** Writer/director Lawrence Kasdan creates another ensemble gem in this story of small town psychologist Mumford (Dean), who uses unusual methods to help the quirky townsfolk deal with their problems. His ability to actually listen to people helps out the young skateboarding millionaire (Lee) who employs most of the town, a shopaholic wife (McDonnell), her loutish husband (Danson), and nearly everyone else in town whose screws are a bit loose. Everyone except a slimy lawyer (Short) who the good doctor fires as a patient. He begins to dig up facts that may prove that Mumford isn't even a doctor. Since there's no big plot payoff or mind-boggling twists, some viewers may find it a bit boring. Those who enjoy deeper character development will love it, however. **112m/C VHS, DVD.** Loren Dean, Alfre Woodard, Hope Davis, Jason Lee, Mary McDonnell, Pruitt Taylor Vince, Zooey Deschanel, Martin Short, David Paymer, Jane Adams, Dana Ivey, Kevin Tighe, Ted Danson, Jason Ritter, Elisabeth (Elissabeth, Elizabeth, Liz) Moss, Robert Stack; ***D:*** Lawrence Kasdan; ***W:*** Lawrence Kasdan; ***C:*** Ericson Core; ***M:*** James Newton Howard.

The Mummy 1/2 **1932** A group of scientists examine a sarcophagus taken from an unmarked grave at an archeological dig in 1921 Egypt. There is a warning on the box that it should not be opened. Does this stop anyone? Of course not! So Im-Ho-Tep (Karloff), a 4000-year-old priest who was disgraced and buried alive, is now revived. Then, of course, ther's his objective—heroine Helen (Johann) whom the wrapped one believes is the reincarnation of his long-gone love Anck-es-en-Amon. Eerie chills mark this classic horror tale that found Karloff undergoing eight hours of extraordinary makeup (by Jack Pierce) to transform him into the macabre mummy. Marked the directing debut of famed German cinematographer Freund. The first in the Universal series. **72m/B VHS, DVD.** Boris Karloff, Zita Johann, David Manners, Edward Van Sloan, Arthur Byron, Bramwell Fletcher, Noble Johnson, Leonard Mudie, Henry Victor; ***D:*** Karl Freund; ***W:*** John Lloyd Balderston; ***C:*** Charles Stumar.

The Mummy **1959** A group of British archaeologists discover they have made a grave mistake when a mummy kills off those who have violated his princess' tomb. A summation of all the previous "mummy" films, this one has a more frightening mummy (6'4" Lee) who is on screen much of the time. Additionally, there is pathos in this monster, not merely murder and revenge. An effective remake of the 1932 classic. **88m/C VHS, DVD.** *GB* Peter Cushing, Christopher Lee, Felix Aylmer, Yvonne Furneaux, Eddie Byrne, Raymond Huntley, George Pastell, Michael Ripper, John Stuart; ***D:*** Terence Fisher; ***W:*** Jimmy Sangster; ***C:*** Jack Asher.

The Mummy 1/2 **1999 (PG-13)** Cheesy fun in the Saturday matinee tradition, this horror tale is a loose remake of the 1932 Boris Karloff-starrer. In the 1920s, American adventurer Rick O'Connell (Fraser) is hired by British librarian Evelyn (Weisz) and her Egyptologist brother Jonathan (Hannah) to escort them to the ancient Egyptian city of the dead. Unfortunately, their meddling results in the release of cursed mummified priest Imhotep (Vosloo), who manages to regenerate into living flesh and who wants to use Evelyn to resurrect his dead girlfriend. Lots of zombies, mummies, skeletons, and flesh-eating beetles as well as spooky tombs. **124m/C VHS, DVD, HD DVD.** Brendan Fraser, Rachel Weisz, Arnold Vosloo, John Hannah, Kevin J. O'Connor, Jonathan Hyde, Oded Fehr, Erik Avari, Tuc Watkins, Stephen Dunham, Corey Johnson, Bernard Fox, Aharon Ipale, Omid Djalili, Patricia Velasquez; ***D:*** Stephen Sommers; ***W:*** Stephen Sommers; ***C:*** Adrian Biddle; ***M:*** Jerry Goldsmith.

Mummy & Curse of the Jackal
WOOF! 1967 Upon opening the tomb of female mummy, a man is cursed to roam the streets of Las Vegas as a werejackal. Impossibly inept. **86m/C VHS.** Anthony Eisley, Martina Pons, John Carradine, Saul Goldsmith; ***D:*** Oliver Drake.

The Mummy Lives **1993 (PG-13)** Vegeance-minded mummy goes on a murderous rampage against the defilers of his tomb and becomes obsessed with a woman he believes is his reincarnated lost love. **97m/C VHS.** Tony Curtis, Greg Wrangler, Muhamad Bakri, Leslie Hardy; ***D:*** Gerry O'Hara; ***W:*** Nelson Gidding; ***C:*** Avi Koren; ***M:*** Dov Seltzer.

The Mummy Returns 1/2 **2001 (PG-13)** Bombastic sequel to the 1999 hit is set a decade later and finds marrieds Rick (Fraser) and Evelyn (Weisz) living in London with their 8-year-old son, Alex (Boath). Unfortunately, a reincarnated Anck-Su-Namun (Velasquez) manages to bring crispy Inhotep (Vosloo) back again to rule the world. Fehr returns as desert warrior Ardeth Bay, as does Hannah as Evelyn's ne'er-do-well brother. Wrestler Dwayne "The Rock" Johnson briefly shows up as a new villain—The Scorpion King, who's already going to have his own film. As usual there's too much going on—it's loud and crowded, sacrificing the original's unexpected charm for visual overkill. **129m/C VHS, DVD, HD DVD.** *US* Brendan Fraser, Rachel Weisz, Oded Fehr, John Hannah, Patricia Velasquez, Dwayne "The Rock" Johnson, Arnold Vosloo, Flip Kobler, Adewale Akinnuoye-Agbaje, Shaun Parkes, Alun Armstrong; ***D:*** Stephen Sommers; ***W:*** Stephen Sommers; ***C:*** Adrian Biddle; ***M:*** Alan Silvestri.

The Mummy: Tomb of the Dragon Emperor **2008 (PG-13)** Third time around for overly-experienced mummy battler Rick O'Connell (Fraser), joined by his wife Evelyn (Bello) in aiding their son Alex (Ford), who has accidentally awakened the evil Dragon Emperor (Li). The emperor resurrects an undead army of 10,000 to conquer the world, but luckily the emperor's archenemy, the fierce sorceress Zi Juan (Yeoh), doesn't approve, bringing her own CGI soldiers into the mix. Bigger than its predecessors, but still little more than a poor man's Indy flick (on steroids). **114m/C DVD, Blu-ray Disc.** *US* Brendan Fraser, Jet Li, Maria Bello, Luke Ford, John Hannah, Michelle Yeoh, Isabella Leong, Anthony Wong, Liam Cunningham, Russell Wong; ***D:*** Rob Cohen; ***W:*** Alfred Gough, Miles Millar; ***C:*** Simon Duggan; ***M:*** Randy Edelman.

The Mummy's Curse **1944** Sequel to "The Mummy's Ghost" and Chaney's last outing as Kharis. Construction by a government order causes Kharis and Ananka (Christine) to be dug up in a Louisiana bayou (how they got there from a New England swamp is anyone's guess) and taken to Cajun country for study by archaeologists. The usual havoc ensues. Includes lots of stock footage from earlier mummy movies. Based on a story by Leon Abrams and Dwight V. Babcock. **61m/B VHS, DVD.** Lon Chaney Jr., Peter Coe, Virginia Christine, Kay Harding, Dennis Moore, Martin Kosleck, Kurt Katch; ***D:*** Leslie Goodwins; ***W:*** Bernard Schubert; ***C:*** Virgil Miller.

The Mummy's Ghost **1944** The fourth in the Universal series and the sequel to "The Mummy's Tomb" has Kharis (Chaney Jr.) searching for the reincarnation of his ancient love, Princess Ananka, who just happens to be New England college coed Amina (Ames). The high priest (Zucco) sends fellow priest Yousef Bey (Carradine) along to assist but he makes the mistake of declaring his own love for Amina and the mummy gets very, very mad. Oh, and both Kharis and Amina sink into a swamp, thus setting up the next (and last) film in the series. **61m/B VHS, DVD.** Lon Chaney Jr., John Carradine, Ramsay Ames, Robert Lowery, Barton MacLane, George Zucco; ***D:*** Reginald LeBorg; ***W:*** Griffin Jay, Henry Sucher, Brenda Weisberg; ***C:*** William Sickner; ***M:*** Hans J. Salter.

The Mummy's Hand 1/2 **1940** Although this is the followup to 1932's "The Mummy," it actually has little to do with the original film. Archaeologists Steve Banning (Foran) and Babe Jensen (Ford) are searching for the tomb of ancient Egyptian Princess Ananka. Crazy high priest Andoheb (Zucco) sends mummy Kharis (Tyler), who is the tomb's guardian, to kill anyone who defiles her rest. So Kharis shuffles off but finds Marta (Moran) instead. And being a guy, albeit a long-dead guy, wants to make the beauty his bride. Low-budget but the mix of scares and comedy make this worth watching. **70m/B VHS, DVD.** Dick Foran, Wallace Ford, Peggy Moran, Cecil Kellaway, George Zucco, Tom Tyler, Eduardo Ciannelli, Charles Trowbridge; ***D:*** Christy Cabanne; ***W:*** Griffin Jay, Maxwell Shane; ***C:*** Elwood "Woody" Bredell; ***M:*** Hans J. Salter.

The Mummy's Revenge *La Venganza de la Momia* **1973** A fanatic revives a mummy with virgin blood. The first mummy movie to feature open gore. **91m/C VHS.** *SP* Paul Naschy, Jack Taylor, Maria Silva, Helga Line, Luis Davila, Eduardo Calvo; ***D:*** Carlos Aured; ***W:*** Paul Naschy.

The Mummy's Shroud **1967** Hammer's next-to-last Mummy horror is a handsomely produced but tepid affair. The plot trots out the familiar elements—British archeological dig led by Sr. Basil Walden (Morell) discovers the remains of Pharaoh Kah-to-Bey; hieroglyphics from the shroud are read aloud...you know the drill. Lots of talk, comparatively little action. **90m/C DVD.** *GB* Andre Morrell, John Phillips, David Buck, Elizabeth Sellars; ***D:*** John Gilling; ***W:*** John Gilling; ***C:*** Arthur Grant; ***M:*** Don Banks.

The Mummy's Tomb **1942** Chaney Jr. is in wraps for the first time in this sequel to "The Mummy's Hand." Kharis is transported to America by a crazed Egyptian high priest to kill off surviving members of the expedition. Weakened by a lame script and too much stock footage. Based on a story by Neil P. Varnick. **71m/B VHS, DVD.** Jack Arnold, Lon Chaney Jr., Dick Foran, John Hubbard, Elyse Knox, George Zucco, Wallace Ford, Turhan Bey; ***D:*** Harold Young; ***W:*** Griffin Jay, Henry Sucher; ***C:*** George Robinson.

Munchie 1/2 **1992 (PG)** A forgotten alien critter is discovered in a mine shaft by young Gage. Munchie turns out to be a good friend, protecting Gage from bullies and granting other wishes. Frequent sight gags help keep the film moving but it's still awfully slow. Sequel to "Munchies" (1987). **80m/C VHS, DVD.** Loni Anderson, Andrew Stevens, Arte Johnson, Jamie McEnnan; ***D:*** Jim Wynorski; ***V:*** Dom DeLuise.

Munchies **1987 (PG)** "Gremlins" rip-off about tiny aliens who love beer and fast food, and invade a small town. Lewd and ribald. **83m/C VHS, DVD.** Harvey Korman, Charles Stratton, Nadine Van Der Velde, Alix Elias, Jon Stafford, Charlie Phillips, Hardy Rawls, Robert Picardo, Wendy Schaal, Paul Bartel; ***D:*** Bettina Hirsch; ***W:*** Lance Smith; ***C:*** Jonathan West.

Munich 1/2 **2005 (R)** Back in "Schindler's List" mode, Spielberg explores in horrifying magnification the politics and far-reaching aftermath of the real-life shocking murders of 11 Israeli athletes at the 1972 Munich Olympics. However, the film is primarily about a team of Israeli agents (Bana, Craig, Hinds, Kassovitz) hired to exact revenge on the Palestinian assassins. Gold standard screenwriters Kushner and Roth draw liberally from George Jonas's nonfiction tome "Vengeance," and, like his other fact-based dramas, Spielberg delivers a thought-provoking and intense experience, making us cringe at the transforming power of revenge. **164m/C DVD.** *US* Eric Bana, Daniel Craig, Ciaran Hinds, Mathieu Kassovitz, Hanns Zischler, Geoffrey Rush, Michael (Michel) Lonsdale, Mathieu Amalric, Lynn Cohen, Marie Josee Croze, Makram Khoury, Moritz Bleibtreu, Gila Almagor, Moshe Ivgi, Yvan Attal, Hiam Abbass, Valeria Bruni-Tedeschi, Meret Becker, Ayelet Zurer, Igal Naor, Omar Metwally, Mostefa Djadjam; ***D:*** Steven Spielberg; ***W:*** Tony Kushner, Eric Roth; ***C:*** Janusz Kaminski; ***M:*** John Williams.

Munster, Go Home! 1/2 **1966** Herman learns he's inherited the stately manor Munster Hall so he and the family head for jolly old England to claim their family history. Will the Brits ever recover? **96m/C VHS, DVD.** Fred Gwynne, Yvonne De Carlo, Al Lewis, Butch Patrick, Debbie Watson, Terry-Thomas, Hermione Gingold, Robert Pine, John Carradine, Bernard Fox, Richard Dawson, Arthur Malet; ***D:*** Earl Bellamy; ***W:*** Joe Connelly, Bob Mosher, George Tibbles; ***C:*** Benjamin (Ben H.) Kline; ***M:*** Jack Marshall.

The Munsters' Revenge **1981** Based on the continuing adventures of the 1960s comedy series characters. Herman, Lily, and Grandpa have to contend with robot replicas of themselves that were created by a flaky scientist. **96m/C VHS, DVD.** Fred Gwynne, Yvonne De Carlo, Al Lewis, Jo McDonnell, Sid Caesar, Ezra Stone, Howard Morris, Bob Hastings, K.C. Martel; ***D:*** Don Weis; ***M:*** Vic Mizzy. **TV**

The Muppet Christmas Carol 1/2 **1992 (G)** Christmas classic features all the muppet favorites together and in Victorian garb. Storyline is more or less faithful to Dickens original, with pleasant special effects. Gonzo the Great as Dickens narrates the tale as Scrooge (Caine) takes his legendary Christmas Eve journey escorted by three (flannel) spirits. The Cratchits are led by Kermit and Miss Piggy. Directed by Brian Henson, Jim's son, the film is as heartwarming as the Cratchit's crackling fire, but doesn't quite achieve the former muppet magic. Also features some sappy songs by Williams, including "Love is Like a Heatwave" and "Island in the Sun." **120m/C VHS, DVD.** Michael Caine; ***D:*** Brian Henson; ***C:*** John Fenner; ***M:*** Paul Williams, Miles Goodman; ***V:*** Dave Goetz, Steve Whitmire, Jerry Nelson, Frank Oz.

The Muppet Movie **1/2 1979 (G)** Seeking fame and footlights, Kermit the Frog and his pal Fozzie Bear travel to Hollywood, and along the way are joined by sundry human and muppet characters, including the lovely Miss Piggy. A delightful cult favorite filled with entertaining cameos, memorable (though somewhat pedestrian) songs and crafty special effects—Kermit rides a bike and rows a boat! A success for the late Jim Henson. ♫The Rainbow Connection; Frog's Legs So Fine; Movin Right Along; Can You Picture That?; Never Before; Something Better; This Looks Familiar; I'm Going Back There Someday. **94m/C VHS, DVD.** *GB* ***Cameos:*** Edgar Bergen, Milton Berle, Mel Brooks, Madeline Kahn, Steve Martin, Carol Kane, Paul Williams, Charles Durning, Bob Hope, James Coburn, Dom DeLuise, Elliott Gould, Cloris Leachman, Telly Savalas, Orson Welles; ***D:*** James Frawley; ***W:*** Jack Burns, Jerry Juhl; ***C:*** Isidore Mankofsky; ***M:*** Paul Williams; ***V:*** Jim Henson, Frank Oz, Jerry Nelson, Richard Hunt, Dave Goetz. Natl. Film Reg. '09.

Muppet Treasure Island **1/2 1996 (G)** Literary classic gets its first coat of felt as Kermit the Frog, Miss Piggy and the entire Muppet gang hit the high seas in an adaptation of Robert Louis Stevenson's 1883 well-worn adventure tale. Delightful settings, from an old English tavern to an exotic south sea island, frame the journey of young Jim Hawkins (flesh and blood Bishop), who along with tavern owners Rizzo the Rat (Whitmire) and the Great Gonzo (Goelz) search for buried treasure. Long John Silver is played to the hilt by Curry, master of the over-the-top villain. Helmer Henson steers a steady ship, with over 400 Muppet critters making an appearance. **99m/C VHS, DVD.** Tim Curry, Kevin Bishop, Billy Connolly, Jennifer Saunders; ***D:*** Brian Henson; ***W:*** Jerry Juhl, James V. Hart, Kirk R. Thatcher; ***C:*** John Fenner; ***M:*** Hans Zimmer; ***V:*** Steve Whitmire, Frank Oz, Dave Goetz.

Muppets from Space **1/2 1999 (G)** The sixth full-length movie featuring Jim Henson's uberpuppets centers on Gonzo and his search for his real family. He discovers that he is an alien from a distant planet and announces his findings on Miss Piggy's talk show. Soon, government bad guy K. Edgar Singer (Tambor) is after him. After escaping Singer, Gonzo must decide whether to stay on earth with his friends or leave on the family spaceship. Features cameos by Ray Liotta, F. Murray Abraham, Andie MacDowell, and Hulk Hogan. Perfect for the sippy-cup set. **88m/C VHS, DVD.** Jeffrey Tambor, F. Murray Abraham, David Arquette, Ray Liotta, Andie MacDowell, Rob Schneider, Josh Charles, Kathy Griffin, Pat Hingle; ***D:*** Timothy Hill; ***W:*** Jerry Juhl, Joseph Mazzarino; ***C:*** Alan Caso; ***V:*** Frank Oz, Dave Goetz, Steve Whitmire.

The Muppets Take Manhattan **1984 (G)** Following a smashing success with a college musical, the Muppets take their show and talents to Broadway, only to face misfortune in the form of an unscrupulous producer. A less imaginative script than the first two Muppet movies, yet an enjoyable experience with numerous major stars making cameo appearances. **94m/C VHS, DVD.** ***Cameos:*** Dabney Coleman, James Coco, Art Carney, Joan Rivers, Gregory Hines, Linda Lavin, Liza Minnelli, Brooke Shields, John Landis; ***D:*** Frank Oz; ***W:*** Frank Oz; ***C:*** Robert Paynter; ***M:*** Ralph Burns; ***V:*** Frank Oz, Tom Patchett, Jim Henson.

The Muppets' Wizard of Oz **2005 (PG)** The sock-puppets that made the world fall in love with the "Rainbow Connection" find themselves somewhere over the rainbow in this made-for-TV feature. Granted, the Muppets have been much, much funnier in the past, but after stinkers like "Muppets Christmas Carol" and "Muppets Treasure Island," it's nice to see the folks at the Henson Company trying to return their creations to their comedic roots. Sure, Ashanti is a pretty dull lead, but the supporting cast is strong and the humor is surprisingly adult. The Muppets might be owned by Disney now, but you can still enjoy Wizard's Quentin Tarantino cameos and jokes about Gonzo's nipples. (Honestly.) **100m/C DVD.** Ashanti, Queen Latifah, David Alan Grier, Jeffrey Tambor; ***Cameos:*** Quentin Tarantino; ***D:*** Kirk R. Thatcher; ***W:*** Debra Frank, Steve Hayes, Adam F. Goldberg, Tom Martin; ***C:*** Tony Westman; ***V:*** Steve Whitmire, Dave Goelz, Bill Barretta, Eric Jacobson. **VIDEO**

Murda Muzik **1/2 2003** Up-and-coming rapper Fresh can't keep the hard life on the mean Queens' streets behind him, risking more than just his big recording contract. Music from popular hip-hop and rap stars, including 50 Cent, Snoop Dogg, and Mobb Deep, are the main draw. **72m/C VHS, DVD.** Nas, Big Noyd, Havoc, Cormega, Chinky, Prodigy; ***D:*** Lawrence Page; ***W:*** Prodigy. **VIDEO**

Murder **1930** Believing in a young woman's innocence, one jurist begins to organize the pieces of the crime in order to save her. Fine early effort by Hitchcock based on play "Enter Sir John," by Clemense Dane and Helen Simpson. **92m/B VHS, DVD.** *GB* Herbert Marshall, Nora Baring, Phyllis Konstam, Miles Mander; ***D:*** Alfred Hitchcock; ***W:*** Alfred Hitchcock; ***C:*** Jack Cox; ***M:*** John Reynders.

Murder Ahoy **1/2 1964** Miss Marple looks perplexed when dead bodies surface on a naval cadet training ship. Dame Marge is the dottie detective in the final, and least appealing, of her four Agatha Christie films of the '60s (although it was released in the States prior to "Murder Most Foul"). **74m/B VHS, DVD.** Margaret Rutherford, Lionel Jeffries, Charles "Bud" Tingwell, William Mervyn, Francis Matthews; ***D:*** George Pollock.

Murder at Devil's Glen **1/2** ***What We Did That Night*** **1999** Henry (Schroder) is a manipulative ex-con who returns to his hometown with a proposition for three of his former college buddies, who have all become successful. They all share a secret—during a frat party hazing incident a young woman accidentally died and the foursome buried her body in an isolated area in the woods. Now Henry wants to develop that particular piece of property, so they have to go back and dig up the evidence of their crime. Ah, if only it were that easy. The sweet-faced Schroder makes a remarkably capable and creepy bad guy. **90m/C VHS, DVD.** Rick Schroder, Jack Noseworthy, Michael Easton, Jayce Bartok, Jennifer Jostyn, Tara Reid; ***D:*** Paul Shapiro; ***W:*** Eric Harlacher; ***C:*** Brian Reynolds; ***M:*** Dana Kaproff. **TV**

Murder at 45 R.P.M. *Meurtre en 45 Tours* **1965** A singer and her lover suspect each other of her husband's murder. Things become sticky when she receives a recorded message from her dead husband. Average. **98m/C VHS.** *FR* Danielle Darrieux, Michel Auclair, Jean Servais, Henri Guisol; ***D:*** Etienne Perier.

Murder at Midnight **1931** The killings begin with a game of charades in which the gun wasn't supposed to be loaded, and continue as members of English high society die one by one. "Blondie" director Strayer still working on his change of pace. **69m/B VHS, DVD.** Alice White, Leslie Fenton, Aileen Pringle, Hale Hamilton, Robert Elliott, Clara Blandick, Brandon Hurst; ***D:*** Frank Strayer.

Murder at 1600 **1997 (R)** Jaded D.C. detective Harlan Regis (Snipes) is called to investigate the murder of Carla Town (Moore), a secretary found dead in a White House bathroom. He's reluctantly assisted by hard-boiled Secret Service agent Chance (Lane), while head of security Nick Spikings (Benzali) wants the whole matter wrapped up quickly and quietly—justice not being his main concern. Cliche-fest script gives stereotypical characters a little more development than you may be used to seeing, but doesn't give them anything new or interesting to say or do. Snipes and Lane make a good team, however, and Miller fulfills his usual wise-cracking sidekick role effortlessly. **107m/C VHS, DVD.** Wesley Snipes, Diane Lane, Daniel Benzali, Dennis Miller, Alan Alda, Ronny Cox, Tate Donovan, Diane Baker, Mary Moore, Harris Yulin, Richard Blackburn; ***D:*** Dwight Little; ***W:*** Wayne Beach, David Hodgin; ***C:*** Steven Bernstein; ***M:*** Christopher Young.

Murder at the Baskervilles *Silver Blaze; Sherlock Holmes: The Silver Blaze* **1937** Sherlock Holmes is invited to visit Sir Henry Baskerville at his estate, but then finds that Baskerville's daughter's fiance is accused of stealing a race horse and murdering its keeper. Based on Sir Arthur Conan Doyle's story "Silver Blaze." Remade in 1977. **67m/B VHS, DVD.** *GB* Arthur Wontner, Ian Fleming, Lyn Harding; ***D:*** Thomas Bentley.

Murder at the Gallop **1/2 1963** Snooping Miss Marple doesn't believe a filthy rich old-timer died of natural causes, despite the dissenting police point of view. Wheedling her way into the police investigation, she discovers the secret of the Gallop club, a place where people bounce up and down on top of horses. Much mugging between Dame Margaret and Morley. Marple's assistant, Mr. Stringer, is the real life Mr. Dame Margaret. Based on Christie's Poirot mystery "After the Funeral." **81m/B VHS, DVD.** Margaret Rutherford, Robert Morley, Flora Robson, Charles "Bud" Tingwell, Duncan Lamont, Stringer Davis; ***D:*** George Pollock; ***W:*** James P. Cavanagh; ***C:*** Arthur Ibbetson; ***M:*** Ronald Goodwin.

Murder at the Vanities **1/2 1934** Vintage murder mystery set against a musical revue format, in which a tough detective must find a killer before the Earl Carroll-based cabaret ends and he or she will escape with the exiting crowd. Also featured is a mind-boggling production number based on the song "Marijuana." ♫Marijuana; Lovely One; Where Do They Come From Now; Live and Love Tonight; Cokctails for Two; Ebony Rhapsody. **91m/B VHS.** Victor McLaglen, Kitty Carlisle Hart, Jack Oakie, Duke Ellington, Carl Brisson, Dorothy Stickney, Gertrude Michael, Jessie Ralph, Charles Middleton, Gail Patrick, Donald Meek, Toby Wing, Lucille Ball, Ann Sheridan; ***D:*** Mitchell Leisen; ***W:*** Sam Hellman; ***C:*** Leo Tover; ***M:*** Arthur Johnston.

Murder by Contract **1958** Cold-blooded hitman Claude (Edwards) goes to L.A. to take out ex-moll Billie (Toriel) who's going to testify against his never-seen boss Mr. Brink in a federal trial. Billie is heavily guarded and Claude blows two attempts. Realizing his boss won't forgive and forget even if he finally succeeds, Claude does the unexpected. **81m/B DVD.** Vince Edwards, Phillip Pine, Michael Granger, Herschel Bernardi, Caprice Toriel; ***D:*** Irving Lerner; ***W:*** Benjamin Simcoe; ***C:*** Lucien Ballard; ***M:*** Perry Botkin.

Murder by Death **1/2 1976 (PG)** Capote is an eccentric millionaire who invites the world's greatest detectives to dinner, offering $1 million to the one who can solve the evening's murder. Entertaining and hammy spoof of Agatha Christie's "And Then There Were None" and the earlier "Ten Little Indians." **95m/C VHS, DVD.** Peter Falk, Alec Guinness, David Niven, Maggie Smith, Peter Sellers, Eileen Brennan, Elsa Lanchester, Nancy Walker, Estelle Winwood, Truman Capote, James Coco; ***D:*** Robert Moore; ***W:*** Neil Simon; ***C:*** David M. Walsh; ***M:*** Dave Grusin.

Murder by Decree **1979 (PG)** Realistic and convincing version of the Jack the Ripper story. Sherlock Holmes and Dr. Watson find a vast web of conspiracy when they investigate the murders of Whitechapel prostitutes. Based partially on facts, it's a highly detailed suspenser with interesting camera work and fine performances. **120m/C VHS, DVD.** *CA* Christopher Plummer, James Mason, Donald Sutherland, Genevieve Bujold, Susan Clark, David Hemmings, Frank Finlay, John Gielgud, Anthony Quayle; ***D:*** Bob (Benjamin) Clark; ***W:*** John Hopkins. Genie '80: Actor (Plummer), Director (Clark), Support. Actress (Bujold).

Murder by Moonlight **1991 (PG-13)** Rival agents investigate a mysterious murder in a prosperous mining colony on the moon. Not only do they discover a dastardly trail that leads all the way back to Earth, but a strange romantic attraction for each other. Originally broadcast on British TV. **94m/C VHS.** *GB* Julian Sands, Brigitte Nielsen, Gerald McRaney, Jane Lapotaire, Brian Cox; ***D:*** Michael Lindsay-Hogg; ***M:*** Trevor Jones.

Murder by Natural Causes **1979** A made-for-TV brain teaser in which a woman and her lover plot to kill her mind-reader husband. Lots of twists make this fun for viewers who enjoy a challenge. **96m/C VHS.** Hal Holbrook, Barry Bostwick, Katharine Ross, Richard Anderson; ***D:*** Robert Day.

Murder by Night **1/2 1989 (PG-13)** Amnesia victim Urich is found next to a dead body, the result of a gruesome murder. Urich is the only witness and thinks he may be the next victim. Others think he's the killer. Mystery with enough twists to make it worthwhile. **95m/C VHS.** Robert Urich, Kay Lenz, Jim Metzler, Richard Monette, Michael Ironside, Michael Williams; ***D:*** Paul Lynch. **CABLE**

Murder by Numbers **1/2 1989 (PG-13)** Murder in the art world stumps a detective. What might have been a good suspense story is ruined by bad editing and a lack of continuity, resulting in confusion rather than suspense. **91m/C VHS.** Sam Behrens, Shari Belafonte, Ronee Blakley, Stanley Kamel, Jayne Meadows, Debra Sandlund, Dick Sargent, Cleavon Little; ***D:*** Paul Leder; ***W:*** Paul Leder.

Murder by Numbers **1/2 2002 (R)** Homicide detective Cassie Mayweather (Bullock) is a crime scene specialist saddled with a by-the-book new partner, Sam Kennedy (Chaplin). This isn't good since she has to prove that two wealthy young men (Gosling, Pitt) have committed what they think is the perfect murder (shades of Leopold and Loeb and with nods to Hitchcock). Naturally, Cassie has baggage and must come to terms with her past in order to solve the crime. Gosling's downright scary while Pitt well-plays his weaker partner; Bullock works against being likeable as a loner toughie. **120m/C VHS, DVD.** *US* Sandra Bullock, Ben Chaplin, Ryan Gosling, Michael Pitt, Christopher Penn, R.D. Call, Agnes Bruckner; ***D:*** Barbet Schroeder; ***W:*** Tony Gayton; ***C:*** Luciano Tovoli; ***M:*** Clint Mansell.

Murder by Phone *Bells; The Calling* **1982 (R)** A deranged technician has turned his phone into an instrument of electronic death. Chamberlain is the visiting professor trying to discover who's permanently disconnecting the numbers of his students. Good cast decides to test schlock meter. **79m/C VHS.** *CA* Richard Chamberlain, John Houseman, Sara Botsford; ***D:*** Michael Anderson Sr.; ***W:*** Michael Butler, John Kent Harrison; ***M:*** John Barry.

Murder by Television **1/2** *The Houghland Murder Case* **1935** Low-budget murder mystery with Lugosi in a dual role as twins—one good, one not so. When a professor and the evil twin are murdered, the instrument of death suspected is...television. Still an exotic and misunderstood invention when this was made, TV sometimes invoked fear and suspicion in the general public. Historically interesting and Lugosi fans will appreciate seeing him in a non-vampiric role. **55m/B VHS, DVD.** Bela Lugosi, George Meeker; ***D:*** Clifford Sanforth.

Murder by the Book **1/2** *Alter Ego* **1987** A mystery writer finds that his fictional character, a hard-boiled private eye, has taken control of his life. With his new macho persona the writer solves a crime and saves the obligatory dame. Based on the novel "Alter Ego" by Mel Arrighi. **100m/C VHS.** Robert Hays, Catherine Mary Stewart, Celeste Holm, Fred Gwynne, Christopher Murney; ***D:*** Mel Damski. **TV**

Murder Czech Style *Vrazda Po Cesky* **1966** Chubby and boring office clerk Frantisek (Hrusinsky) is amazed when a colleague, the beautiful Alice (Fialova), agrees to marry him. He can't believe his good fortune—and he's right—Frantisek soon discovers his wife has a married lover. So, he plots to murder her in several increasingly silly fantasies. Czech with subtitles. **87m/C VHS.** *CZ* Rudolf Hrusinsky, Kveta Fialova, Vaclav Voska, Vladimir Mensik; ***D:*** Jiri Weiss; ***W:*** Jiri

Weiss, Jan Otcenasek; ***C:*** Jan Nemecek; ***M:*** Zdenek Liska.

Murder Elite 🦴 1/2 **1986** A murdering maniac terrorizes the rural English countryside, where MacGraw has returned after losing all her money in America. Poor acting and direction make this one a dust-gatherer. **98m/C VHS.** Ali MacGraw, Billie Whitelaw, Hywel Bennett; ***D:*** Claude Whatham.

Murder for Sale 🦴 *OSS 177 - Double Agent* **1968** Secret Agent 117 stages an elaborate scam in order to infiltrate a ring of terrorists and criminals. Ask for Bond next time. **90m/C VHS.** *FR* John Gavin, Margaret Lee, Curt Jurgens, Luciana Paluzzi, Robert Hossein, Rosalba Neri; ***D:*** Renzo Cerrato; ***W:*** Renzo Cerrato; ***C:*** Tonino Delli Colli; ***M:*** Piero Piccioni.

Murder, He Says 🦴🦴 1/2 **1945** Sinister comedy finds insurance salesman Peter Marshall (MacMurray) sent to gather statistics in the Ozarks and encountering the murderous hillbilly Fleagle family and various other looney characters. Naturally, the prettiest girl in the area, Claire (Walker), also happens to be the only sane person, which is lucky for Peter. **91m/B VHS.** Fred MacMurray, Helen Walker, Marjorie Main, Peter Whitney, Barbara Pepper, Jean Heather, Mabel Paige, Porter Hall; ***D:*** George Marshall; ***W:*** Lou Breslow; ***C:*** Theodor Sparkuhl; ***M:*** Robert Emmett Dolan.

Murder in a Small Town 🦴🦴 1/2 **1999** It's the 1930s and Broadway director Wilder has moved to Connecticut after his wife's murder and runs the community theatre. But soon he finds himself surrounded by dead bodies and, with the aid of an opera-loving cop (Starr), Wilder decides to do some detecting. **100m/C VHS.** Gene Wilder, Mike Starr, Cherry Jones, Frances Conroy, Deirdre O'Connell, Terry O'Quinn; ***D:*** Joyce Chopra; ***W:*** Gene Wilder; ***C:*** Bruce Surtees; ***M:*** John Morris. **CABLE**

Murder in Coweta County 🦴🦴 1/2 **1983** Griffith and Cash are strong in this true-crime drama based on the book by Margaret Anne Barnes. Griffith is a Georgia businessman who thinks he's gotten away with murder; Cash is the lawman who tenaciously pursues him. Based on an actual 1948 case. **100m/C VHS, DVD.** Johnny Cash, Andy Griffith, Earl Hindman, June Carter Cash, Cindi Knight, Ed Van Nuys; ***D:*** Gary Nelson; ***W:*** Dennis Nemec; ***C:*** Larry Pizer; ***M:*** Brad Fiedel. **TV**

Murder in Greenwich 🦴🦴 *Dominick Dunne Presents Murder in Greenwich* **2002 (R)** Based on former LAPD detective Mark Fuhrman's book. Fuhrman (Meloni) investigates the unsolved 25-year-old murder of 15-year-old Martha Moxley (Grace), which happened in Greenwich, CT in the 1970's. This is the case that eventually led to the arrest and conviction of Kennedy nephew Michael Sakal for the crime. **88m/C VHS, DVD.** Christopher Meloni, Robert Forster, Maggie Grace, Toby Moore, Jon Foster, Andrew Mitchell; ***D:*** Tom McLoughlin; ***W:*** Dave Erickson; ***C:*** Mark Wareham; ***M:*** Don Davis. **CABLE**

Murder in Greenwich Village 🦴🦴 **1937** Heiress Kay Cabot (Wray) is accused of a murder that she naturally didn't commit and it's up to her defense attorney, Steve Jackson (Arlen), to get her off so that they can live happily ever after. **68m/B VHS.** Fay Wray, Richard Arlen, Raymond Walburn, Scott Kolk, Thurston Hall, Marc Lawrence, Leon Ames, Marjorie Reynolds, Wyn Cahoon, Mary Russell; ***D:*** Albert Rogell; ***W:*** Michael L. Simmons; ***C:*** Henry Freulich.

Murder-in-Law 🦴 **1992 (R)** Graphic slasher flick about a mother-in-law from hell who escapes from an insane asylum and terrorizes her son-in-law (Estevez) and his family in a series of gruesome killings. **97m/C VHS.** Marilyn Adams, Joe Estevez, Sandy Snyder, Darrel Guilbeau; ***D:*** Tony Jiti Gill.

Murder in Mind 🦴🦴 1/2 **1997 (R)** Caroline Walker's (Parker) accused of murdering her husband (Smits) but can't remember doing so. She tries to figure out the truth by undergoing regression therapy with a hynotherapist (Hawthorne). But what she supposedly uncovers are a lot of ugly secrets that were better left hidden. Adapted by Cooney from his play. **89m/C VHS.** *GB* Nigel Hawthorne, Mary-Louise Parker, Jimmy Smits, Jason Scott Lee, Gailard Sartain; ***D:*** Andrew Morahan; ***W:*** Michael Cooney; ***C:*** John Aronson; ***M:*** Paul Buckmaster.

Murder in New Hampshire: The Pamela Smart Story 🦴🦴 1/2 **1991 (PG-13)** A sleazy true story about a young high school teacher who seduces an impressionable student into murdering her husband. Hunt's fine as the seductress but this TV fare is just average. **93m/C VHS, DVD.** Helen Hunt, Chad Allen, Larry Drake, Howard Hesseman, Ken Howard, Michael Learned; ***D:*** Joyce Chopra; ***M:*** Gary Chang. **TV**

Murder in Space 🦴 1/2 **1985** Nine multinational astronauts are stranded aboard a space station when they discover one of them is a murderer. This creates anxiety, particularly since the killer's identity is unknown. Oatmeal salesman Brimley is the earth-bound mission control chief trying desperately to finger a spaceman while the bodies pile up. **95m/C VHS.** Wilford Brimley, Martin Balsam, Michael Ironside; ***D:*** Steven Hilliard Stern. **TV**

Murder in Texas 🦴🦴🦴 **1981** Docudrama looks at the strange but true events surrounding the death of society woman Joan Robinson Hill, first wife of prominent plastic surgeon, Dr. John Hill, and daughter of wealthy oilman Ash Robinson. Well-crafted script and effective performances keep your interest. Griffith was Emmy nominated. From the book "Prescription Murder," written by the doctor's second wife. **200m/C VHS.** Farrah Fawcett, Katharine Ross, Andy Griffith, Sam Elliott, Craig T. Nelson, Barbara Sammeth; ***D:*** William (Billy) Hale. **TV**

Murder in the First 🦴🦴 1/2 **1995 (R)** Hours after leaving a three-year stint in solitary confinement at Alcatraz, petty thief Henri Young (Bacon) kills the inmate he thinks ratted him out. Young, eager-puppy lawyer James Stamphill (Slater) defends Young by claiming that inhumane and brutal prison treatment turned him into a murderer. Heavy-handed and uneven despite excellent performances by top-notch cast. Oldman does his usual fine job with yet another unsympathetic character, the sadistic warden. Major professional landmark for both Slater and Bacon. Loosely based on a true story that led to the closing of Alcatraz. **123m/C VHS, DVD.** Christian Slater, Kevin Bacon, Gary Oldman, Embeth Davidtz, William H. Macy, Stephen Tobolowsky, Brad Dourif, R. Lee Ermey, Mia Kirshner, Stefan Gierasch, Kyra Sedgwick; ***D:*** Marc Rocco; ***W:*** Dan Gordon; ***C:*** Fred Murphy; ***M:*** Christopher Young. Broadcast Film Critics '95: Actor (Bacon).

Murder in the Footlights 🦴🦴 *The Trojan Brothers* **1946** Murder drama involving a socialite and a vaudeville team. **85m/B VHS.** *GB* Lesley Brook, David Hutcheson, Patricia Burke, David Farrar, Bobby Howes, Barbara Mullen, Finlay Currie; ***D:*** Maclean Rogers; ***W:*** Maclean Rogers; ***C:*** Moray Grant, Ernest Palmer.

Murder in the Old Red Barn 🦴 *Maria Marten* **1936** Based on the real murder of an unassuming girl by a randy squire. Stiff, melodramatic performances are bad enough, but the play-style production, unfamiliar to modern viewers, is the last nail in this one's coffin. **67m/B VHS, DVD.** *GB* Tod Slaughter, Sophie Stewart, D.J. Williams, Eric Portman; ***D:*** Milton Rosmer.

Murder, Inc. 🦴🦴 **1960** Brisk (if familiar) crime drama based on the killers-for-hire crime syndicate that operated out of Brooklyn in the 1930s. Crusading DA Turkus (Morgan) is after racketeer Louis "Lepke" Buchalter (Stewart). Killer Abe "Kid Twist" Reles (Falk) sucks Joey Collins (Whitman) and his wife Eadie (Britt) into the gang and forces them to hide an on-the-lam Lepke, who gets ratted out by his own men. Both Collins and Reles turn up as witnesses for the state (although Reles managed to "fall" out of a window before the trial). **103m/B DVD.** Peter Falk, Stuart Whitman, Harry (Henry) Morgan, David J. Stewart, May Britt, Simon Oakland, Morey Amsterdam; ***D:*** Stuart Rosenberg, Burt Balaban; ***W:*** Mel Barr, Irve Tunick; ***C:*** Gayne Rescher; ***M:*** Frank DeVol.

A Murder Is Announced 🦴🦴 *Agatha Christie's Miss Marple: A Murder Is Announced* **1987** From the critically acclaimed BBC series. While on holiday, super-sleuth Marple encounters a murder that was advertised in the local newspaper one week prior to its occurrence. Based on the 1952 Agatha Christie novel, Hickson shines once again as Christie's detective extraordinaire. **155m/C VHS, DVD.** *GB* Joan Hickson; ***D:*** David Giles. **TV**

Murder Is My Business 🦴 1/2 **1946** Private eye Michael Shayne (Beaumont) is tasked with catching the murderer of his client, a wealthy woman who hired Shayne to protect her from blackmailers. **64m/B DVD.** Hugh Beaumont, Cheryl Walker, Lyle Talbot, George Meeker, Pierre Watkin; ***D:*** Sam Newfield; ***W:*** Brett Halliday, Fred Myton; ***C:*** Jack Greenhalgh.

Murder Mansion 🦴 1/2 **1970** Some decent scares ensue when a group of travelers is stranded in an old haunted mansion. **84m/C VHS, DVD.** *SP* Evelyn Stewart, Analia Gade; ***D:*** Francisco Lara Polop.

Murder Most Foul 🦴🦴🦴 **1965** Erstwhile school marm Dame Margaret is excellent as the only jury member to believe in the accused's innocence. Posing as a wealthy actress to insinuate herself into the local acting troupe, she sniffs out the true culprit. Based on the Poirot mystery "Mr. McGinty's Dead." **90m/B VHS, DVD.** Francesca Annis, Margaret Rutherford, Ron Moody, Charles "Bud" Tingwell, Megs Jenkins, Dennis Price, Ralph Michael; ***D:*** George Pollock.

Murder Motel 🦴 **1974** Inept spine-tingler about a motel keeper who makes a practice of killing his customers. There's always a vacancy at the Murder Motel, at least until the fiancee of one of his victims decides to look into the matter. **80m/C VHS.** *GB* Robyn Millan, Derek Francis, Ralph Bates, Edward Judd; ***D:*** Malcolm Taylor; ***W:*** Brian Clemens. **TV**

Murder, My Sweet 🦴🦴🦴 1/2 *Farewell, My Love* **1944** Down-on-his-luck private detective Philip Marlowe (Powell) searches for an ex-convict's missing girlfriend through a dark world of murder, mayhem, and ever-twisting directions. Classic film noir screen version of Raymond Chandler's tense novel "Farewell, My Lovely," which employs flashback fashion using that crisp Chandler narrative. A breakthrough dramatically for singer Powell; Chandler's favorite version. Remade using the novel's title in 1975. **95m/B VHS, DVD.** Dick Powell, Claire Trevor, Mike Mazurki, Otto Kruger, Anne Shirley, Miles Mander, Douglas Walton, Esther Howard, Donald "Don" Douglas; ***D:*** Edward Dmytryk; ***W:*** John Paxton; ***C:*** Harry Wild; ***M:*** Roy Webb.

A Murder of Crows 🦴🦴 1/2 **1999 (R)** Alcoholic, disbarred New Orleans attorney Lawson Russell (Gooding Jr.) decides to write a book. He happens to meet an elderly man who lets him read his own murder mystery manuscript and when the man unexpectedly dies, Lawson gets the book published as his own. It's a success—only it seems the the story about five lawyers being murdered is real and a detective (Berenger) thinks that since Russell knows so much about the crimes, he must be the killer. **102m/C VHS, DVD.** Cuba Gooding Jr., Tom Berenger, Marianne Jean-Baptiste, Eric Stoltz; ***D:*** Rowdy Herrington; ***W:*** Rowdy Herrington.

The Murder of Mary Phagan 🦴🦴🦴 1/2 **1987 (PG)** Lemmon stars as John Slaton, governor of Georgia during one of America's most notorious miscarriages of justice. In 1913, timid, Jewish factory manager Leo Frank is accused of the brutal murder of a female worker. Prejudice and a power hungry prosecuting attorney conspire to seal the man's fate at the end of the hangman's noose. Sensing the injustice, Slaton re-opens the case, causing riots in Atlanta. Top-notch TV drama, featuring a superb re-creation of turn-of-the-century atmosphere and a compelling, true story which was not finally resolved until the 1970s. **251m/C VHS.** Jack Lemmon, Peter Gallagher, Richard Jordan, Robert Prosky, Paul Dooley, Rebecca Miller, Kathryn Walker, Charles S. Dutton, Kevin Spacey, Wendy J. Cooke; ***D:*** William (Billy) Hale; ***M:*** Maurice Jarre. **TV**

A Murder of Quality 🦴🦴 1/2 **1990** Spymaster George Smiley (Elliott) comes to aid of colleague Ailsa Brimley (Jackson) when he agrees to investigate the nefarious goings-on at the Carne School for boys. It seems a schoolmaster's wife predicted her murder and named her husband as the killer. Now she's dead but her husband has a very solid alibi. Based on the novel by John Le Carre. **103m/C VHS, DVD.** *GB* Denholm Elliott, Glenda Jackson, Joss Ackland, Billie Whitelaw, David Threlfall, Ronald Pickup, Christian Bale, Matthew Scurfield; ***D:*** Gavin Millar; ***C:*** Denis Crossan; ***M:*** Stanley Myers. **TV**

The Murder of Stephen Lawrence 🦴🦴🦴 **1999** Institutional racism is explored in this fact-based drama about the 1993 murder of black teenager Stephen Lawrence (Black) in London. Lawrence is waiting at a bus stop when he is attacked by five teenaged neo-Nazis. His Jamaican-born parents (Baptiste and Quarshie) seek justice but are treated indifferently by the police. Then the charges against the suspects are thrown out for lack of evidence and the Lawrences insist on a private prosecution (civil suit) that studies the incompetent police investigation. **120m/C VHS.** *GB* Marianne Jean-Baptiste, Hugh Quarshie, Leon Black, Joseph Kpobie, Kenneth Cranham, David Calder; ***D:*** Paul Greengrass; ***W:*** Paul Greengrass; ***C:*** Ivan Strasburg. **TV**

Murder on Approval 🦴 *Barbados Quest* **1956** Conway is a carbon-copy Sherlock Holmes, called in to verify the authenticity of a stamp and finds himself involved in murder. Slow-paced, weak and transparent. **70m/B VHS.** Tom Conway, Delphi Lawrence, Brian Worth, Michael Balfour, John Colicos; ***D:*** Bernard Knowles.

Murder on Flight 502 🦴🦴 **1975** A crisis arises on a 747 flight from New York to London when a terrorist runs amuck. Big cast of TV stars and Stack as the pilot keep this stale flick from getting lost in the ozone. **97m/C VHS, DVD.** Farrah Fawcett, Sonny Bono, Ralph Bellamy, Theodore Bikel, Dane Clark, Polly Bergen, Laraine Day, Fernando Lamas, George Maharis, Hugh O'Brian, Molly Picon, Walter Pidgeon, Robert Stack; ***D:*** George McCowan. **TV**

Murder on Lenox Avenue 🦴🦴 1/2 **1941** When the leader of the Harlem Better Business Bureau is overthrown, he swears revenge. **60m/C VHS.** Mamie Smith, Norman Astwood, Augustus Smith, Alberta Perkins, Alec Lovejoy; ***D:*** Arthur Dreifuss; ***W:*** Vincent Valentini; ***C:*** George Webber; ***M:*** Donald Heywood.

Murder on Line One 🦴🦴 **1990** A London murderer films his crimes for his later viewing pleasure. The police arrest a suspect, but the killings continue. Both the police and viewer are soon aware that they've made a mistake. **103m/C VHS.** Emma Jacobs, Peter Blake, Simon Shepherd, Allan Surtees, Andrew Wilde, Dirkan Tulane, Neil Duncan, Brett Forrest; ***D:*** Anders Palm; ***W:*** Anders Palm.

Murder on the Bayou 🦴🦴🦴 *A Gathering of Old Men* **1991 (PG)** Down on the L'siana bayou, a white guy who thinks civil rights are color coded is murdered, and an elderly black man is accused of the crime. Made for TV, well performed, engaging. From the novel by Ernest J. Gaines. **91m/C VHS, DVD.** Louis Gossett Jr., Richard Widmark, Holly Hunter, Woody Strode, Joe Seneca, Papa John Creach, Julius W. Harris, Will Patton; ***D:*** Volker Schlondorff. **TV**

Murder on the Campus 🦴🦴 *Out of the Shadow* **1952** A reporter investigates the apparent suicide of his brother at Cambridge University. He discovers that a number of other mysterious deaths have occurred as well. Interesting characterizations hampered by predictability. **61m/B VHS, DVD.** *GB* Terence Longdon, Donald Gray, Diane Clare, Robertson Hare, Dermot Walsh; ***D:*** Michael Winner; ***W:*** Michael Winner.

Murder on the High Seas 🦴🦴 **1932** Infidelity and murder aboard a cruise ship. **65m/B VHS.** Natalie Moorhead, Jack Mulhall, Edmund Breese, Montagu Love, Clara Kimball Young, Alice Day, Roy D'Arcy; ***D:*** Robert F. "Bob" Hill; ***W:*** Robert F. "Bob" Hill, George Plympton; ***C:*** E. Fox Walker.

Murder on the Midnight Express 🦴 1/2 *Night is the Time for Killing* **1974** Mystery about spies, thieves, honeymooners, and a corpse aboard an all-night train. All aboard. **70m/C VHS.** Judy Geeson, James Smilie, Charles Gray, Alister Williamson; *W:* Brian Clemens. **TV**

Murder on the Orient Express 🦴🦴🦴 **1974 (PG)** An Agatha Christie mystery lavishly produced with an all-star cast. In 1934, a trainful of suspects and one murder victim make the trip from Istanbul to Calais especially interesting. Super-sleuth Hercule Poirot sets out to solve the mystery. An entertaining whodunit, ably supported by the remarkable cast. Followed by "Death on the Nile." **128m/C VHS, DVD.** *GB* Albert Finney, Martin Balsam, Ingrid Bergman, Lauren Bacall, Sean Connery, Richard Widmark, Anthony Perkins, John Gielgud, Jacqueline Bisset, Jean-Pierre Cassel, Wendy Hiller, Rachel Roberts, Vanessa Redgrave, Michael York, Colin Blakely, George Coulouris, Denis Quilley, Vernon Dobtcheff, Jeremy Lloyd; *D:* Sidney Lumet; *W:* Paul Dehn; *C:* Geoffrey Unsworth; *M:* Richard Rodney Bennett. Oscars '74: Support. Actress (Bergman); British Acad. '74: Support. Actor (Gielgud), Support. Actress (Bergman).

Murder on the Yukon 🦴 ½ **1940** An installment in the "Renfrew of the Royal Mounted" series. Newill and O'Brien's vacation plans are ruined when they find a corpse in a canoe and must investigate. Lots of action, but a somewhat threadbare production. Based on "Renfrew Rides North" by Lauri York Erskine. **57m/B VHS, DVD.** James Newill, Dave O'Brien, Polly Ann Young; *D:* Louis Gasnier.

Murder Once Removed 🦴 ½ **1971** A private eye discovers that a respectable doctor has a bedside manner that women are dying for. **74m/C VHS, DVD.** John Forsythe, Richard Kiley, Barbara Bain, Joseph Campanella; *D:* Charles S. Dubin; *M:* Robert Jackson Drasnin. **TV**

Murder One 🦴 **1988 (R)** Two half-brothers escape from a Maryland prison and go on a killing spree, dragging their younger brother with them. Low-budget and it shows. Based on a true story. **83m/C VHS, DVD.** Henry Thomas, James Wilder, Stephen Shellen, Errol Slue; *D:* Graeme Campbell.

Murder 101 🦴🦴 **1991 (PG-13)** Brosnan plays Charles Lattimore, an author and English professor who specializes in murder mysteries. He gives his students a rather unique assignment of planning the perfect murder. When a student is killed right before his eyes and a fellow teacher turns up dead, Lattimore realizes he's being framed for murder. Surprising twists abound in this stylish thriller. **93m/C VHS, DVD.** Pierce Brosnan, Dey Young, Raphael Sbarge, Kim Thomson; *D:* Bill Condon; *W:* Bill Condon.

Murder or Mercy 🦴🦴 ½ **1974** Still timely story of a famous doctor accused of killing his terminally ill wife. Focuses on the morality of mercy killing. **78m/C VHS.** Melvyn Douglas, Bradford Dillman, David Birney, Denver Pyle, Mildred Dunnock; *D:* Harvey Hart. **TV**

Murder Ordained 🦴🦴 ½ **1987** Yet another true-crime network miniseries, this time about a Kansas minister and her lover plotting the demise of their spouses. Good acting for this sort of thing. In two-cassette package. **183m/C VHS.** Keith Carradine, JoBeth Williams, Terry Kinney, Guy Boyd, Terence Knox, Darrell Larson, M. Emmet Walsh, Kathy Bates; *D:* Mike Robe.

Murder over New York 🦴🦴 **1940** Episode in the Charlie Chan mystery series. Chan visits New York City and becomes involved in an investigation at the airport. With the aid of his klutzy son, he sleuths his way through a slew of suspects until the mystery is solved. Standard fare for the Chan fan. **65m/B VHS.** Sidney Toler, Marjorie Weaver, Robert Lowery, Ricardo Cortez, Donald MacBride, Melville Cooper, Victor Sen Yung; *D:* Harry Lachman.

Murder Rap 🦴 **1987** An aspiring musician/sound technologist becomes involved with a mysterious woman and her plot to kill her husband. Complications galore, especially for the viewer. **90m/C VHS, DVD.** John Hawkes, Seita Kathleen Feigny; *D:* Kliff Keuhl.

Murder She Purred: A Mrs. Murphy Mystery 🦴🦴 ½ **1998** Mrs. Murphy is a cat, who along with her doggie housemate Tucker, a Welsh Corgi who complains about his short legs, assists their human owner, postmistress Mary "Harry" Haristeen (Lake), in investigating a murder in their small Virginia town. Based on the mystery series by Rita Mae Brown. **88m/C VHS.** Ricki Lake, Linden Ashby, Bruce McGill, Ed Begley Jr., Christina Pickles, Judith Scott, Wayne Robson, Edie McClurg; *D:* Simon Wincer; *W:* Jim Cox; *V:* Blythe Danner, Anthony Clark. **TV**

Murder She Said 🦴🦴 ½ *Meet Miss Marple* **1962** Dame Margaret, playing the benign Miss M for the first time, witnesses a murder on board a train, but the authorities don't seem inclined to believe her. Posing as a maid at an estate near where she thought the body was dropped, she solves the murder and lands three more Miss Marple movies. Based on Christy's "4:50 From Paddington," it features Marple-to-be Hickson as the cook. **87m/B VHS, DVD.** Margaret Rutherford, Arthur Kennedy, Muriel Pavlow, James Robertson Justice, Thorley Walters, Charles "Bud" Tingwell, Conrad Phillips; *D:* George Pollock.

Murder So Sweet 🦴🦴 ½ *Poisoned by Love: The Kern County Murders* **1993** Hamlin stars as a slick small-town loser, with an apparently limitless appeal to women. He marries five of them but two wives and his mother mysteriously die of poisoning. Then an ex gets suspicious and tries to make certain it'll never happen again. Based on a true story. **94m/C VHS.** Harry Hamlin, Helen Shaver, Faith Ford, Daphne Ashbrook, Eileen Brennan, K.T. Oslin, Terence Knox, Ed Lauter; *D:* Larry Peerce; *W:* Caliope Brattlestreet, Tony Imi, Stephen Glantz; *M:* Steve Dorff. **TV**

Murder Story 🦴🦴 ½ **1989 (PG)** An aspiring mystery writer finds himself mixed up in a real murder and winds up involving his mentor as well. An overdone story, but a reasonably enjoyable film. **90m/C VHS, DVD.** Christopher Lee, Bruce Boa; *D:* Eddie Arno, Markus Innocenti; *W:* Eddie Arno.

Murder: Ultimate Grounds for Divorce 🦴 **1984** A quiet weekend of camping turns into a night of horror for two couples when one of them plans an elaborate murder scheme. **90m/C VHS.** *GB* Roger Daltrey, Toyah Willcox, Leslie Ash, Terry Raven; *D:* Morris Barry; *W:* Tim Purcell; *C:* Charles Tookey; *M:* Harlan Cockburn, Robin Langridge.

Murder with Music 🦴🦴 **1945** A musical drama featuring an all-black cast. **60m/B VHS.** Bob Howard, Noble Sissle, Nellie Hill; *D:* George P. Quigley.

Murder With Pictures 🦴🦴 **1936** Crime boss Nate Girard (Stevens) gets off on a murder rap but his mouthpiece Redfield (Cossart) is murdered soon after. Snappy newspaper photog Murdock (Ayres) is on the story, especially when a mystery dame (Patrick) begs for his help. A photo holds the key to the increasingly convoluted plot. **69m/B DVD.** Lew Ayres, Gail Patrick, Onslow Stevens, Joyce Compton, Benny Baker, Paul Kelly, Ernest Cossart, Joseph (Joe) Sawyer; *D:* Charles T. Barton; *W:* Sidney Salkow, John Moffitt; *C:* Ted Tetzlaff.

Murder Without Conviction 🦴🦴 ½ **2004** When ex-nun Christine Bennett (Ward) visits her cousin in a mental facility, she meets savant James Talley (Proval). He and his twin, Edward, have been separated for 30 years, ever since they were accused, but not convicted, of their mother's murder on Good Friday, 1974, and a judge sent them to separate hospitals. Christine becomes suspicious and teams up with handsome detective Jack Brooks (Weisser) to have the case re-opened. But someone is deadly serious about wanting Christine to mind her own business. **90m/C DVD.** Megan Ward, Morgan Weisser, David Proval, Rutanya Alda, Matt Lutz, Patty Duke; *D:* Kevin Connor; *W:* Bruce Franklin Singer; *C:* Dane Peterson; *M:* Roger Bellon. **CABLE**

Murder Without Motive 🦴🦴 ½ **1992** When two African American teenagers harrass an undercover cop, a struggle ensues and one teen ends up dead. Was the struggle racially motivated, or did the police act justifiably? **93m/C VHS, DVD.** Curtis McClaren, Anna Maria Horsford, Carla Gugino, Christopher Daniel Barnes, Cuba Gooding Jr., Georg Stanford Brown; *D:* Kevin Hooks.

Murderball 🦴🦴🦴🦴 **2005 (R)** Fast-paced yet fluid film catches the warriors of Quad Rugby on and off the court. Quadriplegics candidly answer the questions people are afraid to ask them and boast about sexual escapades. Joe Soares has been a fierce American team leader until being cut from the roster due to his age. His revenge is to coach the Canadian team to their first victory over the U.S. in 12 years. Mark Zupan is the best U.S. player. We also witness breakthroughs for motorcross champ Keith Cavill as he returns home after months of rehabilitation. Attending a quad rugby demonstration, the thought of learning a new sport recharges Cavill. Powerful, must see film. **85m/C DVD.** *US US D:* Henry Alex Rubin, Dana Adam Shapiro; *C:* Henry Alex Rubin; *M:* Jamie Saft.

Murdered Innocence 🦴🦴 **1994 (R)** In 1972, a rookie New York cop is called to a crime scene where a woman has been stabbed to death. Her young son is hysterical and her husband is holding the knife. When the husband panics and tries to flee, the cop shoots him in the back. Now, it's 1992, the convicted killer is out of prison and out for revenge (seems the son said his mother's lover committed the crime but there was a police coverup). **88m/C VHS.** Jason Miller, Ellen Greene, Fred Carpenter; *D:* Frank Coraci; *W:* Frank Coraci, Diego Matamoros.

Murderers Among Us: The Simon Wiesenthal Story 🦴🦴🦴 **1989** Powerful re-enactment of concentration camp survivor Simon Wiesenthal's search for war criminals. Kingsley's gripping performance drives this cable film. Be prepared for disturbing death camp scenes. **157m/C VHS.** Ben Kingsley, Renee Soutendijk, Craig T. Nelson, Paul Freeman, Louisa Haigh, Jack Shepherd; *D:* Brian Gibson; *W:* Abby Mann; *M:* Bill Conti. **CABLE**

The Murderers Are Among Us 🦴🦴 *Die Morder Sind Unter Uns* **1946** In post WWII Germany, Suzanne Wallner (Knef) returns from a concentration camp to her apartment in Berlin only to find it occupied by Dr. Hans Mertens (Borchert). Haunted by his wartime experiences, Mertens has turned to women and alcohol. Suzanne refuses to give up her claim and moves in with Hans, eventually falling in love with him. In turn, Hans decides to face his demons by going after his former superior, Colonel Otto Bruckner (Paulsen), who's living an untroubled life despite the war crimes he committed. German with subtitles. **84m/B VHS, DVD.** *GE* Hildegarde Knef, Ernst Borchert, Arno Paulsen; *D:* Wolfgang Staudte; *W:* Wolfgang Staudte; *C:* Friedl Behn-Grund, Eugen Klagemann; *M:* Ernst Roters.

Murderer's Keep WOOF! *Maxie; The Butchers* **1970** Secret ingredients used in the Central Meat Market's hamburger are discovered by a young, deaf girl. Beware of filler, she learns, particularly if it's someone you know. **89m/C VHS, DVD.** Vic Tayback, Talia Shire, Robert Walden; *D:* Paulmichel Miekhe.

Murderers' Row 🦴 ½ **1966** Daredevil bachelor and former counter-espionage agent Matt Helm is summoned from his life of leisure to ensure the safety of an important scientist. Martin's attempt as a super-spy doesn't wash, and Margret is implausible as the kidnapped scientist's daughter. Unless you want to hear Martin sing "I'm Not the Marrying Kind," don't bother. Second in the "Matt Helm" series. **108m/C VHS, DVD.** Dean Martin, Ann-Margret, Karl Malden, Beverly Adams, James Gregory, Camilla Sparv; *D:* Henry Levin; *W:* Herbert Baker; *C:* Sam Leavitt; *M:* Lalo Schifrin, Lalo Schifrin.

Murderlust WOOF! **1986** Employers in search of a security guard make a poor choice in offering the position to a sexually frustrated man whose hobbies include strangling prostitutes. Poor hiring decisions come into play later when he secures a job at an adolescent crisis center. **90m/C VHS.** Eli Rich, Rochelle Taylor, Dennis Gannon, Bonnie Schneider, Lisa Nichols; *D:* Donald M. Jones.

Murderous Intent 🦴🦴🦴 ½ *Like Minds* **2006** Psychotic thriller set in an all-boys' prep school includes a great mix of twists, flashbacks, investigative details and touches of the occult topped off with a totally unanticipated ending. Alex, (Redmayne) the headmaster's son, gets new student Nigel (Sturridge) as his new roommate despite major objections. The latest arrival is obsessed with history and necrophilia, which leads to a series of ritual-influenced deaths. Although Alex is sickened by what he observes, he's also oddly fascinated. Then Nigel ends up dead. As the forensic psychologist (Collette) interviews Alex she pieces together behavioral clues that lead her on an intuitive case-solving mission. From script to score, acting to set design this Australian/British creation is a fine piece of film art. **110m/C DVD.** *GB AU* Toni Collette, Eddie Redmayne, Thomas Sturridge, Richard Roxburgh, Patrick Malahide, Kate Maberly; *D:* Gregory J. Read; *W:* Gregory J. Read; *C:* Nigel Bluck; *M:* Carlo Giacco.

Murderous Vision 🦴🦴 **1991 (R)** Television fixture Boxleitner is a bored detective in this outing. But one day, while tracking a young mother in the missing persons bureau, he stumbles upon the trail of a serial killer. Enter a beautiful psychic who wants to help, add a race to catch the murderer, and Bruce suddenly has his hands full. **93m/C VHS.** Bruce Boxleitner, Laura Johnson, Robert Culp; *D:* Gary Sherman. **TV**

Murders at Lynch Cross **1985** Mystery about a weird, isolated hotel on the Yorkshire moors. **60m/C VHS.** *GB* Jill Bennett, Joanna David, Barbara Jefford, Sylvia Syms; *D:* Patrick Lau; *W:* Frances Galleymore; *M:* Paul Lewis. **TV**

Murders in the Doll House 🦴 ½ *Midare Karakuri; Crazy Doll Trick* **1979** Private detective must find out who is systematically killing off the family of a Japanese toy executive. With English subtitles. **92m/C VHS.** *JP* Yusaku Matsuda, Shin Kishida, Hirako Shiro; *D:* Susumu Kodama; *W:* Shuichi Nagahara; *C:* Masaharu Ueda; *M:* Yuji Ono.

Murders in the Rue Morgue 🦴🦴 ½ **1932** Lugosi stars as a deranged scientist (what a stretch) who wants to find a female companion for his pet gorilla. He kidnaps a beautiful woman and prepares to make her the gorilla's bride. Very loosely based on the story by Edgar Allan Poe, which has been remade several times. **61m/B VHS, DVD.** Bela Lugosi, Sidney (Sydney) Fox, Leon Ames, Brandon Hurst, Arlene Francis, Noble Johnson; *D:* Robert Florey; *W:* John Huston, Tom Reed, Dale Van Every; *C:* Karl Freund.

Murders in the Rue Morgue 🦴🦴 ½ **1971 (PG)** A young woman has frightening dreams inspired by a play that her father is producing in Paris at the turn of the century. After many people associated with the production become murder victims, the girl becomes involved with one of her father's former associates, a man who killed her mother years ago and then faked his own suicide. The fourth film based on Edgar Allan Poe's classic horror story. **87m/C VHS, DVD.** Jason Robards Jr., Lilli Palmer, Herbert Lom, Michael Dunn, Christine Kaufmann, Adolfo Celi; *D:* Gordon Hessler.

The Murders in the Rue Morgue 🦴🦴🦴 **1986 (PG)** The fifth filmed version of the Edgar Allan Poe story. Set in 19th-century Paris; actors in a mystery play find their roles coming to life. Scott is terrific, with good supporting help. **92m/C VHS, DVD.** George C. Scott, Rebecca De Mornay, Val Kilmer, Ian McShane, Neil Dickson; *D:* Jeannot Szwarc; *C:* Bruno de Keyzer. **TV**

Murders in the Zoo 🦴🦴 ½ **1933** Zoologist Atwill has a reason to be insanely jealous since his wife (Burke) has been having lots of extramarital affairs. But his way of dealing with these other men is certainly unique—he feeds them to various zoo animals (after first sewing the victims' lips shut). Censors were outraged and the film underwent various edits for its theatrical release. **62m/B VHS.** Lionel Atwill, Kathleen Burke, Charlie Ruggles, Randolph Scott, Gail Patrick, John Lodge, Harry Beresford; *D:* Edward Sutherland; *W:* Philip Wylie, Seton I. Miller.

Muriel 🦴🦴🦴 ½ *Muriel, Ou le Temps d'Un Retour; The Time of Return; Muriel, Or the Time of Return* **1963** A complex, mosaic drama about a middle-aged woman who meets an old lover at Boulogne, and her stepson who cannot forget the needless suffering he caused a young woman named Muriel while he was a soldier at war. Throughout, director Alain Resnais plumbs the essential meanings of memory, age, and the anxieties created from the tension between personal and public actions. Acclaimed; in French with subtitles. **115m/C VHS, DVD.** *FR IT* Delphine Seyrig, Jean-Pierre Kerien, Nita Klein, Jean-Baptiste Thierree; ***D:*** Alain Resnais; ***W:*** Jean Cayrol; ***C:*** Sacha Vierny; ***M:*** Georges Delerue. Venice Film Fest. '63: Actress (Seyrig).

Muriel's Wedding **1994 (R)** Muriel (Collette) can catch a bridal bouquet, but can she catch a husband? Her blonde, bitch-goddess friends don't think so. But dowdy, pathetic, overweight Muriel dreams of a fairy tale wedding anyway. How she fulfills her obsessive fantasy is the basis for this quirky, hilarious, and often touchingly poignant ugly duckling tale with the occasional over-the-top satiric moment. Strong cast is led by sympathetic and engaging performances from Collette (who gained 40-plus pounds for the role) and Griffiths as her best friend, Rhonda. '70s pop supergroup ABBA lends its kitschy but catchy tunes to the plot and soundtrack. Not released in the U.S. until 1995. **105m/C VHS, DVD.** *AU* Toni Collette, Bill Hunter, Rachel Griffiths, Jeanie Drynan, Gennie Nevinson Brice, Matt(hew) Day, Daniel Lapaine, Sophie Lee, Rosalind Hammond, Belinda Jarrett; ***D:*** P.J. Hogan; ***W:*** P.J. Hogan; ***C:*** Martin McGrath; ***M:*** Peter Best. Australian Film Inst. '94: Actress (Collette), Film, Sound, Support. Actress (Griffiths).

Murmur of the Heart 1/2 *Dearest Love; La Souffle au Coeur* **1971 (R)** Honest treatment of a 14-year-old's coming of age. After his older brothers take him to a prostitute for his first sexual experience, he comes down with scarlet fever. He then travels to a health spa with his mom to recover. There they find that their mother-son bond is stronger than most. Music by Charlie Parker is featured in the score. In French with English subtitles. **118m/C VHS, DVD.** *FR* Benoit Ferreux, Daniel Gelin, Lea Massari, Corinne Kersten, Jacqueline Chauveau, Marc Wincourt, Michael (Michel) Lonsdale; ***D:*** Louis Malle; ***W:*** Louis Malle; ***C:*** Ricardo Aronovich; ***M:*** Charlie Parker.

Murph the Surf 1/2 *Live a Little, Steal a Lot; You Can't Steal Love* **1975 (PG)** Fact-based, engrossing story of two beach bums turned burglars who grow bored with small-time robbery and plan a trip to New York City to steal the Star of Africa sapphire. Notable among the many action scenes is a boat chase through the inland waterways of Miami, Florida. **102m/C VHS, DVD.** Robert Conrad, Don Stroud, Donna Mills, Luther Adler, Robyn Millan, Paul Stewart; ***D:*** Marvin J. Chomsky.

Murphy's Fault **1988 (PG-13)** Dark comedy about a night watchman/writer plagued by a series of bad luck incidents. **94m/C VHS.** Patrick Dollaghan, Anne Curry, Stack Pierce; ***D:*** Robert J. Smawley.

Murphy's Law **1986 (R)** A hard-headed cop gets framed for his ex-wife's murder and embarks on a mission to find the actual killer. He is slowed down by a smart-mouthed prostitute who is handcuffed to him during his search. Casting a female in the role of a psycho-killer is unique to the genre. **101m/C VHS, DVD.** Charles Bronson, Carrie Snodgress, Kathleen Wilhoite, Robert F. Lyons, Richard Romanus, Angel Tompkins, Bill Henderson, James Luisi, Janet MacLachlan, Lawrence Tierney; ***D:*** J. Lee Thompson; ***C:*** Alex Phillips Jr.; ***M:*** Marc Donahue.

Murphy's Romance **1985 (PG-13)** A young divorced mother with an urge to train horses pulls up the stakes and heads for Arizona with her son. There she meets a pharmacist who may be just what the doctor ordered to help her build a new life. **107m/C VHS, DVD.** James Garner, Sally Field, Brian Kerwin, Corey Haim, Dennis Burkley, Charles Lane, Georgann Johnson; ***D:*** Martin Ritt; ***W:*** Harriet Frank Jr., Irving Ravetch; ***M:*** Carole King.

Murphy's War **1971 (PG)** In WWII, the Germans sink an English ship and gun down most of its crew. An Irishman, however, survives and returns to health with the help of a nurse. He then seeks revenge on those who killed his crewmates, even after he learns the war has ended. O'Toole is interesting as the revenge-minded seaman though saddled with a mediocre script. **106m/C VHS, DVD.** *GB* Peter O'Toole, Sian Phillips, Philippe Noiret; ***D:*** Peter Yates; ***W:*** Stirling Silliphant; ***M:*** John Barry.

Murrow 1/2 **1986** Biography of the renowned chain-smoking journalist who changed broadcasting history by fearlessly voicing his liberal ideas on the air waves. His life was more interesting though Travanti does his best to breathe some life into the script. **114m/C VHS.** Daniel J. Travanti, Dabney Coleman, Edward Herrmann, David Suchet, John McMartin, Robert Vaughn, Kathryn Leigh Scott; ***D:*** Jack Gold; ***W:*** Ernest Kinoy; ***M:*** Carl Davis. **CABLE**

Muscle Beach Party **1964** Sequel to "Beach Party" finds Frankie and Annette romping in the sand again. Trouble invades teen nirvana when a new gym opens and the hardbodies try to muscle in on surfer turf. Meanwhile, Paluzzi tries to muscle in on Funicello's turf. Good clean corny fun, with the usual lack of script and plot. Lorre appeals in a cameo, his final screen appearance. Watch for "Little" Stevie Wonder in his debut. Rickles' first appearance in the "BP" series; Lupus was credited as Rock Stevens. Followed by "Bikini Beach." ♫ Muscle Beach Party; Runnin' Wild; Muscle Bustle; My First Love; Surfin' Woodie; Surfer's Holiday; Happy Street; A Girl Needs a Boy; A Boy Needs a Girl. **94m/C VHS, DVD.** Frankie Avalon, Annette Funicello, Buddy Hackett, Luciana Paluzzi, Don Rickles, John Ashley, Jody McCrea, Morey Amsterdam, Peter Lupus, Candy Johnson, Dolores Wells, Peter Lorre, Stevie Wonder, Donna Loren, Amadee Chabot, Dick Dale; ***D:*** William Asher; ***W:*** William Asher, Robert Dillon; ***C:*** Harold E. Wellman; ***M:*** Les Baxter.

The Muse 1/2 **1999 (PG-13)** Brooks plays Steven, a screenwriter who finds he's unable to get a job when his creative well runs dry. He is introduced by fellow scribe Jack (Bridges) to Sarah (Stone, showing off some surprising comedy chops), who may actually be one of the Greek goddesses of inspiration. Of course, she may be a total lunatic too. After he discovers that some of the biggest names in Hollywood swear by her mojo, Steven is thrilled when he's deemed worthy of her service. Unfortunately for him, Sarah's inspiration requires a fancy hotel room, expensive gifts, and boatloads of cash, which draws the suspicion of his wife Laura (MacDowell). As he begins writing, Steven discovers that Sarah has also inspired his wife to start a career of her own and kick him out of bed. Lots of movie in-jokes and cameos from big shots like Rob Reiner, James Cameron and Martin Scorsese. **97m/C VHS, DVD.** Albert Brooks, Sharon Stone, Jeff Bridges, Andie MacDowell, Steven Wright, Mark Feuerstein, Bradley Whitford, Dakin Matthews, Concetta Tomei, Stacey Travis; ***Cameos:*** James Cameron, Rob Reiner, Martin Scorsese, Jennifer Tilly, Lorenzo Lamas; ***D:*** Albert Brooks; ***W:*** Albert Brooks, Monica Johnson; ***C:*** Thomas Ackerman; ***M:*** Elton John.

Music & Lyrics 1/2 **2007 (PG-13)** The somewhat smarmy, frequently self-deprecating charm of Grant is on full display, opposite Barrymore as his sunny romantic foil. Alex (Grant) is the less-successful half (he wrote the music) of a long-disbanded '80s pop duo. Making a decent living on the nostalgia circuit, Alex gets another chance at a hit when current teen queen Cora (newcomer Bennett) wants her one-time crush to write a duet for them. Alex then stumbles onto insecure, would-be lyricist Sophie (Barrymore) and puts her to work. Grant and Barrymore don't make the most convincing romantic couple (she's too young and ditsy) but it's light-hearted fluff, and the pseudo-80s music videos are hysterical. **106m/C DVD, Blu-ray Disc, HD DVD.** *US* Hugh Grant, Drew Barrymore, Brad Garrett, Kristen Johnston, Aasif Mandvi, Campbell Scott, Haley Bennett; ***D:*** Marc Lawrence; ***W:*** Marc Lawrence; ***C:*** Xavier Perez Grobet; ***M:*** Adam Schlesinger.

Music Box 1/2 **1989 (R)** An attorney defends her father against accusations that he has committed inhumane Nazi war crimes. If she loses, her father faces deportation. As the case progresses, she must struggle to remain objective in the courtroom and come to terms with the possibility that her father is guilty. Lange's portrayal of an ethnic character is highly convincing. **126m/C VHS, DVD.** Jessica Lange, Frederic Forrest, Lukas Haas, Armin Mueller-Stahl, Michael Rooker, Donald Moffat, Cheryl Lynn Bruce; ***D:*** Constantin Costa-Gavras; ***W:*** Joe Eszterhas; ***C:*** Patrick Blossier; ***M:*** Philippe Sarde.

Music from Another Room 1/2 **1997 (PG-13)** Danny (Law) is a hopeless romantic who decided, at five, to marry Anna, whose birth he assisted. But the icy adult Anna (Mol) doesn't seem to be Danny's ideal when he happens to meet her again—and she's got a fiance. **104m/C VHS, DVD.** Jude Law, Gretchen Mol, Brenda Blethyn, Jennifer Tilly, Martha Plimpton, Jon Tenney, Jeremy Piven, Vincent Laresca, Jane Adams, Kevin Kilner, Jan Rubes, Judith Malina, Jon Polito; ***D:*** Charlie Peters; ***W:*** Charlie Peters; ***C:*** Richard Crudo; ***M:*** Richard Gibbs.

Music in My Heart 1/2 **1940** Two taxi cabs crash and spur the love of Martin and Hayworth. She proceeds to break off her engagement to save Martin from deportation. Hayworth's last low-budget film before becoming a Hollywood goddess. **69m/B VHS, DVD.** Rita Hayworth, Tony Martin, Edith Fellows, Alan Mowbray, Eric Blore, George Tobias, Joseph Crehan, George Humbert, Phil Tead; ***D:*** Joseph Santley; ***M:*** Robert Wright, Chet Forrest.

The Music Lovers 1/2 **1971 (R)** Russell's version of Tchaikovsky's tormented life and glorious achievements is a shocker, a movie that infuriates professed music lovers but, nonetheless, has introduced many a neophyte to the world of classical music via its sensationalism. Homosexual Tchaikovsky marries an admirer to appease the Russian government and his financial benefactor. Stunned when he discovers his wife is a nymphomaniac, he banishes her to a netherworld of prostitution and eventual insanity which Russell mercilessly explores. Tchaikovsky's own squalid life is hardly better, though he does enjoy success before the bottom falls out. **122m/C VHS.** *GB* Richard Chamberlain, Glenda Jackson, Max Adrian, Christopher Gable, Kenneth Colley, Izabella Telezynska, Maureen Pryor; ***D:*** Ken Russell; ***W:*** Melvyn Bragg; ***C:*** Douglas Slocombe; ***M:*** Andre Previn.

The Music Man **1962 (G)** Con man in the guise of a traveling salesman gets off the train in River City, Iowa. After hearing about plans to build a pool hall, he argues it would be the gateway to hell for the young, impressionable males of the town. He then convinces the River Cityzens to look toward the future of the community and finance a wholesome children's marching band. Although the huckster plans to take their money and run before the instruments arrive, his feelings for the town librarian cause him to think twice about fleeing the Heartland. This isn't just a slice of Americana; it's a whole pie. Acting and singing are terrific "with a capital 'T' and that rhymes with 'P' and that stands for" Preston, who epitomizes the charismatic pitchman. ♫ Seventy-six Trombones; Trouble; Till There Was You; The Wells Fargo Wagon; Being in Love; Goodnight, My Someone; Rock Island; Iowa Stubborn. **151m/C VHS, DVD.** Robert Preston, Shirley Jones, Buddy Hackett, Hermione Gingold, Paul Ford, Pert Kelton, Ron Howard; ***D:*** Morton DaCosta; ***W:*** Marion Hargrove; ***C:*** Robert Burks; ***M:*** Meredith Willson, Ray Heindorf. Oscars '62: Adapt. Score; Golden Globes '63: Film—Mus./Comedy, Natl. Film Reg. '05.

The Music of Chance 1/2 **1993 (R)** Convoluted story about a smalltime gambler (Spader) and a drifter (Patinkin) who wind up involved in a bizarre high stakes poker game with a Laurel and Hardyish pair (Durning and Grey) who live in an isolated mansion. When Spader and Patinkin lose, their debt forces them into an indentured servitude where they must construct a brick wall around their new masters' estate. Bloated with symbolism, this adaptation from cult fave novelist Auster (who has a small part), loses its eclectic significance in the translation to the big screen. Nonetheless, valiant effort by rookie director Haas. **98m/C VHS, DVD.** James Spader, Mandy Patinkin, Joel Grey, Charles Durning, M. Emmet Walsh, Samantha Mathis, Christopher Penn, Pearl Jones, Paul Auster; ***D:*** Philip Haas; ***W:*** Philip Haas, Belinda Haas; ***C:*** Bernard Zitzermann; ***M:*** Philip Johnston.

Music of the Heart 1/2 *50 Violins* **1999 (PG)** Based on the true story of violin teacher Roberta Guaspari, who was also the subject of the 1996 documentary, "Small Wonders." A divorced Guaspari (Streep) leaves suburbia with her two young sons and a dream to teach music to children, using the 50 violins she had purchased. Roberta finds herself working with a group of Harlem students on what will become the landmark East Harlem Violin Program. Despite numerous obstacles, their determination eventually leads to a performance at Carnegie Hall. Streep gives her usual professionally winning performance in this sentimental heart-tugger. **124m/C VHS, DVD.** Meryl Streep, Angela Bassett, Aidan Quinn, Gloria Estefan, Cloris Leachman, Kieran Culkin, Charlie Hofheimer, Jay O. Sanders, Josh Pais; ***D:*** Wes Craven; ***W:*** Pamela Gray; ***C:*** Peter Deming; ***M:*** Mason Daring.

The Music Teacher 1/2 *Le Maitre de Musique* **1988 (PG)** A Belgian costume drama dealing with a famed singer who retires to devote himself to teaching two students exclusively. In time, he sees his prized pupils lured into an international competition by an old rival of his. Although the singing is sharp, the story is flat. In French with yellow English subtitles. **95m/C VHS, DVD.** *BE* Patrick Bauchau, Sylvie Fennec, Philippe Volter, Jose Van Dam, Johan Leysen, Anne Roussel; ***D:*** Gerard Corbiau.

Music Within 1/2 **2007 (R)** True story plays like an inspirational movie of the week but is not without its appeal. Richard Pimentel (Livingston) has always wanted to be a public speaker; instead he winds up fighting in Vietnam where he loses most of his hearing in a bomb blast. He returns home, goes to college, and makes an unlikely connection with acerbic Art Honeyman (Sheen), who's wheelchair-bound because of cerebral palsy. Both are discriminated against and ostracized because of their disabilities, which leads Richard to his work as a motivational speaker and one of the leading advocates for what will become the Americans With Disabilities Act. **94m/C DVD.** Ron Livingston, Michael Sheen, Melissa George, Yul Vazquez, Rebecca De Mornay, Hector Elizondo; ***D:*** Steven Sawalich; ***W:*** Brett McKinney, Mar Andrew Olsen, Kelly Kennemer; ***C:*** Irek Hartowicz; ***M:*** James T. Sale.

Musica Proibita 1/2 **1943** A serious opera-spiced drama about a young romance crushed by adultery in the teenage couple's ancestry. In Italian with English subtitles. **93m/B VHS.** Tito Gobbi, Maria Mercader; ***D:*** Carlo Campogalliani; ***W:*** Carlo Campogalliani, Carlo Duse; ***C:*** Enzo Serafin; ***M:*** Ettore Campogalliani.

The Musketeer **2001 (PG-13)** Very, very loose adaptation of Dumas's "The Three Musketeers" features fight choreography from Hong Kong stunt master Xin-Xin Xiong. Unfortunately, the direction is murky and the action sequences are too cramped to be effective. In this version of the musketeer-go-round, D'Artagnan (Chambers) is motivated to join the famed battalion to avenge the murder of his parents by the evil Febre (Roth). He is disappointed to find that the musketeers have been decommissioned by the scheming Cardinal Richelieu (Rea), so he forms an alliance with Athos (Gregor), Porthos (Speirs) and Aramis (Moran) to set things aright. Along the way he falls for Francesca (Suvari), a close confidant of the queen (Deneuve). Despite the shortcomings of the fight scenes, the scenic French countryside is filmed beautifully and the actors do their best with the garbled yet overly familiar material. **105m/C VHS, DVD.** *US* Justin Chambers, Mena Suvari, Tim Roth, Catherine Deneuve, Stephen Rea, Daniel Mesguich, David Schofield, Nick Moran, Jeremy Clyde, Michael Byrne, Steve Spiers, Jan Gregor Kremp, Jean-Pierre Castaldi; ***D:*** Peter Hyams; ***W:*** Gene Quintano; ***C:*** Peter Hyams; ***M:*** David Arnold.

Mussolini & I 1/2 *Mussolini: The Decline and Fall of Il Duce* **1985** Docudramatization of the struggle for power between Italy's Benito Mussolini and his son-in-law, Galeazzo Ciano. Narrated by Sarandon in the role of Il Duce's daughter. **130m/C VHS, DVD.** Bob Hoskins, Anthony Hopkins, Susan Sarandon, Annie Girardot, Barbara DeRossi, Fabio Testi, Kurt Raab; *D:* Alberto Negrin. **CABLE**

Must Be Santa 1/2 **1999 (G)** Santa is about to retire (three days before Christmas!) and Tuttle (Coleman), the CEO of the North Pole, is in desperate need of a replacement. And who does he find? Why classic loser Floyd (Pinnock), who decides that having the job will certainly get him his daughter's attention. **92m/C VHS.** *CA* Dabney Coleman, Arnold Pinnock, Deanna Milligan; *D:* Brad Turner; *W:* Douglas Bowie; *C:* Albert J. Dunk; *M:* Jonathan Goldsmith. **VIDEO**

Must Love Dogs **2005 (PG-13)** Recently-divorced Sarah (Lane), a 40ish preschool teacher, is thrown into the online dating world by her family, a large group of cackling Irish Americans. But first Sarah meets Bob (Mulroney), the separated father of one of her students, and later Jake (super-witty Cusack), a romantic who builds wooden boats by hand, and the triangle ensues. Former TV director Goldberg and a star-loaded cast don't quite make a love connection, but a passable date movie is in here somewhere. The title is a good motto to live by, though. **98m/C DVD.** *US* Diane Lane, John Cusack, Dermot Mulroney, Christopher Plummer, Stockard Channing, Elizabeth Perkins, Ben Shenkman, Julie Gonzalo, Brad Hall, Brad William Henke, Ali Hillis, Steve Schirripa, Laura Kightlinger, Jordana Spiro; *D:* Gary David Goldberg; *W:* Gary David Goldberg; *C:* John Bailey; *M:* Craig Armstrong.

Must Read After My Death **2009** Writer/director Dews' discovered more than 200 hours of home movies, 50 hours of Dictaphone and tape recordings, and 300 pages of transcripts after the death of his maternal grandmother Allis in 2001. They reveal a family history of an unhappy 'open' marriage between Allis and alcoholic husband Charley and Allis' dissatisfaction with her lot as a 1950s housewife, which had her turning to therapy for help. It eventually ensnares their four children, who also come under some dubious psychiatric care. Dews' POV is generally limited to that of his grandmother, which protects the identity of his other family members but makes you wonder what they thought of Allis' revelations. **73m/C DVD.** *US* *D:* Morgan Dewes, Peter Dews; *W:* Morgan Dewes, Peter Dews; *M:* Paul Hogan.

Mutant 1/2 *Night Shadows* **1983 (R)** Another argument for the proper disposal of toxic waste. Hazardous materials transform the people of a southern town into monsters. **100m/C VHS, DVD.** Wings Hauser, Bo Hopkins, Jennifer Warren, Lee Montgomery; *D:* John Cardos; *W:* Michael Jones; *C:* Alfred Taylor; *M:* Richard Band.

Mutant Chronicles 1/2 **2008 (R)** In the year 2707 Earth's resources are dwindling with four giant corporations picking over the pieces. Amidst the combat an ancient seal is shattered, releasing a mutant army that carries a plague that threatens humanity with extinction. But a religious order keeps a chronicle that tells how to defeat the threat. You'll root for the mutants because the humans tend to be boring and/or dumb. **100m/C DVD.** Thomas Jane, Ron Perlman, Devon Aoki, Sean Pertwee, Benno Furmann, John Malkovich; *D:* Simon Hunter; *W:* Philip Eisner; *C:* Geoff Boyle; *M:* Richard Wells.

Mutant Hunt WOOF! *Matt Riker* **1987** Story of a battle between robots gone haywire and an all-American hero. The detective cyborgs are set free while high on a sexual stimulant called Euphoron to wreak their technological havoc on a rampage in Manhattan. **90m/C VHS.** Rick Gianasi, Mary-Anne Fahey; *D:* Tim Kincaid; *W:* Tim Kincaid. **VIDEO**

Mutant on the Bounty 1/2 **1989** A musician, lost in space as a beam of light for 23 years, is transported aboard a spaceship. Once he materializes, it becomes apparent that he has undergone some incredible physical changes. As if that's not enough, the crew then must flee from a couple of thugs who are trying to steal a vial of serum they have on board. A space spoof that never gets into orbit. **93m/C VHS.** John Roarke, Deborah Benson, John Furey, Victoria Catlin, John Fleck, Kyle T. Heffner; *D:* Robert Torrance.

Mutant Species *Bio-Force I* **1995 (R)** Soldier is accidentally exposed to altered DNA and begins to mutate into a remorseless and terrifying killer. **100m/C VHS.** Leo Rossi, Ted Prior, Grant Gelt, Denise Crosby, Powers Boothe, Wilford Brimley; *D:* David A. Prior; *W:* David A. Prior, William Vigil; *C:* Carlos Gonzalez.

Mutants WOOF! 2008 (R) If a flick is going to be called "Mutants" then it should show lots of mutants and this lame talky tale apparently couldn't stretch its low-budget that far. A corporate conspiracy adds chemical enhancements to common sugar to make it more addictive but instead turns consumers into zombies. **84m/C DVD.** Michael Ironside, Steven Bauer, Louis Herthum, Tony Senzamici; *D:* Amir Valinia; *W:* Jodie Jones; *C:* Barry Strickland; *M:* Sammy Huen. **VIDEO**

Mutants In Paradise WOOF! 1984 Comedy about a human guinea-pig who always gets involved in some sort of mishap. **78m/C VHS.** Brad Greenquist, Robert Ingham, Anna Nicholas; *D:* Scott Apostolou; *W:* Scott Apostolou.

Mutator *Time of the Beast* **1990 (R)** A corporation makes a tiny genetic mistake and winds up creating a new life form...a demonic pussycat who preys on humans. **91m/C VHS.** Brion James, Carolyn Ann Clark, Milton Raphiel Murrill; *D:* John R. Bowey; *W:* Lynn Rose Higgins.

Mute Witness 1/2 **1995 (R)** Low-budget British thriller, lensed in Moscow film studio, about U.S. filmers making a cheap thriller in Moscow film studio. Billy (Sudina) is the mute make-up artist of the title who, returning to the studio for a forgotten item, witnesses some of the crew shooting a snuff film with a real-life stabbing. First-timer Waller mocks both thriller genre and film biz, sometimes relying on, rather than spoofing, cliched elements. Highlight is 20-minute long chase scene with the killers pursuing Billy in the cavernous studio. Guinness makes a surprise appearance in a cameo. **100m/C VHS, DVD.** *GB* Marina Sudina, Fay Ripley, Evan Richards, Oleg (Yankovsky) Jankowsky, Igor Volkow, Sergei Karlenkov; ***Cameos:*** Alec Guinness; *D:* Anthony Waller; *W:* Anthony Waller; *C:* Egon Werdin; *M:* Wilbert Hirsch.

The Muthers **1976 (R)** Women prisoners escape from their confinement in a South American jungle. **101m/C VHS, DVD.** Jeannie Bell, Rosanne Katon, Jayne Kennedy, Trina Parks; *D:* Cirio H. Santiago.

The Mutilator WOOF! *Fall Break* **1985 (R)** After accidentally bumping off his mother, a young man stalks five high school students wanting to cut them up into tiny bits. An unedited version is also available. Bloody boredom. **85m/C VHS.** Jack Chatham, Trace Cooper, Frances Raines, Bill Hitchcock; *D:* Buddy Cooper.

Mutiny **1952** In the War of 1812, the crew of an American ship carrying $10 million in gold fight among themselves for a part of France's donation to the war effort. The beautiful photography doesn't make up for the predictability of the storyline. **76m/C VHS, DVD.** Mark Stevens, Gene Evans, Angela Lansbury, Patric Knowles; *D:* Edward Dmytryk; *W:* Philip Yordan.

Mutiny 1/2 **1999 (PG-13)** On July 17, 1944, a Victory ship anchored near San Francisco exploded, killing 323 sailors and injuring 390 (most of them black) in the worst homefront disaster of WWII. Three weeks later, 50 of the primarily untrained munition loaders who refused to continue working without safety equipment and proper training were charged with mutiny by the Navy. The men were defended by a young Thurgood Marshall (Morton) in a controversial case. **90m/C VHS.** Michael Jai White, Duane Martin, Joe Morton, Matthew Glave, Adrian Pasdar, James B. Sikking, Troy Winbush, David Ramsey; *D:* Kevin Hooks; *W:* James Henerson; *C:* Ron Garcia; *M:* Lee Holdridge. **TV**

Mutiny in the Big House 1/2 **1939** A man is sent to prison for writing a bad $10 check and must choose between seeking salvation with the prison chaplain or toughing it out with a hardened convict. Surprisingly good low-budget programmer. **83m/B VHS.** Charles Bickford, Barton MacLane, Pat Moriarity, Dennis Moore, William Royle, Charles Foy, George Cleveland; *D:* William Nigh.

The Mutiny of the Elsinore **1939** A writer on board an old sailing ship fights mutineers and wins back both the helm and the captain's daughter. Tedious British flotsam that made hash of an oft-filmed Jack London tale, and made news even in 1939 for its use of modern-day slang and clothing in the period setting. **74m/B VHS.** Paul Lukas, Lyn Harding, Kathleen Kelly, Clifford Evans, Ben Soutten, Jiro Soneya; *D:* Roy Lockwood.

Mutiny on the Blackhawk 1/2 **1939** A swashbuckling western that deals with slave-running between Hawaii and California in 1840, including a shipboard mutiny. To top it off, there's a battle between the Mexican army and small town California settlers that has the cavalry coming to the rescue! **66m/B VHS.** Richard Arlen, Andy Devine, Constance Moore, Guinn "Big Boy" Williams, Thurston Hall, Paul Fix, Richard Lane, Sandra Kane; *D:* Christy Cabanne; *W:* Michael L. Simmons; *C:* John Boyle.

Mutiny on the Bounty **1935** Compelling adaptation of the true story of sadistic Captain Bligh, Fletcher Christian and their turbulent journey aboard the HMS Bounty and the subsequent mutiny in 1788. No gray here: Laughton's Bligh is truly a despicable character and extremely memorable in this MGM extravaganza. Remade twice, in 1962 and again in 1984 as "The Bounty." Much, much better than the 1962 remake. **132m/B VHS, DVD.** Clark Gable, Franchot Tone, Charles Laughton, Donald Crisp, Dudley Digges, Spring Byington, Henry Stephenson, Eddie Quillan, Herbert Mundin, Movita, Ian Wolfe; *D:* Frank Lloyd; *W:* Talbot Jennings, Jules Furthman, Carey Wilson; *M:* Herbert Stothart. Oscars '35: Picture; AFI '98: Top 100; N.Y. Film Critics '35: Actor (Laughton).

Mutiny on the Bounty 1/2 **1962** Based on the novel by Charles Nordhoff and James Norman Hall, this account of the 1789 mutiny led by Fletcher Christian against Captain Bligh of the Bounty is highlighted by lavish photography and an eccentric, though interesting, portrayal of the mutiny leader by Brando. Though overshadowed by Laughton's compelling performance in the original 1935 masterpiece, Howard's Bligh is shipshape as the cold-hearted, single-minded captain determined to reach Tahati and return with a hold full of breadfruit trees. Brando is all knickers and attitude as the peeved Mr. Christian, who finally can take no more of Bligh's social criticism. The other actors, especially Harris, join in the slightly over the top spirit of things. **177m/C VHS, DVD, HD DVD.** Marlon Brando, Trevor Howard, Richard Harris, Hugh Griffith, Richard Haydn, Percy Herbert, Noel Purcell; *D:* Lewis Milestone; *W:* Charles Lederer; *C:* Robert L. Surtees.

Mutual Needs **1997 (R)** Man hires an escort to pose as his wife at a high school reunion. **90m/C VHS.** Richard Grieco, Charlotte Lewis, Christopher Atkins, Robert Davi, Dee Wallace, Rochelle Swanson; *D:* Robert Angelo; *W:* Dode Levenson, George Ayvas; *C:* Carl Oakwood; *M:* Bill Rogers. **VIDEO**

Mutual Respect 1/2 *Shimmering Light* **1977 (PG)** A dying wealthy man sets out to find the son he never knew. **88m/C VHS.** Lloyd Bridges, Beau Bridges; *D:* Don Chaffey.

MVP (Most Valuable Primate) 1/2 **2000 (PG)** Predictable and lackluster tale about a hockey-playing chimp and the team of lovable losers that he helps to the inevitable "big game." Jack is a chimp with very human characteristics thanks to training from animal behavior professor Dr. Kendall (Study). After Dr. Kendall dies, Jack mistakenly ends up in Nelson, British Columbia. He then makes contact with Tara (Smith), a deaf girl who is picked on by her classmates, and her older brother Steven, a hockey player on the worst team in the league. They discover that Jack has natural hockey skills, and recruit him for Steven's team. Unfortunately, the slimy Dr. Peabody (Muirhead) is searching for Jack due to his value as a lab animal, setting up a showdown between the kids and the evil grown-up. Hockey footage of the chimp was actually shot using three honest-to-God skating chimps named Mac, Bernie, and Louie. **91m/C VHS, DVD.** Kevin Zegers, Ric(k) Ducommun, Oliver Muirhead, Jamie Renee Smith, Lomax Study; *D:* Robert Vince; *W:* Robert Vince, Anne Vince; *C:* Glen Winter; *M:* Brahm Wenger.

MVP2: Most Vertical Primate 1/2 **2001** Takes up where those "Air Bud" movies left off. In this equally dumb sequel, Jack the chimp is thrown out of the ZHL hockey league and goes on the lam from authorities. He meets homeless boy Ben (Goodman), who introduces the hairy one to amateur skateboarding. Of course, the chimp is a natural and many monkeyshines ensue. **97m/C VHS, DVD.** Richard Karn, Cameron Bancroft, Scott Goodman, Bob Burnquist; *D:* Robert Vince; *W:* Robert Vince, Anne Vince, Elan Mastai. **VIDEO**

MXP: Most Xtreme Primate *MVP 3* **2003 (G)** Jack the chimp is at it again. This time he finds himself in Colorado, befriending lonely kid Pete, who's having trouble adjusting to a new town. Of course, Pete is an avid snowboarder, and teaches Jack some moves (Why wouldn't you?). They team up for a tournament while trying to avoid kidnappers. Third in the series again proves the comedy axiom "Monkeys are funny." Plot isn't great, but Jack's monkeyshines will keep the whole family amused anyway. **71m/C VHS, DVD.** *CA* Robby Benson, Devin Douglas Drewitz, Gwynyth Walsh, Trevor Wright, Nicole McKay, Ian Bagg; *D:* Robert Vince; *W:* Robert Vince, Anne Vince, Anna McRoberts; *C:* Mike Southon; *M:* Brahm Wenger. **VIDEO**

My African Adventure WOOF! 1987 Silly tale of an ambassador's son discovering a talking monkey in Africa and meeting a slew of opportunistic misfits in his travels. A comedy unfortunately short on laughs. Based on Tamar Burnstein's book. **93m/C VHS.** Dom DeLuise, Jimmie Walker; *D:* Sam Firstenberg.

My American Cousin **1985 (PG)** Award-winning autobiographical Canadian coming-of-age comedy set in 1959 on a British Columbia farm. 12-year-old Sandy (Langrick) exasperates her parents and has just discovered the appeal of boys when her rebellious, fun-loving, runaway 17-year-old American cousin Butch (Wildman) shows up (in a red Cadillac convertible) over summer vacation. Followed by "American Boyfriends" (1989) **94m/C VHS.** *CA* Margaret Langrick, John Wildman, Richard Donat, Jane Mortifee; *D:* Sandy Wilson; *W:* Sandy Wilson. Genie '86: Actor (Wildman), Actress (Langrick), Director (Wilson), Film.

My Antonia 1/2 **1994 (PG)** Orphaned teenaged farm boy Jim Burden (Harris) discovers first romance with poor immigrant girl Antonia (Lowensohn) in 1886 Nebraska. They fall in love, separate, but maintain a 30-year friendship. Based on the book by Willa Cather. **92m/C VHS.** Neil Patrick Harris, Jason Robards Jr., Eva Marie Saint, Elina Lowensohn, Norbert Weisser, Travis Fine, Jan Triska, Anne Tremko, Mira Furlan, Boris Krutonog; *D:* Joseph Sargent; *C:* Robert Primes.

My Apprenticeship **1939** The second film of Donskoi's trilogy on Maxim Gorky has the writer earning his living, at the age of eight, as an apprentice to a bourgeois family. Although they promise him an education, Gorky is forced to learn to read on his own and eventually sets off on a series of land and sea voyages. He recognizes that the poverty and abuse he has suffered is typical of the lives of most Russians and he encounters the beginnings of revolution. In Russian with English subtitles. Preceded by "My Childhood" and followed by "My Universities." **100m/C VHS.** *RU* Varvara O. Massalitinova, Aleksei Lyarsky, Irina Zarubina, Ivan Kudryavtsev; *D:* Mark Donskoi; *W:* Mark Donskoi; *C:* Pyotr Yermolov; *M:* Lev Shvarts.

My Architect: A Son's Journey 1/2 **2003** Slow but moving documentary about the life of famed architect Louis Kahn, written and directed by his son, Nathaniel. The movie begins with Kahn's death in 1974, when Nathaniel discovers in the obituary that his father had children by two other women. From there, he tries to uncover the mystery of Kahn's secretive life while highlighting his public achievements. What results is a film as much about a son trying to find his place in his father's life as Kahn's life itself. A depressing, poignant film only occasionally marred by Nathaniel's focus on his personal relationship, he still creates a bittersweet but empathetic portrait of his complex father. **116m/C VHS, DVD.** ***D:*** Nathaniel Kahn; ***W:*** Nathaniel Kahn; ***C:*** Robert Richman; ***M:*** Joseph Vitarelli; ***Nar:*** Nathaniel Kahn.

My Baby's Daddy 2004 **(PG-13)** Three irresponsible doofuses end up fathers in this hip-hop rehash of an old formula. Lonnie (Griffin) and his buddies G (Anderson) and Dominic (Imperioli) struggle with how new fatherhood will affect their lives as South Philly small-time players with big dreams. Sweet attitude, but the laughs are intermittent in this bland, dumb story that's basically "Three Playaz and Some Shorties." **86m/C VHS, DVD.** *US* Eddie Griffin, Anthony Anderson, Michael Imperioli, John Amos, Method Man, Bai Ling, Marsha Thomason, Paula Jai Parker, Amy Sedaris, Tommy (Tiny) Lister, Denis Akayama, Scott Thompson, Joanna Bacalso, Dee Freeman; ***D:*** Cheryl Dunye; ***W:*** Eddie Griffin, Brent Goldberg, David T. Wagner, Damon "Coke" Daniels; ***C:*** Glen MacPherson; ***M:*** Richard Gibbs.

My Beautiful Laundrette 1985 **(R)** Omar (Warnecke), the nephew of a Pakistani businessman, is given the opportunity to better himself by turning his uncle's rundown laundry into a profitable business. He reunites with Johnny (Day Lewis), a childhood friend and a working-class street punk, and they go into the business together. They find themselves battling the prejudice of each other's families and friends in order to succeed. An intelligent look at the sexuality, race relations and economic problems of Thatcher's London. Great performances by a relatively unknown cast (for contrast, note Day Lewis' performance in "Room with a View," released in the same year.) **93m/C VHS, DVD.** Gordon Warnecke, Daniel Day-Lewis, Saeed Jaffrey, Roshan Seth, Shirley Anne Field, Derrick Branche, Rita Wolf, Souad Faress, Richard Graham, Dudley Thomas, Garry Cooper, Charu Bala Choksi, Neil Cunningham, Walter Donohue, Stephen Marcus, Badi Uzzaman; ***D:*** Stephen Frears; ***W:*** Hanif Kureishi; ***C:*** Oliver Stapleton; ***M:*** Ludus Tonalis, Stanley Myers. Natl. Bd. of Review '86: Support. Actor (Day-Lewis); N.Y. Film Critics '86: Screenplay, Support. Actor (Day-Lewis); Natl. Soc. Film Critics '86: Screenplay.

My Best Friend 1/2 *Mon Meilleur Ami* **2006 (PG-13)** Arrogant loner art dealer Francois (Auteuil) bets his business partner (Gayet) that he has a friend, and he is willing to do anything to win. He recruits taxi driver Bruno (Boon) to help him find a friend, only to discover that friendship isn't as easy to pin down (or buy) as he thought. Director Leconte thoughtfully takes the buddy comedy premise and turns it into an examination of friendship and loneliness in a world of consumerism. **94m/C DVD.** *FR* Daniel Auteuil, Dany Boon, Julie Gayet, Julie Durand; ***D:*** Patrice Leconte; ***W:*** Patrice Leconte, Jerome Tonnerre; ***C:*** Jean-Marie Dreujou; ***M:*** Xavier Demerliac.

My Best Friend Is a Vampire **1988 (PG)** Another teenage vampire story, about trying to cope with certain changes that adolescence and bloodsucking bring. Good supporting cast. **90m/C VHS.** Robert Sean Leonard, Evan Mirand, Cheryl Pollak, Rene Auberjonois, Cecilia Peck, Fannie Flagg, Kenneth Kimmins, David Warner, Paul Willson, Kathy Bates; ***D:*** Jimmy Huston; ***W:*** Tab Murphy; ***C:*** James Bartle; ***M:*** Steve Dorff.

My Best Friend's Girl 1/2 *La Femme De Mon Pote* **1984** Coy, sardonic French romance about a woman who slaloms between two buddies working at a ski resort. Despite fine performances from all, it never quite makes it to the top of the hill. In French with English subtitles. **99m/C VHS.** *FR* Isabelle Huppert, Thierry Lhermitte, Coluche, Francois Perrot; ***D:*** Bertrand Blier; ***W:*** Bertrand Blier, Gerard Brach.

My Best Friend's Girl 2008 **(R)** Supposed romcom that's misogynistic, not romantic, and plays like a practical joke, not a comedy. Tank (Cook) is a professional "rebound guy" hired by ex-boyfriends to date their ex-girlfriends, show them an evening of such disgust that they go running back to the arms of their former lover. Right. Things get ugly when Tank's roommate Dustin (Biggs) hires him to work his magic on Alexis (Hudson), Dustin's beautiful co-worker who "just wants to be friends." Somehow Tank's sleazy tactics do not repulse her and the two hit it off. Cook has never been more annoying. A mean-spirited script filled with unlikable characters sets off a chain reaction of poor judgments by director Deutch. **101m/C DVD, Blu-ray Disc.** *US* Kate Hudson, Dane Cook, Jason Biggs, Lizzy Caplan, Alec Baldwin, Nate Torrence, Diora Baird, Jenny Mollen, Riki Lindhome, Taram Killam, Kate Albrecht, Amanda Brooks, Mini Anden, Faye Grant; ***D:*** Howard Deutch; ***W:*** Jordan Cahan; ***C:*** Jack N. Green; ***M:*** John Debney.

My Best Friend's Wedding 1/2 **1997 (PG-13)** Yes, it's a romantic comedy, but like director Hogan's previous effort, "Muriel's Wedding," there's some snap among the smiles. Restaurant critic Julianne (Roberts) and sports writer Michael (Mulroney) are best friends who have a pact that they'll marry each other if neither has found someone else by the age of 28. Michael finds sweet, wealthy Kimmy (Diaz) and invites Julianne to his nuptials. Naturally, Julianne realizes she's in love with Michael and she'll stop at nothing to break up the wedding, even enlisting gay friend George (Everett) to pose as her new beau. Roberts appears as the critics prefer her (long hair and smiling) while she extends her range of physical comedy. Diaz gets to be nice, Everett gets to steal every scene he's in, and Mulroney gets to be the lucky object of two lovely women's affections. Shot on location in Chicago. **105m/C VHS, DVD.** Julia Roberts, Dermot Mulroney, Cameron Diaz, Rupert Everett, Philip Bosco, M. Emmet Walsh, Rachel Griffiths, Susan Sullivan, Paul Giamatti; ***D:*** P.J. Hogan; ***W:*** Ronald Bass; ***C:*** Laszlo Kovacs; ***M:*** James Newton Howard.

My Best Girl 1927 Plucky Maggie (Pickford) is a store clerk who is the main support for her eccentric family. She falls in love with the store owner's son (future hubby Rogers) but his father is skeptical of the match. A gentle satire on middle-American life in the 1920s. **88m/B VHS, DVD.** Mary Pickford, Charles "Buddy" Rogers, Lucien Littlefield, Carmelita Geraghty, Sunshine Hart, Hobart Bosworth; ***D:*** Sam Taylor; ***W:*** Hope Loring, Tim Whelan, Allen McNeil; ***C:*** Charles Rosher, David Keeson.

My Big Fat Greek Wedding 1/2 **2002 (PG)** This is a big fat wet smooch of a movie—the kind you get from an enthusiastic older relative at a spare-no-expense wedding. Toula (Vardalos) is a frumpy 30-year-old waitress at her Greek parents' Chicago restaurant. They expect her to marry a Greek boy, have babies, and feed everyone. Then she meets handsome Ian Miller (Corbett), a non-Greek vegetarian schoolteacher who really, really likes her. Enough to want to marry her—if Toula's family can ever recover from the shock of her marrying outside their heritage. Every cliche imaginable is trotted out and you won't care as you'll laugh and groan at the too-recognizable family behavior (no matter what your ethnicity). Based on Vardalos' stage monologue. **95m/C VHS, DVD.** *US* Nia Vardalos, John Corbett, Lainie Kazan, Michael Constantine, Gia Carides, Louis Mandylor, Andrea Martin, Joey Fatone, Bruce Gray, Fiona Reid, Bess Meisler, Ian Gomez; ***D:*** Joel Zwick; ***W:*** Nia Vardalos; ***C:*** Jeffrey Jur; ***M:*** Chris Wilson, Alexander Janko. Ind. Spirit '03: Debut Perf. (Vardalos).

My Blood Runs Cold 1965 Your blood will be frozen stiff from boredom by the blonde blandness of the leads. Julie (Heatherton) gives motorcyclist Ben Gunther (Donahue) a lift but is puzzled when he insists on calling her 'Barbara.' Julie's Aunt Sarah (Nolan) says an ancestral Barbara had an affair with a Ben Gunther. Ben insists that he and Julie are reincarnations of the past lovers and Julie decides to elope with him. Ben is a psycho and Julie doesn't have two working brain cells. **103m/B DVD.** Troy Donahue, Joey Heatherton, Barry Sullivan, Nicolas Coster, Jeannette Nolan, Russ Thorson; ***D:*** William Conrad; ***W:*** John Mantley; ***C:*** Sam Leavitt; ***M:*** George Duning.

My Bloody Roommates *Roommates: 4 Horror Tales; D-Day-Eonneunal kabjagi cheotbeonjjae iyagi; Destination Hell* **2006** Ghost stories set in exclusive girls schools are a common (some would say cliche) part of Korean horror cinema, and this third of the "4 Horror Tales" films ventures there once again. The horrific pressure of prep schools designed to get students into the best college possible are common tropes in Asian films, and this one is no different. The students must endure fear and punishment at the hands of the bullying staff while ominous signs that the school is haunted appear. **94m/C DVD.** *KN* Eun-Seong, Jin-yong Heo, Joo-ryeong Kim, Ri-na Kim, Yeong-jin Sin, Joo-hee Yoo; ***D:*** Eun-kyung Kim; ***W:*** Il-han Yoo; ***C:*** Hoon-Gwang Kim; ***M:*** Bong-jun Oh.

My Bloody Valentine 1981 **(R)** Psychotic coal miner visits the peaceful little town of Valentine Bluffs on the night of the yearly Valentine Ball. Many of the townspeople have their hearts removed with a pick axe and sent to the sheriff in candy boxes. The bloodiest scenes were cut out to avoid an X-rating. **91m/C VHS, DVD.** *CA* Paul Kelman, Lori Hallier, Neil Affleck, Keith Knight, Alf Humphreys, Cynthia Dale, Terry Waterland, Peter Cowper, Don Francks, Jack Van Evera; ***D:*** George Mihalka; ***W:*** John Beaird; ***C:*** Rodney Gibbons.

My Bloody Valentine 3D 2009 **(R)** Tom returns to his hometown of Harmony on the 10th anniversary of the Valentine's Day slaughter of 22 people, for which he feels responsible despite the actual killer's death. Hoping to make amends, Tom instead becomes the prime suspect when the killing starts again. An unnecessary remake of an original that isn't very old and wasn't very good in 1981, this version follows the same old horny-teens-systematically-slaughtered-mid-coitus-formula, complete with gratuitous nudity, sex and violence. The halfway decent use of the latest 3-D technology is the only thing that makes this stinker worth mention, but how many flying eyeballs and projectile streams of blood can one endure? **101m/C DVD.** *US* Jensen Ackles, Jaime (James) King, Kerr Smith, Edi Gathegi, Kevin Tighe, Rich Walters, Betsy Rue, Tom Atkins, Megan Boone, Karen Baum; ***D:*** Patrick Lussier; ***W:*** Todd Farmer, Zane Smith; ***C:*** Brian Pearson; ***M:*** Michael Wandmacher.

My Blue Heaven 1/2 **1950** Sentimental musical comedy-drama has successful husband and wife showbiz team Grable and Dailey try to start a family. When pregnant Molly (Grable) loses her baby in a car accident, she and husband/partner Jack (Dailey) decide to adopt, as they also try to make the transition from a popular radio show to TV. Some dialogue considered risque at the time of release wouldn't raise an eyebrow today. **96m/C DVD.** Betty Grable, Dan Dailey, David Wayne, Jane Wyatt, Mitzi Gaynor, Una Merkel, Dan Hicks, Louise Beavers, Mae Marsh, Elinor Donahue; ***D:*** Henry Koster; ***W:*** Claude Binyon, Lamar Trotti; ***C:*** Arthur E. Arling.

My Blue Heaven 1990 **(PG-13)** After agreeing to rat on the Mafia, Martin is dropped into suburbia as part of the witness protection program. Moranis plays the FBI agent assigned to help the former mobster become an upstanding citizen. Adjusting to life in the slow lane isn't easy for an ex con who has grown accustomed to the big time. Not the typical role for Martin, who plays a brunette with a New York accent and is handcuffed by bad writing. **96m/C VHS, DVD.** Steve Martin, Rick Moranis, Joan Cusack, Melanie Mayron, Carol Kane, Bill Irwin, William Hickey, Daniel Stern; ***D:*** Herbert Ross; ***W:*** Nora Ephron; ***C:*** John Bailey; ***M:*** Ira Newborn.

My Blueberry Nights 2007 **(PG-13)** Director Wong Kar Wai's first English-language feature sets up as a bit of a road movie. New Yorker Elizabeth (crooner Jones), in the wake of an ugly breakup, happens into a Manhattan cafe where she orders a piece of blueberry pie and meets waiter/cook Jeremy (Law). Elizabeth is headed out of town to get over her painful split but promises to stay in touch with her new pal. While on the road, she works various jobs and encounters other wandering souls, including an alcoholic cop (Strathairn) and his gorgeous ex-wife (Weisz) in Memphis, and a hard-luck card shark (Portman) in Las Vegas who cons her out of her savings. Finally she heads back to New York, perhaps hungry for another slice of blueberry pie. Don't look for any real plot here—Wong has just artfully strung together a series of vignettes, which works if that's your thing. **90m/C DVD.** *FR HK* Jude Law, David Strathairn, Rachel Weisz, Natalie Portman, Norah Jones, Chan Marshall; ***D:*** Wong Kar-Wai; ***W:*** Larry Block, Wong Kar-Wai; ***C:*** Darius Khondji; ***M:*** Ry Cooder.

My Bodyguard 1980 **(PG)** An undersized high school student fends off attacking bullies by hiring a king-sized, withdrawn lad as his bodyguard. Their "business" relationship, however, develops into true friendship. An adolescent coming of age with more intelligence and sensitivity than most of its ilk, and a pack of up and coming stars as well as old stand-bys Houseman and Gordon. **96m/C VHS, DVD.** Chris Makepeace, Adam Baldwin, Martin Mull, Ruth Gordon, Matt Dillon, John Houseman, Joan Cusack, Craig Richard Nelson, Tim Kazurinsky, George Wendt, Jennifer Beals; ***D:*** Tony Bill; ***W:*** Alan Ormsby; ***C:*** Michael D. Margulies; ***M:*** Dave Grusin.

My Boss's Daughter 2003 **(PG-13)** Spoof-meister Zucker should have let this one stay on the shelf where someone had wisely left it. Instead, Kutcher and Reid are at the center of a gaggle of tasteless and largely unfunny mishaps and gags. Tom (Kutcher) is a clueless schlub who works for Jack (Stamp), a tough-as-nails publishing exec. Wanting to further his career and get in good with Jack's party-hearty but pretty daughter Lisa (Reid), Tom takes a job house-sitting for his cantankerous, and very particular, boss. You can just smell the comic possibilities. Unfortunately, that's not the odor emanating here, despite a solid supporting cast, which includes a typically pneumatic appearance from Dimension Films icon Electra. The whirlwind of destructive disaster, and Kutcher's deer-in-the-headlights routine runs as thin as Electra's t-shirts. **84m/C VHS, DVD.** *US* Ashton Kutcher, Tara Reid, Terence Stamp, Jeffrey Tambor, Andy Richter, Michael Madsen, Jon Abrahams, David Koechner, Carmen Electra, Molly Shannon, Kenan Thompson; ***D:*** David Zucker; ***W:*** David Dorfman; ***C:*** Martin McGrath; ***M:*** Teddy Castellucci.

My Boy 1/2 **1921** Coogan stars as a foreign orphan who faces deportation. Instead he escapes and follows an old man home. This rare film includes an organ score. **56m/B VHS.** Jackie Coogan, Claude Gillingwater, Mathilde Brundage; ***D:*** Albert Austin; ***W:*** Victor Heerman.

My Boy Jack 1/2 **2007** British author Rudyard Kipling (Haig, who also wrote the 1997 play the TV movie is based on) pulls strings that allow his only son, teenager Jack (Radcliffe), to enlist in the army in WWI in spite of the boy's bad eyesight. This is done over the objections of his American wife Caroline (Cattrall). When Jack is reported missing in 1915 in his first battle, the patriotic Kipling is overwhelmed by guilt and grief and spends years searching for answers before Jack's death is confirmed. **120m/C DVD.** *GB* David Haig, Daniel Radcliffe, Kim Cattrall, Carey Mulligan, Julian Wadham, Martin McCann, Richard Dormer; ***D:*** Brian Kirk; ***W:*** David Haig; ***C:*** David Odd; ***M:*** Adrian Johnston. **TV**

My Boyfriend's Back *Johnny Zombie* **1993 (PG-13)** Embarassingly dumb flick about a teenage boy who wants to take the prettiest girl in the school to the prom. The only problem is that he's become a zombie. Bits of him keep falling off (his girl thoughtfully glues them back on) and if he wants to stay "alive" long enough to get to the dance he has to munch on human flesh. Yuck. **85m/C VHS, DVD.** Andrew Lowery, Traci Lind, Edward Herrmann, Mary Beth Hurt, Danny Zorn, Austin Pendleton, Jay O. Sanders, Paul Dooley, Bob (Robert) Dishy, Cloris Leachman, Matthew Fox, Paxton Whitehead; ***D:*** Bob Balaban; ***W:*** Dean Lorey; ***C:*** Mac Ahlberg.

My Boys Are Good Boys 1978 **(PG)** A young foursome steal from an armored car and have to face the consequences. Quirky with an implausible storyline. **90m/C VHS, DVD.** Ralph Meeker, Ida Lupino, Lloyd Nolan, David Doyle; ***D:*** Bethel Buckalew.

My Brilliant Career 1/2 **1979 (G)** Sybella (Davis) is a poor, headstrong young woman spurns the social expectations of turn-of-the-century Australia and pursues opportunities to broaden her intellect and preserve her independence. This despite the fact that she loves Harry (Neill), a handsome, wealthy farmer. Davis is wonderful as the energetic and charismatic community trendsetter, especially in the scenes transforming her from a tomboy to a "lady." Has an excellent supporting cast. Based on an autobiographical novel by Miles Franklin which has been marvelously transferred to the screen. Armstrong deserves credit for her fine direction. **101m/C VHS, DVD.** *AU* Judy Davis, Sam Neill, Wendy Hughes, Robert Grubb, Patricia Kennedy, Aileen Britton, Peter Whitford, Alan Hopgood, Julia Blake; ***D:*** Gillian Armstrong; ***W:*** Eleanor Witcombe; ***C:*** Donald McAlpine; ***M:*** Nathan Waks. Australian Film Inst. '79: Film; British Acad. '80: Actress (Davis).

My Brother 🦴🦴 **2006 (PG-13)** Dying mom L'Tisha is desperate to have her two sons, Isaiah and developmentally disabled James, adopted together. Though that doesn't happen, the brothers' unshakeable bond stays with them into adulthood even when Isaiah gets involved with some hoods in a rather obvious subplot. **90m/C DVD.** Vanessa L(ynne) Williams, Fredro Starr, Tatum O'Neal, Nashawn Kearse, Rodney Henry, Christopher Scott, Donovan Jennings; ***D:*** Anthony Lover; ***W:*** Anthony Lover; ***C:*** John Sawyer; ***M:*** John Califra. **VIDEO**

My Brother Has Bad Dreams 🦴 *Scream Bloody Murder* **1972** Young man with sibling tosses and turns in bed. **97m/C VHS.** Nick Kleinholz, Marlena Lustic; ***D:*** Robert Emery; ***W:*** Robert Emery; ***C:*** Jack L. Richards; ***M:*** James Guglielmo.

My Brother Is an Only Child 🦴🦴 *Mio Fratello e Figlio Unico* **2007** Sibling rivalry mixes with social and political upheaval in the 1960s. Manrico (Scamarcio) follows his father into factory work and communism while his skeptical younger brother Accio (Germano) heads towards fascism. Both also become rivals for the affections of Francesca (Fleri), who leaves her bourgeoisie family for left-wing radicalism. Italian with subtitles. **104m/C DVD.** *FR IT* Elio Germano, Angela Finocchiaro, Riccardo Scarmarcio, Diane Fleri, Alba Rohrwacher, Massimo Popolizio; ***D:*** Daniele Luchetti; ***W:*** Daniele Luchetti, Sandro Petraglia, Stefano Rulli; ***C:*** Claudio Collepiccolo; ***M:*** Franco Piersanti.

My Brother Tom 🦴🦴 **½ 1986** The rural village of St. Helens is scarcely disturbed by WWII. But a burgeoning love affair between young Peggy MacGibbon and Tom Quayle, and the conflict between their two religions, does threaten to tear their country town apart. Based on the novel by James Aldridge. On three cassettes. **200m/C VHS.** Gordon Jackson, Keith Michell, Catherine McClements, Tom Jennings, Christopher Mayer, Christopher Cummings; ***D:*** Pino Amenta. **TV**

My Brother's Keeper 🦴🦴🦴 **1995** Twin brothers, Bob and Tom Bradley, fight for an experimental procedure when Tom is declared HIV positive. **94m/C DVD.** John Lithgow, Annette O'Toole, Veronica Cartwright, Ellen Burstyn, Richard Masur, Zeljko Ivanek, Brian Doyle-Murray, Amy Aquino, Julie Fulton, Mark Harelik; ***D:*** Glenn Jordan; ***W:*** Gregory Goodell.

My Brother's War 🦴🦴 **½ 1997 (R)** Brothers Gerry (Foy) and Liam (Xuereb) find themselves on opposite sides of the troubles in Ireland. Then, CIA operative Hall (Brolin) arrives to prevent Liam kidnapping three politicians who are trying to reach a peace accord. Some plot twists help out this standard actioner. **85m/C VHS, DVD.** Salvator Xuereb, Patrick Foy, James Brolin, Josh Brolin, Jennie Garth, Cristi Conaway; ***D:*** James Brolin; ***W:*** Alex Simon; ***C:*** Michael Bucher; ***M:*** John Graham.

My Brother's Wife 🦴🦴 **½ 1989 (PG)** Barney (Ritter), the black sheep of a wealthy family, spends two decades pursuing Eleanor (Harris), the woman of his dreams. Unfortunately, she's already married—to the brother he despises. Adapted from the play "The Middle Ages" by A.R. Gurney. **94m/C VHS, DVD.** John Ritter, Mel Harris, Polly Bergen, Dakin Matthews, David Byron, Lee Weaver; ***D:*** Jack Bender; ***W:*** Percy Granger. **TV**

My Champion 🦴 *Ritoru Champion* **1981** Chance meeting propels Mike Gorman and Miki Tsuwa into a relationship based on the strong bonds of love and athletic competition. **101m/C VHS.** *JP* Yoko Shimada, Chris Mitchum; ***D:*** Gwen Arner; ***W:*** Richard Martini.

My Chauffeur 🦴🦴 **½ 1986 (R)** When a wise-cracking female is hired on as a chauffeur at an all-male chauffeur service, sparks fly. And when the owner takes a definite liking to her work, things take a turn for the worse. As these sort of sexploitation flicks go, this is one of the better ones. **94m/C VHS, DVD.** Deborah Foreman, Sam Jones, Howard Hesseman, E.G. Marshall, Sean McClory; ***D:*** David Beaird; ***W:*** David Beaird.

My Childhood 🦴🦴🦴 *Childhood of Maxim Gorky* **1938** The first of director Donskoi's trilogy on the life of Maxim Gorky, based on Gorky's autobiographical stories. In this first film, Donskoi depicts Gorky's childhood of abuse and poverty with his grandparents in the 1870s. Eventually, Gorky is forced into the streets and he becomes a wandering beggar. In Russian with English subtitles. Followed by "My Apprenticeship" and "My Universities." **100m/C VHS.** *RU* Varvara O. Massalitinova, Aleksei Lyarsky, Mikhail Troyanovsky, Yelizaveta Alekseyeva; ***D:*** Mark Donskoi; ***W:*** Ilya Gruzdev; ***C:*** Pyotr Yermolov; ***M:*** Lev Shvarts.

My Cousin Vinny 🦴🦴🦴 **1992 (R)** Vinny Gambini (Pesci), a lawyer who took the bar exam six times before passing, goes to Wahzoo City, Alabama to get his cousin and a friend off the hook when they're accused of killing a store clerk. Leather jackets, gold chains, Brooklyn accents, and his fiancee Tomei's penchant for big hair and bold clothing don't go over well with conservative judge Gwynne, causing plenty of misunderstandings. Surprising hit with simplistic story reaches popular heights via entertaining performances by the entire cast. Tomei in particular steals every scene she's in and has an Oscar to prove it. **120m/C VHS, DVD.** Joe Pesci, Ralph Macchio, Marisa Tomei, Mitchell Whitfield, Fred Gwynne, Lane Smith, Austin Pendleton, Bruce McGill; ***D:*** Jonathan Lynn; ***W:*** Dale Launer; ***C:*** Peter Deming; ***M:*** Randy Edelman. Oscars '92: Support. Actress (Tomei); MTV Movie Awards '93: Breakthrough Perf. (Tomei).

My Darling Clementine 🦴🦴🦴 **½ 1946** One of the best Hollywood westerns ever made, this recounts the precise events leading up to and including the gunfight at the O.K. Corral. Fonda's the lawman, with Bond, Holt, and Garner as his brothers, and Mature co-stars as best friend, Doc Holliday. Schoolteacher Clementine (Downs) is Earp's gal, but the real revelation should be Brennan as old man Clanton—he's chilling not folksy. Ford allegedly knew Wyatt Earp and used his stories to recount the details vividly, though not always accurately. Remake of 1939's "Frontier Marshal." **97m/B VHS, DVD.** Henry Fonda, Victor Mature, Walter Brennan, Linda Darnell, Tim Holt, Ward Bond, John Ireland, Cathy Downs, Alan Mowbray, Don Garner, Jane Darwell, Grant Withers; ***D:*** John Ford; ***W:*** Sam Hellman, Winston Miller, Samuel G. Engel; ***C:*** Joe MacDonald; ***M:*** David Buttolph, Cyril Mockridge. Natl. Film Reg. '91.

My Date With Drew 🦴🦴🦴 **2005 (PG)** That would be actress Drew Barrymore, whom struggling filmmaker Herzlinger idolizes. He gives himself 30 days (since Herzlinger must return his video camera to the electronics store in that time in order to get a refund—yes, it's really low-budget). He must also attract her attention and not have her think he's a crazed stalker (he's actually kind of funny in an insecure way). And in the case of this documentary, it's all about the quest and not the outcome, which will not be revealed. **90m/C DVD.** *US* Brian Herzinger; ***D:*** Jon Gunn, Brian Herzinger, Brett Winn; ***C:*** Jon Gunn, Brian Herzinger, Brett Winn; ***M:*** Steven Stern, Stuart Hart.

My Date with the President's Daughter 🦴🦴 **½ 1998** Hallie, the President's sheltered daughter, just wants to go out with a boy and have a little fun. But between her father's re-election campaign and those darn Secret Service agents, what's a teen to do? **89m/C VHS.** Will Friedle, Dabney Coleman, Elisabeth Harnois, Ron Reagan; ***D:*** Alex Zamm. **TV**

My Daughter's Keeper 🦴🦴 **1993 (R)** The apparently perfect nanny of an unsuspecting family reveals her deadly agenda of murder, adultery, and more. **94m/C VHS.** Nicholas Guest, Jocelyn Broderick, Ana Padrao; ***D:*** Heinrich Dahms; ***W:*** Heinrich Dahms.

My Dear Secretary 🦴🦴 **½ 1949** After she marries her boss, a woman grows jealous of the secretary that replaces her. Comedic dialogue and antics result. **94m/B VHS, DVD.** Kirk Douglas, Laraine Day, Keenan Wynn, Rudy Vallee, Florence Bates, Alan Mowbray, Charles Halton; ***D:*** Charles Martin; ***W:*** Charles Martin.

My Demon Lover 🦴🦴 **1987 (PG-13)** This sex comedy is complicated by the hero's transformation into a demon whenever he is aroused. Saved from complete mediocrity by Family Ties's Valentine in a likable performance. **90m/C VHS.** Scott Valentine, Michelle Little, Arnold Johnson, Gina Gallego; ***D:*** Charles Loventhal; ***M:*** David Newman, Ed Alton.

My Dinner with Andre 🦴🦴🦴 **½ 1981** Two friends talk about their lives and philosophies for two hours over dinner one night. A wonderful exploration into storytelling, the conversation juxtaposes the experiences and philosophies of nerdish, bumbling Shawn and the globe-trotting spiritual pilgrimage of Gregory, in this sometimes poignant, sometimes comic little movie that starts you thinking. **110m/C VHS, DVD.** Andre Gregory, Wallace Shawn, Roy Butler, Jean Lenauer; ***D:*** Louis Malle; ***W:*** Andre Gregory, Wallace Shawn; ***C:*** Jeri Sopanen; ***M:*** Allen Shawn.

My Dog Shep 🦴 **½ 1946** An orphan and his dog run away and are pursued diligently when it is discovered that he is a wealthy heir. **71m/B VHS.** Tom Neal, William Farnum, Lannie Rees, Russell Simpson, Sarah Padden, Al "Fuzzy" St. John, Helen Chapman, Douglas Evans, Reed Howes, Grady Sutton; ***D:*** Ford Beebe; ***W:*** Ford Beebe; ***C:*** Fred Mandl.

My Dog Skip 🦴🦴🦴 **1999 (PG)** This is just the kind of movie people are talking about when they complain that there's no family friendly movies being made anymore. In 1940s Mississippi, awkward only child Willie (Muniz) sees his life change when, over the protests of his overprotective father (Bacon), he gets a puppy, Skip, for his ninth birthday. Amid much nostalgia and sentiment, Willie learns to be more outgoing and has many coming-of-age moments. Even if some of the plot elements are weak, the look and feel of the period is captured well, and Muniz does a fine job, although no human is likely to compete with the pooch, anyway. Kids will love the antics of Skip, and adults will enjoy having their hearts, and memories, tugged. Based on the book by Willie Morris. **95m/C VHS, DVD.** Frankie Muniz, Diane Lane, Kevin Bacon, Luke Wilson, Caitlin Wachs, Bradley Coryell, Daylan Honeycutt, Cody Linley; ***D:*** Jay Russell; ***W:*** Gail Gilchriest; ***C:*** James L. Carter; ***M:*** William Ross; ***Nar:*** Harry Connick Jr.

My Dog, the Thief 🦴 **1969** A helicopter weatherman is unaware that the lovable St. Bernard he has adopted is a kleptomaniac. When the dog steals a valuable necklace from a team of professional jewel thieves, the fun begins. **88m/C VHS, DVD.** Joe Flynn, Elsa Lanchester, Roger C. Carmel, Mickey Shaughnessy, Dwayne Hickman, Mary Ann Mobley; ***D:*** Robert Stevenson.

My Dream Is Yours 🦴🦴 **½ 1949** Day plays an up-and-coming radio star in this Warner Bros. musical comedy with a cameo from Bugs Bunny in a dream sequence. This fresh, fun remake of "Twenty Million Sweethearts" is often underrated, but is well worth a look. ♫My Dream is Yours; Some Like You; Tic, Tic, Tic; Love Finds a Way; I'll String Along with You; Canadian Capers; Freddie Get Ready; You Must Have Been a Beautiful Baby; Jeepers, Creepers. **101m/C VHS, DVD.** Jack Carson, Doris Day, Lee Bowman, Adolphe Menjou, Eve Arden, S.Z. Sakall, Selena Royle, Edgar Kennedy; ***D:*** Michael Curtiz.

My Effortless Brilliance 🦴 **½ 2008** If you like improvised dialogue and situations that basically go nowhere, then Shelton's mumblecore effort may be for you. Narcissistic writer Eric Lambert Jones and his childhood friend Dylan have inevitably drifted apart because of differing personalities and choices. Eric still isn't willing to let go and when he's on a book tour, he decides to intrude on Dylan's manly cabin-in-the-woods lifestyle for a drunken weekend with Dylan and his new best bud Jim. **79m/C DVD.** Sean Nelson, Basil Harris, Calvin Reeder, Jeanette Maus; ***D:*** Lynn Shelton; ***W:*** Sean Nelson, Lynn Shelton, Basil Harris, Calvin Reeder, Jeanette Maus; ***C:*** Benjamin Kasulke; ***M:*** Ted Speaker.

My Fair Lady 🦴🦴🦴 **½ 1964 (G)** Colorful production of Lerner and Loewe's musical version of "Pygmalion," about ill-mannered cockney Eliza (Hepburn) who is plucked from her job as a flower girl by Professor Henry Higgins (Harrison). Higgins makes a bet with a colleague that he can turn this rough diamond into a "lady." Winner of eight Academy Awards. Hepburn's singing voice is dubbed by Marni Nixon, who was also responsible for the singing in "The King and I" and "West Side Story"; the dubbing may have undermined Hepburn's chance at an Oscar nomination. Typecasting role for Harrison as the crusty, egocentric Higgins. A timeless classic. ♫Why Can't the English?; Wouldn't It Be Loverly?; I'm an Ordinary Man; With a Little Bit of Luck; Just You Wait, 'Enry 'Iggins; The Servant's Chorus; The Rain in Spain; I Could Have Danced all Night; Ascot Gavotte. **170m/C VHS, DVD.** Audrey Hepburn, Rex Harrison, Stanley Holloway, Wilfrid Hyde-White, Theodore Bikel, Mona Washbourne, Jeremy Brett, Robert Coote, Gladys Cooper; ***D:*** George Cukor; ***W:*** Alan Jay Lerner; ***C:*** Harry Stradling Sr.; ***M:*** Frederick Loewe, Alan Jay Lerner. Oscars '64: Actor (Harrison), Adapt. Score, Art Dir./Set Dec., Color, Color Cinematog., Costume Des. (C), Director (Cukor), Picture, Sound; AFI '98: Top 100; British Acad. '65: Film; Directors Guild '64: Director (Cukor); Golden Globes '65: Actor—Mus./Comedy (Harrison), Director (Cukor), Film—Mus./Comedy; N.Y. Film Critics '64: Actor (Harrison), Film.

My Family 🦴🦴🦴 **½** *Mi Familia* **1994 (R)** Patriarch Jose Sanchez (Rojas) comes to America in the early 1900s from Mexico and soon finds that the grass is not always greener on the other side. Thus begins the multigenerational saga of the Sanchez family in L.A., which chronicles their struggles and hopes over a time span of 60 years. Overlooked in the glut of Hispanic-themed movies released, featuring soulful performances from the ensemble cast, especially Smits and Morales as troubled men from separate generations. Their deep-seated need to assimilate matched by a disdain for authority provide most of the family's heartaches. English and Spanish dialogue. **126m/C VHS, DVD.** Jimmy Smits, Esai Morales, Eduardo Lopez Rojas, Jenny Gago, Elpidia Carrillo, Lupe Ontiveros, Jacob Vargas, Jennifer Lopez, Scott Bakula, Edward James Olmos, Michael Delorenzo, Maria Canals, Leon Singer, Jonathan Hernandez, Constance Marie, Enrique Castillo, Mary Steenburgen; ***D:*** Gregory Nava; ***W:*** Gregory Nava, Anna Thomas; ***C:*** Edward Lachman; ***M:*** Pepe Avila, Mark McKenzie; ***Nar:*** Edward James Olmos.

My Family Treasure 🦴🦴 **½ 1993** Mother tells her children about her dangerous trip into Russia to recover a family legacy—a priceless Faberge egg. **95m/C VHS.** Dee Wallace, Theodore Bikel, Alex Vincent, Bitty Schram; ***D:*** Rolfe Kanefsky, Edward Staroselsky.

My Faraway Bride 🦴🦴 *My Bollywood Bride* **2006** Genial cross-cultural rom com with a leading man who's handsome but is easily shown up by his co-stars. Adventure novelist Alex (Lewis) spends several days in L.A. with Indian tourist Reena (Shah), who cuts her trip short and heads back home without any explanation. Desperate to reunite with his love, Alex flies to Mumbai to track Reena down, finally learning she's a Bollywood star about to marry a powerful producer (Grover). Reena fobs Alex off on fellow actor Bobby (Suri) while she tries to figure out what's best. **95m/C DVD.** *US IN* Kashmira Shah, Jason Lewis, Gulshan Grover, Sanjay Suri, Neha Debey; ***D:*** Rajeev Manoj, Brad Listermann; ***W:*** Richard Martini; ***C:*** John Drake; ***M:*** Anu Malik.

My Father Is Coming 🦴🦴 **1991** German immigrant, Vicky, is trying to get an acting career off the ground in New York. She shares her apartment with Ben, a gay man, and generally does more work as a waitress than actress. Vicky's alarmed when her father, Hans, arrives for a visit. She's told him she's married (Vicky's also gay), so Ben agrees to pose as her husband. The rest of the film details Vicky's complicated love life, unsuccessful career tryouts, and her father's increasing bewilderment. It's meant as a sort of reverse, and perverse, innocents abroad, with the two Germans adrift in zany New York but this only works fitfully. **82m/C VHS.** *GE* Shelley Kastner, Alfred Edel, David Bronstein, Mary Lou Graulau, Michael Massee, Annie Sprinkle, Bruce Benderson; ***D:*** Monika Treut; ***W:*** Monika Treut.

My Father, My Mother, My Brothers and My Sisters *Mon Pere, Ma Mere, Mes Freres et Mes Soeurs* **1999** Free-spirit Anne (Abril) has three children by three different men and has never bothered to inform any of them about their offspring. She's surprised when her young son Victor expresses an interest in meeting his dad, which just happens to be possible since Anne and her brood are vacationing at the same Mexican resort where all three of her ex-lovers happen to also be staying with their significant others. French with subtitles. **95m/C VHS, DVD.** *FR* Victoria Abril, Alain Bashung, Pierre-Jean Cherit, Charlotte de Turckheim; ***D:*** Charlotte de Turckheim; ***W:*** Charlotte de Turckheim, Philippe Giangreco; ***C:*** Javier Salmones; ***M:*** Cyril de Turckheim.

My Father, My Rival **1985** A high school student's crush on his teacher leads to emotional complications when his widowed father becomes romantically involved with her. **60m/C VHS.** Wendy Crewson, Thomas Hauff, Helen Hughes, Andrew Gunn, Lance Guest; ***D:*** Claude Jutra; ***W:*** Marissa Griben.

My Father the Hero **1993 (PG)** Another adaptation of a French film ("Mon Pere, Ce Heroes") finds 14-year-old Heigl on an island paradise with divorced dad Depardieu, passing him off as her boyfriend (without his knowledge) to impress a cute boy, causing obvious misunderstandings. Depardieu shows a flair for physical comedy, but his talent is wasted in a role that's vaguely disturbing; one of the few funny moments finds him unwittingly singing "Thank Heaven For Little Girls" to a horrified audience. For the pre-teen set only, others will probably find it a waste of time. Top notch actress Thompson's surprising (uncredited) cameo is due to her friendship with Depardieu. **90m/C VHS, DVD.** Gerard Depardieu, Katherine Heigl, Dalton James, Lauren Hutton, Faith Prince; ***Cameos:*** Emma Thompson; ***D:*** Steve Miner; ***W:*** Francis Veber, Charlie Peters; ***M:*** David Newman.

My Father's Glory *La Gloire de Mon Pere* **1991 (G)** Based on Marcel Pagnol's tales of his childhood, this is a sweet, beautiful memory of a young boy's favorite summer in the French countryside of the early 1900s. Not much happens, yet the film is such a perfect evocation of the milieu that one is carried swiftly into the dreams and thoughts of all the characters. One half of a duo, followed by "My Mother's Castle." In French with English subtitles. **110m/C VHS, DVD.** *FR* Julien Ciamaca, Philippe Caubere, Nathalie Roussel, Therese Liotard, Didier Pain; ***D:*** Yves Robert; ***W:*** Lucette Andrei; ***C:*** Robert Alazraki; ***M:*** Vladimir Cosma.

My Father's House **1975** Magazine editor recounts his youth while recovering from a heart attack. He measures his own quality of life against the life that his father led and begins to question his own choices with regard to his family. **96m/C VHS.** Cliff Robertson, Robert Preston, Eileen Brennan, Rosemary Forsyth; ***D:*** Alex Segal; ***W:*** David Seltzer; ***C:*** David M. Walsh; ***M:*** Charles Fox. **TV**

My Favorite Blonde **1942** Beautiful British spy Carroll convinces Hope to aid her in carrying out a secret mission. Lots of fun as Hope and his trained penguin, along with Carroll, embark on a cross-country chase to elude the Nazis. Hope's behavior is hilarious and the pacing of the film is excellent. Based on a story by Melvin Frank and Norman Panama. **78m/B VHS, DVD.** Bob Hope, Madeleine Carroll, Gale Sondergaard, George Zucco, Lionel Royce, Walter Kingsford, Victor Varconi, Bing Crosby; ***D:*** Sidney Lanfield; ***W:*** Frank Butler, Don Hartman; ***C:*** William Mellor; ***M:*** David Buttolph.

My Favorite Brunette **1/2 1947** Detective parody starring Hope as a photographer turned grumbling private eye. He becomes involved with a murder, a spy caper, and a dangerous brunette (Lamour). **85m/B VHS, DVD.** Bob Hope, Dorothy Lamour, Peter Lorre, Lon Chaney Jr., Alan Ladd, Reginald Denny, Bing Crosby; ***D:*** Elliott Nugent; ***W:*** Edmund Beloin, Jack Rose; ***C:*** Lionel Lindon; ***M:*** Robert Emmett Dolan.

My Favorite Martian **1/2 1998 (PG)** This retread of the semi-successful '60s TV sitcom adds to the growing pile of evidence that the words "original" and "thought" are not used in the same sentence in Hollywood anymore. Tim (Daniels) is a TV producer cajoled into hiding his "Uncle Martin." Martin (Lloyd) is actually an alien whose spaceship has crashed, and he's on the run from a government agency and the prying press. Tim must throw racy reporter Hurley off the trail as well, although he has a crush on her. Numerous animated and computer morphed sight gags, including a horny wisecracking spacesuit named Zoot (who brings new meaning to the term "skirt chasing"), take the place of a plot. Sets new standards for mediocrity, but the kiddies might enjoy it. **93m/C VHS, DVD.** Jeff Daniels, Christopher Lloyd, Elizabeth Hurley, Daryl Hannah, Wallace Shawn, Christine Ebersole, Ray Walston, Michael Lerner; ***D:*** Donald Petrie; ***W:*** Sherri Stoner, Deanna Oliver; ***C:*** Thomas Ackerman; ***M:*** John Debney.

My Favorite Wife **1940** Handsome widower Nick (Grant) has just married Bianca (Patrick) only to discover that first wife Ellen (Dunne), shipwrecked seven years earlier and presumed dead, has reappeared. Ellen wants Nick back and makes him jealous by revealing that she spent her island sojourn with fellow survivor, Stephen (Scott). Eventually, a judge must decide what to do about their most unusual situation. Farcical and hilarious story filled with a clever cast. The 1963 remake "Move Over Darling" lacks the style and wit of this presentation. **88m/B VHS, DVD.** Ann Shoemaker, Granville Bates, Irene Dunne, Cary Grant, Randolph Scott, Gail Patrick, Scotty Beckett; ***D:*** Garson Kanin; ***W:*** Samuel Spewack, Bella Spewack, Leo McCarey; ***C:*** Rudolph Mate; ***M:*** Roy Webb.

My Favorite Year *My Favourite Year* **1982 (PG)** A young writer on a popular live TV show in the 1950s is asked to keep a watchful eye on the week's guest star—his favorite swashbuckling movie hero. Through a series of misadventures, he discovers his matinee idol is actually a drunkard and womanizer who has trouble living up to his cinematic standards. Sterling performance from O'Toole, with memorable portrayal from Bologna as the show's host, King Kaiser (a take-off of Sid Caesar from "Your Show of Shows"). **92m/C VHS, DVD.** Peter O'Toole, Mark Linn-Baker, Joseph Bologna, Jessica Harper, Lainie Kazan, Bill Macy, Anne DeSalvo, Lou Jacobi, Adolph Green, Cameron Mitchell, Gloria Stuart; ***D:*** Richard Benjamin; ***W:*** Norman Steinberg; ***M:*** Ralph Burns.

My Fellow Americans **1996 (PG-13)** Political "Odd Couple" pits cantankerous conservative Kramer (Lemmon) against womanizing liberal Douglas (Garner) when current President Aykroyd frames his two predecessors for a White House scandal. The age-old adversaries must set aside their differences long enough to clear their names by reaching Kramer's presidential library, where he has vindicating papers. Along the way, they encounter adventure, danger and "the people," the average Americans they used to work for. "Grumpy Old Men" veteran Lemmon is plenty cranky while Garner's charisma is a suitable foil. The ironic "charm" of course banter from the mouths of two ex-Presidents is supposed to carry much of the humor, but instead wears thin. Supporting characters (Aykroyd, Bacall) aren't as well used as the two main characters. Mainly for Lemmon, Garner, and "Grumpy" fans. **96m/C VHS, DVD.** Dan Aykroyd, James Garner, Jack Lemmon, John Heard, Sela Ward, Wilford Brimley, Everett McGill, Bradley Whitford, Lauren Bacall, James Rebhorn, Esther Rolle, Conchata Ferrell, Jack Kehler, Tom Everett, Jeff Yagher; ***D:*** Peter Segal; ***W:*** E. Jack Kaplan, Richard Chapman, Peter Tolan; ***C:*** Julio Macat; ***M:*** William Ross.

My First Mister **1/2 2001 (R)** Explores the delicate friendship between two lost and lonely souls. Teenaged Jennifer (Sobieski) is a goth girl whose look and attitude alienates both school and family members. Looking for a job, she is unexpectedly hired as a stock clerk by men's clothing salesman, Randall (Brooks), a middle-aged conservative in both dress and manner. They discover they have a number of feelings in common, although Randall is careful never to let their relationship get out of control. Film does take an unfortunate turn towards the maudlin when we learn that Randall is dying but the leads keep sentimentality fairly well-checked. **109m/C VHS, DVD.** *US* Albert Brooks, Leelee Sobieski, Desmond Harrington, Carol Kane, Michael McKean, Mary Kay Place, John Goodman, Lisa Jane Persky; ***D:*** Christine Lahti; ***W:*** Jill Franklyn; ***C:*** Jeffrey Jur; ***M:*** Steve Porcaro.

My First Wedding WOOF! **2004 (PG-13)** Disastrous and raunchy would-be rom-com with unlikable characters and ridiculous situations. Bride-to-be Vanessa (Cook) is having sex fantasies about other men just days before her wedding and heads to confession. Horndog carpenter Nick (Doughty) happens to be fixing the confessional booth and is mistaken for the priest. Vanessa pleads with the faker to save her from sin. Of course Nick wants to sin big time and does his best to persuade Vanessa to call off the nuptials. **100m/C DVD.** Rachael Leigh Cook, Kenny Doughty, Paul Hopkins, Valerie Mahaffey; ***D:*** Laurent Firode; ***W:*** Joan Carr-Wiggin; ***C:*** Vernon Layton; ***M:*** Michel Cusson.

My First Wife **1/2 1984 (PG)** Strong drama about a self-indulgent man's devastation when his wife abruptly leaves him after ten years of marriage. Realistic and well-acted. **95m/C VHS.** *AU* John Hargreaves, Wendy Hughes, Lucy Angwin, Anna Maria Monticelli, David Cameron; ***D:*** Paul Cox; ***W:*** Paul Cox, Bob Ellis. Australian Film Inst. '84: Actor (Hargreaves).

My 5 Wives **2000 (R)** Dangerfield is a thrice-divorced real estate tycoon who discovers the Utah land he's invested in comes complete with five wives. **100m/C VHS, DVD.** Rodney Dangerfield, Andrew (Dice Clay) Silverstein, John Byner, Molly Shannon, Jerry Stiller, John Pinette, Emmanuelle Vaugier, Fred Keating, Kate Luyben, Judy Tylor, Angelika Baran, Anita Brown; ***D:*** Sidney J. Furie; ***W:*** Rodney Dangerfield, Harry Basil; ***C:*** Curtis Petersen; ***M:*** Robert Carli. **VIDEO**

My Foolish Heart **1/2 1949** Women's weepie starred Hayward as Eloise Winters, the tippling and unhappily married wife of Lew Wengler (Smith). Eloise stole Lew away from her college roommate, Mary Jane (Wheeler), when she got pregnant by another man. Lew has asked Eloise for a divorce so he and Mary Jane can finally get hitched. But an old evening dress has Eloise remembering her true love and the father of her daughter—Walt Dreiser (Andrews)—whom she fatefully met in 1941. Eloise finally owns up to the unhappiness her deception has caused and at least someone is happy by the closing credits. Based on the short story "Uncle Wiggily in Connecticut" by J.D. Salinger. **98m/B VHS.** Dana Andrews, Susan Hayward, Kent Smith, Lois Wheeler, Jessie Royce Landis, Robert Keith, Gigi Perreau, Karin (Karen, Katharine) Booth; ***D:*** Mark Robson; ***W:*** Julius J. Epstein, Philip G. Epstein; ***C:*** Lee Garmes; ***M:*** Victor Young.

My Forbidden Past **1/2 1951** Melodrama set in 1890 New Orleans centers on a young woman (Gardner) with an unsavory past who unexpectedly inherits a fortune and vows to break up the marriage of the man (Mitchum) she loves. His wife is murdered and he is charged with doing the deed until Gardner, exposing her past, wins his love and helps to extricate him. **81m/B VHS.** Ava Gardner, Melvyn Douglas, Robert Mitchum; ***D:*** Robert Stevenson.

My Friend Flicka **1943** Boy makes friends with four-legged beast. Dad thinks the horse is full of wild oats, but young Roddy trains it to be the best gosh darned horse in pre-Disney family faredom. Based on Mary O'Hara book, followed by "Thunderhead, Son of Flicka," and TV series. **89m/C VHS, DVD.** Roddy McDowall, Preston Foster, Rita Johnson, James Bell, Jeff Corey; ***D:*** Harold Schuster.

My Friend Irma **1/2 1949** An adaptation of the radio series, featuring Wilson as the dumb blonde with boyfriend trouble and Lynn as her sensible pal. The film debut of Martin (singing) and Lewis (mugging) as juice-bar operators. Followed by a sequel, "My Friend Irma Goes West," and later by a TV series. **103m/B VHS.** Marie Wilson, Diana Lynn, John Lund, Don DeFore, Dean Martin, Jerry Lewis, Hans Conried; ***D:*** George Marshall; ***W:*** Cy Howard; ***C:*** Leo Tover; ***M:*** Roy Webb.

My Friend Walter **1/2 1993** Bess Throckmorten attends a family reunion in London with her Aunt Ellie and discovers one of her ancestors is Sir Walter Raleigh. Visiting the Tower of London, Bess finds Sir Walter's ghost who wants to follow her home to Devon to see how the family is doing. He finds that the Throckmorten's are about to lose the family farm but Sir Walter comes up with a plan to restore their fortunes. Shot on location in England and based on the book by Michael Morpurgo. **87m/C VHS.** *GB* Polly Grant, Ronald Pickup, Prunella Scales, Louise Jameson, James Hazeldine, Lawrence Cooper, Constance Chapman; ***D:*** Gavin Millar.

My Fuhrer **1/2** *My Fuhrer: The Truly Truest Truth About Adolf Hitler; Mein Fuhrer: Die Wirklich Wahrste Wahrheit Ueber Adolf Hitler* **2007** Scattershot German comedy about Hitler's last days, set in Berlin in December 1944. Realizing the war is lost, a morose Fuhrer (Schneider) is hiding out with Goebbels (Groth) trying to rally his leader. His idea is to haul out famous Jewish acting teacher Adolf Gruenbaum (Muehe) from a labor camp (promising also to release his family) to coach Hitler into regaining that old Nazi zeal. Though writer-director Levi is himself Jewish, he received criticism about the film's suitability. German with subtitles. **89m/C DVD.** *GE* Helge Schneider, Ulrich Muehe, Sylvester Groth, Ulrich Noethen, Adriana Altaras, Stefan Kurt, Udo Kroschwald, Katja Riemann; ***D:*** Dani Levy; ***W:*** Dani Levy; ***C:*** Carl F. Koschnick, Carsten Thiele; ***M:*** Niki Reiser.

My Geisha **1/2 1962** MacLaine and husband experience bad karma because she wants to be in his new film. In pancake makeup and funny shoes, she poses as a geisha girl and is cast as Madame Butterfly. Her husband, however, is one sharp cookie. Filmed in Japan. **120m/C VHS, DVD.** Shirley MacLaine, Yves Montand, Edward G. Robinson, Robert Cummings; ***D:*** Jack Cardiff.

My Giant **1998 (PG)** Billy Crystal plays a short, annoying, Hollywood-type guy and Romanian-born NBA player Gheorghe Muresan plays a really tall Romanian guy, so you know there's not exactly an Olivier thing happening here. Crystal is the brutish showbiz agent Sammy, who accidently stumbles onto Muresan's Max. The gentle Max is at peace in his monastery; but Sammy, being an agent, quickly finds a way to make money off of him. Max is talked into a movie career so he can be reunited with his childhood crush Lillianna (Pacula). The odd couple schtick is milked until bone dry, and then the sentimentality floodgates open when it's discovered that Max has a serious medical condition. Warning: although presented as a family film, unless you want to recreate that whole "Why did Bambi's mom have to die?" scene (with you as the parent this time), you might want to reconsider renting this movie for small children. **103m/C VHS, DVD.** Michael (Mike) Papajohn, Billy Crystal, Gheorghe Muresan, Kathleen Quinlan, Joanna Pacula, Rider Strong, Harold Gould, Doris Roberts, Philip Sterling, Heather Thomas, Zane Carney; ***Cameos:*** Steven Seagal; ***D:*** Michael Lehmann; ***W:*** David Seltzer; ***C:*** Michael Coulter; ***M:*** Marc Shaiman.

My Girl **1/2 1991 (PG)** Chlumsky is delightful in her film debut as an 11-year-old tomboy who must come to grips with the realities of life. Culkin plays her best friend Thomas, who understands her better than anyone else, including her father, a mortician, and his girlfriend, the makeup artist at the funeral parlor. Some reviewers questioned whether young children would be able to deal with some unhappy occurrences in the film, but most seemed to classify it as a movie the whole family would enjoy. **102m/C VHS, DVD.** Dan Aykroyd, Jamie Lee Curtis, Macaulay Culkin, Anna Chlumsky, Griffin Dunne, Raymond Buktenica, Richard Masur, Ann Nelson, Peter Michael Goetz, Tom Villard; ***D:*** Howard Zieff; ***W:*** Laurice Elehwany; ***C:*** Paul Elliott; ***M:*** James Newton Howard. MTV Movie Awards '92: Kiss (Macaulay Culkin/Anna Chlumsky).

My Girl 2 **1/2 1994 (PG)** It's 1974 and Chlumsky is back as Vada (this time without Culkin, given the killer bee attack in

MG1) in this innocent coming-of-ager. Portly Aykroyd and flaky Curtis return as parental window dressing who encourage Vada's search for information on her long-dead mother. She tracks down old friends of her mom's (Masur and Rose) who are having difficulties with their obnoxious adolescent son (O'Brien). Predictable, but enjoyable. Certain to fail the credibility test of nit-pickers who may wonder why the only thing Aykroyd can remember of his first wife is that she left behind a paper bag with a date scribbled on it. **99m/C VHS, DVD.** Anna Chlumsky, Dan Aykroyd, Jamie Lee Curtis, Austin O'Brien, Richard Masur, Christine Ebersole, Ben Stein; ***D:*** Howard Zieff; ***W:*** Janet Kovalcik; ***C:*** Paul Elliott; ***M:*** Cliff Eidelman.

My Girl Tisa ✓✓ 1/2 **1948** Chronicles the experiences of a young immigrant woman who struggles to survive in the U.S. at the turn of the century and hopes to bring her father over from their home country. Based on a play by Lucille S. Prumbs and Sara B. Smith. **95m/B VHS.** Lilli Palmer, Sam Wanamaker, Akim Tamiroff, Alan Hale, Hugo Haas, Gale Robbins, Stella Adler; ***D:*** Elliott Nugent; ***M:*** Max Steiner.

My Grandpa Is a Vampire ✓ 1/2 **1992 (PG)** When 12 year-old Lonny and his pal visit Grandpa Cooger in New Zealand Lonny discovers a long-hidden family secret—Grandpa's a vampire! This doesn't stop either boy from joining with Grandpa in lots of scary adventures. **90m/C VHS.** Al Lewis, Justin Gocke, Milan Borich, Noel Appleby; ***D:*** David Blyth.

My Heroes Have Always Been Cowboys ✓✓ 1/2 **1991 (PG)** An aging rodeo rider returns to his hometown to recuperate and finds himself forced to confront his past. His ex-girlfriend, his dad and his sister all expect something from him. He learns how to give it, and gains the strength of purpose to get back on the bull that stomped him. Excellent rodeo footage, solid performances, but the story has been around the barn too many times to hold much interest. **106m/C VHS.** Scott Glenn, Kate Capshaw, Ben Johnson, Balthazar Getty, Mickey Rooney, Gary Busey, Tess Harper, Clarence Williams III, Dub Taylor, Clu Gulager, Dennis Fimple; ***D:*** Stuart Rosenberg; ***W:*** Joel Don Humphreys; ***M:*** James Horner.

My House in Umbria ✓✓✓ **2003** Quality HBO production adapted from the novella by William Trevor. Romance writer Emily Delahunty (Smith) is aboard a Milan-bound train when her peace is shattered by a bomb. Emily invites the other survivors from her train car to recuperate at her house in Umbria, including young American Aimee (Clarke), whose parents were killed in the explosion. Aimee begins to lean on Emily (who loves having a ready-made family) and then the snake appears in their Garden of Eden; Aimee's frosty Uncle Thomas (Cooper) has come to pick up his unknown niece. Emily's voiceover ramblings are sometimes distracting but Smith finds the pathos in her character without going overboard. The versatile Cooper also offers excellent support in an unsympathetic role. And, naturally, the scenes at the villa, shot on the Tuscany-Umbria border, are entrancing. **103m/C VHS, DVD.** Maggie Smith, Chris Cooper, Timothy Spall, Emmy Clarke, Benno Furmann, Ronnie Barker, Giancarlo Giannini, Libero De Rienzo; ***D:*** Richard Loncraine; ***W:*** Hugh Whitemore; ***C:*** Marco Pontecorvo; ***M:*** Claudio Capponi. **CABLE**

My Husband's Double Life ✓✓ 1/2 *The Familiar Stranger* **2001** Men are scum. Cable drama based on a true story finds Elizabeth Welsh (Sanders) trying to cope with the apparent suicide of her embezzling husband Patrick (Sanders). She has to sell the house and get a job to support their kids. Then, 10 years later, the Social Security Department informs Elizabeth that the weasel is alive and living in Maine. Naturally, Elizabeth heads off to confront the two-timer. **96m/C VHS, DVD.** Margaret Colin, Jay O. Sanders, Will Estes, Aaron Ashmore, Gary Hudson, Victoria Snow; ***D:*** Alan Metzger; ***W:*** Alan Hines. **CABLE**

My Husband's Secret Life ✓✓ **1998 (PG-13)** Nonsensical thriller about cop's widow Archer who discovers her late hubby had a mistress (Alonso). Unlikely as it seems, the two pair up to investigate police corruption after it seems their mutual honey was also taking payoffs from the mob. The two actresses are much classier than their material. Based on the novel "Tin Wife" by Joe Flaherty. **93m/C VHS.** Anne Archer, Maria Conchita Alonso, Garry Chalk, James Russo, Gerard Plunkett; ***D:*** Graeme Clifford; ***W:*** Georgia Jeffries; ***C:*** David Geddes; ***M:*** Roger Bellon. **CABLE**

My Lady of Whims ✓ **1925** Clara Bow's dad disapproves of debutante daughter's desire to hang out with the girls who just want to have fun. **42m/B VHS.** Clara Bow, Betty Baker, Carmelita Geraghty, Donald Keith, Lee Moran; ***D:*** Dallas Fitzgerald; ***W:*** Doris Schroeder; ***C:*** Jack Young.

My Left Foot ✓✓✓✓ **1989 (R)** A gritty, unsentimental drama based on the life and autobiography of cerebral-palsy victim Christy Brown. Considered an imbecile by everyone but his mother (Fricker, in a stunning award-winning performance) until he teaches himself to write. He survives his impoverished Irish roots to become a painter and writer using his left foot, the only appendage over which he has control. He also falls in love and finds some heartaches along the way. Day-Lewis is astounding; the supporting cast, especially Shaw and Cusack, match him measure for measure. **103m/C VHS, DVD.** *IR* Daniel Day-Lewis, Brenda Fricker, Ray McAnally, Cyril Cusack, Fiona Shaw, Hugh O'Conor, Adrian Dunbar, Ruth McCabe, Alison Whelan; ***D:*** Jim Sheridan; ***W:*** Shane Connaughton, Jim Sheridan; ***C:*** Jack Conroy; ***M:*** Elmer Bernstein. Oscars '89: Actor (Day-Lewis), Support. Actress (Fricker); British Acad. '89: Actor (Day-Lewis), Support. Actor (McAnally); Ind. Spirit '90: Foreign Film; L.A. Film Critics '89: Actor (Day-Lewis), Support. Actress (Fricker); Montreal World Film Fest. '89: Actor (Day-Lewis); N.Y. Film Critics '89: Actor (Day-Lewis), Film; Natl. Soc. Film Critics '89: Actor (Day-Lewis).

My Life ✓✓ 1/2 **1993 (PG-13)** Maudlin, sometimes depressing production preaches the power of a well-examined life. Public relations exec Keaton is diagnosed with cancer and the doctors predict he will most likely die before the birth of his first child. Film follows his transition from uncommunicative and angry to acceptance, a role to which Keaton brings a sentimental strength. Kidman is window dressing as the ever-patient, nobly suffering wife, a cardboard character notable mainly for her beauty. **114m/C VHS, DVD.** Michael Keaton, Nicole Kidman, Haing S. Ngor, Bradley Whitford, Queen Latifah, Michael Constantine, Toni Sawyer, Rebecca Schull, Lee Garlington; ***D:*** Bruce Joel Rubin; ***W:*** Bruce Joel Rubin; ***C:*** Peter James; ***M:*** John Barry.

My Life and Times with Antonin Artaud ✓✓✓ *En Compagnie d'Antonin Artaud; Artaud* **1993** Postwar Parisian bohemia is depicted in the obsessive friendship between ambitious young poet Jacques Prevel (Barbe) and famed intellectual/poet/impressario Antonin Artaud (Frey), who founded the Theatre of Cruelty. Artaud has returned to Paris after spending nine years in an asylum and is suffering from terminal cancer, the misery of which is partially alleviated by the opiates that Prevel can provide. Delusional and paranoid, Artaud makes his self-destruction into genius while Prevel documents Artaud's last two years in diaries, hoping to gain some measure of fame for himself. French with subtitles. Based on Prevel's "En Compagnie d'Antonin Artaud." **93m/B VHS, DVD.** *FR* Sami Frey, Marc Barbe, Valerie Jeannet, Julie Jezequel, Charlotte Valandrey; ***D:*** Gerard Mordillat; ***W:*** Gerard Mordillat, Jerome Prieur; ***C:*** Francois Catonne; ***M:*** Jean-Claude Petit.

My Life As a Dog ✓✓✓✓ *Mitt Liv Som Hund* **1985** A troublesome boy is separated from his brother and is sent to live with relatives in the country when his mother is taken ill. Unhappy and confused, he struggles to understand sexuality and love and tries to find security and acceptance. Remarkable Swedish film available with English subtitles or dubbed. **101m/C VHS, DVD.** *SW* Anton Glanzelius, Tomas von Bromssen, Anki Liden, Melinda Kinnaman, Kicki Rundgren, Ingmari Carlsson; ***D:*** Lasse Hallstrom; ***W:*** Lasse Hallstrom, Per (Pelle) Berglund, Brasse Brannstrom; ***C:*** Jorgen Persson, Rolf Lindstrom; ***M:*** Bjorn Isfalt. Golden Globes '88: Foreign Film; Ind. Spirit '88: Foreign Film; N.Y. Film Critics '87: Foreign Film.

My Life in Ruins ✓✓ **2009 (PG-13)** Moderately amusing comedy relies on too many tourist cliches with a slimmed-down, glammed-up Vardalos not particularly believable as a romantically-challenged tour guide who's lost her zest for life. Greek-American Georgia (Vardalos), a would-be classics professor, is not a particularly popular guide in Athens. She gets stuck with the dilapidated bus, the sullen driver (Georgoulis), and the most stereotypical tourists because she provides pedantic lectures rather than shopping excursions. Her latest week's tour offers gorgeous Greek scenery, bonding situations, a chance at romance, and too much that's tired and obvious. **95m/C DVD.** *US* Nia Vardalos, Richard Dreyfuss, Rachel Dratch, Maria Botto, Harland Williams, Alexis Georgoulis, Sheila Bernette, Ralph Nossek, Bernice Stegers, Maria Adanez; ***D:*** Donald Petrie; ***W:*** Mike Reiss; ***C:*** Jose Luis Alcaine; ***M:*** David Newman.

My Life on Ice ✓✓ *The True Story of My Life in Rouen; Ma Vraie Vie a Rouen* **2002** Sixteen-year-old Etienne (Tavares) has two obsessions: figure skating and filming everything that happens around him with the video camera he got for his birthday. He films his mom, Caroline (Ascaride), and her new boyfriend Laurent (Zaccai), his grandmother (Surgere), and his best friend Ludovic (Bonnifait)—few of whom are happy to constantly be in the camera's eye. The viewer also becomes aware (although those around him seem oblivious) to the virginal Etienne's sexuality—he has a crush on both Laurent, who happens to be his history teacher, and pal Ludovic, who can't deal with any sexual revelations. French with subtitles. **100m/C VHS, DVD.** *FR* Jimmy Tavares, Ariane Ascaride, Helene Surgere, Jonathan Zaccai, Lucas Bonnifait; ***D:*** Olivier Ducastel, Jacques Martineau; ***W:*** Olivier Ducastel, Jacques Martineau; ***C:*** Mathieu Poirot-Delpech, Pierre Milon; ***M:*** Philippe Miller.

My Life So Far ✓✓ 1/2 **1998 (PG-13)** In the 1920s, the Pettigrews live on the family estate of Gamma Macintosh (Harris) in the Scottish Highlands. Eccentric would-be inventor Edward (Firth) ineffectually manages the property, with wife Moira (Mastrantonio) and his children, including mischievious 10-year-old Fraser (Norman). Fraser's safe world is rocked by the arrival of his businessman Uncle Morris (McDowell) and his uncle's seductive French fiancee, Heloise (Jacob), who draws the immediate and overly attentive gaze of Edward. Based on the autobiographical book "Son of Adam" by Sir Denis Forman. **93m/C VHS, DVD.** *GB* Colin Firth, Mary Elizabeth Mastrantonio, Irene Jacob, Malcolm McDowell, Rosemary Harris, Tcheky Karyo, Robert Norman, Kelly Macdonald; ***D:*** Hugh Hudson; ***W:*** Simon Donald; ***C:*** Bernard Lutic; ***M:*** Howard Blake.

My Life to Live ✓✓✓✓ *Vivre Sa Vie; It's My Life* **1962** A woman turns to prostitution in this probing examination of sexual, and social, relations. Idiosyncratic Godard has never been more starstruck than in this vehicle for the endearing Karina, his wife at the time. A classic. In French with English subtitles. **85m/B VHS, DVD.** *FR* Anna Karina, Sady Rebbot, Andre S. Labarthe, Guylaine Schlumberger; ***D:*** Jean-Luc Godard; ***W:*** Jean-Luc Godard; ***C:*** Raoul Coutard; ***M:*** Michel Legrand. Venice Film Fest. '62: Special Jury Prize.

My Life Without Me ✓✓ 1/2 **2003 (R)** Writer/director Coixet delivers a weepy drama about a young, married woman who keeps her impending death a secret from her family. Diagnosed with inoperable ovarian cancer, the happily married 23-year-old Ann (Polley) decides against telling husband Don (Speedman) and their two daughters about her condition. With only a few months to live, Ann draws up a list of things to do before dying, one of which is to really fall in love with another man. She soon finds a cooperative lover in Lee (Ruffalo), who falls for her too. She also tries to set her husband up with a replacement wife, also named Ann (Watling). Despite the far-fetched, soap operatic script and less than sympathetic main character, earnest performances (especially from the likeable Polley) ratchet up the believability factor. **106m/C VHS, DVD.** *CA SP* Sarah Polley, Scott Speedman, Mark Ruffalo, Deborah Harry, Alfred Molina, Leonor Watling, Amanda Plummer, Julian Richings, Maria De Medeiros; ***D:*** Isabel Coixet; ***W:*** Isabel Coixet; ***C:*** Jean-Claude Larrieu; ***M:*** Alfonso de Villalonga.

My Life's in Turnaround ✓✓ **1994 (R)** Amusing low-budget comedy takes a behind-the-scenes, semi-autobiographical look at the lives of two would-be filmmakers. They try for cool but manage only goofy. **84m/C VHS, DVD.** Eric Schaeffer, Donal Lardner Ward, Lisa Gerstein, Dana Wheeler-Nicholson, Debra Clein, Sheila Jaffe; ***Cameos:*** Casey Siemaszko, John Sayles, Martha Plimpton, Phoebe Cates; ***D:*** Eric Schaeffer, Donal Lardner Ward; ***W:*** Eric Schaeffer, Donal Lardner Ward; ***M:*** Reed Hays.

My Little Assassin ✓✓ **1999** In 1959, idealistic 19-year-old Marita Lorenz is in Cuba with her CIA operative mother (Clayburgh), when she falls for revolutionary leader Fidel Castro (Mantegna). She winds up pregnant and alone in New York, where the CIA tries to convince her that Fidel's a bad guy. So, she decides to return to Cuba and assassinate him. In 1993, Lorenz wrote a book detailing her affair, the birth of their daughter, and Lorenz's involved in a failed plot to poison the dictator in 1960. If you can suspend your credulity, you'll discover a watchable potboiler with Mantegna as a charismatic Cuban leader. **90m/C VHS, DVD.** Joe Mantegna, Gabrielle Anwar, Jill Clayburgh, Robert Davi, Scott Paulin, Tony Plana, Reiner Schone, Mike Moroff, Glenn Morshower, Dean Norris; ***D:*** Jack Bender; ***W:*** Howard Korder; ***M:*** David Schwartz. **CABLE**

My Little Chickadee ✓✓✓ **1940** Classic comedy about a gambler and a fallen woman who marry for convenience so they can respectably enter an unsuspecting town. Sparks fly in their adventures together. Fields and West are both at their best playing their larger-than-life selves. **91m/B VHS, DVD.** W.C. Fields, Mae West, Joseph Calleia, Dick Foran, Margaret Hamilton, Donald Meek, Ruth Donnelly, Fuzzy Knight; ***D:*** Edward F. (Eddie) Cline; ***W:*** W.C. Fields, Mae West; ***C:*** Joseph Valentine; ***M:*** Frank Skinner.

My Little Girl ✓✓ **1987 (R)** A rich Philadelphia girl idealistically volunteers her time to help local institutionalized orphans, but meets with opposition. **118m/C VHS.** Mary Stuart Masterson, James Earl Jones, Geraldine Page, Anne Meara, Peter Gallagher, George Newbern; ***D:*** Connie Kaiserman.

My Louisiana Sky ✓✓ 1/2 **2002** Twelve-year-old Tiger Ann (Keel) lives with her grandma Jewel (Knight) and her "slow" parents in Saitler, Louisiana. She's looking forward to the summer when her glamorous aunt, Dorie Kay (Lewis), will visit but Jewel's unexpected death has Tiger Ann re-thinking what matters to her after she goes to live with her aunt in the city. Based on the book by Kimberly Willis Holt. **99m/C VHS, DVD.** Kelsey Keel, Shirley Knight, Juliette Lewis, Karen Robinson, Amelia Campbell, Chris Owens, Michael Cera; ***D:*** Adam Arkin; ***W:*** Anna Sandor; ***C:*** Gavin Smith; ***M:*** Mader. **CABLE**

My Love For Yours ✓✓ 1/2 *Honeymoon in Bali* **1939** The romantic tale of a young man hoping to win the love of a beautiful but icy girl. A tad silly in parts, but the clever dialogue moves the story along. **99m/B VHS, DVD.** Fred MacMurray, Madeleine Carroll; ***D:*** Edward H. Griffith.

My Lucky Star ✓✓ 1/2 **1938** Skating star Henie plays a department store clerk that gets sent off to college to model clothes from the store's sports line. She somehow manages to convince school officials to stage their winter ice show in the department store, where she gets to show off her stuff. Don't miss the grand finale, a performance of "Alice in Wonderland Ice Ballet." Based on the story "They Met in Chicago" by Karl Tunberg and Don Ettlinger. ♫I've Got a Date With a Dream; Could You Pass in Love; This May Be the Night; The All-American Swing; Plymouth University Song. **81m/B VHS.** Sonja Henie, Richard Greene, Joan Davis, Cesar Romero, Buddy Ebsen, Arthur Treacher, George Barbier, Gypsy Rose Lee; ***D:*** Roy Del Ruth; ***W:*** Harry Tugend, Jack Yellen.

My Magic Dog ✓✓ 1/2 **1997** Lucky is eight-year-old Toby's dog. Lucky happens to be invisible. Which turns out to be a good thing when evil Aunt Violet tries to steal Toby's inheritance. **98m/C VHS, DVD.** Leo Millbrook, Russ Tamblyn, John Phillip Law; ***D:*** John Putch. **VIDEO**

My Man Adam ✓✓ **1986 (R)** A dreamy, Mitty-esque high schooler falls in love with a girl (Daryl's auburn-haired sister, Page Hannah), and becomes ensnared in a real life crime, leaving his friend to bail him out. Typical boy-meets-girl, boy-gets-in-trouble yarn. **84m/C VHS.** Raphael Sbarge, Veronica Cartwright, Page Hannah, Larry B. Scott, Charlie Barnett, Arthur Pendleton, Dave Thomas; ***D:*** Roger L. Simon.

My Man Godfrey ✓✓✓✓ **1936** Spoiled rich girl Irene Bullock (Lombard) picks up someone she assumes is a bum (Powell) as part of a scavenger hunt and decides to keep him on as her family's butler. In the process, Godfrey teaches her about life, money, and happiness—and that everything is not as it seems. Top-notch screwball comedy defines the genre. Lombard is a stunner alongside the equally charming Powell. Watch for Jane Wyman as an extra in the party scene. From the novel by Eric Hatch. Remade in 1957 with June Allyson and David Niven. **95m/B VHS, DVD.** William Powell, Carole Lombard, Gail Patrick, Alice Brady, Mischa Auer, Eugene Pallette, Alan Mowbray, Franklin Pangborn, Jane Wyman; ***D:*** Gregory La Cava; ***W:*** Gregory La Cava, Morrie Ryskind; ***C:*** Ted Tetzlaff; ***M:*** Charles Previn. Natl. Film Reg. '99.

My Man Godfrey ✓✓ **1/2 1957** Inferior remake of the sophisticated screwball comedy of the '30s about a butler who brings a touch of the common man to the filthy rich. Niven stars as the butler and Allyson plays the rich girl, but nothing compares to the original roles created by Powell and Lombard. **92m/C VHS, DVD.** June Allyson, David Niven, Martha Hyer, Jessie Royce Landis, Robert Keith, Eva Gabor, Jay Robinson, Jeff Donnell; ***D:*** Henry Koster; ***W:*** Everett Freeman, Peter Berneis, William Bowers; ***C:*** William H. Daniels.

My Michael ✓✓✓ **1975** Sensitive adaptation of Amos Oz's novel set in Jerasalem in the late 1950s. A young woman is stifled by marriage and the conventions of her bourgeois life and her fantasies begin to take over. In Hebrew with English subtitles. **90m/C VHS.** *IS* Efrat Lavie, Oded Kotler; ***D:*** Dan Wolman.

My Mom's a Werewolf ✓ **1/2 1989 (PG)** An average suburban mother gets involved with a dashing stranger and soon, to her terror, begins to turn into a werewolf. Her daughter and companion must come up with a plan to regain dear, sweet mom. **90m/C VHS, DVD.** Susan Blakely, John Saxon, John Schuck, Katrina Caspary, Ruth Buzzi, Marilyn McCoo, Marcia Wallace, Diana Barrows; ***D:*** Michael Fischa; ***W:*** Mark Pirro; ***C:*** Bryan England; ***M:*** Dana Walden, Barry Fasman.

My Mom's New Boyfriend ✓ **1/2 2008 (PG-13)** Oh Meg, how embarrassing. Widowed Martha (Ryan) had been fat and depressed when her uptight FBI son Henry (Hanks) left for an undercover assignment. Returning to Shreveport three years later with his fiancee Emily (Blair) in tow, Henry discovers Martha—now Marty—has transformed herself into a high-spirited (albeit not-too-bright) hottie. She also has a suave but suspicious boyfriend, Tommy (Banderas), whom Henry learns is an international art thief. The Bureau wants Henry to set up surveillance and stop Tommy's latest heist, which means spying on his mom and learning way more than any son should about her personal life. **97m/C DVD.** Meg Ryan, Antonio Banderas, Colin Hanks, Selma Blair, Eli Danker, Enrico Colantoni; ***D:*** George Gallo; ***W:*** George Gallo; ***C:*** Michael Negrin; ***M:*** Chris Boardman. **VIDEO**

My Mother Likes Women ✓✓ *A mi madre le gustan las mujeres* **2002** Screwy, somewhat strained, Spanish comedy has successful, middle-aged classical pianist Sofia (Sarda) introducing her younger, female lover Eliska (Sirova), a shy Czech immigrant, to her three shocked daughters. Conservative, married Jimena (Pujalte) is the eldest, would-be writer Elvira (Watling) is the neurotic middle child, and the youngest, Sol (Abascal), is a breezy pop singer willing to follow her sisters' opinion. Which is that Eliska is a gold-digger and has to be gotten rid of. Czech and Spanish with subtitles. **96m/C DVD.** *SP* Leonor Watling, Rosa Maria Sarda, Silvia Abascal, Chisco Amado, Alex Angulo, Maria Pujalte, Eliska Sirova, Xabier Elorriaga, Aitor Mazo, Sergio Otegui; ***D:*** Ines Paris, Daniela Fejerman; ***W:*** Ines Paris, Daniela Fejerman; ***C:*** David Omedes; ***M:*** Juan Bardem.

My Mother's Castle ✓✓✓ **1/2** *Le Chateau de Ma Mere* **1991 (PG)** The second half of the two part film series based on the autobiography of Marcel Pagnol. Picking up where "My Father's Glory" left off, the family begins a series of vacations in a beautiful country home. Dynamically acted and tenderly directed, charming and suitable for the entire family. In French with English subtitles. **98m/C VHS, DVD.** *FR* Philippe Caubere, Nathalie Roussel, Didier Pain, Therese Liotard, Julien Ciamaca, Victorien Delmare; ***D:*** Yves Robert; ***M:*** Vladimir Cosma.

My Mother's Courage ✓✓ *Mutters Courage* **1995** Based on writer George Tabori's memoir of his Jewish mother, Elsa (Collins), who managed to escape deportation from Budapest in 1944. Her husband is in prison, her sons have left the country, but an unwavering Elsa remains to care for her asthmatic sister. Finally, she is detained and sent to the railyard to be deported—until she confronts a Nazi official and manages to obtain her release. German with subtitles. **88m/C VHS, DVD.** *GE GB* Pauline Collins, Ulrich Tukur, Natalie Morse; ***D:*** Michael Verhoeven; ***W:*** Michael Verhoeven; ***C:*** Michael Epp, Theo Bierkes; ***M:*** Julian Nott, Simon Verhoeven.

My Mother's Secret Life ✓ **1/2 1984** Dull drama focusing on a long-forgotten daughter who suddenly appears on her mother's doorstep and discovers that mom makes a living as a high-priced hooker. **100m/C VHS.** Loni Anderson, Paul Sorvino, Amanda Wyss, James Sutorius, Sandy McPeak; ***D:*** Robert Markowitz; ***M:*** Brad Fiedel.

My Mother's Smile ✓✓ *L'ora di religione; Il sorriso di mia madre* **2002** Controversial drama about religion and family. Artist—and atheist—Ernesto (Castellitto) is disdainful when he learns from a church emissary that his deceased mother (Conti) is a candidate for canonization. Ernesto loathed his pious, cold mother, who was murdered by his mentally unstable brother, and his attitude deepens the rift with his family, who are looking at monetary and social gains should the beatification take place. Both melodramatic and mystical, the narrative is also sometimes puzzling. Italian with subtitles. **103m/C DVD.** *IT* Sergio Castellitto, Jacqueline Lustig, Chiara Conti, Alberto Mondini, Gianni Schicchi, Maurizio Donadoni, Gigio Alberti; ***D:*** Marco Bellocchio; ***W:*** Marco Bellocchio; ***C:*** Pasquale Mari; ***M:*** Riccardo Giagni.

My Name Is Bill W. ✓✓✓ **1989** Woods gave an Emmy-winning performance as Bill Wilson, a successful stockbroker who loses everything in the 1929 crash. Bill turns to alcohol for solace and, after realizing his life is in a downward spiral, forms a support group with Dr. Bob (Garner), which will become Alcoholics Anonymous. **100m/C DVD.** James Woods, James Garner, JoBeth Williams, Gary Sinise, Fritz Weaver; ***D:*** Daniel Petrie; ***W:*** William G. Borchert; ***C:*** Neil Roach; ***M:*** Laurence Rosenthal. **TV**

My Name Is Bruce ✓ **1/2 2008 (R)** Cult movie fave Bruce Campbell mocks his career and B-movie hero status in this stupid horror comedy (which he also directed). The deadbeat drunk and womanizer (who's living in a trailer) is kidnapped by teen fan Jeff, who believes all those movie heroics. Seems while desecrating a cemetery, Jeff and his buds released a Chinese demon that's now terrorizing the mining town of Gold Lick, Oregon. Campbell thinks it's some prank until he comes face-to-demon. **86m/C DVD.** Bruce Campbell, Theodore (Ted) Raimi, Taylor Sharpe, Grace Thorsen, James J. Peck; ***D:*** Bruce Campbell; ***W:*** Mark Verheiden; ***C:*** Kurt Rauf; ***M:*** Joseph LoDuca.

My Name Is Ivan ✓✓✓ **1/2** *Ivan's Childhood; The Youngest Spy* **1962** Tarkovsky's first feature film is a vivid, wrenching portrait of a young Soviet boy surviving as a spy behind enemy lines during WWII. Technically stunning, heralding the coming of modern cinema's greatest formalist. In Russian with English subtitles. **84m/B VHS.** *RU* Kolya Burlyayev, Valentin Zubkov, Ye Zharikov, S. Krylov; ***D:*** Andrei Tarkovsky. Venice Film Fest. '62: Film.

My Name Is Joe ✓✓ **1998 (R)** Set in Glasgow, the Scots accents prove a distinct challenge in this story of working-class romance. Unemployed alcoholic Joe Kavanagh (Mullan) is 10 months sober and does odd jobs to get by, while coaching the local no-hoper football team. By chance he meets community health worker Sarah (Goodall) and the two are drawn together by their similar outlooks on life and begin a cautious romance. But Joe's loyalty to his mates and his efforts to get his friend Liam (McKay) out of trouble, helps to put a strain on the relationship. **105m/C VHS.** *GB* Peter Mullan, Louise Goodall, David McKay, Annemarie Kennedy, David Hayman, Gary Lewis, Loraine McIntosh; ***D:*** Ken Loach; ***W:*** Paul Laverty; ***C:*** Barry Ackroyd; ***M:*** George Fenton. Cannes '98: Actor (Mullan).

My Name is Modesty: A Modesty Blaise Adventure ✓ *Modesty Blaise: The Beginning* **2004 (R)** Based on the comic strip/novels by Peter O'Donnell, this cheap quickie (filmed in Romania) was turned out by Miramax so it could retain its rights to the potential franchise. So what we get is mighty Modesty's backstory as an orphan learning to survive in the war-torn Balkans, who winds up working at a small casino in Tangiers. Her criminal boss Louche is killed by bad guy Miklos, who wants what's in Louche's safe and doesn't care how he gets it. Modesty plays roulette with Miklos to save the day (and her fellow workers who are being held hostage). There's little action and Staden is a mannequin in a role that calls for beauty, brains, and butt-kicking. **77m/C DVD.**

My Name Is Nobody ✓✓ **1/2** *Il Mio Nome e Nessuno* **1974 (PG)** Fast-paced spaghetti-western wherein a cocky, soft-hearted gunfighter is sent to kill the famous, retired outlaw he reveres, but instead they band together. **115m/C VHS, DVD.** *IT* Henry Fonda, Terence Hill, R.G. Armstrong; ***D:*** Tonino Valerii; ***M:*** Ennio Morricone.

My Neighbor Totoro ✓✓ **1/2 1988 (G)** Rather gooey Japanese animated movie about Satsuki and her younger sister Lucy, whose new house in the country is filled with magic, including a friendly creature named Totoro. Totoro is a cuddly, if weird, mix of bear, owl, and seal, with whiskers and a gentle roar. He can fly, has a magic bus, and can only be seen by children. Naturally, every time the two girls get into mischief Totoro is there to rescue them. Dubbed into English. **76m/C VHS, DVD.** *JP* ***D:*** Hayao Miyazaki; ***W:*** Hayao Miyazaki; ***V:*** Frank Welker, Lea Salonga, Timothy Daly, Paul Butcher, Pat Carroll.

My New Gun ✓✓ **1/2 1992 (R)** Uneven, restless dark comedy about Debbie and Gerald Bender, yuppified suburban couple whose lives are disrupted by a gun. When their newly engaged friends get a gun, Gerry decides they need a gun as well. Debbie is very uncomfortable about having a weapon in the house and doesn't want anything to do with it. When mysterious neighbor LeGros steals the gun, it sets off a bizarre chain of events that culminate at the wedding of their friends. Impressive first effort for writer/director Cochran. **99m/C VHS, DVD.** Diane Lane, Stephen Collins, James LeGros, Tess Harper, Bill Raymond, Bruce Altman, Maddie Corman; ***D:*** Stacy Cochran; ***W:*** Stacy Cochran; ***M:*** Pat Irwin. Cannes '92: Film.

My New Partner ✓✓ **1/2** *Les Ripoux* **1984 (R)** Amiable French comedy in which cynical veteran cop is saddled with straight arrow rookie partner. French Cesars for best film and best director, but remember: They like Jerry Lewis too. In French with English subtitles. **106m/C VHS.** *FR* Philippe Noiret, Thierry Lhermitte, Regine, Grace de Capitani, Claude Brosset, Julien Guiomar; ***D:*** Claude Zidi; ***W:*** Claude Zidi; ***C:*** Jean-Jacques Tarbes; ***M:*** Francis Lai.

My Night at Maud's ✓✓✓ *My Night with Maud; Ma Nuit Chez Maud* **1969** Typically subtle Rohmer entry concerns quandary of upright fellow who finds himself drawn to comparatively carefree woman. Talky, somewhat arid film is one of director's Six Moral Tales. You'll either find it fascinating or wish you were watching "Rocky XXIV" instead. In French with English subtitles. **111m/B VHS, DVD.** *FR* Jean-Louis Trintignant, Francoise Fabian, Marie-Christine Barrault, Antoine Vitez; ***D:*** Eric Rohmer; ***W:*** Eric Rohmer; ***C:*** Nestor Almendros. N.Y. Film Critics '70: Screenplay; Natl. Soc. Film Critics '70: Cinematog., Screenplay.

My Old Man ✓✓ **1/2 1979** Plucky teen and her seedy horsetrainer father come together over important horse race. Oates makes this one worth watching on a slow evening. Based on a Hemingway story. **102m/C VHS, DVD.** Kristy McNichol, Warren Oates, Eileen Brennan; ***D:*** John Erman. **TV**

My Old Man's Place ✓ **1/2 1971 (R)** A veteran, with two war buddies and a girl, returns to his father's run-down farm, hoping to fix it up. Sexual tensions arise and violence erupts. **93m/C VHS.** Arthur Kennedy, Michael Moriarty, Mitchell Ryan, William Devane, Topo Swope; ***D:*** Edwin Sherin.

My One and Only ✓✓ **1/2 2009 (PG-13)** Well-tanned actor George Hamilton offers an affectionate memoir of his aging southern belle mother Ann (Zellweger) in Loncraine's sweetly indulgent 1950s-set family comedy. When Ann finds her husband Dan (Bacon) indulging in yet another infidelity she decides on divorce, packs ups teenaged sons George (Lerman) and Robbie (Rendall), and buys a baby blue Cadillac Eldorado convertible. The three head west, with stops along the way as Ann decides she needs a wealthy new husband but her quest increasingly frustrates George who wants some stability in his life. **108m/C DVD.** *US* Renee Zellweger, Logan Lerman, Kevin Bacon, Troy Garity, Mark Rendall, David Koechner, Eric McCormack, Christopher Noth, Nick Stahl, Steven Weber, Robin Weigert, Molly C. Quinn; ***D:*** Richard Loncraine; ***W:*** Charlie Peters; ***C:*** Marco Pontecorvo; ***M:*** Mark Isham.

My Other Husband ✓✓ **1/2** *Attention! Une Femme Peut en Cacher une Autre* **1985 (PG-13)** A woman has two husbands and families, one in Paris and one in Trouville, who eventually meet each other. Seems silly but grows into a sensitive and sad portrait of married life. In French with English subtitles. **110m/C VHS.** *FR* Miou-Miou, Rachid Ferrache, Roger Hanin; ***D:*** Georges Lautner.

My Outlaw Brother ✓✓ *My Brother, the Outlaw* **1951** A man travelling West to visit his brother in Mexico meets a Texas Ranger on the train. The man discovers that his brother is an outlaw, and teams up with the Ranger to capture him. Based on the novel "South of the Rio Grande" by Max Brand. **82m/B VHS, DVD.** Mickey Rooney, Wanda Hendrix, Robert Preston, Robert Stack, Jose Torvay; ***D:*** Elliott Nugent; ***W:*** Gene Fowler Jr.; ***C:*** Jose Ortiz Ramos.

My Own Country ✓✓ **1/2 1998 (R)** Abraham Verghese (Andrews) is an Indian immigrant who becomes the head of infectious diseases at the rural Johnson City, Tennessee hospital, where he had interned, in 1985. Considered an outsider, the doctor also finds himself dealing with the area's first AIDS cases, and his patients who are discriminated against. In fact, Verghese becomes so obsessed with their care that he neglects his own wife and children. Based on Verghese's memoirs. **106m/C VHS, DVD.** Naveen Andrews, Glenne Headly, Marisa Tomei, Hal Holbrook, Swoosie Kurtz, Sean Hewitt, William Webster; ***D:*** Mira Nair; ***W:*** Sooni Taraporevala, Jim Leonard Jr. **CABLE**

My Own Private Idaho ✓✓✓ **1991 (R)** Director Van Sant of "Drugstore Cowboy" returns to the underworld to examine another group of outsiders, this time young, homosexual hustlers. On the streets of Seattle, narcoleptic hustler Mike meets slumming rich boy Scott, and together they begin a search for Mike's lost mother, which leads them to Idaho and Italy. Stunning visuals, an elliptical plot, and a terrific performance by Phoenix highlight this search for love, the meaning of life, and power. Van Sant couples these activities with scenes from Shakespeare's "Henry IV" for a sometimes inscrutable, but always memorable film. Look for director Richert's Falstaff role as an aging chickenhawk. **105m/C VHS, DVD.** River Phoenix, Keanu Reeves, James Russo, William Richert,

Rodney Harvey, Michael Parker, Flea, Chiara Caselli, Udo Kier, Grace Zabriskie, Tom Troupe; ***D:*** Gus Van Sant; ***W:*** Gus Van Sant; ***C:*** John Campbell, Eric Alan Edwards. Ind. Spirit '92: Actor (Phoenix), Screenplay; Natl. Soc. Film Critics '91: Actor (Phoenix).

My Pal, the King 1/2 **1932** Amusing western with Rooney as the boy king of Ruritania, who's bored with his official duties. He meets Mix, the proprietor of a traveling wild west show which just happens to be performing in the country. Good thing too because Rooney has an evil prime minister who wants the throne for himself and kidnaps the kid. Naturally, Mix and his friends arrive to save him in the nick of time. **62m/B VHS.** Tom Mix, Mickey Rooney, Stuart Holmes, Paul Hurst, Noel Francis, James Kirkwood, Jim Thorpe, Clarissa Selwynne; ***D:*** Kurt Neumann; ***W:*** Jack Natteford, Thomas J. Crizer; ***C:*** Daniel B. Clark.

My Pal Trigger **1946** Roy is unjustly imprisoned in this high adventure on the plains. Better than usual script and direction makes this is one of the more entertaining of the singing cowboy's films. **79m/B VHS, DVD.** Roy Rogers, George "Gabby" Hayes, Dale Evans, Jack Holt; ***D:*** Frank McDonald.

My Pleasure Is My Business **1974 (R)** Cinematic autobiography of Xaveria Hollander, the world's most renowned prostitute of the '70s, and the zany occurrences which abound in her profession. **85m/C VHS.** *CA* Xaviera Hollander, Henry Ramer, Colin Fox, Ken Lynch, Jayne (Jane) Eastwood; ***D:*** Al Waxman.

My Reputation **1946** Dated melodrama. Jessica Drummond (Stanwyck) is an attractive young widow who's lonely and chafing under the restrictions of her overbearing long-widowed mother (Watson). While vacationing with friends, Jess meets Major Scott Landis (Brent) and sparks are struck, though Landis makes it clear he's not interested in marriage. Nevertheless, Jess sees him back in Chicago and gossip follows, thanks to some busybodies, though nothing has actually happened. Jess sets the record straight, Landis has a change of heart, and the ending is rather abrupt and sappy even for the times. Ah yes, the old "wave goodbye at the train station" scenario. Actually filmed in 1944. **94m/B DVD.** Barbara Stanwyck, George Brent, Warner Anderson, Lucile Watson, Eve Arden, John Ridgely, Jerome Cowan; ***D:*** Curtis Bernhardt; ***W:*** Catherine Turney; ***C:*** James Wong Howe; ***M:*** Max Steiner.

My Samurai 1/2 **1992 (R)** When young Peter McCrea witnesses a gang murder he turns to his martial-arts expert friend Young Park to help him. On the run from both the gang and the police Peter learns self-defense and the courage to face his fears. **87m/C VHS.** Julian Lee, Mako, Terry O'Quinn, Bubba Smith, Jim Turner, Carlos Palomino, John Kallo; ***D:*** Fred Dresch.

My Sassy Girl 1/2 **2008 (PG-13)** This remake of the 2001 Korean hit isn't sassy at all. Hapless Midwestern Charlie (Bradford) has his life planned out until he falls in love with free-spirited beauty Jordan (Cuthbert), who's going to break his heart. Jordan's keeping secrets and Charlie has to convince her not only to trust him but to believe that it's their destiny to be together. **95m/C DVD.** Jesse Bradford, Elisha Cuthbert, Joanna Gleason, Austin Basis, William Abadie; ***D:*** Yann Samuell; ***W:*** Victor Levin; ***C:*** Eric Schmidt; ***M:*** David Kitay.

My Science Project 1/2 **1985 (PG)** Teenager Stockwell stumbles across a crystal sphere with a funky light. Unaware that it is an alien time-travel device, he takes it to school to use as a science project in a last-ditch effort to avoid failing his class. Chaos follows and Stockwell and his chums find themselves battling gladiators, mutants, and dinosaurs. Plenty of special effects and a likeable enough, dumb teenage flick. **94m/C VHS, DVD.** John Stockwell, Danielle von Zerneck, Fisher Stevens, Raphael Sbarge, Richard Masur, Barry Corbin, Ann Wedgeworth, Dennis Hopper, Candace Silvers, Beau Dremann, Pat Simmons, Pamela Springsteen; ***D:*** Jonathan Betuel; ***W:*** Jonathan Betuel; ***C:*** David M. Walsh; ***M:*** Peter Bernstein.

My Sex Life... Or How I Got into an Argument *Ma Vie Sexuelle...Comment Je Me Suis Dispute* **1996** Paul (Amalric) is unhappy personally and professionally. He's a bored grad student/assistant professor of philosophy and breaking up with lover of ten years, Esther (Devos). Soon Paul's romancing other women, one of whom, Sylvia (Denicourt), is already involved with Paul's best friend Nathan (Salinger). Very talky and Frenchly intellectual. French with subtitles. **178m/C VHS, DVD.** *FR* Mathieu Amalric, Marianne (Cuau) Denicourt, Emmanuelle Devos, Emmanuel Salinger, Jeanne Balibar, Michel Vuillermoz; ***D:*** Arnaud Desplechin; ***W:*** Arnaud Desplechin, Emmanuel Bourdieu; ***C:*** Eric Gautier; ***M:*** Krishna Levy.

My Side of the Mountain 1/2 **1969 (G)** A 13-year-old boy decides to emulate his idol, Henry David Thoreau, and gives up his home and his family to live in the Canadian mountains. **100m/C VHS, DVD.** *CA* Teddy Eccles, Theodore Bikel; ***D:*** James B. Clark.

My Sister Eileen 1/2 **1942** Sisters Ruth (Russell) and Eileen (Blair) leave small-town Ohio for a basement apartment in Greenwich Village with a shady landlord and crazy neighbors. Aspiring writer Ruth tries to sell stories to magazine editor Baker (Aherne) while ditzy aspiring actress Eileen just attracts every man in sight. Based on a series of autobiographical magazine articles by Ruth McKenney, adapted into a Broadway play. The Three Stooges have cameos as subway drillers. **96m/B DVD.** Rosalind Russell, Janet Blair, Brian Aherne, George Tobias, Allyn Joslyn, Elizabeth Patterson, Grant Mitchell, June Havoc, Richard Quine, Clyde Fillmore, Gordon Jones; ***D:*** Alexander Hall; ***W:*** Jerome Chodorov, Joseph Fields; ***C:*** Joseph Walker.

My Sister Eileen **1955** Ruth and Eileen are two small-town Ohio sisters who move to Manhattan seeking excitement. They live in a basement apartment in Greenwich Village with an assortment of oddball tenants as they pursue success and romance. Everyone is daffy and charming, as is the film. Fun, but unmemorable songs, however the terrific choreography is by Fosse, who also appears as one sister's suitor. Remake of a 1942 film which was based on a Broadway play, which was based on a series of autobiographical stories published in the New Yorker. The play was later turned into a Broadway musical known as "Wonderful Town," which has nothing to do with this version of the original stories. ♫ Give Me a Band and My Baby; It's Bigger Than You and Me; There's Nothing Like Love; As Soon As They See Eileen; I'm Great; Conga; Atmosphere. **108m/C VHS, DVD.** Janet Leigh, Betty Garrett, Jack Lemmon, Bob Fosse, Kurt Kasznar, Dick York, Lucy Marlow, Tommy (Thomas) Rall, Barbara Brown, Horace McMahon; ***D:*** Richard Quine; ***W:*** Blake Edwards, Richard Quine; ***M:*** Jule Styne.

My Sister, My Love 1/2 *The Cage; The Mafu Cage* **1978 (R)** Odd tale of two sisters' incestuous relationship and what happens when one of them takes another lover. The cage of the alternate titles refers to the place where their pet apes are kept and seems to symbolize the confining nature of their life together. **102m/C VHS, DVD.** Lee Grant, Carol Kane, Will Geer, James Olson; ***D:*** Karen Arthur.

My Sister's Keeper 1/2 **2002** Christina (Bates) and her sister Judy (Perkins) couldn't have more different lives. Christina struggles to cope with her schizophrenia and her dependence on others while Judy is a work-obsessed art editor in New York. When their mother Helen (Redgrave) dies, Judy is suddenly responsible for Christina's care and they must struggle to accept and support one another. Based on the memoir by Margaret Moorman. **98m/C VHS, DVD.** Kathy Bates, Elizabeth Perkins, Lynn Redgrave, Bobby Harwell, Kimberly J. Brown, Hallee Hirsh, Kathleen Wilhoite, Jascha Washington; ***D:*** Ron Lagomarsino; ***W:*** Susan Tarr; ***C:*** Lloyd Ahern II; ***M:*** Lawrence Shragge. **TV**

My Sister's Keeper **2009 (PG-13)** When their beloved daughter Kate is diagnosed with a rare form of leukemia, Sara (Diaz) and Brian (Patric) conceive another child to be a genetic match to save Kate's life. After undergoing countless procedures throughout the years, rebellious teen Anna (Breslin) decides that, despite her love for her sister (Vassilieva), she's had enough. So she goes to court to become an emancipated minor and make her own decisions about her body. Based on the novel by Jodi Picoult. **m/C DVD.** *US* Cameron Diaz, Abigail Breslin, Sofia Vassilieva, Jason Patrick, Alec Baldwin, Nick Cassavetes, Evan Ellingson; ***D:*** Jeremy Leven; ***W:*** Jeremy Leven; ***C:*** Caleb Deschanel; ***M:*** Aaron Zigman.

My Son, My Son 1/2 **1940** The spoiled son (Hayward) of a successful businessman (Aherne) doesn't think twice about making everyone miserable in his quest to get everything he wants. He even goes as far as trying to steal his dad's new bride. When world war comes, he has a chance to redeem himself. Melodrama is kept from sinking to overwrought soap opera by Hayward and Aherne. **115m/B VHS.** Louis Hayward, Brian Aherne, Scotty Beckett, Lionel Belmore, Laraine Day, Madeleine Carroll, Henry Hull, Howard Davies, Pat Flaherty, Leyland Hodgson, Josephine Hutchinson, Sophie Stewart, Stanley Logan; ***D:*** Charles Vidor; ***W:*** Lenore Coffee; ***C:*** Harry Stradling Sr.

My Son the Fanatic **1997 (R)** Pakistani immigrant Parvez (Puri) has been driving a cab in Bradford, England and trying to fit in his new country for 25 years. He ekes out a living driving prostitutes around town, which leads to a relationship with hooker Bettina (Griffiths). His working-class life is disrupted when Parvez realizes his son, Farid (Kurtha) is exploring his cultural roots by turning to Islamic fundamentalism. Moral and religious tensions lead to a climactic conflict between father and son. **86m/C VHS, DVD.** *GB* Om Puri, Rachel Griffiths, Stellan Skarsgard, Akbar Kurtha; ***D:*** Udayan Prasad; ***W:*** Hanif Kureishi; ***C:*** Alan Almond; ***M:*** Stephen Warbeck.

My Son, the Vampire 1/2 *Old Mother Riley Meets the Vampire; The Vampire and the Robot; Vampire Over London; Mother Riley Meets the Vampire* **1952** Last of Britain's Old Mother Riley series in which Lucan plays the Irish housekeeper in drag. Lugosi is a crazed scientist who thinks he's a vampire and wants to take over the world with his giant robot. Mother Riley interferes. Theme song by Alan Sherman. **72m/B VHS, DVD.** *GB* Bela Lugosi, Arthur Lucan, Dora Bryan, Richard Wattis; ***D:*** John Gilling; ***W:*** Val Valentine; ***C:*** Stanley Pavey.

My Song Goes Round the World 1/2 **1934** Chronicles the romantic foibles of a singing trio and the one girl they decide they all love. **68m/B VHS.** Joseph Schmidt, John Loder, Charlotte Ander; ***D:*** Richard Oswald.

My Stepmother Is an Alien **1988 (PG-13)** When eccentric physicist Aykroyd sends a message beam to another galaxy on a stormy night, the last thing he expects is a visit from beautiful alien Basinger. Unfortunately, he does not realize that this gorgeous blonde is an alien and he continues to court her despite her rather odd habits. Only the daughter seems to notice the strange goings on, and her dad ignores her warnings, enabling Basinger's evil sidekick to continue in its plot to take over the Earth. **108m/C VHS, DVD.** Dan Aykroyd, Kim Basinger, Jon Lovitz, Alyson Hannigan, Joseph Maher, Seth Green, Wesley Mann, Adrian Sparks, Juliette Lewis, Tanya Fenmore; ***D:*** Richard Benjamin; ***W:*** Jerico Stone, Herschel Weingrod, Timothy Harris, Jonathan Reynolds; ***C:*** Richard H. Kline; ***M:*** Alan Silvestri.

My Summer of Love 1/2 **2005 (R)** Teenaged Mona (Press) lives with her ex-con brother, Phil (Considine), over the closed family pub in a dull Yorkshire village. Phil has become a born-again Christian, much to Mona's confusion, and she turns for companionship to wealthy Tamsin (Blunt), who's summering at the family mansion. They soon indulge in a hothouse romance that's part crush, part loneliness, and part boredom. The young women have certain secrets and Tamsin has a streak of cruelty. A dangerous and unsettling atmosphere prevails, along with satisfying performances. Based on the novel by Helen Cross. **85m/C DVD.** *GB* Emily Blunt, Paddy Considine, Nathalie Press, Dean Andrews, Michelle Byrne, Paul Antony-Barber, Lynette Edwards, Kathryn Sumner; ***D:*** Pawel Pawlikowski; ***W:*** Pawel Pawlikowski, Michael Wynne; ***C:*** Ryszard Lenczewski; ***M:*** Alison Goldfrapp, Will Gregory.

My Summer Story 1/2 *It Runs in the Family* **1994 (PG)** Humorist Shepherd and director Clark re-team for another period family comedy in the tradition of their first collaboration, "A Christmas Story," now a video classic. This time the Parkers find themselves battling their crazy new neighbors, the Bumpus family, Ralphie (Kieran Culkin) has troubles with a neighborhood bully and tries to bond with his dad (Grodin) while fishing, and mom (Steenburgen) goes loopy over gravy boats. Charming family fun. Based on Shepherd's novels "In God We Trust, All Others Pay Cash" and "Wanda Hickey's Night of Golden Memories and Other Disasters." **85m/C VHS, DVD.** Charles Grodin, Mary Steenburgen, Kieran Culkin, Chris Culkin, Al Mancini, Troy Evans, Glenn Shadix, Dick O'Neill, Wayne Grace; ***D:*** Bob (Benjamin) Clark; ***W:*** Jean Shepherd, Bob (Benjamin) Clark, Leigh Brown; ***C:*** Stephen M. Katz; ***M:*** Paul Zaza; ***Nar:*** Jean Shepherd.

My Super Ex-Girlfriend **2006 (PG-13)** "Fatal Attraction" meets "Wonder Woman" in this weak effort from veteran director Ivan Reitman. Uma Thurman plays the dual role of Jenny Johnson, Manhattan art curator by day, and G-Girl, crime-fighting superheroine at night, who, unfortunately for her unsuspecting new boyfriend, Matt (Luke Wilson), is super-insecure as well. When Matt makes the mistake of dumping the possessive Jenny, she unleashes the fury of her powers on him. Reitman doesn't know what he wants—comedy, girl-power statement, relationship/date movie—and fails on all fronts as a result. **96m/C DVD.** *US* Uma Thurman, Luke Wilson, Anna Faris, Rainn Wilson, Eddie Izzard, Wanda Sykes, Mark Consuelos; ***D:*** Ivan Reitman; ***W:*** Don Payne; ***C:*** Don Burgess; ***M:*** Teddy Castellucci.

My Sweet Charlie 1/2 **1970** Unwed, pregnant white woman hides out with black lawyer in backwater Texas. Better than it sounds, with nice performances by Duke and Freeman. **97m/C VHS.** Patty Duke, Al Freeman Jr., Ford Rainey, William Hardy, Chris Wilson, Archie Moore, Noble Willingham; ***D:*** Lamont Johnson. **TV**

My Sweet Little Village 1/2 *Vesnicko Ma Strediskova* **1986** Gentle comedy set in a rural village and dealing with everyday events, including a romantic teenager who develops a crush on a schoolteacher, an adulterous wife and her boyfriend, the accident-prone doctor, a Laurel and Hardy duo of truck drivers, and others. Czech with subtitles. **100m/C VHS.** *CZ* Rudolf Hrusinsky, Janos Ban, Marian Labuda, Milena Dvorska, Ladislav Zupanic, Petr Cepek; ***D:*** Jiri Menzel; ***W:*** Zdenek Sverak; ***C:*** Jaromir Sofr; ***M:*** Jiri Sust.

My Sweet Suicide **1998** Very low-budget comedy about staging the perfect suicide. Depressed Kevin (Aldrich) can't even manage to kill himself. He confides his dilemma to eccentric bookstore clerk Thompson, who agrees to help him out. **78m/C VHS.** Matthew Aldrich, Michelle Leigh Thompson, Eric Wheeler; ***D:*** David Michael Flanagan; ***W:*** David Michael Flanagan.

My Sweet Victim *Murder: By Reason of Insanity* **1985** A young couple who recently moved to the United States from Poland try to make a go of their own business. The business fails, and so does their marriage. Will it end in murder? **92m/C VHS.** Candice Bergen, Jurgen Prochnow, Hector Elizondo, Eli Wallach, Wendy Crewson; ***D:*** Anthony Page; ***W:*** Scott Swanton; ***C:*** Alexander Grusynski; ***M:*** John Cacavas.

My Teacher Ate My Homework *Shadow Zone: My Teacher Ate My Homework* **1998 (PG)** Jesse is convinced that his teacher Mrs. Fink has it in for him. When he finds a doll that looks just like her, Jesse can live out all his revenge fantasies but bad things start happening when the doll takes on an attitude of its own. Based on J.R. Black's "Shadowzone" books. **91m/C VHS, DVD.** *CA* MacKenzie Gray, Gregory Edward Smith, Shelley Duvall, Dara Perlmutter, Tim Progosh, Sheila McCarthy, Edwin Hodge, Dan Warry-Smith, Diana Theodore, John Neville, Karen Robinson, Margot Kidder, Damon D'Oliveira; ***D:*** Stephen Williams; ***W:*** Garfield

Reeves-Stevens, Judith Reeves-Stevens; ***C:*** Curtis Petersen; ***M:*** John McCarthy. **VIDEO**

My Teacher's Wife 🦴🦴 ½ **1995 (R)** High-schooler London has big college plans, which won't get anywhere if he doesn't pass math. So he asks Carrere to tutor him, only the problems they study become more personal. **90m/C VHS, DVD.** Tia Carrere, Jason London, Christopher McDonald, Leslie Lyles, Zak Orth, Jeffrey Tambor; ***D:*** Bruce Leddy; ***W:*** Bruce Leddy, Seth Greenland; ***C:*** Zoltan David; ***M:*** Kevin Gilbert. **VIDEO**

My Therapist WOOF! **1984** A sex therapist's boyfriend cannot bear the thought of her having intercourse with other men as part of her work. Soft core. **81m/C VHS.** Marilyn Chambers; ***D:*** Gary Legon.

My Tutor 🦴 ½ **1982 (R)** When a high school student is in danger of flunking French, his parents hire a private tutor to help him learn the lessons. It becomes clear that his studies will involve many more subjects, however. Standard teen sex comedy. **97m/C VHS, DVD.** Caren Kaye, Matt Lattanzi, Kevin McCarthy, Clark Brandon, Bruce Bauer, Arlene Golonka, Crispin Glover, Shelley Taylor Morgan, Amber Denyse Austin, Francesca "Kitten" Natividad, Jewel Shepard, Marilyn Tokuda; ***D:*** George Bowers; ***W:*** Joe Roberts; ***C:*** Mac Ahlberg; ***M:*** Webster Lewis.

My Twentieth Century 🦴🦴🦴 *Az en XX. Szazadom* **1990** This quirky gem of a movie is a charming, sentimental journey through the early 1900s. Twins Dora and Lili are separated in early childhood. They reunite as grown, very different women on the Orient Express after they both (unknowingly) have sex with the same man. Dora is a sex kitten, while Lili is a radical equipped with explosives. When the two sisters come together, they both lose their destructive, dependent selves (Dora on men, Lili on politics) and become independent women. Lots of sidelights and subplots that are sure to amuse the viewer. In Hungarian with English subtitles. **104m/B VHS.** *HU CA* Dortha Segda, Oleg (Yankovsky) Jankowsky, Peter Andorai, Gabor Mate, Paulus Manker, Laszlo Vidovszky; ***D:*** Ildiko Enyedi; ***W:*** Ildiko Enyedi.

My Uncle Silas 🦴🦴🦴 **2001** Finney certainly has fun in the title role as an aging reprobate (with an eye for the ladies) who teaches his 10-year-old grandnephew Edward (Prospero) how to enjoy life. Based on five short stories by H.E. Bates and set during a rural English summer in the early 1900s. **120m/C VHS.** *GB* Albert Finney, Charlotte Rampling, Joe Prospero, Annabelle Apsion; ***D:*** Philip Saville; ***C:*** John Kenway. **TV**

My Uncle: The Alien 🦴🦴 ½ **1996 (PG)** Kelly, President Sullivan's teenaged daughter, travels to L.A. to visit a children's shelter at Christmas. When she finds out the shelter needs money to stay open, she eludes the Secret Service and hatches a plan to raise the funds. But she does have someone watching out for her—no, not a guardian angel, a guardian alien! **90m/C VHS, DVD.** Hailey Foster; ***D:*** Henri Charr.

My Universities 🦴🦴🦴 **1940** In the final part of Donskoi's trilogy on Maxim Gorky, Gorky is a young man at university who is introduced to radical politics by several liberal intellectuals. He makes his first attempts at writing and joins the revolution as he leaves his painful past behind. In Russian with English subtitles. Preceded by "My Childhood" and "My Apprenticeship." **100m/C VHS.** *RU* Nikolai Valbert, Stepan Kayukov, Nikolai Dorokin, Nikolai Plotnikov; ***D:*** Mark Donskoi; ***W:*** Mark Donskoi, Ilya Gruzdev; ***C:*** Pyotr Yermolov; ***M:*** Lev Shvarts.

My Very Best Friend 🦴🦴 **1996 (PG)** Former model Dana Griffin (Smith) likes the good life and seems to have latched onto the prize when a multi-millionaire (Mason) proposes marriage. But Dana has a nasty habit of lying and when things fall, she turns to her oldest friend, Barbara (Eikenberry), to help rebuild her life. But instead of rebuilding her own life, Dana decides she'd just rather take over Barbara's. **92m/C VHS.** Jaclyn Smith, Jill Eikenberry, Tom Mason, Tom Irwin, Mary Kay Place, Garwin Sanford, Robert Lewis, Beverley Elliott; ***D:*** Joyce Chopra; ***W:*** John Robert Bensink; ***C:*** James Glennon; ***M:*** Patrick Williams. **TV**

My Wicked, Wicked Ways 🦴🦴 ½ **1984** Cleverly cast, low-budget drama based on the autobiography of Errol Flynn. **95m/C VHS.** Duncan Regehr, Barbara Hershey, Hal Linden, Darren McGavin; ***D:*** Don Taylor. **TV**

My Wife is an Actress 🦴🦴 ½ *Ma Femme est une Actrice* **2001 (R)** Yvan (Attal) is a TV sports journalist married to famous actress Charlotte (Gainsbourg). He's irritated by the public demands celebrity makes on their relationship and jealous of her co-stars when she films sex scenes. Charlotte's off to London for her latest project, with a courtly and seductive older leading man, John (Stamp). Charlotte can't understand her husband's neuroses and Yvan's fretting increases. Self-mocking and frequently charming although the sub-plot concerning Yvan's pregnant sister is an annoying distraction. French with subtitles. **93m/C VHS, DVD.** *FR* Yvan Attal, Charlotte Gainsbourg, Terence Stamp, Noemie Lvovsky, Ludivine Sagnier, Keith Allen, Lionel Abelanski, Laurent Bateau, Jo McInnes; ***D:*** Yvan Attal; ***W:*** Yvan Attal; ***C:*** Remy Chevrin.

My Wonderful Life 🦴 **1990 (R)** Softcore gristle about a beautiful tramp climbing the social ladder via the boudoir. **107m/C VHS.** *IT* Pierre Cosso, Jean Rochefort, Massimo Venturiello, Carol Alt, Elliott Gould; ***D:*** Carlo Vanzina.

My Zinc Bed 🦴🦴 **2008** Three-character piece adapted by David Hare from his play. Recovering alcoholic Paul (Considine) is unexpectedly befriended by wealthy Victor (Pryce), who offers him a job. Elsa (Thurman), Victor's younger wife, is also a drinker but resists admitting it and going to AA as Paul does. Over the summer, a romantic triangle develops, leading to examinations of friendship and fidelity. **75m/C DVD.** *GB* Jonathan Pryce, Uma Thurman, Paddy Considine; ***D:*** Anthony Page; ***W:*** David Hare; ***C:*** Brian Tufano; ***M:*** Simon Boswell. **CABLE**

Myra Breckinridge WOOF! **1970 (R)** A tasteless version of the Gore Vidal novel. An alleged satire of a film critic who undergoes a sex change operation and then plots the destruction of the American male movie star stereotype. Created an outcry from all sides, and hung out to dry by studio where it's reportedly still blowing in the wind. **94m/C VHS, DVD.** Mae West, John Huston, Raquel Welch, Rex Reed, Farrah Fawcett, Jim Backus, John Carradine, Andy Devine, Tom Selleck; ***D:*** Michael Sarne; ***W:*** Michael Sarne, David Giler; ***C:*** Richard Moore; ***M:*** Lionel Newman.

Myrt and Marge 🦴 ½ **1933** Vail and daughter Dameral repeat their radio serial roles as sisters Myrt Minter and Marge Spear, two chorus girls in a popular Broadway show. The Three Stooges provide some laughs. **62m/B VHS.** Myrtle Vail, Eddie Foy Jr., Trixie Friganza, Ted Healy, Donna Dameral, Curly Howard, Moe Howard, Larry Fine; ***D:*** Al Boasberg; ***W:*** Al Boasberg, Beatrice Banyard; ***C:*** Joseph Valentine.

The Mysterians 🦴🦴 ½ *Earth Defense Forces; Chikyu Boelgun* **1958** A race of gigantic scientific intellects from a doomed planet attempts to conquer Earth. They want to rebuild their race by reproducing with earth women. Earth fights back. From the director of "Godzilla." Dubbed in English from Japanese. **85m/C VHS, DVD.** *JP* Kenji Sahara, Yumi Shirakawa, Takashi Shimura; ***D:*** Inoshiro Honda.

Mysteries 🦴 ½ **1984** A rich tourist becomes obsessed by a beautiful local girl. As his obsession grows, his behavior becomes stranger. Interesting and well-acted. The film is an adaptation of the famous love story by Nobel-laureate Knut Hamsun. Suffers from poor dubbing. **100m/C VHS.** Rutger Hauer, Sylvia Kristel, David Rappaport, Rita Tushingham; ***D:*** Paul de Lussanet.

The Mysteries of Pittsburgh 🦴 **2008 (R)** Poor adaptation of Michael Chabon's 1988 debut novel that takes considerable liberties with the story, making it conventional and dull. Wishy-washy Art Bechstein (Foster) prefers a less criminal life than going to work for his mobster father Joe (Nolte), so he decides to remain in Pittsburgh after college graduation in order to study for his stockbroker's exam (film is set in the '80s). He gets a job working at a bookstore, where his manager Phlox (Suvari) uses Art for sex, and then meets aspiring musician Jane (Miller) at a party. She is already involved with bad boy Cleveland (Sarsgaard), who befriends Art who is then drawn into Cleveland's gambling problems and criminal activities. **95m/C DVD.** Jon Foster, Sienna Miller, Peter Sarsgaard, Mena Suvari, Nick Nolte, Omid Abtahi; ***D:*** Rawson Marshall Thurber; ***W:*** Rawson Marshall Thurber; ***C:*** Michael Barrett; ***M:*** Theodore Shapiro.

Mysterious Desperado 🦴 ½ **1949** Young man, about to inherit a large estate, is framed on a murder charge by land grabbers. **61m/B VHS, DVD.** Tim Holt, Richard Martin, Edward Norris, Movita, Frank Wilcox, William Tannen, Robert "Bob" Livingston, Robert B. Williams; ***D:*** Lesley Selander; ***W:*** Norman Houston; ***C:*** Nicholas Musuraca; ***M:*** Paul Sawtell.

The Mysterious Dr. Fu Manchu 🦴 ½ **1929** Early talkie with Oland starring as evil Fu Manchu. Fu vows vengeance on the English Petrie family, whom he holds responsible for the deaths of his loved ones during the Boxer Rebellion. He hypnotizes sweet Lia (Arthur) to do his fiendish bidding but the Petries are warned by Scotland Yard to be on the lookout. Based on the novel by Sax Rohmer. Followed by "The Return of Dr. Fu Manchu." **80m/B VHS.** Warner Oland, Jean Arthur, O.P. Heggie, William Austin, Claude King; ***D:*** Rowland V. Lee; ***W:*** Lloyd Corrigan, Florence Ryerson; ***C:*** Harry Fischbeck.

Mysterious Doctor Satan 🦴🦴 **1940** A mad satanic scientist builds an army of mechanical robots to rob and terrorize the nation. In 15 episodes. **250m/B VHS.** William "Billy" Newell, C. Montague Shaw, Dorothy Herbert, Charles Trowbridge, Eduardo Ciannelli, Robert Wilcox, Ella Neal; ***D:*** John English, William Witney; ***W:*** Frank (Franklyn) Adreon, Joseph Poland, Barney A. Sarecky; ***C:*** William Nobles.

Mysterious Island 🦴🦴🦴 ½ **1961** Exhilirating sci-fi classic adapted from Jules Verne's novel about escaping Civil War soldiers who go up in Verne balloon and come down on a Pacific island populated by giant animals. They also encounter two shipwrecked English ladies, pirates, and Captain Nemo (and his sub). Top-rate special effects by master Ray Harryhausen. **101m/C VHS, DVD.** *GB* Michael Craig, Joan Greenwood, Michael Callan, Gary Merrill, Herbert Lom, Beth Rogan, Percy Herbert, Dan Jackson, Nigel Green; ***D:*** Cy Endfield; ***W:*** John Prebble, Daniel Ullman, Crane Wilbur; ***C:*** Wilkie Cooper; ***M:*** Bernard Herrmann.

Mysterious Island of Beautiful Women 🦴 **1979** A male sextet is stranded on a South Sea island, where they must endure the trials of an angry tribe of conveniently bikini-clad women. **100m/C VHS, DVD.** Jamie Lyn Bauer, Jayne Kennedy, Kathryn Davis, Deborah Shelton, Susie Coelho, Peter Lawford, Steven Keats, Clint Walker; ***D:*** Joseph Pevney.

Mysterious Jane 🦴 **1981** Amid soft-focus nudity, a husband and his lover conspire to institutionalize his wife. **90m/C VHS.** Amber Lee, Sandy Carey; ***D:*** Harry Flynn.

The Mysterious Lady 🦴🦴 ½ **1928** Pre-Ninotchka Garbo plays Russian spy who betrays her mother country because she does not want to be alone. **99m/B VHS, DVD.** Greta Garbo, Conrad Nagel, Gustav von Seyffertitz, Richard Alexander, Albert Pollet, Edward Connelly; ***C:*** William H. Daniels.

The Mysterious Magician 🦴🦴 ½ **1965** Entertaining suspense story of the mad murderer known as "The Wizard," who was thought by Scotland Yard to be dead, but the current murderwave in London suggests otherwise. Based on an Edgar Wallace story. **95m/C VHS.** *GE* Joachim Fuchsberger, Eddi Arent, Sophie Hardy, Karl John, Heinz Drache; ***D:*** Alfred Vohrer.

Mysterious Mr. Moto 🦴🦴 **1938** Mr. Moto (Lorre) poses as a criminal to escape with killer Paul Brissac (Ames) from Devil's Island. Brissac is part of a gang of assassins, operating out of London, and Moto is not only after their leader but must protect industrialist Anton Darvak (Wilcoxon) who is being blackmailed by the gang. 5th in the series. **63m/B DVD.** Peter Lorre, Leon Ames, Henry Wilcoxon, Mary Maguire, Erik Rhodes, Harold Huber, Frederick Vogeding; ***D:*** Norman Foster; ***W:*** Norman Foster, Philip MacDonald; ***C:*** Virgil Miller; ***M:*** Samuel Kaylin.

Mysterious Mr. Nicholson 🦴 ½ **1947** A burglar (Hulme) is suspected of murder and discovers he has a doppelganger who's actually committed the crime. So he teams up with messenger Peggy (Osmond) to prove his innocence. **78m/B DVD.** *GB* Anthony Hulme, Andy Laurence, Douglas Day Stewart, Lesley Osmond, Frank Hawkins; ***D:*** Oswald Mitchell; ***W:*** Oswald Mitchell, Frances Miller; ***C:*** S.D. Onions; ***M:*** Isaac Snoek.

Mysterious Mr. Wong 🦴 ½ **1935** The Thirteen Coins of Confucius put San Francisco's Chinatown in a state of terror until Mr. Wong arrives. **56m/B VHS, DVD.** Bela Lugosi, Arline Judge, Wallace Ford, E. Alyn (Fred) Warren, Lotus Long; ***D:*** William Nigh; ***W:*** Nina Howatt; ***C:*** Harry Neumann.

The Mysterious Rider 🦴🦴 ½ *The Fighting Phantom* **1933** A cowboy tries to prevent unscrupulous homesteaders from cheating farmers out of their land. **59m/B VHS, DVD.** Kent Taylor, Lona Andre, Gail Patrick, Warren Hymer, Berton Churchill; ***D:*** Fred Allen.

The Mysterious Rider 🦴 ½ *Mark of the Avenger* **1938** A man framed for murder must help innocent homesteaders from being cheated out of their land. **75m/B VHS.** Douglass Dumbrille, Sidney Toler, Russell Hayden, Charlotte Field; ***D:*** Lesley Selander.

The Mysterious Rider 🦴🦴 **1942** Routine oater has Crabbe and St. John helping a couple of kids protect their inheritance. **56m/B VHS.** Buster Crabbe, Al "Fuzzy" St. John, Caroline Burke, John Merton, Kermit Maynard, Jack Ingram, Charles "Slim" Whitaker; ***D:*** Sam Newfield.

Mysterious Skin 🦴🦴🦴 **2004 (NC-17)** As 8-year-olds in 1981, clumsy Brian and athletic Neil both play for the same Kansas Little League team. They have something else in common; both are sexually abused by their Coach (Sage). By 1991, Neil (Gordon-Levitt) has become a reckless hustler—first in his dull hometown and later in New York, where he's followed his best friend Wendy (Trachtenberg). Brian (Corbet) has grown into an awkward misfit who (having suppressed the abuse) believes he was abducted and experimented upon by aliens. He has a vague memory of Neil and decides to track the other teen down to find out what really happened—a confrontation that takes place in a challenging scene set on Christmas Eve. Araki displays a fearless candor in showing the damage that was wrought without exploiting his inflammatory subject matter Both leads give strong, gut-wrenching performances. Based on the 1995 novel by Scott Heims. **103m/C DVD.** *US* Brady Corbet, Joseph Gordon-Levitt, Michelle Trachtenberg, Elisabeth Shue, Jeff(rey) Licon, Mary Lynn Rajskub, Chris Mulkey, Richard Riehle, Lisa Long, Billy Drago, William Sage, George Webster, Chase Ellison; ***D:*** Gregg Araki; ***W:*** Gregg Araki; ***C:*** Steve Gainer; ***M:*** Harold Budd, Robin Guthrie.

The Mysterious Stranger 🦴🦴 **1982** Printer's apprentice is given to bouts of daydreaming about a magic castle in Austria. Based on Twain tale. **89m/C VHS.** Chris Makepeace, Lance Kerwin, Fred Gwynne; ***D:*** Peter H. Hunt.

Mysterious Two 🦴🦴 ½ **1982** Two aliens visit the Earth in an effort to enlist converts to travel the universe with them. **100m/C VHS, DVD.** John Forsythe, Priscilla Pointer, Noah Beery Jr., Vic Tayback, James Stephens, Karen Werner, Robert Englund, Robert Pine; ***D:*** Gary Sherman.

Mystery, Alaska 🦴🦴 ½ **1999 (R)** Amiable sports comedy that plays like a TV movie (with a little more sex and language). Journalist and ex-local Charles Danner (Azaria) does a Sports Illustrated feature on his hometown's weekly cutthroat hockey game. Danner's story draws NHL interest and, for a publicity stunt, the New York Rangers fly in for an exhibition game. This leads to hurt feelings since aging team captain (and local sheriff) John Biebe (Crowe) is asked to step aside for young phenom Stevie Weeks (Northcott). Expect cliches. **118m/C VHS, DVD.** Russell Crowe, Hank Azaria, Mary McCormack, Burt Reynolds, Ron Eldard, Lolita (David) Davidovich, Colm Meaney, Maury Chaykin, Ryan Northcott, Scott Grimes, Judith Ivey, Rachel Wilson, Mike Myers; ***Cameos:*** Little Richard; ***D:*** Jay Roach; ***W:*** David E. Kelley, Sean O'Byrne; ***C:*** Peter Deming; ***M:*** Carter Burwell.

Mystery Date **1991 (PG-13)** A sort of teen version of "After Hours," in which a shy college guy gets a date with the girl of his dreams, only to be mistaken for a master criminal and pursued by gangsters, police and a crazed florist. Not terrible, but if you're old enough to drive you're probably too old to watch with amusement. **98m/C VHS, DVD.** Ethan Hawke, Teri Polo, Brian McNamara, Fisher Stevens, B.D. Wong; ***D:*** Jonathan Wacks; ***W:*** Terry Runte, Parker Bennett; ***M:*** John Du Prez.

Mystery in Swing **1940** An all-black mystery with music, about a trumpet player who has snake venom put on his mouthpiece. **66m/B VHS.** F.E. (Flourney) Miller, Monte Hawley, Marguerite Whitten, Tommie Moore, Ceepee Johnson; ***D:*** Arthur Dreifuss.

Mystery Island 1/2 **1981** Beautifully filmed underwater scenes in this children's film about four youths who discover a deserted island which they name Mystery Island, and a retired pirate who lives there. When the children find counterfeit money and the bad guys return for it, the old pirate's clever plans keep the kids safe. **75m/C VHS.** *AU* Jayson Duncan, Niklas Juhlin, Michael McGlinchey, Melissa Woodhams; ***D:*** Gene W. Scott; ***W:*** Clifford Green, Geoff Beak; ***C:*** Phil Pike.

Mystery Kids 1/2 *Finding Kelly* **1999 (PG)** Preteens Herford and Baltes spend their summer snooping into the disappearance of high school girl Lakin in order to claim a reward. They first think her boyfriend killed her but then discover Lakin has just run away and is working as a singer in a local bar. So the kids decide to try and reconcile the troubled teen with her family. Innocuous family fare but the two would-be sleuths are good. **88m/C VHS, DVD.** Brighton Hertford, Jameson Baltes, Christine Lakin; ***D:*** Lynn Hamrick. **VIDEO**

Mystery Liner 1/2 *The Ghost of John Holling* **1934** Dead bodies are found aboard ocean liner and passengers are concerned about it. Slow-moving sea cruise. **62m/B VHS, DVD.** Noah Beery Sr., Astrid Allwyn, Cornelius Keefe, Gustav von Seyffertitz, Edwin Maxwell, Boothe Howard, George "Gabby" Hayes; ***D:*** William Nigh.

The Mystery Man 1/2 **1935** A Chicago reporter goes on a drinking binge and ends up in St. Louis. There he stumbles upon a mystery which may involve the paper for which he works. He teams up with a beautiful woman to try to crack the case. **65m/B VHS, DVD.** Robert Armstrong, Maxine Doyle, Henry Kolker, Leroy Mason, James Burke; ***D:*** Ray McCarey.

Mystery Man 1/2 **1944** Below-average episode has rancher Hoppy being bothered by rustlers. Boyd solves things in the usual way, while Clyde provides the laughs. **58m/B VHS, DVD.** William Boyd, Andy Clyde, Jimmy Rogers, Don Costello, Francis McDonald, Forrest Taylor, Eleanor Stewart; ***D:*** George Archainbaud.

Mystery Mansion **1983 (PG)** Fortune in gold and a hundred-year-old mystery lead three children into an exciting treasure hunt. Family fare. **95m/C VHS, DVD.** Dallas McKennon, Greg Wynne, Jane Ferguson, Barry Hostetler; ***D:*** David S. Jackson; ***W:*** David S. Jackson; ***C:*** Milas C. Hinshaw; ***M:*** William Loose.

Mystery Men 1/2 **1999 (PG-13)** A cast of quirky comedy all-stars, including Garafalo, Stiller and Macy, help deflate the superhero genre by playing a team of bush league crimefighters. The superhero washouts use their dubious powers to save Champion City from party monster villain Casanova Frankenstein (Rush), who has kidnapped real superhero Captain Amazing (Kinnear). Great concept and dialogue are stretched a bit thin over the long running time. Based on the Dark Horse comic book. **120m/C VHS, DVD, HD DVD.** Ben Stiller, Hank Azaria, William H. Macy, Paul (Pee-wee Herman) Reubens, Claire Forlani, Wes Studi, Janeane Garofalo, Kel Mitchell, Geoffrey Rush, Lena Olin, Greg Kinnear, Tom Waits, Eddie Izzard, Ricky Jay, Louise Lasser, Stacey Travis, Artie Lange, Jenifer Lewis, Pras, Dane Cook; ***D:*** Kinka Usher; ***W:*** Neil Cuthbert; ***C:*** Stephen Burum; ***M:*** Stephen Warbeck.

Mystery Mountain 1/2 **1934** Twelve episodes depict the villain known as the "Rattler" attempting to stop the construction of a railroad over Mystery Mountain. **156m/B VHS, DVD.** Ken Maynard, Gene Autry, Smiley Burnette; ***D:*** Otto Brower, B. Reeves Eason.

The Mystery of Alexina 1/2 *Mystere Alexina* **1986** True story of Herculine Adelaide Barbin, a 19th-century French hermaphrodite, who, after growing up a woman, fell in love with another woman and was actually revealed to be a man. Subtitled. **86m/C VHS.** *FR* Vuillemin, Valeri Stroh; ***D:*** Rene Feret; ***W:*** Jean Gruault.

The Mystery of Edwin Drood 1/2 **1935** Nicely creepy gothic atmosphere highlights this version of Charles Dickens' final novel, which was unfinished at the time of his death. English choirmaster and opium addict John Jasper (Rains) is visited by his nephew Edwin Drood (Manners), who's soon to enter into an arranged marriage with Rosa (Angel). Unbeknownst to anyone, Jasper has long desired Rosa for himself and kills his nephew in a jealous rage. Now that Drood's disappeared, will Jasper have Rosa to himself? **85m/B VHS.** Claude Rains, Heather Angel, Douglass Montgomery, Valerie Hobson, David Manners, Francis L. Sullivan, Ethel Griffies, E.E. Clive; ***D:*** Stuart Walker; ***W:*** John Lloyd Balderston, Gladys Unger; ***C:*** George Robinson; ***M:*** Edward Ward.

The Mystery of Edwin Drood 1/2 **1993** When Edwin Drood vanishes on Christmas Eve, his disappearance leads to a terrifying mystery that unfolds amidst the slums of Victorian England. Adapted from Charles Dickens' last novel, which was left unfinished at his death. **98m/C VHS.** *GB* Robert Powell, Michelle Evans, Jonathan Phillips, Finty Williams, Rupert Rainsford, Nanette Newman, Freddie Jones, Rosemary Leach, Ronald Fraser; ***D:*** Timothy Forder; ***W:*** Timothy Forder.

Mystery of Mr. Wong 1/2 **1939** The largest star sapphire in the world, the "Eye of the Daughter of the Moon," is stolen from a museum in its home country of China. Mr. Wong becomes involved in trying to trace its trail and the perpetrator of the murders that follow in its wake. One in the series of detective films. **67m/B VHS, DVD.** Boris Karloff, Grant Withers, Dorothy Tree, Lotus Long; ***D:*** William Nigh.

The Mystery of Rampo **1994 (R)** Visually dazzling fantasy that propels mystery writer Edogawa Rampo (Takenaka) into his own stories. Set just before WWII, Rampo is despondent when his latest novel (about a woman suffocating her husband in a trunk) is censored by the government and then amazed when a newspaper story reveals a similar crime. So Rampo decides to meet the widow Shizuko (Hada) and discovers she's a double for his fictional character. He then writes a sequel, again featuring Shizuko, and once again finds reality and fiction blending into the bizarre. Rampo was the pseudonym for renowned writer Hirai Taro, regarded as the Japanese Edgar Allan Poe. The film had its own complications when the version filmed by original director Rentaro Mayusumi was rejected by producer Okuyama, who then reshot much of the film himself. Japanese with subtitles. **96m/C VHS, DVD.** *JP* Naoto Takenaka, Michiko Hada, Masahiro Motoki, Teruyuki Kagawa, Mikijiro Hira; ***D:*** Kazuyoshi Okuyama; ***W:*** Kazuyoshi Okuyama, Yuhei Enoki; ***C:*** Yasushi Sasakibara; ***M:*** Akira Senju.

Mystery of the Hooded Horseman **1937** Tex finds himself pitted against a very strange adversary. **61m/B VHS, DVD.** Tex Ritter, Iris Meredith, Charles "Blackie" King, Joseph Girard, Lafe (Lafayette) McKee; ***D:*** Ray Taylor.

The Mystery of the Mary Celeste *The Phantom Ship; The Mystery of the Marie Celeste* **1935** Tale of terror based on the bizarre case of the "Marie Celeste," an American ship found adrift off the coast of England with her sails set but minus any of her crew on December 5, 1872. **64m/B VHS, DVD.** Bela Lugosi, Shirley Grey, Edmund Willard, Arthur Margetson, Dennis Hoey, George Mozart, Ben Welden, Clifford McLaglen; ***D:*** Denison Clift; ***W:*** Denison Clift; ***C:*** Eric Cross, Geoffrey Faithfull.

Mystery of the Million Dollar Hockey Puck 1/2 **1975** Sinister diamond smugglers learn a lesson on ice from a pair of orphan lads. Features the National Hockey League's Montreal Canadians in one of their few film appearances. **88m/C VHS.** Michael MacDonald, Angele Knight; ***D:*** Jean LaFleur, Peter Svatek.

Mystery of the Riverboat 1/2 **1944** Louisiana and the Mississippi River are the background for these 13 episodes of mystery and murder. **90m/B VHS.** Robert Lowery, Eddie Quillan, Lyle Talbot, Francis McDonald, Arthur Hohl; ***D:*** Ray Taylor, Lewis D. Collins.

Mystery of the Wax Museum **1933** Rarely seen, vintage horror classic about a wax-dummy maker who, after a disfiguring fire, resorts to murder and installs the wax-covered bodies of his victims in his museum. Famous for its pioneering use of two-strip Technicolor. Remade in 1953 in 3-D as "House of Wax." **77m/C VHS.** Lionel Atwill, Fay Wray, Glenda Farrell, Frank McHugh, Allen Vincent, Holmes Herbert; ***D:*** Michael Curtiz; ***W:*** Carl Erickson, Don Mullaly; ***C:*** Ray Rennahan.

Mystery Plane 1/2 **1939** An inventor devises a new bomb-dropping mechanism, and must evade secret agents on his way to deliver it to the government. **60m/B VHS, DVD.** John Trent, Marjorie Reynolds, Milburn Stone, Peter George Lynn, Polly Ann Young; ***D:*** George Waggner.

Mystery Ranch 1/2 **1934** A cowboy finds himself in strange predicaments out on the range. **52m/B VHS, DVD.** George O'Brien, Charles Middleton, Cecilia Parker; ***D:*** David Howard.

Mystery Science Theater 3000: The Movie 1/2 **1996 (PG-13)** Mad scientist Dr. Clayton Forrester (Beaulieu) maroons Mike Nelson on the Satellite of Love, forces him to watch bad movies, and monitors his reactions. Mike and his robotic pals, Tom Servo and Crow T. Robot, save their sanity by wisecracking their way through the movies. Today's experiment is "This Island Earth," an uncharacteristically semi-respectable flick. As regular viewers know, the jokes and snide remarks come fast and in bunches. Not all of them work, but the ones that do will be remembered and repeated often. Audience participation is inevitable. Weekend theme-party status is virtually assured. **73m/C VHS, DVD.** Trace Beaulieu, James "Jim" Mallon, Michael J. Nelson, Kevin Murphy, John Brady; ***D:*** James "Jim" Mallon; ***W:*** Trace Beaulieu, James "Jim" Mallon, Michael J. Nelson, Kevin Murphy, Mary Jo Pehl, Paul Chaplin, Bridget Jones; ***C:*** Jeff Stonehouse; ***M:*** Billy Barber.

Mystery Squadron **1933** Twelve chapters, 13 minutes each. Daredevil air action in flight against the masked pilots of the Black Ace. **240m/B VHS, DVD.** Bob Steele, Guinn "Big Boy" Williams, Lucille Browne, Jack Mulhall, J. Carrol Naish, Jack Mower; ***D:*** Colbert Clark.

Mystery Street **1950** Unusual for two reasons: an immigrant detective who ignores race baiting for a shot at his first big case and the use of forensics (then a new science) to solve it. Bar girl Vivian (Sterling) gets the brush-off from her married lover and decides to confront him. She persuades drunken Henry (Thompson) to loan her his car so she can meet the louse. Months later a skeleton turns up on a Cape Cod beach and Portuguese-American detective Peter Morales (Montalban) gets his chance to move up the cop ladder. He enlists the aid of Harvard forensic expert Dr. McAdoo (Bennett) to identify the bones. Then the car turns up, putting foolish Henry (who reported it stolen) in the hot seat. McAdoo insists forensics show Henry is the wrong guy but Morales is skeptical. **93m/B DVD.** Ricardo Montalban, Bruce Bennett, Marshall Thompson, Jan Sterling, Elsa Lanchester, Edmon Ryan, Sally Forrest, Wally Maher; ***D:*** John Sturges; ***W:*** Richard Brooks, Sydney (Sidney) Boehm; ***C:*** John Alton; ***M:*** Rudolph Kopp.

Mystery Train **1989 (R)** A run down hotel in Memphis is the scene for three vignettes concerning the visit of foreigners to the U.S. Themes of mythic Americana, Elvis, and life on the fringe pervade this hip and quirky film. The three vignettes all tie together in clever and funny overlaps. Waits fans should listen for his performance as a DJ. **110m/C VHS, DVD.** Masatoshi Nagase, Youki Kudoh, Screamin' Jay Hawkins, Cinque Lee, Joe Strummer, Nicoletta Braschi, Elizabeth Bracco, Steve Buscemi, Tom Noonan, Rockets Redglare, Rick Aviles, Rufus Thomas, Vondie Curtis-Hall; ***D:*** Jim Jarmusch; ***W:*** Jim Jarmusch; ***C:*** Robby Muller; ***M:*** John Lurie; ***V:*** Tom Waits.

Mystery Trooper *Trail of the Royal Mounted* **1932** Adventures in the great wilderness full of prospecting, greed, and Indians all being observed by the Royal Mounties. Ten chapters of the serial at 20 minutes each. **200m/B VHS.** Blanche Mehaffey, Al Ferguson, Charles King, William Bertram, Robert Frazer, Buzz Barton; ***D:*** Stuart Paton; ***W:*** Harry S. Webb, Carl Krusada; ***C:*** Edward Kull, William Nobles.

Mystery Woman: Mystery Weekend 1/2 **2005** Samantha Kinsey (Martin) inherits a struggling mystery bookstore and tries to boost business by inviting three successful authors to speak as part of a mystery weekend. Only the mystery really begins when one of the writers is murdered. Originally shown on the Hallmark Channel. **87m/C DVD.** Kellie Martin, Clarence Williams III, Nina Siemaszko, Colleen Camp, Casey Sander, Deborah Van Valkenburgh, Paul Satterfield, Beth Broderick; ***D:*** Mark Griffiths; ***W:*** Joyce Burdett; ***C:*** Maximo Munzi; ***M:*** Joe Kraemer. **CABLE**

Mystic Circle Murder *Religious Racketeers* **1939** Reporter sets out to uncover phony mediums, particularly the Great La Gagge, whose fake apparitions are so convincing that it caused one of his clients to have a heart attack. Cheaply made, and it's obvious. Watch for a cameo by Harry Houdini's wife, who talks about life after death. Based on a story by director O'Connor. **69m/B VHS, DVD.** Betty Compson, Robert (Fisk) Fiske, Helene Le Berthon, Arthur Gardner; ***D:*** Frank O'Connor.

The Mystic Masseur 1/2 **2001 (PG)** Ganesh (Mandvi), a disgruntled schoolteacher, is part of the Indian community of Trinidad. He longs to become a writer and is inspired when he returns to his rural village for the funeral of his father, a famed masseur and healer. Ganesh discovers he also has a talent for healing, finds success as a writer, and even tries his hand at politics before finding a private contentment. Based on a novel by V.S. Naipaul. **117m/C VHS, DVD.** *GB IN* Aasif Mandvi, Om Puri, Ayesha Dharker, Jimi Mistry, Zohra Sehgal, James Fox; ***D:*** Ismail Merchant; ***W:*** Caryl Phillips; ***C:*** Ernest Vincze; ***M:*** Richard Robbins, Zakir Hussain.

Mystic Pizza **1988 (R)** Intelligent coming of age drama centers on two sisters and their best friend as they struggle with their hopes, loves, and family rivalries in the small town of Mystic, Connecticut. At times predictable, there are enough unexpected moments to keep interest high; definite appeal to young women, but others may not relate. The relatively unknown Roberts got most of the attention, but is the weakest of the three leads, so watch this one for the strong performances from Gish and Taylor. **101m/C VHS, DVD.** Annabeth Gish, Julia Roberts, Lili Taylor, Vincent D'Onofrio, William R. Moses, Adam Storke, Conchata Ferrell, Joanna Merlin, Matt Damon, Arthur Walsh; ***D:*** Donald Petrie; ***W:*** Amy Holden Jones, Perry Howze, Alfred Uhry; ***C:*** Tim Suhrstedt; ***M:*** David McHugh. Ind. Spirit '89: First Feature.

Mystic River 1/2 **2003 (R)** Complex drama is right up the controlled Eastwood's directorial alley (it's his 24th film)—especially with his three leads giving their all. Jimmy (Penn), Dave (Robbins), and Sean (Bacon) have grown up together in a working-class Irish neighborhood in Boston. As a child, Dave was kidnapped as his buddies looked on helplessly and he's never completely recovered from his ordeal. Decades later, Sean is now a homicide detective; Dave, a subdued loser; and Jimmy, an ex-con who manages a local market. Tragedy brings the guys back in close contact when Jimmy's beloved 19-year-old daughter Katie (Rossum) is murdered and he wants to get the killer before the cops do. There are some strange circumstances surrounding Katie's death and suspicion soon falls on Dave, leading to a climax filled with irony, regret, loss, and the perils of vigilante justice. Based on the novel by Dennis Lehane. **137m/C VHS, DVD.** *US* Sean Penn, Tim Robbins, Kevin Bacon, Laurence Fishburne, Marcia Gay Harden, Laura Linney, Tom Guiry, Kevin Chapman, Emmy Rossum, Spencer (Treat) Clark, Adam Nelson, Jenny O'Hara, Andrew Mackin, Robert Wahlberg; ***D:*** Clint Eastwood; ***W:*** Brian Helgeland; ***C:*** Tom Stern; ***M:*** Clint Eastwood. Oscars '03: Actor (Penn), Support. Actor (Robbins); Golden Globes '04: Actor—Drama (Penn), Support. Actor (Robbins); Natl. Bd. of Review '03: Actor (Penn), Film; Natl. Soc. Film Critics '03: Director (Eastwood); Screen Actors Guild '03: Support. Actor (Robbins).

The Myth of Fingerprints 1/2 **1997 (R)** Four adult siblings and their various partners return to their New England home to spend Thanksgiving with their parents. As with most movie families of upper-middle class status, old resentments and issues abound. Dad (Scheider), a sullen, misanthropic near-recluse, isn't thrilled about the reunion. Younger son Warren (Wyle) hopes to reconcile with his high school sweetheart. Older sister Mia (Moore) can't think of anything nice to say about anyone, and tomboy sister Leigh (Holloman) does the sibling rivalry dance with her. Subdued and interesting, Freundlich's debut doesn't go for a grand conclusion or startling revelation. Depending on your taste for pat endings and easy answers, that could be it's greatest asset or a reason not to bother. Excellent performances by a great cast should have a bearing on the decision. **91m/C VHS, DVD.** Blythe Danner, Roy Scheider, Julianne Moore, Noah Wyle, Michael Vartan, Laurel Holloman, Hope Davis, Brian Kerwin, James LeGros; ***D:*** Bart Freundlich; ***W:*** Bart Freundlich; ***C:*** Stephen Kazmierski; ***M:*** David Bridie, John Phillips.

Nabonga *Gorilla; Jungle Woman* **1944** The daughter of an embezzler, whose plane crashes in the jungle, befriends a gorilla who protects her. Soon a young man comes looking for the embezzler's cash, meets the woman and the ape, and together they go on a wonderful journey. **72m/B VHS, DVD.** Buster Crabbe, Fifi d'Orsay, Barton MacLane, Julie London, Herbert Rawlinson; ***D:*** Sam Newfield.

Nacho Libre 1/2 **2006 (PG)** Surprising misfire offers a few chuckles and the chance to see Black in spandex and a cape but not much else. Ignacio is a cook at a Mexican orphanage who assumes the alter ego of masked wrestler Nacho Libre in order to help out the tykes. He even has a tag-team buddy, skinny Esqueleto (Jimemez), and they somewhat resemble a cheap version of Laurel and Hardy. It's also not nearly as outrageous as the actual Lucha Libre wrestling it features. **91m/C DVD, Blu-ray Disc, HD DVD.** *US* Jack Black, Peter Stormare, Ana de la Reguera, Hector Jimenez, Richard Montoya, Darius A. Rose, Moises Arias, Diego Eduardo Gomez, Carlos Maycotte, Cesar Gonzalez; ***D:*** Jared Hess; ***W:*** Jared Hess, Jerusha Hess, Mike White; ***C:*** Xavier Perez Grobet; ***M:*** Danny Elfman.

Nadia 1/2 **1984** Entertaining account of the life of Nadia Comaneci, the Romanian gymnast who earned six perfect tens with her stunning performance at the 1976 Olympic Games. **100m/C VHS, DVD.** Talia Balsam, Jonathan Banks, Simone Blue, Johann Carlo, Carrie Snodgress; ***D:*** Alan Cooke. **TV**

Nadine 1/2 **1987 (PG)** In Austin circa 1954, an almost divorced beautician witnesses a murder and goes undercover with her estranged husband to track down the murderer, before he finds her. Plenty of low-key humor. Well-paced fun; Basinger is terrific. **83m/C VHS, DVD.** Jeff Bridges, Kim Basinger, Rip Torn, Gwen Verdon, Glenne Headly, Jerry Stiller, Jay Patterson; ***D:*** Robert Benton; ***W:*** Robert Benton; ***C:*** Nestor Almendros; ***M:*** Howard Shore.

Nadja **1995 (R)** Fresh, modern comic take on the vampire tale is about family ties and the power of home, with the required AIDS analogy and lesbian sex scenes. Tired of nightly blood-letting, the daughter of the now-deceased Count, Nadja (Lowensohn), lives in New York's East Village, hoping to change her life. She seduces and falls in love with Lucy (Craze), whose husband is the nephew of old family nemesis Van Helsing (Fonda, in a surprisingly comedic role). Manic Fonda Van Helsing sets out to save Lucy and steal the film. Meanwhile, Nadja finds her long lost twin brother (Harris, son of Richard) and Lucy discovers sex with Nadja is draining. Innovative camera work (vampire point-of-view scenes shot with a toy Pixelvision camera and blown up to 35mm for a moody, grainy look) and a great score keep "Nadja" very watchable despite some missteps in the plot. (Director Almereyda pioneered use of the Pixel-vision camera in "Another Girl, Another Planet.") Executive producer David Lynch contributes a cameo as a guard at the morgue where Nadja claims her father's body. **92m/B VHS, DVD.** Elina Lowensohn, Suzy Amis, Galaxy Craze, Martin Donovan, Peter Fonda, Karl Geary, Jared Harris; ***Cameos:*** David Lynch; ***D:*** Michael Almereyda; ***W:*** Michael Almereyda; ***C:*** Jim Denault; ***M:*** Simon Fisher Turner.

Nail Gun Massacre WOOF! **1986** A crazed killer with a penchant for nailing bodies to just about anything goes on a hammering spree. In horrific, vivid color. **90m/C VHS, DVD.** Rocky Patterson, Ron Queen, Beau Leland, Michelle Meyer; ***D:*** Bill Lesley.

Nails 1/2 **1992 (R)** Harry "Nails" Niles (Hopper) is a tough, experienced cop whose partner has been killed by drug dealers. Harry doesn't take this well and decides to go on a violent search for revenge. Archer is wasted as Harry's estranged wife and Hopper can sleepwalk through this type of cliched wildman role. **96m/C VHS.** Dennis Hopper, Anne Archer, Tomas Milian, Cliff DeYoung; ***D:*** John Flynn. **CABLE**

Nairobi Affair **1988 (PG)** Savage and Heston fight poachers and each other in Kenya, when the father has an affair with his son's ex-wife. Mediocre, derivative script, but beautiful scenery. **95m/C VHS.** Charlton Heston, John Savage, Maud Adams, John Rhys-Davies, Connie Booth; ***D:*** Marvin J. Chomsky. **TV**

Nais **1945** Vintage Pagnolian peasant drama. A hunchback sacrifices himself for the girl he loves. She escapes to another man's arms. Adapted from the Emile Zola novel "Nais Micoulin." In French with English subtitles. **105m/B VHS.** *FR* Fernandel; ***D:*** Fernand Lauterier; ***W:*** Marcel Pagnol.

Naked *Mike Leigh's Naked* **1993 (R)** Existential angst in a '90s London filled with Leigh's usual eccentrics. The unemployed Johnny (Thewlis) comes to London and bunks with former girlfriend Louise (Sharp). After seducing her flatmate Sophie (Cartlidge), Johnny leaves to wander the streets, exchanging philosophical, if foul-mouthed, dialogues with a variety of odd characters. Thewlis gives an explosive performance as the calculatingly brutal and desolate Johnny. Chaotic shifts in mood from comedy to violence to love prove a challenge and the pervasive abuse of all the women characters is very disturbing. Critically acclaimed; see it as a reflection on the mess of modern England. **131m/C VHS, DVD.** *GB* David Thewlis, Lesley Sharp, Katrin Cartlidge, Greg Cruttwell, Claire Skinner, Peter Wight, Ewen Bremner, Susan Vidler, Deborah MacLaren, Gina McKee; ***D:*** Mike Leigh; ***W:*** Mike Leigh; ***C:*** Dick Pope; ***M:*** Andrew Dickson. Cannes '93: Actor (Thewlis), Director (Leigh); N.Y. Film Critics '93: Actor (Thewlis); Natl. Soc. Film Critics '93: Actor (Thewlis).

The Naked and the Dead 1/2 **1958** Sanitized adaptation of Norman Mailer's bestselling novel about army life in the Pacific during WWII. Resentment between officers and enlisted men proves to be almost as dangerous as the Japanese. Uneven acting and cliched characterizations make this an average outing. Don't expect to hear the profane language that sensationalized the book, because most of it was edited out of the screenplay. **131m/C VHS.** Aldo Ray, Cliff Robertson, Joey Bishop, Raymond Massey, Lili St. Cyr, James Best; ***D:*** Raoul Walsh; ***C:*** Joseph LaShelle.

The Naked Angels **1969 (R)** Rape, mayhem, beatings, and road-hogging streetbikes highlight this biker film, acted, in part, by actual bikers, and in part by others who were actually (almost) actors. The gang war rages from Los Angeles to Las Vegas. Roger Corman was the executive producer. **83m/C VHS.** Michael Greene, Richard Rust, Felicia Guy; ***D:*** Bruce (B.D.) Clark; ***W:*** Bruce (B.D.) Clark.

Naked Cage WOOF! **1986 (R)** Brutal women's prison film that is borderline softcore, about an innocent country woman, a horseriding fanatic, who is framed for a robbery and sent to the slammer. There, she contends with lesbian wardens and inmates. Disgusting. **97m/C VHS.** Shari Shattuck, Angel Tompkins, Lucinda Crosby, Christina Whitaker; ***D:*** Paul Nicholas.

The Naked City 1/2 **1948** Film noir classic makes spectacular use of its NYC locations. Beautiful playgirl is murdered and police detectives Fitzgerald and Taylor are left without clues. They spend most of their time running down weak leads and interviewing various suspects and witnesses. When they finally get a break, it leads to playboy Duff. Spectacular ending on the Williamsburg Bridge between cops and killer. Producer Hellinger provided the hard-boiled narration, patterned after the tabloid newspaper stories he once wrote. Served as the impetus for the TV show of the same name, where Hellinger's film postscript also became the show's noted tagline: "There are eight million stories in the naked city, this has been one of them." **96m/B VHS, DVD.** Barry Fitzgerald, Don Taylor, Howard Duff, Ted de Corsia, Dorothy Hart; ***D:*** Jules Dassin; ***W:*** Albert (John B. Sherry) Maltz; ***C:*** William H. Daniels; ***M:*** Miklos Rozsa; ***Nar:*** Mark Hellinger. Oscars '48: B&W Cinematog., Film Editing, Natl. Film Reg. '07.

Naked City: A Killer Christmas 1/2 **1998** Cops Muldoon (Glenn) and Halloran (Vance) are on the case of a serial killer who's sent New York into a panic, thanks to the media efforts of an ambitious newscaster. **92m/C VHS.** Scott Glenn, Courtney B. Vance, Laura Leighton, Barbara Williams, Nigel Bennett, Lisa Vidal, Al Waxman, Jason Blicker, Richard McMillan; ***D:*** Peter Bogdanovich; ***W:*** Christopher Trumbo, Jeff Freilich; ***C:*** James Gardner; ***M:*** Hummie Mann. **CABLE**

Naked City: Justice with a Bullet **1998** Undercover NYC detectives Scott Muldoon (Glenn) and James Halloran (Vance) come to the rescue of naive tourists Sarah (Erbe) and Merri (Tunney) who unwittingly become involved in a drug dealer's murder. And then Halloran has to deal with a boyhood pal from the 'hood who isn't the friend he seems. Based on the 1948 film "The Naked City." **107m/C VHS.** Scott Glenn, Courtney B. Vance, Giancarlo Esposito, Robin Tunney, Kathryn Erbe, Eli Wallach, Tony Bill, Sebastien Roche, Barbara Williams; ***D:*** Jeff Freilich; ***W:*** Jeff Freilich; ***C:*** Miroslaw Baszak; ***M:*** Ashley Irwin. **CABLE**

The Naked Civil Servant 1/2 **1975** Remarkable film, based on the life of flamboyant homosexual Quentin Crisp, who came out of the closet in his native England, long before his lifestyle would be tolerated by Britains. For mature audiences. **80m/C VHS, DVD.** John Hurt; ***D:*** Jack Gold; ***M:*** Carl Davis.

The Naked Country 1/2 **1985 (R)** In the untamed frontier of Australia rancher bigoted Lance Dillion and his sensual wife Mary are determined to make their way. But when Lance finds out that the neglected Mary is fooling around with a local cop, he goes on a killing spree on land sacred to the Aborigines. Plodding plot. **90m/C VHS.** *AU* John Stanton, Rebecca Gilling, Ivar Kants; ***D:*** Tim Burstall; ***C:*** David Eggby; ***M:*** Bruce Smeaton.

The Naked Edge **1961** Cooper stars as a middle-aged businessman whose wife suspects him of murder after she begins snooping into his business affairs. Cooper's last film and far from his best. Poor direction and holes in the screenplay divert from what could have been a tight thriller. **99m/C VHS.** *GB* Gary Cooper, Deborah Kerr, Eric Portman, Diane Cilento, Hermione Gingold, Peter Cushing, Michael Wilding, Ronald Howard; ***D:*** Michael Anderson Sr.; ***W:*** Joseph Stefano.

Naked Evil 1/2 **1966** Two rival West Indian street gangs are causing problems in their Midlands community and one of them has turned to Jamaican voodoo to release a demon. Violent deaths follow. **85m/B DVD.** *GB* Basil Dignam, Olaf Pooley, Anthony Ainley, Suzanne Neve, Richard Coleman, John Ashley Hamilton, Brylo Forde; ***D:*** Stanley Goulder; ***W:*** Stanley Goulder; ***C:*** Geoffrey Faithfull; ***M:*** Bernard Ebbinghouse.

The Naked Face **1984 (R)** A psychiatrist tries to find out why his patients are being killed. He gets no help from police, who suspect he is the murderer. A dull affair featuring unusual casting of Moore, while Steiger's suspicious police captain character provides spark. From the novel by Sidney Sheldon. **105m/C VHS.** Roger Moore, Rod Steiger, Elliott Gould, Art Carney, Anne Archer, David Hedison; ***D:*** Bryan Forbes.

The Naked Flame WOOF! **1968 (R)** O'Keefe plays an investigator in a strange town inhabited by weird, religious fanatics. After he arrives, the womenfolk shed their clothes in this pitiful, pathetic hilarity. **90m/C VHS.** *CA* Dennis O'Keefe, Kasey Rogers, Al Ruscio, Linda Bennett, Tracey Roberts, Barton Heyman, Robert Howay; ***D:*** Larry Matanski; ***W:*** Al Everett Dennis; ***C:*** Paul Ivano.

The Naked Gun: From the Files of Police Squad **1988 (PG-13)** More hysterical satire from the creators of "Airplane!" The short-lived TV cop spoof "Police Squad" moves to the big screen and has Lt. Drebin uncover a plot to assassinate Queen Elizabeth while she is visiting Los Angeles. Nearly nonstop gags and pratfalls provide lots of laughs. Nielsen is perfect as Drebin and the supporting cast is strong; cameos abound. **85m/C VHS, DVD.** Leslie Nielsen, Ricardo Montalban, Priscilla Presley, George Kennedy, O.J. Simpson, Nancy Marchand, John Houseman; ***Cameos:*** Weird Al Yankovic, Reggie Jackson, Dr. Joyce Brothers; ***D:*** David Zucker; ***W:*** Jerry Zucker, Jim Abrahams, Pat Proft, David Zucker; ***M:*** Ira Newborn.

Naked Gun 33 1/3: The Final Insult **1994 (PG-13)** Ever dumb, crass, and crude, Lt. Drebin returns to the force from retirement to lead an investigation into terrorist activities in Hollywood. Lots of current events jokes—dated as soon as they hit the screen. Sure to satisfy genre fans with a taste for bad puns. Watch for the cameos, especially at the "Oscars." **90m/C VHS, DVD.** Leslie Nielsen, Priscilla Presley, O.J. Simpson, Fred Ward, George Kennedy, Gary Cooper, Kathleen Freeman, Raquel Welch; ***Cameos:*** Pia Zadora, James Earl Jones, Weird Al Yankovic, Ann B. Davis; ***D:*** Peter Segal; ***W:*** Robert Locash, David Zucker, Pat Proft; ***M:*** Ira Newborn. Golden Raspberries '94: Worst Support. Actor (Simpson), Worst New Star (Smith).

Naked Gun 2 1/2: The Smell of Fear 1/2 **1991 (PG-13)** Lt. Drebin returns to rescue the world from a faulty energy policy devised by the White House and oil-lords. A notch down from the previous entry but still hilarious cop parody. Nielsen has this character down to a tee, and there's a laugh every minute. **85m/C VHS, DVD.** Leslie Nielsen, Priscilla Presley, George Kennedy, O.J. Simpson, Robert Goulet, Richard Griffiths, Jacqueline Brookes, Lloyd Bochner, Tim O'Connor, Peter Mark Richman; ***Cameos:*** Mel Torme, Eva Gabor, Weird Al Yankovic; ***D:*** David Zucker; ***W:*** David Zucker, Pat Proft; ***M:*** Ira Newborn.

Naked Hills 1/2 **1956** Meandering tale about a man (Wayne) who, suffering from gold fever, searches for 40 years in 19th Century California and ends up out of luck, losing his wife and family. **72m/C VHS, DVD.** David Wayne, Keenan Wynn, James Barton, Marcia Henderson, Jim Backus, Denver Pyle, Myrna Dell, Frank Fenton, Fuzzy Knight; ***D:*** Josef Shaftel; ***W:*** Josef Shaftel.

Naked in New York 1/2 **1993 (R)** Aspiring New York playwright Jake Briggs (Stoltz) and his girlfriend Joanne (Parker), an aspiring photographer, find their relationship in jeopardy when their respective careers start to take off. Offspring from the "Annie Hall" school of neurotic romance examines a number of issues, including ambition, commitment, and the societal dynamics of theatre and art. Celebrity appearances abound, including Styron as himself and Goldberg as a tragedy mask on a wall. Directorial debut of Scorsese protege Algrant is uneven but charming. Parker is particularly strong, and Turner's a riot as a sexpot soap star on the prowl for Jake. **89m/C VHS, DVD.** Eric Stoltz, Mary-Louise Parker, Ralph Macchio, Jill Clayburgh, Tony Curtis, Kathleen Turner, Timothy Dalton, Lynne Thigpen, Roscoe Lee Browne; ***Cameos:*** Whoopi Goldberg, William Styron, Eric Bogosian, Quentin Crisp; ***D:*** Dan Algrant; ***W:*** Dan Algrant, John Warren; ***M:*** Angelo Badalamenti; ***V:*** David Johansen.

Naked in the Night *Madeleine Tel. 13 62 11* **1958** Cheap German exploitation film about the dangers of promiscuous women. Dubbed in English. **85m/B VHS.** *GE* Eva Bartok, Alexander Kerst, Heinz Drache, Ilse Steppat, Sabine Sesselmann; ***D:*** Kurt Meisel; ***W:*** Will Berthold; ***C:*** Kurt Grigoleit; ***M:*** Willy Mattes.

Naked in the Sun **1957** The true story of events leading to the war between the Osceola and Seminole Indians and a slave trader. Somewhat slow. **95m/C VHS.** James Craig, Lita Milan, Barton MacLane, Tony Hunter; ***D:*** R. John Hugh.

Naked Is Better *Los Doctores las Prefieren Desnudas* **1973** A couple of buffoons pose as hospital workers so they can play doctor with a hospitalized actress. **93m/C VHS.** *AR* Mariquita Gallegos, Alberto Olmedo, Jorge Porcel, Jorge Barreiro, Moria Casan; ***D:*** Gerardo Sofovich; ***W:*** Gerardo Sofovich; ***C:*** Americo Hoss; ***M:*** Buddy McCluskey.

Naked Jungle **1954** Suspenseful, well-done jungle adventure of a plantation owner (Heston) in South America and his North American mail-order bride (Parker), who do battle with a deadly, miles-long siege of red army ants. Realistic and worth watching. Produced by George Pal, shot by Ernest Laszlo and based on the story "Leiningen vs. the Ants" by Carl Stephenson. **95m/C VHS, DVD.** Charlton Heston, Eleanor Parker, Abraham Sofaer, William Conrad; ***D:*** Byron Haskin; ***W:*** Philip Yordan; ***C:*** Ernest Laszlo.

Naked Killer *Chiklo Gouyeung* **1992** Kitty (Ching) turns to a female assassin to learn the art of killing so that she may avenge her father's death. When her teacher is herself unceremoniously murdered, Kitty and her policeman boyfriend (Yam) have two scores to settle. Sex and violence. Subtitled in English. **86m/C VHS, DVD.** *HK* Chingmy Yau, Simon Yam, Carrie Ng, Kelly Yao, Svenvara Madoka; ***D:*** Clarence Fok Yiu Leung; ***W:*** Jing Wong; ***C:*** Peter Pau, William Yim; ***M:*** Lowell Lo.

Naked Kiss **1/2** *The Iron Kiss* **1964** Fuller's most savage, hysterical film noir. A brutalized prostitute escapes her pimp and tries to enter respectable small-town society. She finds even more perversion and sickness there. **92m/B VHS, DVD.** Constance Towers, Anthony Eisley, Michael Dante, Virginia Grey, Patsy Kelly, Betty Bronson, Edy Williams, Marie Devereux, Karen Conrad, Linda Francis, Barbara Perry, Walter Matthews, Betty Robinson; ***D:*** Samuel Fuller; ***W:*** Samuel Fuller; ***C:*** Stanley Cortez; ***M:*** Paul Dunlap.

Naked Lie **1989** A District Attorney and a judge engage in an ultra-steamy affair and inevitably clash when she is assigned as a prosecutor on the politically explosive case over which he is presiding. **89m/C VHS, DVD.** Victoria Principal, James Farentino, Glenn Withrow, William Lucking, Dakin Matthews; ***D:*** Richard A. Colla; ***M:*** Robert Alcivar.

Naked Lies **1998 (R)** FBI agent Cara Landry (Tweed) gets transferred to treasury after a drug bust goes bad and is assigned to work an undercover operation that reunites Cara with ex-lover Mitch Kendall (Baker). Kendall has been trying to bust international counterfeiter Damian Medina (Allende) and sends Cara in to work one of Medina's casinos. But Cara finds herself drawn to the bad guy, putting both her career and her life in jeopardy. **93m/C VHS, DVD.** Shannon Tweed, Jay Baker, Fernando Allende, Steven Bauer, Hugo Stiglitz; ***D:*** Ralph Portillo. **VIDEO**

Naked Lunch **1991 (R)** Whacked-out movie based on William S. Burroughs's autobiographical account of drug abuse, homosexuality, violence, and weirdness set in the drug-inspired land called Interzone. Hallucinogenic images are carried to the extreme: typewriters metamorphose into beetles, bloblike creatures with sex organs scurry about, and characters mainline insecticide. Some of the characters are clearly based on writers of the Beat generation, including Jane and Paul Bowles, Allen Ginsberg, and Jack Kerouac. **117m/C VHS, DVD.** *CA GB* Peter Weller, Judy Davis, Ian Holm, Julian Sands, Roy Scheider, Monique Mercure, Nicholas (Nick) Campbell, Michael Zelniker, Robert A. Silverman, Joseph Scorsiani; ***D:*** David Cronenberg; ***W:*** David Cronenberg; ***C:*** Peter Suschitzky; ***M:*** Howard Shore. Genie '92: Adapt. Screenplay, Art Dir./Set Dec., Cinematog., Director (Cronenberg), Film, Sound, Support. Actress (Mercure); N.Y. Film Critics '91: Screenplay, Support. Actress (Davis); Natl. Soc. Film Critics '91: Director (Cronenberg), Screenplay.

The Naked Maja **1959** Elaborate, yet dull drama about the tumultous romance between a Spanish duchess and the legendary painter Francisco Goya. Even the gorgeous costumes and spectacular sets can't overcome the weak script and poor direction that plague the film. Based on a story by Oscar Saul and Talbot Jennings. **111m/C VHS.** Ava Gardner, Anthony (Tony) Franciosa, Amedeo Nazzari, Gino Cervi, Lea Padovani, Massimo Serato, Carlo Rizzo, Renzo Cesana; ***D:*** Henry Koster, Mario Russo; ***W:*** Norman Corwin, Giorgio Prosperi.

The Naked Man **1998 (R)** When a pharmaceutical conglomerate muscles into his small town, chiropractor Rapaport decides to take action to save the livelihood of his family's drugstore—by becoming a professional wrestler. **98m/C VHS.** Michael Rapaport, Michael Jeter, Rachael Leigh Cook, Joe Grifasi, John Slattery; ***D:*** J. Todd Anderson; ***W:*** J. Todd Anderson, Ethan Coen.

Naked Obsession **1/2 1991 (R)** A city councilman running for mayor is mugged in one of the seedier parts of the city. He's found by a homeless man who takes him to a kinky nightclub where the councilman is promptly seduced by a topless bar hostess with secrets of her own. Also available in an unrated version. **93m/C VHS.** William Katt, Maria Ford, Rick Dean; ***D:*** Dan Golden.

Naked Paradise *Black Emmanuelle, White Emmanuelle; Black Velvet* **1978 (R)** A young woman moves in with her mother and step-sister and finds difficulty in adjusting. **86m/C VHS.** *IT* Al Cliver, Gabriele Tinti, Feodor Chaliapin Jr., Laura Gemser, Annie Belle; ***D:*** Brunello Rondi; ***W:*** Brunello Rondi; ***C:*** Gastone Di Giovanni; ***M:*** Alberto Baldan Bembo.

The Naked Prey **1966** Unnerving African adventure which contains some unforgettably brutal scenes. A safari guide (Wilde), leading a hunting party, must watch as an indigenous tribe murders all his companions, and according to their customs, allows him to be set free, sans clothes or weapons, to be hunted by the best of the tribe. **96m/C VHS.** Cornel Wilde, Gertrude Van Der Berger, Ken Gampu; ***D:*** Cornel Wilde.

Naked Souls **1995 (R)** Artist Brit Clark (Anderson) must save scientist fiance Edward (Krause) from the evil experiments of murderous scientist Longstreet (Warner). Like you'll care as long as the Anderson bod is on display. **90m/C VHS.** Michael (Mike) Papajohn, Pamela Anderson, Brian Krause, Clayton Rohner, Justina Vail, David Warner; ***Cameos:*** Dean Stockwell; ***D:*** Lyndon Chubbuck; ***W:*** Frank Dietz; ***C:*** Eric Goldstein; ***M:*** Nigel Holton.

The Naked Spur **1/2 1953** A compulsive bounty hunter tracks down a vicious outlaw and his beautiful girlfriend. An exciting film from the Mann-Stewart team and considered one of their best, infusing the traditional western with psychological confusion. Wonderful use of Rockies locations. **93m/C VHS, DVD.** James Stewart, Robert Ryan, Janet Leigh, Millard Mitchell, Ralph Meeker; ***D:*** Anthony Mann; ***W:*** Sam Rolfe, Harold Jack Bloom; ***C:*** William Mellor; ***M:*** Bronislau Kaper. Natl. Film Reg. '97.

Naked Tango **1/2 1991 (R)** A lurid recreation of the Argentinian underworld in 1924. Stephanie is a bored wife with an older husband who, while traveling with her husband on a cruise ship, pretends to fall overboard in order to establish a new identity. The problem is she becomes the supposed mail-order bride of a young man who promptly sells her into white slavery. One of her customers is a charismatic killer named Cholo who isn't interested in Stephanie for sex, he just wants to dance the tango with her. This is meant to be taken seriously but is one of the many pretensions, erotic and otherwise, that hamper the film. **90m/C VHS.** Mathilda May, Vincent D'Onofrio, Esai Morales, Fernando Rey; ***D:*** Leonard Schrader; ***W:*** Leonard Schrader; ***M:*** Thomas Newman.

The Naked Truth **1/2** *Your Past is Showing* **1958** A greedy publisher tries to get rich quick by publishing a scandal magazine about the "lurid" lives of prominent citizens. Well-drawn characters in an appealing offbeat comedy. **92m/C VHS, DVD.** *GB* Peter Sellers, Terry-Thomas, Shirley Eaton, Dennis Price; ***D:*** Mario Zampi.

Naked Vengeance WOOF! *Satin Vengeance* **1985 (R)** A woman's husband is murdered, she is beaten and raped, and she becomes a vengeful, vicious killing machine. Gratuitous violence, distasteful to the max. **97m/C VHS.** Deborah Tranelli, Kaz Garas, Bill McLaughlin; ***D:*** Cirio H. Santiago.

Naked Venus **1/2 1958** Ulmer's last film is a slow-paced tale about an American artist, married to a model who poses in the nude and belongs to a nudist camp, whose wealthy mother tries to tear the marriage apart. Discrimination and intolerance of nudist camps is explored. **80m/B VHS, DVD.** Patricia Conelle; ***D:*** Edgar G. Ulmer.

Naked Weapon *Chek law dak gung* **2003 (R)** A one-of-a-kind female assassin is slain, and her employer decides the easiest way to replace her is to kidnap 40 middle school girls and spend six years training them. Eventually they will all fight each other to the death to determine who will succeed to their predecessor's job. One of the most improbable exploitation films of all time. **92m/C DVD.** *HK* Daniel Wu, Maggie Q, Pei Pei Cheng, Dennis Chan, Marit Thoresen, Almen Wong Piu-Ha, Anya, Jewel Lee, Hoi Lin; ***D:*** Siu-Tung Ching; ***W:*** Jing Wong; ***C:*** Sung Fai Choi; ***M:*** Ken Chan, Kwong Wing Chan.

Naked Wishes **2000** Sex therapist Taj inherits a trunk from his uncle that contains only a dusty old bottle. When he cleans it up, very sexy genie Samathia is released and she lets Taj knows that they were lovers in a previous life and she's ready to resume their affair, besides granting his every wish. Taj, silly guy, wavers because he's engaged but then Samthia disturbs his therapy sessions by having his patients act out their deepest sexual fantasies. **99m/C VHS.** Jennifer Marks, Jeff Kueppers, Chanda Marie, Lance Moseley; ***D:*** Mike Sedan. **VIDEO**

The Naked Witch **1964** College students researching witchcraft dig up the grave of a long-dead witch. She comes back to life to take revenge on the descendants of the villagers who killed her. Nude shots feature a finger over the camera lens to cover up the witch's, uh, vital organs. **60m/C VHS, DVD.** Jack Herman, Libby Hall, Robert Short, Jo Maryman, Denis Adams, Charles West, Marilyn Pope; ***D:*** Larry Buchanan, Claude Alexander; ***W:*** Larry Buchanan, Claude Alexander.

Naked Youth WOOF! *Wild Youth* **1959** Seedy drive-in cheapie about two punks breaking out of juvenile prison and heading south of the border on a trail filled with crime, drugs, and loose women. **80m/B VHS, DVD.** Robert Hutton, John Goddard, Carol Ohmart, Jan Brooks, Robert Arthur, Steve Rowland, Clancy Cooper; ***D:*** John F. Schreyer.

Nam Angels **1988 (R)** Hell's Angels enter Southeast Asia and rescue POWs. **91m/C VHS, DVD.** *PH* Brad Johnson, Vernon Wells, Kevin Duffis, Fred Bailey, Archie Adamos, Rick Dean, Jeff Griffith, Eric Hahn, Ken Metcalfe, Tonichi Fructuoso, Leah Navarro, Ruben Ramos; ***D:*** Cirio H. Santiago; ***C:*** Ricardo Remias, Chris Squires; ***M:*** Jaime Fabregas.

A Name for Evil **1970 (R)** Having grown tired of city living, a couple moves to an old family estate out in the country near the Great Lakes. Strange sounds in the night are the first signs of the terror to come. **74m/C VHS, DVD.** Robert Culp, Samantha Eggar, Sheila Sullivan, Mike Lane; ***D:*** Bernard Girard.

The Name of the Rose **1/2 1986 (R)** An exhaustive, off-center adaptation of the bestselling Umberto Eco novel about violent murders in a 14th-century Italian abbey. An English monk struggles against religious fervor in his quest to uncover the truth. **128m/C VHS, DVD.** *IT GE FR* Sean Connery, F. Murray Abraham, Christian Slater, Ron Perlman, William Hickey, Feodor Chaliapin Jr., Elya Baskin, Michael (Michel) Lonsdale; ***D:*** Jean-Jacques Annaud; ***W:*** Andrew Birkin, Gerard Brach, Howard Franklin; ***C:*** Tonino Delli Colli; ***M:*** James Horner. British Acad. '87: Actor (Connery); Cesar '87: Foreign Film.

The Namesake **2006 (PG-13)** Nair's thoughtful and emotional adaptation of Jhumpa Lahiri's novel about two generations of a Bengali family living in the U.S. Ashoke (Khan) enters into an arranged marriage with Ashima (Tabu) and they move to New York, settling uneasily into their new lives. The couple's first child, Nikhil, is nicknamed Gogol after Ashoke's favorite writer. The name confusion will continue as the boy accepts and then rejects his various monikers, growing into a young man (Penn) torn between tradition and pursuing his own life. Naturally, he's also torn (at least at first) between WASP princess Maxine (Barrett) and fellow Bengali Moushumi (Robinson). Penn has true dramatic presence to go along with his more familiar comic gifts. **122m/C DVD.** *US* Kal Penn, Tabu, Irfan Khan, Jacinda Barrett, Zuleikha Robinson; ***D:*** Mira Nair; ***W:*** Sooni Taraporevala; ***C:*** Frederick Elmes; ***M:*** Nitin Sawhney.

Namu, the Killer Whale **1/2** *Namu, My Best Friend* **1966** Based on the true story of a marine biologist (Lansing) who gets the perfect opportunity to study killer whales when one is confined to a small cove. The local fisherman want to kill the creature because it feeds on the salmon they catch but they are persuaded against their baser instincts. Filmed on location in the San Juan Islands of Puget Sound. The real Namu lived at the Seattle Public Aquarium. **89m/C VHS, DVD.** Robert Lansing, John Anderson, Robin Mattson, Richard Erdman, Lee Meriwether, Joe Higgins; ***D:*** Laszlo Benedek.

Nana **1955** French version of Emile Zola's novel about an actress-prostitute who seduces the high society of Paris in the late 1880s, and suffers a heart-breaking downfall and death. Film has three remakes of the original 1926 version. **118m/C VHS.** *FR* Charles Boyer, Martine Carol, Jacques Castelot, Paul Frankeur, Noel Roquevert, Walter Chiari, Jean Debucourt, Elisa Cegani; ***D:*** Christian-Jaque; ***W:*** Christian-Jaque, Jean Ferry, Henri Jeanson; ***C:*** Christian Matras; ***M:*** Georges Van Parys.

Nana **1/2 1982** A lavishly photographed, graphic adaptation of the Emile Zola novel about a Parisian whore who acquires power by seducing the richest and politically formidable men. Dubbed. **92m/C VHS.** *IT* Katya Berger, Jean-Pierre Aumont; ***D:*** Dan Wolman; ***W:*** Marc Behm; ***M:*** Ennio Morricone.

Nancy Drew **1/2 2007 (PG)** Poor Nancy! this effort to modernize the teen sleuth is awkward and dull. Nancy (the appealing but rather stiff Roberts) accompanies her lawyer dad Carson (Donovan) to L.A. She discovers that their rented home was the scene of movie star Dehlia Draycott's (Harring) murder, an unsolved case that Nancy can't resist. However, the story really falls apart with Nancy in high school, where her anachronisms make her an object of popular girl scorn (too bad Nancy wasn't doing her sleuthing on vacation). But Nancy's sheer perky tenaciousness can overcome any obstacle (okay, except this script). Based on the Carolyn Keene character. **98m/C DVD.** *US* Emma Roberts, Tate Donovan, Josh Flitter, Max Thieriot, Rachael Leigh Cook, Amy Bruckner, Kay

Panabaker, Laura Elena Harring, Kelly Vitz, Marshall Bell, Caroline Aaron, David Doty, Kay Panabaker, Daniella Monet, Barry Bostwick, Daniella Monet; *D:* Andrew Fleming; *W:* Andrew Fleming, Tiffany Paulsen; *C:* Alexander Grusynski; *M:* Ralph Sall.

Nancy Drew and the Hidden Staircase 1939 Nancy Drew (Granville) and trusty Ted Nickerson (Thomas) are charged with both solving a murder and saving a couple of elderly women from losing their family home, which, by coincidence, seems haunted by some mysteries of its own, like moving walls and hidden staircases. **60m/B VHS.** Bonita Granville, Frankie Thomas Jr., John Litel, Frank Orth, Renie Riano; *D:* William Clemens; *W:* Mildred Wirt Benson, Kenneth Gamet.

Nancy Drew—Detective 1938 Nancy Drew (Granville) and Ted Nickerson (Thomas) are on the case of a kidnapping, or, well-to-do elderly lady napping. Ted fakes it as a nurse and Nancy plays the part of a widow to find both the nappee and the nappers. **66m/B VHS.** Bonita Granville, John Litel, James Stephenson, Frankie Thomas Jr., Frank Orth, Helena Phillips Evans, Renie Riano; *D:* William Clemens; *W:* Kenneth Gamet, Mildred Wirt Benson.

Nancy Drew, Reporter 1939 The young sleuth gets to play reporter after winning a newspaper contest. In no time at all, she's involved in a murder mystery. **68m/B VHS, DVD.** Bonita Granville, John Litel, Frankie Thomas Jr., Mary Lee, Sheila (Manors) Mannors, Betty Amann, Dick(ie) Jones, Olin Howlin, Charles Halton; *D:* William Clemens.

Nancy Drew—Trouble Shooter 1939 Nancy Drew's (Granville) uncle Matt gets slapped with a murder charge, only he's no murderer and it takes Nancy and Ted Nickerson (Thomas) to clear him. They have to find the real murderer, and they're stuck in some perilous situations in order to do just that. **66m/B VHS.** Bonita Granville, Frankie Thomas Jr., John Litel, Aldrich Bowker, Charlotte Wynters, Renie Riano, Edgar Edwards; *D:* William Clemens; *W:* Kenneth Gamet, Mildred Wirt Benson.

Nancy Goes to Rio 1/2 **1950** Actresses Powell and Sothern compete for the same part in a play and for the same man. Catch is, they're mother and daughter. Zany consequences ensue. Sothern's last film for MGM. ♫Time and Time Again; Shine On Harvest Moon; Cha Bomm Pa Pa; Yipsee-I-O; Magic is the Moonlight; Musetta's Waltz; Love is Like This; Nancy Goes to Rio. **99m/C VHS.** Ann Sothern, Jane Powell, Barry Sullivan, Carmen Miranda, Louis Calhern, Scotty Beckett, Hans Conried, Glenn Anders; *D:* Robert Z. Leonard; *W:* Sidney Sheldon.

The Nanny 1/2 **1965** Creepfest stars Davis as a seemingly proper nameless nanny who's been accused by her young charge Joey (Dix) of drowning his sister in the bathtub. But it's Joey who's sent away to a home for disturbed children and when he returns two years later (and just why is the nanny still around a childless home?) it's a battle of wills between the duo over who's responsible for some evil goings-on. Based on a novel by Evelyn Piper. **93m/B VHS.** *GB* Bette Davis, William Dix, Wendy Craig, Jill Bennett, James Villiers, Pamela Franklin, Jack Watling, Alfred Burke, Maurice Denham; *D:* Seth Holt; *W:* Jimmy Sangster; *C:* Henry Waxman; *M:* Richard Rodney Bennett.

The Nanny Diaries **2007 (PG-13)** Recent NYU graduate Annie (Johansson), unsure of herself after bombing a job interview, accepts a nanny job from Manhattan power-mommy extraordinaire Mrs. X (Linney), whose number one priority is herself, and her husband, uptight jerk Mr. X (Giamatti). Meanwhile, she's got the hots for a Harvard man (Adams), the neighbor upstairs. Johansson somehow manages not to give Annie any depth or humor, which is sorely missed amid the other superficial stereotypes. Aspires to satire, but the result is weak social commentary about the class divide between insanely rich Manhattanites and white, college educated upwardly mobile wannabes. Based on a novel fictionalizing its authors' real life Manhattan nanny experiences. **105m/C DVD.** *US* Scarlett Johansson, Laura Linney, Paul Giamatti, Chris Evans, Nicholas Reese Art, Alicia Keys, Donna Murphy, Judith Anna Roberts, Nathan Corddry; *D:* Shari Springer Berman; *W:* Shari Springer Berman; *C:* Terry Stacey; *M:* Mark Suozzo.

Nanny Insanity 1/2 *Domestic Import* **2006 (PG-13)** Over-the-top sitcom situations. Overwhelmed marrieds David (Dorf) and Marsha (Preston) decide to hire an experienced housekeeper/nanny since they're about to have their first child. But somehow they wind up with crazy Ukrainian immigrant Sophia (Korot), who's soon inviting her equally wacky family to move in as well. **94m/C DVD.** Cynthia (Cyndy, Cindy) Preston, Mindy Sterling, Howard Hesseman, Stephanie Patton, Larry Dorf, Alla Korot, Lauri Johnson; *D:* Kevin Connor; *W:* Andrea Malamut; *C:* Barry M. Wilson; *M:* Adam Malamut. **VIDEO**

Nanny McPhee 1/2 **2006 (PG)** Thompson wrote the screenplay and stars as the spectacularly ugly title character, who comes complete with magical abilities and a no-nonsense manner destined to overcome the horrors wrought by the seven motherless Brown children. Their clueless father, Cedric (Firth), counts on a stipend from Aunt Adelaide (Lansbury) to support the unruly brood but she has now demanded that he marry in 30 days or lose the money. Cedric is in love with unsuitable scullery maid Evangeline (Macdonald) but decides on garish, greedy widow Mrs. Quickly (Imrie) instead. Naturally, Nanny will put everything right. Loosely based on Christianna Brand's 1960s "Nurse Matilda" series. **97m/C DVD.** *US GB* Emma Thompson, Colin Firth, Kelly Macdonald, Derek Jacobi, Pat Barlow, Celia Imrie, Imelda Staunton, Thomas Sangster, Angela Lansbury, Jenny Daykin, Eliza Bennett, Raphael Coleman, Samuel Honywood, Holly Gibbs, Hebe Barnes, Zinnia Barnes; *D:* Kirk Jones; *W:* Emma Thompson; *C:* Henry Braham; *M:* Patrick Doyle.

Nanny McPhee 2 *Nanny McPhee and the Big Bang* **2010 (PG)** Nanny McPhee (Thompson) appears at the door of harried mom Isabel Green (Gyllenhaal) who's trying to run the family farm while her husband is away at war. However, Nanny discovers the Green children have their own war going on with their spoiled city cousins who have moved in. **m/C DVD.** Emma Thompson, Maggie Gyllenhaal, Rhys Ifans, Ralph Fiennes, Maggie Smith, Asa Butterfield; *D:* Susanna White; *W:* Emma Thompson; *C:* Mike Eley.

Napoleon **1927** A vivid, near-complete restoration of Gance's epic silent masterpiece about the famed conqueror's early years, from his youth through the Italian Campaign. An innovative, spectacular achievement with its use of multiple split screens, montage, color, and triptychs. Given a gala theatrical re-release in 1981. Remade in 1955. **235m/B VHS.** *FR* Albert Dieudonne, Antonin Artaud, Pierre Batcheff, Gina Manes, Armand Bernard, Harry Krimer, Albert Bras, Abel Gance, Georges Cahuzac, Annabella, Georges Lampin, Max Maxudian, Maurice Schutz, Marguerite Gance, Conrad Veidt, Edmond Van Daele, Alexandre Koubitzky, W. Percy Day, Yvette Dieudonne, Nicolas Koline, Vladimir Roudenko, Suzy Vernon, Robert Vidalin, Paul Amiot, Suzanne Bianchetti, Louis Sance; *D:* Abel Gance; *W:* Abel Gance; *C:* Leonce-Henri Burel, Roger Hubert, Jules Kruger; *M:* Carmine Coppola, Arthur Honegger, Carl Davis.

Napoleon **1955** Depicts life story of Napoleon from his days as a soldier in the French army to his exile on the Island of Elba. Falls short of the fantastic 1927 silent classic as it attempts to delve into Napoleon the man, as opposed to his conquests. Some might find it too slow for their tastes. **123m/C VHS, DVD.** *FR* Raymond Pellegrin, Orson Welles, Maria Schell, Yves Montand, Erich von Stroheim, Jean Gabin, Jean-Pierre Aumont; *D:* Sacha Guitry.

Napoleon 1/2 **1996 (G)** Cute pic for young kiddies who like animals. A very curious golden retriever puppy named Muffin manages to slip into a balloon-covered basket and finds himself airborne across Australia. Deciding he likes the idea of adventuring, Muffin renames himself Napoleon because it sounds braver. He lands unexpectedly near Sydney Harbor and is befriended by Birdo, who becomes his guide when Napoleon decides he wants to meet his wild dog cousins, the dingoes. And it's off into the bush, with kangaroos, koalas, snakes, and lizards to help or hinder along the way. **81m/C VHS, DVD.** *AU JP* *D:* Mario Andreacchio; *W:* Mario Andreacchio, Mark Saltzman; *C:* Roger Dowling; *M:* Bill Conti; *V:* Jamie Croft, Philip Quast, Carole Skinner, Anne Louise Lambert, David Argue, Joan Rivers, Steven Vidler, Susan Lyons.

Napoleon 1/2 **2003** Epic miniseries starts off with a bedraggled general Napoleon Bonaparte (Clavier) managing to make both personal and professional marks in 1794 Paris: he thwarts a royalist riot at the end of the French Revolution and he meets Josephine (Rossellini). Soon, Napoleon is rising through the military ranks, winning the loyalty of the people, and proclaiming himself Emperor. But since Josephine can't give him a child, he has to make some dynastic decisions and begins to lose control. A lavish spectacle and a charismatic titular performance by Clavier. Based on the biography by Max Gallo. **360m/C VHS, DVD.** Christian Clavier, Isabella Rossellini, Gerard Depardieu, John Malkovich, Anouk Aimee, Heino Ferch, Ennio Fantastichini, Guillaume Depardieu, Sebastian Koch, Julian Sands, Toby Stephens, John Wood, Mavie Horbiger, Yves Jacques; *D:* Yves Simoneau; *W:* Didier Decoin; *C:* Guy Dufaux; *M:* Richard Gregoire. **CABLE**

Napoleon and Samantha **1972** Disney adventure about Napoleon, an orphan (Whitaker), who is befriended by Danny, a college student (Douglas). After the death of his grandfather, Napoleon decides to take Major, his elderly pet lion, and follow Danny, who is herding goats for the summer, across the American northwest mountains and they are joined by Samantha (Foster in her film debut). Worth watching. **91m/C VHS, DVD.** Jodie Foster, Johnny Whitaker, Michael Douglas, Will Geer, Henry Jones; *D:* Bernard McEveety; *W:* Stewart Raffill; *C:* Monroe Askins; *M:* Buddy (Norman Dale) Baker.

Napoleon Dynamite **2004 (PG)** Filmed in Preston, Idaho, the debut of director Hess (co-written by his wife) is a small-budget, small-scale, overreaching effort about the unfortunately named title character (Heder), an awkward, frizzy-haired, high school uber-nerd whose life is one exasperation after another. He's beaten up by the jocks, can't score with the babes, and his only friend is a shy Mexican immigrant, Pedro (Ramirez), whom Napoleon assists in his campaign for class president against popular blonde goddess, Summer (Duff, Hilary's sister). His much-older brother Kip (Ruell) is even more of a misfit and his creepily macho Uncle Rico (Gries) is looking after the family since Grandma (Martin) had an ATV-riding accident. You should want to root for the underdog but you may become just as exasperated as Napoleon watching this flick. **86m/C VHS, DVD, UMD.** Jon(athan) Gries, Tina Majorino, Diedrich Bader, Jon Heder, Aaron Ruell, Efren Ramirez, Haylie Duff, Trevor Snarr, Shondrella Avery; *D:* Jared Hess; *W:* Jared Hess, Jerusha Hess; *C:* Munn Powell; *M:* John Swihart.

Narc 1/2 **2002 (R)** Patric is Det. Nick Tellis, an undercover narcotics cop on suspension for a bust that went tragically wrong. He seeks a desk job, but the suits want him to investigate the murder of another undercover cop. He's teamed with the deceased's former partner, Henry Oak (Liotta), who's out to nail the killers, procedures be damned, although his motives may be more than just revenge. As the investigation continues, and the dead end leads mount, the tension and suspense become palpable. Carnahan's tale is brutal, dark, and full of dread, but it is always gripping, and he uses cop drama conventions to great effect. Both Patric and Liotta take well to their roles, with Patric embodying Nick's tortured cop looking for redemption and Liotta swallowing scenes whole with Oak's barely (and sometimes unsuccessfully) suppressed rage. **105m/C VHS, DVD.** *US* Ray Liotta, Jason Patric, Chi McBride, Busta Rhymes, Richard Chevolleau, John Ortiz, Alan Van Sprang, Krista Bridges, Anne Openshaw; *D:* Joe Carnahan; *W:* Joe Carnahan; *C:* Alex Nepomniaschy; *M:* Cliff Martinez.

The Narcotics Story WOOF! *The Dreaded Persuasion* **1958** Bad film on the same vein as "Reefer Madness." Originally intended as a police training film, this shows the evils and destruction of heroin addiction. Portrayals of drug addicts are hilarious. **75m/C VHS.** Sharon Strand, Darlene Hendricks, Herbert Crisp, Fred Marratto; *D:* Robert W. Larsen; *Nar:* Art Gilmore.

The Narrow Margin **1952** Well-made, harrowing adventure about a cop who is in charge of transporting a gangster's widow to a trial where she is to testify. On the train he must try to keep her safe from the hit-men who would murder her. A real cat and mouse game—one of the best suspense movies of the '50s. **71m/B VHS, DVD.** Charles McGraw, Marie Windsor, Jacqueline White, Queenie Leonard, Gordon Gebert, Don Beddoe, Harry Harvey; *D:* Richard Fleischer.

Narrow Margin **1990 (R)** Archer reluctantly agrees to testify against the mob after witnessing a murder, and Los Angeles D.A. Hackman is assigned to protect her on the train through the Rockies back to L.A. Bad idea, she finds out. No match for its '52 predecessor. **99m/C VHS, DVD.** Gene Hackman, Anne Archer, James B. Sikking, J.T. Walsh, M. Emmet Walsh; *D:* Peter Hyams; *W:* Peter Hyams; *M:* Bruce Broughton.

Narrow Trail 1/2 **1917** A silent classic that still stands as one of the best Westerns ever made. A tough cowboy with a troubled past hopes a good woman can save him. But she's seen trouble, too. They meet up again in San Francisco's Barbary Coast. A horse race might hold the answer. **56m/B VHS.** William S. Hart, Sylvia Bremer, Milton Ross; *D:* William S. Hart.

Nashville **1975 (R)** Altman's stunning, brilliant film tapestry that follows the lives of 24 people during a political campaign/music festival in Nashville. Seemingly extemporaneous vignettes, actors playing themselves (Elliott Gould and Julie Christie), funny, touching, poignant character studies concerning affairs of the heart and despairs of the mind. Repeatedly blurs reality and fantasy. ♫I'm Easy; Two Hundred Years; Keep A'Goin'; One, I Love You; Let Me Be the One; The Day I Looked Jesus in the Eye; For the Sake of the Children; I Never Get Enough; It Don't Worry Me. **159m/C VHS, DVD.** Allan Nicholls, Keith Carradine, Lily Tomlin, Henry Gibson, Ronee Blakley, Keenan Wynn, David Arkin, Geraldine Chaplin, Lauren Hutton, Shelley Duvall, Barbara Harris, Allen (Goorwitz) Garfield, Karen Black, Christina Raines, Michael Murphy, Ned Beatty, Barbara Baxley, Scott Glenn, Jeff Goldblum, Gwen Welles, Bert Remsen, Robert DoQui, Elliott Gould, Julie Christie; *D:* Robert Altman; *W:* Joan Tewkesbury; *C:* Paul Lohmann; *M:* Richard Baskin. Oscars '75: Song ("I'm Easy"); Golden Globes '76: Song ("I'm Easy"); Natl. Bd. of Review '75: Director (Altman), Support. Actress (Blakley), Natl. Film Reg. '92;; N.Y. Film Critics '75: Director (Altman), Film, Support. Actress (Tomlin); Natl. Soc. Film Critics '75: Director (Altman), Film, Support. Actor (Gibson), Support. Actress (Tomlin).

Nashville Beat **1989** Gang targets the citizens of Nashville, Tennessee, until two tough cops stomp the gang's delusion that Southern folk are easy marks. **110m/C VHS.** Kent McCord, Martin Milner; *D:* Bernard L. Kowalski.

Nashville Girl *Country Music Daughter; New Girl in Town* **1976 (R)** Innocent country girl who wants to make good in the country music scene, rises to the top of the Nashville success ladder, by compromising everything and hanging out with stereotyped no-goods in the show biz world. It's as good as a yawn. **90m/C VHS.** Monica Gayle, Johnny Rodriguez; *D:* Gus Trikonis.

The Nasty Girl 1/2 *Das Schreckliche Madchen* **1990 (PG-13)** A bright young German model plans to enter a national essay contest on the topic of her hometown's history during the Third Reich. While researching the paper, she's harassed and even brutalized, but refuses to cease her sleuthing. Excellent performances, tight direction, with comedic touches that charmingly imparts an important message. Based on a true story. In German with English subtitles. **93m/C VHS, DVD.** *GE* Lena Stolze, Monika Baumgartner, Michael Gahr; *D:* Michael Verhoeven; *W:* Michael Verhoeven; *C:* Axel de Roche. British Acad. '91: Foreign Film; N.Y. Film Critics '90: Foreign Film.

Nasty Habits 1977 (PG) Broad farce depicting a corrupt Philadelphia convent as a satiric parallel to Watergate, with nuns modeled on Nixon, Dean and Mitchell. Includes cameo appearances by various media personalities. Based on the British novel "The Abbess of Crewe" by Muriel Spark. **92m/C VHS, DVD.** *GB* Glenda Jackson, Geraldine Page, Anne Jackson, Melina Mercouri, Sandy Dennis, Susan Penhaligon, Anne Meara, Edith Evans, Rip Torn, Eli Wallach, Jerry Stiller; ***Cameos:*** Mike Douglas, Bill Jorgensen, Jessica Savitch, Howard K. Smith; ***D:*** Michael Lindsay-Hogg.

Nasty Hero 1/2 1989 (PG-13) Hard-boiled ex-con comes to Miami to get revenge on the car thieves who framed him and got him sent to the slammer. This is car-chase scene heaven—little plot or drama. **79m/C VHS.** Robert Sedgwick, Carlos Palomino, Scott Feraco, Mike Starr, Rosanna DaVon, Jon Tenney, Raymond Serra; ***D:*** Nick Barwood; ***C:*** Oliver Wood.

Nasty Rabbit *Spies-A-Go-Go* 1964 Ridiculous spoof about Soviet spies intent on releasing a rabbit with a hideous Communist disease into the U.S. Everyone gets in on the chase: Nazi forces, cowboys and Indians, sideshow freaks, banditos—what is the point? **88m/C VHS, DVD.** Arch Hall Jr., Micha(el) Terr, Liz Renay, John Akana; ***D:*** James Landis.

The Natalee Holloway Story 2009 Lifetime movie about the 2005 disappearance of Alabama teenager Natalee Holloway while on spring break in Aruba. Her mother Beth and her stepfather Jug Twitty head to the island when the case drags on and remains unsolved (Natalee's body is not found), suspects change their stories, and it seems that the police are involved in a cover-up to hide their incompetence. **96m/C DVD.** Tracy Pollan, Grant Show, Catherine Dent, Amy Gumenick, Jacques Strydom, Sean Higgs, Sean Cameron Michael; ***D:*** Mikael Salomon; ***W:*** Teena Booth; ***C:*** Paul Gilpin; ***M:*** Christopher Ward. **CABLE**

Natas... The Reflection 1983 (PG) A reporter persists in validating an Indian demon myth. **90m/C VHS.** Randy Mulkey, Pat Bolt, Craig Hensley, Kelli Kuhn; ***D:*** Jack Dunlap; ***W:*** Jack Dunlap.

Nate and Hayes 1/2 1983 (PG) Set during the mid-1800s in the South Pacific, the notorious real-life swashbuckler Captain "Bully" Hayes ("good pirate") helps young missionary Nate recapture his fiancee from a cutthroat gang of evil slave traders. Entertaining "jolly rogers" film. **100m/C VHS, DVD.** *NZ* Tommy Lee Jones, Michael O'Keefe, Max Phipps, Jenny Seagrove; ***D:*** Ferdinand Fairfax; ***M:*** Trevor Jones.

Nathalie 1/2 2003 Remarkably dull psycho-sexual tease finds Catherine (Ardant) distressed to learn that Bernard (Depardieu), her husband of 25 years, has been cheating. So Catherine hires a beautician/prostitute named Marlene (Beart) to become Bernard's sex partner and report back to her. In great detail. Oh, and Marlene should call herself Nathalie. French with subtitles. **105m/C DVD.** *FR* Fanny Ardant, Emmanuelle Beart, Gerard Depardieu; ***D:*** Anne Fontaine; ***W:*** Anne Fontaine, Jacques Fieschi; ***C:*** Jean-Marc Fabre; ***M:*** Michael Nyman.

Nathalie Granger 1/2 1972 Maybe Duras was trying to bore her audience to death with this experimental drama. Isabelle (Bose) and her nameless friend (Moreau) go through their dull daily housekeeping rituals moderately worried about getting Isabelle's apparently troubled young daughter Nathalie (Mascolo) into a new school. Depardieu shows up as a door-to-door salesman. French with subtitles. **79m/B DVD.** *FR* Lucia Bose, Jeanne Moreau, Gerard Depardieu, Luce Garcia-Ville, Valerie Mascolo; ***D:*** Marguerite Duras; ***W:*** Marguerite Duras; ***C:*** Ghislan Cloquet.

A Nation Aflame 1/2 1937 Anti-Klan film is based on a story by Thomas L. Dixon, the author of "The Clansman," from which D.W. Griffith made "The Birth of a Nation." In this story, a con man gains control of the state's government through an ultra-nationalistic secret society, and eventually pays for his corruption. **70m/B VHS.** Lila Lee, Noel Madison, Snub Pollard, Norma Trelvar; ***D:*** Victor Halperin.

National Lampoon Goes to the Movies 1981 Parodies of popular Hollywood genres, including cop thrillers, melodramas, and inspirational biographies, done in goofy "Lampoon" style. **89m/C VHS, DVD.** Robby Benson, Candy Clark, Diane Lane, Christopher Lloyd, Peter Riegert, Richard Widmark, Henny Youngman, Bobby DiCicco; ***D:*** Henry Jaglom.

National Lampoon Presents Cattle Call WOOF! *Cattle Call* 2006 (R) Like having a root canal without anesthetic. Losers Sherman, Glenn, and Richie live in L.A. so what better way to meet chicks than to pretend to be casting agents for an indie film and taking their pick from the actresses who show up? After a number of raunchy auditions, the guys each find their special someone, but when the ladies in question discover it was all a scam they are out for male body parts. **87m/C DVD.** Diedrich Bader, Thomas Ian Nicholas, Jenny Mollen, Nicole Eggert, Andrew Kates, Jonathan Winters, Paul Mazursky, Chelsea Handler; ***D:*** Martin Guigui; ***W:*** Martin Guigui; ***C:*** Massimo Zeri; ***M:*** Cody Westheimer. **VIDEO**

National Lampoon Presents RoboDoc *RoboDoc* 2008 (R) Another lame effort from the franchise. Jason Dockery (Faustino) is hired by a healthcare company to build a robot doctor that can never make a misdiagnosis or medical mistake, all to thwart obnoxious lawyer Jake Gorman (Babel), who specializes in medical malpractice. But Jake thinks he can find a way to sue even a mechanical man. **90m/C DVD.** David Faustino, Alan Thicke, Corin "Corky" Nemec, David DeLuise, Michael Winslow, Kenny Babel, William Haze; ***D:*** Stephen Maddocks; ***W:*** Doug Gordon; ***C:*** Stephen Campbell. **VIDEO**

National Lampoon's Adam & Eve *Adam & Eve* 2005 (R) Raunchy, gross, yet amusing and occasionally intelligent sex comedy. Adam (Douglas) falls for virginal sorority babe Eve (Chriqui), who doesn't believe in putting out to keep some horny frat dude around. She's after true love and Adam waits... and waits. But both are pressured by their so-called friends (not to mention hormonal urges) to either consummate the relationship or break up. **91m/C DVD.** Cameron Douglas, Emmanuelle Chriqui, Chad Lindberg, Courtney Peldon, Jake Hoffman, George Dzundza, Lisa Wilhoit; ***D:*** Jeff Kanew; ***W:*** Justin Kanew; ***C:*** John Darbonne. **VIDEO**

National Lampoon's Animal House 1/2 *Animal House* 1978 (R) Classic Belushi vehicle running amuck. Set in 1962 and responsible for launching Otis Day and the Knights and defining cinematic food fights. Every college tradition from fraternity rush week to the homecoming pageant is irreverently and relentlessly mocked in this wild comedy about Delta House, a fraternity on the edge. Climaxes with the homecoming parade from hell. Sophomoric, but very funny, with a host of young stars who went on to more serious work. Remember: "Knowledge is good." **109m/C VHS, DVD, UMD, HD DVD.** John Belushi, Tim Matheson, John Vernon, Donald Sutherland, Peter Riegert, Stephen Furst, Bruce McGill, Mark Metcalf, Verna Bloom, Karen Allen, Tom Hulce, Mary Louise Weller, James Widdoes, Kevin Bacon, Doug Kenney, Martha Smith, Cesare Danova, Stephen Bishop, Sarah Holcomb; ***D:*** John Landis; ***W:*** Harold Ramis, Chris Miller, Doug Kenney; ***C:*** Charles Correll; ***M:*** Elmer Bernstein. Natl. Film Reg. '01.

National Lampoon's Attack of the 5 Ft. 2 Women *Attack of the 5 Ft. 2 Women* 1994 (R) Brown parodies two of 1994's most notorious tabloid queens in "Tonya: The Battle of Wounded Knee" and "He Never Give Me Orgasm: The Lenora Babbitt Story." **82m/C VHS.** Julie Brown, Sam McMurray, Adam Storke, Priscilla Barnes, Lauren Tewes, Dick Miller, Rick Overton, Stanley DeSantis, Anne DeSalvo, Liz Torres, Vicki Lawrence, Stella Stevens, Peter DeLuise, Stacey Travis; ***D:*** Richard Wenk, Julie Brown; ***W:*** Charlie Coffey, Julie Brown; ***M:*** Christopher Tyng. **CABLE**

National Lampoon's Christmas Vacation 1/2 *Christmas Vacation* 1989 (PG-13) The third vacation for the Griswold family finds them hosting repulsive relatives for Yuletide. The sight gags, although predictable, are sometimes on the mark. Quaid is a standout as the slovenly cousin. **93m/C VHS, DVD, Blu-ray Disc.** Chevy Chase, Beverly D'Angelo, Randy Quaid, Diane Ladd, John Randolph, E.G. Marshall, Doris Roberts, Julia Louis-Dreyfus, Mae Questel, William Hickey, Brian Doyle-Murray, Juliette Lewis, Johnny Galecki, Nicholas Guest, Miriam Flynn; ***D:*** Jeremiah S. Chechik; ***W:*** John Hughes; ***C:*** Thomas Ackerman; ***M:*** Angelo Badalamenti.

National Lampoon's Christmas Vacation 2: Cousin Eddie's Big Island Adventure *National Lampoon's Cousin Eddie's Christmas Vacation Lost; Christmas Vacation 2: Cousin Eddie; Christmas Vacation 2: Cousin Eddie's Island Adventure* 2003 Quaid is back as boorish Cousin Eddie. This time his nutty gaggle gets to spend the holidays on a South Pacific island as a payoff from his old boss for a monkey mishap. But their fateful trip instead ends up on an uncharted desert isle. Again, the lessons of "Caddyshack 2" and "Blues Brothers 2000" go tragically unheeded. **83m/C VHS, DVD.** Randy Quaid, Miriam Flynn, Dana Barron, Jake Thomas, Beverly Garland, Stephen Furst, Eric Idle, Fred Willard, Ed Asner, Sung Hi Lee, Julian Stone, Kate Bradley; ***D:*** Nick Marck; ***W:*** Matty Simmons; ***M:*** Nathan Furst. **TV**

National Lampoon's Class of '86 1/2 *Class of '86* 1986 This is a live stage comedy show written and sponsored by the infamous adult humor magazine, featuring a new cast of comics. **86m/C VHS.** Rodger Bumpass, Veanne Cox, Annie Golden, John Michael Higgins, Tommy Koenig.

National Lampoon's Class Reunion WOOF! *Class Reunion* 1982 (R) Class reunion with some very wacky guests and a decided lack of plot or purpose. Things go from bad to worse when a crazed killer decides to join in on the festivities. Disappointing with very few laughs. **85m/C VHS, DVD.** Shelley Smith, Gerrit Graham, Michael Lerner; ***D:*** Michael Miller; ***W:*** John Hughes; ***C:*** Philip Lathrop; ***M:*** Peter Bernstein.

National Lampoon's Dad's Week Off *Dad's Week Off* 1997 (R) Jack (Winkler) is a stressed-out salesman who decides he needs time away from both his job and his family. His wife agrees to take their kids camping while Jack spends a week peacefully at home. But before he knows it, Jack's bud (Jeni) has introduced him to kooky Cherice (d'Abo) and it's party-time at Jack's place. **92m/C VHS.** Henry Winkler, Olivia D'Abo, Richard Jeni, Justin Louis, Ken Pogue, Wendel Meldrum; ***D:*** Neal Israel; ***W:*** Neal Israel; ***C:*** Jan Kiesser; ***M:*** Marc Bonilla. **CABLE**

National Lampoon's European Vacation 1/2 *European Vacation* 1985 (PG-13) Sappy sequel to "Vacation" that has witless Chase and his family bumbling around in the land "across the pond." The Griswolds nearly redefine the term "ugly American." Stonehenge will never be the same. **94m/C VHS, DVD.** Chevy Chase, Beverly D'Angelo, Dana Hill, Jason Lively, Victor Lanoux, John Astin, William Zabka, Robbie Coltrane, Mel Smith; ***Cameos:*** Eric Idle; ***D:*** Amy Heckerling; ***W:*** John Hughes, Robert Klane, Eric Idle; ***M:*** Charles Fox.

National Lampoon's Favorite Deadly Sins 1/2 1995 (R) Three sketches about greed, anger, and lust. In "Lust," Leary plays a security guard who spies on a neighbor; "Anger" finds Clay as an irate convenience store shopper; and Mantegna, in "Greed," stars as a sleazoid producer who helps a young woman kill her wicked stepmother and stepsisters in order to make a movie about it. **99m/C VHS.** Joe Mantegna, Denis Leary, Annabella Sciorra, Andrew (Dice Clay) Silverstein, Cassidy Rae, Brian Keith, William Ragsdale, Farrah Forke, Tanya Pohlkotte; ***D:*** Denis Leary, David Jablin; ***W:*** Michael Barrie, Jim Mulholland, Lee Biondi, Ann Lembeck.

National Lampoon's Gold Diggers WOOF! *Lady Killers* 2004 (PG-13) Why does anyone bother releasing this tripe on the big screen when it barely qualifies for basic cable or direct-to-video? The gold diggers of the title are a couple of inept twenty-something con men (Friedle, Owen) who plot to marry two elderly sisters (Taylor, Lasser) who are supposed to be wealthy Beverly Hills heiresses. Only the gals (who are, of course, broke) have their own insurance scam in mind. Can't even be enjoyed as trash. **82m/C DVD.** Will Friedle, Chris Owen, Louise Lasser, Renee Taylor, Nikki Ziering; ***D:*** Gary Preisler; ***W:*** Gary Preisler; ***C:*** Thomas Callaway.

National Lampoon's Golf Punks 1/2 1999 (PG-13) Innocuous comedy finds luckless former golf pro Al Oliver (Arnold) in desperate need of cash to pay off his gambling debts. So, he becomes an instructor to a bunch of teen misfits and decides to enter the uncoordinated group in a prestigious tournament. **95m/C VHS, DVD.** *CA* Tom Arnold, James Kirk, Rene Tardif; ***D:*** Harvey Frost; ***W:*** Jill Mazursky; ***C:*** Patrick Williams; ***M:*** Richard Bronskill. **VIDEO**

National Lampoon's Holiday Reunion *Thanksgiving Family Reunion* 2003 (PG-13) Think "Christmas Vacation" but without the Griswolds, or the funny. Thanksgiving stands in for Wally World, Europe, Christmas, and Vegas. Cousin Woodward—you, sir, are no Cousin Eddie! **90m/C VHS, DVD.** Bryan Cranston, Judge Reinhold, Reece Thompson, Penelope Ann Miller, Hallie Todd, Brittney Irvin, Anthony Holland, Noel Fisher, Noel Fisher, David Paetkau; ***D:*** Neal Israel; ***W:*** Marc Warren; ***M:*** Robert Folk, Brad Segal. **TV**

National Lampoon's Last Resort 1/2 1994 (PG-13) Retired film actor finds his long-time movie nemesis can't separate screen life from the real thing anymore and is planning an invasion of the actor's private island. So, he calls on his nephew (who brings along a friend) to help him out. **91m/C VHS, DVD.** Corey Feldman, Corey Haim, Geoffrey Lewis, Robert Mandan; ***D:*** Rafal Zielinski.

National Lampoon's Loaded Weapon 1 1/2 *Loaded Weapon 1* 1993 (PG-13) Cop Jack Colt (Estevez) and partner Wes Luger (Jackson) attempt to recover a microfilm which contains a formula for turning cocaine into cookies. Essentially a sendup of the popular "Lethal Weapon" series, although other movies and themes make an appearance, well sort of. Short on plot and long on slapstick, but that's the whole point. Tired formula creates nostalgia for the granddaddy of them all, "Airplane." Lots of cameos, including one from sibling spoof star Sheen. The magazine folded while the movie was in production, an ominous sign. **83m/C VHS, DVD.** Emilio Estevez, Samuel L. Jackson, Jon Lovitz, Tim Curry, Kathy Ireland, William Shatner, Dr. Joyce Brothers, James Doohan, Richard Moll, F. Murray Abraham, Denis Leary, Corey Feldman, Phil Hartman, J.T. Walsh, Erik Estrada, Larry Wilcox, Allyce Beasley, Charlie Sheen; ***D:*** Gene Quintano; ***W:*** Don Holley, Gene Quintano; ***C:*** Peter Deming; ***M:*** Robert Folk.

National Lampoon's Senior Trip *Senior Trip* 1995 (R) According to the promotion, "they came, they saw, they passed out." Good dumb fun is hard to come by, particularly here. Latest lesser "Lampoon" effort in a long line of lesser Lampoons is about midwestern high school seniors who take a bus trip to Washington to meet the President. Along the way they have hijinks, including manipulation by a stereotypically corrupt senator out to embarrass his politcal opponent. Frewer is the inept principal who leads the hopelessly cliched group of misfits through the dopey corridors of power. Somehow, even the Coreys avoided this one. **91m/C VHS, DVD.** Matt Frewer, Valerie Mahaffey, Lawrence Dane, Thomas Chong, Kevin McDonald; ***D:*** Kelly Makin; ***W:*** I. Marlene King, Roger Kumble.

National Lampoon's The Don's Analyst *The Don's Analyst* 1997 (R) Don Vito (Loggia) has lots of problems—his wife has left him, his sons are too stupid to take over the business, and his mob rival wants both his business and his wife. The Don's so upset he's thinking of going legit. Instead, his sons kidnap therapist Dr. Riceputo (Pollak) to straighten the Don out. **103m/C VHS.** Robert Loggia, Kevin Pollak, Joseph Bologna, Angie Dickinson, Sherilyn Fenn;

D: David Jablin. **CABLE**

National Lampoon's The Stoned Aged WOOF! *Homo Erectus* **2007 (R)** No one actually expects a watchable film from anything slapped with this franchise label anymore, and this is no exception. Meek caveman Ishbo (Rifkin) tries to persuade his tribe to evolve (using tools and stuff) but they're not big on his radical ideas. And while Ishbo is angsting over his dream cavegirl Fardart (Larter), his big, dumb older brother Thudnik (MacArthur) just clubs the chick on the head and drags her back to the cave. **88m/C DVD.** Adam Rifkin, Ali Larter, Hayes Macarthur, David Carradine; *D:* Adam Rifkin; *W:* Adam Rifkin; *C:* Scott Billups; *M:* Alex Wurman. **VIDEO**

National Lampoon's Vacation *Vacation* **1983 (R)** The Clark Griswold (Chase) family of suburban Chicago embarks on a westward cross-country vacation via car to the renowned "Wally World." Ridiculous and hysterical misadventures, including a falling asleep at the wheel sequence and the untimely death of Aunt Edna. **98m/C VHS, DVD, HD DVD.** Chevy Chase, Beverly D'Angelo, Imogene Coca, Randy Quaid, Christie Brinkley, James Keach, Anthony Michael Hall, John Candy, Eddie Bracken, Brian Doyle-Murray, Eugene Levy, Dana Barron, Jane Krakowski, Miriam Flynn, Frank McRae, John Diehl, Mickey Jones; *D:* Harold Ramis; *W:* John Hughes, Harold Ramis; *C:* Victor Kemper; *M:* Ralph Burns.

National Lampoon's Van Wilder *Van Wilder* **2002 (R)** Cliched and crass college comedy of suave coed Van Wilder (Reynolds) who gets cut off by his dad (Matheson, in a nice bit of ironic casting), who realizes his son's seven college years have not yielded a degree. The universally adored, high-profile, frat house toastmaster then uses his charm to helps fund his education by helping the underprivileged undergrads meet women and have fun—for a price, of course. A circus of gross-out jokes and sight gags that would make the Farrelly brothers blush ensue. Reid is typically vapid as the lackluster Lois Lane college reporter and love interest. An unrated version is also available. **92m/C VHS, DVD, Blu-ray Disc, UMD.** *US* Ryan Reynolds, Tara Reid, Tim Matheson, Kal Penn, Teck Holmes, Daniel Cosgrove, Deon Richmond, Alex Burns, Paul Gleason, Tom Everett Scott, Chris Owen, Curtis Armstrong, Kim Smith, Erik Estrada, Michelle Rene Thomas; *D:* Walt Becker; *W:* Brent Goldberg, David T. Wagner; *C:* James R. Bagdonas; *M:* David Lawrence.

National Lampoon's Van Wilder 2: The Rise of Taj WOOF! *Van Wilder 2: The Rise of Taj* **2006 (R)** Despite the title, Ryan Reynolds' Van Wilder is completely—and smartly—MIA as his former underling Taj Mahal Badalandabad (Penn) is all grown up and ready to tackle the countless and pointless sexual innuendo jokes that make up this aimless sequel. Taj goes off to Camford University in England as a student-teacher and gets his own crew of flunkies to whip into shape. They must prove themselves to the school's elite in order to win the coveted Camford Cup. Shamelessly—and poorly—rips off scenes from too many other movies to keep track of. So bad it makes the original look good. **95m/C DVD.** *US* Lauren Cohan, Daniel Percival, Glen Barry, Kal Penn, Anthony Cozens, Steven Rathman, Holly Davidson; *D:* Mort Nathan; *W:* David Gallagher; *C:* Hubert Taczanowski; *M:* Robert Folk.

National Security ½ **2003 (PG-13)** Earl Montgomery (Lawrence, seeming surprisingly bored) is a police academy reject and Hank Rafferty (Zahn) is a disgraced cop. Working as security guards, they uncover a smuggling operation in standard buddy-cop fashion. What the problem is? Car chases and Lawrence's rapid-fire "comic" rantings replace any semblance of plot or direction to make a mess that wastes the time of all involved. But at least it has spiteful racial politics played for laughs. **90m/C VHS, DVD.** *US* Martin Lawrence, Steve Zahn, Eric Roberts, Bill Duke, Colm Feore, Timothy Busfield, Robine Lee, Matt McCoy, Brett Cullen, Stephen Tobolowsky, Joe Flaherty; *D:* Dennis Dugan; *W:* Jay Scherick, David Ronn; *C:* Oliver Wood; *M:* Randy Edelman.

National Treasure **2004 (PG)** Old-fashioned and underwhelming adventure tale. Once upon a time, the Knights Templar unearthed the legendary treasure of King Solomon during a crusade. After being hidden in Europe, the treasure supposedly made its way to colonial-era America where the Freemasons, who included many of the Founding Fathers, protected it. The treasure is a longtime obsession for the Gates family, including Benjamin Franklin Gates (Cage), who thinks his best clue is concealed on the reverse side of the Declaration of Independence. When his sinister benefactor Howe (Bean) plots to steal the document, patriotic Ben and his techie sidekick Riley (Bartha) try to alert the authorities, including hottie conservator Abigail (Kruger). Many uninvolving twists and less-than-exciting action sequences follow. **130m/C DVD, Blu-ray Disc, UMD.** *US* Nicolas Cage, Diane Kruger, Justin Bartha, Sean Bean, Jon Voight, Harvey Keitel, Christopher Plummer; *D:* Jon Turteltaub; *W:* Jim Kouf, Marianne S. Wibberley, Cormac Wibberley; *C:* Caleb Deschanel; *M:* Trevor Rabin.

National Treasure: Book of Secrets ½ **2007 (PG)** Equally old-fashioned sequel to the 2004 treasure hunt. Ben Gates (Cage) and dad Patrick (Voight) defend the family honor from dastardly southerner Mitch Wilkinson (Harris), who insists a Gates ancestor was actually behind Lincoln's assassination. Interesting historical clues combine with a presidential book of secrets and a global hunt for missing gold to create an enjoyable adventure. Includes all the players from the original, along with new addition, Gates matriarch Emily (an admirably game Mirren). **124m/C DVD, Blu-ray Disc.** *US* Nicolas Cage, Jon Voight, Diane Kruger, Justin Bartha, Helen Mirren, Harvey Keitel, Ed Harris, Bruce Greenwood, Alicia Coppola, Michael Maize, Timothy Murphy, Joel Gretsch; *D:* Jon Turteltaub; *W:* Cormac Wibberley, Marianne S. Wibberley; *C:* John Schwartzman, Amir M. Mokri; *M:* Trevor Rabin.

The National Tree ½ **2009** In this Hallmark Channel holiday drama, widower Corey Burdock plants a tree in honor of his late wife. When Corey decides to sell his Oregon property years later, the tree is to be bulldozed until it's chosen to be the official White House Christmas tree. Corey and his sullen teenaged son Rock are driving a big rig to deliver the tree in person accompanied by Faith, whose company bought Corey's land and is reaping the publicity, and Katie, Rock's video chat room friend who's blogging about their trip. **88m/C DVD.** Andrew McCarthy, Evan Williams, Kari Matchett, Paula Brancati; *D:* Graeme Campbell; *W:* J.B. White; *C:* Francois Dagenais; *M:* Ian Thomas. **CABLE**

National Velvet **1944 (G)** Velvet Brown (Taylor) wins a horse in a raffle and is determined to train it to compete in the famed Grand National race with the help of her best friend, Mi (Rooney). Taylor, only 12 at the time, is superb in her first starring role. Rooney also gives a fine performance. Filmed with a loving eye on lushly decorated sets, this is a masterpiece version of the story of affection between a girl and her pet. Based on the novel by Enid Bagnold and followed by the dismal "International Velvet" in 1978. **124m/C VHS, DVD.** Elizabeth Taylor, Mickey Rooney, Arthur Treacher, Donald Crisp, Anne Revere, Angela Lansbury, Reginald Owen, Norma Varden, Jackie "Butch" Jenkins, Terence (Terry) Kilburn; *D:* Clarence Brown; *W:* Theodore Reeves, Helen Deutsch; *C:* Leonard Smith; *M:* Herbert Stothart. Oscars '45: Film Editing, Support. Actress (Revere), Natl. Film Reg. '03.

Native Son ½ **1951** A young black man from the ghettos of Chicago is hired as a chauffeur by an affluent white family. His job is to drive their head-strong daughter anywhere she wants to go. Unintentionally, he kills her, tries to hide, and is ultimately found guilty. Based on the classic novel by Richard Wright, who also stars. Remade in 1986. Unprofessional direction and low budget work against the strong story. **91m/B VHS.** Richard Wright, Jean Wallace, Nicholas Joy, Gloria Madison, Charles Cane; *D:* Pierre Chenal.

Native Son ½ **1986 (R)** This second film adaptation of the classic Richard Wright novel is chock full of stars and tells the story of a poor black man who accidentally kills a white woman and then hides the body. Changes in the script soft-soap some of the novel's disturbing truths and themes—so-so drama for those who have not read the book. **111m/C VHS.** Geraldine Page, Oprah Winfrey, Matt Dillon, John Karlen, Elizabeth McGovern, Akosua Busia, Carroll Baker, Victor Love, John McMartin, Art Evans, Willard Pugh, David Rasche; *D:* Jerrold Freedman; *W:* Richard Wesley; *C:* Thomas Burstyn; *M:* James Mtume.

Nativity **1978** Unmemorable, made-for-TV portrayal of the romance between Mary and Joseph (of the Bible story), Joseph's response to Mary's pregnancy, and the birthing of Jesus. Not exactly a Bible epic, the direction and acting are uninspired. **97m/C VHS.** John Shea, Madeleine Stowe, Jane Wyatt, John Rhys-Davies, Kate O'Mara; *D:* Bernard L. Kowalski.

The Nativity Story ½ **2006 (PG)** Faithful retelling of the events leading to the birth of Jesus, from the arrangement of Mary's (Castle-Hughes) marriage to Joseph (Isaac) to the Immaculate Conception to their journey to Bethlehem. A sort of kinder, gentler companion to Mel Gibson's "The Passion of the Christ," it conveys the hope that Jesus' arrival brings amid the mayhem caused by King Herod (Hinds). Though it plays mostly as a Sunday school lesson, director Hardwicke uses her skills as a former production designer to make the scenery gorgeous and detailed, and the teenage Castle-Hughes' performance is solid and mature. **102m/C DVD.** *US* Keisha Castle-Hughes, Shohreh Aghdashloo, Hiam Abbass, Shaun Toub, Oscar Isaac, Stanley Townsend, Ciaran Hinds, Alexander Siddig, Alessandro Giuggioli, Nadim Sawalha, Eriq Ebouaney; *D:* Catherine Hardwicke; *W:* Mike Rich; *C:* Elliot Davis; *M:* Mychael Danna.

The Natural **1984 (PG)** A beautifully filmed movie about baseball as myth. A young man, whose gift for baseball sets him apart, finds that trouble dogs him, particularly with a woman. In time, as an aging rookie, he must fight against his past to lead his team to the World Series, and win the woman who is meant for him. From the Bernard Malamud story. **134m/C VHS, DVD.** Robert Redford, Glenn Close, Robert Duvall, Kim Basinger, Wilford Brimley, Barbara Hershey, Richard Farnsworth, Robert Prosky, Darren McGavin, Joe Don Baker, Michael Madsen; *D:* Barry Levinson; *W:* Roger Towne, Phil Dusenberry; *C:* Caleb Deschanel; *M:* Randy Newman.

Natural Born Killers **1994 (R)** An old script by Tarantino is resurrected by Stone and invested with its own unique subtle nuance and style. Controversial (natch, considering the director and writer) look at the way the media portrays criminals. Harrelson and Lewis are the lovestruck, white-trash serial killers who become tabloid-TV darlings, thanks to a sensationalistic press led by Downey Jr. Stone's dark and manic comment on America's fascination and revulsion with violence is strictly of the love it or leave it variety. Bloodshed galore, dazzling photography, and a dynamite soundtrack (with over 75 selections) add up to sensory overload. **119m/C VHS, DVD, Blu-ray Disc.** Woody Harrelson, Robert Downey Jr., Juliette Lewis, Tommy Lee Jones, Richard Lineback, Tom Sizemore, Rodney Dangerfield, Rachel Ticotin, Arliss Howard, Russell Means, Denis Leary, Steven Wright, Pruitt Taylor Vince, Dale Dye, Louis Lombardi, O-lan Jones, Edie McClurg, Evan Handler, Kirk Baltz, Maria Pitillo, Jared Harris, Balthazar Getty, Joe Grifasi, James Gammon, Mark Harmon; *D:* Oliver Stone; *W:* Oliver Stone; *C:* Robert Richardson; *M:* Trent Reznor.

Natural Causes ½ **1994 (PG-13)** Muddled political thriller finds Dr. Jessie McCarthy (Purl) traveling to Thailand to visit her estranged mother Rachel (Paige), only to discover she's just been murdered. Then Jessie learns Rachel had a secret life aiding Vietnamese refugees and a scheme is afoot to sabotage a reconciliation treaty between the U.S. and Vietnam. However, none of this makes much sense, though the Bangkok settings provide a pleasant distraction. **90m/C VHS.** Linda Purl, Cary-Hiroyuki Tagawa, Will Patton, Tim Thomerson, Janis Paige, Ali MacGraw; *D:* James Becket; *W:* Jake Raymond Needham; *C:* Denis Maloney; *M:* Nathan Wang.

Natural City *Mo* **2003 (R)** It's now 2080, and the world has been painfully rebuilt after a devastating war. Humans are now served by cyborgs, but they are beginning to want rights of their own and are rebelling, so an elite military squad has been tasked with squashing them. But the squad's leader R (Ji-tae Yu) has fallen in love with his own cyborg, and is using AI chips stolen from dead cyborgs to save her life without the knowledge of his employers. **113m/C DVD.** *KN* Ji-tae Yu, Jae-un Lee, Rin Seo; *D:* Byung-chun Min; *W:* Byung-chun Min; *C:* Byung-chun Min; *M:* Jun-kyu Lee.

Natural Enemies ½ **1979 (R)** A successful publisher begins to consider suicide and murder as the cure for his family's increasing alienation and despair. Dark and depressing drama. **100m/C VHS.** Hal Holbrook, Louise Fletcher, Jose Ferrer, Viveca Lindfors; *D:* Jeff Kanew; *W:* Jeff Kanew.

Natural Enemy **1996 (R)** Unsuspecting married couple become the target of a disturbed man with a big secret. **88m/C VHS, DVD.** Donald Sutherland, William McNamara, Lesley Ann Warren, Joe Pantoliano, Tia Carrere; *D:* Douglas Jackson; *W:* Kevin Bernhardt; *C:* Rodney Gibbons; *M:* Alan Reeves. **CABLE**

The Natural History of Parking Lots **1990** What's a rich L.A. father to do when his teenage son hot-wires antique cars for kicks? Why pay his gun-running older brother to keep an eye on him. And the whackiness is just beginning. **92m/C VHS.** Charlie Bean, B. Wyatt, Eli Guralnick; *D:* Everet Lewis; *W:* Everet Lewis; *C:* Hisham Abed; *M:* Johannes Hammers.

Nature of the Beast **1994 (R)** A businessman and a drifter are both hiding deadly secrets as police search for both a serial killer and the $1 million missing in a Vegas casino robbery. Just which man is involved in which crime? **91m/C VHS, DVD.** Eric Roberts, Lance Henriksen, Brion James; *D:* Victor Salva; *W:* Victor Salva.

Nature of the Beast ½ **2007 (PG)** Silly ABC Family Channel flick about a young man with a hairy secret. Rich works for Animal Control but once a month—at the full moon—he retires to his cabin in the woods so he can turn into a werewolf in seclusion. Rich has managed to keep his secret from his overly-understanding fiance Julia but there's a problem since their wedding date is too close to his next transformation for comfort. **90m/C DVD.** Eddie Kaye Thomas, Autumn Reeser, Eric Mabius; *D:* Rodman Flender; *W:* Bob Young, David Kendall; *C:* Kim Derko; *M:* Charles Sydnor. **CABLE**

Nature's Grave ½ *Long Weekend* **2008 (R)** Aussie horror/thriller is a misguided, overly-respectful remake of the far more terrifying 1978 film "Long Weekend." Sniping marrieds Peter (Caviezel) and Carla (Karvan) go camping on a holiday weekend. Their isolated beach campsite proves treacherous when their carelessness causes the local wildlife to go all eco-vengeance on their human butts. **88m/C DVD.** *AU* James (Jim) Caviezel, Claudia Karvan; *D:* Jamie Blanks; *W:* Everett De Roche; *C:* Karl Von Moller; *M:* Jamie Blanks.

Nature's Playmates **1962** A beautiful private eye tours Florida nudist camps in search of a missing man with a distinctive tattoo on his posterior. One of H.G. Lewis' obscure "nudie" flicks, sexually tame by modern standards, awful by any standards. **56m/B VHS.** Vicki (Allison Louise Downe) Miles, Allison Louise Downe, Scott Osborne, Terry Stevens, Peter Lathrop, Fred Gordon, Al Glick; *D:* Herschell Gordon Lewis; *W:* Ben T. Williams; *C:* William R. Johnson.

Naughty Knights *Up the Chastity Belt* **1971 (PG)** Soft-core romp in a medieval setting. Toss it in the moat. **94m/C VHS.** Frankie Howerd, Graham Crowden, Bill Fraser, Roy Hudd, Hugh Paddick, Anna Quayle, Eartha Kitt, Dave King, Fred Emney; *D:* Bob Kellett; *M:* Carl Davis.

Naughty Marietta ½ **1935** A French princess switches identities with a mail-order bride to escape from her arranged marriage, and is captured by pirates. When she's saved by a dashing Indian scout, it's love at first sight. The first MacDonald-Eddy match-up and very popular in its day. ♫ Italian Street Song; Chansonette; Antoinette and Anatole; Prayer; Tramp, Tramp, Tramp; The Owl and the Bobcat; Neath the Southern Moon; Mon Ami Pierrot; Ship Ahoy. **106m/B VHS.** Jeanette MacDonald, Nelson Eddy, Frank Morgan, Elsa Lanchester, Douglass Dumbrille, Cecilia Parker; ***D:*** Woodbridge S. Van Dyke; ***C:*** William H. Daniels. Oscars '35: Sound, Natl. Film Reg. '03.

The Naughty Nineties **1945** Bud and Lou help a showboat owner fend off crooks in the 1890s. Usual slapstick shenanigans, but highlighted by verbal banter. Includes the first on-screen rendition of the classic "Who's on First?" routine. ♫ Rolling Down the River; Uncle Tom's Cabin; I Can't Get You Out of My Mind; On a Sunday Afternoon; I'd Leave My Happy Home for You; Nora Malone; Ma Blushin' Rosie; The Showboat's Comin' to Town; A Blarney from Killarney. **72m/B VHS, DVD.** Bud Abbott, Lou Costello, Henry Travers, Alan Curtis, Joseph (Joe) Sawyer, Rita Johnson, Joe (Joseph) Kirk, Lois Collier; ***D:*** Jean Yarbrough.

Nautilus **1999 (R)** In the year 2100, the planet has been destroyed by a series of cataclysims caused by a scientific experiment, so a scientist decides to go back in time aboard a futuristic submarine in order to change the past and save the future. **90m/C VHS, DVD.** Richard Norton, Hannes Jaenicke, Miranda Wolfe; ***D:*** Rodney McDonald; ***W:*** C. Courtney Joyner; ***M:*** David Wurst, Eric Wurst. **VIDEO**

Navajo Blues **1997 (R)** Police detective Nicholas Epps is installed in the federal witness protection program after seeing a mob hit on his partner. He's sent to a Native American reservation to hide out until the trial but can't resist investigating a series of local murders. **99m/C VHS, DVD.** Steven Bauer, Irene Bedard, Charlotte Lewis, Ed O'Ross, Michael Horse, Tom Fridley; ***D:*** Joey Travolta; ***C:*** Dan Heigh.

Navajo Joe 1/2 **1967** The sole survivor of a massacre single-handedly kills each person involved in the atrocity, and aids a terrorized, though unappreciative, town in the process. Low-budget Spanish-Italian western only worth watching because of Reynolds. Filmed in Spain. **89m/C VHS.** *IT SP* Burt Reynolds, Aldo Sambrel, Tanya Lopert, Fernando Rey; ***D:*** Sergio Corbucci; ***M:*** Ennio Morricone.

The Navigator **1924** Ever the quick thinker, Keaton actually bought a steamer headed for the scrap heap and used it to film an almost endless string of sight gags. Rejected by a socialite, millionaire Keaton finds himself alone with her on the abandoned boat. As he saves her from various and sundry perils, the gags and thrills abound—including one stunt that was inspired by a near-accident on the set. Too bad they don't make 'em like this anymore. Silent. **60m/B VHS, DVD.** Buster Keaton, Kathryn McGuire, Frederick Vroom, Noble Johnson, Clarence Burton, H. M. Clugston; ***D:*** Donald Crisp, Buster Keaton; ***W:*** Clyde Bruckman, Jean C. Havez, Joseph A. Mitchell; ***C:*** Byron Houck, Elgin Lessley.

The Navigator **1988 (PG)** A creative time-travel story of a 14th-century boy with visionary powers who leads the residents of his medieval English village away from a plague by burrowing through the earth's core and into late-20th-century New Zealand. Quite original and refreshing. **92m/C VHS, DVD.** *NZ* Hamish McFarlane, Bruce Lyons, Chris Haywood, Marshall Napier, Noel Appleby, Paul Livingston, Sarah Pierse; ***D:*** Vincent Ward; ***W:*** Vincent Ward. Australian Film Inst. '88: Cinematog., Director (Ward), Film.

The Navigators **2001 (R)** In 1995, British Rail is privatized and a portion of the South Yorkshire line is now serviced by two competing companies. The new owners break up the union system—some of the former workers decide to retire while others, including four friends, have to stick it out. Since fewer men are employed in maintaining the railway depot and lines, accidents increase and the increased stress just isn't professional but personal as well. **92m/C VHS, DVD.** *GB GE SP* Steve Huison, Dean Andrews, Tom Craig, Joe Duttine, Venn Tracey; ***D:*** Ken Loach; ***W:*** Rob Dawber; ***C:*** Barry Ackroyd, Mike Eley; ***M:*** George Fenton.

Navy Blue and Gold 1/2 **1937** Three football-playing midshipmen (Young, Stewart, and Brown) at Annapolis share a friendship. Stewart has registered under a false name since his dad was unfairly cashiered from the service. When he hears some slander about his old man he stands up and tells the truth and gets suspended, just before the big game with Army. Naturally, he's reinstated just in time to make the big play and carry the team to victory. Well-done, old-fashioned hokum. **94m/B VHS.** James Stewart, Robert Young, Tom Brown, Lionel Barrymore, Florence Rice, Billie Burke, Samuel S. Hinds, Paul Kelly, Frank Albertson, Minor Watson; ***D:*** Sam Wood; ***W:*** George Bruce.

The Navy Comes Through **1942** Salty sailors aboard a mangy freighter beat the odds and sink Nazi warships and subs with the greatest of ease. Boy meets girl subplot is added for good measure. Morale booster includes newsreel footage. **81m/B VHS.** Pat O'Brien, George Murphy, Jane Wyatt, Jackie Cooper, Carl Esmond, Max Baer Sr., Desi Arnaz Sr., Ray Collins, Lee Bonnell, Frank Jenks, Helmut Dantine; ***D:*** Edward Sutherland.

Navy SEALS 1/2 **1990 (R)** A group of macho Navy commandos, whose regular work is to rescue hostages from Middle Eastern underground organizations, finds a stash of deadly weapons. They spend the balance of the movie attempting to destroy the arsenal. Sheen chews the scenery as a crazy member of the commando team. Lots of action and violence, but simplistic good guys-bad guys philosophy and plot weaknesses keep this from being more than below average. **113m/C VHS, DVD.** Charlie Sheen, Michael Biehn, Joanne Whalley, Rick Rossovich, Cyril O'Reilly, Bill Paxton, Dennis Haysbert, Paul Sanchez, Ron Joseph, Nicholas Kadi; ***D:*** Lewis Teague; ***W:*** Gary Goldman; ***C:*** John A. Alonzo; ***M:*** Sylvester Levay.

Navy vs. the Night Monsters **WOOF!** *Monsters of the Night* **1966** When horrifying, acid-secreting plant monsters try to take over the world, Van Doren and the Navy must come to the rescue, with the action taking place in a tropical South Pole setting. Amazing deployment of talents. **87m/C VHS.** Mamie Van Doren, Anthony Eisley, Pamela Mason, Bobby Van, Russ Bender; ***D:*** Michael Hoey; ***W:*** Michael Hoey.

Navy Way **1944** Hurriedly produced war propaganda film in which a boxer gets inducted into the Navy just before his title shot. **74m/B VHS, DVD.** Robert Lowery, Jean Parker, Roscoe Karns, William Henry, Robert Armstrong, Tom Keene; ***D:*** William Berke; ***W:*** Maxwell Shane; ***C:*** Fred H. Jackman Jr.; ***M:*** Willy Stahl.

Nazarin **1958** Bunuel's scathing indictment of Christianity finds its perfect vehicle in the adventures of a defrocked priest attempting to relive Christ's life. Gathering a group of disciples, he wanders into the Mexican desert as a cross between Christ and Don Quixote. Filmed in Mexico, this is Bunuel at his grimmest. Based on a novel by Benito Perez Galdos; Spanish with subtitles. **92m/B VHS.** *MX* Francisco Rabal, Rita Macedo, Margo Lopez, Rita McLedo, Ignacio Lopez Tarso, Jesus Fernandez; ***D:*** Luis Bunuel.

Nea 1/2 **1978 (R)** Comic drama about a young girl from a privileged home who writes a best selling pornographic novel anonymously. When her book writing talents are made public through betrayal, she gets even in a most unique way. Subtitled "A Young Emmanuelle." Kaplan also performs. Appealing and sophisticated. **101m/C VHS, DVD.** Sami Frey, Ann Zacharias, Heinz Bennent; ***D:*** Nelly Kaplan.

Neapolitan Carousel *Carosello Napoletano* **1954** Musical structured after the Commedia del 'Arte, featuring ballet, opera, mime, and popular songs and dances. A family of street musicians travels to various towns where patriarch Salvatore (Stoppa) introduces the different pieces. These include Loren as a model of naughty postcards who falls in love with a soldier in WWI and a ballet starring Massine. Italian with subtitles. **124m/C DVD.** *FR* Paolo Stoppa, Clelia Matania, Sophia Loren, Leonide Massine, Maria Fiore, Giacomo Rondinella; ***D:*** Ettore Giannini, Ettore Giannini; ***W:*** Ettore Giannini, Ettore Giannini, Remigio del Grosso, Guiseppe Marotta; ***C:*** Piero Portalupi, Piero Portalupi; ***M:*** Raffaele Gervasio.

Near Dark **1987 (R)** Southwestern farm boy Caleb (Pasdar) is attracted to the pretty Mae (Wright) and falls in unwillingly with a family of thirsty, outlaw-fringe vampires who roam the West in a van. The first mainstream effort by Bigelow, and a rollicking, blood-saturated, slaughterhouse of a movie, with enough laughs and stunning imagery to revive the genre. **95m/C VHS, DVD, UMD.** Adrian Pasdar, Jenny Wright, Bill Paxton, Jenette Goldstein, Lance Henriksen, Tim Thomerson, Joshua John Miller; ***D:*** Kathryn Bigelow; ***W:*** Kathryn Bigelow, Eric Red; ***C:*** Adam Greenberg; ***M:*** Tangerine Dream.

Near Misses 1/2 **1991** Missable farce with Reinhold as a bigamist in the foreign service. To make time for a mistress he swaps identities with a young Marine in Paris, but then the KGB kidnaps the imposter. Doors slam in hallways all over the place as the performers crank up the mixups to maximum frenzy, but with little effect since you really don't care much about these fools. **93m/C VHS.** Judge Reinhold, Casey Siemaszko, Kasia (Katarzyna) Figura, Muriel Combeau; ***D:*** Baz Taylor; ***W:*** Peter Baloff, Dave Wollert.

Near the Rainbow's End 1/2 **1930** Cattle rancher Steele (in his first talking western) finds out that rustlers are aggravating the trouble between the cattlemen and the sheep herders. So he goes after the bad guys and then settles the feud by marrying a sheep herder's daughter. **57m/B VHS, DVD.** Bob Steele, Lafe (Lafayette) McKee, Louise Lorraine, Al Ferguson, Al Hewston; ***D:*** J(ohn) P(aterson) McGowan.

Nearing Grace **2005 (R)** In 1978, responsible high school senior Henry Nearing (Smith) is trying to cope with the death of his mother, while his dad (Morse) and older brother (Moscow) take to drink, drugs, and reckless behavior. Henry can't see that his gal pal Merna (Johnson) is perfect for him and instead he pants after sexy tease Grace (Brewster), until he learns better. Smith and Johnson are a cute twosome but the story's familiar. Based on Scott Sommers' 1979 novel. **105m/C DVD.** Gregory Edward Smith, Jordana Brewster, Ashley Johnson, David Moscow, David Morse, Chad Faust, Brian Murray, Logan Bartholomew; ***D:*** Rick Rosenthal; ***W:*** Jacob Aaron Estes; ***C:*** David Geddes; ***M:*** John E. Nordstrom.

'Neath Brooklyn Bridge **1942** The Boys from the Bowery get tangled up in crime when they try to help a young girl whose guardian was murdered. **61m/B VHS, DVD.** Leo Gorcey, Huntz Hall, Bobby Jordan, Sammy (Earnest) Morrison, Ann Gillis, Noah Beery Jr., Marc Lawrence, Gabriel Dell; ***D:*** Wallace Fox.

'Neath Canadian Skies **1946** Mounted lawman who says "eh" a lot tracks murdering gang of mine looters. **41m/B VHS.** *CA* Russell Hayden, Inez Cooper, Cliff Nazarro, Kermit Maynard, Jack Mulhall; ***D:*** B. Reeves Eason; ***W:*** Arthur V. Jones; ***C:*** Marcel Le Picard; ***M:*** Carl Hoefle.

'Neath the Arizona Skies **1934** Low budget oater epic about a cowhand who finds all the action he and his friends can handle as they try to rescue a young Indian girl (and oil heiress) who has been kidnapped. 'Nuff said. **54m/B VHS, DVD.** John Wayne, George "Gabby" Hayes, Sheila Terry; ***D:*** Harry Fraser.

Necessary Parties **1988** Based on Barbara Dana's book that has a 15-year-old boy filing a lawsuit to stop his parents' divorce. Originally aired on PBS as part of the "Wonderworks" family movie series. **120m/C VHS, DVD.** Alan Arkin, Mark Paul Gosselaar, Barbara Dana, Adam Arkin, Donald Moffat, Julie Hagerty, Geoffrey Pierson, Taylor Fry; ***D:*** Gwen Arner.

Necessary Roughness **1991 (PG-13)** After losing their NCAA standing, the Texas Southern University (passing for the real Texas State) Armadillos football team looks like it's headed for disaster. The once proud football factory is now composed of assorted goofballs instead of stud players. But hope arrives in the form of a 34-year-old farmer with a golden arm, ready to recapture some lost dreams as quarterback. Can this unlikey team rise above itself and win a game, or will their hopes be squashed all over the field? **108m/C VHS, DVD.** Scott Bakula, Robert Loggia, Harley Jane Kozak, Sinbad, Hector Elizondo, Kathy Ireland, Jason Bateman; ***D:*** Stan Dragoti; ***W:*** Rick Natkin, David Fuller; ***C:*** Peter Stein; ***M:*** Bill Conti.

Necromancer: Satan's Servant **1988 (R)** After a woman is brutally raped, she contacts a sorceress and makes a pact with the devil to ensure her successful revenge. Plenty of graphic violence and nudity. **90m/C VHS, DVD.** Elizabeth Kaitan, Russ Tamblyn, Rhonda Dorton; ***D:*** Dusty Nelson; ***W:*** William T. Naud; ***C:*** Eric Cayla, Richard Clabaugh; ***M:*** Kevin Klinger, Bob Mamet, Gary Stockdale.

Necropolis **1987 (R)** A witch burned at the stake 300 years ago is brought back to life as a motorcycle punkette in New York searching for a sacrificial virgin (in New York?). New wave horror should have been watchable. **77m/C VHS.** Leeanne Baker, Michael Conte, Jacquie Fritz, William Reed, Paul Ruben; ***D:*** Tim Kincaid.

Ned Kelly 1/2 *Ned Kelly, Outlaw* **1970 (PG)** Dramatizes the life of Australia's most notorious outlaw. Kelly (Jagger) and his family start off as horse thieves and proceed from there. A manhunt results in death and the eventual capture and execution of Kelly. The very contemporary British Jagger was miscast as a period Australian and British director Richardson seems to have lacked an empathy for the material, given his lethargic direction. **100m/C VHS, DVD.** *GB* Mick Jagger, Allen Bickford, Geoff Gilmour, Mark McManus, Serge Lazareff, Peter Sumner, Ken Shorter, James Elliott, Diane Craig, Sue Lloyd, Clarissa Kaye; ***D:*** Tony Richardson; ***W:*** Ian Jones, Tony Richardson; ***M:*** Shel Silverstein.

Ned Kelly 1/2 **2003 (R)** Another telling of the legend of Australian outlaw Ned Kelly (Ledger), based on the novel "Our Sunshine" by Robert Drewe. Kelly was falsely imprisoned for three years and faced such harassment from corrupt law officers that he took up bank robbery with a gang of four others and became a folk hero for the lower class. Ledger fits the role well but Orlando Bloom (as Kelly's Gang member Joe Byrne) is a true scene-stealer. Very genuine, well-made effort with a brutal final showdown between the police and the gang, but the presentation doesn't always flow well. **109m/C DVD.** *AU* Heath Ledger, Orlando Bloom, Geoffrey Rush, Naomi Watts, Joel Edgerton, Laurence Kinlan, Kris McQuade, Emily Browning, Kiri Paramore, Rachel Griffiths, Charles "Bud" Tingwell, Peter Phelps, Russell Dykstra, Phil Barantini, Kerry Condon, Saskia Burmeister; ***D:*** Gregor Jordan; ***W:*** John M. McDonagh; ***C:*** Oliver Stapleton; ***M:*** Klaus Badelt.

Needful Things 1/2 **1993 (R)** Stephen King film adaptations are becoming as prolific as his novels, though few seem to improve in the transition from page to screen. This time a scheming Maine shopkeeper (Von Sydow) sells unsuspecting small towners peculiar items that, not surprisingly, begin to cause horror and mayhem. Harris is the town sheriff who tries to warn everyone that he's the devil in disguise. Big screen directorial debut for Heston (yes, Charlton's son). **120m/C VHS, DVD.** Ed Harris, Bonnie Bedelia, Max von Sydow, Amanda Plummer, J.T. Walsh, William Morgan Sheppard; ***D:*** Fraser Heston; ***W:*** W.D. Richter; ***C:*** Tony Westman; ***M:*** Patrick Doyle.

Nefertiti, Queen of the Nile **1964** Woman, married against her will, turns into Nefertiti. For fans of Italo-Biblical epics only. **97m/C VHS.** *IT* Jeanne Crain, Vincent Price, Edmund Purdom, Amedeo Nazzari, Liana Orfei; ***D:*** Fernando Cerchio.

Negadon: The Monster from Mars 1/2 *Wakusei daikaiju Negadon* **2005** In 2025 a Japanese expedition to Mars returns with a rock formation that hatches into a giant crustacean of some sort that begins destroying Tokyo. The city's only hope is a robotics constructor devastated by an accident that cost him his daughter and his left eye. An homage to classic Japanese science fiction and giant robot films, containing many nods to films from the 1950s (especially "Godzilla"). The creators even take pains to make the animated film (one of the first films done completely in cgi) look like a grainy film from that era. Too bad it's so darn short. **70m/C DVD.** *JP* Masafumi Kishi, Takuma Sasahara, Dai Shimizu, Akane Yumoto; ***D:*** Jun Awazu; ***W:*** Jun Awazu; ***C:*** Jun Awazu; ***M:*** Shingo Terasawa.

Negatives **1968** A couple indulge in sexual fantasies to dangerous extremes, with the man first impersonating Dr. Crippen, the early 1900s murderer, and later a WWI flying ace. When a photographer friend joins the fun, the action careens off the deep end. **90m/C VHS.** *GB* Peter McEnery, Diane Cilento, Glenda Jackson, Maurice Denham, Norman Rossington; ***D:*** Peter Medak.

The Negotiator ½ **1998 (R)** Police hostage negotiator Danny Roman (Jackson) has had his life destroyed by false accusations of theft and murder. So he decides to go after his accusers by taking the Chicago Internal Affairs Bureau staff (what else?) hostage. Chris Sabian (Spacey), a negotiator from another precinct, is Roman's only hope to save himself and find the real culprits. Jackson and Spacey are excellent in their scenes together, and the supporting cast does a fine job. Nice action sequences and suspenseful storyline make for a thrilling ride, as long as you don't contemplate the details for too long. **115m/C VHS, DVD.** Samuel L. Jackson, Kevin Spacey, David Morse, Ron Rifkin, John Spencer, Regina Taylor, J.T. Walsh, Siobhan Fallon Hogan, Paul Giamatti, Paul Guilfoyle, Carlos Gomez, Nestor Serrano; ***D:*** F. Gary Gray; ***W:*** James DeMonaco, Kevin Fox; ***C:*** Russell Carpenter; ***M:*** Graeme Revell.

The Neighbor ½ **1993 (R)** See nice city couple John and Mary move to small town Vermont. See their nice retired obstetrician neighbor Myron welcome them. See Mary get pregnant and Myron take an obsessional interest. See John arrested for murder. See Mary left alone—except for Myron's tender care. **93m/C VHS, DVD.** Linda Kozlowski, Ron Lea, Rod Steiger, Frances Bay, Bruce Boa, Jane Wheeler; ***D:*** Rodney Gibbons; ***W:*** Kurt Wimmer.

The Neighbor ½ **2007 (PG-13)** Jeff's (Modine) life starts unraveling when he learns his ex-wife is marrying his best friend and his apartment neighbor, real estate developer Christine (Laroque), is determined to drive him out so she can combine their spaces. Jeff finally agrees to move if Christine will attend the wedding with him and pretend to be his new girlfriend, but the festivities just happen to change their opinion of each other. **98m/C DVD.** Matthew Modine, Michele Laroque, Edward Quinn, Gina Mantegna, Ann Cusack, Richard Kind, Krysten Leigh Jones; ***D:*** Eddie O'Flaherty; ***W:*** Eddie O'Flaherty, J.P. Davis; ***C:*** Michael Fimognari; ***M:*** Stephen (Steve) Edwards.

The Neighbor No. Thirteen ½ *Rinjin 13-go* **2005 (R)** Excessively horrific violence abounds when a Japanese man, Juzo (Oguri), meets up with his childhood tormentor Akai (Arai). Seeing that Akai's brutish behavior hasn't changed and that he doesn't even recall Juzo or the suffering he endured causes Juzo's maniacal side to emerge and seek vengeance. **115m/C DVD.** Hirofumi Arai, Takashi Miike, Shido Nakamura, Shun Oguri, Yumi Yoshimura, Tomoya Ishii; ***D:*** Yasou Inoue; ***W:*** Hajime Kado; ***C:*** Taro Kawazu; ***M:*** Riji Kitazato.

Neighbors **1981 (R)** The Keeses (Belushi and Walker) live in a quiet, middle-class suburban neighborhood where life is calm and sweet. But their new neighbors, Ramona and Vic (Aykroyd and Moriarty), prove to be loud, obnoxious, crazy, and freeloading. Will Earl and Enid Keese mind their manners as their neighborhood disintegrates? Some funny moments, but as the script fades, so do the laughs. Belushi's last waltz is based on Thomas Berger's novel. **90m/C VHS.** John Belushi, Dan Aykroyd, Kathryn Walker, Cathy Moriarty; ***D:*** John G. Avildson; ***W:*** Larry Gelbart; ***M:*** Bill Conti.

Neil Gaiman's NeverWhere ½ *NeverWhere* **1996** Ordinary Londoner Richard Mayhew never before realized there's an extraordinary world beneath his feet. Until he helps an injured mystery woman named Door. The next morning Richard's world is turned upside down—no one he knows remembers him and he's now jobless and homeless. When Richard finds his way into London Below, he sees Door again and discovers a feudal society and much strangeness as he tries to get back to his old reality. **180m/C DVD.** *GB* Gary Bakewell, Laura Fraser, Hywel Bennett, Clive Russell, Paterson Joseph, Trevor Peacock, Freddie Jones, Peter Capaldi, Stratford Johns; ***D:*** Dewi Humphreys; ***W:*** Neil Gaiman, Lenny Henry; ***C:*** Steve Murray, Steve Saunderson; ***M:*** Brian Eno. **TV**

Neil Simon's The Odd Couple 2 ½ *The Odd Couple 2* **1998 (PG-13)** In the not-too-grand tradition of "Caddyshack II," "Son of the Pink Panther," and "Blues Brothers 2000" they waited too long. And like the others, they shouldn't have even bothered. Oscar (Matthau) and Felix (Lemmon) reunite when their respective kids (Silverman as Oscar's son, Waltz as Felix's daughter) marry. Meeting at LAX, the duo immediately falls into the old routine of annoying each other and, this time out, the audience. Simon fills his script with leftover road movie cliches and vaudeville jokes, leaving Lemmon and Matthau nothing to do but mug and yell. Since almost everything these two have done together since the original has been a de facto sequel, it's a shame that the real thing falls so flat. **96m/C VHS, DVD.** Jack Lemmon, Walter Matthau, Jonathan Silverman, Lisa Waltz, Christine Baranski, Jean Smart, Barnard Hughes, Doris Belack, Ellen Geer, Jay O. Sanders, Rex Linn, Mary Beth Peil, Alice Ghostley, Rebecca Schull, Florence Stanley, Lou (Cutel) Cutell; ***D:*** Howard Deutch; ***W:*** Neil Simon; ***C:*** Jamie Anderson; ***M:*** Alan Silvestri.

Neil Young: Heart of Gold **2006 (R)** Demme shot two acoustic concert performances by Young at Nashville's fabled Ryman Auditorium on August 18 and 19, 2005, where Young featured songs from his new album "Prairie Wind" as well as some old favorites. In April of that year, Young had been diagnosed with a life-threatening brain aneurysm and wrote and recorded the album before his surgery. The concerts were the first after his recovery. **103m/C DVD.** *US* ***D:*** Jonathan Demme; ***C:*** Ellen Kuras; ***M:*** Neil Young.

Neither the Sea Nor the Sand ½ **1973** Unhappily married Anna takes a holiday on the Isle of Jersey where she falls in love with the local lighthouse keeper. He suddenly dies, but returns to haunt Anna. Or maybe she's just crazy. **116m/C DVD.** *GB* Susan Hampshire, Frank Finlay, Jack Lambert, Michael Petrovitch; ***D:*** Fred Burnley; ***W:*** Gordon Honeycombe; ***C:*** David Muir; ***M:*** Nachum Heiman.

Nekromantik **1987** How much can we say—not to everyone's taste? How's this: a romantic story of necrophilia. Followed by "Nekromantik 2." In German with English subtitles. **74m/C VHS, DVD.** *GE* Monika M., Daktari Lorenz, Harald Lundt, Henri Boeck, Clemens Schwenter, Holger Suhr, Jorg Buttgereit; ***D:*** Jorg Buttgereit; ***W:*** Franz Rodenkirchen, Jorg Buttgereit; ***C:*** Uwe Bohrer; ***M:*** Herman Kopp.

Nekromantik 2 ½ **1991** Includes highlights from the first "Nekro"; the sequel picks up with a new nekro-chick who obtains the head of Rob, the jilted necrophile of the previous movie. Slicker than its predecessor, with less non-stop shock and a little more plot. In German with English subtitles. **100m/C VHS, DVD.** *GE* Monika M., Mark Reeder, Simone Sporl, Wolfgang Muller; ***D:*** Jorg Buttgereit; ***W:*** Jorg Buttgereit, Franz Rodenkirchen; ***C:*** Manfred O. Jelinski; ***M:*** Herman Kopp, Daktari Lorenz.

Nell ½ **1994 (R)** "Wild child" story—adult version. When illiterate, barely verbal backwoods Nell (Foster) is discovered after her stroke-afflicted mother's death, she's placed in the care of a doctor (Neeson) and psychologist (Richardson) who have different ideas about how to bring her into society. Unfairly dismissed by some as self-indulgent, Foster's raw, physical performance is truly mesmerizing; dull script, unconvincingly tidy ending, and gross over-sentimentality are what disappoint. From the play "Idioglossia" by Mark Handley. **114m/C VHS, DVD.** Jodie Foster, Liam Neeson, Natasha Richardson, Richard Libertini; ***D:*** Michael Apted; ***W:*** William Nicholson. Screen Actors Guild '94: Actress (Foster).

Nelly et Monsieur Arnaud *Nelly and Mr. Arnaud* **1995** Chatty adult May/December would-be romance between 25-year-old secretary Nelly (Beart) and Pierre Arnaud (Serrault), the mid-60s retired magistrate for whom she's working. The arrogant divorced Arnaud is intrigued by the independent Nelly, whom he finds he can't control, while she comes to appreciate their emotional ties (altogether different from the selfishness of the younger men she knows). Conclusion avoids a neat resolution to a situation beset by bad timing. French with subtitles. **105m/C VHS, DVD.** *IT GE FR* Emmanuelle Beart, Michel Serrault, Jean-Hugues Anglade, Francoise Brion, Claire Nadeau, Michael (Michel) Lonsdale, Charles Berling, Michele Laroque; ***D:*** Claude Sautet; ***W:*** Jacques Fieschi, Claude Sautet; ***C:*** Jean-Francois Robin; ***M:*** Philippe Sarde. Cesar '96: Actor (Serrault), Director (Sautet).

Nemesis ½ **1993 (R)** Futuristic thriller that combines cybernetics and cyborgs in post-nuclear Los Angeles. Gruner plays a human (although he's mostly composed of mechanical replacement parts) in a world overwrought with system cowboys, information terrorists, bio-enhanced gangsters, and cyborg outlaws. Film's biggest flaw is the extremely confusing script that makes no attempt at logic whatsoever. Special visual effects are good despite the obviously low f/x budget. **95m/C VHS, DVD.** Olivier Gruner, Tim Thomerson, Cary-Hiroyuki Tagawa, Merle Kennedy, Yuji Okumoto, Marjorie Monaghan, Nicholas Guest, Vincent Klyn; ***D:*** Albert Pyun; ***W:*** Rebecca Charles; ***C:*** George Mooradian; ***M:*** Michel Rubini.

Nemesis 2: Nebula ½ **1994 (R)** Cyborg goes on a rampage across time with a superhuman in pursuit. **83m/C VHS.** Sue Price, Tina Cote, Earl White, Jahi JJ Zuri, Tracy Davis; ***D:*** Albert Pyun.

Nemesis 3: Time Lapse ½ *Nemesis 3: Prey Harder* **1996 (R)** Superhuman mutant Alex is the last hope for mankind as the cyborgs once again prepare to destroy civilization. **90m/C VHS.** Sue Price, Tim Thomerson, Norbert Weisser, Xavier DeClie, Sharon Bruneau, Debbie Muggli; ***D:*** Albert Pyun; ***W:*** Albert Pyun; ***C:*** George Mooradian; ***M:*** Tony Riparetti.

Nemesis 4: Cry of Angels **1997 (R)** Alex (Price) is an assassin in the year 2082. When she mistakenly kills the son of crimelord Bernardo (Divoff), a bounty is placed on her head. Cartoonish dreck. **80m/C VHS, DVD.** Sue Price, Norbert Weisser, Andrew Divoff, Simon Poland, Nicholas Guest; ***D:*** Albert Pyun; ***W:*** Albert Pyun; ***C:*** George Mooradian. **VIDEO**

Nemesis Game ½ **2003 (R)** Vern (Paul) is a comic-book store owner who introduces introverted college student Sara (Pope) to a mysterious game that involves finding various riddles located in out-of-the-way places and answering them to move on to the next clue. But then Sara notices when she solves a riddle, people start to die. **91m/C VHS, DVD.** *CA* Adrian Paul, Carly Pope, Brendan Fehr, Jay Baruchel, Ian McShane, Rena Owen, Vanessa Guy, Brian Rhodes; ***D:*** Jesse Warn; ***W:*** Jesse Warn; ***C:*** Aaron Morton; ***M:*** Matthew Fletcher. **VIDEO**

Nenette and Boni **1996** Boni (Colin) is a 19-year-old pizza chef in Marseilles who likes to have sexual fantasies about the local baker's sensuous wife (Bruni-Tedeschi). His life is basically carefree until his pregnant, rebellious 15-year-old sister Nenette (Houri) shows up at his door, having run away from school. Nenette really doesn't want to deal with the pregnancy until Boni forces her to do so and, just to make the teens lives more complicated, their estranged small-time gangster dad (Nolot) has learned about Nenette's condition and wants to help her out. Fine performances. French with subtitles. **103m/C VHS.** *FR* Gregoire Colin, Alice Houri, Valeria Bruni-Tedeschi, Jacques Nolot, Vincent Gallo, Gerard Meylan, Alex Descas, Jamila Farah, Christine Gaya; ***D:*** Claire Denis; ***W:*** Claire Denis, Jean-Pol Fargeau; ***C:*** Agnes Godard.

The Neon Bible **1995** Beautifully crafted, yet thin telling of the struggles of a rural family in 1940s Georgia. The stories unfold in a series of flashbacks, as a 15-year-old boy travels alone on a train, reflecting on his dysfunctional early adolescence. An abusive father (Leary) who dies in the war, suicidal mom (Scarwid), and ex-showgirl visiting aunt (Rowlands) provide plenty of opportunities for familial angst. Starts out strong, with some stunning scenes sprinkled throughout, but director Davies never ventures far from the narrative territory he's covered thoroughly in his other films ("Distant Voices, Still Lives" and "The Long Day Closes"). Adapted from the novel by Pulitzer Prize winning author John Kennedy Toole. **92m/C VHS, DVD.** Gena Rowlands, Jacob Tierney, Diana Scarwid, Drake Bell, Denis Leary, Leo Burmester, Frances Conroy, Peter McRobbie, Joan Glover, Dana Dick, Virgil Graham Hopkins; ***D:*** Terence Davies; ***W:*** Terence Davies; ***C:*** Michael Coulter.

Neon City **1991 (R)** Title refers to a rumored city of refuge in the year 2053, where eight misfit adventurers in an armored transport seek safety from the Earth's toxic environment and "Mad Max" cliches. **99m/C VHS.** Michael Ironside, Vanity, Lyle Alzado, Valerie Wildman, Nick Klar, Juliet Landau, Arsenio "Sonny" Trinidad, Richard Sanders; ***D:*** Monte Markham.

The Neon Empire ½ **1989 (R)** Tepid tale of two gangsters battling inner mob opposition and backstabbing to build Las Vegas. Ostensibly based on the story of Bugsy Siegel and Meyer Lansky. **120m/C VHS.** Martin Landau, Ray Sharkey, Gary Busey, Harry Guardino, Julie Carmen, Linda Fiorentino, Dylan McDermott; ***D:*** Larry Peerce; ***W:*** Pete Hamill. **CABLE**

Neon Maniacs WOOF! **1986 (R)** An even half-dozen fetish-ridden zombies stalk the streets at night, tearing their victims into teensy weensy bits. Brave teenagers try to stop the killing. Brave viewers will stop the tape. **90m/C VHS, DVD.** Allan Hayes, Leilani Sarelle Ferrer, Bo Sabato, Donna Locke, Victor Elliot Brandt; ***D:*** Joseph Mangine.

The Nephew **1997** Part culture clash, part melodrama. Teenager Chad (Harper) heads to Inis Dora, a small island off the Irish coast, in order to fulfill his mother Karen's last request—that her ashes be scattered in her homeland. Karen was long estranged from her family and they're shocked to discover that Chad's father is black. Everyone tries to make the best of the situation but Chad's would-be romance with Aislin (McGuckin), whose father Joe (Brosnan) once loved Karen, causes a lot of friction. **104m/C VHS.** *IR* Hill Harper, Aislin McGuckin, Pierce Brosnan, Donal McCann, Sinead Cusack, Lorraine Pilkington; ***D:*** Eugene Brady; ***W:*** Jacqueline O'Neill, Sean P. Steele; ***C:*** Jack Conroy; ***M:*** Stephen McKeon.

Neptune Factor *The Neptune Disaster; An Underwater Odyssey* **1973 (G)** Scientists board a special new deep-sea sub to search for their colleagues lost in an undersea earthquake. Diving ever deeper into the abyss that swallowed their friend's Ocean Lab II, they end up trapped themselves. The plot's many holes sink it. **94m/C VHS.** Ben Gazzara, Yvette Mimieux, Walter Pidgeon, Ernest Borgnine; ***D:*** Daniel Petrie; ***W:*** Jack DeWitt.

Neptune's Daughter **1949** A swim-happy bathing suit designer finds romance and deep pools of studio water to dive into. Typically lavish and ridiculous Williams aqua-parade. ♫Baby It's Cold Outside; I Love Those Men; My Heart Beats Faster. **92m/C VHS, DVD.** Esther Williams, Red Skelton, Ricardo Montalban, Betty Garrett, Keenan Wynn, Xavier Cugat, Ted de Corsia, Mike Mazurki, Mel Blanc, Juan Duvall, George Mann, Joi Lansing; ***D:*** Edward Buzzell; ***C:*** Charles Rosher. Oscars '49: Song ("Baby It's Cold Outside").

Nerolio **1996** Three imagined episodes depicting the final months of an unnamed poet/director (Cavicchioli), who is actually based on homosexual writer/filmmaker Pier Paolo Pasolini. The contradictory, hypocritical, aging Poet is shown buying sex, while extolling the virtues of male beauty in voiceover, and as the maker of his own doom (Pasolini was murdered in 1975). "Nerolio" is a contraction of "nero" (black) and "Petrolio" (oil), which refers to Pasolini's posthumous novel "Petrolio." Italian with subtitles. **82m/B VHS, DVD.** *IT* Marco Cavicchioli, Vincenzo Crivello, Salvatore Lazzaro; ***D:*** Aurelio Grimaldi; ***W:*** Aurelio Grimaldi; ***C:*** Maurizio Calvesi; ***M:*** Maria Soldatini.

Nervous Ticks 1/2 **1993 (R)** Ninety minutes in the life of airline employee York Daley. All he needs to do is get off work, go home, grab his luggage, pick up his married girlfriend, and get back to the airport for a flight to Rio De Janeiro. Simple, right? Not in this movie. **95m/C VHS.** Bill Pullman, Julie Brown, Peter Boyle, James LeGros, Brent Jennings; ***D:*** Rocky Lang; ***W:*** David Frankel.

The Nervous Wreck **1926** Harrison Ford (not the one from "Indiana Jones") heads West, seeking a cure for what he believes is a terminal illness. Once there, he becomes romantically entangled with the sheriff's fiancee, uses a wrench to hold up a gas station, and gets involved in other shenanigans. And then he discovers he's going to live after all. **70m/B VHS.** Harrison Ford, Phyllis Haver, Chester Conklin, Mack Swain, Hobart Bosworth, Charles Gerrard; ***D:*** Scott Sidney.

The Nest 1/2 *El Nido* **1980** Tragic romance of an elderly man and a 13-year-old girl is helped along by superior script and directing. **109m/C VHS.** *SP* Ana Torrent, Hector Alterio, Patricia Adriani, Luis Politti, Augustin Gonzalez; ***D:*** Jaime de Arminan; ***W:*** Jaime de Arminan; ***C:*** Teodoro Escamilla.

The Nest 1/2 **1988 (R)** A small island is overcome by giant cockroaches created by, you guessed it, a scientific experiment gone wrong. Special effects make it watchable. **89m/C VHS, DVD.** Robert Lansing, Lisa Langlois, Franc Luz, Terri Treas, Stephen Davies, Diana Bellamy, Nancy Morgan; ***D:*** Terence H. Winkless; ***W:*** Robert King; ***C:*** Ricardo Jacques Gale; ***M:*** Rick Conrad.

The Nesting 1/2 **1980 (R)** Too-long tale of a neurotic author who rents a haunted Victorian manor and finds herself a pawn in a ghostly plan for revenge. Features Grahame's last performance. **104m/C VHS.** Robin Groves, John Carradine, Gloria Grahame, Christopher Loomis, Michael David Lally; ***D:*** Armand Weston; ***C:*** Joao Fernandes.

The Net 1/2 **1995 (PG-13)** The ever-spunky Bullock gets stuck behind a computer screen rather than the wheel of a bus as reclusive computer systems analyst Angela Bennett. She's puzzled by a mysterious Internet program, which Angela finds can easily access highly classified databases. It's soon apparent that someone knows she knows because every record of her identity has been erased and the conspirators decide to take care of one last detail by eliminating her as well. Miller's the ex she turns to for help and Northam's a seductive British hacker. Techno paranoia. **114m/C VHS, DVD.** Sandra Bullock, Jeremy Northam, Dennis Miller, Diane Baker, Ken Howard, Wendy Gazelle, Ray McKinnon; ***D:*** Irwin Winkler; ***W:*** John Brancato, Michael Ferris; ***C:*** Jack N. Green; ***M:*** Mark Isham.

The Net 2.0 **2006 (R)** Computer systems analyst Hope (DeLoach) takes a job in Istanbul where her identity is stolen and she's framed for criminal activities that land her in prison. But no, it's not a babes-behind-bars flick (more's the pity), it's a lame go-on-the-run-and-prove-you're-innocent adventure. **93m/C DVD.** Nikki Deloach, Keegan Connor Tracy, Demet Akbag, Neil Hopkins; ***D:*** Charles Winkler; ***W:*** Rob Cowan; ***C:*** S. Douglas Smith; ***M:*** Stephen Endelman. **VIDEO**

Net Games **2003 (R)** Married Adam (Howell) is just looking for a little fantasy fun when he logs on to a website called cyber-chat. He thinks it's all eye candy and no risk—especially when he meets seductive Angel (Sloatman). Too bad she's your basic psycho-babe, who soon has Adam involved in blackmail and murder. **97m/C VHS, DVD.** C. Thomas Howell, Lala Sloatman, Ed Begley Jr., Marina Sirtis, Samuel Ball, Lochlyn Munro, Maeve Quinlan, Monique Demers, Joan Van Ark; ***D:*** Andrew Van Slee; ***W:*** Andrew Van Slee; ***C:*** Kristian Bernier; ***M:*** William Richter. **VIDEO**

Netherbeast Incorporated **2007** A horror comedy set in the corporate world. Berm-Tech Industries is run by vampires who have kept their secret for more than 100 years. But when the head of the firm falls ill, he decides to hire some humans, who are soon wondering about their co-workers (the stake through the heart may be a give-away). **93m/C DVD.** Dave Foley, Jason Mewes, Darrell Hammond, Judd Nelson, Steven Burns, Amy Davidson, Robert Wagner; ***D:*** Dean Ronalds; ***W:*** Bruce Dellis; ***C:*** Stefan von Bjorn; ***M:*** Tim Clark. **VIDEO**

Netherworld 1/2 **1990 (R)** A young man investigating his mysterious, dead father travels to his ancestral plantation in the bayou. To his horror, he discovers that his father was involved in the black arts. Now two beautiful young witches are after him. Can he possibly survive this madness? **87m/C VHS, DVD.** Michael C. Bendetti, Denise Gentile, Anjanette Comer, Holly Floria, Robert Burr, Robert Sampson; ***D:*** David Schmoeller; ***W:*** Billy Chicago; ***C:*** Adolfo Bartoli; ***M:*** Edgar Winter.

Network 1/2 **1976 (R)** As timely now as it was then; a scathing indictment of the TV industry and its propensity towards self-prostitution. A television newscaster's mental breakdown turns him into a celebrity when the network tries to profit from his illness. The individual characters are startlingly realistic and the acting is excellent. **121m/C VHS, DVD.** Faye Dunaway, Peter Finch, William Holden, Robert Duvall, Wesley Addy, Ned Beatty, Beatrice Straight, Lane Smith, Conchata Ferrell, William Prince, Ted (Theodore) Sorel, Lance Henriksen, Marlene Warfield; ***D:*** Sidney Lumet; ***W:*** Paddy Chayefsky; ***C:*** Owen Roizman. Oscars '76: Actor (Finch), Actress (Dunaway), Orig. Screenplay, Support. Actress (Straight); AFI '98: Top 100; British Acad. '77: Actor (Finch); Golden Globes '77: Actor—Drama (Finch), Actress—Drama (Dunaway), Director (Lumet), Screenplay; L.A. Film Critics '76: Director (Lumet), Film, Natl. Film Reg. '00;; N.Y. Film Critics '76: Screenplay; Writers Guild '76: Orig. Screenplay.

Neurotic Cabaret 1/2 **1990** Would-be actress dances exotically and finds more exotic ways to roll in dough. **90m/C VHS.** Edwin Neal, Tammy Stone; ***D:*** John Woodward; ***W:*** John Woodward; ***C:*** Daniel Anaya; ***M:*** John Mills.

Neutron and the Black Mask **1961** Man wears mask with lightning bolts and gains comic book style powers to do deathly battle with a scientist with a neutron bomb up his sleeve. First Neutron feature. **80m/B VHS.** *MX* Wolf Ruvinskis, Julio Aleman, Armando Silvestre, Rosita (Rosa) Arenas, Claudio Brook; ***D:*** Frederick Curiel.

Neutron vs. the Amazing Dr. Caronte **1961** Dr. Caronte from "Neutron and the Black Mask" just won't give up that neutron bomb and let the series die. **80m/B VHS.** *MX* Wolf Ruvinskis, Julio Aleman, Armando Silvestre, Rosita (Rosa) Arenas, Rodolfo Landa; ***D:*** Frederick Curiel.

Neutron vs. the Death Robots **1962** Guy with a mask takes on army of killer robots and neutron bomb to protect the world from future sequels. **80m/B VHS.** *MX* Wolf Ruvinskis, Julio Aleman, Armando Silvestre, Rosita (Rosa) Arenas; ***D:*** Frederick Curiel.

Neutron vs. the Maniac **1962** Man in mask hunts guys who kill people. **80m/B VHS.** *MX* Gina Romand, Rodolfo Landa, Wolf Ruvinskis; ***D:*** Alfredo B. Crevenna.

Nevada 1/2 **1927** Entertaining silent western with a great cast finds gunslinger Cooper running from the law and winding up on a ranch where he falls for Todd, the rancher's daughter. Naturally, Cooper redeems himself by going after a gang of cattle rustlers, led by Powell. Based on a novel by Zane Grey. **67m/B VHS.** Gary Cooper, Thelma Todd, William Powell, Ernie Adams, Philip Strange, Christian J. Frank, Ivan Christy, Guy Oliver; ***D:*** John S. Waters; ***W:*** Jon Stone, L.G. Rigby; ***C:*** Charles E. Schoenbaum.

Nevada 1/2 **1944** Cowpoke Mitchum is mistaken for the killer of a homesteader and narrowly escapes the rope by finding the real killer. First leading role for Mitchum as the tough but laconic hero. Based on a story by Zane Grey. **62m/B VHS, DVD.** Robert Mitchum, Anne Jeffreys, Nancy Gates, Craig Reynolds, Guinn "Big Boy" Williams, Richard Martin, Harry Woods; ***D:*** Edward Killy.

Nevada 1/2 **1997 (R)** Women run a small Nevada town Monday through Friday while their men work at a dam several hours away, returning only on the weekends. When stranger Chrysty (Brenneman) shows up, the townswomen become curiously unsettled in their normally placid lives—accusing her of being a troublemaker or seeing her as a hopeful sign of change. **108m/C VHS.** Amy Brenneman, Kirstie Alley, Gabrielle Anwar, Saffron Burrows, Angus MacFadyen, Kathy Najimy, Dee Wallace, James Wilder, Bridgette Wilson-Sampras; ***D:*** Gary Tieche; ***W:*** Gary Tieche; ***C:*** Nancy Schreiber; ***M:*** Robert Perry.

The Nevada Buckaroo **1931** The hero starts out as a bad guy. Thanks to a clever forgery by sidekick Cherokee (Hayes), outlaw Buck "The Nevada Kid" Hurley (Steele) is released from prison with a full pardon. Vowing to go straight, he returns to the town of Rattlesnake Gulch to make amends but the townsfolk aren't too happy to see him. He takes a job protecting the stagecoach but when it's robbed by his old gang, the Kid decides to bring them to justice. **54m/B DVD.** Bob Steele, George "Gabby" Hayes, Dorothy Dix, Glen Cavender, Ed(ward) Brady, Arthur Millett, Gordon DeMain, Artie Ortego; ***D:*** John P. McCarthy; ***W:*** Wellyn Totman; ***C:*** Faxon M. Dean.

Nevada City 1/2 **1941** Roy outwits a financier who is trying to monopolize transportation in California. **54m/B VHS, DVD.** Roy Rogers, George "Gabby" Hayes, Sally Payne, George Cleveland, Billy Lee, Joseph Crehan, Fred Kohler Jr., Pierre Watkin; ***D:*** Joseph Kane; ***W:*** James R. Webb; ***C:*** William Nobles; ***M:*** Cy Feuer.

Nevada Smith **1966** The half-breed Nevada Smith (previously introduced in Harold Robbins' story "The Carpetbaggers" and film of same name) seeks the outlaws who killed his parents. Standard western plot, characters. Later remade as a TV movie. **135m/C VHS, DVD.** Steve McQueen, Karl Malden, Brian Keith, Arthur Kennedy, Raf Vallone, Suzanne Pleshette, Paul Fix, Pat Hingle, Janet Margolin, Howard da Silva, John Doucette, Gene Evans, Val Avery, Lyle Bettger; ***D:*** Henry Hathaway; ***W:*** John Michael Hayes; ***C:*** Lucien Ballard; ***M:*** Alfred Newman.

The Nevadan 1/2 *The Man From Nevada* **1950** A marshal goes in search of an outlaw's gold cache, only to be opposed by a crooked rancher. Good scenery and action, but not one of Scott's best. **81m/C VHS.** Randolph Scott, Dorothy Malone, Forrest Tucker, Frank Faylen, George Macready, Charles Kemper, Jeff Corey, Tom Powers, Jock Mahoney; ***D:*** Gordon Douglas; ***W:*** Rowland Brown, George W. George; ***C:*** Charles Lawton Jr.; ***M:*** Arthur Morton.

Never a Dull Moment **1950** New York songwriter falls for rodeo Romeo, moves out West, and finds welcome wagon deficient. Mediocre songs; many dull moments. ♫ Once You Find Your Guy; Sagebrush Lullaby; The Man With the Big Felt Hat. **89m/B VHS.** Irene Dunne, Fred MacMurray, William Demarest, Andy Devine, Gigi Perreau, Natalie Wood, Philip Ober, Jack Kirkwood, Ann Doran, Meg Gibson; ***D:*** George Marshall.

Never a Dull Moment **1968 (G)** Mobsters mistake an actor for an assassin in this gag-filled adventure. They threaten the thespian into thievery, before the trouble really starts when Ace, the actual assassin, arrives. **90m/C VHS, DVD.** Dick Van Dyke, Edward G. Robinson, Dorothy Provine, Henry Silva, Joanna Moore, Tony Bill, Slim Pickens, Jack Elam; ***D:*** Jerry Paris; ***W:*** A.J. Carothers; ***M:*** Robert F. Brunner.

Never Again **2001 (R)** The best thing is seeing a radiant fiftysomething Clayburgh back on the big screen. Divorcee Grace (Clayburgh) winds up meeting cute with exterminator/jazz musician Christopher (Tambor). Both vow to maintain a no-strings relationship, no matter how great the sex is, though they can't help becoming emotionally involved. Unfortunately, the film is often more contrived and crude than romantic. **97m/C VHS, DVD.** *US* Jill Clayburgh, Jeffrey Tambor, Michael McKean, Caroline Aaron, Sandy Duncan, Bill Duke; ***D:*** Eric Schaeffer; ***W:*** Eric Schaeffer; ***C:*** Tom Ostrowski; ***M:*** Amanda Kravat.

Never Back Down **2008 (PG-13)** Mild-mannered teen Jake Tyler (Faris) is set off by the school bully's trash talk, exploding into an ugly fist fight. Soon after, boxing trainer Jean (Honsou) takes Jake under his wing, teaching him the ways of the sport and the meaning of self-respect, eventually leading to an inevitable rematch with the bully. And, yes, he wins the girl, rehashing "The Karate Kid" and countless other underdog sports dramas. Oddly preaches a message of non-violence while cheering on Jake's bloody bare-knuckle beat-downs. **110m/C DVD.** *US* Sean Faris, Amber Heard, Djimon Hounsou, Leslie Hope, Cam Gigandet, Evan Peters, Wyatt Smith; ***D:*** Jeff Wadlow; ***W:*** Chris Hauty; ***C:*** Lukas Ettlin; ***M:*** Michael Wandmacher.

Never Been Kissed **1999 (PG-13)** Lightweight and logic-defying, Barrymore's producing debut hypothesizes that the people who were unpopular in high school want another chance at it. Not. Still-nerdy newspaper copy editor Josie is assigned to go undercover as a student and write about high school life. She see it as a chance to be a big-time journalist and one of the "cool kids." When it turns that not much has changed for her, she enlists the help of her brother (Arquette) and a coworker (Shannon), and eventually falls for sensitive teacher Sam (Vartan). Barrymore is sweet, but doesn't exactly stretch here, and the script sounds a lot like the John Hughes comedies of the '80s. Probably more enjoyable if you're actually high school age. **107m/C VHS, DVD.** Drew Barrymore, David Arquette, Leelee Sobieski, Michael Vartan, Molly Shannon, John C. Reilly, Garry Marshall, Sean M. Whalen, Jeremy Jordan, Marley Shelton, Jordan Ladd, Jessica Alba, Carmen (Lee) Llywelyn; ***D:*** Raja Gosnell; ***W:*** Abby Kohn, Marc Silverstein; ***C:*** Alex Nepomniaschy; ***M:*** David Newman.

Never Been Thawed **2005** Mockumentary follows the obsessions of the members of the Mesa Frozen Entree Enthusiasts' Club (frozen food addicts) and their leader, Shawn Anderson (Anders). Besides his obsession with frozen entrees, Shawn has converted to Christianity and fronts a once hardcore punk band that has turned into a Christian rock group so they can increase their music sales. Easy targets, lame humor. **87m/C DVD.** *US* John Morris, Sean Anders; ***W:*** John Morris, Sean Anders, Le Vinus Chuck; ***C:*** Sean Anders; ***M:*** Sean Anders, Thomas Laufenberg.

Never Cry Werewolf **2008** List how many other movies this flick reminds you of (it'll keep you from nodding off from boredom). Sixteen-year-old Loren becomes obsessed with spying on her new neighbor Jared, especially when it seems all his dates go missing. Suspecting Jared turns furry at the full moon, Loren goes to Redd Tucker, the host of a cheesy local TV hunting show, for help in tracking Jared. **87m/C DVD.** Kevin Sorbo, Peter Stebbings, Nina Dobrev, Spence Van Wyck, Sean O'Neill, Melanie Leishmann; ***D:*** Brenton Spencer; ***W:*** David Benullo; ***C:*** Curtis Petersen; ***M:*** Michael Richard Plowman. **VIDEO**

Never Cry Wolf 1/2 **1983 (PG)** A young biologist is sent to the Arctic to study the behavior and habitation of wolves, then becomes deeply involved with their sub-society. Based on Farley Mowat's book. Beautifully photographed. **105m/C VHS, DVD.** Charles Martin Smith, Brian Dennehy, Samson Jorah; ***D:*** Carroll Ballard; ***W:*** Curtis Hanson, Sam Hamm; ***C:*** Hiro Narita; ***M:*** Mark Isham. Natl. Soc. Film Critics '83: Cinematog.

Never Die Alone 1/2 **2004 (R)** King David (DMX) is a drug dealer and a vicious dude to boot, and the opening scene shows him paying the price for his deeds as he is fatally stabbed. This is where Paul (Arquette), a struggling writer desperate for a story to tell, comes in. When King David passes on he gives Paul all of his possessions, including a stack of audiotapes he'd made detailing the events of his wretched life (which provide the means for the at-times tedious narrative), but Paul doesn't realize how dangerous a predicament this really is. Director Dickerson presents powerful images and purposefully avoids garnering sympathy for King David. DMX is engrossing as the suave seducer/violent hoodlum. Based on the 1974 novel by ex-convict Donald Goines. **88m/C DVD, UMD.** *US* DMX, Michael Ealy, Antwon Tanner, David Arquette, Clifton Powell, Tommy (Tiny) Lister, Aisha Tyler, Michele Shay, Reagan Gomez-Preston, Damion Poitier, Jennifer Sky, Drew Sidora; ***D:*** Ernest R. Dickerson; ***W:*** James Gibson; ***C:*** Matthew Libatique; ***M:*** DMX, George Duke.

Never Down ♂♂ **2006** Latino con Rico (LaSardo) is fresh out of the joint after a five-year stint. He's hoping his ex-wife will allow him access to their young daughter but new forces conspire to send him back down that criminal path. Vonnegut (in his last role) makes a brief appearance as a benefactor. **82m/C DVD.** Robert LaSardo, Mary Kelsey; ***Cameos:*** Kurt Vonnegut Jr., James Toback; ***D:*** Robert Oppel. **VIDEO**

Never Forever ♂♂ 1/2 **2007 (R)** New York housewife Sophie (Farmiga) is married to Korean-American lawyer Andrew (McInnis), though there has always been tension within his family over their mixed-marriage and the pressure for them to have a child. Andrew is probably sterile and, after his father dies, he attempts suicide. A desperate Sophie meets poor illegal immigrant Jihah (Ha) and impulsively says she'll pay him for sex until she conceives. Jihah resents Sophie's businesslike attitude but she can't really suppress her emotional needs for long. Lots of nudity but writer/director Kim never makes her story salacious. English and Korean with subtitles. **104m/C DVD.** *KN* Vera Farmiga, Jung-woo Ha, David L. McInnis; ***D:*** Gina Kim; ***W:*** Gina Kim; ***C:*** Matthew Clark; ***M:*** Michael Nyman.

Never Forget ♂♂ **1991** True story of California resident Mel Mermelstein (played by Nimoy), a survivor of Hitler's death camps who accepted a pro-Nazi group's challenge to prove in court that the Holocaust of six million Jews really happened. A sincere, well-meaning courtroom drama that just can't surmount the uncinematic nature of the source material. **94m/C VHS.** Leonard Nimoy, Blythe Danner, Dabney Coleman; ***D:*** Joseph Sargent; ***M:*** Henry Mancini. **CABLE**

Never Forget ♂ 1/2 **2008 (R)** But Frank (Phillips) already did, which is the problem. He wakes up alone and bloodied in the woods without any idea of how he got there. But when his best friend Andy (Holden-Ried) accuses him of a vicious murder, Frank better find the answers. **83m/C DVD.** Lou Diamond Phillips, Kris Holden-Ried, Sarah Manninen, Jonathan Whittaker, James Byron; ***D:*** Leo Scherman; ***W:*** Mark Steinberg; ***C:*** Marcus Elliott; ***M:*** Eric Cadesky, Nick Dyer. **VIDEO**

Never Give a Sucker an Even Break ♂♂♂ 1/2 *What a Man* **1941** An almost plotless comedy, based on an idea reputedly written on a napkin by Fields (he took screenplay credit as Otis Criblecoblis), and features Fields at his most unleashed. It's something of a cult favorite, but not for all tastes. Classic chase scene ends it. Fields' last role in a feature-length film. **71m/B VHS, DVD.** W.C. Fields, Gloria Jean, Franklin Pangborn, Leon Errol, Margaret Dumont, Susan Miller; ***D:*** Edward F. (Eddie) Cline; ***W:*** John Thomas "Jack" Neville, Prescott Chaplin, W.C. Fields; ***C:*** Charles Van Enger; ***M:*** Frank Skinner.

Never Let Go ♂♂ **1960** A man unwittingly tracks down the mastermind of a gang of racketeers. Sellers sheds his comedic image to play the ruthless and brutal gang boss, something he shouldn't have done. **91m/C VHS, DVD.** *GB* Peter Sellers, Richard Todd, Elizabeth Sellars, Carol White; ***D:*** John Guillermin; ***M:*** John Barry.

Never Let Me Go ♂♂ 1/2 **1953** Implausible yet entertaining account of American newsman Gable trying to smuggle ballerina wife Tierney out of Russia. Hard to believe Gable as a one-man assault force infiltrating Russia, but enjoyable nonetheless. Based on the novel "Came the Dawn" by Roger Bax. **94m/B VHS.** Clark Gable, Gene Tierney, Richard Haydn, Bernard Miles, Kenneth More, Karel Stepanek, Theodore Bikel; ***D:*** Delmer Daves; ***W:*** Ronald Millar, George Froeschel.

Never Love a Stranger ♂♂ **1958** A young man becomes a numbers runner for a mobster and ultimately winds up heading his own racket. Later he finds himself in conflict with his old boss and the district attorney. No surprises here. Based on the Harold Robbins' novel. **93m/B VHS, DVD.** John Drew (Blythe) Barrymore Jr., Steve McQueen, Lita Milan, Robert Bray; ***D:*** Robert M. Stevens.

Never Met Picasso ♂♂ 1/2 **1996** Thirty-year-old artist Andrew (Arquette) lives with self-absorbed actress/mom Genna (Kidder) in Boston, struggling with both his lack of work and romantic prospects. Andrew's one consolation is gay Uncle Alfred (Epstein), who serves as a role model. Until, unexpectedly, Andrew meets confident Jerry (McKellar) at his mother's dreadful opening night bash. After Alfred dies suddenly, Andrew discovers some hidden photos of his uncle's lover and seeks to make connections between the past and the present. **97m/C VHS.** Alexis Arquette, Margot Kidder, Don McKellar, Alvin Epstein, Georgia Ringsdale; ***D:*** Stephen Kijak; ***W:*** Stephen Kijak; ***C:*** David Tames; ***M:*** Kristen Hersh.

Never on Sunday ♂♂♂ **1960** An American intellectual tries to turn a Greek prostitute into a refined woman. Fine performances and exhilarating Greek photography. Fun all around. ♫ Never on Sunday. **91m/B VHS, DVD.** *GR* Melina Mercouri, Titos Vandis, Jules Dassin, Mitsos Liguisos; ***D:*** Jules Dassin; ***W:*** Jules Dassin; ***M:*** Manos Hadjidakis. Oscars '60: Song ("Never on Sunday"); Cannes '60: Actress (Mercouri).

Never on Tuesday ♂ 1/2 **1988 (R)** Two jerks from Ohio head to California and find themselves stuck midway in the desert with a beautiful girl, who has plans of her own. **90m/C VHS.** Claudia Christian, Andrew Lauer, Peter Berg; ***Cameos:*** Charlie Sheen, Emilio Estevez; ***D:*** Adam Rifkin; ***W:*** Adam Rifkin.

Never Pick Up a Stranger ♂ 1/2 *Bloodrage* **1979** When a local hooker is murdered, her cop boyfriend, who never gives up on a case, hunts her killer with a vengeance. Extremely graphic. **82m/C VHS.** Ian Scott, Judith-Marie Bergan, James Johnston, Lawrence Tierney; ***D:*** Joseph Bigwood.

Never Say Die ♂♂ 1/2 **1939** Wealthy John Kidley (Hope) is at the Swiss spa of Bad Gasswasser, thinking he only has a few weeks to live. So he marries Mickey Hawkins (Raye) to save her from a crazy Russian, Prince Smirnov (Mowbray), and ends up fighting a duel! Oh, and Mickey thinks she's in love with bus driver Henry Munch (Devine), who accompanies the duo on their honeymoon. Much silliness. Based on the play by William H. Post. **82m/B VHS.** Bob Hope, Martha Raye, Alan Mowbray, Andy Devine, Gale Sondergaard, Monty Woolley, Sig Rumann; ***D:*** Elliott Nugent; ***W:*** Preston Sturges, Don Hartman, Frank Butler; ***C:*** Leo Tover.

Never Say Die ♂ 1/2 **1990** Two innocents are thrown into a web of international intrigue and acquit themselves rather well. Lots of explosions and car crashes for a film shot in New Zealand. **98m/C VHS.** *NZ* George Wendt, Lisa Eilbacher; ***D:*** Geoff Murphy.

Never Say Die ♂♂ **1994 (R)** Ex-Special Forces soldier John Blake (Zagarino), ambushed and left to die, returns to seek vengeance on the renegade commander who betrayed him. And he has the perfect opportunity when his nemesis kidnaps a general's daughter. **99m/C VHS.** Frank Zagarino, Billy Drago, Todd Jensen, Jenny (Jennifer) McShane, Robin Smith; ***D:*** Yossi Wein; ***W:*** Jeff Albert; ***M:*** Wendy Oldfield, Adrian Levy.

Never Say Goodbye ♂♂ **1946** Cliche-ridden story about a man trying to win back his divorce-bound wife. Flynn tries hard, but the material just isn't up to par. Based on the story "Don't Ever Leave Me" by Ben and Norma Barzman. Co-screenwriter Diamond later became famous when he teamed up with Billy Wilder to script "Some Like it Hot" and "The Apartment." **97m/B VHS.** Errol Flynn, Eleanor Parker, Lucile Watson, S.Z. Sakall, Forrest Tucker, Donald Woods, Peggy Knudsen, Tom D'Andrea, Hattie McDaniel; ***D:*** James V. Kern; ***W:*** James V. Kern, I.A.L. Diamond, Lewis R. Foster.

Never Say Macbeth ♂♂ 1/2 **2007** Actors believe that saying the name of Shakespeare's Scottish play will bring about bad luck and nebbish science teacher Danny (Gold) doesn't need any more of that. Lovelorn, he heads to L.A. to reunite with his ex-girlfriend, actress Ruth (Turner), who's been cast as Lady Macbeth. Eccentric director Jason (Enberg) thinks Danny is auditioning for a role and hires him, but Danny has already doomed the production by uttering the "M" word. Oh, and he can suddenly see that the theater is haunted by the ghosts of actors who died in a fire when—you guessed it—that play was last performed. It may sound dopey but it's actually charming and funny. **87m/C DVD.** Joe Tyler Gold, Ilana Turner, Tania Getty, Alexander Enberg, Tammy Caplan, Mark Deklin; ***D:*** Christopher J. Prouty; ***W:*** Joe Tyler Gold; ***C:*** Michael Millikan; ***M:*** Tim Labor. **VIDEO**

Never Say Never Again ♂♂ 1/2 **1983 (PG)** James Bond matches wits with a charming but sinister tycoon who is holding the world nuclear hostage as part of a diabolical plot by SPECTRE. Connery's return to the world of Bond after 12 years is smooth in this remake of "Thunderball" hampered by an atrocious musical score. Carrera is stunning as Fatima Blush. Although Connery is back, purists will have qualms considering this part of the "official" Bond series since longtime Bond producer, Albert "Cubby" Broccoli, had nothing to do with this endeavor. **134m/C VHS, DVD.** Sean Connery, Klaus Maria Brandauer, Max von Sydow, Barbara Carrera, Kim Basinger, Edward Fox, Bernie Casey, Pamela Salem, Rowan Atkinson, Valerie Leon, Prunella Gee, Saskia Cohen Tanugi; ***D:*** Irvin Kershner; ***W:*** Lorenzo Semple Jr.; ***C:*** Douglas Slocombe; ***M:*** Michel Legrand.

Never So Few ♂♂ 1/2 **1959** A military commander and his outnumbered troops overcome incredible odds against the Japanese. There is a lot of focus on romance, but the script and acting make a strong impression nonetheless. Based on the novel by Tom T. Chamales. **124m/C VHS, DVD.** Frank Sinatra, Gina Lollobrigida, Peter Lawford, Steve McQueen, Richard Johnson, Paul Henreid, Charles Bronson; ***D:*** John Sturges; ***C:*** William H. Daniels.

Never Steal Anything Small ♂ 1/2 **1959** A tough union boss pushes everyone as he battles the mob for control of the waterfront. A strange musical-drama combination that will be of interest only to the most ardent Cagney and Jones fans. Based on the Maxwell Anderson/Rouben Mamoulian play "The Devil's Hornpipe." Largely forgettable songs. ♫ I'm Sorry, I Want a Ferrari; I Haven't Got a Thing to Wear; It Takes Love to Make a Home; Never Steal Anything Small; Helping Out Friends. **94m/C VHS.** James Cagney, Shirley Jones, Cara Williams, Wendell Holmes, Nehemiah Persoff, Anthony Caruso, Jack Albertson, Roger Smith, Royal Dano, Horace McMahon, Virginia Vincent, Robert J. Wilke; ***D:*** Charles Lederer; ***M:*** Henry Mancini.

Never Talk to Strangers ♂♂ **1995 (R)** Sarah Taylor (DeMornay) is an uptight criminal psychologist who gets involved with handsome stranger Tony Ramirez (Banderas) while working on the case of a serial killer (Stanton). Then Sarah finds herself the target of an increasingly malevolent stalker—and she has lots of suspects to choose from. Typical woman-in-peril film with equally standard frights but the leads certainly look good (and Banderas is a fine sex object in a bit of role reversal). Filmed in Toronto. **86m/C VHS, DVD.** Rebecca De Mornay, Antonio Banderas, Harry Dean Stanton, Dennis Miller, Len Cariou, Beau Starr; ***D:*** Peter Hall; ***W:*** Lewis Green, Jordan Rush; ***C:*** Elemer Ragalyi; ***M:*** Pino Donaggio.

Never Too Late ♂ 1/2 **1965** Very silly comedy has middle-aged Edith (O'Sullivan) delighted to discover she's pregnant. Her grumbling husband Harry (Ford) and married daughter Kate (Stevens) don't share her happy mood, especially since Kate and her hubby Charlie (Hutton) have infertility issues hampering their own baby plans. A fed-up Edith eventually leaves until everyone can accept the situation and behave sensibly. **105m/C DVD.** Maureen Sullivan, Paul Ford, Connie Stevens, Jim Hutton, Jane Wyatt, Henry Jones, Lloyd Nolan; ***D:*** Bud Yorkin; ***W:*** Sumner Arthur Long; ***C:*** Philip Lathrop; ***M:*** David Rose.

Never Too Late to Mend ♂♂ **1937** Victorian British play about the abuses of the penal system which had, upon its initial London West End run, caused Queen Victoria to institute a sweeping program of prison reform. The movie caused considerably less stir. **67m/B VHS, DVD.** *GB* Tod Slaughter, Marjorie Taylor, Jack Livesey, Ian Colin; ***D:*** David MacDonald.

Never Too Young to Die ♂ **1986 (R)** A young man is drawn into a provocative espionage adventure by his late father's spy associates. Together they try to discover who killed the young man's father. High point may be Simmons as a crazed hermaphrodite plotting to poison L.A. **97m/C VHS.** John Stamos, Vanity, Gene Simmons, George Lazenby; ***D:*** Gil Bettman; ***W:*** Gil Bettman; ***M:*** James Newton Howard, Lennie Niehaus.

Never 2 Big ♂♂ **1998 (R)** A young record company exec wants to prove that someone at the company murdered his singer sister in order to prevent her from leaving and signing with another label. Only he's been framed for the crime and has to stay out of jail and prove his own innocence. **100m/C VHS, DVD.** Ernie Hudson, Nia Long, Tony Todd, Donnie Wahlberg, Terrence Howard, Donald Adeosun Faison, Tommy (Tiny) Lister, Salli Richardson, Shemar Moore; ***D:*** Peter Gathings Bunche; ***W:*** Peter Gathings Bunche; ***C:*** Nancy Schreiber; ***M:*** Joseph Williams. **VIDEO**

Never Wave at a WAC ♂♂ 1/2 *The Private Wore Skirts* **1952** A Washington socialite joins the Women's Army Corps hoping for a commission that never comes. She has to tough it out as an ordinary private. A reasonably fun ancestor of "Private Benjamin," with a cameo by Gen. Omar Bradley as himself. **87m/B VHS, DVD.** Rosalind Russell, Paul Douglas, Marie Wilson, William Ching, Arleen Whelan, Leif Erickson, Hillary Brooke, Regis Toomey; ***Cameos:*** Omar Bradley; ***D:*** Norman Z. McLeod; ***M:*** Elmer Bernstein.

The NeverEnding Story ♂♂♂ 1/2 **1984 (PG)** A lonely young boy helps a warrior save the fantasy world in his book from destruction by the Nothing. A wonderful, intelligent family movie about imagination, with swell effects and a sweet but not overly sentimental script. Petersen's first English-language film, based on the novel by Michael Ende. **94m/C VHS, DVD.** Barret Oliver, Noah Hathaway, Gerald McRaney, Moses Gunn, Tami Stronach, Patricia Hayes, Sydney Bromley, Thomas Hill; ***D:*** Wolfgang Petersen; ***W:*** Wolfgang Petersen, Herman(n) Weigel; ***C:*** Jost Vacano; ***M:*** Klaus Doldinger, Giorgio Moroder.

NeverEnding Story 2: The Next Chapter ♂♂ **1991 (PG)** Disappointing sequel to the first story that didn't end. Bastian (Brandis) must again save Fantasia, this time from the evil sorceress Xayride (Burt). So dull, the kids may wander away. But wait: contains the first Bugs Bunny theatrical cartoon in 26 years, "Box Office Bunny." **90m/C VHS, DVD.** Jonathan Brandis, Kenny Morrison, Clarissa Burt, John Wesley Shipp, Martin Umbach; ***D:*** George Miller; ***W:*** Karin Howard; ***C:*** David Connell; ***M:*** Robert Folk.

The NeverEnding Story 3: Escape from Fantasia ♂♂ **1994 (G)** The third time was not the charm in this case. Bastian, on the edge of puberty, is being bullied by a group at school called the Nasties. He seeks refuge in the library and enters the world of Fantasia through the "Neverending Story" tome. When the book is stolen by the Nasties, it is up to Bastian to return it. Unfortunately, the story does not have the charm of the original, trying to incorporate too much reality and not enough of dreamland. **95m/C VHS, DVD.** Jason James Richter, Melody Kay, Freddie Jones, Jack Black, Ryan Bollman, Tracey Ellis, Kevin McNulty; ***D:*** Peter Macdonald; ***C:*** Robin Vidgeon; ***M:*** Peter Wolf.

Nevermore ♂♂ **2007** Well it certainly sounds like someone has been looking through those Poe stories for a plot. Wealthy Jonathan Usher (Nelson) isolates himself in his childhood home, living on the brink of sanity. Having forced his trophy wife Lydia (O'Dell) to give up her social pleasures, he's now convinced she wants to drive him over the edge to get his money. So Jonathan asks his friend Devin Bayliss (Spano) to visit and confirm or deny his suspicions. Of course paranoid Jonathan is soon questioning Devin's loyalty. **95m/C DVD.** Judd Nelson, Jennifer O'Dell, Vincent Spano, Sidi Henderson; ***D:*** Thomas Zambeck; ***W:*** Thomas Zambeck; ***C:*** Oren Goldenberg; ***M:*** Mark Krench. **VIDEO**

Nevil Shute's The Far Country ♂♂ 1/2 *The Far Country* **1985** Carl Zlintner (York), once a doctor in

Hitler's army, escapes to Australia from post-war Europe to begin a new life with a new identity. Falling in love with the beautiful Jennifer Morton (Thornton), Carl hopes he's left his past behind. But nothing is every that simple. Adaptation of the Shute novel. **200m/C VHS.** *AU* Michael York, Sigrid Thornton, Fred Steele; ***D:*** George Miller. **TV**

The New Adventures of Pippi Longstocking 🦴 1/2 **1988 (G)** Decent cast is trapped in another musical rehashing of the Astrid Lindgren children's books about a precocious red-headed girl and her fantastic adventures with horses, criminals, and pirates. **101m/C VHS, DVD.** Tami Erin, Eileen Brennan, Dennis Dugan, Dianne Hull, George DiCenzo, John Schuck, Dick Van Patten; ***D:*** Ken Annakin; ***W:*** Ken Annakin; ***C:*** Roland Smith; ***M:*** Misha Segal.

The New Adventures of Tarzan 🦴🦴 *Tarzan and the Green Goddess* **1935** Twelve episodes, each 22 minutes long, depict the adventures of Edgar Rice Burrough's tree-swinging character—Tarzan. **260m/B VHS, DVD.** Bruce Bennett, Ula Holt, Frank Baker, Dale Walsh, Lewis Sargent; ***D:*** Edward Kull.

The New Age 🦴🦴 **1994 (R)** Illusions in L.A. centering on talent agent Peter (Weller) and art designer Katherine (Davis) Witner. Katherine loses her job the same day Peter decides to quit his and suddenly the caustic duo are dependent upon each other. The trendy couple decide to open a boutique and quickly find themselves in a fiscal sinkhole and on a downhill slide. The acting is fine but the story is empty. **106m/C VHS.** Peter Weller, Judy Davis, Adam West, Patrick Bauchau, Corbin Bernsen, Jonathan Hadary, Samuel L. Jackson, Patricia Heaton, Audra Lindley, Paula Marshall, Maureen Mueller, Bruce Ramsay, Sandra Seacat, Susan Traylor; ***D:*** Michael Tolkin; ***W:*** Michael Tolkin, Mark Mothersbaugh.

New Best Friend 🦴 1/2 *Depraved Indifference; Mary Jane's Last Dance* **2002 (R)** Obvious and sleazy whodunnit wastes its cast. Alicia (Kirshner) is in a cocaine-induced coma after getting in with the wrong college crowd. Working-class mom Connie (O'Connor) raises a stink with new sheriff Bonner (Diggs) to investigate, though the school wants all the sordid details swept under the rug since it involves some wild partying by rich and vapid students. **91m/C VHS, DVD.** Mia Kirshner, Dominique Swain, Rachel True, Meredith Monroe, Scott Bairstow, Taye Diggs, Glynnis O'Connor, Eric Michael Cole, Oliver Hudson; ***D:*** Zoe Clarke-Williams; ***W:*** Victoria Strouse; ***C:*** Tom Priestley; ***M:*** David A. Hughes, John Murphy.

New Blood 🦴🦴 **1999 (R)** Violent thriller that has a few nifty twists. After seven years, Danny White (Moran) turns up on the doorstep of his estranged father, Alan (Hurt). Danny is bleeding from a gunshot wound and makes the devil's own deal with dad: Danny's twin sister needs a heart transplant and Danny offers his own organ if dad will participate in a mob ordered kidnapping that's gone wrong once already. Solid performances are an asset. **92m/C VHS, DVD.** *GB* Nick Moran, John Hurt, Carrie-Anne Moss, Shawn Wayans, Joe Pantoliano, Eugene Robert Glazer, Richard Fitzpatrick, Rob Freeman; ***D:*** Michael Hurst; ***W:*** Michael Hurst; ***C:*** David Pelletier; ***M:*** Jeff Danna.

The New Centurions 🦴🦴 1/2 **1972 (R)** Rookies training for the Los Angeles Police Department get the inside info from retiring cops. Gritty and realistic drama based on the novel by former cop Joseph Wambaugh. Tends to be disjointed at times, but overall is a good adaptation of the bestseller. Scott, excellent as the retiring beat-walker, is supported well by the other performers. **103m/C VHS.** George C. Scott, Stacy Keach, Jane Alexander, Scott Wilson, Erik Estrada, James B. Sikking; ***D:*** Richard Fleischer; ***W:*** Stirling Silliphant; ***M:*** Quincy Jones.

New Crime City: Los Angeles 2020 🦴 1/2 **1994 (R)** Prisoner Tony Ricks (Rossovich) is executed and then revived thanks to technology. But there's a price to pay for his life and freedom—he must retrieve a biowarfare weapon from a prison gang and he only has 24 hours to do it. **95m/C VHS, DVD.** Rick Rossovich, Stacy Keach, Sherrie Rose; ***W:*** Rick Rossovich.

New Eden 🦴🦴 **1994 (R)** In the year 2237 wartime prisoners are condemned to a desert planet where they are preyed upon by brutal Sand Pirates. An idealistic engineer falls in love and seeks to protect his new family from a deadly confrontation. **89m/C VHS.** Stephen Baldwin, Lisa Bonet, Tobin Bell, Michael Bowen, Janet Hubert-Whitten, Kate McGregor-Stewart; ***D:*** Alan Metzger; ***W:*** Dan Gordon.

The New Eve 🦴🦴🦴 *La Nouvelle Eve* **1998 (R)** Camille (Viard in an astonishing performance) is a hard-partying Parisienne whose hedonistic life is changed when she meets Alexis (Rajot). He's a political activist, married with a couple of kids—not at all the sort of drugged-up playboy she is used to. Their rocky relationship is both sexual and emotional. French with subtitles. **90m/C VHS, DVD.** *FR* Karin Viard, Pierre-Loup Rajot, Catherine Frot, Sergi Lopez, Mireille Roussel, Nozha Khouadra; ***D:*** Catherine Corsini; ***W:*** Catherine Corsini, Marc Syrigas; ***C:*** Agnes Godard.

New Faces of 1952 🦴🦴 1/2 **1954** Based on the hit Broadway revue. The plot revolves around a Broadway show that is about to be closed down, and the performers who fight to keep it open. Lots of hit songs. Mel Brooks is credited as a writer, under the name Melvin Brooks. ♫ C'est Si Bon; Santa Baby; Uskadara; Monotonous; Bal Petit Bal; Boston Beguine; I'm in Love with Miss Logan; Penny Candy; Time for Tea. **98m/C VHS.** Ronny Graham, Eartha Kitt, Robert Clary, Alice Ghostley, June Carroll, Carol Lawrence, Paul Lynde; ***D:*** Harry Horner.

New Fist of Fury 🦴 *Xin Ching-wu Men* **1976** During WWII, a former pickpocket becomes a martial arts whiz with the assistance of his fiancee, and fights the entire Imperial Army. **120m/C VHS, DVD.** Jackie Chan; ***D:*** Lo Wei; ***W:*** Lo Wei.

The New Frontier 🦴 1/2 **1935** Wayne is a small-town sheriff whose predecessor, his father, was murdered. The local saloon-keeper and his gang do everything they can to prevent Wayne from bringing the culprit to justice. **59m/B VHS.** John Wayne, Muriel Evans, Murdock MacQuarrie, Mary MacLaren, Warner Richmond; ***D:*** Carl Pierson.

The New Gladiators WOOF! **1983** In the future, criminals try to kill each other on TV for public entertainment. Two such gladiators discover that the network's computer is using the games in order to take over mankind, and they attempt to stop it. Even if the special effects were any good, they couldn't save this one. **90m/C VHS, DVD.** *IT* Jared Martin, Fred Williamson, Eleanor Gold, Howard (Red) Ross, Claudio Cassinelli; ***D:*** Lucio Fulci; ***W:*** Elisa Briganti, Dardano Sacchetti; ***C:*** Guiseppe Pinori; ***M:*** Riz Ortolani.

The New Guy 🦴 1/2 **2002 (PG-13)** Dorky high school senior Dizzy (Qualls) wants to transform himself into a cool guy—by getting expelled and transferring to another school. Instead, he winds up in prison where he meets Luther (Griffin), who gives him an attitude makeover. Once he hits the new school, his newfound popularity has him winning a hottie cheerleader (Dushku) and uniting the school. Long (but not quite long enough)-delayed high school flick shows a certain lack of effort on most everyone's part, most notably the director, writer, and cinematographer. Qualls is likable, Deschanel is better than flick deserves, and Dushku supplies the expected sexual spark. **88m/C VHS, DVD.** *US* DJ Qualls, Eddie Griffin, Eliza Dushku, Zooey Deschanel, Lyle Lovett, Jerod Mixon, Parry Shen, Sunny Mabrey, Ross Patterson, Matt Gogin, Illeana Douglas, Kurt Fuller, M.C. Gainey, Julius J. Carry III, Horatio Sanz, Geoffrey Lewis; ***Cameos:*** Henry Rollins, Gene Simmons, Vanilla Ice, Tommy Lee; ***D:*** Edward Decter; ***W:*** David Kendall; ***C:*** Michael D. O'Shea; ***M:*** Ralph Sall.

New in Town 🦴🦴 *Chilled in Miami* **2009 (PG-13)** Fast-track corporate exec Lucy Hill (Zellweger) is sent from big-city Miami to rural New Ulm, Minnesota to oversee the downsizing of her company's processing plant, a cornerstone of employment in the community. She arrives smack dab in the middle of the harsh "sotan" winter in fashionable coat and heels, giving the locals lots to laugh about (of course she knows how to make a fire in her rental house—where's the switch?). When the company's plans change, Lucy's career aspirations are at odds with her unexpected fondness for her new north country friends, particularly hunky widower dad Ted (Connick), the plant union rep and town's sole eligible bachelor. A fish-out-of-water formula flick with all the cliched Minnesota practical jokes, don'tcha know! **96m/C DVD.** *US* Renee Zellweger, Harry Connick Jr., Siobhan Fallon Hogan, J.K. Simmons, Rashida Jones, Frances Conroy; ***D:*** Jonas Elmer; ***W:*** C. Jay Cox, Kenneth Rance; ***C:*** Chris Seager; ***M:*** John Swihart.

The New Invisible Man 🦴🦴 *H.G. Wells' New Invisible Man* **1958** A so-so Mexican adaptation of the popular H.G. Wells novel has a prisoner receiving a vanishing drug from his brother, who created it—perhaps to aid an escape attempt. **95m/B VHS.** *MX* Arturo de Cordova, Ana Luisa Peluffo, Jorge Mondragon; ***D:*** Alfredo B. Crevenna.

New Jack City 🦴🦴 1/2 **1991 (R)** Just say no ghetto-melodrama. Powerful performance by Snipes as wealthy Harlem drug lord sought by rebel cops Ice-T and Nelson. Music by Johnny Gill, 2 Live Crew, Ice-T and others. **101m/C VHS, DVD.** Wesley Snipes, Ice-T, Mario Van Peebles, Chris Rock, Judd Nelson, Tracy C. Johns, Allen Payne, Kim Park, Vanessa Williams, Nick Ashford, Thalmus Rasulala, Michael Michele, Bill Nunn, Russell Wong; ***D:*** Mario Van Peebles; ***W:*** Keith Critchlow, Barry Michael Cooper; ***C:*** Francis Kenny; ***M:*** Roger Bourland, Michel Colombier.

New Jersey Drive 🦴🦴 1/2 **1995 (R)** Jason (Corley) has dreams of life outside the mean streets of Newark, but he jeopardizes his future by stealing cars and joyriding around the neighborhood with his friends. Unblinking realism, provided by credible actors (especially Corley, a former gang member), dialogue, and filming in the projects of Brooklyn and Queens, is neutralized by stereotypical characters (especially the lily-white, sadistically brutal cops) and lack of a sympathetic point of view. Loosely based on a series of articles by Michel Mariott, a reporter for the "New York Times." **98m/C VHS, DVD.** Sharron Corley, Gabriel Casseus, Saul Stein, Andre Moore, Donald Adeosun Faison, Conrad Meertin Jr., Deven Eggleston, Gwen McGee, Koran C. Thomas, Samantha Brown, Christine Baranski, Robert Jason Jackson, Roscoe Orman, Dwight Errington Myers, Gary DeWitt Marshall; ***D:*** Nick Gomez; ***W:*** Nick Gomez, Michel Marriott; ***C:*** Adam Kimmel; ***M:*** Wendy Blackstone.

The New Kids 🦴🦴 **1985 (R)** An orphaned brother and sister find out the limitations of the good neighbor policy. A sadistic gang terrorizes them after their move to a relatives' home in Florida. They go after expected revenge. **90m/C VHS, DVD.** Shannon Presby, Lori Loughlin, James Spader, Eric Stoltz; ***D:*** Sean S. Cunningham; ***W:*** Brian Taggert, Stephen Gyllenhaal.

A New Kind of Love 🦴🦴 1/2 **1963** Romantic fluff starring real-life couple Newman and Woodward who meet en route to Paris and end up falling in love. Newman plays a reporter and Woodward is a fashion designer in this light comedy set amidst the sights of Paris. **110m/C VHS, DVD.** Paul Newman, Joanne Woodward, Thelma Ritter, Eva Gabor, Maurice Chevalier, George Tobias; ***D:*** Melville Shavelson; ***W:*** Melville Shavelson; ***C:*** Daniel F. Fapp.

The New Land 🦴🦴🦴 *Nybyggarna* **1973 (PG)** Sequel to "The Emigrants" follows Von Sydow and his family as they struggle to make their new home in the new world. Hardships include severe weather which devastates the farm, a Sioux indian uprising, and a disastrous trek to the Southwest to search for gold. Sensitive performances and direction. Based on the novels by Vilhelm Moberg. Dubbed into English. **161m/C VHS.** *SW* Max von Sydow, Liv Ullmann, Allan Edwall, Eddie Axberg, Hans Alfredson, Halvar Bjork, Peter Lindgren, Monica Zetterlund, Pierre Lindstedt, Per Oscarsson; ***D:*** Jan Troell; ***W:*** Jan Troell, Bengt Forslund; ***C:*** Jan Troell; ***M:*** Bengt Ernryd, George Oddner. Natl. Bd. of Review '73: Actress (Ullmann); Natl. Soc. Film Critics '73: Actress (Ullmann).

A New Leaf 🦴🦴 1/2 **1971 (G)** A playboy who has depleted his financial resources tries to win the hand of a clumsy heiress. May was the first woman to write, direct and star in a movie. She was unhappy with the cuts that were made by the studio, but that didn't seem to affect its impact with the public. Even with the cuts, the film is still funny and May's performance is worth watching. **102m/C VHS.** Walter Matthau, Elaine May, Jack Weston, George Rose, William Redfield, James Coco; ***D:*** Elaine May; ***W:*** Elaine May.

A New Life 🦴🦴 1/2 **1988 (PG-13)** An uptight stockbroker is abandoned by his wife. The New York singles scene beckons both of them to a new chance at life. Appealing performances cannot completely mask the old story line, but it's definitely worth a look. **104m/C VHS.** Alan Alda, Ann-Margret, Hal Linden, Veronica Hamel, John Shea, Mary Kay Place, Cynthia Belliveau, Beatrice Alda; ***D:*** Alan Alda; ***W:*** Alan Alda; ***M:*** Joseph Turrin.

New Mafia Boss 🦴 1/2 *Crime Boss* **1972 (PG)** Italian-made plodder has Savalas taking over a huge Mafia family and all hell breaking loose. **90m/C VHS, DVD.** *IT* Telly Savalas, Lee Van Cleef, Antonio (Tony) Sabato, Paola Tedesco; ***D:*** Alberto De Martino.

New Moon 🦴🦴 1/2 **1940** An adaptation of the operetta by Sigmund Romberg and Oscar Hammerstein II. A French heiress traveling on a boat that is captured by pirates falls in love with their leader. Remake of the 1930 film. Includes the 1935 Robert Benchley MGM short "How to Sleep." ♫ Dance Your Cares Away; Stranger in Paris; The Way They Do It in Paris; Lover Come Back; Shoes; Softly as in a Morning Sunrise; One Kiss; Troubles of the World; No More Weeping. **106m/B VHS.** Jeanette MacDonald, Nelson Eddy, Buster Keaton, Joe Yule, Jack Perrin, Mary Boland; ***D:*** Robert Z. Leonard.

New Orleans 🦴🦴 1/2 **1947** The great legends of jazz re-enact its birth in this song-filled tribute to the town where it all began. When the proprietor (de Cordova) of a Bourbon Street gambling joint (and haven for musicians) falls for an opera-singing socialite, he realizes that only through music will he gain responsibility. He begins a campaign to bring jazz to the highbrow American stage. **90m/B VHS, DVD.** Arturo de Cordova, Dorothy Patrick, Louis Armstrong, Billie Holiday, Woody Herman, Richard Hageman; ***D:*** Arthur Lubin; ***W:*** Elliot Paul, Dick Irving Hyland; ***C:*** Lucien N. Andriot.

New Orleans After Dark 🦴🦴 **1958** A pair of New Orleans detectives tour the city, crime-buster style, and bag a dope ring. Average crime tale, shot on location in the Big Easy. **69m/B VHS.** Stacy Harris, Louis Sirgo, Ellen Moore; ***D:*** John Sledge.

New Pastures 🦴🦴 1/2 **1962** Three ex-convicts run into some humorous situations when they go back to their small hometown. A semi-acclaimed Czech comedy, with subtitles. **92m/B VHS.** *CZ* ***D:*** Vladimir Cech.

New Police Story 🦴🦴 1/2 *San Ging Chaat Goo Si* **2004 (R)** Of course it's the action that carries these pics and 19 years after the 1985 original, star Chan still made it work. Inspector Wing hits the bottle after his team is killed in a shootout with evil Joe (Wu) and his gang. But rookie Frank (Tse) dries Wing out so he can return to the force and finally settle the score. Chinese with subtitles. **123m/C DVD.** *HK* Jackie Chan, Nicholas Tse, Daniel Wu, Charlene (Cheuk-Yin) Choi, Charlie Yeung; ***D:*** Benny Chan; ***W:*** Alan Yuen; ***C:*** Anthony Pun; ***M:*** Tommy Wai.

New Rose Hotel 🦴 1/2 **1998 (R)** Corporate raider Fox (Walken) and his assistant X (Dafoe) are hired to get scientific genius Hiroshi (Amano) into working for another company. Slinky Sandii (Argento) is the lure. She succeeds but double-crosses her employers who now expect to be killed for not fulfilling their contract. (Industrial espionage is apparently quite hazardous.) Frustrating as director Ferrara repeats scenes with minor variations, leaving viewers bewildered if nothing else. Based on a story by William Gibson. **92m/C VHS, DVD.** Christopher Walken, Willem Dafoe, Asia Argento, Yoshitaka Amano, Annabella Sciorra, Gretchen Mol, John Lurie, Ryuichi Sakamoto; ***D:*** Abel Ferrara; ***W:*** Abel Ferrara, Chris Zois; ***C:*** Ken Kelsch.

The New Twenty **2008** Rather ruthlessly unsentimental ensemble piece about the lives of five college pals several years after graduation. Mainly there's the romantic/business triangle between investment banker Andrew (Locke), who's engaged to Julie (Bilderback), and Louie (Serpico), the obnoxious venture capitalist who's repressing his attraction to Andrew. Other players include Julie's brother Tony (Wei Lin), lonely Ben (Fickes), and druggie Felix (Sadoski), although their stories remain sketchy. **92m/C DVD.** Ryan Locke, Nicole Bilderback, Andrew Lin, Colin Fickes, Terry Serpico, Tom Sadoski, Bill Sage; ***D:*** Chris Mason Johnson; ***W:*** Chris Mason Johnson, Ishmael Chawla; ***C:*** David Tumblety; ***M:*** Jeff Toyne.

New Waterford Girl 1/2 **1999** Mooney Pottie (Balaban) is a 15-year-old stuck in a small coal-mining community in Nova Scotia in the 1970s. Mooney has won a scholarship to a prestigious arts school and is desperate to attend but her parents refuse to let her. But careful observation has shown Mooney that girls who get themselves into "trouble" leave the community to have their babies in secret and she decides to transform herself into a slut (while keeping her virginity) and get out of town. Sweetly amusing with a compelling debut performance from Balaban. **97m/C VHS, DVD.** *CA* Liane Balaban, Tara Spencer-Nairn, Andrew McCarthy, Nicholas (Nick) Campbell, Mary Walsh, Cathy Moriarty; ***D:*** Allan Moyle; ***W:*** Tricia Fish; ***C:*** Derek Rogers.

A New Wave **2007 (R)** Bank teller Desmond (Keegan) hates his job and allows his movie-obsessed pal Rupert (Krasinski) to talk him into being the inside man in a heist he's lifted from the plots of favorite flicks. Surprise! Things start to go wrong when Desmond begins having second thoughts and the heist is botched. **94m/C DVD.** Andrew Keegan, Lacey Chabert, John Krasinski, William Sadler, Dean Edwards; ***D:*** Jason Carvey; ***W:*** Jason Carvey; ***C:*** Kambui Olujimi; ***M:*** Chris Blackburn. **VIDEO**

New World 1/2 *Le Nouveau Monde* **1995 (R)** Unflattering portrait of American soldiers in postwar France in the 1950s. Their presence is resented by most of the locals, who are still suffering the depredations caused by WWII unlike their American counterparts, who won't even learn a little French to get by. Young Patrick (Chatel), however, is smitten with American culture, thanks to his meeting with soldier Will (Gandolfini) and All-American girl Trudy (Silverstone). President DeGaul would eventually force the American bases to close. English and French dialogue with subtitles. **117m/C VHS, DVD.** *FR* Nicolas Chatel, James Gandolfini, Alicia Silverstone, Sarah Grappin, Guy Marchand; ***D:*** Alain Corneau; ***C:*** William Lubtchansky.

The New World **2005 (PG-13)** Malick's vision offers the story of Pocahontas (Kilcher), stripped of its revisionist history and cartoon-fantasy world and elevated to a mythic retelling of the establishment of an American colony by the London based Virginia Co., which brought Captain John Smith (Ferrell) in contact with the Powhatan Indians. As the story surrounding Fort James unfolds, Malick brings into question the motives and desires of Pocahontas, Smith, and later John Rolfe (Bale), the tobacco farmer who eventually marries Pocahontas and brings her back home to England. Ends up as a beautifully crafted metaphor for the effect Europe had on the new world and vice versa. **160m/C DVD.** *US* Colin Farrell, Christopher Plummer, Christian Bale, August Schellenberg, Wes Studi, David Thewlis, Yorick Van Wageningen, Ben Mendelsohn, Raoul Trujillo, Brian F. O'Byrne, Irene Bedard, John Savage, Jamie Harris, Alex Rice, Michael Greyeyes, Noah Taylor, Jonathan Pryce, Q'orianka Kilcher, Klanai Queypo, Alexandra Malick; ***D:*** Terrence Malick; ***W:*** Terrence Malick; ***C:*** Emmanuel Lubezki; ***M:*** James Horner. Natl. Bd. of Review '05: Breakthrough Perf. (Kilcher).

New World Disorder **1999 (R)** Action thriller combines familiar elements of the formula with high-tech computer jargon. A gang of thieves led by the bestudded Bishop (McCarthy) blasts into a computer chip company and steals the Rosetta encryption program. Young computer-savvy FBI agent Paddock (Fitzgerald) winds up working with old-fashioned local cop Marx (Hauer) to catch the bad guys. The action scenes are fairly ambitious for a video premiere. **94m/C VHS, DVD.** Rutger Hauer, Andrew McCarthy, Tara Fitzgerald; ***D:*** Richard Spence; ***W:*** Ehren Kruger, Jeffrey Smith; ***C:*** Ivan Strasburg; ***M:*** Gast Waltzing. **VIDEO**

New Year's Day **1989 (R)** Jaglom continues his look at modern relationships in this story of a man reclaiming his house from three female tenants. Introspective character study lightened by humor and insight. **90m/C VHS, DVD.** Maggie Jakobson, Gwen Welles, Melanie Winter, Milos Forman, Michael Emil, David Duchovny, Tracy Reiner, Henry Jaglom; ***D:*** Henry Jaglom; ***W:*** Henry Jaglom.

New Year's Evil WOOF! **1978 (R)** Every hour during a New Year's Eve concert, a madman kills an unsuspecting victim. After each killing, the murderer informs a local disc jockey of his deed. Little does the disc jockey know that she will soon be next on his list. No suspense, bad music makes this slash and crash a holiday wrecker. **88m/C VHS.** Roz Kelly, Kip Niven, Chris Wallace, Louisa Moritz, Grant Cramer, Jed Mills; ***D:*** Emmett Alston; ***W:*** Emmett Alston; ***M:*** W. Michael Lewis.

New York Cop 1/2 **1994 (R)** Japanese martial arts expert Toshi (Nakamura) joins the NYPD and is given an undercover assignment to infiltrate a gun-running gang that supplies both drug lords and Japanese mobsters. But internal rivalries force Toshi to bond with gang leader Hawk (McQueen) and the duo to do battle together. **88m/C VHS, DVD.** Toru Nakamura, Chad McQueen, Mira Sorvino; ***D:*** Toru Murakawa.

New York Doll **2005 (PG-13)** Arthur "Killer" Kane was the bassist for the 1970s glam-rock band the New York Dolls, going from the excesses of rock 'n' roll (the Dolls broke up in 1975) to obscurity and battling a variety of demons (chemical and otherwise) until a belated recovery and his adoption of the Mormon faith. In 2004, die-hard fan Morrissey persuaded Kane to reunite with his two remaining bandmates for a London music festival. Whiteley follows Kane from his settled life in LA to the Dolls' bittersweet reunion. Kane died of leukemia shortly after the concert. **73m/C DVD.** *US* ***D:*** Greg Whiteley; ***C:*** Rod Santiano, Seth Gordon.

New York, I Love You 1/2 **2009 (R)** An American follow-up to 2006's "Paris, Je T'Aime" with 10 filmmakers directing vignettes about love in New York's five boroughs. The stories don't intersect, and each director was only given two days to shoot and one week to edit. Some have ironic twist endings, others are small slices of life with a classic New York vibe. As expected, the results are uneven, but with a maximum eight-minute runtime per story, there's always something new coming shortly. **103m/C DVD.** *US* Natalie Portman, Shia LaBeouf, Cloris Leachman, Blake Lively, Hayden Christensen, Christina Ricci, Anton Yelchin, Orlando Bloom, Rachel Bilson, Robin Wright Penn, Ethan Hawke, Drea De Matteo, James Caan, Julie Christie, Bradley Cooper, John Hurt, Maggie Q, Olivia Thirlby, Andy Garcia, Chris Cooper, Eli Wallach; ***D:*** Natalie Portman, Fatih Akin, Yvan Attal, Shunji Iwai, Joshua Marston, Allen Hughes, Shekhar Kapur, Mira Nair, Brett Ratner, Wen Jiang; ***W:*** Natalie Portman, Fatih Akin, Yvan Attal, Shunji Iwai, Joshua Marston, Anthony Minghella, Alexandra Cassavetes, Jeff Nathanson; ***C:*** Benoit Debie, Pawel Edelman, Declan Quinn, Mauricio Rubinstein.

New York Minute 1/2 **2004 (PG)** Sporting different hair color, way too much make-up, and a sheen only multi-millions from straight-to-video hits can bring, the Olsen twins take New York City in this dumb semi-screwball, wanna-be action comedy. Blonde do-gooder Jane (Ashley) and dark-haired rebel Roxy (Mary-Kate) have recently lost their mom and live with their dad (Pinsky) in the Long Island suburbs. The couldn't-be-more-different twins share a ride into The City in search of their respective dreams (Jane's is an Oxford fellowship; Roxy's a career in rock) when things go awry and they end up running amok to marginal comic effect, while being tailed by truant officer Levy. The twins' TV dad Saget shows up in an amusing cameo. **91m/C VHS, DVD.** *US* Ashley (Fuller) Olsen, Mary-Kate Olsen, Eugene Levy, Andy Richter, Riley Smith, Jared Padalecki, Darrell Hammond, Andrea Martin, Alannah Ong; ***Cameos:*** Bob Saget; ***D:*** Dennie Gordon; ***W:*** Emily Fox, Adam Cooper, Bill Collage; ***C:*** Greg Gardiner; ***M:*** George S. Clinton.

New York, New York **1977 (PG)** Tragic romance evolves between a saxophonist and an aspiring singer/actress in this salute to the big-band era. A love of music isn't enough to hold them together through career rivalries and life on the road. Fine performances by De Niro and Minnelli and the supporting cast. Re-released in 1981 with the "Happy Endings" number, which was cut from the original. Look for "Big Man" Clarence Clemons on sax. ♫New York, New York; There Goes the Ball Game; Happy Endings; But the World Goes 'Round; Night in Tunisia; Opus One; Avalon; You Brought a New Kind of Love to Me; I'm Getting Sentimental Over You. **163m/C VHS, DVD.** Robert De Niro, Liza Minnelli, Lionel Stander, Barry Primus, Mary Kay Place, Dick Miller, Diahnne Abbott; ***D:*** Martin Scorsese; ***W:*** Mardik Martin; ***M:*** Ralph Burns.

New York Nights **1984 (R)** The lives of nine New Yorkers intertwine in a treacherous game of passion and seduction. Liberal borrowing from plot of "La Ronde." **104m/C VHS.** Corinne Alphen, George Auyer, Bobbi Burns, Peter Matthey, Cynthia Lee, Willem Dafoe; ***D:*** Simon Nuchtern.

New York Ripper WOOF! *Lo Squartatore de New York; The Ripper* **1982** A New York cop tracks down a rampaging murderer in this dull, mindless slasher flick. **88m/C VHS, DVD.** *IT* Jack Hedley, Antonella Interlenghi, Howard (Red) Ross, Andrea Occhipinti, Alessandra Delli Colli, Paolo Malco; ***D:*** Lucio Fulci; ***W:*** Lucio Fulci, Gianfranco Clerici, Vincenzo Mannino, Dardano Sacchetti; ***C:*** Luigi Kuveiller; ***M:*** Francesco De Masi.

New York Stories **1989 (PG)** Entertaining anthology of three separate short films by three esteemed directors, all set in New York. In "Life Lessons" by Scorsese, an impulsive artist tries to prevent his live-in girlfriend from leaving him. "Life Without Zoe" by Coppola involves a youngster's fantasy about a wealthy 12-year-old who lives mostly without her parents. Allen's "Oedipus Wrecks," generally considered the best short, is about a 50-year-old man who is tormented by the specter of his mother. **124m/C VHS, DVD.** Nick Nolte, Rosanna Arquette, Woody Allen, Mia Farrow, Mae Questel, Julie Kavner, Talia Shire, Giancarlo Giannini, Don Novello, Patrick O'Neal, Peter Gabriel, Paul Herman, Deborah Harry, Steve Buscemi, Heather McComb, Chris Elliott, Carole Bouquet, Edward I. Koch; ***D:*** Woody Allen, Martin Scorsese, Francis Ford Coppola; ***W:*** Woody Allen, Francis Ford Coppola, Richard Price, Sofia Coppola; ***C:*** Sven Nykvist, Nestor Almendros; ***M:*** Carmine Coppola.

The New Yorker **1998** Frenchman Alfred (Demy) fell for American Alice (Phillips) while she was vacationing in Paris. So he impulsively flies to New York after her, only to be told to go away. Thinking he can win Grace back, Alfred decides to stick around and gets a job with a thug (Elliott) to tide him over, which turns out to be a problem. English and French with subtitles. **75m/C DVD.** *FR* Mathieu Demy, Grace Phillips, Shawn Elliott, Gretchen Cleevely; ***D:*** Benoit Graffin; ***W:*** Benoit Graffin, David Block; ***C:*** Antoine Herberte.

New York's Finest **1987 (R)** Three prostitutes are determined to leave their calling and marry very eligible millionaires. But becoming society ladies is more difficult than they thought. Would-be sophisticated comedy misfires. **80m/C VHS.** Ruth (Coreen) Collins, Jennifer Delora, Scott Thompson Baker, Heidi Paine, Jane (Veronica Hart) Hamilton, Alan Naggar, John Altamura, Alan Fisler, Josey Duval; ***D:*** Chuck Vincent.

Newcastle **2008** Seventeen-year-old Jesse and his brothers live in the small town of Newcastle, Australia where Jesse is a rising surf star. Jesse fights with resentful older brother Victor and plans a weekend off with his mates that is crashed by his trouble-bringing sibling. Meanwhile, Jesse's twin brother Fergus is battling his attraction to Jesse's best pal, Andy. **107m/C DVD.** *AU* Anthony Hayes, Barry Otto, Gigi Edgley, Lachlan Buchanan, Xavier Samuel, Reshad Strik, Kirk Jenkins, Shane Jacobson; ***D:*** Dan Castle; ***W:*** Dan Castle; ***C:*** Richard Michalak; ***M:*** Michael Yezerski.

The Newlydeads 1/2 **1987** An uptight, conservative, honeymoon resort owner murders one of his guests and finds out that "she" is really a he. Fifteen years later, on his wedding night, all of his guests are violently murdered by the transvestite's vengeful ghost. Oddball twist to the usual slasher nonsense. **84m/C VHS, DVD.** Scott Kaske, Jim Williams, Jean Levine, Jay Richardson; ***D:*** Joseph Merhi; ***W:*** Joseph Merhi, Sean Dash; ***C:*** Richard Pepin; ***M:*** John Gonzalez.

Newman's Law **1974 (PG)** A city detective is implicated in a corruption investigation. While on suspension, he continues with his own investigation of a large drug ring and finds corruption is closer than he thought. Director Heffron's first feature film. **98m/C VHS.** George Peppard, Roger Robinson, Eugene Roche, Gordon Pinsent, Louis Zorich, Abe Vigoda; ***D:*** Richard T. Heffron.

News at Eleven **1986** A fading news anchorman is pressured by his ambitious young boss to expose a touchy local sex scandal, forcing him to consider the public's right to know versus the rights of the individual. About average for TV drama. **95m/C VHS, DVD.** Martin Sheen, Peter Riegert, Barbara Babcock, Sheree J. Wilson, Sydney Penny, David S. Sheiner, Christopher Allport; ***D:*** Mike Robe. **TV**

News from Home **1976** Scenes of life in New York are juxtaposed with voiceover from the letters of a mother to her young daughter. Plotless narrative deals with the small details of life. **85m/C VHS.** ***D:*** Chantal Akerman; ***W:*** Chantal Akerman; ***Nar:*** Chantal Akerman.

Newsbreak **2000 (R)** Reckless and arrogant reporter John McNamara (Rooker) has made a lot of enemies. When he decides to investigate the disappearance of a fellow journalist, John uncovers citywide corruption that involves the president of a construction company (Reinhold) and his own father (Culp), a judge with a sterling reputation. **95m/C VHS, DVD.** Michael Rooker, Judge Reinhold, Robert Culp, Kelly Miller, Kim Darby, Noelle Parker; ***D:*** Serge Rodnunsky; ***W:*** Serge Rodnunsky, Paul Tarantino; ***C:*** Howard Wexler; ***M:*** Evan Evans. **VIDEO**

Newsfront **1978** A story about two brothers, both newsreel filmmakers, and their differing approaches to life and their craft in the 1940s and '50s. Tribute to the days of newsreel film combines real stories and fictionalized accounts with color and black and white photography. Noyce's feature film debut. **110m/C VHS, DVD.** *AU* Bill Hunter, Gerard Kennedy, Angela Punch McGregor, Wendy Hughes, Chris Haywood, John Ewart, Bryan Brown; ***D:*** Phillip Noyce. Australian Film Inst. '78: Actor (Hunter), Film.

Newsies 1/2 **1992 (PG)** An unfortunate attempt at an old-fashioned musical with a lot of cute kids and cardboard characters and settings. The plot, such as it is, concerns the 1899 New York newsboys strike against penny-pinching publisher Joseph Pulitzer. Bale plays the newsboy's leader and at least shows some charisma in a strictly cartoon setting. The songs are mediocre but the dancing is lively. However, none of it moves the story along. Add a bone for viewers under 12. Choreographer Ortega's feature-film directorial debut. **121m/C VHS, DVD.** Christian Bale, Bill Pullman, Robert Duvall, Ann-Margret, Michael Lerner, Kevin Tighe, Charles Cioffi, Luke Edwards, Max Casella, David Moscow; ***D:*** Kenny Ortega; ***W:*** Bob Tzudiker; ***C:*** Noni White; ***M:*** Alan Menken, Jack Feldman. Golden Raspberries '92: Worst Song ("High Times, Hard Times").

The Newton Boys 1/2 **1997 (PG-13)** Fact-based drama chronicling the careers and love lives of the bank robbing Newton brothers, who robbed their way from Texas to Toronto during the '20s and '30s. They lived and worked by a romantic credo: no killing, stealing from women or children, and no ratting each other out. McConaughey and Ulrich lead the group as Willis and Joe, respectively, and both prove likeable gangsters. Hawke and D'Onfrio do their best in less developed roles. Highlight is the great train robbery, which garnered the outlaws $3 million and eventually landed the boys in court. Though well-acted with interesting material, Linklater's departure lacks precise angle, which keeps the story from really humming. Stealing the show is the real-life footage of a 1980 "Tonight Show" where Johnny Carson interviews the personable Joe. **122m/C VHS, DVD.** Matthew McConaughey, Skeet Ulrich, Ethan Hawke, Vincent D'Onofrio, Julianna Margulies, Dwight Yoakam, Gail Cronauer, Chloe Webb, Charles Gunning, Becket Gremmels, Richard Jones; ***D:*** Richard Linklater; ***W:*** Claude Stanush, Clark Lee Walker; ***C:*** Peter James; ***M:*** Edward D. Barnes.

Next 𝒮𝒮 **2007 (PG-13)** Struggling Vegas magician Cris (Cage) has the ability to see two minutes into the future. Somehow, FBI agent Ferris (Moore) becomes aware of his ability and wants him to help them find a nuclear weapon that's been smuggled into L.A. Cris would rather focus on meeting his dream girl, Liz (Biel), but the two plot points soon cross paths. Cage stays low-key, Biel is beautiful and bewildered, and director Tamahori handles the action well, but it's ultimately a forgettable gimmick. Adapted from a story by Philip K. Dick. **96m/C DVD, Blu-ray Disc, HD DVD.** *US* Nicolas Cage, Jessica Biel, Julianne Moore, Thomas Kretschmann, Tory Kittles, Peter Falk, Jose Zuniga, Jim Beaver, Michael Trucco, Jason Butler Harner; ***D:*** Lee Tamahori; ***W:*** Gary Goldman, Jonathan Hensleigh, Paul Bernbaum; ***C:*** David Tattersall; ***M:*** Mark Isham.

The Next Best Thing 𝒮 ½ **2000 (PG-13)** L.A. yoga instructor Abbie (Madonna) manages to get preggers thanks to a drunken one-nighter with gay best friend, Robert (Everett). She has the kid, they decide to live together and share parental responsibilities (but nothing more), and for six years things just go along swimmingly. Then Abbie meets the perfect guy—investment banker Ben (Bratt). But Ben is planning to relocate to New York and suddenly sole custody is all that matters to Abbie—even it means a court case. Sappy, predictable story falls prey to Madonna's limited acting ability though both Everett and Bratt supply charm galore. **108m/C VHS, DVD.** Madonna, Rupert Everett, Benjamin Bratt, Michael Vartan, Josef Sommer, Lynn Redgrave, Malcolm Stumpf, Neil Patrick Harris, Illeana Douglas, Mark Valley, Stacy Edwards; ***D:*** John Schlesinger; ***W:*** Tom Ropelewski; ***C:*** Elliot Davis; ***M:*** Gabriel Yared. Golden Raspberries '00: Worst Actress (Madonna).

The Next Big Thing 𝒮 ½ **2002 (R)** Gus Bishop (Eigeman) is a struggling New York artist who meets con man Deech Scumble (Harris) when Deech steals his wallet and, later, a painting. Deech sells the painting, signed "GB," to art gallery owner Arthur (Granger) by inventing a tragic background for the artist he's renamed Geoff Buonardi. Deech manages to convince Gus to continue the scam since his new artistic persona is making them a lot of money. But soon more and more people become aware of the deception. **85m/C VHS, DVD.** *US* Christopher Eigeman, Jamie Harris, Connie Britton, Janet Zarish, Farley Granger, Mike Starr, Marin Hinkle; ***D:*** P.J. Posner; ***W:*** P.J. Posner, Joel Posner; ***C:*** Oliver Bokelberg; ***M:*** Ferdinand Jay Smith.

Next Day Air 𝒮 ½ **2009 (R)** Stoned deliveryman Leo (Faison) drops off a package at the wrong apartment where inept criminals Brody (Epps) and Guch (Harris) discover it contains 10 kilos of cocaine. They immediately decide to sell their unexpected bounty but the merchandise was intended for their hot-headed neighbor (Reyes) and was sent by his drug kingpin boss (Rivera) and neither are happy it's gone astray. Offers a few streetwise yuks, and has cult hit potential. **90m/C DVD.** *US* Mike Epps, Wood Harris, Elilio Rivera, Donald Adeosun Faison, Omari Hardwick, Darius McCrary, Mos Def, Debbie Allen, Cisco Reyes, Yasmin Deliz; ***D:*** Beeny Boom; ***W:*** Blair Cobbs; ***C:*** David Armstrong; ***M:*** The Elements.

Next Door 𝒮𝒮 ½ **1994 (R)** College professors Matt (Woods) and Karen (Capshaw) have the perfect suburban home—complete with the perfect suburban garden. Then their boorish blue-collar neighbor Lenny (Quaid) takes to enthusiastic lawn watering and ruins their flowers. One thing leads to a full-scale feud. **95m/C VHS.** James Woods, Randy Quaid, Kate Capshaw, Lucinda Jenney; ***D:*** Tony Bill; ***W:*** Barney Cohen; ***C:*** Thomas Del Ruth. **CABLE**

Next Friday 𝒮𝒮 **2000 (R)** Amiable, meandering sequel to 1995's surprise hit "Friday" finds Craig (Ice Cube) fleeing to the suburbs to escape Debo (Lister), who's out of prison and looking for payback. Uncle Elroy (Curry) has hit the lotto and moved to the 'burbs, giving Craig, and a whole new bunch of central casting characters a new place to hang out and cause some mischief. The original's biggest success came on home video and cable, and this one's likely to duplicate that pattern. **93m/C VHS, DVD.** Ice Cube, Tommy (Tiny) Lister, John Witherspoon, Justin Pierce, Jacob Vargas, Lobo Sebastian, Rolando Molina, Tamala Jones, Mike Epps, Don "DC" Curry, Lisa Rodriguez, Kym E. Whitley, Amy Hill, Robin Allen, Kirk "Sticky Fingaz" Jones; ***D:*** Steve Carr; ***W:*** Ice Cube; ***C:*** Christopher Baffa; ***M:*** Terence Blanchard.

The Next Karate Kid 𝒮𝒮 ½ **1994 (PG)** Fourth installment in the "Kid" series finds martial arts expert Miyagi (Morita) training Julie Pierce (Swank), the orphaned tomboy daughter of an old war buddy who saved his life 50 years earlier. He even teaches her the waltz, just in time for the prom, but she's still tough enough to scrap with a guy. A must-see for "Karate Kid" fans, if there are any left. **107m/C VHS, DVD.** Noriyuki "Pat" Morita, Hilary Swank; ***D:*** Christopher Cain; ***W:*** Mark Lee; ***M:*** Bill Conti.

Next of Kin 𝒮 **1982** A daughter moves into her dead mother's retirement home and discovers an unspeakable evil that lurks there. Typical horror stuff has some very creepy moments; filmed in New Zealand. **90m/C VHS.** *AU* Jackie Kerin, John Jarratt, Gerida Nicholson, Alex Scott; ***D:*** Tony Williams.

Next of Kin 𝒮𝒮 **1984** A young man experiencing familial difficulties undergoes experimental video therapy where he views a videotape of an Armenian family who gave their son up for adoption. When he discovers the actual family he insinuates himself into their life, determined to be their long-lost son. **72m/C VHS, DVD.** *CA* Patrick Tierney; ***D:*** Atom Egoyan; ***W:*** Atom Egoyan.

Next of Kin 𝒮𝒮 **1989 (R)** A Chicago cop returns to his Kentucky home to avenge his brother's brutal murder. Swayze's return to action films after his success in "Dirty Dancing" is unimpressive. **108m/C VHS, DVD.** Patrick Swayze, Adam Baldwin, Bill Paxton, Helen Hunt, Andreas Katsulas, Ben Stiller, Michael J. Pollard, Liam Neeson; ***D:*** John Irvin; ***C:*** Steven Poster; ***M:*** Jack Nitzsche.

Next One 𝒮 ½ **1984** Mysterious visitor from another time winds up on an isolated Greek island as the result of a magnetic storm. The local inhabitants are amazed when the visitor displays some Christ-like characteristics. **105m/C VHS, DVD.** Keir Dullea, Adrienne Barbeau, Jeremy Licht, Peter Hobbs; ***D:*** Nico Mastorakis.

The Next Step 𝒮𝒮 ½ **1995** Nick Mendez (Negron) is a 35-year-old Broadway dancer who's feeling the wear and tear of his profession. A practiced seducer, Nick does have a devoted girlfriend in ex-dancer turned physical therapist, Amy (Moreu). Amy gets a job offer in Connecticut just as Nick's confidence is shaken when he's rejected for a dance role he originated in favor of a younger performer. Amy wants Nick to retire and move away with her but life away from Broadway leaves Nick wondering what he'd do. Negron is a former Broadway dancer and offers a compelling performance in a film that's ripe with showbiz cliches. **97m/C VHS, DVD.** Rick Negron, Kristin Moreu, Denise Faye, Taylor Nichols; ***D:*** Christian Faber; ***W:*** Aaron Reed; ***C:*** Zack Winestine; ***M:*** Mio Morales, Brian Otto, Roni Skies.

Next Stop, Greenwich Village 𝒮𝒮𝒮 **1976 (R)** An affectionate, autobiographical look by Mazursky at a Brooklyn boy with acting aspirations, who moves to Greenwich Village in 1953. Good performances, especially by Winters as the overbearing mother. **109m/C VHS, DVD.** Lenny Baker, Christopher Walken, Ellen Greene, Shelley Winters, Lou Jacobi, Mike Kellin; ***D:*** Paul Mazursky; ***W:*** Paul Mazursky; ***M:*** Bill Conti.

Next Stop, Wonderland 𝒮𝒮 ½ **1998 (R)** Charming romance, set in Boston, about a couple of odd ducks who are totally right for each other. Waifish Eric (Davis) is a nurse whose boyfriend Sean (Hoffman) has just left her. So her meddling mom Piper (Taylor) secretly places a personal ad to get her daughter some dates. They're a bunch of losers but plumber/marine-biology student Alan (Gelfant), whom Erin keeps seeing on the subway is Mr. Right. If only the duo could get together. Intelligent characters and a terrific bossa nova soundtrack. Title refers to the name of an actual subway stop. **96m/C VHS, DVD.** Hope Davis, Alan Gelfant, Holland Taylor, Robert Klein, Cara Buono, Jose Zuniga, Phil Hoffman, Lyn Vaus, Larry (Lawrence) Gilliard Jr., Victor Argo, Roger Rees, Robert Stanton, Pamela Hart; ***D:*** Brad Anderson; ***W:*** Brad Anderson, Lyn Vaus; ***C:*** Uta Briesewitz; ***M:*** Claudio Ragazzi.

Next Summer 𝒮𝒮𝒮 *L'Ete Prochain* **1984** A large, character-studded French family pursues power, love and beauty. Excellent performances. In French with English subtitles. **120m/C VHS.** *FR* Jean-Louis Trintignant, Claudia Cardinale, Fanny Ardant, Philippe Noiret, Marie Trintignant; ***D:*** Nadine Trintignant.

Next Time 𝒮𝒮 ½ **1999** Offbeat romance tells the story of the relationship between Matt (Campbell), a young white guy, and Evelyn (Allen), a 39-year-old black woman, who meet at a laundrette. **97m/C DVD.** Jonelle Allen, Christian Campbell, Ishtar Robert Harper, Iona Morris; ***D:*** L. Alan Fraser; ***W:*** L. Alan Fraser; ***C:*** William Hooke; ***M:*** James S. Mulhollan Jr.

Next Time I Marry 𝒮 ½ **1938** Lucy fraternizes with ditch digger Ellison because she needs to hitch a Yankee in order to inherit $20 mill. Seems she really loves a foreigner, though. Not much to bobaloo about. Director Kanin's second effort. **65m/B VHS.** Lucille Ball, James Ellison, Lee Bowman, Granville Bates, Mantan Moreland, Florence Lake; ***D:*** Garson Kanin.

Next Time We Love 𝒮𝒮 ½ **1936** Ambitious reporter Chris Tyler (Stewart) and actress Cicely (Sullavan) impulsively marry. With the help of their best friend Tommy (Milland), Cicely gets a shot on Broadway while Chris is assigned to his paper's Rome bureau. Cecily learns she's pregnant and Chris comes back to New York, losing his job. Tommy pulls some strings but Chris' new position is overseas again and Cecily basically raises their son alone while becoming a Broadway star. Eventually, Tommy admits he loves her and Cecily goes to Europe to settle things with Chris only to learn that he's dying. Romantic melodrama also suffers because Cecily isn't a particularly likeable character. An uncredited Preston Sturges worked on the first draft of the script. **87m/B DVD.** James Stewart, Margaret Sullavan, Ray Milland, Grant Mitchell, Robert McWade, Anna Demetrio; ***D:*** Edward H. Griffith; ***W:*** Melville Baker; ***C:*** Joseph Valentine; ***M:*** Franz Waxman.

The Next Victim 𝒮 *Lo Strano Vizio Della Signora Wardh* **1971 (PG)** The unfaithful wife of an Austrian diplomat attempts to find out who has been slicing up beautiful jet-setters. Tepid mystery. **87m/C VHS.** George Hilton, Edwige Fenech, Christina Airoldi, Ivan Rassimov; ***D:*** Sergio Martino.

Next Victim 𝒮 **1974** A beautiful woman confined to a wheelchair is stalked by a lunatic killer. You've seen it before, and done better. **80m/C VHS.** *GB* Carroll Baker, T.P. McKenna, Ronald Lacey, Maurice Kaufmann; ***D:*** James Ormerod.

The Next Voice You Hear 𝒮𝒮 ½ **1950** Lives are changed forever when a group of people hear the voice of God on the radio. Interesting premise presented seriously. **84m/B VHS.** James Whitmore, Nancy Davis, Gary Gray, Lillian Bronson, Art Smith, Tom D'Andrea, Jeff Corey, George Chandler; ***D:*** William A. Wellman.

Next Year If All Goes Well 𝒮𝒮 ½ **1983** Two young lovers struggle to overcome insecurities while establishing a relationship. Dubbed. **95m/C VHS.** *FR* Isabelle Adjani, Thierry Lhermitte, Mariann (Marie-Anne) Chazel; ***D:*** Jean-Loup Hubert.

Next Year in Jerusalem 𝒮𝒮 **1998** Charlie is openly gay—but what he's hiding is his Orthodox Jewish background. Pressured by his mother, Charlie shows up at the family Passover seder, where he meets Manny. Devout Manny is supposed to marry the Rabbi's daughter, only he's got a secret too. The duo soon begin a relationship they keep from their families but it becomes clear that Charlie and Manny need to be honest about who they truly are. **103m/C VHS.** Peter J. Byrnes, Reed McGowan, Georgina Spelvin, Louis Edmonds; ***D:*** David Nahmod; ***W:*** David Nahmod; ***C:*** Kelvin Walker; ***M:*** Richard Barone.

Nezulla the Rat Monster 𝒮 ½ **2002** A small town is being overrun by plague, which a defunct local chemical company fesses up to causing when infected rats escaped during experiments for the American military. But a giant rubber rat monster may have the cure locked within its DNA. So a joint team of Japanese and American Special Forces (all of whom look Japanese) storm the company's facility and get locked inside, and a self-destruct countdown begins. While backstabbing each other the troops find out rat monsters only laugh it off when you shoot them. **90m/C DVD.** *JP* Daisuke Ryu, Mika Katsumura, Yoshiyuki Kubota, Ayumi Tokitou; ***D:*** Kanta Tagawa; ***W:*** Kanta Tagawa; ***C:*** Gen Kobayashi; ***M:*** Takashi Nakagawa.

Niagara 𝒮𝒮 ½ **1952** During their honeymoon in Niagara Falls, a scheming wife (Monroe) plans to kill her crazed war-vet husband (Cotten). Little does she know that he is plotting to double-cross her. Steamy, quasi-Hitchcockian mystery ably directed, with interesting performances. Monroes sings "Kiss." **89m/B VHS, DVD.** Joseph Cotten, Jean Peters, Marilyn Monroe, Max (Casey Adams) Showalter, Don Wilson, Denis O'Dea, Lurene Tuttle, Harry Carey Jr., Russell Collins, Minerva Urecal; ***D:*** Henry Hathaway; ***W:*** Charles Brackett, Walter Reisch; ***C:*** Joe MacDonald; ***M:*** Sol Kaplan.

Niagara Motel 𝒮𝒮 **2006** A run-down motel in Niagara Falls houses the usual malcontents and oddballs, beginning with its drunken Scottish manager, Phillie (Ferguson). Lily (Crewson) is thinking about turning tricks since her husband can't find a job; waitress and wannabe actress Caroline (Dhavernas) is being pushed into filming porn by her sleazy agent Michael (Pollak); and drug addict Denise (Friel) wants to reclaim her daughter from foster care. **88m/C DVD.** *CA* Craig Ferguson, Anna Friel, Wendy Crewson, Caroline Dhavernas, Kevin Pollak, Peter Keleghan, Kris Holden-Ried, Tom Barnett, Gary Yates, Dani Romain; ***W:*** George F. Walker; ***C:*** Ian Wilson; ***M:*** Guy Fletcher.

Niagara, Niagara 𝒮𝒮 **1997 (R)** Marcy (Tunney) is a victim of Tourette's Syndrome, which causes the sufferer to twitch and unleash strings of profanity that would make a longshoreman blush. She meets shy, introverted Seth (Thomas) while they're both shoplifting, and it's love at first sight. They hit the road, supposedly for a doll that Marcy believes can be found in Toronto, but in reality because they are already outcasts at home. When Seth is injured in a botched pharmacy robbery, they're taken in by fellow oddball Walter, a tow truck driver who dotes on a pet chicken named after his dead wife. All of these lost characters are on a road to nowhere, and are pulled apart by Marcy's bourbon-fueled tics and tantrums. Compelling performance by Tunney carries the rest of this dull, flat movie on its back. **96m/C VHS, DVD.** Robin Tunney, Henry Thomas, Michael Parks, Stephen Lang, John MacKay; ***D:*** Bob Gosse; ***W:*** Matthew Weiss; ***C:*** Michael Spiller; ***M:*** Michael Timmins, Jeff Bird.

Nice Girl? 𝒮𝒮 ½ **1941** Jane (Durbin) develops a crush on visiting professor Richard Calvert (Tone), much to his embarassment. But her steady beau Don (Stack) sticks around to provide support while Calvert seeks a way to let Jane down easy. The video includes a 3-minute alternate ending. **96m/B VHS.** Deanna Durbin, Franchot Tone, Robert Stack, Robert Benchley, Walter Brennan, Ann Gillis, Helen Broderick, Anne Gwynne; ***D:*** William A. Seiter; ***W:*** Richard Connell, Gladys Lehman; ***C:*** Joseph Valentine.

Nice Girl Like Me 𝒮𝒮 **1969 (PG)** An orphaned young girl roams Europe, getting pregnant twice by two different men. She eventually finds love in the form of a kind caretaker. Harmless fluff. Based on Anne Piper's novel "Marry At Leisure." **91m/C VHS.** *GB* Harry Andrews, Barbara Ferris, Gladys Cooper, Bill Hinnant, James Villiers; ***D:*** Desmond Davis.

Nice Girls Don't Explode ✌✌ **1987 (PG)** A girl telekinetically starts fires when sexually aroused. This puts a bit of a damper on her relationship with O'Leary, much to her mother's delight. Matchless entertainment. **92m/C VHS.** Barbara Harris, Wallace Shawn, Michelle Meyrink, William O'Leary; ***D:*** Chuck Martinez; ***M:*** Brian Banks.

Nice Guys Sleep Alone ✌✌✌ **1999 (R)** Overachieving independent romantic comedy finds nice guy Carter (O'Bryan) hearing those three dreaded words "let's be friends" at the end of each date. He has resolved to take a new approach when he meets Maggie (Temchen), a vet recently arrived in Louisville from New York. The complications that keep the plot moving are familiar, and Carter's rival Robert (Murray) is such a swine that it's impossible any intelligent woman would pay attention to him, no matter how rich he is. But the characters are engaging, especially Carter's stepsister Erin (Marcil), and the film has its heart in the right place. **92m/C DVD.** Sean O'Bryan, Sybil Temchen, Vanessa Marcil, Blake Steury, Christopher Murray, Morgan Fairchild, William Sanderson; ***D:*** Stu Pollard; ***W:*** Stu Pollard; ***C:*** Nathan Hope.

Nice Neighbor ✌✌✌ **1979** An acclaimed film about an outwardly self-sacrificing neighbor who cold-bloodedly manipulates his fellow rooming house tenants for his own ends. In Hungarian with English subtitles. **90m/C VHS.** *HU* Laszlo Szabo, Margit Dayka, Agi Margittay; ***D:*** Zsolt Kedzi-Kovacs.

Nicholas and Alexandra ✌✌ ½ **1971 (PG)** Epic chronicling the final years of Tsar Nicholas II, Empress Alexandra, and their children. Their lavish royal lifestyle gives way to imprisonment and eventual execution under the new Lenin government. Beautiful, but overlong costume epic that loses steam in the second half. Based on the biography by Robert Massie. **183m/C VHS, DVD.** Michael Jayston, Janet Suzman, Tom Baker, Laurence Olivier, Michael Redgrave, Harry Andrews, Jack Hawkins, Alexander Knox, Curt Jurgens; ***D:*** Franklin J. Schaffner; ***W:*** James Goldman; ***C:*** Frederick A. (Freddie) Young; ***M:*** Richard Rodney Bennett. Oscars '71: Art Dir./Set Dec., Costume Des.

Nicholas Nickleby ✌✌✌ *The Life and Adventures of Nicholas Nickleby* **1946** An ensemble cast works hard to bring to life Charles Dickens' novel about an impoverished family dependent on their wealthy but villainous uncle. Young Nicholas is an apprentice at a school for boys, and he and a student run away to a series of exciting adventures. An enjoyable film, though it is hard to tell the entire story in such a small amount of time. **108m/B VHS.** *GB* Cedric Hardwicke, Stanley Holloway, Derek Bond, Alfred Drayton, Sybil Thorndike, Sally Ann Howes, Bernard Miles, Mary Merrall, Cathleen Nesbitt; ***D:*** Alberto Cavalcanti; ***C:*** Georges Perinal.

Nicholas Nickleby ✌✌✌ **2002 (PG)** Director McGrath reliably takes on another period piece with this sprawling Dickens classic, which he nicely condenses for mass consumption. Nicholas (Hunnam) is a 19 year-old in England forced to grow up quickly when his father dies and he takes over as head of the family. Well acted, with Hunnam able but not outstanding in an overall lighthearted and lively production. **130m/C VHS, DVD.** *US* Charlie Hunnam, Christopher Plummer, Jamie Bell, Jim Broadbent, Juliet Stevenson, Tom Courtenay, Alan Cumming, Edward Fox, Romola Garai, Anne Hathaway, Timothy Spall, Nathan Lane, Barry Humphries, Gerard Horan, Stella Gonet; ***D:*** Douglas McGrath; ***W:*** Douglas McGrath; ***C:*** Dick Pope; ***M:*** Rachel Portman.

Nick and Jane ✌✌ **1996 (R)** See John sleep with another woman. See Jane see John sleep with another woman. See Jane run out of the building to catch a cab. See Nick pick her up in the cab. This is just a glimpse of all the hilarious fun you'll see when New Yorker Jane (Wheeler-Nicholson) gets a fake boyfriend, Nick (McCaffrey), to upset two-timing John (Dossett). Predictable romantic comedy does have something to offer in sparks between the leads, but they're buried amid the bizarre subplots and off-beat supports. The opening scene where Jane catches her boyfriend cheating is the lone unique and funny segment. Cost-saving camera work, devoid of close-ups and reaction shots, shows. **94m/C VHS.** Dana Wheeler-Nicholson, James McCaffrey, Lisa Gay Hamilton, John Dossett, David Johansen, Gedde Watanabe, Saundra Santiago, George Coe, Clinton Leupp; ***D:*** Rich Mauro; ***W:*** Rich Mauro, Peter Quigley, Neil Alumkal; ***C:*** Christopher Norr; ***M:*** Mark Suozzo.

Nick & Norah's Infinite Playlist ✌✌✌ **2008 (PG-13)** Recently dumped Jersey kid Nick (Cera) tries to woo back too-hot-for-him mean girl Tris (Dziena) with one mix CD after another, but she's oblivious to his geeky-cool charm. Nora (Dennings) and her ridiculously wasted sidekick Caroline (Graynor) bump into Nick when they're all in Manhattan for Nick's alt-rock band's gig. After Nora asks Nick to help her tick off ex-boyfriend Tal (Baruchel), she realizes Nick's the one who made all the mix CDs she got from Tris, and they embark on a search for an indie band playing a show so secret that they have to criss-cross the city in Nick's yellow Yugo, picking up clues about the location. What they really find is that all along they were looking for each other. Following the classic formula, director Sollett tosses in enough updated twists to keep it fresh. About as cool as it gets for a teen rom-com. **90m/C DVD, Blu-ray Disc.** *US* Michael Cera, Kat Dennings, Alexis Dziena, Aaron Yoo, Rafi Gavron, Ari Graynor, Jay Baruchel, Zachary Booth; ***D:*** Peter Sollett; ***W:*** Lorene Scafaria; ***C:*** Tom Richmond; ***M:*** Mark Mothersbaugh.

Nick Knight ✌✌ **1989** An L.A. cop on the night beat is really a good-guy vampire, who quaffs cattle blood as he tracks down another killer who's draining humans of their plasma. A gimmicky pilot for a would-be TV series that eventually morphed into "Forever Knight." **92m/C VHS, DVD.** Rick Springfield, Michael Nader, Laura Johnson, John Kapelos; ***D:*** Farhad Mann; ***W:*** James D. Parriott; ***C:*** Frank Beasoechea; ***M:*** Joseph Conlan. **TV**

Nick of Time ✌ ½ **1995 (R)** A malicious stranger (Walken) and his cohort give ordinary accountant Gene Watson (Depp) 90 minutes to assassinate the governor of California (Mason) or his little girl will be killed. Walken as an evil psycho..now there's a stretch. On the other hand, Depp as a button-down, conservative widower is a bit of a switch after his usually quirky roles of the recent past. This may be the first time Depp's picked up a gun since "21 Jump Street." Illogical scenarios (even for an action flick) and curiously uneven pacing do this one in. Shot almost entirely in L.A's Bonaventure Hotel in real time with a handheld camera. **98m/C VHS, DVD.** Johnny Depp, Christopher Walken, Charles S. Dutton, Peter Strauss, Roma Maffia, Gloria Reuben, Marsha Mason, Courtney Chase, Bill Smitrovich, G.D. Spradlin; ***D:*** John Badham; ***W:*** Patrick Duncan; ***C:*** Roy Wagner; ***M:*** Arthur B. Rubinstein.

Nickel & Dime ✌✌ **1992 (PG)** A con artist's luck turns bad when the IRS catches up with him, impounds all his worldly goods, and sticks him with an officious auditor. But if Jack can find the heiress to a fortune, within 48 hours, he can claim a hefty finder's fee and his money worries will be a thing of the past. **96m/C VHS.** C. Thomas Howell, Wallace Shawn, Lise Cutter, Lynn Danielson-Rosenthal, Roy Brocksmith; ***D:*** Ben Moses; ***W:*** Seth Front, Eddy Polon, Ben Moses.

The Nickel Children ✌✌ **2005** Two 14-year-old runaways become prostitutes to survive in L.A. The story focuses more on street-savvy Cat, who only softens her attitude around the puppyish Nolan, who has a shy romantic interest in her. When Cat finds out she's pregnant, and after the murder of a hooker friend, she makes a decision to return home. **95m/C DVD.** Tamara Hope, Tom Sizemore, Jeremy Sisto, Marsha Thomason, John Billingsley, Maeve Quinlan; ***D:*** Glenn Klinker; ***W:*** Eric Litra; ***C:*** John Bartley; ***M:*** Rich Ragsdale.

Nickel Mountain ✌✌ ½ **1985** Heartwarming story of a suicidal 40-year-old man who finds a new reason to live when he falls in love with a pregnant 16-year-old girl who works at his diner. Langenkamp is particularly appealing. Based on a John Gardner novel. **88m/C VHS.** Michael Cole, Heather Langenkamp, Ed Lauter, Brian Kerwin, Patrick Cassidy, Grace Zabriskie, Don Beddoe; ***D:*** Drew Denbaum.

Nico and Dani ✌✌ ½ *Krampack* **2000** Best buddies Nico (Vilches) and Dani (Ramallo) are 17-year-old virgins who hope to change that situtaion while on a Spanish beach vacation. Nico has the hots for pretty Elena (Orozco), who returns his interest, which leaves her cousin Berta (Nubiola) pining for Dani. Too bad Dani realizes that he not only loves Nico, he's IN love with him and that Nico doesn't share his sexual feelings. Dani finds a mentor in an older gay man (Amado) but the situation remains tangled in an all-too realistic (if somewhat overly sunny) way. Based on the play "Krampack" by Jordi Sanchez. Spanish with subtitles. **90m/C VHS, DVD.** *SP* Fernando Ramallo, Jordi Vilches, Marieta Orozco, Esther Nubiola, Chisco Amado, Ana Gracia; ***D:*** Cesc Gay; ***W:*** Cesc Gay, Tomas Aragay; ***C:*** Andreu Rebes; ***M:*** Riqui Sabates, Joan Diaz, Jordi Prats.

Nico Icon ✌✌✌ **1995 (R)** Documentary probes the life of Velvet Underground sensation and Warhol superstar Nico. A pastiche showing V.U. concert footage and movie clips from Nico's most famous film appearances: Fellini's "La Dolce Vita" and Warhol's "The Chelsea Girls." Also features interviews from Warhol's Factory inhabitants, band members, and Nico's grown son Ari. Visually as interesting as the subject herself, film manages to bring the viewer closer to the untouchable Teutonic figure without being sensational or overly flashy. Director Paul Morrissey and musician Jackson Browne make appearances. Some French and German language; subtitled. **75m/C VHS, DVD.** *GE* ***D:*** Susanne Ofteringer; ***W:*** Susanne Ofteringer; ***C:*** Judith Kaufmann.

Nicole ✌ **1972 (R)** The downfall of a wealthy woman who is able to buy everything she wants except love. **91m/C VHS.** Leslie Caron, Catherine Bach, Ramon Bieri; ***D:*** Itsvan Ventilla.

Nicotina ✌ ½ **2003 (R)** Hacker Lolo is commissioned to get Swiss account info for a Russian mobster. But Lolo is a voyeur who has been using spy cams to watch neighbor Andrea and his obsession leads to his supplying the wrong discs to the Russian, causing all sorts of complications. Plot takes place over one night in Mexico City and features debates about smoking and frustrated smokers (hence the title). Spanish with subtitles. **90m/C DVD.** *MX* Diego Luna, Lucas Crespi, Jesus Ochoa, Norman Sotolongo, Marta Belaustegui, Rafael Inclan, Daniel Gimenez Cacho, Rosa Maria Bianchi, Carmen Madrid, Jose Maria Yazpik; ***D:*** Hugo Rodriguez; ***W:*** Martin Salinas; ***C:*** Marcelo Iacarino; ***M:*** Fernando Corona.

The Night After Halloween ✌ *Snapshot* **1979 (R)** A young woman gets the shock of her life when she discovers that her boyfriend is a crazed killer. **90m/C VHS, DVD.** *AU* Chantal Contouri, Robert Bruning, Sigrid Thornton; ***D:*** Simon Wincer; ***W:*** Everett De Roche, Chris De Roche; ***C:*** Vincent Monton; ***M:*** Brian May.

Night After Night ✌✌ ½ **1932** West's screen debut finds her in an unaccustomed secondary role, although a prime scene-stealer. In Raft's first starring role, he's a monied low-life who opens a fancy nightclub and becomes infatuated with Park Avenue beauty Cummings. His problems are compounded by the arrival of raucous ex-flames West and Gleason. When a hatcheck girl cries "Goodness!" over West's diamonds, she replies, in suggestive West-style, "Goodness had nothing to do with it, dearie." Adapted from the novel "Single Night" by Louis Bromfield. **73m/B VHS, DVD.** George Raft, Constance Cummings, Mae West, Wynne Gibson, Alison Skipworth, Roscoe Karns, Louis Calhern; ***D:*** Archie Mayo; ***W:*** Mae West, Kathryn Scola, Vincent Lawrence.

Night Alarm ✌ ½ **1934** Newshound Hal Ashby wants to leave his gardening column behind for investigative journalism but he objects when the column is given over to Helen Smith, the daughter of a wealthy but shady industrialist who's in with city officials. After popping off about Helen's dad, Hall starts investigating a series of arson fires at Smith's factories and even rescues Helen from danger. **65m/B DVD.** Bruce Cabot, Judith Allen, H.B. Warner, Sam Hardy, Harry Holman; ***D:*** Spencer Gordon Bennett; ***W:*** Earle Snell; ***C:*** James S. Brown Jr.

Night Ambush ✌✌ ½ *Ill Met By Moonlight* **1957** A Nazi general is kidnapped on Crete by British agents, who embark on a dangerous trip to the coast where a ship awaits to take them to Cairo. The general tries to thwart their plans, but they outwit him at every turn. Based on a novel by W. Stanley Moss that details a similar real-life event. **100m/B VHS.** *GB* Dirk Bogarde, Marius Goring, David Oxley, Cyril Cusack, Christopher Lee; ***D:*** Michael Powell, Emeric Pressburger.

Night and Day ✌✌ ½ **1946** Sentimental musical about the life of bon-vivant composer-extraordinaire Cole Porter. His intensity and the motivations for his music are dramatized, but this film succeeds best as a fabulous showcase for Porter's songs. ♫ Begin the Beguine; My Heart Belongs to Daddy; You're the Top; I've Got You Under My Skin; Just One of Those Things; I Get a Kick Out of You; Night and Day; What Is This Thing Called Love; Do I Love You. **128m/C VHS, DVD.** Cary Grant, Alexis Smith, Jane Wyman, Eve Arden, Mary Martin, Alan Hale, Monty Woolley, Ginny Simms, Dorothy Malone; ***D:*** Michael Curtiz; ***M:*** Max Steiner.

Night and Day ✌✌✌ *Nuit et Jour* **1991** Charming adult romance about Jack and Julie, young lovers newly arrived in Paris. When Jack gets a night job driving a cab, Julie finds her evenings lonely. But not for long. She meets Joseph, a cab driver on the day shift. Soon, Julie is juggling sexual affairs with both men and everything gets increasingly complicated. Her lovers find out about each other but Julie doesn't want to fully commit to either of them. In French with English subtitles. **90m/C VHS.** *FR BE SI* Guilaine Londez, Thomas Langmann, Francois Negret; ***D:*** Chantal Akerman; ***W:*** Pascal Bonitzer, Chantal Akerman; ***M:*** Marc Herouet.

Night and the City ✌✌✌ ½ **1950** A film noir classic about a hustler's money-making schemes. Widmark is Harry Fabian, a small-time promoter working for slimy nightclub owner Sullivan, whose job is to hustle the marks into the club where his girlfriend Tierney is the singer. Widmark also happens to be romancing Sullivan's wife, Withers, and wants her to back his latest con. But his schemes go awry and Fabian's on the run for his life. Widmark gives a riveting performance of a lowlife whose brains don't match his ambitions. Filmed in London with appropriate brooding tawdriness. Adapted from the novel by Gerald Kersh; remade in 1992. **95m/B VHS, DVD.** *GB* Richard Widmark, Gene Tierney, Googie Withers, Francis L. Sullivan, Hugh Marlowe, Herbert Lom, Mike Mazurki, Charles Farrell; ***D:*** Jules Dassin; ***W:*** Jo Eisinger; ***M:*** Franz Waxman.

Night and the City ✌✌✌ **1992 (R)** Harry Fabian (De Niro), a con-artist/ambulance-chaser, concocts a scheme to make it big, and approaches an old boxing great (Warden) to come out of retirement and revive a local boxing night. Problem is, although Harry has energy and ambition, he also has a talent for making enemies out of the wrong people, like the boxer's brother (King), a neighborhood mobster. Filled with details more interesting than the plot; more about fast-living, fast-talking New Yorkers, a fine showcase for De Niro's talent. Winkler's remake of the 1950 Jules Dassin film. **98m/C VHS, DVD.** Joseph (Joe) D'Onofrio, Michael Badalucco, Michael Rispoli, Robert De Niro, Jessica Lange, Cliff Gorman, Alan King, Jack Warden, Eli Wallach, Barry Primus, Gene Kirkwood, Pedro Sanchez; ***Cameos:*** Regis Philbin, Joy Philbin, Richard Price; ***D:*** Irwin Winkler; ***W:*** Richard Price; ***C:*** Tak Fujimoto; ***M:*** James Newton Howard.

The Night and the Moment ✌ ½ **1994 (R)** Dull, mishmashy costume drama (set in the 17th century) about an imprisoned author (Dafoe) who became intrigued with the mystery woman who had occupied the next cell. They exchanged notes, and he vows to find her when he's released from prison. But first he spends a seductive night, exchanging stories about past conquests, at the chateau of the Marquise (Olin), who, of course, turns out to be the mystery lady. Based on the novel "La Nuit er le Moment" by Claude-Prosper de Jolyot Crebillon. **89m/C VHS, DVD.** *GB FR IT* Willem Dafoe, Lena Olin, Miranda Richardson, Jean-Claude Carriere, Carole Richert; ***D:*** Anna Maria Tato; ***W:*** Anna Maria Tato, Jean-Claude Carriere; ***C:*** Giuseppe Rotunno; ***M:*** Ennio Morricone.

Night Angel 🦴 **1990 (R)** A beautiful seductress lures men into a deadly trap from which only true love can free them. **90m/C VHS.** Isa Anderson, Linda Ashby, Debra Feuer, Helen Martin, Karen Black, Doug Jones, Gary Hudson, Sam Hennings; ***D:*** Dominique Othenin-Girard; ***W:*** Joe Augustyn.

Night at the Golden Eagle 🦴🦴 **2002 (R)** As bleak as the Tom Waits song on the soundtrack. Tommy (Montemarno) is an aging small-time crook fresh out of a seven year prison stint. He meets up with old partner Mic (Agiro) and is dismayed to find out that Mic has gone legit and wants them to move from L.A. to Vegas to work in a casino. Mic takes his pal back to the sleazy Golden Eagle hotel where he's been living. Unfortunately, their plans are soon derailed by a dead hooker (Lyonne) who works for vicious pimp Rodan (Jones). Paralelling the Tommy/Mic friendship is that of veteran whore Sally (Magnuson) to whom Rodan gives runaway teenager Lori Ann (Jacobs) for training. **87m/C VHS, DVD.** Donnie Montemarano, Vinny Argiro, Ann Magnuson, Vinnie Jones, Nicole Jacobs, Natasha Lyonne, Fayard Nicholas, Sam Moore, Francesca "Kitten" Natividad; ***Cameos:*** James Caan; ***D:*** Adam Rifkin; ***W:*** Adam Rifkin; ***C:*** Checco Varese; ***M:*** Tyler Bates.

Night at the Museum 🦴🦴 **2006 (PG)** Wanting to impress his 10-year-old son (Cherry) when his ex-wife's (Raver) new fiance (Rudd)—a successful businessman—proves to be a better role model, Larry (Stiller) decides to change his flighty ways and takes a night guard job at NYC's Museum of Natural History. He gets more than he bargained for when the displays, from the giant T-Rex to a wax figure of Teddy Roosevelt (Williams) to an Old West cowboy (an uncredited Owen Wilson), come alive at night, a minor detail left unrevealed by his predecessors (the comic-legend trio of Rooney, Van Dyke, and Cobbs). But it's not as fun as it sounds—the hyper CGI effects, combined with the weak tale of Larry's life woes, chase away the charm of Milan Trenc's original children's book. **108m/C DVD, Blu-ray Disc.** *US* Ben Stiller, Carla Gugino, Dick Van Dyke, Mickey Rooney, Bill Cobbs, Kim Raver, Ricky Gervais, Robin Williams, Jake Cherry, Owen Wilson, Steve Coogan, Patrick Gallagher, Mizuo Peck, Paul Rudd, Anne Meara, Rami Malek; ***D:*** Shawn Levy; ***W:*** Robert Ben Garant, Thomas Lennon; ***C:*** Guillermo Navarro; ***M:*** Alan Silvestri.

Night at the Museum: Battle of the Smithsonian 🦴🦴 **1/2 2009 (PG)** Follow-up (and more of the same) to the successful 2006 film finds Larry Daley (Stiller) is now an ex-security guard turned entrepreneur. While visiting the Natural History Museum, Larry learns that the old exhibits have been packed up and shipped to the Smithsonian's federal archives. In an effort to secure the Egyptian tablet that brings the exhibits to life, Larry finagles his way into the Smithsonian to stop lisping pharaoh Kahmunrah (Azaria) and his cohorts from committing evil. Adams plays helpful Amelia Earhart as a brash screwball comedy dame. **105m/C DVD.** *US* Ben Stiller, Owen Wilson, Steve Coogan, Amy Adams, Bill Hader, Ricky Gervais, Dick Van Dyke, Hank Azaria, Christopher Guest, Eugene Levy, Jake Cherry, Jon Bernthal, Robin Williams, Jonah Hill, Alain Chabat; ***D:*** Shawn Levy; ***W:*** Robert Ben Garant, Thomas Lennon, Scott Frank; ***C:*** John Schwartzman; ***M:*** Alan Silvestri.

A Night at the Opera 🦴🦴🦴🦴 **1935** The Marx Brothers get mixed up with grand opera in their first MGM-produced epic and their first without Zeppo. Jones, as a budding opera singer warbles "Alone" and "Cosi Cosa." One of their best films, blessed with a big budget—used to reach epic anarchic heights. Some scenes were tested on live audiences before inclusion, including the Groucho/Chico paper-tearing contract negotiation and the celebrated stateroom scene, in which the boys are joined in a small closet by two maids, the ship's engineer, his assistant, a manicurist, a young woman, a cleaning lady, and four food-laden waiters. **92m/B VHS, DVD.** Groucho Marx, Chico Marx, Harpo Marx, Allan Jones, Kitty Carlisle Hart, Sig Ruman, Margaret Dumont, Walter Woolf King, Edward (Ed Kean, Keene) Keane, Robert Emmett O'Connor; ***D:*** Sam Wood; ***W:*** George S. Kaufman, Morrie Ryskind, Bert Kalmar, Harry Ruby, Al Boasberg; ***C:*** Merritt B. Gerstad; ***M:*** Herbert Stothart. Natl. Film Reg. '93.

A Night at the Roxbury 🦴 **1/2 1998 (PG-13)** The Bubati brothers, like so many Saturday Night Live veterans before them, make the leap to the big screen with limited success. Steve and Doug (Ferrell and Kattan) continue their fruitless quest to gain entrance into the hallowed Roxbury night club. Their luck changes when they get into a fender bender with former "21 Jump Street" star Richard Grieco (playing himself), who gets them in. Typical of the SNL skits-to-big-screen formula, the bit works as a three-minute sketch but isn't funny or interesting enough to sustain even its meager 82 minute running time. **83m/C VHS, DVD.** Will Ferrell, Chris Kattan, Molly Shannon, Dan Hedaya, Loni Anderson, Richard Grieco, Elisa Donovan, Lochlyn Munro, Dwayne Hickman, Mark McKinney; ***D:*** John Fortenberry; ***W:*** Steve Koren, Will Ferrell, Chris Kattan; ***C:*** Francis Kenny; ***M:*** David Kitay.

Night Beast 🦴 **1983** Alien creature lands his spaceship near a small town and begins a bloody killing spree. Recycled plot. **90m/C VHS, DVD.** Tom Griffith, Richard Dyszel, Jaimie Zemarel, George Stover; ***D:*** Donald M. Dohler.

Night Beat 🦴 **1/2 1948** A labored crime drama from postwar Britain. Two army pals pursue diverging careers. One becomes a cop, the other a crook. Want to bet that they meet again? **95m/B VHS.** *GB* Anne Crawford, Maxwell Reed, Ronald Howard, Christine Norden; ***D:*** Harold Huth.

The Night Before 🦴🦴 **1/2 1988 (PG-13)** Snobby high school beauty Loughlin loses a bet and has to go to the prom with the school geek Reeves. On the way, they get lost on the wrong side of the tracks, and become involved with pimps, crime, and the police. A drunken Reeves loses Loughlin as well as his father's car. Typical teen farce. **90m/C VHS.** Keanu Reeves, Lori Loughlin, Trinidad Silva, Michael Greene, Theresa Saldana, Suzanne Snyder, Morgan Lofting, Gwil Richards; ***D:*** Thom Eberhardt; ***W:*** Gregory Scherick, Thom Eberhardt.

Night Birds 🦴 **1931** Early British thriller about a notorious crook named "Flash Jack," who heads a gang of top-hated criminals that rob the wealthy. Poor production quality and Raine's standoffish screen presence contribute to this below-average film. **76m/B VHS.** *GB* Jameson Thomas, Jack Raine, Muriel Angelus, Eve Gray; ***D:*** Richard Eichberg; ***W:*** Miles Malleson.

The Night Brings Charlie 🦴 **1/2 1990** A disfigured tree surgeon is the prime suspect in some grisly murders committed with a tree trimming saw. Obviously, everyone in the town fears him as a result. Not a sequel to "Roots." **90m/C VHS.** Kerry Knight, Joe Fishback, Aimee Tenalia, Monica Simmons; ***D:*** Tom Logan.

Night Call Nurses 🦴🦴 *Young L.A. Nurses 2* **1972 (R)** Three gorgeous nurses find danger and intrigue on the night shift at a psychiatric hospital. Third in the "nurse" quintet is back on target, shrugging off the previous film's attempts at "serious" social commentary. Miller provides comic relief. Preceded by "The Student Nurses" and "Private Duty Nurses," and followed by "The Young Nurses" and "Candy Stripe Nurses." **85m/C VHS, DVD.** Patricia T. Byrne, Alana Collins, Mittie Lawrence, Clinton Kimbrough, Felton Perry, Stack Pierce, Richard Young, Dennis Dugan, Dick Miller; ***D:*** Jonathan Kaplan; ***W:*** George Armitage.

The Night Caller 🦴🦴 **1997 (R)** Radio psychologist attracts the attentions of a deranged listener. **94m/C VHS, DVD.** Shanna Reed, Tracy Nelson, Mary Crosby, Cyndi Pass; ***D:*** Rob Malenfant; ***W:*** Frank Rehwaldt; ***C:*** M. David Mullen.

Night Caller from Outer Space 🦴 **1/2** *Blood Beast from Outer Space; The Night Caller* **1966** When a woman-hunting alien arrives in London, women begin to disappear. At first, incredibly, no one makes the connection, but then the horrible truth comes to light. **84m/B VHS, DVD.** *GB* John Saxon, Maurice Denham, Patricia Haines, Alfred Burke, Jack Watson, Aubrey Morris; ***D:*** John Gilling; ***W:*** James O'Connolly; ***C:*** Stephen Dade; ***M:*** Johnny Gregory.

Night Children 🦴 **1989 (R)** Tough L.A. cop teams with a parole officer to battle a nasty gang leader. The battle is quite violent and senseless. **90m/C VHS.** David Carradine, Nancy Kwan, Griffin O'Neal, Tawny (Ellis) Fere; ***D:*** Norbert Meisel.

The Night Club 🦴🦴 **1/2 1925** Swinging single stands to gain fortune if he weds a certain girl, and, as luck would have it, he falls for her. When the usual hearts and roses don't convince her he's earnest, he tries to prove his love is true by attempting suicide and hiring a hit man. **62m/B VHS.** Raymond Griffith, Vera Reynolds, Wallace Beery, Louise Fazenda; ***D:*** Frank Urson.

Night Creature 🦴 *Out of the Darkness; Fear* **1979 (PG)** A tough, Hemingway-type writer is determined to destroy the man-eating black leopard which nearly killed him once before. Filmed in Thailand. **83m/C VHS, DVD.** Donald Pleasence, Nancy Kwan, Ross Hagen; ***D:*** Lee Madden.

Night Cries 🦴🦴 **1/2 1978** After a woman's baby dies at birth, she has persistent dreams that he is alive and in trouble. No one will believe her when she tells them that something is wrong. **100m/C VHS.** Susan St. James, Michael Parks, William Conrad; ***D:*** Richard Lang. **TV**

Night Crossing 🦴🦴 **1/2 1981 (PG)** The fact-based story of two East German families who launch a daring escape to the West in a homemade hot air balloon. Exciting action for the whole family. **106m/C VHS, DVD.** John Hurt, Jane Alexander, Glynnis O'Connor, Doug McKeon, Beau Bridges; ***D:*** Delbert Mann; ***W:*** John McGreevey; ***M:*** Jerry Goldsmith.

The Night Cry 🦴🦴 **1926** Silent canine melodrama has sheep-murdering dog sentenced to death row until he saves little girl from unbelievably big bird. **65m/B VHS.** John Harron, June Marlowe, Mary Louise Miller; ***D:*** Herman C. Raymaker.

Night Divides the Day 🦴🦴 **2001** A serial killer is stalking the students at Hollow Pointe University. The exceptionally low-budget film is more of a serious independent effort than exploitation. **125m/C DVD.** Tiffany Richards, John Stump, David Strowell, Jeff Burton, Michael McCallum, Lynn Wolfbrandt; ***D:*** Jeff Burton; ***W:*** Alex Hencken, Joe Cottonmouth, Jeff Burton; ***M:*** Jeff Burton.

The Night Evelyn Came Out of the Grave 🦴 **1/2** *La Notte Che Evelyn Usca Dalla Tomba* **1971 (R)** A wealthy Italian playboy, obsessed with his dead, flame-haired wife, lures living redheads into his castle, where he tortures and kills them. Standard '70s Euro/horror/sex stuff enlivened by the presence of the incredible Erika Blanc as a stripper who works out of a coffin. **99m/C VHS, DVD.** *IT* Anthony Steffen, Marina Malfatti, Rod Murdock, Erika Blanc, Giacomo "Jack" Rossi-Stuart, Umberto Raho; ***D:*** Emilio P. Miraglio.

Night Eyes 🦴 *Hidden Vision* **1990 (R)** Surveillance can be a dangerous profession, especially when your boss happens to be the jealous husband of a very sexy woman. Watching turns to yearning for this professional peeper, but he may just get more than he bargained for. Roberts is worth watching. **95m/C VHS.** Andrew Stevens, Tanya Roberts, Warwick Sims, Cooper Huckabee; ***D:*** Emilio P. Miraglio; ***W:*** Tom Citrano.

Night Eyes 2 🦴 **1/2 1991 (R)** A security expert assigned to protect the sultry wife of a foreign diplomat finds himself spending a little too much time eyeing her through his hidden cameras. Soon he can no longer control his desire and he makes a move on her that may have international implications. Also available in an unrated version. **97m/C VHS.** Andrew Stevens, Shannon Tweed, Tim Russ, Richard Chaves, Geno Silva; ***D:*** Rodney McDonald.

Night Eyes 3 🦴🦴 **1993 (R)** Night Eyes Security boss Stevens' latest assignment is to protect the superstar lead (Shannon Tweed) of a top TV cop show from a stalker. They wind up in very close contact but someone is videotaping their private moments which don't stay private for long. Maybe on-screen partner Tracy (Shannon's sister) has something to do with it. Also available in an unrated version. **97m/C VHS.** Andrew Stevens, Shannon Tweed, Tracy Tweed, Tristan Rogers; ***D:*** Andrew Stevens; ***W:*** Andrew Stevens, Michel W. Potts.

Night Eyes 4: Fatal Passion 🦴 **1/2 1995 (R)** Beverly Hills shrink Angela Cross (Barbieri) gets involved with bodyguard Steve Caldwell (Trachta), who's been hired to protect her from a stalker, who may also be the same person who stole some sexual explosive patient files. Also available unrated. **101m/C VHS.** Casper Van Dien, Chick Vennera, Paula Barbieri, Jeff Trachta, Andrew Stevens; ***D:*** Rodney McDonald; ***W:*** John Eubanks, Henry Krinkle; ***C:*** Gary Graver; ***M:*** Patrick Seymour.

Night Falls on Manhattan 🦴🦴🦴 **1996 (R)** One man's search for truth runs into serious problems in this adaptation of "Tainted Evidence" by Robert Daley. Former cop turned junior DA, Sean Casey (Garcia), is chosen to lead the prosecution in a sensational NY trial involving a drug dealer/cop killer, who also seriously wounded Sean's long-time cop father, Liam (Holm). He wins but allegations of police corruption dog the trial, thanks to liberal defense lawyer Vigoda (Dreyfuss), and when Sean rather unexpectedly becomes the new district attorney, the issue becomes a full-blown scandal, leading the naive Sean very close to home. Veteran director Lumet knows this scandal-ridden territory very well and is aided by fine performances from his leads. **114m/C VHS, DVD.** Dominic Chianese, Andy Garcia, Ian Holm, Richard Dreyfuss, Lena Olin, James Gandolfini, Ron Leibman, Colm Feore, Shiek Mahmud-Bey, Paul Guilfoyle; ***D:*** Sidney Lumet; ***W:*** Sidney Lumet; ***C:*** David Watkin; ***M:*** Mark Isham.

Night Fire 🦴 **1/2 1994 (R)** Barry wants wife Lydia to try to rekindle the passion in their marriage by getting away for the weekend at their remote ranch. But they're interrupted in their leisure by the stranded Cal and Gwen. Only it turns out Barry has hired the duo, who like kinky games, to peak Lydia's interest. She's merely disgusted and Barry gets nasty. Also available unrated. **93m/C VHS, DVD.** Shannon Tweed, John Laughlin, Martin Hewitt, Rochelle Swanson; ***D:*** Mike Sedan; ***W:*** Catherine Tavel, Helen Haxton; ***C:*** Zoran Hochstatter; ***M:*** Miriam Cutler.

Night Flight 🦴🦴 **1/2 1933** Riviere (John Barrymore) is obsessively devoted to his air delivery service, Trans Andean European Air Mail, putting prompt delivery over the safety of his own men. His best pilot, Jules (Gable), tries to satisfy Riviere's schedule, which includes dangerous night flights over the Andes Mountains. Based on the novel by Antoine de Saint-Exupery. Lionel Barrymore manages to steal scenes from his brother as an airline mechanic. **84m/B VHS.** John Barrymore, Clark Gable, Helen Hayes, Lionel Barrymore, Robert Montgomery, Myrna Loy, William Gargan; ***D:*** Clarence Brown; ***W:*** Oliver H.P. Garrett; ***C:*** Elmer Dyer, Oliver Marsh, Charles A. Marshall; ***M:*** Herbert Stothart.

Night Flight from Moscow 🦴🦴 **1/2** *The Serpent* **1973 (PG)** A Soviet spy defects with a fistful of secret documents that implicate every free government. Then the CIA must decide if he's telling the truth. Complex espionage thriller. **113m/C VHS, DVD.** *FR IT GE* Yul Brynner, Henry Fonda, Dirk Bogarde, Virna Lisi, Philippe Noiret, Farley Granger, Robert Alda, Marie DuBois, Elga Andersen; ***D:*** Henri Verneuil; ***M:*** Ennio Morricone.

A Night for Crime 🦴🦴 **1942** A movie star disappears during the filming of a movie. When she turns up dead, a bumbling cop suspects everyone on the set. **75m/B VHS.** Glenda Farrell, Lyle Talbot, Lena Basquette, Donald Kirke, Ralph Sanford; ***D:*** Alexis Thurn-Taxis.

Night Friend 🦴 **1987 (R)** A priest sets out to help a young woman caught up in a world of drug abuse and prostitution. Exploitation morality flick. **94m/C VHS.** Art Carney, Chuck Shamata, Jayne (Jane) Eastwood, Heather Kjollesdal; ***D:*** Peter Gerretsen.

A Night Full of Rain 🦴 1/2 *End of the World (in Our Usual Bed in a Night Full of Rain)* **1978 (R)** Italian communist tries unsuccessfully to seduce vacationing American feminist. They meet again in San Francisco and wedding bells chime. They argue. They argue more. They put all but rabid Wertmuller fans to sleep. The director's first English-language film. **104m/C VHS.** *IT* Giancarlo Giannini, Candice Bergen, Anne Byrne, Flora Carabella; ***D:*** Lina Wertmuller; ***W:*** Lina Wertmuller.

Night Gallery 🦴🦴🦴 **1969** Serling is the tour guide through an unusual art gallery consisting of portraits that reflect people's greed, desire, and guilt. Pilot for the 1969-1973 TV series. Three stories, including "Eyes," which saw novice Spielberg directing veteran Crawford. **95m/C VHS, DVD.** Joan Crawford, Roddy McDowall, Tom Bosley, Barry Sullivan, Ossie Davis, Sam Jaffe, Kate Greenfield, Richard Kiley, George Macready, Norma Crane, Barry Atwater; ***D:*** Steven Spielberg, Boris Sagal, Boris Shear; ***W:*** Rod Serling; ***C:*** Richard Batcheller; ***M:*** Billy Goldenberg. **TV**

Night Game 🦴 1/2 **1989 (R)** A cop links a string of serial killings to the night games won by the Houston Astros. Brave cast tries hard, but is retired without a hit. **95m/C VHS.** Roy Scheider, Karen Young, Paul Gleason, Lane Smith, Carlin Glynn; ***D:*** Peter Masterson; ***M:*** Pino Donaggio.

Night Games 🦴 **1980 (R)** Raped as a child, California girl Pickett has trouble relating to her husband. To overcome her sexual anxieties, she engages in a number of bizarre fantasies. **100m/C VHS.** Cindy Pickett, Joanna Cassidy, Barry Primus, Gene Davis; ***D:*** Roger Vadim; ***M:*** John Barry.

The Night God Screamed WOOF! *Scream* **1971 (PG)** A fanatical cult leader is convicted of murder and the cult goes wild. **85m/C VHS.** Michael Sugich, Jeanne Crain, James B. Sikking; ***D:*** Lee Madden.

The Night Has Eyes 🦴🦴 1/2 *Terror House* **1942** Tense melodrama concerns a young teacher who disappears on the Yorkshire moors at the same spot where her girlfriend had vanished the previous year. Early film appearance for Mason. **79m/B VHS, DVD.** *GB* James Mason, Joyce Howard, Wilfred Lawson, Mary Clare; ***D:*** Leslie Arliss.

The Night Heaven Fell 🦴🦴 1/2 *Les Bijoutiers du Clair de Lune* **1957** Ursula (Bardot) returns from the convent to the Spanish town where her Aunt Florentine (Valli) lives unhappily with Count Ribera (Nieto), a macho brute and womanizer. A local malcontent, Lambert (Boyd) has returned from political exile to find his sister dead by suicide over the Count; and a deadly feud is reignited. Complicating matters is Aunt Florentine's unwillingness to admit her love for Lambert, and virgin Ursula's instantaneous attraction to him. It's serious, overheated melodrama in a commercial package that reveals Vadim to be basically the sex merchant everyone accuses him of being. **95m/C DVD.** *FR IT* Brigitte Bardot, Stephen Boyd, Alida Valli, Pepe Nieto; ***D:*** Roger Vadim; ***W:*** Roger Vadim, Peter Viertel, Jacques Remy; ***C:*** Armand Thirard; ***M:*** Georges Auric.

Night Hunter 🦴🦴 **1995 (R)** Jack Cutter's (Wilson) vampire-hunting parents were killed by a group of bloodsuckers so he teams up with a tabloid reporter (Smith) to eliminate the last nine vampires who have gathered together in Los Angeles and plan to multiply. **86m/C VHS, DVD.** Don "The Dragon" Wilson, Melanie Smith, Nicholas Guest, Maria Ford; ***D:*** Rick Jacobson.

A Night in Casablanca 🦴🦴🦴 **1946** Groucho, Harpo and Chico find themselves in the luxurious Hotel Casablanca, going after some leftover Nazis searching for treasure. One of the later Marx Brothers' films, but still loaded with the familiar wisecracks and mayhem. **85m/B VHS, DVD.** Groucho Marx, Harpo Marx, Chico Marx, Charles Drake, Dan Seymour, Sig Rumann, Lisette Verea, Lois Collier, Paul Harvey, Lewis L. Russell; ***D:*** Archie Mayo; ***W:*** Roland Kibbee, Frank Tashlin, Joseph Fields; ***C:*** James Van Trees; ***M:*** Werner Janssen.

A Night in Heaven WOOF! 1983 (R) A college teacher gets involved with one of her students, who moonlights as a male stripper. Will he earn that extra credit he needs to pass? Uninspired, overly explicit. Look for Denny Terrio of "Dance Fever" fame. **85m/C VHS, DVD.** Christopher Atkins, Lesley Ann Warren, Carrie Snodgress, Andy Garcia; ***D:*** John G. Avildsen; ***W:*** Joan Tewkesbury. Golden Raspberries '83: Worst Actor (Atkins).

A Night in the Life of Jimmy Reardon 🦴 1/2 **1988 (R)** A high school Casanova watches his friends leave for expensive schools while he contemplates a trip to Hawaii with his rich girlfriend, a ruse to avoid the dull business school his father has picked out. Well photographed, but acting leaves something to be desired. Based on Richert's novel "Aren't You Even Going to Kiss Me Good-bye?" **95m/C VHS, DVD.** River Phoenix, Meredith Salenger, Matthew Perry, Louanne, Ione Skye, Ann Magnuson, Paul Koslo, Jane Hallaren, Jason Court; ***D:*** William Richert; ***W:*** William Richert; ***C:*** John J. Connor; ***M:*** Elmer Bernstein, Bill Conti.

Night Is My Future 🦴🦴 1/2 *Music in Darkness* **1947** A young musician, blinded in an accident, meets a girl who tries to bring him happiness. Usual somber Bergman, but unimportant story. In Swedish with English subtitles. **89m/B VHS, DVD.** *SW* Mai Zetterling, Birger Malmsten, Naima Wifstrand, Olof Winnerstrand, Hilda Borgstrom; ***D:*** Ingmar Bergman.

Night Junkies 🦴🦴 **2007 (R)** Twist on the familiar vampire genre makes this one worth watching. Exotic dancer Ruby is turned by her philosophical vampire lover Vincent and the two hunt for victims along London's seedy waterfront while dealing with their blood addiction. **90m/C DVD.** *GB* Katia Winter, Giles Anderson, Jonathan Coyne, Sasha Jackson; ***D:*** Lawrence Pearce; ***W:*** Lawrence Pearce; ***C:*** Sadik Ahmed; ***M:*** Michael England. **VIDEO**

Night Life 🦴🦴 **1990 (R)** A teenager gets the all-out, high-stakes ride of his life when four cadavers are re-animated in his uncle's mortuary. **92m/C VHS.** Scott Grimes, John Astin, Cheryl Pollak, Alan Blumenfeld; ***D:*** David Acomba; ***W:*** Keith Critchlow; ***M:*** Roger Bourland.

Night Life in Reno 🦴🦴 **1931** When a man leaves his wife, she sets out for Reno and falls in love with a married man. When her new love is killed by his jealous wife, the woman returns to her husband and they begin their marriage anew. Watchable melodrama. **58m/B VHS.** Jameson Thomas, Dorothy Christy, Virginia Valli, Carmelita Geraghty, Dixie Lee, Pat O'Malley, Clarence Wilson; ***D:*** Raymond Cannon; ***W:*** Arthur Hoerl; ***C:*** M.A. Anderson.

The Night Listener 🦴🦴 1/2 **2006** Williams does drama in this adaptation of Maupin's novel. New York radio show host Gabriel Noone is distracted by his break-up with longtime lover, Jess (Cannavale), which is affecting his work. His outlook changes when a friend gives him a memoir purportedly written by dying teenaged fan, Pete. Gabriel begins a telephone relationship with Pete (Culkin) and his foster mother, Donna (Collette), but becomes suspicious about Pete's actual existence when Donna won't let them meet. **90m/C DVD.** *US* Robin Williams, Toni Collette, Bobby Cannavale, Joe Morton, Rory Culkin, Sandra Oh, John Cullum; ***D:*** Patrick Stettner; ***W:*** Patrick Stettner, Armistead Maupin, Terry Anderson; ***C:*** Lisa Rinzler; ***M:*** Peter Nashel.

Night Master 🦴 **1987** A handful of karate students practice their homework with much higher stakes away from the classroom. For them, deadly Ninja games are the only way to study. **87m/C VHS, DVD.** Tom Jennings, Nicole Kidman, Vince Martin; ***D:*** Mark Joffe.

Night Monster 🦴🦴 1/2 *House of Mystery* **1942** A maniac wears artifical limbs to hunt down and murder the doctors responsible for amputating his legs. Picture was shot in 11 days. Fire scene was stock footage from "The Ghost of Frankenstein." **80m/B VHS.** Bela Lugosi, Ralph Morgan, Lionel Atwill, Leif Erickson, Don Porter, Irene Hervey, Nils Asther; ***D:*** Ford Beebe; ***W:*** Clarence Upson Young; ***C:*** Charles Van Enger.

'night, Mother 🦴🦴 1/2 **1986 (PG-13)** A depressed woman, living with her mother, announces one evening that she is going to kill herself. Her mother spends the evening reliving their lives and trying to talk her out of it, but the outcome seems inevitable. Well acted, though depressing. Based on Marsha Norman's Pulitzer Prize-winning novel. **97m/C VHS.** Sissy Spacek, Anne Bancroft, Ed Berke, Carol Robbins, Jennifer Roosendahl; ***D:*** Tom (Thomas R.) Moore; ***W:*** Marsha Norman; ***M:*** David Shire.

Night Moves 🦴🦴🦴 1/2 **1975 (R)** Small-time L.A. detective Harry Moseby (Hackman) is hired by fading actress Arlene Iverson (Ward) to find her wild teenaged daughter Delly (Griffith) who has taken off for the Florida Keys. Delly winds up dead and Harry uncovers a bizarre smuggling ring. Hackman is realistic as the detective whose own life is unraveling and Penn and screenwriter Sharp tweaked the detective convention with Harry being an ultimately ineffectual hero. Underrated when released and worth a view. **100m/C VHS, DVD.** Gene Hackman, Susan Clark, Jennifer Warren, Melanie Griffith, Harris Yulin, Edward Binns, Kenneth Mars, James Woods, Dennis Dugan, Max Gail, Janet Ward; ***D:*** Arthur Penn; ***W:*** Alan Sharp; ***C:*** Bruce Surtees; ***M:*** Michael Small.

Night Must Fall 🦴🦴🦴 **1937** Effective thriller based on the play by Emlyn Williams. Wheelchair-bound grand dame Mrs. Branson (Whitty) hires personable Danny (Montgomery) as a handyman for the cottage she lives in with niece, Olivia (Russell). Danny is, of course, too good to be true. He's a creepy killer after moolah, which Olivia discerns but does nothing about until he strikes again. Oh yeah, he also keeps a suspicious hatbox in his room. Remade in 1964 with Albert Finney as the killer. **101m/B VHS.** Robert Montgomery, May Whitty, Rosalind Russell, Merle Tottenham, Alan Marshal, Kathleen Harrison, Matthew Boulton; ***D:*** Richard Thorpe; ***W:*** John Van Druten; ***C:*** Ray June; ***M:*** Edward Ward.

Night Nurse 🦴🦴🦴 **1931** Stanwyck is a nurse who uncovers a sordid plot involving the murder of two young children for an inheritance. An entertaining, overlooked crime-drama, initially notorious for Stanwyck and roommate Blondell's continual onscreen dressings and undressings. Gable is compelling in an early, villainous role. **72m/B VHS.** Barbara Stanwyck, Ben Lyon, Joan Blondell, Charles Winninger, Charlotte Merriam, Eddie Nugent, Blanche Frederici, Allan "Rocky" Lane, Walter McGrail, Ralf Harolde, Clark Gable; ***D:*** William A. Wellman.

Night Nurse 🦴 **1977** Young nurse signs on to care for an aging, wheelchair-ridden opera star, only to find that the house is haunted. **80m/C VHS, DVD.** Davina Whitehouse, Kay Taylor, Gary Day, Kate Fitzpatrick; ***D:*** Igor Auzins.

Night of a Thousand Cats 🦴🦴 *La Noche de los Mil Gatos; Blood Feast; Cats* **1972 (R)** A reclusive playboy cruises Mexico City in his helicopter, searching for beautiful women. It seems he needs their bodies for his cats who, for some reason, eat only human flesh. He keeps the heads, for some reason, for his private collection. A really odd '70s cannibal cat entry, but it moves along nicely and features some truly groovy fashions (floppy hats, translucent blouses, etc.). Not to be confused with the 1963 film of the same name. From the director of "Night of the Bloody Apes" and "Survive!" **83m/C VHS.** *MX* Anjanette Comer, Zulma Faiad, Hugo Stiglitz, Christa Linder, Teresa Velazquez, Barbara Ange; ***D:*** Rene Cardona Jr.

Night of Bloody Horror 🦴 1/2 **1969 (R)** Tale of a former mental patient who is believed to be responsible for the brutal murders of his ex-girlfriends. A night of bloody horror indeed, as the gore is liberally spread. **89m/C VHS, DVD.** Gaye Yellen, Evelyn Hendricks, Gerald McRaney, Michael Anthony; ***D:*** Joy Houck Jr.; ***W:*** Joy Houck Jr., Robert A. Weaver; ***C:*** Robert A. Weaver.

Night of Dark Shadows 🦴🦴🦴 *Curse of Dark Shadows* **1971 (PG)** Underrated, atmospheric follow-up to "House of Dark Shadows." When newlyweds Quentin (Selby) and Tracy Collins (Jackson) move into the family mansion, they find the place haunted by a ghostly woman named Angelique (Parker). As Quentin is disturbed by visissss of the past, he finds himself possessed by the spirit of Angelique's lover (also Selby) and Tracy's life in danger from the vengeful specter. Though occasionally muddled due to last-minute cuts ordered by the studio, the film still delivers a surplus of chills and is beautifully photographed. **94m/C VHS.** David Selby, Kate Jackson, Lara Parker, Grayson Hall, John Karlen, Nancy Barrett, James Storm, Thayer David; ***D:*** Dan Curtis; ***W:*** Sam Hall; ***C:*** Richard Shore. **TV**

Night of Evil 🦴 1/2 **1962** Girl is released from reform school and promptly wins a beauty contest. Her bid to win the Miss America title is blown to smithereens however, when it is discovered that she has been secretly married all along. From there she resorts to working in strip joints and attempts to pull off an armed robbery. As exploitation fare goes, a winner. **88m/B VHS.** Lisa Gaye, William Campbell; ***D:*** Richard Galbreath; ***Nar:*** Earl Wilson.

Night of Horror 🦴 1/2 **1978 (R)** Zombies attack four young people stranded in the wilderness. **76m/C VHS.** Steve Sandkuhler, Gae Schmitt, Rebecca Bach, Jeff Canfield; ***D:*** Tony Malanowski; ***W:*** Rebecca Bach; ***C:*** Jeff Canfield.

Night of January 16th 🦴 1/2 **1941** Tycoon Bjorn Faulkner (Asther) is accused of embezzlement by his board of directors. When he's apparently murdered, his secretary Kit Lane (Drew) becomes the prime suspect. But good guy Steve Van Ruyle (Preston) sets out to prove that Kit is innocent. Adapted from a play by Ayn Rand. **80m/B VHS.** Robert Preston, Ellen Drew, Clarence (C. William) Kolb, Willard Robertson, Cecil Kellaway, Donald "Don" Douglas, Paul Stanton, Nils Asher; ***D:*** William Clemens; ***W:*** Delmer Daves, Robert Pirosh; ***C:*** John Mescall.

A Night of Love 🦴🦴 1/2 *Manifesto* **1987 (R)** Because of an assassination threat on the new king, Inspector Avanti (Molina) is charged with rounding up the town's troublemakers. Among them is a beguiling debutante (Soeberg) whose sexual appetites are matched only by her passion to kill the king. Based on a story by Emile Zola. **97m/C VHS.** Alfred Molina, Camilla Soeberg, Eric Stoltz, Gabrielle Anwar; ***D:*** Dusan Makavejev.

The Night of Nights 🦴🦴 *Heaven on a Shoestring* **1939** Drunk Broadway show producer Dan O'Farrell (O'Brien) makes his comeback after a long hiatus. **86m/B VHS.** Pat O'Brien, Olympe Bradna, Roland Young; ***D:*** Lewis Milestone; ***W:*** Donald Ogden Stewart.

Night of Terror 🦴 1/2 *He Lived to Kill* **1933** A swami, a couple of Hindu servants, a pretty heroine, a reporter, and all stalked by a killer who's after a formula that can put people in a state of suspended animation. Lame chiller. **64m/B VHS.** Bela Lugosi, Sally Blane, Wallace Ford, Tully Marshall, George Meeker, Edwin Maxwell; ***D:*** Ben Stoloff; ***C:*** Joseph Valentine.

Night of Terror 1987 A bizarre family conducts brain experiments on themselves and then begins to kill each other. Bloodshed for the whole family. **105m/C VHS.** Renee Harmon, Henry Lewis; ***D:*** Felix Girard.

Night of the Assassin 🦴 **1977** Priest leaves his pulpit to become a terrorist. He plans a surprise for a U.N. secretary visiting Greece that would put the U.S. and Greek governments in the palm of his hand. Hard to believe. **98m/C VHS, DVD.** Klaus Kinski, Michael Craig, Eva Renzi; ***D:*** Robert McMahon.

Night of the Blood Beast 🦴 1/2 *Creature from Galaxy 27* **1958** An astronaut comes back from space with an alien growing inside his body. The low-budget defeats a valiant attempt at a story. **65m/B VHS, DVD.** Michael Emmet, Angela Greene, John Baer, Ed Nelson, Georgianna Carter, Tyler McVey; ***D:*** Bernard L. Kowalski; ***W:*** Martin Varno; ***C:*** John M. Nickolaus Jr.; ***M:*** Alexander Laszlo.

Night of the Bloody Apes WOOF! *Gomar the Human Gorilla; La Horriplante Bestia Humana* **1968 (R)** When a doctor transplants an ape's heart into his dying son's body, the son goes berserk. Gory Mexican-made horror at its finest. **84m/C VHS, DVD.** *MX* Jose Elias Moreno, Armando Silvestre, Norma Lazarendo, Augustin Martinez Solares, Gina Moret, Noelia Noel, Gerard Zepeda, Carlos Lopez Moctezuma; *D:* Rene Cardona Jr.; *W:* Rene Cardona Jr.; *C:* Raul Martinez Solares; *M:* Antonio Diaz Conde.

Night of the Bloody Transplant WOOF! **1986 (R)** A lunatic scientist switches hearts from one person to another in this bloody gorefest. Footage of real surgery adds authenticity, but not believeability. **90m/C VHS.** Dick Grimm; *D:* David W. Hanson.

Night of the Cobra Woman **1972 (R)** A woman who can turn herself into a cobra needs constant sex and snake venom to keep her eternally young. Shot on location in the Philippines. One-time underground filmmaker Meyer co-wrote the script, for the Corman factory. **85m/C VHS.** *PH* Joy Bang, Marlene Clark, Roger Garrett, Slash Marks, Vic Diaz; *D:* Andrew Meyer; *W:* Andrew Meyer.

Night of the Comet 1/2 **1984 (PG-13)** After surviving the explosion of a deadly comet, two California girls discover that they are the last people on Earth. When zombies begin to chase them, things begin to lose their charm. Cute and funny, but the script runs out before the movie does. **90m/C VHS, DVD.** Catherine Mary Stewart, Kelli Maroney, Robert Beltran, Geoffrey Lewis, Mary Woronov, Sharon Farrell, Michael Bowen; *D:* Thom Eberhardt; *W:* Thom Eberhardt; *C:* Arthur Albert.

Night of the Creeps 1/2 *Creeps; Homecoming Night* **1986 (R)** In 1958 an alien organism lands on earth and infects a person who is then frozen. Thirty years later he is accidentally unfrozen and starts spreading the infection throughout a college town. B-movie homage contains every horror cliche there is. Director Dekker's first film. **89m/C VHS.** Jason Lively, Jill Whitlow, Tom Atkins, Steve Marshall, Wally Taylor, Bruce Solomon, Kenneth Tobey, Dick Miller, David Oliver; *D:* Fred Dekker; *W:* Fred Dekker; *C:* Robert New; *M:* Barry DeVorzon.

Night of the Cyclone **1990 (R)** A complex but not overly interesting thriller about a big city cop who goes to an island paradise in search of his missing daughter and finds murder. **90m/C VHS.** Kris Kristofferson, Jeffrey Meek, Marisa Berenson, Winston Ntshona, Gerrit Graham; *D:* David Irving.

Night of the Death Cult *Night of the Seagulls* **1975** After moving to a quiet seaside community, a young couple is plagued by cult practising human sacrifice in order to appease the Templars, a zombie-like pack of ancient clergymen who rise from the dead and torture the living. Last in a four film series about the Templars. **90m/C VHS, DVD.** *SP* Victor Petit, Julie James, Maria Kosti, Sandra Mozarowsky; *D:* Armando de Ossorio.

Night of the Demon WOOF! **1980** Anthropology students are attacked by the legendary Bigfoot. Later they discover that he has raped and impregnated a young woman. Gore and sex prevail. **97m/C VHS.** Jay Allen, Michael J. Cutt, Bob Collins, Jodi Lazarus; *D:* James C. Watson.

Night of the Demons **1988 (R)** A gory, special-effects-laden horror farce about teenagers calling up demons in a haunted mortuary. On Halloween, of course. **92m/C VHS, DVD.** Linnea Quigley, Cathy Podewell, Alvin Alexis, William Gallo, Mimi Kinkade, Lance Fenton; *D:* Kevin S. Tenney; *W:* Joe Augustyn.

Night of the Demons **2009** An apparent remake of the 1988 flick. Maddie, Lily, and Suzanne are going to a Halloween party thrown by their friend Angela at the creepy Broussard Mansion in New Orleans. Hooking up with Colin, Dex, and Jason, they all party on until the police break up the festivities. However, the gang find themselves trapped in the house, dealing with demons who need to possess them to break an ancient curse. **m/C DVD.** *US* Shannon Elizabeth, Monica Keena, Diora Baird, Bobbi Sue (Bobby Sue) Luther, Edward Furlong, John Beach, Michael Copon; *D:* Adam Gierasch; *W:* Adam Gierasch; *C:* Yaron Levy; *M:* Joseph Bishara.

Night of the Demons 2 **1994 (R)** Some humor and reasonable special effects help this rise above the usual teen-slasher horror sequels. The demonic Angela (complete with her skull-shaped lollipops) lives on in legend, handily haunting her creepy old house where a group of dumb teens end up on Halloween (and soon wind up dead). With each casualty, a new victim also joins the ranks of the undead. Funniest parts come with heroic rescuer, yardstick-wielding Sister Gloria, who's not about to let any of Satan's helpers get the better of her. **96m/C VHS.** Amelia Kinkade, Jennifer Rhodes, Merle Kennedy, Bobby Jacoby, Rod McCary, Zoe Trilling, Cristi Harris, Johnny Moran, Rick Peters, Christine Taylor, Ladd York, Darin Heames; *D:* Brian Trenchard-Smith; *W:* Joe Augustyn; *M:* Jim Manzie.

Night of the Demons 3 WOOF! *Demon House* **1997 (R)** Yet another bunch of moronic teenagers take refuge in Hull House funeral home on Halloween. Don't they know the mansion houses a bloodthirsty demon by now? May the demon win. **85m/C VHS, DVD.** Amelia Kinkade, Kris Holden-Ried, Vlasta Vrana; *D:* Jim Kaufman.

The Night of the Following Day **1969 (R)** Four professional criminals kidnap a young girl at France's Orly airport, demanding a large ransom from her wealthy father. Each kidnapper turns out to be beset by personal demons, hindering their plans and leading to a bloody climax. Then, there's a final twist to the entire story. Brando and Boone are properly chilling but the plot is muddled and melodramatic. From the novel "The Snatchers" by Lionel White. **93m/C VHS, DVD.** Marlon Brando, Richard Boone, Rita Moreno, Pamela Franklin, Jess Hahn, Jacques Marin, Gerard Buhr, Hughes Wanner; *D:* Hubert Cornfield; *W:* Robert Phippeny, Hubert Cornfield.

Night of the Fox **1990 (R)** An American officer with top secret knowledge is captured by Germans on the brink of D-Day. His home team plans to kill him if he cannot be rescued before spilling the beans. On-location filming adds much. **95m/C VHS.** Michael York, Deborah Raffin, George Peppard; *D:* Charles Jarrott. **CABLE**

Night of the Generals *La Nuit de Generaux* **1967 (R)** A Nazi intelligence officer is pursuing three Nazi generals who may be involved in the brutal murder of a Warsaw prostitute. Dark and sinister, may be too slow for some tastes. Based on Hans Helmut Kirst's novel. **148m/C VHS.** Peter O'Toole, Omar Sharif, Tom Courtenay, Joanna Pettet, Donald Pleasence, Christopher Plummer, Philippe Noiret, John Gregson, Charles Gray; *D:* Anatole Litvak; *M:* Maurice Jarre.

Night of the Ghouls WOOF! *Revenge of the Dead* **1959** Second to last in Wood's celebrated series of inept horror films that began with "Bride of the Monster" and "Plan 9 from Outer Space." This one tells of a phony spiritualist who swindles the grieving by pretending to raise the dead. To his great surprise he actually does enliven some cadavers, who then go after him. Unreleased for over 20 years because Wood couldn't pay the film lab. Not quite as classically bad as his other films, but still a laugh riot. **69m/B VHS, DVD.** Paul Marco, Tor Johnson, Duke Moore, Kenne Duncan, John Carpenter, Criswell, Bud Osborne, Anthony Cardoza, Vampira, Valda Hansen, Karl Johnson; *D:* Edward D. Wood Jr.; *W:* Edward D. Wood Jr.; *C:* William C. Thompson.

Night of the Grizzly **1966** An ex-lawman's peaceful life as a rancher is threatened when a killer grizzly bear goes on a murderous rampage terrorizing the residents of the Wyoming countryside. **99m/C VHS.** Clint Walker, Martha Hyer; *D:* Joseph Pevney.

Night of the Howling Beast *La Maldicion de la Bestia; The Werewolf and the Yeti* **1975 (R)** The selling point of this one is an epic, first-time battle between a werewolf and a Yeti. Unfortunately it lasts about 15 seconds. Naschy's eighth stint as the wolfman. **87m/C VHS.** *SP* Paul Naschy, Grace Mills, Castillo Escalona, Silvia Solar, Gil Vidal, Luis Induni; *D:* Miguel Iglesias Bonns; *W:* Paul Naschy; *C:* Tomas Pladevall.

The Night of the Hunter **1955** The nightmarish story of psychotic bogus preacher Harry Powell (Mitchum) who has the words H-A-T-E tattooed on the knuckles of his left hand and L-O-V-E on his right. He marries lonely widow Willa Harper (Winters), who has two children, in the hopes of finding the cache of money her thieving husband (Graves) had stashed. Gish plays Rachel, the shotgun-wielding, Bible-reading old lady who defends the kids when Harry threatens them. A dark, terrifying tale, completely unique in Hollywood's history. Mitchum is terrific. From novel by Davis Grubb and, sadly, Laughton's only directorial effort. **93m/B VHS, DVD.** Robert Mitchum, Shelley Winters, Lillian Gish, Don Beddoe, Evelyn Varden, Peter Graves, James Gleason, Billy Chapin, Sally Jane Bruce, Gloria Castillo, Mary Ellen Clemons, Cheryl Callaway, Corey Allen, Paul Bryar; *D:* Charles Laughton; *W:* James Agee; *C:* Stanley Cortez; *M:* Walter Schumann. Natl. Film Reg. '92.

The Night of the Iguana **1964** An alcoholic ex-minister acts as a tour guide in Mexico, becoming involved with a spinster and a hotel owner. Based on Tennessee Williams' play. Excellent performances from Burton and Gardner. **125m/B VHS, DVD.** Richard Burton, Deborah Kerr, Ava Gardner, Grayson Hall, Sue Lyon, Emilio Fernandez, Cyril Delevanti; *D:* John Huston; *W:* John Huston, Anthony Veiller; *C:* Gabriel Figueroa; *M:* Benjamin Frankel. Oscars '64: Costume Des. (B&W).

Night of the Juggler 1/2 **1980 (R)** An ex-cop encounters countless obstacles in trying to track down his daughter's kidnapper in NYC. Just a tad too complicated for some tastes. **101m/C VHS.** James Brolin, Cliff Gorman, Richard S. Castellano, Mandy Patinkin, Julie Carmen; *D:* Robert Butler; *W:* William W. Norton Sr.

Night of the Kickfighters **1991** A mighty band of martial artists takes on a terrorist group that has in their possession a secret weapon that could destroy the world. **87m/C VHS.** Andy Bauman, Adam West, Marcia Karr; *D:* Buddy Reyes.

Night of the Laughing Dead 1/2 *Crazy House; House in Nightmare Park* **1975** Veteran British comedy cast perform unthinkable spoof. Man stands to inherit lotsa money as his family members kick the bucket one by one. **90m/C VHS.** *GB* Ray Milland, Frankie Howerd, Rosalie Crutchley, Kenneth Griffith; *D:* Peter Sykes.

Night of the Lepus **1972 (PG)** Giant mutant bunny wabbits lay waste to the countryside after a failed hormone experiment goes horribly awry. Where's Elmer Fudd when you need him? Debate still rages about whether this is an incompetent B-movie horror flick, or an intentionally campy spoof of giant critter flicks. Watch it as the latter to get maximum enjoyment out of it. **88m/C DVD.** Stuart Whitman, Janet Leigh, Rory Calhoun, DeForest Kelley, Paul Fix, William (Bill) Elliott; *D:* William Claxton; *W:* Don Holliday, Gene R. Kearney; *C:* Ted Voightlander; *M:* Jimmie Haskell.

Night of the Living Babes WOOF! **1987** Two yuppie men go looking for fun at a brothel. They get their just deserts in the form of sex-seeking female zombies. **60m/C VHS.** Michelle (McClellan) Bauer, Connie Woods, Andrew Nichols, Louie Bonanno; *D:* Jon Valentine.

Night of the Living Dead 1/2 *Night of the Flesh Eaters; Night of the Anubis* **1968** Cult favorite is low budget but powerfully frightening. Space experiments set off a high level of radiation that makes the newly dead return to life, with a taste for human flesh. Handful of holdouts find shelter in a farmhouse. Claustrophobic, terrifying, gruesome, extreme, and yes, humorous. Followed by "Dawn of the Dead" (1979) and "Day of the Dead" (1985). Romero's directorial debut. Available in a colorized version. **90m/B VHS, DVD.** Judith O'Dea, Duane Jones, Karl Hardman, Marilyn Eastman, Keith Wayne, Judith Ridley, Russell Streiner, Bill "Chilly Billy" Cardille, John A. Russo, Kyra Schon, Bill (William Heinzman) Hinzman, John Simpson, Vincent Survinski, George A. Romero; *D:* George A. Romero; *W:* John A. Russo, George A. Romero; *C:* George A. Romero. Natl. Film Reg. '99.

Night of the Living Dead **1990 (R)** A bunch of people are trapped in a farmhouse and attacked by ghouls with eating disorders. Remake of the '68 classic substitutes high tech blood 'n' guts for bona fide frights. **92m/C VHS, DVD.** Tony Todd, Patricia Tallman, Tom Towler, William Butler, Bill Moseley, McKee Anderson, Kate Finneran, Bill "Chilly Billy" Cardille; *D:* Tom Savini; *W:* George A. Romero, John A. Russo; *C:* Frank Prinzi; *M:* Paul McCollough.

Night of the Living Dead, 25th Anniversary Documentary 1/2 **1993** Features behind the scenes look at low-budget 1968 classic film about legions of dead people who stalk the earth looking for live humans to feed on. **83m/C VHS.**

Night of the Running Man 1/2 **1994 (R)** Las Vegas cab driver McCarthy finds $1 million stolen from a casino and goes on the run from hit man Glenn, who's been hired to recover the loot. **93m/C VHS.** Scott Glenn, Andrew McCarthy, John Glover; *D:* Mark L. Lester.

Night of the Scarecrow 1/2 **1995 (R)** Hundreds of years before a small town makes a pact with a warlock (Lazar) to ensure prosperity. After regretting the deal, the townspeople kill him and bury the body in a field where it's eventually uncovered. Now the warlock's ghost inhabits the frame of a scarecrow and is off on a murderous rampage. Formula horror with some decent production values. Based on a comic book. **90m/C VHS.** Elizabeth Barondes, John Mese, Stephen (Steve) Root, Bruce Glover, Dirk Blocker, Howard Swain, Gary Lockwood, John Lazar, John Hawkes, Martine Beswick; *D:* Jeff Burr; *W:* Reed Steiner, Dan Mazur; *C:* Thomas Callaway; *M:* Jim Manzie.

Night of the Sharks WOOF! **1987** Mercenaries in a downed plane go after a jewel-ridden shipwreck despite a plethora of sharks. **87m/C VHS, DVD.** Treat Williams, Christopher Connelly, Antonio Fargas, Janet Agren; *D:* Anthony Richmond.

The Night of the Shooting Stars *The Night of San Lorenzo; La Notte di San Lorenzo* **1982 (R)** Set in an Italian village during the last days of WWII, this film highlights the schism in the village between those who support the fascists and those who sympathize with the Allies. This division comes to a head in the stunning final scene. A poignant, deeply moving film. **106m/C VHS, DVD.** *IT* Omero Antonutti, Margarita Lozano, Claudio Bigagli, Massimo Bonetti, Norma Martel; *D:* Paolo Taviani, Vittorio Taviani; *W:* Tonino Guerra, Giuliani G. De Negri, Paolo Taviani, Vittorio Taviani; *C:* Franco Di Giacomo; *M:* Nicola Piovani. Cannes '82: Grand Jury Prize; Natl. Soc. Film Critics '83: Director (Taviani), Director (Taviani), Film.

Night of the Sorcerers WOOF! **1970** An expedition to the Congo uncovers a bizarre tribe of vampire leopard women who lure young girls to their deaths. **85m/C VHS, DVD.** Jack Taylor, Simon Andreu, Kali Hansa; *D:* Armando de Ossorio.

Night of the Strangler **1973 (R)** A love affair between a white society girl and a young black man causes a chain of events that end with brutal murders in New Orleans. **88m/C VHS.** Mickey Dolenz, James Ralston, Susan McCullough; *D:* Joy Houck Jr.

Night of the Twisters 1/2 **1995** Teenager Dan (Sawa) and his new stepfather Jack (Schneider) must work together to protect the family when tornadoes rip through their small Nebraska town. Based on the book by Ivy Ruckman. **91m/C VHS, DVD.** John Schneider, Devon Sawa, Lori Hallier, Helen Hughes; *D:* Timothy Bond; *M:* Lawrence Shragge. **CABLE**

Night of the Warrior **1991 (R)** Music videos and martial arts don't mix...not here, anyway. A hunky exotic-dance-club owner pays his disco bills by fighting in illegal, underground blood matches, but not enough to make it exciting. Lamas stars with real life wife Kinmont and mom Dahl. **96m/C VHS, DVD.** Lorenzo Lamas, Anthony Geary, Kathleen Kinmont, Arlene Dahl, Wilhelm von Homburg; *D:*

Rafal Zielinski; *W:* Thomas Ian Griffith; *C:* Edward Pei; *M:* Ed Tomney.

The Night of the White Pants ½ **2006 (R)** Takes family dysfunction to a not terribly exciting level. Dallas good ole boy Max Hagan (Wilkinson) and his brood are left in the cold one night when his nearly-ex trophy wife Barbara (Turner) claims the property and kicks everyone out. Max (in his white pants) tags along with daughter Beth (Blair) and her punk rocker boyfriend Raff (Stahl) on a round of drugs and debauchery until some semblance of family values reasserts itself when the Hagans finally reunite at the same hotel. **87m/C DVD.** Tom Wilkinson, Nick Stahl, Selma Blair, Frances Fisher, Geri Jewell, Fran Kranz, Janine Turner, Laura Jordan; *D:* Amy Talkington; *W:* Amy Talkington; *C:* Jim Denault, David Daniel; *M:* Tony Tisdale.

Night of the Wilding **1990** Very, very loosely based on the story of the female jogger who was gang-raped and left for dead in New York's Central Park. Made soon after the actual incident occurred. **90m/C VHS, DVD.** Erik Estrada, Kathrin Lautner; *D:* Joseph Merhi. **TV**

Night of the Zombies *Gamma 693; Night of the Wehrmacht Zombies* **1981 (R)** WWII soldiers with eating disorders shuffle through 88 minutes of gratuitous gore, while pursued by porn star cum intelligence agent. From the director of "Bloodsucking Freaks." **88m/C VHS, DVD.** James Gillis, Ryan Hilliard, Samantha Grey, Joel M. Reed; *D:* Joel M. Reed; *W:* Joel M. Reed.

Night on Earth **1991 (R)** Jarmusch's "road" movie comprises five different stories taking place on the same night in five different cities—Los Angeles, New York, Paris, Rome, and Helsinki—between cabbies and their passengers. As with any anthology some stories work better than others but all have their moments in this ambitious film with its outstanding international cast. Subtitled in English for the three foreign segments. **125m/C VHS.** Winona Ryder, Gena Rowlands, Giancarlo Esposito, Armin Mueller-Stahl, Rosie Perez, Beatrice Dalle, Roberto Benigni, Paolo Bonacelli, Matti Pellonpaa, Kari Vaananen, Sakari Kuosmanen, Tomi Salmela, Lisanne Falk, Isaach de Bankole, Alan Randolph Scott, Anthony Portillo, Richard Boes, Pascal Nzonzi, Emile Abossolo-M'Bo; *D:* Jim Jarmusch; *W:* Jim Jarmusch; *C:* Frederick Elmes; *M:* Tom Waits, Kathleen Brennan. Ind. Spirit '93: Cinematog.

Night Orchid **1997 (R)** Filmmaker Mark Atkins heads for Stephen King territory with the story of a young psychic (Paris) who arrives in a rural hamlet and has visions of murders. For a low-budget video premiere, this one looks very good. It's made with a degree of style and originality. Fans have seen worse. **93m/C DVD.** Dale Paris, Alyssa Simon, Mary Ellen O'Brien; *D:* Mark Atkins; *C:* Paul Atkins; *M:* C.C. Adcock.

Night Partners ½ **1983** Bored housewives assist the police to patrol the streets after the kids have gone to bed. Originally a TV pilot, but the script doesn't hold water. **100m/C VHS.** Yvette Mimieux, Diana Canova, Arlen Dean Snyder, M. Emmet Walsh, Patricia (Patti) Davis, Larry Linville; *D:* Noel Nosseck. **TV**

Night Passage ½ **1957** Stewart is Grant McLaine, an ex-lawman hired to protect a railroad's payroll from a band of outlaws who've heisted previous attempts to get the payroll through. Unbeknownst to Grant, the gang is led by his brother (Murphy), who's known as the "Utica Kid." Eventually Grant and the Kid will have to have a showdown, unless Grant can convince him to go straight. Anthony Mann was set to direct, at Stewart's request, but declined, damaging his relationship with Stewart. Fans of the stars and the genre will enjoy this solid outing, but will also wonder how much better it could've been with Mann at the helm. Stewart plays accordian and sings two songs. **90m/C DVD.** James Stewart, Audie Murphy, Dan Duryea, Dianne Foster, Elaine Stewart, Brandon de Wilde, Jay C. Flippen, Herbert Anderson, Robert J. Wilke, Hugh Beaumont, Jack Elam, Tommy Cook, Paul Fix, Olive Carey, James Flavin, Donald Curtis, Ellen Corby; *D:* James Neilson; *W:* Borden Chase; *C:* William H. Daniels; *M:* Dimitri Tiomkin.

The Night Patrol ½ **1926** Talmadge is a cop who winds up arresting his girlfriend's brother for murder. Convinced the boy is innocent, Talmadge disguises himself in order to infiltrate the gang he thinks is actually responsible for the crime. Lots of derring-do and a last-minute rescue from the electric chair. **53m/B VHS.** Richard Talmadge, Mary Carr, Rose Blossom, Josef Swickard, Gardner James; *D:* Noel Mason Smith.

Night Patrol **WOOF! 1985 (R)** The streets of Hollywood will never be the same after the night patrol runs amuck in the town. Crude imitation of "Police Academy." **87m/C VHS, DVD.** Linda Blair, Pat Paulsen, Jaye P. Morgan, Jack Riley, Murray Langston, Billy Barty, Noriyuki "Pat" Morita, Sydney Lassick, Andrew (Dice Clay) Silverstein; *D:* Jackie Kong; *C:* Hanania Baer. Golden Raspberries '85: Worst Actress (Blair).

The Night Porter *Il Portiere de Notte* **1974 (R)** Max, an ex-SS concentration camp officer, unexpectedly meets his former lover-victim at the Viennese hotel where he works as the night porter. After they get reacquainted, the couple must hide from the porter's ex-Nazi friends who want the women dead because they fear she will disclose their past. A sado-masochistic voyage not for the faint-hearted. **115m/C VHS, DVD.** *IT* Dirk Bogarde, Charlotte Rampling, Phillippe LeRoy, Gabriele Ferzetti, Isa Miranda; *D:* Liliana Cavani; *W:* Liliana Cavani; *C:* Alfio Contini; *M:* Daniele Paris.

Night Rhythms ½ **1992 (R)** Nick West is a radio talk show host with a sexy voice that causes his women listeners to reveal their most intimate fantasies and problems to him on the air. When one listener goes too far, it's murder, and Nick must work to prove his innocence in the crime if he intends to save his career—and his life. Also available in an unrated version. **99m/C VHS.** Martin Hewitt, Delia Sheppard, David Carradine, Terry Tweed, Sam Jones, Deborah Driggs, Julie Strain; *D:* Alexander Gregory (Gregory Dark) Hippolyte.

Night Ride Home ½ **1999** Nora Mahler (DeMornay) loves running the family ranch with her teenaged children Clea (Birch) and Simon (Brower) and her somewhat indifferent husband, Neil (Carradine). Then Simon is killed in a riding accident and Nora falls apart. Neil thinks the family needs to make a fresh start but Nora's too shattered to make decisions until her mother, Maggie (Burstyn), comes to visit and help her daughter cope with the family's tragedy—and failing marriage. **94m/C VHS.** Rebecca De Mornay, Keith Carradine, Ellen Burstyn, Thora Birch, Lynne Thigpen, Jordan Brower; *D:* Glenn Jordan. **TV**

Night Rider **1932** A cowboy posing as a gunman ends a trail of murder and violence in a small western town. **54m/B VHS.** Elinor Fair, Julian Rivero, Harry Carey Sr., George "Gabby" Hayes; *D:* William Nigh; *W:* Harry Fraser; *C:* James Diamond.

Night Riders of Montana **1950** A state ranger helps a group of ranchers to fight off a band of rustlers. **60m/B VHS.** Roy Barcroft, Claudia Barrett, Arthur Space, Chubby Johnson, Allan "Rocky" Lane; *D:* Fred Brannon; *W:* M. Coates Webster; *C:* John MacBurnie; *M:* Stanley Wilson.

Night Ripper **1986** A psychopathic killer stalks high fashion models and kills them by carving them up. Lots of violence. **88m/C VHS.** James Hansen, April Anne, Larry Thomas; *D:* Jeff Hathcock.

Night School *Terror Eyes* **1981 (R)** A police detective must find out who has been decapitating the women attending night school at Wendell College. Ward's first film. **89m/C VHS.** Leonard Mann, Rachel Ward, Drew Snyder, Joseph R. Sicari, Nicholas Cairis, Bill McCann, Margo Skinner; *D:* Ken Hughes; *W:* Ruth Avergon; *C:* Mark Irwin; *M:* Brad Fiedel.

Night Screams **1987** Violent scaremonger about two escaped convicts who crash a high school house party. Kids and convicts start getting killed, one by one. **85m/C VHS, DVD.** Joe Manno, Ron Thomas, Randy Lundsford, Megan Wyss; *D:* Allen Plone.

Night Shade **1997 (R)** Recent widower Scott Travers (Abell) is still grieving over the death of his wife, although his friends are persistent that he should get out and mingle. So he goes to a club and notices one of the dancers looks very familiar—yep, it's the missus, and she's only kinda dead: she's become a vampire. **90m/C VHS.** Tim Abell, Tane McClure, Teresa Langley; *D:* Fred Olen Ray; *W:* Sean O'Bannon; *C:* James Lawrence Spencer.

Night Shadow **1990 (R)** A woman, returning home after being away for years, picks up a hitchhiker. Soon after her arrival, terrible serial killings begin, and only she has the nerve to track down the killer. **90m/C VHS, DVD.** Brenda Vance, Dana Chan, Tom Boylan; *D:* Randolph Cohlan; *W:* Randolph Cohlan.

Night Shift **1982 (R)** Two morgue attendants, dull Winkler and manic Keaton, decide to spice up their latenight shift by running a call-girl service on the side. Keaton turns in a fine performance in his film debut, and Howard's sure-handed direction almost overcomes the silly premise. Watch closely for Costner in the morgue frat party scene. **106m/C VHS, DVD.** Henry Winkler, Michael Keaton, Shelley Long, Kevin Costner, Pat Corley, Bobby DiCicco, Nita Talbot, Richard Belzer, Shannen Doherty, Clint Howard, Joe Spinell; *D:* Ron Howard; *W:* Babaloo Mandel, Lowell Ganz; *C:* James A. Crabe; *M:* Burt Bacharach; *V:* Vincent Schiavelli.

Night Siege Project: Shadowchaser 2 ½ *Project Shadowchaser 2* **1994 (R)** Smooth actioner finds a terrorist android taking over a nuclear arsenal and threatening to make Washington, D.C. a mushroom cloud. Naturally, there's a hero (and a heroine) to take care of the evildoers. **97m/C VHS, DVD.** Bryan Genesse, Frank Zagarino, Beth Toussaint; *D:* John Eyres; *W:* Nick Davis; *M:* Stephen (Steve) Edwards.

Night Skies **2007 (R)** Allegedly based on a UFO incident reported in Arizona in 1997, this silly low-budget sci-fier is a yawn. Friends in an RV get in a wreck after staring at strange lights in the sky, which then leads to alien abductions. **84m/C DVD.** Jason Connery, A.J. Cook, Gwendoline Yeo, Ashley Peldon, George Stults, Joe Sikora, Michael Dorn; *D:* Roy Knyrim; *W:* Eric Miller; *C:* Steve Adcock; *M:* Paul D'Amou, Brad Laner.

Night Slasher *Night After Night After Night* **1969** A madman enjoys spilling the innards of London prostitutes with his dagger. **87m/C VHS.** Justine Lord, Gilbert Wynne, Jack May, Linda Marlowe; *D:* Lindsay Shonteff; *W:* Dail Ambler; *C:* Douglas Hill; *M:* Douglas Gamley.

Night Stage to Galveston ½ **1952** Autry leads his Texas Rangers on a mission to uncover corruption in the Texas State Police during the turbulent post-Civil War era. **61m/B VHS.** Gene Autry, Pat Buttram, Virginia Huston, Thurston Hall; *D:* George Archainbaud.

The Night Stalker ½ **1971** Pilot movie for the TV series finds veteran reporter Carl Kolchak (McGavin) investigating a series of murders that lead him to believe a modern-day vampire is stalking the streets of Vegas. **73m/C VHS, DVD.** Darren McGavin, Carol Lynley, Simon Oakland, Ralph Meeker, Claude Akins, Kent Smith, Larry Linville, Barry Atwater; *D:* John Llewellyn Moxey; *W:* Richard Matheson; *M:* Robert Cobert. **TV**

Night Stalker **1987 (R)** A bloodthirsty serial killer is tracked by a detective through the streets in New York. The usual rigamarole of fisticuffes, gunplay, and car chases ensure. Impressive acting from Napier raises the film from the run-of-the-mill. **91m/C VHS, DVD.** Charles Napier, John Goff, Robert Viharo, Robert Z'Dar, Joseph Gian, Gary Crosby, Joan Chen, Michelle Reese; *D:* Max Cleven; *C:* Don Burgess.

The Night Strangler ½ **1972** Still creepy sequel to 1971's "The Night Stalker" finds reporter Carl Kolchak (McGavin) investigating of series of murders with female victims. He discovers that similar crimes have been committed in Seattle every 21 years for more than a century and the killer's description is always the same. **90m/C VHS, DVD.** Darren McGavin, Richard Anderson, Simon Oakland, Wally Cox, Margaret Hamilton, John Carradine, Al Lewis; *D:* Dan Curtis; *W:* Richard Matheson; *M:* Robert Cobert. **TV**

Night Sun ½ *Il Sole Anche di Notte; Sunshine Even by Night* **1990** Sergio (Sands) is an 18th-century nobleman who discovers his fiance was once the king's mistress. He abandons worldly pursuits to become a monk and find some peace but temptation follow him. Based on the Tolstoy story "Father Sergius." Sands' voice was dubbed by Italian actor Giancarlo Giannini. Italian with subtitles. **112m/C VHS, DVD.** *IT* Julian Sands, Charlotte Gainsbourg, Massimo Bonetti, Margarita Lozano, Ruediger Vogler; *D:* Paolo Taviani, Vittorio Taviani; *W:* Tonino Guerra, Paolo Taviani, Vittorio Taviani; *C:* Giuseppe Lanci; *M:* Nicola Piovani.

Night Terror **1976** Everyone's after a hausfrau who saw a highway patrolman murdered on an expressway...including the psychotic murderer. Pretty standard fare. **73m/C VHS.** Valerie Harper, Richard Romanus, Michael (Lawrence) Tolan, Beatrice Manley, John Quade, Quinn Cummings, Nicholas Pryor; *D:* E.W. Swackhamer. **TV**

Night Terror **1989** A man wakes up from a nightmare only to find that his terrors are still present. **90m/C VHS.** Lloyd B. Mote, Jeff Keel, Guy Ecker, Jon Hoffman, Michael Coopet; *D:* Michael Weaver, Paul Howard.

The Night the City Screamed ½ **1980 (PG)** It's the hottest day of the year, the city experiences a massive blackout, and nighttime brings out less-than-noble emotions amongst the citizenry. **96m/C VHS.** Raymond Burr, Georg Stanford Brown, Linda Purl, Robert Culp, Clifton Davis, David Cassidy, George DiCenzo, Gary Frank, Don Meredith, Shelley Smith, Vic Tayback, Dick Anthony Williams; *D:* Harry Falk; *W:* Larry Brody. **TV**

The Night the Lights Went Out in Georgia **1981 (PG)** Loosely based on the popular hit song, the film follows a brother and sister as they try to cash in on the country music scene in Nashville. McNichol is engaging. **112m/C VHS, DVD.** Kristy McNichol, Dennis Quaid, Mark Hamill, Don Stroud; *D:* Ronald F. Maxwell; *W:* Bob Bonney; *C:* Bill Butler; *M:* David Shire.

The Night They Raided Minsky's *The Night They Invented Striptease* **1969 (PG)** Chaotic but interesting period comedy about a young Amish girl who leaves her tyrannical father to come to New York City in the 1920s. She winds up at Minsky's Burlesque and accidentally invents the striptease. Lahr's last performance—he died during filming. ♫ The Night They Raided Minsky's; Take Ten Terrific Girls But Only 9 Costumes; How I Love Her; Perfect Gentleman; You Rat, You; Penny Arcade; Wait For Me. **97m/C VHS.** Jason Robards Jr., Britt Ekland, Elliott Gould, Bert Lahr, Norman Wisdom, Denholm Elliott; *D:* William Friedkin; *W:* Norman Lear, Arnold Schulman.

The Night They Robbed Big Bertha's **1975 (R)** Bungling burglar attempts to knock off Big Bertha's massage parlor. **87m/C VHS.** Robert Nichols, Doug Hale, Gary Allen, Hetty Galen; *D:* Peter Kares; *W:* Albert T. Viola.

The Night They Saved Christmas ½ **1987** A Christmas special in which Santa's North Pole headquarters are endangered by the progress of an expanding oil company. Will the attempts of three children be enough to save the day? **94m/C VHS.** Art Carney, Jaclyn Smith, Paul Williams, Paul LeMat; *D:* Jackie Cooper.

Night Tide ½ **1963** Hopper in another off the wall character study, this time as a lonely sailor. He falls for a mermaid (Lawson) who works at the dock. She may be a descendent of the man-killing Sirens. Interesting and different little love story, sometimes advertised as horror, which it is not. **84m/B VHS, DVD.** Dennis Hopper, Gavin Muir, Linda Lawson, Luana Anders, Marjorie Eaton, Tom Dillon, Bruno VeSota; *D:* Curtis Harrington; *W:* Curtis Harrington; *C:* Vilis Lapenieks; *M:* David Raksin.

Night Time in Nevada ½ **1948** Young woman heads West to claim $50,000 trust left by dear old dad, but his crooked lawyer and associate have their hands in the pot. Cowboy Roy rides horse and flexes dimples while helping helpless girl. **67m/B VHS, DVD.** Roy Rogers, Adele Mara, Andy Devine, Grant Withers, Joseph Crehan; ***D:*** William Witney.

A Night to Remember **1942** A murder-mystery writer's wife convinces him to move to a new apartment because she thinks the change might help him finish a novel he started long ago. When they find a dead body behind their new building, they try their hands at sleuthing. A clever and witty mystery, indeed, supported by likeable performances. **91m/B VHS.** Loretta Young, Brian Aherne, Sidney Toler, Gale Sondergaard, William Wright, Donald MacBride, Blanche Yurka; ***D:*** Richard Wallace.

A Night to Remember **1958** Gripping tale of the voyage of the Titanic with an interesting account of action in the face of danger and courage amid despair. Large cast is effectively used. Adapted by Eric Ambler from the book by Walter Lord. **119m/B VHS, DVD.** Kenneth More, David McCallum, Anthony Bushell, Honor Blackman, Michael Goodliffe, George Rose, Laurence Naismith, Frank Lawton, Alec McCowen, Jill Dixon, John Cairney, Joseph Tomelty, Jack Watling, Richard Clarke, Ralph Michael, Kenneth Griffith; ***D:*** Roy Ward Baker; ***W:*** Eric Ambler; ***C:*** Geoffrey Unsworth. Golden Globes '59: Foreign Film.

Night Train ½ **2009 (R)** On Christmas Eve, travelers Chloe and Peter discover a dead body in a train compartment and also find a fortune in diamonds in a wooden box. They convince conductor Miles that they should dump the body and split the gems three ways—until greed gets the better of them. A supernatural element about the mysterious nature of the box itself prove problematic in what seems to be a more straightforward suspenser. (And why is O'Brien in drag?) **91m/C DVD.** Danny Glover, Leelee Sobieski, Steve Zahn, Richard O'Brien; ***D:*** Brian King; ***W:*** Brian King; ***C:*** Christopher Popp; ***M:*** Henning Lohner. **VIDEO**

Night Train Murders WOOF! *L'Ultimo Treno della Notte; The Last Train of the Night* **1975** If you're a fan of the Italian giallo genre then this is the horror for you—if you're not, then ick, ick, ick, ick, ick. Lisa (D'Angelo) and Margaret (Miracle) are taking the train from Germany to Italy to visit Lisa's family. On board, they encounter a sicko trio (DeGrassi, Bucci, Meril) who torture, rape, and eventually kill the girls. The sickos then wind up at the home of Lisa's parents, who enact an equally violent revenge when they discover who their visitors are. The only comic relief is the completely ridiculous English dubbing of the Italian dialogue. **94m/C DVD.** *IT* Flavio Bucci, Macha Meril, Irene Miracle, Enrico Maria Salerno, Marina Berti, Gianfranco de Grassi, Laura D'Angelo; ***D:*** Aldo Lado; ***W:*** Aldo Lado, Renato Izzo; ***C:*** Gabor Pogany; ***M:*** Ennio Morricone.

The Night Train to Kathmandu **1988** A young girl accompanies her parents on a research expedition to Nepal, where her head is turned by an exotically handsome young Sherpa. Old story without much help from actors or director. **102m/C VHS.** Milla Jovovich, Pernell Roberts, Eddie Castrodad; ***D:*** Robert Wiemer. **CABLE**

Night Train to Munich *Night Train; Gestapo* **1940** There's Nazi intrigue galore aboard a big train when a scientist's daughter joins allied intelligence agents in retrieving some secret documents. From the book "Report on a Fugitive" by Gordon Wellesley. **93m/B VHS, DVD.** *GB* Margaret Lockwood, Rex Harrison, Paul Henreid, Basil Radford, Naunton Wayne, James Harcourt, Felix Aylmer, Roland Culver, Raymond Huntley, Austin Trevor, Kenneth Kent, C.V. France, Frederick Valk, Morland Graham, Wally Patch, Irene Handl, Albert Lieven, David Horne; ***D:*** Carol Reed; ***W:*** Frank Launder, Sidney Gilliat; ***C:*** Otto Kanturek.

Night Train to Terror WOOF! *Shiver* **1984 (R)** Strange things start happening on the train where a rock band makes its last appearance. Clips from other horror flicks were pieced together to make this film that's so bad it's almost good. **98m/C VHS, DVD.** John Phillip Law, Cameron Mitchell, Marc Lawrence, Charles Moll, Ferdinand "Ferdy" Mayne; ***D:*** Jay Schlossberg-Cohen; ***W:*** Philip Yordan.

Night Train to Venice ½ **1993 (R)** Martin (Grant) is aboard the Orient Express on his way to Venice to deliver his book about the rise of neo-Nazism. He meets a mystery man (McDowell) and an actress (Welch) with ties to a neo-Nazi group, who also happen to be aboard the train and anxious to stop Martin from delivering his expose. Extended dream sequences and flashbacks tend to stop the story cold but Grant is a draw (and probably the only reason this mishmash has been released to video). **98m/C VHS.** Hugh Grant, Malcolm McDowell, Tahnee Welch, Kristina Soderbaum; ***D:*** Carlo U. Quinterio; ***W:*** Leo Tichat, Toni Hirtreiter; ***M:*** Alexander Bubenheim.

Night Vision **1987** A young writer in the big city is given a video monitor by a street thief which is equipped with some remarkable features, including the ability to present scenes of future murders and demon worship. **102m/C VHS.** Ellie Martins, Stacy Carson, Shirley Ross, Tony Carpenter; ***D:*** Michael Krueger.

Night Vision **1997 (R)** Burned-out detective Dak Smith (Williamson) has been demoted to motorcycle cop on the graveyard shift. But he unexpectedly becomes involved with the case of a serial killer who likes to stalk and videotape his victims. Now Dak and his new partner Kristen O'Conner (Rothrock) are working to capture this psychopath. **95m/C VHS, DVD.** Fred Williamson, Cynthia Rothrock, Robert Forster, Frank Pesce, Willie Gault, Amanda Welles, Nina Richardson; ***D:*** Gil Bettman; ***W:*** Michael Thomas Montgomery; ***C:*** Trey Smith. **VIDEO**

The Night Visitor ½ **1970 (PG)** A man in a prison for the criminally insane seeks violent vengeance on those he believes have set him up. Heavily detailed, slow moving. Ullman and von Sydow can do better. **106m/C VHS, DVD.** *GB DK* Max von Sydow, Liv Ullmann, Trevor Howard, Per Oscarsson, Andrew Keir; ***D:*** Laszlo Benedek; ***M:*** Henry Mancini.

Night Visitor *Never Cry Devil* **1989 (R)** A retired police detective teams up with a teenage peeping tom to disclose the identity of a satanic serial killer. The killer, of course, is one of the youth's teachers. **95m/C VHS, DVD.** Derek Rydall, Shannon Tweed, Elliott Gould, Allen (Goorwitz) Garfield, Michael J. Pollard, Richard Roundtree, Henry Gibson; ***D:*** Rupert Hitzig; ***W:*** Randal Viscovich.

The Night Walker ½ **1964** Stanwyck is always worth watching and she has the best moments in this psycho-thriller which suffers from a low-budget and confused script. The basic story has Stanwyck as a rich widow with a recurring nightmare featuring a faceless lover. There's also a too-helpful lawyer (Taylor), a suspicious private detective (Bochner)—and maybe her husband isn't so dead after all. Taylor and Stanwyck, who had once been married, worked together for the first time in 27 years. **86m/B VHS.** Barbara Stanwyck, Robert Taylor, Lloyd Bochner, Hayden Rorke, Judith Meredith, Rochelle Hudson; ***D:*** William Castle; ***W:*** Robert Bloch.

Night Warning *Nightmare Maker; Butcher Baker (Nightmare Maker)* **1982 (R)** A slasher gorefest redeemed by Tyrrell's go-for-broke performance. She plays a sexually repressed aunt who makes up for her problems by going on murderous rampages. Hide the kitchen knives! **96m/C VHS.** Bo Svenson, Jimmy (James Vincent) McNichol, Susan Tyrrell, Julia Duffy; ***D:*** William Asher; ***W:*** Stephen Breimer.

Night Wars ½ **1988** Two ex-POWs who are plagued by their memories turn to dream therapy to relive their escape. Eventually, they rescue a buddy they left behind. **90m/C VHS.** Dan Haggerty, Brian O'Connor, Cameron Smith; ***D:*** David A. Prior.

Night Watch ½ *Le Trou; Il Buco* **1972** A woman recovering from a nervous breakdown witnesses a murder, but no one will believe her. **100m/C VHS.** *GB* Elizabeth Taylor, Laurence Harvey, Billie Whitelaw; ***D:*** Brian G. Hutton; ***C:*** Billy Williams.

Night Watch *Nochnoi Dozor* **2004 (R)** Russian take on the battle between the forces of good and evil, set in present-day Moscow. A prologue establishes that a diplomatic truce exists between the two: the Night Watch keeps a check on the dark side and the Day Watch on the light. But after centuries, a prophecy about the Great Other, who will tip the balance, seems about to come true. Somewhat chaotic and convoluted but still intense. The first in a trilogy based on the novels of co-writer Lukyanenko. Russian with subtitles. **114m/C DVD.** *RU* Vladimir Menshov, Viktor Verzhbitsky, Konstantin Khabensky, Maria Poroshina, Galina Tyunina, Gosha Kytsenko, Alexsei Chadov, Zhanna Friske, Ilya Larutenko, Rimma Markova, Maria Mironova, Alexei Maklakov, Anna Dubrovskaya, Aleksandr Samojlenko, Anna Slyusaryova, Dmitry Martynov; ***D:*** Timur Bekmambetov; ***W:*** Timur Bekmambetov, Sergei Lukyanenko; ***C:*** Sergei Trofimov; ***M:*** Yuri Potyeyenko, Valera Viktorov, Mukstar Mirzakeev.

The Night Watchman **2002** Decent yet flawed thriller that borrows a bit too much from its acknowledged influences ("Magnolia," "American Beauty," and "Talk Radio"). Strong characterization makes the story of a burned-out, bitter talk show host struggling to come to terms with his failures and save a suicidal caller during his last broadcast a cut above other thrillers. Cheap sets and not-so-adequate performances keep it from becoming anything more. Canadian music video director Eldridge uses very little visual style, which heightens the bare-bones look of the film, as well as the nostalgia for the above mentioned influences. **103m/C VHS.** Christopher Healey, Cory Diamond; ***D:*** Scott Eldridge; ***W:*** Jeff Caulfield. **VIDEO**

The Night We Called It a Day ½ *All the Way* **2003** Taken-from-reality tale finds Frank Sinatra (Hopper) in Australia doing a tour in 1974 with struggling producer Rod Blue (Edgerton). Ol' Blue Eyes barely gets off the airplane before mouthing off at reporter Hilary Hunter (de Rossi) when asked some too-personal questions. The resulting countrywide brouhaha keeps him captive in his hotel as unions protest outside and demand that he apologize. Hopper is a natural at doing Sinatra, though Tom Burlinson—often a Sinatra impersonator—performed the vocals. **97m/C VHS, DVD.** *AU US* Dennis Hopper, Melanie Griffith, Portia de Rossi, Joel Edgerton, Rose Byrne, David Hemmings, David Field, Nicholas Hope; ***D:*** Paul Goldman; ***W:*** Peter Clifton, Michael Thomas; ***C:*** Danny Ruhlmann; ***M:*** Rupert Gregson-Williams. **VIDEO**

The Night We Never Met ½ **1993 (R)** Three yuppies bring different visions of romance and a case of mistaken identity to a time-share apartment in New York's Greenwich Village. Sam (Broderick) needs a quiet space to get over being dumped by a flaky performance artist (Tripplehorn). Ellen (Sciorra) is looking for space to paint away from the confines of her thick-headed spouse (Mantell). Brian, the organizer of the living arrangement, wants a space where he can be one of the boys and escape from his cloying fiancee (Bateman). Fairly predictable but enjoyable romantic comedy. **98m/C VHS.** Matthew Broderick, Jeanne Tripplehorn, Kevin Anderson, Justine Bateman, Annabella Sciorra, Christine Baranski, Doris Roberts, Dominic Chianese, Michael Mantell, Tim Guinee, Greg Germann, Dana Wheeler-Nicholson, Louise Lasser, Billy Campbell, Ranjit (Chaudry) Chowdhry, Garry Shandling, Katharine Houghton, Brooke Smith, Paul Guilfoyle, Lewis Black; ***D:*** Warren Leight; ***W:*** Warren Leight; ***M:*** Evan Lurie.

Night Zoo *Un Zoo, La Nuit* **1987** A confusing story about a father/son reconciliation and the lurid underworld of drugs and sex in Montreal. The graphic sex and violence undermines the sensitive aspects of the film. **115m/C VHS.** *CA* Gilles Maheu, Roger Le Bel, Lynne Adams, Germain Houde; ***D:*** Jean-Claude Lauzon. Genie '88: Actor (Le Bel), Director (Lauzon), Film, Support. Actor (Houde).

Nightbreaker **1989** Revelation of the U.S. government's deliberate exposure of servicemen to atomic bomb tests and the resulting radiation, in order to observe the effects on humans. Sheen and his son, Estevez, portray a U.S. doctor in the 1980s and the 1950s, respectively. **100m/C VHS.** Martin Sheen, Emilio Estevez, Lea Thompson, Melinda Dillon, Nicholas Pryor, Joe Pantoliano; ***D:*** Peter Markle; ***W:*** T.S. Cook; ***M:*** Peter Bernstein.

Nightbreed ½ **1990 (R)** A teenager flees a chaotic past to slowly become a member of a bizarre race of demons that live in a huge, abandoned Canadian graveyard; a place where every sin is forgiven. Based on Barker's novel "Cabal," and appropriately gross, nonsensical and strange. Good special effects almost save this one. **102m/C VHS, DVD.** *CA* Craig Sheffer, Anne Bobby, David Cronenberg, Charles Haid; ***D:*** Clive Barker; ***W:*** Clive Barker; ***C:*** Robin Vidgeon; ***M:*** Danny Elfman.

The Nightcomers **1972 (R)** A pretend "prequel" to Henry James's "The Turn of the Screw," wherein an Irish gardener trysts with the nanny of two watchful children who believe that lovers unite in death. Don't be fooled: stick to the original. **96m/C VHS.** *GB* Marlon Brando, Stephanie Beacham, Thora Hird, Harry Andrews, Christopher Ellis, Verna Harvey, Anna Palk; ***D:*** Michael Winner; ***W:*** Michael Hastings; ***C:*** Robert Paynter; ***M:*** Jerry Fielding.

Nightfall **1956** Ray, accused of a crime he didn't commit, is forced to flee from both the law and the underworld. Classic example of film noir, brilliantly filmed by Tourneur. **78m/B VHS.** Aldo Ray, Brian Keith, Anne Bancroft, Jocelyn Brando, James Gregory, Frank Albertson; ***D:*** Jacques Tourneur; ***W:*** Stirling Silliphant.

Nightfall **1988 (PG-13)** Adaptation of the classic Isaac Asimov short story. A planet that has two suns (and therefore no night) experiences an eclipse and its inhabitants go mad. **87m/C VHS, DVD.** David Birney, Sarah Douglas, Alexis Kanner, Andra Millian; ***D:*** Paul Mayersberg; ***C:*** Darius Wolski. **TV**

Nightflyers ½ **1987 (R)** Aboard a weathered space freighter, the crew experience a series of deadly accidents caused by an unknown evil presence. From a novella by George R.R. Martin; T.C. Blake is better known as Robert Collector. **88m/C VHS.** Michael Praed, Michael Des Barres, Catherine Mary Stewart, John Standing, Lisa Blount; ***D:*** T.C. Blake.

Nightforce **1986 (R)** Five buddies plunge into Central American jungles to rescue a young girl held by terrorists. **87m/C VHS.** Linda Blair, James Van Patten, Chad McQueen, Richard Lynch, Cameron Mitchell; ***D:*** Lawrence Foldes.

Nighthawks **1978** Jim (Robertson) is a geography teacher in London who lives a closeted life. His quiet daily routine is separate from his cruising of the city's gay pleasure spots until his two worlds converge when he's confronted by his students. **113m/C VHS, DVD.** *GB* Ken Robertson; ***D:*** Ron Peck; ***W:*** Ron Peck, Paul Hallam; ***C:*** Johanna Davis; ***M:*** David Graham Ellis.

Nighthawks ½ **1981 (R)** NYC cops scour Manhattan to hunt down an international terrorist on the loose. They race from disco to subway to an airborne tramway. Exciting and well paced. Hauer's American film debut. **100m/C VHS, DVD.** Robert Pugh, Sylvester Stallone, Billy Dee Williams, Rutger Hauer, Lindsay Wagner, Nigel Davenport, Persis Khambatta, Catherine Mary Stewart, Joe Spinell; ***D:*** Bruce Malmuth; ***W:*** David Shaber; ***C:*** James A. Contner; ***M:*** Keith Emerson.

The Nightingale **1983** From "Faerie Tale Theatre" comes the story of an Emperor who discovers the value of true friendship and loyalty from his palace kitchen maid who gives him a nightingale. **60m/C VHS, DVD.** Mick Jagger, Barbara Hershey, Bud Cort, Mako; ***D:*** Ivan Passer. **CABLE**

Nightjohn ½ **1996 (PG-13)** Nightjohn (Lumbly) is the new slave purchased by Southern plantation owner Clel Walker (Bridges). He moves into the cabin shared by 12-year-old Sarny (Jones) and Delie (Toussaint). When Sarny finds out that Nightjohn can read and write (illegal for slaves), she's determined to learn from him. And with her new knowledge, Sarny looks for ways to help her fellow slaves. Based on Gary Paulsen's 1993 novel; filmed on location at Rip Raps Plantation in Sumter, South Carolina. **96m/C VHS, DVD.** Carl Lumbly, Allison Jones, Beau Bridges, Lorraine Toussaint, Bill Cobbs, Kathleen York, Gabriel Casseus, Tom Nowicki, Monica Ford, Joel Thomas Traywick; ***D:*** Charles Burnett; ***W:*** Bill Cain; ***C:*** Elliot Davis; ***M:*** Stephen James Taylor. **CABLE**

Nightkill 1/2 **1980 (R)** Simple love affair turns into a deadly game of cat and mouse when a bored wife plots to do away with her wealthy, powerful husband with the aid of her attractive lover. Mitchum is the reluctant investigator pulled into the game. **104m/C VHS.** Jaclyn Smith, Mike Connors, James Franciscus, Robert Mitchum, Sybil Danning; ***D:*** Ted Post.

Nightlife 1/2 **1990** An ancient vampiress who rises from the dead spends her time haunting a blood clinic, where the Jewish hematologist starts to fall for her. **93m/C VHS.** Ben Cross, Maryam D'Abo, Keith Szarabajka, Jesse Corti, Oliver Clark, Glenn Shadix, Camille Saviola; ***D:*** Daniel Taplitz. **CABLE**

The Nightman **1993 (R)** Ex-soldier Marcoux becomes the night manager of a failing southern resort, run by sexy, and lonely, Kerns. They begin an affair, which turns sour when Robertson, Kerns's teenaged daughter, also falls for the stud. Then mom is murdered and Marcoux goes to prison. But 18 years later Robertson's past comes back to haunt her. Just what did happen all those years ago? Made-for-TV thriller with additional footage. **96m/C VHS, DVD.** Ted Marcoux, Jenny Robertson, Joanna Kerns; ***D:*** Charles Haid; ***W:*** James Poe; ***M:*** Gary Chang. **TV**

Nightmare 1/2 **1963** As a child, Janet sees her insane mother stab her father to death. Left in the care of two guardians, the now-grown Janet has recurring nightmares and fears she's inherited her mother's madness. Routine, with red herrings galore. **83m/B VHS, DVD.** *GB* Jennie Linden, David Knight, Moira Redmond, Brenda Bruce; ***D:*** Freddie Francis; ***W:*** Jimmy Sangster; ***C:*** John Wilcox; ***M:*** Don Banks.

Nightmare WOOF! *Blood Splash; Nightmare in a Damaged Brain* **1982 (R)** Boring splatterthon has a young boy hacking his father and his aggressive mistress to pieces when he discovers them in bed. He grows up to be a psycho who continues along the same lines. Humorless and dreadful, the original ads claimed Tom Savini did the special effects. He had nothing to do with it. **97m/C VHS.** Baird Stafford, Sharon Smith, C.J. Cooke, Mik Cribben, Kathleen Ferguson, Danny Ronan; ***D:*** Romano Scavolini; ***W:*** Romano Scavolini; ***C:*** Gianni Fiore; ***M:*** Jack Eric Williams.

Nightmare **1991 (PG-13)** Single mom Linda Hemmings (Principal) takes matters into her own hands when her daughter Dana (Harris) is kidnapped. Though Dana escapes and her assailant, Edward Ryter (Banks), is arrested, he's soon released and threatening Dana to prevent her testifying. So mom teams up with police detective Jake Wilman (Sorvino) to get the goods on the psycho before he can do further harm. **84m/C VHS, DVD.** Victoria Principal, Jonathan Banks, Paul Sorvino, Danielle Harris; ***D:*** John Pasquin; ***W:*** Rich Husky; ***C:*** Denis Lewiston; ***M:*** Dana Kaproff.

Nightmare 1/2 *Gawi; Gawi: The Nightmare; Horror Game Movie* **2000** Somewhere between an American slasher movie and a Japanese ghost story: a young woman named Seon-ae returns to Korea after a long absence, and she learns from a girlfriend that a dead pal (another woman, why are Asian ghosts always women?) has returned from the grave and is killing everyone they know, one by one. Pretty soon Seon-ae gains a female stalker who looks like the aforementioned dead friend as she tries to figure out why everyone is being killed. Pale spooky Asian women and knives abound. **97m/C DVD.** *KN* Gyu-ri Kim, Jun-sang Yu, Ji-won Ha, Jeong-yun Choi, Ji-tae Yu, Jun Jeong, Hye-yeon Jo; ***D:*** Byeong-ki Ahn; ***W:*** Brian O'Hara, Byeong-ki Ahn; ***C:*** Seok-hyeon Lee; ***M:*** Tae-beon Lee.

Nightmare Alley 1/2 **1947** Dark and disturbing noir has Power, in one of his best roles, as con man/carny who learns the secrets of a mentalist act and turns it into fame and fortune. When a femme fatale shrink persuades him to join a scheme to bilk the rich, it leads to a fascinating and precipitous downfall. Power fought to get the film made, and for the chance to play against his matinee idol type. **111m/B DVD.** Tyrone Power, Joan Blondell, Coleen Gray, Helen Walker, Taylor Holmes, Ian Keith, Mike Mazurki; ***D:*** Edmund Goulding; ***W:*** Jules Furthman; ***C:*** Lee Garmes; ***M:*** Cyril Mockridge.

Nightmare at Bittercreek **1991 (PG-13)** Four babes and a tour guide are pursued by psycho gang in the Sierra mountains. Made for TV nightmare in your living room. **92m/C VHS, DVD.** Tom Skerritt, Joanna Cassidy, Lindsay Wagner, Constance McCashin, Janne Mortil; ***D:*** Tim Burstall. **TV**

Nightmare at 43 Hillcrest **1974** A family's life becomes a living hell when the police mistakenly raid their house. Based on a true story. **72m/C VHS.** Jim Hutton, Mariette Hartley; ***D:*** Dan Curtis; ***W:*** William Katz; ***M:*** Robert Cobert.

Nightmare at Noon **1987 (R)** Watered-down thriller about a small desert town beset by violent terrorists (who are really locals gone mad from a chemical experiment dumped into the water system). Only the sheriff's small staff is there to stop them. **96m/C VHS, DVD.** Wings Hauser, George Kennedy, Bo Hopkins, Brion James, Kimberly Beck, Kimberly Ross; ***D:*** Nico Mastorakis.

The Nightmare Before Christmas *Tim Burton's The Nightmare Before Christmas* **1993 (PG)** Back when he was a animator trainee at Disney, Burton came up with this adventurous idea but couldn't get it made; subsequent directorial success brought more clout. Relies on a painstaking stop-motion technique that took more than two years to film and is justifiably amazing. The story revolves around Jack Skellington, the Pumpkin King of the dangerously weird Halloweentown. Suffering from ennui, he accidentally discovers the wonders of Christmastown and decides to kidnap Santa and rule over this peaceable holiday. Fast pace is maintained by the equally breathless score. Not cuddly, best appreciated by those with a feel for the macabre. **75m/C VHS, DVD, UMD.** ***D:*** Henry Selick; ***W:*** Caroline Thompson, Tim Burton, Michael McDowell; ***C:*** Pete Kozachik; ***M:*** Danny Elfman; ***V:*** Danny Elfman, Chris Sarandon, Catherine O'Hara, William Hickey, Ken Page, Ed Ivory, Paul (Pee-wee Herman) Reubens, Glenn Shadix, Greg Proops.

Nightmare Castle *Amanti d'Oltretomba; Night of the Doomed; The Faceless Monsters; Lovers from Beyond the Tomb* **1965** Jealous mad scientist murders his wife and her lover. Then he conducts a bizarre experiment, using the dead couple's blood to rejuvenate an old servant. Not quite satisfied with his revenge, he then seeks to marry his late wife's sister after realizing that she has been left the inheritance. In time, the perturbed ghosts of the late lovers appear and seek revenge. A real nightmare. **90m/B VHS, DVD.** *IT* Barbara Steele, Paul Muller, Helga Line; ***D:*** Allan Grunewald; ***M:*** Ennio Morricone.

Nightmare Detective *Akumu Tantei* **2006** A surprisingly non-offensive and mainstream film from the director of "Tetsuo the Iron Man." An older man sitting in a creepy apartment learns from a younger man named Kagenuma that he's being haunted by the soul of an aborted daughter his wife never told him about. The older man thanks Kagenuma, who leaves what turns out to be a dream for the real world, where the older man is on life support. Eventually he is drawn into a police case where an unknown person appears to be causing sleeping people to kill themselves. The director is a busy guy: he's also the writer and cinematographer, and he plays the main bad guy. **106m/C DVD.** *JP* Ryuhei Matsuda, Mansanobu Ando, Shinya Tsukamoto, Hitomi; ***D:*** Shinya Tsukamoto; ***W:*** Shinya Tsukamoto; ***C:*** Shinya Tsukamoto; ***M:*** Chu Ishikawa, Tadashi Ishikawa.

Nightmare in Badham County *Nightmare* **1976** Two girls get arrested on trumped-up charges in a small backwoods town. They soon discover that the prison farm is a front for a slavery ring. **100m/C VHS.** Deborah Raffin, Lynne Moody, Chuck Connors, Della Reese, Robert Reed, Ralph Bellamy, Tina Louise; ***D:*** John Llewellyn Moxey; ***M:*** Charles Bernstein. **TV**

Nightmare in Blood 1/2 *Horror Convention* **1975** Vampires lurk in San Francisco and wreak havoc on the night life. **90m/C VHS, DVD.** Kerwin Mathews, Jerry Walter, Barrie Youngfellow; ***D:*** John Stanley.

Nightmare in Wax 1/2 *Crimes in the Wax Museum* **1969** After suffering disfigurement in a fight with a studio boss, a former make-up man starts a wax museum. For fun, he injects movie stars with a formula that turns them into statues. **91m/C VHS, DVD.** Cameron Mitchell, Anne Helm; ***D:*** Bud Townsend.

Nightmare Man **2006 (R)** Ellen (Metz) is being haunted by the title character, which resembles an exotic fertility mask she recently purchased. Husband Bill (Szafir) just thinks she's crazy and needs a little stay in the loony bin. As he's driving through the woods, the car runs out of gas, and Bill leaves Ellen alone. Sure enough, she gets attacked by her nightmare demon. Ellen escapes to a nearby cabin where the occupants should never have let a bloody, screaming woman inside. The women seem to spend a lot of time topless or in their underwear and there is a twist ending, but it's still bad. **90m/C DVD.** Tiffany Shepis, Blythe Metz, Hanna Putnam, James Ferris, Jack Sway, Luciano Szafir, Aaron Sherry; ***D:*** Rolfe Kanesky; ***W:*** Rolfe Kanesky; ***C:*** Paul Deng; ***M:*** Christopher Farrell.

A Nightmare on Elm Street 1/2 **1984 (R)** Feverish, genuinely frightening horror film about Freddy Krueger (Englund), a scarred maniac in a fedora and razor-fingered gloves who kills neighborhood teens in their dreams and, subsequently, in reality. Of the children-fight-back genre, in which the lead victim (Langenkamp) ingeniously goes to great lengths to destroy Freddy. In the tradition of "Friday the 13th"'s Jason and "Halloween"'s Michael Myers, "Elm Street" spawned a "Freddy" phenomenon: seven sequels (including the upcoming "Freddy Vs. Jason," linking "Elm Street, Part 8" with "Friday the 13th, Part 10"); a TV series ("Freddy's Nightmares," a horror anthology show hosted by Englund to capitalize on his character); and an army of razor-clawed trick or treaters at Halloween. **92m/C VHS, DVD.** John Saxon, Heather Langenkamp, Ronee Blakley, Robert Englund, Amanda Wyss, Jsu Garcia, Johnny Depp, Charles Fleischer; ***D:*** Wes Craven; ***W:*** Wes Craven; ***C:*** Jacques Haitkin; ***M:*** Charles Bernstein.

A Nightmare on Elm Street **2010** A relaunch of the venerable horror series with Haley taking on the role of serial killer Freddy Krueger. We're certain dumb high schoolers are just waiting to be slaughtered in their dreams. **m/C DVD.** Jackie Earle Haley, Rooney Mara, Kyle Gallner, Thomas Dekker, Kellan Lutz, Katie Cassidy, Connie Britton, Clancy Brown; ***D:*** Samuel Bayer; ***W:*** Wesley Strick; ***C:*** Jeff Cutter; ***M:*** Steve Jablonsky.

A Nightmare on Elm Street 2: Freddy's Revenge 1/2 **1985 (R)** Mediocre sequel to the popular horror film. Freddy, the dream-haunting psychopath with the ginsu knife hands, returns to possess a teenager's body in order to kill again. Nothing new here, however praise is due for the stunning high-tech dream sequence. **87m/C VHS, DVD.** Mark Patton, Hope Lange, Clu Gulager, Robert Englund, Kim Myers, Robert Rusler, Marshall Bell, Sydney Walsh; ***D:*** Jack Sholder; ***W:*** David Chaskin; ***C:*** Jacques Haitkin.

A Nightmare on Elm Street 3: Dream Warriors **1987 (R)** Chapter three in this slice and dice series. Freddy Krueger is at it again, haunting the dreams of unsuspecting suburban teens. Langenkamp, the nightmare-freaked heroine from the first film, returns to counsel the latest victims of Freddy-infested dreams. Noted for the special effects wizardry but little else, Part Three was produced on a $4.5 million shoe string and took in more than $40 million, making it one of the most successful independently produced films in Hollywood. Followed by "A Nightmare on Elm Street 4: Dream Master." **96m/C VHS, DVD.** Patricia Arquette, Robert Englund, Heather Langenkamp, Craig Wasson, Laurence Fishburne, Priscilla Pointer, John Saxon, Brooke Bundy, Jennifer Rubin, Rodney Eastman, Nan Martin, Dick Cavett, Zsa Zsa Gabor; ***D:*** Chuck Russell; ***W:*** Chuck Russell, Bruce Wagner, Wes Craven, Frank Darabont; ***C:*** Roy Wagner; ***M:*** Angelo Badalamenti.

A Nightmare on Elm Street 4: Dream Master 1/2 **1988 (R)** Freddy Krueger is still preying on people in their dreams, but he may have met his match as he battles for supremacy with a telepathically talented girl. What Part 4 lacks in substance, it makes up for in visual verve, including scenes of a kid drowning in his waterbed, and a pizza covered with pepperoni-like faces of Freddy's previous victims. This boxoffice bonanza set a new record as the most successful opening weekend of any independently released film. Followed by "A Nightmare on Elm Street 5: Dream Child." **99m/C VHS, DVD.** Robert Englund, Rodney Eastman, Danny Hassel, Andras Jones, Tuesday Knight, Lisa Wilcox, Ken Sagoes, Toy Newkirk, Brooke Theiss, Brooke Bundy; ***D:*** Renny Harlin; ***W:*** Brian Helgeland, Scott Pierce; ***C:*** Steven Fierberg; ***M:*** Craig Safan.

A Nightmare on Elm Street 5: Dream Child **1989 (R)** The fifth installment of Freddy Krueger's never-ending adventures. Here, America's favorite knife-wielding burn victim, unable to best the Dream Master from the previous film, haunts the dreams of her unborn fetus. Gore fans may be disappointed to discover that much of the blood and guts ended up on the cutting room floor. **90m/C VHS, DVD.** Robert Englund, Lisa Wilcox, Kelly Jo Minter, Danny Hassel, Erika Anderson, Nicholas Mele, Beatrice Boepple; ***D:*** Stephen Hopkins; ***W:*** Leslie Bohem; ***C:*** Peter Levy; ***M:*** Jay Ferguson. Golden Raspberries '89: Worst Song ("Bring Your Daughter to the Slaughter").

Nightmare on the 13th Floor **1990 (PG-13)** A travel writer at an old hotel glimpses murder on a supposedly non-existent floor. Nasty devil-worshippers are afoot, but the chills in this mild cable throwaway seldom dip below room temperature. **85m/C VHS.** Michael Greene, John Karlen, Louise Fletcher, Alan Fudge, James Brolin; ***D:*** Walter Grauman. **CABLE**

Nightmare Sisters WOOF! **1987 (R)** Three sorority sisters become possessed by a demon and then sexually ravage a nearby fraternity. **83m/C VHS, DVD.** Brinke Stevens, Michelle (McClellan) Bauer, Linnea Quigley; ***D:*** David DeCoteau.

Nightmare Weekend **1986 (R)** A professor's evil assistant lures three young women into his lab and performs cruel and vicious experiments that transform the girls and their dates into crazed zombies. **86m/C VHS, DVD.** Dale Midkiff, Debbie Laster, Debra Hunter, Lori Lewis; ***D:*** Henry Sala.

The Nightmare Years 1/2 **1989** An American reporter in Nazi Germany dares to report the truth to an unbelieving world. Based on a true story. Two cassettes. **237m/C VHS.** Sam Waterston, Marthe Keller, Kurtwood Smith; ***D:*** Anthony Page; ***M:*** Vladimir Cosma.

Nightmares **1983 (PG)** A less-than-thrilling horror anthology featuring four tales in which common, everyday occurrences take on the ingredients of a nightmare. In the same vein as "Twilight Zone" and "Creepshow." **99m/C VHS, DVD.** Christina Raines, Emilio Estevez, Moon Zappa, Lance Henriksen, Richard Masur, Veronica Cartwright; ***D:*** Joseph Sargent; ***W:*** Christopher Crowe, Jeffrey Bloom; ***C:*** Mario DiLeo, Gerald Perry Finnerman; ***M:*** Craig Safan.

Nights and Days 1/2 **1976** Adaptation of writer Maria Dabrowska's tale about a Polish family chronicles the persecution, expulsions, and land grabbing that occurred after the unsuccessful Uprising of 1864. In Polish with English subtitles. **255m/C VHS, DVD.** *PL* Jadwiga Baranska, Jerzy Binczycki; ***D:*** Jerzy Antczak.

Nights and Weekends **2008** Honestly, does anybody really want to watch a couple of dullards break up their long-distance relationship? Writer/director/stars Gerwig and Swanberg do their improvisational mumblecore indie thing as Mattie lives in New York and James lives in Chicago. They yak a lot on the phone and get together sometimes for graphic but decidedly uninteresting sex until they realize absence does not make the heart grow fonder. **80m/C DVD.** Greta Gerwig, Joe Swanberg; ***D:*** Greta Gerwig, Joe Swanberg; ***W:*** Greta Gerwig, Joe Swanberg; ***C:*** Matthias Grunsky, Benjamin Kasulke.

Nights in Rodanthe **2008 (PG-13)** Adrienne Willis (Lane) needs some peace and quiet to ponder her chaotic personal life, so she decides to spend a weekend at a friend's coastal North Carolina inn. A major storm is forecast so the only guest is Dr. Paul Flanner (Gere), who's trying to reconcile with his estranged son Mark (Franco). Naturally, the unhappy (but impossibly attractive) pair turns to each other for advice, and soon they're cooing and wooing against the swoony Outer Banks setting. Too bad it's sappy as a freshly cut pine tree. The completely predictable and contrived story feels engineered simply to jerk tears. Based on the 2002 Nicholas Sparks novel. **96m/C DVD.** *US* Diane Lane, Richard Gere, James Franco, Scott Glenn, Christopher Meloni, Mae Whitman, Viola Davis, Pablo Schreiber, Charlie Tahan, Betty Ann Baker; ***D:*** George C. Wolfe; ***W:*** Ann Peacock, John Romano; ***C:*** Alfonso Beato; ***M:*** Jeanine Tesori.

Nights in White Satin **1/2 1987** A made-for-video Cinderella story about the growing love between a fashion photographer and a young model whose boyfriend has just been murdered. **96m/C VHS.** Kenneth Gilman, Priscilla Harris; ***D:*** Michael Bernard.

Nights of Cabiria **1/2** *Le Notti de Cabiria; Cabiria* **1957** Fellini classic which details the personal decline of a naive prostitute who thinks she's found true love. In Italian with English subtitles or dubbed. Basis for the musical "Sweet Charity." **117m/B VHS, DVD.** *IT* Giulietta Masina, Amedeo Nazzari, Francois Perier, Franca Marzi, Dorian Gray, Aldo Silvani, Ennio Girolami; ***D:*** Federico Fellini; ***W:*** Federico Fellini, Tullio Pinelli, Ennio Flaiano; ***C:*** Aldo Tonti; ***M:*** Nino Rota. Oscars '57: Foreign Film; Cannes '57: Actress (Masina).

Nightscare *Night Scare; Beyond Bedlam* **1993 (R)** When Dr. Stephanie Lyell's (Hurley) drug behavior-modification experiment goes wrong it allows serial killer Marc Gilmour (Allen) to get to his victims through their dreams. The doc tries to prove to Detective Inspector Terry Hamilton (Fairbrass) that the drug is safe by injecting them both but things get out of hand. Adapted from the novel by Harry Adam Knight. **89m/C VHS.** *GB* Craig Fairbrass, Elizabeth Hurley, Keith Allen, Jesse Birdsall, Craig Kelly; ***D:*** Vadim Jean; ***W:*** Vadim Jean.

NightScreams **1/2 1997** Cameron is having terrible nightmares and also sees the ghost of a young woman—the same woman involved in the unexplained murder/suicide that caused the death of Cameron's boyfriend. **90m/C VHS, DVD.** Casper Van Dien, Teri Garr, Candace Cameron; ***D:*** Noel Nosseck; ***W:*** Raymond Singer, Eugenia Singer; ***C:*** Paul Maibaum; ***M:*** Garry Schyman. **VIDEO**

Nightstalker **WOOF!** *Don't Go Near the Park* **1981** A brother and sister who were condemned to eternal death 12,000 years ago must eat virgins to keep their bodies from rotting. Trouble is, while they search for dinner, the movie decomposes. For mature audiences with no fantasies of celluloid nirvana. **90m/C VHS, DVD.** Meeno Peluce, Tamara Taylor, Linnea Quigley, Aldo Ray; ***D:*** Lawrence Foldes; ***W:*** Lawrence Foldes; ***C:*** William de Diego.

Nightstalker **2002 (R)** Based on the '80s true crime saga of L.A. serial killer Robert Ramirez, aka the Nightstalker. Cop Gabriella Martinez (Sanchez), who discovered some of the victims, is offered a promotion to the task force investigating the murders. But she makes a judgement error when she leaks info to reporter Adrianne Deloia (Emma) and is suspended. However, Gabriela's old partner Frank Luis (Trejo) has some info of his own and Gabriela learns that she's become one of the Nightstalker's targets. **95m/C VHS, DVD.** Roselyn Sanchez, Danny Trejo, Evan Dexter Parke, Bret Roberts, Derek Hamilton, Douglas Spain, Brandi Emma; ***D:*** Chris Fisher; ***W:*** Chris Fisher; ***C:*** Eliot Rockett; ***M:*** Ryan Beveridge.

Nightstick **1/2** *Calhoun* **1987 (R)** New York vigilante cop fights nasties who threaten to blow the lid off the city. Worse, they kidnap super cop's girl forcing him to save her along with the city. Lots of violence, predictable plot, and mediocre acting leave this one without much bang. **90m/C VHS.** Bruce Fairbairn, Kerrie Keane, John Vernon, Robert Vaughn, Isaac Hayes, Leslie Nielsen; ***D:*** Joseph L. Scanlan.

Nightwatch **1996 (R)** Law student Martin (McGregor) takes a job as a night watchman in a morgue at the same time a serial killer is killing prostitutes and gouging out their eyes. As if that weren't enough, he has to deal with a cop (Nolte) who suspects him, a sadistic best friend (Brolin) who likes to scare him on the job, and a creepy boss (Dourif) who doesn't like him. Adapted by director Bornedal from his Danish film "Nattevagten," this one's effectively creepy, but disjointed. Excellent cast is misused, as hardly any of the characters are developed beyond simple types. If you enjoyed the murky, depressing atmosphere of "Seven," you'll probably like this. **101m/C VHS, DVD.** Ewan McGregor, Nick Nolte, Patricia Arquette, Josh Brolin, John C. Reilly, Brad Dourif, Lonny (Lonnie) Chapman, Alix Koromzay, Lauren Graham; ***D:*** Ole Bornedal; ***W:*** Ole Bornedal, Steven Soderbergh; ***C:*** Dan Laustsen; ***M:*** Joachim Holbek.

Nightwaves **2003 (PG-13)** A car accident cripples and widows Shelby, who battles pain and boredom by picking up the sorted details of her rich, married neighbors' lives via their phone calls on her police scanner. But when a woman winds up in a body bag Shelby is shoved into a mess that is more than what it seems and makes her a target. **99m/C VHS, DVD.** Sherilyn Fenn, David Nerman, Bruce Dinsmore, Francis X. (Frank) McCarthy, Joanna Noyes, Frank Fontaine, Emma Campbell, Jennifer Morehouse, Kevin Jubinville; ***D:*** Jim Kaufman; ***W:*** Melissa Jo Peltier; ***C:*** Georges Archambault; ***M:*** Simon Carpentier. **TV**

Nightwing **1/2 1979 (PG)** Suspense drama about three people who risk their lives to exterminate a colony of plague-carrying vampire bats in New Mexican Indian community. From the novel by Martin Cruz Smith and adapted by Smith, Steve Shagan, and Bud Shrake. O.K. viewing for those who aren't choosy about their rabid bat movies. **103m/C VHS.** Nick Mancuso, David Warner, Kathryn Harrold, Strother Martin, Stephen Macht, Pat Corley, Charles Hallahan, Ben Piazza, George Clutesi; ***D:*** Arthur Hiller; ***W:*** Steve Shagan, Bud Shrake, Martin Cruz Smith; ***C:*** Charles Rosher Jr.; ***M:*** Henry Mancini.

Nightwish **1/2 1989 (R)** Students do more than homework when a professor leads them into their own horrifying dreams. Soon it becomes impossible to distinguish dreams from reality. **96m/C VHS.** Jack Starrett, Robert Tessier, Clayton Rohner, Elizabeth Kaitan, Alisha Das, Tom Dugan, Brian Thompson, Artur Cybulski; ***D:*** Bruce Cook Jr.; ***W:*** Bruce Cook Jr.

Nijinsky **1980 (R)** An opulent biography of the famous ballet dancer. His exciting and innovative choreography gets little attention. The film concentrates on his infamous homosexual lifestyle and his relationship with impresario Sergei Diaghilev (Bates, in a tour-de-force performance). Lovely to look at, but slow and unconvincing. **125m/C VHS.** Alan Bates, George de la Pena, Leslie Browne, Alan Badel, Carla Fracci, Colin Blakely, Ronald Pickup, Ronald Lacey, Vernon Dobtcheff, Jeremy Irons, Frederick Jaeger, Janet Suzman, Sian Phillips; ***D:*** Herbert Ross.

Nikki, the Wild Dog of the North **1/2 1961 (G)** When a Malemute pup is separated from his Canadian trapper master, he teams up with a bear cub for a series of adventures. Later the pup is reunited with his former master for still more adventures. Adapted from a novel by James Oliver Curwood for Disney. **73m/C VHS, DVD.** *CA* Jean Coutu, Emile Genest, Uriel Luft, Robert Rivard; ***D:*** Jack Couffer, Don Haldane; ***W:*** Winston Hibler, Ralph Wright; ***C:*** Lloyd Beebe; ***M:*** Oliver Wallace.

Nil by Mouth **1996 (R)** Oldman draws on his own dysfunctional working-class London background for his impressive writer/director debut, which casually puts you into the middle of one Cockney family's life. There's brutal Ray (Winstone), husband to Val (Burke) and brother-in-law to young addict Billy (Creed-Miles), as well as his tough mother-in-law Janet (Morse) and her mother, Kath (Dore). Billy gets kicked out of the house by Ray and struggles to survive outside his family while a drunken Ray beats the pregnant Val, prompting a display of female solidarity. Formless pic drops into characters' lives at random, showcasing family loyalty and generosity amidst the violence. **128m/C VHS, DVD.** *GB* Ray Winstone, Kathy Burke, Charlie Creed-Miles, Laila Morse, Edna Dore, Steve Sweeney, Chrissie Cotterill, Jon Morrison, Jamie Foreman; ***D:*** Gary Oldman; ***W:*** Gary Oldman; ***C:*** Ron Fortunato; ***M:*** Eric Clapton. British Acad. '97: Film, Orig. Screenplay; Cannes '97: Actress (Burke).

Nim's Island **1/2 2008 (PG)** A sweet fantasy adventure for kids featuring some excellent special effects, although adult viewers may find the limited plausibility too distracting to buy into the story of Nim (Breslin), who lives on a tropical isle with her scientist dad Jack (Butler). They have a dreamy life with the friendly wildlife and Nim's beloved books, especially those by Alex Rover (Foster), who in real life is a hermit. Then Jack leaves on an ocean journey but doesn't return, leaving poor Nim to fend for herself. Through an unlikely series of events, the author learns of Nim's plight and musters the courage to leave her house to save Nim, who is afraid she might lose her island to developers in a cruise ship. It's a little dizzying, but there is enough charm to satisfy young viewers. **95m/C DVD.** *US* Abigail Breslin, Jodie Foster, Gerard Butler; ***D:*** Marc Levin, Jennifer Flackett; ***W:*** Marc Levin, Jennifer Flackett, Joseph Kwong, Paula Mazur; ***C:*** Stuart Dryburgh; ***M:*** Patrick Doyle.

Nina Takes a Lover **1994 (R)** Romantic comedy finds Nina (San Giacomo) deciding that the passion is gone from her three-year marriage so, while her husband is out of town, she picks up a nameless Welsh photographer (Rhys) and begins an affair. The affair is over as the movie begins but Nina tells her story to a tabloid journalist (O'Keefe) who's writing about adultery. Gimmicky, with shallow if attractive characters and an equally attractive San Francisco setting. **100m/C VHS.** Laura San Giacomo, Paul Rhys, Michael O'Keefe, Cristi Conaway, Fisher Stevens; ***D:*** Alan Jacobs; ***W:*** Alan Jacobs; ***C:*** Phil Parmet; ***M:*** Todd Boekelheide.

Nina's Heavenly Delights **1/2 2006 (PG-13)** Nina Shah (Conn) is an Indo-Scot who left her Glasgow home after an argument with her father. She returns for his funeral, intending to stay to help run the family's curry restaurant, only to learn that it may have to be sold because of her dad's gambling debts. Nina decides to brush up on her culinary skills, with the help of pretty chef Lisa (Fraser), and enter the televised "Best of the West" curry competition. Not very spicy romance with some embarrassingly amateurish scenes. **94m/C DVD.** *GB* Laura Fraser, Art Malik, Ronny Jhutti, Raji James, Veena Sood, Atta Yaqub, Pratibha Parmar; ***W:*** Andrea Gibb; ***C:*** Simon Dennis; ***M:*** Steve Isles.

Nine **1/2 2009 (PG-13)** Adaptation of the 1982 Broadway musical, which was itself inspired by Fellini's 1963 film, "8 1/2." Famous film director Guido Contini (Day-Lewis) is in the midst of working on his latest movie while struggling with his complicated personal life, which includes a number of women, including his sultry and vulgar mistress (Cruz). The music that needs to be onstage, is, instead playing over and over inside his head. A massive challenge to bring this to screen, which, unfortunately collapses under its own grandeur. Devoid of Felliniesque surrealism, and even fails to deliver a single show-stopping number. Disappointing follow-up for "Chicago" director Rob Marshall. **110m/C DVD.** Daniel Day-Lewis, Nicole Kidman, Kate Hudson, Penelope Cruz, Judi Dench, Marion Cotillard, Sophia Loren, Stacy "Fergie" Ferguson; ***D:*** Rob Marshall; ***W:*** Anthony Minghella, Michael Tolkin; ***C:*** Dion Beebe; ***M:*** Andrea Guerra.

9 **1/2 2009 (PG-13)** In this spectacularly animated post-apocalyptic, post-human world, nine numbered doll creatures (known by the number stitched into their backs) must battle for survival against machines intent on the annihilation of any remaining life. 9 (Wood), the youngest and most brave of the group is also the inspirational hero of the film's story. Director Acker uses the small band of survivors as a proxy for the range of characteristics found in humankind, from the most heroic and caring to the basest and most destructive, to hold a mirror up to current human condition. The dialogue and story development are both a little light but the detailed animated action more than compensates for it. **79m/C DVD.** ***D:*** Shane Acker; ***W:*** Pamela Pettler, Shane Acker; ***M:*** Deborah Lurie; ***V:*** Elijah Wood, Jennifer Connelly, Crispin Glover, Martin Landau, Christopher Plummer, John C. Reilly.

Nine Ages of Nakedness **1969** The story of a man whose ancestors have been plagued by a strange problem: beautiful, naked women who create carnal chaos. **88m/C VHS, DVD.** George Harrison Marks; ***D:*** George Harrison Marks; ***W:*** George Harrison Marks; ***Nar:*** Charles Gray.

9 1/2 Ninjas **1/2 1990 (R)** A cautious and disciplined martial artist trains a young and flirtatious woman in the ways of the ninja. His life becomes exciting in more ways than one, when he realizes she's being followed by ninjas with more on their minds than her training—they want to assassinate her! Crazy mixture of sex, kung fu and humor make this film one surprise after another. **88m/C VHS.** Michael Phenicie, Andee Gray, Tommy (Tiny) Lister; ***D:*** Aaron Worth; ***W:*** Bill Crounse.

9 1/2 Weeks **1/2 1986 (R)** Chance meeting between a Wall Street exec and an art gallery employee evolves into an experimental sexual relationship bordering on sado-masochism. Video version is more explicit than the theatrical release, but not by much. Strong characterizations by both actors prevent this from being strictly pornography. Well-written, with strength of male and female personalities nicely balanced. Intriguing, but not for all tastes. **114m/C VHS, DVD.** Mickey Rourke, Kim Basinger, Margaret Whitton, Karen Young, David Margulies, Christine Baranski, Roderick Cook, Dwight Weist; ***D:*** Adrian Lyne; ***W:*** Patricia Louisianna Knop, Zalman King; ***C:*** Peter Biziou; ***M:*** Jack Nitzsche.

Nine Days a Queen *Lady Jane Grey; Tudor Rose* **1936** An historical drama based on the life of Lady Jane Grey, proclaimed Queen of England after the death of Henry VIII of England and summarily executed for treason by Mary Tudor after a nine-day reign. An obscure tragedy with good performances and absorbing story line. Remade as "Lady Jane" (1985). **80m/B VHS.** *GB* John Mills, Cedric Hardwicke, Nova Pilbeam, Sybil Thorndike, Leslie Perrins, Felix Aylmer, Miles Malleson, Frank Cellier, Desmond Tester, Gwen Francon-Davies, Martita Hunt, John Laurie, Roy Emerton, John Turnbull, J.H. Roberts; ***D:*** Robert Stevenson; ***W:*** Robert Stevenson, Miles Malleson; ***C:*** Mutz Greenbaum.

Nine Deaths of the Ninja **WOOF!** **1985 (R)** Faceless ninja warrior Kosugi leads a team of commandos on a mission to rescue a group of political prisoners held captive in the Philippine jungles. Features Ozone-depleted plot, incongruous performances, and inane dialogue, not to mention two main villains—a neurotic Nazi in a wheelchair and a black lesbian amazon—who chew jungle and bring bad art to a new level of appreciation. Amazing in its total badness. Produced by Cannon. **93m/C VHS, DVD.** Sho Kosugi, Brent Huff, Emelia Lesniak, Regina Richardson, Kane (Takeshi) Kosugi, Vijay Amritraj, Blackie Dammett, Sonny Erang, Bruce Fanger; ***D:*** Emmett Alston; ***W:*** Emmett Alston; ***M:*** Cecile Calayco.

Nine Lives **2005 (R)** Character study that captures brief but intense moments in the lives of nine women, ranging from a pregnant married woman (Wright Penn) running into a former lover (Isaacs) at a supermarket to a teenager's (Seyfried) attentiveness to her disabled father (McShane), to cancer, romance, adultery, divorce, death, and mothers and daughters. Writer/director Garcia (the son of famed writer Gabriel Garcia Marquez) showcases his leading ladies while not forgetting to support his equally talented supporting males. **115m/C DVD.** *US* Kathy Baker, Amy Brenneman, Elpidia Carrillo, Glenn Close, Stephen (Dillon) Dillane, Dakota Fanning, William Fichtner, Lisa Gay Hamilton, Holly Hunter, Jason Isaacs, Joe Mantegna, Ian McShane, Molly Parker, Mary Kay Place, Sydney Tamiia Poitier, Aidan Quinn, Miguel (Michael) Sandoval, Amanda Seyfried, Sissy Spacek, Robin Wright Penn; ***W:*** Rodrigo Garcia; ***C:*** Xavier Perez Grobet; ***M:*** Ed Shearmur.

The Nine Lives of Elfego Baca **1958** Venerable Western hero Loggia faces a veritable army of gunfighters and bandits. Action-packed but not too violent; family fun. **78m/C VHS.** Robert Loggia, Robert F. Simon, Lisa Montell, Nestor Paiva; ***D:*** Norman Foster.

Nine Lives of Fritz the Cat **1974** Fritz feels that life's too square in the '70s, so he takes off into some of his other lives for more adventure. Cleaner but still naughty sequel to the X-rated "Fritz the Cat," featuring neither the original's writer/director Ralph Bakshi nor cartoonist Robert Crumb. Tame and lame. Animated. **77m/C VHS, DVD.** ***D:*** Robert Taylor; ***W:*** Robert Taylor, Eric Monte; ***V:*** Skip Hinnant.

Nine Men 1/2 **1943** Nine British troops must fend for themselves in the African desert when their supply convoy truck is destroyed. Besieged by Axis forces, they find a decrepit fort and attempt to hold out by making it seem as if they have more men and ammo than they do. Well-done British production has suspense aplenty. Similarly set and themed "Sahara" would make a nice complement for a double feature. **68m/B VHS.** *GB* Jack Lambert, Gordon Jackson, Frederick Piper, Grant Sutherland, Eric Micklewood, John Varley, Harry Watt, Bill Blewitt, Jack Horseman, Richard Wilkinson; ***C:*** Roy Kellino; ***M:*** John Grenwood.

Nine Months 1/2 **1995 (PG-13)** Happily single Samuel (Grant) gets girlfriend Rebecca (Moore) pregnant and promptly wigs out. He makes amends to the lovely Rebecca, they marry, and true to writer/director Columbus' style, live happily ever after. Bachelor pal Sean (Goldblum) and an expectant couple (Arnold and Cusack) with three kids round out the cast, with Williams offering his usual manic flair as a Russian obstetrician, improvising his scenes with glee. Grant's knack for clumsy befuddlement fits well with the warm, fuzzy style of Columbus. "Nine" doesn't go out on any limbs, but is a pleasant diversion anyway. Remake of the French film "Neuf Mois." **103m/C VHS, DVD.** Hugh Grant, Julianne Moore, Tom Arnold, Joan Cusack, Jeff Goldblum, Robin Williams, Alexa Vega, Ashley Johnson, Mia Cottet, Kristin Davis, Joey Simmrin; ***D:*** Chris Columbus; ***W:*** Chris Columbus; ***C:*** Donald McAlpine; ***M:*** Hans Zimmer.

$9.99 **2008 (R)** Clay nudity and sex! That'll draw in the crowds! Yep this oddball Australian/Israeli co-production is done in a deliberately crude stop-motion animation style with an adult story. Title refers to the price of a self-help, mail-order booklet that purports to reveal the meaning of life. The denizens of a Sydney apartment building find meaning in entirely different ways, including a homeless man—a suicide—who returns as a surly guardian angel. **78m/C DVD.** *AU IS* ***D:*** Tatia Rosenthal; ***W:*** Tatia Rosenthal, Etgar Keret; ***C:*** Susan Stitt, James Lewis, Richard Bradshaw; ***V:*** Geoffrey Rush, Anthony LaPaglia, Samuel Johnson, Ben Mendelsohn, Joel Edgerton, Claudia Karvan, Barry Otto, Jamie Katsamatsas, Leanna (Leeanna) Walsman.

Nine Queens *Nueve Reinas* **2000 (R)** Juan (Pauls) is a rookie con man in Buenos Aries, who is taken under the wing of the more-experienced Marcos (Darin). Marcos stumbles across an opportunity to fence the Nine Queens, a famous set of defectively printed stamps from Weimar Germany. Actually, Marcos's ruse is peddle a counterfeit set to a stamp-collecting patsy named Gandolfo (Abadal). Things get complicated when Marcos needs his angry sister Valeria's (Bredice) help, the stamps are stolen, and even Argentina's economic woes come to play a significant role. Just who's scamming who? Spanish with subtitles. **115m/C VHS, DVD.** *AR* Ricardo Darin, Gaston Pauls, Leticia Bredice, Ignasi Abadal, Tomas Fonzi; ***D:*** Fabian Bielinsky; ***W:*** Fabian Bielinsky; ***C:*** Marcelo Camorino; ***M:*** Cesar Lerner.

9 Souls 1/2 *Nine Souls* **2003** Surreal film begins as a slapstick comedy and ends up as a brutally depressing nightmare drama. Nine prisoners escape from lockup because they know of the location of hidden loot that they hope will give them all a second chance at life so they can start over. Lots of symbolism and metaphor that might be lost on native audiences let alone American ones, so it's definitely not for everyone. But it has prison midgets; can't go wrong with that. **120m/C DVD.** *JP* Yoshio Harada, Ryuhei Matsuda, Kiyohiko Shibukawa, Mame Yamada, Asami Imajuku, Onimaru; ***D:*** Toshiyaki Toyoda; ***W:*** Toshiyaki Toyoda; ***C:*** Junichi Fujisawa.

9 to 5 1/2 **1980 (PG)** In this caricature of large corporations and women in the working world, Coleman plays the male chauvinist boss who calls the shots and keeps his employees, all female, under his thumb. Three of the office secretaries daydream of Coleman's disposal and rashly kidnap him after a silly set of occurrences threaten their jobs. While they have him under lock and key, the trio take office matters into their own hands and take a stab at running things their own way, with amusing results. Basis for a TV series. **111m/C VHS, DVD.** Jane Fonda, Lily Tomlin, Dolly Parton, Dabney Coleman, Sterling Hayden, Norma Donaldson; ***D:*** Colin Higgins; ***W:*** Patricia Resnick; ***C:*** Reynaldo Villalobos; ***M:*** Charles Fox.

976-EVIL **1988 (R)** Englund (the infamous Freddy from the Nightmare on Elm Street epics) directs this horror movie where a lonely teenager dials direct to demons from hell. **102m/C VHS, DVD.** Stephen Geoffreys, Jim Metzler, Maria Rubell, Sandy Dennis, Robert Picardo, Lezlie (Dean) Deane, Pat O'Bryan, J.J. (Jeffrey Jay) Cohen; ***D:*** Robert Englund; ***W:*** Brian Helgeland, Rhet Topham; ***C:*** Paul Elliott; ***M:*** Tom Chase, Steve Rucker.

976-EVIL 2: The Astral Factor 1/2 **1991 (R)** Satan returns the call in this supernatural thriller that sequels the original film. **93m/C VHS.** Pat O'Bryan, Rene Assa, Debbie James; ***D:*** Jim Wynorski; ***W:*** Erik Anjou.

The Nines **2007 (R)** Three stars play three roles in three different, interconnected stories in this ambitious puzzle of a movie whose twists and turns mostly succeed. Each story features Reynolds, McCarthy, and Davis dealing with conflicts internal and external that all seem to come back to "the nines," whatever that may be. Each story connects to the other while the actors' relationships change from episode to episode. Keeps you guessing throughout the build-up but the resolution doesn't entirely pay off. **99m/C DVD.** *US* Ryan Reynolds, Hope Davis, Melissa McCarthy; ***D:*** John August; ***W:*** John August; ***C:*** Nancy Schreiber; ***M:*** Alex Wurman.

1900 *Novecento* **1976 (R)** Bertolucci's impassioned epic about two Italian families, one land-owning, the other, peasant. Shows the sweeping changes of the 20th century begun by the trauma of WWI and the onslaught of Italian socialism. Edited down from its original 360-minute length and dubbed in English from three other languages, the film suffers somewhat from editing and from its nebulous lack of commitment to any genre. **255m/C VHS, DVD.** *FR IT GE* Robert De Niro, Gerard Depardieu, Burt Lancaster, Donald Sutherland, Dominique Sanda, Sterling Hayden, Laura Betti, Francesca Bertini, Werner Bruhns, Stefania Sandrelli, Anna Henkel, Alida Valli; ***D:*** Bernardo Bertolucci; ***W:*** Giuseppe Bertolucci, Bernardo Bertolucci; ***C:*** Vittorio Storaro.

1915 **1982** Aussie mates Billy and Walter decide to leave their country homes and enlist in the army, dreaming of heroics in WWI, only to be shocked by the realities of war. Based on the novel by Roger MacDonald. **352m/C DVD.** *AU* Scott Burgess, Bill Hunter, Sigrid Thornton, Bill Kerr, Scott McGregor, Lorraine Bayly, Jackie Woodburne; ***D:*** Di Drew, Chris Thomson; ***W:*** Peter Yeldham; ***C:*** Peter Hendry; ***M:*** Bruce Smeaton. **TV**

1918 1/2 **1985** An adaptation of the Horton Foote play about the effects of WWI and an influenza epidemic on a small Texas town. Slow-moving but satisfying. Score by Willie Nelson. Originally produced for PBS's "American Playhouse." Prequelled by "On Valentine's Day." **89m/C VHS, DVD.** Matthew Broderick, Hallie Foote, William Converse-Roberts, Rochelle Oliver, Michael Higgins, Horton Foote Jr., William (Bill) McGhee, Jeannie McCarthy; ***D:*** Ken Harrison; ***W:*** Horton Foote; ***M:*** Willie Nelson.

1931: Once Upon a Time in New York **1972** Prohibition-era gangsters war, beat each other up, make headlines, and drink bathtub gin. **90m/C VHS, DVD.** *IT* Tony Anthony, Richard Conte, Adolfo Celi, Lionel Stander, Irene Papas; ***D:*** Luigi Vanzi; ***W:*** Tony Anthony; ***C:*** Riccardo (Pallton) Pallottini.

1941 1/2 **1979 (PG)** Proved to be the most expensive comedy of all time with a budget exceeding $35 million when originally produced, the film was considered a flop when put up against Spielberg's other films. The depiction of Los Angeles in the chaotic days after the bombing of Pearl Harbor combines elements of fantasy and black humor—sometimes effectively. **120m/C VHS, DVD.** John Belushi, Dan Aykroyd, Patti LuPone, Ned Beatty, Slim Pickens, Murray Hamilton, Christopher Lee, Tim Matheson, Toshiro Mifune, Warren Oates, Robert Stack, Nancy Allen, Elisha Cook Jr., Lorraine Gary, Treat Williams, Mickey Rourke, John Candy, Wendie Jo Sperber, Lucille Benson, Eddie Deezen, Bobby DiCicco, Dianne Kay, Perry Lang, Frank McRae, Lionel Stander, Dub Taylor, Joe Flaherty, David Lander, Michael McKean, Samuel Fuller, Audrey Landers, John Landis, Walter Olkewicz, Donovan Scott, Penny Marshall; ***D:*** Steven Spielberg; ***W:*** Robert Zemeckis, Bob Gale, John Milius; ***C:*** William A. Fraker; ***M:*** John Williams.

1969 1/2 **1989 (R)** Three teenage friends during the 1960s become radicalized by the return of one of their friends from Vietnam in a coffin. Critically lambasted directorial debut for "On Golden Pond" author Ernest Thompson. **96m/C VHS, DVD.** Kiefer Sutherland, Robert Downey Jr., Winona Ryder, Bruce Dern, Joanna Cassidy, Mariette Hartley, Christopher Wynne; ***D:*** Ernest Thompson; ***W:*** Ernest Thompson; ***C:*** Jules Brenner; ***M:*** Michael Small.

1984 **1956** Winston Smith and Julia struggle to find happiness through forbidden love in a dystopian totalitarian future ruled by omnipresent dictator Big Brother. Excellently dreary adaptation of the George Orwell novel was made only seven years after the novel's debut, and at the height of the noir age and Cold War, making it that much scarier to contemporary audiences. Seen today, it still captures the dread and paranoia of the novel. **90m/B VHS, DVD.** *GB* Edmond O'Brien, Jan Sterling, Michael Redgrave, David Kossoff, Mervyn Johns, Donald Pleasence, Carol Wolveridge, Ernest Clark, Ronan O'Casey, Kenneth Griffith; ***D:*** Michael Anderson Sr.; ***W:*** William Templeton, Ralph Gilbert Bettinson; ***C:*** N. Peter Rathvon.

1984 1/2 **1984 (R)** A very fine adaptation of George Orwell's infamous novel, this version differs from the overly simplistic and cautionary 1954 film because of fine casting and production design. The illegal love affair of a government official becomes his attempt to defy the crushing inhumanity and lack of simple pleasures of an omniscient government. Filmed in London, it skillfully visualizes our time's most central prophetic nightmare. **117m/C VHS, DVD.** *GB* John Hurt, Richard Burton, Suzanna Hamilton, Cyril Cusack, Gregor Fisher, Andrew Wilde, Rupert Baderman; ***D:*** Michael Radford; ***C:*** Roger Deakins.

1990: The Bronx Warriors WOOF! *1990 I Guerrieri del Bronx; Bronx Warriors* **1983 (R)** Good street gang members combat evil corporate powers in a semi-futuristic South Bronx. Lame copy of "Escape from New York." **86m/C VHS, DVD.** *IT* Vic Morrow, Christopher Connelly, Fred Williamson; ***D:*** Enzo G. Castellari.

1991: The Year Punk Broke 1/2 **1992** Documents a grunge rock tour of European festivals in 1991 when the alternative bands were largely unknown to all but hardcore fans. Follows Sonic Youth, Nirvana, Dinosaur Jr., Babes in Toyland, Gumball, and grandaddy punk idols, The Ramones, behind-the-scenes and through their performances. **95m/C VHS.** ***D:*** David Markey.

1999 **1998 (R)** On New Year's Eve, Rufus King (Futterman) is partying like it's 1999 (which it is), deciding it's the perfect opportunity to make some life-changing decisions. Like dumping his sweet girlfriend for the office sexpot (Peet). **93m/C VHS, DVD.** Dan Futterman, Jennifer Garner, Matt McGrath, Amanda Peet, Steven Wright, Sandrine Holt, Buck Henry, Margaret Devine, Daniel Lapaine, David Gelb, Nick Davis; ***D:*** Nick Davis; ***W:*** Nick Davis; ***C:*** Howard Krupa; ***M:*** Sue Jacobs, Lynne Geller.

90 Days **1986** Charming independently made Canadian comedy about two young men handling their respective romantic dilemmas—one awaiting an oriental fiancee he's never met, the other who is being kicked out of his house by his wife. **99m/C VHS.** *CA* Stefan Wodoslowsky, Sam Grana, Christine Pak; ***D:*** Giles Walker.

92 in the Shade **1976 (R)** Based upon McGuane's novel, the film deals with a bored, wealthy rogue who becomes a fishing guide in the Florida Keys, and battles against the competition of two crusty, half-mad codgers. Sloppy, irreverent comedy as only a first-time writer-turned-director can fashion. **91m/C VHS.** Peter Fonda, Warren Oates, Margot Kidder, Burgess Meredith, Harry Dean Stanton; ***D:*** Thomas McGuane; ***W:*** Thomas McGuane.

99 & 44/100 Dead *Call Harry Crown* **1974 (PG)** Frankenheimer falters with this silly gangster flick. Harris is hired to kill Dillman, by local godfather O'Brien. Originally written as a satirical look at gangster movies, but it doesn't stick to satire, and as a result is disappointing. **98m/C VHS.** Richard Harris, Chuck Connors, Edmond O'Brien, Bradford Dillman, Ann Turkel; ***D:*** John Frankenheimer; ***W:*** Robert Dillon; ***M:*** Henry Mancini.

99 Women 1/2 *Isle of Lost Women* **1969 (R)** Sympathetic prison warden attempts to investigate conditions at a women's prison camp. Thin and exploitative view of lesbianism behind bars that sensationalizes the subject. **90m/C VHS, DVD.** *GB SP GE IT* Maria Schell, Herbert Lom, Mercedes McCambridge, Luciana Paluzzi; ***D:*** Jess (Jesus) Franco.

Ninja 3: The Domination **1984 (R)** Ninja master must remove the spirit of a deadly ninja assassin from a young woman intent on wreaking havoc among the Phoenix police department. Extremely silly super ninja epic utterly uninhibited by the usual plot conventions. **92m/C VHS.** Lucinda Dickey, Sho Kosugi; ***D:*** Sam Firstenberg; ***W:*** James R. Silke; ***C:*** Hanania Baer.

Ninja Academy 1/2 **1990 (R)** Seven wimps, losers, and spoiled brats come to the Ninja Academy to learn the art. Will they make it? **93m/C VHS, DVD.** Will Egan, Kelly Randall, Gerald Okomura, Michael David, Robert Factor, Jeff Robinson; ***D:*** Nico Mastorakis.

Ninja: American Warrior 1/2 **1990** An evil ninja takes on the U.S. Drug Enforcement Agency when the authorities threaten to shut him down. **90m/C VHS.** Joff Houston, John Wilford; ***D:*** Godfrey Ho.

Ninja Assassin **2009 (R)** The vicious Ozunu Clan adopts the orphaned Raizo (Rain) and raises him to be the most deadly, wicked ninja of all time. But after the clan executes his sweetheart, he flees seeking revenge, eventually joining up with Interpol agent Mika Coretti (Harris). Connecting a money-for-political-murders scheme to Far East assassins, Mika defies orders to discontinue her investigation making her a target to be saved by Raizo. Its thin plot is nothing more than an excuse to repeatedly show off sweet gore effects and carefully choreographed ninja fight scenes. Made specifically for its target audience, nothing more, nothing less. **99m/C DVD.** Rain, Naomie Harris, Rick Yune, Ben Miles, Sho Kosugi; ***D:*** James McTeigue; ***W:*** Matthew Sand, J. Michael Straczynski; ***C:*** Karl Walter Lindenlaub; ***M:*** Ilan Eshkeri.

Ninja Brothers of Blood **1989** A guy falls for a rival gang member's girl. Neither the gang nor the guy's former girlfriend take kindly to this! **90m/C VHS.** Marcus Gibson, Fonda Lynn, Brian McClave, Jonathan Soper; ***D:*** Raymond Woo.

Ninja Champion WOOF! 1980 White-clad and masked ninja heros come to the aid of some Interpol agents tracking down a sleazy diamond smuggler. Invisible storyline features very little actual ninja. Extremely unconvincing and poorly dubbed. **90m/C VHS, DVD.** *HK* Bruce Baron, Richard Harrison; ***D:*** Godfrey Ho; ***W:*** Godfrey Ho.

Ninja Commandments 1987 Everything is at stake when an evil warrior takes on the greatest fighter in the land: the winner will rule the empire! **90m/C VHS.** Richard Harrison, Dave Wheeler; ***D:*** Joseph Lai.

Ninja Condors 1987 A young man grows up to avenge the murder of his father. **85m/C VHS.** Alexander Lou, Stuart Hugh; ***D:*** James Wu.

Ninja Connection 1990 Ninja terrorism is employed as a scare tactic to deter a group who wants to break up an international drug ring. **90m/C VHS, DVD.** Patricia Greenford, Jane Kingsly, Joe Nelson, Louis Roth, Henry Steele, Stuart Steen; ***D:*** York Lam.

Ninja Death Squad 1987 A team specializing in political assassinations is hunted down by a special agent. **89m/C VHS.** Glen Carson, Patricia Goodman, Joff Houston, Billy "Red" Jones, Wallace Jones, John Wilford; ***D:*** Godfrey Ho.

Ninja Destroyer 1970 (R) Ninja warriors battle over an emerald mine. **92m/C VHS.** *HK* Bruce Baron, Stuart Smith; ***D:*** Godfrey Ho; ***W:*** Godfrey Ho.

Ninja Fantasy WOOF! 1986 Ninja drug smugglers and government officials battle over a large drug shipment. Everybody go chop socky. Not much in way of ninja fantasy. Dubbed. **95m/C VHS, DVD.** *HK* Adam Nell, Ian Frank, Jordan Heller, Ken Ashley, Jenny Mills, Jack Rodman; ***D:*** Godfrey Ho; ***W:*** Anthony Green.

Ninja Hunt WOOF! 1986 This time, ninjas kick international terrorists in the head while searching for secret formula. Poorly dubbed pseudo ninja developed by Godfrey Ho. **92m/C VHS.** *HK* Bruce Baron, Stuart Smith; ***D:*** Joseph Lai; ***W:*** Stephen Saul.

Ninja in the U.S.A. ½ 1988 Evil drug kingpin Tyger McFerson (Albergo) is acquitted of murder charges because all witnesses against him have been killed by his ninja army. Cops Rodney Kuen and Jerry Wong (Lou) give McFerson the benefit of the doubt because he saved their lives in Viet Nam. But when Jerry's reporter wife is kidnapped by Tyger's ninjas to suppress evidence against him, Jerry suits up with all his ninja gear and storms McFerson's compound. Despite the video release title, there's no reason to believe any of this takes place anywhere in the United States. **93m/C VHS, DVD.** *TW* Alexander Lou, George Nicholas Albergo, Eugene Thomas, Alex Yip; ***D:*** Dennis Wu; ***W:*** Ed Jones; ***C:*** Owen Casey; ***M:*** Sherman Chow.

Ninja Masters of Death 1985 Terrorists reign supreme until the white ninja saves the city. **90m/C VHS.** Mick Jones, Chris Petersen, Daniel Wells, Richard Young; ***D:*** Godfrey Ho.

Ninja Mission ½ 1984 (R) First Scandinavian ninja epic follows CIA agent and his group of ninja fighters as they embark on a hazardous mission to rescue two people from a Soviet prison. They use their fighting skills (Swedish ninjas favor guns more than ninjutsu) against Russian soldiers. Dubbed. **95m/C VHS.** *SW* Christopher Kohlberg, Curt Brober, Hanna Pola; ***D:*** Mats Helge.

Ninja of the Magnificence ½ 1989 When the ninja master is killed, factions within his group battle for control. **90m/C VHS, UMD.** Sam Baker, Patrick Frbezar, Clive Hadwen, Tim Michael, Renato Sala; ***D:*** Godfrey Ho.

Ninja Operation: Licensed to Terminate 1987 Two warriors risk broken noses and twisted limbs to take on the Black Ninja Empire. **89m/C VHS.** Richard Harrison, Paul Marshall, Jack McPeat, Grant Temple; ***D:*** Joseph Lai.

Ninja Phantom Heroes 1987 Two Vietnam vets are imprisoned for war crimes. One escapes and forms his own secret ninja society. **90m/C VHS.** Glen Carson, George Dickson, Allen Leung, Christine Wells; ***D:*** Godfrey Ho.

Ninja Powerforce ½ 1990 Two childhood friends end up as members of rival ninja gangs in the midst of a bloody war. Usual assortment of ninja-inflicted injuries result. **90m/C VHS.** Jonathan Bould, Richard Harrison; ***D:*** Joseph Lai.

Ninja Showdown 1990 A warrior must take on a number of vicious bandits in order to defend his small town. He vows revenge on anyone who threatens his people. **92m/C VHS.** Richard Harrison; ***D:*** Joseph Lai.

Ninja Strike Force ½ 1988 The Black Ninjas steal the powerful "spirit sword," and go on a bloody rampage. **89m/C VHS.** Richard Harrison, Gary Carter; ***D:*** Joseph Lai.

Ninja the Battalion 1990 Agents from America, the Soviet Union, and China try to recover germ warfare secrets stolen by the Japanese secret service. **90m/C VHS.** Roger Crawford, Sam Huxley, Alexander Lou, Dickson Warn; ***D:*** Victor Sears.

Ninja, the Violent Sorcerer ½ 1986 Murderer, with the help of Chinese vampires, does battle with the ghost of a dead gambling lord's wife and the gambling lord's living brother. Often tedious even with above average production and incredible plot. **90m/C VHS.** ***D:*** Godfrey Ho; ***W:*** Daniel Clough.

Ninja Vengeance ½ 1993 (R) The corrupt sheriff of a small Texas town, who also leads the KKK, is terrorizing a young African-American local. Then our lone hero rides into town on his trusty motorcycle to save the day. Only this time instead of your average gunman, he's a ninja. **87m/C VHS.** Stephen K. Hayes, Janet K. Pawlak, Craig Boyett, David Paul Lord; ***D:*** Karl Armstrong; ***W:*** Carrie Armstrong, Karl Armstrong.

Ninotchka ½ 1939 Delightful romantic comedy. Garbo is a cold Russian agent sent to Paris to check up on her comrades, who are being seduced by capitalism. She inadvertently falls in love with a playboy, who melts her communist heart. Garbo talks and laughs. Satirical, energetic, and witty. Later a Broadway musical called "Silk Stockings." **110m/B VHS, DVD.** Greta Garbo, Melvyn Douglas, Ina Claire, Sig Rumann, Felix Bressart, Bela Lugosi; ***D:*** Ernst Lubitsch; ***W:*** Billy Wilder; ***C:*** William H. Daniels. Natl. Film Reg. '90.

The Ninth Configuration *Twinkle, Twinkle, Killer Kane* **1979 (R)** Based on Blatty's novel "Twinkle, Twinkle, Killer Kane" (also the film's alternate title), this is a weird and surreal tale of a mock rebellion of high-ranking military men held in a secret base hospital for the mentally ill. Keach is good as the commander who is just as insane as the patients. Available in many different lengths, this is generally considered to be the best. **115m/C VHS, DVD.** Stacy Keach, Scott Wilson, Jason Miller, Ed Flanders, Neville Brand, Alejandro Rey, Robert Loggia, George DiCenzo; ***D:*** William Peter Blatty; ***W:*** William Peter Blatty. Golden Globes '81: Screenplay.

The Ninth Day *Der Neunte Tag* **2004** Examines Nazism from the side of its victims through the plight of Rev. Henri Kremer, a Roman Catholic priest from Luxembourg imprisoned at Dachau. The cruel logic behind totalitarian power is revealed in the plot to use Kremer in coercing his bishop to declare Nazism compatible with church doctrine, upon which they will 'grant' him a nine-day furlough. Failure will result in the execution of 18 Luxembourg priests in his Dachau block and will also bring harm to his family. All performances, in German with English subtitles, are stellar. Scholondorff lays out the theological and ethical debates of potent themes without over-dramatizing them. **90m/C DVD.** *GE* Ulrich Matthes, August Diehl, Germain Wagner, Bibiana Beglau, Jean-Paul Raths, Ivan Jirik, Karel Hromadka, Miroslav Sichman, Adolf Filip, Vladimir Fiser, Petr Varga, Petr Janis, Zdenek Pechacek, Karel Dobry, Goetz Burger, Hilmar Thate; ***D:*** Volker Schlondorff; ***W:*** Eberhard Goerner, Andreas Pflueger; ***C:*** Tomas Erhart; ***M:*** Alfred Schnittke.

The Ninth Gate 1999 (R) Less-than-scrupulous rare-book dealer Dean Corso (Depp) is hired by wealthy publishing mogul Balkan (Langella) to find and authenticate three copies of a 17th-century book that supposedly holds the secrets to conjuring up the devil. Naturally, he encounters many spooky and deadly people along the way. Depp is perfectly cast as the sleazy bookworm and every scene is appropriately atmospheric, but Polanski's glacial pace and lack of any dramatic tension keeps this flick from getting its due. **127m/C VHS, DVD.** *FR SP* Johnny Depp, Frank Langella, Lena Olin, Emmanuelle Seigner, Barbara Jefford, Jack Taylor, James Russo, Jose Lopez Rodero; ***D:*** Roman Polanski; ***W:*** Roman Polanski, John Brownjohn, Enrique Urbizu; ***C:*** Darius Khondji; ***M:*** Wojciech Kilar.

Nirvana 1997 (R) Jimi Dini (Lambert) is a computer game designer whose latest creation, Nirvana, has a lead character called Solo (Abatantuono). But when Jimi plays the game, he finds out that a computer virus has imparted self-awareness to Solo who pleads to be deleted from his virtual world. Jimi's agreeable but this doesn't turn out to be so easy. **108m/C VHS, DVD.** *FR IT* Christopher Lambert, Diego Abatantuono, Emmanuelle Seigner, Sergio Rubini; ***D:*** Gabriele Salvatores; ***W:*** Gabriele Salvatores.

Nitti: The Enforcer 1988 (PG-13) Made-for-TV saga about Al Capone's brutal enforcer and right-hand man, Frank Nitti. Diversified cast (Moriarty in particular) do their best to keep things moving along, and the atmosphere is consistently and appropriately violent. Made to capitalize on the success of 1987's "The Untouchables." **94m/C VHS, DVD.** Anthony LaPaglia, Vincent Guastaferro, Trini Alvarado, Michael Moriarty, Michael Russo, Louis Guss, Bruno Kirby; ***D:*** Michael Switzer.

Nixon 1995 (R) Stone again "interprets" historical events of the '60s and '70s with a sprawling, bold bio of Richard Nixon. Covering all the highlights of Nixon's public life, and speculating on his private one, Hopkins convincingly portrays "Tricky Dick" as an embattled, lonely political genius. Gigantic all-star cast is lead by Oscar-caliber performance of Joan Allen as Pat Nixon. Even at over three hours, there isn't nearly enough time to explore the significance of all the events covered here. As usual, Stone has taken some creative license, which lead to the Nixon daughters publicly trashing the film, and Walt Disney's daughter expressing "shame" at being affiliated with it. **192m/C VHS, DVD.** Anthony Hopkins, Joan Allen, Ed Harris, Bob Hoskins, David Paymer, Paul Sorvino, J.T. Walsh, James Woods, Madeline Kahn, Brian Bedford, Mary Steenburgen, Powers Boothe, E.G. Marshall, David Hyde Pierce, Kevin Dunn, Annabeth Gish, Tony Goldwyn, Larry Hagman, Edward Herrmann, Saul Rubinek, Tony LoBianco, Kamar De Los Reyes, Michelle Krusiec; ***D:*** Oliver Stone; ***W:*** Oliver Stone, Christopher Wilkinson, Stephen J. Rivele; ***C:*** Robert Richardson; ***M:*** John Williams. L.A. Film Critics '95: Support. Actress (Allen); Natl. Soc. Film Critics '95: Support. Actress (Allen).

No 1998 Based on a segment of writer-director Lepage's play "The Seven Branches of the River Ota," which juxtaposes events at the 1970 World's Fair in Osaka, Japan with an infamous event in Canadian history, as separatist terrorists in Quebec kidnap a British diplomat and a Quebec cabinet minister. Montreal actress Sophie (Cadieux) is performing in Osaka while her boyfriend Michel (Martin) is back home watching the political upheaval on TV. Sophie has a number of personal crises to contend with, while Michel gets so wrapped up in politics he contemplates taking radical actions of his own. The cultural and political differences won't necessarily travel well outside French-speaking Canada. **85m/C VHS.** *CA* Anne-Marie Cadieux, Alexis Martin, Marie Brassard, Richard Frechette, Marie Gignac, Eric Bernier; ***D:*** Robert Lepage; ***W:*** Robert Lepage, Andre Morency; ***C:*** Pierre Mignot; ***M:*** Michael F. Cote, Bernard Falaise. Toronto-City '98: Canadian Feature Film.

No Alibi ½ 2000 (R) Upstanding businessman Bob Valenz (Cain) becomes involved with beautiful Camille (Doig), who also has something kinky going on with Bob's smalltime crook brother, Phil (Stebbings). Phil gets dead and it leads back not only to Camille but to the third man in her life, criminal slickster Vic (Roberts). But by then Bob and Camille are married and she's pregnant. But Bob won't stop investigating his brother's death and he's not going to like what he finds out. **94m/C VHS, DVD.** *CA* Dean Cain, Eric Roberts, Lexa Doig, Peter Stebbings, Richard Chevolleau, Frank Schorpion, Melissa Di Marco; ***D:*** Bruce Pittman; ***W:*** Ivan Kane, John Schafer; ***C:*** Michael Storey; ***M:*** Marty Simon. **VIDEO**

No Big Deal ½ 1983 (PG-13) Dillon is a streetwise teenager who makes friends at his new school. Blah promise; bad acting makes this no big deal. **86m/C VHS, DVD.** Kevin Dillon, Sylvia Miles, Tammy Grimes, Jane Krakowski, Christopher Gartin, Mary Joan Negro; ***D:*** Robert Charlton.

No Blood No Tears *Pido nunmuldo eobshi* **2002** Gyeong-seon (Lee Hye-eun) is a tough butt-kicking female cab driver who worries about how she will pay her deadbeat ex husband's debts to the local mob. Her cab is hit by Su-Jin (Jeon Doyeon), who is the unwilling bed partner of a local gangster named Bulldog. Together they concoct a scheme to rob him. It's sort of a Korean version of "Lock, Stock, and Two Smoking Barrels," but with more martial arts chicks. **120m/C DVD.** *KN* Do-yeon Jeon, Hyeyeong Lee, Jae-yeong Jong, Goo Shin, Doohong Jung; ***D:*** Seung-wan Ryoo; ***W:*** Seung-wan Ryoo, Jin-wan Jeong; ***C:*** Yeong-hwon Choi; ***M:*** Jawe-kwon Han.

No Code of Conduct 1998 (R) Veteran cop Bill Peterson (Sheen) is working with the DEA on a sting operation to recover millions in heroin but when things go wrong, Bill suspects corruption within his own department. So he calls on hot-headed cop son Jake (Charlie Sheen) for help. **90m/C VHS, DVD.** Mark Dacascos, Joe Estevez, Charlie Sheen, Martin Sheen, Courtney Gains, Paul Gleason, Joe Lando, Meredith Salenger, Bret Michaels; ***D:*** Bret Michaels; ***W:*** Charlie Sheen, Bret Michaels, Bill Gucwa, Ed Masterson; ***C:*** Adam Kane; ***M:*** Bret Michaels. **VIDEO**

No Contest 1994 (R) International terrorists, lead by Oz (Clay), hold the TV host (Tweed) and contestants of the Ms. Galaxy beauty pageant hostage with a $10 million ransom demand. **98m/C VHS, DVD.** Andrew (Dice Clay) Silverstein, Shannon Tweed, Robert Davi, Roddy Piper, Nicholas (Nick) Campbell; ***D:*** Paul Lynch; ***W:*** Robert Cooper.

No Country for Old Men 2007 (R) When cowboy Llewelyn Moss (Brolin) happens upon a drug deal gone bad in the West Texas wilderness and grabs a case holding more than $2 million, it's up to world-weary sheriff Ed Tom Bell (Jones) to track him down. However, both men find themselves tangled up with cold-blooded killer Anton Chigurh (Bardem), who's determined to track down the missing money and willing to kill anyone in his way. Expertly adapted from the Cormac McCarthy novel, writers/directors/producers Joel and Ethan Coen have crafted a masterpiece: a painstakingly intense, dark thriller that doubles as a meditation on the role of violence in American society. **122m/C DVD.** *US* Tommy Lee Jones, Javier Bardem, Josh Brolin, Woody Harrelson, Kelly Macdonald, Tess Harper, Garret Dillahunt, Barry Corbin; ***D:*** Joel Coen, Ethan Coen; ***W:*** Joel Coen, Ethan Coen; ***C:*** Roger Deakins; ***M:*** Carter Burwell. Oscars '07: Adapt. Screenplay, Director (Coen, Coen), Film, Support. Actor (Bardem); British Acad. '07: Cinematog., Director (Coen, Coen), Support. Actor (Bardem); Directors Guild '07: Director (Coen), Director (Coen); Golden Globes '08: Screenplay, Support. Actor (Bardem); Screen Actors Guild '07: Support. Actor (Bardem), Cast; Writers Guild '07: Adapt. Screenplay.

No Dead Heroes 1987 Green Beret Vietnam war hero succumbs to Soviet scheming when they plant a computer chip in his brain. Unoriginal and unworthy. **86m/C VHS.** Max (Michael) Thayer, John Dresden, Toni Nero; ***D:*** J.C. Miller.

No Deposit, No Return *Double Trouble* **1976 (G)** Tedious, silly, pointless Disney action comedy. Rich brats persuade bumbling crooks to kidnap them, offer them for ransom to millionaire grandfather. **115m/C VHS, DVD.** David Niven, Don Knotts, Darren McGavin, Barbara Feldon, Charles Martin Smith; ***D:*** Norman Tokar; ***W:*** Arthur Alsberg; ***M:*** Buddy (Norman Dale) Baker.

No Dessert Dad, 'Til You Mow the Lawn 1/2 **1994 (PG)** Suburban parents Ken and Carol Cochran (Robert Hays and Joanna Kerns) are harassed at home by their annoying offspring, Justin, Monica, and Tyler. When they try hypnosis tapes to quit smoking, the kids discover by doctoring the tapes, they can plant suggestions resulting in parental perks. **80m/C VHS, DVD.** Robert Hays, Joanna Kerns, Joshua Schaefer, Allison Meek, Jimmy Marsden, Richard Moll, Larry Linville; ***D:*** Howard McCain.

No Drums, No Bugles 1/2 **1971 (G)** A West Virginia farmer and conscientious objector leaves his family to live alone in a cave for three years during the Civil War. Bad direction spoils Sheen's good performance. **85m/C VHS.** Martin Sheen, Davey Davison, Denine Terry, Rod McCary; ***D:*** Clyde Ware.

No End *Bez Konca* **1984** The ghost of a dead lawyer watches as his wife and young son struggle to survive without him, including the widow getting involved in her husband's last case about a worker arrested for organizing a strike. Well-acted but overly solemn and slow; set during Poland's martial law in 1982. In Polish with English subtitles. **108m/C VHS, DVD.** *PL* Grazyna Szapolowska, Jerzy Radziwilowicz, Maria Pakulnis, Aleksander Bardini, Artur Barcis, Michal Bajor; ***D:*** Krzysztof Kieslowski; ***W:*** Krzysztof Piesiewicz, Krzysztof Kieslowski.

No End in Sight 1/2 **2007** Brookings Institute scholar and political science PhD Charles Ferguson's documentary of the war in Iraq is a powerful, compelling analysis and critique of U.S. policy. Rather than criticize the war as a whole, Ferguson focuses in on the period immediately following the overthrow of Saddam and the Bush Administration's lack of a plan to rebuild Iraq. Most compelling are the interviews with individuals such as Ambassador Barbara Bodine and Major General Paul Eaton, who were hands-on involved in that initial post-Saddam period and found their efforts hindered by disorganization and ideological agendas. By focusing on experts involved in the war rather than outside critics, Ferguson skips partisanship to create a sharp, hard to ignore film. **102m/C DVD.** *US* ***D:*** Charles Ferguson; ***W:*** Charles Ferguson; ***C:*** Antonio Rossi; ***M:*** Peter Nashel.

No Escape 1/2 **1994 (R)** In 2022, Captain Robbins (Liotta) has been banished to a prison colony island inhabited by the most dangerous criminals. With no walls and no guards, the prisoners are left to kill each other. Then Robbins discovers a relatively peaceful community of prisoners who help each other. But this group is soon bedeviled by the evil nasties on the other side of the island. Attempts at escape define the plot, so the film is filled with superhuman feats of sheer courage, determination, and guts. Adapted from the book "The Penal Colony" by Richard Herley. **118m/C VHS, DVD.** Ray Liotta, Lance Henriksen, Stuart Wilson, Kevin Dillon, Kevin J. O'Connor, Michael Lerner, Ernie Hudson, Ian McNeice, Jack Shepherd; ***D:*** Martin Campbell; ***W:*** Joel Gross; ***C:*** Phil Meheux; ***M:*** Graeme Revell.

No Escape, No Return 1/2 **1993 (R)** An FBI agent (Nouri) and a police captain (Saxon) force three renegade cops (Nguyen, Caulfield, and Loveday) to infiltrate a drug syndicate. But things go from bad to worse when a war breaks out between rival drug gangs, leaving a lot of bodies, and a large chunk of money gone missing. Now the trio is sought by both the cops and the crooks. **93m/C VHS, DVD.** Maxwell Caulfield, Dustin Nguyen, Denise Loveday, John Saxon, Michael Nouri, Kevin Benton; ***D:*** Charles Kanganis; ***W:*** Charles Kanganis; ***M:*** Jim Halfpenny.

No Fear, No Die **1990** To make some quick cash two black immigrants in France train and sell birds for illegal cockfights at a roadside restaurant. Jocelyn, who trains the cocks, pays them lavish, obsessive attention. But cultural conflicts and repressed passions are just waiting to explode. In French with English subtitles. **97m/C VHS.** *FR* Alex Descas, Isaach de Bankole, Jean-Claude Brialy, Solveig Dommartin, Christopher Buchholz; ***D:*** Claire Denis; ***W:*** Claire Denis, Jean-Pol Fargeau; ***M:*** Abdullah Ibrahim.

No Good Deed 1/2 *The House on Turk Street* **2002 (R)** Fairly mild thriller adapted from the Dashiell Hammett story, "The House on Turk Street." Diabetic, cello-playing cop Jack Friar (Jackson) postpones his vacation to look for a neighbor's runaway daughter. While checking around Turk Street, he comes to the aid of elderly Mrs. Quarre (Zabriskie) and winds up the hostage of a gang planning a bank robbery: mastermind Tyrone (Skarsgard), hothead Hoop (Hutchinson), inside man David (Higgins), and Tyrone's sexy and duplicitious girlfriend Erin (Jovovich), who's given the job of guarding Jack. Naturally, Jack's diabetes and his cello-playing will both come into play. **97m/C VHS, DVD.** Samuel L. Jackson, Milla Jovovich, Stellan Skarsgard, Doug Hutchison, Grace Zabriskie, Joss Ackland, Jonathan Higgins; ***D:*** Bob Rafelson; ***W:*** Christopher Canaan, Steve Barancik; ***C:*** Juan Ruiz-Anchia; ***M:*** Jeff Beal.

No Greater Love 1/2 **1943** Capraesque Soviet war movie. A peasant woman mobilizes her village against the Nazis to avenge her family's death. Dubbed into English by the Soviets for Western circulation during WWII. **74m/B VHS.** *RU* Vera Maretskaya; ***D:*** Frederic Ermler.

No Highway in the Sky **1951** Eccentric scientist Theodore Honey (Stewart) works for the Royal Aircraft Establishment, which has just produced a new plane, the Reindeer. But Honey tells his boss Dennis Scott (Hawkins) that the plane has a serious defect. While flying to examine a Reindeer crash site, Honey befriends Monica (Dietrich), a musical star, and stewardess Marjorie (Johns), who support him when his company accuses him of maliciously damaging the aircraft's reputation. Dietrich steals every scene with her Christian Dior wardrobe and star attitude. Based on the novel "No Highway" by Nevil Shute. **98m/B VHS.** *GB* James Stewart, Marlene Dietrich, Glynis Johns, Jack Hawkins, Ronald Squire, Niall MacGinnis, Elizabeth Allan, Kenneth More, David Hutcheson; ***D:*** Henry Koster; ***W:*** R.C. Sherriff, Oscar Millard; ***M:*** Malcolm Arnold.

No Holds Barred 1/2 **1989 (PG-13)** Cheesy, campy remake of cheesy, campy 1952 wrestling movie. Hulk Hogan on the big screen, at last. **98m/C VHS.** Hulk Hogan, Kurt Fuller, Joan Severance, Tommy (Tiny) Lister; ***D:*** Thomas J. Wright.

No Kidding 1/2 *Beware of Children* **1960** Weak Brit com. David (Phillips) and Catherine (McEwan) Robinson inherit a large country home and, needing money for upkeep, decide to turn it into a summer camp for rich kids neglected by their parents. Naturally, most of the youngsters are little horrors or hormonal teens, the help is drunk and/or inept, and busy-body alderwoman Mrs. Spicer (Handl) wants to take the property for a community center. **83m/B DVD.** *GB* Leslie Phillips, Geraldine McEwan, Irene Handl, Joan Hickson, Noel Purcell, Julia Lockwood, June Jago; ***D:*** Gerald Thomas; ***W:*** Norman Hudis, Robin Estridge; ***C:*** Alan Hume; ***M:*** Bruce Montgomery.

No Laughing Matter 1/2 **1997 (PG-13)** The widow of a policeman, outgoing Emma (Somers) is especially close to her teenaged son Charlie (Christ), who feels protective of his mother. And Emma needs protection since she has a long-standing drinking problem she refuses to admit to. Her ability to function becomes increasingly impaired just as Charlie needs her most—seems his girlfriend Lauren (Blair) is pregnant. Finally, Emma seeks help but as she pulls herself together, Charlie turns hostile over his own volatile situation. **90m/C VHS.** Suzanne Somers, Chad Christ, Selma Blair, Robert Desiderio; ***D:*** Michael Elias; ***W:*** Michael Elias, Ted Kristian. **TV**

No Looking Back *Long Time, Nothing New* **1998 (R)** Small-town 30ish waitress Claudia (Holly) is about to settle for a boring life with decent-but-dull Michael (Bon Jovi) when her ne'er-do-well former boyfriend Charlie (Burns) comes home looking to relive the glory days. Burns stays with the working-class, northeastern setting, but goes for drama this time. With themes that cover economic hopelessness and a yearning to escape, Burns seems to be trying for a cinematic distillation of Bruce Springsteen's (very cinematic) music. In fact, many Springsteen songs are used to set scenes. Like Bruce, Burns knows the working class vernacular, and uses it well. But this time, all traces of sublety are gone, and the story plays out pretty much as expected. Holly doesn't help much, barely registering in the crucial role. She also looks too damn good to be a washed-up waitress with no options. **96m/C VHS, DVD.** Lauren Holly, Edward Burns, Jon Bon Jovi, Blythe Danner, Connie Britton; ***D:*** Edward Burns; ***W:*** Edward Burns; ***C:*** Frank Prinzi; ***M:*** Joe Delia.

No Love for Johnnie **1960** Well acted if unoriginal political drama. Finch is a British M.P. who fails in both public and private life. Based on the novel by Wilfred Fienburgh. **105m/B VHS.** *GB* Peter Finch, Stanley Holloway, Donald Pleasence, Mary Peach, Mervyn Johns, Dennis Price, Oliver Reed, Billie Whitelaw; ***D:*** Ralph Thomas; ***W:*** Mordecai Richler; ***M:*** Malcolm Arnold. British Acad. '61: Actor (Finch).

No Man Is an Island 1/2 **1962** Wartime adventure based on the exploits (Hollywoodized) of U.S. Naval radio operator George R. Tweed (Hunter), who is stationed on Guam when the Japanese invade. He hides out in the jungle to avoid capture and is aided by the natives for nearly three years until he's able to contact some American warships. Thanks to Tweed's info, the Americans are able to recapture the island. **114m/C VHS, DVD.** Jeffrey Hunter, Marshall Thompson, Ronald Remy, Rolf Bayer, Barbara Perez, Joseph de Cordova; ***D:*** John Monks Jr., Richard Goldstone; ***W:*** John Monks Jr., Richard Goldstone; ***C:*** Carl Kayser; ***M:*** Restie Umali.

No Man of Her Own 1/2 **1932** Gable and Lombard in their only screen pairing. Gambler Babe Stewart (Gable) marries small town librarian (Lombard) on a bet and attempts to hide his secret life from her. Neither star's best film. **81m/B VHS.** Carole Lombard, Clark Gable, Grant Mitchell, Elizabeth Patterson, Dorothy Mackaill, George Barbier, J. Farrell MacDonald, Walter Walker, Paul Ellis; ***D:*** Wesley Ruggles; ***W:*** Benjamin Glazer, Edmund Goulding, Maurine Watkins; ***C:*** Leo Tover; ***M:*** W. Franke Harling.

No Man's Land **1987 (R)** Undercover cop Sweeney tails playboy car thief Sheen but is seduced by wealth and glamour. Flashy surfaces, shiny cars, little substance. **107m/C VHS, DVD.** Charlie Sheen, D.B. Sweeney, Lara Harris, Randy Quaid; ***D:*** Peter Werner; ***W:*** Dick Wolf; ***M:*** Basil Poledouris.

No Man's Land 1/2 **2001 (R)** Let's talk about the futility and stupidity of war. In Bosnia in 1993, Croatian soldier Ciki (Branko Djuric) and Serbian Nino (Rene Bitorajac) wind up sharing the same trench between enemy lines, which is booby-trapped by a land mine. Laying on the mine is injured Croat Cera (Filip Sovagovic) and if he moves, they all die. Reluctantly brought into the already tense situation is ineffectual U.N. officer Col. Soft (Callow) and then journalist Jane (Cartlidge) also shows up. Bosnian with subtitles. **98m/C VHS, DVD.** *BS FR IT BE GB* Branko Djuric, Rene Bitorajac, Filip Sovagovic, Georges Siatidis, Serge-Henri Valcke, Simon Callow, Katrin Cartlidge; ***D:*** Danis Tanovic; ***W:*** Danis Tanovic; ***C:*** Walther Vanden Ende; ***M:*** Danis Tanovic. Oscars '01: Foreign Film; Cannes '01: Screenplay; L.A. Film Critics '01: Foreign Film.

No Man's Law 1/2 **1927** Hardy plays the depraved villian desperate to get the goldmine owned by an old prospector and his beautiful daughter. But the mine is protected by Rex the Wonder Horse! **?m/B VHS.** Oliver Hardy, Barbara Kent, James Finlayson, Theodore von Eltz; ***D:*** Fred W. Jackman.

No Man's Range *No Man's Land* **1935** Unremarkable, typical, predictable Western: good guys, bad guys, guns, bullets, horses. **56m/B VHS, DVD.** Buck Connors, Steve Clark, Charles French, Roberta Gale, Bob Steele; ***D:*** Robert North Bradbury; ***W:*** Forbes Parkhill; ***C:*** William Nobles.

No Marriage Ties 1/2 **1933** Reporter Bruce Foster (Dix) loses his job because he's a boozer but finds his way with words appeals to ad man Perkins (Dinehart). The two partner up successfully but Perkins begins to disapprove of the way Foster does business, especially when Bruce goes after a cosmetics account and its owner (Deane). **72m/B VHS.** Richard Dix, Alan Dinehart, Doris Kenyon, Elizabeth Allan, David Landau; ***D:*** J. Walter Ruben; ***W:*** Sam Mintz; ***C:*** Henry Cronjager.

No Mercy **1986 (R)** A Chicago cop (Gere) plunges into the Cajun bayou in order to avenge the murder of his partner. He falls for a beautiful girl enslaved by the killer, but that doesn't stop him from using her to flush out the powerful swamp-inhabiting crime lord. Absurd story without much plot. **108m/C VHS, DVD.** Richard Gere, Kim Basinger, Jeroen Krabbe, George Dzundza, William Atherton, Ray Sharkey, Bruce McGill; ***D:*** Richard Pearce; ***W:*** James (Jim) Carabatsos; ***C:*** Michel Brault; ***M:*** Alan Silvestri.

No Money Down *The Definite Maybe* **1997 (R)** When Eric (Lucas) needs a new place to live, his best pal Ziggy (Beuhl) takes him to the Hamptons for the weekend to look at houses and enjoy the cocktails parties and other amenities—such as fraud, adultery, and attempted murder. **90m/C DVD.** Josh(ua) Lucas, Bob Balaban, Jeffrey Beuhl, Claudia Rocafort; ***D:*** Sam Sokolow, Rob Rollins Lobl; ***W:*** Sam Sokolow, Rob Rollins Lobl; ***C:*** Elia Lyssy; ***M:*** Tree Adams, Billy Jay Stein.

No More Women 1/2 **1934** A beautiful young woman inherits a boat employing two divers. When she decides to keep only one in her employ, it leads to fights, attempted murder, jail time, and broken hearts. **76m/B VHS.** Edmund Lowe, Victor McLaglen, Sally Blane, Minna Gombell; ***D:*** Albert Rogell; ***W:*** Lou Breslow, Delmer Daves, Grant Leenhouts, John Mikale Strong.

No Name on the Bullet **1959** Aloof gunman John Gant (Murphy) is seeking revenge from someone in the town of Lordsburg, only none of the inhabitants know who the intended victim is. And slowly the town's citizens begin to panic. Great final showdown. **77m/C VHS, DVD.** Audie Murphy, Charles Drake, Joan Evans, Edgar Stehli, Warren Stevens, R.G. Armstrong, Whit Bissell, Karl Swenson; ***D:*** Jack Arnold; ***W:*** Gene L. Coon; ***C:*** Harold Lipstein.

No News from God *Sin Noticias de Dios; Don't Tempt Me!* **2001 (R)** Angel Lola (Abril) is a nightclub singer in heaven who is sent by her boss Marina (Ardant) to Earth to save the soul of boxer Many (Bechir). But when Jack (Garcia Bernal), Marina's counterpart in hell, hears the news, he sents devil waitress Carmen (Cruz) to do the deed first. To Many, Lola appears to be his ex, while Carmen is a cousin. Naturally, Lola tries to get Many to be good and Carmen wants him to be bad—and Many is well on his way to the latter. Starts out offbeat but then goes conventional. Spanish, French, and English dialogue. **115m/C VHS, DVD.** *SP FR IT MX* Victoria Abril, Penelope Cruz, Damian Bechir, Fanny Ardant, Gael Garcia Bernal, Juan Echanove, Bruno Bichir, Emilio Gutierrez-Caba; ***D:*** Agustin Diaz Yanes; ***W:*** Agustin Diaz Yanes; ***C:*** Paco Femenia; ***M:*** Bernardo Bonezzi.

No, No Nanette 1/2 **1940** Lackluster filming of the Broadway production which fared better on the stage. Stock story of a young woman (Neagle) who rescues her uncle from financial ruin and finds romance in the process. **96m/B VHS.** Anna Neagle, Richard Carlson, Victor Mature, Roland Young, Zasu Pitts, Eve Arden, Billy Gilbert, Keye Luke; ***D:*** Herbert Wilcox; ***C:*** Russell Metty.

No One Cries Forever WOOF! **1985** When a prostitute breaks away from a gangster-madam after finding love, she is tracked down and disfigured. Swedish; dubbed. **96m/C DVD.** Elke Sommer, Howard Carpendale, Zoli Marks; ***D:*** Jans Rautenbach.

No One Man **1932** Palm Beach socialite Penelope (Lombard) is a bored divorcee who marries ne'er-do-well Bill

(Cortez) who, fortunately, soon drops dead. (Must have been all that extramarital activity.) Thus leaving her free to pursue old flame and idealistic doctor, Karl Bemis (Lukas). Adapted from the novel "No One Man" by Rupert Hughes. **73m/B VHS.** Carole Lombard, Ricardo Cortez, Paul Lukas, George Barbier, Juliette Compton, Virginia Hammon; ***D:*** Lloyd Corrigan; ***W:*** Sidney Buchman, Percy Heath, Alice Leahy; ***C:*** Charles B(ryant) Lang Jr.

No One Sleeps 2001 Berlin medical researcher Stefan Hein (Wlaschiha) is attending an AIDS conference in San Francisco just as a serial killer is targeting men who are HIV positive. Stefan also wants to investigate his late father's theory that U.S. researchers used prisoners to test a virus that created HIV by trying to find an alleged list of the injected prisoners. Along the way Stefan meets detective Louise Tolliver (Levi) and discovers the two investigations may be linked. **108m/C VHS, DVD.** Tom Wlashchiha, Irit Levi, Jim Thalman, Kalene Parker; ***D:*** Jochen Hick; ***W:*** Jochen Hick; ***C:*** Thomas M. Harting, Michael Maley; ***M:*** James Hardway.

No Other Woman ½ 1933 Stand by your man despite the fact that he's a cheating, lying louse. Pittsburgh steelworker Jim Stanley (Bickford) is persuaded by wife Anna (Dunne) to invest in a dyeworks that brings them big bucks. Instead of staying home, Jim takes up with a gold-digging blonde (Andre) and causes lots of heartache for his faithful spouse. Adapted from Eugene Walter's play "Just a Woman." **58m/B VHS.** Irene Dunne, Charles Bickford, Christian Rub, J. Carrol Naish, Gwili Andre, Eric Linden, Leila Bennett; ***D:*** J. Walter Ruben; ***W:*** Bernard Schubert, Wanda Tuchock; ***C:*** Edward Cronjager.

No Place to Hide ½ 1981 A girl's father drowns and she blames herself. Her mother and psychologist try to convince the girl that her father's spirit isn't stalking her, but she doesn't believe them. **120m/C VHS.** Keir Dullea, Mariette Hartley, Kathleen Beller, Arlen Dean Snyder, Gary (Rand) Graham, John Llewellyn Moxey; ***D:*** John Llewellyn Moxey. **TV**

No Place to Hide ½ 1993 (R) Barrymore is the target of a psycho who's already killed her sister. Kristofferson plays the hard-edged cop who's out to protect her and trap the killer. **90m/C VHS.** Drew Barrymore, Kris Kristofferson, Martin Landau, O.J. Simpson, Dey Young, Bruce Weitz; ***D:*** Richard Danus; ***W:*** Richard Danus.

No Place to Run 1972 An elderly man fights for custody of his grandson, then kidnaps him and flees with him to Canada. Made for TV. **78m/C VHS.** Herschel Bernardi, Larry Hagman, Stefanie Powers, Neville Brand; ***D:*** Delbert Mann. **TV**

No Prince for My Cinderella 1978 A schizophrenic girl who has turned to prostitution is sought desperately by her social worker. **100m/C VHS.** Robert Reed.

No Problem *Pas de Probleme!* 1975 A man is pursued, shot, and drops dead in the apartment of an unsuspecting man who doesn't know what to do with the body. Dubbed in English. **94m/C VHS.** *FR* Miou-Miou, Bernard Menez, Jean (Lefevre) Lefebvre, Henri Guybet, Anny (Annie Legras) Duperey, Renee (Raymonde-Renee Vittoret) Saint-Cyr; ***D:*** Georges Lautner; ***W:*** Jean-Marie Poire; ***C:*** Roger Fellous; ***M:*** Philippe Sarde.

No Regrets for Our Youth 1946 A feminist saga depicting the spiritual growth of a foolish Japanese girl during the tumultuous years of WWII. In Japanese with English subtitles. **110m/B VHS.** *JP* Setsuko Hara, Susumu Fujita, Denjiro Okochi, Haruko Sugimura, Eiko Miyoshi; ***D:*** Akira Kurosawa; ***W:*** Akira Kurosawa; ***C:*** Asakazu Nakai; ***M:*** Tadashi Hattori.

No Reservations ½ 2007 (PG) Uptight, temperamental chef Kate (Zeta-Jones) meets her match romantically and professionally in laid back sous chef Nick (Eckhart). He's perfect, but she's too neurotic to recognize it, and just for a touch of extra conflict she's saddled with an orphaned pre-teen niece (Breslin). Aspires to be the romantic comedy version of fine dining but the end result is a bland and uninspired dish. Remake of popular German film "Mostly Martha." **105m/C DVD, Blu-ray Disc, HD DVD.** *US* Catherine Zeta-Jones, Aaron Eckhart, Abigail Breslin, Patricia Clarkson, Jenny Wade, Bob Balaban, Brian F. O'Byrne, Lily Rabe, Celia Weston, John McMartin, Stephanie Barry; ***D:*** Scott Hicks; ***W:*** Carol Fuchs; ***C:*** Stuart Dryburgh; ***M:*** Philip Glass.

No Retreat, No Surrender 1986 (PG) A young American kick-boxer battles a formidable Russian opponent and wins, quite improbably, after having been tutored by the ghost of Bruce Lee in an abandoned house. Notable as Van Damme's debut, but little else recommends this silly "Rocky" rehash. Followed by "No Retreat, No Surrender II." **85m/C VHS.** Kurt McKinney, J.W. Fails, Jean-Claude Van Damme; ***D:*** Corey Yuen.

No Retreat, No Surrender 2 1989 (R) With help from two karate experts, a man sets out to find his girlfriend who has been kidnapped by Soviets. Has little or nothing to do with the movie to which it is ostensibly a sequel. High level kick-boxing action sequences. **92m/C VHS.** Loren Avedon, Max (Michael) Thayer, Cynthia Rothrock; ***D:*** Corey Yuen; ***W:*** Maria Elene Cellino.

No Retreat, No Surrender 3: Blood Brothers 1991 (R) Sibling martial arts rivals decide to bond in a manly way when CIA agent dad is most heinously slain by terrorists. Answers the burning question: "Whatever became of Joseph Campanella?" **97m/C VHS.** Keith Vitali, Loren Avedon, Joseph Campanella; ***D:*** Lucas Lowe; ***W:*** Keith W. Strandberg; ***C:*** John Huneck; ***M:*** Richard Huen.

No Room to Run ½ 1978 Concert promoter's life turns into a nightmare of deadly corporate intrigue when he arrives in Australia. Luckily, he finds time to fall in love. **101m/C VHS.** *AU* Richard Benjamin, Paula Prentiss, Barry Sullivan; ***D:*** Robert Lewis. **TV**

No Safe Haven 1987 (R) A government agent seeks revenge for his family's death. **92m/C VHS, DVD.** Wings Hauser, Marina Rice, Robert Tessier; ***D:*** Ronnie Rondell; ***W:*** Nancy Locke, Wings Hauser; ***C:*** Steve McWilliams; ***M:*** Joel Goldsmith.

No Secrets ½ 1991 (R) A young man on the run seeks refuge with three girls in an isolated house. His dread secret isn't so dread, leaving this mild teen-oriented thriller starved for lack of menace. **92m/C VHS.** Adam Coleman Howard, Amy Locane, Heather Fairfield, Traci Lind; ***D:*** Dezso Magyar.

No Sex Please—We're British ½ 1973 Silly—and now dated—sex farce finds a postman accidentally delivering a parcel of pornography to a conservative bank. The contents inflame the bank's stuffy employees and suddenly it's a sexual free-for-all! Based on the play by Anthony Marriott and Alistair Foot. **90m/C VHS.** *GB* Ronnie Corbett, Beryl Reid, Arthur Lowe, Ian Ogilvy, Susan Penhaligon, Michael Bates, Gerald Sim, David Swift; ***D:*** Cliff Owen; ***W:*** John Mortimer, Anthony Marriott, Brian Cooke; ***C:*** Ken Hodges; ***M:*** Eric Rogers.

No Sleep 'Til Madison ½ 2002 Thirty-something Owen (Gaffigan) rounds up his old high school buddies for their yearly trek back to sweet home Wisconsin for their alma mater's hockey tournament. Along the way, he discovers that growing up is hard to do as his chums desert him when adulthood beckons. The message in this lighthearted flick is as subtle as a crosscheck to the face, but the likeable Gaffigan won't be sent to the penalty box for his efforts. **89m/C VHS, DVD.** Jim Gaffigan, Rebekah Louise Smith, Ian Brennan, T.J. Jagodowski, Michael Gilio, Jed Resnik, Molly Glynn, Jason Wells, David Fleer, Erik Moe; ***D:*** David Fleer, Erik Moe, Peter Rudy; ***W:*** David Fleer, Erik Moe, Peter Rudy; ***C:*** Bradley W. Milsap; ***M:*** Stephen (Steve) Edwards. **VIDEO**

No Small Affair 1984 (R) A 16-year-old aspiring photographer becomes romantically involved with a sultry 22-year-old rock star. **102m/C VHS, DVD.** Jon Cryer, Demi Moore, George Wendt, Peter Frechette, Elizabeth (E.G. Dailey) Daily, Tim Robbins, Jennifer Tilly, Ric(k) Ducommun, Ann Wedgeworth; ***D:*** Jerry Schatzberg; ***C:*** John A. Alonzo; ***M:*** Rupert Holmes.

No Smoking ½ 1955 Scientist Reg Bates (Dixon) discovers a successful formula to cure nicotine addiction. Of course when he tries to manufacture and distribute his new pill, he runs into serious opposition from the tobacco industry. **72m/B DVD.** *GB* Reg Dixon, Peter Martyn, Belinda Lee, Lionel Jeffries, Myrtle Rowe, Ruth Trouncer, Alexander Gauge; ***D:*** Lionel Jeffries, Henry Cass; ***C:*** Monty Berman; ***M:*** Ivor Slaney.

No Strings Attached 1998 (R) Mark Demetrius (Spano) is a reporter working on a story about women's sexual fantasies. To the distress of his fiancee, he enters a relationship with a mysterious woman he knows only through telephone conversations. To nobody's surprise, murder ensues. **97m/C VHS, DVD.** Vincent Spano, Cheryl Pollak, Traci Lind, David Packer, Michael McKean; ***D:*** Josef Rusnak; ***W:*** Nicholas Bogner, Michael Holden; ***C:*** Wedigo von Schultzendorff; ***M:*** Eric Lundmark.

No Such Thing 2001 (R) This "Beauty and the Beast" fairytale for grownups doesn't always work but it's at least intriguing. Burke stars as an ill-tempered, drunken, ageless, nameless monster who has been terrorizing the remote areas of Iceland. When timid Beatrice (Polley) learns that her fiance, part of a news crew, has been slaughtered by the beast, she persuades her ratings-driven TV news show boss (Mirren) to send her to follow up on the story. Monster and Beatrice develop an unexpected rapport and she brings him back to New York where he's exploited, not unknowingly, as the lastest celeb. **103m/C VHS, DVD.** *US* Sarah Polley, Robert John Burke, Helen Mirren, Julie Christie, Baltasar Kormakur; ***D:*** Hal Hartley; ***W:*** Hal Hartley; ***C:*** Michael Spiller; ***M:*** Hal Hartley.

No Surrender 1986 (R) An unpredictable, darkly charming comedy about a Liverpool nightclub newly managed by Angelis. On New Year's Eve, a small drunken war is triggered when two groups of irate senior citizens are booked into the club and clash over their beliefs. The group is made up of Protestants and Catholics and the fight resembles the ongoing conflicts in modern-day Northern Ireland, although most of the action takes place in the loo. Watch for Costello as an inept magician. **100m/C VHS.** *GB* Ray McAnally, Michael Angelis, Avis Bunnage, James Ellis, Tom Georgeson, Mark Mulholland, Joanne Whalley, Elvis Costello, Bernard Hill, Michael Ripper; ***D:*** Peter Smith; ***W:*** Alan Bleasdale; ***C:*** Michael Coulter; ***M:*** Daryl Runswick.

No Survivors, Please ½ *Der Chef Wuenscht Keine Zeugen; The Chief Wants No Survivors* 1963 Aliens from Orion take over politicians in order to rule the Earth. Bizarre, obscure, based on true story. **92m/B VHS.** *GE* Maria Perschy, Uwe Friedrichsen, Robert Cunningham, Karen Blanguernon, Gustavo Rojo; ***D:*** Hans Albin, Peter Berneis.

No Time for Romance 1948 A sprightly musical with an all-black cast. First such film to be shot in color. **?m/C VHS.** Joel Fluellen, Eunice Wilson, Austin McCoy, Shirley Haven, Bill Walker.

No Time for Sergeants 1958 Hilarious film version of the Broadway play by Ira Levin, which was based on the novel by Mac Hyman. Griffith is excellent as Georgia farm boy Will Stockdale, who gets drafted into the service and creates mayhem among his superiors and colleagues. Of course, Griffith had already played the role both on stage and in a TV version. McCormick was also repeating his Broadway role of Sgt. King. Note Don Knotts in a small role along with Jameel Farah who went on to star in TV's "M*A*S*H" after changing his name to Jamie Farr. **119m/B VHS.** Andy Griffith, Nick Adams, Murray Hamilton, Myron McCormick, Howard Smith, Will Hutchins, Sydney Smith, Don Knotts, Jamie Farr; ***D:*** Mervyn LeRoy; ***W:*** John Lee Mahin; ***C:*** Harold Rosson; ***M:*** Ray Heindorf.

No Time to Die 1984 In Indonesia, two corporate pawns and a beautiful reporter battle for the possession of a new laser cannon. **87m/C VHS.** *GE* Chris Mitchum, John Phillip Law, Grazyna Dylong; ***D:*** Helmut Ashley; ***W:*** Helmut Ashley; ***C:*** Wolfgang Grasshoff; ***M:*** Hans Hammerschmidt.

No Tomorrow ½ 1999 (R) Criminal Busey works with shipping-company employee Daniels to broker a multimillion-dollar arms deal. As word of the deal spreads, both a gangster (Master P) and an FBI agent (Grier) get involved as well. Lots of shootouts and explosions cover the threadbare plot. **99m/C VHS, DVD.** Gary Busey, Gary Daniels, Pam Grier, Jeff Fahey, Master P; ***D:*** Master P. **VIDEO**

No Trace 1950 A writer who broadcasts his crime stories as part of a radio show is the victim of blackmail. It seems a former associate is aware that the stories are all based in fact. A Scotland Yard detective investigates when murder rears its ugly head. **76m/B VHS.** *GB* Hugh Sinclair, Dinah Sheridan, John Laurie, Barry Morse, Michael Brennan, Dora Bryan; ***D:*** John Gilling.

No Turning Back ½ 2001 (R) Intriguing based-on-real-events story of Pablo Hernandez (Nebot), an illegal immigrant who came to southern California after losing everything except his six-year-old daughter, Cristina (Rendon), during 1998's Hurricane Mitch in Honduras. After Pablo unintentionally mows down a well-to-do young girl with a borrowed truck, the pair is on the run with Soid (Price), a struggling journalist who agrees to aid the desperate man in exchange for filming the getaway. Along with playing the lead role, Nebot also co-wrote and makes his debut as co-director. **98m/C VHS, DVD.** Jesus Nebot, Lindsay Price, Vernee Watson-Johnson, Susan Haskell, Chelsea Rendon, Joe Estevez, Niki Botelho, Kenya Moore, Gage Hunter Bebank; ***D:*** Jesus Nebot, Julia Montejo; ***W:*** Jesus Nebot, Julia Montejo; ***C:*** Ian Fox; ***M:*** Steven Chesne. **VIDEO**

No Vacancy ½ 1999 (R) LA's Pink Motel may be a dump but it feels like home to the kooky folks who are hanging out there, such as Lillian (Ricci), who's shook up to see that the man in her bed isn't her fiance. Also, there's two druggies who stiff their working girls andhave to deal with the gals' super-slick pimp (Wagner). **83m/C VHS, DVD.** Olek Krupa, Lolita (David) Davidovich, Timothy Olyphant, Christina Ricci, Ryan Bollman, Steven Schub, Tracy Tutor, Joaquim de Almeida, Patricia Velasquez, Graham Beckel, Gabriel Mann, Robert Wagner, Rhona Bennett, June Velar, Tracey Minner, Micaela Lockridge, Irina Gasanova, Tom Todoroff; ***D:*** Marius Balchunas; ***W:*** Marius Balchunas; ***C:*** Denis Maloney; ***M:*** Jeff Marsh, Alex Wurman. **VIDEO**

No Way Back 1974 (R) Way. Writer, director, and producer Williamson portrays Jess Crowder, a man-for-hire who is an expert with guns, fists, and martial arts. An angry look at the white establishment. **92m/C VHS.** Fred Williamson, Charles Woolf, Tracy Reed, Virginia Gregg, Don Cornelius; ***D:*** Fred Williamson.

No Way Back WOOF! *Ain't No Way Back* 1990 (R) Two men find themselves in a trashy mess when they come to the aid of a damsel in distress while hunting the backwoods. One man dies and the other, Fletcher (Scott), must stop a family feud if he hopes to survive. Actually filmed in 1989, this terrible terror movie sat on the shelf for 16 years before our good friends at Troma decided to rescue it. **90m/C DVD.** Campbell Scott, Virginia Lantry, Bernie (Bernard) White, John Durbin, Sean McGuirk, Dennis Ott; ***D:*** Michael Borden; ***W:*** Morgan Sloane; ***C:*** Nastaran Dibai; ***M:*** Murielle Hamilton. **VIDEO**

No Way Back 1996 (R) FBI agent Zack Grant (Crowe) has never dealt with the death of his wife in childbirth and his career has suffered. His last professional chance is a sting operation involving the Mafia and the Yakuza. But when the operation goes wrong, Grant has a vendetta on his hands. Mafia boss Serlano (Lerner) kidnaps Zack's young son so Zack will turn over his prisoner—Yuji (Toyokawa), a Yakuza whom Serlano believes is responsible for his own son's death. Zack's only interest is to rescue his son and he doesn't care who gets in his way, including his fellow feds and the gangsters. **92m/C VHS, DVD.** Kelly Hu, Russell Crowe, Helen Slater, Michael Lerner, Etsushi Toyokawa, Ian Ziering; ***D:*** Frank Cappello; ***W:*** Frank Cappello; ***C:*** Richard Clabaugh; ***M:*** David Williams.

No Way Home 1996 (R) Joey (Roth), who's mentally a little slow, returns to his tough Staten Island neighborhood after being paroled from prison. He goes to live with his low-level drug dealer older brother Tommy (Russo) and Tommy's wife, Lorrain (Unger), who's not too happy about the situation—at first. But Joey's basically a decent guy and Lorrain begins to respond to his consideration. Meanwhile, desperate Tommy's in debt to a loan shark and his behavior may once again find Joey taking the rap for his brother's misdeeds. The story's predictable but the cast definitely rises above the material. **101m/C VHS, DVD.** Catherine Kellner, Joe Ragno, Tim Roth, James Russo, Deborah Kara Unger; ***D:*** Buddy Giovinazzo; ***W:*** Buddy Giovinazzo; ***C:*** Claudia Raschke; ***M:*** Ricky Giovinazzo.

No Way Out 🦴🦴 1/2 **1950** When bigoted bad guy Roy Biddle (Widmark) and his brother George (Bellaver) are shot, they're taken to a small hospital run by Dr. Wharton (McNally), who believes in giving all his doctors a fair chance. So black doctor Luther Brooks (Poitier) works on George, who dies. Naturally, Roy blames the doctor and gets his hoodlum pals to cause some bloody confrontations. **105m/B VHS, DVD.** Sidney Poitier, Richard Widmark, Stephen McNally, Linda Darnell, Harry Bellaver, Stanley Ridges, Ruby Dee, Ossie Davis; ***D:*** Joseph L. Mankiewicz; ***W:*** Joseph L. Mankiewicz, Lesser Samuels; ***C:*** Milton Krasner; ***M:*** Alfred Newman.

No Way Out 🦴🦴🦴 **1987 (R)** Career Navy man Tom Farrel (Costner) is involved with a beautiful, sexy party girl, Susan (Young), who gets killed. Turns out she was also the mistress of Secretary of Defense Brice (Hackman), Tom's boss. Assigned to investigate her suspicious death, Tom suddenly finds himself set up as the chief suspect. A tight thriller based on 1948's "The Big Clock," with a new surprise ending. Costner looks fine in his Navy whites and there's a backseat limousine sex scene that's quite steamy. **114m/C VHS, DVD.** Kevin Costner, Sean Young, Gene Hackman, Will Patton, Howard Duff, George Dzundza, Iman, Chris D, Marshall Bell, Jason Bernard, Fred Dalton Thompson, David Paymer, Eugene Robert Glazer; ***D:*** Roger Donaldson; ***W:*** Robert Garland; ***C:*** John Alcott; ***M:*** Maurice Jarre.

No Way to Treat a Lady 🦴🦴🦴 **1968** Steiger is a psychotic master of disguise who stalks and kills various women in this suspenseful cat-and-mouse game. Segal, as the detective assigned to the case, uncovers clues, falls in love, and discovers that his new girl may be the killer's next victim. **108m/C VHS, DVD.** Rod Steiger, Lee Remick, George Segal, Eileen Heckart, Murray Hamilton; ***D:*** Jack Smight; ***W:*** John Gay; ***C:*** Jack Priestley.

No Witness 🦴 1/2 **2004 (R)** Shady Senator Gene Haskell (Fahey) is having some problems staying on the right side of the law and makes his gopher Leiter (Feldman) his pawn in covering up the misdeeds. The thorough hit man Paul (Barnes) hired by gives even the senator the willies. All-too-familiar thriller-wannabe includes some familiar faces who don't further the cause. **95m/C DVD.** Jeff Fahey, Corey Feldman, Michael Damian, Steve Barnes, Marisa Petroro; ***D:*** Michael Valverde; ***W:*** Michael Valverde, Steve Antczak. **VIDEO**

Noa at Seventeen 🦴🦴🦴 **1982** The political/social turmoil of Israel in 1951 is allegorically depicted by the school vs. kibbutz debate within a young girl's middle-class family. In Hebrew with English subtitles. **86m/C VHS, DVD.** *IS* Dalia Shimko, Idit Zur, Shmuel Shilo, Moshe Havazelet; ***D:*** Isaac Yeshurun.

The Noah 🦴🦴 1/2 **1975** Bourla's only film, filmed in 1968 with a brief appearance on the festival circuit in 1975, is a murky B&W post-apocalyptic nightmare. Former soldier Noah (character actor Strauss) is the only survivor of a nuclear holocaust. He finds himself marooned on an island that once housed a Communist Chinese military facility, thus offering him shelter. Unable to cope with his solitude, Noah begins hearing voices that grow into an imaginary civilization complete with problems, including a war, which Noah must battle. A definite cinematic oddity. **107m/B DVD.** Robert Strauss; ***D:*** Daniel Bourla; ***W:*** Daniel Bourla; ***C:*** Jerry Kalogeratos; ***V:*** Geoffrey Holder, Sally Kirkland, Jim Blackmore.

Noah 🦴🦴 **1998** Contemporary update of the biblical story of Noah and his ark, retold for laughs (and morals). Busy widowed contractor Norman Waters (Danza) has three sons to provide for and can't spend as much time with them as he may like. Then a heavenly bureaucrat (Shawn) comes down and tells Norman to build an ark in the usual 40 days. At least it brings the family together. **90m/C VHS.** Tony Danza, Wallace Shawn, Jane Sibbett; ***D:*** Ken Kwapis. **TV**

Noah's Arc: Jumping the Broom 🦴🦴 1/2 **2008 (R)** This feature film, based on the Logo network series, follows the preparations for the Martha's Vineyard nuptials of Noah and Wade. Of course the attendees indulge in the usual round of flirtations, secrets, jealousies, and sexual situations, with a satisfying happy ending for at least some. **101m/C DVD.** Darryl Stephens, Jensen Atwood, Douglas Spearman, Christian Vincent, Rodney Chester, Gary LeRoi Gray, Jonathan Julian, Jason Steed; ***D:*** Patrik-Ian Polk; ***W:*** Patrik-Ian Polk, John R. Gordon; ***C:*** Christopher Porter; ***M:*** Adam S. Goldman, Julian Wass.

Noah's Ark 🦴🦴 **1999** Made-for-TV biblical epic of the Old Testament story that doesn't exactly stay close to its biblical roots. It's eccentric, special effects-laden, and borders on the irreverent. Noah builds his ark, gathers the animals (and his family), watches as the world is destroyed, and survives the 40 days and nights of flooding. **178m/C VHS, DVD.** Jon Voight, Mary Steenburgen, F. Murray Abraham, Carol Kane, James Coburn, Jonathan Cake, Alexis Denisof, Emily Mortimer, Sydney Tamiia Poitier, Sonya Walger; ***D:*** John Irvin; ***W:*** Peter Barnes; ***C:*** Mike Molloy; ***M:*** Paul Grabowsky. **TV**

Nobel Son 🦴 1/2 **2008 (R)** Professor Eli Michaelson (Rickson) was an egomaniacal jerk before being awarded the Nobel Prize in chemistry. Now, he's completely insufferable. So much so that he is uncaring when his only son Barkley (Greenberg), whom Eli regards as a complete disappointment, is kidnapped, and he won't pay the ransom. The abductor is no secret—Thaddeus James (Hatosy) is a mechanical genius claiming to be Eli's illegitimate son and he tries to force Barkley into aiding him in his revenge/extortion plot. However the characters are so tedious (as is the unfolding of the action) that it's hard to stay interested. **102m/C DVD.** *US* Alan Rickman, Bryan Greenberg, Shawn Hatosy, Mary Steenburgen, Eliza Dushku, Bill Pullman, Danny DeVito, Ted Danson; ***D:*** Randall Miller; ***W:*** Randall Miller, Jody Slavin; ***C:*** Michael Ozier; ***M:*** Paul Oakenfold, Mark Adler.

Noble House 🦴🦴 1/2 **1988** Continuation of James Clavell's Hong Kong series, following "Tai-Pan," and set in the present day. Ian Dunross (Brosnan) is the head of Struan and Company, Hong Kong's leading trading company, which is being undermined by the nefarious Quillan Gornt (Rhys-Davies) who plots to destroy his archrival. American businesswoman Casey Tcholok (the bland Raffin) serves as Dunross' love interest. Originally a four-part TV miniseries partially filmed on location. **350m/C VHS.** Pierce Brosnan, John Rhys-Davies, Deborah Raffin, Ben Masters, Julia Nickson-Soul, Khigh (Kaie Deei) Deigh, Tia Carrere, Gordon Jackson; ***D:*** Gary Nelson; ***W:*** Eric Bercovici; ***C:*** Cristiano Pogany; ***M:*** Paul Chihara.

Nobody 🦴🦴 **1999** Three businessmen get involved in a bar fight that isn't your average brawl. In fact, the situation begins to take over their lives and they're no longer certain even who they're fighting. Japanese with subtitles. **100m/C VHS, DVD.** *JP* Masaya Kato, Jinpachi Nezu, Riki Takeuchi, Hideo Nakano; ***D:*** Shundo Ohkawa, Toshimichi Ohkawa; ***W:*** Shundo Ohkawa.

Nobody 🦴 1/2 **2007** Repetitious modern noir about an assassin who claims success on a kill to his mobster boss Toles. But Toles wants proof and it seems the dead man isn't so dead after all. Non-linear timeline and the lack of a coherent ending make this more of an indie experiment than cohesive storytelling. **88m/C DVD.** *CA* Costas Mandylor, Ed O'Ross, Darren Wall, Dawn Johnson; ***D:*** Shawn Linden; ***W:*** Shawn Linden; ***M:*** James Robertson.

Nobody Knows 🦴🦴 1/2 *Dare mo shiranai* **2004 (PG-13)** Inspired by a true story that happened in 1988, Koreeda's overly-long drama follows the lives of four abandoned children. Irresponsible Keiko (You) smuggles her brood into a Tokyo apartment, refusing to let them attend school and giving them bizarre rules to follow so they won't be discovered. 12-year-old Akira (Yuya) is the de facto head of the family, especially when mom leaves a little cash and takes off with her latest boyfriend. Akira soon realizes she isn't returning and struggles to keep the family together under increasingly dire circumstances. Japanese with subtitles. **141m/C DVD.** Yuya Yagira, Ayu Kitaura, Momoko Shimizu, Hanae Kan, Hiei Kimura; ***D:*** Hirokazu Kore-eda; ***W:*** Hirokazu Kore-eda; ***C:*** Yutaka Yamazaki; ***M:*** Gontiti.

Nobody's Baby 🦴🦴 **2001 (R)** Poor man's "Raising Arizona" with Ulrich and Oldman playing hick vs. hick in the battle for an orphaned baby. Orphaned themselves at a young age, hillbilly brothers Billy and Buford have turned to crime, facing hard prison time and a court-ordered separation from one another until they escape from the paddy wagon on the way to the big house. Splitting up, dim Billy triggers a car crash which kills everyone aboard except a baby. Absconding with the child, Billy gets aid caring for the tot from truck stop waitress Shauna (Mitchell). Buford joins the party with the plan to ransom the kid off to still-living relatives, only to discover Billy has grown attached to the young-un. Slapstick antics ensue as the two attempt to secure funds to raise the child as their own. Only Ulrich is able to bring any interest to the weak, patchy script and unmemorable performances. **113m/C VHS, DVD.** Skeet Ulrich, Gary Oldman, Radha Mitchell, Mary Steenburgen, Gordon Tootoosis, Anna Gunn, Peter Greene, Ed O'Neill, Matthew Modine; ***D:*** David Seltzer; ***W:*** David Seltzer; ***C:*** Christopher Taylor; ***M:*** Brian Tyler, Joseph Vitarelli.

Nobody's Daughter 🦴🦴 1/2 **1976** The tragedy of an eight-year-old orphan shuttled from one family to another, all of whom are only interested in the money the government will pay for her care. In Hungarian with English subtitles. **90m/C VHS.** *HU* Zsuzsi Czinkoczi; ***D:*** Lazlo Ranody.

Nobody's Fool 🦴🦴 **1986 (PG-13)** Another entry in the genre of quirky Americana, this romantic comedy concerns a hapless Midwestern waitress suffering from low-self esteem who falls in love with a traveling stage-hand. **107m/C VHS, DVD.** Rosanna Arquette, Eric Roberts, Mare Winningham, Louise Fletcher, Jim Youngs, Gwen Welles, Stephen Tobolowsky, Charlie Barnett, Lewis Arquette; ***D:*** Evelyn Purcell; ***W:*** Beth Henley; ***C:*** Misha (Mikhail) Suslov; ***M:*** James Newton Howard.

Nobody's Fool 🦴🦴🦴 1/2 **1994 (R)** Newman shines as 60-year-old Donald "Sully" Sullivan, a construction worker who, in spite of himself, begins mending his many broken relationships over the course of the holiday season. Seemingly plotless scenario is sprinkled with enough humor, hope, and understated inspiration to become a delightfully modest celebration of a perfectly ordinary man. Character-driven story is blessed with commendable performances by supporting players—obviously inspired by Newman's brilliant portrayal. Based on the novel by Richard Russo. **110m/C VHS, DVD.** Paul Newman, Jessica Tandy, Bruce Willis, Melanie Griffith, Dylan Walsh, Pruitt Taylor Vince, Gene Saks, Josef Sommer, Philip Seymour Hoffman, Philip Bosco, Margo Martindale, Jay Patterson; ***D:*** Robert Benton; ***W:*** Robert Benton; ***C:*** John Bailey; ***M:*** Howard Shore. Berlin Intl. Film Fest. '94: Actor (Newman); N.Y. Film Critics '94: Actor (Newman); Natl. Soc. Film Critics '94: Actor (Newman).

Nobody's Perfect 🦴 **1990 (PG-13)** Where "Tootsie" and "Some Like It Hot" collide (or more likely crash and burn). A lovesick teenager masquerades as a girl and joins the tennis team to be near his dream girl. Takes its title from Joe E. Brown's famous last line in "Some Like It Hot." **90m/C VHS.** Chad Lowe, Gail O'Grady, Patrick Breen, Kim Flowers, Robert Vaughn; ***D:*** Robert Kaylor; ***W:*** Joel Block.

Nobody's Perfekt **WOOF!** **1979 (PG)** Supposed comedy about three psychiatric patients who decide to extort $650,000 from the city of Miami when their car is wrecked. Lacks laughs and generally considered a turkey. **95m/C VHS.** Gabe Kaplan, Robert Klein, Alex Karras, Susan Clark; ***D:*** Peter Bonerz.

Nocturna **WOOF!** *Nocturna, Granddaughter of Dracula* **1979 (R)** Hard times have fallen upon the house of Dracula. To help pay the taxes on the castle, the owners have converted it to the Hotel Transylvania. In order to increase business and the blood supply at the hotel, Nocturna books a disco group to entertain the guests. Hard times fell on this script, too. It's no wonder that director Tampa hid behind the alias Harry Hurwitz. **82m/C VHS.** Yvonne De Carlo, John Carradine, Antony (Tony) Hamilton, Nai Bonet; ***D:*** Harry (Hurwitz) Tampa; ***C:*** Mac Ahlberg.

Nocturne 🦴🦴 1/2 **1946** A police lieutenant investigates the supposed suicide of a famous composer and uncovers dark secrets that suggest murder is afoot. An overlooked RKO production shines thanks to Raft's inimitable tough guy performance and some offbeat direction. For film noir completists. **88m/B VHS.** George Raft, Lynn Bari, Virginia Huston, Joseph Pevney, Myrna Dell, Edward Ashley, Walter Sande, Mabel Paige; ***D:*** Edwin L. Marin; ***W:*** Rowland Brown, Jonathan Latimer; ***C:*** Harry Wild; ***M:*** Leigh Harline.

Noel 🦴 1/2 **2004 (PG)** Not designed for Christmas cheer, this coal-in-your-stocking drama (Palminteri's directorial debut) follows the intertwined stories of several lonely New Yorkers searching for happiness on Christmas Eve. Rose (Sarandon) is a divorced, workaholic book editor desperately trying for a final reconciliation with a mother who's in the last stages of Alzheimer's. Nina (Cruz) and Mike (Walker) are engaged but Mike's pathological jealousy is about to destroy the relationship. Waiter Artie (Arkin) thinks Mike is the reincarnation of his dead wife(!) and follows him around constantly. And homeless Jules's (Thomas) one happy holiday memory was a party in the hospital emergency room so he decides to have an "emergency." When Robin Williams shows up (unbilled) to give advice, you know you're in trouble. **96m/C DVD.** *US* Penelope Cruz, Susan Sarandon, Paul Walker, Alan Arkin, Marcus Thomas, Chazz Palminteri, Robin Williams; ***D:*** Chazz Palminteri; ***W:*** David Hubbard; ***C:*** Russell Carpenter; ***M:*** Alan Menken.

Noi 🦴🦴 *Noi Albinoi; Noi the Albino* **2003 (PG-13)** Feature debut of Kari is set in a remote Icelandic fjord village cut off from the world by winter weather. Noi (Lemarquis) is a misfit 17-year-old who lives with his eccentric grandma (Fridriksdottir) and gets expelled from school for being a smart-ass. He begins a diffident romance with newcomer Iris (Hansdottir) and wants to escape the constraints of his life, but just can't manage to get anywhere-much like the film. Icelandic with subtitles. **90m/C DVD.** *IC GE GB DK* Tomas Lemarquis, Throstur Leo Gunnarsson, Elin Hansdottir, Anna Fridriksdottir, Hjalti Rognvaldsson; ***D:*** Dagur Kari; ***W:*** Dagur Kari; ***C:*** Rasmus Videbaek.

Noir et Blanc 🦴🦴 **1986** Antoine (Frappat) is a shy accountant who takes a job in a health club and begins an increasingly sadomasochistic relationship with black masseur, Jacques (Martial). The violence is inferred not actually shown but still makes for some kinky adult fare. Based on a short story by Tennessee Williams; debut film for director Devers. French with subtitles. **82m/B VHS.** *FR* Francis Frappat, Jacques Martial, Josephine Fresson, Marc Berman, Claire Rigollier; ***D:*** Claire Devers; ***W:*** Claire Devers.

Noise 🦴 1/2 **2007** A recognizable situation turns one-note (and just what's the Russian chick all about?). Manhattanite David Owen (Robbins) is driven crazy by the city's noise pollution and starts taking a baseball bat to cars with constantly shrieking car alarms. He becomes a popular vigilante known as "The Rectifier" but blowhard Mayor Schneer (Hurt) is not one of his fans, and David's defiance becomes a real problem for City Hall. **88m/C DVD.** Tim Robbins, William Hurt, Bridget Moynahan, Margarita Levieva, William Baldwin; ***D:*** Henry Bean; ***W:*** Henry Bean; ***C:*** Andrij Parekh; ***M:*** Philip Johnston.

Noises Off 🦴🦴 1/2 **1992 (PG-13)** An Americanization of a British farce about a group of second-rate actors touring in a sex comedy and their convoluted private lives. Wretched rehersals and equally disasterous preformances, backstage sniping, lovers' quarrels, and a beleaguered director all bumble along together. It worked better on stage, where it was a Broadway hit, but the actors at least have some fun with the material. Based on the play by Michael Frayn.

101m/C VHS, DVD. Michael Caine, Carol Burnett, Denholm Elliott, Julie Hagerty, Marilu Henner, Mark Linn-Baker, Christopher Reeve, John Ritter, Nicolette Sheridan; ***D:*** Peter Bogdanovich; ***W:*** Marty Kaplan; ***M:*** Phil Marshall.

Nomad Riders 🦴 **1981** A la "Mad Max," (though with an even smaller budget and a decided lack of originality) one rugged man goes after the bikers who killed his wife and daughter. **82m/C VHS.** Wayne Chema, Richard Cluck, Ron Gregg; ***D:*** Frank Roach.

Nomads 🦴🦴 ½ **1986 (R)** A supernatural thriller set in Los Angeles about a French anthropologist who is mysteriously killed, and the woman doctor who investigates and becomes the next target of a band of strange street people with nomadic spirits. Nomad notables include pop stars Adam Ant and Josie Cotton. **91m/C VHS, DVD.** Pierce Brosnan, Lesley-Anne Down, Adam Ant, Anna Maria Monticelli, Mary Woronov, Hector Mercado; ***D:*** John McTiernan; ***W:*** John McTiernan; ***C:*** Stephen Ramsey; ***M:*** Bill Conti.

Nomads of the North 🦴 ½ **1920** Vintage silent melodrama set in the North Woods with the requisite young girl beset by evil villians, a climactic forest fire, and a dashing Mountie who allows a man wrongly sought by the law to be reunited with the woman he secretly loves. Also available at 75 minutes. **109m/B VHS, DVD.** Lon Chaney Sr., Lewis Stone, Betty Blythe; ***D:*** David M. Hartford.

Nomugi Pass 🦴🦴 ½ **1979** A young woman working in a Japanese silk mill in the early 1900s must endure hardship and abuse. English subtitles. **154m/C VHS.** *JP* Shinobu Otake, Meiko Harada, Rentaro Mikuni, Takeo Jii; ***D:*** Satsuo Yamamoto; ***W:*** Satsuo Yamamoto; ***C:*** Setsuo Kobayashi; ***M:*** Masaru Sato.

Non-Stop New York 🦴🦴 ½ **1937** Mystery tale with interesting twist. A wealthy woman can give an alibi for a murder suspect, but no one will listen, and she is subsequently framed. Pays homage to Hitchcock with its photography and humor. Quick and charming. **71m/B VHS.** Anna Lee, John Loder, Francis L. Sullivan, Frank Cellier, Desmond Tester, Athene Seyler, William Dewhurst, Drusilla Wills, Jerry Verno, James Pirrie, Ellen Pollock, Arthur Goullet, James Carew, Alf Goddard, Danny Green; ***D:*** Robert Stevenson; ***W:*** Curt Siodmak, Roland Pertwee, Derek Twist, J.O.C. Orton, E.V.H. Emmett; ***C:*** Mutz Greenbaum.

None But the Brave 🦴🦴 **1965** During WWII, an American bomber plane crash-lands on an island already inhabited by stranded Japanese forces. After a skirmish, the two groups initiate a fragile truce, with the understanding that fighting will resume if one or the other sends for help. The Americans repair their radio unit and must decide on their next actions. Sinatra's directorial debut is a poor effort. **105m/C VHS.** Frank Sinatra, Clint Walker, Tommy Sands, Brad Dexter, Tony Bill, Tatsuya Mihashi, Takeshi Kato, Sammy Jackson; ***D:*** Frank Sinatra; ***M:*** John Williams.

None But the Lonely Heart 🦴🦴🦴 **1944** In the days before WWII, a Cockney drifter (Grant) wanders the East End of London. When his get-rich-quick schemes fail, his dying shopkeeper-mother tries to help and lands in prison. Interesting characterization of life in the slums. Odets not only directed, but wrote the screenplay. **113m/B VHS, DVD.** Cary Grant, Ethel Barrymore, Barry Fitzgerald, Jane Wyatt, Dan Duryea, George Coulouris, June Duprez; ***D:*** Clifford Odets; ***W:*** Clifford Odets; ***C:*** George Barnes. Oscars '44: Support. Actress (Barrymore).

Noon Sunday 🦴 **1975 (PG)** A cold war situation in the Pacific islands explodes into an orgy of death. **104m/C VHS.** Mark Lenard, John Russell, Linda Avery, Keye Luke; ***D:*** Terry Bourke; ***W:*** Terry Bourke; ***C:*** Akira Mimura; ***M:*** Nick Demuth.

Noon Wine 🦴🦴🦴 **1984** Dramatization of Katherine Anne Porter's classic story about a Swedish worker on a Texas farm who becomes the center of a family battle. Made for PBS' American Playhouse. **60m/C VHS.** Fred Ward, Lise Hilboldt, Stellan Skarsgard, Jon Cryer; ***D:*** Michael Fields. **TV**

The Noose Hangs High 🦴🦴🦴 **1948** This broad comedy has our heroes as window washers mistaken for gamblers and getting involved with a bunch of gangsters. Much physical and verbal shenanigans as only these two can do it. The bits may be a bit old, but they're done with a fresh twist. Some good word play with the phrase "You can't be here" runs in the same vein as their classic "Who's on first?" routine. Genuinely funny. **77m/B VHS, DVD.** Bud Abbott, Lou Costello, Cathy Downs, Joseph Calleia, Leon Errol, Mike Mazurki, Jack Overman, Fritz Feld, Vera Martin, Joe (Joseph) Kirk, Matt Willis, Benny Rubin; ***D:*** Charles T. Barton.

Nora 🦴🦴 ½ **2000 (R)** In a film about the passionate relationship between two people, there's actually little heat to be found, although the leads are effective. Ambitious would-be writer James Joyce (McGregor) and hotel maid Nora Barnacle (Lynch) meet in Dublin in 1904. Nora soon becomes his muse, common-law wife, and the mother of his children but insecure Joyce is mistrustful of her faithfulness and the two are locked in a constant battle as they travel between Italy and Ireland and Joyce seeks to find a publisher for his work. Based on the book by Brenda Maddox. **106m/C VHS, DVD.** *IR GB GE* Ewan McGregor, Susan Lynch, Peter McDonald, Roberto Citran, Andrew Scott, Vincent McCabe, Veronica Duffy, Aedin Moloney, Darragh Kelly; ***D:*** Pat Murphy; ***W:*** Gerard Stembridge, Pat Murphy; ***C:*** Jean-Francois Robin; ***M:*** Stanislas Syrewicz.

Nora Prentiss 🦴🦴 ½ **1947** Staid San Francisco doctor Richard Talbot (Smith) is in a boring marriage and ripe to have an affair with nightclub singer Nora (Sheridan). When he dithers about a divorce, she moves to New York and the depressed Richard comes up with a radical idea when a patient unexpectedly dies in his office. Richard assumes another identity, fakes his own death, and goes to Nora. Unfortunately, the doctor's death is investigated as a murder and Richard later becomes paranoid, thinking the successful Nora is cheating on him. **111m/B DVD.** Ken Smith, Ann Sheridan, Bruce Bennett, Robert Alda, Rosemary DeCamp, John Ridgely; ***D:*** Vincent Sherman; ***W:*** N. Richard Nash; ***C:*** James Wong Howe; ***M:*** Franz Waxman.

Nora's Hair Salon 🦴🦴 **2004 (R)** Girlfriends get together and dish the dirt at Nora's (Lewis) L.A. salon in this lively yet not quite as folksy female take on "Barbershop" where Nora plays mom to her staff and customers. Whitney Houston cameos. **84m/C VHS, DVD.** Jenifer Lewis, Tatyana Ali, Bobby Brown, Christine Carlo, Tamala Jones, Pras, Kimberly (Lil' Kim) Jones; ***D:*** Jerry LaMothe; ***W:*** Jean-Claude La Marre; ***C:*** Robert Humphreys. **VIDEO**

Nora's Hair Salon 2: A Cut Above 🦴🦴 **2008 (PG-13)** Nora willed her beauty salon to her two nieces, but the estranged cousins have very different ideas for the business: Lilliana (Ali) wants to keep the shop open and Simone (Dash) wants to sell. There's some sassiness, some romance, and some thoughts on what it means to be family. **80m/C DVD.** Stacey Dash, Tatyana Ali, Bobby Brown, Mekhi Phifer, Christine Carlo, Lucille Soong, Malik Barnhardt; ***D:*** Jill Maxcy; ***W:*** Jill Maxcy, Chanel Capra; ***C:*** Laura Beth Love; ***M:*** John "Flexx" Simeus. **VIDEO**

Norbit 🦴 ½ **2007 (PG-13)** Eddie does triple duty as meek Norbit, raised in an orphanage by Mr. Wong (Murphy as the worst Asian stereotype since Mickey Rooney in "Breakfast at Tiffany's"), who is bullied into marriage with gargantuan Rasputia (yeah, it's Murphy inside the fat suit). But he's really in love with slender beauty Kate (Newton), whose fiance (Gooding Jr.) is in shady cahoots with Rasputia's intimidating brothers. Like you care, as long as Eddie delivers the predictable laughs. Rick Baker does the special effects makeup. **95m/C DVD, Blu-ray Disc, HD DVD.** *US* Eddie Murphy, Thandie Newton, Terry Crews, Clifton Powell, Cuba Gooding Jr., Eddie Griffin, Katt Micah Williams, Marlon Wayans, Lester "Rasta" Speight; ***D:*** Brian Robbins; ***W:*** Charles Murphy, Jay Scherick, David Ronn; ***C:*** Clark Mathis; ***M:*** David Newman. Golden Raspberries '07: Worst Actor (Murphy), Worst Support. Actor (Murphy), Worst Support. Actress (Murphy).

Noriega: God's Favorite 🦴🦴 ½ **2000** Hoskins is the reason to watch this cable drama about Panamanian strongman Gen. Manuel "Tony" Noriega who was deposed in 1989 after the U.S. invasion. He has a complicated private life and an even more complicated political existence that includes Castro, the CIA, Colombian drug cartels, and various rivals for power. **115m/C VHS.** Bob Hoskins, Jeffrey DeMunn, Richard Masur, Nestor Carbonell, Tony Plana, Luis Avalos, Edward Edwards, David Marshall Grant, Rosa Blasi, Denise Blasor, John Verea, Michael Sorich; ***D:*** Roger Spottiswoode; ***W:*** Lawrence Wright; ***C:*** Pierre Mignot. **CABLE**

The Norliss Tapes 🦴🦴 **1973** This failed NBC TV pilot is best viewed for its nostalgia value (especially those special effects). Troubled journalist David Norliss (Thinnes) disappears while investigating an attack by an alleged dead man. When his publisher (Porter) investigates, he finds only the recordings that Norliss left behind, which point to some supernatural forces at work. Curtis and Nolan were also responsible for "Kolchak: The Night Stalker." **72m/C DVD.** Roy Thinnes, Don Porter, Angie Dickinson, Claude Akins, Vonetta McGee, Nick Dimitri; ***D:*** Dan Curtis; ***W:*** William F. Nolan; ***C:*** Ben Colman; ***M:*** Robert Cobert. **TV**

Norma Jean and Marilyn 🦴🦴 ½ **1995 (R)** Blonde screen goddess Marilyn Monroe (Sorvino) is haunted by her past, literally, since she never escapes the legacy of ambitious Norma Jean Baker (Judd). As her relationships and career falter, Norma Jean is always there (thanks to drug-induced hallucinations) to remind Marilyn how worthless she is. Drama deals with Norma Jean's troubled past and how she was willing to do anything to be in the movies, although it (apparently) brought her little happiness. The dual stars work surprisingly well and director Fywell offers the proper camp flair. **133m/C VHS, DVD.** Mira Sorvino, Ashley Judd, Josh Charles, Peter Dobson, Ron Rifkin, David Dukes, Taylor Nichols, Lindsay Crouse, John Rubinstein, Steven Culp, Perry Stephens, Earl Boen; ***D:*** Tim Fywell; ***W:*** Jill Isaacs; ***C:*** John Thomas; ***M:*** Christopher Young. **CABLE**

Norma Rae 🦴🦴🦴 **1979 (PG)** A poor, uneducated textile worker joins forces with a New York labor organizer to unionize the reluctant workers at a Southern mill. Field was a surprise with her fully developed character's strength, beauty, and humor; her Oscar was well-deserved. Ritt's direction is top-notch. Jennifer Warnes sings the theme song, "It Goes Like It Goes," which also won an Oscar. ♫It Goes Like It Goes. **114m/C VHS, DVD.** Sally Field, Ron Leibman, Beau Bridges, Pat Hingle; ***D:*** Martin Ritt; ***W:*** Harriet Frank Jr., Irving Ravetch; ***C:*** John A. Alonzo; ***M:*** David Shire. Oscars '79: Actress (Field), Song ("It Goes Like It Goes"); Cannes '79: Actress (Field); Golden Globes '80: Actress—Drama (Field); L.A. Film Critics '79: Actress (Field); Natl. Bd. of Review '79: Actress (Field); N.Y. Film Critics '79: Actress (Field); Natl. Soc. Film Critics '79: Actress (Field).

Normal 🦴🦴 **2003** No guts, no glory. And both Wilkinson and Lange had to have guts to make this story work. Roy and Irma Applewood (Wilkinson, Lange) have been married for 25 years and are respected church-going members of their small Illinois farming community. Chronic headaches and stress have Roy seeking counseling—and finally admitting that he has always felt like a woman trapped in a man's body. He's determined to undergo sex-change surgery and tells Irma that he still loves her and wants them to continue living together. Irma's not unreasonably confused, resentful, angry, and, ultimately, loving and supportive as the community turns its back on Roy and his family. Adapted from Anderson's play "Looking for Normal." **108m/C VHS, DVD.** Tom Wilkinson, Jessica Lange, Hayden Panettiere, Joe Sikora, Clancy Brown, Richard Bull, Randall Arney, Mary Seibel; ***D:*** Jane Anderson; ***W:*** Jane Anderson; ***C:*** Alar Kivilo; ***M:*** Alex Wurman.

Normal 🦴 **2007** University prof Walt (Rennie) drives drunk and gets involved in a car crash that kills a teenaged boy, but is acquitted of any wrongdoing. The dead boy's mother, Catherine (Moss), can't cope with her grief and ignores her remaining family. Troubled Jordie (Zegers), who was driving a stolen car and involved in the same accident, starts an affair with his stepmother to help him cope. There's a bunch of other people peripherally involved and a lot of overwrought guilt. **100m/C DVD.** *CA* Carrie-Anne Moss, Kevin Zegers, Callum Keith Rennie, Lauren Lee Smith, Andrew Airlie, Tygh Runyan, Cameron Bright, Camille Sullivan; ***D:*** Carl Bessai; ***W:*** Travis McDonald; ***C:*** Carl Bessai; ***M:*** Clinton Shorter.

Normal Life 🦴🦴 **1996 (R)** Straight-arrow, smalltown Illinois rookie cop Chris Anderson (Perry) comes to the aid of sexy, impetuous biker chick Pam (Judd) and they impulsively marry. Fast forward two years and the willfully irresponsible Pam has turned their lives into a disaster but for some reason Chris (now a security guard) sticks it out, even pulling bank jobs to afford Pam's luxuries. When she finds out what Chris has been doing, Pam insists on joining in, leading to a bitter end. Based on the true story of Jeffrey and Jill Erickson, who went on a bank robbing spree and were killed in 1991. Great lead performances though character motivation is lacking. **108m/C VHS, DVD.** Luke Perry, Ashley Judd, Bruce A. Young, Jim True-Frost, Dawn Maxey, Penelope Milford, Tom Towler, Kate Walsh; ***D:*** John McNaughton; ***W:*** Bob Schneider, Peg Haller; ***C:*** Jean De Segonzac.

Norman Conquest 🦴 *Park Plaza* **1953** Conway finds himself drugged and framed for murder in this bargain-basement thriller. Bartok is the leader of a diamond-smuggling operation who may be involved. **75m/B VHS.** *GB* Tom Conway, Eva Bartok, Joy Shelton, Sidney James, Richard Wattis, Robert Adair, Ian Fleming; ***D:*** Bernard Knowles; ***W:*** Bernard Knowles.

The Norman Conquests, Part 1: Table Manners 🦴🦴🦴 **1978** Part one of playwright Alan Ayckbourn's comic trilogy of love unfulfilled, as the charmingly unreliable Norman (Conti) works his amorous wiles on three women. **108m/C VHS.** *GB* Tom Conti, Richard Briers, Penelope Keith, David Troughton, Fiona Walker, Penelope Wilton; ***D:*** Herbert Wise; ***W:*** Alan Ayckbourn; ***C:*** Peter Coombs.

The Norman Conquests, Part 2: Living Together 🦴🦴🦴 **1978** Part two concerns the happenings in the living room during Norman's disastrous weekend of unsuccessful seduction. **93m/C VHS.** *GB* Tom Conti, Penelope Keith, Richard Briers, Fiona Walker, David Troughton, Penelope Wilton; ***D:*** Herbert Wise; ***W:*** Alan Ayckbourn; ***C:*** Peter Coombs.

The Norman Conquests, Part 3: Round and Round the Garden 🦴🦴🦴 **1978** Part three concerns Norman's furtive appearance in the garden, which suggests that the weekend is going to misfire. **106m/C VHS.** *GB* Tom Conti, Penelope Keith, Richard Briers, David Troughton, Fiona Walker, Penelope Wilton; ***D:*** Herbert Wise; ***W:*** Alan Ayckbourn; ***C:*** Mike Hobbs.

Norman, Is That You? 🦴 ½ **1976** Unsuccessful film adaptation based on the unsuccessful Broadway play about one family's sexual revolution. Revamped by a host of black stars, it's basically a one-joke affair when Foxx discovers his son is gay and living with his white lover. Shot on videotape and transferred to film. **91m/C VHS.** Redd Foxx, Pearl Bailey, Dennis Dugan, Michael Warren, Tamara Dobson, Vernee Watson-Johnson, Jayne Meadows, George Furth; ***D:*** George Schlatter; ***W:*** George Schlatter, Ron Clark, Sam Bobrick; ***M:*** William Goldstein.

Norman Loves Rose 🦴 ½ **1982 (R)** A precocious 13-year-old and his married sister-in-law join forces in this substandard comedy. When Rose tries to help Norman by teaching him about sex, she learns a little too—she's pregnant. **95m/C VHS.** *AU* Carol Kane, Tony Owen, Warren Mitchell, Myra de Groot; ***D:*** Henri Safran.

Norman's Awesome Experience WOOF! **1988 (PG-13)** Three adolescents are transported back in time to the Roman Empire. Bill and Ted, anyone? **90m/C VHS.** Tom McCamus, Laurie Paton, Jaques Lussier; ***D:*** Paul Donovan.

Norseman 🦴 ½ **1978 (PG)** Leader of a band of Norsemen sets sail for the New World in search of his missing royal father.

Low-budget Viking adventure. **90m/C VHS.** Lee Majors, Cornel Wilde, Mel Ferrer, Christopher Connelly, Jack Elam; ***D:*** Charles B. Pierce; ***W:*** Charles B. Pierce.

North 1/2 **1994 (PG)** Some laughs with a message in family fare from Reiner. Eleven-year-old ace kid actor Wood divorces his workaholic parents Alexander and Louis-Dreyfus and searches the world for a functional family (good luck). Willis, who's a treat in a pink bunny suit, acts as guardian angel/narrator and shows the kid what's really important. Illustrious comedic cast inhabits story based on a book by original "Saturday Night Live" screenwriter (and "Gary Shandling Show" co-creator) Zweibel, who put things in motion ten years ago when he asked Reiner to write a book jacket quote for the novel. **87m/C VHS.** Elijah Wood, Jason Alexander, Julia Louis-Dreyfus, Bruce Willis, Jon Lovitz, Alan Arkin, Dan Aykroyd, Kathy Bates, Faith Ford, Graham Greene, Reba McEntire, John Ritter, Abe Vigoda, Kelly McGillis, Alexander Godunov, Noriyuki "Pat" Morita, Ben Stein; ***D:*** Rob Reiner; ***W:*** Andrew Scheinman, Alan Zweibel; ***M:*** Marc Shaiman.

North and South Book 1 **1985** Lavish spectacle about a friendship tested by the turbulent times leading up to Civil War. Orry Main (Swayze) is a South Carolina plantation owner while his best friend George Hazard (Read) comes from a Pennsylvania industrial family. Orry is also involved in a doomed romance with the beautiful Madeline (Down), who's forced to marry the odious Justin LaMotte (Carradine). Lots of intrigue and excitement. Based on the novel by John Jakes. Filmed on location in Charleston, South Carolina. Originally broadcast as a six-part TV miniseries. Available on six cassettes. **561m/C VHS.** Patrick Swayze, James Read, Lesley-Anne Down, David Carradine, Kirstie Alley, Jean Simmons, Inga Swenson, Jonathan Frakes, Genie Francis, Terri Garber, Georg Stanford Brown, Olivia Cole, David Ogden Stiers, Robert Guillaume, Hal Holbrook, Gene Kelly, Robert Mitchum, Johnny Cash, Elizabeth Taylor; ***M:*** Bill Conti.

North and South Book 2 **1986** Equally dramatic sequel follows the southern Main clan and the northern Hazard family into the Civil War as friendship and romance struggle to survive the fighting. Casnoff is a notable presence as the aptly named Bent, who will go to any length to settle old scores with both families. Based on the John Jakes novel "Love and War." Originally broadcast as a six-part TV miniseries; on six cassettes. The last of the Jakes trilogy, "Heaven and Hell," was finally filmed for TV in '94 but proved a major disappointment. **570m/C VHS.** Patrick Swayze, James Read, Lesley-Anne Down, Terri Garber, Genie Francis, Jean Simmons, Kirstie Alley, Philip Casnoff, Hal Holbrook, Lloyd Bridges, James Stewart, Morgan Fairchild, Nancy Marchand, Parker Stevenson, Lewis Smith; ***M:*** Bill Conti.

The North Avenue Irregulars 1/2 **1979 (G)** Slapstick Disney comedy along the same lines as some of their earlier laugh-fests. A priest and three members of the local ladies' club try to bust a crime syndicate. Though the premise is silly, there are still lots of laughs in this family film. **99m/C VHS, DVD.** Edward Herrmann, Barbara Harris, Susan Clark, Karen Valentine, Michael Constantine, Cloris Leachman, Melora Hardin, Alan Hale Jr., Ruth Buzzi, Patsy Kelly, Virginia Capers; ***D:*** Bruce Bilson; ***W:*** Don Tait; ***C:*** Leonard J. South; ***M:*** Robert F. Brunner.

North by Northwest **1959** Self-assured Madison Avenue ad exec Roger Thornhill (Grant) inadvertently gets involved with international spies when they mistake him for someone else. His problems are compounded when he's framed for murder and winds up on a cross-country train trip with pretty Eve Kendall (Saint) who offers her help. The movie where Grant and Saint dangle from the faces of Mount Rushmore and a plane chases Grant through farm fields. Exceptional performances, particularly Grant's. Plenty of plot twists are mixed with tongue-in-cheek humor. **136m/C VHS, DVD.** Cary Grant, Eva Marie Saint, James Mason, Leo G. Carroll, Martin Landau, Jessie Royce Landis, Philip Ober, Adam Williams, Josephine Hutchinson, Edward Platt; ***D:*** Alfred Hitchcock; ***W:*** Ernest Lehman; ***C:*** Robert Burks; ***M:*** Bernard Herrmann. AFI '98: Top 100, Natl. Film Reg. '95.

North Country 1/2 **2005 (R)** Theron de-glamorizes once again to play Josey Aimes, a hard luck single mom who returns to her Minnesota home town to make a new start. Since the best-paying jobs are working in the mines, Josey decides to become a miner. Eventually fed up with the blatant sexual harassment of her male co-workers and the indifference of her employer, Josey files the first class action lawsuit for sexual harassment in the country (the actual plaintiff, Lois Jenson, sued her employer in 1984). An old-fashioned exercise in social responsibility and the search for justice. **123m/C DVD.** *US* Charlize Theron, Frances McDormand, Sean Bean, Richard Jenkins, Jeremy Renner, Michelle Monaghan, Woody Harrelson, Sissy Spacek, Rusty Schwimmer, Jillian Armenante, Thomas Curtis, Elizabeth Peterson, Linda Emond, Amber Heard, Cole Williams; ***D:*** Niki Caro; ***W:*** Michael Seitzman; ***C:*** Chris Menges; ***M:*** Gustavo Santaolalla.

North Dallas Forty 1/2 **1979 (R)** Based on the novel by former Dallas Cowboy Peter Gent, the film focuses on the labor abuses in pro-football. One of the best football movies ever made, it contains searing commentary and very good acting, although the plot is sometimes dropped behind the line of scrimmage. **119m/C VHS, DVD.** Nick Nolte, Mac Davis, Charles Durning, Bo Svenson, John Matuszak, Dayle Haddon, Steve Forrest, Dabney Coleman, G.D. Spradlin; ***D:*** Ted Kotcheff; ***W:*** Ted Kotcheff, Frank Yablans; ***C:*** Paul Lohmann; ***M:*** John Scott.

North Face *Nordwand* **2008** Icy period piece loosely based on the 1936 attempt to climb the north face of Switzerland's Eiger Mountain. Hoping to gain publicity before the Olympic games, the Third Reich recruits small-town Bavarian mountaineers Toni (Furmann) and Andi (Lukas) to climb the last unconquered peak of the Alps. Their struggles and setbacks are contrasted with the luxury and ease of the propaganda brigade sent to cover the ascent, which includes Toni's former girlfriend Luise (Wokalek). Director Stolzl plays rather fast-and-loose with the facts to heighten the tension and tie his story in with the Nazi ideology that's pervading Germany at the time. The action and drama are riveting when focused on the men on the mountain, however. German with subtitles. **126m/C DVD.** *GE* Benno Furmann, Florian Lukas, Johanna Wokalek, Simon Schwarz, Georg Friedrich, Ulrich Tukur; ***D:*** Philipp Stolzl; ***W:*** Philipp Stolzl, Christoph Silber, Rupert Henning, Johannes Naber; ***C:*** Kolja Brandt; ***M:*** Christian Kolonovits.

North of the Great Divide 1/2 **1950** Standard Rogers programmer, with Roy as a half-breed mediator between salmon fisherman and Indians. **67m/C VHS, DVD.** Roy Rogers, Penny Edwards, Gordon Jones, Roy Barcroft, Jack Lambert, Douglas Evans, Noble Johnson; ***D:*** William Witney.

North Shore 1/2 **1987 (PG)** A young surfer from Arizona hits the beaches of Hawaii and discovers love, sex, and adventure. Only redeeming quality is surfing footage. **96m/C VHS, DVD.** Matt Adler, Nia Peeples, John Philbin, Gregory Harrison, Christina Raines; ***D:*** Will Phelps.

North Shore Fish **1997 (R)** North Shore Fish is a failing Massachusetts fish-packing factory with various cynical managers and employees, including divorcee Flo (Ruehl), who's just found out she's pregnant by her married boss Sal (Danza); 60ish Arlyne (Baker), who regards her co-workers as family; and Josie (Schwimmer), whose husband has left her for a younger woman. It's on this one day that they realize how uncertain all their futures are. Based on the play by Israel Horovitz. **95m/C VHS.** Mercedes Ruehl, Peter Riegert, Carroll Baker, Tony Danza, Rusty Schwimmer, Wendie Malick, Cordelia Richards; ***D:*** Steve Zuckerman; ***W:*** Israel Horovitz; ***C:*** Levie Isaacks. **CABLE**

The North Star *Armored Attack* **1943** Gripping war tale of Nazis over-running an eastern Russian city, with courageous villagers fighting back. Colorized version available. **108m/B VHS, DVD.** Dana Andrews, Walter Huston, Anne Baxter, Farley Granger, Walter Brennan, Erich von Stroheim, Jack Perrin, Dean Jagger; ***D:*** Lewis Milestone; ***W:*** Lillian Hellman; ***C:*** James Wong Howe; ***M:*** Aaron Copland.

North Star 1/2 **1996 (R)** Formulaic actioner where no one seems very enthusiastic. Half-breed trapper Hudson Ipsehawk (Lambert) refuses to mine the gold on his Alaskan property because the land is considered sacred. This doesn't concern greedy miner Sean McLennon (Caan) who wants the property for himself. Oh yeah, there's also a babe, Sarah (McCormack), that both men are interested in. Norway substitutes for Alaska. Based on the novel by Will Henry. **89m/C VHS.** Christopher Lambert, James Caan, Catherine McCormack, Burt Young; ***D:*** Nils Gaup; ***W:*** Paul Ohl, Sergio Donati, Lorenzo Donati; ***C:*** Bruno de Keyzer; ***M:*** Bruce Rowland.

North to Alaska **1960** A gold prospector encounters many problems when he agrees to pick up his partner's fiancee in Seattle to bring her home to Nome, Alaska, in the 1890s. Overly slapstick at times, but great fun nonetheless. Loosely based on Laszlo Fodor's play "The Birthday Gift." **120m/C VHS, DVD.** John Wayne, Stewart Granger, Ernie Kovacs, Fabian, Capucine; ***D:*** Henry Hathaway; ***C:*** Leon Shamroy.

Northanger Abbey 1/2 **1987** Catherine is a young woman whose head is turned by her romance readings of dark secrets, sinister castles, dashing heroes, and helpless women. When the handsome Henry Tilney invites her to visit his ancestral home, Northanger Abbey, it seems all her fancies have come to life. A somewhat tepid adaptation of Jane Austen's parody of the popular Gothic romances of her day. **90m/C VHS, DVD.** *GB* Peter Firth, Katherine Schlesinger, Googie Withers, Robert Hardy; ***D:*** Giles Foster; ***W:*** Maggie Wadey; ***C:*** Nat Crosby; ***M:*** Ilona Sekacz.

Northanger Abbey 1/2 **2007** Spirited teenager Catherine Morland (Jones) has an over-active imagination, fueled by the popular gothic romances she reads. Taken to fashionable Bath by family friends, Catherine falls in with two different families: the Thorpes and the Tilneys. Catherine becomes romantically interested in gentle Henry Tilney (Field) and is invited to their rather sinister family estate. Carried away by her surroundings, Catherine thoughtlessly upsets Henry and is then left to wonder about her future. Based on the novel by Jane Austen. **90m/C DVD.** *GB* Felicity Jones, J.J. Feild, Carey Mulligan, Catherine Walker, Liam Cunningham, Hugh O'Connor, Sophie Vavasseur, Sylvestria Le Touzel, William Beck, Mark Dymond, Shauna Taylor, Desmond Barrit, Julia Dearden; ***D:*** Jon Jones; ***W:*** Andrew Davies; ***C:*** Ciaran Tanham; ***M:*** Sue Wyatt; ***Nar:*** Geraldine James. **TV**

Northeast of Seoul **1972 (PG)** Three people will stop at nothing to steal a legendary jewel-encrusted sword out of Korea. **84m/C VHS.** Anita Ekberg, John Ireland, Victor Buono; ***D:*** David Lowell Rich.

Northern Extremes 1/2 *Buried on Sunday* **1993 (PG)** Silly comedy about an eccentric Canadian island village whose fishing livelihood is threatened. So the town mayor captures an errant nuclear submarine and uses it as a big bargaining chip. Filmed in Nova Scotia, Canada. **80m/C VHS, DVD.** *CA* Paul Gross, Denise Virieux, Henry Czerny, Jeff Leder, Tommy Sexton, Louis Del Grande, Maury Chaykin; ***D:*** Paul Donovan; ***W:*** Bill Fleming.

Northern Lights **1979** A small, black-and-white independent drama depicting the struggle of a lowly farmer combating governmental forces in the 1915 heartland. Subtitled. **85m/B VHS.** Robert Behling, Susan Lynch, Joe Spano, Rob Nilsson, Henry Martinson, Marianne Astrom-DeFina, Ray Ness, Helen Ness; ***D:*** Rob Nilsson, John Hanson; ***W:*** Rob Nilsson.

Northern Passage 1/2 **1995 (PG-13)** Cowboy tries to protect a young Native American woman from harm in the wilderness. **97m/C VHS.** *CA* Jacques Weber, Lorne Brass, Jeff Fahey, Neve Campbell; ***D:*** Arnaud Selignac; ***W:*** Jonathan Hales; ***C:*** Michel Mandero; ***M:*** Alain Chamfort.

Northern Pursuit 1/2 **1943** A Canadian Mountie disguises himself to infiltrate a Nazi spy ring in this exciting adventure film. Based on Leslie White's "Five Thousand Trojan Horses." **94m/B VHS.** Errol Flynn, Helmut Dantine, Julie Bishop, Gene Lockhart, Tom Tully; ***D:*** Raoul Walsh.

Northfork **2003 (PG-13)** Surrealistic fairy tale, with pretensions of examining death and the afterlife, crossed with comical Americana circa 1955. The town of Northfolk is being evacuated to make way for an incoming hydroelectric plant, as a band of strange gypsy angels search for the "unknown angel," thought to be a sick orphan boy who has been left to the town preacher. Patchwork script is a jumble of pompous spiritual pronouncements, kitschy sitcom catch-phrasery, and Lynchian confusion. At least the beautifully-filmed landscape gives you something nice to look at while wondering what the heck is going on. **103m/C VHS, DVD.** *US* James Woods, Nick Nolte, Claire Forlani, Duel Farnes, Mark Polish, Daryl Hannah, Ben Foster, Anthony Edwards, Robin Sachs, Graham Beckel, Peter Coyote, Jon(athan) Gries, Marshall Bell, Kyle MacLachlan, Michele Hicks, Josh Barker; ***D:*** Michael Polish; ***W:*** Mark Polish, Michael Polish; ***C:*** M. David Mullen; ***M:*** Stuart Matthewman.

Northville Cemetery Massacre *The Northfield Cemetery Massacre* **1976 (R)** Gang of bikers comes to town and all hell breaks loose. The result is a horribly bloody war between the townsfolk and the gang. Yup, it was a massacre. **81m/C VHS, DVD.** David Hyry, Craig Collicott, Jan Sisk, Carson Jackson; ***D:*** William Dear, Thomas L. Dyke; ***C:*** William Dear, Thomas L. Dyke; ***M:*** Michael Nesmith.

Northwest Outpost 1/2 *End of the Rainbow* **1947** Eddy is a California cavalry officer in this lightweight operetta. He helps a young woman who is trying to free her husband from jail, and after his death they are able to pursue their relationship. Eddy's last film. ♫ Weary; Raindrops on a Drum; Tell Me With Your Eyes; One More Mile to Go; Russian Easter Hymn; Love is the Time; Nearer and Dearer. **91m/B VHS.** Nelson Eddy, Ilona Massey, Hugo Haas, Elsa Lanchester, Lenore Ulric; ***D:*** Allan Dwan.

Northwest Passage **1940** The lavish first half of a projected two-film package based on Kenneth Roberts' popular novel, depicting the troop of Rogers' Rangers fighting the wilderness and hostile Indians. Beautifully produced; the second half was never made and the passage itself is never seen. **126m/C VHS.** Spencer Tracy, Robert Young, Ruth Hussey, Walter Brennan, Nat Pendleton, Robert Barrat, Lumsden Hare; ***D:*** King Vidor.

Northwest Trail **1946** Royal Canadian Mountie Steele's assignment is to escort Woodbury across the wilderness. She's carrying a large sum of money to save her uncle's business. Problem is, killers are on their trail. **75m/C VHS, DVD.** Bob Steele, Joan Woodbury, John Litel, Raymond Hatton, Madge Bellamy, Charles Middleton; ***D:*** Derwin Abrahams.

Nosferatu *Nosferatu, Eine Symphonie des Grauens; Nosferatu, A Symphony of Terror; Nosferatu, A Symphony of Horror; Nosferatu, the Vampire; Terror of Dracula; Die Zwolfte Stunde* **1922** The first film adaptation of Bram Stoker's "Dracula" remains one of the creepiest and most atmospheric versions. Murnau knew how to add just the right touches to make this one of the best vampire films ever made. All it lacks is the name of Dracula, which was changed due to copyright problems with Stoker's widow. Filmed in Bavaria. Silent with music and English titles. Remade by Werner Herzog in 1979. **63m/B VHS, DVD.** *GE* Max Schreck, Alexander Granach, Gustav von Wagenheim, Greta Schroder, John Gottowt, Ruth Landshoff, G.H. Schnell; ***D:*** F.W. Murnau; ***W:*** Henrik Galeen; ***C:*** Fritz Arno Wagner, Gunther Krampf.

Nosferatu the Vampyre *Nosferatu: Phantom der Nacht* **1979** Herzog's tribute to fellow countryman's F.W. Murnau's 1922 silent film interpretation of Bram Stoker's "Dracula" story. It features Kinski as the disgustingly rodent-like Count, with Ganz as Jonathan Harker, and Adjani as Harker's wife and the beautiful object of the Count's lust. Released in a German language version with subtitles and an English language version. **107m/C VHS, DVD.** *FR GE* Klaus Kinski, Isabelle Adjani, Bruno Ganz, Roland Topor, Walter Ladengast; ***D:*** Werner Herzog; ***W:*** Werner Herzog; ***C:*** Jorge Schmidt-Reitwein; ***M:*** Popul Vuh, Florian Fricke.

Nostalghia **1983** Russian academic Jankovsky comes to Tuscany to research the life of an 18th-century composer and meets the mysterious Josephson, who's convinced the end of the world is near. And soon the homesick Russian is in a search for himself. Filled with Christian iconography and some extraordinary images. Tarkovsky's first film outside his native Russia. Russian and Italian with subtitles; the Russian sequences are filmed in B&W. **126m/C VHS, DVD.** *IT* Oleg (Yankovsky) Jankowsky, Erland Josephson, Domiziana Giordano, Delia Boccardo; ***D:*** Andrei Tarkovsky; ***W:*** Andrei Tarkovsky, Tonino Guerra; ***C:*** Giuseppe Lanci.

Nostradamus **1993 (R)** Historical soap opera about unconventional 16th-century French physician and astrologer Michel de Nostradame. Persecuted by the Inquisition, he comes under the protection of Queen Catherine de Medici of France, although his visions of destruction and death continue to haunt him. Nostradamus' prophecies, first published in 1555, have continued to fascinate, being used to predicate everything from the death of historical leaders to WWI. The film, however, is slow going and fails to hold much interest. **118m/C VHS.** *FR* Tcheky Karyo, F. Murray Abraham, Julia Ormond, Rutger Hauer, Amanda Plummer, Assumpta Serna, Anthony (Corlan) Higgins, Diana Quick, Michael Gough; ***D:*** Roger Christian; ***W:*** Knut Boeser, Piers Ashworth.

The Nostradamus Kid **1992 (R)** Young man, convinced the world is about to end, decides his last goal will be to make love (for the first time) with his girlfriend. **120m/C VHS.** Noah Taylor, Miranda Otto, Arthur Dignam; ***D:*** Bob Ellis.

Nostromo *Joseph Conrad's Nostromo* **1996** Tediously drawn-out TV adaptation of the 1904 novel by Joseph Conrad takes place in the 1890s in the fictional South American country of Costaguana. Englishman Charles Gould (Firth) is determined to reopen his family's silver mine—a plan supported by the local regime, which is, however, soon to be overthrown. Amidst the revolution is the title character Nostromo (Amendola), a contraction of "nostro uomo" or "our man," an enigmatic Italian immigrant who organizes the dockworkers and is thrust into the role of hero. Filmed on location in Cartagena, Colombia. On three cassettes. **360m/C VHS.** Colin Firth, Albert Finney, Claudio Amendola, Serena Scott Thomas, Claudia Cardinale, Brian Dennehy, Lothaire Bluteau, Ruth Gabriel, Joaquim de Almeida; ***D:*** Alastair Reid; ***W:*** John Hale; ***M:*** Ennio Morricone. **TV**

Not Another Teen Movie 1/2 **2001 (R)** Unsuccessful parody of the recent proliferation of bad teen movies and the better John Hughes films of the '80s. Teen moviedom's stereotypes are hammed up to the extreme, from the bitchy teenager to the dumb jock, nerdy beauty-in-waiting and fat guy for comic relief. Which is okay if you like really obvious, unoriginal humor. Film's self-awareness is sometimes amusing but more often sinks to the level of what it's supposed to be satirizing, and of course, there's enough bodily-function and base sexual jokes to fill three Tom Green flicks. If there was ever a genre begging to be parodied, it's teen movies, but this entry flunks. Entertaining cameos by Molly Ringwald and John Vernon, though. **90m/C VHS, DVD, UMD.** *US* Chyler Leigh, Chris Evans, Eric Jungmann, Eric Christian Olsen, Cody McMains, Sam Huntington, Ron Lester, Samm Levine, Deon Richmond, Jaime Pressly, Mia Kirshner, Riley Smith, Lacey Chabert, Cerina Vincent, Beverly Polcyn, Joanna Garcia, Randy Quaid, Ed Lauter, Mr. T, Paul Gleason, Molly Ringwald; ***D:*** Joel Gallen; ***W:*** Michael G. Bender, Adam Jay Epstein, Andrew Jacobson, Phil Beauman, Buddy Johnson; ***C:*** Reynaldo Villalobos; ***M:*** Theodore Shapiro.

Not as a Stranger 1/2 **1955** Glossy film about the medical profession and the varying degrees of dedication shown by doctors. Mitchum stars as an medical student who can't afford to pay his tuition, so he marries nurse de Havilland and continues going to school on her money, although their relationship is far from being a loving one. Producer Kramer's directorial debut. Based on the book by Morton Thompson. **135m/B VHS.** Olivia de Havilland, Robert Mitchum, Frank Sinatra, Gloria Grahame, Broderick Crawford, Charles Bickford, Myron McCormick, Lon Chaney Jr.; ***D:*** Stanley Kramer; ***W:*** Edward Anhalt.

Not Easily Broken 1/2 **2009 (PG-13)** Wounded by the promise of an athletic career derailed by injury, Dave Johnson (Chestnut) now toils as a remodeling contractor in the shadow of his wife Clarice (Henson), a successful real estate agent garnering a hefty salary. Clarice and her live-in mom (Lewis) don't miss a beat in pointing out Dave's shortfalls, which places the marriage under constant strain. To escape, Dave coaches Little League and hangs out with his buddies until Clarice is injured in an auto accident, and Dave finds himself smitten by Clarice's single-mom physical therapist. Based on the book by T.D. Jakes, this marriage melodrama's attempt in spreading the bishop's theological message into the mainstream falls flat with zip for character development and a plodding, predictable plot. **100m/C DVD.** *US* Morris Chestnut, Taraji P. Henson, Maeve Quinlan, Cannon Jay, Jenifer Lewis, Kevin Hart, Wood Harris, Eddie Cibrian, Niecy Nash, Albert Hall; ***D:*** Bill Duke; ***W:*** Brian Bird; ***C:*** Geary McLeod; ***M:*** Kurt Farquhar.

Not for Publication **1984 (R)** A woman working as both a tabloid reporter and a mayoral campaign worker uncovers governmental corruption with the help of a shy photographer and a midget. Meant to be on par with older screwball comedies but lacking the wit and subtlety. **87m/C VHS, DVD.** Nancy Allen, David Naughton, Richard Paul, Alice Ghostley, Laurence Luckinbill; ***D:*** Paul Bartel; ***W:*** Paul Bartel.

Not in This Town 1/2 **1997 (PG-13)** Fact-based drama stars Baker as Billings, Montana, housewife Tammie Schnitzer, who is shocked when white supremacists, led by Henry Whitcomb (Begley Jr.), begin harassing religious and ethnic minorities in her town. She forms the Montana Coalition for Human Rights and begins a public appeal to rally the community but soon Tammie and her family need some protection of their own. **95m/C VHS.** Kathy Baker, Adam Arkin, Ed Begley Jr., Bradford Tatum, Max Gail; ***D:*** Donald Wrye; ***W:*** Adam Gilad; ***M:*** Don Davis. **CABLE**

Not Like Us 1/2 **1996 (R)** Bored Anita's (Pacula) tired of life in her small town and glad to make a new friend in Janet (Grant). But she's shocked to discover Janet may be involved in several mysterious deaths (oh yeah, and she happens to be an alien). **87m/C VHS.** Joanna Pacula, Annabelle Gurwitch, Peter Onorati, Morgan Englund, Rainer Grant; ***D:*** Dave Payne; ***W:*** Daniella Purcell.

Not My Kid 1/2 **1985** The 15-year-old daughter of a surgeon brings turmoil to her family when she becomes heavily involved in drugs. Producer Polson, along with Dr. Miller Newton, wrote the original book for this emotional story that is one of the better treatments of this important subject. **120m/C VHS.** George Segal, Stockard Channing, Viveka Davis, Andrew (Andy) Robinson, Gary Bayer, Nancy Cartwright, Tate Donovan; ***D:*** Michael Tuchner; ***W:*** Christopher Knopf. **TV**

Not of This Earth 1/2 **1988 (R)** In a remake of the 1957 Roger Corman quickie, an alien wearing sunglasses makes an unfriendly trip to Earth. In order to save his dying planet he needs major blood donations from unsuspecting Earthlings. Not a match for the original version, some may nevertheless want to see ex-porn star Lords in her role as the nurse. **92m/C VHS, DVD.** Traci Lords, Arthur Roberts, Lenny Juliano, Rebecca Perle, Ace Mask, Roger Lodge, Michael Delano, Monique Gabrielle, Becky LeBeau; ***D:*** Jim Wynorski; ***W:*** Jim Wynorski, R.J. Robertson, Charles B. Griffith, Mark Hanna; ***C:*** Zoran Hochstatter; ***M:*** Chuck Cirino.

Not of This Earth **1996 (R)** Corman remake of his own 1957 cheapie is both camp and sexy. Sunglass-wearing mystery millionaire Paul Johnson (York) apparently suffers from a rare condition and must have constant blood transfusions, so he hires a sexy live-in nurse (Barondes) to be at his beck-and-call. Yes, he does turn out to be a vampire but of the space alien-with-telepathic-powers variety who has a particular purpose for coming to earth. **92m/C VHS, DVD.** Michael York, Elizabeth Barondes, Richard Belzer, Parker Stevenson; ***D:*** Terence H. Winkless; ***W:*** Charles Philip Moore. **CABLE**

Not of This World 1/2 *Fuori dal Mondo* **1999** Sister Caterina (Buy) is a novice, about to take her final vows, when she discovers a baby abandoned in a park. Although she takes the baby to a hospital and learns the child will be put up for adoption, Caterina can't ignore her surge of maternal feelings and decides to search for the baby's parents. When she traces a cleaning tag from the sweater the baby was wrapped in, Caterina meets Ernesto (Orlando), the middle-aged owner of a local laundry who suspects he may be the baby's father. The duo both take long looks at their lives and wonder if they should may some changes. Italian with subtitles. **100m/C VHS, DVD.** *IT* Margherita Buy, Silvio Orlando, Carolina Freschi, Maria Cristina Minerva; ***D:*** Giuseppe Piccioni; ***W:*** Gualtiero Rosella, Giuseppe Piccioni, Lucia Maria Zei; ***C:*** Luca Bigazzi; ***M:*** Ludovico Einaudi.

Not One Less 1/2 *Yi Ge Dou Bu Neng Shao* **1999 (G)** Gao is teaching in a run-down rural Chinese school when he is called away to visit his dying mother. The only substitute he can find is 13-year-old Wei Minzhi, who's scarcely older than her would-be students. Because so many children are forced to leave school because of their poverty-stricken families, Gao promises the girl extra money if she will keep all the pupils in class until he returns. When Zhang Huike must go to work in the city, Wei Minzhi is stubbornly determined to find and bring him back. Mandarin with subtitles. **106m/C VHS, DVD.** *CH* Wei Minzhi, Zhang Huike, Gao Enman; ***D:*** Yimou Zhang; ***W:*** Shi Xiangsheng; ***C:*** Hou Yong; ***M:*** San Bao.

Not Quite Human **1987** When Jonas Carson builds himself an android teenage son, he must keep the technology from falling into the hands of an evil toy manufacturer with plans of his own. Humorous hijinks abound. Based on the book series "Not Quite Human" by Seth McEvoy. Followed by two sequels. **91m/C VHS.** Alan Thicke, Robin (Robyn) Lively, Robert Harper, Joseph Bologna, Jay Underwood; ***D:*** Steven Hilliard Stern. **CABLE**

Not Quite Human 2 1/2 **1989** In this sequel, Dr. Jonas Carson sends his cyber-son off to college where Chip meets the not-quite-human girl of his dreams. Followed by "Still Not Quite Human." **91m/C VHS.** Alan Thicke, Jay Underwood, Robin (Robyn) Lively, Greg Mullavey, Katie Barberi, Mark Arnott; ***D:*** Eric Luke. **CABLE**

Not Quite Paradise *Not Quite Jerusalem* **1986 (R)** A young American medical student falls in love with a young Israeli girl living on a kibbutz. **106m/C VHS.** Sam Robards, Joanna Pacula; ***D:*** Lewis Gilbert.

Not So Dusty 1/2 **1956** Director Rogers remade his own 1936 comedy but it's a tired affair the second time around. Cockney dustbin collectors Dusty (Owen) and Nobby (Dwyer) find a book in the trash that turns out to be quite valuable. Apparently thrown away by accident, its owners want it back before it can be sold but it's finders-keepers as far as the workers are concerned. **80m/B DVD.** *GB*

Not Tonight Darling **1972 (R)** A bored suburban housewife becomes involved with a fast-talking businessman who leads her into a web of deceit and blackmail. **90m/C VHS, DVD.** *GB* Luan Peters, Vincent Ball, Jason Twelvetrees, James Hayter; ***D:*** Anthony Slocombe; ***W:*** Christopher Gregory, James Pillock; ***C:*** Harry Waxman.

Not Without My Daughter 1/2 **1990 (PG-13)** Overwrought drama shot in Israel about American Field, who travels with her Arab husband and their daughter to his native Iran, where (he must have forgotten to tell her) she has no rights. He decides the family will stay, using beatings and confinement to persuade his uncooperative wife, but she risks all to escape with daughter. Based on the true story of Betty Mahmoody. **116m/C VHS, DVD.** Sally Field, Alfred Molina, Sheila Rosenthal, Roshan Seth, Sarah Badel, Mony Rey, Georges Corraface; ***D:*** Brian Gilbert; ***W:*** David W. Rintels; ***C:*** Peter Hannan; ***M:*** Jerry Goldsmith.

The Note 1/2 **2007** Widowed newspaper columnist Peyton Macgruder (Francis) may get the axe unless her readership picks up. When an airplane crashes nearby, Peyton goes to the site but is uncomfortable trying to get a story. Later she returns and finds a note in the debris that seems to have been written by a passenger to his child. Peyton wants to give the note to the intended recipient and makes her search the subject of her increasingly popular columns. Where the truth leads her, however, turns out to be very personal indeed. A Hallmark Channel original. **87m/C DVD.** Genie Francis, Ted McGinley, Richard Leacock, Rick Roberts, Maria Ricossa, Katie Boland, Heather Hanson, Ginelle Williams; ***D:*** Douglas Barr; ***W:*** Paul W. Cooper; ***C:*** Derick Underschultz; ***M:*** Eric Allaman. **CABLE**

The Note 2: Taking a Chance on Love 1/2 *Taking a Chance on Love* **2009** In this sequel to 2007's "The Note," sports writer King (McGinley) proposes to relationship-columnist Peyton (Francis) who tells him she needs to think about it. Peyton has commitment and family issues but swapping stories with a regretful reader who didn't follow her heart may help her make up her mind. **88m/C DVD.** Genie Francis, Ted McGinley, Katie Boland, Genelle Williams, Maria Ricossa; ***D:*** Douglas Barr; ***W:*** Douglas Barr; ***C:*** Peter Benison; ***M:*** Eric Allaman. **CABLE**

The Notebook **2004 (PG-13)** An elderly man (Garner) tries patiently to reawaken beloved wife's (Rowlands) failing memory of their life together by reading the story to her. Couple is seen in flashback of youth and follows them through the struggles of romance. There are two stories here: one very interesting, the other rehashed saccharine. Story of the young lovers is harlequin romance cliche in which noble blue collar overreaches his station, but pretty rich girl just can't help herself. They love, they lose one another, they're reunited again. Sure to make many tender hearts quiver. When Garner and Rowlands share the screen there's true magic. Their chemistry is genuine and finally heartbreaking, and too little time is spent exploring it. A frustrating schizophrenic letdown. **120m/C DVD, Blu-ray Disc.** *US* Rachel McAdams, Ryan Gosling, Gena Rowlands, James Garner, Joan Allen, James Marsden, Kevin Connolly, Sam Shepard; ***D:*** Nick Cassavetes; ***W:*** Jan Sardi, Jeremy Leven; ***C:*** Robert Fraisse; ***M:*** Aaron Zigman.

Notes from Underground **1995** Modern adaptation of the Dostoevsky novella has Czerny starring as a nameless, alienated civil servant who can only find pleasure in the petty torments his job allows him to inflict on others. Everything he does to broaden his world backfires in humiliating ways. Most of the film consists of monologues that Czerny records on a homevideo camera as he recalls the worst moments in his life. Fortunately, Czerny is up to the nearly one-man task of carrying this odd film. **90m/C VHS, DVD.** Henry Czerny, Sheryl Lee, Jon Favreau, Charles Stratton; ***D:*** Gary Walkow; ***W:*** Gary Walkow; ***C:*** Dan Gillham; ***M:*** Mark Governor.

Notes on a Scandal **2006 (R)** Compelling look at obsession based on Zoe Heller's 2003 novel. Attractive Sheba Hart (Blanchett) is a novice art teacher who's given guidance by acerbic veteran Barbara Covett (Dench). Sheba has a much older husband (Nighy), two children, and a vague dissatisfaction with her comfortable life, which soon leads her into a relationship with her very willing 15-year-old pupil Steven (Simpson). When the bitter, lonely Barbara discovers Sheba's indiscretion, she ruthlessly uses emotional blackmail to tether the younger woman to her. But as Barbara's neediness grows, even the self-destructive Sheba finally has enough until the inevitable showdown. Disturbing and dazzling, thanks to the no-holds-barred performances of both Dench and Blanchett. **91m/C DVD.** *GB US* Judi Dench, Cate Blanchett, Bill Nighy, Andrew Simpson, Juno Temple, Max Lewis; ***D:*** Richard Eyre; ***W:*** Patrick Marber; ***C:*** Chris Menges; ***M:*** Philip Glass.

Nothin' 2 Lose 🦴 ½ **2000** Kwame (Hooks) can't bring him himself to commit to marriage with his girlfriend, Yasmine (Bayete). He prefers to spend his time hanging with his friends, gambling on playground basketball games, and chattering illiterate gibberish about all things inane. Racist language serves for humor and women serve as objects in what proves to be a sad excuse for an urban comedy. **100m/C DVD.** Brian Hooks, Shani Bayete, Cedric Pendleton, Crystal Sessoms, Michael A. LeMelle, Martin C. Jones, Rodney J. Hobbs, Sekenia Williams, Malik Jones; ***D:*** Barry Bowles; ***W:*** Barry Bowles.

Nothing but a Man 🦴🦴 ½ **1964** Duff Anderson (Dixon) is a black laborer trying to make a life in a small Alabama town. He falls for the daughter of a minister, they marry, and he gets a job at a local sawmill. When he won't bend to his racist white employers, he's fired and labeled a troublemaker. Unsentimental depiction of the times. **95m/B VHS, DVD.** Ivan Dixon, Abbey Lincoln, Gloria Foster, Julius W. Harris, Martin Priest, Yaphet Kotto, Leonard Parker, Stanley Greene, Helen Lounck, Helene Arrindell; ***D:*** Michael Roemer; ***W:*** Michael Roemer, Robert M. Young; ***C:*** Robert M. Young. Natl. Film Reg. '93.

Nothing But the Night 🦴 ½ *The Devil's Undead; The Resurrection Syndicate* **1972 (PG)** Lee's company produced this convoluted story of orphans who are victims of a cult that uses them in their quest for immortality. **90m/C VHS.** *GB* Christopher Lee, Peter Cushing, Diana Dors, Georgia Brown, Keith Barron, Fulton Mackay, Gwyneth Strong, John Robinson; ***D:*** Peter Sasdy.

Nothing But the Truth 🦴🦴🦴 **2008 (R)** Very loosely based on the courtroom spectacle following the leak of CIA operative Valerie Plame's identity after her husband, a U.S. ambassador, publicly refuted President Bush's claim that Saddam Hussein was trying to buy uranium for nuclear weapons. Here, journalist Rachel (Beckinsale) leaks the classified CIA identity and is heavily prosecuted by the feds, represented in court by lawyer Patton Dubois (Dillon). Jailed for refusing to reveal her source, much like real-life New York Times reporter Judith Miller, her newspaper hires hotshot defense attorney Albert Burnside (Alda). Focused docudrama keeps to the cold, hard plot-points and excels with its veteran cast. **108m/C DVD.** *US* Kate Beckinsale, Matt Dillon, Alan Alda, Vera Farmiga, Angela Bassett, David Schwimmer, Courtney B. Vance, Noah Wyle, Floyd Abrams; ***D:*** Rod Lurie; ***W:*** Rod Lurie; ***C:*** Alik Sakharov; ***M:*** Lawrence Nash Groupe.

Nothing But Trouble 🦴🦴 ½ **1944** Laurel & Hardy's last film for MGM is a complicated tale of two servants who wind up protecting an exiled boy king from the machinations of his power-mad uncle. **70m/B VHS, DVD.** Stan Laurel, Oliver Hardy, Henry O'Neill, Mary Boland, David Leland, John Warburton, Connie Gilchrist, Philip Merivale; ***D:*** Sam Taylor.

Nothing But Trouble 🦴 **1991 (PG-13)** Yuppie couple out for weekend drive find themselves smoldering in small town hell thanks to a traffic ticket. Horror and humor mix like oil and water in Aykroyd's debut as director. **93m/C VHS, DVD.** Dan Aykroyd, Demi Moore, Chevy Chase, John Candy, Taylor Negron, Bertila Damas, Valri Bromfield; ***D:*** Dan Aykroyd; ***W:*** Dan Aykroyd, Peter Aykroyd; ***C:*** Dean Cundey. Golden Raspberries '91: Worst Support. Actor (Aykroyd).

Nothing in Common 🦴🦴 ½ **1986 (PG)** In his last film, Gleason plays the abrasive, diabetic father of immature advertising agency worker Hanks. After his parents separate, Hanks learns to be more responsible and loving in caring for his father. Comedy and drama are blended well here with the help of satirical pokes at the ad business and Hanks turns in a fine performance, but the unorganized, lengthy plot may lose some viewers. **119m/C VHS, DVD.** Tom Hanks, Jackie Gleason, Eva Marie Saint, Bess Armstrong, Hector Elizondo, Barry Corbin, Sela Ward, John Kapelos, Jane Morris, Dan Castellaneta, Tracy Reiner; ***D:*** Garry Marshall; ***W:*** Rick Podell; ***C:*** John A. Alonzo; ***M:*** Patrick Leonard.

Nothing Like the Holidays 🦴🦴 ½ **2008 (PG-13)** The holidays bring together the boisterous Puerto Rican Rodriguez clan at Mama Anna (Pena) and Papa Edy's (Molina) old family home in Chicago's Humboldt Park, only to be shocked by Anna's asking Edy for a divorce over dinner, as she suspects he's two-timing her. She also openly pines for a grandchild from her son Mauricio (Leguizamo) and his Jewish wife Sarah (Messing)—a New York power couple—but Sarah won't comply. Daughter Roxanna (Ferlito)—given the least interesting storyline of the bunch—is home from L.A. where her dreams of being an actress have only minimally come true. While the youngest Jesse (Rodriguez) can't quite overcome the traumas of his service in Iraq and resists Edy's desire that he take over the family bodega, or grocery store. Sure, it's a typical family reunion but with an ethnic kick and a believable cast that meshes well. **98m/C DVD.** *US* Luis Guzman, John Leguizamo, Debra Messing, Freddy Rodriguez, Alfred Molina, Melonie Diaz, Vanessa Ferlito, Jay Hernandez, Elizabeth Pena; ***D:*** Alfredo de Villa; ***W:*** Rick Najera, Alison Swan; ***C:*** Scott Kevan; ***M:*** Paul Oakenfold.

Nothing Personal 🦴 ½ **1980 (PG)** Confused mix of romantic comedy and environmental themes. Lawyer (?) Somers attempts to help college professor Sutherland prevent the slaughter of seals. Enter romance (hey, but what about the baby seals?). Enlivened by appearances of Canadian SCTV vets and Somers's first starring theatrical role. **96m/C VHS.** Donald Sutherland, Suzanne Somers, Dabney Coleman, John Dehner, Roscoe Lee Browne, Catherine O'Hara; ***D:*** George Bloomfield.

Nothing Personal 🦴🦴🦴 *All Our Fault* **1995 (R)** Uncompromising drama about the sectarian violence in northern Ireland that engulfs even the innocent. The IRA bombing of a Protestant pub sets a Loyalist unit, led by dedicated Kenny (Frain) and psychotic Ginger (a terrifying Hart), on an increasingly deadly 24-hour rampage through Belfast (in 1975). Catholic single father Liam Kelly (Lynch) finds himself in the wrong part of town and only wants to return to his two children but is inexorably drawn into the violence, which leads to tragedy for all. Adapted from the novel "All Our Fault" by Mornin, who wrote the screenplay. **86m/C VHS.** *GB IR* Ian Hart, John Lynch, James Frain, Michael Gambon, Ruaidhri Conroy, Jeni Courtney, Gary Lydon, Maria Doyle Kennedy, Gerard McSorley, Gareth O'Hare; ***D:*** Thaddeus O'Sullivan; ***W:*** Daniel Mornin; ***C:*** Dick Pope; ***M:*** Philip Appleby.

Nothing Sacred 🦴🦴🦴 ½ **1937** Slick, overzealous reporter takes advantage of a small-town girl's situation. As a publicity stunt, his newspaper brings her to the Big Apple to distract her from her supposedly imminent death in order to manipulate the public's sentiment as a means to sell more copy. Innocent young Lombard, however, is far from death's door, and deftly exploits her exploitation. Scathing indictment of the mass media and bovine mentality of the masses. Both hysterically funny and bitterly cynical; boasts Lombard's finest performance as the small-town rube who orchestrates the ruse. Remade in 1954 as "Living It Up." DVD version includes home movie footage of a Lombard-Gable hunting trip and two Mack Sennett shorts—"Campus Vamp" (1928) and "Matchmaking Mama." **75m/C VHS, DVD.** Fredric March, Carole Lombard, Walter Connolly, Sig Rumann, Charles Winninger, Margaret Hamilton; ***D:*** William A. Wellman; ***W:*** Ben Hecht; ***C:*** William Howard Greene; ***M:*** Oscar Levant.

Nothing to Lose 🦴🦴 ½ **1996 (R)** Ad exec Nick Beam (Robbins) is having a very bad day. He loses his job, finds his wife is having an affair, then gets carjacked by street-wise but dim-witted thief T-Paul (Lawrence). T-Paul picked the wrong day to rob Nick, who ironically takes T-Paul hostage. The unlikely pair find they have more in common than realized. Screwball buddy comedy shows its originality in casting, and not much else. Robbins and Lawrence are an inspired pair with great comedic potential but are trapped in a mundane story. Filming was delayed due, in part, to Lawrence's constant run-ins with the law. **97m/C VHS, DVD.** Tim Robbins, Martin Lawrence, John C. McGinley, Giancarlo Esposito, Kelly Preston, Michael McKean, Irma P. Hall, Susan Barnes, Rebecca Gayheart, Patrick Cranshaw; ***D:*** Steve Oedekerk; ***W:*** Steve Oedekerk; ***C:*** Donald E. Thorin; ***M:*** Robert Folk.

Nothing to Lose 🦴🦴 *TBS* **2008** Johan was convicted of murdering his father though he claimed self-defense. Escaping after years in a mental institution, Johan decides to find his mother whose testimony he believes will finally clear him. And to have some leverage with the police, he kidnaps 13-year-old Tessa to hold as a hostage. Dutch with subtitles. **87m/C DVD.** *NL* Theo Maassen, Lisa Smit, Bob Schwarze; ***D:*** Peter Kuijpers; ***W:*** Peter Kuijpers, Paul Jan Nelissen; ***C:*** Bert Pot; ***M:*** Paleis Van Boem.

Nothing Underneath 🦴 ½ **1985** An American guy goes to Rome to search for his model twin sister, who may be one of the victims of a series of scissor killings. **95m/C VHS.** Tom Schanley, Renee Simonsen, Nicola Perring, Donald Pleasence; ***D:*** Carlo Vanzina.

Notorious 🦴🦴🦴🦴 **1946** Post-WWII story of beautiful playgirl Alicia (Bergman), who's sent by the U.S. government to marry a suspected spy (Rains) living in Brazil. Cynical agent Devlin (Grant) is assigned to watch her. Duplicity and guilt are important factors in this brooding, romantic spy thriller. Suspenseful throughout, with a surprise ending. The acting is excellent all around and Hitchcock makes certain that suspense is maintained throughout this classy and complex thriller. **101m/B VHS, DVD.** Cary Grant, Ingrid Bergman, Claude Rains, Louis Calhern, Leopoldine Konstantin, Reinhold Schunzel, Moroni Olsen; ***D:*** Alfred Hitchcock; ***W:*** Ben Hecht; ***C:*** Ted Tetzlaff; ***M:*** Roy Webb. Natl. Film Reg. '06.

Notorious 🦴🦴 **2009 (R)** That would be "Notorious" as in the rapper The Notorious B.I.G. (aka Christopher Wallace), his rise from the Brooklyn streets to fame in the 1990s, his rivalry with Tupac Shakur, and ultimately his murder. Biopic faithfully follows the all too familiar underdog-beats-odds, becomes-rich-star, dies-premature-death formula. Convincing, engaging performance by Woolard, who channels the bigger-than-life Biggie is the best part of an otherwise forgettable pic. Seen one rags-to-riches music biopic, seen this one. **122m/C DVD.** *US* Derek Luke, Anthony Mackie, Angela Bassett, Marc John Jefferies, Jamal Woodard, Naturi Naughton, Antonique Smith, Sean Ringgold; ***D:*** George Tillman Jr.; ***W:*** Reggie Rock Bythewood, Cheo Hodari Coker; ***C:*** Michael Grady; ***M:*** Danny Elfman.

The Notorious Bettie Page 🦴🦴 ½ **2006 (R)** The ultimate 50s fetish pinup, Bettie (Mol) is a sweet, religious Southern gal with a rocky past (bad childhood, bad men), who comes to the Big Apple to be an actress. She can't act, but Bettie looks great—dark hair, curvy body, come-hither smile, and an open sexuality that soon has her doing nude photo shoots. After Bettie meets the Klaws, Irving (Bauer) and his sister Paula (Taylor), she becomes a sensation in the specialty market of leather and bondage. This being the 50s, morality soon wags a disapproving finger when Senator Estes Kefauver (Strathairn) convenes his indecency hearings and Bettie gets caught in the crossfire. Mol is charming but Bettie remains a cipher. **91m/C DVD.** *US* Gretchen Mol, Chris Bauer, Jared Harris, Sarah Paulson, Cara Seymour, Lili Taylor, David Strathairn, John Cullum, Matt McGrath, Austin Pendleton, Norman Reedus, Dallas Roberts, Victor Slezak, Tara Subkoff, Kevin Carroll, Ann Dowd, Michael Gaston, Jefferson Mays, Peter McRobbie, Jonathan M. Woodward; ***D:*** Mary Harron; ***W:*** Mary Harron, Guinevere Turner; ***C:*** W. Mott Hupfel III; ***M:*** Mark Suozzo.

The Notorious Lady 🦴🦴 ½ **1927** Englishman Stone kills the man he finds in Bedford's room, believing him to be his wife's lover. He's mistaken but she lies to save him and Stone takes off for the diamond mines in Africa. Bedford hears he's dead and sets out, seeking the truth. **79m/B VHS.** Lewis Stone, Barbara Bedford, Earl Metcalfe, Francis McDonald; ***D:*** King Baggot; ***C:*** Gaetano Antonio "Tony" Gaudio.

The Notorious Landlady 🦴🦴 ½ **1962** State Department employee William Gridley (Lemmon) is transferred to London and rents a flat from Carlye Hardwicke (Novak). Her shady husband Miles (Reed) is missing and Gridley's boss Ambruster (Astaire) and Scotland Yard Inspector Oliphant (Jeffries) ask Gridley to snoop around. When Miles turns up, he threatens Carlye over some stolen jewels and she kills him and goes on trail. There's also a pawn ticket, a blackmail scheme, and an old lady (Winwood) who saw too much. Fast paced comic mystery. **123m/B DVD.** Kim Novak, Jack Lemmon, Fred Astaire, Lionel Jeffries, Estelle Winwood, Maxwell Reed, Philippa Bevans; ***D:*** Richard Quine; ***W:*** Blake Edwards, Larry Gelbart; ***C:*** Arthur E. Arling; ***M:*** George Duning.

Notre Histoire 🦴 ½ *Our Story; Separate Rooms* **1984** Confusing and frequently surreal drama. Middle-aged alcoholic Robert (Delon) is in despair about his life as he sits alone in a train compartment. Suddenly, beautiful Donatienne (Baye) enters and just as suddenly leaves (after they have sex, of course) with Robert soon obsessively chasing after her. French with subtitles. **110m/C DVD.** *FR* Alain Delon, Nathalie Baye; ***D:*** Bernard Blier; ***W:*** Bernard Blier; ***C:*** Jean Penzer; ***M:*** Laurent Rossi.

Notting Hill 🦴🦴🦴 **1999 (PG-13)** Romantic comedy that can coast by on charm alone. Roberts is not playing herself (okay, so there are, possibly, some similarities). She is playing a famous and neurotic movie star, Anna Scott, who's filming on location in London. She meets cute with shy travel bookstore owner William Thacker (Grant) and the unexpected twosome are soon spending a lot of time together. Trouble immediately begins when the paparazzi find out about their affair and William finds his face splashed all over the tabloids and reporters camped out in his garden. Ifans is a scene stealer as William's grubby and crazy housemate. **123m/C VHS, DVD, HD DVD.** Julia Roberts, Hugh Grant, Hugh Bonneville, Rhys Ifans, Tim (McInnerny) McInnery, Gina McKee, James Dreyfus, Richard McCabe, Emma Chambers; ***D:*** Roger Michell; ***W:*** Richard Curtis; ***C:*** Michael Coulter; ***M:*** Trevor Jones.

Nous N'Irons Plus au Bois 🦴🦴 **1969** On the outskirts of a forest held by the Germans, a small group of French resistance fighters capture a German soldier during WWII. He actually wants to join forces with them, however, after falling in love with a lovely young French girl. In French; subtitled in English. **98m/C VHS.** *FR* Marie-France Pisier, Siegfried Rauch, Richard Leduc; ***D:*** Georges Dumoulin.

Nouvelle Vague 🦴🦴 ½ *New Wave* **1990** Delon is a philosopher king and Giordano a wealthy countess involved in Godard's usual sexual and political themes, which has society geared toward support of the rich. Dialogue is composed entirely of quotations. In French with English subtitles. **89m/C VHS.** *SI FR* Alain Delon, Domiziana Giordano, Roland Amstutz, Laurence Cote, Christophe Odent; ***D:*** Jean-Luc Godard; ***W:*** Jean-Luc Godard.

Novel Desires 🦴 ½ **1992 (R)** Brian Freedman is a best-selling author who teams up with his writing rival, Vicky Chance. But it isn't just their imaginations they give free reign to, it's all their desires as well. **80m/C VHS, DVD.** Tyler Gains, Caroline Monteith, Mitchell Clark, Lisa Hayland; ***D:*** Lawrence Unger.

Novel Romance 🦴🦴 **2006 (R)** Hearing her biological clock ticking very loudly, magazine editor Max (Lord) decides to have a baby and looks for a sperm donor. She picks a suitably charismatic unpublished writer (Johansson) and offers to make him a literary success if he will do his part (baby-making wise) and then get lost. He does, she does, and Max raises their daughter while he moves to France. But they just can't quite let go completely. **92m/C DVD.** Traci Lords, Paul Johansson, Sherilyn Fenn, Mariette Hartley, Jacqueline Pinol; ***D:*** Emily Skopov; ***W:*** Emily Skopov; ***C:*** David Klein; ***M:*** Raney Shockne. **VIDEO**

November 🦴🦴🦴 **2005 (R)** A young man (Le Gros) enters an L.A. convenience store to buy ice cream for his girlfriend Sophie (Cox) who is waiting in the car, but unwittingly walks into a holdup and is shot dead. The fateful date is replayed in three sections, "Denial," "Despair," and "Acceptance," each offering clues to what's behind the actual event, as Sophie begins to question her grip on her life and reality. Answers are beside the point in this psychological thriller—it's all about the quest. Fine acting by all and mindfully filmed. **73m/C DVD.** *US* Courteney Cox, James LeGros, Nora Dunn, Anne Archer, Michael

Ealy, Nick Offerman, Matthew Carey; *D:* Greg Harrison; *W:* Benjamin Brand; *C:* Nancy Schreiber; *M:* Lew Baldwin.

November Conspiracy 1/2 **1996 (R)** Journalist Jenny Baron (Turco) is covering the presidential campaign of a senator (Segal) when she uncovers a conspiracy linking a number of assassinations and murder attempts. A computer disk reveals more information but when her lover (Benedict) is murdered during an attempted political assassination, Baron goes on the run to save her own life. **103m/C VHS.** Paige Turco, George Segal, Elliott Gould, Bo Hopkins, Dirk Benedict, Conrad Janis; *D:* Conrad Janis; *W:* Maria Grimm; *M:* Tony Humecke.

The November Men 1/2 **1993 (PG)** In 1992, liberal Hollywood director Arthur Gwenlyn (Williams) begins filming a thriller about an assassin after a presidential candidate. But cinematographer Elizabeth (Bevis) begins to suspect that Gwenlyn's actually serious about killing off some right-wing politicos and is using the production as a cover. Doesn't make a lot of sense. **98m/C VHS.** Paul W. Williams, James Andronica, Leslie Bevis, Robert Davi; *D:* Paul W. Williams; *W:* James Andronica.

November Moon *Novembermond* **1985** On the eve of WWII, Jewish November Messing (Osburg) flees Germany for what she hopes will be safety in Paris. She meets Ferial (Millet) and the two become lovers, but Ferial must hide November when the Nazis occupy the city. Ferial also decides to take a position on a Nazi-run newspaper in order to gather information and protect them both. German with subtitles. **106m/C VHS, DVD.** *GE* Gabriele Osburg, Christiane Millet, Gerhard Olschewski, Daniele Delorme, Bruno Pradal, Werner Stocker; *D:* Alexandra von Grote; *W:* Alexandra von Grote; *C:* Bernard Zitzermann.

Novocaine **2001 (R)** Ambitious, occasionally successful blend of black comedy and film noir framed in toothy imagery. Frank (Martin) is a humdrum dentist with a thriving practice and perfect, if nutty, hygienist/fiancee (Dern). The normalcy is crushing and dread is palpable. Enter Susan (Carter), a seductive, if grungy, first-time patient with a need for painkillers. She appeals to Frank's latent desire for danger by allowing a cavity search of another kind right in the dentist's chair. From there, playing the classic noir role of the stooge, Frank makes a lot of really bad decisions. Story is pretty unbelievable, but the screwball quality keeps it afloat to a point. Ultimately the plot stumbles and dueling tones bump into each other. Martin has some funny moments but Carter is still in "Fight Club" mode and falls into caricature. Laughing gas would've been preferable to the numbness of the film's ending, but points given for originality. **95m/C VHS, DVD.** *US* Steve Martin, Helena Bonham Carter, Laura Dern, Elias Koteas, Scott Caan, Keith David, Lynne Thigpen, Kevin Bacon; *D:* David Atkins; *W:* David Atkins; *C:* Vilko Filac; *M:* Steve Bartek.

Now and Forever 1/2 **1934** Penny (Temple) is the young daughter of charming widower and con man Jerry Day (Cooper). Penny's been in the care of her uncle but Jerry's decided to settle down in Paris with his lady love Toni (Lombard) and figures he can give the tyke a home. But the hard-up Jerry can't resist stealing a valuable necklace and there's much trouble ahead (and not your average happy ending). Temple steals the film from her elders. Adapted from the story "Honor Bright" by Jack Kirkland and Melville Baker. Colorized. **82m/C VHS, DVD.** Gary Cooper, Carole Lombard, Shirley Temple, Guy Standing, Charlotte Granville, Gilbert Emery; *D:* Henry Hathaway; *W:* Vincent Lawrence, Sylvia Thalberg; *C:* Harry Fischbeck.

Now and Forever 1/2 **1982 (R)** Young wife's life is shattered when her unfaithful husband is wrongly accused and convicted of rape. After he is sent to prison, she begins drinking and taking drugs. From the novel by Danielle Steel, it will appeal most to those who like their romances a la Harlequin. **93m/C VHS, DVD.** *AU* Cheryl Ladd, Robert Coleby, Carmen Duncan, Christine Amor, Aileen Britton; *D:* Adrian Carr.

Now & Forever **2002** Childhood friends Angela Wilson and John Myron live in small-town Saskatchewan and come from different backgrounds (he's Cree, she's white). Angela's plagued by major family woes and longs to be an actress; John is mystical and grounded by his culture, and has loved Angela from the moment he met her. She takes up with a jerk who does the unthinkable (we're not spoiling it) and she leaves town. But the connection between Angela and John proves strong enough to bring them back together. Too many elements make the film too convoluted, but it is earnest. **101m/C DVD.** *CA* Mia Kirshner, Adam Beach, Theresa Russell, Gordon Tootoosis, Gabriel Olds, Callum Keith Rennie, Alexandra Purvis, Simon Baker; *D:* Bob (Benjamin) Clark, Billy Boyle; *C:* Jan Kiesser; *M:* Paul Zaza.

Now and Then **1995 (PG-13)** Four women hold a reunion 25 years after their most eventful childhood summer to relive the good ol' days of prepubescent triumphs and tragedies. Flashback, which thankfully comprises about 85% of the movie, explores first kisses, budding breasts, death and divorce. Despite good intentions, this nostalgic coming-of-ager for the girls is a jumbled mass of borrowed formulas that just can't shake that feeling of forced sentimentality. The young actresses are talented and charming, but their less convincing adult counterparts serve mostly as big names to draw crowds and studio support. **97m/C VHS, DVD.** Rosie O'Donnell, Melanie Griffith, Demi Moore, Rita Wilson, Christina Ricci, Thora Birch, Gaby Hoffman, Ashleigh Aston Moore, Cloris Leachman, Lolita (David) Davidovich, Bonnie Hunt, Brendan Fraser; *D:* Leslie Linka Glatter; *W:* I. Marlene King; *C:* Ueli Steiger; *M:* Cliff Eidelman.

Now, Voyager 1/2 **1942** Davis plays a lonely spinster who is transformed into a vibrant young woman by therapy. She comes out of her shell to have a romantic affair with a suave European (who turns out to be married) but still utters the famous phrase "Oh, Jerry, we have the stars. Let's not ask for the moon." Definitely melodramatic, but an involving story nonetheless. Based on a novel by Olive Higgins Prouty. **117m/B VHS, DVD.** Bette Davis, Gladys Cooper, Claude Rains, Paul Henreid, Bonita Granville, Ilka Chase; *D:* Irving Rapper; *W:* Casey Robinson; *C:* Sol Polito; *M:* Max Steiner. Oscars '42: Orig. Dramatic Score, Natl. Film Reg. '07.

Now You Know **2002 (R)** But you won't want to. Jeremy's (Sisto) fiancee Keri (Jones) suddenly calls off their wedding while he's at his bachelor party. He drowns his sorrows with buds Gil (Anderson) and Biscuit (Fehrman) while Keri talks it out with gal pal Marti (Kent). Finally, Jeremy just decides to ask Keri what went wrong. Lame comedy attempt from "Clerks" sidekick Anderson, making his directorial debut. **102m/C DVD.** Jeremy Sisto, Rashida Jones, Trevor Fehrman, Paget Brewster, Heather Paige Kent, Anthony John (Tony) Denison, Jeff Anderson; *D:* Jeff Anderson; *W:* Jeff Anderson; *C:* Marco Cappetta; *M:* Lanny Cordola, Matt Sorum. **VIDEO**

Now You See Him, Now You Don't **1972 (G)** Light Disney comedy involving a gang of crooks who want to use a college student's invisibility formula to rob a local bank. Sequel to Disney's "The Computer Wore Tennis Shoes." **85m/C VHS, DVD.** Kurt Russell, Joe Flynn, Cesar Romero, Jim Backus, Kelly Thordsen; *D:* Robert Butler; *M:* Robert F. Brunner.

Nowhere **1996 (R)** Third in Araki's teen trilogy, following "Totally F***ed Up" and "The Doom Generation" is a basic day-in-the-life look at alienated L.A. 18-year-old Dark Smith (Duval), adrift in a world of consumerism and looking for love. He loves Mel (True) but she's torn between Dark and girlfriend Lucifer (Robertson), so Dark turns to Montgomery (Bexton). His friends have their own trials with drugs and sex (in various combos), and violence. Angst to the Nth degree, with Araki's imagination in wild disarray. **82m/C VHS.** James Duval, Rachel True, Kathleen Robertson, Nathan Bexton, Guillermo Diaz, Alan Boyce, Christina Applegate, Jeremy Jordan, Chiara Mastroianni, Debi Mazar, Jordan Ladd, Thyme Lewis, Sarah Lassez, Ryan Phillippe, Heather Graham, Scott Caan, Jaason Simmons, Mena Suvari, Christopher Knight, Eve Plumb, Beverly D'Angelo, David Leisure, Traci Lords, Shannen Doherty, John Ritter, Rose McGowan, Charlotte Rae, Denise Richards, Teresa Hill, Lauren Tewes, Staci Keanan, Joshua Gibran Mayweather; *D:* Gregg Araki; *W:* Gregg Araki; *C:* Arturo Smith.

Nowhere Boy **2009** Conventional bio of the early life of John Lennon (Johnson) set in a 1950s Liverpool. There's lots of family drama as John reunites with his free-spirited mother Julia (Duff), who abandoned him as a baby to be raised by her stern, middle-class older sister, Mimi (Scott Thomas). Lennon escapes into music to avoid the tug of war for his affections (a lifelong theme), and the film goes on to depict his first meeting with a 15-year-old Paul McCartney (Sangster), the formation of The Quarrymen, and their first gigs. **98m/C DVD.** *GB* Aaron Johnson, Kristin Scott Thomas, Anne-Marie Duff, Thomas Sangster, David Threlfall, David Morrissey, Sam Bell; *D:* Sam Taylor Wood; *W:* Matt Greenhalgh; *C:* Seamus McGarvey; *M:* Alison Goldfrapp.

Nowhere in Africa 1/2 *Nirgendwo in Afrika* **2002 (R)** Walter Redlich (Ninidze), a German Jew, has fled Breslau for a job as a farm manager in British-colonized Kenya. In 1938, his wife Jettel (Koehler) and their 5-year-old daughter Regina (Kurka) join him. Jettel is unhappy with their harsh new life and isolation but Regina quickly adapts. When war is declared, Walter is briefly interned and eventually joins the British Army, leaving Jettel behind to manage things. As Regina (Eckertz) grows up, she becomes ever-more adapted to life in Kenya and is dismayed when, in 1947, her father is offered a prestigious job and wants to return "home" to Germany. German with subtitles. From the novel by Stefanie Zweig. **141m/C VHS, DVD.** *GE* Juliane Kohler, Merab Redlich, Karoline Eckertz, Lea Kurka, Matthias Habich, Sidede Onyulo; *D:* Caroline Link; *W:* Caroline Link; *C:* Gernot Roll; *M:* Niki Reiser. Oscars '02: Foreign Film.

Nowhere in Sight 1/2 **2001** Rehash of "Wait until Dark" has little to add that masterpiece of suspense/horror. This time, Carly Bauer (Slater) is the blind woman who's tormented in her apartment by a couple of nasty thugs. The cast does credible work with familiar material. **94m/C DVD.** Helen Slater, Mark Camacho, Richard Jutras, Max Perlus, Andrew McCarthy; *D:* Douglas Jackson; *W:* James (Momel) Lemmo; *C:* Bruno Philip; *M:* Helen Slater, David Findlay.

Nowhere Land **1998 (R)** If the feds want to make a case against the mob, they need to keep their witness alive and the dangerous beauty sent to provide protection is more than anyone bargained for. **88m/C VHS, DVD.** Peter Dobson, Dina Meyer, Francesco Quinn, Jon Polito, Martin Kove; *D:* Rupert Hitzig; *W:* Dennis Manuel; *M:* Russ Landau.

Nowhere to Hide *On the Run* **1983 (R)** A widow whose Marine officer husband has been assassinated is chased by some bad guys who are after a helicopter part (say what?) and she must fight for survival for herself and her six-year-old son. **91m/C VHS, DVD.** Beau Cox, Ray Meagher, Amy Madigan, Daniel Hugh-Kelly, Michael Ironside; *D:* Mende Brown, Mario Azzopardi; *W:* Michael Fisher; *C:* Paul Onorato; *M:* Laurie Lewis, Brad Fiedel.

Nowhere to Land 1/2 **2000** Familiar plotline still manages to be suspenseful. A bomb filmed with nerve gas is stashed aboard a Boeing 747 flying from Australia to California. It's up to pilot John Prescott (Wagner) and the feds to get the situation under control. **90m/C VHS.** Jack Wagner, Christine Elise, James B. Sikking, Ernie Hudson, Mark Lee, Helen Thomson; *D:* Armand Mastroianni. **CABLE**

Nowhere to Run **1988 (R)** Slipshod version of a true story about a series of murders in Caddo, Texas in 1960. Carradine, parolled from prison, murders for revenge while six high school seniors get involved in the chase and in the seedy side of politics, police, and their own puberty. **87m/C VHS.** David Carradine, Jason Priestley, Kieran Mulroney, Henry Jones; *D:* Carl Franklin.

Nowhere to Run 1/2 **1993 (R)** Kickboxer with heart seeks cross-over movie to establish real acting career. Unfortunately, even if such a movie existed, Van Damme wouldn't know what to do with it. Arquette plays the damsel in distress, facing eviction from the family farm with her two small children. Fortunately for Van Damme's escaped convict character, she is also a very lonely widow (nudge, nudge). He saves the day by abusing the daylights out of the big bad bankers, yet also finds time to play surrogate dad. Whatta guy. **95m/C VHS, DVD.** Jean-Claude Van Damme, Rosanna Arquette, Kieran Culkin, Tiffany Taubman, Joss Ackland, Ted Levine; *D:* Robert Harmon; *W:* Joe Eszterhas, Leslie Bohem, Randy Feldman; *C:* David Gribble, Doug Milsome, Michael A. Benson; *M:* Mark Isham.

Nuclear Conspiracy 1/2 **1985** A reporter disappears while investigating a huge nuclear waste shipment, and his wife searches for him. **115m/C VHS.** *GE* Birgit Doll, Albert Fortell; *D:* Rainer Erler; *W:* Rainer Erler; *C:* Wolfgang Grasshoff; *M:* Eugen Thomass.

The Nude Bomb 1/2 *The Return of Maxwell Smart* **1980 (PG)** Proof that old TV shows never die—they just get made into big screen movies. Maxwell Smart from "Get Smart" (would you believe?) tries to save the world from a bomb intended to destroy clothing and leave everyone in the buff. Old hat lines. Followed by the TV movie "Get Smart, Again!" **94m/C VHS.** Don Adams, Dana Elcar, Pamela Hensley, Sylvia Kristel, Norman Lloyd, Rhonda Fleming, Joey Forman; *D:* Clive Donner; *W:* Bill Dana; *M:* Lalo Schifrin.

Nude on the Moon **WOOF!** **1961** Lunar expedition discovers moon inhabited by people who bare skin as hobby. Groovy theme song, "I'm Mooning Over You, My Little Moon Doll." Part of Joe Bob Brigg's "Sleaziest Movies in the History of the World" series. **83m/C VHS, DVD.** Shelby Livingston, Pat Reilly; *D:* Doris Wishman; *W:* Doris Wishman; *C:* Raymond Phelan; *M:* Daniel Hart.

Nudity Required **1990** Two pals use the casting couch, pretending to be Hollywood producers, to seduce young women. Silly comedy with gratuitous nudity (Ms. Newmar included). Hardly a laugh to be found. **90m/C VHS.** Julie Newmar, Troy Donahue, Brad Zutaut, Billy Frank, Mindi Miller, Alvin Silver, Eli Rich, Phil Hock; *D:* John Bown.

Nudo di Donna *Portrait of a Woman, Nude* **1983** A witty comedy about a Venetian bookseller who is becoming tired of marital struggles with his sexy wife of 16 years. He wanders into a fashion photography shop, sees a backside nude photo of a model who looks like his wife, and he takes off in fiery pursuit to find the subject of the photo. Venetian location photography is quite nice. In Italian with English subtitles. **112m/C VHS.** *IT* Nino Manfredi, Jean-Pierre Cassel, Georges Wilson, Elenora Giorgi; *D:* Nino Manfredi.

Nueba Yol **1995** Balbuena (Marti) is a recent widower with nothing much to look forward to in his native Dominican Republic, so he's easily persuaded by fast-talking friend Fellito (Carbonell) into immigrating to New York (illegally). He has trouble finding any kind of work, is confused and intimidated by the city, and finds himself at odds with more acclimated immigrants from his homeland. Spanish with subtitles. **105m/C VHS.** Luisito Marti, Caridad Ravelo, Raul Carbonell, Joel Garcia; *D:* Angel Muniz; *W:* Angel Muniz; *C:* Christopher Norr.

The Nugget 1/2 **2002 (R)** Aussie-made comedy's jokes may be better understood by the locals. Three working-class blokes spend their weekends out in the bush allegedly gold prospecting but mostly sitting around drinking beer. But on one trip, they finally find a huge nugget, and their greed leads to a disruption in their friendship, until their windfall gets stolen. **90m/C DVD.** *AU* Eric Bana, Alan Brough, Max Cullen, Dave O'Neil, Stephen Currie, Peter Moon, Belinda Emmett, Sallyanne Ryan, Karen Pang; *D:* Bill Bennett; *W:* Bill Bennett; *C:* Danny Ruhlmann; *M:* Nigel Westlake.

Nukie 1/2 **1993 (G)** Brothers from another planet crash land on Earth. The first one is subjected to a dizzying array of scientific experiments in Florida involving electric cattle prods. The other one, Nukie, lands in Africa and is befriended by twins from a remote tribal village. They join him in his quest to free his brother from the sadistic clutches of suntanned professionals who have lost all compassion. Important message for our youth about the dangers of a runaway technocracy. **99m/C VHS.** Glynis Johns, Steve Railsback; ***D:*** Sias Odendal.

Numb 1/2 **2007 (R)** Screenwriter Hudson Milbank (Perry) suffers from depersonalization disorder (DPD), a mental illness where the person cannot feel normal human emotion. Hudson feels neither love nor fear, just a depressed blank nothingness that permeates his life. He's tried many different drugs and therapies with no success until Sarah (Collins) enters his life. Hudson knows there's an attraction but cannot demonstrate it despite his desire to get better and Sarah's supportiveness. Funny rather than mawkish, and personal as director/writer Goldberg suffers from DPD himself. **94m/C DVD.** Matthew Perry, Lynn Collins, Kevin Pollak, Mary Steenburgen, Bob Gunton, Helen Shaver, William B. Davis; ***D:*** Harris Goldberg; ***W:*** Harris Goldberg; ***C:*** Eric Steelberg; ***M:*** Ryan Shore.

Number One Fan 1/2 **1994 (R)** Hollywood action star Zane Barry (McQueen) is stalked by Blair (Ammann), a fan with whom he had a brief romance. Zane manages to patch things up when fiancee Holly (Stewart) finds out but Blair's determined to be the only woman in his life. **93m/C VHS.** Chad McQueen, Catherine Mary Stewart, Renee Griffin, Hoyt Axton, Paul Bartel, Eric (DaRe) Da Re, Charles Matthau; ***D:*** Jane Simpson; ***W:*** Anthony Laurence Greene.

Number 1 of the Secret Service **1977 (PG)** A handsome secret agent must foil the plans of a millionaire industrialist to destroy the economy. Spy spoof that's marginally interesting. **87m/C VHS.** *GB* Nicky Henson, Geoffrey Keen, Sue Lloyd, Aimi MacDonald, Richard Todd; ***D:*** Lindsay Shonteff.

Number One with a Bullet **1987 (R)** Two unorthodox "odd couple" detectives are demoted after losing a key witness, but still set out on their own to unearth a drug czar. Carradine and Williams are better than this standard action material. **103m/C VHS.** Bobby DiCicco, Doris Roberts, Mykelti Williamson, Jon(athan) Gries, Vanessa Bell Calloway, Shari Shattuck, Robert Carradine, Billy Dee Williams, Peter Graves, Valerie Bertinelli; ***D:*** Jack Smight; ***W:*** James Belushi, Andrew Kurtzman, Rob Riley; ***C:*** Alex Phillips Jr.; ***M:*** Alf Clausen.

No. 17 **1932** A humorous early thriller by the Master Hitchcock, filmed before the likes of "The 39 Steps." An unsuspecting hobo accidentally discovers a jewel thief's cache. The chase is on—superb final chase sequence involving a bus and a train. Based on the play by J. Jefferson Farjeon. **64m/B VHS, DVD.** *GB* Leon M. Lion, Anne Grey, John Stuart, Donald Calthrop; ***D:*** Alfred Hitchcock; ***W:*** Alfred Hitchcock; ***C:*** Jack Cox, Bryan Langley.

No. 3 1/2 *Number Three* **1997** Gangster Tae-ju (suk-kyu Han) is a young triad member who resents being number three in the pecking order of his gang. His rival is a dumb guy who beats people with ashtrays, and his wife is cheating on him with a poet. This simply will not stand. **109m/C DVD.** *KN* Min-Sik Choi, Suk-kyu Han, Mi-yeon Lee, Kang-ho Song, Kwang-jung Park, Sang-Myeon Park; ***D:*** Neung-han Song; ***W:*** Neung-han Song; ***C:*** Seung-bae Park; ***M:*** Dong-Ik Cho.

The Number 23 1/2 **2007 (R)** Disappointing, gimmicky, and generally incoherent effort stars Carrey as dog catcher Walter Sparrow, who's given a mystery novel by wife Agatha (Madsen in another supportive wife role). It's about a noirish detective (also played by Carrey), and all the significant events in the book are oddly connected to the number 23. Walter also becomes obsessive about the number and begins to fear that he will follow the book's plot, which includes murder. Walter eventually gets a grip but the film never recovers. **95m/C DVD.** *US* Jim Carrey, Virginia Madsen, Logan Lerman, Danny Huston, Rhona Mitra, Lynn Collins, Mark Pellegrino, Ed Lauter; ***D:*** Joel Schumacher; ***W:*** Fernley Phillips; ***C:*** Matthew Libatique; ***M:*** Harry Gregson-Williams.

Numero Deux *Number Two* **1975** Godard explores politics, sex, and the trials of the modern family. A dissatisfied wife suffers from chronic constipation, her exhausted husband is impotent, they, their children, and grandparents all try to cope with daily life. For nine-tenths of the film Godard only used small portions of the screen (the upper left and lower right corners) to manipulate his message of frustration. It's only at the end that the full-screen is used to offer some sort of relief. In French with English subtitles. **90m/C VHS.** *FR* Sandrine Battistella, Pierre Oudry, Alex(andre) Rignault, Rachel Stefanopol; ***D:*** Jean-Luc Godard; ***W:*** Anne-Marie Mieville, Jean-Luc Godard.

The Nun 1/2 **1966** A young woman, unable to meet financial obligations, is forced into a convent. Victimized by the mother superior and betrayed by a clergyman who befriends her, she escapes from the convent and eventually ends up in a bordello, despairing and suicidal. Not a cheery story. Banned in France for two years. In French with English subtitles. **155m/C VHS.** *FR* Anna Karina, Lilo (Liselotte) Pulver, Micheline Presle, Christine Lenier, Francine Berge, Francisco Rabal, Wolfgang Reichmann, Catherine Diamant, Yori Bertin; ***D:*** Jacques Rivette.

Nuns on the Run **1990 (PG-13)** Idle and Coltrane are two nonviolent members of a robbery gang who double-cross their boss during a hold-up and disguise themselves as nuns while on the run from both the Mob and the police. Catholic humor, slapstick, and much fun with habits dominate. Idle and Coltrane do their best to keep the so-so script moving with its one-joke premise. **95m/C VHS, DVD.** Eric Idle, Robbie Coltrane, Janet Suzman, Camille Coduri, Robert Patterson, Tom Hickey, Doris Hare, Lila Kaye; ***D:*** Jonathan Lynn; ***W:*** Jonathan Lynn; ***C:*** Mike Garfath.

The Nun's Story 1/2 **1959** The melancholy tale of a young nun working in the Congo and Belgium during WWII, and struggling to reconcile her free spirit with the rigors of the order. Gabrielle (Hepburn) is the daughter of a Belgian doctor (Jagger), who leaves the convent as Sister Luke. Her assignment in the Congo is at a European hospital where's she influenced by dedicated surgeon, Dr. Fortunai (Finch). But Sister Luke comes to question her vocation as the Nazis rise to power and invade her homeland. Highly acclaimed; from the Kathryn Hulme novel. **152m/C VHS, DVD.** Audrey Hepburn, Peter Finch, Edith Evans, Peggy Ashcroft, Mildred Dunnock, Dean Jagger, Beatrice Straight, Colleen Dewhurst; ***D:*** Fred Zinnemann; ***W:*** Robert Anderson; ***C:*** Franz Planer; ***M:*** Franz Waxman. British Acad. '59: Actress (Hepburn); Natl. Bd. of Review '59: Director (Zinnemann), Support. Actress (Evans); N.Y. Film Critics '59: Actress (Hepburn), Director (Zinnemann).

Nuremberg 1/2 **2000** A decent but not overly compelling intro to the allied prosecution of Nazi war criminals at Nuremberg, Germany in 1945/46. Supreme Court Justice Robert H. Jackson (Baldwin) is asked to take a leave from the bench to head up the prosecution and he decides to try a representative sample of Third Reich leaders, including Hitler's No. 2 man, Hermann Goering (the always chilling Cox). The trial scenes generally work but there's also the needless byplay of a romance between Jackson and his secretary Elsie (Hennessy). Based on the book "Nuremberg: Infamy on Trial" by Joseph E. Persico. **240m/C VHS, DVD.** Alec Baldwin, Jill(ian) Hennessey, Brian Cox, Michael Ironside, Christopher Plummer, Matt Craven, Max von Sydow, Len Cariou, Len Doncheff, Herbert Knaup; ***D:*** Yves Simoneau; ***W:*** David W. Rintels; ***C:*** Alan Dostie; ***M:*** Richard Gregoire. **CABLE**

Nurse 1/2 **1980** A recently widowed woman resumes her career as a nurse in a large urban hospital, after her son leaves for college. Based on Peggy Anderson's book. Pilot for a TV series. **105m/C VHS.** Michael Learned, Robert Reed, Antonio Fargas; ***D:*** David Lowell Rich. **TV**

The Nurse 1/2 **1997 (R)** Nurse Laura Harriman (Zane) seeks revenge from the man she holds responsible for her father's suicide by destroying his family. **94m/C VHS, DVD.** Lisa Zane, John Stockwell, Janet Gunn, William R. Moses, Nancy Dussault, Sherrie Rose, Jay Underwood, Michael Fairman; ***D:*** Rob Malenfant; ***W:*** Richard Brandes; ***C:*** Feliks Parnell; ***M:*** Richard Bowers.

Nurse Betty **2000 (R)** Small-time waitress Betty (Zellweger) fantasizes about her favorite soap opera doc David Ravell (Kinnear). But she confuses fantasy and reality after witnessing the murder of her sleazoid husband (Eckhart) over a drug deal and thinks she's a character in the soap herself. So she travels to Hollywood to be reunited with her true love, trailed by her husband's two killers (Rock and Freeman). LaBute's unpredictable black comedy represents a departure from his previous claustrophobic, misanthropic work, but retains a cynical edge. Zellweger and Freeman stand out in a stellar cast that includes Kinnear at his smarmy best. **110m/C VHS, DVD.** Renee Zellweger, Morgan Freeman, Chris Rock, Greg Kinnear, Aaron Eckhart, Crispin Glover, Allison Janney, Pruitt Taylor Vince, Kathleen Wilhoite, Harriet Sansom Harris, Susan Barnes, Sheila Kelley, Tia Texada; ***D:*** Neil LaBute; ***W:*** John C. Richards; ***C:*** Jean-Yves Escoffier; ***M:*** Rolfe Kent. Golden Globes '01: Actress—Mus./Comedy (Zellweger).

Nurse Edith Cavell **1939** Fine performances in this true story of Britain's famous nurse who aided the Belgian underground during WWI, transporting wounded soldiers out of the German-occupied country. Decidedly opposes war and, ironically, was released just as WWII began to heat up in 1939. **95m/B VHS, DVD.** George Sanders, Edna May Oliver, Zasu Pitts, Robert Coote, May Robson, Anna Neagle; ***D:*** Herbert Wilcox.

Nurse Marjorie **1920** Aristocratic nurse Marjorie (Minter) falls in love and marries the leader of the Labor Party, much to her family's dismay. Based on the play by Israel Zangwill. Minter made four films with director Taylor, whose murder in 1922 has never been solved. **88m/B VHS.** Mary Miles Minter, Clyde Fillmore, George Periolat, Mollie McConnell, Frank Leigh, Vera Lewis; ***D:*** William Desmond Taylor; ***W:*** Julia Crawford Ivers.

Nurse on Call **1988** A bevy of trampy nurses cavort throughout a big city hospital. Softcore. **80m/C VHS.** Anne Tilson, Jennie Martinez, Christopher Floyd.

The Nut 1/2 **1921** Charlie Jackson (Fairbanks) is a wacky, wealthy inventor who falls for Estrell Wynn (De La Motte), a society gal dedicated to improving the lives of underprivileged children. He tries to aid her in a variety of ways—none of which work out as he expects. The usually swashbuckling Fairbanks does get to rescue the heroine. **61m/B VHS.** Douglas Fairbanks Sr., Marguerite de la Motte, William E. (W.E., William A., W.A.) Lowery; ***D:*** Theodore Reed; ***W:*** William Parker.

Nutcase **1983** A trio of young children in New Zealand attempt to thwart a group of terrorists who threaten to reactivate a large city's volcanoes unless they are given a large sum of money. Novel twist there. **49m/C VHS.** *NZ* Nevan Rowe, Ian Watkin, Michael Wilson; ***D:*** Roger Donaldson.

Nutcracker: Money, Madness & Murder **1987** Remick is chillingly effective as sociopathic socialite Frances Bradshaw Schreuder in this true crime miniseries that's based on the book by Shana Alexander. Mentally unstable Frances comes from a wealthy family but impulsively marries outside her social strata. After divorcing two husbands, she takes her sons Marc and Larry and tries to establish herself in New York, using them to swindle money from her father. Frances eventually pressures a teenaged Marc (Donovan) into murder, leading to her own arrest and sensational trial. **286m/C DVD.** Lee Remick, Tate Donovan, Frank Military, John Glover, Linda Kelsey, G.D. Spradlin, Elizabeth Wilson, Inga Swenson; ***D:*** Paul Bogart; ***W:*** William Hanley; ***C:*** Isidore Mankofsky; ***M:*** Billy Goldenberg. **TV**

The Nutcracker Prince **1991** The classic children's Christmas tale comes alive in this feature-length animated special. **75m/C VHS, DVD.** *CA* ***D:*** Paul Schibli; ***V:*** Kiefer Sutherland, Megan Follows, Michael McDonald, Phyllis Diller, Peter O'Toole.

Nutcracker Sweet **1984** Ridiculous drama about a beautiful and powerful socialite (Collins) who runs a renowned ballet company with an iron fist. A Russian ballerina defects and infiltrates Collins's company to try out her own treacherous motives. **101m/C VHS.** Joan Collins, Finola Hughes, Paul Nicholas; ***D:*** Anwar Kawadri.

Nutcracker: The Motion Picture 1/2 **1986** A lavish, stage-bound filmization of the Tchaikovsky ballet, designed by Maurice Sendak. **82m/C VHS.** ***D:*** Carroll Ballard.

Nuts **1987 (R)** A high-priced prostitute attempts to prove her sanity when she's accused of manslaughter. Ashamed of her lifestyle, and afraid of her reasons for it, her parents attempt to institutionalize her. A filmed version of Tom Topor's play that manages to retain its mesmerizing qualities. Fine performances, although the funnygirl goes over the top on several occasions. **116m/C VHS, DVD.** Barbra Streisand, Richard Dreyfuss, Maureen Stapleton, Karl Malden, James Whitmore, Robert Webber, Eli Wallach, Leslie Nielsen, William Prince, Dakin Matthews, Hayley Taylor Block; ***D:*** Martin Ritt; ***W:*** Tom Topor, Darryl Ponicsan, Alvin Sargent; ***C:*** Andrzej Bartkowiak; ***M:*** Barbra Streisand.

Nuts in May **1976** Two smug, middle-aged, middle-class vegetarians go on a camping trip and totally alienate their cynical, working-class fellow campers. **84m/C VHS, DVD.** *GB* Alison Steadman, Anthony O'Donnell, Roger Sloman; ***D:*** Mike Leigh; ***W:*** Mike Leigh; ***C:*** Michael Williams. **TV**

The Nutt House 1/2 **1995 (PG-13)** Identical twins—separated at birth—grow up to be a slimy politician and a nutcase (living up to the family name) with multiple personalities. Naturally, when the two are reunited it makes for lots of outrageous complications. **90m/C VHS, DVD.** Stephen Kearney, Traci Lords, Amy Yasbeck; ***Cameos:*** Stella Stevens, Robert Mandan, Catherine Bach; ***D:*** Adam Rifkin; ***W:*** Ron Zwang, Scott Spiegel, Sam Raimi; ***C:*** Bernd Heinl; ***M:*** Cameron Allan.

The Nutty Professor **1963** A mild-mannered chemistry professor creates a potion that turns him into a suave, debonair, playboy type with an irresistible attraction to women. Lewis has repeatedly denied the slick character is a Dean Martin parody, but the evidence is quite strong. Easily Lewis's best film. **107m/C VHS, DVD.** Jerry Lewis, Stella Stevens, Del Moore, Kathleen Freeman, Howard Morris, Les Brown, Med Flory, Norman Alden, Milton Frome, Buddy Lester, Henry Gibson; ***D:*** Jerry Lewis; ***W:*** Bill Richmond, Jerry Lewis; ***C:*** Wallace Kelley; ***M:*** Walter Scharf. Natl. Film Reg. '04.

The Nutty Professor **1996 (PG-13)** Remake of the 1963 Jerry Lewis comedy stars Murphy as Professor Sherman Klump, a severely overweight but bright man whose heft gets in the way of his love life. He takes a swig of his own secret potion and is transformed into the slim and suave Buddy Love. Only the formula isn't perfect and seems to wear off at the worst possible times. After a string of bad movies, Murphy may have stumbled upon his own formula for a comeback by relinquishing creative control and concentrating on the comedy. Reminiscent of "Coming to America," Murphy plays eight different roles. The fat and fart jokes are plentiful and so are the laughs. **96m/C VHS, DVD, HD DVD.** Eddie Murphy, Jada Pinkett Smith, James Coburn, Dave Chappelle; ***D:*** Tom Shadyac; ***W:*** David Sheffield, Barry W. Blaustein, Steve Oedekerk, Tom Shadyac; ***C:*** Julio Macat; ***M:*** David Newman. Oscars '96: Makeup; Natl. Soc. Film Critics '96: Actor (Murphy).

Nutty Professor 2: The Klumps 1/2 **2000 (PG-13)** Sequel to the 1996 hit finds Murphy working overtime as Sherman Klump attempts to remove the DNA of his alter ego Buddy Love from his system. Once Buddy escapes, he steals Sherman's latest experiment, a youth serum. Buddy also complicates Sherman's relationship with a beautiful colleague (Jackson) and the entire Klump clan. Expanding a one-joke scene from the original is risky, but Murphy and the writers manage to pull it off rather impressively. Yes, the humor is crude, (the more uptight may even say offensive) but the story is funny and interesting while the characters, if not always appealing, are sympathetic and genuine. **105m/C VHS, DVD, HD DVD.** Eddie Murphy, Janet Jackson, Anna Maria Horsford, Melinda McGraw, Richard Gant, John Ales, Larry Miller, Chris Elliott, Earl Boen, Kathleen Freeman, Charles Napier, Jamal Mixon, Nikki Cox; ***D:*** Peter Segal; ***W:*** Barry W. Blaustein, David Sheffield, Chris Weitz, Paul Weitz, Steve

Oedekerk; ***C:*** Dean Semler; ***M:*** David Newman.

A Nymphoid Barbarian in Dinosaur Hell WOOF! 1994 Nuclear holocaust survivors, human and otherwise, vie for the affections of the last woman alive, a voluptuous nymphoid barbarian. **90m/C VHS, DVD.** Linda Corwin, Paul Guzzi; ***D:*** Bret Piper; ***W:*** Bret Piper.

Nyoka and the Tigermen *Nyoka and the Lost Secrets of Hippocrates; Perils of Nyoka* **1942** The adventures of the jungle queen Nyoka and her rival Vultura in their search for the lost tablets of Hippocrates. In 15 episodes. **250m/B VHS.** Kay Aldridge, Clayton Moore; ***D:*** William Witney.

O **2001 (R)** Apparently Hollywood has discovered that this Shakespeare fella can do some writin'. An exclusive South Carolina high school serves as background for this updated teen "Othello," which substitutes basketball for battle. Odin (Phifer) is the sole black student at Palmetto Grove Academy due to his hoops prowess. He has an intimate relationship with Desi (Stiles, in her third Bard adaptation in as many years), the daughter of the school's dean. Hugo (Hartnett), the envious son of the basketball coach (Sheen), plots Odin's disgrace and destruction by poisoning his mind against Desi. Although blasted by some critics as full of skimpy plot devices, there's not much that's not taken straight from the source material. Filmed in 1999, it was pulled by skittish studio bigwigs following the Columbine shootings and not released until 2001. **94m/C VHS, DVD.** *US* Mekhi Phifer, Josh Hartnett, Julia Stiles, Elden (Ratliff) Henson, Andrew Keegan, Rain Phoenix, John Heard, A.J. (Anthony) Johnson, Martin Sheen; ***D:*** Tim Blake Nelson; ***W:*** Brad Kaaya; ***C:*** Russell Fine; ***M:*** Jeff Danna.

O Brother Where Art Thou? **1/2 2000 (PG-13)** Clooney stars as chain gang escapee Ulysses Everett McGill, who, along with fellow escapees Pete and Delmar (Turturro and Nelson), sets out on an "Odyssey"-like journey through Depression-era Mississippi bound for home, where waits McGill's wife, Penny (Hunter). What the trio encounter along the way are a number of Coenesque situations and characters that, when all is said and done, seem like just that—individual situations that never really add up to a cohesive whole. They fit well enough to comprise a pretty enjoyable film, though. Fine performances by Clooney, Nelson, and Coen regulars Goodman and Turturro. **103m/C VHS, DVD.** George Clooney, Tim Blake Nelson, John Turturro, Holly Hunter, John Goodman, Charles Durning, Del Pentacost, Michael Badalucco, Brian Reddy, Wayne Duvall, Ed Gale, Ray McKinnon, Daniel von Bargen, Royce D. Applegate, Frank Collison, Lee Weaver, Stephen (Steve) Root, Musetta Vander, Chris Thomas King, Mia Tyler, Christy Taylor; ***D:*** Joel Coen; ***W:*** Ethan Coen, Joel Coen; ***C:*** Roger Deakins; ***M:*** T-Bone Burnett, Chris Thomas King, Carter Burwell. Golden Globes '01: Actor—Mus./Comedy (Clooney).

O Fantasma *Phantom* **2000** The darker side of sexuality is explored as lonely, twentysomething trash collector Sergio (Menses) drifts through his life in a dreamline haze, indulging in anonymous sexual encounters. He discovers a taste for the sexual extreme and becomes obsessed with the unobtainable Joao (Barbosa)—stalking him until Sergio can act on his desires. Explicit sex—fuzzy narrative. Portuguese with subtitles. **90m/C VHS, DVD.** *PT* Ricardo Menses, Andre Barbosa, Beatriz Torcato, Eurico Vieira; ***D:*** Joao Pedro Rodrigues; ***W:*** Joao Pedro Rodrigues, Jose Neves, Paulo Rebelo, Alexandre Melo; ***C:*** Rui Pocas.

O Jerusalem **1/2 2007 (R)** Clunky retelling of the founding of Israel in 1948 that's based on the 1972 book by Dominique Lapierre and Larry Collins. When they lived in New York, Jewish Bobby (Feild) and Arab Said (Taghamaoui) were the best of friends. But in 1946 both travel to Palestine and find themselves in increasing opposition in a clash between the Brits, the Arabs, and the Jews for territory and legitimacy. **101m/C DVD.** J.J. Feild, Said Taghmaoui, Ian Holm, Tovah Feldshuh, Tom Conti, Patrick Bruel, Maria Papas, Mel Raido, Jamie Harding; ***D:*** Elie Chouraqui; ***W:*** Elie Chouraqui; ***C:*** Giovanni Fiore Coltellacci; ***M:*** Stephen Endelman.

O Lucky Man! **1973 (R)** Surreal, black comedy following the rise and fall and eventual rebirth of a modern British coffee salesman. Several actors play multiple roles with outstanding performances throughout. Price's excellent score combines with the hilarity for an extraordinary experience. **178m/C VHS.** *GB* Malcolm McDowell, Ralph Richardson, Rachel Roberts, Arthur Lowe, Alan Price, Helen Mirren, Mona Washbourne, Warren Clarke; ***D:*** Lindsay Anderson; ***M:*** Alan Price. British Acad. '73: Support. Actor (Lowe).

O Pioneers! **1/2 1991 (PG)** Lange plays Alexandra Bergson, an unmarried woman at the turn of the century, who inherits her family's Nebraska homestead because her father knows how much she loves the land. Although the family has prospered through Alexandra's smart investments, her brothers come to resent her influence. When her first love returns after 15 years and the romance is rekindled, family resentments surface once again. Based on the novel by Willa Cather. A Hallmark Hall of Fame presentation. **99m/C VHS, DVD.** Jessica Lange, David Strathairn, Tom Aldredge, Reed Edward Diamond, Anne Heche, Heather Graham, Josh Hamilton, Leigh Lawson, Graham Beckel; ***D:*** Glenn Jordan; ***W:*** Glenn Jordan. **TV**

O Quatrilho **1995** Two young couples from Italy immigrate to southern Brazil in the 1910s, hoping to find their fortunes. Thrifty peasant Angelo (Paternost) marries romantic Teresa (Pillar) and goes into business with the equally romantic Massimo (Campos), who's married to the thrifty Pierina (Pires). The grain mill thrives but the romantic half of each couple delve into some illicit amore and decide to flee while their left-behind spouses discover their own attractions. A happy ending is had by all (this must be a fairytale). Lots of high-gloss gush. Based on the novel by Jose Clemente Pozenat. Portuguese and Italian with subtitles. **120m/C VHS.** *BR* Gloria Pires, Patricia Pillar, Bruno Campos, Alexandre Paternost; ***D:*** Fabio Barreto; ***W:*** Leopoldo Serran; ***C:*** Felix Monti; ***M:*** Caetano Veloso.

The Oak **1/2 1993** Morgenstern grieves over the loss of her father until she realizes she can't get rid of the body. Her difficulties in locating adequate medical facilities reflect the nightmarish realities of pre-1990 communist Romania. Potentially farcical aspects of storyline are successfully removed by violence in following scene involving Morgenstern and a band of roaming soldiers. A tragicomic look at obstinate communist bureaucrats and the wily, willful peasants who overcome them. Based on a novel by Ion Baiesu. In Romanian with English subtitles. **105m/C VHS.** *RO* Maia Morgenstern, Razvan Vasilescu, Victor Rebengiuc, Dorel Visan, Mariana Mihut, Dan Condurache, Virgil Andriescu, Leopoldina Balanuta, Matei Alexandru, Gheorghe Visu, Magda Catone, Ionel Mahailescu; ***D:*** Lucian Pintilie; ***W:*** Lucian Pintilie.

Oasis of the Zombies *Bloodsucking Nazi Zombies; Treasure of the Living Dead* **1982** European students set out to find buried treasure in Saharan oasis but instead find bevy of hungry Nazis with eating disorders. Franco directed under the name "A.M. Frank." **75m/C VHS, DVD.** *SP FR* Manuel Gelin, France Jordan, Jeff Montgomery, Miriam Landson, Eric Saint-Just, Caroline Audret, Henry Lambert; ***D:*** Jess (Jesus) Franco; ***W:*** Jess (Jesus) Franco.

Oath of Vengeance **1/2 1944** Billy the Kid rides the West once more. **50m/B VHS, DVD.** Buster Crabbe, Al "Fuzzy" St. John, Jack Ingram, Charles "Blackie" King; ***D:*** Sam Newfield.

The Object of Beauty **1991 (R)** Two Americans, trapped in Europe by their love of pleasure and their lack of money, bicker over whether to sell their one object of value—a tiny Henry Moore sculpture. When it disappears, their relationship is challenged. Excellent acting and telling direction. Forces an examination of one's own value placement. **105m/C VHS, DVD.** Andie MacDowell, John Malkovich, Joss Ackland, Lolita (David) Davidovich, Peter Riegert, Bill Paterson, Rudi Davies, Ricci Harnett; ***D:*** Michael Lindsay-Hogg; ***W:*** Michael Lindsay-Hogg; ***C:*** David Watkin; ***M:*** Tom Bahler.

The Object of My Affection **1/2 1998 (R)** Nina (Aniston) is a Brooklyn social worker with an overbearing boyfriend, Vince (Pankow), she doesn't really love. Unfortunately, the man she does fall for is handsome gay teacher George (Rudd), who's just broken up with his pretentious boyfriend Joley (Daly), and who winds up renting Nina's spare room. When Nina discovers she's pregnant, she decides George would make a terrific father and asks him to raise the baby with her. But both turn out to have very unrealistic expectations about friendship and romance. Mix of humor and tears, with good performances, particularly by the appealing leads. Adapted from the novel by Stephen McCauley. **112m/C VHS, DVD.** Jennifer Aniston, Paul Rudd, John Pankow, Timothy Daly, Alan Alda, Nigel Hawthorne, Allison Janney, Amo Gulinello, Steve Zahn, Daniel Cosgrove; ***D:*** Nicholas Hytner; ***W:*** Wendy Wasserstein; ***C:*** Oliver Stapleton; ***M:*** George Fenton.

Object of Obsession **1/2 1995 (R)** One wrong phone call propels divorcee Margaret into an affair with a stranger that leads to kinky psycho/sexual games and revenge. **91m/C VHS, DVD.** Erika Anderson, Scott Valentine; ***D:*** Alexander Gregory (Gregory Dark) Hippolyte; ***W:*** Brad (Sean) Marlowe; ***C:*** Wally Pfister.

The Objective **1/2 2008** Stale and cliched supernatural thriller. CIA agent Benjamin Keynes (Ball) is sent on a secret mission to Afghanistan to figure out if a mysterious radioactive heat signal means Al Qaeda has nuclear weapons. Keynes heads into the mountains with a special forces team only to discover that their enemy isn't even human. **90m/C DVD.** Jonas Ball, Jon Huertas, Michael C. Williams, Sam Hunter, Jeff Prewett, Chems-Eddine Zinoune, Matthew R. Anderson; ***D:*** Daniel Myrick; ***W:*** Daniel Myrick, Mark Patton, Wes Clark Jr.; ***C:*** Stephanie Martin; ***M:*** Kays Al-Atrakchi.

Objective, Burma! **1945** Deemed by many to be the greatest and most moving WWII production released during the war. American paratroopers are dropped over Burma where their mission is to destroy a Japanese radar station. The Americans led by Flynn are successful in wiping out the station, but they are spotted and descended upon by Japanese forces. Impeded from returning to Allied lines, the American soldiers must try to survive enemy encounters, exhaustion, starvation, and the elements until they are rescued. Splendid performance by Flynn and exceptional direction from Walsh; excellent performances enhanced by energetic score. **142m/B VHS, DVD.** Errol Flynn, James Brown, William Prince, George Tobias, Henry Hull, Warner Anderson, Richard Erdman, Mark Stevens, Anthony Caruso, Hugh Beaumont, John Alvin, William (Bill) Hudson, Lester Matthews, George Tyne, Erville Alderson; ***D:*** Raoul Walsh; ***W:*** Ranald MacDougall, Lester Cole; ***C:*** James Wong Howe; ***M:*** Franz Waxman.

Oblivion **1/2 1994 (PG-13)** In this sci-fi western, set in the year 3031, its cowboys versus the aliens. A sheriff's son (Paul) returns to the town of Oblivion to avenge his father's murder and finds a reptilian extraterrestrial (Divoff) terrorizing the community. **94m/C VHS, DVD.** Richard Joseph Paul, Andrew Divoff, Jackie Swanson, Meg Foster, Isaac Hayes, Julie Newmar, Carel Struycken, George Takei; ***D:*** Sam Irvin; ***W:*** Peter David; ***M:*** Pino Donaggio.

Oblomov **1/2** *A Few Days in the Life of I.I. Oblomov; Neskolko Dnel iz Zhizni I.I. Oblomov* **1981** A production of the classic Goncharov novel about a symbolically inert Russian aristocrat whose childhood friend helps him find a reason for action. Well made, with fine performances. In Russian with English subtitles. **145m/C VHS, DVD.** *RU* Oleg Tabakov, Elena Solovei; ***D:*** Nikita Mikhalkov.

The Oblong Box *Edgar Allen Poe's The Oblong Box* **1969 (PG)** Coffins, blood, and live corpses fill drawn-out and lifeless adaptation of Edgar Allan Poe story. English aristocrat Price attempts to hide his disfigured brother in an old tower. Brother predictably escapes and rampages through town before being killed. **91m/C VHS, DVD.** *GB* Vincent Price, Christopher Lee, Alister Williamson, Hilary Dwyer, Peter Arne, Harry Baird, Carl Rigg, Sally Geeson, Maxwell Shaw; ***D:*** Gordon Hessler; ***W:*** Lawrence Huntington; ***C:*** John Coquillon.

Observe and Report **1/2 2009 (R)** Head of security Ronnie Barnhard (Rogen) patrols his shopping mall jurisdiction with an iron fist, combating skateboarders, shoplifters, and the occasional unruly customer while dreaming of the day when he can swap his flashlight for a badge and a gun. Ronnie's delusions of grandeur are tested when the mall is struck by a flasher. Plays it way more dark than you'd expect from the cast and the ad campaign. Rogen works against his everyman-likability by relying on sexist, racist, homophobic, and sterotypical rent-a-cop mentality, so it's definitely not for everyone. On the heel of Kevin James' "Paul Blart: Mall Cop", this one plays like "Travis Bickle: Mall Cop." Faris is genuinely funny as the ditzy blond object of Rogen's misguided affection. **86m/C DVD.** *US* Seth Rogen, Ray Liotta, Anna Faris, Patton Oswalt, Michael Pena, Jesse Plemons; ***D:*** Jody Hill; ***W:*** Jody Hill; ***C:*** Tim Orr; ***M:*** Joey Stephens.

The Obsessed *The Late Edwina Black* **1951** Uninspiring story with Farrar suspected of murdering his wife. Competent performances, but this mystery isn't developed with any sense of style and the killer's real identity will be obvious to anyone watching. Cliches and stereotyped situations don't add anything. **77m/B VHS.** *GB* David Farrar, Geraldine Fitzgerald, Roland Culver, Jean Cadell, Mary Merrall, Harcourt Williams, Charles Heslop, Ronald Adam, Sydney Monkton; ***D:*** Maurice Elvey; ***W:*** Charles Frank, David Evans; ***C:*** Stephen Dade.

Obsessed **1/2 1988 (PG-13)** Semi-realistic tale of a woman's exhausting desire for revenge against hit-and-run driver who killed her son. Cast acceptable but lack of psychological foundation weakens plot. **100m/C VHS.** Allan Nicholls, Kerrie Keane, Alan Thicke, Colleen Dewhurst, Saul Rubinek, Daniel Pilon, Lynne Griffin; ***D:*** Robin Spry. Genie '89: Support. Actress (Dewhurst).

Obsessed **2009 (PG-13)** Cat fights between hot chicks! Successful L.A. businessman Derek (Elba) finds his idyllic married life with beautiful wife Sharon (Knowles) threatened when office temp Lisa (Larter) becomes obsessed and starts stalking him. Derek resists Lisa's vixenish charms but she makes certain that the jealous Sharon thinks something happened. But when Sharon comes to her senses she isn't about to let a delusional Lisa have her man. **101m/C DVD.** *US* Idris Elba, Beyonce Knowles, Ali Larter, Christine Lahti, Bruce McGill, Scout Taylor-Compton, Jerry O'Connell, Matthew Humphreys; ***D:*** Steve Shill; ***W:*** David Loughery; ***C:*** Ken Seng; ***M:*** James Dooley.

Obsession **1949** A decent British noir creeper. Dr. Clive Riordan (Newton) goes crazy when he discovers his wife Storm (Gray) has taken yet another lover. He kidnaps Bill (Brown) and holds him captive, planning a protracted and grisly end (involving an acid bath) for the unfortunate fellow. However, Storm's curious poodle Monty and a Scotland Yard detective (Wayne) foil the plot. **96m/B DVD.** *GB* Robert Newton, Phil Brown, Sally Gray, Naunton Wayne, James Harcourt; ***D:*** Edward Dmytryk; ***W:*** Alec Coppel; ***C:*** C.M. Pennington-Richards; ***M:*** Nino Rota.

Obsession **1/2 1976 (PG)** A rich, lonely businessman meets a mysterious young girl in Italy, the mirror image of his late wife who was killed by kidnappers. Intriguing suspense film that's not quite up to comparisons with Hitchcock thrillers. Music by Hitchcock-collaborator Herrmann. **98m/C VHS, DVD.** Cliff Robertson, Genevieve Bujold, John Lithgow; ***D:*** Brian De Palma; ***W:*** Paul Schrader; ***C:*** Vilmos Zsigmond; ***M:*** Bernard Herrmann.

Obsession **1/2 1997** Pierre (Berling) is Miriam's (Makatsch) longtime lover. They seem happy until Miriam has a chance encounter at the Berlin train station with Jack McHale (Craig), who's investigating a family secret. The romantic triangle is inexplicable (Pierre's accepting, Jack's suddenly obsessed, and Miriam waffles) and John's family quest is confusing and ends in an unsatisfying manner. **105m/C DVD.** *FR GE* Heike Makatsch, Charles Berling, Daniel Craig, Seymour Cassel, Allen (Goorwitz) Garfield, Marie-Christine Barrault, Daniel Gelin; ***D:*** Peter Sehr; ***W:*** Peter Sehr, Marie Noelle; ***C:*** David Watkin; ***M:*** Micki Meuser.

Obsession: A Taste for Fear 🦴 ½ **1989 (R)** Diane's high fashion models are being killed and although there are plenty of suspects, she can't find the killer. **90m/C VHS.** Virginia Hey, Gerard Darmon, Carlo Mucari; ***D:*** Piccio Raffanini.

Obsessive Love 🦴🦴 ½ **1984** A lonely, mentally unstable typist (Mimieux) becomes obsessed with her soap opera hero and decides to go to Hollywood to seduce him. She transforms herself into a sleek and stunning Hollywood temptress to woo him, and at first he goes along with her—until he realizes that she is insane. An average made-for-TV movie of the older woman/younger man genre. **97m/C VHS.** Yvette Mimieux, Simon MacCorkindale, Kin Shriner, Constance McCashin, Allan Miller, Lainie Kazan; ***D:*** Steven Hilliard Stern.

O.C. and Stiggs 🦴 ½ **1987 (R)** Two teens spend a summer harassing a neighbor and his family. Flimsy attempts at comedy fall flat. A failed adaptation of a National Lampoon short story, it was held for three years before release. **109m/C VHS, DVD.** Daniel H. Jenkins, Neill Barry, Jane Curtin, Tina Louise, Jon Cryer, Dennis Hopper, Paul Dooley, Ray Walston, Louis Nye, Martin Mull, Melvin Van Peebles; ***D:*** Robert Altman; ***W:*** Donald Cantrell.

An Occasional Hell 🦴🦴 ½ **1996 (R)** Ernest DeWalt (Berenger) is an ex-cop turned writer and college professor. He investigates the death of a fellow professor (Lang) at the behest of the beautiful widow (Golino) and then learns the lady is the prime suspect. Filmed in South Carolina and based on the novel by Silvis, who wrote the screenplay. **93m/C VHS, DVD.** Tom Berenger, Valeria Golino, Kari Wuhrer, Robert Davi, Stephen Lang, Richard Edson, Geoffrey Lewis; ***D:*** Salome Breziner; ***W:*** Randall Silvis; ***C:*** Mauro Fiore; ***M:*** Anton Sanko.

The Occultist WOOF! 1989 Satan worshippers do the dance of death as they skin men alive for their evil purposes. **82m/C VHS, DVD.** Rick Gianasi; ***D:*** Tim Kincaid; ***W:*** Tim Kincaid.

Occupation: Dreamland 🦴🦴🦴 **2005** Documentary directors Scott and Olds spent six weeks in 2004 in the very dangerous city of Fallujah, following an eight-man squad of the Army's 82nd Airborne as they deal with hostile fire, isolation, bewildering customs, and whether their presence really will make any difference to the Iraqis. **78m/C DVD.** *US* ***D:*** Garrett Scott, Ian Olds.

An Occurrence at Owl Creek Bridge/Coup de Grace 1962 "Occurrence at Owl Creek Bridge" (1962), from a story by Ambrose Bierce documents the last moments of a man about to be hanged for sabotage. "Coup de Grace" (1978) tells the story of a group of friends who are caught up amongst the turmoil of the Bolshevik revolution. **123m/B VHS, DVD.** Margarethe von Trotta, Matthias Habich, Rudiger Kirschstein, Matthieu Carriere, Valeska Gert; ***D:*** Volker Schlondorff, Robert Enrico.

Ocean Drive Weekend WOOF! 1985 (PG-13) Several college students congregate at "Ocean Drive" for a weekend of beer, sex, and dancing. Stereotypical characters, lack of plot, and poor versions of 1960 classics combine for boring and inane comedy. **98m/C VHS.** Robert Peacock, Charles Redmond, Tony Freeman; ***D:*** Brian Thomas Jones.

Oceans 2009 (G) Specially designed cameras follow a vast variety of sea creatures in this nature documentary that took four years of filming in some 54 locations. **102m/C DVD.** *FR SP SI* ***D:*** Jacques Perrin, Jacques Cluzaud; ***W:*** Jacques Perrin, Jacques Cluzaud; ***M:*** Bruno Coulais; ***Nar:*** Jacques Perrin.

Ocean's 11 🦴🦴 ½ **1960** A Rat Pack romp. Spyros Acebos (Tamiroff) comes up with a plan to simultaneously rob five Las Vegas casinos on New Year's Eve. Danny Ocean (Sinatra) will lead his buddies—all of whom are veterans of the 82nd Airborne Division—in the action by shutting off all the electricity. The planning's elaborate but the plan itself goes wrong (so what else is new) and the gang can't get their stolen loot out of the city. **148m/C VHS, DVD.** Frank Sinatra, Dean Martin, Sammy Davis Jr., Angie Dickinson, Peter Lawford, Richard Conte, Cesar Romero, Joey Bishop, Akim Tamiroff, Henry Silva, Buddy Lester, Norman Fell, Red Skelton, Shirley MacLaine, George Raft; ***D:*** Lewis Milestone; ***W:*** Harry Brown, Charles Lederer; ***C:*** William H. Daniels; ***M:*** Nelson Riddle.

Ocean's Eleven 🦴🦴🦴 **2001 (PG-13)** Stylish, fun remake of the 1960 Rat Pack caper flick measures up to the original in Cool Factor and surpasses it in plot and action. In this version, Danny Ocean (Clooney) is an ex-con with a taste for the grift and a grudge against powerful casino owner Benedict (Garcia). Backed by an eclectic, amusingly quirky crew, he encounters complications when his ex (Roberts) turns out to be involved with Benedict. Great cast looks like they're having a blast (especially Gould and Reiner, who make the most of small but showy roles) as Soderburgh's "Midas touch" streak continues. **116m/C VHS, DVD, UMD.** *US* George Clooney, Brad Pitt, Andy Garcia, Matt Damon, Julia Roberts, Don Cheadle, Casey Affleck, Scott Caan, Elliott Gould, Bernie Mac, Carl Reiner, Edward Jemison, Shaobo Qin; ***Cameos:*** Henry Silva, Angie Dickinson, Holly Marie Combs, Joshua Jackson, Topher Grace, Steve Lawrence, Eydie Gorme, Wayne Newton; ***D:*** Steven Soderbergh; ***W:*** Ted Griffin; ***C:*** Steven Soderbergh; ***M:*** David Holmes.

Oceans of Fire 🦴 **1986 (PG)** Average rehash of the tension-filled world of oil riggers. Lives of two ex-cons are threatened when they hire on as divers for world's deepest undersea oil rig. **100m/C VHS, DVD.** Gregory Harrison, Billy Dee Williams, Cynthia Sikes, Lyle Alzado, Tony Burton, Ray "Boom Boom" Mancini, David Carradine, Ken Norton; ***D:*** Steve Carver.

Ocean's Thirteen 🦴🦴🦴 **2007 (PG-13)** The neo-Rat Pack returns to Vegas, baby, where they belong. Reuben (Gould) has been screwed out of his share of the strip's newest luxury hotel/casino by double-dealing egomaniac Willie Banks (Pacino). So Danny (Clooney) and Rusty (Pitt) assemble their usual team and concoct an elaborate plan (including simulating an earthquake) to sabotage the opening, bankrupt the casino, and ruin Banks. Old nemesis Garcia gets to join in on the fun this time out. Barkin comes in to cherchez la femme the boys club and everyone just has a cool, wink-wink good time. So should you. **122m/C DVD, Blu-ray Disc, HD DVD.** *US* George Clooney, Brad Pitt, Matt Damon, Andy Garcia, Al Pacino, Bernie Mac, Ellen Barkin, Casey Affleck, Scott Caan, Elliott Gould, Shaobo Qin, Don Cheadle, Edward Jemison, Carl Reiner, Eddie Izzard, Michael Mantell, David Paymer, Vincent Cassel, Julian Sands, Bob Einstein, Noureen DeWulf; ***D:*** Steven Soderbergh; ***W:*** Brian Koppelman, David Levien; ***C:*** Steven Soderbergh; ***M:*** David Holmes.

Ocean's Twelve 🦴🦴 ½ **2004 (PG-13)** The gang's all back, enjoying themselves mightily in this undemanding but fun sequel. It's taken three years but casino boss Terry Benedict (Garcia) has tracked down Danny Ocean (Clooney), who's now remarried to Tess (Roberts), and demands repayment of his $160 mil or else. Having spent his share of the dough, Danny gets the boys together and he and partner Rusty (Pitt) come up with a plan that takes them all a-thieving in various picturesque European cities. New to the adventure are Interpol agent Isabel Lahiri (Zeta-Jones), who has an amorous past with Rusty, and top Euro thief Francois Toulour (Cassel) out to prove just who's the best criminal. A frivolous, good-looking romp all the way. **125m/C VHS, DVD.** *US* George Clooney, Brad Pitt, Matt Damon, Catherine Zeta-Jones, Andy Garcia, Don Cheadle, Bernie Mac, Casey Affleck, Scott Caan, Vincent Cassel, Edward Jemison, Shaobo Qin, Carl Reiner, Elliott Gould, Robbie Coltrane, Eddie Izzard, Cherry Jones, Jeroen Krabbe, Julia Roberts, Jared Harris; ***D:*** Steven Soderbergh; ***W:*** George Nolfi; ***C:*** Steven Soderbergh; ***M:*** David Holmes.

Octagon 🦴🦴 **1980 (R)** Norris protects a woman from threatening Ninja warriors in average kung-fu adventure. Enough action and violence for fans of the genre. **103m/C VHS, DVD, UMD.** Chuck Norris, Karen Carlson, Lee Van Cleef, Kim Lankford, Art Hindle, Jack Carter; ***D:*** Eric Karson; ***W:*** Paul Aaron, Leigh Chapman.

Octaman 🦴 ½ **1971** Comical thriller featuring non-threatening octopus-man discovered by scientists in Mexico. Rip-off of director Essex's own "Creature from the Black Lagoon." Not without its curiosity factor: young Rick Baker designed the octopus man, while actress Angeli died of a drug overdose during filming. **79m/C VHS, DVD.** Kerwin Mathews, Pier Angeli, Harry Guardino, David Essex, Jeff Morrow, Norman Fields; ***D:*** Harry Essex; ***W:*** Harry Essex; ***C:*** Robert Caramico.

Octane 🦴 ½ *Dolphins* **2007 (R)** Brighton bad boy Brent Black discovers the adrenaline rush of illegal street racing but his success is challenged by the Bling London Boy Racers. Then Brent's car is mysteriously destroyed just a week before the big grudge match. **89m/C DVD.** *GB* Frank Harper, Karl Davies, Lauren Steventon, Layke Anderson, Gemma Baker, Amy Blackburn, Roots Manuva; ***D:*** Mark Jay; ***W:*** Mark Jay; ***C:*** Simon Dennis, Brendan McGinty; ***M:*** Sacha Puttnam.

Octavia 🦴 **1982 (R)** A contemporary fable about a blind girl who befriends a convict and learns about life and love. **93m/C VHS.** Susan Curtis; ***D:*** David Beaird; ***W:*** David Beaird.

The October Man 🦴🦴🦴 **1948** When a model is found murdered, a stranger with mental problems must prove his innocence to others and himself. Strong characters make good, suspenseful mystery reminiscent of Hitchcock. **95m/B VHS.** *GB* John Mills, Joan Greenwood, Edward Chapman, Joyce Carey, Kay Walsh, Felix Aylmer, Juliet Mills; ***D:*** Roy Ward Baker; ***W:*** Eric Ambler.

October Sky 🦴🦴🦴 **1999 (PG)** Relates the true story of young Homer Hickam Jr. (Gyllenhaal), who rose from a gloomy West Virginia mining town to become a NASA engineer. Spurred by the launch of Sputnik and a supportive teacher (Dern), Homer and three of his friends experiment with rockets with the hope of winning college scholarships. The boys battle the skepticism of their peers and families as well as the looming possibility of a future in the mines. Entertaining and uplifting without resorting to melodrama and sentimentality. Adapted from Hickam's memoir "Rocket Boys." **108m/C VHS, DVD.** Jake Gyllenhaal, Chris Cooper, Laura Dern, Chris Owen, William Lee Scott, Chad Lindberg, Natalie Canerday, Scott Miles, Randy Stripling, Chris Ellis; ***D:*** Joe Johnston; ***W:*** Lewis Colick; ***C:*** Paul Murphy; ***M:*** Mark Isham.

Octopus 🦴🦴 **2000 (PG-13)** Giant mutant octopus lurking in the ocean depths is disturbed by a U.S. Navy submarine and decides to make it lunch. This, however, is not the only bad news. Seems the sub was transporting a terrorist who escapes in the confusion, and winds up on a cruise ship. He thinks he's safe but our eight-legged horror is just getting started. Special effects are pretty lame but the film doesn't take itself serously and the humor covers a lot of holes. **99m/C VHS, DVD.** Carolyn Lowery, David Beecroft, Jay Harrington, Ravil Isyanov; ***D:*** John Eyres; ***W:*** Michael D. Weiss; ***C:*** Adolfo Bartoli; ***M:*** Marco Marinangelo. **VIDEO**

Octopus 2: River of Fear 🦴🦴 **2002 (R)** After two Russian tourists are killed on the waterfront off the Hudson River, scuba diver cop Nick (Burke) discovers a giant man-eating octopus. Not wanting to spoil the city's 4th of July celebrations, the mayor refuses to do anything. So Nick and his partner Walter (Lane) must stop the rampaging creature—who attacks the Statue of Liberty! That's just wrong. **95m/C VHS, DVD.** Michael Reilly Burke, Frederic Lehne, Duncan Fraser, Meredith Morton, John Thaddeus; ***D:*** Yossi Wein; ***W:*** Michael D. Weiss; ***C:*** Peter Belcher; ***M:*** Bill Wandel. **VIDEO**

Octopussy 🦴🦴 **1983 (PG)** The Bond saga continues as Agent 007 is on a mission to prevent a crazed Russian general from launching a nuclear attack against the NATO forces in Europe. Lots of special effects and gadgets keep weak plot moving. **140m/C VHS, DVD.** *GB* Roger Moore, Maud Adams, Louis Jourdan, Kristina Wayborn, Kabir Bedi, Steven Berkoff, Robert Brown; ***D:*** John Glen; ***W:*** Michael G. Wilson; ***C:*** Alan Hume; ***M:*** John Barry.

The Odd Angry Shot 🦴🦴 ½ **1979** Australian soldiers fighting in Vietnam discover the conflict is not what they expected. Ironic perspective of men struggling with their feelings about the war. More of an unremarkable drama with comic overtones than a combat film, it will appeal to those who prefer good direction to bloodshed. **90m/C VHS.** *AU* Graham Kennedy, John Hargreaves, John Jarratt, Bryan Brown, Graeme Blundell, Richard Moir, Ian Gilmour, John Allen, Brandon Burke, Graham Rouse, Tony Barry, Max Cullen, John Fitzgerald, Ray Meagher; ***D:*** Tom Jeffrey; ***W:*** Tom Jeffrey; ***C:*** Donald McAlpine; ***M:*** Walter (Wendy) Carlos.

Odd Birds 🦴🦴 ½ **1985** Coming of age drama set in 1965 California. Shy 15-year-old Joy Chan is a Chinese-American dreaming of becoming an actress. Her widowed immigrant mother wants Joy to have a practical profession—like nursing. Longing for someone to understand Joy meets Brother Murphy, a math teacher at the local boys school. Murphy's been trying to reconcile his religious commitment with his unorthodox views. It isn't long before these two individualists recognize a fellow kindred spirit. **87m/C VHS.** Michael Moriarty, Donna Lai Ming Lew, Nancy Lee, Bruce Gray, Karen Maruyama, Scott Crawford; ***D:*** Jeanne Collachia; ***W:*** Jeanne Collachia.

The Odd Couple 🦴🦴🦴 ½ **1968 (G)** Two divorced men with completely opposite personalities move in together. Lemmon's obsession with neatness drives slob Matthau up the wall, and their inability to see eye-to-eye results in many hysterical escapades. A Hollywood rarity, it is actually better in some ways than Neil Simon's original Broadway version. Simon based the characters on brother Danny and his roommates. Basis for the hit TV series. **106m/C VHS, DVD.** Jack Lemmon, Walter Matthau, Herb Edelman, John Fiedler, Monica Evans, Carol(e) Shelley; ***D:*** Gene Saks; ***W:*** Neil Simon; ***C:*** Robert B. Hauser.

The Odd Job 🦴🦴 **1978** Insurance salesman Chapman, depressed after his wife leaves him, hires a hit man to kill him. Chapman then has a hard time shaking his stalker after deciding he wants to live. Monty Python fans will enjoy seeing ex-troupe member Chapman again, but the comic's heart isn't in this unoriginal story. **100m/C VHS.** *GB* Graham Chapman; ***D:*** Peter Medak; ***M:*** Howard Blake.

Odd Jobs 🦴🦴 **1985 (PG-13)** When five college friends look for jobs during summer break, they wind up running their own moving business with the help of the mob. Good comic talent, but a silly slapstick script results in only a passable diversion. **89m/C VHS, DVD.** Paul Reiser, Scott McGinnis, Rick Overton, Robert Kevin Townsend; ***D:*** Mark Story; ***W:*** Robert Conte; ***C:*** Arthur Albert, Peter Lyons Collister; ***M:*** Robert Folk.

Odd Man Out 🦴🦴🦴 ½ *Gang War* **1947** An Irish revolutionary is injured during a robbery attempt. Suffering from gunshot wounds and closely pursued by the police, he must rely on the help of others who could betray him at any moment. A gripping tale of suspense and intrigue that will keep the proverbial seat's edge warm until the final credits. Adapted from F.L. Green's novel, previously filmed as "The Last Man." **111m/B VHS, DVD.** *GB* James Mason, Robert Newton, Dan O'Herlihy, Kathleen Ryan, Cyril Cusack; ***D:*** Carol Reed; ***W:*** F.L. Green, R.C. Sherriff; ***C:*** Robert Krasker; ***M:*** William Alwyn. British Acad. '47: Film.

Odd Obsession 🦴🦴 ½ *The Key* **1960** One of Ichikawa's first films, about an elderly Japanese gentleman with a young wife whose feelings of jealousy and impotence eventually wreak havoc on the marriage. In Japanese with English subtitles. **96m/C VHS.** *JP* Machiko Kyo, Ganjiro Nakamura; ***D:*** Kon Ichikawa. Golden Globes '60: Foreign Film.

The Odd Squad 🦴 **1986 (R)** Five GIs in WWII defend a bridge from the enemy, and manage in doing so to have loads of laughs. **82m/C VHS.** Johnny Dorelli, Vincent Gardenia; ***D:*** E.B. (Enzo Barboni) Clucher.

Oddball Hall 🦴🦴 **1991 (PG)** Two aging jewel thieves hide out in the African wilds, masquerading as powerful "wizards." When they head back to civilization, an African tribe beseeches the phony sorcerers to cure their long drought. **87m/C VHS.** Don Ameche, Burgess Meredith; ***D:*** Jackson Hunsicker; ***W:*** Jackson Hunsicker.

Oddballs WOOF! 1984 (PG-13) In another attempt to capitalize on the success of Bill Murray's "Meatballs," this summer camp story follows three campers and their pathetic attempts to lose their virginity. Brooks has his moments, but there is little else to recommend here. **92m/C VHS, DVD.** Foster Brooks, Jason Sorokin, Wally Wodchis, Konnie Krome; ***D:*** Miklos Lente.

Odds Against Tomorrow
1959 Compulsive gambler/nightclub singer Johnny Ingram (Belafonte) owes big money to gangster Bacco (Kuluva). He hooks up with racist ex-con Earl Slater (Ryan) and former policeman Dave Burke (Begley) to rob a bank but everything goes wrong. Ingram and Slater manage to escape to a nearby oil storage area but the racial tensions between the two are proving deadlier than the cops on their trail. Based on the novel by William P. McGivern; because of the blacklist screenwriter Polonsky was "fronted" by John O. Killens. Polonsky officially received credit for his work in 1996. **120m/B VHS, DVD.** Harry Belafonte, Robert Ryan, Shelley Winters, Ed Begley Sr., Gloria Grahame, Will Kuluva, Richard Bright; ***D:*** Robert Wise; ***W:*** Abraham Polonsky, Nelson Gidding; ***C:*** Joseph Brun; ***M:*** John Lewis.

Odds and Evens 1/2 **1978 (PG)** Italian supercops pretend they don't have badges in order to clean up illegal betting and gambling rings in sunny Miami. Odds are this spaghetti cop-o-rama won't keep Morpheus at bay. **109m/C VHS.** *IT* Terence Hill, Bud Spencer; ***D:*** Sergio Corbucci.

Ode to Billy Joe **1976 (PG)** The 1967 Bobby Gentry hit song of the same title is expanded to tell why a young man jumped to his death off the Tallahatchie Bridge. The problems of growing up in the rural South and teenage romance do not match the appeal of the theme song. Benson and O'Connor, however, work well together. **106m/C VHS.** Robby Benson, Glynnis O'Connor, Joan Hotchkis, Sandy McPeak, James Best; ***D:*** Max Baer Jr.

The Odessa File 1/2 **1974 (PG)** During 1963, a German journalist attempts to track down some SS war criminals who have formed a secret organization called ODESSA. The story, from Frederick Forsyth's novel, drags in some places, but the scene where bad guy Schell and reporter Voight finally confront each other is a high point. **128m/C VHS, DVD.** *GB GE* Jon Voight, Mary Tamm, Maximilian Schell, Maria Schell, Derek Jacobi, Peter Jeffrey, Klaus Lowitsch, Kurt Meisel, Hannes Messemer, Garfield Morgan, Shmuel Rodensku, Ernst Schroder, Noel Willman, Hans Caninenberg, Towje Kleiner, Gunnar Moiler; ***D:*** Ronald Neame; ***W:*** Kenneth Ross, George Markstein; ***C:*** Oswald Morris; ***M:*** Andrew Lloyd Webber.

The Odyssey 1/2 **1997 (PG-13)** Lavish TV miniseries based on Homer's 2,700-year-old epic poem, relating the adventures of King Odysseus of Ithaca. On the day his son is born to faithful wife Penelope (Scacchi), Odysseus (Assante) is commanded by the goddess Athena (Rossellini) to leave his home and travel to battle the Trojans. Little does he realize that this is the beginning of a 20-year sojourn, where additional trials include sea monsters, the Cyclops, the Kingdom of the Dead, enchantress Circe (Peters), and getting shipwrecked on the isle of Calypso (Williams), who wants to keep the hunk around. But even Odysseus realizes there's no place like home. **203m/C VHS, DVD.** Armand Assante, Greta Scacchi, Geraldine Chaplin, Eric Roberts, Bernadette Peters, Irene Papas, Vanessa L(ynne) Williams, Christopher Lee, Isabella Rossellini, Jeroen Krabbe, Nicholas Clay, Ron Cook, Michael J. Pollard, Paloma Baeza, Alan Cox, Heathcote Williams; ***D:*** Andrei Konchalovsky; ***W:*** Andrei Konchalovsky, Chris Solimine; ***C:*** Sergei Kozlov; ***M:*** Eduard Artemyev. **TV**

The Odyssey of the Pacific 1/2 *The Emperor of Peru* **1982** Three young Cambodian refugees encounter retired train engineer Rooney living in the woods where a railway station once thrived. Together they work to restore an old locomotive. The ordinary, inoffensive script will not endanger quality family time. **82m/C VHS.** *CA* Mickey Rooney, Monique Mercure; ***D:*** Fernando Arrabal.

Oedipus Rex *Edipo Re* **1967** A new twist on the famous tragedy as Pasolini gives the story a modern prologue and epilogue. The classic plot has Oedipus spiraling downward into moral horror as he tries to avoid fulfilling the prophecy that he will murder his father and sleep with his mother. Cross-cultural curiosities include Japanese music and Lenin-inspired songs, some written by Pasolini, who also stars as the high priest. In Italian with English subtitles. **110m/C VHS, DVD.** *IT* Franco Citti, Silvana Mangano, Alida Valli, Julian Beck, Pier Paolo Pasolini; ***D:*** Pier Paolo Pasolini.

Of Freaks and Men *Pro Urodov i Lyudej* **1998** Kinky Russian melodrama set in pre-revolutionary St. Petersburg. Pornographer Johann and his assistant Viktor specialize in selling photos and films featuring half-naked women getting flogged. They manage to insinuate themselves into two upper class Russian households and involve the families in some secret sadomasochistic games. Russian with subtitles. **93m/C VHS, DVD.** *RU* Tatiana Polonskaia, Sergei Makovetsky, Dinara Drukarova, Anzhelika Nevolina, Viktor Sukhorukov, Aleksei De, Chingiz Tsydendabayev, Vadim Prokhorov, Aleksandr Mezentsev, Igor Shibanov, Darya Lesnikova; ***D:*** Alexsei Balabanov; ***W:*** Alexsei Balabanov; ***C:*** Sergei Astakhov; ***M:*** Eric Neveux.

Of Human Bondage **1934** The first movie version of W. Somerset Maugham's classic novel in which a young, handicapped medical student falls in love with a crude cockney waitress, in a mutually destructive affair. Established Davis's role as the tough, domineering woman. Remade in 1946 and 1964. **84m/B VHS, DVD.** Bette Davis, Leslie Howard, Frances Dee, Reginald Owen, Reginald Denny, Alan Hale; ***D:*** John Cromwell; ***W:*** Lester Cohen; ***C:*** Henry W. Gerrard; ***M:*** Max Steiner.

Of Human Bondage **1964** An essentially decent man falls fatally in love with an alluring but heartless waitress, who subtly destroys him. Based on the W. Somerset Maugham novel. Miscast and least interesting of the three film versions, although Novak gives a good performance. **100m/B VHS.** *GB* Kim Novak, Laurence Harvey, Robert Morley, Roger Livesey, Siobhan McKenna; ***D:*** Henry Hathaway, Ken Hughes; ***W:*** Bryan Forbes; ***C:*** Oswald Morris.

Of Human Hearts 1/2 **1938** Rural life just before the Civil War sets up this cornpone tale of family strife. Huston is a stern preacher who has his family living in near poverty as an example of sacrifice to his flock. Son Stewart wants to study medicine and Bondi, defying her husband, manages to fund his dream. Only Stewart becomes so engrossed by his ambitions that he ignores the family, even after his father dies and his mother is left poor and alone. Then Stewart joins the Civil War as a doctor where he meets President Lincoln (Carradine), who tells him he should never neglect his mother. Oy. Well, the cast is good. Adapted from the story "Benefits Forgot" by Honore Morrow. **100m/B VHS.** James Stewart, Beulah Bondi, Walter Huston, John Carradine, Guy Kibbee, Charles Coburn, Ann Rutherford, Charley Grapewin, Gene Lockhart; ***D:*** Clarence Brown; ***W:*** Bradbury Foote; ***C:*** Clyde De Vinna.

Of Love and Shadows **1994 (R)** Political photojournalist Francisco (Banderas) begins investigating the disappearance of a self-proclaimed saint after the bloody 1973 coup in Chile. He's aided by aristocratic Chilean Irene (Connelly), who's engaged to her Army captain cousin Gustavo (Gallardo) but can't resist Francisco's ever-smoldering charms. The intrepid duo naturally find lots of corruption. Based on the novel by Isabel Allende; shot on location in Argentina. **103m/C VHS, DVD.** Antonio Banderas, Jennifer Connelly, Stefania Sandrelli, Camillo Gallardo, Patricio Contreras; ***D:*** Betty Kaplan; ***W:*** Donald Freed; ***C:*** Felix Monti; ***M:*** Jose Nieto.

Of Mice and Men **1939** A powerful adaptation of the classic Steinbeck tragedy about the friendship between two itinerant Southern ranch hands during the Great Depression. Chaney is wonderful as the gentle giant and mentally retarded Lenny, cared for by migrant worker Meredith. They both get into an irreversible situation when a woman is accidentally killed. **107m/C VHS, DVD.** Lon Chaney Jr., Burgess Meredith, Betty Field, Bob Steele, Noah Beery Jr., Charles Bickford; ***D:*** Lewis Milestone; ***W:*** Eugene Solow; ***C:*** Norbert Brodine; ***M:*** Aaron Copland.

Of Mice and Men **1981** TV remake of the classic Steinbeck tale, casting TV's Baretta (Blake) as George and Quaid as Lenny. Worth watching. **150m/C VHS, DVD.** Robert (Bobby) Blake, Randy Quaid, Lew Ayres, Mitchell Ryan, Ted Neeley, Cassie Yates, Pat Hingle, Whitman Mayo, Dennis Fimple, Pat Corley; ***D:*** Reza Badiyi. **TV**

Of Mice and Men 1/2 **1992 (PG-13)** Set on the migratory farms of California, John Steinbeck's novel covers the friendship of the simple-minded Lenny, his protector George, and a flirtatious farm wife who doesn't know Lenny's strength. Director Sinise got permission from Steinbeck's widow to film the novel (actually the third adaptation). **110m/C VHS, DVD.** John Malkovich, Sherilyn Fenn, Casey Siemaszko, Joe Morton, Ray Walston, Gary Sinise, John Terry, Richard Riehle; ***D:*** Gary Sinise; ***W:*** Horton Foote; ***C:*** Kenneth Macmillan; ***M:*** Mark Isham.

Of Time and the City **2008** Autobiographical filmmaker Terence Davies does a poetic visual memoir about his hometown of Liverpool. It's a free-association collage of archive material, original footage, and Davies' narration of his history and that of the city from the 1940s through approximately the 1960s, which often link up to his own feature films. **72m/C DVD.** *GB* ***D:*** Terence Davies; ***W:*** Terence Davies; ***C:*** Tim Pollard; ***M:*** Ian Neil; ***Nar:*** Terence Davies.

Of Unknown Origin 1/2 **1983 (R)** Weller encounters a mutated rampaging rat in his New York townhouse while his family is away on vacation. His house becomes the battleground in a terror-tinged duel of survival. A well-done rat thriller not for those with a delicate stomach. Based on the novel "The Visitor." **88m/C VHS, DVD.** *CA* Peter Weller, Jennifer Dale, Lawrence Dane, Kenneth Welsh, Louis Del Grande, Shannon Tweed; ***D:*** George P. Cosmatos; ***W:*** Brian Taggert; ***C:*** Rene Verzier.

Off and Running 1/2 **1990 (PG-13)** Struggling actress Cyd (Lauper) is working as a mermaid at a Miami hotel lounge when her horse trainer boyfriend Woody is suddenly murdered by a psycho thug (Belzer). Turns out he's after a key hidden in a necklace now in Cyd's possession. Cyd goes on the run and gets some help from failed golf pro Jack (Keith) as they try to stay one step ahead of the killer and discover what the key unlocks. **91m/C VHS.** Cyndi Lauper, David Keith, Richard Belzer, David Thornton, Anita Morris; ***D:*** Edward Bianchi; ***W:*** Eugene Robert Glazer; ***C:*** Andrzej Bartkowiak; ***M:*** Mason Daring.

Off Beat 1/2 **1986 (PG)** A shy librarian unluckily wins a spot in a police benefit dance troupe, and then falls in love with a tough police woman. With a screenplay by playwright Medoff, and a good supporting cast, it still manages to miss the mark. **92m/C VHS.** Judge Reinhold, Meg Tilly, Cleavant Derricks, Fred Gwynne, John Turturro, Jacques D'Amboise, James Tolkan, Joe Mantegna, Harvey Keitel, Amy Wright, Christopher Noth; ***D:*** Michael Dinner; ***W:*** Mark Medoff; ***C:*** Carlo Di Palma; ***M:*** James Horner.

Off Limits 1/2 **1953** When a boxing manager is drafted into the Army, he freely breaks regulations in order to train a fighter as he sees fit. Hope and Rooney, while not in peak form, make a snappy duo in this amusing romp. **89m/B VHS.** Bob Hope, Mickey Rooney, Marilyn Maxwell, Marvin Miller; ***D:*** George Marshall.

Off Limits 1/2 **1987 (R)** A spree of murders involving Vietnamese hookers draws two cops from the Army's Criminal Investigation Department into the sleazy backstreets of 1968 Saigon. There is little mystery as to who the killer is in this tale that seems written more for the sake of foul language and gratuitous gunfights than actual plot. **102m/C VHS, DVD.** Willem Dafoe, Gregory Hines, Fred Ward, Scott Glenn, Amanda Pays, Keith David, David Alan Grier; ***D:*** Christopher Crowe; ***W:*** Christopher Crowe, Jack Thibeau; ***M:*** James Newton Howard.

Off Season 1/2 **2001** A Christmas movie set in July or, rather, a spirit of Christmas movie set in July. Recently orphaned Jackson (Culkin) is now living with his Aunt Patty in Florida. She tends bar in a tacky hotel where they also live and Jackson likes to make up stories about the guests. He decides that cranky Sam Clausner (Cronyn) is actually Santa Claus on vacation, although the elderly man is more Scrooge-like than jolly. Then hotel manager Mel Breskin (McBeath) gets the idea to use Jackson's tall tale in a tasteless promotion scheme and things just snowball from there. **95m/C VHS, DVD.** Rory Culkin, Hume Cronyn, Sherilyn Fenn, Tom McBeath, Adam Arkin, Bruce Davison; ***D:*** Bruce Davison; ***W:*** Glen Gers; ***C:*** Tony Westman; ***M:*** Daniel Licht. **CABLE**

Off the Lip 1/2 **2004 (R)** Rookie reporter Kat gets to rove the wilds of Hawaii when her first beat puts her in pursuit of slippery surfing legend The Monk. While the search might have stalled, what she learns about herself means so golly gosh more. **88m/C VHS, DVD.** Marguerite Moreau, MacKenzie Astin, Adam Scott, Mark Fite, David Rasche, Jim Turner, Rick Overton, Matty Liu; ***D:*** Robert Mickelson; ***W:*** Shem Bitterman; ***C:*** Joey Forsyte; ***M:*** Andrew Gross. **VIDEO**

Off the Map **2003 (PG-13)** Folksy, quirky melodrama gets an extra bone for the strength of its performances. In 1974, eccentric IRS agent William Gibbs (True-Frost) is assigned to audit the Groden family and manages to stumble across their isolated New Mexico desert house. The Grodens, who live off the grid, are in the midst of a crisis. Grizzled Charley (Elliott) has slipped into clinical depression and hasn't spoken in months while free-spirited, unsentimental wife Arlene (Allen) gardens in the nude, and their preteen daughter Bo (de Angelis) longs for friends and a "normal" life. Gibbs becomes so involved with the Grodens that he throws his job aside to stay with them and his presence alters the family's precarious balance. Film is narrated by the grown-up Bo (Brenneman); Ackermann adapted from her play. **111m/C DVD.** *US* Joan Allen, Sam Elliott, J.K. Simmons, Amy Brenneman, Valentina de Angelis, Jim True-Frost; ***D:*** Campbell Scott; ***W:*** Joan Ackermann; ***C:*** Juan Ruiz-Anchia; ***M:*** Gary DeMichele.

Off the Mark **1987 (R)** Neely is a young athlete suffering from a childhood affliction that causes spasms in his legs. Facing the ultimate challenge, he must overcome his handicap and defeat a talented woman athlete and a Russian student in a triathalon competition. An unremarkable effort, it had a limited one-week run in theatres. **89m/C VHS.** Mark Neely, Terry Farrell, Jon Cypher, Clarence Gilyard Jr.; ***D:*** Bill Berry; ***C:*** Arledge Armenaki.

Off the Wall **1982 (R)** Two hitchhikers wind up in a southern maximum security prison after being accused of a crime they did not commit. What follows is a series of shenanigans as they try to escape. This supposed comedy falls flat in every way with the possible exception of Arquette's portrayal of the governor's daughter. **86m/C VHS.** Paul Sorvino, Rosanna Arquette, Patrick Cassidy, Billy Hufsey, Monte Markham, Mickey Gilley; ***D:*** Rick Friedberg.

Off Your Rocker 1/2 **1980** Representatives of a corporate conglomerate find that the residents of Flo Adler's Mapleview Nursing Home can still muster stiff resistance to a threatened takeover. **99m/C VHS.** Milton Berle, Red Buttons, Lou Jacobi, Dorothy Malone, Helen Shaver, Sharon Acker, Helen Hughes; ***D:*** Morley Markson, Larry Pall.

The Offence *Something Like the Truth* **1973 (R)** Connery plays a London detective who beats a suspected child molester to death during a police interrogation. Turns out he's reacting to a long-buried molestation incident from his own childhood. A chilling psycho-drama highlighted by a strong lead performance by Connery. **108m/C VHS.** *GB* Sean Connery, Trevor Howard, Vivien Merchant, Ian Bannen, Derek Newark, John Hallam, Peter Bowles; ***D:*** Sidney Lumet; ***W:*** John Hopkins.

Offerings **1989 (R)** After a boy is tormented by a gang of children who cause him to fall down a well, his resulting brain injuries turn him into a psychopathic killer. Seeking revenge ten years later, he systematically murders his oppressors, offering bits of their anatomy to the one girl who treated him kindly. A typical slasher movie, the plot is only slightly better than the worst examples of the genre. **96m/C VHS, DVD.** G. Michael Smith, Loretta L. Bowman; ***D:*** Christopher Reynolds.

Office Killer **1997 (R)** Just when you thought it was safe to run with scissors! Dorine (Kane) is a meek copy editor who is in danger of losing her job. After securing her position by accidentally electrocuting a fellow employee, Dorine begins some downsizing of her own. Pent up frustrations cause her sanity to take a personal leave of absence, and she begins to streamline her department by folding, spindling and mutilating her co-workers. Office tramp Kim (Ringwald) suspects the truth, but no one believes her. Stab at horror-black comedy isn't very scary or very funny. First directorial effort by still photographer Cindy Sherman, who didn't adapt very well to people moving around. **83m/C VHS, DVD.** Carol Kane, Molly Ringwald, Jeanne Tripplehorn, Barbara Sukowa, Michael Imperioli, David Thornton, Alice Drummond, Mike Hodge; ***Cameos:*** Eric Bogosian; ***D:*** Cindy Sherman; ***W:*** Tom Kalin, Todd Haynes, Elise MacAdam; ***C:*** Russell Fine; ***M:*** Evan Lurie.

Office Romances **1986** A woman who has moved to London from the country is seduced by her employer. Because of her plain appearance, she is flattered by his attention even though he is married and has no real feelings for her. Competently made, nonetheless hard to watch because of the slow pace. **60m/C VHS.** *GB* Judy Parfitt, Ray Brooks, Suzanne Burden; ***D:*** Mary McMurray; ***W:*** Hugh Whitemore.

Office Space 1/2 **1998 (R)** Cartoon bigwig Mike Judge tries his hand at live action in this satire of white collar corporate drudgery. Peter (Livingston) is a drone for a software company well on his way to a nervous breakdown when a hypnosis mishap opens his eyes. He becomes so apathetic toward his job that he can't even muster up the energy to quit. His new no-work ethic is mistaken by a pair of corporate headhunters as "middle-management potential," and he is promoted as his pals Michael (Herman) and Samir (Naidu) are laid off. Frustrated in his attempts to be down-sized, Peter hatches a plot to embezzle the company. Stephen Root, as disgruntled nerd Milton, steals scenes like they were office supplies in an unlocked cabinet. Adapted from animated shorts made by Judge before the Beavis and Butthead gravy train rolled into the station. **89m/C VHS, DVD, Blu-ray Disc, UMD.** Mike Judge, John C. McGinley, Paul Willson, Orlando Jones, Alexandra Wentworth, Michael McShane, Ron Livingston, Jennifer Aniston, David Herman, Ajay Naidu, Gary Cole, Diedrich Bader, Stephen (Steve) Root, Richard Riehle; ***D:*** Mike Judge; ***W:*** Mike Judge; ***C:*** Tim Suhrstedt; ***M:*** John (Gianni) Frizzell.

An Officer and a Gentleman 1/2 **1982 (R)** Young drifter Gere, who enters Navy Officer Candidate School because he doesn't know what else to do with his life, becomes a better person almost despite himself. Winger is the love interest who sets her sights on marrying Gere, and Gossett is the sergeant who whips him into shape. Strong performances by the whole cast made this a must-see in 1982 that is still appealing, despite the standard Hollywood premise. ♫Up Where We Belong; Hungry for Your Love; An Officer and a Gentleman; Treat Me Right; Tunnel of Love. **126m/C VHS, DVD.** Richard Gere, Louis Gossett Jr., David Keith, Lisa Eilbacher, Debra Winger, David Caruso, Robert Loggia, Lisa Blount; ***D:*** Taylor Hackford; ***W:*** Douglas Day Stewart; ***C:*** Donald E. Thorin; ***M:*** Jack Nitzsche. Oscars '82: Song ("Up Where We Belong"), Support. Actor (Gossett); Golden Globes '83: Song ("Up Where We Belong"), Support. Actor (Gossett).

Official Denial 1/2 **1993** A victim of an alien abduction becomes the only hope for a captured space being. Can Paul help the alien escape from a special Air Force UFO group and what secrets will he uncover if he does? **86m/C VHS.** Parker Stevenson, Erin Gray, Dirk Benedict, Chad Everett; ***D:*** Brian Trenchard-Smith; ***W:*** Bruce Zabel; ***M:*** Garry McDonald, Laurie Stone. **TV**

The Official Story 1/2 *La Historia Oficial; The Official History; The Official Version* **1985 (R)** A devastating drama about an Argentinian woman who realizes her young adopted daughter may be a child stolen from one of the thousands of citizens victimized by the country's repressive government. A powerful, important film. In Spanish with English subtitles or dubbed. **112m/C VHS, DVD.** *AR* Norma Aleandro, Hector Alterio, Chunchuna Villafane, Patricio Contreras; ***D:*** Luis Puenzo; ***W:*** Luis Puenzo, Aida Bortnik. Oscars '85: Foreign Film; Cannes '85: Actress (Aleandro); Golden Globes '86: Foreign Film; L.A. Film Critics '85: Foreign Film; N.Y. Film Critics '85: Actress (Aleandro).

The Offspring *From a Whisper to a Scream* **1987 (R)** In four stories of past evils Price reveals his hometown can force folks to kill. Not the usual Price material: dismemberment, cannibalism, and necrophilia clash with his presence. Strong yuk factor. **99m/C VHS, DVD, UMD.** Vincent Price, Cameron Mitchell, Clu Gulager, Terry Kiser, Susan Tyrrell, Harry Caesar, Rosalind Cash, Martine Beswick, Angelo Rossitto, Lawrence Tierney; ***D:*** Jeff Burr; ***W:*** Jeff Burr, C. Courtney Joyner; ***M:*** Jim Manzie.

The Ogre *Der Unhold* **1996** Misfit Abel (Malkovich) desperately believes in his own personal power to change the world around him. He winds up captured by the Germans in 1939 and is held in a POW camp until chance lands him in the service of a group of high-ranking Nazis, including Hermann Goring (Spengler). Goring sends Abel out to recruit young boys into becoming military conscripts and he gains the nickname of the Ogre, the mythic devourer of children. Adapted from Michael Tournier's novel "The Erl King." **117m/C VHS, DVD.** *GE FR GB* John Malkovich, Volker Spengler, Armin Mueller-Stahl, Gottfried John; ***D:*** Volker Schlondorff; ***W:*** Volker Schlondorff, Jean-Claude Carriere; ***C:*** Bruno de Keyzer; ***M:*** Michael Nyman.

Oh, Alfie *Alfie Darling* **1975 (R)** In every man's life, there comes a time to settle down... but never when you're having as much fun as Alfie! Inadequate sequel to "Alfie." **99m/C VHS, DVD.** *GB* Joan Collins, Alan Price, Jill Townsend; ***D:*** Ken Hughes; ***W:*** Ken Hughes.

Oh, Bloody Life! 1/2 **1988** Young actress faces deportation during the Stalin era in Hungary because of her aristocratic family ties. In Hungarian with English subtitles. **115m/C VHS.** *HU* Udvaros Dorottya, Szacsvay Laszlo, Kern Andras, Bezeredi Zoltan, Oze Lajos, Lukacs Margit; ***D:*** Peter Bacso; ***W:*** Peter Bacso. Montreal World Film Fest. '88: Actress (Dorottya).

Oh! Calcutta! 1/2 **1972** Film version of the first nude musical to play on Broadway, which caused a sensation in the late 1960s. It's really a collection of skits, some of which were written by such notables as John Lennon, Sam Shepard, and Jules Feiffer. And it's really not that funny or erotic. **105m/C VHS, DVD.** Bill Macy, Mark Dempsey, Raina Barrett, Samantha Harper, Patricia Hawkins, Mitchell McGuire; ***D:*** Guillaume Martin Aucion; ***W:*** Robert Benton, Jules Feiffer, Dan Greenberg, John Lennon, Jacques Levy, Sam Shepard, Leonard Melfi, David Newman, Clovis Trouille, Sherman Yellen; ***C:*** Frank Biondo, Arnold Giordano, Jerry Sarcone; ***M:*** Prof. Peter Schickele, Robert Dennis.

Oh Dad, Poor Dad (Momma's Hung You in the Closet & I'm Feeling So Sad) **1967** Cult fave black comedy about a bizarre family on a vacation in Jamaica. The domineering mother travels with a coffin containing the stuffed body of her late husband. Additional corpses abound. Based on the play by Arthur L. Kopit. **86m/C VHS.** Rosalind Russell, Robert Morse, Barbara Harris, Hugh Griffith, Lionel Jeffries, Jonathan Winters, Cyril Delevanti, Hiram Sherman, George Kirby, Janis Hansen; ***D:*** Richard Quine; ***W:*** Herbert Baker, Pat McCormick, Ian Bernard; ***C:*** Geoffrey Unsworth; ***M:*** Neal Hefti.

Oh, God! 1/2 **1977 (PG)** God, in the person of Burns, recruits Denver as his herald in his plan to save the world. Despite initial skepticism, Denver, in his film debut, keeps faith and is rewarded. Sincere performances and optimistic end make for satisfying story. Followed by "Oh God! Book 2" and "Oh God! You Devil." **104m/C VHS, DVD.** George Burns, John Denver, Paul Sorvino, Ralph Bellamy, Teri Garr, William Daniels, Donald Pleasence, Barnard Hughes, Barry Sullivan, Dinah Shore, Jeff Corey, David Ogden Stiers; ***D:*** Carl Reiner; ***W:*** Larry Gelbart. Writers Guild '77: Adapt. Screenplay.

Oh, God! Book 2 **1980 (PG)** Burns returns as the "Almighty One" in strained sequel to "Oh God!" This time he enlists the help of a young girl to remind others of his existence. The slogan she concocts saves God's image, but not the movie. Followed by "Oh, God! You Devil." **94m/C VHS.** George Burns, Suzanne Pleshette, David Birney, Louanne, Conrad Janis, Wilfrid Hyde-White, Hans Conried, Howard Duff, Anthony Holland; ***D:*** Gilbert Cates; ***M:*** Charles Fox.

Oh, God! You Devil **1984 (PG)** During his third trip to earth, Burns plays both the Devil and God as he first takes a struggling musician's soul, then gives it back. A few zingers and light atmosphere save unoriginal plot. The second sequel to "Oh, God!" **96m/C VHS, DVD.** George Burns, Ted Wass, Roxanne Hart, Ron Silver, Eugene Roche, Robert Desiderio; ***D:*** Paul Bogart; ***W:*** Andrew Bergman; ***M:*** David Shire.

Oh, Heavenly Dog! **1980 (PG)** A private eye returns from the dead as a dog to solve his own murder. Man's best friend and intelligent to boot. The famous dog Benji's third film, and his acting improves with each one. Adults may find this movie slow, but kids will probably love it. **104m/C VHS, DVD.** Chevy Chase, Jane Seymour, Omar Sharif, Robert Morley, Susan Kellerman; ***D:*** Joe Camp; ***W:*** Joe Camp, Rod Browning.

The Oh in Ohio **2006 (R)** Naughty trifle of an indie comedy with the 'oh' standing for orgasm. Frigid Priscilla (Posey) may say she's satisfied with the sex in her 10-year marriage to Jack (Rudd) but he isn't and she's lying. He's a high school teacher who succumbs to nubile student Kristen (Barton) while Priscilla finally decides to go to sex guru Alyssa (Minnelli) for advice. Once past the vibrator stage, Priscilla finds an unlikely sexual healer in lusty (and surprisingly sweet) swimming pool mogul Larry (DeVito). **88m/C DVD.** Parker Posey, Paul Rudd, Danny DeVito, Mischa Barton, Liza Minnelli, Miranda Bailey, Keith David, Tim Russ, Linda Watkins, John McNamara; ***D:*** Danny DeVito, Billy Kent, Dan Milner; ***W:*** Billy Kent, Sarah Bird, Richard Bernstein; ***C:*** Ramsay Nickell, Brydon Baker; ***M:*** Darrell Calker.

Oh, Mr. Porter **1937** Billeted at an obscure railway post, the stationmaster hero renovates the place and hires a special train to transport the area soccer team. Trouble arises when the train is hijacked by gun smugglers. **85m/B VHS.** *GB* Will Hay, Moore Marriott, Graham Moffatt, Frederick Piper; ***D:*** Marcel Varnel.

Oh! My Zombie Mermaid *A! Ikkenya puroresu; Ah! House Collapses; Ah! House of Pro Wrestling* **2004** Bizarre Japanese cult film. Shishioh (Hashimoto) is on top of the world as one of Japan's best wrestlers as well as having just built his wife's dream house. But a housewarming party is crashed by a rival looking for revenge and is blown up with Shishioh's wife in it. While recovering, she catches the 'mermaid disease,' which turns her into a zombie mermaid leaving him to challenge all comers to a fight to the death in order to raise money to cure her. **100m/C DVD.** *JP* Sonim, Shiro Sano, Nicholas Pettas, Shinya Hashimoto; ***D:*** Terry Ito, Naoki Kudo; ***W:*** Izo Hashimoto, Naoki Kudo.

Oh Susannah 1/2 **1938** Robbed and thrown from a train, Autry and the two drifters who rescue him follow the thieves to Mineral Springs. Their journey is plagued by too many songs and the bad guys are predictably punished in the end. **59m/B VHS, DVD.** Gene Autry, Boothe Howard, Smiley Burnette, Frances Grant, Donald Kirke, Clara Kimball Young; ***D:*** Joseph Kane.

Oh! What a Lovely War 1/2 **1969** Scathing musical re-creation of British soldiers in WWI using the era's popular songs and presenting the story as a music hall review as seen through the eyes of the working-class Smith family. All their sons are seduced into enlisting and get killed, while the generals and the politicians are safely behind the lines or complaining at home. Attenborough's directorial debut features an all-star cast but comes off as somewhat disjointed and obvious due to its adaptation from a stage production. Filmed on location in and around Brighton. **144m/C DVD.** *GB* Colin Farrell, John Rae, Corin Redgrave, Maurice Roeves, Kim Smith, Angela Thorne, Mary Wimbush, Paul Daneman, Laurence Olivier, Michael Redgrave, Vanessa Redgrave, John Gielgud, Ralph Richardson, Maggie Smith, Susannah York, John Mills, Isabel Dean, Vincent Ball, Christian Doermer, Robert Flemyng, Ian Holm, David Lodge, Guy Middleton, Juliet Mills, Nanette Newman, Cecil Parker, Natasha Parry, Gerald Sim, Thorley Walters, Penelope Allen, Michael Bates, Edward Fox, Peter Gilmore, Ben Howard, Dirk Bogarde, Phyllis Calvert, Jean-Pierre Cassel, John Clements, Jack Hawkins, Kenneth More, Jane Seymour, Pippa Steele, Wendy Alnutt, Malcolm McFee, Paul Shelley; ***D:*** Richard Attenborough; ***W:*** Len Deighton; ***C:*** Gerry Turpin; ***M:*** Alfred Ralston. British Acad. '69: Art Dir./Set Dec., Cinematog., Costume Des., Support. Actor (Olivier); Golden Globes '70: Foreign Film.

Oh, What a Night **1992 (PG-13)** Bittersweet coming of age tale about a lonely 17-year-old (Haim) who has moved with his father and stepmother to a chicken farm in 1955 Ontario. After struggling with the untimely death of his mother, Haim falls in love with an older woman who has a husband and two kids. Features a great '50s soundtrack and beautiful scenes of the Canadian countryside. **93m/C VHS.** *CA* Corey Haim, Barbara Williams, Keir Dullea, Genevieve Bujold, Robbie Coltrane; ***D:*** Eric Till.

O'Hara's Wife 1/2 **1982** Loving wife Harley continues to care for her family even after her untimely death. Only husband Asner, however, can see her ghost. Lightweight drama traps good cast. **87m/C VHS, DVD.** Ed Asner, Mariette Hartley, Jodie Foster, Tom Bosley, Perry Lang, Ray Walston; ***D:*** William S. Bartman; ***W:*** William S. Bartman; ***M:*** Artie Butler. **TV**

O.H.M.S. 1/2 **1937** Convoluted story about a New York hood (Ford) who flees to England where he joins the British Army by posing as a Canadian. He buddies up with Mills and they both fall for Lee. His regiment is sent to China, via ship, and Lee just happens to be a stowaway. In China, Ford manages to prove his worth by saving Lee from bandits. Maybe it's not supposed to make sense. **71m/B VHS.** *GB* Wallace Ford, John Mills, Anna Lee, Frank Cellier, Frederick Leister, Peter Croft; ***D:*** Raoul Walsh.

O'Horten **2009 (PG-13)** At 67, train engineer Odd Horten is forced into retirement and realizes that without his orderly existence he doesn't know what to do with his life. Norwegian with subtitles. **89m/C DVD.** *FR GE NO* Baard Owe, Espen Skjonberg, Ghita Norby, Henry Moan; ***D:*** Bent Hamer; ***W:*** Bent Hamer; ***C:*** John Christian Rosenlund; ***M:*** Kaada.

Oil **1978 (PG)** Seven men fight a raging oil fire that threatens to destroy an entire country. Unfortunately, the movie is unable to ignite any interest at all. **95m/C VHS, DVD.** Ray Milland, Woody Strode, Stuart Whitman, Tony Kendall, William Berger; ***D:*** Mircea Dragan.

The O.J. Simpson Story **1994** Tacky tabloid TV movie follows incredibly exploited story about former gridiron star Simpson (Hosea) who's accused of murdering blonde babe ex-wife Nicole (Tuck). Mainly stolid performances though Weitz is slick as Simpson lawyer Robert Shapiro. Told in flashbacks, the actual murder is never depicted. Director Jerry Friedman took his name off the credits, leaving the standard Smithee pseudonym as a replacement. **90m/C VHS.** Bobby Hosea, Jessica Tuck, James Handy, Kimberly Russell, David Roberson, Bruce Weitz; ***D:*** Alan Smithee; ***W:*** Stephen Harrigan; ***M:*** Harald Kloser.

Oklahoma! 1/2 **1955 (G)** Jones's film debut; a must-see for musical fans. A cowboy and country girl fall in love, but she is tormented by another unwelcomed suitor. At over two hours, cuteness wears thin for some. Actually filmed in Arizona. Adapted from Rodgers and Hammerstein's broadway hit with original score; choreography by Agnes de Mille. ♫Oh, What a Beautiful Morning; Surrey with the Fringe on Top; I Cain't Say No; Many a New Day; People Will Say We're in Love; Poor Jud Is Dead; All 'Er Nuthin'; Everything's Up to Date in Kansas City; The Farmer and the Cowman. **145m/C VHS, DVD.** Gordon MacRae, Shirley Jones, Rod Steiger, Gloria Grahame, Eddie Albert, Charlotte Greenwood, James Whitmore, Gene Nelson, Barbara Lawrence, Jay C. Flippen; ***D:*** Fred Zinnemann; ***W:*** Sonya Levien, William Ludwig; ***C:*** Robert L. Surtees; ***M:*** Richard Rodgers, Oscar Hammerstein. Oscars '55: Sound, Scoring/Musical, Natl. Film Reg. '07.

Oklahoma Annie **1951** Storekeeper Canova joins the new sheriff in booting undesirables out of town, and tries to sing her way into his heart. Amazingly, it works—not for delicate ears. **90m/C VHS.** Judy Canova, Fuzzy Knight, Grant Withers, John Russell, Denver Pyle, Allen Jenkins, Almira Sessions; ***D:*** R.G. Springsteen.

Oklahoma Badlands ½ **1948** Lane and his horse outsmart a corrupt newspaper publisher trying to steal land from a female rancher. An early directorial work for veteran stuntman Canutt. **59m/B VHS.** Allan "Rocky" Lane, Mildred Coles; ***D:*** Yakima Canutt.

Oklahoma Bound **1981** A feisty farmer tries to save his failing farm through a series of ostensibly comedic, unsuccessful schemes. **92m/C VHS.** F.E. Bowling, Dan (Daniel) Jones; ***D:*** Patrick C. Poole.

Oklahoma Crude ½ **1973 (PG)** Sadistic oil trust rep Palence battles man-hating Dunaway for her well. Drifter Scott helps her resist on the promise of shared profits. In this 1913 setting, Dunaway tells Scott she wishes she could avoid men altogether, but later settles for him. **108m/C VHS.** George C. Scott, Faye Dunaway, John Mills, Jack Palance, Harvey Jason, Woodrow Parfrey; ***D:*** Stanley Kramer; ***W:*** Marc Norman; ***C:*** Robert L. Surtees; ***M:*** Henry Mancini.

Oklahoma Cyclone ½ **1930** A group of bronco busters find action and adventure on the prairie. Second of eight talkies in Steele series, includes his first of few singing roles. **64m/B VHS, DVD.** Bob Steele, Al "Fuzzy" St. John, Nita Ray, Charles "Blackie" King; ***D:*** John P. McCarthy.

Oklahoma Frontier ½ **1939** Jeff McLeod and his pal Frosty have decided to join in the Cherokee Strip land rush, agreeing to help the Rankins stake out a certain claim with good water. The tract is also wanted by bad guys Frazier and Saunders, who are not above murder and framing an innocent man (that would be Jeff) for the crime in order to get the property. **58m/B DVD.** Johnny Mack Brown, Robert F. (Bob) Kortman, Anne Gwynne, Bob Baker, Fuzzy Knight, Charles King, Harry Tenbrook, James Blaine; ***D:*** Ford Beebe; ***W:*** Ford Beebe; ***C:*** Jerome Ash.

Oklahoma Kid **1939** Offbeat, hilarious western with Bogie as the villain and gunfighter Cagney seeking revenge for his father's wrongful death. Highlight is Cagney's rendition of "I Don't Want To Play In Your Yard," complete with six-shooter accompaniment. **82m/B VHS.** James Cagney, Humphrey Bogart, Rosemary Lane, Ward Bond, Donald Crisp, Charles Middleton, Harvey Stephens; ***D:*** Lloyd Bacon; ***C:*** James Wong Howe; ***M:*** Max Steiner.

Oklahoma Renegades ½ **1940** The Three Mesquiteers return home after having fought in the Spanish-American War and send word to their fellow vets about homestead property being offered by the government in the Oklahoma Territory. However, the veterans are greeted by hostile cattlemen determined to get the property for themselves. Both the cattlemen and the homesteaders are about to be swindled unless the Mesquiteers can do something. The 31st film in the series. **57m/B DVD.** Robert "Bob" Livingston, Raymond Hatton, Duncan Renaldo, Lee White, Florine McKinney, Harold Daniels, William Ruhl; ***W:*** Nate Watt, Doris Schroeder, Earle Snell; ***C:*** Reggie Lanning.

The Oklahoman **1956** A routine western with some trivia value. Town doc McCrea helps Indian Pate keep his land. Talbott plays Indian maiden in same year as her title role in Daughter of Jekyll. Continuity buffs will note Hale wears the same outfit in most scenes. **80m/C VHS.** Joel McCrea, Barbara Hale, Brad Dexter, Gloria Talbott, Verna Felton, Douglas Dick, Michael Pate, Scotty Beckett; ***D:*** Francis D. Lyon.

Okoge *Fag Hag* **1993** Rueful sexual comedy about a triangular friendship. Sayoko is a single young working woman living in a tiny Tokyo apartment. She meets the gay Noh and his older married lover Tochi and when they become friendly, Sayoko lets them use her apartment as their love nest—to the complications of all concerned. Title is a slang term used to refer to women who prefer the company of gay men. In Japanese with English subtitles. **120m/C VHS.** *JP* Misa Shimizu, Takehiro Murata, Takeo Nakahara, Masayuki Shionoya, Noriko Sengoku, Kyozo Nagatsuka, Toshie Negishi; ***D:*** Takehiro Nakajima; ***W:*** Takehiro Nakajima; ***C:*** Yoshimasa Hakata; ***M:*** Hiroshi Ariyoshi.

Oktober **1998** A multinational pharmaceutical company is behind a sinister plot for global domination as a young teacher becomes both a walking experiment and a marked target in this medical thriller. **90m/C DVD.** *GB* Stephen Tompkinson, Maria Lennon, James McCarthy, Lydzia Englert; ***D:*** Stephen Gallagher; ***W:*** Stephen Gallagher; ***C:*** Bruce McGowan; ***M:*** Alan Parker. **TV**

Old Barn Dance ½ **1938** Autry and his singing cowboys are selling horses until a crooked tractor company puts them out of business. They join a radio program, discovers that it is owned by the same company that put them out of the horse-selling business, and runs the crooks out of town. **54m/B VHS, DVD.** Gene Autry, Smiley Burnette, Roy Rogers; ***D:*** Joseph Kane.

Old Boyfriends **1979 (R)** Shire is weak as a psychologist searching for old boyfriends in order to analyze her past. Strange combination of Carradine and Belushi may draw curious fans. **103m/C VHS, DVD.** Talia Shire, Richard Jordan, John Belushi, Keith Carradine, John Houseman, Buck Henry; ***D:*** Joan Tewkesbury; ***W:*** Leonard Schrader, Paul Schrader; ***M:*** David Shire.

Old Corral *Texas Serenade* **1936** Sheriff Autry protects his love interest, a girl fleeing the Mob. **54m/B VHS, DVD.** Gene Autry, Roy Rogers, Smiley Burnette; ***D:*** Joseph Kane.

The Old Curiosity Shop ½ **1935** Webster and Benson are an old gambler and his daughter in this well-made film adaptation of the Dickens tale. Their miserly landlord tries to ruin their lives by evicting them and forcing them into a life of poverty. Remade as "Mr. Quilp" in 1957. **90m/B VHS.** Ben Webster, Elaine Benson, Hay Petrie, Beatrix Thompson, Gibb McLaughlin, Reginald Purdell; ***D:*** Thomas Bentley.

The Old Curiosity Shop *Mr. Quilp* **1975 (G)** Flat musical version of the Charles Dickens story about an evil man who wants to take over a small antique shop run by an elderly man and his granddaughter. ♫When a Felon Needs a Friend; Somewhere; Love Has the Longest Memory; Happiness Pie; The Sport of Kings; What Shouldn't Happen to a Dog; Quilp. **118m/C VHS.** *GB* Anthony Newley, David Hemmings, David Warner, Jill Bennett, Peter Duncan, Michael Hordern; ***D:*** Michael Tuchner; ***M:*** Elmer Bernstein.

The Old Curiosity Shop ½ **1994 (PG)** Another adaptation of Charles Dickens's 1840 tale about Grandfather Trent (Ustinov), an antiques dealer who has lost his fortune through gambling and makes matters worse by borrowing money from the miserable Mr. Quilp (Courtenay). Unable to repay the debt, Trent and young granddaughter Sally (Walsh) try to escape London, which turns Quilp's wrath upon them. Fine performances and a colorful production. **280m/C VHS, DVD.** Peter Ustinov, Tom Courtenay, James Fox, Sally Walsh, William Mannering, Christopher Ettridge, Julia McKenzie, Anne White, Jean Marlow, Cornelia Hayes O'Herlihy, Michael Mears; ***D:*** Kevin Connor; ***W:*** John Goldsmith; ***C:*** Doug Milsome; ***M:*** Mason Daring. **CABLE**

The Old Curiosity Shop ½ **2007** Truncated BBC presentation of the Dickens novel. Ruthless moneylender Daniel Quilp (Jones) hounds the debt-ridden owner of the London antiques shop, causing the old man (Jacobi) and his teenaged granddaughter Little Nell (Vayasseur) to flee after their eviction. Since Quilp would rather see them in debtor's prison, they're relentlessly pursued as Grandfather's inveterate gambling makes their situation ever more dire. And then the ending gets changed! It's still tragic but not nearly so poignant. **100m/C DVD.** *GB* Derek Jacobi, Toby Jones, Gina McKee, Bryan Dick, Martin Freeman, Adam Godley, Anna Madeley, Adrian Rawlins, Sophie Vayasseur, Geoff Breton, Zoe Wanamaker, George MacKay; ***D:*** Brian Percival; ***W:*** Martyn Hesford; ***C:*** Peter Greenhalgh; ***M:*** Stephen McKeon. **TV**

The Old Dark House **1932** An atmospheric horror film, with more than a touch of comedy, well-directed by Whale. In an old haunted house live the bizarre Femm family: the 102 year-old patriarch (Dudgeon), an atheist son (Thesinger), a religious fanatic daughter (Moore), and a crazed pyromanic son (Wills), all watched over by the mute, scarred, and psychotic butler (Karloff's first starring role). Into this strange group wander five unsuspecting, stranded travelers who set all sorts of dastardly plots in motion. Based on the novel "Benighted" by J.B. Priestley. John Dudgeon is actually actress Elspeth Dudgeon who's playing in drag. Remade in 1963 by William Castle. **71m/B VHS, DVD.** Boris Karloff, Melvyn Douglas, Charles Laughton, Gloria Stuart, Ernest Thesiger, Raymond Massey, Lillian Bond, Eva Moore, Brember Wills, Elspeth (John) Dudgeon; ***D:*** James Whale; ***W:*** Benn W. Levy, R.C. Sherriff; ***C:*** Arthur Edeson.

Old Dogs WOOF! **2009 (PG)** Divorcee Dan (Williams) and happy bachelor Charlie (Travolta) are best buds and business partners who have their lives upended when they suddenly become the guardians of mischievous 7-year-old twins. At this stage in their career, these two actors should've known better—as should the other veteran stars, such as Dillon, Ann-Margaret, and Wilson. Hacked together, in a failed attempt to salvage any type of laughs, complete with four camera angles of Williams falling into a pond. Sad to say that none of them are funny. Regrettably, Travolta drags daughter Ella Bleu and wife Kelly Preston into this disastrous Disney flop. **88m/C DVD.** *US* Robin Williams, John Travolta, Conner Rayburn, Ella Bleu Travolta, Kelly Preston, Bernie Mac, Seth Green, Lori Loughlin, Matt Dillon, Rita Wilson, Laura Allen, Ann-Margret, Amy Sedaris; ***D:*** Walt Becker; ***W:*** David Diamond, David Weissman; ***C:*** Jeffrey L. Kimball; ***M:*** John Debney.

Old Enough **1984 (PG)** Slow-moving coming-of-age comedy on the rich kid-poor kid friendship theme. Silver's directing debut. **91m/C VHS.** Sarah Boyd, Rainbow Harvest, Neill Barry, Danny Aiello, Susan Kingsley, Roxanne Hart, Alyssa Milano, Fran Brill, Anne Pitoniak; ***D:*** Marisa Silver; ***W:*** Marisa Silver; ***C:*** Michael Ballhaus. Sundance '84: Grand Jury Prize.

Old Explorers ½ **1990 (PG)** Two old friends refuse to let old age lessen their want for excitement, so they get together on a regular basis to set out on dangerous, imaginary adventures. They search for Atlantis, explore the Himalayan Mountains, and visit the Bermuda Triangle. After one of the men survives a stroke, the two set out on a real-life adventure on a tugboat cruising down the Mississippi River. Although the leads put in strong performances, they can't hide the slow-moving plot or the thin action sequences. Based on the play by James Cada and Mark Keller. **91m/C VHS.** Jose Ferrer, James Whitmore, Jeffrey Gadbois, Caroline Kaiser, William Warfield, Christopher Pohlad, Storm Richardson, William M. Pohlad; ***D:*** William M. Pohlad; ***W:*** William M. Pohlad; ***C:*** William F. Carlson.

An Old-Fashioned Thanksgiving ½ **2008** Hallmark Channel movie that's very loosely based on a short story by Louisa May Alcott and set after the Civil War. Wealthy Isabella (Bisset) has been estranged from her daughter Mary (Joy) ever since she ran away to marry a stablehand. With her husband dead, the widow and her children live in poverty so granddaughter Mathilda (Maslany) concocts a story to get Isabella to visit. **88m/C DVD.** Jacqueline Bisset, Tatiana Maslany, Ted Atherton, Kristopher Turner, Helene Joy, Gage Munroe, Vivien Endicott Douglas, Paula Boudreau; ***D:*** Graeme Campbell; ***W:*** Shelley Evans; ***C:*** Mitchell Ness; ***M:*** James Gelfand. **CABLE**

Old Gringo ½ **1989 (R)** Adapted from Carlos Fuentes' mysterious novelization of writer Ambrose Bierce's mysterious disappearance in Mexico during the revolution of 1913. Features Fonda in the unlikely role of a virgin schoolteacher, Smits as her revolutionary lover, and Peck as her hero. Soggy acting by all but Peck, whose presence is wasted in a sketchy character. Technical problems and cheesy sets and costumes—look for the dusk backdrop in the dance scene and Smits' silly moustache. Better to read the book. **119m/C VHS, DVD.** Jane Fonda, Gregory Peck, Jimmy Smits, Patricio Contreras, Jenny Gago, Gabriela Roel, Sergio Calderon, Guillermo Rios, Anne Pitoniak, Pedro Armendariz Jr., Jim Metzler; ***D:*** Luis Puenzo; ***W:*** Aida Bortnik, Luis Puenzo; ***M:*** Lee Holdridge.

Old Gun *Vengeance One by One; Le Vieux Fusil* **1976** A grief-plagued doctor finds he must seek out and kill each Nazi involved in the slaughter of his wife and child to ease his pain. Excellent directing and a fully formed main character. **141m/C VHS.** *FR GE* Philippe Noiret, Romy Schneider, Jean Bouise; ***D:*** Robert Enrico; ***W:*** Robert Enrico; ***C:*** Etienne Becker; ***M:*** Francois de Roubaix.

Old Ironsides **1926** Silent, black-and-white version of the big budget/important director and stars action-adventure. Merchant marines aboard the famous Old Ironsides battle 19th century Barbary pirates in rousing action scenes. Home video version features an engaging organ score by Gaylord Carter. Based on the poem "Constitution" by Oliver Wendell Holmes. **111m/B VHS.** Esther Ralston, Wallace Beery, Boris Karloff, Charles Farrell, George Bancroft; ***D:*** James Cruze; ***M:*** Gaylord Carter.

Old Joy **2006** Two 30-something buddies who spent their younger days smoking pot and fighting the system embark on a reunion road trip to an Oregon natural hot springs. While their time together is pleasant enough, the pair doesn't quite reconnect—Kurt (Oldham) is still living in the past, while Mark (London) has a career, wife, and child on the way. Not much in the way of action but their talks—or, even, what isn't talked about—show how the glory days of friendship can't always be recaptured. Drawn from Jonathan Raymond's short story. **76m/C DVD.** *US* William Oldham, Daniel London, Tanya Smith; ***D:*** Kelly Reichardt; ***W:*** Kelly Reichardt, Jonathan Raymond; ***C:*** Peter Sillen.

The Old Lady Who Walked in the Sea *La Vieille qui Marchait dans la Mer* **1991** Eccentric Lady M (Moreau) and her equally aging ex-lover Pompilius (Serrault) have spend their lives conning the rich. Summering on the French Riviera, Lady M spots handsome beach boy/thief Lambert (Thuiller) and decides to groom him for their latest caper, a jewel heist. Meanwhile, Pompilius pursues the young Noemie (Danon) and brings her into their menage, where Lambert is instantly smitten. Their lust leads to some unexpected complications but the real drama in the film is watching old pros Moreau and Serrault at work. Based on the novel by San Antonio; French with subtitles. **95m/C VHS.** *FR* Jeanne Moreau, Michel Serrault, Luc Thuillier, Geraldine Danon; ***D:*** Laurent Heynemann; ***W:*** Dominique Roulet; ***C:*** Robert Alazraki; ***M:*** Philippe Sarde.

The Old Maid **1939** After her beau is killed in the Civil War, a woman allows her cousin to raise her illegitimate daughter, and therein begins a years-long struggle over the girl's affections. High grade soaper based on Zoe Adkin's stage adaptation of Edith Wharton's novel. **96m/B VHS.** Bette Davis, Miriam Hopkins, George Brent, Donald Crisp, Jane Bryan, Louise Fazenda, Henry Stephenson; ***D:*** Edmund Goulding; ***C:*** Gaetano Antonio "Tony" Gaudio; ***M:*** Max Steiner.

The Old Man and the Sea ½ **1958** Cuban fisherman Santiago hooks a giant marlin and battles sharks and the sea to bring his trophy home. Tracy's performance as the tough, aging fisherman garnered him his sixth Academy Award nomination and Tiomkin's beautiful score was an Oscar winner. **86m/C DVD.** Spencer Tracy, Felipe Pazos, Harry Bellaver, Don Diamond, Don Blackman, Joey Ray; ***D:*** John Sturges; ***W:*** Peter Viertel; ***C:*** James Wong Howe, Floyd Crosby; ***M:*** Dimitri Tiomkin. Oscars '58: Orig. Dramatic Score.

The Old Man and the Sea 𝒮𝒮 1/2 **1990** Quinn is wonderful as Hemingway's aging Cuban fisherman, Santiago, who battles a band of marauding sharks for a giant marlin in the Gulf Stream. Unfortunately, this made-for-TV adaptation is ordinary. **97m/C VHS, DVD.** Anthony Quinn, Gary Cole, Alexis Cruz, Patricia Clarkson, Francesco Quinn; ***D:*** Jud Taylor; ***W:*** Roger O. Hirson; ***C:*** James Wong Howe; ***M:*** Bruce Broughton. **TV**

Old Mother Riley, Headmistress 𝒮 1/2 **1950** Irish washerwoman Mrs. Riley (Lucan) winds up the headmistress of a girls' school that is threatened when a railroad line is planned to go through the property. **76m/B VHS.** *GB* Arthur Lucan, Kitty McShane, Enid Hewitt, Jenny Mathot, Cyril Smith; ***D:*** John Harlow; ***W:*** Jack Marks, Con West; ***C:*** Ken Talbot.

Old Mother Riley's Ghosts 𝒮𝒮 **1941** A group of spies "haunt" Mother Riley's castle home in a futile attempt to scare her out; she turns the tables. Some good scares and laughs. Part of the Old Mother Riley series. Look for similarities to later Monty Python films. **82m/B VHS, DVD.** *GB* Arthur Lucan, Kitty McShane, John Stuart; ***D:*** John Baxter.

Old Mother Riley's Jungle Treasure 𝒮 1/2 **1951** Mother Riley (Lucan) and daughter Kitty (McShane) are working in an antiques shop where they discover a treasure map. So they head for the South Seas and find a pirate's ghost as well. **75m/B VHS.** *GB* Arthur Lucan, Kitty McShane, Sebastian Cabot, Garry Marsh, Roddy Hughes; ***D:*** Maclean Rogers; ***W:*** Val Valentine; ***C:*** James Wilson.

Old Mother Riley's New Venture 𝒮 1/2 **1949** Old Mother Riley (Lucan) is hired as the manager of a hotel that's been victimized by a series of robberies. But she's soon framed for a hotel jewel heist by the real thief. **80m/B VHS.** *GB* Arthur Lucan, Kitty McShane, Chili Bouchier, Willer Neal, Sebastian Cabot; ***D:*** John Harlow; ***W:*** Jack Marks, Con West; ***C:*** James Wilson.

Old San Francisco 𝒮 1/2 **1927** The Spanish Vasquez family was one of the original settlers of the San Francisco area, but now they are in financial difficulties. The evil and powerful Buckwell (Oland)—who is hiding a secret about his own origins—becomes interested in Dolores Vasquez (Costello) but she is in love with Irishman Terrence (Mack). When Dolores learns Buckwell's secret and threatens to expose him, he kidnaps her and Terrence. The 1906 San Francisco earthquake proves providential in their escape. The film's racial stereotyping of the Chinese community will appear offensively racist to modern eyes. **88m/B DVD.** Dolores Costello, Warner Oland, Charles Emmet Mack, Josef Swickard, Anders Randolf, Anna May Wong; ***D:*** Alan Crosland; ***W:*** Anthony Coldeway; ***C:*** Hal Mohr.

Old School 𝒮𝒮 1/2 **2003 (R)** Thirty-something pals Mitch (Wilson), Frank (Ferrell), and Beanie (Vaughn) start a frat at the nearby college so they can have a place to escape their everyday troubles. Mitch's girlfriend hosts orgies during his business trips, the recently-married Frank longs for beery bachelor freedom, and Beanie has never grown up despite having a nice family and owning an electronics store chain. Nonsensical plot threads lead only to frat-boy fun and confrontation with the dean, a stereotypical villain who used to be the butt of their jokes. Despite the plot breakdowns and generally one-dimensional characters, everyone, including the audience, manages to have a pretty good time, thanks largely to the likeability of the cast. Vaughn plays Beanie as if Trent from "Swingers" had ended up with a wife and two kids. **90m/C VHS, DVD, Blu-ray Disc, HD DVD.** *US* Luke Wilson, Will Ferrell, Vince Vaughn, Ellen Pompeo, Juliette Lewis, Leah Remini, Perrey Reeves, Elisha Cuthbert, Jeremy Piven, Rick Gonzalez, Terry O'Quinn, Artie Lange, Matthew Carey, Harve Presnell, Seann William Scott, Craig Kilborn; ***Cameos:*** Andy Dick, Snoop Dogg; ***D:*** Todd Phillips; ***W:*** Todd Phillips, Scot Armstrong; ***C:*** Mark Irwin; ***M:*** Theodore Shapiro.

The Old Settler 𝒮𝒮 1/2 **2001** Elizabeth Barney (Rashad) is middleaged and has never been married, thus making her an old settler according to sister Quilly (Allen). Quilly has been abandoned by her husband and is living with Elizabeth in her Harlem apartment because times are hard. In fact to make a little extra cash, Elizabeth rents a room to handsome country boy Husband Witherspoon (Robinson), fresh off the bus from South Carolina. Eventually Husband, who's been disappointed in love, turns his attentions to Elizabeth, much to the bitter Quilly's astonishment. Based on the play by John Henry Redwood. **90m/C VHS, DVD.** Phylicia Rashad, Debbie Allen, Bumper Robinson, Eartha D. Robinson, Crystal Fox, Randy J. Goodwin; ***D:*** Debbie Allen; ***W:*** Shauneille Perry. **TV**

Old Spanish Custom 𝒮 *The Invader* **1936** Only a Keaton fan could love this comedy, set in Spain and filmed in England. One of his rarest—and poorest—sound films. He plays a bumbling rich yachtsman smitten with Tovar, a Spanish maiden who uses him to make her lover jealous. **58m/B VHS.** *GB* Buster Keaton, Lupita Tovar, Lyn Harding, Esme Percy; ***D:*** Adrian Brunel.

Old Swimmin' Hole 𝒮𝒮 *When Youth Conspires* **1940** Small-town friends Moran and Jones try to bring their single parents together; his mother can't afford to finance his dream to be a doctor. Dull, melodramatic ode to heartland America, reminiscent of "Our Town." **78m/B VHS, DVD.** Marcia Mae Jones, Jackie Moran, Leatrice Joy, Charles D. Brown; ***D:*** Robert McGowan.

Old Yeller 𝒮𝒮𝒮 1/2 **1957 (G)** Disney Studios' first and best boy-and-his-dog film, set in Texas in 1969. 15-year-old Travis Coates (Kirk) is left in charge of the family farm while dad Jim (Parker) is away on a cattle drive. When his younger brother Arliss (Corcoran) brings home a stray dog, Travis is displeased but lets him stay. Yeller saves Travis's life, but contracts rabies in the process. Keep tissue handy, especially for the kids. Strong acting, effective scenery—all good stuff. Based on the novel by Fred Gipson. Sequel "Savage Sam" released in 1963. **84m/C VHS, DVD.** Dorothy McGuire, Fess Parker, Tommy Kirk, Kevin Corcoran, Jeff York, Beverly Washburn, Chuck Connors; ***D:*** Robert Stevenson; ***W:*** Fred Gipson, William Tunberg; ***C:*** Charles P. Boyle; ***M:*** Oliver Wallace.

Oldboy 𝒮𝒮𝒮𝒮 **2003 (R)** Winner of the 2004 Cannes Grand Jury Award, this Korean thriller takes the emotionally charged terror of a David Fincher film and multiples it by a factor of ten. After a drunken evening, Oh Dae-su (Choi, in a brilliant performance) awakens to find himself trapped inside a small room, barred from escape by a thick steel door. Oh spends the next fifteen years in captivity, with no explanation ever offered from his jailers. With no warning, Oh—now half crazy from isolation and his thirst for vengeance—is suddenly freed and a mysterious figure gives him five days to figure out why he's been imprisoned. Park should be applauded for his vicious, unflinching insight into human sexuality and violence in this sad, surrealistic mystery. **120m/C DVD, Blu-ray Disc, UMD.** *KN* Min-Sik Choi, Yu Ji-tae, Hye-jeong Kang; ***D:*** Chan-wook Park; ***W:*** Chan-wook Park, Hwang Jo-yun, Lim Jun-hyeong; ***C:*** Jeong-hun Jeong; ***M:*** Yeong-wook Jo, Shim Hyeon-jeong, Lee Ji-su, Choi Sung-hyeon.

Oldest Confederate Widow Tells All 𝒮𝒮𝒮 **1995** TV drama starts with the recollections of 99-year-old Lucy Marsden (Bancroft), the widow of the title, as she revisits her marriage to troubled Civil War veteran Capt. William Marsden (Sutherland, sporting an impressive set of whiskers). In 1899, the teenaged Lucy (played by Lane) marries the eccentric 50-year-old, who constantly relives battlefield horrors and the loss of his boyhood friend, while she deals with family and various domestic crises. Somewhat meandering story with fine performances and subtle details. Based on Allan Gurganus' novel. **180m/C VHS, DVD.** Diane Lane, Donald Sutherland, Anne Bancroft, Cicely Tyson, Blythe Danner, E.G. Marshall, Gwen Verdon, Maureen Mueller, Wil Horneff; ***D:*** Ken Cameron; ***W:*** Joyce Eliason; ***M:*** Mark Snow.

Oldest Living Graduate 𝒮𝒮𝒮 1/2 **1980** Fonda is memorable in his last stage role as the oldest graduate of a Texas military academy. He and his son clash when Fonda refuses to give up his land. Teleplay features strong performances from Leachman and other big-name cast members. **75m/C VHS.** Cloris Leachman, Henry Fonda, John Lithgow, Timothy Hutton, Harry Dean Stanton, David Ogden Stiers, George Grizzard, Penelope Milford; ***D:*** Jack Hofsiss. **TV**

Oldest Profession 𝒮 *Le Plus Vieux Metier du Monde* **1967** A study of prostitution from prehistoric times to the future. Generally unexciting and unfunny. In six segments meant as vehicles for their directors. **97m/C VHS.** *FR GE IT* Raquel Welch, Jeanne Moreau, Elsa Martinelli, Michele Mercier; ***D:*** Jean-Luc Godard, Philippe de Broca, Claude Autant-Lara, Franco Indovina, Mauro Bolognini, Michael Pfleghar; ***W:*** Jean-Luc Godard.

Oleanna 𝒮 1/2 **1994** Mamet directs the big-screen version of his controversial play about political correctness, sexual harrassment, and the gender gap. Pompous, burned-out college professor (Macy) is accused of sexual harassment by dense, shrill, academically weak student (Eisenstadt) after she misconstrues a self-important speech as a come-on. Unbalanced perspective, obvious stereotyping of unsympathetic characters, and weak performances remove any hint of the intended drama. **90m/C VHS, DVD.** William H. Macy, Debra Eisenstadt; ***D:*** David Mamet; ***W:*** David Mamet; ***C:*** Andrzej Sekula; ***M:*** Rebecca Pidgeon.

Olga's Girls 𝒮𝒮 *Mme. Olga's Massage Parlor; Olga's Massage Parlor; Olga's Parlor* **1964** Sadistic Olga deals in narcotics and white slavery in New York's Chinatown. Her drug addicted girls turn to each other for comfort but Olga suspects there's a snitch in her outfit. She'll stop at nothing to get the informant but the girls think it's about time for revenge. Campy sexploitation. **72m/B VHS, DVD.** Audrey Campbell, Alice Linville; ***D:*** Joseph P. Mawra; ***M:*** Claude Otis.

Oliver! 𝒮𝒮𝒮 1/2 **1968 (G)** Splendid big-budget musical adaptation of Dickens' "Oliver Twist." An innocent orphan is dragged into a life of crime when he is befriended by a gang of pickpockets. ♫ Food, Glorious Food; Oliver; Boy For Sale; Where Is Love?; Consider Yourself; Pick a Pocket or Two; I'd Do Anything; Be Back Soon; As Long As He Needs Me. **145m/C VHS, DVD.** *GB* Mark Lester, Jack Wild, Ron Moody, Shani Wallis, Oliver Reed, Hugh Griffith; ***D:*** Carol Reed; ***W:*** Vernon Harris; ***C:*** Oswald Morris; ***M:*** Lionel Bart. Oscars '68: Adapt. Score, Art Dir./Set Dec., Director (Reed), Picture, Sound; Golden Globes '69: Actor—Mus./Comedy (Moody), Film—Mus./Comedy.

Oliver & Company 𝒮𝒮 1/2 **1988 (G)** Animated animal retelling of Dicken's "Oliver Twist"—Disney style. Kitten Oliver (Lawrence) is left to fend for himself on the mean streets of New York until he's taken under the paw of Dodger (Joel) the dog. Dodger heads up a gang of doggy thieves, who help down-and-out human Fagin (DeLuise), who owes money to ruthless loan shark Sykes (Loggia). Out on his first job, Oliver's found by rich little Jenny (Gregory) and happily adopted. But his pals think he's been kidnapped and are off to rescue him. ♫ Once Upon a Time in New York City; Why Should I Worry?. **72m/C VHS, DVD.** ***D:*** George Scribner; ***W:*** Jim Cox, James Mangold; ***V:*** Joey Lawrence, Billy Joel, Richard "Cheech" Marin, Bette Midler, Dom DeLuise, Roscoe Lee Browne, Richard Mulligan, Sheryl Lee Ralph, Robert Loggia, Taurean Blacque, Carl Weintraub, Natalie Gregory, William Glover.

Oliver Twist 𝒮𝒮𝒮 **1922** Silent version of the Dickens classic is a vehicle for young Jackie Coogan. As orphan Oliver Twist, he is subjected to many frightening incidents before finding love and someone to care for him. Remade numerous times, most notably in 1933 and 1948 and as the musical "Oliver!" in 1968. **77m/B VHS, DVD.** Jackie Coogan, Lon Chaney Sr., Gladys Brockwell, George Siegmann, Esther Ralston, James A. Marcus, Aggie Herring, Nelson McDowell, Lewis Sargent, Joan Standing, Carl Stockdale, Edouard Trebaol, Lionel Belmore; ***D:*** Frank Lloyd; ***W:*** Frank Lloyd, Henry Weil; ***C:*** Glen MacWilliams, Robert Martin.

Oliver Twist 𝒮𝒮 **1933** The first talking version of Dickens's classic about an ill-treated London orphan involved with youthful gang of pickpockets. Moore was too young—at seven—to be very credible in the lead role. The 1948 version is much more believable. **70m/B VHS, DVD.** Dickie Moore, Irving Pichel, William "Stage" Boyd, Barbara Kent; ***D:*** William J. Cowen.

Oliver Twist 𝒮𝒮𝒮𝒮 **1948** Charles Dickens' immortal story of a workhouse orphan who is forced into a life of crime with a gang of pickpockets. The best of many film adaptations, with excellent portrayals by the cast. **116m/C VHS, DVD.** *GB* Robert Newton, John (Howard) Davies, Alec Guinness, Francis L. Sullivan, Anthony Newley, Kay Walsh, Diana Dors, Henry Stephenson; ***D:*** David Lean; ***W:*** David Lean; ***C:*** Guy Green; ***M:*** Arnold Bax.

Oliver Twist 𝒮𝒮𝒮 **1982** Good version of the classic Dicken's tale of a boy's rescue from a life of crime. Scott's Fagin is a treat, and period details are on the mark. **100m/C VHS.** George C. Scott, Tim Curry, Michael Hordern, Timothy West, Lysette Anthony, Eileen Atkins, Cherie Lunghi; ***D:*** Clive Donner; ***W:*** James Goldman; ***M:*** Nick Bicat. **TV**

Oliver Twist 1985 Miniseries adaptation of the Charles Dickens classic about an orphan boy plunging into the underworld of 19th-century London. **333m/C VHS, DVD.** *GB* Ben Rodska, Eric Porter, Frank Middlemass, Gillian Martell; ***D:*** Gareth Davies; ***W:*** Alexander Baron; ***C:*** Dudley Simpson. **TV**

Oliver Twist 𝒮𝒮 1/2 **1997** Lavish TV version of the Dickens tale finds orphaned Oliver (Trench) escaping to 1837's London and being befriended by the wicked Fagin (Dreyfuss) and his gang of pickpocketing youngsters, including the Artful Dodger (Wood). **92m/C VHS, DVD.** Alex Trench, Richard Dreyfuss, Elijah Wood, David O'Hara, Antoine Byrne, Olivia Caffrey; ***D:*** Tony Bill; ***W:*** Monte Merrick; ***C:*** Keith Wilson; ***M:*** Van Dyke Parks. **TV**

Oliver Twist 𝒮𝒮𝒮 **2000** The umpteenth version of the Dickens saga is a well-done British miniseries that includes the backstory of Oliver's parents, an inheritance, scheming relatives, and finally young Oliver (Smith) himself and his adventures with Fagin (Lindsay) and the criminal elements of London. **360m/C VHS, DVD.** Sam Smith, Robert Lindsay, Andy Serkis, Emily Woof, Julie Walters, Michael Kitchen, Annette Crosbie, Alex Crowley, David Ross, Tim Dutton, Lindsay Duncan, Sophia Myles, Keira Knightley; ***D:*** Renny Rye; ***W:*** Alan Bleasdale; ***C:*** Walter McGill; ***M:*** Elvis Costello, Paul Pritchard. **TV**

Oliver Twist 𝒮𝒮𝒮 **2005 (PG-13)** Hey, what would happen if Roman Polanski took on a classic Charles Dickens' tale? Already a dark enough story, Polanski adds what he always adds: depth and details. What's new, or perhaps simply fitting, is Polanski's take, using his own experiences in a Jewish ghetto to inform his interpretation of 19th century London slums. Lavish sets and costumes are set to a lush orchestral score, Ben Kingsley portrays the suitably frightening Fagin. **130m/C DVD.** *GB CZ FR IT* Ben Kingsley, Jamie Foreman, Harry Eden, Leanne Rowe, Edward Hardwicke, Ian McNeice, Mark Strong, Jeremy Swift, Frances Cuka, Alun Armstrong, Peter Copley, Liz Smith, Barney Clark, Michael Heath, Gillian Hanna, Andy De La Tour; ***D:*** Roman Polanski; ***W:*** Ronald Harwood; ***C:*** Pawel Edelman; ***M:*** Rachel Portman.

Oliver Twist 𝒮𝒮 1/2 **2007** This grittier version of the Dickens saga is a typically well-done presentation from the BBC with the roles of criminal Fagin (Spall), violent Bill Sikes (Hardy), and tragic Nancy (Okonedo) particularly well-cast. Born in a workhouse, plucky orphan Oliver (Miller) has many misadventures in London, falls into bad company, is rescued, and has his true past and family revealed. **176m/C DVD.** *GB* Timothy Spall, Thomas (Tom) Hardy, Sophie Okonedo, Edward Fox, Morven Christie, Julian Rhind-Tutt, Sarah Lancashire, Gregor Fisher, Anna Massey, John Sessions, Michelle Gomez, Adam Arnold; ***D:*** Coky Giedroyc; ***W:*** Sarah Phelps; ***C:*** Matt Gray; ***M:*** Martin Phipps. **TV**

Oliver's Story **1978 (PG)** A "not so equal" sequel to "Love Story," where widower O'Neal wallows in grief until rich heiress Bergen comes along. He falls in love again, this time with money. **90m/C VHS, DVD.** Ryan O'Neal, Candice Bergen, Ray Milland, Edward Binns, Nicola Pagett, Charles Haid; ***D:*** John Korty; ***W:*** Erich Segal.

Olivia 1/2 **1983** Abused housewife moonlights as a prostitute and begins killing her customers. She falls in love with an American businessman and flees to America when her husband finds out about the affair. Revenge and murder are the result. **90m/C VHS, DVD.** Suzanna Love, Robert Walker Jr., Jeff Winchester; ***D:*** Ulli Lommel.

Olivier, Olivier **1992 (R)** Holland's directorial follow-up to "Europa, Europa" is based on a 1984 French newspaper story and evokes "The Return of Martin Guerre" and its update, "Sommersby." Beloved nine-year-old boy disappears from his home in a small French town and his dysfunctional family falls apart. Mom obsesses and falls into trances, dad escapes to North Africa, and sister Nadine develops telekinetic powers in order to cope. Six years later a detective brings an amnesiac teenager, who has been working as a hustler in Paris, to the boy's family. Is it the missing Olivier? Spooky, provocative, and emotionally resonate. In French with English subtitles. **110m/C VHS.** *FR* Francois Cluzet, Brigitte Rouan, Gregoire Colin, Marina Golovine, Jean-Francois Stevenin, Emmanuel Morozof, Faye Gatteau, Frederic Quiring; ***D:*** Agnieszka Holland; ***W:*** Agnieszka Holland. L.A. Film Critics '93: Score.

Ollie Hopnoodle's Haven of Bliss 1/2 **1988** Humorist Jean Shepherd (of "A Christmas Story" fame) spins another tale of frantic family life with his alter ego, Ralphie. This time the family is off on a summer vacation—with all its inherent problems. **90m/C VHS.** James B. Sikking, Dorothy Lyman, Jerry O'Connell; ***D:*** Richard Bartlett. **TV**

Olly Olly Oxen Free *The Great Balloon Adventure* **1978** Junkyard owner Hepburn helps two boys fix up and fly a hot-air balloon, once piloted by McKenzie's grandfather, as a surprise for the man's birthday. Beautiful airborne scenes over California and a dramatic landing to the tune of the "1812 Overture," but not enough to make the whole film interesting. **89m/C VHS, DVD.** Katharine Hepburn, Kevin McKenzie, Dennis Dimster-Denk, Peter Kilman; ***D:*** Richard A. Colla; ***M:*** Robert Alcivar.

Omaha (the movie) **1995** Gen-Xer Simon (Walkinshaw) flees his native Nebraska and eccentric, dsyfunctional family for enlightenment in Tibet. He's instructed in Buddhism and returns home but doesn't find the peace he's seeking and decides to hit the road with former girlfriend Gina (Anderson). **85m/C VHS.** Hughston Walkinshaw, Jill Anderson; ***D:*** Dan Mirvish; ***W:*** Dan Mirvish; ***C:*** Oslo Anderson.

Omar Khayyam **1957** In medieval Persia, Omar (Wilde) becomes involved in a romance with the Shah of Persia's fiancee, while trying to fight off a faction of assassins trying to overthrow the Shah. Although this film has a great cast, the script is silly and juvenile, defeating the cast's fine efforts. **101m/C VHS.** Cornel Wilde, Michael Rennie, Debra Paget, Raymond Massey, John Derek, Yma Sumac, Margaret (Maggie) Hayes, Joan Taylor, Sebastian Cabot; ***D:*** William Dieterle.

The Omega Code 1/2 **1999 (PG-13)** This entry in the God vs. Devil steel cage apocalypse smackdown genre was actually financed by the Christian cable network TBN. Therefore, you can be sure that it's not evil, although it's plenty bad. In this corner, representing good, is motivational speaker Gillen Lane (Van Dien), who believes that hidden truths may be discovered by applying mathematical equations to sections of the Bible or by overacting. In that corner, representing evil, is Stone Alexander (York), AKA The Antichrist, who uses the hidden codes for nefarious purposes such as taking over the world government and overacting. In the stunning climax stolen from "Raiders of the Lost Ark," evil is overthrown and we find that the whole thing was a fix from the beginning. Caused a minor stir with semi-big boxoffice numbers, but much of the business was a case of preaching to the choir of fervent TBN viewers in its opening weeks. **99m/C VHS, DVD.** Casper Van Dien, Michael York, Catherine Oxenberg, Michael Ironside, Jan Triska, William Hootkins, Robert Ito, Janet Carroll, Gregory Wagrowski, Devon Odessa, George Coe, Robert F. Lyons; ***D:*** Robert Marcarelli; ***W:*** Stephan Bliss, Hollis Barton; ***C:*** Carlos Gonzalez; ***M:*** Harry Manfredini.

Omega Cop *John Travis, Solar Survivor* **1990 (R)** In a post-apocalyptic future, there's only one cop left. He uses his martial arts skills and tons of guns attempting to rescue three women, but the violence doesn't cover the poor acting and shoddy production. Fans of TV's Batman might enjoy this for West's presence. **89m/C VHS, DVD.** Ron Marchini, Adam West, Stuart Whitman, Troy Donahue, Meg Thayer, Jennifer Jostyn, Chrysti Jimenez, D.W. Landingham, Chuck Katzakian; ***D:*** Paul Kyriazi.

Omega Doom **1996 (PG-13)** Four hundred years after an apocalyptic war the most organic thing around are the cyborgs, who exist along with androids and robots in a world where humans no longer matter. Omega Doom (Hauer) is an android developed as a fighter who has no function except to kill. In a ruined amusement park, the Roms and Droids, two rival cyborg groups, maintain an uneasy truce and when Doom wanders in they unite to destroy the intruder. But they don't know what they're up against. **84m/C VHS, DVD.** Rutger Hauer, Anna (Katerina) Katarina, Norbert Weisser, Jahi JJ Zuri, Shannon Whirry, Earl White, Tina Cote, Jill Pierce; ***D:*** Albert Pyun; ***W:*** Ed Naha; ***C:*** George Mooradian; ***M:*** Tony Riparetti.

Omega Man 1/2 **1971 (PG)** In post-holocaust Los Angeles, Heston is immune to the effects of a biologically engineered plague and battles those who aren't—an army of albino victims bent on destroying what's left of the world. Strong suspense with considerable violence, despite the PG rating. Based on the science fiction thriller "I Am Legend" by Richard Matheson, which is also the basis for the film "The Last Man on Earth." **98m/C VHS, DVD, Blu-ray Disc.** Charlton Heston, Anthony Zerbe, Rosalind Cash, Paul Koslo, Eric Laneuville, Lincoln Kilpatrick, Anna Aries, John Dierkes, Monika Henreid; ***D:*** Boris Sagal; ***W:*** John W. Corrington, Joyce H. Corrington; ***C:*** Russell Metty; ***M:*** Ron Grainer.

Omega Syndrome 1/2 **1987 (R)** Neo-Nazis kidnap Wahl's daughter. He and Vietnam buddy DiCenzo get her back. Ho hum. DiCenzo's is the best performance. Tolerable for vigilante film fans. **90m/C VHS.** Ken Wahl, Ron Kuhlman, George DiCenzo, Doug McClure; ***D:*** Joseph Manduke.

The Omen 1/2 *Birthmark* **1976 (R)** American diplomat's family adopts a young boy who always seems to be around when bizarre and inexplicable deaths occur. Of course, what else would you expect of Satan's son? The shock and gore prevalent in "The Exorcist" is replaced with more suspense and believable effects. Well-done horror film doesn't insult the viewer's intelligence. Followed by three sequels: "Damien: Omen 2," "The Final Conflict," and "Omen 4." **111m/C VHS, DVD.** Gregory Peck, Lee Remick, Harvey Stephens, Billie Whitelaw, David Warner, Holly Palance, Robert Rietty, Patrick Troughton, Martin Benson, Leo McKern, Richard Donner; ***D:*** Richard Donner; ***W:*** David Seltzer; ***C:*** Gilbert Taylor; ***M:*** Jerry Goldsmith. Oscars '76: Orig. Score.

The Omen 1/2 **2006 (R)** Robert Thorn (Schreiber), American ambassador to England, adopts an orphaned newborn after his own son dies, without telling his fragile wife Katherine (Stiles). Damien (newcomer Davey-Fitzpatrick) grows into a spooky little boy looked after by overprotective nanny Mrs. Baylock (Farrow). Sinister happenings lead Thorn to believe he's raising the antichrist. The remake uses the same screenwriter—David Seltzer—as the 1976 original with some modest updates so nothing's very surprising. But it's still pretty scary (and bloody). **110m/C DVD, Blu-ray Disc.** *US* Liev Schreiber, Julia Stiles, Mia Farrow, David Thewlis, Pete Postlethwaite, Michael Gambon, Seamus Davey-Fitzpatrick; ***D:*** John Moore; ***W:*** David Seltzer; ***C:*** Jonathan Sela; ***M:*** Marco Beltrami.

Omen 4: The Awakening **1991** It turns out Damien of Omens past had a daughter, Delia, who takes up where dear old devilish Dad left off. Delia is adopted by your basic clueless couple and proceeds to wreak havoc wherever she goes, including getting rid of several interfering adults. She also plans to make her adoptive father, a U.S. senator, President, so that his delightful child anti-Christ can have him carry out all her evil plans. **97m/C VHS, DVD.** Faye Grant, Michael Woods, Michael Lerner, Asia Vieira; ***D:*** Jorge Montesi, Dominique Othenin-Girard. **TV**

Omoo Omoo, the Shark God **1949** A sea captain is cursed when he removes the black pearls from a stone shark god in this extremely cheap adventure. **58m/B VHS, DVD.** Ron Randell, Devera Burton, Trevor Bardette, Pedro de Cordoba, Richard Benedict, Rudy Robles, Michael Whalen, George Meeker; ***D:*** Leo Leonard.

On a Clear Day 1/2 **2005 (PG-13)** Frank (Mullan) is a 55-year-old Glasgow shipbuilder who has been laid off after 35 years. At odds with himself and his family, Frank regularly meets his mates at the local swimming pool, where an offhand remark sets him on his new goal—to swim the English Channel. He begins training in secret, thus causing his anxious wife Joan (Blethyn) to suspect he's having an affair. Frank also grapples with some past sorrows that have caused a rift between himself and son Rob (Sives). Mullan portrays Frank as such a gruff bloke that the mawkishness is kept at bay. **99m/C DVD.** *GB* Peter Mullan, Brenda Blethyn, Sean McGinley, Jamie Sives, Billy Boyd, Ron Cook, Jodhi May, Benedict Wong, Shaun Dingwall, Anne-Marie Timoney, Tony Roper, Paul Ritter; ***D:*** Gaby Dellal; ***W:*** Alex Rose; ***C:*** David Johnson; ***M:*** Stephen Warbeck.

On a Clear Day You Can See Forever **1970 (G)** A psychiatric hypnotist helps a girl stop smoking and finds that in trances she remembers previous incarnations. He falls in love with one of the women she used to be. Alan Jay Lerner of "My Fair Lady" and "Camelot" wrote the lyrics and the book. Based on a musical by Lerner and Burton Lane. ♫ On a Clear Day, You Can See Forever; Come Back to Me; What Did I Have That I Don't Have?; He Isn't You; Hurry, It's Lovely Up Here; Go To Sleep; Love with All the Trimmings; Melinda. **129m/C VHS, DVD.** Barbra Streisand, Yves Montand, Bob Newhart, Jack Nicholson, Simon Oakland; ***D:*** Vincente Minnelli; ***C:*** Harry Stradling Sr.

On an Island with You 1/2 **1948** Williams plays a movie star who finds romance on location in Hawaii in this musical extravaganza. Contains many of Williams' famous water ballet scenes and a bevy of bathing beauties. ♫ On an Island with You; If I Were You; Taking Miss Mary to the Ball; Dog Song; Buenas Noches, Buenos Aires; Wedding Samba; I Can Do Without Broadway, But Can Broadway Do Without Me?. **107m/C VHS, DVD.** Esther Williams, Peter Lawford, Ricardo Montalban, Jimmy Durante, Cyd Charisse, Leon Ames; ***D:*** Richard Thorpe.

On Approval **1944** Hilarious British farce in which two women trade boyfriends. Lillie's performance provides plenty of laughs. Brook runs the show as leading man, co-author, director, and co-producer. Based on the play by Frederick Lonsdale. **80m/B VHS, DVD.** *GB* Clive Brook, Beatrice Lillie, Googie Withers, Roland Culver, O.B. Clarence, Lawrence Hanray, Elliot Mason, Hay Petrie, Marjorie Munks, Molly Munks; ***D:*** Clive Brook; ***W:*** Terence Young, Clive Brook; ***C:*** Claude Friese-Greene; ***M:*** William Alwyn.

On Borrowed Time **1939** Engrossing tale of Death (Hardwicke) coming for an old man (Barrymore) who isn't ready to die so he traps him in his backyard apple tree. Performances are first rate in this good adaptation of the stage success (originally by Eugene O'Neill). Hardwicke is especially a standout; he gave up theatre for Hollywood after making this film. **99m/B VHS.** Lionel Barrymore, Cedric Hardwicke, Beulah Bondi, Una Merkel, Bobs Watson, Henry Travers; ***D:*** Harold Bucquet; ***C:*** Joseph Ruttenberg.

On Dangerous Ground **1951** A world-weary detective is sent to the country-side to investigate a murder. He encounters the victim's revenge-hungry father and the blind sister of the murderer. In the hateful father the detective sees a reflection of the person he has become, in the blind woman, he learns the redeeming qualities of humanity and compassion. A well-acted example of film noir that features the composer Herrman's favorite score. **82m/B VHS.** Robert Ryan, Ida Lupino, Ward Bond, Ed Begley Sr., Cleo Moore, Charles Kemper; ***D:*** Nicholas Ray; ***M:*** Bernard Herrmann.

On Deadly Ground **WOOF!** **1994 (R)** Seagal nearly destroys Alaska in an effort to save it in this inane, preachy story of an oil-rig roughneck out to protect the landscape from an evil oil company's drilling habits. Directorial debut for Seagal lumbers from scene to scene. Violence is expected, as is silly dialogue—just try to keep from laughing when stoneyfaced Steven intones "What does it take to change the essence of man?" A better script, for one. **102m/C VHS, DVD.** Steven Seagal, Michael Caine, Joan Chen, John C. McGinley, Billy Bob Thornton, R. Lee Ermey; ***D:*** Steven Seagal; ***W:*** Ed Horowitz; ***C:*** Ric Waite; ***M:*** Basil Poledouris. Golden Raspberries '94: Worst Director (Seagal).

On Each Side *A Cada Lado* **2007** An exploration of past and future through interconnected stories of characters affected by the building of the Rosario-Victoria Bridge across the Parana River in Argentina. Photographer Abel, hired to document the bridge's construction, meets a pair of thieves; two young boys grow into teenagers as the bridge building continues; an old man is constantly irritated by construction noise; and two elderly sisters take in a boarder—a German engineer secretly meeting a transvestite singer across the river. German and Spanish with subtitles. **95m/C DVD.** *AR* Miguel Franchi, Miguel Bosco, Milagros Alacron, Julian Knab, Juan Pablo Garetto, Monica Alfonso, Monica Galan, Hector Bidonde; ***D:*** Hugo Grosso; ***W:*** Hugo Grosso; ***C:*** Sergio Garcia; ***M:*** Carlos Casazza.

On Edge **2003 (R)** Figure skaters Wendy (Winokur), Veda (Swatek), and J.C. (Langer) are three Olympic hopefuls vying for the Southern California regional figure skating championship amidst the usual jealousies and craziness. Alexander is the Zamboni driver who observes it all and a number of professional skaters play skating judges. **93m/C VHS, DVD.** A.J. (Allison Joy) Langer, Jason Alexander, Barret Swatek, Marissa Jaret Winokur, John Glover, Kathy Griffin, Chris Hogan, Wallace (Wally) Langham, Sabrina Lloyd, Wendie Malick; ***D:*** Karl Slovin; ***W:*** Karl Slovin, Laura Wolf; ***C:*** Chris Squires; ***M:*** Jim Latham. **VIDEO**

On Golden Pond 1/2 **1981 (PG)** Henry Fonda won his first—and long overdue—Oscar for his role as the curmudgeonly patriarch of the Thayer family. He and his wife have grudgingly agreed to look after a young boy while at their summer home in Maine. Through his gradually affectionate relationship with the boy, Fonda learns to allay his fears of mortality. He also gains an understanding of his semi-estranged daughter. Jane Fonda plays his daughter and Hepburn is his loving wife in this often funny adaptation of Ernest Thompson's 1978 play. Predictable but deeply moving. Henry Fonda's final screen appearance. **109m/C VHS, DVD.** Henry Fonda, Jane Fonda, Katharine Hepburn, Dabney Coleman, Doug McKeon, William Lanteau; ***D:*** Mark Rydell; ***W:*** Ernest Thompson; ***C:*** Billy Williams; ***M:*** Dave Grusin. Oscars '81: Actor (Fonda), Actress (Hepburn), Adapt. Screenplay; British Acad. '82: Actress (Hepburn); Golden Globes '82: Actor—Drama (Fonda), Film—Drama, Screenplay; Natl. Bd. of Review '81: Actor (Fonda); Writers Guild '81: Adapt. Screenplay.

On Guard! 1/2 *Le Bossu; En Garde* **2003** Thrilling story of revenge and swordplay set in 18th century France. Lagardere (Auteuil) attempts to kill the Duke of Nevers (Perez) for money and ends up being taken in and trained by him. Nevers' cousin, the evil Gonzague (Luchini), murders him to grab the family fortune and Lagardere is forced to go into hiding and raise Nevers' daughter Aurore. 16 years later, Lagardere and grown Aurore (Gillain) find themselves in the court of Gonzague, where they put their plot for vengeance into effect. Fantastic swordfighting scenes, complex intrigue, and excellent acting make this a world-class swashbuckler. Based on the frequently adapted 1857 French serial "Le Bossu" by Paul Feval. In French with subtitles. **128m/C VHS, DVD.** *FR IT GE* Daniel Auteuil, Fabrice Luchini, Vincent Perez, Marie Gillain, Jean-Francois Stevenin, Didier Pain, Claire Nebout, Philippe Noiret, Yann Collette; ***D:*** Philippe de Broca; ***W:*** Philippe de Broca, Jean Cosmos, Jerome Tonnerre; ***C:*** Jean-Francois Robin; ***M:*** Philippe Sarde.

On Her Majesty's Secret Service **1969 (PG)** In the sixth 007 adventure, Bond again confronts the infamous Blofeld, who is planning a germ-warfare assault on the entire world. Australian Lazenby took a crack at playing the super spy, with mixed results. Many feel this is the best-written of the Bond films and might have been the most famous, had Sean Connery continued with the series. Includes the song "We Have All the Time In the World," sung by Louis Armstrong. **144m/C VHS, DVD.** *GB* George Lazenby, Diana Rigg, Telly Savalas, Gabriele Ferzetti, Ilse Steppat, Bernard Lee, Lois Maxwell, Desmond Llewelyn, Catherine Schell, Julie Ege, Joanna Lumley, Mona Chong, Anouska (Anoushka) Hempel, Jenny Hanley; ***D:*** Peter Hunt; ***W:*** Richard Maibaum; ***M:*** John Barry.

On Moonlight Bay 1/2 **1951** Set in small-town Indiana in 1917 with Day as the tomboyish Marjorie who falls for college man MacRae. Her father (Ames) doesn't approve but the trouble really begins when Marjorie's younger brother gets into trouble at school. The incorrigible Wesley (Gray) blames everything on dear old dad and MacRae feels he must come to Marjorie's rescue! Gray steals the movie as the bratty brother—otherwise its business as usual. Based on Booth Tarkington's "Penrod" stories and followed by "By the Light of the Silvery Moon." ♫ Love Ya; On Moonlight Bay; Till We Meet Again; Pack Up Your Troubles In Your Old Kit Bag; I'm Forever Blowing Bubbles; Christmas Story; Tell Me Why Nights Are Lonely; Cuddle Up a Little Closer; Every Little Movement Has a Meaning All Its Own. **95m/C VHS, DVD.** Doris Day, Gordon MacRae, Leon Ames, Billy Gray, Rosemary DeCamp, Mary Wickes, Ellen Corby, Esther Dale; ***D:*** Roy Del Ruth; ***W:*** Melville Shavelson, Jack Rose; ***M:*** Max Steiner.

On My Own **1992** Fifteen-year-old Simon Henderson (Ferguson) struggles to cope with his life when he's sent away to school after his mother (Davis) suffers a nervous breakdown. Just as he begins to adjust and make friends, his mother pays a disturbing visit and reveals the source of her troubles. **96m/C VHS.** *CA* Judy Davis, Matthew Ferguson, David McIlwraith; ***D:*** Antonio Tibaldi.

On Our Merry Way 1/2 *A Miracle Can Happen* **1948** Episodic comedy with Meredith starring as Oliver Pease, a would-be newspaper reporter (he actually works on the classifieds), asking the question "How has a child changed your life?" Among those queried are a couple of jazz musicians (Fonda, Stewart), Hollywood bit players (Lamour, Moore), and con men (Demerest, MacMurray). Goddard, who was married to Meredith at the time, plays his wife in the film. **107m/B VHS, DVD.** Burgess Meredith, Paulette Goddard, Dorothy Lamour, Victor Moore, James Stewart, Henry Fonda, Fred MacMurray, William Demarest, Hugh Herbert, Eilene Janssen, Dorothy Ford, David Whorf; ***D:*** King Vidor, Leslie Fenton; ***W:*** Laurence Stallings, Lou Breslow; ***C:*** John Seitz, Ernest Laszlo, Gordon Avil, Joseph Biroc, Edward Cronjager; ***M:*** Heinz Roemheld.

On the Air *En el Aire* **1995** DJ Alberto (Gimenez Cacho) is facing job loss with the shutdown of the radio station where he does his psychedelic music show. This isn't his only loss as Alberto's marriage to Laura (Heredia) is also failing. He explores his problems on air as he flashes back to his life growing up in the '60s and '70s. Spanish with subtitles. **90m/C VHS, DVD.** *MX* Daniel Gimenez Cacho, Dolores Heredia, Angelica Aragon, Alberto Estrella; ***D:*** Juan Carlos de Llaca; ***W:*** Juan Carlos de Llaca; ***C:*** Claudio Rocha; ***M:*** Alejandro Giacoman.

On the Air Live with Captain Midnight 1/2 *Captain Midnight* **1979** Socially challenged teen finds hipness as a rebel DJ operating an illegal radio station from his van. Leading actor is the son of the director/writer/producer but nepotism does not a good film make. **90m/C VHS.** Tracy Sebastian; ***D:*** Ferd Sebastian.

On the Avenue **1937** Broadway showman Powell opens up a new musical, starring Faye as the richest girl in the world, in this musical-comedy satirizing upper-crust society. Debutante Carroll is outraged because she realizes it's mocking her actual life. Carroll tries to get Powell to change the show, they fall in love, Faye gets her nose out of joint, and after lots of fuss everything ends happily. Fine Berlin score. ♫ He Ain't Got Rhythm; You're Laughing at Me; This Year's Kisses; Slumming on Park Avenue; The Girl on the Police Gazette; I've Got My Love to Keep Me Warm. **90m/B VHS, DVD.** Dick Powell, Madeleine Carroll, Alice Faye, George Barbier, Al Ritz, Harry Ritz, Jimmy Ritz, Alan Mowbray, Cora Witherspoon, Walter Catlett, Stepin Fetchit, Sig Rumann, Douglas Fowley, Joan Davis; ***D:*** Roy Del Ruth; ***W:*** Gene Markey; ***M:*** Irving Berlin.

On the Beach 1/2 **1959** A group of survivors attempt to live normal lives in post-apocalyptic Australia, waiting for the inevitable arrival of killer radiation. Astaire is strong in his first dramatic role. Though scientifically implausible, still a good anti-war vehicle. Based on the best-selling novel by Nevil Shute. **135m/B VHS, DVD.** Gregory Peck, Anthony Perkins, Donna Anderson, Ava Gardner, Fred Astaire; ***D:*** Stanley Kramer; ***W:*** John Paxton; ***C:*** Daniel F. Fapp; ***M:*** Ernest Gold. Golden Globes '60: Score.

On the Beach 1/2 **2000** Remake of the 1959 anti-nuke film (based on the 1957 novel by Nevil Shute) is well-acted but so low-key that it never generates real tension. In 2006, the bomb has been dropped and Australia is the current refuge and the destination of sub commander Dwight Towers (Assante). A radio transmission from Alaska offers some hope but Towers needs the help of Melbourne scientist Julian Osborne (Brown), who happens to be the ex- of Towers' sultry love, Moira (Ward). **180m/C VHS, DVD.** Armand Assante, Rachel Ward, Bryan Brown, Jacqueline McKenzie, Grant Bowler; ***D:*** Russell Mulcahy; ***W:*** David Williamson, Bill Kerby; ***C:*** Martin McGrath; ***M:*** Anna Borghesi. **CABLE**

On the Border 1/2 **1998 (R)** Familiar neo-noir revolves around a bank heist. Ex-bank robber Jake (Van Dien) is now a security guard. Kristin (Roos) entices him into a plot involving Brown, Baldwin, and Mitchum. The humor is intentional, and the Texas locations are well utilized. Overall, this is an overachieving video premiere. **103m/C DVD.** Casper Van Dien, Bryan Brown, Bentley Mitchum, Camilla Overbye Roos, Rochelle Swanson, Daniel Baldwin; ***D:*** Bob Misiorowski; ***W:*** Josh Olson; ***C:*** Lawrence Sher; ***M:*** Serge Colbert. **VIDEO**

On the Borderline 1/2 **2001 (R)** On their way to California with their new baby, Luke (Mabius) and Nicole (Shelton) find themselves short of funds in a border town. She takes work as a waitress while he becomes involved with transporting Mexican aliens. Curious little road thriller actually works pretty well. The leads and a solid supporting cast handle the material well. Some scenes are curiously tinted to disguise the less-than-lavish production values. **93m/C DVD.** Eric Mabius, Marley Shelton, Elizabeth Pena, R. Lee Ermey; ***D:*** Michael Oblowitz; ***W:*** Kevin R. Frech; ***C:*** Michael Barrow; ***M:*** Michael Wandmacher.

On the Comet *Na Komete; Hector Servadac's Ark* **1968** Zeman's fourth fantasy based on Jules Verne stories, about a chunk of the Earth's crust suddenly becoming a comet and giving its passengers a ride through the galaxy. Complete with Zeman's signature animation fantasias. In English. **76m/C VHS.** *CZ* Emil Horvath Jr., Magda Vasarykova, Frantisek Filipovsky; ***D:*** Karel Zeman.

On the Doll 1/2 **2007** Jimmy (Ben-Victor) has a small-time sleaze business in L.A., including a strip club and a peep-show arcade. Tara (Sarafyan) owes Jimmy a lot of dough so she works the peep while boyfriend Jaron (Janowicz) tries to figure out a way to pay off her debt. To make some quick cash, he helps out hooker Balery (Snow) with an abusive client. Meanwhile, high schoolers Courtney (Domont) and Melody (Accola) get lured into Internet "modeling" for Jimmy, and streetwalker Chantal (Collins) works to provide for her unsuccessful musician boyfriend Wes (Crawford). **102m/C DVD.** Brittany Snow, Josh Janowicz, Paul Ben-Victor, Marcus Giamatti, Edward Jemison, Clayne Crawford, Shanna Collins, Angela Sarafyan, Chloe Domont, Candice Accola; ***D:*** Thomas Mignone; ***W:*** Thomas Mignone; ***C:*** Nicole Hirsch; ***M:*** Paul D'Amour. **VIDEO**

On the Edge 1/2 **1986 (PG-13)** A drama about the inevitable Rocky-esque triumph of Dern as an aging marathon runner. Simultaneous to his running endeavor, Dern is trying to make up for lost time with his father. Available in two versions, one rated, the other unrated with a racy appearance by Pam Grier as the runner's interracial lover. **86m/C VHS, DVD.** Bruce Dern, John Marley, Bill Bailey, Jim Haynie, Pam Grier; ***D:*** Rob Nilsson; ***W:*** Rob Nilsson.

On the Edge 1/2 **2000 (R)** Troubled 19-year-old Jonathan Breech (Murphy) deals with his depression over his father's death by stealing a car and driving it over a cliff. Surviving with very minor injuries, Jonathan is faced with prison or spending time in a mental institution. He chooses the latter, where he meets his caring therapist, Dr. Figure (Rea), and some fellow patients to bond with—Rachel (Vessey) and Toby (Jackson). Much teen angst is explored before the resolution and the material may not be fresh but it is heartfelt. **86m/C VHS, DVD.** *IR* Cillian Murphy, Tricia Vessey, Jonathan Jackson, Stephen Rea; ***D:*** John Carney; ***W:*** Daniel James, John Carney; ***C:*** Eric Alan Edwards.

On the Edge 1/2 **2002 (R)** Community do-gooder Dakota Smith (Williamson) comes to the aid of basketball phenom Willie Jo Harris (Franklin) when he crosses drug dealer Slim Jim (Ice-T). Slim's goons mistakenly hit the family of Rex Stevens (Casey) so he teams up with Smith and Willie Jo's dad Frank (O'Neal) to start cleaning up the 'hood by first getting rid of hitman Felix (Busey). Fellow blaxploitation star Brown also makes an appearance. **90m/C DVD.** Fred Williamson, Bernie Casey, Ron O'Neal, Gary Busey, Ice-T, Jim Brown, Derrick Franklin; ***D:*** Fred Williamson; ***W:*** Linda Williamson; ***C:*** John Dirlam. **VIDEO**

On the Edge: The Survival of Dana **1979** Another entry from the world of low-quality made-for-TV films. A young girl moves with her family to a new town. When she falls in with the "bad" crowd, her ethical standards are challenged. A stinker that may appeal to those with campy tastes. Not for the discriminating palate. **92m/C VHS.** Melissa Sue Anderson, Robert Carradine, Marion Ross, Talia Balsam, Michael Pataki, Kevin Breslin, Judge Reinhold, Barbara Babcock; ***D:*** Jack Starrett. **TV**

On the Fiddle 1/2 *Operation Snafu; Operation Warhead* **1961** Conniving Horace Pope (Lynch) gets his mate Pedlar Pascoe (Connery) to join the Royal Air Force with him during WWII. Horace sets up a number of rackets but, despite their larceny, they become unintentional heroes. Based on the novel "Stop at a Winner" by R.F. Delderfield. **93m/B VHS.** *GB* Alfred Lynch, Sean Connery, Cecil Parker, Stanley Holloway, Wilfrid Hyde-White; ***D:*** Cyril Frankel; ***W:*** Harold Buchman; ***C:*** Edward Scaife; ***M:*** Malcolm Arnold.

On the Line 1/2 **1983** Two Mexico-US border guards, one hard-bitten, the other sympathetic to the illegal immigrants' plight, battle it out over a beautiful Mexican whore. Disjointed and confusing. **95m/C VHS, DVD.** *SP* David Carradine, Victoria Abril, Scott Wilson, Sam Jaffe, Jesse Vint; ***D:*** Jose Luis Borau; ***W:*** Jose Luis Borau.

On the Line 1/2 **2001 (PG)** Insipid romance featuring Bass and Fatone from the teenybopper group 'N Sync. Kevin (Bass) meets Abbey (Chriqui), the girl of his dreams, on a train in Chicago. How does he know she's the one for him? Well, they can both name all the presidents in order and they both like the Cubs. Gee! Ain't that sweet? Unfortunately, Kevin is too shy to ask for her number, and he lets her slip away. He laments to his friends Rod (Fatone), Eric (GQ) and Randy (Bulliard) and they decide to help him find her by posting flyers all over town. A local reporter (Montgomery) picks up the story and a gaggle of girls claiming to be "The L Girl" respond. Further plot contrivances keep the two apart. Love wins out in the end, however, much to the delight of squealing 12-year-old girls everywhere. **90m/C VHS, DVD.** *US* Lance Bass, Joey Fatone, Emmanuelle Chriqui, GQ, Al Green, Tamala Jones, Dave Foley, Dan Montgomery Jr., Jerry Stiller; ***D:*** Eric Bross; ***W:*** Paul Stanton, Eric Aronson; ***C:*** Michael Bernard; ***M:*** Stewart Copeland.

On the Nickel **1980 (R)** An ex-alcoholic returns to Fifth Street in Los Angeles to save his friend from a life of despair. Waits' musical score enhances this sentimental skid row drama. Scripted, directed, and produced by "The Waltons'" Waite. **96m/C VHS.** Ralph Waite, Donald Moffat, Hal Williams, Jack Kehoe; ***D:*** Ralph Waite; ***W:*** Ralph Waite; ***M:*** Tom Waits.

On the Night Stage **1915** Gruff bandit (legendary Hart) loses his girl-of-questionable-values to town preacher. One of the first feature length westerns. **83m/B VHS.** William S. Hart, Robert Edeson, Rhea Mitchell, Shorty Hamilton; ***D:*** Reginald Barker.

On the Old Spanish Trail 1/2 **1947** Rogers becomes a singing cowboy with a traveling tent show in order to pay off a note signed by the Sons of the Pioneers. **56m/B VHS, DVD.** Roy Rogers, Jane Frazee, Andy Devine, Tito Guizar; ***D:*** William Witney.

On the Other Hand, Death 1/2 **2008 (R)** Albany PI Donald Strachey (Allen) returns in this third mystery based on the Richard Stevenson series. Donald's husband Tim (Spence) is asked for help by ex-boyfriend Andrew (Runyan) when lesbian couple Dorothy (Kidder) and Edith (Rose) are apparently the targets of a hate crime. Strachey soon decides it's business rather than sexuality that's the issue since the women are the only ones who won't sell out to a rapacious developer, but it may not be that simple either. **85m/C DVD.** Chad Allen, Sebastian Spence, Margot Kidder, Gabrielle Rose, Nelson Wong, Daryl Shuttleworth, Damon Runyan; ***D:*** Ron Oliver; ***W:*** Ron McGee, Gillian Horvath; ***C:*** C. Kim Miles; ***M:*** Peter Allen. **CABLE**

On the Outs **2005 (R)** Three teen girls find the mean streets more than they can handle. Suzette (Mariano) is pregnant by a crack dealer who leaves her literally holding the gun that killed a rival. Crack addict Marisol (Mendoza) is a single mom who loses her daughter to child welfare and learns that even if she stays clean it could take years to regain parental custody. Oz (Marte) is herself a crack dealer, trying to raise her mentally retarded younger brother. Based on case studies of young women who were held in a Jersey City juvenile detention center. **86m/C DVD.** Judy Marte, Anny Mariano, Paola Mendoza, Dominic Colon; ***D:*** Lori Silverbush, Michael Skolnik; ***W:*** Lori Silverbush; ***C:*** Mariana Sanchez du Antunano; ***M:*** Richard Leigh, Brian Satz.

On the Right Track 1/2 **1981 (PG)** Young orphan living in Chicago's Union Station has the gift of being able to pick winning race horses. May be appealing to fans of Coleman and "Different Strokes" TV show, but lacks the momentum to keep most viewers from switching tracks. **98m/C VHS.** Gary Coleman, Lisa Eilbacher, Michael Lembeck, Norman Fell, Maureen Stapleton, Herb Edelman; ***D:*** Lee Philips.

On the Run *Country Blue; One for the Money, Two for the Show* **1973 (R)** An ex-con and his gal cut a law-defying swath through the Bayou. **110m/C VHS, DVD.** Jack Conrad, Rita George, Dub Taylor, David Huddleston; ***D:*** Jack Conrad; ***W:*** Jack Conrad; ***C:*** Emmett Alston.

On the Run **1983** A hitman is hired to kill a young boy who witnesses a brutal murder. The hitman, however, decides he's already killed too many people and wants to get out of the business. Will he become the next murder target? **101m/C VHS.** Paul Winfield, Rod Taylor, Shirley Cameron, Beau Cox; ***D:*** Mende Brown; ***W:*** Michael Fisher; ***C:*** Paul Onorato; ***M:*** Laurie Lewis.

On the Sunny Side 1/2 **1942** English boy Hugh Aylesworth (McDowall) is sent to live with the American Andrew family in order to escape the Nazi blitz. His politeness endears him to the parents but causes friction with son Tom (Clements) until the two boys unite against the neighborhood bully. **69m/B VHS.** Roddy McDowall, Katherine Alexander, Stanley Clements, Jane Darwell, Donald "Don" Douglas, William Benedict, Jill Esmond, Freddie Mercer; ***D:*** Harold Schuster; ***W:*** Lillie Hayward, George Templeton; ***C:*** Lucien N. Andriot.

On the Sunny Side *Auf der Sonnenseite* **1962** Martin, who works as a steel worker, wants to become an actor and tries his hand at drama school, where his anarchic ways eventually get him expelled. This doesn't seem to bother Martin much, probably because he's fallen in love with Ottilie, an architect who's immune to his charms. German with subtitles. **97m/B VHS.** *GE* Manfred Krug, Marita Bohme, Heinz Schubert; ***D:*** Ralf Kirsten; ***W:*** Ralf Kirsten; ***C:*** Hans Heinrich; ***M:*** Andre Asriel.

On the Third Day **1983** A headmaster finds a mysterious stranger in his house who turns out to be his long-lost illegitimate son. **101m/C VHS.** Richard Marant, Catherine Schell, Paul Williamson; ***D:*** Stanley O'Toole; ***W:*** Stanley O'Toole; ***C:*** Alec Mills; ***M:*** Michael Lewis.

On the Town ½ **1949** Kelly's directorial debut features three sailors on a one day leave search for romance in the Big Apple. Filmed on location in NYC, with uncompromisingly authentic flavor. Based on the successful Broadway musical. ♫ New York, New York; I Feel Like I'm Not Out of Bed Yet; Come Up to My Place; Miss Turnstiles Ballet; Main Street; You're Awful; On the Town; You Can Count on Me; Pearl of the Persian Sea. **98m/C VHS, DVD.** Gene Kelly, Frank Sinatra, Vera-Ellen, Ann Miller, Betty Garrett, Jules Munshin; ***D:*** Stanley Donen, Gene Kelly; ***W:*** Betty Comden, Adolph Green; ***M:*** Leonard Bernstein. Oscars '49: Scoring/Musical.

On the Town ½ **1991** Bernstein's first big Broadway success in 1944, recorded in a live performance June 1992, at London's Barbican Centre. Follows the story of three sailors on a 24-hour leave in New York City during WWII. This version includes numbers which never made it into the original Broadway show. **110m/C VHS.** Frederica von Stade, Tyne Daly, Marie McLaughlin, David Garrison, Thomas Hampson, Kurt Ollman, Evelyn Lear, Samuel Ramey, Cleo Laine; ***M:*** Leonard Bernstein, Betty Comden, Adolph Green.

On the Waterfront **1954** A trend-setting, gritty portrait of New York dock workers embroiled in union violence. Cobb is the gangster union boss, Steiger his crooked lawyer, and Brando, Steiger's ex-fighter brother who "could've been a contender!" Intense performances and excellent direction stand up well today. The picture was a huge financial success. **108m/B VHS, DVD.** Marlon Brando, Rod Steiger, Eva Marie Saint, Lee J. Cobb, Karl Malden, Pat Henning, Leif Erickson, Tony Galento, John Hamilton, Nehemiah Persoff; ***D:*** Elia Kazan; ***W:*** Budd Schulberg; ***C:*** Boris Kaufman; ***M:*** Leonard Bernstein. Oscars '54: Actor (Brando), Art Dir./Set Dec., B&W, B&W Cinematog., Director (Kazan), Film Editing, Picture, Story & Screenplay, Support. Actress (Saint); AFI '98: Top 100; British Acad. '54: Actor (Brando); Directors Guild '54: Director (Kazan); Golden Globes '55: Actor—Drama (Brando), Director (Kazan), Film—Drama, Natl. Film Reg. '89;; N.Y. Film Critics '54: Actor (Brando), Director (Kazan), Film.

On the Yard **1979 (R)** An attempt to realistically portray prison life. Focuses on a murderer who runs afoul of the leader of the prisoners and the system. A fairly typical prison drama with above average performances from Heard and Kellin. **102m/C VHS.** Dominic Chianese, John Heard, Thomas G. Waites, Mike Kellin, Joe Grifasi; ***D:*** Raphael D. Silver; ***W:*** Malcolm Braly.

On Top of Old Smoky ½ **1953** Autry and the Cass County Boys are mistaken for Texas Rangers by a gang of land poachers. **59m/B VHS.** Gene Autry, Smiley Burnette, Gail Davis, Sheila Ryan; ***D:*** George Archainbaud.

On Top of the Whale **1982** Two scholars move onto the estate of strange but wealthy benefactor to conduct research on the few survivors of a disappearing clan of Indians. Two tribesmen speak bizarre dialect which utilizes only one word while others confound the researchers with stories of ghosts and graveyards. Dutch comedy subtitled in English. **93m/C VHS.** *NL* Willeke Van Ammelrooy, Fernando Bordeu, Jean Badin, Herbert Curiel; ***D:*** Raul Ruiz; ***W:*** Raul Ruiz; ***C:*** Henri Alekan; ***M:*** Jorge Arriagada.

On Valentine's Day ½ *Story of a Marriage* **1986 (PG)** Author Horton Foote based this story loosely on his parents' lives. A wealthy young Southern girl marries a poor but decent young man and finds herself ostracized from her family. A prequel to the same author's "1918." Produced with PBS for "American Playhouse." **106m/C VHS, DVD.** Hallie Foote, Matthew Broderick, Michael Higgins, Steven Hill, William Converse-Roberts, Rochelle Oliver, Richard Jenkins, Horton Foote Jr., Carol Goodheart; ***D:*** Ken Harrison; ***W:*** Horton Foote; ***M:*** Jonathan Sheffer.

On Wings of Eagles ½ **1986** During the 1979 Iranian revolution two American executives are imprisoned by Islamic radicals. Help arrives in the form of covert agents of their boss—Texas tycoon H. Ross Perot (played by Crenna). Don't expect strict historical veracity or insight from this network miniseries (based on the "nonfiction novel" by Ken Follett), an okay but lengthy "mission impossible." It came out in a two-cassette set, just in time for Perot's 1992 presidential campaign. **221m/C VHS.** Burt Lancaster, Richard Crenna, Paul LeMat, Esai Morales, Constance Towers, Jim Metzler, James Sutorius, Lawrence Pressman, Karen Carlson, Cyril O'Reilly; ***D:*** Andrew V. McLaglen.

On with the Show ½ **1929** A frantic backstage—and onstage—musical that cuts between the behind the scenes efforts to manage the make-or-break production that is in rehearsals during an out-of-town tryout. Has a classic showbiz cliche of the diva leading lady refusing to perform so the chorus girl goes on instead. Ethel Waters debuts what would become her signature tune 'Am I Blue?' Filmed in two-strip Technicolor but those prints have been lost. **104m/B DVD.** Betty Compson, Louise Fazenda, Sally O'Neil, Joe E. Brown, Arthur Lake, William "Billy" Bakewell, Purnell Pratt, Wheeler Oakman, Lee Moran, Sam Hardy; ***D:*** Alan Crosland; ***W:*** Robert Lord; ***C:*** Antonio Gaudio.

Onassis ½ *The Richest Man in the World: The Story of Aristotle Onassis* **1988** Romanticized biography of Greek shipping magnate Aristotle Onassis, from the poverty of his youth to his later wealth and family and romantic liaisons and tragedies. Julia is adequate as the title character but English actress Annis is badly miscast as Jackie Kennedy Onassis. However, Seymour is terrific as Onassis's lover, opera star Maria Callas. Quinn, who played Onassis in "The Greek Tycoon," plays Onassis's father in this one. Miniseries based on the novel by Peter Evans. **120m/C VHS, DVD.** Raul Julia, Jane Seymour, Francesca Annis, Anthony Quinn, Anthony Zerbe, Lorenzo Quinn; ***D:*** Waris Hussein. **TV**

Once **2006 (R)** Simple story, cool soundtrack. A nameless guy (singer-songwriter Hansard) works at his dad's vacuum repair shop and busks on the Dublin streets, still hoping to make his musical dreams come true. He meets a young Czech immigrant (Irglova), also a musician-songwriter, who wants them to team up. There's a hint of romance but it's the music that really draws them together. **86m/C DVD.** *IR* Glen Hansard, Marketa Irglova; ***D:*** John Carney; ***W:*** John Carney; ***C:*** Tim Fleming; ***M:*** Glen Hansard, Marketa Irglova. Oscars '07: Song ("Falling Slowly"); Ind. Spirit '08: Foreign Film.

Once a Hero **1988** The dregs of society, the Cicero Gang, have taken Captain Justice's number one fan and his mother hostage. Is it really curtains for rosy cheeks, bubble gum, and apple pie? But wait, it's Captain Justice, the man, the myth, to the rescue! **74m/C VHS.** Jeff Lester, Robert Forster, Milo O'Shea; ***D:*** Claudia Weill.

Once a Thief *Zong Heng Si Hai* **1990 (R)** Minor Woo. Three orphaned children are raised to be thieves by crime boss/surrogate father Chow (Tsang). As adults, Joe (Chow), Jim (Cheung), and Cherie (Chung) have just completed another successful art heist and Cherie thinks it's time they retire. Instead, they agree to one last job—stealing a painting from a heavily guarded French villa. But it turns out to be a set-up and Joe is apparently killed. He returns, in a wheelchair, two years later—seeking revenge against Chow, who betrayed them. Chinese with subtitles. Woo went on to use a variation of this premise for his TV movie/series of the same name. **108m/C VHS, DVD.** *HK* Chow Yun-Fat, Leslie Cheung, Cherie Chung, Kenneth Tsang; ***D:*** John Woo; ***W:*** John Woo.

Once a Thief **1996 (R)** A fun and action-packed TV movie finds adopted children Li Ann (Holt) and Mac (Sergei) being raised along with natural son Michael (Wong) by Hong Kong crime head Tang (Ito) and trained as daring professional thieves. A falling out finds Li Ann in Vancouver, involved with ex-cop Victor (Lea), and both of them working for a covert crime-fighting agency headed by a very tough director (Dale). Then Mac is forced to join the duo in an elaborate heist to bring down Michael and his family's criminal empire. Woo's director's cut contains additional footage. **101m/C VHS, DVD.** Ivan Sergei, Sandrine Holt, Nicholas Lea, Michael Wong, Robert Ito, Jennifer Dale, Alan Scarfe; ***D:*** John Woo; ***W:*** Glenn Davis, William Laurin; ***C:*** Bill Wong; ***M:*** Amin Bhatia.

Once Around ½ **1991 (R)** 30ish, lonely Renata Bella (Hunter) meets boisterous, self-assured (read utterly obnoxious) Lithuanian salesman Sam Sharpe (Dreyfuss). He sweeps her off her feet, showers her with affection and gifts, and then tries hard—too hard—to please her close-knit Italian family. Casting doesn't get much better than the group assembled here and Hallstrom steers everyone to wonderful performances in his American directorial debut. The major flaw is the script, a light romantic comedy that sometimes swerves into heavy drama, so much so that you may need Kleenex. **115m/C VHS, DVD.** Richard Dreyfuss, Holly Hunter, Danny Aiello, Gena Rowlands, Laura San Giacomo, Roxanne Hart, Danton Stone, Tim Guinee, Greg Germann, Griffin Dunne; ***D:*** Lasse Hallstrom; ***W:*** Malia Scotch Marmo; ***M:*** James Horner.

Once Before I Die ½ **1965** Army soldiers caught in the Philippines during WWII struggle to survive and elude the Japanese. A single woman traveling with them becomes the object of their spare time considerations. A brutal, odd, and gritty war drama. Director/actor Derek was Andress' husband at the time. **97m/C VHS.** *PH* Ursula Andress, John Derek, Richard Jaeckel, Rod Lauren, Ron Ely; ***D:*** John Derek.

Once Bitten **1985 (PG-13)** Centuries-old though still remarkably youthful vampiress comes to LA to stalk male virgins. That may be the wrong city, but she needs their blood to retain her young countenance. Vampire comedy theme was more effectively explored in 1979s "Love at First Bite," notable, however for the screen debut of comic Carrey who would later gain fame for TV's "In Living Color" and "Ace Ventura, Pet Detective." **94m/C VHS, DVD.** Lauren Hutton, Jim Carrey, Cleavon Little, Karen Kopins, Thomas Balltore, Skip Lackey; ***D:*** Howard Storm; ***W:*** Jonathan Roberts, David Hines, Jeffrey Hause; ***C:*** Adam Greenberg; ***M:*** John Du Prez.

Once in Paris... ½ **1979 (PG)** A bittersweet romance about a scriptwriter working in Paris, the chauffeur who befriends him, and the aristocratic British woman with whom the writer falls in love. Beautiful French scenery and the engaging performance of Lenoir as the chauffeur make this film a diverting piece of entertainment. **100m/C VHS.** Wayne Rogers, Gayle Hunnicutt, Jack Lenoir; ***D:*** Frank D. Gilroy; ***W:*** Frank D. Gilroy.

Once in the Life ½ **2000 (R)** Fishburne transfers his 1995 Off Broadway play "Riff Raff" to the big screen but its stage antecedents are apparent. 20/20 Mike (Fishburne) has hooked up with his heroin-addicted white half-brother Torch (Welliver) and they have trouble over a drug score gone wrong that has enraged local boss Manny (Calderon). Manny has sent henchman Tony the Tiger (Walker) to take care of things, even though Tony and Mike are old prison buddies. The film basically turns into a talky, one-set triangle leading to inevitable tragedy. **107m/C VHS, DVD.** Laurence Fishburne, Titus Welliver, Eamonn Walker, Paul Calderon, Dominic Chianese, Gregory Hines, Annabella Sciorra, Michael Paul Chan, Nicholas Chinlund, Jim Breuer; ***D:*** Laurence Fishburne; ***W:*** Laurence Fishburne; ***C:*** Richard Turner; ***M:*** Branford Marsalis.

Once Is Not Enough ½ *Jacqueline Susann's Once is Not Enough* **1975 (R)** Limp trash-drama concerning the young daughter of a has-been movie producer who has a tempestuous affair with a writer who reminds her of her father. Based on the novel by Jacqueline Susann. **121m/C VHS.** Kirk Douglas, Deborah Raffin, David Janssen, George Hamilton, Brenda Vaccaro, Alexis Smith, Melina Mercouri; ***D:*** Guy Green; ***W:*** Julius J. Epstein; ***C:*** John A. Alonzo; ***M:*** Henry Mancini. Golden Globes '76: Support. Actress (Vaccaro).

Once Upon a Brothers Grimm **1977** An original musical fantasy in which the Brothers Grimm meet a succession of their most famous storybook characters including Hansel and Gretel, the Gingerbread Lady, Little Red Riding Hood, and Rumpelstiltskin. **102m/C VHS.** Dean Jones, Paul Sand, Cleavon Little, Ruth Buzzi, Chita Rivera, Teri Garr; ***D:*** Norman Campbell; ***M:*** Mitch Leigh. **TV**

Once Upon a Crime ½ **1992 (PG)** Extremely disappointing comedy featuring a high profile cast set in Europe. The plot centers around Young and Lewis finding a dachshund and travelling from Rome to Monte Carlo to return the stray and collect a $5,000 reward. Upon arrival in Monte Carlo, they find the dog's owner dead and they end up getting implicated for the murder. Other prime suspects include Belushi, Candy, Hamilton, and Shepherd. Weak script is made bearable only by the comic genius of Candy. **94m/C VHS, DVD.** John Candy, James Belushi, Cybill Shepherd, Sean Young, Richard Lewis, Ornella Muti, Giancarlo Giannini, George Hamilton, Joss Ackland, Elsa Martinelli; ***D:*** Eugene Levy; ***M:*** Richard Gibbs.

Once Upon a Forest **1993 (G)** Animated tale of three woodland creatures in a daring race against time when their young friend's life is at stake. Ecologically correct story by "American Tail" creator David Kirschner is light on humor and heavy on gloom, as little animals encounter oppressive human society and their big, bad machines. Servicable animation, though not up to Don Bluth standards (and a long, long way from Disney). Crawford, the voice of the wise old uncle, has a song, while Vereen breaks into a fervent gospel number as a marsh bird with a yen for preaching. For an evening of anti-pollution, treat the earth kindly animation, see it with "Ferngully." **80m/C VHS, DVD.** ***D:*** Charles Grosvenor; ***W:*** Mark Young, Kelly Ward; ***V:*** Michael Crawford, Ben Vereen.

Once Upon a Honeymoon ½ **1942** Set in 1938, Grant is an American radio broadcaster reporting on the oncoming war. Rogers is the ex-showgirl who unknowingly marries a Nazi. In this strange, uneven comedy, Grant tries to get the goods on him and also rescue Rogers. The plot is basic and uneven with Grant attempting to expose the Nazi and save Rogers. However, the slower moments are offset by some fairly surreal pieces of comedy. **116m/B VHS.** Ginger Rogers, Cary Grant, Walter Slezak, Albert Dekker; ***D:*** Leo McCarey; ***C:*** George Barnes.

Once Upon a Midnight Scary **1990** Price narrates a collection of three tales of terror, "The Ghost Belonged to Me," "The Legend of Sleepy Hollow," and "The House with a Clock in Its Walls." Aimed at the kiddies. **50m/C VHS.** Rene Auberjonois, Severn Darden; ***D:*** Neil Cox; ***Nar:*** Vincent Price.

Once Upon a Scoundrel ½ **1973 (G)** A ruthless Mexican land baron arranges to have a young woman's fiancee thrown in jail so he can have her all to himself. **90m/C VHS.** Zero Mostel, Katy Jurado, Titos Vandis, Priscilla Garcia, A. Martinez; ***D:*** George Schaefer; ***M:*** Alex North.

Once Upon a Time in America ½ **1984 (R)** The uncut, original version of Leone's epic saga of five friends from a rough Jewish neighborhood in Brooklyn who grow up to be powerful Mob figures during Prohibition and try to keep their friendships and loyalties intact. Told, mostly in flashback, from the persepective of "Noodles" Aaronson (De Niro) as an old man looking back on a lifetime of crime, love, and death, with a sweeping and violent elegance. **229m/C VHS, DVD.** Robert De Niro, James Woods, Elizabeth McGovern, Tuesday Weld, Treat Williams, James Hayden, Joe Pesci, Danny Aiello, William Forsythe, Burt Young, Darlanne Fluegel, Robert Harper, Richard Bright, Mario Brega, Frank Gio, Jennifer Connelly, Brian Bloom, James Russo, Tandy Cronyn, Marcia Jean Kurtz, Estelle Harris; ***D:*** Sergio Leone; ***W:*** Sergio Leone, Leonardo Benvenuti, Piero De Bernardi, Enrico Medioli, Franco Arcalli, Franco Ferrini; ***C:*** Tonino Delli Colli; ***M:*** Ennio Morricone. British Acad. '84: Costume Des., Orig. Score.

Once Upon a Time in China *Wong Fei-hung* **1991** Martial arts expert Wong Fei-hung (Li) is dismayed as his country is overrun with western influences and the slave trade that provides labor to the California gold fields. When his aunt is kidnapped by slavers, Wong is determined to get revenge. The DVD edition clocks in at 134 minutes. **100m/C VHS, DVD.** *HK* Jet Li, Yuen Biao, Jacky Cheung, Rosamund Kwan, Kent Cheng; ***D:*** Tsui Hark; ***W:*** Tsui Hark; ***C:*** Arthur Wong Ngok Tai, David Chung; ***M:*** James Wong.

Once Upon a Time in China II *Wong Fei-hung Ji Yi: Naam Yi Dong Ji Keung* **1992 (R)** Wong (Li), his assistant Foon, and his aunt arrive in the city of Canton for a medical conference at which Wong is to demonstrate the Chinese art of acupuncture. But the city is on the brink of anarchy as a crumbling dynasty threatens its stability. So Wong joins the revolutionary Sun Yat Sen when a terrorist group initiates a campaign of violence. Dubbed into English. **112m/C VHS, DVD.** *HK* Jet Li, Rosamund Kwan, Mok Siu Chung, Xin-Xin Xiong, John Chiang, Zhang Tie Lin, Yen Chi Tan; ***D:*** Tsui Hark; ***W:*** Tsui Hark; ***C:*** Wong Ngok Tai; ***M:*** Richard Yuen.

Once Upon a Time in China III *Wong Fei-hung Tsi Sam: Siwong Tsangba* **1993 (R)** Wong Fei-Hung, his young aunt-by-adoption Yee (to whom he is secretly engaged), and his friend Chung arrive in Peking just as the Empress announces an important martial arts contest. Wong faces rivals on two fronts: a brutal martial arts foe and a Russian diplomat who has a history with Yee. **105m/C VHS, DVD.** *HK* Jet Li, Rosamund Kwan, Mok Siu Chung, Xin-Xin Xiong, Shun Lau; ***D:*** Tsui Hark; ***W:*** Tsui Hark; ***C:*** Wai Keung (Andrew) Lau; ***M:*** Wai Lap Wu.

Once Upon a Time in Mexico **2003 (R)** The last in Rodriguez's "El Mariachi" trilogy. El Mariachi (Banderas) is enlisted by corrupt CIA agent Sands to take part in a coup against the President of Mexico. The coup is being planned by vicious cartel leader Barillo (Dafoe) and crooked Gen. Marquez, both of whom want to see El Mariachi dead (and the feeling is mutual). Confusing plot twists and twirls around flashbacks, doublecrosses, triplecrosses, and at least three different subplots to keep you guessing about what's going on and who's on whose side. The top-notch cast keeps it all together (especially Depp, who walks away with every scene he's in), under the playful guidance of Rodriguez, who doesn't disappoint with several spectacular action scenes. **101m/C VHS, DVD, UMD.** *US* Antonio Banderas, Johnny Depp, Willem Dafoe, Salma Hayek, Mickey Rourke, Eva Mendes, Danny Trejo, Enrique Inglesias, Marco Leonardi, Richard "Cheech" Marin, Ruben Blades, Pedro Armendariz Jr., Gerardo Vigil; ***D:*** Robert Rodriguez; ***W:*** Robert Rodriguez; ***C:*** Robert Rodriguez; ***M:*** Robert Rodriguez.

Once Upon a Time in the Midlands **2002 (R)** Small-time criminal Jimmy (Carlyle) decides to take a second chance on romance in this fitfully engaging comedy. Jimmy sees ex-girlfriend Shirley (Henderson) on a TV chat show where she's just turned down the marriage proposal of her current beau Dek (Ifans). He decides to try to win Shirley back—and he needs to get out of town after literally being left holding the bag after a bungled robbery. Jimmy tries to insinuate himself into Shirley's good graces by making like a dad to their daughter Marlene (Atkins) and having several ineffectual showdowns with Dek. Then Jimmy's pissed-off cohorts come to town looking for their share of the loot and more trouble ensues. **104m/C VHS, DVD.** *GB* Robert Carlyle, Rhys Ifans, Shirley Henderson, Kathy Burke, Ricky Tomlinson, Finn Atkins; ***D:*** Shane Meadows; ***W:*** Shane Meadows, Paul Fraser; ***C:*** Brian Tufano; ***M:*** John Lunn.

Once Upon a Time in the West 1/2 **1968 (PG)** The uncut version of Leone's sprawling epic about a band of ruthless gunmen who set out to murder a mysterious woman waiting for the railroad to come through. Filmed in John Ford's Monument Valley, it's a revisionist western with some of the longest opening credits in the history of the cinema. Fonda is cast against type as an extremely cold-blooded villain. Brilliant musical score. **165m/C VHS, DVD.** *IT* Henry Fonda, Jason Robards Jr., Charles Bronson, Claudia Cardinale, Keenan Wynn, Lionel Stander, Woody Strode, Jack Elam; ***D:*** Sergio Leone; ***W:*** Sergio Leone, Bernardo Bertolucci, Dario Argento; ***C:*** Tonino Delli Colli; ***M:*** Ennio Morricone. Natl. Film Reg. '09.

Once Upon a Time ... When We Were Colored **1995 (PG)** Actor Reid makes a fine directorial debut with the story of a black youngster growing up parentless in '50s Mississippi. His family faces the usual troubles of the time, including poor wages and white bigotry, but manages to provide a positive and loving home life for him. Nostalgic, sensitive, and heartwarming adaptation of Clifton Taulbert's autobiographical book. **112m/C VHS, DVD.** Al Freeman Jr., Paula Kelly, Phylicia Rashad, Polly Bergen, Richard Roundtree, Charles Taylor, Willie Norwood, Jr., Damon Hines, Leon; ***D:*** Tim Reid; ***W:*** Paul Cooper; ***C:*** Johnny (John W.) Simmons; ***M:*** Steve Tyrell; ***Nar:*** Phill Lewis.

Once Upon a Wedding **2005 (PG)** Margarita (Ayanna), the daughter of an eccentric Caribbean dictator (Martinez), is just a week away from an arranged marriage to wealthy Manolo (de la Fuente). She accidentally runs over poor-but-handsome Rogelio (Becker) and takes him to the palace to recover. Of course when Margarita realizes she's fallen in love Dad isn't happy. **92m/C DVD.** Charlotte Ayanna, A. Martinez, Kuno Becker, Christian de la Fuente, Esai Morales; ***D:*** Matia Karrell; ***W:*** Reuben Gonzalez; ***C:*** Steven Finestone; ***M:*** Douglas G. Cuomo. **VIDEO**

Once Were Warriors **1994 (R)** Violent story of the struggling Maori Heke family, who have left their rural New Zealand roots to live in the city. Feisty mom Beth (Owen) is struggling with five kids and volatile hubby Jake (Heke), who's continuously out of work, boozing, and fighting. Eldest son Nig (Arahanga) has left home and joined a street gang and the rest of the kids hate Jake for beating up on their mother. They also fall victim to his temper and his habit of bringing his brawling, drunk buddies home-leading to further tragedy. Intense drama showcases great performances, with Owen honored as best actress at the Montreal World Film Festival. Based on the novel by Alan Duff. Feature-film directorial debut of Tamahori. **102m/C VHS, DVD.** *NZ* Rena Owen, Temuera Morrison, Mamaengaroa Kerr-Bell, Julian (Sonny) Arahanga, Taungaroa Emile, Rachael Morris, Joseph Kairau, Pete Smith; ***D:*** Lee Tamahori; ***W:*** Riwia Brown; ***C:*** Stuart Dryburgh; ***M:*** Murray Grindlay, Murray McNabb. Australian Film Inst. '95: Foreign Film; Montreal World Film Fest. '94: Actress (Owen), Film.

The One **2001 (PG-13)** The premise of this action-intensive martial arts flick is that there are 125 parallel universes, and that each person has a counterpart in all of them. Gabriel Yulaw (Li) is a renegade Multiverse Bureau of Investigation agent who is killing his fellow selves in order to absorb their energy. He has fellow MBI agents Roedecker (Lindo) and Funsch (Statham) after him, but he only has one Gabe left to kill, this one a hardworking L.A. deputy sheriff. Bad Gabe kills good Gabe's wife, and the stage is set for a showdown in a grungy factory. Did you follow all of that? Well, it doesn't matter, because it's all just an excuse to have Jet Li kick Jet Li's butt on a catwalk to the sounds of grating techno/metal. Should have added a touch of humor to a completely ludicrous plot instead of concentrating on stealing special effects from "The Matrix." **80m/C VHS, DVD.** *US* Jet Li, Delroy Lindo, Carla Gugino, Jason Statham, Dylan Bruno, Richard Steinmetz, James Morrison; ***D:*** James Wong; ***W:*** Glen Morgan, James Wong; ***C:*** Robert McLachlan; ***M:*** Trevor Rabin.

One Against the Wind **1991 (PG)** A true story of one woman's courage against great odds. British Mary Liddell and her children are living in Paris during the WWII Nazi occupation. Mary's secret agenda is to smuggle downed Allied pilots out of the country to safety without arousing Nazi suspicions. Great performances by Davis as the resourceful Mary and Neill as one of the pilots she rescues. A Hallmark Hall of Fame presentation. **96m/C VHS.** Judy Davis, Sam Neill, Denholm Elliott, Anthony (Corlan) Higgins, Christien Anholt, Kate Beckinsale, Frank Middlemass, Benedick Blythe, Peter Cellier, Stefan Gryff, Mark Wing-Davey, John Savident, David Ryall, Tom Hodgkins, Wolf Kahler, Michael Crossman, Terry Taplin, Mikush Alexander; ***D:*** Larry Elikann; ***W:*** Chris Bryant; ***C:*** Denis Lewiston; ***M:*** Lee Holdridge. **TV**

One A.M. 1/2 **1916** Charlie is a drunk who must first battle a flight of stairs in order to get to bed. Silent with music track. **34m/B VHS, DVD.** Charlie Chaplin, Albert Austin; ***D:*** Charlie Chaplin; ***W:*** Charlie Chaplin; ***C:*** Roland H. Totheroh, William C. Foster.

The One and Only 1/2 **1978 (PG)** An egotistical young man is determined to make it in show business. Instead, he finds himself in the world of professional wrestling. Most of the humor comes from the wrestling scenes, with Winkler and Darby's love story only serving to dilute the film. **98m/C VHS.** Henry Winkler, Kim Darby, Gene Saks, William Daniels, Harold Gould, Herve Villechaize; ***D:*** Carl Reiner.

The One and Only, Genuine, Original Family Band **1968 (G)** A harmonious musical family becomes divided when various members take sides in the presidential battle between Benjamin Harrison and Grover Cleveland, a political era that has been since overlooked. **110m/C VHS, DVD.** Walter Brennan, Buddy Ebsen, Lesley Ann Warren, Kurt Russell, Goldie Hawn, Wally Cox, Richard Deacon, Janet Blair; ***D:*** Michael O'Herlihy.

One Arabian Night *Sumurun* **1921** When an exotic dancer in a traveling carnival troupe is kidnapped into a harem, a dwarf acts on his unrequited love and avenges her death by murdering the sheik who killed her. Secured a place in American filmmaking for director Lubitsch. **85m/B VHS, DVD.** *GE* Pola Negri, Ernst Lubitsch, Paul Wegener; ***D:*** Ernst Lubitsch.

One Armed Executioner **1980 (R)** An Interpol agent seeks revenge on his wife's murderers. **90m/C VHS.** Franco Guerrero, Jody Kay; ***D:*** Bobby A. Auarez.

One Away **1976** Gypsy escapes from a South African prison and the police are in hot pursuit. **83m/C VHS.** Elke Sommer, Bradford Dillman, Dean Stockwell; ***D:*** Sidney Hayers.

One Body Too Many **1944** A mystery spoof about a wacky insurance salesman who's mistaken for a detective. The usual comedy of errors ensues. A contrived mish-mash—but it does have Lugosi going for it. **75m/B VHS, DVD.** Jack Haley, Jean Parker, Bela Lugosi, Lyle Talbot, Blanche Yurka, Douglas Fowley, Fay Helm, Lucien Littlefield, Dorothy Granger; ***D:*** Frank McDonald; ***W:*** Maxwell Shane, Winston Miller; ***C:*** Fred H. Jackman Jr.; ***M:*** Alexander Laszlo.

One Brief Summer **WOOF! 1970 (R)** Love triangles and intrigues abound on a spectacular country manor. An aging woman is mortified by her father's interest in a young seductress, who finds herself attracted to the old man, but not only him. **86m/C VHS.** Clifford Evans, Felicity Gibson, Jennifer Hilary, Jan Holden, Peter Egan; ***D:*** John MacKenzie.

One Christmas 1/2 *Truman Capote's One Christmas* **1995** Conman father uses his estranged son as a pawn to gain access to New Orleans high society. Based on the story "One Christmas" by Truman Capote. **91m/C VHS, DVD.** Katharine Hepburn, Henry Winkler, Swoosie Kurtz, T.J. Lowther, Pat Hingle, Julie Harris; ***D:*** Tony Bill; ***W:*** Duane Poole; ***M:*** Van Dyke Parks. **TV**

One Cooks, the Other Doesn't **1983** A most unlikely story of a man's ex-wife and his son moving back into his house, where he's now living with his new wife. **96m/C VHS.** Suzanne Pleshette, Joseph Bologna, Rosanna Arquette, Oliver Clark; ***D:*** Richard Michaels. **TV**

One Crazy Night 1/2 **1993 (PG-13)** In 1964, five Australian teenagers try to get into the Melbourne hotel where the Beatles are staying on tour. They wind up trapped in the basement, swapping secrets, and finding out how much they have in common. **92m/C VHS.** *AU* Noah Taylor, Beth Champion, Malcolm Kennard, Danni Minogue, Malcolm Braly; ***D:*** Michael Pattinson.

One Crazy Summer 1/2 **1986 (PG)** A group of wacky teens spends a fun-filled summer on Nantucket Island in New England. Follow-up to "Better Off Dead" is offbeat and fairly charming, led by Cusack's perplexed cartoonist and with comic moments delivered by Goldthwait. **94m/C VHS, DVD.** John Cusack, Demi Moore, William Hickey, Curtis Armstrong, Bob(cat) Goldthwait, Mark Metcalf, Joel Murray, Tom Villard, Joe Flaherty; ***D:*** Savage Steve Holland; ***W:*** Savage Steve Holland; ***M:*** Cory Lerios.

One Dark Night 1/2 *Entity Force; Mausoleum* **1982 (R)** Two high school girls plan an initiation rite for one of their friends who is determined to shed her "goody-goody" image. West is the caped crusader of TV series "Batman" fame. **94m/C VHS, DVD.** Meg Tilly, Adam West, David Mason Daniels, Robin Evans, Elizabeth (E.G. Dailey) Daily; ***D:*** Tom McLoughlin.

One Day in the Life of Ivan Denisovich **1971** The film version of Nobel Prize-winner Alexander Solzhenitsyn's novel about a prisoner's experiences in a Soviet labor camp. A testament to human endurance. Photography be Sven Nykvist. **105m/C VHS.** *NO GB* Tom Courtenay, Alfred Burke, Espen Skjonberg, James Maxwell, Eric Thompson; ***D:*** Casper Wrede; ***W:*** Ronald Harwood; ***C:*** Sven Nykvist.

One Day You'll Understand *Later; Plus Tard* **2008** Jewish WII survivor Rivka (Moreau) is quietly living in Paris in 1987 when her son Victor (Girardot) discovers an Aryan declaration among his late father's papers that was designed to protect the family from Nazi persecution. Since Rivka refuses to discuss the past, Victor and his family travel to the small French town where Rivka's parents sheltered before they were deported to Auschwitz. Increasingly agitated, Victor delves into his family's possibly anti-Semitic activities during the war. French with subtitles. **90m/C DVD.** *FR* Jeanne Moreau, Hippolyte Giradot, Emmanuelle Devos, Dominique Blanc; ***D:*** Amos Gitai; ***W:*** Dan Franck, Jerome Clement; ***C:*** Caroline Champetier; ***M:*** Louis Sclavis.

One Deadly Owner **1974** A possessed Rolls-Royce tortures its new owner. Quite a vehicle for the usually respectable set of wheels. **80m/C VHS.** *GB* Donna Mills, Jeremy Brett, Robert Morris, Laurence Payne; ***D:*** Ian Fordyce; ***W:*** Brian Clemens; ***M:*** Laurie Johnson. **TV**

One Deadly Summer *L'Ete Meurtrier* **1983 (R)** Revenge drama about a young girl who returns to her mother's home village to ruin three men who had assaulted her mother years before. Very well acted. From the novel by Sebastien Japrisot. In French with English subtitles. **134m/C VHS.** *FR* Isabelle Adjani, Alain Souchon, Suzanne Flon; ***D:*** Jean Becker; ***M:*** Georges Delerue. Cesar '84: Actress (Adjani), Support. Actress (Flon), Writing.

One Down, Two to Go! **WOOF! 1982 (R)** When the mob is discovered to be rigging a championship karate bout, two dynamic expert fighters join in a climactic battle against the hoods. Example of really bad "blaxploitation" that wastes talent, film, and the audience's time. **84m/C VHS, DVD.** Jim Brown, Fred Williamson, Jim Kelly, Richard Roundtree, Tom Signorelli, Joe Spinell, Paula Sills, Laura Loftus; ***D:*** Fred Williamson; ***W:*** Jeff Williamson; ***C:*** James (Momel) Lemmo; ***M:*** Herb Hetzer, Joe Trunzo.

187 1/2 **1997 (R)** Jackson's a Brooklyn high school teacher who is brutally attacked by one of his students. His physical scars are healed, but his emotional state is marred as he takes some pretty unorthodox teaching methods to a troubled L.A. school. Very dark, psychological drama with a powerful performance by Jackson. Tough film whose title refers to the California penal code number for murder. First film from director Reynolds after his "Waterworld" fiasco. **119m/C VHS, DVD.** Samuel L. Jackson, John Heard, Kelly Rowan, Clifton (Gonzalez) Collins Jr., Tony Plana, Lobo Sebastian, Jack Kehler, Demetrius Navarro, Karina Arroyave; ***D:*** Kevin Reynolds; ***W:*** Scott Yagemann; ***C:*** Ericson Core.

One-Eyed Jacks 1/2 **1961** An often engaging, but lengthy, psychological western about an outlaw who seeks to settle the score with a former partner who became a sheriff. Great acting by all, particularly Brando, who triumphed both as star and director. Stanley Kubrick was the original director, but Brando took over mid-way through the filming. The photography is wonderful and reflects the effort that went into it. **141m/C VHS, DVD.** Marlon Brando, Karl Malden, Katy Jurado, Elisha Cook Jr., Slim Pickens, Ben Johnson, Pina Pellicer, Timothy Carey; ***D:*** Marlon Brando; ***W:*** Calder Willingham; ***C:*** Charles B(ryant) Lang Jr.

One-Eyed Soldiers **1967** Young woman, criminal, and dwarf follow trail to mysterious key to unlock $15 million treasure. Much cheesy intrigue. **83m/C VHS, DVD.** *GB YU* Dale Robertson, Luciana Paluzzi; ***D:*** Jean Christopher.

One-Eyed Swordsman **1963** A handicapped samurai battles shogun warriors. With English subtitles. **95m/C VHS.** *JP* Tetsuro Tamba, Haruko Wanibuchi; ***D:*** Seiichiro Uchikawa.

One False Move **1991 (R)** Black psycho Pluto, his white-trash partner Ray, and Ray's biracial lover Fantasia are three low-level drug dealers on the streets of Los Angeles who get involved in murder. Fleeing the city for Fantasia's small hometown in Arkansas, they come up against the local sheriff and two L.A. cops sent to bring them back. Not a typical crime thriller, first-time feature director Franklin is more interested in a psychological character study of racism and smalltown mores than in your average shoot 'em up action picture. Good performances, especially by Williams as the deceptive bad girl. **105m/C VHS, DVD.** Bill Paxton, Cynda Williams, Michael Beach, Jim Metzler, Earl Billings, Billy Bob Thornton, Natalie Canerday, Robert Ginnaven, Robert Anthony Bell, Kevin Hunter; ***D:*** Carl Franklin; ***W:*** Billy Bob Thornton, Tom Epperson; ***C:*** James L. Carter; ***M:*** Peter Haycock, Derek Holt. Ind. Spirit '93: Director (Franklin); MTV Movie Awards '93: New Filmmaker (Franklin).

One Fine Day 1/2 **1996 (PG)** Marshmallows. That's what this movie is like—light, fluffy, not much substance, but enjoyable when you're in the mood. Nod to the classic screwball comedies of the '40s and '50s throws harried single mom/architect Pfeiffer and political columnist/weekend dad Clooney together when their kids, who attend the same school, miss a class field trip. Naturally, they take an instant dislike to each other, but are forced to cooperate to solve the daycare situation. An accidental switching of cell phones provides the chance for repeated encounters, and growing mutual interest. Predictable, but pleasantly so. No matter how hard she tries, Pfeiffer always looks good, and Clooney has that cocked head, devilish grin thing working overtime. Screenplay by Neil Simon's daughter Ellen supplies all the elements for a fine date movie. **108m/C VHS, DVD.** Michelle Pfeiffer, George Clooney, Alex D. Linz, Mae Whitman, Charles Durning, Jon Robin Baitz, Ellen Greene, Joe Grifasi, Pete Hamill, Anna Maria Horsford, Sheila Kelley, Barry Kivel, Robert Klein, George Martin, Michael Massee, Amanda Peet, Bitty Schram, Holland Taylor, Rachel York; ***D:*** Michael Hoffman; ***W:*** Terrel Seltzer, Ellen Simon; ***C:*** Oliver Stapleton; ***M:*** James Newton Howard.

One Flew Over the Cuckoo's Nest **1975 (R)** Touching, hilarious, dramatic, and completely effective adaptation of Ken Kesey's novel. Nicholson is two-bit crook Randle Patrick McMurphy, who, facing a jail sentence, feigns insanity to be sentenced to a cushy mental hospital. The hospital is anything but cushy, with tyrannical head nurse Ratched (Fletcher) out to squash any vestige of the patients' independence. Nicholson proves to be a crazed messiah and catalyst for these mentally troubled patients and a worthy adversary for the head nurse. Classic performs superbly on numerous levels. **129m/C VHS, DVD.** Jack Nicholson, Brad Dourif, Louise Fletcher, Will Sampson, William Redfield, Danny DeVito, Christopher Lloyd, Scatman Crothers, Vincent Schiavelli, Michael Berryman, Peter Brocco, Louisa Moritz; ***D:*** Milos Forman; ***W:*** Ken Kesey, Bo Goldman; ***C:*** Haskell Wexler, Bill Butler, William A. Fraker; ***M:*** Jack Nitzsche. Oscars '75: Actor (Nicholson), Actress (Fletcher), Adapt. Screenplay, Director (Forman), Picture; AFI '98: Top 100; British Acad. '76: Actor (Nicholson), Actress (Fletcher), Director (Forman), Film, Support. Actor (Dourif); Directors Guild '75: Director (Forman); Golden Globes '76: Actor—Drama (Nicholson), Actress—Drama (Fletcher), Director (Forman), Film—Drama, Screenplay; Natl. Bd. of Review '75: Actor (Nicholson), Natl. Film Reg. '93;; N.Y. Film Critics '75: Actor (Nicholson); Natl. Soc. Film Critics '75: Actor (Nicholson); Writers Guild '75: Adapt. Screenplay.

One for the Road *Against All Hope* **1982** Michael Madsen's screen debut is unwatchable in this atrocious movie. He plays alcoholic Cecil Moe who's trying to straighten himself out. **90m/C VHS, DVD.** Michael Madsen, Maureen McCarthy, Rex Flores, Tim Joosten, Herb Harms, Ron Schultz; ***D:*** Edward T. McDougal.

One Frightened Night 1/2 **1935** An eccentric millionaire informs his family members that he is leaving each of them $1 million...as long as his long-lost granddaughter doesn't reappear. Guess who comes to dinner. **69m/B VHS, DVD.** Mary Carlisle, Wallace Ford, Hedda Hopper, Charley Grapewin; ***D:*** Christy Cabanne.

One from the Heart **1982 (R)** The film more notable for sinking Coppola's Zoetrope Studios than for its cinematic context. Garr and Forrest are a jaded couple who seek romantic excitement with other people. An extravagant (thus Coppola's finance problems) fantasy Las Vegas set, pretty to look at but does little to enhance the weak plot. Score by Waits, a much-needed plus. **100m/C VHS, DVD.** Teri Garr, Frederic Forrest, Nastassja Kinski, Raul Julia, Lainie Kazan, Rebecca De Mornay, Harry Dean Stanton; ***D:*** Francis Ford Coppola; ***W:*** Armyan Bernstein, Francis Ford Coppola; ***M:*** Tom Waits, Robert Alcivar.

One Good Cop 1/2 **1991 (R)** A noble, inconsistent attempt to do a police thriller with a human face, as a young officer and his wife adopt the three little daughters of his slain partner from the force. But it reverts to a routine action wrapup, with 'Batman' Keaton even donning a masked-avenger getup to get revenge. **105m/C VHS, DVD.** Michael Keaton, Rene Russo, Anthony LaPaglia, Kevin Conway, Rachel Ticotin, Grace Johnston, Blair Swanson, Rhea Silver-Smith, Tony Plana, Benjamin Bratt, Charlaine Woodard, Lisa Arrindell Anderson; ***D:*** Heywood Gould; ***W:*** Heywood Gould; ***C:*** Ralf Bode; ***M:*** William Ross.

One Good Turn **1995 (R)** Matt Forrest (Von Dohlen) and his wife Laura (Amis) seemingly have it all only to have their fortunes take a radical turn for the worse. Matt "accidentally" runs into Simon Jury (Remar), the man who saved his life 12 years before. But the seemingly friendly Jury is actually intent on destroying everything they have. **90m/C VHS, DVD.** Lenny Von Dohlen, James Remar, Suzy Amis, John Savage; ***D:*** Tony Randel; ***W:*** Jim Piddock; ***C:*** Jacques Haitkin; ***M:*** Joel Goldsmith.

One Hour Photo **2002 (R)** Creepy thriller with Williams treading new ground as Seymour Parrish, Sy the Photo Guy, a disturbed and disturbing one-hour photo clerk. While seeming the mild Milquetoast, Sy becomes a tad obsessed with the suburban Yorkin family, idealizing them in the process. After years of viewing their happiest moments frozen in time, he decides to get involved in their lives when he sees trouble brewing. A breakthrough performance by Williams, he creates an off-kilter character that is surprisingly sympathetic. Romanek's direction is clever and extremely stylish, avoiding cliche, to craft a gripping psychodrama. **98m/C VHS, DVD.** *US* Robin Williams, Connie Nielsen, Michael Vartan, Gary Cole, Eriq La Salle, Dylan Smith, Erin Daniels, Andy Comeau; ***D:*** Mark Romanek; ***W:*** Mark Romanek; ***C:*** Jeff Cronenweth; ***M:*** Reinhold Heil, Johnny Klimek.

One Hour with You 1/2 **1932** Lubitsch remade his 1924 silent, "The Marriage," into this musical comedy. Parisian doctor Andre Bertier (Chavalier) may be wed to Colette (MacDonald) but that doesn't stop his roving eye. Married Mitzi (Tobin) has designs on Andre and when her suspicious husband (Young) threatens to name him in a divorce suit, Andre is forced to reveal all to the miffed Colette, who decides to get even. Cukor started out as director but quit because of producer Lubitsch's interference and he finished the picture himself. **80m/B DVD.** Maurice Chevalier, Charlie Ruggles, Jeanette MacDonald, Genevieve Tobin, Roland Young, Richard Carle, George Barbier, Joseph Dunn; ***D:*** Ernst Lubitsch, George Cukor; ***W:*** Samson Raphaelson; ***C:*** Victor Milner; ***M:*** Oscar Straus.

One Hundred and One Nights *Les Cent et Une Nuits; Les Cent et Une Nuits de Simon Cinema* **1995** Simon Cinema (Piccoli) is a 100-year-old producer/director whose memory is fading. So he hires young film student Camille (Gayet) to prompt his memory. Numerous celebrities make cameo appearances to talk about film and numerous film clips are shown. **101m/C VHS, DVD.** *FR GB* Michel Piccoli, Marcello Mastroianni, Henri Garcin, Julie Gayet, Mathieu Demy, Emmanuel Salinger; ***D:*** Agnes Varda; ***W:*** Agnes Varda; ***C:*** Eric Gautier.

100 Days Before the Command *Sto Dnej Do Pri Kaza* **1990** Five young Red Army recruits struggle for survival and to preserve their humanity against the violence of their daily lives by leaning on each other. Russian with subtitles. **71m/C VHS, DVD.** *RU* Vladimir Zamansky, Armen Dzhigarkhanyan, Oleg Vasilkov, Roman Grekov, Valeri Troshinl; ***D:*** Hussein Erkenov; ***W:*** Vladimir Kholodov, Yuri Polyakov; ***C:*** Vladislav Menshikov.

100 Feet 1/2 **2008 (R)** Janssen makes a good woman-in-peril in this chiller. Marnie Watson was convicted of manslaughter for killing her abusive NYPD husband Mike (Pare) and must finish out her sentence under house arrest tethered to an ankle monitor. Her late husband's partner Shanks (Cannavale) still thinks the murder was deliberate and he's keeping a close eye on Marnie, hoping she screws up. Then Marnie starts getting abused again—from Mike's very vengeful ghost. She can't get away so Marnie has to get rid of Mike for good this time (which turns out to be the weakest part of the plot). **101m/C DVD.** Famke Janssen, Bobby Cannavale, Michael Pare, Ed Westwick, John Fallon, Patricia Charbonneau, Kevin Geer; ***D:*** Eric Red; ***W:*** Eric Red; ***C:*** Ken Kelsch; ***M:*** John (Gianni) Frizzell. **VIDEO**

100 Girls **2000 (R)** College freshman Tucker (Tucker) scores an unexpected sexual encounter with a co-ed in the girls' dorm elevator during a blackout. He can't see her face and doesn't know her name, so he spends the semester investigating the 100 possibles in search of his mystery girl. Actually funny and not as sleazy as it may sound. **95m/C VHS, DVD.** Jonathan Tucker, James DeBello, Emmanuelle Chriqui, Larisa Oleynik, Jaime Pressly, Katherine Heigl; ***D:*** Michael Davis; ***W:*** Michael Davis; ***C:*** James Lawrence Spencer; ***M:*** Kevin Bassinson.

100 Men and a Girl **1937** Charming musical features Durbin as the daughter of an unemployed musician, who decides she will try to persuade Leopold Stokowski to help her launch an orchestra that will employ her father and his musician friends. Beautiful mix of classical and pop music. Based on a story by Hans Kraly. ♫Hungarian Rhapsody No. 2; Symphony No. 5; Alleluja; It's Raining Sunbeams; A Heart That's Free. **85m/B VHS, DVD.** Deanna Durbin, Leopold Stokowski, Adolphe Menjou, Alice Brady, Eugene Pallette, Mischa Auer, Billy Gilbert, Alma Kruger, Christian Rub, Jed Prouty, Jack Mulhall; ***D:*** Henry Koster; ***W:*** Charles Kenyon, Bruce Manning; ***C:*** Joseph Valentine. Oscars '37: Score.

100 Mile Rule 1/2 **2002 (R)** Dark comedy has a trio of salesman from Detroit discussing the "100 Mile Rule" en route to a business meeting in L.A. The rule states that a man is free to cheat on his girlfriend/spouse if he's over 100 miles away. Jerry is all for it, while family man Bobby wants no part of it. Bobby changes his tune when he meets Monica (Bello). After she seduces him, she blackmails him with a tape of the encounter, leading to murder and corporate backstabbing. Think "Very Bad Things" on business. Standard fare is helped along by McKean and Bello. **98m/C VHS, DVD.** Jake Weber, Maria Bello, David Thornton, Michael McKean, Nicholas Chinlund, David Dorfman, Shawn Huff; ***D:*** Brent Huff; ***W:*** Drew Pillsbury; ***C:*** Giovani Lampassi; ***M:*** Tor Hyams.

100 Monsters *Yokai hyaku monogatari; The Hundred Monsters; Yokai Monsters 2: 100 Monsters* **1968** The second film in the Yokai Monsters trilogy is a little more serious than the first. An evil magistrate decides to demolish a shrine and some adjacent apartments to build a brothel. The peasants try fighting back, but their landlord is murdered. A lone samurai agrees to help them, and he summons the Yokai to teach the magistrate a lesson. Not as well done as the first, but still different enough to be worth attention. One of the few known horror films starring an umbrella monster. **90m/C DVD.** *JP* Mikiko Tsubouchi, Ryutaro Gomi, Jun Fujimaki, Jun Hamamura, Tatsuo Hananuno, Masaru Hiraizumi, Takashi Kanda, Keiko Kayanagi, Koichi Ogura, Teruko Oumi, Rookie Shin-ichi, Shosaku Sugiyama, Miwa Takada, Yoshio Yoshida; ***D:*** Kimiyoshi Yasuda; ***W:*** Tetsuro Yoshida; ***C:*** Yasukazu Takemura; ***M:*** Michiaki Watanabe.

101 Ways (The Things a Girl Will Do to Keep Her Volvo) 1/2 **2000** Actually, struggling writer Watson (Hoopes) doesn't seem to be trying too hard to keep that car, which her mother insisted she purchase because of its safety record. Watson has moved from the bright lights of the Big Apple to the suburbs of Connecticut in order to concentrate on her career but since she has to pay the bills, she works ineffectually at a couple of nothing jobs. The flick itself is ineffectual and Watson isn't terribly likeable so who cares what happens to her. **100m/C DVD.** *US* Wendy Hoopes, Glenn Fitzgerald, Jamie Harrold, Jack Gilpin, Patricia Elliott, Gabriel Macht; ***D:*** Jennifer B. Katz; ***W:*** Jennifer B. Katz; ***C:*** Jeffrey A. Splett; ***M:*** John Hodian.

100 Proof **1996** Based on a 1986 murder rampage in Lexington, Kentucky. Rae (Stewart) and her compliant sidekick, Carla (Bellando), are a couple of smalltime, smalltown hustlers, with drug/booze habits, who turn tricks to get by. The day begins in its usual bleak fashion until Rae encounters her degenerate father (Varney), who routinely abused her. Rae's anger grows, fueled by cocaine and alcohol, until she snaps and begins shooting people. **94m/C VHS.** Pamela Stewart, Tara Bellando, Larry Brown, Jim Varney; ***D:*** Jeremy Horton; ***W:*** Jeremy Horton; ***C:*** Harold McNeese.

100 Rifles **1969 (R)** Native American bank robber and Black American lawman join up with a female Mexican revolutionary to help save the Mexican Indians from annihilation by a despotic military governor. What it lacks in political correctness it makes up for in fits of action. Although quite racy in its day for its interracial sex sizzle of Brown and Rachel, it's tame and overblown by today's standards. **110m/C VHS, DVD.** Jim Brown, Raquel Welch, Burt Reynolds, Fernando Lamas; ***D:*** Tom Gries; ***M:*** Jerry Goldsmith.

101 Dalmatians 1/2 **1961 (G)** Disney classic is one of the highest-grossing animated films in the history of Hollywood. Dogowners Roger and Anita, and their spotted pets Pongo and Perdita are shocked when their puppies are kidnapped by Cruella de Vil, villainess extraordinaire, to make a simply fabulous spotted coat. The aid of various animals including a dog named Colonel, a horse, a cat, and a goose is enlisted to rescue the doomed pups. Imagine their surprise when they find not only their own puppies, but 84 more as well. You can expect a happy ending and lots of spots—6,469,952 to be exact. Based on the children's book by Dodie Smith. Technically notable for the first time use of the Xerox process to transfer the animator's drawings onto celluloid, which made the film's opening sequence of dots evolving into 101 barking dogs possible. ♫ Remember When; Cruella de Vil; Dalmation Plantation; Kanine Krunchies Kommercial. **79m/C VHS, DVD.** ***D:*** Clyde Geronimi, Wolfgang Reitherman, Hamilton Luske; ***W:*** Bill Peet; ***M:*** George Bruns; ***V:*** Rod Taylor, Betty Lou Gerson, Lisa Davis, Ben Wright, Frederick Worlock, J. Pat O'Malley.

101 Dalmatians 🦴🦴 1/2 **1996 (G)** Yes, it's the live-action Disney version of their own 1961 animated feature (based on the book by Dodie Smith) about dog-napping villainess Cruella De Vil (Close) and lots of spotted pups. They're absolutely adorable, of course, Cruella's costumes (and hair) are certainly eye-catching, and the bumbling crooks get their proper comeuppance. Daniels and Richardson have the thankless role of the dogs' human owners, Roger and Anita, and get upstaged at every opportunity. Kids familiar with the cartoon pups may be surprised that the live pups don't talk—and keep in mind that Close, while terrific, may be too scary for the little ones. The Hound is always happy to see another dog movie but still feels some classics should be left alone. **103m/C VHS, DVD.** Glenn Close, Jeff Daniels, Joely Richardson, Joan Plowright, Hugh Laurie, Mark Williams; ***D:*** Stephen Herek; ***W:*** John Hughes; ***C:*** Adrian Biddle; ***M:*** Michael Kamen.

102 Dalmatians 🦴 1/2 **2000 (G)** Lackluster sequel to the 1996 live-action Disney film finds Cruella De Vil (Close) being released from prison and teaming up with fur designer Jean Pierre Le Pelt (Depardieu). She still wants that dalmatian fur coat (and this time a hood as well). The puppies are as cute as ever, with the addition of digitally de-spotted Oddball, but this one just seems like another excuse for Disney to print money and Close to chew scenery. Stick with the original (the 1961 cartoon version, that is). **100m/C VHS, DVD.** Glenn Close, Gerard Depardieu, Ioan Gruffudd, Tim (McInnerny) McInnery, Ian Richardson, Ben Crompton, Jim Carter, Ron Cook, David Horovitch, Timothy West, Alice Evans, Carol MacReady; ***D:*** Kevin Lima; ***W:*** Bob Tzudiker, Noni White, Kristen Buckley, Brian Regan; ***C:*** Adrian Biddle; ***M:*** David Newman; ***V:*** Eric Idle.

125 Rooms of Comfort 🦴🦴 **1983** A mental patient has bizarre fantasies that create the havoc among those who stand in his way. **82m/C VHS.** Tim Henry, Jackie Burroughs, Bob Warner, Bob Silverman, Les Barker; ***D:*** Patrick Loubert; ***W:*** Patrick Loubert, Bill Freut.

One in a Million 🦴🦴🦴 **1936** Debut film of Norwegian skating star Henie centers around a Swiss girl whose father is training her for the Olympics. Features good comedy by the Ritz Brothers and Sparks, as well as the beautiful skating of Henie. ♫ One in a Million; We're Back in Circulation Again; Who's Afraid of Love; Lovely Lady in White; The Moonlight Waltz. **95m/B VHS.** Sonja Henie, Adolphe Menjou, Jean Hersholt, Al Ritz, Harry Ritz, Jimmy Ritz, Arline Judge, Don Ameche, Ned Sparks, Montagu Love, Leah Ray; ***D:*** Sidney Lanfield; ***W:*** Leonard Praskins, Mark Kelly.

One in a Million: The Ron LeFlore Story 🦴🦴 1/2 **1978** The true story of Detroit Tigers' star Ron LeFlore, who rose from the Detroit ghetto to the major leagues. Adaptation of LeFlore's autobiography, "Breakout." A well-acted and compelling drama with Burton in a standout performance. **90m/C VHS.** LeVar Burton, Madge Sinclair, Billy Martin, James Luisi; ***D:*** William A. Graham; ***C:*** Jordan Cronenweth.

One Kill 🦴🦴🦴 **2000 (PG-13)** Fact-based drama focuses on a murder and a trial. Mary Jane O'Malley (Heche) is a decorated Marine captain and divorced mom who is having an affair with her troubled senior officer, Maj. Nelson Gray (Shepard). Mary Jane breaks things off when she finds out Nelson is married but he's obsessed and when he breaks into her home, she shoots him in self-defense. At least, the D.A. says justifiable homicide but the military has other ideas and decides to try O'Malley itself. Good performances by the leads. **93m/C VHS.** Anne Heche, Sam Shepard, Eric Stoltz, Bill MacDonald, Kate McNeil, Carl Marotte; ***D:*** Christopher Menaul; ***W:*** Shelley Evans; ***C:*** Michael Storey; ***M:*** Eric Allaman. **CABLE**

One Last Ride 🦴🦴 **2003 (R)** Hard slice-of-life look at L.A. gambling addict Michael (Cupo), who's in deep to loan shark Tweat (Palminteri). Tweat tells the fabric salesman to do what he says or he and his unsuspecting pregnant wife Gina (Barone) will be harmed. Despite the threats, Michael is still sure he is just one win from everything going his way. Low-budget with a familiar story; Cupo adapted from his play. **90m/C DVD.** *US* Chazz Palminteri, Anita Barone, Mario Roccuzzo, Robert Davi, Charles Durning, Jack Carter, Pat Cupo, Joe Marinelli; ***D:*** Tony Vitale; ***W:*** Pat Cupo; ***C:*** Mark Doering-Powell; ***M:*** Josh G. Abrahams.

One Last Run 🦴 1/2 **1989** It's drama on the slopes as a variety of individuals confront their pasts/fears/personal demons via extreme skiing. Features the performances of champion skiers Franz Weber and Scot Schmidt. **82m/C VHS.** Russell Todd, Ashley Laurence, Craig Branham, Jimmy Aleck, Tracy Scoggins, Nels Van Patten, Chuck Connors; ***D:*** Peter Winograd, Glenn Gebhard; ***W:*** Peter Winograd, Glenn Gebhard.

One Last Thing 🦴🦴 1/2 **2005 (R)** Dylan (Angarano) is 16 and dying from brain cancer. When a charity chooses to grant his final wish, he decides that rather than spending time with his football hero Jason O'Malley (Messner), he wants to meet supermodel Nikki Sinclair (Mabrey). Well, duh. Self-destructive Nikki needs the good publicity but bails as quickly as possible. Still, Jason offers Dylan and his buddies Ricky (Bush) and Slap (Glick) a luxury weekend in New York during which Nikki is given a chance to redeem herself. Ping-pongs between sentiment and reality. Ethan Hawke appears uncredited in flashbacks as Dylan's dead father. **93m/C DVD.** *US* Cynthia Nixon, Michael Angarano, Sunny Mabrey, Michael Rispoli, Brian Stokes Mitchell, Gina Gershon, Nelust Wyclef Jean, Matthew Bush, Gideon Glick; ***D:*** Alex Steyermark; ***W:*** Barry Stringfellow; ***C:*** Christopher Norr; ***M:*** Anton Sanko.

One Little Indian 🦴🦴 **1973** AWOL cavalry man Garner and his Indian ward team up with a widow (Miles) and her daughter (Foster) in an attempt to cross the New Mexican desert. A tepid presentation from the usually high quality Disney studio. **90m/C VHS, DVD.** James Garner, Vera Miles, Jodie Foster, Clay O'Brien, Andrew Prine, Bernard McEveety; ***D:*** Bernard McEveety; ***M:*** Jerry Goldsmith.

One Long Night 🦴 1/2 **2007** In 1994 (after the governor of California signs a controversial immigration bill), Mexican-American businessman Richard Macedo (Seda) is sent to Mexico City, witnesses a murder, goes on the run from a gang leader, gets attacked by drag queens, and tries to make it home all the while wondering about his Mexican heritage. **90m/C DVD.** Jon Seda, Paul Rodriguez, Ed Begley Jr., Karen Black, Alison Eastwood, Mircea Monroe, Hector Suarez Gomez, Itati Cantoral; ***D:*** David Siqueiros; ***W:*** David Siqueiros, Chris Smernes; ***C:*** Reynaldo Villalobos; ***M:*** Gustavo Farias.

One Magic Christmas 🦴🦴 1/2 **1985 (G)** Disney feel-good film about a disillusioned working woman whose faith in Christmas is restored when her guardian angel descends to Earth and performs various miracles. Somewhat cliched and tiresome, but partially redeemed by Stanton and Steenburgen's presence. **88m/C VHS, DVD.** Mary Steenburgen, Harry Dean Stanton, Gary Basaraba, Michelle Meyrink, Arthur Hill, Elisabeth Harnois, Robbie Magwood; ***D:*** Phillip Borsos; ***W:*** Thomas Meehan; ***C:*** Frank Tidy; ***M:*** Michael Conway Baker.

One Man Army 🦴 1/2 **1993 (R)** Kickboxer goes to visit gramps in small town, only to discover the old guy has been murdered and corruption and cover-ups abound. So he decides to kick some butt and set things right. **95m/C VHS, DVD.** Jerry Trimble; ***D:*** Cirio H. Santiago.

One Man Force 🦴🦴 **1989 (R)** L.A. narcotics cop Jake Swan goes on a vigilante spree. Huge in body and vengeful in spirit, he makes his partner's murderers pay! **92m/C VHS, DVD.** John Matuszak, Ronny Cox, Charles Napier, Sharon Farrell, Sam Jones, Chance Boyer, Richard Lynch, Stacey Q; ***D:*** Dale Trevillion; ***W:*** Dale Trevillion; ***M:*** Charles Fox.

One Man Jury 🦴 **1978 (R)** LAPD lieutenant, wearied by an ineffective justice system, becomes a one-man vigilante avenger. Pale Dirty Harry rip-off with over acting and an overdose of violence. **95m/C VHS.** Jack Palance, Chris Mitchum, Joe Spinell, Pamela Shoop; ***D:*** Charles Martin.

One Man Out 🦴 **1989 (R)** An ex-CIA agent diverts his psychological problems into his new job: assassin for a South American despot. His jaded view of life changes when he meets and falls in love with an American journalist. Trouble in paradise when he is ordered to kill her. One man out was not enough, they should have done away with the entire crew of this stinker. **90m/C VHS.** Stephen McHattie, Deborah Van Valkenburgh, Aharon Ipale, Ismael Carlo, Michael Champion, Dennis A. Pratt; ***D:*** Michael Kennedy.

One Man's Hero 🦴 1/2 **1998 (R)** Heavy-handed retelling of the U.S.-Mexican war of the 1840s. Irish Catholic Army Sgt. John Riley (Berenger) is tired of the constant harassment he and his fellow Irishmen are subjected to. After disobeying an officer, Riley leads his men into Mexico where they eventually join the Mexican army as the St. Patrick's Battalion just in time to battle the U.S. troops of Gen. Zachary Taylor (Gammon). The history's confusing and isn't helped when the action stops for romantic interludes between Riley and rebel girl, Marta (Romo). **122m/C VHS, DVD.** Tom Berenger, Joaquim de Almeida, Daniela Romo, James Gammon, Mark Moses, Stuart Graham, Stephen Tobolowsky, Carlos Carrasco, Patrick Bergin; ***D:*** Lance Hool; ***W:*** Milton S. Gelman; ***C:*** Joao Fernandes; ***M:*** Ernest Troost.

One Man's Journey 🦴🦴 1/2 **1933** Barrymore plays it noble as widowed small town doctor Eli Watt. He's completely devoted to his practice though he doesn't make any money and sometimes feels unappreciated. But the doc comes to professional notice when he saves the town from a smallpox epidemic. Remade as "A Man to Remember" (1939). **72m/B DVD.** Lionel Barrymore, May Robson, Dorothy Jordan, Joel McCrea, Frances Dee, David Landau, Hale Hamilton, James Rush; ***D:*** John S. Robertson; ***W:*** Lester Cohen, Samuel Ornitz; ***C:*** Jack MacKenzie.

One Man's Justice 🦴🦴 1/2 **1995 (R)** Army drill sergeant John North (Bosworth) heads for the streets of Venice, California to get the drug-dealing, gun-running scum who killed his wife and daughter. And a streetwise 10-year-old may be his best chance for finding them. **100m/C VHS, DVD.** Brian Bosworth, Bruce Payne, Jeff Kober, DeJuan Guy, Hammer, M.C. Gainey; ***D:*** Kurt Wimmer; ***W:*** Steven Selling; ***C:*** Jurgen Baum, John Huneck; ***M:*** Anthony Marinelli.

One Man's War 🦴🦴 1/2 **1990 (PG-13)** A human-rights crusader in repressive Paraguay won't be silenced, even after government thugs torture and murder his son. He fights obsessively to bring the killers to justice. The true story of the Joel Filartiga family is heartfelt but ultimately a dramatic letdown; an epilogue proves that full story hasn't been told. **91m/C VHS, DVD.** Anthony Hopkins, Norma Aleandro, Fernanda Torres, Ruben Blades; ***D:*** Sergio Toledo.

One Man's Way 🦴🦴 1/2 **1963** Murray is appropriately devout as charasmatic religious leader Norman Vincent Peale. With the support of his wife (Hyland), he survives the adulations and accusations of blasphemy for his rather unorthodox theological ideas and his book, "The Power of Positive Thinking." Based on the book "Norman Vincent Peale: Minister to Millions" by Arthur Gordon. **105m/B VHS.** Don Murray, Diana Hyland, William Windom, Virginia Christine, Carol Ohmart, Veronica Cartwright, Liam Sullivan, June Dayton, Ian Wolfe; ***D:*** Denis Sanders; ***W:*** Eleanore Griffin, John W. Bloch.

One Million B.C. 🦴🦴 1/2 *The Cave Dwellers; Cave Man; Man and His Mate* **1940** The strange saga of the struggle of primitive cavemen and their battle against dinosaurs and other monsters. Curiously told in flashbacks, this film provided stock footage for countless dinosaur movies that followed. Portions of film rumored to be directed by cinematic pioneer D. W. Griffith. **80m/B VHS, DVD.** Victor Mature, Carole Landis, Lon Chaney Jr.; ***D:*** Hal Roach, Hal Roach Jr.

One Million Years B.C. 🦴🦴 1/2 **1966 (R)** It's Welch in a fur bikini and special FX expert Ray Harryhausen doing dinosaurs so who cares about a plot (which involves Welch and her boyfriend, who's from a rival clan). Remake of the 1940 film "One Million B.C." **100m/C VHS, DVD.** *GB* Raquel Welch, John Richardson, Percy Herbert, Robert Brown, Martine Beswick; ***D:*** Don Chaffey.

One Minute to Zero 🦴🦴 **1952** Korean War action film divides its time between an army romance and war action. The lukwarm melodrama features Mitchum as a colonel in charge of evacuating American civilians but who ends up bombing refugees. **105m/B VHS.** Robert Mitchum, Ann Blyth, William Talman, Charles McGraw, Margaret Sheridan, Richard Egan, Eduard Franz, Robert Osterloh, Robert Gist; ***D:*** Tay Garnett.

One Missed Call 🦴🦴🦴 *Chakushin ari* **2003 (R)** A young girl named Yoko receives a telephone message from 72 hours in the future, hearing herself in her last moments alive. The phone says the call comes from Yoko's own number, and sure enough 72 hours later she's dead. Investigating her friend's death, Yumi finds that Yoko isn't the only one to receive these calls. A vengeful spirit has been creeping onto people's cell phones, and killing the numbers listed in their internal phone books. As Yumi struggles to find out why the killings are occurring, it begins to look like she herself is somehow involved. A surprisingly straightforward Japanese horror film, considering the director is Takashi Miike, usually known for more surreal works. **111m/C DVD.** *JP* Yutaka Matsushige, Goro Kishitani, Kou Shibasaki, Shin'ichi Tsutsumi, Kazue Fukiishi, Anna Nagata, Atsushi Ida, Mariko Tsutsui, Azusa, Karen Oshima, Yuna Mikuni, Renji Ishibashi; ***D:*** Takashi Miike; ***W:*** Yasushi Akimoto, Minako Daira; ***C:*** Hideo Yamamoto; ***M:*** Koji Endo.

One Missed Call WOOF! **2008 (PG-13)** Yet another technophobic Japanese horror remake, this one looking for scares from college students who receive cell phone calls from their future selves that capture the sounds of their own looming deaths. Burns and Cho are cringe-worthy as the good cop/bad cop tandem investigating at the behest of the dewy and earnest co-ed (Sossamon), who also brings a child-abuse subplot into play. Meanwhile, director Valette fails to conjure much oogidy-boogidy, and even the gore is boring. **87m/C DVD.** *GE JP US GB* Shannyn Sossamon, Edward Burns, Ana Claudia Talancon, Ray Wise, Azura Skye, Jason Beghe, Margaret Cho, Meagan Good; ***D:*** Eric Valette; ***W:*** Andrew Klavan; ***C:*** Glen MacPherson; ***M:*** Reinhold Heil, Johnny Klimek.

One Missed Call 2 🦴🦴 1/2 *Chakushin ari 2* **2005 (R)** The survivors of the first film realize they haven't stopped the curse, which has now achieved urban legend status throughout Asia due to the live television death of a victim in the first film. Instead it has begun to spread like wildfire, and they begin to track its origins to the country of Taiwan in an effort to stop the ghost a second time before it manages to kill them. Unfortunately the film suffers form the curse of being a horror movie sequel, and the infamous director of the original didn't return to do this one as well. **106m/C DVD.** *JP* Haruko Wanibuchi, Kathryn Adams, Joseph H. Lewis, Asako Seto, Karen Oshima, Renji Ishibashi, Peter Ho; ***D:*** Renpei Tsukamoto; ***W:*** Yasushi Akimoto, Minako Daira; ***C:*** Tokusho Kikumura.

One Missed Call 3: Final 🦴 1/2 *Final Call; One Missed Call Final; Chakushin ari Final* **2006** Asuka (Maki Horikita) is a young schoolgirl bullied heavily by her classmates, and on a trip to Korea all of them get a cell phone message from her saying to pass the message on and their life will be spared. No one takes much notice until people start dying then it's a mad rush to betray each other in order to live. Billed as the finale of the One Missed Call series, it's done well enough to ensure that one day we'll probably see a One Missed Call Final Part 2. **104m/C DVD.** *JP* Maki Horikita, Meisa Kuroki, Yun-seok Jang, Erika Asakura, Yu Kamiwaki, Rie Tsuneyoshi, Arisa Naito, Rakuto Tochihara, Kazuma Yamane, Takashi Yamagata, Takanori Kawamoto, Yuta Ishida, Mami Hashimoto, Miho Amakawa, Sora Matsumoto, Ayumi Taahashi, Suna Ikeda, Ryu Morioka, Kenichi Okana, Haruki Itagashi, Chika Yada, Haruno Inoue, Mayu Sato, Yuki Takayasu, Mina Obata, Yuta Murakami, Ryoto Iwai; *D:* Manabu Asao.

One More Chance 𝒥 1/2 **1990** While he's in jail, an ex-con's family moves away without leaving a forwarding address. When he's released he strikes up a friendship with a woman from the neighborhood who knows where they've gone. **102m/C VHS.** Kirstie Alley, John Lamotta, Logan Clarke, Michael Pataki, Hector Maisonette; *D:* Sam Firstenberg.

One More Kiss 𝒥𝒥 **1999** Scottish immigrant Sarah (Edmond) leaves New York to return to her hometown when she learns she's dying from cancer. On her to-do list is getting closer to her father Frank (Cosmo) and spending time with old flame Sam (Butler), which doesn't please his wife Charlotte (Gogan). Tear-jerker, although Sarah comes across as selfish rather than your standard noble character. **98m/C DVD.** *GB* Valerie Edmond, Gerard Butler, James Cosmo, Valerie Gogan, Carl Proctor; *D:* Vadim Jean; *W:* Suzie Halewood; *C:* Mike J. Fox; *M:* David A. Hughes, John Murphy.

One More Saturday Night 𝒥 **1986 (R)** Franken and Davis, "Saturday Night Live" alumni, wrote this film about a small town going wild on the weekend. Dry, taxing, and unfunny. Averages about one laugh per half hour—at one-and-a-half hours, that's way too long. **96m/C VHS.** Al Franken, Tom Davis, Nan Woods, Dave Reynolds; *D:* Dennis Klein; *W:* Al Franken, Tom Davis.

One More Time 𝒥 1/2 **1970 (PG)** Lewis' directorial effort is an uneven comedy follow-up to 1968's "Salt & Pepper." Salt (Davis Jr.) and Pepper's (Lawford) nightclub is having money trouble so Pepper goes to his wealthy twin brother Sydney (who lives in the family castle) for some dough. When Sydney is murdered, Pepper assumes his identity and learns that his brother was posing as a smuggler on behalf of Interpol. Then the duo gets chased through the countryside by Interpol agents and crooks after stolen diamonds. **95m/C DVD.** Peter Lawford, Sammy Davis Jr., John Wood, Maggie Wright, Leslie Sands, Esther Anderson, Edward Evans, Sydney Arnold; ***Cameos:*** Peter Cushing, Christopher Lee; *D:* Jerry Lewis; *W:* Michael Pertwee; *C:* Ernest Steward; *M:* Les Reed.

One Night at McCool's 𝒥𝒥 **2001 (R)** Quirky and inventive, this poor man's "Rashomon" gets points for effort, but the execution doesn't always live up to the ambition. Easygoing bartender Randy (Dillon) is involved in a murder by aggressively materialistic con artist Jewel (Tyler) and before he knows it, he's in love. Somehow his sleazy lawyer cousin (Reiser) becomes involved, as well as Det. Dehling (Goodman) who is investigating the murder of Jewel's former partner (Clay). Of course, all three fall in love, and we see the preceding night's events through each set of love-struck eyes as they spill their guts to a hitman (Douglas), a shrink (McIntire), and a priest (Jenkins), respectively. Douglas's outlandish toupee and understated portrayal of the hitman, as well as some fine comic touches by Dillon, are highlights. **93m/C VHS, DVD.** *US* Liv Tyler, Matt Dillon, Paul Reiser, John Goodman, Michael Douglas, Reba McEntire, Richard Jenkins, Andrew (Dice Clay) Silverstein, Leo Rossi, Eric Schaeffer; *D:* Harald Zwart; *W:* Stan Seidel; *C:* Karl Walter Lindenlaub; *M:* Marc Shaiman.

One Night in the Tropics 𝒥𝒥 1/2 **1940** The film debut of radio stars Abbott & Costello who play secondary roles to a love triangle (set to music). Jones is an insurance salesman who falls in love with Kelly, the fiance of Cummings. Based on the novel "Love Insurance" by Earl Derr Biggers. ♫Back in My Shell; Remind Me; You and Your Kiss; Your Dream is the Same as My Dream. **83m/B VHS, DVD.** Allan Jones, Robert Cummings, Nancy Kelly, Bud Abbott, Lou Costello, Mary Boland, Peggy Moran, William Frawley, Leo Carrillo; *D:* Edward Sutherland; *W:* Kathryn Scola, Gertrude Purcell, Charles Grayson, Francis Martin.

One Night of Love 𝒥𝒥𝒥 1/2 **1934** Moore's best quasi-operetta, about a young American diva rebelling in response to her demanding Italian teacher. "Pygmallion"-like story has her falling in love with her maestro. Despite being nearly 60 years old, this film is still enchanting and fresh. ♫One Night of Love; Ciri-Biri-Bin; Sempre Libera; Sextet; Indian Love Call; 'Tis the Last Rose of Summer; Habanera; Un bel di; None But the Lonely Heart. **95m/B VHS.** Grace Moore, Tullio Carminati, Lyle Talbot, Jane Darwell, Nydia Westman, Mona Barrie, Jessie Ralph, Luis Alberni; *D:* Victor Schertzinger. Oscars '34: Sound, Score.

One Night Only **1984** A gorgeous law student decides to make big money by hiring herself and her friends out as hookers to the school football team. **87m/C VHS.** Lenore Zann, Jeff Braunstein, Grant Alianak; *D:* Timothy Bond.

One Night Stand 𝒥𝒥 **1978** Woman's chance encounter with a man in a singles bar leads to an evening of unexpected terror. Billed as a horror flick, it is really more of a drama. **90m/C VHS.** *CA* Chapelle Jaffe, Brent Carver, Susan Hogan, Len Doncheff; *D:* Allan King; *W:* Carol Bolt; *C:* Kenneth Gregg. **TV**

One Night Stand 𝒥𝒥𝒥 **1984** Four young people attempt to amuse themselves at the empty Sydney Opera House on the New Year's Eve, that night WWIII begins. An odd commentary on nuclear war that sees the bomb as the ultimate bad joke. Features an appearance by alternative rock group Midnight Oil. **94m/C VHS.** Tyler Coppin, Cassandra Delaney, Jay Hackett, Saskia Post; *D:* John Duigan.

One Night Stand 𝒥𝒥 1/2 **1995 (R)** Lonely Michelle (Sheedy) visits a nightclub and allows herself to be picked up by your basic handsome stranger, Jack (Martinez) in this case. She wakes up alone and learns from building owner Josslyn (Forrest) that the apartment is up for lease. Obsessed with finding her mystery man, Michelle discovers Jack's wife was murdered—possibly by him or maybe by Josslyn, who turns out to be the dead woman's father. Debut feature for director Shire covers familiar territory, with Sheedy giving a strong performance. **92m/C VHS, DVD.** Ally Sheedy, A. Martinez, Frederic Forrest, Don Novello, Diane Salinger, Millie Slavin; *D:* Talia Shire; *W:* Marty Casella; *C:* Arthur Albert; *M:* David Shire.

One Night Stand 𝒥𝒥𝒥 **1997 (R)** Max (Snipes) is a commercial director in New York on business. While visiting his friend Charlie (Downey), a choreographer dying of AIDS, he meets willowy beauty Karen (Kinski). This chance meeting leads to, you guessed it, a one night stand. When Max returns home to L.A., he realizes how empty and stale his life is. One year later, he and wife Mimi (Wen) return to visit the quickly fading Charlie. They meet Charlie's brother Vernon (McLachlan) and his wife..Karen. Good performances (especially by Downey) and characterization make this more than a morality play about the ramifications of a sexual fling. Although paid for his original material, Joe Eszterhas didn't take any writing credit after Figgis totally rewrote the script. **103m/C VHS, DVD.** Mike Figgis, Wesley Snipes, Nastassja Kinski, Ming Na, Robert Downey Jr., Kyle MacLachlan, Glenn Plummer, Amanda Donohoe, Thomas Haden Church, Julian Sands, John Ratzenberger, Annabelle Gurwitch, Donovan Leitch, Zoe Nathenson, Vincent Ward, Susan Barnes; ***Cameos:*** Ione Skye, Xander Berkeley; *D:* Mike Figgis; *W:* Mike Figgis; *C:* Declan Quinn; *M:* Mike Figgis.

1-900 𝒥𝒥 **1994** Based on the play "06" by Doesburg, which refers to the Dutch exchange for phone-sex numbers. Sarah (Schluter) and Thomas (van Kempen) are both lonely professionals who "meet" when Thomas answers Sarah's personal ad. Their weekly phone chats lead to descriptions of sexual fantasies but relationship issues begin to intrude as time passes. Dutch with subtitles. **80m/C VHS, DVD.** *NL* Ariane Schluter, Ad van Kempen; *D:* Theo van Gogh; *W:* Ariane Schluter, Ad van Kempen, Johan Doesburg, Marcel Otten; *C:* Tom Erisman; *M:* Ruud Bos.

One of Her Own 𝒥𝒥 1/2 **1997** Based on the true story of a police officer (Laughlin) who decides to press charges against the fellow cop (Evigan) who raped her, despite the consequences to her career. **91m/C VHS.** Lori Loughlin, Greg Evigan, Martin Sheen, Vel Johnson; *D:* Armand Mastroianni; *W:* Pablo F. Fenjves, Valerie West. **TV**

One of My Wives Is Missing 𝒥𝒥 1/2 **1976** An ex-New York cop tries to solve the mysterious disappearance of a newlywed socialite. Things become strange when she reappears but is discovered as an imposter. Above-average acting in a film adapted from the play "The Trap for a Lonely Man." **97m/C VHS.** Jack Klugman, Elizabeth Ashley, James Franciscus; *D:* Glenn Jordan. **TV**

One of Our Aircraft Is Missing 𝒥𝒥𝒥 1/2 **1941** The crew of an R.A.F. bomber downed in the Netherlands, struggle to escape Nazi capture. A thoughtful study of wars and the men who fight them, with an entertaining melodramatic plot. Look for the British version, which runs 106 minutes. Some of the American prints only run 82 minutes. **103m/B VHS.** *GB* Godfrey Tearle, Eric Portman, Hugh Williams, Pamela Brown, Googie Withers, Peter Ustinov; *D:* Emeric Pressburger, Michael Powell.

One of Our Dinosaurs Is Missing 𝒥𝒥 **1975 (G)** An English nanny and her cohorts help British Intelligence retrieve a microfilm—concealing dinosaur fossil from the bad guys that have stolen it. Disney film was shot on location in England. **101m/C VHS.** Peter Ustinov, Helen Hayes, Derek Nimmo, Clive Revill, Robert Stevenson, Joan Sims; *D:* Robert Stevenson.

One of Them WOOF! **2003 (R)** Really bad dead teen flick. Elizabeth (Carmichael) and her friends are trapped in a school of horrors (Satanism is involved). Uncle Don (Crenna) tries to come to the rescue. **93m/C DVD.** Richard Anthony Crenna, Kelly Carmichael, Brian Sheridan, Erin Byron, Paul Geffre; *D:* Ralph Portillo; *W:* David Ciesielski; *C:* Keith Holland; *M:* Geoff Levin. **VIDEO**

One on One 𝒥𝒥 1/2 **1977 (PG)** A Rocky-esque story about a high school basketball star from the country who accepts an athletic scholarship to a big city university. He encounters a demanding coach and intense competition. Light weight drama that is economically entertaining. **100m/C VHS.** Robby Benson, Annette O'Toole, G.D. Spradlin, Gail Strickland, Melanie Griffith; *D:* Lamont Johnson; *W:* Robby Benson; *M:* Charles Fox.

One Plus One 𝒥 *Exploring the Kinsey Report* **1961** A dramatization, believe it or not, of the Kinsey sex survey of the 1950s. Participants in a sex lecture talk about and demonstrate various "risque" practices, such as premarital sex and extramarital affairs. Despite this film, the sexual revolution went on as planned. **114m/B VHS.** *CA* Leo G. Carroll, Hilda Brawner, William Traylor, Kate Reid, Ernest Graves; *D:* Arch Oboler; *W:* Arch Oboler.

One-Punch O'Day 𝒥 **1926** Boxing boy tries to buy back hometown's oil livelihood by winning prizefight. Much patient waiting by his honey. **60m/B VHS.** Billy Sullivan, Jack Herrick, Charlotte Merriam; *D:* Harry Joe Brown.

One Rainy Afternoon 𝒥𝒥 **1936** A bit-player kisses the wrong girl in a Paris theatre causing a massive uproar that brands him as a notorious romantic "monster." Patterned after a German film, the story lacks depth and zest. **80m/B VHS, DVD.** Francis Lederer, Ida Lupino, Hugh Herbert, Roland Young, Donald Meek; *D:* Rowland V. Lee.

One Russian Summer WOOF! **1973 (R)** During the Russian Revolution, a cripple seeks revenge on the corrupt land baron who murdered his parents. An unfortunate attempt to dramatize a novel by M. Lermontov. **112m/C VHS.** Oliver Reed, Claudia Cardinale, John McEnery, Carole Andre, Ray Lovelock; *D:* Antonio Calenda.

One Shoe Makes It Murder 𝒥𝒥 **1982** A shady casino owner hires ex-cop Mitchum to investigate the disappearance of his unfaithful wife. Adapted from Eric Bercovici's novel, the story does little to enhance Mitchum's TV debut. **100m/C VHS.** Robert Mitchum, Angie Dickinson, Mel Ferrer, Howard Hesseman, Jose Perez; *D:* William (Billy) Hale; *M:* Bruce Broughton.

One Sings, the Other Doesn't 𝒥𝒥 1/2 *L'Une Chante, l'Autre Pas* **1977** Seeking contentment, a conservative widow and a liberal extrovert help each other cope in a man's world. Endearing characters, but a superficial treatment of dated feminist issues. In French with English subtitles. **105m/C VHS.** *FR BE* Valerie Mairesse, Therese Liotard, Robert Dadies, Ali Affi, Jean-Pierre Pellegrin; *D:* Agnes Varda; *W:* Agnes Varda; *C:* Charlie Van Damme; *M:* Francois Wertheimer.

One Small Hero 𝒥 1/2 **1999 (PG)** Dopey family entertainment might not be a complete waste of time for easygoing viewers. Joey Cooper (Kiley) can't pass the tests to become a member of the Wilderness Club and go on their camping trip. He fails once again (he's physically too small) but can't tell his mom after she surprises Joey with camping gear. So, he trails behind the campers and is the only one who can save them from kidnappers. **90m/C VHS, DVD.** Nathan Kiley, Matthew Peters, Lindsay Lewis, Bonnie Burroughs; *D:* Jennifer Malchese; *C:* Denis Maloney; *M:* Herman Beeftink. **CABLE**

One Special Night 𝒥𝒥 1/2 **1999 (PG)** Robert (Garner) is visiting his Alzheimer's-stricken wife in the hospital and is unable to get a taxi home because of a snowstorm. Doctor Catharine (Andrews) offers him a ride but her car gets stuck on a deserted road and they find shelter in a small cabin. The twosome are drawn to each other during their snowy refuge but will a romance be possible when they rejoin the real world? **90m/C VHS, DVD.** Julie Andrews, James Garner, Patricia Charbonneau, Stacy Grant, Stewart Bick; *D:* Robert M. Young; *W:* Nancy Silvers; *C:* Guy Dufaux; *M:* Richard Bellis. **TV**

One Step to Hell 𝒥 1/2 *Caccia Ai Violenti; King of Africa* **1967** Good cop rescues gold-miner's widow from three escaped convicts. Beautiful African scenery helps save an otherwise mediocre film. **90m/C VHS.** Ty Hardin, Rossano Brazzi, Pier Angeli, George Sanders, Helga Line, Jorge (George) Rigaud; *D:* Sandy Howard; *W:* Sandy Howard; *C:* Julio Ortas; *M:* Gianni Marchetti.

One Summer Love 𝒥 1/2 *Dragonfly* **1976** Man checks out from loony bin, searches for family ties and befriends beautiful woman who works in a moviehouse. **95m/C VHS.** Beau Bridges, Susan Sarandon, Mildred Dunnock, Ann Wedgeworth, Michael B. Miller, Linda Miller, James Noble, Frederick Coffin; *D:* Gilbert Cates; *W:* N. Richard Nash.

One Sunday Afternoon 𝒥𝒥 **1933** Told in flashbacks. Biff Grimes (Cooper) and Hugo Barnstead (Hamilton) are romantic rivals for selfish beauty Virginia Brush (Wray) while sweet Amy Lind (Fuller) pines for Biff to notice her. When Virginia and Hugo elope, Biff impulsively marries Amy. The rivalry takes a turn and one of the men goes to jail. Remade in 1941 as "The Strawberry Blonde" and again in 1948 under the original title. **90m/B DVD.** Gary Cooper, Fay Wray, Frances Fuller, Neil Hamilton, Roscoe Karns, Jane Darwell; *D:* Stephen Roberts; *W:* Grover Jones, William Slavens McNutt; *C:* Victor Milner.

One That Got Away 𝒥𝒥𝒥 **1957** A loyal German Luftwaffe pilot captured by the British becomes obsessed with escape. Fast paced and exciting. Based on a true story. **111m/B VHS, DVD.** Hardy Kruger, Colin Gordon, Alec Gordon; *D:* Roy Ward Baker.

The One That Got Away 𝒥𝒥 **1996** A badly prepared SAS patrol is dropped 300 miles behind enemy lines during the Gulf War to destroy Scud missile launchers that are aimed at Israel. Only when they are under fire, the soldiers discover that they cannot call for reinforcements and things get very bad indeed. Based on a true story. **104m/C DVD.** *GB* Paul McGann, David Morrissey, Nick Brimble, Simon Burke, Steven Waddington; *D:* Paul Greengrass; *W:* Paul Greengrass; *M:* Barrington Pheloung. **TV**

One Third of a Nation 🦴🦴 1/2 **1939** Depression era film contrasts the conditions of slum life with those in high society. A young entrepreneur inherits a city block in ruins, only to fall in love with a young woman who lives there and help her crippled brother. Timely social criticism. **79m/B VHS.** Sylvia Sidney, Leif Erickson, Myron McCormick, Sidney Lumet; ***D:*** Dudley Murphy.

1001 Arabian Nights 🦴🦴 1/2 **1959** In this Arabian nightmare, the nearsighted Mr. Magoo is known as "Azziz" Magoo, lamp dealer and uncle of Aladdin. **76m/C VHS.** ***D:*** Jack Kinney; ***M:*** George Duning; ***V:*** Jim Backus, Kathryn Grant, Hans Conried, Herschel Bernardi.

One to Another 🦴 1/2 *Chacun sa Nuit* **2006** Lucie investigates the beating death of her troubled bisexual brother Pierre, a member of a rock band made up of equally beautiful and bored teenagers. More of an excuse for bed-hopping and showing off good-looking bodies than a true murder mystery. French with subtitles. **95m/C DVD.** *FR* Pierre Perrier, Valerie Mairesse, Lizzie Brochere, Arthur Dupont, Guillame Bache, Nicolas Nollet; ***D:*** Jean-Marc Barr, Pascal Arnold; ***W:*** Pascal Arnold; ***C:*** Jean-Marc Barr; ***M:*** Irina Decermic.

One Too Many 🦴 *The Important Story of Alcoholism; Killer With a Label* **1951** Exploitation film depicting the evils of alcoholism. Campy, but slick. **110m/B VHS.** Ruth Warrick, Richard Travis, Victor Kilian, Onslow Stevens, Lyle Talbot; ***D:*** Erle C. Kenton; ***W:*** Malcolm Stuart Boylan; ***C:*** Carl Berger; ***M:*** Bert Shefter.

One Touch of Venus 🦴🦴 1/2 **1948** Love fills a department store when a window dresser kisses a statue of the goddess Venus—and she comes to life. Appealing adaptation of the Broadway musical. ♫ Speak Low; The Trouble with Women; That's Him; Don't Look Now But My Heart Is Showing; My Week. **82m/B VHS.** Ava Gardner, Robert Walker, Eve Arden, Dick Haymes, Olga San Juan, Tom Conway; ***D:*** William A. Seiter; ***W:*** Frank Tashlin, Harry Kurnitz; ***C:*** Franz Planer; ***M:*** Kurt Weill.

One Tough Cop 🦴🦴 **1998 (R)** Baldwin proves he's more than just a goofy face in a potential breakthrough role as headstrong NYPD detective Bo Dietl. Together with partner Finnerty (Penn), Dietl investigates a brutal rape and mutilation of a nun in East Harlem. Despite Brazilian director Barreto's good eye for the mean streets of New York and Baldwin's stellar performance, this is just one more derivative police drama without distinction. Barreto's wife Irving makes an appearance as a mean-spirited federal agent. Based on the autobiography on real-life retired cop Bo Dietl. **94m/C VHS, DVD.** Stephen Baldwin, Gina Gershon, Christopher Penn, Mike McGlone, Paul Guilfoyle, Amy Irving, Victor Slezak, Luis Guzman; ***D:*** Bruno Barreto; ***W:*** Jeremy Iacone; ***C:*** Ron Fortunato; ***M:*** Bruce Broughton.

One Trick Pony 🦴🦴 1/2 **1980 (R)** Once-popular rock singer/songwriter struggles to keep his head above water in a turbulent marriage and in the changing currents of popular taste. Simon wrote the autobiographical screenplay and score, but let's hope he is more sincere in real life. A good story. **100m/C VHS.** Paul Simon, Blair Brown, Rip Torn, Joan Hackett, Mare Winningham, Lou Reed, Harry Shearer, Allen (Goorwitz) Garfield, Daniel Stern; ***D:*** Robert M. Young; ***C:*** Dick Bush.

One True Thing 🦴🦴🦴 **1998 (PG-13)** Better check for the family-sized box of tissues before you take home this tearjerker about cancer-stricken mother Kate (Streep) and her relationship with arrogant, career-oriented daughter Ellen (Zellweger). After being guilted by her stuffy college professor dad (Hurt), Ellen agrees to care for Kate as the disease progresses, and the two bridge their emotional distance. Lifted above the disease-of-the-week Lifetime TV material by the presence of stars Streep and Hurt, and by the stellar performance of Zellweger. Based on the novel by Anna Quindlen. **128m/C VHS, DVD.** Meryl Streep, Renee Zellweger, William Hurt, Tom Everett Scott, Nicky Katt, Lauren Graham, James Eckhouse, Patrick Breen, Gerrit Graham; ***D:*** Carl Franklin; ***W:*** Karen Croner; ***C:*** Declan Quinn; ***M:*** Cliff Eidelman.

One, Two, Three 🦴🦴🦴 1/2 **1961** Cagney, an American Coca-Cola exec in Germany, zealously pursues any opportunity to run Coke's European operations. He does this by promising to keep an eye on the boss's wild daughter, who promptly falls for an East German Communist. Fast-paced laughs, wonderful cinematography, and a fine score. **110m/B VHS, DVD.** James Cagney, Horst Buchholz, Arlene Francis, Pamela Tiffin; ***D:*** Billy Wilder; ***W:*** Billy Wilder, I.A.L. Diamond; ***C:*** Daniel F. Fapp; ***M:*** Andre Previn.

One Way 🦴 1/2 **2006** Ad exec Eddie Schneider (Schweiger) is a womanizer despite his engagement to his boss' daughter Judy (von Pfetten). He's also always ready to put his career first even if it means lying so that his friend Angelina's (Smith) rapist Anthony (Roberts) is acquitted since Anthony is Judy's psycho brother. **117m/C DVD.** Til Schweiger, Lauren Lee Smith, Stefanie von Pfetten, Sebastien Roberts, Art Hindle, Eric Roberts, Sonja Smits, Michael Clarke Duncan; ***D:*** Reto Salimbeni; ***W:*** Reto Salimbeni; ***C:*** Paul Sarossy, Mark Willis; ***M:*** Dirk Reichardt, Stefan Hansen.

One Way Out 🦴🦴 **1995** Frank (Gwaltney) gets out of jail, teams up with Bobby (Monahan) and his stripper girlfriend Eve (Golden), and the trio go to visit Frank's brother, Snooky (Turano). When Frank learns that Snooky's lowlife boss (Ironside) has been ripping him off, they plan to even the score. Naturally, the heist goes wrong and they wind up with a hostage (Gillies) and on the lam. **106m/C VHS.** Jack Gwaltney, Jeff Monahan, Annie Golden, Robert Turano, Michael Ironside, Isabel Gillies; ***D:*** Kevin Lynn.

One Way Out 🦴🦴 **2002 (R)** Detective Harry Woltz (Belushi) is lax on the morality issues and has some gambling debts to the wrong people. They suggest Harry show unhappy hubby John Farrow (Bateman) how to murder his wife and get away with it. As an added incentive, they threaten Harry's girlfriend and partner, Gwen (Featherstone). But the subsequent murder investigation finds the evidence pointing Harry's way. **87m/C VHS, DVD.** *CA* James Belushi, Jason Bateman, Angela Featherstone, Jack Langedijk; ***D:*** Allan Goldstein; ***W:*** John Salvati; ***C:*** Sylvain Brault. **VIDEO**

One Way Passage 🦴🦴 1/2 **1932** Joan Ames (Francis) is dying and decides to spend her last days having fun aboard a cruise ship. She meets cute Dan Hardesty (Powell) but keeps her illness a secret from him. Dan's got a big secret of his own: he's an escaped killer being returned to San Francisco for execution by Steve (Hymer), who begins his own flirtation with con woman Betty (MacMahon). Betty and fellow con man Skippy (McHugh) hope to help Dan escape but when he learns of Joan's condition, he refuses to abandon her. **68m/B VHS.** Kay Francis, William Powell, Aline MacMahon, Frank McHugh, Warren Hymer, Frederick Burton; ***D:*** Tay Garnett; ***W:*** Robert Lord, Wilson Mizner, Joe Jackson; ***C:*** Robert B. Kurrle.

One Wild Moment 🦴🦴 1/2 **1978 (R)** Comic complications arise when a divorced man is seduced by his best friend's daughter while vacationing. Warm and charming. Later re-made as "Blame It on Rio." In French with English subtitles. **88m/C VHS.** *FR* Jean-Pierre Marielle, Victor Lanoux, Agnes Soral, Christine Dejoux, Martine Sarcey; ***D:*** Claude Berri; ***W:*** Claude Berri.

One Wish Too Many 🦴🦴 1/2 **1955** A young boy finds a marble that grants wishes. He has the time of his life with his teachers and the school bullies, but runs into trouble when he creates a giant steam roller which overruns London. Winner of Best Children's Film, 1956 Venice Film Festival, but it is hard to say why. **55m/B VHS.** *GB* Anthony Richmond, Rosalind Gourgey, John Pike; ***D:*** John Durst.

One Woman or Two 🦴🦴 1/2 *Une Femme ou Deux* **1985 (PG-13)** Paleontologist Depardieu is duped by beautiful ad-exec who plans to use his findings to push perfume. Remake of "Bringing Up Baby," this screwball comedy has a few screws loose. Dubbed. **100m/C VHS.** *FR* Gerard Depardieu, Sigourney Weaver, Dr. Ruth Westheimer, Michel Aumont, Zabou; ***D:*** Daniel Vigne; ***W:*** Elisabeth Rappeneau, Daniel Vigne.

One Wonderful Sunday 🦴🦴 *Subarashiki Nichiyobi* **1947** It's postwar Tokyo, so just how wonderful can things be? Well, perky Masako (Nakakita) is determined to make the day as bright as possible for her depressed fiance, Yuzo (Numasaki), despite the fact they have no money and can't afford to do much more than walk around together. More of a curiosity in Kurosawa's oeuvre than a substantial work. Japanese with subtitles. **108m/B VHS.** *JP* Chieko Nakakita, Isao Numasaki; ***D:*** Akira Kurosawa; ***W:*** Akira Kurosawa, Keinosuke Uegusa; ***C:*** Asakazu Nakai; ***M:*** Tadashi Hattori.

Onegin 🦴🦴 **1999** Fiennes family affair, with Martha assuming directorial duties, brother Magnus providing the score, and Ralph starring as the titular 18th-century Russian aristocrat. The cynical sophisticate inherits a vast country estate in the 1820s, where Onegin befriends his young neighbor Lensky (Stephens) and his featherbrained fiancee, Olga (Headey). But Onegin is intrigued by Olga's older sister, lovely innocent Tatyana (Tyler), though he rejects her impulsive romantic gestures. This isn't the only mistake that Onegin makes—all of which cost him dearly. Film looks beautiful but doesn't have much soul. Based on the Aleksandr Pushkin novel "Eugene Onegin." **106m/C VHS, DVD.** *GB* Ralph Fiennes, Liv Tyler, Toby Stephens, Lena Headey, Martin Donovan, Alun Armstrong, Harriet Walter, Irene Worth, Francesca Annis; ***D:*** Martha Fiennes; ***W:*** Peter Ettedgui, Michael Ignatieff; ***C:*** Remi Adefarasin; ***M:*** Magnus Fiennes.

101 Reykjavik 🦴🦴 **2000** Icelandic comedy about a slacker and his mom. The slacker is the pushing 30 Hlynur (Gudnason) who lives with indulgent mom Berglind (Karlsdottir). He's cynical, jobless and unambitious (though not unintelligent). Then Berglind invites her Spanish friend Lola (Abril), who's teaching flamenco at the local dance school, to stay. Hylnur falls for the hottie bigtime and they have a drunken New Year's Eve fling while Berglind is away—and before she manages to tell her son that Lola is her own lover. And then Lola finds out she's pregnant. Oh, the complications! Icelandic and English dialogue. **90m/C VHS, DVD.** *IC DK FR NO* Hilmir Snaer Guonason, Victoria Abril, Baltasar Kormakur, Hanna Maria Karlsdottir, Olafur Darri Olafsson, Pruour Vilhjalmsdottir; ***D:*** Baltasar Kormakur; ***W:*** Baltasar Kormakur; ***C:*** Peter Stueger; ***M:*** Damon Albarn, Einar Orn Benediktsson.

Ong-Bak 🦴🦴🦴 **2003 (R)** Over-the-top action is the centerpiece of this breakthrough Thai martial arts film. Loose-cannon Thai kickboxer Ting (Jaa) travels to Bangkok in search of the stolen head to his tiny village's Buddha. Mayhem ensues. What little plot exists is just a vehicle for superb action sequences that are exceptionally violent yet highly inventive, especially when one considers that all the action was filmed without digital effects, wires, or other modern-day trickery. The result is a 70's-style martial-arts movie for the modern era, refreshingly real and a heck of a lot of fun. Thai with English subtitles. **107m/C DVD.** *TH* Tony Jaa, Wannakit Siriput, Sukhaaw Phongwilai, Petchthai Wongkamlao, Pumwaree Yodkamol, Rungrawee Borrijindakul; ***D:*** Prachya Pinkaew; ***W:*** Suphachai Sithiamphian; ***C:*** Nattawut Kittihun; ***M:*** Atomix Clubbing.

Ong Bak 2 🦴🦴 *Ong Bak: The Beginning* **2008 (R)** Given its production problems (which included the director/star disappearing for over a month) it's amazing this prequel made it to film. Set several hundred years in Thailand's past, when it was still known as Siam, Tien (Jaa) is a young orphan whose parents have been murdered. After beating up a crocodile he is adopted by a band of thieves/martial arts masters and taught various fighting styles with the goal of merging them into one superior style. Eventually he learns of an opportunity for revenge, and it's bone-crunching time. There's no real plot or character development, but no one is really looking for those in a martial arts revenge movie. There are more than enough money shots for fighting fans to cheer for, though. **115m/C DVD, Blu-ray Disc.** *TH* Tony Jaa, Sorapong Chatree, Sarunyu Wongkrachang, Nirut Sirichanya, Dan Chupong, Santisuk Promsiri, Primorata Dejudom; ***D:*** Tony Jaa, Panna Rittikrai; ***W:*** Panna Rittikrai; ***C:*** Nattawhut Khittikhun; ***M:*** Terdsak Janpan.

Onibaba 🦴🦴🦴 *The Demon; The Devil Woman* **1964** A brutal parable about a mother and her daughter-in-law in war-ravaged medieval Japan who subsist by murdering stray soldiers and selling their armor. One soldier beds the daughter, setting the mother-in-law on a vengeful tirade. Review of the film varied widely, hailed by some as a masterpiece and by others as below average; in Japanese with subtitles. **103m/B VHS, DVD.** *JP* Nobuko Otowa, Jitsuko Yoshimura, Kei Sato; ***D:*** Kaneto Shindo.

The Onion Field 🦴🦴🦴 1/2 **1979 (R)** True story about the mental breakdown of an ex-cop who witnessed his partner's murder. Haunted by the slow process of justice and his own feelings of insecurity, he is unable to get his life together. Based on the novel by Joseph Wambaugh, who also wrote the screenplay. Compelling script and excellent acting. **126m/C VHS, DVD.** John Savage, James Woods, Ronny Cox, Franklyn Seales, Ted Danson, David Huffman, Christopher Lloyd, Dianne Hull, Priscilla Pointer, Richard Venture, William Sanderson, Michael Pataki; ***D:*** Harold Becker; ***W:*** Eric Roth; ***C:*** Charles Rosher Jr.; ***M:*** Eumir Deodato.

On_Line 🦴🦴 **2001 (R)** Neurotic John Roth (Hamilton) and his partner Moe Curley (Perrineau) run an online sex site called InterconX. John is obsessive about documenting his life via a daily Webcam and becomes mesmerized by watching the beautiful Jordan (Ferlito), who does her own erotic fantasy thing on the website. He tries a real-live date with her but finds reality too much to handle. Other characters wander into the online world and Weintrob shows them (usually in split screen) interacting in various ways via computer and in person, but the characters aren't particularly appealing and it all seems dated. **87m/C VHS, DVD.** Josh Hamilton, Harold Perrineau Jr., Isabel Gillies; Vanessa Ferlito, John Fleck, Eric Millegan, Liz Owens; ***D:*** Jed Weintrob; ***W:*** Andrew Osborne, Jed Weintrob; ***C:*** Toshiaki Ozawa; ***M:*** Roger Neill.

Only Angels Have Wings 🦴🦴🦴🦴 **1939** Melodramatic adventure about a broken-down Peruvian air mail service. Large cast adds to the love tension between Grant, a pilot, and Arthur, a showgirl at the saloon. Nominated for special effects, a category recognized by the Academy that year for the first time. William Rankin and Eleanor Griffin are uncredited writers. **121m/B VHS, DVD.** Cary Grant, Thomas Mitchell, Richard Barthelmess, Jean Arthur, Noah Beery Jr., Rita Hayworth, Sig Rumann, John Carroll, Allyn Joslyn; ***D:*** Howard Hawks; ***W:*** Jules Furthman; ***C:*** Joseph Walker; ***M:*** Dimitri Tiomkin.

Only Love 🦴 1/2 *Erich Segal's Only Love* **1998** Sappy made for TV romance adapted from the Segal novel. Neurosurgeon Matthew Heller (Morrow) is shocked by the reappearance of former fiancee Silvia Rinaldi (May) some 15 years after they broke up. She's dying of a brain tumor and needs his medical help. His longtime (platonic) female friend Evie (Tomei) can't understand his obsession and you won't either. (The scenery's nice though). **130m/C VHS.** Rob Morrow, Marisa Tomei, Mathilda May, Jeroen Krabbe, Paul Freeman, Georges Corraface; ***D:*** John Erman; ***W:*** Gerald Christopher; ***M:*** John Morris. **TV**

Only Once in a Lifetime 🦴 **1979** A love story about an Hispanic immigrant painter looking for success in America. **90m/C VHS.** Miguel Robelo, Estrellita Lopez, Sheree North; ***D:*** Alejandro Grattan; ***C:*** Turner Browne; ***M:*** Robert O. Ragland.

Only One Night 🦴🦴 *En Enda Natt* **1942** Upon finding out that he's the illegitimate son of an aristocrat, a happy-go-lucky carousel operator in a circus joins high society and is promptly matched with a beautiful but repressed woman. In Swedish with English subtitles. **87m/B VHS.** *SW* Ingrid Bergman, Edvin Adolphson, Alno Taube, Olof Sandborg, Erik "Bullen" Berglund, Marianne Lofgren, Magnus Kesster; ***D:*** Gustaf Molander.

Only the Brave 🦴🦴 **1994** Gay coming-of-age story about two teenaged, working-class girls living on the seedy fringes of Melbourne. Alex (Manadalis), her wild best friend Vicki (Kaskanis), and their equally tough girlfriends seem to spend most of their time hanging out, smoking dope, and getting into trouble. But Alex slowly recognizes her feelings for Vicki are also sexual, and their friendship drastically changes. **62m/C VHS.** *AU* Elena Mandalis, Dora Kaskanis, Moudo Davey, Bob Bright; ***D:*** Ana Kokkinos; ***W:*** Ana Kokkinos, Mira Robertson.

Only the Brave 🦴🦴 **2006 (R)** Patriotism triumphs over social prejudice in Nishikawa's feature directorial debut about a heroic all-volunteer WWII infantry unit, comprised of Hawaiian Nisei and Japanese-American internment camp residents, who were sent to North Africa, Italy, and France to fight. A tight budget and some too-modern dialogue as well as cliched war situations lessen the inspirational impact. **97m/C DVD.** Jason Scott Lee, Mark Dacascos, Yuji Okumoto, Tamlyn Tomita, Greg Watanabe, Lane Nishikawa, Ken Narasaki; ***D:*** Lane Nishikawa; ***W:*** Lane Nishikawa; ***C:*** Michael G. Wojciechowski; ***M:*** Dan Kuramato, Kimo Cornwell. **VIDEO**

Only the Lonely 🦴🦴 ½ **1991 (PG)** Middle-aged cop, Candy, falls in love with a shy undertaker's assistant, Sheedy, and is torn between love and dear old Mom, O'Hara, in her first role in years. Candy is an unlikely leading man and even the jokes are forced. But the restaurant scene makes the whole thing well worth seeing. **104m/C VHS, DVD.** John Candy, Ally Sheedy, Maureen O'Hara, Anthony Quinn, Kevin Dunn, James Belushi, Milo O'Shea, Bert Remsen, Macaulay Culkin, Joe V. Greco; ***D:*** Chris Columbus; ***W:*** Chris Columbus; ***M:*** Maurice Jarre.

Only the Strong 🦴 ½ **1993 (PG-13)** Louis (Dacascos) is a special forces officer who has mastered capoeira, a Brazilian form of kung fu. In Miami, he works with his old teacher (Lewis) to instill discipline in the 12 toughest punks in school by teaching them his martial arts skills. A neighborhood drug lord, related to two of the students, decides to cause trouble for Louis. Dascascos displays some charm along with his physical abilities but the story's ridiculous and the movie hastily put together. **96m/C VHS, DVD.** Mark Dacascos, Stacey Travis, Todd Susman, Geoffrey Lewis, Paco Christian Prieto; ***D:*** Sheldon Lettich; ***W:*** Sheldon Lettich, Luis Esteban; ***M:*** Harvey W. Mason.

Only the Strong Survive 🦴🦴🦴 **2003 (PG-13)** Documentary filmmakers Hegedus and Pennebaker showcase R&B and soul legends of the late fifties to the early seventies in where-are-they-now features and in concert performances, including a number of performers from Memphis and Stax-Volt Records. Featured are Carla and Rufus Thomas, Issac Hayes, William Bell, the Chi-Lites, Jerry Butler, Sam Moore, Ann Peebles, Wilson Pickett, and Mary Wilson. **95m/C DVD.** *US* ***D:*** Chris Hegedus, D.A. Pennebaker; ***C:*** Chris Hegedus, D.A. Pennebaker, James Desmond, Nick Doob, Jehane Noujaim.

Only the Valiant 🦴🦴 **1950** Action-packed story of a cavalry officer who struggles to win his troops respect while warding off angry Apaches. Fast-paced Western fun requires little thought. **105m/B VHS.** Gregory Peck, Ward Bond, Gig Young, Lon Chaney Jr., Barbara Payton, Neville Brand; ***D:*** Gordon Douglas; ***C:*** Lionel Lindon.

The Only Thrill 🦴🦴 ½ *Tennessee Valley* **1997** Old-fashioned small town romance based on Ketron's play "The Trading Post." In 1966, Reece McHenry (Shepard) decides to open a used clothing store in his Tennessee hometown and hires widowed seamstress Carol Fitzsimmons (Keaton) to help him out. Reece is married but his wife is in an irreversible coma and soon the aw-shucks storekeeper is interested in romancing his new employee. Meanwhile, Reece's son Tom (Patrick) and Carol's daughter Katherine (Lane) have also discovered a reciprocated love. However, neither romance runs smoothly. **108m/C VHS.** Sam Shepard, Diane Keaton, Robert Patrick, Diane Lane, Tate Donovan, Sharon Lawrence, Stacey Travis; ***D:*** Peter Masterson; ***W:*** Larry Ketron; ***C:*** Don E. Fauntleroy; ***M:*** Peter Melnick.

Only Two Can Play 🦴🦴🦴 **1962** Sellers is a hilarious Casanova librarian who puts the moves on a society lady to get a promotion. Funny, of course, and based on Kingsley Amis' novel "That Uncertain Feeling." **106m/C VHS.** *GB* Peter Sellers, Virginia Maskell, Mai Zetterling, Richard Attenborough; ***D:*** Sidney Gilliat; ***M:*** Richard Rodney Bennett.

The Only Way 🦴🦴 ½ **1970 (G)** A semi-documentary account of the plight of the Jews in Denmark during the Nazi occupation. Despite German insistence, the Danes succeeded in saving most of their Jewish population from the concentration camps. **86m/C VHS.** Jane Seymour, Martin Potter, Benjamin Christiansen; ***M:*** Carl Davis.

The Only Way Home 🦴🦴 **1972 (PG)** Two bikers end up in big trouble when one of them kills a wealthy man, and they kidnap his wife. Filmed entirely in Oklahoma. **86m/C VHS.** Bo Hopkins, Beth Brickell, Steve Sandor, G.D. Spradlin; ***D:*** G.D. Spradlin.

Only When I Laugh 🦴🦴🦴 *It Hurts Only When I Laugh* **1981 (R)** Neil Simon reworked his Broadway flop "The Gingerbread Lady" to produce this poignant comedy about the relationship between an aging alcoholic actress and her teenage daughters. **120m/C VHS.** Marsha Mason, Kristy McNichol, James Coco, Joan Hackett, David Dukes, Kevin Bacon, John Bennett Perry; ***D:*** Glenn Jordan; ***W:*** Neil Simon; ***M:*** David Shire. Golden Globes '82: Support. Actress (Hackett).

Only with Married Men 🦴 **1974** Carne's hassle-free dating routine is disrupted when a sly bachelor pretends that he's married to get a date. A middle-aged persons answer to a teenage sex comedy. Pretty bad. **74m/C VHS, DVD.** David Birney, Judy Carne, Gavin MacLeod, John Astin; ***D:*** Jerry Paris.

Only You 🦴 ½ **1992 (PG-13)** A shy guy has always searched for true romance. But his cup runneth over when he meets, and must choose between, two beautiful women—your basic beach babe and a sensible beauty. What's a guy to do? **85m/C VHS.** Andrew McCarthy, Kelly Preston, Helen Hunt; ***M:*** Wendy Blackstone.

Only You 🦴🦴 ½ *Him; Just in Time* **1994 (PG)** According to her ouija board, young Faith's (Tomei) soul mate is named Damon Bradley. But as the years pass, Faith is about to settle for a podiatrist—until an old school friend of her fiance's calls from Venice, Italy, with best wishes. Guess what his name is. So Faith and best friend Kate (Hunt) hop on a plane in search of Mr. Right. Then Faith meets charming shoe salesman Peter Wright (Downey) and wonders if ouija got things wrong. Slight romantic comedy with Jewison creating satisfactory chemistry with charming Downey and the somewhat miscast Tomei (and the Venetian scenery is gorgeous). **108m/C VHS, DVD.** Marisa Tomei, Robert Downey Jr., Bonnie Hunt, Fisher Stevens, Billy Zane, Joaquim de Almeida; ***D:*** Norman Jewison; ***W:*** Diane Drake; ***C:*** Sven Nykvist; ***M:*** Rachel Portman.

Onmyoji 🦴🦴 *Onmyoji: The Yin Yang Master; The Yin Yang Masters; Yin Yang Masters* **2001 (R)** Onmyodo is a traditional Japanese form of occultism based on Chinese philosophy and influenced by Japanese culture and religion. Its professional practitioners were called the Onmyoji, and this film is about one of the most famous, Abe no Seimei. Abe is asked by a bumbling court noble to defend the emperor from an evil Onmyoji who is unleashing a horde of Yokai (spirit monsters) to bring about the government's downfall. Originally a novel, it became a comic and then a highly stylized film. A hit in Japan, it has strong cultural overtones, meaning most Western audiences will miss a lot of subtext if they aren't familiar with the Heian period of Japanese history. **116m/C DVD, UMD.** *JP* Kenichi Yajima, Kenjiro Ishimaru, Houka Kinoshita, Akira (Tsukamoto) Emoto, Ittoku Kishibe, Hiroyuki (Henry) Sanada, Mansai Nomura, Hideaki Ito, Eriko Imai, Yui Natsukawa, Mai Hosho, Kenichi Ishii, Sachiko Kokubu, Kenji Yamaki, Masato Hagiwara, Kyoko Koizumi; ***D:*** Yojiro Takita; ***W:*** Baku Yumemakura; ***C:*** Naoke Kayano, Naoki Kayano; ***M:*** Shigeru Kumebayashi.

Onmyoji 2 🦴🦴 **2003** The forces of the Daimyo brutally slaughter a small village, and a hidden priest invokes an ancient god to take revenge. Many years later, after a solar eclipse, mysterious events happen in the Heian capital. Demons are murdering members of the nobility by biting off parts of their body, and once again the famous Abe no Seimei is called upon to solve the problem. This sequel is more cinematic, and probably more accessible to viewers who aren't natives of Japan. **113m/C DVD.** *JP* Mansai Nomura, Hideaki Ito, Eriko Imai, Kenji Yamaki, Kiichi Nakai, Kyoko Fukada, Hayato Ichihara, Yuko Kategawa; ***D:*** Yojiro Takita; ***W:*** Yojiro Takita, Baku Yumemakura; ***C:*** Harry Henderson; ***M:*** Shigeru Kumebayashi.

Open Cam 🦴 ½ *OpenCam* **2005** Lots of skin, but not too much mystery or plot logic in this gay crime thriller. A D.C. serial killer finds his victims through an adult webcam site, all of whom are somehow connected to aspiring artist Manny. Police detective Hamilton is investigating while behaving in a decidedly unprofessional manner with his protagonist. **100m/C DVD.** Andreau Thomas, Amir Darvish, Ben Green, J. Matthew Miller, Christian Jones; ***D:*** Robert Gaston; ***W:*** Robert Gaston; ***C:*** Doug Gritzmacher; ***M:*** Jerry Walterick.

Open City 🦴🦴🦴🦴 *Roma, Citta Aperta; Rome, Open City* **1945** A leader in the Italian underground resists Nazi control of the city. A stunning film, making Rossellini's realistic style famous. In Italian with English subtitles. **103m/B VHS, DVD.** *IT* Anna Magnani, Aldo Fabrizi, Marcel Pagliero, Maria Michi, Vito Annicchiarico, Nando (Fernando) Bruno, Harry Feist; ***D:*** Roberto Rossellini; ***W:*** Federico Fellini, Sergio Amidei; ***C:*** Ubaldo Arata; ***M:*** Renzo Rossellini. N.Y. Film Critics '46: Foreign Film.

Open Doors 🦴🦴🦴 ½ *Porte Aperte* **1989 (R)** Bitter review of Fascist rule and justice. The Fascist regime promises security, safety, and tranquility. So, on the morning that a white collar criminal murders his former boss, murders the man who got his job, and then rapes and murders his wife, tensions rise and the societal structures are tested. The people rally for his death. A judge and a juror struggle to uphold justice rather than serve popular passions. Winner of four Donatello Awards, Italian Golden Globes for Best Film, Best Actor, and Best Screenplay, and many international film awards. In Italian with English subtitles. **109m/C VHS.** *IT* Gian Marie Volonte, Ennio Fantastichini, Lidia Alfonsi; ***D:*** Gianni Amelio; ***W:*** Gianni Amelio.

Open Fire 🦴🦴 **1994 (R)** Alex McNeil (Wincott) is an ex-FBI agent, haunted by the death of his partner. But when a group of terrorists threaten to release a cloud of nerve gas over L.A. and hold McNeil's father hostage, he comes back full force. **93m/C VHS.** Jeff Wincott, Patrick Kilpatrick, Lee DeBroux, Mimi (Meyer) Craven, Arthur Taxier; ***D:*** Kurt Anderson; ***W:*** Thomas Ritz; ***C:*** Jurgen Baum; ***M:*** Richard Bowers.

Open House 🦴 **1986** Radio psychologist and beautiful real estate agent search for the killer of real estate agents and their clients. A mystery-thriller for the very patient. **95m/C VHS.** Joseph Bottoms, Adrienne Barbeau, Mary Stavin, Rudy Ramos; ***D:*** Jag Mundhra.

Open Range 🦴🦴🦴 ½ **2003 (R)** Proving definitively that he should stick to sports and cowboys, Costner revives the glory of the classic Western with overwhelming success. Cowpokes Boss (Duvall) and Charley (Costner) peacefully graze their cattle on the open range during the late 1800s. That is, until they run up against cranky, land-grabbing rancher Baxter (Gambon) who dislikes the free-spirited, free-grazers and Boss's posse in particular. Bening is excellent as Costner's love interest. Their chemistry is only slightly less palpable than that of lone rangers Costner and a superb Duvall. Actor Costner handles familiar role with aplomb, while director Costner displays an eye for detail and a reverence for the genre. Alberta, Canada subs for the Wild West. Based on the novel by Lauran Paine. **135m/C VHS, DVD.** *US* Robert Duvall, Kevin Costner, Annette Bening, Michael Gambon, Michael Jeter, Diego Luna, James Russo, Abraham Benrubi, Dean McDermott, Kim Coates; ***D:*** Kevin Costner; ***W:*** Craig Storper; ***C:*** J.(James) Michael Muro; ***M:*** Michael Kamen.

The Open Road 🦴🦴 ½ **2009 (PG-13)** Predictable reconciliation plot with some strong performances by leads Bridges and Timberlake. Kyle Garrett (Bridges) was a baseball superstar and a lousy family man. Retired, Kyle is thrown when his estranged son Carlton (Timberlake) shows up at an Ohio baseball convention to inform his dad that Carlton's mom Katherine (Steenburgen) insists on seeing Kyle before having a risky operation at a Houston hospital. It turns into a road trip—that gives them plenty of time to talk—thanks to Kyle's irresponsibility but director Meredith (whose dad is football legend Don Meredith) doesn't resort to melodrama to get his story across. **90m/C DVD.** Jeff Bridges, Justin Timberlake, Kate Mara, Mary Steenburgen, Harry Dean Stanton; ***Cameos:*** Lyle Lovett, Ted Danson; ***D:*** Michael Meredith; ***W:*** Michael Meredith; ***C:*** Yaron Orbach; ***M:*** Christopher Lennertz.

Open Season 🦴🦴 **1995 (R)** Stuart Sain (Wuhl) is an ambitious executive at Fielding, a TV ratings company (think Nielsen) whose boxes turn out to be defective. The ratings error causes public television programming to be number one, forcing the networks to counter-program culturally in order to regain their market share. Meanwhile, the public TV executives get overconfident and everything's just up for grabs. Flawed satire. **97m/C VHS.** Robert Wuhl, Rod Taylor, Gailard Sartain, Maggie Han, Joe Piscopo, Helen Shaver, Dina Merrill, Saul Rubinek, Steven C. White, Timothy Arrington, Barry Flatman, Tom Selleck, Alan Thicke, Jimmie Walker; ***D:*** Robert Wuhl; ***W:*** Robert Wuhl; ***C:*** Stephen Lighthill; ***M:*** Marvin Hamlisch.

Open Season 🦴🦴 ½ **2006 (PG)** Harmless animated flick about the plight of animals vs. man. Boog (Lawrence) is a grizzly bear, raised in captivity, who's released into the woods a few days before the opening of hunting season. He relies on the help of his friend Elliot (Kutcher), a spastic mule deer, to find his way to safety, which means returning to human civilization since Boog really doesn't like this life-in-the-wild stuff. Abounds with standard bathroom humor, with sprinkles of wit for the grown-ups. **99m/C DVD, Blu-ray Disc.** *US* ***D:*** Roger Allers, Jill Culton; ***W:*** Steve Bencich, Maurizio Merli, Nat Maudlin; ***M:*** Paul Westerberg, Ramin Djawadi; ***V:*** Martin Lawrence, Ashton Kutcher, Gary Sinise, Debra Messing, Billy Connolly, Jon Favreau, Georgia Engel, Jane Krakowski, Gordon Tootoosis, Patrick Warburton.

Open Secret 🦴🦴 **1948** Jewish residents are plagued by a gang of anti-semitic thugs. Violence and destruction escalate until a fed up police lieutenant, tenaciously played by Ireland, and a victimized shop owner (Tyne) join forces to just say no more. When the gang learns the shopkeeper has caught their dastardly deeds on camera, the battle begins in earnest. Fast-paced and intriguing suspense. **70m/B VHS, DVD.** John Ireland, Jane Randolph, Roman Bohnen, Sheldon Leonard, George Tyne, Morgan Farley, Ellen Lowe, Anne O'Neal, Arthur O'Connell; ***D:*** John Reinhardt.

Open Water 🦴🦴🦴 **2003 (R)** Daniel (Travis) and Susan (Ryan) are an overworked couple who badly need a vacation. Little do they realize what they're in for when they go on a group scuba diving excursion in the Caribbean. Somehow, the boat crew screws up, and the two resurface to find the boat has left without them. Fighting cold, hunger, dehydration, sharks (which were real) and worst of all, their own fear and insecurities, the couple stay afloat for more than 24 hours hoping the boat will discover they are missing. Kentis and his wife Laura Lua shot on location in the Bahamas using a digital camera. The resulting visceral images add to the realism, and, subsequently, the fear and tension. Based on actual events. **79m/C DVD, UMD.** *US* Saul Stein, Blanchard Ryan, Daniel Travis, Estelle Lau, Michael E. Williamson, John Charles, Christina Zenaro; ***D:*** Chris Kentis; ***W:*** Chris Kentis; ***C:*** Chris Kentis, Laura Lau; ***M:*** Graeme Revell.

Open Window 🦴🦴 **2006 (R)** Peter (Edgerton) leaves the window open after fixing up a backyard studio for his photographer fiance Izzy (Tunney). She's working late one night and is raped by an intruder who enters through the open window. A guilt-ridden Peter feels helpless while trying to support a traumatized and deeply-depressed Izzy, and their relationship is soon at a breaking point. **98m/C DVD.** Robin Tunney, Joel Edgerton, Cybill Shepherd, Elliott Gould, Scott Wilson, Shirley Knight, Matt Keeslar; ***D:*** Mia Goldman; ***W:*** Mia Goldman; ***C:*** Denis Maloney; ***M:*** Cliff Eidelman.

Open Your Eyes *Abre Los Ojos* **1997 (R)** Reality gets taken for a mind-bending spin in this Spanish thriller. Gorgeous womanizer, Cesar (Noriega), meets equally gorgeous Sofia (Cruz) and thinks he's finally found the one. Only his crazy ex-girlfriend Nuria (Nimri) causes a car crash that kills her and disfigures Cesar. He awakens in a prison hospital wearing a mask, accused of murder, and with confused memories. But maybe he's had an operation to restore his looks and is actually back together with Sofia but then Cesar keeps seeing Nuria's ghost. So just what is going on? Spanish with subtitles. **117m/C VHS, DVD.** *SP* Eduardo Noriega, Penelope Cruz, Najwa Nimri, Chete Lera, Fele Martinez, Gerard Barray; ***D:*** Alejandro Amenabar; ***W:*** Alejandro Amenabar, Mateo Gil; ***C:*** Hans Burman; ***M:*** Alejandro Amenabar, Mariano Marin.

Opening Night 1/2 **1977 (PG-13)** Very long study about an actress (Rowlands) and the play she's about to open in on Broadway. Backstage turmoil increases her own insecurities and the bad luck persists when an adoring fan is struck by a car while the play is in try-outs in New Haven. Performances carry this neurotic epic along, including Cassavettes as Rowland's co-star and Blondell as the playwright. **144m/C VHS, DVD.** Gena Rowlands, John Cassavetes, Joan Blondell, Ben Gazzara, Paul Stewart, Zohra Lampert, Laura Johnson; ***D:*** John Cassavetes; ***W:*** John Cassavetes; ***C:*** Frederick Elmes; ***M:*** Bo Harwood.

Opera 1/2 *Terror at the Opera* **1988 (R)** A bizarre staging of Verdi's "Macbeth" is plagued by depraved gore murders. But the show must go on, as one character chirps in badly dubbed English. Italian horrormeister Argento's ever-fluid camera achieves spectacular shots, but the lurid, ludicrous script make this one for connoisseurs only. The operatic scenes employ the voice of Maria Callas. Available in an edited "R" rated version. **107m/C VHS, DVD.** *IT* Christina Marsillach, Ian Charleson, Urbano Barberini, William McNamara, Antonella Vitale, Barbara Cupisti, Coralina Cataldi-Tassoni, Daria Nicolodi; ***D:*** Dario Argento; ***W:*** Dario Argento, Franco Ferrini; ***C:*** Ronnie Taylor; ***M:*** Claudio Simonetti.

Opera do Malandro 1987 A lavish Brazilian take off of "The Threepenny Opera." Married hustler falls for a beautiful entrepreneur longing to get rich off of American goods. Based on Chico Buarque's musical play. In Portuguese, with subtitles. **106m/C VHS, DVD.** *BR* Edson Celulari, Claudia Ohana, Elba Ramalho, Ney Latorraca; ***D:*** Ruy Guerra.

Operation Amsterdam **1960** Four agents have 14 hours to snare $10 million in diamonds from under the noses of local Nazis. Based on a true story. Full of 1940s wartime action and suspense. **103m/B VHS, DVD.** Peter Finch, Eva Bartok, Tony Britton, Alexander Knox; ***D:*** Michael McCarthy.

Operation Bikini 1/2 **1963** Although set in WWII, this AIP flick was aimed at the teen market with Avalon pop-singing his way through the unlikely action as part of a naval demolition team. Old salt Brady and his submarine crew must deliver Frankie and his pals to Bikini Island for a super-secret mission. **83m/C VHS.** Frankie Avalon, Tab Hunter, Scott Brady, Jim Backus, Gary Crosby, Jody McCrea, Michael Dante, Eva Six; ***D:*** Anthony Carras; ***W:*** John Tomerlin; ***C:*** Gilbert Warrenton; ***M:*** Les Baxter.

Operation C.I.A. *Last Message From Saigon* **1965** A plot to assassinate the U.S. ambassador in Saigon inspires brave CIA agent Reynolds to wipe out the bad guys. Action-packed and somewhat exciting. **90m/C VHS.** Burt Reynolds, John Hayt, Kieu Chinh, Danielle Aubry; ***D:*** Christian Nyby.

Operation Condor **1991 (PG-13)** Secret agent Jackie (Chan) is sent by the United Nations to retrieve 240 tons of gold buried by the Nazis in a Moroccan desert during WWII. Naturally, he's not the only one after the treasure. Lots of typically exuberant stunts and laughable dialogue (dubbed into English from Cantonese). **92m/C VHS, DVD.** *HK* Jackie Chan, Carol Cheng, Eva Cabo De Garcia, Ikeda Shoko; ***D:*** Jackie Chan; ***W:*** Edward Tang, Jackie Chan; ***C:*** Wong Ngok Tai; ***M:*** Stephen Endelman.

Operation Condor 2: The Armour of the Gods *Armour of God; Longxiong Hudi* **1986 (R)** Prequel to "Operation Condor" was re-released in 1997. Chan plays an adventurous treasure-hunter who is asked by his ex-girlfriend's new fiancee Alan (Tam), who used to be Jackie's best friend, to rescue her from an evil cult. The kidnappers want Jackie and Alan to deliver a priceless medieval set of armour, thought to contain mysterious powers, to them. Naturally, Chan must come up with some spectacular saves of both the armour and the girl. In Cantonese with English subtitles. **88m/C VHS, DVD.** *HK* Jackie Chan, Alan Tam, Rosamund Kwan, Lola Forner; ***D:*** Jackie Chan; ***W:*** Jackie Chan, Edward Tang, John Sheppard; ***C:*** Peter Ngor; ***M:*** Michael Lai.

Operation Cross Eagles *Unakrsna Vatra* **1969** Routine WWII military thriller with Conte and Calhoun on a mission to rescue an American general in exchange for their German prisoner. Their mission is complicated by a traitor in the group. Conte's only directorship. **90m/C VHS, DVD.** *YU* Richard Conte, Rory Calhoun, Aili King, Phil Brown; ***D:*** Richard Conte.

Operation Crossbow *The Great Spy Mission; Code Name: Operation Crossbow* **1965** Action-packed espionage tale in which a trio of agents are assigned to destroy a Nazi munitions installation. Exciting ending and sensational pyrotechnics. **116m/C VHS, DVD.** Sophia Loren, George Peppard, Trevor Howard, John Mills, Richard Johnson, Tom Courtenay, Jeremy Kemp, Anthony Quayle, Helmut Dantine; ***D:*** Michael Anderson Sr.; ***W:*** Ray Rigby, Duilio Coletti.

Operation Dames 1/2 **1959** A squadron of soldiers must go behind Korean enemy lines to locate a missing U.S.O. troupe and bring them to safety. Low budget and not very funny for a supposed comedy. **73m/B VHS.** Eve Meyer, Chuck Henderson, Don Devlin, Ed Craig, Cindy Girard; ***D:*** Louis Clyde Stouman.

Operation: Delta Force **1997 (R)** Nash (Lara) and his South African terrorist band have stolen two vials of the Ebola virus in order to provide some cleansing of the population. So the Delta Force, lead by Lang (Fahey), are flown into Mozambique to stop 'em. Macho guys and lots of firepower. **93m/C VHS.** Jeff Fahey, Ernie Hudson, Frank Zagarino, Joe Lara, Todd Jensen, Hal Holbrook; ***D:*** Sam Firstenberg; ***W:*** David Sparling; ***C:*** Yossi Wein; ***M:*** Serge Colbert.

Operation Delta Force 2: Mayday 1/2 **1997 (R)** Russian terrorist Lukash (Campbell) is threatening atomic mayhem unless he's paid $25 billion and it's up to the elite combat unit, the Delta Force, to stop him. Standard actioner is less than memorable. **98m/C VHS, DVD.** Michael McGrady, J. Kenneth Campbell, Dale Dye, Simon Jones; ***D:*** Yossi Wein; ***W:*** David Sparling; ***C:*** Peter Belcher; ***M:*** Russell Stirling, Wessel Van Rensburg. **VIDEO**

Operation Delta Force 3: Clear Target 1/2 **1998 (R)** When the Delta Force destroys a billion-dollar cocaine operation, the drug cartel is out for revenge. Drug lord Umberto Salvatore steals a submarine and programs its warheads to fire on New York City. Of course, Delta Force has to get to the sub first. **96m/C VHS, DVD.** Bryan Genesse, Danny Keogh, Jim (James) Fitzpatrick, Greg Collins, Darcy La Pier; ***D:*** Mark Roper; ***W:*** David Sparling; ***C:*** John Scheepers; ***M:*** Serge Colbert. **VIDEO**

Operation Dumbo Drop 1/2 *Dumbo Drop* **1995 (PG)** It's 1968 and tough Green Beret captain (Glover), rescued by Vietnamese villagers, promises to replace their prized elephant, which was killed during his mission. He and a group of commandos use land, sea, and air to transport the reluctant beast, learning way more about elephant hygiene and eating habits than they ever wanted to know in the process. Wincer, who also directed "Free Willy," seems to be going for the title of "greatest large mammal director of all time." Anything with good-guy U.S. troops, a paratrooper elephant, and a family-friendly plot should be a Bob Dole favorite. **107m/C VHS, DVD.** Danny Glover, Ray Liotta, Doug E. Doug, Denis Leary, Corin "Corky" Nemec, Thein Le Dihn; ***D:*** Simon Wincer; ***W:*** Jim Kouf, Gene Quintano; ***C:*** Russell Boyd; ***M:*** David Newman.

Operation Golden Phoenix **1994 (R)** A security specialist (Mehri) is betrayed in his assignment is to protect one half of a valuable medallion. Seems the medal reveals the location in Lebanon of a ancient mountain of gold—desired by a ruthless warlord (Hong). Martial arts fights are well done in this routine actioner. **95m/C VHS.** Jalal Merhi, James Hong, Al Waxman, Loren Avedon; ***D:*** Jalal Merhi.

Operation Haylift **1950** The true story of the U.S. Air Force's efforts to rescue starving cattle and sheep herds during Nevada's blizzards of 1949. The Air Force provided realism for the film with planes, equipment, and servicemen. **73m/B VHS.** Bill Williams, Tom Brown, Ann Rutherford, Jane Nigh, Joseph (Joe) Sawyer, Dean Riesner, Richard Travis, Raymond Hatton, Jimmy Conlin, Tommy "T.V." Ivo; ***D:*** William Berke; ***W:*** Joseph (Joe) Sawyer, Dean Riesner; ***C:*** Benjamin (Ben H.) Kline.

Operation Intercept 1/2 **1995 (R)** Francesca (Andreichenko) suspects that the government is behind her father's murder after he develops technology that causes enemy planes to crash. So she threatens to destroy civilian aircraft until the killer is brought to justice. **94m/C VHS.** Natasha Andreichenko, Bruce Payne, John Stockwell, Lance Henriksen, Dennis Christopher, Michael Champion, Curt Lowens, Corbin Bernsen; ***D:*** Paul Levine; ***W:*** Paul Levine; ***C:*** John Newby.

Operation Julie 1/2 **1985** A detective searches out a huge drug ring that manufactures LSD. **100m/C VHS.** Colin Blakely, Lesley Nightingale, Clare Powney; ***D:*** Bob Mahoney.

Operation Mad Ball 1/2 **1957** Lemmon plays a conniving enlisted man in this military comedy. Bored WWII GIs, stationed at an Army medical unit in France, decide to liven things up by throwing a party for the nurses at a local hotel. Fast-talking Pvt. Hogan (Lemmon) must sneak around by-the-book Capt. Locke (Kovacs) since the nurses are officers and the enlisted men can't fraternize with them. Kovacs's screen debut. **105m/B DVD.** Jack Lemmon, Ernie Kovacs, Kathryn Grant, Mickey Rooney, Arthur O'Connell, Dick York, James Darren, Roger Smith, L.Q. Jones, Jeanne Manet; ***D:*** Richard Quine; ***W:*** Blake Edwards, Arthur Carter, Jed Harris; ***C:*** Charles Lawton Jr.; ***M:*** George Duning.

Operation 'Nam **1985** A group of bored Vietnam vets return to 'Nam to rescue their leader from a POW camp. Nothing special, but features John Wayne's son. De Angelis used the pseudonym Larry Ludman. **85m/C VHS.** Oliver Tobias, Christopher Connelly, Manfred Lehman, John Steiner, Ethan Wayne, Donald Pleasence; ***D:*** Fabrizio de Angelis.

Operation Orient 1/2 **1978** A statue laden with drugs is stolen when an international drug smuggler tries to bring it to the U.S. **94m/C VHS.** *GR* Gianni Gori, Gordon Mitchell; ***D:*** Ilias Milonakos.

Operation Petticoat 1/2 **1959** Submarine captain Grant teams with wheeler-dealer Curtis to make his sub seaworthy. They're joined by a group of Navy women, and the gags begin. Great teamwork from Grant and Curtis keeps things rolling. Jokes may be considered sexist these days. Later remake and TV series couldn't hold a candle to the original. **120m/C VHS, DVD.** Cary Grant, Tony Curtis, Joan O'Brien, Dina Merrill, Gene Evans, Arthur O'Connell, Virginia Gregg; ***D:*** Blake Edwards; ***W:*** Stanley Shapiro, Maurice Richlin; ***C:*** Russell Harlan; ***M:*** David Rose.

Operation Sandman: Warriors in Hell **2000 (R)** Scientist Perlman develops a serum for the military that allows soldiers to remain awake for weeks with heightened senses. Only there turns out to be a disturbing side effect—the soldiers eventually begin hallucinating and turn violent. Very disturbing. **89m/C VHS.** Ron Perlman, Richard Tyson, Mary B. Ward, John Haymes Newton; ***D:*** Nelson McCormick; ***W:*** Nelson McCormick; ***C:*** Larry Blanford. **TV**

Operation Thunderbolt 1/2 *Entebbe: Operation Thunderbolt* **1977** Israeli-produced depiction of Israel's July 14, 1976 commando raid on Entebbe, Uganda to rescue the passengers of a hijacked plane. Better than the American versions "Raid on Entebbe" and "Victory at Entebbe" in its performances as well as the information provided, much of it unavailable to the American filmmakers. **120m/C VHS, DVD.** Yehoram Gaon, Assaf Dayan, Ori Levy, Klaus Kinski; ***D:*** Menahem Golan.

Operation Valkyrie 1/2 *Stauffenberg* **2004** German television movie based on the true story of a 1944 plot to assassinate Hitler by placing a bomb in his war office. The plot is hatched by decorated Army Colonel Claus von Stauffenberg but we all know how it ends. German with subtitles. The same incident was filmed with Tom Cruise as 2008's "Valkyrie." **92m/C DVD.** *GE* Sebastian Koch, Christopher Buchholz, Hardy Kruger, Stefania Rocca, Ulrich Tukur, Nina Kunzendorf, Olli Dittrich, Axel Milberg; ***D:*** Jo Baier; ***W:*** Jo Baier; ***C:*** Gunnar Fuss; ***M:*** Enjott Schneider. **TV**

Operation Warzone **1989** A platoon of soldiers uncovers a plot by corrupt officers to continue the Vietnam war and sell weapons. **86m/C VHS.** Joe Spinell, John Cianetti, Sean Holton, William Zipp, David Marriott; ***D:*** David A. Prior; ***W:*** David A. Prior, Ted Prior; ***C:*** Andy Parke.

The Operator **2001** Scumdog lawyer Gary Whelan (Laurence) gets his comeuppance when he insults the wrong telephone operator (Kim). Calling herself Shiva (the Hindu goddess of destruction), she decides to even the karmic balance by stripping Gary of all his worldly possessions, breaking up his marriage, and framing him for murder. Set in Dallas, Texas. **102m/C VHS, DVD.** Jacqueline Kim, Michael Laurence, Christa Miller, Stephen Tobolowsky, Brion James, Frances Bay; ***D:*** Jon Dichter; ***W:*** Jon Dichter.

Operator 13 **1934** Implausible plot, and the title role is not a good fit for natural comedienne Davies as she plays an actress turned Union spy during the Civil War. Gail assumes a couple of identities (including that of a mulatto washerwoman) to get information and later discovers a mutual attraction with Confederate captain, Jack Gailliard (Cooper). The Oscar-nominated cinematography by George Folsey is the best thing about the film. **86m/B DVD.** Marion Davies, Gary Cooper, Douglass Dumbrille, Katherine Alexander, Jean Parker, Sidney Toler, William Robertson; ***D:*** Richard Boleslawski; ***W:*** Eve Greene, Zelda Sears, Harvey Thew; ***C:*** George J. Folsey; ***M:*** William Axt.

Opium and Kung-Fu Master *Hung Kuen Dai See; Lightning Fists of Shaolin; Hong quan da shi* **1984** Martial arts hero Ti Lung (Chao-San) and his students have long protected the local village they dwell in. But the arrival of a rival Kung Fu school does not bode well, as its master pushes Opium on the local populace who initially don't realize just how bad it truly is. Even Ti Lung himself becomes an addict, and must go cold turkey if he is to fight off the growing menace. **86m/C DVD, Blu-ray Disc.** *HK* Master Teih Chao-san, Kuan Tai Chen, Philip Ko, Shen Chan, Ying Huang; ***D:*** Chia Tang; ***C:*** Hui-chi Tsao; ***M:*** Chin Yung Shing, Chen-hou Su.

Opium: Diary of a Madwoman 1/2 **2007** A perverse look at addiction, madness, and obsession that's set in 1913 in a remote and nightmarish mental institution for women. Morphine-addicted Dr. Joszef Brenner comes to the clinic under the guise of psychoanalyzing the patients. The beautiful Gizella attracts his attention as she is convinced that the devil has possessed her and she compulsively fills diaries with her ramblings. Suffering from writer's block himself, Brenner is both jealous and sexually obsessed with Gizella. Based on the diaries of Hungary's first neurologist, writing under the pen name Geza Csath. **109m/C DVD.** *HU GE* Ulrich Thomsen, Kirsti Stubo, Zsolt Laszlo; ***D:*** Janos Szasz; ***W:*** Andras Szeker; ***C:*** Tibor Mathe.

The Oppermann Family 1/2 *Die Geschwister Oppermann* **1982** Long epic (made for German TV) about a family trying to survive in Berlin during the rise of Hitler. In German with subtitles. **238m/C VHS.** *GE* Peter Fitz, Wolfgang Kieling, Rosel Zech, Andrea Dahmen, Michael Degen, Til Topf; ***D:*** Egon Monk; ***C:*** Wolfgang Treu; ***M:*** Alexander Goehr. **TV**

The Opponent 1989 **(R)** A young boxer saves a young woman's life, not realizing that she has mob connections, thus embroiling him in a world of crime. **102m/C VHS.** *IT* Daniel Greene, Ernest Borgnine, Julian Gemma, Mary Stavin, Kelly Shaye Smith; ***D:*** Sergio Martino.

The Opponent 1/2 **2001 (R)** After years of domestic violence, Patty (Eleniak) finds an outlet for her anger in the boxing ring of the community center. With the encouragement of her trainer (Colby), she decides to take it to the next level and go for a pro career. But when Patty embarks on a romance with the guy, she also gets distracted from her goals. **90m/C VHS, DVD.** Erika Eleniak, Aunjanue Ellis, James Colby, John Doman; ***D:*** Eugene Jarecki; ***W:*** Eugene Jarecki; ***C:*** Joe Di Gennaro. **VIDEO**

Opportunity Knocks 1/2 **1990 (PG-13)** Carvey's first feature film has him impersonating a friend of a rich suburbanite's family while hiding from a vengeful gangster. They buy it, and give him a job and the daughter. Not hilarious, but not a dud either. **105m/C VHS, DVD.** Dana Carvey, Robert Loggia, Todd Graff, Milo O'Shea, Julia Campbell, James Tolkan, Doris Belack, Sally Gracie, Del Close; ***D:*** Donald Petrie; ***W:*** Mitchel Katlin, Nat Bernstein; ***M:*** Miles Goodman.

Opposing Force 1/2 *Hellcamp* **1987 (R)** The commander of an Air Force camp simulates prisoner-of-war conditions for realistic training, but he goes too far, creating all too real torture situations. He preys on the only female in the experiment, raping her as part of the training. A decent thriller. **97m/C VHS.** Tom Skerritt, Lisa Eichhorn, Anthony Zerbe, Richard Roundtree, Robert Wightman, John Considine, George Kee Cheung, Paul Joynt, Jay Louden, Ken Wright, Dan Hamilton; ***D:*** Eric Karson; ***W:*** Gil Cowan; ***M:*** Marc Donahue.

Opposite Corners **1996 (R)** Bryant Donatello (Warlock) is looking for a shot at the Golden Gloves boxing championship, something his father (Dennison) has been obsessed about ever since his own chance was taken away. Then Bryant realizes just what kind of "connections" his dad has. **106m/C VHS.** Billy Warlock, Cathy Moriarty, Anthony John (Tony) Denison, Jay Acovone, Robert Miano; ***D:*** Louis D'Esposito.

The Opposite of Sex 1/2 **1998 (R)** Teenaged terror Dedee (Ricci) wreaks havoc with the life of gay half-brother Bill (Donovan). She seduces his boyfriend Matt (Sergei), gets pregnant, steals his savings, and nearly costs him his high school teacher's job. Then she takes off for L.A., with Bill, his best friend Lucia (Kudrow), and sheriff Carl (Lovett) in pursuit. Quirky black comedy isn't shy, especially when Ricci's vamping across the screen, and features fine work by Kudrow (in a welcome departure from the dumb blonde roles) and Ricci (who can definitely remove the words "child actress" from her resume). Dedee's acerbic narration is another highlight. **105m/C VHS, DVD.** Christina Ricci, Martin Donovan, Lisa Kudrow, Ivan Sergei, Lyle Lovett, Johnny Galecki, William Lee Scott, Colin Ferguson; ***D:*** Don Roos; ***W:*** Don Roos; ***C:*** Hubert Taczanowski; ***M:*** Mason Daring. Ind. Spirit '99: First Feature, Screenplay; Natl. Bd. of Review '98: Support. Actress (Ricci); N.Y. Film Critics '98: Support. Actress (Kudrow).

The Opposite Sex **1956** Bevy of women battle mediocre script in adaptation of 1939's "The Women." ♫The Opposite Sex; Dere's Yellow Gold on de Trees (De Banana); A Perfect Love; Rock and Roll Tumbleweed; Now! Baby, Now; Jungle Red; Young Man with a Horn. **115m/C VHS.** June Allyson, Joan Collins, Dolores Gray, Ann Sheridan, Ann Miller, Leslie Nielsen, Agnes Moorehead, Joan Blondell; ***D:*** David Miller; ***W:*** Fay Kanin, Michael Kanin.

The Opposite Sex and How to Live With Them **1993 (R)** Yuppies (Gross and Cox) from different backgrounds (he's Jewish, she's a WASP) meet, fall in love, fight, break up, and reunite, inspiring yawning disinterest. All this while their two best buddies (Pollak and Brown) offer what are meant to be "candid insights" delivered directly to the camera. Flat and formulaic romantic comedy wants to sparkle, but script lacks both purpose and point, and worse, takes way too much time not getting there. Winner of the annual Grammar Police award for the worst example of a semantically incorrect title in recent years. **86m/C VHS.** Arye Gross, Courteney Cox, Kevin Pollak, Julie Brown, Mitchell Ryan, Philip Bruns, Mitzi McCall, B.J. Ward; ***D:*** Matthew Meshekoff; ***W:*** Noah Stern; ***M:*** Ira Newborn.

Optic Fiber *Fibra Optica* **1997** Marco (Sosa) is an unemployed journalist in Mexico who is hired by an anonymous telephone caller to investigate the murder of a labor union leader. The man's mistress, a Brazilian, has been framed for the crime. Marco enlists the help of his photographer girlfriend Maria (Cavazos) and they both plunge into a world of corruption and coverups. Spanish with subtitles. **105m/C VHS, DVD.** *MX* Roberto Sosa, Lumi Cavazos, Angelica Aragon, Alberto Estrella; ***D:*** Francisco Athie; ***W:*** Francisco Athie; ***C:*** Rodrigo Prieto.

The Optimists 1/2 **1973** Sentimental story finds Sam (Sellers), an old vaudeville performer, reduced to performing with his dog on London street corners. He befriends young Liz (Mullane) and her brother Mark (Chaffey), offering friendship and an optimistic view to their poverty-stricken lives on the wrong side of the tracks. Simmons directed from his novel "The Optimists of Nine Elms." **110m/C DVD.** Peter Sellers, David Daker, Marjorie Yates, Donna Mullane, John Chaffey; ***D:*** Anthony Simmons; ***W:*** Anthony Simmons, Tudor Gates; ***C:*** Larry Pizer; ***M:*** Lionel Bart, George Martin.

Options **1988 (PG)** Nerdy Hollywood agent Salinger treks to Africa to "option" a princess's life story—hence the title. He gets mixed up with her kidnapping and with her. Misplaced cameos by Roberts and Anton drag down the overall comedy content, which isn't to high to begin with. **105m/C VHS.** Matt Salinger, Joanna Pacula, John Kani, James Keach; ***Cameos:*** Susan Anton, Eric Roberts; ***D:*** Camilo Vila; ***W:*** Edward Decter.

Or (My Treasure) *Mon tresor* **2004** Feature debut of Israeli director Yedaya is naive, irritating, and compelling. Set in a modern-day, working-class neighborhood of Tel Aviv, it follows the struggles of prostitute Ruthie (Elkabetz) and her teenage daughter Or (Ivgy). Or is the responsible one—going to school, working, and looking after her self-destructive mother. Ruthie makes promises to go straight but inevitably goes back to the streets, thus breaking the heart of the daughter she refers to as "my treasure." Hebrew with subtitles. **100m/C DVD.** *IS* Ronit Elkabetz, Dana Ivgy, Meshar Cohen; ***D:*** Keren Yedaya; ***W:*** Sari Ezouz, Keren Yedaya; ***C:*** Laurent Brunet.

The Oracle **1985** A woman takes a new apartment only to find that the previous occupant's spirit is still a resident. The spirit tries to force her to take revenge on his murderers. Not bad for a low-budget thriller, but bad editing is a distraction. **94m/C VHS, DVD.** Caroline Capers Powers, Roger Neil; ***D:*** Roberta Findlay.

Orange County 1/2 **2002 (PG-13)** Pedigreed star Hanks (son of Tom) enters the world of leading men alongside character-meister Black in this pleasant buddy comedy. Equally credible Tinseltown offspring continue aplenty with love-interest Fisk (daughter of Sissy Spacek and Jake Fisk) and director Jake Kasdan (son of Lawrence). Typical Orange County, California teen Shaun Brumder trades his surf board for a pen when he accidentally discovers the joys of literature via a Marcus Skinner (an uncredited Kline) novel on the beach. Determined to study under Skinner at Stanford, Brumder is bummed when the wrong test scores are submitted to the college who summarily rejects him. Enter stoner brother Lance, to help him straighten everything out. Dynamic comedy with character development of a surprisingly sophisticated nature for this type of film. **81m/C VHS, DVD.** *US* Colin Hanks, Jack Black, Schuyler Fisk, Catherine O'Hara, John Lithgow, Harold Ramis, Jane Adams, Garry Marshall, Dana Ivey, Chevy Chase, Lily Tomlin, George Murdock, Leslie Mann, Kyle Howard, Kevin Kline; ***D:*** Jake Kasdan; ***W:*** Mike White; ***C:*** Greg Gardiner; ***M:*** Michael Andrews.

Oranges Are Not the Only Fruit 1/2 **1989** Lesbian coming of age story about young Jess (Coleman), who must escape her evangelical religious upbringing and mother (McEwan) in order to be true to herself. When the teenaged Jess gets a schoolgirl crush on her friend Melanie, the congregation finds out and condemns the girls until Jess finds the strength to break away. Based on the novel by Winsterson, who also wrote the screenplay. Made for TV. **165m/C VHS, DVD.** *GB* Charlotte Coleman, Geraldine McEwan, Cathryn Bradshaw, Kenneth Cranham, Freda Dowie, Richard Henders, Elizabeth Spriggs, Sophie Thursfield; ***D:*** Beeban Kidron; ***W:*** Jeanette Winterson; ***M:*** Rachel Portman. **TV**

Orca **WOOF!** *Orca—Killer Whale; The Killer Whale* **1977 (PG)** Ridiculous premise has a killer whale chasing bounty hunter Harris to avenge the murder of its pregnant mate. Great for gore lovers, especially when the whale chomps Derek's leg off. **92m/C VHS, DVD.** Richard Harris, Charlotte Rampling, Bo Derek, Keenan Wynn, Will Sampson, Robert Carradine; ***D:*** Michael Anderson Sr.; ***W:*** Sergio Donati, Luciano Vincenzoni; ***C:*** Ted Moore; ***M:*** Ennio Morricone.

Orchestra Rehearsal *Prova d'Orchestra* **1978** Italian orchestra musicians gather in a 13th-century chapel to film a TV documentary, protest the increasing authoritarianism of their German conductor, but are eventually persuaded to play amidst the chaos. Rota's last score. Italian with subtitles. **72m/C VHS, DVD.** *IT* Balduin Baas, Clara Colosimo, Elisabeth Labi, Ronaldo Bonacchi, Ferdinando Villella, Giovanni Javarone, David Mauhsell, Francesco Aluigi; ***D:*** Federico Fellini; ***W:*** Federico Fellini, Brunello Rondi; ***C:*** Giuseppe Rotunno; ***M:*** Nino Rota.

Orchestra Wives **1942** A drama bursting with wonderful Glenn Miller music. A woman marries a musician and goes on the road with the band and the other wives. Trouble springs up with the sultry singer who desperately wants the woman's new husband. The commotion spreads throughout the group. ♫People Like You and Me; At Last; Serenade in Blue; I've Got a Gal in Kalamazoo. **98m/B VHS, DVD.** George Montgomery, Glenn Miller, Lynn Bari, Carole Landis, Jackie Gleason, Cesar Romero, Ann Rutherford, Virginia Gilmore, Mary Beth Hughes, Harry (Henry) Morgan; ***D:*** Archie Mayo.

Orde Wingate **1976** Capable biography of Orde Wingate (Foster), who was one of Britain's most celebrated and unorthodox commanders during WWII. While serving in Palestine, Wingate becomes a passionate Zionist and develops guerrilla tactics he teaches to the future leaders of the Israeli Defense Force. **174m/C DVD.** *GB* Barry Foster, James Cosmo, Denholm Elliott, Bernard Hepton, Sheila Ruskin, Arnold Diamond; ***D:*** Bill Hays; ***W:*** Don Shaw. **TV**

Ordeal by Innocence 1/2 **1984 (PG-13)** Sutherland is an amateur sleuth in 1950s England convinced he has proof that a convicted murderer is innocent, but no one wishes to reopen the case. Big-name cast is essentially wasted. Based on an Agatha Christie story. **91m/C VHS.** Donald Sutherland, Christopher Plummer, Faye Dunaway, Sarah Miles, Ian McShane, Diana Quick, Annette Crosbie, Michael Elphick; ***D:*** Desmond Davis; ***C:*** Billy Williams; ***M:*** Pino Donaggio.

Ordeal in the Arctic 1/2 **1993 (PG)** Military transport plane, piloted by Capt. John Couch (Chamberlain), crashes into the remote glaciers of the Arctic. The survivors face a blizzard and freezing to death unless a rescue team can get to them quickly. Based on the book "Death and Deliverance" by Robert Mason Lee. **93m/C VHS, DVD.** *CA* Richard Chamberlain, Melanie Mayron, Catherine Mary Stewart, Scott Hylands, Page Fletcher, Christopher Bolton, Richard McMillan; ***D:*** Mark Sobel; ***W:*** Paul F. Edwards; ***C:*** Miklos Lente; ***M:*** Amin Bhatia. **CABLE**

The Ordeal of Dr. Mudd **1980** His name was Mudd—a fitting moniker after he unwittingly aided President Lincoln's assassin. Dr. Mudd set John Wilkes Boothe's leg, broken during the assassination, and was jailed for conspiracy. He became a hero in prison for his aid during yellow fever epidemics and was eventually released. A strong and intricate performance by Weaver keeps this TV drama interesting. Mudd's descendants are still trying to completely clear his name of any wrongdoing in the Lincoln assassination. **143m/C VHS, DVD.** Dennis Weaver, Susan Sullivan, Richard Dysart, Michael McGuire, Nigel Davenport, Arthur Hill; ***D:*** Paul Wendkos. **TV**

The Order *Sin Eater* **2003 (R)** Dark and logy religious thriller stars a dour and underwhelming Ledger as Alex, a Catholic priest investigating the death of his mentor (Carnelutti). His sleuthing eventually leads to a character known as a "Sin Eater" (Furmann), who literally ingests a wide range of normally unforgivable sins. These sins are represented by creatures similar to those in "Alien," as they also come bursting out of the chests of the unfortunate, but soon to be forgiven, souls. Upbeat subplot involves Alex's roll in the hay with a mentally deranged girl (Sossamon) who once attempted to kill him. What this poor man's "Exorcist" lacks in action, sufficient pacing, and a believable story line, it more than makes up for in gloomy lethargy, heavy-handed dialogue, loopy plotting, and humorless characters. **102m/C VHS, DVD.** *US* Heath Ledger, Shannyn Sossamon, Benno Furmann, Mark Addy, Peter Weller, Francesco Carnelutti; ***D:*** Brian Helgeland; ***W:*** Brian Helgeland; ***C:*** Nicola Pecorini; ***M:*** David Torn.

Order of the Black Eagle 1/2 **1987 (R)** A Bond-ish spy and his sidekick, Typhoon the Baboon, battle neo-Nazis planning to bring Hitler back to life in this silly tongue-in-cheek thriller. **93m/C VHS.** *GB* Ian Hunter, Charles K. Bibby, William T. Hicks, Jill Donnellan; ***D:*** Worth Keeter.

Order of the Eagle 1/2 **1989** An innocent scouting trip turns into a non-stop nightmare when an Eagle Scout uncovers some dangerous information. **88m/C VHS.** Frank Stallone; ***D:*** William Zipp; ***W:*** William Zipp.

Order to Kill 1/2 **1973** A gambling boss puts out a contract on a hit man. **110m/C VHS, DVD.** Jose Ferrer, Helmut Berger, Sydne Rome, Kevin McCarthy; ***D:*** Jose Maesso.

Ordet 1/2 *The Word* **1955** A man who believes he is Jesus Christ is ridiculed until he begins performing miracles, which result in the rebuilding of a broken family. A statement on the nature of religious faith vs. fanaticism by the profoundly religious Dreyer, and based on the play by Kaj Munk. In Danish with English subtitles. **126m/B VHS, DVD.** *DK* Henrik Malberg, Birgitte Federspiel, Cay Kristiansen, Emil Hass Christiansen; ***D:*** Carl Theodor Dreyer; ***W:*** Carl Theodor Dreyer, Kaj Munk; ***C:*** Henning Bendtsen. Golden Globes '56: Foreign Film; Venice Film Fest. '55: Film.

Ordinary Decent Criminal **1999 (R)** Lightweight caper flick loosely based on the life of Irish thief Martin Cahill was shot in 1998 but only recently received limited runs abroad. Spacey is Michael Lynch, a self-styled blue collar criminal who enjoys high-profile heists and making the local cops look bad. When he steals a Caravaggio painting worth $45 million, he gets caught up with the IRA and an obsessive cop (Dillane) bent on catching him. Passes the time pleasantly enough, with a jovial performance by Spacey, but John Boorman's "The General" tells this story better. **90m/C VHS, DVD.** *IR GB* Kevin Spacey, Linda Fiorentino, Helen Baxendale, Stephen (Dillon) Dillane, Peter Mullan, Patrick Malahide, Gerard McSorley, Colin Farrell; ***D:*** Thaddeus O'Sullivan; ***W:*** Gerard Stembridge; ***C:*** Andrew Dunn; ***M:*** Damon Albarn.

Ordinary Heroes 1/2 **1985** The story is familiar but the leads make it worthwhile. Anderson is strong as a blinded Vietnam vet readjusting to life at home. Bertinelli's portrayal of his former girlfriend is eloquent. Nice work on an overdone story. **105m/C VHS.** Richard Dean Anderson, Doris Roberts, Valerie Bertinelli; ***D:*** Peter H. Cooper.

Ordinary Magic 1/2 **1993** Teenaged Jeffrey was raised in India, picking up more than a little eastern wisdom along the way. After the death of his parents Jeffrey comes to the U.S. to live with his aunt where he sticks out not only as the new kid but as a decided oddball. But he manages to make some new friends and teach a few lessons about individuality along the way. Adapted from the novel by Malcolm Bosse. **96m/C VHS.** David Fox, Glenne Headly, Heath Lamberts, Ryan Reynolds; ***Cameos:*** Paul Anka; ***D:*** Giles Walker; ***W:*** Jefferson Lewis.

Ordinary People ½ **1980 (R)** Powerful, well-acted story of a family's struggle to deal with one son's accidental death and the other's subsequent guilt-ridden suicide attempt. Features strong performances by all, but Moore is especially believable as the cold and rigid mother. McGovern's film debut as well as Redford's directorial debut. Based on the novel by Judith Guest. **124m/C VHS, DVD.** Mary Tyler Moore, Donald Sutherland, Timothy Hutton, Judd Hirsch, M. Emmet Walsh, Elizabeth McGovern, Adam Baldwin, Dinah Manoff, James B. Sikking, Frederic Lehne; ***D:*** Robert Redford; ***W:*** Alvin Sargent; ***C:*** John Bailey; ***M:*** Marvin Hamlisch. Oscars '80: Adapt. Screenplay, Director (Redford), Picture, Support. Actor (Hutton); Directors Guild '80: Director (Redford); Golden Globes '81: Actress—Drama (Moore), Director (Redford), Film—Drama, Support. Actor (Hutton); L.A. Film Critics '80: Support. Actor (Hutton); Natl. Bd. of Review '80: Director (Redford); N.Y. Film Critics '80: Film; Writers Guild '80: Adapt. Screenplay.

Ordinary Sinner ½ **2002** Peter (Hines) has dropped out of an Episcopal seminary, having had his faith shaken while working as a teen counselor. He's come to a small Vermont college town where his shy childhood friend Alex (Park) is going to school. Alex has a crush on sexy student Rachel (Banks), who's more interested in the depressed Peter. Meanwhile, Peter's one-time mentor Father Ed (Martinez) publicly reveals he's gay when a series of gay-bashing incidents strike the campus. A death causes more emotional upheaval and adds some unnecessary whodunit elements to an already overstuffed plot. Well-meaning plea for tolerance does border on the preachy. **92m/C VHS, DVD.** Brendan P. Hines, Kris Park, Elizabeth Banks, A. Martinez, Peter Onorati, Nathaniel Marston; ***D:*** John Henry Davis; ***W:*** William Mahone; ***C:*** Mathieu Roberts; ***M:*** Brian Adler.

Orfeu **1999** Diegues's musical drama is adapted from the Vinicius de Moraes play that also inspired Marcel Camus's, 1959 film "Black Orpheus." The retelling of the Greek Orpheus and Eurydice tragedy is set during carnivale in Rio and features pop singer Garrido as egotistical songwriter Orfeu who becomes smitten with country girl Eurydice (Franca). Portuguese with subtitles. **112m/C VHS, DVD.** *BR* Toni Garrido, Patricia Franca, Murilo Benicio, Zeze Motta, Milton Goncalves, Isabel Fillardis; ***D:*** Carlos Diegues; ***W:*** Carlos Diegues; ***C:*** Alfonso Beato; ***M:*** Caetano Veloso.

The Organization **1971 (PG)** Poitier's third and final portrayal of Detective Virgil Tibbs, first seen in "In the Heat of the Night." This time around he battles a drug smuggling ring with a vigilante group. Good action scenes and a realistic ending. **108m/C VHS, DVD.** Sidney Poitier, Barbara McNair, Sheree North, Raul Julia; ***D:*** Don Medford; ***W:*** James R. Webb; ***C:*** Joseph Biroc; ***M:*** Gil Melle.

Organized Crime & Triad Bureau *Chungon Satluk Linggei* **1993** Determined Lee and his cop team seal off crowded Hong Kong island Cheung Chai to trap mob boss Tung and his tootsie. And the bystanders better just get out of the way. Lots of action; Chinese with subtitles. **91m/C VHS, DVD.** *HK* Danny Lee, Anthony Wong, Cecilia Yip, Roy Cheung, Elizabeth Lee; ***D:*** Kirk Wong; ***W:*** Winky Wong; ***C:*** Wing-Hung Wong, Kwong-Hung Chan; ***M:*** Danny Chung, Ding-Yat Tsung.

The Organizer *I Compagni; Comrades* **1964** In 19th-century Turin, impoverished aristocratic professor Mastroianni unites a group of textile workers striking against unsafe working conditions. Italian with subtitles. **127m/B VHS.** *IT* Marcello Mastroianni, Annie Girardot, Renato Salvatori, Bernard Blier, Francois Perier, Folco Lulli; ***D:*** Mario Monicelli; ***W:*** Mario Monicelli; ***C:*** Giuseppe Rotunno.

Organizm ½ *Living Hell* **2008 (R)** Typically underwhelming Sci-Fi Channel original. When Frank Sears was a kid, his dad worked at a New Mexico army base doing weird experiments that his crazy mom ranted about. She knew they kept something dangerous locked in an underground lab and carved the section's numbers into the palms of Frank's hands. When the adult Frank (Schaech) learns the base is to be demolished, he finally gets someone to look in the lab and they accidentally unleash a deadly organism that feeds on light and energy. Naturally, Frank is the only one that can stop the creature. **92m/C DVD.** Johnathon Schaech, Erica Leerhsen, James McDaniel, Jason Wiles, Frederick Lopez; ***D:*** Richard Jefferies; ***W:*** Richard Jefferies; ***C:*** Eric Leach; ***M:*** Terence Jay. **CABLE**

Orgazmo ½ **1998 (NC-17)** "South Park" co-creator Trey Parker plays Morman porn star Joe Young in this tale of sinners and Latter Day Saints in the dirty movie biz. When his sidekick (Bachar) invents an orgasm ray gun, they become superheroes and ride the one-joke premise like a rented Ferrari. Although hung with an NC-17 rating, it's guilty of bad humor more than bad taste. Parker is likeable, however, and provides intermittent laughs. **95m/C VHS.** Trey Parker, Dian Bachar, Ron Jeremy, Matt Stone, Robyn Lynne, Michael Dean Jacobs, Andrew W. Kemler, David Dunn; ***D:*** Trey Parker; ***W:*** Trey Parker; ***C:*** Kenny Gioseffi; ***M:*** Paul Robb.

Orgy of the Dead **WOOF! 1965** Classic anti-canon film scripted by Ed Wood Jr., from his own novel. Two innocent travelers are forced to watch an even dozen nude spirits dance in a cardboard graveyard. Hilariously bad. **90m/C VHS, DVD.** Criswell, Fawn Silver, William Bates, Pat (Barringer) Barrington, John Andrews, Colleen O'Brien; ***D:*** A.C. (Stephen Apostoloff) Stephen; ***W:*** Edward D. Wood Jr.; ***C:*** Robert Caramico.

Orgy of the Vampires *Vampire's Night Orgy* **1973 (R)** Tourists wander into village during cocktail hour. **86m/C VHS, DVD.** *SP IT* Jack Taylor, Charo Soriano, Dianik Zurakowska, John Richard; ***D:*** Leon Klimovsky.

Oriana **1985** Marie (Silverio) learns that her Aunt Oriana (Wells) has willed her the family estate, a remote Venezuelan hacienda she visited as a girl. While preparing the house for sale and going through her aunt's things, Marie remembers her long-ago stay and tries to discover why Oriana never left the property, what happened to her first love, and what other secrets she kept. Spanish and French with subtitles. **88m/C DVD.** *FR VZ* Daniela Silverio, Doris Wells, Rafael Briceno, Luis Armando Castillo, Maya Oloe, Mirtha Borges; ***D:*** Fina Torres; ***W:*** Fina Torres, Antoine Lacomblez; ***C:*** Jean-Claude Larrieu; ***M:*** Eduardo Marturet.

The Original Fabulous Adventures of Baron Munchausen ½ *The Fabulous Baron Munchausen* **1961** An adventure fantasy that takes the hero all over, from the belly of a whale, eventually landing him on the surface of the moon. **84m/C VHS.** *CZ* Milos Kopecky, Hana Brejchova, Rudolf Jelinek, Jan Werich; ***D:*** Karel Zeman.

Original Gangstas **1996 (R)** In Hollywood everything old eventually becomes new again. John Bookman (Williamson) returns to his old neighborhood in Gary, Indiana, after his father is brutally shot by a gang leader. Things have changed from Bookman's days of gang banging, with the streets swarming with young machine guntoting lowlifes. Bent on revenge, cigar-chewing Bookman, aided by childhood friends Jake (Brown), Slick (Roundtree), and Bubba (O'Neal), decide to take back their streets with a little help from Foxy Brown herself (Grier), as a greiving mother. The nostalgia quotient is high watching these '70s blaxploitation stars together in one movie, older, more gray and a little wider, but still able to kick butt. Serious topic (gang violence) is lost in a conventional vigilante vehicle, which sacrifices a message for an all-too-familiar and bloody showdown. **98m/C VHS, DVD.** Jim Brown, Fred Williamson, Pam Grier, Ron O'Neal, Richard Roundtree, Paul Winfield; ***D:*** Larry Cohen; ***W:*** Aubrey Rattan; ***C:*** Carlos Gonzalez; ***M:*** Vladimir Horunzhy.

Original Intent **1991 (PG)** A successful lawyer, facing a mid-life crisis, jeopardizes both his family and career when he decides to defend a homeless shelter from eviction proceedings. What might have been a powerful drama about one man's crusade to help the homeless instead merely melodramtic. Actor/activist Sheen appears briefly as a homeless man. **97m/C VHS.** Jay Richardson, Candy Clark, Kris Kristofferson, Vince Edwards, Cindy Pickett, Robert DoQui, Joseph Campanella; ***Cameos:*** Martin Sheen; ***D:*** Robert Marcarelli; ***W:*** Robert Marcarelli.

Original Sin **2001 (R)** 1880s Cuban coffee-plantation owner Luis (Banderas) sends to America for a mail-order bride, seeking only someone loyal and of childbearing years. To discourage gold diggers, he describes himself as a clerk. When his bride-to-be Julia (Jolie) shows up, Luis discovers that she's much more attractive than her picture. She claims that she wanted to be desired for something other than her beauty. With a start like that, what could go wrong? Well, betrayal, murder and theft for starters. An American private detective arrives on the scene, hired by Julia's family to report on her well-being. This fuels doubts in Luis, but a little too late. Soon he's cleaned out, shamed and on the trail of his former "wife." Banderas and Jolie torch the scenes as the couple in lust, but the ham-handed dialogue and direction derail this period potboiler. Loosely based on the Cornell Woolrich novel "Waltz Into Darkness," which was also the source for Truffaut's "Mississippi Mermaid." **112m/C VHS, DVD.** *US* Antonio Banderas, Angelina Jolie, Thomas Jane, Jack Thompson, Gregory Itzin, Joan Pringle, Allison Mackie, Cordelia Richards, Pedro Armendariz Jr.; ***D:*** Michael Cristofer; ***W:*** Michael Cristofer; ***C:*** Rodrigo Prieto; ***M:*** Terence Blanchard.

Orlando **1992 (PG-13)** Potter's sumptuous film adaptation of Virginia Woolf's 1928 novel, which covers 400 years in the life of an English nobleman, who not only defies death but evolves from a man to a woman in the intervening years. Orlando (Swinton) is first seen as a young man in the court of Queen Elizabeth I (Crisp) but after a deep sleep it's suddenly 40 years later. Things like this just keep happening and by 1750 he is now a she (and remains so), finding and losing love, and eventually gaining fulfillment in the 20th century. Elaborate productions never overwhelm Swinton's serene, self-assured performance. **93m/C VHS, DVD.** *GB* Tilda Swinton, Charlotte Valandrey, Billy Zane, Lothaire Bluteau, John Wood, Quentin Crisp, Heathcote Williams, Dudley Sutton, Thom Hoffman, Peter Eyre, Jimmy Somerville; ***D:*** Sally Potter; ***W:*** Sally Potter; ***C:*** Alexei Rodionov; ***M:*** Bob Last.

Orloff and the Invisible Man *Orloff Against the Invisible Man; The Invisible Dead; Dr. Orloff's Invisible Monster* **1970** So many invisible man movies, so little time. A scientist creates an invisible man, imprisons and tortures him. A bit miffed with his host, he who can't be seen escapes, and vents his invisible spleen. **76m/C VHS, DVD.** *IT FR* Howard Vernon, Brigitte Carva, Fernando (Fernand) Sancho, Isabel Del Rio, Paco Valladares; ***D:*** Pierre Chevalier; ***W:*** France Villon; ***M:*** Camile Sauvage.

Orochi, the Eight Headed Dragon ½ *Yamato Takeru* **1994** Based on Japanese myth, with similarities to the old Ray Harryhausen films that were also loosely based on the same mythology. Prince Yamato is born under an evil sign. Saved from execution at birth by the intervention of the Bird of Heaven, his bad luck ends up killing his family before he is exiled. Eventually he learns he is destined to seek out the ultimate weapon and use it to put a stop to the destruction being caused by the evil god Tsukiyomi. The giant rubber monsters are okay, but beyond that the effects are pretty bad. **100m/C DVD.** *JP* Masahiro Takashima, Yasuka Sawaguchi, Hiroshi Abe, Kenpachiro Satsuma; ***D:*** Takao Okawara; ***W:*** Waturu Mimura; ***C:*** Yoshinori Sekiguchi; ***M:*** Yoko Kanno.

The Orphan ½ **1979** A young orphaned boy seeks revenge against his cruel aunt who is harassing him with sadistic discipline. **80m/C VHS.** Mark Evans, Joanna Miles, Peggy (Margaret) Feury; ***D:*** John Ballard.

Orphan ½ **2009 (R)** Gory and somewhat repulsive killer kiddie flick. When their third child is stillborn it takes a toll on John (Sarsgaard) and Kate's (Farmiga) marriage and Kate's sanity as well, tipping her farther over the edge into alcoholism. So of course it makes sense (only in movie plot land) to decide it would be a great time to adopt. They choose extremely polite but obviously odd nine-year-old orphan Esther (Fuhrman) but Kate becomes increasingly alarmed that something evil lurks beneath the girl's prim facade. Passive-aggressive John (and everyone else) seems to think Kate is the one needing a timeout. **101m/C DVD.** *US* Vera Farmiga, Peter Sarsgaard, Jimmy Bennett, Isabelle Fuhrman, Aryana Engineer, CCH Pounder, Margo Martindale, Karel Roden, Rosemary Dunsmore; ***D:*** Jaume Collet-Serra; ***W:*** David Leslie Johnson; ***C:*** Jeff Cutter; ***M:*** John Ottman.

An Orphan Boy of Vienna ½ **1937** A homeless street urchin with a beautiful singing voice is accepted into the wonderful world of the Choir, but is later unjustly accused of stealing. Performances by the Vienna Boys' Choir redeem the melodramatic plot. In German with English subtitles. **87m/B VHS.** *GE* ***D:*** Max Neufeld.

Orphan Train **1979** A woman realizes her New York soup kitchen can't do enough to help the neighborhood orphans, so she takes a group of children out West in hopes of finding families to adopt them. Their journey is chronicled by a newspaper photographer and a social worker. Based on the actual "orphan trains" of the mid- to late 1800s. From the novel by Dorothea G. Petrie. **150m/C VHS.** Jill Eikenberry, Kevin Dobson, Glenn Close, Linda Manz; ***D:*** William A. Graham. **TV**

The Orphanage *El Orfanato* **2007 (R)** Laura (Rueda) returns to the orphanage of her youth with husband Carlos (Cayo) and adopted son Simon (Princep) three decades after leaving with her adoptive parents. Laura and Carlos have purchased the abandoned building with plans to establish a home for sick and disabled children. Their plans are preempted by the arrival of an imaginary playmate for Simon, which forces long-repressed frightening memories to the surface for Laura and leads to Simon's disappearance. What follows is Laura's nightmarish attempt to sort reality from haunting fantasy as she desperately tries to simultaneously find her son and cling to sanity. Well acted and well crafted, this terrifying ghost story is gripping, anxious, and truly scary, and an antidote to the torture porn that passes for horror of late. **100m/C DVD.** *SP* Belen Rueda, Geraldine Chaplin, Mabel Rivera, Fernando Cayo, Roger Princep, Montserrat Carulla; ***D:*** Juan Antonio Bayona; ***W:*** Sergio G. Sanchez; ***C:*** Oscar Fauna; ***M:*** Fernando Velazquez.

The Orphans *Podranki* **1977** A sensitive edge-of-glasnost portrait of a young boy's discovery of love, friendship, and literature. In Russian with English subtitles. **97m/C VHS.** *RU* Nikolai Gubenko, Y. Boudraitis, A. Tcherstvov, A. Kaliaguine, E. Bourkov, J. Bolotova, R. Bikov, E. Evstigneev; ***D:*** Nikolai Gubenko; ***W:*** Nikolai Gubenko; ***C:*** Alexander Kniajinsky.

Orphans **1987 (R)** A gangster on the run is kidnapped by a tough New York orphan but soon takes control by befriending his abductor's maladjusted brother. Eventually each brother realizes his need for the older man, who has become a father figure to them. This very quirky film is salvaged by good performances. Based on the play by Lyle Kessler. **116m/C VHS.** Albert Finney, Matthew Modine, Kevin Anderson; ***D:*** Alan J. Pakula; ***W:*** Lyle Kessler; ***M:*** Michael Small.

Orphans **1997** Three brothers and their handicapped sister come unraveled in the 24-hour period following their mother's death. The four Flynn siblings head for the pub the night before the funeral where eldest brother Thomas (Lewis) takes to singing, drawing amusement from the onlookers. This upsets Michael (Henshall), who then gets stabbed in the subsequent bar fight, leading youngest brother John (McCole) to vow to get revenge. Meanwhile, angry, wheelchair-bound Sheila (Stevenson) is bored and decides to take a little roll around Glasgow on her own. Frustrated characters all lash out at one another. Feature directorial debut of actor Mullan. **102m/C VHS, DVD.** *GB* Douglas Henshall, Gary Lewis, Stephen McCole, Rosemarie Stevenson, Alex Norton, Frank Gallagher, Malcolm Shields; ***D:*** Peter Mullan; ***W:*** Peter Mullan; ***C:*** Grant Scott Cameron; ***M:*** Craig Armstrong.

Orphans of the North **1940** The story of Bedrock Brown's search for gold and his lost partner. Filmed on location in Alaska with non-professional actors. Impressive footage of America's "last frontier," including the flora and fauna. **56m/C VHS.** ***D:*** Norman Dawn; ***W:*** Susan Denis; ***Nar:*** Norman Dawn.

Orphans of the Storm 1/2 **1921** Two sisters are separated and raised in opposite worlds—one by thieves, the other by aristocrats. Gish's poignant search for her sister is hampered by the turbulent maelstrom preceding the French Revolution. Silent. Based on the French play "The Two Orphans." **190m/B VHS, DVD.** Lillian Gish, Dorothy Gish, Monte Blue, Joseph Schildkraut; ***D:*** D.W. Griffith; ***W:*** D.W. Griffith; ***C:*** Billy (G.W.) Bitzer, Hendrik Sartov; ***M:*** Louis F. Gottschalk, William F. Peters.

Orpheus 1/2 *Orphee* **1949** Cocteau's fascinating, innovative retelling of the Orpheus legend in a modern, though slightly askew, Parisian setting. Classic visual effects and poetic imagery. In French with English subtitles. **95m/B VHS, DVD.** Jean Marais, Francois Perier, Maria Casares, Marie Dea, Edouard Dermithe, Juliette Greco; ***D:*** Jean Cocteau; ***W:*** Jean Cocteau; ***C:*** Nicolas Hayer; ***M:*** Georges Auric.

Orpheus Descending 1/2 **1991** Lust and hatred in small Southern town. Confusing, poorly paced, but interesting for Anderson as Elvis-style drifter and Redgrave as woman addicted to love. Cable version of the 1989 Broadway revival of Tennessee Williams play. **117m/C VHS.** Vanessa Redgrave, Kevin Anderson, Anne Twomey, Miriam Margolyes, Brad Sullivan, Sloane Shelton, Patti Allison; ***D:*** Peter Hall; ***W:*** Peter Hall, Tennessee Williams. **CABLE**

Orwell Rolls in His Grave **2003** Wordy talking-head dominated movie parallels George Orwell's Big Brother totalitarianism in "1984" with the current relationship of U.S. media and government. Interviews conducted in dull settings and comically ominous soundtrack music detract from the main objective. Basically a poor rehashing of other Republication-bashing docs like "Fahrenheit 9/11," "The Corporation," and "Outfoxed." **95m/C DVD.** ***D:*** Robert Kane Pappas; ***W:*** Robert Kane Pappas, Tom Blackburn; ***C:*** Robert Kane Pappas, Alan Hostetter; ***M:*** Eric Wood.

Osa 1/2 **1985** Yet another post-nuke flick with the usual devastated landscape, leather-clad survivors, and hokey dialog. It's sometimes funny, despite everyone's effort to make it dramatic. The supposed plot centers on one woman's efforts to break up a man's monopoly on clean water. **94m/C VHS.** Kelly Lynch, Daniel Grimm, Phillip Vincent, Etienne Chicot, John Forristal, Pete Walker, David Hausman, Bill Moseley; ***D:*** Oleg Egorov; ***M:*** Mason Daring.

Osaka Elegy 1/2 *Woman of Osaka* **1936** A study of Japanese cultural rules when society condemns a woman for behavior that is acceptable for a man. In Japanese with English subtitles. **71m/B VHS.** *JP* Isuzu Yamada; ***D:*** Kenji Mizoguchi.

Osama **2003** First post-Taliban movie produced in Afghanistan shows the oppression suffered by women under that regime in the story of a young girl forced to pose as a boy. Osama (Golbahari) breaks the law, disguising herself to work in a grocery to support her family after her father and brother are killed. This ends quickly as she's rounded up with all the boys of her village and forced into the local religious/military training camp run by the Taliban, where she does everything she can to keep her disguise from being discovered. Director Barmak has an exceptional eye for detail and uses handheld cameras and nonprofessional actors on the streets of Kabul to create a brutally realistic portrait of Afghanistan under the Taliban. A brilliant, intense portrait of one girl's quest to survive hopelessness, horrible cruelty, and overbearing oppression. In Dari with English subtitles. **82m/C DVD.** *JP IR* Marina Golbahari, Arif Herati, Zubaida Sahar; ***D:*** Siddiq Barmak; ***W:*** Siddiq Barmak; ***C:*** Ebraheem Ghafouri; ***M:*** Mohammad Reza Darvishi.

The Oscar 1/2 **1966 (R)** Unless you enjoy razzing bad acting, this is not for you. Meant as a comeuppance for Hollywood, by Hollywood, this story of movie star Frank Fane (Boyd), climbing the ladder of success and squashing fingers on every rung is too schlocky to succeed. The climax, when the scumbag star thinks he's won an Oscar and stands up, only to find it's for someone else, was based on Frank Capra's embarrassing experience in 1932 with the same situation. Adapted from the novel by Richard Sale. **119m/C VHS.** Stephen Boyd, Elke Sommer, Jill St. John, Tony Bennett, Milton Berle, Eleanor Parker, Joseph Cotten, Edie Adams, Ernest Borgnine, Ed Begley Sr., Walter Brennan, Broderick Crawford, James Dunn, Peter Lawford, Merle Oberon, Bob Hope, Frank Sinatra; ***D:*** Russell Rouse; ***W:*** Russell Rouse, Harlan Ellison, Clarence Greene; ***C:*** Joseph Ruttenberg.

Oscar **1991 (PG)** The improbable casting of Stallone in a 1930s style crime farce (an attempt to change his image) is hard to imagine, and harder to believe. Stallone has little to do as he plays the straight man in this often ridiculous story of a crime boss who swears he'll go straight. Cameos aplenty, with Curry's the most notable. Based on a French play by Claude Magnier. **109m/C VHS, DVD.** Sylvester Stallone, Ornella Muti, Peter Riegert, Vincent Spano, Marisa Tomei, Kirk Douglas, Art LaFleur, Ken Howard, Chazz Palminteri, Tim Curry, Don Ameche, Richard Romanus; ***D:*** John Landis; ***W:*** Michael Barrie, Jim Mulholland; ***C:*** Mac Ahlberg; ***M:*** Elmer Bernstein.

Oscar and Lucinda 1/2 **1997 (R)** A priest and a glassworks heiress are united by a shared passion for gambling; together they attempt to transport a glass church through 1860s Australian wilderness. Fiennes' performance as the vulnerable and flailing Oscar is particularly good. Narrated by Geoffrey Rush. Based on the Booker Prize-winning novel by Peter Carey. **131m/C VHS, DVD.** Ralph Fiennes, Cate Blanchett, Ciaran Hinds, Tom Wilkinson, Richard Roxburgh, Clive Russell, Bille Brown, Josephine Byrnes, Barnaby Kay, Barry Otto, Linda Bassett; ***D:*** Gillian Armstrong; ***W:*** Laura Jones; ***C:*** Geoffrey Simpson; ***M:*** Thomas Newman; ***Nar:*** Geoffrey Rush. Australian Film Inst. '98: Cinematog., Score.

Osmosis Jones 1/2 **2001 (PG-13)** Combo of animation and live-action concerns a slob named Frank (Murray) who's suffering from an evil virus (Fishburne) that's taking over his body. To the rescue are white blood cell Osmosis Jones (Rock) and cold tablet Drix (Pierce). The Farrellys once again push the envelope of gross-out humor, but this time it's a PG envelope, and the live-action sequences suffer for it, especially when compared to the funny, clever, and high-energy animated sequences. Luckily, the animation comprises about two-thirds of the movie. Kids will enjoy the lively animation and the gross stuff, while the adults should have a good enough time picking out the puns and references to other movies. Murray goes to heroic lengths to portray Frank's devotion to self-degradation. **95m/C VHS, DVD.** *US* Bill Murray, Molly Shannon, Chris Elliott, Elena Franklin; ***D:*** Bobby Farrelly, Peter Farrelly, Piet Kroon, Tom Sito; ***W:*** Marc Hyman; ***C:*** Mark Irwin; ***M:*** Randy Edelman; ***V:*** Chris Rock, Laurence Fishburne, David Hyde Pierce, Brandy Norwood, William Shatner, Ron Howard.

O.S.S. **1946** John Martin (Ladd) has been recruited by Commander Brady (Knowles) as a would-be spy for the new Office of Strategic Services. Martin's teamed with Ellen Rogers (Fitzgerald) and they parachute into France with orders to obtain information on German troop movements and destroy an important railroad tunnel. A turncoat Gestapo agent sells them information but German colonel Meister (Hoyt) is after them and it's a race to see if their mission can be completed before they're caught. The O.S.S. allowed Paramount studio a look at their WWII files for story purposes and numerous ex-agents served as technical advisors. **108m/B VHS.** Alan Ladd, Geraldine Fitzgerald, Patric Knowles, John Hoyt, Richard Benedict, Gloria Saunders, Bobby Driscoll, Don Beddoe, Richard Webb, Gavin Muir, Onslow Stevens, Joseph Crehan, Leslie Denison; ***D:*** Irving Pichel; ***W:*** Richard Maibaum; ***C:*** Lionel Lindon; ***M:*** Daniele Amfitheatrof.

OSS 117: Cairo, Nest of Spies *OSS 117: Le Caire Nid d'Espions* **2006** This spy spoof has a long history in France, beginning with Jean Bruce's first novel in 1949 (pre-James Bond), with the character previously appearing in seven films. A suavely deadpan OSS 117 (Dujardin) is sent to Cairo in 1955 to protect French interests in the Suez crisis and investigate the murder of a fellow agent. He's condescending to the locals, thinks he's irresistible to women, and his dumb luck is surpassed only by his ignorance. French with subtitles. **99m/C DVD.** *FR* Berenice Bejo, Philippe Lefebvre, Aure Atika, Jean Dujardin, Constantin Alexandrev; ***D:*** Michel Hazanavicius; ***W:*** Jean-Francois Halin; ***C:*** Guillaume Schiffman; ***M:*** Ludovic Bource.

Ossessione 1/2 **1942** An adaptation of "The Postman Always Rings Twice," transferred to Fascist Italy, where a drifter and an innkeeper's wife murder her husband. Visconti's first feature, which initiated Italian neo-realism, was not released in the U.S. until 1975 due to a copyright dispute. In Italian with English subtitles. **135m/B VHS, DVD.** *IT* Massimo Girotti, Clara Calamai, Juan deLanda, Elio Marcuzzo; ***D:*** Luchino Visconti; ***W:*** Guiseppe de Santis, Mario Alicata; ***C:*** Aldo Tonti, Domenico Scala.

The Osterman Weekend **1983 (R)** Peckinpah was said to have disliked the story and the script in this, his last film, which could account for the convoluted and confusing end result. Adding to the problem is the traditional difficulty of adapting Ludlum's complex psychological thrillers for the screen. The result: cast members seem to not quite "get it" as they portray a group of friends, one of whom has been convinced by the CIA that the others are all Soviet spies. **102m/C VHS, DVD.** Burt Lancaster, Rutger Hauer, Craig T. Nelson, Dennis Hopper, John Hurt, Chris Sarandon, Meg Foster, Helen Shaver; ***D:*** Sam Peckinpah; ***M:*** Lalo Schifrin.

Otaku No Video *Fan's Video* **1991** The title of this satirized bio of Gainax animation studio and its founders can be read as "Fan's Video." The tape contains two installments, one made in 1982 and one in 1985. In 1982, college freshman Kubo is reunited with his old friend Tanaka and slowly gets sucked into the world of hopelessly obsessed anime and science fiction fans or "otaku." Both the fun and social costs of his new hobby are examined (in Japan, like the U.S., the coolest guys aren't sitting inside watching TV all day). The second installment finds Kubo and Tanaka starting two different businesses that are directly related to their beloved hobby. As if the animated stories weren't hilarious enough (and, perhaps, all-too familiar to some anime fans), there are live-action, fake documentary segments. These examine different aspects of "otakudom." People less familiar with the world of anime should be able to understand the basic story which is very funny (keeping in mind that practically nothing about this video is to be taken seriously). More experienced anime fans will have the added fun of trying to spot all the anime references and in-jokes liberally woven into the script. **100m/C VHS, DVD.** *JP* ***D:*** Takeshi Mori; ***W:*** Toshio Okada; ***C:*** Tadashi Sano; ***M:*** Kohei Tanaka; ***V:*** Kohi Tsujitani, Toshiharu Sakurai.

Otello 1/2 **1986 (PG)** An uncommon film treat for opera fans, with a stellar performance by Domingo as the troubled Moor who murders his wife in a fit of jealous rage and later finds she was never unfaithful. Be prepared, however, for changes from the Shakespeare and Verdi stories, necessitated by the film adaptation. Highly acclaimed and awarded; in Italian with English subtitles. **123m/C VHS, DVD.** *IT* Placido Domingo, Katia Ricciarelli, Justino Diaz; ***D:*** Franco Zeffirelli.

Othello 1/2 **1922** A silent version of Shakespeare's tragedy, featuring Jannings as the tragic Moor. Titles are in English; with musical score. **81m/B VHS, DVD.** *GE* Emil Jannings, Lya de Putti, Werner Krauss; ***D:*** Dimitri Buchowetzki.

Othello *Orson Welles's Othello; The Tragedy of Othello: The Moor of Venice* **1952** Welles's striking adaptation of the Shakespeare tragedy casts him as the self-deluding Moor, with MacLiammoir as the despicable Iago and Cloutier as innocent victim, Desdemona. Welles filmed his epic over a four-year period due to budget difficulties, which also resulted in his filming in a number of different countries and settings. The film underwent a $1 million restoration, supervised by Welles's daughter, prior to its limited theatrical re-release in 1992. **90m/B VHS, DVD.** Orson Welles, Michael MacLiammoir, Suzanne Cloutier, Robert Coote, Hilton Edwards, Michael Lawrence, Nicholas Bruce, Fay Compton, Doris Dowling, Jean Davis, Joseph Cotten, Joan Fontaine; ***D:*** Orson Welles; ***W:*** Orson Welles; ***C:*** Anchise Brizzi, George Fanto, Alberto Fusi, Aldo (G.R. Aldo) Graziatti, Oberdan Troiani; ***M:*** Alberto Barberis, Angelo Francesco Lavagnino. Cannes '52: Film.

Othello 1/2 **1965** Olivier (in blackface) gives another towering performance as Shakespeare's tragic Moor, led to disaster by his own jealousy. He's ably supported by Finlay's insinuating performance as Iago, Smith as a sweetly vulnerable Desdemona, and Jacobi as unwitting rival Cassio. The production, however, doesn't stray far from its stage-bound roots. **150m/C VHS.** Laurence Olivier, Frank Finlay, Maggie Smith, Derek Jacobi, Joyce Redman, Anthony Nicholls, Sheila Reid, Roy Holder; ***D:*** Stuart Burge; ***W:*** Margaret Unsworth; ***C:*** Geoffrey Unsworth; ***M:*** Richard Hampton.

Othello **1995 (R)** Fishburne stars as Shakespeare's tragic Moor, with Branagh as silken agitator Iago, and Jacob as the tragic Desdemona. First time director Oliver Parker (brother Nathaniel is also in the film) drastically cut the play, rearranging scenes (and even adding material)—purists will no doubt scream, but performances carry the production. Through the clever use of asides directed at the camera, Branagh's Iago makes the viewer feel like an accomplice in the plot. French-speaking Jacob, however, seems to have a hard time pronouncing the Shakespearean dialogue. **125m/C VHS, DVD.** Laurence Fishburne, Irene Jacob, Kenneth Branagh, Nathaniel Parker, Michael Maloney, Anna Patrick, Nicholas Farrell, Indra Ove, Michael Sheen, Andre Oumansky, Philip Locke, John Savident, Gabriele Ferzetti, Pierre Vaneck; ***D:*** Oliver Parker; ***W:*** Oliver Parker; ***C:*** David C(lark) Johnson; ***M:*** Charlie Mole.

Othello **2001** Updated version (with modern dialogue) of Shakespeare's "Othello" set in contemporary London. John Othello (Walker) is a respected police officer who has just been installed as the first black commissioner of the Metropolitan force. His promotion comes at the expense of his mentor/friend Ben Jago (Eccleston) who does not handle the slight well as he is now second-in-command. So Ben plays the race card and works on John's jealousy of his heiress white wife, Dessie (Hawley), by suggesting that she is unfaithful. Walker is convincingly impassioned but Eccleston's slimy manipulation is rather too obvious. **96m/C VHS, DVD.** *GB* Eamonn Walker, Christopher Eccleston, Keeley Hawes, Richard Coyle, Del Synnott, Christopher Fox, Allan Cutts, Patrick Myers; ***D:*** Geoffrey Sax; ***W:*** Andrew Davies; ***C:*** Daf Hobson; ***M:*** Debbie Wiseman. **TV**

The Other **1972 (PG)** Eerie, effective thriller adapted by Tyron from his supernatural novel. Twin brothers represent good and evil in a 1930s Connecticut farm town beset with gruesome murders and accidents. A good scare. **100m/C VHS, DVD.** Martin Udvarnoky, Chris Udvarnoky, Uta Hagen, Diana Muldaur, Norma Connolly, Victor French, John Ritter, Loretta Leversee, Lou Frizzell, Portia Nelson, Jenny Sullivan; ***D:*** Robert Mulligan; ***W:*** Tom Tryon; ***C:*** Robert L. Surtees; ***M:*** Jerry Goldsmith.

The Other Boleyn Girl **2003** Truncated, low-budget TV version of Philippa Gregory's novel about Mary Boleyn (McElhone), who first won the favor of King Henry VIII (Harris) while a young married woman at court. When Mary becomes pregnant, the restless Henry turns his attentions to Mary's older and much-more ambitious sister Anne

(May), who refuses to give in until Henry is free to marry her. **90m/C DVD.** *GB* Natascha (Natasha) McElhone, Jodhi May, Jared Harris, Jack Shepherd, Philip Glenister, John Woodvine, Ron Cook, Anthony Howell, Yolanda Vazquez, Steven Macintosh, Jane Gurnett; ***C:*** Graham Smith; ***M:*** Peter Salem. **TV**

The Other Boleyn Girl 1/2 **2008 (PG-13)** Big-budget Elizabethan period piece that comes off more like a Hollywood soap opera, starring three non-British leads that seem too hip and contemporary for this kind of melodramatic material. Divided into two sections: the first depicting two sisters, Anne (Portman) and Mary Boleyn (Johansson) competing for the love of King Henry VIII (Bana), and the second being a fast-forward through history showing Anne's ascent to the throne. The costumes and scenery are expectedly great, and script is surprisingly tight (even if it's occasionally anachronistic), but the execution is often confusing and awkward, reducing what could have been excellent to just plain old good. Based on the novel by Phillipa Gregory. **115m/C DVD, Blu-ray Disc.** *GB US* Eric Bana, Natalie Portman, Scarlett Johansson, David Morrissey, Mark Rylance, Jim Sturgess, Eddie Redmayne, Benedict Cumberbatch, Ana Torrent, Juno Temple, Oliver Coleman, Kristin Scott Thomas; ***D:*** Justin Chadwick; ***W:*** Peter Morgan; ***C:*** Kieran McGuigan; ***M:*** Paul Cantelon.

The Other Brother 1/2 **2002 (R)** Nice guy Martin (Phifer) is shocked to discover his girlfriend in bed with another woman. Uncertain about his judgement of the fair sex, he reluctantly agrees to listen to his player brother Junnie's (Blake) advice, which results in some awkward pickup moments. Of course, Martin has already meet the perfect new girlfriend, his new upstairs neighbor Paula (Miller), if only he would listen to what his own heart says. **94m/C VHS, DVD.** Mekhi Phifer, Andre B. Blake, Michele Morgan, Tangi Miller, Ebony Jo-Ann, Regina Hall, Collette Wilson; ***D:*** Mandel Holland; ***W:*** Mandel Holland; ***C:*** Matthew Clark.

The Other End of the Line 1/2 **2008 (PG-13)** Charming cross-cultural romantic comedy. Priya (Saran) has the best American accent of all the Indian employees at the Bangalore call center. Good enough to fool regular client Granger Woodruff (Metcalfe) who thinks Priya also lives in San Francisco. A series of contrivances takes Priya to the city by the bay and a chance for true love. **106m/C DVD.** Jesse Metcalfe, Austin Basis, Larry Miller, Anupam Kher, Shriya Saran; ***D:*** James Dodson; ***W:*** Tracey Jackson; ***C:*** Harlan Bosmajian; ***M:*** B.C. Smith.

The Other Guys **2010** New York detective and forensic accountant Allen Gamble (Ferrell) prefers to work a desk rather than the streets while his new partner is trigger-happy Terry Hoitz (Wahlberg). They decide to emulate top cops Danson (Johnson) and Highsmith (Jackson) but things don't work out as they planned. **m/C DVD.** *US* Will Ferrell, Mark Wahlberg, Dwayne "The Rock" Johnson, Samuel L. Jackson, Steve Coogan, Eva Mendes, Lindsay Sloane, Michael Keaton, Anne Heche, Damon Wayans Jr., Paris Hilton, Rob Riggle; ***D:*** Adam McKay; ***W:*** Adam McKay, Chris Henchy; ***C:*** Oliver Wood.

The Other Half **2006** Englishman Mark surprises his American bride Holly with her dream honeymoon in Portugal. Then Holly discovers that the country is hosting an international soccer tournament and the English national team just happens to be playing. Mark protests his innocence but Holly is convinced her soccer-mad hubby is lying, which isn't a great way to start a marriage. **101m/C DVD.** *GB* Danny Dyer, Gillian Kearney, Vinnie Jones, Mark Lynch, Jonathan Broke, Katie Cromer; ***D:*** Marlowe Fawcett, Richard Nockles; ***W:*** Marlowe Fawcett, Richard Nockles; ***C:*** John Behrens.

Other Hell **1985 (R)** Schlocky Italian-made chiller has the devil inhabiting a convent where he does his damnest to upset the nuns. Gross, but not scary—lots of cliche dark-hallway scenes and fright music. **88m/C VHS, DVD.** *IT* Carlo De Mejo, Francesca Carmeno; ***D:*** Stefan Oblowsky.

The Other Man **2008 (R)** Fussy, minor romantic melodrama/thriller with silly plot twists. Successful software exec Peter (Neeson) and his longtime wife, upscale shoe designer Lisa (Linney), live with their daughter Abigail (Garai) in Cambridge, England. Lisa apparently disappears after dropping hints about marital infidelity and Peter learns by snooping on her computer that she's having an affair with Ralph (Banderas), who lives in Milan. Jealous, Peter heads to Italy, befriends Ralph over chess games in a local cafe, and tries to press him for details on the affair without divulging who he is. **89m/C DVD.** *GB* Liam Neeson, Antonio Banderas, Laura Linney, Romola Garai; ***D:*** Richard Eyre; ***W:*** Richard Eyre, Charles Wood; ***C:*** Haris Zambarloukos; ***M:*** Stephen Warbeck.

Other Men's Women **1931** Railroad engineer Jack (Toomey) and his wife Lily (Astor) agree to let his pal Bill (Withers) stay with them. The flirtatious Bill starts up with Lily, which leads to a quarrel with Jack and a train accident that leaves Jack blind. Unwilling to be a burden to Lily, Jack comes up with a radical solution when a railroad bridge is threatened with collapse during a flood. **70m/B DVD.** Regis Toomey, Mary Astor, Grant Withers, Joan Blondell, James Cagney, Fred Kohler Sr., J. Farrell MacDonald; ***D:*** William A. Wellman; ***W:*** Maude Fulton, William K. Wells; ***C:*** Barney McGill.

Other People's Money 1/2 **1991 (R)** DeVito is "Larry the Liquidator," a corporate raider with a heart of stone and a penchant for doughnuts. When he sets his sights on a post-smokestack era, family-owned cable company, he gets a taste of love for the first time in his life. He and Miller, the daughter of the company president and also its legal advisor, court one another while sparring over the fate of the company. Unbelievably clipped ending mars otherwise enterprising comedy about the triumph of greed in corporate America. Based on the off-Broadway play by Jerry Sterner. **101m/C VHS, DVD.** Danny DeVito, Penelope Ann Miller, Dean Jones, Gregory Peck, Piper Laurie, Tom Aldredge, R.D. Call; ***D:*** Norman Jewison; ***W:*** Alvin Sargent; ***C:*** Haskell Wexler; ***M:*** David Newman.

The Other Side of Heaven **2002 (PG)** Well-meaning if heavy-handed biodrama based on Groberg's memoir "In the Eye of the Storm." John Groberg (Gorham) is a Mormon college student at Brigham Young University in 1953, who's pining for Jean (Hathaway), the girl of his dreams. Then he receives his missionary assignment—to Tonga in the South Seas. Groberg has to struggle with native culture, the language barrier, and various hardships and natural disasters before he can accomplish his goals. Film's sincere although you never get much of an idea of how Groberg feels about all that befalls him except for his enduring faith. Picture was filmed in the Cook Islands. **113m/C VHS, DVD.** *US* Christopher Gorham, Anne Hathaway, Joe Folau, Miriama Smith, Nathaniel Lees, Whetu Fala; ***D:*** Mitch Davis; ***W:*** Mitch Davis; ***C:*** Brian J. Breheny; ***M:*** Kevin Kiner.

The Other Side of Midnight WOOF! **1977 (R)** The dreary, depressingly shallow life story of a poor French girl, dumped by an American GI, who sleeps her way to acting stardom and a profitable marriage, then seeks revenge for the jilt. Based on Sidney Sheldon's novel, it's not even titillating—just a real downer. **160m/C VHS, DVD.** Susan Sarandon, Marie-France Pisier, John Beck, Raf Vallone, Clu Gulager, Sorrell Booke; ***D:*** Charles Jarrott; ***W:*** Daniel Taradash; ***C:*** Fred W. Koenekamp.

The Other Side of Sunday *Sondagsengler* **1996** A small town in 1959 Norway is the setting for this coming of age comedy. Maria (Thiesen) is the eldest daughter of conservative priest Johannes (Sundquist). Fun doesn't seem to be part of their religion but puberty is hitting Maria hard and she longs to join in with the livelier crowd of her school friend Brigit (Salvesen), who listens to rock 'n' roll, wears makeup, and makes out with boys. Maria does find a compassionate listener in Mrs. Tunheim (Riise), who urges the teenager to learn how to think for herself. Based on the novel "Sunday" by Reidun Nortvedt. Norwegian with subtitles. **103m/C VHS, DVD.** *NO* Marie Theisen, Bjorn Sundquist, Hildegunn Riise, Sylvia Salvesen; ***D:*** Berit Nesheim; ***W:*** Berit Nesheim, Lasse Glomm; ***C:*** Arne Borsheim; ***M:*** Geir Bohren, Bent Aserud.

The Other Side of the Bed *El Otro Lado de la Cama* **2003 (R)** Two sexy and self-absorbed Madrid couples slyly swap partners—yet still find time to break out in song and dance when the mood strikes—in this lively, sex-packed high-camp Spanish import. In Spanish, with subtitles. **114m/C VHS, DVD.** *SP* Ernesto Alterio, Guillermo Toledo, Maria Esteve; ***W:*** David Serrano; ***C:*** Juan Molina; ***M:*** Roque Banos. **VIDEO**

The Other Side of the Law **1995 (R)** Man makes a wilderness hideout with his son after killing his wife's murderer. But when the boy grows up, dad decides to send him back into civilization for education, leading to nothing but trouble. **96m/C VHS.** *CA* Johnny Morina, Maggie Castle, Yves Renier, Xavier DeLuc, Jurgen Prochnow; ***D:*** Gilles Carle; ***W:*** Gilles Carle; ***M:*** Jean Delorme.

The Other Side of the Mountain *A Window to the Sky* **1975 (PG)** Tear-jerking true story of Olympic hopeful skier Jill Kinmont, paralyzed in a fall. Bridges helps her pull her life together. A sequel followed two years later. Based on the book "A Long Way Up" by E. G. Valens. **102m/C VHS.** Marilyn Hassett, Beau Bridges, Dabney Coleman, John David Garfield, Griffin Dunne; ***D:*** Larry Peerce; ***W:*** David Seltzer; ***M:*** Charles Fox.

The Other Side of the Mountain, Part 2 **1978 (PG)** Quadriplegic Jill Kinmont, paralyzed in a skiing accident that killed her hopes for the Olympics, overcomes depression and the death of the man who helped her to recover. In this chapter, she falls in love again and finds happiness. More tears are jerked. **99m/C VHS.** Marilyn Hassett, Timothy Bottoms; ***D:*** Larry Peerce.

The Other Sister **1998 (PG-13)** Carla (Lewis) is the mentally challenged but exuberant member of the repressed Tate family. After leaving a "special school," she convinces her uptight parents Elizabeth (Keaton) and Radley (Skerritt) to let her enroll in a vocational program. She meets and falls for fellow retarded student Danny (Ribisi), much to her parents' dismay. Love wins out, but the script is so sappy that a maple syrup factory could be built on it. Lewis and Ribisi do an admirable job of rising above the material, which was co-written by schmaltz-meister director Garry Marshall. **129m/C VHS, DVD.** Juliette Lewis, Giovanni Ribisi, Diane Keaton, Tom Skerritt, Poppy Montgomery, Linda Thorson, Juliet Mills, Hector Elizondo, Sarah Paulson, Joe Flanigan, Dina Merrill; ***D:*** Garry Marshall; ***W:*** Garry Marshall, Bob Brunner; ***C:*** Dante Spinotti; ***M:*** Rachel Portman.

Other Voices, Other Rooms 1/2 **1995** Adaptation of Truman Capote's 1948 novel (his first) is the semi-autobiographical story of a young boy's search for his father set against the backdrop of a decaying Bayou mansion. Southern saga, narrated by Capote sound-alike Kingdom, starts when 12-year-old Joel's mother dies and he is sent by his aunts to live with his father. Instead of being greeted by his father, Joel (Speck) instead meets an odd collection of guests, including Amy (Thomson), a fragile and pretty Southern belle and her cousin Randolph (Bluteau), a sensitive, effete, and charming alcoholic. Pic deals with the secrets of the father's illness and what lies behind the unhappiness of the two cousins, who try to keep the child from fleeing the wacky "family." Lacks the danger and suspense of Capote's novel, but sets proper mood and shows off actors talents. Best known as a documentary director/producer, this is Rocksavage's feature debut. **98m/C VHS, DVD.** Lothaire Bluteau, Anna Thomson, David Speck, April Turner, Aubrey Dollar; ***D:*** David Rocksavage; ***W:*** David Rocksavage, Sara Flanigan; ***C:*** Paul Ryan; ***M:*** Chris Hajian; ***Nar:*** Bob Kingdom.

The Other Woman 1/2 **1992 (R)** Investigative reporter Jessica is working on a murder case when she finds incriminating sex photos showing her husband with another woman. She becomes obsessed with finding the woman in the pictures but it would be dangerous for Jessica to forget there's still a murderer on the loose. **90m/C VHS.** Adrian Zmed, Lee Ann Beaman, Daniel Moriarty, Jenna Persaud, Sam Jones; ***D:*** Jag Mundhra.

The Others **2001 (PG-13)** Twisting Gothic haunt-fest centers on Grace (Kidman) and her two children Anne (Mann) and Nicholas (Bentley), living in a mansion on Britain's remote Isle of Jersey. She waits for her husband's return from WWII, although she fears he may be dead. After her servants disappear in the middle of the night, she's surprised when a trio of domestics show up, claiming to have worked in the house before. They're hired on the spot, but the help soon discovers why their predecessors took off. Grace is demanding and high-strung to the point of mania. Because of rare allergies, the kids must be kept out of the sunlight. Maybe the solitude is preying on Grace's mind, maybe she's crazy, or maybe their house is haunted. Kidman is at her chilly best as the audience is kept guessing. **101m/C VHS, DVD.** *US* Nicole Kidman, Fionnula Flanagan, Alakina Mann, James Bentley, Christopher Eccleston, Elaine Cassidy, Eric Sykes, Renee Asherson; ***D:*** Alejandro Amenabar; ***W:*** Alejandro Amenabar; ***C:*** Javier Aguirresarobe; ***M:*** Alejandro Amenabar.

Otto: Or, Up with Dead People **2008** A sexually explicit gay zombie film from provocateur LaBruce that's not for the squeamish. Young zombie Otto lives in Berlin and subsists on roadkill. He gets a role in a queer zombie movie, directed by pretentiously avant-garde Medea Yarn, and his fellow cast members think Otto's taking his 'method acting' quite seriously. English and German with subtitles. **95m/C DVD.** *CA GE* Jay Crisfar, Katharina Klewinghaus, Marcel Schlutt, Christophe Chemin; ***D:*** Bruce LaBruce; ***W:*** Bruce LaBruce; ***C:*** James Carman.

Oubliette 1/2 **1914** A peripheral version of Francois Villon, in what is a recently discovered and restored film, the earliest extant Chaney film. **35m/B VHS.** Lon Chaney Sr., Murdock MacQuarrie, Pauline Bush, Doc (Harry F.) Crane, Chester Withey; ***D:*** Charles Giblyn; ***W:*** H.G. Stafford; ***C:*** Lee Bartholomew.

Our America 1/2 **2002 (R)** In 1993, Chicago teens LeAlan Jones (Pannell) and Lloyd Newman (Hammond) are living in a notorious southside housing project. They are approached by white NPR producer David Isay (Charles) to record an audio diary of their daily lives, which becomes the radio series "Ghetto Life 101." Stung by the controversy the program receives, the boys pull back until the death of a five-year-old boy has them looking into neighborhood problems once again. Camille Robert (Miller) and her boyfriend steal a priceless artifact from Ghana and have numerous officials on their trail. The manipulative Camille wants to doublecross her beau and keep all the profits for herself but she needs some help, so she comes whining to big sister Riana (Williams) that she's in trouble. **95m/C DVD, DVD.** Brandon Hammond, Josh Charles, Vanessa Williams, Mykelti Williamson, Peter Paige, Irma P. Hall, Roderick Pannell, Serena Lee; ***D:*** Ernest R. Dickerson; ***W:*** Gordon Rayfield; ***C:*** Ernest R. Dickerson; ***M:*** Patrice Rushen. **CABLE**

Our Brand Is Crisis **2005** Unsettling documentary follows the American political consultancy firm of Greenberg Carville and Shrum as they work on the 2002 Bolivian presidential campaign. Their candidate is unpopular former president Gonzalo Sanchez de Lozada, and the consultants work to spin him as the new and improved version, with the focus ("brand") being that Bolivia is in crisis and needs an experienced politico at the helm. English and Spanish with subtitles. **87m/C DVD.** *US* ***D:*** Rachel Boynton; ***C:*** Michael Anderson, Tom Hurwitz, Christine Burrill, Jerr Risius; ***M:*** Marcelo Zarvos.

Our Daily Bread *Miracle of Life* **1934** Vidor's sequel to the 1928 "The Crowd." A young couple inherit a farm during the Depression and succeed in managing the land. A near-classic, with several sequences highly influenced by directors Alexander Dovshenko and Sergei Eisenstein. Director Vidor also co-scripted this film, risking bankruptcy to finance it. **80m/B VHS, DVD.** Karen Morley, Tom Keene, John Qualen, Barbara Pepper, Addison Richards; ***D:*** King Vidor; ***W:*** King Vidor, Elizabeth Hill; ***C:*** Robert Planck.

Our Dancing Daughters 1/2 **1928** Flapper (Crawford on the brink of stardom) falls hard for millionaire who's forced into arranged marriage, but obliging little missus kicks bucket so Crawford can step in. **98m/B VHS.** Joan Crawford, Johnny Mack Brown, Nils Asther, Dorothy Sebastian, Anita Page; *D:* Harry Beaumont; *C:* George Barnes.

Our Family Business ♪♪ **1981** TV pilot; this generally plodding "Godfather"-type story is saved by good performances by Wanamaker and Milland. **74m/C VHS.** Sam Wanamaker, Vera Miles, Ray Milland, Ted Danson, Chip (Christopher) Mayer; *D:* Robert E. Collins. **TV**

Our Family Wedding ♪ ½ *Family Wedding* **2010 (PG-13)** Playing like an over-long sitcom episode, this ham-fisted tale of interracial marriage is a wedding album best left unseen. Lucia (Ferrara) and Marcus (Gross) are two college grads who are itching to tie the knot. The problem is that she's Mexican-American and he's African-American. At least that's a problem for her father Miguel (Mencia) and his father Brad (Whitaker). The two dads engage in a battle of stereotypes and slapstick until the inevitable "kiss-and-make-up" ending. You may return to the video store seeking an annulment. **101m/C DVD.** Forest Whitaker, Carlos Mencia, America Ferrera, Lance Gross, Regina King, Lupe Ontiveros, Anna Maria Horsford, Warren Sapp; *D:* Rick Famuyiwa; *W:* Rick Famuyiwa; *C:* Julio Macat.

Our Hospitality ♪♪♪♪ **1923** One of Keaton's finest silent films, with all the elements in place. William McKay (Keaton) travels to the American South on a quaint train (a near-exact replica of the Stephenson Rocket), to claim an inheritance as the last survivor of his family. En route, a young woman traveler informs him that her family has had a long, deadly feud with his, and that they intend to kill him. McKay resolves to get the inheritance, depending on the Southern rule of hospitality to guests to save his life until he can make his escape. Watch for the river scene where, during filming, Keaton's own life was really in danger. By the way, Keaton married his leading lady in real life. **74m/B VHS, DVD.** Buster Keaton, Natalie Talmadge, Joe Keaton, Buster Keaton Jr., Kitty Bradbury, Joe Roberts, Monte (Monty) Collins; *D:* John Blystone, Buster Keaton; *W:* Jean C. Havez, Joseph A. Mitchell, Clyde Bruckman; *C:* Elgin Lessley, Gordon Jennings.

Our Italian Husband ♪ ½ **2004 (PG-13)** Lame comedy. Vincenzo is a struggling artist living with his pregnant American wife Charlene in New York. Except Vincenzo is a bigamist, as everyone discovers when his Italian wife Maria arrives with their two kids. **?m/C DVD.** *IT* Brooke Shields, Maria Grazia Cucinotta, Chevy Chase, Pierfrancesco Favino; *D:* Ilaria Berrelli; *W:* Ilaria Berrelli; *C:* Benjamin Morgan; *M:* Brian Burnam.

Our Lady of the Assassins ♪♪ *La Virgen de los Sicarios* **2001 (R)** Based on Vallejo's 1994 autobiographical novel, the film follows Fernando (Jaramillo), an older gay man and a writer who has returned to his hometown of Medellin, Colombia to die. After 30 years away, Fernando discovers a crime-ridden city with drug trafficking, gangs, and violence to be the norm. At a party, Fernando is introduced to 16-year-old street tough Alexis (Ballesteros), who soon moves in with him. But when Alexis's past catches up with him, Fernando seeks the truth in a city of lies. Not for the faint-hearted; Spanish with subtitles. **98m/C VHS, DVD.** *CO FR* German Jaramillo, Anderson Ballesteros, Juan David Restrepo, Manuel Busquets; *D:* Barbet Schroeder; *W:* Fernando Vallejo; *C:* Rodrigo Lalinde; *M:* Jorge Arriagada.

Our Little Girl ♪♪ **1935 (PG)** A precocious little tyke tries to reunite her estranged parents by running away to their favorite vacation spot. Sure to please Shirley Temple fans, despite a lackluster script. **65m/B VHS.** Shirley Temple, Joel McCrea, Rosemary Ames, Lyle Talbot, Erin O'Brien-Moore; *D:* John S. Robertson.

Our Man Flint ♪♪ **1966** James Bond clone Derek Flint uses gadgets and his ingenuity to save the world from an evil organization, GALAXY, that seeks world domination through control of the weather. The plot moves quickly around many bikini-clad women, but still strains for effect. Spawned one sequel: "In Like Flint." **107m/C VHS, DVD.** James Coburn, Lee J. Cobb, Gila Golan, Edward Mulhare, Benson Fong, Shelby Grant, Sigrid Valdis, Gianna Serra, James Brolin, Helen Funai, Michael St. Clair; *D:* Daniel Mann; *W:* Hal Fimberg, Ben Starr; *C:* Daniel F. Fapp; *M:* Jerry Goldsmith.

Our Man in Havana ♪♪♪ **1959** Excellent noir—with plenty of veddy British black comedy—has ordinary, but not very successful, Havana-based vacuum salesman Guinness joining the British spy service to make some extra money. He begins spinning elaborate tails of intrigue to justify himself, and his lies eventually spiral out of control and into some very real, very dangerous situations. Kovacs, Richardson, and Coward stand out among a great cast. See "The Tailor of Panama" for a post-Cold War re-telling of the tale, but see this one first. **111m/B VHS, DVD.** *GB* Alec Guinness, Burl Ives, Maureen O'Hara, Noel Coward, Ernie Kovacs, Ralph Richardson, Jo Morrow, Paul Rogers, Gregoire Aslan, Joseph Prieto, Timothy Bateson, Duncan MacRae, Maurice Denham, Raymond Huntley, Ferdinand "Ferdy" Mayne, Rachel Roberts; *D:* Carol Reed; *W:* Graham Greene; *C:* Oswald Morris.

Our Miss Brooks ♪♪ ½ **1956** Quietly pleasing version of the TV series. Miss Brooks pursues the "mother's boy" biology professor. The father of the child she begins tutoring appears taken with her. The professor takes notice. **85m/B VHS.** Eve Arden, Gale Gordon, Nick Adams, Richard Crenna, Don Porter; *D:* Al Lewis.

Our Modern Maidens ♪♪ ½ **1929** Scandalous jazz-age drama in which Crawford and Fairbanks both fall in love with other people before their wedding is to take place. This sequel to "Our Dancing Daughters" features beautiful gowns and lush, opulent Art Deco interiors. Based on a story by Josephine Lovett. **75m/B VHS.** Joan Crawford, Rod La Rocque, Douglas Fairbanks Jr., Anita Page, Josephine Dunn; *D:* Jack Conway; *W:* Josephine Lovett.

Our Mother's Murder ♪♪ ½ **1997 (PG-13)** Title says it all in this drama based on the true story of publishing heiress Anne Scripps Douglas (Hart) who, in 1989, marries volatile young carpenter, Scott (Wilder), and begins an abusive four-year marriage that will end with her beating death in 1993. Scripps Douglas's two daughters by her first marriage, Alexandra and Annie (portrayed on screen by Clarke and Combs), cooperated with the production. **92m/C VHS.** Roxanne Hart, Holly Marie Combs, Sarah Chalke, James Wilder, Jonathan Scarfe; *D:* Bill W.L. Norton; *W:* Richard DeLong Adams. **CABLE**

Our Music ♪♪ *Our Music* **2004** Godard divides his film into three kingdoms, using Dante's "The Divine Comedy" as his structure. First there's Hell, with a montage showing war and genocide throughout history. Next is the longest section, Purgatory, set in Sarajevo and featuring Godard at a literary conference where we meet Israeli journalist Judith (Adler), and Olga (Dieu), a Russian Jew now living in Israel, and the theme is reconciliation and sacrifice. Then we get to Heaven, which again features Olga under very different circumstances. If you're a Godard fan, you'll know what strangeness you're getting into: others beware. French with subtitles. **80m/C DVD.** *FR SI* Nade Dieu, Sarah Adler; *D:* Jean-Luc Godard; *W:* Jean-Luc Godard; *C:* Julien Hirsch, Jean-Christophe Beauvallet.

Our Mutual Friend ♪♪ ½ **1998** Charles Dickens' last completed novel follows the complicated saga of John Harmon (Mackintosh), who must consent to a prearranged marriage if he's to inherit a fortune. But when fate allows Harmon to assume a new identity, he decides to see what anonymity will bring him. Meanwhile, Harmon's life and death also brings together low-born Lizzie Hexum and wastrel lawyer Eugene Wrayburn, who develops an unexpected affection for the lovely young woman. On 3 cassettes. **339m/C VHS.** *GB* Steven Mackintosh, Anna Friel, Paul McGann, Keeley Hawes, David Morrissey, Dominic Mafham, Peter Vaughan, Pam Ferris, Kenneth Cranham, Timothy Spall, David Bradley, Margaret Tyzack; *D:* Julian Farino; *W:* Sandy Welch; *C:* David Odd; *M:* Adrian Johnston. **TV**

Our Relations ♪♪♪ ½ **1936** Confusion reigns when Stan and Ollie meet the twin brothers they never knew they had, a pair of happy-go-lucky sailors. Laurel directs the pair through madcap encounters with their twins' wives and the local underworld. One of the pair's best efforts, though not well-remembered. Based on a story by W.W. Jacobs. **94m/B VHS.** Stan Laurel, Oliver Hardy, Alan Hale, Sidney Toler, James Finlayson, Daphne Pollard; *D:* Harry Lachman.

Our Song ♪♪♪ **2001 (R)** Not your average teen drama. McKay's second dramatic feature concerning the troubled lives of adolescent girls faced with tough choices is a quietly affecting, poetic and solid effort. First-time actors Washington, Simpson and Martinez bring poignancy and realism to their roles as high school friends living in the Brooklyn projects and rehearsing for a marching band competition. The expected issues are present, but the film's treatment of them is what makes it unique. Bold in its way of forgoing major plot drama in favor of finding powerful moments in small places and offering food for thought. Real-life marching band the Jackie Robinson Steppers, who were the inspiration for the film, provide a focal point for the story and punch to the mostly languid pacing. **96m/C VHS, DVD.** *US* Kerry Washington, Anna Simpson, Melissa Martinez, Marlene Forte, Rosalyn Coleman, Ray Anthony Thomas, D'Monroe, Kim Howard, Carmen Lopez; *D:* Jim McKay; *W:* Jim McKay; *C:* Jim Denault.

Our Sons ♪♪ ½ **1991** Two middle-aged moms strike up an unlikely friendship over their gay sons in this TV weeper. Arkansas waitress Luanna (Ann Margret) hasn't talked to son Donald (Ivanek) in years—now he's dying of AIDS. Successfull career woman Audrey (Andrews in her TV-movie debut) has seemingly accepted son James' (Grant) life with Donald and it's James who urges his mother to make contact with Luanna and persuade her to see Donald one last time. **100m/C VHS, DVD.** Julie Andrews, Ann-Margret, Hugh Grant, Zeljko Ivanek, Tony Roberts; *D:* John Erman; *W:* John Erman, William Hanley.

Our Time ♪♪ ½ *Death of Her Innocence* **1974** An exclusive girls finishing school in the '50s is the setting for the friendship of Abby (Martin) and Muffy (Slade) and their first stirrings of romance. But when Muffy gets pregnant, tragedy awaits. Sappy. **91m/C VHS.** Pamela Sue Martin, Betsey Slade, Parker Stevenson, George O'Hanlon Jr., Roderick Cook, Edith Atwater, Meg Wyllie, Debralee Scott, Nora Heflin, Kathryn Holcomb, Robert Walden, Helene Winston; *D:* Peter Hyams; *W:* Jane C. Stanton.

Our Town ♪♪♪ **1940** Small-town New England life in Grover's Corners in the early 1900s is celebrated in this well-performed and directed adaptation of the Pulitzer Prize-winning play by Thornton Wilder. Film debut of Scott. **90m/B VHS, DVD.** Martha Scott, William Holden, Thomas Mitchell, Fay Bainter, Guy Kibbee, Beulah Bondi, Frank Craven; *D:* Sam Wood; *W:* Harry Chandlee, Frank Craven; *C:* Bert Glennon; *M:* Aaron Copland.

Our Town ♪♪♪ **1977** TV version of Thornton Wilder's classic play about everyday life in Grovers Corners, a small New England town at the turn of the century. It hews more closely to the style of the stage version than the earlier film version. **120m/C VHS, DVD.** Ned Beatty, Sada Thompson, Ronny Cox, Glynnis O'Connor, Robby Benson, Hal Holbrook, John Houseman; *D:* Franklin J. Schaffner. **TV**

Our Town ♪♪ ½ **1989** Filmed TV version of the Tony Award-winning Lincoln Center production of the Thornton Wilder play focusing on small-town life in Grover's Corners, New Hampshire. Gray is the omniscient Stage Manager, with Stolz and Miller as the young couple brought together by the everyday cycle of happiness and hardship. **104m/C VHS, DVD.** Eric Stoltz, Penelope Ann Miller, Spalding Gray; *D:* Gregory Mosher.

Our Town ♪♪ ½ **2003** Filmed version of the 1938 Thornton Wilder play as staged by the Westport County Playhouse. Newman makes his first stage appearance in nearly 40 years as the Stage Manager, who narrates the story of the townspeople of Grover's Corners, New Hampshire at the turn of the 20th century. At the play's heart are Emily Webb and George Gibbs, who will grow up, marry, and start a family with tragic results as the ghosts of the town watch the lives of those they've left behind. **120m/C DVD.** Paul Newman, Margaret Lacey, Frank Converse, Jayne Atkinson, Jeffrey DeMunn, Jane Curtin, Stephen Spinella, Mia Dillon; *D:* James Naughton; *W:* Thornton Wilder. **CABLE**

Our Very Own ♪♪ **1950** At 18, and about to graduate from high school, Gail (Blyth) discovers she was adopted. So she decides to find her birth mother and then comes to realize what her foster parents really mean to her. Pretty sappy all the way 'round. **93m/B VHS.** Ann Blyth, Jane Wyatt, Donald Cook, Farley Granger, Ann Dvorak, Joan Evans, Natalie Wood, Martin Milner, Phyllis Kirk; *D:* David Miller; *W:* F. Hugh Herbert; *C:* Lee Garmes; *M:* Victor Young.

Our Vines Have Tender Grapes ♪♪♪ ½ **1945** A change of pace role for the volatile Robinson who plays a kind Norwegian farmer, living in Wisconsin with his daughter, the spunky O'Brien. The film is made-up of small-town moments as O'Brien learns a few of life's lessons, eased by the thoughtful compassion of Robinson. Based on the novel "For Our Vines Have Tender Grapes" by George Victor Martin. **105m/B VHS.** Edward G. Robinson, Margaret O'Brien, James Craig, Agnes Moorehead, Jackie "Butch" Jenkins, Morris Carnovsky, Frances Gifford, Sara Haden, Louis Jean Heydt; *D:* Roy Rowland; *W:* Dalton Trumbo; *C:* Robert L. Surtees.

Out ♪♪ ½ *Deadly Drifter* **1982** A drifter's travels throughout the U.S. from the '60s to the '80s. Successfully manages to satirize just about every conceivable situation but keeps from posturing by not taking itself too seriously. Adapted from an experimental novel by Ronald Sukenick. **88m/C VHS, DVD.** Peter Coyote, Danny Glover, O-Lan Shepard, Jim Haynie, Scott Beach, Semu Haute; *D:* Eli Hollander; *W:* Eli Hollander; *M:* David Cope.

Out at the Wedding ♪♪ **2007** Alex Houston tells her Jewish, African-American fiance Dana that her family is dead because she believes they'll disapprove. Then she quietly heads home to South Carolina to be a bridesmaid in her sister Jeannie's wedding, taking along her gay best friend Jonathan. Jonathan mentions Dana to her family and they think Dana is a woman. Alex is so surprised by their supportive attitude that she lets the lie stand. But things spin out of control when Jeannie decides to come to New York to meet her sister's 'girlfriend.' **96m/C DVD.** Charlie Schlatter, Mystro Clark, Mike Farrell, Mink Stole, Andrea Marcellus, Desi Lydic, Cathy DeBuono, Jill Bennett; *D:* Lee Friedlander; *W:* Paula Goldberg; *C:* Alex Vendler; *M:* Laura Karpman.

Out Cold ♪ ½ **1989 (R)** Black comedy follows the misadventures of a butcher who believes he has accidentally frozen his business partner; the iced man's girlfriend, who really killed him; and the detective who tries to solve the crime. Too many poor frozen body jokes may leave the viewer cold. **91m/C VHS, DVD.** John Lithgow, Teri Garr, Randy Quaid, Bruce McGill; *D:* Malcolm Mowbray; *M:* Michel Colombier.

Out Cold ♪ ½ **2001 (PG-13)** Dumb snowboarding comedy (the snowboarding scenes are the only cool things about the movie) focuses on a ragged ski resort in Bull Mountain, Alaska that developer Jack Majors (Majors) wants to turn into a family-oriented resort. That means getting rid of the resort's raucous loser employees, including Rick (London) and his buddies. **90m/C VHS, DVD.** Jason London, Willie Garson, Lee Majors, A.J. Cook, Derek Hamilton, Zach Galifianakis, Flex Anderson, Caroline Dhavernas, Victoria Silvstedt; *D:* Brendan Malloy, Emmett Malloy; *W:* Jon Zack; *C:* Richard Crudo; *M:* Michael Andrews.

Out for Blood ♪♪ **1993 (R)** Attorney John Decker is living a happy life until his family is murdered by drug dealers. He turns vigilante, dubbed "Karateman" by the press, and finds himself hunted by the cops and the criminals. **90m/C VHS, DVD.** Don "The Dragon" Wilson, Shari Shattuck, Michael Delano,

Kenneth McLeod, Todd Curtis, Timothy Baker, Howard Jackson, Bob Schott, Eric Lee; *D:* Richard W. Munchkin; *W:* David S. Green.

Out for Justice 1/2 **1991 (R)** A psycho Brooklyn hood goes on a murder spree, and homeboy turned lone-wolf cop Seagal races other police and the mob to get at him. Bloodthirsty and profane, it does try to depict N.Y.C.'s Italian-American community—but 90 percent of them are dead by the end so what's the point? Better yet, why does it open with a quote from Arthur Miller? Better still, what's Daffy Duck doing on this tape peddling Warner Bros. T-shirts to kid viewers?! **91m/C VHS, DVD, Blu-ray Disc, HD DVD.** Dominic Chianese, Steven Seagal, William Forsythe, Jerry Orbach, Julianna Margulies, Gina Gershon, John Leguizamo, Julie Strain; *D:* John Flynn; *W:* David Lee Henry; *C:* Ric Waite; *M:* David Michael Frank.

Out in Fifty 1/2 **1999 (R)** Con is released from prison only to be pursued by a psycho detective who wants him back in the slammer and a mystery babe who has her own plans for the guy. **95m/C VHS, DVD.** Mickey Rourke, Bojesse Christopher, Christina Applegate, Scott Leet, Balthazar Getty, Peter Greene; *D:* Bojesse Christopher, Scott Leet. **VIDEO**

Out of Africa **1985 (PG)** An epic film of the years spent by Danish authoress Isak Dinesen (her true name is Karen Blixen) on a Kenya coffee plantation. She moved to Africa to marry, and later fell in love with Denys Finch-Hatten, a British adventurer. Based on several books, including biographies of the two lovers. Some critics loved the scenery and music; others despised the acting and the script. A definite "no" for those who love action. **161m/C VHS, DVD.** Meryl Streep, Robert Redford, Klaus Maria Brandauer, Michael Kitchen, Malick Bowens, Michael Gough, Suzanna Hamilton, Rachel Kempson, Graham Crowden, Shane Rimmer, Donal McCann, Iman, Joseph Thiaka, Stephen Kinyanjui; *D:* Sydney Pollack; *W:* Kurt Luedtke; *C:* David Watkin; *M:* John Barry. Oscars '85: Adapt. Screenplay, Art Dir./Set Dec., Cinematog., Director (Pollack), Picture, Sound, Orig. Score; British Acad. '86: Adapt. Screenplay; Golden Globes '86: Film—Drama, Support. Actor (Brandauer), Score; L.A. Film Critics '85: Actress (Streep), Cinematog.; Natl. Bd. of Review '85: Support. Actor (Brandauer); N.Y. Film Critics '85: Cinematog., Support. Actor (Brandauer).

Out of Annie's Past 1/2 **1994 (R)** Successful career woman Annie Carver (Stewart) has managed to hide a dreadful secret from family and co-workers for some 10 years. But now the past is back to haunt her—seems Annie was once the prime suspect in a murder. **91m/C VHS.** Catherine Mary Stewart, Dennis Farina, Scott Valentine, Carsten Norgaard, Michael Flynn; *D:* Stuart Cooper; *W:* Pablo F. Fenjves. **CABLE**

Out of Bounds 1/2 **1986 (R)** An Iowa farmboy picks up the wrong bag at the Los Angeles airport, and is plunged into a world of crime, drugs, and murder. Plenty of action, but the fast pace can't hide huge holes in the script or the silliness of Hall playing a tough kid on the run from the law. **93m/C VHS.** Anthony Michael Hall, Jenny Wright, Jeff Kober; *D:* Richard Tuggle; *C:* Bruce Surtees; *M:* Stewart Copeland.

Out of Control **1985 (R)** A plane full of rich teenagers crash on a secluded island and must battle a gang of vicious smugglers to survive. A teen sex theme keeps working its way in, leaving the viewer as confused as the actors and actresses appear to be. **78m/C VHS.** Betsy Russell, Martin Hewitt, Claudia Udy, Andrew J. Lederer; *D:* Allan Holzman; *W:* Vicangelo Bulluck; *C:* John A. Alonzo.

Out of Order 1/2 **1984** A German-made film about people stuck in an office building's malevolent, free-thinking elevator. Dubbed. **87m/C VHS.** *GE* Renee Soutendijk, Goetz George, Wolfgang Kieling, Hannes Jaenicke; *D:* Carl Schenkel.

Out of Order **2003 (R)** The pilot episode of the Showtime series finds Stoltz and Huffman starring as a long-married, successful Hollywood screenwriting couple Mark and Lorna Colm. Lorna is going through a deep depression, which leaves Mark caring for their son and vulnerable to the unhappily married Danni (Dickens). Meanwhile, Lorna finds some solace with bitter best pal Steven (Macy), a not very successful producer. **97m/C VHS, DVD.** Eric Stoltz, Felicity Huffman, Kim Dickens, William H. Macy, Justine Bateman, Peter Bogdanovich; *D:* Wayne Powers; *W:* Wayne Powers, Donna Powers. **CABLE**

Out of Season *Winter Rates* **1975 (R)** Mother and teenage daughter compete for the attentions of the mother's mysterious ex-lover. We never know who wins the man in this enigmatic drama set in an English village, and hints of incest make the story even murkier. Had only a short run in the U.S. **90m/C VHS, DVD.** *GB* Cliff Robertson, Vanessa Redgrave, Susan George; *D:* Alan Bridges.

Out of Sight **1998 (R)** Cerebral director Soderbergh turns up the heat in this fine adaptation (with fine performances) of the Elmore Leonard crime caper. Jack Foley (Clooney) is a charming bank robber with bad luck and three prison terms—his current one being served in a Florida pen from which he escapes with the aid of partner Buddy (Rhames). Even the escape doesn't go as planned since federal marshal Karen Sisco (Lopez) becomes an unexpected (temporary) hostage. Sparks fly between the duo but Karen's still determined to bring Jack to justice, even as he plans his next heist. A heist involving shady financier Richard Ripley (Brooks) that will take Jack and Buddy to Detroit and more complications. **122m/C VHS, DVD, HD DVD.** George Clooney, Jennifer Lopez, Ving Rhames, Don Cheadle, Albert Brooks, Steve Zahn, Dennis Farina, Catherine Keener, Luis Guzman, Isaiah Washington IV, Keith Loneker, Nancy Allen; ***Cameos:*** Michael Keaton, Samuel L. Jackson; *D:* Steven Soderbergh; *W:* Scott Frank; *C:* Elliot Davis; *M:* Cliff Martinez. Natl. Soc. Film Critics '98: Director (Soderbergh), Film, Screenplay; Writers Guild '98: Adapt. Screenplay.

Out of Sight, Out of Her Mind *Out of Sight, Out of Mind* **1989 (R)** After witnessing her daughter burned alive, Alice is released from a mental institution. She tries to start a new life, but her daughter won't let her—she keeps appearing, crying out for help. **94m/C VHS.** Susan Blakely, Eddie Albert, Wings Hauser; *D:* Greydon Clark; *W:* Roy Langsdon, John Platt; *C:* Nicholas Josef von Sternberg.

Out of Sync 1/2 **1995 (R)** Deejay Jason St. Julian gets in trouble with his bookies and L.A. detectives, one of whom forces him into an undercover job with a drug-dealing club owner. Then Jason falls for the dealer's girlfriend. Hip-hop soundtrack may provide the only interest. **105m/C VHS, DVD.** LL Cool J, Victoria Dillard, Howard Hesseman, Ramy Zada, Don Yesso, Yaphet Kotto; *D:* Debbie Allen; *W:* Robert E. Dorn; *C:* Isidore Mankofsky; *M:* Steve Tyrell.

Out of the Ashes 1/2 **2003 (R)** Based on actual events. Dr. Gisella Perl (Lahti) is a Hungarian Jew who is sent to Auschwitz, along with her family, in 1944. Perl survives by working as a doctor in the camp, but when she tries to immigrate to the U.S. in 1947 she is accused of being a Nazi collaborator by immigration officials. **113m/C DVD.** Christine Lahti, Beau Bridges, Richard Crenna, Bruce Davison, Jonathan Cake, Jolyon Baker, Jessica Beitchman; *D:* Joseph Sargent; *W:* Anne Meredith; *C:* Donald M. Morgan; *M:* Charles Bernstein. **CABLE**

Out of the Black 1/2 **2001** In 1976, 10-year-old Cole Malby is told to forget everything he thinks he saw regarding the death of his Pennsylvania coal miner father and the shooting that paralyzed his mother (Kirkland). Thirteen years later, Cole (Christopher) and his younger brother Patrick (Widener) struggle on the family farm and decide it's past time to find out the truth. Naturally, there are a lot of people determined to make the brothers sorry for their interference. **105m/C VHS, DVD.** Tyler Christopher, Sally Kirkland, Dee Wallace, Jason Widener, Jacqueline Aries, Jack Conley, Michael J. Pollard, Miles O'Keeffe, Sally Struthers, Allison Lange, John Capodice, Tom Atkins; *D:* Karl Kozak; *W:* Karl Kozak, Joel Eisenberg; *C:* Maximo Munzi; *M:* Lawrence Nash Groupe.

Out of the Blue 1/2 **1947** There's trouble in paradise for a married man when a shady lady passes out in his apartment. Thinking she is dead, he tries to get rid of the body. The antics with his neighbor and wife provide plenty of laughs. **86m/B VHS.** George Brent, Virginia Mayo, Carole Landis, Turhan Bey, Ann Dvorak; *D:* Leigh Jason.

Out of the Blue **1980 (R)** A harsh, violent portrait of a shattered family. When an imprisoned father's return fails to reunite this Woodstock-generation family, the troubled teenage daughter takes matters into her own hands. "Easy Rider" star Hopper seems to have reconsidered the effects of the 1960s. **94m/C VHS, DVD.** Dennis Hopper, Linda Manz, Raymond Burr; *D:* Dennis Hopper; *W:* Gary Jules Jouvenat, Brenda Nielson, Leonard Yakir; *C:* Marc Champion; *M:* Tom Lavin.

Out of the Body **1988 (R)** A man is possessed by a spirit that likes to kill young, beautiful women. This makes him (and the viewer) uncomfortable. **91m/C VHS.** *AU* Mark Hembrow, Tessa Humphries, John Clayton, John Ley, Carrie Zivetz, Linda Newton; *D:* Brian Trenchard-Smith; *W:* Kenneth Ross; *C:* Kevan Lind; *M:* Peter Westheimer.

Out of the Cold 1/2 **1999 (R)** Jewish tap dancer Dan Scott (Carradine) decides to take his fading cabaret act to his family's homeland of Estonia on the eve of WWII. Bad idea. Trapped between the Nazis and the Soviets, Dan still finds time to romance local beauty Deborah (Kirshner), although their love affair is cut short by tragedy. Blah film whose plot goes nowhere quickly. **111m/C VHS, DVD.** Keith Carradine, Mia Kirshner, Judd Hirsch, Brian Dennehy, Mercedes Ruehl, Bronson Pinchot, Kim Hunter, Mark Sheppard; *D:* Aleksandr (Sasha) Buravsky; *W:* Aleksandr (Sasha) Buravsky, Alex Kustanovich; *C:* Vladimir Klimov; *M:* Maksim Dunayevsky.

Out of the Dark 1/2 **1988 (R)** The female employees of a telephone-sex service are stalked by a killer wearing a clown mask in this tongue-in-cheek thriller. A few laughs amid the slaughter. Look for Divine. **98m/C VHS.** Cameron Dye, Divine, Karen Black, Bud Cort, Lynn Danielson-Rosenthal, Geoffrey Lewis, Paul Bartel, Tracey Walter, Silvania Gallardo, Starr Andreeff, Lainie Kazan, Tab Hunter, John DeBello; *D:* Michael Schroeder; *W:* James DeFelice, Zane W. Levitt; *C:* Julio Macat; *M:* Paul Antonelli, David Wheatley.

Out of the Darkness **1985 (R)** TV movie about the personal life of the New York detective who hunted and arrested sexual killer Son of Sam. Sheen shines in a tight suspenser. **96m/C VHS.** Martin Sheen, Hector Elizondo, Matt Clark, Jennifer Salt, Eddie Egan, Robert Trebor; *D:* Jud Taylor; *W:* T.S. Cook. **TV**

Out of the Fog **1941** Garfield stars as an irredeemable racketeering louse who shakes down the fishermen of Sheepshead Bay. Elderly friends Jonah (Mitchell) and Olaf (Qualen) have big dreams and small means but pay protection money to Harold Goff for safety's sake. Harold woos Jonah's bored daughter Stella (Lupino) and continues to threaten the two men so they plot Harold's death. Fate intervenes so the good guys don't become bad guys. Based on the Irwin Shaw play "The Gentle People." **93m/B DVD.** John Garfield, Thomas Mitchell, John Qualen, Ida Lupino, Eddie Albert, George Tobias, Aline MacMahon, Leo Gorcey, Paul Harvey; *D:* Anatole Litvak; *W:* Jerry Wald, Robert Rossen, Richard Macaulay; *C:* James Wong Howe.

Out of the Past 1/2 *Build My Gallows High* **1947** A private detective gets caught in a complex web of love, murder, and money in this film noir classic. The plot is torturous but clear thanks to fine directing. Mitchum became an overnight star after this film, which was overlooked but now considered one of the best in its genre. Based on Geoffrey Homes's novel "Build My Gallows High." Remade in 1984 as "Against All Odds." **97m/B VHS, DVD.** Robert Mitchum, Kirk Douglas, Jane Greer, Rhonda Fleming, Steve Brodie, Dickie Moore, Richard Webb, Virginia Huston, Ken Niles, Paul Valentine; *D:* Jacques Tourneur; *W:* Daniel Mainwaring; *C:* Nicholas Musuraca; *M:* Roy Webb. Natl. Film Reg. '91.

Out of the Rain 1/2 **1990 (R)** A small town becomes a hotbed of deceit and lies due to the influence of drugs. A man and a woman engage in a passionate struggle to free themselves from the town's grip. **91m/C VHS.** Bridget Fonda, Michael O'Keefe, John E. O'Keefe, John Seitz, Georgine Hall, Al Shannon; *D:* Gary Winick; *W:* Shem Bitterman.

Out of the Shadows 1/2 **1988** Scotland Yard Chief Inspector Michael Hayden (Dance) investigates a series of international art thefts that lead him to believe the goods are being smuggled out of the country through diplomatic channels. **95m/C VHS.** *GB* Charles Dance, Alexandra Paul, Wanda Ventham; *D:* Willi Patterson. **TV**

Out of Time 1/2 **2000** Dull update of the Rip Van Winkle legend. While walking in the woods outside his small Oregon town, Jack Epson (McDaniels) takes a drink from a spring and falls asleep for 20 years. He wakes up to find his natural surroundings are under siege from developers and his now-grown daughter has a child of her own. **94m/C VHS, DVD.** James McDaniel, Mel Harris, August Schellenberg, Ken Pogue; *D:* Ernest Thompson; *W:* Ernest Thompson, Rob Gilmer; *C:* Stephen McNutt; *M:* Terry Frewer. **CABLE**

Out of Time 1/2 **2003 (PG-13)** Far-fetched thriller gets by on the charms of its lead. Matt Lee Whitlock (Washington) is an easy-going police chief in a sleepy Florida town who is having an affair with Ann (Lathan), who's married to jealous Chris (Cain). Ann reveals she has cancer and Matt decides to "borrow" money he recovered in a drug bust and give it to Ann to help with her treatment. Then, there's a mysterious fire, a couple of charred bodies, and soon Matt is trying to stay one step ahead of a criminal investigation being lead by his estranged wife Alex (Mendes). He may not be an innocent but Matt's not a murderer either, and he has to figure out who's setting him up. **114m/C VHS, DVD.** *US* Denzel Washington, Eva Mendes, Sanaa Lathan, Dean Cain, Robert Baker, Alex Carter, John Billingsley; *D:* Carl Franklin; *W:* Dave Collard; *C:* Theo van de Sande; *M:* Graeme Revell.

The Out-of-Towners **1970 (G)** A pair of Ohio rubes travels to New York City and along the way everything that could go wrong does. Lemmon's performance is excellent and Simon's script is, as usual, both wholesome and funny. **98m/C VHS, DVD.** Jack Lemmon, Sandy Dennis, Anne Meara, Sandy Baron, Billy Dee Williams; *D:* Arthur Hiller; *W:* Neil Simon. Writers Guild '70: Orig. Screenplay.

The Out-of-Towners **1999 (PG-13)** Hawn and Martin are Nancy and Henry Clark, middle-aged Ohio empty-nesters headed for Henry's job interview in New York. Along the way, they're thwarted by every tourist nightmare obstacle imaginable: rerouting to Boston, missed trains, rental car mishaps, muggings, maxed credit cards, snooty hotel personnel, etc, etc. Martin's seen all this before (in "Planes, Trains, and Automobiles") and so have we, in any number of movies, including the original 1970 Neil Simon script. Mostly uninspired and inconsistent, with flashes of fine physical comedy from Hawn and Martin. Cleese plays a familiar role as a needlessly pompous hotel manager. **92m/C VHS, DVD.** Mark McKinney, Goldie Hawn, Steve Martin, John Cleese, Oliver Hudson; *D:* Sam Weisman; *W:* Marc Lawrence; *C:* John Bailey; *M:* Marc Shaiman.

Out on a Limb **1987** MacLaine plays herself in this miniseries based on her best-selling book by the same name. In the midst of love affairs with an unnamed British politician and a mysterious teacher, she learns about her past, present, and future through meditation and her beliefs in reincarnation. Features footage of psychics performing spiritual channeling. Beautiful scenery filmed on location in California, Hong Kong, London, Hawaii, Sweden, and Peru, but the acting is just average, and the movie is slow in some parts. **160m/C VHS.** Shirley MacLaine, Charles Dance, John Heard, Anne Jackson, Jerry Orbach; *D:* Robert Butler. **TV**

Out on a Limb **1992 (PG)** Lame comedy follows the misadventures of financial whiz Bill Campbell (Broderick). His young sister is convinced their stepfather is a criminal and persuades her brother to return home. On his way, Bill is robbed and abandoned by a woman hitchhiker, then found by two moronic brothers. It also turns out his stepfather has a twin brother who wants revenge for past crimes. Frantic chase scenes and lots of noise do not a comedy make. Broderick and Jones also appeared together in "Ferris Bueller's Day Off." **82m/C VHS.** Matthew Broderick, Jeffrey Jones, Heidi Kling, John C. Reilly, Marian Mercer, Larry Hankin, David Margulies; ***D:*** Francis Veber.

Out on Bail 🦴 ½ **1989 (R)** A law-abiding citizen witnesses a murder, only to discover the crooked town council is behind the slaying. **102m/C VHS.** Robert Ginty, Kathy Shower, Tom Badal, Sydney Lassick; ***D:*** Gordon Hessler; ***W:*** Tom Badal, Jason Booth.

Out There 🦴🦴 ½ **1995 (PG-13)** Cable sci-fi comedy finds photographer Delbert Mosley (Campbell) buying a Brownie camera at a garage sale and discovering the 25-year-old film shows pictures of a UFO encounter. Mosley then tries to verify the photos with a supermarket tabloid, the military, and UFO fanatics all on his trail. Fast-paced amusement with appealing performances. **98m/C VHS.** Richard Speight Jr., Billy Campbell, Wendy Schaal, Julie Brown, David Rasche, Paul Dooley, Bill Cobbs, Bob(cat) Goldthwait, Rod Steiger, June Lockhart, Jill St. John, Carel Struycken, Billy Bob Thornton, P.J. Soles; ***D:*** Sam Irvin; ***W:*** Thomas Strelich, Alison Nigh; ***C:*** Gary Tieche; ***M:*** Deborah Holland, Frankie Blue. **CABLE**

Out to Sea 🦴🦴 ½ **1997 (PG-13)** Charlie (Matthau) persuades brother-in-law Herb (Lemmon) to become a dance instructor aboard a cruise ship so they can meet women and con them out of money. Charlie sets his sights on feisty socialite Liz (Cannon), while Herb romances Vivian (DeHaven), who's tagging along on her daughter's honeymoon. Both of these "salty old dogs" have to avoid the wrath of militaristic cruise director Gil (Spiner). The duo still has great comic timing, as they continue to defy the odds that this is the one that's gonna flop. Great supporting cast, which includes O'Connor in a couple of nifty dance scenes, seems to be having a great time. **109m/C VHS, DVD.** Joe (Johnny) Viterelli, Walter Matthau, Jack Lemmon, Dyan Cannon, Gloria De Haven, Brent Spiner, Elaine Stritch, Hal Linden, Donald O'Connor, Edward Mulhare, Rue McClanahan; ***D:*** Martha Coolidge; ***W:*** Robert Nelson Jacobs, Danny Jacobson; ***C:*** Lajos Koltai; ***M:*** David Newman.

Outbreak 🦴🦴🦴 **1994 (R)** Smuggled African monkey spits on someone who kisses someone else who sneezes on a bunch of people, thus initiating the spread of a highly infectious mystery disease in a northern California 'burb. Hoffman leads a team of scientists in a search for the anti-serum, but it's a secret government plot to exterminate the victims that literally sends Hoffman and crew into action movie cliche overdrive (add "helicopter" to the list of chase scene vehicles). Not that that's so bad—if the beat-the-clock tempo doesn't grab you, paranoia certainly will. But Hoffman's hardly a threat to Arnold or Sylvester as the next action hero, and the talented Russo remains suspiciously ravishing even with festering pustules. Based on two books: Richard Preston's "The Hot Zone" and Laurie Garrett's "The Coming Plague." **128m/C VHS, DVD.** Dustin Hoffman, Rene Russo, Morgan Freeman, Donald Sutherland, Cuba Gooding Jr., Kevin Spacey, J.T. Walsh, Dale Dye; ***D:*** Wolfgang Petersen; ***W:*** Laurence Dworet, Robert Roy Pool; ***C:*** Michael Ballhaus; ***M:*** James Newton Howard. N.Y. Film Critics '95: Support. Actor (Spacey).

The Outcast 🦴🦴 **1954** A young tough heads west to seize the family ranch wrongfully held by a conniving uncle. Of course he finds love as well, and enjoys gun and fistfights in this exciting though unspectacular western. **90m/C VHS.** John Derek, Jim Davis, Joan Davis; ***D:*** William Witney.

The Outcast 🦴 ½ **1984** Story of three brothers who live by the ax, love from the heart, hate with passion, and die violently. Trouble is they have to recite from a script written in crayon. **86m/C VHS.** *SA* Anthony H. Wilson, Marcel Van Heerden, Ben Dekker, Sandra Prinsloo; ***D:*** Gray Hofmeyr; ***W:*** Gray Hofmeyr; ***C:*** James Robb; ***M:*** Barry Bekker.

The Outcasts 🦴🦴🦴 **1986** A Taiwanese film about young gay boys in an urban jungle who are given shelter and protection by an aging photographer. In Chinese with English subtitles. **102m/C VHS.** *TW* ***D:*** Yu Kan-Ping.

Outcasts of the City 🦴🦴 **1958** The sort of negligible film filler that TV killed off. An American officer in post-WWII Germany romances a German girl, then gets blamed for the death of her Boche beau. **61m/B VHS.** Osa Massen, Robert Hutton, Maria Palmer, Nestor Paiva, John Hamilton, George Neise, Norbert Schiller, George Sanders; ***D:*** Boris L. Petroff.

Outcasts of the Trail 🦴 ½ **1949** When Tom White (Gallaudet) is jailed for robbing the stage, his children are shunned by the town even after Tom decides to return the stolen cash after his release. So, it's up to stagecoach driver Pat Garrett (Hale) to clear up the family's trouble. **61m/B VHS.** Monte Hale, John Gallaudet, Roy Barcroft, Jeff Donnell, Tommy "T.V." Ivo, Paul Hurst; ***D:*** Philip Ford; ***W:*** Olive Cooper, Stanley Wilson; ***C:*** Bud Thackery.

The Outer Limits: Sandkings 🦴🦴🦴 *Sandkings* **1995** Cable revival of the '60s sci-fi series is creepier than ever with this tale of loony scientist Simon Kress (Bridges). He discovers tiny alien eggs while doing an analysis of Martian soil samples and decides to take his research home with him when the government cuts off funding. Big mistake—the critters he successfully hatches in his barn are mean and hungry. Features both dad Lloyd and Beau's 10-year-old son, Dylan, in roles. **93m/C VHS.** Beau Bridges, Lloyd Bridges, Helen Shaver, Dylan Bridges, Kim Coates; ***D:*** Stuart Gillard; ***W:*** Melinda M. Snodgrass. **CABLE**

The Outfit 🦴🦴 ½ **1993 (R)** It's the 1930s and a mob war is brewing between Lucky Luciano, Legs Diamond and Dutch Schultz. A maverick FBI agent gets in good with Diamond and works to end their reign of crime—only he winds up being the spark to light a war between the rival bosses. **92m/C VHS.** John Christian, Billy Drago, Lance Henriksen, Martin Kove, Josh Moby, Rick Washburne; ***D:*** J. Christian Ingvordsen; ***W:*** J. Christian Ingvordsen, Steven Kaman, Whitney Ransick.

Outfoxed: Rupert Murdoch's War on Journalism 🦴🦴🦴 **2004** Greenwald's doc rails against what he views as manipulation, political bias, and smear-campaign tactics used to further the conservative agenda of Fox News Channel. Uses internal Fox News Department memos to illustrate and ask hard questions about the line between news coverage and commentary. **77m/C DVD.** ***D:*** Robert Greenwald; ***C:*** Bob Sullivan, James Curry, Will Miller, Glen Pearcy, Richard Perez, Luke Riffle, Eugene Thompson; ***M:*** Nicholas O'Toole.

The Outing 🦴🦴 *The Lamp* **1987 (R)** A group of high school kids sneaks into a museum at night to party, and get hunted down by a 3,000-year-old genie-in-a-lamp. The genie idea is original enough to make things interesting. Mediocre special effects and run-of-the-mill acting. **87m/C VHS.** Deborah Winters, James Huston, Andra St. Ivanyi, Scott Bankston, Mark Mitchell, Andre Chimene, Damon Merrill, Barry Coffing; ***D:*** Tom Daley; ***W:*** Warren Chaney; ***C:*** Herbert Raditschnig.

Outing Riley 🦴🦴 **2004** Chicago architect Bobby Riley (Jones) is a regular guy in his thirties from an Irish-Catholic family. At the urging of his sister (Pearl) and his boyfriend (McDonald), Bobby finally decides to come out to his three brothers. Only they don't believe him. **86m/C DVD.** Pete Jones, Nathan Fillion, Michael McDonald, Stoney Westmoreland, Dev Kennedy, Julie R. Pearl, Dana Gilhooley; ***D:*** Pete Jones; ***W:*** Pete Jones; ***C:*** Pete Biagi.

Outland 🦴🦴 **1981 (R)** On a volcanic moon of Jupiter, miners begin suffering from spells of insanity. A single federal marshal begins an investigation that threatens the colony's survival. No more or less than a western in space, and the science is rather poor. Might make an interesting double feature with "High Noon," though. **109m/C VHS, DVD.** Kika Markham, Clarke Peters, Steven Berkoff, John Ratzenberger, Manning Redwood, Angus MacInnes, Sean Connery, Peter Boyle, Frances Sternhagen, James B. Sikking; ***D:*** Peter Hyams; ***W:*** Peter Hyams; ***C:*** Stephen Goldblatt; ***M:*** Jerry Goldsmith.

Outlander 🦴 ½ **2008 (R)** We're in aliens vs. Vikings territory. In 709 AD, human-looking alien Kainan (Caviezel) crashes his spacecraft in a Norwegian fjord. Unbeknownst to him, a vicious alien called a Moorwen was hiding aboard and promptly decides to destroy the local Norse settlements. Kainan convinces the Viking king Rothgar (Hurt) that he can kill the monster. Some flashbacks explain the Kainan/Moorwen connection and there's finally some action in the last half of the pic but it's a slow slog to get there. **115m/C DVD.** *US GE* James (Jim) Caviezel, John Hurt, Sophia Myles, Jack Huston, Ron Perlman, Cliff Saunders, Patrick Stevenson; ***D:*** Howard McCain; ***W:*** Howard McCain, Dirk Blackman; ***C:*** Pierre Gill; ***M:*** Geoff Zanelli.

The Outlaw 🦴🦴 **1943** Hughes's variation on the saga of Billy the Kid, which spends more time on Billy's relationship with girlfriend Rio than the climactic showdown with Pat Garrett. The famous Russell vehicle isn't as steamy as it must have seemed to viewers of the day, but the brouhaha around it served to keep it on the shelf for six years. Also available colorized. **123m/B VHS, DVD.** Jane Russell, Jack Buetel, Walter Huston, Thomas Mitchell, Mimi Aguglia, Gene Rizzi, Joseph (Joe) Sawyer; ***D:*** Howard Hughes; ***W:*** Jules Furthman; ***C:*** Gregg Toland; ***M:*** Victor Young.

Outlaw 🦴 ½ **2007 (R)** Good Brit cast in a revenge flick with lots and lots (and lots) of violence. Embittered ex-soldier Danny Bryant (Bean) forms a vigilante group after becoming disgusted by the brazenness of the city's criminals and the weakness of the PC judicial system. His recruits have all been victimized by violence and Danny has an inside man with longtime copper Lewis (Hoskins), who passes along information on the whereabouts of various scum that need dealing with. **105m/C DVD.** *GB* Sean Bean, Bob Hoskins, Danny Dyer, Rupert Friend, Sean Harris, Lennie James; ***D:*** Nick Love; ***W:*** Nick Love; ***C:*** Sam McCurdy; ***M:*** David Julyan.

The Outlaw and His Wife 🦴🦴 ½ **1917** An early silent film about a farmer, accused of a petty crime, who flees with his wife into the mountains to escape the police. This powerful drama was a breakthrough film for the early Swedish movie industry. **73m/B VHS.** *SW* Victor Sjostrom, Edith Erastoff; ***D:*** Victor Sjostrom.

The Outlaw Bikers—Gang Wars 🦴 **1970** The original road warriors take it to the streets as rival biker gangs square off. **90m/C VHS.** Clancy Syrko, Des Roberts, John King III, Linda Jackson; ***D:*** Laurence Merrick.

Outlaw Blues 🦴🦴 **1977 (PG)** An ex-convict becomes a national folk hero when he sets out to reclaim his stolen hit song about prison life. St. James is charming in her first major movie role. A grab bag of action, drama, and tongue-in-cheek humor. **101m/C VHS.** Peter Fonda, Susan St. James, Johnny Crawford, Michael Lerner, James Callahan; ***D:*** Richard T. Heffron; ***M:*** Charles Bernstein.

Outlaw Country 🦴🦴 ½ **1949** LaRue has a dual role as the marshal who is after a band of counterfeiters and an outlaw who's part of the gang. **72m/B VHS.** Lash LaRue, Al "Fuzzy" St. John, House Peters Jr., Ted Adams, Dan(iel) White, Steve Dunhill; ***D:*** Ray Taylor.

The Outlaw Deputy 🦴 ½ **1935** The law-abiding McCoy as an outlaw! It's really a mistake and Lane helps him clear his name. Based on the story "King of Cactusville" by Johnston McCulley. **55m/B VHS, DVD.** Tim McCoy, Nora Lane, Bud Osborne, Si Jenks, George Offerman Jr.; ***D:*** Otto Brower.

Outlaw Express 🦴 ½ **1938** After the annexing of California, a U.S. marshall is sent to stop a gang of outlaws who have been raiding Spanish landowners. **57m/B VHS.** Bob Baker, Cecilia Callejo, Leroy Mason, Don Barclay, Carleton Young; ***D:*** George Waggner.

Outlaw Force 🦴 **1987 (R)** A Vietnam veteran country singer tracks down the vicious rednecks that kidnapped his daughter and raped and killed his wife. Heavener did all the work in this low-budget, low-quality take-off on "Death Wish." **95m/C VHS.** David Heavener, Frank Stallone, Paul Smith, Robert Bjorklund, Devin Dunsworth; ***D:*** David Heavener.

Outlaw Fury 🦴 ½ *Hostile Country* **1950** Another Shamrock Ellison epic, this time dealing with a coward proving himself by killing the bad guys. **55m/B VHS.** James Ellison, Russell Hayden, Julie Adams, Raymond Hatton, Tom Tyler, George Lewis, John Cason, Stanley Price, I. Stanford Jolley; ***D:*** Thomas Carr; ***W:*** Ron Ormond, Maurice Tombragel; ***C:*** Ernest Miller.

Outlaw Gang 🦴 ½ *The Dalton Gang* **1949** A marshal investigates a rash of rancher killings, leading to a conflict between Indians and local land and water companies. **59m/B VHS, DVD.** Donald (Don "Red") Barry, Robert Lowery, Betty Adams, James Millican, Byron Foulger, J. Farrell MacDonald, Greg McClure, George Lewis, Stanley Price, Tom Tyler; ***D:*** Ford Beebe; ***W:*** Ford Beebe; ***C:*** Ernest Miller.

The Outlaw Josey Wales 🦴🦴🦴🦴 **1976 (PG)** Eastwood plays a farmer with a motive for revenge—his family was killed by Union guerillas, and he was betrayed and hunted. His desire to play the lone killer is, however, tempered by his need for family and friends. He kills plenty, but in the end finds peace. Considered one of the last great Westerns, with many superb performances. Eastwood took over directorial chores during filming from Kaufman, who co-scripted. Adapted from "Gone To Texas" by Forest Carter. **135m/C VHS, DVD.** Clint Eastwood, Chief Dan George, Sondra Locke, Matt Clark, John Vernon, Bill McKinney, Sam Bottoms, Will Sampson, Woodrow Parfrey, Royal Dano, John Quade, John Russell, John Mitchum, Kyle Eastwood; ***D:*** Clint Eastwood; ***W:*** Philip Kaufman; ***C:*** Bruce Surtees; ***M:*** Jerry Fielding. Natl. Film Reg. '96.

Outlaw Justice 🦴🦴 **1932** Worn oater plot has our hero infiltrating a gang of outlaws to bring them to justice and save the heroine. **56m/C VHS.** Jack Hoxie, Dorothy Gulliver, Donald Keith, Kermit Maynard, Charles "Blackie" King, Tom London; ***D:*** Armand Schaefer.

Outlaw Justice 🦴🦴 ½ **1998 (R)** Aging gunslingers Nelson and Kristofferson meet up with buddy Tritt in order to avenge the death of their old partner. Nothing new storywise but the cast is certainly comfortable with the material. **94m/C VHS, DVD.** Kris Kristofferson, Willie Nelson, Sancho Garcia, Travis Tritt, Chad Willet, Waylon Jennings; ***D:*** Bill Corcoran; ***W:*** Gene Quintano; ***C:*** Federico Ribes; ***M:*** Jay Gruska. **TV**

Outlaw of Gor 🦴 ½ **1987 (PG)** Once again, the mild professor is transported to Gor, where he has new, improved, bloody adventures. Lots of sword-play, but no magic. Sequel to "Gor." From the novel by John Norman. **89m/C VHS.** Rebecca Ferratti, Urbano Barberini, Jack Palance, Donna Denton; ***D:*** John Cardos; ***W:*** R.J. Marx.

Outlaw of the Plains 🦴 **1946** Another of Crabbe's cowboy pictures in which he played hero Billy Carson, now bailing his trouble-prone sidekick out of a land swindle. Very plain indeed. **56m/B VHS.** Buster Crabbe, Al "Fuzzy" St. John, Patti McCarty, Charles "Blackie" King, Karl Hackett, John Cason, Bud Osborne, Budd Buster, Charles "Slim" Whitaker; ***D:*** Sam Newfield.

Outlaw Riders 🦴 **1972 (PG)** Three outlaw bikers take it on the lam after committing a series of disastrous bank robberies. **84m/C VHS.** Bryan (Sonny) West, Darlene Duralia, Bambi Allen, Bill Bonner; ***D:*** Tony Houston.

Outlaw Roundup 🦴 **1944** The Texas Rangers battle an outlaw gang. Guess who wins. **51m/B VHS.** Tex O'Brien, James Newill, Guy Wilkerson, Helen Chapman, Jack Ingram, I. Stanford Jolley; ***D:*** Harry Fraser.

Outlaw Rule 🦴 ½ **1936** Standard action-packed western adventure pitting outlaws against the law of the West. **61m/B VHS.** Reb Russell, Betty Mack, Yakima Canutt, Jack Rockwell, John McGuire, Alan Bridge; ***D:*** S. Roy Luby.

The Outlaw Tamer 🦴 **1933** Even though Chandler is on the run he still helps capture some horse thieves. **56m/B VHS, DVD.** Lane Chandler, J(ohn) P(aterson) McGowan, Janet Morgan, George "Gabby" Hayes; ***D:*** J(ohn) P(aterson) McGowan.

Outlaw Trail 🦴 ½ **1944** The Trail Blazers put an end to a counterfeiter's evil ways.

53m/B VHS. Hoot Gibson, Bob Steele, Chief Thundercloud, Jennifer Holt, Cy Kendall; *D:* Robert Emmett Tansey.

Outlaw Trail ♪♪ 1/2 **2006 (PG)** In 1951, teenager Roy Parker (Kelley) sets out to prove that his late great-uncle was actually Butch Cassidy, who survived a Bolivian ambush to return to the States with a fortune in gold. Roy wants to clear the family name and, thanks to a handy map, find Butch's missing treasure, but he's not the only one looking. Lively family fare. **90m/C DVD.** Ryan Kelley, Arielle Kebbel, Dan Byrd, Bruce McGill, Brent Weber, James Gammon, James Karen, Brian Wimmer; *D:* Ryan Little; *W:* David Pliler; *C:* Geno Salvatori; *M:* J Bateman.

Outlaw Women ♪ **1952** A western town is run by a woman who won't let male outlaws in—until one wins her heart. **76m/C VHS.** Marie Windsor, Jackie Coogan, Carla Balenda; *D:* Sam Newfield.

The Outlaws Is Coming! ♪♪ 1/2 **1965** Three magazine staffers (Larry, Moe, and Curly Joe) and their editor (West) encounter Wyatt Earp, Wild Bill Hickock, Jesse James, and Annie Oakley when they journey out West to save the buffalo. Last, and one of the best, of the Three Stooges feature films. **90m/B VHS, DVD.** Moe Howard, Larry Fine, Joe DeRita, Adam West, Nancy Kovack, Emil Sitka, Henry Gibson; *D:* Norman Maurer.

Outlaws of Sonora ♪ 1/2 **1938** A man transports money to a neighboring town while his outlaw double tries to steal it from him. **58m/B VHS, DVD.** Robert "Bob" Livingston, Ray Corrigan, Max Terhune, Jack Mulhall, Otis Harlan; *D:* George Sherman.

Outlaws of the Cherokee Trail ♪ 1/2 **1941** The Three Mesquiteers join the Texas Rangers. Outlaw Lemar operates from the Cherokee Strip where the Rangers have no jurisdiction. But when his brother is captured and sentenced to hang, Lemar's gang kidnaps the daughter of Captain Sheldon as a bargaining chip and the boys must rescue her. The 39th film in the series. **56m/B DVD.** Bob Steele, Rufe Davis, Tom Tyler, Lois Collier, Tom Chatterton, Roy Barcroft, Joel Friedkin; *D:* Les(ter) Orlebeck; *W:* Albert DeMond; *C:* Ernest Miller.

Outlaws of the Desert ♪ 1/2 **1941** Having run out of bad guys in the Old West, Hoppy and his pals head to Arabia to buy some horses. Once there, they get involved in a kidnapping. Russell Hayden is replaced as Hoppy's sidekick by Brad King. Duncan ("The Cisco Kid") Renaldo plays the sheik. **66m/B VHS, DVD.** William Boyd, Brad King, Andy Clyde, Forrest Stanley, Jean Phillips, Duncan Renaldo, George Lewis; *D:* Howard Bretherton.

Outlaws of the Range ♪ 1/2 **1936** Action western featuring outlaws who terrorize the countryside. **60m/B VHS, DVD.** Bill Cody, Marie Burton, William (Bill, Billy) McCall, Gordon Griffith; *D:* Al(bert) Herman.

Outlaws of the Rio Grande ♪ 1/2 **1941** Marshal Tim Barton's (McCoy) friend is murdered and he tracks the killers into Mexico. Rita (Carpenter) is forced to help trap Barton since the bad guys have kidnapped her father. **63m/B DVD.** Tim McCoy, Charles King, Ralph Peters, Kenne Duncan, Rex Lease, Thornton Edwards; *D:* Sam Newfield; *W:* George Plympton; *C:* Jack Greenhalgh.

Outlaw's Paradise ♪♪ **1939** Cowboy hero McCoy plays not only a lawman out to catch mail thieves, but also the chief outlaw he's hunting! That's one way to keep the budget low. **62m/B VHS.** Tim McCoy, Ben (Benny) Corbett, Joan Barclay, Ted Adams, Forrest Taylor, Bob Terry; *D:* Sam Newfield.

Outpost in Morocco ♪ 1/2 **1949** A desert soldier is sent to quiet the restless natives and falls for the rebel leader's daughter. The good guys win, but the love interest is sacrificed. Glory before love boys, and damn the story. **92m/B VHS, DVD.** George Raft, Marie Windsor, Akim Tamiroff, John Litel, Eduard Franz; *D:* Robert Florey; *W:* Charles Grayson, Paul de Sainte-Colombe; *C:* Lucien N. Andriot; *M:* Michel Michelet.

The Outrage ♪ 1/2 **1964** Paul Newman plays a Mexican bandit with a bad accent in this dreary western remake of "Rashomon." A con man (Robinson), preacher (Shatner), and prospector (Da Silva) wait at a railway station. They were all witnesses at the trial of bandit Juan (Newman), who was convicted of rape and murder. But the three men give divergent accounts as to what happened (shown in flashbacks). **95m/B DVD.** Paul Newman, Laurence Harvey, Claire Bloom, Edward G. Robinson, William Shatner, Howard da Silva, Albert Salmi, Paul Fix, Thomas Chalmers; *D:* Martin Ritt; *W:* Michael Kanin; *C:* James Wong Howe; *M:* Alex North.

Outrage! ♪♪ 1/2 **1986** An upstanding citizen guns down his daughter's killer and turns himself in to police. His ambitious lawyer fights an open-and-shut homicide case with both fair and foul means. Not a shootout like the cassette box suggests, but an okay courtroom drama attacking excesses of the legal system. From a novel by Henry Denker, made for TV by producer Irwin Allen. **96m/C VHS.** Robert Preston, Beau Bridges, Anthony Newley, Mel Ferrer, Burgess Meredith, Linda Purl, William Allen Young; *D:* Walter Grauman. **TV**

Outrage ♪♪ *Dispara* **1993 (R)** Journalist Marco Vallez's (Banderas) latest assignment is a story about a traveling circus. Bored with the usual acts, he's intrigued by equestrian/sharpshooter Anna (Neri) and asks her for an interview, which leads to passion. While Marco is on assignment in Barcelona, Anna is attacked and raped in her trailer. Rather than calling the police, Anna decides to take her own revenge. Spanish with subtitles or dubbed. **108m/C VHS, DVD.** *SP* Antonio Banderas, Francesca Neri, Eulalia Ramon, Walter Vidarte, Coque Malla; *D:* Carlos Saura; *W:* Carlos Saura; *C:* Javier Aguirresarobe; *M:* Alberto Iglesias.

Outrage ♪♪ 1/2 **1998** Average guy Tom Casey (Lowe) thinks he's being a good citizen when he reports some teens stealing from cars to the cops. Instead, he and wife Sally (Grey) are terrorized by the punks and Tom decides the best solution is to take care of the miscreants himself. **90m/C VHS, DVD.** Rob Lowe, Jennifer Grey, Eric Michael Cole, Shane Meier, Nathaniel DeVeaux, Kathryn Harrold, Robert Wisden; *D:* Robert Allan Ackerman; *W:* Ellen Weston; *C:* Tobias Schliessler; *M:* David Mansfield. **TV**

Outrage ♪♪ **2009 (R)** Controversial documentarian Kirby Dick focuses on politicians (mainly Republicans) who campaign and vote against gay rights legislation while living closeted lives. Dick offers interviews (such as with gay blogger Michael Rogers who specializes in outing politicos), television clips, and commercials although it can come across as manipulative, including Dick's presumptions of a media conspiracy. **98m/C DVD.** *D:* Kirby Dick; *C:* Thaddeus Wadleigh; *M:* Peter Golub.

Outrageous! ♪♪♪ **1977 (R)** An offbeat, low-budget comedy about the strange relationship between a gay female impersonator and his pregnant schizophrenic friend. The pair end up in New York, where they feel right at home. Russell's impersonations of female film stars earned him the best actor prize at the Berlin Film Festival. **100m/C VHS, DVD.** *CA* Craig Russell, Hollis McLaren, Richard Easley, Allan Moyle, Helen Shaver, Martha Gibson, Helen Hughes, David McIlwraith, Andree Pelletier; *D:* Richard Benner; *W:* Richard Benner; *C:* James Kelly; *M:* Paul Hoffert.

Outrageous Fortune ♪♪ **1987 (R)** Two would-be actresses—one prim and innocent and one wildly trampy—chase after the same two-timing boyfriend and get involved in a dangerous CIA plot surrounding a deadly bacteria. Tired plot. Mediocre acting and formula jokes, but somehow still funny. Disney's first foray into comedy for grown-ups. **112m/C VHS, DVD.** Shelley Long, Bette Midler, George Carlin, Peter Coyote; *D:* Arthur Hiller; *W:* Leslie Dixon; *C:* David M. Walsh; *M:* Alan Silvestri.

Outside Chance ♪ **1978** A soapy, sanitized remake of Mimieux's film, "Jackson County Jail," wherein an innocent woman is persecuted in a small Southern jail. **92m/C VHS.** Yvette Mimieux, Royce D. Applegate; *D:* Michael Miller. **TV**

Outside Chance of Maximillian Glick ♪♪ **1988 (G)** A sentimental Canadian comedy about a boy's dreams and his tradition-bound Jewish family. **94m/C VHS.** *CA* Noam Zylberman, Fairuza Balk, Saul Rubinek; *D:* Allan Goldstein; *C:* Ian Elkin. Toronto-City '88: Canadian Feature Film.

The Outside Man ♪♪ *Un Homme Est Mort* **1973 (PG)** A French hit man is called to Los Angeles to knock off a crime boss, which he does. But then an American hit man is hired to do in the Frenchman. The climatic showdown is set around the crime boss' body, which happens to be embalmed in a sitting position. Decidely offbeat. **104m/C VHS.** *FR* Jean-Louis Trintignant, Roy Scheider, Ann-Margret, Angie Dickinson, Georgia Engel, Carlo De Mejo, Umberto Orsini, Ted de Corsia, Felice Orlandi, John Hillerman; *D:* Jacques Deray.

Outside Ozona ♪♪ **1998 (R)** Three sets of couples listen to a ranting all-night DJ (Taj Mahal) as they drive through the desolate Southwest. Wit Roy (Pollak) is an unemployed circus clown driving with his ex-stripper girlfriend, Earlene (Miller), trucker Odell Parks (Forster) comes to the aid of stranded Reba Twosalt (Walker) and her grandmother, while feuding sisters Marcy (Fenn) and Bonnie (Styne) are driving to their father's funeral. Oh yeah, there's also a backroads serial killer on the loose. Looks good but doesn't make much of an impression. **100m/C VHS.** Robert Forster, Kevin Pollak, Penelope Ann Miller, David Paymer, Sherilyn Fenn, Beth Ann Styne, Lois Red Elk, Kateri Walker, Swoosie Kurtz, Taj Mahal, Meat Loaf Aday, Lucy Webb; *D:* J.S. Cardone; *W:* J.S. Cardone; *C:* Irek Hartowicz; *M:* Taj Mahal, Johnny Lee Schell.

Outside Providence ♪♪ 1/2 **1999 (R)** Although heavily promoted as created "by the makers of 'There's Something About Mary'" upon its release to draw fans of low-brow humor, this coming-of-age comedy is actually a bit more sensitive. Based on Peter Farrelly's semi-autobiographical novel, it tells the story of Dunph (Hatosy), a stoner teen from Pawtucket who's sent to a snooty prep school by his father (Baldwin) after he and his high-on friends crash into a police car. He has immediate trouble fitting in, although he manages to hook up with coed Jane (Smart), whose book smarts help his anemic GPA. Unfortunately, his pranks put her Ivy League hopes in danger. Baldwin gives a good performance as the gruff-but-loving dad, but too many of the characters are merely skimmed over before they have a chance to develop. **103m/C VHS, DVD.** Shawn Hatosy, Alec Baldwin, George Wendt, Jonathan Brandis, Amy Smart, Gabriel Mann, Jon Abrahams, Adam LaVorgna, Mike Cerrone, Richard Jenkins; *D:* Michael Corrente; *W:* Peter Farrelly, Michael Corrente, Bobby Farrelly; *C:* Richard Crudo; *M:* Sheldon Mirowitz.

Outside the Law ♪♪ **1921** Lon Chaney plays dual roles of the underworld hood in "Black Mike Sylva," and a Chinese servant in "Ah Wing." Silent. **77m/B VHS, DVD.** Lon Chaney Sr., Priscilla Dean, Ralph Lewis, Wheeler Oakman; *D:* Tod Browning; *W:* Lucien Hubbard; *C:* William Fildew.

Outside the Law ♪ 1/2 **1995 (R)** Maverick cop Brad Kingsbury (Bradley) crosses the line when he falls for luscious Tanya Borgman (Thomson), who's the prime suspect in a murder investigation. Also available unrated. **94m/C VHS.** David Bradley, Anna Thomson, Ashley Laurence; *D:* Boaz Davidson; *W:* Dennis Dimster-Denk; *C:* Avi (Avraham) Karpik; *M:* Blake Leyh.

The Outsider ♪♪ 1/2 **2002 (R)** Rebecca Yoder (Watts) is part of a relgious community that has settled in Montana in 1886, hoping to escape the prejudice that plagued them in Ohio. But the local cattle ranchers are angry over a land dispute and kill Rebecca's husband, hoping to force her to sell her farm. Then, a wounded stanger staggers onto her property, whom Rebecca nurses back to health. Of course, Johnny Gault (Daly) is not only worldly but dangerous and Rebecca may be forced to choose between her new man and the religious community that disapproves. Adapted from the book by Penelope Williamson. **119m/C VHS, DVD.** Timothy Daly, Naomi Watts, Keith Carradine, David Carradine, Jason Clarke, Grant Piro; *D:* Randa Haines; *W:* Jenny Wingfield; *C:* Ben Nott; *M:* Todd Boekelheide. **CABLE**

The Outsiders ♪♪ 1/2 **1983 (PG)** Based on the popular S.E. Hinton book, the story of a teen gang from the wrong side of the tracks and their conflicts with society and each other. Melodramatic and over-done, but teenagers still love the story. Good soundtrack and cast ripples with up and coming stars. Followed by a TV series. Coppola adapted another Hinton novel the same year, "Rumble Fish." **91m/C VHS, DVD.** C. Thomas Howell, Matt Dillon, Ralph Macchio, Patrick Swayze, Diane Lane, Tom Cruise, Emilio Estevez, Rob Lowe, Tom Waits, Leif Garrett; *D:* Francis Ford Coppola; *W:* Kathleen Rowell; *C:* Stephen Burum; *M:* Carmine Coppola.

Outsourced ♪♪ 1/2 **2006 (PG-13)** Romantic comedy makes it cultural points with a light touch. Todd Anderson (Hamilton) manages a Seattle call center filling orders for cheap novelties. Told his department is being shut down because the jobs have been outsourced to India, Todd is then informed he's expected to travel to the country and train his replacements. He reluctantly labors to instruct his confused new employees until he finds a bittersweet romance with co-worker Asha (Dharker), who introduces him to her culture. **103m/C DVD.** Josh Hamilton, Ayesha Dharker, Larry Pine, Matt Smith, Asif Basra; *D:* John Jeffcoat; *W:* John Jeffcoat, George Irving; *C:* Teodoro Maniaci; *M:* B.C. Smith.

Outta Time ♪♪ *The Courier* **2001 (R)** Tijuana native David Morales (Lopez) has gottan an athletic scholarship to the University of San Diego but loses it because of a knee injury. Needing cash to pay his tuition, David doesn't ask a lot of questions when ex-professor Darabont (Saxon) asks David to transport some sealed packages of serum for testing across the border. Naturally, this job isn't as easy as David has been told. **90m/C VHS, DVD.** Mario Lopez, John Saxon, Ali Landry, Nancy O'Dell, Tava Smiley, Tim Sitarz; *D:* Lorena David; *W:* Scott Duncan, Ned Kerwin; *C:* Lisa Wiegand; *M:* Scott Gilman.

The Oval Portrait ♪ 1/2 **1988** An adaptation of the Edgar Allan Poe suspense tale about a Civil War-era maiden, her illicit love for a Confederate soldier and her eventual death. **89m/C VHS.** Giselle MacKenzie, Barry Coe; *D:* Regelio A. Gonzalez Jr.

Over Her Dead Body ♪ 1/2 **2008 (PG-13)** Henry (Rudd) and Kate (Longoria Parker) are about to tie the knot at their perfectly orchestrated wedding when a freak ice sculpture accident leads to the bee-otchy bridezilla's untimely demise. A year later, the still-mourning Henry is encouraged by his sister Chloe (Sloane) to see her psychic friend Ashley (Bell) to help him get over his grief. Of course sparks fly, but ghostly Kate shows up to put the kibosh on Henry's new romance. Bell's charming and Rudd's likable in a premise that's been done to death, but the inexplicably top-billed Longoria Parker grates in every scene she stomps through. **95m/C DVD.** *US* Eva Longoria, Paul Rudd, Lake Bell, Jason Biggs, Lindsay Sloane, Stephen (Steve) Root, William Morgan Sheppard; *D:* Jeff Lowell; *W:* Jeff Lowell; *C:* John Bailey; *M:* David Kitay.

Over Indulgence ♪♪ **1987 (R)** A young woman witnesses a murder in an affluent society in British East Africa. **95m/C VHS.** Denholm Elliott, Holly Aird, Michael Byrne, Kathryn Pogson; *D:* Ross Devenish.

Over the Brooklyn Bridge ♪♪ *My Darling Shiksa* **1983 (R)** A young Jewish man (Gould) must give up his Catholic girlfriend (Hemingway) in order to get his uncle (Caesar) to lend him the money he needs to buy a restaurant in Manhattan. Nowhere near as funny as it should be, and potentially offensive to boot. **100m/C VHS.** Elliott Gould, Sid Caesar, Shelley Winters, Margaux Hemingway, Carol Kane, Burt Young; *D:* Menahem Golan; *M:* Pino Donaggio.

Over the Edge ♪♪♪ 1/2 **1979 (PG)** The music of Cheap Trick, The Cars, and The Ramones highlights this realistic tale of alienated suburban youth on the rampage. Dillon makes his screen debut in this updated, well-done "Rebel Without a Cause." Shelved for several years, the movie was finally released after Dillon made it big. Sleeper with excellent direction and dialogue. **91m/C VHS, DVD.** Michael Kramer, Matt Dillon, Pamela Ludwig, Vincent Spano, Tom Fergus, Harry

Northrup, Andy Romano, Ellen Geer, Richard Jamison, Julia Pomeroy, Tiger Thompson; ***D:*** Jonathan Kaplan; ***W:*** Charles F. Haas, Tim Hunter; ***C:*** Andrew Davis; ***M:*** Sol Kaplan.

Over the Hedge **2006 (PG)** Hilarious, somewhat shallow comedy has a group of woodland creatures awakening from their winter hibernation, surprised to see a subdivision has sprouted up just beyond a hedge. Opportunistic raccoon RJ (Willis) tells his pals, including cautious turtle Verne (Shandling), that humans equal the good life and that they should venture into this strange new world. Of course, the humans, in the form of harpie Gladys (Janney) and "Verminator" Dwayne (Church) view these new neighbors as pests. Plenty of laughs and excellent voice performances, especially from Carell and Shatner, but trades some of the satire of Michael Fry and T. Lewis's source comic strip for fuzzy sentimentality. **84m/C DVD.** *US* ***D:*** Tim Johnson, Karey Kirkpatrick; ***W:*** Karey Kirkpatrick, Len Blum, Lorne Cameron, David Hoselton; ***M:*** Rupert Gregson-Williams; ***V:*** Bruce Willis, Garry Shandling, Steve Carell, William Shatner, Catherine O'Hara, Eugene Levy, Wanda Sykes, Nick Nolte, Thomas Haden Church, Allison Janney, Avril Lavigne, Omid Djalili, Sami Kirkpatrick, Shane Baumel, Madison Davenport.

Over the Hill **1/2 1993 (PG)** Dukakis stars as Alma, an eccentric widow who decides to leave her well-meaning son's restrictive home in Maine to visit her estranged daughter Elizabeth in Sydney, Australia. Embarassed by her peculiarities Elizabeth arranges a holiday away but Mom has her own plans. She wants to "loop the loop," and make a complete circuit around the Australian continent. Soon Alma is on the road, meeting fellow eccentrics and experiencing a variety of adventures. **102m/C VHS.** Olympia Dukakis, Sigrid Thornton, Derek Fowlds, Pippa Grandison; ***D:*** George Miller; ***W:*** Robert Caswell; ***C:*** David Connell.

Over the Hill Gang **1969** A quirky cast is the only real reason to watch this made-for-TV western about a retired Texas Ranger and his pals who clean up a corrupt town. **75m/C DVD.** Walter Brennan, Edgar Buchanan, Andy Devine, Jack Elam, Gypsy Rose Lee, Kristin Harmon, Ricky Nelson, Chill Wills, Edward Andrews; ***D:*** Jean Yarbrough; ***W:*** Jameson Brewer; ***C:*** Henry Cronjager Jr. **TV**

Over the Summer **1/2 1985** Strong drama about a troubled teen who escapes the city for a summer with her grandparents. No cliches here—the grandfather lusts after the granddaughter and eventually kills himself, and problems remain at the end. Intelligent and entertaining, though marred by needless nude scenes. **97m/C VHS.** Laura Hunt, Johnson West, Catherine Williams, David Romero; ***D:*** Teresa Sparks.

Over the Top **1/2 1986 (PG)** The film that started a nationwide arm-wrestling craze. A slow-witted trucker decides the only way he can retain custody of his estranged son, as well as win the boy's respect, is by winning a big arm-wrestling competition. Stallone is an expert at grinding these movies out by now, and the kid (General Hospital's Mikey) is all right, but the end result is boredom, as it should be with an arm-wrestling epic. **94m/C VHS, DVD.** Sylvester Stallone, Susan Blakely, Robert Loggia, David Mendenhall; ***D:*** Menahem Golan; ***W:*** Sylvester Stallone, Gary Conway, Stirling Silliphant. Golden Raspberries '87: Worst Support. Actor (Mendenhall), Worst New Star (Mendenhall).

Over the Wire **1/2 1995** Telephone lineman Bruce (Christensen) accidentally overhears a conversation where a woman hires a hitman to kill her sister. He finds out that the sisters live together and tries to figure out just who the target is before it's too late (of course, he has to seduce both of them to accomplish this). Ray used the pseudonym Nicholas Medina. **90m/C VHS, DVD.** David Christensen, Shauna O'Brien, Landon Hall, Tim Abell, John Lazar, Bob Dole; ***D:*** Fred Olen Ray; ***W:*** Pete Slate; ***C:*** Howard Wexler.

Overboard **1987 (PG)** A wealthy, spoiled woman falls off of her yacht and into the arms of a low-class carpenter who picks her up and convinces her she is in fact his wife, and mother to his four brats. Just when she learns to like her life, the tables are turned again. Even though it's all been done before, you can't help but laugh at the screwy gags. **112m/C VHS, DVD.** Goldie Hawn, Kurt Russell, Katherine Helmond, Roddy McDowall, Edward Herrmann; ***D:*** Garry Marshall; ***W:*** Leslie Dixon; ***C:*** John A. Alonzo; ***M:*** Alan Silvestri.

The Overcoat **1/2** *The Cloak; Shinel* **1959** An adaptation of Nikolai Gogol's classic story about the dehumanizing life endured in 20th-century bureaucracy. All a menial civil servant wants is a new overcoat. When he finally gets one, this treasured article not only keeps him warm but makes him feel self-satisfied as well. In Russian with English subtitles. **93m/B VHS.** *RU* Rolan Bykov, Yuri Tolubeyev; ***D:*** Alexei Batalov; ***W:*** L. Solovyov; ***C:*** Heinrich Marandzhjan; ***M:*** N. Sidelnikov.

Overdrawn at the Memory Bank **1983** In a futuristic tyranny, a romantic rebel becomes somehow fused with the spirit of Humphrey Bogart in the milieu of "Casablanca," and lives out a cliched version of the film character's adventures. **84m/C VHS.** Raul Julia, Linda Griffiths, Wanda Cannon, Louis Negin, Chapelle Jaffe, Jackie Burroughs, Maury Chaykin, Shiela Moore, Bill Smitrovich; ***D:*** Douglas Williams; ***W:*** John Varley.

Overexposed **1990 (R)** All the wackos love the sultry soap star Oxenburg; one is a killer. Eighty minutes and a bunch of bodies later the killer is unmasked. Plenty of suspense and some original gore. Based on the true stories of fans who stalk celebrities. **83m/C VHS.** Catherine Oxenberg, David Naughton, Jennifer Edwards, Karen Black; ***D:*** Larry Brand; ***W:*** Larry Brand.

Overkill **1986 (R)** A detective and the vengeance-minded brother of a dead Japanese-American fight back against the controlling Yakuza in Little Tokyo. **81m/C** Steve Rally, John Nishio, Laura Burkett, Roy Summerset; ***D:*** Ulli Lommel.

Overkill **1996 (R)** Burnt-out cop Jack Hazard (Norris) heads for vacation in Costa Rica and winds up being the prey for demented hunter Lloyd Wheeler (Nouri). **92m/C VHS.** Aaron Norris, Michael Nouri; ***D:*** Dean Ferrandini; ***W:*** Dean Ferrandini.

Overland Mail **1942** Fifteen episodes of the vintage serial filled with western action. **225m/B VHS, DVD.** Lon Chaney Jr., Helen Parrish, Don Terry, Bob Baker, Noah Beery Sr., Noah Beery Jr., Tom Chatterton, Charles Stevens; ***D:*** Ford Beebe, John Rawlins; ***W:*** Paul Huston; ***C:*** George Robinson, William Sickner.

Overland Stage Raiders **1938** The "Three Mesquiteers" ride again, this time to guard a Greyhound bus! The trio must protect a shipment of gold from hijackers. This is the last film for Brooks, who had starred in the German masterpiece "Pandora's Box" in 1929. **55m/B VHS.** John Wayne, Ray Corrigan, Max Terhune, Louise Brooks, John Archer, Frank LaRue, Yakima Canutt; ***D:*** George Sherman.

Overlanders **1946** The Japanese may invade, but rather than kill 1,000 head of cattle, these Aussies drive the huge herd across the continent, facing danger along the way. Beautifully photographed, featuring the "Australian Gary Cooper" and a stampede scene to challenge "Dances with Wolves." **91m/B VHS.** *AU* Chips Rafferty, Daphne Campbell, Jean Blue, John Nugent Hayward; ***D:*** Harry Watt.

Overnight **2003 (R)** Troy Duffy's "The Boondock Saints" has garnered a cult following on video, but this documentary about the story behind the film will make viewers recoil in disbelief at how one man's hubris and self-delusion can sink a promising career. During the indie film boom of the 1990s, Miramax offered Duffy $1 million for his "Boondock" script and signed his band to a record deal. Convinced of his own greatness, Duffy alienates and bullies everyone around him until he loses every opportunity he's been handed. It's hard to sympathize with Duffy, particularly because he originally hired Montana and Smith to direct the doc as a chronicle of his rise to the top. Weak in spots, but it's still schadenfreude at its best. **81m/C DVD.** *US* ***D:*** Mark Smith; ***C:*** Mark Smith; ***M:*** Troy Duffy.

Overnight Delivery **1996 (PG-13)** Convinced his girlfriend (Taylor) has been cheating on him, Wyatt (Rudd) sends her a nasty breakup letter via overnight mail. But when he realizes he's been wrong, Wyatt enlists the aid of friendly stripper Ivy (Witherspoon) to help him retrieve the letter. **87m/C VHS, DVD.** Larry Drake, Tobin Bell, Reese Witherspoon, Paul Rudd, Christine Taylor; ***D:*** Jason Bloom; ***W:*** Steven L. Bloom; ***C:*** Edward Pei; ***M:*** Andrew Gross.

Overseas: Three Women with Man Trouble **1990** Three beautiful sisters in French colonial Algeria surround themselves in a life of luxury to avoid the incredible social changes going on around them. Each sister has a different perspective on her life, and the perspectives are graphically revealed. Lush photography set in the Mediterranean. In French with English subtitles. **96m/C VHS.** *FR* Nicole Garcia, Marianne Basler, Philippe Galland, Pierre Doris, Brigitte Rouan; ***D:*** Brigitte Rouan; ***W:*** Brigitte Rouan. Cannes '90: Film.

Overthrow **1/2 1982 (R)** American sportswriter finds himself caught up in violence and intrigue in Buenos Aires. De Angelis used the pseudonym Larry Ludman. **90m/C VHS.** John Phillip Law, Lewis Van Bergen, Roger Wilson; ***D:*** Fabrizio de Angelis.

Overture to Glory **1/2** *Der Vilner Shtot Khazn* **1940** A Jewish cantor longs for the world of opera. He leaves his wife and son to fulfill his passion, but eventually he loses his voice and humbly returns home on Yom Kippur, the Jewish Day of Atonement. He learns that his son has passed away. Grief-stricken, he goes to the synagogue. There, the cantor regains his voice as he performs Kol Nidre in a passionate and melodious rendering. In Yiddish with English subtitles. **85m/B VHS.** Helen Beverly, Florence Weiss.

The Owl and the Pussycat **1970 (PG)** Nerdy author gets the neighborhood hooker evicted from her apartment. She returns the favor, and the pair hit the street—and the sack—in Buck Henry's hilarious adaptation of the Broadway play. Streisand's first non-singing role. **96m/C VHS, DVD.** Barbra Streisand, George Segal, Robert Klein, Allen (Goorwitz) Garfield; ***D:*** Herbert Ross; ***W:*** Buck Henry; ***C:*** Harry Stradling Sr., Andrew Laszlo; ***M:*** Dick Halligan.

Owning Mahowny **1/2 2003 (R)** Dan Mahowny (Hoffman) is a vice president at a Toronto bank. He is also a compulsive gambler and in order to clear his gambling debts, he embezzles (millions of dollars as it turns out). Even Dan's fiancee Belinda (Driver) can't pull him away from the casino tables when they are supposed to be on a romantic getaway (why she's so loyal is something of a mystery). Hoffman excels as an everyday schlub who's completely absorbed in his addiction and Hurt is fascinatingly reptilian as the Atlantic City casino boss who is happy to enable Mahowny's addiction. Based on a true story; adapted from the book "Stung: The Incredible Obsession of Brian Molony" by Gary Ross. **107m/C VHS, DVD.** *CA GB* Philip Seymour Hoffman, Minnie Driver, Maury Chaykin, John Hurt, Sonja Smits, Ian Tracey, Roger Dunn, Jason Blicker, Chris Collins; ***D:*** Richard Kwietniowski; ***W:*** Richard Kwietniowski, Maurice Chauvet; ***C:*** Oliver Curtis; ***M:*** Richard Grassby-Lewis.

The Ox **1/2 1991** Slow-moving, simple tale, set in rural Sweden in the 1860s during a famine. Desperate to feed his family a tenant farmer kills his employer's ox. Consumed by guilt, the man is quickly found out and sentenced to life imprisonment. Pardoned after six years, the farmer returns to his family, to find out his wife has survived by doing things he finds difficult to forgive. Based on a true story. Directorial debut of Nykvist, the longtime cinematographer for Ingmar Bergman, well displays his familiarity with composition and lighting to heighten mood. In Swedish with English subtitles. **93m/C VHS.** *SW* Stellan Skarsgard, Ewa Froling, Lennart Hjulstrom, Max von Sydow, Liv Ullmann, Bjorn Granath, Erland Josephson; ***D:*** Sven Nykvist; ***W:*** Lasse Summanen, Sven Nykvist.

The Ox-Bow Incident *Strange Incident* **1943** A popular rancher is murdered, and a mob of angry townspeople can't wait for the sheriff to find the killers. They hang the young man, despite the protests of Fonda, a cowboy with a conscience. Excellent study of mob mentality with strong individual characterizations. A brilliant western based on a true story by Walter Van Tilburg Clark. Also see "Twelve Angry Men"—less tragic but just as moving. **75m/B VHS, DVD.** Henry Fonda, Harry (Henry) Morgan, Dana Andrews, Anthony Quinn, Frank Conroy, Harry Davenport, Jane Darwell, William Eythe, Mary Beth Hughes; ***D:*** William A. Wellman; ***W:*** Lamar Trotti; ***C:*** Arthur C. Miller; ***M:*** Cyril Mockridge. Natl. Bd. of Review '43: Director (Wellman), Natl. Film Reg. '98.

Oxford Blues **1984 (PG-13)** An American finagles his way into England's Oxford University and onto the rowing team in pursuit of the girl of his dreams. Beautiful scenery, but the plot is wafer-thin. Remake of "Yank at Oxford." **98m/C VHS.** Rob Lowe, Ally Sheedy, Amanda Pays, Julian Sands, Michael Gough, Gail Strickland, Cary Elwes, Jeffrey S. (Jeff) Perry; ***D:*** Robert Boris; ***W:*** Robert Boris; ***M:*** John Du Prez.

Oxygen **1999 (R)** Madeline (Tierney) is a troubled police detective who's married to another cop (Kinney) and involved in a kinky extramarital affair. Harry (Brody) is an escape artist who fancies himself the new Houdini—he kidnaps the wife (Robbins) of wealthy Clarke Hannon (Naughton) and buries her alive. Madeline's assigned to the case and Harry takes to taunting her and their dangerous game could have more than one victim. **92m/C VHS, DVD.** Adrien Brody, Maura Tierney, Terry Kinney, James Naughton, Laila Robins, Dylan Baker; ***D:*** Richard Shepard; ***W:*** Richard Shepard; ***C:*** Sarah Cawley; ***M:*** Rolfe Kent.

P **1/2** *The Possessed* **2004** Dau (Jaturaphut) is a simple country girl tormented by her peers. One day her Grandmother saves her from an attacker using the family magic, and teaches it to her as long as she never violates the rules. When Grandmother falls ill, Dau accepts a sex bar job in Thailand to get money for her, quickly forgetting the rules. This causes a bloodthirsty demon to grow within her, and it begins eating people around her. Banned temporarily in Thailand for its expose of underage prostitution, it is also the only Thai film to have a foreign director. **109m/C DVD, Blu-ray Disc.** *TH* Suangporn Jaturaphut; ***D:*** Paul Spurrier; ***W:*** Paul Spurrier, Preeyaporn Chareonbutra; ***C:*** Rich B. Moore Jr.; ***M:*** Paul Spurrier.

P2 **2007 (R)** Late on Christmas Eve, Angela (Nichols) decends to level PS of her office's parking garage, only to find that her car won't start and the parking lot attendant Thomas (Bentley) is a homicidal maniac obsessed with her. After she initially escapes, she again finds herself trapped, with Thomas menacingly creeping her out. Standard gory "woman in danger" thriller fare with the occasional imaginative twist. **98m/C DVD.** *US* Wes Bentley, Rachel Nichols; ***D:*** Franck Khalfoun; ***W:*** Franck Khalfoun, Alexandre Aja, Gregory Levasseur; ***C:*** Maxime Alexandre; ***M:*** Tomandandy.

Pace That Kills **1928** An anti-drug cautionary drama from the Roaring '20s, one of many now marketed on cassette as campy fun. Beware, though, a little bit of this stuff goes a long way. A young man goes to the big city to find his missing sister and winds up hooked on heroin. **87m/B VHS.** Owen Gorin, Virginia Roye, Florence Turner; ***D:*** William A. O'Connor, Norton S. Parker; ***W:*** Ruth Todd; ***C:*** Ernest Laszlo.

The Pacific and Eddy **1/2 2007** Eddy (Donowho) skips out of his seaside hometown after the death of a friend for which he feels responsible. After living life as a struggling musician, he decides to return and tries to reconnect with the people he left behind, but they aren't that interested in making nice. **87m/C DVD.** Ryan Donowho, Dominique Swain, James Duval, Baelyn Neff, Mark Gregg, Nikki Sudden; ***D:*** Matthew Nourse; ***W:*** Matthew Nourse; ***C:*** Aaron Platt; ***M:*** Kelli Scarr.

Pacific Heights 1990 (R) Young San Francisco couple takes on mammoth mortgage assuming tenants will write their ticket to the American dream, but psychopathic tenant Keaton moves in downstairs and redecorates. He won't pay the rent and he won't leave. Creepy psycho-thriller has lapses but builds to effective climax. It's a treat to watch mother/daughter actresses Hedren and Griffith work together. Watch for D'Angelo as Keaton's lover. **103m/C VHS, DVD.** Melanie Griffith, Matthew Modine, Michael Keaton, Mako, Nobu McCarthy, Laurie Metcalf, Carl Lumbly, Dorian Harewood, Luca Bercovici, Tippi Hedren, Sheila McCarthy, Dan Hedaya, Beverly D'Angelo, Nicholas Pryor, Miriam Margolyes, D.W. Moffett, Tracey Walter, Dabbs Greer, O-lan Jones; ***D:*** John Schlesinger; ***W:*** Daniel Pyne; ***C:*** Amir M. Mokri; ***M:*** Hans Zimmer.

Pacific Inferno 1985 During WWII, American POWs endeavor to break out of a Japanese prison camp in the Philippines. Their goal is to prevent their captors from retrieving millions of dollars worth of sunken U.S. gold. **90m/C VHS, DVD.** Jim Brown, Richard Jaeckel, Timothy Brown; ***D:*** Rolf Bayer. **CABLE**

The Pacifier 1/2 2005 (PG) Schwarzenegger had "Kindergarten Cop," Hulk Hogan had "Mr. Nanny," and wooden Diesel has this. Shane Wolfe is a Navy SEAL who fails to prevent the death of a scientist at the hands of terrorists and is then assigned to protect the scientist's five kids and find some top-secret disk hidden in their home. Mom Ford is conveniently absent for much of the time. He retrofits his gadgets to hold baby formula and other child-friendly necessities and tries to promote military discipline on the bratty, unwilling clan. There's also a pet duck who doesn't like the new babysitter. It's all obvious and silly. **95m/C VHS, DVD.** *US* Vin Diesel, Lauren Graham, Faith Ford, Brittany Snow, Max Thieriot, Chris Potter, Morgan York, Scott Thompson, Carol Kane, Brad Garrett, Tate Donovan, Denis Akiyama, Mung-Ling Tsui; ***D:*** Adam Shankman; ***W:*** Robert Ben Garant; ***C:*** Peter James; ***M:*** John Debney.

The Pack 1/2 *The Long, Dark Night* 1977 (R) A group of dogs become wild when left on a resort island. A marine biologist leads the humans who fight to keep the dogs from using vacationers as chew toys. Fine production valves keep it from going to the dogs. Made with the approval of the American Humane Society who helped with the treatment of stage hands. **99m/C VHS.** Joe Don Baker, Hope Alexander-Willis, R.G. Armstrong, Richard B. Shull; ***D:*** Robert Clouse; ***W:*** Robert Clouse.

The P.A.C.K. 1996 The P.A.C.K. are alien warriors who mistakenly land on earth, which doesn't prevent them from killing all but one of a team of government agents sent to investigate. Now lone agent Rachel (Bergman) reluctantly teams up with a second alien who's been sent to destroy the P.A.C.K. **90m/C VHS.** Sandahl Bergman, Ted Prior, Red West.

Pack of Lies 1/2 1987 In the early 1960s, MI5 agents manipulate a British family, quietly living in the suburbs, into allowing them to use their home for a surveillance mission. Only it turns out they're watching the Jackson's neighbors and best friends, who are actually Soviet spies. Based on a true story. **100m/C DVD.** Ellen Burstyn, Teri Garr, Alan Bates, Ronald Hines, Daniel Benzali, Sammi Davis, Clive Swift; ***D:*** Anthony Page; ***W:*** Hugh Whitemore; ***C:*** Kenneth Macmillan; ***M:*** Stanley Myers. **TV**

Pack Up Your Troubles 1/2 *We're in the Army Now* 1932 Laurel and Hardy make good on a promise to help find the grandfather of a girl whose father was killed in WWI. All they know is the grandfather's last name though—Smith. Wholesome R and R. **68m/B VHS, DVD.** Stan Laurel, Oliver Hardy, James Finlayson, Jacquie Lyn; ***D:*** George Marshall.

The Package 1/2 1989 (R) An espionage thriller about an army sergeant who loses the prisoner he escorts into the U.S. When he tries to track him down, he uncovers a military plot to start WWIII. Hackman is believable in his role as the sergeant. **108m/C VHS, DVD.** Gene Hackman, Tommy Lee Jones, Joanna Cassidy, Dennis Franz, Pam Grier, John Heard, Reni Santoni, Thalmus Rasulala, Ike Pappas, Kevin Crowley, Wilhelm von Homburg; ***D:*** Andrew Davis; ***W:*** John Bishop; ***M:*** James Newton Howard.

Packin' It In 1983 A Los Angeles family is in for a rude awakening when they leave the city for a quieter life in the Oregon woods. There they encounter a band of survivalists with semi-comedic results. **92m/C VHS.** Richard Benjamin, Paula Prentiss, Molly Ringwald, Tony Roberts, Andrea Marcovicci; ***D:*** Jud Taylor.

Paco 1/2 1975 (G) A young, South American boy heads for the city, where he meets his uncle. He discovers his uncle is the leader of a gang of youthful thieves. Predictable and sluggish. **89m/C VHS, DVD.** Jose Ferrer, Panchito Gomez, Allen (Goorwitz) Garfield, Pernell Roberts, Andre Marquis; ***D:*** Robert Vincent O'Neil.

The Pact *The Secret Pact* 1999 (R) When teenager Greg (Frost) witnesses his parents' murder by the mob, he's sent to a private school in Montreal as part of the witness protection program. He makes a new best friend with a fellow student (Strong) but discovers his fellow teen is actually a hit man sent to kill him. Only they come to a strange sort of deal instead. **94m/C VHS, DVD.** *CA* Rider Strong, Adam Frost, John Heard, Nick Mancuso, Jack Langedijk, Lisa Zane; ***D:*** Rodney Gibbons; ***W:*** William Lee, Brian Cameron Fuld; ***C:*** Bert Tougas; ***M:*** Antonio Battista. **VIDEO**

Paddy *Goodbye to the Hill* 1970 (PG) A young Irish lad realizes his sexual potential by seducing every woman he can find. Freudians will have a field day. **97m/C VHS.** *IR* Des Cave, Milo O'Shea, Dearbhla Molloy, Peggy Cass; ***D:*** Daniel Haller.

Padre Nuestro 1/2 1985 Religious satire about a dying priest who wishes to reunite his family, who include an atheist brother, a mistress from his youth, and his illegitimate daughter who's a notorious prostitute. In Spanish with English subtitles. **91m/C VHS.** *SP* Fernando Rey, Francisco Rabal, Victoria Abril; ***D:*** Francisco Regueiro.

Padre Padrone 1/2 *Father Master; My Father, My Master* 1977 The much acclaimed adaptation of the Gavino Ledda autobiography about his youth in agrarian Sardinia with a brutal, tyrannical father. Eventually he overcomes his handicaps, breaks the destructive emotional ties to his father and successfully attends college. Highly regarded although low budget; in an Italian dialect (Sardinian) with English subtitles. **113m/C VHS, DVD.** *IT* Omero Antonutti, Saverio Marconi, Marcella Michelangeli, Fabrizio Forte; ***D:*** Paolo Taviani, Vittorio Taviani; ***W:*** Paolo Taviani, Vittorio Taviani; ***C:*** Mario Masini; ***M:*** Egisto Macchi. Cannes '77: Film.

Pagan Island 1960 A man is stranded on a desert island with 30 beautiful girls who tie him up and abandon him. Maki, to be sacrificed by the rest, saves Dew and they fall in love. They go off in search of a reputed treasure, which they find, but at a deadly cost. **67m/B VHS, DVD.** Eddie Dew, Nani Maka, Yanka (Doris Keating) Mann; ***D:*** Barry Mahon; ***W:*** Clelle Mahon; ***C:*** Mark Dennis.

Pagan Love Song 1950 A dull musical which finds Keel in Tahiti taking over his uncle's coconut plantation and falling in love with Williams. Surprise! Williams performs one of her famous water ballets, which is the only saving grace in this lifeless movie. ♫ The House of Singing Bamboo; Singing in the Sun; Etiquette; Why is Love So Crazy; Tahiti; The Sea of the Moon; Pagan Love Song; Coconut Milk. **76m/C VHS.** Esther Williams, Howard Keel, Minna Gombell, Rita Moreno; ***D:*** Robert Alton.

The Page Turner *La Tourneuse de Pages* 2006 As a child, aspiring pianist Melanie has her dreams carelessly ruined by concert pianist Ariane (Frot). She nurses a grudge and when Melanie (Francois) grows up, she puts her plan for revenge into action by insinuating herself into Ariane's family life. Okay thriller, but nothing that hasn't been seen before. French with subtitles. **85m/C DVD.** *FR* Deborah Francois, Catherine Frot, Pascal Greggory, Clothilde Mollet; ***D:*** Denis Dercourt; ***W:*** Denis Dercourt, Jacques Sotty; ***C:*** Jerome Peyrebrune; ***M:*** Jacques Lemonnier.

The Pagemaster 1/2 1994 (G) Timid Richard (Macauley) is basically scared of his own shadow but, during a storm, he's forced to take refuge in a mysterious library with an even odder librarian, Mr. Dewey (Lloyd). Richard's intrigued by the library's mural, which turns out to be the doorway to an animated universe where the wizardlike Pagemaster (voiced by Lloyd) and other literary characters help Richard discover his strengths and overcome his fears. Mildly amusing but kids may not know who the characters refer to unless they're readers (a good intro, perhaps?) **76m/C VHS, DVD.** Macaulay Culkin, Christopher Lloyd, Ed Begley Jr., Mel Harris; ***D:*** Joe Johnston, Maurice Hunt; ***W:*** David Casci, David Kirschner, Ernie Contreras; ***M:*** James Horner; ***V:*** Christopher Lloyd, Whoopi Goldberg, Patrick Stewart, Frank Welker, Leonard Nimoy.

Paid 2006 French hooker Paula Gireaux is working in Amsterdam where she gets involved with young hitman Michel. Both of them would like to start new lives together but Paula made a deal with drug lord Rudi Dancer. Now Rudi's rivalry with fellow drug baron William Montague threatens Paula and Michel's futures. **91m/C DVD.** Annie Charrier, Murilo Benicio, Tom Conti, Corbin Bernsen, Guy Marchand, Marie-France Pisier, Beppe Chierici; ***D:*** Laurence Lamers; ***W:*** Laurence Lamers; ***C:*** Tom Erisman; ***M:*** Jaques Morelembaum. **VIDEO**

Paid in Full 1/2 2002 (R) Based on the true story of the rise and fall of three Harlem drug dealers in the mid '80s during the height of the crack cocaine trade and the beginnings of "Gangsta" culture. The trio rises to the top of their dubious profession dealing with the issues of staying friends while also becoming rivals and making obscene amounts of money. Story hinges on Ace (Harris, who also narrates), a good kid who quickly goes bad after seeing the money to be made on the streets. Phifer is excellent as his best friend whose business he takes over after he's been busted. Cam'ron is the third friend, who may end up as Ace's replacement. Highlights the unsavory side of a business that makes Ace a fortune, but steals his soul. Acting all around is admirable and story is well told but revisits too-familiar territory about the price of greed and the politics of poverty. **93m/C VHS, DVD.** Wood Harris, Mekhi Phifer, Kevin Carroll, Esai Morales, Chi McBride, Cynthia Martells, Elise Neal, Cam'ron, Regina Hall, Remo Greene, Anthony Clark; ***D:*** Charles Stone III; ***W:*** Azie Faison Jr., Austin Phillips, Matthew Cirulnick, Thulani Davis; ***C:*** Paul Sarossy; ***M:*** Vernon Reid, Frank Fitzpatrick.

Paid to Kill *Five Days* 1954 A failing businessman hires a thug to kill him in order to leave his family insurance money, but when the business picks up, he can't contact the thug to cancel the contract. The actors' lack of talent is matched only by the characters' lack of motivation. **71m/B VHS, DVD.** *GB* Dane Clark, Paul Carpenter, Thea Gregory, Howard Marion-Crawford, Peter Gawthorne; ***D:*** Montgomery Tully; ***W:*** Paul Tabori; ***C:*** Walter J. (Jimmy W.) Harvey.

Pain in the A— 1977 (PG) A hit man helps a suicidal shirt salesman solve his marital problems in this black comedy that was later Americanized as "Buddy, Buddy." Not for all tastes, but has acquired a reputation for its dark wit. In French with English subtitles. **90m/C VHS.** *FR IT* Lino Ventura, Jacques Brel, Caroline Cellier; ***D:*** Edouard Molinaro; ***W:*** Edouard Molinaro, Francis Veber.

Paint It Black 1/2 1989 (R) A violent/steamy mystery and action flick from the director of "River's Edge," in which a young man from the silver-spoon set develops a fascination for an artist. **101m/C VHS.** Sally Kirkland, Rick Rossovich, Martin Landau, Doug Savant, Peter Frechette, Jason Bernard, Julie Carmen, Monique Van De Ven; ***D:*** Tim Hunter.

The Paint Job 1993 (R) Wesley, the lonely house painter, falls in love with his neighbor, Margaret. Unfortunately, Margaret is married—to Wesley's boss Willy. Margaret is drawn to Wesley and bored with Willy. But one of the men turns out to be a serial killer. What's a gal in love to do? **90m/C VHS.** Will Patton, Bebe Neuwirth, Robert Pastorelli; ***D:*** Micheal Taav; ***W:*** Micheal Taav; ***M:*** John Wesley Harding.

Paint Your Wagon 1/2 1969 (PG) Big-budget western musical-comedy about a gold mining boom town, and two prospectors sharing the same Mormon wife complete with a classic Lerner and Lowe score. Marvin chews up the sagebrush and Eastwood attempts to sing, although Seberg was mercifully dubbed. Overlong, with patches of interest, pretty songs, and plenty of panoramic scenery. Adapted from the L & L play. ♫ I Talk to the Trees; I Still See Elisa; I'm on My Way; Hand Me Down That Can o' Beans; Whoop-Ti-Ay; They Call the Wind Maria; There's a Coach Comin' In; Wandrin' Star; Best Things. **164m/C VHS, DVD.** Lee Marvin, Clint Eastwood, Jean Seberg, Harve Presnell; ***D:*** Joshua Logan; ***W:*** Paddy Chayefsky; ***M:*** Frederick Loewe, Andre Previn, Alan Jay Lerner.

Painted Desert 1931 Gable's first film role of any consequence came in this early sound western. Gable plays a villain opposite "good guy" William Boyd. **80m/B VHS, DVD.** William Boyd, Helen Twelvetrees, George O'Brien, Clark Gable, William Farnum; ***D:*** Howard Higgin.

Painted Hero 1/2 1995 (R) Rodeo clown Virgil Kidder (Yoakum) has to watch out for more than rampaging bulls when he returns to Waco, where he's accused of murder and reunites with the mother of his now-dead son. **105m/C VHS, DVD.** Dwight Yoakam, Bo Hopkins, Cindy Pickett, Michelle Joyner; ***D:*** Terry Benedict; ***W:*** Terry Benedict; ***C:*** David Bridges; ***M:*** Rick Marotta.

The Painted Hills 1/2 1951 (G) Lassie outsmarts crooked miners and rescues her friends. Surprise, Surprise! Overly sentimental, but action packed and beautifully shot. Lassie's last outing with MGM. **70m/C VHS, DVD.** Paul Kelly, Bruce Cowling, Gary Gray, Art Smith, Ann Doran; ***D:*** Harold F. Kress.

A Painted House 2003 Loose adaptation of the John Grisham novel finds 10-year-old Luke Chandler (Lerman) living on a struggling Arkansas farm in 1952 with his parents and grandparents. The family needs to hire local "hill" people and Mexican migrant workers to pick their cotton crop and there's trouble between the groups as well as with Luke and his family. Title refers to the fact that the Chandler's bare clapboard farmhouse gets mysteriously painted (they can't afford to do it themselves). **110m/C DVD.** Scott Glenn, Melinda Dillon, Robert Sean Leonard, Logan Lerman, Geoffrey Lewis, Arija Bareikis, Pablo Schreiber, Luis Esteban Garcia, Luke Eberl, Diane Delano, Audrey Marie Anderson; ***D:*** Alfonso Arau; ***W:*** Patrick Sheane Duncan; ***C:*** Xavier Perez Grobet; ***M:*** Ruy Folguera. **TV**

The Painted Lady 1997 Maggie Sheridan (Mirren) is a hard-living ex-blues singer with some destructive habits. After bottoming out some years before, she was taken in by Sir Charles Stafford (Cuthbertson), the father of childhood friend Sebastian (Glen). Sir Charles is murdered during a botched robbery, a 16th-century painting stolen, and Sebastian becomes the victim of a brutal attack, so Maggie decides to get involved. And finds herself deeply enmeshed in the illegal art trade, posing as a collector, and romancing a very dangerous man (Nero). **204m/C VHS.** *GB* Helen Mirren, Franco Nero, Iain Glen, Michael Maloney, Lesley Manville, Roland Gift, Iain Cuthbertson, Michael Liebman, Indro Montanelli; ***D:*** Julian Jarrold. **TV**

Painted Skin *Hua Pi Zhi Yinyang Fawang* 1993 Historical supernatural tale concerns a ghost (Joey Wang) who's trapped on Earth and must paint her skin to pass among humans. The evil Demon King is responsible. Sammo Hung co-stars as a monk. **93m/C DVD.** *HK* Adam Cheng, Joey Wang, Sammo Hung; ***D:*** King Hu; ***W:*** King Hu, Chang A. Cheng; ***C:*** Stephen Yip; ***M:*** Ng Tai Kong.

The Painted Stallion 1937 This 12-chapter serial features a mysterious figure on a painted stallion who attempts to maintain peace between Mexicans and Indians. **212m/B VHS, DVD.** Ray Corrigan, Hoot Gibson, Duncan Renaldo, Leroy Mason, Yakima Canutt; ***D:*** William Witney, Ray Taylor.

The Painted Trail 1/2 **1938** Lawman Tom Gray poses as the Pecos Kid to break up a smuggling ring in Mexico. But when the real Kid shows up, you know there's going to be a showdown. **51m/B DVD.** Tom Keene, Leroy Mason, Eleanor Stewart, Walter Long, Frank Campeau, James Eagles, Glenn Strange; ***D:*** Robert F. "Bob" Hill; ***W:*** Robert Emmett Tansey; ***C:*** Bert Longenecker.

The Painted Veil 1/2 **1934** Adaptation of a W. Somerset Maugham story. Garbo, once again the disillusioned wife turning to the affections of another man, is magnificent, almost eclipsing the weak script. Lost money at the box office, but for Garbo fans, an absolute must. **83m/B VHS.** Greta Garbo, Herbert Marshall, George Brent, Warner Oland, Jean Hersholt; ***D:*** Richard Boleslawski; ***C:*** William H. Daniels.

The Painted Veil **2006 (PG-13)** The third film version of Maugham's 1925 novel takes some liberties and the leads can't engender much sympathy for their self-absorbed characters, although the locations are eye-catching. Flirty Kitty (Watts) impulsively marries serious bacteriologist Walter Fane (Norton) to get away from her family—far away, all the way to Shanghai. Bored, Kitty begins an affair with British consul Charlie Townsend (Schreiber); upon discovering her infidelity, Walter forces Kitty to join him in a remote area beset by a cholera outbreak, where he'll do medical research. Kitty finds herself helping out a group of nuns at their orphanage amidst the rise of Chinese nationalism (as if an epidemic and problematic marriage aren't trouble enough). **125m/C DVD.** *CH US* Naomi Watts, Edward Norton, Liev Schreiber, Toby Jones, Diana Rigg, Anthony Wong; ***D:*** John Curran; ***W:*** Ron Nyswaner; ***C:*** Stuart Dryburgh; ***M:*** Alexandre Desplat. Golden Globes '07: Orig. Score.

Painting the Clouds With Sunshine **1951** Average MGM musical comedy has Abby (Norman) dumping her gambler boyfriend Vince (Morgan) to join friends Carol (Mayo) and June (Gibson) in Vegas in a search for rich husbands. The girls get a job as a singing trio and Abby is pursued by dancer Ted Lansing (Nelson)—only he's really a millionaire in disguise. Then Ted's banker cousin Bennington (Conway) shows up and Ted tries to keep him quiet until he can get Abby to the altar but Vince isn't ready to give up his claim to her heart. **86m/C DVD.** Dennis Morgan, Lucille Norman, Virginia Mayo, Virginia Gibson, Gene Nelson, S.Z. Sakall, Tom Conway, Wallace Ford; ***D:*** David Butler; ***W:*** Roland Kibbee, Peter Milne, Harry Clork; ***C:*** Wilfrid M. Cline.

Pair of Aces 1/2 **1990** Kristofferson is a Texas Ranger who's on the trail of a serial killer. His only other problem is being saddled with Nelson, a philosophical safecracker who's awaiting trial and in the reluctant cop's custody. Low-key western with good buddy pairing of Nelson and Kristofferson. **94m/C VHS.** Willie Nelson, Kris Kristofferson, Rip Torn, Helen Shaver, Jane Cameron, Sonny Carl Davis, Lash LaRue, Emily Warfield, Michael Marich; ***D:*** Aaron Lipstadt. **TV**

Paisan **1946** Six episodic tales of life in Italy, several featuring Allied soldiers and nurses during WWII. One of the stories tells of a man who tries to develop a relationship without being able to speak Italian. Another focuses on a young street robber who is confronted by one of his victims. Strong stories that covers a wide range of emotions. In Italian with English subtitles. **115m/B VHS.** *IT* Maria Michi, Carmela Sazio, Gar Moore, William Tubbs, Harriet White, Robert Van Loon, Dale Edmonds, Carlo Pisacane, Dots Johnson; ***D:*** Roberto Rossellini; ***W:*** Federico Fellini, Roberto Rossellini. Natl. Bd. of Review '48: Director (Fellini); N.Y. Film Critics '48: Foreign Film.

The Pajama Game 1/2 **1957** A spritely musical about the striking workers of the Sleeptite Pajama Ffactory and their plucky negotiator, Katie (Day), who falls in love with the new foreman, Sid (Raitt). Based on the hit Broadway musical, which was based on Richard Bissell's book "Seven and a Half Cents" and adapted for the screen by Bisell and Abbott. Bob Fosse choreographed the dance numbers. ♫ I'm Not at All in Love; Small Talk; There Once Was a Man; Steam Heat; Hernando's Highway; Hey There; Once-a-Year Day; Seven and a Half Cents; I'll Never Be Jealous Again. **101m/C VHS, DVD.** Doris Day, John Raitt, Eddie Foy Jr., Reta Shaw, Carol Haney; ***D:*** Stanley Donen, George Abbott; ***W:*** George Abbott, Richard Bissell; ***C:*** Harry Stradling Sr.

Pajama Party **1964** Followup to "Bikini Beach" takes the party inside in this fourth entry in the popular "Beach Party" series. Plot is up to beach party realism. Funicello is Avalon-less (although he does have a cameo) so she falls for Martian Kirk instead. He's scouting for an alien invasion, but after he falls into Annette's lap decides to save the planet instead. Typical fluff with the usual beach movie faces present; look for a young Garr as a dancer. Followed by the classic "Beach Blanket Bingo." ♫ It's That Kind of Day; There Has to Be a Reason; Where Did I Go Wrong?; Pajama Party; Beach Ball; Among the Young; Stuffed Animal. **82m/C VHS, DVD.** Tommy Kirk, Annette Funicello, Elsa Lanchester, Harvey Lembeck, Jesse White, Jody McCrea, Donna Loren, Susan Hart, Bobbi Shaw, Cheryl Sweeten, Luree Holmes, Candy Johnson, Dorothy Lamour, Toni Basil, Frankie Avalon, Don Rickles, Teri Garr, Ben Lessy; ***Cameos:*** Buster Keaton; ***D:*** Don Weis; ***W:*** Louis M. Heyward; ***C:*** Floyd Crosby; ***M:*** Les Baxter.

Pajama Tops 1/2 **1983** A stage production of the classic French bedroom farce, taped live at the Music Hall Theatre in Toronto, Canada. Includes all the trials of marriage including adultery and deceit. **105m/C VHS.** Robert Klein, Susan George, Pia Zadora.

Pal Joey **1957** Musical comedy about an opportunistic singer who courts a wealthy socialite in hopes that she will finance his nightclub. His play results in comedic complications. Stellar choreography, fine direction, and beautiful costumes complement performances headed by Hayworth and Sinatra. Oscar overlooked his pal Joey when awards were handed out. Songs include some of Rodgers and Hart's best. Based on John O'Hara's book and play. ♫ Zip; Bewitched, Bothered and Bewildered; I Could Write a Book; That Terrific Rainbow; Whad Do I Care for a Dame?; Happy Hunting Horn; Plant You Now, Dig You Later; Do It the Hard Way; Take Him. **109m/C VHS, DVD.** Frank Sinatra, Rita Hayworth, Kim Novak, Barbara Nichols, Hank Henry, Elizabeth Patterson; ***D:*** George Sidney; ***W:*** Dorothy Kingsley; ***C:*** Harold Lipstein; ***M:*** Richard Rodgers. Golden Globes '58: Actor—Mus./Comedy (Sinatra).

Palais Royale 1/2 **1988** Craven plays an ad exec who gets involved in the world of gangsters in the late 50s. **100m/C VHS.** *CA* Matt Craven, Kim Cattrall, Dean Stockwell; ***D:*** Martin Lavut; ***M:*** Jonathan Goldsmith.

Pale Blood 1/2 **1991 (R)** A serial killer in Los Angeles is leaving his victims drained of blood. Could it be that a vampire is stalking the modern American metropolis, or is this merely the workings of a bloodthirsty psychopath? **93m/C VHS.** George Chakiris, Wings Hauser, Pamela Ludwig, Diana Frank, Darcy Demoss, Earl Garnes; ***D:*** V.V. Dachin Hsu; ***W:*** V.V. Dachin Hsu, Takashi Matsuoka.

Pale Rider **1985 (R)** A mysterious nameless stranger rides into a small California gold rush town to find himself in the middle of a feud between a mining syndicate and a group of independent prospectors. Christ-like Eastwood evokes comparisons to "Shane." A classical western theme treated well complemented by excellent photography and a rock-solid cast. **116m/C VHS, DVD.** Clint Eastwood, Michael Moriarty, Carrie Snodgress, Sydney Penny, Richard Dysart, Richard Kiel, Christopher Penn, John Russell, Charles Hallahan, Douglas McGrath, Fran Ryan; ***D:*** Clint Eastwood; ***W:*** Michael Butler, Dennis Shryack; ***C:*** Bruce Surtees; ***M:*** Lennie Niehaus.

Pale Saints 1/2 **1997 (R)** Small-time hoods Louis (Flanery) and Dody (Riley) decide that they will do one last job for crime broker Quick Vic and use their share of the money to head off to California. They travel to Montreal and wind up with a botched heist, a case of mistaken identity, and a lot of double-dealing. The plot gets too convoluted, although it's so fast-paced you may not notice the holes. **98m/C VHS, DVD.** *CA* Sean Patrick Flanery, Michael Riley, Saul Rubinek, Maury Chaykin, Rachael Crawford, Gordon Pinsent; ***D:*** Joel Wyner; ***W:*** Joel Wyner; ***C:*** Barry Stone; ***M:*** Michel Theriault.

The Paleface **1948** A cowardly dentist becomes a gunslinging hero when Calamity Jane starts aiming for him. A rip-roarin' good time as the conventions of the Old West are turned upside down. Includes the Oscar-winning song "Buttons and Bows." The 1952 sequel is "Son of Paleface." Remade in 1968 as "The Shakiest Gun in the West." ♫ Buttons and Bows; Get a Man!; Meetcha 'Round the Corner. **91m/C VHS, DVD.** Jane Russell, Bob Hope, Robert Armstrong, Iris Adriah, Robert Watson; ***D:*** Norman Z. McLeod; ***C:*** Ray Rennahan. Oscars '48: Song ("Buttons and Bows").

The Palermo Connection **1991 (R)** Not the action-thriller the cassette box claims, but a cynical study of a crusading N.Y.C. mayoral candidate who honeymoons in Mafia-haunted Sicily and learns that the war on crime has already been lost. Remote adaptation of "To Forget Palermo" by Edmonde Charles-Roux. **100m/C VHS.** James Belushi, Mimi Rogers, Joss Ackland, Philippe Noiret, Vittorio Gassman, Carolina Rosi; ***D:*** Francesco Rosi; ***W:*** Francesco Rosi, Gore Vidal, Tonino Guerra; ***C:*** Pasqualino De Santis; ***M:*** Ennio Morricone.

Palindromes **2004** As if having abortion as his central topic wasn't challenging enough, Solondz raises the art-house ante exponentially by having his protagonist, Aviva, played by eight different actors, including Jennifer Jason Leigh, an African-American woman, and a boy. Thirteen-year-old Aviva dreams of motherhood, but after she's impregnated, her overbearing parents insist she get an abortion. To keep the baby, Aviva runs away, meeting an eccentric cast of characters on the road. Solondz masterfully conducts this postmodern morality play, showing the pitfalls of both sides of the abortion issue until the audience's moral compass is helplessly askew. May be too esoteric for most, but that's half the fun anyway. **100m/C DVD.** *US* Jennifer Jason Leigh, Ellen Barkin, Richard Masur, Debra Monk, Emani Sledge, Valerie Shusterov, Hannah Freiman, Rachel Corr, Will Denton, Shayna Levine, Sharon Wilkins, Stephen Adly Guirgis, Matthew Faber, Steve Singer, Richard Riehle, Robert Agri, John Gemberling, Alexander Brickel, Walter Bobbie; ***D:*** Todd Solondz; ***W:*** Todd Solondz; ***C:*** Tom Richmond; ***M:*** Nathan Larson.

The Pallbearer 1/2 **1995 (PG-13)** You probably liked this one better when it was called "The Graduate," as this one shares some key plot points with, but lacks the edge and cultural impact of the 1967 classic. Basset-faced Schwimmer plays Tom, who is asked to be a pallbearer for an old high school classmate whom he can't quite remember. He is then seduced by the mother (Hershey) of the deceased, while trying to kindle a romance with the fabulous Julie DeMarco (Paltrow), an old classmate who can't quite remember him. The spurned older woman then begins to exact her revenge, while Tom tries to figure out how to court Julie while living at home with his mom. Good performances make it watchable. **98m/C VHS, DVD.** Joseph (Joe) D'Onofrio, David Schwimmer, Gwyneth Paltrow, Barbara Hershey, Michael Rapaport, Carol Kane, Toni Collette, Michael Vartan; ***D:*** Matt Reeves; ***W:*** Matt Reeves, Jason Katims; ***C:*** Robert Elswit; ***M:*** Stewart Copeland.

Palm Beach **1979** The lives of two petty thieves, a runaway, and a private detective intertwine at Palm Beach Down Under. Best appreciated by fans of things Aussie. **90m/C VHS.** *AU* Bryan Brown, Nat Young, Ken Brown, Amanda Berry; ***D:*** Albie Thomas.

The Palm Beach Story **1942** Young architect Tom Jeffers (McCrea) dreams of building an airport and his adoring wife Gerry (Colbert) decides to help him out—by divorcing him. That way she can head to Palm Beach, marry rich, and finance Tom's ambitions. So Gerry sets her considerable charms on catching eccentric J.D. Hackensacker (Vallee). When Tom follows, he becomes prey for J.D.'s tart-tongued sister (Astor). Takes amusing aim at the idle rich with Sturges's trademark witty, sophisticated dialogue. **88m/B VHS, DVD.** Claudette Colbert, Joel McCrea, Mary Astor, Rudy Vallee, William Demarest, Franklin Pangborn; ***D:*** Preston Sturges; ***C:*** Victor Milner.

Palm Springs Weekend 1/2 **1963** A busload of love-hungry kids head south and get involved in routine hijinks. Actually shot in Palm Springs with above average performances by a handful of stars. **100m/C VHS.** Troy Donahue, Ty Hardin, Connie Stevens, Stefanie Powers, Robert Conrad, Jack Weston, Andrew Duggan; ***D:*** Norman Taurog.

Palmetto 1/2 **1998 (R)** Contempo-noir that misses the mark has bitter ex-con Harry (Harrelson) partnered with seductress Rhea (Shue) in a phony kidnapping of her step-daughter Odette (Sevigny). Newly released from the joint after a rotten frame-up job, Harry is lured back by ex Nina (Gershon), to the backwater town that sent him up, where he once again winds up in trouble as all three women go to work on him. Originality and character development go AWOL, as the normally adept Harrelson flounders for an identity alongside Shue's broad characterization of a vamp who teeters on high heels and the brink of satire. Feels like Tennessee Williams as written by Joe Eszterhas. From Rene Raymond's (a.k.a. James Hadley Chase) novel, "Just Another Sucker." **114m/C VHS, DVD.** Angela Featherstone, Woody Harrelson, Elisabeth Shue, Michael Rapaport, Gina Gershon, Chloe Sevigny, Rolf Hoppe, Tom Wright; ***D:*** Volker Schlondorff; ***W:*** E. Max Frye; ***C:*** Thomas Kloss; ***M:*** Klaus Doldinger.

Palmy Days 1/2 **1931** Shy Eddie (Cantor) is involved with a phony medium, a scam involving a bakery, theft, romance, singing, and a disguise as a woman (the other bakery workers are the Goldwyn Girls, including Betty Grable). Silly fun, with choreography by Busby Berkeley. ♫ Bend Down, Sister; Goose Pimples; Dunk Dunk Dunk; My Honey Said Yes, Yes; There's Nothing Too Good for My Baby. **77m/B VHS.** Eddie Cantor, Charlotte Greenwood, Charles Middleton, George Raft, Harry Woods, Spencer Charters, Barbara Weeks, Paul Page; ***D:*** Edward Sutherland; ***W:*** Morrie Ryskind, Keene Thompson, Eddie Cantor; ***C:*** Gregg Toland.

Palo Alto **2007 (R)** Not the trashy teens-gone-wild flick you might expect from the rating. Four longtime buds, who have gone off to separate colleges, reunite at their first Thanksgiving break to catch up. They not only discover how much they're changing but how much their hometown actually does mean to them. **95m/C DVD.** Ben Savage, Aaron Ashmore, Johnny Lewis, Autumn Reeser, Justin Mentell, Tom Arnold; ***D:*** Brad Leong; ***W:*** Tony Vallone; ***C:*** Rachel Morrison.

Palombella Rossa **1989** Political comedy about the fate of Italian communism. When communist politician Michele loses his memory in a car crash, he finds himself trying to reconstruct his life during a game of water polo as well as trying to answer political questions and keep track of the people from his life who randomly appear and disappear. In Italian with English subtitles. **87m/C VHS.** *IT* Nanni Moretti, Silvio Orlando, Asia Argento; ***D:*** Nanni Moretti; ***W:*** Nanni Moretti; ***C:*** Giuseppe Lanci; ***M:*** Nicola Piovani.

Palooka 1/2 ***Joe Palooka; The Great Schnozzle*** **1934 (G)** Based on the comic strip, this film portrays a fast-talking boxing manager and his goofy, lovable protege. The young scrapper fights James Cagney's little brother. Durante sings his classic tune, "Inka-Dinka-Doo," and packs a punch in the lead. A two-fisted comedy with a witty dialogue and fine direction. Not a part of the Palooka series of the 1940s. **86m/B VHS, DVD.** Jimmy Durante, Stuart Erwin, Lupe Velez, Robert Armstrong, Thelma Todd, William Cagney; ***D:*** Ben Stoloff.

Palookaville **1995 (R)** Nostalgic comedy of three under-employed friends who take up crime, temporarily, just until they can secure legit work. Using a little-known 1950s crime movie as their tutor, the trio of criminal cretins encounter a variety of setbacks on their way to financial security. Planning an elaborate scheme to rob an armored car, they decide to use toy guns, so Jerry (Trese) rounds up a most intimidating assortment of the neon orange plastic variety. Later, while chiseling through a wall to a jewelry store, they find themselves in the bakery next door, with Jerry delighted to score some pastries instead. The other two aren't much brighter—Russ (Gallo) is the leader of the three and a small-time ladies man while Sid (Forsythe) is a devout dog lover whose dreams of a taxi service for the aged are shattered when customers are driven away by his kennel on wheels. Adapted from short stories written in the 1940s by the Italian Italo Calvino, modern adaptation manages to retain a '40s feel and charm. **92m/C VHS, DVD.** William Forsythe, Vincent Gallo, Adam Trese, Lisa Gay Hamilton, Frances McDormand, Davis Boulton, James David Hilton, Gareth Williams, Bridget Ryan, Kim Dickens, Suzanne Shepherd, Robert LuPone; ***D:*** Alan Taylor; ***W:*** David Epstein; ***C:*** John Thomas; ***M:*** Rachel Portman.

Pals 🦴🦴 **1987** Old friends stumble across $3 million in cash and learn the predictable lesson that money can't buy happiness. A terribly trite TV-movie with an exceptional cast. **90m/C VHS, DVD.** Don Ameche, George C. Scott, Sylvia Sidney, Susan Rinell, James Greene; ***D:*** Lou Antonio.

Pals of the Range 🦴 **1935** A framed ranch owner breaks out of jail in order to catch the real cattle thieves. Ho hum in the Old West. **55m/B VHS.** Frances Morris, Yakima Canutt, George Chesebro, Robert "Blackie" Whiteford, Rex Lease; ***D:*** Elmer Clifton; ***W:*** Elmer Clifton; ***C:*** Edward Linden.

Pals of the Saddle 🦴🦴 ½ **1938** The intrepid trio go after enemy agents who are trying to smuggle chemicals for poisonous gas into Mexico. This is the first of the series in which the Duke played the part of Stony Brooke. Somewhat convoluted plot, but nevertheless enjoyable. **55m/B VHS.** John Wayne, Ray Corrigan, Max Terhune, Doreen McKay, Josef Forte, Ted Adams, Curley Dresden; ***D:*** George Sherman.

The Pamela Principle 🦴🦴 **1991 (R)** A bored, middle-aged man thinks his prayers are answered when he meets a sexy 20-year-old model and begins a sordid affair with her. Soon, however, he finds himself in a tense situation when he must choose between his family or his fantasy. Also available in an unrated version. **94m/C VHS.** J.K. Dumont, Veronica Cash, Shelby Lane, Troy Donahue, Frank Pesce; ***D:*** Paul Thomas.

Panama Flo 🦴 ½ **1932** While stranded in Panama, honky-tonk chanteuse Flo (Twelvetrees) steals the wallet of mining engineer Don McTeague (Bickford), but gets caught. Instead of calling the cops, the mark insists Flo go with him to his mining camp and work off the debt as his housekeeper. Eventually, Flo's louse of a boyfriend (Armstrong) shows up to cause more trouble and ruin a budding romance. **72m/B VHS.** Helen Twelvetrees, Charles Bickford, Robert Armstrong, Maude Eburne, Paul Hurst, Marjorie Peterson; ***D:*** Ralph Murphy; ***W:*** Garrett Fort; ***C:*** Arthur C. Miller.

Panama Hattie 🦴🦴 **1942** Screen adaptation of Cole Porter's delightful Broadway musical. Unfortunately, something (like a plot) was lost in transition. Southern runs a saloon for our boys down in Panama. Among the musical numbers and vaudevillian acts some spies show up. Several screenwriters and directors, including Vincente Minnelli, worked uncredited on this picture, to no avail. Horne's second screen appearance. ♫It Was Just One of Those Things; Fresh as a Daisy; I've Still Got My Health; Let's Be Buddies; Make It Another Old Fashioned; Hattie from Panama; Good Neighbors; I'll Do Anything for You; The Son of a Gun Who Pick on Uncle Sam. **79m/B VHS.** Ann Sothern, Dan Dailey, Red Skelton, Virginia O'Brien, Rags Ragland, Alan Mowbray, Ben Blue, Carl Esmond, Lena Horne; ***D:*** Norman Z. McLeod; ***C:*** George J. Folsey; ***M:*** George Bassman, Cole Porter.

Panama Lady 🦴 ½ **1939** Ball stars as the sexy, sultry "Panama Lady" in this old-fashioned romance. She gets involved in some shady business south of the border. A lackluster remake of "Panama Flo." **65m/B VHS.** Lucille Ball, Evelyn Brent, Allan "Rocky" Lane, Steffi Duna, Don Briggs, Bernadene Hayes; ***D:*** Jack B. Hively; ***W:*** Michael Kanin; ***C:*** J. Roy Hunt.

Panama Menace 🦴 *South of Panama* **1941** An agent heads to Panama to thwart spies who are after a special paint that makes things invisible. Poor effort all around, in spite of Beaumont's presence. **68m/B VHS.** Roger Pryor, Virginia Vale, Lionel Royce, Lucien Prival, Duncan Renaldo, Lester Dorr, Hugh Beaumont; ***D:*** Jean Yarbrough.

Panama Patrol 🦴🦴 ½ **1939** Just as they are about to be married, two Army officers are called to duty in Panama. It seems that the Chinese have infiltrated the area with spies and something's got to be done. Too much attention to minor parts of the plot slows the story occasionally, but performances and photography compensate for some of the sluggishness. **67m/B VHS, DVD.** Leon Ames, Charlotte Wynters, Weldon Heyburn, Adrienne Ames, Abner Biberman, Hugh McArthur, Donald (Don "Red") Barry; ***D:*** Charles Lamont.

Panamint's Bad Man 🦴 **1938** Ballaw is a poor man's Gary Cooper fighting for justice against stagecoach robbers. Almost as much flavor as tumbleweed. **59m/B VHS, DVD.** Smith Ballew, Evelyn Daw,, Noah Beery Sr.; ***D:*** Ray Taylor.

Pancho Barnes 🦴🦴 ½ **1988 (PG)** Routine biography of one of the first female pilots of the 1920s. Barnes is a bored debutante who finds her challenge in life when she learns to fly, becoming a barnstormer and movie stunt pilot. Her ambitions naturally get in the way of her romantic life. Good flying scenes. **150m/C VHS.** Valerie Bertinelli, Ted Wass, Sam Robards, James Stephens, Cynthia Harris, Geoffrey Lewis; ***D:*** Richard T. Heffron; ***W:*** John Michael Hayes. **TV**

Pancho Villa 🦴 ½ **1972 (PG)** Savalas has the lead in this fictional account of the famous Mexican, He leads his men in a raid on an American fort after being hoodwinked in an arms deal. Connors tries to hold the fort against him. The finale, in which two trains crash head on, is the most exciting event in the whole darn movie. **92m/C VHS, DVD.** *SP* Telly Savalas, Clint Walker, Anne Francis, Chuck Connors, Angel Del Pozo, Luis Davila; ***D:*** Eugenio (Gene) Martin; ***W:*** Julian Zimet; ***C:*** Alejandro Ulloa; ***M:*** Anton Abril.

Pancho Villa Returns 🦴🦴 **1950** It's 1913, and noble Mexican General Pancho Villa leads his merry men against the assassins of President Madera. This Mexican production (filmed in English) paints a partisan portrait of title character as a good-hearted revolutionary folk hero, not the roving bandit later notorious north of the border. **95m/B VHS.** *MX* Leo Carrillo, Esther Fernandez, Jeanette Comber, Rodolfo Acosta; ***D:*** Miguel Contreras Torres; ***W:*** Miguel Contreras Torres.

Pandaemonium 🦴🦴 ½ **2000 (PG-13)** Friendship, rivalry, and jealousy between 19th century English romanticists William Wordsworth (Hannah) and Samuel Taylor Coleridge (Roache). In 1813, debilitated by opium abuse, Coleridge attends a reception for the now-distant Wordsworth and flashes back to their first meeting some 20 years before. Coleridge and his wife Sara (Morton) move to a country cottage with Wordworth and his sister Dorothy (Woof) living nearby as the two men collaborate on a poetry collection. Coleridge becomes (mutually) attracted to Dorothy and finds inspiration in drugs. A rift between the two men deepens when Wordsworth marries and Coleridge dependency on drugs worsens—even as his poetry soars. **125m/C VHS, DVD.** *GB* Linus Roache, John Hannah, Samantha Morton, Emily Woof, Emma Fielding, Andy Serkis, Samuel West, Guy Lankester; ***D:*** Julien Temple; ***W:*** Frank Cottrell-Boyce; ***C:*** John Lynch; ***M:*** Dario Marianelli.

Pandemic 🦴 ½ **2007** Dr. Kayla Martin (Thiessen) and her partner Carl (Stewart) fear the frightening effects of a biological attack when a young man dies on a plane following a fever and violent convulsions. Other passengers on board are now filtering into the city and infecting areas of Los Angeles. The virus and panic continue to spread. Fairly entertaining but overly saturated with unsupported improbability (starting with Thiessen as a doctor). **170m/C DVD.** Tiffani(-Amber) Thiessen, Vincent Spano, Eric Roberts, Faye Dunaway, French Stewart, Bruce Boxleitner, Bob Gunton, Renee Taylor, Tamlyn Tomita, Clyde Kusatsu; ***D:*** Armand Mastroianni; ***W:*** Bruce Zabel, Jackie Zabel; ***C:*** Amit Bhattacharya. **CABLE**

Pandemic 🦴 ½ **2009 (R)** Action-thriller about a New Mexico community where humans and animals are both stricken with a gory contagious virus. The area is quarantined by the military and all outside communication is cut off so veterinarian Sydney Stevens teams up with conspiracy theorist Spenser to figure out what's going on and reveal the truth. **90m/C DVD.** Alesha Rucci, Peter Holden, Ray Wise, Graham McTavish, Kristi Culbert; ***D:*** Jason Connery; ***W:*** Aaron Pope; ***C:*** Miguel Bunster; ***M:*** Christian Henson. **VIDEO**

Pandemonium 🦴🦴 ½ *Thursday the 12th* **1982 (PG)** A spoof of teen slasher films involving murder at Bambi's Cheerleading School. Seems that nationwide, cheerleaders have been brutally eliminated from their squads, leaving Bambi's as the last resort for the terminally perky. Smothers is interesting and more intelligent than his TV persona (although not by much) as the Mountie hero, assisted by Paul Reubens in a pre-Pee-Wee role. Kane steals the show as Candy, a pleasant lass with hyperkinetic powers. **82m/C VHS.** *CA* Tom Smothers, Carol Kane, Miles Chapin, Paul (Pee-wee Herman) Reubens, Judge Reinhold, Tab Hunter, Marc McClure, Donald O'Connor, Eve Arden, Eileen Brennan, Edie McClurg, Lenny Montana; ***D:*** Alfred Sole.

Pandora and the Flying Dutchman 🦴🦴 ½ **1951** Feverish romantic fantasy has playgirl/nightclub singer Pandora Reynolds (Gardner) living in '30s Spain and being romanced by every man in sight. Naturally, she cares for none of them until she meets enigmatic Dutch captain Hendrick van der Zee (Mason) who is, in fact, the legendary Flying Dutchman—condemned to wander the seas forever unless a woman is willing to give up her life for him. Gardner is, as usual, exotically lovely. **123m/C VHS, DVD.** Ava Gardner, James Mason, Nigel Patrick, Sheila Sim, Harold Warrender, Mario Cabre; ***D:*** Albert Lewin; ***W:*** Albert Lewin; ***C:*** Jack Cardiff; ***M:*** Alan Rawsthorne.

Pandora's Box 🦴🦴🦴🦴 *Die Buechse der Pandora; Lulu* **1928** This silent classic marked the end of the German Expressionist era and established Brooks as a major screen presence. She plays the tempestuous Lulu, who destroys everyone she comes in contact with, eventually sinking to prostitution and a fateful meeting with Jack the Ripper. Silent with orchestral score. **110m/B VHS, DVD.** *GE* Louise Brooks, Fritz Kortner, Francis Lederer, Carl Goetz, Alice Roberts, Gustav Diesl; ***D:*** G.W. Pabst; ***W:*** G.W. Pabst; ***C:*** Gunther Krampf.

Pandora's Clock 🦴🦴 **1996** Over-extended but often suspenseful disaster flick. Quantum Airlines flight 66 is traveling from Frankfurt to New York when a passenger dies. Capt. Holland (Anderson) radios to make an emergency landing in London but is informed that the passenger was infected with a doomsday virus and the plane must be quarantined. No country will let them land and then the CIA and various shady government types get involved, proposing much more drastic solutions. Based on the novel by John J. Nance. **178m/C DVD.** Richard Dean Anderson, Daphne Zuniga, Jane Leeves, Richard Lawson, Edward Herrmann, Robert Guillaume, Robert Loggia, Stephen (Steve) Root; ***D:*** Eric Laneuville; ***W:*** David Israel; ***C:*** Paul Pollard; ***M:*** Don Davis. **TV**

Pandorum 🦴 ½ **2009 (R)** Two space shuttle crew members, Payton (Quaid) and Bower (Foster), awake from a cryogenic snooze to find that they have no memory of why they're in outer space and little recollection of their own identity. While trying to piece together their mystery they realize they're sharing quarters with flesh-eating alien rodents. Any shot at being a genuine sci-fi thriller is undone by these unimaginative creatures that push it into nothing more than "Alien" knock-off territory. **108m/C DVD.** *US* Dennis Quaid, Ben Foster, Norman Reedus, Cam Gigandet, Cung Le, Eddie Rouse, Antje Traue; ***D:*** Christian Alvart; ***W:*** Christian Alvart, Travis Milloy; ***C:*** Wendigo von Schultzendorff; ***M:*** Michi Britsch.

Panhandle 🦴🦴 **1948** Trading post owner John Sands (Cameron) wound up in Mexico after he went from lawman to gunslinger. Learning his brother was murdered, Sands heads north to hunt down the killers but old adversary Matt Garson (Hadley) has no intention of making it a fair fight. Co-star (and co-writer) Edwards, playing a gunfighter, became better-known as a writer-director. **85m/B DVD.** Rod Cameron, Reed Hadley, Anne Gwynne, Cathy Downs, Blake Edwards, J. Farrell MacDonald, Dick Crockett; ***D:*** Lesley Selander; ***W:*** Blake Edwards, John C. Champion; ***C:*** Harry Neumann; ***M:*** Rex Dunn.

Panic 🦴 ½ *Bakterion* **1976** A scientist terrorizes a small town when he becomes hideously deformed by one of his bacteria experiments. He should have known better. **90m/C VHS.** *IT SP* David Warbeck, Janet Agren; ***D:*** Tonino Ricco; ***W:*** Victor Andres Catena, Jaime Comas Gil; ***C:*** Giovanni Bergamini; ***M:*** Marcello Giombini.

Panic 🦴🦴 ½ **2000 (R)** Hangdog Macy is perfect as middle-aged Alex, who is not having your usual midlife crisis since he's a hit man. As a matter of fact, he learned his trade from his ruthless dad Michael (Sutherland), who still calls the shots. But Alex has been keeping the truth from his wife Martha (Ullman) and his beloved son Sammy (Dorfman) and he needs to talk. So he goes to shrink Josh Parks (Ritter) and, in the waiting room, Alex meets neurotic Sarah (Campbell), with whom he contemplates an affair. Alex wants to make some changes but when you're a professional killer, it's not that easy. **93m/C VHS, DVD.** William H. Macy, John Ritter, Neve Campbell, Donald Sutherland, Tracey Ullman, Barbara Bain, David Dorfman; ***D:*** Henry Bromell; ***W:*** Henry Bromell; ***C:*** Jeffrey Jur; ***M:*** Brian Tyler.

Panic Button 🦴 ½ **1962** Mel Brooks took the plot from this film and made "The Producers," which was much better. Italian gangsters produce a TV show and stack the deck so that it will fail. Unbeknownst to them, the star has figured out what they are doing and works to make it a success. Shot in Italy, mainly in Venice and Rome. **90m/B VHS.** *IT* Maurice Chevalier, Eleanor Parker, Jayne Mansfield, Mike Connors, Akim Tamiroff; ***D:*** George Sherman.

Panic in Echo Park 🦴🦴 **1977** A doctor races against time to find the cause of an epidemic that is threatening the health of a city. Good performances compensate for a predictable plot. **78m/C VHS, DVD.** Dorian Harewood, Robin Gammell, Catlin Adams, Ramon Bieri, Movita; ***D:*** John Llewellyn Moxey. **TV**

Panic in Needle Park 🦴🦴🦴 **1971 (R)** Drugs become an obsession for a young girl who goes to New York for an abortion. Her new boyfriend is imprisoned for robbery in order to support both their habits. She resorts to prostitution to continue her drug habit, and trouble occurs when her boyfriend realizes she was instrumental in his being sent to jail. Strikes a vein in presenting an uncompromising look at drug use. May be too much of a depressant for some. Pacino's first starring role. **90m/C VHS.** Al Pacino, Kitty Winn, Alan Vint, Richard Bright, Kiel Martin, Warren Finnerty, Raul Julia, Paul Sorvino; ***D:*** Jerry Schatzberg; ***W:*** Joan Didion, John Gregory Dunne; ***C:*** Adam Holender. Cannes '71: Actress (Winn).

Panic in the Skies 🦴🦴 **1996** The cockpit of a Boeing 747 is struck by lightning in mid-flight, killing the pilot and co-pilot. Flight attendant Jackson and passenger Marinaro try to figure out a way to safely land the passenger-filled jet. **90m/C VHS, DVD.** Kate Jackson, Ed Marinaro, Erik Estrada, Maureen McCormick, Billy Warlock, Robert Guillaume; ***D:*** Paul Ziller; ***W:*** Robert Hamilton; ***C:*** Rod Parkhurst; ***M:*** Todd Hayen. **TV**

Panic in the Streets 🦴🦴🦴 **1950** The Black Death threatens New Orleans in this intense tale. When a body is found on the waterfront, a doctor (Widmark) is called upon for a diagnosis. The carrier proves to be deadly in more ways than one. Fine performances, taut direction (this was one of Kazan's favorite movies). Filmed on location in New Orleans. **96m/B VHS, DVD.** Richard Widmark, Jack Palance, Barbara Bel Geddes, Paul Douglas, Zero Mostel; ***D:*** Elia Kazan; ***W:*** Edward Anhalt. Oscars '50: Story.

Panic in the Year Zero! 🦴🦴 ½ *End of the World* **1962** Milland and family leave Los Angeles for a fishing trip just as the city is hit by a nuclear bomb. Continuing out into the wilderness for safety, the family now must try to survive as their world crumbles around them. Generally considered the best of Milland's five directorial efforts. **92m/B VHS,**

DVD. Ray Milland, Jean Hagen, Frankie Avalon, Mary Mitchell, Joan Freeman, Richard Garland, Rex Holman, Richard Bakalyan, Willis Bouchey, Neil Nephew; *D:* Ray Milland; *W:* Jay Simms, John Morton; *C:* Gilbert Warrenton; *M:* Les Baxter.

Panic on the 5:22 1974 Wealthy commuters are kidnapped and held hostage by terrorist hoodlums in a suburban train club car. **78m/C VHS.** Lynda Day George, Laurence Luckinbill, Ina Balin, Bernie Casey; *D:* Harvey Hart. **TV**

Panic Room 1/2 **2002 (R)** Recently divorced mom Meg (Foster) moves with daughter Sarah (Stewart) into a huge, ominous four-story brownstone in New York. The house comes equipped with a "panic room" a fortress-like room the paranoid billionaire previous occupant had built. Before the night is over, the room comes into play as three intruders come looking for something. The three happen to be looking for something that's in the room, where the women have holed themselves up. And thus the cat-and-mouse game begins. Fincher's talents for visual style, creative camera work, and squirmy set pieces are well-used here as the tension mounts with each scene. The plot isn't especially original, but the twists are well-done the performers acquit themselves nicely. **112m/C VHS, DVD.** *US* Jodie Foster, Forest Whitaker, Dwight Yoakam, Jared Leto, Kristen Stewart, Ann Magnuson, Patrick Bauchau, Ian Buchanan, Paul Schulze; *D:* David Fincher; *W:* David Koepp; *C:* Conrad W. Hall, Darius Khondji; *M:* Howard Shore.

Panic Station *The Plains of Heaven* **1982** Two guys get lonely at remote satellite relay station. **90m/C VHS.** *AU* Richard Moir, Reg Evans, Gerard Kennedy; *D:* Ian Pringle.

Panique *Panic* **1947** A study of mob psychology in slums of post-WWII Paris. Two lovers frame a stranger for murder. Dark and tautly paced thriller taken from the novel by Georges Simenon. In French with English subtitles. **87m/B VHS.** *FR* Michel Simon, Viviane Romance; *D:* Julien Duvivier.

Pan's Labyrinth *El Laberinto del Fauno* **2006 (R)** When her loving soldier father dies in combat during Spain's civil war, young Ofelia (Baquero) is stuck with Captain Vidal (Lopez), a brute of a stepfather, when her mother, Carmen (Gil), remarries. Ofelia sees an escape from her miserable situation when she stumbles upon a garden labyrinth that leads to a freakish-yet-bewitching underground fantasy world inhabited by strange creatures led by Pan (Jones), who is part goat, part man. He tells Ofelia that she might be their lost princess but must perform three tasks in order to prove herself worthy of the crown. Despite feeling guilty about abandoning her mother, whose difficult pregnancy leaves her bedridden, Ofelia takes on the risky, off-the-wall missions. Eventually the line between the two worlds blurs, causing dire consequences. Complex and entertaining fairy tale mixes vivid scenery with computer-generated effects, but its violence and adult themes are too intense for the kiddies. In Spanish with subtitles. **112m/C DVD, Blu-ray Disc, HD DVD.** *MX SP* Sergi Lopez, Maribel Verdu, Doug Jones, Alex Angulo, Ivana Baquero, Ariadna Gil, Roger Casamajor; *D:* Guillermo del Toro; *W:* Guillermo del Toro; *C:* Guillermo Navarro; *M:* Javier Navarrete. Oscars '06: Art Dir./Set Dec., Cinematog., Makeup; British Acad. '06: Costume Des., Foreign Film, Makeup; Ind. Spirit '07: Cinematog.

Pantaloons **1957** A man who fancies himself to be irresistible chases women for sport. A quaint and lively period film. **93m/C VHS.** *FR* Fernandel, Carmen Sevilla, Fernando Rey; *D:* John Berry.

Panther **1995 (R)** The Van Peebles family teaches Oliver Stone History 101 with a fictionalized account of the Black Panthers' emergence as a voice for African Americans and as a fixture on the FBI's most wanted list in the late '60s. Judge (Hardison), a Vietnam vet forced by the FBI to become an informant, chronicles the activities of leaders Bobby Seale (Vance) and Huey P. Newton (Chong) and serves as witness to the Panthers' rise and subsequent fall into corruption and disintegration. Scatter-shot editing is meant to signify the chaos of the times, but instead adds to the action-flick feel and further detracts from the professed intent of being a message movie. **124m/C VHS, DVD.** Kadeem Hardison, Marcus Chong, Courtney B. Vance, Bokeem Woodbine, Joe Don Baker, Anthony Griffith, Nefertiti, James Russo, Richard Dysart, M. Emmet Walsh, Mario Van Peebles; *D:* Mario Van Peebles; *W:* Melvin Van Peebles; *C:* Edward Pei; *M:* Stanley Clarke.

Panther Squad **1984** Litter of sex kittens led by Danning get into major scraps to save world. **77m/C VHS.** *FR* Jack Taylor, Analia Ivars, Jean-Rene Gossart, Karin Schubert, Sybil Danning; *D:* Pierre Chavalier; *W:* Georges Friedland; *C:* Max Monteillet; *M:* Douglas Cooper.

The Panther's Claw **1942** Murder befalls an opera troupe, but a sleuth with the memorable name of Thatcher Colt is on the case. A quick-moving mystery quickie that delivers on its own modest terms. **72m/B VHS, DVD.** Sidney Blackmer, Byron Foulger, Rick Vallin, Herbert Rawlinson; *D:* William Beaudine.

Paparazzi 1/2 **2004 (PG-13)** An actor's revenge? Produced by Mel Gibson (who has a cameo) and his Icon production company, this overheated melodrama follows newly-crowned action star Bo Laramie (Hauser), whose celebrity has led to his being stalked by those degenerate paparazzi. When Bo's family is critically injured in a car crash caused by the relentless shutterbug pursuit, Bo turns vigilante to get revenge. Sizemore is at his slimy nastiest as the lead sleazy photog. **85m/C VHS, DVD.** *US* Cole Hauser, Robin Tunney, Dennis Farina, Daniel Baldwin, Tom Hollander, Kevin Gage, Tom Sizemore, Duane Davis, Blake Bryan, Andrea Baker, Jordan Baker; ***Cameos:*** Mel Gibson, Chris Rock, Matthew McConaughey, Vince Vaughn; *D:* Paul Abascal; *W:* Forrest Smith; *C:* Daryn Okada; *M:* Brian Tyler.

Papa's Angels **2000 (PG)** Sappy Christmas drama set in the 1930s. The Jenkins family, headed by gruff furniture maker Grins (Bakula), live a hard-but-happy life in the Appalachia mountains, with mom Sharon (Nixon) raising their four kids. Then Sharon is diagnosed with tuberculosis and is sent to a sanatorium. But Grins builds a glass room onto the house so she can see the children without infecting them, and brings her home to die. After her death, Grins takes to the moonshine and the kids are left to fend for themselves—he doesn't even want to celebrate Christmas! Based on the book by Collin Wilcox Paxton and Gary Carden. **95m/C VHS.** Scott Bakula, Cynthia Nixon, Eva Marie Saint, Kimberly Warnat, Brandon James Olson, Jenny Lynn Hutcheson, Lachlan Murdoch, Kirsten Bishopric; *D:* Dwight Little; *W:* Bill Cain. **TV**

Papa's Delicate Condition **1963** Based on the autobiographical writings of silent screen star Corinne Griffith. Gleason is Papa whose "delicate condition" is a result of his drinking. His antics provide a constant headache to his family. A paean to turn-of-the-century family life. No I.D.s required as the performances are enjoyable for the whole family. Features the Academy Award-winning song "Call Me Irresponsible." ♫ Call Me Irresponsible; Bill Bailey, Won't You Please Come Home?. **98m/C VHS, DVD.** Jackie Gleason, Glynis Johns, Charlie Ruggles, Laurel Goodwin, Elisha Cook Jr., Murray Hamilton, Ned Glass, Charles Lane, Don Beddoe, Juanita Moore, Trevor Bardette, Ken Renard; *D:* George Marshall; *W:* Jack Rose; *C:* Loyal Griggs; *M:* Joseph J. Lilley. Oscars '63: Song ("Call Me Irresponsible").

The Paper **1994 (R)** Another crowd pleaser from director Howard follows a red letter day in the life of an editor at the tabloid New York Sun (modeled on the trashy Post). Fresh, fast-moving script by the Koepp brothers (who appear as reporters) offers a fairly accurate portrayal of the business of journalism (including the "brisk" language), with a few Hollywood exceptions. Pace suffers from cutaways to life outside, while script and direction sometimes coast past targets. Propelled by a fine cast, with cola-swigging editor Keaton the focus as he juggles his personal and professional lives. As a managing editor married to her work and ready to run over anyone in her way, Close is both funny and scary. Duvall contributes salt as the old newsroom warhorse. Tons of cameos, though those outside of the business may not notice them. **112m/C VHS, DVD.** Michael Keaton, Robert Duvall, Marisa Tomei, Glenn Close, Randy Quaid, Jason Robards Jr., Jason Alexander, Spalding Gray, Catherine O'Hara, Lynne Thigpen; *D:* Ron Howard; *W:* David Koepp, Steven Koepp; *C:* John Seale; *M:* Randy Newman.

The Paper Brigade 1/2 **1996 (PG)** Fifteen-year-old Gunther (Howard) gets a paper route to pay for the concert tickets he bought to impress a girl. Now he has to contend with his crazy neighbor (Englund) and a gang of bullies, as well as other obstacles. **89m/C VHS.** Kyle Howard, Robert Englund, Travis Wester; *D:* Blair Treu.

Paper Bullets **1999 (R)** Cop John Rourke's son is kidnapped by a Chinese drug lord and, naturally, he'll do anything to get his boy back. Including aligning himself with a beautiful woman who has an equal obsession for revenge. **95m/C VHS, DVD.** James Russo, William McNamara, Ernie Hudson, Nicole Bilderback, Jeff Wincott, Francois Chan; *D:* Serge Rodnunsky; *W:* Serge Rodnunsky; *C:* Greg Patterson; *M:* Jeff Walton. **VIDEO**

The Paper Chase **1973 (PG)** Students at Harvard Law School suffer and struggle through their first year. A realistic, sometimes acidly humorous look at Ivy League ambitions, with Houseman stealing the show as the tough professor. Wonderful adaptation of the John Jay Osborn novel which later became the basis for the acclaimed TV series. **111m/C VHS, DVD.** Timothy Bottoms, Lindsay Wagner, John Houseman, Graham Beckel, Edward Herrmann, James Naughton, Craig Richard Nelson, Bob Lydiard; *D:* James Bridges; *W:* James Bridges; *C:* Gordon Willis; *M:* John Williams. Oscars '73: Support. Actor (Houseman); Golden Globes '74: Support. Actor (Houseman); Natl. Bd. of Review '73: Support. Actor (Houseman).

Paper Clips **2004 (G)** A middle school class in Whitwell, Tennessee, a small rural town with virtually no Jews, few minorities, and within 100 miles of the KKK's headquarters inspires the world through a class project in this powerful documentary. During their studies of the Holocaust, the students discovered that in Norway, where the paper clip was invented, citizens wore paper clips on their lapels in protest of the Nazis. They begin writing letters to public figures asking for one paper clip each, in hopes of collecting 6 million to match the number of Jews that lost their lives. They receive an overwhelming response from around the world, eventually collecting 29 million. At times a little too tedious and self-congratulatory for its own good, but makes a great tool for discussing diversity education. **87m/C DVD.** *US* *D:* Jeffrey Ventimilia, Elliot Berlin; *W:* Jeffrey Ventimilia; *C:* Michael Marton; *M:* Charlie Barnett.

Paper Heart **2009 (PG-13)** What's fake and what's real and do you care? What started out as an alleged documentary turned into something else as skeptical, chipmunk-cheeked performance artist Yi takes a road trip to ask the question 'Does true love really exist?' Her director/crew is played by an actor (Johnson) who is portraying the actual co-writer/director (Jasenovec). Then Yi meets actor Michael Cera and just might have the answer to her own question, although they act like a couple of grade-school kids playing at romance without any actual understanding of adult relationships. And then there are the puppets. We don't get it either. **88m/C DVD.** *US* Michael Cera, Charlyne Yi, Jake M. Johnson; *D:* Nicholas Jasenovec; *W:* Charlyne Yi, Nicholas Jasenovec; *C:* Jay Hunter; *M:* Michael Cera, Charlyne Yi.

Paper Lion 1/2 **1968** A comedy "documentary" about bestselling writer George Plimpton's tryout game as quarterback with the Detroit Lions. Film debut of Alan Alda. Helped Karras make the transition from the gridiron to the silver screen. Moves into field goal range but doesn't quite score. **107m/C VHS.** Alan Alda, Lauren Hutton, Alex Karras, Ann Turkel, John Gordy, Roger Brown, "Sugar Ray" Robinson, Roy Scheider, David Doyle; *D:* Alex March.

Paper Man **1971** A group of college students create a fictitious person in a computer for a credit card scam. The scheme snowballs, resulting in murder and hints of possible artificial intelligence. But it's just standard network TV fare, with a creepy performance by Stockwell as a computer whiz. **90m/C VHS.** Dean Stockwell, Stefanie Powers, James Stacy, Elliot Street, Tina Chen, James Olson, Ross Elliott; *D:* Walter Grauman.

Paper Marriage 1/2 **1988** In Canada, a less-than-successful Chinese boxer agrees to marry a Hong Kong girl for a promise of payment in order that she may become a citizen. The money never comes, but the nearly betrothed pair discover that they love each other, after all. In Cantonese with English subtitles. **102m/C VHS.** *CH* Sammo Hung, Maggie Cheung; *D:* Alfred Cheung.

Paper Marriage 1/2 **1993** Yet another variation on the marriage in order to gain citizenship but yes we're going to fall in love films. A young Polish woman has fallen for an upper-crust English doctor she's met in Warsaw. When Alicja arrives in England, she's promptly dumped by the cad. She's ambitious and wants to stay in England so Alicja arranges a marriage of convenience with small-time crook Aiden, who finds his new bride is more than he bargained for. **88m/C VHS.** *GB PL* Gary Kemp, Joanna Trepechinska, Rita Tushingham, Richard Hawley, David Horovitch, William Ilkley, Mark McKellen, Ann Mitchell, Sadie Frost; *D:* Krzysztof Lang; *W:* Marek Kreutz, Krzysztof Lang.

Paper Mask 1/2 **1991 (R)** When a promising young doctor is killed in an auto accident, an unscrupulous, psychotic porter assumes his identity. He uses said identity to, among other things, initiate an affair with a sultry co-worker. How long will this madman play his unholy game, and at what cost? **105m/C VHS.** *GB* Paul McGann, Amanda Donohoe, Frederick Treves, Barbara Leigh-Hunt, Jimmy Yuill, Tom Wilkinson; *D:* Christopher Morahan; *W:* John Collee; *C:* Nat Crosby; *M:* Richard Harvey.

Paper Moon 1/2 **1973 (PG)** Award-winning story set in depression-era Kansas with Ryan O'Neal as a Bible-wielding con who meets up with a nine-year-old orphan. During their travels together, he discovers that the orphan (his daughter, Tatum) is better at "his" game than he is. Irresistible chemistry between the O'Neals, leading to Tatum's Oscar win (she is the youngest actor ever to take home a statue). Cinematically picturesque and cynical enough to keep overt sentimentalism at bay. Based on Joe David Brown's novel, "Addie Pray." The director's version contains a prologue by director Bogdanovich. **102m/B VHS, DVD.** Ryan O'Neal, Tatum O'Neal, Madeline Kahn, John Hillerman, Randy Quaid; *D:* Peter Bogdanovich; *W:* Alvin Sargent. Oscars '73: Support. Actress (O'Neal); Writers Guild '73: Adapt. Screenplay.

Paper Tiger **1974** Niven plays an imaginative English tutor who fabricates fantastic yarns fictionalizing his past in order to impress his student, the son of the Japanese ambassador to a Southeast Asian country. Poorly executed karate, misdirection, and a simplistic story line work against it. **104m/C VHS.** *GB* David Niven, Toshiro Mifune, Eiko Ando, Hardy Kruger; *D:* Ken Annakin; *W:* Jack Davies.

A Paper Wedding *Les Noces de Papier* **1989** A middle-aged literature professor with a dead-end career and equally dead-end romance with a married man is persuaded by her lawyer sister to marry a Chilean political refugee to avoid his deportation. Of course, they must fool an immigration official and their fake marriage does turn into romance, but this is no light-hearted "Green Card." Bujold shines. In French and Spanish with English subtitles. **90m/C VHS, DVD.** *CA* Genevieve Bujold, Manuel Aranguiz, Dorothee Berryman; *D:* Michel Brault; *C:* Sylvain Brault.

Paperback Hero **1973** A hot-shot hockey player turns to crime when his team loses its financial backing. Choopy storyline could use a Zamboni, while Dullea should be penalized for occasionally losing his rustic accent. Still the supporting actors skate through their roles and, for periods, it works. A slapshot that ultimately clangs off the goal post. **94m/C VHS.** *CA* Keir Dullea, Elizabeth Ashley, John Beck, Dayle Haddon; ***D:*** Peter Pearson.

Paperback Hero 1/2 **1999** Engaging leads help carry a weak story in this fluffy romantic comedy. Studly Jack (Jackman) is a long-distance trucker who makes his home in a remote outback community and is the secret author of a bodice-ripper that has become a bestseller. What Jack has neglected to tell his best friend, Ruby (karvan), is that he used her name as his nom de plume. Now the book's publisher wants Ruby to come to Sydney for a face-to-face meeting and Jack has a tough time getting her to go along with the deception. **96m/C VHS.** *AU* Hugh Jackman, Claudia Karvan, Andrew S. Gilbert, Angie Milliken, Jeanie Drynan, Tony Barry, Ritchie Singer, Bruce Venables, Charlie Little; ***D:*** Antony J. Bowman; ***W:*** Antony J. Bowman; ***C:*** David Burr; ***M:*** Burkhard Dallwitz.

Paperback Romance 1/2 *Lucky Break* **1996 (R)** Sophie (Carides) is a writer of erotica who doesn't act on her own impulses because she's embarassed by her polio-crippled leg. But when she breaks her leg, the cast allows her to pass the injury off as a skiing accident and Sophie decides to go after the man of her dreams, a charmingly shady jewelry dealer named Eddie (LaPaglia)—who just happens to be engaged. **99m/C VHS, DVD.** *AU* Gia Carides, Anthony LaPaglia, Rebecca Gibney; ***D:*** Ben Lewin; ***W:*** Ben Lewin; ***C:*** Vincent Monton; ***M:*** Paul Grabowsky.

The Paperboy **1994 (R)** Melissa Thorpe (Paul) returns to her small hometown to settle her mother's estate, only to become the obsession of Johnny (Marut), the 12-year-old paperboy she mistakenly befriends. Seems he becomes psychotically jealous when Melissa takes up with an old flame (Katt) and dead bodies become as common as old newspapers. **93m/C VHS.** Alexandra Paul, Marc Marut, William Katt, Brigid Tierney; ***D:*** Douglas Jackson; ***W:*** David Peckinpah; ***M:*** Milan Kymlicka.

Paperhouse **1989** An odd fantasy about a young girl plagued by recurring dreams that begin to influence real life. Very obtuse, British-minded film with "Twilight Zone" feel that manages to capture genuine dream-ness. Not for all audiences, but intriguing nontheless. Based on the novel "Marianne Dreams" by Catherine Storr. **92m/C VHS.** *GB* Glenne Headly, Ben Cross, Charlotte Burke, Elliott Spiers, Gemma Jones, Sarah Newbold; ***D:*** Bernard Rose; ***W:*** Matthew Jacobs; ***M:*** Hans Zimmer, Stanley Myers.

Papillon **1973 (PG)** McQueen is a criminal sent to Devil's Island in the 1930s determined to escape from the Lemote prison. Hoffman is the swindler he befriends. A series of escapes and recaptures follow. Boxoffice winner based on the autobiographical writings of French thief Henri Charriere. Excellent portrayal of prison life and fine performances from the prisoners. Certain segments would have been better left on the cutting room floor. The film's title refers to the lead's butterfly tattoo. **150m/C VHS, DVD.** Steve McQueen, Dustin Hoffman, Victor Jory, George Coulouris, Anthony Zerbe; ***D:*** Franklin J. Schaffner; ***W:*** Dalton Trumbo, Lorenzo Semple Jr.; ***C:*** Fred W. Koenekamp; ***M:*** Jerry Goldsmith.

Paprika 1/2 **2006 (R)** "Tokyo Godfathers" creator Satoshi Kon is back with the warped tale of a company that has created a machine that allows therapists to enter their patient's dreams. Head researcher Dr. Chiba—known to her patients as Paprika—enlists the help of a police detective because a madman has stolen a prototype and is mucking about with the minds of her colleagues. The animation is mind-blowing, but the surreal and disturbing nature of the dream sequences will make it too spicy for some. **90m/C DVD.** *JP* ***D:*** Seishi Minakimi; ***W:*** Seishi Minakimi, Seishi Minakimi; ***C:*** Michiya Kato; ***M:*** Susumu Hirasawa; ***V:*** Akio Ohtsuka, Toru Furuya, Satoshi Kon.

Parade **1974** A series of vignettes in a circus, "Parade" is actually a play within a play, meshing the action with events offstage. **85m/C VHS.** *FR* Jacques Tati; ***D:*** Jacques Tati; ***W:*** Jacques Tati.

The Paradine Case 1/2 **1947** A passable Hitchcock romancer about a young lawyer who falls in love with the woman he's defending for murder, not knowing whether she is innocent or guilty. Script could be tighter and more cohesive. $70,000 of the $3 million budget were spent recreating the original Bailey courtroom. Based on the novel by Robert Hichens. **125m/B VHS, DVD.** Gregory Peck, Alida Valli, Ann Todd, Louis Jourdan, Charles Laughton, Charles Coburn, Ethel Barrymore, Leo G. Carroll; ***D:*** Alfred Hitchcock; ***W:*** David O. Selznick; ***C:*** Lee Garmes; ***M:*** Franz Waxman.

Paradise **1982 (R)** Young American boy and beautiful English girl on a 19th-century jaunt through the Middle East are the sole survivors when their caravan is massacred. Left to their own devices, they discover a magnificent oasis and the joys of frolicking naked and experience (surprise) their sexual awakening. Do a double-take: it's the "Blue Lagoon" all over, with a bit more nudity and a lot more sand. **96m/C VHS.** Phoebe Cates, Willie Aames, Richard Curnock, Tuvio Tavi; ***D:*** Stuart Gillard.

Paradise **1991 (PG-13)** Young boy is sent to the country to live with his pregnant mother's married friends (real life husband and wife Johnson and Griffith). From the outset it is clear that the couple are experiencing marital troubles, making the boy's assimilation all the more difficult. Help arrives in the form of a sprightly ten-year-old girl, with whom he forms a charming relationship. Largely predictable, this remake of the French film "Le Grand Chemin" works thanks to the surprisingly good work of its ensemble cast, and the gorgeous scenery of South Carolina, where the movie was filmed. **112m/C VHS, DVD.** Melanie Griffith, Don Johnson, Elijah Wood, Thora Birch, Sheila McCarthy, Eve Gordon, Louise Latham, Greg Travis, Sarah Trigger; ***D:*** Mary Agnes Donoghue; ***W:*** Mary Agnes Donoghue; ***M:*** David Newman.

Paradise Alley **1978 (PG)** Rocky tires of boxing, decides to join the WWF. Three brothers brave the world of professional wrestling in an effort to strike it rich and move out of the seedy Hell's Kitchen neighborhood of New York, circa 1946. Stallone wrote, stars in, and makes his directorial debut in addition to singing the title song. He makes a few good moves as director, but is ultimately pinned to the canvas. **109m/C VHS, DVD.** Sylvester Stallone, Anne Archer, Armand Assante, Lee Canalito, Kevin Conway; ***D:*** Sylvester Stallone; ***W:*** Sylvester Stallone; ***M:*** Bill Conti.

Paradise Canyon 1/2 **1935** Early Wayne "B" thriller, in which he plays an undercover government agent sent to track down a group of counterfeiters. **59m/B VHS, DVD.** John Wayne, Yakima Canutt, Marion Burns; ***D:*** Carl Pierson; ***W:*** Lindsley Parsons, Robert Emmett Tansey; ***C:*** Archie Stout.

Paradise, Hawaiian Style 1/2 **1966 (G)** Out-of-work pilot returns to Hawaii, where he and a buddy start a charter service with two helicopters. Plenty of gals are wooed by "the Pelvis." Filmed four years after Elvis's first Pacific piece, "Blue Hawaii." Presley, showing the first signs of slow-down, displays no surprises here. ♫ Paradise, Hawaiian Style; Scratch My Back (Then I'll Scratch Yours); Stop Where You Are; This Is My Heaven; House of Sand; Queenie Wahine's Papaya; Datin'; Drums of the Islands; A Dog's Life. **91m/C VHS, DVD.** Elvis Presley, Suzanna Leigh, James Shigeta, Donna Butterworth, Irene Tsu, Julie Parrish, Philip Ahn, Mary Treen, Marianna Hill, John Doucette, Grady Sutton; ***D:*** Michael D. Moore; ***W:*** Anthony Lawrence, Allan Weiss; ***C:*** Wallace Kelley; ***M:*** Joseph J. Lilley.

Paradise in Harlem 1/2 **1940** All-black musical in which a cabaret performer witnesses a gangland murder, sees his sick wife die, and is pressured into leaving town by the mob. Have a nice day. **83m/B VHS, DVD.** Frank Wilson, Mamie Smith, Edna Mae Harris, Juanita Hall; ***D:*** Joseph Seiden.

Paradise Island **1930** Down-scale musical romance about an ingenue on her way to join her fiance in the South Seas, only to find that he has gambled away his money. The opportunistic saloon owner tries to put the moves on her. Will the two lovers be reunited? ♫ I've Got a Girl In Every Port; Drinking Song; Lazy Breezes; Just Another Dream. **68m/B VHS, DVD.** Kenneth Harlan, Marceline Day, Thomas Santschi, Paul Hurst, Victor Potel, Gladden James, Will Stanton; ***D:*** Bert Glennon.

Paradise Motel 1/2 **1984 (R)** Teen exploitation film centered around a local motel predominantly used for one-night rendezvous. High school heroes and jocks battle for the affections of a beautiful classmate. **87m/C VHS.** Bob Basso, Gary Hershberger, Jonna Leigh Stack, Robert Krantz; ***D:*** Cary Medoway; ***C:*** James L. Carter.

Paradise Now *Al-Jenna-An* **2005 (PG-13)** Recounts how two young Palestinians go from garage mechanics to suicide bombers preparing for a mission to Tel Aviv. Best friends Said (Nashef) and Khaled (Suliman) live in Nablus on the West Bank and apparently have guerrilla ties. They are informed that they have been chosen and have 24 hours to prepare; the men seem more resigned than fanatical. Director Abu-Assad pays close attention to the details. **90m/C DVD.** Lubna Azabal, Hiam Abbass, Kais Nashef, Ali Suliman, Amer Hlehel, Ashraf Barhoum; ***D:*** Hany Abu-Assad; ***W:*** Hany Abu-Assad, Bero Beyer; ***C:*** Antoine Heberle. Golden Globes '06: Foreign Film; Ind. Spirit '06: Foreign Film; Natl. Bd. of Review '05: Foreign Film.

Paradise Road **1997 (R)** Fleeing Singapore during WWII, a group of British, American, and Australian women straggle to the shore of Sumatra after their ship is bombed, where they're taken prisoner by the Japanese. Headed by Close, the prisoners form a vocal ensemble that crosses their collective national differences and attempts to lift the spirits of the brutalized women. Familiar ground is trod in this prisoner-of-war saga, but the music is genuinely moving, and excellent performances from the cast help sustain interest. The symphonic choral pieces were taken from actual sheet music used by a similar group of real-life WWII prisoners. **115m/C VHS, DVD.** Glenn Close, Frances McDormand, Julianna Margulies, Pauline Collins, Jennifer Ehle, Elizabeth Spriggs, Tessa Humphries, Sab Shimono, Cate Blanchett, Wendy Hughes, Johanna Ter Steege, Pamela Rabe, Clyde Kusatsu, Stan(ford) Egi, Susie Porter, Lisa Hensley, Penne Hackforth-Jones, Pauline Chan; ***D:*** Bruce Beresford; ***W:*** Bruce Beresford, David Giles, Martin Meader; ***C:*** Peter James; ***M:*** Margareth Dryburgh, Ross Edwards.

Paradise, Texas **2005 (PG)** Mack Cameron (Bottoms) is an action actor whose career has faded, which is why he agrees to star in an indie drama being made in his Texas hometown. Mack also hopes that bringing his family along will help him reestablish the bonds with his wife (Baxter) and sons. He even mentors his star-struck young co-star (Estus), until a professional setback turns Mack into a morose drunk who needs some tough love (personal and professional). **90m/C DVD.** Timothy Bottoms, Meredith Baxter, Sheryl Lee, Polly Bergen, Ben Estus, Rider Strong, Brandon Smith; ***D:*** Lorraine Senna; ***W:*** Joe Conway; ***C:*** Shane F. Kelley; ***M:*** Jay Ferguson.

A Paradise Under the Stars *Un Paraiso Bajo las Estrellas* **1999** Sissy wants to perform at Cuba's Tropicana nightclub, just as her mother did, but her strict father Candido forbids it. But Sissy has more problems when she discover her new lover Sergio may also be her brother! Spanish with subtitles. **90m/C VHS, DVD.** *CU SP* Vladimir Cruz, Thais Valdes, Enrique Molina, Amparo Munoz, Daisy Granados, Litico Rodriguez, Satiago Alfonso, Jacqueline Arenal; ***D:*** Gerardo Chijona; ***W:*** Gerardo Chijona, Senel Paz; ***C:*** Raul Perez Ureta; ***M:*** Carlos Faruolo.

Paradisio 1/2 **1961 (R)** Dying inventor wills Oxford professor an authentic pair of X-ray specs. Spies come gunning for the professor, chasing him through Europe. Doc keeps forgetting he's being chased while using the special specs to see (sometimes in 3-D) through the clothing of young women. Meager plot does not get in way of 3-D nudie exploitation. **82m/C VHS.** Arthur Howard, Eva Waegner; ***D:*** Jacques Henrici; ***W:*** Jacques Henrici; ***M:*** John Bath.

The Parallax View 1/2 **1974 (R)** Lee (Prentiss) was a witness to the assassination of a senator and is worried for her own safety, so she goes to newspaper reporter Joe Frady (Beatty) with her fears. He becomes suspicious after her alleged suicide and starts to investigate, discovering a mysterious corporation that hires assassins. As Joe digs deeper and deeper, he uncovers more than he bargained for and becomes a pawn in the conspirators' further plans. Beatty is excellent and the conspiracy is never less than believable. A lesser-known, compelling political thriller that deserves to be more widely seen. Based on the novel by Loren Singer. **102m/C VHS, DVD.** Warren Beatty, Hume Cronyn, William Daniels, Paula Prentiss, Kenneth Mars, Bill McKinney, Anthony Zerbe, Walter McGinn, Kelly Thordsen; ***D:*** Alan J. Pakula; ***W:*** David Giler, Lorenzo Semple Jr.; ***C:*** Gordon Willis; ***M:*** Michael Small. Natl. Soc. Film Critics '74: Cinematog.

Parallel Corpse **1983** A mortuary attendant finds a murder victim hidden in a coffin and blackmails the remorseless killer. **89m/C VHS.** Buster Larsen, Jorgen Kiil, Agneta Ekmanner, Masja Dessau; ***D:*** Hans-Erik Philip, Soren Melson; ***W:*** Hans-Erik Philip, Soren Melson; ***C:*** Henning Kristiansen; ***M:*** Hans-Erik Philip.

Parallel Lives 1/2 **1994 (R)** Sorority sisters and frat brothers (and their various spouses and lovers), from the classes of both 1948 and 1973, gather for an on-campus weekend reunion and discover old and new jealousies, rivalries, and lots of lust (requited and not). There's also an unexpected death and a police investigation as well. Director Yellen had her cast improvise much of their dialogue—the same method she used in "Chantilly Lace." **105m/C VHS.** James Belushi, James Brolin, LeVar Burton, Lindsay Crouse, Jill Eikenberry, Ben Gazzara, Jack Klugman, David Lansbury, Liza Minnelli, Dudley Moore, Gena Rowlands, Ally Sheedy, Helen Slater, Mira Sorvino, Paul Sorvino, Robert Wagner, Patricia Wettig, JoBeth Williams, Treat Williams; ***D:*** Linda Yellen; ***W:*** Gisella Bernice; ***M:*** Patrick Seymour. **CABLE**

Parallel Sons **1995** No-budget first feature from Young has an awkward construction but a couple of fine performances. Teen Seth (Mick) lives in a conservative upstate New York farming community—exactly the wrong place for a young white man with a penchant for black culture and both artistic and homosexual desires. He's working at the local diner, which just happens to get held up by Knowledge (Mason), a black con shot during an escape from the local prison. Seth shelters Knowledge, whose hostility is gradually overcome by both Seth's concern and a mutual sexual attraction. However, more plot complications lead to melodrama. **93m/C VHS, DVD.** Heather Gottlieb, Gabriel Mick, Laurence Mason, Murphy Guyer, Graham Alex Johnson; ***D:*** John G. Young; ***W:*** John G. Young; ***C:*** Matt Howe; ***M:*** E.D. Menasche.

Paramedics 1/2 **1988 (PG-13)** A motley crew of cavorting paramedics battle their evil captain. Another parody of people in uniform. A comedy with little pulse. **91m/C VHS.** George Newbern, Christopher McDonald, John P. Ryan, Ray Walston, Lawrence-Hilton Jacobs; ***D:*** Stuart Margolin.

Paranoia *Orgasmo; A Beautiful Place to Kill; A Quiet Place to Kill* **1969** Beautiful jet-set widow is trapped in her own Italian villa by a young couple who drug her to get her to perform in various sex orgies, which are probably the most interesting part of this muddled affair. **94m/C VHS.** *IT* Carroll Baker, Lou Castel, Colette Descombes; ***D:*** Umberto Lenzi.

Paranoia **1998 (R)** An imprisoned killer uses a computer to harass the surviving member of the family he murdered. **86m/C VHS, DVD.** Larry Drake, Sally Kirkland, Scott Valentine, Brigitte Bako; ***D:*** Larry Brand; ***W:*** Larry Brand; ***M:*** Martin Trum. **VIDEO**

Paranoia 1.0 *One Point O* **2004 (R)** Computer programmer Simon J (Sisto) keeps finding mysterious empty packages left in his rundown apartment. Are the boxes really empty? (Maybe they contain an airborne contaminant.) Is one of his freaky neighbors leaving them? Is Simon J just nuts? Well, he's paranoid and having hallucinations, so he's got a reason. Note the tagline: "Are you infected?" **92m/C DVD.** *RO IC US* Jeremy Sisto, Deborah Kara Unger, Lance Henriksen, Udo Kier, Eugene Byrd, Bruce

Payne, Richard Rees; *D:* Jeff Renfroe, Marteinn Thorsson; *W:* Jeff Renfroe, Marteinn Thorsson; *C:* Christopher Soos; *M:* Terry Huud.

Paranoiac 🦴🦴 1/2 **1962** Greed and terror set in a country mansion. Simon (Reed) wants the family inheritance all to himself even if it means driving sister Eleanor (Scott) insane. This may not be so hard—she's claiming to see their dead brother Tony. Surprise! Tony (Davion) shows up (really throwing Simon for a loop). Reed's evil is tinged with humor although the numerous plot twists can get confusing. First directorial effort for cinematographer Francis. **80m/B VHS, DVD.** *GB* Oliver Reed, Janette Scott, Alex Davion, Liliane Brousse, Sheila Burrell, Maurice Denham; *D:* Freddie Francis; *W:* Jimmy Sangster; *C:* Arthur Grant; *M:* Elisabeth Lutyens.

Paranoid Park 🦴🦴 1/2 **2007 (R)** A security guard is murdered at Portland, Oregon's famous skater hangout, Paranoid Park, and police hone in on high school student Alex (Nevins) as a suspect. But that's just one of Alex's problems; he has schoolwork, his girlfriend (Momsen), his social life, and the fallout of his parents' divorce to deal with as well. As the investigation continues, the pieces fall into place both for viewers and for Alex, who finds his own outlets to cope with the consequences of his actions. Clean 35-millimeter is interspersed with grainy Super-8 footage of Alex and friends at the skate park, and a mostly newcomer cast is a plus, giving the teen characters a natural, easy credibility. But with its dark, ambivalent tone, it's hardly the usual teen skating flick. **90m/C DVD.** *US* Taylor Momsen, Scott Green, Gabe Nevins, Lauren McKinney, Jake Miller, Richard Lu; *D:* Gus Van Sant; *W:* Gus Van Sant; *C:* Christopher Doyle, Rain Kathy Li.

Paranormal Activity 🦴🦴🦴 **2009 (R)** Katie (Featherston) and Micah (Sloat) are an otherwise boring, argumentative young couple—except when night comes around and bizarre otherworldly things start happening. A skeptical and ornery Micah sets up a camera to basically shut Katie up, and Katie's admission that this isn't the first supernatural episode in her lifetime doesn't help matters. While obviously inspired by "The Blair Witch Project," director Peli used his low budget (only $15,000), low special effects, and low gore to go higher on the scare factor. At times slow-moving, the "found" footage and the unknown leads more than make up for the pace. A clever online marketing campaign got the flick off college campuses and into mainstream theaters and probable cult classic status. **99m/C DVD.** Katie Featherston, Micah Sloat, Michael Bayouth, Amber Armstrong, Mark Fredrichs, Ashley Palmer, Randy McDowell, Tim Piper, Crystal Cartwright; *D:* Oren Peli; *W:* Oren Peli.

Parasite WOOF! **1982 (R)** A small town is beset by giant parasites. An "Alien" ripoff originally filmed in 3-D, during that technique's brief return in the early '80s. Bad films like this killed it both the first and second times. An unpardonable mess that comes off as a stinky sixth-grade film project. **90m/C VHS, DVD.** Bob Glaudini, Demi Moore, Luca Bercovici, Cherie Currie, Gale Robbins, James Davidson, Al Fann, Cheryl "Rainbeaux" Smith, Vivian Blaine; *D:* Charles Band; *W:* Alan J. Adler, Frank Levering, Michael Shoob; *C:* Mac Ahlberg; *M:* Richard Band.

Parasite 🦴 1/2 **2003 (R)** Ah, the far reaches of the North Sea...what a perfect spot to gather a team of engineers on an old oil rig to test out some cleaning fluid. But those pesky environmental do-gooders have to come and ruin the fun by hijacking the rig and holding them captive. Then to really top things off there's the parasite that's absolutely famished and happy to see so many items on the menu. **93m/C VHS, DVD.** *GB* Saskia Gould, Conrad Whitaker, G.W. Stevens, Gary Condes, Margaret Thompson, Oliver Price, Michell Acuna; *D:* Andrew Prendergast; *W:* Andrew Prendergast, Alan Coulson, Paul Mackman; *C:* Tom Wright; *M:* Tom Bible. **VIDEO**

Parasite Eve 🦴🦴🦴 **1997** Hiroshi Mikami stars as Dr. Nagashima, a scientist who has discovered that mitochondria, the organisms which provide energy for cells, appear to have their own DNA and life-cycle. Nagashima has put this theory to work in his research, as he attempts to cure diseases in lab animals, using the mitochondrian energy. When Nagashima's young wife Kiyomi (Riona Hakuzi) is killed in an auto accident, Nagashima takes her liver in order to try and clone her, once again, using the energy of the mitochondria. He doesn't realize is that her death may be the first step in an evolutionary leap, in which the mitochondria will rise up and dominate the world. **120m/C DVD.** *JP* Hiroshi Mikami, Riona Hakuzi, Tomoko Nakajima; *D:* Masayuki Ochiai.

Pardners 🦴🦴 1/2 **1956** Spoiled New York millionaire (Lewis) becomes the sheriff of small western town, with Martin as a ranch foreman. The two team up to rid the town of bad guys and romance two local cuties. Western spoof (with music) is a remake of 1936's "Rhythm on the Range." ♫ Buckskin Beauty; Pardners; The Wind! The Wind!; Me 'N You 'N the Moon. **88m/C VHS, DVD.** Jerry Lewis, Dean Martin, Lori Nelson, Jackie Loughery, Jeff Morrow, John Baragrey, Agnes Moorehead, Lon Chaney Jr., Milton Frome, Lee Van Cleef, Jack Elam, Bob Steele, Emory Parnell; *D:* Norman Taurog; *W:* Sidney Sheldon, Jerry Davis.

Pardon Mon Affaire 🦴🦴🦴 *Un Elephant a Trompe Enormement* **1976 (PG)** When a middle-aged civil servant gets a look at a model in a parking garage, he decides it's time to cheat on his wife. Enjoyable French farce. Re-made as in the United States "The Woman in Red" and followed by "Pardon Mon Affair, Too!" Subtitled. **107m/C VHS.** *FR* Jean Rochefort, Claude Brasseur, Guy Bedos, Victor Lanoux, Daniele Delorme, Martine Sarcey, Anny (Annie Legras) Duperey; *D:* Yves Robert; *M:* Vladimir Cosma. Cesar '77: Support. Actor (Brasseur).

Pardon Mon Affaire, Too! 🦴🦴 1/2 *We Will All Meet in Paradise* **1977** Pale sequel to the first popular French comedy, "Pardon Mon Affair." This time the four fantasy-minded buddies withstand the trials of marriage and middle-class life. With English subtitles or dubbed. **105m/C VHS.** *FR* Jean Rochefort, Claude Brasseur, Guy Bedos; *D:* Yves Robert; *M:* Vladimir Cosma.

Pardon My Gun 🦴 1/2 **1930** Cowpoke falls for the boss' daughter but has a rival in a wealthy rancher, who isn't above sabotage to get the girl. **64m/B VHS.** Tom Keene, Harry Woods, Sally Starr, Lee Moran, Mona Ray; *D:* Robert De Lacy; *W:* Hugh Cummings.

Pardon My Sarong 🦴🦴 1/2 **1942** Bud and Lou star as Chicago bus drivers who end up shipwrecked on a South Pacific island when they get involved with notorious jewel thieves. The island natives think Lou is a god! Standard Abbott & Costello fare. **83m/B VHS, DVD.** Bud Abbott, Lou Costello, Virginia Bruce, Robert Paige, Lionel Atwill, Leif Erickson, William Demarest, Samuel S. Hinds; *D:* Erle C. Kenton; *C:* Milton Krasner.

Pardon My Trunk 🦴🦴 *Hello Elephant; Bvongiorno, Elefante* **1952** Struggling against poverty on his teacher's salary, a man and his family receive a gift from a Hindu prince—an elephant. De Sica carries this silly premise beyond mere slapstick. Dubbed. **85m/B VHS.** *IT* Sabu, Vittorio De Sica; *D:* Gianni Franciolini.

Pardon Us 🦴🦴 1/2 *Jail Birds* **1931** Laurel and Hardy are thrown into prison for bootlegging. Plot meanders along aimlessly, but the duo have some inspired moments. The first Laurel and Hardy feature. **78m/B VHS, DVD.** Stan Laurel, Oliver Hardy, June Marlowe, James Finlayson; *D:* James Parrott.

The Parent Trap 🦴🦴 1/2 **1961** Mills plays a dual role in this heartwarming comedy as twin sisters Susan and Sharon, who were separated at birth by their divorcing parents Mitch (Keith) and Maggie (O'Hara), discover each other during a stay a summer camp. They decide to switch lives and when they realize that dear old dad is about to get married to just the wrong woman (Barnes), the twins conspire to bring their divorced parents back together. Well-known Disney fluff. Followed by several made-for-TV sequels featuring the now grown-up twins (Mills reprised her role). **127m/C VHS, DVD.** Hayley Mills, Maureen O'Hara, Brian Keith, Charlie Ruggles, Una Merkel, Leo G. Carroll, Joanna Barnes, Cathleen Nesbitt, Ruth McDevitt; *D:* David Swift; *W:* David Swift; *C:* Lucien Ballard; *M:* Paul J. Smith.

The Parent Trap 🦴🦴 1/2 **1998 (PG)** Updated remake of Disney's 1961 family film about long-separated identical twins, Hallie and Annie (both played by Lohan), who meet accidentally at camp and decide to reunite their divorced parents. Quaid is Napa vineyard-owning dad while Richardson is London fashion designer mom. The twins switch places and foil gold digging publicist Meredith (Hendrix) in order to get their parents back together. Since it's both Disney and a remake, you can assume that it works. However, it's doubtful that parents that don't even tell their kid that they have a twin are going to be winning any PTA awards. "Let's Get Together," the song that the guitar strummin' Hayley Mills made popular with the original, makes a cameo in an elevator. **128m/C VHS, DVD.** Dennis Quaid, Natasha Richardson, Lindsay Lohan, Polly Holliday, Elaine Hendrix, Joanna Barnes, Ronnie Stevens, Lisa Ann Walter, Simon Kunz, Maggie Wheeler; *D:* Nancy Meyers; *W:* Nancy Meyers, Charles Shyer, David Swift; *C:* Dean Cundey; *M:* Alan Silvestri.

Parental Guidance 🦴🦴 *Kinfolks* **1998 (R)** Sean (Lee) is part of a crazy extended family in South Central L.A. who is reluctant to bring his upscale girlfreind Lisa (Johnson) home for the family's Christmas dinner. **87m/C VHS, DVD.** Maia Campbell, Stacii Jae Johnson, Casey Lee; *D:* A.M. Cali; *W:* A.M. Cali; *C:* Scott Edelstein; *M:* Horace Washington.

Parenthood 🦴🦴🦴 **1989 (PG-13)** Four grown siblings and their parents struggle with various levels of parenthood. From the college drop-out, to the nervous single mother, to the yuppie couple raising an overachiever, every possibility is explored, including the perspective from the older generation, portrayed by Robards. Genuinely funny with dramatic moments that work most of the time, with an affecting performance from Martin and Wiest. Director Howard has four kids and was inspired to make this film when on a European jaunt with them. **124m/C VHS, DVD.** Steve Martin, Mary Steenburgen, Dianne Wiest, Martha Plimpton, Keanu Reeves, Tom Hulce, Jason Robards Jr., Rick Moranis, Harley Jane Kozak, Joaquin Rafael (Leaf) Phoenix, Paul (Link) Linke, Dennis Dugan; *D:* Ron Howard; *W:* Ron Howard, Lowell Ganz, Babaloo Mandel; *C:* Donald McAlpine; *M:* Randy Newman.

Parents 🦴🦴🦴 **1989 (R)** Dark satire of middle class suburban life in the '50s, centering on a young boy who discovers that his parents aren't getting their meat from the local butcher. Gives new meaning to leftovers and boasts a very disturbing barbecue scene. Balaban's debut is a strikingly visual and creative gorefest with definite cult potential. The eerie score is by Badalamenti, who also composed the music for "Blue Velvet," "Wild at Heart," and "Twin Peaks." **81m/C VHS, DVD.** Randy Quaid, Mary Beth Hurt, Bryan Madorsky, Sandy Dennis, Kathryn Grody, Deborah Rush, Graham Jarvis, Juno Mills-Cockell; *D:* Bob Balaban; *W:* Christopher Hawthorne; *C:* Robin Vidgeon, Ernest Day; *M:* Angelo Badalamenti, Jonathan Elias, Sherman Foote.

Paris **2008 (R)** Professional chorus dancer Pierre (Duris) is forced to quit his cabaret job because of heart problems. His frumpy social worker sister Elise (Binoche) agrees to help him out while Pierre tries to decide what to do next. Mostly he either stares out his window or interacts with various Parisian characters while wandering the streets. English and French with subtitles. **128m/C DVD.** *FR* Melanie Laurent, Francois Cluzet.

Paris Belongs to Us 🦴🦴 1/2 *Paris Nous Appartient; Paris is Ours* **1960** An early entry in the French "new wave" of naturalistic cinema, this psychological mystery drama has a woman investigating a suicide linked to a possible worldwide conspiracy. Interesting, if somewhat dated by Cold War elements. **120m/B VHS.** *FR* Jean-Claude Brialy, Betty Schneider, Gianni Esposito, Francoise Prevost; *D:* Jacques Rivette; *W:* Jacques Rivette, Jean Gruault.

Paris Blues 🦴🦴 1/2 **1961** Two jazz musicians, one white, one black, strive for success in Paris and become involved with American tourists who want to take them back to the States. Score by Duke Ellington and an appearance by Armstrong make it a must-see for jazz fans. **100m/B VHS.** Paul Newman, Sidney Poitier, Joanne Woodward, Diahann Carroll, Louis Armstrong, Barbara Lange; *D:* Martin Ritt; *W:* Jack Sher, Walter Bernstein; *M:* Duke Ellington.

Paris Express 🦴🦴 1/2 *The Man Who Watched Trains Go By* **1953** When a man steals money from his employer, he boards the Paris Express to escape from the police. A bit convoluted, but well acted. Based on the George Simenon novel. **82m/C VHS.** Claude Rains, Herbert Lom, Felix Aylmer, Marius Goring, Anouk Aimee, Marta Toren; *D:* Harold French; *W:* Paul Jarrico.

Paris, France 🦴🦴 **1994 (NC-17)** Lucy (Hope) is a frustrated writer, living in Toronto, who decides the pursuit of sexual passion will unleash her blocked creative urges. Her main partner is poet Sloan (Outerbridge), the young man Lucy is trying to fashion in the image of a deceased Parisian lover, and also the man whose poetry her husband (and publisher) Michael (Ertmanis) is promoting. Lots of self-delusion and literary pretensions as well as erotic grappling. Adapted from the novel by Tom Walmsley. **111m/C VHS, DVD.** *CA* Leslie Hope, Peter Outerbridge, Victor Ertmanis, Raoul Trujillo, Dan Lett; *D:* Gerard Ciccoritti; *W:* Tom Walmsley; *M:* John McCarthy.

Paris Holiday 🦴🦴 1/2 **1957** An actor heading for Paris to buy a noted author's latest screenplay finds mystery and romance. Entertaining chase scenes as the characters try to find the elusive script. **100m/C VHS, DVD.** Bob Hope, Fernandel, Anita Ekberg, Martha Hyer, Preston Sturges; *D:* Gerd Oswald; *W:* Edmund Beloin, Dean Reisner; *C:* Roger Hubert.

Paris in Spring 🦴🦴 1/2 **1935** Romance, Paris, springtime... ahhhh. But love in the air leads to heartbreak when Simone (Ellis) breaks it off with Paul de Lille (Carminati) because she's not into the whole marriage thing. Meanwhile Mignon (Lupino) and Albert (Blakely) call it splits for exactly the same reason. **82m/B VHS.** Mary Ellis, Tullio Carminati, Ida Lupino, Lynne Overman, James Blakely, Jessie Ralph; *D:* Lewis Milestone; *W:* Franz Schulze, Samuel Hoffenstein.

Paris Is Burning 🦴🦴🦴 **1991 (R)** Livingston's documentary portrayal of New York City's transvestite balls where men dress up, dance, and compete in various categories. Filmed between 1985 and 1989, this is a compelling look at a subculture of primarily black and Hispanic men and the one place they can truly be themselves. Madonna noted this look and attitude (much watered down) in her song "Vogue." **71m/C VHS.** Dorian Corey, Pepper Labeija, Venus Xtravaganza, Octavia St. Laurant, Willi Ninja, Anji Xtravaganza, Freddie Pendavis, Junior Labeija; *D:* Jennie Livingston; *C:* Paul Gibson. Natl. Soc. Film Critics '91: Feature Doc.; Sundance '91: Grand Jury Prize.

Paris, je t'aime 🦴🦴 *Paris, I Love You* **2006 (R)** Eighteen—count 'em—eighteen uneven vignettes by 20 international directors all set in various Parisian neighborhoods. Some are little slice of life tales while others are fantasies (vampires?). Some are about love and some about friendship and some are serious while some are lighthearted. All are so brief that if one doesn't strike your fancy, the next one may, especially given the variety of the cast. English and French with subtitles. **120m/C DVD.** *FR SI* Leila Bekhti, Marianne Faithfull, Elias McConnell, Gaspard Ulliel, Steve Buscemi, Catalina Sandino Moreno, Barbet Schroeder, Sergio Castellitto, Miranda Richardson, Leonor Watling, Juliette Binoche, Willem Dafoe, Hippolyte Girardot, Yolande Moreau, Nick Nolte, Ludivine Sagnier, Bob Hoskins, Fanny Ardant, Maggie Gyllenhaal, Aissa Maiga, Elijah Wood, Emily Mortimer, Rufus Sewell, Natalie Portman, Melchior Beslon, Gerard Depardieu, Ben Gazzara, Gena Rowlands, Margo Martindale, Bruno Podalydes, Florence Muller, Cyril Descours, Julie Bataille, Axel Kiener, Li Xin, Paul Putner, Lionel Dray, Seydou Boro, Olga Kurylenko; *D:* Gerard Depardieu, Gurinder Chadha, Gus Van Sant, Joel Coen, Ethan Coen, Walter Salles, Daniela Thomas, Christopher Doyle, Isabel Coixet, Sylvain Chomet, Alfonso Cuaron, Richard LaGravenese, Olivier Assayas, Oliver Schmitz, Vincenzo Natali, Wes Craven, Alexander Payne, Tom Tykwer, Noburhiro Suwa; *W:* Gurinder Chadha, Gus Van Sant, Joel Coen, Ethan Coen, Walter Salles, Daniela Thomas,

Christopher Doyle, Isabel Coixet, Sylvain Chomet, Alfonso Cuaron, Richard LaGravenese, Olivier Assayas, Oliver Schmitz, Vincenzo Natali, Wes Craven, Alexander Payne, Tom Tykwer, Noburhiro Suwa; ***C:*** Christopher Doyle, Mathieu Poirot-Delpech, Pascal Rabaud, Bruno Delbonnel, Eric Gautier, Jean-Claude Larrieu, Pascal Marti, Eric Guichard, Gerard Sterin, Michel Amathieu, Michael Seresin, Pierre Aim, J. Eddie Peck, Tetsuo Nagata, David Quesemand, Frank Greibe; ***M:*** Tom Tykwer, Michael Andrews, Reinhold Heil, Johnny Klimek.

Paris, Texas ½ **1983 (PG)** After four years a drifter returns to find his son is being raised by his brother because the boy's mother has also disappeared. He tries to reconnect with the boy. Introspective script acclaimed by many film critics, but others found it to be too slow. **145m/C VHS, DVD.** *FR GE* Harry Dean Stanton, Nastassja Kinski, Dean Stockwell, Hunter Carson, Aurore Clement; ***D:*** Wim Wenders; ***W:*** Sam Shepard, L.M. Kit Carson; ***M:*** Ry Cooder. British Acad. '84: Director (Wenders); Cannes '84: Film.

Paris 36 ½ *Faubourg 36* **2008 (PG-13)** Old-fashioned musical drama about workers' rights and politics in 1930s Paris. Labor/management tensions escalate after the Popular Front left-wing party is elected. Working-class stage manager Germain Pigoli (Jugnot) is distraught when scheming bigwig Galapiat (Donnadieu) closes down the theater but he manages to reopen it with the help of a couple of performers and a political activist. French with subtitles. **120m/C DVD.** *FR* Gerard Jugnot, Barnard Pierre Donnadieu, Kad Merad, Clovis Cornillac, Elisabeth Vitali, Maxence Perrin, Nora Arnezeder; ***D:*** Christophe Barratier; ***W:*** Christophe Barratier; ***C:*** Tom Stern.

Paris Trout ½ **1991 (R)** Believing himself above the law, southern Trout (Hopper) shoots the mother and sister of a young black man who reneged on his IOU. Lawyer Harris is forced to defend a man he knows deserves to be punished, and wife Hershey suffers long. Adapted by Pete Dexter from his National Book Award-winning novel. **98m/C VHS.** Dennis Hopper, Barbara Hershey, Ed Harris, Tina Lifford, Darnita Henry, Eric Ware, Ray McKinnon; ***D:*** Stephen Gyllenhaal; ***W:*** Pete Dexter; ***C:*** Robert Elswit. **CABLE**

Paris When It Sizzles **1964** A screenwriter and his secretary fall in love while working on a film in Paris, confusing themselves with the script's characters. Star-studded cast deserves better than this lame script. Shot on location in Paris. Holden's drinking—he ran into a brick wall while under the influence—and some unresolved romantic tension between him and Hepburn affected shooting. Dietrich, Sinatra, Astaire, Ferrer, and Curtis show up for a party on the set. **110m/C VHS, DVD.** William Holden, Audrey Hepburn, Gregoire Aslan, Raymond Bussieres, Tony Curtis, Fred Astaire, Frank Sinatra, Noel Coward, Marlene Dietrich, Mel Ferrer; ***D:*** Richard Quine; ***W:*** George Axelrod; ***C:*** Charles B(ryant) Lang Jr.; ***M:*** Nelson Riddle.

Parisian Love **1925** Marie (Bow) is a streetwise Paris urchin who makes her living by fleecing the tourists. When her lover Armand (Keith) is shot, Marie vows revenge on the culprit, wealthy Pierre Marcel (Tellegen). With the help of some underworld friends, Marie transforms herself into a beauty in order to seduce Pierre. **62m/B VHS, DVD.** Clara Bow, Donald Keith, Lou Tellegen, Lillian (Lillianne, Lyllian) Leighton; ***D:*** Louis Gasnier; ***W:*** Lois Hutchinson; ***C:*** Allen Siegler.

Park Avenue Logger ½ **1937** Silly story has blue-blood Ingraham believing son O'Brien is a panty-waist, so he sends him to a lumber camp to prove his manhood. But junior is actually a wrestling champ (known as The Masked Marvel) and manages just fine, even winning the gal. **65m/B VHS.** George O'Brien, Beatrice Roberts, Lloyd Ingraham, Ward Bond, Willard Robertson, Bert Hanlon; ***D:*** David Howard.

The Park Is Mine **1985** A deranged and desperate Vietnam vet takes hostages in Central Park. Semi-infamous film, notable for being the first movie made for HBO, and for being filmed in Toronto, before the inexpensive practice of filming in Canada became widespread. **102m/C VHS.** Tommy Lee Jones, Yaphet Kotto, Helen Shaver; ***D:*** Steven Hilliard Stern; ***M:*** Tangerine Dream. **CABLE**

Parker **1984** An executive is kidnapped, then released, but does not know why. Unable to live with the mystery, he tracks his kidnappers down into a world of blackmail, drugs, and intrigue. **100m/C VHS.** *GB* Cherie Lunghi, Elizabeth Spriggs, Bob Peck, Bryan Brown, Kurt Raab; ***D:*** Jim Goddard; ***W:*** Trevor Preston; ***C:*** Peter Jessop; ***M:*** Richard Hartley.

Parlor, Bedroom and Bath *Romeo in Pyjamas* **1931** A family tries to keep a young woman from seeing that her love interest is flirting with other prospects. Doesn't live up to the standard Keaton set in his silent films. Keaton spoke French and German for foreign versions. **75m/B VHS, DVD.** Buster Keaton, Charlotte Greenwood, Cliff Edwards, Reginald Denny; ***D:*** Edward Sedgwick.

Parole, Inc. **1949** FBI takes on the underground in this early crime film. Criminals on parole have not served their sentences, and the mob is responsible. A meagerly financed yawner. **71m/B VHS, DVD.** Michael O'Shea, Evelyn Ankers, Turhan Bey, Lyle Talbot; ***D:*** Alfred Zeisler.

Paroled to Die ½ **1937** A man frames a young rancher for a bank robbery and a murder he committed in this wild west saga. Predictable and bland. **66m/B VHS, DVD.** Karl Hackett, Horace Murphy, Steve Clark, Bob Steele, Kathleen Elliott; ***D:*** Sam Newfield; ***W:*** George Plympton; ***C:*** Robert E. Cline.

Parrish ½ **1961** Parrish McLean (Donohue) is a very ambitious young man, determined to make it in the rich world of the tobacco growers of the Connecticut River Valley. But his ruthless tobacco king stepfather (Malden) would like to thwart his plans. As befits Donohue's teen idol status, he also gets to romance three beautiful girls. Very silly and much too long. Based on the novel by Mildred Savage. **138m/C VHS.** Troy Donahue, Claudette Colbert, Karl Malden, Dean Jagger, Diane McBain, Connie Stevens, Sharon Hugueny, Dub Taylor, Hampton Fancher, Bibi Osterwald, Madeline Sherwood, Sylvia Miles, Carroll O'Connor, Vincent Gardenia; ***D:*** Delmer Daves; ***W:*** Delmer Daves; ***C:*** Harry Stradling Sr.; ***M:*** Max Steiner.

Parting Glances **1986 (R)** Low-budget but acclaimed film shows the relationship between two gay men and how they deal with a close friend's discovery of his exposure to the AIDS virus. Touching and realistic portrayals make this a must see. In 1990 Sherwood died of AIDS without completing any other films. **90m/C VHS, DVD.** John Bolger, Richard Ganoung, Steve Buscemi, Adam Nathan, Patrick Tull, Kathy Kinney; ***D:*** Bill Sherwood; ***W:*** Bill Sherwood; ***C:*** Jacek Laskus.

Parting Shots ½ **1998** Harry's feeling like a bunch of folks have done him wrong—from his ex-wife to his thieving best buddy to the local chef—so once he learns he's only got six weeks to live, he aims to settle the score...with a gun. "Death Wish" director Winner shoots for edgy humor but misses. **98m/C VHS, DVD.** Chris Rea, Felicity Kendal, Bob Hoskins, Ben Kingsley, Joanna Lumley, Oliver Reed, Diana Rigg, John Cleese, Gareth Hunt, Peter Davison, Patrick Ryecart, Edward Hardwicke, Nicholas Gecks, Ruby Snape, Nicola Bryant, Brian Poyser, Nicky Henson, Caroline Langrishe, Taryn Kay, Alison Reynolds, Roland Curram, Craig Jelley, Jenny Logan, Sarah Reeves, Anthony Smee, Donald Standen, Nathan Weaver; ***D:*** Michael Winner; ***W:*** Michael Winner, Nick Mead; ***C:*** Ousama Rawi; ***M:*** Chris Rea, Chris Rea, Les Reed. **VIDEO**

Partition **2007** Predictable historical romance/drama. Gian Singh (Mistry) is an ex-soldier from a Sikh regiment who fought for the Brits in WWII. In 1947, when India and Pakistan have become separate countries, Gian watches the violent upheavals from his Punjab village and then rescues Muslim refugee Naseem (Kruek) from an angry mob. The two fall in love and marry despite the religious complications but Naseem eventually hears word of her family in Pakistan and goes to see them. Her brothers are horrified that she's married an enemy and hold her prisoner, which causes more trouble when Gian travels to bring his wife home. **115m/C DVD.** *CA* Jimi Mistry, Kristin Kreuk, Neve Campbell, John Light, Madhur Jaffrey, Irfan Khan, Jesse Moss; ***D:*** Vic Sarin; ***W:*** Vic Sarin, Patricia Finn; ***C:*** Vic Sarin; ***M:*** Brian Tyler.

Partner **1968** An extremely shy young man invents a strong alter ego to cope with the world but this second personality comes to dominate—with tragic results. In Italian with English subtitles. **110m/C VHS, DVD.** *IT* Pierre Clementi, Stefania Sandrelli, Tina Aumont; ***D:*** Bernardo Bertolucci; ***M:*** Ennio Morricone.

Partners **1982 (R)** A straight, macho cop must pose as the lover of a gay cop to investigate the murder of a gay man in Los Angeles' homosexual community. Sets out to parody "Cruising"; unfortunately, the only source of humor the makers could find was in ridiculous homosexual stereotypes that are somewhat offensive and often unfunny. **93m/C VHS.** Ryan O'Neal, John Hurt, Kenneth McMillan, Robyn Douglass, Jay Robinson, Rick Jason; ***D:*** James Burrows; ***W:*** Francis Veber; ***M:*** Georges Delerue.

Partners **1999 (R)** All of the usual suspects are rounded up for this action comedy. Mild-mannered Bob (Paymer) steals a super-secret computer program from his company. Then it's stolen from him by hunky thief Axel (Van Dien). A series of double-crosses and chases—involving the obligatory Caddy convertible—ensue. Toss in the sexy girlfriend (Angel) and a cheap L.A. motel with a heart-shaped bed. **90m/C VHS, DVD.** Casper Van Dien, Vanessa Angel, David Paymer, Jenifer Lewis, Yuji Okumoto, Donna Pescow; ***D:*** Joey Travolta; ***W:*** Jeff Ferrell; ***C:*** Kristian Bernier; ***M:*** Jeff Lass.

Partners in Crime **1999 (R)** Local detective Gene Reardon (Hauer) is assigned to investigate the kidnapping of a wealthy man from a small town. But soon the FBI is called in, including Reardon's ex-wife Wallis Longworth (Porizkova). Then the victim turns up dead on Reardon's property and he's suddenly suspect numero uno. Since Wallis doesn't think Gene's guilty, she decides to secretly help him prove who really done it. **90m/C VHS, DVD.** Rutger Hauer, Paulina Porizkova, Michael Flynn, Andrew Dolan; ***D:*** Jennifer Warren; ***W:*** Brett Lewis; ***C:*** Stevan Larner. **VIDEO**

Partners of the Trail ½ **1944** U.S. marshals Brown and Hatton try to find out who's murdering ranchers which leads them to gunplay with Ingraham's band of outlaws. **57m/B VHS.** Johnny Mack Brown, Raymond Hatton, Lloyd Ingraham, Christine McIntyre, Robert Frazer; ***D:*** Lambert Hillyer.

The Party **1968** Disaster-prone Indian actor wreaks considerable havoc at a posh Hollywood gathering. Laughs come quickly in this quirky Sellers vehicle. **99m/C VHS, DVD.** Peter Sellers, Claudine Longet, Marge Champion, Sharron Kimberly, Denny Miller, Gavin MacLeod, Carol Wayne; ***D:*** Blake Edwards; ***W:*** Blake Edwards; ***C:*** Lucien Ballard; ***M:*** Henry Mancini.

Party **1996** Leonor (Silveira) and Rogerio (Samora) are having a 10th anniversary party at their seaside villa. As the celebration continues, Leonor is pursued by aging playboy Michel (Piccoli) while her husband stands idly by. Maybe that has something to do with the secret Rogerio's about to reveal. French and Portuguese with subtitles. **91m/C VHS, DVD.** *FR PT* Leonor Silveira, Michel Piccoli, Rogerio Samora, Irene Papas; ***D:*** Manoel de Oliveira; ***W:*** Manoel de Oliveira, Augustina Bessa-Luis; ***C:*** Renato Berta.

Party Animal **1983 (R)** A college stud teaches a shy farm boy a thing or two about the carnal aspects of campus life. **78m/C VHS, DVD.** Timothy Carhart, Matthew Causey, Robin Harlan; ***D:*** David Beaird; ***W:*** David Beaird; ***C:*** Bryan England.

Party Camp **1987 (R)** A rowdy summer camp counselor endeavors to turn a tame backwoods camp into a non-stop party. Late entry in the "Meatballs"-spawned genre fails to do anything of even minor interest. **96m/C VHS.** Andrew Ross, Billy Jacoby, April Wayne, Kirk Cribb; ***D:*** Gary Graver.

Party Favors WOOF! **1989 (R)** Erotic dancing, strip tease acts, and general hilarity are featured in this party tape. **83m/C VHS.** Jeannie Winters, Marjorie Miller, Gail Thackray; ***D:*** Ed Hansen.

Party Girl ½ **1958** A crime drama involving an attorney representing a 1920s crime boss and his henchmen when they run afoul of the law. The lawyer falls in love with a nightclub dancer who successfully encourages him to leave the mob, but not before he is wounded in a gang war attack, arrested, and forced to testify against the mob as a material witness. The mob then takes his girlfriend hostage to prevent his testifying, leading to an exciting climax. Must-see viewing for Charisse's steamy dance numbers. **99m/C VHS.** Robert Taylor, Cyd Charisse, Lee J. Cobb, John Ireland, Kent Smith, Claire Kelly, Corey Allen; ***D:*** Nicholas Ray.

Party Girl ½ **1994 (R)** In the "girls just wanna have fun" category comes this spritely saga of 20-something Manhattan club gal Mary (Posey), who needs some steady income after the cops bust her for throwing an illegal rent party. So, since Mary's godmother is a librarian, she gets a job as a library clerk and discovers the wonders of the Dewey Decimal system (no, I'm not joking but presumably director Mayer is). Parker's Mary is a properly flaunting poseur but a little nightlife tends to go a long way. **94m/C VHS, DVD.** Parker Posey, Omar Townsend, Anthony De Sando, Guillermo Diaz, Sasha von Scherler, Liev Schreiber; ***D:*** Daisy von Scherler Mayer; ***W:*** Harry Birckmayer, Daisy von Scherler Mayer; ***C:*** Michael Slovis; ***M:*** Anton Sanko.

Party Girls ½ **1929** Escort service girls run afoul of the law in this hokey melodrama. **67m/B VHS, DVD.** Douglas Fairbanks Jr., Jeanette Loff, Judith Barrie, Marie Prevost, John St. Polis, Lucien Prival; ***D:*** Victor Halperin.

Party Girls for Sale *Violated; Mannequins for Rio* **1954** Mystery thriller in which a young girl's body is found on the beach in Rio de Janeiro. **80m/B VHS.** *US GE* Raymond Burr, Scott Brady, Johanna (Hannerl) Matz, Kurt Meisel, Gert Frobe; ***D:*** Kurt Neumann; ***W:*** Kurt Neumann; ***C:*** Ekkehard Kyrath; ***M:*** Michael Jary.

Party Incorporated *Party Girls* **1989 (R)** Marilyn Chambers (of "Behind the Green Door" fame) stars as a young widow with a huge tax load who gives parties to pay it off. Also known as "Party Girls." **80m/C VHS.** Marilyn Chambers, Kurt Woodruff, Christine Veronica, Kimberly Taylor; ***D:*** Chuck Vincent.

Party Line **1988 (R)** A veteran police captain and a district attorney team up to track down a pair of killers who find their victims through party lines. **90m/C VHS.** Richard Hatch, Shawn Weatherly, Richard Roundtree, Leif Garrett, Greta Blackburn; ***D:*** William Webb; ***W:*** Richard Brandes.

Party Monster ½ **2003 (R)** Culkin impressively crosses over into on-screen adulthood, starring as Michael Alig, the real-life club kid turned murderer. Alig, a misunderstood kid from Indiana, travels to the Big Apple where he quickly finds his niche in the decadent and flamboyant club scene of NYC circa 1990s. There, he hooks up with mentor James St. James (Green), also a former Midwesterner, who teaches him the ropes. Alig quickly surpasses his master, becoming a celebrated party promoter at the famed disco Limelight. As Michael spirals out of control both in his addictions and emotionally, St. James, as his best friend, attempts to intervene to little avail. Green provides superb support to Culkin's lead. Based on the book "Disco Bloodbath" by St. James. **98m/C VHS, DVD.** *US* Macaulay Culkin, Seth Green, Chloe Sevigny, Natasha Lyonne, Wilson Cruz, Wilmer Valderrama, Dylan McDermott, Justin Hagan, Diana Scarwid, Marilyn Manson; ***D:*** Fenton Bailey, Randy Barbato; ***W:*** Fenton Bailey, Randy Barbato; ***C:*** Teodoro Maniaci; ***M:*** Jimmy Harry.

Party! Party! **1983** A bunch of kids go nuts and have a party when their parents leave. **100m/C VHS.** *GB* Daniel Peacock, Karl Howman, Perry Fenwick, Sean Chapman, Phoebe Nicholls; ***D:*** Terry Winsor; ***W:*** Daniel Peacock, Terry Winsor; ***C:*** Syd Macartney; ***M:*** Sting, David

Bowie, Joe Jackson, Elvis Costello.

Party Plane 🦴 **1990** Softcore fun-fest about a plane full of oversexed stewardesses. **81m/C VHS.** Kent Stoddard, Karen Annarino, John Goff; ***D:*** Ed Hansen.

Party 7 🦴🦴 ½ **2000** A portrait of seven people who are too disturbed to be out running around free, let alone employed by organized crime. In one hotel room is a yakuza goon who has stolen money from his bosses, his girlfriend, her new boyfriend (oops!), a gangster pursuing the stolen money, two peeping toms (one of whom is known as Captain Banana), and an assassin obsessed with plastic models. **104m/C DVD.** *JP* Masatoshi Nagase, Keisuke Horibe, Yoshinori Okada, Tadanobu Asano, Yoshio Harada, Tatsuya Gashuin, Akemi Kobayashi; ***D:*** Katushito Ishii; ***W:*** Katushito Ishii; ***C:*** Hiroshi Machida; ***M:*** James Shimoji.

Pas Tres Catholique 🦴🦴 *Something Fishy* **1993** Pleasant comedy finds 40ish, chain-smoking, unconventional P.I. Maxine (Anemone) investigating her ex-husband for an insurance scam, drawing closer to her estranged son, and trying to decide romantically between long-time friend Florence and handsome economist Jacques. French with subtitles. **100m/B VHS.** *FR* Anemone, Christine Boisson, Michel Didym, Gregoire Colin, Denis Podalydes, Roland Bertin, Bernard Verley, Michel Roux; ***Cameos:*** Micheline Presle; ***D:*** Tonie Marshall; ***W:*** Tonie Marshall; ***C:*** Dominique Chapuis.

Pascali's Island 🦴🦴🦴 ½ **1988 (PG-13)** A Turkish spy becomes involved with an adventurer's plot to steal rare artifacts, then finds himself ensnared in political and personal intrigue. Superior tragedy features excellent performances from Kingsley, Dance, and Mirren. **106m/C VHS.** *GB* Ben Kingsley, Helen Mirren, Charles Dance, Sheila Allen, Vernon Dobtcheff; ***D:*** James Dearden; ***W:*** James Dearden; ***C:*** Roger Deakins; ***M:*** Loek Dikker.

Pass the Ammo 🦴🦴 ½ **1988 (R)** Entertaining comedy about a young couple who attempt to steal back $50,000 of inheritance money that a televangelist swindled from the family. One of the more creative satires on this religious TV phenomenon. **93m/C VHS.** Bill Paxton, Tim Curry, Linda Kozlowski, Annie Potts, Anthony Geary, Dennis Burkley, Glenn Withrow, Richard Paul; ***D:*** David Beaird; ***W:*** Neil Cohen, Joel Cohen; ***M:*** Carter Burwell.

A Passage to India 🦴🦴🦴 **1984 (PG)** An ambitious adaptation of E.M. Forster's complex novel about relations between Brits and Indians in the 1920s. Drama centers on a young British woman's accusations that an Indian doctor raped her while serving as a guide in some rather ominous caves. Film occasionally flags, but is usually compelling. Features particularly strong performances from Bannerjee, Fox, and Davis. **163m/C VHS, DVD, Blu-ray Disc.** *GB* Peggy Ashcroft, Alec Guinness, James Fox, Judy Davis, Victor Banerjee, Nigel Havers; ***D:*** David Lean; ***W:*** David Lean; ***C:*** Ernest Day; ***M:*** Maurice Jarre. Oscars '84: Support. Actress (Ashcroft), Orig. Score; British Acad. '85: Actress (Ashcroft); Golden Globes '85: Foreign Film, Support. Actress (Ashcroft), Score; L.A. Film Critics '84: Support. Actress (Ashcroft); Natl. Bd. of Review '84: Actor (Banerjee), Actress (Ashcroft), Director (Lean); N.Y. Film Critics '84: Actress (Ashcroft), Director (Lean), Film.

Passage to Marseilles 🦴🦴🦴 **1944** Hollywood propaganda in which convicts escape from Devil's Island and help French freedom fighters combat Nazis. Routine but entertaining. What else could it be with Bogart, Raines, Greenstreet, and Lorre, who later made a pretty good film set in Casablanca? **110m/B VHS, DVD.** Humphrey Bogart, Claude Rains, Sydney Greenstreet, Peter Lorre, Helmut Dantine, George Tobias, John Loder, Eduardo Ciannelli, Michele Morgan; ***D:*** Michael Curtiz; ***C:*** James Wong Howe; ***M:*** Max Steiner.

Passed Away 🦴 ½ **1992 (PG-13)** Family patriarch Jack Scanlan dies and his entire family gets together for the funeral and a big Irish wake. The family, of course, is made up of a weird group of characters, good steadfast son Hoskins, dim-witted but good-looking son Petersen, rebellious daughter Reed, and a left-wing nun who works in Central America and is accompanied by an illegal alien (McDormand). Throw in a mysterious female mourner and a pregnant granddaughter who goes into labor at the graveside and you come up with a movie that manages to use every comic death cliche ever imagined. Talented cast is wasted in a movie that should have passed away. **96m/C VHS.** Bob Hoskins, Jack Warden, William L. Petersen, Helen Lloyd Breed, Maureen Stapleton, Pamela Reed, Tim Curry, Peter Riegert, Blair Brown, Patrick Breen, Nancy Travis, Teri Polo, Frances McDormand; ***D:*** Charlie Peters; ***W:*** Charlie Peters; ***C:*** Arthur Albert; ***M:*** Richard Gibbs.

Passenger 🦴🦴🦴 *Pasazerka* **1961** While on a cruise ship Lisa (Slaska), a former camp guard at Auschwitz, realizes that fellow passenger Martha (Ciepielewska) was once one of her prisoners. Their meeting triggers a series of flashbacks to the Holocaust and to domination, suffering, and resistance. Director Munk was killed in a car crash during filming, which was completed by his colleague Witold Lesiewicz. Based on the novel by Zofia Posmysz-Piasecka; Polish with subtitles. **63m/B VHS.** *PL* Aleksandra Slaska, Anna Ciepielewska, Marek Walezewski, Jan Kreczewski, Irena Malkiewicz; ***D:*** Andrzej Munk; ***W:*** Andrzej Munk, Zofia Posmysz-Piasecka; ***C:*** Krzysztof Winiewicz; ***M:*** Tadeusz Baird.

The Passenger 🦴🦴🦴 ½ *Profession: Reporter* **1975 (PG)** A dissatisfied TV reporter changes identities with a dead man while on assignment in Africa, then learns that he is posing as a gunrunner. Mysterious, elliptical production from Italian master Antonioni, who co-wrote. Nicholson is fine in the low-key role, and Schneider is surprisingly winning as the woman drawn to him. The object of much debate, hailed by some as quintessential cinema and by others as slow and unrewarding. **119m/C VHS, DVD.** *IT* Jack Nicholson, Maria Schneider, Ian Hendry, Jenny Runacre, Steven Berkoff; ***D:*** Michelangelo Antonioni; ***W:*** Mark Peploe, Michelangelo Antonioni; ***M:*** Claude Bolling.

Passenger 57 🦴 **1992 (R)** Classic movie-of-the-week fare. Anti-terrorist specialist John Cutter (Snipes) leaves his profession because of his wife's murder, and coincidentally boards the same plane as Charles Rane (Payne), an apprehended evil terrorist headed to trial in L.A. Somehow, Rane's thugs have also sneaked aboard with plans to hijack the plane, and it's up to Cutter to use his skills and save the day. Athletic Snipes is convincing in his role but can't make up for the plot's lack of premise. **84m/C VHS, DVD.** Wesley Snipes, Bruce Payne, Tom Sizemore, Alex Datcher, Bruce Greenwood, Robert Hooks, Elizabeth Hurley, Michael Horse; ***D:*** Kevin Hooks; ***W:*** Dan Gordon, David Loughery; ***C:*** Mark Irwin; ***M:*** Stanley Clarke.

Passengers 🦴 ½ **2008 (PG-13)** Grief counselor Claire Summers (Hathaway) is assigned to treat a group of plane crash survivors, who she suspects are involved in a cover-up. The life-long lonely workaholic soon finds romance with her patient Eric (Wilson), who begins to reveal the mystery behind the crash. Marketed as a horror/thriller, but the obvious absence of both horrors and thrills plainly put it in drama territory. Be warned, the twist ending isn't very twisted. **92m/C DVD.** *US* Anne Hathaway, Patrick Wilson, David Morse, Andre Braugher, Clea DuVall, Dianne Wiest, Chelah Horsdal, Ryan Robbins; ***D:*** Rodrigo Garcia; ***W:*** Ronnie Christensen; ***C:*** Igor Jadue-Lillo; ***M:*** Ed Shearmur.

The Passing 🦴🦴 ½ **1988** Two men find themselves trapped in the darker vicissitudes of life. The two lead almost parallel lives until an extraordinary event unites them. **96m/C VHS, DVD.** James Plaster, Welton Benjamin Johnson, Lynn Dunn, Albert B. Smith; ***D:*** John Huckert.

Passing Glory 🦴🦴🦴 **1999** The script may not be a three-pointer but the acting is a slam-dunk in this fact-based drama. Joseph Verrett (Braugher) is a black priest in segregationist New Orleans in the early '60s, teaching at St. Augustine High and coaching the school's unbeaten varsity basketball squad. Verrett is a go-getter who wants to integrate the league now, while his boss, Father Robert Grant (Torn) preaches patience. Despite numerous obstacles, Verrett manages to challenge white Jesuit High to an unofficial city championship game. **94m/C VHS.** Andre Braugher, Rip Torn, Bill Nunn, Sean Squire, Ruby Dee, Daniel Hugh-Kelly, Anderson Bourell, Khalil Kain; ***D:*** Steve James; ***W:*** Harold Sylvester; ***C:*** Bill Butler; ***M:*** Stephen James Taylor. **CABLE**

The Passing of Evil 🦴🦴 ½ *The Grasshopper; Passions* **1970 (R)** Bisset is a starstruck Canadian undone by the bright lights and big cities of America. By age 22, she's a burnt-out prostitute in Las Vegas. Cheerless but compelling. **96m/C VHS.** Jacqueline Bisset, Jim Brown, Joseph Cotten, Corbett Monica, Ramon Bieri, Christopher Stone, Roger Garrett, Stanley Adams, Dick Richards, Tim O'Kelly, Ed Flanders; ***D:*** Jerry Paris; ***C:*** Sam Leavitt; ***M:*** Billy Goldenberg.

The Passing of the Third Floor Back 🦴🦴 **1936** Boarding house tenants improve their lives after being inspired by a mysterious stranger. They revert, though, when he leaves. Now you know. Based on a Victorian morality play. **80m/B VHS, DVD.** *GB* Conrad Veidt, Rene Ray, Frank Cellier, Anna Lee, John Turnbull, Cathleen Nesbitt; ***D:*** Berthold Viertel.

Passion 🦴🦴 ½ **1919** Paris, and the decadent Louis XV falls for the lovely Jeanne, making her his mistress, much to the scandal of the nation. Respectable silent version of "Madame DuBarry" is a relatively realistic costume drama, but it doesn't rate with the best German films of this period. **135m/B VHS.** *GE* Pola Negri, Emil Jannings, Harry Liedtke; ***D:*** Ernst Lubitsch.

Passion 🦴🦴 **1954** When a rancher's young family falls victim to rampaging desperadoes, he enlists an outlaw's aid to avenge the murders of his loved ones. **84m/C VHS, DVD.** Raymond Burr, Cornel Wilde, Yvonne De Carlo, Lon Chaney Jr., John Qualen; ***D:*** Allan Dwan.

Passion 🦴🦴 **1982 (R)** A Polish film director (Radziwilowicz) is making a movie called "Passion" and practicing what he's filming by having an affair with the motel owner (Schygulla) where the film crew are staying. Then the money for the film begins to run out. Meanwhile, Schygulla's husband, Piccoli, is having problems at his factory because of a labor dispute called by worker Huppert. French with subtitles. **88m/C VHS.** *FR* Jerzy Radziwilowicz, Hanna Schygulla, Michel Piccoli, Isabelle Huppert, Laszlo Szabo; ***D:*** Jean-Luc Godard; ***W:*** Jean-Luc Godard; ***C:*** Raoul Coutard.

Passion 🦴 ½ **1992** Linda decides she married the wrong brother. So she plots to kill her husband and marry her in-law instead. **90m/C VHS.** Kristine Rose, Robert Labrosse, Kristine Frischhertz, Jack Ciolini; ***D:*** Joe D'Amato.

Passion 🦴🦴 **1999** Over-the-top bio of Aussie-born composer Percy Grainger (1882-1961). Although born in Melbourne and starting his career as a concert pianist, Grainger (Roxburgh) spent most of his life in Europe and the U.S. and was involved in recovering English and Celtic folk songs. But his home life is a twisted psychosexual drama as his devoted mother, Rose (Hershey), suffers from syphilitic fits amid rumors of their incestuous relationship and Grainger's own masochistic impulses, which are catered to by his piano student, Karen (Woof). **98m/C VHS, DVD.** *AU* Richard Roxburgh, Barbara Hershey, Emily Woof, Claudia Karvan, Simon Burke, Linda Cropper, Julia Blake; ***D:*** Peter Duncan; ***W:*** Don Watson; ***C:*** Martin McGrath. Australian Film Inst. '99: Art Dir./Set Dec., Cinematog., Costume Des.

Passion Fish 🦴🦴🦴 **1992 (R)** McDonnell plays May-Alice, a soap opera actress who is paralyzed after a taxi accident in New York. Confined to a wheelchair, the bitter woman moves back to her Louisiana home and alienates a number of live-in nurses until Chantelle (Woodard), who has her own problems, comes along. Blunt writing and directing by Sayles overcome the story's inherent sentimentality as do the spirited performances of the leads, including Curtis-Hall as the rogue romancing Chantelle and Strathairn as the Cajun bad boy McDonnell once loved. **136m/C VHS, DVD.** Mary McDonnell, Alfre Woodard, David Strathairn, Vondie Curtis-Hall, Nora Dunn, Sheila Kelley, Angela Bassett, Mary Portser, Maggie Renzi, Leo Burmester, Shauntisa Willis, John Henry, Michael Laskin; ***D:*** John Sayles; ***W:*** John Sayles; ***C:*** Roger Deakins; ***M:*** Mason Daring. Ind. Spirit '93: Support. Actress (Woodard).

Passion Flower 🦴🦴 **1986 (PG-13)** A tropical romantic melodrama made for network TV and set in Singapore, where an ambitious banker falls in love with the daughter of island's wealthiest smuggler. The mixture of high finance, low-dealing and lust only proves moderately passionate. **95m/C VHS.** Bruce Boxleitner, Barbara Hershey, Nicol Williamson; ***D:*** Joseph Sargent; ***M:*** Miles Goodman. **TV**

Passion for Life 🦴🦴 ½ *L'Ecole Buissonniere; I Have a New Master* **1948** A new teacher uses revolutionary methods to engage students, but draws ire from staid parents in rural France. Worthwhile drama. In French with English subtitles. **89m/B VHS.** Bernard Blier, Juliette Faber, Edouard Delmont; ***D:*** Jean-Paul LeChanois.

Passion for Power **1985** Two men involved in a drug-smuggling syndicate attempt to take over the business. Complications arise when they both fall for a beautiful, deceitful woman who turns them against one another. **94m/C VHS.** *SP* Hector Suarez, Sasha Montenegro, Manuel Capetillo, Alejandra Peniche.

Passion in Paradise 🦴🦴 ½ **1989** Fact-based mystery set in the Bahamas in 1943. Stewart is a spoiled rich girl who marries a handsome gigolo (Assante), much to daddy big bucks' (Steiger) displeasure. Then daddy is murdered and the son-in-law becomes the key suspect. Trashy, but Assante's fine. **100m/C VHS.** Armand Assante, Catherine Mary Stewart, Rod Steiger, Mariette Hartley, Wayne Rogers; ***D:*** Harvey Hart. **TV**

Passion in the Desert 🦴🦴 *Simoom: A Passion in the Desert* **1997 (PG-13)** Definitely one of the stranger plots going. Augustin Roberts (Daniels) is a French officer in Napoleon's Egyptian campaign. He's escorting artist Venture de Paradis (Piccoli), who's been commissioned to record the country's monuments. The duo are lost and separated in a desert sandstorm, with Roberts eventually finding shelter in the ruins of an ancient city. But he's not alone—his dangerous companion is a female leopard, who decides to help out the two-legged interloper. Based on a novella by Honore de Balzac. **93m/C VHS, DVD.** Ben Daniels, Michel Piccoli; ***D:*** Lavinia Currier; ***W:*** Lavinia Currier, Martin Edmunds; ***C:*** Alexei Rodionov; ***M:*** Jose Nieto.

The Passion of Anna 🦴🦴🦴 **1970 (R)** A complicated psychological drama about four people on an isolated island. Von Sydow is an ex-con living a hermit's existence when he becomes involved with a crippled widow (Ullmann) and her two friends—all of whom have secrets in their pasts. Brutal and disturbing. Wonderful cinematography by Sven Nykvist. Filmed on the island of Faro. In Swedish with English subtitles. **101m/C VHS, DVD.** *SW* Max von Sydow, Liv Ullmann, Bibi Andersson, Erland Josephson, Erik Hell; ***D:*** Ingmar Bergman; ***W:*** Ingmar Bergman; ***C:*** Sven Nykvist. Natl. Soc. Film Critics '70: Director (Bergman).

The Passion of Ayn Rand 🦴🦴 ½ **1999** Warts-and-all bio of the Russian-born novelist/philosopher that focuses on the 20-year friendship between Rand (Mirren) and psychoanalyst Nathaniel Branden (Stoltz). When the pic opens in 1951, self-important Rand is already famous for "The Fountainhead" and has a longtime marriage to the overshadowed Frank (Fonda). Nathaniel and Barbara (Delpy) are college students pushed to marry by mentor Rand, who soon becomes Nathaniel's lover and encourages his ambitions—to the dismay of both spouses. Based on the 1986 memoir by Barbara Branden, so there's an axe to grind. **104m/C VHS, DVD.** Helen Mirren, Eric Stoltz, Julie Delpy, Peter Fonda, Tom McCamus, Sybil Temchen, Don McKellar, David Ferry; ***D:*** Christopher Menaul; ***W:*** Howard Korder, Mary Gallagher; ***C:*** Ronald Orieux; ***M:*** Jeff Beal. **CABLE**

The Passion of Darkly Noon 🦴 ½ **1995** Strange religious/sexual allegory. Running through the woods, Darkly Noon

(Fraser) stumbles across the rural home of Callie (Judd) and Clay (Mortensen). Callie sees that the young man is ill and allows him to stay, discovering his parents have recently died and he's escaped from the ultra-religious community where he was raised. The sexy Callie is an uncomfortable attraction for the naive lad and when he meets a crazy old woman, Roxy (Zabriskie), in the woods, he's inclined to listen to her ravings against Callie, leading Darkly to believe he's been sent to punish the transgressors. **106m/C VHS.** *GB GE BE* Brendan Fraser, Ashley Judd, Viggo Mortensen, Grace Zabriskie, Loren Dean; ***D:*** Philip Ridley; ***W:*** Philip Ridley; ***C:*** John de Borman; ***M:*** Nick Bicat.

Passion of Joan of Arc **1928** Dreyer's version of the life of France's Joan of Arc ignores all the battlefield dramatics and confines itself to showing Joan in her cell and at her trial, with only one exterior shot—that of Joan (stage actress Falconetti in her only film role) on her way to the stake. The script is drawn from the Latin text of the heresy trial itself and Dreyer uses numerous close-ups (the actors wore no makeup) to show the bewilderment, fear, and anger of the participants. Dreyer refused to have his film shown with musical accompaniment but the tape includes Richard Einhron's oratoria, "Voices of Light." **114m/B VHS, DVD.** *FR* Renee (Marie) Falconetti, Eugena Sylvaw, Maurice Schutz, Antonin Artaud, Michel Simon; ***D:*** Carl Theodor Dreyer; ***W:*** Carl Theodor Dreyer, Joseph Delteil; ***C:*** Rudolph Mate.

Passion of Love *Passione d'Amore* **1982** Military captain becomes the obsession of his commander's mysterious cousin when he reports to an outpost far from home. Daring and fascinating. An unrelentingly passionate historical romance guaranteed to heat up the VCR. Available dubbed or with subtitles. **117m/C VHS.** *IT FR* Laura Antonelli, Bernard Giraudeau, Valeria (Valerie Dobson) D'Obici, Jean-Louis Trintignant; ***D:*** Ettore Scola; ***W:*** Ettore Scola.

Passion of Mind 1/2 **2000 (PG-13)** Moore plays two roles: Marie is an American widow and mother living in France while Marty is a hard-charging single New York literary agent. Marie falls asleep and wakes up as Marty and vice versa. Marie/Marty can't tell anymore which of her two worlds is real and things get even more complicated when each persona falls for an appealing man (Skarsgard in France, Fichtner in New York). It's not really confusing since the script is so simplistic and both her lives turn out to be remarkably dull (as is Moore's performance). English-language debut for Berliner and Moore's first film since 1997's "G.I. Jane." **105m/C VHS, DVD.** Demi Moore, Stellan Skarsgard, William Fichtner, Peter Riegert, Joss Ackland, Sinead Cusack; ***D:*** Alain Berliner; ***W:*** Ronald Bass, David Field; ***C:*** Eduardo Serra; ***M:*** Randy Edelman.

The Passion of the Christ **2004 (R)** Calling Gibson's record-breaking, graphic version of the last 12 hours in the life of Jesus Christ "controversial" is an understatement on par with calling the Sahara Desert "warm." Film begins as Jesus (Caveizel) is arrested and taken before Hebrew and Roman authorities for crimes of heresy. Although some backstory is told in flashback, the movie assumes the viewer's knowledge of Jesus's life and focuses on giving as graphic a portrayal of his torture and crucifixion as possible (including a 45 minute flogging scene) in a movie as painful and intense to watch as any put on film. Very bold and well-crafted, but the obsessive focus on gore and violence will leave many asking where the spirituality is supposed to be. Endorsed by many church leaders but drew complaints for its negative depiction of the Hebrew leaders, as well as some violent scenes that Gibson invented. Gibson funded the film with $30 million of his own money. In Aramaic, Latin, and Hebrew with English subtitles. **126m/C DVD, Blu-ray Disc.** *US* James (Jim) Caviezel, Monica Bellucci, Maia Morgenstern, Claudia Gerini, Sergio Rubini, Toni Bertorelli, Mattia Sbragia, Luca Lionello, Hristo Naumov Shopov, Giancinto Ferro, Rosalinda Celentano, Francesco De Vito, Hristo Jivkov, Roberto Bestazzoni, Adel Ben Ayed, Fabio Sartor, Luca De Dominicis, Pietro (Pedro) Sarubbi, Chokri Ben Zagden, Jarreth Merz, Matt Patresi, Francesco Cabras, Giovanni Capalbo, Olek Mincer; ***D:*** Mel Gibson; ***W:*** Mel Gibson, Benedict Fitzgerald; ***C:*** Caleb Deschanel; ***M:*** John Debney.

A Passion to Kill 1/2 *Rules of Obsession* **1994 (R)** Formulaic thriller finds psychologist David (Bakula) getting sexually involved with his best friend Jerry's (Getz) wife, who has a lurid past. Seems Diana (Field) stuck a kitchen knife into her abusive first husband and now Jerry's prospects don't look too good. **93m/C VHS.** Scott Bakula, Chelsea Field, Sheila Kelley, John Getz, Rex Smith, France Nuyen, Michael Warren; ***D:*** Rick King; ***W:*** William F. Delligan.

Passionate Thief 1/2 *Risate de Gioia; Joyous Laughter* **1960** Two pickpockets and a bumbling actress plan to rip off the guests at a posh New Year's Eve party with slightly comic results. Not much to recommend in this slow moving flick. **100m/C VHS.** *IT* Anna Magnani, Ben Gazzara, Fred Clark, Toto, Edy Vessel; ***D:*** Mario Monicelli; ***C:*** Leonida Barboni.

The Passover Plot **1975 (PG)** A controversial look at the crucifixion of Christ which depicts him as a Zealot leader who, aided by his followers, faked his death and then "rose" to win new converts. **105m/C VHS.** Harry Andrews, Hugh Griffith, Zalman King, Donald Pleasence, Scott Wilson; ***D:*** Michael Campus; ***M:*** Alex North.

Passport to Pimlico 1/2 **1949** Farce about a London neighborhood's residents who discover an ancient charter proclaiming their right to form their own country within city limits. Passable comedy. **81m/B VHS, DVD.** *GB* Stanley Holloway, Margaret Rutherford, Hermione Baddeley, Naunton Wayne, Basil Radford; ***D:*** Henry Cornelius.

Past Midnight **1992 (R)** Richardson plays a social worker who believes recently paroled killer Hauer was wrongly convicted. She attempts to prove his innocence while also falling in love—a dangerous combination. Richardson's beautiful and Hauer's making a successful career out of playing handsome psychos. **100m/C VHS, DVD.** Natasha Richardson, Rutger Hauer, Clancy Brown, Guy Boyd; ***D:*** Jan Eliasberg; ***W:*** Frank Norwood; ***M:*** Steve Bartek.

Past Perfect 1/2 **1998 (R)** Gun battles, car chases, and fights move this actioner right along. Cop Dylan Cooper's (Roberts) job is made harder because his city is overrun with juvenile crime. But even he's shocked when the young criminals start turning up dead. Then Cooper discovers a group of futuristic bounty hunters have been sent back in time to eliminate these violent delinquents before they become adult killers. **92m/C VHS.** Eric Roberts, Nick Mancuso, Saul Rubinek, Laurie Holden; ***D:*** Jonathan Heap; ***W:*** John Penney; ***C:*** John Houtman; ***M:*** Christophe Beck.

Past Tense 1/2 **1994 (R)** Complicated thriller about a cop with a gorgeous but mysterious neighbor, a murder to solve, and problems separating reality from his nightmares. **91m/C VHS.** Scott Glenn, Lara Flynn Boyle, Anthony LaPaglia, David Ogden Stiers, Sheree J. Wilson, Marita Geraghty, Stephen Graziano; ***D:*** Graeme Clifford. **CABLE**

Past the Bleachers 1/2 **1995 (PG)** Sentimental TV movie finds Anderson starring as Bill Parish—a man still lost by the death of his 11-year-old son. Reluctantly, he agrees to coach the Little League team his son had played on, with the help of an opinionated senior citizen (scene-stealer Hughes), and is drawn to the boy who turns out to be the team's star player. The appropriately named Lucky Diamond (Fricke) is both mute and of a mysterious family background, and bonding proves therapeutic for both Bill and the youngster. Based on a novel by Christopher A. Bohjalian. **120m/C VHS.** Richard Dean Anderson, Barnard Hughes, Grayson Fricke, Glynnis O'Connor, Ken Jenkins; ***D:*** Michael Switzer; ***W:*** Don Rhymer; ***M:*** Stewart Levin.

Pastime *One Cup of Coffee* **1991 (PG)** A bittersweet baseball elegy set in the minor leagues in 1957. A boyish 41-year-old pitcher can't face his impending retirement and pals around with the team pariah, a 17-year-old black rookie. Splendidly written and acted, it's a melancholy treat whether you're a fan of the game or not, and safe for family attendance. The only drawback is a grungy, low-budget look. **94m/C VHS, DVD.** William Russ, Scott Plank, Glenn Plummer, Noble Willingham, Jeffrey Tambor, Deirdre O'Connell, Ricky Paull Goldin; ***Cameos:*** Ernie Banks, Harmon Killebrew, Duke Snider, Bob Feller, Bill Mazeroski, Don Newcombe; ***D:*** Robin B. Armstrong; ***W:*** David Eyre; ***C:*** Tom Richmond. Sundance '91: Aud. Award.

Pat and Mike **1952** War of the sexes rages in this comedy about a leathery sports promoter who futilely attempts to train a woman for athletic competition. Tracy and Hepburn have fine chemistry, but supporting players contribute too. Watch for the first on-screen appearance of Bronson (then Charles Buchinski) as a crook. **95m/B VHS, DVD.** Spencer Tracy, Katharine Hepburn, Aldo Ray, Jim Backus, William Ching, Sammy White, Phyllis Povah, Charles Bronson, Chuck Connors, Mae Clarke, Carl "Alfalfa" Switzer; ***D:*** George Cukor; ***W:*** Garson Kanin, Ruth Gordon; ***C:*** William H. Daniels; ***M:*** David Raksin.

Pat Garrett & Billy the Kid **1973** Coburn is Garrett, one-time partner of Billy the Kid (Kristofferson), turned sheriff. He tracks down and eventually kills the outlaw. The uncut director's version released on video is a vast improvement over the theatrical and TV versions. Dylan's soundtrack includes the now famous "Knockin' on Heaven's Door." **106m/C VHS, DVD.** Kris Kristofferson, James Coburn, Bob Dylan, Richard Jaeckel, Katy Jurado, Chill Wills, Charles Martin Smith, Slim Pickens, Harry Dean Stanton; ***D:*** Sam Peckinpah; ***W:*** Rudy Wurlitzer; ***M:*** George Duning.

Patch Adams **1998 (PG-13)** Maverick medical student Hunter "Patch" Adams (Williams) takes the expression "laughter is the best medicine" literally and treats terminally ill patients with slapstick routines. Naturally, his stodgy old boss, not to mention the rest of the medical establishment, frown on his antics and prefer more conventional treatments (like medicine). But Patch thumbs his nose at The Man and tries to defend his unorthodox ways to fellow students, including the requisite love interest (Potter). Director Shadyac and screenwriter Oedekerk seem to let Williams unleash his rapid-fire wackiness without much direction. Ultimately, flick is brought down by sappy melodrama and emotional manipulation under the guise of sincere emotion. **115m/C VHS, DVD, HD DVD.** Robin Williams, Philip Seymour Hoffman, Monica Potter, Bob Gunton, Josef Sommer, Irma P. Hall, Daniel London, Frances Lee McCain, Harve Presnell, Peter Coyote, Michael Jeter, Harold Gould, Richard Kiley, Alan Tudyk, Barry (Shabaka) Henley; ***D:*** Tom Shadyac; ***W:*** Steve Oedekerk; ***C:*** Phedon Papamichael; ***M:*** Marc Shaiman.

A Patch of Blue 1/2 **1965** A kind-hearted blind girl falls in love with a black man without acknowledging racial differences. Good performances from Hartman and Poitier are film's strongest assets. **108m/C VHS, DVD.** Sidney Poitier, Elizabeth Hartman, Shelley Winters, Wallace Ford, Ivan Dixon, John Qualen, Elisabeth Fraser, Kelly Flynn; ***D:*** Guy Green; ***C:*** Robert Burks; ***M:*** Jerry Goldsmith. Oscars '65: Support. Actress (Winters).

Patchwork Girl of Oz **1914** You wonder what Baum might have been imbibing when he wrote some of his Oz books. In this story a mysterious Emerald City doctor is working on a powder of life that his wife accidentally tests on a patchwork servant doll that suddenly comes alive. **80m/B VHS, DVD.** Frank Moore, Violet MacMillan, Raymond Russell, Leontine Dranet, Pierre Couderc, Richard Rosson, Bobbie Gould, Marie Wayne; ***D:*** J. Farrell MacDonald; ***W:*** L. Frank Baum; ***C:*** James A. Crosby.

Paternity **1981 (PG)** Routine comedy about middle-aged manager of Madison Square Gardens (Reynolds) who sets out to find a woman to bear his child, no strings attached. The predictability of the happy ending makes this a yawner. Steinberg's directorial debut. **94m/C VHS.** Burt Reynolds, Beverly D'Angelo, Lauren Hutton, Norman Fell, Paul Dooley, Elizabeth Ashley; ***D:*** David Steinberg; ***W:*** Charlie Peters; ***M:*** David Shire. Golden Raspberries '81: Worst Song ("Baby Talk").

Path to Paradise **1997 (R)** Based on the true story of the 1993 World Trade Center bombing, which focuses on both the terrorists and the FBI investigators. FBI agent John Anticev (Gallagher) is investigating a rabbi's murder, which leads him to Islamic extremists. An informant warns Anticev that the group are planning terroritst activities in Manhattan but the conspirators are closer to their target than the FBI imagine. **95m/C VHS.** Peter Gallagher, Art Malik, Ned Eisenberg, Marcia Gay Harden, Paul Guilfoyle, Andreas Katsulas, Shiek Mahmud-Bey, Mike Starr; ***D:*** Larry Williams, Leslie Libman; ***W:*** Ned Curren; ***C:*** Jean De Segonzac. **CABLE**

Path to War 1/2 **2002** Covers the period from the night of President Lyndon B. Johnson's (Gambon) inauguration in 1965 to his 1968 decision not to seek re-election because of the escalating war in Vietnam. While the British Gambon has Johnson's mannerisms down, he can't manage the Texas drawl, which is a real handicap. Baldwin plays Defense Secretary Robert McNamara and Sutherland is Johnson adviser Clark Clifford. **160m/C VHS, DVD.** Michael Gambon, Alec Baldwin, Donald Sutherland, John Aylward, Cliff DeYoung, Christopher Eigeman, Frederic Forrest, James Frain, Philip Baker Hall, Felicity Huffman, Patricia Kalember, Bruce McGill, Tom Skerritt, Diana Scarwid, Gary Sinise; ***D:*** John Frankenheimer; ***W:*** Daniel Giat; ***C:*** Stephen Goldblatt, Nancy Schreiber; ***M:*** Gary Chang. **CABLE**

Pather Panchali *The Song of the Road; The Saga of the Road; The Lament of the Path* **1954** Somber, moving story of a young Bengali boy growing up in impoverished India. Stunning debut from India's master filmmaker Ray, who continued the story in "Aparajito" and "World of Apu." A truly great work. In Bengali with English subtitles. **112m/B VHS, DVD.** *IN* Kanu Bannerjee, Karuna Bannerjee, Uma Das Gupta, Subir Banerji, Runki Banerji, Chunibala Devi; ***D:*** Satyajit Ray; ***W:*** Satyajit Ray; ***M:*** Ravi Shankar.

Pathfinder 1/2 **1987** A young boy in Lapland of 1,000 years ago comes of age prematurely after he falls in with cutthroat nomads who already slaughtered his family and now want to wipe out the rest of the village. Gripping adventure in the ice and snow features stunning scenery. In Lappish with English subtitles and based on an old Lapp fable. **88m/C VHS.** *NO* Mikkel Gaup, Nils Utsi, Svein Scharffenberg, Helgi Skulason, Sara Marit Gaup, Sverre Porsanger; ***D:*** Nils Gaup; ***W:*** Nils Gaup.

The Pathfinder 1/2 **1994 (PG-13)** TV adaptation of the 1840 James Fenimore Cooper novel that finds legendary woodsman Natty Bumppo, his adoptive Indian father Chingachgook, and lovely Mabel Dunham trying to aid a beseiged British fort during the French and Indian wars. If this sounds familiar, it's because Cooper's "Leatherstocking Tales" were also the basis for "The Last of the Mohicans." **104m/C VHS, DVD.** Kevin Dillon, Graham Greene, Jaimz Woolvett, Laurie Holden, Russell Means, Stacy Keach; ***D:*** Donald Shebib; ***W:*** James Mitchell Miller, Thomas W. Lynch; ***M:*** Reg Powell.

Pathfinder **2007 (R)** Shelved for a year and then released after blockbuster "300." Coincidence? We think not. Violent and gory (although with fewer ripped abs), this epic wannabe doesn't even have the camp factor to save it. Abandoned by his father during a North American raid, a Viking lad is raised by a peaceful Native American tribe. When the Vikings return for more pillaging and slaughter, now-grown Ghost (Urban) takes on the intruders. Soon all the action cliches commence. Loosely inspired by the 1988 Norwegian pic "Ofelas." **99m/C DVD, Blu-ray Disc.** *US* Karl Urban, Russell Means, Moon Bloodgood, Clancy Brown, Ralph (Ralf) Moeller, Jay Tavare, Clancy Brown; ***D:*** Marcus Nispel; ***W:*** Laeta Kalogridis; ***C:*** Daniel Pearl; ***M:*** Jonathan Elias.

Pathology **2008 (R)** Grisly, perverse horror thriller finds amoral young doctor Ted Grey (Ventimiglia) beginning his residency in pathology. His fellow docs are a sex-and-drugs crazed bunch led by loony Jack (Weston). Jack has devised a game in which one of the team commits a murder and then the others perform an autopsy to decide how it was done (so much for the Hippocratic

Oath). Ted's soon involved up to his scalpel but discovers getting out of Jack's band of merry killers isn't so easy. **93m/C DVD.** *US* Milo Ventimiglia, Michael Weston, Alyssa Milano, Lauren Lee Smith, Johnny Whitworth, John de Lancie, Mei Melancon, Keir O'Donnell; ***D:*** Marc Schoelermann; ***C:*** Ekkehart Pollack; ***M:*** Johannes Kobilke, Robert Williamson.

Paths of Glory 🦴🦴🦴🦴 **1957** Classic anti-war drama set in WWI France. A vain, ambitious officer imposes unlikely battle strategy on his hapless troops, and when it fails, he demands that three soldiers be selected for execution as cowards. Menjou is excellent as the bloodless French officer, with Douglas properly heroic as the French officer who knows about the whole disgraceful enterprise. Fabulous, wrenching fare from filmmaking great Kubrick, who co-wrote. Based on a true story from Humphrey Cobb's novel of the same name. **86m/B VHS, DVD.** Kirk Douglas, Adolphe Menjou, George Macready, Ralph Meeker, Richard Anderson, Wayne Morris, Timothy Carey, Susanne Christian, Bert Freed, Joe Turkel, Peter Capell; ***D:*** Stanley Kubrick; ***W:*** Stanley Kubrick, Calder Willingham, Jim Thompson; ***C:*** Georg Krause; ***M:*** Gerald Fried. Natl. Film Reg. '92.

Paths to Paradise 🦴🦴🦴 **1925** Compson and Griffith share criminal past, reunite at gala event to snatch priceless necklace, and head south of the border. World-class chase scene. **78m/B VHS.** Raymond Griffith, Betty Compson, Thomas Santschi, Bert Woodruff, Fred Kelsey; ***D:*** Clarence Badger.

Patrick 🦴 ½ **1978 (PG)** Coma patient suddenly develops strange powers and has a weird effect on the people he comes in contact with. **115m/C VHS, DVD.** *AU* Robert Helpmann, Susan Penhaligon, Rod Mullinar; ***D:*** Richard Franklin; ***M:*** Brian May.

The Patriot 🦴 ½ **1986 (R)** An action film about an ex-Navy commando who battles a band of nuclear-arms smuggling terrorists. Edited via George Lucas' electronic editor, Edit Droid. **88m/C VHS, DVD.** Jeff Conaway, Michael J. Pollard, Leslie Nielsen, Gregg Henry, Simone Griffeth; ***D:*** Frank Harris; ***W:*** Andy Ruben, Katt Shea; ***M:*** Jay Ferguson.

The Patriot 🦴🦴 **1999 (R)** Wesley McClaren (Seagal) is a former government immunologist who's now the local doctor for a small ranching community. The peaceful community becomes a plague town when an extremist militia group take over and turn out to be carriers of a mysterious disease. McClaren might be a healer but he also can kick some extremist butt when necessary. **90m/C VHS, DVD.** Steven Seagal, Gailard Sartain, L.Q. Jones; ***D:*** Dean Semler; ***C:*** Stephen Windon; ***M:*** Stephen (Steve) Edwards.

The Patriot 🦴🦴 ½ **2000 (R)** Bloody, long, and melodramatic Revolutionary War revenge pic with a strong lead by Gibson and a notably hissable villain in Isaacs. Benjamin Martin (Gibson) is a former guerilla soldier in the French and Indian wars who just wants to raise his family in peace. Unfortunately, local redcoat leader, Col. Tavington (Isaacs), has other ideas and when Martin's idealistic soldier son Gabriel (Ledger) is captured, dad gets caught up in the action. Producing partners Roland Emmerich and Dean Devlin did "Independence Day" and "Godzilla," so spectacle is their middle name. Film gave the British critics apoplexy with its inaccuracies. But who won, anyway? **164m/C VHS, DVD, Blu-ray Disc.** Mel Gibson, Heath Ledger, Jason Isaacs, Chris Cooper, Tcheky Karyo, Joely Richardson, Tom Wilkinson, Donal Logue, Rene Auberjonois, Adam Baldwin, Leon Rippy, Jay Arlen Jones, Gregory Edward Smith, Logan Lerman, Mika Boorem, Skye McCole Bartusiak, Trevor Morgan, Mary Jo Deschanel, Joey D. Viera, Bryan Chafin; ***D:*** Roland Emmerich; ***W:*** Robert Rodat; ***C:*** Caleb Deschanel; ***M:*** John Williams.

Patriot Games 🦴🦴🦴 **1992 (R)** Jack Ryan, retired CIA analyst, takes his wife and daughter to England on a holiday and ends up saving a member of the Royal Family from assassination by IRA extremists. Ryan, who has killed one of the terrorists, then becomes the target of revenge by the dead man's brother. Good action sequences but otherwise predictable adaptation of the novel by Tom Clancy. Companion to "The Hunt for Red October," with Ford taking over the role of Ryan from Alec Baldwin. Since this movie did well, we can probably expect two more from Ford, who's becoming the king of trilogies. Followed by "Clear and Present Danger." **117m/C VHS, DVD.** Harrison Ford, Anne Archer, Patrick Bergin, Thora Birch, Sean Bean, Richard Harris, James Earl Jones, James Fox, Samuel L. Jackson, Polly Walker, Theodore (Ted) Raimi; ***D:*** Phillip Noyce; ***W:*** Donald Stewart, W. Peter Iliff; ***C:*** Donald McAlpine; ***M:*** James Horner.

The Patriots 🦴🦴🦴 **1933** A German prisoner works as a shoemaker in a small village during WWI. A lyrical drama in German and Russian with English titles. **82m/B VHS, DVD.** *RU* Sergei Komarov, Nikolai Kryuchkov, Aleksandr Chistyakov, Yelena Kuzmina; ***D:*** Boris Barnet; ***W:*** Boris Barnet; ***C:*** Mikhail Kirillov; ***M:*** Sergei Vasilenko.

The Patsy 🦴🦴 ½ **1928** Patricia (Davies) has fallen for glamorous older sister Grace's (Winton) boyfriend Tony (Caldwell). Grace seems more interested in rich playboy Bill (Gray), but she's stringing Tony along and she and their domineering mother (Dressler) want baby sis to butt out. Tony unwittingly gives Patricia romantic advice that she uses on him although not quite as intended. Davies was a charming comedienne and her character's attempts to act sophisticated are amusing. **78m/B DVD.** Marion Davies, Jane Winton, Marie Dressler, Orville Caldwell, Lawrence Gray, Dell Henderson; ***D:*** King Vidor; ***W:*** Ralph Spence; ***C:*** John Seitz.

The Patsy 🦴🦴 **1964** Shady producers attempt to transform a lowly bellboy into a comedy superstar. Not one of Lewis's better efforts; Lorre's last film. **101m/C VHS, DVD.** Jerry Lewis, Ina Balin, Everett Sloane, Phil Harris, Keenan Wynn, Peter Lorre, John Carradine, Hans Conried, Richard Deacon, Scatman Crothers, Del Moore, Neil Hamilton, Buddy Lester, Nancy Kulp, Norman Alden, Jack Albertson; ***D:*** Jerry Lewis; ***W:*** Jerry Lewis.

Pattern for Plunder 🦴 ½ *The Bay of Saint Michel* **1962** Ex-commando leader rounds up his former comrades to head back to Normandy in search of buried Nazi plunder. **73m/B VHS.** *GB* Keenan Wynn, Mai Zetterling, Ronald Howard, Edward Underdown; ***D:*** John Ainsworth; ***W:*** Christopher Davis.

Patterns 🦴🦴🦴 *Patterns of Power* **1956** Realistic depiction of big business. Heflin starts work at a huge New York office that is under the ruthless supervision of Sloane. Serling's astute screenplay (adapted from his TV play) is adept at portraying ruthless, power-struggling executives and the sundry workings of a large corporation. Film has aged slightly, but it still has some edge to it. Originally intended for television. **83m/B VHS, DVD.** Van Heflin, Everett Sloane, Ed Begley Sr., Beatrice Straight, Elizabeth Wilson; ***D:*** Fielder Cook; ***W:*** Rod Serling; ***C:*** Boris Kaufman.

Pattes Blanches 🦴🦴 ½ *White Paws* **1949** A reclusive aristocrat always wears white spats, causing ridicule in the small fishing village where he lives. Trouble comes when a local saloon-keeper becomes resentful of the rich man's advances on his girlfriend. Moody, sensual French melodrama exploring class, money and sex. Adaptation of a play by Jean Anouilh. In French with English subtitles. **92m/B VHS.** *FR* Suzy Delair, Fernand Ledoux, Paul Bernard, Michel Bouquet; ***D:*** Jean Gremillon.

Patti Rocks 🦴🦴🦴 **1988 (R)** Offbeat, realistic independent effort concerns a foul chauvinist who enlists a friend to accompany him on a visit to a pregnant girlfriend who turns out to be less than the bimbo she's portrayed as en route. Mulkey shines as the sexist. Same characters featured earlier in "Loose Ends." **86m/C VHS.** Chris Mulkey, John Jenkins, Karen Landry, David L. Turk, Stephen Yoakam; ***D:*** David Burton Morris; ***W:*** Chris Mulkey, John Jenkins, Karen Landry, David Burton Morris; ***M:*** Doug Maynard.

Patton 🦴🦴🦴 ½ *Patton—Lust for Glory; Patton: A Salute to a Rebel* **1970 (PG)** Lengthy but stellar bio of the vain, temperamental American general who masterminded significant combat triumphs during WWII. "Old Blood and Guts," who considered himself an 18th-century commander living in the wrong era, produced victory after victory in North Africa and Europe, but not without a decided impact upon his troops. Scott is truly magnificent in the title role, and Malden shines in the supporting role of General Omar Bradley. Not a subtle film, but neither is its subject. Interesting match-up with the 1986 TV movie "The Last Days of Patton," also starring Scott. **171m/C VHS, DVD, Blu-ray Disc.** George C. Scott, Karl Malden, Stephen Young, Michael Strong, Frank Latimore, James Edwards, Lawrence (Larry) Dobkin, Michael Bates, Tim Considine, Edward Binns, John Doucette, Morgan Paull, Siegfried Rauch, Paul Stevens, Richard Muench; ***D:*** Franklin J. Schaffner; ***W:*** Francis Ford Coppola, Edmund H. North; ***C:*** Fred W. Koenekamp; ***M:*** Jerry Goldsmith. Oscars '70: Actor (Scott), Art Dir./Set Dec., Director (Schaffner), Film Editing, Picture, Sound, Story & Screenplay; AFI '98: Top 100; Directors Guild '70: Director (Schaffner); Golden Globes '71: Actor—Drama (Scott); Natl. Bd. of Review '70: Actor (Scott), Natl. Film Reg. '03;; N.Y. Film Critics '70: Actor (Scott); Natl. Soc. Film Critics '70: Actor (Scott); Writers Guild '70: Orig. Screenplay.

Patty Hearst 🦴 ½ **1988 (R)** Less than fascinating, expressionistic portrait of Hearst from her kidnapping through her brainwashing and eventual criminal participation with the SLA. An enigmatic film that seems to only make Hearst's transformation into a Marxist terrorist all the more mysterious. Based on Hearst's book, "Every Secret Thing." **108m/C VHS.** Natasha Richardson, William Forsythe, Ving Rhames, Frances Fisher, Jodi Long, Dana Delany; ***D:*** Paul Schrader; ***W:*** Nicholas Kazan; ***C:*** Bojan Bazelli.

Paul and Michelle 🦴 **1974 (R)** The equally dull sequel to "Friends" finds the two lovers a little older but no wiser. Paul has graduated from his British school and returns to France to seek out Michelle and their child. They try to rekindle their romance but the stresses of everyday life cause them problems. **102m/C VHS.** *GB FR* Sean Bury, Anicee Alvina, Keir Dullea, Ronald Lewis, Catherine Allegret, Georges Beller; ***D:*** Lewis Gilbert; ***M:*** Michel Colombier.

Paul Bartel's The Secret Cinema 🦴🦴 ½ *The Secret Cinema* **1969** Long before "The Truman Show" or "Ed TV," there was this little Bartel short of a woman who can't determine whether her life is real or a film by a maniacal director. Offbeat, creative, and a little disturbing. Followed by Bartel's short "Naughty Nurse." **37m/B VHS.** Amy Vane, Gordon Felio, Connie Ellison, Phillip Carlson, Estelle Omens, Barry Dennen, Mara Lepmanis, Camille Fife, Mimi Randolph, Glenn Johnson; ***D:*** Paul Bartel; ***W:*** Paul Bartel; ***C:*** Fred Wellington.

Paul Blart: Mall Cop 🦴 ½ **2009 (PG)** Mild-mannered single dad and security guard Paul Blart must save the day when a gang of crooks (dressed as Santa's helpers) takes over his New Jersey shopping mall with a plan to rob all the stores. Like the comedy of the 3 Stooges, flick relies upon slapstick and pratfalls to pry loose a few mindless laughs, which get old after the first 20 minutes, not coincidently the approximate running time of a TV sitcom, a venue more suited to James' limited range. **91m/C DVD.** *US* Kevin James, Keir O'Donnell, Jayma Mays, Erik Avari, Shirley Knight, Peter Gerety, Bobby Cannavale, Adam Ferrara, Raini Rodriguez, Stephen Rannazzisi; ***D:*** Steve Carr; ***W:*** Kevin James, Nicky Bakay; ***C:*** Russ T. Alsobrook; ***M:*** Waddy Wachtel.

Paul Robeson 🦴🦴 **1977** Major events in the life of the popular actor are recounted in this one-man performance. Originally staged by Charles Nelson Reilly. **118m/C VHS, DVD.** James Earl Jones; ***D:*** Lloyd Richards.

Paulie 🦴🦴 ½ **1998 (PG)** Dreamworks follows up "Mouse Hunt" with this tale of a conversant parrot (voiced by Mohr) whose mouth keeps getting him in trouble. Trapped in a dingy basement, Paulie tells a lonely Russian janitor (Shalhoub) the story of his cross-country quest to return to his original owner, the little girl (Eisenberg) who raised him from a fledgling. After the girl's parents send him away, Paulie goes through a procession of owners: a smart-aleck pawn shop owner (Hackett); a kindly old woman (Rowlands) who drives him to L.A in her RV; a petty criminal (Mohr again); a taco stand owner (Marin) who manages a parrot dancing act; and a scientist (Davison) looking to cash in on the bird's talent. Not a whole lot of action for a kiddie movie, and some of the jokes may go over their heads, but fine performances all around and a charming story keep pic aloft. **91m/C VHS, DVD.** Jay Mohr, Gena Rowlands, Tony Shalhoub, Richard "Cheech" Marin, Hallie Kate Eisenberg, Bruce Davison, Trini Alvarado, Buddy Hackett, Matt Craven, Bill Cobbs, Laura Harrington, Tia Texada; ***D:*** John Roberts; ***W:*** Laurie Craig; ***C:*** Tony Pierce-Roberts; ***M:*** John Debney; ***V:*** Jay Mohr.

Pauline and Paulette 🦴🦴 **2001 (PG)** Pauline (van der Groen) is a 66-year-old mentally retarded woman living happily with her sister Martha (De Bruyn) is a Flemish town near Brussels. When Martha dies, her will states that her estate will be divided in thirds on condition that one of the two remaining sisters, Paulette (Petersen) or Cecile (Bergmans), must take in Pauline. Otherwise the money will go to set Pauline up in a special care facility. Paulette agrees to care for Pauline, at least temporarily, and finds there are some obligations that aren't easy to get rid of. French and Flemish with subtitles. **78m/C VHS, DVD.** *BE FR NL* Dora van der Groen, Ann Petersen, Rosemarie Bergmans, Julienne De Bruyn, Idwig Stephane; ***D:*** Lieven Debrauwer; ***W:*** Lieven Debrauwer, Jacques Boon; ***C:*** Michael Van Laer; ***M:*** Frederic Devreese.

Pauline at the Beach 🦴🦴🦴 ½ *Pauline a la Plage* **1983 (R)** Fifteen-year-old Pauline (Langlet) accompanies her more experienced divorced cousin Marion (Dombasle) to the French coast for a summer of sexual hijinks. Contemplative, not coarse, though the leads look great in—and out—of their swimsuits. Breezy, typically talky fare from small-film master Rohmer. Third film in the director's Comedies & Proverbs series. French with subtitles. **95m/C VHS, DVD.** *FR* Amanda Langlet, Arielle Dombasle, Pascal Greggory, Rosette, Feodor Atkine, Simon de la Brosse; ***D:*** Eric Rohmer; ***W:*** Eric Rohmer; ***C:*** Nestor Almendros.

Pavilion of Women 🦴 ½ **2001 (R)** Dull adaptation of the 1946 Pearl S. Buck novel. As the Japanese prepare to invade Manchuria in 1938, Madame Wu (Luo), tired of her husband's brutality, decides to give him a peasant girl concubine, Chiuming (Ding), whom he promptly rejects. However, the pretty girl attracts the interest of the Wu's youngest son, Fengmo (Cho), just as Madame becomes interested in American missionary doctor, Father Andre (Dafoe), who runs the local orphanage. The film is in English and the Chinese actors do struggle with their dialogue which doesn't help the emotional balance of the production. **120m/C VHS, DVD.** Luo Yan, Willem Dafoe, John Cho, Yi Ding, Shek Sau, Amy Hill, Anita Loo, Kate McGregor-Stewart; ***W:*** Luo Yan, Paul R. Collins; ***C:*** Hang-Seng Poon; ***M:*** Conrad Pope.

The Pawnbroker 🦴🦴🦴 ½ **1965** A Jewish pawnbroker in Harlem is haunted by his grueling experiences in a Nazi camp during the Holocaust. Powerful and well done. Probably Steiger's best performance. Adapted from a novel by Edward Lewis Wallant. **120m/B VHS, DVD.** Rod Steiger, Brock Peters, Geraldine Fitzgerald, Jaime Sanchez, Thelma Oliver; ***D:*** Sidney Lumet; ***C:*** Boris Kaufman; ***M:*** Quincy Jones. Berlin Intl. Film Fest. '65: Actor (Steiger); British Acad. '66: Actor (Steiger), Natl. Film Reg. '08.

Pawnshop 🦴🦴 ½ **1916** Charlie is employed as a pawnbroker's assistant. Silent with music track. **32m/B VHS, DVD.** Charlie Chaplin, Henry Bergman, Edna Purviance, John Rand; ***D:*** Charlie Chaplin; ***W:*** Charlie Chaplin; ***C:*** Roland H. Totheroh.

Pay It Forward 🦴🦴 **2000 (PG-13)** Seventh-grade student Trevor (Osment) takes his social studies assignment very seriously. His teacher Eugene (Spacey) has his students think of an idea to change the world and tells them to put it into action. Trevor comes up with the idea of doing a good deed for someone who is then supposed to do a favor for someone else as a way to "pay the favor forward." Trevor's cocktail waitress/recovering alcoholic mom Arlene (Hunt) finds herself wary of both the project and the teacher. Trevor, however, has decided to use the two of them as his first "pay it forward" subjects. Cloyingly emotional and more than a little manipulative. Based on the novel by

Catherine Ryan Hyde. **122m/C VHS, DVD.** Haley Joel Osment, Kevin Spacey, Helen Hunt, Jay Mohr, James (Jim) Caviezel, Jon Bon Jovi, Angie Dickinson, David Ramsey, Gary Werntz; ***D:*** Mimi Leder; ***W:*** Leslie Dixon; ***C:*** Oliver Stapleton; ***M:*** Thomas Newman.

Pay Off **1989** A lunatic psychiatrist seeks murderous revenge on his ex-patient/ girlfriend and her family. **87m/C VHS.** Michael Fitzpatrick, Veronika Mattson, Margareta Krook; ***D:*** Jiri (George) Tirl.

Pay or Die **1983 (R)** A crime boss' men turn on him and kidnap his daughter, prompting the intervention of an unusual martial arts team. **92m/C VHS.** Dick Adair, Johnny Wilson; ***D:*** Bobby Suarez.

Payback **1989** A brawny young man uses firepower to avenge those who have wronged him. **90m/C VHS.** Jean Carol, Alex Meneses; ***D:*** Addison Randall.

Payback 1/2 **1990 (R)** A convict sets out to avenge his brother's death, and creates all sorts of mayhem in the process. Produced by Bob "Newlywed Game" Eubanks and scored by Daryl "Captain and Tenille" Dragon. **94m/C VHS.** Corey Michael Eubanks, Michael Ironside, Teresa Blake, Bert Remsen, Vincent Van Patten, Don Swayze; ***D:*** Russell Solberg; ***M:*** Daryl Dragon.

Payback 1/2 **1994 (R)** An old, dying con (Armstrong) tells fellow inmate Oscar Bonsetter (Howell) the whereabouts of a fortune if he'll promise to kill cruel jail guard Gully (Bell) who made the geezer's life a misery. Years later, the now ex-con finds the ex-guard running a diner near the spot where the money is buried and decides to carry out his plan for revenge. If Oscar doesn't get too distracted by Gully's hot-to-trot wife, Rose (Severance), first. Also available in an unrated version. **92m/C VHS.** C. Thomas Howell, Joan Severance, Marshall Bell, R.G. Armstrong; ***D:*** Anthony Hickox; ***W:*** Sam Bernard; ***C:*** David Bridges.

Payback **1998 (R)** Mel's very, very mean. Of course, his character has every reason to be in this loose remake of 1967's "Point Blank" and the novel "The Hunter" by Richard Stark. Porter (Gibson) is double-crossed by partner Val (Henry), who steals the loot from their latest heist as well as Porter's junkie wife, Lynn (Unger), and then leaves Porter for dead. Porter becomes obsessed with getting his money back, and he'll take on anyone who gets in his way. Very cold, violent neo-noir with a pro lead and interesting supporting cast. **110m/C VHS, DVD, Blu-ray Disc, HD DVD.** Mel Gibson, Gregg Henry, Maria Bello, David Paymer, Deborah Kara Unger, William Devane, Kris Kristofferson, Bill Duke, Jack Conley, John Glover, Lucy Liu, James Coburn; ***D:*** Brian Helgeland; ***W:*** Brian Helgeland, Terry Hayes; ***C:*** Ericson Core; ***M:*** Chris Boardman.

Paycheck **2003 (PG-13)** Michael Jennings (Affleck) is a brilliant engineer hired by his old friend Jimmy Rethrick (Echkart) to work on a top-secret project. The one condition is that he gets his mind erased after his job is completed. Three years later, Jennings, sans memories, finds that he had forfeited his fee of $90 million in exchange for a manila envelope full of seemingly random objects. It turns out that he was framed for murder and his former employers want him dead. The objects become clues to figuring out what the heck is going on. Surprisingly lackluster adaption of a Phillip K. Dick short story, considering that John Woo is the director. **110m/C DVD.** *US* Ben Affleck, Aaron Eckhart, Uma Thurman, Paul Giamatti, Colm Feore, Joe Morton, Michael C. Hall; ***D:*** John Woo; ***W:*** Dean Georgaris; ***C:*** Jeffrey L. Kimball; ***M:*** John Powell. Golden Raspberries '03: Worst Actor (Affleck).

Payday 1/2 **1973** Torn stars as a declining country music star on tour in this portrayal of the seamy side of show business, from groupies to grimy motels. Well-written script and fine performances make this an engaging, if rather draining, drama not easily found on the big screen. **98m/C VHS, DVD.** Sonny Shroyer, Rip Torn, Ahna Capri, Michael C. Gwynne, Jeff Morris; ***D:*** Daryl Duke; ***W:*** Don Carpenter; ***C:*** Richard C. Glouner; ***M:*** Ed Bogas, Shel Silverstein, Ian Tyson.

Payment on Demand 1/2 **1951** Bette plays social climbing bitch Joyce Ramsey who, nonetheless, is stunned when David (Sullivan), her husband of 20 years, calmly asks her for a divorce. She's livid when she learns that he has been seeing another woman (Dee) and threatens a scandal unless David coughs up a large settlement. While taking a cruise, Joyce gets a glimpse into the lonely life of a divorcee so before the final decree can be granted, she asks David for another chance. Definitely a movie suited to the conservative Hollywood times. **90m/B DVD.** Bette Davis, Frances Dee, Kent Taylor, John Sutton, Jane Cowl, Barry Sullivan, Betty Lynn, Peggy Castle, Otto Kruger, Richard Anderson; ***D:*** Curtis Bernhardt; ***W:*** Curtis Bernhardt; ***C:*** Bruce Manning, Leo Tover; ***M:*** Victor Young.

The Payoff 1/2 **1943** The old-fashioned newspaper-reporter-as-crime-fighter routine. When the city's special prosecutor is murdered a daring newshawk investigates and tracks the bad guys. But will he spell their names right? **74m/B VHS, DVD.** Lee Tracy, Tom Brown, Tina Thayer, Evelyn Brent, Jack La Rue, Ian Keith, John Maxwell; ***D:*** Arthur Dreifuss.

Payoff **1991 (R)** An ex-cop discovers the identity of gangsters who killed his parents. He traces them to a Lake Tahoe resort and plots revenge. Familiar crime story with a good cast. **111m/C VHS.** Keith Carradine, Kim Greist, Harry Dean Stanton, John Saxon, Jeff Corey; ***D:*** Stuart Cooper; ***W:*** Douglas S. Cook; ***M:*** Charles Bernstein.

P.C.U. **1994 (PG-13)** Satire on campus political correctness follows freshman Tom Lawrence's (Young) adventures as he navigates the treacherous waters of Port Chester University (PCU). He falls in with the gang from the Pit, the militantly non-PC dorm, who encourage bizarre and offensive behavior. Essentially a modern update of "National Lampoon's Animal House," but without the brilliance; add half a bone for tackling the thorny sensitivity issue in a humorous way that parodies, but shouldn't offend. Actor Bochner's directorial debut. **81m/C VHS, DVD.** Jeremy Piven, Chris Young, David Spade, Sarah Trigger, Jessica Walter, Jon Favreau, Megan Ward, Jake Busey, Alex Desert; ***Cameos:*** George Clinton; ***D:*** Hart Bochner; ***W:*** Adam Leff, Zak Penn; ***M:*** Steve Vai.

P.D. James: Death in Holy Orders 1/2 *Death in Holy Orders* **2003** When murder and suicide overtake St. Anselm's, a remote theological college, one victim's wealthy father pressures Scotland Yard to investigate. Adam Dalgleish (Shaw), who spent childhood summers at the school, is sent and discovers that the Church of England wishes to close the school, and Archdeacon Matthew Crampton (Wood) is particularly interested in seeing that its valuable art works have more suitable settings. What the widowed Dalgleish doesn't expect to encounter is potential romance with visiting professor Emma Lavenham (Dee). **180m/C DVD.** *GB* Martin Shaw, Jesse Spencer, Alan Howard, Clive Wood, Hugh Fraser, Robert Hardy, Janie Dee; ***D:*** John Campbell; ***W:*** Robert C. Jones; ***C:*** Martin Fuhrer; ***M:*** Julian Nott. **TV**

P.D. James: The Murder Room 1/2 *The Murder Room* **2004** A macabre family legacy leads to murder and other crimes. London's Dupayne Museum houses exhibits from some of Britain's most gruesome real-life homicides. When Neville (Maloney), one of the Dupayne heirs, dies in a terrible fire, Adam Dalgleish (Shaw) investigates and discovers that the killing is similar to a notorious case on display. But there are also family secrets the remaining Dupaynes don't want exposed. **180m/C DVD.** *GB* Martin Shaw, Samantha Bond, Michael Maloney, Nicholas Le Prevost, Sian Phillips, Kerry Fox, Janie Dee; ***D:*** Diarmuid Lawrence; ***W:*** Robert C. Jones; ***C:*** Simon Richards; ***M:*** John Lunn. **TV**

Peace, Propaganda & the Promised Land **2004** Expose lashing out at the American media's coverage of the Israeli-Palestinian conflict. Another long-winded attempt at a Michael Moore-style "documentary." Cites twists on terms, such as "retaliate" when Israel makes a move, but using the word "attack" when describing Palestinian operations. On-camera interviews come from unabashedly biased academics and advocates. Makes some stirring observations, but its lack of humor and tunnel-visioned hoopla will turn off most audiences. Ironically, it falls into the category it sets out to derail: juicy propaganda. **80m/C DVD.** *US* ***D:*** Sut Jhally, Bathsheba Ratzkoff; ***C:*** Kelli Garner; ***M:*** Thom Monahan.

Peaceful Warrior **2006 (PG-13)** It's not quite the new "Karate Kid" despite that whole Zen mentor aspect that Nolte brings to the role of Socrates. Dan (Mechlowicz) is a hotshot college gymnast who is told his dreams are over after a bad motorcycle crash. Socrates offers his own spiritual take on Dan's dilemma and Dan goes on to—well, the actual Dan Millman goes on to write a 1980 New Age memoir called "Way of the Peaceful Warrior," which this film is based on. **121m/C DVD.** *US* Nick Nolte, Scott Mechlowicz, Amy Smart, Tim DeKay, Paul Wesley, Ashton Holmes, Agnes Bruckner, Ray Wise, B. J. Britt; ***D:*** Victor Salva; ***W:*** Victor Salva, Kevin Bernhardt; ***C:*** Sharon Meir; ***M:*** Bennett Salvay.

The Peacekeeper **1998 (R)** Frank Cross (Lundgren) is one unlucky man. While guarding the president (Scheider), he manages to lose the briefcase containing nuclear launch codes to a terrorist group. Now, they're blackmailing the government and Cross needs to breach the terrorist's stronghold to save the day. **98m/C VHS, DVD.** *CA* Dolph Lundgren, Roy Scheider, Michael Sarrazin, Montel Williams, Monica Schnarre; ***D:*** Frederic Forestier; ***W:*** James H. Stewart, Robert Geoffrion; ***C:*** John Berrie; ***M:*** Francois Forestier.

Peacekillers 1/2 **1971** A mean bunch of bikers visit a commune to kidnap a young woman. The gang has a big surprise in store for them when the girl escapes. **86m/C VHS.** Michael Ontkean, Clint Ritchie, Paul Krokop; ***D:*** Douglas Schwartz.

Peacemaker **1990 (R)** Two aliens masquerading as human cops stalk each other through a major city. **90m/C VHS, DVD.** Robert Forster, Lance Edwards, Hilary Shepard, Bert Remsen, Robert Davi; ***D:*** Kevin S. Tenney; ***W:*** Kevin S. Tenney.

The Peacemaker 1/2 **1997 (R)** First-time feature director Leder teams up with fellow "ER" vet Clooney on the first theatrical release for Dreamworks SKG. Clooney's Army Intel officer Lt. Col. Thomas Devoe works with White House nuke expert Dr. Julia Kelly (Kidman) when a renegade Russian colonel diverts some nuclear warheads, scheduled for dismantling, into the hands of a Bosnian diplomat (Iures) with a grudge against the West. Plenty of well-constructed action set pieces and a reasonably plausible plot overcome a lack of snappy dialogue. Extra credit for making the terrorist human instead of the usual evil caricature, and for letting the two leads work together without having to sleep together. **123m/C VHS, DVD.** George Clooney, Nicole Kidman, Armin Mueller-Stahl, Marcel Iures, Alexander Baluyev, Randall Batinkoff, Jim Haynie, Michael Boatman, Gary Werntz, Holt McCallany, Joan Copeland, Carlos Gomez, Rene Medvesek, Alexander Strobele; ***D:*** Mimi Leder; ***W:*** Michael Schiffer; ***C:*** Dietrich Lohmann; ***M:*** Hans Zimmer.

The Peacock Fan 1/2 **1929** The Peacock Fan is protected by a deadly curse, with certain death to anyone who possesses it. **50m/B VHS.** Lucian Preval, Dorothy Dwan, Rosemary Theby, Gladden James; ***D:*** Phil Rosen; ***W:*** Arthur Hoerl; ***C:*** M.A. Anderson.

The Peanut Butter Solution 1/2 **1985 (PG)** An imaginative 11-year-old boy investigates a strange old house which is haunted by friendly ghosts who are in possession of a magic potion. **96m/C VHS.** Matthew Mackay, Siluck Saysanasy, Alison Podbrey, Michael Maillot, Griffith Brewer, Michael Hogan, Helen Hughes; ***D:*** Michael Rubbo; ***W:*** Michael Rubbo; ***M:*** Lewis Furey.

The Pearl **1948** Based on a John Steinbeck story, a Mexican fisherman, living in poverty, finds a magnificent pearl and he thinks it will improve the lives of his family. He is bewildered by what this pearl really brings—liars and thieves. Simple, yet larger-than-life film, beautifully photographed; a timeless picture capturing human nature. **77m/B VHS.** *MX* Pedro Armendariz Sr., Maria Elena Marques, Fernando Wagner, Charles Rooner; ***D:*** Emilio Fernandez. Natl. Film Reg. '02.

Pearl 1/2 **1978** Sweeping miniseries covers the careers and private lives of those who live and work at the naval base at Pearl Harbor, Hawaii, from right before the Japanese attack to its aftermath. **233m/C VHS.** Robert Wagner, Dennis Weaver, Lesley Ann Warren, Brian Dennehy, Max Gail, Mary Crosby, Gregg Henry, Katherine Helmond, Angie Dickinson, Tiana Alexandra, Richard Anderson, Adam Arkin, Marion Ross, Allan Miller, David Elliott; ***D:*** Hy Averback, Alexander Singer; ***W:*** Stirling Silliphant; ***C:*** Gayne Rescher; ***M:*** John Addison; ***Nar:*** Joseph Campanella. **TV**

Pearl Diver **2004** Sisters Hannah and Marian were raised on the family's farm in a Mennonite community in rural Indiana. Their mother's murder has caused them to drift apart as Hannah has moved to the city and become a writer and Marian has married and stayed at home. When Marian's daughter is severely injured in a farm accident, Hannah returns to help out and the two sisters also attempt to confront what really happened the night their mother died. **90m/C DVD.** Eugene (Yevgeny) Lazarev, Joey Honja, Amy Jean Johnson, Kim Stauffer, Brian Boland, Maddie Abshire, Christopher Collard; ***D:*** Sidney King; ***W:*** Sidney King; ***C:*** John Rotan; ***M:*** Jay Lapp, Frances Miller.

Pearl Harbor **2001 (PG-13)** Director Bay has also done "The Rock" and "Armageddon" so he knows his way around big-budget, action-packed event movies. The problem, besides his usual difficulties with characterization and sublety, is that we have to wade through the trite romantic triangle between U.S. Army Air aviator Hartnett, flyboy Affleck, and Navy nurse Beckinsale before we get to the well-done spectacle of the bombing on December 7, 1941, as well as the subsequent U.S. raid on Tokyo led by James Doolittle (Baldwin). It's probably quicker, and more enjoyable, to skip to the attack sequence between a rented double feature of "From Here to Eternity" and "Thirty Seconds Over Tokyo." **183m/C VHS, DVD.** *US* Ben Affleck, Josh Hartnett, Kate Beckinsale, Alec Baldwin, Cuba Gooding Jr., Dan Aykroyd, Mako, Tom Sizemore, Jon Voight, William Lee Scott, Colm Feore, Michael Shannon, Peter Firth, Jennifer Garner, Catherine Kellner, Jaime (James) King, Scott Wilson, William Fichtner, Ewen Bremner, Leland Orser, Graham Beckel, Tomas Arana, Guy Torry, Brian Haley, Tony Curran, Kim Coates, Glenn Morshower, John Fujioka, Tim Choate, John Diehl, Ted McGinley, Raphael Sbarge; ***D:*** Michael Bay; ***W:*** Randall Wallace; ***C:*** John Schwartzman; ***M:*** Hans Zimmer.

The Pearl of Death 1/2 **1944** Holmes and Watson investigate the theft of a precious pearl. **69m/B VHS, DVD.** Basil Rathbone, Nigel Bruce, Dennis Hoey, Miles Mander, Rondo Hatton, Evelyn Ankers; ***D:*** Roy William Neill.

Pearl of the South Pacific *South Sea Woman* **1955** A trio of adventurers destroy a quiet and peaceful island when they ransack it for pearl treasures. **85m/C VHS, DVD.** Dennis Morgan, Virginia Mayo, David Farrar; ***D:*** Allan Dwan; ***W:*** Edwin Blum; ***C:*** John Alton; ***M:*** Louis Forbes.

Peau D'Ane **1971** Charming fairy tale about a widowed king in search of a beautiful wife. Gorgeous color production. In French with English subtitles. **90m/C VHS, DVD.** *FR* Catherine Deneuve, Jacques Perrin, Jean Marais, Delphine Seyrig; ***D:*** Jacques Demy.

The Pebble and the Penguin 1/2 **1994 (G)** Animated musical about a shy, romantic penguin named Hubie (Short), who must present his lady love Marina (Golden) with a beautiful pebble to win her hand forever before the villainous Drake (Curry) can claim her. Hubie is helped along the way by a cantankerous new friend (Belushi) he meets when stranded on a boat to Tahiti. Together the two race back to Antarctica fighting enemies and the elements along the way. Based on a true mating custom of the Adeli penguins, the story is satisfying for younger viewers, but does not have the animation magic of other recents films to keep adults interested. Beware of the sugary Manilow tunes. **74m/C VHS, DVD.** ***D:*** Don Bluth; ***W:*** Rachel Koretsky, Steve Whitestone; ***M:*** Barry Manilow, Bruce Sussman, Mark Watters; ***V:*** Martin Short, Annie Golden, Tim Curry, James Belushi; ***Nar:*** Shani Wallis.

Pecker 1/2 **1998 (R)** A kinder, gentler Waters? To be sure, he doesn't laugh at, but with, his working-class Baltimoreans. Still, you've got strippers (of both sexes), a "talking" statue of the Virgin Mary, and rats having sex, so this isn't a Disney film. Pecker (Furlong), who gets his name from pecking at his food, is a sweet teenager and amateur photog, who takes pictures of what's around him. His work catches the eye of New York art dealer Rorey Wheeler (Taylor), who wants to showcase the next hot trend, and Pecker becomes an overnight superstar in the fickle art world. But his celeb status has unexpected repercussions on his hometown friends and family. **87m/C VHS, DVD.** Edward Furlong, Lili Taylor, Christina Ricci, Martha Plimpton, Mary Kay Place, Brendan Sexton III, Mark Joy, Mink Stole, Bess Armstrong, Patty (Patricia Campbell) Hearst, Mary Vivian Pearce, Lauren Hulsey, Jean Schertler; ***D:*** John Waters; ***W:*** John Waters; ***C:*** Robert M. Stevens; ***M:*** Stewart Copeland; ***V:*** John Waters. Natl. Bd. of Review '98: Support. Actress (Ricci).

Peck's Bad Boy **1921** Impudent, precocious brat causes his parents considerable grief. Someone should lock this kid in a room with W.C. Fields or the Alien. Silent film based on the stories by George Wilbur Peck. **51m/B VHS, DVD.** Jackie Coogan, Thomas Meighan, Raymond Hatton, Wheeler Oakman, Lillian (Lillianne, Lyllian) Leighton; ***D:*** Sam Wood.

Peck's Bad Boy 1/2 **1934** A wedge is driven between a young boy and his adoptive father when the man's sister and her son move in. The aunt wants her son to be number one, causing much discord. Cooper is excellent in his role as the adopted son. **70m/B VHS, DVD.** Thomas Meighan, Jackie Cooper, Dorothy Peterson, Jackie Searl, O.P. Heggie, Harvey Clark, Lloyd Ingraham; ***D:*** Edward F. (Eddie) Cline.

Peck's Bad Boy with the Circus **1938** The circus will never be the same after the mischievous youngster and his buddies get done with it. Gilbert and Kennedy provide the high points. **67m/B VHS, DVD.** Tommy Kelly, Ann Gillis, George "Spanky" McFarland, Edgar Kennedy, Billy Gilbert; ***D:*** Edward F. (Eddie) Cline.

Pecos Bill **1986** Meet the man who used the Grand Canyon for a swimmin' hole, dug the Rio Grande, and used the Texas panhandle for a fryin' pan. From Shelly Duvall's "Tall Tales and Legends" cable series. **50m/C VHS, DVD.** Steve Guttenberg, Martin Mull, Claude Akins, Rebecca De Mornay. **CABLE**

Pecos Kid **1935** A child has his parents killed, and grows up embittered, vengeful and thirsty for blood. **56m/B VHS.** Roger Williams, Edward Cassidy, Wally Wales, Ruth Findlay, Earl Dwire, Fred Kohler Jr.; ***D:*** Harry Fraser; ***W:*** Henry Hess.

Pedale Douce 1/2 *What a Drag* **1996** Irreverant comedy features a romantic triangle involving content gay businessman Adrien (Timsit), whose confidante is the liberal Eva (Ardant), owner of a trendy Paris eatery with an all-gay staff and predominatly gay clientele. Adrien persuades Eva to pose as his wife in order to close a deal with conservative, married banker Alexandre (Berry). Alexandre becomes enchanted with Eva and begins to pursue her, causing a comedy of errors and unexpected jealousy for Adrien, who tries to derail their affair. French with subtitles. **102m/C VHS.** *FR* Patrick Timsit, Fanny Ardant, Richard Berry, Michele Laroque, Jacques Gamblin; ***D:*** Gabriel Aghion; ***W:*** Patrick Timsit, Gabriel Aghion, Pierre Palmade; ***C:*** Fabio Conversi; ***M:*** Herve Masini, Philippe Chopin. Cesar '97: Actress (Ardant).

Peddlin' in Society *Da Bancarella a Bancarotta* **1947** A fruit vendor makes it big on the black market and lives the good life, until poor investments force her back to her old means. Strong perfomances by Magnani and De Sica. In Italian with English subititles. **85m/B VHS.** *IT* Anna Magnani, Vittorio De Sica, Virgilio Riento, Laura Gore; ***D:*** Gennaro Righelli.

The Pedestrian 1/2 *Der Fussgaenger* **1973 (PG)** A prominent German industrialist is exposed as a Nazi officer who supervised the wholesale devastation of a Greek village during WWII. Impressive debut for director Schell, who also appears in a supporting role. **97m/C VHS.** *GE SI* Maximilian Schell, Peggy Ashcroft, Lil Dagover, Francoise Rosay, Elisabeth Bergner; ***D:*** Maximilian Schell; ***M:*** Manos Hadjidakis. Golden Globes '74: Foreign Film.

The Pee-wee Herman Show 1/2 **1982** The original HBO special which introduced Pee-wee to the world. Hilarious stuff, with help from Captain Carl (Hartman), Miss Yvonne, and other assorted pals. Warning: Not to be confused with Pee-wee's children's show. **60m/C VHS, DVD.** Paul (Pee-wee Herman) Reubens, John Moody, John Paragon, Tito Larriva, Nicole Panter, Phil Hartman, Lynne Stewart, Edie McClurg; ***D:*** Marty Callner; ***W:*** Bill Steinkellner; ***M:*** Jay Condom. **CABLE**

Pee-wee's Big Adventure 1/2 **1985 (PG)** Zany, endearing comedy about an adult nerd's many adventures while attempting to recover his stolen bicycle. Chock full of classic sequences, including a barroom encounter between Pee-wee and several ornery bikers, and a tour through the Alamo. A colorful, exhilarating experience. **92m/C VHS, DVD.** Paul (Pee-wee Herman) Reubens, Elizabeth (E.G. Dailey) Daily, Mark Holton, Diane Salinger, Judd Omen, Cassandra Peterson, James Brolin, Morgan Fairchild, Tony Bill, Jan Hooks, Phil Hartman, Jason Hervey, John Paragon; ***D:*** Tim Burton; ***W:*** Michael Varhol, Paul (Pee-wee Herman) Reubens, Phil Hartman; ***C:*** Victor Kemper; ***M:*** Danny Elfman.

Peephole **1993** Prison psychiatrist is asked by the DA to keep Rick, who committed a sex crime against a little girl, in jail any way he can. So he visits Rick's prostitute girlfriend Sheena for info but instead winds up one of her clients. Meanwhile, Rick has been released and a little girl has been found dead, but nothing's that clear cut. Based on director/writer Bitterman's play. **90m/C VHS.** Patrick Husted, Rick Dean, William Dennis Hunt, Kristen Trucksess, Peter Crook; ***D:*** Shem Bitterman; ***W:*** Shem Bitterman.

Peeping Tom 1/2 *Face of Fear; The Fotographer of Panic* **1960** Controversial, unsettling thriller in which psychopath Mark Lewis (Boehm) lures women before his film camera, then records their deaths at his hand. Unnerving subject matter is rendered impressively by British master Powell, who plays the part of Mark's abusie father who's shown in home movies tormenting the boy. A classic of its kind, but definitely not for everyone. Critical brickbats effectively derailed Powell's career and the original uncut version was not released until 1979. **88m/C VHS, DVD.** *GB* Karl-Heinz Boehm, Moira Shearer, Anna Massey, Maxine Audley, Esmond Knight, Shirley Anne Field, Brenda Bruce, Pamela Green, Jack Watson, Nigel Davenport, Susan Travers, Veronica Hurst, Martin Miller, Miles Malleson, Michael Powell; ***D:*** Michael Powell; ***W:*** Leo Marks; ***C:*** Otto Heller; ***M:*** Brian Easdale.

Peg o' My Heart **1922** Taylor portrays the motherless Irish charmer sent to live with her mother's English relatives during the Irish rebellion. Of course, she must overcome their upper-class English snobbery to become a part of the family. **85m/B VHS.** Laurette Taylor, Mahlon Hamilton, Russell Simpson, Ethel Grey, D.R.O. Hatswell; ***D:*** King Vidor; ***C:*** George Barnes.

Peggy Sue Got Married 1/2 **1986 (PG-13)** Uneven but entertaining comedy about an unhappily married woman seemingly unable to relive her life when she falls unconscious at a high school reunion and awakens to find herself back in school. Turner shines, but the film flags often, and Cage isn't around enough to elevate entire work. O'Connor scores, though, as a sensitive biker. Look for musician Marshall Crenshaw as part of the reunion band. **103m/C VHS, DVD.** Kathleen Turner, Nicolas Cage, Catherine Hicks, Maureen O'Sullivan, John Carradine, Helen Hunt, Lisa Jane Persky, Barbara Harris, Joan Allen, Kevin J. O'Connor, Barry Miller, Don Murray, Leon Ames, Sofia Coppola, Sachi (MacLaine) Parker, Jim Carrey; ***D:*** Francis Ford Coppola; ***W:*** Jerry Leichtling, Arlene Sarner; ***C:*** Jordan Cronenweth; ***M:*** John Barry. Natl. Bd. of Review '86: Actress (Turner).

The Peking Blond 1/2 *The Blonde From Peking; Le Blonde de Pekin* **1968** French-fried spyfilm boasts lousy acting unencumbered by plot. Amnesiac may or may not hold secrets coveted by Americans, Russians and Chinese. **80m/C VHS.** *FR* Mireille Darc, Claudio Brook, Edward G. Robinson, Pascale Roberts; ***D:*** Nicolas Gessner; ***W:*** Nicolas Gessner, Marc Behm.

The Pelican Brief 1/2 **1993 (PG-13)** Tulane law student Darby Shaw (Roberts) writes a speculative brief on the murders of two Supreme Court justices that results in more murder and sends her running for her life. Fairly faithful to the Grisham bestseller, but the multitude of characters is confusing. Pakula adds style and star-power, but much will depend on your tolerance for paranoid political thrillers and ability to accept Roberts as the smart cookie who hits on the right answer and then manages to keep herself alive while bodies are dropping all around her. Washington is sharp as reporter Gray Grantham, the guy Roberts looks like she falls hard for (but the book's romance is nowhere to be seen). **141m/C VHS, DVD, Blu-ray Disc.** Julia Roberts, Denzel Washington, John Heard, Tony Goldwyn, Stanley Tucci, James B. Sikking, William Atherton, Robert Culp, John Lithgow, Sam Shepard, Hume Cronyn; ***D:*** Alan J. Pakula; ***W:*** Alan J. Pakula; ***C:*** Stephen Goldblatt; ***M:*** James Horner.

Pelle the Conqueror **1988** Overpowering tale of a Swedish boy and his widower father who serve landowners in late 19th-century Denmark. Compassionate saga of human spirit contains numerous memorable sequences. Hvenegaard is wonderful as young Pelle, but von Sydow delivers what is probably his finest performance as a sympathetic weakling. American distributors foolishly trimmed the film by some 20 minutes (140 minute version). From the novel by Martin Anderson Nexo. In Swedish with English subtitles. **160m/C VHS, DVD.** *SW DK* Max von Sydow, Pelle Hvenegaard, Erik Paaske, Bjorn Granath, Axel Strobye, Astrid Villaume, Troels Asmussen, John Wittig, Anne Lise Hirsch Bjerrum, Kristina Tornqvist, Morten Jorgensen; ***D:*** Bille August; ***W:*** Bille August. Oscars '88: Foreign Film; Cannes '88: Film; Golden Globes '89: Foreign Film.

The Penalty 1/2 **1920** Legless madman Blizzard (Chaney) is after revenge on his family, doctor, and society. Chaney's properly creepy. **93m/B VHS, DVD.** Lon Chaney Sr., Claire Adams, Kenneth Harlan, Charles Clary; ***D:*** Wallace Worsley II; ***W:*** Charles Kenyon, Philip Lonergan; ***C:*** Don Short.

Penalty Phase **1986** An up-for-election judge must decide a murder case in which his future, as well as the defendant's, is in question. **94m/C VHS.** Peter Strauss, Melissa Gilbert, Jonelle Allen; ***D:*** Tony Richardson; ***M:*** Ralph Burns. **TV**

Pendulum **1969 (PG)** A police captain struggles to prove himself innocent of his wife's—and his wife's lover's—murders. Wow. **106m/C VHS.** George Peppard, Jean Seberg, Richard Kiley, Madeline Sherwood, Charles McGraw, Marj Dusay; ***D:*** George Schaefer; ***C:*** Lionel Lindon.

Penelope 1/2 **2006 (PG)** Modern-day retelling of an old fairy tale casts Ricci as Penelope, the lonely girl cursed with a pig's snout. Raised by overbearing and bizarre upper-crust parents (O'Hara and Grant), Penelope is presented with a long line of suitors, all of whom hope to marry into the family's wealth but immediately bail at the sight of their daughter's schnoz. Penelope soon flees to the Big Apple in search of a companion equally cursed and reviled, but instead meets Max (McAvoy), a sweet and charming rocker who sees her inner beauty instead. First-time director Mark Palansky successfully blends a sense of fantasy with the modern world, even throwing a few political jabs along the way. Still, as hard as he may try, he's no Tim Burton. **101m/C DVD.** *GB* Christina Ricci, James McAvoy, Catherine O'Hara, Peter Dinklage, Richard E. Grant, Reese Witherspoon, Simon Woods, Michael Feast, Nigel Havers, Lenny Henry, Ronni Ancona; ***D:*** Mark Palansky; ***W:*** Leslie Caveny; ***C:*** Michel Amanthieu; ***M:*** Joby Talbot.

The Penitent **1988 (PG-13)** A remote village's annual reenactment of the crucifixion of Christ serves as the backdrop for Assante's affair with his friend's (Julia) wife. Quirky little tale that focuses a shade too much on the romantic problems of the trio rather than the intriguing religious practices going on around them. **94m/C VHS.** Raul Julia, Armand Assante, Rona Freed, Julie Carmen; ***D:*** Cliff Osmond; ***M:*** Alex North.

Penitentiary 1/2 **1979 (R)** A realistic story of a black fighter who survives his prison incarceration by winning bouts against the other prisoners. Well-made and executed, followed by two progressively worse sequels. **99m/C VHS, DVD.** Leon Isaac Kennedy, Jamaa Fanaka, Badja (Medu) Djola, Chuck "Porky" Mitchell; ***D:*** Jamaa Fanaka; ***W:*** Jamaa Fanaka; ***C:*** Marty Ollstein.

Penitentiary 2 **1982 (R)** A welterweight fighter is after the man who murdered his girlfriend, who, luckily, is incarcerated in the same prison as Our Hero. Sometimes things just work out right. **108m/C VHS, DVD.** Leon Isaac Kennedy, Mr. T, Leif Erickson, Ernie Hudson, Glynn Turman; ***D:*** Jamaa Fanaka; ***W:*** Jamaa Fanaka; ***C:*** Stephen Posey; ***M:*** Jack Wheaton.

Penitentiary 3 1/2 **1987 (R)** Once again, Kennedy as the inmate boxer extraordinaire punches his way out of various prison battles. Another punch-drunk sequel. **91m/C VHS.** Leon Isaac Kennedy, Anthony Geary, Steve Antin, Ric Mancini, Kessler Raymond, Jim Bailey, Mindi Miller; ***D:*** Jamaa Fanaka; ***W:*** Jamaa Fanaka.

Penn and Teller Get Killed **1990 (R)** The comedy team with a cult following are pursued by an assassin through dozens of pratfalls in this dark comedy. **91m/C VHS.** Penn Jillette, Teller, Caitlin Clarke, Leonardo Cimino, David Patrick Kelly; ***D:*** Arthur Penn.

Pennies from Heaven 1/2 **1936** Bing plays Larry, a singer wrongly imprisoned, who promises to help the family of a man killed by a death row inmate Larry has befriended. Once on the outside, Larry finds the family, sassy little girl Patsy (Fellows) and her grandfather (Meek), enduring hard times. A social worker (Evans) is trying to keep Patsy out of the orphanage, and the gift of a home that Larry brings may help accomplish that. Complications arrive, however, when they try to turn the place into a cafe and find it may even be haunted. Typical of Crosby's 1930s work, it's pleasant enough and relies on Bing's charm and singing. He sings the Oscar-nominated title song no less than three times. Louis Armstrong appears to great effect, for the film and his subsequent career. **80m/C DVD.** Bing Crosby, Madge Evans, Edith Fellows, Donald Meek, Louis Armstrong, John Gallaudet, Tom Dugan, Nana Bryant, Charles C. Wilson, Harry Tyler, William Stack; ***D:*** Norman Z. McLeod; ***W:*** Jo Swerling; ***C:*** Robert Pittack; ***M:*** Johnny Burke, Arthur Johnston, John Scott Trotter. Oscars '36: Song ("Pennies from Heaven").

Pennies from Heaven 1/2 **1981 (R)** Underrated, one-of-a-kind musical about a horny sheet-music salesman in Chicago and his escapades during the Depression. Extraordinary musical sequences have stars lip-synching to great effect. Martin is only somewhat acceptable as the hapless salesman, but Peters and Harper deliver powerful performances as the women whose lives he ruins. Walken brings down the house in a stunning song-and-dance sequence. Adapted by Dennis Potter from his British TV series. ♫ The Clouds Will Soon Roll By; Did You Ever See A Dream Walking?; Yes, Yes; Pennies From Heaven; Love Is Good for Anything That Ails You; I Want to Be Bad; Let's Misbehave; Life Is Just a Bowl of Cherries; Let's Face the Music and Dance. **107m/C VHS, DVD.** Steve Martin, Bernadette Peters, Christopher Walken, Jessica Harper, Vernel Bagneris; ***D:*** Herbert Ross; ***W:*** Dennis Potter; ***C:*** Gordon Willis; ***M:*** Ralph Burns, Marvin Hamlisch. Golden Globes '82: Actress—Mus./Comedy (Peters); Natl. Soc. Film Critics '81: Cinematog.

Penny Serenade **1941** Newlyweds adopt a child, but tragedy awaits. Simplistic story nonetheless proves to be a moving experience. They don't make 'em like this anymore, and no one plays Grant better than Grant. Dunne is adequate. Also available colorized. **120m/B VHS, DVD.** Cary Grant, Irene Dunne, Beulah Bondi, Edgar Buchanan, Ann Doran, Wallis (Clarke) Clark; ***D:*** George Stevens; ***W:*** Morrie Ryskind; ***C:*** Joseph Walker; ***M:*** W. Franke Harling.

The Pentagon Wars ½ **1998 (R)** Based on the true story of Air Force Col. James G. Burton (Elwes) whose mandate in the 1980s was to monitor weapons testing. What he discovers is the ultimate in white elephants—the Bradley Fighting Vehicle, an armored troop transport project that cost the taxpayers $14 billion over 17 years. Grammer is the scheming and pompous Army General Patridge (a composite character) who'll brook no interference. Adapted from the book "The Pentagon Wars" by James Burton. **104m/C VHS, DVD.** Cary Elwes, Kelsey Grammer, Olympia Dukakis, Richard Benjamin, John C. McGinley, Tom Wright, Clifton Powell, Richard Schiff; ***D:*** Richard Benjamin; ***W:*** Martyn Burke, Jamie Malanowski; ***C:*** Robert Yeoman; ***M:*** Joseph Vitarelli. **CABLE**

Pentathlon ½ **1994 (R)** East German Olympic athlete Eric Brogar (Lundgren) defects to the U.S. a year before the crash of the Berlin Wall, causing embarassed German authorities to seek revenge on him and his family. **101m/C VHS.** Dolph Lundgren, David Soul, Roger E. Mosley, Renee Coleman; ***D:*** Bruce Malmuth.

Penthouse *Crooks in Clover* **1933** Baxter is a corporation lawyer who, for a change of pace, defends a gangland boss (Pendleton). His success loses him his high-society clientele but wins him Pendleton's respect and protection. But Baxter then gets involved in a further series of gang-related crimes, which nearly cost him his life. Also aiding Baxter is Loy, playing a smart-cookie gun moll, who would take her wisecracks to "The Thin Man" the following year. Good combo of melodrama, suspense, and humor. **90m/B** Warner Baxter, Myrna Loy, Nat Pendleton, C. Henry Gordon, Mae Clarke, Charles Butterworth, Phillips Holmes; ***D:*** Woodbridge S. Van Dyke.

The Penthouse **1992** Givens stars as a wealthy young woman stalked by an old boyfriend who just happens to have escaped from a mental institution. When he traps her in her home, she has two choices—love him or die. Based on the novel by Elleston Trevor. **93m/C VHS, DVD.** Robin Givens, David Hewlett, Cedric Smith, Donnelly Rhodes, Robert Guillaume; ***D:*** David Greene.

The People ½ **1971** A young teacher takes a job in a small town and finds out that her students have telepathic powers and other strange qualities. Adapted from a novel by Zenna Henderson. Good atmosphere, especially for a TV movie. **74m/C VHS, DVD.** Kim Darby, Dan O'Herlihy, Diane Varsi, William Shatner; ***D:*** John Korty; ***M:*** Carmine Coppola.

People **2004** Charles (Everett) is party planner for the jet set in Paris until a jealous rival brings him down. Desperate, Charles heads off to hedonistic Ibiza in order to persuade flamboyant club owner John John (Garcia) to join forces so Charles can restore his reputation. French with subtitles. **88m/C DVD.** *FR SP* Rupert Everett, Jose Garcia, Ornella Muti, Lambert Wilson, Rossy de Palma, Marisa Berenson, Jean-Claude Brialy, Patrice Cols; ***D:*** Fabien Onteniente; ***W:*** Fabien Onteniente; ***C:*** Josep Civit; ***M:*** Joachim Garraud, Bernard Grimaldi, David Guetta, Pascal Lemaire.

People Are Funny **1946** Battling radio producers vie to land the big sponsor with an original radio idea. Comedy ensues when one of them comes up with a great idea—stolen from a local station. **94m/B VHS, DVD.** Jack Haley, Rudy Vallee, Ozzie Nelson, Art Linkletter, Helen Walker; ***D:*** Sam White.

People I Know ½ **2002 (R)** Pacino forgoes the over-the-top style that's been his forte lately for a more restrained, meticulous portrayal of burned-out publicist Eli Wurman, and his performance saves the intriguing but muddled character study/political caper. Wurman's down to his last bigtime client, movie star Cary Launer (O'Neal), a shallow, womanizing, preening actor trying to break into politics. His bid for office is endangered when an actress with whom Launer had a drug-fueled fling is arrested. Eli is sent to bail her out, but becomes entangled in her murder and mysterious political hijinks, all while trying to stage a benefit for African refugees. Fine supporting cast delivers but plot gets a little busy for its own good when not focused on Eli's inner struggle. **95m/C VHS, DVD.** *US* Al Pacino, Kim Basinger, Ryan O'Neal, Tea Leoni, Richard Schiff, Bill Nunn, Robert Klein, Mark Webber, Polly Adams; ***D:*** Dan Algrant; ***W:*** Jon Robin Baitz; ***C:*** Peter Deming; ***M:*** Terence Blanchard.

The People Next Door **1970** Seventies attempt at exposing the drug problems of suburban youth. Typical middle-class parents Wallach and Harris are horrified to discover that daughter Winters is strung out on LSD. They fight to expose the neighborhood pusher while struggling to understand their now-alien daughter. Based on J.P. Miller's television play. **93m/C VHS.** Deborah Winters, Eli Wallach, Julie Harris, Stephen McHattie, Hal Holbrook, Cloris Leachman, Nehemiah Persoff; ***D:*** David Greene; ***W:*** J(ames) P(inckney) Miller.

The People That Time Forgot ½ **1977 (PG)** Sequel to "The Land That Time Forgot," based on the Edgar Rice Burroughs novel. A rescue team returns to a world of prehistoric monsters to rescue a man left there after the first film. **90m/C VHS, DVD.** *GB* Doug McClure, Patrick Wayne, Sarah Douglas, Dana Gillespie, Thorley Walters, Shane Rimmer; ***D:*** Kevin Connor; ***W:*** Patrick Tilley; ***C:*** Alan Hume; ***M:*** John Scott.

The People under the Stairs ½ **1991 (R)** Adams is part of a scheme to rob a house in the slums owned by a mysterious couple (Robie and McGill, both of "Twin Peaks" fame). After his friends are killed off in a gruesome fashion, he discovers that the couple aren't the house's only strange inhabitants—homicidal creatures also lurk within. **102m/C VHS, DVD.** Everett McGill, Wendy Robie, Brandon Adams, Ving Rhames, A.J. (Allison Joy) Langer, Sean M. Whalen, Kelly Jo Minter; ***D:*** Wes Craven; ***W:*** Wes Craven; ***C:*** Sandi Sissel; ***M:*** Don Peake.

The People vs. Jean Harris **1981** Follows the trial of Jean Harris. Shortly before this film was released, she had been convicted of murder in the death of Dr. Herman Tarnower, the author of "The Scarsdale Diet." Harris was headmistress in a private school all the while. Burstyn was nominated for an Emmy Award for best actress. **147m/C VHS, DVD.** Ellen Burstyn, Martin Balsam, Richard Dysart, Peter Coyote, Priscilla Morrill, Sarah Marshall, Millie Slavin; ***D:*** George Schaefer; ***M:*** Brad Fiedel. **TV**

The People vs. Larry Flynt **1996 (R)** Controversy surrounded director Forman's look at unrepentant pornographer and Hustler Magazine publisher, Larry Flynt (Harrelson). While feminists decried what they saw as a whitewash of Flynt's career, Forman insisted his movie was about Flynt's legal battles concerning the First Amendment and freedom of speech. If you can set aside your prejudices, you'll find a master storyteller at work and some great performances from Harrelson as Flynt, Love as his drug-addicted and ultimately tragic wife Althea, and Norton as Flynt's sometimes impatient attorney, Alan Isaacman, who does get his big moment before the U.S. Supreme Court (his speeches are taken from actual court transcripts). **130m/C VHS, DVD.** Woody Harrelson, Courtney Love, Edward Norton, James Cromwell, Crispin Glover, Brett Harrelson, James Carville, Vincent Schiavelli, Richard Paul, Donna Hanover, Norm MacDonald, Miles Chapin, Jan Triska; ***Cameos:*** Larry Flynt; ***D:*** Milos Forman; ***W:*** Larry Karaszewski, Scott M. Alexander; ***C:*** Philippe Rousselot; ***M:*** Thomas Newman. Golden Globes '97: Director (Forman), Screenplay; L.A. Film Critics '96: Support. Actor (Norton); Natl. Bd. of Review '96: Support. Actor (Norton); N.Y. Film Critics '96: Support. Actress (Love).

People Who Own the Dark WOOF! **1975 (R)** A group of wealthy men and a coterie of call girls are having an orgy in the basement of an old home when a nuclear war breaks out. Everyone outside is blinded by the blast but some survivors manage to make their way to the house where they try to attack the inhabitants. Don't bother. **87m/C VHS.** Paul Naschy, Tony Kendall, Maria Perschy, Terry Kemper, Tom Weyland, Anita Brock, Paul Mackey; ***D:*** Armando de Ossorio; ***W:*** Armando de Ossorio.

People Will Talk ½ **1951** Grant plays Dr. Noah Praetorius, a doctor and educator who believes that the mind is a better healer than medicine. Archenemy Cronyn is the fellow instructor with a vengeance. Sickened by Grant's goodwill and the undying attention he receives, Cronyn reports Grant's unconventional medical practices to the higher-ups in hopes of ruining his reputation as doctor/educator. Witty and satirical, this well-crafted comedy-drama is chock-full of interesting characters and finely tuned dialogue. Adapted from the play "Dr. Praetorius" by Curt Goetz. **110m/B VHS, DVD.** Cary Grant, Jeanne Crain, Finlay Currie, Hume Cronyn, Walter Slezak, Sidney Blackmer, Basil Ruysdael, Katherine Locke, Margaret Hamilton, Carleton Young, Billy House, Stuart Holmes; ***D:*** Joseph L. Mankiewicz; ***W:*** Joseph L. Mankiewicz; ***C:*** Milton Krasner.

People's Choice **1946** A small town boy suffers laryngitis, becomes a radio personality via his new huskiness, and claims he's a notorious criminal. **68m/B VHS.** Drew Kennedy, Louise Arthur, George Meeker, Rex Lease, Fred Kelsey, Bill Kennedy; ***D:*** Harry Fraser.

Pep Squad ½ **1998 (R)** Director Steve Balderson does a John Waters riff with the story of evil Cherry (Brooke Balderson) who reacts inappropriately when she's not chosen for the high school pep squad. The Kansas production is driven by broad, nasty slapstick humor. **97m/C DVD.** Brooke Balderson, Jennifer Dreiling, Adrian Pujoi, Summer Makovkin; ***D:*** Steve Balderson; ***W:*** Steve Balderson; ***C:*** Rhet W. Bear; ***M:*** Johnette Napolitano.

Pepe Le Moko **1937** An influential French film about a notorious gangster holed up in the Casbah, emerging at his own peril out of love for a beautiful woman. Stirring film established Gabin as a matinee idol. Cinematography is particularly fine too. Based upon the D'Ashelbe novel. The basis for both "Algiers," the popular Boyer-Lamarr melodrama, and the musical "The Casbah." In French with English subtitles. **87m/B VHS, DVD.** *FR* Jean Gabin, Mireille Balin, Gabriel Gabrio, Lucas Gridoux; ***D:*** Julien Duvivier; ***W:*** Julien Duvivier, Henri Jeanson; ***C:*** Jules Kruger; ***M:*** Vincent Scotto.

Pepi, Luci, Bom and Other Girls on the Heap ½ *Pepi, Luci, Bom y Otras Chicas del Monton* **1980** Almodovar's low-budget directorial debut will be of interest primarily to the director's aficionadoes. Pepi (Maura's debut role) is a Madrid heiress who gets in trouble when her neighbor, a policeman, notices her marijuana plants. She offers sexual favors in return for silence but is raped instead. Pepi later decides on revenge by seducing Luci, the policeman's wife, aided by her girlfriend, Bom. There's lots of partying, drugs, promiscuity, and violence, none of it very involving. In Spanish with English subtitles. **80m/C VHS.** *SP* Carmen Maura, Eva Siva, Olivido Gara, Felix Rotaeta; ***D:*** Pedro Almodovar; ***W:*** Pedro Almodovar.

Pepper and His Wacky Taxi ½ **1972 (G)** Father of four buys a '59 Cadillac and starts a cab company. Time-capsule fun. **79m/C VHS.** John Astin, Frank Sinatra Jr., Jackie Gayle, Alan Sherman; ***D:*** Alex Grasshof.

Peppermint Soda **1977** Kurys' affecting directorial debut is a semi-autobiographical tale of two teenaged sisters set in 1963 Paris. Seen through the eyes of the 13-year-old Anne, who lives with 15-year-old sister Frederique and their divorced mother, this is the year of first loves, strict teachers, dreaded family vacations, and a general awareness of growing up. Sweet look at adolescence and all its embarassing tribulations. In French with English subtitles. **97m/C VHS.** *FR* Eleonore Klarwein, Odile Michel, Anouk Ferjac, Tsilla Chelton, Coralie Clement, Marie-Veronique Maurin, Puterflam; ***D:*** Diane Kurys; ***W:*** Diane Kurys; ***C:*** Philippe Rousselot.

Perception **2006** The perception is that this comedy pretty much stinks. Weirdo Jen (Perabo) lives with her equally weird parents (Hurt, Rasche) in Brooklyn. She also has a weird possessive girlfriend, Ramona (Burns); during an argument, Jen runs into the street and gets hit by a car, which leaves her in a wheelchair. There's also something about Jen's ex-boyfriend who's back from Iraq and her befriending an ex-heroin addict but the story is so incoherent, you probably won't care. **101m/C DVD.** *US* Piper Perabo, Heather Burns, Aunjanue Ellis, Mary Beth Hurt, Seth Meyers, Kate Mulgrew, Ajay Naidu, David Rasche, Nick Scotti, Mark Dobies, Carolina Hoyos; ***D:*** Irving Schwartz; ***W:*** Irving Schwartz; ***C:*** John Darbonne; ***M:*** Joel Someillan.

Perceval *Perceval Le Gallois* **1978** Rohmer's extremely stylized version of Chretien de Troyes unfinished 12th century poem. Young Welsh knight Perceval (Luchini) comes to a mysterious castle where he sees a vision of the Holy Grail, although he doesn't recognize it. In the morning, the castle is deserted and Perceval resumes his wanderings. When he finally realizes what he has seen, the castle has disappeared and Perceval continues with his search for the Grail. French with subtitles. **140m/C VHS, DVD.** *FR* Fabrice Luchini, Andre Dussollier, Arielle Dombasle, Marie-Christine Barrault; ***D:*** Eric Rohmer; ***W:*** Eric Rohmer; ***C:*** Nestor Almendros.

Percy & Thunder ½ **1993** Percy Banks (Jones) is an old-school boxing trainer who believes in hard work and he sees a likely prospect in Wayne "Thunder" Carter (Vance), a middleweight with a chance to be a champ. That is, if big time boxing promotion doesn't get in the way. **90m/C VHS.** James Earl Jones, Billy Dee Williams, Courtney B. Vance, Robert Wuhl, Gloria Foster, Zakes Mokae, Gloria Reuben; ***D:*** Ivan Dixon; ***W:*** Art Washington; ***M:*** Tom Scott.

Percy Jackson & The Olympians: The Lightning Thief **2010 (PG)** Based on a popular series of children's books, this tale of Greek gods and awkward teens can't escape comparison to the Harry Potter movies. Percy (Lerman) is a student struggling with learning disabilities when he discovers that he is the son of the sea god Poseidon and a mortal woman. He is sent to a special school for demi-gods along with his pal Grover (Jackson). When his mother (Keener) disappears and he is accused of stealing the lightning bolt of Zeus (Bean), Percy must go on a quest to return Zeus' property and prevent civil war between the gods. Director Columbus, who also directed the first two Potter films, makes some significant changes to the story and tone of Rick Riordan's novel, which may bother fans of the book. **118m/C DVD.** Logan Lerman, Pierce Brosnan, Uma Thurman, Sean Bean, Kevin McKidd, Melina Kanakaredes, Catherine Keener, Steve Coogan; ***D:*** Chris Columbus; ***W:*** Craig Titley; ***C:*** Stephen Goldblatt; ***M:*** Christophe Beck.

Perestroika **2009** In 1992, middle-aged astrophysicist Sasha Greenberg (Robards) returns to Moscow after the fall of communism and after spending 17 years in New York working for the U.S. military. He's scheduled to give the keynote address at a physics conference but his time is taken up by old friends and ex-lovers who are both happy and suspicious to see him. His mentor was/is Professor Gross (Abraham), an American defector who helped the Soviets develop nuclear weapons much as Greenberg did for the Americans. Sasha's life is depicted with numerous flashbacks while director Tsukerman overstuffs the plot as Sasha is beset by his past and present. **116m/C DVD.** Sam Robards, F. Murray Abraham, Oksana Stashenko, Ally Sheedy, Maria Andreyeva, Jicky Schnee; ***D:*** Slava Tsukerman; ***W:*** Ally Sheedy, Slava Tsukerman; ***C:*** Mikhail Iskandarov; ***M:*** Alexander Zhurbin. **VIDEO**

The Perez Family ½ **1994 (R)** Juan Paul Perez (Molina) has spent 20 years in Cuban jails, dreaming of being reunited with wife Carmela (Huston) and daughter Teresa (Alvarado) who successfully escaped to Miami. Part of the 1980 Mariel exodus, Juan meets exuberant Dottie (Tomei), who learns families get sponsored first at the refugee camps. She convinces Juan to pose as her husband, while Carmela, who's being wooed by cop Pirelli (Palminteri), mistakenly believes Juan has literally missed the boat. Tomei's spunky (but with a garish accent), Huston's regal, Palminteri courtly, and Molina morose. The film's inconsistently whimsical, wistful, and clunky. From the novel by Christine Bell. **135m/C VHS, DVD.** Marisa Tomei, Alfred Molina, Anjelica Huston, Chazz Palminteri, Trini Alvarado, Celia Cruz; ***D:*** Mira Nair; ***W:*** Robin Swicord; ***C:*** Stuart Dryburgh; ***M:*** Alan Silvestri.

Perfect 🦴 1/2 **1985 (R)** A "Rolling Stone" reporter goes after the shallowness of the Los Angeles health club scene, and falls in love with the aerobics instructor he is going to write about. "Rolling Stone" publisher Wenner plays himself. As bad as it sounds. **120m/C VHS, DVD.** John Travolta, Jamie Lee Curtis, Carly Simon, Marilu Henner, Laraine Newman, Jann Wenner, Anne DeSalvo; ***D:*** James Bridges; ***W:*** James Bridges, Aaron Latham; ***C:*** Gordon Willis; ***M:*** Ralph Burns.

Perfect Alibi 🦴🦴 1/2 **1994** Woman's suspicions of her husband's affair leads to murder. **90m/C VHS.** Teri Garr, Hector Elizondo, Kathleen Quinlan, Anne Ramsey, Rigg Kennedy; ***D:*** Kevin Meyer.

Perfect Assassins 1998 FBI profiler pursues a killer on a murder spree. **100m/C VHS.** Andrew McCarthy, Robert Patrick, Nick Mancuso, Portia de Rossi, Matthew Laurance, Lisa Jane Persky, Aki Aleong; ***D:*** H. Gordon Boos; ***W:*** John Penney; ***C:*** Bruce Douglas Johnson; ***M:*** Geoff Levin. **VIDEO**

The Perfect Bride 🦴 1/2 **1991 (R)** A pretty young nurse prepares to marry her fiance, but his sister thinks she is hiding a secret. Could the bride-to-be have murder on her mind? **95m/C VHS.** John Agar, Sammi Davis, Kelly Preston, Linden Ashby, Marilyn Rockafellow, Ashley Tillman; ***D:*** Terrence O'Hara; ***M:*** Richard Bronskill. **CABLE**

The Perfect Clown 🦴 1/2 **1925** Hardly perfect since this is a rather labored silent comedy. Hapless clerk Bert (Semon) is forced to keep a large bank deposit safe overnight. Because he was evicted from his boardinghouse, Bert takes refuge in a barn but he's not the only man needing a place to stay that night. Note the presence of Oliver Hardy as Semon's best pal. **52m/B DVD.** Larry Semon, Oliver Hardy, Kate Price, Dorothy Dwan, Otis Harlan, Spencer Bell; ***D:*** Fred Newmeyer; ***W:*** Thomas J. Crizer; ***C:*** Nicholas T. Barrows, George Baker.

Perfect Crime 🦴🦴 *Indagine su un Delitto Perfetto* **1979** A Scotland Yard inspector must find out who has been killing off executives of a powerful world trust. **90m/C VHS.** *IT* Joseph Cotten, Anthony Steel, Janet Agren, Leonard Mann, Alida Valli, Adolfo Celi; ***D:*** Giuseppe Rosati; ***W:*** Giuseppe Rosati; ***M:*** Carlo Savina.

Perfect Crime 🦴🦴 **1997 (PG-13)** Navy investigator Joanne Jensen (Kapture) is assigned to look into the disappearance of a black Marine captain (Guy) and all fingers point to her white, alcoholic, ex-Marine estranged husband (Searcy). Though Jensen doesn't have a body, murder weapon, or confession, she stills decides to take the case to trial. Based on a 1989 true story. **92m/C VHS.** Mitzi Kapture, Nick Searcy, Jasmine Guy, Andrew Masset; ***D:*** Robert M. Lewis; ***W:*** Selma Thompson; ***C:*** Irek Hartowicz; ***M:*** Joseph Conlan. **CABLE**

The Perfect Daughter 🦴🦴 1/2 **1996 (PG-13)** A near-fatal hit-and-run accident reintroduces Alexandra Michelson (Gold) to her family—mother, Jill (Armstrong), father, Tom (Joy), and younger brother, Josh (Shulman). They'd cut the ties to the troubled drug abuser and runaway but the accident has erased Alexandra's memory of her recent life. Unfortunately for them all, Alex's sordid and dangerous past will leave neither her nor her family alone. **90m/C VHS.** Tracey Gold, Bess Armstrong, Mark Joy, Michael Shulman, Harold P. Pruett, Jay Edward Anthony, Brian Gamble; ***D:*** Harry S. Longstreet; ***W:*** Sean Silas; ***C:*** Stephen Lighthill; ***M:*** Don Davis. **CABLE**

A Perfect Day 🦴🦴 **2006** Rather maudlin story based on the novel by Richard Paul Evans. Author Rob Harlan (Lowe) writes an unexpected bestseller and his fame has him ignoring his wife and daughter. Then his supposed guardian angel (Lloyd) appears to show Mr. Selfish the error of his ways, especially when he tells Rob that if he doesn't change his attitude, he dies on Christmas. Fear—what an incentive to become a better person. **91m/C DVD.** Rob Lowe, Christopher Lloyd, Paget Brewster, Frances Conroy, Jude Ciccolella, Rowena King, Kevin Dunn; ***D:*** Peter Levin; ***W:*** Joyce Eliason; ***C:*** Kees Van Oostrum; ***M:*** Jeff Beal. **CABLE**

Perfect Family 🦴🦴 **1992 (R)** Standard woman-and-kids-in-peril-from-psycho tale. Maggie is a recent widow with two young daughters who's looking for a nanny and a handyman. She hires brother and sister combo Janice and Alan, who, of course, are too good to be true. One is a sociopath who has murdered a family once before. Guess along with Maggie who the nut might be. **92m/C VHS.** Jennifer O'Neill, Bruce Boxleitner, Joanna Cassidy, Juliana Hansen, Shiri Appleby; ***D:*** E.W. Swackhamer; ***W:*** Christian Stoianovich, Phoebe Dorin; ***M:*** Nicholas Pike.

The Perfect Furlough 🦴🦴 1/2 *Strictly for Pleasure* **1959** Paul Hodges (Curtis) is an Army corporal who wins three weeks in Paris with a movie star (Cristal) as a publicity gimmick. It's the idea of a female Army psychologist (Leigh), who thinks the guys need a morale booster, and she accompanies Hodges on his trip. Pretty bizarre, but it works. **93m/C VHS.** Tony Curtis, Janet Leigh, Keenan Wynn, Linda Cristal, Elaine Stritch, Marcel Dalio, King Donovan; ***D:*** Blake Edwards; ***W:*** Stanley Shapiro.

Perfect Game 🦴🦴 1/2 **2000** Kanin Crosby (Finley) and his equally uncoordinated friends are determined to make it into the winning park league baseball team, the Bulldogs, but they're all surprised when they're chosen by the team's arrogant coach, Bobby Geiser (Duffy). Eventually the kids learn that Geiser is only playing and coaching his best players, leaving the others to warm the bench. A confrontation leads to Kanin's mom Diane (Nelson) taking over along with grumbling retired coach Billy Hicks (Asner) and the kids are on their way once again. **99m/C VHS, DVD.** Cameron Finley, Tracy Nelson, Patrick Duffy, Ed Asner; ***D:*** Dan Guntzelman; ***W:*** Dan Guntzelman; ***M:*** David Benoit. **VIDEO**

A Perfect Getaway 🦴🦴 **2009 (R)** A Hawaiian honeymoon hike to a remote beach turns into a nightmare for newlyweds Cliff (Zahn) and Cydney (Jovovich) when they're joined by fellow hikers Nick (Olyphant) and Gina (Sanchez) and confronted by belligerent hitchhikers Cleo (Shelton) and Kale (Hemsworth). Screenwriter Cliff and survivalist Nick discuss movie red herrings (or 'red snappers' as Nick calls them) and viewers will probably want a second look at Twohy's flick to check them out. Offers cheap and mindless B-movie thrills with gratuitous nudity and violence. Really, what more could you want? **98m/C DVD.** *US* Milla Jovovich, Steve Zahn, Timothy Olyphant, Kiele Sanchez, Marley Shelton, Chris Hemsworth; ***D:*** David N. Twohy; ***W:*** David N. Twohy; ***C:*** Mark Plummer; ***M:*** Boris Elkis.

The Perfect Gift 🦴🦴 **1995 (R)** Suzanne decides to fulfill her boyfriend's menage-a-trois fantasy and discovers that the partner they involve just may be the woman of her dreams. **90m/C VHS.** John McCafferty, Kim (Kimberly Dawn) Dawson, Monique Parent; ***D:*** Michael Paul Girard; ***W:*** Michael Paul Girard; ***M:*** Michael Paul Girard.

Perfect Harmony 🦴🦴 1/2 **1991** Racial conflict at an exclusive Southern boys school in 1950s South Carolina is overcome through friendship and the love of music in this sentimental tale. **93m/C VHS, DVD.** Peter Scolari, Darren McGavin, Catherine Mary Stewart, Moses Gunn, Cleavon Little, Justin Whalin, David Faustino, Richie Havens, Eugene Boyd; ***D:*** Will MacKenzie. **CABLE**

Perfect Hideout 🦴 1/2 **2008** Nick and Celia are lovers on the lam who take a hostage after they invade a remote villa. He says he's Victor, the homeowner, but then the twosome notice the dead bodies and realize that they're trapped with a killer while the police surround the property. **93m/C DVD.** Billy Zane, Cristian Solimeno, Ken Bones, Melinda Y. Cohen, Scarlett Sabet; ***D:*** Stephen Manuel; ***W:*** Andreas Brune, Sven Frauenhoff; ***C:*** Oliver Staack; ***M:*** Eckart Gadow. **VIDEO**

The Perfect Holiday 🦴 1/2 **2007 (PG)** Nancy (Union), a struggling single mother of three who is desperately searching for a good man, finds love in Benjamin (Chestnut), a mall Santa and aspiring songwriter. The only problem is that Nancy's ex-husband and famous rapper, J-Jizzy (Murphy), is recording one of Benjamin's songs and doesn't know Nancy and Benjamin have fallen in love. Benjamin doesn't know J-Jizzy is Nancy's ex and Nancy is just plain clueless. A predictable and lukewarm romantic comedy saved in part by Queen Latifah's cameo appearance. Despite the marketing ploy, this is not a sequel to "The Last Holiday." **96m/C DVD.** *US* Gabrielle Union, Morris Chestnut, Queen Latifah, Terrence Howard, Charlie (Charles Q.) Murphy, Faizon Love, Katt Micah Williams, Jill Jones, Malik Hammond, Khail Bryant, Jeremy Gumbs, Rachel True; ***D:*** Lance Rivera; ***W:*** Lance Rivera, Nat Mauldin, Jeff Stein, Marc Calixte; ***C:*** Teodoro Maniaci; ***M:*** Christopher Lennertz.

The Perfect Husband 🦴🦴 *El Marido Perfecto* **1992** Womanizing 19th-century opera singer Milan (Roth) finally falls in love—only it's to a woman he can't have. **90m/C VHS, DVD.** *SP GB* Tim Roth, Peter Firth, Aitana Sanchez-Gijon, Ana Belen; ***D:*** Beda Docampo Feijoo; ***W:*** Beda Docampo Feijoo, Juan Bautista Stagnaro; ***C:*** Frantisek Uldrich; ***M:*** Jose Nieto.

Perfect Killer 🦴 1/2 *Satanic Mechanic* **1977 (R)** Van Cleef stars as a world weary Mafia hit-man who is double-crossed by his girl, set up by his best friend, and hunted by another hired assassin. **85m/C VHS, DVD.** Lee Van Cleef, Tita Barker, John Ireland, Robert Widmark; ***D:*** Marlon Sirko.

Perfect Lies 🦴 1/2 **1997** Trying to pull her life back together, private eye Toby Merck (Friese) winds up being blackmailed by her former lover, an FBI agent, who wants her to infilitrate a drug kingpin's operation. **94m/C VHS.** Brettanya Friese, Charis Michelsen, Eric Leffler, William Laney, Geoff Thompson, Carolyn Smith; ***D:*** Bret Stern; ***W:*** Steve Arthur. **VIDEO**

A Perfect Little Murder 🦴🦴 1/2 *A Quiet Little Neighborhood, A Perfect Little Murder* **1990** Marsha is expecting an uneventful life of barbecues and Little League when her family settles down in the suburbs. But then she overhears a murder plot and someone finds out she knows. **94m/C VHS.** Teri Garr, Robert Urich, Susan Ruttan, Jeffrey Tambor, Tom Poston, Florence Stanley, Gail Edwards, Alex Rocco; ***D:*** Anson Williams; ***W:*** Mark Stein. **TV**

Perfect Love 🦴🦴 *Parfait Amour* **1996** Divorced Frederique (Renauld) has an affair with volatile younger man, Christophe (Renaud). When she realizes he's also seeing other women, she's angry and the tension builds as each seeks to psychologically wound the other. The only thing they still agree upon is sex but then Christophe loses control. French with subtitles. **110m/C VHS, DVD.** *FR* Isabelle Renauld, Francis Renaud, Laura Saglio; ***D:*** Catherine Breillat; ***W:*** Catherine Breillat; ***C:*** Laurent Dailland.

The Perfect Man 🦴 **2005 (PG)** Whenever 16-year-old Holly's (Duff) single mom, the gloomy Jean (Locklear), loses at love she packs up Holly and younger sister Zoe to a brand new city in a desperate search for a fresh start. Fed up with the chaos, Holly concocts a secret admirer—based on her best friend Amy's suave Uncle Ben (Noth)—when she sees another potentially lame suitor on the horizon in the form of Styx-loving Lenny (O'Malley). Naturally the ruse gets dicey and Holly must scurry to cover her you-know-what. Feeble humor, plus it's hard to believe the knockout Locklear would have trouble finding a decent man. **100m/C DVD.** *US* Hilary Duff, Heather Locklear, Christopher Noth, Vanessa Lengies, Aria Wallace, Ben Feldman, Michael O'Malley, Caroline Rhea, Kym E. Whitley; ***D:*** Mark Rosman; ***W:*** Gina Wendkos; ***C:*** John R. Leonetti; ***M:*** Christophe Beck.

The Perfect Marriage 🦴🦴 **1946** Tired comedy about a perfect couple who decide they can't stand each other anymore after ten years of marriage. Good cast makes the most of weak script. Based on the play by Samuel Raphaelson. **88m/B VHS.** Loretta Young, David Niven, Eddie Albert, Charlie Ruggles, Zasu Pitts, Jerome Cowan, Rita Johnson; ***D:*** Lewis Allen; ***W:*** Leonard Spigelgass.

Perfect Match 🦴🦴 **1988 (PG)** A timid young woman and an unambitious young man meet each other through the personal ads and then lie to each other about who they are and what they do for a living. **93m/C VHS.** Marc McClure, Jennifer Edwards, Diane Stilwell, Rob Paulsen, Karen Witter; ***D:*** Mark Deimel.

A Perfect Murder 🦴🦴 **1998 (R)** Steven Taylor (Douglas), a rich commodities trader about to lose his fortune, is married to young, rich, Emily (Paltrow), who's having a torrid affair with hippie artist David (Mortensen). The love triangle gets shaken when Steven devises a solution to both his wife's infidelities and his financial woes by paying David to kill Emily. Things go a little bit astray, and the psychological cat and mouse game begins. Glossy production is only eye candy while the unsympathetic characters (led by a weak protagonist in Paltrow) march to the beat of many plot points that all come together in a rushed and dull climax. Douglas, the aged yet sturdy centerpiece of the film, shines as the pompous rich dude devoid of morals, and overpowers his youthful supporting players. Inspired by Hitchcock's 1954 film, "Dial M for Murder." **105m/C VHS, DVD.** Michael Douglas, Gwyneth Paltrow, Viggo Mortensen, David Suchet, Sarita Choudhury, Constance Towers, Novella Nelson; ***D:*** Andrew Davis; ***W:*** Patrick Smith Kelly; ***C:*** Darius Wolski; ***M:*** James Newton Howard.

Perfect Murder, Perfect Town 🦴🦴 **2000** Re-telling of the (still unsolved) murder of six-year-old JonBenet Ramsey in Boulder, Colorado, the subsequent investigation and the media frenzy that descended on the community. Miniseries is based on the book by director Schiller. **178m/C VHS, DVD.** Marg Helgenberger, Ronny Cox, Kris Kristofferson, Ken Howard, John Heard, Ann-Margret, Scott Cohen, John Rubinstein, Dennis Boutsikaris, Sean M. Whalen; ***D:*** Lawrence Schiller; ***W:*** Tom Topor; ***C:*** Peter Sova; ***M:*** John Cacavas. **TV**

The Perfect Nanny 🦴🦴 **2000** Andrea McBride (Nelson) gets released from a mental institution and manages to get a job as a nanny to the children of a wealthy widower (Boxleitner). But Andrea expects a fairy-tale life and will do anything to make her romantic happy ending come true. **90m/C VHS, DVD.** Tracy Nelson, Bruce Boxleitner, Dana Barron, Susan Blakely, Katherine Helmond; ***D:*** Rob Malenfant; ***W:*** Victor Schiller, Christine Conradt, Richard Gilbert Hill; ***C:*** Don E. Fauntleroy; ***M:*** Richard Bowers. **VIDEO**

Perfect Parents 🦴🦴 1/2 **2006** After learning about the violence their 10-year-old daughter Lucy (Garrood) has witnessed at her public school, Stuart (Eccleston) and Allison (Harker) are anxious to get her into a respected private Catholic school despite being atheists. Willing to lie, they enlist the aid of a dodgy priest (Warner) and others to vouch for them, but that first fib spirals into fraud, blackmail, and murder. **92m/C DVD.** *GB* Christopher Eccleston, Susannah Harker, Lesley Manville, David Warner, Brendan Coyle, Maddy Garrood, Michelle Joseph, Isha Joseph; ***D:*** Joe Ahearne; ***W:*** Joe Ahearne; ***C:*** Peter Greenhalgh; ***M:*** Murray Gold. **TV**

The Perfect Score 🦴🦴 1/2 **2004 (PG-13)** Anxious high school seniors stressing about the SATs decide to steal the answers in this slightly above-average teen movie of the "Breakfast Club" variety. Kyle (Chris Evans), worried that his lousy test scores will prevent him from becoming an architect, assembles a crew of high school stereotypes to do the crime, including Chris's slacker buddy Matty (Greenberg), angry rich girl Francesca (Johansson), whose dad is a testing company executive, overachiever Anna (Christiansen), star athlete Desmond (hoopster Miles) and stoner Roy (Nam), who happens to be the smartest of the bunch. The plot takes a backseat to the interaction between the misfits, but none of it adds up to much more than average fare, with the exception of scene-stealers Johansson and Nam. **93m/C DVD.** *US* Erika Christensen, Chris Evans, Scarlett Johansson, Tyra Ferrell, Bryan Greenburg, Darius Miles, Leonardo Nam, Matthew Lillard, Vanessa Angel, Fulvio Cecere; ***D:*** Brian Robbins; ***W:*** Mark Schwahn, Marc Hyman, Jon Zack; ***C:*** Clark Mathis; ***M:*** John Murphy.

The Perfect Sleep 🦴 **2008 (R)** Pretentious film noir homage. An unnamed man (Pardue) returns to being an assassin to save the woman (Sanchez) he loves but can never have. There's revenge, a Russian crime boss, a sinister doctor, and way too much narration in a plot that ultimately makes no sense. **90m/C DVD.** Roselyn Sanchez, Patrick Bauchau, Peter J. Lucas, Tony Amendola, Cameron Daddo, Michael Pare, Sam Thakur, Sam Thakur, Anton Pardue; ***D:*** Jeremy Alter; ***W:*** Anton Pardue; ***C:*** Charles Papert; ***M:*** David Vanian.

The Perfect Son ✓✓ 1/2 **2000** When their father dies, estranged brothers Theo (Cubitt) and Ryan (Feore) are reluctantly reunited. Theo is out of rehab and hoping to make a fresh start with ex-lover Sarah (West) but it's his "perfect brother" Ryan who has some revelations. The overly responsible, successful lawyer reveals to his younger bro that he is gay and dying of AIDS. They try to set aside old rivalries as one struggles to start over and the other struggles with facing his mortality. Strong drama with two exceptional lead performances, although the story is simple and somewhat old-fashioned. **93m/C VHS, DVD.** *CA* David Cubitt, Colm Feore, Chandra West; ***D:*** Leonard Farlinger; ***W:*** Leonard Farlinger; ***C:*** Barry Stone; ***M:*** Ron Sures.

A Perfect Spy ✓✓ 1/2 *John Le Carre's A Perfect Spy* **1988** In this BBC miniseries, John Le Carre takes a break from the world of George Smiley to take a look at spying from a personal view. Magnus Pym (Evan) would seem to be the perfect English gentleman; having gone to the right schools he proceeds to join the covert world of espionage. But Magnus hides the secret that his estranged father is a con man par excellence and it leads him to his own betrayals. Adapted from the novel, which Le Carre is said to have drawn from his own past. On three cassettes. **360m/C VHS, DVD.** *GB* Peter Egan, Ray McAnally, Frances Tomelty, Benedict Taylor, Tim Healy; ***W:*** Arthur Hopcraft.

The Perfect Storm ✓✓ 1/2 **2000 (PG-13)** Based on the true story of the Andrea Gail, a swordfishing boat lost at sea in 1991 during a freak storm—one of the biggest of the century—off the coast of Newfoundland. Film briefly sets up the backgrounds of the six men who will be the captain and crew on the tragic voyage, but not even Clooney and Wahlberg can compete with the watery special effects and it turns into a stereotypical disaster flick. Adapted from Sebastian Junger's bestselling nonfiction account of the tragedy. **129m/C VHS, DVD, Blu-ray Disc, HD DVD.** George Clooney, Mark Wahlberg, Mary Elizabeth Mastrantonio, John C. Reilly, Diane Lane, William Fichtner, Allen Payne, John Hawkes, Karen Allen, Bob Gunton, Cherry Jones, Christopher McDonald, Dash Mihok, Josh Hopkins, Michael Ironside, Janet Wright, Rusty Schwimmer; ***D:*** Wolfgang Petersen; ***W:*** William D. Wittliff; ***C:*** John Seale; ***M:*** James Horner.

Perfect Stranger ✓✓ 1/2 **2007 (R)** Efficient, if routine, thriller. Rowena (Berry) is an investigative reporter whose childhood friend Grace (Aycox) is murdered shortly after admitting to an affair with married corporate hotshot Harrison Hill (Willis). She goes undercover at Hill's ad firm, with the help of sorta creepy/geeky tech whiz Miles (Ribisi), to get to the truth and double-plays Hill by also posing as an online tart (which is how Grace met him). Rowena is unethical, Hill is smug, but at least director Foley won't leave viewers frustrated. **109m/C DVD, Blu-ray Disc.** *US* Halle Berry, Bruce Willis, Giovanni Ribisi, Richard Portnow, Nicki Aycox, Gary Dourdan, Kathleen Chalfant, Florencia Lozano; ***D:*** James Foley; ***W:*** Todd Komarnicki; ***C:*** Anastas Michos; ***M:*** Antonio Pinto.

Perfect Strangers ✓✓ **1950** Divorcee Terry (Rogers) and unhappily married David (Morgan) fall for each other when they're sequestered jurors on an L.A. murder trial. But will the romance last once the verdict is reached? **88m/B DVD.** Ginger Rogers, Dennis Morgan, Thelma Ritter, Margalo Gillmore, Anthony Ross, Howard Freeman, Paul Ford; ***D:*** Bretaigne Windust; ***W:*** Edith Sommer; ***C:*** J. Peverell Marley; ***M:*** Leigh Harline.

Perfect Strangers ✓✓ *Blind Alley* **1984 (R)** Thriller develops around a murder and the child who witnesses it. The killer attempts to kidnap the young boy, but problems arise when he falls in love with the lad's mother. **90m/C VHS, DVD.** Anne Carlisle, Brad Rijn, John Woehrle, Matthew Stockley, Ann Magnuson, Stephen Lack; ***D:*** Larry Cohen; ***W:*** Larry Cohen.

Perfect Strangers ✓✓ 1/2 **2003** It's too bad when a girl (Blake) can't go out on the town, get plastered, and pick up an honorable, upstanding guy. No, he (Neill) has to turn out to be a charming kidnapper (aren't those the worst kind?) who holds her hostage at his shack on a desolate island (off of New Zealand's west coast). But, this captivating yet contorted tale might just reveal that there's just no escaping the true bliss that demented love brings. **96m/C VHS, DVD.** Sam Neill, Rachael Blake, Joel Tobeck, Robyn Malcolm, Madeleine Sami; ***D:*** Gaylene Preston; ***W:*** Gaylene Preston; ***C:*** Alun Bollinger; ***M:*** Neil Finn. **VIDEO**

Perfect Target ✓ 1/2 **1998 (R)** An ex-CIA agent is forced to work as a mercenary, protecting the president of Santa Brava. Naturally, this assignment doesn't go well and he becomes the fall guy for the politico's murder. Only he doesn't intend to stay that way. **97m/C VHS, DVD.** Daniel Bernhardt, Robert Englund, Brian Thompson, Dara Tomanovich; ***D:*** Sheldon Lettich. **VIDEO**

Perfect Tenant ✓ 1/2 **1999 (R)** Overly familiar thriller. Because of financial problems Jessica (Purl) is forced to rent out her guesthouse. She thinks she's found the perfect tenant in Bryan (Caulfield) since he's not only handsome but polite and tidy. But it's all a facade since Bryan actually wants revenge on the woman he blames for his father's suicide. **93m/C VHS, DVD.** Linda Purl, Maxwell Caulfield, Tracy Nelson, Earl Holliman, Melissa Behr, Stacy Hogue; ***D:*** Doug Campbell; ***W:*** Jim Vines, M. Todd Bonin; ***C:*** M. David Mullen. **VIDEO**

Perfect Timing WOOF! **1984** Soft-core film about a fledgling photographer who can't turn his orgy-like photo sessions into anything profitable. **87m/C VHS.** Stephen Markle, Michelle Scarabelli; ***D:*** Rene Bonniere.

Perfect Victims ✓ *Hidden Rage* **1987 (R)** Beautiful models are being hunted by a killer, and a police officer wants to catch the psychopath before he strikes again. **100m/C VHS.** John Agar, Deborah Shelton, Clarence Williams III, Lyman Ward; ***D:*** Shuki Levy.

The Perfect Weapon ✓✓ **1991 (R)** Kenpo karate master Speakman severs family ties and wears funny belt in order to avenge underworld murder of his teacher. **85m/C VHS.** Jeff Sanders, Jeff Speakman; ***D:*** Mark DiSalle; ***W:*** David Wilson; ***C:*** Russell Carpenter; ***M:*** Gary Chang.

The Perfect Wife ✓✓ **2000** Liza (Sturges) is another of those vengeful blondes who, in the wake of "Hand that Rocks the Cradle," thrive on video premieres. She goes after everyone she blames for her beloved brother's death, including the doctor (King) who did not save his life after an auto accident. How does she get close to the good doctor? She marries him, of course, and sets about to ruin everyone he cares for. The pace moves along briskly while production values are strictly of the made-for-TV level. **92m/C DVD.** Shannon Sturges, Perry King, Lesley-Anne Down, William R. Moses; ***D:*** Don E. Fauntleroy; ***W:*** Frank Rehwaldt, George Saunders.

Perfect Witness ✓✓ 1/2 **1989** A restaurant owner witnesses a mob slaying and resists testifying against the culprit to save his family and himself. Filmed in New York City. **104m/C VHS, DVD.** Brian Dennehy, Aidan Quinn, Stockard Channing, Laura Harrington, Joe Grifasi; ***D:*** Robert Mandel; ***M:*** Brad Fiedel. **CABLE**

The Perfect Witness ✓ *The Ungodly* **2007 (R)** Wannabe documentary filmmaker Mickey thinks he's gotten his big break when he accidentally tapes serial killer James in the act. Mickey doesn't go the cops but to James; he'll interview him and film his crimes until James is either caught or killed. (Way to be a good citizen, Mickey!) But it's the serial killer who turns out to have the upper hand. **100m/C DVD.** Kenny Johnson, Mark Borkowski, Wes Bentley, Joanne Baron, Beth Grant; ***D:*** Thomas Dunn; ***W:*** Mark Borkowski, Thomas Dunn; ***C:*** Paco Fremenia.

A Perfect World ✓✓ 1/2 **1993 (PG-13)** Butch Haynes (Costner) is an escaped con who takes eight-year-old fatherless Phillip (Lowther) as a hostage in 1963 Texas and is pursued by Texas Ranger Red Garnett (Eastwood). Butch is a bad guy and the film never tries to make him heroic but it also allows him to grow attached to Phillip and acknowledge him as a surrogate son. Costner gives a quiet and strong performance and the remarkable Lowther never goes wrong in his role as the needy little boy. Eastwood's role is strictly secondary as the well tested lawman who understands justice without seeking vengeance. Somewhat draggy—especially the protracted final scene. **138m/C VHS, DVD.** Kevin Costner, T.J. Lowther, Clint Eastwood, Laura Dern, Keith Szarabajka, Leo Burmester, Paul Hewitt, Bradley Whitford, Ray McKinnon, Wayne Dehart, Jennifer Griffin, Linda Hart; ***D:*** Clint Eastwood; ***W:*** John Lee Hancock; ***C:*** Jack N. Green; ***M:*** Lennie Niehaus.

Perfectly Normal ✓✓ **1991 (R)** Two friends end up in hilarious situations when one opens an eccentric restaurant with a mysterious, newly found fortune. **106m/C VHS.** Michael Riley, Robbie Coltrane, Kenneth Welsh, Eugene Lipinski; ***D:*** Yves Simoneau; ***W:*** Eugene Lipinski, Paul Quarrington.

Performance ✓✓✓ 1/2 **1970 (R)** Grim and unsettling psychological account of a criminal who hides out in a bizarre house occupied by a peculiar rock star and his two female companions. Entire cast scores high marks, with Pallenberg especially compelling as a somewhat mysterious and attractive housemate to mincing Jagger. A cult favorite, with music by Nitzsche under the direction of Randy Newman. **104m/C VHS, DVD.** *GB* James Fox, Mick Jagger, Anita Pallenberg, Michele Breton, Ann Sidney, John Bindon, Stanley Meadows, Allan Cuthbertson, Antony Morton; ***D:*** Donald Cammell, Nicolas Roeg; ***W:*** Donald Cammell; ***C:*** Nicolas Roeg; ***M:*** Jack Nitzsche.

Perfume ✓ 1/2 **1991** Five beautiful, black childhood friends join together to conquer the cosmetics industry with their new perfume, Sassy. But can they resist all the temptations success brings and keep both their company and their friendship? **98m/C VHS.** Cheryl Francis Harrington, Kathleen Bradley Overton, Shy Jefferson, Lynn Marlin, Eugina Wright, Ted Lange; ***D:*** Roland S. Jefferson.

Perfume ✓✓ **2001 (R)** Rymer worked from an outline rather than a complete script and had his actors improvise this satire on the fashion world but the film fumbles on fuzzy plots and characters. English photog Anthony (Harris) deals with professional and personal crises; gay fashion mogul Lorenzo (Sorvino) learns he has terminal cancer and draws closer to his family and lover; magazine editor Janice (Baron) is suddenly confronted by the daughter (Williams) she hasn't seen in years; and various designers (Epps, Wilson, Mann) have various problems. **106m/C VHS, DVD.** Rita Wilson, Leslie Mann, Jared Harris, Michelle Forbes, Paul Sorvino, Peter Gallagher, Sonia Braga, Omar Epps, Jeff Goldblum, Harris Yulin, Michelle Williams, Joanne Baron, Mariel Hemingway, Carmen Electra, Coolio, Harry Hamlin, Mariska Hargitay, Gaby Hoffman, Robert Joy, Chris Sarandon, Angela Bettis, Kyle MacLachlan; ***D:*** Michael Rymer; ***W:*** Michael Rymer, L.M. Kit Carson; ***C:*** Rex Nicholson; ***M:*** Adam Plack.

The Perfume of Yvonne ✓ 1/2 *Le Parfum d'Yvonne; The Scent of Yvonne* **1994** Pretty but languid story told in flashbacks. Victor (Giradot) is staying at a Swiss hotel in 1958 and begins a flirtation with aspiring actress Yvonne (Majani), who's there with her gay companion, Dr. Meinthe (Mareille). To Victor it turns into an unforgettable romance, but the only person Yvonne loves is herself. French with subtitles. **90m/C DVD.** *FR* Richard Bohringer, Hippolyte Giradot, Sandra Majani, Jean-Pierre Mareille; ***D:*** Patrice Leconte; ***W:*** Patrice Leconte; ***C:*** Eduardo Serra; ***M:*** Pascal Esteve.

Perfume: The Story of a Murderer ✓✓ **2006 (R)** Patrick Susskind's "unfilmable" 1985 novel offered a unique challenge to director Tykwer: how do you visualize the sense of smell? Jean-Baptiste Grenouille (Whishaw), orphaned in filthy, smelly 18th-century Paris, has two unique characteristics: he has no natural body odor and he possesses an unparalleled sense of smell that leads to an apprenticeship with perfumer Baldini (Hoffman). Grenouille soon becomes obsessed with the natural scent of young women and turns to serial killing in order to preserve that smell and turn it into the perfect perfume. Ironically, the flick may be too faithful to the book and could have used some judicious editing; it also appeals more to the intellect than to the heart or any of the other senses. **145m/C DVD.** *SP FR GE* Ben Whishaw, Dustin Hoffman, Alan Rickman, Rachel Hurd-Wood, Corinna Harfouch; ***D:*** Tom Tykwer; ***W:*** Tom Tykwer, Andrew Birkin, Bernd Eichinger; ***C:*** Frank Griebe; ***M:*** Tom Tykwer, Johnny Klimek, Reinhold Heil; ***Nar:*** John Hurt.

Perfumed Nightmare ✓✓✓ **1989** Unique, appealing fable about a Filipino youth who discovers the drawbacks of social and cultural progress when he moves to Paris. Director Tahimik also plays the lead role. Imaginative, yet remarkably economical, this film was produced for $10,000 and received the International Critics Award at the Berlin Film Festival. In Tagalog with English dialogue and subtitles. **93m/C VHS.** *PH* Kidlat Tahimik, Dolores Santamaria, Georgette Baudry, Katrin Muller, Harmut Lerch; ***D:*** Kidlat Tahimik.

Perhaps Love ✓✓ *Ruguo Ai* **2005** Marketed as the first Chinese musical in 40 years, the premise is that everyone's life is a film, and they are the star only in that film. In the "life movies" of others they are at best a bit part. Famous director Nie Wen (Jacky Cheung) is directing a musical about a romantic triangle starring his lover Sun (Zhou) and her former lover Lin (Kaneshiro). **108m/C DVD, Blu-ray Disc.** *CH HK* Takeshi Kaneshiro, Jacky Cheung, Xun Zhou, Jin-hee Ji; ***D:*** Peter Chan; ***W:*** Oi Wah Lam, Raymond To; ***C:*** Christopher Doyle, Peter Pau; ***M:*** Peter Kam, Leon Ko.

Peril ✓✓ 1/2 *Peril en la Demeure* **1985 (R)** From the novel "Sur La Terre Comme Au Ciel" by Rene Belletto. Deals with a music teacher's infiltration into a wealthy family and the sexually motivated, back-stabbing murder plots that ensue. DeVille does poorly with avant-garde technique. In French with English subtitles. **100m/C VHS.** *FR* Michel Piccoli, Christophe MaLavoy, Richard Bohringer, Nicole Garcia, Anais Jeanneret; ***D:*** Michel DeVille; ***W:*** Michel DeVille. Cesar '86: Director (DeVille).

Peril ✓ **2000 (R)** Out-of-control plot dooms this women-in-peril saga. Terry (Fairchild) and her semi-disabled hubby Scott (James) are facing financial ruin but have one chance to save themselves. Unfortunately, Scott falls and gets trapped in a storm drain and when Terry goes for help, she gets captured by an escaped mental patient (Pare) who uses her as a hostage against the cops. Oh, and the water is rising in the storm drain, so Scott's gonna drown unless Terry can get free. Very dumb. **90m/C VHS, DVD.** Morgan Fairchild, Michael Pare, John James, Steve Eastin, Thom Christopher; ***D:*** David Giancola. **VIDEO**

The Perils of Gwendoline ✓✓ 1/2 *Gwendoline; The Perils of Gwendoline in the Land of the Yik-Yak* **1984 (R)** A young woman leaves a convent to search for her long-lost father, in this adaptation of a much funnier French comic strip of the same name. What ends up on the screen is merely a very silly rip-off of the successful "Raiders of the Lost Ark," and of primary interest for its numerous scenes of amply endowed Kitaen in the buff. **88m/C VHS, DVD.** *FR* Tawny Kitaen, Brent Huff, Zabou, Bernadette LaFont, Jean Rougerie; ***D:*** Just Jaeckin; ***M:*** Pierre Bachelet.

The Perils of Pauline ✓✓ 1/2 **1934** All 12 episodes of this classic melodrama/adventure serial in one package, featuring dastardly villains, cliff-hanging predicaments, and worldwide chases. **238m/B VHS, DVD.** Evalyn Knapp, Robert "Tex" Allen, James Durkin, Sonny Ray, Pat O'Malley; ***D:*** Ray Taylor.

The Perils of Pauline ✓✓ **1947** A musical biography of Pearl White, the reigning belle of silent movie serials. Look for lots of silent film stars. **96m/C VHS, DVD.** Betty Hutton, John Lund, Constance Collier, William Demarest, Billy DeWolfe; ***D:*** George Marshall; ***C:*** Ray Rennahan; ***M:*** Frank Loesser.

Perils of the Darkest Jungle ✓✓ 1/2 *The Tiger Woman; Jungle Gold* **1944** Tiger Woman battles money-mad oil profiteers to protect her tribe. This 12-episode serial comes on two tapes. **180m/B VHS.** Linda Stirling, Allan "Rocky" Lane, Duncan Renaldo, George Lewis; ***D:*** Spencer Gordon Bennet.

Period of Adjustment ☆☆☆ **1962** Heartwarming comedy about young newlyweds adjusting to the pressures of domestic life and trying to help the troubled marriage of an older couple. Based on the play by Tennessee Williams. **112m/B VHS.** Anthony (Tony) Franciosa, Jane Fonda, Jim Hutton, Lois Nettleton, John McGiver, Jack Albertson; ***D:*** George Roy Hill; ***W:*** Isobel Lennart.

Permanent Midnight ☆ ½ **1998 (R)** Stiller stars as TV writer Jerry Stahl in this film version of his 1995 autobiography, which follows his plunge from a guy who has it all to a loser junkie who's as unlikable as this movie itself. At its real-life peak, Stahl's heroine habit reached $6,000 a week. There are some great flashes of dark humor—Jerry is obsessed with exercising and eating right even while pumping himself full of drugs—and some truly horrific sequences (at one low point, Stahl both scores and shoots up with his baby daughter by his side). The problem is that we don't care. Stiller's comic timing makes most of the bleak jokes work, and it's the only thing that makes the movie bearable; however, his brooding performance (possibly due to writer/director Veloz) lacks any charisma. Watch for Stahl himself as a pessimistic doctor at a methadone clinic. **85m/C VHS, DVD.** Ben Stiller, Elizabeth Hurley, Maria Bello, Owen Wilson, Lourdes Benedicto, Peter Greene, Cheryl Ladd, Fred Willard, Charles Fleischer, Janeane Garofalo, Jerry Stahl; ***D:*** David Veloz; ***W:*** David Veloz; ***C:*** Robert Yeoman; ***M:*** Daniel Licht.

Permanent Record ☆☆ ½ **1988 (PG-13)** Hyper-sincere drama about a popular high schooler's suicide and the emotional reactions of those he left behind. Great performance from Reeves. **92m/C VHS, DVD.** Alan Boyce, Keanu Reeves, Michelle Meyrink, Jennifer Rubin, Pamela Gidley, Michael Elgart, Richard Bradford, Barry Corbin, Kathy Baker, Dakin Matthews; ***D:*** Marisa Silver; ***W:*** Jarre Fees, Alice Liddle, Larry Ketron; ***C:*** Frederick Elmes; ***M:*** Joe Strummer.

Permanent Vacation ☆☆ ½ **1984** A young man disenchanted with New York City decides to escape to Europe to forget about his problems. **80m/C VHS.** John Lurie, Chris Parker; ***D:*** Jim Jarmusch; ***W:*** Jim Jarmusch; ***M:*** John Lurie.

Permission To Kill ☆☆ ½ **1975 (PG)** Grim spy drama features Bogard as an agent determined to prevent the return of a third-world radical to a totalitarian state. **96m/C VHS.** *GB* Dirk Bogarde, Ava Gardner, Timothy Dalton, Frederic Forrest; ***D:*** Cyril Frankel; ***C:*** Frederick A. (Freddie) Young; ***M:*** Richard Rodney Bennett.

Perpetrators of the Crime ☆☆ **1998 (R)** Dumb criminals—dumb crime. Jones (Burgess) comes up with a kidnapping scheme but his sidekicks, Phil (Strong) and Ed (Devine), kidnap the wrong girl (Spelling) and take her to the wrong hideout. That makes things difficult when Jones tries to shake down their mark (Davis) for the ransom. **85m/C VHS, DVD.** *CA* Danny Strong, Tori Spelling, Mark Burgess, Sean Devine, William B. Davis; ***D:*** John Hamilton; ***W:*** Max Sartor.

Perry Mason Returns ☆☆☆ **1985** Perry Mason returns to solve another baffling mystery. This time he must help his longtime assistant, Della Street, when she is accused of killing her new employer. **95m/C VHS.** Raymond Burr, Barbara Hale, William Katt, Patrick O'Neal, Richard Anderson, Cassie Yates, Al Freeman Jr.; ***D:*** Ron Satlof.

Perry Mason: The Case of the Lost Love ☆☆ ½ **1987** Super-lawyer Mason defends the husband of a former lover he hadn't seen in 30 years. The solution to the mystery may catch viewer off guard. **98m/C VHS.** Raymond Burr, Barbara Hale, William Katt, Jean Simmons, Gene Barry, Robert Walden, Stephen Elliott, Robert Mandan, David Ogden Stiers; ***D:*** Ron Satlof. **TV**

Persepolis ☆☆☆ **2007 (PG-13)** Animated universal coming-of-age tale spans the life of a young Iranian girl beginning at the tumultuous period from the end of the rule of the Shah through the abrupt transition to the fundamentalist Muslim regime that followed. The profound impact of the many changes Marjane (Mastroianni) endures is heartrending. Although she is part of a modern and progressive Iranian family, she is forced to don a face-covering veil; she then flees to Austria, where she is an outsider stereotyped as a fanatical Muslim. When she finally returns to Iran, she finds that she is an outsider in her native land, and she is forced yet again to flee. Adapted from the semi-autobiographical graphic novel by Marjane Satrapi, the characters are expressed as rather low-tech line drawings when compared to other contemporary animation, but the resulting images and storyline are relatable. **95m/B DVD, Blu-ray Disc.** *FR* ***D:*** Marjane Satrapi, Vincent Paronnauel; ***W:*** Marjane Satrapi, Vincent Paronnaud; ***M:*** Olivier Bernet; ***V:*** Chiara Mastroianni, Danielle Darrieux, Simon Abkarian, Gabrielle Lopes, Catherine Deneuve, Francois Jerosme.

Persona ☆☆☆☆ **1966** A famous actress turns mute and is treated by a talkative nurse at a secluded cottage. As their relationship turns increasingly tense, the women's personalities begin to merge. Memorable, unnerving—and atypically avant garde—fare from cinema giant Bergman. First of several collaborations between the director and leading lady Ullman. In Swedish with English subtitles. **100m/C VHS, DVD.** *SW* Bibi Andersson, Liv Ullmann, Gunnar Bjornstrand, Margareta Krook, Jorgen Lindstrom; ***D:*** Ingmar Bergman; ***W:*** Ingmar Bergman; ***C:*** Sven Nykvist; ***M:*** Lars Johan Werle. Natl. Soc. Film Critics '67: Actress (Andersson), Director (Bergman), Film.

Personal Best ☆☆☆ **1982 (R)** Lesbian lovers compete while training for the 1990 Olympics. Provocative fare often goes where few films have gone before, but overly stylized direction occasionally overwhelms characterizations. It gleefully exploits locker-room nudity, with Hemingway in her pre-implant days. Still, an ambitious, often accomplished production. Towne's directorial debut. **126m/C VHS, DVD.** Mariel Hemingway, Scott Glenn, Patrice Donnelly; ***D:*** Robert Towne; ***W:*** Robert Towne; ***C:*** Michael Chapman; ***M:*** Jack Nitzsche.

Personal Effects ☆ ½ **2009 (R)** A clumsily-told combo of tragedy and romance. Kutcher goes from comedy to drama (with middling success) as a college wrestler whose life is upended when his twin sister is murdered. Walter meets equally grief-stricken Linda (Pfeiffer) at a support group and the two are bonded by circumstance as well as Linda's deaf teen son Clay (Hudson) who is heading down a dangerous path of his own. **110m/C DVD.** Ashton Kutcher, Michelle Pfeiffer, Kathy Bates, John Mann, David Lewis, Spencer Hudson; ***D:*** David Hollander; ***W:*** David Hollander; ***C:*** Elliot Davis; ***M:*** Johann Johannsson. **VIDEO**

Personal Exemptions ☆ ½ **1988 (PG)** In this stock comedy a frenzied IRS auditor learns that her daughter is smuggling aliens into the country, her son is brokering with some businessmen she's targeted for tax fraud, and her husband is having an affair with a high-school girl. **100m/C VHS.** Nanette Fabray, John Cotton; ***D:*** Peter Rowe.

Personal Maid ☆☆ **1931** Poor Irish lassie, Nora Ryan (Carroll), dreams of bettering herself and decides to start by becoming a maid for New York's wealthy Gary family and seeing how the other half lives. Wayward son Dick Gary (Raymond) immediately starts flirting with Nora but true love has some bumps in the road. **74m/B VHS.** Nancy Carroll, Gene Raymond, Pat O'Brien, Mary Boland, Donald Meek, George Fawcett, Lewis Drayton, Jessie Busley, Hugh O'Connell; ***D:*** Monta Bell, Lothar Mendes; ***W:*** Adelaide Heilbron; ***C:*** Karl Freund.

Personal Property ☆☆ ½ *The Man in Possession* **1937** Taylor tries every trick in the book to win Harlow over in this MGM romantic fluff. Not that big on laughs, but plenty of good shots of Harlow and a beefcake scene of Taylor in a bathtub, who was the darling of the MGM lot and worked with every leading lady. This was the only film Harlow and Taylor made together. Remake of the 1931 film "The Man in Possession." **84m/B VHS.** Robert Taylor, Jean Harlow, Reginald Owen, Una O'Connor, E.E. Clive, Henrietta Crosman, Cora Witherspoon; ***D:*** Woodbridge S. Van Dyke; ***W:*** Hugh Mills.

Personal Services ☆☆ ½ **1987 (R)** A bawdy satire loosely based on the life and times of Britain's modern-day madam, Cynthia Payne, and her rise to fame in the world of prostitution. Payne's earlier years were featured in the film "Wish You Were Here." **104m/C VHS, DVD.** *GB* Julie Walters, Alec McCowen, Shirley Stelfox, Tim Woodward, Dave Atkins, Danny Schiller, Victoria Hardcastle; ***D:*** Terry Jones; ***W:*** David Leland; ***C:*** Roger Deakins; ***M:*** John Du Prez.

Personal Velocity: Three Portraits ☆☆☆ **2002 (R)** Fictional triptych of three New York women undergoing moments of epiphany. Delia (Sedgwick) summons the courage to take her children and leave her broke, abusive spouse and Catskill trailer life. Greta (Posey), a Manhattan cookbook editor realizes that her work does have merit but in order to really move forward in life she needs to leave her slouch of a husband. And finally Paula (Balk), a pregnant, misdirected young woman driving nowhere in particular, connects with her maternal instincts through an encounter with a hitchhiker. Ellen Kuras's cinematography is notable in its attention to detail and Miller (playwright Arthur's daughter) mixes great storytelling with flashbacks, montages, and narrator commentary to provides a well-rounded understanding of each situation, leaving final judgment to the audience. **86m/C VHS, DVD.** *US* Kyra Sedgwick, David Warshofsky, Leo Fitzpatrick, Brian Tarantina, Mara Hobel, Parker Posey, Tim Guinee, Joel de la Fuente, Wallace Shawn, Ron Leibman, Josh Weinstein, Ben Shankman, Fairuza Balk, Seth Gilliam, David Patrick Kelly, Lou Taylor Pucci, Patti D'Arbanville; ***D:*** Rebecca Miller; ***W:*** Rebecca Miller; ***C:*** Ellen Kuras; ***M:*** Michael Rohatyn; ***Nar:*** John Ventimiglia.

The Personals ☆☆ ½ **1983 (PG)** A recently divorced young man takes out a personal ad in a newspaper to find the woman of his dreams. But it isn't quite that simple in this independent comedy shot entirely in Minneapolis. **90m/C VHS, DVD.** Bill Schoppert, Karen Landry, Paul Eiding, Michael Laskin, Vickie Dakil; ***D:*** Peter Markle.

Personals ☆☆ **1990** Chilling drama that casts O'Neill as an unnoticed librarian, until she begins to meet (and kill) the men who answer her ads. Zimbalist is a widow who is determined to learn the truth. **93m/C VHS.** Stephanie Zimbalist, Jennifer O'Neill, Robin Thomas, Clark Johnson, Gina Gallego, Rosemary Dunsmore, Colm Feore; ***D:*** Steven Hilliard Stern. **TV**

The Personals ☆☆ ½ **1998** Fed up with her boring love life, Dr. Du Jia-zhen (Liu) takes out a personal ad and gets 100 responses. The body of the film is made up of the interviews she conducts with these men—well, most of them are men. Other filmmakers have made more of the same premise, but director Kuo-fu Chen keeps his camera squarely on his characters. The Taiwan setting is a bit exotic. Liu's performance is a model of restraint. Mandarin with subtitles. **104m/C VHS, DVD.** *TW* Rene Liu, Wu Bai; ***D:*** Kuo-fu Chen, Shih-chich Chen; ***W:*** Kuo-fu Chen, Shih-chich Chen; ***C:*** Nan-hong Ho.

Personals ☆☆ ½ **2000** New Yorker Keith (Yoba) is juggling two girlfriends and a writing job and sucking at all three endeavors. So it's no big surprise when he loses it all. Keith then decides to write an expose of personal ads but finds out more about himself then the women who answer his ad. Entertaining debut for filmmaker Sargent. **91m/C VHS, DVD.** Malik Yoba, Stacey Dash, Sheryl Lee Ralph, Rhonda Ross Kendrick, Monteria Ivey; ***D:*** Mike Sargent; ***W:*** Mike Sargent. **VIDEO**

Persons Unknown ☆☆ **1996** Melodramatic noir with a decent cast. Disgraced ex-cop Jim Holland (Mantegna) now runs a security firm in Long Beach, CA. He has a one-nighter with foxy Amanda (Lynch) and wakes up to discover she's stolen confidential files. So, with colleague Cake (Walsh), he tracks Amanda down and discovers that she and her wheelchair-bound sister, Molly (Watts), are planning a robbery that involves ripping off Columbian drug lords. But, as usual, nothing works out as intended. **99m/C VHS.** Joe Mantegna, Kelly Lynch, J.T. Walsh, Naomi Watts, Xander Berkeley, Jon Favreau, Channon Roe, Michael Nicolosi; ***D:*** George Hickenlooper; ***W:*** Craig Smith; ***C:*** Richard Crudo; ***M:*** Ed Tomney.

Persuasion ☆☆ ½ **1971** Practical Anne Elliott is always at the beck-and-call of her snobbish and helpless family. She even turned down a marriage proposal for their sake. Now Captain Wentworth has come back into Anne's life and she has a second chance. But will she be strong enough to take it? Made for BBC TV. **225m/C VHS, DVD.** *GB* Ann(e) Firbank, Basil Dignam, Valerie Gearon, Marian Spence, Charlotte Mitchell; ***D:*** Howard E. Baker; ***W:*** Julian Mitchell. **TV**

Persuasion ☆☆☆ ½ **1995 (PG)** Charming British costume romance, based on Jane Austen's final novel, deals with the constricted life of practical, plain, put-upon Anne Elliot (Root). Thanks to well-meaning interference, Anne refused the marriage proposal of the manly Frederick Wentworth (Hinds) and instead stuck by her snobbish and demanding family. Eight years later, Anne is given a second chance at love when the now-wealthy Wentworth happens back into her life—but she still has her obnoxious relations to contend with. It's wonderful to see Anne blossom from mouse to lioness although the swirl of supporting players (and settings) provide some confusion. **104m/C VHS, DVD.** *GB* Amanda Root, Ciaran Hinds, Susan Fleetwood, Corin Redgrave, Fiona Shaw, John Woodvine, Phoebe Nicholls, Samuel West, Sophie Thompson, Judy Cornwell, Felicity Dean, Simon Russell Beale, Victoria Hamilton, Emma Roberts; ***D:*** Roger Mitchell; ***W:*** Nick Dear, Jeremy Sams; ***C:*** John Daly; ***M:*** Jeremy Sams.

Persuasion ☆☆ ½ **2007** Poor, put-upon spinster Anne Elliot (Hawkins)! Some years before, having respected the wishes of family and friends, she turned down the marriage proposal of Captain Wentworth (Penry-Jones) to care for her selfish and self-centered family. But Wentworth unexpectedly re-enters the scene—now a wealthy, rather dashing, and very eligible bachelor. Can Anne still catch his eye? And will she allow her own feelings to rule what's still expected of her? Based on the novel by Jane Austen. **90m/C DVD.** *GB* Sally Hawkins, Rupert Penry-Jones, Anthony Head, Julia Davis, Amanda Halle, Sam Hazeldine, Alice Krige, Michael Fenton-Stevens, Mary Stockley, Maisie Dimbelby; ***D:*** Adrian Shergold; ***W:*** Simon Burke; ***C:*** David Odd; ***M:*** Martin Phipps. **TV**

The Perverse Countess ☆ *La Comtesse Perverse* **1973** Romay is a bored tourist who spends a free weekend on a fling with Woods, who procures human flesh for the cannibalistic Count and Countess Zaroff (Vernon and Arno). Romay accompanies her lover to the haunted castle on a delivery, not realizing she is the package. When the Countess sees what a succulent bon-bon Romay is, she faces difficult choices. Subtitled in English. **86m/C VHS.** *FR* Lina Romay, Robert Woods, Howard Vernon, Alice Arno, Caroline Riviere; ***D:*** Jess (Jesus) Franco.

The Pest ☆ **1996 (PG-13)** Movie certainly lives up to its title. A hyperkinetic Leguizamo stars as Pestario (Pest) Vargas, a small-time Miami con man, who owes 50 large to the mob. Eccentric German businessman Gustav Shank (Jones) offers the money to Pest—the catch being that Pest will become the human prey for Gustav's private island hunting party. You'll be rooting for the hunter. **85m/C VHS, DVD.** John Leguizamo, Jeffrey Jones, Edoardo Ballerini, Freddy Rodriguez, Joe Morton, Charles Hallahan, Tammy Townsend, Aries Spears; ***D:*** Paul Miller; ***W:*** David Bar Katz; ***C:*** Roy Wagner; ***M:*** Kevin Kiner.

Pet Sematary ☆☆ **1989 (R)** A quirky adaptation of Stephen King's bestseller about a certain patch of woods in the Maine wilderness that rejuvenates the dead, and how a newly located college MD eventually uses it to restore his dead son. Mildly creepy. **103m/C VHS, DVD.** Dale Midkiff, Fred Gwynne, Denise Crosby, Blaze Berdahl, Brad Greenquist, Miko Hughes, Stephen King; ***D:*** Mary Lambert; ***W:*** Stephen King; ***C:*** Peter Stein; ***M:*** Elliot Goldenthal.

Pet Sematary 2 ☆ ½ **1992 (R)** Lame sequel to original Stephen King flick. After seeing his mother electrocuted, a teen and his veterinarian father move to the Maine town where the legendary Pet Sematary is located. Horror begins when the boy's friend's dog is shot by his stepfather, and the boys bury the dog in the "sematary." King wasn't involved with this film, so the story isn't very coherent, but shock value and special effects are great. Not recommended for those with a weak stomach. **102m/C VHS, DVD.** Anthony Edwards, Edward Furlong, Clancy Brown, Jared Rushton, Darlanne Fluegel, Lisa Waltz, Jason McGuire, Sarah Trigger; ***D:*** Mary Lambert; ***W:*** Richard Outten; ***C:*** Russell Carpenter.

Pet Shop 🦴🦴 ½ **1994 (PG)** Pair of evil, galaxy-travelling aliens take over the local pet store in a remote desert town and plan to abduct all the kids by bewitching them with a spaceship full of intergalactic creatures. Only Dena (aided by the good alien furballs) can stop the bad guys from making space pets of the earthlings. **88m/C VHS.** Leigh Ann Orsi, Spencer Vrooman, David Wagner, Joanne Baron, Jane Morris, Terry Kiser, Jeff Michalski, Shashawnee Hall, Sabrina Wiener, Cody Burger; ***D:*** Hope Perello; ***W:*** Mark Goldstein, Greg Suddeth, Brent Friedman; ***M:*** Reg Powell.

Pete Kelly's Blues 🦴🦴 **1955** A jazz musician in a Kansas City speakeasy is forced to stand up against a brutal racketeer. The melodramatic plot is brightened by a nonstop flow of jazz tunes sung by Lee and Fitzgerald and played by an all-star lineup that includes Dick Cathcart, Matty Matlock, Eddie Miller and George Van Eps. ♫ Sugar; Sombody Loves Me; Bye Bye Blackbird; What Can I Say After I Say I'm Sorry?; He Needs Me; Sing a Rainbow; Pete Kelly's Blues. **96m/C VHS.** Jack Webb, Janet Leigh, Edmond O'Brien, Lee Marvin, Martin Milner, Peggy Lee, Ella Fitzgerald, Jayne Mansfield; ***D:*** Jack Webb.

Pete 'n' Tillie 🦴🦴 ½ **1972 (PG)** Amiable comedy turns to less appealing melodrama as couple meets, marries, and endures tragedy. Film contributes little to director Ritt's hitt-and-miss reputation, but Matthau and Burnett shine in leads. Adapted by Julius J. Epstein from a Peter de Vries' story. **100m/C VHS.** Walter Matthau, Carol Burnett, Geraldine Page, Barry Nelson, Rene Auberjonois, Lee Montgomery, Henry Jones, Kent Smith; ***D:*** Martin Ritt; ***W:*** Julius J. Epstein; ***C:*** John A. Alonzo; ***M:*** John Williams. British Acad. '73: Actor (Matthau).

Peter and Paul 🦴🦴 ½ **1981** TV miniseries follows the lives of the two apostles, Peter (Foxworth) and Paul (Hopkins), from the Crucifixion through the next three decades as they travel spreading the word of Christ, until both are executed in Rome. Tries valiantly, but falls a bit short. **194m/C VHS.** Anthony Hopkins, Robert Foxworth, Eddie Albert, Raymond Burr, Jose Ferrer, Jon Finch, David Gwillim, Herbert Lom, Jean Peters; ***D:*** Robert Day; ***W:*** Christopher Knopf.

Peter and Vandy 🦴 ½ **2009** New Yorker Peter (Ritter) is constantly apologizing for all his actions, which annoys his girlfriend Vandy (Weixler). Of course he needs to since his insecurities cause Peter to behave like a jerk although Vandy's a passive-aggressive pill so maybe they deserve each other. They bicker—a lot—in a non-linear timeframe that gets old really, really quickly. Some romance. DiPetro adapted his own two-character play. **78m/C DVD.** *US* Jason Ritter, Jess Weixler, Jesse L. Martin, Noah Bean, Zak Orth, Dana Ekelson, Bruce Altman, Maryann Plunkett; ***D:*** Jay DiPietro; ***W:*** Jay DiPietro; ***C:*** Frank DeMarco.

Peter Gunn 🦴🦴 **1989** Detective Peter Gunn returns, only to find himself being hunted by both the mob and the Feds. A TV movie reprise of the vintage series that has none of the original cast members. **97m/C VHS, DVD.** Peter Strauss, Barbara Williams, Jennifer Edwards, Charles Cioffi, Pearl Bailey, Peter Jurasik, David Rappaport; ***D:*** Blake Edwards; ***M:*** Henry Mancini. **TV**

Peter Lundy and the Medicine Hat Stallion 🦴🦴 ½ *The Medicine Hat Stallion; Pony Express* **1977** A teenaged Pony Express rider must outrun the Indians and battle the elements in order to carry mail from the Nebraska Territory to the West Coast. Good family entertainment. **85m/C VHS, DVD.** Leif Garrett, Mitchell Ryan, Bibi Besch, John Quade, Milo O'Shea; ***D:*** Michael O'Herlihy. **TV**

Peter Pan 🦴🦴 ½ **1924** The first film adaptation of James M. Barrie's children's classic stars Bronson as the title character (in a performance endorsed by Barrie himself) that of an adventurous boy who refuses to grow up. Torrence is a scene-stealer as Captain Hook. A little on the stagy side but it still shines. **102m/B VHS, DVD.** Betty Bronson, Ernest Torrence, Mary Brian, Virginia Brown Faire, Anna May Wong, Esther Ralston, Cyril Chadwick, Philippe De Lacey, Jack Murphy; ***D:*** Herbert Brenon; ***W:*** Willis Goldbeck; ***C:*** James Wong Howe; ***M:*** Philip Carli. Natl. Film Reg. '00.

Peter Pan 🦴🦴🦴 **1953 (G)** Disney classic about a boy who never wants to grow up. Based on J.M. Barrie's book and play. Still stands head and shoulders above any recent competition in providing fun family entertainment. Terrific animation and lovely hummable music. **76m/C VHS, DVD.** ***D:*** Hamilton Luske; ***W:*** Milt Banta, William Cottrell, Winston Hibler, Bill Peet, Erdman Penner, Joe Rinaldi, Ted Sears, Ralph Wright; ***M:*** Edward Plumb, Oliver Wallace; ***V:*** Bobby Driscoll, Kathryn Beaumont, Hans Conried, Heather Angel, Candy Candido, Bill Thompson; ***Nar:*** Tom Conway.

Peter Pan 🦴🦴🦴 ½ **1960** A TV classic, this videotape of a performance of the 1954 Broadway musical adapted from the J.M. Barrie classic features Mary Martin in one of her most famous incarnations, as the adolescent Peter Pan. Songs include "I'm Flying," "Neverland," and "I Won't Grow Up." **100m/C VHS, DVD.** Mary Martin, Cyril Ritchard, Sondra Lee, Heather Halliday, Luke Halpin; ***D:*** Vincent J. Donehue. **TV**

Peter Pan 🦴🦴 ½ **2003 (PG)** Much more literal adaptation of the J.M. Barrie novel is surprisingly serious in its tone. Peter Pan (Sumpter), played by an actual boy this time around, teaches the Darling children how to fly and leads them to Neverland. Newcomer Rachel Hurd-Wood shines as Wendy Darling. Goes deeper into the relationships and emotions between the characters, including Peter and Hook, than in previous versons. **113m/C VHS, DVD.** *US* Jason Isaacs, Jeremy Sumpter, Rachel Hurd-Wood, Olivia Williams, Ludivine Sagnier, Richard Briers, Lynn Redgrave, Geoffrey Palmer, Harry Newell, Freddie Popplewell; ***D:*** P.J. Hogan; ***W:*** P.J. Hogan, Michael Goldenberg; ***C:*** Donald McAlpine; ***M:*** James Newton Howard; ***Nar:*** Saffron Burrows.

Peter the First: Part 1 🦴🦴 **1937** The first half of Petrov's Soviet epic about the early years of Tsar Peter I's reign. Lavish, in Russian with English subtitles. **95m/B VHS.** *RU* Nikolai Simonov, Nikolai Cherkassov, Mikhail Zharov, Mikhail Tarkanov; ***D:*** Vladimir Petrov; ***W:*** Vladimir Petrov; ***C:*** Vyacheslav Gordanov; ***M:*** Vladimir Scherbachov.

Peter the First: Part 2 🦴🦴 *The Conquests of Peter the Great* **1938** The second half of Petrov's epic, covering the triumphs and final years of the famous Tsar. In Russian with English subtitles. **104m/B VHS.** *RU* Nikolai Simonov, Mikhail Zharov, Nikolai Cherkassov, Mikhail Tarkanov, Alla Tarasova, Irina Zarubina, Vladimir Gardin; ***D:*** Vladimir Petrov; ***C:*** Vyacheslav Gordanov; ***M:*** Vladimir Scherbachov.

Peter the Great 🦴🦴🦴 **1986** Dry but eye-pleasing TV miniseries follows the life of Russia's colorful, very tall ruler, from childhood on. Much of the interesting cast is wasted in tiny roles. **371m/C VHS.** Maximilian Schell, Laurence Olivier, Omar Sharif, Vanessa Redgrave, Ursula Andress; ***D:*** Marvin J. Chomsky; ***W:*** Edward Anhalt; ***C:*** Vittorio Storaro; ***M:*** Laurence Rosenthal. **TV**

Peter's Friends 🦴🦴 ½ **1992 (R)** Peter has recently inherited a grand manor house located outside London and invites some chums to celebrate a New Year's Eve weekend, ten years after they've been at university together. So begins another nostalgic trip down memory lane ala "The Big Chill," but unlike other clones, this one can stand on its own, with a lightweight and sly script by talented comedienne Rudner (in her film debut) and her husband Bergman. If the script sometimes falls a little flat, the fine cast will make up for it. Thompson's mother, actress Law, plays the housekeeper. **102m/C VHS, DVD.** *GB* Kenneth Branagh, Rita Rudner, Emma Thompson, Stephen Fry, Hugh Laurie, Imelda Staunton, Alphonsia Emmanuel, Tony Slattery, Alex Lowe, Alex Scott, Phyllida Law, Richard Briers; ***D:*** Kenneth Branagh; ***W:*** Rita Rudner, Martin Bregman.

Pete's Dragon 🦴🦴 ½ **1977 (G)** Elliot, an enormous, bumbling dragon with a penchant for clumsy heroics, becomes friends with poor orphan Pete. Combines brilliant animation with the talents of live actors for an interesting effect. **128m/C VHS, DVD.** Helen Reddy, Shelley Winters, Mickey Rooney, Jim Dale, Red Buttons, Sean Marshall, Jim Backus, Jeff Conaway; ***D:*** Don Chaffey; ***W:*** Malcolm Marmorstein; ***C:*** Frank Phillips; ***M:*** Irwin Kostal; ***V:*** Charlie Callas.

Pete's Meteor 🦴🦴 ½ **1998 (R)** A meteor lands in the Dublin backyard where Mickey and his two siblings are living with their grandmother (Fricker) after the death of their parents. They think the rock is a gift from mom and dad (who now live up in the stars). But when the government takes the meteor and sends it to a university scientist (Molina) for study, the kids decide to get it back. And if this wasn't plot enough, the trio's junkie Uncle Pete (Myers), who promised to look after them, is in trouble with the mob. Don't be fooled—this is a gritty and thoughtful drama, not a kid flick or a comedy despite Myers presence. **103m/C VHS, DVD.** Mike Myers, Brenda Fricker, Alfred Molina, Ian Costello; ***D:*** Joe O'Byrne; ***W:*** Joe O'Byrne; ***C:*** Paul Sarossy.

Petit Con 🦴🦴 ½ **1984 (R)** A live-action version of the popular French comic strip wherein a young rebel drops out of society to live with aging hippies. With English subtitles. **90m/C VHS.** *FR* Guy Marchand, Michel Choupon, Caroline Cellier, Bernard Brieux, Soudad Amidou; ***D:*** Gerard Lauzier.

Petits Freres 🦴🦴 ½ *Little Fellas* **2000** Troubled 13-year-old Talia (Touly) takes her pitbull Kim and runs away from her brutal stepfather. She hangs out in the projects with a group of boys her own age whom she warily befriends, only to be victimized when they steal and sell Kim to a dogfighting ring. Despite their denials, Talia knows what they did, even when they promise to help her rescue the dog. Kids, who are non-professionals, do fine but the story meanders it's way to a predictable ending. French with subtitles. **92m/C VHS, DVD.** *FR* Stephanie Touly, Ilies Sefraoui, Mustapha Goumane, Nassim Izem, Rachid Mansouri, Gerald Dantsoff; ***D:*** Jacques Doillon; ***W:*** Jacques Doillon; ***C:*** Manuel Teran.

Petrified Forest 🦴🦴🦴 **1936** Writer Alan Squier (Howard) is hitchhiking through the Arizona desert when he stops at a rundown gas station/diner run by Maple (Hall) and his daughter Gabrielle (Davis). Once an idealist, Alan now feels he has little to live for, which may explain his attitude when the diner patrons and employees are held hostage by on the lam gangster Duke Mantee (Bogart) and his boys. Often gripping, with memorable performances from Davis, Howard, and Bogart. Based on the play by Robert Sherwood with Howard and Bogart re-creating their stage roles. **83m/B VHS, DVD.** Bette Davis, Leslie Howard, Humphrey Bogart, Dick Foran, Charley Grapewin, Porter Hall, Genevieve Tobin, Joseph (Joe) Sawyer; ***D:*** Archie Mayo; ***W:*** Delmer Daves; ***C:*** Sol Polito; ***M:*** Bernhard Kaun.

Petty Crimes 🦴🦴 *Aller-Simple Pour Manhattan* **2002** Evading jail time in France, two-bit thief Michel immigrates to the Big Apple and falls for the zesty Zoe who works on his deportation battle when his visa expires. But he needs to scrounge up some major coinage pronto. Enter the persistent old partner tempting him back into his rotten ways of yore. All goes pleasantly enough until the Frenchman faces a puzzling, perturbing twist at the end—mais non! **78m/C VHS, DVD.** *FR* Andrew Pang, Ann Hu, Jeremie Covillault, Sarah Zoe Canner; ***D:*** Michel Ferry; ***W:*** Sarah Zoe Canner, Michel Ferry; ***C:*** Jean Coudsi; ***M:*** Jean-Claude Ghrenessia. **VIDEO**

Petulia 🦴🦴🦴🦴 **1968 (R)** Overlooked, offbeat drama about a flighty woman who spites her husband by dallying with a sensitive, recently divorced surgeon. Classic '60s document and cult favorite offers great performance from the appealing Christie, with Scott fine as the vulnerable surgeon. Onscreen performances by the Grateful Dead and Big Brother. Among idiosyncratic director Lester's best. From the novel "Me and the Arch Kook Petulia" by John Haase. **105m/C VHS, DVD.** George C. Scott, Richard Chamberlain, Julie Christie, Shirley Knight, Arthur Hill, Joseph Cotten, Pippa Scott, Richard Dysart, Kathleen Widdoes, Austin Pendleton, Rene Auberjonois, Roger Bowen, Ellen Geer; ***D:*** Richard Lester; ***W:*** Lawrence B. Marcus; ***C:*** Nicolas Roeg; ***M:*** John Barry.

Peyton Place 🦴🦴🦴 **1957** Passion, scandal, and deception in a small New England town set the standard for passion, scandal, and deception in soap operadom. Shot on location in Camden, Maine. Performances and themes now seem dated, but produced a blockbuster in its time. Adapted from Grace Metalious' popular novel and followed by "Return to Peyton Place." **157m/C VHS, DVD.** Lana Turner, Hope Lange, Lee Philips, Lloyd Nolan, Diane Varsi, Lorne Greene, Russ Tamblyn, Arthur Kennedy, Terry Moore, Barry Coe, David Nelson, Betty Field, Mildred Dunnock, Leon Ames, Alan Reed Jr.; ***D:*** Mark Robson; ***W:*** John Michael Hayes; ***C:*** William Mellor; ***M:*** Franz Waxman.

Phaedra 🦴🦴 **1961** Loose and updated adaptation of Euripides' "Hipploytus." Mercouri, the second wife of a rich Greek shipping magnate, is dispatched to London to convince her husband's adult son (Perkins) to come home to Greece. Mercouri and Perkins immediately begin a steamy affair but their return home brings problems for all. Dubbed. **116m/B VHS.** *GR FR* Melina Mercouri, Anthony Perkins, Raf Vallone, Elizabeth Ercy; ***Cameos:*** Jules Dassin; ***D:*** Jules Dassin; ***W:*** Jules Dassin, Margarita Liberaki; ***M:*** Mikis Theodorakis.

Phantasm 🦴🦴 ½ *The Never Dead* **1979 (R)** A small-budgeted, hallucinatory horror fantasy about two parentless brothers who discover weird goings-on at the local funeral parlor, including the infamous airborne, brain-chewing chrome ball. Creepy, unpredictable nightmare fashioned on a shoestring by young independent producer Coscarelli. Scenes were cut out of the original film to avoid "X" rating. Followed by "Phantasm II." **90m/C VHS, DVD.** Michael Baldwin, Bill Thornbury, Reggie Bannister, Kathy Lester, Terrie Kalbus, Kenneth V. Jones, Susan Harper, Lynn Eastman, David Arntzen, Angus Scrimm, Bill Cone; ***D:*** Don A. Coscarelli; ***W:*** Don A. Coscarelli; ***C:*** Don A. Coscarelli; ***M:*** Fredric Myrow, Malcolm Seagrave.

Phantasm 2 🦴🦴 **1988 (R)** Teen psychic keeps flashing on villainous Tall Man. A rehash sequel to the original, cultishly idiosyncratic fantasy, wherein more victims are fed into the inter-dimensional abyss and Mike discovers that the horror is not all in his head. Occasional inspired gore; bloodier than its predecessor. More yuck for the buck. **97m/C VHS.** James LeGros, Reggie Bannister, Angus Scrimm, Paula Irvine, Samantha (Sam) Phillips, Ken Tigar; ***D:*** Don A. Coscarelli; ***W:*** Don A. Coscarelli; ***C:*** Daryn Okada.

Phantasm 3: Lord of the Dead 🦴 ½ **1994 (R)** Murderous mortician The Tall Man and his killer silver spheres return once again in this continuing gore fest. Mike, whose brother Jody was one of The Tall Man's victims, teams up with the cynical Reggie and martial arts expert Rocky to try to defeat the creep. That's if they can get past his zombie cohorts and flesh-eating ghouls. **91m/C VHS, DVD.** Reggie Bannister, A. Michael Baldwin, Bill Thornbury, Gloria Lynne Henry, Kevin Connor, Angus Scrimm; ***D:*** Don A. Coscarelli; ***W:*** Don A. Coscarelli.

Phantasm 4: Oblivion 🦴 ½ **1998 (R)** At least this sequel can boast the original's lead actors, which allows for footage from the first movie to be used in telling a familiar story. The Tall Man (Scrimm) is still transporting corpses and Mike (Baldwin) is now becoming one of the evil guy's minions. But some time travel takes Mike back to the Tall Man's origins and he tries to take care of the problem at the source. **90m/C VHS, DVD.** Angus Scrimm, A. Michael Baldwin, Reggie Bannister, Bill Thornbury, Bob Ivy; ***D:*** Don A. Coscarelli; ***W:*** Don A. Coscarelli; ***C:*** Chris Chomyn; ***M:*** Christopher Stone. **VIDEO**

Phantom 🦴🦴 **1922** A mild-mannered clerk, dreaming of bettering himself by becoming a famous poet, becomes obsessed with a wealthy beauty. Restored and hand-tinted silent from legendary German director Murnau with a 2003 orchestral score by Israel. **120m/B DVD.** *GE* Alfred Abel, Lya de Putti, Lil Dagover; ***D:*** F.W. Murnau; ***W:*** Thea von Harbou; ***C:*** Axel Graatkjaer, Theophan Ouchakoff; ***M:*** Robert Israel.

The Phantom **1931** Rare cheapie of a hooded killer terrorizing a group of people in a haunted house. **62m/C VHS, DVD.** Guinn "Big Boy" Williams, Wilfrid Lucas, Sheldon Lewis, William (Bill) Gould; ***D:*** Alan James.

The Phantom 1/2 **1996 (PG)** Based on the Lee Falk comic created in 1936. Deep in the Bengalla jungle, a mysterious costumed figure honors a 400-year-old legacy by fighting piracy, greed, and cruelty. With the help of a beautiful newspaper heiress (Swanson), the latest guardian (Zane) must keep an American industrialist (Williams) and a secret brotherhood of pirates from finding three sacred skulls that contain the power to dominate the world. Old-fashioned swashbuckling story is helped along by Zane's enthusiastic portrayal of the stalwart hero. Action set pieces, while done more dynamically elsewhere, are fun and exciting. Older kids (read: teenagers) may find the proceedings a bit hokey, but everyone seems to be having a good time. **100m/C VHS, DVD.** Billy Zane, Kristy Swanson, Treat Williams, Catherine Zeta-Jones, James Remar, Jon Tenney, Patrick McGoohan, Samantha Eggar, Cary-Hiroyuki Tagawa, Robert Coleby, David Proval; ***D:*** Simon Wincer; ***W:*** Jeffrey Boam; ***C:*** David Burr; ***M:*** David Newman.

The Phantom Broadcast 1/2 *Phantom of the Air* **1933** A popular radio crooner is murdered. The main suspect is his hunchbacked accompanist and manager. A tightly plotted minor thriller that holds up surprisingly well. **63m/B VHS, DVD.** Ralph Forbes, Gail Patrick, Vivienne Osborne, Guinn "Big Boy" Williams, George "Gabby" Hayes; ***D:*** Phil Rosen.

Phantom Brother 1/2 **1988** A semi-spoof about a teenager left orphaned by a car crash that wiped out his entire family, and who is subsequently haunted by his dead brother. Even thinner than it sounds. **92m/C VHS.** Jon Hammer, Patrick Molloy, John Gigante, Mary Beth Pelshaw; ***D:*** William Szarka.

The Phantom Bullet 1/2 **1926** Hoot wants to holler at his father's murderers. **60m/B VHS.** Eileen (Elaine Persey) Percy, Alan Forrest, Nelson McDowell, Pat Harmon, Hoot Gibson; ***D:*** Cliff(ord) Smith; ***W:*** Curtis Benton; ***C:*** Harry Neumann.

The Phantom Chariot 1/2 **1920** A fantasy depicting the Swedish myth about how Death's coach must be driven by the last man to die each year. Silent. **89m/B VHS.** *SW* Hilda Borgstrom, Tore Svennberg, Astrid Holm; ***D:*** Victor Sjostrom; ***W:*** Victor Sjostrom; ***C:*** Julius Jaenzon.

The Phantom Creeps **1939** Evil Dr. Zorka, armed with a meteorite chunk which can bring an army to a standstill, provides the impetus for this enjoyable serial in 12 episodes. **235m/B VHS, DVD.** Bela Lugosi, Dorothy Arnold, Robert Kent, Regis Toomey; ***D:*** Ford Beebe, Saul Goodkind.

The Phantom Empire *Radio Ranch* **1935** Autry faces the futuristic "Thunder Riders" from the subterranean city of Murania, located 20,000 feet beneath his ranch. A complete serial in 12 episodes. If you only see one science-fiction western in your life, this is the one. Also available in an edited theatrical version at 80 minutes. **245m/B VHS, DVD.** Gene Autry, Frankie Darro, Betsy King Ross, Smiley Burnette; ***D:*** B. Reeves Eason, Otto Brower.

Phantom Empire **1987 (R)** A woman who rules over a lost city takes a bunch of scientists prisoner and forces them to be slaves. **85m/C VHS, DVD.** Ross Hagen, Jeffrey Combs, Dawn Wildsmith, Robert Quarry, Susan Stokey, Michelle (McClellan) Bauer, Russ Tamblyn, Sybil Danning; ***D:*** Fred Olen Ray; ***W:*** Fred Olen Ray, T.L. Lankford.

Phantom Express **1932** Experienced old engineer is dismissed from his job because no one believes his explanation that a mysterious train caused the wreck of his own train. He aims to find justice. **65m/B VHS, DVD.** J. Farrell MacDonald, Sally Blane, William "Buster" Collier Jr., Hobart Bosworth; ***D:*** Emory Johnson.

Phantom Fiend 1/2 **1935** A gentle musician becomes a suspect when a series of Jack-the-Ripper type murders terrorize London. Is he the nice guy known by his girlfriend and the people in his lodging house, or is the musician really JTR? Based on the novel "The Lodger" by Marie Belloc-Lowndes. **70m/B VHS, DVD.** *GB* Ivor Novello, Elizabeth Allan, A.W. Baskcomb, Jack Hawkins, Barbara Everest, Peter Gawthorne, Kynaston Reeves; ***D:*** Maurice Elvey.

The Phantom Flyer 1/2 **1928** Stunt pilot helps out a cattle-owning frontier family bedeviled by rustlers. Silent. **54m/B VHS.** Al Wilson, Buck Connors, Billy "Red" Jones, Lillian Gilmore, Myrtis Crinley, Larry Steers; ***D:*** Bruce Mitchell; ***W:*** Bruce Mitchell; ***C:*** William S. Adams.

Phantom from Space 1/2 **1953** An invisible alien lands on Earth, begins killing people, and is pursued by a pair of scientists. **72m/B VHS, DVD.** Ted Cooper, Rudolph Anders, Noreen Nash, James Seay, Harry Landers; ***D:*** W. Lee Wilder; ***C:*** William Clothier.

The Phantom from 10,000 Leagues **1956** Slimy sea monster attacks swimmers and fishermen; investigating oceanographer pretends not to notice monster is hand puppet. Early AIP release, when still named American Releasing Company. **80m/B VHS, DVD.** Kent Taylor, Cathy Downs, Michael Whalen, Helene Stanton, Phillip Pine; ***D:*** Dan Milner; ***W:*** Lou Rusoff; ***C:*** Brydon Baker; ***M:*** Ronald Stein.

Phantom Gold 1/2 **1938** The wicked Whitaker claims to have struck it rich but it's really a scam to lure unsuspecting miners to the claim and then rob and murder them. Luden's suspicious and proves Whitaker's a bad guy. **56m/B VHS.** Jack Luden, Charles "Slim" Whitaker, Beth Marion, Hal Taliaferro, Art Davis; ***D:*** Joseph Levering.

The Phantom in the House **1929** A woman commits a murder and has her inventor husband take the rap. While he's in prison, she gets rich off of his work. Things get hairy when he is released 15 years later and is introduced to his daughter as a friend of the family. Melodramatic film was originally made with and without sound. **64m/B VHS, DVD.** Ricardo Cortez, Nancy Welford, Henry B. Walthall, Grace Valentine; ***D:*** Phil Rosen.

Phantom Killer **1942** A district attorney tries to hang a murder rap on a most improbable suspect. When the man is aquitted, the DA quits his job to find the truth, which takes a disturbing twist. The plot is a thinly veiled rehash of "The Sphinx" (1933). **61m/B VHS, DVD.** Dick Purcell, Joan Woodbury, John Hamilton, Warren Hymer, Kenneth Harlan, J. Farrell MacDonald, Mantan Moreland; ***D:*** William Beaudine.

Phantom Lady **1944** After an argument with his wife Scott Henderson (Curtis) walks into a bar and chats up a mystery woman (Helm). When he returns home, the police are there and his wife has been strangled with his necktie. Since he doesn't know his bar mate's name and no one professes to remember her, Scott is quickly convicted of the crime. Only his loyal secretary Carol (Raines) believes him and she sets out to solve the crime. Based on the novel by Cornell Woolrich. **87m/B VHS.** Ella Raines, Alan Curtis, Franchot Tone, Thomas Gomez, Elisha Cook Jr., Fay Helm, Aurora Miranda, Andrew Tombes, Regis Toomey, Joseph Crehan, Virginia Brissac, Milburn Stone; ***D:*** Robert Siodmak; ***W:*** Bernard C. Schoenfeld; ***C:*** Elwood "Woody" Bredell.

The Phantom Light 1/2 **1935** A lighthouse keeper is murdered under strange circumstances and a mysterious light keeps appearing at the scene. Detective Hale joins up with a navy man and another lighthouse keeper to solve the crime. A low-budget mystery with good atmosphere and some humor. **75m/B VHS.** *GB* Binnie Hale, Gordon Harker, Ian Hunter, Donald Calthrop; ***D:*** Michael Powell.

The Phantom Lover 1/2 *Ye Bang Ge Sheng* **1995** It's "The Phantom of the Opera" Hong Kong style, although it's a adult fairytale rather than a horror story. In 1936 a theatrical troupe hopes to restore a burned-out opera house for their performances. Legendary singer Sung Dan-Ping (Cheung) was thought to have died in the fire, instead, horribly disfigured, he hides out in the ruins and dreams of his lost love (Chein-Lien). Chinese with subtitles or dubbed. **102m/C VHS, DVD.** *HK* Leslie Cheung, Chien-Lien Wu, Philip Kwok, Roy Szeto; ***D:*** Ronny Yu; ***W:*** Roy Szeto, Raymond Wong; ***C:*** Peter Pau; ***M:*** Chris Babida.

Phantom of Chinatown **1940** Mr. Wong is called in to solve another murder in the final entry in the series. The first to have an Asian actor portray the lead, as Luke replaced Boris Karloff. **61m/B VHS, DVD.** Keye Luke, Lotus Long, Grant Withers, Paul McVey, Charles F. Miller; ***D:*** Phil Rosen; ***W:*** George Waggner; ***C:*** Fred H. Jackman Jr.; ***M:*** Edward Kay.

Phantom of Death 1/2 **1987 (R)** A brilliant pianist, stricken by a fatal disease that causes rapid aging, goes on a murderous rampage. **95m/C VHS.** *IT* Michael York, Donald Pleasence, Edwige Fenech; ***D:*** Ruggero Deodato; ***M:*** Pino Donaggio.

The Phantom of 42nd Street **1945** An actor and a cop team up to find the killer of a wealthy uncle. **58m/B VHS, DVD.** Dave O'Brien, Kay Aldridge, Alan Mowbray, Frank Jenks; ***D:*** Al(bert) Herman.

Phantom of Liberty 1/2 *Le Fantome de la Liberte; The Specter of Freedom* **1974** Master surrealist Bunuel's episodic film wanders from character to character and from event to event. Animals wander through a man's bedroom, soldiers conduct military exercises in an inhabited area, a missing girl stands before her parents even as they futilely attempt to determine her whereabouts, and an assassin is found guilty, then applauded and led to freedom. They don't get much more surreal than this. If you think you may like it, you'll probably love it. Bunuel, by the way, is among the firing squad vicitms in the film's opening enactment of Goya's May 3, 1808. In French with English subtitles. **104m/C VHS, DVD.** *FR* Adriana Asti, Jean-Claude Brialy, Michel Piccoli, Adolfo Celi, Monica Vitti, Milena Vukotic, Michael (Michel) Lonsdale, Claude Pieplu, Julien Bertheau, Paul Frankeur, Paul Le Person, Bernard Verley; ***D:*** Luis Bunuel; ***W:*** Luis Bunuel, Jean-Claude Carriere; ***C:*** Edmond Richard.

The Phantom of Paris 1/2 **1931** Bibi (Gilbert), a world-class French escape artist, attempts to escape a false murder charge trumped up by an evil marquis (Keith) who has murdered the wealthy father of Bibi's fiancee (Hyams) in a plot to lay claim to her and her father's wealth. Bibi uses his talent for escape to elude the law while he attempts to clear his name. Featuring one of John Gilbert's first talking roles after a successful career in silent film. **73m/B DVD.** John Gilbert, Leila Hyams, Lewis Stone, Jean Hersholt, Sir C. Aubrey Smith, Ian Keith; ***D:*** John S. Robertson; ***W:*** Gaston Leroux; ***C:*** Oliver Marsh.

The Phantom of Soho *Das Phantom von Soho* **1964** A Scotland Yard detective investigates the murders of several prominent businessmen and is assisted by a beautiful mystery writer. **92m/B VHS, DVD.** *GE* Dieter Borsche, Barbara Rutting, Hans Sohnker, Peter Vogel, Helga Sommerfeld, Werner Peters; ***D:*** Franz Gottlieb.

Phantom of the Air **1933** Twelve chapters of high-flying adventure with Tom Tyler! **230m/B VHS, DVD.** Tom Tyler, Gloria Shea, William Desmond, Leroy Mason, Walter Brennan; ***D:*** Ray Taylor.

Phantom of the Mall: Eric's Revenge **1989** A murderous spirit haunts the local mall. Gore flows like water. **91m/C VHS, DVD.** Morgan Fairchild, Kari Whitman, Jonathan Goldsmith, Derek Rydall, Pauly Shore, Robert Estes, Brinke Stevens; ***D:*** Richard Friedman; ***W:*** Robert King; ***C:*** Harry Mathias; ***M:*** Stacy Widelitz.

The Phantom of the Opera **1925** Deranged, disfigured music lover haunts the sewers of a Parisian opera house and kills to further the career of an unsuspecting young soprano. First of many film versions still packs a wallop, with fine playing from Chaney Sr. Silent with two-color Technicolor "Bal Masque" sequence. Versions with different running times are also available, including 79 and 88 minutes. **101m/B VHS, DVD.** Lon Chaney Sr., Norman Kerry, Mary Philbin, Gibson Gowland, Arthur Edmund Carewe, John St. Polis, Snitz Edwards, Virginia Pearson; ***D:*** Rupert Julian, Edward Sedgwick, Lon Chaney Sr.; ***W:*** Elliot J. Clawson, Raymond L. Schrock, Frank M. McCormack; ***C:*** Virgil Miller, Charles Van Enger, Milton Bridenbecker. Natl. Film Reg. '98.

The Phantom of the Opera **1943** Second Hollywood version (following the 1925 silent) of Gaston Leroux's novel, remade by the same studio (Universal), suffers by dispersing the chills with too many opera scenes (no doubt to give Eddy something to do) and weak comedy. Enrique (a sympathetic Rains) is a disfigured musician in the Paris Opera who sacrifices himself for the love of young singer Christine (DuBois), who doesn't even know he exists. Rains is only briefly seen in his horror visage. **92m/C VHS, DVD.** Nelson Eddy, Susanna Foster, Claude Rains, Edgar Barrier, Leo Carrillo, Hume Cronyn, J. Edward Bromberg; ***D:*** Arthur Lubin; ***W:*** Samuel Hoffenstein, Eric Taylor; ***C:*** Hal Mohr, William Howard Greene; ***M:*** Edward Ward. Oscars '43: Color Cinematog.

The Phantom of the Opera 1/2 **1962** Hammer version of the Gaston Leroux novel transfers the action from Paris to London but keeps the basic story of a young singer (Sears) and her masked benefactor (Lom), who lives in the sewers beneath the opera house. There's also the wimpy fiance (De Souza) to come between them. Good gothic melodrama. Sears' singing was dubbed by opera performer Pat Clark; producer Hinds used the pseudonym John Elder for his screenplay. **85m/C VHS, DVD.** Herbert Lom, Heather Sears, Edward De Souza, Thorley Walters, Michael Gough, Martin Miller, Ian Wilson; ***D:*** Terence Fisher; ***W:*** John (Anthony Hinds) Elder; ***C:*** Arthur Grant; ***M:*** Edwin Astley.

The Phantom of the Opera 1/2 **1989 (R)** A gory, "Elm Street"-ish version of the Gaston Leroux classic, attempting to cash in on the success of the Broadway musical. **93m/C VHS, DVD.** Robert Englund, Jill Schoelen, Alex Hyde-White, Bill Nighy, Terence Harvey, Stephanie Lawrence, Nathan Lewis, Peter Clapham, Molly Shannon; ***D:*** Dwight Little; ***W:*** Duke Sandefur; ***C:*** Elemer Ragalyi; ***M:*** Misha Segal.

The Phantom of the Opera 1/2 **1990** Yet another version of the tragic tale of a disfigured mask-wearing opera lover, who lurks in the depths of the Paris Opera House, and his desire for lovely young singer, Christine. Dance plays the Phantom as doomed romantic, with Lancaster his protective father. Kopit adapted from his 1983 play. Made for TV drama, originally shown in two parts. **200m/C VHS, DVD.** *GB* Charles Dance, Burt Lancaster, Teri Polo, Ian Richardson, Andrea Ferreol, Adam Storke, Jean-Pierre Cassel; ***D:*** Tony Richardson; ***W:*** Arthur Kopit; ***C:*** Steve Yaconelli; ***M:*** John Addison. **TV**

The Phantom of the Opera 1/2 *Dario Argento's Phantom of the Opera; Il Fantasma dell'Opera* **1998 (R)** Campy excess (and lots of gore) overwhelms Gaston Leroux's often-filmed chiller. This Phantom (Sands) doesn't have a facial disfigurement and goes unmasked but he's weird nonetheless. Abandoned as a baby, he's raised by rats (ewwww) beneath the Paris Opera where he becomes smitten by young singer, Christine (Argento), and does his best to make her his alone. **100m/C VHS, DVD.** *IT* Julian Sands, Asia Argento, Andrea Di Stefano, Nadia Rinaldi, Coralina Cataldi-Tassoni, Istvan Bubik, Zoltan Barabas; ***D:*** Dario Argento; ***W:*** Dario Argento, Gerard Brach; ***C:*** Ronnie Taylor; ***M:*** Ennio Morricone.

The Phantom of the Opera **2004 (PG-13)** Andrew Lloyd Webber's London musical finally hit the big-screen in this extravagant version from director Schumacher. This umpteenth adaptation ramps up the romance over the hideousness of the title character. As played here by brawny Scottish actor Butler, the Phantom is positively swoon-worthy. Story is simple: Paris Opera engenue Christine (Rossum) gets her big chance when diva Carlotta (Driver) huffs off the stage. Christine is then torn between two would-be loves; well-mannered opera patron Vicompte Raoul de Chagny (Wilson) and that mystery man. Some changes are made from stage to screen but fans won't be unduly alarmed although the film's cheesy romanticism is unlikely to find new converts. Sets and costumes are eye-catching. **143m/C VHS, DVD, Blu-ray Disc, HD DVD.** Gerard Butler, Emmy Rossum, Patrick Wilson, Miranda Richardson, Minnie Driver, Simon Callow, Ciaran Hinds, James Fleet, Kevin McNally, Murray Melvin, Victor McGuire, Jennifer Ellison; ***D:*** Joel Schumacher; ***W:*** Joel Schumacher, Andrew Lloyd Webber; ***C:*** John Mathieson; ***M:*** Andrew Lloyd Webber.

Phantom of the Paradise **1974 (PG)** A rock 'n' roll parody of "Phantom of the Opera." Splashy, only occasionally horrific spoof in which cruel music executive Williams, much to his everlasting regret, swindles a songwriter. Violence ensues. Not for most, or even many, tastes. Graham steals the film as rocker Beef. A failure at the boxoffice, and now a cult item (small enthusiastic cult with few outside interests) for its oddball humor and outrageous rock star parodies. Williams also wrote the turgid score. ♫ Goodbye, Eddie, Goodbye; Faust; Upholstery; Special to Me; Old Souls; Somebody Super Like You; Life At Last; The Hell of It; The Phantom's Theme (Beauty and the Beast). **92m/C VHS, DVD.** Paul Williams, William Finley, Jessica Harper, Gerrit Graham, George Memmoli, Archie Hahn; ***D:*** Brian De Palma; ***W:*** Brian De Palma; ***C:*** Larry Pizer; ***M:*** George Aliceson Tipton, Paul Williams.

The Phantom of the Range 1/2 **1938** Marion is trying to sell her grandfather's ranch only his "ghost" is scaring everyone away. She and cowpoke Tyler find out a group of evil treasure hunters are searching the property for hidden gold. **59m/B VHS, DVD.** Tom Tyler, Beth Marion, Charles "Blackie" King, Forrest Taylor, John Elliott, Soledad Jiminez, Sammy Cohen; ***D:*** Robert F. "Bob" Hill.

Phantom of the Ritz **1988 (R)** Bizarre accidents begin to take place when Ed Blake and his girlfriend start renovating the old Ritz Theatre. It seems the theatre is inhabited by a rather angry ghost and somebody's got to deal with it before the Ritz can rock and roll. Features the fabulous sounds of the '50s. **89m/C VHS.** Peter Bergman, Deborah Van Valkenburgh; ***D:*** Allen Plone.

Phantom of the West **1931** Ten-episode serial about a rancher who becomes "The Phantom of the West" in order to smoke out his father's killer. **166m/B VHS, DVD.** William Desmond, Thomas Santschi, Tom Tyler; ***D:*** David Ross Lederman.

Phantom Patrol 1/2 **1936** A mystery writer is kidnapped and someone impersonates him. Mountie Maynard must come to the rescue. **60m/B VHS.** Kermit Maynard, Joan Barclay, Paul Fix, Julian Rivero, Eddie (Edward) Phillips, Roger Williams; ***D:*** Charles (Hutchison) Hutchinson.

The Phantom Pinto *Buzzy and the Phantom Pinto* **1941** Henry and O'Brien try to discover the secret of Black Mountain Cut where a rancher was shot. Before dying, the man claims he saw a phantom black pinto. **55m/B DVD.** Robert "Buzzy" Henry, Dave O'Brien, Dorothy Short, George Morrell; ***D:*** Richard C. Kahn; ***W:*** E.G. Robertson.

The Phantom Planet 1/2 **1961** An astronaut crash-lands on an asteroid and discovers a race of tiny people living there. Having breathed the atmosphere, he shrinks to their dimunitive size and aids them in their war against brutal invaders. Infamously peculiar. **82m/B VHS, DVD.** Dean Fredericks, Coleen Gray, Tony Dexter, Dolores Faith, Francis X. Bushman, Richard Kiel; ***D:*** William Marshall; ***W:*** Fred De Gorter, Fred Gebhardt, William Telaak; ***C:*** Elwood J. Nicholson; ***M:*** Hayes Pagel.

Phantom Rancher 1/2 **1939** Roaring melodrama finds Maynard donning a mask to find the real Phantom, who is causing havoc. **61m/B VHS, DVD.** Ken Maynard, Dorothy Short, Harry Harvey, Ted Adams, Dave O'Brien, Tom London, John Elliott, Reed Howes; ***D:*** Harry Fraser; ***W:*** William Lively; ***C:*** William (Bill) Hyer; ***M:*** Lew Porter.

Phantom Ranger 1/2 **1938** A federal agent masquerades as a crook to catch a band of counterfeiters. **54m/B VHS, DVD.** Tim McCoy, Suzanne Kaaren, Karl Hackett, John St. Polis, John Merton, Harry Strang; ***D:*** Sam Newfield.

The Phantom Rider **1936** Mystery fills the old West in this serial composed of 15 chapters. **152m/B VHS.** Buck Jones, Marla Shelton, Joey Ray, Diana Gibson, Harry Woods, Frank LaRue, George Cooper, Eddie Gribbon; ***D:*** Ray Taylor; ***W:*** Basil Dickey, George Plympton, Ella O'Neill; ***C:*** John Hickson, Allen Q. Thompson.

The Phantom Rider 1/2 *Ghost Riders of the West* **1946** The masked do-gooder rides the plains protecting the local Indians from some surly settlers. A 12-episode serial. **167m/C VHS.** Robert Kent, Peggy Stewart, Leroy Mason, Chief Thundercloud; ***D:*** Fred Brannon, Spencer Gordon Bennet; ***W:*** Barney A. Sarecky, Basil Dickey, Jesse Duffy, Lynn Perkins; ***C:*** Bud Thackery.

Phantom Stallion 1/2 **1954** Routine oater has a ranch owner believing a wild stallion is enticing away horses from his herd. But Rex thinks the answer is human and lies close to home. **54m/B VHS.** Rex Allen, Slim Pickens, Carla Balenda, Harry Shannon; ***D:*** Harry Keller; ***W:*** Gerald Geraghty; ***C:*** Bud Thackery; ***M:*** R. Dale Butts.

Phantom Thunderbolt 1/2 **1933** A man who has falsely spread the rumor that he's a gunfighter is hired to chase away some good-for-nothings. **62m/B VHS, DVD.** Ken Maynard, Frances Lee, Frank Rice, William (Bill) Gould, Robert F. (Bob) Kortman; ***D:*** Alan James.

Phantom Tollbooth **1969 (G)** A young boy drives his car into an animated world, where the numbers are at war with the letters and he has been chosen to save Rhyme and Reason, to bring stability back to the Land of Wisdom. Completely unique and typically Jonesian in its intellectual level and interests. Bright children will be interested, but this is really for adults who will understand the allegory. Based on Norman Justers' metaphorical novel. **89m/C VHS.** ***D:*** Chuck Jones; ***V:*** Mel Blanc, Hans Conried.

Phantom 2040 Movie: The Ghost Who Walks 1/2 **1995** Teenager Kit Walker discovers his destiny when a mysterious stranger tells him about his late father and how Kit must carry on his father's legacy as a superhero called the Phantom. A purple suit renders Kit invisible and he finds himself battling his dad's old nemesis, Rebecca Madison, who's out to destroy the Earth's resources. Based on the TV and comic book series. **97m/C VHS, DVD.** ***V:*** Scott Valentine, Margot Kidder, Ron Perlman, Carrie Snodgress, Mark Hamill.

Phantoms **1997 (R)** Dr. Jennifer Pailey (Going) and her sister Lisa (McGowan) arrive in a Colorado resort town and discover that the entire population has been wiped out by a mysterious force. They team up with local sheriff Hammond (Affleck) and his odd deputy (Schrieber) to battle the evil force thingie, which also seems to have an adverse affect on acting ability. Peter O'Toole appears as an expert on ancient plagues, and to show the rest of the cast what a real actor looks like. Schrieber plays the part of the squirmy deputy very well, but the rest of the characters are cheap plywood. Will they stop the amorphous monster who is taking over the corpses of its victims? Will they remember their lines if someone drops the cue card? Based on the novel by Dean Koontz, who also adapted it for the screen and produced. **91m/C VHS, DVD.** Peter O'Toole, Joanna Going, Rose McGowan, Ben Affleck, Liev Schreiber, Nicky Katt, Clifton Powell, Adam Nelson, John Hammil, John Scott Clough; ***D:*** Joe Chappelle; ***W:*** Dean Koontz; ***C:*** Richard Clabaugh; ***M:*** David Williams.

Phar Lap 1/2 *Phar Lap: Heart of a Nation* **1984 (PG)** Saga of a legendary Australian racehorse who rose from obscurity to win nearly 40 races in just three years before mysteriously dying in 1932. American version runs 10 minutes shorter than the Aussie one. **107m/C VHS.** *AU* Ron Leibman, Tom Burlinson, Judy Morris, Celia de Burgh; ***D:*** Simon Wincer; ***W:*** David Williamson; ***C:*** Russell Boyd.

Pharaoh **1966** An expensive Polish epic about the power plays of royalty in ancient Egypt. Dubbed. **125m/B VHS.** *PL* Wieslawa Mazurkiewicz, Barbara Brylska, Krstyna Mikolajewska, Jerzy Zelnick; ***D:*** Jerzy Kawalerowicz; ***W:*** Jerzy Kawalerowicz; ***C:*** Jerzy Wojcik; ***M:*** Adam Walacinski.

Pharmacist 1/2 **1932** A day in the life of a hapless druggist undone by disgruntled customers and robbers. Typical Fields effort. **19m/B VHS, DVD.** Elise Cavanna, Marjorie "Babe" Kane, W.C. Fields, Grady Sutton; ***D:*** Arthur Ripley.

Pharoah's Army 1/2 **1995 (PG-13)** Five Union soldiers are foraging for food at a small Kentucky farm when one young soldier (Fox) is badly injured and his captain, John Abston (Cooper), is forced to stay put while he treats the wounds. The farm is home to Sarah Anders (Clarkson) and her young son (Lucas), while her husband is off fighting for the Confederates. Sarah isn't happy about the arrangement but the decent Alston, a farmer himself in peacetime, begins slowly to win her over. Their friendship, however, doesn't sit well with either his men nor Sarah's son. Fine performances in a restrained drama. **90m/C VHS, DVD.** Chris Cooper, Patricia Clarkson, Kris Kristofferson, Richard Tyson, Huckleberry Fox, Will Lucas; ***D:*** Robby Henson; ***W:*** Robby Henson; ***C:*** Doron Schlair.

Phase 4 **1974 (PG)** A tale of killer ants retaliating against the humans attempting to exterminate them. **84m/C VHS.** Nigel Davenport, Michael Murphy, Lynne Frederick; ***D:*** Saul Bass; ***C:*** Dick Bush.

Phat Beach 1/2 **1996 (R)** Generic but basically harmless buddies-at-the-beach comedy with a hip-hop beat. Fast-talking, slickster Durrell (Hooks) manipulates sensitive, overweight pal Benny (Hopkins, who's real life nickname is "Huggy") into emptying his savings, "borrowing" his dad's Mercedes convertible, and taking off for some Southern California fun. Scores of scantily clad beach bunnies aren't the only ones threadbare—so's the whole premise of this flick—but that's not the point of this lighthearted romp. The likable Hopkins/Hooks comedy team is a hit with precise, lowbrow humor. Coolio, prominent in the ads, is barely window dressing with minimal screen time. Kickin' soundtrack includes E-40, Biz Markie, and SugaT featuring The Click. **99m/C VHS, DVD.** Jermaine "Huggy" Hopkins, Brian Hooks, Jennifer Lucienne, Claudia Kaleem, Gregg D. Vance, Tommy (Tiny) Lister, Erick Fleeks, Alma Collins, Candice Merideth, Sabrina De Pina, Coolio; ***D:*** Doug Ellin; ***W:*** Doug Ellin, Brian E. O'Neal, Ben Morris; ***C:*** Jurgen Baum; ***M:*** Paul Stewart.

Phat Girlz **2006 (PG-13)** Sassy, plus-sized comedienne Mo'Nique stars as Jazmin, a salesclerk at a store catering to the snooty skinny with designs on creating her own plus-sized fashion line. Her self-esteem a little battered, Jazmin and her equally-fleshy best friend Stacey (Johnson) are happy to indulge themselves at a Palm Springs resort, especially when they meet a couple of buff Nigerian doctors (Jean-Louis and Godfrey) who happen to like their ladies with some extra curves. Thus inspired, Jazmin decides to pursue her fashion dream. **99m/C DVD.** *US* Mo'Nique, Jimmy Jean-Louis, Godfrey, Jack Noseworthy, Kendra C. Johnson, Joyful Drake, Eric Roberts; ***D:*** Nnegest Likke; ***W:*** Nnegest Likke; ***C:*** Dean Lent, John L. (Ndiaga) Demps Jr.; ***M:*** Stephen Endelman.

Phedre 1/2 **1968** Jean Racine's adaptation of the Greek legend involving Phedre, Theseus, and Hippolyte. Bell is the only one worth watching in this weak and stagy picture. In French with English subtitles. **93m/C VHS.** Claude Giraud, Jacques Dacqmine, Jean Chevrier, Marie Bell; ***D:*** Pierre Jourdan; ***C:*** Michel Kelber.

Phenomenon 1/2 **1996 (PG)** Average small town schmoe George Malley (Travolta) is turned into a genius when he's struck by a bright light on his 37th birthday. This development brings him to the attention of the scientific community and, of course, the military. The locals scorn him, thus fulfilling the Hollywood stereotype of rural folks fearing anything they don't understand. Good-natured weeper plays the Gump card (but turns too paranoid) and wins as Travolta gets to be the nice guy, while attractive Sedgwick is fine as romantic interest Lace. **123m/C VHS, DVD.** John Travolta, Robert Duvall, Kyra Sedgwick, Forest Whitaker, Richard Kiley, Brent Spiner; ***D:*** Jon Turteltaub; ***W:*** Gerald Di Pego; ***C:*** Phedon Papamichael; ***M:*** Thomas Newman.

Phffft! 1/2 **1954** Holliday and Lemmon are a bored couple who decide to divorce, date others, and take mambo lessons. By no stretch of plausibility, they constantly run into each other and compete in the same mambo contest. **91m/B VHS.** Judy Holliday, Jack Lemmon, Jack Carson, Kim Novak, Luella Gear, Merry Anders; ***D:*** Mark Robson; ***W:*** George Axelrod; ***C:*** Charles B(ryant) Lang Jr.

Philadelphia 1/2 **1993 (PG-13)** AIDS goes Hollywood as hot-shot corporate attorney Andrew Beckett (Hanks), fired because he has the disease, hires brilliant but homophobic personal injury attorney Washington as his counsel when he sues for discrimination. Boxoffice winner was criticized by some gay activists as too mainstream, which is the point. It doesn't probe deeply into the gay lifestyle, focusing instead on justice and compassion. Boasts a good script, make-up that transforms Hanks, sure direction, great soundtrack, and a strong supporting cast, but all would mean little without Hanks' superb performance, his best to date. ♫ Streets of Philadelphia. **125m/C VHS, DVD.** Tom Hanks, Denzel Washington, Antonio Banderas, Jason Robards Jr., Joanne Woodward, Mary Steenburgen, Ron Vawter, Robert Ridgely, Obba Babatunde, Robert Castle, Daniel Chapman, Roger Corman, John Bedford Lloyd, Roberta Maxwell, Warren Miller, Anna Deavere Smith, Kathryn Witt, Andre B. Blake, Ann Dowd, Bradley Whitford, Chandra Wilson, Charles Glenn, Peter Jacobs, Kathryn Witt, Dan Olmstead, Joey Perillo, Lauren Roselli, Bill Rowe, Lisa Talerico, Daniel von Bargen, Tracey Walter; ***Cameos:*** Karen Finley, David Drake, Quentin Crisp; ***D:*** Jonathan Demme; ***W:*** Ron Nyswaner; ***C:*** Tak Fujimoto; ***M:*** Howard Shore. Oscars '93: Actor (Hanks), Song ("Streets of Philadelphia"); Berlin Intl. Film Fest. '94: Actor (Hanks); Golden Globes '94: Actor—Drama (Hanks), Song ("Streets of Philadelphia"); MTV Movie Awards '94: Male Perf. (Hanks); Blockbuster '95: Drama Actor, V. (Hanks).

The Philadelphia Experiment 1/2 **1984 (PG)** A WWII sailor falls through a hole in time and lands in the mid-1980s, whereupon he woos a gorgeous woman. Sufficient chemistry between Pare and Allen, but PG rating is an indication of the film's less-than-graphic love scenes. **101m/C VHS, DVD.** Michael Pare, Nancy Allen, Eric Christmas, Bobby DiCicco; ***D:*** Stewart Raffill; ***W:*** Don Jakoby; ***C:*** Dick Bush; ***M:*** Kenneth Wannberg.

Philadelphia Experiment 2 1/2 **1993 (PG-13)** Melodramatic sci-fi what-ifer has Germany winning WWII by dropping a bomb on Washington. So southern California is now one big labor camp with an evil mad scientist (Graham) and a beleagured hero (Johnson) who must time-travel back to 1943 to prevent the Germans from dropping that bomb. **98m/C VHS, DVD.** Brad Johnson, Gerrit Graham, Marjean Holden, James Greene, Geoffrey Blake, John Christian Grass, Cyril O'Reilly; ***D:*** Stephen Cornwell; ***W:*** Kevin Rock, Nick Paine; ***M:*** Gerald Gouriet.

The Philadelphia Story **1940** A woman's plans to marry again go awry when her dashing ex-husband arrives on the scene. Matters are further complicated when a loopy reporter—assigned to spy on the nuptials—falls in love with the blushing bride. Classic comedy, with trio of Hepburn, Grant, and Stewart all serving aces. Based on the hit Broadway play by Philip Barry, and remade as the musical "High Society" in 1956 (stick to the original). Also available colorized. **112m/B VHS, DVD.** Katharine Hepburn, Cary Grant, James Stewart, Ruth Hussey, Roland Young, John Howard, John Halliday, Virginia Weidler, Henry Daniell, Hillary Brooke, Mary Nash; ***D:*** George Cukor; ***W:*** Donald Ogden Stewart; ***C:*** Joseph Ruttenberg; ***M:*** Franz Waxman. Oscars '40: Actor (Stewart), Screenplay; AFI '98: Top 100, Natl. Film Reg. '95;; N.Y. Film Critics '40: Actress (Hepburn).

Philby, Burgess and MacLean: Spy Scandal of the Century 1/2 **1984** The true story of the three infamous British officials who defected to the Soviet Union in 1951, after stealing some vital British secrets for the KGB. **83m/C VHS.** *GB* Derek Jacobi, Anthony Bate, Michael Culver; ***D:*** Gordon Flemyng; ***W:*** Ian Curteis.

Phobia **WOOF!** **1980 (R)** Patients at a hospital are mysteriously being murdered. Stupid and unpleasant story that lasts too long and probably should never have started. **91m/C VHS.** *CA* Paul Michael Glaser, Susan Hogan; ***D:*** John Huston; ***W:*** Peter Bellwood, Lew Lehman, Gary Sherman, Ronald Shusett, Jimmy Sangster.

Phoebe in Wonderland **2008 (PG-13)** Nine-year-old Phoebe (Fanning) is bright but troubled, though her protective mother (Huffman) prefers to believe her child is merely high-spirited and imaginative. Phoebe's imagination works to her advantage when she's cast in the lead role in her school's production of "Alice in Wonderland" and taken under the wing of charismatic, nonconformist drama teacher Miss Dodger (Clarkson). But as Phoebe's fantasies get more self-destructive, it becomes clear she needs serious help and not adults mouthing platitudes. Fanning and Clarkson are compelling but the story suffers from shrillness and a tendency towards artistic preaching. **96m/C DVD.** *US* Elle Fanning, Felicity Huffman, Bill Pullman, Patricia Clarkson, Campbell Scott, Peter Gerety, Caitlin Sanchez, Tessa Albertson; ***D:*** Daniel Barnz; ***W:*** Daniel Barnz; ***C:*** Bobby Bukowski; ***M:*** Christophe Beck.

Phoenix 1/2 *Hi No Tori; The Firebird* **1978** Aging queen summons her marksman to find the Phoenix, a mythical bird that she believes will bring her eternal life. With English subtitles. **137m/C VHS, DVD.** *JP* Tomisaburo Wakayama, Ken Tanaka, Reiko Ohara, Micko Takamine, Tatsuya Nakadai; ***D:*** Kon Ichikawa; ***W:*** Shuntaro Kanigawa; ***C:*** Kiyoshi Hasegawa; ***M:*** Jun Fukamachi.

Phoenix **1995** The Titus 4 deep-space outpost has problems when the creators of a killing machine are targeted for death by their creation, which has begun to think for itself. **94m/C VHS, DVD.** Stephen Nichols, Billy Drago, William Sanderson, Brad Dourif; ***D:*** Troy Cook; ***W:*** Troy Cook, Jimmy Lifton.

Phoenix **1998 (R)** With a cast like this, you hope for a bit more than the usual cliched crime drama. Gambling addict/Phoenix cop Harry Collins (Liotta) is in big debt to loanshark. He decides the best way to get the money is to rob the nightclub of a local sleaze where fellow corruptible officer Mike Henshaw (LaPaglia) moonlights. But beyond the inherent stupidity of such a plan is the lurking presence of internal affairs officer Clyde Webber (Berkely). **104m/C VHS, DVD.** Ray Liotta, Anthony LaPaglia, Daniel Baldwin, Jeremy Piven, Xander Berkeley, Giancarlo Esposito, Anjelica Huston, Tom Noonan, Kari Wuhrer, Brittany Murphy; ***D:*** Danny Cannon; ***W:*** Eddie Richey; ***C:*** James L. Carter; ***M:*** Graeme Revell.

The Phoenix and the Magic Carpet 1/2 **1995 (PG)** Visiting England to settle her father's estate, Mrs. Wilson and her three children discover an egg from which a phoenix emerges. This mythical firebird proceeds to take the children on a magic adventure. Adapted from the book by Edith Nesbit. **80m/C VHS.** Dee Wallace, Timothy Hegeman, Nick Klein, Laura Kamrath, Peter Ustinov; ***D:*** Zoran Perisic; ***W:*** Florence Fox; ***M:*** Alan Parker.

Phoenix the Warrior **1988** Sometime in the future, female savages battle each other for control of the now ravaged earth. A newcomer seeks the tribe most worthy of receiving the last man on the planet, thereby continuing the human race. **90m/C VHS.** Persis Khambatta, James H. Emery, Peggy Sands, Kathleen Kinmont; ***D:*** Robert Hayes; ***W:*** Robert Hayes.

Phone 1/2 *Pon* **2002 (R)** After writing a series of articles on pedophiles, a journalist begins receiving threatening calls. So she changes her number and moves. Her phone then inadvertently curses her friend's daughter, who suddenly becomes a little too attached to her father. Everyone else who has ever had the new phone number she is now using has apparently died under less than explainable circumstances. Often accused of ripping off "Ringu," this pic is strong enough to stand apart from other vengeful ghost movies. **102m/C DVD.** *KN* Ji-won Ha, Yu-mi Kim, Woo-jae Choi, Ji-yeon Choi, Seo-woo Eun; ***D:*** Byeong-ki Ahn; ***C:*** Yong-shik Mun; ***M:*** Sang-ho Lee.

Phone Booth **2002 (R)** Stu (Farrell), a slimy Broadway publicist, uses a phone booth to call a would-be actress he's been stringing along. After he hangs up, the phone rings and he answers it, only to be informed that if he hangs up or runs, he'll be shot. To prove his point, the unseen sniper (voiced by Sutherland), kills a pimp who's been wanting the booth for himself. After the interesting premise and set-up, what follows is a disappointing mix of suspense thriller cliches and Schumacher's trademark visual stunts. It all adds up to nothing more than a showcase for Farrell, who does a great job as the weasel who must face and confess the fact that he hasn't been a very nice guy. Whitaker, Holmes and Mitchell are wasted in one-dimensional roles. Cohen has been trying to get the script, filmed in real time, made for about 30 years. **81m/C VHS, DVD, Blu-ray Disc.** *US* Colin Farrell, Forest Whitaker, Katie Holmes, Radha Mitchell, Kiefer Sutherland, Richard T. Jones, Keith Nobbs, John Enos, James MacDonald, Josh Pais, Paula Jai Parker, Tia Texada; ***D:*** Joel Schumacher; ***W:*** Larry Cohen; ***C:*** Matthew Libatique; ***M:*** Harry Gregson-Williams.

The Phone Call **1989 (R)** 900-number morality tale about high-powered executive who calls phone sex line and is connected with escaped homicidal maniac who takes a toll on him and his family. **95m/C VHS.** Michael Sarrazin, Linda Smith, Ron Lea, Lisa Jakub; ***D:*** Allan Goldstein.

Phone Call from a Stranger 1/2 **1952** After a plane crash, a survivor visits the families of three of the victims whom he met during the flight. **96m/B VHS.** Bette Davis, Gary Merrill, Michael Rennie, Shelley Winters, Hugh Beaumont, Keenan Wynn, Eve Arden, Craig Stevens; ***D:*** Jean Negulesco; ***W:*** Nunnally Johnson; ***C:*** Milton Krasner.

Photographer **1975 (PG)** A photographer turns into a murderer, showing the negative side of his personality. **94m/C VHS.** Michael Callan; ***D:*** William B. Hillman.

Photographing Fairies **1997 (R)** Haunting story that's not quite as compelling as it could be. After Anne-Marie (Shelley), the bride of photographer Charles Castle (Stephens), is killed on their honeymoon, Charles shuts down emotionally, and the horrors he photographs in WWI only numb him further. After the war, Charles sets up a studio in London and becomes an expert in unmasking doctored photos. When Beatrice (Barber) shows him photos of fairies taken by her young daughters, Charles travels to her country home to expose them as fakes. Instead, Charles comes to believe that the fairies represent the "Other Side" and if he can photograph their spirit world, he can enter it and be reunited with his lost love. Based on the novel by Steve Szilagyi. The premise involving the young girls and the faked fairy photos is also the basis of the film "Fairytale: A True Story." **107m/C VHS.** *GB* Toby Stephens, Frances Barber, Ben Kingsley, Emily Woof, Philip Davis, Rachel Shelley, Edward Hardwicke, Hannah Bould, Miriam Grant, Clive Merrison; ***D:*** Nick Willing; ***W:*** Nick Willing, Chris Harrald; ***C:*** John de Borman; ***M:*** Simon Boswell.

Physical Evidence **1989 (R)** A lawyer finds herself falling for an ex-cop turned murder suspect while she tries to defend him for a crime he doesn't remember committing. **99m/C VHS, DVD.** Burt Reynolds, Theresa Russell, Ned Beatty, Kay Lenz, Ted McGinley; ***D:*** Michael Crichton; ***W:*** Bill Phillips; ***C:*** John A. Alonzo; ***M:*** Henry Mancini.

Pi **1998 (R)** Definitely a first—a religious/mathematical thriller about a man obsessed with decoding the real name of God. Max (Gullette) is a genius mathematician who believes everything can be understood in terms of numbers, so he works on his homebuilt supercomputer to unravel the stock market. Max begins to suffer hallucinations and blackouts just as his work draws the interest of both a high-powered Wall Street firm and a Hasidic cabalistic sect. **85m/B VHS, DVD.** Sean Gullette, Mark Margolis, Ben Shenkman, Pamela Hart, Stephen Pearlman, Samia Shoaib, Ajay Naidu; ***D:*** Darren Aronofsky; ***W:*** Darren Aronofsky, Eric Watson, Sean Gullette; ***C:*** Matthew Libatique; ***M:*** Clint Mansell. Ind. Spirit '99: First Screenplay; Sundance '98: Director (Aronofsky).

P.I. Private Investigations **1987 (R)** Corrupt, drug-dealing cops stalk another cop who can finger them. **91m/C VHS.** Clayton Rohner, Ray Sharkey, Paul LeMat, Talia Balsam, Phil Morris, Martin Balsam; ***D:*** Nigel Dick; ***W:*** John Dahl, David Warfield; ***C:*** David Bridges, Bryan Duggan; ***M:*** Murray Munro.

Piaf **1981 (PG)** Musical drama chronicles the life of Edith Piaf, France's legendary singer of the Roaring '20s. Her rise from the streets, bout with temporary blindness, and many self-destructive attempts at experiencing life are retold in music. **114m/C VHS.** Judith Ivey, Jean Smart, Robert Chisholm, Jane Lapotaire; ***Nar:*** Patti LuPone.

The Pianist **1991** As teenagers in Toronto, sisters Jean (Travers) and Colette (Grenon) become infatuated with Yoshi Takahashi (Okuda), a Japanese concert pianist who lived across the street. Ten years later, they have a family reunion in Vancouver and learn Yoshi is giving a concert in the city. Jean is excited to renew their ties but Colette is reluctant—and Jean reveals that she knows her sister and the pianist had a sexual relationship. Is Jean jealous? Or does she plan on establishing her own claims? Based on Ann Ireland's novel "A Certain Mr. Takahashi." **90m/C VHS, DVD.** *CA* Gail Travers, Macha Grenon, Eiji Okuda, Maury Chaykin, Dorothee Berryman, Carl Alacchi; ***D:*** Claude Gagnon; ***W:*** Claude Gagnon.

The Pianist 1/2 **2002 (R)** Polanski effectively turns his personal knowledge of the Holocaust into a spellbinding portrait of fellow Holocaust survivor Wladyslaw Szpilman, the renowned Polish-Jewish pianist of the title. Brody's dead-on portrayal of Szpilman, who as a gifted artist scarcely believes he will be affected by the war, effectively registers the horrifying transition from life of luxury to ending up in the Warsaw ghetto. An interesting feeling of hopefulness that lies beneath the barbarism shows Polanski's attention to the humanity and kindness that still may be found in the most savage conditions, and winningly captures the feel of one of recent history's darkest times. Based on the autobiography of Wladyslaw Szpilman. **148m/C VHS, DVD, HD DVD.** *FR PL GE GB* Adrien Brody, Thomas Kretschmann, Frank Finlay, Maureen Lipman, Emilia Fox, Ed Stoppard, Julia Rayner, Jessica Kate Meyer, Ruth Platt; ***D:*** Roman Polanski; ***W:*** Ronald Harwood; ***C:*** Pawel Edelman; ***M:*** Wojciech Kilar. Oscars '02: Actor (Brody), Adapt. Screenplay, Director (Polanski); British Acad. '02: Director (Polanski), Film; Cannes '02: Film; Natl. Soc. Film Critics '02: Actor (Brody), Director (Polanski), Film, Screenplay.

The Piano 1/2 **1993 (R)** In the 1850s, Ada (Hunter), a mute Scottish widow with a young daughter, agrees to an arranged marriage with Stewart (Neill), a colonial landowner in New Zealand. The way she expresses her feelings is by playing her cherished piano, left behind on the beach by her new husband. Another settler, George (Keitel), buys it, arranges for lessons with Ada, and soon the duo begin a grand passion leading to a cruelly calculated revenge. Fiercely poetic and well acted (with Keitel in a notably romantic role), though the film may be too dark and intense for some. Fine original score with Hunter doing her own piano playing. **120m/C VHS, DVD.** *AU* Holly Hunter, Harvey Keitel, Sam Neill, Anna Paquin, Kerry Walker, Genevieve Lemon; ***D:*** Jane Campion; ***W:*** Jane Campion; ***C:*** Stuart Dryburgh; ***M:*** Michael Nyman. Oscars '93: Actress (Hunter), Orig. Screenplay, Support. Actress (Paquin); Australian Film Inst. '93: Actor (Keitel), Actress (Hunter), Cinematog., Costume Des., Director (Campion), Film, Film Editing, Screenplay, Sound, Score; British Acad. '93: Actress (Hunter); Cannes '93: Actress (Hunter), Film; Golden Globes '94: Actress—Drama (Hunter); Ind. Spirit '94: Foreign Film; L.A. Film Critics '93: Actress (Hunter), Cinematog., Director (Campion), Screenplay, Support. Actress (Paquin); Natl. Bd. of Review '93: Actress (Hunter); N.Y. Film Critics '93: Actress (Hunter), Director (Campion), Screenplay; Natl. Soc. Film Critics '93: Actress (Hunter), Screenplay; Writers Guild '93: Orig. Screenplay.

A Piano for Mrs. Cimino **1982** Declared senile and incompetent, a widowed woman fights for control of her own life. Good script helps this made for TV soaper. **100m/C VHS.** Bette Davis, Keenan Wynn, Alexa Kenin, Penny Fuller, Christopher Guest, George Hearn; ***D:*** George Schaefer; ***M:*** James Horner. **TV**

The Piano Lesson **1994 (PG)** The prized heirloom of the Charles family is an 80-year-old, ornately carved upright piano, jealously guarded by widowed Berniece (Woodard), and housed in the Pittsburgh home of Uncle Doaker (Gordon). When Berniece's brother Willie Boy (Dutton) visits from Mississippi, it's to persuade her to sell the piano in order to buy some land that their grandfather had worked as a slave. But the past, carved into the piano's panels, has a strong hold—one that Berniece refuses to give up. Set in 1936. Adaptation by Wilson of his 1990 Pulitzer Prize-winning play. **99m/C VHS, DVD.** Alfre Woodard, Charles S. Dutton, Courtney B. Vance, Carl Gordon, Tommy Hollis, Zelda Harris, Lou Myers, Rosalyn Coleman, Tommy La Fitte; ***D:*** Lloyd Richards; ***W:*** August Wilson; ***M:*** Stephen James Taylor, Dwight Andrews. **TV**

Piano Man 1/2 **1996** The police have begun to discover bodies so horribly mutilated that they've become unidentifiable—along with small toy pianos stuffed in them. Eventually the killer gets tired of waiting for the police to quit fumbling and figure things out and begins sending them clues. Unfortunately what follows is all too predictable despite a promising start. **120m/C DVD.** *KN* Seung-yeon Lee, Kyoung-In Hong, Cheol Park, Min-su Choi; ***D:*** Sang-wook Yu; ***W:*** Sang-wook Yu, Jae-ho Heo; ***C:*** Jeong-min Seo; ***M:*** Baek-sang Nam.

The Piano Teacher *La Pianiste* **2001** Middle-aged Erika (Huppert) teaches piano at the Vienna Conservatory where she is demanding—if not cruel—to her students. Erika lives with her controlling mother (Girardot) and spends her off hours mutiliating herself, watching porn, and engaging in other bizarre behavior. Which doesn't improve when she agrees to a questionable sexual relationship (on her masochistic terms) with hot new student Walter (Magimel). Not for the faint-hearted; adapted from the 1983 novel by Elfriede Jelinek. French with subtitles. **130m/C VHS, DVD.** *FR AT* Isabelle Huppert, Benoit Magimel, Annie Girardot, Udo Samel, Susanne Lothar, Anna Sigalenteh; ***D:*** Michael Haneke; ***W:*** Michael Haneke; ***C:*** Christian Berger. Cannes '01: Actor (Magimel), Actress (Huppert), Grand Jury Prize.

Piano Tuner of Earthquakes *L'Accordeur de tremblements de terre* **2005** Appropriately bizarre but unfortunately stale experimental film from the Quay brothers has beautiful opera star Malvina (Casar) killed before her weding by the evil Dr. Droz (John), who then steals her corpse to revive it. He then hires piano tuner Felsiberto (Sasachu) to write and choreograph an opera depicting the events. Since he resembles her former love, Malvina falls in love with him and he plots their escape. Interesting staging and visuals can't make up for the many weaknesses. **99m/C DVD.** *FR GB GE* Amira Casar, Gottfried John, Assumpta Serna, Cesar Sarachu; ***D:*** Stephen Quay, Timothy Quay; ***W:*** Stephen Quay, Timothy Quay; ***C:*** Nicholas D. Knowland; ***M:*** Christopher Slaski.

Picasso Trigger **1989 (R)** An American spy tries to catch an elusive murderer. The sequel to "Hard Ticket to Hawaii" and "Malibu Express." **99m/C VHS, DVD.** Steve Bond, Dona Speir, John Aprea, Hope Marie Carlton, Guich Koock, Roberta Vasquez, Bruce Penhall, Harold Diamond, Rodrigo Obregon; ***D:*** Andy Sidaris; ***W:*** Andy Sidaris; ***C:*** Howard Wexler; ***M:*** Gary Stockdale.

Pick a Card *Afula Express* **1997 (PG-13)** David (Hadar) is an unemployed mechanic who dreams of becoming a magician while his girlfriend Batla (Zakheim) just wants to get married. So how can they reconcile their dreams with their reality? **94m/C VHS, DVD.** *IS* Zvika Hadar, Esti Zakheim, Aryeh Moskona, Orli Perl; ***D:*** Julie Shles; ***W:*** Amit Leor; ***C:*** Itzik Portal; ***M:*** Yuval Shafrir.

Pick a Star *Movie Struck* **1937** Lawrence is a small-town girl who wins a contest and is off to Hollywood. Only no one pays any attention to her except for publicity man Haley, who arranges her screen test. Naturally, she knocks the studio bosses for a loop and becomes a star. Laurel & Hardy are featured in a couple of comedy segments showing the newcomer some backstage silliness and movie business on the set of a Western they're filming (with Finlayson, better known as a director, cast as the duo's director). **70m/B VHS.** Rosina Lawrence, Jack Haley, Patsy Kelly, Mischa Auer, Stan Laurel, Oliver Hardy, Charles Halton, Tom Dugan, Russell Hicks, James Finlayson; ***D:*** Edward Sedgwick.

The Pick-Up Artist 1/2 **1987 (PG-13)** The adventures of a compulsive Don Juan who finds he genuinely loves the daughter of an alcoholic who's in debt to the mob. Standard story with no surprises. **81m/C VHS, DVD.** Robert Downey Jr., Molly Ringwald, Dennis Hopper, Harvey Keitel, Danny Aiello, Vanessa L(ynne) Williams, Robert Towne, Mildred Dunnock, Lorraine Bracco, Joe Spinell, Victoria Jackson, Polly Draper, Brian Hamill, Christine Baranski, Bob Gunton, G. Anthony "Tony" Sirico, Victor Argo, Reni Santoni; ***D:*** James Toback; ***W:*** James Toback; ***C:*** Gordon Willis; ***M:*** Georges Delerue.

Pick-Up Summer *Pinball Summer; Pinball Pick-Up* **1979 (R)** Two suburban boys cruise their town after school lets out, chasing a pair of voluptuous sisters. **99m/C VHS, DVD.** *CA* Michael Zelniker, Carl Marotte; ***D:*** George Mihalka.

Picking Up the Pieces **1999 (R)** Tex (Allen) is a kosher cowboy in a New Mexico town, who's also a butcher. This trade comes in handy when he dismembers unfaithful wife, Candy (Stone), and scatters her remains in the desert. When a blind woman stumbles on Candy's severed hand and miraculously has her sight restored, she delivers the hand to the local church where it becomes a shrine for pilgrims seeking miracle cures. Meanwhile, Tex just wants to rebury the evidence. If you can buy Allen as any kind of cowboy, you can buy the rest of this would-be comedy. **95m/C VHS, DVD.** Woody Allen, David Schwimmer, Maria Grazia Cucinotta, Kiefer Sutherland, Sharon Stone, Alfonso Arau, Richard "Cheech" Marin, Lou Diamond Phillips, Danny De La Paz, Andy Dick, Fran Drescher, Joseph Gordon-Levitt, Elliott Gould, Eddie Griffin, Lupe Ontiveros; ***D:*** Alfonso Arau; ***W:*** Bill Wilson; ***C:*** Vittorio Storaro; ***M:*** Ruy Folguera.

The Pickle **1993 (R)** Self-indulgent comedy about a midlife crisis. Aiello stars as a middle-aged manic-depressive director certain that his new film is going to be an abysmal flop (as have all his recent pictures). He seeks comfort and reassurance from various ex-wives, children, lovers, and others, though he abuses them all. This dispirited tale also shows clips of the director's dreadful film about children who launch a giant pickle into space. It couldn't possibly be worse that what Mazursky actually put up on the screen. **103m/C VHS, DVD.** Danny Aiello, Dyan Cannon, Clotilde Courau, Shelley Winters, Barry Miller, Jerry Stiller, Christopher Penn, Rebecca Miller; ***Cameos:*** Ally Sheedy, Little Richard, Spalding Gray, Griffin Dunne, Isabella Rossellini, Dudley Moore; ***D:*** Paul Mazursky; ***W:*** Paul Mazursky; ***M:*** Michel Legrand.

Pickpocket 1/2 **1959** Slow moving, documentary-like account of a petty thief's existence is a moral tragedy inspired by "Crime and Punishment." Ending is particularly moving. Classic filmmaking from Bresson, France's master of austerity. In French with English subtitles. **75m/B VHS, DVD.** *FR* Martin LaSalle, Marika Green, Pierre Leymarie, Pierre Etaix, Jean Pelegri, Dolly Scal; ***D:*** Robert Bresson; ***W:*** Robert Bresson; ***C:*** Leonce-Henri Burel.

Pickup on South Street **1953** Petty thief Widmark lifts woman's wallet only to find it contains top secret Communist micro-film for which pinko agents will stop at nothing to get back. Intriguing look at the politics of the day. The creme of "B" movies. **80m/B VHS, DVD.** Richard Widmark, Jean Peters, Thelma Ritter, Murvyn Vye, Richard Kiley, Milburn Stone; ***D:*** Samuel Fuller; ***W:*** Samuel Fuller; ***C:*** Joe MacDonald; ***M:*** Leigh Harline.

The Pickwick Papers 1/2 **1954** Comedy based on the Dickens classic wherein Mrs. Bardell sues the Pickwick Club for breach of promise. **109m/B VHS.** *GB* James Hayter, James Donald, Nigel Patrick, Hermione Gingold, Hermione Baddeley, Kathleen Harrison; ***D:*** Noel Langley.

Picnic 1/2 **1955** Drifter Hal Carter (Holden) arrives in a small town and immediately wins the love of his friend's girl, Madge (Novak). The other women in town seem interested too. Strong, romantic work, with Holden excelling in the lead. Novak provides a couple pointers too. Lavish Hollywood adaptation of the William Inge play, including the popular tune "Moonglow/Theme from Picnic." Remade for TV in 2000 with Josh Brolin in the Holden role. **113m/C VHS, DVD.** William Holden, Kim Novak, Rosalind Russell, Susan Strasberg, Arthur O'Connell, Cliff Robertson, Betty Field, Verna Felton, Reta Shaw, Nick Adams, Phyllis Newman, Raymond Bailey; ***D:*** Joshua Logan; ***W:*** Daniel Taradash; ***C:*** James Wong Howe; ***M:*** George Duning. Oscars '55: Art Dir./Set Dec., Color, Film Editing; Golden Globes '56: Director (Logan).

Picnic at Hanging Rock **1975 (PG)** School outing in 1900 into a mountainous region ends tragically when three girls disappear. Eerie film is strong on atmosphere, as befits mood master Weir. Lambert is extremely photogenic—and suitable subdued—as one of the girls to disappear. Otherwise beautifully photographed on location. From the novel by Joan Lindsey. **110m/C VHS, DVD.** *AU* Margaret Nelson, Rachel Roberts, Dominic Guard, Helen Morse, Jacki Weaver, Vivean Gray, Anne Louise Lambert; ***D:*** Peter Weir; ***W:*** Clifford Green; ***C:*** Russell Boyd; ***M:*** Bruce Smeaton.

Picnic on the Grass *Le Dejeuner sur l'Herbe; Lunch on the Grass* **1959** A strange, whimsical fantasy heavily evocative of the director's Impressionist roots; a science-minded candidate for the president of Europe throws a picnic as public example of his earthiness, and falls in love with a peasant girl. In French with English subtitles. **92m/C VHS.** *FR* Paul Meurisse, Catherine Rouvel, Fernand Sardou, Jacqueline Morane, Jean-Pierre Granval; ***D:*** Jean Renoir.

Picture Bride 1/2 **1994 (PG-13)** Familiar immigrant saga finds 17-year-old Japanese Riyo (Kudoh) setting off for Hawaii in 1918 as a "picture bride" to a husband she's never met but with whom she's exchanged photos (hence the title). Riyo's shocked to discover her intended, sugar-cane worker Matsuji (Takayama), has deceived her with an out-of-date picture and is at least 25 years older than she. She refuses to consummate the marriage and goes to work in the fields, intending to earn money for her passage home but of course things don't work out quite as Riyo intends. Japanese with subtitles. **95m/C VHS, DVD.** *JP* Yoko Sugi, Youki Kudoh, Akira Takayama, Tamlyn Tomita, Cary-Hiroyuki Tagawa; ***Cameos:*** Toshiro Mifune; ***D:*** Kayo Hatta; ***W:*** Kayo Hatta, Mari Hatta, Diane Mark; ***C:*** Claudio Rocha; ***M:*** Cliff Eidelman. Sundance '95: Aud. Award.

Picture Claire **2001 (R)** Lewis is miscast as the independent French-speaking Claire, who leaves Montreal for Toronto to find a one-time boyfriend. Instead, Claire gets in the middle of a diamond heist between shady lady Lily (Gershon), sleazy Eddie (Rourke), and sadistic thug Laramie (Rennie)—all because she can't speak English. Bleech. English and French with subtitles. **90m/C VHS, DVD.** *CA* Juliette Lewis, Callum Keith Rennie, Gina Gershon, Mickey Rourke; ***D:*** Bruce McDonald; ***W:*** Semi Chellas; ***C:*** Miroslaw Baszak; ***M:*** Paul Haslinger.

Picture Mommy Dead **1966** Well acted melodrama involving a scheming shrew who struggles to drive her mentally disturbed stepdaughter insane for the sake of cold, hard cash. **85m/C VHS.** Don Ameche, Zsa Zsa Gabor, Martha Hyer, Susan Gordon; ***D:*** Bert I. Gordon; ***C:*** Ellsworth Fredericks.

Picture of Dorian Gray **1945** Hatfield plays the rake who stays young while his portrait ages in this adaptation of Oscar Wilde's classic novel. Lansbury steals this one. **110m/B VHS.** Hurd Hatfield, George Sanders, Donna Reed, Angela Lansbury, Peter Lawford, Lowell Gilmore, Miles Mander; ***D:*** Albert Lewin; ***W:*** Albert Lewin; ***C:*** Harry Stradling Sr. Oscars '45: B&W Cinematog.; Golden Globes '46: Support. Actress (Lansbury).

Picture of Dorian Gray **1974** Another version of Wilde's renowned novel about a man who retains his youthful visage while his portrait shows the physical ravages of aging. Davenport is particularly appealing in the lead. **130m/C VHS, DVD.** Shane Briant, Nigel Davenport, Charles Aidman, Fionnula Flanagan, Linda Kelsey, Vanessa Howard; ***D:*** Glenn Jordan. **TV**

Picture Perfect 1/2 **1996 (PG-13)** While trying to impress her new boss, ad exec Kate (Aniston) claims Nick (Mohr), the man standing with her in a photo, is her fiance. Unfortunately, the boss now wants to meet the guy (a stranger who was at the same party) and she must find him and get him to play along. The story's cliched, but Aniston's appealing screen presence perks things up a bit. **100m/C VHS, DVD.** Jennifer Aniston, Jay Mohr, Kevin Bacon, Illeana Douglas, Olympia Dukakis, Kevin Dunn, Faith Prince, Anne Twomey; ***D:*** Glenn Gordon Caron; ***W:*** Glenn Gordon Caron; ***C:*** Paul Sarossy; ***M:*** Carter Burwell.

Picture Snatcher **1933** Former gangster Danny Kean (Cagney) tries to make himself over as a photographer for a tabloid, using his criminal know-how to get scoops. But his sometimes underhanded ways cause problems when Danny romances Patricia (Ellis), who happens to be the daughter of the cop (O'Connor) who once put Danny behind bars. **76m/B DVD.** James Cagney, Patricia Ellis, Ralph Bellamy, Alice White, Robert Emmett O'Connor, Ralf Harolde; ***D:*** Lloyd Bacon; ***W:*** P.J. Wolfson, Allen Rivkin; ***C:*** Sol Polito.

Picture This! 1/2 **2008 (PG-13)** High school senior Mandy (chipper blonde Tisdale) isn't one of the popular girls but she does know what she wants. And it's within reach when very popular guy Drew (Amell) asks her to the biggest party of the year. Too bad Mandy's over-protective dad (Pollak) has grounded her. But with some help from her friends and her new video phone, Mandy is determined to go to the ball—uh, party. **?m/C DVD.** Ashley Tisdale, Maxim Roy, Lauren Collins, Robbie Amell, Kevin Pollak, Shenae Grimes, Cindy Busby; ***D:*** Stephen Herek; ***W:*** Temple Mathews; ***C:*** Bernard Couture; ***M:*** Richard (Rick) Marvin. **VIDEO**

Picture Windows **1995 (R)** Three short cable movies inspired by works of art. "Lightning," based on Frederic Remington sketches and a Zane Grey short story, finds western codger Keith striking gold with the help of his trusty mule. A David Hockney painting suggested "Armed Response," which features a confrontation between a wealthy lawyer (Loggia) and a burglar (Zahn). And an anonymous 16th-century canvas "Two Nudes Bathing" is given an imaginative history. **95m/C VHS, DVD.** Brian Keith, Robert Loggia, Steve Zahn, Charley Boorman; ***D:*** Joe Dante, Bob Rafelson, John Boorman. **CABLE**

Pictures 1/2 **1981** The silent-film era in England is spoofed in this look at ambitious waitress Ruby Sears, who's determined to be a film star, and writer Bill Trench, who winds up a novice screenwriter. Bill's first movie script is based on Ruby's life and she desperately wants to star in the production, if only she can convince the producer and the drunken male lead that she has the talent. **208m/C VHS.** *GB* Wendy Morgan, Peter McEnery, Harry Towb, Anton Rodgers, Annette Badland, Malcom Jamieson, Marc Smith; ***W:*** Roy Clarke. **TV**

Pictures of Hollis Woods 1/2 **2007** Twelve-year-old Hollis Woods (Ferland) was found abandoned as a baby and has spent her life in various foster homes. Her dedicated social worker Edna (Woodard) had hoped that Hollis' last family, the Reagans, would be permanent but an incident put Hollis on the move again and into the care of retired schoolteacher Josie (Spacek). Only Josie's forgetfulness turns out to be the early stages of Alzheimer's—a fact Hollis tries to cover up so she won't be moved again. Adapted from Patricia Reilly Giff's novel. **110m/C DVD.** Jodelle Ferland, Sissy Spacek, Alfre Woodard, Judith Ivey, James Tupper, Julie Ann Emery, Ridge Canipe; ***D:*** Tony Bill; ***W:*** Ann Peacock, Daniel Petrie Jr.; ***C:*** Camille Thomasson; ***M:*** Paul Sarossy, Van Dyke Parks. **TV**

Pie in the Sky 1/2 **1995 (R)** Charles Dunlap (Charles) is a traffic geek, fascinated by the flow of cars on the nearby freeway, whose hero is local traffic reporter Alan Davenport (Goodman), with whom he eventually gets a job in L.A. Charles' other interest is dancer/waitress Amy (Heche)—their first attempt at romance goes awry but persistence pays off. Optimistic and corny. **94m/C VHS, DVD.** Josh Charles, Anne Heche, John Goodman, Christine Lahti, Peter Riegert, Christine Ebersole, Wil Wheaton, Bob Balaban, Dey Young; ***D:*** Bryan Gordon; ***W:*** Bryan Gordon; ***C:*** Bernd Heinl; ***M:*** Michael Covertino.

Piece of Cake 1/2 **1988** Adaptation of the Derek Robinson novel follows the flyboys of the RAF Hornet Squadron during the early years of WWII. They have trouble taking the war seriously but tangles with the Luftwaffe and increasing casualties put a strain on everyone. Great aerial photography and the British planes are vintage Spitfires not repros. Made for British TV miniseries on six cassettes. **312m/C VHS, DVD.** *GB* Tom Burlinson, Tim Woodward, Boyd Gaines, Nathaniel Parker, Neil Dudgeon, David Horovitch, Richard Hope, Jeremy Wortham, Michael Elwyn, Corinne Dacla, Helena Michell; ***D:*** Ian Toynton; ***W:*** Leon Griffiths; ***C:*** Peter Jessop; ***M:*** Peter Martin. **TV**

A Piece of Pleasure *Un Partie de Plaisir* **1974** Marriage declines due to a domineering husband in this familiar domestic study from French master Chabrol. Good, but not among the director's best efforts. In French with English subtitles. **100m/C VHS, DVD.** *FR* Paul Gegauff, Danielle Gegauff, Clemence Gegauff, Paula Moore, Michel Valette, Cecile Vassort; ***D:*** Claude Chabrol; ***W:*** Paul Gegauff; ***C:*** Jean Ralsier; ***M:*** Pierre Jansen.

Piece of the Action 1/2 **1977 (PG)** An ex-cop beats two con men at their own game when he convinces them to work for a Chicago community center. **135m/C VHS, DVD.** Sidney Poitier, Bill Cosby, James Earl Jones, Denise Nicholas, Hope Clarke, Tracy Reed, Titos Vandis, Ja'net DuBois; ***D:*** Sidney Poitier; ***M:*** Curtis Mayfield.

Pieces WOOF! **1983 (R)** Chain-saw wielding madman roams a college campus in search of human parts for a ghastly jigsaw puzzle. Gory and loathsome. **90m/C VHS, DVD.** *IT SP* Christopher George, Lynda Day George, Paul Smith; ***D:*** J(uan) Piquer Simon.

Pieces of April 1/2 **2003 (PG-13)** Delightfully dysfunctional family meets for a chaotic Thanksgiving when tattooed New Yorker April (Holmes) has her suburban family join her for holiday dinner. The family trip to NYC is rife with humorous dramas and sidetracks involving roadkill and Mom bogarting little bro's stash. Meanwhile in the city, domestically-challenged April's oven breaks down while seemingly nice new boyfriend Bobby's behavior hints that something dark is afoot. Despite a misleading and slightly disturbing subplot involving Bobby (Luke) and a somewhat hasty ending, film is entertaining and original. Completed in three weeks on a limited budget ($200,000) with surprisingly slick digital camerawork. **81m/C VHS, DVD.** *US* Katie Holmes, Patricia Clarkson, Oliver Platt, Derek Luke, Alison Pill, Alice Drummond, Sean P. Hayes, John Gallagher Jr., Sisqo, Isiah Whitlock Jr., Lillias White; ***D:*** Peter Hedges; ***W:*** Peter Hedges; ***C:*** Tami Reiker; ***M:*** Stephin Merritt. Natl. Bd. of Review '03: Support. Actress (Clarkson); Natl. Soc. Film Critics '03: Support. Actress (Clarkson).

Pied Piper 1/2 **1972** Weird and violent not-for-the-kiddies retelling of the legend of the Pied Piper of Hamelin. Donovan minimally stars as the mysterious musical rat catcher who offers to rid the grubby 14th-century town of Hamelin of its plague-carrying rodents for a price. When the town reneges, the piper plays his tunes for the town's children instead. **90m/C DVD.** *GB* Jack Wild, Donald Pleasence, John Hurt, Michael Hordern, Roy Kinnear, Peter Vaughan, Diana Dors, Cathryn Harrison, Donovan; ***D:*** Jacques Demy; ***W:*** Jacques Demy, Andrew Birkin, Mark Peploe; ***C:*** Peter Suschitzky; ***M:*** Donovan.

The Pied Piper of Hamelin 🦴🦴 **1957** The evergreen classic of the magical piper who rids a village of rats and then disappears with the village children into a mountain when the townspeople fail to keep a promise. **90m/C VHS, DVD.** Van Johnson, Claude Rains, Jim Backus, Kay Starr, Lori Nelson; ***D:*** Bretaigne Windust.

The Pied Piper of Hamelin 🦴🦴 ½ **1984** From Shelley Duvall's "Faerie Tale Theatre" comes the story of how a man with a magic flute charmed the rats out of Hamelin. **60m/C VHS, DVD.** Eric Idle; ***D:*** Nicholas Meyer. **CABLE**

Pier 23 🦴🦴 **1951** A private eye is hired to bring a lawless ex-convict to a priest's custody, but gets an imposter instead. A web of intrigue follows. **57m/B VHS.** Hugh Beaumont, Ann Savage, David Bruce, Raymond Greenleaf, Joi Lansing, Edward Brophy, Richard Travis, Peter Mamakos, Mike Mazurki, Margia Dean, Harry Hayden, Richard Monahan; ***D:*** William Berke; ***W:*** Julian Harmon, Herbert Margolis, Louis Morheim; ***C:*** Jack Greenhalgh; ***M:*** Bert Shefter.

Pierrot le Fou 🦴🦴🦴 ½ **1965** A woman fleeing a gangster joins a man leaving his wife in this stunning, occasionally confusing classic from iconoclast Godard. A hallmark in 1960s improvisational filmmaking, with rugged Belmondo and always-photogenic Karina effortlessly excelling in leads. In French with English subtitles. **110m/C VHS, DVD.** *FR IT* Samuel Fuller, Jean-Pierre Leaud, Jean-Paul Belmondo, Anna Karina, Dirk Sanders; ***D:*** Jean-Luc Godard; ***W:*** Jean-Luc Godard; ***C:*** Raoul Coutard; ***M:*** Antoine Duhamel.

Pigalle 🦴🦴 **1995** Dridi's feature debut focuses on the red light district of Paris and the company of various lowlifes, including pickpocket Fifi (Renaud), who's involved with both stripper Vera (Brile) and transvestite hooker Divine (Li). There's also an increasingly violent turf war between a couple of drug dealers that takes in everyone around. Violent and sordid melodrama. French with subtitles. **93m/C VHS, DVD.** *FR* Francis Renaud, Vera Briole, Bianca Li, Raymond Gil, Younesse Boudache, Philippe Ambrosini, Jean-Claude Grenier; ***D:*** Karim Dridi; ***W:*** Karim Dridi; ***C:*** John Mathieson.

Piglet's Big Movie 🦴🦴 ½ **2003 (G)** An adaptation of three stories by A.A. Milne. Piglet (voiced by Fielder) is a very small animal and something of a fraidy pig. He's feeling too small to be of help to his friends and decides to take a little hike into the Hundred Acre Woods when he's ignored once again. However, when best bud Pooh (Cummings) thinks Piglet is missing, he organizes a search party and everyone realizes how important Piglet is to them. Best for the wee ones with its gentle lessons on friendship, even if it can't live up to the original shorts of the '60s and early '70s. **75m/C VHS, DVD.** *US* ***D:*** Francis Glebas; ***W:*** Brian Hohlfield; ***M:*** Carly Simon, Carl Johnson, Carly Simon; ***V:*** John Fiedler, Jim (Jonah) Cummings, Kath Soucie, Nikita Hopkins, Andre Stoja, Thomas Wheatley, Peter Cullen, Ken Sansom.

Pigs 🦴 ½ *Daddy's Deadly Darling; The Killers* **1973** Young woman who has escaped from a mental hospital teams up with an evil old man to go on a murdering spree. They complement each other beautifully. She kills them and he disposes of the bodies by making pig slop out of them. **90m/C VHS, DVD.** Toni Lawrence, Marc Lawrence, Jesse Vint, Katharine Ross; ***D:*** Marc Lawrence; ***M:*** Charles Bernstein.

Pigs 🦴 **2007** In this lame oink-fest about young men behaving, well, like pigs, Miles (Brown) takes a bet from his best buddy Cleaver (Lucio) that he can have sex with 26 girls, alphabetically A-Z. Only he doesn't intend to fall for Miss X—Gaby Xeropolus (Marden). Tries to go from wacky sex romp to heartfelt romance but can't really pull it off. **85m/C DVD.** Chris Elliott, Jefferson Brown, Melanie Marden, Darryn Lucio; ***D:*** Karl DiPelino; ***W:*** Karl DiPelino, Chris Ragonetti; ***C:*** Gurjeet Mann; ***M:*** John Jamieson. **VIDEO**

A Pig's Tale 🦴 ½ *Summer Camp* **1994 (PG)** Rich kids rule at Kamp Kipperman but one 13-year-old forms the Pig Pen club and the club members decide to turn the tables on their overbearing rivals. **94m/C VHS.** Joe Flaherty, Graham Sack; ***D:*** Paul Tassie.

Pigskin Parade 🦴🦴 ½ **1936** Fifteen-year-old Garland's first feature is a light-hearted musical combining college and football. Winston Winters (Haley) coaches the Texas State U team, which has been mistakenly invited to play Yale, and goes to great lengths to give his team a chance by recruiting a farmboy (Erwin) who's a natural phenom. (Garland's the boy's singing sister.) ♫ Balboa; The Texas Tornado; It's Love I'm After; You're Simply Terrific; You Do the Darndest Things, Baby; T.S.U. Alma Mater; Hold That Bulldog; Down with Everything; We'd Rather Be In College. **95m/B VHS, DVD.** Jack Haley, Patsy Kelly, Stuart Erwin, Judy Garland, Johnny Downs, Betty Grable, Arline Judge, Tony Martin, Fred Kohler Jr., Elisha Cook Jr.; ***D:*** David Butler; ***W:*** Harry Tugend, Jack Yellen; ***C:*** Arthur C. Miller.

Pilgrim, Farewell 🦴🦴 ½ **1982** Dramatic story about a dying woman who needs to tie up loose ends before her death and goes looking for her estranged teenage daughter. Made for PBS's "American Playhouse." **110m/C VHS.** Elizabeth Huddle, Christopher Lloyd, Laurie Pranage, Lesley Paxton, Shelley Wyant, Robert Brown; ***D:*** Michael Roemer. **TV**

Pilgrimage 🦴🦴 **1933** Overbearing Hannah Jessop (Crosman) is horrified when her son Jim (Foster) takes up with the unsuitable Mary (Nixon), so she sends him off to fight in WWI. Jim doesn't know Mary is pregnant and after he is killed, Hannah refuses to have anything to do with her grandson. It's not until she takes a trip to France to visit her son's grave that she realizes her heartlessness and makes amends. Crosman was a grand dame of the theater and well-suited to her part. **96m/B DVD.** Henrietta Crosman, Marion (Marian) Nixon, Norman Foster, Heather Angel, Charley Grapewin, Lucille La Verne, Maurice Murphy, Hedda Hopper; ***D:*** John Ford; ***W:*** Philip Klein, Barry Connors, Dudley Nichols; ***C:*** George Schneiderman; ***M:*** R. H. Bassett.

The Pillow Book 🦴🦴 **1995 (NC-17)** Greenaway's usual chilliness gives way to some true erotic heat that still keeps to arcane subjects, violence, and dazzling visuals. Japanese model Nagiko (Wu) longs for the childhood rituals enacted by her calligrapher father (Ogata) as he literally painted birthday greetings on her face with brush and ink. As an adult, Nagiko searches out calligrapher/lovers willing to use her body as their paper but she's still unsatisfied until she meets bisexual Englishman Jerome (McGregor) and he insists Nagiko write on him. When Nagiko learns Jerome's male lover is the publisher (Oida) who was once involved with her father, her jealousy triggers tragic consequences. Title refers to the 10th century diary "The Pillow Book of Sei Shonagon." Some subtitled Japanese dialogue. **126m/C VHS, DVD.** *NL FR GB* Vivian Wu, Ewan McGregor, Yoshi Oida, Ken Ogata, Hideko Yoshida, Judy Ongg, Ken Mitsuishi, Yutaka Honda, Ronald Guttman; ***D:*** Peter Greenaway; ***W:*** Peter Greenaway; ***C:*** Sacha Vierny.

Pillow of Death 🦴🦴 ½ **1945** Attorney Chaney is accused of smothering various family members to death. Based on radio's "The Inner Sanctum Mysteries." **66m/B DVD.** Lon Chaney Jr., Brenda Joyce, Rosalind Ivan, Clara Blandick, George Cleveland, Wilton Graff, Bernard B. Thomas; ***D:*** Wallace Fox; ***W:*** Dwight V. Babcock, George Bricker; ***C:*** Jerome Ash; ***M:*** Frank Skinner.

Pillow Talk 🦴🦴🦴 ½ **1959** Sex comedy in which a man woos a woman who loathes him. By the way, they share the same telephone party line. Narrative provides minimal indication of the film's strengths, which are many. Classic '50s comedy with masters Day and Hudson exhibiting considerable rapport, even when fighting. Lighthearted, constantly funny. **102m/C VHS, DVD.** Rock Hudson, Doris Day, Tony Randall, Thelma Ritter, Nick Adams, Lee Patrick; ***D:*** Michael Gordon; ***W:*** Maurice Richlin, Stanley Shapiro; ***C:*** Arthur E. Arling; ***M:*** Frank DeVol. Oscars '59: Story & Screenplay, Natl. Film Reg. '09.

The Pilot's Wife 🦴🦴 **2001 (PG-13)** Kathryn Lyons (Lahti) learns that her husband Jack (Heard), a commercial airline pilot, has died in a crash over Ireland. She's angry when she discovers investigators think he caused the crash and bewildered when she finds out Jack led a double life. Accompanied by union rep Robert Hart (Scott), Kathryn heads to England and Ireland to get some answers. Shreve co-scripted the teleplay from her own novel. **89m/C VHS, DVD.** Christine Lahti, Campbell Scott, John Heard, Alison Pill, Nigel Bennett; ***D:*** Robert Markowitz; ***W:*** Anita Shreve, Christine Berardo; ***C:*** Rudolf Blahacek; ***M:*** Lee Holdridge. **TV**

Pimpernel Smith 🦴🦴 ½ *Mister V* **1942** Seemingly scatterbrained archaeology professor is actually a dashing agent rescuing refugees from evil Nazis in WWII France. Howard is well cast, but the film is somewhat predictable, and it's too long. Wonderful scene, though, in which a Nazi officer champions Shakespeare as Aryan. **121m/B VHS.** *GB* Leslie Howard, Mary Morris, Francis L. Sullivan, David Tomlinson; ***D:*** Leslie Howard.

Pin... 🦴🦴 ½ **1988 (R)** A boy's imaginary friend assists in the slaying of various enemies. Horror effort could be worse. **103m/C VHS, DVD.** Cynthia (Cyndy, Cindy) Preston, David Hewlett, Terry O'Quinn, Bronwen Mantel, Helene Udy, Patricia Collins, Steven Bednarski, Katie Shingler, Jacob Tierney, Michelle Anderson; ***D:*** Sandor Stern; ***W:*** Sandor Stern; ***C:*** Guy Defaux.

Pin Down Girls 🦴 *Racket Girls; Pin Down Girl* **1951** Great schlock about girl wrestlers. **81m/B VHS, DVD.** Clara Mortensen, Rita Martinez, Peaches Page, Timothy Farrell; ***D:*** Robert Derteno; ***W:*** Robert Derteno; ***C:*** William C. Thompson.

Pin-Up Girl 🦴🦴 **1944** Grable plays a secretary who becomes an overnight sensation during WWII. Loosely based on her famous pinup poster that was so popular at the time, the movie didn't even come close to being as successful. The songs aren't particularly memorable, although Charlie Spivak and his Orchestra perform. ♫ Once Too Often; Yankee Doodle Dandy; I'll Be Marching to a Love Song; You're My Little Pin Up Girl; Story of the Very Merry Widow; Time Alone Will Tell; Don't Carry Tales Out of School; Red Robins, Bob Whites and Blue Birds. **83m/C VHS, DVD.** Betty Grable, Martha Raye, Jon Harvey, Joe E. Brown, Eugene Pallette, Mantan Moreland; ***D:*** H. Bruce Humberstone; ***C:*** Ernest Palmer.

Pineapple Express 🦴🦴🦴 **2008 (R)** After scoring some super-robust dope—the "Pineapple Express" of the title—from his buddy/dealer Saul (a high-spirited Franco), process server/burnout Dale (Rogen, also a co-writer) heads to subpoena Ted (Cole), who coincidentally is Saul's supplier. Panicked by the sight of a cop car outside the house, Dale catches sight of Ted and corrupt policewoman Carol (Perez) in the middle of a murder. When Ted makes the reefer connection, the constantly stoned buddies end up on the run. Think Cheech and Chong, but with more consistent laughs and lots of action-movie violence. And explosions. **111m/C DVD, Blu-ray Disc.** *US* Seth Rogen, James Franco, Gary Cole, Rosie Perez, Amber Heard, James Remar, Bill Hader, Danny McBride, Nora Dunn, Kevin Corrigan, Ed Begley Jr., Bobby Lee, Craig Robinson, Jack Kehler, Ken Jeong; ***D:*** David Gordon Green; ***W:*** Seth Rogen, Evan Goldberg; ***C:*** Tim Orr; ***M:*** Graeme Revell.

Pinero 🦴🦴 **2001 (R)** Change of pace role for Bratt, best known for clean-cut characters on the right side of the law. Although he physically did not resemble the Puerto Rican poet/playwright/actor Miguel Pinero, Bratt gives a dynamic performance as the street smart hustler/heroin addict who died at age 40 in 1988. An ex-con who did time at Sing-Sing, Pinero put his experience to use with the Tony Award-nominated play, "Short Eyes," and was one of the founders of the Nuyorican Cafe. Film is non-chronological, which can get confusing, and few of the secondary characters have enough screen time to make strong impressions. **103m/C VHS, DVD.** Benjamin Bratt, Talisa Soto, Giancarlo Esposito, Rita Moreno, Mandy Patinkin, Michael Irby, Michael Wright, Nelson Vasquez, Jaime Sanchez, Rome Neal; ***D:*** Leon Ichaso; ***W:*** Leon Ichaso; ***C:*** Claudio Chea.

Ping! 🦴🦴 **1999 (PG)** Silly family comedy that gets an extra half-bone from the Hound for being about a dog—in this case, smart little chihuahua Ping who's been rescued from the pound by Ethel. And the little guard dog is not about to let a couple of inept burglars (Reinhold, Howard) cause problems on his new turf. **93m/C VHS, DVD.** Judge Reinhold, Clint Howard, Shirley Jones, Lou Ferrigno; ***D:*** Chris Baugh; ***W:*** Albert Ruis. **VIDEO**

Ping Pong 🦴🦴 ½ **1987 (PG)** A Chinese patriarch drops dead in London's Chinatown, leaving a young law student to disentangle his will, and get mixed up with his cross-cultured family. **100m/C VHS.** David Yip, Lucy Sheen, Robert Lee, Lam Fung, Victor Kan, Ric Young; ***D:*** Po-Chih Leung.

Ping Pong 🦴🦴🦴 **2002** Based on the comic by Taiyo Matsumoto, this is the story of two friends (and polar opposites) who are competitive ping pong players. Peco (Yosuke Kubozuka) is arrogant and always trash talks his opponents. Smile (Arata) is a quiet player who let's his opponents win so they don't feel bad. After both are beaten soundly in a tournament they must pick themselves back up and train for their inevitable rematch with their opponents. **114m/C DVD.** *JP* Arata, Sam Lee, Shido Nakamura, Naoto Takenaka, Mari Natsuki, Yosuke Kobuzuka, Koji Ookura; ***D:*** Fumihiko Sori; ***W:*** Kankuro Kudo, Taiyo Matsumoto; ***C:*** Akira Sakoh.

Pink Cadillac 🦴🦴 ½ **1989 (PG-13)** A grizzled, middle-aged bondsman is on the road, tracking down bail-jumping crooks. He helps the wife and baby of his latest target escape from her husband's more evil associates. Eastwood's performance is good and fun to watch, in this otherwise lightweight film. **121m/C VHS, DVD.** Clint Eastwood, Bernadette Peters, Timothy Carhart, Michael Des Barres, William Hickey, John Dennis Johnston, Geoffrey Lewis, Jim Carrey, Tiffany Gail Robinson, Angela Louise Robinson; ***D:*** Buddy Van Horn; ***W:*** John Eskow; ***M:*** Steve Dorff.

The Pink Chiquitas 🦴 **1986 (PG-13)** Sci-fi spoof about a detective battling a mob of meteorite-traveling Amazons. **86m/C VHS, DVD.** Frank Stallone, Eartha Kitt, Bruce Pirrie, McKinlay Robinson, Elizabeth Edwards, Claudia Udy; ***D:*** Anthony Currie.

The Pink Conspiracy 🦴 **2007** David thinks his girlfriend Jamie is cheating on him so he follows her and discovers the truth is worse. She has teamed up with his ex-girlfriends to make David's life miserable. Since David doesn't seem like that bad a guy and since Jamie targeted her previous boyfriend Frank before, the chicks just come across as crazy. **98m/C DVD.** Mercedes McNab, Sarah Thompson, MacKenzie Firgens, James Russo, Chad Everett, Bradley Snedeker, Frank Krueger; ***D:*** Brian Scott Miller, Marc Clebanoff; ***W:*** Brian Scott Miller, Marc Clebanoff; ***C:*** Tim Otholt; ***M:*** Vashi Nedomansky.

Pink Flamingos 🦴🦴 **1972 (NC-17)** Divine, the dainty 300-pound transvestite, faces the biggest challenge of his/her career when he/she competes for the title of World's Filthiest Person. Tasteless, crude, and hysterical film; this one earned Waters his title as "Prince of Puke." If there are any doubts about this honor—or Divine's rep—watch through to the end to catch Divine chewing real dog excrement, all the time wearing a you-know-what-eating grin. **95m/C VHS, DVD.** Divine, David Lochary, Mary Vivian Pearce, Danny Mills, Mink Stole, Edith Massey, Cookie Mueller, Channing Wilroy, Paul Swift, Susan Walsh, Linda Olgierson, Elizabeth Coffey, Steve Yeager, Pat Moran, George Figgs; ***D:*** John Waters; ***W:*** John Waters; ***C:*** John Waters; ***Nar:*** John Waters.

Pink Floyd: The Wall 🦴🦴 ½ **1982 (R)** Film version of Pink Floyd's 1979 LP, "The Wall." A surreal, impressionistic tour-de-force about a boy who grows up numb from society's pressures. The concept is bombastic and overwrought, but Geldof manages to remain somewhat likeable as the cynical rock star and the Gerald Scarfe animation perfectly complements the film. **95m/C VHS, DVD.** *GB* Bob Geldof, Christine Hargreaves, Bob Hoskins, James Laurenson, Eleanor David, Kevin McKeon, David Bingham, Jenny Wright, Alex McAvoy, Nell Campbell, Joanne Whalley; ***D:*** Alan Parker; ***W:*** Roger Waters; ***C:*** Peter Biziou; ***M:*** Michael Kamen, David Gilmour, Roger Waters.

The Pink Jungle 🦴🦴 1/2 **1968** Ben Morris (Garner) is a fashion photographer on assignment with model Alison (Renzi) in South America where they become entangled with eccentric Sammy Ryderbeit (Kennedy) who's searching for a lost diamond mine. Caught up in the adventure, the duo accompany Sammy and find the mine, only to discover Raul Ortega (Ansara) and his band of revolutionaries have gotten there first. Based on the novel "Snake Water" by Alan Williams. **104m/C VHS.** James Garner, Eva Renzi, George Kennedy, Michael Ansara, Nigel Green, George Rose; ***D:*** Delbert Mann; ***W:*** Charles Williams; ***C:*** Russell Metty; ***M:*** Ernie Freeman.

Pink Motel WOOF! *Motel* **1982 (R)** Several people spend a night meant to be romantic at a pink stucco motel which caters to couples. Comic stiff with Diller and Pickens as the owners of said pink motel. **90m/C VHS.** Phyllis Diller, Slim Pickens, Terri Berland, Squire Fridell; ***D:*** Mike MacFarland.

Pink Nights 🦴 **1987 (PG)** A high school nebbish is suddenly pursued by three beautiful girls, and his life gets turned upside-down. **87m/C VHS.** Shaun Allen, Kevin Anderson, Larry King, Johnathan Jamcovic Michaels; ***D:*** Philip Koch.

The Pink Panther 🦴🦴🦴 **1964** Bumbling, disaster-prone inspector invades a Swiss ski resort and becomes obsessed with capturing a jewel thief hoping to lift the legendary "Pink Panther" diamond. Said thief is also the inspector's wife's lover, though the inspector doesn't know it. Slick slapstick succeeds on strength of Sellers' classic portrayal of Clouseau, who accidentally destroys everything in his path while speaking in a funny French accent. Followed by "A Shot in the Dark," "Inspector Clouseau" (without Sellers), "The Return of the Pink Panther," "The Pink Panther Strikes Again," "Revenge of the Pink Panther," "Trail of the Pink Panther," and "Curse of the Pink Panther." Memorable theme supplied by Mancini. **113m/C VHS, DVD, Blu-ray Disc.** *GB* Peter Sellers, David Niven, Robert Wagner, Claudia Cardinale, Capucine, Brenda de Banzie; ***D:*** Blake Edwards; ***W:*** Blake Edwards; ***C:*** Philip Lathrop; ***M:*** Henry Mancini.

The Pink Panther 🦴🦴 **2006 (PG)** Martin returns to his slapstick roots as he takes over the character of bumbling Inspector Jacques Clouseau. When soccer coach Gluant (Statham) is murdered, the Pink Panther diamond he was about to give his girlfriend, hottie pop diva Xania (Knowles), disappears. Ambitious Inspector Dreyfus (Kline) assigns the case to Clouseau and his partner Ponton (Reno), knowing they will botch it and he can take over and save the day. Martin maintains a ridiculous accent and leaves destruction in his wake, but the effort is wasted in a tired retread. Clive Owen has a cameo as Agent 006, spoofing superspy James Bond. **92m/C DVD, Blu-ray Disc, UMD.** *US* Steve Martin, Kevin Kline, Jean Reno, Emily Mortimer, Henry Czerny, Kristin Chenoweth, Roger Rees, Beyonce Knowles, Clive Owen; ***D:*** Shawn Levy; ***W:*** Steve Martin, Len Blum; ***C:*** Jonathan Brown, George Folsey Jr.; ***M:*** Christophe Beck, Randall Poster.

The Pink Panther 2 🦴 1/2 **2009 (PG)** Martin returns as the bumbling French inspector Clouseau to stop an international artifacts thief who's out for France's prized Pink Panther diamond. Along for the wacky ride is his new assistant Nicole (Mortimer), who's head-over-heels (literally) for the inspector. John Cleese replaces Kevin Kline as Dreyfus, Clouseau's boss, with too many other stars vying for screen time with not enough material for any of them. The sight gags and language barrier jokes are still there, and much like the first, Martin never lives up to his potential. **92m/C DVD.** *US* Steve Martin, Jean Reno, Emily Mortimer, John Cleese, Andy Garcia, Alfred Molina, Aishwarya Rai, Yuki Matsuzaki, Lily Tomlin, Geoffrey Palmer, Jeremy Irons, Johnny Hallyday; ***D:*** Harald Zwart; ***W:*** Steve Martin, Scott Neustadter, Michael H. Weber; ***C:*** Denis Crossan, Rick Butler; ***M:*** Christophe Beck.

The Pink Panther Strikes Again 🦴🦴🦴 **1976 (PG)** Fifth in the series has the incompetent inspector tracking his former boss, who has gone insane and has become preoccupied with destroying the entire world. A must for Sellers buffs and anyone who appreciates slapstick. **103m/C VHS, DVD.** *GB* Peter Sellers, Herbert Lom, Lesley-Anne Down, Colin Blakely, Leonard Rossiter, Burt Kwouk; ***D:*** Blake Edwards; ***W:*** Edwards Waldman, Frank Waldman; ***C:*** Harry Waxman; ***M:*** Henry Mancini. Writers Guild '76: Adapt. Screenplay.

Pink String and Sealing Wax 🦴🦴 **1945** A brutish pub owner in Victorian England is poisoned by his abused wife. She tries to involve the son of a chemist with the idea of blackmailing the father. Fine period flavor. **89m/B VHS.** *GB* Mervyn Johns, Mary Merrall, Gordon Jackson, Googie Withers, Sally Ann Howes, Catherine Lacey, Garry Marsh, Frederick Piper, Don Stannard, Valentine Dyall; ***D:*** Robert Hamer; ***W:*** Robert Hamer; ***C:*** Richard S. Pavey.

Pinky 🦴🦴🦴 **1949** Early Hollywood treatment of the tragic choice made by some black Americans to pass as white in order to attain a better life for themselves and their families. The story is still relevant today. Waters and Barrymore also star, but the lead black character is portrayed by a white actress. Based on the novel "Quality" by Cyd Ricketts Sumner. **102m/B VHS, DVD.** Jeanne Crain, Ethel Barrymore, Ethel Waters, Nina Mae McKinney, William Lundigan; ***D:*** Elia Kazan; ***W:*** Philip Dunne, Dudley Nichols; ***M:*** Alfred Newman.

Pinocchio 🦴🦴🦴🦴 **1940 (G)** Second Disney animated film featuring Pinocchio, a little wooden puppet, made with love by the old woodcarver Geppetto, and brought to life by a good fairy. Except Pinocchio isn't content to be just a puppet—he wants to become a real boy. Lured off by a sly fox, Pinocchio undergoes a number of adventures as he tries to return safely home. Has some scary scenes, including Geppetto, Pinocchio, and their friend Jiminy Cricket getting swallowed by a whale, and Pleasure Island, where naughty boys are turned into donkeys. An example of animation at its best and a Disney classic that has held up over time. ♫ When You Wish Upon a Star; Give a Little Whistle; Turn on the Old Music Box; Hi-Diddle-Dee-Dee (An Actor's Life For Me); I've Got No Strings. **87m/C VHS, DVD.** ***D:*** Hamilton Luske, Ben Sharpsteen; ***W:*** Aurelius Battaglia, William Cottrell, Otto Englander, Erdman Penner, Joseph Sabo, Ted Sears, Webb Smith; ***V:*** Dick(ie) Jones, Cliff Edwards, Evelyn Venable, Walter Catlett, Frankie Darro, Charles (Judel, Judells) Judels, Don Brodie, Christian Rub. Oscars '40: Song ("When You Wish Upon a Star"), Orig. Score, Natl. Film Reg. '94.

Pinocchio 🦴🦴🦴 **1983** Pee-wee Herman is the puppet who wants to be a real little boy in this "Faerie Tale Theatre" adaptation of this children's classic. **60m/C VHS, DVD.** James Belushi, Paul (Pee-wee Herman) Reubens, James Coburn, Carl Reiner, Lainie Kazan; ***D:*** Peter Medak. **CABLE**

Pinocchio 🦴 1/2 **2002 (G)** Benigni's faithful version of Carlo Collodi's Italian fairy tale suffers from a disastrous decision to dub the dialogue for an American audience and Benigni's self-consciously manic and forced portrayal of the little wooden boy. Set against this wall-to-wall performance, the rest of the proceedings seem lifeless and dull, with the exception of the opening sequence (before Benigni shows up). By the time you read this, a subtitled version could be around, which may help with the humor, but will still leave the other problems. One thing that is not a problem is Spinotti's wonderful cinematography. Production is the most expensive in Italian history, at $45 million. **108m/C VHS, DVD.** *IT* Roberto Benigni, Nicoletta Braschi, Mino Bellei, Carlo Guiffre, Peppe Barra, Max Cavallari, Bruno Arena, Kim Rossi-Stuart; ***D:*** Roberto Benigni; ***W:*** Roberto Benigni, Vincenzo Cerami; ***C:*** Dante Spinotti; ***M:*** Nicola Piovani; ***V:*** Breckin Meyer, Glenn Close, Eric Idle, David Suchet, John Cleese, Richard "Cheech" Marin, Eddie Griffin, Topher Grace. Golden Raspberries '02: Worst Actor (Benigni).

Pinocchio 964 🦴 1/2 *964 Pinocchio* **1992** Japanese cyberpunk films like "Tetsuo" or "Rubber's Lover" are an acquired taste, and usually difficult to watch. This one is no exception. A malfunctioning sex android is thrown into the street by its lesbian owners, and it takes up with an amnesiac homeless woman in a quest to confront its creators. Their journey is anything but pretty, and decay and madness swiftly overcome them as everything in their path dies. As with most Japanese cyberpunk, dialogue and explanation are minimal. Also famous for having what may be the most disturbing vomit scene on film. **97m/C DVD.** *JP* Hage Suzuki, Onn Chan; ***D:*** Shozin Fukui; ***W:*** Shozin Fukui; ***M:*** Hiroyuki Nagashima.

Pinocchio's Revenge 🦴 **1996 (R)** Man murders his child and buries the body with a wooden Pinocchio puppet. Somehow before his execution, his lawyer, Jennifer Garrick (Allen), and her cute daughter Zoe (Smith) wind up with the grisly toy and Jennifer allows her daughter to keep it. Naturally, this is not a good thing. **96m/C VHS, DVD.** Rosalind Allen, Brittany Alyse Smith, Todd Allen, Lewis Van Bergen, Aaron Lustig, Ron Canada; ***D:*** Kevin S. Tenney; ***W:*** Kevin S. Tenney; ***M:*** Dennis Michael Tenney.

Pinochet's Last Stand 🦴🦴 *Pinochet in Suburbia* **2006** In 1973, General Augusto Pinochet took control of Chile in a violent coup and ruled as a dictator for 17 years. But in 1998, in a surprise move, the elderly ex-leader (Jacobi) was arrested in Britain (where he was seeking medical treatment) and charged with crimes against humanity. Confined to a house in a London suburb, Pinochet waited in exile while government ministers vacillated and the judicial system took over. **77m/C DVD.** *GB* Derek Jacobi, Peter Capaldi, Phyllida Law, Michael Maloney, Jessica Stevenson, Pip Torrens, Yolanda Vasquez, Anna Massey, Susan Woolridge; ***D:*** Richard Curson Smith; ***W:*** Richard Curson Smith; ***C:*** Jeff Baynes; ***M:*** Jeff Beal.

Pinto Canyon 🦴 1/2 **1940** An honest sheriff does away with a band of cattle rustlers. **55m/B VHS.** Bob Steele, Louise Stanley, Kenne Duncan, Ted Adams, Steve Clark, Budd Buster; ***D:*** Bernard B. Ray.

Pinto Rustlers 🦴 1/2 **1936** A cowboy left orphaned by a gang of rustlers seeks revenge. **52m/C VHS.** Tom Tyler, George Walsh, Marie Burton, Earl Dwire, Al "Fuzzy" St. John, George Chesebro, William (Bill) Gould, Roger Williams, Charles "Slim" Whitaker, Murdock MacQuarrie; ***D:*** Harry S. Webb; ***W:*** Robert Emmett Tansey; ***C:*** William (Bill) Hyer.

Pioneer Marshal 🦴 **1949** Lawman Hale disguises himself as a criminal to track down an embezzler. **60m/B VHS.** Nan Leslie, Roy Barcroft, Monte Hale, Paul Hurst; ***D:*** Philip Ford; ***W:*** Robert Creighton Williams; ***C:*** John MacBurnie; ***M:*** Stanley Wilson.

Pioneer Woman 🦴🦴 *Pioneers* **1973** A family encounters hostility when they set up a frontier homestead in Nebraska in 1867. Told from the feminine perspective, the tale is strewn with hurdles, both personal and natural. **74m/C VHS, DVD.** Joanna Pettet, William Shatner, David Janssen, Helen Hunt; ***D:*** Buzz Kulik. **TV**

The Pioneers 🦴 1/2 **1941** Ritter sets out to protect a wagon train. **59m/B VHS.** Tex Ritter, Red Foley, Wanda McKay, George Chesebro, Slim Andrews; ***D:*** Al(bert) Herman; ***W:*** Charles E. Anderson; ***C:*** Marcel Le Picard; ***M:*** Frank Sanucci.

Pioneers of the West 🦴 1/2 **1940** Judge Platt and his cronies cheated new settlers by selling them worthless land. Having prospered through hard work, the settlers are then beset by exorbitant taxes because Platt wants to sell their property to the railroad. The Mesquiteers arrange to get the tax money but Platt's henchmen have other ideas. The 28th film in the series. **56m/B DVD.** Robert "Bob" Livingston, Raymond Hatton, Duncan Renaldo, Noah Beery Sr., Beatrice Roberts, Lane Chandler, George Cleveland, Hal Taliaferro, Joe McGuinn, Yakima Canutt; ***D:*** Les(ter) Orlebeck; ***W:*** Gerald Geraghty, Karen DeWolf, Jack Natteford; ***C:*** Jack Marta; ***M:*** Cy Feuer.

Pipe Dream 🦴🦴 1/2 **2002 (R)** David (Donovan) is a New York City plumber who is tired of being taken for granted by snobs. So he steals the unproduced screenplay of writer/neighbor Toni (Parker) and pretends to be a casting director with the help of industry pal R.J. (Carroll). He holds auditions for his nonexistant movie and suddenly the buzz is that the film is hot and everyone wants a piece of the action, including Toni, who feeds the clueless David appropriate showbiz lines. The cast is good but the film turns out to be mildly amusing rather than satiric. **94m/C VHS, DVD.** *US* Martin Donovan, Mary-Louise Parker, Kevin Carroll, Rebecca Gayheart, Peter Jacobson, Cynthia Kaplan, Tim Hopper, Guinevere Turner, Marla Sucharetza; ***D:*** John C. Walsh; ***W:*** Cynthia Kaplan, John C. Walsh; ***C:*** Peter Nelson; ***M:*** Alexander Lasarenko.

Pipe Dreams 🦴🦴 **1976 (PG)** A couple tries to repair their broken marriage against the backdrop of the Alaskan pipeline's construction. **89m/C VHS.** Gladys Knight, Barry Hankerson, Bruce French, Sally Kirkland, Sherry Bain; ***D:*** Stephen Verona.

Pippi Goes on Board 🦴🦴 1/2 **1969 (G)** The fourth and last film in the Swedish series finds Pippi's father arriving one day to take her sailing to Taka-Kuka, his island kingdom. She can't bear to leave her friends and jumps off the ship to return home. The series is poorly dubbed and technically flawed, which the kids probably won't notice. Based on the books by Astrid Lindgren. Preceded by "Pippi Longstocking," "Pippi in the South Seas," and "Pippi on the Run." **83m/C VHS, DVD.** *SW* Maria Persson, Par Sundberg, Margot Trooger, Hans Clarin, Inger Nilsson; ***D:*** Olle Hellbom; ***W:*** Astrid Lindgren; ***C:*** Kalle Bergholm; ***M:*** Christian Bruhn.

Pippi in the South Seas 🦴🦴 1/2 *Pippi Langstrump Pa de Sju Haven* **1970 (G)** Pippi, a fun-loving, independent, red haired little girl, and her two friends decide to rescue her father, who is being held captive by a band of pirates on a South Sea island. Naturally, clever Pippi saves the day. Poorly dubbed and edited. Based on the children's book by Astrid Lindgren. Follows "Pippi Longstocking" and precedes "Pippi on the Run" and "Pippi Goes on Board." **99m/C VHS, DVD.** *SW* Maria Persson, Par Sundberg, Beppe Wolgens, Inger Nilsson; ***D:*** Olle Hellbom; ***W:*** Olle Hellbom; ***C:*** Kalle Bergholm; ***M:*** Jan Johansson.

Pippi Longstocking 🦴🦴 1/2 **1969 (G)** This little red-headed, pigtailed terror is left alone by her sailor father as he heads out to sea. Not that Pippi minds, since it gives her the chance to create havoc in her town through the antics of her pets, a monkey and a horse. Pippi's antics may amuse the kiddies but adults will find her obnoxious. Poorly dubbed and technically somewhat shaky. Based on the children's book by Astrid Lindgren. Followed by "Pippi in the South Seas," "Pippi on the Run," and "Pippi Goes on Board." **99m/C VHS, DVD.** *SW* Maria Persson, Par Sundberg, Margot Trooger, Hans Clarin, Inger Nilsson; ***D:*** Olle Hellbom; ***W:*** Astrid Lindgren; ***C:*** Kalle Bergholm; ***M:*** Konrad Elfers.

Pippi on the Run 🦴🦴 1/2 **1970 (G)** The third film in the series finds Pippi on the trail of two friends who have run away from home. The three have many adventures before deciding home is best. Preceded by "Pippi Longstocking" and "Pippi in the South Seas," followed by "Pippi Goes on Board." Films lacks technical and dubbing skills. Based on the children's book by Astrid Lindgren. **99m/C VHS, DVD.** *SW* Inger Nilsson, Hans Alfredson, Maria Persson, Par Sundberg; ***D:*** Olle Hellbom; ***W:*** Astrid Lindgren; ***C:*** Kalle Bergholm; ***M:*** Christian Bruhn.

Pippin 🦴🦴🦴 **1981** Video version of the stage musical about the adolescent son of Charlemagne finding true love. Adequate record of Bob Fosse's Broadway smash. Features Vereen re-creating his original Tony Award-winning role. **120m/C VHS, DVD.** Ben Vereen, William Katt, Martha Raye, Chita Rivera, Leslie Denniston, Benjamin Rayson; ***D:*** David Sheehan; ***W:*** Roger O. Hirson; ***M:*** Stephen Schwartz. **TV**

Piranha 🦴🦴 1/2 **1995 (R)** Genetically enhanced piranha terrorize the resort community of Lost River. Scientists Paul (Katt) and Maggie (Paul) have accidentally released the vicious fishies but everyone ignores their warnings until some swimmers become din-din. Remake of Roger Corman's 1978 cult item and based on John Sayles' original screenplay. **81m/C VHS, DVD.** Alexandra Paul, William Katt, Soleil Moon Frye, Monte Markham, Darlene Carr, James Karen, Lincoln Kilpatrick; *D:* Scott Levy; *W:* Alex Simon; *C:* Christopher Baffa; *M:* Christopher Lennertz.

Piranha ✓✓ 1/2 **1978 (R)** A rural Texas resort area is plagued by attacks from ferocious man-eating fish which a scientist created to be used as a secret weapon in the Vietnam War. Spoofy horror film features the now-obligatory Dante film in-jokes in the background. **90m/C VHS, DVD.** Bradford Dillman, Heather Menzies, Kevin McCarthy, Keenan Wynn, Barbara Steele, Dick Miller, Paul Bartel, John Sayles, Richard Deacon; *D:* Joe Dante; *W:* John Sayles; *C:* Jamie Anderson; *M:* Pino Donaggio.

Piranha 2: The Spawning ✓ 1/2 *Piranha 2: Flying Killers; The Spawning* **1982 (R)** Diving instructor and a biochemist seek to destroy piranha mutations that are murdering tourists at a club. Early Cameron exercise in gore tech that's a step down from original "Piranha." **88m/C VHS, DVD.** Tricia O'Neil, Steve Marachuk, Lance Henriksen, Ricky Paul; *D:* James Cameron; *W:* H.A. Milton; *C:* Roberto D'Ettorre Piazzoli.

Piranha 3D 2010 An underwater tremor opens up a fault line and sets loose prehistoric man-eating fish into Lake Victoria over a wild 4th of July weekend that sees the town also invaded by tourists. Since becoming fish food would be bad for business, the townspeople must band together to stop the hungry critters. **m/C DVD.** Elisabeth Shue, Adam Scott, Jerry O'Connell, Jessica Szohr, Dina Meyer, Cody Longo, Christopher Lloyd, Ving Rhames, Richard Dreyfuss; *D:* Alexandre Aja; *W:* Alexandre Aja, Josh Stolberg; *M:* Michael Wandmacher.

The Pirate ✓✓✓ **1948** A traveling actor poses as a legendary pilot to woo a lonely woman on a remote Caribbean island. Minnelli always scores with this type of fare, and both Garland and Kelly make the most of the Cole Porter score. ♫ Be a Clown; Nina; Mack the Black; You Can Do No Wrong; Sweet Ices, Papayas, Berry Man; Sea Wall; Serafin; The Ring; Judy Awakens. **102m/C VHS.** Judy Garland, Gene Kelly, Walter Slezak, Gladys Cooper, George Zucco, Reginald Owen; *D:* Vincente Minnelli; *C:* Harry Stradling Sr.

Pirate Movie ✓✓ 1/2 **1982 (PG)** Gilbert and Sullivan's "The Pirates of Penzance" is combined with new pop songs in this tale of fantasy and romance. Feeble attempt to update a musical that was fine the way it was. **98m/C VHS, DVD.** Kristy McNichol, Christopher Atkins, Ted Hamilton, Bill Kerr, Garry McDonald; *D:* Ken Annakin; *M:* Tony Britten. Golden Raspberries '82: Worst Director (Annakin), Worst Song ("Pumpin' and Blowin'").

Pirate Radio ✓✓ 1/2 *The Boat That Rocked* **2009 (R)** Rocking tale of rebellious broadcasters fighting the staid BBC radio programming of '60s England. Quentin (Nighy) and his crew of raucous deejays (Hoffman, Ifans, Frost) set up a ship in the North Sea to beam rock songs back to Blighty in defiance of uptight government minister Dormandy (Branagh). Most of the action revolves around the hijinks of the outlaw band, but a coming-of-age plotline is shoehorned in as naive teen Carl (Sturridge) attempts to find love and the identity of his father. The story drags at times, but the excellent cast and soundtrack keeps the good times rolling. Released in Great Britain as "The Boat That Rocked," this love letter to rock and roll was trimmed substantially for American release. **134m/C DVD, DVD.** *US GB US* Philip Seymour Hoffman, Bill Nighy, Rhys Ifans, Nick Frost, Kenneth Branagh, Rhys Darby, Katharine Parkinson, Tom Wisdom, Thomas Sturridge, Jack Davenport, Emma Thompson, Tom Brooke, Chris O'Dowd; *D:* Richard Curtis; *W:* Richard Curtis; *C:* Danny Cohen.

Pirate Ship ✓ 1/2 *The Mutineers* **1949** Slow-moving story has sailor Hall discovering new captain Reeves is involved with a gang of gun-runners and counterfeiters. **60m/C VHS.** Jon Hall, George Reeves, Adele Jergens, Noel Cravat, Tom Kennedy, Lyle Talbot; *D:* Jean Yarbrough.

Pirate Warrior ✓✓ **1964** Grade-B pirate flick about slavery and the evil Tortuga. **86m/C VHS.** Ricardo Montalban, Vincent Price, Liana Orfei; *D:* Mary Costa.

Pirates ✓ 1/2 **1986 (PG-13)** Blustery, confused effort at a big-budgeted retro-adventure, about a highly regarded pirate and his gains and losses on the high seas. Broad comedy, no story to speak of. **124m/C VHS.** Walter Matthau, Cris Campion, Damien Thomas, Richard Pearson, Charlotte Lewis, Olu Jacobs, David Patrick Kelly, Roy Kinnear, Bill Fraser, Jose Santamaria; *D:* Roman Polanski; *W:* Gerard Brach, Roman Polanski. Cesar '87: Art Dir./Set Dec., Costume Des.

Pirates of Blood River ✓✓ **1962** Pirate story is mostly land-locked since it's a low-budget Hammer production but Lee gets a lot of mileage out of his role as the evil, eye-patch wearing LaRoche. The pirate leader forces exiled Jonathan Standing (Mathews) to take him to his island home to find reputed buried treasure. LaRoche kills many in his search and Standing finally escapes to gather support. **87m/C DVD.** *GB* Christopher Lee, Kerwin Mathews, Glenn Corbett, Marla Landi, Oliver Reed, Andrew Keir, Michael Ripper, Peter Arne; *D:* John Gentil; *W:* John Gentil, John Hunter; *C:* Arthur Grant; *M:* Gary Hughes.

The Pirates of Penzance ✓✓ **1983 (G)** Gilbert and Sullivan's comic operetta is the story of a band of fun-loving pirates, their reluctant young apprentice, the "very model of a modern major general," and his lovely daughters. An adaptation of Joseph Papp's award-winning Broadway play. **112m/C VHS, DVD.** Kevin Kline, Angela Lansbury, Linda Ronstadt, Rex Smith, George Rose; *D:* Wilford Leach.

The Pirates of Silicon Valley ✓✓ 1/2 **1999** Fact-based docudrama covering the early days of Apple and Microsoft. The partners in both companies tend to get the short end of the story as the telepic focuses on charismatic manipulator Steve Jobs (Wyle) and shrewd geek kingpin Bill Gates (Hall), who not only kept an eye on each other but outmanuevered industry giants such as IBM and Xerox to virtually begin the personal computer market. **95m/C VHS, DVD.** Noah Wyle, Anthony Michael Hall, Joey Slotnick, John DiMaggio, Josh Hopkins, Gema Zamprogna, Allan Royal, Bodhi (Pine) Elfman, Gailard Sartain; *D:* Martyn Burke; *W:* Martyn Burke; *C:* Ousama Rawi; *M:* Frank Fitzpatrick. **CABLE**

Pirates of the Caribbean: At World's End ✓✓ 1/2 **2007 (PG-13)** Like a good captain, this latest (and last?) entry in the "Pirates" franchise goes down with the ship. Familiar heroes and villains must band together to fight even worse villains, perform rescues, and go head-to-head with Chow-Yun Fat, mostly to serve up 168 minutes of non-stop spectacle. Lord Cutler Beckett (Hollander) and tentacle-faced Davy Jones (Nighy) are trying to wipe out pirates, and only Captain Jack Sparrow (Depp), Will (Bloom), and Elizabeth (Knightley) can stop him. Oh, and Captain Barbossa (Rush, who steals every scene) is back, and Captain Jack's been swallowed by a sea monster, and Keith Richards is his dad. The plot is largely nonsensical, characters switch sides of the conflict from scene to scene, and much is lost to the hectic pace and CGI effects that jump off the screen. Still, the swashbuckling and action are excellent, and it all adds up to a fun, if overstuffed, mess of a movie. Enjoy it, just don't expect it to make sense. **168m/C DVD, Blu-ray Disc.** *US* Johnny Depp, Keira Knightley, Orlando Bloom, Geoffrey Rush, Bill Nighy, Chow Yun-Fat, Jack Davenport, Stellan Skarsgard, Jonathan Pryce, Naomie Harris, Tom Hollander, Kevin McNally, Mackenzie Crook, Martin Klebba, Lee Arenberg, Marshall Manesh; *D:* Gore Verbinski; *W:* Terry Rossio, Ted Elliott; *C:* Darius Wolski; *M:* Hans Zimmer.

Pirates of the Caribbean: Dead Man's Chest ✓✓ 1/2 **2006 (PG-13)** The second installment of Disney's amusement-park-ride-turned-flick finds Capt. Jack Sparrow (Depp) swishing and swashbuckling in and out of one perilous predicament after another. This time he must contend with a ghost ship full of half-men/half-sea creatures in an attempt to repay a debt. This absurdly long chapter serves up plenty of Depp hamming up one scene more than the next, with little substance nor a meaningful story, and seems to aspire merely to showing off the tens of millions likely spent on CGI and special effects. Somewhat effective follow-up doesn't have the charm of the first. This and the third installment were shot back-to-back. **150m/C DVD, Blu-ray Disc.** *US* Johnny Depp, Orlando Bloom, Keira Knightley, Stellan Skarsgard, Bill Nighy, Naomie Harris, Jack Davenport, Jonathan Pryce, Kevin McNally, Tom Hollander, Mackenzie Crook, Lee Arenberg, Alex Norton, David Bailie, Martin Klebba, David Schofield; *D:* Gore Verbinski; *W:* Ted Elliott, Terry Rossio; *C:* Darius Wolski; *M:* Hans Zimmer. Oscars '06: Visual FX; British Acad. '06: Visual FX.

Pirates of the Caribbean: The Curse of the Black Pearl ✓✓✓ **2003 (PG-13)** Yes, the film was inspired by the Disney theme park ride but unlike "The Country Bears," this one is a lot of fun, thanks primarily to star Depp. He swashes his buckle with addled glee as pirate captain Jack Sparrow—a cross, Depp said, between Keith Richards and Pepe Le Pew—whose ship, the Black Pearl, has been commandeered by Capt. Barbossa (Rush, having an equally good teeth-gnashing time). Barbossa and his crew are cursed and need a gold medallion, unwittingly held by feisty Governor's daughter Elizabeth (Knightley), to break the spell. This involves kidnapping the girl and a rescue mission led by her true love, blacksmith Will (Bloom), and Sparrow, who has a score to settle. There's a few too many plot twists and extended sword fights but the action and humor keep things moving along with relative ease. **134m/C VHS, DVD, Blu-ray Disc, UMD.** *US* Johnny Depp, Geoffrey Rush, Orlando Bloom, Keira Knightley, Jonathan Pryce, Jack Davenport, Kevin McNally, Zoe Saldana, Treva Etienne, Lee Arenberg, Trevor Goddard, David Bailie, Mackenzie Crook, Isaac C. Singleton Jr., Brye Cooper; *D:* Gore Verbinski; *W:* Ted Elliott, Terry Rossio; *C:* Darius Wolski; *M:* Klaus Badelt. British Acad. '03: Actor (Depp), Makeup; Screen Actors Guild '03: Actor (Depp).

Pirates of the Coast ✓ 1/2 **1961** A Spanish naval commander teams up with a group of pirates to even the score with an evil governor during the 1500s. **102m/C VHS.** Lex Barker, Estella Blain, Livio Lorenzon, Liana Orfei; *D:* Domenico Paolella.

Pirates of the High Seas ✓ 1/2 **1950** Crabbe helps a friend save his shipping line from sabotage. A serial in 15 chapters. **?m/C VHS.** Buster Crabbe, Lois Hall, Tommy Farrell, Gene Roth, Tristram Coffin; *D:* Spencer Gordon Bennet, Thomas Carr.

Pirates of the Seven Seas ✓ 1/2 **1962** In the further tales of "Sandokan the Great," the pirate hero helps save the heroine's father from an evil English Imperialist. **90m/C VHS.** Steve Reeves, Jacqueline Sassard, Andrea Bosic; *D:* Umberto Lenzi.

The Pirates Who Don't Do Anything: A VeggieTales Movie ✓✓ **2008 (G)** Three produce-aisle pals—a cucumber, a gourd, and a giant grape—find themselves transformed from dinner theater waiters into 17th-century pirates charged with the task of saving a princess and thwarting the bad guy. The faith-based, kid-friendly franchise backs off on its usual religiosity in favor of a more Oz-like tone to convey the virtues of moral fortitude, but the young'uns will be too into the bright colors, silly voices, and funny faces to care about the message, let alone the fact that the characters are fresh from the middle strata of the food pyramid. **85m/C DVD.** *US* *M:* Kurt Heinecke; *V:* Cam(eron) Clarke, Mike Nawrocki, Phil Vischer, Laura Gerow, Yuri Lowenthal.

Pistol Opera ✓ 1/2 *Pisutoru opera* **2002** Director Suzuki simultaneously does a remake, sequel, and parody of his 1967 film "Branded to Kill." Stray Cat is a female assassin, ranked as the Number 3 killer in her organization. She befriends Number 0 (the assassin from the original film) after she realizes all the hitmen are being manipulated into a contest to kill each other off to see who truly is the best. More art film than action movie, with so many surreal dream sequences that distinguishing them from the plot eventually becomes tricky. **112m/C DVD.** *JP* Makiko Esumi, Sayaka Yamaguchi, Hanae Kan, Mikijiro Hira, Kirin Kiki, Haruko Kato, Yoji Tanaka; *D:* Seijun Suzuki; *W:* Kazunori Ito, Takeo Kimura; *C:* Yonezo Maeda; *M:* Kodama Kzufumi.

Pistol: The Birth of a Legend ✓✓ 1/2 **1990 (G)** Biography of "Pistol" Pete Maravich, the basketball star who defied age limitations in the 1960s to play on his varsity team. **104m/C VHS, DVD.** Adam Guier, Nick Benedict, Boots Garland, Millie Perkins; *D:* Frank C. Schroeder; *W:* Darrel A. Campbell.

Pistol Whipped ✓ **2008 (R)** Seagal lumbers through with his usual inexpressiveness. Alcoholic ex-cop Matt has a gambling problem and big debts. So when a stranger (Henriksen) offers to take care of Matt's money issues in exchange for his assassinating some mobsters, he's not as unwilling as you might imagine. Of course, it's just not that simple. The real problem is that there's not enough Henriksen onscreen. **96m/C DVD.** Steven Seagal, Lance Henriksen, Paul Calderon, Blanchard Ryan, Renee Goldsberry, Lydia Grace Jordan; *D:* Roel Reine; *W:* J.D. Zeik; *C:* Richard Crudo; *M:* Jerry Brunskill.

Pistoleros Asesinos ✓✓ **1987** Plenty of action, plus a little romance, when a man falls in love with a crooked landowner's daughter and must battle her father's henchmen for her hand. **83m/C VHS.** *SP* Maria de Lourdes, Federico Villa, Victor Alcocer, Arturo Benavides, Polo Ortin, Rosa Gloria; *D:* Angel Rodriguez Vazquez.

The Pit ✓ 1/2 **1981 (R)** Autistic boy gets his chance for revenge. The townspeople who humiliate him are in for a surprise after he stumbles across a huge hole in the forest, at the bottom of which are strange and deadly creatures. **96m/C VHS, DVD.** Sammy Snyders, Sonja Smits, Jeannie Elias, Laura Hollingsworth; *D:* Lew Lehman.

The Pit and the Pendulum ✓✓✓ **1961** A woman and her lover plan to drive her brother mad, and he responds by locking them in his torture chamber, which was built by his loony dad, whom he now thinks he is. Standard Corman production only remotely derived from the classic Poe tale, with the cast chewing on a loopy script. A landmark in Gothic horror. **80m/C VHS, DVD.** Vincent Price, John Kerr, Barbara Steele, Luana Anders, Antony Carbone, Charles Victor, Lynn Bernay, Patrick Westwood; *D:* Roger Corman; *W:* Richard Matheson; *C:* Floyd Crosby; *M:* Les Baxter.

The Pit & the Pendulum ✓✓ 1/2 **1991 (R)** Retelling of the classic Poe short story, mixed with his "A Cask of Amantillado" and set during the Spanish Inquisition. Great special effects and professional scary guy, Lance Henriksen. **97m/C VHS, DVD.** Lance Henriksen, Rona De Ricci, Jonathan Fuller, Jeffrey Combs, Tom Towler, Stephen Lee, Frances Bay, Oliver Reed; *D:* Stuart Gordon; *W:* Dennis Paoli; *M:* Richard Band.

Pit Fighter ✓✓ **2005 (R)** A pit fighter suffering from amnesia, now living in Mexico, comes under the gun once old enemies find out he's not dead. Over-the-top low budget fight flick manages to pack a decent punch/dropkick combo. Its exaggerated style whoops its doofus plot. **84m/C DVD.** Steven Bauer, Stephen Graham, Stana Katic, Dominiquie Vandenberg; *D:* Jesse Johnson; *W:* Jesse Johnson; *C:* Robert Hayes; *M:* Marcello De Francisci. **VIDEO**

Pit Stop ✓✓✓ **1967** On the DVD commentary track, director Jack Hill admits that he made this movie quickly to capitalize on the short-lived phenomenon of figure-8 racing, where the shape of the track guarantees many crashes. Brian Donlevy is the promoter who involves young racers Sid Haig and Dick Davalos in his plans. **91m/B DVD.** Brian Donlevy, Richard (Dick) Davalos, Ellen Burstyn, Sid Haig, Beverly Washburn; *D:* Jack Hill; *W:* Jack Hill; *C:* Austin McKinney.

Pitch Black ✓✓✓ **2000 (R)** Scary sci-fier with some familiar elements. Freak meteor storm causes a spaceship to make a crash landing on an unknown planet with three suns and apparently no life. Hah! In this version of "they only come out at night," the survivors discover that very nasty hunting creatures attack after dark—and the planet is in for a total eclipse. Diesel gives a hard-ass performance as a convicted murderer who has nothing to lose. Shot in Queensland, Australia. **108m/C VHS, DVD, UMD, HD DVD.** Vin Diesel, Radha Mitchell, Cole Hauser, Keith David, Lewis Fitz-Gerald, John Moore, Simon Burke, Claudia Black, Rhiana Griffith; ***D:*** David N. Twohy, Jim Wheat, Ken Wheat; ***W:*** David N. Twohy; ***C:*** David Eggby; ***M:*** Graeme Revell.

Pitfall **1948** Gritty tale in which an insurance salesman, bored with his routine suburban life and family, follows his less noble instincts—and finds himself up to his ears in stolen goods, adultery and murder. **85m/B VHS.** Dick Powell, Jane Wyatt, Lizabeth Scott, Raymond Burr, John Litel, Byron Barr, Ann Doran, Jimmy Hunt, Selmer Jackson, Margaret Wells, Dick Wessel; ***D:*** Andre de Toth; ***W:*** Karl Kamb; ***C:*** Harry Wild; ***M:*** Louis Forbes.

Pittsburgh **1942** Slow-moving drama about a love triangle combined with class differences. Dietrich loves Wayne, but he's more interested in the coal and steel business, so rival Scott steps in. Although limited by standard plot, picture works because of excellent performances by leads. Based on a screen story by George Owen and Tom Reed. **98m/B VHS, DVD.** Marlene Dietrich, Randolph Scott, John Wayne, Frank Craven, Louise Allbritton, Shemp Howard, Thomas Gomez, Ludwig Stossel; ***D:*** Lewis Seiler; ***W:*** Kenneth Gamet, Tom Reed, John Twist.

Pittsburgh 1/2 **2006** Actor Goldblum (playing himself) agrees to do a two-week regional theater production of "The Music Man" in his Pennsylvania hometown, because he's in love with the young actress (Wreford) who's cast as Marion the Librarian. He drags a bunch of friends into the production as well and, since Goldblum is hardly a natural for the singing/dancing title role, he undergoes quite a bit of humiliation before opening night. **84m/C DVD.** Jeff Goldblum, Illeana Douglas, Ed Begley Jr., Moby, Catherine Wreford, Richard Sabellico; ***D:*** Christopher Bradley, Kyle LaBrache; ***C:*** Christopher Bradley, Kyle LaBrache; ***M:*** David Byrne.

Pixote *Pixote: A Lei do Mais Fraco* **1981** Wrenching, documentary-like account of an orphan-boy's life on the streets in a Brazil metropolis. Graphic and depressing, it's not for all tastes but nonetheless masterfully done. In Portuguese with English subtitles. **127m/C VHS, DVD.** *BR* Fernando Ramos Da Silva, Marilia Pera, Jorge Juliao, Gilberto Moura, Jose Nilson dos Santos, Edilson Lino; ***D:*** Hector Babenco; ***W:*** Hector Babenco; ***C:*** Rodolfo Sanchez; ***M:*** John Neschling. L.A. Film Critics '81: Foreign Film; N.Y. Film Critics '81: Foreign Film; Natl. Soc. Film Critics '81: Actress (Pera).

Pizza 1/2 **2005** This pizza has a lot of extra cheese. An overweight misfit, Cara-Ethyl (Sparks) throws herself an 18th birthday party, but none of the guests show up. Finally, pizza delivery guy Matt (Embry) arrives. Maybe he feels sorry for her, 'cause Matt invites C-E to come along on his pizza runs. Misadventure and strangeness ensue while the two bond. **82m/C DVD.** *US* Kylie Sparks, Ethan (Randall) Embry, Julie Hagerty, Joey Kern, Alexis Dziena, Mary Birdsong, Marylouise Burke, Richard Easton, Miriam Shor, Judah Friedlander; ***D:*** Mark Christopher; ***W:*** Mark Christopher; ***C:*** Ken Ferris; ***M:*** John Kimbrough.

Pizza Man 1/2 **1991 (PG-13)** Pizza deliveryman Elmo Bunn is minding his own business, delivering an extra large with anchovies and sausage, when he finds himself mixed up in a political scandal. Lawton directed under alias "J.D. Athens." **90m/C VHS.** Bill Maher, Annabelle Gurwitch; ***D:*** J.F. Lawton; ***W:*** J.F. Lawton.

Pizzicata **1996** When an American fighter plane is shot down over southern Italy in 1943, the pilot, Italian-American Tony Marciano (Frascaro), is rescued by peasant family, the Panaleos, who nurse the wounded man despite the danger. When Tony is discovered by a neighbor, he pretends to be a family cousin and tries to fit into the community—all the while falling for young Cosima Panaleo (Torelli), even though she's engaged to Paquale (Massafra). During a community dance, everyone's feelings become dramatically clear. Italian with subtitles. **93m/C VHS.** *IT* Fabio Frascaro, Chiara Torelli, Cosimo Cinieri, Paolo Massafra; ***D:*** Edoardo Winspeare; ***W:*** Edoardo Winspeare; ***C:*** Paolo Carnera.

P.K. and the Kid **1985** A runaway kid meets up with a factory worker on his way to an arm wrestling competition and they become friends. **90m/C VHS.** Molly Ringwald, Paul LeMat, Alex Rocco, John Madden, Esther Rolle; ***D:*** Lou Lombardo; ***W:*** Neal Barbera; ***M:*** James Horner.

A Place Called Glory *Die Holle von Manitoba* **1966** Barker comes to the aid of the local townsfolk in Glory city who have their hands full with a gang of bloodthirsty outlaws. **92m/C VHS.** *GE SP* Lex Barker, Pierre Brice, Marianne Koch; ***D:*** Sheldon Reynolds; ***W:*** Edward Di Lorenzo; ***C:*** Federico G. Larraya; ***M:*** Angel Arteaga.

A Place Called Today *City in Fear* **1972** Sordid tale of big city politics where violence and fear in the streets is at the heart of the campaign. **105m/C VHS.** Cheri Caffaro, J. Herbert Kerr Jr., Lana Wood, Richard Smedley, Timothy Brown; ***D:*** Don Schain.

A Place Called Truth 1/2 **1998 (R)** A millionaire's daughter has an affair with the hired help, which incites the jealousy of her best friend and the wrath of her father. **95m/C VHS.** Audie England, Brion James, Jacqueline Lovell, Chris Browning, Joseph Whipp, Valerie Perrine, Anthony Addabbo; ***D:*** Rafael Eisenman. **VIDEO**

A Place for Annie 1/2 **1994 (PG)** Lots of tears in this drama of devoted pediatrics nurse Susan Lansing (Spacek) who decides to become the foster mother of abandoned baby girl Annie, who's been diagnosed as HIV-positive. Then Annie's destitute birth mom (Parker), a former junkie dying of AIDS, resurfaces and decides she wants her daughter back. Sputters into melodrama but good performances by strong women, including Plowright as the nanny and Merkerson as a concerned hospital social worker. Based on a true story. **98m/C VHS.** Sissy Spacek, Mary-Louise Parker, Joan Plowright, S. Epatha Merkerson, Jack Noseworthy; ***D:*** John Gray; ***W:*** Cathleen Young, Lee Guthrie. **TV**

Place in Hell 1/2 **1969** The Japanese armed forces camouflage a Pacific island beach which they are holding and invite the American forces to invade it during WWII. **106m/C VHS.** *IT* Guy Madison, Helene Chanel, Monty Greenwood; ***D:*** Giuseppe Vari; ***W:*** Adriano Bolzoni; ***C:*** Stelvio Massi; ***M:*** Roberto Pregadio.

A Place in the Sun **1951** Melodramatic adaptation of "An American Tragedy," Theodore Dreiser's realist classic about an ambitious laborer whose aspirations to the high life with a gorgeous debutante are threatened by his lower-class lover's pregnancy. Clift is magnificent in the lead, and Taylor and Winters also shine in support. Burr, however, grossly overdoes his role of the vehement prosecutor. Still, not a bad effort from somewhat undisciplined director Stevens. **120m/B VHS, DVD.** Montgomery Clift, Elizabeth Taylor, Shelley Winters, Raymond Burr, Anne Revere, Keefe Brasselle, Shepperd Strudwick, Herbert (Hayes) Heyes, Frieda Inescort; ***D:*** George Stevens; ***W:*** Harry Brown, Michael Wilson; ***C:*** William Mellor; ***M:*** Franz Waxman. Oscars '51: B&W Cinematog., Costume Des. (B&W), Director (Stevens), Film Editing, Screenplay, Orig. Dramatic Score; AFI '98: Top 100; Directors Guild '51: Director (Stevens); Golden Globes '52: Film—Drama, Natl. Film Reg. '91.

A Place in the World **1992** Returning from exile to their native Argentina during a military dictatorship, Mario and Ana (Luppi and Roth) work to help the less advantaged in their society, determined to make a difference. Story is seen as a flashback from point-of-view of the couples' son Ernesto (Batyi). Well-crafted, finely acted piece exploring political, social, and interpersonal themes. 1993 Oscar bid retracted due to controversy over country of film's origin. **120m/C VHS.** *AR* Jose Sacristan, Federico Luppi, Cecilia (Celia) Roth, Leonor Benedetto, Gaston Batyi, Lorena Del Rio; ***D:*** Adolfo Aristarain; ***W:*** Alberto Lecchi, Adolfo Aristarain; ***C:*** Ricardo De Angelis; ***M:*** Emilio Kauderer.

Place of Execution 1/2 **2009** In 1963, 13-year-old Alison goes missing from the village of Scardale and young inspector George Bennett (Ingleby) becomes obsessed with the case. Alison's bloody clothing is eventually found (but no body) and her wealthy, pervy stepfather Philip Hawkin (Wise) is accused of her murder after Bennett finds porn photos of Alison. Forty years later, filmmaker Catherine Heathcote (Stevenson) is making a documentary about the case with extensive interviews with the retired Bennett (Jackson) who suddenly withdraws his cooperation. Obsessive herself, Catherine starts digging deeper and discovers a miscarriage of justice may have occurred that leads back to George. Based on the novel by Val McDermid. **140m/C DVD.** *GB* Juliet Stevenson, Lee Ingleby, Philip Jackson, Greg Wise, Emma Cunniffe, Tony Maudsley, David Hill, Elizabeth Day, Zoe Telford, Danny Sapani; ***D:*** Daniel Percival; ***W:*** Patrick Harbinson; ***C:*** Steve Lawes; ***M:*** The Insects. **TV**

Place of Weeping 1/2 **1986 (PG)** Early entry in the anti-apartheid sweepstakes (made in South Africa, no less). A South African woman opposes her nation's racist policies. A reporter supports her. **88m/C VHS.** *SA* James Whylie, Geini Mhlophe; ***D:*** Darrell Roodt.

Place Vendome **1998** Deneuve stars as elegant alcoholic Marianne Malivert, who finds a new interest after her husband's (Fresson) suicide. A prominent jeweler with a shop on the fashionable Place Vendome, he was unable to confess that the business is bankrupt and his connections shady. Instead, he leaves Marianne with seven priceless diamonds that turn out to be stolen, which rekindles her business instincts (she's a former gem broker) and places her in danger. French with subtitles; originally released at 117 minutes. **105m/C VHS, DVD.** *FR* Catherine Deneuve, Jean-Pierre Bacri, Emmanuelle Seigner, Jacques Dutronc, Bernard Fresson, Francois Berleand, Philippe Clevenot; ***D:*** Nicole Garcia; ***W:*** Nicole Garcia, Jacques Fieschi; ***C:*** Laurent Dailland; ***M:*** Richard Robbins.

Places in the Heart **1984 (PG)** A young widow determines to make the best of a bad situation on a small farm in Depression-era Texas, fighting poverty, racism, and sexism while enduring back-breaking labor. Support group includes a blind veteran and a black drifter. Hokey but nonetheless moving film is improved significantly by strong performances by virtually everyone in the cast. In his debut, Malkovich shines through this stellar group. Effective dust-bowl photography by Nestor Almendros. **113m/C VHS, DVD.** Sally Field, John Malkovich, Danny Glover, Ed Harris, Lindsay Crouse, Amy Madigan, Terry O'Quinn, Ned Dowd, Ray Baker; ***D:*** Robert Benton; ***W:*** Robert Benton; ***C:*** Nestor Almendros; ***M:*** Howard Shore. Oscars '84: Actress (Field), Orig. Screenplay; Golden Globes '85: Actress—Drama (Field); Natl. Bd. of Review '84: Support. Actor (Malkovich); N.Y. Film Critics '84: Screenplay; Natl. Soc. Film Critics '84: Support. Actor (Malkovich).

The Plague 1/2 **1992 (R)** An outbreak of bubonic plague has turned the South American city of Oran into a prison, with no one permitted to leave until the disease has run its course. Hurt is the doctor trying to balance his duties with his own fears. Necessarily bleak adaptation of the Albert Camus novel is also slow-moving and long-winded—an equally deadly combination for the viewer. **105m/C VHS.** *FR SP* William Hurt, Robert Duvall, Raul Julia, Sandrine Bonnaire, Jean-Marc Barr; ***D:*** Luis Puenzo.

The Plague Dogs **1982** Two dogs carrying a plague escape from a research center and are tracked down in this unlikely animated film. A bit ponderous. And yes, that is Hurt's voice. From the novel by Richard Adams, author of "Watership Down." **99m/C VHS, DVD.** ***D:*** Martin Rosen; ***W:*** Martin Rosen; ***M:*** Patrick Gleeson; ***V:*** John Hurt, Christopher Benjamin, Judy Geeson, Barbara Leigh-Hunt, Patrick Stewart.

Plague of the Zombies 1/2 **1966** The local doctor in a Cornish village gets suspicious when its inhabitants begin suddenly dying off and the local squire refuses to allow any autopsies. That's because he's learned voodoo rites while staying in Haiti and is turning the dead locals into zombies. **90m/C VHS, DVD.** *GB* Andre Morell, John Carson, Diane Clare, Alex Davion, Jacqueline Pearce, Brook Williams, Michael Ripper, Marcus Hammond, Roy Royston; ***D:*** John Gilling; ***W:*** Peter Bryan, John (Anthony Hinds) Elder; ***C:*** Arthur Grant; ***M:*** James Bernard.

Plain Clothes 1/2 **1988 (PG)** An undercover cop masquerades as a high school student to solve the murder of a teacher. He endures all the trials that made him hate high school the first time around. **98m/C VHS.** Arliss Howard, George Wendt, Suzy Amis, Diane Ladd, Abe Vigoda, Robert Stack, Seymour Cassel, Larry Pine, Jackie Gayle, Alexandra Powers, Peter Dobson, Harry Shearer, Loren Dean, Reginald VelJohnson, Max Perlich; ***D:*** Martha Coolidge; ***W:*** Scott Frank; ***M:*** Scott Wilk.

Plain Dirty *Briar Patch; Killing Edgar* **2004 (R)** Abused wife Inez (Swain) has smitten local hermit Flowers (Verveen) help kill her husband (Thomas) then runs of with a rich lawyer (Urbaniak). Well, Flowers is none too pleased with that development, and sets out to vent his displeasure. Allusions to Shakespeare's MacBeth somehow work for this literate Southern Gothic tale, and the cinematography makes great use of the Virginia setting. **103m/C VHS, DVD.** Dominique Swain, Henry Thomas, Arie Verveen, James Urbaniak, Karen Allen, Debra Monk, Blake Lindsley; ***D:*** Zev Berman; ***W:*** Christian Carion; ***C:*** Scott Kevan; ***M:*** Nathan Barr. **VIDEO**

Plain Jane 1/2 **2001** In 1911, David Bruce (Whately) has just moved to London with his wife (Manville) and baby daughter. Newly prosperous, the family can afford to hire live-in maid, Jane (Cunniffe). But David begins to take too much of an interest in Jane (and doesn't realize that his grown son is also involved with her) and sexual obsession leads to murder. **150m/C VHS, DVD.** *GB* Kevin Whately, Emma Cunniffe, Lesley Manville, Jason Hughes; ***D:*** John Woods; ***W:*** Lucy Gannon; ***M:*** Ray Russell. **TV**

Plain Truth 1/2 **2004** Lifetime movie based on the book by Jodi Picoult. Amish teenager Katie Finch is accused of killing her baby and Philadelphia defense attorney Ellie Harrison is called in to represent her. In order to get Katie out of jail, Ellie becomes her legal guardian and moves into the Fitch family home. Ellie also needs Katie to open up about her pregnancy, which Katie has been denying. **90m/C DVD.** Mariska Hargitay, Alison Pill, Jan Niklas, Kate Trotter, Robert Bockstael, Jonathan LaPaglia, Alex McClure; ***D:*** Paul Shapiro; ***W:*** Matthew Tabak; ***C:*** David (Robert) A. Greene; ***M:*** Yves Laferriere. **CABLE**

The Plainsman 1/2 **1937** Western legends Wild Bill Hickock, Buffalo Bill, and Calamity Jane team up for adventure in this big, empty venture. Just about what you'd expect from splashy director DeMille. **113m/B VHS, DVD.** Gary Cooper, Jean Arthur, Charles Bickford, Anthony Quinn, George "Gabby" Hayes, Porter Hall, James Mason; ***D:*** Cecil B. DeMille; ***C:*** Victor Milner.

Plan B 1/2 **1997** Comedy, set between Halloween and New Year's Eve, about a group of 30-ish friends who realize their lives aren't going the way they'd planned. Waiter Stuart (Cryer) despairs of being a serious writer and has instead penned a lurid serial killer novel; aspiring actor Ricky (Matheison) freaks about growing older; Gina (Mornell) is successful in business but unlucky in love; while Gina's older sister Clare (Darr) is happily married to Jack (Guest) but fretting over not being a mother yet. It's pretty familiar but not a complete waste of time, thanks to the appealing cast. **102m/C VHS.** Jon Cryer, Mark Matheison, Sara Mornell, Lisa Darr, Lance Guest; ***D:*** Gary Leva; ***W:*** Gary Leva; ***C:*** Yoram Astrakhan; ***M:*** Andrew Rose.

Plan 9 from Outer Space WOOF! *Grave Robbers from Outer Space* **1956** Two or three aliens in silk pajamas conspire to resurrect several slow-moving zombies from a cardboard graveyard in order to conquer the Earth. Spaceships that look suspiciously like paper plates blaze across the sky. Pitiful, inadvertently hilarious fright worth a look if you're desperate to kill time since it's in the running for the "dumbest movie ever made" award. Lugosi's actual screen time is under two minutes, since he had the good sense to die before the film was complete. Enjoy the taller and younger replacement (the chiropractor of Wood's wife) they found for Lugosi, who remains hooded to protect his identity. **78m/B VHS, DVD.** Bela Lugosi, Tor Johnson, Lyle Talbot, Vampira, Gregory Walcott, Tom Keene, Dudley Manlove, Mona McKinnon, Duke Moore, Joanna Lee, Bunny Breckinridge, Criswell, Carl Anthony, Paul Marco, Norma McCarty, David DeMering, Bill Ash, Conrad Brooks, Karl Johnson, Edward D. Wood Jr.; ***D:*** Edward D. Wood Jr.; ***W:*** Edward D. Wood Jr.; ***C:*** William C. Thompson; ***M:*** Trevor Duncan, Van Phillips, James Stevens, Bruce Campbell.

Plan 10 from Outer Space 1/2 **1995** The play on the infamous Ed Wood title is the only connection between the two fringe features as director Harris takes aim at his hometown of Salt Lake City, Utah. Heroine Lucinda (Russell) discovers a mysterious bronze plaque buried near the Great Salt Lake and uncovers a UFO conspiracy loosely conforming to Mormon mythology. There's a basic mass hysteria/alien invasion scene, cheesy special effects, dumb sexual humor, and not much else. **82m/C VHS.** Stefene Russell, Pat Collins, Curtis James, Karen Black; ***D:*** Trent Harris; ***W:*** Trent Harris; ***C:*** Bryan Duggan; ***M:*** Fredric Myrow.

Planes, Trains & Automobiles 1/2 **1987 (R)** One-joke Hughes comedy saved by Martin and Candy. Strait-laced businessman Neal Page (played straight by Martin) on the way home for Thanksgiving meets up with a oafish, bad-luck-ridden boor Del Griffith (Candy) who turns his efforts to get home upside down. Martin and Candy both turn in fine performances, and effectively straddle a thin line between true pathos and hilarious buffoonery. Bacon and McClurg, both Hughes alumni, have small but funny roles. **93m/C VHS, DVD.** Steve Martin, John Candy, Edie McClurg, Kevin Bacon, Michael McKean, William Windom, Laila Robins, Martin Ferrero, Charles Tyner, Dylan Baker, Ben Stein, Lyman Ward; ***D:*** John Hughes; ***W:*** John Hughes; ***C:*** Don Peterman; ***M:*** Ira Newborn.

Planet Burg 1/2 **1962** A classic Soviet sci-fi flick about a space exploration team landing on Venus. Their job becomes a rescue mission when one of the crew is stranded. Although there are some silly moments, some good plot twists and acting make up for them. In Russian with English subtitles. **90m/C VHS.** *RU* Vladimir Temelianov, Gennadi Vernov, Kyunna Ignatova; ***D:*** Pavel Klushantsev.

Planet Earth 1/2 **1974** In the year 2133, a man who has been in suspended animation for 154 years is revived to lead the troops against a violent group of women (and mutants, too!). **78m/C VHS.** John Saxon, Janet Margolin, Ted Cassidy, Diana Muldaur, Johana DeWinter, Christopher Gary; ***D:*** Marc Daniels.

Planet 51 1/2 **2009 (PG)** American astronaut Chuck Baker (voiced by Johnson, aka The Rock) thinks he's the first to walk on Planet 51, but quickly discovers he's not alone. The green inhabitants are nice, suburban families who live with only one fear—being invaded by aliens, like Chuck. Now all he wants to do is avoid capture and get his spaceship back to Earth. Luckily a friendly teen named Lem (Long) helps him out when General Grawl (Oldman) and wacky scientist professor Kipple (Cleese) tell the locals that Chuck is out to get them and the pursuit begins. A 1950s Hollywood sci-fi idea turned into a vice-versa animated family cartoon. Nice and cute, though loaded with '50s pop references that most kids won't get. **91m/C DVD.** *US* ***D:*** Jorge Blanco, Javier Abad, Marcos Martinez; ***W:*** Joe Stillman; ***M:*** James Seymour Brett; ***V:*** Dwayne "The Rock" Johnson, Jessica Biel, Justin Long, Seann William Scott, Gary Oldman, John Cleese.

Planet of Blood *Queen of Blood* **1966** Space opera about an alien vampire discovered on Mars by a rescue team. If you've ever seen the Soviet film "Niebo Zowiet," don't be surprised if some scenes look familiar; the script was written around segments cut from that film. **81m/C VHS, DVD.** John Saxon, Basil Rathbone, Judi Meredith, Dennis Hopper, Florence Marly, Forrest J Ackerman; ***D:*** Curtis Harrington; ***W:*** Curtis Harrington; ***C:*** Vilis Lapenieks; ***M:*** Leonard Morand.

Planet of the Apes 1/2 **1968 (G)** Astronauts crash land on a planet where apes are masters and humans are merely brute animals. Superior science fiction with sociological implications marred only by unnecessary humor. Heston delivers one of his more plausible performances. Superb ape makeup creates realistic pseudo-simians of McDowall, Hunter, Evans, Whitmore, and Daly. Adapted from Pierre Boulle's novel "Monkey Planet." Followed by four sequels and two TV series. **112m/C VHS, DVD, Blu-ray Disc.** Charlton Heston, Roddy McDowall, Kim Hunter, Maurice Evans, Linda Harrison, James Whitmore, James Daly; ***D:*** Franklin J. Schaffner; ***W:*** Rod Serling, Michael Wilson; ***C:*** Leon Shamroy; ***M:*** Jerry Goldsmith. Natl. Film Reg. '01.

Planet of the Apes **2001 (PG-13)** Burton's "re-imagining" of the story looks more to the original novel by Pierre Boulle than it does to the 1968 classic. Wahlberg, as generic action hero Leo Davidson, takes over the Heston role, but with nowhere near the bravado or screen presence. Roth excels as Gen. Thade, an angry militarist with a loathing for all humans and a contempt for polite ape society. Needless to say, Leo becomes the focus for his rage. Come to think of it, all of the actors in the ape makeup do a fine job. The makeup effects, courtesy of Rick Baker, are astounding (and light-years ahead of where they were in '68), and the action moves along at a satisfyingly brisk pace. The screenplay provides plenty of sly and clever references to the original, but doesn't have its sense of social commentary (this is, after all, a summer blockbuster). What it does have is a twist ending that seems tacked on for the purpose of setting up a sequel. **125m/C VHS, DVD, Blu-ray Disc, UMD.** *US* Mark Wahlberg, Tim Roth, Helena Bonham Carter, Michael Clarke Duncan, Paul Giamatti, Estella Warren, Cary-Hiroyuki Tagawa, David Warner, Kris Kristofferson, Erik Avari, Luke Eberl, Charlton Heston, Evan Dexter Parke, Michael Jace; ***D:*** Tim Burton; ***W:*** William Broyles Jr., Larry Konner, Mark Rosenthal; ***C:*** Philippe Rousselot; ***M:*** Danny Elfman. Golden Raspberries '01: Worst Remake/Sequel, Worst Support. Actor (Heston), Worst Support. Actress (Warren).

Planet of the Dinosaurs 1/2 **1980 (PG)** Survivors from a ruined spaceship combat huge savage dinosaurs on a swampy uncharted planet. **85m/C VHS, DVD.** James Whitworth, Max (Michael) Thayer, Louie Lawless, Pamela Bottaro, Charlotte Speer; ***D:*** James K. Shea; ***W:*** Ralph Lucas.

Planet of the Vampires 1/2 *The Demon Planet; The Haunted Planet; The Outlawed Planet; Planet of Blood; Planet of Terror; Planet of the Damned; Space Mutants; Terror in Space; Terrore nello Spazio; Terreur dans l'Espace* **1965** Astronauts search for missing comrades on a planet dominated by mind-bending forces. Acceptable atmospheric filmmaking from genre master Bava, but it's not among his more compelling ventures. **86m/C VHS, DVD.** *IT SP* Barry Sullivan, Norma Bengell, Angel Aranda, Evi Marandi, Stelio Candelli, Ivan Rassimov, Fernando Villena; ***D:*** Mario Bava; ***W:*** Mario Bava, Alberto Bevilacqua, Callisto Cosulich, Louis M. Heyward, Ib Melchior, Antonio Roman, Rafael J. Salvia; ***C:*** Antonio Rinaldi; ***M:*** Gino Marinuzzi Jr.

Planet on the Prowl *War Between the Planets* **1965** A fiery planet causes earthly disasters, so a troop of wily astronauts try to destroy it with the latest technology. They fail, leading one sacrificial soul to do it himself. **80m/C VHS, DVD.** *IT* Giacomo "Jack" Rossi-Stuart, Amber Collins, Peter Martellanza, John Bartha, Halina Zalewska, James Weaver; ***D:*** Anthony M. Dawson.

Planet Terror 1/2 *Robert Rodriguez's Planet Terror; Grindhouse: Planet Terror* **2007** For the first time in his career, Rodriguez trumps his pal Quentin Tarantino by directing the better half of the Weinstein Bros. B-movie double-feature "Grindhouse." Almost every schlock-film cliche makes an appearance, which is the point, really. After a rogue military team sets loose a nerve gas that turns people into surprisingly gross zombies, it's up to El Wray (Rodriguez), his gal Cherry Darling (McGowan), and a gaggle of terrified Texans to try to stop the gas from spreading. McGowan steals the show with her M16-prosthetic leg, but the flurry of cheap thrills starts to feel... well... "cheap" after an hour or so. **105m/C DVD, Blu-ray Disc.** Rose McGowan, Freddy Rodriguez, Josh Brolin, Marley Shelton, Jeff Fahey, Michael Biehn, Bruce Willis, Naveen Andrews, Julio Oscar Mechoso, Stacy "Fergie" Ferguson, Nicky Katt, Tom Savini, Carlos Gallardo, Michael Parks, Quentin Tarantino, Rebel Rodriguez; ***D:*** Robert Rodriguez; ***W:*** Robert Rodriguez; ***C:*** Robert Rodriguez; ***M:*** Graeme Revell.

Planets Against Us 1/2 *I Pianeti Contro di Noi; The Man with the Yellow Eyes; Hands of a Killer; The Monster with Green Eyes* **1961** Science fiction tale of escaped alien humanoid robots who take refuge on Earth, but whose touch is fatal. Good special effects. **85m/B VHS.** *IT FR* Michel Lemoine, Maria Pia Luzi, Jany Clair; ***D:*** Romano Ferrara.

The Plastic Age 1/2 **1925** Cynthia (Bow) is a flapper college babe who likes boys and parties. She easily manages to charm naive newcomer Hugh (Keith), who pays more attention to her than his athletic career. But Cynthia's not heartless—when she sees that Hugh is ruining his chances, she decides to give him up. **73m/B VHS, DVD.** Clara Bow, Donald Keith, Gilbert Roland, Henry B. Walthall, Mary Alden; ***D:*** Wesley Ruggles; ***W:*** Eve Unsell, Frederica Sagor; ***C:*** Gilbert Warrenton, Allen Siegler.

Platinum Blonde **1931** Screwball comedy in which a newspaper journalist (Williams) marries a wealthy girl (Harlow) but finds that he doesn't like the restrictions and confinement of high society. Yearning for a creative outlet, he decides to write a play and hires a reporter (Young) to collaborate with him. The results are funny and surprising when Young shows up at the mansion flanked by a group of hard-drinking, fun-loving reporters. **86m/B VHS, DVD.** Loretta Young, Robert Williams, Jean Harlow, Louise Closser Hale; ***D:*** Frank Capra; ***W:*** Jo Swerling, Dorothy Howell.

Platinum High School 1/2 *Trouble at 16; Rich, Young, and Deadly* **1960** Divorced father Rooney is appalled when his son is "accidentally" killed while off at an exclusive military academy. His suspicions are aroused by the prevaricating school commander and he discovers some horrible truths about his son's death and life at the school. **91m/B VHS.** Mickey Rooney, Terry Moore, Dan Duryea, Conway Twitty, Warren Berlinger, Yvette Mimieux, Jimmy Boyd, Richard Jaeckel, Harold Lloyd Jr., Elisha Cook Jr., Jimmy Murphy; ***D:*** Charles F. Haas; ***W:*** Robert Smith; ***M:*** Van Alexander.

Platoon 1/2 **1986 (R)** A grunt's view of the Vietnam War is provided in all its horrific, inexplicable detail. Sheen is wooden in the lead, but both Dafoe and Berenger are resplendent as, respectively, good and bad soldiers. Strong, visceral filmmaking from fearless director Stone, who based the film on his own GI experiences. Highly acclaimed; considered by many to be the most realistic portrayal of the war on film. **113m/C VHS, DVD.** Charlie Sheen, Willem Dafoe, Tom Berenger, Francesco Quinn, Forest Whitaker, John C. McGinley, Kevin Dillon, Richard Edson, Reggie Johnson, Keith David, Johnny Depp, Dale Dye, Mark Moses, Chris Pederson, David Neidorf, Tony Todd, Ivan Kane, Paul Sanchez, Corey Glover, Oliver Stone; ***D:*** Oliver Stone; ***W:*** Oliver Stone; ***C:*** Robert Richardson; ***M:*** Georges Delerue. Oscars '86: Director (Stone), Film Editing, Picture, Sound; AFI '98: Top 100; British Acad. '87: Director (Stone); Directors Guild '86: Director (Stone); Golden Globes '87: Director (Stone), Film—Drama, Support. Actor (Berenger); Ind. Spirit '87: Cinematog., Director (Stone), Film, Screenplay.

Platoon Leader **1987 (R)** A battle-drenched portrait of a West Point lieutenant in Vietnam. When he first arrives, he must win the trust of his men, who have been on their tours for a much longer time. As time goes on, he slowly becomes hardened to the realities of the brutal life in the field. Made on the heels of the widely acclaimed "Platoon," but it doesn't have the same power. Norris is martial arts king Chuck Norris' brother. **97m/C VHS.** Michael Dudikoff, Brian Libby, Robert F. Lyons, Rick Fitts, Jesse Dabson, William (Bill) Smith, Michael Delorenzo; ***D:*** Aaron Norris; ***W:*** R.J. Marx; ***M:*** George S. Clinton.

Platoon the Warriors **1988** The underworld rages with violence when two kingpins, Rex and Bill, become bitter and declare war over a botched drug deal. **90m/C VHS.** David Coley, Dick Crown, James Miller, Don Richard, Alex Sylvian; ***D:*** Philip Ko.

Plato's Run **1996 (R)** Ex-CIA agent agrees to free a Cuban who's been falsely imprisoned. But once the job is done, the agent learns he's been doublecrossed and the prisoner turns out to be a professional assassin. **96m/C VHS, DVD.** Gary Busey, Roy Scheider, Steven Bauer, Jeff Speakman; ***D:*** James Becket; ***W:*** James Becket; ***C:*** Richard Clabaugh; ***M:*** Robert O. Ragland.

Platypus Cove **1986** An adopted boy tracks down the culprits responsible for the sabotage of his family's boat, a crime for which he was suspected. Australian. **72m/C VHS.** Paul Smith; ***D:*** Peter Maxwell.

Play Dead *Satan's Dog* **1981** Poor Yvonne De Carlo plays a psychotic woman who trains a dog to rip people to shreds. **89m/C VHS.** Yvonne De Carlo, Stephanie Dunham, David Culliname, Glenn Kezer, Ron Jackson, Carolyn Greenwood; ***D:*** Peter Wittman.

Play for Me *Toca Para Mi* **2001** Punk rock drummer Carlos goes on a search for identity after his adoptive father dies. He travels to the town of his birth in the Argentine pampas and meets hooker Fabiana who helps him on his journey. Spanish with subtitles. **101m/C VHS, DVD.** *AR* Hermes Gaido, Maria Laura Frigerio, Alejandro Fiore, Emilio Urdapilleta; ***D:*** Rodrigo Furth; ***W:*** Rodrigo Furth, Eduardo Ruderman; ***C:*** Paula Grandio; ***M:*** Fernando Manuel Dieguez.

Play It Again, Sam 1/2 **1972 (PG)** Allen is—no surprise—a nerd, and this time he's in love with his best friend's wife. Modest story line provides a framework of endless gags, with Allen borrowing heavily from "Casablanca." Bogey even appears periodically to counsel Allen on the ways of wooing women. Superior comedy isn't hurt by Ross directing instead of Allen, who adapted the script from his own play. **86m/C VHS, DVD.** Woody Allen, Diane Keaton, Tony Roberts, Susan Anspach, Jerry Lacy, Jennifer Salt, Joy Bang, Viva, Herbert Ross; ***D:*** Herbert Ross; ***W:*** Woody Allen; ***C:*** Owen Roizman; ***M:*** Billy Goldenberg.

Play It to the Bone **1999 (R)** Harrelson and Banderas are fading boxers and best friends Vince and Cesar, who unexpectedly wind up in an undercard bout against each other. Since they need to get to Vegas, and didn't think to get travel money from the promoter, Cesar's girlfriend (and Vince's ex) Grace (Davidovich) agrees to drive them. Along the way, she uses her wiles to whip up their competitive juices to use in the fight. It works, as the excessively brutal fight sequence shows. Shelton's fifth attempt at sports movie success doesn't quite connect, as it's mostly an uninteresting road movie with boxing-movie cliches tacked onto both ends. **124m/C VHS, DVD.** Woody Harrelson, Antonio Banderas, Lolita (David) Davidovich, Lucy Liu, Tom Sizemore, Robert Wagner, Richard Masur, Willie Garson, Cylk Cozart, Jack Carter; ***D:*** Ron Shelton; ***W:*** Ron Shelton; ***C:*** Mark Vargo; ***M:*** Alex Wurman.

Play Misty for Me **1971 (R)** A radio deejay obliges a psychotic woman's song request and suddenly finds himself the target of her obsessive behavior, which rapidly turns from seductive to murderous. Auspicious directorial debut for Eastwood, borrowing from the Siegel playbook (look for the director's cameo as a barkeep). Based on a story by Heims. **102m/C VHS, DVD.** Jessica Walter, Donna Mills, John Larch, Irene Hervey, Jack Ging, Clint Eastwood; ***Cameos:*** Donald Siegel; ***D:*** Clint Eastwood; ***W:*** Jo Heims, Dean Riesner; ***C:*** Bruce Surtees; ***M:*** Dee Barton.

Play Murder for Me **1991 (R)** Saxophonist performing in a seedy Buenos Aires nightclub has his world turned upside down when a former lover suddenly re-enters his life. She still has her eye on him, but she's now the woman of a notorious mobster. Soon the musician finds himself drawn into the usual deadly world of crime, deceit, and unharnessed passion. **80m/C VHS.** Jack Wagner, Tracy Scoggins; ***D:*** Hector Olivera.

Play Nice 1/2 **1992 (R)** A detective hunts down a murderous psychopath but is shocked when he discovers his suspect is a woman—and someone he knows. Also available in an unrated version. **90m/C VHS, DVD.** Ed O'Ross, Michael Zand, Bruce McGill, Ron Canada, Louise Robey; ***D:*** Terri Treas; ***W:*** Michael Zand, Chuck McCollum; ***M:*** Gary Stevan Scott.

Play Time **1994** Jeannie, Lindsay, and their husbands are on vacation in Palm Springs where they get up to some naughty sexual games that test the limits of friendship. Available in an unedited version at 95 minutes. **90m/C VHS, DVD.** Monique Parent, Craig Stepp, Jennifer Burton, Elliot David, Julie Strain, Tammy Parks, Ashlie Rhey; ***D:*** Dale Trevillion; ***W:*** Mary Ellen Hanover; ***C:*** Sven Kirsten; ***M:*** Joel Derouin.

Playback 1/2 **1995 (R)** Young couple think they've finally captured the gold ring when hubby David (Grant) gets a chance at a million dollar merger deal. But David's set-up by sexy co-worker Karen (Whirry) and his slimy boss Gil (Hamilton) tries to seduce his wife Sara (Kitaen). **91m/C VHS.** Charles Grant, Shannon Whirry, George Hamilton, Tawny Kitaen, Harry Dean Stanton; ***D:*** Oley Sassone; ***W:*** Oley Sassone, David DuBos; ***C:*** Russ Brandt.

Playboy of the Western World 1/2 **1962** An innkeeper's daughter is infatuated with a young man who says he murdered his father. Adapted from the classic play by John Millington Synge. **96m/C VHS.** *IR* Siobhan McKenna, Gary Raymond; ***D:*** Brian Desmond Hurst.

The Playboys **1992 (PG-13)** In 1957 in a tiny Irish village, unmarried Tara Maguire (Wright Penn) causes a scandal by having a baby. Her beauty attracts lots of men—there's a former beau who kills himself, the obsessive, middle-aged Sergeant Hegarty (Finney), and the newest arrival, Tom Castle (Quinn), an actor with a rag-tag theatrical troupe called the Playboys. Slow-moving and simple story with particularly good performances by Wright as the strong-willed Tara and Finney as Hegarty, clinging to a last chance at love and family. The Playboys' hysterically hammy version of "Gone With the Wind" is a gem. Directorial debut of Mackinnon. Filmed in the village of Redhills, Ireland, the hometown of co-writer Connaughton. **114m/C VHS, DVD.** Albert Finney, Aidan Quinn, Robin Wright Penn, Milo O'Shea, Alan Devlin, Niamh Cusack, Ian McElhinney, Niall Buggy, Adrian Dunbar; ***D:*** Gilles Mackinnon; ***W:*** Shane Connaughton, Kerry Crabbe; ***C:*** Jack Conroy; ***M:*** Jean-Claude Petit.

Played **2006 (R)** Dull, low-budget crime drama that the name actors seem to have done as a favor to Rossi. Ray (Rossi), the fall guy for a botched heist, gets out of prison and is hired by London crime boss Rawlings (Dotrice) to take out rival gangster Riley (Bergin) who was behind the bungled job. **87m/C DVD.** *GB* Patrick Bergin, Roy Dotrice, Val Kilmer, Gabriel Byrne, Mick Rossi, Vinnie Jones, Anthony LaPaglia, Bruno Kirby, Joanne Whalley, Patsy Kensit; ***D:*** Sean Stanek; ***W:*** Mick Rossi, Sean Stanek; ***C:*** Michael Pavlisan; ***M:*** Danny Saber.

The Player 1/2 **1992 (R)** Clever, entertaining, and biting satire of the movie industry and the greed that controls it. Robbins is dead-on as Griffin Mill, a young studio exec who becomes the chief suspect in a murder investigation. He personifies Hollywood's ethics (or lack thereof) in a performance both cold and vulnerable, as he looks for the right buttons to push and the proper back to stab. Strong leading performances are supplemented by 65 star cameos. Some viewers may be put off by the inside-Hollywood jokes, but Altman fans will love it. **123m/C VHS, DVD.** Michael Tolkin, Louise Fletcher, Dennis Franz, Malcolm McDowell, Ray Walston, Rene Auberjonois, David Alan Grier, Jayne Meadows, Michael Bowen, Steve James, Brian Tochi, Natalie Strong, Tim Robbins, Greta Scacchi, Fred Ward, Whoopi Goldberg, Peter Gallagher, Brion James, Cynthia Stevenson, Vincent D'Onofrio, Dean Stockwell, Richard E. Grant, Dina Merrill, Sydney Pollack, Lyle Lovett, Randall Batinkoff, Gina Gershon, Nick Nolte, Jack Lemmon, Lily Tomlin, Marlee Matlin, Julia Roberts, Bruce Willis, Anjelica Huston, Elliott Gould, Sally Kellerman, Steve Allen, Richard Anderson, Harry Belafonte, Shari Belafonte, Karen Black, Gary Busey, Robert Carradine, James Coburn, Cathy Lee Crosby, John Cusack, Brad Davis, Peter Falk, Teri Garr, Leeza Gibbons, Scott Glenn, Jeff Goldblum, Joel Grey, Buck Henry, Kathy Ireland, Sally Kirkland, Andie MacDowell, Martin Mull, Mimi Rogers, Jill St. John, Susan Sarandon, Rod Steiger, Joan Tewkesbury, Robert Wagner; ***Cameos:*** Burt Reynolds, Cher; ***D:*** Robert Altman; ***W:*** Michael Tolkin; ***C:*** Jean Lepine; ***M:*** Thomas Newman. British Acad. '92: Adapt. Screenplay; Cannes '92: Actor (Robbins), Director (Altman); Golden Globes '93: Actor—Mus./Comedy (Robbins), Film—Mus./Comedy; Ind. Spirit '93: Film; N.Y. Film Critics '92: Cinematog., Director (Altman), Film; Writers Guild '92: Adapt. Screenplay.

Player 5150 1/2 **2008 (R)** Bookie Tony (McDonald) gives all his bettors a number and that's the one given to gambling addict Joey (Embry). He's a day-trader who likes risky investment strategies and he owes Tony a lot of money. Vegas denizen Nick (Gunton) leaves a duffle bag of cash for Joey to discreetly invest but of course he's going to put the money to another use. **91m/C DVD.** Ethan (Randall) Embry, Bob Gunton, Christopher McDonald, Kelly Carlson, Bob Sapp, Kathleen Roberson; ***D:*** David Michael O'Neill; ***W:*** David Michael O'Neill; ***C:*** Patrice Lucien Cochet; ***M:*** Michael Muhlfriedel. **VIDEO**

Players **1979 (PG)** Young tennis hustler touring Mexico hooks up with beautiful and mysterious older woman. They seem to be from different worlds yet their love grows. She inspires him enough to enter Wimbledon. Several tennis pros appear, including Guillermo Vilas, John McEnroe, and Ilie Nastase. Almost as boring as watching a real tennis game. **120m/C VHS.** Ali MacGraw, Dean Paul (Dino Martin Jr.) Martin, Maximilian Schell, Pancho Gonzales; ***D:*** Anthony Harvey; ***W:*** Arnold Schulman; ***M:*** Jerry Goldsmith.

Players 1/2 *Pledge of Allegiance* **2003 (R)** Star high school football player Sean (Rodriguez) dates Sophia (Marsala), the daughter of local Nevada wiseguy Salvi (Dobson). Then Sean discovers that having dad's friendship means throwing some championship games to help the sports betting line. Trouble follows. **90m/C DVD.** Freddy Rodriguez, Peter Dobson, Rena Owen, Carmine D. Giovinazzo, Melissa Marsala, Joseph Bologna, John Doe, Theodore (Ted) Raimi, James DeBello, James Duval; ***D:*** Lee Madsen; ***W:*** Lee Madsen; ***C:*** Ben Kufrin; ***M:*** Adam Sanborne.

The Players Club **1998 (R)** Rapper-turned-auteur Ice Cube directs this look at the seamy and steamy world of strip clubs from his own screenplay. Diana (LisaRaye) is a single mom and college student by day, and a dancer at a strip club owned by the bombastic Dollar Bill (Mac) by night. When her naive cousin Ebony (Calhoun) is lured into turning tricks by fellow stripper Ronnie (Wilson), trouble starts. Blue (Foxx) is the deejay who falls for Diana, and is persuaded to act honorably by Diana's disapproving (and target shooting) father (Williams). Ice Cube appears as a customer who inadvertently lights the fuse for the movie's climax. While not in Woody Allen territory yet, Mr. Cube brings both humor and reality to the seedy world of strip joints. **103m/C VHS, DVD.** LisaRaye, Bernie Mac, Monica Calhoun, A.J. (Anthony) Johnson, Jamie Foxx, Ice Cube, Dick Anthony Williams, Tommy (Tiny) Lister, John Amos, Faizon Love, Alex Thomas, Chrystale Wilson, Adele Givens, Larry McCoy; ***D:*** Ice Cube; ***W:*** Ice Cube; ***C:*** Malik Hassan Sayeed; ***M:*** Hidden Faces.

Playgirl Killer *Decoy for Terror* **1966** After impulsively murdering a restless model, an artist continues to kill indiscriminately, keeping his spoils on ice. Sedaka croons between kills and luxuriates poolside—seemingly oblivious to the plot of the film—while a female decoy is sent to bait the killer for the police. For adult viewers. **86m/C VHS, DVD.** *CA* Allan Nicholls, William Kerwin, Jean Christopher, Andree Champagne, Neil Sedaka; ***D:*** Erick Santamaria.

Playing Around 1/2 **1930** Flapper Sheba Miller (White) is bored with poor good guy boyfriend Jack (Bakewell) and all-too eager to spend time with flashy playboy Nickey Solomon (Morris). Only Nickey can't afford his lavish spending without resorting to armed robbery and Sheba learns the error of her ways. **66m/B VHS.** Alice White, Chester Morris, William "Billy" Bakewell, Richard Carlyle; ***D:*** Mervyn LeRoy; ***W:*** Harvey Thew; ***C:*** Sol Polito.

Playing Away **1987** A team of Caribbean cricket players meet a team of stuffy Brits on the field in a clash of the cultures. **100m/C VHS.** *GB* Norman Beaton, Robert Urquhart; ***D:*** Horace Love.

Playing by Heart *Dancing about Architecture* **1998 (R)** Excellent ensemble cast doesn't save this episodic film about several L.A. couples falling in and out of love. Theatre director Anderson tries to avoid becoming involved with architect Stewart; loud-mouthed night-clubber Jolie won't give up on Phillippe; Quaid uses bad lines and lies on Kinski and Clarkson, while his wife, Stowe, fools around with Edwards; Connery and Rowlands (in the best-acted segments) find their 40-year marriage threatened by emotional and health problems; and Burstyn tries to comfort her son Mohr, in the last stages of AIDS. Writer/director Carroll claims he was inspired by the saying "talking about love is like dancing about architecture," and appropriately the working title was "Dancing about Architecture." **121m/C VHS, DVD.** Sean Connery, Gena Rowlands, Ryan Phillippe, Angelina Jolie, Ellen Burstyn, Gillian Anderson, Dennis Quaid, Jay Mohr, Anthony Edwards, Madeleine Stowe, Jon Stewart, Patricia Clarkson, Nastassja Kinski, Jeremy Sisto; ***D:*** Willard Carroll; ***W:*** Willard Carroll; ***C:*** Vilmos Zsigmond; ***M:*** John Barry.

Playing Dangerous 1/2 **1995 (PG-13)** Eleven-year-old computer whiz must outsmart computer thieves with the aid of a water gun and a remote-controlled car. **86m/C VHS.** David Keith Miller; ***D:*** Lawrence Lanoff.

Playing Dead 1/2 **1915** Drew and his wife portray a married couple in this silent farce. The insecure husband decides to fake his death so his wife can be with the man he thinks she loves. **58m/B VHS.** Sidney Drew, Lucille Drew, Alice Lake, Donald Hall, Harry English, Isadore Marcil; ***D:*** Sidney Drew.

Playing for Keeps **1986 (PG-13)** Three high school grads turn a dilapidated hotel into a rock 'n' roll resort. Music by Pete Townshend, Peter Frampton, Phil Collins, and others. **103m/C VHS, DVD.** Daniel Jordano, Matthew Penn, Leon Grant, Harold Gould, Jimmy Baio; ***D:*** Bob Weinstein.

Playing for Time **1980** Compelling, award-winning TV drama based on actual experiences of a Holocaust prisoner who survives by leading an inmate orchestra. Strong playing from Redgrave and Mayron. Pro-Palestinian Redgrave's political beliefs made her a controversial candidate for the role of Jewish Fania Fenelon, but her stunning performance is on the mark. **148m/C VHS.** Vanessa Redgrave, Jane Alexander, Maud Adams, Verna Bloom, Melanie Mayron; ***D:*** Daniel Mann; ***M:*** Brad Fiedel. **TV**

Playing God 1/2 **1996 (R)** Eugene (Duchovny), a disgraced junkie doctor who has lost his license, saves the life of a hood in a bar while trying to score more drugs. This brings him to the attention of Raymond (Hutton), the head of a counterfeiting and smuggling ring, who hires Eugene as his own personal emergency room. While patching up crooks so they don't get arrested at the hospital, Eugene develops more than a doctor-patient relationship with Raymond's pillow-lipped girlfriend Claire (Jolie). Things begin to get a little slicey and dicey for Eugene, until he saves the life of an undercover cop. While sufficiently bloody and nasty, flick tries too hard to be offbeat and hip. **94m/C VHS, DVD.** Stacey Travis, David Duchovny, Timothy Hutton, Angelina Jolie, Michael Massee, Peter Stormare, Andrew Tiernan, John Hawkes, Gary Dourdan; ***D:*** Andy Wilson; ***W:*** Mark Haskell Smith; ***C:*** Anthony B. Richmond; ***M:*** Richard Hartley.

Playing Mona Lisa 1/2 **2000 (R)** Piano prodigy Claire (Witt) gets dumped by her boyfriend on the night of her college graduation and then is humiliated at a piano competition. So, while trying to cope with her problems, Claire decides to adopt a Mona Lisa smile and see what life has to offer. **97m/C VHS, DVD.** Alicia Witt, Ivan Sergei, Brooke Langton, Johnny Galecki, Elliott Gould, Marlo Thomas, Harvey Fierstein, Molly Hagan, Estelle Harris, Sandra Bernhard, Shannon Finn; ***D:*** Matthew Huffman; ***W:*** Marni Freedman, Carlos De Los Rios; ***C:*** James Glennon.

Playmaker 1/2 **1994 (R)** Jaime (Rubin) is a struggling actress whose coach Talbert (Firth) guarantees success as long as she follows his bizarre training methods, which include seduction, abuse, and betrayal. Good chemistry between the leads but a mishmash of a script. **91m/C VHS.** Jennifer Rubin, Colin Firth, John Getz, Jeff(rey) Perry; ***D:*** Yuri Zeltser; ***W:*** Yuri Zeltser; ***C:*** Ross Berryman; ***M:*** Mark Snow.

Playmates **1941** Barrymore is practically wasted in his last film as a down-on-his-luck actor who agrees to turn bandleader Kyser into a Shakespearean actor. Bizarre comedy is funny at times, but leaves the audience wondering what Barrymore thought he was doing. ♫ Humpty Dumpty Heart; How Long Did I Dream?; Que Chica?; Romeo Smith and Juliet Jones; Thank Your Lucky Stars and Stripes. **96m/B VHS.** Kay Kyser, John Barrymore, Ginny Simms, Lupe Velez, May Robson, Patsy Kelly, Peter Lind Hayes, George Cleveland; ***D:*** David Butler.

Playmates 1/2 **1972** Two divorced buddies fall in love with each other's ex-wives. Typical Alda vehicle isn't bad. **78m/C VHS.** Doug McClure, Alan Alda, Connie Stevens, Barbara Feldon, Eileen Brennan, Tiger Williams, Severn Darden; ***D:*** Theodore J. Flicker. **TV**

Playroom **1990 (R)** Archaeologist McDonald is completing his father's search for the tomb of a medieval boy-prince. But someone, or something, has been waiting for him for a long, long time. When he finally reaches the long-sought-after tomb, he discovers that it is a torture chamber where his worst nightmares become realities. The demonic prince who was buried in the tomb has picked Chris as his playmate, and the rest of the staff as his personal toys. **87m/C VHS.** Lisa Aliff, Aron Eisenberg, Christopher McDonald, James Purcell, Jamie Rose, Vincent Schiavelli; ***D:*** Manny Coto; ***C:*** James L. Carter.

Playtime **1967** Occasionnally enterprising comedy in which the bemused Frenchman Hulot tries in vain to maintain an appointment in an urban landscape of glass and steel. The theme of cold, unfeeling civilization is hardly unique, but the film is nonetheless enjoyable. The third in the Hulot trilogy, preceded by "Mr. Hulot's Holiday" and "Mon Oncle." In French with English subtitles. **108m/C VHS, DVD.** *FR* Jacques Tati, Barbara Dennek, Jacqueline Lecomte, Jack Gautier; ***D:*** Jacques Tati.

Plaza Suite **1971 (PG)** Three alternating skits from Neil Simon's play about different couples staying at the New York hotel. Matthau shines in all three vignettes. Some of Simon's funnier stuff, with the first sketch being the best: Matthau and Stapleton are a couple celebrating their 24th anniversary. She's sentimental, while he's yearning for his mistress. Number two has producer Matthau putting the make on old flame Harris, while the finale has father Matthau coaxing his anxious daughter out of the bathroom on her wedding day. **114m/C VHS, DVD.** Walter Matthau, Maureen Stapleton, Barbara Harris, Lee Grant, Louise Sorel; ***D:*** Arthur Hiller; ***W:*** Neil Simon; ***M:*** Maurice Jarre.

Pleasantville 1/2 **1998 (PG-13)** Nerdy David (Maguire) and his slut wanna-be sister Jennifer (Witherspoon) are sucked into the sterile and innocent world of Pleasantville, a 1950s B/W TV show in constant reruns, where they find themselves in the roles of Bud and Mary Sue, the blandly adorable children of George and Betty Parker (Macy and Allen). After Jennifer shows a classmate what lovers' lane is really for, the townspeople begin to lose their innocence; the black-and-white world becomes more colorful as each new human passion is realized. The performances are dead-on, particularly Allen as the sexually awakening mom. The transition from straight comedy to social commentary is adeptly handled. The great character actor J. T. Walsh gives his usual excellent (and sadly, last) performance as the stubborn head of the chamber of commerce bitterly fighting change. **124m/C VHS, DVD.** Tobey Maguire, Reese Witherspoon, William H. Macy, Joan Allen, Jeff Daniels, J.T. Walsh, Don Knotts, Paul Walker, Jane Kaczmarek, Marley Shelton; *D:* Gary Ross; *W:* Gary Ross; *C:* John Lindley; *M:* Randy Newman. L.A. Film Critics '98: Support. Actress (Allen); Broadcast Film Critics '98: Support. Actress (Allen).

Please Don't Eat My Mother
WOOF! *Hungry Pets; Glump* **1972** A softcore remake of "Little Shop of Horrors" in which a lonely voyeur plays host to a human-eating plant. **95m/C VHS, DVD.** Buck Kartalian, Lynn Lundgren, Art Hedberg, Alice Fredlund, Adam Blair, Flora Wiesel, Ric Lutze, Renee Bond, Dash Fremont; *D:* Carl Monson; *W:* Eric Norden; *C:* Jack Beckett; *M:* Dan Foly.

Please Don't Eat the Daisies 1/2 **1960** City couple and kids leave the Big Apple for the country and are traumatized by flora and fauna. Goofy '60s fluff taken from Jean Kerr's book and the basis for the eventual TV series. **111m/C VHS, DVD.** Doris Day, David Niven, Janis Paige, Spring Byington, Richard Haydn, Patsy Kelly, Jack Weston, Margaret Lindsay; *D:* Charles Walters; *W:* Isobel Lennart; *C:* Robert J. Bronner; *M:* David Rose.

Please Not Now! *Only for Love; La Bride sur le Cou* **1961** Parisian model Bardot discovers her boyfriend Riberolles is cheating on her and she decides to shoot him. He's warned by Subor, who wants Bardot for himself, and takes off with new gal pal James, but Bardot and Subor are in pursuit. Then Bardot and James commiserate over the fact that men are scum and decide to team up against their lovers. French with subtitles. **74m/B VHS, DVD.** *FR IT* Brigitte Bardot, Josephine James, Michel Subor, Jacques Riberolles, Mireille Darc, Serge Marquand, Claude Brasseur, Jean Tissier, Bernard Fresson, Claude Berri; *D:* Roger Vadim, J(ack) D(unn) Trop; *W:* Roger Vadim, Claude Brule, J(ack) D(unn) Trop; *C:* Robert Lefebvre; *M:* James Campbell.

Pleasure **1931** A saga of love, treachery, and melodrama in English society in which a married author begins an affair with a model, unaware that she also has someone on the side, and it turns out to be his brother. **53m/B VHS.** Conway Tearle, Roscoe Karns, Carmel Myers, Lena Basquette, Frances Dade, Paul Page, Harold Goodwin, George "Gabby" Hayes; *D:* Otto Brower; *W:* Jo Van Ronkel, Thomas Thiteley, John Varley.

A Pleasure Doing Business **1979 (R)** Three high school buddies, now in their 40s, are reunited at a stag party, where they decide to go into business as managers in "the oldest profession." **86m/C VHS.** Conrad Bain, John Byner, Alan Oppenheimer, Misty Rowe, Phyllis Diller, Tom Smothers; *D:* Steve Vagnino.

The Pleasure Drivers 1/2 **2005** Disjointed plot follows the efforts of caregiver Daphne (Holly) to get what's due from cult leader Marvin (Zane), who refuses to pay for his son's care. Daphne decides to kidnap her patient's mentally unstable sister to get dad's attention. Meanwhile, psychology professor Bill (Macfadyen) takes a road trip with sex-obsessed student Faruza (Chabert) after his wife leaves him for another woman. Somehow a lesbian hitwoman (Bennett) becomes involved. All ultimately meet in the desert where justice is meted out. **99m/C DVD.** Lauren Holly, Lacey Chabert, Billy Zane, Jill Bennett, Angus MacFadyen, Steffany Huckaby, Angelo Spizzirri, Meat Loaf Aday, Jason Mewes, Rachel Dratch, Harrison Young; *D:* Andrzej Sekula; *W:* Adam Haynes; *C:* Andrzej Sekula; *M:* Steve Gutheinz. **VIDEO**

Pleasure Palace **1980** A gambling ladies' man (Sharif) meets his match when he helps a woman casino owner (Lange). **96m/C VHS.** Omar Sharif, Victoria Principal, J.D. Cannon, Gerald S. O'Loughlin, Jose Ferrer, Hope Lange, Alan King; *D:* Walter Grauman. **TV**

The Pledge **2000 (R)** Retired Reno homicide detective Nicholson is obsessed with the unsolved murder of a little girl, which bares a resemblance to past unsolved child murders. Unconventional thriller's dark subject matter will no doubt dissuade some potential viewers, but Penn's third (and best) directorial outing is impressive, thanks in large part to Nicholson's subtle, intense work. **124m/C VHS, DVD.** *US* Jack Nicholson, Robin Wright Penn, Aaron Eckhart, Vanessa Redgrave, Patricia Clarkson, Benicio Del Toro, Costas Mandylor, Helen Mirren, Tom Noonan, Michael O'Keefe, Mickey Rourke, Sam Shepard, Lois Smith, Harry Dean Stanton, Dale Dickey, Pauline Roberts; *D:* Sean Penn; *W:* Jerzy Kromolowski, Mary Olson-Kromolowski; *C:* Chris Menges; *M:* Hans Zimmer.

The Pledge 1/2 **2008** Sheriff Matt Austin (Perry) goes after the escaped criminal who murdered his wife and son and finds he's been hired by greedy land developer Horn (Howell) to harass widowed Gail (Brenner) until she sells. Pretty standard stuff, done better elsewhere. **85m/C DVD.** Luke Perry, C. Thomas Howell, Lisa Brenner, Kim Coates, Francesco Quinn; *D:* Armand Mastroianni; *W:* Jim Byrnes; *C:* James W. Wrenn. **CABLE**

Pledge Night **1990 (R)** Tale of horror and revenge. Killed years before in a fraternity hazing, Sid returns for the brothers who did him in. Gory and violent. **90m/C VHS.** Will Kempe, Shannon McMahon, Todd Eastland; *D:* Paul Ziller.

Plenty 1/2 **1985 (R)** Difficult but worthwhile film with Streep in top form as a former member of the French Resistance, who upon returning to England finds life at home increasingly tedious and banal and begins to fear her finest hours may be behind her. Gielgud is flawless as the aging career diplomat. Adapted by David Hare from his play, an allegory to British decline. **119m/C VHS, DVD.** Meryl Streep, Tracey Ullman, Sting, John Gielgud, Charles Dance, Ian McKellen, Sam Neill, Burt Kwouk; *D:* Fred Schepisi; *W:* David Hare; *C:* Ian Baker; *M:* Bruce Smeaton. L.A. Film Critics '85: Support. Actor (Gielgud); Natl. Soc. Film Critics '85: Support. Actor (Gielgud).

The Plot Against Harry **1969** Jewish racketeer Harry Plotnik checks out of prison, and finds the outside world ain't what it used to be. Attempting to lead an honest life only makes matters worse. Completely overlooked when first released in 1969 (and quickly shelved) because it was considered to have no commercial potential, Roemer's crime comedy found an enthusiastic audience when it was rediscovered 20 years later. **81m/B VHS, DVD.** Martin Priest, Ben Lang, Maxine Woods, Henry Nemo, Jacques Taylor, Ellen Herbert, Sandra Kazan; *D:* Michael Roemer; *W:* Michael Roemer; *C:* Robert M. Young; *M:* Frank Lewin.

The Ploughman's Lunch **1983** A BBC news reporter claws and lies his way to the top. He then discovers that he is the victim of a far more devious plan. Engrossing and well made, although some of the political views are simplistic. **107m/C VHS, DVD.** Jonathan Pryce, Charlie Dore, Tim Curry, Rosemary Harris, Frank Finlay, Bill Paterson; *D:* Richard Eyre.

Plucking the Daisy 1/2 *Please! Mr. Balzac; While Plucking the Daisy; En Effeuillant la Marguerite; Mademoiselle Striptease* **1956** Agnes Dumont (Bardot) anonymously writes a scandalous romantic novel that becomes a best-seller and causes her straitlaced father to send Agnes to a convent school. Only she escapes to her brother's in Paris instead, where she decides to earn some money by entering a striptease contest (which serves to put enticing Bardot's ample charms on display). French with subtitles. **100m/B VHS, DVD.** *FR* Brigitte Bardot, Robert Hirsch, Daniel Gelin, Jacques Dumesnil; *D:* Marc Allegret; *W:* Marc Allegret, Roger Vadim; *C:* Louis Page; *M:* Paul Misraki.

Plughead Rewired: Circuitry Man 2 *Circuitry Man 2* **1994 (R)** Earth's atmosphere has been destroyed and survivors are forced underground, where they're terrorized by the humanoid Plughead, who likes to literally plug into the minds of his victims. Plughead wants to rule what's left of life on Earth and all that stands in his way is the android Circuitry Man and FBI agent Kyle. Special effects are strictly bargain basement level. **97m/C VHS, DVD.** Vernon Wells, Deborah Shelton, Jim Metzler, Dennis Christopher, Nicholas Worth, Traci Lords; *D:* Steven Lovy, Robert Lovy; *W:* Steven Lovy, Robert Lovy; *C:* Stephen Timberlake; *M:* Tim Kelly.

Plum Role 1/2 **2007** Struggling actor Jacob (Hardie) lives in Perth in western Australia, where gigs aren't so plentiful. He's just gotten his big break by getting cast in a cop show filming in Sydney. The week before he leaves, Jacob meets vulnerable Cheryl (Henderson) and a series of unexpected complications threaten not only his potential career but his life. **80m/C DVD.** *AU* Matt Hardie, Laura Henderson, Luke Jago, Adam McGurk, Tom Stokes; *D:* Zak Hilditch; *W:* Zak Hilditch; *C:* Antony Webb; *M:* Ash Gibson Greig.

Plumber 1/2 **1979** A plumber who makes a house call extends his stay to psychologically torture the woman of the house. Originally made for Australian TV. **76m/C VHS.** *AU* Judy Morris, Ivar Kants, Robert Coleby; *D:* Peter Weir; *W:* Peter Weir. **TV**

A Plumm Summer 1/2 **2008 (PG)** You try saying no to a cute five-year-old when he needs your help. Young Elliott (Massaglia) is heartbroken when his favorite local children's TV show is forced off the air when Happy Herb's (Winkler) sidekick puppet Froggy Doo is kidnapped. Elliott insists his teen brother Rocky (Pearce) help him investigate but Rocky doesn't agree until pretty neighbor Haley (Flynn) wants to help with their sleuthing. The story takes a strange turn because the Plumm's dad (Baldwin) is a bitter alcoholic constantly fighting with their mother (Guerrero) but gets back on track by the third act. **101m/C DVD.** William Baldwin, Brenda Strong, Henry Winkler, Peter Scolari, Rick Overton, Tim Quill, Chris Massoglia, Owen Pearce, Morgan Flynn, Lisa Guerrero; *D:* Caroline Zelder; *W:* Caroline Zelder, T.J. Lynch, Frank Antonelli; *C:* Mark Vargo; *M:* Tom Hiel.

Plump Fiction **1997 (R)** The movie that proves beyond a doubt that when you make fun of Quentin Tarantino, you should stick to his truly horrible acting. Instead, this spoof attacks his already over-the-top characters from "Pulp Fiction" and "Natural Born Killers." Julius (Davidson) and Jimmy (Dinello) are the loser hit men, and Mimi (Brown) is the gangster's wife. You see, Mimi has a substance abuse problem, but it's not cocaine. It's food! She's fat, get it? Ha! Ha ha. Ha? Hmm. Intersecting storylines feature Nicky (Glave) and Vallory (Segall, doing a dead-on Juliette Lewis) as "Natural Blonde Killers." The only redeeming scene is that of Kane Picoy as "Christopher Walken character," doing an uncanny impersonation of the king of the psychos. **82m/C VHS, DVD.** Tommy Davidson, Julie Brown, Sandra Bernhard, Paul Dinello, Dan Castellaneta, Colleen Camp, Pamela Segall, Kevin Meaney, Matthew Glave, Jennifer Rubin, Robert Costanzo, Phillipe Bergerone; *D:* Bob Koherr; *W:* Bob Koherr; *C:* Rex Nicholson; *M:* Michael Muhlfriedel.

Plunder Road 1/2 **1957** Eddie (Raymond)masterminds a plan to rob a train bound for the San Francisco Mint that's carrying a fortune in gold bullion. The heist's a success but actually getting away with the loot becomes a problem. Top notch B-film noir. **76m/B VHS.** Gene Raymond, Jeanne Cooper, Wayne Morris, Elisha Cook Jr., Stafford Repp, Steven Ritch; *D:* Hubert Cornfield; *W:* Steven Ritch; *C:* Ernest Haller; *M:* Irving Gertz.

The Plunderers 1/2 **1960** Four young toughs try to terrorize a small western town but bitter one-armed Civil War hero-turned-rancher Sam (Chandler) finds the courage to oppose them. **94m/B DVD.** Jeff Chandler, John Saxon, Ray Stricklyn, Dee Pollock, Marsha Hunt, Dolores Hart, Jay C. Flippen, Joseph Pevney, Roger Torrey; *D:* Joseph Pevney; *W:* Bob Barbash; *C:* Gene Polito; *M:* Leonard Rosenman.

Plunge Into Darkness 1/2 **1977** Quiet weekend in the mountains turns into a nightmare for an ex-Olympic runner and his family. **77m/C VHS.** Bruce Barry, Olivia Hamnett, Ashley Greenville, Wallace (Wallas) Eaton, Tom Richards; *D:* Peter Maxwell.

Plunkett & Macleane **1998 (R)** Will Plunkett (Carlyle) is a lower-class thief who teams up with wastrel aristocrat Macleane (Miller) for careers as highwaymen in 18th-century London. The rogues are aided by hedonistic Lord Rochester (Cumming) and opposed by Lord Chief Justice Gibson (Gambon), whose vixenish niece, Lady Rebecca (Tyler), becomes Macleane's inamorata. Carlyle and Miller make a fine criminal duo but the film has lots of flaws to distract the viewer. (Son of Ridley) Scott's directorial debut. **102m/C VHS, DVD.** *GB* Robert Carlyle, Jonny Lee Miller, Liv Tyler, Michael Gambon, Alan Cumming, Ken Stott, Terence Rigby, Claire Rushbrook, Iain Robertson, Dave Atkins; *D:* Jake Scott; *W:* Robert Wade, Neal Purvis, Charles McKeown; *C:* John Mathieson; *M:* Craig Armstrong.

Plutonium Baby **1987** A mutated kid, whose mother was killed by the same radiation exposure that infected him, tracks down the guilty party in New York in this comic-book style film. **85m/C VHS.** Patrick Molloy, Danny Guerra; *D:* Ray Hirschman.

Plutonium Incident **1982** A female technician at a nuclear power plant suspects the facility to be less safe than it appears, and faces a diabolical plan of harassment when she attempts to bring attention to the hazards. **90m/C VHS.** Janet Margolin, Powers Boothe, Bo Hopkins, Joseph Campanella; *D:* Richard Michaels.

Pocahontas **1995 (G)** It's 1607 and spirited Powhatan maiden Pocahontas and British settler Captain John Smith strike an unlikely but doomed romance in Disney's 33rd animated feature, its first based on the life of a historical figure. Lovely Poca, a virtual post-adolescent Native American superbabe, introduces the roguish captain (spoken and sung by Gibson) to the wonders of unspoiled nature and serves as peacemaker in the clash of European and Native American cultures. Disney puts its spin on history but maintains cultural sensitivity: several characters are voiced by Native American performers, including Chief Powhatan, spoken by American Indian activist Means, who led the 1973 siege at Wounded Knee, and Bedard as Pocahantas. Just don't tell the kids the real Pocahontas married someone else, moved to England, and died of smallpox at 21. Stunningly animated, but its mediocre soundtrack and decidedly somber tone leave it lacking in typical Disney majesty and charm. Premiered at New York's Central Park, for the usual theatre crowd of 100,000 or so. **90m/C VHS, DVD.** *D:* Mike Gabriel, Eric Goldberg; *W:* Carl Binder, Susannah Grant, Philip LaZebnik; *M:* Alan Menken, Stephen Schwartz; *V:* Irene Bedard, Judy Kuhn, Mel Gibson, Joe Baker, Christian Bale, Billy Connolly, James Apaumut Fall, Linda Hunt, John Kassir, Danny Mann, Bill Cobbs, David Ogden Stiers, Michelle St. John, Gordon Tootoosis, Frank Welker. Oscars '95: Song ("Colors of the Wind"), Orig. Score; Golden Globes '96: Song ("Colors of the Wind").

Pocahontas: The Legend 1/2 **1995** Live-action version of the increasingly familiar story of the Native American girl who aids Virginia settler, John Smith. **101m/C VHS, DVD.** *CA* Sandrine Holt, Miles O'Keeffe, Tony Goldwyn, Gordon Tootoosis; *D:* Daniele Suissa; *W:* Daniele Suissa.

The Pocatello Kid 1/2 **1931** Maynard stretches in a dual role as the wrongly convicted Kid and the Kid's no-good sheriff brother. **60m/B VHS, DVD.** Ken Maynard, Marceline Day, Charles "Blackie" King, Lafe (Lafayette) McKee; *D:* Phil Rosen.

Pocket Money **1972 (PG)** Down-on-their-luck cowpokes foolishly do business with crooked rancher in attempt to make comeback in faltering acting careers. Star-powered, moderately entertaining modern western-comedy based on the novel "Jim Kane" by J.K.S. Brown. **100m/C VHS, DVD.** Paul Newman, Lee Marvin, Strother Martin, Christine Belford, Wayne Rogers, Hector Elizondo, Gregory Sierra; *D:* Stuart Rosenberg; *W:* Terrence Malick; *M:* Alex North.

Pocketful of Miracles **1961** Capra's final film, a remake of his 1933 "Lady for a Day," is just as corny and sentimental but doesn't work quite as well. Davis is delightful as Apple Annie, a down-on-her-luck street vendor who will go to any extreme to hide her poverty from the well-married daughter she adores. Ford is terrific as the man who transforms Annie into a lady in time for her daughter's visit. Touching. Maybe too touching. Also marks Ann-Margret's film debut. **136m/C VHS, DVD.** Bette Davis, Glenn Ford, Peter Falk, Hope Lange, Arthur O'Connell, Ann-Margret, Thomas Mitchell, Jack Elam, Edward Everett Horton, David Brian, Mickey Shaughnessy; *D:* Frank Capra; *W:* Hal Kanter, Harry Tugend; *C:* Robert J. Bronner; *M:* Walter Scharf. Golden Globes '62: Actor—Mus./Comedy (Ford).

A Pocketful of Rye 🦴🦴 *Agatha Christie's Miss Marple: A Pocketful of Rye* **1987** Based on Agatha Christie's novel featuring the sleuthing Miss Marple. She faces another murderous puzzle, this one based on an old nursery rhyme. **101m/C VHS, DVD.** *GB* Joan Hickson; ***D:*** Guy Slater. **TV**

Poco 🦴 **1977** The story of Poco, a shaggy little dog who travels across the country to search for the young girl who owns him. **88m/C VHS.** Chill Wills, Michelle Ashburn, John Steadman; ***D:*** Dwight Brooks; ***W:*** William Carville; ***C:*** Dwight Brooks.

Poetic Justice 🦴🦴 ½ **1993 (R)** Justice (Jackson in her movie debut, for better or worse) gives up college plans to follow a career in cosmetology after her boyfriend's brutal murder. She copes with her loss by dedicating herself to poetry writing (provided by no less than poet Maya Angelou) and meets postal worker Shakur. Singleton's second directorial effort is about the girlz n the hood and boasts a lighter script (well, it is about a hairdresser) focusing less on the Boyz-style morality and more on the trials and tribulations of Justice. Production stopped on the South Central L.A. set during the '92 riots, but the aftermath provided poignant pictures for later scenes. **109m/C VHS, DVD.** Janet Jackson, Tupac Shakur, Tyra Ferrell, Regina King, Joe Torry, Norma Donaldson; ***D:*** John Singleton; ***W:*** John Singleton; ***C:*** Peter Lyons Collister; ***M:*** Stanley Clarke. MTV Movie Awards '94: Female Perf. (Jackson), Most Desirable Female (Jackson); Golden Raspberries '93: Worst New Star (Jackson).

Poil de Carotte 🦴🦴 ½ *The Red Head* **1931** A semi-famous French melodrama about a young boy harassed by his overbearing mother to the point of disaster, redeemed finally by the love of his father. In French with English subtitles. **90m/B VHS.** *FR* Harry Baur, Robert Lynen, Catherine Fontenoy; ***D:*** Julien Duvivier.

The Point 🦴🦴 ½ **1971** Charming and sincere animated feature about the rejection and isolation of a round-headed child in a world of pointy-headed people. Excellent score. **74m/C VHS, DVD.** ***D:*** Fred Wolf; ***M:*** Harry Nilsson; ***V:*** Paul Frees; ***Nar:*** Ringo Starr. **TV**

Point Blank 🦴🦴 ½ **1967** Adapted from Stark's "The Hunter." The film's techniques are sometimes compared to those of Resnais and Godard. Double-crossed and believed dead, gangster Marvin returns to claim his share of the loot from the Organization. Hard-nosed examination of the depersonalization of a mechanized urban world. **92m/C VHS, DVD.** Lee Marvin, Angie Dickinson, Keenan Wynn, Carroll O'Connor, Lloyd Bochner, Michael Strong, James B. Sikking; ***D:*** John Boorman.

Point Blank 🦴 ½ **1998 (R)** A bus carrying death-row convicts is ambushed but the cons don't go their separate ways. Instead, they take over a shopping mall and begin fighting among themselves. **90m/C VHS, DVD.** Mickey Rourke, Danny Trejo, Kevin Gage, Michael Wright, Frederic Forrest, James Gammon; ***D:*** Matt Earl Beesley. **VIDEO**

Point Break 🦴🦴 ½ **1991 (R)** If you can suspend your disbelief—and you'd need a crane—then this crime adventure is just dandy. Reeves is a young undercover FBI kid sent to infiltrate a gang of bank-robbing surfer dudes. Swayze is the leader of the beach subculture, a thrillseeker who plays cat-and-mouse with the feds in a series of excellent action scenes. Silly brain candy. **117m/C VHS, DVD, Blu-ray Disc.** Jack Kehler, Lee Tergesen, Christopher Pettiet, Elizabeth Berkley, Tom Sizemore, Anthony Mangano, Patrick Swayze, Keanu Reeves, Gary Busey, Lori Petty, John C. McGinley, Chris Pederson, Bojesse Christopher, Julian Reyes, Daniel Beer, Sydney Walsh, Vincent Klyn, James LeGros, John Philbin; ***D:*** Kathryn Bigelow; ***W:*** W. Peter Iliff; ***C:*** Don Peterman; ***M:*** Mark Isham. MTV Movie Awards '92: Most Desirable Male (Reeves).

Point of Impact 🦴🦴 *Spanish Rose* **1993 (R)** A Miami customs officer is killed in an explosion and his partner is blamed. He knows a Cuban crime boss was actually behind it and goes undercover to bring the criminal organization down. But there's also the temptation of the the criminal's sexy ladyfriend. Also available in an unrated version. **96m/C VHS.** Michael Pare, Barbara Carrera, Michael Ironside; ***D:*** Bob Misiorowski; ***W:*** George Fernandez; ***C:*** Yossi Wein; ***M:*** Vladimir Horunzhy.

Point of No Return 🦴🦴 ½ **1993 (R)** Fonda is Maggie, a drugged-out loser condemned to death for her part in a murder spree, but if she agrees to work as a government assassin, she'll be given a reprieve. Fonda displays a certain perkiness as the assassin and is better in her early surly scenes; Keitel is creepy as another assassin. Flashy, exacting, but ultimately innocuous remake of the 1990 French thriller "La Femme Nikita." **108m/C VHS, DVD.** Bridget Fonda, Gabriel Byrne, Dermot Mulroney, Miguel Ferrer, Anne Bancroft, Olivia D'Abo, Harvey Keitel, Richard Romanus, Lorraine Toussaint, Geoffrey Lewis, Calvin Levels; ***D:*** John Badham; ***W:*** Robert Getchell, Alexandra Seros; ***C:*** Michael Watkins; ***M:*** Hans Zimmer.

Point of Origin 🦴🦴 ½ **2002** Captain John Orr (Liotta) is an arson investigator with the Glendale fire department. He's investigating a six-year string of fires in southern California (in the 1980s) along with protege/inspector Keith Lang (Leguizamo). Everyone's a suspect, including the firefighters themselves. Based on a true story. **86m/C VHS, DVD.** Ray Liotta, John Leguizamo, Colm Feore, Clifford Curtis, Bai Ling, Illeana Douglas, Ronny Cox; ***D:*** Newton Thomas (Tom) Sigel; ***W:*** Matthew Tabak; ***C:*** Anthony G. Nakonechnyi; ***M:*** John Ottman. **CABLE**

Point of Terror 🦴 **1971 (R)** A handsome rock singer seduces a record company executive's wife in order to further his career. **88m/C VHS, DVD.** Peter Carpenter, Dyanne Thorne, Lory Hansen, Leslie Simms; ***D:*** Alex Nicol.

The Pointsman 🦴🦴 ½ *De Wisselwachter* **1986 (R)** A quirky, small film based on the novel by Jean Paul Franssens. A beautiful Scandinavian woman accidentally gets off a train in Northern Scotland, where the only shelter is a small railway outpost, and the only company is a mysterious pointsman who lives by the comings and goings of the trains. The couple's increasing isolation as winter falls and their lack of a common language persists is portrayed with both humor and poignancy. **95m/C VHS.** *NL* Jim Van Der Woude, Stephane Excoffier, John Kraaykamp, Josse De Pauw, Ton Van Dort; ***D:*** Jos Stelling.

Poison 🦴🦴🦴 **1991 (R)** A controversial, compelling drama weaving the story of a seven year-old boy's murder of his father with two other tales of obsessive, fringe behavior. From the director of the underground hit "Superstar: The Karen Carpenter Story," which was shot using only a cast of "Barbie" dolls. **85m/C VHS, DVD.** Edith Meeks, Larry Maxwell, Susan Norman, Scott Renderer, James Lyons, Millie White, Buck Smith, Anne Giotta, Al Quagliata, Michelle Sullivan, John R. Lombardi, Tony Pemberton, Andrew Harpending; ***D:*** Todd Haynes; ***W:*** Todd Haynes; ***C:*** Maryse Alberti; ***M:*** James Bennett. Sundance '91: Grand Jury Prize.

Poison *Thy Neighbor's Wife* **2001 (R)** Ann believes that an ordinary housewife is responsible for the death of her husband. So Ann disguises herself, gets a job with the family, and decides to extract the proper revenge. Of course, Ann's crazy. **92m/C VHS, DVD.** Kari Wuhrer, Jeff Trachta, Barbara Crampton, Michael Cavanaugh, Larry Poindexter; ***D:*** Jim Wynorski; ***W:*** Sean O'Bannon; ***C:*** Andrea V. Rossotto. **VIDEO**

Poison Ivy 🦴🦴 **1985** A routine comedy about a chaotic and lusty summer camp. **97m/C VHS.** Michael J. Fox, Nancy McKeon, Robert Klein, Caren Kaye; ***D:*** Larry Elikann; ***M:*** Miles Goodman. **TV**

Poison Ivy 🦴🦴 **1992 (R)** Barrymore is right on target as a junior femme fatale in this trashy tale of a wayward teenager and her takeover of her best friend's family. Ivy has no discernable family life and quickly attaches herself to the lonely, neglected Cooper (Gilbert) who ends up watching as she systematically seduces both her mother (emotionally) and her father (physically). But when Ivy's homewrecking turns lethal, Cooper must fight her "friend" to save herself. Glossy, over-done pulp. An unrated version is also available. **91m/C VHS, DVD.** Drew Barrymore, Sara Gilbert, Tom Skerritt, Cheryl Ladd; ***D:*** Katt Shea; ***W:*** Katt Shea, Andy Ruben; ***C:*** Phedon Papamichael; ***M:*** David Michael Frank.

Poison Ivy 2: Lily 🦴 ½ **1995 (R)** Art student Lily (Milano) finds the provocative Ivy's diary and becomes intrigued enough to decide to take a walk on the wild side herself, which gets her into all sorts of trouble. Also available unrated. **110m/C VHS, DVD.** Alyssa Milano, Xander Berkeley, Johnathon Schaech, Belinda Bauer; ***D:*** Anne Goursaud; ***W:*** Chloe King; ***C:*** Suki Medencevic; ***M:*** Joseph Williams.

Poison Ivy 3: The New Seduction 🦴 ½ **1997 (R)** Now Ivy has a long-lost sister, appropriately named Violet (Pressly), who heads to their childhood home to get revenge on those she believes betrayed them. Naturally, it's all sex and men being led around by their...zippers. Also available unrated. **93m/C VHS, DVD.** Jaime Pressly, Megan Edwards, Michael Des Barres, Greg Vaughan; ***D:*** Kurt Voss; ***W:*** Karen Kelly; ***C:*** Feliks Parnell; ***M:*** Reg Powell.

Poison Ivy 4: The Secret Society 🦴 **2008** Has no connection to the previous trashy flicks except for that whole flower name thing. Freshman Daisy Brooks is really enjoying her time at Beckshire College, especially when she is invited to join the exclusive Ivy Society. But Daisy soon learns the members have no scruples when it comes to getting what they want, including blackmail and murder. **96m/C DVD.** Miriam McDonald, Shawna Waldron, Ryan Kennedy, Greg Evigan, Catherine Hicks; ***D:*** Jason Hreno; ***W:*** Peter Sullivan, Liz Maverick; ***C:*** Kamal Derkaoui. **VIDEO**

Pokemon 3: The Movie 🦴🦴 **2001 (G)** As opposed to what, "Pokemon 3: The Dinner Theater?" This installment of the interminable franchise has a young girl, who's father has disappeared, turning her surroundings into a land of icy crystal. Ash, Pikachu and the other Pokemon (Pokemen?) show up to save the day with various pocket monster battles. Lessons are learned, battles are fought and won or lost, and days are saved, except for the days wasted by parents who have to sit throught it all. **88m/C VHS, DVD.** ***D:*** Kunihiko Yuyama, Michael Haigney; ***W:*** Michael Haigney, Norman Grossfeld, Takeshi Shudo, Hideki Sonoda; ***V:*** Veronica Taylor, Eric Stuart, Rachael Lillis, Maddie (Maddeleine) Blaustein, Ikue Otani.

Pokemon: The First Movie 🦴🦴 **1999 (G)** If your kid is saying things like "Pikachu," "Squirtle," and "Charizard," then you've already been introduced to the multimedia (and mucho dollar) world of Pokemon. In that case, you'll be forced to rent or buy this movie regardless of any criticism (unless by the time you read this the craze has gone the way of the Teenage Mutant Ninja Turtle). In this full-length version of the popular cartoon series (video game, trading card game, toy line, etc...), hero Ash and his pals Misty and Brock go to New Island to do battle with a twisted genetically engineered Pokemon called Mewtwo. Mewtwo defeats all the Pokemon trainers in battle, and is ready to clone hideous monsters from the defeated critters when he is challenged by the mysterious and rare Mew. Several new characters are introduced along with clever marketing ties, because apparently the gigantic pile of money this stuff is generating is not yet the size of Mt. Fuji. Also contains the short "Pikachu's Vacation." **75m/C VHS, DVD.** ***D:*** Kunihiko Yuyama, Michael Haigney; ***W:*** Michael Haigney, Takeshi Shudo; ***C:*** Hisao Shirai; ***V:*** Veronica Taylor, Rachael Lillis, Eric Stuart, Philip Bartlett.

Pokemon the Movie 2000: The Power of One 🦴🦴 *Poketto Monsutaa: Maboroshi No Pokemon X: Lugia Bakudan* **2000 (G)** As with the first Pokemon movie, considerations such as quality, plot, characterization, or dialogue do not matter. If you have kids under ten years old, you will be forced to rent (or more likely buy) this movie and watch it repeatedly. If you don't have any kids under ten, you most likely don't know or care what a Pokemon is anyway. If you do, for some strange reason, need to know the plot, here it is: Ash must stop the Collector from capturing Pokemon. If the kiddies like the Pokemon, they'll enjoy this little exercise in media overkill. **103m/C VHS, DVD.** *JP* ***D:*** Kunihiko Yuyama, Michael Haigney; ***W:*** Michael Haigney, Takeshi Shudo; ***M:*** Ralph Schuckett, John Loeffler; ***V:*** Ikue Ootani, Rica Matsumoto, Mayumi Iizuka, Tomokazu Seki.

Poker Alice 🦴🦴 **1987** A lively Western starring Elizabeth Taylor as a sometime gambler who wins a brothel in a poker game. **100m/C VHS, DVD.** Elizabeth Taylor, George Hamilton, Tom Skerritt, Richard Mulligan, David Wayne, Susan Tyrrell, Pat Corley; ***D:*** Arthur Allan Seidelman; ***W:*** James Lee Barrett.

The Poker Club 🦴 **2008 (R)** For years, Aaron and his three buds have been getting together for a Monday night poker game that's an excuse to get drunk and high. On this night, a burglar tries to break into the house and is accidentally bashed to death. The guys panic and dump the body in the river but someone witnessed their crime and the cops eventually come into the picture as well. Clumsy twists in a story you've seen before. Adapted from the Ed Gorman novel. **82m/C DVD.** Johnathon Schaech, Johnny Messner, Loren Dean, Michael Risley, Lori Heuring, Judy Reyes, Lenny Levi; ***D:*** Tim McCann; ***W:*** Johnathon Schaech; ***C:*** Frank Barrera; ***M:*** Evan Evans. **VIDEO**

The Poker House 🦴 ½ **2009 (R)** In 1976, 14-year-old Agnes is living in a rundown house with her two young sisters, her druggie, drunk hooker mom Sarah, and Sarah's pimp Duval, who runs poker games in the living room. Agnes tries to protect her sisters while struggling to find a way to get them a better life. Petty's directorial debut is allegedly based on incidents from her own childhood. **93m/C DVD.** Jennifer Lawrence, Selma Blair, Bokeem Woodbine, David Alan Grier; ***D:*** Lori Petty; ***W:*** David Alan Grier, Lori Petty; ***C:*** Ken Seng; ***M:*** Mike Post. **VIDEO**

Pola X 🦴🦴 **1999** French film continues to push the sexual envelope even when it's inspired by Herman Melville's 1852 novel, "Pierre, or, the Ambiguities." Rich boy Pierre (Depardieu) lives with his beautiful widowed mother, Marie (Deneuve), in a country chateau. He's about to marry his faithful girlfriend, Lucie (Chuillot), when a strange woman named Isabelle (Golubeva) shows up, claiming to be Pierre's half-sister. Soon Pierre is living the grunge life with Isabelle in Paris and the two are involved in an incestuous relationship (some of which is explicitly displayed). Another bizarre film from auteur Carax. French with subtitles. **134m/C VHS, DVD.** *FR* Guillaume Depardieu, Yekaterina (Katia) Golubeva, Catherine Deneuve, Delphine Chuillot, Laurent Lucas; ***D:*** Leos Carax; ***W:*** Leos Carax, Jean-Pol Fargeau, Lauren Sedofsky; ***C:*** Eric Gautier; ***M:*** Scott Walker.

The Polar Bear King 🦴🦴 ½ **1994 (PG)** When a handsome prince refuses to marry the evil witch of Summerland, the wicked woman uses her power to turn him into a polar bear. The polar bear prince embarks on a journey to Winterland where he meets and falls in love with a beautiful princess. Together they return to Summerland and try to break the witch's spell. Filmed on location in Norway and Sweden. **87m/C VHS, DVD.** Maria Bonnevie, Jack Fjeldstad, Tobias Hoesl, Anna-Lotta Larsson; ***D:*** Ola Solum.

The Polar Express 🦴🦴 ½ **2004 (G)** Your capacity to enjoy this Christmas story will depend on whether or not you find the so-called performance or motion capture animation technique (think Gollum from "Lord of the Rings") enthralling or creepy. An extended version of Chris Van Allsburg's popular children's book, the story opens on Christmas Eve when nameless skeptic Hero Boy is suddenly awakened by the steam train of the title, which appears outside his window. The train is leaving for the North Pole and Hero Boy, encouraged by a kindly conductor (one of Hanks' many roles), joins the passengers on their journey to meet Santa. There are various adventures intended to offer life-affirming lessons but this is a rather melancholy tale with which to entertain the tykes. **100m/C DVD, Blu-ray Disc, HD DVD.** *US* Tom Hanks, Michael Jeter, Nona Gaye, Peter Scolari, Eddie Deezen, Charles Fleischer, Steven Tyler, Daryl Sabara, Leslie Zemeckis, Andre Sogliuzzo, Jimmy Bennett, Isabella Peregrina; ***D:***

Robert Zemeckis; *C:* Don Burgess, Robert Presley; *M:* Alan Silvestri; *V:* Daryl Sabara.

Poldark **1975** Tempestuous love, political intrigue, and family struggles all set in 18th-century Cornwall, then the copper-producing center of England. Heroic Ross Poldark has just returned from fighting upstart Americans in the Revolutionary War only to discover that his father has died and the family mines are about to be sold to the scheming Warleggan family. Ross struggles to pay off family debts, reclaim his heritage, resolve his feelings for an old love, and fight his attraction to the beguiling, but completely unsuitable, Demelza. Adapted from the novels by Winston Graham. **720m/C VHS.** *GB* Robin Ellis, Angharad Rees, Jill Townsend, Judy Geeson, Ralph Bates, Richard Morant, Clive Francis, John Baskcomb, Paul Curran, Tilly Tremayne, Mary Wimbush; *D:* Paul Annett, Christopher Barry, Kenneth Ives; *W:* Paul Wheeler, Peter Draper, Jack Pulman. **TV**

Poldark **1996** Picks up the story of Ross and Demelza Poldark and their family from where the 1970s BBC series ended. It's 1810 and Ross is spending most of his time in London as a Member of Parliament while at their Cornwall home, Demelza deals with the continuing Warleggan feud. Poldark son, Jeremy, struggles to keep the mine going and daughter Clowance is in the throes of her first romance. Based on the novel "The Stranger from the Sea" by Winston Graham. **105m/C VHS, DVD.** *GB* John Bowe, Mel Martin, Ioan Gruffudd, Michael Attwell, Kelly Reilly, Hans Matheson, Amanda Ryan, Nicholas Gleaves, Gabrielle Lloyd, Sarah Carpenter; *D:* Richard Laxton; *W:* Robin Mukbarjee; *M:* Ian Hughes. **TV**

Poldark 2 **1975** The further adventures of Ross Poldark, wife Demelza, and assorted family, friends, and enemies, all set in 18th-century Cornwall. Demelza's two meddlesome younger brothers come to live at Nampara, enemy George Warleggan and Ross' old love Elizabeth move too close for comfort, and the uncertainties of the copper mining economy all bring their share of trouble. Adapted from the novels by Winston Graham. Made for British TV; six cassettes. **720m/C VHS.** *GB* Robin Ellis, Angharad Rees, Jill Townsend, Judy Geeson, Ralph Bates, Kevin McNally, Brian Stirner, Michael Cadman, Jane Wymark, David Delve, Christopher Biggins, Trudie Styler; *D:* Philip Dudley, Roger Jenkins; *W:* Alexander Baron, John Wiles, Martin Worth. **TV**

Police 1/2 **1985** French police drama with the intense Depardieu as a cop hunting an Algerian drug boss. Matters grow complicated when he falls for the elusive crook's girlfriend. Sometimes gripping, but unveven; the actors were encouraged to improvise. Inspired by the novel "Bodies Are Dust" by P.J. Wolfson. In French with English subtitles. **113m/C VHS.** *FR* Gerard Depardieu, Sophie Marceau, Sandrine Bonnaire, Richard Anconina, Pascale Rocard; *D:* Maurice Pialat; *W:* Catherine Breillat. Venice Film Fest. '85: Actor (Depardieu).

Police Academy 1/2 **1984 (R)** In an attempt to recruit more cops, a big-city police department does away with all its job standards. The producers probably didn't know that they were introducing bad comedy's answer to the "Friday the 13th" series, but it's hard to avoid heaping the sins of its successors on this film. Besides, it's just plain dumb. **96m/C VHS, DVD.** Steve Guttenberg, Kim Cattrall, Bubba Smith, George Gaynes, Michael Winslow, Leslie Easterbrook, Georgina Spelvin, Debralee Scott; *D:* Hugh Wilson; *W:* Hugh Wilson, Pat Proft, Neal Israel; *C:* Michael D. Margulies; *M:* Robert Folk.

Police Academy 2: Their First Assignment **1985 (PG-13)** More predictable idiocy from the cop shop. This time they're determined to rid the precinct of some troublesome punks. No real story to speak of, just more high jinks in this mindless sequel. **87m/C VHS, DVD.** Steve Guttenberg, Bubba Smith, Michael Winslow, Art Metrano, Colleen Camp, Howard Hesseman, David Graf, George Gaynes; *D:* Jerry Paris; *W:* Barry W. Blaustein.

Police Academy 3: Back in Training **1986 (PG)** In yet another sequel, the bumbling cops find their alma mater is threatened by a budget crunch and they must compete with a rival academy to see which school survives. The "return to school" plot allowed the filmmakers to add new characters to replace those who had some scruples about picking up yet another "Police Lobotomy" check. Followed by three more sequels. **84m/C VHS, DVD.** Steve Guttenberg, Bubba Smith, David Graf, Michael Winslow, Marion Ramsey, Art Metrano, Bob(cat) Goldthwait, Leslie Easterbrook, Tim Kazurinsky, George Gaynes, Shawn Weatherly; *D:* Jerry Paris; *W:* Gene Quintano; *M:* Robert Folk.

Police Academy 4: Citizens on Patrol **1987 (PG)** The comic cop cutups from the first three films aid a citizen's patrol group in their unnamed, but still wacky, hometown. Moronic high jinks ensue. Fourth in the series of five (or is it six?) that began with "Police Academy." **88m/C VHS, DVD.** James Carroll, Steve Guttenberg, Bubba Smith, Michael Winslow, David Graf, Tim Kazurinsky, George Gaynes, Colleen Camp, Bob(cat) Goldthwait, Sharon Stone; *D:* Jim Drake; *W:* Gene Quintano; *M:* Robert Folk.

Police Academy 5: Assignment Miami Beach **WOOF!** **1988 (PG)** The fourth sequel, wherein the misfits-with-badges go to Miami and bumble about in the usual manner. It's about time these cops were retired from the force. **89m/C VHS, DVD.** Bubba Smith, David Graf, Michael Winslow, Leslie Easterbrook, Rene Auberjonois, Marion Ramsey, Janet Jones, George Gaynes, Matt McCoy; *D:* Alan Myerson; *W:* Stephen J. Curwick; *M:* Robert Folk.

Police Academy 6: City under Siege **1989 (PG)** In what is hoped to be the last in a series of bad comedies, the distinguished graduates pursue three goofballs responsible for a crime wave. **85m/C VHS, DVD.** Bubba Smith, David Graf, Michael Winslow, Leslie Easterbrook, Marion Ramsey, Matt McCoy, Bruce Mahler, G.W. Bailey, George Gaynes; *D:* Peter Bonerz; *W:* Stephen J. Curwick; *M:* Robert Folk.

Police Academy 7: Mission to Moscow **1994 (PG)** The seventh in the series is another inept comedy, which finds the chaotic crew tackling a Russian mobster on his Moscow turf—all because of a popular computer game with some sinister software. Like you'll care about the plot anyway. **83m/C VHS, DVD.** George Gaynes, Michael Winslow, David Graf, Leslie Easterbrook, G.W. Bailey, Charlie Schlatter, Ron Perlman, Christopher Lee; *D:* Alan Metter; *W:* Michele S. Chodos, Randolph Davis; *M:* Robert Folk.

Police, Adjective *Politist, Adj* **2009** Undercover cop Cristi (Bacur) is on a dull surveillance assignment, following alleged pot-selling teen Victor (Costin) through the streets of the stagnating, post-communist city of Vasliu. Cristi's officious boss Nelu (Stoica) wants to know who's supplying the teen's drugs but Victor turns out to be just indulging his own tastes. However, Nelu is unwilling to let the situation drop. Cristi and Nelu actually have a linguistic discussion (hence the title) about conscience and justice and the job of the police. Romanian with subtitles. **113m/C DVD.** *RO* Vlad Ivanov, Dragos Bucur, Ion Stoica, Irina Saulescu, Cosmin Selesi, George Remes, Dan Cogalniceanu, Radu Costin; *D:* Corneliu Porumboiu; *W:* Corneliu Porumboiu; *C:* Marius Panduru; *M:* Mirabela Dauer, Yan Raiburg.

Police Court **1932** The son of a faded, alcoholic screen star tries to bring the old fellow back to prominence. **62m/B VHS.** Henry B. Walthall, Leon Janney, Al "Fuzzy" St. John, Aileen Pringle, King Baggot, Lionel Belmore, Edmund Breese, Walter James; *D:* Louis King; *W:* Stuart Anthony; *C:* Archie Stout.

Police Story 1/2 *Jackie Chan's Police Force; Police Force; Jackie Chan's Police Story; Ging Chaat Goo Si* **1985 (PG-13)** Chopsocker Chan's assigned to protect a witness in a drug case. Faced by unsavory thugs, he flies through the air with the greatest of ease. Very cool stunts. **92m/C VHS, DVD.** *HK* Jackie Chan, Brigitte Lin, Maggie Cheung, Cho Yuen, Bill Tung, Kenneth Tong; *D:* Jackie Chan; *C:* Yiu-tsou Cheung.

Policewoman Centerfold **1983** Exploitative rendering based on the true story of a cop who posed for a pornographic magazine. Anderson is appealing in the lead. **100m/C VHS.** Melody Anderson, Ed Marinaro, Donna Pescow, Bert Remsen, David Spielberg; *D:* Reza Badiyi. **TV**

Policewomen 1/2 **1973 (R)** Female undercover agent must stop a ring of gold smugglers. **99m/C VHS, DVD.** Sondra Currie, Tony Young, Phil Hoover, Elizabeth Stuart, Jeanie Bell; *D:* Lee Frost.

A Polish Vampire in Burbank **1980** A shy vampire in Burbank tries again and again to find blood and love. Wacky. **84m/C VHS, DVD.** Mark Pirro, Lori Sutton, Eddie Deezen; *D:* Mark Pirro.

Polish Wedding 1/2 **1997 (PG-13)** Strong-willed teenager Hala (Danes) throws her working-class Polish/American family into a tizzy when she becomes pregnant and the family decides she must get married. But Hala's not the only one whose life is romntically complicated—her mom Jadzia's (Olin) had a longtime affair with Roman (Serbedzja), which husband Bolek (Byrne) tolerates because he's afraid of losing her. Too slapsticky but the cast is game and it does have heart. **107m/C VHS, DVD.** Claire Danes, Lena Olin, Gabriel Byrne, Adam Trese, Rade Serbedzija, Mili Avital, Daniel Lapaine, Kristen Bell; *D:* Theresa Connelly; *W:* Theresa Connelly; *C:* Guy Dufaux; *M:* Luis Bacalov.

Politics **1931** Widowed Hattie (Dressler) decides to run for mayor because the incumbent is doing nothing about the town's crime problem with bootleggers and other gangsters. Unbeknownst to Hattie, her daughter Myrtle (Morley) is involved with Benny (Bakewell), who wants to get out of the mob. Hattie persuades the town's married women to withhold domestic services so they can influence their husbands (shades of Lysistrata). Her campaign is going fine until the Benny problem comes to light. **73m/B DVD.** Marie Dressler, Karen Morley, William "Billy" Bakewell, Polly Moran, Roscoe Ates, John Miljan, Tom McGuire, Joan Marsh, Kane Richmond; *D:* Charles Reisner; *W:* Wells Root; *C:* Clyde De Vinna.

Pollock **2000 (R)** First-time director Harris (who also stars) scores a personal triumph with his bio of abstract expressionist artist Jackson Pollock (whom the actor resembles quite astonishingly). Pollock is a troubled soul, beset by alcoholism and insecurity, who leads himself down a self-destructive path. The film covers 1941-1956 as Pollock struggles to find his artistic breakthrough and marries fellow artist Lee Krasner (Harden), a tough New Yorker who takes his career in hand, but his success only exacerbates Pollock's problems. Solid production with a couple of great leading performances; based on the book by Steven Naifeh and Gregory White Smith. **122m/C VHS, DVD.** Ed Harris, Marcia Gay Harden, Amy Madigan, Jennifer Connelly, Jeffrey Tambor, Bud Cort, John Heard, Val Kilmer; *D:* Ed Harris; *W:* Barbara Turner, Susan J. Emshwiller; *C:* Lisa Rinzler; *M:* Jeff Beal. Oscars '00: Support. Actress (Harden); N.Y. Film Critics '00: Support. Actress (Harden).

Pollyanna 1/2 **1920** A young orphan girl is adopted by her cold, embittered aunt and does her best to bring joy and gladness to all the new people she meets. Silent with music score. **60m/B VHS.** Katherine Griffith, Helen Jerome Eddy, Wharton James, George Berrell, Howard Ralston, Mary Pickford; *D:* Paul Powell; *W:* Frances Marion; *C:* Charles Rosher.

Pollyanna 1/2 **1960** Based on the Eleanor Porter story about an enchanting young girl whose contagious enthusiasm and zest for life touches the hearts of all she meets. Mills is perfect in the title role and was awarded a special Oscar for outstanding juvenile performance. A distinguished supporting cast is the icing on the cake in this delightful Disney confection. Original version was filmed in 1920 with Mary Pickford. **134m/C VHS, DVD.** Hayley Mills, Jane Wyman, Richard Egan, Karl Malden, Nancy Olson, Adolphe Menjou, Donald Crisp, Agnes Moorehead, Kevin Corcoran; *D:* David Swift; *W:* David Swift; *C:* Russell Harlan; *M:* Paul J. Smith.

Poltergeist **1982 (PG)** This production has Stephen Spielberg written all over it. A young family's home becomes a house of horrors when they are terrorized by menancing spirits who abduct their five-year-old daughter...through the TV screen! Roller-coaster thrills and chills, dazzling special effects, and perfectly timed humor highlight this stupendously scary ghost story. **114m/C VHS, DVD.** JoBeth Williams, Craig T. Nelson, Beatrice Straight, Heather O'Rourke, Zelda Rubinstein, Dominique Dunne, Oliver Robins, Richard Lawson, James Karen, Michael McManus; *D:* Tobe Hooper; *W:* Steven Spielberg, Michael Grais, Mark Victor; *C:* Matthew F. Leonetti; *M:* Jerry Goldsmith.

Poltergeist 2: The Other Side 1/2 **1986 (PG-13)** Adequate sequel to the Spielburg-produced venture into the supernatural, where demons follow the Freeling family in their efforts to recapture the clairvoyant young daughter Carol Anne. The film includes sojourns into Indian lore and a four-foot high agave worm designed by H.R. Giger. The movie was followed by "Poltergeist 3" in 1988. **92m/C VHS, DVD.** Craig T. Nelson, JoBeth Williams, Heather O'Rourke, Will Sampson, Julian Beck, Geraldine Fitzgerald, Oliver Robins, Zelda Rubinstein; *D:* Brian Gibson; *W:* Mark Victor, Michael Grais; *C:* Andrew Laszlo; *M:* Jerry Goldsmith.

Poltergeist 3 1/2 **1988 (PG-13)** Wrestling with the supernatural has finally unnerved Carol Ann and she's sent to stay with her aunt and uncle in Chicago where she attends a school for gifted children with emotional disorders. Guess who follows her? Uninspired acting, threadbare premise, and one ghastly encounter too many. Oddly, O'Rourke died suddenly four months before the film's release. **97m/C VHS, DVD.** Tom Skerritt, Nancy Allen, Heather O'Rourke, Lara Flynn Boyle, Zelda Rubinstein; *D:* Gary Sherman; *W:* Gary Sherman, Brian Taggert; *C:* Alex Nepomniaschy.

Poltergeist: The Legacy 1/2 **1996** Pilot for the cable series about a secret international society, the Legacy, which is devoted to the paranormal and to protecting mankind from supernatural evil. Derek Rayne (De Lint), the head of the San Francisco Legacy house, must find the last of five sepulchers containing the evil spirits of five fallen angels. This takes him and his cohorts to Ireland where Rachel Corrigan (Shaver) and her young psychic daughter Kat (Purvis) come into unwitting possession of the fifth box and untold danger. **86m/C VHS, DVD.** Derek de Lint, Helen Shaver, Alexandra Purvis, Martin Cummins, Robbi Chong, Patrick Fitzgerald, Jordan Bayne, William Sadler, Daniel Pilon, Chad Krowchuk; *D:* Stuart Gillard; *W:* Brad Wright; *C:* Manfred Guthe. **CABLE**

Polyester 1/2 **1981 (R)** Amusing satire on middle-class life, described by producer, director and writer Waters as "'Father Knows Best' gone berserk." Forlorn housewife Divine pines for the man of her dreams while the rest of her life is falling apart at the seams. Filmed in "Odorama," a hilarious gimmick in which theatre goers were provided with scratch-n-sniff cards, containing specific scents corresponding to key scenes. Video watchers will have to use their imagination in experiencing a wide range of smells. The first of Waters' more mainstream films. Features songs by Murray and Harry. **86m/C VHS, DVD.** Divine, Tab Hunter, Edith Massey, Mink Stole, Stiv Bators, David Samson, Mary Garlington, Kenneth King, Joni-Ruth White, Jean Hill, Hans Kramm, Mary Vivian Pearce, Cookie Mueller, Susan Lowe, George Stover, George Figgs, Steve Yeager; *D:* John Waters; *W:* John Waters; *C:* David Insley; *M:* Deborah Harry, Michael Kamen.

Pom Poko 1/2 *Heisei tanuki gassen pompoko; The Raccoon War* **1994 (PG)** Despite being referred to as the Raccoon War, this film actually stars Tanuki—a sort of wild dog native to Japan that resembles a raccoon. The humans are encroaching upon the Tanuki's forest realm with new urban development, and they've decided to fight for their forest homes any way they can. Not necessarily a children's film despite being animated, and surprisingly lightly censored given that Disney translated it. A working knowledge of Japanese myth will also aid greatly in understanding. **112m/C DVD.** *JP* *D:* Isao Takahata; *W:* Isao Takahata; *V:* Maurice LaMarche, Jonathan Taylor Thomas, J.K. Simmons, Tress MacNeille, Clancy Brown, Jess Harnell, Kevin M. Richardson, Olivia D'Abo, Marc Donato, Brian George, Brian Posehn, Jillian Bowen, David Oliver Cohen, John Di Maggio, Wally Kurth.

Pom Pom Girls 🦴 1/2 **1976 (R)** High school seniors, intent on having one last fling before graduating, get involved in crazy antics, clumsy romances, and football rivalries. **90m/C VHS, DVD.** Robert Carradine, Jennifer Ashley, Michael Mullins, Cheryl "Rainbeaux" Smith, Dianne Lee Hart, Lisa Reeves, Bill Adler; ***D:*** Joseph Ruben; ***W:*** Joseph Ruben; ***C:*** Stephen M. Katz; ***M:*** Michael Lloyd.

The Pompatus of Love 🦴🦴 1/2 **1995 (R)** Remember Steve Miller's song "The Joker"?—well, that's where the title comes from—and we still don't know what it means. But the film's about four New York guys and the mystery of women. They may be (reasonably) bright and literate but they still don't have a clue about love or how to grow-up. Naturally, the women they know—or meet—are all too smart for them. **99m/C VHS, DVD.** Jon Cryer, Tim Guinee, Adrian Pasdar, Adam Oliensis, Kristen Wilson, Dana Wheeler-Nicholson, Paige Turco, Mia Sara, Kristin Scott Thomas, Arabella Field, Jennifer Tilly, Roscoe Lee Browne; ***D:*** Richard Schenkman; ***W:*** Jon Cryer, Adam Oliensis, Richard Schenkman; ***C:*** Russell Fine; ***M:*** John Hill. **VIDEO**

The Ponder Heart 🦴🦴 1/2 **2001** Eccentric Daniel Ponder (MacNicol) wants to give all his inherited fortune away. So folks in his Mississippi community considered him a mite peculiar, especially after he suddenly marries the teenaged Bonnie Dee (Bettis). Then Bonnie disappears and Ponder is put on trial for the alleged murder of his bride. Easy-going southern charm and smalltown craziness. Based on the novel by Eudora Welty. **120m/C VHS.** Peter MacNichol, JoBeth Williams, Angela Bettis; ***D:*** Martha Coolidge. **TV**

Ponette 🦴🦴 **1995** Four-year-old Ponette (Thivisol) is hard-pressed to understand what's happening to her family after her mother is killed in a car accident. Her father can't seem to explain it properly, so Ponette comes to her own acceptance with the help of some school friends. Film drew some controversy when the very young Thivisol was awarded the best actress award at the Venice Film Festival—since Thivisol was thought by some critics to be too young to "act," director Doillon was accused of manipulating the youngster in order to get a performance. French with subtitles. **92m/C VHS, DVD.** *FR* Victorie Thivisol, Marie Trintignant, Claire Nebout, Xavier Beauvois; ***D:*** Jacques Doillon; ***W:*** Jacques Doillon; ***C:*** Caroline Champetier; ***M:*** Philippe Sarde. N.Y. Film Critics '97: Foreign Film; Venice Film Fest. '96: Actress (Thivisol).

Pontiac Moon 🦴 1/2 **1994 (PG-13)** Danson plays a high school teacher who takes his son on a road trip to Spires of the Moon National Park hoping to arrive simultaneously with the astronauts' first lunar landing. His wife (Steenburgen) decides to follow them, although she's phobic about leaving the house and hasn't set foot outside in seven years. Sincere yet tedious film about father-son bonding has a few heartfelt moments, but not enough to sustain interest for entire viewing period. Best (and only) reason for watching: Monument Valley scenery. **108m/C VHS, DVD.** Ted Danson, Mary Steenburgen, Ryan Todd, Eric Schweig, Cathy Moriarty, Max Gail, Lisa Jane Persky; ***D:*** Peter Medak; ***W:*** Finn Taylor, Jeffrey Brown; ***M:*** Randy Edelman.

Pontypool 🦴 1/2 **2009** The staff of radio station CLSY broadcasts from a church basement in the rural Ontario town of the title. On Valentine's Day, the station is besieged by callers reporting cases of extreme violence in the town and it turns out tainted English language (especially endearments) is making zombies out of the listeners. So to prevent the spread of the infection, hard-drinking DJ Grant (McHattie) and his cohorts resort to broken French to get by (only in bilingual Canada). Burgess adapted from his novel "Pontypool Changes Everything." English and French with subtitles. **95m/C DVD.** *CA* Stephen McHattie, Rick Roberts, Grant Alianak, Lisa Houle, Georgina Reilly; ***D:*** Bruce McDonald; ***W:*** Tony Burgess; ***C:*** Miroslaw Baszak; ***M:*** Claude Foisy.

The Pony Express 🦴🦴 1/2 **1925** Melodramatic western about an evil senator (Hart) who's out to establish his own empire. His scheme is thwarted by pony express rider Cortez. Based on the novel by Henry James Forman and Walter Woods. **67m/B VHS.** Ricardo Cortez, Al Hart, Betty Compson, Ernest Torrence, Wallace Beery, George Bancroft, Frank Lackteen; ***D:*** James Cruze; ***W:*** Walter Woods.

Pony Express 🦴🦴🦴 **1953** Buffalo Bill Cody and Wild Bill Hickok join forces to extend the Pony Express mail route west to California through rain and sleet, snow and hail. Far from a factual account but good for extending the myth of the Old West. **101m/C VHS.** Charlton Heston, Rhonda Fleming, Jan Sterling, Forrest Tucker; ***D:*** Jerry Hopper; ***C:*** Ray Rennahan.

Pony Express Rider 🦴🦴🦴 **1976 (G)** Young man with a mission joins up with the Pony Express hoping to bag the male responsible for killing his pa. The well-produced script boasts a bevy of veteran western character actors, all lending, solid, rugged performances. **100m/C VHS.** Stewart Petersen, Henry Wilcoxon, Buck Taylor, Maureen McCormick, Joan Caulfield, Ken Curtis, Slim Pickens, Dub Taylor, Jack Elam; ***D:*** Robert Totten.

Pony Post 🦴 1/2 **1940** Standard horse opera has Brown running a pony express station where he battles Indians and typical villains. **59m/B VHS.** Johnny Mack Brown, Fuzzy Knight, Nell O'Day, Dorothy Short, Kermit Maynard, Lane Chandler; ***D:*** Ray Taylor; ***W:*** Sherman Lowe.

Ponyo 🦴🦴🦴 *Gake no Ue no Ponyo; Ponyo on the Cliff by the Sea* **2008 (G)** Miyazaki's wonderfully joyous animated story (a variation of "The Little Mermaid") finds young fish princess Ponyo so curious about the surface world that she goes exploring and needs to be rescued by Sosuke, a five-year-old boy who promises to protect her. So Ponyo decides to become human and stay awhile, but Ponyo's sorcerer father eventually takes her home, only to have his willful daughter escape again. This time she causes ecological havoc by accidentally releasing one of her dad's magic potions and it's Sosuke and his village that will need saving. The Japanese film was redone with an English-language cast. **100m/C DVD.** *JP* ***D:*** Hayao Miyazaki; ***W:*** Hayao Miyazaki; ***M:*** Joe Hisaishi; ***V:*** Cate Blanchett, Tina Fey, Liam Neeson, Betty White, Lily Tomlin, Cloris Leachman, Noah Lindsey Cyrus, Matt Damon, Frankie Jonas.

The Pooch and the Pauper 🦴🦴 **1999 (G)** This may be the first film where dogs switch identities. So the Presidential pooch has been replaced by a lookalike and the confused interloper can only be considered a, well, bad dog. Meanwhile, the First Pup is being pursued by a dogcatcher on those mean D.C. streets. Hey, it's Disney, so every dog has its day. **88m/C VHS.** Fred Willard, George Wendt, Richard Karn, Vincent Schiavelli; ***D:*** Alex Zamm; ***W:*** Mark Steilen, Bennett Yellin; ***C:*** Albert J. Dunk; ***M:*** Chris Hajian; ***V:*** Peter MacNichol, Daryl (Chill) Mitchell. **VIDEO**

Poodle Springs 🦴🦴 **1998** In 1963, Philip Marlowe (Caan) has a wealthy young wife (Meyer) and is living in Palm Springs. Bored, he decides to get back into the PI biz and is soon dealing with land swindlers and dead bodies (and a confusing plot) that lead to a political conspiracy. Raymond Chandler died before finishing his novel and his estate eventually hired Robert B. Parker to complete it from Chandler's outline. **96m/C DVD.** James Caan, Dina Meyer, David Keith, Brian Cox, Julia Campbell, Nia Peeples, Joe Don Baker; ***D:*** Bob Rafelson; ***W:*** Tom Stoppard; ***C:*** Stuart Dryburgh; ***M:*** Michael Small. **CABLE**

Pooh's Heffalump Movie 🦴🦴 **2005 (G)** Another addition to Disney's Winnie-the-Pooh collection. The Hundred Acre gang suspects that a heffalump has been wandering the forest. Pooh, Piglet, Eeyore, Tigger, Rabbit and Kanga all decided to go capture what they think is a fearsome creature. Roo wants to join, too, but is told he is too young. He decides to go on his own adventure, where in the course of events, he meets and befriends Lumpy, the not-so-fearsome heffalump. Mild story has a nice moral about accepting differences in people, which should please the parents. Not Disney glory days great, but kids will like it. **63m/C VHS, DVD.** *US* ***D:*** Frank Nissen; ***W:*** Brian Hohlfield, Evan Spiliotopolos; ***M:*** Joel McNeely; ***V:*** Jim (Jonah) Cummings, John Fiedler, Nikita Hopkins, Kath Soucie, Ken Sansom, Peter Cullen, Brenda Blethyn, Kyle Stanger.

Pool Hustlers 🦴 1/2 **1983** A romantic comedy about an amateur billiards whiz who finds love and successfully defeats the national champ. In Italian with English subtitles. **101m/C VHS.** *IT* Francesco Nuti, Guiliana de Sio, Marcello Loti; ***D:*** Maurizio Ponzi.

Pool Sharks 🦴🦴 1/2 **1915** W.C. Fields' first film features the comedian's antics while playing a pool game to win the love of a woman. Silent. **10m/B VHS, DVD.** W.C. Fields; ***D:*** Edwin Middleton; ***W:*** W.C. Fields.

Poolhall Junkies 🦴🦴 1/2 **2002 (R)** Johnny Doyle (writer-director Callahan) is a pool hustler who always aspired to greatness, and could've had it. His mentor/backer Joe (Palminteri) sabotaged his chance at the pro tour a while back. When Johnny left him, Joe broke his wrist and found himself a new boy, Brad (Schroder). Johnny impresses his girlfriend's uncle Mike (Walken) who agrees to bankroll his road to the final showdown with Brad and Joe. Gritty but enthusiastic debut for Callahan doesn't wallow in cliches, it revels in 'em. Fortunately, it all works because of Callahan's obvious joy at getting to make the movie, the work of the elder actors (including Steiger in his last role), and the good sense of the younger ones to stay out of their way. Walken's performance alone is worth the price of a rental. Excellent pool hall action makes up for the times Walken's not on screen. **94m/C VHS, DVD.** *US* Mars Callahan, Michael Rosenbaum, Chazz Palminteri, Rod Steiger, Christopher Walken, Rick Schroder, Alison Eastwood, Glenn Plummer, Ernie Reyes Jr., Peter Mark Richman, Anson Mount; ***D:*** Mars Callahan; ***W:*** Mars Callahan, Chris Corso; ***C:*** Robert Morris; ***M:*** Richard Glasser.

Poor Girl, a Ghost Story 🦴🦴 **1974** A young girl takes a job as a governess at an English mansion and is besieged by all manner of strange goings-on. **52m/C VHS.** *AU* Lynn Miller, Angela Thorne; ***D:*** Michael Apted.

A Poor Little Rich Girl 🦴🦴🦴 **1917** Mary Pickford received raves in this film, in which she portrayed Gwendolyn, with everything money could buy, except the attention of her family. Gwendolyn has a bizarre dream in which she sees a number of horrors and is tempted by death. Elaborate sets and special effects, as well as Pickford's delicate performance, make this one special. Organ score. **64m/B VHS.** Mary Pickford, Madeline Traverse, Charles Wellesley, Gladys Fairbanks; ***D:*** Maurice Tourneur. Natl. Film Reg. '91.

The Poor Little Rich Girl 🦴🦴 1/2 **1936** A motherless rich girl wanders away from home and is "adopted" by a pair of struggling vaudevillians. With her help, they rise to the big time. ♫ Oh My Goodness; Buy a Bar of Barry's; Wash Your Neck With a Cake of Peck's; Military Man; When I'm with You; But Definitely; You've Gotta Eat Your Spinach, Baby. **79m/B VHS.** Shirley Temple, Jack Haley, Alice Faye, Gloria Stuart, Michael Whalen, Sara Haden, Jane Darwell; ***D:*** Irving Cummings.

Poor Little Rich Girl: The Barbara Hutton Story 🦴🦴 1/2 **1987** Biodrama of the one-time richest woman in America, Woolworth heiress Hutton (Fawcett), and her extravagant lifestyle. She married seven times (including actor Cary Grant) until falling into self-destructive alcohol and drug addictions. Lavishly presented but superficial. Based on the book by C. David Heymann. **98m/C VHS.** Farrah Fawcett, Bruce Davison, Kevin McCarthy, Burl Ives, James Read, Stephane Audran, Anne Francis, David Ackroyd, Tony Peck, Zoe Wanamaker, Amadeus August; ***D:*** Charles Jarrott; ***W:*** Dennis Turner; ***M:*** Richard Rodney Bennett. **TV**

Poor Man's Game 🦴🦴🦴 *Poor Boy's Game* **2006 (R)** Provocative look at racism and redemption. White working-class Donnie Rose (Sutherland, son of Donald) is released from prison after serving 10 years for the brutal beating of a black man named Keith Carvery, who was left brain damaged. The racially-motivated incident has continued to divide the black and white communities of Halifax. Having boxed in the joint, Donnie agrees to a grudge match with local fisticuffs star Ossie (Alexander), a violent friend of the Carvery family. After much soul-searching, George Carvery (a strong Glover) decides that an eye-for-an-eye has to stop and he offers to become Donnie's trainer so he'll have a chance to survive. **104m/C DVD.** *CA* Danny Glover, Rossif Sutherland, Flex Alexander, Stephen McHattie, Tonya Lee Williams, Greg Bryk, K.C. Collins, Laura Reagan; ***D:*** Clement Virgo; ***W:*** Chaz Thorne, Clement Virgo; ***C:*** Luc Montpellier; ***M:*** Bryon Kent Wong.

Poor Pretty Eddie 🦴 1/2 *Black Vengeance; Heartbreak Motel; Redneck County* **1973 (R)** A young black singer gets waylaid and taken in by a twisted white Southern clan. An incredibly sleazy movie which boasts Shelly Winters performing a strip act. **90m/C DVD.** Leslie Uggams, Shelley Winters, Michael Christian, Ted Cassidy, Slim Pickens, Dub Taylor; ***D:*** Richard Robinson.

Poor White Trash 🦴 1/2 *Bayou* **1957** An architect arrives in bayou country with plans to design a new building. He meets with resistance from the locals but falls for the sensual daughter of one of his staunchest detractors. **83m/B VHS.** Peter Graves, Lita Milan, Douglas Fowley, Timothy Carey, Jonathan Haze; ***D:*** Harold Daniels.

Poor White Trash 🦴 1/2 **2000 (R)** One-note comedy. Buddies Mike (Denman) and Lennie's (Tierney) prank on a local store owner backfires and the boys are in bigtime trouble that could be eased if they had money for defense attorney Ron (Devane). So Mike's trailer-trash mom, Linda (Young), and her boy toy Brian (London) agree to help the dummies raise the money through some burglaries that, of course, get botched. The gags are repeated so often that they lose what humor they initially possessed. **85m/C VHS, DVD.** Jacob Tierney, Sean Young, Jason London, Tony Denman, William Devane, Jaime Pressly, M. Emmet Walsh, Tim Kazurinsky; ***D:*** Michael Addis; ***W:*** Michael Addis; ***C:*** Peter Kowalski; ***M:*** Tree Adams.

Poor White Trash 2 🦴 *Scum of the Earth* **1975 (R)** A young couple, vacationing in Louisiana's bayou country, are introduced to an unusual brand of southern hospitality by the eponymous group of locals. **90m/C VHS.** Gene Ross, Ann Stafford, Norma Moore, Camilla Carr; ***D:*** S.F. Brownrigg.

Pootie Tang 🦴 1/2 **2001 (PG-13)** The gibberish-babbling Pootie Tang (Crouther) was mildly amusing as a three-minute one-joke sketch on "The Chris Rock Show." Stretched to 80 minutes, it turns into "It's Pat 2: Electric Boogaloo." The premise here is that Pootie talks so cool, no one wants to admit they don't have a clue what he's saying. He's also a role model to all the kids and fights crime with his whip-crackin' belt, which he wields like a kung-fu master. Evil captain of industry Lecter (Vaughn) tricks Pootie into endorsing his empire of cigarettes, booze and junk food by using the feminine wiles of slinky Ireenie (Coolidge). Pootie retires in disgrace to his hometown before he can come back and make everything wambly again. Or something like that. It really is hard to figure out what that dude is saying. **81m/C VHS, DVD.** *US* Lance Crouther, Jennifer Coolidge, Robert Vaughn, Chris Rock, Reg E. Cathey, Wanda Sykes, Dave Attell, Mario Joyner, JB Smoove, Cathy Trien, Andy Richter, Kristen Bell; ***Cameos:*** Bob Costas; ***D:*** Louis CK; ***W:*** Louis CK; ***C:*** Willy Kurant.

Pop Always Pays 🦴🦴 **1940** A father gets in a jam when he has to make good on a bet with his daughter's boyfriend. **67m/B VHS.** Walter Catlett, Dennis O'Keefe, Leon Errol, Pamela Blake; ***D:*** Leslie Goodwins.

Popcorn 🦴🦴 **1989 (R)** A killer stalks a movie audience who is unaware that his crimes are paralleling those in the very film they are watching. **93m/C VHS, DVD.** Jill Schoelen, Tom Villard, Dee Wallace, Derek Rydall, Elliott Hurst, Kelly Jo Minter, Malcolm Danare, Ray Walston, Tony Roberts, Karen Witter; ***D:*** Mark Herrier, Alan Ormsby; ***W:*** Alan Ormsby; ***C:*** Ronnie Taylor.

Pope Dreams 🦴🦴 1/2 **2006** Quiet, aimless teenager Andy works for his dad and drums in a garage band. His devoutly Catholic mother Kristina is dying and Andy (who's closest to her) is trying to come up with a way to fulfill her dream of seeing the Vatican. Meanwhile, might-be girlfriend Brady discovers the guy she chose to date because she thought it would upset her dad is really a keeper. **105m/C DVD.** Marne Patterson, Stephen Tobolowsky, Noel Fisher, Rex Smith, Phillip Vaden, Julie Haggerty, David Shatraw, Larisa Oleynik; ***D:*** Patrick Hogan; ***W:*** Patrick Hogan; ***C:*** John Ealer; ***M:*** Joel J. Richard. **VIDEO**

Pope John Paul II 1984 Biography of the Pontiff, from childhood to world eminence. **150m/C VHS.** Albert Finney, Michael Crompton, Nigel Hawthorne, John McEnery, Brian Cox; ***D:*** Herbert Wise. **TV**

The Pope Must Diet 1/2 *The Pope Must Die* **1991 (R)** Coltrane stars as a misfit who accidentally becomes Pope Dave I. Living up to the benevolence suggested by his title, Pope Dave proposes to use Vatican money to create a children's fund. But there are those in the organization who have different, less noble plans for the cash, and soon Dave finds himself the target of a mob hit. Frantic comedy caused a stir with its original title "The Pope Must Die," with many newspapers refusing to run ads for the film. This, coupled with lukewarm critical reviews, led to a very brief stint at the boxoffice. **87m/C VHS.** *GB* Robbie Coltrane, Alex Rocco, Beverly D'Angelo, Herbert Lom, Paul Bartel, Salvatore Cascio, Balthazar Getty; ***D:*** Peter Richardson; ***M:*** Anne Dudley.

The Pope of Greenwich Village 1/2 **1984 (R)** Two Italian-American cousins (Rourke and Roberts) struggle to escape the trap of poverty in New York's Greenwich Village. When a small crime goes wrong in a big way, the two must learn about deception and loyalty. Mostly character study; Page is exceptional. Inferior re-run of the "Mean Streets" idea does have its moments. **122m/C VHS, DVD.** Eric Roberts, Mickey Rourke, Daryl Hannah, Geraldine Page, Tony Musante, M. Emmet Walsh, Kenneth McMillan, Burt Young, Jack Kehoe, Philip Bosco, Val Avery, Joe Grifasi, Tony DiBenedetto; ***D:*** Stuart Rosenberg; ***W:*** Vincent Patrick; ***C:*** John Bailey; ***M:*** Dave Grusin.

Popeye **1980 (PG)** The cartoon sailor brought to life is on a search to find his long-lost father. Along the way, he meets Olive Oyl and adopts little Sweet Pea. Williams accomplishes the near-impossible feat of physically resembling the title character, and the whole movie does accomplish the maker's stated goal of "looking like a comic strip," but it isn't anywhere near as funny as it should be. **114m/C VHS, DVD.** Ned Dowd, Allan Nicholls, Robin Williams, Shelley Duvall, Ray Walston, Paul Dooley, Bill Irwin, Paul Smith, Linda Hunt, Richard Libertini; ***D:*** Robert Altman; ***W:*** Jules Feiffer; ***M:*** Harry Nilsson.

Popeye's Voyage: The Quest for Pappy 1/2 **2004** Popeye's searching the seas for his Pappy with Olive Oyl and Sweet Pea in tow so they don't miss any happy holiday family time. Old standbys Bluto, Wimpy, and the Sea Hag all pop up in this animated romp. **44m/C VHS, DVD.** Kathy Bates, Marcel Jonker, Garry Chalk, Billy West, Tabitha St. Germain, Sanders Whiting; ***D:*** Ezekiel Norton; ***W:*** Paul Reiser, Jim Hardison. **VIDEO**

Popi **1969 (G)** Arkin is the heart and soul of this poignant charmer in his role as a Puerto Rican immigrant hell-bent on securing a better life outside the ghetto for his two sons. His zany efforts culminate in one outrageous scheme to set them adrift off the Florida coast in hopes they will be rescued and raised by a wealthy family. Far fetched, but ultimately heartwarming. **115m/C VHS, DVD.** Alan Arkin, Rita Moreno, Miguel Alejandro, Reuben Figueroa; ***D:*** Arthur Hiller.

The Poppy Is Also a Flower 1/2 *Poppies Are Also Flowers; Opium Connection* **1966 (PG)** A star-laden, anti-drug drama produced by the United Nations. Filmed on location in Iran, Monaco, and Italy. Based on a drug trade thriller by Ian Fleming that explains how poppies, converted into heroin, are brought into the United States. **100m/C VHS.** E.G. Marshall, Trevor Howard, Gilbert Roland, Eli Wallach, Marcello Mastroianni, Angie Dickinson, Rita Hayworth, Yul Brynner, Trini Lopez, Bessie Love; ***D:*** Terence Young. **TV**

Population 436 **2006 (R)** Census investigator Steve Kady (Sisto) is sent to the reclusive town of Rockwell Falls, where the population has remained unchanged at 436 people for more than 100 years. The town seems idyllic although excess residents have a tendency to succumb to a strange fever. Can Steve stay alive long enough to figure out what's really going on? Sisto plays the horror straight and Limp Bizkit frontman Durst is amiable as the town law. **92m/C DVD.** *CA* Jeremy Sisto, Fred Durst, R.H. Thomson, Peter Outerbridge, Charlotte Sullivan, David Ames, David Fox; ***D:*** Michelle Maxwell MacLaren; ***W:*** Michael Kingston; ***C:*** Thomas Burstyn. **VIDEO**

Porcile *Pigsty; Porcherie* **1969** Pasolini intertwines the story of a soldier cannibal living in a medieval age with the son of an ex-Nazi industrialist in present day Germany. Both the soldier and the young German (who prefers pigs to his fiance) become sacrificial victims of their differing societies. A grotesque fable on Pasolini's hatred of middle class mores and the 20th century. In Italian with English subtitles. **90m/C VHS, DVD.** *IT FR* Pierre Clementi, Franco Citti, Jean-Pierre Leaud, Anna Wiazemsky, Ugo Tognazzi, Alberto Lionello; ***D:*** Pier Paolo Pasolini; ***W:*** Pier Paolo Pasolini; ***C:*** Armando Nannuzzi, Giuseppe Ruzzolini, Tonino Delli Colli.

Pork Chop Hill **1959** A powerful, hard-hitting account of the last hours of the Korean War. Peck is totally believable as the man ordered to hold his ground against the hopeless onslaught of Chinese Communist hordes. A chilling, stark look in the face of a no-win situation. Top notch cast and masterful directing. **97m/B VHS, DVD.** Gregory Peck, Harry Guardino, Rip Torn, George Peppard, James Edwards, Bob Steele, Woody Strode, Robert (Bobby) Blake, Martin Landau, Norman Fell, Bert Remsen, George Shibata, Biff (Elliott) Elliot, Barry Atwater, Martin Garth, Lew Gallo, Charles Aidman, Leonard Graves, Ken Lynch, Paul Comi, Cliff Ketchum, Abel Fernandez, Gavin MacLeod; ***D:*** Lewis Milestone; ***W:*** James R. Webb; ***C:*** Sam Leavitt; ***M:*** Leonard Rosenman.

Porky's 1/2 **1982 (R)** Investigation of teen horniness set in South Florida during the fab '50s. Irreverent comedy follows the misadventures of six youths imprisoned in Angel Beach High School who share a common interest: girls. Their main barrier to sexual success: the no-touch babes they lust after and the incredibly stupid adults who run the world. Fairly dumb and tasteless with occasional big laughs that earned mega bucks at the drive-in and created perceived popular outcry for more porky: "Porky's II: The Next Day" (1983) and "Porky's Revenge" (1985). **94m/C VHS, DVD.** *CA* Dan Monahan, Wyatt Knight, Scott Colomby, Tony Ganios, Mark Herrier, Cyril O'Reilly, Roger Wilson, Alex Karras, Kim Cattrall, Kaki Hunter, Nancy Parsons, Boyd Gaines, Douglas McGrath, Susan Clark, Art Hindle, Wayne Maunder, Chuck "Porky" Mitchell, Eric Christmas, Bob (Benjamin) Clark; ***D:*** Bob (Benjamin) Clark; ***W:*** Bob (Benjamin) Clark; ***C:*** Reginald Morris; ***M:*** Paul Zaza, Carl Zittrer.

Porky's 2: The Next Day **1983 (R)** More tame tomfoolery about teenage sex drives, Shakespeare, fat high school teachers, the Ku Klux Klan, and streaking in the Florida high school where it all began. Outright caricature shares the stage with juvenile humor, some of which may induce laughter. **100m/C VHS, DVD.** *CA* Bill Wiley, Dan Monahan, Wyatt Knight, Cyril O'Reilly, Roger Wilson, Tony Ganios, Mark Herrier, Scott Colomby, Kaki Hunter, Nancy Parsons, Eric Christmas, Art Hindle; ***D:*** Bob (Benjamin) Clark; ***W:*** Alan Ormsby, Bob (Benjamin) Clark, Roger E. Swaybill; ***C:*** Reginald Morris; ***M:*** Carl Zittrer.

Porky's Revenge **1985 (R)** The Angel Beach High School students are out to get revenge against Porky who orders the school basketball coach to throw the championship game. The second of the "Porky's" sequels. **95m/C VHS.** *CA* Dan Monahan, Wyatt Knight, Tony Ganios, Nancy Parsons, Chuck "Porky" Mitchell, Kaki Hunter, Kimberly Evenson, Scott Colomby, Mark Herrier, Eric Christmas, Rose McVeigh; ***D:*** James Komack; ***W:*** Ziggy Steinberg; ***C:*** Robert C. Jessup; ***M:*** Dave Edmunds.

The Pornographer **2000 (R)** In his introduction, director Atchison says that the inspiration for this story of lonely guy Paul Ryan (Degood) who becomes a porno filmmaker almost by accident came from his own situation. While trying to raise money for his own legitimate movies, Atchison briefly considered trying to make skin flicks to raise money. Instead, he came up with an intriguing little video premiere. **88m/C VHS, DVD.** Michael Degood, Craig Wasson, Monique Parent, Katheryn Cain; ***D:*** Doug Atchison; ***W:*** Doug Atchison; ***C:*** Christopher Mosio; ***M:*** Warner David Jansen.

The Pornographers **1966** Bizzare, black comedy focuses on a part-time porno filmmaker lusting after the daughter of the widow he lives with and trying to cope with his family, the world, and himself. A perversely fascinating exploration of contemporary Japanese society and the many facets of sexual emotion. In Japanese with English subtitles. **128m/B VHS, DVD.** *JP* Shoichi Ozawa, Massaomi Konda, Sumiko Sakamoto, Haruo Tanaka, Keiko Sagowa; ***D:*** Shohei Imamura.

Porridge *Doing Time* **1991** A British comedy inspired by the popular BBC situation comedy of the title, about a habitual criminal and convict who makes the most of his time in prison. **105m/C VHS, DVD.** *GB* Ronnie Barker, Fulton Mackay, Peter Vaughan, Julian Holloway, Geoffrey Bayldon; ***D:*** Dick Clement.

Port of Call **1948** Early Bergman drama about a seaman on the docks who falls for a troubled woman whose wild, unhappy past has earned her an unsavory reputation. The hopeful, upbeat tone seems incongruous with the grim harbor/slum setting. It's minor Bergman but the seeds of his trademark themes can be seen taking shape, making it a must-see for avid fans. In Swedish with English subtitles. **100m/B VHS, DVD.** *SW* Ivine-Christine Jonsson, Bengt Eklund, Erik Hell, Berta Hall, Mimi Nelson; ***D:*** Ingmar Bergman.

The Port of Missing Girls **1938** A young woman implicated in a murder stows away on a freighter. There she becomes caught up in a waterfront world of pirates, smugglers and other assorted undesirables. **56m/B VHS.** Harry Carey Sr., Judith Allen, Milburn Stone, Betty Compson; ***D:*** Karl Brown.

Port of New York **1949** A narcotics gang is smuggling large quantities of drugs into New York. A government agent poses as a gang member in order to infiltrate the mob and get the goods on them. Brynner's film debut. **82m/B VHS, DVD.** Scott Brady, Yul Brynner, K.T. Stevens; ***D:*** Laszlo Benedek.

Portfolio **1988 (R)** Real-life models star in this gritty drama about rising to the top of the fashion heap. Music by Eurythmics, Fun Boy Three and others. **83m/C VHS.** Paulina Porizkova, Julie Wolfe, Carol Alt, Kelly Emberg; ***D:*** Robert Guralnick; ***C:*** Edward Lachman.

Portland Expose 1/2 **1957** Stilted noir supposedly based on an actual expose of mob/union corruption. George Madison owns a Portland, Oregon tavern and is being pressured by mobsters and corrupt union members to add some sleazy action to his joint. When his daughter is attacked by a goon, George decides to get evidence to put them all in jail. **72m/B DVD.** Edward Binns, Carolyn Craig, Virginia Gregg, Frank Gorshin, Lawrence (Larry) Dobkin, Joseph Marr; ***D:*** Harold Schuster; ***W:*** Jack DeWitt; ***C:*** Carl Berger; ***M:*** Paul Dunlap.

Portnoy's Complaint 1/2 **1972 (R)** Limp screen adaptation of Philip Roth's novel follows the frustrating experiences of a sexually obsessed young man as he relates them to his psychiatrist. **101m/C VHS.** Richard Benjamin, Karen Black, Lee Grant, Jeannie Berlin, Jill Clayburgh; ***D:*** Ernest Lehman; ***W:*** Ernest Lehman.

The Portrait **1993** Longtime real-life friends Bacall and Peck on-screen together for the first time in 37 years prove they are still shining stars as they play aging parents to Peck's real-life daughter, Cecilia Peck. The younger Peck is an artist preparing for a exhibition and asks her parents to sit for a portrait. This is the pole around which their relationships and reconciliations swing in this emotional drama based loosely on Tina Howe's 1983 off-Broadway play, "Painting Churches." **89m/C VHS.** Lauren Bacall, Gregory Peck, Cecilia Peck, Paul McCrane, Joyce O'Connor, Donna Mitchell, Mitchell Laurance, William Prince, Augusta Dabney; ***D:*** Arthur Penn; ***W:*** Lynn Roth, Jack Darcus; ***M:*** Michael Conway Baker. **CABLE**

The Portrait 1/2 **1999 (R)** A distaff version of "The Picture of Dorian Gray." Beautiful woman meets strange photographer whose work is weird. Nevertheless, she poses for him and, after seeing the results, unwittingly vows to remain as eternally youthful as her portrait. But the photo shows the real story as time passes by. **85m/C VHS, DVD.** Gabriella Hall, Jenna Bodnar, Avalon Anders, Christopher Johnston; ***D:*** David Goldner; ***W:*** David Goldner; ***C:*** Rocky Dijon. **VIDEO**

Portrait in Black 1/2 **1960** Invalid shipping magnate Matthew Cabot (Nolan) is contemptuous of second wife Sheila (Turner), who can't leave the marriage because of young son Peter (Kohler). She finds comfort in the arms of her husband's doctor, David Rivera (Quinn), and the duo decide the only way to find happiness is to kill off Cabot, which they do. Then Sheila begins to get anonymous letters accusing her of murder. Turner's glamor can't hide the gaping holes in the contrived plot. Adapted from the Goff/Roberts play. **113m/C VHS.** Lana Turner, Lloyd Nolan, Anthony Quinn, Richard Basehart, Sandra Dee, John Saxon, Ray Walston, Anna May Wong, Virginia Grey, Dennis Kohler; ***D:*** Michael Gordon; ***W:*** Ivan Goff, Ben Roberts; ***C:*** Russell Metty; ***M:*** Frank Skinner.

Portrait in Terror 1/2 **1966** A master thief and a deranged artist plan a heist of a Titian painting in an oddball suspense piece. Not a great success, but atmospheric and weird. **81m/B VHS, DVD.** Patrick Magee, William Campbell, Anna Pavane; ***D:*** Jack Hill.

Portrait of a Hitman *Jim Buck* **1977** Aspiring painter leads a double life as a professional hitman. Ragged feature feels more abandoned than finished, as if most of the movie had been shot and then the money ran out. All leads turn in paycheck performances, no more. **85m/C VHS, DVD.** Jack Palance, Rod Steiger, Richard Roundtree, Bo Svenson, Ann Turkel; ***D:*** Allan A. Buckhantz.

Portrait of a Lady 1/2 **1967** A spirited young American woman is taken to England and insists on complete freedom to choose her own future and make her own choices. Based on the 1881 novel by Henry James. On two cassettes. **240m/C VHS, DVD.** *GB* Richard Chamberlain, Suzanne Neve, Edward Fox; ***D:*** James Cellan Jones; ***W:*** Jack Pulman.

Portrait of a Lady **1996 (PG-13)** Adapted from the century-old Henry James novel, "Portrait" paints the story of independent and newly wealthy American, Isabel Archer (Kidman). Abroad in Europe, she falls under the influence of the bitter, opportunistic Madame Merle (Hershey, in a strong portrayal), who manages to steer the innocent Isabel into a disastrous marriage with Gilbert Osmond (Malkovich). From there, film deals with Isabel's efforts to flee the domineering Osmond and find herself again. Kidman plays her role with never-before-seen efficiency. Malkovich is suitably evil but plays his villain card a bit too early. Director Campion's modern voice carries the film through, but is sometimes out of place, as in the opening segment. Filmed in England and Italy. **142m/C VHS, DVD.** *GB* Nicole Kidman, John Malkovich, Barbara Hershey, Martin Donovan, Christian Bale, Shelley Winters, Shelley Duvall, Mary-Louise Parker, Richard E. Grant, John Gielgud, Viggo Mortensen; ***D:*** Jane Campion; ***W:*** Laura Jones; ***C:*** Stuart Dryburgh; ***M:*** Wojciech Kilar. L.A. Film Critics '96: Support. Actress (Hershey); Natl. Soc. Film Critics '96: Support. Actor (Donovan), Support. Actress (Hershey).

Portrait of a Rebel: Margaret Sanger 1/2 **1982** TV docudrama about the struggle of Margaret Sanger to repeal the Comstock Act of 1912, which prohibited the distribution of birth control information. **96m/C VHS.** Bonnie Franklin, David Dukes, Milo O'Shea; ***D:*** Virgil W. Vogel.

Portrait of a Showgirl **1982** Inexperienced showgirl learns the ropes of Las Vegas life from a veteran of the Vegas stages. **100m/C VHS, DVD.** Lesley Ann Warren, Rita Moreno, Tony Curtis, Dianne Kay, Howard Morris; ***D:*** Steven Hilliard Stern. **TV**

Portrait of a Stripper 🦴 **1979** A widowed mother works part-time as a stripper to support her son. Trouble arises when her father-in-law attempts to prove that she is an unfit mother. **100m/C VHS.** Lesley Ann Warren, Edward Herrmann, Vic Tayback, Sheree North; ***D:*** John A. Alonzo.

Portrait of a White Marriage 🦴🦴 ½ **1988** An extended cable comedy special revamping certain old "Mary Hartman, Mary Hartman" and "Fernwood 2-Night" conventions; a moronic talk show host moves his cheap show to his hometown of Hawkins Falls in order to boost the ratings. **81m/C VHS.** Martin Mull, Mary Kay Place, Fred Willard, Michael McKean, Harry Shearer, Jack Riley, Conchata Ferrell; ***D:*** Harry Shearer. **CABLE**

Portrait of an Assassin 🦴🦴 **1949** Unhappy with his marriage to a nagging wife (Arletty), carnival daredevil Fabius (Brasseur) goes so far as to tell her that he killed a woman by mistake, thinking it was her. Can this marriage be saved? Before it's over, more infidelity and the paralyzed Eric (the inimitable Von Stroheim) have come into play. French with subtitles. **86m/B VHS, DVD.** *FR* Pierre Brasseur, Arletty, Maria Montez, Erich von Stroheim; ***D:*** Bernard Roland; ***W:*** Marcel Rivet; ***C:*** Roger Hubert; ***M:*** Maurice Hiriet.

Portrait of Jennie 🦴🦴🦴 ½ *Jennie; Tidal Wave* **1948** In this haunting, romantic fable, a struggling artist is inspired by and smitten with a strange and beautiful girl who he also suspects may be the spirit of a dead woman. A fine cast works wonders with what could have been a forgettable story. The last reel was tinted green in the original release with the last scene shot in technicolor. Oscar-winning special effects. Based on a novella by Robert Nathan. **86m/B VHS, DVD.** Joseph Cotten, Jennifer Jones, Cecil Kellaway, Ethel Barrymore, David Wayne, Lillian Gish, Henry Hull, Florence Bates, Felix Bressart, Anne Francis; ***D:*** William Dieterle; ***W:*** Leonardo Bercovici, Peter Berneis, Paul Osborn; ***C:*** Joseph August; ***M:*** Dimitri Tiomkin. Venice Film Fest. '49: Actor (Cotten).

Portrait of Teresa 🦴🦴🦴 **1979** Havana housewife has to balance motherhood, textile job, and cultural group activities without the cooperation of her husband. Vega skillfully portrays the lingering archaic attitudes and insulting assumptions that still confront post-revolution women. A fine eye for the revealing moments and movements of everyday life. In Spanish with English subtitles. **115m/C VHS.** Daisy Granados, Aldolfo Llaurado, Alina Sanchez, Alberto Molina; ***D:*** Pastor Vega.

Portraits Chinois 🦴🦴 ½ *Shadow Play* **1996** Uneven romantic drama finds English fashion designer Ada (Bonham Carter) living in Paris with her screenwriter boyfriend Paul (Ecoffey). They have just moved into an apartment together though dissatisfaction looms. Paul's writing parter, Guido (Castellito), has broken up with his girlfriend thus complicating their latest assignment, and Ada's fellow designer Lise (Bohringer) has not only impressed their boss Rene (Brialy) but has fallen for Paul. Various other friends interact and everything breaks apart and re-forms over the course of several months. French with subtitles. **105m/C VHS, DVD.** *FR* Helena Bonham Carter, Jean-Philippe Ecoffey, Romane Bohringer, Sergio Castellitto, Marie Trintignant, Elsa Zylberstein, Yvan Attal, Miki (Predrag) Manojlovic, Jean-Claude Brialy; ***D:*** Martine Dugowson; ***W:*** Martine Dugowson, Peter Chase; ***C:*** Vincenzo Marano; ***M:*** Peter Chase.

Portraits of a Killer 🦴🦴 *Portraits of Innocence* **1995** Attorney Elaine Taylor (Grey) is getting all hot and bothered by her client—photographer George Kendell (Mandylor), who's suspected in the murders of five hookers. But the detective (Ironside) on the case thinks she's just asking for trouble. **93m/C VHS.** Jennifer Grey, Costas Mandylor, Michael Ironside, Patricia Charbonneau, Kenneth Welsh, M. Emmet Walsh; ***D:*** Bill Corcoran.

Posed for Murder 🦴🦴 **1989 (R)** A young centerfold is stalked by a psycho who wants her all for himself. **90m/C VHS.** Charlotte J. Helmkamp, Carl Fury, Rick Gianasi, Michael Merrins; ***D:*** Brian Thomas Jones.

Poseidon 🦴 ½ **2006 (PG-13)** Uninspired remake of 1972's "The Poseidon Adventure" sunk faster at the box office than the flick's luxury cruise ship. A rogue wave capsizes the liner on New Year's Eve but a few of the passengers defy the captain's orders to remain in the ballroom and await rescue and decide to make their own way to the surface through the treacherous wreckage. The cast is stuck with recognizable genre types (hero, coward, protective parent) but no one stands out amidst the watery rubble. **99m/C DVD, HD DVD.** *US* Josh(ua) Lucas, Kurt Russell, Emmy Rossum, Jacinda Barrett, Jimmy Bennett, Mia Maestro, Andre Braugher, Richard Dreyfuss, Mike Vogel, Kevin Dillon, Freddy Rodriguez, Gabe Jarret, Stacy "Fergie" Ferguson; ***D:*** Wolfgang Petersen; ***W:*** Mark Protosevich; ***C:*** John Seale; ***M:*** Klaus Badelt.

The Poseidon Adventure 🦴🦴 ½ **1972 (PG)** The cruise ship Poseidon is on its last voyage from New York to Athens on New Year's Eve when it is capsized by a tidal wave. The ten survivors struggle to escape the water-logged tomb. Oscar-winning special effects, such as Shelley Winters floating in a boiler room. Created an entirely new genre of film making—the big cast disaster flick. ♫The Morning After. **117m/C VHS, DVD.** Gene Hackman, Ernest Borgnine, Shelley Winters, Red Buttons, Jack Albertson, Carol Lynley, Roddy McDowall; ***D:*** Ronald Neame; ***W:*** Wendell Mayes, Stirling Silliphant; ***C:*** Harold E. Stine; ***M:*** John Williams. Oscars '72: Song ("The Morning After"), Visual FX; Golden Globes '73: Support. Actress (Winters).

Posers 🦴 ½ *Viperes* **2002 (R)** An unwary woman is fatally pummeled in a nightclub bathroom by four jealous party chicks. When the leader of the pack is suspiciously AWOL the terrible trio just totally freaks out thinking that—gasp!—someone is after them to avenge the killing. Cue the customary finger-pointing as the girls disintegrate along with this tale of woe. **85m/C VHS, DVD.** *CA* Jessica Pare, Stefanie von Pfetten, Emily Hampshire, Adam Beach, Sarain Boylan, Chad Connell, Danielle Kind, Adrian Langley, Alexandra Sinclair; ***D:*** Katie Tallo; ***W:*** Katie Tallo; ***C:*** Claudine Sauve; ***M:*** Serge Cote. **VIDEO**

Positive I.D. 🦴🦴 **1987 (R)** A troubled housewife learns that the man who raped her years before is getting released on parole. She devises a second persona for herself with which to entrap him and get her revenge. **96m/C VHS, DVD.** Stephanie Rascoe, John Davies, Steve Fromholz; ***D:*** Andy Anderson; ***W:*** Andy Anderson; ***C:*** Paul Barton.

The Positively True Adventures of the Alleged Texas Cheerleader-Murdering Mom 🦴🦴🦴 ½ **1993 (R)** Satirical melodrama about Texas housewife Wanda Holloway (Hunter), accused of hiring a hitman to murder the mother of her daughter's chief cheerleading rival. She figures the girl will be so distraught that her own daughter can easily replace her. Ruthless and hilarious, this fact-based cable movie goes way over the top in satirizing suburban lifestyle excess and media overkill. Hunter, complete with whiney Texas twang, is perfect in her role as self-absorbed Wanda and Bridges is great as her loopy ex-brother-in-law and partner in planned homicide. A riot compared to the usual dramatic movies served up by the networks. **99m/C VHS, DVD.** Andy Richter, Jack Kehler, Holly Hunter, Beau Bridges, Swoosie Kurtz, Gregg Henry, Matt Frewer, Frankie Ingrassia, Elizabeth Ruscio, Megan Berwick; ***D:*** Michael Ritchie; ***W:*** Jane Anderson; ***M:*** Lucy Simon. **CABLE**

Posse 🦴🦴🦴 **1975 (PG)** There's a hidden agenda, fueled by political ambition, in a lawman's (Douglas) dauntless pursuit of an escaped bandit (Dern). An interesting contrast between the evil of corrupt politics and the honesty of traditional lawlessness. Well performed, well photographed, and almost insightful. **94m/C VHS, DVD.** Kirk Douglas, Bruce Dern, James Stacy, Bo Hopkins, Luke Askew, David Canary, Alfonso Arau, Kate Woodville, Mark Roberts; ***D:*** Kirk Douglas; ***W:*** William Roberts; ***M:*** Maurice Jarre.

Posse 🦴🦴🦴 **1993 (R)** Big, brawny western shot with MTV in mind that tells the tale in part of how more than 8,000 black cowboys helped tame the American frontier. Or, as the advertising put it, "The untold story of the wild West." Or, spaghetti western meets blaxploitation meets the magnificent seven meets the L.A. riots, with characters actually saying, "No justice, no peace" and "Can't we all get along." However categorized, the intent is to show a side of Americana seldom seen, a goal realized. Strode, perhaps the greatest black Western star, appears at both the beginning and ending, while several other veteran black performers, including Russell, appear in cameos. Hunky Van Peebles is the leader of the usual misfits in the "Dirty Dozen" tradition, infantry deserters holding a load of gold. Between them and freedom is a gang of goons led by Zane. Lots of flash and dash, but lacking soul. **113m/C VHS, DVD.** Mario Van Peebles, Stephen Baldwin, Charles Lane, Tommy (Tiny) Lister, Big Daddy Kane, Billy Zane, Blair Underwood, Tone Loc, Salli Richardson, Reginald (Reggie) Hudlin, Richard Edson, Reginald VelJohnson, Warrington Hudlin; ***Cameos:*** Melvin Van Peebles, Pam Grier, Isaac Hayes, Robert Hooks, Richard Jordan, Paul Bartel, Nipsey Russell, Woody Strode, Aaron Neville, Stephen J. Cannell; ***D:*** Mario Van Peebles; ***W:*** Sy Richardson, Dario Scardapane; ***C:*** Peter Menzies Jr.; ***M:*** Michel Colombier.

Possessed 🦴🦴 ½ **1931** A poor factory girl becomes a wealthy Park Avenue sophisticate when she falls in love with a rich lawyer who wants to be governor. Not to be confused with Crawford's 1947 movie of the same name, but worth a look. Gable and Crawford make a great couple! **77m/B VHS.** Joan Crawford, Clark Gable, Wallace Ford, Richard "Skeets" Gallagher, John Miljan; ***D:*** Clarence Brown.

The Possessed 🦴🦴🦴 **1947** Crawford is at her melodramatic best as a crazed gal who can't find happiness with either hunk Heflin or bland Massey. First film for Brooks. From the story "One Man's Secret" by Rita Weiman. **109m/B VHS, DVD.** Joan Crawford, Van Heflin, Raymond Massey, Geraldine Brooks, Stanley Ridges, John Ridgely, Nana Bryant, Moroni Olsen; ***D:*** Curtis Bernhardt; ***C:*** Joseph Valentine.

The Possessed 🦴 ½ **1977 (PG-13)** Farentino is a priest who loses his faith, but regains it after an apparently fatal auto accident. Hackett is the headmistress of a private girls' school which is in need of an exorcist, since one of her student's appears to be possessed, and Farentino seems just the man for the job. Fairly tame, since originally made for TV. **75m/C VHS.** James Farentino, Joan Hackett, Diana Scarwid, Claudette Nevins, Eugene Roche, Ann Dusenberry, Dinah Manoff, P.J. Soles; ***D:*** Jerry Thorpe. **TV**

The Possessed 🦴🦴 *Les Possedes* **1988** Based on the Dostoevsky novel which follows a young aristocrat who's torn between love and politics during the failed Russian revolution of the 1870s. French with subtitles. **124m/C VHS.** *FR* Lambert Wilson, Jean-Philippe Ecoffey, Isabelle Huppert, Jutta Lampe, Laurent Malet, Remi Martin, Omar Sharif, Bernard Blier; ***D:*** Andrzej Wajda; ***W:*** Jean-Claude Carriere, Agnieszka Holland; ***C:*** Witold Adamek; ***M:*** Zygmunt Konieczny.

Possessed 🦴🦴 **2000** William Bowdern (Dalton) is a troubled priest in 1949 St. Louis, who has taken to drink because of his WWII nightmares. He's called on to help 11-year-old Robbie (Malen) who is apparently possessed by a demon. Will reluctant Archbishop Hume (Plummer) allow Bowdern to performan an arcane exorcism and does Robbie's strange Aunt Hanna (Laurie) have anything to do with his condition? Based on the true story of the only documented exorcism performed by the Catholic Church in the U.S. **111m/C VHS, DVD.** Timothy Dalton, Christopher Plummer, Henry Czerny, Jonathan Malen, Shannon Lawson, Piper Laurie, Michael Rhoades; ***D:*** Steven E. de Souza; ***W:*** Steven E. de Souza, Michael Lazarou; ***C:*** Edward Pei; ***M:*** John (Gianni) Frizzell. **CABLE**

Possessed 🦴🦴 *Deadly Visions* **2005** After being blinded in a car accident, Anne Culver (Sheridan) is given a new pair of eyes from a donor. The only problem is that now she's seeing visions of her donor's murder. Ho-hum thriller with few surprises. Should please fans of the genre. **95m/C VHS, DVD.** Nicolette Sheridan, Gordon Currie, Sarah Deakins, Philip Granger; ***D:*** Michael Scott; ***W:*** John Murlowski; ***C:*** Adam Sliwinski; ***M:*** Sophia Morizet. **VIDEO**

Possessed by the Night 🦴🦴 **1993 (R)** Kinky sex games ensue between a married writer and a sexy other woman thanks to a mysterious fetish object. Unrated version also available. **84m/C VHS.** Ted Prior, Shannon Tweed, Sandahl Bergman, Chad McQueen, Henry Silva; ***D:*** Fred Olen Ray.

Possession 🦴 **1981 (R)** Returned from a long mission, a secret agent notices that his wife is acting very strangely. She's about to give birth to a manifestation of the evil within her! Gory, hysterical, over-intellectual and often unintelligible. **123m/C VHS, DVD.** *FR GE* Johanna Hofer, Isabelle Adjani, Sam Neill, Heinz Bennent, Margit Carstensen, Shaun Lawtor; ***D:*** Andrzej Zulawski; ***W:*** Andrzej Zulawski, Frederic Tuten; ***C:*** Bruno Nuytten; ***M:*** Andrzej Korzynski, Art Phillips. Cesar '82: Actress (Adjani).

Possession 🦴🦴 **2002 (PG-13)** English lit lite in this uninvolving romance from LaBute, based on the 1990 novel by A.S. Byatt. Brash and scruffy (doesn't the man own a razor?) American scholar Roland Michell (Eckhart) finds letters from 19th-century poet Randolph Henry Ash (Northam)—possibly to feminist poet Christabel LaMotte (Ehle). Michell hooks up with repressed Brit scholar Maud Bailey (bun-wearing Paltrow), an expert on Christabel, to investigate the connection. They discover the married Ash and LaMotte had a brief, passionate affair that changed their lives. The modern-day duo are too wary to get involved the same way—at least at first. Looks beautiful but is utterly predictable. **102m/C VHS, DVD.** *US GB* Gwyneth Paltrow, Aaron Eckhart, Jeremy Northam, Jennifer Ehle, Lena Headey, Toby Stephens, Tom Hickey, Trevor Eve, Tom Hollander, Graham Crowden, Anna Massey, Holly Aird, Georgia Mackenzie; ***D:*** Neil LaBute; ***W:*** Neil LaBute, David Henry Hwang, Laura Jones; ***C:*** Jean-Yves Escoffier; ***M:*** Gabriel Yared.

Possession **2009 (PG-13)** Gellar is starring in another Asian horror remake, this time of the Korean film "Jungdok." A car accident sends both Jessica's husband Ryan and brother-in-law Roman into comas. When Roman does wake up, he thinks he's his brother and Jessica starts wondering if Ryan's spirit is possessing him. **m/C DVD.** *US* Sarah Michelle Gellar, Lee Pace, Michael Landes; ***D:*** Joel Bergvall, Simon Sandquist; ***W:*** Michael Petroni; ***C:*** Gregory Middleton; ***M:*** Christian Sandquist.

The Possession of Joel Delaney 🦴🦴 ½ **1972 (R)** Blend of occult horror and commentary on social mores works for the most part, but some viewers may be put off by the low production values and spottiness of the script. MacLaine is a wealthy divorcee who must deal with the mysterious transformations affecting her brother. Skeptical at first, she begins to suspect he is the victim of Caribbean voodoo. **105m/C VHS, DVD.** Shirley MacLaine, Perry King, Michael Hordern, David Elliott, Robert Burr; ***D:*** Waris Hussein; ***W:*** Matt Robinson; ***C:*** Arthur Ornitz; ***M:*** Joe Raposo.

Possession: Until Death Do You Part 🦴 **1990** When one man's attraction for a beautiful young woman becomes an obsession, a bizarre series of inexplicable events unravels a terrifying account of passion and revenge. **93m/C VHS.** Monica Marko, John R. Johnston, Sharlene Martin, Cat Williamson; ***D:*** Michael Mazo, Lloyd A. Simandl.

Possible Loves 🦴🦴🦴 *Amores Possiveis* **2000** Romantic comedy with a Brazilian beat and three possible outcomes. College student Carlos (Benicio) is waiting for his girlfriend Julia (Ferraz) outside a Rio cinema. Fifteen years later, the viewer learns what happens if she does—or doesn't—show up. In the first, Julia doesn't, so Carlos has a dull marriage to Maria (Goulart) until he and Julia have a chance meeting. Scenario two has Julia and Carlos married but he leaves his wife and son for Pedro (de Mello) as he tries to decide whom he loves. In the third plot, Julia doesn't show again and Carlos is a swinging bachelor looking for the perfect woman. Guess who. Portuguese with subtitles. **98m/C VHS, DVD.** *BR* Murilo Benicio, Carolina Ferraz, Beth Goulart, Emilio de

Mello, Irene Ravache; *D:* Sandra Werneck; *W:* Paulo Halm; *C:* Walter Carvalho; *M:* Chico Buarque, Joao Nabuco.

Possums 1/2 **1999 (PG)** Beat-up small town can't endure the local high school football team's quarter-century of losing seasons and pulls the plug on the pathetic Possums. But their announcer, Will (Davis), breathes new life into the downtrodden fans by calling fictional wins. It's all high-fives until the real champs want to square off and Will has to assemble a first-rate squad. **97m/C VHS, DVD.** Mac Davis, Cynthia Sikes, Greg Coolidge, Andrew Prine, Dennis Burkley, Monica Creel, Jay Underwood, Clive Revill; *D:* J. Max Burnett; *W:* J. Max Burnett; *C:* Christopher Duskin; *M:* Justin Caine Burnett. **VIDEO**

Post Concussion **1999 (PG-13)** Matthew (Yoon) is a ruthless corporate "consultant" who specializes in downsizing and layoffs until he's hit by a car and suffers a severe head injury. Unable to work because of lingering symptoms, he re-evaluates his life, starts a romance with a neighbor, and explores New Age remedies. Writer-director Yoon based his refreshing, inventive, and gently humorous debut on his own experience with a brain-injuring accident and its subsequent effect on his own life and career. **82m/C VHS, DVD.** Daniel Yoon, Michael Hohmeyer, Destry Miller, Niloufar Talebi, Jennifer Welch; *D:* Daniel Yoon; *W:* Daniel Yoon; *C:* Daniel Yoon.

Post Grad 1/2 *Ticket to Ride; The Post Grad Survival Guide* **2009 (PG-13)** Mediocre comedy finds overachieving Ryden Malby (Bledel) getting a rude awakening to the real world when she graduates from college, misses out on the perfect job (which goes to a rival), and so must move back in with her eccentric family. One thing that does seem to make sense is maybe Ryden and her platonic buddy Adam (Gilford) shouldn't be so platonic anymore only Ryden is more interesting in ogling flirty, hunky Brazilian neighbor David (Santoro). Flick features the protracted burial arrangements for a squished cat (it's funny in a sick sorta way). **88m/C DVD.** *US* Alexis Bledel, Michael Keaton, Jane Lynch, Rodrigo Santoro, Zach Gilford, Craig Robinson, Carol Burnett, Fred Armisen, Andrew Daly, Catherine Reitman, Bobby Coleman; *D:* Victoria Jenson; *W:* Kelly Fremon; *C:* Charles Minsky; *M:* Christophe Beck.

Post Mortem **1999** Single mom Linda (Moreau) will do anything to safeguard her daughter Charlotte, which in reality means Linda robs every man she dates after whacking him with some heavy object. Then there's lonely Ghislain (Arcand), who is abruptly arrested by the cops and accused of a crime. Naturally, his life and Linda's intersect. French with subtitles. **92m/C VHS.** *CA* Gabriel Arcand, Sylvie Moreau, Helene Loiselle; *D:* Louis Belanger; *W:* Louis Belanger; *C:* Jean-Pierre St.-Louis; *M:* Guy Belanger. Genie '99: Actress (Moreau), Screenplay.

Postal **WOOF!** **2007 (R)** Energetically tasteless, fitfully amusing farce, adapted from the videogame, satirizes our post-9/11 world and skewers its targets equally. Unemployed Dude (Ward) turns to his Uncle Dave (Foley), the leader of an apocalyptic cult, for money, and the two plot to steal a truckload of dirty dolls—a must-have toy in short supply. The same idea has occurred to Osama bin Laden follower Mohammed (Benyaer), and the two factions collide at the Third Reich-themed amusement park Little Germany (with director Boll appearing as the park's manager). **109m/C DVD.** *US CA GE* Zack (Zach) Ward, Dave Foley, Christopher Coppola, J.K. Simmons, Larry Thomas, Verne Troyer, Michael Benyaer, Brent Mendenhall; ***Cameos:*** Uwe Boll; *D:* Uwe Boll; *W:* Uwe Boll, Bryan C. Knight; *C:* Mathias Neumann; *M:* Jessica de Rooij. Golden Raspberries '08: Worst Director (Boll).

Postal Inspector **1936** An extraordinary tale of a postal inspector's life. Crime, romance, and natural disaster all overtake this civil servant. Catch the song "Let's Have Bluebirds On All Our Wallpaper." **58m/B VHS, DVD.** Carlos Cortez, Patricia Ellis, Michael Loring, Bela Lugosi, David Oliver, Wallis (Clarke) Clark; *D:* Otto Brower; *W:* Robert Presnell Sr., Horace McCoy; *C:* George Robinson.

Postcards from America **1995 (R)** Traces the non-artistic aspects of the life of writer/artist David Wojnarowicz, who died of AIDS. Neophyte McLean concentrates on troubled childhood with an abusive father and teen years spent as a street hustler years. Choppy narrative uses little of Wojnarowicz's dialogue, save the voice-over narration by the lead character. Based on two semi-autobiographical novels by the artist. **93m/C VHS, DVD.** James Lyons, Michael Tighe, Olmo Tighe, Michael Imperioli, Michael Ringer, Maggie Low; *D:* Steve McLean; *W:* Steve McLean; *C:* Ellen Kuras; *M:* Stephen Endelman.

Postcards from the Edge 1/2 **1990 (R)** Fisher adapted her best-selling novel, tamed and tempered, for the big screen with a tour-de-force of talent. Streep very fine as a delightfully harried actress struggling with her career, her drug dependence, and her competitive, overwhelming show-biz mother. Autobiographical script is bitingly clever and filled with refreshingly witty dialogue. Lots of cameos by Hollywood's hippest. **101m/C VHS, DVD.** Meryl Streep, Shirley MacLaine, Dennis Quaid, Gene Hackman, Richard Dreyfuss, Rob Reiner, Mary Wickes, Conrad Bain, Annette Bening, Michael Ontkean, Dana Ivey, Robin Bartlett, Anthony Heald, Oliver Platt, CCH Pounder; *D:* Mike Nichols; *W:* Carrie Fisher; *C:* Michael Ballhaus; *M:* Shel Silverstein, Carly Simon, Stephen Sondheim, Howard Shore, Paul Shaffer, Gilda Radner.

Poster Boy **2004 (R)** Right-wing senator Jack Kray (Lerner) decides to use his college- student son Henry (Newton) in his reelection campaign in order to attract the youth vote. Except Henry's gay, and while he's living it up within his college confines, he's not out to the rest of the world, including his parents. Over-the-top soapiness and preachiness ensue as secrets and truth affect the dynamics of family, friendship, and public image. Allen is excellent as the smile-and-wave political wife who likes a cocktail, but the good performances are crushed by a heavy-handed script. **98m/C DVD.** *US* Matt Newton, Karen Allen, Michael Lerner, Jack Noseworthy, Valerie Geffner, Ian Reed Kesler, Sheff Stevens; *D:* Zak Tucker; *W:* Ryan Shiraki, Lecia Rosenthal; *C:* Wolfgang Held; *M:* Mark Garcia.

The Postman 1/2 *Il Postino* **1994 (PG)** Bittersweet, charming film about Mario (Troisi), a shy villager who winds up the personal postman of poet Pablo Neruda (Noiret), who is exiled from his beloved Chile in 1952, granted asylum by the Italian government, and who finds himself living in the tiny Italian community of Isla Negra. The tongue-tied Mario has fallen in love with barmaid Beatrice (Cucinotta) and asks the poet's help in wooing the dark-eyed beauty, striking up an unlikely friendship with the worldly Neruda. Based on the novel "Burning Patience" by Antonio Skarmeta. Italian with subtitles. Troisi, a beloved comic actor in his native Italy, was gravely ill, needing a heart transplant, during the making of the film (all-too apparent from his gaunt appearance) and died the day after filming was completed. **115m/C VHS, DVD.** *IT* Massimo Troisi, Philippe Noiret, Maria Grazia Cucinotta, Linda Moretti, Renato Scarpa, Anna Buonaiuto, Mariana Rigillo; *D:* Michael Radford; *W:* Massimo Troisi, Michael Radford, Furio Scarpelli, Anna Pavignano, Giacomo Scarpelli; *C:* Franco Di Giacomo; *M:* Luis Bacalov. Oscars '95: Orig. Dramatic Score; British Acad. '95: Director (Radford), Foreign Film, Score; Broadcast Film Critics '95: Foreign Film.

The Postman **1997 (R)** It's post-apocalypse time (the year's 2013), with a nameless drifter (Costner) assuming the role of a postal carrier in order to bring hope to a devasted town terrorized by maruading hooligans, led by General Bethlehem (Patton). If you fancy deadpan dialogue and can swallow the image of a mail carrier as the symbol for patriotism, then this one's for you. Overall, Costner offers nothing new to the genre of the stranger offering hope, and soon flick becomes a cornball exercise and extravagant waste of time for all involved. Costner's first directing effort since "Dances with Wolves." It's time someone told Kevin to get out of the epic business and stick to the "everyday Joe" roles. **170m/C VHS, DVD.** Kevin Costner, Larenz Tate, Will Patton, Olivia Williams, James Russo, Tom Petty, Daniel von Bargen, Scott Bairstow, Giovanni Ribisi, Roberta Maxwell, Joe Santos, Peggy Lipton, Ron McLarty, Rex Linn, Todd Allen, Shawn Hatosy; *D:* Kevin Costner; *W:* Brian Helgeland, Eric Roth; *C:* Stephen Windon; *M:* James Newton Howard. Golden Raspberries '97: Worst Picture, Worst Actor (Costner), Worst Director (Costner), Worst Screenplay, Worst Song (Entire Song Score).

The Postman Always Rings Twice 1/2 **1946** Even without the brutal sexuality of the James M. Cain novel, Garfield and Turner sizzle as the lust-laden lovers in this lurid tale of fatal attraction. Garfield steals the show as the streetwise drifter who blows into town and lights a fire in Turner. As their affair steams up the two conspire to do away with her husband and circumstances begin to spin out of control. Tense and compelling. A classic. **113m/B VHS, DVD.** Lana Turner, John Garfield, Cecil Kellaway, Hume Cronyn, Leon Ames, Audrey Totter, Alan Reed; *D:* Tay Garnett; *W:* Harry Ruskin, Niven Busch; *C:* Sidney Wagner; *M:* George Bassman.

The Postman Always Rings Twice **1981 (R)** It must be true because he's ringing again in Mamet's version of James M. Cain's depression-era novel. This time Nicholson plays the drifter and Lange the amoral wife with an aged husband. Truer to the original story than the 1946 movie in its use of brutal sex scenes, it nevertheless lacks the power of the original. Nicholson works well in this time era and Lange adds depth and realism to the character of Cora. But in the end it remains dreary and easily forgettable. **123m/C VHS, DVD.** Jack Nicholson, Jessica Lange, John Colicos, Anjelica Huston, Michael Lerner, John P. Ryan, Christopher Lloyd; *D:* Bob Rafelson; *W:* David Mamet; *C:* Sven Nykvist; *M:* Michael Small.

Postman's Knock **1962** Chaotic comic Milligan is stuck in a conventional slapstick comedy. Village postman Harold Petts (Milligan) is so efficient he gets transferred to London. He meets pretty art student Jean (Shelley) and thwarts an attempted mail train robbery but becomes a suspect despite his alibi. And while Harold is being trailed by the coppers, the inept gang decides to try again. **87m/B DVD.** *GB* Spike Milligan, Barbara Shelley, John Wood, Warren Mitchell, Archie Duncan, Lance Percival, Arthur Mullard, John Bennett; *D:* Robert Lynn; *W:* John Briley, Jack Trevor Story, Robert Kinnoch; *C:* Gerald Moss; *M:* Ronald Goodwin.

Postmark for Danger 1/2 *Portrait of Alison* **1956** Detectives do their best to smash a diamond smuggling ring that operates between Britain and the U.S. Along the way a number of people are killed. **84m/B VHS.** *GB* Terry Moore, Robert Beatty, William Sylvester, Josephine Griffin, Geoffrey Keen, Henry Oscar; *D:* Guy Green.

Postmortem **1998 (R)** Sheen is an FBI serial killer profiler who leaves the job to become a novelist and find peace in a small town. But his quiet life is shattered by a murderer who writes the obituaries of his victims before he kills. **105m/C VHS, DVD.** Charlie Sheen, Michael Halsey, Stephen McCole, Gary Lewis, Hazel Ann Crawford; *D:* Albert Pyun; *W:* John Lamb; *C:* George Mooradian; *M:* Tony Riparetti.

Pot o' Gold *The Golden Hour* **1941** Stewart plays a wealthy young man who signs on with a struggling band. He convinces his uncle, who has a radio program, to let the band perform during a radio giveaway show he has concocted. Slight comedy, Stewart notwithstanding. **87m/B VHS, DVD.** Paulette Goddard, James Stewart, Charles Winninger, Horace Heidt, Art Carney; *D:* George Marshall; *W:* Walter DeLeon; *C:* Hal Mohr.

Pot, Parents, and Police *The Cat Ate the Parakeet* **1971** A 13-year-old boy goes crazy when his dog dies and soon gets in with a hippie crowd, drops acid, and gets in trouble with the cops. **86m/C VHS.** Phillip Pine, Robert Mantell, Madelyn Keen, Arthur Battanides, Martin Margulies; *D:* Phillip Pine; *W:* Phillip Pine.

Pound Puppies and the Legend of Big Paw **1988** The Pound Puppies, known for breaking dogs out of pounds and delivering them to safe and secure homes, are featured in their first full-length musical (and merchandising effort). Fifties music. **76m/C VHS, DVD.** *D:* Pierre de Celles; *W:* Jim Carlson; *V:* Nancy Cartwright, George Rose, B.J. Ward, Ruth Buzzi, Brennan Howard.

Pouvoir Intime 1/2 **1987 (PG-13)** What happens when robbers of an armored car lock the guard in the vehicle, and he decides to fight back? This film offers one possible scenario. Available in dubbed or subtitled versions. **86m/C VHS.** *FR* Marie Tifo, Pierre Curzi, Yvan Ponton, Jaques Lussier; *D:* Yves Simoneau.

P.O.W. Deathcamp **1989** A combat unit is captured and tortured by the Vietcong in this typical Vietnam story. **92m/C VHS.** Charles Black, Bill Balbridge, Rey Malonzo; *D:* Jett C. Espirtu.

The P.O.W. Escape 1/2 *Behind Enemy Lines* **1986 (R)** The adventures of a surly American commander captured as a POW during the final days of the Vietnam War. **90m/C VHS.** David Carradine, Mako, Charles R. Floyd, Steve James; *D:* Gideon Amir; *W:* Malcolm Barbour, James Bruner, Jeremy Lipp, John Langley.

Powaqqatsi: Life in Transformation 1/2 **1988 (G)** Director Reggio's follow-up to "Koyaanisqatsi" doesn't pack the wallop of its predecessor. Still, the cinematography is magnificent and the music of Philip Glass is exquisitely hypnotic as we are taken on a spellbinding video collage of various third world countries and see the price they've paid in the name of progress. Part 2 of a planned trilogy. **95m/C VHS, DVD.** *D:* Godfrey Reggio; *M:* Philip Glass.

Powder **1995 (PG-13)** An electromagnetic albino with an I.Q. off the charts is discovered living in his grandparents' cellar and brought to live in a school for troubled teens. Despite harrassment from the crude locals, Powder (Flanery) manages to exude compassion and electricity all over the place with the help of sensitive school director Steenbergen and wacky science teacher Goldblum. Hyper-sentimentality, convoluted and contradictory writing, absurd messianic overtones, and a cop-out climax barely scratch the surface of film's problems. Revelations of Salva's criminal conviction for child molestation cast some scenes in a disturbing light and caused major headaches for Disney's publicity department. **111m/C VHS, DVD.** Sean Patrick Flanery, Mary Steenburgen, Lance Henriksen, Jeff Goldblum, Brandon Smith, Bradford Tatum, Susan Tyrrell, Missy (Melissa) Crider, Ray Wise, Esteban Louis Powell; *D:* Victor Salva; *W:* Victor Salva; *C:* Jerzy Zielinski; *M:* Jerry Goldsmith.

Powder Blue **2009 (R)** Manages to make Jessica Biel as a stripper boring. Intersecting drama, set during Christmas, about said stripper, an ex-priest, an ex-con, and a mortician who are all in crisis. It sounds like a bad bar joke and it is. It not only snows in L.A. but the snow is blue-colored. **106m/C DVD.** Jessica Biel, Eddie Redmayne, Forest Whitaker, Ray Liotta, Lisa Kudrow, Patrick Swayze, Kris Kristofferson, Sanaa Lathan; *D:* Timothy Linh Bui; *W:* Stephane Gauger, Timothy Linh Bui; *C:* Jonathan Sela; *M:* Didier Rachou.

Powder Burn 1/2 **1996** Detective Jack Becker seeks to protect a Beverly Hills client's young daughter when he uncovers unsavory goings-on at her home. And then discovers he's being set up to be the patsy for a murder. **92m/C VHS.** Jay Irwin, Elizabeth Barry; *D:* Serge Rodnunsky; *W:* Serge Rodnunsky; *C:* Pierre Chemaly; *M:* Jimmy Lifton.

Powder Keg **1970** Railroad company hires a rowdy team of investigators to retrieve a hijacked train. Action never quits. Inspired the TV pilot "The Bearcats." **93m/C VHS.** Rod Taylor, Dennis Cole, Michael Ansara, Fernando Lamas, Tisha Sterling; *D:* Douglas Heyes.

Powdersmoke Range 1/2 **1935** Crooked frontier politician plots to steal valuable ranch property. The new owners, however, have other ideas. First in "The Three Mesquiteer" series. **71m/B VHS.** Harry Carey Sr., Hoot Gibson, Tom Tyler, Guinn "Big Boy" Williams, Bob Steele, Sam Hardy, Patricia "Boots" Mallory, Franklyn Farnum, William Desmond, William Farnum, Buzz Barton, Wally Wales, Art Mix, Buffalo Bill Jr., Buddy Roosevelt; *D:* Wallace Fox.

Power 🦴🦴 1/2 **1928** Two dam-building construction workers vie with each other for the local girls. Silent. **60m/B VHS.** William Boyd, Alan Hale, Carole Lombard, Joan Bennett; *D:* Howard Higgin.

Power 🦴🦴 1/2 *Jew Suss* **1934** A Jewish ghetto inhabitant in 18th-century Wurtemburg works his way out of the gutter and into some authority by pleasing the whims of an evil duke. Based on the novel by Leon Fuechtwangler. **105m/B VHS.** *GB* Conrad Veidt, Benita Hume, Frank Vosper, Cedric Hardwicke, Gerald du Maurier, Pamela Ostrer, Joan Maude, Paul Graetz, Mary Clare, Percy Parsons, Dennis Hoey, Gibb McLaughlin, Francis L. Sullivan; *D:* Lothar Mendes.

The Power 🦴 1/2 **1980 (R)** An ancient clay idol that was created by the Aztecs and possesses incredible destructive power is unleashed on modern man. **87m/C VHS.** Warren Lincoln, Susan Stokey, Lisa Erickson, Jeffrey Obrow, Chad Christian, Ben Gilbert, Chris Morrill, Rod Mays; *D:* Stephen Carpenter, Jeffrey Obrow; *W:* Stephen Carpenter, John Penney, Jeffrey Obrow; *C:* Stephen Carpenter; *M:* Christopher Young.

Power 🦴🦴 1/2 **1986 (R)** A study of corporate manipulations. Gere plays a ruthless media consultant working for politicians. Fine cast can't find the energy needed to make this great, but it's still interesting. Lumet did better with same material in "Network." **111m/C VHS, DVD.** Richard Gere, Julie Christie, E.G. Marshall, Gene Hackman, Beatrice Straight, Kate Capshaw, Denzel Washington, Fritz Weaver, Michael Learned, E. Katherine Kerr, Polly Rowles, Matt Salinger, J.T. Walsh; *D:* Sidney Lumet; *W:* David Himmelstein; *C:* Andrzej Bartkowiak; *M:* Cy Coleman.

Power and Beauty 🦴 1/2 **2002** A titillating topic turns into a dull telepic. Judith Campbell Exner (Henstridge) is a beauty who, afer a fling with Frank Sinatra (Ralston), becomes the mistress of JFK (Anderson). Sinatra is also the one who introduced Judith to wiseguy Sam Giancana (Friedman) and FBI honcho Herbert Hoover is convinced that the babe is some kind of messenger service between the White House and the Chicago crime boss. (In 1975, the real Exner is subpoenaed by a Senate committee who wants details and is briefly in the public eye.) **94m/C VHS, DVD.** Natasha Henstridge, Kevin Anderson, Peter Friedman, Grant Nickalls, John Ralston; *D:* Susan Seidelman; *W:* William Bast, Dave Erickson, Paul Huson; *C:* Derick Underschultz; *M:* Patrick Williams. **CABLE**

Power Dive 🦴🦴 **1941** Test pilot Brad (Arlen) must show that a new plane commissioned by the army that was designed and constructed of plastic by Professor Blake (Ross) is safe to fly. Brad's gal is Blake's daughter Carol (Parker) and Brad has a romantic rival in his own brother, engineer Doug (Castle), which makes things sticky on and off the ground. **71m/B DVD.** Richard Arlen, Jean Parker, Don Castle, Thomas Ross W., Roger Pryor, Cliff Edwards, Helen Mack, Louis Jean Heydt; *D:* James Hogan; *W:* Edward Churchill, Maxwell Shane; *C:* John Alton; *M:* C. Bakaleinikoff.

Power 98 🦴 **1996 (R)** L.A. shock-jock Karlin Pickett (Roberts) takes inexperienced Jon Price (Gedrick) as his protege, much to the dismay of girlfriend Sharon (Garth). Since Pickett will do anything to get higher ratings, she's right to worry, especially after a caller confesses to murder during Pickett's show. Roberts refrains from scenery-chewing but co-stars Gedrick and Garth give new meaning to bland. **89m/C VHS.** Eric Roberts, Jason Gedrick, Jennie Garth, Larry Drake, Stephen Tobolowsky; *D:* Jaime Hellman; *W:* Jaime Hellman; *C:* Kent Wakeford; *M:* Jeff Beal.

Power of Attorney 🦴🦴 **1994 (R)** Ambitious up-from-the-streets lawyer Paul Diehl (Koteas) decides to defend Mafia don Joseph Scassi (Aiello) against federal charges of murder and extortion, convincing himself that the mobster is telling the truth. But Scassi decides to make certain his lawyer will do his best by threatening Diehl's drug-dealing brother Frankie (Wilson). **97m/C VHS, DVD.** Danny Aiello, Elias Koteas, Nina Siemaszko, Rae Dawn Chong, Roger Wilson; *D:* Howard Himelstein; *W:* George Erschbamer, Jeff Barmash; *M:* Hal Beckett.

The Power of One 🦴🦴 **1992 (PG-13)** Good cast is generally wasted in liberal white look at apartheid. Set in South Africa during the 1940s, P.K. is a white orphan of British descent who is sent to a boarding school run by Afrikaaners (South Africans of German descent). Humiliated and bullied, particularly when England and Germany go to war, P.K. is befriended by a German pianist and a black boxing coach who teach him to box and stand up for his rights. Preachy and filled with stereotypes. Based on the novel by Bryce Courtenay. **126m/C VHS, DVD.** Stephen Dorff, Armin Mueller-Stahl, Morgan Freeman, John Gielgud, Fay Masterson, Marius Weyers, Tracy Brooks Swope, John Osborne, Daniel Craig, Dominic Walker, Alois Mayo, Ian Roberts, Maria Marais; *D:* John G. Avildsen; *W:* Robert Mark Kamen; *C:* Dean Semler; *M:* Hans Zimmer.

The Power of the Ninjitsu 🦴 **1988** A young man inherits the leadership of a martial arts crime gang, the Scorpions, but the elder members muscle him out of his place. He returns for revenge and has the old ones running scared. Power to the Ninjitsu! **90m/C VHS.** Britton Lee, Adam Frank, Peter Ujaer; *D:* Joseph Lai.

Power of the Press 🦴 1/2 **1943** Villainous propagandist newspaper publisher Rankin (Kruger) hires gangsters to bump off anyone who annoys him. Honest managing editor Thompson (Tracy) eventually exposes him. Badly-paced, low-budget production. **64m/C DVD.** Lee Tracy, Otto Kruger, Guy Kibbee, Gloria Dickson, Victor Jory, Larry Parks; *D:* Lew Landers; *W:* Robert D. (Robert Hardy) Andrews; *C:* John Stumar.

Power, Passion & Murder 🦴 1/2 **1983** A young, glamorous movie star has an affair with a married man which begins the end of her career in 1930s Hollywood. **104m/C VHS, DVD.** Michelle Pfeiffer, Darren McGavin, Stella Stevens; *D:* Paul Bogart, Leon Ichaso.

Power Play 🦴 1/2 *Operation Overthrow; A State of Shock* **1978** Young army colonel from a small European country joins forces with rebels to overthrow the government. After the coup, the group discovers that in their midst is a traitor. So who is it? Suspense never builds adequately. **95m/C VHS, DVD.** *CA GB* Peter O'Toole, David Hemmings, Donald Pleasence, Barry Morse; *D:* Martyn Burke; *W:* Martyn Burke.

Power Play 🦴 1/2 **2002 (R)** Connecting an energy company's greed to massive earthquakes in southern California is no small feat but reporter Matt Nash puts his life on the line to do just that. B-movie disaster flick is decidedly low-energy. **100m/C VHS, DVD.** Dylan Walsh, Alison Eastwood, Tobin Bell, Julia Davis, Jaimz Woolvett; *D:* Joseph Zito; *W:* B.J. Davis, Brent Huff, Adrian Fulle; *C:* Gideon Porath. **VIDEO**

The Power Within 🦴 1/2 **1979** An electrified stuntman finds he can send electrical shocks from his hands and becomes the victim of a kidnapping plot. **90m/C VHS.** Eric (Hans Gudegast) Braeden, David Hedison, Susan Howard, Art Hindle; *D:* John Llewellyn Moxey.

The Power Within 🦴🦴 1/2 **1995 (PG-13)** Evil Raymond Vonn has stolen an ancient ring of power but to acquire its complete strength he needs to find a second, matching ring. This is in the possession of teenaged Stan Dryer (Roberts), who must discover the ring's power if he expects to defeat Vonn. **97m/C VHS, DVD.** Ted Jan Roberts, Karen Valentine, Keith Coogan, John O'Hurley, Gary Morgan, Sean Fitzgerald, William Zabka; *D:* Art Camacho; *W:* Jacobsen Hart, Susan Bowen; *M:* Jim Halfpenny.

The Powerpuff Girls Movie 🦴🦴🦴 **2002 (G)** Blossom, Buttercup, and Bubbles hit the big screen. The big-eyed trio of superpowered kindergartners came into existence after a botched science experiment by Professor Utonium, who mixed his sugar, spice, and everything nice recipe with a little Chemical X (thanks to Jojo the lab chimp). The "X" factor has left the seemingly normal tots with super powers. After a mishap leaves their father/creator in jail, the girls join up with Jojo (voice of Jackson), who since has been genetically altered by Chemical X himself and acquired a taste for world domination, unbeknownst to the Power Pack. Runs a bit long, but creator/director McCracken's cool retro animation, fast-paced editing, and satiric fun makes the spunky girls' action-packed film debut a winner with kids and adults alike. **74m/C VHS, DVD.** *US D:* Craig McCrackin; *W:* Craig McCrackin, Charlie Bean, Lauren Faust, Paul Rudish, John Roarke; *V:* Catherine Cavadini, Tara Strong, Elizabeth (E.G. Dailey) Daily, Roger L. Jackson, Tom Kane, Tom Kenny, Jennifer Hale, Jennifer Martin; *Nar:* Tom Kenny.

Powwow Highway 🦴🦴🦴 1/2 **1989 (R)** Remarkably fine performances in this unusual, thought-provoking, poorly titled foray into the plight of Native Americans. Farmer shines as the unassuming, amiable Cheyenne traveling to New Mexico in a beat-up Chevy with his Indian activist buddy, passionately portrayed by Martinez. On the journey they are constantly confronted with the tragedy of life on a reservation. A sobering look at government injustice and the lingering spirit of a people lost inside their homeland. **105m/C VHS, DVD.** Gary Farmer, A. Martinez, Amanda Wyss, Sam Vlahos, Joanelle Romero, Graham Greene; *D:* Jonathan Wacks; *W:* Janet Heaney, Jean Stawarz; *C:* Toyomichi Kurita; *M:* Barry Goldberg. Sundance '89: Filmmakers Trophy.

Practical Magic 🦴🦴 1/2 **1998 (PG-13)** Gillian (Kidman) and Sally (Bullock) are modern-day witch sisters whose family suffers from an unfortunate 100-year-old curse. Any man they fall in love with is doomed to an early death. One more dead body, Gillian's abusive boyfriend Jimmy (Visnjic), brings out detective Gary Hallet (Quinn) and his charms prove mighty attractive to the frantic Sally. Good cast, weak story. Based on the 1995 novel by Alice Hoffman. **105m/C VHS, DVD.** Sandra Bullock, Nicole Kidman, Aidan Quinn, Stockard Channing, Dianne Wiest, Goran Visnjic; *D:* Griffin Dunne; *W:* Robin Swicord, Akiva Goldsman, Adam Brooks; *C:* Andrew Dunn; *M:* Alan Silvestri.

The Practice of Love 🦴🦴 **1984** A woman journalist's investigation of a murder casts suspicion on her two male lovers. The film raises the question of whether love is even possible in a world dominated by men's struggles for power. In German with English subtitles. **90m/C VHS.** *GE D:* Valie Export.

Prairie Fever 🦴🦴 **2008** Grieving the death of his wife, former sheriff Preston Biggs (Sorbo) has become a drunk. Needing money to pay his debts, Biggs takes a job transporting several rejected mail-order brides said to be suffering from "prairie fever" (or mental illness) to the train depot in Carson City. Meanwhile, card cheat Olivia (Allman) has dumped partner Monte (Henriksen) and stolen their money. Needing a way out of town, she takes a place with Biggs. The women turn out to have been abused and Olivia is a calming influence. They're trailed by some outlaws with a grudge against Biggs and Olivia hasn't seen the last of Monte either. **80m/C DVD.** Kevin Sorbo, Jillian Armenante, Dominique Swain, Lance Henriksen, Silas Weir Mitchell, Don Swayze, Chris(topher) McKenna, Felecia Day, Jamie Anne Allman; *D:* Stephen Bridgewater, David S. Cass Sr.; *W:* Steven H. Berman; *C:* Al Lopez. **TV**

A Prairie Home Companion 🦴🦴 1/2 **2006 (PG-13)** Leisurely-paced adaptation of Keillor's radio show begins at the Fitzgerald Theater in St. Paul on a Saturday night. Only this night is the program's last broadcast because the radio station has been sold. Emcee Keillor (more or less playing himself) doesn't want to spoil things by making a fuss so the show goes on with the singing Johnson sisters—ditsy Yolanda (Streep) and caustic Rhonda (Tomlin)—and risque cowboy duo Lefty (Reilly) and Dusty (Harrelson), while backstage P.I. Guy Noir (Kline) wonders about the mysterious blonde in white (Madsen). Ensemble master Altman just lets his 39th feature meander gently along. **105m/C DVD.** *US* Meryl Streep, Lily Tomlin, Lindsay Lohan, Woody Harrelson, John C. Reilly, Kevin Kline, Tommy Lee Jones, L.Q. Jones, Virginia Madsen, Maya Rudolph, Garrison Keillor, Marylouise Burke; *D:* Robert Altman; *W:* Garrison Keillor; *C:* Edward Lachman.

The Prairie King 🦴 1/2 **1927** Will grants three people the same gold mine but stipulates only one may own it. Silent quandary. **58m/B VHS.** Hoot Gibson, Barbara Worth, Charles Sellon, Albert Priscoe; *D:* B. Reeves Eason; *W:* Frank Howard Clark; *C:* Harry Neumann.

Prairie Moon 🦴 1/2 **1938** Autry becomes the guardian of three tough kids from Chicago after they inherit a ranch. The kids help Autry round up a gang of rustlers. **58m/B VHS.** Gene Autry, Smiley Burnette, Shirley Deane, Tommy Ryan, David Gorcey, Jack Rockwell, Tom London; *D:* Ralph Staub; *W:* Betty Burbridge, Stanley Roberts; *C:* William Nobles.

Prairie Pals 🦴 1/2 **1942** Deputies go undercover to rescue a kidnapped scientist. **60m/B VHS.** William Boyd, Lee Powell, Art Davis, Charles "Blackie" King, John Merton, Kermit Maynard, Al "Fuzzy" St. John; *D:* Sam Newfield.

The Prairie Pirate 🦴🦴 1/2 **1925** Carey is the western hero tracking down the dirty dogs who murdered his sister. Fast-paced. **59m/B VHS.** Harry Carey Sr., Lloyd Whitlock, Jean Dumas, Trilby Clark; *D:* Edmund Mortimer.

Praise 🦴🦴🦴 **1998** First-time director Curran scores big with this downbeat sex-and-drugs saga. Gordan (Fenton) has quit his convenience store job to spend his time drinking with his mates in his grubby Brisbane apartment. Former co-worker Cynthia (Holder) invites Gordon to her parents' empty house where the duo spend their time with various chemical substances, alcohol, and sex. They wind up sticking together out of mutual need and never rise above their marginal existence. Still, both director and actors deliver a powerful production. Adapted from the novel by McGahan, who wrote the screenplay. **97m/C VHS, DVD.** *AU* Peter Fenton, Sacha Horler; *D:* John Curran; *W:* Andrew McGahan; *C:* Dion Beebe. Australian Film Inst. '99: Actress (Horler), Adapt. Screenplay.

Prancer 🦴🦴 **1989 (G)** An eight-year-old girl whose mother has recently died thinks an injured reindeer she has found belongs to Santa. She lovingly nurses him back to health. Harmless family entertainment. **102m/C VHS, DVD.** Sam Elliott, Rebecca Harrell, Cloris Leachman, Rutanya Alda, John Joseph Duda, Abe Vigoda, Michael Constantine, Ariana Richards, Mark Rolston; *D:* John Hancock; *W:* Greg Taylor; *C:* Misha (Mikhail) Suslov; *M:* Maurice Jarre.

Prancer Returns 🦴🦴 1/2 **2001 (G)** When dad cuts out, 8-year-old Charlie, his mom and his brother move to a small Michigan town where Charlie hears about a local legend. Seems a young girl nursed a wounded deer back to health and set it free on Christmas Eve. The deer turned out to be Prancer and he rejoined Santa just in time to help pull the sleigh. So when Charlie finds a baby reindeer in the woods, he decides it must be a new Prancer and he has to make sure that the deer gets to Santa in time for Christmas. **90m/C VHS, DVD.** Jack Palance, John Corbett, Stacy Edwards, Gavin Fink, Michael O'Keefe; *D:* Joshua Butler; *W:* Greg Taylor. **CABLE**

Pray 🦴🦴 *Purei* **2005 (R)** A couple decides their need for money can be met by kidnapping a young girl and holding her for ransom. It's either that or find themselves offed for not repaying money they owe from a drug deal gone bad. So they swipe a girl, hole up in a school, and wait for their friends to join them. When making the ransom call, they are informed the girl they kidnapped has been dead for a year and told not to call back. So who do they have locked up in the building with them? **92m/C DVD.** *JP* Asami Mizukawa, Mitsuyoshi Shinoda, Tetsuji Tamayama, Toshiyuki Toyonaga; *D:* Yuichi Sato; *W:* Tomoko Ogawa.

Pray for Death 🦴🦴 **1985 (R)** When a mild-mannered Japanese family is victimized by a crime syndicate in L.A., a master ninja comes to the rescue. Higher quality production than most ninja adventures. **93m/C VHS, DVD.** James Booth, Robert Ito, Sho Kosugi, Shane Kosugi, Kane (Takeshi) Kosugi, Donna Kei Benz; *D:* Gordon Hessler; *W:* James Booth.

Pray for the Wildcats 🦴 1/2 **1974** Three advertising executives' promotional trip from (or to?) Hell. Anything to please a client. **96m/C VHS.** Andy Griffith, William Shatner, Angie Dickinson, Janet Margolin, Marjoe Gortner, Lorraine Gary; ***D:*** Robert Lewis.

Pray TV 🦴🦴 *KGOD* **1980 (PG)** A sly con man turns a failing TV station into a profitable one when the station starts to broadcast around-the-clock religious programming. **92m/C VHS, DVD.** Dabney Coleman, Archie Hahn, Joyce Jameson, Nancy Morgan, Roger E. Mosley, Marcia Wallace; ***D:*** Rick Friedberg; ***W:*** Nick Castle. **TV**

Pray TV 🦴🦴 **1982** Expose of broadcast religion in which a young preacher chooses between orthodox religion and lots of money. Not as cutting an indictment as it could have been. **100m/C VHS.** John Ritter, Ned Beatty, Madolyn Smith, Richard Kiley, Louise Latham, Jonathan Prince, Michael Currie, Lois Areno; ***D:*** Robert Markowitz. **TV**

A Prayer for Katarina Horovitzova 🦴🦴🦴 1/2 **1969** Stunning tale of a Polish singer who struggles to find the meaning and beauty of life while working to trade Nazi prisoners in U.S. jails for Jews hoping to emigrate. Based on the Arnost Lustig novel. Confiscated by the Czech Communist government and kept from the screen for 21 years. In Czechoslovakian with English subtitles. **60m/C VHS.** *CZ* Jiri Adamira, Lenka Fiserova, Cestmir Randa; ***D:*** Arnost Lustig; ***W:*** Arnost Lustig; ***C:*** Jiri Kadanka; ***M:*** Lubos Fiser.

Prayer for the Dying 🦴🦴 1/2 **1987 (R)** An IRA hitman longs to quit, but he has to complete one last assignment. The hit is witnessed by a priest who becomes an unwitting associate when the hitman hides out at the church. Fine performances from Bates and Rourke, though Hodges and Rourke were not satisfied with finished film. **104m/C VHS, DVD.** Mickey Rourke, Alan Bates, Bob Hoskins, Sammi Davis, Liam Neeson, Alison Doody, Christopher Fulford; ***D:*** Mike Hodges; ***W:*** Edmund Ward, Martin Lynch; ***M:*** Bill Conti.

A Prayer in the Dark 🦴🦴 1/2 **1997 (PG-13)** Pious Quaker wife and mother, Emily Hayworth (Carter), is taken hostage in her own home by a former Quaker friend, Jimmy (Ferguson). He's escaped from prison with two armed cons, demanding that Emily steal $4 million from the bank where she works. Since they're also holding her family, she agrees. But when Emily's out of the house, she and others in the Quaker community try to find a peaceful solution to the volatile situation. **91m/C VHS.** Lynda Carter, Colin Ferguson, Teri Polo; ***D:*** Jerry Ciccoritti; ***W:*** Andrew Laskos; ***C:*** Ron Tannett; ***M:*** David Michael Frank. **CABLE**

Prayer of the Rollerboys 🦴🦴 1/2 **1991 (R)** Violent, futuristic, funky action as Haim infiltrates a criminal gang of syncopated roller-blading neo-nazi youth with plans for nationwide domination. Though routinely plotted and predictable, it's got great skating stunts and a wry vision of tomorrow's shattered USA—broke, drug-soaked, homeless, foreign-owned; even sharper when you realize this is a Japanese-American co-production. **94m/C VHS, DVD.** Corey Haim, Patricia Arquette, Christopher Collet, Julius W. Harris, J.C. Quinn, Jake Dengel, Devin Clark, Mark Pellegrino, Morgan Weisser; ***D:*** Rick King; ***W:*** W. Peter Iliff; ***C:*** Phedon Papamichael; ***M:*** Stacy Widelitz.

Praying Mantis 🦴🦴 **1983 (PG-13)** The professor's scheming nurse murdered his family and plans to marry him for his money. She enlists the aid of the professor's assistant in her evil plot. **119m/C VHS.** Jonathan Pryce, Cherie Lunghi, Anna Cropper, Carmen (De Sautoy) Du Sautoy, Pinkas Braun; ***D:*** Jack Gold; ***M:*** Carl Davis.

Praying Mantis 🦴🦴 1/2 **1993 (PG-13)** Seymour stars as a femme fatale who likes to get married and then, in a rage against her own abusive childhood, kill her new husbands off. So far her total is five dead hubbies with number six (Bostwick) in her sights. Only this time, her almost-sister-in-law (Fisher) is very suspicious of the bride-to-be. **90m/C VHS.** Jane Seymour, Barry Bostwick, Frances Fisher, Chad Allen; ***D:*** James Keach; ***W:*** Duane Poole, William F. Delligan; ***M:*** John Debney. **CABLE**

Pre-Madonnas: Rebels Without a Clue 🦴🦴 1/2 *Social Suicide* **1995 (PG-13)** Kim Sterling (Sturges) decides to rig the Beverly Hills Las Madonnas debutante ball to teach the snobs a lesson. **98m/C VHS.** Shannon Sturges, Bobbie Bresee, Peter Anthony Elliott, Kenn Cooper; ***D:*** Lawrence Foldes.

Preacherman 🦴 1/2 **1983 (R)** Phony preacher travels through the South, fleecing gullible congregations (and providing for their sexual desires) wherever he goes. **90m/C VHS, DVD.** Amos Huxley, Marian Brown, Adam Hesse, Ilene Kristen, W. Henry Smith; ***D:*** Albert T. Viola; ***W:*** Albert T. Viola, Harvey Flaxman; ***M:*** W. Henry Smith, Roland Pope.

The Preacher's Wife 🦴🦴 **1996 (PG)** Remake of 1947's "The Bishop's Wife" finds troubled Newark minister Henry Biggs (Vance) praying for heavenly intervention. His prayers are answered with angel Dudley (Washington)—who isn't so holy that he can't appreciate the minister's choir-leading wife Julia (Houston). While trying to save his cash-strapped church from a greedy developer (Hines), Rev. Biggs is so mired in material problems that he is unable to believe that Dudley is actually an angel. Washington is the dictionary definition of debonair as the angel with a touch of the devil in his eye. All problems are, of course, wrapped up neatly with a bow on top in the end. The real stars of this Christmas tale, however, are Houston's vocal cords. Fans of her singing will love this movie, while others may want to rent the original. **124m/C VHS, DVD.** Shari Headley, Denzel Washington, Whitney Houston, Courtney B. Vance, Gregory Hines, Jenifer Lewis, Loretta Devine, Lionel Richie, Paul Bates, Justin Pierre Edmund, Darvel Davis Jr., William James Stiggers Jr.; ***D:*** Penny Marshall; ***W:*** Nat Mauldin, Allan Scott; ***C:*** Miroslav Ondricek; ***M:*** Hans Zimmer.

Preaching to the Choir 🦴🦴 **2005 (PG-13)** Twin brothers Teshawn (Greene) and Wesley (Sills-Evans) Tucker have been estranged since the death of their parents. Te is the gangsta hip hop star Zulu while Wes is a minister at a Harlem church. When Te gets into big trouble with his LA record producer Bull Sharkey (Akinnoyye-Agbaje), he flees to Harlem to hide out and he and Wes try to reconcile their differences, especially when Te offers to whip the church's raggedy gospel choir into shape in time for a competition. **100m/C DVD.** Darien Sills-Evans, Billoah Greene, Tichina Arnold, Adewale Akinnuoye-Agbaje, Eartha Kitt, Patti LaBelle, Novella Nelson, Janine Green; ***D:*** Olga San Juan; ***W:*** Kevin Heffernan, Peter E. Lengyel; ***C:*** Robert Barocci; ***M:*** Nona Hendryx.

Preaching to the Perverted 🦴 **1997 (R)** Silly sex comedy finds politician Henry Harding (Bell) crusading against smut with his intention to close down London's S&M clubs. First up is the House of Thwax, run by New York fetish queen, Tanya (Turner). To get evidence of naughtiness, Henry sends in virginal volunteer Peter (Anholt), who becomes obsessed with Tanya. Tanya's intrigued by his innocence and teaches Peter a few sexual tricks, which soon means he has to choose between his job and his newly acquired interest in kink. **99m/C DVD.** *GB* Guinevere Turner, Christien Anholt, Tom Bell, Julie Graham, Julian Wadham, Georgina Hale, Ricky Tomlinson, Don Henderson; ***D:*** Stuart Urban; ***W:*** Stuart Urban; ***C:*** Sam McCurdy; ***M:*** Magnus Fiennes.

Precious: Based on the Novel by Sapphire 🦴🦴🦴 1/2 **2009 (R)** Multi-award winning drama is a graphic and uncompromising urban nightmare that offers a sliver of hope. In 1987 Harlem, obese, 16-year-old African-American Claireece "Precious" Jones (Sidibe) is precious to no one—certainly not to her monster mom Mary (Mo'Nique), who treats her like a slave and uses her for her welfare benefits, or the unseen father who raped her and got Precious pregnant again. Withdrawn Precious has her fantasies, which the audience sees and hears, about being a movie or singing star while being nearly illiterate. She enrolls at an alternative school with the prerequisite caring teacher (Patton) and also comes to the attention of a welfare counselor (Carey) who tries to show her something more. There's no magical moment that changes Precious' life completely but there's quiet progress. As the title states, based on the 1996 novel by Sapphire. **109m/C DVD.** *US* Gabourney "Gabby" Sidibe, Mo'Nique, Paula Patton, Mariah Carey, Lenny Kravitz, Sherri Shepherd; ***D:*** Lee Daniels; ***W:*** Geoffrey "Damien Paul" Fletcher; ***C:*** Andrew Dunn; ***M:*** Mario Grigorov. Oscars '09: Adapt. Screenplay, Support. Actress (Mo'Nique); British Acad. '09: Support. Actress (Mo'Nique); Golden Globes '10: Support. Actress (Mo'Nique); Ind. Spirit '10: Actress (Sidibe), Director (Daniels), Film, Support. Actress (Mo'Nique), First Screenplay; Screen Actors Guild '09: Support. Actress (Mo'Nique), Support. Actress (Mo'Nique).

Precious Find 🦴🦴 **1996 (R)** In 2049 there's a new gold rush—this time into outer space. The moon's enclosed city is a staging area for mining operations throughout the solar system and draws the attention of three prospectors: Ben, who can "smell" gold, Crille (Hauer), who has a high-tech treasure map, and Sam (James), who owns a space hauler. They're all anxious to cash in when a newly discovered asteroid turns out to be a literal gold mine as is claim jumper Camilla (Chen). **90m/C VHS.** Rutger Hauer, Brion James, Harold P. Pruett, Joan Chen; ***D:*** Philippe Mora; ***W:*** Jane Ubell, John Remark; ***C:*** Walter Bal; ***M:*** Roy Hay.

Predator 🦴🦴 1/2 **1987 (R)** Schwarzenegger leads a team of CIA-hired mercenaries into the Central American jungles to rescue hostages. They encounter an alien force that begins to attack them one by one. Soon it's just Arnold and the Beast in this attention-grabbing, but sometimes silly, suspense film. **107m/C VHS, DVD, UMD.** Arnold Schwarzenegger, Jesse Ventura, Sonny Landham, Bill Duke, Elpidia Carrillo, Carl Weathers, R.G. Armstrong, Richard Chaves, Shane Black, Kevin Peter Hall; ***D:*** John McTiernan; ***W:*** Jim Thomas, John Thomas; ***C:*** Donald McAlpine; ***M:*** Alan Silvestri.

Predator 2 🦴🦴 **1990 (R)** Tough cop takes time away from battling drug dealers to deal with malicious extraterrestrial who exterminated Arnold's band of commandos in "Predator." Miss-billed as sequel, its only resemblance to the original is that the predator has inexplicably returned (this time to the thick of L.A.). Gory action aplenty, little logic. Fine cast dominated by minority performers can't save this one. **105m/C VHS, DVD.** Danny Glover, Gary Busey, Ruben Blades, Maria Conchita Alonso, Bill Paxton, Robert Davi, Adam Baldwin, Kent McCord, Morton Downey Jr., Calvin Lockhart, Teri Weigel, Kevin Peter Hall, Steve Kahan, Michael (Mike) Papajohn, Jsu Garcia; ***D:*** Stephen Hopkins; ***W:*** John Thomas, Jim Thomas; ***C:*** Peter Levy; ***M:*** Alan Silvestri.

Predator Island 🦴 *Hell's Beacon* **2005 (R)** Teens and aliens-what could be more fun? A group of teens head off for a lovely weekend boat trip off the New England Coast. A meteor crash spurs bad weather and throws the crew off-course, stranding them on an island inhabited only by a creepy lighthouse keeper and his wife. The aliens, presumably having hitched a ride on the meteor, terrorize all. **75m/C DVD.** Daniel Gordon, Hank Torrance, Libby Krall, Tom Dahl, Ilana Becker, Michael Wrann; ***D:*** Steven Charles Castle; ***W:*** Steven Charles Castle; ***C:*** Andrew Gernhard; ***M:*** Tony Bitten. **VIDEO**

Predators 2010 A group of elite warriors are hunted by alien trackers called Predators in this franchise reboot/sequel from producer Robert Rodriguez (he also wrote the screen story). **m/C DVD.** *US* Adrien Brody, Laurence Fishburne, Topher Grace, Alice Braga, Danny Trejo, Walton Goggins, Mahershalhashbaz Ali, Oleg Nikolai; ***D:*** Nimrod Antal; ***W:*** Michael Finch, Alex Litvak; ***C:*** Gyula Pados; ***M:*** John Debney.

Prefontaine 🦴🦴 1/2 **1996 (PG-13)** Sports bio has appeal, thanks to lead actor Leto, in covering the brief career of early '70s runner Steve Prefontaine. Cocky and outspoken, the charismatic University of Oregon star soon owns every American record for distances between 2,000 and 10,000 meters. He's expected to gold at the 1972 Munich Olympics but falters, thanks in part to the tragedy surrounding the games. Returning home, the flamboyant Pre becomes a sports activist for athletes' rights before dying in a car crash in 1975 at the age of 24. Relatively straight narrative and little psychological insight make for few lasting impressions. **107m/C VHS, DVD.** Jared Leto, R. Lee Ermey, Ed O'Neill, Amy Locane, Lindsay Crouse, Laurel Holloman, Breckin Meyer, Kurtwood Smith, Brian McGovern, Peter Anthony Jacobs; ***D:*** Steve James; ***W:*** Steve James, Eugene Corr; ***C:*** Peter Gilbert; ***M:*** Mason Daring.

Prehistoric Bimbos in Armageddon City **WOOF! 1993** Trianna and her tribe of Prehistoric Bimbos must prevent post-nuclear domination in Old Chicago City, the last remaining civilization after WWIII, by defeating the evil ruler Nemesis and his cyborgs. "Enough bimbos to fill two post-nuclear action comedies." So bad its gotta be good. **70m/C VHS.** Robert Vollrath, Tonia Monahan, Deric Bernier; ***D:*** Todd Sheets; ***W:*** Roger Williams.

Prehistoric Women **WOOF! 1950** A tribe of prehistoric women look for husbands the old-fashioned way—they drag them back to their caves from the jungle. So bad it's almost good. **74m/C VHS, DVD.** Laurette Luez, Allan Nixon, Mara Lynn, Joan Shawlee, Judy Landon; ***D:*** Gregg Tallas.

Prehistoric Women 🦴 *Slave Girls* **1967** Essentially, an equally tacky remake of the 1950 woofer. Great white hunter David Marchant (Latimer) gets lost in a jungle where the local tribe worship the white rhino. He escapes from one group, only to recapture by some Amazons, who take the hunter to their queen, Kari (Beswick—the only reason to waste your time), who gives him two options—satisfy her or die. **90m/C VHS, DVD.** *GB* Michael Latimer, Martine Beswick, Edina Ronay, Carol White; ***D:*** Michael Carreras; ***W:*** Henry Younger; ***C:*** Michael Reed; ***M:*** Carlo Martelli.

Prehysteria 🦴🦴 1/2 **1993 (PG)** Fantasy/adventure about a widower, his 11-year-old son and teenage daughter, and what happens when some mysterious eggs from South America accidentally wind up at their farm. Imagine their surprise when the eggs hatch and out pop a brood of pygmy dinosaurs. The dinosaurs are cute (as is the family), the villain is dumb, and the violence minimal. **84m/C VHS.** Brett Cullen, Austin O'Brien, Samantha Mills, Colleen Morris, Tony Longo, Stuart Fratkin, Stephen Lee; ***D:*** Albert Band, Charles Band; ***W:*** Greg Suddeth, Mark Goldstein.

Prehysteria 2 🦴🦴 1/2 **1994 (PG)** While their adoptive family is on vacation the pygmy dinosaurs get loose and aid a lonely rich boy whose governess is plotting to send him to military boarding school. **81m/C VHS.** Kevin R. Connors, Jennifer Harte, Dean Scofield, Bettye Ackerman, Larry Hankin, Greg Lewis, Alan Palo, Michael Hagiwara, Owen Bush; ***D:*** Albert Band; ***W:*** Brent Friedman, Michael Davis; ***M:*** Richard Band.

Prehysteria 3 🦴🦴 1/2 **1995 (PG)** The mini-dinos take up miniature golf. Seems Thomas MacGregor's (Willard) putt-putt business is about to sink when his daughter Ella (Anderson) finds the pygmy dinosaurs and a promotional bonanza is born. But Thomas' evil brother Hal (Weitz) hatches a plot to take over the now-successful enterprize. DeCoteau used the pseudonym Julian Breen. **85m/C VHS.** Fred Willard, Bruce Weitz, Whitney Anderson, Pam Matteson; ***D:*** David DeCoteau; ***W:*** Michael Davis, Neil Ruttenberg.

Prelude to a Kiss 🦴🦴 **1992 (PG-13)** Disappointing screen adaptation of Craig Lucas' hit play features Baldwin and Ryan as young lovers in this romantic fantasy. Ryan is Rita, a free-spirited bartender and Baldwin is Peter, a conservative writer, who decide to marry after a whirlwind courtship. At their wedding reception, Rita obligingly kisses one of their guests, an old man (Walker). Then, on their honeymoon, Peter begins to notice a number of changes to Rita's character and comes to realize this is truly not the girl he married. The delicate fantasy which worked on stage struggles to survive the "opening up" of the screen adaptation though Baldwin (who reprises his stage role) and Ryan are appealing. **106m/C VHS, DVD.** Alec Baldwin, Meg Ryan, Sydney Walker, Ned Beatty, Patty Duke, Kathy Bates, Stanley Tucci; ***D:*** Norman Rene; ***W:*** Craig Lucas; ***C:*** Stefan Czapsky; ***M:*** Howard Shore.

Prelude to War 🦴🦴 ½ **1942** A compact look at the events of 1931-39; includes a series of contrasts between free societies and totalitarian governments. From the "Why We Fight" series. **53m/B VHS, DVD.** ***D:*** Frank Capra. Oscars '42: Feature Doc.

Premature Burial 🦴🦴 **1962** A cataleptic Englishman's worst fears come true when he is buried alive. He escapes and seeks revenge on his doctor and his greedy wife. Based upon the story by Edgar Allan Poe. **81m/C VHS, DVD.** Ray Milland, Richard Ney, Hazel Court, Heather Angel, Alan Napier, John Dierkes, Dick Miller, Brendan Dillon Jr., Clive Halliday; ***D:*** Roger Corman; ***W:*** Charles Beaumont, Ray Russell; ***C:*** Floyd Crosby; ***M:*** Ronald Stein.

Premonition 🦴 ½ **1971 (PG)** Three drug-riddled '60s college students experience similar premonitions of death, and subsequently either die or become tormented. **83m/C VHS.** Carl Crow, Tim Ray, Winfrey Hester Hill, Victor Izay; ***D:*** Alan Rudolph; ***W:*** Alan Rudolph; ***C:*** John Bailey.

The Premonition 🦴🦴 ½ **1975 (PG)** Parapsychologist searching for a missing child is drawn into a frightening maze of dream therapy and communication with the dead. Well-done paranorm tale filmed in Mississippi. **94m/C VHS, DVD.** Richard Lynch, Sharon Farrell, Jeff Corey, Ellen Barber, Edward Bell, Danielle Brisebois; ***D:*** Robert Allen Schnitzer; ***W:*** Anthony Mahon.

Premonition 🦴🦴 **1998 (R)** Lloyd and Preston are tabloid reporters who investigate supernatural phenomena. Their latest find is a mental patient who predicts events that wind up leading back to a past they both share. Unfortunately, the film is more a series of horror cliches and makes little sense. **93m/C VHS, DVD.** Christopher Lloyd, Adrian Paul, Cynthia (Cyndy, Cindy) Preston, Blu Mankuma; ***D:*** Gavin Wilding; ***W:*** Gavin Wilding, Raul Inglis, John Fairley; ***C:*** Glen Winter. **VIDEO**

Premonition 🦴🦴 *Yogen; J joraa shiataa 2; J-Horror Theater Vol. 2* **2004 (R)** Based on the comic strip "Newspaper of Terror" and second in the J-Horror Theatre series (six films commissioned to be done by famous directors after the success of "Ringu"). While waiting in a phone booth to upload a file, a high school professor sees a newspaper from a future date foretelling the death of his daughter, which occurs in short order. She dies as expected, and the film picks up years later as the professor has become obsessed with finding the legendary newspaper that foretells death and destruction. Eventually he begins trying to change the events it prophesizes, and his life begins to unravel. **95m/C DVD.** *JP* Hiroshi Mikami, Noriko Sakai, Hana Inoue; ***D:*** Norio Tsuruta; ***W:*** Norio Tsuruta, Jiro Tsunoda, Noboru Takagi; ***C:*** Naoki Kayano.

Premonition 🦴🦴 ½ **2007 (PG-13)** He's dead! No, he's not! He's in the shower! He's being buried! Whew—no wonder Linda (Bullock) thinks she's going nuts. Seems every time she wakes up the fate of her husband Jim (McMahon) has changed. Linda finally realizes her days are mysteriously out of order and if she can figure out the pattern (or have a little faith), maybe she can save her man. It's confusing however you look at it, though Bullock tries her best. **97m/C DVD, Blu-ray Disc.** *US* Sandra Bullock, Julian McMahon, Nia Long, Kate Nelligan, Amber Valletta, Peter Stormare, Courtney Taylor Burness, Shyann McClure; ***D:*** Mennan Yapo; ***W:*** Bill Kelly; ***C:*** Torsten Lippstock; ***M:*** Klaus Badelt.

Prep School 🦴 **1981 (PG-13)** A very proper New England prep school is turned topsy-turvy by two rambunctious co-eds. They're determined to break every one of the school's cardinal rules. **97m/C VHS.** Leslie Hope, Andrew Sabiston; ***D:*** Paul Almond.

The Preppie Murder 🦴🦴 ½ **1989** Made for TV crime drama based on the killing of Jennifer Levin in New York City's Central Park in 1987, with Baldwin cast as prep school grad Robert Chambers. Amid sensational headlines, the story told of drugs, sexual games, and idle and disaffected youth. **100m/C VHS.** William Baldwin, Lara Flynn Boyle, Danny Aiello, Joanna Kerns, Dorothy Fielding, James Handy, William Devane; ***D:*** John Herzfeld. **TV**

Preppies 🦴 ½ **1982 (R)** Yet another teen sex comedy, but this time Ivy Leaguer Drake must pass his exams to receive his $50 million inheritance. Lots of skirt chasing as his conniving cousin leads him astray. **83m/C VHS, DVD.** Dennis Drake, Peter Brady Reardon, Steven Holt, Nitchie Barrett, Cindy Manion, Katt Shea, Lynda Wiesmeier; ***D:*** Chuck Vincent.

Prescott Kid 🦴🦴 **1936** Legendary western star McCoy plays a law-abiding cowboy mistaken for the new Marshall in the outlaw town of San Lorenzo, which has been targeted by a gang of cattle rustling killers. **58m/B VHS.** Tim McCoy, Sheila (Manors) Mannors, Alden Chase, Hooper Atchley, Walter Brennan; ***D:*** David Selman; ***W:*** Ford Beebe.

Presenting Lily Mars 🦴🦴 **1943** A small-town girl comes to New York to make it on Broadway. Based on the Booth Tarkington novel. ♫ When I Look at You; Three O'Clock in the Morning; Kulebiaka; Is It Love? (Or The Gypsy in Me); Broadway Rhythm; Sweethearts of America; Where There's Music; Every Little Movement Has a Meaning All Its Own; Tom, Tom the Piper's Son. **105m/B VHS, DVD.** Judy Garland, Van Heflin, Fay Bainter, Richard Carlson, Tommy Dorsey; ***D:*** Norman Taurog; ***C:*** Joseph Ruttenberg.

The President's Analyst 🦴🦴🦴 ½ **1967** A superbly written, brilliantly executed satire from the mind of Theodore J. Flicker, who wrote as well as directed. Coburn steals the show as a psychiatrist who has the dubious honor of being appointed "secret shrink" to the President of the U.S. Pressures of the job steadily increase his paranoia until he suspects he is being pursued by agents and counter agents alike. Is he losing his sanity or...? Vastly entertaining. **104m/C VHS, DVD.** James Coburn, Godfrey Cambridge, Severn Darden, Joan Delaney, Pat Harrington, Will Geer, William Daniels, Barry McGuire, Jill Banner, Arte Johnson; ***D:*** Theodore J. Flicker; ***W:*** Theodore J. Flicker; ***C:*** William A. Fraker; ***M:*** Lalo Schifrin.

President's Mistress 🦴 ½ **1978** A security agent searches for his sister's murderer, while trying to obscure the fact that she was having an affair with the President. **97m/C VHS.** Beau Bridges, Susan Blanchard, Larry Hagman, Joel Fabiani, Karen Grassle; ***D:*** John Llewellyn Moxey.

The President's Mystery 🦴 ½ *One For All* **1936** A lawyer decides to turn his back on society by giving up his practice and his marriage. Eventually he meets and falls in love with another woman. The most interesting aspect of the film is that it is based on a story by Franklin D. Roosevelt, which was published in "Liberty" magazine. The story was supposedly better than its screen adaptation. **80m/B VHS, DVD.** Henry Wilcoxon, Betty Furness, Sidney Blackmer, Evelyn Brent; ***D:*** Phil Rosen.

The President's Plane Is Missing 🦴🦴 **1971** When Air Force One disappears, the less than trustworthy Vice President takes control. Could there be a dire plot in the making? Based on a novel by Rod Serling's brother Robert J. Serling. **100m/C VHS.** Buddy Ebsen, Peter Graves, Arthur Kennedy, Rip Torn, Louise Sorel, Raymond Massey, James Wainwright, Mercedes McCambridge, Dabney Coleman, Joseph Campanella; ***D:*** Daryl Duke.

President's Target 🦴🦴 **1993** An anti-drug mission in South America is ambushed and CIA operative Peter Caine is the only survivor. Now he's out to see who planned the double-cross and how best to get his revenge. **82m/C VHS.** John Coleman, Martin Kove, Bo Hopkins, Brigitte Audrey; ***D:*** Yvan Chiffre.

The Presidio 🦴🦴 **1988 (R)** An easy going police detective must investigate a murder on a military base where he and the base commander have sparred before. The commander becomes downright nasty when his daughter shows an interest in the detective. Good action scenes in San Francisco almost covers up script weaknesses, but not quite. **97m/C VHS, DVD.** Sean Connery, Mark Harmon, Meg Ryan, Jack Warden, Mark Blum, Jenette Goldstein; ***D:*** Peter Hyams; ***W:*** Larry Ferguson; ***M:*** Bruce Broughton.

Pressure 🦴🦴 ½ **2002 (R)** Med students Steve (Smith) and Patrick (Munro) find themselves on a road trip to hell when they make a stop in a smalltown bar. Patrick spends his time dancing with the cheerleaders inhabiting the premises while Steve is lured outside by vampy Amber (Featherstone). He's then knocked unconscious and set-up by her beau, Bo (Dorval), who accidentally shoots himself. This puts our boys in big trouble since Bo is the local corrupt sheriff's (Rhodes) kid. Then the chase is on! **90m/C VHS, DVD.** Kerr Smith, Lochlyn Munro, Angela Featherstone, Adrien Dorval, Donnelly Rhodes, Michelle Harrison; ***D:*** Richard Gale; ***W:*** Richard Gale, Craig Brewer; ***M:*** Christopher Brady. **VIDEO**

Pressure Point 🦴🦴🦴 **1962** Poitier stars as a prison psychiatrist treating an inmate who is a racist and a member of the Nazi party. Darin gives an excellent performance as the Nazi patient in this intelligent drama based on a true case. **87m/B VHS, DVD.** Sidney Poitier, Bobby Darin, Peter Falk, Carl Benton Reid, Barry J. Gordon, Howard Caine, Mary Munday; ***D:*** Hubert Cornfield; ***M:*** Ernest Gold.

The Prestige 🦴🦴🦴 **2006 (PG-13)** Nolan reunites with his "Batman Begins" stars Bale and Caine in this perplexing, complicated, and lavish period mystery that focuses on the increasingly violent rivalry between two London magicians. Posh Robert Angier (Jackman) is the more natural showman while Cockney Alfred Borden (Bale) is the risk taker; both are mentored by the conciliatory Cutter (Caine). One of Borden's risks causes the death of Robert's wife Julia (Perabo) and their feud is on. Eventually it will involve Alfred's unhappy missus, Sarah (Hall), lush magician's assistant Olivia (Johansson), reclusive inventor Nikola Tesla (Bowie), and murder. Situations turn fantastical but clues are apparent if you pay attention. Definitely worth a second look. **128m/C DVD, Blu-ray Disc.** *GB US* Christian Bale, Hugh Jackman, Michael Caine, Scarlett Johansson, Piper Perabo, Rebecca Hall, David Bowie, Andy Serkis, Roger Rees, Ricky Jay, Samantha Mahurin, William Morgan Sheppard; ***D:*** Christopher Nolan; ***W:*** Christopher Nolan, Jonathan Nolan; ***C:*** Wally Pfister; ***M:*** David Julyan.

Presumed Guilty 🦴 **1991** An innocent man is released from prison only to find he is once again a wanted man! So he gets his gal, who happens to be the sheriff's daughter, is beaten up and in the end winds up living happily ever after. **91m/C VHS, DVD.** Jack Vogel, Holly Floria, Sean Holton, Wayne Zanelotti, Bradley Rockwell, Sharon Young, Al Schuerman; ***D:*** Lawrence L. Simeone; ***W:*** Lawrence L. Simeone.

Presumed Innocent 🦴🦴🦴 **1990 (R)** Assistant district attorney is the prime suspect when a former lover turns up brutally murdered. Cover-ups surround him, the political climate changes, and friends and enemies switch sides. Slow-paced courtroom drama with excellent performances from Ford, Julia, and Bedelia. Skillfully adapted from the best-seller by Chicago attorney Scott Turow. **127m/C VHS, DVD.** Harrison Ford, Brian Dennehy, Bonnie Bedelia, Greta Scacchi, Raul Julia, Paul Winfield, John Spencer, Joe Grifasi, Anna Maria Horsford, Sab Shimono, Christine Estabrook, Michael (Lawrence) Tolan, Tom Mardirosian, Bradley Whitford, Jesse Bradford, Joseph Mazzello, Jeffrey Wright, Ron Frazier; ***D:*** Alan J. Pakula; ***W:*** Alan J. Pakula, Frank Pierson; ***C:*** Gordon Willis; ***M:*** John Williams.

Pretty Baby 🦴🦴 **1950** Silly workplace comedy. All Patsy (Drake) wants is a seat on the subway and a chance to advance at the ad agency where she works. When a baby food campaign fails, Patsy takes the life-sized baby doll from the ad and uses it to pass herself off as a young mother so she can finally sit down. Baby food manufacturer Baxter (Gwenn) just happens to sit next to Patsy and her subterfuge leads to his insisting that she take over his ad campaign much to the dismay of her bosses. **92m/B DVD.** Betsy Drake, Edmund Gwenn, Dennis Morgan, Zachary Scott, William Frawley; ***D:*** Bretaigne Windust; ***W:*** Everett Freeman, Harry Kurnitz; ***C:*** J. Peverell Marley; ***M:*** David Buttolph.

Pretty Baby 🦴🦴🦴 **1978 (R)** Shield's launching pad and Malle's first American film is a masterpiece of cinematography and style, nearly upstaged by the plodding story line. Carradine manages to be effective but never succeeds at looking comfortable as the New Orleans photographer besotted with, and subsequently married to, an 11-year-old prostitute (Shields). Low key, disturbingly intriguing story, beautifully photographed by Sven Nykvist. **109m/C VHS, DVD.** Brooke Shields, Keith Carradine, Susan Sarandon, Barbara Steele, Diana Scarwid, Antonio Fargas, Frances Faye, Gerrit Graham, Mae Mercer; ***D:*** Louis Malle; ***W:*** Polly Platt; ***C:*** Sven Nykvist; ***M:*** Jerry Wexler.

Pretty in Pink 🦴🦴 ½ **1986 (PG-13)** More teen angst from the pen of Hughes. Poor girl falls for a rich guy. Their families fret, their friends are distressed, and fate conspires against them. If you can suspend your disbelief that a teenager with her own car and answering machine is financially inferior, then you may very well be able to accept the entire premise. Slickly done and adequately, if not enthusiastically, acted. In 1987, Hughes essentially rewrote this film with "Some Kind of Wonderful," the same story with the rich/pauper characters reversed by gender. **96m/C VHS, DVD.** Molly Ringwald, Andrew McCarthy, Jon Cryer, Harry Dean Stanton, James Spader, Annie Potts, Andrew (Dice Clay) Silverstein, Margaret Colin, Alexa Kenin, Gina Gershon, Dweezil Zappa, Kristy Swanson; ***D:*** Howard Deutch; ***W:*** John Hughes; ***C:*** Tak Fujimoto; ***M:*** Michael Gore.

Pretty Persuasion 🦴 **2005** Nasty girls. Toxic Kimberly (Wood) rules her private high school roost, dragging along airhead best pal Brittany (Harnois) and new student Randa (Schnall) in her wake. The vicious teen targets her English teacher, Mr. Anderson (Livingston), who harbors fantasies about his female students, accusing him of sexual abuse and persuading her friends to back her up. The ensuing scandal and trial are played up by preening tabloid reporter Emily Klein (Krakowski). Woods is around as Kimberly's wealthy, aggressively nasty dad. Smug and offensive. **104m/C DVD.** *US* Evan Rachel Wood, Ron Livingston, James Woods, Jane Krakowski, Elisabeth Harnois, Selma Blair, Danny Comden, Stark Sands, Michael Hitchcock, Robert Joy, Jaime (James) King, Adi Schnall, Alex Desert; ***D:*** Marcos Siega; ***W:*** Skander Halim; ***C:*** Ramsay Nickell; ***M:*** Gilad Benamram.

Pretty Poison 🦴🦴🦴 ½ **1968** You won't need an antidote for this one. Original, absorbing screenplay, top-notch acting, and on target direction combine to raise this low-budget, black comedy above the crowd. Perkins at his eerie best as a burned-out arsonist who cooks up a crazy scheme and enlists the aid of a hot-to-trot high schooler, only to discover too late she has some burning desires of her own. Weld is riveting as the turbulent teen. **89m/C VHS, DVD.** Anthony Perkins, Tuesday Weld, Beverly Garland, John Randolph, Dick O'Neill, Joe (Joseph) Bova, Ken Kercheval; ***D:*** Noel Black; ***W:*** Lorenzo Semple Jr.; ***C:*** David Quaid; ***M:*** Johnny Mandel. N.Y. Film Critics '68: Screenplay.

Pretty Smart **WOOF!** **1987 (R)** Two diametrically opposed sisters at a European finishing school team up against a drug-dealing, voyeuristic teacher. Pretty lame. **84m/C VHS.** Tricia Leigh Fisher, Patricia Arquette, Dennis Cole, Lisa Lorient; ***D:*** Dimitri Logothetis; ***M:*** Eddie Arkin.

Pretty Village, Pretty Flame 🦴🦴🦴 *Lepa Sela, Lepo Gore* **1996** Powerful story of the Bosnian conflict that is loosely based on a true incident. Story flashes from the days of Yugoslavian unity under Marshal Tito to 1992 when members of a Serbian patrol are trapped (along with an American journalist) by Muslim militiamen in a tunnel connecting Zagreb and Belgrade with no hope for escape. Serbo-Croatian with subtitles. **125m/C VHS, DVD.** Dragan Bjelogric, Nikola Kojo, Bata Zivojinovic, Dragan Maksimovic, Zoran Cvijanovic, Nikola Pejakovic, Lisa Moncure; ***D:*** Srdjan Dragojevic; ***W:*** Srdjan Dragojevic, Vanja Bulic, Nikola Pejakovic; ***C:*** Dusan Joksimovic; ***M:*** Lazar Ristovski.

Pretty Woman 🦴🦴🦴 **1990 (R)** An old story takes a fresh approach as a successful but stuffy business man hires a fun-loving, energetic young hooker to be his companion for a week. The film caused some controversy over its upbeat portrayal of prostitution, but its popularity at the boxoffice catapulted

Roberts to stardom. **117m/C VHS, DVD, Blu-ray Disc.** Richard Gere, Julia Roberts, Ralph Bellamy, Jason Alexander, Laura San Giacomo, Hector Elizondo, Alex Hyde-White, Elinor Donahue, Larry Miller, Jane Morris; ***D:*** Garry Marshall; ***W:*** J.F. Lawton; ***C:*** Charles Minsky; ***M:*** James Newton Howard. Golden Globes '91: Actress—Mus./Comedy (Roberts).

Prettykill WOOF! **1987 (R)** A confusing storyline with numerous subplots involves detective with a paramour/prostitute (Hubley) attempting to stalk a mad killer while contending with her split personality. **95m/C VHS.** David Birney, Susannah York, Season Hubley, Yaphet Kotto, Suzanne Snyder, Germane Honde; ***D:*** George Kaczender; ***W:*** Sandra K. Bailey; ***C:*** Joao Fernandes.

The Prey **1980 (R)** Poorly done horror show about a predator who is looking for a mate in the Colorado Rockies and kills five campers in the process. **80m/C VHS.** Debbie Thurseon, Steve Bond, Lori Lethin, Jackie Coogan; ***D:*** Edwin Scott Brown; ***W:*** Edwin Scott Brown, Summer Brown.

Prey for Rock and Roll **2003 (R)** Jacki (Gershon) is a punk rocker who heads the all-girl band Clam Dandy in the L.A. club scene. She's been trying to make it big for the past twenty years, and, fast approaching 40, wonders if it's time to call it quits. While the movie has heart and an authentic rock and roll attitude, it falls on some conventional tactics. That doesn't undermine the raw performance of Gershon, who co-produced the film, and sang her own songs, but it does have a buzz-killing effect on the rest of the proceedings. Adapted from the autobiographical play by Cheri Lovedog. **104m/C VHS, DVD.** *US* Gina Gershon, Drea De Matteo, Lori Petty, Shelly Cole, Marc Blucas, Ivan Martin; ***D:*** Alex Steyermark; ***W:*** Cheri Lovedog, Robin Whitehouse; ***C:*** Antonio Calvache.

Prey for the Hunter **1992 (R)** Four businessmen on a big-game hunt decide they're bored with their usual prey. They persuade a photojournalist to join them in a game with paint pellet guns except they decide to use real bullets and the journalist becomes their new target. An old and tired plot with nothing new to distinguish it. **90m/C VHS.** Todd Jensen, Andre Jacobs, Michelle Bestbier, Evan J. Klisser, David Butler, Allan Granville; ***D:*** John H. Parr.

Prey of the Chameleon **1991 (R)** A female serial killer escapes from her asylum, ready to rip more men to shreds. However a tough lady cop has other ideas and goes all out to put an end to the madwoman's doings. Can she stop this fiend before the man she loves becomes the next victim? **91m/C VHS.** Daphne Zuniga, James Wilder, Alexandra Paul, Don Harvey; ***D:*** Fleming Fuller.

Prey of the Jaguar 1/2 **1996 (R)** Derek Leigh (Caulfield) is an ex-Special Ops agent who's the target of revenge-minded drug lord Damien Bandera (Goddard). When Bandera slaughters his family, Leigh transforms himself into costumed avenger, the Jaguar (after his son's drawing), and first goes after Bandera's drug network before hunting the man himself. Dopey costume but this vigilante prefers putting people to sleep (via a dart) rather than killing them so there's reduced gore and the violence is more martial-arts than slice-and-dice. **96m/C VHS, DVD.** Maxwell Caulfield, Trevor Goddard, Linda Blair, Stacy Keach, Paul Regina; ***D:*** David DeCoteau; ***W:*** Rory Johnston, Bud Robertson, Nick Spagnoli; ***C:*** Howard Wexler; ***M:*** Jeff Walton.

A Price above Rubies 1/2 **1997 (R)** Evils of patriarchal society are exposed in this tale of an Orthodox Jewish wife who seeks fulfillment outside the lonely and oppressive world in which she lives. Zellweger shines as Sonia, who defies her frigid Hasidic husband Mendel (Fitzgerald) to take a job as a jeweler, then falls in love with a Puerto Rican artist (Payne). Eccleston is Mendel's brother, who has a strange relationship with Sonia, and Margulies is his more traditional wife who tries to help Sonia fit in with their way of life. Interesting, though not earth-shatteringly deep, characterization beyond film's female lead is scanty, with one-dimensional male models on display here. Second feature from writer/director Yakin. **117m/C VHS, DVD.** Renee Zellweger, Christopher Eccleston, Glenn Fitzgerald, Allen Payne, Julianna Margulies, Kim Hunter, John Randolph, Kathleen Chalfant, Edie Falco, Tim Jerome, Phyllis Newman; ***D:*** Boaz Yakin; ***W:*** Boaz Yakin; ***C:*** Adam Holender; ***M:*** Lesley Barber.

Price of Glory **2000 (PG-13)** After seeing hs promising boxing career destroyed by an unscrupulous manager, Arturo Ortega (Smits) tries to live his dreams through his three sons. Sonny (Seda) is the best boxer but can't please his father, Jimmy (Collins) is the rebel, and Johnny (Hernandez) shares his dad's passion and has talent. Complicating matters are a powerful promoter (Perlman) and Arturo's self-destructive tendencies. You've seen this story before, even if the setting is changed to the Southwest, and except for excellent performances by Smits and Seda, there's nothing here to cover for the lack of originality and less-than-stellar execution. **118m/C VHS, DVD.** Jimmy Smits, Jon Seda, Clifton (Gonzalez) Collins Jr., Maria Del Mar, Sal Lopez, Louis Mandylor, Paul Rodriguez, Ron Perlman, Danielle Camastra, Ernesto Hernandez; ***D:*** Carlos Avila; ***W:*** Phil Berger; ***C:*** Alfonso Beato; ***M:*** Joseph Julian Gonzalez.

The Price of Milk **2000 (PG-13)** Quirky modern fairy tale has Rob and Lucinda living a happy idyllic life on a New Zealand dairy farm when Lucinda becomes worried that they've become too happy. She decides, on the advice of her best friend Drosophilia, to test Rob's love. She does this by first jumping into a vat of fresh cow's milk worth $1,500. Rob forgives her, but things are about to get strange. Lucinda accidently runs over a local Maori woman named "Auntie." The woman is unharmed but upset. Later, Auntie has her golf-playing nephews steal Lucinda's prized patchwork quilt, demanding the entire dairy herd in exchange for its return. Sinclair worked from a 30-page "outline" instead of a script, and it shows. Robust performances and the beautiful scenery do help make up for it, though. **87m/C VHS, DVD.** *NZ* Danielle Cormack, Karl Urban, Willa O'Neill, Michael Lawrence, Rangi Motu; ***D:*** Harry Sinclair; ***W:*** Harry Sinclair; ***C:*** Leon Narbey.

Priceless 1/2 *Hors de Prix* **2006 (PG-13)** French fluff. Slinky/sweet gold digger Irene (Tautou) mistakes soulful hotel employee Jean (Elmaleh) for a wealthy mark and they spend a night together before she realizes her mistake. But Jean is smitten and circumstances eventually lead to another meeting in Monte Carlo where a rich widow (Adam) wants to make Jean her boy toy. So Jean asks for gigolo lessons from Irene, who's surprised to find herself miffed that someone else wants him. French with subtitles. **106m/C DVD.** *FR* Audrey Tautou, Gad Elmaleh, Vernon Dobtcheff, Annelise Hesme, Marie-Christine Adam, Jacques Spiesser; ***D:*** Pierre Salvadori; ***W:*** Pierre Salvadori, Benoit Graffin; ***C:*** Gilles Henry; ***M:*** Camille Bazbaz.

Priceless Beauty 1/2 **1990 (R)** Musician Lambert was only looking when he spotted the bottle which changed his life. Beautiful genie (Lane) lives inside, and is waiting just for him! Fun premise, good score, nice chemistry between the actors. **94m/C VHS.** Christopher Lambert, Diane Lane, Francesco Quinn, J.C. Quinn, Claudia Ohana, Monica Scattini, Joaquim de Almeida; ***D:*** Charles Finch.

Prick Up Your Ears **1987 (R)** Film biography of popular subversive playwright Joe Orton depicts his rise to fame and his eventual murder at the hands of his homosexual lover in 1967. Acclaimed for its realistic and sometimes humorous portrayal of the relationship between two men in a society that regarded homosexuality as a crime, the film unfortunately pays scant attention to Orton's theatrical success. The occasional sluggishness of the script detracts a bit from the three leads' outstanding performances. **110m/C VHS, DVD.** *GB* Gary Oldman, Alfred Molina, Vanessa Redgrave, Julie Walters, Lindsay Duncan, Wallace Shawn, James Grant, Frances Barber, Janet Dale, Dave Atkins; ***D:*** Stephen Frears; ***W:*** Alan Bennett; ***C:*** Oliver Stapleton; ***M:*** Stanley Myers. N.Y. Film Critics '87: Support. Actress (Redgrave).

Pride 1/2 **2007 (PG)** Yet another inspirational true sports flick. Jim Ellis (Howard) experiences racism as a black collegiate swimmer in the 1960s and the same problem when he tries to get a job coaching in the early '70s. He finally accepts work at a dismal Philly rec center that does have an unused pool (the kids prefer basketball). Jim decides to pull a team together, instilling discipline and a winning attitude in his kids. It's predictable and is more Hollywood than factual, but you can't fault the performances. **108m/C DVD.** *US* Terrence Howard, Bernie Mac, Kimberly Elise, Tom Arnold, Alphonso McAuley, Nathaniel Parker, Kevin Phillips, Scott Reeves, Brandon Fobbs, Regine Nehy, Evan Ross, Gary Sturgis; ***D:*** Sunu Gonera; ***W:*** J. Mills Goodloe, Norman Vance Jr., Kevin Michael Smith, Michael Gozzard; ***C:*** Matthew F. Leonetti; ***M:*** Aaron Zigman.

Pride and Glory **2008 (R)** Ray Tierney (Norton) is from an Irish-American family of NYC cops. Reluctantly, the detective is assigned to a task force investigating a drug bust gone awry that cost the lives of four cops, which also involves his bad-guy brother-in-law Jimmy (Farrell). Lots of drinking and swearing ensues amid the angst and double-crossing that threatens both family ties and the Thin Blue Line. Norton's talent is wasted in this paint-by-numbers rehash, but his presence makes the pic watchable. **129m/C DVD.** *US* Edward Norton, Colin Farrell, Jon Voight, Noah Emmerich, Jennifer Ehle, John Ortiz, Shea Whigham, Frank Grillo, Lake Bell, Rick Gonzalez, Wayne Duvall, Carmen Ejogo; ***D:*** Gavin O'Connor; ***W:*** Gavin O'Connor, Joe Carnahan; ***C:*** Declan Quinn; ***M:*** Mark Isham.

Pride and Prejudice 1/2 **1940** Classic adaptation of Austen's classic novel of manners as a young marriageable woman spurns the suitor her parents choose for her. Excellent cast vividly re-creates 19th-century England, aided by the inspired set design that won the film an Oscar. **114m/B VHS, DVD.** Greer Garson, Laurence Olivier, Edmund Gwenn, Edna May Oliver, Mary Boland, Maureen O'Sullivan, Ann Rutherford, Frieda Inescort; ***D:*** Robert Z. Leonard; ***C:*** Karl Freund.

Pride and Prejudice 1/2 **1985** BBC miniseries adaptation of Jane Austen's novel about 19th-century British mores and the attempts of five sisters to get married. **226m/C VHS, DVD.** *GB* Elizabeth Garvie, David Rintoul; ***D:*** Cyril Coke. **TV**

Pride and Prejudice **1995** Lavish TV adaptation of the Jane Austen novel finds bright Elizabeth Bennet (Ehle) unwillingly smitten by the wealthy, mysterious, and arrogant Mr. Darcy (Firth). Her family, filled with unmarried daughters, is rather silly and, of course, Elizabeth should be looking to get married (or at least not hinder her sisters' chances). Filmed on location in Derbyshire. On six cassettes. **300m/C VHS, DVD.** *GB* Jennifer Ehle, Colin Firth, Susannah Harker, Alison Steadman, Julia Sawalha, Benjamin Whitrow, Crispin Bonham Carter, Anna Chancellor, David Bamber, David Bark-Jones, Polly Maberly, Lucy Briers, Barbara Leigh-Hunt, Adrian Lukis; ***D:*** Simon Langton; ***W:*** Andrew Davies; ***C:*** John Kenway; ***M:*** Carl Davis.

Pride and Prejudice **2005 (PG)** In 19th century England, Mrs. Bennet (Blethyn) must marry her daughters off to the right men, but headstrong daughter Elizabeth (Knightley) proves difficult. More manageable in scope than the BBC miniseries, this version is gorgeous and classic nonetheless, losing none of the essence of the story. Knightley brings a welcomed force and passion to her portrayal of Lizzie that, for some reason, brought mixed reviews. Sutherland is excellent as the brood's bemused patriarch. **127m/C DVD, HD DVD.** Keira Knightley, Matthew MacFadyen, Brenda Blethyn, Donald Sutherland, Tom Hollander, Judi Dench, Rosamund Pike, Jena Malone, Kelly Reilly, Claudie Blakley, Peter Wight, Penelope Wilton, Simon Woods, Rupert Friend, Carey Mulligan, Talulah Riley, Tamzin Merchant; ***D:*** Joe Wright; ***W:*** Deborah Moggach; ***C:*** Roman Osin; ***M:*** Dario Marianelli.

The Pride and the Passion **1957** A small group of resistance fighters battling for Spanish independence in 1810 must smuggle a 6-ton cannon across the rugged terrain of Spain. Miscasting, especially of Sinatra as a Spanish peasant, hurts this film. **132m/C VHS, DVD.** Cary Grant, Frank Sinatra, Sophia Loren, Theodore Bikel, John Wengraf, Jay Novello, Philip Van Zandt; ***D:*** Stanley Kramer; ***W:*** Edward Anhalt; ***C:*** Franz Planer; ***M:*** George Antheil.

Pride of Jesse Hallum 1/2 **1981** An illiterate man (played by country singer Cash) learns, after much trial and tribulation, to read. **105m/C VHS, DVD.** Johnny Cash, Brenda Vaccaro, Eli Wallach; ***D:*** Gary Nelson. **TV**

Pride of St. Louis **1952** A romanticized and humorous portrait of famed baseball player-turned-commentator Dizzy Dean. **93m/B VHS.** Dan Dailey, Joanne Dru, Richard Crenna, Richard Haydn, Hugh Sanders; ***D:*** Harmon Jones; ***W:*** Herman J. Mankiewicz; ***C:*** Leo Tover; ***M:*** Arthur Lange.

Pride of the Bowery *Here We Go Again* **1941** The Dead End Kids versus a boxing hopeful in training camp. **60m/B VHS, DVD.** Leo Gorcey, David Gorcey, Huntz Hall, Gabriel Dell, Billy Halop, Bobby Jordan; ***D:*** Joseph H. Lewis.

Pride of the Clan 1/2 **1918** Silent drama with Pickford and Moore as Scottish sweethearts battling a bit of adversity. When Pickford's father is lost at sea, she moves onto his fishing boat. She meets Moore, a fishing boy, and falls in love. But, he inherits a fortune and his parents forbid him to see Pickford. He goes off to live the good life but comes back to dramatically rescue Pickford. **80m/B VHS.** Mary Pickford, Matt Moore; ***D:*** Maurice Tourneur.

Pride of the Marines **1945** This true story is notable for its war scenes and for its depiction of returning wounded vets (as well as Garfield's outstanding performance). Al Schmid (Garfield) meets Ruth (Parker) on a blind date and becomes engaged to her just before enlisting in the Marines and getting shipped off to Guadalcanal. His machine gun crew defeats a Japanese assault but Al is blinded by a grenade. Hospitalized, depressed, and bitter, Al tells Ruth the engagement is off and can't be persuaded to try rehab until he gets told some hard truths by buddy Lee (Clark) and Ruth reassures him of her love. Director Daves uses a number of visual techniques to showcase Al's blindness and recovery. **119m/B DVD.** John Garfield, Eleanor Parker, Dane Clark, John Ridgely, Ann Doran, Anthony Caruso, Rosemary DeCamp, Ann E. Todd; ***D:*** Delmer Daves; ***W:*** Albert (John B. Sherry) Maltz; ***C:*** J. Peverell Marley; ***M:*** Franz Waxman.

The Pride of the Yankees 1/2 **1942** Excellent portrait of baseball great Lou Gehrig. Beginning as he joined the Yankees in 1923, the film follows this great American through to his moving farewell speech as his career was tragically cut short by the disease that bears his name. Cooper is inspiring in the title role. **128m/B VHS, DVD.** Vinton (Hayworth) Haworth, Gary Cooper, Teresa Wright, Babe Ruth, Walter Brennan, Dan Duryea; ***D:*** Sam Wood; ***W:*** Herman J. Mankiewicz, Jo Swerling; ***C:*** Rudolph Mate; ***M:*** Leigh Harline. Oscars '42: Film Editing.

Priest **1994 (R)** Father Greg (an intense performance by Roache) is a young, idealistic priest who gets a rude awakening when he's assigned to a tough inner-city Liverpool parish. His superior, Father Matthew (Wilkinson), is a middle-aged rabble rouser who's openly having an affair with their black housekeeper Maria (Tyson). But Father Greg has a secret of his own—despite struggles with his sexuality he gets involved with Graham (Carlyle), a man he meets in the local gay bar. Greg's inner turmoil is heightened when a young parishoner confesses that her father is sexually abusing her but, because of the seal of the confessional, the priest cannot report the problem. Director Bird walks a fine line between criticism and condemnation of Catholic doctrine. British TV feature provoked a storm of controversy in the U.S.; originally released at 105 minutes. **98m/C VHS, DVD.** *GB* Linus Roache, Tom Wilkinson, Cathy Tyson, Robert Carlyle, James Ellis, John Bennett, Rio Fanning, Jimmy Coleman, Lesley Sharp, Robert Pugh, Christine Tremarco; ***D:*** Antonia Bird; ***W:*** Jimmy McGovern; ***C:*** Fred Tammes; ***M:*** Andy Roberts.

Priest of Love 1/2 **1981 (R)** Arty account of the final years of the life of then-controversial author D.H. Lawrence, during which time he published "Lady Chatterly's Lover." A slow-moving but interesting portrayal of this complex man and his wife as they grapple with his imminent death from tuberculosis. **125m/C VHS.** *GB* Ian McKellen, Janet Suzman, John Gielgud, Helen Mirren, Jorge (George) Rivero; *D:* Christopher Miles; *W:* Alan Plater; *C:* Ted Moore.

Primal Fear 1996 (R) Chicago defense attorney Martin Vail (Gere) is torn between the fight for justice and the lure of fame. He seems to have found the spotlight when a gentle altar boy (newcomer Norton is a standout) is accused of savagely murdering an archbishop. This leads to some courtroom fireworks due, in part, to the fact that the prosecutor (Linney) is Vail's former lover. Gere turns in a satisfying performance but, except when he's with his client, can't keep the script afloat. Lame plot revelations and an obvious "shocker" ending don't help matters. Feature directorial debut of Hoblit, Emmy winner for TV's "Hill Street Blues," "L.A. Law," and "NYPD Blue." Adapted from the book by William Diehl. **130m/C VHS, DVD.** Richard Gere, Laura Linney, Edward Norton, John Mahoney, Alfre Woodard, Frances McDormand, Terry O'Quinn, Andre Braugher, Steven Bauer, Joe Spano, Tony Plana, Stanley Anderson, Maura Tierney, Jon Seda; *D:* Gregory Hoblit; *W:* Steve Shagan, Ann Biderman; *C:* Michael Chapman; *M:* James Newton Howard. Golden Globes '97: Support. Actor (Norton); L.A. Film Critics '96: Support. Actor (Norton); Natl. Bd. of Review '96: Support. Actor (Norton).

Primal Impulse 1/2 *Footprints* 1974 An astronaut, stranded on the moon because of a sinister experimental double-cross, unleashes a mental scream which possesses a young woman's mind back on earth. **90m/C VHS.** *IT* Florinda Bolkan, Peter McEnery, Lila Kedrova, Nicoletta Elmi, Klaus Kinski; *D:* Luigi Bazzoni; *W:* Mario Fanelli; *C:* Vittorio Storaro; *M:* Nicola Piovani.

Primal Rage 1990 (R) A student is bitten by an experimental monkey, and begins to manifest his primal urges physically. Special effects by Carlo Rimbaldi. **92m/C VHS.** Bo Svenson, Patrick Lowe, Mitch Watson, Cheryl Arutt, Sarah Buxton; *D:* Vittoria Rambaldi.

Primal Scream 1/2 *Hellfire* 1987 (R) The Year is 1993. Earth's fuel sources are rapidly decaying and the top secret project to mine a revolutionary new energy source is underway—independently managed by a corrupt corporation. **95m/C VHS, DVD.** Kenneth John McGregor, Sharon Mason, Julie Miller, Jon Maurice, Mickey Shaughnessy; *D:* William Murray.

Primal Secrets 1/2 *Trick of the Eye* 1994 Artist Tilly, who specializes in illusionary trompe l'oeil paintings, is commissioned to paint a mural for reclusive socialite/widow Burstyn but there's a lot of mystery surrounding the job, especially when Burstyn begins to take an overly avid interest in Tilly's life. Based on the novel by Jane Stanton Hitchcock. Made for TV. **93m/C VHS, DVD.** Meg Tilly, Ellen Burstyn, Barnard Hughes; *D:* Ed Kaplan. **TV**

Primary Colors 1/2 1998 (R) Joe Klein's anonymously published political satire is adapted for the big screen, starting off humorously and shifting into somber. Southern good ole boy, Gov. Jack Stanton (Travolta), and his savvy wife (Thompson) are after the presidential nomination and surrounded by crazy associates, including skeptical first-time campaign manager Henry Burton (Lester). More about Henry's political baptism by fire than anything else, as he tries to accommodate his conscience to the continuous scandals and double-dealing. It really doesn't matter whether Travolta's channeling Clinton or if Thompson acts like Hilary, since the film has bigger problems. The change in tone is jarring, characters and situations disappear without warning. And given that the press act like salivating wolverines at the merest hint of scandal, the situation surrounding opponent Fred Picker (Hagman) seems far-fetched at best. Still the goings-on will hold your attention until they're over—and you realize it's all smoke-and-mirrors. **138m/C VHS, DVD.** John Travolta, Emma Thompson, Adrian Lester, Kathy Bates, Billy Bob Thornton, Larry Hagman, Maura Tierney, Stacy Edwards, Diane Ladd, Gia Carides, Paul Guilfoyle, Tommy Hollis, Robert Klein, J.C. Quinn, Rob Reiner, Caroline Aaron, Allison Janney, Mykelti Williamson, Tony Shalhoub, John Vargas, Ben Jones, Bonnie Bartlett; *D:* Mike Nichols; *W:* Elaine May; *C:* Michael Ballhaus; *M:* Ry Cooder. British Acad. '98: Adapt. Screenplay; Screen Actors Guild '98: Support. Actress (Bates); Broadcast Film Critics '98: Support. Actress (Bates).

Primary Motive 1992 (R) Taut political thriller with Nelson as Andy Blumenthal, a press secretary who finds that an opposing candidate's campaign is covered by a web of lies. Blumenthal exposes the lies, but the candidate denies them and pulls further ahead in the polls. When the candidate's wife gives Blumenthal an extremely damaging piece of information, will the polls finally turn against him? **93m/C VHS.** Judd Nelson, Richard Jordan, Sally Kirkland, Justine Bateman, John Savage; *D:* Daniel Adams; *W:* William Snowden III, Daniel Adams; *M:* John Cale.

Primary Target 1989 (R) A mercenary reunites his 'Nam guerilla unit to rescue a diplomat's wife kidnapped by a Laotian jungle lord. **85m/C VHS.** John Calvin, Miki Kim, Joey Aresco, Charles (Chip) Lucia, John Ericson, Colleen Casey; *D:* Clark Henderson.

Prime 1/2 2005 (PG-13) Streep plays Lisa, an interfering Jewish mama, fretting over her handsome 23-year-old son, David (Greenberg). Lisa's a shrink; one of her needier patients is newly divorced Rafi (Thurman) who's beautiful but insecure. Rafi is happy but fretful over a new romance with a much-younger guy, who, of course, turns out to be Lisa's son David. Lisa is the first to realize this and suffers agonies of embarrassment as Rafi enthusiastically describes her rejuvenated sex life. Lots more embarrassment is to come for all concerned. Harmless comedic fluff. **105m/C DVD.** *US* Meryl Streep, Uma Thurman, Bryan Greenberg, Jon Abrahams, Zak Orth, Annie Parisse; *D:* Ben Younger; *W:* Ben Younger; *C:* William Rexer; *M:* Ryan Shore.

Prime Cut 1/2 1972 (R) Veritable orgy of drug trafficking, prostitution, extortion, loan sharking, fisticuffs and gangsters getting ground into mincemeat. Sleazy but well-made crime melodrama has its followers, but is best known as Spacek's film debut. **86m/C VHS, DVD.** Lee Marvin, Gene Hackman, Sissy Spacek, Angel Tompkins, Gregory Walcott; *D:* Michael Ritchie; *W:* Robert Dillon; *M:* Lalo Schifrin.

Prime Evil 1988 (R) A brave and determined nun infiltrates a sect of devil worshipping monks in an attempt to end their demonic sacrifices. The question is, will this sister slide beneath Satan's cleaver? **87m/C VHS, DVD.** William Beckwith, Christine Moore; *D:* Roberta Findlay.

The Prime Gig 2000 Wise (Vaughn) works a telephone scam for a rundown company manafed by Mick (Tobolowsky) that soon goes under. He's then recruited by Caitlin (Ormond) for a telemarketing scheme involving selling stocks in a gold mine for guru Kelly Grant (Harris), whose previous schemes cost him jail time. Wise is a success but despite the money (and the girl) you know there's trouble ahead. Predictable plot with Harris giving the strong performance. **96m/C VHS, DVD.** Vince Vaughn, Julia Ormond, Ed Harris, Rory Cochrane, Wallace Shawn, George Wendt, Stephen Tobolowsky; *D:* Gregory Mosher; *W:* William Wheeler; *C:* John A. Alonzo; *M:* David Robbins.

The Prime of Miss Jean Brodie 1969 (PG) Oscar-winning performance by Smith as a forward-thinking teacher in an Edinburgh girls' school in 1932. She captivates her impressionable young students with her fascist ideals and free-thinking attitudes in this adaptation of the play taken from Muriel Spark's novel. **116m/C VHS, DVD.** *GB* Maggie Smith, Pamela Franklin, Robert Stephens, Celia Johnson, Gordon Jackson, Jane Carr; *D:* Ronald Neame; *W:* Jay Presson Allen; *C:* Ted Moore. Oscars '69: Actress (Smith); British Acad. '69: Actress (Smith), Support. Actress (Johnson); Golden Globes '70: Song ("Jean"); Natl. Bd. of Review '69: Support. Actress (Franklin).

Prime Risk 1/2 1984 (PG-13) A young engineer who discovers an electronic method to break into automated teller machines finds that it leads to more trouble when she discovers that foreign agents are hot on her trail. **98m/C VHS.** Toni Hudson, Lee Montgomery, Sam Bottoms; *D:* W. Farkas; *C:* Mac Ahlberg.

Prime Suspect 1982 An honest citizen becomes the prime suspect after the coverage of a murder by an over-ambitious television reporter. **100m/C VHS, DVD.** Mike Farrell, Teri Garr, Veronica Cartwright, Lane Smith, Barry Corbin, James Sloyan, Charles Aidman; *D:* Noel Black; *C:* Reynaldo Villalobos; *M:* Charles Gross. **TV**

Prime Suspect 1988 A young man escapes from a mental institution to clear his name after being wrongfully accused of murdering his girlfriend. **89m/C VHS, DVD.** Susan Strasberg, Frank Stallone, Billy Drago, Doug McClure; *D:* Mark Rutland.

Prime Suspect 1992 Mirren stars as Detective Chief Inspector Jane Tennison in this British TV police procedural. When a male inspector dies of a heart attack while investigating a rape-murder, Tennison, the only women of senior police status, wants the case. But she runs into multiple obstructions, not the least being the smug male police system. Then the case really takes a turn when it appears Tennison is searching for a serial killer. But Jane is no quitter and she has both the brains and the guts to back up her orders. Adapted from the book by Lynda La Plante, who also wrote the teleplay. Several other TV movies followed. **240m/C VHS, DVD.** *GB* Helen Mirren, Tom Bell, Zoe Wanamaker, John Bowe, Tom Wilkinson, Ralph Fiennes; *D:* Christopher Menaul; *W:* Lynda La Plante. **TV**

Prime Target 1991 (R) Small-town cop John Bloodstone (Heavener) is recruited by the FBI to transfer a mafia boss (Curtis) from a safehouse to the courthouse. He has to keep the former mobster alive long enough to testify against the "family." Their cross-country adventure is heightened by a murderous confrontation with evil forces that want them both dead. **87m/C VHS.** David Heavener, Tony Curtis, Isaac Hayes, Jenilee Harrison, Robert Reed, Andrew (Andy) Robinson, Don Stroud; *D:* David Heavener; *W:* David Heavener; *M:* Chris Boardman.

The Prime Time WOOF! 1960 Horrid film about a teen girl who leaves home and gets involved with a teen gang and a slimy detective. She's also kidnapped by a weird beatnik artist who forces her to pose nude. Black's film debut. Also known as "Hellkitten." **76m/B VHS.** JoAnn LeCompte, Frank Roche, James Brooks, Ray Gronwold, Maria Pavelle, Robert Major, Karen Black; *D:* Herschell Gordon Lewis.

Prime Time 1/2 *American Raspberry* 1977 (R) Forgotten satirical comedy about what would happen if the censors took a day off from American TV. **73m/C VHS.** Warren Oates, David Spielberg, Robert Ridgely, Joanna Cassidy, Harry Shearer, Harris Yulin, Dick O'Neill, George Furth, Stephen Furst, Larry Gelman, Fred (John F.) Dryer; *D:* Bradley R. Swirnoff; *W:* Steve Feinberg, Bradley R. Swirnoff; *C:* Matthew F. Leonetti; *M:* Ken Lauber.

Prime Time Murder 1/2 1992 (R) Freelance TV journalist hooks up with eccentric ex-cop to trail a psycho stalking street people. **95m/C VHS, DVD.** Tim Thomerson, Sally Kirkland, Anthony Finetti, Laura Reed; *D:* Gary Skeen Hall.

Primer 1/2 2004 (PG-13) Writer/director Carruth's debut film might be the world's first thinking-man's time travel movie, beautifully shot for an absurdly low $7,500. Winner of the 2004 Sundance Grand Jury Prize, the plot revolves around two engineers, Aaron (Carruth) and Abe (Sullivan), who, while trying to develop a patentable invention, accidentally construct a box that allows them to move backwards through time. Carruth piles on the technical jargon, which will either hopelessly confuse viewers or make them love the director for respecting their intelligence. (No character ever whines, "Tell it to me in English, Doc!") At its core, Carruth's film is a meditation on trust, obsession, power, and the chaos surrounding innovation, combined with a nonlinear storyline that should inspire more repeated viewings than "Donnie Darko." **80m/C DVD.** Shane Carruth, David Sullivan, Casey Gooden, Anand Upadhyaya, Carrie Crawford, Samantha Thomson, Brandon Blagg; *D:* Shane Carruth; *W:* Shane Carruth; *C:* Shane Carruth, Anand Upadhyaya; *M:* Shane Carruth.

Primeval 2007 (R) What a croc—literally. Weird fact-based combo of horror and politics set in pre-2005, war-torn Burundi. Cynical reporter Tim (Purcell) is pressured into a tabloid story—capture a 25-foot croc, nicknamed Gustave, that has been eating the locals for years. The area is also the province of a vicious warlord who has nicknamed himself after the beastie. Brooding guide Jacob (Prochnow) takes Tim and his crew to the croc's favorite dining spot, but things don't go as planned. Neither as campy nor as gruesome as most of its ilk. **94m/C DVD, Blu-ray Disc.** *US* Dominic Purcell, Orlando Jones, Brooke Langton, Jurgen Prochnow, Gideon Emery, Dumisani Mbebe, Gabriel Malema; *D:* Michael Katleman; *W:* John Brancato, Michael Ferris; *C:* Edward Pei; *M:* John (Gianni) Frizzell.

The Primitive Lover 1916 Early silent comedy about young wife who decides she deserves more than her marriage is giving her. **67m/B VHS.** Constance Talmadge, Kenneth Harlan, Harrison Ford; *D:* Sidney Franklin.

Primrose Path 1/2 1940 Melodramatic soaper with comedic touches about a wrong-side-of-the-tracks girl falling for and then losing an ambitious young go-getter running a hamburger stand. **93m/B VHS.** Ginger Rogers, Joel McCrea, Marjorie Rambeau, Henry Travers, Miles Mander, Queenie Vasser, Joan Carroll, Vivienne Osborne; *D:* Gregory La Cava.

The Prince 1995 Young toy company executive Roy (Riley) is given cutthroat corporate advice by a sinister bartender (Williams) who uses the treatise on power by Machiavelli as his bible. Soon Roy is manipulating with the best of them and will do anything to get ahead. **89m/C VHS.** *CA* Billy Dee Williams, Michael Riley, Henry Silva, Lou Rawls, Timothy Bottoms, Liat Goodson, Edie McClurg; *D:* Pinchas Perry; *W:* Pinchas Perry; *C:* Hanania Baer; *M:* David Michael Frank.

The Prince & Me 1/2 2004 (PG) Dairy farmer's daughter Paige (Stiles) is a driven pre-med student who dreams of a future with Doctors Without Borders until Prince Charming shows up disguised as an average Joe. In this case his name is Eddie—actually Prince Edvard of Denmark (Mably)—and they fall in love, but as these young romance stories go the truth inevitably surfaces and the inner conflict begins. Should she give up on her life's passion? Or live the supposed fairy tale life of a princess? Of course in this modern day the larger question should be why does she have to choose? Only Stiles' engaging performance makes this sweet-yet-typical story at all worth watching. **110m/C VHS, DVD.** Julia Stiles, Luke Mably, Ben Miller, James Fox, Miranda Richardson, Eliza Bennett, Alberta Watson, John Bourgeois, Joanne Baron; *D:* Martha Coolidge; *W:* Mark Amin, Jack Amiel, Katherine Fugate, Michael Begler; *C:* Alex Nepomniaschy; *M:* Jennie Muskett.

The Prince & Me 2: Royal Wedding 2006 (PG) In this dull fluff sequel, Danish Prince Edvard (Mably) runs into a problem with his wedding plans to American commoner Paige (Heskin). Conniving cousin Albert (Holt) uses an ancient obscure law to proclaim that Edvard must marry someone of royal blood or he can't become king—and Albert offers his daughter, the equally sly Princess Kirsten (Burton-Hill), as a substitute. Apparently, Edvard is just too stupid to ask the Danish parliament to change the law, so Paige must find a loophole. **97m/C DVD.** Luke Mably, Kam Heskin, Jim Holt, Maryam D'Abo, Clemency Burton-Hill, Jonathan Firth; *D:* Catherine Cyran; *W:* Allison Robinson; *C:* Blake T. Evans; *M:* Andrew Gross. **VIDEO**

The Prince & Me 3: A Royal Honeymoon 1/2 2008 (PG) They met, they married, and finally newly crowned Danish king Edvard (Geere) and his American bride Paige (Heskin) can take their honeymoon. To avoid the paparazzi, Edvard takes them to a resort at Belaria, a remote Danish protectorate. Too bad that evil Prime Minister Polonius' (Jensen) flunky Oliver (Rubin) is already there and they suspiciously run into Paige's ex-fiance Scott (Croasdell). Edward learns that Polonius is planning to bulldoze the local forest to drill for oil and he and Paige intend to stop the nefarious plot. **92m/C DVD.** Kam Heskin, Todd Jensen, Jonathan Firth, Chris Geere, Joshua Rubin, Adam Croasdell; ***D:*** Catherine Cyran; ***W:*** Blayne Weaver; ***C:*** Emil Topuzov; ***M:*** Andrew Gross. **VIDEO**

Prince and the Great Race 1/2 *Bush Christmas* **1983** Three Australian children search the outback to find their kidnapped horse who is scheduled to run in the big New Year's Day Race. **91m/C VHS.** *AU* John Ewart, John Howard, Nicole Kidman; ***D:*** Henri Safran; ***W:*** Ted Roberts; ***C:*** Ross Berryman; ***M:*** Mike Perjanik.

The Prince and the Pauper **1937** Satisfying adaptation of the classic Mark Twain story of a young street urchin who trades places with the young king of England. Wonderful musical score by noted composer Korngold who provided the music for many of Flynn's adventure films. Also available in a computer-colorized version. **118m/B VHS, DVD.** Errol Flynn, Claude Rains, Alan Hale, Billy Mauch, Montagu Love, Henry Stephenson, Barton MacLane, Anne Howard; ***D:*** William Keighley; ***M:*** Erich Wolfgang Korngold.

The Prince and the Pauper **1962** A prince and a poor young boy swap their clothes and identities, thus causing a lot of confusion for their families. Based on the story by Mark Twain. **93m/C VHS.** Guy Williams, Laurence Naismith, Donald Houston, Jane Asher, Sean Scully; ***D:*** Don Chaffey; ***W:*** Jack Whittingham; ***C:*** Paul Beeson; ***M:*** Tristram Cary. **TV**

The Prince and the Pauper 1/2 *Crossed Swords* **1978 (PG)** Remake of the 1937 Errol Flynn film employing lavish sets and a tongue-in-cheek attitude among the all-star cast, who occasionally wander adrift when the director stops for tea. When an English prince and a pauper discover that they have identical appearances, they decide to trade places with each other. From Mark Twain's classic. **113m/C VHS, DVD.** *GB* Oliver Reed, Raquel Welch, Mark Lester, Ernest Borgnine, George C. Scott, Rex Harrison, Charlton Heston, Sybil Danning; ***D:*** Richard Fleischer; ***W:*** Berta Dominguez, George MacDonald Fraser, Pierre Spengler; ***C:*** Jack Cardiff; ***M:*** Maurice Jarre.

The Prince and the Pauper 1/2 **2001** Yet another version of the Mark Twain classic covers all the familiar bases but is briskly paced and has a good cast. Prince Edward (Jonathan Timmins) exchanges identities with peasant Tom Canty (Robert Timmins) and both learn that whether you're rich or poor life will always be a challenge. **90m/C VHS, DVD.** Jonathan Timmins, Robert Timmins, Aidan Quinn, Alan Bates, Jonathan Hyde; ***D:*** Giles Foster; ***W:*** Duke Fenady, Dominic Minghella. **CABLE**

The Prince and the Pauper 1/2 **2007 (PG)** A modern-day retelling of the Mark Twain classic, starring the Sprouse twins. Tom Canty wants to be an actor so he sneaks onto the set of his favorite show to meet its lead, Eddie Tutor. A spoiled child star, Eddie is about to get fired for his antics until the look-alikes decide to trade places and see how the other half lives. But neither of the boys expects the TV production to suddenly go on location to Miami, leaving the duo in their assumed identities. **92m/C DVD.** Dylan Sprouse, Cole Sprouse, Vincent Spano, Kay Panabaker, Dedee Pfeiffer, Ed Lauter, Sally Kellerman, Nick Vallelonga; ***D:*** James Quattrochi; ***W:*** Amanda Moresco; ***C:*** Jeff Baustert; ***M:*** Dennis McCarthy. **VIDEO**

The Prince and the Showgirl 1/2 **1957** An American showgirl in 1910 London is wooed by the Prince of Carpathia. Part of the "A Night at the Movies" series, this tape simulates a 1957 movie evening, with a Sylvester the Cat cartoon, "Greedy for Tweety," a newsreel and coming attractions for "Spirit of St. Louis." **127m/C VHS, DVD.** Laurence Olivier, Marilyn Monroe, Sybil Thorndike, Jeremy Spenser, Richard Wattis; ***D:*** Laurence Olivier; ***W:*** Terence Rattigan; ***C:*** Jack Cardiff.

The Prince and the Surfer 1/2 **1999 (PG)** A modern young prince, Edward, wants a chance to be a regular guy and changes places with his surfer teen double, Cash. Updated version of the Mark Twain story. **90m/C VHS, DVD.** Vincent Schiavelli, Arye Gross, Robert Englund, Timothy Bottoms, C. Thomas Howell, Linda Cardellini; ***D:*** Gregory Gieras. **VIDEO**

Prince Brat and the Whipping Boy *The Whipping Boy* **1995 (G)** Orphaned Jemmy (Munro) is living on the streets of the 18th-century German town of Brattenburg with his younger sister Annyrose (Salt). Neglected, spoiled Prince Horace (Knight) has been causing mischief in the castle but instead of being punished himself, the king's men catch Jemmy and use him as a punishment stand-in. Jemmy escapes the castle to get back to his sister and the Prince decides to go along for the adventure. Filmed on location in North Rhine-Westphalia and Burgundy, Germany. Adventurous TV movie with spunky leads; adapted from Sid Fleischman's novella. **96m/C VHS.** Truan Munro, Nic Knight, Karen Salt, George C. Scott, Kevin Conway, Vincent Schiavelli, Andrew Bicknell, Jean Anderson, Mathilda May; ***D:*** Syd Macartney; ***W:*** Max Brindle; ***M:*** Lee Holdridge.

Prince Jack **1983** Profiles the turbulent political career of President John F. Kennedy. **100m/C VHS.** Lloyd Nolan, Dana Andrews, Robert Guillaume, Cameron Mitchell; ***D:*** Bert Lovitt; ***M:*** Elmer Bernstein.

Prince of Bel Air 1/2 **1987 (R)** A pool-cleaning playboy who makes a habit of one night stands meets a woman and starts falling in love with her. **95m/C VHS, DVD.** Mark Harmon, Kirstie Alley, Robert Vaughn, Patrick Laborteaux, Deborah Harmon; ***D:*** Charles Braverman; ***M:*** Robert Folk. **TV**

The Prince of Central Park **1977** Two young orphans are forced by circumstance to live in a tree in New York's Central Park until they are befriended by a lonely old woman. An above-average adaptation of the novel by Evan H. Rhodes, the story was later used for a Broadway play. **76m/C VHS.** Ruth Gordon, T(imothy) J(ohn) Hargrave, Lisa Richards, Brooke Shields, Marc Vahanian, Dan Hedaya; ***D:*** Harvey Hart. **TV**

Prince of Central Park 1/2 **2000 (PG-13)** JJ Somerled (Nasso) is a 12-year-old stuck in the abusive foster home of Mrs. Ardis (Moriarty). Fed up, he takes off for the carousel at Central Park, where he had his last happy memory of his long-gone mother. In the park, JJ is befriended by all sorts of do-gooders and eccentrics. Bland non-musical reworking of a musical play. **105m/C VHS, DVD.** Frank Nasso, Kathleen Turner, Danny Aiello, Harvey Keitel, Cathy Moriarty, Lauren Velez, Jerry Orbach, Tina Holmes; ***D:*** John Leekley; ***W:*** John Leekley; ***C:*** Jonathan Herron; ***M:*** Theodore Shapiro.

Prince of Darkness 1/2 **1987 (R)** University students release Satan, in the form of a mysterious chemical, unwittingly on the world. Written by Martin Quatermass (a pseudonym of Carpenter). Strong personnel does not save this dreary and slow-moving cliche plot. **102m/C VHS, DVD.** Alice Cooper, Donald Pleasence, Lisa Blount, Victor Wong, Jameson Parker, Dennis Dun, Susan Blanchard, Anne Marie Howard, Ken Wright, Dirk Blocker; ***D:*** John Carpenter; ***W:*** John Carpenter; ***C:*** Gary B. Kibbe; ***M:*** John Carpenter.

Prince of Egypt **1998 (PG)** First animated musical from Dreamworks manages to tell the story of the Exodus without turning it into Mickey Moses. Kilmer voices the young Moses, who is adopted by the royal family: imperious pharaoh Seti (Stewart), his stately Queen (Mirren) and jockish son Rameses (Fiennes). Happily wed to Tzipporah (Pfeiffer), he's living it up at the dawn of civilization until a chance meeting with his real sister Miriam (Bullock) twists his conscience and destiny. Steve Martin and Martin Short provide a short comic break, but overall the joking is kept to a minimum. Successful in combining epic feeling with stylized animation. **93m/C VHS, DVD.** ***D:*** Simon Wells, Brenda Chapman, Steve Hickner; ***M:*** Hans Zimmer; ***V:*** Val Kilmer, Michelle Pfeiffer, Helen Mirren, Steve Martin, Martin Short, Ralph Fiennes, Sandra Bullock, Jeff Goldblum, Danny Glover, Patrick Stewart, Ofra Haza, James Avery, Eden Riegel. Oscars '98: Song ("When You Believe"); Broadcast Film Critics '98: Song ("When You Believe").

Prince of Foxes 1/2 **1949** In 16th-century Italy, rascally Orsini (Power) is sent by his boss, the power-hungry Cesare Borgia (Welles), to seduce Camilla (Hendrix), the insipid young wife of an old duke (Aylmer), and turn the town over to the Borgias. But Orsini likes Count Varano and decide to switch sides, which doesn't please his now ex-boss. The story is plodding, the dialogue is deadly, and although it's lavishly picturesque (and filmed on location), it's a shame that Fox didn't shoot the film in Technicolor. Based on the novel by Samuel Shellabarger. **107m/B DVD.** Tyrone Power, Orson Welles, Wanda Hendrix, Felix Aylmer, Everett Sloane, Marina Berti, Katina Paxinou; ***D:*** Henry King; ***W:*** Milton Krims; ***C:*** Leon Shamroy; ***M:*** Alfred Newman.

Prince of Pennsylvania 1/2 **1988 (R)** A mild comedy about a spaced-out youth who kidnaps his own father in hopes of nabbing a family inheritance. **113m/C VHS, DVD.** Keanu Reeves, Fred Ward, Amy Madigan, Bonnie Bedelia, Jeff Hayenga; ***D:*** Ron Nyswaner; ***W:*** Ron Nyswaner; ***M:*** Thomas Newman.

Prince of Persia: The Sands of Time **2010 (PG-13)** A rogue prince (a considerably bulked-up Gyllenhaal) joins forces with a feisty princess (Tamina) to safeguard an ancient dagger from evil forces. The dagger can release a 'gift' from the gods that can reverse time and allow the possessor unimagined power as well as turn the locals into demons. Jerry Bruckheimer-produced adaptation of the videogame (for Disney). **m/C DVD.** *US* Jake Gyllenhaal, Gemma Arterton, Ben Kingsley, Alfred Molina; ***D:*** Mike Newell; ***W:*** Doug Miro, Carlo Bernard; ***C:*** John Seale; ***M:*** Harry Gregson-Williams.

Prince of Poisoners: The Life and Crimes of William Palmer 1/2 **1998** A true crime story set in mid-19th century England. Dr. William Palmer (Allen) appears to be a successful surgeon with a devoted wife, Annie (Ashbourne), and happy family. But the doctor has a secret passion for racehorses and gambling and his good life is about to crumble because of his debts. So what's his solution? Why, murder of course, so Palmer can collect on various insurance policies and dispose of his gambling rivals. **180m/C VHS.** *GB* Keith Allen, Jayne Ashbourne, Judy Cornwell, Richard Coyle, Freddie Jones, Stephen Moore; ***D:*** Alan Dossor; ***W:*** Glenn Chandler; ***C:*** Allan Pyrah; ***M:*** Christopher Gunning. **TV**

Prince of the City **1981 (R)** Docu-drama of a police officer who becomes an informant in an effort to end corruption within his narcotics unit, but finds he must pay a heavy price. Based on the true story told in Robert Daly's book, the powerful script carries the tension through what would otherwise be an overly long film. Excellent performances make this a riveting character study. **167m/C VHS, DVD.** Treat Williams, Jerry Orbach, Richard Foronjy, Don Billett, Ken Marino, Lindsay Crouse, Lance Henriksen; ***D:*** Sidney Lumet; ***W:*** Jay Presson Allen, Sidney Lumet; ***C:*** Andrzej Bartkowiak. N.Y. Film Critics '81: Director (Lumet).

The Prince of Thieves **1948** Robin Hood helps Lady Marian extricate herself from a forced marriage in this adventure made with younger audiences in mind. **72m/C VHS.** Jon Hall, Patricia Morison, Adele Jergens, Alan Mowbray, Michael Duane; ***D:*** Howard Bretherton; ***W:*** Charles Schnee, Maurice Tombragel; ***C:*** Fred H. Jackman Jr.

The Prince of Tides 1/2 **1991 (R)** Conroy's sprawling southern-fried saga is neatly pared down to essentials in this tale of the dysfunctional Wingo family, whose dark tragedies are gradually revealed as twins Tom and Savannah come to grips with personal demons under the ministering aid of psychiatrist Streisand. Bravura performance by Nolte in what may be his best role to date; Streisand is restrained in both her performance and direction although a subplot dealing with her bad marriage and rebellious son is a predictable distraction. The South Carolina low country, and even New York City, never looked better. Conroy adapted the screenplay from his novel of the same name with Johnston's help. **132m/C VHS, DVD.** Nick Nolte, Barbra Streisand, Blythe Danner, Kate Nelligan, Jeroen Krabbe, Melinda Dillon, George Carlin, Jason Gould, Brad Sullivan; ***D:*** Barbra Streisand; ***W:*** Pat Conroy, Becky Johnston; ***C:*** Stephen Goldblatt; ***M:*** James Newton Howard. Golden Globes '92: Actor—Drama (Nolte); L.A. Film Critics '91: Actor (Nolte).

Prince Valiant 1/2 **1954 (PG-13)** When his royal dad is exiled by an evil tyrant, brave young Wagner brushes aside bangs and journeys to Camelot to seek the help of King Arthur. Based on Harold Foster's classic comic strip. **100m/C VHS, DVD.** James Mason, Janet Leigh, Robert Wagner, Debra Paget, Sterling Hayden, Victor McLaglen, Donald Crisp, Brian Aherne, Barry Jones, Mary (Phillips) Philips; ***D:*** Henry Hathaway; ***W:*** Dudley Nichols.

Prince Valiant 1/2 **1997 (PG-13)** We're back at Camelot with a lot of colorful pageantry and old-fashioned action. Young orphaned Valiant (Moyer) is the squire to Sir Gawain (Hickox), one of King Arthur's (Fox) knights. He is given the task of escorting Princess Ilene (Heigl) to her home in Wales and naturally the young twosome fall in love. Meanwhile, the sword Excalibur has been stolen by Viking leader Thagnar (Kretschmann) and somehow become embedded in his castle's stone floor. Then Ilene gets kidnapped and it's up to Valiant to rescue both Ilene and Excalibur. Based on the comic strip created by Harold R. Foster. **91m/C VHS.** *GB GE IR* Stephen Moyer, Katherine Heigl, Thomas Kretschmann, Edward Fox, Benjamin Pullen, Anthony Hickox, Udo Kier, Warwick Davis, Zach Galligan, Ron Perlman, Joanna Lumley, Gavan O'Herlihy, Walter Gotell; ***D:*** Anthony Hickox; ***W:*** Michael Frost Beckner, Anthony Hickox; ***C:*** Roger Lanser; ***M:*** David Bergeaud.

Princes in Exile 1/2 **1990 (PG-13)** Young people struggle with their life-threatening illnesses at a special summer camp. They find that love and friendship hold the key to dreams about the future. Excellent cast of newcomers. Based on a novel of the same name by Mark Schreiber. **103m/C VHS.** *CA* Zachary Ansley, Nicholas Shields, Stacy Mistysyn, Alexander Chapman, Chuck Shamata; ***D:*** Giles Walker.

Princess: A Modern Fairytale 1/2 **2008** Cute ABC Family movie. Mysterious Princess Ithaca makes her annual appearance at a fund-raising ball where William Humphrey hopes to get a date with her. But Ithaca must pass on the power of speech to a bunch of CGI animals as well as find a new princess to take over her duties when Ithaca turns 25 so she doesn't think she has time to fall in love as well. **88m/C DVD.** Nora Zehetner, Kip Pardue; ***D:*** Mark Rosman; ***W:*** Heidi Ferrer; ***C:*** David Makin; ***M:*** Richard (Rick) Marvin. **CABLE**

Princess Academy **1987 (R)** A self-respecting young debutante battles the ways of her elitist finishing school. **91m/C VHS.** *FR* Eva Gabor, Lu Leonard, Richard Paul, Lar Park-Lincoln, Carole (Raphaelle) Davis; ***D:*** Bruce Block; ***M:*** Paul Antonelli, Roger Bellon.

The Princess & the Call Girl **1984** Call girl Lucy Darling asks her look-alike college girlfriend Audrey Swallow (Levy in a dual role) to take her place in Monaco for a lavishly erotic weekend. Then when Audrey gets delayed, Lucy winds up taking her place in New York—at Audrey's engagement party. Weaker than Metzger's usual sexual romps. **90m/C VHS, DVD.** Carol Levy, Shannah Hall, Victor Bevine; ***D:*** Radley Metzger.

The Princess and the Frog **2009 (G)** Hand-drawn animated musical comedy featuring Disney's first African-American heroine aspires to the greatness of classic Disney and (mostly) succeeds. Living in New Orleans during the Jazz Age, orphan and aspiring chef Tiana (Rose) finds a talking frog in the bayou who claims to be Prince Naveen (Campos), under a curse until a kiss can break the spell and turn him human again. Of course, there's a twist, and with the help of some bayou animals, the two must find a way to stop sinister voodoo priest Dr. Facilier (David) and break the curse before it's too late. Kids and adults will like this charming story supported by animation in the old Disney style and inspiring musical numbers. **97m/C DVD.** *US D:* Ron Clements, John Musker; *W:* Ron Clements, John Musker; *M:* Randy Newman; *V:* Anika Noni Rose, Bruno Campos, Terrence Howard, John Goodman, Keith David, Jim (Jonah) Cummings, Jenifer Lewis, Oprah Winfrey, Jennifer Cody.

The Princess and the Goblin 🦴🦴 1/2 **1994 (G)** Little kiddies may enjoy this animated adventure but it's a bland story with mediocre animation. Groups of ugly, underground-dwelling goblins like nothing better than to scare humans, especially castle-dwelling Princess Irene. Brave working-class Curdie helps to save the day. Based on a book by George MacDonald. **82m/C VHS, DVD.** *GB HU D:* Jozsef Gemes; *W:* Robin Lyons; *M:* Istvan Lerch; *V:* Sally Ann Marsh, Peter Murray, Claire Bloom.

The Princess and the Pea 🦴🦴🦴 **1983** From "Faerie Tale Theatre" comes the story of a princess who tries to prove that she's a blueblood by feeling the bump of a tiny pea under the thickness of 20 mattresses. **60m/C VHS, DVD.** Liza Minnelli, Tom Conti, Tim Kazurinsky, Pat McCormick, Beatrice Straight; *D:* Tony Bill. **CABLE**

The Princess and the Pirate 🦴🦴🦴 **1944** Hope at his craziest as a vaudvillian who falls for a beautiful princess while on the run from buccaneers on the Spanish Main. Look for Crosby in a closing cameo performance. Available in digitally remastered stereo with original movie trailer. **94m/C VHS, DVD.** Bob Hope, Walter Slezak, Walter Brennan, Virginia Mayo, Victor McLaglen, Bing Crosby; *D:* David Butler; *W:* Everett Freeman, Don Hartman, Melville Shavelson; *C:* Victor Milner; *M:* David Rose.

The Princess and the Warrior 🦴🦴🦴 *Der Krieger und die Kaiserin* **2000 (R)** Writer/director Twyker reunites with Potente, the star of his breakthrough feature "Run Lola Run." Potente plays Sissi, a mental institution nurse whose life is saved by small-time crook Bodo (Furmann). On the way to the bank (which he was about to rob), she is run over by a truck (in an accident that he helped cause). He crawls under the truck to avoid the police, but ends up saving her as she's about to choke to death on her own blood. After she recovers, she sets out to find Bodo, feeling that he is her one true love. Bodo, still grieving the loss of his wife, resists. Impossible to pigeonhole in one genre, as Twyker is clearly more concerned with his characters than with shoving them into a conveniently labeled plot. **130m/C VHS, DVD.** *GE* Franka Potente, Benno Furmann, Joachim Krol, Marita Breuer, Lars Rudolph, Jurgen Tarrach, Melchior Beslon, Ludger Pistor; *D:* Tom Tykwer; *W:* Tom Tykwer; *C:* Frank Griebe; *M:* Tom Tykwer, Johnny Klimek, Reinhold Heil.

The Princess Blade 🦴🦴 1/2 *Shura Yukihime* **2002 (R)** It is the future in Japan, and the reigning monarchy employs a group of sword fighting samurai assassins to hunt down the rebels opposing them. Yuki (Shaku) is the last of a noble line, and an assassin herself. She quits the clan after finding out they killed her mother, and ends up hiding with the rebels in a gas station awaiting the inevitable bloody showdown. **95m/C DVD.** *JP* Hideaki Ito, Shiro Sano, Yoichi Numata, Yoko Chosokabe, Yoko Maki, Naomasa Musaka, Yutaka Matsushige, Yumiko Shaku, Kyusaku Shimada; *D:* Shinsuke Sato; *W:* Kazuo Kamimura, Kazuo Koike, Shinsuke Sato, Kei Kunii; *C:* Taro Kawazu; *M:* Kenji Kawai.

The Princess Bride 🦴🦴🦴 1/2 **1987 (PG)** A modern update of the basic fairy tale crammed with all the cliches, this adventurously irreverent love story centers around beautiful maiden Buttercup (Wright Penn) and her young swain Westley (Elwes) as they battle the evils of the mythical kingdom of Florin to be reunited with one another. Great dueling scenes and offbeat satire of the genre make this fun for adults as well as children. Based on William Goldman's cult novel. **98m/C VHS, DVD, Blu-ray Disc, UMD.** Cary Elwes, Mandy Patinkin, Robin Wright Penn, Wallace Shawn, Peter Falk, Andre the Giant, Chris Sarandon, Christopher Guest, Billy Crystal, Carol Kane, Fred Savage, Peter Cook, Mel Smith; *D:* Rob Reiner; *W:* William Goldman; *C:* Adrian Biddle; *M:* Mark Knopfler.

Princess Caraboo 🦴🦴 1/2 **1994 (PG)** Fluffy quasi-fairy tale (but based on a true story) finds an exotic beauty (Cates) appearing in an English village in 1817. She speaks a language no one understands and is taken under the wing of the local gentry, the Worralls, who believe she is an Asian princess washed ashore during a shipwreck. Meanwhile, the local jouralist (Rea) is suspicious but protective, an Oxford linguist (Lithgow) is determined to prove her a fraud, and she must put up with the Worrall family's pompous Greek butler (Cate's husband Kline at his showy best). **97m/C VHS, DVD.** Phoebe Cates, Stephen Rea, John Lithgow, Kevin Kline, Jim Broadbent, Wendy Hughes, Peter Eyre, Jacqueline Pearce, John Lynch, John Sessions, Arkie Whiteley, John Wells; *D:* Michael Austin; *W:* Michael Austin, John Wells; *C:* Freddie Francis; *M:* Richard Hartley.

The Princess Comes Across 🦴🦴🦴 **1936** Deft comedy-mystery finds Brooklyn actress Lombard deciding to take an ocean voyage and pass herself off as a Swedish princess in the hopes of furthering her career. Bandleader MacMurray is smitten but an old beau recognizes the ruse and demands hush money. Then he turns up dead and the duo fall under the suspicious eye of a German passenger (Rumann) who happens to be a detective. From the novel by Louis Lucien Rogger. **77m/B VHS, DVD.** Carole Lombard, Fred MacMurray, Alison Skipworth, Sig Rumann, Douglass Dumbrille, William Frawley, Porter Hall, George Barbier, Lumsden Hare, Mischa Auer, Tetsu Komai; *D:* William K. Howard; *W:* Walter DeLeon, Francis Martin, Frank Butler, Don Hartman; *C:* Ted Tetzlaff.

Princess Daisy 🦴 **1983** A beautiful model claws her way to the top of her profession while trying to find true love and avoid the clutches of her rotten half-brother. Adapted from Judith Krantz's glitzy best-selling novel. **200m/C VHS, DVD.** Merete Van Kamp, Lindsay Wagner, Claudia Cardinale, Stacy Keach, Ringo Starr, Barbara Bach; *D:* Waris Hussein. **TV**

The Princess Diaries 🦴🦴 1/2 **2001 (G)** Gently amusing comedy perfect for tweenies who worry about being misfits. Modern-day Cinderella story finds brainy-but-clumsy San Francisco teen Mia (newcomer Hathaway, who's a real find) learning that she's the heir to the European kingdom of Genovia after the death of her long-absent dad. And to teach her the ways of royalty is her very regal grandmama (Andrews). Think Henry Higgins and Eliza Doolittle. Of course, Mia has her doubts about being a princess, especially when the kids at school learn her secret. There's even a little first romance thrown in for good measure. Based on the novel by Meg Cabot. **114m/C VHS, DVD.** *US* Anne Hathaway, Julie Andrews, Hector Elizondo, Heather Matarazzo, Erik von Detten, Mandy Moore, Robert Schwartzman, Caroline Goodall, Larry Miller, Sandra Oh, Sean O'Bryan; *D:* Garry Marshall; *W:* Gina Wendkos; *C:* Karl Walter Lindenlaub; *M:* John Debney.

The Princess Diaries 2: Royal Engagement 🦴🦴 **2004 (G)** Princess Mia (Hathaway), still sweet and klutzy, is now a college grad and on her way to Genovia to live with grandma, Queen Clarisse (Andrews), and assume her royal duties. But Clarisse is being forced to abdicate, and ancient law dictates that Mia must marry before she can become queen and she only has 30 days to find a suitable royal consort. If she can't, sneaky Viscount Mabrey's (Rhys-Davies) plastic-handsome nephew, Nicholas (Pine), is the next rightful heir. Nicholas tries to charm Mia while she dutifully agrees to marry affable British nobleman Andrew (Blue). Hathaway's a charmer, Andrews offers class and wisdom and gets to continue her discreet romance with suave security chief Joe (Elizondo), and Matarazzo returns as Mia's acerbic best friend. There's a little too much slapstick but it's all very nice and innocent, and little princesses should be enchanted once again. **120m/C VHS, DVD.** *US* Anne Hathaway, Julie Andrews, Hector Elizondo, John Rhys-Davies, Heather Matarazzo, Chris Pine, Callum Blue, Kathleen Marshall, Tom Poston, Joel McCrary, Kim Thomson, Larry Miller, Raven, Caroline Goodall, Sean O'Bryan, Matthew (Matt) Walker, Elinor Donahue, Paul Williams, Lorraine Nicholson; *D:* Garry Marshall; *W:* Shonda Rhimes; *C:* Charles Minsky; *M:* John Debney.

Princess Mononoke 🦴🦴🦴 **1998 (PG-13)** Stunning animated feature by Japanese master Hayao Miyazaki is a bit too long and graphic for small children, but is a must-see for fans of anime. Dubbed into English by an all-star cast, the tale follows the plight of Ashitaka (Crudup), who tries to find some way to lift a curse inflicted upon him after he accidentally kills a rampaging forest spirit. He discovers the cause is the encroaching civilization of Iron Town, led by the cold Lady Eboshi (Driver) and its conflict with the forest spirits and their champion San (Danes)—the princess of the title. Also lending their voices are Billy Bob Thornton as a mischievous monk and Gillian Anderson as San's wolf protector. Became the first feature of any kind to gross over $150 million at the box office in its native Japan. **133m/C VHS, DVD.** *D:* Hayao Miyazaki; *W:* Neil Gaiman; *M:* Joe Hisaishi; *V:* Claire Danes, Billy Crudup, Minnie Driver, Gillian Anderson, Jada Pinkett Smith, Billy Bob Thornton.

The Princess of Nebraska 🦴 **2007** Meandering indie sketch from Wang with an ambiguous ending. Sasha, a sullen Chinese exchange student studying in Omaha, travels to San Francisco to look up her Beijing one-night stand's American lover. Sasha's pregnant and thinks she wants an abortion but she seems to spend most of her time wandering aimlessly around the city doing stuff she shouldn't. **77m/C DVD.** Li Ling, Brian Danforth, Pamelyn Chee; *D:* Wayne Wang; *W:* Michael Ray; *C:* Richard Wong; *M:* Kent Sparling.

Princess of Thieves 🦴🦴 1/2 **2001** An aging Robin Hood and Will Scarlett return to England with a mortally wounded King Richard. Robin knows that Prince John will stop at nothing to assume the throne, including killing Richard's son Phillip. Unfortunately, the duo are captured by the Sheriff of Nottingham and it's up to Robin's feisty daughter Gwyn, who disguises herself as a boy, to rescue her father and Will and stop the bad guys from taking over the kingdom. **88m/C VHS, DVD.** Malcolm McDowell, Keira Knightley, Roger Ashton-Griffiths, Jonathan Hyde, Del Synnott, Stephen Moyer, Stuart Wilson; *D:* Peter Hewitt; *W:* Sally Robinson, Robin Lerner. **TV**

Princess O'Rourke 🦴🦴 1/2 **1943** European diplomat Holman (Coburn) is living in wartime exile in New York with his royal niece Maria (de Havilland). He's determined to marry her off because their country needs a male heir and an incident with sleeping pills has Maria chastely spending the night in the apartment of flyboy Eddie O'Rourke (Cummings). Eddie thinks Maria is some kind of war refugee and they fall in love. Uncle Holman is happy to see them together and arranges a White House wedding but things get a little complicated. FDR makes a cameo appearance and his Scottie dog Fala actually has a part as a romantic go-between. **95m/B DVD.** Olivia de Havilland, Robert Cummings, Charles Coburn, Jack Carson, Jane Wyman, Gladys Cooper, Minor Watson, Curt Bois, Harry Davenport; *D:* Norman Krasna; *W:* Norman Krasna; *C:* Ernest Haller; *M:* Frederick "Friedrich" Hollander.

Princess Protection Program 🦴🦴 1/2 **2009 (G)** Charming Disney cable flick about an imperiled young princess and the tomboyish teen who befriends her. Princess Rosalinda Marie Montoya Fiore (Lovato) must go into hiding when her island home of Costa Luna is threatened by a neighboring dictator's political coup. Unbeknownst to his daughter Carter (Gomez), Joe Mason (Verica) is an agent for the Princess Protection Program and spirits the newly-named Rosie to his home in Lake Monroe, Louisiana for safekeeping. She doesn't exactly fit in so Carter, despite some hesitation, helps Rosie navigate high school and typical teen life. **89m/C DVD.** Selena Gomez, Demi Lovato, Tom Verica, Nicholas Braun, Jamie Chung, Samantha Droke, Robert Adamson; *D:* Allison Liddi-Brown; *W:* Annie DeYoung; *C:* David Makin; *M:* John Van Tongeren. **CABLE**

Princess Tam Tam 🦴🦴🦴 **1935** Pleasing French adaptation of Shaw's "Pygmalion," as a beautiful native African woman is "westernized" by a handsome writer and then introduced to high society as an exotic princess. A musical notable for its spectacular choreography and on-location Tunisian scenery. Story by Pepito Abatino, who was then Baker's husband. In French with English subtitles. **77m/B VHS, DVD.** *FR* Josephine Baker, Albert Prejean, Germaine Aussey, Viviane Romance; *D:* Edmond T. Greville.

The Princess Who Never Laughed 🦴🦴🦴 **1984** A stern king holds a laugh-off contest to make his morose daughter happy in this adaptation of the Brothers Grimm story from the "Faerie Tale Theatre" series. **60m/C VHS, DVD.** Ellen Barkin, Howard Hesseman, Howie Mandel, Mary Woronov.

Princess Yang Kwei Fei 🦴🦴🦴 *Yokihi; The Empress Yang Kwei Fei* **1955** Set in 8th-century China and based on the life of the last T'ang emperor and the beautiful servant girl he loves and makes his bride. She falls victim to court jealousies and he to his greedy family, though even death cannot end their love. Beautifully filmed and acted romantic tragedy. In Japanese with English subtitles. **91m/C VHS.** *JP* Machiko Kyo, Masayuki Mori, Eitaro (Sakae, Saka Ozawa) Ozawa, So Yamamura; *D:* Kenji Mizoguchi.

The Principal 🦴🦴 1/2 **1987 (R)** A tough, down-on-his-luck high school teacher is hired as the principal of a relentlessly violent, uncontrollable high school. Naturally he whips it into shape. **109m/C VHS, DVD.** James Belushi, Louis Gossett Jr., Rae Dawn Chong, Michael Wright, Esai Morales, J.J. (Jeffrey Jay) Cohen, Troy Winbush, Jacob Vargas; *D:* Christopher Cain; *W:* Frank Deese; *C:* Arthur Albert; *M:* Jay Gruska.

The Principal Takes a Holiday 🦴🦴 1/2 **1998** John's (Bryan) parents threaten to deprieve him of his grandmother's inheritance if he doesn't keep out of trouble during his senior year. But his latest prank is already underway and when the principal is mistakenly hospitalized because of it, John decides to manipulate the situation and sets up anti-establishment drifter Franklin (Nealon) as the school's temporary replacement. **89m/C VHS.** Kevin Nealon, Zachery Ty Bryan, Jessica Steen; *D:* Robert King; *W:* Mark Amin. **VIDEO**

Prison 🦴 1/2 **1988 (R)** The zombified body of an unjustly executed inmate haunts Creedmore Prison, stalking the guard that killed him. His search is aided by the terrified inmates. **102m/C VHS.** Lane Smith, Chelsea Field, Viggo Mortensen, Lincoln Kilpatrick, Tom Everett, Tommy (Tiny) Lister; *D:* Renny Harlin; *W:* C. Courtney Joyner; *C:* Mac Ahlberg; *M:* Richard Band.

Prison Break 🦴🦴 **1938** A convict plans a daring prison escape in order to clear his name for a murder he did not commit. **72m/B VHS, DVD.** Barton MacLane, Glenda Farrell, Paul Hurst, Constance Moore, Edmund MacDonald, Ward Bond, Guy Usher, Victor Kilian; *D:* Arthur Lubin; *W:* Dorothy Davenport Reid; *C:* Harry Neumann; *M:* Frank Sanucci, Hayes Pagel.

Prison Break: The Final Break 🦴🦴 **2009** Takes place in the time frame of the TV series' fourth season finale after the company is defeated and before the four year flash-forward coda. Pregnant Sara is now in prison (for the murder of Christina Scofield) and Michael reunites with his cohorts to break her out. Explains some of the questions left hanging in the last TV episode but some of the silly plot points won't please fans. **88m/C DVD.** Wentworth Miller, Sarah Wayne Callies, Dominic Purcell, Amaury Nolasco, William Fichtner, Robert Knepper, Jodi Lyn O'Keefe, Leon Russom, Kim Coates, Chris Bruno; *D:* Brad Turner; *W:* Nick Santora, Christian Trokey; *C:* Jeffrey Mygatt; *M:* Ramin Djawadi. **VIDEO**

Prison for Children 🦴🦴 1/2 **1993** Sixteen-year-old Chris is orphaned and put into a boys home where a supervisor sees his potential and helps him achieve it. **96m/C VHS.** Raphael Sbarge, Kenny Ransom, Jonathan Chapin, Josh Brolin, James Callahan, Betty Thomas, John Ritter; *D:* Larry Peerce.

Prison of Secrets 🦴🦴 1/2 **1997** Mom Zimbalist gets convicted of racketeering and sent to the big house where she learns that some of the prison guards are pimping the inmates. After suffering degradation herself, Zimbalist finally decides to expose the abuse but she needs the other women to testify as well. **91m/C VHS, DVD.** Stephanie Zimbalist, Dan Lauria, Finola Hughes, Rusty Schwimmer, Gary Frank, Kimberly Russell; ***D:*** Fred Gerber; ***W:*** Layce Gardner; ***C:*** John Fleckenstein; ***M:*** Nan Miskin. **CABLE**

Prison on Fire **1987** A mobster sent to prison for murdering his wife becomes friends with an innocent prisoner who has been framed. Violent portrayal of prison life. In Cantonese with English subtitles. **98m/C VHS, DVD.** *HK* Chow Yun-Fat, Tony Leung Ka-Fai; ***D:*** Ringo Lam; ***W:*** Yin Nam; ***M:*** Lowell Lo.

Prison on Fire 2 *Tao Fan; Jian Yu Feng Yun Xu Ji* **1991** Ching is a hard-timer in a Hong Kong prison troubled by an ongoing battle between local inmates and those from Mainland China. He manages to escape to see his young son but is soon returned to prison where evil security chief Zau sets him up against the Mainland gang, led by Dragon. There are more escapes, a riot, revenge, and lots of action. Subtitled. **107m/C DVD.** *HK* Chow Yun-Fat, Elvis Tsui, Kam-Kong Tsui, Yu Li; ***D:*** Ringo Lam; ***M:*** Lowell Lo.

Prison Planet **1/2 1992 (R)** In the year 2200 Earth is under the dictatorship of an evil king, with only a band of intrepid rebels to oppose him. Blaine, one of the rebels, gets himself arrested and sent to prison in search of the true ruler, the king's brother. But the prison is protected by a brutal warlord and his equally sadistic warriors, whom Blaine must battle if he ever hopes to find truth and justice. **90m/C VHS.** James Phillips, Jack Willcox, Michael Foley, Deborah Thompson-Carlin; ***D:*** Armand Gazarian; ***W:*** Armand Gazarian.

Prison Shadows **1936** Contrived programmer about a fighter (Nugent) who attempts to make a comeback after having served three years of a five-year sentence for killing an opponent in the boxing ring. He makes his comeback, but deals yet another mortal blow. Turns out that a gambling ring is behind the bizarre murders of the fighters and Nugent is their next victim. **67m/B VHS.** Eddie Nugent, Lucille Lund, Joan Barclay, Forrest Taylor, Syd Saylor, Monte Blue; ***D:*** Robert F. "Bob" Hill; ***W:*** Al Martin.

Prison Stories: Women on the Inside **1991** Three short dramatic stories depict the life of women inside prison walls. "New Chicks," directed by Spheeris, tells the story of two lifelong friends and partners in crime. "Esperanza," directed by Deitch, tells the story of a woman on the inside trying to prevent her family from following the same destructive path. Silver's "Parole Board" features Davidovich as a murderess up for parole but reluctant to leave the security of the prison. Blunt and gritty portrayal of prison gangs, the lifestyle of female inmates, and their fears of returning to life on the outside. **94m/C VHS.** Rae Dawn Chong, Annabella Sciorra, Lolita (David) Davidovich, Talisa Soto, Rachel Ticotin, Grace Zabriskie, Silvania Gallardo, Francesca Roberts; ***D:*** Donna Deitch, Penelope Spheeris, Joan Micklin Silver; ***W:*** Dick Beebe. **CABLE**

Prison Train **1/2** *People's Enemy* **1938** Travelogue of a convicted murderer's cross-country journey to begin his prison sentence at Alcatraz. **84m/B VHS, DVD.** Fred Keating, Dorothy Comingore, Clarence Muse, Faith Bacon, Alexander Leftwich, Nestor Paiva, Franklyn Farnum; ***D:*** Gordon Wiles.

The Prisoner **1955** Gritty drama about a Cardinal imprisoned in a Soviet bloc country as his captors attempt to break his determination not to be used as a propaganda tool. Interactions between the prisoner and his interogator are riveting. Based on the real-life experiences of Cardinal Mindszenty, a Hungarian activist during and after WWII. **91m/B VHS, DVD.** *GB* Alec Guinness, Jack Hawkins, Raymond Huntley, Wilfred Lawson; ***D:*** Peter Glenville.

The Prisoner *Jackie Chan Is the Prisoner; Huo Shao Dao* **1990 (R)** Even though the cover of this bizarre import says "Jackie Chan Is The Prisoner," he doesn't even show up for the first 20 minutes or so. Actually, the film is something of an ensemble piece that cheerfully borrows from American prison movies (most blatantly "Cool Hand Luke") between action scenes. The free-wheeling plot has Jackie, Sammo Hung, and Tony Leung battling fellow prisoners and corrupt officials. **94m/C DVD.** *HK* Jackie Chan, Sammo Hung, Tony Leung Ka-Fai; ***D:*** Yen Ping Chu; ***W:*** Fu Lai, Yeh Yuen Chiao; ***C:*** Chan Wing Su; ***M:*** Eckart Seeber.

Prisoner **1/2 2007** Controversial director Derek Plato (McMahon) checks out the location for his next violent film—an abandoned prison that's not so empty when a deranged man locks Derek up in a cell on death row. His jailer (Koteas) then starts filming Derek and asking him questions about his sordid past and career. Every unanswered question moves Derek closer to a presumably-working electric chair. **94m/C DVD.** Julian McMahon, Elias Koteas, Dagmara Dominczyk, Tom Guiry; ***D:*** David Alford, Robert Lynn; ***W:*** David Alford, Robert Lynn; ***C:*** Armanda Costanza. **VIDEO**

The Prisoner **2009** If you are unfamiliar with the surreal 1967 British cult series, which was co-created by and starred a powerful Patrick McGoohan, you may be moderately interested in Bill Gallagher's reinterpretation of the material. Otherwise, this miniseries is self-conscious, somewhat incoherent, and frustrating. Weak lead Caviezel is overshadowed by McKellan's silkily sinister Two. After abruptly resigning from some giant corporation, Michael (Caviezel) awakens in someplace called the Village where everyone has numbers instead of names. He's now Six and Two runs the show. Naturally a baffled, angry Six doesn't want to be there, wants to know what's going on, and wants to escape. You'll probably feel the same way yourself. **276m/C DVD.** *GB* James (Jim) Caviezel, Ian McKellen, Jamie Campbell, Hayley Atwell, Lennie James, Ruth Wilson, Rachael Blake; ***D:*** Nick Hurran; ***W:*** Bill Gallagher; ***C:*** Florian Hoffmeister. **CABLE**

Prisoner in the Middle **1974 (PG)** Janssen is the only man who can stop a nuclear warhead from falling into the hands of rival Middle East factions. Originally released as "Warhead." **87m/C VHS, DVD.** David Janssen, Karin Dor, Christopher Stone, Turia Tan, David Semadar, Art Metrano; ***D:*** John O'Conner.

Prisoner of Honor **1991 (PG)** A cable retelling of notorious Dreyfus Affair, in which a Jewish officer in the 19th-century French military was accused of treason based on little evidence and lots of bigotry. George Piquart (Dreyfuss), the anti-semitic counterintelligence head, grows to realize Dreyfuss's innocence and fights zealously for the truth. Russell's flamboyant direction takes the heroic tale into the realm of the surreal; this may not be a thoroughly accurate account, but it's one of the more eye-filling. **90m/C VHS, DVD.** Richard Dreyfuss, Oliver Reed, Peter Firth, Jeremy Kemp, Brian Blessed, Peter Vaughan, Kenneth Colley, Lindsay Anderson; ***D:*** Ken Russell. **CABLE**

Prisoner of Love **1/2 1999 (R)** After bartender Tracy (Campbell) witnesses a shakedown gone wrong, low-level stooge Jonny (Thal) is told to get rid of her. But since he's fallen in lust with Tracy after flirting with her in a nightclub, Jonny kidnaps her and holds her prisoner in a warehouse until he can figure out how to keep them both alive. Not nearly as kinky as it sounds—in fact the sheer blandness makes this a miss. **100m/C VHS, DVD.** Eric Thal, Naomi Campbell, Beau Starr, Carl Marotte; ***D:*** Steve DiMarco; ***M:*** Norman Orenstein.

Prisoner of Paradise **2002** Stark PBS documentary profiling German singer/actor/director Kurt Gerron who gained fame during the 1920s and 1930s in "The Blue Angel," but, as a Jew, was not allowed to work with the Nazis in power and oddly declined a chance to escape. After being captured while touring with gypsies and sent to a camp, the Nazis forced him to create a pro-Nazi film, "The Fuhrer Gives a City to the Jews." His 23-minute work is curiously omitted. **96m/C DVD.** ***D:*** Malcolm Clarke, Stuart Sender; ***W:*** Malcolm Clarke, Ian Holm. **TV**

Prisoner of Rio **1989** Satire of scruple-less TV evangelists and their nefarious schemes at acquiring their audience's money. **90m/C VHS.** Steven Berkoff, Paul Freeman; ***D:*** Lech Majewski; ***M:*** Hans Zimmer. **CABLE**

Prisoner of Second Avenue **1/2 1974 (PG)** A New Yorker in his late 40s faces the future, without a job or any confidence in his ability, with the help of his understanding wife. Based on the Broadway play by Neil Simon. **98m/C VHS, DVD.** Jack Lemmon, Anne Bancroft, Gene Saks, Elizabeth Wilson, Sylvester Stallone, F. Murray Abraham; ***D:*** Melvin Frank; ***W:*** Neil Simon; ***M:*** Marvin Hamlisch.

The Prisoner of Shark Island **1/2 1936** Dr. Samuel Mudd (Baxter) is wrongly convicted of conspiring to assassinate President Lincoln after he unwittingly sets the broken leg of assassin John Wilkes Booth (McDonald). He's sent to the titular island where Mudd cares for the inmates and guards, saving many during a yellow fever epidemic. Thanks to his heroism, Mudd's case is then re-opened. Baxter elicits audience sympathy without over-playing his role. **86m/B DVD.** Warner Baxter, Gloria Stuart, Claude Gillingwater, Frank McGlynn, Francis McDonald, Harry Carey Sr., John Carradine, Fred Kohler Jr., Douglas Wood, Paul Fix; ***D:*** John Ford; ***W:*** Nunnally Johnson; ***C:*** Bert Glennon.

Prisoner of the Mountains *Kavkazsky Plennik; Prisoner of the Caucasus* **1996 (R)** A modern-day, freely adapted version of Leo Tolstoy's novella "Prisoner of the Caucasus." Two Russian soldiers find themselves taken hostage in a remote Muslim village high in the Caucasus Mountains. Their captor, Abdul-Mourant (Sikharulidze), wishes to exchange them for his own captive son. Seasoned veteran Sacha (Menshikov) and young recruit Vanya (Bodrov Jr.) slowly form a bond, not only with each other but gradually with their captors. But there's a tragic inevitability to the entire untenable situation. Russian with subtitles. **98m/C VHS, DVD.** *RU* Sergei Bodrov Jr., Oleg Menshikov, Djemal Sikharulidze, Susanna Mekhralieva, Alexander Burejev, Alexei Zharkov, Valentina Fedotova; ***D:*** Sergei Bodrov; ***W:*** Sergei Bodrov, Arif Aliev, Boris Giller; ***C:*** Pavel Lebeshev; ***M:*** Leonid Desyatnikov.

The Prisoner of Zenda **1/2 1922** The third silent film adaptation of Anthony Hope's popular adventure novel. Stone stars in the dual role of King Rudolf of Ruritania and his lookalike English cousin, Rudolf Rassendyll. The King is drugged and thrown into the dungeon of Zenda by his evil half-brother Michael (Holmes) who wants the throne. Imagine Michael's surprise when the imposter shows up for the coronation. Novarro steals the flick as monocle-wearing baddie Rupert. **115m/B DVD.** Lewis Stone, Stuart Holmes, Ramon Novarro, Alice Terry, Barbara La Marr, Robert Edeson; ***D:*** Rex Ingram; ***W:*** Mary O'Hara; ***C:*** John Seitz.

Prisoner of Zenda **1/2 1937** An excellent cast and splendid photography make this the definitive film adaptation of Anthony Hope's swashbuckling novel. A British commoner is forced to pose as his cousin, the kidnapped king of a small European country, to save the throne. Complications of the romantic sort ensue when he falls in love with the queen. Excellent acting, robust sword play, and beautifully designed costumes make this an enjoyable spectacle. **101m/B VHS.** Ronald Colman, Douglas Fairbanks Jr., Madeleine Carroll, David Niven, Raymond Massey, Mary Astor, Sir C. Aubrey Smith, Montagu Love, Byron Foulger, Alexander D'Arcy, Charles Halton; ***D:*** John Cromwell; ***W:*** Donald Ogden Stewart, John Lloyd Balderston, Wells Root; ***C:*** James Wong Howe. Natl. Film Reg. '91.

Prisoner of Zenda **1/2 1952** Less-inspired remake of the 1937 version of Anthony Hope's novel, of a man resembling the monarch of a small country who is forced to pose as King during the coronation ceremony, becomes enamored with the queen, and finds himself embroiled in a murder plot. Worth watching for the luxurious costumes and lavish sets. Cast as a Cardinal here, Stone starred in the 1922 version. **101m/C VHS, DVD.** Stewart Granger, Deborah Kerr, Louis Calhern, James Mason, Jane Greer, Lewis Stone; ***D:*** Richard Thorpe; ***C:*** Joseph Ruttenberg.

Prisoner of Zenda **1979 (PG)** Flat comedic interpretation of Anthony Hope's swashbuckling tale of two identical men who switch places, only to find things complicated by a murder. Sellers stars in the double role of Prince Rudolph of Ruritania and Syd, the cockney cab driver who doubles for Rudolph when the Prince is imprisoned by his jealous brother Michael. **108m/C VHS.** Peter Sellers, Jeremy Kemp, Lynne Frederick, Lionel Jeffries, Elke Sommer; ***D:*** Richard Quine; ***W:*** Dick Clement, Ian La Frenais; ***M:*** Henry Mancini.

Prisoners of Inertia **1/2 1989 (R)** Two newlyweds travel to New York city and find themselves caught up in a whirlwind adventure in this well-acted but lazily scripted comedy drama. **92m/C VHS.** Amanda Plummer, Christopher Rich, John C. McGinley; ***D:*** Jay Noyles Seles.

Prisoners of the Lost Universe **1/2 1984** Talk-show hostess and her buddy are transported to a hostile universe by a renegade scientist. The two terrified humans search desperately for the dimensional door that is their only hope of escape. **94m/C VHS, DVD.** Richard Hatch, Kay Lenz, John Saxon; ***D:*** Terry Marcel. **TV**

Prisoners of the Sun *Blood Oath* **1991 (R)** Right after WWII an Australian captain fights to convict Japanese officers for atrocities against Allied POWs, but he's stonewalled by both the U.S. military and still-defiant enemy prisoners. This fiery drama from Down Under packs a punch as it questions whether wartime justice even exists; similar in that way to Brown's earlier "Breaker Morant." Takei (Sulu of the original "Star Trek") makes an imposing Japanese admiral. **109m/C VHS, DVD.** *AU* Bryan Brown, George Takei, Terry O'Quinn, John Back, Toshi Shioya, Deborah Kara Unger; ***D:*** Stephen Wallace.

Private Affairs **1989 (R)** The mistress of a well-known surgeon becomes jealous when the doctor decides to have a fling with a gorgeous young swim instructor. Italian-made cheapie. **83m/C VHS.** *IT* Guiliana de Sio, Kate Capshaw, David Naughton, Luca Barbareschi, Michele Placido; ***D:*** Francesco Massaro.

The Private Affairs of Bel Ami **1947** "This is the story of a scoundrel," proclaims the opening. Sanders is ideally cast as a suave cad who rises in 1880s Parisian society, largely through the strategic seduction of prominent women. Moralistically minded Old Hollywood toned down the talky adaptation of the Guy de Maupassant novel, but it's still drama of a high order. **112m/B VHS.** George Sanders, Angela Lansbury, Ann Dvorak, Frances Dee, John Carradine, Susan Douglas, Hugo Haas, Marie Wilson, Albert Bassermann, Warren William, Katherine Emery, Richard Fraser; ***D:*** Albert Lewin; ***W:*** Albert Lewin.

Private Benjamin **1/2 1980 (R)** Lighthearted fare about a pampered New York Jewish princess who impulsively enlists in the U.S. Army after her husband dies on their wedding night. Hawn, who also produced, creates a character loveable even at her worst moments and brings a surprising amount of depth to this otherwise frivolous look at high society attitudes. Basis for a TV series. **110m/C VHS, DVD.** Goldie Hawn, Eileen Brennan, Albert Brooks, Robert Webber, Armand Assante, Barbara Barrie, Mary Kay Place, Sally Kirkland, Craig T. Nelson, Harry Dean Stanton, Sam Wanamaker; ***D:*** Howard Zieff; ***W:*** Nancy Meyers, Charles Shyer, Harvey Miller; ***C:*** David M. Walsh; ***M:*** Bill Conti. Writers Guild '80: Orig. Screenplay.

Private Buckaroo **1942** War time entertainment in which Harry James and his orchestra get drafted. They decide to put on a show for the soldiers and get help from the Andrews Sisters. ♫ Don't Sit Under the Apple Tree with Anyone Else But Me; Three Little Sisters; Private Buckaroo; Johnny Get Your Gun Again; We've Got a Job to Do; You Made Me Love You; Six Jerks in a Jeep; That's the Moon My Son; I Love the South. **70m/B VHS, DVD.** The Andrews Sisters, Harry James, Joe E. Lewis, Dick Foran, Shemp

Howard, Mary Wickes, Donald O'Connor; ***D:*** Edward F. (Eddie) Cline.

Private Confessions **1998** Continues Bergman's exploration of his parents' unhappy marriage (following "The Best Intentions"), set mostly in 1925. Restless Anna (August) is constantly at odds with her clergyman husband, Henrik (Froler), and she has an affair with divinity student Tomas (Hanzon). Anna confesses the affair to Pastor Jacob (von Sydow), who she regards as a surrogate uncle, and he advises her to tell Henrik. Anna's confrontation with Henrik will leave lasting scars—as Anna once again reveals to Jacob some ten years later. Swedish with subtitles. **127m/C VHS.** *SW* Pernilla August, Samuel Froler, Max von Sydow, Thomas Hanzon; ***D:*** Liv Ullmann; ***W:*** Ingmar Bergman; ***C:*** Sven Nykvist.

Private Contentment **1983** This is a drama about a young soldier's experiences before he goes off to war in 1945. **90m/C VHS.** Trini Alvarado, Peter Gallagher, John McMartin, Kathryn Walker; ***D:*** Vivian Matalon.

Private Duty Nurses **1/2** *Young L.A. Nurses 1* **1971 (R)** Three nurses take on racism, war wounds, and a menage-a-trois (between one nurse, a doctor, and a drug addict). Second in Roger Corman's "nurse" quintet takes itself too seriously to be entertaining, but the gals make good use of those exciting new inventions, waterbeds. Preceded by "The Student Nurses" and followed by "Night Call Nurses," "The Young Nurses," and "Candy Stripe Nurses." **80m/C VHS, DVD.** Katherine (Kathy) Cannon, Joyce Williams, Pegi Boucher, Joseph Kaufmann, Dennis Redfield, Herbert Jefferson Jr., Paul Hampton, Paul Gleason; ***D:*** George Armitage; ***W:*** George Armitage; ***C:*** John McNichol; ***M:*** Sky.

The Private Eyes **1/2** **1980 (PG)** Light and uneven comedic romp with Knotts and Conway as bungling sleuths engaged to investigate two deaths. They're led on a merry chase through secret passages to a meeting with a ghostly adversary. **91m/C VHS, DVD.** Don Knotts, Tim Conway, Trisha Noble, Bernard Fox; ***D:*** Lang Elliott; ***W:*** John Myhers, Tim Conway; ***C:*** Jacques Haitkin; ***M:*** Peter Matz.

Private Fears in Public Places **1/2** *Coeurs* **2006** Many short scenes make for a fitful stop-and-start story about six essentially lonely people in Paris. Nicole (Morante) is looking for a new apartment for herself and fiance Dan (Wilson) with the help of broker Thierry (Dussollier). Thierry works with Charlotte (Azema), who knows bartender Lionel (Arditi) at the hotel where Dan likes to drink. Dan's drinking causes him to split with Nicole and he meets Gaelle (Carre), who happens to be Thierry's unhappy younger sister. The actors are pros but the production feels flat and constricted. French with subtitles. **120m/C DVD.** *FR IT* Laura Morante, Lambert Wilson, Pierre Arditti, Isabelle Carre, Andre Dussollier, Azema; ***D:*** Alain Resnais; ***W:*** Alain Resnais, Alan Ayckbourn, Jean-Michel Ribes; ***C:*** Eric Gautier; ***M:*** Mark Snow.

The Private Files of J. Edgar Hoover **1/2** **1977 (PG)** Scandalmongering "biography" of J. Edgar Hoover's private, sex-filled life. **112m/C VHS.** Broderick Crawford, Dan Dailey, Jose Ferrer, Rip Torn, Michael Parks, Raymond St. Jacques, Ronee Blakley; ***D:*** Larry Cohen; ***W:*** Larry Cohen.

A Private Function **1/2** **1984 (PG)** A ribald gag-fest dealing with Palin as a Yorkshireman who steals and fattens a wily contraband pig against the backdrop of post-WWII rationing. The satire ranges from biting to downright nasty, but Palin is always likeable in the center of it all. **96m/C VHS, DVD.** *GB* Michael Palin, Maggie Smith, Denholm Elliott, Bill Paterson, Liz Smith, Richard Griffiths, Tony Haygarth, John Normington, Alison Steadman, Pete Postlethwaite; ***D:*** Malcolm Mowbray; ***W:*** Alan Bennett; ***C:*** Tony Pierce-Roberts; ***M:*** John Du Prez. British Acad. '84: Actress (Smith), Support. Actor (Elliott), Support. Actress (Smith).

Private Hell 36 **1954** Two detectives become guilt-ridden after keeping part of some stolen money recovered after a robbery. Co-produced by Lupino. **81m/B VHS.** Ida Lupino, Howard Duff, Steve Cochran, Dean Jagger, Dorothy Malone, Bridget Duff, Jerry Hausner, Dabbs Greer, Chris O'Brien, Kenneth Patterson, George Dockstader, Jimmy Hawkins, King Donovan; ***D:*** Donald Siegel; ***W:*** Ida Lupino; ***C:*** Burnett Guffey; ***M:*** Leith Stevens.

The Private History of a Campaign That Failed **1/2** **1981** Adaptation of the Mark Twain story about a cowardly troop of Confederate soldiers. **89m/C VHS.** Pat Hingle, Edward Herrmann; ***D:*** Peter Hunt; ***W:*** Philip Reisman Jr.; ***C:*** Walter Lassally; ***M:*** William Perry.

Private Investigations **1/2** **1987 (R)** A made-for-video thriller about a nosey reporter who gets himself and his adult son in trouble while investigating drug-pushing cops. **91m/C VHS.** Ray Sharkey, Clayton Rohner, Talia Balsam, Anthony Zerbe, Paul LeMat; ***D:*** Nigel Dick; ***W:*** John Dahl, David Warfield.

Private Lessons **1975 (R)** Teenage boy is left alone for the summer in the care of an alluring maid and a scheming chauffeur. **83m/C VHS, DVD.** *IT* Eric Brown, Sylvia Kristel, Howard Hesseman, Ed Begley Jr.; ***D:*** Alan Myerson, Vittorio De Sisti; ***W:*** Vittorio De Sisti; ***C:*** Jan De Bont, Mario Masini; ***M:*** Franco Micalizzi.

Private Lessons, Another Story **1/2** **1994 (R)** A New York photographer (Morgan) is sick of her philandering husband and decides to experience some sexual excitement of her own by heading off to Miami. All that tropical heat inspires passion with her Cuban chauffeur (Garaza). **86m/C VHS.** Mariana Morgan, Ray Garaza, Theresa Morris; ***D:*** Dominique Othenin-Girard; ***W:*** William Mernit.

Private Life **1/2** *Chastnaya Zhizn* **1982** Suddenly with time on his hands, a Soviet official scrutinizes his relationships. After a number of revelations, he is forced to make new choices based on what he has learned. Oscar nominee in 1983. In Russian with English subtitles. **103m/C VHS.** *RU* Mikhail Ulyanov, Ita Sanvina, Irina Gubanova; ***D:*** Edgar Ryazanov; ***W:*** Andrew Davies.

Private Life of Don Juan *Don Juan* **1934** Appropriately slow-moving British costume drama set in 17th-century Spain finds an aging Don Juan struggling to maintain his usual antics in the pursuit of beautiful women. Furthermore, his reputation is being upstaged by a young imposter. Notable only as the last film appearance by Douglas Fairbanks Sr., and based on the play by Henri Bataille. **87m/B VHS.** *GB* Douglas Fairbanks Sr., Merle Oberon, Binnie Barnes, Melville Cooper, Joan Gardner, Benita Hume, Athene Seyler; ***D:*** Alexander Korda; ***C:*** Georges Perinal.

The Private Life of Henry VIII **1933** Lavish historical spectacle lustily portraying the life and lovers of notorious British Monarch, King Henry VIII. A tour de force for Laughton as the robust 16th-century king, with outstanding performances by the entire cast. **97m/B VHS, DVD.** *GB* Charles Laughton, Binnie Barnes, Elsa Lanchester, Robert Donat, Merle Oberon, Miles Mander, Wendy Barrie, John Loder, Lady Tree, Franklin Dyall, Claud Allister, William Austin, Gibb McLaughlin, Sam Livesey, Lawrence Hanray, Everley Gregg, Judy Kelly, John Turnbull, Frederick Culley, Hay Petrie, Wally Patch; ***D:*** Alexander Korda; ***W:*** Arthur Wimperis, Lajos Biro; ***C:*** Georges Perinal. Oscars '33: Actor (Laughton).

The Private Life of Sherlock Holmes **1/2** **1970 (PG-13)** A unique perspective on the life of the famous detective reveals a complex character. Beautifully photographed, with fine performances by the supporting cast, the film boasts a haunting musical score but received suprisingly little recognition despite Wilder's high caliber direction. **125m/C VHS, DVD.** *GB* Robert Stephens, Colin Blakely, Genevieve Page, Irene Handl, Stanley Holloway, Christopher Lee, Clive Revill, Catherine Lacey, Tamara Toumanova, Mollie Maureen, Michael Balfour; ***D:*** Billy Wilder; ***W:*** Billy Wilder, I.A.L. Diamond; ***C:*** Christopher Challis; ***M:*** Miklos Rozsa.

Private Lives **1/2** **1931** Stylish adaptation of Noel Coward play starring Shearer and Montgomery as a couple with a tempestuous relationship. Although once married, they have since divorced and married other mates. While honeymooning at the same french hotel (Quelle coincidence!), they have trouble showing affection to their new spouses and realize they still feel passionately about one another. Excellent acting combined with Coward's witty dialogue makes this film a treat. **92m/B VHS.** Norma Shearer, Robert Montgomery, Reginald Denny, Una Merkel, Jean Hersholt; ***D:*** Sidney Franklin; ***W:*** Hans Kraly, Richard Schayer; ***C:*** Ray Binger.

The Private Lives of Elizabeth & Essex **1939** Cast reads like a Who's Who in Hollywood in this lavishly costumed dramatization of the love affair between Queen Elizabeth I (Davis) and Robert Devereaux (Flynn), the second Earl of Essex. Forced to choose between her Kingdom and her lover, Davis' monarch is the epitome of a regal women. Fabray made her first film appearance as an adult in this adaptation of Maxwell Anderson's 1930 play "Elizabeth the Queen." **106m/C VHS, DVD.** Bette Davis, Errol Flynn, Vincent Price, Nanette Fabray, Olivia de Havilland, Alan Hale, Donald Crisp, Leo G. Carroll; ***D:*** Michael Curtiz.

The Private Lives of Pippa Lee **2009 (R)** Miller adapted her own novel for this mild dysfunctional family drama. At 50, placid Pippa Lee (Wright) thought she has the perfect life. Then her dominating, 30-years-older husband Herb (Arkin) moves them from their Manhattan apartment into a Connecticut retirement community because of his failing health. Pippa thinks about her troubled past with her drug addict mom (Bello), which lead to her own druggie-runaway youth in New York and starts confiding in neighbor's son Chris (Reeves) that she's lost her own identity while devoting her life to placating everyone else. Now she wonders just where it got her. **93m/C DVD.** *US* Robin Wright Penn, Alan Arkin, Keanu Reeves, Shirley Knight, Robin Weigert, Julianne Moore, Blake Lively, Maria Bello, Tim Guinee, Winona Ryder, Monica Bellucci, Zoe Kazan, Ryan McDonald; ***D:*** Rebecca Miller; ***W:*** Rebecca Miller; ***C:*** Declan Quinn; ***M:*** Michael Rohatyn.

Private Manoeuvres **WOOF!** *Sababa* **1983** A comely Swiss military adviser gives her all to uplift the morale of the men at Camp Samantha. **79m/C VHS.** *GE IS* Zachi Noy, Joseph Shiloah, Dvora Bekon; ***D:*** Tzvi Shissel; ***W:*** Boaz Davidson; ***C:*** Adam Greenberg; ***M:*** Jose Padilla.

A Private Matter **1992 (PG-13)** Based on the true story of Sherri Finkbine (hostess of TV's "Romper Room") and the controversy surrounding her decision to terminate her pregnancy in 1962. Pregnant with her fifth child, she discovered her sleeping medication contained thalidomide, known to cause severe birth defects. Although technically illegal, her doctor agreed to quietly perform an abortion. Sherri warned a local newspaper reporter about the drug's dangers and her identity was mistakenly revealed. A storm of adverse publicity forced her to Sweden for the abortion. Great performances highlight this complex and traumatic issue. **89m/C VHS, DVD.** Sissy Spacek, Aidan Quinn, Estelle Parsons, Sheila McCarthy, Leon Russom, William H. Macy; ***D:*** Joan Micklin Silver; ***W:*** William Nicholson. **CABLE**

Private Navy of Sgt. O'Farrell **1968** Serviceable World War II service comedy casts Hope as the titular NCO who must salvage a cargo ship full of beer that was sunk by the Japanese. He also tries to get some nurses assigned to the remote Pacific island where he's stationed. But Phyllis Diller proves to be a poor morale booster. The film doesn't come close to the "Road" comedies, but it's still worth a mild recommendation to the star's fans. **92m/C DVD.** Bob Hope, Phyllis Diller, Jeffrey Hunter, Dick Sargent, Mako, Gina Lollobrigida; ***D:*** Frank Tashlin; ***W:*** Frank Tashlin; ***C:*** Alan Stensvold.

Private Obsession **1/2** **1994 (R)** Model Emanuelle Griffith (Whirry) is missing—kidnapped by obsessed admirer Richard (Christian) who wants the beauty for himself alone. Emanuelle may be blonde but she's not dumb and she decides to turn the tables on her captor. **93m/C VHS, DVD.** Shannon Whirry, Michael Christian, Bo Svenson, Rip Taylor; ***D:*** Lee Frost; ***W:*** Lee Frost; ***C:*** William Boatman; ***M:*** Dean Andre.

Private Parts **1972 (R)** A bizarre first attempt at feature length for Bartel. Black comedy featuring a runaway, a voyeuristic photographer and a hotel full of strange people who participate in murder and a variety of freakish sexual acts. **87m/C VHS, DVD.** Ayn Ruymen, Lucille Benson, John Ventantonio, Laurie Main, Stanley Livingston, Charles Woolf, John Lupton, Dorothy Neumann, Gene Simms; ***D:*** Paul Bartel; ***W:*** Philip Kearney, Les Rendelstein; ***C:*** Andrew Davis; ***M:*** Hugo Friedhofer.

Private Parts **1/2** *Howard Stern's Private Parts* **1996 (R)** Stern makes his movie debut as...himself! Self-effacing yet self-aggrandizing bio traces Stern's rise from gawky kid to gawky college student to awkward small-market DJ to New York madman to inauguration as self-proclaimed King of All Media. Funny, and at times, touching flick features good performances by the rookie actors in Stern's inner circle, as well as by the pros. Giamatti is exceptional as the young WNBC exec assigned to tame Howard. Script manages to show Stern's outrageousness and still make him likeable. While this is clearly a whitewash job, and under other circumstances Stern himself might make fun of its sentimentality, pic should please everyone but the most rabid Stern-hater. **109m/C VHS, DVD.** Howard Stern, Robin Quivers, Mary McCormack, Paul Giamatti, Fred Norris, Gary Dell'Abate, Bobby Boriello, Michael Maccarone, Matthew Friedman, Jackie Martling, Carol Alt, Richard Portnow, Kelly Bishop, Henry Goodman, Jonathan Hadary, Paul Hecht, Allison Janney, Michael Murphy, James Murtaugh, Reni Santoni, Lee Wilkof, Theresa Lynn, Amber Smith; ***D:*** Betty Thomas; ***W:*** Len Blum, Michael Kalesniko; ***C:*** Walt Lloyd; ***M:*** Van Dyke Parks.

Private Passions **1985** A sultry woman gives her teenaged cousin a lesson in love during his European vacation. **86m/C VHS, DVD.** Sybil Danning, David J. Siegel, Susanne Ashley, Gavin Brennan; ***D:*** Kikuo Kawasaki; ***W:*** Kikuo Kawasaki; ***C:*** Ramon Suarez.

Private Property **1/2** *Nue Propriete* **2006** Unpleasant dysfunctional family drama. Pascale lives with her lay-about twin sons Francois and Thierry in a rundown farmhouse that was part of her acrimonious divorce settlement. She and her sons have never cut those apron strings and the boys are appalled when Pascale hints at selling the dump, in part because she's found a boyfriend. Lots of bickering (and more) follows. French with subtitles. **95m/C DVD.** *BE FR LU* Isabelle Huppert, Jeremie Renier, Patrick Descamps, Yannick Renier, Kris Cuppens; ***D:*** Joachim Lafosse; ***W:*** Joachim Lafosse, Francois Pirot; ***C:*** Hichame Alaouie.

Private Resort **1984 (R)** Curious house detective and a bumbling thief interrupt the highjinks of two girl-crazy teens on a quest for fun at an expensive Miami hotel. Occasionally funny plodder. **82m/C VHS, DVD.** Johnny Depp, Rob Morrow, Karyn O'Bryan, Emily Longstreth, Tony Azito, Hector Elizondo, Dody Goodman, Leslie Easterbrook, Andrew (Dice Clay) Silverstein; ***D:*** George Bowers.

Private Road: No Trespassing **1987 (R)** A stock car racer and a top engineer compete over a military project, cars and a rich heiress. **90m/C VHS.** George Kennedy, Greg Evigan, Mitzi Kapture; ***D:*** Raphael Nussbaum.

Private School **1/2** **1983 (R)** Two high school girls from the exclusive Cherryvale Academy for Women compete for the affections of a young man from nearby Freemount Academy for Men, while Cherryvale's headmistress is trying to raise funds to build a new wing. Banal teen sexploitation comedy with better-than-average cast. **89m/C VHS, DVD.** Phoebe Cates, Betsy Russell, Kathleen Wilhoite, Sylvia Kristel, Ray Walston, Matthew Modine, Michael Zorek, Fran Ryan, Jonathan Prince, Kari Lizer, Richard Stahl; ***D:*** Noel Black; ***C:*** Walter Lassally.

The Private Secretary **1/2** **1935** Horton is a mild-mannered clergyman who finds out his identity has been usurped by a young man with a great many angry creditors. Horton has some amusing comic bits but the film, based on a popular Victorian farce "Der Bibliotheker" by Van Moser, did not translate well to the screen. **70m/B VHS.** *GB* Edward Everett Horton, Barry Mackay, Oscar Asche, Judy Gunn, Michael Shepley, Alastair Sim; ***D:*** Henry Edwards.

Private Valentine: Blonde & Dangerous 🦴 *Major Movie Star* **2008 (PG-13)** Simpson pulls a Goldie Hawn/ "Private Benjamin" moment with a lot less talent involved but an amiable presence. Megan Valentine is a fluff bunny movie star whose latest effort is a flop. Adding to her woes is a bad breakup and a crooked accountant who's left her broke. So what's a busty blonde to do? Hey, Megan is a nice girl—so she decides to join the Army. **98m/C DVD.** Jessica Simpson, Vivica A. Fox, Steve Guttenberg, Cheri Oteri, Bryce Johnson; ***D:*** Steve Miner; ***W:*** April Blair, Kelly Bowe; ***C:*** Patrick Cady; ***M:*** Dennis Smith.

Private War 🦴 ½ **1990 (R)** Training for an elite force turns deadly when the commanding officer makes the rules. Now it's a private war between two brutal fighting machines. Adapted from a Jan Guillou story. **95m/C VHS.** Martin Hewitt, Joe Dallesandro, Kimberly Beck; ***D:*** Frank De Palma; ***W:*** Frank De Palma, Terry Borst.

The Private War of Major Benson 🦴🦴 ½ **1955** Tough Army officer Major Bernard Benson (Heston) has his work cut out for him when he's ordered to take over an ROTC program at a military academy. First he finds out the school's run by nuns and then he treats his young cadets as he would adult troops, which naturally makes him very unpopular. But he manages to unbend enough to try for a romance with the school's doctor (Adams). And of course the kids teach him how to become a human being. Remade in 1995 as "Major Payne." **104m/C VHS.** Charlton Heston, Julie Adams, Milburn Stone, Nana Bryant, William Demarest, Tim Considine, Sal Mineo; ***D:*** Jerry Hopper; ***W:*** William Roberts, Richard Alan Simmons; ***C:*** Harold Lipstein.

Private Wars 🦴🦴 **1993 (R)** A law-abiding community falls victim to gangland violence until the inhabitants hire a down-and-out private eye (Railsback) to show them how to fight back. He finds out that a greedy land developer (Whitman) has bribed the Chief of Police (Champion) to let his goons do anything to get the people out so he can redevelop the land. **94m/C VHS, DVD.** Steve Railsback, Michael Champion, Stuart Whitman, Holly Floria, Dan Tullis Jr., Michael Delano, James Lew, Brian Patrick Clarke; ***D:*** John Weidner; ***W:*** Ken Lamplugh, John Weidner.

Privates on Parade 🦴🦴 ½ **1984 (R)** Film centering around the comic antics of an Army song-and-dance unit entertaining the troops in the Malayan jungle during the late '40s. Occasionally inspired horseplay based on Peter Nichols play. **107m/C VHS, DVD.** *GB* John Cleese, Denis Quilley, Simon Jones, Joe Melia, Nicola Pagett, Julian Sands; ***D:*** Michael Blakemore.

Privilege 🦴🦴 **1967** The acting's poor but the situations are still relevant. British pop star Steve Shorter (debut of singer Jones) is immensely popular but also easily manipulated and exploited. In this nightmare future oddity, the government decides to use Steve as a symbol of national unity and conformity. Artist Vanessa (model Shrimpton in her only film role) becomes Steve's lover and makes him see how he's been used so he'll stage a social revolt. **103m/C DVD.** *GB* Paul Jones, Mark London, Jeremy Child, William Job, Jean Shrimpton, Max Bacon; ***D:*** Peter Watkins; ***W:*** Peter Watkins, Norman Bogner; ***C:*** Peter Suschitzky; ***M:*** Mike Leander.

Prix de Beaute 🦴 ½ *Miss Europe* **1930** A woman's boyfriend does not know that she has won a beauty contest. Brooks' last starring role and the only film she did in France. In French with English subtitles. **93m/B VHS, DVD.** *FR* Louise Brooks, Jean Bradin, George Charlia, Gaston Jacquet; ***D:*** Augusto Genina.

The Prize 🦴🦴🦴 **1963** Gripping spy story laced with laughs based on a novel by Irving Wallace (adapted by Lehman). In Stockholm, writer accepts the Nobel prize for dubious reasons and then finds himself in the midst of political intrigue. Newman and Sommer turn in great performances in this action drama. **136m/C VHS.** Paul Newman, Edward G. Robinson, Elke Sommer, Leo G. Carroll, Diane Baker, Micheline Presle, Gerard Oury, Sergio Fantoni; ***D:*** Mark Robson; ***W:*** Ernest Lehman; ***C:*** William H. Daniels; ***M:*** Jerry Goldsmith.

Prize Fighter 🦴🦴 **1979 (PG)** Comedy team of Knotts and Conway take on Depression-era boxing. Fight manager Knotts and his pugilistic protege Conway unknowingly get involved with a powerful gangster, who convinces them to fight in a fixed championship match. Most enjoyable if intelligence is suspended at onset. **99m/C VHS, DVD.** Tim Conway, Don Knotts; ***D:*** Michael Preece; ***W:*** Tim Conway.

Prize of Peril 🦴🦴 **1984** A French TV game show rewards it winners with wealth and its losers with execution. Not always the best policy to learn what's behind Door #1. **95m/C VHS.** *FR* Michel Piccoli, Marie-France Pisier; ***D:*** Yves Boisset.

The Prize Pulitzer 🦴🦴 *Roxanne: The Prize Pulitzer* **1989** Watered-down account of the scandalous divorce between publishing heir Herbert "Pete" Pulitzer and his young wife Roxanne. Based on the book "The Prize Pulitzer" by Roxanne Pulitzer. **95m/C VHS, DVD.** Perry King, Chynna Phillips, Courteney Cox, Betsy Russell, Sondra Blake, Caitlin Brown; ***D:*** Richard A. Colla. **TV**

The Prize Winner of Defiance, Ohio 🦴🦴🦴 **2005 (PG-13)** Based on a memoir by Terry Adams. The "prize winner" is Terry's mother Evelyn (Moore, who filmmakers seem to love casting as a 1950s housewife). The mother of ten children and the wife of a drunk (Harrelson), ever-cheerful Evelyn figures out how to (barely) hold it all together by becoming a successful jingle writer, winning money and prizes for her catchy advertising tunes. Maybe a little heavy and nostalgic at moments, but charming nonetheless. **99m/C DVD.** *US* Julianne Moore, Woody Harrelson, Laura Dern, Trevor Morgan, Simon Reynolds; ***D:*** Jane Anderson; ***W:*** Jane Anderson; ***C:*** Jonathan Freeman; ***M:*** John (Gianni) Frizzell.

The Prizefighter and the Lady 🦴🦴🦴 *Every Woman's Man* **1933** In his first film role boxer Baer (who won the heavyweight boxing crown in 1934) is a natural as a fighter who falls for a beautiful nightclub singer (Loy). Baer and Loy get, but don't stay, together but she does turn out to be his lucky charm in the big fight finale. Fellow professional boxer Carnera, Baer's opponent in the climatic fight scene, refused to lose as the script indicated and the film ending was eventually rewritten. The likeable Baer later earned his living as an actor. **102m/B** Max Baer Sr., Myrna Loy, Otto Kruger, Primo Carnera, Walter Huston, Vince Barnett, Muriel Evans; ***D:*** Woodbridge S. Van Dyke.

Prizzi's Honor 🦴🦴🦴 **1985 (R)** Highly stylized, sometimes leaden black comedy about Vharley Partana (Nicholson), an aging and none-to-bright hit man from a New York mob family who breaks with family loyalties when he falls for Irene Walker (Turner), an upwardly mobile tax consultant who's also a hired killer. Skirting caricature in every frame, Nicholson is excellent in his portrayal of the thick-skulled mobster, as are Angelica Huston as the hot-to-trot Mafia daughter Maerose and Hickey as Don Prizzi. Adapted by Condon and Roach from Condon's novel. **130m/C VHS, DVD.** Jack Nicholson, Kathleen Turner, Robert Loggia, John Randolph, Anjelica Huston, Lawrence Tierney, William Hickey, Lee Richardson, Michael Lombard, Joseph Ruskin, CCH Pounder; ***D:*** John Huston; ***W:*** Richard Condon, Janet Roach; ***C:*** Andrzej Bartkowiak; ***M:*** Alex North. Oscars '85: Support. Actress (Huston); British Acad. '85: Adapt. Screenplay; Golden Globes '86: Actor—Mus./ Comedy (Nicholson), Actress—Mus./ Comedy (Turner), Director (Huston), Film—Mus./Comedy; L.A. Film Critics '85: Support. Actress (Huston); N.Y. Film Critics '85: Actor (Nicholson), Director (Huston), Film, Support. Actress (Huston); Natl. Soc. Film Critics '85: Actor (Nicholson), Director (Huston), Support. Actress (Huston); Writers Guild '85: Adapt. Screenplay.

Probable Cause 🦴🦴 **1995 (R)** A knife-wielding serial killer specializes in murdering cops and the clues seem to point to a troubled veteran cop (Ironside), newly paired with a beautiful detective (Vernon). Some unexpected twists and a surprise ending. **90m/C VHS.** Michael Ironside, Kate Vernon, Kirk Baltz, Craig T. Nelson, M. Emmet Walsh; ***D:*** Paul Ziller; ***W:*** Hal Salwen; ***C:*** Danny Nowak.

Probation 🦴🦴 *Second Chances* **1932** A dashing young man in trouble with the law receives an unusual sentence; he must become a chauffeur for a spoiled society girl. Grable's first film role is a small one. **60m/B VHS.** Sally Blane, J. Farrell MacDonald, Eddie (Edward) Phillips, Clara Kimball Young, Betty Grable; ***D:*** Richard Thorpe.

Probe 🦴🦴 ½ **1972** A detective uses computer-age technology to apprehend criminals. Pilot for the TV series "Search." **95m/C VHS.** Hugh O'Brian, Elke Sommer, John Gielgud, Burgess Meredith, Angel Tompkins, Lilia Skala, Kent Smith, Alfred Ryder, Jaclyn Smith; ***D:*** Russ Mayberry; ***W:*** Leslie Stevens. **TV**

Problem Child 🦴 ½ **1990 (PG)** Ritter decides to adopt Oliver out of the goodness of his heart, but it seems young Oliver's already got a father figure named Beelzebub. Potential for laughs is unmet. **81m/C VHS, DVD.** John Ritter, Michael Oliver, Jack Warden, Amy Yasbeck, Gilbert Gottfried, Michael Richards, Peter Jurasik; ***D:*** Dennis Dugan; ***W:*** Scott M. Alexander, Larry Karaszewski; ***C:*** Peter Lyons Collister; ***M:*** Miles Goodman.

Problem Child 2 🦴 **1991 (PG-13)** Ritter and his nasty adopted son are back, but this time there's an equally malevolent little girl. They team up to prevent Ritter's upcoming marriage to a socialite. Low slapstick junk. **91m/C VHS, DVD.** John Ritter, Michael Oliver, Laraine Newman, Amy Yasbeck, Jack Warden, Ivyann Schwan, Gilbert Gottfried, James Tolkan, Charlene Tilton, Alan Blumenfeld, Paul Sutera; ***D:*** Brian Levant; ***W:*** Scott M. Alexander, Larry Karaszewski.

The Prodigal 🦴🦴 ½ **1955** Luke's New Testament Bible story of the son seduced by greed slickly transfered to the silver screen by MGM. A colorful cast is the main attraction. **113m/C DVD.** Lana Turner, Edmund Purdom, Louis Calhern, Audrey Dalton, Neville Brand, Walter Hampden, Taina Elg, Francis L. Sullivan, Joseph Wiseman, Sandy Descher, John Dehner, Cecil Kellaway, Henry Daniell, Paul Cavanagh, Tracey Roberts, Jay Novello, Dorothy Adams, Richard Devon; ***D:*** Richard Thorpe; ***C:*** Joseph Ruttenberg.

The Prodigal 🦴🦴 **1983 (PG)** A born-again family drama in which a sundered family is brought together by the return of a once-estranged son. **109m/C VHS.** John Hammond, Hope Lange, John Cullum, Morgan Brittany, Ian Bannen, Arliss Howard, Joey Travolta, Billy Graham; ***M:*** Bruce Broughton.

The Prodigal Planet 🦴 **1988** Small group of believers continue their struggle against the world government UNTIE by disrupting their communication network. Sequel to "Thief in the Night," "A Distant Thunder," and "Image of the Beast." **67m/C VHS, DVD.** William Wellman Jr., Linda Beatie, Cathy Wellman, Thom Rachford; ***D:*** Donald W. Thompson.

The Prodigal Son 🦴🦴 ½ **1982** Small-town martial arts champ Biao learns all his fights were fixed by his wealthy father. Determined to prove himself fairly, Biao learns the true wisdom and skills of kung fu from traveling entertainer Ying. Typically over-the-top fight scenes. Chinese with subtitles or dubbed. **100m/C VHS, DVD.** *HK* Yuen Biao, Ching-Ying Lam, Sammo Hung; ***D:*** Sammo Hung; ***W:*** Jing Wong.

The Prodigy 🦴🦴 **1998** Well-intentioned but far-fetched drama posits that Nathan Jones (Earl), an illiterate 12-year-old black boy, is "adopted" by a fraternity and enrolled as a student as a child prodigy. Sounds like an after-school special gone tragically awry. **104m/C DVD.** Robert Foreman, Jeremy Isiah Earl, Jennifer Rochester; ***D:*** Edward T. McDougal; ***W:*** Edward T. McDougal, Dale Chapman, Christopher Panneck; ***C:*** Ben Kufrin.

The Producers 🦴🦴🦴 ½ **1968** A hilarious farce follows an attempted swindle by theater producer/con artist Max Bialystock (Mostel), who convinces his meek accountant Leo Bloom (Wilder) to go along with a scheme to deliberately stage a Broadway flop and abscond with the investors' money. They pick what they believe will be a surefire disaster, a musical entitled "Springtime for Hitler," only to see their plan backfire. Film achieved cult status and is considered one of Brooks' best. The phony play was later actually produced by Alan Johnson. **90m/C VHS, DVD.** Zero Mostel, Gene Wilder, Dick Shawn, Kenneth Mars, Estelle Winwood, Lee Meredith, Frank Campanella, Mel Brooks; ***D:*** Mel Brooks; ***W:*** Mel Brooks; ***C:*** Joseph Coffey; ***M:*** John Morris. Oscars '68: Story & Screenplay, Natl. Film Reg. '96;; Writers Guild '68: Orig. Screenplay.

The Producers 🦴🦴 ½ **2005 (PG-13)** The wildly funny Mel Brooks 1968 film showed up in 2001 as a hit Broadway musical—this is the film version of that, cast with most of the originals from Broadway. Shifty producer Max (Lane) and his accountant Leo (Broderick) hatch a scheme to get rich by producing a flop and pocketing the leftover investor money after the show surely closes. Hideous Nazi musical "Springtime for Hitler" not only doesn't flop, it's a major success, which means trouble. Yes, it's all rehashed, and old-schoolers will go back to the original film with a renewed fondness. Fun cast and hilarious musical numbers help to somewhat mask the weaknesses. **129m/C DVD.** *US* Nathan Lane, Matthew Broderick, Uma Thurman, Will Ferrell, Roger Bart, Eileen Essell, David Huddleston, Michael McKean, Debra Monk, Andrea Martin, Jon Lovitz, Mel Brooks, Gary Beach; ***D:*** Susan Stroman; ***W:*** Mel Brooks, Thomas Meehan; ***C:*** John Bailey, Charles Minsky; ***M:*** Mel Brooks.

The Professional 🦴🦴 *Leon; The Cleaner* **1994 (R)** Leon (Reno) is an eccentric French hit man, working New York's mean streets, when his 12-year-old neighbor Mathilda (Portman) comes knocking. Seems her family has been murdered by minions of crooked drug enforcement agent Stansfield (Oldman) and she'd like Leon to teach her how to be a "cleaner" so she can get revenge. And Leon obliges. The lovely young Portman (in her film debut) is a little too Lolita-ish for comfort as she manipulates the stolid Reno, with Oldman suitably extravagant in the role of sadistic psycho. **109m/C VHS, DVD.** *FR* Jean Reno, Natalie Portman, Gary Oldman, Danny Aiello, Michael Badalucco, Ellen Greene; ***D:*** Luc Besson; ***W:*** Luc Besson; ***C:*** Thierry Arbogast; ***M:*** Eric Serra.

The Professionals 🦴🦴🦴 ½ **1966 (PG-13)** Action and adventure count for more than a story line in this exciting western about four mercenaries hired by a wealthy cattle baron to rescue his young wife from Mexican kidnappers. Breathtaking photography recreates turn-of-the-century Mexico in this adaptation of the Frank O'Rourke novel. **117m/C VHS, DVD.** Burt Lancaster, Lee Marvin, Claudia Cardinale, Jack Palance, Robert Ryan, Woody Strode, Ralph Bellamy; ***D:*** Richard Brooks; ***W:*** Richard Brooks; ***C:*** Conrad L. Hall; ***M:*** Maurice Jarre.

The Professor 🦴🦴 **1958** Rare sci-fi thriller featuring a werewolf, an eccentric scientist and a communist plot. Also includes several 'werewolf' oriented movie trailers. **30m/C VHS.** Doug Hobart, John Copeland, Irene Barr; ***D:*** Tom McCain.

Profile 🦴🦴 ½ **1954** A newsman gets an editorial job for a magazine called "Profile," and promptly falls in love with the boss's daughter. Complications arise when the boss's wife puts the moves on him. As if that isn't trouble enough, he finds himself accused of embezzlement. Average entertainment with some notable performances and an interesting chase scene. **65m/B VHS.** John Bentley, Kathleen Byron, Thea Gregory, Stuart Lindsell; ***D:*** Francis Searle.

Profile for Murder 🦴🦴 *The Fifth Season* **1996 (R)** Criminal profiler Hanna Carras (Severance) and Detective Andy Sachs (Michael) are assigned by DA Michael Weinberg (Wincott) to investigate investment banker Adrian Cross (Henriksen), the primary suspect in a series of grisly murders of young women. Cross likes to play mind games and soon Carras is very personally involved with the suspect but does that also make him the killer? **95m/C VHS.** Joan Severance, Lance Henriksen, Jeff Wincott, Ryan

Michael; *D:* David Winning; *W:* Steve(n) Fisher; *C:* Bruce Worrall; *M:* Barron Abramovitch.

Progeny **1998** Familiar horror ground with some scary creatures. Craig (Vosloo) and Sherry (McWhirter) are zapped by a bright light while in bed and don't remember what happened until a shrink (Crouse) and UFO investigator Clavell (Douriff) hypnotize them. Then Sherry remembers she was abducted and apparently impregnated by some slimy, tentacled aliens and it's all just kind of predictably gross from there on out. **100m/C VHS, DVD.** Arnold Vosloo, Jillian McWhirter, Brad Dourif, Lindsay Crouse, Wilford Brimley; *D:* Brian Yuzna; *W:* Aubrey Solomon; *C:* James Hawkinson; *M:* Steven Morrell. **VIDEO**

The Program 1/2 **1993 (R)** Sensitive tearjerker about college football players getting caught up in the drive for a championship. As the season takes its toll on both mind and body, players prepare for the Big Game. Caan is the team's gruff coach, who's willing to look the other way as long as his boys are winning. Film sparked controversy when the Disney studio pulled and recut it after release because one scene, where Sheffer's character lies down in traffic, sparked copy-cat actions and several deaths. The scene was not restored for the video version. **110m/C VHS, DVD.** James Caan, Craig Sheffer, Kristy Swanson, Halle Berry, Omar Epps, Duane Davis, Abraham Benrubi, Jon Maynard Pennell, Andrew Bryniarski, Joey Lauren Adams; *D:* David S. Ward; *W:* David S. Ward, Aaron Latham; *M:* Michel Colombier.

Programmed to Kill *Retaliator* **1986 (R)** A beautiful terrorist is captured by the CIA and transformed into a buxom bionic assassin. **91m/C VHS.** Robert Ginty, Sandahl Bergman, James Booth, Louise Caire Clark; *D:* Allan Holzman.

Project A 1/2 *Jackie Chan's Project A; A Gai Waak* **1983 (PG-13)** This period piece has several excellent physical routines. As Dragon Ma, a coast guard officer in 19th-century Hong Kong, Jackie Chan (who also directed) performs some of his most ingenious stunts, and pays overt homage to one of his greatest influences, Harold Lloyd. **105m/C VHS, DVD.** *HK* Jackie Chan, Sammo Hung, Yuen Biao; *D:* Jackie Chan; *W:* Edward Tang, Jackie Chan; *M:* Nicholas Rivera.

Project A: Part 2 *Jackie Chan's Project A2* **1987** Dragon Ma, the only honest cop in Hong Kong on the high seas at the turn of the century is back with a new set of adventures. In Cantonese with English subtitles. **101m/C VHS, DVD.** *HK* Jackie Chan, Maggie Cheung, Carina Lau, David Lam; *D:* Jackie Chan; *W:* Edward Tang, Jackie Chan.

Project: Alien **1989 (R)** Science fiction fans in search of a good extraterrestrial flick should avoid this teaser, for it has nothing to do with aliens. As the film begins, Earth is allegedly being attacked by beings from space, and a vast array of scientists, militia and journalists track the aliens. What's actually happening revolves around the testing of deadly biological weapons. Shot in Yugoslavia. **92m/C VHS.** Michael Nouri, Darlanne Fluegel, Maxwell Caulfield, Charles Durning; *D:* Frank Shields; *W:* Anthony Able.

Project: Eliminator 1/2 **1991 (R)** A group of terrorists kidnap a designer of "smart" weapons, and it's up to a hard-hitting special forces unit to get him back. Filmed in New Mexico. **89m/C VHS, DVD.** David Carradine, Frank Zagarino, Drew Snyder, Hilary English, Vivian Schilling; *D:* H. Kaye Dyal; *W:* H. Kaye Dyal, Morris Asgar; *C:* Gerry Lively; *M:* Jon McCallum.

Project: Genesis 1/2 **1993** Pascal and a beautiful Alien Woman are shipwrecked on a desolate planet in the 23rd century. As they watch the worlds around them clash in war, they know it is up to them to create a new beginning at the end of the Universe. **79m/C VHS.** David Ferry, Olga Prokhorova; *D:* Philip Jackson; *W:* Philip Jackson; *M:* Andy McNeill.

Project: Kill! **1977** Head of a murder-for-hire squad suddenly disappears and his former assistant is hired to track him down dead or alive. **94m/C VHS, DVD.** Leslie Nielsen, Gary Lockwood, Nancy Kwan, Vic Silayan, Vic Diaz, Donald G. Thompson; *D:* William Girdler; *W:* Donald G. Thompson; *C:* Frank Johnson; *M:* Robert O. Ragland.

Project Metalbeast: DNA Overload 1/2 **1994 (R)** A CIA agent, cryogenically frozen for 10 years, becomes the guinea pig when a group of scientists decide to unthaw him for a DNA experiment involving living metallic skin. Too bad he turns into a metal beast by the light of the full moon. Sci-fi take on the werewolf saga. **92m/C VHS.** Kim Delaney, Barry Bostwick; *D:* Allessandro DeGaetano; *W:* Timothy E. Sabo; *M:* Conrad Pope.

Project Moon Base 1/2 **1953** Espionage runs rampant on a spaceship headed by a female officer. Eventually the ship is stranded on the moon. Actually filmed for the TV series "Ring Around the Moon." A cold-war sexist relic. **64m/B VHS, DVD.** Donna (Dona Martel) Martell, Hayden Rorke, Ross Ford, Larry Johns, Herb Jacobs; *D:* Richard Talmadge; *W:* Robert Heinlein, Jack Seaman; *C:* William C. Thompson; *M:* Herschel Burke Gilbert. **TV**

Project: Nightmare 1/2 **1985** Seems not all dreams are wish fulfillment, when these nightmares start coming true. **75m/C VHS.** Elly Koslo, Lance Dickson; *D:* Donald M. Jones.

Project: Shadowchaser 1/2 **1992 (R)** Action-packed would-be thriller about a billion dollar android who escapes from a top secret government laboratory. Programmed with superhuman strength and no human emotions the android and five terrorists take over a hospital (located in a skyscraper no less). Their hostages include the President's daughter and the terrorists demand a $150 million ransom. With a four-hour deadline the FBI calls in the hospital architect to advise them—only they've got the wrong man—and the android's creator, who wants his creation back—no matter what the cost. A low-budget Terminator clone. **97m/C VHS.** Martin Kove, Meg Foster, Frank Zagarino, Paul Koslo, Joss Ackland; *D:* John Eyres.

Project Shadowchaser 3000 1/2 **1995 (R)** Deep space satellite station collides with a mining vessel carrying a killer android. The seven surviving crew are then hunted by the android as the ship's nuclear core is also threatening to explode. **99m/C VHS.** Frank Zagarino, Sam Bottoms, Christopher Atkins, Musetta Vander, Christopher Neame; *D:* John Eyres; *W:* Nick Davis; *M:* Stephen (Steve) Edwards.

Project Vampire 1/2 **1993** Vampire concocts a serum that will change humans into vampires within three days. His first guinea pig fights to stop the evil from succeeding. **90m/C VHS, DVD.** Brian Knudson, Mary-Louise Gemmill, Christopher Cho, Myron Natwick; *D:* Peter Flynn.

Project X 1/2 **1987 (PG)** A bemused Air Force pilot is assigned to a special project involving chimpanzees. He must decide where his duty lies when he realizes the semi-intelligent chimps are slated to die. **107m/C VHS, DVD.** Matthew Broderick, Helen Hunt, William Sadler, Johnny Rae McGhee, Jonathan Stark, Robin Gammell, Stephen Lang, Jean Smart, Dick Miller; *D:* Jonathan Kaplan; *W:* Stanley Weiser, Lawrence Lasker; *C:* Dean Cundey; *M:* James Horner.

The Projectionist **1971 (PG)** A must-see for movie buffs, Dangerfield made his screen debut in this story about a projectionist in a seedy movie house whose real-life existence begins to blur into the films he continuously watches. Made on a limited budget, this creative effort by Hurwitz was the first film to utilize the technique of superimposition. **84m/C VHS, DVD.** Rodney Dangerfield, Chuck McCann, Ina Balin, Jara Kohout, Harry Hurwitz, Stephen Phillips, Clara Rosenthal, Jacquelyn Glenn, Robert Staats; *D:* Harry Hurwitz; *W:* Harry Hurwitz; *C:* Victor Petrashevich; *M:* Igo Kantor, Erma E. Levin.

Prom Night **1980 (R)** A masked killer stalks four high school girls during their senior prom as revenge for a murder which occurred six years prior. Sequelled by "Hello Mary Lou: Prom Night 2," "Prom Night 3: The Last Kiss," and "Prom Night 4: Deliver Us from Evil." **91m/C VHS, DVD.** *CA* Jamie Lee Curtis, Leslie Nielsen, Casey Stevens, Eddie Benton, Antoinette Bower, Michael Tough, Pita Oliver, David Mucci, Joy Thompson, Mary Beth Rubens; *D:* Paul Lynch; *W:* William Gray; *C:* Robert New; *M:* Paul Zaza.

Prom Night **2008 (PG-13)** Scream, run, die. Director McCormick's feature debut is a watered-down but slick sorta remake of the R-rated 1980 slasher with Snow a merely adequate substitute in the Jamie Lee Curtis scream queen role. Donna's (Snow) family was slain by obsessed teacher Richard Fenton (Schaech) and, three years later, he's escaped from prison to finish his work while Donna and her friends party in their hotel suite on prom night. **88m/C DVD.** *US* Brittany Snow, Johnathon Schaech, Idris Elba, Dana Davis, Jessica Stroup, Scott Porter, Collins Pennie, Kelly Blatz; *D:* Nelson McCormick; *W:* J.S. Cardone; *C:* Checco Varese; *M:* Paul Haslinger.

Prom Night 3: The Last Kiss **1989 (R)** The second sequel, in which the reappearing high school ghoul beguiles a lucky teenager. **97m/C VHS, DVD.** Tim Conlon, Cynthia (Cyndy, Cindy) Preston, Courtney Taylor, David Stratton, Dylan Neal, Jeremy Ratchford; *D:* Ron Oliver, Peter Simpson; *W:* Ron Oliver; *C:* Rhett Morita.

Prom Night 4: Deliver Us from Evil **1991 (R)** Yet another gory entry in the Prom series (one would hope it will be the last). Another group of naive teens decide that they can have more fun at a private party than at the prom. They host the party in a summer home that was once a monastery, but the festive affair soon turns into a night of terror when an uninvited guest crashes the party. For true fans of slasher flicks. **95m/C VHS, DVD.** *CA* Nikki de Boer, Alden Kane, Joy Tanner, Alle Ghadban, James Carver; *D:* Clay Borris; *W:* Richard Beattie.

Prom Queen **2004** Based on the actual 2002 Canadian Supreme Court case of Ontario gay teen Marc Hall (Ashmore). An out blue-haired rebel in a small town who attends Catholic school, Marc is a popular student who only wants to take his boyfriend Jason (Fyfe) to the senior prom. When he's denied by the homophobic school board, Marc and his lawyer (Thompson) decide to sue the Catholic Church for discrimination. **92m/C DVD.** *CA* Dave Foley, Tamara Hope, Fiona Reid, Aaron Ashmore, Scott Thompson, Mak Fyfe, Marie Tifo, Peter Zabriskie, Victoria Adilman; *D:* John L'Ecuyer; *W:* Kent Staines; *C:* Glenn Warner; *M:* Gary Koftinoff. **TV**

The Promise 1/2 *Face of a Stranger* **1979 (PG)** Weepie outdated story about star-crossed lovers Michael (Collins) and Nancy (Quinlan). A car accident leaves Michael comatose and Nancy badly disfigured. Michael's mother (Straight), who loathes Nancy, sees her chance to finally break them up. She offers to pay for Nancy's plastic surgery if she'll leave Michael forever, then Mom tells her son his girlfriend's dead. A year later Nancy, with her new face and new identity, and Michael meet. From the novel by Danielle Steele. **97m/C VHS.** Stephen Collins, Kathleen Quinlan, Beatrice Straight, Laurence Luckinbill, William Prince, Michael O'Hare; *D:* Gilbert Cates; *W:* Garry Michael White; *M:* David Shire.

The Promise 1/2 *Das Versprechen* **1994 (R)** Young lovers Konrad (Zoller and Zirner) and Sophie (Harfouch and Becker) find themselves separated by the Berlin Wall after a botched escape attempt in 1961. The estranged lovers meet only four times during the next three decades as they adjust to the systems under which they're forced to live. Somewhat contrived and cliched, this bittersweet romance uses Konrad and Sophie as symbols of the social and political turmoil and triumphs of the divided Germany. Received some criticism from East Germans who found the film's severe portrayal of Communist rule too harsh. Gets points for being the first post-fall film to explore the Wall's legacy. **115m/C VHS.** *GE* Corinna Harfouch, Meret Becker, August Zirner, Anian Zollner, Jean-Yves Gautier, Eva Mattes, Suzanne Uge, Hans Kremer, Pierre Besson, Tina Engel, Otto Sander, Hark Bohm; *D:* Margarethe von Trotta; *W:* Peter Schneider, Margarethe von Trotta; *C:* Franz Rath; *M:* Jurgen Knieper.

The Promise 1/2 *Wu Ji; Master of the Crimson Armor* **2005 (PG-13)** Complicated and stylized martial arts fantasy in which a young orphan is offered a life of riches by a goddess (Hong) with the caveat that she will lose every man she loves. Qingcheng (Cheung) lives with her bargain until she falls for General Guangming (Sanada), he of the crimson armor. Except it was his slave, Kunlun (Dong-Gun), who was wearing the armor and actually rescued the princess. Never really makes any sense (at least to Westerners). Mandarin with subtitles; also released at 121 minutes. **103m/C DVD.** *CH US* Hiroyuki (Henry) Sanada, Dong-Kun Jang, Cecilia Cheung, Nicholas Tse, Liu Yeh, Chen Hong, Qian Bo, Yu Xiaowei, Cheng Qian; *D:* Chen Kaige, Zhang Tan; *W:* Chen Kaige; *C:* Peter Pau; *M:* Klaus Badelt.

Promise Her Anything **1966** A widow (Caron) with a baby decides to make her boss (Cummings), a child psychologist who hates kids, her new husband. So she stashes the kid with her upstairs neighbor (Beatty), a would-be filmmaker who earns his living making blue movies. But the filmmaker has romantic designs on the widow and decides the baby may be his way to make a good impression. Beatty isn't very believable in this type of light-romantic comedy and the farcical situations are forced. **98m/C VHS.** *GB* Warren Beatty, Leslie Caron, Robert Cummings, Hermione Gingold, Lionel Stander, Keenan Wynn, Cathleen Nesbitt; *D:* Arthur Hiller; *W:* William Peter Blatty.

Promise to Murder 1/2 **1956** An early murder-drama episode from the "Climax" TV series. **60m/B VHS.** Peter Lorre, Louis Hayward, Ann Harding.

Promised a Miracle 1/2 **1988 (PG)** Based on the true story of a religious couple who sought help for their diabetic son through prayer rather than conventional medical means. Following the boy's death in 1974, the couple were charged with manslaughter. From the non-fiction account "We Let Our Son Die" by Larry Parker. **94m/C VHS.** Rosanna Arquette, Judge Reinhold, Tom Bower, Gary Bayer, Maria O'Brien, Giovanni Ribisi; *D:* Stephen Gyllenhaal; *W:* David Hill; *C:* Thomas Burstyn. **TV**

Promised Land *Young Hearts* **1988 (R)** Two high school friends from the rural northwestern U.S. come together several years after graduation under tragic circumstances. Writer Hoffman's semi-autobiographical, disillusioned look at the American Dream was re-discovered by movie goers due to its excellent dramatic performances, notable also as the first film produced by Robert Redford's Sundance Institute. **110m/C VHS, DVD.** Kiefer Sutherland, Meg Ryan, Tracy Pollan, Jason Gedrick, Googy Gress, Deborah Richter, Sandra Seacat, Jay Underwood, Oscar Rowland; *D:* Michael Hoffman; *W:* Michael Hoffman; *M:* James Newton Howard.

Promises in the Dark 1/2 **1979 (PG)** Drama focusing on the complex relationship between a woman doctor and her 17-year-old female patient who is terminally ill with cancer. Hellman's directorial debut. **118m/C VHS.** Marsha Mason, Ned Beatty, Kathleen Beller, Susan Clark, Paul Clemens, Donald Moffat, Michael Brandon; *D:* Jerome Hellman.

Promises! Promises! 1/2 *Promise Her Anything* **1963** Having difficulty getting pregnant, a woman goes on a cruise with her husband. While on board, they meet another couple, all get drunk, and change partners. Of course, both women find themselves pregnant, leaving the paternity in doubt. Famous primarily as the movie Mansfield told "Playboy" magazine she appeared "completely nude" in. **90m/B VHS, DVD.** Jayne Mansfield, Marie McDonald, Tommy Noonan, Fritz Feld, Claude Stroud, Mickey Hargitay, Marjorie Bennett, Vic Lundin; *D:* King Donovan; *W:* William Welch, Tommy Noonan; *C:* Joseph Biroc.

The Promoter *The Card* **1952** Horatio Alger comedy stars Guinness as an impoverished student who gives himself a surreptitious leg up in life by altering his school entrance exam scores. Outstanding performances enliven this subtle British comedy of morals. **87m/B VHS.** *GB* Alec Guinness, Glynis Johns, Petula Clark, Valerie Hobson, Michael Hordern; *D:* Ronald Neame; *W:* Eric Ambler.

The Promotion 2008 (R) Murky comedy focusing on two down-and-out supermarket employees desperate to win the managerial spot at a new store. Doug (Scott) is convinced he'll get the promotion and invests all his money in a non-refundable deposit on a new house, while Richard (Reilly), a recovering addict, fights for the position to prove to his wife he's a trustworthy husband and father. A human story at its core, but only mildly amusing as a comedy. Reilly and Scott are good, but never seem to find their groove. Directorial debut for writer Conrad, who penned "The Pursuit of Happyness." **85m/C DVD.** *US* Seann William Scott, John C. Reilly, Jenna Fischer, Lili Taylor, Fred Armisen, Gil Bellows, Bobby Cannavale, Rick Gonzalez, Chris Conrad; ***D:*** Steve Conrad; ***W:*** Steve Conrad; ***C:*** Lawrence Sher; ***M:*** Alex Wurman.

Pronto 1/2 **1997 (R)** Semi-retired bookie Harry Arno (Falk) is forced to head out of Miami when his mobster boss realizes Harry's been skimming. So he takes off for the Italian Riviera with ex-stripper girlfriend Joyce (Headly), while being trailed by doofus U.S. Marshal Raylan Givens (LeGros), who's trying to keep Harry alive so the feds can get his testimony against his gangster cohorts. Falk's gruff, Headly's smart, LeGros is a laugh, and the movie's vivid since it's taken from Elmore Leonard's 1993 novel. **100m/C VHS.** Peter Falk, Glenne Headly, James LeGros, Sergio Castellitto, Bradford Tatum, Walter Olkewicz, Glenn Plummer, Luis Guzman; ***D:*** Jim McBride; ***W:*** Michael Butler; ***C:*** Alfonso Beato; ***M:*** John Altman. **CABLE**

Proof **1991 (R)** Directorial debut of Moorhouse tells a tale of manipulation, friendship, and obsessive love between a blind photographer, Martin, his housekeeper, and the young man he befriends. Martin, mistrustful of the world around him, takes photographs as "proof" of the reality of his life. A chance meeting with Andy provides Martin with his "eyes" and the opportunity to expand his world and emotions—something his housekeeper, Celia, would be only too happy to help him with. Unhealthy triangle leads all three to a re-evaluation of their lives. Propelled by terrific performances and enough humor to balance its emotional content. **90m/C VHS, DVD.** *AU* Hugo Weaving, Genevieve Picot, Russell Crowe, Heather Mitchell, Jeffrey Walker, Frank Gallacher; ***D:*** Jocelyn Moorhouse; ***W:*** Jocelyn Moorhouse. Australian Film Inst. '91: Actor (Weaving), Director (Moorhouse), Film, Film Editing, Screenplay, Support. Actor (Crowe).

Proof 1/2 **2005 (PG-13)** Film adaptation of David Auburn's award-winning Broadway play makes the most of its four-character construct. Catherine (Paltrow), the gifted daughter of a once-brilliant mathematician (Hopkins), who in the final years of his life suffered with dementia, sits at the center of the film. A brainy introvert by nature, Catherine is forced in the wake of her father's death to seek redeeming personal value as both an academic and a daughter, while contemplating her own fragile grip on sanity. **99m/C DVD.** *US* Gwyneth Paltrow, Anthony Hopkins, Jake Gyllenhaal, Hope Davis, Roshan Seth, Gary Houston; ***D:*** John Madden; ***W:*** David Auburn; ***C:*** Alwin Kuchler; ***M:*** Stephen Warbeck.

Proof of Life 1/2 **2000 (R)** When Alicia's (Ryan) engineer husband (Morse) is kidnapped by anti-government guerrillas in South America, she hires professional negotiator Terry Thorne (Crowe) to get him back. Complications arise when Terry falls for the wife. Complications also arose when Ryan fell for Crowe and her marriage to Dennis Quaid fell apart. Crowe and Ryan subsequently broke up just in time for the marketing push, leaving director Hackford without his two biggest stars to promote the film. Despite the offscreen heat, the movie's a lot better when dealing with the husband's predicament and the rescue operations than when exploring Ryan's angst and the budding romance. **135m/C VHS, DVD.** Russell Crowe, Meg Ryan, David Morse, David Caruso, Pamela Reed, Anthony Heald, Stanley Anderson, Gottfried John, Alun Armstrong, Michael Kitchen, Margo Martindale, Mario Ernesto Sanchez, Pietro Sibille, Vicky Hernandez, Norma Martinez, Diego Trujillo; ***D:*** Taylor Hackford; ***W:*** Tony Gilroy; ***C:*** Slawomir Idziak; ***M:*** Danny Elfman.

Proof of the Man **1977** A Japanese co-production about a murder in Tokyo that takes on international importance. **100m/C VHS.** *JP* George Kennedy, Broderick Crawford, Toshiro Mifune; ***D:*** Junya Sato; ***W:*** Zenzo Matsuyama; ***C:*** Sinsaku Himeda; ***M:*** Yuji Ono.

Prophecy 1/2 **1979 (PG)** A doctor and his wife travel to Maine to research the effects of pollution caused by the lumber industry. They encounter several terrifying freaks of nature and a series of bizarre human deaths. Laughable horror film. **102m/C VHS, DVD.** Talia Shire, Robert Foxworth, Armand Assante, Victoria Racimo, Richard Dysart, George Clutesi; ***D:*** John Frankenheimer; ***W:*** David Seltzer; ***C:*** Harry Stradling Jr.

The Prophecy 1/2 **1995 (R)** Modern variation of "Paradise Lost" carries a heavy load including possession, Native American mythology, and Walken as the archangel Gabriel. Not surprisingly, it stumbles under the weight. Gabriel is at odds with good angel Simon (Stolz) over the souls of humans, a battle that has its final showdown in a small Arizona community and crosses the paths of homicide detective Thomas Dagget (Koteas) and school teacher Katherine (Madsen). Successfully mixes humor and horror, but biblical jargon can lose horror fans just looking for a cheap thrill. Directorial debut of screenwriter Widen. **97m/C VHS, DVD.** Christopher Walken, Eric Stoltz, Elias Koteas, Virginia Madsen, Amanda Plummer, Viggo Mortensen; ***D:*** Gregory Widen; ***W:*** Gregory Widen; ***C:*** Bruce Douglas Johnson, Richard Clabaugh; ***M:*** David Williams.

The Prophecy 2: Ashtown 1/2 **1997 (R)** It's post-apocalyptic L.A. and power-hungry fallen angel Gabriel (Walken) returns from hell to stop the creation of a half-human/half-angelic child who's prophesized as the new savior of mankind. Angel Danyael (Wong) is intended as the dad while nurse Valerie (Beals) is the woman chosen as the mother. The good guys get some help from angel Michael (Roberts). Lots of action and good special effects, though viewers who haven't seen the first film may be confused. **83m/C VHS, DVD.** Christopher Walken, Russell Wong, Eric Roberts, Jennifer Beals, Bruce Abbott, Brittany Murphy, Steve Hytner, Glenn Danzig; ***D:*** Greg Spence; ***W:*** Greg Spence, Matt Greenberg; ***C:*** Richard Clabaugh; ***M:*** David Williams. **VIDEO**

The Prophecy 3: The Ascent **1999 (R)** Half-human/half-angel Danyael (Buzzotta) has grown up to be an anti-religious street preacher and is out to destroy new angel, Piriel (Cleverdon). This doesn't sit well with angel Zophael (Spano) who decides to stop him. Walken seems to be having the most fun as he once again appears as Gabriel, who's become content in his mortal guise and with human pleasure. **83m/C VHS, DVD.** Christopher Walken, Vincent Spano, Brad Dourif, Dave Buzzotta, Steve Hytner, Scott Cleverdon, Kayren Ann Butler; ***D:*** Patrick Lussier; ***W:*** Joel Soisson, Carl DuPre; ***C:*** Nathan Hope. **VIDEO**

A Prophet *Un Prophete* **2009 (R)** Audiard's powerful coming-of-age prison drama finds illiterate, 19-year-old French-Arab Malik (Rahim) sentenced to six years in prison, which is where he truly gets his education in life in a continual effort to survive. Malik is forced by Cesar Luciani (Arestrup), the Corsican crime boss who runs one of the two prison gangs, to kill a fellow Arab. He does so but is still regarded as an outsider by both the Corsicans and the prison's Muslim bloc. However, Malik is nothing if not a quick study and gradually gains some power of his own as the time passes. French, Arabic, and Corsican with subtitles. **155m/C DVD.** *FR IT* Niels Arestrup, Tahar Rahim, Adel Bencherif, Gilles Cohen, Antoine Basler, Reda Kateb, Hichem Yacoubi, Jean-Philippe Ricci, Pierre Leccia; ***D:*** Jacques Audiard; ***W:*** Jacques Audiard, Thomas Bidegain; ***C:*** Stephane Fontaine; ***M:*** Alexandre Desplot. British Acad. '09: Foreign Film.

The Prophet's Game **1999 (R)** Retired Seattle detective Vincent Swan (Hopper) gets a message from the Prophet, a serial killer that Swan supposedly killed years before. Then new victims turn up in L.A., killed in the Prophet's distinctive manner. So Swan heads south to help with the investigation and figure out is he dealing with a copycat—or did he just kill the wrong man? **107m/C VHS, DVD.** Dennis Hopper, Geoffrey Lewis, Stephanie Zimbalist, Joe Penny, Greg Lauren, Shannon Whirry, Michael Dorn, Don Swayze, Robert Ginty, Sondra Locke; ***D:*** David Worth; ***W:*** Carol Chrest; ***C:*** David Worth. **VIDEO**

The Proposal 1/2 **2000 (R)** Moran is an undercover cop who's forced to take on partner Esposito, who has no such experience, because he needs someone to pose as his wife in order to trap crime boss Lang. Only Esposito and Lang are starting to get a little too friendly, so Moran wonders how much she can be trusted. **90m/C VHS, DVD.** Nick Moran, Jennifer Esposito, Stephen Lang, William B. Davis; ***D:*** Richard Gale; ***W:*** Maurice Hurley; ***C:*** Curtis Petersen; ***M:*** Joseph Conlan.

The Proposal 1/2 **2009 (PG-13)** Tyrannical New York book editor Margaret Tate (Bullock) has overstayed her visa and is going to be deported back to Canada. She decides on a green card marriage to her put-upon younger assistant Andrew Paxton (Reynolds). Andrew agrees, in exchange for a promotion, although immigration official Gilbertson (O'Hare) is suspicious. To make things look good, Andrew takes Margaret to meet his wealthy family in Sitka, Alaska so they can celebrate his wacky grandma Annie's (White) 90th birthday and tell his parents (Nelson, Steenburgen) the news. Familiar rom-com situations are given a light touch by director Fletcher through likeable leads (and their chemistry together) as well as pro supporting players. **107m/C DVD.** *US* Sandra Bullock, Ryan Reynolds, Craig T. Nelson, Mary Steenburgen, Betty White, Denis O'Hare, Malin Akerman, Osmar Nunez, Michael Nouri, Aasif Mandvi; ***D:*** Anne Fletcher; ***W:*** Peter Chiarelli; ***C:*** Oliver Stapleton; ***M:*** Aaron Zigman.

The Proposition 1/2 **1996 (R)** Unless widow Catherine Morgan (Russell) can find the money to pay her late husband's gambling debts, she and her two daughters will be evicted from their Welsh farm. She refuses to take the easy way and marry local sheriff Huw (Lynch), instead making a bargain with his rakish, drunken bastard brother Rhys (Bergin) to drive her cattle to Gloucester market. Huw takes exception to this plan and tries every dirty trick he can to thwart them and naturally, Catherine and Rhys become more than antagonistic allies along the rough journey. **99m/C VHS, DVD.** Theresa Russell, Patrick Bergin, Richard Lynch, Richard Harrington, Jennifer Vaughan, Ifan Huw Dafydd, Nick McGaughey, Owen Garmon; ***D:*** Strathford Hamilton; ***W:*** Paul Matthews; ***C:*** David Lewis; ***M:*** Ben Heneghan, Ian Lawson.

The Proposition *Tempting Fate; Shakespeare's Sister* **1997 (R)** Convoluted and clunky story centering on wealthy-but-sterile Boston industrialist Hurt and his feminist writer wife Stowe, who decide to hire a surrogate (Harris) to get Stowe pregnant. But faltering priest Branagh, whom the couple consult, has some concerns. After the surrogate is murdered, the melodrama starts to fly and the movie plays out like a daytime soap opera, complete with dirty little secrets and earth-shaking revelations dropped with the sublety usually reserved for an anvil on Wile E. Coyote. Hurt and Stowe give their characters a little fire, but everybody else seems to be wandering around on their own little acting planet. **115m/C VHS, DVD.** Pamela Hart, Kenneth Branagh, William Hurt, Madeleine Stowe, Blythe Danner, Neil Patrick Harris, Robert Loggia, Josef Sommer, David Byrd; ***D:*** Leslie Linka Glatter; ***W:*** Rick Ramage; ***C:*** Peter Sova; ***M:*** Stephen Endelman.

The Proposition **2005 (R)** Brutal Aussie western set in the outback in the 1880s. Capt. Stanley (Winstone) is obsessed with bringing law to his patch of dirt, which means getting rid of the Burns brothers and their gang. He gets a break when he captures Charlie Burns (Pearce) and his younger brother, Mikey (Wilson). Stanley offers Charlie a devil's bargain—he will spare both brothers if Charlie will track and kill vicious older brother Arthur (a poetically psychotic Huston). Charlie has no choice but to agree but all that can be expected is more violence, blood, and death. **104m/C DVD, Blu-ray Disc.** *AU GB* Guy Pearce, Ray Winstone, Emily Watson, Danny Huston, John Hurt, David Wenham, Noah Taylor, David Gulpilil, Leah Purcell, Tommy (Tom E.) Lewis, Richard Wilson; ***D:*** John Hillcoat; ***W:*** Nick Cave; ***C:*** Benoit Delhomme; ***M:*** Warren Ellis.

The Proprietor **1996 (R)** Thinly disguised as a returning-to-your-roots and facing-your-ghosts drama, film is actually a celluloid shrine to its Gallic star, the legendary Moreau, who plays a legendary Gallic novelist, Adrienne Mark. Mark, after residing in New York for 30 years, reclaims her Jewish identity and returns to Paris to buy the home in which she grew up with her mother, who was killed in WWII. Famous for writing the novel "Call Me French," which became a highly acclaimed French film and a current American remake, Mark's primary struggle to come to grips with her mother's death is overshadowed by a bevy of subplots that compete with one another. Young as a sassy and somewhat stereotypical Hollywood producer; Carter as Milly the loyal housekeeper; Waterston, an antique dealer; and Billy, NYC video artist and adoring Mark fan, all add to the confusion. Moreau tries her best to give life to the saintly lead figure, but the coma-inducing sugar level of her character's goodness is overwhelming. Director Merchant's sophomore effort, though well-acted, is a good idea, poorly told. **105m/C VHS.** Jeanne Moreau, Sean Young, Sam Waterston, Nell Carter, Austin Pendleton, Pierre Vaneck, Christopher Cazenove, Jean-Pierre Aumont, Josh Hamilton, Marc Tissot; ***D:*** Ismail Merchant; ***W:*** Jean-Marie Besset, George Trow; ***C:*** Larry Pizer; ***M:*** Richard Robbins.

Pros & Cons **1999 (R)** Opposites help each other out as new cellmates Davidson and Miller (both doing time for crimes they didn't commit) bumble their way into the good graces of convict kingpin Lindo. **103m/C VHS, DVD.** Larry Miller, Tommy Davidson, Delroy Lindo; ***D:*** Boris Damast; ***W:*** Larry Miller; ***C:*** Jonathan Brown; ***M:*** Michel Colombier.

Prospero's Books **1991 (R)** Greenaway's free-ranging adaptation of Shakespeare's "The Tempest" has all his usual hallmarks of the bizarre. Gielgud is the aged Propsero, exiled to a magical island with his innocent daughter Miranda, and 24 beloved books containing the magician's recipe for life, each of which becomes a separate chapter in the film. Greenaway mixes film and high-definition video to create, with cinematographer Sacha Vierny, dazzling visuals that threaten to overwhelm but don't quite, thanks to both Greenaway's skill and the astonishing performance of the then 87-year-old Gielgud. **129m/C VHS.** John Gielgud, Michel Blanc, Erland Josephson, Isabelle Pasco, Tom Bell, Kenneth Cranham, Michael Clark, Mark Rylance; ***D:*** Peter Greenaway; ***W:*** Peter Greenaway; ***C:*** Sacha Vierny; ***M:*** Michael Nyman.

Protecting the King **2007** When he was four, David Stanley's mother married widower Vernon Presley and the boy became Elvis's (Dobson) stepbrother. In 1972, David (Barr) began working as the singer's bodyguard until Presley's death five years later. In this biographical take, David witnesses the King's ever-increasing drug use and watches hopelessly as the singer's life spirals downward. **90m/C DVD.** Peter Dobson, John Bennett Perry, Tom Sizemore, Brian Krause, Matt Barr, Max Perlich, Mark Rolston, Dey Young; ***D:*** David Edward Stanley; ***W:*** David Edward Stanley; ***C:*** Philip Lee; ***M:*** Joe Cruz.

Protection 1/2 **2001 (R)** Mobster Sal (Baldwin) and his family are relocated into the witness protection program and Sal gets a job with real estate broker Ted (Gallagher), who's putting together a low-income housing project. But Sal can't resist using his past and brings in local crime boss Lujack (Tager) to finance the deal. **97m/C VHS, DVD.** Stephen Baldwin, Peter Gallagher, Katie Griffin, Deborah Odell, Vlasta Vrana, Aron Tager; ***D:*** John Flynn; ***W:*** Jack Kelly; ***C:*** Marc Charlebois; ***M:*** Richard (Rick) Marvin. **VIDEO**

Protector **1985 (R)** A semi-martial arts cops 'n' robbers epic about the cracking of a Hong Kong-New York heroin route. **94m/C VHS, DVD.** Jackie Chan, Danny Aiello; ***D:*** James Glickenhaus.

Protector *Valentine's Day* **1997 (R)** Undercover cop Jack Valentine (Van Peebles) is supposed to be protecting a witness, who winds up being murdered. The cop is given 10 days to solve the crime or lose his badge. **97m/C VHS, DVD.** Mario Van

Peebles, Randy Quaid, Rae Dawn Chong, Ben Gazzara; *D:* Duane Clark. **VIDEO**

Proteus **1995 (R)** Survivors of a boat wreck wash up on an off-shore oil rig that's actually a secret lab financed by loony millionaire Brinkstone (Bradley), who's seeking immortality. His DNA experiments have led to the creation of a disgusting parasite that travels from body to body. Naturally, the boat survivors also seek to survive this latest health threat. Based on the novel "Slimer" by Harry Adam Knight. **97m/C VHS.** *GB* Doug Bradley, Craig Fairbrass, Toni Barry; *D:* Bob Keen.

Protocol **1984 (PG)** A series of comic accidents lead a Washington cocktail waitress into the U.S. State Department's employ as a protocol official. Once there she is used as a pawn to make an arms deal with a Middle Eastern country. Typical Hawn comedy with an enjoyable ending. **100m/C VHS, DVD.** Goldie Hawn, Chris Sarandon, Andre Gregory, Cliff DeYoung, Ed Begley Jr., Gail Strickland, Richard Romanus, Keith Szarabajka, James Staley, Kenneth Mars, Kenneth McMillan, Archie Hahn, Amanda Bearse; *D:* Herbert Ross; *W:* Nancy Meyers, Harvey Miller, Charles Shyer, Buck Henry; *C:* William A. Fraker; *M:* Basil Poledouris.

Protocols of Zion **2005** Filmmaker Levin structures his documentary around "The Protocols of the Elders of Zion," a 19th-century screed that purports to reveal a Jewish plan to rule the world. Although exposed as a forgery (written by aides to the Russian czar to foment anti-Semitism), extremists of all persuasions still use the material for their own agendas. Levin examines recent examples of anti-Semitic propaganda, including the ridiculous belief that Jews were behind 9/11, and quizzes a wide variety of interviewees from skinheads to Holocaust survivors. **92m/C DVD.** *US D:* Marc Levin; *C:* Mark Benjamin; *M:* John Zorn.

Prototype **1983** TV revision of the Frankenstein legend has award-winning scientist Plummer as the creator of the first android. Fearful of the use the military branch of government has in mind for his creation, he attempts to steal back his discovery, in this suspenseful adventure. **100m/C VHS, DVD.** Christopher Plummer, David Morse, Frances Sternhagen, James Sutorius; *D:* David Greene; *M:* Billy Goldenberg. **TV**

Prototype X29A 1/2 **1992 (R)** The year is 2057 in a desolate, lawless Los Angeles. A research scientist is conducting experiments on a crippled ex-soldier named Hawkins when they suddenly go awry, turning him into a half-man, half-machine robot. Known as Prototype, the creature goes on a hunting and killing spree. Lame "Terminator" & "Robocop" takeoff. **98m/C VHS.** Brenda Swanson, Robert Tossberg, Lane Lenhart; *D:* Phillip J. Roth; *W:* Phillip J. Roth.

The Proud and the Damned *Proud, Damned, and Dead* **1972 (PG)** Five Civil-War-veteran mercenaries wander into a Latin American war and get manipulated by both sides. **95m/C VHS, DVD.** Chuck Connors, Aron Kincaid, Cesar Romero; *D:* Ferde Grofe Jr.

The Proud Family Movie **2005 (G)** The Disney Channel's original television series featuring an animated African American family gets a feature-length storyline. Teenager Penny Proud's parents treat her like a kid, banning her from dancing in a hip-hop half time show and dragging her off to a tropical island for a family vacation. The family finds themselves in trouble when their "vacation" turns out to be an excuse for the evil Dr. Carver to get his hands on dad's hot sauce recipe. Hijinks abound as Penny saves the recipe-and the day. Short enough to sit through with most pre-teens. **91m/C VHS, DVD.** *D:* Bruce Smith; *W:* Calvin Brown Jr.; *M:* Elik Alvarez; *V:* Kyla Pratt, Tommy Davidson, Paula Jai Parker, Soleil Moon Frye, Omari (Omarion) Grandberry, Arsenio Hall, Orlando Brown, Jo Maria Payton. **CABLE**

Proud Men **1987** A cattle rancher and his expatriate son are separated by bitterness toward each other. Good acting from Heston and Strauss, and good action sequences, but ordinary script. **95m/C VHS.** Charlton Heston, Peter Strauss, Nan Martin, Alan Autry, Belinda Balaski, Red West; *D:* William A. Graham.

The Proud Ones 1/2 *Les Orgueilleux* **1953** An aristocratic French woman and her husband are traveling through Mexico when he suddenly dies of a mysterious illness. Left penniless in a decaying seaside town, she falls for the local doctor who is mourning the death of his wife. Adaptation of the Satre novel "L'Amour Redempteur." In French with English subtitles. **105m/B VHS.** *FR* Gerard Philipe, Michele Morgan, Victor Manuel Mendoza; *D:* Yves Allegret.

Proud Rebel **1958** A character study of a stubborn widower who searches for a doctor to aid him in dealing with the problems of his mute son, and of the woman who helps to tame the boy. Ladd's real-life son makes his acting debut. **99m/C VHS, DVD.** Alan Ladd, Olivia de Havilland, Dean Jagger, Harry Dean Stanton; *D:* Michael Curtiz; *W:* Lillie Hayward, Joseph Petracca; *C:* Ted D. McCord; *M:* Jerome Moross.

Providence **1977 (R)** An interesting score highlights this British fantasy drama of a dying writer envisioning his final novel as a fusion of the people from his past with the circumstances he encounters on a daily basis. The first English-language effort by French director Resnais. **104m/C VHS.** *GB* John Gielgud, Dirk Bogarde, Ellen Burstyn, David Warner, Elaine Stritch; *D:* Alain Resnais; *W:* David Mercer; *C:* Ricardo Aronovich; *M:* Miklos Rozsa. Cesar '78: Art Dir./Set Dec., Director (Resnais), Film, Sound, Writing, Score; N.Y. Film Critics '77: Actor (Gielgud).

Provincial Actors **1979** Ambitious Christopher is the leading actor of a rural theatre troupe, who dreams of moving to the city and becoming a star. But his wife Anna is fed up with his dreams and leaves him and Christopher must make a choice between his career and his marriage. Polish with subtitles. **104m/C VHS.** *PL* Tadeysz Huk, Halina Labonarska, Ewa Dalkowska, Jerzy Stuhr; *D:* Agnieszka Holland.

Provocateur *Agent Provocateur* **1996 (R)** Story revolves around the 1994 power struggle in North Korea. Spy Sook Hee (March), with close ties to dictator Kim Il Sung, takes a job as a nanny in South Korea in order to get access to sensitive info from her boss, a U.S. colonel. But her loyalties are torn when she befriends her young charge and then falls in love with the colonel's teenaged son Chris (Brancato). When her true identity is revealed, there's trouble for all. **104m/C VHS.** Jane March, Nick Mancuso, Lillo Brancato, Cary-Hiroyuki Tagawa; *D:* Jim Donovan.

Provoked 1/2 **1989** What would you do if your husband were being held hostage by a gang of ruthless, but stupid, escaped cons? Well, Maranne actually wants her husband back (maybe 'cause they're newleyweds) and no by-the-book police chief (Jones) is gonna stop her. This bride gets her hands on some automatic weaponry and look out! Shot in eight days with a $130,000 budget. **90m/C VHS.** Cindy Maranne, McKeiver Jones III, Harold W. Jones, Sharon Blair, Bob Fall, Joe Sprosty, Phyllis Durant, Tara Untiedt; *D:* Rick Pamplin; *W:* Tara Untiedt, Steve Pake.

Prowler 1/2 **1951** Heflin is a cop who responds to a prowler scare and finds the beautiful married Keyes worried about an intruder. He learns she will inherit a lot of money if anything happens to her husband so he seduces her and then "accidentally" kills her husband, supposedly mistaking him for a prowler. Keyes then marries Heflin but when she learns the truth her own life is in danger. Tidy thriller with Heflin doing a good job as the unpredictable villain. **92m/B VHS.** Van Heflin, Evelyn Keyes, Katherine Warren, John Maxwell, Emerson Treacy, Madge Blake, Wheaton Chambers, Sherry Hall, Robert Osterloh, Matt Dorff; *D:* Joseph Losey; *W:* Hugo Butler, Dalton Trumbo; *C:* Arthur C. Miller; *M:* Lyn Murray.

The Prowler *Rosemary's Killer* **1981 (R)** A soldier returns from duty during WWII, only to find his girl in bed with another guy. He kills them, and for unclear reasons, returns to the same town 35 years later to kill more people. An effects-fest for Tom Savini. **87m/C VHS, DVD.** Vicky Dawson, Christopher Goutman, Cindy Weintraub, Farley Granger, John Seitz, Lawrence Tierney; *D:* Joseph Zito; *W:* Neal Barbera; *M:* Richard Einhorn.

Proximity 1/2 **2000 (R)** William Conroy (Lowe) gets prison time for vehicular manslaughter and learns that the big house is hazardous to his health. Seems the inmates have a bad habit of getting killed and Conroy is next when he learns too much about what's going on. Conroy manages to escape and seeks help to expose the whole sleazy situation. Unfortunately, the movie is really dopey and dull. **86m/C VHS, DVD.** Rob Lowe, James Coburn, Kelly Rowan, Sonya A. Avakian; *D:* Scott Ziehl; *W:* Ben Queen, Seamus Ruane; *M:* Stephen Cullo.

Prozac Nation 1/2 **2001 (R)** Drama based on Elizabeth Wurtzel's (Ricci) memoir of her depression, drug, and booze fueled college breakdown, which led her to seek the help of therapist Dr. Sterling (Heche). Unfocused script detracts from fine performance by Ricci, Williams and Biggs. **99m/C DVD.** Christina Ricci, Michelle Williams, Jason Biggs, Anne Heche, Jonathan Rhys Meyers, Jessica Lange, Nicholas (Nick) Campbell, Emily Perkins; *D:* Erik Skjoldbjaerg; *W:* Frank Deasy; *C:* Erling Thurmann-Andersen; *M:* Nathan Larson.

P.S. **2004 (R)** Linney is a treasure but the same can't be said about this film, which is based on co-screenwriter Schulman's novel, "P.S. I Love You." Louise (Linney) is a quiet divorcee who works as a Columbia University admissions officer. She's intrigued by a young grad school applicant who bears the same name, F. Scott Feinstadt, as her lost first love. The young man (a game Grace) is bewildered but flattered by this attractive, lonely woman's attentions. F. Scott is basically a cipher, since it's Louise's emotional baggage we're supposed to be interested in, and she's got a lot of it (dysfunctional family, sex addict ex, backbiting best friend). Unfortunately, neither the movie nor the viewer can really handle all that weight without buckling. **97m/C DVD.** *US* Laura Linney, Topher Grace, Paul Rudd, Lois Smith, Gabriel Byrne, Marcia Gay Harden; *D:* Dylan Kidd; *W:* Dylan Kidd, Helen Schulman; *C:* Joaquin Baca-Asay; *M:* Craig (Shudder to Think) Wedren.

P.S. I Love You **2007 (PG-13)** In this painfully sappy romantic drama, happily marrieds Holly (Swank) and Gerry (Butler) soon aren't so happy when Gerry dies of a brain tumor. Ah, but good ol' Gerry had enough time to plot out his widow's life for the next year—sending her a series of letters with various instructions to, you know, get out there and live! Kudrow and Gershon are gal pals while Connick and Morgan are potential new romances. Swank is game but Butler looked a lot more comfortable in leather and muscles in "300." **126m/C DVD, Blu-ray Disc.** *US* Hilary Swank, Gerard Butler, Lisa Kudrow, Gina Gershon, Harry Connick Jr., Jeffrey Dean Morgan, Kathy Bates, James Marsters; *D:* Richard LaGravenese; *W:* Richard LaGravenese, Steven Rogers; *C:* Terry Stacey; *M:* John Powell.

P.S. Your Cat is Dead! 1/2 **2002 (R)** A moldy oldie. James Kirkwood's 1975 off-Broadway play was based on his 1972 novel and its attitudes towards gays appear quaint at best if not outright insulting. Jimmy Zoole (Guttenberg) is a failed actor/writer with a dead cat and a girlfriend, Kate (Watros), who's just dumped him. This leaves Jimmy alone in his L.A. apartment on New Year's Eve. Except for gay burglar Eddie (Boyar), who has the misfortune to be caught by a distraught Jimmy, who takes his gun and ties the man face down on a kitchen counter. Eddie proceeds to taunt Jimmy about his manhood, various humiliating things happen, and somehow male bonding occurs. **92m/C VHS, DVD.** Steve Guttenberg, Lombardo Boyar, Cynthia Watros, Shirley Knight, Tom Wright, A.J. Benza; *D:* Steve Guttenberg; *W:* Steve Guttenberg, Jeff Korn; *C:* David Armstrong; *M:* Dean Grinsfelder.

PSI Factor 1/2 **1980** A civilian researcher working at the NASA space track station observes and records signals coming from planet Serius B. **91m/C VHS.** Peter Mark Richman, Gretchen Corbett, Tommy Martin; *D:* Bryan Trizers; *W:* Quentin Masters.

Psych-Out 1/2 **1968** A deaf girl searches Haight-Ashbury for her runaway brother. She meets hippies and flower children during the Summer of Love. Psychedelic score with Strawberry Alarm Clock and The Seeds. Somewhere in the picture, Nicholson whangs on lead guitar. **95m/C VHS, DVD.** Jack Nicholson, Bruce Dern, Susan Strasberg, Dean Stockwell, Henry Jaglom; *D:* Richard Rush; *W:* Richard Rush.

The Psychic **WOOF!** *Copenhagen's Psychic Loves* **1968** An ad executive gains psychic powers after he falls off a ladder and tries to conquer the world. A later effort by gore-king Lewis, notable only for sex scenes inserted by Lewis to make the movie salable. **90m/C VHS.** Dick Genola, Robin Guest, Bobbi Spencer, Carol Saenz, Sandra Wolsfeld; *D:* Herschell Gordon Lewis, James F. Hurley; *C:* Herschell Gordon Lewis; *M:* Vincent Oddo.

The Psychic **1978 (R)** A psychic envisions her own death and attempts to alter the prediction. **90m/C VHS.** Jennifer O'Neill, Marc Porel, Evelyn Stewart, Gabriele Ferzetti, Gianni "John" Garko; *D:* Lucio Fulci.

Psychic 1/2 **1991 (R)** A college student with psychic powers believes he knows who the next victim of a demented serial killer will be. The problem is: no one will believe him. And the victim is the woman he loves. **92m/C VHS.** Michael Nouri, Catherine Mary Stewart, Zach Galligan; *D:* George Mihalka; *W:* Paul Koval; *C:* Ludek Bogner; *M:* Milan Kymlicka.

Psychic Killer 1/2 **1975 (PG)** A wrongfully committed asylum inmate acquires psychic powers and decides to use them in a deadly revenge. Good cast in cheapie horror flick. **89m/C VHS, DVD.** Jim Hutton, Paul Burke, Julie Adams, Neville Brand, Aldo Ray, Rod Cameron, Della Reese; *D:* Ray Danton; *W:* Ray Danton, Mikel Angel, Greydon Clark; *C:* Herb Pearl; *M:* William Craft.

Psycho **1960** Hitchcock counted on his directorial stature and broke all the rules in this story of violent murder, transvestism, and insanity. Based on Robert Bloch's novelization of an actual murder, Leigh plays a fleeing thief who stops at the secluded Bates Motel where she meets her death in Hitchcock's classic "shower scene." Shot on a limited budget in little more than a month, "Psycho" changed the Hollywood horror film forever. Followed by "Psycho 2" (1983), "Psycho 3" (1986), "Psycho 4: The Beginning" (1990), and a TV movie. **109m/B VHS, DVD.** Anthony Perkins, Janet Leigh, Vera Miles, John Gavin, John McIntire, Martin Balsam, Simon Oakland, Ted (Edward) Knight, John Anderson, Frank Albertson, Patricia Hitchcock, Alfred Hitchcock; *D:* Alfred Hitchcock; *W:* Joseph Stefano; *C:* John L. "Jack" Russell; *M:* Bernard Herrmann; *V:* Virginia Gregg, Jeannette Nolan. AFI '98: Top 100; Golden Globes '61: Support. Actress (Leigh), Natl. Film Reg. '92.

Psycho 1/2 **1998 (R)** Since Hitchcock's "Psycho" is one of the most famous movies of all time, it would seem redundant to summarize the plot here. Although, redundant is a fitting description of Gus Van Sant's shot-for-shot recreation. Wisely, Van Sant doesn't meddle with a good thing. On the other hand, ya pretty much have to ask, "what's the point?" Significant to the success of the original was that it pushed the envelope in 1960. (A shot of a toilet flushing! A woman taking a shower! Blasphemy!) But by today's standards, "Psycho" is utterly tame. Performances are excellent all around. As talented as Vaughn is, however, the inevitable comparison between him and Anthony Perkins reveals that Vaughn is just too cool for this role. Perkins' Norman Bates was geeky and frail, Vaughn just isn't. As the saying goes, "if it ain't broke, don't fix it." **106m/C VHS, DVD.** Vince Vaughn, Anne Heche, Julianne Moore, William H. Macy, Viggo Mortensen, Robert Forster, Philip Baker Hall, Anne Haney, Chad Everett, Rance Howard, Rita Wilson, James Remar, James LeGros; *D:* Gus Van Sant; *W:* Joseph Stefano; *C:* Christopher Doyle. Golden Raspberries '98: Worst Remake/Sequel, Worst Director (Van Sant).

Psycho 2 **1983 (R)** This sequel to the Hitchcock classic finds Norman Bates returning home after 22 years in an asylum to find himself haunted by "mother" and caught up in a series of murders. In a surprisingly good horror film, Perkins and Miles reprise their roles from the original "Psycho." Perkins went on to direct yet another sequel, "Psycho 3." **113m/C VHS, DVD.** Claudia Bryar, Oz (Osgood) Perkins II, Anthony Perkins, Vera Miles, Meg Tilly, Robert Loggia, Dennis Franz; ***D:*** Richard Franklin; ***W:*** Tom Holland; ***C:*** Dean Cundey; ***M:*** Jerry Goldsmith.

Psycho 3 **1986 (R)** The second sequel to Hitchcock's "Psycho" finds Norman Bates drawn into his past by "mother" and the appearance of a woman who reminds him of this original victim. Perkins made his directorial debut in this film that stretches the plausibility of the storyline to its limits, but the element of parody throughout makes this an entertaining film for "Psycho" fans. **93m/C VHS, DVD.** Anthony Perkins, Diana Scarwid, Jeff Fahey, Roberta Maxwell, Robert Alan Browne, Hugh Gillin, Lee Garlington; ***D:*** Anthony Perkins; ***W:*** Charles Edward Pogue; ***C:*** Bruce Surtees; ***M:*** Carter Burwell.

Psycho 4: The Beginning **1990 (R)** Prequels "Psycho" when, at the behest of a radio talk show host, Norman Bates recounts his childhood and reveals the circumstances that aided in the development of his peculiar neuroses. Stefano wrote the original screenplay and the original score is used, but this doesn't even come close to the original. **96m/C VHS.** Anthony Perkins, Henry Thomas, Olivia Hussey, CCH Pounder, Warren Frost, Donna Mitchell; ***D:*** Mick Garris; ***W:*** Joseph Stefano; ***C:*** Rodney Charters; ***M:*** Graeme Revell.

Psycho Beach Party **1/2 2000** Busch adapted his own play—a spoof of 60s teen beach movies and pyscho/thrillers. Perky teen tomboy Florence (Ambrose) desperately wants to fit into her SoCal ocean lifestyle by becoming the first female accepted into the local surfers who are led by hipster Kanaka (Gibson). The newly christened "Chicklet" has a dark side, however, a separate sultry personality named Anne that she fears is responsible for a series of murders that are thinning out the teen population. Busch plays the investigating officer, and former Kanaka girlfriend, Capt. Monica Stark. **95m/C VHS, DVD.** Lauren Ambrose, Thomas Gibson, Nicholas Brendon, Charles Busch, Kimberly Davies, Matt Keeslar, Nathan Bexton, Buddy Quaid, Beth Broderick, Amy Adams, Danni Wheeler, Kathleen Robertson; ***D:*** Robert Lee King; ***W:*** Charles Busch; ***C:*** Arturo Smith; ***M:*** Ben Vaughn.

Psycho Cop **1/2 1988** Six college undergrads on a weekend retreat are menaced and picked off one at a time by a crazed local cop. **89m/C VHS.** Robert (Bobby Ray) Shafer, Barbara Niven, Rod Sweitzer, Julie Strain; ***D:*** Wallace Potts.

Psycho Cop 2 **1/2 1994 (R)** Four buddies plan a raunchy bachelor party, commandeering the company conference room for an after-hours orgy. Only Psycho Cop is on their case. Gore. Rifkin used the pseudonym Rif Coogan. **80m/C VHS, DVD.** Robert (Bobby Ray) Shafer, Barbara Lee (Niven) Alexander, Julie Strain; ***D:*** Adam Rifkin.

Psycho from Texas *The Butcher* **1975 (R)** Quiet Southern town is disrupted by the kidnapping of a wealthy oil man, followed by a string of meaningless murders. **85m/C VHS.** John King III, Candy Dee, Janel King, Herschel Mays; ***D:*** Jim Feazell, Jack Collins; ***W:*** Jim Feazell; ***C:*** Paul Hipp; ***M:*** Jaime Mendoza-Nava.

Psycho Girls **1986 (R)** Very low budget horror flick redeemed by spurts of weird black humor. Crazed woman is released from institution to seek out sister who should have been put away in the first place. She crashes anniversary celebration and, well, let's just say she's not the life of the party. Never released theatrically. **87m/C VHS.** *CA* John Haslett Cuff, Darlene Mignacco, Agi Gallus, Rose Graham, Silvio Oliviero, Michael Hoole, Pier Giorgia DiCicco, Fernne Kane; ***D:*** Gerard Ciccoritti; ***W:*** Gerard Ciccoritti, Michael Boekner.

Psycho Sisters **1/2 1998** As children, Jackie (North) and Jane (Lynn) witness shocking events that traumatize them into the titular killers. Actually, after seeing so many young women pursued by homicidal maniacs, it's nice that a couple of them get to turn the tables. This low-budget horror has developed a strong cult following. **90m/C DVD.** J.J. North, Theresa Lynn; ***D:*** Pete Jacelone; ***W:*** Pete Jacelone, James L. Edwards; ***C:*** Timothy Healy.

Psychomania **1/2** *Violent Midnight* **1963** Semi-limpid mystery thriller about a former war hero and painter who is suspected of being the demented killer stalking girls on campus. To prove his innocence, he tracks the killer himself. **95m/C VHS, DVD.** Lee Philips, Shepperd Strudwick, Jean Hale, Dick Van Patten, Sylvia Miles, James Farentino; ***D:*** Richard Hilliard.

Psychomania *The Death Wheelers* **1973 (R)** A drama of the supernatural, the occult, and the violence which lies just beyond the conventions of society for a group of dead motorcyclists, the Living Dead, who all came back to life after committing suicide with the help of the devil. **89m/C VHS, DVD.** *GB* George Sanders, Beryl Reid, Nicky Henson, Mary Laroche, Patrick Holt; ***D:*** Don Sharp; ***W:*** Arnaud d'Usseau; ***C:*** Ted Moore.

Psychopath **1/2 1968** A film about a modern-day, slightly unhinged, Robin Hood and his escapades, stealing from other thieves and giving to the victimized. **90m/C VHS.** *GB* Klaus Kinski, George Martin, Ingrid Schoeller; ***D:*** Guido Zurli.

Psychopath *An Eye for an Eye* **1973 (PG)** A nutso children's TV personality begins to murder abusive parents. Fairly gory, and definitely not for family viewing. **85m/C VHS.** Tom Basham, Gene Carlson, Gretchen Kanne; ***D:*** Larry G. Brown; ***M:*** John Williams.

Psychopath **1/2** *Twist of Fate* **1997 (R)** D.A. Rachel Dwyer (Amick) needs the help of serial killer Lennox (Mulkey), who targets female law students, in solving another crime. Low on the histrionics and high on the courtroom drama as well as being well-acted. **95m/C VHS, DVD.** Madchen Amick, Chris Mulkey, Bruce Dinsmore, Don Jordan, Lynne Adams, Cas Anvar, Tara Slone, James Bradford; ***D:*** Max Fischer; ***W:*** Cameron Kent, William Lee; ***C:*** Guy Kinkead; ***M:*** Normand Corbeil. **CABLE**

Psychos in Love **WOOF!** **1987** A psychotic murderer who hates grapes of any kind finds the woman of his dreams—she's a psychotic murderer who hates grapes! Together they find bliss—until the plumber discovers their secret! **90m/C VHS.** Carmine Capobianco, Debi Thibeault, Frank Stewart; ***D:*** Gorman Bechard.

The Psychotronic Man **1/2 1991** An innocent man suddenly finds he possesses amazing and dangerous powers, enabling him to control outside events with a thought. **88m/C VHS.** Peter Spelson, Christopher Carbis, Curt Colbert, Robin Newton, Paul Marvel; ***D:*** Jack M. Sell.

PT 109 **1963** The WWII exploits of Lieutenant (j.g.) John F. Kennedy in the South Pacific. Part of the "A Night at the Movies" series, this tape simulates a 1963 movie evening, with a Foghorn Leghorn cartoon ("Banty Raids"), a newsreel on the JFK assassination, and coming attractions for "Critic's Choice" and "Four for Texas." **159m/C VHS.** Cliff Robertson, Ty Hardin, Ty Hardin, Robert (Bobby) Blake, Robert Culp, James Gregory; ***D:*** Leslie Martinson.

P.T. Barnum **1/2 1999** Bio of Phineas Taylor Barnum (Beau Bridges) and his development of "The Greatest Show on Earth." A shopkeeper from Connecticut, P.T. was determined to make his fortune in New York, eventually purchasing Scudder's American Museum and its exhibits, which he turned into a traveling big top event, thanks to his promotional skills. Barnum's zest for work, however, made for a less than happy home life. Beau's son Jordan plays the young Barnum. Filmed in Montreal and Vancouver, Canada. **138m/C VHS, DVD.** Beau Bridges, Cynthia Dale, Natalie Radford, Jordan Bridges, George Hamilton, Henry Czerny, Charles Martin Smith, Josh Ryan Evans, R.H. Thomson, Stephanie Morgenstern, Isabelle Cyr, Michelle-Barbara Pelletier, Victoria Sanchez; ***D:*** Simon Wincer; ***W:*** Lionel Chetwynd; ***C:*** Pierre Mignot. **CABLE**

Pterodactyl Woman from Beverly Hills **1997 (R)** California housewife Pixie Chandler (D'Angelo) is the victim of an eccentric witch doctor (James) when her paleontologist husband Dick (Wilson) disturbs an ancient burial site and the doc curses Pixie by turning her into a dinosaur. This is the first so-called family release from those madcap Troma people who brought you the Toxic Avenger. **97m/C VHS, DVD.** Beverly D'Angelo, Brion James, Brad Wilson, Moon Zappa, Aron Eisenberg; ***D:*** Philippe Mora; ***W:*** Philippe Mora; ***C:*** Walter Bal; ***M:*** Roy Hay.

PU-239 **1/2** *The Half Life of Timofey Berezin* **2006** Nuclear plant worker Timofey Berezin (Considine) is dosed with a lethal amount of radiation and becomes the victim of an administrative cover-up. To provide for his family, Timofey steals a tube of plutonium and turns to smalltime Moscow gangster Shiv (Isaac) to help him sell it on the black market. But Shiv's general ineptitude just gets them into trouble with mob boss Starkov (Berkoff). Set in 1995. **107m/C DVD.** *GB* Paddy Considine, Radha Mitchell, Oscar Isaac, Jason Flemyng, Steven Berkhoff, Nikolaj Lie Kaas, Michael Fisher; ***D:*** Scott Burns; ***W:*** Scott Burns; ***C:*** Eigil Bryld; ***M:*** Abel Koreniowski.

Puberty Blues **1/2 1981 (R)** Two Australian girls become part of the local surfing scene in order to be accepted by the "in crowd" at their high school. **86m/C VHS.** *AU* Neil Schofield, Jad Capelja; ***D:*** Bruce Beresford.

Public Access **1993 (R)** Newcomer Whiley Pritcher (Marquette) manages to cause trouble in the small town of Brewster when he begins broadcasting a call-in program over a public-access cable station that encourages complaining about the town's problems. Skeletons start falling out of closets, leading to unexpected tragedy. Feature-film directorial debut of Singer. **90m/C VHS, DVD.** Ron Marquette, Dina Brooks, Burt Williams, Charles Kavanaugh, Larry Maxwell, Brandon Boyce; ***D:*** Bryan Singer; ***W:*** Bryan Singer, Christopher McQuarrie, Michael Feit Dougan; ***C:*** Bruce Douglas Johnson; ***M:*** John Ottman. Sundance '93: Grand Jury Prize.

A Public Affair **1/2 1962** Exposes the evils and abuses of collection agencies without even a shred of humor. Certainly gets its point across, but will bore any audience to tears or spontaneous naps. **71m/B VHS.** Myron McCormick, Edward Binns, Harry Carey Jr.; ***D:*** Bernard Girard; ***W:*** Bernard Girard; ***C:*** Howard Schwartz; ***M:*** Joe "Mean Joe" Greene.

Public Cowboy No. 1 **1/2 1937** Cattle thieves use a radio, airplanes, and refrigerator trucks in their updated rustling schemes. **54m/B VHS, DVD.** Gene Autry, William Farnum, Smiley Burnette, Ann Rutherford, Arthur Loft, House Peters Jr.; ***D:*** Joseph Kane; ***W:*** Oliver Drake; ***C:*** Jack Marta.

Public Enemies **1996 (R)** It's nefarious Ma Barker (Russell) and her boys on a '30s crime spree that gets even bigger when they hook up with criminal Alvin Karpis (Stallone). But when Ma's lover Arthur (Roberts) dreams up a kidnapping plot, it's a fast road to ruin. **95m/C VHS.** Theresa Russell, Eric Roberts, Frank Stallone, Alyssa Milano, Joseph Lindsey, Richard Eden, James Marsden, Dan Cortese; ***D:*** Mark L. Lester; ***W:*** C. Courtney Joyner; ***M:*** Christopher Franke.

Public Enemies **2009 (R)** Stylish but cold crime drama from Mann centers on Depression-era gangster John Dillinger (Depp), here an enigmatic guy who likes to rob banks. The director dispenses with background and psychological insights so it's all meticulous surface (though what a handsome surface it is). Pic hops from 1933 when Dillinger led a daring mass prison break of old cohorts from the Indiana State Penitentiary to his 1934 death outside a Chicago movie theater, taking some time out for Dillinger to romance hat check girl Billie (Cotillard) and draw the unwanted notice of the feds. In an effort to bring attention to his fledging FBI operation, ambitious J. Edgar Hoover (Crudup) assigns his top agent, tightly-wound Melvin Purvis (Bale), to get Dillinger, the Bureau's first 'Public Enemy.' **140m/C DVD.** *US* Christian Bale, Johnny Depp, Stephen Graham, Channing Tatum, Billy Crudup, Leelee Sobieski, Stephen Dorff, Giovanni Ribisi, David Wenham, Marion Cotillard, Emilie de Ravin, Rory Cochrane, Shawn Hatosy, Jason Clarke, Stephen Lang, Bill Camp, Peter Gerety, Branka Katic, James Russo; ***D:*** Michael Mann; ***W:*** Ronan Bennett, Ann Biderman; ***C:*** Dante Spinotti; ***M:*** Elliot Goldenthal.

Public Enemy **1/2** *Enemies of the Public* **1931** Cagney's acting career was launched by this story of two Irish boys growing up in a Chicago shantytown to become hoodlums during the prohibition era. Tom (Cagney) and Matt (Woods) work their way up the criminal ladder, hooking up with molls Kitty (Clarke) and Mamie (Blondell) on their rise to the top. Harlow's a tough blonde who knows how to handle Cagney when he gets tired of Clarke. Considered the most realistic "gangster" film, Wellman's movie is also the most grimly brutal due to its release prior to Hollywood censorship. The scene where Cagney smashes a grapefruit in Clarke's face was credited with starting a trend in abusing film heroines. **85m/B VHS, DVD.** James Cagney, Edward (Eddie) Woods, Leslie Fenton, Joan Blondell, Mae Clarke, Jean Harlow, Donald Cook, Beryl Mercer; ***D:*** William A. Wellman; ***W:*** Harvey Thew, John Bright, Kubec Glasmon; ***C:*** Devereaux Jennings. Natl. Film Reg. '98.

Public Enemy **1/2** *Gonggongui jeog* **2002** Detective Kang (Sol Kyung-gu) is a corrupt officer whose partner has committed suicide in shame after Internal Affairs announces they are being investigated for criminal activities. While on a stakeout a young man he bumps into slashes Kang's face with a knife. Later on he realizes the man may be responsible for a horrible double murder nearby. He becomes obsessed with bringing the man to justice, and puts aside his own illegal activities to hunt him down. **138m/C DVD.** *KN* Kyung-gu Sol, Shin-il Kang, Sung-jae Lee, Jeong-hak Kim, Yong-gu Do; ***D:*** Woo-suk Kang; ***W:*** Hyeong-jeon Kim; ***C:*** Sung-bok Kim; ***M:*** Yeong-wook Jo.

The Public Eye **1/2 1992 (R)** Underappreciated film noir homage casts Pesci as a crime photographer with an unsuspected romantic streak. It's 1942 in NYC and cynical freelancer Leon "Bernzy" Bernstein's always looking for the perfect shot. Hershey's the recent widow whose nightclub-owner husband had mob ties and decides Pesci would be a likely patsy for helping her out. Hershey seems decorative and the romantic angle never quite develops, but Pesci delivers a rich, low-key performance as the visionary, hard-boiled artist. Climatic mob shootout is cinematic bullet ballet. Based loosely on the career of '40s photog Weegee, who defined New York and its times in his work. **98m/C VHS.** Joe Pesci, Barbara Hershey, Stanley Tucci, Richard Foronjy, Richard Riehle, Jared Harris, Jerry Adler, Dominic Chianese, Gerry Becker; ***D:*** Howard Franklin; ***W:*** Howard Franklin; ***M:*** John Barry.

Puccini for Beginners **2006** Snappy, droll, if occasionally labored comedy. Opera-loving Allegra (Reaser) breaks up with girlfriend Samantha (Nicholson) and drunkenly decides to have an affair after meeting appealing Philip (Kirk), who's dumped girlfriend Grace (Mol), who soon has her own rebound romance—with Allegra. Obviously, New York is a very small town. **82m/C DVD.** *US* Elizabeth Reaser, Justin Kirk, Gretchen Mol, Jennifer (Jennie) Dundas Lowe, Julianne Nicholson, Tina Benko, Brian Letscher; ***D:*** Maria Maggenti; ***W:*** Maria Maggenti; ***C:*** Mauricio Rubinstein; ***M:*** Terry Dame.

Pucker Up and Bark Like a Dog **1989 (R)** A young artist and his inspirationally lovely actress girl-friend find themselves in strange and crazy situations. Good cast gives this potential. **94m/C VHS.** Lisa Zane, Jon(athan) Gries, Paul Bartel, Robert Culp; ***D:*** Paul S. Parco.

Pudd'nhead Wilson **1/2 1984** An adaptation of a Mark Twain story about a small-town lawyer who discovers the illicit exchange of a white infant for a light-skinned negro infant by a slave woman. Made as an "American Playhouse" presentation on PBS. **87m/C VHS.** Lise Hilboldt, Dick Latessa, James Pritchett, Tom Aldredge, Steven Weber, Ken Howard; ***D:*** Alan Bridges; ***W:*** Philip Reisman Jr.; ***C:*** Walter Lassally. **TV**

Pueblo Affair **1973** A dramatization of the capture of the American spy ship "Pueblo" by the North Koreans, during which time the crew was tortured, imprisoned, and all intelligence documents were confiscated.

99m/C VHS. Hal Holbrook, Andrew Duggan, Richard Mulligan, George Grizzard, Gary Merrill, Mary Fickett; *D:* Anthony Page. TV

Puerto Vallarta Squeeze ⚡⚡ 1/2 **2004 (R)** Failed American writer Danny Paster (Wasson) is living in Mexico with his girlfriend Maria (Zacarias). Needing money, Danny agrees to drive Clayton Price (Glenn) to the border though he knows something is off and that officials are on high alert following two assassinations. Seems Price is a government hitman gone rogue and CIA operative Walter McGrane (Keitel) has been sent in to clean up the mess, which includes getting rid of Price. Based on the novel by Robert James Waller. **120m/C DVD.** Scott Glenn, Harvey Keitel, Craig Wasson, Jonathan Brandis, Giovanna Zacarias; *D:* Arthur Allan Seidelman; *W:* Richard Alfieri; *C:* Chuy Chavez; *M:* Lee Holdridge.

Puff, Puff, Pass WOOF! **2006 (R)** Excretal comedy about a couple of tokers who get locked out of their apartment for nonpayment of rent and then get into various unpleasant situations as they seek a place to hang out. Not even worth watching stoned. **95m/C DVD.** *US* Danny Masterson, Mekhi Phifer, Ronnie Warner; *D:* Mekhi Phifer; *W:* Ronnie Warner, Kent George; *C:* Arthur Albert.

Pufnstuf ⚡⚡ 1/2 **1970 (G)** Surreal theatrical feature based on the "H.R. Pufnstuff" children's series by Sid and Marty Kroft. Jimmy (Wild) takes his talking flute to Living Island, where objects, plants, and animals can speak and where he meets mayor Pufnstuf, a dragon. But Jack's magic flute is stolen by Witchiepoo (Hayes) who wants to be named "Witch of the Year" at the annual witches convention. **95m/C VHS.** Jack Wild, Billie Hayes, Martha Raye, "Mama" Cass Elliott, Billy Barty; *D:* Hollingsworth Morse; *W:* John Fenton Murray; *C:* Kenneth Peach Sr.; *M:* Charles Fox.

Pulp ⚡⚡ 1/2 **1972 (PG)** Caine, playing a mystery writer, becomes a target for murder when he ghostwrites the memoirs of a movie gangster from the 1930s, played deftly by Rooney. **95m/C VHS, DVD.** *GB* Michael Caine, Mickey Rooney, Lionel Stander, Lizabeth Scott, Nadia Cassini, Dennis Price, Al Lettieri; *D:* Mike Hodges; *W:* Mike Hodges.

Pulp Fiction ⚡⚡⚡⚡ **1994 (R)** Tarantino moves into the cinematic mainstream with his trademark violence and '70s pop culture mindset intact in this stylish crime trilogy. A day in the life of a criminal community unexpectedly shifts from outrageous, esoteric dialogue to violent mayhem with solid scripting that takes familiar stories to unexplored territory. Offbeat cast offers superb performances, led by Travolta in his best role to date as a hit man whose adventures with partner Jackson tie the seemingly unrelated stories together. Clever, almost gleeful look at everyday life on the fringes of mainstream society. Inspired by "Black Mask" magazine. **154m/C VHS, DVD, UMD.** Paul Calderon, Bronagh Gallagher, Stephen Hibbert, Angela Jones, Phil LaMarr, Duane Whitaker, Kathy Griffin, John Travolta, Samuel L. Jackson, Uma Thurman, Harvey Keitel, Tim Roth, Amanda Plummer, Maria De Medeiros, Ving Rhames, Eric Stoltz, Rosanna Arquette, Christopher Walken, Bruce Willis, Frank Whaley, Steve Buscemi, Peter Greene, Alexis Arquette, Julia Sweeney, Quentin Tarantino, Dick Miller; *D:* Quentin Tarantino; *W:* Roger Avary, Quentin Tarantino; *C:* Andrzej Sekula; *M:* Karyn Rachtman. Oscars '94: Orig. Screenplay; AFI '98: Top 100; British Acad. '94: Orig. Screenplay, Support. Actor (Jackson); Cannes '94: Film; Golden Globes '95: Screenplay; Ind. Spirit '95: Actor (Jackson), Director (Tarantino), Film, Screenplay; L.A. Film Critics '94: Actor (Travolta), Director (Tarantino), Film, Screenplay; MTV Movie Awards '95: Film, Dance Seq. (John Travolta/ Uma Thurman); Natl. Bd. of Review '94: Director (Tarantino), Film; N.Y. Film Critics '94: Director (Tarantino), Screenplay; Natl. Soc. Film Critics '94: Director (Tarantino), Film, Screenplay.

Pulse ⚡⚡ **1988 (PG-13)** Electricity goes awry in this science-fiction thriller about appliances and other household devices that become super-charged and destroy property and their owners. **90m/C VHS, DVD.** Cliff DeYoung, Roxanne Hart, Joey Lawrence, Charles Tyner, Dennis Redfield, Robert Romanus, Myron Healey; *D:* Paul Golding; *C:* Peter Lyons Collister; *M:* Jay Ferguson.

Pulse ⚡⚡ 1/2 *Kairo* **2001** Set in dirty and industrial Tokyo, a great example of Japanese horror. Don't look for logic because its not here. Instead there's tension and dread surrounding disquieting images hosted by a malevolent website. A group of friends are shocked by the suicide of another friend and are then haunted by ghostly computer images. Other people continue to die or disappear in strange ways, as Tokyo becomes an increasingly desolate place. **118m/C DVD.** *JP* Kumiko Aso, Koyuki, Shun Sugata, Masayuki Shionoya, Shinji Takeda, Koji Yakusho, Haruhiko Kato, Kurume Arisaka, Masatoshi Matsuo, Kenji Mizuhashi, Jun Fubuki; *D:* Kiyoshi Kurosawa; *W:* Kiyoshi Kurosawa; *C:* Junichiro Hayashi; *M:* Takefumi Haketa.

Pulse ⚡⚡ *Octane* **2003 (R)** Weirdo traveling vampire cult kidnaps teenage girl causing her anguished mom to descend into their world to attempt her rescue. **90m/C VHS, DVD.** Madeleine Stowe, Norman Reedus, Bijou Phillips, Mischa Barton, Jonathan Rhys Meyers, Samuel Froler, Tom Hunsinger, Leo Gregory, Amber Batty, Jenny Jules, Patrick O'Kane, Martin McDougall, Shauna Shim, David Menkin, Nigel Whitmey, Stephen Lord, Dean Gregory, Sarah Drews, Raffaello Degruttola, Glenn Wrage, Monika Hudgins, Emma Drews, Marcus Adams; *D:* Marcus Volk; *W:* Stephen Volk; *C:* Robin Vidgeon; *M:* Paul Hartnoll, Phil Hartnoll, Orbital. VIDEO

Pulse ⚡ 1/2 **2006 (R)** Remake of the 2001 Japanese horror flick "Kairo" that features an evil website. When the unsuspecting click on the creepy images of the dead, the supernatural force behind the site invades the lives of those who log on and makes them commit suicide. Technology is bad, but not as bad as this watered-down version, which forgoes creepy atmospherics and conceptualized plot for the occasional scare. **90m/C DVD, HD DVD.** *US* Kristen Bell, Ian Somerhalder, Christina Milian, Rick Gonzalez, Zach Grenier, Ron Rifkin, Jonathan Tucker, Brad Dourif, Samm Levine; *D:* Jim Sonzero; *W:* Wes Craven, Ray Wright; *C:* Mark Plummer; *M:* Elia Cmiral.

Pulse 2: Afterlife ⚡ 1/2 *Pulse: Afterlife and Invasion* **2008 (R)** After the events of the first film, what little is left of the world's population is hiding out in the woods or mountains to escape the soul-eating phantoms that have been using technology to access our world. One of the survivors, a divorced executive, must protect his daughter from his ex-wife's spirit and fend off the jealous, possessive girlfriend who inspired the divorce. What seems like a sound premise is ruined by the cinematography, which makes it look like a student film with a decent budget. And it's not like the first film was all that great. **89m/C DVD.** Jamie Bamber, Boti Ann Bliss, Laura Cayouette, Noureen DeWulf, Jackie Arnold, Karley Scott Collins, Georgina Rylance, Brittany Renee Finamore, Todd Giebenhain, Diane Goldner, Grant James, Robin McGee, Claudia Templeton; *W:* Joel Soisson; *C:* Brandon Trost; *M:* Elia Cmiral. VIDEO

Pulsebeat WOOF! **1985** Flick about warring health club owners. As boring as it sounds unless you're in the mood for lots of on-screen aerobics. If so, rent Jane Fonda instead. Dubbed. **92m/C VHS.** *SP* Daniel Greene, Lee Taylor Allen, Bob Small, Alice Moore, Helga Line, Alex Intriago, Peter Lupus; *D:* Marice Tobias.

The Puma Man WOOF! **1980** Puma Man is a super hero who must stop the evil Dr. Kobras from using an ancient mask in his attempt to become ruler of the world. Unreleased theatrically in the U.S., this low budget sci-fi/horror mix is so bad one wonders why an actor like Pleasence would sign on. Special effects these days are so extraordinary that the ones employed here are laughable. **80m/C VHS.** *IT* Donald Pleasence, Walter George Alton, Sydne Rome, Miguel Angel Fuentes; *D:* Alberto De Martino.

Pump Up the Volume ⚡⚡ 1/2 **1990 (R)** High school newcomer leads double life as Hard Harry, sarcastic host of an illegal radio broadcast and Jack Nicholson soundalike. Anonymously popular with his peers, he invites the wrath of the school principal due to his less than flattering comments about the school administration. Slater seems to enjoy himself as defiant deejay while youthful cast effectively supports. **105m/C VHS, DVD.** Christian Slater, Scott Paulin, Ellen Greene, Samantha Mathis, Cheryl Pollak, Annie Ross, Andy Romano, Mimi Kennedy; *D:* Allan Moyle; *W:* Allan Moyle; *C:* Walt Lloyd; *M:* Cliff Martinez.

Pumpkin ⚡⚡ **2002 (R)** Ambitious but over-reaching satire. California blonde sorority sister Carolyn McDuffy (Ricci) is a reluctant participant in the group's charity activity—helping to coach "special" athletes. Then Carolyn gets to know Pumpkin (Harris), who's confined to a wheelchair and seems to be mentally retarded as well (this isn't very clear). Soon, Pumpkin is smitten and Carolyn falls for his inner beauty—thus alienating her boyfriend, sorority sisters, and Pumpkins's mother. Too bad all the characters are little more than stereotypes. **118m/C VHS, DVD.** *US* Christina Ricci, Brenda Blethyn, Dominique Swain, Hank Harris, Marisa Coughlan, Samuel Ball, Harry J. Lennix, Nina Foch, Caroline Aaron, Lisa Banes, Julio Oscar Mechoso, Amy Adams, Michelle Krusiec; *D:* Adam Larson Broder, Tony R. Abrams; *W:* Adam Larson Broder; *C:* Tim Suhrstedt; *M:* John Ottman.

The Pumpkin Eater ⚡⚡⚡ **1964** British housewife Jo (Bancroft) has seemingly found contentment with her third husband, famous and wealthy writer Jake (Finch), and her eight children. But as Jo struggles to face middle age she discovers Jake is chronically unfaithful and goes into an emotional tailspin. Last film for Hardwicke. Slow-paced film with fine performances; based on the novel by Penelope Mortimer. **110m/C VHS.** *GB* Anne Bancroft, Peter Finch, James Mason, Richard Johnson, Cedric Hardwicke, Maggie Smith, Alan Webb, Eric Porter; *D:* Jack Clayton; *W:* Harold Pinter; *C:* Oswald Morris; *M:* Georges Delerue. British Acad. '64: Screenplay.

Pumpkinhead ⚡⚡ 1/2 *Vengeance: The Demon* **1988 (R)** A farmer evokes a demon from the earth to avenge his son's death. When it continues on its murdering rampage, the farmer finds he no longer has any control over the vicious killer. **89m/C VHS, DVD.** Lance Henriksen, John DiAquino, Kerry Remsen, Matthew Hurley, Jeff East, Kimberly Ross, Cynthia Bain, Joel Hoffman, Florence Schauffler, George "Buck" Flower, Tom Woodruff Jr.; *D:* Stan Winston; *W:* Mark Patrick Carducci, Gary Gerani; *C:* Bojan Bazelli; *M:* Richard Stone.

Pumpkinhead 2: Blood Wings ⚡ 1/2 **1994 (R)** Five typically stupid teenagers resurrect a demon and the creature goes on a bloodthirsty rampage. His leaves his signature, a calling card in the shape of wings, at each murder scene. **88m/C VHS, DVD.** Ami Dolenz, Andrew (Andy) Robinson, Kane Hodder, R.A. Mihailoff, Linnea Quigley, Steve Kanaly, Caren Kaye, Gloria Hendry, Soleil Moon Frye, Mark McCracken, Roger Clinton; *D:* Jeff Burr; *W:* Ivan Chachornia, Constantin Chachornia.

Pumpkinhead 3: Ashes to Ashes ⚡ **2006 (R)** Cheapie forgettable franchise entry starts 20 years after the original although dead Ed Harley (Henriksen) still manages to return. Local mortician Doc Frasier (Bradley) has been stealing body parts from the dead and throwing the remains in the swamp rather than giving them a proper burial. After his desecration is discovered, outraged townsfolk turn to Haggis the witch to summon the demonic Pumpkinhead to give them revenge. **95m/C DVD.** Doug Bradley, Lance Henriksen, Douglas Roberts, Lisa McAllister, Tess Panzer; *D:* Jake West; *W:* Jake West; *C:* Erik Wilson; *M:* Robert Lord. VIDEO

Pumpkinhead 4: Blood Feud ⚡ 1/2 **2007 (R)** Jody Hatfield and Ricky McCoy fall in love despite their families' ongoing feud. But when Ricky's younger sister dies, he decides to get the local witch to call up Pumpkinhead to kill all the Hatfields except for lover Jody. A ghostly Ed Harley tries to convince 'em that this is a bad idea since Pumpkinhead isn't going to check IDs before he starts his slaughter. Better than the previous entry but still standard monster fare. **95m/C DVD.** Rob Freeman, Richard Durden, Lance Henriksen, Bradley Taylor, Amy Manson, Claire Lams; *D:* Michael Hurst; *W:* Michael Hurst; *C:* Eric Wilson; *M:* Robert Lord. VIDEO

Punch-Drunk Love ⚡⚡⚡ **2002 (R)** Enjoy Adam Sandler's doofus americanus roles? Then don't put this on your "to see" list. Looking for a new twist on the romantic comedy featuring Adam Sandler's best performance to date? Here's your flick. Barry Egan (Sandler), owner of a novelty toilet-plunger company, prone to sudden outbreaks of physical violence (mostly to glass doors and public bathrooms) serendipitously finds a woman (Watson) attracted to him. Amid the budding love stuff, Egan battles with a phone sex company's extortion attempts, and his discovery of a marketing mistake allowing him to obtain millions of frequent flyers miles for the price of some pudding cups (based on a true incident). Anderson arranges scenes like musical numbers, escalating sound and spectacle to a dizzying point, to good effect. **97m/C VHS, DVD.** *US* Adam Sandler, Emily Watson, Philip Seymour Hoffman, Luis Guzman, Mary Lynn Rajskub, Ashley Clark; *D:* Paul Thomas Anderson; *W:* Paul Thomas Anderson; *C:* Robert Elswit; *M:* Jon Brion.

Punch the Clock ⚡⚡ **1990 (R)** Attractive female thief finds her bail bondsman very exciting; he's ready to help her any way he can. **88m/C VHS.** Michael Rogen, Chris Moore, James Lorinz; *D:* Eric L. Schlagman.

Punchline ⚡⚡ **1988 (R)** A look at the lives of stand-up comics, following the career ups-and-downs of an embittered professional funny-man and a frustrated housewife hitting the stage for the first time. Some very funny and touching moments and some not-so-funny and touching as the movie descends into melodrama without a cause. **100m/C VHS, DVD.** Tom Hanks, Sally Field, John Goodman, Mark Rydell, Kim Greist, Barry Sobel, Paul Mazursky, Pam Matteson, George Michael McGrath, Taylor Negron, Damon Wayans; *D:* David Seltzer; *W:* David Seltzer; *C:* Reynaldo Villalobos. L.A. Film Critics '88: Actor (Hanks).

The Punisher ⚡ **1990 (R)** Lundgren portrays Frank Castle, the Marvel Comics anti-hero known as the Punisher. When his family is killed by the mob Castle set his eyes on revenge. Filmed in Australia. **92m/C VHS, DVD.** Dolph Lundgren, Louis Gossett Jr., Jeroen Krabbe, Kim Miyori; *D:* Mark Goldblatt; *W:* Boaz Yakin; *C:* Ian Baker; *M:* Dennis Dreith.

The Punisher ⚡⚡ **2004 (R)** What this brutal revenger lacks in humor and cheeriness, it more than makes up for in gloomy, dour punishment, drunken brooding, and grisly deaths. The Punisher a.k.a. Frank Castle (Jane) is an FBI agent turned vigilante after an FBI sting which kills a wealthy mobster's son triggers the systematic murder of his entire family. Said mobster is the ironically named Mr. Saint (an uninspired Travolta). Despite a severe battering, Castle survives the slaughter. Rest of pic is his revenge plot against Saint, his right hand man (Patton) and assorted evil cohorts. Adding a touch of humanity are Castle's fellow rooming house residents, including Romjin-Stamos, Pinette and Foster, who futilely attempt to socialize Castle. Based on the Marvel comic books. **124m/C VHS, DVD, Blu-ray Disc, UMD.** *US* Thomas Jane, John Travolta, Edward Jemison, Samantha Mathis, Will Patton, Laura Elena Harring, Roy Scheider, Rebecca Romijn, Geoff Wallace, Mark Collie, John Pinette, Russell Andrews, Marc Macaulay, Ben Foster, Eduardo Yanez, Marcus Johns, Bonnie Johnson, Omar Avila; *D:* Jonathan Hensleigh; *W:* Jonathan Hensleigh, Michael France; *C:* Conrad W. Hall; *M:* Carlo Siliotto.

Punisher: War Zone ⚡⚡ 1/2 **2008 (R)** In this third rendering of the Marvel Comics' vigilante justice-seeker Frank Castle, or The Punisher (Stevenson, taking over for Thomas Jane), full-length director newbie Alexander gleefully surpasses her predecessors in the how-many-different-gory-ways-can-they-die category. When Castle unwittingly knocks off an undercover FBI agent during one of his anti-mob slaughter sessions, his guilty conscience forces him to protect the widow and her daughter from one of the escaped mobsters, Billy Russoti (West) and his brother Loony Bin Jim (Hutchison). It seems that Russoti is a little upset that the Punisher caused him to have a horribly disfiguring encounter with a glass-crushing machine during the melee, and he reemerges as the aptly named Jigsaw—and recruits a criminal army. **107m/C DVD.** *US GE* Ray Stevenson, Dominic West, Julie Benz, Wayne Knight, Doug Hutchison, Dash Mihok, Doug Hutchison, Colin Salmon; *D:* Lexi Alexander; *W:* Nick Santora, Art

Marcum, Mat Holloway; ***C:*** Steve Gainer; ***M:*** Michael Wandmacher.

Punk Love 1/2 **2006** Sarah is an aimless 15-year-old, living in a bad home situation in a dreary factory town. She hooks up with drug addicted musician Spike and they turn to petty crime to support themselves. Things start looking up when Spike's band audition actually pays off but they head downwards soon enough. **96m/C DVD.** Chad Lindberg, Max Perlich, Emma Bing; ***D:*** Nick Lyon; ***W:*** Nick Lyon; ***C:*** Rene Richter; ***M:*** Miles Mosley. **VIDEO**

Punk Vacation **1990** A gang of motorcycle mamas terrorize a small town. The usual biker stuff. **90m/C VHS.** Stephen Falchi, Roxanne Rogers, Don Martin, Sandra Bogan; ***D:*** Stanley Lewis.

P.U.N.K.S. 1/2 **1998 (PG)** Preteen Drew (Redwine) and his friends are regularly beaten up by school bullies. Then they realize that evil industrialist Edward Crow (Winkler) has stolen an invention that turns weaklings into hulks and they decide to steal it back. **99m/C VHS.** Randy Quaid, Cathy Moriarty, Henry Winkler, Ted Redwine, Patrick Renna; ***D:*** Sean McNamara. **VIDEO**

Puppet Master 1/2 **1989 (R)** Four psychics are sent to investigate a puppet maker who they think may have discovered the secret of life. Before they know it, they are stalked by evil puppets. Great special effects, not-so-great script. **90m/C VHS, DVD.** Paul LeMat, Jimmie F. Skaggs, Irene Miracle, Robyn Frates, Barbara Crampton, William Hickey, Matt Roe, Kathryn O'Reilly; ***D:*** David Schmoeller; ***W:*** Joseph G. Collodi; ***C:*** Sergio Salvati; ***M:*** Richard Band.

Puppet Master 2 **1990 (R)** Puppets on a rampage turn hotel into den of special effects. Less effective string pulling than in original. Long live Pinocchio. **90m/C VHS, DVD.** Elizabeth MacLellan, Collin Bernsen, Greg Webb, Charlie Spradling, Nita Talbot, Steve Welles, Jeff Weston; ***D:*** Dave Allen; ***W:*** David Pabian; ***C:*** Thomas Denove; ***M:*** Richard Band.

Puppet Master 3: Toulon's Revenge **1990 (R)** Prequel about the origin of the whole gory Puppet Master shebang, set in Nazi Germany. The weapon-hungry Third Reich tries to wrest secrets of artificial life from sorceror Andre Toulon, who sics his deadly puppets on them. Toulon's a good guy here, one of many contradictions in the series. Fine cast, but strictly for the followers. **86m/C VHS, DVD.** Guy Rolfe, Ian Abercrombie, Sarah Douglas, Richard Lynch, Walter Gotell; ***D:*** David DeCoteau; ***W:*** C. Courtney Joyner; ***C:*** Adolfo Bartoli; ***M:*** Richard Band.

Puppet Master 4 **1993 (R)** It's the puppets versus the totems, equally loathsome midget creatures who derive their power from the same eternal force as the puppets. No one wants to share and there's lots of gore while they battle for supremacy. **80m/C VHS, DVD.** Gordon Currie, Chandra West, Jason Adams, Teresa Hill, Guy Rolfe; ***D:*** Jeff Burr; ***W:*** Todd Henschell, Steven E. Carr, Jo Duffy, Douglas Aarniokoski, Keith Payson; ***M:*** Richard Band.

Puppet Master 5: The Final Chapter 1/2 **1994** Greedy Dr. Jennings has come to Bodega Bay Inn to capture the puppets and discover the secret formula for their animation so he can sell it to the highest bidder. But he's not the only threat, it seems the demonic Eyad, a being from another dimension, also wants the secret and has sent his own evil puppet to kill the puppet master and steal their magic. **81m/C VHS, DVD.** Gordon Currie, Chandra West, Ian Ogilvy, Teresa Hill, Nicholas Guest, Willard Pugh, Diane McBain, Kaz Garas, Guy Rolfe; ***D:*** Jeff Burr; ***W:*** Douglas Aarniokoski, Jo Duffy, Todd Henschell, Keith Payson, Steven E. Karr; ***C:*** Adolfo Bartoli; ***M:*** Richard Band.

The Puppet Masters *Robert A. Heinlein's The Puppet Masters* **1994 (R)** Government official (Sutherland) discovers aliens are taking over the bodies of humans and if he doesn't find a way to stop the parasites they'll soon rule the Earth. Yes, it does sound like "Invasion of the Body Snatchers" but the film is based on Robert A. Heinlein's 1951 novel, written five years before. The parasites are sufficiently yucky but, unfortunately, this adaptation is mediocre and generally wastes a talented cast. **109m/C VHS, DVD.** Donald Sutherland, Eric Thal, Julie Warner, Keith David, Will Patton, Richard Belzer, Yaphet Kotto, Dale Dye; ***D:*** Stuart Orme; ***W:*** Terry Rossio, David S. Goyer, Ted Elliott; ***M:*** Colin Towns.

Puppet on a Chain **1972 (PG)** American narcotics officer busts an Amsterdam drug ring and the leader's identity surprises him. Slow-moving thriller based on the Alistair MacLean novel. **97m/C VHS.** *GB* Sven-Bertil Taube, Barbara Parkins, Alexander Knox, Patrick Allen, Geoffrey Reeve; ***D:*** Geoffrey Reeve; ***C:*** Jack Hildyard.

The Puppetoon Movie **1987 (G)** A compilation of George Pal's famous Puppetoon cartoons from the 1940s, marking his stature as an animation pioneer and innovator. Hosted by Gumby, Pokey, Speedy Alka Seltzer and Arnie the Dinosaur in newly directed scenes. **80m/C VHS, DVD.** ***D:*** Arnold Leibovit; ***M:*** Buddy (Norman Dale) Baker.

Pups **1999** Surburban 13-year-old Stevie (Van Hoy) finds his mom's gun, which he shows to equally young girlfriend, Rocky (Barton). Instead of going to school, Stevie impulsively decides to rob a nearby bank, and nearly gets away with it until the cops and the FBI show up. Now the kids have hostages and no clue as to what they're doing, while hostage negotiator Daniel Bender (Reynolds) tries to get a volatile Stevie to listen to reason. **103m/C VHS, DVD.** Cameron Van Hoy, Mischa Barton, Burt Reynolds, Darling Narita; ***D:*** Ash; ***W:*** Ash; ***C:*** Carolos Arguello.

Purana Mandir *The Old Temple* **1984** The Ramsay brothers are considered the fathers of Bollywood horror, and this is one of their better efforts. A demon is ordered beheaded by the Raja, but before dying he curses the Raja and his family for all time. Flash forward to modern day India, where the Raja's great great grandson has a daughter who wishes to marry, and he doesn't know how to explain why she can't. Be aware Bollywood films tend to follow a very different formula than Hollywood, and their style may not make sense to a western audience as they shift from one genre to another effortlessly (and this pic includes a comic parody of "Sholay," the biggest hit in Bollywood history). **145m/C DVD.** *IN* Mohnish Bahl, Arti Gupta, Puneet Issar, Sadashiv Amrapurkar, Ajay Agarwal, Satish Shah, Rajendra Nath, Pradeep Kumar, Dheeraj Kumar, Leen Das, Ashalata, Lalita Pawar, Jagdeep; ***D:*** Shyam Ramsay, Tulsi Ramsay; ***W:*** J. K. Ahuja, Dr. Gurdeep, Siddiqui M.S. Rahman, Kumar Ramsay; ***C:*** Gangu Ramsay; ***M:*** Ajit Singh.

The Purchase Price **1932** After a less than amorous beginning, farmer Brent and mail order bride Stanwyck fall into love and financial despair in this drama bordering on comedy. Good neighbor Landau is willing to help the poor agriculturalist out in exchange for Stanwyck. Tragedy strikes again when Stanwyck's bootlegger ex-boyfriend shows up and further disasters continue to test the couple's commitment. Based on the story "The Mud Lark" by Arthur Stringer. **70m/B VHS.** Barbara Stanwyck, George Brent, Lyle Talbot, Hardie Albright, David Landau; ***D:*** William A. Wellman; ***W:*** Robert Lord.

Pure **2002 (R)** Sentimental and brutal tale about Paul (Eden), a 10-year-old boy trying to stay in control of his life and save his mother from her addiction to heroin. Everyone around him is either an addict, a prostitute, or a pusher, yet he remains in confident denial of his true situation. The bad choices and ludicrous behavior of the adults in his life are perpetual and heartbreaking. Fine acting, especially by Eden; well shot but story on the whole is emotionally unsatisfying. **94m/C DVD.** *GB GB* Molly Parker, David Wenham, Geraldine McEwan, Keira Knightley, Kate Ashfield, Gary Lewis, Marsha Thomason, Karl Johnson, Harry Eden, Nitin Ganatra, Levi Hayes, Vinni Hunter; ***D:*** Gilles Mackinnon; ***W:*** Alison Hume; ***C:*** John de Borman; ***M:*** Nitin Sawhney.

Pure Country 1/2 **1992 (PG)** An easygoing movie about a familiar subject is held together by the charm of Strait (in his movie debut) and the rest of the cast. Strait plays a country music superstar, tired of the career glitz, who decides to get out and go back to his home in Texas. He falls in love with the spunky Glasser and decides to run his career his own way. Warren is effective as his tough manager and old-time cowboy Calhoun is finely weathered as Glasser's gruff dad. **113m/C VHS, DVD.** George Strait, Isabel Glasser, Lesley Ann Warren, Rory Calhoun, Kyle Chandler, John Doe, Molly McClure; ***D:*** Christopher Cain; ***W:*** Rex McGee; ***C:*** Rick Bota; ***M:*** Steve Dorff.

Pure Danger 1/2 **1996 (R)** Short order cook Johnny (Howell) and his waitress girlfriend Becky (Linn) stumble upon a bag of diamonds and think all their troubles are over. Wrong—they're just beginning, since some very nasty men want the jewels and don't care who they kill to get them. Howell keeps his directorial debut fast-paced and surprisingly entertaining. **99m/C VHS, DVD.** C. Thomas Howell, Teri Ann Linn, Leon, Michael Russo; ***D:*** C. Thomas Howell; ***W:*** William Applegate Jr., Joseph John Barmettler Jr.; ***C:*** Ken Blakey; ***M:*** K. Alexander (Alex) Wilkinson.

A Pure Formality *Una Pura Formalita; Une Pure Formalite* **1994 (PG-13)** Murky psycho-drama finds a disheveled man (Depardieu) winding up at an isolated police station in a nameless country (in the middle of a rainstorm, no less). The Inspector (Polanski) suspects him of a local murder, especially after he claims to be a famous writer named Onoff, yet, can remember nothing. The Inspector wants a confession and spends the night trying to exact one from his guileful suspect. French with subtitles. Film is rated at a much younger level than will possibly understand or enjoy it. **111m/C VHS.** *FR IT* Gerard Depardieu, Roman Polanski, Sergio Rubini; ***D:*** Giuseppe Tornatore; ***W:*** Giuseppe Tornatore, Pascal Quignard; ***C:*** Blasco Giurato; ***M:*** Ennio Morricone.

The Pure Hell of St. Trinian's 1/2 **1961** In this sequel to "Blue Murder at St. Trinian's," a sheik who desires to fill out his harem tries recruiting at a rowdy girls' school. Although it isn't as funny as the first, due to the lack of Alistair Sim, it is still humorous. Followed by "The Great St. Trinian's Train Robbery." Based on the cartoon by Ronald Searle. **94m/B VHS.** *GB* Cecil Parker, Joyce Grenfell, George Cole, Thorley Walters; ***D:*** Frank Launder; ***M:*** Malcolm Arnold.

Pure Luck 1/2 **1991 (PG)** A who-asked-for-it remake of a 1981 Franco-Italian film called "La Chevre." The premise is the same: an accident-prone heiress disappears in Mexico, and her father tries to locate her using an equally clumsy accountant. The nebbish and an attendant tough private eye stumble and bumble south of the border until the plot arbitrarily ends. Pure awful. **96m/C VHS.** Martin Short, Danny Glover, Sheila Kelley, Scott Wilson, Sam Wanamaker, Harry Shearer; ***D:*** Nadia Tass; ***W:*** Herschel Weingrod, Timothy Harris.

Purgatory **1989** While travelling abroad, two innocent women find themselves unjustly jailed. During their confinement they are tortured and raped. **90m/C VHS.** Tanya Roberts, Julie Pop; ***D:*** Ami Artzi; ***W:*** Paul Aratow.

Purgatory 1/2 **1999** A group of desperadoes head for what they think is the defenseless town of Refuge, where the sheriff (Shepard) doesn't carry a gun or allow cussing. But the town and its inhabitants are not what they seem and these cowpoke bad guys are in for quite a surprise. **94m/C VHS.** Sam Shepard, Eric Roberts, Randy Quaid, Peter Stormare, Donnie Wahlberg; ***D:*** Uli Edel; ***W:*** Gordon Dawson. **CABLE**

Purgatory House 1/2 **2004 (R)** Unable to bear her miserable drug-addled and Goth-wannabe existence, 14-year-old Silver Strand (Davis) offs herself, only to become stranded with other similarly-troubled teens between heaven and hell, where she is made to attend daily group sessions while watching the televised earthly sufferings of the loved ones she left behind. With the help of Saint James (Hanks) she must either cope with the fallout or be stuck there. Frank discussion of teen angst by first-time director Baer and written by lead Davis, who was 14 years old at the time. **95m/C DVD.** Celeste Davis, Jim Hanks, Johnny Pacar, Devin Witt, Cindy Baer; ***D:*** Cindy Baer; ***W:*** Celeste Davis. **VIDEO**

The Purifiers **2004 (R)** In a near-future Glasgow, rival gangs like to show off by holding martial arts battles. Crime boss Moses (McKidd) wants to organize the gangs but the Purifiers, led by John (Alexander), are eager to keep crime out of their 'hood and don't want to go along. Chop-socky with a Scottish brogue. **85m/C DVD.** Kevin McKidd, Dominic Monaghan, Gordon Alexander, Rachel Grant; ***D:*** Richard Jobson; ***W:*** Richard Jobson; ***C:*** John Rhodes; ***M:*** Steven Severin.

Purlie Victorious 1/2 *Gone are the Days!; The Man from C.O.T.T.O.N* **1963** Preacher Purlie (Davis) returns to Georgia and tries to get an inheritance from the plantation owner, "Ol' Cap'n" Cotchipee (Booke), he used to serve. Cotchipee's progressive son (Alda) unexpectedly helps him in his cause. Presentation of Davis's award-winning Broadway hit. **93m/C VHS.** Ossie Davis, Ruby Dee, Godfrey Cambridge, Alan Alda, Sorrell Booke, Beah Richards; ***D:*** Nicholas Webster; ***W:*** Ossie Davis; ***C:*** Boris Kaufman.

Purple Butterfly 1/2 *Zi Hudie* **2003 (R)** Stunning political thriller/noir set in 1930s Shanghai. Zhang stars as Cynthia/Ding Hui, an operative in the anti-Japanese underground Purple Butterfly. She's a fearless and dedicated patriot driven by the assassination of her brother years before. Her past comes to haunt her in the form of former lover Itami (Nakamura), who is now a Japanese agent assigned to bring down Purple Butterfly. Soon enough, the two are caught in a delicate balancing act, struggling between their duty and the love that may still exist between them, while all around them the conflict between Japanese and Chinese threatens not only them but innocent people as well. Director Lou mixes Western noir style with a distinct, dreamlike moodiness that ensnares while shocking with interesting twists in the complex plot. Chinese with English subtitles. **127m/C DVD.** Ziyi Zhang, Toru Nakamura, Ye Liu, Yuanzheng Feng; ***D:*** Ye Lou; ***W:*** Ye Lou; ***C:*** Yu Wang; ***M:*** Jorg Lemberg.

The Purple Heart 1/2 **1944** An American Air Force crew is shot down over Tokyo and taken into brutal POW camps. Intense wartime melodramatics. **99m/B VHS, DVD.** Dana Andrews, Richard Conte, Farley Granger, Donald (Don "Red") Barry, Sam Levene, Kevin O'Shea, Tala Birell, Nestor Paiva, Benson Fong, Marshall Thompson, Richard Loo; ***D:*** Lewis Milestone; ***C:*** Arthur C. Miller.

Purple Heart **2005 (R)** What obligation does the military have to care for its damaged soldiers while simultaneously hiding the truth about its operations? Colonel Allen (Sadler) leads a covert unit into Iraq with orders to kill Saddam Hussein prior to the 2003 invasion. Marine sniper Oscar Padilla (Navarro) is chosen for the job, but he's captured and tortured. After his rescue, the troubled Padilla is locked in a military psych ward from which he escapes. Allen is sent after him since if word of their illegal mission gets out it would cause a political firestorm. **91m/C DVD.** William Sadler, Demetrius Navarro, Mel Harris; ***D:*** Bill Birrell; ***W:*** Russell Gannon, Bill Birrell; ***C:*** Guy Livneh; ***M:*** Ralph Rieckermann. **VIDEO**

Purple Hearts 1/2 **1984 (R)** Wahl stars as a Navy doctor who falls in love with nurse Ladd against the backdrop of the Vietnam war. Overlong and redundant. **115m/C VHS.** Cheryl Ladd, Ken Wahl, Stephen Lee, Annie McEnroe, Paul McCrane, Cyril O'Reilly; ***D:*** Sidney J. Furie; ***W:*** Sidney J. Furie, Ron Nyswaner; ***M:*** Robert Folk.

The Purple Monster Strikes *D-Day on Mars; The Purple Shadow Strikes* **1945** A martian plots to conquer Earth to save his dying planet. Serial in 15 episodes. **188m/B VHS.** Dennis Moore, Linda Stirling, Roy Barcroft; ***D:*** Spencer Gordon Bennet, Fred Brannon; ***W:*** Barney A. Sarecky, Basil Dickey, Lynn Perkins, Joseph Poland, Albert DeMond; ***C:*** Bud Thackery.

Purple Noon *Plein Soleil; Lust for Evil* **1960 (PG-13)** Don't let the ratings fool you, this isn't teen fodder. The gorgeous

Delon stars as opportunistic Tom Ripley, who's hired by the father of his rich, arrogant playboy friend Philippe (Ronet) to persuade him to return home to San Francisco. Instead, Ripley covets the man's yacht, beautiful girlfriend Marge (Laforet), and money, so when Philippe pushes Tom too far he disposes of him and tries to divert police suspicions. Film noir set in the hedonistic Mediterranean sun. Based on the novel "The Talented Mr. Ripley" by Patricia Highsmith, although the ending of novel and film differ greatly. French with subtitles. **118m/C VHS, DVD.** *FR* Alain Delon, Maurice Ronet, Marie Laforet, Erno Crisa, Billy Kearns; ***D:*** Rene Clement; ***W:*** Rene Clement, Paul Gegauff; ***C:*** Henri Decae; ***M:*** Nino Rota.

Purple People Eater **1988 (PG)** The alien of the title descends to earth to mix with young girls and rock 'n' roll. Based on the song of the same name whose performer, Sheb Wooley, appears in the film. Harmless, stupid fun for the whole family. **91m/C VHS.** Ned Beatty, Shelley Winters, Neil Patrick Harris, Kareem Abdul-Jabbar, Little Richard, Chubby Checker, Peggy Lipton; ***D:*** Linda Shayne.

Purple Rain 1/2 **1984 (R)** A quasi-autobiographical video showcase for the pop-star Prince. Film tells the tale of his struggle for love, attention, acceptance, and popular artistic recognition in Minneapolis. Not a bad film, for such a monumentally egotistical movie. **113m/C VHS, DVD, Blu-ray Disc, HD DVD.** Prince, Apollonia, Morris Day, Olga Karlatos, Clarence Williams III; ***D:*** Albert Magnoli; ***W:*** William Blinn; ***C:*** Donald E. Thorin; ***M:*** Michel Colombier. Oscars '84: Orig. Song Score and/or Adapt.

The Purple Rose of Cairo **1985 (PG)** A diner waitress, disillusioned by the Depression and a lackluster life, escapes into a film playing at the local movie house where a blond film hero, tiring of the monotony of his role, makes a break from the celluloid to join her in the real world. The ensuing love story allows director-writer Allen to show his knowledge of old movies and provide his fans with a change of pace. Farrow's film sister is also her real-life sister Stephanie, who went on to appear in Allen's "Zelig." **82m/C VHS, DVD.** Mia Farrow, Jeff Daniels, Danny Aiello, Dianne Wiest, Van Johnson, Zoe Caldwell, John Wood, Michael Tucker, Edward Herrmann, Milo O'Shea, Glenne Headly, Karen Akers, Deborah Rush; ***D:*** Woody Allen; ***W:*** Woody Allen; ***C:*** Gordon Willis; ***M:*** Dick Hyman. British Acad. '85: Film, Orig. Screenplay; Cesar '86: Foreign Film; Golden Globes '86: Screenplay; N.Y. Film Critics '85: Screenplay.

The Purple Taxi 1/2 **1977 (R)** Romantic drama revolving around several wealthy foreigners who have taken refuge in beautiful southern Ireland. From Michel Deon's bestselling novel. **93m/C VHS.** *FR* Fred Astaire, Charlotte Rampling, Peter Ustinov, Philippe Noiret, Edward Albert; ***D:*** Yves Boisset.

Purple Vigilantes 1/2 *The Purple Riders* **1938** The Three Mesquiteers uncover a gang of vigilantes. Part of the series. **54m/B VHS, DVD.** Robert "Bob" Livingston, Ray Corrigan, Max Terhune, Joan Barclay, Earl Dwire, Earle Hodgins, George Chesebro, Robert (Fisk) Fiske; ***D:*** George Sherman; ***W:*** Betty Burbridge, Oliver Drake; ***C:*** Ernest Miller.

Purple Violets 1/2 **2007** Yet another of Burns' New York-set comedy-dramas, but this time he takes a supporting role to the somewhat more appealing story of Blair and Wilson. Patti (Blair) is a failed novelist in a bad marriage, unhappily working as a real estate agent. Out for a drink with girlfriend Kate (Messing), she runs into her college beau Brian (Wilson), a successful writer of crime fiction who has just had a professional setback. Along with Brian is his best friend, Murph (Burns), who used to be Kate's college love until an incident she refuses to forgive him for, though he keeps trying to charm her. Meanwhile, Patti and Brian decide to explore the possibilities of renewing their romance. **93m/C DVD.** Selma Blair, Patrick Wilson, Debra Messing, Edward Burns, Donal Logue, Elizabeth Reaser, Dennis Farina; ***D:*** Edward Burns; ***W:*** Edward Burns; ***C:*** William Rexer; ***M:*** P.T. Walkley. **VIDEO**

Purpose 1/2 **2002 (R)** College dropout turned Internet entrepreneur John Elias (Light) finds fame and fortune during the dot.com boom but things turn rough when his girlfriend (Dodds) and dad (Coyote) question his business ethics and John must prevent a hostil takeover of his company. **96m/C VHS, DVD.** John Light, Megan Dodds, Peter Coyote, Jeffrey Donovan, Hal Holbrook, Mia Farrow, Paul Reiser; ***D:*** Alan Ari Lazar; ***W:*** Alan Ari Lazar; ***M:*** Alan Ari Lazar.

Pursued **1947** Excellent performances by Mitchum and Wright mark this suspenseful Western drama of a Spanish-American war veteran in search of his father's killer. **105m/B VHS, DVD.** Teresa Wright, Robert Mitchum, Judith Anderson, Dean Jagger, Alan Hale, Harry Carey Jr., John Rodney; ***D:*** Raoul Walsh; ***C:*** James Wong Howe; ***M:*** Max Steiner.

Pursuit **1972** A terrorist threatens to release a toxic nerve gas throughout a city hosting a political convention. Tension mounts as federal agents must beat the extremists' countdown to zero. Based on the novel by Crichton. **73m/C VHS, DVD.** Ben Gazzara, E.G. Marshall, Martin Sheen, Joseph Wiseman, William Windom; ***D:*** Michael Crichton; ***M:*** Jerry Goldsmith.

Pursuit **1990 (R)** A mercenary comes out of retirement to join a renegade team recovering stolen gold. But they turn on him, stealing the treasure and taking a hostage. Now he must track them down, or there's no movie. **94m/C VHS.** James Ryan, Andre Jacobs; ***D:*** John H. Parr.

The Pursuit of D.B. Cooper **1981 (PG)** Based on an actual hijacking that occurred on Thanksgiving Eve in 1971 in which J.R. Meade (alias D.B. Cooper) parachuted out of an airliner with $200,000 of stolen money. Although his fate and whereabouts have remained a mystery, this story speculates about what may have happened. **100m/C VHS.** Robert Duvall, Treat Williams, Kathryn Harrold, Ed Flanders; ***D:*** Roger Spottiswoode; ***C:*** Harry Stradling Jr.; ***M:*** James Horner.

The Pursuit of Happiness 1/2 **1970 (PG)** An idealistic man is convicted of manslaughter after accidentally running down a woman. Once in prison, he's faced with the decision to try to escape. **85m/C VHS.** Michael Sarrazin, Arthur Hill, E.G. Marshall, Barbara Hershey, Robert Klein; ***D:*** Robert Mulligan.

Pursuit of Happiness 1/2 **2001** L.A. ad exec Alan Oliver (Whaley) always has his longtime best platonic friend Marissa (Gish) to turn to when his life spins out of control. And it's about to—his boss (Stapleton) takes him off his biggest account, his girlfriend moves out, and he's suddenly in a rebound romance with Tracy (Johnson). What Alan fails to realize is that Marissa is also having trouble since her marriage is falling apart. Oh, and as Alan pursues happiness, he should also realize that it's closer than he thinks. **93m/C VHS, DVD.** Frank Whaley, Annabeth Gish, Amy Jo Johnson, Patrick Van Horn, Jean Stapleton, Alex Hyde-White, Cress Williams, Liz Vassey, Kieran Mulroney, Anne-Marie Johnson, Michelle Krusiec, Adam Baldwin, Tom Wright; ***D:*** John Putch; ***W:*** John Robert Zaring; ***C:*** Ross Berryman.

The Pursuit of Happyness 1/2 **2006 (PG-13)** Smith and too-cute son Jaden (in his film debut) easily fill the shoes of real-life father and son as Chris Gardner and 5-year-old Christopher. When Chris' bad decisions leave the family broke and mom (Newton) bails, father and son are soon homeless, until Chris pins his hopes on a six-month unpaid competitive internship at a brokerage firm that could lead to a full-time job and a stable life. The usual feel-good, never-give-up path ensues, and the Smiths make it a worthwhile journey. A misspelling on a mural at Christopher's daycare center supplied the film's title. **120m/C DVD, Blu-ray Disc.** *US* Will Smith, Thandie Newton, Brian Howe, James Karen, Jaden Smith, Dan Castellaneta, Kurt Fuller; ***D:*** Gabriele Muccino; ***W:*** Steve Conrad; ***C:*** Phedon Papamichael; ***M:*** Andrea Guerra.

Pursuit of the Graf Spee 1/2 *The Battle of the River Plate* **1957** Three small British ships destroy the mighty Graf Spee, a WWII German battleship. **106m/C VHS.** *GB* Anthony Quayle, Peter Finch, Ian Hunter; ***D:*** Michael Powell.

Pursuit to Algiers 1/2 **1945** The modernized Holmes and Watson guard over the King of fictional Rovenia during a sea voyage, during which assassins close in. **65m/B VHS, DVD.** Basil Rathbone, Nigel Bruce, Martin Kosleck, Marjorie (Reardon) Riordan, Rosalind Ivan, John Abbott; ***D:*** Roy William Neill.

Push **2006 (R)** Unoriginal drug story set in Miami. Bartender Joe (Lindberg) gets his greedy pals Micky (DePaolo) and Kevin (Forsythe) involved in a scheme to push Ecstasy for drug lord Paul (Sanchez). Naturally, they get in too deep and bad things happen. **105m/C DVD.** Chad Lindberg, Otto Sanchez, Chazz Palminteri, Charlotte Ayanna, William DePaolo, Pierce Forsythe, Michael Rapaport; ***D:*** Dave Rodriguez; ***W:*** Dave Rodriguez, Ben Carlin; ***C:*** Steve Goodman; ***M:*** Tommy Finno.

Push 1/2 **2009 (PG-13)** Operating in a shadowy spy world of paranormals are the subsequent generations of the subjects of a Nazi experiment gone awry, battling over world supremacy. A government agency known as "the Division" seeks to exploit these gifted individuals to carry out their dastardly plans, but young Cassie (Fanning), a "watcher," teams up with Nick (Evans), a "telekinetic," who is underground in Hong Kong to rescue Kira (Belle). Kira is a "pusher" (one who can push thoughts and beliefs into others' minds) who the Division wants dead. Slick and sophisticated cinematography but the performances and plot fall flat. **111m/C DVD.** *US* Chris Evans, Dakota Fanning, Camilla Belle, Djimon Hounsou, Clifford Curtis, Neil Jackson, Maggie Siff, Ming Na, Nate Mooney; ***D:*** Paul McGuigan; ***W:*** David Bourla; ***C:*** Peter Sova; ***M:*** Neil Davidge.

Pushed to the Limit 1/2 **1992 (R)** Harry Lee, the most feared gangster in Chinatown, is about to meet his match in martial-arts queen Lesseos. She's out for revenge when she learns that Lee is responsible for her brother's murder but first she must get by Lee's lethal bodyguard, the equally skilled Inga. **88m/C VHS, DVD.** Mimi Lesseos, Henry Hayashi, Verrel Reed, Barbara Braverman, Greg Ostrin; ***D:*** Michael Mileham; ***W:*** Mimi Lesseos; ***C:*** Bodo Holst; ***M:*** Miriam Cutler.

Pusher **1996** Violent thriller was the directorial debut of 24-year-old Refn. Frank (Bodnia) and his buddy Tonny (Mikkelsen) sell heroin in Copenhagen. Their drug supplier is a Serbian gangster named Milo (Buric), to whom Frank owes money. Things get worse when Frank dumps his latest supply before being arrested—Milo warns him if he doesn't pay his debts in the next couple of days, he's a dead man. The more Frank tries to get the money, the worse things get for him. Danish with subtitles. **105m/C VHS, DVD.** *DK* Kim Bodnia, Zlatko Buric, Mads Mikkelsen, Laura Drasbaek, Slavko Labovic, Lisbeth Rasmussen; ***D:*** Nicolas Winding Refn; ***W:*** Nicolas Winding Refn, Jens Dahl; ***C:*** Morten Soborg; ***M:*** Povl Kristian Mortensen.

Pushing Hands 1/2 **1992** Aging tai chi master Mr. Chu (Lung) leaves Beijing to live with his son Alex (Wang) and daughter-in-law Martha (Snyder) in suburban New York. High-strung Martha doesn't understand her tranquilly stubborn father-in-law, nor does Chu find disposable American society much to his liking. Naturally, and slowly, some accomodations are made. The title is a tai chi reference to keeping your opponent off-balance while maintaining your own equilibrium. Director Lee's debut feature is also the first in his trilogy of family films—followed by the more accomplished "The Wedding Banquet" and "Eat Drink Man Woman." English and Mandarin Chinese with subtitles. **100m/C VHS, DVD.** Sihung Lung, Deb Snyder, Bo Z. Wang, Lai Wang; ***D:*** Ang Lee; ***W:*** Ang Lee; ***C:*** Jong Lin; ***M:*** Xiao-Song Qu.

Pushing Tin **1999 (R)** Nick (Cusack) and Russell (Thornton) are rival air traffic controllers at the Long Island tower that oversees New York's three main airports (JFK, La Guardia, and Newark). Nick is a cool professional and a family man, with stay-at-home wife Connie (Blanchett) and two kids. Russell is a cowboy whose wife Mary (Jolie)is young, wild, and usually drunk. The guys' rivalry at work is intensified when Nick sleeps with Mary and his paranoia and guilt get to him. The technical and journalistic aspects (it's based on a New York Times article) of the tower scenes get things started in surprisingly exciting fashion, and the four leads keep the intensity going with excellent performances despite some script lapses and questionable plot devices at the end. **124m/C VHS, DVD.** John Cusack, Billy Bob Thornton, Cate Blanchett, Angelina Jolie, Vicki Lewis, Jake Weber, Kurt Fuller, Matt Ross, Jerry Grayson, Michael Willis; ***D:*** Mike Newell; ***W:*** Glen Charles, Les Charles; ***C:*** Gale Tattersall; ***M:*** Anne Dudley.

Pushover **1954** It's all because of a dame. Detective Paul Sheridan (MacMurray) is assigned to befriend moll Lona (Novak) in the hopes she'll lead him to her gangster boyfriend Wheeler (Richards), who was involved in a bank robbery. However, Sheridan and Lona get a little too friendly. After Sheridan and two cohorts stake out Lona's apartment, he agrees to the femme's plan to kill Wheeler and keep the dough instead. The plan goes wrong. **88m/B DVD.** Fred MacMurray, Kim Novak, Phil Carey, Paul Richards, Allen Nourse, Dorothy Malone, E.G. Marshall; ***D:*** Richard Quine; ***W:*** Roy Huggins; ***C:*** Lester White; ***M:*** Arthur Morton.

Puss 'n Boots **1984** From "Faerie Tale Theatre" comes the story of a cat who makes his poor master a rich land-owning nobleman. **60m/C VHS, DVD.** Ben Vereen, Gregory Hines; ***D:*** Robert Iscove. **CABLE**

Putney Swope **1969 (R)** Comedy about a token black ad man mistakenly elected Chairman of the board of a Madison Avenue ad agency who turns the company upside-down. A series of riotous spoofs on commercials is the highpoint in this funny, though somewhat dated look at big business. **84m/B VHS, DVD.** Arnold Johnson, Laura Greene, Stanley Gottlieb, Mel Brooks; ***D:*** Robert Downey; ***W:*** Robert Downey; ***C:*** Gerald Cotts; ***M:*** Charles Cura.

Puzzle 1/2 **1978** Franciscus searches for the urn that contains the remains of Buddha but instead finds danger and intrigue. **90m/C VHS.** *AU* James Franciscus, Wendy Hughes, Robert Helpmann, Peter Gwynne, Gerald Kennedy, Kerry McGuire; ***D:*** Gordon Hessler. **TV**

Puzzlehead 1/2 **2005** Hitchcock and Frankenstein collide in this ill-fated fable. Walter creates an android that not only looks like him but also has his psyche downloaded into its hard drive. As Puzzlehead starts to experience more of Walter's emotions, things get complicated and the two find themselves in love with the same Russian woman from the shop down the street. Conceptually and visually stunning with a regrettably flat-lined plot. **81m/C DVD.** Stephen Galaida, Robbie Shapiro; ***D:*** James Bai; ***W:*** James Bai; ***C:*** Jeffrey Scott Lando; ***M:*** Max Lichtenstein.

Pygmalion 1/2 **1938** Oscar-winning film adaptation of Shaw's play about a cockney flower-girl who is transformed into a "lady" under the guidance of a stuffy phonetics professor. Shaw himself aided in writing the script in this superbly acted comedy that would be adapted into the musical, "My Fair Lady," first on Broadway in 1956 and for the screen in 1964. **96m/B VHS, DVD.** *GB* Leslie Howard, Wendy Hiller, Wilfred Lawson, Marie Lohr, Scott Sunderland, David Tree, Everley Gregg, Leueen McGrath, Jean Cadell, Eileen Beldon, Frank Atkinson, O.B. Clarence, Esme Percy, Violet Vanbrugh, Iris Hoey, Viola Tree, Irene Browne, Kate Cutler, Cathleen Nesbitt, Cecil Trouncer, Stephen Murray, Wally Patch, H.F. Maltby; ***D:*** Anthony Asquith, Leslie Howard; ***W:*** W.P. Lipscomb, Anatole de Grunwald, Cecil Lewis, Ian Dalrymple, George Bernard Shaw; ***C:*** Harry Stradling Sr. Oscars '38: Screenplay; Venice Film Fest. '38: Actor (Howard).

Pyrates **1991 (R)** Real life husband-wife team of Bacon and Sedgwick try to provide fireworks as hot, hot lovers in the forgettable one. For the price of this one you can buy a newspaper and chewing gum instead. Use both at the same time and you'll be ahead of everyone involved in this senseless hoot. **98m/C VHS.** Kevin Bacon, Kyra Sedgwick, Bruce Payne, Kristin Dattilo-Hayward; ***D:*** Noah Stern.

A Pyromaniac's Love Story ♂♂ **1995 (PG)** Offbeat tale of romance has a neigborhood bakery burning down and every major character confessing to the crime. Earnest working stiffs, snotty rich kids, and kindly old shop owners all have really confusing reasons for wanting to take the heat, most of which have to do with unrequited love. At times charming, but ultimately too whimsical for its own good. The quirky characters and goofy plot twists sabotage any attempt to ignite much interest. **99m/C VHS, DVD.** John Leguizamo, Sadie Frost, William Baldwin, Erika Eleniak, Michael Lerner, Joan Plowright, Armin Mueller-Stahl, Richard Crenna; ***D:*** Joshua Brand; ***W:*** Morgan Ward; ***C:*** John Schwartzman; ***M:*** Rachel Portman.

Python ♂ 1/2 **2000 (R)** Intelligence organization develops a perfect weapon in a gigantic python. Of course, the government screws up, the snake gets loose, and there's hell to pay. **90m/C VHS, DVD.** Robert Englund, Casper Van Dien, Jenny McCarthy, Wil Wheaton, Frayne Rosenoff; ***D:*** Richard Clabaugh; ***W:*** Chris Neal, Gary Hershberger, Paul J.M. Bogh; ***C:*** Patrick Rousseau; ***M:*** David J. Nelsen. **VIDEO**

Python 2 **WOOF!** **2002 (R)** HISSSSSSSSS!!! No, not the titular snake, the unfortunate viewer who picks up this woofer. American cargo plane carrying a secret weapon is shot down over war-torn Chechnya and Russian scientists go to investigate. The "weapon" turns out to be a biogenetically enhanced python that has a taste for human flesh. **85m/C VHS, DVD.** William Zabka, Dana Ashbrook, Simmone MacKinnon, Alex Jolig; ***D:*** Jeff Rank; ***W:*** Lee McConnell. **CABLE**

Python Wolf ♂♂ *C.A.T. Squad: Python Wolf* **1988 (R)** It's non-stop action in South Africa as a counter-terrorist group sets out to thwart a drug smuggler's plans to export plutonium. As usual, intense pacing from director Friedkin. Sequel to "C.A.T. Squad" (1986). **100m/C VHS.** Joe Cortese, Jack Youngblood, Steve James, Deborah Van Valkenburgh, Miguel Ferrer, Alan Scarfe; ***D:*** William Friedkin; ***M:*** Ennio Morricone. **TV**

The Pyx ♂♂♂ *The Hooker Cult Murders* **1973 (R)** Canadian suspense thriller about the murder of a prostitute with satanic overtones. Poice sergeant investigates the crime and enters a world of devil worship and decadence. Based on the novel by John Buell. **111m/C VHS, DVD.** *CA* Karen Black, Christopher Plummer, Donald Pilon; ***D:*** Harvey Hart.

Q & A ♂♂ **1990 (R)** Semi-taut thriller with Nolte playing a totally corrupt, hair-trigger cop trying to make his murder of a drug dealer look like self-defense. Assigned to the case is an ex-cop turned assistant DA (Hutton) who's supposed to sweep the case under the rug. Then he finds out another dealer (Assante) is a witness and he happens to be romancing Hutton's former girlfriend (film debut of director Lumet's daughter). Lots of violence and raw language. **132m/C VHS, DVD.** Dominic Chianese, Nick Nolte, Timothy Hutton, Armand Assante, Patrick O'Neal, Lee Richardson, Luis Guzman, Charles S. Dutton, Jenny Lumet, Paul Calderon, Fyvush Finkel; ***D:*** Sidney Lumet; ***W:*** Sidney Lumet; ***C:*** Andrzej Bartkowiak; ***M:*** Ruben Blades.

Q Ships ♂♂ 1/2 **1928** Silent German drama about a submarine commander who has inner conflicts with his country's war effort. Uses actual WWI footage. **78m/B VHS.** *GE* J.P. Kennedy, Roy Travers, Johnny Butt, Philip Hewland; ***D:*** Geoffrey Barkas, Michael Barringer.

Q (The Winged Serpent) ♂♂♂ *Q; The Winged Serpent* **1982 (R)** A cult of admirers surrounds this goony monster flick about dragonlike Aztec god Quetzlcoatl, summoned to modern Manhattan by gory human sacrifices, and hungry for rooftop sunbathers and construction teams. Direction and special effects are pretty ragged, but witty script helps the cast shine, especially Moriarty as a lowlife crook who's found the beast's hidden nest. **92m/C VHS, DVD.** Michael Moriarty, Candy Clark, David Carradine, Richard Roundtree, Malachy McCourt, James Dixon, Eddie Jones, Bruce Carradine, Tony Page, Fred J. Scollay, Mary Louise Weller; ***D:*** Larry Cohen; ***W:*** Larry Cohen; ***C:*** Fred Murphy; ***M:*** Robert O. Ragland.

QB VII ♂♂♂ 1/2 **1974** A knighted physician brings a suit for libel against a novelist for implicating him in war crimes. Hopkins as the purportedly wronged doctor and Gazzara as the writer are both superb. Ending is stunning. Adapted from the novel by Leon Uris. **313m/C VHS, DVD.** Anthony Hopkins, Ben Gazzara, Lee Remick, Leslie Caron, Juliet Mills, John Gielgud, Anthony Quayle; ***D:*** Tom Gries; ***W:*** Edward Anhalt; ***M:*** Jerry Goldsmith. **TV**

Quackser Fortune Has a Cousin in the Bronx ♂♂♂ *Fun Loving* **1970 (R)** An Irish fertilizer salesman meets an exchange student from the U.S., who finds herself attracted to this unlearned, but not unknowing, man. An original love story with drama and appeal. **88m/C VHS, DVD.** *IR* Gene Wilder, Margot Kidder, Eileen Colgan, May Ollis, Seamus Ford, Danny Cummins, Liz Davis; ***D:*** Waris Hussein; ***W:*** Gabriel Walsh; ***C:*** Gilbert Taylor; ***M:*** Michael Dress.

Quadrophenia ♂♂♂ **1979 (R)** Pete Townshend's excellent rock opera about an alienated youth looking for life's meaning in Britain's music scene circa 1963. Jimmy (Daniels) and his pals are Mods who brawl with their rivals, the Rockers. Music by The Who is powerful and apt. Fine performance by Sting in his acting debut as The Ace Face. **115m/C VHS, DVD.** *GB* Phil Daniels, Mark Wingett, Philip Davis, Leslie Ash, Sting, Garry Cooper, Gary Shail, Toyah Willcox, Trevor Laird, Ray Winstone; ***D:*** Franc Roddam; ***W:*** Franc Roddam, Martin Stellman, Dave Humphries, Pete Townshend; ***C:*** Brian Tufano; ***M:*** John Entwhistle, Pete Townshend.

Quake ♂ 1/2 **1992 (R)** Railsback stars as a stalker who takes advantage of the 1990 San Franscisco earthquake to finally obtain the woman of his dreams. A surveillance expert, he's after a beautiful lawyer (Anderson) and when the earthquake leaves her trapped he rushes to rescue her—only to hold her captive himself. **83m/C VHS.** Steve Railsback, Erika Anderson, Eb Lottimer, Dick Miller; ***D:*** Louis Morneau; ***W:*** Mark Evan Schwartz.

Quality Street ♂♂ **1937** English lovers Tone and Hepburn are separated when he leaves to fight in the Napoleonic Wars. When Tone returns years later, he's forgotten his erstwhile heartthrob. He also fails to recognize that the 16-year old coquette who's caught his eye is his old beloved in disguise. Cast works hard to overcome the absurd premise, based on the play by Sir James Barrie. **84m/B VHS.** Katharine Hepburn, Franchot Tone, Fay Bainter, Eric Blore, Cora Witherspoon, Estelle Winwood, Florence Lake, Bonita Granville; ***D:*** George Stevens; ***W:*** J.M. Barrie.

Quantum of Solace ♂♂ 1/2 **2008 (PG-13)** The latest Bond picks up where "Casino Royale" left off as 007 seeks answers to the late Vesper Lynd's betrayal. An MI6 traitor leads Bond to Dominic Greene, a ruthless businessman who's part of the mysterious Quantum organization, although this time the quest for world domination isn't the issue; it's the water supply that's in jeopardy. As the best Bond since George Lazenby, Craig gives another excellent performance, lending greater depth and emotion to the character with his steely, angst-ridden depiction. The usual Bond requisites (the gadgets, the car, the explosions, and of course, the femme fatale) are also top-shelf and very nice to watch for one hundred or so minutes. **105m/C DVD.** *US* Daniel Craig, Judi Dench, Mathieu Amalric, Olga Kurylenko, Jeffrey Wright, Giancarlo Giannini, Jesper Christensen, Stana Katic, Gemma Arterton, Joaquin Cosio, David Harbour; ***D:*** Marc Foster; ***W:*** Paul Haggis, Neal Purvis, Robert Wade; ***C:*** Roberto Schaefer; ***M:*** David Arnold.

Quarantine ♂♂ 1/2 **1989 (R)** Quarantine camps for carriers of a fatal virus are the serious measures taken by the nation. The solution is clear to a rebel and an inventor; all must be liberated or exterminated. **92m/C VHS.** Beatrice Boepple, Garwin Sanford, Jerry Wasserman, Charles Wilkinson; ***D:*** Charles Wilkinson; ***W:*** Charles Wilkinson.

Quarantine ♂ **2008 (R)** TV reporter Angela Vidal (Carpenter) and her faithful cameraman Scott (Harris) have been assigned to follow two veteran L.A. firefighters, Jake (Hernandez) and Fletcher (Schaech), to capture the essence of these heroes. After responding to a 911 call at a run-down apartment building, the four are suddenly locked inside, trapped with the residents, all of whom are now bloodthirsty zombies, thanks to a mutant virus. And, you guessed it, cameraman Scott films the entire thing, "Blair Witch"-style, with the nauseating handheld camera and panicked confessionals. Supposedly a remake of the terrifying Spanish horror flick "Rec," but plays more like a cheap knock-off. **89m/C DVD.** *US* Jennifer Carpenter, Dania Ramirez, Johnathon Schaech, Jay Hernandez, Columbus Short, Marin Hinkle, Rade Serbedzija, Denis O'Hare, Greg Germann, Steve Harris; ***D:*** John Erick Dowdle; ***W:*** John Erick Dowdle, Drew Dowdle; ***C:*** Ken Seng.

The Quare Fellow ♂♂ **1962** Thomas Crimmin (McGoohan), the new warden in a Dublin prison, believes in capital punishment. Two condemned men ("quares" in prison slang) are on death row and one kills himself. Crimmin visits Kathleen (Syms), the other prisoner's wife, and learns the real circumstances behind her husband's crime. He then tries to get the man a reprieve after finding his own views changing. Based on a play by Brendan Behan. **85m/B DVD.** *GB* Patrick McGoohan, Sylvia Syms, Jack Cunningham, Hilton Edwards, Dermot Kelly, Philip O'Flynn, Walter Macken; ***D:*** Arthur Dreifuss; ***W:*** Jacqueline Sundstrom; ***C:*** Peter Hennessy; ***M:*** Alexander Faris.

The Quarrel ♂♂ 1/2 **1993** Chaim Kovler is a New York poet visiting Montreal in 1948. In a park he notices a group of Orthodox Jews and discovers one is his childhood friend Hersh. Fifteen years earlier their friendship broke over Chaim's decision to give up the religious life for his writing. Having lost their families to the Holocaust in Poland, both men have immigrated to new lives in North America. They immediately pick up their quarrel over religious faith and its value, particularly in light of the Holocaust. The two characters serve too much as careful ideologues to be compelling and the story turns cloyingly sentimental. Based on a short story by Yiddish writer Chaim Grade. **88m/C VHS, DVD.** *CA* Saul Rubinek, R.H. Thomson, Arthur Grosser; ***D:*** Eli Cohen; ***W:*** David Brandes; ***M:*** William Goldstein.

The Quarry ♂♂ **1998** A nameless fugitive (Lynch) accepts a ride from a minister, whom he accidentally kills. He takes over the man's identity and possessions and journeys to the minister's new posting in a nearby isolated South African town. When his goods are in turn stolen by a poor young black man, Valentine, the town's racist white police chief not only arrests Valentine for the theft but links him to the murder when the minister's body is discovered. The original fugitive is consumed by guilt but will justice prevail? Based on the novel by Damon Galgut. English and Afrikaans with subtitles. **112m/C VHS, DVD.** *SA* John Lynch, Serge-Henri Valcke, Jonny Phillips, Oscar Petersen, Jody Abrahams, Sylvia Esau; ***D:*** Marion Hansel; ***W:*** Marion Hansel; ***C:*** Bernard Lutic; ***M:*** Takashi Kako.

Quarterback Princess ♂♂ **1985** Workaday telling of the real-life girl who goes out for football and becomes homecoming queen. Heartwarming, if you like that kinda stuff, but not exciting, except for the early appearances of such '90s stars as Helen Hunt (as said quarterback), Daphne Zuniga as her sister, and Tim Robbins as a teammate. **96m/C VHS.** Helen Hunt, Don Murray, John Stockwell, Barbara Babcock, Daphne Zuniga, Kathleen Wilhoite, Tim Robbins; ***D:*** Noel Black. **TV**

Quartet ♂♂♂ **1981 (R)** A young French woman is taken in by an English couple after her husband goes to prison. The husband seduces her, and she becomes trapped emotionally and socially. Superbly acted, claustrophobic drama based on a Jean Rhys novel. **101m/C VHS, DVD.** *GB FR* Isabelle Adjani, Alan Bates, Maggie Smith, Anthony (Corlan) Higgins; ***D:*** James Ivory; ***W:*** Ruth Prawer Jhabvala. Cannes '81: Actress (Adjani).

Quartier Mozart ♂♂ **1992** Sexual farce presenting the assimilation of African American pop-culture into African traditions. A local sorceress uses witchcraft to give Queen of the 'Hood a first-hand look at sexual politics. The young girl enters the body of a boy struggling to find his place in the male hierarchy established by neighborhood Casanovas. In French with English subtitles. **80m/C VHS.** Pauline Andela, Jimmy Niyona, Essindi Mindja, Sandrine Ola'a; ***D:*** Jean-Pierre Bekolo; ***W:*** Jean-Pierre Bekolo; ***C:*** Regis Blondeau.

Quatermass 2 ♂♂♂ *Enemy from Space* **1957** In the well made sequel to "Quatermass Experiment," (also known as "The Creeping Unknown") Professor Quatermass battles blobs and brainwashed zombies to rescue government officials whose bodies have been invaded by aliens. "Five Million Years to Earth" concluded the trilogy. **84m/B VHS, DVD.** *GB* Brian Donlevy, John Longden, Sidney James, Bryan Forbes, William Franklyn, Vera Day, John Van Eyssen, Michael Ripper, Michael Balfour; ***D:*** Val Guest; ***W:*** Val Guest, Nigel Kneale; ***C:*** Gerald Gibbs; ***M:*** James Bernard.

Quatermass and the Pit ♂♂ 1/2 **1958** From the original BBC production. Professor Quatermass is up to his ears in trouble as a Martian spacecraft is found by subway workers. Not long after a monster stalks the streets of London. Remade cinematically in 1968 as "Five Million Years to Earth." **180m/B VHS.** *GB* Andre Morell, Cec Linder; ***D:*** Rudloph Carier; ***W:*** Nigel Kneale.

Quatermass Conclusion ♂♂ **1979** An elderly British scientist comes out of retirement to stop an immobilizing death ray from outer space from destroying Earth. Edited version of a TV miniseries continues earlier adventures of Quatermass on film and television. **105m/C VHS, DVD.** *GB* John Mills, Simon MacCorkindale, Barbara Kellerman, Margaret Tyzack; ***D:*** Piers Haggard. **TV**

The Quatermass Experiment ♂♂♂ *The Creeping Unknown* **1956** Excellent British production about an astronaut who returns to Earth carrying an alien infestation that causes him to turn into a horrible monster. Competent acting and tense direction. Followed by "Enemy From Space." **78m/B VHS.** *GB* Brian Donlevy, Margia Dean, Jack Warner, Richard Wordsworth, Frank Phillips; ***D:*** Val Guest; ***M:*** James Bernard.

Quatorze Juliet ♂♂ 1/2 **1932** A taxi driver and a flower girl meet on Bastille Day and fall in love. When he becomes involved with gangsters, she steers him back to virtue in this minor French relic from director Clair. **85m/B VHS.** *FR* Anabella Rigaud, Jorge (George) Rigaud; ***D:*** Rene Clair.

Que Viva Mexico ♂♂♂ *Da Zdravstvuyet Meksika* **1932** Eisenstein's grand unfinished folly on the history of Mexico, reconstructed and released in 1979 by his protege, Grigori Alexandrov. Divided into four sections: "Sandunga" covers the Tehuantepec jungles and its inhabitants; "Manguel" is about a peasant and his bride; "Fiesta" devotes itself to bullfighting and romance; and "Soldadera" depicts the 1910 Mexican revolution through frescoes. Along with "Greed" and "Napoleon," it remains as one of cinema's greatest irrecoverable casualties. Russian narration with English subtitles. **85m/B VHS, DVD.** *RU* ***D:*** Sergei Eisenstein; ***W:*** Sergei Eisenstein, Grigori Alexandrov; ***C:*** Eduard Tisse.

Queen ♂♂♂ **1993** Epic miniseries from Pulitzer Prize-winner Alex Haley chronicles the life of his paternal great-grandmother, who bore a baby girl, Queen, to her white slave master. At the heart is Queen's quest for identity as she experiences unique problems due to her mixed race. She finally finds love with a ferry operator (Glover) whose role is powerful but unfortunately brief. It is this union that produces Alex's father, Simon. Although Haley died during production, he had spent considerable time sharing his vision with the staff, who also worked with him on the original "Roots." Good casting and a nice interpretation of Haley's tale is above average. Worth a watch. **360m/C VHS.** Halle Berry, Ann-Margret, Jasmine Guy, Timothy Daly, Danny Glover, Madge Sinclair, Martin Sheen, Paul Winfield, Ossie Davis, Raven, Victor Garber, Lonette McKee, Sada Thompson, Elizabeth Wilson; ***D:*** John Erman; ***W:*** David Stevens. **TV**

The Queen ♂♂♂ **2006 (PG-13)** Mirren is royalty personified as Britain's Queen Elizabeth II, who maintains her regal authority while dealing with her gossip-prone family and those annoying politicians. The timeline begins in 1997 with the election of Tony Blair (Sheen) as Labor prime minister and moves onto what happens when Princess Diana is killed in that car crash a few months later. Frankly, the Queen can't understand the fuss but, thanks to her professionalism, when she realizes the effect the tragedy has on the country, its politics, and, ultimately, her family, she rallies to put the best royal face on the public grief. **101m/C DVD, Blu-ray Disc.** *GB FR IT* Helen Mirren, Michael Sheen, James Cromwell, Helen McCrory, Alex Jennings, Sylvia Sims; ***D:*** Stephen Frears; ***W:*** Peter Morgan; ***C:*** Alfonso Beato; ***M:*** Alexandre Desplat. Oscars '06: Actress (Mirren); British Acad. '06: Actress (Mirren), Film; Golden Globes '07: Actress—Drama (Mirren), Screenplay; Screen Actors Guild '06: Actress (Mirren).

Queen Bee ℒℒ ½ **1955** Crawford is at her manipulative best as Southern belle Eva Phillips, married to wealthy Georgia mill owner Avery (Sullivan). The ruthless Eva is despised by her bitter, tippling husband who finds a chance at romance when cousin Jennifer (Marlow) comes to visit. Naturally, Eva can't stand any competition, though she doesn't care about Avery, and tries to break up the duo even as she seeks to renew her own affair with a former lover (Ireland). Based on the novel by Edna Lee. **94m/B VHS, DVD.** Joan Crawford, Barry Sullivan, John Ireland, Lucy Marlow, Betsy Palmer, Fay Wray; ***D:*** Ranald MacDougall; ***W:*** Ranald MacDougall; ***C:*** Charles B(ryant) Lang Jr.; ***M:*** George Duning.

Queen Christina ℒℒℒ ½ **1933** A stylish, resonant star vehicle for Garbo, portraying the 17th-century Swedish queen from ascension to the throne to her romance with a Spanish ambassador. Alternately hilarious and moving, it holds some of Garbo's greatest and most memorable moments. Gilbert's second to last film and his only successful outing after the coming of sound. **101m/B VHS, DVD.** Greta Garbo, John Gilbert, Lewis Stone, Sir C. Aubrey Smith, Ian Keith, Reginald Owen, Elizabeth Young; ***D:*** Rouben Mamoulian; ***C:*** William H. Daniels.

Queen for a Day ℒℒ ½ *Horsie* **1951** Three differing vignettes, based on a rather notorious radio and TV game show of the time, in which "deserving" (or sufficiently pathetic) working-class women were rewarded for their selflessness. Part one concerns a perfect suburban family whose son contracts polio. Part two has a teen spooking his immigrant parents by working as a carnival high diver to earn college cash. The finale is a Dorothy Parker farce about a homely but kindhearted nurse caring for the child of an unappreciative couple. So popular was this segment that the film was retitled after the main character. Overall, not bad considering the source. **107m/B VHS.** Phyllis Avery, Darren McGavin, Tristram Coffin, Adam Williams, Tracey Roberts, Jack Bailey, Jim Morgan, Fort Pearson; ***D:*** Arthur Lubin.

Queen Kelly ℒℒℒ **1929** The popularly known, slapdash version of von Stroheim's famous final film, in which an orphan goes from royal marriage to white slavery to astounding wealth. Never really finished, the film is the edited first half of the intended project, prepared for European release after von Stroheim had been fired. Even so, a campy, extravagant and lusty melodrama. Silent. **113m/B VHS, DVD.** Gloria Swanson, Walter Byron, Seena Owen, Tully Marshall, Madame Sul Te Wan; ***D:*** Erich von Stroheim; ***W:*** Erich von Stroheim; ***C:*** Paul Ivano, Gordon Pollock.

Queen Margot ℒℒℒ ½ *La Reine Margot* **1994 (R)** Blood-soaked period of French history is duly rendered on screen in big-budget costume epic. Beautiful Catholic Princess Marguerite de Valois (Adjani), is the pawn of her devious mother, the widowed queen Catherine de Medici (Lisi). Mom skillfully manipulates unstable son Charles IX (Anglade), the nominal ruler of 1570s France, while she plots to marry Margot off to Protestant Henri de Navarre (Auteuil). Margot is contemptuous of her new husband, preferring to find her amatory amusements in the Paris streets, where she takes a handsome lover de la Mole (Perez). But both Margot and Henri are united against the Queen when Catherine's minions order the murder of the rival Huguenots—a notably violent affair known as the St. Bartholomew's Day Massacre. The history's confusing, the violence graphic, the acting flamboyant, and the visuals top-notch. Based on the novel by Alexandre Dumas. French with subtitles; originally released at 161 minutes. **135m/C VHS, DVD.** *FR* Isabelle Adjani, Daniel Auteuil, Virna Lisi, Jean-Hugues Anglade, Vincent Perez, Pascal Greggory, Miguel Bose, Dominique Blanc, Claudio Amendola, Asia Argento, Julien Rassam, Jean-Claude Brialy; ***D:*** Patrice Chereau; ***W:*** Patrice Chereau, Daniele Thompson; ***C:*** Philippe Rousselot; ***M:*** Goran Bregovic. Cannes '94: Special Jury Prize, Actress (Lisi); Cesar '95: Actress (Adjani), Cinematog., Costume Des., Support. Actor (Anglade), Support. Actress (Lisi).

Queen of Diamonds ℒℒ *Popsy Pop; The Butterfly Affair* **1970 (PG)** A woman pulls off the biggest diamond heist of all time. **90m/C VHS.** *FR IT* Claudia Cardinale, Stanley Baker, Henri Charriere; ***D:*** Jean Herman; ***W:*** Jean Herman, Henri Charriere; ***C:*** Jean-Jacques Tarbes; ***M:*** Frederic Botton.

Queen of Diamonds ℒℒ **1991** The "Queen of Diamonds" is an alienated blackjack dealer in Vegas who, in between dealing cards, casually searches for her missing husband and looks after an old man in a motel. **77m/C VHS.** Tinka Menkes; ***D:*** Nina Menkes; ***W:*** Nina Menkes.

Queen of Hearts ℒℒℒ ½ **1989 (PG)** Excellent, original romantic comedy is a directorial triumph for Amiel in his first feature. An Italian couple defy both their families and marry for love. Four children later, we find them running a diner in England. Humorous, dramatic, sad—everything a movie can and should be. Fine performances. **112m/C VHS.** *GB* Anita Zagaria, Joseph Long, Eileen Way, Vittorio Duse, Vittorio Amandola, Ian Hawkes; ***D:*** Jon Amiel; ***M:*** Michael Convertino.

The Queen of Mean ℒ ½ *Leona Helmsley: The Queen of Mean* **1990** Tabloid TV-movie based on Ransdell Pierson's scandal-sheet bio of the hotel magnate and convicted tax cheat. See Leona connive. See Leona bitch. See Leona get hers. What's the point? If you ask that you're too bright to watch. **94m/C VHS.** Suzanne Pleshette, Lloyd Bridges, Bruce Weitz, Joe Regalbuto; ***D:*** Richard Michaels; ***C:*** Hanania Baer. **TV**

Queen of Outer Space WOOF! **1958** Notorious male-chauvinist sci-fi cheapie starts out slow, but then the laughs keep coming as the cast plays the hyperdumb material straight. Space cadets crash on Venus, find it ruled by women—and the dolls have wicked plans in store for mankind. Don't be surprised if you've seen the sets before since they were borrowed from "Forbidden Planet," "World Without End," and "Flight to Mars." **80m/C VHS, DVD.** Zsa Zsa Gabor, Eric Fleming, Laurie Mitchell, Paul Birch, Barbara Darrow, Dave Willcock, Lisa Davis, Patrick Waltz, Marilyn Buferd, Marjorie Durant, Lynn Cartwright, Gerry Gaylor; ***D:*** Edward L. Bernds; ***W:*** Charles Beaumont; ***C:*** William F. Whitley; ***M:*** Marlin Skiles.

The Queen of Spades ℒℒℒ **1949** Mystical drama about a Russian soldier who ruins his life searching for winning methods of card playing. Well-made version of the Pushkin story. **95m/B VHS, DVD.** *GB* Anton Walbrook, Edith Evans, Ronald Howard, Mary Jerrold, Yvonne Mitchell, Anthony Dawson; ***D:*** Thorold Dickinson.

Queen of the Amazons ℒ ½ **1947** A girl searches for her fiance and finds him reluctantly held captive by a tribe of women who rule the jungle. **60m/B VHS, DVD.** Robert Lowery, Patricia Morison, J. Edward Bromberg, John Miljan, Keith Richards, Bruce Edwards, Wilson Benge, Amira Moustafa; ***D:*** Edward Finney; ***W:*** Roger Merton; ***C:*** Robert Pittack.

Queen of the Damned ℒℒ **2002 (R)** Adaptation of the third book in Anne Rice's "Vampire Chronicles" resurrects vampire Lestat (Townsend) to rock the new millennium after a 200-year nap. He's awakened to become the singing sensation of a goth band (what's more goth than a vampire?). He soon meets up with Jesse (Moreau) a reckless vampire researcher and fellow vampires Marius (Perez), and Maharet (Olin). Lestat's new lady love, however, is Akasha (late pop star Aaliyah), the mother of all the vampires, who has big plans for her and her bloodsucking beau, to (what else?) rule the world. Her followers feel differently, however. Camp, but not camp enough to excuse its lameness and host of lifeless performances. One dimensional characters and lackluster plot leave this drag of a "Queen" to Rice and vampire fans only. **101m/C VHS, DVD.** *US AU* Aaliyah, Stuart Townsend, Marguerite Moreau, Vincent Perez, Lena Olin, Paul McGann, Claudia Black, Bruce Spence, Christian Manon; ***D:*** Michael Rymer; ***W:*** Scott Abbott; ***C:*** Ian Baker; ***M:*** Richard Gibbs, Jonathan Davis.

Queen of the Jungle ℒ **1935** Re-edited adventure serial featuring a white woman cast off in a hot-air balloon and landing in Africa, where she is hailed as a Queen. High camp, starring ex-Our Ganger Kornman. **85m/B VHS.** Mary Kornman, Reed Howes; ***D:*** Robert F. "Bob" Hill.

Queen of the Road ℒℒ **1984** A feisty Aussie schoolteacher starts a new life as a tractor-trailer driver. **96m/C VHS.** *AU* Joanne Samuel, Amanda Muggleton; ***D:*** Bruce Best.

Queen of the Stardust Ballroom ℒℒℒ **1975** Well-made drama about a lonely widow who goes to a local dance hall, where she meets a man and begins an unconventional late love. **98m/C DVD.** Maureen Stapleton, Charles Durning, Michael Strong, Charlotte Rae, Sam O'Steen; ***D:*** Michael Brandon; ***M:*** Billy Goldenberg. **TV**

Queen Sized ℒℒ **2008** Maggie (Blonsky) is a fat (which she prefers to plus-sized) high school senior constantly humiliated by the popular clique. She's also nagged about her weight by her worried mom (Potts) since her overweight dad died of diabetes. As a cruel prank, Maggie is nominated for homecoming queen but her friend Casey (Holleman) encourages her to let the other social outcasts organize a real campaign. Blonsky shines in a predictable but fact-based story, letting her insecurities and triumphs all show on her expressive face. **120m/C DVD.** Nicole Blonsky, Annie Potts, Lilly Holleman, Jackson Pace, Fabian Morena, Kimberly Matula, Liz McGeever, Kelsey Schultz; ***D:*** Peter Levin; ***W:*** Richard Kletter, Rodney Johnson, Nora Kletter; ***C:*** Neil Roach. **CABLE**

Queenie ℒℒ ½ **1987** Miniseries loosely based on the life of actress Merle Oberon, exploring her rise to stardom. Based on the best-selling novel by Michael Korda, Oberon's nephew by marriage. Many long, dry passages fit for leaving the room for snacks. **233m/C VHS.** Mia Sara, Kirk Douglas, Martin Balsam, Claire Bloom, Chaim Topol, Joel Grey, Sarah Miles, Joss Ackland; ***D:*** Larry Peerce; ***M:*** Georges Delerue. **TV**

Queens Logic ℒℒ ½ **1991 (R)** Ensemble comedy in the tradition of "The Big Chill" featuring the trials and tribulations of the "old-neighborhood" gang, who gather again on hometurf and reminisce. Most of the film centers around Olin and girlfriend Webb and whether or not he will chicken out of their wedding. Not bad comedy, with Mantegna delivering most of the good lines. **116m/C VHS, DVD.** John Malkovich, Kevin Bacon, Jamie Lee Curtis, Linda Fiorentino, Joe Mantegna, Ken Olin, Tom Waits, Chloe Webb, Ed Marinaro, Kelly Bishop, Tony Spiridakis; ***D:*** Steve Rash; ***W:*** Tony Spiridakis; ***C:*** Amir M. Mokri; ***M:*** Joe Jackson.

Queen's Messenger II ℒℒ *Witness to a Kill* **2001 (R)** Super-suave-James-Bond-wannabe Captain Strong's mission is to free two gorgeous women from their captors while cracking an international smuggling ring and preventing an African country's government from being overthrown. **90m/C VHS, DVD.** Gary Daniels, Norman Anstey, Vusi Kunene, Ron Smerczak, Nick Boraine, Lindelani Buthelezi, Isaac Chokwe, Gideon Emery, Moagi Modise, Robert Whitehead, John Whiteley; ***D:*** Darrell Roodt, Mark Roper; ***W:*** Peter Jobin, Harry Alan Towers, Michael Swan; ***C:*** Adolfo Bartoli, Giulio Biccari; ***M:*** Rene Veldsman. **VIDEO**

Queens of Comedy ℒℒ ½ **2001 (R)** This "sort of" companion piece to Spike Lee's "Original Kings of Comedy" is a concert recorded at the Orpheum Theatre in Memphis starring four black stand-up comediennes—Miss Laura Hayes, Adel Givens, Sommore, and Mo'Nique. **79m/C DVD.** Adele Givens, Mo'Nique, Miss Laura Hayes, Sommore; ***D:*** Steve Purcell.

The Queen's Sister ℒℒ **2005** The queen would be the never-seen Elizabeth and the sister would be perennial tabloid fodder, Princess Margaret (Cohu), a fun-loving sort who never let royal restrictions impinge on her having a good time. Unable to marry her true love (a divorced man), Margaret settles for photographer Anthony Armstrong-Jones (Stephens), eventually leading to her own divorce (the first in the royal family) and a series of controversial liaisons. Cohu is properly flamboyant but, ultimately, Margaret's life is a sad decline. **155m/C DVD.** Toby Stephens, David Threlfall, Simon Woods, Meredith MacNeill, Lucy Cohu, Aden Gillet; ***D:*** Simon Cellan Jones; ***W:*** Craig Warner; ***C:*** David Katznelson; ***M:*** John Altman. **TV**

Queer Duck: The Movie ℒℒ **2006** An extension of the Showtime cartoons featuring a gay duck. Queer Duck breaks up with his partner Openly Gator for an unlikely love interest—aging diva Lola Buzzard. But this turn towards heterosexuality proves to be a mistake. Raucous humor and musical numbers further liven the rude proceedings. **72m/C DVD.** ***D:*** Xeth Feinberg; ***W:*** Mike Reiss; ***M:*** Sam Elwitt; ***V:*** Kevin M. Richardson, Maurice LaMarche, Billy West, Jackie Hoffman, Tim Curry, Conan O'Brien, David Duchovny, Jim J. Bullock. **VIDEO**

Quentin Durward ℒℒ ½ **1955** In 1465, dashing Quentin (Taylor) is sent from Scotland by his elderly uncle (Thesinger) to pick up his French bride-to-be Isabelle (Kendall). She is a pawn at Louis XI's (Morley) court because of her previous association with the power-hungry Duke of Burgundy (Clunes) and gets kidnapped. Quentin, who has nobly refrained from expressing his own love for the lovely, comes to her rescue and much swashbuckling follows. Based on a novel by Sir Walter Scott. **100m/C DVD.** Robert Taylor, Kay Kendall, Robert Morley, Alec Clunes, George Cole, Duncan Lamont, Marius Goring, Wilfrid Hyde-White, Ernest Thesiger; ***D:*** Richard Thorpe; ***W:*** Robert Ardrey, George Froeschel; ***C:*** Christopher Challis; ***M:*** Bronislau Kaper.

Querelle ℒℒ ½ **1983 (R)** Querelle, a handsome sailor, finds himself involved in a bewildering environment of murder, drug smuggling, and homosexuality in the port of Brest. Highly stylized and erotic sets, along with a dark look, give the film an interesting feel. Nice performances by Davis, Nero, and Moreau. Fassbinder's controversial last film, based on the story by Jean Genet. Strange, difficult narrative (such as it is), alternately boring and engrossing. **106m/C VHS, DVD.** *GE* Brad Davis, Jeanne Moreau, Franco Nero, Laurent Malet; ***D:*** Rainer Werner Fassbinder; ***W:*** Rainer Werner Fassbinder, Burkhard Driest; ***C:*** Xaver Schwarzenberger, Josef Vavra; ***M:*** Peer Raben.

The Quest ℒℒ **1986 (PG)** Australian film never released theatrically in the United States. A young boy (Thomas, of "E.T." fame) raised in the outback investigates a local Aboriginal superstition about a monster living in an ancient cemetery. Not bad, just dull. **94m/C VHS.** *AU* Henry Thomas, Tony Barry, John Ewart, Rachel Friend, Tamsin West, Dennis Miller, Katya Manning; ***D:*** Brian Trenchard-Smith.

The Quest ℒℒ **1996 (PG-13)** In his directorial debut, Van Damme plays pickpocket Christopher Dubois, who finds his adventures just beginning when he hops a freighter heading for the Far East in order to escape police trouble. He learns about a prestigious martial arts competition, where the prize could set him up for life, if he can manage to get into the invitation-only event. After many films set in the future, Van Damme chose to set this one in the '20s, with fairly good results. He piles on the beautiful location shots until the inevitable martial arts melee toward the end. Pacing is sketchy but Van Damme does display directorial talent. **95m/C VHS, DVD.** Jean-Claude Van Damme, Roger Moore, Aki Aleong, James Remar, Jack McGee, Janet Gunn, Abdel Qissi, Louis Mandylor; ***D:*** Jean-Claude Van Damme; ***W:*** Stuart Klein, Paul Mones; ***C:*** David Gribble; ***M:*** Randy Edelman.

Quest for Camelot ℒℒ ½ **1998 (G)** Camelot's future lies in the hands of heroine Kayley, who sees an opportunity to win a spot at King Arthur's roundtable when Excalibur is stolen by evil knight Ruber (Oldman). On her quest to recover the sword, she meets blind hermit Garrett and two-headed dragon Devon and Cornwall (Idle and Rickles). With an all-star cast, this first full-length animated feature from Warner Bros. wants to be a contender for the Disney animation crown, but can't quite overcome its familar story, one-dimensional villain, and forgettable songs. However, Kayley and Garrett are strong, non-stereotypical characters that children and adults will welcome. Based on the children's novel "The King's Damosel" by Vera Chapman. **85m/C VHS, DVD.** ***D:*** Frederick Du Chau; ***W:*** Kirk De Micco, William Schifrin, David Seidler; ***M:*** Patrick Doyle; ***V:*** Jessalyn Gilsig, Cary Elwes, Gary Oldman, Eric Idle, Don Rickles, Jane Seymour, Pierce Brosnan, Gabriel Byrne, Bronson Pinchot, Jaleel White, John Gielgud. Golden Globes '99: Song ("The Prayer").

Quest for Fire **1982 (R)** An interesting story sans the usual dialogue thing. A group of men (McGill, Perlman, El-Kadi) during the Ice Age must wander the land searching for fire after they lose theirs fending off an attack. During their quest, they encounter and battle various animals and tribesmen in order to survive. The special language they speak was developed by Anthony Burgess, while the primitive movements were Desmond "The Naked Ape" Morris. Perlman went on to become the Beast in TV's "Beauty and the Beast"; Chong, as a primitive babe, is the daughter of Tommy Chong of the comic duo Cheech and Chong. **75m/C VHS, DVD.** *FR* Everett McGill, Ron Perlman, Nameer El-Kadi, Rae Dawn Chong; ***D:*** Jean-Jacques Annaud; ***W:*** Gerard Brach. Oscars '82: Makeup; Genie '83: Actress (Chong).

Quest for Love **1/2 1971** Quirky sci-fi story of a man who passes through a time warp and finds himself able to maintain two parallel lives. Based on John Wyndham's short story. **90m/C VHS.** *GB* Joan Collins, Tom Bell, Denholm Elliott, Laurence Naismith; ***D:*** Ralph Thomas.

Quest for the Mighty Sword **1990 (PG-13)** A warrior battles dragons, demons and evil wizards. D'Amato used the pseudonym David Hills. **94m/C VHS.** Eric Allen Kramer, Margaret Lenzey, Donald O'Brien, Dina Marrone, Chris Murphy; ***D:*** Joe D'Amato.

Quest of the Delta Knights **1/2 1993 (PG)** Swashbuckling fantasy about a kingdom suffering under an evil ruler and his equally sinister queen. They are opposed by the heroic Delta Knights whose only chance to defeat the fiendish powers of darkness is by unearthing a legendary storehouse containing technology from the age of Atlantis and all the powers of the Ancients. **97m/C VHS.** David Warner, Olivia Hussey, Corbin Allred, Brigid Brannah, David Kriegel; ***D:*** James Dodson; ***W:*** Redge Mahaffey.

A Question of Attribution **1/2 1991** Sir Anthony Blunt (Fox) is an internationally respected art expert who also serves as an art adviser to Queen Elizabeth II. His life unravels when an on-going British Intelligence investigation reveals him to be the fourth man in the Burgess-Maclean-Philby scandal involving Englishmen who spied for, and eventually defected to, the USSR. The investigation of Blunt's covert past is paralleled with his own art investigation of a painting attributed to Titian. Three men are depicted in the art work—with a fourth male figure discovered to have been painted over. Alan Bennett adapted his play for this TV drama. **90m/C VHS.** *GB* James Fox, David Calder, Geoffrey Palmer, Prunella Scales, Mark Payton, Jason Flemyng, Edward De Souza, Ann Beach; ***D:*** John Schlesinger; ***W:*** Alan Bennett. **TV**

Question of Faith **1/2 1993** A happily married woman is diagnosed with a rare form of cancer. Much to her family's dismay, she turns to some unconventional medical therapies in order to heal herself. Based on a true story. Basically noble, Archer and Neill lift this tearjerker out of most of its maudlin aspects. **90m/C VHS.** Anne Archer, Sam Neill, Frances Lee McCain, James Tolkan, James Hong, CCH Pounder, Louis Giambalvo, Norman Parker, Michael Constantine; ***D:*** Stephen Gyllenhaal; ***W:*** Bruce Hart.

A Question of Guilt **1978** When her child turns up dead, a free-wheeling divorcee is the prime suspect. **100m/C VHS.** Tuesday Weld, Ron Leibman, Peter Masterson, Alex Rocco, Viveca Lindfors, Lana Wood; ***D:*** Robert Butler. **TV**

Question of Honor **1/2 1980** Under governmental pressures, an honest narcotics cop decides to inform on his department's corruption. Co-written and produced by ex-cop Sonny Grosso, on whom "The French Connection" was based. Based on the book "Point Blank," by Grosso and Philip Rosenberg. **134m/C VHS.** Ben Gazzara, Paul Sorvino, Robert Vaughn, Tony Roberts, Danny Aiello, Anthony Zerbe; ***D:*** Jud Taylor; ***W:*** Budd Schulberg. **TV**

A Question of Love **1978** Fine performances in this well-done TV movie about two lesbians—one of whom is fighting her ex-husband for custody of their child. **100m/C VHS.** Gena Rowlands, Jane Alexander, Ned Beatty, Clu Gulager, Bonnie Bedelia, James Sutorius, Jocelyn Brando; ***D:*** Jerry Thorpe; ***M:*** Billy Goldenberg. **TV**

Question of Silence *De Stilte Rond Christine M* **1983 (R)** Three women, strangers to each other, stand trial for a murdering a man. Intricately analyzed courtroom drama with much to say about male domination. In Dutch with English subtitles or dubbed. **92m/C VHS.** *NL* Cox Habrema, Nelly Frijda, Henriette Tol, Edda Barends; ***D:*** Marleen Gorris.

Qui Etes Vous, Mr. Sorge? **1961** The story of German journalist Richard Sorge, who was hanged by the Japanese in 1944 for being a Soviet spy. Uninteresting docudrama which focuses on the opinions of various witnesses as to the accuracy of the espionage charge. In French with English subtitles. **130m/B VHS.** *FR* Thomas Holtzman, Keiko Kishi; ***D:*** Andre Girard.

Quick **1/2 1993 (R)** Polo stars as Quick, a professional assassin whose latest job is Herschel (Donovan), a mob accountant turned federal witness. When Quick is double-crossed, she takes off with Herschel as her insurance and a couple of bad guys (Fahey and Davi) on her trail. Not too much sex and lots of violence to go along with the fast pacing. **99m/C VHS, DVD.** Teri Polo, Martin Donovan, Jeff Fahey, Robert Davi, Tia Carrere; ***D:*** Rick King; ***W:*** Frederick Bailey; ***M:*** Robert Sprayberry.

The Quick and the Dead **1987** Based on a Louis L'Amour story, this cable western features a lone gunslinger who protects a defenseless settler's family from the lawless West, only to become a source of sexual tension for the wife. **91m/C VHS, DVD.** Sam Elliott, Tom Conti, Kate Capshaw, Kenny Morrison, Matt Clark; ***D:*** Robert Day; ***C:*** Dick Bush; ***M:*** Steve Dorff. **CABLE**

The Quick and the Dead **1/2 1995 (R)** Stone is a tough gal gunslinger out to avenge the murder of her father. Ellen arrives in the frontier town of Redemption where arch-villain Herod (Hackman) rules by means of violence and intimidation. Director Raimi packs in so many cliches that you're amazed that it's not a parody of the spaghetti westerns it tries to emulate. Maybe if Stone and Raimi didn't take this film so seriously, it would have been a better movie, but it's still an entertaining one. Just sit back and enjoy the wildly staged gunfights, interesting camera angles, and excellent work by Hackman and Crowe. **105m/C VHS, DVD.** Sharon Stone, Gene Hackman, Leonardo DiCaprio, Russell Crowe, Kevin Conway, Lance Henriksen, Roberts Blossom, Pat Hingle, Keith David, Michael Stone, Stacey Linn Ramsower, Gary Sinise; ***D:*** Sam Raimi; ***W:*** Simon Moore; ***C:*** Dante Spinotti; ***M:*** Alan Silvestri.

Quick Change **1/2 1990 (R)** Murray, Davis, and Quaid form bumbling trio of New York bank robbers who can't seem to exit the Big Apple with loot. Based on Jay Cronley's book, it's Murray's directing debut (with help from screenwriter Franklin). Engaging minor caper comedy displaying plenty of NYC dirty boulevards. **89m/C VHS, DVD.** Tony Shalhoub, Stanley Tucci, Jack Gilpin, Reg E. Cathey, Bill Murray, Geena Davis, Randy Quaid, Jason Robards Jr., Bob Elliott, Victor Argo, Kathryn Grody, Philip Bosco, Phil Hartman, Kurtwood Smith, Jamey Sheridan; ***D:*** Bill Murray, Howard Franklin; ***W:*** Howard Franklin; ***C:*** Michael Chapman; ***M:*** Randy Edelman, Howard Shore.

Quick, Let's Get Married **WOOF!** *Seven Different Ways; The Confession* **1971** Quick, let's not watch this movie. Even the people who made it must have hated it: they waited seven years to release it. Rogers runs a whorehouse; Eden is a gullible, pregnant prostitute; Gould in his big-screen debut(!) is a deaf-mute. A must-not see. **96m/C VHS.** Ginger Rogers, Ray Milland, Barbara Eden, Carl Schell, Michael Ansara, Walter Abel, Scott Meyer, Cecil Kellaway, Elliott Gould; ***D:*** William Dieterle.

Quick Trigger Lee **1/2 1931** Rancher Phil Lee (Custer) is known for his quick temper and quicker trigger finger. Crook Jeremy Wales (Cordova) tricks old miner Saunders (Carlyle) into signing a large promissory note and Saunders brings his problems to Lee. Lee takes it back to Wales and his sneering son Sam (Montague) and gets the best of them. Then he "rescues" Rose Campbell (Lincoln) from danger, only to find out she was filming a movie scene. The smitten Rose invites Lee out and he learns that she's looking for her long-lost granddad who happens to be Saunders. But Sam Wales isn't done yet and decides to smear Lee's good name. **57m/B DVD.** Bob Custer, Monte Montague, Richard Carlyle, Frank Ellis, Al Taylor, Caryl Lincoln, Lee Cordova; ***D:*** J(ohn) P(aterson) McGowan; ***W:*** George Morgan; ***C:*** Edward Kull.

Quicker Than the Eye **1988** When a magician gets mixed up in an assassination plot, he must use his wit, cunning, and magic to get out of it. **94m/C VHS.** Ben Gazzara, Mary Crosby, Catherine Jarrett, Ivan Desny, Eb Lottimer, Sophie Carle, Wolfram Berger, Dinah Hinz, Jean Yanne; ***D:*** Nicolas Gessner.

The Quickie **1/2 2001 (R)** Get your minds out of the gutter! Actually, this mob soap opera would have been a lot more fun if it had wallowed in the gutter itself. Conflicted Russian mobster Oleg (Mashkov) is celebrating his retirement with his family on New Year's Eve at their Malibu beach house. But Oleg has been targeted for extermination and maybe exterminator Lisa (Leigh), who is supposedly at the house to get rid of the vermin, is there to do the job. Bodrov's first English-language venture. **95m/C VHS, DVD.** Vladimir Mashkov, Jennifer Jason Leigh, Dean Stockwell, Lesley Ann Warren, Henry Thomas, Sergei Bodrov Jr., Brenda Bakke, Jsu Garcia; ***D:*** Sergei Bodrov; ***W:*** Sergei Bodrov, Carolyn Cavallero; ***C:*** Sergei Kozlov; ***M:*** Gia Kancheli.

Quicksand **1/2 1950** Mechanic Rooney borrows $20 from his boss's cash register, intending to return it. One thing leads to another, the plot thickens, and it's downhill (for Rooney) from there. Good, tense suspense drama. **79m/B VHS, DVD.** Mickey Rooney, Peter Lorre, Jeanne Cagney; ***D:*** Irving Pichel; ***W:*** Robert Smith; ***C:*** Lionel Lindon; ***M:*** Louis Gruenberg.

Quicksand **2001 (R)** Bill Turner (Dudikoff) is the new shrink on a marine base and one of his patients is Randi Stewart (Theiss), who's not only a sergeant but the commanding officer's (Hedaya) daughter. When General Stewart is murdered, Randi becomes the prime suspect. Turner, who has taken more than a professional interest in his patient, begins investigating and learns that the base has had an unusually high number of suicides as well. **92m/C VHS, DVD.** Michael Dudikoff, Brooke Theiss, Dan Hedaya, Michael O'Hagan, Douglas Weston, Richard Kind, Pamela Salem; ***D:*** Sam Firstenberg; ***W:*** Steve Schoenberg, Ruben Gordon; ***C:*** Sameer Reddy; ***M:*** Curt Harpel. **VIDEO**

Quicksand **2001 (R)** Bank exec Martin (Keaton) is sent to Monaco to investigate some questionable offshore accounts. Apparently the money is being laundered through financing various film productions—one of which is the currently filming "Quicksand" that stars washed-up actor Jake (Caine). Soon both are in over their heads in some real-life drama. **93m/C VHS, DVD.** *GB FR* Michael Caine, Michael Keaton, Rade Serbedzija, Judith Godreche, Xander Berkeley, Elina Lowensohn, Kathleen Wilhoite; ***D:*** John MacKenzie; ***W:*** Tim Prager; ***C:*** Walter McGill; ***M:*** Hal Lindes, Anthony Marinelli. **VIDEO**

Quicksand: No Escape **1991 (PG-13)** Scott Reinhardt (Matheson) is a successful architect whose partner decides to secure a building contract by bribing a city official. When his partner is murdered Reinhardt is approached by a former cop (Sutherland) asking a lot of money for some incriminating evidence. Reinhardt is then drawn ever deeper into the illicit dealings, endangering his life. **93m/C VHS.** Tim Matheson, Donald Sutherland, Jay Acovone, Timothy Carhart, John Finn, Marc Alaimo, Felicity Huffman, Al Pugliese; ***D:*** Michael Pressman; ***W:*** Peter Baloff, Dave Wollert.

Quicksilver **1/2 1986 (PG)** A young stockbroker loses all, then quits his job to become a city bicycle messenger. Pointless, self-indulgent yuppie fantasy. **106m/C VHS, DVD.** Kevin Bacon, Jami Gertz, Paul Rodriguez, Rudy Ramos, Andrew Smith, Gerald S. O'Loughlin, Laurence Fishburne, Louie Anderson; ***D:*** Thomas Michael Donnelly; ***W:*** Thomas Michael Donnelly; ***M:*** Tony Banks.

Quicksilver Highway **1/2 1998 (R)** Storyteller Aaron Quicksilver (Lloyd) entertains with two horror tales, based on the stories "The Body Politic" by Clive Barker and "Chattery Teeth" by Stephen King. The Barker story has been re-set in America and now features a plastic surgeon whose hands decide to become independent from the rest of his body, while the King story is about a traveling salesman who purchases a pair of steel teeth at a Arizona gas station, which turn out to be lifesavers when he makes the mistake of picking up a nightmarish hitchhiker. **90m/C VHS.** Christopher Lloyd, Matt Frewer, Raphael Sbarge, Missy (Melissa) Crider, Veronica Cartwright, Bill Nunn, Amelia Heinle; ***Cameos:*** Clive Barker; ***D:*** Mick Garris; ***W:*** Mick Garris; ***C:*** Shelly Johnson; ***M:*** Mark Mothersbaugh. **TV**

Quid Pro Quo **2008 (R)** Kinky drama with a stunning performance by Farmiga. Isaac Knott (Stahl) has been in a wheelchair since a childhood car accident. Now a reporter for a New York public radio station, Isaac gets a tip about a fetish group whose members suffer from paralysis envy and will pay to become disabled. His informer is slinky femme Fiona (Farmiga), who finds his wheelchair a turn-on. As they begin a edgy romance, things really turn weird when Isaac starts regaining feeling in his legs while he encourages Fiona to live out her fantasies. **82m/C DVD.** Nick Stahl, Vera Farmiga, Kate Burton, Dylan Bruno, Aimee Mullins; ***D:*** Carlos Brooks; ***W:*** Carlos Brooks; ***C:*** Michael McDonough; ***M:*** Mark Mothersbaugh.

The Quiet **2005 (R)** Dot (Belle), an orphaned deaf-mute teen, goes to live with her godparents (Donovan and Falco), much to the disdain of their catty cheerleader daughter Nina (Cuthbert). Dad twitches and mom self-medicates, Nina snarks, and Dot sulks, but then the otherwise socially rejected Dot becomes a convenient confessor for Nina and others, and the secrets they reveal are doozies. Too heavy to be a teen sex farce, too outlandish and gross to be poignant, the movie melts into cheesy ick despite good turns by the main players. **96m/C DVD.** *US* Camilla Belle, Elisha Cuthbert, Martin Donovan, Edie Falco, Shawn Ashmore, Katy Mixon; ***D:*** Jamie Babbit; ***W:*** Abdi Nazemian, Micah Schraft; ***C:*** M. David Mullen; ***M:*** Jeff Rona.

The Quiet American **2002 (R)** Caine well-deserves accolades in this role of a lifetime, portraying the aging and cynical English journalist Thomas Fowler, a long-time correspondent based in 1950s Saigon. He's obsessed with his beautiful young Vietnamese mistress Phuong (Yen) who also becomes a romantic object for brash American Alden Pyle (Fraser). There's something about this do-gooder, who's supposedly on a medical mission, that makes Fowler both suspicious and jealous. Set amidst the communist insurgence of Ho Chi Minh into French-held Indo-China, which will then lead to American involvement. Based on the novel by Graham Greene. **118m/C VHS, DVD.** *US* Michael Caine, Brendan Fraser, Do Thi Hai Yen, Rade Serbedzija, Tzi Ma, Robert Stanton, Holmes Osborne, Pham Thai Mai Hoa, Quang Hai, Ferdinand Hoang; ***D:*** Phillip Noyce; ***W:*** Christopher Hampton, Robert Schenkkan; ***C:*** Christopher Doyle; ***M:*** Craig Armstrong. Natl. Bd. of Review '02: Director (Noyce).

Quiet Chaos 1/2 *Caos Calmo* **2008** While on vacation, Pietro (Moretti) rescues a woman from drowning only to learn on his return home that his wife has died in an accident. Grief-stricken, Pietro must adjust to being a single dad to 10-year-old Claudia (Yoshimi) and can scarcely bear to let his daughter out of his sight. So he begins spending his days in a park by her school while quietly attempting to come to terms with his loss. Italian with subtitles. **105m/C DVD.** *IT* Nanni Moretti, Valeria Golino, Isabella Ferrari, Blu Yoshimi, Alessandro Gassman, Hippolyte Girardot, Kasia Smutniak; *D:* Antonello Grimaldi; *W:* Nanni Moretti, Francesco Piccolo, Laura Paolucci; *C:* Alessandro Pesci; *M:* Paolo Buonvino.

Quiet Cool **1986 (R)** When his former girlfriend's family is killed, a New York cop travels to a sleepy California town run by a pot-growing tycoon. He subsequently kills the bad guys in a Rambo-like fit of vengeance. Dopey exercise in sleepy-eyed bloodshed. **80m/C VHS, DVD.** James Remar, Daphne Ashbrook, Adam Coleman Howard, Jared Martin, Fran Ryan; *D:* Clay Borris; *W:* Clay Borris; *M:* Jay Ferguson.

Quiet Day in Belfast **1974** Tragedy occurs when northern Irish patriots and British soldiers clash in an Irish betting parlor. Kidder plays a duel role: an Irish woman in love with a British soldier (Foster) and the woman's twin sister, newly arrived from Canada, who becomes the victim of a case of mistaken identity. Convincingly adapted from a Canadian stage play by Andrew Dalrymple. **92m/C VHS.** *CA* Barry Foster, Margot Kidder, Leo Leyden, Emmet Bergin, Joyce Campion, Sean McCann; *D:* Milad Bessada; *W:* Jack Gray.

Quiet Days in Clichy *Jours Tranquilles a Clichy* **1990** Chabrol's ludicrous adaptation (previously filmed in 1970) of Henry Miller's autobiographical novel, which followed the sexually obsessed writer (young and poor at the time) and his friend through various exploits in the French town of Clichy in the 1930s. Chabrol's version features the horrendously miscast McCarthy as Miller, who now has money to throw around, as he and his pal Alfred (Havers) spend most of their time in a fancy brothel with various girls. French with subtitles. **100m/C VHS.** *FR* Andrew McCarthy, Nigel Havers, Stephane Audran, Isolde Barth, Eva Grimaldi, Stephanie Cotta, Barbara De Rossi; *D:* Claude Chabrol; *W:* Claude Chabrol, Ugo Leonzio; *C:* Jean Rabier; *M:* Matthieu Chabrol.

Quiet Days in Hollywood *The Way We Are* **1997 (R)** Sexual roundelay in Hollywood involves a prostitute, an actor, a crook, a waitress, a rape, a gay triangle, various affairs, and related sexual experimentation. Less titillating than it sounds; German director Rusnak was making his U.S. feature debut. Maybe something got lost in the translation. **95m/C VHS, DVD.** Peter Dobson, Chad Lowe, Steven Mailer, Daryl (Chill) Mitchell, Bill Cusack, Meta Golding, Hilary Swank, Natasha Gregson Wagner; *D:* Josef Rusnak; *W:* Josef Rusnak; *C:* Dietrich Lohmann; *M:* Harald Kloser.

A Quiet Duel *Akira Kurosawa's The Quiet Duel; Shizuka Naru Ketto* **1949** Kyoji (Mifune), a young, idealistic doctor working as an army surgeon, contracts syphillis from the blood of a patient during an operation. Because the disease was virtually incurable at the time, the tormented Kyoji abandons his fiance and decides to dedicate himself to his work. Based on a play by Kazuo Kikuta. Japanese with subtitles. **95m/B VHS, DVD.** *JP* Toshiro Mifune, Takashi Shimura, Kenjiro Uemura; *D:* Akira Kurosawa; *W:* Senkichi Taniguchi, Akira Kurosawa; *M:* Akira Ifukube.

The Quiet Earth **1985 (R)** Serious science fiction film about a scientist who awakens to find himself seemingly the only human left on earth as the result of a misfired time/space government experiment. He later finds two other people, a girl and a Maori tribesman, and must try to repair the damage in order to save what's left of mankind. **91m/C VHS, DVD.** *NZ* Bruno Lawrence, Alison Routledge, Peter Smith, Norman Fletcher, Tom Hyde; *D:* Geoff Murphy; *W:* Sam Pillsbury, Bill Baer, Bruno Lawrence; *C:* James Bartle; *M:* John Charles.

The Quiet Family *Choyonghan kajok* **1998** The Kang family buy a mountain lodge after hearing a major road will be getting built there. But there's a problem: no customers. And they've spent all the money they have on the lodge. One night a guest finally arrives, but commits suicide and the family buries him in the woods to avoid bad publicity. Unfortunately their soon-to-be arriving waves of guests all inexplicably snuff it in the night (willingly or not). The Kangs continue to bury them all, wondering how long they can keep it up. Eventually remade as "The Happiness of the Katakuris" by Takashi Miike. **105m/C DVD.** *KN* Kang-ho Song, Min-Sik Choi, In-hwan Park, Mun-hee Na, Ho-kyung Go, Yun-seong Lee; *D:* Ji-woon Kim; *W:* Ji-woon Kim; *C:* Kwang-Seok Jeong.

Quiet Fire 1/2 **1991 (R)** A health-club owner tries to get the goods on the arms-dealing congressman who killed his best friend. Hilton-Jacobs looks properly pumped up since his sweathog days on TV's "Welcome Back Kotter." **100m/C VHS, DVD.** Lawrence-Hilton Jacobs, Robert Z'Dar, Nadia Marie, Karen Black, Lance Lindsay; *D:* Lawrence-Hilton Jacobs.

The Quiet Man **1952** The classic incarnation of Hollywood Irishness, and one of Ford's best, and funniest films. Wayne is Sean Thornton, a weary American ex-boxer who returns to the Irish hamlet of his childhood and tries to take spirited lass Mary Kate (O'Hara) as his wife, despite the strenuous objections of her brawling brother Red Will (McLaglen). Thornton's aided by the leprechaun-like Michaleen Flynn (Fitzgerald) and the local parish priest (Bond). A high-spirited and memorable film filled with Irish stew, wonderful banter, and shots of the lush countryside. Listen for the Scottish bagpipes at the start of the horse race, a slight geographic inaccuracy. **129m/C VHS, DVD.** John Wayne, Maureen O'Hara, Barry Fitzgerald, Victor McLaglen, Arthur Shields, Jack MacGowran, Ward Bond, Mildred Natwick, Ken Curtis, Mae Marsh, Sean McClory, Francis Ford, D.R.O. Hatswell; *D:* John Ford; *W:* Frank Nugent; *C:* Archie Stout; *M:* Victor Young. Oscars '52: Color Cinematog., Director (Ford); Directors Guild '52: Director (Ford); Venice Film Fest. '52: Director (Ford)..

The Quiet Room **1996 (PG)** A nameless seven-year-old girl (Chloe Ferguson) refuses to speak when she learns her constantly quarreling parents are separating. Film is shown from only the child's perspective and her fantasies of a different life as she goes about her daily routine. Although the girl remains silent, she answers her parents in her thoughts (the voiceover lets the viewer into the girl's world) and she has flashbacks to her younger self (played by Ferguson's sister Phoebe) and when her parents loved each other. **91m/C VHS.** *AU* Chloe Ferguson, Celine O'Leary, Paul Blackwell, Phoebe Ferguson; *D:* Rolf de Heer; *W:* Rolf de Heer; *C:* Tony Clark; *M:* Graham Tardif.

Quiet Thunder **1987 (PG-13)** A hard-drinking bush pilot in Africa and a beautiful senator's wife are thrown together on the run after both witness an assassination. Mindless, thoroughly derivative "adventure." **94m/C VHS.** Wayne Crawford, June Chadwick, Victor Steinbach; *D:* David Rice.

Quigley 1/2 **2003 (G)** When a ruthless, stinking-rich businessman suddenly dies, the powers-that-be won't let him into heaven unless he goes back and fixes his wrongdoings—as a cutesy pup named Quigley. **89m/C VHS, DVD.** Gary Busey, Oz (Osgood) Perkins II, Curtis Armstrong, Christopher Atkins, P.J. Ochlan, Kieran Mulroney, Bill Fagerbakke, Jessica Ferrarone, Caryn Greenhut; *D:* William B. Hillman; *W:* William B. Hillman; *C:* Gary Graver; *M:* Eric Lundmark. **VIDEO**

Quigley Down Under 1/2 **1990 (PG-13)** A Western sharpshooter moves to Australia in search of employment. To his horror, he discovers that he has been hired to kill aborigines. Predictable action is somewhat redeemed by the terrific chemistry between Selleck and San Giacomo and the usual enjoyable theatrics from Rickman as the landowner heavy. **121m/C VHS, DVD.** *AU* Tom Selleck, Laura San Giacomo, Alan Rickman, Chris Haywood, Ron Haddrick, Tony Bonner, Roger Ward, Ben Mendelsohn, Jerome Ehlers, Conor McDermottroe; *D:* Simon Wincer; *W:* John Hill; *C:* David Eggby; *M:* Basil Poledouris.

The Quiller Memorandum **1966** An American secret agent travels to Berlin to uncover a deadly neo-Nazi gang. Refreshingly different from other spy tales of its era. Good screenplay adapted from Adam Hall's novel, "The Berlin Memorandum." **103m/C VHS, DVD.** George Segal, Senta Berger, Alec Guinness, Max von Sydow, George Sanders; *D:* Michael Anderson Sr.; *W:* Harold Pinter; *M:* John Barry.

Quills 1/2 **2000 (R)** Follows the last years of the life of the Marquis de Sade (played by Rush), which he spent in an insane asylum as punishment for his erotic writings. Sade continues to write while imprisoned, and with the help of his secret courier, Madeleine (played by Winslet), is able to distribute his stories to the public. Unfortunately, the movie uses Sade's imprisonment to put forth lessons about the importance of freedom of expression and perils of censorship, thereby sacrificing a closer investigation of the real story—the man's boiling imagination. Worth viewing for the performances and for the glimpse into the life of one of histories most fascinating authors. Based on the off-Broadway play by David Wright. **123m/C VHS, DVD.** Geoffrey Rush, Kate Winslet, Joaquin Rafael (Leaf) Phoenix, Michael Caine; *D:* Philip Kaufman; *W:* Doug Wright; *C:* Rogier Stoffers; *M:* Stephen Warbeck. Natl. Bd. of Review '00: Film, Support. Actor (Phoenix).

Quilombo 1/2 **1984** The title refers to a legendary settlement of runaway slaves in 17th-century Brazil; an epic chronicles its fortunes as leadership passes from a wise ruler to a more militant one who goes to war against the government. Stunning scenery, tribal images, and folk songs, but the numerous characters seldom come to life as personalities. One of Brazil's most expensive films, in Portuguese with English subtitles. **114m/C VHS, DVD.** *BR* Vera Fischer, Antonio Pompeo, Zeze Motta, Toni Tornado; *D:* Carlos Diegues; *W:* Carlos Diegues.

Quinceanera **2006 (R)** Quinceanera is a traditional celebration that marks a coming-of-age at 15 for Mexican American girls. Magdalena (newcomer Rios) reaches this milestone with the revelation that she's pregnant (even though she swears she's a virgin). Banished from her home by her devout father, she takes refuge with her Uncle Tomas (Gonzalez), a wise octogenarian who is also sheltering his gay nephew Carols (Garcia). Meanwhile, Tomas's modest but longstanding home is threatened by his new landlords, thus unfolding a complex story of tradition versus change, the definition of family, and gentrification. Effective docu-stylings illuminate life in L.A.'s Echo Park community and make the flick's ending utterly satisfying. **90m/C DVD.** *US* David W. Ross, Emily Rios, Jesse Garcia, Chalo Gonzalez, J.R. Cruz, Jason L. Wood, Araceli Guzman-Rico, Jesus Castanos-Chima; *D:* Richard Glatzer, Wash Westmoreland; *W:* Richard Glatzer, Wash Westmoreland; *C:* Eric Steelberg; *M:* Victor Block.

Quintet **1979** Atypical Altman sci-fi effort. The stakes in "Quintet," a form of backgammon, are high—you bet your life. Set during the planet's final ice age. Newman and wife Fossey wander into a dying city and are invited to play the game, with Fossey losing quickly. Bizarre and pretentious, with heavy symbolic going. **118m/C VHS, DVD.** Paul Newman, Bibi Andersson, Fernando Rey, Vittorio Gassman, David Langton, Nina Van Pallandt, Brigitte Fossey; *D:* Robert Altman; *W:* Lionel Chetwynd, Patricia Resnick, Robert Altman, Frank Barhydt.

Quiz Show **1994 (PG-13)** Redford's intelligent, entertaining, and morally complex film about the TV game show scandals of the late '50s is his most accomplished work to date. At the center of the film is Charles Van Doren (Fiennes), an intellectual, golden boy who dethrones Herbert Stempel (Turturro), the reigning champion of the rigged "Twenty-One." The program's sponsor felt Stempel, a nerdy Jewish grad's everyman qualities were wearing thin and wanted a more polished image, which they found in handsome, sophisticated Van Doren. Federal investigator Goodwin (Morrow) suspects Van Doren's reign is a sham and sets out to expose him as a fraud. Acting is of the highest caliber with Fiennes, Turturro, and Morrow all giving beautiful performances. Notable among supporting cast is Scofield as Van Doren's Pulitzer prize-winning father. With strong script and gorgeous lensing, this modern Faust story is a brilliant reflection on corporate greed, class rivalry, and the powers of television. Based on the book "Remembering America: A Voice From the Sixties" by Richard N. Goodwin. **133m/C VHS, DVD.** John Turturro, Rob Morrow, Ralph Fiennes, Paul Scofield, David Paymer, Hank Azaria, Christopher McDonald, Johann Carlo, Elizabeth Wilson, Mira Sorvino, Griffin Dunne, Martin Scorsese, Barry Levinson; *D:* Robert Redford; *W:* Paul Attanasio; *C:* Michael Ballhaus; *M:* Mark Isham. British Acad. '94: Adapt. Screenplay; N.Y. Film Critics '94: Film.

Quo Vadis 1/2 **1912** One of the first truly huge Italian silent epics. The initial adaptation of the Henryk Sienkiewicz novel about Nero and ancient Rome. Probably the cinema's first great financial success. **45m/B VHS.** Amleto Novelli, Gustavo Serena, Amelia Vattaneo, Carlo Cattaneo, Lea Giunchi; *D:* Enrico Guazzoni; *W:* Enrico Guazzoni; *C:* Eugenio Bava.

Quo Vadis **1951** Larger-than-life production about Nero and the Christian persecution. Done on a giant scale: features exciting fighting scenes, romance, and fabulous costumes. Definitive version of the classic novel by Henryk Siekiewicz. Remade for Italian TV in 1985. **171m/C VHS, Blu-ray Disc.** Robert Taylor, Deborah Kerr, Peter Ustinov, Patricia Laffan, Finlay Currie, Abraham Sofaer, Marina Berti, Buddy Baer, Felix Aylmer, Nora Swinburne, Elspeth March; ***Cameos:*** Sophia Loren, Elizabeth Taylor; *D:* Mervyn LeRoy; *C:* Robert L. Surtees; *M:* Miklos Rozsa; ***Nar:*** Walter Pidgeon. Golden Globes '52: Support. Actor (Ustinov).

Quo Vadis 1/2 **1985 (R)** Third screen version of Henryk Sienkiewicz's book. See the other two first. This one is slow and perfunctory. Brandauer is memorable as Nero; Quinn (in the lead) is the son of Anthony. **122m/C VHS.** *IT* Klaus Maria Brandauer, Frederic Forrest, Christina Raines, Maria Therese Relin, Francesco Quinn, Barbara DeRossi, Phillippe LeRoy, Max von Sydow, Gabriele Ferzetti, Massimo Girotti, Leopoldo Trieste; *D:* Franco Rossi.

R-Point 1/2 *Arpointeau* **2004 (R)** A South Korean military base in Vietnam receives a radio signal from a missing, presumed-dead platoon from a strategic location known as R-Point. The high command sends in a decorated lieutenant and eight men to rescue the troops, but all they find is a crazy woman with a machine gun, a ruined fort, and a temple dedicated to the massacre of the Vietnamese at the hands of China 100 years ago, leading them to the very astute conclusion that something is amiss. **107m/C DVD.** *KN* Byeong-ho Son, Woo-seong Kam, Tae-kying Oh, Won-sang Park, Seon-gyun Lee, Jin-ho Song, Byeong-cheol Kim, Kyeong-ho Jeong, Yeong-dong Mun, Ju-Bong Gi; *D:* Su-chang Kong; *W:* Su-chang Kong; *C:* Hyeong-jin Seok; *M:* Palan Dal.

'R Xmas **2001** Brancato and de Matteo star as the unnamed husband and wife whose idyllic Manhattan days disguise their shady heroin dealings by night in the Bronx. It's Christmas time and everything is just swell for the mom and pop drug dealers until they attempt to illegally obtain a hard-to-find toy for their daughter (Valens), which ends in dad getting kidnapped by a thug (Ice-T) who wants a huge ransom and asks that they refrain from dealing drugs in the future. They're then left to decide between their tarnished American Dream and going straight and being poor. Some racial issues are explored (she's Puerto Rican, he's Dominican), as well as the obvious moral and financial issues. De Matteo makes her character complex and eminently watchable through somewhat predictable and tired material. **83m/C VHS, DVD.** *US FR* Lillo Brancato, Drea De Matteo, Ice-T, Victor Argo, Lisa Valens; *D:* Abel Ferrara; *W:* Abel Ferrara, Scott Pardo; *C:* Ken Kelsch.

The Rabbit Is Me *Das Kaninchen Bin Ich; I Am the Rabbit* **1965** Maria's life in East Germany is tainted when her brother is jailed for subversive political activity. She has an affair with an older man, only to discover he's the judge who sent her brother to prison. This doesn't help her self-esteem. German with subtitles. **109m/B DVD.** *GE* Angelika Waller, Alfred Muller, Irma Munch; Ilse Voight, Wolfgang Winkler, Willi Narloch; ***D:*** Kurt Maetzig; ***W:*** Manfred Bieler; ***C:*** Erich Gusko; ***M:*** Reiner Bredemeyer, Gerhard Rosenfeld.

Rabbit-Proof Fence 1/2 **2002 (PG)** Fascinating, true story of three mixed-race Aboriginal girls in 1930s Australia, who escape their forced incarceration at an institution designed to train such children, snatched from their parents by the government, as domestic workers. Embarking on an incredible 1,500 mile journey to return home, Molly (Sampi), Daisy (Sansbury) and Gracie (Monaghan), follow the line of a fence—the longest unbroken piece of fence ever created—built by the government to keep out the rabbits that had overrun the farmlands. Hunted by the authorities, the girls struggle to survive in a heartbreaking and riveting adventure. Mailman is a sympathetic white woman who helps the girls along the way while Branagh plays Neville, a first-class bigot who oversaw the racist policies that the Australian government enforced until 1970. Neophyte leads are appealingly natural. Based on a book by Doris Pilkington, daughter of one of the girls. **95m/C VHS, DVD.** *AU GB* Everlyn Sampi, Tianna Sansbury, Laura Monaghan, Kenneth Branagh, David Gulpilil, Deborah Mailman, Jason Clarke, Garry McDonald, Ningali Lawford, Myarn Lawford; ***D:*** Phillip Noyce; ***W:*** Christine Olsen; ***C:*** Christopher Doyle; ***M:*** Peter Gabriel. Natl. Bd. of Review '02: Director (Noyce).

Rabbit Test 1/2 **1978 (PG)** In Rivers' first directorial effort, a clumsy virginal guy becomes the world's first pregnant man. So irreverent it's almost never in good taste, and so poorly written it's almost never funny. **86m/C VHS.** Sab Shimono, Billy Crystal, Roddy McDowall, Imogene Coca, Paul Lynde, Alex Rocco, George Gobel; ***D:*** Joan Rivers.

Rabid 1/2 *Rage* **1977 (R)** A young girl undergoes a radical plastic surgery technique and develops a strange and unexplained lesion in her armpit. She also finds she has an unusual craving for human blood. **90m/C VHS, DVD.** *CA* Marilyn Chambers, Frank Moore, Joe Silver, Howard Ryshpan, Patricia Gage, Susan (Suzan) Roman, Roger Periard, Victor Desy; ***D:*** David Cronenberg; ***W:*** David Cronenberg; ***C:*** Rene Verzier.

Rabid Grannies WOOF! **1989 (R)** Wicked satire about two aging sisters who receive a surprise birthday gift from their devilworshipping nephew. The gift turns their party into a gorefest as they rip into various family members—literally. Any humor will be lost on any but the most diehard Troma fans. Dubbed. **89m/C VHS, DVD.** *BE* Catherine Aymerie, Caroline Brackman, Danielle Daven, Raymond Lescot, Anne Marie Fox, Richard Cotica, Patricia Davie; ***D:*** Emmanuel Kervyn; ***W:*** Emmanuel Kervyn; ***C:*** Hugh Labye; ***M:*** Jean-Bruno Castelain, Pierre-Damien Castelain.

Race 1/2 **1999 (R)** Serious low-budget film attempts to take a serious look at practical politics on the local level. L.A. councilman Durman (Robertson) comes in third in the primary after redistricting. Tied for first are Lucinda Davis (Pounder), a black woman, and Gustavo Alvarez (Rodriguez), a Latino house painter. Their race touches all of the Southern California racial and ethnic hot buttons, and quickly turns nasty. **103m/C VHS, DVD.** Paul Rodriguez, CCH Pounder, Cliff Robertson, Annette Murphy; ***D:*** Tom Musca; ***W:*** Tom Musca, Mark Kemble; ***C:*** Arturo Smith; ***M:*** Stan Ridgway.

Race Against Time **2000** Another bleak futuristic thriller but with fast-paced and suspenseful action. When Gabriel's (Roberts) son is diagnosed with a deadly virus, Gabirel learns that the vaccine will cost him mucho dinero—and he has only 12 hours to come up with the cash. So he agrees to sell his organs to Lifecorps for harvesting in a year's time, then it's bye-bye for Gabe. But when his son dies anyway, Gabriel tries to get out of the agreement, especially when it seems his son's death wasn't so straightforward. **90m/C VHS, DVD.** Eric Roberts, Cary Elwes, Sarah Wynter, Chris Sarandon; ***D:*** Geoff Murphy. **CABLE**

Race for Glory 1/2 **1989 (R)** A young motorcyclist builds a super-bike he hopes will help him win a world championship race. Will he win? Can you stand the suspense? Let's just say there's a happy ending. **102m/C VHS.** Alex McArthur, Peter Berg, Pamela Ludwig; ***D:*** Rocky Lang; ***M:*** Jay Ferguson.

Race for Life 1/2 *Mask of Dust* **1955** A race car driver attempts to make a comeback despite objections from his wife. He races around Europe (great scenery); she leaves him; he tries to win her back and salvage his career. Standard, un-gripping story. Car scenes are great. **69m/B VHS.** *GB* Richard Conte, Mari Aldon, George Coulouris, Alec Mango, Meredith Edwards, Richard Marner, Jeremy Hawk; ***D:*** Terence Fisher; ***W:*** Richard H. Landau; ***C:*** Walter J. (Jimmy W.) Harvey; ***M:*** Leonard Salzedo.

Race for Your Life, Charlie Brown 1/2 **1977 (G)** Another in the popular series of "Peanuts" character films. This one features Charlie Brown, Snoopy, and all the gang spending an exciting summer in the American wilderness. **76m/C VHS.** ***D:*** Bill Melendez, Phil Roman; ***W:*** Charles M. Schulz; ***M:*** Ed Bogas; ***V:*** Gail Davis, Melanie Kohn, Duncan Watson, Gregory Felton, Stuart Brotman, Liam Martin, Ed Bogas.

Race the Sun **1996 (PG)** There's nothin' new under this sun. Tired story of a group of young losers who band together to beat the odds and compete in an unusual contest is trotted out once again for populist amusement. This time it's a Hawaiian high school solar car team traveling to Australia to go for the prize against the big shots and snobs. Based on true events, it features some nice scenery from Berry and the main locations, but not much else. Uninspired but basically harmless, this one's fine for the kids. **100m/C VHS, DVD.** Halle Berry, James Belushi, Casey Affleck, Eliza Dushku, Kevin Tighe, Anthony Michael Ruivivar, J. Moki Cho, Dion Basco, Sara Tanaka, Nadja Pionilla, Steve Zahn, Bill Hunter; ***D:*** Charles Kanganis; ***W:*** Barry Morrow; ***C:*** David Burr; ***M:*** Graeme Revell.

Race to Freedom: The Story of the Underground Railroad 1/2 **1994** Story of four fugitive slaves, in 1850, who struggle to get from North Carolina to the safety of Canada through a network of safe-houses and people willing to risk smuggling them to asylum. **90m/C VHS, DVD.** *CA* Courtney B. Vance, Janet Bailey, Glynn Turman, Tim Reid, Michael Riley, Dawnn Lewis, Ron White, Alfre Woodard; ***D:*** Don McBrearty; ***W:*** Nancy Trite Botkin, Diana Braithwaite; ***M:*** Christopher Dedrick. **CABLE**

Race to Space 1/2 **2001 (PG)** German rocket scientist Wilhelm Von Huber (Woods) and his young son Billy (Linz) move to Cocoa Beach, Florida, in 1960 so dad can work for NASA on the Mercury program. Billy, who's been lonely since his mother's death, is taken under the wing of vet Donni McGuinness (Gish), and bonds with Mac, one of the chimps being trained to go into space, which in turn helps him get closer to his father. The chimp steals the movie, which is heavy on the sentimentality. **104m/C VHS, DVD.** Alex D. Linz, James Woods, William Devane, William Atherton, John O'Hurley, Barry Corbin, Annabeth Gish, Jake Lloyd; ***D:*** Sean McNamara; ***W:*** Eric Gardner, Steven H. Wilson; ***C:*** Christian Sebaldt; ***M:*** John Coda. **VIDEO**

Race to Witch Mountain **2009 (PG)** Reworking of the 1975 Disney classic "Escape from Witch Mountain" adds muscle, firearms, and non-stop action to satisfy the modern young audience. Jack Bruno (Johnson), an ex-con Vegas cabbie, finds sweet-looking teenaged siblings Sara (Robb) and Seth (Ludwig) in the back seat of his cab from out of nowhere—after their spaceship crashes—and needing his help to get to the desert. A wad of cash persuades the skeptical Bruno. Along the way they're harassed by Bruno's former underworld associates, targeted by an especially nasty extraterrestrial terminator, pursued by well-armed agents in black SUVs, and then accompanied by a slightly kooky UFO-seeking astrophysicist (Gugino). Sacrifices plot and character development for its frenetic pace. It's more about "hold on tight, it's gonna be a bumpy ride." **98m/C DVD.** *US* AnnaSophia Robb, Alexander Ludwig, Carla Gugino, Ciaran Hinds, Dwayne "The Rock" Johnson, Tom Everett Scott, Richard "Cheech" Marin, Garry Marshall; ***D:*** Andy Fickman; ***W:*** Matt Lopez, Mark Bomback; ***C:*** Greg Gardiner; ***M:*** Trevor Rabin.

Race with the Devil 1/2 **1975 (PG)** Vacationers are terrorized by devil worshippers after they witness a sacrificial killing. Heavy on car chases; light on plot and redeeming qualities. Don't waste your time. **88m/C VHS, DVD.** Peter Fonda, Warren Oates, Loretta Swit, Lara Parker, R.G. Armstrong; ***D:*** Jack Starrett; ***W:*** Wes Bishop, Lee Frost; ***C:*** Robert C. Jessup.

The Racers 1/2 *Such Men are Dangerous* **1955** Douglas brings power to the role of a man determined to advance to the winners' circle. Exciting European location photography, but not much plot. **112m/C VHS.** Gilbert Roland, Kirk Douglas, Lee J. Cobb, Cesar Romero, Bella Darvi; ***D:*** Henry Hathaway; ***M:*** Alex North.

Rachel and the Stranger **1948** A God-fearing farmer declares his love for his wife when a handsome stranger (Mitchum) nearly woos her away. Well-cast, well-paced, charming Western comedy-drama. **93m/B VHS.** Loretta Young, Robert Mitchum, William Holden, Gary Gray; ***D:*** Norman Foster.

Rachel Getting Married 1/2 **2008 (R)** Rachel (DeWitt) is indeed getting married, but here comes the bride's junkie sister Kym (Hathaway), attending the wedding after her umpteenth rehab stint. The impending nuptials force a reluctant reunion of a family fragmented by the weight of accumulated self-inflicted wounds but held together by a desire to belong. Kym's habit of hogging a spotlight that should finally be on Rachel anchors the sibs' caustic relationship, which is further eroded by father Paul (Irwin) and his second wife (Winger). That this feels so real is the result of an ensemble cast delivering their best work, while director Demme's documentary-like approach provides an at times uncomfortable intimacy. **111m/C DVD.** *US* Anne Hathaway, Rosemarie DeWitt, Bill Irwin, Debra Winger, Tunde Adebimpe, Mather Zickel, Anisa George, Anna Deavere Smith; ***D:*** Jonathan Demme; ***W:*** Jenny Lumet; ***C:*** Declan Quinn; ***M:*** Zafer Tawil, Donald Harrison Jr.

The Rachel Papers **1989 (R)** Based on the Martin Amis novel, this is the funny/sad tale of an Oxford youth who plots via his computer the seduction of a beautiful American girl. For anyone who has ever loved someone just out of their reach. **92m/C VHS, DVD.** Dexter Fletcher, Ione Skye, James Spader, Jonathan Pryce, Bill Paterson, Michael Gambon, Lesley Sharp; ***D:*** Damian Harris; ***W:*** Damian Harris; ***M:*** Chaz Jankel.

Rachel, Rachel 1/2 **1968 (R)** Rachel teaches by day, wearing simple, practical dresses and her hair up. By night she caters to her domineering mother by preparing refreshments for her parties. This sexually repressed, spinster schoolteacher, however, gets one last chance at romance in her small Connecticut town. Woodward mixes just the right amounts of loneliness and sweetness in the leading role. A surprising award-winner that was an independent production of Newman. Based on Margaret Laurence's "A Jest of God." **102m/C VHS.** Joanne Woodward, James Olson, Estelle Parsons, Geraldine Fitzgerald, Donald Moffat; ***D:*** Paul Newman; ***W:*** Stewart Stern. Golden Globes '69: Actress—Drama (Woodward), Director (Newman); N.Y. Film Critics '68: Actress (Woodward), Director (Newman).

Rachel River 1/2 **1987 (PG-13)** A divorced radio personality struggles to make something of her life in her small Minnesota town. **88m/C VHS.** Pamela Reed, Craig T. Nelson, Viveca Lindfors, James Olson, Zeljko Ivanek, Jo Henderson, Alan North, Jon (John) DeVries; ***D:*** Sandy Smolan; ***W:*** Judith Guest; ***M:*** Arvo Part.

Rachel's Man **1975** A big-screen version of the Biblical love story of Jacob and Rachel. **115m/C VHS, DVD.** Mickey Rooney, Rita Tushingham, Leonard Whiting, Michal Bat-Adam; ***D:*** Moshe Mizrahi.

Rachida **2005** Rachida is a young school teacher in terror-stricken 1990s Algeria. When stopped by street kids who demand she place a bomb in her classroom, she refuses. Shot point-blank and left for dead, Rachida miraculously survives. Under the care of her mother, far from the dangers of the city life, she begins to recover. Still, the struggle to find hope in such a violent world proves difficult for everyone. An unflinching portrait of fear with a brave performance from Djouadi; promising debut from writer/director Bachir. Arabic and French with English subtitles. **100m/C DVD.** *FR AL* Ibtissem Djouadi, Bahia Rachedi, Rachida Messaoui En, Zaki Boulenafed, Hamid Remas; ***D:*** Yamina Bachir; ***W:*** Yamina Bachir.

Racing Blood 1/2 **1936** Young jockey Frankie (Darro) buys and nurses a lame horse back to health and is soon winning on the racetrack. Racketeers get involved, kidnapping Frankie before a big race, and his escape attempt naturally puts him in harm's way. **61m/B DVD.** Frankie Darro, James Eagles, Gladys Blake, Kane Richmond, Arthur Housman, Matthew Betz; ***D:*** Victor Halperin; ***W:*** Joseph O'Donnell; ***C:*** Jack Greenhalgh, Robert Doran, William (Bill) Hyer.

Racing Daylight **2007** Sadie Stokes (Leo) is caring for her ill grandma in the family's longtime Hudson River Valley home when a ghostly presence makes itself known. As Sadie starts researching her family's past, she believes that she and handyman Henry (Strathairn) are reincarnations of Stokes ancestors who have unfinished business and are determined to be reunited. **83m/C DVD.** Melissa Leo, David Strathairn, Sabrina Lloyd, Giancarlo Esposito, Jason Downs, Sigrid Heath; ***D:*** Nicole Quinn; ***W:*** Nicole Quinn; ***C:*** Stephen Harris; ***M:*** Sarah Plant. **VIDEO**

Racing Luck *Red Hot Tires* **1935** While working at a race track, a man is framed and forced to work for another stable. **56m/B VHS.** William Boyd, Barbara Worth, George Ernest, Esther Muir, Dick Curtis; ***D:*** Sam Newfield.

Racing Stripes **2005 (PG)** Farmer Nolan Walsh (Greenwood), finds a baby zebra (voiced by Muniz) left by a traveling circus in rural Kentucky and raises him on his farm. Stripes grows up yearning to be a racing horse, just as Channing (Panettiere), the farmer's daughter, yearns to be a jockey. The plot thickens as Walsh is a former horse trainer whose wife died in a riding accident and has since forbidden Channing from racing. Strange combination of "Babe," "National Velvet" and "Charlotte's Web" uses live animals with creepy computer-enhanced mouths for the speaking parts. Kids will enjoy it, but mom and dad might get bored with its routine plotlines. **102m/C DVD.** *US* Bruce Greenwood, Hayden Panettiere, M. Emmet Walsh, Wendie Malick; ***D:*** Frederick Du Chau; ***W:*** Frederick Du Chau, David F. Schmidt; ***C:*** David Eggby; ***M:*** Mark Isham; ***V:*** Frankie Muniz, Mandy Moore, Michael Clarke Duncan, Joshua Jackson, Jeff Foxworthy, Joe Pantoliano, Michael Rosenbaum, Steve Harvey, David Spade, Snoop Dogg, Fred Dalton Thompson, Dustin Hoffman, Whoopi Goldberg.

Racing with the Moon **1984 (PG)** Sweet, nostalgic film about two buddies awaiting induction into the Marines in 1942. They have their last chance at summer romance. Benjamin makes the most of skillful young actors and conventional story. Great period detail. Keep your eyes peeled for glimpses of many rising young stars including Hannah and Carvey. **108m/C VHS, DVD.** Sean Penn, Elizabeth McGovern, Nicolas Cage, John Karlen, Rutanya Alda, Max (Casey Adams) Showalter, Crispin Glover, Page Hannah, Michael Madsen, Carol Kane, Dana Carvey, Michael Talbott, Suzanne Adkinson, Michael Schoeffling, Victor Rendina; ***D:*** Richard Benjamin; ***W:*** Steve Kloves; ***C:*** John Bailey; ***M:*** Dave Grusin.

The Racket **1951** Police captain Mitchum tries to break up mob racket of gangster Ryan. Internecine strife on both sides adds complexity. Mitchum and especially Ryan are super; fine, tense melodrama. **88m/B VHS, DVD.** Robert Ryan, Robert Mitchum, Lizabeth Scott, Ray Collins, William Conrad, Don Porter; ***D:*** John Cromwell.

The Racketeer 1/2 **1929** A racketeer falls in love with a pretty girl and attempts to win her over. As part of his plan, the gangster arranges to help the girl's boyfriend begin his musical career in exchange for the girl's promise to marry him. **68m/B VHS, DVD.** Carole Lombard, Robert Armstrong, Hedda Hopper; ***D:*** Howard Higgin.

Racketeers of the Range 1/2 **1939** Cattleman fights a crooked attorney who wants to sell his client's stock to a large meat packing company. **62m/B VHS.** George O'Brien, Marjorie Reynolds, Chill Wills, Ray Whitley; ***D:*** David Ross Lederman.

Racquet **1979** Tennis pro Convy searches for true love and a tennis court of to call his own in Beverly Hills. Lame, sophomoric, and unfunny. **87m/C VHS.** Bert Convy, Edie Adams, Lynda Day George, Phil Silvers, Bobby Riggs, Bjorn Borg, Tanya Roberts; ***D:*** David Winters.

Rad 1/2 **1986 (PG)** Teenage drama revolving around BMX racing and such dilemmas as: can the good guys beat the bad guys, who's got the fastest bike, must you cheat to win, and should our hero miss his SAT tests to compete in "the big race.." Directed by stunt-expert Needham. **94m/C VHS.** Bill Allen, Bart Conner, Talia Shire, Jack Weston, Lori Loughlin; ***D:*** Hal Needham; ***W:*** Sam Bernard.

Radar Men from the Moon *Retik, the Moon Menace* **1952** Commando Cody, with his jet-pack, fights to defend the earth from invaders from the moon. Twelve-episode serial on two tapes. Silly sci-fi. **152m/B VHS, DVD.** George D. Wallace, Aline Towne, Roy Barcroft, William "Billy" Bakewell, Clayton Moore; ***D:*** Fred Brannon.

Radar Patrol vs. Spy King **1949** Special agent Alyn and his buxom Vargas girl Jean Dean battle the deadly Baroda and his ring of saboteurs, hell-bent on destroying America. 12 episodes of the serial edited onto two cassettes. **167m/B VHS.** Anthony Warde, George Lewis, John Merton, Eve Whitney, Kirk Alyn, Jeanne Dean; ***D:*** Fred Brannon; ***W:*** William Lively, James Lydon, Sol Shor; ***C:*** Ellis W. Carter; ***M:*** Stanley Wilson.

Radar Secret Service 1/2 **1950** Two servicemen witness the hijacking of a truck loaded with nuclear material. **59m/B VHS.** John Howard, Adele Jergens, Tom Neal, Ralph Byrd; ***D:*** Sam Newfield; ***C:*** Ernest Miller; ***M:*** Russell Garcia, Richard Hazard.

Radiance **1998** Three half-sisters reunite in their rundown family home, located in the sugar cane country of Australia's tropical north, to bury their mother. Resentful Mae (Morton-Thomas) feels she was trapped into caring alone for their prematurely senile mother while sophisticated Cressy (Maza) became a successfull opera singer and youngest sister Nona (Mailman) indulged her party girl ways. Old grievances are aired and the trio set off more than one kind of fireworks together. Adapted by Nowra from his play. **83m/C VHS.** *AU* Trisha Morton-Thomas, Rachel Maza, Deborah Mailman; ***D:*** Rachel Perkins; ***W:*** Louis Nowra; ***C:*** Warwick Thornton; ***M:*** Alistair Jones. Australian Film Inst. '98: Actress (Mailman).

Radio 1/2 **2003 (PG)** Feelgooder inspired by the true story of the mentally disabled James "Radio" Kennedy (Gooding Jr.), who befriends the kindly local football coach (Harris) and becomes a beloved mascot of sorts in Anderson, South Carolina circa 1976. Coach Jones finds Radio (so named for his ample, much-loved collection of discarded radios) locked in a storage shed after being taunted by a few players and is determined to help him. Radio, in turn, ends up teaching the town a lesson or two about the Golden Rule. Top notch cast and script can't completely save the somewhat saccharine but nonetheless inspirational story. Based on a "Sports Illustrated" story by Gary Smith. **109m/C VHS, DVD.** *US* Cuba Gooding Jr., Ed Harris, Alfre Woodard, S. Epatha Merkerson, Chris Mulkey, Sarah Drew, Riley Smith, Patrick Breen, Brent Sexton, Debra Winger; ***D:*** Mike Tollin; ***W:*** Mike Rich; ***C:*** Don Burgess; ***M:*** James Horner.

Radio Cab Murder 1/2 **1954** Fred (Hanley) was a safecracker who's trying to go straight by getting a job as a London cabbie. When an anonymous note informs his boss of Fred's past, the police deduce a gang wants Fred fired so they can recruit him. Fred plays along to infiltrate the gang and learn their plans for a bank heist but then his ruse is discovered. **70m/B DVD.** *GB* Lana Morris, Jimmy Hanley, Sam Kydd, Elizabeth Seal, Jack Allen, Rupert Holliday, Bruce Beeby; ***D:*** Vernon Sewell; ***W:*** Vernon Sewell; ***C:*** Geoffrey Faithfull.

Radio Days **1987 (PG)** A lovely, unpretentious remembrance of the pre-TV radio culture. Allen tells his story in a series of vignettes centering around his youth in Brooklyn, his eccentric extended family, and the legends of radio they all followed. The ubiquitous Farrow is a young singer hoping to make it big. **89m/C VHS, DVD.** Mia Farrow, Dianne Wiest, Julie Kavner, Michael Tucker, Wallace Shawn, Josh Mostel, Tony Roberts, Jeff Daniels, Kenneth Mars, Seth Green, William Magerman, Diane Keaton, Renee Lippin, Danny Aiello, Gina DeAngelis, Kitty Carlisle Hart, Mercedes Ruehl, Tito Puente; ***D:*** Woody Allen; ***W:*** Woody Allen; ***C:*** Carlo Di Palma; ***Nar:*** Woody Allen.

Radio Flyer **1992 (PG-13)** It's 1969 and Mike and Bobby have just moved to northern California with their divorced mom. Everything would be idyllic if only their mother hadn't decided to marry a drunken child abuser who beats Bobby whenever the mood strikes him. Mike decides to help Bobby escape by turning their Radio Flyer wagon into a magic rocketship that will carry Bobby to safety, but ultimately proves tragic. Appealing version of childhood dreams sans the child abuse angle (toned down though it was), which is abruptly and unsatisfactorily handled. **114m/C VHS, DVD.** Elijah Wood, Joseph Mazzello, Lorraine Bracco, Adam Baldwin, John Heard, Ben Johnson; ***D:*** Richard Donner; ***Nar:*** Tom Hanks.

Radio Inside 1/2 **1994** Aimless Matthew (McNamara) comes to live with older brother Michael (Walsh) after their dad's death. Matthew needs someone to listen to him but, unfortunately, his picks his brother's neglected girlfriend Natalie (Shue). Aimless story, as well. **91m/C VHS.** William McNamara, Dylan Walsh, Elisabeth Shue, Gil Goldstein; ***D:*** Jeffrey Bell; ***W:*** Jeffrey Bell. **CABLE**

Radio Patrol **1937** Plenty of action and thrills abound in this 12-chapter serial. Pinky Adams, radio cop, is assisted by his trusty canine partner, Irish (Silverwolf). A cop's best friend is his dog. **235m/B VHS.** Mickey Rentschler, Adrian Morris, Monte Montague, Jack Mulhall, Grant Withers, Catherine Hughes; ***D:*** Ford Beebe, Cliff(ord) Smith.

Radioactive Dreams **1986 (R)** Surreal, practically senseless fantasy wherein two men, trapped in a bomb shelter for 15 years with nothing to read but mystery novels, emerge as detectives into a post-holocaust world looking for adventure. **94m/C VHS.** John Stockwell, Michael Dudikoff, Lisa Blount, George Kennedy, Don Murray, Michelle Little; ***D:*** Albert Pyun; ***W:*** Albert Pyun.

Radioland Murders 1/2 **1994 (PG)** Looks overwhelm weak plot in this mystery-comedy about 1939 Chicago radio station WBN. Lots of stock types (befuddled director, preening announcer, lusty vamp) with Masterson as Penny, the secretary holding everything together except for her marriage to head writer Roger (Benben). Then bodies start piling up during the live broadcast and everyone runs around frantically trying to solve the crimes and keep the broadcast going. Tiring and cliched. **112m/C VHS, DVD.** Brian Benben, Mary Stuart Masterson, Ned Beatty, George Burns, Brion James, Michael Lerner, Michael McKean, Jeffrey Tambor, Scott Michael Campbell, Anita Morris, Stephen Tobolowsky, Christopher Lloyd, Larry Miller, Corbin Bernsen; ***Cameos:*** Robert Klein, Harvey Korman, Peter MacNichol, Joey Lawrence, Bob(cat) Goldthwait; ***D:*** Mel Smith; ***W:*** Willard Huyck, Gloria Katz, Jeff Reno, Ron Osborn; ***C:*** David Tattersall; ***M:*** Joel McNeely.

Rafferty & the Gold Dust Twins 1/2 *Rafferty and the Highway Hustlers* **1975 (R)** Two women kidnap a motor vehicle inspector at gunpoint in Los Angeles and order him to drive to New Orleans. En route, they become pals. Wandering, pointless female buddy flick. **91m/C VHS.** Alan Arkin, Sally Kellerman, MacKenzie Phillips, Charles Martin Smith, Harry Dean Stanton; ***D:*** Dick Richards; ***M:*** Artie Butler.

The Raffle 1/2 **1994 (R)** Frank and David travel the globe to find the world's most beautiful woman, who'll be the prize date of the lucky guy with the winning raffle ticket. **100m/C VHS.** Nicholas Lea, Bobby Dawson, Jennifer Clement, Teri-Lynn Rutherford, Jay Underwood, Mark Hamill; ***D:*** Gavin Wilding; ***W:*** John Fairley; ***M:*** Robert O. Ragland.

Raffles **1930** Debonair and dashing gentleman thief A.J. Raffles (Coleman) is a famed cricket player by day and a cat burglar by night, who's always been successful at eluding Scotland Yard. Then he falls for beautiful socialite Lady Gwen Manders (Francis) and gets invited to a weekend house party where Lady Kitty Melrose (Skipworth) just happens to own a very valuable necklace and one of the other guests is suspicious Scotland Yard inspector McKenzie (Torrance). Naturally Raffles goes after the jewels. Based on the novel "The Amateur Cracksman" by Ernest William Hornung. Director D'Arrast was fired by producer Goldwyn and Fitzmaurice finished the film. **72m/B VHS.** Ronald Colman, Kay Francis, Alison Skipworth, David Torrence, Bramwell Fletcher, Frances Dade; ***D:*** Harry D'Abbadie D'Arrast, George Fitzmaurice; ***W:*** Sidney Howard; ***C:*** George Barnes, Gregg Toland.

Rafter Romance 1/2 **1934** When neither Mary (Rogers) nor Jack (Foster) can afford their separate Greenwich Village apartments any longer, landlord Max (Sidney) moves them both into the same attic room. He figures the arrangement will be manageable because Mary works days and Jack nights and they will never see each other. But this doesn't mean they can't snipe with caustic notes and play practical jokes (oh, and fall in love). Remade as "Living on Love" (1937). **72m/B DVD.** Ginger Rogers, Norman Foster, George Sidney, Robert Benchley, Laura Hope Crews, Guinn "Big Boy" Williams, Sidney Miller; ***D:*** William A. Seiter; ***W:*** Sam Mintz, H. W. Hanemann; ***C:*** David Abel.

Rage 1/2 **1972** Never the subtlest of actors, Scott goes over-the-top in this self-directed melodrama. Dan (Logan) and his son Chris (Beauvy) are camping when an Army helicopter accidentally sprays the area with a nerve gas. Dan rushes Chris to the hospital (he's in a coma) where he's separated from his son by Army medico Holliford (Sheen). Chris dies but Holliford keeps the news from Dan because he's not only trying to cover-up the incident but he wants to figure out why Dan survived a supposedly fatal gas. It's just a delayed reaction, and when the terminal Dan discovers the truth, he decides to get some serious revenge. **99m/C DVD.** George C. Scott, Martin Sheen, Richard Basehart, Barnard Hughes, Nicolas Beauvy, Paul Stevens, Stephen Young; ***D:*** George C. Scott; ***W:*** Dan Kleinman, Philip Friedman; ***C:*** Fred W. Koenekamp; ***M:*** Lalo Schifrin.

Rage **1980** Well-acted, well-written, nerve-wracking drama about a convicted rapist who finds help through difficult therapy. Focuses on how the sex-offender discovers the "whys" behind his assaults. **100m/C VHS.** David Soul, James Whitmore, Yaphet Kotto, Caroline McWilliams, Vic Tayback, Sharon Farrell, Craig T. Nelson, Garry Walberg; ***D:*** William A. Graham; ***C:*** Allen Daviau. **TV**

Rage 1/2 **1995 (R)** When Alex Gainer (Daniels) is kidnapped he becomes the target of a high-tech lab experiment. Injected with chemicals that induce blind and killing rages, Alex escapes and unwillingly goes on a murderous rampage. Now he must find the antidote and clear his name before it happens again. **94m/C VHS, DVD.** Gary Daniels, Ken Tigar, Jillian McWhirter, Fiona Hutchinson, Peter Jason, Mark Metcalf; ***D:*** Joseph Merhi; ***W:*** Jacobsen Hart, Joseph John Barmettler Jr.; ***C:*** Ken Blakey; ***M:*** Louis Febre.

The Rage **1996 (R)** Nick Travis (Lamas) is a burned-out FBI agent with a brand new partner Kelly McCord (Cloke), who has no field experience, and a tough assignment. He's after a gang of anti-government killers led by psycho Dacy (Busey). Good action sequences substitute for the lack of plot sense. **95m/C VHS, DVD.** Lorenzo Lamas, Gary Busey, Kristen Cloke, Roy Scheider, David Carradine, Jenny (Jennifer) McShane; ***D:*** Sidney J. Furie; ***W:*** Greg Mellott; ***C:*** Donald M. Morgan; ***M:*** Paul Zaza.

The Rage **2007** Old-fashioned gorefest about a mad scientist and a deadly mutating virus. Russian scientist Viktor (Divoff) get the pharmaceutical shaft after discovering a cancer cure. To get even he develops the rage virus, which turns the infected into flesh-eating mutants. One of his test subjects escapes, dies in the woods, and becomes dinner for vultures. The infected birds then attack any unfortunates they find, some of whom eventually turn up at Viktor's cabin. There's lots of limb-ripping, blood-gushing, and flesh-noshing with some decent special effects. **99m/C DVD.** Andrew Divoff, Misty Mundae, Reggie Bannister, Robert Kurtzman, Ryan Hooks; ***W:*** John Bisson; ***M:*** Edward Douglas. **VIDEO**

Rage and Honor **1992 (R)** Rothrock stars as Kris Fairfield, a high-school teacher who spends her spare time tutoring students in the martial-arts. Her present students are a group of cops, including Aussie visitor Preston Michaels. When Michaels witnesses a drug deal, he gets set-up by the dealers for a murder he didn't commit and only Kris can help him prove his innocence. **93m/C VHS, DVD.** Cynthia Rothrock, Richard Norton, Brian Thompson, Terri Treas, Catherine Bach, Alex Datcher; ***D:*** Terence H. Winkless; ***W:*** Terence H. Winkless.

Rage and Honor 2: Hostile Takeover 1/2 **1993 (R)** Rothrock returns as black-belt CIA operative Kris Fairfield, whose latest assignment takes her to Jakarta where a banker is involved in a large-scale drug money laundering operation. She teams up with Preston Michaels (Norton), a renegade Australian cop, and winds up following a trail that leads to a fortune in diamonds and lots of trouble. **98m/C VHS.** Cynthia Rothrock, Richard Norton, Patrick Muldoon, Frans Tumbuan, Ron Vreeken, Alex Tumundo; ***D:*** Guy Norris; ***W:*** Louis Sun, Steven Reich.

Rage at Dawn 1/2 *Seven Bad Men* **1955** An outlaw gang is tracked by a special agent who must "bend" the rules a little in order to get the bad guys. Not surprisingly, he gets his girl as well. A solid standard of the genre, with some clever plot twists. **87m/C VHS, DVD.** Randolph Scott, Forrest Tucker, Mala Powers, J. Carrol Naish, Edgar Buchanan; ***D:*** Tim Whelan; ***W:*** Horace McCoy; ***C:*** Ray Rennahan; ***M:*** Paul Sawtell.

The Rage: Carrie 2 *Carrie 2* **1999 (R)** You don't need psychic powers to know that things probably aren't going to end well for the tormenting teens in this slightly altered sequel. The heroine this time is Rachel (Bergl), a semi-Goth outcast who has a crush on good guy jock Jesse (London). She also has the ability to rattle and explode things when she's upset. Sue (Irving), the sole survivor from Carrie White's little tantrum years earlier, discovers that Rachel is related to the late telekinetic prom queen and tries to warn her. Too late. Jesse's bitchy girlfriend sets out to humiliate Rachel at a big party held at an all too flammable mansion. Lacks the character development and shock value of the first installment. **97m/C VHS, DVD.** Emily Bergl, Amy Irving, Jason London, J. Smith-Cameron, Zachery Ty Bryan, John Doe, Gordon Clapp, Rachel Blanchard, Mena Suvari, Eddie Kaye Thomas, Dylan Bruno, Charlotte Ayanna, Justin Urich, Elijah Craig; ***D:*** Katt Shea; ***W:*** Rafael Moreu; ***C:*** Donald M. Morgan; ***M:*** Danny P. Harvey.

A Rage in Harlem **1991 (R)** The crime novels of Chester A. Himes were translated into the best movies of the early '70s blaxploitation era. Now, a Himes story gets the big budget Hollywood treatment with juice and aplomb. A voluptuous lady crook enters Harlem circa 1950 with a trunkful of stolen gold sought by competing crooks, and the chase is on, with one virtuous soul (Whitaker) who only wants the girl. Great cast and characters, much humor, but unsparing in its violence. **108m/C VHS, DVD.** Forest Whitaker, Gregory Hines, Robin Givens, Zakes Mokae, Danny Glover, Tyler Collins, Ron Taylor, T.K. Carter, Willard Pugh, Samm-Art Williams, Screamin' Jay Hawkins, Badja (Medu) Djola,

John Toles-Bey, Stack Pierce, George D. Wallace; *D:* Bill Duke; *W:* John Toles-Bey, Bobby Crawford; *M:* Elmer Bernstein.

Rage of Angels 1983 Lengthy miniseries adaptation of the Sidney Sheldon novel about an ambitious female attorney, her furs, and her men. Followed by "Rage of Angels: The Story Continues" (1986). **192m/C VHS.** Jaclyn Smith, Ken Howard, Armand Assante, Ronald Hunter, Kevin Conway, George Coe, Deborah May; *D:* Buzz Kulik; *M:* Billy Goldenberg. **TV**

Rage of Angels: The Story Continues ½ **1986** In this sequel to the Sidney Sheldon trash-with-flash miniseries, Smith reprises her role as the beautiful lady lawyer who always gets involved with the wrong men. This time she tries to hide the fact of her illegitimate son from his father, who's about to become Vice President of the United States. **200m/C VHS.** Jaclyn Smith, Ken Howard, Michael Nouri, Susan Sullivan, Brad Dourif, Angela Lansbury, Mason Adams; *D:* Paul Wendkos; *C:* Jack Priestley; *M:* Billy Goldenberg. **TV**

Rage of Honor 1987 **(R)** A high-kicking undercover cop seeks vengeance on bad guys for his partner's murder. Standard of its type; why bother? **92m/C VHS, DVD.** Sho Kosugi, Lewis Van Bergen, Robin Evans, Gerry Gibson; *D:* Gordon Hessler; *W:* Wallace C. Bennett.

The Rage of Paris 1938 Scheming ex-actress and head waiter hope to gain by helping a beautiful French girl (Darrieux) snag a rich hubby. She comes to her senses, realizing that love, true love, matters more than wealth. Well-acted, quaint comedy. **78m/B VHS, DVD.** Danielle Darrieux, Douglas Fairbanks Jr., Mischa Auer, Helen Broderick; *D:* Henry Koster; *C:* Joseph Valentine.

Rage of the Werewolf ½ **1999** Okay, try to follow this. It's 2010 in New York City after an asteroid has collided with the moon, which somehow causes thousands of people to become werewolves. Now Jake was already a werewolf, so he has more flexibility than these newbies, including evil brother Lazlo who wants to unite all the wolves and destroy humanity. But Jake doesn't want anything to do with this evil plot and goes on the run. And then there's some mystery babe with special powers who can possibly help Jake out. **90m/C VHS.** Santo Marotta, Tom NonDorf, Hollis Granville, Debbie Rochon, Sasha Graham, Michael (Mick) McCleery, Jon Sanborne; *D:* Kevin J. Lindenmuth; *W:* Kevin J. Lindenmuth, Santo Marotta. **VIDEO**

Rage to Kill ½ **1988 (R)** Jingoistic retelling of the 1982 Grenada invasion, complete with helpless American med students. Good-guy race car driver whips them into shape to fight the Soviet-supplied general (he's the bad guy). Guess who wins. **94m/C VHS.** Oliver Reed, James Ryan, Henry Cele, Cameron Mitchell; *D:* David Winters.

Raggedy Man 1981 **(PG)** Spacek in her signature role as a lonely small-town woman. Here she's raising two sons alone in a small Texas town during WWII. Spacek's strong acting carries a well-scripted story, unfortunately marred by an overwrought ending. **94m/C VHS, DVD.** Sissy Spacek, Eric Roberts, Sam Shepard, Tracey Walter, William Sanderson, Henry Thomas; *D:* Jack Fisk; *W:* William D. Wittliff; *C:* Ralf Bode; *M:* Jerry Goldsmith.

The Raggedy Rawney ½ **1990 (R)** A young Army deserter dresses in women's clothing and hides out as a mad woman with a band of gypsies. Good first directing effort by English actor Bob Hoskins. Unpretentious and engaging. **102m/C VHS, DVD.** Bob Hoskins, Dexter Fletcher, Zoe Nathenson, David Hill, Ian Dury, Zoe Wanamaker, J.G. Devlin, Perry Fenwick; *D:* Bob Hoskins; *W:* Bob Hoskins, Nicole De Wilde; *M:* Michael Kamen.

Ragin' Cajun 1990 Retired kickboxer is forced into a death match to save his girlfriend. **91m/C VHS, DVD.** David Heavener, Charlene Tilton, Sam Bottoms, Samantha Eggar; *D:* William B. Hillman.

Raging Angels 1995 **(R)** L.A. couple Chris (Flanery) and Lila (Mazur) are struggling rock 'n' rollers when Lila gets a job as a backup singer to star Colin (Pare), who's part of a cult called the Coalition for World Unity. Turns out they're a recruiting org for Satan and are looking for new souls. Our young duo are aided by flamboyant evangelist Sister Kate (Ladd) but it all comes down to a sky battle over downtown L.A. between a good angel and a satanic creature. Lots of unintentional laughs. The director wisely opted for the industry's Smithee pseudonym. **97m/C VHS.** Sean Patrick Flanery, Monet Mazur, Michael Pare, Diane Ladd, Shelley Winters, Arielle Dombasle; *D:* Alan Smithee; *W:* Kevin Rock, David Markov, Chris Bittler; *C:* Bryan England; *M:* Terry Plumeri.

Raging Bull 1980 **(R)** Scorsese's depressing but magnificent vision of the dying American Dream and suicidal macho codes in the form of the rise and fall of middleweight boxing champ Jake LaMotta, a brutish, dull-witted animal who can express himself only in the ring and through violence. A photographically expressive, brilliant drama, with easily the most intense and brutal boxing scenes ever filmed. De Niro provides a vintage performance, going from the young LaMotta to the aging has-been, and is ably accompanied by Moriarty as his girl and Pesci as his loyal, much beat-upon bro. **128m/B VHS, DVD, Blu-ray Disc.** Robert De Niro, Cathy Moriarty, Joe Pesci, Frank Vincent, Nicholas Colasanto, Theresa Saldana; *D:* Martin Scorsese; *W:* Paul Schrader, Mardik Martin; *C:* Michael Chapman; *M:* Robbie Robertson. Oscars '80: Actor (De Niro), Film Editing; AFI '98: Top 100; Golden Globes '81: Actor—Drama (De Niro); L.A. Film Critics '80: Actor (De Niro), Film; Natl. Bd. of Review '80: Actor (De Niro), Support. Actor (Pesci), Natl. Film Reg. '90;; N.Y. Film Critics '80: Actor (De Niro), Actor (De Niro), Support. Actor (Pesci, Pesci); Natl. Soc. Film Critics '80: Cinematog., Director (Scorsese), Support. Actor (Pesci).

Raging Hormones 1999 Florida teen Peter Broadhurst thinks he's died and gone to hormone heaven when his beautiful neighbor Sally decides to make him her personal sex toy. At least until his mother finds out. Strictly low-budget, amateur night. **93m/C DVD.** Antoni Corone, Topher Hopkins, Della Hobby, Darlene Demko, Rene Orobello; *D:* Michael Dugan; *W:* Michael Dugan; *C:* Anthony Foy. **VIDEO**

Rags to Riches 1987 A wealthy Beverly Hills entrepreneur decides to improve his public image by adopting six orphan girls. TV pilot. **96m/C VHS.** Joseph Bologna, Tisha Campbell; *D:* Bruce Seth Green; *W:* David Garber. **TV**

Ragtime 1981 **(PG)** The lives and passions of a middle class family weave into the scandals and events of 1906 America. A small, unthinking act represents all the racist attacks on one man, who refuses to back down this time. Wonderful period detail. From the E.L. Doctorow novel, but not nearly as complex. Features Cagney's last film performance. **156m/C VHS, DVD.** Howard E. Rollins Jr., Kenneth McMillan, Brad Dourif, Mary Steenburgen, James Olson, Elizabeth McGovern, Pat O'Brien, James Cagney, Debbie Allen, Jeff Daniels, Moses Gunn, Donald O'Connor, Mandy Patinkin, Norman Mailer, Jeffrey DeMunn, Robert Joy, Fran Drescher, Frankie Faison, Samuel L. Jackson, Michael Jeter, John Ratzenberger; *D:* Milos Forman; *W:* Michael Weller; *C:* Miroslav Ondricek; *M:* Randy Newman.

Raid on Entebbe 1977 **(R)** Dramatization of the Israeli rescue of passengers held hostage by terrorists at Uganda's Entebbe Airport in 1976. A gripping actioner all the more compelling because true. Finch received an Emmy nomination in this, his last film. **113m/C VHS, DVD.** Charles Bronson, Peter Finch, Horst Buchholz, John Saxon, Martin Balsam, Jack Warden, Yaphet Kotto, Sylvia Sidney; *D:* Irvin Kershner; *C:* Bill Butler; *M:* David Shire. **TV**

Raid on Rommel ½ **1971 (PG)** A British soldier (Burton) poses as a Nazi and tries to infiltrate Rommel's team with his rag-tag brigade of misfits. Predictable drivel. Contains action footage from the 1967 film "Tobruk." **98m/C VHS, DVD.** Richard Burton, John Colicos, Clinton Greyn, Wolfgang Preiss; *D:* Henry Hathaway; *W:* Richard M. Bluel; *C:* Earl Rath; *M:* Hal Mooney.

Raiders of Atlantis *The Atlantis Interceptors* **1983** Battles break out when the lost continent surfaces in the Caribbean. The warriors in these apocalyptic frays deploy atomic arsenals. **100m/C VHS.** Christopher Connelly; *D:* Roger Franklin.

Raiders of Ghost City ½ **1944** Serial in 13 chapters involves a Union Secret Service Agent after a ring of gold robbers who are posing as Confederate soldiers during the end of the Civil War. **225m/B VHS, DVD.** Dennis Moore, Lionel Atwill, Regis Toomey, Wanda McKay, Joseph (Joe) Sawyer, Virginia Christine; *D:* Lewis D. Collins, Ray Taylor; *W:* Morgan Cox; *C:* Harry Neumann, William Sickner.

Raiders of Leyte Gulf 1963 Long-unavailable Philippine film from the early 1960s is a throwback to the propaganda that Hollywood produced during WWII. This one features sadistic buck-toothed Japanese soldiers. The protagonists are American POWs and Philippine guerrillas who are setting the stage for MacArthur's return. Director Romero would go on to a busy career in horror and other genres. **80m/B VHS, DVD.** *PH* Leopold Salcedo, Michael Parsons, Jennings Sturgeon, Liza Moreno; *D:* Eddie Romero; *W:* Carl Kuntze, E.F. Romero; *C:* Felipe Sacdalan; *M:* Tito Arevalo.

Raiders of Red Gap ½ **1943** A cattle company tries running homesteaders off their land to get control of it. The Lone Rider saves the day. **56m/B VHS.** Robert "Bob" Livingston, Al "Fuzzy" St. John, Myrna Dell, Edward Cassidy, Charles "Blackie" King, Charles "Slim" Whitaker, Kermit Maynard, George Chesebro; *D:* Sam Newfield; *W:* Joseph O'Donnell; *C:* Robert E. Cline.

Raiders of Sunset Pass 1943 Wartime western quickie makes an interesting novelty today. With most cowboys off fighting the Axis, the ladies form the Women's Army of the Plains to watch out for 4-F rustlers. **57m/B VHS.** Eddie Dew, Smiley Burnette, Jennifer Holt, Roy Barcroft, Mozelle Cravens, Beverly Aadland, Nancy Worth, Kenne Duncan, Jack Rockwell, Budd Buster, Jack Ingram; *D:* John English.

Raiders of the Border 1944 A white-hatted cowboy must prevent the take-over of a trading post. **55m/B VHS.** Johnny Mack Brown, Raymond Hatton, Ellen Hall; *D:* John P. McCarthy; *W:* Adele Buffington; *C:* Harry Neumann.

Raiders of the Lost Ark **1981 (PG)** Classic '30s-style adventure reminiscent of early serials spawned two sequels and numerous rip-offs and made Ford a household name as dashing hero and intrepid archeologist Indiana Jones. Set in 1936, Indy battles mean Nazis, decodes hieroglyphics, fights his fear of snakes, and even has time for a little romance in his quest for the biblical Ark of the Covenant. Allen is perfectly cast as his feisty ex-flame Marion, more than a little irritated with the smooth talker who dumped her years earlier. Asks viewers to suspend belief as every chase and stunt tops the last. Unrelated opening sequence does a great job of introducing the character. **115m/C VHS, DVD.** Harrison Ford, Karen Allen, Wolf Kahler, Paul Freeman, John Rhys-Davies, Denholm Elliott, Ronald Lacey, Anthony (Corlan) Higgins, Alfred Molina; *D:* Steven Spielberg; *W:* George Lucas, Philip Kaufman; *C:* Douglas Slocombe; *M:* John Williams. Oscars '81: Art Dir./Set Dec., Film Editing, Sound, Visual FX; AFI '98: Top 100, Natl. Film Reg. '99.

Raiders of the Sun 1992 **(R)** After the Earth has been ruined in a biological disaster, a futuristic warrior arrives to help restore world peace and order. Cheap "Mad Max" ripoff. **80m/C VHS, DVD.** Richard Norton, Rick Dean, William (Bill) Steis, Blake Boyd, Brigitta Stenberg, Ned Hourani, Nick Nicholson, Nigel Hogge, Paul Holmes, Ernie Satana; *D:* Cirio H. Santiago; *W:* Frederick Bailey, Thomas McKelvey Cleaver; *C:* Joe Batac; *M:* Gary Earl, Odette Springer.

Railroaded 1947 The police seek a demented criminal who kills his victims with perfumed-soaked bullets. Tense, excellent noir Anothony Mann crime drama. **72m/B VHS, DVD.** John Ireland, Sheila Ryan, Hugh Beaumont, Ed Kelly, Jane Randolph; *D:* Anthony Mann; *W:* John C. Higgins; *C:* Guy Roe; *M:* Alvin Levin.

Railrodder 1965 Buster Keaton as the railroader in this slapstick short fumbles his way across Canada. As in the days of the silents, he speaks not a word. **25m/C VHS.** Buster Keaton; *D:* Gerald Potterton; *W:* Gerald Potterton; *C:* Robert Humble; *M:* Eldon Rathburn.

Rails & Ties ½ **2007 (PG-13)** Despite some good performances, this drama goes off track with some unbelievable plot machinations in (daughter of Clint) Eastwood's directorial debut. Emotionally distant train engineer Tom Stark (Bacon) can't cope with his wife Megan's (Harden) terminal cancer diagnosis and is glad to escape through work. At a rail crossing, a disturbed young woman (Root) deliberately parks her car on the tracks; the train/car crash kills her but her now-orphaned son Danny (Heizer) survives. Tom gets suspended and is brooding at home when Danny shows up on the Stark's doorstep, having run away from foster care. Childless Megan is happy to take the boy in and Tom and Danny are soon bonding over their mutual love of trains. **101m/C DVD.** Kevin Bacon, Marcia Gay Harden, Marin Hinkle, Eugene Byrd, Miles Heizer, Margo Martindale, Bonnie Root, Micky Levy; *D:* Alison Eastwood; *W:* Micky Levy; *C:* Tom Stern; *M:* Kyle Eastwood, Michael Stevens.

The Railway Children ½ **1970** At the turn of the century in England, the father of three children is framed and sent to prison during Christmas. The trio and their mother must survive on a poverty stricken farm near the railroad tracks. They eventually meet a new friend who helps them prove their father's innocence. Wonderfully directed by Jeffries. From the classic Edith Nesbitt children's novel. **104m/C VHS, DVD.** *GB* Jenny Agutter, William Mervyn, Bernard Cribbins, Dinah Sheridan, Iain Cuthbertson, Sally Thomsett, Peter Bromilow, Ahn Lancaster, Gary Warren, Gordon Whiting, David Lodge; *D:* Lionel Jeffries; *W:* Lionel Jeffries; *C:* Arthur Ibbetson.

The Railway Children 2000 Heart-tugger about the three Waterbury children, who must move to a small village and live in reduced circumstances with their mother (Agutter) when their father (Kitchen) is wrongfully imprisoned. The threesome spend much of their time by the railroad with its stationmaster (Russell) and a kindly railroad tycoon (Attenborough), who takes an interest in their situation. Based on the novel by Edith Nesbitt. Agutter played the role of the eldest daughter in the 1970 film version. **90m/C VHS, DVD.** *GB* Jenny Agutter, Michael Kitchen, Jemima Rooper, Jack Blumenau, Clare Thomas, Richard Attenborough, Clive Russell, David Bamber, Gregor Fisher; *D:* Catherine Morshead; *W:* Simon Nye; *C:* John Daly; *M:* Simon Lacey. **TV**

The Railway Station Man **1992** Set in present-day Ireland. Christie plays a widowed artist struggling to put her life back together after her husband's death in a terrorist bombing. She meets a mysterious American (Sutherland) who's working on restoring the local railway station and finds herself falling in love. When she stumbles upon an IRA bombing plot she also finds out some unpleasant truths about her new lover. Wonderful performances, tragic story. Shot on location in County Donegal, Northern Ireland. Based on the novel by Jennifer Johnston. **93m/C VHS.** Julie Christie, Donald Sutherland, John Lynch, Mark Tandy, Frank McCusker, Niall Cusack; *D:* Michael Whyte; *W:* Shelagh Delaney. **CABLE**

Rain ½ **1932** W. Somerset Maugham's tale of a puritanical minister's attempt to reclaim a "lost woman" on the island of Pago Pago. Crawford and Huston work up some static. Remake of the 1928 silent film "Sadie Thompson." Remade again in 1953 as "Miss Sadie Thompson." **92m/B VHS, DVD.** Joan Crawford, Walter Huston, William Gargan, Guy Kibbee, Beulah Bondi, Walter Catlett; *D:* Lewis Milestone; *W:* Maxwell Anderson; *C:* Oliver Marsh; *M:* Alfred Newman.

Rain 2001 Coming-of-age drama based on the 1994 novel by Kirsty Gunn. In 1972, 13-year-old Janey (Fulford-Wierzbicki) is spending the summer at a New Zealand beach cottage with her depressed mom Kate (Peirse), ineffectual father Ed (Browning), and her younger brother, Jim (Murphy). Trouble comes in the form of too much booze and the attentions of photographer Cady (Csokas), who not only catches Kate's eye but blossoming Janey's as well. Tensions build as the betrayals multiply. **90m/C VHS, DVD.** *AU* Alicia Fulford-Wierzbicki, Sarah Peirse, Marton Csokas, Alistair Browning, Aaron Murphy; ***D:*** Christine Jeffs; ***W:*** Christine Jeffs; ***C:*** John Toon; ***M:*** Neil Finn, Edmund McWilliams.

Rain *V.C. Andrews' Rain* **2006** Rain is a musical prodigy living with her family in the projects. She inadvertently witnesses the gangland slaying of her sister. In order to protect Rain, her mother reveals that the teenager is adopted and her biological mother is white and rich. Rain is taken into the home of her wealthy grandparents and offered a privileged new life but it's not easy. Very loosely based on the V.C. Andrews novel. **99m/C DVD.** Brooklyn Sudano, Faye Dunaway, Robert Loggia, Khandi Alexander, Giancarlo Esposito; ***D:*** Craig De Bona; ***W:*** Andrew Neiderman; ***C:*** Craig De Bona. **VIDEO**

The Rain Killer **1990 (R)** Big city cop and fed don goloshes to track serial killer who slays rich ladies during heavy precipitation. Soggy story. **94m/C VHS.** Ray Sharkey, David Beecroft, Maria Ford, Woody Brown, Tania Coleridge; ***D:*** Ken Stein; ***W:*** Ray Cunneff.

Rain Man **1/2 1988 (R)** When his father dies, ambitious and self-centered Charlie Babbit finds he has an older autistic brother who's been institutionalized for years. Needing him to claim an inheritance, he liberates him from the institution and takes to the road, where both brothers undergo subtle changes. The Vegas montage is wonderful. Critically acclaimed drama and a labor of love for the entire cast. Cruise's best performance to date as he goes from cad to recognizing something wonderfully human in his brother and himself. Hoffman is exceptional. **128m/C VHS, DVD.** Dustin Hoffman, Tom Cruise, Valeria Golino, Jerry Molen, Jack Murdock, Michael D. Roberts, Ralph Seymour, Lucinda Jenney, Bonnie Hunt, Kim Robillard, Beth Grant; ***D:*** Barry Levinson; ***W:*** Ronald Bass, Barry Morrow; ***C:*** John Seale; ***M:*** Hans Zimmer. Oscars '88: Actor (Hoffman), Director (Levinson), Orig. Screenplay, Picture; Berlin Intl. Film Fest. '88: Golden Berlin Bear; Directors Guild '88: Director (Levinson); Golden Globes '89: Actor—Drama (Hoffman), Film—Drama.

The Rain People **1969 (R)** Pregnant housewife Knight takes to the road in desperation and boredom; along the way she meets retarded ex-football player Caan. Well directed by Coppola from his original script. Pensive drama. **102m/C VHS.** Shirley Knight, James Caan, Robert Duvall, Tom Aldredge, Marya Zimmet, Andrew Duncan, Sally Gracie, Alan Manson, Laura Hope Crews; ***D:*** Francis Ford Coppola; ***W:*** Francis Ford Coppola; ***C:*** Bill Butler; ***M:*** Ronald Stein.

Rain Without Thunder **1/2 1993 (PG-13)** Imagine the year 2042, a time when abortion is illegal and a fertilized egg has full Constitutional rights. Now imagine sitting through an 87 minute fake documentary that follows the story of a mother and daughter team who have been jailed for trying to go to Sweden so that the daughter can get an abortion. A one-sided, militant pro-choice effort that is neither entertaining nor informational. **87m/C VHS.** Betty Buckley, Jeff Daniels, Ali Thomas, Frederic Forrest, Carolyn McCormick, Linda Hunt, Robert Earl Jones, Graham Greene, Iona Morris, Austin Pendleton; ***D:*** Gary Bennett; ***W:*** Gary Bennett; ***M:*** Randall Lynch, Allen Lynch.

Rainbow **1978** Broadway's "Annie" is badly miscast as Judy Garland from her early years in vaudeville to her starring years at MGM. Based on the book by Christopher Finch. Directed by sometime-Garland flame Jackie Cooper. **100m/C VHS.** Andrea McArdle, Jack Carter, Don Murray; ***D:*** Jackie Cooper; ***M:*** Charles Fox. **TV**

The Rainbow **1989 (R)** Mature, literate rendering of the classic D.H. Lawrence novel about a young woman's sexual awakening. Beautiful cinematography. Companion/prequel to director Russell's earlier Lawrence adaptation, "Women in Love" (1969). **104m/C VHS.** *GB* Sammi Davis, Amanda Donohoe, Paul McGann, Christopher Gable, David Hemmings, Glenda Jackson, Kenneth Colley; ***D:*** Ken Russell; ***W:*** Vivian Russell, Ken Russell; ***C:*** Billy Williams; ***M:*** Carl Davis.

Rainbow Bridge **1971 (R)** The adventures of a group of hippies searching for their consciousness in Hawaii. Features concert footage from Jimi Hendrix's final performance. **74m/C VHS, DVD.** Chuck Wein, Herbie Fletcher, Pat Hartley; ***D:*** Chuck Wein; ***C:*** Vilis Lapenieks.

Rainbow Drive **1/2 1990 (R)** Cop thriller promises great things but fails to deliver. Weller is a good cop trapped in the political intrigues of Hollywood. He discovers five dead bodies; when the official count is four, he detects funny business. From the novel by Roderick Thorp. **93m/C VHS.** Peter Weller, Sela Ward, Bruce Weitz, David Caruso, James Laurenson, Chris Mulkey, Kathryn Harrold, Tony Jay, Jon(athan) Gries, Henry Sanders, David Neidorf, Chelcie Ross, Rutanya Alda, Megan Mullally, Rob Nilsson; ***D:*** Bobby Roth; ***W:*** Roderick Thorp, Bill Phillips, Bennett Cohen; ***C:*** Tim Suhrstedt; ***M:*** Tangerine Dream. **CABLE**

The Rainbow Gang *Rainbow Boys* **1973** A trio of unlikely prospectors heads into a legendary mine in search of riches and fame. **90m/C VHS.** *CA* Donald Pleasence, Don Calfa, Kate Reid; ***D:*** Gerald Potterton; ***W:*** Gerald Potterton; ***C:*** Robert Saad; ***M:*** Howard Blake.

Rainbow over Broadway **1933** A former Broadway star mother is set against having her son and daughter try their luck on Broadway. **52m/C VHS.** Joan Marsh, Frank Albertson, Lucien Littlefield, Grace Hayes, Dell Henderson, Harry C. (Henry) Myers, Gladys Blake, Glen Boles, Nat Carr; ***D:*** Richard Thorpe.

Rainbow over Texas **1946** Roy and the Sons of the Pioneers head to his hometown on a promotional tour. Roy enters the local Pony Express race but some disgruntled locals try to make certain that he doesn't win. **65m/B VHS.** Roy Rogers, Dale Evans, George "Gabby" Hayes, Sheldon Leonard; ***D:*** Frank McDonald; ***W:*** Gerald Geraghty; ***C:*** Reggie Lanning.

Rainbow Ranch **1/2 1933** A Navy boxer returns home to his ranch to find murder and corruption. Needless to say, he rides off to seek revenge. **54m/B VHS.** Rex Bell, Cecilia Parker, Robert F. (Bob) Kortman, Henry Hall, Gordon DeMain; ***D:*** Harry Fraser.

Rainbow Warrior **1/2 1994 (PG)** True story of the bombing of the Greenpeace vessel and the two men who set out to solve the crime. **90m/C VHS.** Sam Neill, Jon Voight, Kerry Fox, Bruno Lawrence; ***D:*** Michael Tuchner.

Rainbow's End **1935** Gibson must defend Gale, the female rancher, from an evil adversary who is trying to run Gale and her invalid father off of their land. Things get complicated when Gibson discovers that Richmond works for his father! **54m/B VHS.** Hoot Gibson, June Gale, Oscar Apfel, Ada Ince, Charles Hill, Warner Richmond; ***D:*** Norman Spencer.

Raining Stones **1993** A hard-up plumber becomes obsessed with buying an expensive first communion dress for his daughter and gets involved in numerous misadventures trying to get the money. Another of Loach's comedy-dramas about the British working class and their struggle to survive with dignity. **90m/C VHS, DVD.** *GB* Bruce Jones, Julie Brown, Ricky Tomlinson, Tom Hickey, Gemma Phoenix, Jonathan James; ***D:*** Ken Loach; ***W:*** Jim Allen; ***C:*** Barry Ackroyd; ***M:*** Stewart Copeland. Cannes '93: Special Jury Prize.

The Rainmaker **1956** Reminiscent of "Elmer Gantry" in his masterful performance, Lancaster makes it all believable as a con man who comes to a small midwestern town and works miracles not only on the weather but on spinster Hepburn, although both were a little long in the tooth for their roles. Written by Nash from his own play. **121m/C VHS, DVD.** Burt Lancaster, Katharine Hepburn, Wendell Corey, Lloyd Bridges, Earl Holliman, Cameron Prudhomme, Wallace Ford; ***D:*** Joseph Anthony; ***W:*** N. Richard Nash; ***C:*** Charles B(ryant) Lang Jr.; ***M:*** Alex North. Golden Globes '57: Support. Actor (Holliman).

The Rains Came **1/2 1939** Living within a loveless marriage in the mythical Indian city of Ranchipur, English socialite Loy pursues extramarital love interests, including the compassionate doctor Power, potential heir to the maharajah's throne. When an earthquake hits and brings major destruction to the city, Loy aids the doctor in helping the injured. Hankies should be kept handy. Adapted from the Louis Bromfield novel. **104m/B VHS, DVD.** Myrna Loy, Tyrone Power, George Brent, Brenda Joyce, Nigel Bruce, Maria Ouspenskaya, Joseph Schildkraut, Laura Hope Crews, Marilyn Nash, Jane Darwell, Marjorie Rambeau, Henry Travers, H.B. Warner, William Royle, C. Montague Shaw, Harry Hayden, Abner Biberman, George Regas; ***D:*** Clarence Brown; ***W:*** Philip Dunne, Julien Josephson; ***C:*** Arthur C. Miller; ***M:*** Alfred Newman.

Raintree County **1/2 1957** A lavish, somewhat overdone epic about two lovers caught up in the national turmoil of the Civil War. An Indiana teacher (Clift) marries a southern belle (Taylor) just after the outbreak of war. The new wife battles mental illness. Producers had hoped this would be another "Gone with the Wind." Adapted from the novel by Ross Lockridge Jr. Film was delayed in mid-production by Clift's near-fatal and disfiguring car crash. **175m/C VHS, DVD.** Elizabeth Taylor, Montgomery Clift, Eva Marie Saint, Lee Marvin, Nigel Patrick, Rod Taylor, Agnes Moorehead, Walter Abel; ***D:*** Edward Dmytryk; ***C:*** Robert L. Surtees.

Raise the Red Lantern **1/2 1991 (PG)** Set in 1920s China, Zhang explores its claustrophobic world of privilege and humiliation. Songlian, an educated 19-year-old beauty, is forced into marriage as the fourth wife of a wealthy and powerful old man. She discovers that the wives have their own separate quarters and servants, and spend most of their time battling to attract their husband's attention. Over the course of a year, Songlian's fury and resentment grow until self-defeating rebellion is all she has. Gong Li is exquisite as the young woman struggling for dignity in a portrayal which is both haunting and tragic. **125m/C VHS, DVD.** *CH* Gong Li, Ma Jingwu, He Caifei, Cao Cuifeng, Jin Shuyuan, Kong Lin, Ding Weimin; ***D:*** Yimou Zhang. British Acad. '92: Foreign Film; L.A. Film Critics '92: Cinematog.; N.Y. Film Critics '92: Foreign Film; Natl. Soc. Film Critics '92: Cinematog., Foreign Film.

Raise the Titanic **WOOF! 1980 (PG)** A disaster about a disaster. Horrible script cannot be redeemed by purported thrill of the ship's emergence from the deep after 70 years. It's a shame, because the free world's security hangs in the balance. Based on Clive Cussler's best seller. **112m/C VHS.** Jason Robards Jr., Richard Jordan, Anne Archer, Alec Guinness, J.D. Cannon; ***D:*** Jerry Jameson; ***M:*** John Barry.

Raise Your Voice **1/2 2004 (PG)** Contrived tweenie fluff has eager 16-year-old Terri (Duff, blonde and bubbly as usual) longing to expand her singing talents by attending a performing arts summer school in L.A. Terri is encouraged by everyone but her overprotective dad (Keith) but finds the highly competitive atmosphere an eye-opener. Can sweet Terri realize her dreams and find mild romance with nice guy Jay (James)? Since this flick hits every teen cliche the answer should be obvious but it will still appeal to Duff's fans. **103m/C VHS, DVD.** *US* Hilary Duff, Oliver James, David Keith, Rita Wilson, Rebecca De Mornay, John Corbett, Jason Ritter, Robert Trebor, Dana Davis, Johnny Lewis, Kat Dennings, Lauren C. Mayhew; ***D:*** Sean McNamara; ***W:*** Sam Schreiber; ***C:*** John R. Leonetti; ***M:*** Machine Head, Aaron Zigman.

A Raisin in the Sun **1961** Outstanding story of a black family trying to make a better life for themselves in an all-white neighborhood in Chicago. The characters are played realistically and make for a moving story. Each person struggles with doing what he must while still maintaining his dignity and sense of self. Based on the 1959 Broadway play by Hansberry, who also wrote the screenplay. Remade for TV in 1989 with Danny Glover. **128m/B VHS, DVD.** Diana Sands, John Fiedler, Ivan Dixon, Louis Gossett Jr., Sidney Poitier, Claudia McNeil, Ruby Dee; ***D:*** Daniel Petrie; ***W:*** Lorraine Hansberry; ***C:*** Charles Lawton Jr.; ***M:*** Laurence Rosenthal. Natl. Bd. of Review '61: Support. Actress (Dee), Natl. Film Reg. '05.

A Raisin in the Sun **1989** An "American Playhouse" presentation of the Lorraine Hansberry play about a black family threatened with dissolution by the outside forces of racism and greed when they move into an all-white neighborhood in the 1950s. **171m/C VHS, DVD.** Danny Glover, Esther Rolle, Starletta DuPois; ***D:*** Bill Duke. **TV**

A Raisin in the Sun **1/2 2008** The leads reprise their roles from the 2004 Broadway revival of Lorraine Hansberry's 1959 play. The Youngers live in a crowded Chicago tenement: mother Lena (Rashad) is a maid, daughter Beneatha (Lathan) is attending college, and son Walter (Combs) is a chauffeur with a long-suffering wife, Ruth (McDonald), and young son, Travis (Martin). When Lena receives a substantial insurance check, she decides to use the money to buy a house in a nice middle-class—and white—neighborhood. Walter wants to spend the money to open a family business, a liquor store, but Lena disapproves. **87m/C DVD.** Phylicia Rashad, Sean (Puffy, Puff Daddy, P. Diddy) Combs, Audra McDonald, Sanaa Lathan, Justin Martin, Sean Patrick Thomas, David Oyelowo, John Stamos, Bill Nunn; ***D:*** Kenny Leon; ***W:*** Paris Qualles; ***C:*** Ivan Strasburg; ***M:*** Mervyn Warren; ***Nar:*** Morgan Freeman. **TV**

Raising Arizona **1/2 1987 (PG-13)** Hi's an ex-con and the world's worst hold-up man. Ed's a policewoman. They meet, fall in love, marry, and kidnap a baby (one of a family of quints). Why not? Ed's infertile and the family they took the baby from has "more than enough," so who will notice? But unfinished furniture tycoon Nathan Arizona wants his baby back, even if he has to hire an axe murderer on a motorcycle to do it. A brilliant, original comedy narrated in notorious loopy deadpan style by Cage. Innovative camera work by Barry Sonnenfeld. Wild, surreal, and hilarious. **94m/C VHS, DVD.** Nicolas Cage, Holly Hunter, John Goodman, William Forsythe, Randall "Tex" Cobb, Trey Wilson, M. Emmet Walsh, Frances McDormand, Sam McMurray, T.J. Kuhn, Peter Benedek, M. Emmet Walsh; ***D:*** Joel Coen; ***W:*** Ethan Coen, Joel Coen; ***C:*** Barry Sonnenfeld; ***M:*** Carter Burwell.

Raising Cain **1992 (R)** Thriller evoking poor man's Hitchcock about a child psychiatrist who just happens to be nuts features Lithgow in five roles. Seems his supposedly dead Norwegian father has come to the United States and needs his son's help to steal babies for a child development experiment, so the son's alter ego, Cain, shows up to commit the nasty deed. Unfortunately Lithgow also catches his wife with another man, and that's when the bodies start piling up. **95m/C VHS, DVD.** John Lithgow, Lolita (David) Davidovich, Steven Bauer, Frances Sternhagen, Tom Bower, Mel Harris, Gabrielle Carteris, Barton Heyman; ***D:*** Brian De Palma; ***W:*** Brian De Palma; ***C:*** Stephen Burum; ***M:*** Pino Donaggio.

Raising Flagg **2006 (PG-13)** Flagg Purdy (Arkin) is a small-town handyman with a stubborn streak and a continuing feud with his neighbor Gus (Pendleton). Their latest fracas causes a public humiliation and a crisis for Flagg and he takes to his bed, sure he's about to meet his maker. So his family reluctantly gathers to figure out what to do about dad now. **102m/C DVD.** Alan Arkin, Austin Pendleton, Barbara Dana, Lauren Holly, Glenne Headly, Matthew Arkin, Daniel Quinn, Stephanie Lemelin, Dawn Maxey, Richard Kind, Clifton James, Vana O'Brien; ***D:*** Neal Miller; ***W:*** Nancy Miller, Dorothy Velasco; ***C:*** Erich Roland; ***M:*** Alan Barcus, Les Hooper.

Raising Genius **1/2 2004 (R)** Weird teenaged math genius Hal (Long) locks himself in the bathroom to work on an equation that involves watching his cheerleader neighbor Lacy (McKellar) bounce on a trampoline. And it also upsets his overbearing mother Nancy (Malick). But things get out of hand when a burglary brings out the cops who think Hal is being kept prisoner. **83m/C DVD.** Justin Long, Wendie Malick, Stephen (Steve) Root, Danica McKellar, Tippi Hedren, Shirley Jones; ***D:*** Linda Voorhees, Bess Wiley; ***W:*** Linda Voorhees; ***C:*** Chris W. Johnson. **VIDEO**

Raising Helen 🦴🦴 ½ **2004 (PG-13)** Helen (Hudson) has a successful, carefree life as a modeling agency exec, and is the favorite "cool" aunt of her sis Lindsay's (Huffman) three kids. However, Helen's shocked when Lindsay and her husband are killed in a car accident and she is given custody of the kids over perfect homemaker sis Jenny (Cusack). Helen soon gets fired, moves from Manhattan to Queens, finds a new job (working for Elizondo), and enrolls the kids at a nearby school run by the single and hunky Pastor Dan (Corbett). Hudson is as winsome as ever, but this is just another notch in her romantic comedy belt and it's all-too-familiar attire. **119m/C DVD.** *US* Kate Hudson, Joan Cusack, John Corbett, Helen Mirren, Hayden Panettiere, Spencer Breslin, Felicity Huffman, Sean O'Bryan, Hector Elizondo, Sakina Jaffrey, Abigail Breslin, Kevin Kilner; ***D:*** Garry Marshall; ***W:*** Jack Amiel, Michael Begler; ***C:*** Charles Minsky; ***M:*** John Debney.

Raising Heroes 🦴🦴 **1997** Josh (Sistillio) and Paul (White) are about to finalize their adoption of a child when Josh witnesses a mob hit. Now he's a target, trying to stay alive and protect his family as well. **85m/C VHS, DVD.** Troy Sistillio, Henry White; ***D:*** Douglas Langway; ***W:*** Douglas Langway.

Raising the Heights 🦴 ½ **1997 (R)** Tensions escalate in the Brooklyn neighbor of Crown Heights when a drug deal, involving a high school teacher, results in the death of a young girl. So the victim's brother, Michael, decides to take revenge by taking a teacher hostage, with reporter Judy Burke leading a media barrage about the tense situation. Good intentions can't quite make up for the amateur filmmaking. **86m/C VHS.** Gilbert Brown Jr., John Knox, Fia Perera; ***D:*** Max Gottlieb; ***W:*** Max Gottlieb.

Raising Victor Vargas 🦴🦴 ½ *Long Way Home* **2003 (R)** Fifteen-year-old Latino Victor (Rasuk) thinks he's pretty hot stuff in his Lower East Side New York neighborhood as he spends his summer vacation chasing the local hotties. His feisty old-world Grandma (Guzman), who's raising Victor and his two younger siblings, begs to differ but the kids try to keep Grandma in the dark. Then Victor meets Judy (Marte), who's too smart to fall for his lines, and Victor really gets some lessons in love. **87m/C VHS, DVD.** *US* Victor Rasuk, Judy Marte, Melonie Diaz, Altagracia Guzman, Silvestre Rasuk, Krystal Rodriguez, Kevin Rivera; ***D:*** Peter Sollett; ***W:*** Peter Sollett; ***C:*** Tim Orr; ***M:*** Roy Nathanson.

Rally 'Round the Flag, Boys! 🦴 ½ **1958** Badly dated satire (from the novel by Max Shulman) turned slapstick comedy. Harry (Newman) and Grace (Woodward) Bannerman live in the quiet commuter community of Putnam's Landing, CT. When the Air Force chooses the town as the site of a new missile base, civic-minded Grace joins a committee to halt the project, much to the initial embarrassment of reservist Harry, who's chosen as the government's liaison. Local vamp Angela (Collins) regards their marital misunderstandings as her chance to console handsome Harry. Unfortunately, Newman was never good at flat-out comedy and the strain shows. **106m/C DVD.** Paul Newman, Joanne Woodward, Joan Collins, Jack Carson, Tuesday Weld, Dwayne Hickman, Gale Gordon, O.Z. Whitehead; ***D:*** Leo McCarey; ***W:*** Leo McCarey, Claude Binyon, George Axelrod; ***C:*** Leon Shamroy; ***M:*** Cyril Mockridge.

Rambling Rose 🦴🦴🦴 **1991 (R)** Dern is Rose, a free-spirited, sexually liberated before her time young woman taken in by a Southern family in 1935. Rose immediately has an impact on the male members of the clan, father Duvall and son Haas, thanks to her insuppressible sexuality. This causes consternation with the strait-laced patriarch, who attempts to control his desire for the girl. Eventually Rose decides she must try to stick to one man, but this only causes further problems. Dern gives her best performance yet in this excellent period piece, and solid support is offered from the rest of the cast, in particular Duvall and Dern's real-life mother Ladd. **115m/C VHS, DVD.** Laura Dern, Diane Ladd, Robert Duvall, Lukas Haas, John Heard, Kevin Conway, Robert John Burke, Lisa Jakub, Evan Lockwood; ***D:*** Martha Coolidge; ***W:*** Calder Willingham; ***C:*** Johnny E. Jensen; ***M:*** Elmer Bernstein. Ind. Spirit '92: Director (Coolidge), Film, Support. Actress (Ladd).

Rambo 🦴🦴 **2008 (R)** World-weary killing machine John Rambo (Stallone) is back, and this time the body count is higher than ever. Seemingly forgotten by the American military that used him in Vietnam and Afghanistan, Rambo's retired to isolation in the swamps of Thailand, but he's soon sucked back into the life of a mercenary when a group of missionaries recruit him to take them to Myanmar (Burma). Before the group has much time to help the innocents affected by the ongoing civil war, they're kidnapped by Burmese soldiers, and Rambo must swing into action, wiping out anyone in his way in the process. Passable if over-the-top action sequences highlight Stallone's freakishly buff 60-year-old bod. **93m/C DVD, Blu-ray Disc.** *US* Sylvester Stallone, Julie Benz, Paul Schulze, Ken Howard, Tim Kang, Graham McTavish, Rey Gallegos, Jake La Botz, Maung Maung Khin; ***D:*** Sylvester Stallone; ***W:*** Sylvester Stallone, Art Montersatelli; ***C:*** Glen MacPherson; ***M:*** Brian Tyler, Ashley Miller.

Rambo: First Blood, Part 2 🦴🦴 **1985 (R)** If anyone can save Our Boys still held prisoner in Asia it's John Rambo. Along the way he's tortured, flexes biceps, grunts, and then disposes of the bad guys by the dozen in one of filmdom's bigger dead body parades. Mindless action best enjoyed by testosterone-driven fans of the genre. Sequel to "First Blood" (1982); followed by "Rambo 3" (1988). **93m/C VHS, DVD, Blu-ray Disc.** Sylvester Stallone, Richard Crenna, Charles Napier, Steven Berkoff, Julia Nickson-Soul, Martin Kove; ***D:*** George P. Cosmatos; ***W:*** Sylvester Stallone, James Cameron; ***C:*** Jack Cardiff; ***M:*** Jerry Goldsmith. Golden Raspberries '85: Worst Picture, Worst Actor (Stallone), Worst Screenplay, Worst Song ("Peace In Our Life").

Rambo 3 🦴 ½ **1988 (R)** John Rambo, the famous Vietnam vet turned Buddhist monk, this time invades Afghanistan to rescue his mentor. Meets up with orphan and fights his way around the country. Typically exploitative, kill now, ask questions later Rambo attack, lacking the sheer volume of no-brainer action of the first two Rambos. At the time, the most expensive film ever made, costing $58 million. Filmed in Israel. **102m/C VHS, DVD, Blu-ray Disc.** Sylvester Stallone, Richard Crenna, Marc De Jonge, Kurtwood Smith, Spiros Focas; ***D:*** Peter McDonald; ***W:*** Sylvester Stallone; ***C:*** John Stanier; ***M:*** Jerry Goldsmith. Golden Raspberries '88: Worst Actor (Stallone).

The Ramen Girl 🦴🦴 **2008 (PG-13)** Abby (Murphy) gets dumped and stranded just after she's moved to Tokyo. Depressed, she wanders into a noodle shop and decides it's her destiny, pestering Maezumi (Nishida), the demanding chef, until he agrees to teach her his ramen secrets. Abby regains her self-confidence but after meeting Toshi (Park), Abby needs to decide her priorities, especially since he's moving to Shanghai. **102m/C DVD.** Brittany Murphy, Toshiyuki Nishida, Tammy Blanchard, Kimiko Yo, Sohee Park; ***D:*** Robert Allan Ackerman; ***W:*** Becca Topol; ***C:*** Yoshitaka Sakamoto; ***M:*** Carlo Siliotto.

Ramona and Beezus 2010 Adaptation of Beverly Cleary's Newberry Award-winning series about elementary school student Ramona Quimby (King) and her overactive imagination, which is always getting her in trouble and embarrassing her teenaged sister Beezus (Gomez). **m/C DVD.** *US* Joey King, Selena Gomez, John Corbett, Bridget Moynahan, Ginnifer Goodwin, Josh Duhamel, Sandra Oh, Hutch Dano; ***D:*** Elizabeth Allen; ***W:*** Laurie Craig, Nick Pustav; ***C:*** John Bailey; ***M:*** Mark Mothersbaugh.

Rampage 🦴🦴 **1987 (R)** Seemingly all-American guy Charles Reece (McArthur) goes on a murder spree, killing and then mutiliating his victims. Fraser (Biehn) is a liberal district attorney who questions his own views as he argues during the trial that Reece was sane when he committed the murders and deserves the death penalty. Director Friedkin makes no bones about his concerns that the criminal insanity defense often spares the perpetrator while denying justice to the victims. Adapted from the book by William P. Wood and loosely based on killer Richard Chase. Filmed in 1987, the movie wasn't released until 1992 due to the production company's financial difficulties. **92m/C VHS.** Michael Biehn, Alex McArthur, Nicholas (Nick) Campbell, Deborah Van Valkenburgh, John Harkins, Art LaFleur; ***D:*** William Friedkin; ***W:*** William Friedkin; ***M:*** Ennio Morricone.

Rampage: The Hillside Strangler Murders 🦴 **2004 (R)** Has only the most tenuous connection with the true serial killer story involving the rape and strangulation deaths of young women in L.A. in the late 1970s. Detective Jillian Dunne (Bell) calls in troubled shrink Samantha Stone (Daniel) to examine prime suspect Kenneth Bianchi (Collins). Samantha is led to believe that Bianchi is suffering from multiple personalities but the killer is only playing head games. **85m/C DVD.** Clifton (Gonzalez) Collins Jr., Brittany Daniel, Lake Bell, Bret Roberts, Michael G. (Mike) Hagerty, Tomas Arana, Channon Roe; ***D:*** Chris Fisher; ***W:*** Chris Fisher, Aaron Pope; ***C:*** Eliot Rockett; ***M:*** Ryan Beveridge. **VIDEO**

Ramparts of Clay 🦴🦴🦴 **1968 (PG)** A young woman in Tunisia walks the line between her village's traditional way of life and the modern world just after her country's independence from France. Brilliantly shot on location; exquisitely poignant. In Arabic with English subtitles. **87m/C VHS.** *FR* Leila Shenna, Jean-Louis Trintignant; ***D:*** Jean-Louis Bertucelli; ***W:*** Jean-Louis Bertucelli; ***C:*** Andreas Winding.

Ramrod 🦴🦴 **1947** Lake is a tough ranch owner at odds with her father, who is being manipulated by a big-time cattleman into trying to put them out of business. She fights back, and McCrea is caught in the middle as the only good guy. Nothing special. **94m/B VHS.** Veronica Lake, Joel McCrea, Arleen Whelan, Don DeFore, Preston Foster, Charlie Ruggles, Donald Crisp, Lloyd Bridges; ***D:*** Andre de Toth.

Ran 🦴🦴🦴🦴 **1985 (R)** The culmination of Kurosawa's career stands as his masterpiece. Loosely adapting Shakespeare's "King Lear," with plot elements from "Macbeth," he's fashioned an epic, heartbreaking statement about honor, ambition, and the futility of war. Aging medieval warlord Hidetora gives control of his empire to his oldest son, creating conflict with two other sons. Soon he's an outcast, as ambition and greed seize the two sons. Stunning battle scenes illuminate the full-blown tragedy of Kurosawa's vision. Superb acting with a scene-stealing Harada as the revenge-minded Lady Kaede; period costumes took three years to create. Japanese with English subtitles. **160m/C VHS, DVD.** *JP FR* Tatsuya Nakadai, Akira Terao, Jinpachi Nezu, Daisuke Ryu, Meiko Harada, Hisashi Igawa, Peter, Kazuo Kato, Takeshi Kato, Jun Tazaki, Toshiya Ito, Yoshiko Miyazaki, Masayuki Yui, Norio Matsui, Takashi Nomura; ***D:*** Akira Kurosawa; ***W:*** Akira Kurosawa, Hideo Oguni, Masato Ide; ***C:*** Asakazu Nakai, Takao Saito, Masaharu Ueda; ***M:*** Toru Takemitsu. Oscars '85: Costume Des.; British Acad. '86: Foreign Film; L.A. Film Critics '85: Foreign Film; Natl. Bd. of Review '85: Director (Kurosawa); N.Y. Film Critics '85: Foreign Film; Natl. Soc. Film Critics '85: Cinematog., Film.

Rana: The Legend of Shadow Lake 🦴 **1975** Gold at the bottom of a lake is guarded by a frog-monster, but treasure hunters try to retrieve it anyway. **96m/C VHS, DVD.** Alan Ross, Karen McDiarmid, Jerry Gregoris; ***D:*** Bill Rebane; ***W:*** Lyoma Denetz; ***C:*** Bill Rebane; ***M:*** Bruce Malm.

The Ranch 🦴🦴 **1988 (PG-13)** An executive who loses everything inherits a dilapidated ranch and renovates it into a health spa. **97m/C VHS.** Andrew Stevens, Gary Fjellgaard, Lou Ann Schmidt, Elizabeth Keefe; ***D:*** Stella Stevens.

Rancho Deluxe 🦴🦴🦴 **1975** Off-beat western spoof starring Bridges and Waterston as two carefree cowpokes. Cult favorite featuring music by Buffett, who also appears in the film. **93m/C VHS, DVD.** Jeff Bridges, Sam Waterston, Elizabeth Ashley, Charlene Dallas, Clifton James, Slim Pickens, Harry Dean Stanton, Richard Bright, Jimmy Buffett; ***D:*** Frank Perry; ***W:*** Thomas McGuane; ***C:*** William A. Fraker; ***M:*** Jimmy Buffett.

Rancho Notorious 🦴🦴🦴 **1952** Kennedy, on the trail of his girlfriend's murderer, falls for dance hall girl Dietrich. Fine acting. A "period" sample oF '50s westerns, but different. A must for Dietrich fans. **89m/C VHS.** Marlene Dietrich, Arthur Kennedy, Mel Ferrer, William Frawley, Jack Elam, George Reeves; ***D:*** Fritz Lang; ***W:*** Daniel Taradash; ***C:*** Hal Mohr.

Rancid 🦴 ½ **2004 (R)** Not terribly thrilling crime thriller. Failed writer (but successful drunk) James Hayson (Settle) hooks up with former flame Monica (Masterson) at a class reunion. This upsets her wealthy, controlling husband Crispin (Graham) and James winds up in a room with Monica's corpse. He learns he's been set-up but maybe not by who you think. **102m/C DVD.** Matthew Settle, Fay Masterson, Jay Acovone, Patrick Ersgard, Graham Currie, Siena Goines, Jarmo Makinen; ***D:*** Joakim (Jack) Ersgard; ***W:*** Patrick Ersgard, Joakim (Jack) Ersgard, Jesper Ersgard; ***C:*** Kjell Lagerros; ***M:*** Lars Anderson.

Rancid Aluminium 🦴 ½ **2000** Druggie Pete Thompson (Ifans) inherits his family's failing publishing business, which ticks off his friend (and the company's accountant) Sean Deeny (Fiennes). So Sean decides to take over the business by borrowing money from Russian mobster, Mr. Kant (Berkoff). Pete thinks Sean is just getting an additonal source of capital. Pete sleeps around and eventually learns what Sean is really up to. The Russian wants a return on his investment. And the viewer will wonder why he's wasting his time since this movie is dumb. Based on the novel by Hawes, who did the screenplay. **91m/C VHS, DVD.** *GB* Rhys Ifans, Joseph Fiennes, Steven Berkoff, Tara Fitzgerald, Sadie Frost, Dani Behr, Keith Allen, Nick Moran; ***D:*** Edward Thomas; ***W:*** James Hawes; ***C:*** Tony Imi; ***M:*** John E.R. Hardy.

Random Encounter 🦴 ½ **1998** Executive Berkley becomes invovled in extortion and a murder cover-up all because she takes a shine to a mystery man. **100m/C VHS, DVD.** *CA* Elizabeth Berkley, Joel Wyner, Frank Schorpion, Barry Flatman, Mark Walker, Ellen David, Susan Glover, Frank Fontaine; ***D:*** Douglas Jackson; ***W:*** Matt Dorff; ***C:*** Georges Archambault; ***M:*** Daniel Scott. **VIDEO**

Random Harvest 🦴🦴🦴 **1942** A masterful, tearjerking film based on the James Hilton novel. A shell-shocked WWI amnesiac meets and is made happy by a beautiful music hall dancer. He regains his memory and forgets about the dancer and their child. This is Garson's finest hour, and a shamelessly potent sobfest. **126m/B VHS, DVD.** Greer Garson, Ronald Colman, Reginald Owen, Philip Dorn, Susan Peters, Henry Travers, Margaret Wycherly, Bramwell Fletcher; ***D:*** Mervyn LeRoy; ***W:*** Claudine West, George Froeschel, Arthur Wimperis; ***C:*** Joseph Ruttenberg; ***M:*** Herbert Stothart.

Random Hearts 🦴🦴 **1999 (R)** If this film had stuck to overcoming tragedy and finding new love, it could have been a classic romantic weepie. But the addition of some police corruption malarkey and a slow pace undermine the emotional payoff. Congresswoman Kay Chandler (Scott Thomas) and internal affairs cop Dutch Van Den Broeck (Ford) discover that their respective spouses, who were killed in the same airliner crash, had been having an affair. Dutch needs to know all the sordid details when Kay, who's up for re-election, wants the potentially scandalous situation to remain quiet. Based on the novel by Warren Adler. **133m/C VHS, DVD.** Harrison Ford, Kristin Scott Thomas, Sydney Pollack, Charles S. Dutton, Bonnie Hunt, Dennis Haysbert, Richard Jenkins, Paul Guilfoyle, Susanna Thompson, Peter Coyote, Dylan Baker, Lynne Thigpen, Bill Cobbs, Susan Floyd, Edie Falco, Kate Mara; ***D:*** Sydney Pollack; ***W:*** Kurt Luedtke; ***C:*** Philippe Rousselot; ***M:*** Dave Grusin.

Randy Rides Alone 🦴🦴 **1934** Very young Wayne is good in this slappable but pleasant B effort. Wayne single-handedly cleans up the territory and rids the land of a passel o'bad guys. **53m/B VHS, DVD.** John Wayne, Alberta Vaughn, George "Gabby" Hayes; ***D:*** Harry Fraser; ***W:*** Lindsley Parsons.

Range Busters 🦴 **1940** Range Busters are called in to find the identity of the phantom killer. **55m/B VHS, DVD.** Ray Corrigan, Max Terhune, John "Dusty" King, Luana Walters, Leroy Mason, Earle Hodgins, Kermit Maynard, Frank LaRue; ***D:*** S. Roy Luby; ***W:*** John Rathmell;

C: Edward Linden; *M:* Lew Porter.

Range Feud ½ **1931** Wayne is a ranch owner's son falsely accused of murder. Just as he's about to hang, Jones, as the heroic sheriff, saves the day and reveals the real killer's identity. **58m/B VHS.** Buck Jones, John Wayne, Susan Fleming, William Walling, Wallace MacDonald, Harry Woods, Ed LeSaint; *D:* David Ross Lederman.

Range Law **1931** Another entry in the infamous Maynard series of horseplay, cliche, and repetitive plot elements. **60m/B VHS.** Ken Maynard, Charles "Blackie" King, Lafe (Lafayette) McKee; *D:* Phil Rosen; *W:* Earle Snell; *C:* Arthur Reed.

Range Law ½ **1944** Ranchers are being terrorized for their silver mine and its up to Brown and Hatton to catch the villains. **59m/B VHS.** Johnny Mack Brown, Raymond Hatton, Lloyd Ingraham, Sarah Padden, Ellen Hall, Steve Clark, Jack Ingram, Bud Osborne; *D:* Lambert Hillyer.

Range of Motion ½ **2000** After an accident, Lainie Berman's (De Mornay) husband slips into a coma but she's positive he can recover if she has enough faith. Based on the book by Elizabeth Berg. **120m/C VHS, DVD.** Rebecca De Mornay, Henry Czerny, Melanie Mayron, Barclay Hope, Kimberly Roberts; *D:* Donald Wrye; *W:* Grace McKeaney; *C:* Malcolm Cross; *M:* Gary Chang. **CABLE**

Range Renegades ½ **1948** Sheriff Wakely and his pals have their hands full when his deputy gets involved with the leader of a gang of outlaw women. Predictable B oater reflects the then developing trend of using wicked female characters in westerns. Paved the way for films like "Johnny Guitar" and "Rancho Notorious." **54m/B VHS.** Jimmy Wakely, Dub Taylor, Dennis Moore, Jennifer Holt, John James, Steve Clark, Frank LaRue; *D:* Lambert Hillyer; *W:* Ronald Davidson, William Lively.

Range Riders **1935** A gunman poses as a wimp and cleans out an outlaw gang. **46m/B VHS.** Lew Meehan, Merrill McCormick, Horace Carpenter, Barbara Starr, Buddy Roosevelt; *D:* Sam Newfield; *W:* George Plympton; *C:* William (Bill) Hyer; *M:* Lew Porter.

Rangeland Empire *West of the Brazos* **1950** Shamrock and Lucky are at it again, implicated as being members of an outlaw gang until that gang attacks them. **59m/B VHS.** James Ellison, Russell Hayden, Stanley Price, John Cason, Raymond Hatton, Fuzzy Knight, Tom Tyler, George Lewis; *D:* Thomas Carr; *W:* Ron Ormond, Maurice Tombragel, Robert North Bradbury; *C:* Ernest Miller; *M:* Walter Greene.

Ranger and the Lady ½ **1940** Texas Ranger Rogers romances the woman who is the leader of a wagon train. **54m/B VHS, DVD.** Roy Rogers, George "Gabby" Hayes; *D:* Joseph Kane.

Rangers **2000 (R)** McCoy leads an Army Rangers team in capturing a terrorist bomber and while they accomplish their mission, the unit is forced to leave behind Plummer, which turns out to be part of a government setup. Not happy about this, Plummer joins the terrorists to get revenge and goes after his ex-buddies while McCoy realizes there's a conspiracy going on. **100m/C VHS, DVD.** Matt McCoy, Glenn Plummer, Corbin Bernsen, Dartanyan Edmonds, Rene Rivera; *D:* Jim Wynorski; *W:* Steve Latshaw; *C:* Ken Blakey; *M:* David Wurst, Eric Wurst. **VIDEO**

The Rangers' Roundup ½ **1938** Tex (Scott) joins a traveling medicine show as a singer and marksman but he's really a Texas Ranger who's gone undercover to expose a gang robbing stage and express offices. **55m/B DVD.** Fred Scott, Al "Fuzzy" St. John, Christine McIntyre, Earle Hodgins, Steve Ryan, Karl Hackett, Sydney Chatton; *D:* Sam Newfield; *W:* George Plympton; *C:* William (Bill) Hyer; *M:* Lew Porter.

The Rangers Step In ½ **1937** Allen leaves the Texas Rangers when a feud between his family and that of the girl he loves heats up again. Turns out rustlers are stirring things up in order to get some of the disputed land. **56m/B VHS.** Robert "Tex" Allen, Eleanor Stewart, John Merton, Hal Taliaferro, Jack Ingram, Jack Rockwell, Lafe (Lafayette) McKee, Robert F. (Bob) Kortman; *D:* Spencer Gordon Bennet.

Rangers Take Over ½ **1942** Gunlords are driven out by the Texas Rangers. **62m/B VHS.** Dave O'Brien, James Newill, Iris Meredith, Guy Wilkerson, Charles "Blackie" King, Forrest Taylor, I. Stanford Jolley; *D:* Al(bert) Herman; *W:* Elmer Clifton; *C:* Robert E. Cline.

Ransom **1996 (R)** Tight and crafty thriller proves millionaire airline magnate Tom Mullen (Gibson) is a force to be reckoned with when son Sean (Nolte, son of actor Nick) is kidnapped. A vigilante Donald Trump (only gorgeous and brave), Mullen treats this like a high-stakes business deal and decides to get his kid back by announcing on TV that the $2 million ransom demand will instead become a bounty on the kidnappers. Wife Kate (Russo), predictably flips out but Mullen, after a few encounters with the heinous abductors, has sized them up and is convinced he's done the right thing. Lindo is a by-the-book fed with bad dialogue and Sinise is a bad cop playing for the other team. Gibson's emergency appendectomy delayed filming but he was soon leaping over cars for director Howard's well-staged action scenes. Based on the 1956 flick starring Glenn Ford. **121m/C VHS, DVD.** Mel Gibson, Rene Russo, Gary Sinise, Delroy Lindo, Brawley Nolte, Lili Taylor, Liev Schreiber, Evan Handler, Dan Hedaya, Paul Guilfoyle, Jose Zuniga, Donnie Wahlberg, Michael Gaston, Nancy Ticotin; ***Cameos:*** Richard Price; *D:* Ron Howard; *W:* Richard Price, Alexander Ignon; *C:* Piotr Sobocinski; *M:* James Horner.

Ransom Money ½ **1970** A kidnapping scheme involving millions of dollars, in and around the Grand Canyon, backfires. **37m/C VHS, DVD.** Broderick Crawford, Rachel Romen, Gordon Jump, Randy Whipple; *D:* DeWitt Lee; *W:* Verland Whipple; *C:* Vern Piehl.

Ranson's Folly ½ **1926** Barthelmess makes a wager that he can impersonate a famous outlaw well enough to rob a stage with only a pair of scissors. When the army paymaster is killed, guess who gets caught with his swash unbuckled? **80m/B VHS.** Richard Barthelmess, Dorothy Mackaill, Anders Randolf, Pat Hartigan, Brooks Benedict; *D:* Sidney Olcott.

Rapa Nui ½ **1993 (R)** The title refers to the Polynesian name for Easter Island, with the film set in the 17th century (before Dutch explorers discovered the island). It depicts the annual rituals of the mysterious people who built the Island's moai—the famous giant stone statues. Lee plays the heroic Noroinia, with Morales as his rival Make, and Holt as Ramana, the object of their desires. Faux primitive but with some great on-location filming. **107m/C VHS.** Jason Scott Lee, Esai Morales, Sandrine Holt; *D:* Kevin Reynolds; *W:* Kevin Reynolds, Tim Rose Price; *M:* Stewart Copeland.

Rape *Desnuda Inquietud* **1976** Two guys investigate a third pal's mysterious death. They discover that his supernatural-power-imbued girlfriend is at the root of the matter. **90m/C VHS.** *SP* Gaspar Gonzalez, Alfred Lucchetti, Ramiro Oliveros, Luis Induni, Fernando Ulloa, Gil Vidal, Nadiuska; *D:* Miguel Iglesias; *W:* Miguel Iglesias, Enrique Josa; *C:* Tomas Pladevall.

Rape and Marriage: The Rideout Case ½ **1980** The true story of an Oregon wife who accused her husband of rape. Thoughtfully explores the legal and moral questions raised by the case. Interpreted well enough, though not superbly, by a decent cast (although Rourke is a little too intense). **96m/C VHS.** Mickey Rourke, Linda Hamilton, Rip Torn, Eugene Roche, Conchata Ferrell, Gail Strickland, Bonnie Bartlett, Alley Mills; *D:* Peter Levin. **TV**

Rape of Love ½ **1979** The story begins with one of the most chilling rape scenes on film and then attempts to analyze the emotional impact of rape on its victim. Well-acted and directed. In French with English subtitles. **117m/C VHS.** *FR* Nathalie Nell, Alain Foures; *D:* Yannick Bellon.

The Rape of the Sabines **WOOF!** *El Rapto de las Sabinas; The Mating of the Sabine Women; Shame of the Sabine Women* **1961** The story of Romulus, king of Rome, and how he led the Romans to capture the women of Sabina. The battles rage, the women plot, and Romulus fights and lusts. Dubbed in English. **101m/C VHS.** *IT FR* Roger Moore, Mylene Demongeot, Jean Marais; *D:* Richard Pottier.

Rapid Assault **1999 (R)** Terrorist Lars Rynark (Scribner) is set to detonate a biochemical agent in the Atlantic Ocean that will decimate the population—unless he gets paid a lot of cash. Three government ops are sent to get to the terrorist first. Typical action fodder—the plot making any sense is besides the point. **90m/C VHS, DVD.** Tim Abell, Don Scribner, Jeff Rector, Lisa Mazzetti; *D:* Fred Olen Ray. **VIDEO**

Rapid Fire **1989** Cheap, made-for-video quickie about a good guy U.S. agent who battles terrorists. Easy to skip. **90m/C VHS, DVD.** Joe Spinell, Michael Wayne, Ron Waldron; *D:* David A. Prior.

Rapid Fire ½ **1992 (R)** Lee (son of martial arts cult film star Bruce Lee) is a Chinese-American art student who also happens to be a martial arts expert. He's tapped by the police to help stem the violence between the Asian and Italian gangs fighting for control over Chicago's drug trade. Typical martial arts movie is made better by uniquely choreographed action sequences and Lee's attractive presence. **96m/C VHS, DVD.** Brandon Lee, Powers Boothe, Nick Mancuso, Raymond J. Barry, Kate Hodge, Tzi Ma, Tony Longo, Michael Paul Chan, Dustin Nguyen, John Vickery; *D:* Dwight Little; *W:* Alan B. McElroy, Cindy Cirile, Paul Attanasio; *M:* Christopher Young.

Rappin' **1985 (PG)** Ex-con Van Peebles gets into it with the landlord and a street gang leader. Forgettable action/music drivel. ♫Rappin'; Two of a Kind; Call Me; Born to Love; Killer; Itching for a Scratch; Snack Attack; Dodge; Golly Gee. **92m/C VHS, DVD.** Mario Van Peebles, Tasia Valenza, Harry Goz, Charles Flohe; *D:* Joel Silberg.

The Rapture **1991 (R)** A beautiful telephone operator engages in indiscrimate sexual adventures to relieve the boredom of her job and life. She becomes curious by, and eventually converted to, evangelical Christianity, which leads her to a contented marriage and the birth of a daughter. When her husband is tragically killed she becomes convinced that she and her child will be taken by God into heaven if she only waits for the proper sign. **100m/C VHS, DVD.** Mimi Rogers, David Duchovny, Patrick Bauchau, Will Patton; *D:* Michael Tolkin; *W:* Michael Tolkin; *C:* Bojan Bazelli.

Rapturious **2007** Surprisingly entertaining supernatural thriller. White rapper Rapturious (Oppel) takes a new street drug that causes murderous hallucinations, only to discover that the murders are real. As it turns out, the rapper is the reincarnation of a 19th-century western serial killer hanged for his crimes and sent to Hell. And Hell wants him back. **95m/C DVD.** Robert Oppel, Debbie Rochon, Cinque Lee, Joe Bob Briggs, Amin Joseph, Hoya Guerra; *D:* Kamal Ahmed; *W:* Kamal Ahmed; *C:* Tom Agnello; *M:* Kamal Ahmed, Timo Elliston. **VIDEO**

Rapunzel ½ **1982** A beautiful young woman locked in a tall tower is saved by the handsome prince who climbs her golden tresses. Part of Shelly Duvall's "Faerie Tale Theatre" series. **60m/C VHS, DVD.** Shelley Duvall, Gena Rowlands, Jeff Bridges; *D:* Gilbert Cates.

Rare Birds ½ **2001** Quirky Canadian comedy finds Dave Purcell (Hurt) depressed. His restaurant, located in the small town of Cape Spear, Newfoundland, is failing as is his long-distance marriage. But his eccentric neighbor Alphonse (Jones) comes up with a plan—he spreads the word among birders that a rare duck has been sighted and soon the area is flooded with amateur ornithologists, which is certainly good for Dave's business and his love life as he gets together with waitress Alice (Parker). Oh yeah, there's also Alphonse's plans for a cocaine shipment he's salvaged from a sunken boat, if he can keep away from the product himself. Based on the novel by Riche. **101m/C VHS, DVD.** *CA* William Hurt, Molly Parker, Andy Jones, Cathy Jones, Sheila McCarthy, Vicky Hynes, Greg Malone; *D:* Sturla Gunnarsson; *W:* Edward Riche; *C:* Jan Kiesser; *M:* Jonathan Goldsmith.

The Rare Breed ½ **1966** Plodding but pleasant Western. A no-strings ranch hand (Stewart) agrees to escort a Hereford Bull to Texas, where the widow of an English breeder plans to crossbreed the bull with longhorn cattle. The widow (O'Hara) insists that she and her daughter accompany Stewart on the trip, which features every kind of western calamity imaginable. When all others believe the attempt to crossbreed has failed, Stewart sets out to prove them wrong. **97m/C VHS, DVD.** James Stewart, Maureen O'Hara, Brian Keith, Juliet Mills, Jack Elam, Ben Johnson; *D:* Andrew V. McLaglen; *C:* William Clothier; *M:* John Williams.

A Rare Breed ½ **1981 (PG)** Real-life story of a kidnapped horse in Italy and a young girl's quest to retrieve it. Directed by David Nelson of TV's "Ozzie and Harriet" fame, this movie is cute and old-fashioned. **94m/C VHS.** George Kennedy, Forrest Tucker, Tracy Vaccaro, Tom Hallick, Don DeFore; *D:* David Nelson.

The Rascals ½ **1981 (R)** An irrepressible youth at a rural Catholic boys' school comes of age. **93m/C VHS.** *FR* Bernard Brieux, Pascale Rocard, Etienne Draber, Pierre Vial, Thomas Chabrol; *D:* Bernard Revon; *W:* Bernard Revon; *C:* Gerard de Battista; *M:* Roland Romanelli.

Rasen ½ **1998** The original sequel to "Ringu," directed and released at the same time. It is closer to the actual book, and attempts to explain the first film with pseudo science, which is probably why it bombed at the Japanese box office and is largely forgotten. Taking place directly after the first film, the body of Reiko's ex husband is being examined by his longtime friend Dr. Ando, a pathologist. Ando finds a cryptic note in his friend's stomach, which leads him to discover the dreaded video tape that kills all who watch it within a week. Depressed over the death of his own child, Ando watches the tape, only to discover that Sadako has very different plans for him. **90m/C DVD.** *JP* Koichi Sato, Hiroyuki (Henry) Sanada, Yutaka Matsushige, Hitomi Sato, Hinako Saeki, Shingo Tsurumi, Nanako Matsushima, Tomohiro Okada, Koji Suzuki; *D:* Joji Iida; *W:* Koji Suzuki, Joji Iida, Koji Suzuki; *C:* Makoto Watanabe.

Rashomon *In the Woods* **1951** In 12th century Japan, two travelers attempt to discover the truth about an ambush/rape/murder. They get four completely different versions of the incident from the three people involved in the crime and the single witness. An insightful masterpiece that established Kurosawa and Japanese cinema as major artistic forces. Fine performances, particularly Mifune as the bandit. Visually beautiful and rhythmic. Remade as a western, "The Outrage," in 1964. In Japanese with English subtitles. **83m/B VHS, DVD.** *JP* Machiko Kyo, Toshiro Mifune, Masayuki Mori, Takashi Shimura, Minoru Chiaki, Kichijiro Ueda, Daisuke Kato; *D:* Akira Kurosawa; *W:* Akira Kurosawa, Shinobu Hashimoto; *C:* Kazuo Miyagawa; *M:* Fumio Hayasaka. Oscars '51: Foreign Film; Natl. Bd. of Review '51: Director (Kurosawa); Venice Film Fest. '51: Film.

Rasputin *Agoniya* **1985** The long-censored and banned film of the story of the mad monk and his domination of the royal family before the Russian Revolution. Petrenko is superb. First released in the United States in 1988. In Russian with English subtitles. **104m/C VHS.** *RU* Alexei Petrenko, Anatoly Romashin, Velta Linne, Alice Freindlikh; *D:* Elem Klimov; *W:* Semyon Lunghin, Ilya Nusinov; *M:* Alfred Shnitke.

Rasputin and the Empress *Rasputin: The Mad Monk* **1933** Lavish historical epic teamed the three Barrymore sibs for the first and only time, as they vied for scene-stealing honors. Ethel is Empress Alexandra of Russia, tied to the weak-willed Nicholas II (Morgan) and under the spell of Rasputin, played by Lionel. John is a nobleman who seeks to warn the Russian rulers of their perilous perch on the throne, made only worse by Rasputin's spreading power and corruption. Ethel's first talkie and Wynyard's first film role. Uncredited director Charles Brabin was replaced by

Boleslawski due to his incompatability with the imperious Ethel. **123m/B VHS, DVD.** Ethel Barrymore, John Barrymore, Lionel Barrymore, Ralph Morgan, Diana Wynyard, Tad Alexander, C. Henry Gordon, Edward Arnold, Gustav von Seyffertitz, Anne Shirley, Jean Parker, Henry Kolker; *D:* Richard Boleslawski; *W:* Charles MacArthur; *C:* William H. Daniels.

Rasputin: Dark Servant of Destiny ✓✓✓ **1996 (R)** Charismatic Russian peasant/mystic Grigori Rasputin (a mesmerizing Rickman), having received a vision of the Virgin Mary, comes to St. Petersburg in order to relieve the suffering of young hemophiliac, Prince Alexei (Findlay). Tsarina Alexandra (Scacchi) approves of anyone who can help her stricken son while Tsar Nicholas II (McKellen) tentatively agrees to accept the self-proclaimed holy man into the Russian court. Fine performances and beautiful photography. Filmed in St. Petersburg. **120m/C VHS.** Alan Rickman, Ian McKellen, Greta Scacchi, Freddie Findlay, David Warner, John Wood, James Frain, Diana Quick, Ian Hogg, Peter Jeffrey, Ian McDiarmid, Julian Curry; *D:* Uli Edel; *W:* Peter Bruce; *C:* Elemer Ragalyi; *M:* Brad Fiedel. **CABLE**

Rasputin the Mad Monk ✓✓ **1966** Hammer's version of Russian history of course emphasizes the evil powers of the mad Russian monk (Lee) who gains entry into the court of the czar. Poor script but Lee's good. **90m/B VHS, DVD.** *GB* Christopher Lee, Barbara Shelley, Richard Pasco, Francis Matthews, Suzan Farmer, Nicholas Pennell, Renee Asherson, Derek Francis; *D:* Don Sharp; *W:* John (Anthony Hinds) Elder; *C:* Michael Reed; *M:* Don Banks.

The Rat Pack ✓✓ ½ **1998 (R)** Warts-and-all bio of ole blue eyes, Frank Sinatra (Liotta) and his pals, including Dean Martin (Mantegna), Sammy Davis Jr. (Don Cheadle), Joey Bishop (Slayton), and Peter Lawford (McFayden). Story focuses on the time when Sinatra decides to support John F. Kennedy's (Petersen) bid for the presidency but his mobster ties eventually end their would-be association. TV effort is unauthorized and scorned by the late Sinatra's family. **120m/C VHS, DVD.** Ray Liotta, Don Cheadle, Angus MacFadyen, Joe Mantegna, Bobby Slayton, William L. Petersen, Zeljko Ivanek, Robert Miranda, Dan O'Herlihy, Deborah Kara Unger, Phyllis Lyons, Megan Dodds; *D:* Rob Cohen; *W:* Kario Salem; *C:* Shane Hurlbut; *M:* Mark Adler. **CABLE**

Rat Pfink a Boo-Boo **WOOF!** *Rat Pfink and Boo Boo* **1966** Parody on "Batman" in which a bumbling superhero and his sidekick race around saving people. Notoriously inept. Title story is legendary—it was misspelled accidentally and Steckler didn't have the cash to fix it. **72m/B VHS, DVD.** Vin Saxon, Carolyn Brandt, Titus Moede, Mike Kannon, James Bowie, George Caldwell, Keith Wester; *D:* Ray Dennis Steckler; *W:* Ron Haydock; *C:* Ray Dennis Steckler; *M:* Andre Brummer.

The Rat Race ✓✓✓ **1960** A dancer and a musician venture to Manhattan to make it big, and end up sharing an apartment. Their relationship starts pleasantly and becomes romantic. Enjoyable farce. Well photographed and scripted, with the supporting characters stealing the show. **105m/C VHS.** Tony Curtis, Debbie Reynolds, Jack Oakie, Kay Medford, Don Rickles, Joe Bushkin; *D:* Robert Mulligan; *C:* Robert Burks; *M:* Elmer Bernstein.

Rat Race ✓✓ ½ **2001 (PG-13)** Eccentric Las Vegas casino tycoon Cleese sends six ordinary gamblers on a treasure hunt for two million bucks while rich gamblers wager on the outcome. It's all in the tradition of "It's a Mad, Mad, Mad, Mad World" and the "Cannonball Run" movies, which means it's also old-fashioned. But in that good, solidly funny, anything-for-a-laugh way. But it doesn't go for the cheap, bodily-function humor that so many recent comedies have done to death. The mostly B-list cast has a lot of fun with the material, which is well-paced and expertly carried out by writer Breckman and director Zucker, who thankfully returns to the zany wall-to-wall comedy that put him on the map. **92m/C VHS, DVD.** *US* John Cleese, Whoopi Goldberg, Cuba Gooding Jr., Jon Lovitz, Breckin Meyer, Amy Smart, Seth Green, Kathy Najimy, Rowan Atkinson, Wayne Knight, Dean Cain, Vince Vieluf, Lanei Chapman, Paul Rodriguez; *D:* Jerry Zucker; *W:* Andy Breckman; *C:* Thomas Ackerman; *M:* John Powell.

Ratas, Ratones, Rateros ✓✓ *Rodents* **1999** In poverty-stricken Ecuador, young Salvador (Bustos) tries to make his way as a petty thief. His life manages to take a turn for the worse with the arrival of Salvador's ex-con cousin Angel (Valencia) who stays with him and leads the boy down a self-destructive path. Spanish with subtitles. **107m/C VHS, DVD.** Marco Bustos, Carlos Valencia, Simon Brauer, Cristina Davila; *D:* Sebastian Cordero; *W:* Sebastian Cordero; *C:* Matthew Jensen; *M:* Sergio Sacoto-Arias.

Ratatouille ✓✓✓✓ **2007 (G)** Remy the rat (Oswalt) has a very refined palate, too refined for the garbage his colony hoards to survive. So he sneaks into the best restaurant in Paris to forage while he dreams of becoming a chef himself. This makes him odd-rat-out with his dad and the sewer-dwelling rodent community, not to mention the rodent-averse employees of the restaurant. He gets an in when he helps the klutzy new guy, a kitchen helper named Linguini (Romano), to become a renowned chef. Provides plenty to entertain all ages, with beautiful animation, excellent voice work, well-developed characters, and some surprising plot twists. **110m/C DVD, Blu-ray Disc.** *US* *D:* Brad Bird; *W:* Brad Bird, Jan Pinkava, Jim Capobianco; *C:* Sharon Calahan, Robert Anderson; *M:* Michael Giacchino; *V:* Patton Oswalt, Brian Dennehy, Brad Garrett, Janeane Garofalo, Ian Holm, Peter O'Toole, Will Arnett, James Remar, Lou Romano, John Ratzenberger, Brad Bird, Peter Sohn; *Nar:* Stephane Roux. Oscars '07: Animated Film; British Acad. '07: Animated Film; Golden Globes '08: Animated Film.

Ratboy ✓✓ ½ **1986 (PG-13)** An unscrupulous woman attempts to transform a boy with a rat's face into a celebrity, with tragic results. First directorial effort by Locke that gradually loses steam. **105m/C VHS.** Sondra Locke, Sharon Baird, Robert Kevin Townsend; *D:* Sondra Locke; *W:* Rob Thompson; *C:* Bruce Surtees; *M:* Lennie Niehaus.

Ratcatcher ✓✓ ½ **1999** Twelve-year-old James (Eadie) gets into a fight with another boy on the banks of the canal that runs through their 1970s working-class Glasgow neighborhood. Ryan falls in and drowns and James keeps quiet while being endlessly drawn back to the scene. Meanwhile there's trouble at home and the family's hopes for a better life (by moving to new council housing) is also in jeopardy. **93m/C VHS, DVD.** *GB* William Eadie, Tommy Flanagan, Mandy Matthews, Leanne Mullen, John Miller; *D:* Lynne Ramsay; *W:* Lynne Ramsay; *C:* Alwin Kuchler; *M:* Rachel Portman.

Rated X ✓✓ **2000 (R)** True story of smut kings, the Mitchell Brothers, as portrayed by brothers Sheen and Estevez. Porno pioneer Jim (Estevez) sees dollar signs and joins with younger brother Artie (Sheen) to film skin flicks in San Francisco, including their hardcore classic "Behind the Green Door." They get busted a lot on obscenity charges and fall victim to booze and drugs but while Jim finally cleans up his act, Artie just sinks deeper, leading to a deadly confrontation between the two. The brothers do a surprisingly impressive job but it's grim going. Based on the book by David McCumber. **114m/C VHS, DVD.** Emilio Estevez, Charlie Sheen, Megan Ward, Danielle Brett, Rafer Weigel, Terry O'Quinn, Nikki de Boer, Peter Bogdanovich, Tracy Hutson; *D:* Emilio Estevez; *W:* Norman Snider, Anne Meredith, David Hollander; *C:* Paul Sarossy; *M:* Tyler Bates. **CABLE**

A Rather English Marriage ✓✓ ½ **1998** Aging Reggie (Finney) and Roy (Courtenay) meet in a hospital waiting room after their wives have just died. The odd couple (Reggie is blustery ex-military while Roy was a milkman) are further thrown together when a social worker suggests that both should share Reggie's house to help with chores and expenses (and neither man is used to living alone). The rest of the subdued drama is their adjustment to each other and their new situations with flashbacks to their younger selves. Based on the novel by Angela Carter. Finney and Courtenay starred together in 1983's "The Dresser." **104m/C VHS, DVD.** *GB* Albert Finney, Tom Courtenay, Joanna Lumley, Sean Murray; *D:* Paul Seed; *W:* Andrew Davies; *C:* Gavin Finney; *M:* Jim Parker. **TV**

Ratings Game ✓✓ *The Mogul* **1984** A bitter, out-of-work actor and a woman who works at the ratings service manage to mess up the TV industry. Early directorial effort by DeVito is uneven but funny. **102m/C VHS, DVD.** Danny DeVito, Rhea Perlman, Gerrit Graham, Kevin McCarthy, Jayne Meadows, Steve Allen, Ronny Graham, George Wendt, Barry Corbin, Huntz Hall, Louis Giambalvo, Basil Hoffman, Michael Richards, Ron Rifkin, Joe Santos, Vincent Schiavelli, Frank Sivero, Daniel Stern, Randi Brooks, Robert Costanzo, Allyce Beasley, Selma Diamond, Jason Hervey, James LeGros, Jerry Seinfeld, Damon Hines; *D:* Danny DeVito; *W:* Michael Barrie, Jim Mulholland; *C:* Tim Suhrstedt; *M:* Bruce Kimmel, David Spear. **CABLE**

Rats ✓✓ *Rats: Night of Terror* **1983** In 2225, the beleaguered survivors of a nuclear holocaust struggle with a mutant rodent problem. Mattei used the pseudonym Vincent Dawn. **97m/C VHS, DVD.** Ottaviano Dell'Acqua, Richard Cross, Alex McBride; *D:* Bruno Mattei; *W:* Claudio Fragasso.

The Rats ✓✓ **2001 (R)** Manhattan department store manager Susan Costello (Amick) calls in exterminator Jack Carver (Spano) to get rid of some rats but they discover these aren't the usual critters. Turns out these pesky rodents are genetically altered lab rats who have gotten loose and they're very aggressive—and very hungry. **94m/C VHS, DVD.** Vincent Spano, Madchen Amick, Daveigh Chase, Shawn Michael Howard, Sheila McCarthy; *D:* John Lafia; *W:* Frank Deasy; *M:* Elia Cmiral. **TV**

The Rats Are Coming! The Werewolves Are Here! **WOOF!** **1972 (R)** Low-budget schlock revolves around a family of werewolves and the daughter who decides to put an end to the curse. Imaginative title promises much more than movie delivers. The killer rats were thrown in as an afterthought to increase the run time. **92m/C VHS.** Hope Stansbury, Jackie Skarvellis, Noel Collins, Joan Ogden, Douglas Phair, Bernard Kaler; *D:* Andy Milligan; *W:* Andy Milligan; *C:* Andy Milligan.

A Rat's Tale ✓✓ **1998 (G)** "Romeo & Juliet" for rats. A regular Joe, Manhattanite Monty Mad-Rat meets Isabella Noble-Rat, the daughter of the rat President, and soon Monty is a goner for this out-of-reach rodent whose family disapproves of the common sewer creature. Adding to the intrigue, a land developer (Ostendorf) appears with a scheme to obliterate the rat population and build a parking garage. The rats band together to raise money to buy their land and prevent ratricide. Admirably lo-tech, kid pic nonetheless suffers from the cute but expressionless and very much wired marionettes playing the rats—they're no muppets—and the broadly characterized roles of the human actors (Hutton, Stiller and D'Angelo). Marionettes complements of Germany's Augsburger Puppet Theatre. Based on the book by Tor Seidler. **90m/C VHS.** *GE* Lauren Hutton, Jerry Stiller, Beverly D'Angelo, Josef Ostendorf; *D:* Michael F. Huse; *W:* Werner Morganrath, Peter Scheerbaum; *C:* Piotr Lenar; *M:* Frederic Talgorn; *V:* Dee Bradley Baker, Lynsey Bartilson, Donald Arthur, Ray Guth, Scott MacDonald.

Rattle of a Simple Man ✓✓ ½ **1964** A naive, chaste, middle-aged bachelor (Corbett) who lives in London must spend the night with a waitress (Cilento) to win a bet. She knows of the bet and kindly obliges. Enjoyable sex comedy. **91m/B VHS.** *GB* Harry H. Corbett, Diane Cilento, Michael Medwin, Thora Hird; *D:* Muriel Box.

Rattled ✓✓ ½ **1996 (PG-13)** Indiana Jones won't be the only snake-hater after seeing what hundreds of rattlesnakes can do. When their den is disturbed by construction on a new water project, hundreds of rattlers slither down the mountainside ready to attack anyone in their path. Based on the book "Rattlers" by Joseph Gilmore. **90m/C VHS.** William Katt, Shanna Reed, Michael Galeota, Monica Creel, Clint Howard, Ian Abercrombie, Ed Lauter, Bibi Besch, Zack Eginton; *D:* Tony Randel; *W:* Jim Wheat, Ken Wheat.

Rattler Kid ✓ *Un Hombre vino a matar* **1968** Cavalry sergeant wrongly accused of murdering his commanding officer escapes from prison and finds the real killer. **86m/C VHS, DVD.** *IT SP* Richard Wyler, Brad Harris, Jesus Puente, Femi Benussi; *D:* Leon Klimovsky; *W:* Odoardo Fiory; *C:* Julio Ortas; *M:* Francesco De Masi.

Rattlers ✓ **1976 (PG)** TV movie featuring poisonous rattlesnakes who attack at random. **82m/C VHS, DVD.** Sam Chew, Elizabeth Chauvet, Dan Priest; *D:* John McCauley. **TV**

Ratz ✓ ½ **1999** Dumb teen film about best friends Marci and Summer who get involved with a magic ring, an eccentric shopkeeper, and two rats (yes, the rodent kind) who are transformed into a couple of datable young hunks so the girls will have escorts to the big spring dance. **95m/C VHS, DVD.** Caroline Elliott, Vanessa Lengies, Jake Seeley, Levi James, Kathy Baker, Ron Silver, Barbara Tyson; *D:* Thom Eberhardt; *W:* Thom Eberhardt; *C:* Ric Waite. **CABLE**

Ravager ✓ ½ **1997 (R)** When a space transport ship crashlands in the desert, former lovers Cooper Wayne (Payne) and Avedon Hammond (Butler), along with their crew, search for help. They discover an underground storage facility and some leaking hazardous material labeled "Ravenger" that infects one of their technicians. When they return the infected crewman to the ship, they also bring back a contagion that threatens the survival of everyone aboard. **92m/C VHS.** Bruce Payne, Yancy Butler, Juliet Landau, Salvator Xuereb; *D:* James D. Deck; *W:* James D. Deck.

The Ravagers ✓✓ **1965** Capt. Kermit Dowling (Saxon) and ex-con Gaudiel (Poe) led Filipino guerrillas against remnants of the Japanese forces on the Philippines. The Japanese have taken over a convent in their search for a ship of gold bullion and Gaudiel manages to sneak inside where he encounters American Shelia (Fitzsimmons), who's been sheltered by the nuns. In between the action, they take a liking to each other. **80m/B VHS, DVD.** John Saxon, Fernando Poe Jr., Bronwyn Fitzsimons, Robert Arevalo, Mike Parsons; *D:* Eddie Romero; *W:* Eddie Romero, Cesar Amigo; *M:* Tito Arevalo.

Rave Review ✓✓ **1995** Desperate L.A. theatrical director wants to scare a powerful critic into giving his latest production a glowing review so that his small theatre company can remain in business. Too bad he scares the critic to death. **91m/C VHS.** Jeff Seymour, Ed Begley Jr., Leo Rossi, Joe Spano, Bruce Kirby, James Handy; *D:* Jeff Seymour; *W:* Jeff Seymour.

The Raven ✓✓ **1915** An early, eccentric pseudo-biography of author Edgar Allan Poe. The film opens with a look at Poe's ancestors and follows the author to maturity when he turns to alcohol for solace. His drunken stupor produces hallucinations that lead to his tale of "The Raven." Silent with added music track. **80m/B VHS.** Henry B. Walthall, Wanda Howard; *D:* Charles Brabin.

The Raven ✓✓✓ **1935** A lunatic surgeon (Lugosi), who has a dungeon full of torture gadgets inspired by Edgar Allan Poe's stories, is begged by a man to save his daughter's life. The surgeon does, and then falls in love with the girl. But when she rejects his love (she's already engaged), he plans revenge in his chamber of horrors. Karloff plays the criminal who winds up ruining the mad doctor's plans. Lugosi is at his prime in this role, and any inconsistencies in the somewhat shaky script can be overlooked because of his chilling performance. **62m/B VHS, DVD.** Boris Karloff, Bela Lugosi, Irene Ware, Lester Matthews, Samuel S. Hinds; *D:* Lew Landers; *W:* David Boehm, Jim Tully; *C:* Charles Stumar.

The Raven ✓✓✓ **1963** This could-have-been monumental teaming of horror greats Karloff, Lorre, and Price is more of a satire than a true horror film. One of the more enjoyable of the Corman/Poe adaptations, the movie takes only the title of the poem. As for the story line: Price and Karloff play two rival sorcerers who battle for supremacy, with Lorre as the unfortunate associate turned into the bird of the title. **86m/C VHS, DVD.**

Vincent Price, Boris Karloff, Peter Lorre, Jack Nicholson, Hazel Court, Olive Sturgess; *D:* Roger Corman; *W:* Richard Matheson; *C:* Floyd Crosby; *M:* Les Baxter.

Raven ♂ 1/2 **1997 (R)** Covert mercenary team codenamed Raven is after a Soviet satellite decoder. They're double-crossed by renegade CIA agents and their leader Reynolds decides to get his own brand of justice. **93m/C VHS, DVD.** Burt Reynolds, Krista Allen, Matt Battaglia, David Ackroyd, Richard Gant; *D:* Russell Solberg; *W:* Jacobsen Hart; *C:* John Dirlam; *M:* Harry Manfredini.

The Raven ♂♂ **2007** Somewhere in this happily cheesy gay horror film there's an acknowledgement of the Edgar Allan story. Roderick is hosting a masquerade ball in the same house that was the scene of the Ravenswood massacre 50 years before. Soon his guests are being slaughtered by a man wearing a raven costume. **96m/C DVD.** Rick Armando, Ivan Botha, Litha Booi, Traverse Le Goff; *D:* David DeCoteau; *W:* Matthew Jason Walsh; *C:* Vincent Cox; *M:* Richard Band, Joe Silva; *Nar:* Richard Johnson.

Ravenhawk ♂♂ **1995 (R)** Native American Ravenhawk (McLish) is falsely accused of murdering her parents and sent to a maximum security asylum. Twelve years later she returns to her home and learns that corporate slimeball Philip Thorne (Atherton) framed her. Now, he's built a nuclear waste plant on Shoshone land over the objections of the tribe and Ravenhawk is determined to even the score. **88m/C VHS.** Rachel McLish, John Enos, William Atherton, Ed Lauter, Mitch Pileggi; *D:* Albert Pyun; *W:* Kevin Elders; *C:* George Mooradian; *M:* Johnny Harris.

Ravenous ♂♂ 1/2 **1999 (R)** Off-kilter tale of cannibalism in the American West in 1847 (loosely based on the Donner Party) loses its way when it begins to use man-eating as a metaphor for settlers carving up the land. When stringy, twitching Colqhoun (Carlyle) shows up starving and nearly frozen at an army fort in the Sierra Nevadas, he tells Captain John Boyd (Pearce) that he was with a party that resorted to eating their dead when stranded. When a team is sent to investigate, more than the facts are digested. Soon Colqhoun is extolling the virtues of pan-frying your pals to Boyd. The unusual subject and offbeat attempts at humor make this a recipe not for all tastes. **100m/C VHS, DVD.** John Spencer, Stephen Spinella, Neal McDonough, David Arquette, Guy Pearce, Robert Carlyle, Jeremy Davies, Jeffrey Jones; *D:* Antonia Bird; *W:* Ted Griffin; *C:* Anthony B. Richmond; *M:* Michael Nyman, Damon Albarn.

Raven's Ridge ♂♂ 1/2 **1997 (R)** Imagine an exceptionally low-budget combination of Stanley Kubrick's heist movie "The Killing" and "Deliverance." That's essentially what this story boils down to. A group of friends knock over an armored car at a racetrack then stash the loot out in the woods. When they go to retrieve it, they're attacked by a grizzled local. **77m/C DVD.** William Kendall, Dawn Howard, John Rizzi; *D:* Mike Upton.

Ravishing Idiot ♂♂ *Agent 38-24-36; Adorable Idiot; The Warm-Blooded Spy; Bewitching Scatterbrain* **1964** An unemployed bank clerk becomes mixed up with Soviet spies. **99m/B VHS, DVD.** *FR* Brigitte Bardot, Anthony Perkins; *D:* Edouard Molinaro.

Raw Courage ♂ *Courage* **1984** Three long-distance runners relax in New Mexico, but are kidnapped by vigilantes. Loosely based on a James Dickey novel. **90m/C VHS.** Ronny Cox, Lois Chiles, Art Hindle, Tim Maier, M. Emmet Walsh; *D:* Robert L. Rosen.

Raw Deal ♂♂♂ **1948** Sadistic Rick Coyle (Burr) framed one-time associate Joe Sullivan (O'Keefe), who wound up in prison. Joe's moll Pat (Trevor) helps him to escape and they take prison social worker Ann (Hunt), who's befriended Joe, as a hostage. They go after Coyle and Joe begins to fall for the demure dame, who finds the underworld life exciting and even saves Joe from one of Coyle's henchmen. No good guys here but it is fine film noir. **79m/B VHS, DVD.** Dennis O'Keefe, Claire Trevor, Raymond Burr, Marsha Hunt, John Ireland, Curt Conway, Whit Bissell; *D:* Anthony Mann; *W:* John C. Higgins, Leopold Atlas; *C:* John Alton; *M:* Paul Sawtell.

Raw Deal ♂ 1/2 **1986 (R)** Don't ever give Schwarzenegger a raw deal! FBI agent Schwarzie infiltrates the mob and shoots lots of people. **106m/C VHS, DVD.** Arnold Schwarzenegger, Kathryn Harrold, Darren McGavin, Sam Wanamaker, Paul Shenar, Steven Hill; *D:* John Irvin; *W:* Patrick Edgeworth, Gary De Vore; *C:* Alex Thomson.

Raw Force ♂ *Shogun Island* **1981 (R)** Three karate buffs visit an island inhabited by a sect of cannibalistic monks who have the power to raise the dead (it could happen). They fix the villains by kicking them all in the head. **90m/C VHS, DVD.** *PH* Cameron Mitchell, Geoffrey Binney, John Dresden, John Locke, Ralph Lombardi; *D:* Edward Murphy.

Raw Justice ♂♂ **1993 (R)** When the daughter of a powerful Southern mayor is murdered, tough ex-cop Mace (Keith) is hired to get the killer. Mace enlists the reluctant help of call girl Sarah (Anderson) to help him trap Mitch (Hayes), his prime suspect. Only things don't work out as Mace planned and the wary threesome must work together to save themselves from certain death. **92m/C VHS, DVD.** David Keith, Pamela Anderson, Robert Hays, Leo Rossi, Charles Napier, Stacy Keach; *D:* David A. Prior; *W:* David A. Prior.

Raw Meat ♂♂ *Death Line* **1972** British creepfest. Two college students (Ladd, Gurney) find a body on the steps of London's Russell Square subway platform but it has disappeared by the time Scotland Yard shows up. Inspector Calhoun (Pleasence) investigates since it's not the first time something strange has happened there. He learns he's chasing the remaining survivor of a long-ago cave-in who has mutated into a cannibal-zombie creature. **88m/C DVD.** *GB* Donald Pleasence, David Ladd, Sharon Gurney, Norman Rossington, Clive Swift, Christopher Lee, Hugh Armstrong; *D:* Gary Sherman; *W:* Ceri Jones; *C:* Alex Thomson; *M:* Wil Mallone, Jeremy Rose.

Raw Nerve ♂ **1991 (R)** A cast with possibilities can't overcome this poorly reasoned suspenser. A young man has visions of the local serial killer, but when he reports them to police he becomes the suspect. There are a few twists beyond that, none too thrilling. **91m/C VHS.** Glenn Ford, Traci Lords, Sandahl Bergman, Randall "Tex" Cobb, Ted Prior, Jan-Michael Vincent; *W:* David A. Prior.

Raw Nerve ♂♂ 1/2 **1999 (R)** Rogue cop Blair (Van Peebles) has crossed the line one too many times and is being investigated for money laundering. He's in trouble with IAD and the mob, which also puts girlfriend Izabel (Sheridan) in danger. Blair turns for help to ex-cop buddy Ethan (Galligan) but won't change his violent ways and keeps sinking down. **102m/C VHS, DVD.** Mario Van Peebles, Nicolette Sheridan, Zach Galligan; *D:* Avi Nesher. **VIDEO**

Raw Summer ♂♂♂ *Nama-natsu* **2006** Masuo (Yutaka Mishima) is a middle aged man who has become obsessed with a young school girl who rides on the subway with him (played by Japanese adult film actress Sora Aoi). Eventually his obsession leads him to confront her and get rejected which sends him over the edge. **60m/C DVD.** *JP* Aoi Sola, Yutaka Mishima; *D:* Keisuke Yoshida; *W:* Keisuke Yoshida; *C:* Shinya Yamada; *M:* Shin-Ichi Kawahara.

Raw Target ♂ 1/2 **1995 (R)** Ex-kickboxer Johnny Rider (Cook) finds himself a police decoy in a drug bust and then learns that the drug gang's leader Sparks (Hill) was also involved in his brother's death. **92m/C VHS, DVD.** Dale "Apollo" Cook, Ron Hall, Nick (Nicholas, Niko) Hill, Mychelle Charters; *D:* Tim Spring; *W:* Larry Maddox; *C:* Bruce Dorfman; *M:* Jun Lupito.

Rawhead Rex ♂ 1/2 **1987 (R)** An ancient demon is released from his underground prison in Ireland by a plowing farmer, and begins to decapitate and maim at will. Adapted by Clive Barker from his own short story. But Barker later disowned the film, so make your own judgment. **89m/C VHS, DVD.** David Dukes, Kelly Piper, Niall Toibin, Niall O'Brien, Donal McCann, Gladys Sheehan, Cora Lunny, Heinrich von Schellendorf; *D:* George Pavlou; *W:* Clive Barker; *C:* John Metcalfe; *M:* Colin Towns.

Rawhide ♂♂ **1938** Rancher's Protection Association forces landowners to knuckle under resulting in friction. Lou Gehrig plays a rancher in a western released the year before he died. Bandleader Ballew could be more gripping in the lead. **60m/B VHS, DVD.** Lou Gehrig, Smith Ballew, Evalyn Knapp; *D:* Ray Taylor.

Rawhide ♂♂♂ *Desperate Siege* **1950** Four escaped convicts hijack a stagecoach way station and hold hostages while waiting for a shipment of gold. A suspenseful B-grade western with a bang-up ending. Well paced and cast with an abundance of good talent. A remake of "Show Them No Mercy" (1938). **86m/B VHS.** Tyrone Power, Susan Hayward, Hugh Marlowe, Jack Elam, Dean Jagger, George Tobias, Edgar Buchanan, Jeff Corey; *D:* Henry Hathaway; *C:* Milton Krasner.

Rawhide Romance ♂ **1934** Bill finds justice and love in this chap-slappin' opus, which finds him neglecting the thieves operating on the ranch as he romances his girl. Naturally he comes to his senses and goes after the crooks. **47m/B VHS.** Buffalo Bill Jr., Genee Boutell, Lafe (Lafayette) McKee, Si Jenks, William Barrymore, Marin Sais, Clyde McClary; *D:* Victor Adamson; *W:* L.V. Jefferson.

Ray ♂♂♂ **2004 (PG-13)** If imitation is the sincerest form of flattery then Foxx (who did win an Oscar) has it all covered for his depiction of the legendary Ray Charles in an extended biography that covers 1930 to 1966. This detailed, colorful, and straightforward retelling starts with young Ray Charles Robinson being sent away to better himself at a school for the blind. Ray finds musical success in the Seattle jazz scene but also gets firsthand knowledge of the dark side of the biz. While touring, he picks up a 20-year heroin habit and an equally destructive addiction to women, although it's supportive wife Della Bea (Washington) who encourages Ray to develop his own style, a heady fusion of gospel and R&B. Hackford doesn't skimp on Ray's charms or faults and finds a workable balance between showcasing the musician's professional and personal lives. Foxx auditioned for Charles, who gave his approval for what became Foxx's breakout performance. **152m/C VHS, DVD, HD DVD.** *US* Jamie Foxx, Kerry Washington, Regina King, Clifton Powell, Aunjanue Ellis, Harry J. Lennix, Terrence Howard, Larenz Tate, Bokeem Woodbine, Curtis Armstrong, Richard Schiff, Wendell Pierce, Chris Thomas King, David Krumholtz, Warwick Davis, Robert Wisdom, Denise Dowse, Thomas Jefferson Byrd, Rick Gomez, Kurt Fuller, Sharon Warren, C.J. Sanders, Patrick Bauchau; *D:* Taylor Hackford; *W:* James L. White; *C:* Pawel Edelman; *M:* Craig Armstrong. Oscars '04: Actor (Foxx), Sound; British Acad. '04: Actor (Foxx), Sound; Golden Globes '05: Actor—Mus./Comedy (Foxx); Screen Actors Guild '04: Actor (Foxx).

Razor Blade Smile ♂♂ **1998 (R)** Kinky vampire tale with a really killer babe fond of leather fetish wear. She's Lilith Silver (Daley), a vampire hitwoman working in London. Lilith has been hired to murder members of the Illuminati—a secret society that has made inroads into the highest levels of business and government. Turns out the head of the Illuminati is Sethane Blake (Adamson), the vampire who originally made Lilith one of the undead. Low-budget, bloody camp with some watchable twists and turns. Also available in an unrated version. **101m/C VHS, DVD.** *GB* Eileen Daly, Chris(topher) Adamson, Kevin Howarth, Jonathan Coote, Heidi James, David Warbeck; *D:* Jake West; *W:* Jake West; *C:* James Solan; *M:* Richard Wells.

The Razor: Sword of Justice ♂♂ *Hanzo the Razor: Sword of Justice* **1972** Reasonably honest cop Hanzo Itami knows he won't get a promotion under his corrupt boss Inspector Onishi unless he can blackmail him into it. And he finds a way when he discovers condemned prisoner Kanbei is actually living with his mistress Omino, who it turns out is busy with Onishi as well. A little knowledge could get Hanzo killed but he's willing to take the risk. Japanese with subtitles. **90m/C VHS, DVD.** *JP* Shintaro Katsu, Asaoka Yukiji, Atsumi Mari, Nishimura Akira; *D:* Kenji Misumi.

Razorback ♂ **1984 (R)** Young American travels to the Australian outback in search of his missing journalist wife. During his quest, he encounters a giant killer pig that has been terrorizing the area. Firmly establishes that pigs, with little sense of natural timing, make lousy movie villains. **95m/C VHS.** *AU* Gregory Harrison, Bill Kerr, Arkie Whiteley, Judy Morris, Chris Haywood, David Argue; *D:* Russell Mulcahy; *W:* Everett DeRoche; *C:* Dean Semler.

The Razor's Edge ♂♂♂ **1946** Adaptation of the W. Somerset Maugham novel. A rich young man spends his time between WWI & WWII searching for essential truth, eventually landing in India. A satisfying cinematic version of a difficult novel, supported by an excellent cast. Remade in 1984 with Bill Murray in the lead role. **146m/B VHS, DVD.** Tyrone Power, Gene Tierney, Anne Baxter, Clifton Webb, Herbert Marshall, John Payne, Elsa Lanchester, Lucile Watson, Frank Latimore, Cecil Humphreys, Harry Pilcer, Cobina Wright Sr., Noel Cravat, John Wengraf; *D:* Edmund Goulding; *W:* Lamar Trotti; *C:* Arthur C. Miller; *M:* Alfred Newman. Oscars '46: Support. Actress (Baxter); Golden Globes '47: Support. Actor (Webb), Support. Actress (Baxter).

The Razor's Edge ♂♂ 1/2 **1984 (PG-13)** A beautifully filmed but idiosyncratic version of the W. Somerset Maugham novel. WWI-ravaged Larry Darrell combs the world in search of the meaning of life. Murray is a little too old and sardonic to seem really tortured. Russell is great as the loser he rescues. Subtly unique, with real shortcomings. **129m/C VHS, DVD.** Bill Murray, Catherine Hicks, Theresa Russell, Denholm Elliott, James Keach, Peter Vaughan, Saeed Jaffrey, Brian Doyle-Murray; *D:* John Byrum; *W:* John Byrum; *M:* Jack Nitzsche.

Razorteeth **WOOF!** **2005** No budget digital film rip-off of the 1978 cult classic "Piranha." **75m/C DVD.** Todd Carpent, Stevan Anselmi, Brian Berry, Brice Kennedy; *D:* John Polonia; *W:* John Polonia; *C:* Paul Alan Steele; *M:* Jon McBride. **VIDEO**

Re-Animator ♂♂♂ **1984** Black humor cult classic, based on the H.P. Lovecraft story "Herbert West, The Re-Animator." Med student Herbert West (Combs) is determined to make a medical breakthrough by bringing the dead back to life. His experimental green goo is finally successful on a corpse from the med school morgue but, as usual, any resurrected cadaver becomes difficult to control. Grisly if somewhat self-conscious but there's an unforgettable sex scene invovling a lustful severed head and heroine Megan (Crampton). Followed by "Bride of Re-Animator." **86m/C VHS, DVD.** Jeffrey Combs, Bruce Abbott, Barbara Crampton, David Gale, Robert Sampson, Gerry Black, Carolyn Purdy-Gordon; *D:* Stuart Gordon; *W:* Stuart Gordon, Dennis Paoli, William J. Norris; *C:* Mac Ahlberg; *M:* Richard Band.

Re-Cycle ♂♂ 1/2 *Gwai wik; Gui yu* **2006 (R)** A successful romance writer is working on a horror novel as a change of pace, and the creepy things she describes keep happening. Soon she is sucked into another universe in a scene that is sort of like "Alice in Wonderland" meets "Silent Hill." Gore hounds will be disappointed, but Terry Gilliam fans might want to give it a chance. **97m/C DVD, Blu-ray Disc.** Lawrence Chou, Angelica Lee, Yaqi Zeng; *D:* Oxide Pang Chun, Danny Pang; *W:* Oxide Pang Chun, Danny Pang, Cub Chin, SirLaosson Dara, Sam Lung, Thomas Pang; *C:* Decha Srimantra; *M:* Payont Permsith. **VIDEO**

Re-Generation ♂ 1/2 *The Limb Salesman* **2004** Unconvincing, low-budget Canadian sci-fi. After a series of eco disasters, water has become a prized and expensive commodity. Abe Fielder (Johnson) and his family run a remote northern underground mining operation that extracts water from ice. So he's wealthy enough to afford to hire roving genetic specialist Dr. Gabriel Goode (Stebbings) to manufacture legs for Abe's daughter Clara (Veninger) who was born without them. **79m/C DVD.** *CA* Clark Johnson, Peter Stebbings, Ingrid Veninger, Charles Officer, Jackie Burroughs; *D:* Anais Granofsky; *W:* Ingrid Veninger, Anais Granofsky; *C:* D. Gregor Hagey; *M:* John Weisman.

Reach for the Sky ♂♂ 1/2 **1956** WW II flying ace loses both legs in an accident and learns to fly again. He becomes a hero during the Battle of Britain, then is shot down over France and held prisoner by the Germans. At war's end he returns to England to lead 3,000 planes over London in a victory flight. Inspirationally told true story. **123m/B VHS, DVD.** *GB* Kenneth More, Alexander Knox, Nigel Green; ***D:*** Lewis Gilbert; ***M:*** John Addison. British Acad. '56: Film.

Reach the Rock **1998 (R)** Robin (Nivola) is a minor troublemaker who gets tossed into his small hometown jail one hot summer night by Sgt. Quinn (Sadler), who blames Robin for his nephew's accidental drowning. Robin keeps escaping from lockup to cause more minor vandalism but always returns to his cell, since he's hoping his ex-girlfriend Lise (Langton), who's taking off for New York, will come and bail him out so they can have one last heart-to-heart. When she does so, Robin finally seems to reach some mature understanding (but the character is so weakly developed, it's hard to tell). **100m/C VHS.** Alessandro Nivola, William Sadler, Brooke Langton, Bruce Norris, Karen Sillas, Norman Reedus, Richard Hamilton; ***D:*** William Ryan; ***W:*** John Hughes; ***C:*** John Campbell; ***M:*** John McEntire.

Reaching for the Moon ½ **1917** A day-dreaming department store employee finds himself in the unlikely position of ruling a kingdom. Vintage Fairbanks fun, based on a story by Anita Loos. Silent. **62m/B VHS.** Douglas Fairbanks Sr., Eileen (Elaine Persey) Percy, Millard Webb; ***D:*** John Emerson.

Reaching for the Moon ½ **1931** Fairbanks is a businessman who falls for liquor and Daniels on a transatlantic cruise. Dull and cruel; not as light-hearted as it intends. One Irving Berlin song sung by Crosby. **62m/B VHS, DVD.** Douglas Fairbanks Sr., Bebe Daniels, Bing Crosby, Edward Everett Horton; ***D:*** Edmund Goulding.

Reactor *War of the Robots; La Guerra dei Robot* **1978** A low-budget sci-fi film about kidnapped scientists, alien ships and an activated nuclear reactor. **90m/C VHS.** *IT* Yanti Somer, Melissa Long, Giacomo "Jack" Rossi-Stuart, Robert Barnes, Aldo Canti, Antonio (Tony) Sabato; ***D:*** Alfonso Brescia; ***W:*** Alfonso Brescia; ***C:*** Silvio Fraschetti; ***M:*** Marcello Giombini.

Read My Lips ½ *Sur Mes Levres* **2001** Hearing-impaired Carla (Devos) is an office worker for a real-estate firm who is tired of being either ignored or used. When her boss has her hire an assistant, Carla chooses ex-con Paul (Cassel), who has no discernable office skills but does retain his shady criminal associations. He wants to heist some loot from an old associate, she wants revenge on a weaselly co-worker and it seems Carla's lip-reading skills are the key to both plans. French with subtitles. **115m/C VHS, DVD.** *FR* Emmanuelle Devos, Vincent Cassel, Olivier Gourmet, Olivier Perrier, Olivia Bonamy, Pierre Diot; ***D:*** Jacques Audiard; ***W:*** Jacques Audiard, Tonino Beranacquista; ***C:*** Mathieu Vadepied; ***M:*** Alexandre Desplat. Cesar '01: Actress (Devos), Screenplay.

The Reader ½ **2008 (R)** In postwar Germany, middle-aged Hanna (Winslet) and 15-year-old Michael (Kross) become sexually involved after Hanna cares for him during an illness (she insists he read to her before their encounters—hence the title). She breaks off the forbidden relationship abruptly and the story leaps ahead to an older Michael (Fiennes), now a law student, witnessing Hanna on trial for war crimes relating to the Holocaust. Her involvement in atrocities, her concealed illiteracy, and her past relationship with Michael are pressed to the surface and serve as a way to attempt to understand how awful things can be done by seemingly decent people. This film adaptation of the best-selling novel by Bernhard Schlink has high aspirations but proves a somewhat tricky adaptation to screen. Still, Winslet's performance is a somber and convincing treat. **123m/C DVD.** *US GE* Ralph Fiennes, Kate Winslet, Bruno Ganz, Alexandra Maria Lara, Lena Olin, Karoline Herforth, David Kross, Matthias Habich, Susanne Lothar; ***D:*** Stephen Daldry; ***W:*** David Hare; ***C:*** Chris Menges, Roger Deakins; ***M:*** Nico Muhly. Oscars '08: Actress (Winslet); British Acad. '08: Actress (Winslet); Golden Globes '09: Support. Actress (Winslet); Screen Actors Guild '08: Support. Actress (Winslet).

The Reading Room ½ **2005 (PG)** Businessman William Campbell (Jones) fulfills his deceased wife's last wish by opening a free reading room in the gang-ridden inner-city neighborhood where he grew up. But his generosity is resented, and his dream threatened, by some in the neighborhood. **87m/C DVD.** James Earl Jones, Douglas Spain, Joanna Cassidy, Lynne Moody, Spencir Bridges, Tim Reid, Georg Stanford Brown; ***D:*** Georg Stanford Brown; ***W:*** Randy Feldman; ***C:*** James W. Wrenn; ***M:*** Elia Cmiral. **CABLE**

Ready? OK! **2008** Sweet-natured comedy about a young boy who's very sure of what he likes even if the grown-up implications escape him. San Diego single mom Andy is struggling to raise her strong-willed 10-year-old son Joshua with the help of her deadbeat brother Alex and gay neighbor Charlie. Joshua, who likes dolls and dresses, is determined to join the all-girl cheerleading squad at his Catholic school, which results in a number of parent-teacher conferences as Sister Vivian tries to steer Joshua into more manly pursuits with some unexpected results. **91m/C DVD.** Carrie Preston, John Preston, Michael Emerson, Kail Rocha, Lurie Poston, Tara Karsian; ***D:*** James Vasquez; ***W:*** James Vasquez; ***C:*** Elizabeth Santoro; ***M:*** Lance Horne.

Ready to Rumble **2000 (PG-13)** Sanitation workers and best buds Gordie (Arquette) and Sean (Caan) decide to mastermind the comeback of their favorite wrestler, Jimmy "the King" King (Platt). The reason he needs a comeback is that promoter Titus Sinclair (Pantaliano) has decided that he's outlasted his usefulness. Sort of like this movie. Arquette and wrestling are annoying enough individually, but put 'em together and it's almost painful to watch. The two buddies make Bill and Ted look like Rhodes scholars, and it's not like there's any point to further parodying the "sport" of wrestling. Hopefully, this was a worth a few mortgage payments to supporting players Platt, Landau, and Pantaliano. **100m/C VHS, DVD.** David Arquette, Scott Caan, Oliver Platt, Rose McGowan, Joe Pantoliano, Martin Landau, Richard Lineback, Chris Owen, Kathleen Freeman, Lewis Arquette, Diamond Dallas Page; ***D:*** Brian Robbins; ***W:*** Steven Brill; ***C:*** Clark Mathis; ***M:*** George S. Clinton.

Ready to Wear *Pret-a-Porter* **1994 (R)** Altman travels to Paris to take on the fashion industry with his trademark satire, ensemble cast, and cameo players in tow. The untimely death of a major industry player begins a swirl of random subplots involving a head-spinning array of fashion industry stereotypes. Loren and Mastroianni recreate their "Yesterday, Today and Tomorrow" boudoir striptease scene. Coterie of one-dimensional characters is set adrift with no discernable plot, which might make for interesting people watching, but results in a tedious movie. Altman did it better with "The Player" and "Short Cuts." **132m/C VHS, DVD.** Sophia Loren, Marcello Mastroianni, Julia Roberts, Tim Robbins, Kim Basinger, Stephen Rea, Anouk Aimee, Lauren Bacall, Lili Taylor, Sally Kellerman, Tracey Ullman, Linda Hunt, Rupert Everett, Forest Whitaker, Richard E. Grant, Danny Aiello, Teri Garr, Lyle Lovett, Jean Rochefort, Michel Blanc, Anne Canovos, Jean-Pierre Cassel, Francois Cluzet, Rossy de Palma, Kasia (Katarzyna) Figura, Sam Robards, Cher, Harry Belafonte, Issey Miyake, Sonia Rykiel, Jean-Paul Gaultier, Thierry Mugler; ***D:*** Robert Altman; ***W:*** Barbara Shulgasser, Robert Altman; ***C:*** Jean Lepine, Pierre Mignot; ***M:*** Michel Legrand.

The Reagans **2004** Despite it being pulled from network broadcast due to allegations of character assassination, the production presents a compassionate and charitable portrayal of Ronald and Nancy Reagan's assent from Hollywood couple to First Family. Starting with their first date in 1949 and follows them through two White House terms. **180m/C DVD.** James Brolin, Judy David, Zeljko Ivanek, Mary Beth Peil, Bill Smitrovich, Shad Hart, Tom Barnett, Stewart Bick, Sean McCann, John Stamos, Lisa Bronwyn Moore, Zoie Palmer, Claudia Besso; ***D:*** Robert Allan Ackerman; ***W:*** Thomas (Tom) Rickman; ***C:*** James Chressanthis; ***M:*** John Altman. **TV**

A Real American Hero ½ *Hard Stick* **1978** Story of Tennessee sheriff Buford Pusser, the subject of three "Walking Tall" films. Here, he battles moonshiners with the usual violence. **94m/C VHS, DVD.** Brian Dennehy, Brian Kerwin, Forrest Tucker; ***D:*** Lou Antonio. **TV**

The Real Blonde ½ **1997 (R)** Entertaining ensemble pic that daringly exposes the business of show features a disillusioned actor, his beleaguered girlfriend, and a successful soap star (Caulfield) searching for a peroxide-free blonde in New York. On-the-outs couple Joe and Mary (Modine and Keener) is main focus but is undercut by the industry mania that surrounds them. Intelligent writing and caustic wit provide a few memorable scenes, such as the "Il Piano" debate in a crowded restaurant over a thinly veiled "acclaimed independent film" and Bob's resolution to his blonde quest. Modine also revs things up in an emotional improv. Thomas stands out from the crowd as a pretentious fashion photog. DiCillo's latest feature tackles the movie biz from the other side of the camera than his 1995 acclaimed satire, "Living in Oblivion." **105m/C VHS, DVD.** Matthew Modine, Catherine Keener, Daryl Hannah, Maxwell Caulfield, Elizabeth Berkley, Marlo Thomas, Buck Henry, Bridgette Wilson-Sampras, Christopher Lloyd, Kathleen Turner, Denis Leary, Steve Buscemi; ***D:*** Tom DiCillo; ***W:*** Tom DiCillo; ***C:*** Frank Prinzi; ***M:*** Jim Farmer.

Real Bullets **1990** Stunt team performs the real thing when two members get imprisoned in a bad guy's desert castle. **86m/C VHS.** John Gazarian, Martin Landau; ***D:*** Lance Lindsay.

The Real Charlotte ½ **1991** When young, lovely, and flirtatious Francie Fitzpatrick (Roth) is romantically betrayed by a young English officer, she then sets her mind on the one man (Bergin) whom her plain and middle-aged cousin Charlotte (Crowley) has long loved. Set in Victorian-era Ireland; made for British TV. **240m/C VHS, DVD.** *GB* Joanna Roth, Jeananne Crowley, Patrick Bergin; ***D:*** Tony Barry; ***W:*** Bernard MacLaverty; ***M:*** Paul Corbett. **TV**

The Real Dirt on Farmer John **2006** Eccentric John Peterson is the titular Illinois farmer whose life has been documented since the 1950s when his mother, Anna, began shooting Super 8 home movies. John, who embraced the counterculture of the 1960s, later took over filming—and the farm—after his father died. Director Siegel befriended and started filming John in the 1980s after a number of financial crises led him to sell most of the acreage, though the farm eventually rebounded as an organic co-op. **83m/C** *US* ***D:*** Taggart Siegel; ***W:*** John Peterson; ***C:*** Taggart Siegel; ***M:*** Mark Orton.

Real Genius **1985 (PG)** Brainy kids in California work with lasers on a class project that is actually intended for use as an offensive military weapon. When they learn of the scheme, they use their brilliant minds to mount an amusingly elaborate strategic defense initiative of their own. Eccentric characters and an intelligent script provide a bevy of laughs for the family. **108m/C VHS, DVD.** Val Kilmer, Gabe Jarret, Jon(athan) Gries, Michelle Meyrink, William Atherton, Patti D'Arbanville, Severn Darden, Robert Prescott, Deborah Foreman, Ed Lauter, Tommy Swerdlow, Dean Devlin; ***D:*** Martha Coolidge; ***W:*** Peter Torokvei, Neal Israel, Pat Proft; ***M:*** Thomas Newman.

The Real Glory **1939** After the U.S. capture of the Philippine islands during the Spanish-American war, an uprising of Moro tribesmen spreads terror. After most of the islands are evacuated only a small group of Army officers is left to lead the Filipino soldiers against the rebels. Cooper plays the heroic doctor, who is not afraid to fight, especially when he comes to the rescue of the beseiged Army fort. Great action sequences and particularly good performances by Cooper and Niven. **95m/B VHS.** Gary Cooper, David Niven, Andrea Leeds, Reginald Owen, Broderick Crawford, Kay Johnson, Russell Hicks, Vladimir Sokoloff, Rudy Robles, Tetsu Komai, Roy Gordon, Henry Kolker, Soledad Jiminez; ***D:*** Henry Hathaway; ***W:*** Robert Presnell Sr., Jo Swerling; ***C:*** Rudolph Mate; ***M:*** Alfred Newman.

The Real Howard Spitz ½ **1998 (PG)** Cranky has-been detective turned writer Spitz (Grammer) finds unlikely success with a children's book about a crime-solving cow, despite the fact that Howard hates kids. But even he can't resist 8-year-old Samantha's (Tessier) pleas to help her find her missing father. Amusing and Grammer even dresses in a cow costume. **93m/C VHS.** Kelsey Grammer, Amanda Donohoe, Genevieve Tessier, Cathy Lee Crosby; ***D:*** Vadim Jean; ***W:*** Jurgen Wolff; ***C:*** Glen MacPherson; ***M:*** John Murphy. **VIDEO**

Real Life **1979 (R)** Writer/comedian Brooks's first feature sags in places, but holds its own as a vehicle for his peculiar talent. Brooks plays a pompous director whose ambition is to make a documentary of a "typical" American family. Good, intelligent comedy. **99m/C VHS, DVD.** Charles Grodin, Frances Lee McCain, Albert Brooks; ***D:*** Albert Brooks; ***W:*** Monica Johnson, Harry Shearer, Albert Brooks; ***C:*** Eric Saarinen; ***M:*** Mort Lindsey.

The Real Macaw **1998 (G)** Mac (voiced by Goodman) is a 150-year-old parrot who lives with Benjamin Girdis (Robards), who is forced into a retirement home because of serious debt. Mac just happens to know where a pirate treasure is hidden and he's willing to share the info with Ben's grandson, Sam (Croft) and the two set off for the South Pacific. **92m/C VHS.** *AU* Jason Robards Jr., Jamie Croft, Deborra-Lee Furness; ***D:*** Mario Andreacchio; ***W:*** Bruce Hancock; ***C:*** David Foreman; ***M:*** Bill Conti; ***V:*** John Goodman. **VIDEO**

The Real McCoy ½ **1993 (PG-13)** Generally awful crime-caper film about female bank robber Karen McCoy (Basinger). Just out of prison, all Karen wants to do is go straight and raise her young son but her plans are thwarted by former associates who kidnap the child to force her into one last heist. Kilmer is the small-time thief, with a crush on Karen, who tries to help her out. Dumb, slow-moving story with a vapid performance by Basinger. **104m/C VHS, DVD.** Kim Basinger, Val Kilmer, Terence Stamp, Zach English, Gailard Sartain; ***D:*** Russell Mulcahy; ***W:*** William Davies, William Osborne; ***C:*** Denis Crossan; ***M:*** Brad Fiedel.

Real Men ½ **1987 (PG-13)** The junior Belushi brother is a spy forced to recruit ordinary guy Ritter to help him negotiate with aliens to save the world. Bizarre premise shows promise, but spy spoof doesn't fire on all comedic pistons. Nice try. **86m/C VHS, DVD.** James Belushi, John Ritter, Barbara Barrie; ***D:*** Dennis Feldman; ***C:*** John A. Alonzo; ***M:*** Miles Goodman.

The Real Thing *Livers Ain't Cheap* **1997 (R)** Ex-con Rupert (Russo) is trying the straight and narrow while his kid brother James (Buzzotta) continues to be a bad guy. But when James is shot, Rupert gets together with some criminal buddies to pull off a New Year's Eve heist to raise the money needed for James' care. This one's kind of dull until the ending shoot-out. **89m/C VHS.** James Russo, Jeremy Piven, Rod Steiger, Esai Morales, Gary Busey, Emily Lloyd, Dave Buzzotta, Ashley Laurence, Fabrizio Bentivoglio, Robert LaSardo; ***D:*** James Merendino; ***W:*** James Merendino; ***C:*** Greg Littlewood; ***M:*** Peter Leinheiser. **VIDEO**

Real Time **2008 (R)** Andy (Baruchel) is a whiny, chronic screw-up and compulsive gambler who's upset his creditors for the last time. They send thoughtful Aussie hit man Reuben (Quaid) to take care of him but Reuben allows Andy one last hour to settle his affairs. **78m/C DVD.** *CA* Jay Baruchel, Randy Quaid, Jayne (Jane) Eastwood, Jeff Pustil, Ella Chan; ***D:*** Randel Cole; ***W:*** Randel Cole; ***C:*** Rudolf Blahacek; ***M:*** Jim Guthrie.

Real Time: Siege at Lucas Street Market **2000** Deals with an armed robbery at a convenience store, which escalates into a hostage situation. What makes "Real Time" unique is that the story is played out through in-store security video, police-car cameras, and TV news footage. While this approach is interesting, it also depersonalizes the action, deflating the drama. At times, it feels like an extended episode of "Cops." On DVD, every scene can be viewed from a second angle, giving the movie the extra kick that it needs. Unfortunately, the inventiveness behind the camera never matches the on-screen action. **72m/C DVD.** Michael Cornelison, Chadrick Hoch, Tom Keane, Carol German, Sandy Grillet; ***D:*** Max

Allan Collins; *W:* Max Allan Collins; *C:* Phillip W. Dingeldein.

Real Women Have Curves 𝒱𝒱𝒱 **2002 (PG-13)** Coming-of-age comedy marks the debut of Ferrara as the young, headstrong and slightly plump Mexican-American Ana, who has decided to attend college despite her overbearing mother Carmen (Ontiveros), who's decided that Ana would be better off married with children. Ana's plans are put on hold when she has to help her sister Estela (Oliu) meet deadlines in a dress factory. While featuring such themes as the body image of larger women, work in a sweatshop and the rigid roles assigned to ethnic youngsters by their elders, the film manages to avoid cliches and preachiness. **93m/C VHS, DVD.** *US* America Ferrera, Lupe Ontiveros, Ingrid Oliu, George Lopez, Soledad St. Hilaire, Brian Sites, Jorge Cerera Jr.; *D:* Patricia Cardoso; *W:* George LaVoo, Josefina Lopez; *C:* Jim Denault; *M:* Hector Pereira.

A Real Young Girl 𝒱 **1975** Breillat's explicit film was never commercially released—being too weird even for French cinema (at least at the time). It deals with the budding sexuality of the teenaged Alice (Alexandra) during her summer vacation as she becomes infatuated with Jim (Keller), a hunky laborer at her father's saw mill. Based on the director's novel "Le Soupirail" ("The Air Duct"). In French with subtitles. **93m/C VHS, DVD.** *FR* Charlotta Alexandra, Hiram Keller, Rita Meiden, Bruno Balp, Shirley Stoler; *D:* Catherine Breillat; *W:* Catherine Breillat; *C:* Pierre Fattori; *M:* Mort Shuman.

Reality Bites 𝒱𝒱 ½ **1994 (PG-13)** Humorous look at four recent college grads living, working, and slacking in Houston. Script by newcomer Childress is at its best when highlighting the trends: 7-Eleven Big Gulps, tacky '70s memorabilia, and games revolving around episodes of old TV shows like "Good Times," to name a few. Definite appeal for those in their early 20s, but anyone over 25 may encounter a "Generation X-er" gap, a noticeable problem since "Reality" claims to speak for the entire twenty-something generation. Decent directorial debut for Stiller; good cast, particularly Garofalo, in her film debut. **99m/C VHS, DVD.** Winona Ryder, Ethan Hawke, Ben Stiller, Janeane Garofalo, Steve Zahn, Swoosie Kurtz, Joe Don Baker, John Mahoney; ***Cameos:*** David Pirner, Anne Meara, Jeanne Tripplehorn, Karen Duffy, Evan Dando; *D:* Ben Stiller; *W:* Helen Childress; *C:* Emmanuel Lubezki; *M:* Karl Wallinger.

Really Weird Tales 𝒱𝒱 ½ **1986** Several SCTV alumni highlight this three-story movie, which is science fiction with a satirical edge. **85m/C VHS.** John Candy, Martin Short, Joe Flaherty, Catherine O'Hara, Olivia D'Abo, Sheila McCarthy, David McIlwraith; *D:* John Blanchard, Paul Lynch, Don McBrearty.

Reap the Wild Wind 𝒱𝒱 ½ **1942** DeMille epic about salvagers off the Georgia coast in the 1840s featuring Wayne as the captain and Massey and a giant squid as the villains. Good cast, lesser story, fine underwater photography. **123m/C VHS, DVD.** Ray Milland, John Wayne, Paulette Goddard, Raymond Massey, Robert Preston, Lynne Overman, Susan Hayward, Charles Bickford, Walter Hampden, Louise Beavers, Martha O'Driscoll, Elisabeth Risdon, Hedda Hopper, Raymond Hatton, Barbara Britton; *D:* Cecil B. DeMille; *W:* Charles Bennett, Jesse Lasky Jr., Alan LeMay; *C:* Victor Milner; *M:* Victor Young.

The Reaper 𝒱𝒱 **1997 (R)** A crime writer's most famous novel seems to be the basis for a copycat serial killer. Since the author is nearby the scene of every crime as well, he becomes the prime suspect. The investigating detective asks for his help but if the killer stays true to the plot, she's likely to become the next victim. **97m/C VHS, DVD.** *CA* Chris Sarandon, Catherine Mary Stewart, Vlasta Vrana, Joanna Noyes; *D:* John Bradshaw; *W:* Matt Dorff; *C:* Bruce Chun. **TV**

The Reaping 𝒱 ½ **2007 (R)** Southern gothic revisits the 10 plagues from the book of Exodus that are being felt in the Louisiana bayou town of Haven. Having lost her own faith, professor Katherine Winter (Swank), now a professional debunker of alleged miracles and religious phenomena, is called in to offer scientific explanations. Of course, she can't. CGI's decent, Swank's stoic, but the story is so much familiar hooey (and not very scary). **98m/C DVD, Blu-ray Disc, HD DVD.** *US* Hilary Swank, David Morrissey, Idris Elba, AnnaSophia Robb, William Ragsdale, Hilary Swank, David Morrissey, Idris Elba, AnnaSophia Robb, Stephen Rea; *D:* Stephen Hopkins, Stephen Hopkins; *W:* Carey Hayes, Chad Hayes, Carey Hayes, Chad Hayes; *C:* Peter Levy, Peter Levy; *M:* John (Gianni) Frizzell, John Frizzell.

Rear Window 𝒱𝒱𝒱𝒱 **1954** A newspaper photographer with a broken leg (Stewart) passes the time recuperating by observing his neighbors through the window. When he sees what he believes to be a murder, he decides to solve the crime himself. With help from his beautiful girlfriend and his nurse, he tries to catch the murderer without getting killed himself. Top-drawer Hitchcock blends exquisite suspense with occasional on-target laughs. Based on the story by Cornell Woolrich. **112m/C VHS, DVD.** James Stewart, Grace Kelly, Thelma Ritter, Wendell Corey, Raymond Burr, Judith Evelyn; *D:* Alfred Hitchcock; *W:* John Michael Hayes; *C:* Robert Burks; *M:* Franz Waxman. AFI '98: Top 100, Natl. Film Reg. '97.

Rear Window 𝒱𝒱 ½ **1998** Reeve stars as paralyzed architect Jason Kemp, whose wheelchair-bound existence has brought out the voyeur in the man. Kemp becomes convinced one of his neighbors is a murderer and has gotten rid of his drunken wife. Now all he needs to do is convince his friend and fellow architect, Claudia (Hannah), to help him prove his theory to skeptical police detective Moore (Forster). Oh, and keep the murderer from discovering just what Kemp knows. Reeve's first acting role since his own 1995 accident. **89m/C VHS.** Christopher Reeve, Daryl Hannah, Robert Forster, Ruben Santiago-Hudson, Anne Twomey, Allison Mackie, Ritchie Coster; *D:* Jeff Bleckner; *W:* Larry Gross, Eric Overmyer; *C:* Ken Kelsch; *M:* David Shire. **TV**

A Reason to Believe 𝒱𝒱 **1995 (R)** Campus date rape drama filmed at writer/director Tirola's alma mater, Miami University. Charlotte (Smith) goes to her boyfriend Wesley's (Quinn) big frat party, even though he's away and asked her not to. She drinks and flirts (a lot) with his best friend Jim (Underwood) and eventually leaves to collapse in a stupor on Wesley's bed. Jim follows and rapes her, though he'll tell his buddies Charlotte was a willing participant, which Wesley angrily believes. Meanwhile, the traumatized Charlotte is taken up by Linda (Emelin), the leader of the student feminist organization who wants the fraternities disbanded. Somewhat preachy and predicatable. **109m/C VHS, DVD.** Allison Smith, Jay Underwood, Daniel Quinn, Georgia Emelin, Obba Babatunde; *D:* Douglas Tirola; *W:* Douglas Tirola; *C:* Sarah Cawley.

Reason to Die 𝒱 **1990 (R)** Bounty hunter uses his own girlfriend as a decoy to trap a psychotic prostitute killer. **86m/C VHS.** Liam Cundill, Wings Hauser, Anneline Kriel, Arnold Vosloo; *D:* Tim Spring.

A Reason to Live, a Reason to Die 𝒱𝒱 *Massacre at Fort Holman; Una Ragione Per Vivere e Una Per Morire* **1973** A bland Italian-French-German-Spanish western in which a group of condemned men attempt to take a Confederate fort. **90m/C VHS, DVD.** James Coburn, Telly Savalas, Bud Spencer, Guy Mairesse; *D:* Tonino Valerii.

Rebecca 𝒱𝒱𝒱𝒱 **1940** Based on Daphne Du Maurier's best-selling novel about a young unsophisticated girl who marries a moody and prominent country gentleman haunted by the memory of his first wife. Fontaine and Olivier turn in fine performances as the unlikely couple. Suspenseful and surprising. Hitchcock's first American film and only Best Picture Oscar. **130m/B VHS, DVD.** Joan Fontaine, Laurence Olivier, Judith Anderson, George Sanders, Nigel Bruce, Florence Bates, Gladys Cooper, Reginald Denny, Leo G. Carroll, Sir C. Aubrey Smith, Melville Cooper; *D:* Alfred Hitchcock; *W:* Joan Harrison, Robert Sherwood; *C:* George Barnes; *M:* Franz Waxman. Oscars '40: B&W Cinematog., Picture.

Rebecca 𝒱𝒱𝒱 **1997** Daphne du Maurier's tale of marriage and jealousy makes its second TV incarnation. Worldly widower Maxim de Winter (Dance) takes his nameless, shy young bride (Fox) back to Manderley, the family estate. There she must compete with the ghost of the first Mrs. de Winter—the glamorous Rebecca—family secrets, and obsessive housekeeper, Mrs. Danvers (Rigg). The 1980 TV version (with Jeremy Brett as Maxim) starred Joanna David in the title role, coincidentally newcomer Fox's mother. **240m/C VHS, DVD.** *GB* Emilia Fox, Charles Dance, Diana Rigg, Faye Dunaway, Geraldine James, Jonathan Cake; *D:* Jim O'Brien; *W:* Arthur Hopcraft; *C:* Rex Maidment. **TV**

Rebecca of Sunnybrook Farm 𝒱𝒱 **1917** The original film version of the tale about an orphan who spreads sunshine and good cheer to all those around her. Silent with organ score. Based on the popular novel by Kate Douglas Wiggin; remade with Shirley Temple in 1938. **77m/B VHS.** Mary Pickford, Eugene O'Brien, Marjorie Daw, Helen Jerome Eddy; *D:* Marshall Neilan; *M:* Gaylord Carter.

Rebecca of Sunnybrook Farm 𝒱𝒱 ½ **1938** Temple becomes a radio star over her aunt's objections in this bouncy musical that has nothing to do with the famous Kate Douglas Wiggin novel. Temple sings a medley of her hits, and dances the finale with Bill "Bojangles" Robinson. ♫ On the Good Ship Lollipop/When I'm With You/Animal Crackers medley; Crackly Corn Flakes; Alone With You; Happy Ending; Au Revoir; An Old Straw Hat; Come and Get Your Happiness; Parade of the Wooden Soldiers. **80m/B VHS, DVD.** Shirley Temple, Randolph Scott, Jack Haley, Phyllis Brooks, Gloria Stuart, Slim Summerville, Bill Robinson, Helen Westley, William Demarest; *D:* Allan Dwan; *C:* Arthur C. Miller.

Rebel 𝒱 ½ *No Place to Hide* **1970 (PG)** Mumbling student radical must decide between his love for a country girl and his loyalty to an underground terrorist organization. Notable (or not) for display of early Stallone. **80m/C VHS.** Sylvester Stallone, Anthony Page, Vickie Lancaster, Rebecca Grimes; *D:* Robert Allen Schnitzer; *W:* Robert Allen Schnitzer, Larry Beinhart.

Rebel 𝒱 ½ **1985 (R)** A U.S. Marine falls in love with a Sydney nightclub singer and goes AWOL during WWII. Stylish but empty and badly cast. **93m/C VHS.** *AU* Matt Dillon, Debbie Byrne, Bryan Brown, Bill Hunter, Ray Barrett; *D:* Michael Jenkins.

The Rebel 𝒱𝒱𝒱 *Dong Mau Anh Hung* **2008** In 1920's French Colonial Vietnam, a government agent is trying to stop a rebellion caused by the injustices of his masters. Feeling sympathy for the rebel leader's daughter, he sets her free, becoming a wanted man himself. Low budget actioner looks spectacular, and as one of the few Vietnamese martial arts films, it's a treat for fans looking for something beyond kung fu. **103m/C DVD.** *VT* Dustin Nguyen, Stephane Gauger, Johnny Nguyen, Thanh Van Ngo, David Minetti, Thang Nguyen; *D:* Truc 'Charlie' Nguyen; *W:* Truc 'Charlie' Nguyen, Johnny Nguyen, Dominic Pereira; *C:* Dominic Pereira; *M:* Christopher Wong. **VIDEO**

Rebel High 𝒱 ½ **1988 (R)** Hijinks occur at a high school where youngsters study guerilla warfare and teachers wear bulletproof vests. **92m/C VHS.** Harvey Berger, Stu Trivax, Larry Gimple, Shawn Goldwater; *D:* Harry Jacobs.

Rebel Love 𝒱 **1985** Love grows between a northern widow and a Confederate spy. In better hands it might have been a good story. Here, it's overwrought and embarrassing historical melodrama. **84m/C VHS.** Terence Knox, Jamie Rose, Fred Ryan; *D:* Milton Bagby Jr.; *W:* Milton Bagby Jr.

Rebel Rousers 𝒱𝒱 **1969** A motorcycle gang wreaks havoc in a small town where a drag-race is being held to see who will get the pregnant girlfriend of Dern's high-school buddy as the prize. Young Nicholson in striped pants steals the show. **81m/C VHS, DVD.** Jack Nicholson, Cameron Mitchell, Diane Ladd, Bruce Dern, Harry Dean Stanton; *D:* Martin B. Cohen; *W:* Martin B. Cohen, Abe Polsky, Michael Kars; *C:* Laszlo Kovacs, Glen R. Smith; *M:* William Loose.

Rebel Run 𝒱 *Bolt* **1994 (R)** Biker Grieco moves west in order to escape his violent past but is then drawn into a rumble with arch-rival Ironside. **93m/C VHS, DVD.** Richard Grieco, Sean Young, Michael Ironside; *D:* Henri Colline; *W:* Henri Colline; *C:* Gerald Wolfe; *M:* Chris Squire. **VIDEO**

The Rebel Set 𝒱𝒱 ½ *Beatsville* **1959** The owner of a beat generation coffeehouse plans an armed robbery with the help of some buddies. Genuinely suspenseful, competently directed. **72m/B VHS, DVD.** Gregg (Hunter) Palmer, Kathleen Crowley, Edward Platt, John Lupton, Ned Glass, Don Sullivan, Vicki Dougan, I. Stanford Jolley; *D:* Gene Fowler Jr.; *W:* Bernard Girard, Louis Vittes; *C:* Karl Struss; *M:* Paul Dunlap.

Rebel Storm 𝒱 **1990 (R)** A group of freedom fighters team up to rescue America from the totalitarian rulers that are in charge in A.D. 2099. **99m/C VHS.** Zach Galligan, Wayne Crawford, June Chadwick, Rod McCary, John Rhys-Davies, Elizabeth Kiefer; *D:* Francis Schaeffer.

Rebel Vixens WOOF! *The Scavengers* **1969** Even though the war is over, ex-confederate soldiers continue looting and raping, until a brothel-full of prostitutes concoct a plan that has a lot to do with softcore sex. **94m/C VHS, DVD.** Maria Lease, Roda Spain, Jonathan Bliss, Michael Divoka, Wes Bishop, Bruce (Kemp) Kimball; *D:* Lee Frost; *W:* Robert W. Cresse; *C:* Robert Maxwell; *M:* Lee Frost, Robert W. Cresse.

Rebel without a Cause 𝒱𝒱𝒱𝒱 **1955** James Dean's most memorable screen appearance. In the second of his three films (following "East of Eden"), he plays troubled teen Jim Stark, who's alienated from both his parents and peers. He befriends outcasts Judy (Wood) and Plato (Mineo) in a police station and together they find a common ground. Many memorable scenes, including the "chickie run" between Jim and black leather-jacketed Buzz (Allen). Superb young stars carry this in-the-gut story of adolescence. All three leads met with real-life tragic ends. **111m/C VHS, DVD.** James Dean, Natalie Wood, Sal Mineo, Jim Backus, Nick Adams, Dennis Hopper, Ann Doran, William Hopper, Rochelle Hudson, Corey Allen, Edward Platt; *D:* Nicholas Ray; *W:* Irving Shulman, Stewart Stern; *C:* Ernest Haller; *M:* Leonard Rosenman. AFI '98: Top 100, Natl. Film Reg. '90.

The Rebels 𝒱𝒱 **1979** In the sequel to the TV miniseries "The Bastard," Philip Kent (Stevens) continues his Revolutionary War battle on the side of American independence. He is assisted by Southerner Judson Fletcher (Johnson) in thwarting an assassination attempt on George Washington. In addition to Bosley's Ben Franklin, "The Rebels" offers Backus as John Hancock. Followed by "The Seekers"; based on the novel by John Jakes. **190m/C VHS.** Andrew Stevens, Don Johnson, Doug McClure, Jim Backus, Richard Basehart, Joan Blondell, Tom Bosley, Rory Calhoun, MacDonald Carey, Kim Cattrall, William Daniels, Anne Francis, Peter Graves, Pamela Hensley, Wilfrid Hyde-White, Nehemiah Persoff, William (Bill) Smith, Forrest Tucker, Tanya Tucker, Robert Vaughn, Deborah Richter; *D:* Russ Mayberry; *Nar:* William Conrad. **TV**

Rebels of the Neon God 𝒱𝒱 *Cing shao nian nuo jha; Teenage Norcha* **1992 (R)** Hsiao Kang (Kang-sheng Lee) has a lot of anger issues, and argues a lot with his parents. His mother believes he's the reincarnation of a minor Chinese god called Norcha. His father's taxi is vandalized by a pair of petty thieves who live a fairly pitiful life. Hsiao becomes obsessed with them and hunts them down to gain revenge for the slight. Viewers who are unfamiliar with Chinese mythology (or at least the deity in question) will miss much of the subtext of this film. **106m/C DVD.** *HK TW* Kang-sheng Lee, Yi-ching Lu, Tien Miao, Yu-Wen Wang, Chao-jung Chen, Chang-bin Jen; *D:* Ming-liang Tsai; *W:* Ming-liang Tsai; *C:* Pen-jung Liao; *M:* Shu-Jun Huang.

Rebirth of Mothra 𝒱𝒱 *Mosura; Mothra* **1996** A lumber company working in the Hokkaido rain forest accidently unearths the secret lair of Desghidorah, a three-headed monster, who teams up with the evil Belvera. It's up to twins More and Mona to call on

Mothra to rescue the earth from their demonic powers. **106m/C VHS, DVD.** *JP* Megumi Kobayashi, Sayaka Yamaguchi, Hano Aki; ***D:*** Okihiro Yoneda.

Rebirth of Mothra 2 ₰ 1/2 *Mosura 2; Mothra 2* **1997** Garbage-eating monster Degehra and mutant marine lifeforms threaten Earth's oceans and it's up to Mothra and a magical treasure hidden in the underwater city of Nelikani to save the day. **103m/C VHS, DVD.** *JP* Megumi Kobayashi, Sayaka Yamaguchi, Hano Aki; ***D:*** Kunio Miyoshi; ***W:*** Masumi Suetani.

Reborn ₰₰ *Renacer* **1981** A faith healer and a talent scout hire actors to be cured of fake ailments. **105m/C VHS.** *SP* Dennis Hopper, Michael Moriarty, Francisco Rabal, Antonella Murgia; ***D:*** Bigas Luna; ***W:*** Bigas Luna; ***C:*** Juan Ruiz-Anchia; ***M:*** Scott Harper.

Rebound ₰₰ **2005 (PG)** Dumped as a college basketball coach after his usual sideline histrionics lead to the demise of an opposing team's avian mascot, Roy McCormick (Lawrence) decides to accept his old middle school's offer to take over their woeful team. From there, the tired, warm and fuzzy sports tale plays out as hard-nosed Roy becomes a softy while fashioning the losing squad into winners and finding love, too. Lawrence curbs his customary foul language for this family flick. **103m/C DVD.** *US* Martin Lawrence, Steven Anthony Lawrence, Horatio Sanz, Megan Mullally, Patrick Warburton, Wendy Raquel Robinson, Breckin Meyer, Fred Stoller, Oren Williams, Eddy Martin, Alia Shawkat, Steven Christopher Parker, Logan McElroy, Gus Hoffman, Tara Correa, Amy Bruckner; ***D:*** Steve Carr; ***W:*** Jon Lucas, Scott Moore; ***C:*** Glen MacPherson; ***M:*** Teddy Castellucci, Spring Aspers.

Rebound: The Legend of Earl "The Goat" Manigault ₰₰ 1/2 **1996 (R)** Earl "The Goat" Manigault (Cheadle) was a '60s Harlem playground basketball phenom who was taken under the wing of parks director Holcomb Rucker (Whitaker), who tries to steer the young man towards college and a career in the NBA. Unfortunately, the easily influenced Manigault also attracts the attention of local drug dealer Legrand (Beach) and when Manigault's life starts to fall apart, he drops out of college and turns to heroin, eventually winding up in prison. Since this is an inspirational true story, Manigault does turn his life around to found his own basketball tournament in Harlem. **111m/C VHS, DVD.** Don Cheadle, Michael Beach, James Earl Jones, Loretta Devine, Glynn Turman, Clarence Williams III, Ronny Cox, Eriq La Salle, Monica Calhoun, Tamara Tunie, Forest Whitaker; ***Cameos:*** Kareem Abdul-Jabbar; ***D:*** Eriq La Salle; ***W:*** Larry Golin, Alan Swyer; ***C:*** Alar Kivilo; ***M:*** Kevin Eubanks. **CABLE**

Rec ₰₰ **2007 (R)** Spanish horror with TV reporter Angela and her cameraman doing a segment on firemen for a reality show. Angela goes with them on a rescue call at an apartment house and it's zombie time as a flesh-eating disease infects the inhabitants, the building is sealed off, and Angela continues reporting as the camera keeps recording. Spanish with subtitles. Remade as 2008's "Quarantine." **80m/C DVD.** Manuela Velasco, Ferran Terraza, David Vert, Carlos Vicente, Carlos Lesarte; ***D:*** Jaume Balaguero, Paco Plaza; ***W:*** Jaume Balaguero, Paco Plaza, Luis Berdejo; ***C:*** Pablo Rosso; ***M:*** Carlos Ann.

The Reception ₰₰ 1/2 **2005** Jeannette, a wealthy, alcoholic Frenchwoman, lives with African American gay painter, Martin, under sadly codependent circumstances. Sierra, her estranged daughter, shows up one winter day with her new husband, coincidently also African American, to collect on a promised inheritance. What unfolds is a scenario of shifting alliances that shadow the entanglement of racial prejudice, sexual orientation and addiction. Shooting in eight days on a $5,000 budget, Young presents an admirable effort. **75m/C DVD.** *US* Pamela Stewart, Darien Sills-Evans, Wayne Lamont Sims, Margaret Burkwit; ***D:*** John G. Young; ***W:*** John G. Young; ***C:*** Derek Wiesehahn.

Recipe for Disaster ₰₰ 1/2 **2003 (G)** The kids have to save the day when Mom (Warren) and Dad (Larroquette) get lost on their way home on the eve of their new restaurant's grand opening. Snooty owners of a neigboring restaurant complicate matters by trying to sabotage the kids' efforts at keeping the opening night crowd happy. Fun, well-paced family flick should go over well with the young 'uns, especially with the "kids-save-the-day" theme and pop culture references. Younger children may be scared by the villains, who are a little more mean than they have to be for this type of movie. **92m/C VHS, DVD.** Lesley Ann Warren, John Larroquette, Michelle Brookhurst, Margo Harshman, Devon Werkheiser, Bill Dawes, Andrew James Allen, Melissa Peterman; ***D:*** Harvey Frost; ***W:*** William Propp; ***C:*** Christopher Pearson; ***M:*** William Goodrum. **TV**

Recipe for Revenge ₰ 1/2 **1998** Caterer Carly (Huffman) is cooking dinner for her friend Sophie (Hallier) so Sophie can impress her new beau. She shockingly witnesses Sophie's murder by Dr. Winnifield (Bernsen) but he gives the cops a solid alibi and convinces them that Carly is unstable. However, Detective Jack Brannigan (Carter) gives Carly the benefit of the doubt, especially when her own life is threatened. From the Harlequin Romance Series; adapted from the Kristin Gabriel novel. **95m/C DVD.** *CA* Alex Carter, Corbin Bernsen, Lori Hallier, Hugh Thompson, Kim Huffman; ***D:*** Stacey Stewart Curtis; ***W:*** Peter Lauterman, Jennifer Black; ***C:*** Michael Storey; ***M:*** John McCarthy. **TV**

Reckless ₰₰ **1935** Harlow, in a role originally intended for Joan Crawford, plays a showgirl coveted by a millionaire and secretly loved by her manager. Unfortunately, Harlow couldn't pull off the acting (much less the singing and dancing), although the plot strangely paralleled her own life. Songs include "Reckless," "Ev'rything's Been Done Before," "Trocadero," "Hear What My Heart Is Saying" and "Cyclone." **96m/B VHS.** Jean Harlow, William Powell, Franchot Tone, May Robson, Ted Healy, Nat Pendleton, Rosalind Russell; ***D:*** Victor Fleming; ***C:*** George J. Folsey.

Reckless ₰₰ 1/2 **1984 (R)** A sincere movie about a "good" girl who finds herself obsessed with a rebel from the wrong side of her small town. Differs from 1950s' wrong-side-of-the-track flicks only in updated sex and music. **93m/C VHS.** Aidan Quinn, Daryl Hannah, Kenneth McMillan, Cliff DeYoung, Lois Smith, Adam Baldwin, Dan Hedaya, Jennifer Grey, Pamela Springsteen; ***D:*** James Foley; ***W:*** Chris Columbus; ***C:*** Michael Ballhaus; ***M:*** Thomas Newman.

Reckless ₰₰ **1995 (PG-13)** Rachel (Farrow) thinks she has a happy marriage and family but her husband (Goldwyn) informs her that he's hired a hit man to kill her. This startling revelation sends her on a 15-year journey in which she meets many other people who are not what they seem. Rene and Lucas go for an ultra-stylized fable theme, exploring Rachel's (and America's) aversion to dealing with the world as it really is. Quirky characters and situations are at turns amusing and annoying. Adapted by Lucas from his own play. **91m/C VHS.** Mia Farrow, Scott Glenn, Mary-Louise Parker, Tony Goldwyn, Stephen Dorff, Eileen Brennan, Giancarlo Esposito, Deborah Rush; ***D:*** Norman Rene; ***W:*** Craig Lucas; ***C:*** Frederick Elmes; ***M:*** Stephen Endelman.

Reckless ₰₰₰ **1997** British TV production's a combo of farce, romance, and drama that finds young doctor Owen Springer (Green) returning to Manchester to look after his feisty-but-ailing father (Bradley). He has a chance meeting with a beautiful middle-aged woman on the train, and then Anna Fairley (Annis) turns out to be his job interviewer. Reckless Owen falls impulsively in love—before learning Anna is also the wife of his new boss, Dr. Richard Crane (Kitchen). This doesn't deter Owen, and when he learns Crane is having an affair, Owen arranges for Anna to discover her husband's infidelity. Naturally, this leads to Owen and Anna hitting the sheets and things get very complicated. **312m/C VHS, DVD.** *GB* Robson Green, Francesca Annis, Michael Kitchen, David Bradley, Julian Rhind-Tutt, Daniela Nardini, Margery Mason, Conor Mullen; ***D:*** David Richards, Sarah Harding; ***W:*** Paul Abbott. **TV**

Reckless Disregard ₰ 1/2 **1984** A doctor whose career is ruined by a news report accusing him of involvement in a drug scam sues the newscaster. Based on Dan Rather's "60 Minutes" story and ensuing lawsuit. **92m/C VHS.** Leslie Nielsen, Tess Harper, Ronny Cox, Kate Lynch; ***D:*** Harvey Hart. **TV**

Reckless Kelly ₰₰ 1/2 **1993 (PG)** Australian bank robber, pop culture hero, and local video store owner Kelly is upset when his gang's island retreat is about to be sold to a Japanese conglomerate, unless he can come up with a higher offer. So he prepares for a last-ditch defense of his home. Slapstick homage to legendary Australian outlaw Ned Kelly. **81m/C VHS.** *AU* Yahoo Serious, Hugo Weaving, Melora Hardin, Alexei Sayle, Bob Maza, Kathleen Freeman; ***D:*** Yahoo Serious; ***W:*** Yahoo Serious.

Reckless Moment ₰₰₰ **1949** A mother commits murder to save her daughter from an unsavory older man, and finds herself blackmailed. Gripping, intense thriller. **82m/B VHS, DVD.** James Mason, Joan Bennett, Geraldine Brooks; ***D:*** Max Ophuls; ***C:*** Burnett Guffey.

Reckless: The Sequel ₰₰₰ **1998** A year later, Anna (Annis) has divorced philandering Richard (Kitchen) and is living with Owen (Green). The duo decide, somewhat impulsively, to marry, which drives the chronically jealous Richard into a frenzy and he vows to use any dirty trick necessary to break them up. But family interference and Anna and Owen's own doubts may do the job for him. **120m/C VHS.** *GB* Robson Green, Francesca Annis, Michael Kitchen, David Bradley; ***D:*** David Richards; ***W:*** Paul Abbott; ***C:*** Lawrence Jones; ***M:*** Hal Lindes. **TV**

The Reckless Way ₰ 1/2 **1936** A young woman struggles for her big break into the movies. **72m/B VHS.** Marion (Marian) Nixon, Kane Richmond, Inez Courtney, Malcolm McGregor, Harry Harvey, Arthur Howard; ***D:*** Bernard B. Ray.

The Reckoning ₰₰₰ **2003 (R)** Nicholas (Bettany) is a 14th century priest on the run from charges of adultery who joins a band of actors led by the bored Martin (Dafoe). They come upon a town where deaf-mute woman healer Martha is on trial for a boy's murder. The actors decide to perform a play based on the murder (which is a wild departure from performing only Bible-based stories), and find out that other boys have been killed recently in a similar manner. Nicholas becomes obsessed with proving Maria's innocence and uncovering the secrets of the village's "protector" Lord De Guise (Cassel). McGuigan makes excellent use of a deft story and exciting but not intrusive visuals to build suspense for the plot, and development for the interesting character development. Bettany and Dafoe shine. **110m/C VHS, DVD.** Paul Bettany, Sarah Henderson, Thomas (Tom) Hardy, Willem Dafoe, Gina McKee, Stuart Wells, Vincent Cassel, Elvira Minguez, Ewen Bremner; ***D:*** Paul McGuigan; ***W:*** Mark Mills; ***C:*** Peter Sova; ***M:*** Adrian Lee, Mark Mancina.

Recoil ₰₰ **1953** Tense Brit crime drama. Jean Talbot (Sellars) witnesses her father's murder by Nicholas Conway (Moore) during a jewel heist. Nicholas works for gangster Farnborough (Benson), but decides to keep some of the gems for himself although Farnborough soon learns of his thievery. Nicholas also uses his unwitting brother Michael (Underdown) as his alibi. So Jean decides to secretly help the police to get evidence to arrest Nicholas, never expecting that both brothers will fall for her. **79m/B DVD.** *GB* Elizabeth Sellars, Kieron Moore, Edward Underdown, Martin Benson, John Horsley, Robert Reglan, Ian Fleming; ***D:*** John Gilling; ***W:*** John Gilling; ***C:*** Monty Berman; ***M:*** Stanley Black.

Recoil ₰₰ **1997 (R)** L.A. detective Ray Morgan (Daniels) gets in trouble with a crime family and they target his wife and family. So, for Ray it's a kill or be killed situation. **96m/C VHS, DVD.** Gary Daniels, Gregory McKinney; ***D:*** Art Camacho; ***W:*** Richard Preston Jr.; ***C:*** Ken Blakey; ***M:*** Tim Wynn. **VIDEO**

Reconstruction ₰₰ **2003** One evening, photographer Alex (Kaas) dumps girlfriend Simone (Bonnevie) to follow blonde Swedish beauty Aimee (also Bonnevie) through the streets of Copenhagen. She's married to an older author, August (Henriksson), who also serves as narrator. Or is August actually narrating the plot of the book he's currently writing? After a one-night stand, Alex's world is completely changed-no one recognizes him and all he can think to do is find Aimee again. Danish and Swedish with subtitles. **91m/C** Nikolaj Lie Kaas, Maria Bonnevie, Krister Henriksson; ***D:*** Christoffer Boe; ***W:*** Mogens Rukov, Christoffer Boe; ***C:*** Manuel Alberto Claro; ***M:*** Thomas Knak.

Record of a Tenement Gentleman ₰₰ **1947** An abandoned child picks a grumpy, middle-aged widow as a surrogate mother and she and her crazy neighbors come to love the little boy. Surprise ending. Japanese with subtitles. **72m/B VHS.** *JP* Choko Iida, Hohi Aoki, Chishu Ryu, Eitaro (Sakae, Saka Ozawa) Ozawa; ***D:*** Yasujiro Ozu.

Recount ₰₰ 1/2 **2008** Just in time for the 2008 presidential election is a retelling of the 2000 election battle and the infamous hanging chads in Florida. Dern is scary as Florida's secretary of state Katherine Harris and Spacey is effective as Al Gore's chief of staff Ron Klain. Actual broadcast news clips are interspersed to show that the entire farcical situation (which was ultimately decided in Florida's Supreme Court) was really that insane. **116m/C DVD.** Kevin Spacey, Laura Dern, Tom Wilkinson, Bob Balaban, Ed Begley Jr., John Hurt, Denis Leary, Bruce McGill, Bruce Altman, Mitch Pileggi; ***D:*** Jay Roach; ***W:*** Danny Strong; ***C:*** Jim Denault; ***M:*** Dave Grusin. **CABLE**

The Recruit ₰₰ 1/2 **2003 (PG-13)** In a role that should mean leading-man superstardom, Farrell is James Clayton, an MIT graduate on his way to the good life when he's approached by CIA "talent scout" Walter Burke (Pacino). Walter says James has the goods to be a top agent and entices him with the promise of info on his dad, who died in a plane crash in 1990. Once on the Farm, the CIA training center, James learns the ropes and meets beautiful fellow spook-wannabe Layla (Moynahan), who may not be what she appears. Pacino is in full-on scenery-chewing mode, which helps when the plot heads into spy cliche territory near the end. Farrell and Moynihan provide good chemistry, which helps pick up the slack when Pacino's not around. **105m/C VHS, DVD, Blu-ray Disc.** *US* Al Pacino, Colin Farrell, Bridget Moynahan, Gabriel Macht, Karl Pruner, Eugene Lipinski; ***D:*** Roger Donaldson; ***W:*** Roger Towne, Mitch Glazer, Kurt Wimmer; ***C:*** Stuart Dryburgh; ***M:*** Klaus Badelt.

Recruits ₰ **1986 (R)** Sophomoric gagfest about an inept Californian police force. Typical '80s-style mindless "comedy": dumb gags ensue from perfunctory premise. **81m/C VHS.** Alan Deveau, Annie McAuley, Lolita (David) Davidovich; ***D:*** Rafal Zielinski.

The Rector's Wife ₰₰ **1994** Anna Bouverie (Duncan) has spent 20 years as a clergyman's wife, scrimping and slaving to raise a family, serve God, and work for the parish on limited means. Tired of the financial strain she takes a job at a local supermarket causing additional disturbances in her already shaky marriage, disapproval of the parish, and the sudden interest of three different men. Based on the novel by Joanna Trollope; on four cassettes. **208m/C VHS, DVD.** *GB* Lindsay Duncan, Jonathan Coy, Simon Fenton, Lucy Dawson, Joyce Redman, Stephen (Dillon) Dillane, Ronald Pickup, Miles Anderson, Prunella Scales, Jonathan Cecil; ***D:*** Giles Foster; ***W:*** Hugh Whitemore; ***M:*** Richard Hartley.

Red ₰₰₰ **1991** Lawrence Tierney stars in this dramatization of the "Red Tapes," a series of taped phone pranks in which a witty young man phones a bar and asks to speak to "Mike Hunt," "Al Koholic," "Stu, last name, Pid," "Ben Dover," "Pepe, last name, Roney," etc., the prank made most commercially famous by Bart Simpson. Tierney plays Red, the bartender who receives these calls; he responds to the prankster with mounting incoherent expletives and unfavorable references to the caller's mother. Written and directed by "Film Threat" magazine founder Chris Gore. **35m/B VHS, DVD.** Lawrence Tierney, Scott Spiegel, Carmen Von Daacke, Ron Zwang, J. J. Hommel; ***D:*** Christian Gore; ***W:*** Christian Gore; ***C:*** David E. Williams.

Red ₰₰ **2008 (R)** Small-town widowed veteran Avery Ludow's best friend is his dog Red. When three teens kill the dog for kicks,

Avery first turns to the law and when that fails, he decides to mete out his own justice. Based on the Jack Ketchum novel. **98m/C DVD.** Brian Cox, Tom Sizemore, Noel Fisher, Kyle Gallner, Shiloh Fernandez, Robert Englund, Amanda Plummer, Kim Dickens, Richard Riehle; ***D:*** Lucky McKee, Trygve Allister Diesen; ***W:*** Stephen Susco; ***C:*** Harald Gunnar Paalgard; ***M:*** Soren Hyldgaard.

Red Alert ♪♪ 1/2 **1977** Good, suspenseful, topical made for televison thriller about nuclear meltdown. Will Minneapolis be saved? Usually Barbeau's name in the credits is a red alert, but this one is better than most. **95m/C VHS.** William Devane, Ralph Waite, Michael Brandon, Adrienne Barbeau; ***D:*** William (Billy) Hale. **TV**

The Red and the Black ♪♪♪ *Le Rouge et le Noir* **1957** A big budgeted French adaptation of the classic Stendhal novel. A young man from the country seeks success, first in the Church and later in the employment and seduction of the gentry. In French with English subtitles. **134m/B VHS.** *FR* Danielle Darrieux, Gerard Philipe; ***D:*** Claude Autant-Lara.

The Red and the White ♪♪♪ *Csillagosok, Katonak* **1968** Epic war drama about the civil war between the Red Army and the non-communist Whites in Russia in 1918. Told from the perspective of Hungarians who fought alongside the Reds. Little dialogue. In Hungarian with English subtitles. **92m/B VHS, DVD.** *HU* Tibor Molnar, Andras Kozak, Josef Madaras; ***D:*** Miklos Jancso; ***W:*** Miklos Jancso, Gyula Hernadi, Giorgi Mdivani; ***C:*** Tamas Somlo.

The Red Badge of Courage ♪♪♪ 1/2 **1951** John Huston's adaptation of the Stephen Crane Civil War novel is inspired, despite cutting room hatchet job by the studio. A classic study of courage and cowardice. Sweeping battle scenes and intense personal drama. **69m/B VHS, DVD.** Audie Murphy, Bill Mauldin, Douglas Dick, Royal Dano, Andy Devine, Arthur Hunnicutt, John Dierkes, Richard Easton, Tim Durant; ***D:*** John Huston; ***W:*** Albert Band; ***C:*** Harold Rosson; ***M:*** Bronislau Kaper.

Red Ball Express ♪♪ 1/2 **1952** Fast-paced action highlights this WWII story about the transportation corp that must supply the gas, food, and ammunition necessary for General Patton's tank assault on Nazi-held Paris. Tough company leader Lt. Campbell (Chandler) must get the cooperation of both his first sergeant (Nicol), who holds a pre-war grudge, and a black corporal (Poitier), who believes he's the target of racism, in order to accomplish his mission. **84m/B VHS.** Jeff Chandler, Alex Nicol, Sidney Poitier, Charles Drake, Hugh O'Brian, Jack Kelly, Judith Braun, Jacqueline Duval; ***D:*** Budd Boetticher; ***W:*** John Michael Hayes; ***C:*** Maury Gertsman.

The Red Balloon ♪♪♪ 1/2 **1956** The story of Pascal, a lonely French boy who befriends a wondrous red balloon which follows him everywhere. Lovely, finely done parable of childhood, imagination and friendship. **34m/C VHS, DVD.** *FR* Pascal Lamorisse; ***D:*** Albert Lamorisse. Oscars '56: Orig. Screenplay.

Red Barry **1938** A comic strip detective tries to track down criminals who threaten the world. Thirteen episodes on one videotape. **?m/B VHS.** Buster Crabbe, Frances Robinson, Edna Sedgwick, Cyril Delevanti, Frank Lackteen; ***D:*** Ford Beebe, Alan James.

Red Beard ♪♪♪ *Akahige* **1965** An uncharacteristic drama by Kurosawa, about a young doctor in Japan awakening to life and love under the tutelage of a compassionate old physician. Highly acclaimed; in Japanese with English subtitles. **185m/B VHS, DVD.** *JP* Toshiro Mifune, Yuzo Kayama, Yoshio Tsuchiya, Reiko Dan; ***D:*** Akira Kurosawa.

Red Blooded 2 ♪♪ *Hot Blooded* **1996** Sequel to "Red Blooded American Girl" finds all-American college boy Trent Colbert (Winters) peacefully driving home when he's forced to rescue tough babe Miya (Salin) from rape and murder at a truck stop. Miya informs him that her violent trucker father is behind the attack and the duo are chased by 18-wheelers and the cops. However, this doesn't prevent Miya from finding the time to introduce innocent Trent to cheap motels, hot sex, and black leather. **86m/C VHS.** *CA* Kari Salin, Kristoffer Ryan Winters, Burt Young, David Keith, Nicholas Pasco; ***D:*** David Blyth; ***W:*** Nicolas Stiliadis; ***C:*** Edgar Egger; ***M:*** Paul Zaza.

Red Blooded American Girl ♪ **1990 (R)** A scientist develops a virus that turns people into vampires. Those infected hit the streets in search of blood. **89m/C VHS, DVD.** *CA* Christopher Plummer, Andrew Stevens, Heather Thomas, Kim Coates; ***D:*** David Blyth.

Red Cherry ♪♪ *Hong Ying Tao* **1995 (PG-13)** Based on a true story that focuses on the aftermath of the Chinese revolution in 1940 and the horrors of war. The orphaned Chuchu (Ke-Yu) and Luo (Xiaoli) are sent to a Russian school outside of Moscow and begin to settle into their new lives. But their precarious happiness is shattered when German troops invade Russia during WWII. Chinese and Russian with subtitles. **120m/C VHS, DVD.** *CH* Guo Ke-Yu, Xu Xiaoli; ***D:*** Ye Ying.

Red Cliff ♪♪♪ *Chi Bi* **2008 (R)** Woo's epic historical action-drama is based on a 208 A.D. battle foretelling the end of the 400-year-old Han dynasty. General Coa Coa (Zhang) gets the emperor's permission to crush the rebel warlords Bei Liu (You) and Quan Sun (Chang). Bei's military strategist Zhuge (Kaneshiro) knows they must ally with their rival to survive and parlays with Quan's advisor Zhao (Leung Chiu-wai) to mount a campaign against Coa Coa's numerically-superior forces. In Chinese-speaking territories, Woo released a two-part, four-and-a-half-hour version. The subtitled "Red Cliff" will be followed by "The Battle of Red Cliff." Mandarin with subtitles. **131m/C DVD.** *CH JP KN TW US* Tony Leung Chiu-Wai, Takeshi Kaneshiro, Fengyi Zhang, Chang Chen, You Yong, Vicki Zhao, Jun Hu, Shido Nakamura, Ning Wang, Chiling Lin; ***D:*** John Woo; ***W:*** John Woo, Khan Chan, Cheng Kuo, Heyu Sheng; ***C:*** Lu Yue, Li Zhang; ***M:*** Taro Iwashiro.

Red Corner ♪♪ 1/2 **1997 (R)** Wrong-man scenario features Gere as an American entertainment lawyer on business in China who is framed for murdering a Chinese model he spent the night with. A colossal bummer, Jack's beautiful, court-appointed attorney (Ling) explains the Chinese legal process: "If you plead not guilty, you will be shot within a week and the cost of the bullet will be charged to your family." Gruesome jail scenes involving excrement and a hell-on-wheels female judge don't help his case much, either. Pic suffers from some of the usual cliches but is aided by an acclaimed performance by Ling and one of the better recent Gere turns. Beijing was recreated on the DreamWorks studio lot in California. **118m/C VHS, DVD.** Richard Gere, Bai Ling, Byron Mann, Bradley Whitford, Peter Donat, Robert Stanton, Tsai Chin, James Hong, Tzi Ma, Richard Venture; ***D:*** Jon Avnet; ***W:*** Robert King; ***C:*** Karl Walter Lindenlaub; ***M:*** Thomas Newman.

Red Dawn ♪ 1/2 **1984 (PG-13)** During WWIII, Russian invaders overrun America's heartland and take over the country. Eight small-town teenagers, calling themselves the Wolverines, hide out in the rugged countryside and fight the Russians. Swayze and Grey met again in "Dirty Dancing." **114m/C VHS, DVD.** Patrick Swayze, C. Thomas Howell, Harry Dean Stanton, Powers Boothe, Lea Thompson, Charlie Sheen, Ben Johnson, Jennifer Grey, Ron O'Neal, William (Bill) Smith; ***D:*** John Milius; ***W:*** John Milius, Kevin Reynolds; ***C:*** Ric Waite; ***M:*** Basil Poledouris.

Red Desert ♪ **1950** The Pecos Kid is sent to track down the theft of a shipment of gold. **60m/B VHS, DVD.** Jack Holt, Donald (Don "Red") Barry, Tom Neal, Joseph Crehan, Tom London, Margia Dean, Byron Foulger, John Cason; ***D:*** Charles Marquis Warren, Ford Beebe; ***W:*** Ford Beebe, Daniel Ullman, Ron Ormond; ***C:*** Ernest Miller.

The Red Desert ♪♪♪ *Il Deserto Rosso* **1964** Antonioni's first color film, depicting an alienated Italian wife who searches for meaning in the industrial lunar landscape of northern Italy, to no avail. Highly acclaimed, and a masterpiece of visual form. In Italian with English subtitles. **120m/C VHS, DVD.** *IT* Monica Vitti, Richard Harris, Carlos Chionetti; ***D:*** Michelangelo Antonioni; ***W:*** Michelangelo Antonioni, Tonino Guerra; ***C:*** Carlo Di Palma; ***M:*** Giovanni Fusco. Venice Film Fest. '64: Film.

Red Desert Penitentiary **1983** A spoof of movie-making featuring caricatures of industry-types. **104m/C VHS.** James Michael Taylor, Cathryn Bissell, Will Rose; ***D:*** George Sluizer.

Red Dirt ♪ 1/2 **1999** Teenaged cousins Griffith (Montgomery) and Emily (Palladino) spent their days lazying around their Mississippi town, sometimes in the company of their crazy Aunt Summer (Black). That is until the older Lee (Goggins) rents a cottage from the family and Griffith has some confused reactions to the newcomer, much to Emily's dismay. Unfortunately, this coming of age story is tritely told with laborious performances. **111m/C VHS, DVD.** Dan Montgomery Jr., Walton Goggins, Aleksa Palladino, Karen Black, Glenn Shadix, John Mese, Peg O'Keef; ***D:*** Tag Purvis; ***W:*** Tag Purvis; ***C:*** Ted Cohen; ***M:*** Nathan Barr.

Red Doors ♪♪ 1/2 **2005 (R)** A cultural-clash family comedy. A red door is supposed to mean good luck in Chinese culture but it doesn't seem to be working for the Chinese-American Wong family. Dad Ed (Ma) is in a suicidal funk since his retirement, wondering what happened to the three little girls he and his wife (Shen) raised, since they are so absorbed in their own lives and seem oblivious to his pain. Ed suddenly decides to immure himself in a monastery and then the family really gets crazy. **90m/C DVD.** Tzi Ma, Jacqueline Kim, Freda Foh Shen, Sebastian Stan, Kathy Shao-Lin Lee, Elaine Kao, Jayce Bartok, Rossif Sutherland, Mia Riverton; ***D:*** Georgia Lee; ***W:*** Georgia Lee; ***C:*** Zeus Morand; ***M:*** Robert Miller.

Red Dragon ♪♪ 1/2 **2002 (R)** Prequel to "Silence of the Lambs" with filmdom's favorite man-eater pitted against former FBI agent Will Graham (Norton). Graham needs the charismatic cannibal to crack the case of a serial killer (Fiennes) dubbed the Tooth Fairy. Graham and Lecter have a history, as Graham helped to put Hannibal away after coming this close to becoming a plate-mate of some fava beans. As usual, Hopkins steals the show. While the plot is better than in "Hannibal," with good character development and a rare look at Lecter before incarceration, the franchise may have reached its expiration date. Second movie telling of Harris's first Lecter novel, following 1986's "Manhunter." **124m/C VHS, DVD, HD DVD.** *US* Anthony Hopkins, Edward Norton, Ralph Fiennes, Harvey Keitel, Emily Watson, Mary-Louise Parker, Philip Seymour Hoffman, Anthony Heald, Bill Duke, Stanley Anderson, Ken Leung, Azura Skye, Frankie Faison, Tyler Patrick Jones, Tom Verica, Dwier Brown, Conrad Palmisano, Mary Beth Hurt, Frank Whaley; ***D:*** Brett Ratner; ***W:*** Ted Tally; ***C:*** Dante Spinotti; ***M:*** Danny Elfman; ***V:*** Ellen Burstyn, Alex D. Linz.

Red Dust ♪♪♪ **1932** Dennis Carson (Gable) is the overseer of a rubber plantation in Indochina who causes all kinds of trouble when he falls in love with an engineer's (Raymond) new wife, Barbara (Astor). Harlow's the tart Vantine also interested in the big lug. Filled with free-spirited humor and skillfully directed; remarkably original. Remade in 1940 as "Congo Maisie" and Gable did his own remake with 1954's "Mogambo," co-starring Ava Gardner and Grace Kelly. **83m/B VHS.** Tully Marshall, Clark Gable, Jean Harlow, Mary Astor, Gene Raymond, Donald Crisp; ***D:*** Victor Fleming; ***W:*** John Lee Mahin. Natl. Film Reg. '06.

The Red Dwarf ♪♪ **1999 (R)** Somewhat mawkish melodramatic fantasy about love-starved dwarf Lucien Lhotte (Thual) who works as a law clerk. He's summoned by aging opera singer Countess Paola Bendoni (Ekberg), who wants a divorce. The duo become improbable lovers, although he's humiliated (and vengeful) when the Countess returns to her husband. Lucien is also innocently loved by young circus acrobat, Isis (Gauzy), and her profession leads Lucien to an unexpected escape from his restricted world. French with subtitles. **101m/B VHS, DVD.** *FR* Anita Ekberg, Jean-Yves Thual, Dyna Gauzy, Arno Chevrier; ***D:*** Yvan Le Moine; ***W:*** Yvan Le Moine; ***C:*** Danny Elsen; ***M:*** Alexei Shelegin, Daniel Brandt.

Red Earth ♪♪ *Voros Fold* **1982** A satire about life under Hungarian socialism. Szanto is a bauxite mixer whose pigs have rooted out high quality bauxite from his backyard. Only the local bauxite prospectors don't want to believe in luck (and pigs) and credit, instead, careful planning. When Szanto's village is turned into a vast open mine, he's blamed. In Hungarian with English subtitles. **105m/C VHS.** *HU* Imre Nemeth, Sandor Kocsis, Kalman Toronyi, Ferenc Togh, Vilmos Gadori; ***D:*** Laszlo Vitezy; ***W:*** Istvan Darday.

Red Ensign ♪ 1/2 **1934** A low-budget British quota quickie that served as a good apprenticeship for director Powell. Obsessed ship builder David Barr (Banks) is determined to launch a new kind of vessel and save the industry despite the company's board of directors refusing financing. When Barr runs out of his own money, he's caught forging a check and goes to jail while fiancee June (Goodner) stands loyally by, waiting for his release and eventual triumph. **69m/B DVD.** *GB* Leslie Banks, Carol Goodner, Frank Vosper, Alfred Drayton, Donald Calthrop, Allan Jeayes; ***D:*** Michael Powell; ***W:*** Michael Powell, Jerome Jackson; ***C:*** Leslie Rowson.

Red Eye ♪♪♪ **2005 (PG-13)** Lisa (McAdams) deftly handles calls, questions, and customers at the front desk of the high-end Miami hotel where she works. Jackson Rippner (Murphy) appears to be like any other guest—until he shows up next to her on her red-eye flight. Turns out she's his target, and Lisa's dad Joe (Cox) and an official of the Department of Homeland Security are at stake if Lisa doesn't figure out how to deal with the high-flying madman. Psychological thrills and chills at high-altitude don't disappoint, with McAdams scoring as a feisty and crafty heroine. **85m/C DVD, UMD.** *US* Rachel McAdams, Cillian Murphy, Brian Cox, Kyle Gallner, Brittany Oaks, Jack Scalia; ***Cameos:*** Wes Craven, Carl Ellsworth; ***D:*** Wes Craven; ***W:*** Carl Ellsworth, Dan Foos; ***C:*** Robert Yeoman; ***M:*** Marco Beltrami.

Red Firecracker, Green Firecracker ♪♪ 1/2 *Paoda Shuang Deng* **1993 (R)** Set in northern China before the 1911 revolution, this gorgeous saga focuses on the fortunes of the Cai family. The family, whose wealth depends on their fireworks business, has no male heirs and is headed by daughter Chun Zhi (Jing). To assume this lofty position, Chun Zhi must dress like a man and is forbidden to marry but that doesn't stop her from falling in love with bold young travelling artist Nie Bao (Gang). The household is thrown into a frenzy by their affair and it's decided that all Chun Zhi's potential suitors must undergo a firecracker ritual in order to win her hand. Mandarin Chinese with subtitles. **111m/C VHS, DVD.** *HK CH* Ning Jing, Wu Gang, Zhao Xiaorui, Gai Yang; ***D:*** He Ping; ***W:*** Da Ying; ***C:*** Yang Lun.

Red Flag: The Ultimate Game ♪♪ 1/2 **1981** Pilots rival for success in battle simulation training with terrible consequences. Fine performances cover plot weaknesses. Well-written dialogue. **100m/C VHS.** Barry Bostwick, William Devane, Joan Van Ark, Fred McCarren, Debra Feuer, George Coe, Linden Chiles, Arlen Dean Snyder; ***D:*** Don Taylor. **TV**

The Red Fury ♪♪ **1984** Young Indian boy struggles to overcome prejudice and caring for his horse shows him the way. Good family viewing. **105m/C VHS, DVD.** William Jordan, Katherine (Kathy) Cannon; ***D:*** Lyman Dayton; ***W:*** Joe Elliott; ***C:*** Arch Bryant; ***M:*** Merrill Jenson.

Red Garters ♪♪ 1/2 **1954** A musical parody of old-time westerns which doesn't quite come off. Mitchell palys the cowpoke who comes to town to avenge the death of his brother with Clooney as the saloon singer who uses him to make boyfriend Carson jealous. The adequate songs include "Red Garters," "Man and Woman," "A Dime and a Dollar," and "Vaquero." **91m/C VHS, DVD.** Guy Mitchell, Rosemary Clooney, Jack Carson, Gene Barry, Pat(ricia) Crowley, Joanne Gilbert, Frank Faylen, Reginald Owen, Buddy Ebsen; ***D:*** George Marshall; ***W:*** Michael Fessier; ***M:*** Jay Livingston, Ray Evans.

The Red Half-Breed ♪ 1/2 **1970** A lonely half-breed Indian, wrongly accused of murder, discovers the real killer while running from the law. **103m/C VHS.** Daniel Pilon, Genevieve Deloir; ***D:*** Gilles Carle.

Red Headed Stranger 🦴 ½ **1987 (R)** Willie Nelson vehicle based on his 1975 album. Nelson is a gun-totin' preacher who kills his wife and is led to salvation by a good farm woman. But honestly: Morgan Fairchild as Willie Nelson's wife? Please. **108m/C VHS.** Willie Nelson, Katharine Ross, Morgan Fairchild; ***D:*** William D. Wittliff; ***W:*** William D. Wittliff.

Red Headed Woman 🦴🦴🦴 **1932** Unscrupulous Lil (sultry Harlow in a red wig) vamps her boss Bill Legendre (Morris) into divorcing his wife (Hyams) and marrying her. But then she gets bored and takes up with the wealthier Gaerste (Stephenson), while keeping his chauffeur Albert (Boyer) on the side. Bill finally divorces her and Lil heads for Europe (with Albert) to play among the nobility. Audiences loved the scandalous material, but the Hays Office objected to the fact that the immoral woman goes unpunished. Boyer took the small but notable role in his third American film because of studio MGM's prestige and it made his career. **79m/B VHS, DVD.** Jean Harlow, Chester Morris, Lewis Stone, Leila Hyams, Una Merkel, Henry Stephenson, May Robson, Charles Boyer, Harvey Clark; ***D:*** Jack Conway; ***W:*** Anita Loos; ***C:*** Harold Rosson.

Red Heat 🦴 ½ **1985** Blair is a tourist in East Germany mistakenly arrested and sent to a rough women's prison. Her fiance tries to free her. Meanwhile, she has to deal with tough-lady fellow jail bird Kristel. Familiar and marginal. **104m/C VHS.** Linda Blair, Sylvia Kristel, Sue Kiel, William Ostrander; ***D:*** Robert Collector.

Red Heat 🦴🦴 **1988 (R)** Two cops—one from the Soviet Union, one from Chicago—team up to catch the Eastern Bloc's biggest drug czar. Lots of action, but at times it seems too similar to Hill's earlier hit "48 Hours." Film claims to be the first major U.S. production shot in Red Square, Moscow. **106m/C VHS, DVD.** Arnold Schwarzenegger, James Belushi, Peter Boyle, Ed O'Ross, Laurence Fishburne, Gina Gershon, Richard Bright; ***D:*** Walter Hill; ***W:*** Walter Hill; ***C:*** Matthew F. Leonetti; ***M:*** James Horner.

Red Hot 🦴🦴 ½ **1995 (PG)** Alexi (Getty), a young Russian classical musician, is secretly smuggled American rock 'n' roll music (it's 1959) by his uncle. He immediately decides to form a band and plots the first underground Soviet rock concert. Too bad girlfriend Valentina's (Gugino) dad is a disapproving highly ranked Communist Party official and the KGB are giving Alexi the evil eye. **95m/C VHS.** Balthazar Getty, Carla Gugino, Donald Sutherland, Armin Mueller-Stahl; ***D:*** Paul Haggis; ***W:*** Paul Haggis, Michael Maurer.

The Red House 🦴🦴🦴 **1947** Robinson plays a crippled farmer who, after his daughter brings home a suitor, attempts to keep everyone from a mysterious red house located on his property. Madness and murder prevail. Strange film noir about tangled relationships and unsuccessful attempts to bury the horrid past. Based on the novel by George Agnew Chamberlain. **100m/B VHS, DVD.** Edward G. Robinson, Lon (Bud) McCallister, Judith Anderson, Allene Roberts, Rory Calhoun, Ona Munson, Julie London, Harry Shannon, Arthur Space, Walter Sande, Pat Flaherty; ***D:*** Delmer Daves; ***W:*** Delmer Daves; ***C:*** Bert Glennon; ***M:*** Miklos Rozsa.

The Red Inn 🦴🦴 *L'Auberge Rouge* **1951** Yes, it is a comedy. An innkeeper and his wife have a second career involving the robbery and murder of stagecoach travellers staying at their isolated inn. And it's up to a monk (Fernandel) to stop the mayhem. French with subtitles. Yves Montand sings on the soundtrack. **95m/B VHS.** *FR* Fernandel, Francoise Rosay, Julien Carette, Gregoire Aslan, Marie-Claire Olivia, Lud Germain; ***D:*** Claude Autant-Lara; ***W:*** Jean Aurenche, Pierre Bost; ***C:*** Andre Bac; ***M:*** Rene Cloerec.

Red Kimono 🦴🦴 **1925** Exploitative silent melodrama about a young woman ditched by her husband. She becomes a prostitute, but is redeemed by true love. Interesting slice of its period. **95m/B VHS.** Tyrone Power Sr., Priscilla Boner, Nellie Bly Baker, Mary Carr; ***D:*** Walter Lang.

Red King, White Knight 🦴🦴 ½ **1989 (R)** An assassin tries to kill Mikhail Gorbachev during superpower peace talks. Ex-spook Skerritt returns to duty to thwart him. Better than most "topical" thrillers. **106m/C VHS.** Tom Skerritt, Max von Sydow, Helen Mirren; ***D:*** Geoff Murphy. **CABLE**

Red Kiss 🦴🦴🦴 *Rouge Baiser* **1985** In 1952 Paris, Nadia, a 15-year-old French-Jewish Stalinist of Polish descent falls in love with Stephane, an older, apolitical photographer. She's torn between love and politics; he's worried (rightly) about her being underage; and to make matters more complicated, her Polish mother has been reunited with her first love and Nadia's family may be split apart. The sensual Valandrey is a real find in her difficult coming-of-age role. In French with English subtitles. **110m/C VHS.** *FR* Charlotte Valandrey, Lambert Wilson, Marthe Keller, Gunter Lamprecht, Laurent Terzieff; ***D:*** Vera Belmont; ***W:*** Vera Belmont, David Milhaud, Guy Konopnicki; ***C:*** Ramon Suarez; ***M:*** Jean-Marie Senia. Berlin Intl. Film Fest. '86: Actress (Valandrey).

Red Letters 🦴🦴 **2000 (R)** The plot veers wildly but the performances are worth a watch. Widowed college prof Dennis Burke (Coyote) has an eye for the ladies. He flirts with the dean's sexy young daughter, Gretchen (Balk), and is so taken with the imprisoned Lydia (Kinski) that he helps her escape so she can prove her innocence in a murder conviction. Not a good idea. **102m/C VHS, DVD.** Peter Coyote, Nastassja Kinski, Fairuza Balk, Jeremy Piven, Ernie Hudson, Udo Kier; ***D:*** Bradley Battersby; ***W:*** Bradley Battersby, Tom Hughes; ***C:*** Steven Fierberg. **VIDEO**

The Red Light Sting 🦴 **1984** A Justice Department rookie (Bridges) and a call girl (Fawcett) reluctantly team up to con the Mafia in order to convict a San Francisco rackets czar. Goes down easy, but also easily forgotten or skipped. **96m/C VHS.** Farrah Fawcett, Beau Bridges, Harold Gould, Paul Burke, Sunny Johnson; ***D:*** Rod Holcomb.

Red Lights 🦴🦴🦴 *Feux rouges* **2004** Troubled couple embarks on a trip to pick up their children from camp. They argue viciously as hubby repeatedly stops to drink along the way. When the missus finally ditches him and takes the train, the volatile and smashed husband continues by car but picks up an ominous stranger. Story of a man who regains his dignity through surprisingly violent twist of fate. Terrific French thriller in the vein of Hitchcock, with solid acting and direction. **106m/C VHS, DVD.** *FR* Jean-Pierre Darroussin, Carole Bouquet, Jean-Pierre Gros; ***D:*** Cedric Kahn; ***W:*** Cedric Kahn; ***C:*** Patrick Blossier; ***M:*** Arvo Part.

Red Lights Ahead 🦴🦴 **1936** Grandpa tries to save the day as he fights against spiritualism and crystal balls to help a friend prove that he is not running a scam. **63m/C VHS, DVD.** Andy Clyde, Paula Stone, Roger Imhof, Frank "Junior" Coghlan, Ben Alexander, Matty Kemp, Sam Flint, Addison "Jack" Randall, Lucile Gleason, Dann Doran; ***D:*** Roland D. Reed.

The Red Lily 🦴🦴 **1924** Marise La Noue (Bennett) is a poor cobbler's daughter while her beau, Jean Leonnec (Navarro), is the son of the mayor. To be together they must run away to Paris and Jean promises to meet Marise at the train station so they can be married. But fate intervenes and they are destined to spend years apart with Marise forced into prostitution while Jean falls in with thief Bo-Bo (Beery). When they finally reunite, both are bitterly disappointed although Marise still comes to Jean's aid when the police come after him. **80m/B DVD.** Enid Bennett, Ramon Novarro, Wallace Beery, Frank Currier, Mitchell Lewis; ***D:*** Fred Niblo Jr.; ***W:*** Bess Meredyth; ***C:*** Victor Milner.

Red Line 🦴 ½ **1996 (R)** Stock-car racer Jim (McQueen) loses his sponsorship, turns to petty crime to settle his debts, and winds up in trouble with the mob when he hooks up with a couple of hoods to steal some diamonds. **102m/C VHS, DVD.** Chad McQueen, Michael Madsen, Corey Feldman, Jan-Michael Vincent, Roxana Zal, Dom DeLuise, Julie Strain, Robert Z'Dar; ***D:*** John Sjogren; ***W:*** John Sjogren, Scott Ziehl, Rolfe Kanefsky; ***C:*** Kevin McKay; ***M:*** Craig Carothers, Junior Walker.

Red Line 7000 🦴🦴 **1965** High stakes auto racers drive fast cars and date women. Excellent racing footage in otherwise routine four-wheel fest. **110m/C VHS, DVD.** James Caan, Laura Devon, Gail Hire, Charlene Holt, Marianna Hill, George Takei; ***D:*** Howard Hawks; ***C:*** Milton Krasner.

Red Lion 🦴🦴 ½ *Akage* **1969** A bumbling horse-tender in feudal Japan impersonates a military officer to impress his family, only to be swept into leading a liberating revolution. In Japanese with English subtitles. **115m/C VHS, DVD.** *JP* Toshiro Mifune, Shima Iwashita; ***D:*** Kihachi Okamoto.

Red Meat 🦴🦴 ½ **1998** Stefan (Slattery) and Chris (Mailer) are the last remaining members of the Red Meat Club, buddies who get together for macho posturing over steak dinners. This time, they run into Victor (Frain) who's been out of touch. Stefan and Chris boast of their dating games (which are shown in flashback) and then it's Victor's turn to regale them with a lurid sexual saga. Only Victor's story involves his tender relationship with a dying woman, Ruth (Boyle). **94m/C VHS, DVD.** James Frain, John Slattery, Steven Mailer, Lara Flynn Boyle, Jennifer Grey, Traci Lind; ***D:*** Allison Burnett; ***W:*** Allison Burnett; ***C:*** Charlie Lieberman.

The Red Menace **WOOF!** **1949** Anti-Communist propaganda, made with unknown actors in documentary style has little to offer today's viewers other than unintentional laughs. Picture the Commies offering naive Americans money and sex to join the party, and you'll have an idea of the intellectual talent that went into this one. **87m/B VHS.** Robert Rockwell, Hannelore Axman, Shepard Menken, Betty Lou Gerson, Barbara Fuller; ***D:*** R.G. Springsteen.

Red Mercury 🦴 ½ **2005 (R)** Three Islamic terrorists, planning a London bombing, have their cover blown and flee into a Greek restaurant, taking hostages. They're still carrying materials for their dirty bomb but the tension heightens as time passes and the bombers are forced to interact with their hostages as the police and government officials await the outcome. Rather too talky and obvious. **113m/C DVD.** *GB* Stockard Channing, Ron Silver, Pete Postlethwaite, Juliet Stevenson, David Bradley, Nigel Terry, Navin Chowdhry, Honeysuckle Weeks, Alex Caan, San Shella; ***D:*** Roy Battersby; ***W:*** Farrukh Dhondy; ***C:*** Colin Towns, Uday Tiwari. **VIDEO**

The Red Mill 🦴🦴 **1927** Makes good use of Davies' comedic talents as she portrays Cinderella-like Dutch barmaid Tina, who hopes that handsome newcomer Dennis (Moore) will be her Prince Charming. Instead, he falls for her friend Gretchen (Faenda), the burgomaster's daughter, who is being forced into an arranged marriage. When Tina and Dennis interfere, the burgomaster locks all three into the haunted mill of the title. Loosely based on the Victor Herbert operetta. Davies championed the hiring of a post-scandal Arbuckle as director, through he used the pseudonym "William Goodrich" for the film's release. **73m/B DVD.** Marion Davies, Owen Moore, George Siegmann, Karl (Daen) Dane, Snitz Edwards, Louise Faenda; ***D:*** Fatty Arbuckle; ***W:*** Frances Marion; ***C:*** Hendrik Sartov.

Red Nights 🦴 **1987** A country boy goes to Hollywood seeking success and finds instead corruption, decadence, and dishonesty. Excellent soundtrack by Tangerine Dream. **90m/C VHS.** Chris Parker, Jack Carter, Brian Matthews; ***D:*** Izhak Hanooka.

Red Planet 🦴🦴 ½ **2000 (PG-13)** It's 2050, Earth is dying, and the crew of the Mars-1 has been sent to the red planet to find out what went wrong with a previous colonization mission. Alas, something goes wrong with this mission, too (those pesky gamma rays), and some of the crew are forced to shuttle to the surface of Mars, where yet another mishap leaves them stranded without means of communication or escape. To make matters worse, the crew's AMEE (Autonomous Mapping Evaluation and Evasion) robot has turned nasty and intends to further endanger them and their mission. Heavy with visual effects, yet the film tries to keep the focus on the human elements. Follows the unexceptional "Mission to Mars" in exploring the big red one. **110m/C VHS, DVD.** Val Kilmer, Tom Sizemore, Carrie-Anne Moss, Benjamin Bratt, Simon Baker, Terence Stamp; ***D:*** Antony Hoffman; ***W:*** Jonathan Lemkin, Chuck Pfarrer.

Red Planet Mars 🦴🦴 **1952** Anti-communist, pro-Christianity story about scientists discovering that the Voice of Radio Free Mars belongs to God. Incoherent film overburdened with messages about politics, religion, and science was ahead of its time. Based on the play "Red Planet" by John L. Balderson and John Hoare. **87m/B VHS, DVD.** Peter Graves, Andrea King, Marvin Miller, Herbert Berghof, House Peters Jr., Vince Barnett; ***D:*** Harry Horner; ***W:*** Anthony Veiller, John Lloyd Balderston.

The Red Pony 🦴🦴🦴 **1949** A young boy escapes from his family's fighting through his love for a pet pony. Based on the novel by John Steinbeck. Timeless classic that the whole family can enjoy. **89m/C VHS, DVD.** Myrna Loy, Robert Mitchum, Peter Miles, Louis Calhern, Shepperd Strudwick, Margaret Hamilton, Beau Bridges; ***D:*** Lewis Milestone; ***C:*** Gaetano Antonio "Tony" Gaudio; ***M:*** Aaron Copland.

The Red Pony 🦴🦴🦴 **1976** Excellent TV remake of a classic 1949 adaptation of John Steinbeck. Fonda is superb as a troubled young boy's difficult father. **101m/C VHS.** Henry Fonda, Maureen O'Hara, Clint Howard, Jack Elam, Ben Johnson; ***D:*** Robert Totten. **TV**

The Red Raiders 🦴🦴 **1927** Cavalry officer Scott (Maynard) must stop young renegade Lone Wolf (Chief Yowlachie) and his braves from a confrontation with the Army over moving to a new reservation. Filmed on location in Montana, allegedly on the site of the Little Bighorn battlefield. **64m/B DVD.** Ken Maynard, Chief Yowlachie, Anne Drew, Harry Shutan, J(ohn) P(aterson) McGowan, Paul Hurst; ***D:*** Albert Rogell; ***W:*** Marion Jackson; ***C:*** Ross Fisher.

The Red Raven Kiss-Off 🦴 **1990 (R)** A seedy Hollywood detective becomes the key suspect in a movie-making murder. Based on the 1930s' Dan Turner mystery stories. **93m/C VHS.** Marc Singer, Tracy Scoggins, Nicholas Worth, Arte Johnson; ***D:*** Christopher Lewis. **VIDEO**

Red Riding Hood 🦴🦴 ½ **1988** Musical version of story of wolf who has little girl fetish. **81m/C VHS, DVD.** Isabella Rossellini, Craig T. Nelson, Rocco Sisto; ***D:*** Adam Brooks; ***W:*** Carole Lucia Satrina; ***C:*** Yuri Neyman; ***M:*** Stephen Lawrence.

Red Riding Hood 🦴 **2003 (R)** Freak-show fairytale. Jenny (Satta) is a 12-year-old American who has been abandoned in a Rome apartment by her mother. She watched her politician father get assassinated, which obviously twisted her little psyche since Jenny roams the streets handing out her own brand of vigilante justice. She's accompanied by a big bad wolf named George (Dipascasio), who could be a figment of her crazy imagination. Then Granny (Archebald) shows up to take the little darling home, but Jenny's got other plans. English and Italian with subtitles. **90m/C DVD.** *IT* Susan Satta, Kathleen Archebald, Simone K. Dipascasio, Iaon Gunn, Roberto Purvis, Marco Firini, Justine Powell; ***D:*** Giacomo Cimini; ***W:*** Ovidio G. Assonitis, Andrew Benker; ***C:*** Sergio Salvati, Roberto Benvenuti; ***M:*** Alessandro Molinari.

Red River 🦴🦴🦴🦴 **1948** The classic Hawks epic about a gruelling cattle drive and the battle of wills between father and son. Tom Dunston (Wayne), who owns a sprawling cattle empire, decides to make a difficult trek north, refusing to listen to any advice from his adopted son, Matthew Garth (Clift, in his first film). Matt is eventually forced to take over the drive from the obsessed Dunston, who swears revenge. Generally regarded as one of the best westerns ever made, with a great supporting cast headed by Brennan and Ireland, although Dru is a very nominal love interest. Restored version has eight minutes of previously edited material. Remade for TV in 1988 with James Arness and Bruce Boxleitner. **133m/B VHS, DVD.** John Wayne, Montgomery Clift, Walter Brennan, Joanne Dru, John Ireland, Noah Beery Jr., Paul Fix, Coleen Gray, Harry Carey Jr., Harry Carey Sr., Chief Yowlachie, Hank Worden; ***D:*** Howard Hawks; ***W:*** Borden Chase, Charles Schnee; ***C:***

Russell Harlan; ***M:*** Dimitri Tiomkin. Natl. Film Reg. '90.

Red River Valley *Man of the Frontier* **1936** Autry and partner Burnette go undercover to find out who's plaguing a dam construction site with explosions. Not to be confused with a 1941 Roy Rogers pic bearing the same title. **60m/B VHS, DVD.** Gene Autry, Smiley Burnette, Frances Grant, Boothe Howard, Sam Flint, George Chesebro, Charles "Blackie" King, Eugene Jackson, Frank LaRue, Lloyd Ingraham; ***D:*** B. Reeves Eason.

Red River Valley **1941** Rogers helps the local ranchers get enough money together to build a much-needed water reservoir. Only gambler Bardette cons them out of the money, until Roy comes to the rescue. **62m/B VHS.** Roy Rogers, George "Gabby" Hayes, Trevor Bardette, Sally Payne; ***D:*** Joseph Kane; ***W:*** Malcolm Stuart Boylan; ***C:*** Jack Marta.

Red Road **2006** Debut feature for Brit helmer Arnold heightens suspense but fumbles the ending. Widowed Jackie (Dickie) works for a private security firm monitoring cameras that maintain surveillance on a rough North Glasgow neighborhood. She becomes obsessed watching ex-con Clyde (Curran) and his friends, who live in the decrepit Red Road housing estate. She contrives to meet him but it turns out Jackie has specific reasons for her interest in Clyde and they aren't going to make him happy. **113m/C DVD.** *GB CZ* Tony Curran, Martin Compston, Nathalie Press, Kate Dickie, Andrew Armour; ***D:*** Andrea Arnold; ***W:*** Andrea Arnold; ***C:*** Robbie Ryan.

Red Rock Outlaw **1947** A sleazy character tries to kill his twin brother and takes his place as an honest rancher. **56m/B VHS.** Billy Dix, Bob Gilbert, Ione Nixon, Forrest Matthews, Lee White; ***D:*** Elmer Clifton; ***W:*** Elmer Clifton; ***C:*** Darlan Cunha.

Red Rock West ½ **1993 (R)** Nothing is what it seems in this stylish and entertaining film noir set in a desolate Wyoming town. Perennial loser and nice guy Michael (Cage) is headed to a job at an oil rig, but blows his chance by admitting he has a bad leg. Landing in the tiny burg of Red Rock, he's mistaken for the hit man hired by local barkeep Walsh to kill his pretty wife (Boyle). Then Boyle doubles Walsh's offer—what's a film noir boy to do? And Hopper, the real killer, strides into town. Full of twists, turns, and shades of "El Mariachi," this enjoyable, well-acted thriller is a real gem that escaped directly to cable before being rescued by a San Francisco exhibitor. **98m/C VHS, DVD.** Nicolas Cage, Dennis Hopper, Lara Flynn Boyle, J.T. Walsh, Timothy Carhart, Dan Shor, Dwight Yoakam, Bobby Joe McFadden, Craig Reay, Vance Johnson, Robert Apel, Dale Gibson, Ted Parks, Babs Bram, Robert Guajardo, Sarah Sullivan; ***D:*** John Dahl; ***W:*** John Dahl, Rick Dahl; ***C:*** Marc Reshovsky; ***M:*** William Olvis.

The Red Rope ½ **1937** A Western hero cuts his honeymoon short to track down some villains. **56m/B VHS.** Bob Steele, Lois January, Forrest Taylor, Charles "Blackie" King, Karl Hackett, Bobby Nelson; ***D:*** S. Roy Luby; ***W:*** George Plympton; ***C:*** Bert Longenecker.

Red Roses and Petrol ½ **2003 (R)** Flashbacks and home videos are used to fill in details of the life of patriarch Enda Doyle (McDowell) as his widow and estranged children reunite at his Dublin wake. Dysfunctional family revelations are all too commonplace. Based on a play by Joseph O'Connor. **97m/C DVD.** Malcolm McDowell, Olivia Tracey, Heather Jurgenson, Max Beesley, Greg Ellis, Susan Lynch, Arie Verveen, Sean Lawlor, Catherine Farrell; ***D:*** Tamar Simon Hoffs; ***W:*** Tamar Simon Hoffs, Gail Wager Stayden; ***C:*** Nancy Schreiber; ***M:*** Seth Pedowitz.

Red Salute **1935** Screwball comedy in the "It Happened One Night" tradition (only not as good) with an anti-Communist message. General's daughter Drue (Stanwyck) falls in love with a young communist. Patriotic dad tries to divert her attention by sending her on a Mexican vacation, where she meets an AWOL soldier. When the pair tries to sneak back into the U.S., he's arrested and she heads back to her leftist lover, whereupon dad releases her AWOL beau and causes more confusion. Film caused much consternation among the left-leaning intelligensia at the time of its release. **88m/B VHS.** Barbara Stanwyck, Robert Young, Hardie Albright, Ruth Donnelly, Cliff Edwards, Gordon Jones, Lester Dorr; ***D:*** Sidney Lanfield; ***W:*** Manuel Seff, Elmer Harris, Humphrey Pearson; ***C:*** Robert Planck.

Red Sands *The Stone House* **2009 (R)** In Afghanistan, a group of soldiers is dispatched to take control of a road that runs past an abandoned house. They find an ancient stone statue and destroy the relic by using it for target practice but they've released a supernatural force that proves to be deadly. **89m/C DVD.** Callum Blue, Noel Guglielmi, Shane West, Brendan Miller, Leonard Roberts, Aldis Hodge, Theo Rossi; ***D:*** Alex Turner; ***W:*** Simon Barrett; ***C:*** Sean O'Dea; ***M:*** Luke Rothschild. **VIDEO**

Red Scorpion **1989 (R)** A Soviet soldier journeys to Africa where he is to assassinate the leader of a rebel group. Will he succeed or switch allegiances? Poor acting and directing abound. **102m/C VHS, DVD, UMD.** Dolph Lundgren, M. Emmet Walsh, Al White, T.P. McKenna, Carmen Argenziano, Brion James, Regopstann; ***D:*** Joseph Zito; ***W:*** Arne Olsen, Jack Abramoff, Robert Abramoff; ***C:*** Joao Fernandes; ***M:*** Jay Chattaway.

Red Scorpion 2 ½ **1994 (R)** Another "Dirty Dozen" rip-off finds your average ethnically mixed good guys brought together by a government agency to be heroic. In this case the enemy is a neo-fascist businessman who uses skinheads to cause mayhem in minority communities. **90m/C VHS.** Matt McColm, John Savage, Jennifer Rubin, Michael Ironside, Michael Covert, Real Andrews, George Touliatos; ***D:*** Michael Kennedy; ***W:*** Troy Bolotnick, Barry Victor; ***M:*** George Blondheim.

Red Shoe Diaries **1992 (R)** After a woman's suicide her grieving lover discovers her diaries and finds out she led a secret erotic life, revolving around her shoe-salesman lover and a pair of sexy red shoes. Also available in an unrated version. **105m/C VHS, DVD.** David Duchovny, Billy Wirth, Brigitte Bako; ***D:*** Zalman King. **CABLE**

Red Shoe Diaries 2: Double Dare **1992 (R)** The erotic sequel to "Red Shoe Diaries" follows the libidinous fancies of three women. Severance begins a sexual affair with a stranger only to be torn between love and lust. Johnson gets naked to tease an office worker in the building next door. Crosby is a cop who is rejected by the man she desires—so she arrests and handcuffs him in order to play some kinky games. Also available in an unrated version. **92m/C VHS.** Joan Severance, Laura Johnson, Denise Crosby, Steven Bauer, Arnold Vosloo, David Duchovny; ***D:*** Zalman King, Tibor Takacs. **CABLE**

Red Shoe Diaries 3: Another Woman's Lipstick **1993 (R)** Another sexual anthology focusing on three stories of desire. In "Another Woman's Lipstick" Zoey finds out her husband is having an affair and follows him to his liaison—only to become intrigued with his lover herself. "Just Like That" finds the up-tight Trudie falling for two very opposite men. "Talk to Me Baby" finds Ida and her lover Bud caught up in a very obsessional relationship. Also available in an unrated version. **90m/C VHS.** Nina Siemaszko, Matt LeBlanc, Tcheky Karyo, Maryam D'Abo, Richard Tyson, Lydie Denier, Christina (Kristina) Fulton, Kevin Haley, David Duchovny; ***D:*** Ted Kotcheff, Rafael Eisenman, Zalman King; ***W:*** Zalman King, Chloe King. **CABLE**

Red Shoe Diaries 4: Auto Erotica **1993 (R)** Yet another compilation of erotic tales courtesy of the Zalman King series. The first story finds a maid finding her employer's secret chamber and uncovering a very private fantasy. The second has an architect lured by a mystery woman into a game of seduction and the third finds a couple engaged in competitive obsessions. Also available in an unrated version. **83m/C VHS.** Ally Sheedy, Scott Plank, David Duchovny, Sheryl Lee, Nicholas Chinlund; ***D:*** Zalman King. **CABLE**

Red Shoe Diaries 5: Weekend Pass **1995 (R)** Yet another erotic saga from the cable series that features a model (Barbieri) hustling a pool hustler, a bounty hunter (Stansfield) becoming captivated by her prey, and an army recruit (Pouget) whose furlough involves a sexy drifter. **85m/C VHS.** Paula Barbieri, Claire Stansfield, Ely Pouget, Francesco Quinn, Ron Marquette, Anthony Addabbo; ***D:*** Ted Kotcheff. **CABLE**

Red Shoe Diaries 6: How I Met My Husband **1995 (R)** Three more erotic vignettes from the cable series. "How I Met My Husband" finds Alice enrolling in a course on becoming a domanitrix and falling for Giuseppe, who's one of the training objects. Camille has inherited her father's vast fortune in "Naked in the Moonlight" on the condition that she take special care of his '57 Cadillac convertible—and the one mechanic allowed to work on the car. In "Midnight Bells," Claire reminisces about the mystery lover she meets on only one night of the year—New Year's Eve. **85m/C VHS.** Luigi Amodeo, Neith Hunter, Raven Snow, Carsten Norgaard, John Enos, Charlotte Lewis, David Duchovny; ***D:*** Anne Goursaud, Philippe Angers, Bernard Auroux. **CABLE**

Red Shoe Diaries 7: Burning Up **1996 (R)** Yet another trilogy of TV eroticism. "Burning Up" finds Lynn becoming obsessed with a handsome fireman, "Kidnap" features the workaholic Sara taken hostage during a bank robbery and finding out that her captor has decided to marry her, Alia is a top model in "Runway," who falls in lust with a cabby. **90m/C VHS.** Udo Kier, Ron Marquette, Jennifer Ciesar, Amber Smith, Anthony Guidera, Daniel Blasco, Alexandra Tydings, David Duchovny; ***D:*** Rafael Eisenman. **CABLE**

Red Shoe Diaries 8: Night of Abandon **1997 (R)** Three more erotic adventures from the cable series. "Night of Abandon" finds Isabelle visiting her grandma in Rio de Janeiro and indulging in Carnival. "Liar's Table" has photojournalist Corey assigned to record L.A.'s sex scene and becoming intrigued by a very expensive call girl. Married Kathryn's life changes "In the Blink of an Eye" when she meets a young boxer who's in training with her husband. **86m/C VHS.** Erika Anderson, Audie England, Daniel Leza, Ann Cockburn, Terrence Sheahan, Laurie Simpson, Julien Maurel, Brian Edwards, David Duchovny; ***D:*** Rafael Eisenman, Rene Manzor, James Gavin Bedford. **CABLE**

Red Shoe Diaries: Four on the Floor **1996** The late-night cable series continues with three more stories concerning a psychiatrist and her patient, two couples stranded on a rainy night, and the meeting of a rap star and a dancer. Contents:" The Psychiatrist," "Four on the Floor," "Emily's Dance." **85m/C DVD.** Denise Crosby, Georges Corraface, Christopher Atkins, Jsu Garcia, David Duchovny, Demetra Hampton, Rachel Palieri, Freedom Williams, Marry Morrow, Kent Masters-King; ***D:*** Rafael Eisenman, Zalman King, David Womark; ***W:*** Richard Baskin, Nellie Allard, Joelle Bentolila; ***C:*** Etienne Fauduet, Manuel Teran, Marco Mazzei; ***M:*** George S. Clinton. **CABLE**

Red Shoe Diaries: Luscious Lola ½ **2000** In these three stories, shy Mimi (Phillips) fantasizes about winning her dream guy; a sailor on shore leave winds up with more women than he can handle; and a young woman toys with men. **87m/C DVD.** Bobbie Phillips, Michael C. Bendetti, Christina (Kristina) Fulton, Perrey Reeves, Ernie Banks, John Enos, Joseph Whipp, David Duchovny, Andrew Bilgore, Heidi Mark, Michael Reilly Burke; ***D:*** Zalman King, Stephen Halbert; ***W:*** John Enos, Chloe King, Pascal Franchot, Elize D'Haene; ***C:*** Eagle Egilsson, David Stockton; ***M:*** George S. Clinton. **CABLE**

Red Shoe Diaries: Strip Poker **1996** Contains the episodes "Strip Poker," "Slow Train," "Hard Labor". **87m/C DVD.** Athena Massey, Jennifer Ciesar, Carolyn Seymour, David Duchovny, Anfisa Nezinskaya, Larisa Tipikina, Andrew Calder, Mark Suelke, Maximo Morrone; ***D:*** Zalman King, Rafael Eisenman; ***W:*** Zalman King, Patricia Louisianna Knop, Julie Marie Myatt, Elize D'Haene; ***C:*** Eagle Egilsson, Alexei Rodionov; ***M:*** George S. Clinton. **CABLE**

Red Shoe Diaries: Swimming Naked ½ **2000** The mother of all late-night cable series is still the artsiest. As such, these stories about a lifeguard, a skydiver, and a dancer are told with lots of smoke and gauzy focus. Contents: "Swimming Naked," "Jump," "Tears." **83m/C DVD.** Michael Woods, Cyia Batten, Carolyn Seymour, Arabella Holzbog, David Duchovny, Kristi Frank, Omry Reznik, Sonya Ryzy-Ryski, Todd Gordon, Daniel Ezralow; ***D:*** Zalman King, Rafael Eisenman; ***W:*** Zalman King, Melanie Finn, Chloe King, Katarina Wittich, Kathryn MacQuarrie; ***C:*** Eagle Egilsson, David Knaus; ***M:*** George S. Clinton. **CABLE**

The Red Shoes **1948** British classic about a young ballerina torn between love and success. Boris Lermontov (Walbrook) is the impresario of a ballet company who hires dancer Victoria Page (Shearer) and composer Julian Craster (Goring), giving them the chance at a new ballet inspired by the Hans Christian Andersen fairy tale. But when the endeavor becomes a major success, Boris become jealous over the closeness that develops between his proteges. Noted for the 20-minute ballet at the heart of the film and for the lavish use of Technicolor. **136m/C VHS, DVD.** *GB* Anton Walbrook, Moira Shearer, Marius Goring, Leonide Massine, Robert Helpmann, Albert Bassermann, Ludmilla Tcherina, Esmond Knight; ***D:*** Emeric Pressburger, Michael Powell; ***W:*** Emeric Pressburger, Michael Powell; ***C:*** Jack Cardiff; ***M:*** Brian Easdale. Oscars '48: Art Dir./Set Dec., Color, Orig. Dramatic Score; Golden Globes '49: Score.

The Red Shoes *Bunhongsin* **2005** Korean horror film based on a fairy tale by Hans Christian Andersen, though you wouldn't know that by watching it. Sun Jae leaves her cheating husband and moves with her daughter into an old apartment building. She finds a pair of red high heels on the subway and takes them home, not knowing they are cursed to destroy anyone they come in contact with. The race is on to discover the origin of the shoes and somehow end the curse before everyone dies. **103m/C DVD.** *KN* Hye-su Kim, Seong-su Kim, Yeon-ah Park; ***D:*** Yong-gyun Kim; ***W:*** Yong-gyun Kim, Ma Sang-Ryeol; ***M:*** Byung-woo Lee.

Red Signals **1927** Mystery criminal makes trains collide. **70m/B VHS.** Wallace MacDonald, Earl Williams, Eva Novak, J(ohn) P(aterson) McGowan, Frank Rice; ***D:*** J(ohn) P(aterson) McGowan.

The Red Sneakers ½ **2001** Reggie Reynolds (Pappion) is a high-school math whiz who figures he'll get more respect as a basketball star. He meets junkman Zeke (Hines), who gives Reggie a pair of worn red high-tops that he insists were worn by a legendary Harlem hoopster. When Reggie puts the shoes on, he suddenly seems to have inherited all the skill of their former owner and is suddenly drawing lots of attention as a star player. But there's a price to be paid. **109m/C VHS, DVD.** Gregory Hines, Vincent D'Onofrio, Vanessa Bell Calloway, Dempsey Pappion, Ruben Santiago-Hudson, Philip Akin; ***D:*** Gregory Hines; ***W:*** Mark Saltzman; ***C:*** John Berrie; ***M:*** Stanley Clarke. **CABLE**

Red Snow **1991** High in the Cascade Mountains, Kyle Lewis is the new snowboard instructor for the Hurricane Ridge Ski Resort. The job is fine in the beginning, until Kyle learns of the tragic fate of the last instructor. Before he knows it, Kyle is the next target and is framed for two murders. He secures the help of his fellow snowboard buddies in hopes of solving the mystery and getting the girl, too. High speed ski scenes and dangerous stunts are the film's only redeeming qualities. **86m/C VHS.** Carlo Scandiuzzi, Scott Galloway, Darla Haun, Mitchell Cox, Tamar Tibbs, Brian Mahoney; ***D:*** Phillip J. Roth.

Red Sonja ½ **1985 (PG-13)** Two warriors join forces against an evil queen in this sword and sorcery saga. Big, beautiful bodies everywhere, with Bergman returning from her Conan adventures. Little humor, few special effects, and weak acting make this a poor outing. **89m/C VHS, DVD.** Arnold Schwarzenegger, Brigitte Nielsen, Sandahl Bergman, Paul Smith; ***D:*** Richard Fleischer; ***M:*** Ennio Morricone. Golden Raspberries '85: Worst New Star (Nielsen).

Red Sorghum ½ **1987** A stunning visual achievement, this new wave Chinese film (and Yimou's directorial debut) succeeds on many levels—as an ode to the color red, as dark comedy, and as a sweeping epic with fairy tale overtones. Set in rural China in the 1920s, during the period of the Japanese invasion. The sorghum plot nearby is a symbolic playing field in the movie's most stunning scenes. Here, people make love, murder, betray, and commit acts of bravery, all under the watchful eye of nature. In Mandarin with English subtitles. **91m/C VHS.** *CH* Gong Li, Jiang Wen, Ji Cun Hua; ***D:*** Yimou Zhang; ***C:*** Gu Changwei.

The Red Spectacles 🦴🦴 *Jigoku no banken: akai megane* **1987** First film in Mamoru Oshii's trilogy based on his comic series Kerberos Panzer Cop, and perversely its events take place after the events of the sequel (it helps to watch that one first, with all of the genre-switching and surrealism). The Kerberos were an elite armored police force made to restore order, but they quickly succumbed to corruption. When three of their own decide to stand up to them, only one escapes alive. Years have passed, and the lone survivor has come home for unknown reasons. **116m/B DVD.** *JP* Eisei Amamoto, Shigeru Chiba, Machiko Washio, Hideyuki Tanaka, Tessho Genda; ***D:*** Mamoru Oshii; ***W:*** Mamoru Oshii, Kazunori Ito; ***C:*** Yousuke Mamiya; ***M:*** Kenji Kawai.

The Red Squirrel 🦴🦴 *La Ardilla Roja* **1993** Former pop star Jota (Novo) is distraught over breaking up with his girlfriend and contemplating throwing himself off a bridge when he witnesses a motorcycle accident and rushes to help the young woman (Suarez) involved. After learning she's suffering from amnesia, Jota tells both the woman and the hospital that her name is Lisa and he's her lover. Then Jota invents a fictitious life for her, according to his own desires. Spanish with subtitles. **104m/C VHS, DVD.** *SP* Nancho Novo, Emma Suarez, Maria Barranco, Carmelo Gomez, Ana Garcia; ***D:*** Julio Medem; ***W:*** Julio Medem; ***C:*** Gonzalo F. Berridi; ***M:*** Alberto Iglesias.

The Red Stallion 🦴 ½ **1947** Good film for animal lovers, but it loses something when it comes to human relationships. A young boy raises his pony into an award-winning racehorse that saves the farm when it wins the big race. Good outdoor photography. **82m/B VHS.** Robert Paige, Noreen Nash, Ted Donaldson, Jane Darwell; ***D:*** Lesley Selander.

Red Sun 🦴🦴 **1971** A gunfighter, a samurai, and a French bandit fight each other in various combinations in the 1860s. Ludicrous and boring. **115m/C VHS, DVD.** *FR IT SP* Charles Bronson, Toshiro Mifune, Alain Delon, Ursula Andress; ***D:*** Terence Young; ***W:*** William Roberts; ***M:*** Maurice Jarre.

Red Sun Rising 🦴 ½ **1994 (R)** Kyoto cop Thomas Hoshino (Wilson) heads to L.A. in order to extradite a Japanese gangster, Yamata (Oh), and teams up with local detective Karen Ryder (Ferrell). Seems Yamata wants to start a turf war between two L.A. street gangs so he can sell guns to both sides. **95m/C VHS.** Don "The Dragon" Wilson, Terry Farrell, Soon-Teck Oh, Mako, James Lew, Edward Albert, Michael Ironside; ***D:*** Francis Megahy; ***C:*** John Newby.

Red Surf 🦴🦴 **1990 (R)** Action abounds in this surfer film. A couple of hard-nosed wave-riders get involved with big money drug gangs and face danger far greater than the tide. **104m/C VHS, DVD.** George Clooney, Doug Savant, Dedee Pfeiffer, Gene Simmons, Rick Najera, Philip McKeon; ***D:*** H. Gordon Boos; ***W:*** Vincent Robert; ***C:*** John Schwartzman; ***M:*** Sasha Matson.

Red Tent 🦴🦴🦴 *Krasnaya Palatka* **1969 (G)** A robust, sweeping man-versus-nature epic based on the true story of the Arctic stranding of Italian explorer Umberto Nobile's expedition in 1928. A Russian-Italian co-production. **121m/C DVD.** Sean Connery, Claudia Cardinale, Peter Finch, Hardy Kruger, Massimo Girotti, Luigi Vannucchi; ***D:*** Mikhail Kalatozov; ***M:*** Ennio Morricone.

The Red Violin 🦴🦴 ½ *Le Violon Rouge* **1998 (R)** Spans 300 years in the life of one famed musical instrument that winds up in present-day Montreal on the auction block. Crafted by the Italian master Bussotti (Cecchi) in 1681, the red violin derives its unusual color from the human blood mixed into the finish. With this legacy, the violin travels to Austria, England, China, and Canada, leaving both beauty and tragedy in its wake. Most of the vignettes are dull, with the Montreal-set framing story holding the most interest. **131m/C VHS, DVD.** *CA* Samuel L. Jackson, Don McKellar, Carlo Cecchi, Irene Grazioli, Jean-Luc Bideau, Jason Flemyng, Greta Scacchi, Christoph Koncz, Sylvia Chang, Colm Feore, Monique Mercure, Liu Zi Feng; ***D:*** Francois Girard; ***W:*** Don McKellar, Francois Girard; ***C:*** Alan Dostie; ***M:*** John Corigliano. Oscars '99: Orig. Score; Genie '98: Art Dir./Set Dec., Cinematog., Costume Des., Director (Girard), Film, Screenplay, Score.

Red Water 🦴 **2001 (R)** Sanders is a Louisiana fisherman and ex-oil company worker who hooks up with his scientist wife to find natural gas in a Louisiana river. At the same time, gangsters and an ex-con are heading to the same place looking for buried loot, and a freshwater shark picks the spot as well, looking for a human buffet. The too-complicated plot only serves as a reason for everyone to show up and become shark bait for the ridiculously fake-looking maneater. If you're gonna spend time watching a shark movie, make it "Jaws" instead of this made-for-TV waste. **92m/C VHS, DVD.** Lou Diamond Phillips, Kristy Swanson, Coolio, Jaimz Woolvett; ***D:*** Charles Robert Carner; ***W:*** J.D. Feigelson, Chris Mack; ***C:*** Michael Goi. **TV**

Red, White & Busted 🦴 *Outside In* **1975** Three friends are affected in different ways by the Vietnam War, whether or not they went. One who fled to Canada tries to return home for his father's funeral. **85m/C VHS.** Darrell Larson, Heather Menzies, Dennis Oliveri, John Bill, Peggy (Margaret) Feury, Logan Ramsey; ***D:*** Allen Baron, G.D. Spradlin; ***W:*** Allen Baron; ***C:*** Mario Tosi; ***M:*** Randy Edelman.

Red Wind 🦴🦴 **1991 (R)** Kris Morrow is a psychotherapist whose latest patient, Lila, has a number of disturbing sadomasochistic fantasies. When Kris feels she's getting too close to the situation, she refers Lila to another therapist. But Lila calls and tells Kris she's already acted out one of her fantasies by killing her husband. In order to stop Lila from killing again, Kris goes on a dangerous search for her deadly patient. **93m/C VHS.** Lisa Hartman Black, Deanna Lund, Philip Casnoff, Christopher McDonald; ***D:*** Alan Metzger.

Redacted 🦴🦴 **2007 (R)** A group of soldiers, compromised by the experience of war, find themselves in increasingly brutal and amoral situations, culminating in the group rape and murder of a 15-year-old girl. Izzy Diaz (Salazar), who's filming his experiences in Iraq in hopes of getting into film school, is disgusted by the actions of his comrades but fears retribution if he reports them. DePalma, who addressed similar issues in "Casualties of War," uses true stories from the Iraq War as inspiration and a "fictional documentary" technique, in which the entire film appears to be composed of assembled footage shot by Diaz, documentary makers, or other "real" sources. Story is powerful but ultimately heavy-handed, and the performances are inconsistent. Intense, depressing, and highly divisive, the pic received accusations of anti-American bias and bombed at the box office. **90m/C DVD.** *US CA* Kel O'Neill, Pat Carroll, Izzy Diaz, Rob Devaney, Daniel Stewart Sherman, Ty Jones; ***D:*** Brian De Palma; ***W:*** Brian De Palma; ***C:*** Jonathan Cliff.

Redbelt 🦴🦴🦴 ½ **2008 (R)** Mike Terry (Ejiofor), a Gulf war vet turned small-time jujitsu instructor, lives in modern-day Los Angeles with a strict code of honor of an ancient samurai. Money causes constant ethical dilemmas as both Mike's wife (Braga) and a shady promoter (Jay) urge him to drop his pride and get out of debt. Later, a Hollywood action star (Allen, in a surprisingly venomous role) and his producer (Mantegna) offer to pay Mike for ideas they plan on stealing. Terrific performances all around, especially from Ejiofor. Writer and director David Mamet wisely takes a philosophical approach, rather than making a formulaic fight flick, and shelves his usual twists and trickery for a story that's human and honest. (Still, the fight scenes are pretty cool.) **99m/C DVD.** *US* Chiwetel Ejiofor, Alice Braga, Tim Allen, Emily Mortimer, Rodrigo Santoro, Joe Mantegna, Rebecca Pidgeon, David Paymer, Ricky Jay, Jose Pablo Cantillo, Ray "Boom Boom" Mancini, Maximillian Martini, John Machado; ***D:*** David Mamet; ***W:*** David Mamet; ***C:*** Robert Elswit; ***M:*** Stephen Endelman.

Redeemer 🦴🦴 ½ **2002** Paul Freeman is a writing teacher in a prison program who decides to help inmate Charles Henderson (Babatunde), an articulate ex-Black Panther serving life for murder. After 20 years, Charles wants to write a letter to his victim's sister, Sharon Davidson (Greene), asking her forgiveness. The reaction to the letter turns out to be a catalyst for a second chance for each of them. **90m/C VHS, DVD.** Matthew Modine, Obba Babatunde, Michele Greene; ***D:*** Graeme Clifford; ***W:*** James Ricci; ***C:*** Norayr Kasper; ***M:*** Frankie Blue. **CABLE**

Redemption: Kickboxer 5 🦴 *Kickboxer 5* **1995 (R)** Retired kickboxer Matt Reeves (Dacascos) goes after the scum who murdered a friend. No surprises here. **87m/C VHS, DVD.** Mark Dacascos, James Ryan; ***D:*** Kristine Peterson; ***M:*** John Massari.

The Redhead from Wyoming 🦴🦴 ½ **1953** Spirited sagebrush adventure with fiery-tempered O'Hara as a saloon proprietress with feelings for both a local cattle rustler and the town's sheriff. Based on a story by James. **81m/C VHS, DVD.** Maureen O'Hara, Alex Nicol, William Bishop, Robert Strauss, Alexander Scourby, Jack Kelly, Jeanne Cooper, Dennis Weaver, Stacy Harris; ***D:*** Lee Sholem; ***W:*** Polly James, Herb Meadow.

Redline 🦴🦴 *Deathline* **1997 (R)** John Wade (Hauer) is double-crossed and murdered by his partner Merrick (Dacascos), who's involved with a Russian crime syndicate. But Wade is resurrected as a bionically enhanced creation and hunts for revenge in a seedily futuristic Moscow. **96m/C VHS, DVD.** Rutger Hauer, Mark Dacascos, Yvonne Scio, John Thompson; ***D:*** Tibor Takacs, Brian Irving; ***W:*** Tibor Takacs, Brian Irving; ***C:*** Zoltan David; ***M:*** Guy Zerafa. **VIDEO**

Redline 🦴 **2007 (PG-13)** Self-financed and distributed by real estate tycoon Sadek, this action pic is most notable for its conspicuous consumption. Dissolute Michael (Macfadyen) instigates an illegal $100 million winner-take-all race with high-rollers Infamous (Griffin), a rapper, and movie producer Jerry (Matheson), and such drivers as the vengeful Natasha (Bjorlin) and daredevil Jason (Johnson). Plot—such as it is—is an excuse to watch some of the world's most expensive cars become scrap metal. **95m/C DVD.** *US* Nathan Phillips, Angus MacFadyen, Tim Matheson, Eddie Griffin, Nadia Bjorlin, Jesse Johnson, Barbara Niven, Louis Mandylor, Denyce Lawton, Neill Skylar; ***D:*** Andy Cheng; ***W:*** Richard Foreman; ***C:*** Bill Butler; ***M:*** Ian Honeyman, Andrew Raiher.

Redneck 🦴 **1973** Implausible, distasteful purported "thriller" about criminals on the run. **92m/C VHS.** *IT GB* Telly Savalas, Franco Nero, Mark Lester, Ely Galleani, Dulio Del Prete, Maria Michi; ***D:*** Silvio Narizzano.

Redneck Zombies 🦴 **1988 (R)** A bunch of backwoods rednecks become zombies after chug-a-lugging some radioactive beer. Eating local tourists becomes a hard habit to break. Betcha can't have just one! **83m/C VHS, DVD.** Lisa DeHaven, W.E. Benson, Floyd Piranha, William-Livingston Dekkar, Zoofeet, James Housely, Anthony Burlington-Smith, Martin J. Wolfman, Boo Teasdale, Darla Deans, Tyrone Taylor, Frank Lantz, Pericles Lewnes; ***D:*** Pericles Lewnes; ***W:*** Fester Smellman; ***C:*** Ken Davis; ***M:*** Adrian Bond.

Reds 🦴🦴🦴 **1981 (PG)** The re-creation of the life of author John Reed ("Ten Days that Shook the World"), his romance with Louise Bryant, his efforts to start an American Communist party, and his reporting of the Russian Revolution. A sweeping, melancholy epic using dozens of "witnesses" who reminisce about what they saw. See director Sergei Eisenstein's silent masterpiece "Ten Days that Shook the World," based on Reed's book, for the Russian view of some of the events depicted in Beatty's film. **195m/C VHS, DVD, Blu-ray Disc, HD DVD.** Warren Beatty, Diane Keaton, Jack Nicholson, Edward Herrmann, Maureen Stapleton, Gene Hackman, Jerzy Kosinski, George Plimpton, Paul Sorvino, William Daniels, M. Emmet Walsh, Dolph Sweet, Josef Sommer; ***D:*** Warren Beatty; ***W:*** Warren Beatty; ***C:*** Vittorio Storaro; ***M:*** Dave Grusin, Stephen Sondheim. Oscars '81: Cinematog., Director (Beatty), Support. Actress (Stapleton); British Acad. '82: Support. Actor (Nicholson), Support. Actress (Stapleton); Directors Guild '81: Director (Beatty); Golden Globes '82: Director (Beatty); L.A. Film Critics '81: Cinematog., Director (Beatty), Support. Actress (Stapleton); Natl. Bd. of Review '81: Director (Beatty), Support. Actor (Nicholson); N.Y. Film Critics '81: Film; Natl. Soc. Film Critics '81: Support. Actress (Stapleton); Writers Guild '81: Orig. Screenplay.

Reducing 🦴🦴 **1931** Polly owns a ritzy New York beauty and reducing salon and when her Midwestern sister Marie's family falls on hard times, she offers her a job and the chance to live with Polly and her daughter Joyce. Joyce is dating wealthy Johnnie but Marie's daughter Vivian makes a play for him. **77m/B DVD.** Marie Dressler, Polly Moran, Anita Page, Sally Eilers, William "Buster" Collier Jr., Lucien Littlefield, William "Billy" Bakewell; ***D:*** Charles Reisner; ***W:*** Beatrice Banyard, William Mack; ***C:*** Leonard Smith.

Redwood Curtain 🦴🦴 ½ **1995 (PG)** Geri Riordan (Salonga) is an Amerasian teenager, with a brilliant future as a concert pianist before her, until she becomes obsessed with learning about her past. Her wealthy adoptive father, Laird Riordan (Lithgow), provides understanding but no answers so she turns to her sympathetic Aunt Geneva (Monk), who lives in the redwood forest area of northern California. There Geri encounters homeless Vietnam vet Lyman Fellers (Daniels) and becomes convinced the troubled man is her birth father. Adapted from the play by Lanford Wilson; made for TV. **99m/C VHS.** Lea Salonga, John Lithgow, Jeff Daniels, Debra Monk, Catherine Hicks; ***D:*** John Korty; ***W:*** Ed Namzug; ***M:*** Lawrence Shragge. **TV**

Redwood Forest Trail 🦴🦴 **1950** Environmental-themed oater about a camp for underprivileged city boys. The boys of the camp are blamed for the death of a landowner whose daughter then refuses to renew the camp's mortgage. Allen and Switzer set out to prove that the real culprits are sawmill workers out to control the area timber. Smokey the Bear also makes an appearance to lecture about careless forest fires and the need to preserve the woods. **67m/B VHS.** Rex Allen, Jeff Donnell, Carl "Alfalfa" Switzer, Jane Darwell, Marten Lamont, Pierre Watkin; ***D:*** Philip Ford; ***W:*** Bradford Ropes.

Redwoods 🦴🦴 **2009** Everett (Bradley) and Miles (Coughenour) are long-term partners, raising their son Billy. Everett thinks the relationship has stagnated and when Miles and Billy are away, he stays home and starts a flirtation with writer Chase (Montgomery) who is driving through Northern California. Their attraction is instantaneous but neither man may be able to deal with more than a vacation fling. **90m/C DVD.** Matthew Montgomery, Brendan Bradley, Tad Coughenour, Laurie Burke; ***D:*** David Lewis; ***W:*** David Lewis; ***C:*** Joe Rivera; ***M:*** Jack Curtis Dubowsky. **VIDEO**

Reed: Insurgent Mexico 🦴🦴 *Reed, Mexico Insurgente* **1973** Dramatization of John Reed's newspaper reporting on the Mexican Revolution. Spanish with subtitles. **104m/B VHS.** *MX* Claudio Obregon, Eduardo Lopez Rojas, Eracio Zepeda; ***D:*** Paul Leduc.

Reefer Madness WOOF! *Tell Your Children; Dope Addict; Doped Youth; Love Madness; The Burning Question* **1938 (PG)** Considered serious at the time of its release, this low-budget depiction of the horrors of marijuana has become an underground comedy favorite. Overwrought acting and lurid script contribute to the fun. **67m/B VHS, DVD.** Dave O'Brien, Dorothy Short, Warren McCollum, Lillian Miles, Thelma White, Carleton Young, Josef Forte, Harry Harvey Jr., Pat Royale; ***D:*** Louis Gasnier; ***W:*** Paul Franklin, Arthur Hoerl; ***C:*** Jack Greenhalgh; ***M:*** Abe Meyer.

Reel Paradise 🦴🦴🦴 **2005 (R)** Follows film industry insider, John Pierson, and his family during the final month of a one-year sabbatical in Taveuni, Fiji, from their suburban New York home. In Taveuni, the Piersons established the self-proclaimed "most remote theatre in the world" in the 180 Meridian Cinema, Taveuni's 52-year-old 288-seat theatre. Taps into the unbridled enthusiasm as the local Fijians pack the seats to view such films as "Jackass: The Movie" (later banned in Fiji), "Apocalypse Now Redux," "Bend it Like Beckham" and the Hindi film "Kaante." With free admission, the Piersons received little support from the Local Catholic mission—apparently the films were in competition with attendance at religious services. **110m/C DVD.** *US* ***D:*** Steve James; ***C:*** P.H. O'Brien; ***M:*** Norman Arnold.

Reet, Petite and Gone **1947** All-Black musical featuring the music of neglected jive singer Louis Jordan, and his band, The Tympany Five. A girl's mother dies; sneaky lawyer tries to cheat her. Slick and enjoyable. **75m/B VHS, DVD.** Louis Jordan, June Richmond; ***D:*** William Forest Crouch.

The Ref **1993 (R)** The couple from hell turn the tables on Gus (Leary), a hard-nosed fugitive who takes Caroline (Davis) and her husband Lloyd (Spacey) hostage. Gus then finds himself trapped in the traditional Christmas ordeal of a family suffering from industrial-strength dysfunction. He plots his getaway while masquerading as the couple's marriage counselor, hence the film's title. This sometimes brutal, frequently hysterical satire of male-female relationships, family ties, and compulsory holiday rituals uses consistently sharp dialogue and superb acting to tell an absurd but convincing tale. **97m/C VHS, DVD.** J.K. Simmons, Raymond J. Barry, Richard Bright, Adam LeFevre, Ellie Raab, Bill Raymond, Jim Turner, Robert Ridgely, Vincent Pastore, B.D. Wong, Rutanya Alda, Denis Leary, Judy Davis, Kevin Spacey, Glynis Johns, Robert J. Steinmiller Jr., Christine Baranski; ***D:*** Ted (Edward) Demme; ***W:*** Richard LaGravenese, Marie Weiss; ***M:*** David A. Stewart.

The Reflecting Skin **1991** In a 1950s prairie town a small boy sees insanity, child-murder, and radiation sickness, leading him to fantasize that the tormented young widow next door is a vampire. The pretentious drama/freak show rationalizes its ghastly events as symbolizing the hero's loss of youthful innocence. But the Hound knows the score; this is "Faces of Death" for the arts crowd, a grotesque menagerie that dares you to watch. The exploding-frog opener is already notorious. Beautiful photography, with vistas inspired by the painting of Andrew Wyeth. **116m/C VHS.** *GB* Viggo Mortensen, Lindsay Duncan, Jeremy Cooper, Duncan Fraser, Shiela Moore, David Longworth, Robert Koons, David Bloom, Evan Hall; ***D:*** Philip Ridley; ***W:*** Philip Ridley; ***C:*** Dick Pope; ***M:*** Nick Bicat.

A Reflection of Fear *Labyrinth* **1972 (PG)** Lame psycho-thriller about a young girl's jealously of her father's girlfriend, with family members dying of supernatural causes. **90m/C VHS.** Robert Shaw, Sally Kellerman, Sondra Locke, Mary Ure; ***D:*** William A. Fraker; ***W:*** Lewis John Carlino.

Reflections in a Golden Eye 1/2 **1967** Huston's film adaptation of Carson McCullers novel about repressed homosexuality, madness, and murder at a Southern Army base in 1948. Star-studded cast cannot consistently pull off convoluted lives of warped characters; not for everyone, though it holds some interest. **109m/C VHS.** Elizabeth Taylor, Marlon Brando, Brian Keith, Julie Harris; ***D:*** John Huston; ***C:*** Oswald Morris.

Reflections in the Dark *Reflections on a Crime* **1994 (R)** Beautiful Regina (Rogers) is on death row for murdering her overbearing husband James (Terry). On execution-eve, she relates her tale to young guard Colin (Zane), dispatching hubby by a different method each time she varies her story. Takes itself too seriously though Rogers gives a star performance. **83m/C VHS.** Mimi Rogers, Billy Zane, John Terry, Kurt Fuller, Lee Garlington, Nancy Fish; ***D:*** Jon Purdy; ***W:*** Jon Purdy; ***C:*** Teresa Medina.

Reflections of Murder 1/2 **1974** Evil schoolteacher's wife and mistress decide to kill him off and then are plagued by his phantom. Well-done TV remake of the French film "Diabolique." Suspenseful, with a great ending. **97m/C VHS.** Tuesday Weld, Joan Hackett, Sam Waterston, Lucille Benson, R.G. Armstrong, Michael Lerner, Ed Bernard, Lance Kerwin; ***D:*** John Badham; ***M:*** Billy Goldenberg. **TV**

Reform School Girl **1957** A young girl ends up behind bars when her boyfriend steals a car to go joy-riding and is involved in a hit-and-run murder. Extremely cheap production and incredulous story. Look for Kellerman in a bit part in her first screen appearance. **71m/B VHS.** Gloria Castillo, Ross Ford, Edward Byrnes, Ralph Reed, Jack Kruschen, Sally Kellerman, Luana Anders, Yvette Vickers, Diana Darrin, Edmund Burns, Ross Hunter; ***D:*** Edward L. Bernds; ***W:*** Edward L. Bernds; ***C:*** Floyd Crosby; ***M:*** Ronald Stein.

Reform School Girls **1986 (R)** Satiric raucous women's prison film, complete with tough lesbian wardens, brutal lesbian guards, sadistic lesbian inmates, and a single, newly convicted heterosexual heroine. Wendy O. Williams as a teenager? Come on. Overdone, over-campy, exploitative. **94m/C VHS, DVD.** Linda Carol, Wendy O. Williams, Pat Ast, Sybil Danning, Charlotte McGinnis, Sherri Stoner; ***D:*** Tom De Simone; ***W:*** Tom De Simone; ***C:*** Howard Wexler.

The Refrigerator 1/2 **1991** Filmed on a miniscule budget, this comic/horror flick tells the story of the innocent Batemans of Ohio who move into a grubby New York apartment where they discover their battered Norge refrigerator is actually a doorway to hell. The fridge has a taste for flesh and tends to eat the unwary visitor as well as defrosting blood (very messy). All the previous tenants disappeared without a trace—will the Batemans be next? Cartoon satire is too amateurish to be successful. **86m/C VHS.** David Simonds, Julia McNeal, Angel Caban, Nena Segal, Jaime Rojo, Michelle DeCosta, Phyllis Sanz; ***D:*** Nicholas A.E. Jacobs; ***W:*** Nicholas A.E. Jacobs; ***C:*** Paul Gibson.

Regarding Henry **1991 (PG-13)** A cold-hearted lawyer gets shot in the head during a holdup and survives with memory and personality erased. During recovery the new Henry displays compassion and conscience the old one never had. Though too calculated in its yuppie-bashing ironies, the picture works thanks to splendid acting and low-key, on-target direction. **107m/C VHS, DVD.** Harrison Ford, Annette Bening, Bill Nunn, Mikki Allen, Elizabeth Wilson, Robin Bartlett, John Leguizamo, Donald Moffat, Nancy Marchand; ***D:*** Mike Nichols; ***W:*** J.J. (Jeffrey) Abrams; ***C:*** Giuseppe Rotunno; ***M:*** Hans Zimmer.

Regeneration **1915** Irish hoodlum Owen (Fellowes) is saved from his life of crime by social worker Mamie Rose (Nilsson). Walsh filmed on location in New York's Bowery district and used actual gangsters in roles. Also features the 10-minute 1910 short "The Police Force of New York City," produced by Thomas Edison. **72m/B VHS, DVD.** Rockliffe Fellowes, Anna Q. Nilsson; ***D:*** Raoul Walsh; ***W:*** Raoul Walsh, Carl Harbaugh; ***C:*** Georges Benoit. Natl. Film Reg. '00.

Reggie Mixes In **1916** Wealthy man brawls in bar room and falls for barmaid. Taking a job to be near his beloved, he wipes out local thugs while tending to her welfare. Exhilarating fight scenes in which Fairbanks fists it out with real life boxers. **58m/B VHS.** Douglas Fairbanks Sr., Bessie Love, Joseph Singleton, William E. (W.E., William A., W.A.) Lowery, Wilbur Higby, Frank Bennett; ***D:*** Christy Cabanne.

Regina 1/2 *Regina Roma* **1983** A woman controls all the activities of her husband and son. At age 36, her son is ready to leave home and she refuses to let him. Fine performances in this strange and disturbing film. **86m/C VHS, DVD.** *IT* Anthony Quinn, Ava Gardner, Ray Sharkey, Anna Karina; ***D:*** Jean-Yves Prate.

Reg'lar Fellers **1941** A gang of kids save the town and soften the heart of their grandmother, too. Production is sloppy. Based on a comic strip by Gene Byrnes. **66m/B VHS, DVD.** Billy Lee, Carl "Alfalfa" Switzer, Buddy Boles, Janet Dempsey, Sarah Padden, Roscoe Ates; ***D:*** Arthur Dreifuss.

Regular Guys 1/2 *Echte Kerle; Real Men* **1996** Macho Frankfurt cop Christoph (Ohrt) gets blindingly drunk after discovering his girlfriend with another guy. She kicks him out—sans belongings—and after a very long night, Christoph wakes up in the bed of stud car mechanic, Edgar (Bergmann). Christoph can't remember anything and Edgar won't say if something happened between them, although he agrees to let Christoph stay awhile while he sorts things out. Meanwhile, the cop's new colleague Helen (Tietze) is making eyes at him and rumors are flying at the police station about his living arrangements and sexual orientation. German with subtitles. **102m/C VHS, DVD.** *GE* Christoph M. Ohrt, Tim Bergmann, Carin C. Tietze, Oliver Stokowski; ***D:*** Rolf Silber; ***W:*** Rolf Silber, Rudolf Bergmann; ***C:*** Jurgen Hermann; ***M:*** Peter W. Schmitt.

Rehearsal for Murder 1/2 **1982** Movie star Redgrave is murdered on the night of her Broadway debut. Seems it might have been someone in the cast. Brought to you by the creative team behind "Columbo." Challenging whodunit a twist. Good cast. **96m/C VHS, DVD.** Robert Preston, Lynn Redgrave, Patrick Macnee, Lawrence Pressman, Madolyn Smith, Jeff Goldblum, William Daniels; ***D:*** David Greene; ***W:*** Richard Levinson, William Link; ***C:*** Stevan Larner; ***M:*** Billy Goldenberg. **TV**

Reign of Fire 1/2 **2002 (PG-13)** Your average year 2020 post-apocalyptic world scenario: Fire-breathing dragons rule the earth. Yes, the film has dragons as the bad guys. These long dormant, London tunnel-dwelling beasties are out to incinerate what's left of humankind, which ain't much. Enter multi-tattooed, macho American Van Zan (McConaughey), British fireman (Bale), and a foxy blond helicopter pilot (Scorupco), who hook up to give the nasty critters a taste of their own medicine. By the looks of this rag tag reptile posse, apparently personal grooming has gone by the wayside in the near futuristic world and the filmmakers saw to it that character development and semi-believable plot went along with it, too. Throw-away humor scores points for the humans but after the dust settles, the cool FX dragons definitely come out on top. **101m/C VHS, DVD, Blu-ray Disc, UMD.** *US* Matthew McConaughey, Christian Bale, Izabela Scorupco, Gerard Butler, Scott James Moutter, Alexander Siddig, David Kennedy, Alice Krige, Ned Dennehy, Rory Kennan, Terence Maynard, Ben Thornton; ***D:*** Rob Bowman; ***W:*** Matt Greenberg, Gregg Chabot, Kevin Peterka; ***C:*** Adrian Biddle; ***M:*** Ed Shearmur.

Reign of Terror *The Black Book* **1949** British-made adventure set during the French Revolution, with everyone after the black book that holds the names of those arch-fiend Robespierre plans to guillotine in his ruthless bid for power. Well-mounted, but historical personages and events are reduced to cartoon form. **89m/B VHS, DVD.** Robert Cummings, Arlene Dahl, Richard Hart, Arnold Moss, Richard Basehart; ***D:*** Anthony Mann; ***W:*** Philip Yordan; ***C:*** John Alton.

Reign Over Me 1/2 **2007 (R)** Why is Adam Sandler wearing Bob Dylan's hair? Anyway, it's subtle pro Cheadle you should be watching. Alan (Cheadle), a NYC dentist, is mildly bored with his successful life and perfect family. Then he runs into his old college roommate, Charlie (Sandler), who's acting weird. Turns out his family was killed in 9/11 and Charlie's not dealing. He won't even acknowledge he had a family and flies into a rage whenever the past is brought up. However, Alan's a compassionate guy and tries to do some male bonding that will result in bringing Charlie back to reality. Sandler restrains from doing shtick, although he's done the angry boy-man thing before, and Binder rushes his predictable ending. **128m/C DVD, Blu-ray Disc.** *US* Adam Sandler, Don Cheadle, Jada Pinkett Smith, Liv Tyler, Saffron Burrows, Donald Sutherland, Robert Klein, Melinda Dillon, Jonathan Banks, Mike Binder; ***D:*** Mike Binder; ***W:*** Mike Binder; ***C:*** Russ T. Alsobrook; ***M:*** Rolfe Kent.

Reilly: Ace of Spies **1987** Covers the exploits of the real-life superspy and womanizer Sydney Reilly who uncovers Russian secrets in 1901, allowing the Japanese to sink the Russian fleet and invade China. After a lively spying career for the British, Reilly eventually plots against the Bolsheviks and comes close to overthrowing Lenin and installing himself as the new leader of the Russian government. Eleven episodes on four cassettes. **572m/C VHS, DVD.** *GB* Sam Neill, Sebastian Shaw, Jeananne Crowley; ***D:*** Jim Goddard.

The Reincarnate **1971 (PG)** Cult guarantees lawyer will live forever if he can find a new body. Enter gullible sculptor; lawyer uses skill at persuasion. **89m/C VHS, DVD.** *CA* Jack Creley, Jay Reynolds, Trudy Young, Terry Tweed; ***D:*** Don Haldane.

Reincarnation 1/2 *Rinne* **2005 (R)** Years ago a professor murdered his wife, his young daughter, and nine hotel guests at the Ono Kanko hotel, and someone decides they have to make a horror film about it. The lead actress sees the original murders in a dream, and then all her co-stars die in the same manner as the victim they were to portray. Confusing and bloody. **9m/C DVD.** *JP* Shun Oguri, Yuka, Karina, Kippei Shiina, Tetta Sugimoto, Marika Matsumoto, Atsushi Haruta, Miki Sanjo, Mao Sasaki, Hiroto Ito; ***D:*** Takashi Shimizu; ***W:*** Takashi Shimizu, Masaki Adachi; ***C:*** Takahide Shibanushi; ***M:*** Kenji Kawai.

The Reincarnation of Golden Lotus *Pan Jin Lian Zhi Qian Shi Jin Sheng* **1989** In this highly erotic story of love and revenge, Wong escapes China for decadent Hong Kong by marrying a wealthy but foolish man. She has numerous sadomasochistic affairs and begins having flashbacks, revealing her to be the reincarnation of Golden Lotus, a courtesan of ancient China. In Mandarin Chinese with English subtitles. **99m/C VHS.** *HK* Joi Wong, Eric Tsang, Lam Chen Yen; ***D:*** Clara Law.

The Reincarnation of Peter Proud **1975 (R)** A college professor has nightmares which lead him to believe the spirit of a murdered man is now possessing him. Kinda scary, but predictable. Screenplay by Ehrlich from his novel. **105m/C VHS.** Michael Sarrazin, Jennifer O'Neill, Margot Kidder, Cornelia Sharpe, Paul Hecht; ***D:*** J. Lee Thompson; ***W:*** Max Ehrlich; ***C:*** Victor Kemper; ***M:*** Jerry Goldsmith.

Reindeer Games **2000 (R)** Too much talking and not nearly enough gun-toting action bog down this already inane crime thriller that tries way too hard to impress with loopy plot twists that come at a dizzying pace. A miscast Affleck is Rudy Duncan, a just released convict who takes on the identity of his recently deceased cellmate in order to get cozy with Ashley (Theron), who had established a correspondence with the dead inmate. The couple spends blissful days together via aerobic sex until Ashley's sadistic "brother" Gabriel (Sinise) forces Rudy to help him and his skanky gang rob an Indian casino on Christmas Eve. Pic is surprisingly flat, deadening the impact of the surprise endings that come in rapid succession, which unintentionally transform the film into a parody of itself. **98m/C VHS, DVD.** Ben Affleck, Charlize Theron, Gary Sinise, Clarence Williams III, Dennis Farina, Donal Logue, James Frain, Isaac Hayes, Danny Trejo; ***D:*** John Frankenheimer; ***W:*** Ehren Kruger; ***C:*** Alan Caso; ***M:*** Alan Silvestri.

The Reivers 1/2 **1969 (PG)** Young boy and two adult pals journey from small town Mississippi (circa 1905) to the big city of Memphis in a stolen car. Picaresque tale is delightful onscreen, as in William Faulkner's enjoyable last novel. **107m/C VHS.** Steve McQueen, Sharon Farrell, Will Geer, Michael Constantine, Rupert Crosse; ***D:*** Mark Rydell; ***W:*** Harriet Frank Jr., Irving Ravetch; ***M:*** John Williams.

The Rejuvenator 1/2 *Rejuvenatrix* **1988 (R)** An oft-told film story: an aging actress discovers a "youth" serum but finds out that the serum affects things other than her aging. Well-done. **90m/C VHS.** Marcus Powell, John MacKay, James Hogue, Vivian Lanko, Jessica Dublin; ***D:*** Brian Thomas Jones; ***W:*** Simon Nuchtern; ***M:*** Larry Juris.

Relative Fear 1/2 **1995 (R)** Little Adam has bad luck with his friends and relatives—they keep getting murdered all around him. His mother begins to suspect something unnatural is going on, and discovers Adam is not her natural child, but the son of a homicidal madwoman. Has Adam inherited some deadly traits? **94m/C VHS, DVD.** Darlanne Fluegel, M. Emmet Walsh, James Brolin, Denise

Crosby, Martin Neufeld, Linda Sorensen, Matthew Dupuis; *D:* George Mihalka; *W:* Kurt Wimmer.

Relative Strangers **1999** Newly widowed Maureen Lessing is devastated to learn her husband was a bigamist, maintaining a second household with a wife and young son. Maureen goes to confront the other woman and learns her child is seriously ill. So she tries to set aside her anger when the boy's only chance to live may hinge on Maureen's own children. **178m/C DVD.** *GB IR* Brenda Fricker, Lena Stolze, Harriet Owen, Robin Laing, Adrian Dunbar, Benjamin Butler, Paul Copley; *D:* Giles Foster; *W:* Eric Deacon; *C:* Rex Maidment; *M:* Nick Bicat. **TV**

Relative Strangers ½ **2006 (PG-13)** Ticky-tacky and too familiar. Uptight self-help author Richard Clayton (Livingston) learns from his oh-so-proper parents (Baranski, Herrmann) that he was adopted. But when Richard finds his birth parents, the Menures (Bates, DeVito) turn out to be less-than-couth trailer park denizens. His fiancee Ellen (Campbell) thinks Richard should just roll with it but he's horrified. **86m/C DVD.** Ron Livingston, Neve Campbell, Kathy Bates, Danny DeVito, Christine Baranski, Edward Herrmann, Ed Begley Jr., Beverly D'Angelo; *D:* Greg Glienna; *W:* Greg Glienna, Jeff Baynes; *C:* Jeffrey Greeley, Tim Suhrstedt; *M:* David Kitay, Arnold Diamond.

Relative Values ½ **1999 (PG-13)** The upper crusty Countess of Marshwood (Andrews) is appalled when her son Nigel (Atterton) wants to marry American starlet Miranda (Tripplehorn). And she isn't the only one—Miranda has jilted her Hollywood star boyfriend Don (Baldwin), who shows up at the Marshwood's country house to change her mind, and she also has a long-lost sister, Moxie (Thompson), who happens to be the Countess' maid. Slight but witty confection, based on a 1951 Noel Coward play. **92m/C VHS, DVD.** *GB* Julie Andrews, Edward Atterton, Jeanne Tripplehorn, William Baldwin, Sophie Thompson, Colin Firth, Stephen Fry; *D:* Eric Styles; *W:* Paul Rattigan, Michael Walker; *C:* Jimmy Dibling; *M:* John Debney.

Relax... It's Just Sex! ½ **1998 (R)** Love and sex in the '90s surround gay looking-for-love writer Vincey (Anderson). His self-made extended family include best gal pal Tara (Tilly) and her boyfriend Gus (Perez), whose HIV-positive brother Javi (Garcia) has just attracted the attention of Buzz (Carson), the man Vincey had his eye on. Then there's troubled lesbian couple Megan (Scott Thomas), who has a fling with a guy (Wirth), and girlfriend Sarina (Williams), who's drawn into the arms of Robin (Petty). But romantic complications take a back seat when Javi and Vincey are subjected to a fag bashing in which Vincey violently turns the tables on one of his attackers. **110m/C VHS, DVD.** Mitchell Anderson, Jennifer Tilly, Cynda Williams, Serena Scott Thomas, Lori Petty, Eddie Garcia, Terrence "T.C." Carson, Timothy Paul Perez, Billy Wirth, Susan Tyrrell, Chris Cleveland, Gibbs Toldsdorf, Seymour Cassel, Paul Winfield; *D:* P.J. Castellaneta; *W:* P.J. Castellaneta; *C:* Lon Magdich; *M:* Lori Eschler Frystak.

Relentless **1989 (R)** Twisted psycho Nelson, once rejected by the LAPD Academy on psychological grounds, takes his revenge by murdering people and using his police training to cover his tracks. Good acting keeps sporadically powerful but cliched thriller afloat. **92m/C VHS, DVD.** Edward (Eddie) Bunker, Judd Nelson, Robert Loggia, Meg Foster, Leo Rossi, Pat O'Bryan, Mindy Seeger, Angel Tompkins, Ken Lerner, George "Buck" Flower; *D:* William Lustig.

Relentless 2: Dead On **1991 (R)** Rossi, the detective from the first film, tracks yet another murderer whose occult-style mutilations mask an international political conspiracy. So-so slaughter with artsy camera work. Honestly, how many "Relentless" fans can you name who've been waiting with anticipation? **93m/C VHS, DVD.** Leo Rossi, Ray Sharkey, Meg Foster, Miles O'Keeffe, Dale Dye; *D:* Michael Schroeder.

Relentless 3 **1993 (R)** A serial killer (Forsythe) likes to carve up his women victims and send various body parts to taunt the police. Then this sicko decides to really drive the cops crazy by stalking the beautiful girlfriend of the detective (Rossi) investigating the crimes. **84m/C VHS.** William Forsythe, Leo Rossi, Tom Bower, Robert Costanzo, Signy Coleman; *D:* James (Momel) Lemmo; *W:* James (Momel) Lemmo.

Relentless 4 ½ **1994 (R)** A psychiatrist with a secret (Janssen) is the only clue Detective Sam Dietz (Rossi) has to a serial killer. Seems all the victims knew the shrink but what does she know? **91m/C VHS.** Leo Rossi, Famke Janssen, Ken Lerner, Colleen T. Coffey; *D:* Oley Sassone; *W:* Mark Sevi, Terry Plumeri.

The Relic **1996 (R)** Quiz time! Which is more implausible: a huge reptilian creature from South American mythology who is crazy for decapitations running amok in a Chicago museum, or Miller as an evolutionary biologist? That's right! Both are equally implausible. But we're forced to accept both after a ship from Brazil arrives with crates for the museum and a completely headless crew (extra credit if you said it's implausible for people with no heads to pilot a ship). Superstitious police detective Vincent D'Agosto (Sizemore) decides to close down the museum's exhibit of...Superstition. That does not sit well with museum director Ann Cuthbert (Hunt), who decides she needs grant money (and the movie needs victims). The monster proceeds to suck brains until the sassy scientist decides she's had enough and takes off her high heels, which everyone knows means the end is near for the creature. Sound interesting? Only if you like Lifestyles of the Rich and Headless. **110m/C VHS, DVD.** Penelope Ann Miller, Tom Sizemore, Linda Hunt, James Whitmore, Clayton Rohner, Thomas Ryan, Lewis Van Bergen, Chi Muoi Lo, Robert Lesser; *D:* Peter Hyams; *W:* Amy Holden Jones, John Raffo, Rick Jaffa, Amanda Silver; *C:* Peter Hyams; *M:* John Debney.

Religulous **2008 (R)** Comedian/talk show host Maher and director Charles' documentary (of sorts) revolves around Maher's ultimate disdain of organized religions, including Christianity, Judaism, Islam, Mormonism and Scientology. On the surface, Maher attempts to apply thoughtful reason to issues of faith—but reason is just a launch pad for his typical sharp-witted skewering of willing ignorance and delusional acceptance of what appear to be, to him at least, ridiculous fairy tales. One-sided and at times both hilarious and offensive, it all becomes a little frightening when he begins drawing his larger conclusion: that these absurd belief systems have been responsible for the world's conflict, division, war, and suffering and perhaps will eventually push us into mutually-assured annihilation. A must for Maher fans, although certain to cheese off the devout. **101m/C DVD.** *US* Bill Maher; *D:* Larry Charles; *C:* Anthony Hardwick.

The Reluctant Agent *Double Your Pleasure* **1989** Waitress Linda (Jackee) is persuaded to take the place of injured twin sister Charlene, an FBI agent hot on the trail of shady-but-attractive businessman C. Gabriel Dash (Lawson). So, she goes undercover with the questionable assistance of agent John Fraser (Hedaya) to bring their criminal to justice. **94m/C VHS.** Jackee, Richard Lawson, Dan Hedaya, Bill Fagerbakke, Harold Sylvester, Cynthia Stevenson, Sharon Barr, Eda Reiss Merin; *D:* Paul Lynch; *W:* Jeff Cohn, Kristi Kane; *M:* Tim Truman. **TV**

The Reluctant Astronaut ½ **1967** Roy Fleming (Knotts) is a carnival worker who operates the spaceship ride. Dad's upset the kid has no ambition and sends an application for Roy to NASA. Everyone's surprised when Roy gets accepted and he heads off to Florida but it turns out the job is janitorial. Still Roy does make friends with astronaut Red (Nielsen), who persuades NASA that Roy would be the perfect civilian to send up in an experimental capsule. Too bad Roy's terrified to fly in anything. **103m/C VHS, DVD.** Don Knotts, Leslie Nielsen, Joan Freeman, Arthur O'Connell, Jesse White, Jeannette Nolan, Joan Shawlee; *D:* Edward Montagne; *W:* James Fritzell, Everett Greenbaum; *C:* Rexford Wimpy; *M:* Vic Mizzy.

The Reluctant Debutante **1958** Harrison and Kendall are the urbane parents of Dee who are trying to find a suitable British husband for their girl. It seems their choices just won't do however, and Dee falls for American bad boy musician Saxon. A very lightweight yet extremely enjoyable romantic comedy thanks to Harrison and in particular his real-life wife Kendall, who unfortunately died the following year. **96m/C VHS.** Rex Harrison, Kay Kendall, John Saxon, Sandra Dee, Angela Lansbury, Diane Clare; *D:* Vincente Minnelli; *C:* Joseph Ruttenberg.

The Remains of the Day **1993 (PG)** If repression is your cup of tea then this is the film for you. Others may want to shake British butler par excellence Stevens (Hopkins) and tell him to express an emotion. In the 1930s, Stevens is the rigidly traditional butler to Lord Darlington (Fox). When Miss Kenton (Thompson) the almost vivacious new housekeeper expresses a quietly personal interest in Stevens his loyalty to an unworthy master prevents him from a chance at happiness. A quiet movie, told in flashback. Hopkins' impressive performance gets by strictly on nuance with Thompson at least allowed a small amount of natural charm. Based on the novel by Kazuo Ishiguro. **135m/C VHS, DVD.** *GB* Anthony Hopkins, Emma Thompson, James Fox, Christopher Reeve, Peter Vaughan, Hugh Grant, Michael (Michel) Lonsdale, Tim Pigott-Smith; *D:* James Ivory; *W:* Ruth Prawer Jhabvala; *C:* Tony Pierce-Roberts; *M:* Richard Robbins. British Acad. '93: Actor (Hopkins); L.A. Film Critics '93: Actor (Hopkins); Natl. Bd. of Review '93: Actor (Hopkins).

Rembrandt **1936** Necessarily very visual biography of the great Dutch painter, Rembrandt. Superb acting by Laughton. **86m/B VHS, DVD.** *GB* Charles Laughton, Elsa Lanchester, Gertrude Lawrence, Walter Hudd; *D:* Alexander Korda; *C:* Georges Perinal.

Rembrandt—1669 **1977** A recreation of the controversial artist's last year, with his egotism clashing with his artistic impulses. In Dutch with English subtitles. **114m/C VHS.** *NL* Frans Stelling, Tom de Koff, Aye Fil; *D:* Jos Stelling.

Remedy ½ **2005** Will's life is perfect until his friend is fatally shot while the two are out partying. Too doped up to remember anything, he appears guilty thus forcing him to find the real killers amid New York City's sleaziest players. **82m/C VHS, DVD.** Christian Maelen, Arthur J. Nascarelli, Vincent Pastore, Nicholas Reiner; *D:* Christian Maelen; *W:* Jonathan Hanser; *C:* Brendan Flynt; *M:* Jon Doscher. **VIDEO**

Remedy for Riches **1940** The fourth "Dr. Christian" comedy, has the small-town doctor trying to uncover a real estate fraud before it bankrupts his community. Mildly funny. **66m/B VHS, DVD.** Jean Hersholt, Dorothy Lovett, Edgar Kennedy, Jed Prouty, Walter Catlett; *D:* Erle C. Kenton.

Remember Me **1985** Just as a woman is starting to gain control of her life, her husband returns home from the mental hospital. **95m/C VHS.** Robert Grubb, Wendy Hughes, Richard Moir; *D:* Lex Marinos.

Remember Me **2010 (PG-13)** Pattinson takes a break from playing a mopey vampire to play a mopey hipster in this story of star-crossed love. Tyler (Pattinson) is a chain-smoking, beer-drinking rebel who is arrested by police Sgt. Craig (Cooper) after a drunken brawl. He plans to date Craig's daughter Ally (de Ravin) and dump her as revenge, but true love starts to bloom. The two lovers bond over the fallout of their respective family tragedies, but trouble soon returns. A veritable avalanche of misfortune then befalls nearly every character, including Tyler's cold father Charles (Brosnan) and sensitive little sis Caroline (Jerins). Sighs are then heaved, but at least no one gets all glittery. **113m/C DVD.** Robert Pattinson, Emilie de Ravin, Chris Cooper, Martha Plimpton, Lena Olin, Pierce Brosnan; *D:* Allen Coulter; *W:* Will Fetters, Jenny Lumet; *C:* Jonathan Freeman; *M:* Marcelo Zarvos.

Remember the Daze ½ *The Beautiful Ordinary* **2007 (R)** Starts with four teenaged girls on the last day at their suburban high school in 1999 and expands to include various groups of geeks, jocks, divas, and stoners as they get ready for the first we're-out-of-school summer party. Manafort's debut basically looks back at her own school years (she graduated in 2000) as aimlessly as the kids themselves. **101m/C DVD.** Amber Heard, Melonie Diaz, Alexa Vega, Leighton Meester, Douglas Smith, Wesley Jonathan, Marne Patterson, Christopher Marquette, Sean Marquette, John Robinson, Moira Kelly, Lyndsy Fonseca, Charles Chen; *D:* Jess Manafort; *W:* Jess Manafort; *C:* Steve Gainer; *M:* Dustin O'Halloran.

Remember the Night **1940** Another Sturges-scripted winner in which assistant D.A. MacMurray falls for sophisticated shoplifter Stanwyck, who has stolen a diamond bracelet amidst the Christmas holiday bustle. On a promise that she will return for the trial MacMurray postpones the trial and offers her a ride home for the holidays. Stanwyck is turned away by her mother and MacMurray brings her home for a real family Christmas, where love blooms. A sentimental, funny romance that boisters holiday cheer any time of year. **94m/B VHS.** Barbara Stanwyck, Fred MacMurray, Beulah Bondi, Elizabeth Patterson, Willard Robertson, Sterling Holloway; *D:* Mitchell Leisen; *W:* Preston Sturges; *C:* Ted Tetzlaff; *M:* Frederick "Friedrich" Hollander.

Remember the Titans **2000 (PG)** Black coach Herman Boone (Washington) is hired to lead the football team at racially tense T. C. Williams High School in Alexandria, Virginia, a school that has been forced to integrate in 1971. This forces white coach Bill Yoast (Patton), who was close to reaching an important milestone, into the role of assistant. He and his former players almost sit out the season, but decide warily to show up for the first practices. The team works through initial stages of mistrust and ignorance, but finally learn to work together. As the school year begins, racial tensions are eased by the success of the team, and the unified team goes to the state championship. A bit predictable and cliche-ridden, but heartfelt. Based on a true story. **114m/C VHS, DVD, Blu-ray Disc, UMD.** Denzel Washington, Will Patton, Donald Adeosun Faison, Wood Harris, Ethan Suplee, Nicole Ari Parker, Hayden Panettiere, Kate (Catherine) Bosworth, Ryan Hurst, Kip Pardue, Craig Kirkwood, Burgess Jenkins, Earl C. Poitier, Ryan Gosling; *D:* Boaz Yakin; *W:* Gregory Allen Howard; *C:* Philippe Rousselot; *M:* Trevor Rabin.

Remembering the Cosmos Flower **1999** Teenager Akiko and her mother return to their small town home in Japan after seven years in South America. Akiko has contracted AIDS—a fact the entire community is aware of. While Akiko tries to cope with her illness, her childhood playmate Natsumi confronts the ignorance and fear of the village. Japanese with subtitles. **103m/C VHS, DVD.** *JP* Mari Natsuki, Megumi Matsushita, Akane Oda, Kai Shishido; *D:* Junichi Suzuki; *W:* Junichi Suzuki, Tetsutomo Kosugi; *C:* Kaz Tanaka; *M:* Mamoru Samurakouchi.

Remo Williams: The Adventure Begins *Remo: Unarmed and Dangerous* **1985 (PG-13)** Adaptation of "The Destroyer" adventure novel series with a Bond-like hero who can walk on water and dodge bullets after being instructed by a Korean martial arts master. Funny and diverting, and Grey is excellent (if a bit over the top) as the wizened oriental. The title's assumption is that the adventure will continue. **121m/C VHS, DVD.** Fred Ward, Joel Grey, Wilford Brimley, Kate Mulgrew, J.A. Preston, George Coe, Charles Cioffi, Patrick Kilpatrick, Michael Pataki, Marv Albert, Reginald VelJohnson, William Hickey; *D:* Guy Hamilton; *W:* Warren B. Murphy, Christopher Wood; *C:* Andrew Laszlo; *M:* Craig Safan.

Remolino de Pasiones **1968** A young woman is driven to suicide after succumbing to her mother's persistent lover. **89m/C VHS.** *MX* Amparo Rivelles, Carlos Pinar, Susana Dosamantes; *D:* Alejandro Galindo; *W:* Alejandro Galindo; *C:* Alex Phillips Jr.; *M:* Gustavo Cesar Carrion.

Remote ½ **1993 (PG)** Thirteen-year-old Randy is a whiz designing high-tech remote-control gadgets. When one of his toys wipes out a friend's science project, Randy's parents try to put a halt to his tinkering but the kid has other plans. Innocuous rip-off of "Honey, I Shrunk the Kids" with some "Home Alone" thrown in as well. **80m/C**

VHS. Chris Carrara, Jessica Bowman, John Diehl, Derya Ruggles, Tony Longo, Stuart Fratkin; ***D:*** Ted Nicolaou; ***W:*** Mike Farrow; ***M:*** Richard Band.

Remote Control 🦴 1/2 **1988 (R)** A circulating videotape of a 1950s sci-fi flick is turning people into murderous zombies, thanks to some entrepreneurial aliens. Silly, but performed by young actors with gusto. **88m/C VHS.** Kevin Dillon, Deborah Goodrich, Christopher Wynne, Jennifer Tilly; ***D:*** Jeff Lieberman; ***M:*** Peter Bernstein.

Remote Control 🦴🦴 1/2 **1994** Quiet Axel lives with his mom, whose life revolves around the TV set, and his sister Maeja, who spends most of her time partying in a seedy club called Sodoma. Sodoma is run by three amateur gangsters who are anxious to get rid of a rival, Moli. Meanwhile, Axel falls in love with Moli's sister Unnur (who also happens to be Maeja's best friend). Then the gangsters kidnap Unnur and Axel sets out to rescue her. Icelandic with English subtitles. **85m/C VHS.** *IC* Bjorn Fridbjornsson, Margret H. Gustavsdottir, Helgi Bjornsson, Soley Eliasdottir; ***D:*** Oskar Jonasson; ***W:*** Oskar Jonasson.

Renaissance 🦴🦴 1/2 **2006 (R)** Stark noir/sci-fi animation set in 2054 Paris, a city that has become a gigantic labyrinth run by Avalon, a company and entity more like Big Brother, Inc. A female scientist who works for the company goes missing, setting off a classic noir adventure with the brooding cop hero, femme fatale, and enemies around every corner. The B&W design is striking but the story drags after awhile. The film was originally voiced by French actors and redone for the English-language market. **103m/B DVD.** *GB FR LU* Romola Garai, Ian Holm, Jonathan Pryce; ***D:*** Christian Volckman; ***W:*** Alexandre de la Patelliere, Matthieu Delaporte; ***M:*** Nicholas Dodd; ***V:*** Daniel Craig, Catherine McCormack.

Renaissance Man 🦴🦴 1/2 **1994 (PG-13)** Skeptical new teacher inspires a classroom of underachievers and finds his true calling. Based loosely on the experiences of screenwriter Burnstein at a base in Michigan. Civilian Bill Rago (DeVito) is an unemployed ad exec assigned to teach Shakespeare to a group of borderline Army recruits led by Hardison. Add half a bone for the recruits and their Hamlet rap, a breath of fresh air in an otherwise stale plot. Some funny moments, reminiscent of "Stripes," but not quite as wacky. On the other hand, Marshall does endearing well. Look for rapper Marky Mark with his shirt on (hard to recognize). Shot with the cooperation of the Army. **128m/C VHS, DVD.** Danny DeVito, Gregory Hines, James Remar, Stacey Dash, Ed Begley Jr., Mark Wahlberg, Lillo Brancato, Kadeem Hardison, Richard T. Jones, Khalil Kain, Peter Simmons, Jenifer Lewis; ***Cameos:*** Cliff Robertson; ***D:*** Penny Marshall; ***W:*** Jim Burnstein, Ned Mauldin; ***M:*** Hans Zimmer.

The Rendering 🦴🦴 **2002** Art student Sarah (Doherty) is attacked by a man who's obsessed with her. Recovering in the hospital, she renders a sketch that has Theodore Grey (Outerbridge) arrested and sent to prison. Ten years later, Sarah is married to Boston businessman Michael (Brennan) but has never told him what happened to her and her continued paranoia has caused a rift. Sarah has also continued to help the police as a sketch artist and her latest drawing of a suspect looks suspiciously like Michael. Has he committed a crime or is this a set-up by Grey, who happens to be out on parole. **93m/C VHS, DVD.** *CA* Shannen Doherty, Peter Outerbridge, John Brennan, Tammy Isabell, Conrad Pla, Sean Devine; ***D:*** Peter Svatek; ***W:*** David Amann; ***C:*** Francois Dagenais; ***M:*** James Gelfand. **CABLE**

Rendez-Moi Ma Peau 🦴🦴 1/2 *Give Me Back My Skin* **1981** A modern-day witch gets in a traffic accident with a married couple and, as revenge, she transposes their personalities into the other's body. In French with subtitles. **82m/C VHS.** *FR* Jean-Luc Bideau, Erik Colin, Bee Michelin, Chantal Neuwirth; ***D:*** Patrick Schulmann; ***C:*** Jacques Assuerus, Andre Zarra; ***M:*** Patrick Schulmann.

Rendez-vous 🦴🦴🦴 **1985 (R)** A racy, dark film about the sensitive balance between sex and exploitation, the real world and the stage world. Some may be disturbed by chillingly explicit scenes. Impressive tour de force of imagination, direction, and cinematography. In French with English subtitles. **82m/C VHS, DVD.** *FR* Juliette Binoche, Lambert Wilson, Wadeck Stanczak, Jean-Louis Trintignant; ***D:*** Andre Techine; ***W:*** Olivier Assayas; ***C:*** Philippe Angers. Cannes '85: Director (Techine).

Rendez-vous de Juillet 🦴🦴 1/2 **1949** In postwar Paris Lucien dreams of becoming a documentary filmmaker, with his friends accompanying him to Africa to serve as his production team. His parents want him to get a regular job and Lucien's buddies are more concerned with love affairs, jazz, theatre, and other pleasures to take him too seriously. Includes a performance by American trumpeter Rex Stewart. French with subtitles; follows Becker's "Antoine et Antoinette." **110m/B VHS.** *FR* Daniel Gelin, Brigitte Auber, Nicole Courcel, Maurice Ronet, Bernard Lajarrige; ***D:*** Jacques Becker; ***W:*** Jacques Becker, Maurice Griffe; ***C:*** Claude Renoir; ***M:*** Jean Wiener.

Rendezvous in Paris 🦴🦴 *Les Rendez-vous de Paris* **1995** Includes three stories by Rohmer about the complications and disappointments of love. "Le Rendez-vous de 7 heures" finds Esther (Bellar) upset when boyfriend Horace (Basler) is spotted with another girl at a cafe. She decides to make him jealous by showing up at the same cafe with another man. A woman (Rauscher) decides to leave her boring fiance in "Les Bancs de Paris" and tries to decide on a possible new romance with a provincial professor (Renko). In "Mere et Enfant 1907," a painter (Kraft) goes to an art gallery where he spots a woman (Loyen) admiring Picasso's painting "Mother and Child" and he decides to pursue her. French with subtitles. **100m/C VHS.** *FR* Clara Bellar, Antoine Basler, Mathias Megard, Judith Chancel, Aurore Rauscher, Serge Renko, Michael Kraft, Benedicte Loyen, Veronika Johansson; ***D:*** Eric Rohmer; ***W:*** Eric Rohmer; ***C:*** Diane Baratier; ***M:*** Sebastien Erms.

Rendition 🦴 1/2 **2007 (R)** Egyptian-born, assimilated American citizen Anwar El-Ibrahimi (Metwally) is ripped from his suburban Chicago existence to the confusion of his pregnant wife Isabella (Witherspoon), who worries when he doesn't return from a business trip. She turns to old boyfriend Alan Smith (Sarsgaard), a congressional aide, for access to Senator Hawkins (Arkin), although her pleas fall on deaf ears. Turns out Anwar's in North Africa being tortured by the local authorities (with Washington's secret blessing) for what they believe is his involvement in a terrorist bombing. Meanwhile, newly-promoted CIA analyst Douglas Freeman (Gyllenhaal) is privy to Anwar's interrogation and begins to have second thoughts. Corrinne Whitman (Streep) runs the whole rendition program (an actual government policy that allows suspected terrorists to be extradited for interrogation) with a steely resolve. Unfortunately it all fails to convince, and even an otherwise brilliant cast can't pull this topical nugget out of the trash bin. **120m/C DVD.** *US* Meryl Streep, Reese Witherspoon, Jake Gyllenhaal, Peter Sarsgaard, Alan Arkin, Omar Metwally, Igal Naor, Moa Khouas, Zineb Oukach; ***D:*** Gavin Hood; ***W:*** Kelley Sane; ***C:*** Dion Beebe; ***M:*** Paul Hepker, Mark Killian.

Renegade Girl 🦴 **1946** A special agent is sent west to capture the female head of a band of outlaws. **65m/B VHS, DVD.** Alan Curtis, Ann Savage, Edward Brophy, Ray Corrigan, Jack Holt, Russell Wade, Claudia Drake, John "Dusty" King, Chief Thundercloud, Edmund Cobb; ***D:*** William Berke; ***W:*** Edwin Westrate; ***C:*** James S. Brown Jr.; ***M:*** Darrell Calker.

Renegade Trail 🦴🦴 **1939** Hopalong Cassidy helps a marshall and a pretty widow round up ex-cons and rustlers. The King's Men, radio singers of the era, perform a fistful of songs. **61m/B VHS.** William Boyd, George "Gabby" Hayes, Russell Hayden, Charlotte Wynters, Russell Hopton, Sonny Bupp, Jack Rockwell, Roy Barcroft, Eddie Dean; ***D:*** Lesley Selander; ***W:*** Harrison Jacobs, John Rathmell; ***C:*** Russell Harlan; ***M:*** Phil Ohman.

Renegades 🦴🦴 **1989 (R)** A young cop from Philadelphia and a Lakota Indian begrudgingly unite to track down a gang of ruthless crooks. Good action, and lots of it; not much story. **105m/C VHS, DVD.** Kiefer Sutherland, Lou Diamond Phillips, Robert Knepper, Jami Gertz, Bill Smitrovich; ***D:*** Jack Sholder; ***C:*** Phil Meheux; ***M:*** Michael Kamen.

Renfrew of the Royal Mounted 🦴🦴 **1937** A Canadian Mountie goes after counterfeiters and sings a few songs in this mild adaptation of a popular kids' radio serial. Newill was a popular tenor of the day, but the Hound thinks Renfrew's dog 'Lightning' should have been the star. **57m/B VHS, DVD.** Carol Hughes, James Newill, Kenneth Harlan; ***D:*** Al(bert) Herman.

Renfrew on the Great White Trail 🦴 1/2 *On the Great White Trail; Renfrew of the Royal Mounted on the Great White Trail* **1938** A frustrated fur trader takes off after a pack of thieves. **58m/B VHS, DVD.** James Newill, Terry Walker, Robert Frazer, Richard Alexander; ***D:*** Al(bert) Herman.

Reno 911! Miami 🦴🦴 **2007 (R)** If you're a fan of the Comedy Central TV show, you'll enjoy this expanded version in all its raunchy, silly glory. The Reno sheriffs go to a police convention in Miami and are left to patrol the city's streets (with their usual complete incompetence) when all the other cops are quarantined at the hotel. Improv is hit-or-miss and involves alligators, topless beaches, crazy mobsters, sexual frustration—and Lt. Dangle (Lennon) in his short-shorts. **84m/C DVD.** *US* Thomas Lennon, Robert Ben Garant, Niecy Nash, Nick Swardson, Kerri Kenney-Silver, Carlos Alazraqui, Mary Birdsong, Wendi McLendon-Covery, Cedric Yarbrough, Paul Rudd; ***Cameos:*** Danny DeVito, Dwayne "The Rock" Johnson; ***D:*** Robert Ben Garant; ***W:*** Thomas Lennon, Robert Ben Garant, Kerri Kenney-Silver; ***C:*** Joe Kessler; ***M:*** Craig (Shudder to Think) Wedren.

Reno and the Doc 🦴🦴 1/2 **1984** Enjoyable comedy about two endearingly cranky middle-aged men battling mid-life crises join together and test their mettle in the world of professional skiing. **88m/C VHS.** *CA* Kenneth Welsh, Henry Ramer, Linda Griffiths; ***D:*** Charles Dennis.

Renoir Shorts 🦴🦴🦴 **1927** Two early silent Renoir fantasies: "The Little Matchgirl," a lyrical adaptation of the Hans Christian Anderson fairy tale, and "Charleston," in which a space-traveling African and Parisian girl dance comically. **50m/B VHS.** Catherine Hessling; ***D:*** Jean Renoir.

Rent 🦴🦴 **2005 (PG-13)** Hit Broadway show makes its screen debut, though it all feels just a bit too late. For the uninitiated, the story follows a group of New York squatters and struggling artists in an update of La Boheme. The passion isn't an act—the film cast is the same group that developed the characters on stage. If you dug the musical or have ever been a little lost, young, and broke in a big city, the timing and uber-sentimentality won't matter. Themes of AIDS, homosexuality and drugs may be too much for stuffier viewers. **128m/C DVD, Blu-ray Disc, UMD.** *US* Anthony Rapp, Adam Pascal, Rosario Dawson, Taye Diggs, Jesse L. Martin, Wilson Jermaine Heredia, Idina Menzel, Tracie Thoms; ***D:*** Chris Columbus; ***C:*** Stephen Goldblatt; ***M:*** Rob Cavallo.

Rent-A-Cop 🦴🦴 **1988 (R)** A cop (Reynolds) is bounced from the force after he survives a drug-bust massacre under suspicious circumstances. He becomes a security guard and continues to track down the still-at-large killer with help from call girl Minnelli. **95m/C VHS, DVD.** Burt Reynolds, Liza Minnelli, James Remar, Richard Masur, Bernie Casey, John Stanton, John P. Ryan, Dionne Warwick, Robby Benson; ***D:*** Jerry London; ***W:*** Michael Blodgett; ***C:*** Giuseppe Rotunno; ***M:*** Jerry Goldsmith. Golden Raspberries '88: Worst Actress (Minnelli).

Rent-A-Kid 🦴🦴 1/2 **1995 (G)** Businessman Harry Haber (Nielsen) is asked by his son to keep an eye out on the Mid-Valley Orphanage for a week. Then Harry meets a young couple who are unsure about having a family so, since Harry's business is renting all sorts of things, he decides to rent the couple three orphans so they can get a taste of parenting. **89m/C VHS.** Leslie Nielsen, Christopher Lloyd, Matt McCoy, Sherry Miller, Amos Crawley, Cody Jones, Tabitha Lupien, Tony Rosato; ***D:*** Fred Gerber; ***W:*** Paul Bernbaum; ***C:*** Rene Ohashi; ***M:*** Ron Ramin.

Rentadick 🦴🦴 **1972** A precursor to the Monty Python masterpieces, written by future members Chapman and Cleese. Private eye spoof isn't as funny as later Python efforts; but it is an indication of what was yet to come and fans should enjoy it. **94m/C VHS.** *GB* James Booth, Julie Ege, Ronald Fraser, Donald Sinden, Michael Bentine, Richard Briers, Spike Milligan, Tsai Chin, Kenneth Cope, John Wells; ***D:*** Jim Clark; ***W:*** Graham Chapman, John Cleese; ***C:*** John Coquillon; ***M:*** Carl Davis.

Rented Lips 🦴 **1988 (R)** Two documentary filmmakers sell out, taking over the production of a porno film at the request of a public television producer who promises to help their careers. Mull and Shawn are well supported by an impressive cast, but everyone's effort is wasted in unfunny attempt at comedy. **82m/C VHS.** Martin Mull, Dick Shawn, Jennifer Tilly, Kenneth Mars, Edy Williams, Robert Downey Jr., June Lockhart, Shelley Berman, Mel Welles, Pat McCormick, Eileen Brennan; ***D:*** Robert Downey.

Repentance 🦴🦴🦴 *Pokayaniye; Confession* **1987 (PG)** A popular, surreal satire of Soviet and Communist societies. A woman is arrested for repeatedly digging up a dead local despot, and put on trial. Wickedly funny and controversial; released under the auspices of glasnost. In Russian with English subtitles. **151m/C VHS, DVD.** *RU* Avtandil Makharadze, Zeinab Botsvadze, Ia Ninidze, Edisher Giorgobiani, Ketevan Abuladze, Kakhi Kavsadze; ***D:*** Tengiz Abuladze. Cannes '87: Grand Jury Prize.

The Replacement Killers 🦴🦴 1/2 **1998 (R)** Hong Kong action star Chow Yun-Fat makes his American debut in this somewhat disappointing first feature from director Antoine Fuqua. Chow stars as John Lee, an assassin working for crime boss Mr. Wei (Tsang). When Lee decides not to carry out a hit on a cop's (Rooker) son, he becomes the target of the men sent to replace him. Needing a passport to get back to China, Lee goes to forger Meg Coburn (Sorvino). Before she can finish the papers, Wei's men begin the first of many high body count gun battles. Fuqua, who was heavily influenced by John Woo (one of the film's exec producers), does a passable job of conveying the style of Chow and Woo's Hong Kong work, but doesn't leave much room for the substance. Chow's sublety and charisma are crammed into a mechanical action plot, and only his talent saves the whole thing from imploding. **86m/C VHS, DVD, Blu-ray Disc, UMD.** Chow Yun-Fat, Mira Sorvino, Michael Rooker, Kenneth Tsang, Jurgen Prochnow, Danny Trejo, Til Schweiger, Clifton (Gonzalez) Collins Jr., Carlos Gomez, Frank Medrano; ***D:*** Antoine Fuqua; ***W:*** Ken Sanzel; ***C:*** Peter Lyons Collister; ***M:*** Harry Gregson-Williams.

The Replacements 🦴 1/2 **2000 (PG-13)** An NFL players' strike finds coach Hackman stuck with a bunch of replacement players, including washed-up quarterback Shane Falco (Reeves) and never-was receiver Clifford Franklin (Jones). If you can get past the fact that the heroes are scabs, this silly cliche-fest still isn't very good. It's better than it oughta be, but only because of Hackman's presence and Jones's comic talents. The odd assortment of misfits and goofballs is occasionally amusing, but nothing you haven't seen in all the other "rag-tag-team-fights-the-odds" sports comedies. Based on the 1987 strike when players filling in for the Washington Redskins won three straight games. **105m/C VHS, DVD.** Keanu Reeves, Gene Hackman, Jon Favreau, Orlando Jones, Jack Warden, Brooke Langton, Rhys Ifans, Brett Cullen, Gailard Sartain, Art LaFleur, Faizon Love, Michael "Bear" Taliferro, Troy Winbush, Michael Jace, Ace Yonamine, David Denman, Keith David, Pat Summerall, John Madden, Evan Dexter Parke; ***D:*** Howard Deutch; ***W:*** Vince McKewin; ***C:*** Tak Fujimoto; ***M:*** Alan Silvestri.

Repli-Kate 🦴🦴 1/2 **2001 (R)** Reporter Kate (Landry) is accidentally cloned by grad student Max (Roday) while she's doing a story on his professor's (Levy) genetic experiments. Since Kate is a hot babe, Max's pal Henry (Askew) thinks this is a wonderful thing and promptly teaches Repli-Kate about the important things in every guy's life—sports, beer, and sex. **90m/C VHS, DVD.** Ali Landry, James Roday, Desmond Askew, Eugene Levy; ***D:*** Frank Longo; ***W:*** Stuart Gibbs; ***C:*** Alan Caso; ***M:*** Teddy Castellucci. **VIDEO**

Replicant ½ **2001 (R)** It takes a killer to catch a killer. In this case Van Damme is cloned by the government so he can go after himself (the original is a vicious serial killer). Cop Rooker, who's been unsuccessfully hunting the psycho for several years, teams up with the duplicate to get results. Lots of chases, fights, and high-tech thrills. **100m/C VHS, DVD.** Jean-Claude Van Damme, Michael Rooker, Ian Robinson, Catherine Dent; ***D:*** Ringo Lam; ***W:*** Lawrence Riggins, Les Weldon; ***C:*** Mike Southon; ***M:*** Guy Zerafa. **VIDEO**

Replikator: Cloned to Kill ½ **1994 (R)** In the 21st century, a ruthless criminal gets hold of replication techology that can duplicate anything, including people. So it's up to a cop and two cyberpunks to stop the destruction. **96m/C VHS.** Michael St. Gerard, Brigitte Bako, Ned Beatty; ***D:*** G. Philip Jackson; ***W:*** Tony Johnston, Michelle Bellerose, John Dawson.

Repo Jake ½ **1990** Jake Baxter learns the myth of the carefree life of a repossession man in this action thriller. His illusion is destroyed by angry clients, pornography, a deadly underworld racetrack, and a sinister crime boss. **90m/C VHS.** Dan Haggerty, Robert Axelrod; ***D:*** Joseph Merhi; ***W:*** Joe Hart; ***C:*** Richard Pepin; ***M:*** John Gonzalez.

Repo Man ½ **1983 (R)** An inventive, perversely witty portrait of sick modern urbanity, following the adventures of punk stock boy Otto (Estevez), who takes a job as a car repossessor under the jaundiced eye of veteran Bud (Stanton). Then there's the lobotomized physicist Parnell (Harris), who carries around a strang glowing object in the trunk of his car that's wanted by the government. The L.A. landscape is filled with pointless violence, no-frills packaging, media hypnosis, and aliens. Executive producer: none other than ex-Monkee Michael Nesmith. **93m/C VHS, DVD.** Emilio Estevez, Harry Dean Stanton, Sy Richardson, Tracey Walter, Olivia Barash, Fox Harris, Jennifer Balgobin, Vonetta McGee, Angelique Pettyjohn, Biff Yeager; ***D:*** Alex Cox; ***W:*** Alex Cox; ***C:*** Robby Muller; ***M:*** Tito Larriva, Iggy Pop.

Repo Men **2010 (R)** In the near future, a giant corporation supplies the world with artificial organs but they're pricey, and not covered by medical insurance. And just like buying a house or a car, if payments aren't made, then the merchandise gets repossessed. After a fall out with his employer, ex-repo man Remy (Law) joins forces with drugged-out singer Beth (Braga), going up against his former partner Jake (Whitaker) to protect his own artificial parts. While lifting a generic hyper-active style from Guy Ritchie, first-time director Sapochnik isn't as confident with the film's mood or purpose, wobbling along as part sci-fi, part satire, part action, but never committing to much of anything. **111m/C DVD.** Jude Law, Forest Whitaker, Alice Braga, Carice van Houten, Liev Schreiber; ***D:*** Miguel Sapochnik; ***W:*** Eric Garcia, Garrett Lerner; ***C:*** Enrique Chediak; ***M:*** Marco Beltrami.

Repo! The Genetic Opera **2008 (R)** Truly awful although it may pass muster for inclusion in the midnight movie madness genre. Sometime in the future, organs may be bought for transplantation purposes—and repossessed if you're late with your payments. Villainous Rotti Largo (Sorvino) has manipulated guilt-ridden scientist Nathan (Head) into becoming a repo man so Nathan can care for his sickly daughter, the angelic Shilo (Vega). **98m/C DVD, Blu-ray Disc.** *US* Anthony Head, Alexa Vega, Paul Sorvino, Bill Moseley, Paris Hilton, Sarah Brightman, Terrance Zdunich, Nivek Ogre; ***D:*** Darren Lynn Bousman; ***W:*** Darren Smith; ***C:*** Joseph White; ***M:*** Darren Smith. Golden Raspberries '08: Worst Support. Actress (Hilton).

The Report on the Party and the Guests **1966** A controversial, widely banned political allegory, considered a masterpiece from the Czech new wave. A picnic/lawn party deteriorates into brutality, fascist intolerance and persecution. Many Czech film makers, some banned at the time, appear. Based on a story by Ester Krumbachova, who also co-wrote the screenplay. In Czech with English subtitles. **71m/B VHS.** *CZ* Jiri Nemec, Evald Schorm, Ivan Vyskocil, Jan Klusak, Zdena Skvorecka, Pavel Bosek; ***D:*** Jan Nemec; ***W:*** Jan Nemec.

Report to the Commissioner *Operation Undercover* **1974 (R)** A rough, energetic crime-in-the-streets cop thriller. A young detective accidentally kills an attractive woman who turns out to have been an undercover cop, then is dragged into the bureaucratic cover-up. **112m/C VHS.** Michael Moriarty, Yaphet Kotto, Susan Blakely, Hector Elizondo, Richard Gere, Tony King, Michael McGuire, Stephen Elliott; ***D:*** Milton Katselas; ***W:*** Abby Mann; ***M:*** Elmer Bernstein.

Repossessed **1990 (PG-13)** A corny, occasionally funny takeoff on the human-possessed-by-the-devil films with Blair, as usual, as the afflicted victim. Nielsen, in another typecast role, plays the goofy man of the cloth who must save the day. Numerous actors appear in brief comedy sequences which lampoon current celebrities and constitute the film's highlights. For fans of "Airplane" and "The Naked Gun"; not necessarily for others. **89m/C VHS, DVD.** Linda Blair, Ned Beatty, Leslie Nielsen, Anthony Starke, Jesse Ventura; ***D:*** Bob Logan; ***W:*** Bob Logan; ***M:*** Charles Fox. Golden Raspberries '90: Worst Song ("He's Comin' Back (The Devil!)").

Reprise **2006 (R)** Feature film debut of Trier follows the fortunes of two 20-something childhood buds, Erik (Klouman-Hoiner) and Phillip (Lie). They share the same literary ambitions but only Phillip's first novel gets published and becomes a success. However, he can't deal with the attention, develops an obsession with girlfriend Kari (Winge), and has a breakdown that lands him in a mental hospital. Meanwhile, Erik neglects his girlfriend Lillian (Hagen) for his literary pursuits and tries to remain loyal to Phillip. Norwegian with subtitles. **105m/C DVD.** *NO SW* Anders Danielsen Lie, Espen Klouman-Hoiner, Viktoria Winge, Silje Hagen, Sigmund Saeverud; ***D:*** Joachim Trier; ***W:*** Joachim Trier, Eskil Vogt; ***C:*** Jakob Ihre; ***M:*** Ola Flottum, Knut Schreiner.

The Reptile **1966** The inhabitants of yet another Cornish village are turning up dead—mysteriously from snakebite. When Harry (Barrett) investigates his brother's death, he finds out Anna (Pearce) is the victim of a curse, which causes her to turn into a snake. Rather sympathetic characters for the horror genre. **90m/C VHS, DVD.** *GB* Jacqueline Pearce, Ray Barrett, Noel Willman, Jennifer Daniel, Michael Ripper, John Laurie, Marne Maitland, Charles Lloyd-Pack, George Woodbridge, David Baron; ***D:*** John Gilling; ***W:*** John (Anthony Hinds) Elder; ***C:*** Arthur Grant; ***M:*** Don Banks.

Reptilian **1999 (PG-13)** Archeologists Campbell (Livingston) and Hughes (Young) are searching for remains of a gigantic dinosaur. But guess who gets to them first? Evil aliens! Who want to take over the earth! So they ray-zap the dino remains back to life and the creature goes on a rampage until the military puts him down. But it doesn't end there—although you'll certainly wish it had. **99m/C VHS, DVD.** *KN* Harrison Young, Donna Philipson, Richard B. Livingston; ***D:*** Hyung Rae Shim; ***W:*** Marty Poole; ***C:*** Hong Kim An; ***M:*** Chris Desmong, Seung Woo Cho.

Reptilicus **1962** Oil drillers in Lapland bring up a sample of prehistoric flesh from a frozen bog deep below the earth, which is transported to Copenhagen. It proves to be alive and growing; eventually a lightning storm frees it from its holding tank. Soon thereafter the army has a real problem on its hands when it reappears as a completely regenerated monster, crawling across the landscape, crushing buildings and eating farmers. The authorities have no luck ridding themselves of the scaly, snake-like dragon, until they corner it in the main square in downtown Copenhagen. This alternative epic comes in dead last in the list of movies where giant monsters attack cities. The several hundred extras who run politely through the streets in "panic" look bored or amused. Most of Reptilicus's scenes are artlessly shot in broad daylight, making its general artificiality even more obvious. **90m/C DVD.** *DK* Carl Ottosen, Ann Smyrner, Mimi Heinrich, Asbjorn Andersen, Bodil Miller, Bent Mejding, Dirch Passer, Ole Wisborg; ***D:*** Sidney W. Pink; ***W:*** Sidney W. Pink, Ib Melchior; ***C:*** Aage Wiltrup; ***M:*** Sven Gyldmark.

The Republic of Love ½ **2003** Set in Toronto and based on the novel by Carol Shields. Late-night radio talk show host Tom had an unconventional upbringing that has led to his being impulsive about love and marriage (including three ex-wives). Academician Fay views her parents' 40-year marriage as perfect so she has impossibly high standards for her own relationships. When their lives finally intersect, there is instant attraction and a lot of unrealistic expectations. **96m/C DVD.** *CA* Bruce Greenwood, Emilia Fox, Edward Fox, Martha Henry, Lloyd Owen, Jackie Burroughs, Gary Farmer, Jan Rubes; ***D:*** Deepa Mehta; ***W:*** Deepa Mehta, Esta Spalding; ***C:*** Douglas Koch; ***M:*** Talvin Singh.

Repulsion ½ **1965** Character study of a young French girl who is repulsed and attracted by sex. Left alone when her sister goes on vacation, her facade of stability begins to crack, with violent and bizarre results. Polanski's first film in English and his first publicly accepted full-length feature. Suspenseful, disturbing and potent. **105m/B VHS, DVD.** *GB* Catherine Deneuve, Yvonne Furneaux, Ian Hendry, John Fraser, Patrick Wymark, James Villiers, Renee Houston, Helen Fraser, Mike Pratt, Valerie Taylor; ***D:*** Roman Polanski; ***W:*** Roman Polanski, Gerard Brach, David Stone; ***C:*** Gilbert Taylor.

Requiem for a Dream ½ **2000** Amazing performances from the entire cast, particularly Burstyn, propel this harrowing story of drug addiction and crumbled dreams. Harry (Leto) and his friend Tyrone (Wayans) decide to become small-time drug dealers in order to raise the cash needed to help his designer girlfriend Marion (Connelly) open a clothing store. Unfortunately, they begin to sample the merchandise, and their plans slip away until all they can plan is how to get the next fix. In a parallel storyline, Harry's mother Sara (Burstyn) receives a call that she may be a contestant on her favorite game show. She begins gobbling diet pills to improve her appearance and soon can't live without them. Director Aronofsky has stated that addiction is the hero of this movie. Based on the novel by Hubert Selby, Jr. **102m/C VHS, DVD.** Jared Leto, Ellen Burstyn, Jennifer Connelly, Marlon Wayans, Christopher McDonald, Louise Lasser, Keith David, Sean Gullette; ***D:*** Darren Aronofsky; ***W:*** Darren Aronofsky, Hubert Selby Jr.; ***C:*** Matthew Libatique; ***M:*** Clint Mansell. Ind. Spirit '01: Actress (Burstyn), Cinematog.

Requiem for a Heavyweight **1956** Original TV version of the story about an American Indian heavyweight boxer played by Palance who risks blindness in order to help his manager pay off bookies. Highly acclaimed teleplay written for "Playhouse 90." **90m/B VHS.** Jack Palance, Keenan Wynn, Ed Wynn, Kim Hunter, Ned Glass; ***D:*** Ralph Nelson; ***W:*** Rod Serling. **TV**

Requiem for a Heavyweight *Blood Money* **1962** After 17 years, Mountain Rivera (Quinn) is a washed-up heavyweight risking his life if he continues boxing. He tries to find another job but his manager, Maish Rennick (Gleason), owes the mob big, and persuades the fighter to help him pay off his debts by joining the wrestling circuit, so Mountain humiliates himself to help out his old friend. The 1956 TV version is still more compelling but the film's performances are all first-rate. **100m/B VHS, DVD.** Anthony Quinn, Jackie Gleason, Mickey Rooney, Julie Harris, Stanley Adams, Spivy Levoe, Muhammad Ali, Jack Dempsey; ***D:*** Ralph Nelson; ***W:*** Rod Serling; ***C:*** Arthur Ornitz; ***M:*** Laurence Rosenthal.

Requiem for Dominic ½ *Requiem fur Dominic* **1991 (R)** A Communist-bloc country in the midst of revolution accuses a man of terrorist activities. Can his friend, exiled for years, help him discover the truth? Interesting and timely premise matched with outstanding ensemble acting make for a superior thriller. Amnesty International receives partial proceeds from all sales of this video. In German with English subtitles. **88m/C VHS.** *GE* Felix Mitterer, Viktoria Schubert, August Schmolzer, Angelica Schutz; ***D:*** Robert Dornhelm.

Requiem for Murder ½ **1999 (PG-13)** Psychotic fan of a classical radio DJ decides to murder her competition. **95m/C VHS, DVD.** Molly Ringwald, Chris Heyerdahl, Lynne Adams, Chris Mulkey, Jayne Heitmeyer; ***D:*** Douglas Jackson; ***W:*** Matt Dorff; ***C:*** Barry Gravelle; ***M:*** Milan Kymlicka. **VIDEO**

The Rescue ½ **1988 (PG)** An elite team of U.S. Navy Seals is captured after destroying a disabled submarine. When the U.S. government writes off the men, their children decide to mount a rescue. Puerile, empty-headed trash for teens. **97m/C VHS.** Marc Price, Charles Haid, Kevin Dillon, Christina Harnos, Edward Albert; ***D:*** Ferdinand Fairfax; ***W:*** Jim Thomas, John Thomas; ***C:*** Russell Boyd; ***M:*** Bruce Broughton.

Rescue Dawn **2006 (PG-13)** Brutal true survival story of Dieter Dengler, the only American POW to ever escape from a prison camp in the Laotian jungle and return alive to his own side. Director Herzog—who also helmed a documentary version of Dengler's epic experience a decade earlier with "Little Dieter Needs to Fly"—forgoes the flashy effects and plot complications of most modern war films in favor of raw storytelling. Funny guy Zahn is notable in a rare non-comic screen role. **125m/C DVD, Blu-ray Disc.** Christian Bale, Steve Zahn, Jeremy Davies, Evan Jones, Marshall Bell, Zach Grenier, Toby Huss, Abhijati Jusakul, Pat Healy, Galen Yuen, Chaiyan Chunsuttiwat; ***D:*** Werner Herzog; ***W:*** Werner Herzog; ***C:*** Peter Zietleinger; ***M:*** Klaus Bartle.

Rescue from Gilligan's Island ½ **1978** Fifteen years after the cancellation of "Gilligan's Island" came this TV movie that reunited the principal cast (minus Tina Louise's original Ginger) and finally depicted the rescue of the castaways. When a tsunami sweeps the group's huts into the sea, they're discovered by the Coast Guard and return to civilization. Somewhat changed by their experiences on the island, the castaways face difficulties assimilating with modern life, while at the same time Gilligan is pursued by Russian spies sent to retrieve an information disc that landed on the island. This awkward return to the lame jokes and Keaton-inspired slapstick of the TV series seemed out of date even during the original broadcast, but the cast's chemistry is still evident. **92m/C VHS, DVD.** Bob Denver, Alan Hale Jr., Russell Johnson, Jim Backus, Natalie Schafer, Dawn Wells, Judith Baldwin; ***D:*** Leslie Martinson; ***W:*** David Harmon, Sherwood Schwartz, Elroy Schwartz, Al Schwartz; ***C:*** Robert Primes; ***M:*** Gerald Fried. **TV**

Rescue Me ½ **1993 (PG-13)** Geek photographer Fraser carries a torch for high school honey Ginny and just happens to be on the scene (with camera) when she's kidnapped. So he persuades a scruffy Vietnam vet to help him rescue his damsel in distress. Likeable adventure with lots of chases. **99m/C VHS.** Michael Dudikoff, Stephen Dorff, Peter DeLuise, Ami Dolenz, William Lucking, Dee Wallace; ***D:*** Arthur Allan Seidelman; ***W:*** Michael Snyder; ***C:*** Hanania Baer; ***M:*** Al Kasha, Joel Hirschhorn, David Waters.

The Rescuers **1977 (G)** Bernard and Miss Bianca, two mice who are members of the Rescue Aid Society, attempt to rescue an orphan named Penny from the evil Madame Medusa, who's after the world's biggest diamond. They are aided by comic sidekick, Orville the albatross, and a group of lovable swamp creatures. Very charming in the best Disney tradition. Based on the stories of Margery Sharp. Followed by "The Rescuers Down Under." **76m/C VHS, DVD.** ***D:*** Wolfgang Reitherman, John Lounsbery; ***M:*** Artie Butler; ***V:*** Bob Newhart, Eva Gabor, Geraldine Page, Jim Jordan, Joe Flynn, Jeannette Nolan, Pat Buttram.

The Rescuers Down Under ½ **1990 (G)** "Crocodile" Dundee goes Disney; the followup to "The Rescuers" places its characters in Australia with only mild results for a Magic Kingdom product. Heroic mice Bernard and Bianca protect a young boy and a rare golden eagle from a poacher. The great bird closely resembles the logo of Republic Pictures. **77m/C VHS, DVD.** ***D:*** Hendel Butoy, Mike Gabriel; ***W:*** Jim Cox, Karey Kirkpatrick, Joe Ranft, Byron Simpson; ***M:*** Bruce Broughton; ***V:*** Bob Newhart, Eva Gabor, John Candy, Tristan Rogers, George C. Scott, Frank Welker, Adam Ryen.

Rescuers: Stories of Courage—Two Couples **1998 (PG)** In "Aart and Joht Je Vos," Delaney and Donovan are Dutch newlyweds who turn their home into a refuge for Jews hiding from the Nazis. The second story, "Marie Taquet," features Hamilton in the title role as a Belgian who, along with her husband (Molina), hides Jewish students at their Catholic boarding school. These true stories are based on the book "Rescuers: Portraits of Moral Courage in the Holocaust." **109m/C VHS.** Dana Delany, Martin Donovan, Linda Hamilton, Alfred Molina, Jan Rubes, Nigel Bennett, James Kidnie, Nicholas Kilbertus, Scott Speedman; ***D:*** Tim Hunter, Lynne Littman; ***W:*** Paul Monash, Francine Carroll, Cy Chermack; ***C:*** Miroslaw Baszak; ***M:*** Pino Donaggio, Hummie Mann. **CABLE**

Rescuers: Stories of Courage "Two Women" 🦴🦴🦴 **1997 (PG-13)** Fact-based drama about Gentiles who sheltered Jews from Nazi persecution during WWII. In "Mamusha" Perkins plays Gertruda, a Catholic nanny in Poland, who poses as the mother of her orphaned Jewish charge. "The Woman on the Bicycle" is French-woman Marie-Rose (Ward), who works for the Resistance and hides a Jewish family in the attic of her home. **107m/C VHS.** Elizabeth Perkins, Sela Ward, Fritz Weaver, Anne Jackson, Al Waxman, Gerard Parkes, Michael Landes; ***D:*** Peter Bogdanovich; ***W:*** Ernest Kinoy, Terry Norris; ***C:*** Miroslaw Baszak; ***M:*** Hummie Mann. **CABLE**

Reservation Road 🦴🦴 **2007 (R)** Dwight Arno (Ruffalo) is a small town Connecticut lawyer. Already running late returning his son to his ex-wife's home at the end of a visitation day spent at a Red Sox game, Dwight accidentally strikes and kills a young boy with his car, then in a panic flees the scene. The dead boy's father, Ethan Learner (Phoenix), is a local professor who, expectedly grief stricken and filled with anger, becomes dissatisfied with local law enforcement's inability to find his son's killer and seeks the assistance of an attorney—who ends up being Dwight. Dwight, meanwhile, is obviously conflicted. An unfortunate series of coincidences stretch believability and derail this overly melodramatic story. Fans of Joaquin Phoenix will still enjoy his raw, emotional performance. **102m/C DVD.** *US* Joaquin Rafael (Leaf) Phoenix, Mark Ruffalo, Jennifer Connelly, Christopher Sorvino, Elle Fanning, John Slattery, Antoni Corone, Sean Curley, Eddie Alderson; ***D:*** Terry George; ***W:*** John Burnham Schwartz; ***C:*** John Lindley; ***M:*** Mark Isham.

Reservoir Dogs 🦴🦴🦴 ½ **1992 (R)** Ultraviolent tale of honor among thieves. Six professional criminals known by code names to protect their identities (Misters Pink, White, Orange, Blonde, Blue, and Brown) are assembled by Joe Cabot (Tierney) to pull off a diamond heist. But two of the gang are killed in a police ambush. The survivors regroup in an empty warehouse and try to discover the informer in their midst. In probably the most stomach-churning scene (there is some competition here), a policeman is tortured (by Madsen) just for the heck of it to the tune of the Stealers Wheel "Stuck in the Middle with You." Unrelenting; auspicious debut for Tarantino with strong ensemble cast anchored by Keitel as the very professional Mr. White. **100m/C VHS, DVD, Blu-ray Disc.** Harvey Keitel, Tim Roth, Michael Madsen, Steve Buscemi, Christopher Penn, Lawrence Tierney, Kirk Baltz, Quentin Tarantino, Edward (Eddie) Bunker, Randy Brooks; ***D:*** Quentin Tarantino; ***W:*** Quentin Tarantino; ***C:*** Andrzej Sekula; ***M:*** Karyn Rachtman; ***V:*** Steven Wright. Ind. Spirit '93: Support. Actor (Buscemi).

Resident Evil 🦴🦴 **2002 (R)** Yet another noisy movie adapted from a videogame, which never gets as creepy as a zombie movie should. Umbrella Corp. (AKA the Hive) is the front for a secret military tech and genetics operations. Its security operations are controlled by a A.I. computer known as the Red Queen, which instigates a series of defensive measures to contain a virus (that can reanimate the dead) that has been released. A group of containment specialists (including heroine babe Jovanovich) are sent in and have to battle workers who have been contaminated and turned into flesh-munching creatures. **100m/C VHS, DVD, Blu-ray Disc, UMD.** *GE GB* Milla Jovovich, Michelle Rodriguez, Colin Salmon, Eric Mabius, James Purefoy, Stephen Billington; ***D:*** Paul W.S. Anderson; ***W:*** Paul W.S. Anderson; ***C:*** David C(lark) Johnson; ***M:*** Marco Beltrami.

Resident Evil: Apocalypse 🦴 **2004 (R)** While its predecessor was a moderately successful return to pulp science-fiction films, this outing is nothing of the kind. It's less of a sequel than a regurgitating of the earlier installment but with fewer thrills, less action, and an inconsequential story. Alice and a new batch of survivors are trying to escape the city above The Hive, which has been re-infected with the T-virus. By simply rehashing the first film, any fresh conflict is forgone. Lack of suspense and characterization make for an uninspired, unoriginal, and thoroughly unenjoyable genre pic. **93m/C VHS, DVD, Blu-ray Disc, UMD.** *GB CA* Milla Jovovich, Sienna Guillory, Oded Fehr, Thomas Kretschmann, Sophie Vavasseur, Jared Harris, Mike Epps, Sandrine Holt, Raz Adoti, Zack (Zach) Ward, Iain Glen; ***D:*** Alexander Witt; ***W:*** Paul W.S. Anderson; ***C:*** Christian Sebaldt, Derek Rogers; ***M:*** Jeff Danna.

Resident Evil: Extinction 🦴 ½ **2007 (R)** Video game franchise trades claustrophobic underground sets for "Road Warrior" style wasteland, but star Jovovich is stuck battling the same old zombies. This time super-powered Alice meets up with a convoy of refugees led by Larter and Fehr, trying to stay one step ahead of the zombie virus. Between the zombies and the evil corporation that created them, there's not much hope that they'll make it to safety unscathed. Instead, they must make a stand in a mostly sand-buried Las Vegas (created by Oscar-winning production designer Caballero). Short on originality, the movie depends on its mostly dull action scenes and its franchise status to keep viewers interested. **94m/C DVD, Blu-ray Disc.** *CA GB* Milla Jovovich, Oded Fehr, Ali Larter, Iain Glen, Ashanti, Christopher Egan, Spencer Locke, Matthew Mardsen, Linden Ashby, Mike Epps, Jason O'Mara; ***D:*** Russell Mulcahy; ***W:*** Paul W.S. Anderson; ***C:*** David Johnson; ***M:*** Charlie Clouser.

Resilience 🦴 ½ **2006** Corporate manager Jimmy finds doing a good deed brings lots of trouble. He fakes the work record of his destitute Uncle Hodge to get him a job and then gets blackmailed by his shifty cousin Andrew. Jimmy learns a drug dealer has put a contract out on the troublesome Andrew and he can't decide whether to warn him or let the hit take place, which would solve Jimmy's own problems with the sleazebag. **96m/C DVD.** Henry LeBlanc, Steve Wilcox, Al Rossi, Julie Alexander, Amy Arce; ***D:*** Paul Bojack; ***W:*** Paul Bojack; ***C:*** Michael Parry; ***M:*** Markian Federowycz.

Resistance 🦴🦴 **1992** Apocalytic tale of rebels and soldiers. The poor have been driven from abandoned cities into working as farm hands for a large corporation. When the workers rebel, anti-terrorist squads manage to make the situation worse and a full-scale rebellion begins. **112m/C VHS, DVD.** Jack Thompson, Stephen Leeder, Robyn Nevin, Harold Hopkins, Helen Jones, Kris McQuade, Hugh Keays-Byrne; ***D:*** Paul Elliot.

Resistance 🦴🦴 **2003 (R)** Wartime romance based on the novel by Anita Shreve. American fighter pilot Ted Brice (Paxton) is shot down over Belgium in 1944. He's badly injured but brought to safety by members of the resistance. Hidden and cared for by Claire (Ormond), whose husband Henri (Volter) is away on a mission, they soon find love. When their affair is discovered by Henri, it sets up more than one betrayal. **92m/C DVD.** Bill Paxton, Julia Ormond, Philippe Volter, Sandrine Bonnaire, Jean-Michel Vovk, Antoine Van Lierde; ***D:*** Todd Komarnicki; ***W:*** Todd Komarnicki; ***C:*** Marc Felperlaan; ***M:*** Angelo Badalamenti.

A Respectable Trade 🦴🦴 ½ **1998** Frances Scott (Fielding) has lost her position as a governess in 1788 Bristol, England. A job-search letter gathers Frances a marriage proposal from Josiah Cole (Clarke), an older, earnest, social climbing businessman whose trade happens to be slaves. Josiah wishes Frances to teach English to some of his property so they may be sold as house servants and Frances begins to feel something special for one of the group—Moses (Bakare)—who turns out to be much more of an educated gentleman than her own husband. Based on Gregory's 1995 novel. **240m/C VHS, DVD.** *GB* Emma Fielding, Warren Clarke, Ariyon Bakare, Anna Massey; ***D:*** Suri Krishnamma; ***W:*** Philippa Gregory. **TV**

The Respectful Prostitute 🦴🦴 ½ **1952** Sartre's tale of a hooker who is cajoled into providing false testimony as a witness in the trial of a member of a prominent family. English language version of French drama. **75m/B VHS.** *FR* Ivan Desny, Barbara Laage, Walter Bryan; ***D:*** Marcel Pagliero, Charles Brabant; ***W:*** Jean-Paul Sartre.

Respiro 🦴🦴 *I Breathe; Respiro: Grazia's Island* **2002 (PG-13)** Grazia (Golino—the only professional in the cast) does not fit into the usual life of the small Sicilian fishing village of Lempedusa. Although devoted to her husband Pietro (Amato) and their children, Grazia's emotions are volatile (even by Italian standards)—maybe she needs professional help? When Pietro tries to send his wife to Milan for treatment, she runs away to hide out in a local cave, depending on her 13-year-old son Pasquale (Casisa) to protect her. The film replaces reality (the fact that Grazia has a mental illness) with poetics (she's really just a free-spirit) but you'll be lulled by its charms. Italian with subtitles. **95m/C VHS, DVD.** *IT FR* Valeria Golino, Vincenzo Amato, Francesco Casisa, Veronica D'Agostino, Filippo Pucillo, Muzzi Loffredo, Elio Germano; ***D:*** Emanuele Crialese; ***W:*** Emanuele Crialese; ***C:*** Fabio Zamarion; ***M:*** John Surman.

Rest in Pieces 🦴 **1987 (R)** A young woman inherits a Spanish mansion, and weird things begin to happen. It seems a cult of Satan worshippers is already living on the estate. As one might infer from the title, quite a bit of hacking and slashing ensues. **90m/C VHS.** Scott Thompson Baker, Lorin Jean, Dorothy Malone; ***D:*** Joseph (Jose Ramon Larraz) Braunstein.

Rest Stop 🦴 *Rest Stop: Dead Ahead* **2006** The dumbest woman of all time and her boyfriend pause at a rest stop while en route to California. When she returns from the loo he's gone, and then she finds a torture victim in the restroom who apparently couldn't speak up before. Eventually she gets chased by a psycho, tries to escape by hitching a ride with a family of psychos, and makes other unfortunate choices, including getting drunk and passing out instead of going for help. **85m/C DVD.** Joey Mendicino, Deanna Russo, Joseph Lawrence, Mikey Post, Diane Salinger, Jaimie Alexander, Michael Childers, Nick Orefice; ***D:*** John Shiban; ***W:*** John Shiban; ***C:*** Mark Vargo; ***M:*** Bear McCreary.

Rest Stop: Don't Look Back 🦴 ½ *Rest Stop 2* **2008** One year after the events of the first film, the brother of one of the victims returns from Iraq and goes looking for her. He and his companions immediately find an eyewitness who proceeds to give the stereotypical "y'all wanna leave this place" explanation germane to all bad horror films. The killers from the original return, and once again you have an average torture flick, spiced up only by the appearance of ghosts from the victims killed in the first go-round. **89m/C DVD, Blu-ray Disc.** Richard Tillman, Jessie Ward, Mikey Post, Julie Mond, Joey Mendicino, Graham Norris; ***D:*** Shawn Papazian; ***C:*** Jas Shelton; ***M:*** Bear McCreary. **VIDEO**

Restaurant 🦴 ½ **1998 (R)** Would-be showbiz types all work at the same swanky New Jersey restaurant while exploring their relationships and ambitions. Recovering alcoholic and aspiring playwright Chris (Brody) is still carrying a torch for ex-girlfriend, Leslie (Hill) who slept with actor/co-worker Kenny (Baker), who's been cast in Chris' new play, much to his dismay. Meanwhile, Chris is trying a new romance with singer/waitress Jeanine (Neal). Although race doesn't seem to be a problem in personal relations (Chris is white, both his girlfriends are black), it starts to raise ugly problems at work (and change the tenor of the movie). **107m/C DVD.** Adrien Brody, Elise Neal, David Moscow, Simon Baker, Catherine Kellner, Malcolm Jamal Warner, Lauryn Hill, John Carroll Lynch, Sybil Temchen, Vonte Sweet, Michael Stoyanov; ***D:*** Eric Bross; ***W:*** Tom Cudworth; ***C:*** Horacio Marquinez; ***M:*** Theodore Shapiro.

Restless 🦴 *The Beloved* **1972** A restless homemaker begins an affair with a childhood friend. Director Cosmatos later oversaw "Rambo." **75m/C VHS.** *GR* Raquel Welch, Richard Johnson, Jack Hawkins, Flora Robson; ***D:*** George P. Cosmatos.

The Restless 🦴🦴 ½ *Joong Chun; Joong-cheon* **2006** Yi Gwak (Woo-sung Jung) was born able to see evil spirits and joins a squad of demon hunters after the monsters kill his fiancee. As the squad finally begins to push back the forces of darkness they journey to the worlds beyond to confront them, and Yi Gwak enters a shrine to the Gods, and ends up in Mid Heaven where souls wait their 49 days before Reincarnation. He agrees to help the Goddess Yon-Hwa (Tae-hee Kim) in a quest against the demons not because it's the right thing, but because she is the reincarnation of his fiancee. **102m/C DVD.** *KN CH* Woo-sung Jung, Jun-ho Heo, Tae-hee Kim; ***D:*** Dong-oh Cho, Dong-oh Jo; ***W:*** Dong-oh Cho, Dong-oh Jo, Hee-dae Lee; ***C:*** Young-Ho Kim; ***M:*** Shiroh Sagisu.

The Restless Breed 🦴 **1958** Son is restless after dad, a secret service agent, is slain by gunrunners. Routine oater-revenge epic done in by listless script. **81m/C VHS.** Scott Brady, Anne Bancroft, Jay C. Flippen, Rhys Williams, Jim Davis; ***D:*** Allan Dwan.

Restless Spirits 🦴🦴 ½ *Dead Aviators* **1999** Sullen Katie (Wimbles) and her young brother Simon (Swan) arrive to stay with their grandmother Lydia (Mason) in Porter's Point, Newfoundland. Both children are still grieving over the death of their aviator father in a crash four years before. While exploring a remote pond, Katie encounters the ghosts of French airmen Nungesser (Bluteau) and Coli (Monty). In 1927, they left Paris in a biplane on a nonstop trans-Atlantic flight to New York and disappeared. It seems their plane crashed into Porter's Pond and until the plane can be recovered they are doomed to wander its banks. Katie's determined to help, though no one believes her story. **95m/C VHS, DVD.** *CA* Juliana Wimbles, Lothaire Bluteau, Michel Monty, Marsha Mason, Leslie Hope, Ben Cook, Eugene Lipinski, Nickolas Swan; ***D:*** David Wellington; ***W:*** Semi Chellas; ***C:*** Andre Pienaar; ***M:*** Ron Sures. **CABLE**

Restoration 🦴🦴🦴 **1994 (R)** Set in the 17th century after Charles II is restored to the British throne, the title may instead refer to the restoration of one man's values. After curing one of the king's dogs, physician Downey is elevated to courtier and falls into drunken debauchery. He is soon forced to marry (but not touch) the king's favorite mistress. Unfortunately, he is caught trespassing on his majesty's main squeeze and banished from the court. Cast among the common rabble, he encounters the plague and the Great Fire of London while trying to redeem himself. Strong cast and sumptuous set design help to propel Downey's performance. Adapted from Rose Tremain's 1989 novel. Release was delayed a year because no one could seem to come up with a marketing strategy. **118m/C VHS, DVD.** Robert Downey Jr., Meg Ryan, Sam Neill, Hugh Grant, David Thewlis, Polly Walker, Ian McKellen; ***D:*** Michael Hoffman; ***W:*** Rupert Walters; ***C:*** Oliver Stapleton; ***M:*** James Newton Howard. Oscars '95: Art Dir./Set Dec., Costume Des.

Restraining Order 🦴🦴 **1999 (R)** Lawyer Robert Woodfield (Roberts) witnesses a murder that's committed by a former client. He contacts a friend in the D.A.'s office but when that friend is also murdered and Woodfield's efforts to bring the killer to justice are futile, he decides to personally avenge the crimes. **95m/C VHS, DVD.** Eric Roberts, Hannes Jaenicke, Tatjana Patitz, Dean Stockwell; ***D:*** Lee H. Katzin; ***W:*** John Jarrell; ***M:*** David Wurst, Eric Wurst. **VIDEO**

Restraint 🦴🦴 **2008 (R)** Ron and Dale are a couple of not-so-bright criminals who get into a mess and need a place to hide out. They come across what they think is an abandoned mansion, only wealthy agoraphobic Andrew actually lives there and the duo take him hostage. Except Andrew is really willing and starts telling Dale how much she looks like his ex-fiancee, who just happened to leave all her things behind when she supposedly left him. So who's really got the upper hand? **92m/C DVD.** *AU* Stephen Moyer, Teresa Palmer, Travis Fimmel; ***D:*** David Denneen; ***W:*** David T. Wagner; ***C:*** Simon Duggan; ***M:*** Elliott Wheeler.

Restrepo **2010** Director/cinematographers Junger and Hetherington shadow the 173rd Airborne Brigade through their year-long deployment in Afghanistan's dangerous Korengal Valley. **92m/C DVD.** *US* ***D:*** Tim Hetherington, Sebastian Junger; ***C:*** Tim Hetherington, Sebastian Junger.

The Resurrected 1/2 **1991 (R)** One of the best recent H.P. Lovecraft horror adaptations, a fairly faithful try at "The Case of Charles Dexter Ward." Ward learns he has a satanic ancestor who possessed the secret of resurrection and eternal life—but, as the warlock says, it is very messy. Surprisingly tasteful even with occasional gore and truly ghastly monsters; in fact this pic could have used a bit more intensity. **108m/C VHS, DVD.** John Terry, Jane Sibbett, Chris Sarandon, Robert Romanus; ***D:*** Dan O'Bannon; ***M:*** Richard Band.

Resurrecting the Champ **2007 (PG-13)** Erik Kernan (Hartnett) is a sports reporter looking for a big story. He thinks he's found it in Bob "Champ" Satterfield (Jackson), a former contender now homeless in Denver. Moving from back page to the top of the heap, Erik pursues his big chance to make a name for himself without much concern for Champ. After his feature story is published he realizes that everything might not be what it seems, and of course there's a valuable lesson to be learned. Hartnett tries but ultimately can't give his flawed character depth, and is forced to carry far more weight than he's capable of. Any energy Jackson gives to the movie disappears the second he's not on the screen. Loosely based on a true story about writer J.R. Moehringer and real-life boxer Satterfield. **111m/C DVD.** *US* Samuel L. Jackson, Josh Hartnett, Teri Hatcher, Kathryn Morris, Alan Alda, David Paymer, Rachel Nichols, Dakota Goyo, Harry J. Lennix, Peter Coyote, Ryan McDonald; ***D:*** Rod Lurie; ***W:*** Michael Bortman, Allison Burnett; ***C:*** Adam Kane; ***M:*** Lawrence Nash Groupe.

Resurrection 1/2 **1980 (PG)** After a near-fatal car accident, a woman finds she has the power to heal others by touch. She denies that God is responsible, much to her Bible Belt community's dismay. Acclaimed and well-acted. **103m/C VHS.** Ellen Burstyn, Sam Shepard, Roberts Blossom, Eva LeGallienne, Clifford David, Richard Farnsworth, Pamela Payton-Wright; ***D:*** Daniel Petrie; ***W:*** Lewis John Carlino; ***M:*** Maurice Jarre. Natl. Bd. of Review '80: Support. Actress (LeGallienne).

Resurrection **1999 (R)** Chicago detectives John Prudhomme (Lambert) and Andrew Hollinsworth (Orser) are tracking a serial killer (Joy) who is killing men named after Christ's 12 apostles. He intends to use parts of his victims to reassemble the body of Christ in time for Easter Sunday resurrection. **108m/C VHS, DVD.** Christopher Lambert, Leland Orser, Robert Joy, Rick Fox, Barbara Tyson, James Kidnie, David Cronenberg; ***D:*** Russell Mulcahy; ***W:*** Brad Mirman; ***C:*** Jonathan Freeman; ***M:*** Jim McGrath.

Resurrection Man **1997 (R)** Sociopath Victor Kelly (Townsend) is in his element in 1975's Belfast when he's recruited to lead a group of Loyalist killers known as the "Resurrection Men." The gang's violence draws the attention of journalist Ryan (Nesbitt), who makes them media stars, and local cop Ferguson (Thompson), who wants to bring them down. Soon, though, Victor's capacity for bloodshed begins to worry older hood, McLure (McGinley), who thinks they'll all be better off without Victor. Very creepy atmosphere sustained by some appalling violence. Based on the novel by McNamee, who also wrote the screenplay. **100m/C VHS.** *GB* Stuart Townsend, James Nesbitt, Sean McGinley, Derek Thompson, John Hannah, Geraldine O'Rawe, Brenda Fricker, James Ellis, B.J. Hogg, Zara Turner; ***D:*** Marc Evans; ***W:*** Eoin McNamee; ***C:*** Pierre Aim; ***M:*** David Holmes, Gary Burns, Keith Tenniswood.

Resurrection of Zachary Wheeler 1/2 **1971 (G)** A presidential candidate, who narrowly escaped death in an auto crash, is brought to a mysterious clinic in New Mexico. A reporter sneaks into the clinic and discovers the horrors of cloning. **100m/C VHS.** Angie Dickinson, Bradford Dillman, Leslie Nielsen, Jack Carter, James Daly; ***D:*** Bob Wynn.

Retreat, Hell! **1952** Korean War drama about the retreat from the Changjin Reservoir. Standard gun-ho military orientation with dismal results. **95m/B VHS.** Frank Lovejoy, Richard Carlson, Russ Tamblyn, Anita Louise; ***D:*** Joseph H. Lewis.

Retribution 1/2 **1988 (R)** Struggling artist survives suicide attempt only to find himself possessed by the spirit of a criminal who was tortured to death. Seeing the hood's gruesome demise in his dreams, the survivor sets out to bring his murderers face-to-face with their maker. **106m/C VHS.** Dennis Lipscomb, Hoyt Axton, Leslie Wing, Suzanne Snyder; ***D:*** Guy Magar.

Retribution *Complicity* **1998 (R)** Cameron Colley (Miller) is an investigative journalist who constantly runs into trouble with his editors. He's also addicted to cigarettes, cocaine, computer games, and sex with the married Yvonne (Hawes). Now he's looking into a series of grisly murders that possibly lead back to the youthful protests of a group of activists. Tends to be confusing more than compelling. Based on the novel by Iain Banks. **99m/C VHS, DVD.** *GB* Jonny Lee Miller, Brian Cox, Keeley Hawes, Paul Higgins, Bill Paterson, Samuel West, Rachael Stirling, Jason Hetherington; ***D:*** Gavin Millar; ***W:*** Bryan Elsley; ***C:*** David Odd; ***M:*** Colin Towns.

Retribution 1/2 *Sakebi* **2006 (R)** Yoshioka (Koji Yakusho) is a cop investigating the murder of a local woman. Unfortunately the evidence seems to point to him though he doesn't remember doing it. After being visited by her ghost he assumes he must have did it and then blocked it out. Shortly after this more people die, and the evidence still points to Yoshioka. With any luck he may be able to blame the ghost. **104m/C DVD.** *JP* Koji Yakusho, Manami Konishi, Tsuyoski Ihara, Joe Odagiri, Kaoru Okunuki, Ikuji Nakamura, Hironobu Nomura; ***D:*** Kiyoshi Kurosawa; ***W:*** Kiyoshi Kurosawa; ***C:*** Akiko Ashizawa; ***M:*** Kuniaki Haishima.

Retribution Road 1/2 *Blue Eyes* **2007 (PG-13)** A bank robbery gone wrong lands Wardlaw, Texas sheriff Gimbol with notorious outlaw Johnny Rios as a prisoner in his jail. However, Rios' family will stop at nothing to break him out, even if it means they destroy the town trying. **75m/C DVD.** Michael Gregory, Leslie Easterbrook, Peter Sherayko, John Castellanos, Eduardo Enriquez Jr., Mark Enriquez; ***D:*** Chuck Walker; ***W:*** Chuck Walker. **VIDEO**

Retrievers **1982** Young man and a former CIA agent team up to expose the unsavory practices of the organization. **90m/C VHS, DVD.** Max (Michael) Thayer, Roselyn Royce, Richard Anderson, Shawn Hoskins, Mary McCormick, Lenard Miller; ***D:*** Elliot Hong; ***W:*** Elliot Hong; ***C:*** Stephen Kim; ***M:*** Ted Ashford.

Retro Puppet Master **1999 (PG-13)** Most recent entry in the "Puppet Master" series is officially the first, finding a young Toulon in pre-World War I Paris where he falls in love with the daughter of the Swiss ambassador. Of course, the puppets and other mini-critters are involved too. **90m/C DVD.** Guy Rolfe, Greg Sestero, Brigitta Dau, Jack Donner, Stephen Blackehart; ***D:*** Joseph Tennent; ***W:*** Benjamin Carr; ***C:*** Viorel Sergovici Jr.; ***M:*** John Massari.

Retroactive **1997 (R)** Scientist Brian (Whaley) has been experimenting with reversing time and finally manages to make his project work. Meanwhile, police psychologist Karen (Travis) has has car trouble and been given a ride by Frank (Belushi) and his wife Rayanne (Whirry). Karen soon realizes Frank is a psycho and escapes, stumbling into Brian's lab. But Brian's just reversed time and Karen winds up back in Frank's car, trying to change the sequence of events. **91m/C VHS, DVD.** James Belushi, Kylie Travis, Shannon Whirry, Frank Whaley, Jesse Borrego, M. Emmet Walsh, Guy Boyd; ***D:*** Louis Morneau; ***W:*** Robert Strauss, Phillip Badger; ***C:*** George Mooradian; ***M:*** Tim Truman.

The Return **WOOF!** *The Alien's Return* **1980 (PG)** Vincent and Shepherd meet as adults and discover that they had both, as children, been visited by aliens who had given technology to a cattle-mutilating prospector. A mess with no idea of what sort of film it wants to be. **91m/C VHS.** Cybill Shepherd, Raymond Burr, Jan-Michael Vincent, Martin Landau, Vincent Schiavelli, Zachary Vincent, Farah Bunch, Neville Brand, Susan Kiger; ***D:*** Greydon Clark.

Return **1988 (R)** A woman believes that the man she loves is the reincarnation of her dead grandfather. Interesting concept, but overall, a disappointing mystery. **78m/C VHS.** Frederic Forrest, Anne Francis, Karlene Crockett, John Walcutt, Lisa Richards; ***D:*** Andrew Silver.

The Return 1/2 **2006 (PG-13)** Supernatural thriller that substitutes atmospheric moodiness for actual plot and dialogue. Joanna (Gellar) is a sales rep who uses the constant movement of her job to escape the visions and blackouts that have plagued her since her childhood. When business brings her back to her hometown, her hallucinations intensify. She begins seeing visions of a woman and the mysterious dirtbag who may have murdered her. Soon Joanna is being stalked by the killer, as well as by a jilted ex and a sexy stranger who also seems wrapped up in the mystery. **85m/C DVD.** *US* Sarah Michelle Gellar, Peter O'Brien, Adam Scott, Kate Beahan, Sam Shepard, J.C. MacKenzie, Erinn Allison; ***D:*** Asif Kapadia; ***W:*** Adam Sussman; ***C:*** Roman Osin; ***M:*** Dario Marianelli.

Return Engagement 1/2 **1978** A lonely middle-aged ancient history professor falls in love with one of her students. **76m/C VHS.** Elizabeth Taylor, Joseph Bottoms, Peter Donat, James Ray; ***D:*** Joseph Hardy.

Return Fire 1/2 *Jungle Wolf 2* **1988 (R)** A former employee of the government finds that he must now fight the system if he wants to save his son. Trivial action fare. **97m/C VHS.** Adam West, Ron Marchini, Mindi Miller; ***D:*** Neil Callaghan, Neil Callaghan; ***W:*** Neil Callaghan, Neil Callaghan; ***C:*** Dan Goodman, Dan Goodman.

Return from Witch Mountain 1/2 **1978 (G)** A pair of evil masterminds use a boy's supernatural powers to place Los Angeles in nuclear jeopardy. Sequel to Disney's ever-popular "Escape to Witch Mountain." **93m/C VHS, DVD.** Christopher Lee, Bette Davis, Ike Eisenmann, Kim Richards, Jack Soo, Helene Winston; ***D:*** John Hough; ***W:*** Malcolm Marmorstein.

The Return of a Man Called Horse **1976 (PG)** Sequel to "A Man Called Horse" tells the story of an English aristocrat who was captured and raised by Sioux Indians, and then returned to his native homeland. Contains more of the torture scenes for which this series is famous, but not much of Harris. **125m/C VHS, DVD.** Richard Harris, Gale Sondergaard, Geoffrey Lewis; ***D:*** Irvin Kershner; ***W:*** Jack DeWitt; ***C:*** Owen Roizman.

The Return of Boston Blackie 1/2 **1927** The oft-filmed crook/detective tries to retrieve an heiress's stolen jewels. Silent. **77m/B VHS.** Raymond Glenn, Corliss Palmer, Strongheart, Rosemary Cooper, Coit Albertson; ***D:*** Harry Hoyt.

Return of Captain Invincible 1/2 *Legend in Leotards* **1983 (PG)** Arkin is a derelict superhero persuaded to fight crime again in this unique spoof. One liners fly faster than a speeding bullet. Lee gives one of his best performances as the mad scientist. Musical numbers by Rocky Horror's O'Brien and Hartley sporadically interrupt. Made on a shoe-string budget, offbeat film is entertaining but uneven. **102m/C VHS, DVD.** *AU* Alan Arkin, Christopher Lee, Kate Fitzpatrick, Bill Hunter, Graham Kennedy, Michael Pate, Hayes Gordon, Max Phipps, Noel Ferrier; ***D:*** Philippe Mora; ***W:*** Steven E. de Souza, Andrew Gaty; ***C:*** Louis Irving, Mike Molloy; ***M:*** William Motzing, Richard O'Brien.

The Return of Casey Jones *Train 2419* **1934** Early adventure film featuring lots of great railroad action. **64m/B VHS, DVD.** Charles Starrett, Ruth Hall, George "Gabby" Hayes, Robert Elliott, Margaret Seddon, Jackie Searl; ***D:*** John P. McCarthy.

Return of Chandu **1934** This serial in 12 chapters features Bela Lugosi as Chandu, who exercises his magical powers to conquer a religious sect of cat worshippers inhabiting the island of Lemuria. In the process, he fights to save the Princess Nadji from being sacrificed by them. **156m/B VHS, DVD.** Bela Lugosi, Maria Alba, Clara Kimball Young; ***D:*** Ray Taylor.

The Return of Count Yorga **1971 (R)** The vampire Count returns, taking up residence in a decrepit mansion nearby an orphanage. There he spies the toothsome Cynthia and Yorga decides to make her a vampiric bride. But the Count reckons without Cynthia's noble boyfriend who wants to keep his honey on this side of the grave. Preceded by "Count Yorga, Vampire." **97m/C VHS, DVD.** Robert Quarry, Mariette Hartley, Roger Perry, Yvonne Wilder, Rudy DeLuca, George Macready, Walter Brooke, Tom Toner, Karen Huston, Paul Hansen, Craig T. Nelson; ***D:*** Bob Kelljan; ***W:*** Bob Kelljan, Yvonne Wilder; ***C:*** Bill Butler.

Return of Daimajin 1/2 *Daimajin gyakushu; Majin Strikes Again; Return of Majin; The Return of the Giant Majin* **1966** Once again the great god Daimajin sets atop his mountain. Yet another evil overlord has decided to oppress the peasants, kidnapping the fathers of some local kids to labor in his work camps. Their sons set out to rescue them and evil samurai give chase, awaking Daimajin by not paying him proper respect. Considering the first two films, you'd think they'd see this coming. He of course smashes the work camp, and for once doesn't trample the peasants underfoot as well. Dude's getting soft in his old age. **90m/C DVD.** *JP* Riki Hashimoto, Hideki Ninomiya; ***D:*** Kazuo Mori; ***W:*** Tetsuro Yoshida; ***M:*** Akira Ifukube.

The Return of Dr. Fu Manchu 1/2 **1930** Fu Manchu (Oland) fakes his death and once again goes after Jack Petrie (Hamilton) and Scotland Yard Inspector Smith (Heggie), still determined to find revenge. Based on the novel by Sax Rohmer. Sequel to "The Mysterious Dr Fu Manchu." **73m/B VHS.** Warner Oland, O.P. Heggie, Neil Hamilton, Jean Arthur, Evelyn Hall, William Austin, Margaret Fealy; ***D:*** Rowland V. Lee; ***W:*** Lloyd Corrigan, Florence Ryerson; ***C:*** Archie Stout.

The Return of Dr. Mabuse 1/2 *Im Stahlnetz Des Dr. Mabuse; Phantom Fiend* **1961** The evil doctor is back, this time sending his entranced slaves to attack a nuclear power plant. Frobe, the inspector, and Barker, the FBI man, team up to thwart him. Fun for fans of serial detective stories. **88m/B VHS.** *GE FR IT* Gert Frobe, Lex Barker, Daliah Lavi, Wolfgang Preiss, Fausto Tozzi, Rudolph Forster; ***D:*** Harald Reinl.

Return of Dracula *The Curse of Dracula; The Fantastic Disappearing Man* **1958** Low-budget film about the Count killing a Czech artist and assuming his identity as he makes his way to the States. Once there, he moves in with the dead man's family and begins acting rather strangely. Retitled "The Curse of Dracula" for TV. **77m/C VHS.** Francis Lederer, Norma Eberhardt, Ray Stricklyn, Jimmy Baird, John Wengraf, Virginia Vincent, Greta Granstedt; ***D:*** Paul Landres; ***W:*** Pat Fielder; ***C:*** Jack MacKenzie.

Return of Draw Egan 1/2 **1916** Vintage silent western wherein Hart is an outlaw-turned-greenhorn sheriff of a lawless town. Music score. **64m/B VHS.** William S. Hart, Louise Glaum; ***D:*** William S. Hart.

The Return of Eliot Ness 1/2 **1991 (R)** Ness comes out of retirement in 1947 Chicago to track down a friend's killer. And with Al Capone dead, Chicago mob bosses are fighting for their piece of illegal turf. Stack reprises his "The Untouchables" TV role from the early '60s in this made for TV movie. **94m/C VHS, DVD.** Robert Stack, Charles Durning, Philip Bosco, Jack Coleman, Lisa Hartman Black, Anthony De Sando; ***D:*** James A. Contner. **TV**

Return of Frank Cannon **1980** Portly private eye Frank Cannon comes out of retirement to investigate the alleged suicide of an old friend. **96m/C VHS.** William Conrad, Diana Muldaur, Joanna Pettet, Allison Argo, Arthur Hill, Ed Nelson; ***D:*** Corey Allen; ***M:*** Bruce Broughton. **TV**

Return of Frank James **1940** One of Lang's lesser Hollywood works, this is nonetheless an entertaining sequel to 1939's "Jesse James." Brother Frank tries to go straight, but eventually has to hunt down the culprits who murdered his infamous outlaw sibling. Tierney's first film. **92m/C VHS, DVD.** Henry Fonda, Gene Tierney, Jackie Cooper, Henry Hull, John Carradine, Donald Meek, J. Edward Bromberg; ***D:*** Fritz Lang.

The Return of Grey Wolf 1922 A wild dog must fight for survival in Northern Quebec and is befriended by a fur trapper. An intelligent hound, he repays the trapper's generosity by helping him put the moves on some fur thieves. Silent. **62m/B VHS.** Walter Shumway, Helen Lynch, James Pierce; ***D:*** Jack Rollens.

The Return of Jafar 1/2 **1994 (G)** Clumsy thief Abis Mal inadvertently releases evil sorcerer Jafar from his lamp prison and now the powerful "genie Jafar" plots his revenge. So it's up to Aladdin and friends to save the Sultan's kingdom once again. Contains five new songs. ♫Just Forget About Love; Nothing In the World (Quite Like a Friend); I'm Looking Out for Me; You're Only Second Rate; Arabian Nights. **66m/C VHS, DVD.** ***W:*** Kevin Campbell, Mirith J.S. Colao; ***V:*** Scott Weinger, Linda Larkin, Gilbert Gottfried, Val Bettin, Dan Castellaneta, Jason Alexander.

Return of Jesse James 1950 Look-alike of dead outlaw Jesse James joins in with some former members of the James Gang, leading townsfolk to believe the notorious bank robber never died. It's up to brother Frank James, now an upstanding citizen, to set the record straight. A little slow moving at times, but still worth viewing. **77m/B VHS, DVD.** John Ireland, Ann Dvorak, Reed Hadley, Henry Hull, Hugh O'Brian, Tommy Noonan, Peter Marshall; ***D:*** Arthur Hilton.

The Return of Josey Wales 1986 **(R)** No match for the original featuring Clint Eastwood, the title character is played woodenly by Parks. This installment finds Wales pitted against a bumbling lawman. Sequel to 1976's "The Outlaw Josey Wales." **90m/C VHS.** Michael Parks, Rafael Campos, Bob Magruder, Paco Vela, Everett Sifuentes, Charlie McCoy; ***D:*** Michael Parks.

The Return of Martin Guerre 1/2 *Le Retour de Martin Guerre* **1983** In this medieval tale, a dissolute village husband disappears soon after his marriage. Years later, someone who appears to be Martin Guerre returns, allegedly from war, and appears much kinder and more educated. Starring in a love story of second chances, Depardieu does not disappoint, nor does the rest of the cast. In French with English subtitles. Based on an actual court case. Remade in 1993 as "Sommersby." **111m/C VHS, DVD.** *FR* Gerard Depardieu, Roger Planchon, Maurice Jacquemont, Barnard Pierre Donnadieu, Nathalie Baye; ***D:*** Daniel Vigne; ***W:*** Daniel Vigne, Jean-Claude Carriere; ***C:*** Andre Neau; ***M:*** Michel Portal. Cesar '83: Writing, Score; Natl. Soc. Film Critics '83: Actor (Depardieu).

The Return of Peter Grimm 1/2 **1935** Man returns from death to try to tidy up the mess he left behind. Enjoyable if trite fantasy based on a play by David Belasco. **82m/B VHS.** Lionel Barrymore, Helen Mack, Edward Ellis, Donald Meek, George Breakston, James Bush; ***D:*** George Nicholls Jr.

Return of Sabata 1/2 **1971 (PG)** Van Cleef is back in this thoroughly confusing mishmash. Sabata is working as a trick-shot performer in a circus that arrives in the town of Hobsonville. Robber baron Joe McIntock heavily taxes the community, secretly turning his ill-gotten gains into gold so he can skip town with a fortune. Sabata discovers his plan. **100m/C DVD.** *IT* Lee Van Cleef, Giampiero Albertini, Reiner Schone, Ignazio Spalla, Annabella Incontrera; ***D:*** Gianfranco Parolini; ***W:*** Gianfranco Parolini, Renato Izzo; ***C:*** Sandro Moncori; ***M:*** Marcello Gombini.

The Return of Spinal Tap 1/2 **1992** Cult-fave mock rock group Spinal Tap is back with a feature-length video of performance and backstage footage from its recent reunion concert tour promoting their album "Break Like the Wind." Sequel to "This Is Spinal Tap" features lots of heavy metal songs including the title track, "Majesty of Rock," "Bitch School," "Diva Fever," "Clam Caravan," and "Stinkin' Up the Great Outdoors." Not as great as the original satire, but will appeal to Spinal Tap fans. **110m/C VHS, DVD.** Christopher Guest, Michael McKean, Harry Shearer, Rick Parnell, C.J. Vanston, June Chadwick; ***Cameos:*** Paul Anka, Jeff Beck, Jamie Lee Curtis, Richard Lewis, Martha Quinn, Kenny Rogers, Martin Short, Mel Torme, Rob Reiner, Paul Shaffer, Fred Willard, Bob Geldof; ***W:*** Christopher Guest, Michael McKean, Harry Shearer.

Return of Superfly **1990 (R)** Man with insect moniker pesters drug dealers and cops in Harlem. Long-awaited sequel to urban epic "Superfly," scored again by Mayfield. **94m/C VHS.** Margaret Avery, Nathan Purdee, Samuel L. Jackson; ***M:*** Ice-T, Curtis Mayfield.

The Return of Swamp Thing 1/2 **1989 (PG-13)** The DC Comics creature rises again out of the muck to fight mutants and evil scientists. Tongue-in-cheek, and nothing at all like the literate, ecologically oriented comic from which it was derived. **95m/C VHS, DVD.** Louis Jourdan, Heather Locklear, Sarah Douglas, Dick Durock; ***D:*** Jim Wynorski.

Return of the Aliens: The Deadly Spawn *The Deadly Spawn* **1983 (R)** Aliens infect the earth and violently destroy humans. Extremely violent and gory. Watch out for those officious offspring. **90m/C VHS, DVD.** Charles George Hildebrandt; ***D:*** Douglas McKeown.

Return of the Ape Man 1944 Campy fun with Carradine and Lugosi. A mad scientist transplants Carradine's brain into the body of the "missing link." Hams galore. **51m/B VHS.** Bela Lugosi, John Carradine, George Zucco, Judith Gibson, Michael Ames, Frank Moran, Mary Currier; ***D:*** Phil Rosen.

Return of the Bad Men 1948 Scott is a retired marshall who must fight against a gang of outlaws lead by the Sundance Kid. Sequel to "Badman's Territory." **90m/C VHS.** Randolph Scott, Robert Ryan, Anne Jeffreys, George "Gabby" Hayes, Jason Robards Sr., Jacqueline White; ***D:*** Ray Enright; ***W:*** Charles "Blackie" O'Neal.

The Return of the Beverly Hillbillies 1981 The Clampett clan, along with now-government official Miss Jane help to solve the energy crisis using Granny's 'white lightening.' Adding to the whoops and hollers is Miss Jane's downhome Ozark wedding to her boss Mr. Medford. Entertaining enough but not quite the same with the loss of key players in the parts of Granny, Mr. Drysdale and Jethro. **100m/C VHS.** Buddy Ebsen, Donna Douglas, Nancy Kulp, Ray Young, Imogene Coca; ***D:*** Robert M. Leeds; ***W:*** Paul Henning. **VIDEO**

The Return of the Borrowers **1996** Sweet sequel to 1993's "The Borrowers" finds the six-inch Clock family—father Pod (Holm), mother Homily (Wilton), and teenaged daughter Arrietty (Callard)—having to find a new home. Lots of misadventures ensue as they must avoid nasty humans, a giant bee, a storm, and other dangers on their way to safety. Based on the novels by Mary Norton. **165m/C VHS.** *GB* Ian Holm, Penelope Wilton, Rebecca Callard, Sian Phillips, Tony Haygarth, Judy Parfitt, Ben Chaplin, Paul Cross, Pamela Cundell, Ross McCall, Richard Vernon, Daniel Newman; ***D:*** John Henderson; ***W:*** Richard Carpenter; ***C:*** Clive Tucker; ***M:*** Howard Goodall.

Return of the Dragon 1/2 **1973 (R)** In Lee's last picture, a Chinese restaurant in Rome is menaced by gangsters who want to buy the property. On behalf of the owners, Lee duels an American karate champ in the Roman forum. The battle scenes between Lee and Norris are great and make this a must-see for martial arts fans. **91m/C VHS, DVD.** *CH* Bruce Lee, Nora Miao, Chuck Norris; ***D:*** Bruce Lee; ***W:*** Bruce Lee; ***C:*** Ho Lang Shang; ***M:*** Joseph Koo.

Return of the Evil Dead *Return of the Blind Dead; El Ataque de los Muertos Sin Ojos* **1975** The sightless dead priests return to attack still more 1970s' Europeans in this second installment of the "blind dead" trilogy. Preceded by "Tombs of the Blind Dead" and followed by "Horror of the Zombies." Not to be confused with Raimi's "Evil Dead" slasher flicks. **85m/C VHS, DVD.** *SP PT* Tony Kendall, Esther Roy, Frank Blake, Fernando (Fernand) Sancho, Lone Fleming, Loreta Tovar, Jose Canalejas; ***D:*** Armando de Ossorio; ***W:*** Armando de Ossorio; ***C:*** Miguel Mila; ***M:*** Anton Abril.

Return of the Family Man **1989** A mass murderer seems unstoppable as he continues to slash whole families at a time-...the family man is redefined in this bloody gore-fest. **90m/C VHS.** Ron Smerczak, Liam Cundill, Terence Reis, Michelle Constant; ***D:*** John Murlowski.

Return of the Fly 1959 The son of the scientist who discovered how to move matter through space decides to continue his father's work, but does so against his uncle's wishes. He soon duplicates his dad's experiments with similar results. This sequel to "The Fly" doesn't buzz like the original. Followed by "Curse of the Fly." **80m/B VHS, DVD.** Vincent Price, Brett Halsey, John Sutton, Dan Seymour, David Frankham, Danielle De Metz, Ed Wolff; ***D:*** Edward L. Bernds; ***W:*** Edward L. Bernds, Brydon Baker.

Return of the Frontiersman 1/2 **1950** Sheriff's son Logan Barrett (MacRae) is falsely accused and convicted of numerous crimes and sent to jail. He escapes to find the man who framed him with the help of girlfriend Janie (London). MacRae croons a couple of western ditties to pass the time. **74m/C DVD.** Edwin Rand; ***W:*** Edna Anhalt.

Return of the Jedi 1/2 *Star Wars: Episode 6—Return of the Jedi* **1983 (PG)** Third film in George Lucas' popular space saga. Against seemingly fearsome odds, Luke Skywalker battles such worthies as Jabba the Hut and heavy-breathing Darth Vader to save his comrades and triumph over the evil Galactic Empire. Han and Leia reaffirm their love and team with C3PO, R2-D2, Chewbacca, Calrissian, and a bunch of furry Ewoks to aid in the annihilation of the Dark Side. The special effects are still spectacular, even the third time around. Sequel to "Star Wars" (1977) and "The Empire Strikes Back" (1980). **132m/C VHS, DVD.** Mark Hamill, Carrie Fisher, Harrison Ford, Billy Dee Williams, David Prowse, James Earl Jones, Kenny Baker, Denis Lawson, Anthony Daniels, Peter Mayhew, Sebastian Shaw, Jeremy Bulloch, Toby Philpot; ***D:*** Richard Marquand; ***W:*** George Lucas, Lawrence Kasdan; ***C:*** Alan Hume; ***M:*** John Williams; ***V:*** Alec Guinness, Frank Oz. Oscars '83: Visual FX.

Return of the Killer Tomatoes! **1988 (PG)** The man-eating plant-life from 1977's "Attack of the Killer Tomatoes" is back, able to turn into people due to the slightly larger budget. Astin is mad as the scientist. Not as bad as "Attack," representing a small hurdle in the history of filmdom. Followed by "Killer Tomatoes Strike Back." **98m/C VHS, DVD.** Anthony Starke, George Clooney, Karen Mistal, Steve Lundquist, John Astin, Charlie Jones, Rock Peace, Frank Davis, C.J. Dillon, Teri Weigel; ***D:*** John DeBello; ***W:*** John DeBello, Constantine Dillon, Steve Peace; ***C:*** Stephen Kent Welch; ***M:*** Neal Fox, Rick Patterson.

The Return of the King **1980** The third and final animated episode of J.R.R Tolkien's Middle Earth Trilogy. This saga features Frodo, relative to Hobbit Bilbo Baggins, and his faithful servant, making middle Earth safe from Orcs, Gollums and other ooky creatures. **120m/C VHS, DVD.** ***D:*** Arthur Rankin Jr., Jules Bass; ***M:*** Maury Laws; ***V:*** Orson Bean, Roddy McDowall, John Huston, Theodore Bikel, William Conrad, Glen Yarborough, Paul Frees, Casey Kasem, Sonny Melendrez.

Return of the Lash 1947 Lash LaRue once again defends settlers' rights from ruthless outlaws. **53m/B VHS.** Lash LaRue, Al "Fuzzy" St. John, Mary Maynard, George Chesebro; ***D:*** Ray Taylor.

Return of the Living Dead 1/2 **1985 (R)** Poisonous gas revives a cemetery and a morgue rendering an outrageous spoof on the living-dead sub-genre with fast-moving zombies, punk humor, and exaggerated gore. Its humor does not diminish the fear factor, however. Sequel follows. Directed by "Alien" writer O'Bannon. **90m/C VHS, DVD.** Clu Gulager, James Karen, Linnea Quigley, Don Calfa, Jewel Shepard, Beverly Randolph, Miguel A. Nunez Jr., Brian Peck; ***D:*** Dan O'Bannon; ***W:*** Dan O'Bannon, John A. Russo, Russell Streiner; ***C:*** Jules Brenner.

Return of the Living Dead 2 1/2 **1988 (R)** An inevitable sequel to the original Dan O'Bannon satire about George Romero-esque brain-eating zombies attacking suburbia with zest and vigor. **89m/C VHS, DVD.** Dana Ashbrook, Marsha Dietlein, Philip Bruns, James Karen, Thom Mathews, Suzanne Snyder, Michael Kenworthy, Thor Van Lingen; ***D:*** Ken Wiederhorn; ***W:*** Ken Wiederhorn; ***C:*** Robert Elswit.

Return of the Living Dead 3 1/2 **1993 (R)** When Curt's girlfriend Julie dies in a motorcycle accident you'd think that would be the end of romance. But not when your dad heads a secret project that involves reviving corpses. Only problem is now Julie's a zombie with long metal claws and glass spikes sticking out of various body parts. Hey, if it's true love Curt will get over it. Macabre special effects. Also available unrated. **97m/C VHS, DVD.** Melinda (Mindy) Clarke, J. Trevor Edmond, Kent McCord, Basil Wallace, Fabio Urena; ***D:*** Brian Yuzna; ***W:*** John Penney; ***C:*** Gerry Lively; ***M:*** Barry Goldberg.

Return of the Living Dead: Rave to the Grave **2005 (R)** Don't expect much from the franchise and you won't be disappointed. In this fifth installment, university chemist Garrison (Coyote) creates a toxin that is discovered by a group of buds who made their own designer drug. One pill gets you high but use too many and you become a brain-eating zombie. Just in time to party at the campus Halloween rave. **86m/C DVD.** Peter Coyote, Aimee-Lynn Chadwick, John Keefe, Cory Hardrict, Jenny Mollen; ***D:*** Ellory Elkayem; ***W:*** William Butler, Aaron Strongoni; ***C:*** Gabriel Kosuth. **VIDEO**

Return of the Magnificent Seven *Return of the Seven* **1966** The first sequel to "The Magnificent Seven" features the group liberating a compatriot who is held hostage. Yawn. **97m/C VHS, DVD.** Yul Brynner, Warren Oates, Robert Fuller, Claude Akins, Julian Mateos, Elisa Montes, Emilio Fernandez; ***D:*** Burt Kennedy; ***W:*** Larry Cohen; ***C:*** Paul Vogel; ***M:*** Elmer Bernstein.

Return of the Man from U.N.C.L.E. **1983** Those dashing super agents Napoleon Solo and Illya Kuryakin come out of retirement to settle an old score with their nemesis THRUSH. **96m/C VHS.** Robert Vaughn, David McCallum, Patrick Macnee, Gayle Hunnicutt, Geoffrey Lewis; ***D:*** Ray Austin. **TV**

The Return of the Musketeers 1/2 **1989 (PG)** Lester's third Musketeers film (after his successful double-act in the '70s) is a good-natured but average costume/comedy/buddy film. Twenty years after D'Artagnan, Athos, Porthos, and Aramis saved the French queen from scandal it's time to do it all over again. Milady DeWinter, who hatched the first plot, is dead but her equally devious daughter Justine is more than able to take mama's scheming place. Just to add a little more excitement Athos' adopted son Raoul meets Justine and passions fly amidst the swordplay. Based on the Alexandre Dumas novel "Twenty Years After." **103m/C VHS.** *GB FR SP* Michael York, Oliver Reed, Frank Finlay, Richard Chamberlain, Kim Cattrall, C. Thomas Howell, Geraldine Chaplin, Roy Kinnear, Christopher Lee, Philippe Noiret, Jean-Pierre Cassel, Billy Connolly, Eusebio Lazaro; ***D:*** Richard Lester; ***W:*** George MacDonald Fraser.

The Return of the Native 1/2 **1994 (PG)** Wind-swept moors, a tempestuous heroine, two loves, and requisite tragedy all courtesy of Thomas Hardy's 1878 novel. Beautiful Eustacia Vye (Jones) longs to leave the boredom of Egdon Heath—even though she's involved with the roguish Damon Wildeve (Owen). Then businessman Clym Yeobright (Stevenson) returns from Paris and captures Eustacia's fancy. She marries him in the hope they'll return to the continent but she's bitterly disappointed when Clym wants to remain in Egdon. Meanwhile, Damon has married Clym's gentle cousin Thomasin (Skinner) but he and Eustacia can't seem to stay away from each other, leading to storms for all. **99m/C VHS, DVD.** Catherine Zeta-Jones, Clive Owen, Ray Stevenson, Claire Skinner, Joan Plowright, Steven Mackintosh, Celia Imrie, Paul Rogers; ***D:*** Jack Gold; ***W:*** Robert W. Lenski; ***M:*** Carl Davis. **TV**

Return of the Pink Panther 1/2 **1974 (G)** Bumbling Inspector Clouseau is called upon to rescue the Pink Panther diamond stolen from a museum. Sellers manages to produce mayhem with a vacuum cleaner and other devices that, in his hands, become instruments of terror. Clever opening credits. Fourth installment in the Pink Panther series but the first with Sellers since 1964's "A Shot in the Dark." **113m/C VHS, DVD.** Peter Sellers, Christopher Plummer, Catherine Schell, Herbert Lom, Victor Spinetti; ***D:*** Blake Edwards; ***W:*** Frank Waldman, Blake Edwards; ***C:*** Geoffrey Unsworth; ***M:*** Henry Mancini.

The Return of the Rangers ½ **1943** After saving the life of Anne Miller, Texas Ranger Tex Wyatt takes a job on the ranch that's being run by Anne until the deceased owner's trustee can arrive. There's swindling going on as Tex is accused of murder and a fake trustee tries to sell the property to land-grabbing Frank Martin. But Tex's fellow Rangers Jim and Panhandle come to his rescue. **60m/B DVD.** Dave O'Brien, James Newill, Guy Wilkerson, Nell O'Day, Glenn Strange, Emmett Lynn, I. Stanford Jolley, Robert V. Barron; ***D:*** Elmer Clifton; ***W:*** Elmer Clifton; ***C:*** Robert Cline; ***M:*** Lee Zahler.

Return of the Rebels **1981** TV fluff with Eden as a motorcycle matron whose campground is rid of riff-raff by the crow-lined participants in a 25-year reunion of a biker gang. **100m/C VHS.** Barbara Eden, Robert Mandan, Jamie Farr, Patrick Swayze, Don Murray, Christopher Connelly; ***D:*** Noel Nosseck. **TV**

Return of the Secaucus 7 ½ **1980** Centers around a weekend reunion of seven friends who were activists during the Vietnam War in the turbulent '60s. Now turning 30, they evaluate their present lives and progress. Writer and director Sayles plays Howie in this excellent example of what a low-budget film can and should be. A less trendy predecessor of "The Big Chill" (1983) which, perhaps, was a few years ahead of its time. **110m/C VHS, DVD.** Mark Arnott, Gordon Clapp, Maggie Cousineau-Arndt, David Strathairn, Adam LeFevre, Bruce MacDonald, Maggie Renzi, Jean Passanante, Karen Trott, John Sayles; ***D:*** John Sayles; ***W:*** John Sayles; ***C:*** Austin De Besche; ***M:*** Mason Daring. L.A. Film Critics '80: Screenplay, Natl. Film Reg. '97.

Return of the Soldier **1982** A shell-shocked WWI veteran has no memory of his marriage, leaving his wife, his childhood flame, and an unrequited love to vie for his affections. Adapted from the novel by Rebecca West. **101m/C VHS, DVD.** *GB* Glenda Jackson, Julie Christie, Ann-Margret, Alan Bates, Ian Holm, Frank Finlay; ***D:*** Alan Bridges; ***M:*** Richard Rodney Bennett.

Return of the Street Fighter ½ *Satsujin-ken 2* **1974** Sequel to "The Street Fighter," finds Terry Tsuguri (Chiba) hired by a gang to silence a jailed informer. So, Terry gets arrested, practices his karate and does the guy in, and finds out the gang now wants to silence him. Big mistake! Notice a pattern yet? Followed by "The Street Fighter's Last Revenge" and "Sister Street Fighter." **88m/C VHS, DVD.** *JP* Sonny Chiba, Claude Gannyon; ***D:*** Shigehiro (Sakae) Ozawa; ***W:*** Hajjime Koiwa, Koji Takada; ***C:*** Teiji Yoshida.

Return of the Tall Blond Man with One Black Shoe ½ *Le Retour du Grand Blond* **1974** Sequel to 1972's "The Tall Blond Man With One Black Shoe." Again a "klutz" is mistaken for a master spy and becomes unknowingly involved in the world of international intrigue. In French with English subtitles. Not quite as good as the original. **84m/C VHS.** *FR* Pierre Richard, Mireille Darc, Michel Duchaussoy, Jean Rochefort, Jean Carmet; ***D:*** Yves Robert; ***W:*** Francis Veber; ***M:*** Vladimir Cosma.

Return of the Tiger ½ **1978** The Hovver Night Club in Bangkok fronts the operations of an international narcotics group headed by an American. When a rival Chinese gang tries to dominate the drug market, conflict and lots of kicking ensue. **95m/C VHS, DVD.** Bruce Li, Paul Smith, Chaing I, Angela (Mao Ying) Mao; ***D:*** Jimmy Shaw.

Return of the Vampire **1943** A Hungarian vampire and his werewolf servant seek revenge on the family who drove a spike through his heart two decades earlier. **69m/B VHS, DVD.** Bela Lugosi, Nina Foch, Miles Mander, Matt Willis, Frieda Inescort, Roland Varno, Gilbert Emery, Ottola Nesmith; ***D:*** Lew Landers; ***W:*** Griffin Jay; ***C:*** L.W. O'Connell, John Stumar.

Return of Wildfire ½ **1948** Two sisters are left to run the family horse ranch when their brother is killed. A drifter aids the sisters in bringing the murderer to justice. **83m/B VHS.** Richard Arlen, Patricia Morison, Mary Beth Hughes, James Millican, Reed Hadley, Chris-Pin (Ethier Crispin Martini) Martin, Stanley Andrews, Holly (Mike Ragan) Bane; ***D:*** Ray Taylor; ***W:*** Betty Burbridge; ***C:*** Ernest Miller.

Return to Africa **1989** Rebels threaten the familial paradise of the tightknit Mallory clan. **95m/C VHS.** Stan Brock, Anne Collings, David Tors, Ivan Tors, Peter Tors, Steven Tors; ***D:*** Leslie Martinson.

Return to Boggy Creek **1977 (PG)** Townspeople in a small fishing village learn from a photographer that a "killer" beast, whom they thought had disappeared, has returned and is living in Boggy Creek. Some curious children follow the shutterbug into the marsh, despite hurricane warnings, and the swamp monster reacts with unusual compassion. OK for the kiddies. Fictitious story unlike other "Boggy Creek" films, which are billed as semi-documentaries. Sequel to "Legend of Boggy Creek" and features Mary Ann from "Gilligan's Island." **87m/C VHS.** Dawn Wells, Dana Plato, Louise Belaire, John Hofeus; ***D:*** Tom (Thomas R.) Moore.

Return to Cabin by the Lake ½ **2001** Psychos never die—they always return to do the sequel. Presumed dead writer/serial killer Stanley Caldwell (Nelson) isn't dead at all. In fact, he infiltrates a movie crew making a film adaptation of the circumstances of his killing spree. But Stanley doesn't like the way events are being portrayed, so he bumps off the director (Krause) and takes control. Campy rather than scary. **89m/C VHS, DVD.** Judd Nelson, Brian Krause, Dahlia Salem, Michael P. Northey, Emmanuelle Vaugier; ***D:*** Po-Chih Leung; ***W:*** Jeffrey Reddick; ***C:*** Stephen M. Katz; ***M:*** Frankie Blue. **CABLE**

Return to Cranford ½ **2009** Picks up where "Cranford" left off as Miss Matty (Dench) and her gossiping cronies enjoy the social life of their close-knit mid-Victorian-era village. However, inevitable progress is chugging along just outside of town as the railroad comes ever closer to linking Cranford to the wider world despite some community opposition. The usual mixture of reunions, romance, and tragedy also plays a part. Based on the stories by Elizabeth Gaskell. **175m/C DVD.** *GB* Judi Dench, Julia McKenzie, Barbara Flynn, Imelda Staunton, Jim Carter, Jonathan Pryce, Tom Hiddleston, Michelle Dockery, Lesley Sharp, Jodie Wittaker, Matthew McNulty, Emma Fielding, Alex Etel, Celia Emrie, Francesca Annis, Greg Wise, Nicholas Le Prevost, Tim Curry, Alex Jennings, Claudie Blakley; ***D:*** Simon Curtis; ***W:*** Heidi Thomas; ***C:*** Ben Smithard; ***M:*** Carl Davis. **TV**

Return to Earth **1976** Drama deals with the self-doubts faced by Apollo 11 astronaut Buzz Aldrin after his triumphant return to Earth. Based on Aldrin's own novel. **74m/C VHS.** Cliff Robertson, Shirley Knight, Ralph Bellamy, Stefanie Powers, Charles Cioffi; ***D:*** Jud Taylor. **TV**

Return to Eden **1989** A young woman falls in love with her philosophy tutor, but he can't return her affections. An interesting comparison between the passion of the primitive and the tangle of modern-day romance. **90m/C VHS.** Sam Bottoms, Edward Binns, Renee Coleman; ***D:*** William Olsen.

Return to Fantasy Island ½ **1977** Boss, boss, it's da plane! The second full-length TV treatment of the once-popular series wherein three couples get their most cherished fantasy fulfilled by Mr. Roarke and company. **100m/C VHS, DVD.** Ricardo Montalban, Herve Villechaize, Adrienne Barbeau, Pa-t(ricia) Crowley, Joseph Campanella, Karen Valentine, Laraine Day, George Maharis, Horst Buchholz, France Nuyen, Joseph Cotten, Cameron Mitchell, George Chakiris; ***D:*** George McCowan. **TV**

Return to Frogtown WOOF! **1992 (PG-13)** Sequel to "Hell Comes to Frogtown" finds Texas Rocket Ranger Ferrigno captured by mutant frogs. As unbelievably bad as it sounds. **90m/C VHS, DVD.** Lou Ferrigno, Charles Napier, Robert Z'Dar, Denice Duff, Don Stroud; ***D:*** Donald G. Jackson.

Return to Halloweentown *Halloweentown 4* **2006** Marnie (now played by Paxton) has enrolled at Halloweentown's Witch University along with nerdy brother Dylan and her boyfriend Ethan. But she runs into trouble with the three Sinister sisters and their evil father, who want to take Marnie's powers. **88m/C DVD.** Sara Paxton, Lucas Grabeel, Joey Zimmerman, Keone Young, Kristy Wu, Summer Bishil, Millicent Martin, Judith Hoag, Katie Cockrell, Kellie Cockrell, Debbie Reynolds; ***D:*** David S. Jackson; ***W:*** Max Enscoe, Annie DeYoung; ***C:*** Denis Maloney; ***M:*** Kenneth Burgomaster. **CABLE**

Return to Horror High **1987 (R)** A horror movie producer makes a film in an abandoned and haunted high school, where a series of murders occurred years earlier. As in most "return" flicks, history repeats itself. **95m/C VHS, DVD.** Alex Rocco, Vince Edwards, Philip McKeon, Brendan Hughes, Lori Lethin, Scott Jacoby, George Clooney, Maureen McCormick; ***D:*** Bill Froelich; ***W:*** Bill Froelich, Mark Lisson, Dana Escalante, Greg H. Sims, Nancy Forner; ***C:*** Roy Wagner; ***M:*** Stacy Widelitz.

Return to House on Haunted Hill ½ **2007 (R)** Typical haunted house flick. Sarah survived the massacre at Vanacutt Mansion only to later commit suicide. Now her sister Ariel is investigating, aided by the diary of Dr. Vanacutt, which speaks of a diabolical evil inhabiting the house. But the mansion also contains a relic worth millions, and several treasure-seekers come to claim it, although the house has other ideas. **81m/C DVD, Blu-ray Disc, HD DVD.** Erik Palladino, Cerina Vincent, Tom Riley, Jeffrey Combs, Amanda Righetti, Andrew Lee Potts, Steven Pacey; ***D:*** Victor Garcia; ***W:*** William Massa; ***C:*** Lorenzo Senatore; ***M:*** Frederik Wiedmann. **VIDEO**

Return to Lonesome Dove ½ **1993** Routine sequel to successful western saga "Lonesome Dove" picks up after the burial of Gus McCrae in Texas by his friend, ex-Texas Ranger Woodrow F. Call (now played by Voight). The original dealt with a cattle drive, this one with horses. Along the way you'll run into the usual sidewinders as well as McCrae's lost love Clara (now Hershey) and Schroder, returning as Call's unacknowledged son Newt. Filmed on loction in Montana. TV production was already underway when author Larry McMurtry gave the producers his then unpublished sequel "Streets of Laredo" which differed from the script. Some changes were made but the book and miniseries don't match. **330m/C VHS, DVD.** Jon Voight, William L. Petersen, Rick Schroder, Barbara Hershey, Louis Gossett Jr., Oliver Reed, Reese Witherspoon, Nia Peeples, Dennis Haysbert, Timothy Scott, Barry Tubb, Chris Cooper, CCH Pounder, William Sanderson; ***D:*** Mike Robe; ***W:*** John Wilder. **TV**

Return to Macon County **1975** Tale of three young, reckless youths who become involved with drag racing and a sadistic law enforcement officer. Nolte turns in a good performance in his first film, as does Johnson, despite a mediocre script and dialogue. Sequel to 1974's "Macon County Line." **90m/C VHS.** Nick Nolte, Don Johnson, Robin Mattson; ***D:*** Richard Compton; ***W:*** Richard Compton.

Return to Mayberry **1985** Andy Taylor returns to Mayberry after 20 years to obtain his old job as sheriff. Sixteen of the original actors reappeared for this nostalgiafest. **95m/C VHS.** Andy Griffith, Ron Howard, Don Knotts, Jim Nabors, Aneta Corsaut, Jack Dodson, George Lindsey, Betty Lynn; ***D:*** Bob Sweeney. **TV**

Return to Me ½ **2000 (PG)** Widowed building contractor Bob (Duchovny) is uneasy about getting involved in a new romance (particularly after some pathetic blind dates) but meets waitress Grace (Driver) and suddenly love is in the air. However, Grace is reluctant to reveal that she's had a heart transplant. But what's she going to do when she discovers that the donor heart came from Bob's beloved late wife. The best romance, however, might be between the testily loving marrieds, the Daytons (Hunt, Belushi), who are Grace's best friends. Directorial debut of Hunt is soapy without being sappy. **113m/C VHS, DVD.** David Duchovny, Minnie Driver, James Belushi, Bonnie Hunt, Carroll O'Connor, Robert Loggia, David Alan Grier, Joely Richardson, Eddie Jones, Marianne Muellerleile, William Bronder; ***D:*** Bonnie Hunt; ***W:*** Bonnie Hunt, Don Lake; ***C:*** Laszlo Kovacs; ***M:*** Nicholas Pike.

Return to Never Land ½ **2002 (G)** Losing much of the charm and magic of the 1953 Disney animated classic "Peter Pan," this sequel picks up years after the other left off and finds Peter (Weaver), Tinker Bell, and the rest of the gang in Never Land. Wendy (Soucie), however, is now grown and married with a daughter of her own, the spunky Jane (Owen), whose skepticism about her mother's wild tales fades after she is kidnaped by Captain Hook (Burton), still on a quest for the treasure he believes Pan stole. She then finds her way to Peter and more adventure with her mom's old pals. Innocuous and generic but refined Disney entry works for the youngest viewers but older children and parents won't find anything deeper for them. Nice blend of digital and traditional animation. **72m/C VHS, DVD.** *US* ***D:*** Robin Budd; ***W:*** Temple Mathews; ***M:*** Joel McNeely; ***V:*** Blayne Weaver, Harriet Owen, Corey Burton, Jeff Glenn Bennett, Kath Soucie, Roger Rees, Spencer Breslin, Andrew McDonough.

Return to Oz ½ **1985 (PG)** Picking up where "The Wizard of Oz" left off, Auntie Em and Uncle Ed place Dorothy in the care of a therapist to cure her "delusions" of Oz. A natural disaster again lands her in the land of the yellow brick road, where the evil Nome King and Princess Mombi are spreading terror and squalor. Based on a later L. Frank Baum book. Enjoyable for the whole family although some scenes may frighten very small children. **109m/C VHS, DVD.** Fairuza Balk, Piper Laurie, Matt Clark, Nicol Williamson, Jean Marsh; ***D:*** Walter Murch; ***W:*** Walter Murch, Gill Dennis; ***C:*** David Watkin; ***M:*** David Shire.

Return to Paradise **1953** Cooper is a soldier of fortune wandering through the Polynesian islands in the late 1920s. On a remote atoll he comes across a crazy missionary intent upon subduing the native population. Cooper falls in love with a native beauty (Haynes in her screen debut) and leads the natives in a revolt against authority. Cliched but with nice scenery from the location shoot in Samoa. Loose adaptation of the short story "Mr. Morgan" by James Michener. **100m/C VHS.** Gary Cooper, Roberta Haynes, Barry Jones, John Hudson, Moira MacDonald; ***D:*** Mark Robson; ***W:*** Charles A. Kaufman.

Return to Paradise *All for One* **1998 (R)** Sheriff (Vaughn) and Tony (Conrad), along with their new friend Lewis (Phoenix), take a vice-filled vacation in Malaysia. Done with the partying, the two New Yorkers return home while Lewis stays in Asia to work with orangutans. Two years later, Lewis is in a Malaysian prison, facing execution for a brick of hashish, which Sheriff haphazardly tossed into the garbage. Enter Heche as lawyer Beth, who finds Sheriff and tells him that in order to save Lewis, he and Tony must return and take their share of the responsibility (and serve time in a squalid third-world prison). Despite contributing an important twist to the extremely powerful climax, Pinkett Smith's role feels too contrived and is the biggest flaw in the film. Loose retelling of the 1989 French film "Force Majeure." **112m/C VHS, DVD.** Vince Vaughn, Joaquin Rafael (Leaf) Phoenix, Anne Heche, David Conrad, Jada Pinkett Smith, Vera Farmiga, Nick Sandow; ***D:*** Joseph Ruben; ***W:*** Wesley Strick, Bruce Robinson; ***C:*** Reynaldo Villalobos; ***M:*** Mark Mancina.

Return to Peyton Place ½ **1961** A young writer publishes novel exposing town as virtual Peyton Place, and the townsfolk turn against her and her family. Sequel to the scandalously popular '50s original and inspiration for the just-as-popular soap opera. Astor is excellent as the evil matriarch. **122m/C VHS, DVD.** Carol Lynley, Jeff Chandler, Eleanor Parker, Mary Astor, Robert Sterling, Luciana Paluzzi, Tuesday Weld, Brett Halsey, Bob Crane; ***D:*** Jose Ferrer.

Return to Salem's Lot **1987 (R)** Enjoyable camp sequel to the Stephen King tale, this time involving a cynical scientist and his son returning to the town only to find it completely run by vampires. **101m/C VHS.** Michael Moriarty, Ricky Addison Reed, Samuel Fuller, Andrew Duggan, Evelyn Keyes, Jill Gatsby, June Havoc, Ronee Blakley, James Dixon, David Holbrook; *D:* Larry Cohen; *W:* Larry Cohen, James Dixon; *C:* Daniel Pearl.

Return to Savage Beach 🦴 1/2 **1997 (R)** Top secret government agency L.E-.T.H.A.L. is sent to retrieve a computer disk containing the location of a hidden treasure. Lots of action, babes, and hard-bodies (you're not expecting acting talent, are you?). **98m/C VHS, DVD.** Julie Strain, Julie K. Smith, Shae Marks, Cristian Letelier; *D:* Andy Sidaris; *W:* Andy Sidaris; *C:* Howard Wexler. **VIDEO**

Return to Snowy River 🦴🦴🦴 **1988 (PG)** Continues the love story of the former ranch hand and the rancher's daughter in Australia's Victoria Alps that began in "The Man From Snowy River." Dennehy takes over from Kirk Douglas as the father who aims to keep the lovers apart. The photography of horses and the scenery is spectacular, making the whole film worthwhile. **99m/C VHS, DVD.** *AU* Tom Burlinson, Sigrid Thornton, Brian Dennehy, Nicholas Eadie, Mark Hembrow, Bryan Marshall; *D:* Geoff Burrowes; *W:* Geoff Burrowes.

Return to the Blue Lagoon 🦴 **1991 (PG-13)** Neither the acting nor the premise has improved with age. Another photogenic adolescent couple experiences puberty on that island; for continuity, the young man is the son of the lovers in the first "Blue Lagoon." Breathtaking scenery—just turn down the sound. **102m/C VHS, DVD.** Milla Jovovich, Brian Krause, Lisa Pelikan; *D:* William A. Graham; *C:* Robert Steadman.

Return to the Lost World 🦴🦴 1/2 **1993 (PG)** Rival scientists Challenger and Summerlee set out for the Lost World and find it threatened by oil prospectors. With a volcano about to explode the scientists set out to save their prehistoric paradise and its dinosaur inhabitants. Based on a story by Sir Arthur Conan Doyle. Sequel to "The Lost World." **99m/C VHS, DVD.** John Rhys-Davies, David Warner, Darren Peter Mercer, Geza Kovacs; *D:* Timothy Bond.

Return to Two Moon Junction 🦴 1/2 **1993 (R)** New York supermodel Savannah (Clarke) returns to her family's riverfront home in Georgia and promptly sheds her clothing for local sculptor Jake (Schafer). Must be something about the southern heat. This sequel should have the same video success as its predecessor since it keeps to the minimal plot/maximum teasing sex scenes outline. **96m/C VHS.** Melinda (Mindy) Clarke, John Clayton Schafer, Louise Fletcher; *D:* Farhad Mann.

Return to Waterloo 🦴🦴 **1985 (PG-13)** Experimental musical concept from the Kinks' Ray Davies about an everyman commuter (Colley) who is either having a nervous breakdown or living in a fantasy world or both. As he rides the train between the Guildford and Waterloo stations, his fellow passengers burst into song and things get increasingly violent. Also includes "Come Dancing with the Kinks," with videos of eight songs, including "Lola" and "Come Dancing." **95m/C VHS, DVD.** *GB* Ray Davies, Gretchen Franklin, Tim Roth; *D:* Ray Davies; *W:* Ray Davies; *C:* Roger Deakins; *M:* Ray Davies.

Returner 🦴🦴 1/2 *Ritana* **2002 (R)** Humanity is being decimated by aliens in the year in 2084, and a young woman travels back in time to 2002 to prevent the invasion by getting to a captured alien secretly being held by the Japanese government. She arrives in the middle of a firefight between a young mercenary and the Triad ring he's trying to destroy. Putting an explosive collar around his neck, she forces him to help her as they both outrun the crime gang in a race to stop the world's destruction. Often thought of as the closest a live action film has gotten to anime. **117m/C DVD.** *JP* Takeshi Kaneshiro, Anne Suzuki, Goro Kishitani, Kazuya Shimizu, Masay Takahashi, Kirin Kiki, Yukiko Okamoto, Kisuke Ida, Dean Harrington; *D:* Takashi Yamazaki; *W:* Takashi Yamazaki, Kenya Hirata; *C:* Akira Sakoh, Kozo Shibazaki; *M:* Akihito Matsumoto.

Reuben, Reuben 🦴🦴🦴 **1983 (R)** Brilliant, but drunken poet Conti turns himself around when he falls in love with earthy college girl McGillis in her film debut. The student's dog Reuben unwittingly alters Conti's progress, however, in the film's startling conclusion. Based on the writings of Peter DeVries. **100m/C VHS.** Tom Conti, Kelly McGillis, Roberts Blossom, E. Katherine Kerr, Cynthia Harris, Joel Fabiani, Kara Wilson, Lois Smith; *D:* Robert Ellis Miller; *W:* Julius J. Epstein; *M:* Billy Goldenberg. Natl. Bd. of Review '83: Actor (Conti); Writers Guild '83: Adapt. Screenplay.

Reunion 🦴🦴 **1936** The Chamber of Commerce holds a testimonial dinner for the humble Dr. John Luke at which the Dionne quintuplets and many other townies join in sharing how he's helped them all. **80m/B VHS.** Jean Hersholt, Rochelle Hudson, Helen Vinson; *D:* Norman Tourog; *W:* Bruce Gould. **VIDEO**

Reunion 🦴🦴🦴 **1988 (PG-13)** Robards stars as a Jewish businessman, living in the U.S., who returns to his boyhood home of Stuttgart, Germany some 50 years after his leaving in 1933. He hopes to find out what happened to a boyhood school chum—the son of an artistocractic (and Aryan) German family. Film uses extensive flashbacks to show the the rise of anti-Semitism and how it affects the friendship of both youths. Thoughtfull and well-acted though occasionally plodding drama based on Fred Uhlman's novel. **120m/C VHS.** *FR GE GB* Jason Robards Jr., Christien Anholt, Samuel West, Francoise Fabian, Maureen Kerwin, Barbara Jefford, Alexander Trauner; *D:* Jerry Schatzberg; *W:* Harold Pinter; *C:* Bruno de Keyzer.

Reunion in France 🦴🦴 *Mademoiselle France; Reunion* **1942** Parisian dress designer sacrifices her lifestyle to help an American flier flee France after the Nazis invade. Dated patriotic flag-waver. **104m/B VHS.** Joan Crawford, John Wayne, Philip Dorn, Reginald Owen, Albert Bassermann, John Carradine, Ann Ayars, J. Edward Bromberg, Henry Daniell, Moroni Olsen, Howard da Silva, Ava Gardner, John Considine; *D:* Jules Dassin.

Revak the Rebel 🦴 *The Barbarians* **1960** Giggle-inducing sword and sandal pic filled with stiffs and scenery-chewing. Penda, an island kingdom, is conquered by the Carthaginians during their war against Rome. Prince Revak (Palance) is captured and put on board a slave ship, but he escapes and vows revenge. **84m/C DVD.** Jack Palance, Milly Vitale, Deirdre Sullivan; *D:* Rudolph Mate; *W:* Martin Rackin, John Lee Martin; *C:* Carl Guthrie; *M:* Franco Ferrara.

Revelation 🦴 **2000** In the continuing adventures based on the "Left Behind" novels (a conservative Christian interpretation of the Book of Revelation), a counter-terrorism expert (Fahey) goes up against a Messiah (Mancuso) out to rule the world, etc., etc. **97m/C DVD.** Jeff Fahey, Nick Mancuso, Carol Alt, Leigh Lewis; *D:* Andre Van Heerden; *W:* Peter LaLonde, Paul LaLonde; *C:* Jiri (George) Tirl.

Revenge 🦴 1/2 *Terror under the House; After Jenny Died; Inn of the Frightened People* **1971** The parents of a girl who was brutally killed take the law into their own hands in this bloody, vengeful thriller. **89m/C VHS.** *GB* Joan Collins, James Booth, Ray Barrett, Sinead Cusack, Kenneth Griffith; *D:* Sidney Hayers.

Revenge WOOF! 1986 (R) Sequel to "Blood Cult" about a cult led by horror king Carradine. Seems these dog worshippers want McGowan's land and Senator Carradine will stop at nothing to get it. Woofer filled with gratuitous violence. **104m/C VHS, DVD.** Patrick Wayne, John Carradine, Bennie Lee McGowan, Josef Hanet, Stephanie Kropke; *D:* Christopher Lewis; *W:* Christopher Lewis; *C:* Steve McWilliams; *M:* Rod Slane.

Revenge 🦴🦴 **1990 (R)** Retired pilot Costner makes the mistake of falling in love with another man's wife. Quinn gives a first-rate performance as the Mexican crime lord who punishes his spouse and her lover, beginning a cycle of vengeance. Sometimes contrived, but artfully photographed with tantalizing love scenes. Based on the Jim Harrison novel. **123m/C VHS, DVD, Blu-ray Disc.** Kevin Costner, Anthony Quinn, Madeleine Stowe, Sally Kirkland, Joe Santos, Miguel Ferrer, James Gammon, Tomas Milian; *D:* Tony Scott; *W:* Jim Harrison; *M:* Jack Nitzsche.

Revenge in the House of Usher 🦴🦴 *Neurosis; Zombie 5* **1982** Mad Eric Usher, the last of his equally insane family, lives in a creepy cliffside house with vampire-ghost Helen. Then he invites Alan Harker for a visit, and Alan's accepting is a big mistake on his part. **90m/C VHS, DVD.** *FR* Howard Vernon, Anthony (Jose, J. Antonio, J.A.) Mayans, Dan Villers, Lina Romay; *D:* Jess (Jesus) Franco; *C:* Alain Hardy; *M:* Daniel White.

The Revenge of Frankenstein 🦴🦴 1/2 **1958** Frankenstein (Cushing) is rescued from the guillotine by his dwarf servant and decides to relocate to Carlsbruck where he becomes the popular society physician, Dr. Stein. But the misunderstood doc just can't stop his ghoulish experiments and plans to transfer his servant's brain into another sewn together creature. Nicely macabre sequel to "The Curse of Frankenstein"; followed by "The Evil of Frankenstein." **89m/C VHS, DVD.** *GB* Peter Cushing, Michael Gwynn, Francis Matthews, Oscar Quitak, Lionel Jeffries, Eunice Gayson, John Welsh; *D:* Terence Fisher; *W:* Jimmy Sangster.

Revenge of the Barbarians 🦴 *La Vendetta dei Barbari* **1960** As the barbarians descend on Rome, Olympus must decide whether to save the empire or the beautiful Gallo, the woman he loves. Decisions, decisions. **104m/C VHS.** *IT* Robert Alda, Anthony Steel, Tom Felleghi, Daniela Rocca; *D:* Giuseppe Vari; *W:* Gastone Ramazzotti; *C:* Sergio Pesce; *M:* Roberto Nicolosi.

Revenge of the Barbarians 🦴 *Hrafninn Flygur; When the Raven Flies* **1985** A Scandinavian adventure about a young Celt seeking revenge against the Viking hordes that killed his family. **95m/C VHS, DVD.** *IC* Helgi Skulason, Jakob Thor Einarsson, Edda Bjorgvinsdottir, Egill Olafsson, Flosi Olafsson; *D:* Hrafn Gunnlaugsson; *W:* Hrafn Gunnlaugsson; *C:* Tony Forsberg.

Revenge of the Cheerleaders 🦴 **1976 (R)** The cheerleaders pull out all the stops to save their school from a ruthless land developer. What spirit. **86m/C VHS, DVD.** Jerii Woods, Cheryl "Rainbeaux" Smith, Helen Lang, Patrice Rohmer, Susie Elene, Eddra Gale, William Bramley, Carl Ballantine, David Hasselhoff; *D:* Richard Lerner.

Revenge of the Creature 🦴🦴 **1955** In this follow up to "The Creature from the Black Lagoon," the Gill-man is captured in the Amazon and taken to a Florida marine park. There he is put on display for visitors and subjected to heartless experiments. Growing restless in his captive surroundings, the creature breaks free and makes for the ocean. Includes screen debut of Clint Eastwood as a lab technician. Originally shot in 3-D. Based on a story by William Alland. **82m/B VHS, DVD.** John Agar, Lori Nelson, John Bromfield, Nestor Paiva, Clint Eastwood, Robert B. Williams, Grandon Rhodes, Charles Cane; *D:* Jack Arnold; *W:* Martin Berkeley; *C:* Charles S. Welbourne; *M:* Joseph Gershenson.

Revenge of the Dead 🦴 **1984 (R)** European archeological team discovers the existence of a powerful force that allows the dead to return to life. **100m/C VHS, DVD.** *IT* Gabriele Lavia, Anne Canoras; *D:* Pupi Avati.

Revenge of the Living Zombies 🦴 **1988 (R)** Teens on a Halloween hayride run headlong into flesh-craving zombies. Available in a slightly edited version. **85m/C VHS, DVD.** Bill (William Heinzman) Hinzman, John Mowod, Leslie Ann Wick, Kevin Kindlin; *D:* Bill (William Heinzman) Hinzman.

Revenge of the Musketeers 🦴🦴 *D'Artagnan Contro I Tre Moschettieri* **1963** A lighthearted (dubbed) swashbuckler. D'Artagnan (Lamas) is reunited with his musketeer comrades to help out Charles II (Antonini), the English king who's been exiled to France during Cromwell's rule. Naturally there are evil plots to thwart. **90m/C DVD.** *IT* Fernando Lamas, Gloria Milland, Roberto Risso, Walter Barnes, Franco Fantasia, Gabriel Antonio, Folco Lulli, Andreina Paul; *D:* Fulvio Tului; *W:* Tito Carpi, Robert Gianviti.

Revenge of the Musketeers 🦴🦴 1/2 *D'Artagnan's Daughter; La Fille de D'Artagnan* **1994 (R)** Exciting swashbuckler that finds the beautiful Eloise (Marceau) uncovering a dastardly plot by the Duc of Crassac (Rich) to kill King Louis XIV (Legros). She goes to her father, aging Musketeer D'Artagnan (Noiret), and he seeks the aid of old compatriots Athos (Bideau), Porthos (Billerey), and Aramis (Frey). Since Eloise can handle a sword as well as any of the Musketeers, she gets her own share of dering-do. French with subtitles. **130m/C VHS, DVD.** *FR* Sophie Marceau, Philippe Noiret, Jean-Luc Bideau, Raoul Billerey, Sami Frey, Claude Rich, Nils (Niels) Tavernier, Charlotte Kady, Stephane Legros, Luigi Proietti; *D:* Bertrand Tavernier; *W:* Michel Leviant; *C:* Patrick Blossier; *M:* Philippe Sarde.

Revenge of the Nerds 🦴🦴 1/2 **1984 (R)** When nerdy college freshmen are victimized by jocks, frat boys and the school's beauties, they start their own fraternity and seek revenge. Carradine and Edwards team well as the geeks in this better than average teenage sex comedy. Guess who gets the girls? Sequel was much worse. **89m/C VHS, DVD.** Robert Carradine, Anthony Edwards, Timothy Busfield, Andrew Cassese, Curtis Armstrong, Larry B. Scott, Brian Tochi, Julia Montgomery, Michelle Meyrink, Ted McGinley, John Goodman, Bernie Casey; *D:* Jeff Kanew; *W:* Tim Metcalfe, Jeff Buhai; *C:* King Baggot; *M:* Thomas Newman.

Revenge of the Nerds 2: Nerds in Paradise 🦴 **1987 (PG-13)** The nerd clan from the first film (minus Edwards who only makes a brief appearance) travels to Fort Lauderdale for a fraternity conference. They fend off loads of bullies and jocks with raunchy humor. Boy can Booger belch. Not as good as the first Nerds movie; a few laughs nonetheless. **89m/C VHS, DVD.** Robert Carradine, Curtis Armstrong, Timothy Busfield, Andrew Cassese, Ed Lauter, Larry B. Scott, Courtney Thorne-Smith, Anthony Edwards, James Hong; *D:* Joe Roth; *W:* Dan Guntzelman, Steve Marshall; *C:* Charles Correll; *M:* Mark Mothersbaugh.

Revenge of the Nerds 3: The Next Generation 🦴 1/2 **1992** Adams College has nerd-loathing trustee Downey Jr. mobilizing those frat boys against the bespectacled geeks, who turn to founding nerd Carradine to save them. Cookie-cutter characters and the gags won't hold your attention. Let's hope this is the last in the series. **100m/C VHS.** Robert Carradine, Curtis Armstrong, Ted McGinley, Morton Downey Jr., Julia Montgomery; *D:* Roland Mesa; *W:* Steve Zacharias, Jeff Buhai; *C:* Zoran Hochstatter; *M:* Garry Schyman.

Revenge of the Nerds 4: Nerds in Love 🦴🦴 1/2 **1994** Yes, even nerds deserve a little love. This time the gang get together for Booger's (Armstrong) wedding—complete with nerd bachelor party and wedding shower. Too bad Booger's future father-in-law is so reluctant to have a nerd in the family that he hires a sleazy detective to dig up some dirt. Made for TV. **90m/C VHS.** Curtis Armstrong, Robert Carradine, Ted McGinley, Larry B. Scott, Donald Gibb, Joseph Bologna, Julia Montgomery, Corinne Bohrer, Christina Pickles, Jessica Tuck, Robert Picardo; *D:* Steve Zacharias; *W:* Steve Zacharias, Steve Buhai. **TV**

Revenge of the Ninja 🦴🦴 1/2 **1983 (R)** Ninja Kosugi hopes to escape his past in Los Angeles. A drug trafficker, also ninja-trained, prevents him. The two polish off a slew of mobsters before their own inevitable showdown. Better-than the standard chopsocky fest from Cannon with amusing surreal touches like a battling grandma ninja. Sequel to "Enter the Ninja," followed by "Ninja III." **90m/C VHS, DVD.** Sho Kosugi, Arthur Roberts, Keith Vitali, Virgil Frye, Ashley Ferrare, Kane (Takeshi) Kosugi, John Lamotta, Grace Oshita, Melvin C. Hampton, Mario Gallo; *D:* Sam Firstenberg; *W:* James R. Silke; *M:* Rob Walsh, W. Michael Lewis.

Revenge of the Pink Panther 🦴🦴 1/2 **1978 (PG)** Inspector Clouseau survives his own assassination attempt, but allows the world to think he is dead in order to pursue an investigation of the culprits in his own unique, bumbling way. The last "Pink Panther" film before Sellers died, and perhaps the least funny. **99m/C VHS, DVD.** Peter Sellers, Herbert Lom, Dyan Cannon, Robert Webber, Burt Kwouk, Robert Loggia; ***D:*** Blake Edwards; ***W:*** Frank Waldman, Blake Edwards, Ron Clark; ***C:*** Ernest Day; ***M:*** Henry Mancini.

Revenge of the Radioactive Reporter 🦴🦴 **1991** Nuclear plant honchos don't like journalist who's about to hang their dirty laundry, so they toss him into vat of nuclear waste. He returns as a reporter with a cosmetic peel. **90m/C VHS.** David Scammell, Kathryn Boese, Randy Pearlstein, Derrick Strange; ***D:*** Craig Pryce.

Revenge of the Red Baron 🦴🦴 1/2 **1993 (PG-13)** Jim Spencer (Rooney) is the WWI pilot who shot down Germany's fearsome Red Baron. Now aged and infirm he's tormented by what he thinks is his enemy's ghost. A vengeful ghost who takes after Spencer's family. **90m/C VHS, DVD.** Mickey Rooney, Tobey Maguire, Laraine Newman, Cliff DeYoung; ***D:*** Robert Gordon; ***W:*** Michael James McDonald; ***C:*** Christian Sebaldt.

Revenge of the Stepford Wives 🦴 1/2 **1980** TV sequel to the Ira Levin fantasy about suburban husbands who create obedient robot replicas of their wives. In this installment, the wives are not robots, but are simply made docile by drugs. Strange casting pairs Johnson and Kavner as husband and stepford wife. Begat "The Stepford Children." **95m/C VHS.** Sharon Gless, Julie Kavner, Don Johnson, Audra Lindley, Mason Adams, Arthur Hill; ***D:*** Robert Fuest. **TV**

Revenge of the Teenage Vixens from Outer Space 🦴🦴 **1986** A low-budget film about three sex starved females from another planet who come to earth to find men. When the ones they meet do not live up to their expectations, the frustrated females turn the disappointing dudes are turned into vegetables. **84m/C VHS, DVD.** Lisa Schwedop, Howard Scott; ***D:*** Jeff Ferrell.

Revenge of the Virgins 🦴 **1962** A tribe of topless 'Indian' women protect their sacred land from the white men. Exhumed exploitation for bad-film junkies, narrated by Kenne Duncan, an Ed Wood cohort. **53m/B VHS, DVD.** Jewell Morgan, Charles Veltman, Jodean Russo, Stanton Pritchard; ***D:*** Paul Perri; ***Nar:*** Kenne Duncan.

Revenge of the Zombies 🦴 1/2 **1943** In this sequel of sorts to "King of the Zombies," Carradine is creating an army of the undead for use by an evil foreign entity. **61m/B VHS.** John Carradine, Robert Lowery, Gale Storm, Veda Ann Borg, Mantan Moreland; ***D:*** Steve Sekely.

Revenge Quest 🦴 **1996** In the year 2031, Trent McCormic, L.A.'s most violent serial killer, escapes from a maximum security prison on Mars. He's determined to kill Julie Myers, the woman who testified against him. LAPD detective Rick Castle is equally determined to protect her. **90m/C VHS, DVD.** Brian Gluhak, Christopher Michael Egger, Jennifer Agular; ***D:*** Alan De Herrera; ***W:*** Alan De Herrera; ***C:*** Alan De Herrera; ***M:*** Joseph Andalino. **VIDEO**

The Revenge Rider 🦴🦴 **1935** Orphan McCoy goes after the villains who killed his parents. Good performance from McCoy in an otherwise average film. **60m/B VHS.** Tim McCoy, Robert "Tex" Allen, Billie Seward, Edward Earle, Jack Clifford, Lafe (Lafayette) McKee; ***D:*** David Selman.

The Revenger 🦴 **1990** A framed man returns from prison and finds that a mobster has kidnapped his wife and wants $50,000 to give her back. **91m/C VHS, DVD.** Oliver Reed, Frank Zagarino; ***D:*** Cedric Sundstrom.

Reversal of Fortune 🦴🦴🦴 1/2 **1990 (R)** True tale of wealthy socialite Claus von Bulow (Irons) accused of deliberately giving his wife Sunny (Close) a near-lethal overdose of insulin. Comatose Close narrates history of the couple's courtship and married life, a saga of unhappiness and substance abuse, while Silver (as lawyer Dershowitz) et al prepare von Bulow's defense. An unflattering picture of the idle rich that never spells out what really happened. Irons is excellent as the eccentric and creepy defendant and richly deserved his Best Actor Oscar. From the novel by Dershowitz. **112m/C VHS, DVD.** Jeremy Irons, Glenn Close, Ron Silver, Annabella Sciorra, Uta Hagen, Fisher Stevens, Julie Hagerty, Jack Gilpin, Christine Baranski, John David (J.D.) Cullum; ***D:*** Barbet Schroeder; ***W:*** Nicholas Kazan; ***C:*** Luciano Tovoli; ***M:*** Mark Isham. Oscars '90: Actor (Irons); Golden Globes '91: Actor—Drama (Irons); L.A. Film Critics '90: Actor (Irons), Screenplay; Natl. Soc. Film Critics '90: Actor (Irons).

The Revolt of Job 🦴🦴🦴 *Job Lazadasa* **1984** An elderly Jewish couple adopts an eight-year-old Gentile boy although it is illegal in WWII-torn Hungary and against the beliefs of the orthodox community. Moving story with fine performances. **98m/C VHS.** *GE HU* Fereno Zenthe, Hedi Temessy; ***D:*** Imre Gyongyossy, Barna Kabay.

Revolt of the Barbarians 🦴 *La Rivolta dei Barbari* **1964** Ancient Rome is plagued by barbarian invasion and piracy. A consul travels to Gaul to try to put an end to their misdeeds. **99m/C VHS.** *IT* Roland Carey, Maria Grazia Spina, Mario Feliciani, Mario Feliciani; ***D:*** Guido Malatesta.

Revolt of the Zombies 🦴 **1936** A mad scientist learns the secret of bringing the dead to life and musters the zombies into an unique, gruesome military unit during WWI. Strange early zombie flick looks silly by today's standards. **65m/B VHS, DVD.** Dorothy Stone, Dean Jagger, Roy D'Arcy, Robert Noland, George Cleveland; ***D:*** Victor Halperin; ***W:*** Howard Higgin; ***C:*** Jockey A. Feindel, Arthur Martinelli.

Revolution 🦴 **1985 (R)** The American Revolution is the setting for this failed epic centering on an illiterate trapper and his son who find themselves caught up in the fighting. Long and dull, which is unfortunate, because the story had some potential. The cast is barely believable in their individual roles. Where did you get that accent, Al? **125m/C VHS, DVD.** *GB* Al Pacino, Donald Sutherland, Nastassja Kinski, Annie Lennox, Joan Plowright, Steven Berkoff, Dave King; ***D:*** Hugh Hudson; ***W:*** Robert Dillon.

Revolution! A Red Comedy 🦴🦴🦴 **1991** A group of students are lured away from their revolutionary tendencies by materialistic indulgences. This satirical comedy is in color and black and white. **84m/B VHS.** Kimberly Flynn, Christopher Renstrom, Georg Osterman; ***D:*** Jeff Kahn; ***W:*** Jeff Kahn.

Revolution #9 🦴🦴 1/2 **2001** James Jackson (Risley) is a late twenties worker drone in NYC who's just become engaged to Kim (Shelly) when his behavior undergoes a radical transformation. He's getting subliminal messages via commercials for a perfume called Revolution #9—the kind of messages that lead to worldwide conspiracy theories. His mental breakdown is diagnosed as schizophrenia with Kim bearing the brunt of James's paranoia and self-destructive behavior while she also tries to deal with the bureaucracy and inadequacies of the mental health system. Risley forgoes the histrionics often associated with playing a mentally ill character while Shelly displays the toughness of an ordinary woman confronted by a difficult situation. **91m/C VHS, DVD.** *US* Michael Risley, Adrienne Shelly, Spalding Gray, Callie (Calliope) Thorne, Sakina Jaffrey, Michael Rodrick; ***D:*** Tim McCann; ***W:*** Tim McCann; ***C:*** Tim McCann; ***M:*** Douglas J. Cuomo.

Revolutionary Road 🦴🦴 1/2 **2008 (R)** Young, attractive New Yorkers Frank Wheeler (DiCaprio) and April (Winslet) meet at a Manhattan party, both certain they'll lead lives filled with excitement. Seven years and two kids later, the Wheelers are entrenched in suburban Connecticut leading a typical 1950's suburban life. The oppression eventually leads them to infidelity and a combative relationship. Pressed to the breaking point, Frank agrees to April's plan to flee to Paris to find themselves and their abandoned dreams. But John (Shannon), the mentally ill son of the Wheeler's neighbor (Bates), exposes their failure to address the self-loathing at the root of their problems. Based on Richard Yates' novel of the same title, the film captures the buttoned-up look and feel of mid-1950s America though bypassing the nostalgia. **119m/C DVD.** *US* Leonardo DiCaprio, Kate Winslet, Kathy Bates, Kathryn Hahn, Michael Shannon, David Harbour, Dylan Baker, Richard Easton, Zoe Kazan, Jay O. Sanders, Max Casella; ***D:*** Sam Mendes; ***W:*** Justin Haythe; ***C:*** Roger Deakins; ***M:*** Thomas Newman. Golden Globes '09: Actress—Drama (Winslet).

Revolver 🦴🦴 **1992 (R)** FBI agent Nick Sastro is paralyzed by an assassin's bullet when he tries to stop Aldo Testi, an arms and drug smuggler. But Nick decides to come out of retirement when a chance to nail Testi comes his way. **96m/C VHS.** Robert Urich, Dakin Matthews, Steven Williams, Assumpta Serna, Craig Hill; ***D:*** Gary Nelson.

Revolver 🦴 **2005** Director Ritchie sticks to lowlife criminals with little return. Ex-con Jake Green (Statham) decides to get even with casino-owning baddie Macha (Liotta), who set him up for a prison stint. Jake wins big at the casino and Macha orders a hit to soothe his humiliation. Then Jake is picked up by loan shark Zack (Pastore) and his partner Avi (Benjamin), who dispense a lot of silly psychobabble to no known purpose, which is par for the flick's general incoherence. **115m/C DVD.** *GB FR* Jason Statham, Ray Liotta, Vincent Pastore, Andre Benjamin, Francesca Annis, Terence Maynard, Mark Strong, Andrew Howard; ***D:*** Guy Ritchie; ***W:*** Guy Ritchie; ***C:*** Tim Jones; ***M:*** Nathaniel Mechaly.

RFK 🦴🦴 1/2 **2002** Focuses on the years following the assassination of President John F. Kennedy (Donovan) as his brother Robert (Roache) pursued his own political career until his own assassination. **90m/C VHS, DVD.** Linus Roache, James Cromwell, David Paymer, Martin Donovan, Ving Rhames, Marnie McPhail, Jacob Vargas, Sean Gregory Sullivan, Kevin Hare; ***D:*** Robert Dornhelm; ***W:*** Hank Steinberg; ***C:*** Derick Underschultz; ***M:*** Harald Kloser, Thomas Wanker. **CABLE**

Rhapsody 🦴🦴 1/2 **1954** Taylor plays a wealthy woman torn between a famous young violinist and an equally talented pianist in this long and overdrawn soap opera. Although Taylor gives a superb performance, it's not enough to save this sugarcoated musical romance. Includes lush European scenery and sequences of classical music dubbed in by Claudio Arrau and Michael Rabin. Based on the adaptation of the Henry Handel Richardson novel "Maurice Guest." **115m/C VHS.** Elizabeth Taylor, Vittorio Gassman, John Ericson, Louis Calhern, Michael Chekhov, Barbara Bates, Celia Lovsky; ***D:*** Charles Vidor; ***W:*** Michael Kanin, Fay Kanin.

Rhapsody 🦴🦴 **2001 (R)** In 1986, young hoods Jelly and Roughneck are caught out by an undercover cop in a drug deal. Jelly escapes arrests while Roughneck does time. Released from prison, Roughneck (Plummer) thinks his ex-partner (Phillips), who's now a successful music producer, owes him. **95m/C VHS, DVD.** Glenn Plummer, Fred Williamson, Ice-T, Tee Phillips, Tone Loc, Freda Payne; ***D:*** Don Abernathy; ***W:*** Don Abernathy. **VIDEO**

Rhapsody in August 🦴🦴 1/2 *Hachigatsu no Kyoshikyoku* **1991 (PG)** Talky family drama has four children spending the summer with their grandmother Kane in Nagasaki. They become obsessed with the memorials and bomb sites commemorating the dropping of the atomic bomb in 1945 and their grandmother's experiences. Then Kane's Eurasian nephew (Gere) comes for a visit, inciting more family discussions. Adapted from the novel "Nabe-no-Naka" by Kiyoko Murata. Minor Kurosawa; in Japanese with English subtitles. **98m/C VHS, DVD.** *JP* Sachiko Murase, Narumi Kayashima, Hisashi Igawa, Richard Gere; ***D:*** Akira Kurosawa; ***W:*** Akira Kurosawa; ***C:*** Takao Saito, Masaharu Ueda; ***M:*** Shinichiro Ikebe.

Rhapsody in Blue 🦴🦴🦴 **1945** Standard Hollywood biography of the great composer features whitewashed and non-existent characters to deal with the spottier aspects of George Gershwin's life. Still, the music is the main attraction and it doesn't disappoint. ♫ Rhapsody in Blue; Concerto in F; The Cuban Overture; Fascinatin' Rhythm; The Man I Love; Yankee Doodle Blues; Somebody Loves Me; Swanee; Mine. **139m/B VHS.** Robert Alda, Joan Leslie, Alexis Smith, Charles Coburn, Julie Bishop, Albert Bassermann, Morris Carnovsky, Rosemary DeCamp, Herbert Rudley, Charles Halton, Robert Shayne, Johnny Downs, Al Jolson; ***D:*** Irving Rapper; ***W:*** Howard Koch; ***M:*** Max Steiner, Ira Gershwin.

Rhapsody of Spring 🦴🦴 **1998** Inspired by the life of one of China's most-respected composers. Zhao (Shao) comes of age during the Cultural Revolution and is torn between preserving the past and living in the present. He studies China's indigenous musical forms and becomes determined to compose a new type of opera that will combine traditional songs within a westernized orchestral arrangement, despite any disapproval. Mandarin with subtitles. **120m/C DVD.** *CH* Bing Shao, Ying Qu, Quan Yuan; ***D:*** Wenji Teng; ***W:*** Wenji Teng, Ping He, Wu Hanqing; ***C:*** Lei Zhi; ***M:*** Yuhong Chang.

Rhinestone 🦴 **1984 (PG)** A country singer claims she can turn anyone, even a cabbie, into a singing sensation. Stuck with Stallone, Parton prepares her protege to sing at New York City's roughest country-western club, The Rhinestone. Only die-hard Dolly and Rocky fans need bother with this bunk. Some may enjoy watching the thick, New York accented Stallone learn how to properly pronounce dog ("dawg") in country lingo. Yee-haw. **111m/C VHS, DVD.** Sylvester Stallone, Dolly Parton, Ron Leibman, Richard Farnsworth, Tim Thomerson; ***D:*** Bob (Benjamin) Clark; ***W:*** Sylvester Stallone, Phil Alden Robinson. Golden Raspberries '84: Worst Actor (Stallone), Worst Song ("Drinkenstein").

Rhodes 🦴🦴 1/2 *Rhodes of Africa* **1936** The story of Cecil Rhodes, a man who was instrumental in the Boer War in Africa and established the Rhodes Scholarships with $10 million, is told in this biography. Fine performance by Huston and Homolka. **91m/B VHS.** *GB* Walter Huston, Oscar Homolka, Basil Sydney, Frank Cellier, Peggy Ashcroft, Renne De Vaux, Percy Parsons, Bernard Lee, Ndanisa Kumalo; ***D:*** Berthold Viertel.

Rhodes 🦴🦴 1/2 **1997** British miniseries details the life of 19th-century colonialist, British-born Cecil Rhodes (Shaw), who makes his money in the South African diamond trade and decides to place as much African territory under Britain's flag as possible. Rhodes succeeded in begetting the nation of Rhodesia (now Zimbabwe), became involved in the bloody Boer War, and established the prestigious Rhodes scholarship at Oxford University. On three cassettes. **336m/C VHS.** *GB* Martin Shaw, Frances Barber, Tim Dutton, David Butler, Ken Stott, Raymond Coulthard, Neil Pearson; ***D:*** David Drury; ***W:*** Antony Thomas; ***C:*** Alec Curtis; ***M:*** Alan Parker. **TV**

Rhubarb 🦴🦴 1/2 **1951** Eccentric millionaire T.J. Banner (Lockhart) adopts tough alley cat Rhubarb, making him the mascot of his losing baseball team, the Brooklyn Loons. When Banner dies, he leaves his fortune to the cat, with his lawyer Eric Yeager (Milland) as the feline's guardian. Yeager's also the press agent for the ball club and after he convinces the superstitious players that Rhubarb is good luck, the team starts winning. But then disgruntled gamblers kidnap the fur ball just before the championship game. Leonard Nimoy can be spotted as one of the ball players. **95m/B DVD.** Ray Milland, Jan Sterling, Gene Lockhart, William Frawley, Strother Martin, Taylor Holmes, Elsie Holmes, Leonard Nimoy, Billie Bird, Willard Waterman; ***D:*** Ray Milland, Arthur Lubin; ***W:*** Dorothy Reid, Francis Cockrell; ***C:*** Lionel Lindon; ***M:*** Nathan Van Cleave.

Rhythm on the Range 🦴🦴 1/2 **1936** Crosby stars as a singing cowboy who befriends freight car stowaway Farmer while transporting his prize steer back to his ranch in California. He invites her to his domicile and she falls in love with life on the range and with the rancher himself. Filled with lots of musical numbers, including an appearance from the Sons of the Pioneers featuring Roy Rogers. Comedy from Burns and Raye, who makes her feature film debut here, is as entertaining as always. Remade by Dean Martin and Jerry Lewis in 1956 as "Pardners." ♫ I'm an Old Cowhand; Empty Saddles; I Can't Escape From You; The House That Jack Built for Jill; If You Can't Sing It You'll Have to Swing It; Roundup Lullaby; Drink It Down; Memories; Hang Up My Saddle. **88m/B VHS, DVD.** Bing Crosby, Frances Farmer, Bob Burns, Martha Raye, Samuel S. Hinds, Warren Hymer, Lucile Watson; ***D:***

Norman Taurog; ***W:*** John Moffitt, Sidney Salkow, Walter DeLeon, Francis Martin; ***C:*** Karl Struss.

Rhythm on the River 🦴🦴 ½ **1940** Famous Broadway songwriter Rathbone has lost his magic touch so he hires melody maker Crosby to ghost for him while also hiring Martin to be the wordsmith. When the two fall in love they decide to strike off on their own but can't get their music heard since everyone assumes they've been copying Rathbone. Lots of backstage jokes with Rathbone terrific as an insecure egomaniac. ♫ Rhythm on the River; When the Moon Comes Over Madison Square; Ain't It a Shame About Mame?; What Would Shakespeare Have Said?; Only Forever; That's for Me; I Don't Want to Cry Anymore. **94m/B VHS, DVD.** Bing Crosby, Mary Martin, Basil Rathbone, Oscar Levant, Oscar Shaw, Charley Grapewin, William Frawley, Charles Lane; ***D:*** Victor Schertzinger; ***W:*** Dwight Taylor; ***M:*** Victor Young.

Rhythm Parade 🦴🦴 **1943** A woman takes off for Hawaii, leaving her infant in the care of an L.A. nightclub singer. A jealous rival of the singer takes the opportunity to cause problems. The thin plot serves as a vehicle for lots of singing. ♫ Tootin' My Own Horn; Petticoat Army; Mimi From Tahiti; You're Drafted; Wait Till the Sun Shines Nellie; Sweet Sue; 'Neath the Yellow Moon In Old Tahiti. **68m/B VHS.** Nils T. Granlund, Gale Storm, Robert Lowery, Margaret Dumont, Chick Chandler, Cliff Nazarro, Jan Wiley, Candy Candido, Yvonne De Carlo; ***D:*** Howard Bretherton.

Rhythm Romance 🦴🦴 ½ *Some Like It Hot* **1939** Gene Krupa and his Orchestra are the reason to see this lesser Hope comedy. Nicky Nelson (Hope) is a Coney Island carnival barker, who's latest scheme is to make a buck off the swing craze with Krupa. Meanwhile, Nelson's girl, Lily Racquel (Ross), is miffed at him and decides to take a job as Krupa's girl singer. Based on the play "The Great Magoo" by Ben Hecht and Gene Fowler. ♫ The Lady's in Love with You; Some Like It Hot; Heat and Soul. **65m/B VHS.** Bob Hope, Shirley Ross, Gene Krupa, Una Merkel; ***D:*** George Archainbaud; ***W:*** Lewis R. Foster, Gene Fowler Sr.; ***C:*** Karl Struss.

Rhythm Thief 🦴🦴 **1994** No-budget independent film finds alienated New York hustler Simon (Andrews) eking out a living selling tapes of local underground bands he has illegally recorded. He wants to be left alone but circumstances won't allow it. He's got one of the enraged bands after him, he's pestered by local "admirers," and his eccentric former girlfriend Marty (Daniels) suddenly turns up—severely shaking Simon's emotionally barren existence. Quirky character study gets lots of impact from tiny bucks. **88m/B VHS.** Jason Andrews, Eddie Daniels, Kimberly Flynn, Kevin Corrigan, Sean Haggerty, Mark Alfred, Christopher Cooke; ***D:*** Matthew Harrison; ***W:*** Matthew Harrison, Christopher Grimm; ***C:*** Howard Krupa; ***M:*** Danny Brenner. Sundance '95: Special Jury Prize.

Rica 🦴🦴 *Konketsuji Rika; Rika the Mixed Blood Girl* **1972** A good example of Japan's Pinky violence films in the 1970s. Rica is a half-Japanese girl, whose mother was raped by American G.I.s, who is sent to reform school after murdering a yakuza who left her friend after getting her pregnant (the poor girl soon commits suicide). While in school most of her gang is kidnapped and sold by rivals, so she decides to bust out and raise hell. **90m/C DVD.** *JP* Masami Souda, Ryohei Uchida, Masane Tsukayama, Rika Aoki, Mich Nono, Yasuo Harakayama, Satoshi Moritsuka, Yoshihiro Nakdai, Jun Otomo; ***D:*** Ko Nakahira; ***W:*** Taro Bonten, Kaneto Shindo; ***C:*** Aguri Sugita; ***M:*** Jiro Takemura.

Rica 2: Lonely Wanderer 🦴🦴 ½ *Konketsuji Rika: Hitoriyuku sasuraitabi* **1973** Rica (Rika Aoki) has left her old life behind until a friend dies in a mysterious boat explosion. When she tries to investigate what happened by talking to the survivors they all end up dying. Her only clue is that a drug cartel is behind the killings Pairing with a private detective, the two take the cartel on. **83m/C DVD.** *JP* Taiji Tonoyama, Hitoshi Takagi, Rika Aoki, Ryunosuke Minagishi, Eiji Karasawa, Wolf Otsuki, Haruhiko Tazaki, Kentaro Kaji, Yushi Nishi, Koichi Kubo; ***D:*** Ko Nakahira; ***W:*** Kaneto Shindo, Taro Bonten; ***C:*** Yasushi Sasakibara, Shigenari Hanamura, Tadashi Saijo, Aguri Sugita; ***M:*** Jiro Takemura.

Rica 3: Juvenile's Lullaby 🦴🦴 **1973** In trouble again, Rica is sent to a reform school, and then to a mental institution where the people running things are selling the worst girl delinquents into slavery—where they are forced to produce pornographic films. Yet again, young Rica must use all her Karate skills to defeat an army of intimidating but physically useless goobers. Third film in the series, with a bit more comedy than the rest. **85m/C DVD.** *JP* Taiji Tonoyama, Rika Aoki, Masami Souda, Boss Alstrom, Mammoth Suzuki; ***D:*** Oxide Pang Chun, Kozabura Yoshimura; ***W:*** Kaneto Shindo, Taro Bonten; ***C:*** Aguri Sugita; ***M:*** Jiro Takemura.

Ricco 🦴🦴 *Summertime Killer* **1974 (PG)** A young man swears vengeance against the mobsters who killed his father. He kidnaps the daughter of a mafia kingpin and the battle begins. **90m/C VHS, DVD.** *FR IT SP* Chris Mitchum, Karl Malden, Olivia Hussey, Raf Vallone, Claudine Auger, Gerard Tichy; ***D:*** Antonio (Isasi-Isasmendi) Isasi.

R.I.C.C.O. 🦴 ½ **2002 (R)** When a defense attorney saves a beautiful young woman from the clutches of sinister hitmen, they both become pawns in a deadly game of hide and seek, running from R.I.C.C.O., Detroit's mysterious ganglord. No budget action piece acts more like a decent tour video of Detrot. Other than that, there's not much to look at. Dismal acting and a silly score. **108m/C VHS, DVD.** Walter Harris, Sophia Taylor; ***D:*** Shawn Woodard; ***W:*** Shawn Woodard. **VIDEO**

Rich and Famous 🦴🦴 **1981 (R)** The story of the 25-year friendship of two women, through college, marriage, and success. George Cukor's last film. **117m/C VHS, DVD.** Jacqueline Bisset, Candice Bergen, David Selby, Hart Bochner, Meg Ryan, Steven Hill, Michael Brandon, Matt Lattanzi; ***D:*** George Cukor; ***W:*** Gerald Ayres; ***M:*** Georges Delerue. Writers Guild '81: Adapt. Screenplay.

Rich and Strange 🦴🦴 ½ *East of Shanghai* **1932** Early Hitchcock movie is not in the same class as his later thrillers. A couple inherits a fortune and journeys around the world. Eventually the pair gets shipwrecked. **92m/B VHS, DVD.** *GB* Henry Kendall, Joan Barry, Betty Amann, Percy Marmont, Elsie Randolph; ***D:*** Alfred Hitchcock; ***W:*** Alfred Hitchcock, Alma Reville; ***C:*** Jack Cox, Charles Martin.

Rich Girl 🦴 **1991 (R)** A winsome, wealthy wench hides her millions by going to work in a rock 'n' roll bar and falls in love with the local Bruce Springsteen wanna-be. Despite the thick coating of music, sex, drugs, and profanity, this consists of cliches that were old before talkies. Too earnestly acted to be campy fun. Poor movie. **96m/C VHS.** Jill Schoelen, Don Michael Paul, Ron Karabatsos, Sean Kanan, Willie Dixon, Paul Gleason; ***D:*** Joel Bender.

Rich in Love 🦴🦴 ½ **1993 (PG-13)** Light-hearted look at the changes in a Southern family after matriarch Helen Odom leaves to pursue her own life, shattering the peaceful existence of those around her. Seen through the eyes of 17-year-old daughter Lucille who assumes the role of "mother" for her sister and father while trying to come to terms with her own confused feelings. Nice performances by newcomer Erbe and Finney can't overcome a mediocre script. Based on the novel by Josephine Humphreys. **105m/C VHS.** Albert Finney, Jill Clayburgh, Kathryn Erbe, Kyle MacLachlan, Piper Laurie, Ethan Hawke, Suzy Amis, Alfre Woodard; ***D:*** Bruce Beresford; ***W:*** Alfred Uhry; ***M:*** Georges Delerue.

Rich Kids 🦴🦴 ½ **1979 (PG)** A young girl trying to cope with the divorce of her parents is aided by a boyfriend whose parents have already split. **97m/C VHS.** John Lithgow, Kathryn Walker, Trini Alvarado, Paul Dooley, David Selby, Jill Eikenberry, Olympia Dukakis; ***D:*** Robert M. Young; ***C:*** Ralf Bode.

Rich Man, Poor Man 🦴🦴🦴 **1976** Classic TV miniseries covers 20 (sometimes bitter) years in the lives of the two Jordache brothers. It's 1945 in quiet Port Phillip, New York with embittered German baker Axel (Asner), his unfulfilled wife Mary (McGuire), and sons Tom (Nolte) and Rudy (Strauss). Tom is wild and irresponsible, Rudy is ambitious and college-bound, and Julie Prescott (Blakely), Rudy's girl, overshadows both their lives. Based on the novel by Irwin Shaw. The first series contained 12 episodes. A second series of 21 episodes primarily followed the tribulations of the next generation, although Strauss returned as Rudy. **720m/C VHS.** Peter Strauss, Nick Nolte, Susan Blakely, Ed Asner, Dorothy McGuire, Bill Bixby, Robert Reed, Ray Milland, Kim Darby, Talia Shire, Lawrence Pressman, Kay Lenz; ***M:*** Alex North. **TV**

The Rich Man's Wife 🦴 ½ **1996 (R)** Modern noir strands unhappy wife Josie (Berry) on Martha's Vineyard without her loathsome spouse (McDonald), where she makes the mistake of confiding her marital woes to sympathetic, yet obviously deranged stranger Cole (Greene). She tells Cole sometimes she wishes her husband was dead. Poof! Before you can say "foreshadowing," hubby's murdered and she's the prime suspect. Increasingly nutso Cole stalks our heroine, seemingly innocent, but possibly not as blameless as it appears. Failed mystery/thriller delivers little of either and the attempt at a "Strangers on a Train" premise and a "Usual Suspects" type ending fail miserably. **95m/C VHS, DVD.** Halle Berry, Christopher McDonald, Clive Owen, Peter Greene, Charles Hallahan, Frankie Faison, Clea Lewis; ***D:*** Amy Holden Jones; ***W:*** Amy Holden Jones; ***C:*** Haskell Wexler; ***M:*** John (Gianni) Frizzell.

Rich, Young and Pretty 🦴🦴 ½ **1951** Light-hearted, innocuous musical starring Powell as a Texas gal visiting Paris with her rancher father (Corey). Powell finds romance with Damone (in his screen debut) and a secret—the mother she has never known (Darrieux). Lamas (in his American screen debut) plays Darrieux's new heartthrob. ♫ Dark is the Night; L'Amour Toujours, Tonight For Sure; Wonder Why; I Can See You; Paris; We Never Talk Much; How Do You Like Your Eggs in the Morning?; There's Danger in Your Eyes, Cherie; The Old Piano Roll Blues. **95m/C VHS.** Jane Powell, Danielle Darrieux, Wendell Corey, Vic Damone, Fernando Lamas, Marcel Dalio, Una Merkel, Richard Anderson, Jean Murat, Hans Conried; ***D:*** Norman Taurog; ***W:*** Sidney Sheldon, Dorothy Cooper; ***M:*** Sammy Cahn, Nicholas Brodszky.

Richard Petty Story 🦴 **1972 (G)** The biography of race car driver Petty, played by himself, and his various achievements on the track. **83m/C VHS, DVD.** Richard Petty, Darren McGavin, Kathie Browne, Lynn(e) Marta, Noah Beery Jr., L.Q. Jones; ***D:*** Ed Lasko.

Richard III 🦴🦴 *The Life and Death of King Richard III* **1912** According to the American Film Institute, this is the oldest surviving American feature film and, in 1912, the most ambitious adaptation of Shakespeare ever attempted. Despite changes in conventions, it's still a lively work that's brightened considerably by a new Ennio Morricone score. **58m/B DVD.** Frederick Warde, Robert Gomp, Albert Gardner, Violet Stuart; ***D:*** James Keane.

Richard III 🦴🦴🦴 ½ **1955** This landmark film version of the Shakespearean play features an acclaimed performance by Laurence Olivier, who also directs. The plot follows the life of the mentally and physically twisted Richard of Gloucester and his schemes for the throne of England. **138m/C VHS, DVD.** *GB* Laurence Olivier, Cedric Hardwicke, Ralph Richardson, John Gielgud, Stanley Baker, Michael Gough, Claire Bloom; ***D:*** Laurence Olivier. British Acad. '55: Actor (Olivier), Director (Olivier), Film; Golden Globes '57: Foreign Film.

Richard III 🦴🦴🦴 ½ **1995 (R)** The Brits once again bring the Bard's most notorious monarch to the screen, this time in a new setting. McKellen stars in the title role of the deformed and ruthless English king, now in an imagined 1930s London of swanky Art Deco, Black Shirt thugs and modern media. Purists may resent major dialogue cuts, but famous speeches (such as the "winter of our discontent" opener) are amusingly staged in this modern take. Gorgeously polished visuals are perfect foil for the slimy, evil goings-on. Based on both Shakespeare's play and Richard Eyre's stage adaptation (in which McKellen also starred). **105m/C VHS, DVD.** *GB* Ian McKellen, Annette Bening, Jim Broadbent, Robert Downey Jr., Nigel Hawthorne, Kristin Scott Thomas, Maggie Smith, John Wood; ***D:*** Richard Loncraine; ***W:*** Ian McKellen, Richard Loncraine; ***C:*** Peter Biziou; ***M:*** Trevor Jones.

Richard's Things 🦴🦴 **1980 (R)** A man's wife and his girlfriend find love and comfort in each other after his death. Screenplay by Frederic Raphael, from his novel. Very slow and dreary, with a weak performance from Ullman. **104m/C VHS.** *GB* Liv Ullmann, Amanda Redman; ***D:*** Anthony Harvey; ***W:*** Frederic Raphael; ***C:*** Frederick A. (Freddie) Young; ***M:*** Georges Delerue.

Richie Rich 🦴🦴 ½ **1994 (PG)** Yet another adaptation from the comics. Richie (Culkin), the world's richest boy, takes over the family business when his madcap parents Richard (Herrmann) and Regina (Ebersole) disappear thanks to the devious Laurence Van Dough (Larroquette). But there's kindly valet Cadbury (Hyde) and eccentric live-in inventor Keenbean (McShane) to help Richie save the day. Some silliness but Culkin has clearly outgrown this type of kid role. Biltmore, the 8,000 acre Vanderbilt estate in Asheville, North Carolina, serves as the Rich family home. **94m/C VHS, DVD.** Macaulay Culkin, John Larroquette, Edward Herrmann, Christine Ebersole, Jonathan Hyde, Michael McShane, Stephi Lineburg; ***Cameos:*** Reggie Jackson, Claudia Schiffer; ***D:*** Donald Petrie; ***W:*** Tom S. Parker, Jim Jennewein; ***C:*** Don Burgess; ***M:*** Alan Silvestri.

Rick 🦴🦴 ½ **2003 (R)** Drawing from Verdi's "Rigoletto," the widower Rick is a detestable corporate exec who despises his annoying and much younger boss Duke yet degrades himself to score points. He's pushed past the breaking point when he learns that the punk has been sex-chatting online with his teenage daughter and figures putting a hit out on him is the only answer. **93m/C VHS, DVD.** Bill Pullman, Aaron Stanford, Agnes Bruckner, Sandra Oh, Dylan Baker, Emmanuelle Chriqui, Marianne Hagan, Jamie Harris, Paz de la Huerta, P.J. Brown, Haviland (Haylie) Morris, Dan Moran, Jerome Preston Bates, Marin Rathje, William Ryall, Daniel Handler, Dennis Parlato, Todd A. Kovner, Kimberly Anne Thompson, Vita Haas, Ben Hauck; ***W:*** Daniel Handler; ***C:*** Lisa Rinzler; ***M:*** Ted Reichman. **VIDEO**

Ricky 1 🦴 ½ **1988** Mumbling pugilist spoof. Da Mob wants to make Ricky da fall guy, but uh, he's not as dumb as he looks. **90m/C VHS, DVD.** Michael Michaud, Maggie Hughes, James Herbert, Lane Montano; ***D:*** Bill Naud; ***M:*** Joel Goldsmith.

Ricochet 🦴🦴🦴 **1991 (R)** Rookie cop Washington causes a sensation when he singlehandedly captures notorious psychopath Lithgow. But this particular criminal is a twisted genius, and from his prison cell he comes up with a plan to destroy the young cop. Teaming up with old friend Ice-T, the rookie tries to outwit his evil arch-nemesis. Genuinely scary, tense and violent thriller. **104m/C VHS, DVD.** Denzel Washington, John Lithgow, Ice-T, Jesse Ventura, Kevin Pollak, Lindsay Wagner, Mary Ellen Trainor, Josh Evans, Victoria Dillard, John Amos, John Cothran Jr.; ***D:*** Russell Mulcahy; ***W:*** Steven E. de Souza; ***C:*** Peter Levy; ***M:*** Alan Silvestri.

Ricochet River 🦴🦴 **1998 (R)** High school senior Lorna (Hudson) has big dreams that don't include staying around her tiny Oregon community, even if she is dating hotshot school quarterback Wade. The duo are also the only two to accept newcomer Jesse, a Native American who falls victim to the town's prejudice. **111m/C VHS, DVD.** Kate Hudson, Douglas Spain, Jason James Richter, Matthew Glave, Dan Lauria, John Cullum; ***D:*** Deborah Del Prete. **VIDEO**

The Riddle 🦴🦴 **2007 (PG-13)** Thames-side pub landlady Sadie (Day) is murdered after discovering an unpublished Charles Dickens manuscript in her cellar. But she's already turned it over to her friend, sports reporter Mike (Jones), who's trying to reinvent himself as an investigative journalist. He's willing to hook up with police press officer Kate (Cox) and even a dockside tramp (Jacobi) if they can help him. But a century-old crime described by Dickens (played in flashbacks by Jacobi) might lead Mike to solving Sadie's murder and figuring out who's trying to grab the manuscript from him.

116m/C DVD. *GB* Vinnie Jones, Julie Cox, Derek Jacobi, Vanessa Redgrave, Jason Flemyng, P. H. Moriarty, Mel Smith, Vera Day; ***D:*** Brendan Foley; ***W:*** Brendan Foley; ***C:*** Mark Moriarty; ***M:*** Graham Sack.

The Riddle of the Sands 🦴🦴 ½ **1979** Two English yachtsmen in 1903 inadvertently stumble upon a German plot to invade England by sea. British film based on the Erskine Childers spy novel. **99m/C VHS.** *GB* Michael York, Jenny Agutter, Simon MacCorkindale, Alan Badel; ***D:*** Tony Maylam; ***M:*** Howard Blake.

Ride 🦴🦴 **1998 (R)** This sometimes-amusing but mostly rude road comedy seems to be merely an excuse for getting MTV veejays and rap stars together without actually showing any videos. Freddy B (Campbell) is a superstar looking for street cred, so his director Bleau (Brown) sends Leta (DeSousa) to Harlem to bring a group of young street talents to Miami for a video shoot. There are too many storylines in the busload of passengers to develop fully, so they are skimmed over and defused with a mixture of generic road movie brawls and narrow escapes combined with sexual and scatalogical humor. Yoba does a good job as Poppa, who's trying to watch over reckless little brother Geronimo (Starr) while keeping the rest of the crew in line. **83m/C VHS, DVD.** Malik Yoba, Melissa De Sousa, Fredro Starr, John Witherspoon, Cedric the Entertainer, Kirk "Sticky Fingaz" Jones, Kellie Williams, Idalis de Leon, Julia Garrison, Guy Torry, Reuben Asher, The Lady of Rage, Dartanyan Edmonds, Downtown Julie Brown; ***Cameos:*** Snoop Dogg; ***D:*** Millicent Shelton; ***W:*** Millicent Shelton; ***C:*** Frank Byers; ***M:*** Dunn Pearson Jr.

Ride a Wild Pony 🦴🦴🦴 **1975 (G)** A poor Australian farmer's son is allowed to pick a horse of his own from a neighboring rancher's herd. After he trains and grows to love the pony, the rancher's daughter, a handicapped rich girl, decides to claim it for herself. Enjoyable Disney story is based on the tale "Sporting Proposition," by James Aldridge. **86m/C VHS.** *AU* John Meillon, Michael Craig, Robert Bettles, Eva Griffith, Graham Rouse; ***D:*** Don Chaffey; ***C:*** Jack Cardiff; ***M:*** John Addison.

The Ride Back 🦴🦴 ½ **1957** Well-done western about lawman Hamish (Conrad) who decides to take outlaw Kallen (Quinn) across the Mexican border back to Texas—a four days' journey through hostile territory. At the site of a massacre they discover a lone survivor, a little girl whom they take with them. Then they are attacked by Apaches and when Hamish is wounded, Kallen sees his chance for escape. Good performances by the leads; feature debut for director Miner. **80m/B VHS, DVD.** William Conrad, Anthony Quinn, Lita Milan, Ellen Hope Monroe; ***D:*** Allen Miner; ***W:*** Antony Ellis; ***C:*** Joseph Biroc; ***M:*** Frank DeVol.

Ride Clear of Diablo 🦴🦴 ½ **1954** Crooked Sheriff Kenyon (Birch) and equally crooked lawyer Meredith (Pullen) murder Clay O'Mara's (Murphy) father and brother. He vows to get revenge, aided by gunslinger Whitey Kincade (Duryea). Then Laurie (Cabot), Kenyon's niece and Meredith's fiance, comes to Clay's attention. Macho Technicolor western with a likeable cast. **80m/C VHS.** Audie Murphy, Dan Duryea, Susan Cabot, Paul Birch, William Pullen, Abbe Lane, Russell Johnson, Jack Elam, Lane Bradford, Holly (Mike Ragan) Bane, Denver Pyle; ***D:*** Jesse Hibbs; ***W:*** George Zuckerman, D.D. Beauchamp; ***C:*** Irving Glassberg.

Ride 'Em Cowboy 🦴🦴 ½ **1942** Two peanut and hotdog vendors travel west to try their hand as cowpokes. Usual Abbott and Costello fare with a twist—there are lots of great musical numbers. ♫ A Tisket, A Tasket; I'll Remember April; Wake Up Jacob; Beside the Rio Tonto; Rock 'n' Reelin'; Give Me My Saddle; Cow Boogie. **86m/B VHS, DVD.** Bud Abbott, Lou Costello, Anne Gwynne, Samuel S. Hinds, Dick Foran, Richard Lane, Johnny Mack Brown, Ella Fitzgerald, Douglass Dumbrille; ***D:*** Arthur Lubin.

Ride 'Em Cowgirl 🦴🦴 **1941** Singing cowgirl, Page, enters a horse race to expose the crook who cheated her father. **51m/B VHS.** Dorothy Page, Vince Barnett, Milton Frome; ***D:*** Samuel Diege.

Ride Him, Cowboy 🦴🦴🦴 **1932** Entertaining oater has Wayne saving horse Duke from being sentenced to death. This was the first of six series films Wayne made for Warner's, all of which costarred his white wonder horse, Duke. Remake of the 1926 Ken Maynard silent "The Unknown Cavalier." Based on the story by Kenneth Perkins. **55m/B VHS, DVD.** John Wayne, Ruth Hall, Henry B. Walthall, Harry Gribbon, Otis Harlan, Charles Sellon; ***D:*** Fred Allen; ***W:*** Scott Mason.

Ride in a Pink Car 🦴 **1974 (R)** When a Vietnam vet returns home, he discovers that his welcoming committee is really a lynch mob. **83m/C VHS.** Glenn Corbett, Morgan Woodward, Ivy Jones; ***D:*** Robert Emery.

Ride in the Whirlwind 🦴🦴 **1966** Three cowboys are mistaken for members of a gang by a posse. Screenplay for the offbeat western by Nicholson. **83m/C DVD.** Jack Nicholson, Cameron Mitchell, Millie Perkins, Katherine Squire, Harry Dean Stanton, Rupert Crosse; ***D:*** Monte Hellman; ***W:*** Jack Nicholson; ***C:*** Gregory Sandor; ***M:*** Robert Jackson Drasnin.

Ride Lonesome 🦴🦴 ½ **1959** The heroic Scott is a bounty hunter looking for a killer (Best). It's not just the money, Scott hopes Best will lead him to the man who murdered Scott's wife. Along the trail he meets a pretty widow and two outlaws who hope if they capture Best, they'll get a pardon. A well-done example of a "B" western with good performances; Coburn's film debut. **73m/C VHS.** Randolph Scott, James Best, Karen Steele, Pernell Roberts, Lee Van Cleef, James Coburn; ***D:*** Budd Boetticher; ***W:*** Burt Kennedy.

Ride, Ranger, Ride 🦴 ½ **1936** Texas Ranger Autry is out to stop a group of Comanches from raiding a wagon train. **56m/B VHS.** Gene Autry, Smiley Burnette, Kay Hughes, Max Terhune, Monte Blue, Chief Thundercloud; ***D:*** Joseph Kane.

Ride the High Country 🦴🦴🦴🦴 *Guns in the Afternoon* **1962** The cult classic western about two old friends who have had careers on both sides of the law. One, Joel McCrea, is entrusted with a shipment of gold, and the other, Randolph Scott, rides along with him to steal the precious cargo. Although barely promoted by MGM, the film became a critics' favorite. Grimacing and long in the tooth, McCrea and Scott enact a fitting tribute and farewell to the myth of the grand ol' West. **93m/C VHS, DVD.** Randolph Scott, Joel McCrea, Mariette Hartley, Edgar Buchanan, R.G. Armstrong, Ronald Starr, John Anderson, James Drury, L.Q. Jones, Warren Oates, Jenie Jackson, John Davis Chandler; ***D:*** Sam Peckinpah; ***W:*** N.B. Stone Jr.; ***C:*** Lucien Ballard; ***M:*** George Bassman. Natl. Film Reg. '92.

Ride the Man Down 🦴 ½ **1953** Story of a murderous land war between neighboring landowners tells the same old story: Greed knows no boundaries. **90m/C VHS.** Brian Donlevy, Chill Wills, Jack La Rue, Rod Cameron, Ella Raines, Barbara Britton; ***D:*** Joseph Kane.

Ride the Wild Fields 🦴🦴 ½ **2000** Tender adaptation of Vacarro's play "And the Home of the Brave" finds 11-year-old Opal Miller (Vega) and her mother Ruby (Whalley) struggling to manage their small North Carolina farm while Opal's dad serves overseas during WWII. Ruby is grateful for the help of drifter Tom (Flanery), though others are suspicious of the young man, but complications arise when the adults develop stronger feelings for one another. **101m/C VHS.** Joanne Whalley, Sean Patrick Flanery, Alexa Vega, Cotter Smith; ***D:*** Paul A. Kaufman; ***W:*** Rodney Vaccaro; ***C:*** Thom Best; ***M:*** Laura Kaufman. **CABLE**

Ride the Wild Surf 🦴🦴 ½ **1964** It's fun in the sun when surfers Fabian, Hunter, and Brown head to Hawaii in search of the ultimate waves. Throw in a little romance and a cool title song by Jan and Dean and you've got your better than average beach movie. The surfing footage is excellent. Cowabunga! **101m/C VHS, DVD.** Fabian, Tab Hunter, Barbara Eden, Peter Brown, Susan Hart, Shelley Fabares, Jim Mitchum; ***D:*** Don Taylor.

Ride to Glory 🦴🦴 *The Deserter; La Spina Dorsale del Diavolo* **1971** In 1886, a cavalry officer deserts his troops to seek revenge on the Apaches that brutally killed his family. Hearing this, a general offers to pardon him if he will lead a dangerous group of men on a mission against the Apaches. Fast-paced and very bloody. **90m/C VHS.** Bekim Fehmiu, Richard Crenna, Chuck Connors, Ricardo Montalban, Ian Bannen, Slim Pickens, Woody Strode, Patrick Wayne, John Huston; ***D:*** Burt Kennedy.

Ride with the Devil 🦴🦴 ½ **1999 (R)** Clunky Civil War saga adapted from Daniel Woodrell's novel "Woe to Live On." Lee concentrates on the 1862 Border Wars between the Southern-sympathizers known as the Bushwhackers and the pro-Union Jayhawkers. Best pals Jack Bull Chiles (Ulrich) and Jake Roedel (Maguire) join a group of Bushwhackers and both become involved with a young farm widow, Sue Lee (singer Jewel in her acting debut). After some loses, Jake and the remaining band join in Quantrill's (Ales) infamous raid on the abolitionist stronghold of Lawrence, Kansas. Film serves as a coming-of-age story for the teenaged Jake and Maguire, at least, is up to the challenge. **139m/C VHS, DVD.** Tobey Maguire, Skeet Ulrich, Jeffrey Wright, Jewel, Simon Baker, Jonathan Rhys Meyers, James (Jim) Caviezel, Tom Guiry, Tom Wilkinson, Jonathan Brandis, John Ales, Matthew Faber, Steven Mailer, Zach Grenier, Margo Martindale, Mark Ruffalo, Celia Weston; ***D:*** Ang Lee; ***W:*** James Schamus; ***C:*** Frederick Elmes; ***M:*** Mychael Danna.

Rider from Tucson 🦴🦴 **1950** Two rodeo riders head out to Colorado for a friend's wedding. They find out the bride has been kidnapped by a bunch of claim jumpers after control of a gold mine. **60m/B VHS.** Tim Holt, Richard Martin, Elaine Riley, Douglas Fowley, Veda Ann Borg; ***D:*** Lesley Selander.

The Rider of Death Valley 🦴 ½ **1932** Larribe and Grant plot to steal Bill Joyce's desert gold mine after he dies and leaves the property to his sister Helen and young daughter Betty. Knowing something shady is going on rancher Tom Rigby tries to protect the claim but Helen gets the wrong idea. **78m/B DVD.** Tom Mix, Lois Wilson, Fred Kohler Jr., Forrest Stanley, Edith Fellows, Willard Robertson, Mae Busch; ***D:*** Albert Rogell; ***W:*** Jack Cunningham; ***C:*** Daniel B. Clark.

Rider of the Law 🦴 **1935** A government agent poses as a greenhorn easterner to nab a gang of outlaws. **56m/B VHS.** Gertrude Messinger, Si Jenks, Lloyd Ingraham, John Elliott, Earl Dwire, Bob Steele; ***D:*** Robert North Bradbury; ***W:*** Jack Natteford; ***C:*** Gus Peterson.

Rider on the Rain 🦴🦴🦴 *Lepassager de la Pluie* **1970** A young housewife is viciously raped by an escaped sex maniac. She kills him and disposes of his body, not knowing that he is being relentlessly pursued by mysterious American Bronson. Suspenseful, French-made thriller featuring one of Bronson's best performances. **115m/C VHS, DVD.** *FR* Marlene Jobert, Charles Bronson, Jill Ireland; ***D:*** Rene Clement. Golden Globes '71: Foreign Film.

Riders 🦴 *Jilly Cooper's Riders* **1988** Enemies since childhood, aristocratic Rupert Campbell-Black (Gilbert) and half-gypsy Jake Lovell (Praed) have carried their rivalry into the competitive equestrian field. Of course, there's the added complication of Rupert's wife, whom Jake is also interested in. Based on Jilly Cooper's steamy novel. **210m/C VHS.** *GB* Marcus Gilbert, Michael Praed, Stephanie Beacham, Gabrielle Beaumont, Serena Gordon, John Standing, Anthony Valentine, Cecile Paoli; ***D:*** Gabrielle Beaumont; ***W:*** Charlotte Bingham; ***C:*** Michael J. Davis; ***M:*** Roger Webb.

Riders of Death Valley 🦴🦴 ½ **1941** Splendid western action serial in 15 episodes. Foran, Jones, and Carillo head a passel o'men watching for thieves and claim jumpers in a mining area. **320m/B VHS, DVD.** Dick Foran, Buck Jones, Leo Carrillo, Lon Chaney Jr.; ***D:*** Ford Beebe, Ray Taylor.

Riders of Destiny 🦴🦴 ½ **1933** Wayne plays a government agent sent to find out who is stealing water from the local farmers. Very early Wayne has the Duke looking awfully young as an agent securing water rights for ranchers. **59m/B VHS, DVD.** John Wayne, George "Gabby" Hayes, Cecilia Parker, Forrest Taylor, Al "Fuzzy" St. John; ***D:*** Robert North Bradbury; ***W:*** Robert North Bradbury; ***C:*** Archie Stout.

Riders of Pasco Basin 🦴 ½ **1940** Outlaws are tricking ranchers out of their money by falsely promising to build a dam. So Brown and his cohorts come to set things right. **56m/B VHS.** Johnny Mack Brown, Fuzzy Knight, Bob Baker, Frances Robinson, Arthur Loft, Frank LaRue, Lafe (Lafayette) McKee, Kermit Maynard; ***D:*** Ray Taylor; ***W:*** Ford Beebe.

Riders of the Desert 🦴 ½ **1932** Steele tracks down the loot from a stagecoach robbery. **57m/B VHS, DVD.** Bob Steele, Gertrude Messinger, Al "Fuzzy" St. John, George "Gabby" Hayes, John Elliott; ***D:*** Robert North Bradbury; ***W:*** Wellyn Totman; ***C:*** Archie Stout.

Riders of the Purple Sage 🦴🦴 ½ **1925** When Texas Ranger Jim Lassiter's (Mix) sister and niece are kidnapped by the evil Walters (Oland), he devotes his life to finding them. While working on a ranch (and falling in love with the beautiful ranch owner), he learns Walters has changed his name and is passing himself off as a judge. Promptly shooting the skunk dead, Lassiter and his sweetie must run from a posse. Based on the Zane Grey novel. **63m/B VHS.** Tom Mix, Warner Oland, Mabel Ballin, Beatrice Burnham, Arthur Morrison, Fred Kohler Sr.; ***D:*** Lynn F. Reynolds; ***W:*** Edfrid Bingham.

Riders of the Purple Sage 🦴🦴 ½ **1996** Legendary gunman (are there any other kind?) Lassiter (Harris) helps save Bern (Thomas) from a beating in a town run by a conservative religious sect, led by Deacon Tull (Weisser). Seems Bern's befriended ranch owner (and nonmember) Jane (Madigan) and the Deacon is not only after Jane but her considerable land and cattle holdings. Lassiter rides to the rescue. Properly brooding TV adaptation of the 1912 Zane Grey novel (the Grey novel specifies that the sect are Mormons but this caused considerable fuss). Filmed in Utah. **90m/C VHS.** Ed Harris, Amy Madigan, Henry Thomas, Norbert Weisser, Robin Tunney, G.D. Spradlin; ***D:*** Charles Haid; ***W:*** Gill Dennis; ***C:*** William Wages; ***M:*** Arthur Kempel. **TV**

Riders of the Range 🦴🦴 **1924** Sheep invade the cattle range and a range war flares up between those who would herd and the ranchers. Silent flick of interest because of the stars. **62m/B VHS.** Edmund Cobb, Dolly Dale; ***D:*** Otis Thayer.

Riders of the Range 🦴 **1950** Cowboy rides into town just in time to save a girl's brother from gamblers. **60m/B VHS.** Tim Holt, Richard Martin, Jacqueline White, Reed Hadley, Robert Barrat, Robert Clarke, Tom Tyler, William Tannen; ***D:*** Lesley Selander; ***W:*** Norman Houston; ***C:*** J. Roy Hunt; ***M:*** Paul Sawtell.

Riders of the Rio Grande 🦴 ½ **1943** Banker Pop Owens is ashamed that his son Tom's gambling has led to financial difficulties for the bank. In order to save the bank and his reputation, Pop arranges a contract killing on himself to leave the money from his estate to clear the debts. But he mistakes the Three Mesquiteers for the hired guns. The 51st and last film in the series. **55m/B DVD.** Bob Steele, Tom Tyler, Jimmie Dodd, Edward Van Sloan, Lorraine Miller, Rick Vallin, Harry Worth, Charles King, Roy Barcroft, Jack Ingram; ***D:*** Howard Bretherton; ***W:*** Albert DeMond; ***C:*** Ernest Miller; ***M:*** Mort Glickman.

Riders of the Rockies 🦴🦴 ½ **1937** An honest cowboy turns rustler in order to trap a border gang. One of Ritter's very best cowboy outings; good fun, and a very long fistfight with King. **60m/B VHS, DVD.** Tex Ritter, Yakima Canutt, Louise Stanley, Charles "Blackie" King, Snub Pollard; ***D:*** Robert North Bradbury.

Riders of the Storm 🦴 ½ *The American Way* **1988 (R)** A motley crew of Vietnam vets runs a covert TV broadcasting station from an in-flight B-29, jamming America's legitimate airwaves. Interesting premise with boring result. **92m/C VHS, DVD.** Dennis Hopper, Michael J. Pollard, Eugene Lipinski, James Aubrey, Nigel Pegram; ***D:*** Maurice Phillips; ***W:*** Scott Roberts.

Riders of the Timberline 🦴🦴 **1941** Unusual for a Hopalong Cassidy programmer in that it puts him in timber country. Yes, he's a lumberjack and he's okay, as he fights against land-grabbing crooks all day. **59m/B VHS, DVD.** William Boyd, Brad King, Andy Clyde, J. Farrell MacDonald, Elaine Stewart, Anna Q. Nilsson, Hal Taliaferro, Tom Tyler, Victor Jory; ***D:*** Lesley Selander.

Riders of the West **1942** An honest cowpoke fights off a band of rustlers. **58m/B VHS, DVD.** Buck Jones, Tim McCoy, Raymond Hatton, Sarah Padden, Harry Woods; ***D:*** Howard Bretherton.

Riders of the Whistling Pines **1949** Our ever-so-bland hero solves a murder perpetrated by a passel of lumber thieves and saves the day for yet another damsel in distress. **70m/B VHS, DVD.** Gene Autry, Patricia Barry, Jimmy Lloyd; ***D:*** John English.

Riders of the Whistling Skull 1/2 *The Golden Trail* **1937** The Three Mesquiteers are guiding an expedition to an ancient Indian city. A gang of rustlers looting the city are holding an archeology professor hostage, and the Mesquiteers must rescue him. Swell cast; nifty, creepy plot; solid-as-usual leads. **58m/B VHS, DVD.** Robert "Bob" Livingston, Ray Corrigan, Max Terhune, Yakima Canutt, Roland Winters; ***D:*** Mack V. Wright.

Riders to the Sea 1/2 **1988** A mother envisions the death of her last son in the same manner her other sons died—by drowning. Based on the play by Irish dramatist John Millington Synge. **90m/C VHS.** Geraldine Page, Amanda Plummer, Sachi (MacLaine) Parker, Barry McGovern; ***D:*** Ronan O'Leary.

Ridicule 1/2 **1996 (R)** Fish-out-of-water drama has minor country aristocrat Pondeludon (Berling) enter the depraved world of the 18th-century court at Versailles. There, he hopes, the king will aid him in his quest to drain the disease-ridden swamps at his estate. The naive provincial finds he must master the weapons of choice for success within the court—wit, deadly ridicule, and impeccable lineage. After initial missteps due to lack of finesse, he quickly adapts, and finds some influential allies: the beautiful Madame de Blayac (Ardant) and sympathetic Marquis de Bellegarde (Rochefort). When the Marquis's spirited and attractive daughter, Mathilde (Godreche), shows up, the smitten Pondeludon must stop her loveless marriage of convenience. Perfectly cast, director Leconte's highly lauded period piece has all the emotional and technical elements of an engaging film. In French with subtitles. **102m/C VHS, DVD.** *FR* Charles Berling, Jean Rochefort, Fanny Ardant, Bernard Giraudeau, Judith Godreche, Bernard Dheran, Carlo Brandt, Jacques Mathou; ***D:*** Patrice Leconte; ***W:*** Remi Waterhouse, Michel Fessler, Eric Vicaut; ***C:*** Thierry Arbogast; ***M:*** Antoine Duhamel. Oscars '96: Foreign Film; Cesar '97: Director (Leconte), Film; Broadcast Film Critics '96: Foreign Film.

Ridin' Down the Canyon 1/2 **1942** Standard but entertaining entry in Rogers' popular series. It's Rogers to the rescue when a gang of outlaws are rustling cattle and selling to the government for wartime profits. Roy, along with the Sons of the Pioneers, also manages to croon a few tunes. Based on a story by Robert Williams and Norman Houston. **54m/B VHS, DVD.** Roy Rogers, George "Gabby" Hayes, Linda Hayes, Addison Richards, Adrian Booth, James Seay; ***D:*** Joseph Kane; ***W:*** Albert DeMond.

The Ridin' Fool 1/2 **1931** Steve Kendall (Steele) saves gambler "Boston" Harry Manners (Adams) from hanging after he's falsely accused of robbery. When they both fall for Sally Warren (Morris), her brother Bud (Fetherston) is afraid they'll discover he and his partner Nikkos (Bridge) are the actual criminals. **58m/B DVD.** Bob Steele, Ted Adams, Frances Morris, Alan Bridge, Florence Turner, Eddie Fetherston, Gordon De Main, Josephine Velez; ***D:*** John P. McCarthy; ***W:*** Wellyn Totman; ***C:*** Archie Stout.

Ridin' for Justice 1/2 **1932** Cowpoke Buck Randall (Jones) gets into trouble with Sheriff Slyde (Simpson) when he refuses to surrender his gun in compliance with a town ordinance. Buck escapes the posse by hiding out in the sheriff's own house, given shelter by Slyde's pretty, unhappy wife Mary (Doran). But Buck's troubles are far from over because he's then accused of murdering Slyde's deputy. **61m/B DVD.** Buck Jones, Russell Simpson, Mary Doran, Walter Miller, Robert McKenzie; ***D:*** David Ross Lederman; ***W:*** Harold Shumate; ***C:*** Benjamin (Ben H.) Kline.

Ridin' on a Rainbow 1/2 **1941** Has-been performer on a steamboat decides to rob a bank in the hopes of starting a new life for himself and his daughter. The money he robs had just been deposited by some cattlemen, one of whom joins the steamboat's crew, wins the daughter's heart, and gets to the father. Slow and dull, with too much singing, and too little plot and scenery. **79m/B VHS, DVD.** Gene Autry, Smiley Burnette, Mary Lee; ***D:*** Lew Landers.

Ridin' the Lone Trail WOOF! **1937** Steele attempts to stop some criminals who've been harassing a stagecoach line. Republic was better than this weak western would lead us to believe. Steele, who went on to better things, is a bright spot in a film that sounds and looks bad. Keep your ears open for the sound of airplanes—apparently Newfield forgot they hadn't been invented in the time of the wild west. From a story by E.B. Mann. **56m/B VHS.** Bob Steele, Claire Rochelle, Charles "Blackie" King, Ernie Adams, Lew Meehan, Julian Rivero; ***D:*** Sam Newfield; ***W:*** Charles Francis Royal.

Ridin' the Trail **1940** Scott stars as a cowboy out to rid the countryside of bad guys in this western. **60m/B VHS.** Fred Scott, Iris Lancaster, Harry Harvey, Jack Ingram, John Ward; ***D:*** Bernard B. Ray.

Ridin' Thru **1935** Another Tom Tyler western, in which the hero does battle with unscrupulous villains. **60m/B VHS, DVD.** Tom Tyler, Ruth Hiatt, Lafe (Lafayette) McKee, Philo (Philip, P.H., P.M.) McCullough, Lew Meehan, Bud Osborne; ***D:*** Harry S. Webb.

Riding Alone for Thousands of Miles *Qian Li Zou Dan Ji* **2005 (PG)** Small-scale, compelling human drama from Zhang. Japanese fisherman Gou-ichi Takata (Takakura) is called to Tokyo by his daughter-in-law, where his estranged son Ken-ichi (Nakai) is hospitalized with terminal cancer. Grief-stricken, Gou-ichi vows to fulfill his son's dying dream—to film celebrated Chinese opera star Li Jiamin (appearing as himself) in performance. This involves the elderly man traveling to a remote Chinese province and ultimately reuniting Li with his own illegitimate son. Hope triumphs amidst the hardships. Japanese and Chinese with subtitles. **108m/C DVD.** *CH HK JP* Ken Takakura, Kiichi Nakai, Shinobu Terajima, Li Jiamon; ***D:*** Yimou Zhang; ***W:*** Zou Jingzhi; ***C:*** Xiaoding Zhao; ***M:*** Guo Wenjing.

The Riding Avenger 1/2 **1936** To gain the love of a beautiful lady, a cowboy vows never to fight again, but is forced to break his promise when the town is terrorized. Aw, shucks. **56m/B VHS, DVD.** Hoot Gibson, Ruth Mix, Buzz Barton; ***D:*** Harry Fraser.

Riding Giants **2004 (PG-13)** Director Stacy Peralta does for surfing what she did for skateboarding in "Dogtown and Z-Boys" by capturing the consummate skill and infectious enthusiasm of those who dominate the sport. Includes an animated mini-history that sardonically traces surfing from its Polynesian roots through the 20th century. **105m/C DVD.** *US* Jeff Clark, Darrick Doerner, Mickey Munoz, Brian L. Keaulana, Dick Brewer, Buzzy Kerbox, Ricky Grigg, Pat Curren, Laird Hamilton, Lyon Hamilton, Dave Kalama, Randy Rarick, Buffalo Keaulana, Evan Slater, Kelly Slater; ***Cameos:*** Sam George, Gabrielle Reece, Dr. Mark Renneker, Mike Stange; ***D:*** Stacy Peralta; ***W:*** Sam George, Stacy Peralta; ***C:*** Peter Pilafian; ***M:*** Alan Barker.

Riding High 1/2 **1950** Capra remade his 1934 film "Broadway Bill" as this light-hearted musical. Horse trainer Crosby falls for the wealthy Gray who demands he choose between her and his horse. Bing chooses the horse who proves his loyalty by winning the big race and making Crosby a rich man. ♫Someplace on Anywhere Road; Sunshine Cake; We've Got a Sure Thing; The Horse Told Me; The Whiffenpoof Song; De Camptown Races. **112m/B VHS, DVD.** Bing Crosby, Coleen Gray, Charles Bickford, William Demarest, Frances Gifford, Raymond Walburn, James Gleason, Ward Bond, Percy Kilbride, Harry Davenport, Margaret Hamilton, Douglass Dumbrille, Gene Lockhart, Charles Lane, Frankie Darro, Paul Harvey, Marjorie Lord, Dub Taylor, Max Baer Sr., Oliver Hardy; ***D:*** Frank Capra; ***W:*** Robert Riskin, Melville Shavelson, Jack Rose; ***C:*** George Barnes.

Riding High **1978** It's a battle for supremacy between the kings of the motorcycle stunt world. TV movie's soundtrack includes songs from The Police, Dire Straits, Jerry Lee Lewis, and more. **92m/C VHS.** Murray Salem, Marella Oppenheim, Eddie Kidd, Irene Handl; ***D:*** Ross Cramer. **TV**

Riding in Cars with Boys **2001 (PG-13)** Based on the memoir of Beverly Donofrio, the plot follows Beverly (Barrymore) from 1965, when she becomes pregnant at age 15, to 1986, when her son has grown up and she has completed her book. The story is more concerned with the way parents treat their children, however, and Beverly doesn't emerge as the spunky supermom who prevailed despite the odds. Instead she comes off as a whiner who blames her loser husband Ray (Zahn) for getting her pregnant, her own parents (Woods and Bracco) for not talking to her, and even her son Jason (Garcia) for merely being around. Barrymore gives a good performance, but Zahn outdoes her by breaking his "goofy guy" typecast and adding texture to the woeful Ray. **132m/C VHS, DVD.** *US* Drew Barrymore, Steve Zahn, Brittany Murphy, Adam Garcia, Lorraine Bracco, James Woods, Sara Gilbert, Desmond Harrington, David Moscow, Maggie Gyllenhaal, Peter Facinelli, Marisa Ryan, Mika Boorem, Skye McCole Bartusiak, Logan Lerman; ***D:*** Penny Marshall; ***W:*** Morgan Ward; ***C:*** Miroslav Ondricek; ***M:*** Hans Zimmer.

Riding On **1937** Hayseed falls for the daughter of his father's arch rival. While his father battles it out over cattle, he pines for his enemy's daughter. Lots of action which is typical fare in mediocre western production. **59m/B VHS.** Tom Tyler, Germaine Greer, Rex Lease, John Elliott, Earl Dwire; ***D:*** Harry S. Webb.

Riding on Air **1937** Small-town newspaper editor Brown discovers that his bumbling methods get him the right results. Smugglers and crazy inventions in a ho-hum Brown entry. **58m/B VHS.** Joe E. Brown; ***D:*** Edward Sedgwick.

Riding Speed **1935** Our hero breaks up a gang of smugglers along the Mexican border. **50m/B VHS.** Buffalo Bill Jr., Bud Osborne, Lafe (Lafayette) McKee, Clyde McClary; ***D:*** Buffalo Bill Jr.; ***C:*** Brydon Baker.

Riding the Bullet 1/2 **2004 (R)** A death-obsessed young man (Jackson) keeps running from and into the Grim Reaper and his agents. Lame Garris/King collaboration relying on obvious shocks instead of suspense for its thrills. Tired horror movie cliches abound, so it never gets under your skin the way it should. **98m/C DVD.** *US* Jonathan Jackson, David Arquette, Cliff Robertson, Barbara Hershey, Erika Christensen; ***D:*** Mick Garris; ***W:*** Mick Garris; ***C:*** Robert New; ***M:*** Nicholas Pike.

Riding the California Trail 1/2 **1947** The Cisco Kid is wanted dead or alive in several states. **40m/B VHS.** Gilbert Roland, Martin Garralaga, Frank Yaconelli, Teala Loring, Ted Hecht; ***D:*** William Nigh; ***W:*** Clarence Upson Young; ***C:*** Harry Neumann.

Riding the Sunset Trail **1941** Top-notch tale of Keene trying to stop a con from cashing in on his dead half-brother's fortune. Solid production values and an enthusiastic performance by Keene make this one of his best films after a string of flops. **56m/B VHS.** Tom Keene, Betty Miles, Frank Yaconelli, Sugar Dawn, Slim Andrews, Kenne Duncan; ***D:*** Robert Emmett Tansey; ***W:*** Robert Emmett, Frances Kavanaugh.

The Riding Tornado 1/2 **1932** Bronc rider McCoy takes a job on Grey's ranch, promptly falling for her. Ranch foreman Oakman, who's really the leader of a gang of rustlers, kidnaps Grey and McCoy goes after them. **63m/B VHS.** Tim McCoy, Shirley Grey, Wheeler Oakman, Wallace MacDonald, Russell Simpson, Montagu Love, Lafe (Lafayette) McKee, Bud Osborne; ***D:*** David Ross Lederman.

Riding Wild 1/2 **1935** Stevens is out to start a range war between ranchers and illegal homesteaders. Cowboy Tim Mallory joins the squatters' cause but Stevens happens to find a Mallory look-alike he's going to use to cause trouble. **57m/B DVD.** Tim McCoy, Niles Welch, Ed LeSaint, Richard Alexander, Dick Botiller, Edmund Cobb, Billie Stewart; ***D:*** David Selman; ***W:*** Ford Beebe; ***C:*** Benjamin (Ben H.) Kline.

Riding with Death **1976** A man who can become invisible, thanks to a military experiment, uses his power to uncover a dastardly plot by a mad scientist. So-so TV pilot. **97m/C VHS.** Ben Murphy, Andrew Prine, Katherine Crawford, Richard Dysart; ***D:*** Alan J. Levi. **TV**

Riel **1979** The story of Louis Riel, a half-French, half-Indian visionary who challenged the Canadian army in his fight for equality and self-rule. **150m/C VHS.** Raymond Cloutier, Arthur Hill, William Shatner, Christopher Plummer, Leslie Nielsen; ***D:*** George Bloomfield.

Riff Raff *Riffraff* **1935** Melodramatic story about the relationship of two waterfront workers in the tuna fishing business. Confusing script saddled with too many characters, but there is some good sharp dialogue between the leads. Also features the scenic California waterfront. **80m/B VHS.** Jean Harlow, Spencer Tracy, Joseph Calleia, Una Merkel, Mickey Rooney, Victor Kilian, J. Farrell MacDonald, Roger Imhof; ***D:*** J. Walter Ruben.

Riff-Raff 1/2 **1947** Various dramatic and comic complications arise when a dying man gives Panama City con man O'Brien a map to oil deposits. Interesting and quick-moving melodrama. **80m/B VHS.** Pat O'Brien, Walter Slezak, Anne Jeffreys, Jason Robards Sr., Percy Kilbride, Jerome Cowan; ***D:*** Ted Tetzlaff.

Riff Raff **1992** Unsparing black comedy about the British working class by director Loach. Ex-con Stevie comes to London from Scotland to look for work and escape his thieving past. He finds a nonunion job on a construction site, takes up squatter's rights in an abandoned apartment, and finds a girlfriend in equally struggling singer Susie, who turns out to be a junkie. Loach's characters deal with their unenviable lot in life through rough humor and honest sentiment. Regional accents are so thick that the film is subtitled. **96m/C VHS.** *GB* Robert Carlyle, Emer McCourt, Jimmy Coleman, George Moss, Ricky Tomlinson, David Finch, Bill Jesse; ***D:*** Ken Loach; ***W:*** Bill Jesse; ***M:*** Stewart Copeland.

Rififi 1/2 *Du Rififi Chez les Hommes* **1954** Perhaps the greatest of all "heist" movies. Four jewel thieves pull off a daring caper, only to fall prey to mutual distrust. The long scene of the actual theft, completely in silence, will have your heart in your throat. In French with English subtitles. **115m/B VHS, DVD.** *FR* Jean Servais, Carl Mohner, Robert Manuel, Jules Dassin; ***D:*** Jules Dassin; ***W:*** Jules Dassin; ***C:*** Philippe Agostini; ***M:*** Georges Auric. Cannes '55: Director (Dassin).

Rift 1/2 **1996** Bland romantic triangle set among Manhattan twentysomethings. Shy Tom (Sage) pines for Lisa (Bransford), the wife of his best friend, Bill (Cavanaugh). In fact, Tom begins having overwhelming nightmares, involving murder, about the situation. Not that you'll care since Tom is a mope, Lisa's a whiner, and Bill's a nasty-tempered bore. **87m/C VHS.** William Sage, Timothy Cavanaugh, Jennifer Bransford, Alan Davidson; ***D:*** Edward S. Barkin; ***W:*** Edward S. Barkin; ***C:*** Lee Daniel.

Right at Your Door **2006 (R)** Brad (Cochrane) is forced to seal up his house and lock his wife Lexi (McCormack) outside after she is exposed to deadly toxins caused by dirty bombs hitting Los Angeles. Basically a disaster flick with only two major characters, and that gets dull real fast (especially since Brad is obnoxious). **96m/C DVD.** Rory Cochrane, Mary McCormack, Tony Perez; ***D:*** Chris Gorak; ***W:*** Chris Gorak; ***C:*** Tom Richmond; ***M:*** Tomandandy.

The Right Hand Man 1/2 **1987 (R)** A brother and sister must deal with their crusty patriarch's demise in the Victorian-era Australian outback. Disappointing and overwrought. **101m/C VHS, DVD.** *AU* Rupert Everett, Hugo Weaving, Arthur Dignam; *D:* Di Drew.

Right of Way 1/2 **1984** Stewart plays an elderly man who makes a suicide pact with his wife (Davis) when he learns of her terminal illness. Davis and Stewart's first film together is disappointing and stodgy, with an abrupt ending that looks like bad editing by a frightened studio. Made for TV. **102m/C VHS.** James Stewart, Bette Davis, Priscilla Morrill, Melinda Dillon; *D:* George Schaefer; *M:* Brad Fiedel. **TV**

The Right Stuff **1983 (PG)** A rambunctious adaptation of Tom Wolfe's non-fiction book about the beginnings of the U.S. space program, from Chuck Yeager's breaking of the sound barrier to the last of the Mercury missions. Featuring an all-star cast and an ambitious script. Rowdy, imaginative, and thrilling, though broadly painted and oddly uninvolving. Former astronaut John Glenn was running for president when this was out. **193m/C VHS, DVD.** Ed Harris, Dennis Quaid, Sam Shepard, Scott Glenn, Fred Ward, Charles Frank, William Russ, Kathy Baker, Barbara Hershey, Levon Helm, David Clennon, Kim Stanley, Mary Jo Deschanel, Veronica Cartwright, Pamela Reed, Jeff Goldblum, Harry Shearer, Donald Moffat, Scott Paulin, Lance Henriksen, Scott Wilson, John P. Ryan, Royal Dano; *D:* Philip Kaufman; *W:* Philip Kaufman; *C:* Caleb Deschanel; *M:* Bill Conti. Oscars '83: Film Editing, Sound, Orig. Score.

The Right Temptation 1/2 **2000 (R)** Female PI Derian (De Mornay) is hired by a jealous wife (Delaney) to get the dirt on her adulterous rich husband (Sutherland). Too bad the PI then falls for her target, who may also be in bed with the mob. **93m/C VHS, DVD.** Kiefer Sutherland, Rebecca De Mornay, Dana Delany, Adam Baldwin; *D:* Lyndon Chubbuck.

The Right to Remain Silent **1995 (R)** Rookie cop Christine Paley (Thompson) learns all about human foibles in her job processing incoming suspects. Based on a play by Brent Briscoe and Mark Fauser. **96m/C VHS.** Lea Thompson, Amanda Plummer, Christopher Lloyd, Laura San Giacomo, Judge Reinhold, Carl Reiner, LL Cool J, Patrick Dempsey, Fisher Stevens, Robert Loggia; *D:* Hubert de la Bouillerie.

Righteous Kill **2008 (R)** On paper, this must've looked like the world's greatest buddy-cop flick. Turk (De Niro) and Rooster (Pacino), long-time friends and partners, have been assigned to investigate the recent murders of violent criminals who've gotten off on legal technicalities. Neither is too motivated to solve the case, almost grateful for the vigilante's sense of justice. Keeping them in check are detectives Perez (Leguizamo) and Riley (Wahlberg), who begin to suspect one of the two. Unfortunately, it's a fairly routine police drama that likely would've gone straight to DVD or turned into an episode of "CSI" had it not been for its heavyweight billing. De Niro and Pacino's third film together, but only the second time they've actually shared screen time. **100m/C DVD, Blu-ray Disc.** *US* Robert De Niro, Al Pacino, Brian Dennehy, Carla Gugino, Donnie Wahlberg, John Leguizamo, Curtis "50 Cent" Jackson, Melissa Leo, Trilby Glover, Alan Rosenberg, Barry Primus, Alan Blumenfeld, Oleg Taktarov, Shirly Brener, Ajay Naidu, Saidah Arrika Ekulona; *D:* Jon Avnet; *W:* Russell Gewirtz; *C:* Denis Lenoir; *M:* Ed Shearmur.

Rikisha-Man 1/2 *Rickshaw Man; Muhomatsu no Issho* **1958** A tragic melodrama about a rickshaw puller who helps raise a young boy after his father has died, and loves the boy's mother from afar. Inagaki's remake of his original 1943 version. In Japanese with English subtitles. **105m/B VHS, DVD.** *JP* Toshiro Mifune; *D:* Hiroshi Inagaki.

Rikky and Pete 1/2 **1988 (R)** An engaging Australian comedy about a bizarre, precociously eccentric brother and sister. He's a Rube Goldberg-style mentor; she's a scientist-cum-country singer. They move together to the outback and meet a score of weird characters. A worthy follow-up to director Tass's "Malcolm." **103m/C VHS, DVD.** *AU* Nina Landis, Stephen Kearney, Tetchie Agbayani, Bruce Spence, Bruno Lawrence, Bill Hunter, Dorothy Allison, Don Reid, Lewis Fitz-Gerald; *D:* Nadia Tass; *W:* David Parker; *M:* Phil Judd.

Rikyu **1990** Set in 16th century Japan, Rikyu is a Buddhist priest who elevated the tea ceremony to an art form. To him it is a spiritual experience, to his master, Lord Hideyoshi Toilyotomi, the ruler of Japan, mastery of the ceremony is a matter of prestige. Conflict arises between Rikyu's ideal of profound simplicity, symbolized by the ceremony, and Toilyotomi's planned conquest of China, which Rikyu opposes. In Japanese with English subtitles. **116m/C VHS, DVD.** *JP* Rentaro Mikuni, Tsutomu Yamazaki; *D:* Hiroshi Teshigahara; *W:* Hiroshi Teshigahara, Genpei Akasegawa; *C:* Fujio Morita; *M:* Toru Takemitsu.

Rim of the Canyon 1/2 **1949** Autry has a dual role as a lawman tracking villains who were jailed by his father years before. **70m/B VHS, DVD.** Gene Autry, Nan Leslie, Thurston Hall, Clem Bevans, Walter Sande, Jock Mahoney, Alan Hale Jr., Denver Pyle; *D:* John English.

Rimfire 1/2 **1949** An undercover agent tracks down some stolen U.S. Army gold, aided by the ghost of a wrongly hanged gambler. Fun B western. **65m/B VHS, DVD.** Mary Beth Hughes, Henry Hull, Fuzzy Knight, James Millican, Victor Kilian, Margia Dean, Jason Robards Sr., Reed Hadley, Chris-Pin (Ethier Crispin Martini) Martin, John Cason, George Cleveland, I. Stanford Jolley, Stanley Price; *D:* B. Reeves Eason; *W:* Ron Ormond, Arthur St. Claire, Frank Wisbar; *C:* Ernest Miller; *M:* Walter Greene.

Rin Tin Tin, Hero of the West **1955** In one of his last adventures, the famous German Shepherd proves his courage and hyper-canine intelligence. Colorized. **75m/C VHS.** James Brown, Lee Aaker.

The Ring 1/2 **1927** Very early Hitchcock about boxer who marries carnival girl, loses carnival girl, and wins carnival girl back again. Standard romantic punch and roses yarn interesting as measure of young director's developing authority. **82m/B VHS, DVD.** *GB* Carl Brisson, Lillian Hall-Davis, Ian Hunter, Gordon Harker; *D:* Alfred Hitchcock; *W:* Alfred Hitchcock; *C:* Jack Cox.

The Ring 1/2 **1952** Poignant early fight movie that gives a lesson in prejudice against Chicanos. The main character feels that the only way to get respect from the world is to fight for it. Well-directed and perceptive. **79m/B VHS, DVD.** Gerald Mohr, Rita Moreno, Kiri Te Kanawa, Robert Arthur, Art Aragon, Jack Elam; *D:* Kurt Neumann.

The Ring 1/2 **2002 (R)** American adaptation of the novel and film that took Japan by storm in 1998. Upon hearing of an allegedly lethal videotape in urban legend fashion, teen Katie (Tamblyn) gets her hands on a copy and watches it with three of her friends. Immediately after viewing the tape, she gets a call telling her that she will die in exactly one week. A week later all four teens are dead. Katie's reporter aunt Rachel (Watts) tries to get to the bottom of the mystery, but has only one week to do so after also viewing the tape. She is also racing to save her son (Dorfman) and ex-husband Noah (Henderson), who she has rather stupidly exposed to this Memorex of Mayhem. While the look is suitably atmospheric and creepy, the plot stretches plausibility to the breaking point. **115m/C VHS, DVD.** *US* Naomi Watts, Martin Henderson, David Dorfman, Brian Cox, Jane Alexander, Lindsay Frost, Amber Tamblyn, Rachael Bella, Daveigh Chase, Pauley Perrette, Sara Rue, Shannon Cochran; *D:* Gore Verbinski; *W:* Ehren Kruger; *C:* Bojan Bazelli; *M:* Hans Zimmer.

The Ring 2 1/2 **2005 (PG-13)** Creepy demon-child Samara (Chase) continues to pursue reporter Rachel (Watts) and her son (Dorfman). This time around the killer videotape is dispensed with early on in favor of a more traditional possession theme. Samara wants all the comforts of Mommy and home, and seems to find them in the son's body. Excruciatingly slow, confused, and almost totally unfrightening wreck, this time helmed by the director of the original Japanese film, who should have known better. **111m/C DVD.** *US* Naomi Watts, Simon Baker, David Dorfman, Elizabeth Perkins, Gary Cole, Sissy Spacek, Ryan Merriman, Emily Van Camp, Daveigh Chase, Kelly Overton, Kelly Stables, James Lesure; *D:* Hideo Nakata; *W:* Ehren Kruger, Hideo Nakata; *C:* Gabriel Beristain; *M:* Henning Lohner, Martin Tillman.

The Ring Finger 1/2 *L'Annulaire* **2005** Factory worker Iris loses part of her ring finger on a bottling assembly line and then gets a job as an assistant to a man who preserves people's mementos in such things as glass jars. He also wants her to wear red hooker pumps on the job, which leads to a sexual obsession. Adapted from the Yoko Ogawa novel; French with subtitles. **104m/C DVD.** *FR* Olga Kurylenko, Marc Barbe, Stipe Erceg; *D:* Diane Betrand; *W:* Diane Betrand; *C:* Alain Duplantier; *M:* Beth Gibbons.

Ring of Bright Water **1969 (G)** Well done story of a pet otter from Gavin Maxwell's autobiography. The film stars the couple that made the delightful "Born Free." Beautiful Scottish Highlands photography adds to this captivating and endearing tale of a civil servant who purchases an otter from a pet store and moves to the country. **107m/C VHS, DVD.** *GB* Bill Travers, Virginia McKenna, Peter Jeffrey, Archie Duncan; *D:* Jack Couffer; *W:* Jack Couffer, Bill Travers; *C:* Wolfgang Suschitzky; *M:* Frank Cordell.

Ring of Darkness **WOOF! 2004 (R)** Boy band zombies. Pop singer Shawn (Martines) reluctantly agrees to girlfriend Stacy's (Starr) demands that he try out to be the replacement lead singer of boy band Take Ten. Shawn and two other finalists are whisked away to a secluded island and discover that the band members are zombies who use black magic to stay young and on the charts. An unfortunate Barbeau plays their evil manager. Grating music and no frights—except for that plotline. **85m/C DVD.** Jeremy Jackson, Adrienne Barbeau, Mink Stole, Stephen Martines, Ryan Starr, Eric Dearborn, Greg Cipes; *D:* David DeCoteau; *W:* Matthew Jason Walsh, Ryan Carrasi, Michael Gingold; *C:* Mateo Londono. **CABLE**

Ring of Death 1/2 *The Detective* **1969 (R)** A tough cop investigating a routine case becomes a hunted man after someone kills the man he is following. **103m/C VHS.** *IT* Franco Nero, Florinda Bolkan, Adolfo Celi, Delia Boccardo, Susanna Martinkova; *D:* Romolo Guerrieri; *W:* Massimo D'Avak; *C:* Roberto Gerardi; *M:* Fred Bongusto.

Ring of Death 1/2 **2008** Disgraced ex-cop Burke Wyatt (Messner) is trying to rebuild his life and get back together with estranged wife Mary (Ross). He agrees to go undercover for the feds, getting himself tossed in prison to bust up a crime ring. Then Wyatt finds himself caught up in a deadly underground fight league. **86m/C DVD.** Johnny Messner, Stacy Keach, Charlotte Ross; *D:* Bradford May; *W:* Matthew Chernov, David Rosiak; *C:* Maximo Munzi. **CABLE**

Ring of Fire 1/2 **1991 (R)** Wilson is one of very few modern American kung-fu heroes of Asian descent, and he works messages against prejudice into this interracial Romeo-and-Juliet chopsocky tale. What foot through yonder window breaks? **100m/C VHS, DVD.** Don "The Dragon" Wilson, Maria Ford, Vince Murdocco, Dale Jacoby, Michael Delano, Eric Lee; *D:* Richard W. Munchkin.

Ring of Fire 2: Blood and Steel 1/2 **1992 (R)** Wilson returns as Dr. Johnny Wu in this martial-arts actioner which finds the good doctor the witness to a robbery. When one of the robbers is killed, the gang's leader kidnaps Johnny's fiance and holds her for ransom. He decides to bypass the police and use his own expertise to rescue her. **94m/C VHS, DVD.** Don "The Dragon" Wilson, Maria Ford, Sy Richardson, Michael Delano, Dale Jacoby, Vince Murdocco, Evan Lurie, Charlie Ganis, Ron Yuan; *D:* Richard W. Munchkin.

Ring of Fire 3: Lion Strike 1/2 **1994 (R)** Johnny Wu is supposed to be on vacation with his son and a beautiful forest ranger when they find themselves in the way of a violent group known as the Global Mafia. Seems Johnny has a computer disk that the gangsters want. **90m/C VHS, DVD.** Don "The Dragon" Wilson, Bobbie Phillips, Robert Costanzo; *D:* Rick Jacobson.

Ring of Steel **1994 (R)** Alex, a one-time Olympic hopeful in fencing, is enticed into combat by the mysterious owner of a decadent nightclub where gladiator-type matches are staged for the thrill of the bored and jaded super-rich. Unaware of the high stakes, Alex wins a duel and is showered with money and the attention of a beautiful, yet dangerous woman. When Alex discovers the club's dark secret, he no longer wants to fight, but blackmail draws him in even deeper. **94m/C VHS.** Joe Don Baker, Carol Alt, Robert Chapin, Gary Kasper, Darlene Vogel; *D:* David Frost; *W:* Robert Chapin; *M:* Jeff Beal.

Ring of Terror **1962** College boy who wants to join a fraternity must survive the initiation rights, which include stealing a ring from a corpse. Unfortunately, this seemingly invincible guy has a deadly terror of the dead. Cheaply made flop alledgedly based on a composite of actual hazing incidents. **72m/B VHS, DVD.** George Mather, Esther Furst, Austin Green, Joseph Conway; *D:* Clark Paylow.

Ring of the Musketeers 1/2 **1993 (PG-13)** Contemporary spoof of the Musketeers saga finds three descendants of the swashbuckling heroes carrying on the family tradition of protecting the weak and innocent. They even get stuck with a Musketeer-wanna-be when they come to the rescue of a young boy who is kidnapped to prevent his dad from testifying against mobsters. **86m/C VHS.** David Hasselhoff, Alison Doody, Thomas Gottschalk, Richard "Cheech" Marin, Corbin Bernsen, John Rhys-Davies; *D:* John Paragon; *W:* Joel Surnow.

The Ring Virus **1999** South Korea's remake of "Ringu" is ironically closer to the novel than the Japanese film. On the same day four people die under similar circumstances. A reporter, Sun-Joo, discovers they all knew each other. Believing this can't possibly be a coincidence, she investigates. She ends up watching a supposedly cursed videotape that tells her she has one week to live. With only a week left she teams with a neurologist who has also seen the tape, eventually being led to a remote island and the demonic girl Eun-Suh. Not quite as good as the Japanese version, it still has its moments. And it's worth seeing for purists who want a film closer to the novel. **95m/C DVD.** *KN* Du-na Bae, Eun-Kyung Shin, Jin-yeong Jong, Seung-Hyeon Lee, Chang-wan Kim, Ggoch-ji Kim, Yeon-Su Yu; *D:* Dong-bin Kim; *W:* Koji Suzuki, Dong-bin Kim; *C:* Mauricio Dortona, Chul-hyun Hwang; *M:* Il Won.

The Ringer 1/2 **2005 (PG-13)** Throughout their film careers, the Farrelly Brothers have consistently showcased their un-ironic affection for both toilet humor and the mentally handicapped. However, their attempt to bring the two together in this Johnny Knoxville vehicle (directed by one of their farm-team minions) fails miserably. Steve (Knoxville) is a nice guy who, thanks to money woes, gets talked into posing as a retarded athlete, so his uncle Gary (Cox) can fix the Special Olympics. It sounds like the most "wrong" comedy ever, but the script is completely toothless, vacillating between mocking the handicapped and telling us how awesome they are. Hypocrisy is rarely funny, and this dud is no exception. **94m/C DVD.** *US* Johnny Knoxville, Brian Cox, Katherine Heigl, Geoffrey Arend, Leonard Earl Howze, Jed Rees, John Taylor, Edward Barbanell, Bill Chott, Leonard Flowers; *D:* Barry W. Blaustein; *W:* Ricky Blitt; *C:* Mark Irwin; *M:* Mark Mothersbaugh.

Ringmaster **WOOF!** *Jerry Springer's Ringmaster* **1998 (R)** Okay, this is it. Hug the kids, empty the bank accounts. It's the apocalypse. Jerry Springer's made a movie. And the first question would be: why? To cash in, of course, and to try to justify the show's existence. The second question is: Why should you bother? The answer is a resounding "You shouldn't." In case you couldn't guess the plot, Jerry welcomes a stepdad (Dudikoff) who's doing it with his 15-year-old stepdaughter (Pressly), and a woman (Robinson) who caught her man (White) with her best friend. Sexual escapades and the thrill of being on "the TEE-vee" ensue. **89m/C VHS, DVD.** Jerry Springer, John Capodice,

Jaime Pressly, Molly Hagan, Michael Dudikoff, Michael Jai White, William McNamara, Dawn Maxey, Wendy Raquel Robinson, Tangie Ambrose, Nicki Micheaux, Ashley Holbrook; *D:* Neil Abramson; *W:* Jon Bernstein; *C:* Russell Lyster; *M:* Kennard Ramsey. Golden Raspberries '98: Worst New Star (Springer).

Ringside 1/2 **1949** A concert pianist turns boxer to avenge his brother who was blinded in a fight. **64m/B VHS.** Donald (Don "Red") Barry, Sheila Ryan, Tom Brown, Margia Dean, John Cason, Joseph Crehan, Lyle Talbot; *D:* Frank McDonald; *W:* Ron Ormond, Daniel Ullman; *C:* Ernest Miller.

Ringu **1998** Based on Koji Suzuki's novel, "Ringu" is largely responsible for the resurgence of the Japanese horror genre. Oddly enough the film relies far less on pseudo-science than the novel, and more heavily on the supernatural, making it more effective. Western audiences unfamiliar with Japanese culture may miss several of the film's references to mythology. One week after renting a cabin and watching a strange tape a group of students die. The cousin of one, Reiko Asakawa, is a reporter. She asks her estranged husband for help investigating the deaths due to his psychic abilities. Together they search for the meaning behind the mysterious tape, and the deadly spirit known as Sadako. **96m/C DVD.** *JP* Hiroyuki (Henry) Sanada, Yutaka Matsushige, Hiroyuki Watanabe, Nanako Matsushima, Miki Nakatani, Yuko Takeuchi, Hitomi Sato, Yoichi Numata, Katsumi Muramatsu, Rikiya Otaka, Masako, Daisuke Ban, Kiyoshi Risho, Yurei Yanagi, Yoko Oshima, Kiriko Shimizu, Rie Inou, Miwako Kaji, Takashi Takayama, Toshiliko Takeda, Chihiro Shirai, Mantaro Koichi, Shinkichi Noda, Kazufumi Nakai, Kazu Nagahama; *D:* Hideo Nakata; *W:* Koji Suzuki, Hiroshi Takahashi; *C:* Junichiro Hayashi; *M:* Kenji Kawai.

Ringu 0 1/2 *Ringu 0: Basudei* **2001** In this prequel to "Ringu," a young Sadako has gone off to college. Despite being shy and withdrawn she has joined the drama club. The members hate her, especially when a lead actress dies and the director nominates Sadako to replace her. All of them begin plotting to get rid of her some way, except for Hiroshi who has begun to fall in love with her. To make matters worse a reporter who believes Sadako is responsible for murder begins nosing around, and eventually the cast members assault Sadako before traveling to her home for the apocalyptic finale. Creepy and effective, the only sequel that is on par with the original. **99m/C DVD.** *JP* Seichi Tanabe, Kumiko Aso, Yoshiko Tanaka, Takeshi Wakamatsu, Kazue Tsunogae, Ryuji Mizukami, Kaoru Okunuki, Daisuke Ban, Tsukasa Kimura, Junko Takahata, Masako, Yasuji Kimura, Masami Hashimoto, Chinami Furuya, Go Shimada, Yoshiyuki Morishita, Yukimi Koyanagi, Yoji Tanaka, Shuichiro Idemitsu, Masato Oba, Tasuko Uno; *D:* Norio Tsuruta; *W:* Koji Suzuki, Hiroshi Takahashi; *M:* Shinichiro Ogata.

Ringu 2 **1999** Taking off right after the end of the first film, Reiko and her son have gone into hiding after surviving their encounter with Sadako while the authorities try to explain the deaths. Unfortunately it seems Sadako's spirit has not been laid to rest, and Reiko's son appears to be developing psychic powers like his father. Reiko fears the ghost now has some connection to her son. Like the first film, "Ringu 2" relies on growing suspense as opposed to gore or shocks, but it doesn't do it nearly as well. **92m/C DVD.** *JP* Miki Nakatani, Hitomi Sato, Kyoko Fukada, Fumiyo Kohinata, Kenjiro Ishimaru, Yurei Yanagi, Rikiya Otaka, Yoichi Numata, Nanako Matsushima, Hiroyuki (Henry) Sanada, Masako, Rie Inou, Katsumi Muramatsu, Daisuke Ban, Yoko Chosokabe, Reita Serizawa, Isao Yatsu, Taro Suwa, Yoshiko Yura, Kazu Nagahama, Takashi Nishina, Shiro Namiki, Shinmei Tsuji; *D:* Hideo Nakata; *W:* Hideo Nakata, Koji Suzuki, Hiroshi Takahashi; *C:* Hideo Yamamoto; *M:* Kenji Kawai.

The Rink **1916** Chaplin plays a waiter who spends his lunch hour on roller skates. Silent with musical soundtrack added. **20m/B VHS, DVD.** Charlie Chaplin; *D:* Charlie Chaplin.

Rio Bravo 1/2 **1959** John T. Chance (Wayne) is the sheriff of a Texas border town who takes murderer Joe (Akins) into custody. Since Joe is the brother of powerful local cattle baron Nathan Burdette (Russell), the sheriff faces a blockade of gunmen hired to keep his prisoner from being brought to justice. Chance has to make do with the help of a cripple (Brennan), a drunk (Martin), and a hot-headed kid (Nelson). Long, but continually entertaining film that didn't impress critics at the time but its reputation has improved over the years. Hawks and Wayne basically remade this one with "El Dorado." **140m/C VHS, DVD, Blu-ray Disc, HD DVD.** John Wayne, Dean Martin, Angie Dickinson, Ricky Nelson, Walter Brennan, Ward Bond, Claude Akins, Bob Steele, John Russell, Harry Carey Jr., Pedro Gonzalez-Gonzalez; *D:* Howard Hawks; *W:* Leigh Brackett, Jules Furthman; *C:* Russell Harlan; *M:* Dimitri Tiomkin.

Rio Conchos **1964** Nifty nonstop action in this western set in Texas after the Civil War. Three Army buddies search for 2,000 stolen rifles. Boone is understated, O'Brien is good, and Brown memorable in his debut. **107m/C VHS.** Richard Boone, Stuart Whitman, Edmond O'Brien, Anthony (Tony) Franciosa, Jim Brown; *D:* Gordon Douglas; *M:* Jerry Goldsmith.

Rio Diablo 1/2 **1993** Country Western singers abound in—what else—a made-for-TV Western movie. A bounty hunter (Rogers) and newlywed groom (Tritt) set off after a gang of thieving kidnappers who have snatched the young bride (Harring). Judd shows up as the owner of a desert hostelry, who happens to cross paths with the hunters. Watch out—this could be more fun than a Partridge Family reunion. **120m/C VHS, DVD.** Kenny Rogers, Travis Tritt, Naomi Judd, Stacy Keach, Brion James, Bruce Greenwood, Laura Elena Harring; *M:* Larry Brown.

Rio Grande **1950** The last entry in Ford's cavalry trilogy following "Fort Apache" and "She Wore a Yellow Ribbon." A U.S. cavalry unit on the Mexican border conducts an unsuccessful campaign against marauding Indians. The commander of the lonely outpost, Lt. Col. Kirby Yorke (Wayne), plays no favorites when his only son, Jeff (Jarman Jr.), arrives as a new recruit and is soon followed by Yorke's estranged wife, Kathleen (O'Hara). Featuring an excellent Victor Young score and several songs by the Sons of the Pioneers. **105m/B VHS, DVD.** John Wayne, Maureen O'Hara, Ben Johnson, Claude Jarman Jr., Harry Carey Jr., Victor McLaglen, Chill Wills, J. Carrol Naish; *D:* John Ford; *W:* James Kevin McGuinness; *C:* Bert Glennon; *M:* Victor Young.

Rio Grande Raiders **1946** A Stagecoach driver discovers that his kid brother is working for a crooked rival stage company. **54m/B VHS.** Sunset Carson, Linda Stirling, Bob Steele; *D:* Thomas Carr; *W:* Norton S. Parker; *C:* Alfred S. Keller.

Rio Grande Ranger 1/2 **1937** Texas Ranger Bob (Allen) takes off his badge to chase some bandits across the border into their Mexican hideout. He and his partner Garrick (Taliaferro) come up with a plan so that Bob will join the gang. Then they learn there's a price on Bob's head and take him back to Texas to collect. Only things don't go quite right. **54m/B DVD.** Robert "Tex" Allen, Iris Meredith, Hal Taliaferro, Paul Sutton, Jack Rockwell, Tom London, Slim Whitaker, Robert "Buzzy" Henry, John Elliott; *D:* Spencer Gordon Bennet; *W:* Nate Gatzert; *C:* James S. Brown Jr.

Rio Lobo 1/2 **1970 (G)** Hawks's final film takes place after the Civil War, when Union Colonel Wayne goes to Rio Lobo to take revenge on two traitors. Disappointing. The Duke has to carry weak supporting performances on his brawny shoulders—and nearly does. **114m/C VHS, DVD.** John Wayne, Jorge (George) Rivero, Jennifer O'Neill, Jack Elam, Chris Mitchum, David Huddleston, George Plimpton; *D:* Howard Hawks; *C:* William Clothier; *M:* Jerry Goldsmith.

Rio Rattler 1/2 **1935** Tyler takes the place of a murdered lawman in order to find his killer. **60m/B VHS, DVD.** Tom Tyler, Marion Shilling, Eddie Gribbon, William (Bill) Gould, Tom London; *D:* Franklin Shamray.

Rio Rita 1/2 **1929** RKO's film version of producer Florenz Ziegfeld's 1928 Broadway musical with sequences filmed in two-strip Technicolor. Irish-Mexican ranch owner Rita (Daniels) is being wooed by disguised, singing Texas Ranger Jim (Boles) who thinks her brother (Alvarado) is a notorious bandit. There's also a subplot with comic duo Wheeler & Woolsey with Wheeler hiring shyster lawyer Woolsey to get him a quickie Mexican divorce. Loosely remade in 1942. **102m/C DVD.** Bebe Daniels, John Boles, Bert Wheeler, Robert Woolsey, Don Alvarado, Dorothy Lee, Georges Renavent, Helen Kaiser; *D:* Luther Reed; *W:* Luther Reed; *C:* Robert B. Kurrle.

Rio Rita 1/2 **1942** Abbott & Costello are working on a ranch and somehow become involved with Nazi spies. Provides a few original comic bits for the duo but is otherwise mediocre. An updated remake of the 1929 Wheeler & Woolsey comedy. **91m/B VHS.** Bud Abbott, Lou Costello, Kathryn Grayson, John Carroll, Patricia Dane, Tom Conway, Peter Whitney; *D:* S. Sylvan Simon; *C:* George J. Folsey.

Riot 1/2 **1969 (R)** Men in cages throw tantrums until warden returns from vacation. Filmed in Arizona State Prison with real convicts as extras. Strong performances by fullback Brown and durable Hackman. Based on story by ex-con Frank Elli. Too oft-played theme song sung by Bill Medley of the Righteous Brothers. **97m/C VHS.** Gene Hackman, Jim Brown, Mike Kellin, Ben Carruthers, Frank Eyman; *D:* Buzz Kulik; *W:* James Poe.

Riot **1996 (R)** Dumb actioner set on Christmas Eve, 1999, amidst some L.A. riots. British Special Air Service officer Shane Alcott (Daniels) must rescue his kidnapped ex-girlfriend Anna-Lisa (Rowland), who just happens to be the British ambassador's daughter. She's being held by ghetto gangster Leon (Sanders), whose gang turn out to be pawns for IRA leader O'Flaherty (Kilpatrick), who has a score to settle. Predictable fights, lots of explosions. **95m/C VHS, DVD.** Gary Daniels, Ray "Sugar Ray" Leonard, Patrick Kilpatrick, Paige Rowland, Dex Elliot Sanders, Charles Napier; *D:* Joseph Merhi; *W:* Joseph John Barmettler Jr., William Applegate Jr.; *C:* Ken Blakey; *M:* Jim Halfpenny.

Riot in Cell Block 11 **1954** A convict leads four thousand prisoners in an uprising to improve prison conditions. Based on producer/ex-con Walter Wanger's own experience. Powerful and still timely. Filmed at Folsom Prison. **80m/B VHS.** Neville Brand, Leo Gordon, Emile Meyer, Frank Faylen; *D:* Donald Siegel.

Riot in the Streets *Riot* **1996 (R)** Four intertwined stories revolving around the 1992 Los Angeles riots, on the day the Rodney King verdict was announced. Concerned are an African-American family, a white police officer, a Latino family, and Asian-American shopowners. Documentary footage of the actual riots is also included. **95m/C VHS, DVD.** Mario Van Peebles, Melvin Van Peebles, Cicely Tyson, Luke Perry, Peter Dobson, Dante Basco, Mako, Kieu Chinh, Alexis Cruz, Douglas Spain, Yelba Osorio, John Ortiz; *D:* C. David Johnson, Richard Dilello, Galen Yuen, Alex Munoz; *W:* C. David Johnson, Richard Dilello, Galen Yuen, Joe Vasquez; *C:* Paul Elliott. **CABLE**

Riot Squad **1941** An intern poses as a doctor in order to find out who was responsible for putting a mob hit on a police captain. **55m/B VHS, DVD.** Richard Cromwell, Rita Quigley, John Miljan, Mary Ruth, Herbert Rawlinson, Mary Gordon, Arthur Space; *D:* Edward Finney.

Rip It Off *Beyond the City Limits* **2002 (R)** Lexi (Hannigan) and Misha (Kinski) have a couple of loser thug boyfriends (Denisof, McCardie) who are planning a casino heist with a couple of dirty cops. When the gals get fed up by the way they're treated, they hook up with pal Helena (Esposito) and decide to pull off the heist first and leave the guys out in the cold. Told from the POV of Helena's own dirty cop, Toretti (Field). **91m/C VHS, DVD.** Nastassja Kinski, Alyson Hannigan, Jennifer Esposito, Brian McCardie, Alexis Denisof, Todd Field, Steve Harris, Freddy Rodriguez, Sophie B. Hawkins; *D:* Gigi Gaston; *W:* John McMahon; *C:* David Bridges.

Rip-Off **1977** Two Greek wanderers enter the American way of life via sex, drugs, syndicated crime, and terrorism. **78m/C VHS.** Michael Benet, Michelle Simone, James Masters, Johnny Dark; *D:* Manolis Tsafos.

The Rip Off **1978 (R)** A colorful gang of hoodlums goes for the biggest heist of their lives—six million bucks in diamonds! **99m/C VHS.** Lee Van Cleef, Karen Black, Robert Alda, Edward Albert; *D:* Anthony M. Dawson.

Rip Roarin' Buckaroo **1936** A fighter sets out to avenge himself when he is framed in a dishonest fight. **51m/B VHS, DVD.** Tom Tyler, B.J. Quinn Jr., Beth Marion, Charles "Blackie" King; *D:* Robert F. "Bob" Hill.

Rip van Winkle 1/2 **1985** Sleepy Coppola adaptation of the Washington Irving story about a man who falls asleep for 20 years after a group of ghosts get him drunk. From the "Faerie Tale Theatre" series. **60m/C VHS, DVD.** Harry Dean Stanton, Talia Shire; *D:* Francis Ford Coppola.

Ripe **1997 (R)** Fourteen-year-old fraternal twins Violet (Keena) and Rosie (Eagan) decide to make it on their own after their abusive parents are killed in a car crash. They wind up on a derelict southern army base where they're befriended by caretaker Pete (Currie) and M.P. Ken (Brice), who may not have the most innocent of intentions. **93m/C VHS, DVD.** Monica Keena, Daisy Eagan, Gordon Currie, Ron Brice, Karen (Lynn) Gorney, Vincent Laresca; *D:* Mo Ogrodnik; *W:* Mo Ogrodnik; *C:* Wolfgang Held; *M:* Anton Sanko.

Ripley's Game **2002 (R)** Tom Ripley (Malkovich) is still a sociopath, but now he's older, more refined, icier, married, and (not surprisingly) successful. When he overhears an insult by the host, Trevanny (Scott), of a dinner party, he decides to make him pay. His opportunity comes when British gangster Reeves (Winstone) asks him for an anonymous assassin to take out a Russian mobster. Ripley, knowing Trevanny is terminally ill and broke, suggests him as the hit man. Trevanny accepts, but is betrayed by Reeves, which conflicts with Ripley's sense of honor, who then intervenes. Malkovich is perfect as the steely Ripley, and has good support from the rest of the cast, as well as an enjoyably intricate plot. **100m/C VHS, DVD.** John Malkovich, Dougray Scott, Ray Winstone, Lena Headey, Chiara Caselli; *D:* Liliana Cavani; *W:* Liliana Cavani, Charles McKeown; *C:* Alfio Contini; *M:* Ennio Morricone. **VIDEO**

The Ripper WOOF! **1986** The spirit of Jack the Ripper possesses a university professor's body. Ultra-violent. Shot on videotape for the video market. **90m/C VHS.** Wade Tower, Tom Schreir, Mona Van Pernis, Andrea Adams; *D:* Christopher Lewis.

The Ripper **1997 (R)** Yet another version of the Jack the Ripper saga. In 1888 London, ambitious Scotland Yard inspector Jim Hansen (Bergin) is investigating the murders of several East End prostitutes. Clues direct him to a member of the nobility, in fact, Queen Victoria's grandson, Prince Edward (West), but pursuing his inquiries could lead to the end of Hansen's career. **100m/C VHS.** Patrick Bergin, Gabrielle Anwar, Michael York, Samuel West, Essie Davis, Olivia Hamnett; *D:* Janet Meyers; *W:* Robert Rodat; *C:* Martin McGrath; *M:* Mason Daring. **CABLE**

Ripper: Letter from Hell **2001 (R)** Thankfully, there's more terror than gore in this slasher, which could be a bummer if you prefer the bloodier the better. Molly Keller (Cook) enrolls in a forensic science program taught by criminologist Marshall Kane (Payne). There's a spate of recent campus murders that Molly and her study group are investigating and the modus operandi resembles that of Jack the Ripper. Then they start becoming the killer's next victims. **113m/C VHS, DVD.** A.J. Cook, Bruce Payne, Ryan Northcott, Jurgen Prochnow, Claire Keim, Derek Hamilton, Emmanuelle Vaugier; *D:* John Eyres; *W:* Patrick Bermel; *C:* Thomas M. Harting; *M:* Peter Allen. **VIDEO**

Ripper Man 1/2 **1996 (R)** Ex-cop is accused of murder when he finds a body at a nightclub and then becomes the killer's next target. **93m/C VHS.** Timothy Bottoms, Robert F. Lyons, Charles Napier, Bruce Locke, Mike Norris; *D:* Phil Sears; *W:* Phil Sears; *C:* Blake T. Evans; *M:* Jim Ervin. **VIDEO**

Ripple Effect **2007 (R)** Lebanese-born American fashion mogul Amer Atrash (writer/director Caland) is having money troubles and a bailout by a friend falls through. Convinced that it's karmic payback for covering up a 15-year-old hit-and-run, Amer is determined to make amends to the wheelchair-bound Philip (Whitaker). Except to Philip, his accident was a blessing in disguise. **87m/C DVD.** Forest Whitaker, Virginia Madsen, Minnie Driver, John Billingsley, Philippe Caland, Kip Pardue, Kail Rocha; ***D:*** Philippe Caland; ***W:*** Philippe Caland; ***C:*** Daron Keet; ***M:*** Anthony Marinelli.

Riptide 1934 Shearer is a carefree American married to stuffy English lord Marshall. He goes off to America on a business trip, she's bored and goes to a costume party (everyone dresses as insects!) where she meets old flame Montgomery. He gets drunk, follows her home in an effort to rekindle their passion, and winds up in the hospital after a drunken fall. The returning Marshall is appalled by the scandalous press and instigates divorce proceedings. Eventually, they come to their senses and decide they do love each other. Quality production with an entertaining cast. **90m/B VHS.** Norma Shearer, Herbert Marshall, Robert Montgomery, Richard "Skeets" Gallagher, Ralph Forbes, Lilyan Tashman; ***D:*** Edmund Goulding; ***W:*** Edmund Goulding.

The Rise and Fall of Legs Diamond 1/2 1960 Not quite historically accurate but fast-paced and entertaining gangster bio of legendary booze trafficker Legs Diamond. Danton's debut. **101m/B VHS.** Ray Danton, Karen Steele, Jesse White, Simon Oakland, Robert Lowery, Elaine Stewart; ***D:*** Budd Boetticher.

The Rise & Rise of Daniel Rocket 1986 A exceptional young boy believes he can fly without the aid of a flying machine. From the "American Playhouse" series. **90m/C VHS.** Tom Hulce, Timothy Daly, Valerie Mahaffey; ***D:*** Emile Ardolino.

Rise: Blood Hunter 2007 Reporter Sadie (Liu) becomes a victim of the underground vampire cult she was investigating. She's not happy and, armed with a crossbow, she decides to get revenge on the vamp leader (D'Arcy) and anyone else who brutalized her. Lots of violence, gore, and nakedness. **94m/C DVD.** Lucy Liu, Michael Chiklis, Carla Gugino, James D'Arcy, Nick Lachey, Robert Forster, Mako; ***D:*** Sebastian Gutierrez; ***W:*** Sebastian Gutierrez; ***C:*** John Toll; ***M:*** Nathan Barr.

The Rise of Louis XIV *La Prise de Pouvoir Par Louis XIV* 1966 A masterful docudrama detailing the life and court intrigues of Louis XIV of France. Successfully captures the attitudes and mores of the royalty at the time. One of a series of historical films directed by Rossellini. Made for French TV; subtitled. **100m/C VHS.** *FR* Jean-Marie Patte, Raymond Jourdan, Dominique Vincent, Giorgio Silvagni, Pierre Barrat; ***D:*** Roberto Rossellini. **TV**

Rise of the Footsoldier 2007 (R) Brit crime flick, based on a true story, that has nothing going for it but violence. Carlton Leach goes from football hooligan in the 1980s to criminal muscle and gangster in the 1990s and is ultimately involved in the discovery of three murdered drug dealers who were found in rural Essex. **119m/C DVD.** *GB* Ricci Harnett, Craig Fairbrass, Terry Stone, Roland Manookian; ***D:*** Julian Gilbey; ***W:*** Julian Gilbey, Will Gilbey; ***C:*** Ali Asad.

The Rising Place 2002 (PG-13) Nostalgia and tears. Dying Emily Hodge (Drummond) recalls her sometimes unconventional life to her niece Virginia (Fisher) in a series of flashbacks. The young Emily (Holloman) is a smalltown Southern belle who gets pregnant by her boyfriend who goes off to WWII, never to return. Having scandalized her conventional parents (Harper, Cole), Emily agrees to give her baby up for adoption but refuses to go into hiding. Instead, she becomes a schoolteacher along with her black best friend, Wilma (Neal), who encourages Emily to get involved in the civil rights movement. Based on the novel by David Armstrong. **93m/C VHS, DVD.** Laurel Holloman, Elise Neal, Mark Webber, Billy Campbell, Gary Cole, Tess Harper, Alice Drummond, Frances Fisher; ***D:*** Tom Rice; ***W:*** Tom Rice; ***C:*** Jim Dollarhide; ***M:*** Conrad Pope.

Rising Son 1990 A family man who loves his job faces trauma when his factory closes at the same time his son informs him he's quitting medical school. Solid family drama and parable of economic hard times of the early '80s, sustained by top-drawer performances by Dennehy, Damon, and Laurie. Well directed by Coles. **92m/C VHS.** Brian Dennehy, Matt Damon, Piper Laurie, Graham Beckel, Ving Rhames, Jane Adams, Richard Jenkins, Emily Longstreth; ***D:*** John David Coles; ***W:*** Bill Phillips. **CABLE**

Rising Sun 1993 (R) When a prostitute is found murdered in the boardroom of a powerful Japanese-owned corporation, seasoned cop (and Japanese expert) Connery and new partner Snipes are sent to investigate. Complicated yarn about business, prejudice, cops, and the differences between east and west. Filmed with stylized camera techniques, quick action, and good rapport between the two leads. Based on the book by Crichton, which offered ominous theories about international politics and business. These aspects had the film labeled as Japan-bashing, one of the reasons the script was rewritten to focus more on the murder mystery. **129m/C VHS, DVD.** Dan E. Butler, Stan Shaw, Steve Buscemi, Peter Crombie, Alexandra Powers, Daniel von Bargen, Amy Hill, Clyde Kusatsu, Sean Connery, Wesley Snipes, Tia Carrere, Harvey Keitel, Kevin Anderson, Stan(ford) Egi, Mako, Cary-Hiroyuki Tagawa, Ray Wise, Tatjana Patitz, Michael Chapman; ***D:*** Philip Kaufman; ***W:*** Michael Backes, Michael Crichton, Philip Kaufman; ***C:*** Michael Chapman; ***M:*** Toru Takemitsu.

Risk 1994 Maya (Sillas) is a struggling, emotionally distant, New York artist when she meets overly friendly Joe (Ilku) on a bus. He follows her home and manages to entice Maya into letting him spend the night but Joe has some psychological problems, including criminal behavior, which manifests itself when he steals a car. Maya, nevertheless, agrees to drive with him to his older sister's home in rural Connecticut and finds bad blood and more mental anguish that she knows how to deal with. Terrifically honest performance by Sillas and an equally touching one by Ilku are highlights of this adult attempt at romance. **85m/C VHS.** Karen Sillas, David Ilku, Molly Price, Jack Gwaltney; ***D:*** Deirdre Fishel; ***W:*** Deirdre Fishel; ***C:*** Peter Pearce; ***M:*** John Paul Jones.

Risk 1/2 2000 (R) Shady insurance guy John Kriesky (Brown) is tutoring young Ben (Long) in money, sex, and shifty deals, including involving him in insurance fraud. Then Kriesky's lawyer/girlfriend Louise (Karvan) decides to give Ben a few personal lessons as well. Fast-paced thriller with a cast that's well worth watching. **89m/C VHS, DVD.** *AU* Bryan Brown, Tom Long, Claudia Karvan, Jason Clarke; ***D:*** Alan White; ***W:*** John Armstrong; ***C:*** Simon Duggan; ***M:*** Don Miller-Robinson. **CABLE**

Risky Business 1928 Fortune-seeking mother disapproves of daughter's doctor fiance, and educates girl in marital woes. Video includes early Pollard short "Sold at Auction." **104m/B VHS.** Vera Reynolds, Zasu Pitts, Ethey Clayton; ***D:*** Alan Hale.

Risky Business 1983 (R) With his parents out of town and awaiting word from the college boards, a teenager becomes involved in unexpected ways with a quick-thinking prostitute, her pimp, and assorted others. Cruise is likeable, especially when dancing in his underwear. Funny, well-paced, stylish prototypical '80s teen flick reintroduced Ray-Bans as the sunglasses for the wanna-be hip. What a party! **99m/C VHS, DVD, Blu-ray Disc.** Tom Cruise, Rebecca De Mornay, Curtis Armstrong, Bronson Pinchot, Joe Pantoliano, Kevin Anderson, Richard Masur, Raphael Sbarge, Nicholas Pryor, Janet Carroll; ***D:*** Paul Brickman; ***W:*** Paul Brickman; ***C:*** Reynaldo Villalobos, Bruce Surtees; ***M:*** Tangerine Dream.

Rita Hayworth: The Love Goddess 1/2 1983 Drama details the tragic life of the beautiful film star. Carter, lovely though she is, plays Rita weakly and without depth. **100m/C VHS.** Lynda Carter, Michael Lerner, Alejandro Rey, John Considine; ***D:*** James Goldstone. **TV**

Rita, Sue & Bob Too 1987 (R) A middle-aged Englishman gets involved in a menage a trois with two promiscuous teenagers, until the whole town gets wind of it. A raunchy, amoral British comedy. **94m/C VHS, DVD.** *GB* Michelle Holmes, George Costigan, Siobhan Finneran, Lesley Sharp, Willie Ross, Patti Nicholls, Kulvinder Ghir; ***D:*** Alan Clarke; ***W:*** Andrea Dunbar; ***C:*** Ivan Strasburg; ***M:*** Michael Kamen.

The Rite *The Ritual; Riten* 1969 Members of a famous theatrical troupe are called before a judge to answer charges that a production is obscene. The judge's interrogation exposes their private and painful neuroses until the performers decide to turn on their accuser. Pessimistic even by Bergman standards and the first film the director made specifically for TV. Swedish with subtitles. **75m/B VHS, DVD.** *SW* Ingrid Thulin, Gunnar Bjornstrand, Erik Hell, Anders Ek; ***D:*** Ingmar Bergman; ***W:*** Ingmar Bergman; ***C:*** Sven Nykvist.

Rites of Frankenstein *Erotic Rites of Frankenstein* 1972 (R) Ultra-low budget remake with plenty of blood, sex and perversions required of surreal horrors. Frankenstein (Price) is murdered and his monster creation is stolen by his archenemy Dr. Cagliostro, a mad genius taken to kidnapping girls for their body parts, which he uses in dastardly experiments. Frankenstein's daughter (Savon) seeks to avenge her father's death through unconventional methods, of course. Just wacky enough to become a euro-trash classic. In Spanish with English subtitles. **94m/C DVD.** Jess (Jesus) Franco, Dennis Price, Howard Vernon, Anne Libert, Britt Nichols, Alberto Dalbes, Luis Barboo, Lina Romay, Daniel White, Beatriz Savon; ***D:*** Jess (Jesus) Franco; ***W:*** Jess (Jesus) Franco; ***C:*** Raul Artigot; ***M:*** Daniel White. **VIDEO**

Rites of Passage 1999 (R) Suspenser about fathers, sons, and masculinity has both awkwardness and intensity. Del Farraday (Stockwell) and his son D.J. (Keith) travel to their secluded mountain cabin for a heart-to-heart chat, only to discover the place is being used by Farley's estranged gay son, Campbell (Behr). As if there weren't enough family angst, the trio are joined by violent escaped cons Frank (Remar) and Red (Woolvett). Tempers flare between Del and Frank and the entire situation is worsened by a secret that Campbell is keeping. Good performances. **94m/C VHS, DVD.** Dean Stockwell, James Remar, Jaimz Woolvett, Jason Behr, Robert Keith; ***D:*** Victor Salva; ***W:*** Victor Salva; ***C:*** Don E. Fauntleroy; ***M:*** Bennett Salvay.

Rituals 1/2 *The Creeper* 1979 Group of five calm, rational men suddenly turn desperate after a chain of nightmarish events on a camping trip. Yet another low-budget "Deliverance" rip off. **100m/C VHS.** *CA* Hal Holbrook, Lawrence Dane; ***D:*** Peter Carter.

The Ritz 1976 (R) Weston tries to get away from his gangster brother-in-law by hiding out in a gay bathhouse in New York. Moreno plays a talentless singer Googie Gomez, who performs in the bathhouse while waiting for her big break. Moreno is great reprising her Tony-winning stage role, and Lester's direction is spiffy. Written by Terence McNally from his play. **91m/C VHS, DVD.** Rita Moreno, Jack Weston, Jerry Stiller, Kaye Ballard, Treat Williams, F. Murray Abraham; ***D:*** Richard Lester.

Rivals 1/2 *Deadly Rivals* 1972 (R) Shallow, unconvincing drama about a stepfather challenged by his stepson, who wants to kill this new contender for his mother's love. Nice handling of cast credits, but other details—like acting, directing and photography—leave much to be desired. **103m/C VHS.** Robert Klein, Joan Hackett, Scott Jacoby; ***D:*** Krishna Shah.

The River 1951 A massively lauded late film by Renoir about three British girls growing up in Bengal, India, all developing crushes on a one-legged American vet. Lyrical and heartwarming, with hailed cinematography by Claude Renoir. Rumer Godden wrote the novel, and co-scripted the screenplay with director Renoir. Satyajit Ray, one of India's greatest filmmakers, assisted Renoir. **99m/C VHS, DVD.** *FR* Patricia Walters, Adrienne Corri, Nora Swinburne, Radha, Arthur Shields, Thomas E. Breen, Esmond Knight; ***D:*** Jean Renoir; ***W:*** Jean Renoir; ***C:*** Claude Renoir; ***Nar:*** June Hillman.

The River 1984 (PG) Farmers battle a river whose flood threatens their farm. Spacek, as always, is strong and believable as the wife and mother, but Gibson falters. Beautiful photography. The third in an onslaught of films in the early '80s that dramatized the plight of the small American farmer. "The River" isn't as strong as "Country" and "Places in the Heart" which managed to convey important messages less cloyingly. **124m/C VHS, DVD, HD DVD.** Mel Gibson, Sissy Spacek, Scott Glenn, Billy Green Bush; ***D:*** Mark Rydell; ***W:*** Julian Barry, Robert Dillon; ***C:*** Vilmos Zsigmond; ***M:*** John Williams.

River Beat 1954 A woman aboard an American freighter is unwittingly used as diamond smuggler, and is arrested when the ship docks in London. An inspector does his best to clear the hapless woman. **70m/B VHS.** Phyllis Kirk, John Bentley, Robert Ayres, Lenny White, Glyn Houston, Charles Lloyd-Pack; ***D:*** Guy Green.

The River is Red 1948 (R) Trying to save his younger brother Tom (Moscow) from the beatings Dad regularly gives him, Dave Holden (Scott), stabs their father to death. As a minor (and therefore subject to a lighter sentence), Tom takes the rap and is sent to a juvenile home until he is 21. Dave's guilt (and the debts his father has left him) cause him to become physically violent, leading him into a life of crime. When the brothers reunite, emotions come to a head. Based on Drilling's one-act stage play, film boasts fine performances but nevertheless fails to take advantage of its controversial plot and deep psychological themes. A more thorough examination of the motivations would have made for a heightened outcome and a more interesting film overall. **104m/C VHS.** Tom Everett Scott, David Moscow, Cara Buono, Denis O'Hare, Leo Burmester, Tibor Feldman, James Murtaugh, David Lowery, Michael Kelly; ***D:*** Eric Drilling; ***W:*** Eric Drilling; ***C:*** Steven Schlueter; ***M:*** Johnny Hickman.

The River King 2005 (R) Muddled and dull crime drama based on the novel by Alice Hoffman. Small town police detective Abel Grey (Burns) doesn't believe that the drowning death of a private school student was suicide. His investigation leads him to the boy's photography teacher, Betsy Chase (Ehle), who aids in Abel's sleuthing. **99m/C DVD.** *GB CA* Edward Burns, Jennifer Ehle, Julian Rhind-Tutt, Jaime (James) King, Rachelle Lefevre, Sean McCann; ***D:*** Nick Willing; ***W:*** David Kane; ***C:*** Paul Sarossy; ***M:*** Simon Boswell.

A River Made to Drown In 1997 When wealthy lawyer Thaddeus MacKenzie (Chamberlain) learns he is dying from AIDS, he decides to get in touch with the two people he once loved, Allen and Jaime. Allen (Imperioli) is a struggling artist who once worked the streets and is now involved with gallery owner Eva (Lemper), who knows nothing about his former life. But he agrees to look for the still-hustling Jaime (Duval), even if this means confronting a past he'd rather forget. **98m/C VHS, DVD.** Michael Imperioli, Richard Chamberlain, James Duval, Ute Lemper, Austin Pendleton, Talia Shire, Mike Starr, Michael Saucedo, James Karen, Lewis Arquette; ***D:*** James Merendino; ***W:*** Paul Marius; ***C:*** Thomas Callaway.

The River Niger 1/2 1976 (R) Jones is riveting, and Tyson is good in an otherwise muddling adaptation of the Tony-award winning play about black ghetto life. Realistic emotions and believable characters. **105m/C VHS, DVD.** James Earl Jones, Cicely Tyson, Glynn Turman, Louis Gossett Jr., Roger E. Mosley, Jonelle Allen; ***D:*** Krishna Shah.

River of Death 1/2 1990 (R) Absurd adventure, based on an Alistair McLean novel, about a white man entering the Amazon jungle world of a forgotten tribe in search of wealth, tripping over Neo-Nazi scientists and war criminals. Too complex to be harmlessly enjoyable; too mindless for the complexity to be worth unraveling. **103m/C VHS.** Michael Dudikoff, Robert Vaughn, Donald Pleasence, Herbert Lom, L.Q. Jones, Cynthia Erland, Sarah Maur-Thorp; ***D:*** Steve Carver.

River of Diamonds 1990 A daring adventurer, with the standard beautiful woman at his side, battles evil curses and

Nazis buried alive to find a fortune in diamonds. Yeah, sure. Another miserable "Indiana Jones" rip off. **88m/C VHS.** Dack Rambo, Angela O'Neill, Ferdinand "Ferdy" Mayne, Graham Clark, David Sherwood, Tony Caprari, Dominique Tyawa; ***D:*** Robert J. Smawley.

River of Evil ☙ 1/2 **1964** Action/adventure in which a young girl travels through the Amazon jungle searching for clues to her father's death. **83m/C VHS.** *GE* Barbara Rutting, Harald Leipnitz, Oswaldo Loureiro, Cyl Farney, Tereza Raquel; ***D:*** Franz Eichhorn; ***W:*** Franz Eichhorn; ***C:*** Edgar Eichhorn; ***M:*** Catulo Cearense.

River of Grass ☙ 1/2 **1994** No-budget noirish crime/romance set in the swampy, low-rent Florida area between Miami and the Everglades. Uncaring and frankly dumb housewife/mom Cozy (Bowman) hooks up with the boozing Lee Ray (Fessenden) and the dim duo take an illegal dip in a private pool. Cozy manages to fire off Lee's gun and thinks she hit a man who suddenly appeared. Not bothering to find out if this is true, they decide to hold up in a motel until they can figure out what to do. You won't really care but director Reichardt does have a way with visuals so things aren't a total loss. **80m/C VHS, DVD.** Lisa Bowman, Larry Fessenden, Dick Russell; ***D:*** Kelly Reichardt; ***W:*** Jesse Hartman, Kelly Reichardt; ***C:*** Jim Denault.

River of No Return ☙☙ 1/2 **1954** During the gold rush, an itinerant farmer and his young son help a heart-of-gold saloon singer search for her estranged husband. Rather crummy script is helped by the mere presence of Mitchum and Monroe. Marilyn sings the title song, as well as "Down in the Meadow," and "I'm Going to File My Claim." **91m/C VHS, DVD.** Robert Mitchum, Marilyn Monroe, Tommy Rettig, Rory Calhoun, Murvyn Vye, Douglas Spencer; ***D:*** Otto Preminger; ***W:*** Frank Fenton; ***C:*** Joseph LaShelle; ***M:*** Cyril Mockridge.

River of Unrest ☙☙ 1/2 *Ourselves Alone* **1936** Remarkable visual expressiveness and emotional power mark this depiction of terrorism and open warfare during the Irish Rebellion. Based on a play, hence slow; but good acting pulls it up half a bone. **69m/B VHS.** John Lodge, John Loder, Antoinette Cellier, Clifford Evans; ***D:*** Brian Desmond Hurst; ***W:*** Philip MacDonald; ***C:*** Walter J. (Jimmy W.) Harvey.

The River Pirates ☙☙ 1/2 *Good Ole Boy: A Delta Boyhood* **1988 (PG)** Mississippi boy discovers a lot about life over the summer of his 12th birthday in 1942. He finds the secret hiding place of a band of river thieves, endures a tornado, has some adventures with his friends, and finds out that his crush on the prettiest girl in town is reciprocated. Based on a novel by Willie Morris. **108m/C VHS.** Ryan Francis, Richard Farnsworth, Gennie James, Doug Emerson, Anne Ramsey, Maureen O'Sullivan; ***D:*** Tom G. Robertson.

River Queen ☙ 1/2 **2005 (R)** A wannabe epic that turns out to be a snoozer. In 1854, the native Maori population is clashing with European settlers in New Zealand. At a garrison post, Sarah (Morton) has an affair with the son of a Maori tribal leader and bears his son. Her lover dies and eventually the boy is kidnapped by his grandfather so he can be raised according to Maori tradition. Sarah isn't reunited with her son until he's a teenager torn between the two cultures. **114m/C DVD.** *GB NZ* Samantha Morton, Clifford Curtis, Temuera Morrison, Kiefer Sutherland, Anton Lesser, Stephen Rea, David Rawiri Pene; ***D:*** Vincent Ward; ***W:*** Vincent Ward, Toa Fraser; ***C:*** Alun Bollinger; ***M:*** Karl Jenkins.

The River Rat ☙☙ 1/2 **1984 (PG)** Ex-con Jones is reunited with his daughter after spending 13 years in prison. There's something in there about stashed loot that should have been jettisoned in favor of more getting-to-know-you father-daughter drama, which is good. **93m/C VHS.** Tommy Lee Jones, Brian Dennehy, Martha Plimpton, Shawn Smith, Melissa Davis; ***D:*** Thomas (Tom) Rickman.

A River Runs Through It ☙☙☙ 1/2 **1992 (PG)** Contemplative exploration of family ties and coming of age with impact falling just short of the novel's is another well-crafted American tale directed by Redford. Set in Montana during the early part of the century, a Presbyterian minister teaches his two sons, one troubled and one on his way to success, about life and religion via fly-fishing. Based on the novel by Norman Maclean. **123m/C VHS, DVD.** Craig Sheffer, Brad Pitt, Tom Skerritt, Brenda Blethyn, Emily Lloyd, Edie McClurg, Stephen Shellen, Susan Taylor; ***D:*** Robert Redford; ***W:*** Richard Friedenberg; ***C:*** Philippe Rousselot; ***M:*** Mark Isham. Oscars '92: Cinematog.

River Street ☙☙ **1995** Ambitious real estate agent Ben Egan (Young) is engaged to marry Sharon (MacIntosh), his shady boss Vincent Pierce's (Hunter) daughter. But when he blows a big deal and winds up striking a cop, Ben's sentenced to community service at a dilapidated center for street kids. He takes an interest in good-hearted center director Wendy (Davis) but can't change his ways so easily. The center stands on valuable river front property and if Ben can get the land, he'll get back both his job and Sharon. The relationships don't convince and Ben's change of heart seems forced. **88m/C VHS.** *AU* Aden Young, Bill Hunter, Essie Davis, Tammy MacIntosh, Sullivan Stapleton, Lois Ramsey; ***D:*** Tony Mahood; ***W:*** Philip Ryall; ***C:*** Martin McGrath; ***M:*** David Bridie, John Phillips.

The River Wild ☙☙ 1/2 **1994 (PG-13)** Dissatisfied wife Gail (Streep) plans a family white-water rafting vacation with 10-year-old son Roarke (Mazzello) and workaholic husband Tom (Strathairn). A former guide (and white-water expert) Gail comes to the aid of river novices Wade (boyishly menacing Bacon) and Terry (Reilly), who quickly turn out to be violent criminals needing Gail's help with their escape. Slow start leads to nonstop thrills with Streep an adept action heroine, though undercut by the flic's need to do something with Strathairn's thankless role. Beautiful Montana and Oregon settings. **111m/C VHS, DVD.** Meryl Streep, David Strathairn, Joseph Mazzello, Kevin Bacon, John C. Reilly, Benjamin Bratt; ***D:*** Curtis Hanson; ***W:*** Raynold Gideon; ***C:*** Robert Elswit; ***M:*** Jerry Goldsmith.

Riverbend ☙☙ **1989 (R)** A renegade black Army major escapes a rigged court martial only to be persecuted by racist whites in a small Southern town. **106m/C VHS.** Steve James, Tony Frank, Julius Tennon, Margaret Avery; ***D:*** Sam Firstenberg. **TV**

The Riverman ☙☙ 1/2 **2004 (R)** In 1982, Washington state detective Dave Reichert (Jaeger) is investigating the unsolved murders of 13 women in the Green River area. Needing help, Reichert turns to obsessive homicide detective/profiler Robert Keppel (Greenwood) who worked on the Ted Bundy case. Awaiting execution in Florida, Bundy (Elwes) contacts Keppel, offering his own ideas on the Green River killer but he wants something in exchange. Focuses more on the Keppel/Bundy connection that the Green River case itself but Greenwood and Elwes are excellent and the cable pic (originally shown on A&E) is inevitably disturbing. Based on Keppel's book. **91m/C DVD.** Bruce Greenwood, Cary Elwes, Sam Jaeger, Kathleen Quinlan, David Brown; ***D:*** Bill Eagles; ***W:*** Tom Towler; ***C:*** Steve Cossens; ***M:*** Jeff Rona. **CABLE**

River's Edge ☙☙☙ **1987 (R)** Drug-addled high school student strangles his girlfriend and casually displays the corpse to his apathetic group of friends, who leave the murder unreported for days. Harrowing and gripping; based on a true story. Aging biker Hopper is splendid. **99m/C VHS, DVD.** Keanu Reeves, Crispin Glover, Daniel Roebuck, Joshua John Miller, Dennis Hopper, Ione Skye, Roxana Zal, Tom Bower, Constance Forslund, Leo Rossi, Jim Metzler; ***D:*** Tim Hunter; ***W:*** Neal Jimenez; ***C:*** Frederick Elmes; ***M:*** Jurgen Knieper. Ind. Spirit '88: Film, Screenplay; Sundance '87: Special Jury Prize.

River's End ☙☙ 1/2 *Molding Clay* **2005 (PG)** Texas teen Clay Watkins has gotten into scrapes ever since his father died. When things get too bad, his sheriff grandfather Buster gives Clay a choice: go to jail or make a 60-mile wilderness trip along the Pecos River and do some serious thinking. Clay decides on the latter but his path eventually crosses a couple of fugitive drug dealers who are trying to get to Mexico with Buster tracking them. **94m/C DVD.** Sam Huntington, Barry Corbin, Caroline Goodall, Rudolf Martin, Joe Stephens, Amanda Brooks, Greg Evigan, Charles Durning, Clint Howard, William Katt; ***D:*** William Katt; ***W:*** Samuel Benedict, Glen Stephens; ***C:*** John-Paul Beeghly; ***M:*** Jay Michael Ferguson, Paul Cristo. **VIDEO**

Rize ☙☙☙ **2005 (PG-13)** Intensely up-tempo, hyped-up L.A. dancing form called "clowning" or "krumping" is vividly chronicled in this David LaChappelle documentary. Born from the 1992 riots as a peaceful means of expression by poverty-stricken inner-city dwellers, krumping was the invention of Tom Johnson, or Tommy the Clown, a reformed drug dealer who started the movement by dressing as a clown and, later, reenacting the Rodney King footage. Payoff comes in the form of a grand krumping contest held annually at the Great Western Forum. **85m/C DVD.** *US* ***D:*** David LaChapelle; ***C:*** Morgan Susser; ***M:*** Red Ronin Prods., Amy Marie Beauchamp, Jose Cancella.

RKO 281 ☙☙☙ **1999 (R)** This retelling of Orson Welles' (Schrieber) battles to make 1941's "Citizen Kane" is all about egos. Welles had the arrogance of youth and Hearst the arrogance of power. The film, written with Herman J. Mankiewicz (Malkovich), was a thinly disguised look at newspaper magnate William Randolph Hearst (Cromwell) and his life with longtime mistress, blond actress Marion Davies (Griffith). Hearst was so outraged by Welles' movie that he tried to use his considerable influence with the Hollywood studios to have the film destroyed. Naturally, the story is both streamlined and altered but the leading roles are dramatically well served. **87m/C VHS, DVD.** Liev Schreiber, John Malkovich, James Cromwell, Melanie Griffith, Brenda Blethyn, Roy Scheider, David Suchet, Fiona Shaw, Liam Cunningham, Tim Woodward; ***D:*** Ridley Scott; ***W:*** John Logan; ***C:*** Mike Southon; ***M:*** John Altman. **CABLE**

The Road ☙☙ *El Camino* **2000** Manuel is on his way to a family funeral (by motorcycle) when he meets photographer Caroline on the road. Their romance is tested when Manuel is suddenly arrested and thrown in jail—only to escape after seeing a cop beat an inmate to death. The lovers are on the run but the end of the road is not the end of the journey. Spanish with subtitles. **107m/C VHS, DVD.** *AR* Ezequiel Rodriquez, Antonella Costa, Daniel Valenzuela, Hector Anglada, Alejandro Awada, Ruben Patagonia; ***D:*** Javier Olivera; ***W:*** Hector Olivera, Javier Olivera; ***C:*** Cristian Cottet; ***M:*** Axel Krygier.

The Road ☙☙ **2009 (R)** A post-apocalyptic nightmare road trip taken by a father and son that's based on Cormac McCarthy's Pulitzer Prize-winning novel. An unnamed man (Mortenson) and young boy (Smit-McPhee) trudge along towards the sea in a daily quest for food, shelter, and survival while trying to avoid violent, and probably cannibalistic, roving gangs. Mortensen is haunted and determined and Smit-McPhee convincingly acts fearful and stunned. It's relentlessly grim (although how could it not be?), with limited dialogue, and the appropriately scorched and desolate look but it's also emotionally distancing and as much of a slog as the duo's walk itself. **119m/C DVD.** *US* Viggo Mortensen, Kodi Smit-McPhee, Charlize Theron, Guy Pearce, Robert Duvall, Garret Dillahunt, Michael K. Williams; ***D:*** John Hillcoat; ***W:*** Joe Penhall; ***C:*** Javier Aguirresarobe; ***M:*** Nick Cave.

Road Agent ☙ 1/2 *Texas Road Agent* **1926** Hoxie is the Kansas Kid, a fugitive hired by a crooked lawyer to pose as the long-lost heir to a ranching fortune. Only the Kid develops a soft spot for his "family" and may not be able to go through with the evil plot. **70m/B VHS.** Al Hoxie, Ione Reed, Lew Meehan, Florence Lee, Leon de la Mothe; ***D:*** J(ohn) P(aterson) McGowan; ***W:*** Charles Sexton; ***C:*** Robert Cline.

Road Ends ☙☙ 1/2 **1998 (R)** Small town sheriff Hopper and local innkeeper Hemingway unwittingly offer refuge to runaway FBI informant, Maceda (Sarandon), who's supposed to testify against his drug trafficking boss. FBI agent Gere (Coyote) is after Maceda as well as his ex-employers—and it's just a matter of who catches up to him first. **98m/C VHS, DVD.** Chris Sarandon, Peter Coyote, Dennis Hopper, Mariel Hemingway, Joanna Gleason; ***D:*** Rick King; ***W:*** Bill Mesce Jr.; ***C:*** Bruce Douglas Johnson; ***M:*** David Mansfield.

The Road from Coorain ☙☙ 1/2 **2002** Based on the 1989 memoir by historian Jill Ker Conway who was born and raised on a vast and isolated Australian sheep ranch called Coorain. The story, which opens in the early 1940s, deals with Jill's difficult relationship with her stoical mother Eve (Stevenson), who keeps Coorain even after being widowed and moving her family to Sydney. Jill proves to be an exceptional student and excels at university but family tragedies continue to haunt the Kers. **120m/C VHS.** *AU* Juliet Stevenson, Richard Roxburgh, Katherine Slattery, Alex Tomasetti, Tim Guinee, John Howard, Bernard Curry, Sean Hall; ***D:*** Brendan Maher; ***W:*** Sue Smith; ***C:*** Tristan Milani; ***M:*** Stephen Rae. **TV**

Road Games ☙☙ **1981 (PG)** Trucker Keach is drawn into a web of intrigue surrounding a series of highway "Jack the Ripper"-style murders. Curtis is a hitchhiker. Nothing special. Director Franklin later helmed "Psycho II." **100m/C VHS, DVD.** *AU* Stacy Keach, Jamie Lee Curtis, Marion Edwards, Grant Page, Bill Stacey, Thaddeus Smith, Alan Hopgood; ***D:*** Richard Franklin; ***W:*** Everett DeRoche; ***C:*** Vincent Monton; ***M:*** Brian May.

The Road Home ☙☙ 1/2 **1995 (PG)** Depression-era heart-tugger features two orphaned brothers who ride the rails from New York to Nebraska in search of a new home at Father Flanagan's Boys Town. **90m/C VHS.** Keegan Macintosh, Will Estes, Kris Kristofferson, Charles Martin Smith, Danny Aiello, Dee Wallace, Mickey Rooney; ***D:*** Dean Hamilton.

The Road Home ☙☙☙ *Wo De Fu Qin Mu Qin* **2001 (G)** Sweet story about enduring love. Luo Yuseng (Honglei) returns to his Chinese village to bury his father. He learns his mother wants to have a funeral ritual performed as a mark of respect, which involves carrying the coffin to the cemetery. Flashbacks show how young illiterate beauty Zhao Di (Ziyi) caught the eye of Luo Changyu (Hao), the new schoolteacher, who comes from the city and is of a higher class. But Changyu falls victim to the political climate of the '50s and must leave her behind, promising to return. And she promises to wait. The flashbacks are filmed in color while the present is filmed in B&W. Chinese with subtitles. **89m/C VHS, DVD.** *CH* Zhang Ziyi, Honglei Sun, Zheng Hao, Zhao Yuelin, Bin Li; ***D:*** Yimou Zhang; ***W:*** Bao Shi; ***C:*** Hou Yong; ***M:*** San Bao.

Road House ☙☙ 1/2 **1948** Nightclub singer Lupino inspires noir feelings between jealous road house owner Widmark and his partner Wilde. Widmark sets up Wilde to take the fall for a faked robbery, convinces the law to release him into his custody, then dares him to escape. **95m/B VHS, DVD.** Richard Widmark, Ida Lupino, Cornel Wilde, Celeste Holm, O.Z. Whitehead; ***D:*** Jean Negulesco; ***W:*** Edward Chodorov, Oscar Saul; ***C:*** Joseph LaShelle; ***M:*** Cyril Mockridge.

Road House ☙ 1/2 **1989 (R)** Bouncer Swayze is hired to do the impossible: clean up the toughest bar in Kansas City. When he lays down his rules he makes a lot of enemies, including ex-bar employees and local organized crime. Ample violence; an example of formula filmmaking at its most brain-numbing, with a rock soundtrack. **115m/C VHS, DVD, UMD.** Patrick Swayze, Sam Elliott, Kelly Lynch, Ben Gazzara, Kevin Tighe, Marshall Teague, Julie Michaels, Jeff Healey; ***D:*** Rowdy Herrington; ***C:*** Dean Cundey; ***M:*** Michael Kamen.

Road House 2: Last Call ☙ 1/2 **2006 (R)** Dopey sequel to the 1989 cheese-fest. Nate Tanner (Patton) is the owner of a rowdy Louisiana road house called the Black Pelican. When local drug runner Wild Bill (wildly overacted by Busey) and his minions want to take over the place, Nate's DEA nephew Shane (Schaech) decides to forcibly discourage them. Many brawls follow. **86m/C DVD.** *US* Johnathon Schaech, Jake Busey, Will Patton, William Ragsdale, Ellen Hollman; ***D:*** Scott Ziehl; ***W:*** Johnathon Schaech, Richard Chizmar; ***M:*** Amotz Plessner. **VIDEO**

Road Kill USA ☙☙ 1/2 **1993** Two sleazy drifters on a cross-country murder spree pick up a hitchhiking college student and expect him to join in the fun. When he refuses, he has two choices: kill or be killed. **98m/C VHS.** Andrew Porter, Sean Bridges, Deanna Perry; ***D:*** Tony Elwood.

The Road Killers 1995 (R) Sickening psycho Cliff (well-played by Sheffer) is head of a brutal quartet that terrorizes a family driving along a remote desert highway. Cliff kidnaps the family daughter and her mild-mannered dad (Lambert) must rescue her. **89m/C VHS.** Christopher Lambert, Craig Sheffer, Adrienne Shelly; ***D:*** Deran Sarafian; ***W:*** Tedi Sarafian.

Road Movie 1/2 **1972** Cult favorite about a pair of brutish truck drivers (Bostwick and Drivas) who pick up a prostitute (Baff) on a trip across America. Baff delivers an emotional performance as the beaten and furious hooker who, after being abused and rejected, seeks her revenge. **82m/C DVD.** Barry Bostwick, Robert Drivas, Regina Baff; ***D:*** Joseph Strick; ***W:*** Judith Rascoe; ***C:*** Don Lenzer.

Road Racers **1959** The roar of the engine, fast cars, and family ties combine in this movie about the thrill of speed. **73m/B VHS, DVD.** Joel Lawrence, Marian Collier, Skip Ward; ***D:*** Arthur Swerdloff; ***W:*** Stanley Kallis, Ed Lasko.

Road Rage WOOF! *A Friday Night Date* **2001** The familiar plot wouldn't be so bad if there was some suspense or twists to this flick but there's not. Jim offers Sonia a ride home after breaking up a fight between Sonia and her possessive ex-boyfriend Bo. While driving, Jim cuts off a big rig, whose driver decides to get even. It won't be any surprise to discover the truck's driver is Bo. Blah. **96m/C VHS, DVD.** Casper Van Dien, Danielle Brett, Catherine Oxenberg, Joseph Griffin; ***D:*** Sidney J. Furie; ***W:*** Greg Mellott; ***C:*** Curtis Petersen; ***M:*** Robert Carli. **VIDEO**

Road Show 1/2 **1941** Hubbard stars as a young man wrongfully committed to an insane asylum. He escapes and joins a bankrupt carnival owned by Landis. Some really zany stuff keeps this from being just standard fare. Co-written by silent film comic Langdon. **87m/B VHS, DVD.** Adolphe Menjou, Carole Landis, John Hubbard, Charles Butterworth, Patsy Kelly, George E. Stone, Polly Ann Young, Edward Norris, Marjorie Woodworth, Florence Bates; ***D:*** Hal Roach; ***W:*** Harry Langdon.

The Road to Bali **1953** Sixth Bob-n-Bing road show, the only one in color, is a keeper. The boys are competing for the love of—that's right—Lamour. She must be some gal, cuz they chase her all the way to Bali, where they meet cannibals and other perils, including the actual Humphrey Bogart. Jones's debut, in a bit role. ♫ Moonflowers; Chicago Style; Hoots Mon; To See You; The Merry-Go-Runaround; Chorale for Brass, Piano, and Bongo (instrumental). **90m/C VHS, DVD.** Bob Hope, Bing Crosby, Dorothy Lamour, Murvyn Vye, Ralph Moody, Jane Russell, Jerry Lewis, Dean Martin, Carolyn Jones; ***D:*** Hal Walker; ***W:*** Frank Butler, Hal Kanter, William Morrow; ***C:*** George Barnes.

The Road to El Dorado 1/2 **2000 (PG)** Spanish con men Tulio (Kline) and Miguel (Branagh) search for the legendary Lost City of Gold in this animated mix of the Crosby-Hope "Road" pictures and Kipling's "Man Who Would Be King." The duo hitch a ride with Cortes's expedition to South America, land among the natives, and are mistaken for gods. They also run into a beautiful local (Perez) who's onto their game and agrees to help them, and run afoul of the local priest, who's fond of human sacrifice and wants to overthrow the kindly chief (Olmos). As usual, the animation is superb, and there are enjoyable moments throughout, but a weak plot and nondescript characters add up to a somewhat disappointing outing. **90m/C VHS, DVD.** ***D:*** Eric Bergeron, Don Paul; ***W:*** Ted Elliott, Terry Rossio; ***M:*** Elton John, Hans Zimmer, John Powell, Tim Rice; ***V:*** Kevin Kline, Kenneth Branagh, Rosie Perez, Armand Assante, Edward James Olmos; ***Nar:*** Elton John.

The Road to Galveston **1996 (PG-13)** Texas widow Jordan Roosevelt (Tyson) needs to pay her mortgage so she turns her home into a residence for three Alzheimer patients. When her financial problems only worsen, Jordan decides to fulfill her lifetime goal and takes everyone on a trip to Galveston to see the ocean. Sentimental, fact-based TV movie cuts the saccharine through compelling performances. **93m/C VHS.** Cicely Tyson, Piper Laurie, Tess Harper, Sallie Ellis, Starletta DuPois, James McDaniel, Penny Johnson, Clarence Williams III, Stephen (Steve) Root; ***D:*** Michael Toshiyuki Uno; ***W:*** Tony Lee; ***M:*** Stanley Clarke.

The Road to Guantanamo **2006 (R)** Political docudrama from Winterbottom and Whitecross focuses on the misfortunes of the "Tipton Three." These young British Muslims are in Pakistan for a wedding immediately after 9/11 and then travel to Afghanistan (apparently for humanitarian reasons). Big mistake—they get rounded up by Northern Alliance troops and are guilty until proven innocent, which takes years of military imprisonment and interrogation at Gitmo (film covers 2001-2004). **95m/C DVD.** *GB* Rizwan Ahmed, Farhad Harun, Waqar Siddiqui, Afran Usman; ***D:*** Michael Winterbottom, Mat Whitecross; ***C:*** Marcel Zyskind; ***M:*** Molly Nyman, Harry Escott. Ind. Spirit '07: Feature Doc.

The Road to Hong Kong 1/2 **1962** Last of the Crosby/Hope team-ups shows some wear, but still manages charm and humor. Lamour appears only briefly in this twisted comedy of hustlers caught in international espionage and cosmic goings-on. ♫ Teamwork; Let's Not Be Sensible; It's The Only Way to Travel; We're On the Road to Hong Kong; Warmer Than a Whisper. **91m/B VHS, DVD.** Bob Hope, Bing Crosby, Joan Collins, Dorothy Lamour, Peter Sellers; ***D:*** Norman Panama; ***W:*** Norman Panama; ***C:*** Jack Hildyard.

The Road to Life *Putyovka V Zhizn* **1931** In the turmoil caused by Russia's Revolutionary and Civil wars, thousands of orphans roam the countryside resorting to petty crime to survive. One group is sent to a collective as part of an experimental program where they can be reformed and learn a trade but their criminal pasts seem inescapable. Russian with subtitles. **100m/B VHS.** *RU* Nikolai Batalov, Maria Gonfa, Tsifan Kyria; ***D:*** Nicolai Ekk; ***W:*** Nicolai Ekk; ***M:*** Yakov Stollyar.

The Road to Morocco 1/2 **1942** The third in the road movie series finds Hope and Crosby in Morocco, stranded and broke. To get some money, Crosby sells Hope into slavery to be the princess's (Lamour) personal plaything. Feeling guilty, Crosby returns to the palace to rescue Hope, only to find that he and the princess are getting married because the royal astrologer said it was in the stars. Crosby then tries to woo Lamour and, when the astrologer discovers the stars were mistaken, those two decide to marry. Quinn, however, also wants her and hilarious scenes ensue when the boys rescue Lamour from him. One of the funniest in the series. Watch for the camel at the end. ♫ Constantly; Moonlight Becomes You; Ain't Got a Dime to My Name; Road to Morocco. **83m/C VHS, DVD.** Bing Crosby, Bob Hope, Dorothy Lamour, Anthony Quinn, Dona Drake, Vladimir Sokoloff, Yvonne De Carlo; ***D:*** David Butler; ***W:*** Frank Butler, Don Hartman; ***C:*** William Mellor. Natl. Film Reg. '96.

Road to Nashville **1967 (G)** An agent travels to Nashville to enlist talent for a new musical. Why do so many of these semi-musicals insist on having a plot? Good music. **110m/C VHS, DVD.** Marty Robbins, Johnny Cash, Doodles Weaver, Connie Smith, Richard Arlen; ***D:*** Robert Patrick.

Road to Nhill **1997** Very Aussie comedy filled with eccentric characters. An isolated, rural community is thrown into a tizzy when four female members of the local bowling team are in an accident that traps them in their overturned car. Volunteer emergency services rush into action but head off in the wrong direction and the women finally manage to free themselves, with various local yokels inept aid at the scene. Ensemble cast is fine. **95m/C VHS.** *AU* Lynette Curran, Patricia Kennedy, Lois Ramsey, Monica Maughan, Paul Chubb, Bill Hunter, Kerry Walker, Matthew Dyktynski, Terry Norris, Bill Young, Tony Barry, Alwyn Kurts; ***D:*** Sue Brooks; ***W:*** Alison Tilson; ***C:*** Nicolette Freeman; ***M:*** Elizabeth Drake.

Road to Perdition **2002 (R)** Michael Sullivan (Hanks) is a Depression-era hitman who must take his teenage son Michael Jr. (Hoechlin) on the run as he seeks revenge on the people who betrayed him and killed his wife and youngest son. Dark, atmospheric tale excels on the strength of the brilliantly understated screenplay and outstanding performances, highlighted by Hanks's tormented hitman/father and Newman's conflicted mob boss. Based on the 1998 graphic novel by Max Allan Collins and Richard Piers Rayner. **116m/C VHS, DVD.** *US* Tom Hanks, Paul Newman, Jude Law, Tyler Hoechlin, Jennifer Jason Leigh, Stanley Tucci, Daniel Craig, Liam Aiken, Ciaran Hinds, Dylan Baker, David Darlow, Mina (Badiyi) Badie; ***D:*** Sam Mendes; ***W:*** David Self; ***C:*** Conrad L. Hall; ***M:*** Thomas Newman. Oscars '02: Cinematog.; British Acad. '02: Cinematog.

Road to Riches *Strange Hearts* **2001 (R)** This independent feature by first-timer Gallagher is a happy surprise, thanks especially to McGowan and Forster. Middle-aged Jack (Forster) is very protective of the emotionally disturbed Moira (McGowan). Then cocky, handsome, and exceptionally lucky young Henry (Pardue) comes along and takes Moira away without realizing the extent of her problems. Jack is not about to let her go so easily, but he needs some good luck of his own to get her back. **90m/C VHS, DVD.** Robert Forster, Rose McGowan, Kip Pardue, Harry Hamlin; ***D:*** Michelle Gallagher; ***W:*** Michelle Gallagher; ***C:*** Adam Holender; ***M:*** Fletcher Beasley.

The Road to Rio 1/2 **1947** The wisecracking duo travel to Rio De Janeiro to prevent Spanish beauty Lamour (there she is again) from going through with an arranged marriage. Top-notch entry; fifth in the "Road" series. ♫ But Beautiful; You Don't Have To Know the Language; For What?; Experience; Apalachicola, Florida; Cavaquinho; Brazil. **100m/B VHS, DVD.** Bing Crosby, Bob Hope, Dorothy Lamour, Gale Sondergaard, Frank Faylen, The Andrews Sisters; ***D:*** Norman Z. McLeod; ***W:*** Jack Rose; ***C:*** Ernest Laszlo.

The Road to Ruin **1928** The evils of smoking and drinking plummet a girl into a life of prostitution in this melodramatic, moralistic tale. An unintentional laugh-riot right up there with "Reefer Madness." Silent. **45m/B VHS, DVD.** Helen Foster, Grant Withers, Virginia Roye; ***D:*** Norton S. Parker; ***W:*** Erik Anjou; ***C:*** James Diamond.

Road to Ruin **1991 (R)** A rich playboy pretends to lose all his money to see if his girlfriend loves him for himself or for his wealth. But when his business partner embezzles his fortune, he must regain both his money and his girlfriend's trust. **94m/C VHS.** Peter Weller, Carey Lowell, Michel Duchaussoy; ***D:*** Charlotte Brandstrom.

Road to Salina **1968 (R)** A drifter is mistaken for (and might actually be) a desert-restaurant owner's long-lost son. He plays along, eventually seducing the family's daughter, who might be his sister. **97m/C VHS.** *FR* Robert Walker Jr., Rita Hayworth, Mimsy Farmer, Ed Begley Sr.; ***D:*** Georges Lautner.

The Road to Singapore 1/2 **1940** This is the movie that started it all. Crosby and Hope decide to swear off women and escape to Singapore to enjoy the free life. There they meet Lamour, a showgirl who is abused by Quinn. The boys rescue Lamour, but soon find they are both falling for her. She's in love with one of them, but won't reveal her feelings. Who will get the girl? Not as funny as some of the other road movies, but it's great for a first try. ♫ Captain Custard; The Moon and the Willow Tree; Sweet Potato Piper; Too Romantic; Kaigoon. **84m/C VHS, DVD.** Bing Crosby, Bob Hope, Dorothy Lamour, Charles Coburn, Judith Barrett, Anthony Quinn, Jerry Colonna, Johnny Arthur, Pierre Watkin; ***D:*** Victor Schertzinger; ***W:*** Frank Butler, Don Hartman; ***C:*** William Mellor.

The Road to Utopia **1946** Fourth of the "Road" films, wherein the boys wind up in Alaska posing as two famous escaped killers in order to locate a secret gold mine. One of the series' funniest and most spontaneous entries, abetted by Benchley's dry, upper-crust comments. ♫ Put It There, Pal; Welcome to My Dreams; Would You?; Personality; Sunday, Monday, or Always?; Goodtime Charlie; It's Anybody's Spring. **90m/B VHS, DVD.** Bing Crosby, Bob Hope, Dorothy Lamour, Jack La Rue, Robert Benchley, Douglass Dumbrille, Hillary Brooke, Robert Barrat, Nestor Paiva; ***D:*** Hal Walker; ***W:*** Norman Panama, Melvin Frank; ***C:*** Lionel Lindon; ***M:*** Johnny Burke, Leigh Harline, James Van Heusen.

The Road to Wellville **1994 (R)** Corn flake magnate John Harvey Kellogg takes good health to an intestine-invading extreme in this spa satire featuring Hopkins as the buck-toothed Kellogg. Broderick and Fonda portray a wealthy couple who visit the turn-of-the-century sanitarium in search of Kellogg's cure, but receive only sexual frustration and anal humiliations. Bowel jokes and an essentially plotless scenario overshadow a gifted, but helpless cast. Adapted from T. Coraghessan Boyle's not-so-easily-adaptable novel. **120m/C VHS, DVD.** Anthony Hopkins, Bridget Fonda, Matthew Broderick, John Cusack, Dana Carvey, Michael Lerner, Colm Meaney, John Neville, Lara Flynn Boyle, Traci Lind, Roy Brocksmith, Norbert Weisser; ***D:*** Alan Parker; ***W:*** Alan Parker; ***C:*** Peter Biziou; ***M:*** Rachel Portman.

The Road to Yesterday 1/2 **1925** Two couples together on a crashing train are somehow thrown into the 18th century in roles parallel to their own lives. DeMille's first independent film; intriguing action/melodrama. Silent with musical soundtrack. **136m/B VHS.** Joseph Schildkraut, William Boyd, Jetta Goudal, Vera Reynolds, Iron Eyes Cody; ***D:*** Cecil B. DeMille.

The Road to Zanzibar **1941** After selling a fake diamond mine to a criminal, Crosby and Hope flee to Zanzibar, where they meet up with Lamour and Merkel. The guys put up the money for a safari, supposedly to look for Lamour's brother, but they soon discover that they too have been tricked. Deciding to head back to Zanzibar, Crosby and Hope find themselves surrounded by hungry cannibals. Will they survive, or will they be someone's dinner? Not as funny as the other road movies, but amusing nonetheless. ♫ It's Always You; You're Dangerous; On the Road to Zanzibar; You Lucky People You; Birds of a Feather; African Etude. **92m/C VHS, DVD.** Bing Crosby, Bob Hope, Dorothy Lamour, Una Merkel, Eric Blore, Iris Adrian, Lionel Royce; ***D:*** Victor Schertzinger; ***W:*** Frank Butler, Don Hartman; ***C:*** Ted Tetzlaff.

Road Trip 1/2 **2000 (R)** Extremely low-brow comedy about four college buddies who set out on an 1,800-mile road trip (from New York to Texas) in order to intercept an incriminating videotape Josh (Meyer) has mistakenly mailed to his long-distance girlfriend. Green does disgusting things to a defenseless white mouse, and there's the usual frat-house sexual humor, but like most teen comedies these days, it's quotable, laugh-even-though-you-know-better funny, and basically harmless. **91m/C VHS, DVD.** Breckin Meyer, Seann William Scott, Rachel Blanchard, DJ Qualls, Fred Ward, Andy Dick, Paulo Costanzo, Tom Green, Amy Smart, Anthony Rapp, Ethan Suplee; ***D:*** Todd Phillips; ***W:*** Todd Phillips, Scot Armstrong; ***C:*** Mark Irwin; ***M:*** Mike Simpson.

Road Trip: Beer Pong **2009 (R)** Usual dumb raunchy comedy with Qualls taking over as the framing device narrator from the first flick. Graduate student Kyle is giving a campus tour to prospective students when he relates a story about a legendary road trip (shown in flashbacks). Andy and some buds are headed out to a national beer pong championship with Andy's secondary mission to hook up with hottie ex-girlfriend Jenna. **96m/C DVD.** Preston Jones, Danny Pudi, Michael Trotter, Daniel Newman, Nestor Aaron Absera, DJ Qualls, Julianna Guill, Julia Levy-Boeken; ***D:*** Steve Rash; ***W:*** Brad Riddell; ***C:*** Levie Isaacks. **VIDEO**

The Road Warrior 1/2 *Mad Max 2* **1982 (R)** The first sequel to "Mad Max" takes place after nuclear war has destroyed Australia. Max helps a colony of oil-drilling survivors defend themselves from the roving murderous outback gangs and escape to the coast. The climactic chase scene is among the most exciting ever filmed; this film virtually created the "action-adventure" picture of the 1980s. **95m/C VHS, DVD, Blu-ray Disc, HD DVD.** *AU* Mel Gibson, Bruce Spence, Emil Minty, Vernon Wells, Virginia Hey, Max Phipps,

Mike (Michael) Preston, William Zappa; *D:* George Miller; *W:* George Miller, Terry Hayes; *C:* Dean Semler; *M:* Brian May. L.A. Film Critics '82: Foreign Film.

Roadhouse Girl 🦴 *Marilyn* **1953** A sexy woman kindles a romance with one of her husband's employees and the result is murder. Reminiscent of "The Postman Always Rings Twice," but with poor production values and performances. **70m/B VHS.** *GB* Maxwell Reed, Sandra Dorne, Leslie Dwyer, Vida Hope, Ferdinand "Ferdy" Mayne; *D:* Wolf Rilla; *W:* Wolf Rilla.

Roadhouse 66 🦴 1/2 **1984 (R)** Utterly unoriginal broke-down-in-a-hick-town nonsense. Snooty Reinhold and scruffy Dafoe go through the motions, and of course find a pair of female companions. Soundtrack features Los Lobos, the Pretenders, and Dave Edmunds. **90m/C VHS, DVD.** Willem Dafoe, Judge Reinhold, Karen Lee, Kate Vernon, Stephen Elliott; *D:* John Mark Robinson; *C:* Thomas Ackerman.

Roadie 🦴 1/2 **1980 (PG)** Supposedly a look at the back-stage world of rock 'n' roll, but the performance and direction leave a lot to be desired. Meatloaf is a roadie who desperately wants to meet Alice Cooper, and spends the movie trying to do so. Features Art Carney, and musical names like Blondie, Roy Orbison, Hank Williams Jr., and Don Cornelius (of "Soul Train" fame). **105m/C VHS, DVD.** Meat Loaf Aday, Kaki Hunter, Art Carney, Gailard Sartain, Alice Cooper, Roy Orbison, Hank Williams Jr., Ramblin' Jack Elliot; *D:* Alan Rudolph; *W:* Alan Rudolph, Michael Ventura.

Roadkill 🦴 **1989** Cheap thriller about Ramona (Buhagiar), a concert promoter who tries to find a lost band, "The Children of Paradise," in the Canadian north woods. Along the way, she meets a would-be serial killer and other assorted weirdos. **85m/B VHS, DVD.** *CA* Valerie Buhagiar, Don McKellar, Bruce McDonald; *D:* Bruce McDonald; *W:* Don McKellar. Toronto-City '89: Canadian Feature Film.

Roadracers 🦴🦴 **1994 (R)** Made as part of Showtime's "Rebel Highway" series, Rodriguez basically takes the title from the 1959 AIP low-budgeter and goes his own way. Leather-clad rebel Dude Delaney (Arquette) has a voluptuous Latino dreamgirl named Donna (Hayek) and a gang which faces off against the clique led by rival Teddy Leather (Wiles) in drag races and roller rinks all around town. Great rockabilly soundtrack. **95m/C VHS, DVD.** David Arquette, Jason Wiles, Salma Hayek, John Hawkes, William Sadler, O'Neal Compton, Lance LeGault, Karen Landry, Tommy Nix; *D:* Robert Rodriguez; *W:* Robert Rodriguez, Tommy Nix; *C:* Roberto Schaefer; *M:* Paul Boll, Johnny Reno. **CABLE**

Roads to the South 🦴🦴 1/2 *Les Routes du Sud* **1978** One-time Spanish revolutionary turned screenwriter returns to his homeland to fight fascism, but finds himself attracted to his son's beautiful girlfriend. Much soul searching. In French with English subtitles. **100m/C VHS.** *FR* Yves Montand, Miou-Miou, Laurent Malet, Mario Gonzalez, Jose Luis Gomez, Jeannine Mestre, Roger Planchon, Didier Sauvegrain; *D:* Joseph Losey; *W:* Jorge Semprun; *C:* Gerry Fisher; *M:* Michel Legrand.

Roadside Prophets 🦴🦴 **1992 (R)** Counter-culture road trip, striving to be the '90s version of "Easy Rider," follows factory worker/biker Joe (Doe) on his mission to transport the ashes of a fellow biker to Nevada. He is accompanied by the pesky younger Sam (Horovitz), and together they meet up with lots of eccentrics and stay at lots of cheap motels. Interesting cast meanders through sentimental and slow-moving buddy flick from debut director Wool, who wrote "Sid and Nancy." Cusack completes the cameo hat trick, with appearances here and in 1992's "The Player" and "Shadows and Fog." **96m/C VHS, DVD.** John Doe, Adam Horovitz, David Carradine, Timothy Leary, Arlo Guthrie, Barton Heyman, Jennifer Balgobin, John David (J.D.) Cullum; ***Cameos:*** John Cusack; *D:* Abbe Wool; *W:* Abbe Wool.

The Roamin' Cowboy 🦴🦴 **1937** In a town where the local ranchers are being threatened, a drifter comes to their rescue and wins both a girl and a job. **56m/B VHS.** Fred Scott, Al "Fuzzy" St. John, Lois January, Forrest Taylor, Roger Williams; *D:* Robert F. "Bob" Hill.

Roanoak 🦴🦴 1/2 **1986** A dramatization in three parts of the mysterious fate of the early English settlement of Roanoak in North Carolina, which disappeared without a trace. Long, but intriguing. Made for PBS: "American Playhouse." **180m/C** Will Sampson, Victoria Racimo, Porky White, Adrian Sparks, Patrick Kilpatrick; *D:* Jan Egleson. **TV**

Roarin' Lead 🦴 1/2 **1937** Three Mesquiteers fight with a gang of rustlers while helping the orphans' and cattlemen's associations. **54m/B VHS, DVD.** Robert "Bob" Livingston, Ray Corrigan, Max Terhune, Christine Maple, Hooper Atchley, Yakima Canutt, George Chesebro, Tommy Bupp; *D:* Sam Newfield, Mack V. Wright; *W:* Oliver Drake, Jack Natteford; *C:* William Nobles; *M:* Hugo Riesenfeld.

Roaring City 🦴 1/2 **1951** A hard-boiled detective searches for the person behind the murders of gangsters and prize fighters. **58m/B VHS.** Hugh Beaumont, Edward Brophy, Richard Travis, Joan Valerie, Wanda McKay, Rebel Randall, Greg McClure, Stanley Price, William Tannen, Abner Biberman, Anthony Warde; *D:* William Berke; *W:* Julian Harmon, Herbert Margolis, Louis Morheim; *C:* Jack Greenhalgh.

Roaring Guns 🦴🦴 1/2 **1936** An unflappable McCoy rides in to thwart a despicable landowner trying to drive all the small ranchers out of business. Low-budget fun. **66m/B VHS.** Tim McCoy, Rex Lease, Wheeler Oakman; *D:* Sam Newfield.

Roaring Ranch 🦴 1/2 **1930** Gibson is trying to protect his ranch from the evil Oakman while attempting to care for a baby as well. **65m/B VHS.** Hoot Gibson, Wheeler Oakman, Sally Eilers, Bobby Nelson, Frank Clark; *D:* B. Reeves Eason; *W:* B. Reeves Eason.

The Roaring Road 🦴🦴 1/2 **1919** Romantic comedy about a car salesman named Toodles, who drives for his company in a big race. Vintage racing footage; silent with original organ music. **57m/B VHS.** Wallace Reid, Ann Little, Theodore Roberts; *D:* James Cruze.

Roaring Roads 🦴 **1935** An heir to a fortune acquires a lust for race car driving, and his family thinks, a reckless death wish. **60m/B VHS.** Gertrude Messinger, David Sharpe, Mickey Daniels, Mary Kornman, Jack Mulhall; *D:* Charles E. Roberts; *W:* David Sharpe, Charles E. Roberts; *C:* Robert E. Cline.

Roaring Six Guns 🦴 1/2 **1937** Maynard protects his property against his crooked partner and his fiancee's father. **60m/B VHS, DVD.** Kermit Maynard, Mary Hayes, John Merton, Edward Cassidy, Sam Flint, Budd Buster, Robert (Fisk) Fiske, Charles "Slim" Whitaker; *D:* J(ohn) P(aterson) McGowan; *W:* Arthur Everett; *C:* Jack Greenhalgh.

Roaring Speedboats 🦴 *Mile a Minute Love* **1937** Bakewell is a speedboat racer up against crooks who want to con him out of his money by tinkering with his invention. **62m/B VHS.** William "Billy" Bakewell, Arletta Duncan, Duncan Renaldo, Vivien Oakland, Wilfrid Lucas; *D:* Elmer Clifton.

The Roaring Twenties 🦴🦴🦴 1/2 **1939** Eddie (Cagney), George (Bogart), and Lloyd (Lynn) are three WWI buddies who find their lives intersecting unexpectedly in Prohibition-era New York. Eddie becomes a bootlegger and vies with George for status as crime boss. Lloyd is the attorney working to prosecute them. Great gangster flick was the last time Bogart and Cagney worked together after "Angels with Dirty Faces" (1938) and "The Oklahoma Kid" (1939). Cheesy script delivered with zest by top pros. **106m/B VHS, DVD.** James Cagney, Humphrey Bogart, Jeffrey Lynn, Priscilla Lane, Gladys George, Frank McHugh, Paul Kelly, Joseph (Joe) Sawyer; *D:* Raoul Walsh; *W:* Robert Rossen, Richard Macaulay; *C:* Ernest Haller; *M:* Heinz Roemheld, Ray Heindorf.

Rob Roy 🦴🦴🦴 **1995 (R)** Kilt-raising though overlong tale of legendary Scot Robert Roy MacGregor mixes love and honor with bloodlust and revenge. Neeson's rugged clan leader fends off a band of dastardly nobles led by Cunningham (Roth), a foppish twit with an evil bent. Misty highland scenery and intense romantic interplay between Neeson and Lange as the spirited Mary MacGregor lend a passionate twist to an otherwise earthy, robust adventure of lore capped by one of the best sword fights in years. Both Neeson and Lange provide a gutsy substance to their characters: Neeson's Celtic hero is sexy and steadfast (and generally sports an Irish accent), while Lange inhabits a soulful and tenacious Mary. Roth's delightfully hammy performance as MacGregor's loathsome, bewigged nemesis delivers zip amid the high-minded speeches, plot lulls, and separated body parts. Visually stunning, with on-location shooting in the Scottish Highlands. More ambience is provided by Buswell's evocative score. **144m/C VHS, DVD.** Liam Neeson, Jessica Lange, Tim Roth, John Hurt, Eric Stoltz, Andrew Keir, Brian Cox, Brian McCardie, Gilbert Martin, Vicki Masson, David Hayman, Jason Flemyng, Shirley Henderson, Gilly Gilchrist, John Murtagh, Ewan Stewart; *D:* Michael Caton-Jones; *W:* Alan Sharp; *C:* Karl Walter Lindenlaub, Roger Deakins; *M:* Carter Burwell. British Acad. '95: Support. Actor (Roth).

Rob Roy—The Highland Rogue 🦴 1/2 *Rob Roy* **1953** In the early 18th century, Scottish Highlander Rob Roy must battle against the King of England's secretary, who would undermine the MacGregor clan to enact his evil deeds. Dull Disney drama. **84m/C VHS.** Richard Todd, Glynis Johns, James Robertson Justice, Michael Gough; *D:* Harold French.

Robbers of the Sacred Mountain 🦴🦴 *Falcon's Gold* **1983** TV rip-off of "Raiders of the Lost Ark," loosely based on Arthur Conan Doyle's story "Challenger's Gold." Adventurers seek meteorites in the Mexican jungle. Billed as the first made-for-cable movie. **95m/C VHS.** John Marley, Simon MacCorkindale, Louise Vallance, George Touliatos; *D:* Bob Schulz. **CABLE**

Robbery 🦴🦴 1/2 **1967** Unoriginal but competent rendition of the hackneyed British Royal Mail robbery. Thieves plan and execute a heist of a late-night mail train carrying $10 million. **113m/C VHS.** *GB* Stanley Baker, James Booth, Joanna Pettet, Frank Finlay, Barry Foster; *D:* Peter Yates.

Robbery 🦴 **1985** A six-man platoon of Vietnam war veterans endeavors to assault and rob a mob of shiftless bookies. **91m/C VHS.** John Sheerin, Tony Rickards, Tim Hughes; *D:* Michael Thornhill.

Robbery under Arms 🦴🦴 1/2 **1957** From Australia in the 1800s, similar to the American wild west, comes a tale of love and robbery. Finch is the leader of a band of outlaws. Rather dull story redeemed by excellent photography of beautiful landscape. **83m/C VHS.** *GB* Peter Finch, Ronald Lewis, Laurence Naismith, Maureen Swanson, David McCallum, Jill Ireland; *D:* Jack Lee.

Robby 🦴🦴 **1968** A young white boy and a young black boy shipwrecked on an island form a strong friendship that sees them through a series of adventures. **60m/C VHS.** Warren Raum, Ryp Siani, John Garces; *D:* Ralph Bluemke.

The Robe 🦴🦴 1/2 **1953** This moving, religious portrait follows the career and religious awakening of drunken and dissolute Roman tribune Marcellus (Burton), after he wins the robe of the just-crucified Christ in a dice game. Mature plays Burton's slave surprisingly well, and reprised the role in the sequel, "Demetrius and the Gladiators"; Burton is wooden. "The Robe" was the first movie to be filmed in CinemaScope. Based on the novel by Lloyd C. Douglas. **133m/C VHS, DVD.** Richard Burton, Jean Simmons, Victor Mature, Michael Rennie, Richard Boone, Dean Jagger, Jeff Morrow, Jay Robinson, Dawn Addams, Ernest Thesiger, Torin Thatcher; *D:* Henry Koster; *W:* Albert (John B. Sherry) Maltz, Philip Dunne; *C:* Leon Shamroy. Oscars '53: Art Dir./Set Dec., Color, Costume Des. (C); Golden Globes '54: Film—Drama; Natl. Bd. of Review '53: Actress (Simmons).

The Robert Benchley Miniatures Collection 🦴🦴 1/2 **1935** Writer and humorist Robert Benchley made 30 theatrical shorts for MGM between 1935 and 1944 as he commented on such everyday subjects as training a dog, figuring out income taxes, and enjoying a movie. Also included is Benchley's debut short, "How to Sleep," which won an Academy Award. **267m/B DVD.** Robert Benchley; *D:* Jules White; *W:* Robert Benchley.

Robert et Robert 🦴🦴🦴 **1978** Two 'ineligible' bachelors resort to using a computerized matrimonial agency to find the girls of their dreams. They become friends while they wait for their dates. Sensitive tale of loneliness and friendship. Warm and witty with fine performances throughout. French with English subtitles. **105m/C VHS.** *FR* Charles Denner, Jacques Villeret, Jean-Claude Brialy, Macha Meril, Germaine Montero, Regine; *D:* Claude Lelouch; *W:* Claude Lelouch; *C:* Jacques Lefrancois. Cesar '79: Support. Actor (Villeret).

Robert Kennedy and His Times 🦴🦴 1/2 **1990** Another look at the Kennedy clan, this time from the Bobby angle. Good acting. Based on the book by Arthur Schlesinger. **309m/C VHS.** Brad Davis, Veronica Cartwright, Cliff DeYoung, Ned Beatty, Beatrice Straight, Jack Warden; *D:* Marvin J. Chomsky.

Robert Louis Stevenson's The Game of Death 🦴🦴 1/2 *The Suicide Club; The Game of Death; Robert Louis Stevenson's The Suicide Club* **1999 (R)** This version sticks to the spirit of Stevenson's story (which was filmed in 1936 as "Trouble for Two") but adds plotlines and characters. It's 1899 and Henry Joyce (Morrissey) has decided to kill himself because of his lover's betrayal. He and pal, Captain May (Shuke), meet the equally suicidal Shaw (Bettany), who takes them along to the Suicide Club. Run by the mysterious Bourne (Pryce), its members willingly want to die—and both the next victim and their murderer are selected by a drawing of the cards. And you aren't allowed to change your mind. **89m/C VHS, DVD.** David Morrissey, Jonathan Pryce, Paul Bettany, Neil Stuke, Catherine Siggins; *D:* Rachel Samuels; *W:* Lev L. Spiro; *C:* Chris Manley; *M:* Adrian Johnston.

Roberta 🦴🦴🦴 **1935** A football player inherits his aunt's Parisian dress shop and finds himself at odds with an incognito Russian princess. Dumb plot aside, this is one of the best Astaire-Rogers efforts. A later remake was titled "Lovely to Look At." ♫ Let's Begin; Yesterdays; Smoke Gets in Your Eyes; I'll Be Hard to Handle; I Won't Dance; Lovely to Look At; Back Home Again in Indiana; The Touch of Your Hand; You're Devasting. **85m/B VHS, DVD.** Fred Astaire, Ginger Rogers, Irene Dunne, Lucille Ball, Randolph Scott; *D:* William A. Seiter; *M:* Max Steiner.

Robin and Marian 🦴🦴 **1976 (PG)** After a separation of 20 years, Robin Hood is reunited with Maid Marian, who is now a nun. Their dormant feelings for each other are reawakened as Robin spirits her to Sherwood Forest. In case you wanted to see Robin Hood robbed of all magic, spontaneity, and fun. Connery is dull, dull, dull, working with an uninspired script. **106m/C VHS, DVD.** *GB* Sean Connery, Audrey Hepburn, Robert Shaw, Richard Harris, Denholm Elliott, Ian Holm, Nicol Williamson, Ronnie Barker; *D:* Richard Lester; *C:* David Watkin; *M:* John Barry.

Robin and the 7 Hoods 🦴🦴 1/2 **1964** Runyon-esque Rat Pack version of 1920s Chicago, with Frank and the boys as do-good gangsters in their last go-round. Fun if not unforgettable. ♫ Bang! Bang!; Style; Mister Booze; Don't Be a Do-Badder; My Kind of Town. **124m/C VHS, DVD.** Frank Sinatra, Bing Crosby, Dean Martin, Sammy Davis Jr., Peter Falk, Barbara Rush, Victor Buono, Hank Henry, Robert Foulk, Allen Jenkins, Jack La Rue, Edward G. Robinson, Hans Conried, Tony Randall; *D:* Gordon Douglas; *W:* John Fenton Murray, David R. Schwartz; *C:* William H. Daniels; *M:* Nelson Riddle, James Van Heusen.

Robin-B-Hood 🦴🦴 *Rob-B-Hood* **2006** Goofy two-men-and-a-baby crime comedy. Compulsive gamblers Thongs (Chan) and Octopus (Koo) steal to support their addiction. Their boss wants them to kidnap an infant for big bucks but they have to babysit the tyke until arrangements for transfer can be made. Despite many mishaps, the duo bond with baby and are reluctant to turn him over to a Triad leader, who thinks the boy is his grandson. Cantonese with subtitles. **134m/C DVD.** *CH HK* Jackie Chan, Michael Hui, Yuen Biao, Chen Baoguo, Louis Koo, Yuanyuan Gao; ***D:*** Benny Chan; ***W:*** Jackie Chan, Benny Chan; ***C:*** Anthony Pun; ***M:*** Fai-young Chan.

Robin Cook's Invasion 1/2 *Invasion* **1997** College student Beau Stark (Perry) is one of many sickened by some kind of strange viral infection after being exposed to rocks of interstellar origin. The virus induces mutations and Beau works with scientists to find an antidote to the alien threat. A familiar story slickly done. **180m/C VHS, DVD.** Luke Perry, Kim Cattrall, Rebecca Gayheart, Christopher Orr, Jon Polito, Neal McDonough, Jason Schombing; ***D:*** Armand Mastroianni; ***W:*** Rockne S. O'Bannon; ***C:*** Bryan England; ***M:*** Don Davis. **TV**

Robin Cook's Terminal *Terminal* **1996** Mediocre medical thriller. Cancer researcher Sean O'Grady (Savant) has just gotten an internship at a medical clinic that has a phenomenal cure rate for a particular type of brain cancer. Sean gets suspicious about the treatment and works with ex-girlfriend (and nurse) Janet (Peeples) to find out the truth. Which is always a bad idea in these sorts of movies because then lots of unsavory, suspicious types come after you. **90m/C VHS, DVD.** Doug Savant, Nia Peeples, Michael Ironside, James Eckhouse, Roy Thinnes, Jenny O'Hara, Khandi Alexander, Gregg Henry; ***D:*** Larry Elikann; ***W:*** Nancy Isaak; ***C:*** Eric Van Haren Noman; ***M:*** Garry Schyman. **TV**

Robin Hood 1/2 **1922** Extravagant production casts Fairbanks as eponymous gymnastic swashbuckler who departs for Crusades as Earl of Huntington and returns as the hooded one to save King Richard's throne from the sinister Sheriff of Nottingham. Best ever silent swashbuckling. **110m/B VHS, DVD.** Douglas Fairbanks Sr., Wallace Beery, Sam De Grasse, Enid Bennett, Paul Dickey, William E. (W.E., William A., W.A.) Lowery, Roy Coulson, Bill Bennett, Merrill McCormick, Wilson Benge, Willard Louis, Alan Hale, Maine Geary, Lloyd Talman; ***D:*** Allan Dwan; ***W:*** Douglas Fairbanks Sr.; ***C:*** Arthur Edeson.

Robin Hood **1973** This time the Sherwood Forest crew are portrayed by appropriate cartoon animals, hence, Robin is a fox, Little John a bear, etc. Good family fare, but not as memorable as other Disney features. **83m/C VHS, DVD.** ***D:*** Wolfgang Reitherman; ***M:*** George Bruns; ***V:*** Roger Miller, Brian Bedford, Monica Evans, Phil Harris, Andy Devine, Carol(e) Shelley, Peter Ustinov, Terry-Thomas, Pat Buttram, George Lindsey, Ken Curtis.

Robin Hood **1991** Dark version of the medieval tale. Bergin's Prince of Thieves is well developed and Thurman is a graceful Marion. Three studios announced plans to remake "Robin Hood" in 1990 and two were completed, including this one which was scaled down for cable TV. **116m/C VHS, DVD.** Patrick Bergin, Uma Thurman, Jurgen Prochnow, Edward Fox, Jeroen Krabbe, Jeff Nuttal, David Morrissey, Owen Teale; ***D:*** John Irvin; ***M:*** Geoffrey Burgon. **CABLE**

Robin Hood **2010** In this 5th collaboration between star Crowe and director Ridley Scott they take on the legendary English folk hero in a less-than-swashbuckling manner. Robin (Crowe) is an ex-crusader who has returned home to England after the death of King Richard. The newly-crowned King John (Isaac) is weak and the country is suffering so Robin gathers together a band of mercenaries to confront corruption, beginning with the despotic Sheriff of Nottingham (Macfadyen). The widowed Marian (Blanchett) is suspicious of Robin's motives. **m/C DVD.** Russell Crowe, Cate Blanchett, Matthew MacFadyen, William Hurt, Mark Strong, Mark Addy, Scott Grimes, Kevin Durand, Eileen Atkins, Oscar Isaac, Danny Huston, Alan Doyle; ***D:*** Ridley Scott; ***W:*** Brian Helgeland; ***C:*** John Mathiesen; ***M:*** Marc Streitenfeld.

The Robin Hood Gang 1/2 *Angels in the Attic* **1998 (PG)** Brad (Taylor) and Frankie (Losack) are enterprising youngsters who collect empty soda cans to raise money to buy new bikes. But when they discover a suitcase full of cash in the attic of their apartment, they decide to share the wealth with their equally hard-up neighbors. When they learn that it's stolen bank loot, they must figure out how to catch the criminal and return the money. Nobody's going to mistake this modest kidvid for "Home Alone" but it's an acceptable time-waster for the short set. **86m/C DVD.** Clayton Taylor, Steven Losak, Dalin Christiansen, Brenda Price, Scott Christopher; ***D:*** Eric Hendershot; ***W:*** Eric Hendershot; ***C:*** T.C. Christensen; ***M:*** Allen Williams. **VIDEO**

Robin Hood: Men in Tights 1/2 *Men in Tights* **1993 (PG-13)** Brooksian rendition of the classic legend inspires guffaws, but doesn't hit the bullseye on all it promises. Hood afficionados will appreciate the painstaking effort taken to spoof the 1938 Errol Flynn classic while leaving plenty of room to poke fun at the more recent Costner nonclassic "Robin Hood: Prince of Thieves." Elwes, last seen swinging swords in "The Princess Bride," is well cast as the Flynn lookalike. Expect the usual off-color humor that's so prevalent in all Brooks outings. **105m/C VHS, DVD.** Cary Elwes, Richard Lewis, Roger Rees, Amy Yasbeck, Dave Chappelle, Isaac Hayes, Tracey Ullman, Mark Blankfield, Megan Cavanagh, Eric Allen Kramer, Tony Griffin, Dick Van Patten, Mel Brooks; ***D:*** Mel Brooks; ***W:*** Mel Brooks, J. David Shapiro, Evan Chandler; ***M:*** Hummie Mann.

Robin Hood of Texas 1/2 **1947** Autry finds his calm life disturbed when he is falsely accused of robbing a bank. Pretty good plot for once, in Autry's last Republic western, and plenty of action. **71m/B VHS, DVD.** Gene Autry, Lynne Roberts, Sterling Holloway, Adele Mara; ***D:*** Lesley Selander.

Robin Hood of the Pecos 1/2 **1941** Ex-Confederate soldier takes on northern post-war politicians and carpetbaggers. Decent Rogers/Hayes outing. **56m/B VHS, DVD.** Roy Rogers, George "Gabby" Hayes, Marjorie Reynolds, Jay Novello, Roscoe Ates; ***D:*** Joseph Kane.

Robin Hood: Prince of Thieves 1/2 **1991 (PG-13)** Costner is the politically correct Rebel with a Cause, but a thinker, not a doer—and therein lies the problem. His quiet thoughtfulness doesn't add up to leadership and Rickman easily overpowers him as the wicked, crazed Sheriff of Nottingham. Freeman is excellent as a civilized Moor who finds England, and its people, inhospitable, dangerous, and not a little stupid. Mastrantonio, a last minute choice, excels as the lovely Lady Marian. Great action sequences, a gritty and morbid picture of the Middle Ages, and some fun scenes with the Merry Men. Revisionist in its ideas about the times and people, critics generally disapproved of the changes in the story and Costner's performance, though their comments about his lack of an English accent seem nitpicky in light of some basic plot problems. Still has lots of fun for lovers of action, romance and fairy tales. **144m/C VHS, DVD.** Kevin Costner, Morgan Freeman, Mary Elizabeth Mastrantonio, Christian Slater, Alan Rickman, Geraldine McEwan, Michael McShane, Brian Blessed, Michael Wincott, Nick Brimble, Harold Innocent, Jack Wild; ***Cameos:*** Sean Connery; ***D:*** Kevin Reynolds; ***W:*** Pen Densham, John Watson; ***C:*** Billy Milton; ***M:*** Michael Kamen. British Acad. '91: Support. Actor (Rickman); MTV Movie Awards '92: Song ("(Everything I Do) I Do for You"); Golden Raspberries '91: Worst Actor (Costner).

Robin Hood... The Legend: Herne's Son 1/2 **1985** When Robin Hood is killed by the Sheriff of Nottingham, he begs Robert of Huntington (Connery) to continue his work. Connery refuses, the band dissolves, Maid Marion is kidnapped, and they reunite to save her. Good entry in the BBC series. **101m/C VHS.** *GB* Jason Connery, Oliver Cotton, Michael Craig, Nickolas Grace, George Baker; ***D:*** Robert M. Young. **TV**

Robin Hood... The Legend: Robin Hood and the Sorcerer 1/2 **1983** Robin Hood is chosen by the mystical Herne the Hunter to thwart the evil Sheriff of Nottingham and protect the English peasantry. He must defeat the supernatural powers of a sorcerer and gather together his men in this pilot for British TV. **115m/C VHS.** *GB* Michael Praed, Anthony Valentine, Nickolas Grace, Clive Mantle, Peter Williams; ***D:*** Ian Sharp. **TV**

Robin Hood... The Legend: The Swords of Wayland 1/2 **1983** A wicked sorceress provides a supernatural threat to Robin and his merry men. Second entry in the BBC series. Convoluted, breathless plot makes for swashbuckling fun and much derring-do. **115m/C VHS.** *GB* Michael Praed, Rula Lenska, Nickolas Grace; ***D:*** Robert M. Young. **TV**

Robin Hood... The Legend: The Time of the Wolf 1/2 **1985** Robin Hood finds out that an old enemy is about to release his evil doings on the world and only he can stop him, while Maid Marian comes to a momentous decision. **105m/C VHS.** *GB* Jason Connery, Nickolas Grace, Richard O'Brien; ***D:*** Syd Roberson. **TV**

Robin Hood: The Movie **1955** A colorized and re-mixed version of several episodes of the British TV series adds up to a fine version of the classic tale. Excellent cast, clever editing, and stunning colorization. **90m/C VHS.** *GB* Richard Greene, Bernadette O'Farrell, Alan Wheatley; ***D:*** Ralph Smart, Daniel Birt, Terence Fisher. **TV**

Robin of Locksley 1/2 **1995 (PG)** A modern-day, teenaged Robin Hood (Sawa) battles the bullies at his private boys school (thanks to his archery prowess), meets a girl named Marian, and takes on sinister FBI agent Nottingham. **97m/C VHS, DVD.** Devon Sawa, Sarah Chalke, Joshua Jackson; ***D:*** Michael Kennedy.

Robin's Hood **2003** Robin (Turner) is a black social worker in Oakland who is about to lose her job for caring too much about her clients. She meets thief Brooklyn (Cates) and together they start robbing banks and distributing the money to the neighborhood needy. But their crime spree can't last for long. **81m/C DVD.** *US* Khahtee V. Turner, Clody Cates; ***D:*** Sara Millman; ***W:*** Khahtee V. Turner, Sara Millman; ***C:*** Howard Shack.

Robinson Crusoe **1936** A real oddity: a British silent film originally made in 1927, re-edited ten years later. Music and sound effects were added, along with a narration by children's radio personality Carney. Follows the plot of the famous adventure story by Daniel Defoe. **34m/B VHS.** M.A. Wetherell, Fay Compton, Herbert Waithe; ***D:*** M.A. Wetherell; ***W:*** M.A. Wetherell; ***C:*** J. Rosenthal; ***Nar:*** Uncle Don Carney.

Robinson Crusoe 1/2 *Daniel Defoe's Robinson Crusoe* **1996 (PG-13)** Originally intended as a TV production, film got pushed to the big screen thanks to Brosnan's success as James Bond. He's the shipwrecked seaman and Takaku is Friday. First film to be shot in Papua, New Guinea. **105m/C DVD.** Polly Walker, Ian Hart, Damian Lewis, Lysette Anthony, Pierce Brosnan, William Takaku; ***D:*** George Miller; ***W:*** Tracy Keenan Wynn, Christopher Canaan; ***C:*** David Connell.

Robinson Crusoe & the Tiger 1/2 **1972 (G)** A tiger tells the famous story of how Robinson Crusoe became stranded on a desert island. **109m/C VHS, DVD.** Hugo Stiglitz, Ahui; ***D:*** Rene Cardona Jr.

Robinson Crusoe of Clipper Island **1936** Fourteen-episode serial featuring the investigative expertise of Mala, a Polynesian in the employ of the U.S. Intelligence Service. Each episode runs 16 minutes. Shortened version titled "Robinson Crusoe of Mystery Island." **256m/B VHS, DVD.** Mala, Rex, Buck, Kate Greenfield, John Ward, Tracy Lane, Robert F. (Bob) Kortman, Herbert Rawlinson; ***D:*** Mack V. Wright.

Robinson Crusoe of Mystery Island **1936** A Polynesian employed by the U.S. Intelligence Service investigates saboteurs on a mysterious island. Would-be cliffhanger is a yawner; where are the chills and thrills? Edited from the serial "Robinson Crusoe of Clipper Island." **100m/B VHS.** Mala, Rex, Buck, Herbert Rawlinson, Ray Taylor; ***D:*** Mack V. Wright.

Robinson Crusoe on Mars **1964** Sci-fi interpretation of Defoe classic. West is one of two daring scientists who take a monkey with them on a mission to outer space. When a meteor strikes their ship, it hurtles out of control towards the red planet and only Mantee and Mona survive the wreckage. They meet Lundin, an escaped slave and teach him English until evil slave traders spoil the fun. **109m/C** Adam West, Vic Lundin, Paul Mantee; ***D:*** Byron Haskin; ***W:*** Ib Melchior, John C. Higgins; ***C:*** Winton C. Hoch; ***M:*** Nathan Van Cleave.

Robo-Chic *Cyber-Chic* **1989** A woman who is part cop, part machine, becomes a defender of justice. **90m/C VHS.** Kathy Shower, Jack Carter, Burt Ward, Lyle Waggoner; ***D:*** Ed Hansen, Jeffrey Mandel.

Robo Warriors **1996 (PG-13)** In the year 2036, Earth has been conquered by the Terridaxx, a half-human, half-reptile race. But 12-year-old Zac finds the last high-tech fighting machine, the Robo Warrior (Remar), and convinces him to help destroy the invaders. **94m/C VHS.** James Remar, James Lew, James Tolkan, Kyle Howard, Bernard Kates; ***D:*** Ian Barry; ***W:*** Michael Berlin; ***M:*** Richard Band.

RoboCop **1987 (R)** A nearly dead Detroit cop, Alex Murphy (Weller), is used as the brain for a crime-fighting robot in this bleak vision of the future. Humor, satire, action, and violence keep this moving in spite of its underlying sadness. Slick animation techniques from Phil Tippet. Verhoeven's first American film. **103m/C VHS, DVD, UMD.** Peter Weller, Nancy Allen, Ronny Cox, Kurtwood Smith, Ray Wise, Miguel Ferrer, Dan O'Herlihy, Robert DoQui, Felton Perry, Paul McCrane, Del Zamora; ***D:*** Paul Verhoeven; ***W:*** Michael Miner, Edward Neumeier; ***C:*** Jan De Bont; ***M:*** Basil Poledouris.

RoboCop 2 **1990 (R)** Grimer, more violent sequel to the initial fascinating look at the future, where police departments are run by corporations hungry for profit at any cost. A new and highly addictive drug has made Detroit more dangerous than ever. Robocop is replaced by a stronger cyborg with the brain of a brutal criminal. When the cyborg goes berserk, Robocop battles it and the drug lords for control of the city. Dark humor and graphic savagery, with little of the tenderness and emotion of the original. **117m/C VHS, DVD.** Peter Weller, Nancy Allen, Belinda Bauer, Dan O'Herlihy, Tom Noonan, Gabriel Damon, Galyn Gorg, Felton Perry, Patricia Charbonneau; ***D:*** Irvin Kershner; ***W:*** Walon Green; ***C:*** Mark Irwin; ***M:*** Leonard Rosenman.

RoboCop 3 1/2 **1991 (PG-13)** Robocop's new Japanese owners plan to build a huge, new, ultra-modern city (in place of the decrepit 21st-century Detroit) but first must evict thousands of people in this third installment of the "Robocop" films (which sat on the studio shelf before finally being released in 1993). There's an android Ninja warrior to do battle with Robo, who's gone over to the rebel underground. Plot and action sequences are rehashed from better films. Watch the original. **104m/C VHS, DVD.** Robert John Burke, Nancy Allen, John Castle, CCH Pounder, Bruce Locke, Rip Torn, Remi Ryan, Felton Perry, Stephen (Steve) Root; ***D:*** Fred Dekker; ***W:*** Fred Dekker, Frank Miller; ***C:*** Gary B. Kibbe; ***M:*** Basil Poledouris.

Roboman 1/2 *Who?* **1975 (PG)** American scientist gets in car crash in Soviet Union. When he returns to the States as a cyborg, his friends seem to notice a change. **91m/C VHS.** *GB GE* Elliott Gould, Trevor Howard, Joe (Joseph) Bova, Ed Grover, James Noble, John Lehne; ***D:*** Jack Gold.

Robot Holocaust **1987** Somewhere in the doomed future, after the Earth is laid waste by robots with superior intelligence, a human survivor dares to challenge them. If you're doomed to watch this, you just might survive; it's so-so, unsurprisingly sci-fi. **79m/C VHS.** Norris Culf, Nadine Hart, Joel von Ornsteiner, Jennifer Delora, Andrew Howarth, Angelika Jager, Rick Gianasi; ***D:*** Tim Kincaid; ***W:*** Tim Kincaid.

Robot in the Family **1994** Slapstick comedy about Alex and his wacky but endearing robot who embark on a race against time through the streets of New York to track down a priceless antique that could save Alex's family from financial ruin. **92m/C VHS.** Joe Pantoliano, John Rhys-Davies, Danny Gerard, Amy Wright, Tom Signorelli, Peter Maloney, John Wylie, David Shuman, Matthew Locricchio; ***D:*** Mark Richardson, Jack Shaoul; ***W:*** Jack Shaoul; ***M:*** Papo Gely, Ted Mason; ***V:*** Don Peoples.

Robot Jox 1/2 **1990 (PG)** Two futuristic warriors battle to the finish in giant mechanical robots. Preteen fare. **84m/C VHS, DVD.** Gary (Rand) Graham, Anne-Marie Johnson, Paul Koslo, Robert Sampson, Danny Kamekona, Hilary Mason, Michael Alldredge; ***D:*** Stuart Gordon; ***W:*** Joe Haldeman; ***C:*** Mac Ahlberg.

Robot Monster 1/2 *Monster from Mars; Monsters from the Moon* **1953** Ludicrous cheapie is widely considered one of the worst films of all time, as a single alien dressed in a moth-eaten gorilla suit and diving helmet conspires to take over the Earth from his station in a small, bubble-filled California cave. Available in original 3-D format. **84m/B VHS, DVD.** George Nader, Claudia Barrett, Gregory Moffett, Selena Royle, John (Jack) Mylong, George Barrows; ***D:*** Phil Tucker; ***W:*** Wyott Ordung; ***C:*** Jack Greenhalgh; ***M:*** Elmer Bernstein; ***V:*** John Brown.

Robot Pilot *Emergency Landing* **1941** Tucker stars as a WWII test pilot trying to promote a friend's invention. Along the way, he's involved in a subplot with enemy agents who steal a bomber. He also finds time to become romantically entangled with the boss' spoiled daughter. **68m/B VHS.** Forrest Tucker, Carol Hughes, Evelyn Brent, Emmett Vogan, William (Bill) Halligan; ***D:*** William Beaudine.

Robot Stories 1/2 **2003** Writer-director Pak's first theatrical venture gazes into the future and imagines the impact that robots and artificial intelligence will have on society via four short stories. Though the central theme is sci-fi, at its core each piece is really an intriguing exploration of timeless human emotions such as grief, death, family, and love. **85m/C DVD.** *US* Tamlyn Tomita, James Saito, Joshua Spafford, Rea Tajiri, Vin Knight, Gina Quintos, Karen Tse Lee, Glen Kubota, Norma Fire, Tanisha Eanes, Catherine Carota, Wai Ching Ho, Cindy Cheung, Louis Ozawa Changchien, Angel Desai, Olivia Oguma, Sab Shimono, Antonio Roman, John Cariani, Greg Pak, Bill Coelius, Tim Kang, Julienne Hanzelka Kim, Vivian Bang, Julie Atlas Muz, Brian Nishii; ***D:*** Greg Pak; ***W:*** Greg Pak; ***C:*** Peter Olsen; ***M:*** Rick Knutsen; ***V:*** Ari Garin.

The Robot vs. the Aztec Mummy **WOOF!** *El Robot Humano; La Momia Azteca Contra el Robot Humano* **1959** Grade-Z Mexican horror film pits a jealous mummy who guards a tomb against tomb robbers and the robot they invent. Special effects are laughable today—the robot's ears are lightbulbs—but true mummy movie fans might want to watch this one. Everyone else will probably be better off skipping it. **65m/B VHS, DVD.** *MX* Ramon Gay, Rosita (Rosa) Arenas, Crox Alvarado, Luis Aceves Cantaneda, Emma Rolden; ***D:*** Rafael Portillo; ***W:*** Alfredo Salazar; ***C:*** Enrique Wallace; ***M:*** Antonio Diaz Conde.

Robot Wars **1993 (PG)** When what seems to be the last mega-robot on earth falls into enemy hands, a renegade pilot unearths another with the help of an engineer and archeologist to fight for the future of mankind. **106m/C VHS.** Don Michael Paul, Barbara Crampton, James Staley, Lisa Rinna, Danny Kamekona, Yuji Okumoto, J. Downing, Peter Haskell; ***D:*** Albert Band.

Robots 1/2 **2005 (PG)** Standing in the shadows of Pixar, the makers of "Ice Age" return with this tale of a small-town robot in the big city. Idealistic Rodney Copperbottom (McGregor) travels to Robot City to present his inventions to Bigweld (Brooks), the beloved president of Bigweld Industries. However, Ratchet (Kinnear) and Madame Gasket (Broadbent) have taken over the company and are forcing old robots to upgrade or perish. Rodney organizes a motley band of rejects, including Williams' predictably schticky Fender, to topple the heartless duo and the outcome is as predictable as it sounds. The CGI work is dazzling (the kitschy character design is the highlight), but the generic story and characters fail to inspire. **91m/C VHS, DVD, UMD.** *US* ***D:*** Chris Wedge; ***W:*** Lowell Ganz, Babaloo Mandel, David Lindsay-Abaire; ***M:*** John Powell; ***V:*** Ewan McGregor, Halle Berry, Robin Williams, Greg Kinnear, Mel Brooks, Drew Carey, Jim Broadbent, Amanda Bynes, Jennifer Coolidge, Stanley Tucci, Dianne Wiest, Paul Giamatti, Natasha Lyonne, Lowell Ganz, Dan Hedaya, Jackie Hoffman, James Earl Jones, Harland Williams, Stephen Tobolowsky, Alan Rosenberg, Jay Leno, Terry Bradshaw, Paula Abdul.

Rocco and His Brothers 1/2 *Rocco et Ses Freres; Rocco E I Suoi Fratelli* **1960** A modern classic from top director Visconti, about four brothers who move with their mother from the Italian countryside to Milan. Very long, sometimes ponderous, but engrossing, complex drama. Available shortened to 90 minutes, but the unedited version is much more rewarding. In Italian with English subtitles. **168m/B VHS, DVD.** *IT* Alain Delon, Renato Salvatori, Annie Girardot, Katina Paxinou, Claudia Cardinale, Roger Hanin, Alessandra Panaro, Spiros Focas, Max Cartier; ***D:*** Luchino Visconti; ***W:*** Luchino Visconti, Suso Cecchi D'Amico, Pasquale Festa Campanile, Enrico Medioli, Massimo Franciosa; ***C:*** Giuseppe Rotunno; ***M:*** Nino Rota.

The Rock **1996 (R)** Cage follows up his Oscar win with a big-budget action hero turn, with great results. In an attempt to get benefits for the families of soldiers killed in various covert operations, a decorated general (Harris) and his commando squad occupy Alcatraz island, taking hostages and threatening to unleash a deadly gas bomb on San Francisco. Biochemical weapons expert Stanley Goodspeed (Cage) is called in to disarm the rockets, aided by John Patrick Mason (Connery), only man to successfully escape from the island prison. Like most Simpson/Bruckheimer productions, credibility is stretched to the limit, but the action scenes and crisp pacing don't leave much time for pondering details, anyway. Connery, cool as ever, hasn't lost a step. Cage effectively plays up his character's inexperience at being the hero. Co-producer Don Simpson died of drug overdose during production. **136m/C VHS, DVD, Blu-ray Disc.** Nicolas Cage, Sean Connery, Ed Harris, Michael Biehn, William Forsythe, David Morse, John Spencer, John C. McGinley, Tony Todd, Bokeem Woodbine, Danny Nucci, Claire Forlani, Vanessa Marcil, Gregory Sporleder, Steve Harris, Jim Maniaci, Brendan Kelly, Todd Louiso, Willie Garson, Stuart Wilson, Anthony Clark, James (Jim) Caviezel, Xander Berkeley, Sam Whipple, Raymond Cruz, David Marshall Grant, Philip Baker Hall; ***D:*** Michael Bay; ***W:*** Jonathan Hensleigh; ***C:*** John Schwartzman; ***M:*** Nick Glennie-Smith. MTV Movie Awards '97: On-Screen Duo (Sean Connery/Nicolas Cage).

Rock-A-Bye Baby 1/2 **1957** Clayton Poole (Lewis) is a big fan of glamorous movie star Carla Naples (Maxwell), a recent widow who gives birth to triplets—a fact she wants kept hush-hush since she's starring as a virgin in a religious epic. So Clayton comes to the rescue by agreeing to be the little bundles' babysitter. And as a job bonus he gets to fall in love with Carla's sweet sister, Sandy (Stevens). A very loose adaptation of the Preston Sturges comedy "The Miracle of Morgan's Creek." **103m/C VHS.** Jerry Lewis, Marilyn Maxwell, Connie Stevens, Salvatore Baccaloni, Reginald Gardiner, Hans Conried, Ida Moore, George Sanders, James Gleason; ***D:*** Frank Tashlin; ***W:*** Frank Tashlin; ***C:*** Haskell Boggs; ***M:*** Walter Scharf.

Rock-a-Doodle 1/2 **1992 (G)** Little Edmond is knocked out during a storm and has an Elvis-influenced vision. He sees Chanticleer, the sun-raising rooster, tricked into neglecting his duties by an evil barnyard owl. Humiliated and scorned, the earnest young fowl leaves the farm and winds up in a Las Vegas-like city as an Elvis-impersonating singer (complete with pompadour) where he meets with success and all its trappings. Mildly amusing, but bland by today's standards of animation, with music which is certainly nothing to crow about. **77m/C VHS, DVD.** ***D:*** Don Bluth; ***W:*** David N. Weiss; ***M:*** Robert Folk; ***V:*** Glen Campbell, Christopher Plummer, Phil Harris, Sandy Duncan, Ellen Greene, Charles Nelson Reilly, Eddie Deezen, Toby Scott Granger, Sorrell Booke.

Rock All Night **1957** Typically trashy Corman quickie (filmed in five days on one set) about some wild '50s teens and, in this case, a couple of murderers. Seems Cloud Nine, the local teen hangout, is invaded by a couple of murderers who hold the kids hostage. It's up to the hipster bartender, known as Shorty because he's five-foot-one, to save the day. Unrelated concert footage of the Platters and the Blockbusters opens the film. **62m/B VHS.** Dick Miller, Abby Dalton, Russell Johnson, Jonathan Haze, Robin Morse, Chris Alcaide, Beach Dickerson, Bruno VeSota, Mel Welles; ***D:*** Roger Corman; ***W:*** Charles B. Griffith; ***C:*** Floyd Crosby.

Rock & Roll Cowboys **1992** Set in the near-future. Mickey LaGrange is a roadie who has dreams of playing his own songs and becoming a rock and roll star himself. When he meets the mysterious Damien Shard he just may get the opportunity and a lot more besides. Shard is the inventor of an instrument that taps directly into the brain to transform thought into music. When Mickey uses the instrument he becomes an instant success—until he notices some horrifying side effects. **83m/C VHS.** Peter Phelps, David Franklin, John (Roy Slaven) Doyle; ***D:*** Robert Stewart.

Rock & Rule **1983** Animated sword & sorcery epic with a rock soundtrack. Voices are provided by Deborah Harry, Cheap Trick, Lou Reed, and Iggy Pop. **85m/C VHS, DVD.** ***D:*** Clive A. Smith; ***M:*** Deborah Harry, Lou Reed, Iggy Pop; ***V:*** Paul LeMat, Susan (Suzan) Roman, Don Francks, Dan Hennessey, Chris Wiggins, Catherine Gallant, Catherine O'Hara.

Rock & the Money-Hungry Party Girls **1989** A struggling musician battles against Gabor-sister-worshipping bimbos in an effort to find unpublished songs by a '50s music legend. **90m/C VHS.** Paul Sercu, Adam Small, Judi Durand, Mary Baldwin, Debra Lamb; ***D:*** Kurt MacCarley.

Rock, Baby, Rock It **1957** Weak and silly rock-and-roll crime drama about teens trying to fight the Mafia in Dallas in 1957. Features performances by many regional bands including Kay Wheeler, the Cell Block Seven, Johnny Carroll, Preacher Smith and the Deacons, and the Five Stars. If you grew up in Dallas in the '50s, the musical groups may bring back some fond memories; otherwise, this obscure film probably isn't worth your time. **84m/B VHS, DVD.** Kay Wheeler, John Carroll; ***D:*** Murray Douglas Sporup.

Rock Haven **2007** A devout Christian, 18-year-old Bradley has just moved with his overprotective mother to the titular coastal town in northern California. Settling in, he's surprised to find himself attracted to athletic neighbor Clifford. But will Bradley's beliefs cause him to turn away from his first romance? Sentimental story that doesn't negate the importance of Bradley's spirituality. **78m/C DVD.** Sean Hoagland, Owen Alabado, Laura Jane Coles, Katheryn Hecht, Erin Daly; ***D:*** David Lewis; ***W:*** David Lewis; ***C:*** Christian Bruno; ***M:*** Jack Curtis Dubowsky.

Rock House **1988 (R)** When an L.A. narcotics officer's wife is murdered by drug runners he goes on an obsessive revenge mission to destroy the city's cocaine operations. **98m/C VHS.** Joseph Jennings, Michael Robbin, Alan Shearer; ***D:*** Jack Vacek; ***W:*** Jack Vacek.

Rock Hudson's Home Movies **1992** Farr re-creates the character of the late actor over numerous film clips used to suggest homoerotic themes in Hudson's movies. Low-budget and high camp. **63m/C VHS, DVD.** Eric Farr; ***D:*** Mark Rappaport; ***W:*** Mark Rappaport.

Rock My World *Global Heresy* **2002 (R)** Amazingly bad would-be comedy finds one-hit American band Global Heresy forced to hire new bassist Nat (Silverstone) when their original player suddenly disappears. The group is headed to a English country mansion to relax and rehearse and it turns out the cash-poor aristocratic owners (O'Toole, Plowright) are secretly posing as the butler and cook. Every culture clash cliche is trotted out. **106m/C VHS, DVD.** *GB CA* Peter O'Toole, Joan Plowright, Alicia Silverstone, Jaimz Woolvett, Lochlyn Munro, Martin Clunes; ***D:*** Sidney J. Furie; ***W:*** Mark Mills; ***C:*** Curtis Petersen.

Rock 'n' Roll High School **1979 (PG)** The music of the Ramones highlights this non-stop high-energy cult classic about a high school out to thwart the principal at every turn. If it had been made in 1957, it would have been the ultimate rock 'n' roll teen movie. As it is, its 1970s' milieu works against it, but the performances are perfect for the material and the Ramones are great. Songs include "Teenage Lobotomy," "Blitzkrieg Bop," "I Wanna Be Sedated," and the title track, among others. Followed less successfully by "Rock 'n' Roll High School Forever." ♫Teenage Lobotomy; Blitzkrieg Bop; I Wanna Be Sedated; Rock and Roll High School. **94m/C VHS, DVD, UMD.** P.J. Soles, Vincent Van Patten, Clint Howard, Dey Young, Mary Woronov, Alix Elias, Dick Miller, Paul Bartel, Don Steele, Dee Dee Ramone, Joey Ramone, Johnny Ramone, Marky Ramone; ***D:*** Allan Arkush; ***W:*** Joe Dante, Russ Dvonch, Joseph McBride, Richard Whitley; ***C:*** Dean Cundey; ***M:*** The Ramones.

Rock 'n' Roll High School Forever **1991 (PG-13)** Jesse Davis and his band just want to rock 'n' roll, but the new principal doesn't share their enthusiasm. Way late, way lame sequel to "Rock 'n' Roll High School" doesn't come close to the originality that made it a cult classic. Soundtrack includes music from The Divinyls, Dee Dee Ramone, Mojo Nixon, Will and the Bushmen, The Pursuit of Happiness, and more. **94m/C VHS, DVD.** Corey Feldman, Mary Woronov, Mojo Nixon, Evan Richards, Michael Ceveris, Patrick Malone, Larry Linville, Sarah Buxton, Liane (Alexandra) Curtis, Lewis Arquette, Jason Lively; ***D:*** Deborah Brock; ***W:*** Deborah Brock; ***C:*** James Mathers.

Rock 'n' Roll Nightmare 1/2 *The Edge of Hell* **1985 (R)** A rock band is pursued by demons from another dimension. The usual lame garbage. **89m/C VHS, DVD.** *CA* Jon Mikl Thor, Paula Francescatto, Rusty Hamilton, Jillian Peri, Frank Dietz, David Lane, Teresa Simpson, Liane Abel, Nancy Bush; ***D:*** John Fasano; ***W:*** Jon Mikl Thor; ***C:*** Mark MacKay.

Rock, Pretty Baby **1956** Early rock-'n'-roll movie about a teenage band and high school riots. **89m/B VHS.** Sal Mineo, John Saxon, Rod McKuen, Luana Patten, Fay Wray, Edward Platt, Alan Reed Jr.; ***D:*** Richard Bartlett; ***M:*** Henry Mancini.

Rock River Renegades **1942** The Range Busters capture a band of renegades and restore peace to the territory once more. **59m/B VHS, DVD.** Ray Corrigan, John "Dusty" King, Max Terhune, Christine McIntyre, John Elliott, Weldon Heyburn, Kermit Maynard, Frank Ellis; ***D:*** S. Roy Luby; ***W:*** Earle Snell, John Vlahos; ***C:*** Robert E. Cline.

Rock, Rock, Rock 1/2 **1956** A young girl tries to earn enough money for a prom gown after her father closes her charge account. Screen debut of Tuesday Weld. Ultra-low-budget, but a classic after a fashion. Includes classic musical numbers performed by Chuck Berry and other rock 'n' roll pioneers. **78m/B VHS, DVD.** Alan Freed, Chuck Berry, Fats Domino, Tuesday Weld; ***D:*** Will Price.

Rock School **2005 (R)** Director Argott's dynamic documentary lays bare the life of offbeat and intense music teacher Paul Green and his School of Rock Music, an after-school program in Philadelphia for highly-skilled nine to 17-year-olds. Flipping between cursing and berating his pupils to chumming around with them, Green prepares his most gifted group for an inspired appearance at the annual Zappanale festival in Germany (a tribute to the late rocker Frank Zappa). Green is often thought to be the basis for Jack Black's comedy "School of Rock," though its creators have refuted the claim. **93m/C DVD.** ***D:*** Don Argott; ***C:*** Don Argott.

Rock Star **2001 (R)** Not a number one hit, but thanks to Mark Wahlberg, at least you won't choke on your own vomit. Working class Chris (Wahlberg) spends his off hours as the lead singer in Blood Pollution, a "tribute band" (don't call them a cover band!) to heavy metal demigods Steel Dragon. He gets a little too obsessive in the worship of his heroes, alienates the rest of the band, and is finally replaced for telling guitarist Rob (Olyphant) how to play. In a fantastical twist (and a none-too-subtle reference to real-life rockers Judas Priest), the musicians in Steel Dragon fire their secretly gay lead singer

Bobby Beers (Flemyng) and recruit the amazed Chris to replace him. Real rock musicians and former rock star wives are scattered throughout the cast, but they don't add any glam to a rather bland depiction of a raunchy time period. **106m/C VHS, DVD.** *US* Mark Wahlberg, Jennifer Aniston, Timothy Olyphant, Timothy Spall, Jason Flemyng, Dominic West, Matthew Glave, Beth Grant, Stephan Jenkins, Jason Bonham, Heidi Mark, Michael Shamus Wiles, Dagmara Dominczyk, Rachel Hunter, Colleen (Ann) Fitzpatrick; ***D:*** Stephen Herek; ***W:*** John Stockwell; ***C:*** Ueli Steiger; ***M:*** Trevor Rabin.

Rock the Paint 1/2 **2005 (R)** High school sports pic would work better if co-star Smith wasn't such a blank onscreen. Josh Sendler (Smith) is a white star basketball player from rural Indiana who must move to Newark, New Jersey, with his loud-mouthed younger brother Tim (Stone) when their widowed dad (Innvar) gets a new job. Josh gets some hard lessons learning to deal with his black teammates, despite the help of Antwon (Phillips), amidst the city's overall racial tensions. The team has a shot at the state championship but things go south during the big game when Josh loses his cool and blurts out exactly the wrong thing. **90m/C DVD.** Douglas Smith, Kevin Phillips, John Doman, Christopher Innvar, Sam Oz Stone, Jas Anderson, Tom Brennan; ***D:*** Phil Bertelsen; ***W:*** Dallas Brennan; ***C:*** John Foster; ***M:*** Wyclef Jean. **VIDEO**

Rockabye 1/2 **1986** Single mother Bertinelli is visiting New York with her two-year-old son when she's attacked and her child stolen. In her search for the boy, she discovers a black market in baby selling. **100m/C VHS.** Valerie Bertinelli, Rachel Ticotin, Jason Alexander, Ray Baker, Dick Latessa, James Rebhorn, Lynne Thigpen; ***D:*** Richard Michaels. **TV**

The Rocker **2008 (PG-13)** Aging, bitter, unemployed former rocker Robert "Fish" Fishman (Wilson) gets roped into a drumming gig with his teenage nephew's rock band (aptly named A.D.D.). Fish schools the adolescents in all things rock and A.D.D. gains notoriety, eventually landing an opening gig for Fish's former band, Vesuvius, as headliner. Fish needs to grow up in order to impress A.D.D. bandmate Curtis' (Geiger) hot single mom (Applegate) and outdo Vesuvius. Unapologetically retro and definitely reminiscent of "School of Rock," with the requisite immature gags you'd expect, but plenty fun nonetheless. Hader steals the movie as a slimy manager. Bonus: Dumped Beatles drummer Peter Best cameos. **102m/C DVD.** *US* Rainn Wilson, Christina Applegate, Josh Gad, Emma Stone, Teddy Geiger, Jane Lynch, Jeff Garlin, Jason Sudeikis, Howard Hesseman, Will Arnett, Bradley Cooper, Fred Armisen, Lonny Ross, Jane Krakowski; ***D:*** Peter Cattaneo; ***W:*** Maya Forbes, M. Wallace Wolodarsky; ***C:*** Anthony B. Richmond; ***M:*** Chad Fischer.

The Rocket *Maurice Richard* **2005 (PG)** Inspiring biopic of hockey legend Maurice "The Rocket" Richard (perfectly portrayed by Dupuis), who, in the 1940s and 50s, rises from the Quebec working-class to stardom with the Montreal Canadiens and winner of multiple Stanley Cups. Although his speed and skill make him popular with the fans, Richard has to battle prejudice against French-speaking players from the controlling, Anglo hockey establishment. Injuries lead to constant trade talk and Richard also isn't afraid to push for much-needed NHL reforms, which doesn't endear him to the suits. English and French with subtitles. **124m/C DVD.** *CA* Roy Dupuis, Stephen McHattie, Charles Biname, Ken Scott, Patrice Robitaille, Julie Le Breton, Francois Langlois Vallieres, Ian Laperriere, Vincent Lecavalier, Serge Roude, Ted Dillon; ***C:*** Pierre Gill; ***M:*** Michel Cusson.

Rocket Attack U.S.A. **WOOF! 1958** Antiquated and ridiculous tale of nuclear warfare about the time of Sputnik, with Russia's first strike blowing up New York City and environs. Mercifully short, with time for a little romance. Everything about this movie is so bad it's good for a laugh. **70m/B VHS.** Monica Davis, John MacKay, Dan Kern, Edward Czerniuk, Art Metrano; ***D:*** Barry Mahon.

Rocket Gibraltar **1988 (PG)** On the occasion of a crusty patriarch's birthday, a large family unites on his remote estate to carry out his special birthday wish. Fine performance by Lancaster. Supported by a solid cast, overcomes a slim story, Culkin, later of "Home Alone," is loveable as the precocious five-year-old. Picturesque Long Island scenery. **92m/C VHS, DVD.** Burt Lancaster, Bill Pullman, John Glover, Suzy Amis, Macaulay Culkin, Patricia Clarkson, Frances Conroy, Sinead Cusack, Bill Martin, Kevin Spacey; ***D:*** Daniel Petrie; ***W:*** Amos Poe; ***M:*** Andrew Powell.

Rocket Science **2007 (R)** Hal (Thompson) is having a tough time: his dad (O'Hare) has just walked out on his family, his brother Earl (Piazza) is a domineering bully, and his stutter is so intense that it gets him mocked at school. Along comes ambitious Ginny (Kendrick), who recruits him for the debate club. Hal slowly falls for Ginny, all the time unsure if she likes him or if she's just using him. Sweet and quirky meditation on first love and teenage awkwardness provides plenty of laughs, but director Blitz has a genuine sense of feeling for the characters as well in his first feature film; he previously directed the spelling bee documentary "Spellbound." **98m/C DVD.** *US* Reece Thompson, Anna Kendrick, Margo Martindale, Nicholas D'Agosto, Vincent Piazza; ***D:*** Jeffrey Blitz; ***W:*** Jeffrey Blitz; ***C:*** Jo Willems; ***M:*** Eef Barzelay.

Rocket to the Moon **1986** An adaptation of the Clifford Odets story about the mundane life of a 30-year-old Manhattan dentist and how he comes to terms with his life. From the PBS "American Playhouse" series. **118m/C VHS.** Judy Davis, John Malkovich, Eli Wallach; ***D:*** John Jacobs.

The Rocketeer **1991 (PG)** Light-headed fun. A stunt flyer in the 1930s finds a prototype jet backpack sought by Nazi spies. Donning a mask, he becomes a flying super-hero. Breezy family entertainment with stupendous effects; even better if you know movie trivia, as it brims with Hollywood references, like a great villain (Dalton) clearly based on Errol Flynn. **109m/C VHS, DVD.** Billy Campbell, Jennifer Connelly, Alan Arkin, Timothy Dalton, Paul Sorvino, Melora Hardin, Tiny Ron, Terry O'Quinn, Ed Lauter, James Handy; ***D:*** Joe Johnston; ***W:*** Paul DeMeo, Danny Bilson; ***C:*** Hiro Narita; ***M:*** James Horner.

RocketMan 1/2 *Rocket Man* **1997 (PG)** Houston, we have a gastrointestinal problem. Well, dumb astronaut Fred Z. Randall (Williams) does, anyway. The bumbling computer geek is picked to go on the first manned mission to Mars, much to the dismay of crew commander "Wild Bill" Overbeck (Sadler) and specialist Julie Ford (Lundy). Beau Bridges plays Bud Nesbitt, the veteran astronaut back at NASA headquarters who is Randall's only supporter. While too much of the humor revolves around flatulence, Williams shows some talent while raiding the Disney archive for impressions. Remember, in space no one can hear you...pull my finger. **93m/C VHS, DVD.** Harland Williams, Jessica Lundy, Beau Bridges, William Sadler, Jeffrey DeMunn, James Pickens Jr., Peter Onorati; ***D:*** Stuart Gillard; ***W:*** Craig Mazin, Greg Erb; ***C:*** Steven Poster; ***M:*** Michael Tavera.

Rocketship *Flash Gordon: Rocketship* **1936** Flash Gordon battles sea monsters, ray guns, and robots in this sci-fi adventure, which is an edited version of a Flash serial. **97m/B VHS, DVD.** Buster Crabbe, Jean Rogers, Charles Middleton; ***D:*** Frederick Stephani; ***W:*** Frederick Stephani; ***C:*** Jerome Ash; ***M:*** Clifford Vaughan.

Rocketship X-M 1/2 *Expedition Moon* **1950** A lunar mission goes awry and the crew lands on Mars, where they discover ancient ruins. Well acted and nicely photographed. Contains footage, a tinted sequence and previews of coming attractions from classis science fiction files. **77m/B VHS, DVD.** Lloyd Bridges, Osa Massen, John Emery, Hugh O'Brian, Noah Beery Jr.; ***D:*** Kurt Neumann; ***W:*** Kurt Neumann, Dalton Trumbo; ***C:*** Karl Struss; ***M:*** Ferde Grofe Jr.

Rockin' Road Trip **1985 (PG-13)** A guy meets a girl in a Boston bar, and finds himself on a drunken, slapstick road trip down the Eastern seaboard with a rock band. **101m/C VHS.** Garth McLean, Katherine Harrison, Margeret Currie, Steve Boles; ***D:*** William Olsen; ***W:*** William Olsen; ***C:*** Austin McKinney; ***M:*** Ricky Keller.

The Rocking Horse Winner 1/2 **1949** Poignant tale of a young boy who discovers he can predict racehorse winners by riding his rocking horse. His spendthrift mother's greed leads to tragedy. Based on the short story by D.H. Lawrence. **91m/B VHS, DVD.** *GB* John (Howard) Davies, Valerie Hobson, Hugh Sinclair; ***D:*** Anthony Pelissier.

RocknRolla 1/2 **2008 (R)** Ritchie's usual fast-talking, overly complicated methods are again at work when the London and Russian criminal underworlds go to war with each other over $350 million in real estate that has slipped through the fingers of a major corporation. Motley crews of eclectic gangsters are all out to cheat one another, along with sexy accountant Stella (Newton), who swoops in to turn the con around. And just when things begin to click, drugged-out rock 'n' roller, known simply as Rocker (Bower), enters to mess with everyone. Not as gung-ho and innovative as "Lock, Stock, and Two Smoking Barrels," but still never lets up. **114m/C DVD.** *US* Gerard Butler, Tom Wilkinson, Thandie Newton, Mark Strong, Idris Elba, Thomas (Tom) Hardy, Karel Roden, Toby Kebbell, Jeremy Piven, Chris Bridges, Jimi Mistry; ***D:*** Guy Ritchie; ***W:*** Guy Ritchie; ***C:*** David Higgs; ***M:*** Steve Isles.

Rocktober Blood 1/2 **1985 (R)** A convicted and executed rock star comes back from the grave and starts killing people all over again. Yet another gorefest. **88m/C VHS.** Donna Scoggins, Tray Loren, Nigel Benjamin, Beverly Sebastian; ***D:*** Ferd Sebastian.

Rockula 1/2 **1990 (PG-13)** Teen rock comedy about a young-yet-300-year-old vampire looking to lose his virginity. Recommended only for hard-core Diddley fans. **90m/C VHS.** Dean Cameron, Bo Diddley, Tawny (Ellis) Fere, Susan Tyrrell, Thomas Dolby, Toni Basil; ***D:*** Luca Bercovici; ***W:*** Luca Bercovici.

Rockwell: A Legend of the Wild West 1/2 **1993** Black heroics in the wild west. U.S. Marshall Porter Rockwell and his posse of sharp shooters are after a vicious gang murdering supposed claim jumpers who just happen to be Rockwell's friends. **105m/C VHS, DVD.** Randy Gleave, Karl Malone, Michael Rudd, George Sullivan; ***D:*** Richard Lloyd Dewey; ***W:*** Richard Lloyd Dewey.

Rocky 1/2 **1976 (PG)** Boxoffice smash about a young man from the slums of Philadelphia who dreams of becoming a boxing champion. Stallone plays Rocky, the underdog hoping to win fame and self-respect. Rags-to-riches story seems to parallel Stallone's life; he had been previously virtually unknown before this movie. Intense portrayal of the American Dream; loses strength in the subsequent (and numerous) sequels. **125m/C VHS, DVD, Blu-ray Disc.** Sylvester Stallone, Talia Shire, Burgess Meredith, Burt Young, Carl Weathers, Pedro Lovell, Joe Spinell, Thayer David, Tony Burton, Michael Dorn; ***D:*** John G. Avildsen; ***W:*** Sylvester Stallone; ***C:*** James A. Crabe; ***M:*** Bill Conti. Oscars '76: Director (Avildsen), Film Editing, Picture; AFI '98: Top 100; Directors Guild '76: Director (Avildsen); Golden Globes '77: Film—Drama; L.A. Film Critics '76: Film; Natl. Bd. of Review '76: Support. Actress (Shire), Natl. Film Reg. '06;; N.Y. Film Critics '76: Support. Actress (Shire).

Rocky 2 **1979 (PG)** Time-marking sequel to the boxoffice smash finds Rocky frustrated by the commercialism that followed his match to Apollo, but considering a return bout. Meanwhile, his wife fights for her life. The overall effect is to prepare you for the next sequel. **119m/C VHS, DVD.** Sylvester Stallone, Talia Shire, Burt Young, Burgess Meredith, Carl Weathers; ***D:*** Sylvester Stallone; ***W:*** Sylvester Stallone; ***C:*** Bill Butler; ***M:*** Bill Conti.

Rocky 3 1/2 **1982 (PG)** Rocky is beaten by big, mean Clubber Lang (played to a tee by Mr. T). He realizes success has made him soft, and has to dig deep to find the motivation to stay on top. Amazingly, Stallone regains his underdog persona here, looking puny next to Mr. T, who is the best thing about the second-best "Rocky" flick. **103m/C VHS, DVD.** Sylvester Stallone, Talia Shire, Burgess Meredith, Carl Weathers, Mr. T, Leif Erickson, Burt Young; ***D:*** Sylvester Stallone; ***W:*** Sylvester Stallone; ***C:*** Bill Butler; ***M:*** Bill Conti.

Rocky 4 1/2 **1985 (PG)** Rocky travels to Russia to fight the Soviet champ who killed his friend during a bout. Will Rocky knock the Russkie out? Will Rocky get hammered on the head a great many times and sag around the ring? Will Rocky ever learn? Lundgren isn't nearly as much fun as some of Rocky's former opponents and Stallone overdoes the hyper-patriotism and relies too heavily on uplifting footage from earlier "Rocky" movies. **91m/C VHS, DVD.** Sylvester Stallone, Talia Shire, Dolph Lundgren, Brigitte Nielsen, Michael Pataki, Burt Young, Carl Weathers; ***D:*** Sylvester Stallone; ***W:*** Sylvester Stallone; ***C:*** Bill Butler; ***M:*** Bill Conti, Vince DiCola. Golden Raspberries '85: Worst Actor (Stallone), Worst Support. Actress (Nielsen), Worst Director (Stallone), Worst Screenplay, Worst New Star (Nielsen).

Rocky 5 **1990 (PG)** Brain damaged and broke, Rocky finds himself back where he started on the streets of Philadelphia. Boxing still very much in his blood, Rocky takes in a protege, training him in the style that made him a champ (take a lickin' and keep on tickin'). However an unscrupulous promoter has designs on the young fighter and seeks to wrest the lad from under the former champ's wing. This eventually leads to a showdown between Rocky and the young boxer in a brutal streetfight. Supposedly the last "Rocky" film, it's clear the formula has run dry. **105m/C VHS, DVD.** Sylvester Stallone, Talia Shire, Burt Young, Sage Stallone, Tom Morrison, Burgess Meredith; ***D:*** John G. Avildsen; ***W:*** Sylvester Stallone; ***C:*** Steven Poster; ***M:*** Bill Conti.

Rocky Balboa 1/2 **2006 (PG)** The Italian Stallion finds himself put out to pasture after the demise of his boxing glory days and the death of his wife (whose name graces the restaurant he now runs)—until a computer simulation predicts that the 50-something former champ would beat the current heavyweight title holder, Mason "The Line" Dixon (Tarver). The new bout stirs up all that was good about the olden days—the music, the punching bag, and those infamous museum steps. But what about Rocky's previous brain damage? Why is Rocky Jr. (Ventimiglia) so whiny? Are those muscles or implants? None of it seems to matter in this somewhat cheer-worthy effort that doesn't embarrass the franchise as much as the previous outing did. **101m/C DVD, Blu-ray Disc.** *US* Sylvester Stallone, Burt Young, Milo Ventimiglia, Tony Burton, Antonio Tarver, Geraldine Hughes, A.J. Benza, James Francis Kelly III, Henry Sanders, Lahmard Tate, Pedro Lovell, Ana Gerena; ***D:*** Sylvester Stallone; ***W:*** Sylvester Stallone; ***C:*** Clark Mathis; ***M:*** Bill Conti.

The Rocky Horror Picture Show **1975 (R)** When a young couple take refuge in a haunted castle, they find themselves the unwilling pawns in a warped scientist's experiment. Cult camp classic has been a midnight movie favorite for years and has developed an entire subculture built around audience participation. Includes a seven-minute short detailing the story behind the movie's popularity. May not be as much fun watching it on the little screen unless you bring the rice and squirt guns. ♫The Time Warp; Science Fiction Double Feature; Wedding Song; Sweet Transvestite; The Sword of Damocles; Charles Atlas Song; Whatever Happened to Saturday Night; Touch-a Touch-a Touch-a Touch Me; Eddie's Teddy. **105m/C VHS, DVD.** *GB* Tim Curry, Susan Sarandon, Barry Bostwick, Nell Campbell, Richard O'Brien, Patricia Quinn, Jonathan Adams, Peter Hinwood, Meat Loaf Aday, Charles Gray, Koo Stark; ***D:*** Jim Sharman; ***W:*** Jim Sharman, Richard O'Brien; ***C:*** Peter Suschitzky; ***M:*** Richard Hartley, Richard O'Brien. Natl. Film Reg. '05.

Rocky Jones, Space Ranger: Renegade Satellite 1/2 **1954** Nostalgia freaks may embrace this revived edition of the infamous early live-TV space cadet show. Rocky squares off against enemies of the United Solar System like Dr. Reno and Rudy DeMarco. Really cheap. **69m/B VHS.** Richard Crane, Sally Mansfield, Maurice Cass; ***D:*** Hollingsworth Morse; ***W:*** Warren Wilson; ***C:*** Ernest Miller; ***M:*** Alexander Laszlo.

Rocky Marciano 1/2 **1999 (R)** Boxing biopic about the up-from-poverty Rocky (Favreau) who, as heavyweight champ, had 43 knockouts and who retired in 1956 undefeated. (He was killed in a 1969 plane crash.) Marciano has the usual tribulations—greedy managers and overly interested mobsters—and a climatic bout with his childhood hero, an aging Joe Louis (Davis). LoBianco, who plays a mobster, starred as Marciano in the 1979 TV movie, "Marciano." **90m/C VHS.** Jon Favreau, Judd Hirsch, Penelope Ann Miller, George C. Scott, Tony LoBianco, Duane Davis, Rhoda Gemignani, Rino Romano; ***D:*** Charles Winkler; ***W:*** Charles Winkler, Larry Golin; ***C:*** Paul Sarossy; ***M:*** Stanley Clarke. **CABLE**

Rocky Mountain **1950** The hard-living Flynn was looking mighty weather-beaten by the time he filmed this, his last western, although it suited the part of Lafe Barstow, a Confederate officer who's seen too much. Barstow and some of his men are sent to California to contact southern sympathizers in hopes that the territory can still be claimed for the south. The soldiers come to the aid of a stagecoach besieged by Indians and Barstow is taken with pretty passenger Johanna (Wymore). But his interest doesn't stop him from using her as bait when he learns her fiance is a Union Army commander. Flynn also fell in love with the much-younger Wymore off screen and she became Mrs. Flynn (no. 3) the same year. **83m/B DVD.** Errol Flynn, Patrice Wymore, Scott Forbes, Guinn "Big Boy" Williams, Slim Pickens, Dick(ie) Jones, Chubby Johnson, Howard Petrie; ***D:*** William Keighley; ***W:*** Winston Miller, Alan LeMay; ***C:*** Ted D. McCord; ***M:*** Max Steiner.

Rocky Mountain Rangers **1940** The Three Mesquiteers do what they do best: save a town from bad guys. **58m/B VHS.** Robert "Bob" Livingston, Raymond Hatton, Duncan Renaldo, Leroy Mason, Dennis Moore, John St. Polis; ***D:*** George Sherman.

Rodan *Radon; Radon the Flying Monster* **1956** A gigantic prehistoric bird is disturbed from his slumber by H-bomb tests. He awakens to wreak havoc on civilization. Big bugs also run amok. From the director of "Godzilla" and a host of other nuclear monster movies. **74m/C VHS, DVD.** *JP* Kenji Sahara, Yumi Shirakawa; ***D:*** Inoshiro Honda.

Rodeo Girl **1/2 1980** Ross is a restless housewife who joins the rodeo in this drama based on the life of cowgirl Sue Pirtle. Particularly strong supporting cast of Hopkins, Clark, and Brimley. **100m/C VHS, DVD.** Katharine Ross, Bo Hopkins, Candy Clark, Jacqueline Brookes, Wilford Brimley, Parley Baer; ***D:*** Jackie Cooper. **TV**

Rodeo King and the Senorita **1951** Rex and his horse Koko are hired on to a Wild West show, which DiSimone is struggling to run after the death of her dad. Her situation is more difficult because of a series of accidents that Rex doesn't think are so accidental. Remake of the 1946 Roy Rogers/Trigger movie "My Pal Trigger." **67m/B VHS.** Rex Allen, Buddy Ebsen, Roy Barcroft, Bonnie DeSimone, Mary Ellen Kay, Tristram Coffin; ***D:*** Philip Ford; ***W:*** John K. Butler; ***C:*** Walter Strenge.

Rodeo Rhythm **1942** Scott's last starring role as a singing cowboy is a cheap and terrible grade-Z western slightly redeemed by the riding talents of Roy Knapp's Juvenile Rough Riders. Buck (Scott) tries to prevent mortgage-holding Twitchell (Frank) from foreclosing on his sister Tillie's (Bridge) orphanage, while the kids put on a rodeo to raise money. **72m/B DVD.** Fred Scott, Loie Bridge, Patricia Redpath, John Frank, Pat Dunn; ***D:*** Fred Newmeyer; ***W:*** Eugene Allen, Gene Tuttle; ***C:*** Edward Kull.

Rodgers & Hammerstein's South Pacific **1/2** *South Pacific* **2001** Close may be a little mature to be cockeyed optimist and smalltown nurse Nellie Forbush but she gives it her all (and served as one of the exective producers) in this TV remake of the Rodgers and Hammerstein musical. Filmed in Australia and Tahiti, the scenery, music, and capable cast (who can sing just fine), all contribute. Of course, Connick Jr. (as romantic Lt. Cable) has an advantage in the vocal area but Serbedzija's plantation owner Emile de Becque has charisma to spare. **135m/C VHS, DVD.** Glenn Close, Rade Serbedzija, Harry Connick Jr., Robert Pastorelli, Jack Thompson, Ilene Graff, Lori Tan Chinn, Natalie Mendoza, Simon Burke, Steve Le Marquand, Steve Bastoni, Damon Herriman; ***D:*** Richard Pearce; ***W:*** Lawrence D. Cohen; ***C:*** Stephen Windon; ***M:*** Richard Rodgers. **TV**

Rodrigo D.: No Future **1991** Gritty, realistic portrayal of the youth-killing culture of Medellin, Columbia. Minimal plot involves a young drummer and his drug-running friends. The actors used are actual untrained street kids, several of whom died after the film's completion. In Spanish with English subtitles. **92m/C VHS, DVD.** Ramiro Meneses, Carlos Mario Resrepo; ***D:*** Victor Gaviria.

Roe vs. Wade **1989** Hunter is excellent as the single woman from Texas who successfully challenged the nation's prohibitive abortion laws in a landmark Supreme Court case. Based on the actual 1973 case of Norma McCorvey. **92m/C VHS.** Holly Hunter, Amy Madigan, Terry O'Quinn, Stephen Tobolowsky, Dion Anderson, Kathy Bates, James Gammon, Chris Mulkey; ***D:*** Gregory Hoblit. **TV**

Roger & Me **1/2 1989 (R)** Hilarious, controversial and atypical semi-documentary details Moore's protracted efforts to meet General Motors president Roger Smith and confront him with the poverty and despair afflicting Flint, Michigan, after GM closed its plants there. Includes some emotionally grabbing scenes: a Flint family is evicted just before Christmas; a woman makes a living by selling rabbits for food or pets; and a then soon-to-be Miss America addresses the socioeconomic impact of GM's decision. One of the highest-grossing non-fiction films ever released, and Moore's first. **91m/C VHS, DVD.** Michael Moore, Anita Bryant, Bob Eubanks, Pat Boone; ***D:*** Michael Moore; ***W:*** Michael Moore; ***C:*** Kevin Rafferty, Chris Beaver, John Prusak, Bruce Schermer.

Roger Dodger **2002 (R)** Roger (Scott) is a slightly sleazy ad copywriter who believes he can talk his way into or out of anything, especially when it comes to women. After he's dumped by boss/girlfriend Joyce (Rossellini), however, he realizes that in his attempt to con everyone else, he has cheated himself. While his relationship with Joyce is turning unsavory, his nephew Nick (Eisenberg) arrives unannounced and eager to learn the art of picking up women. Roger tutors Nick in his cynical methods, but the hotties respond more positively to Nick's innocence and honesty than to Roger's bag of tricks. Scott's performance adds a touch of warmth and compassion to a character who could have been totally odious. **104m/C VHS, DVD.** *US* Campbell Scott, Jesse Eisenberg, Isabella Rossellini, Elizabeth Berkley, Jennifer Beals, Ben Shenkman, Mina (Badiyi) Badie, Chris Stack, Colin Fickes; ***D:*** Dylan Kidd; ***W:*** Dylan Kidd; ***C:*** Joaquin Baca-Asay; ***M:*** Craig (Shudder to Think) Wedren. Natl. Bd. of Review '02: Actor (Scott), Actor (Scott); N.Y. Film Critics '02: First Feature.

RoGoPaG **1962** Four episodic films by four European masters (the title refers to their last names), satirizing the human condition. Rossellini's "Virginity" finds an airline stewardess (Schiaffino) fending off an amorous passenger (Balabin). Godard's "The New World" features a post-nuclear Paris and its effect on romance. "La Ricotta" is Pasolini's controversial take on religion with Welles as the director of a religious epic. Gregoretti's "The Range Grown Chicken" finds Tognazzi the frazzled head of a family beset by consumerism. A mixed bag with Pasolini and Godard offering the most disturbing essays. **122m/B VHS.** *IT* Orson Welles, Ugo Tognazzi, Rosanna Schiaffino, Alexandra Stewart, Jean-Mark Bory, Renato Salvatori, Lisa Gastoni, Bruce Balabin; ***D:*** Roberto Rossellini, Jean-Luc Godard, Pier Paolo Pasolini, Ugo Gregoretti; ***W:*** Roberto Rossellini, Jean-Luc Godard, Pier Paolo Pasolini, Ugo Gregoretti; ***M:*** Carlo Ristichelli.

Rogue **1976 (R)** The Rogue is a ruthless man who can make beautiful women do anything that he desires; so, of course, he does. **87m/C VHS.** Milan Galvonic, Barbara Bouchet, Margaret Lee; ***D:*** Gregory Simpson.

Rogue **1/2 2007 (R)** Competent Aussie horror about a killer croc. American travel writer Pete McKell (Vartan) heads to the Northern Territory and joins a river cruise run by Kate Ryan (Mitchell) along with various disposable passengers. The unseen croc rams the vessel, leaving everyone stranded on a tiny river island that's disappearing under a rising tide with the beast just waiting to pick them off. **92m/C DVD.** *AU US* Michael Vartan, Radha Mitchell, Sam Worthington, Stephen Curry, John Jarratt, Heather Mitchell, Geoff Morrell, Mia Wasikowska; ***D:*** Greg Mclean; ***W:*** Greg Mclean; ***C:*** William Gibson; ***M:*** Francois Tetaz.

Rogue Force **1/2 1999 (R)** A renegade SWAT commander (Patrick) leads a vigilante group of ex-police officers in assassinating a number of mobsters. The murders are being investigating by federal agent Rooker and homicide detective DiLascio, who have no idea where their assignment is leading them. Predictable but delivers the action required of the genre. **90m/C VHS, DVD.** Robert Patrick, Michael Rooker, Louis Mandylor, Diane DiLascio; ***D:*** Martin Klinert. **VIDEO**

Rogue Male **1/2 1976** TV movie finds '30s British aristocrat O'Toole plotting to assassinate Hitler. When his plan fails, he's on the run from both the Gestapo and the British police. Based on the novel by Geoffrey Household. **100m/C VHS, DVD.** *GB* Peter O'Toole, Alastair Sim, John Standing, Cyd Hayman; ***D:*** Clive Donner; ***W:*** Frederic Raphael.

Rogue of the Range **1936** A lawman pretends that he is a bandit in order to track down an outlaw gang. **60m/B VHS, DVD.** Lois January, Alden Chase, Phyllis Hume, George Ball, Johnny Mack Brown; ***D:*** S. Roy Luby; ***W:*** Earle Snell; ***C:*** Jack Greenhalgh.

Rogue of the Rio Grande **1/2 1930** Musical western in which the renowned bandit El Malo arrives in the peace-loving town of Sierra Blanca. One of Loy's earlier films. ♫ Argentine Moon; Carmita; Song of the Bandoleros. **60m/B VHS.** Myrna Loy, Jose Bohr, Raymond Hatton, Carmelita Geraghty, Walter Miller, Florence Dudley, Gene Morgan, William P. Burt; ***D:*** Spencer Gordon Bennet; ***W:*** Oliver Drake.

Rogue Trader **1998 (R)** Unremarkable recreation of the true story of futures trader Nick Leeson (McGregor), who singlehandedly brought down the Barings Merchant Bank in 1995. Working the floor of the Singapore International Money Exchange, Leeson quickly realizes he's completely out of his depth but can't admit it, so he hides his losses and continues to gamble until the deficit adds up to a $1 billion. Based on the book by Nicholas Leeson and Edward Whitley. The real Leeson was paroled from a Singapore jail in 1999. **101m/C VHS, DVD.** *GB* Ewan McGregor, John Standing, Anna Friel, Yves Beneyton, Tim (McInnerny) McInnery, Betsy Brantley, Caroline Langrishe; ***D:*** James Dearden; ***W:*** James Dearden; ***C:*** Jean-Francois Robin; ***M:*** Richard Hartley.

Rogue's Gallery **1944** A reporter and photographer covering the story of an inventor and his latest device are caught up in intrigue when he is found murdered. **60m/B VHS, DVD.** Frank Jenks, Robin Raymond, H.B. Warner, Ray Walker, Davison Clark, Robert E. Homans, Frank McGlynn, Pat Gleason, Edward (Ed Kean, Keene) Keane; ***D:*** Al(bert) Herman.

Rogue's Tavern **1936** In this grade B curio, a blood-thirsty killer stalks the occupants of a country inn, bodies are found with their throats crushed, and a psycho psychic is on the loose. Surprise ending. **70m/B VHS, DVD.** Wallace Ford, Joan Woodbury, Clara Kimball Young, Barbara Pepper, Jack Mulhall, John Elliott; ***D:*** Robert F. "Bob" Hill.

Rogue's Yarn **1956** An investigator probes the death of a woman, ostensibly the result of a boating accident. Gradually he uncovers a plot involving the woman's husband and his mistress in this semi-entertaining British mystery. **80m/B VHS.** *GB* Nicole Maurey, Derek Bond, Elwyn Brook-Jones, Hugh Latimer; ***D:*** Vernon Sewell.

Roland the Mighty **1/2 1956** Muscular, Herculeanesque hero takes on all comers in this sword and sandal epic set in the Asian steppes. **98m/C VHS.** *IT* Rick (Rik) Battaglia, Rosanna Schiaffino, Ivo Garrani, Fabrizio Mioni; ***D:*** Pietro Francisci; ***W:*** Ennio de Concini; ***C:*** Mario Bava; ***M:*** Angelo Francesco Lavagnino.

Role Models **2008 (R)** Danny (Rudd) and Wheeler (Scott) choose community service over jail time following an incident involving the truck they drive while working as sales representatives for a super-caffeinated beverage called Minotaur. Their lives are pathetic enough, but when Danny's girlfriend Beth (Banks) ditches him he goes on a Minotaur-fueled rage landing him and Wheeler in the "Sturdy Wings" program as reluctant role models to at-risk kids. The program matches them up with Augie (Mitz-Plasse) an awkward geek whose life is totally immersed in a medieval fantasy play-acting game, and Ronnie (Thompson), a pint-sized troublemaker with the attitude and vocabulary of a hardened convict. The two mentors have their hands full as they stumble from one gaffe to another. In the end they're all the better for the experience as is required by the formula, but this one is funnier than most on the way there. **99m/C DVD.** *US* Paul Rudd, Seann William Scott, Elizabeth Banks, Jane Lynch, Ken Marino, Christopher Mintz-Plasse, Bobb'e J. Thompson; ***D:*** David Wain; ***W:*** Paul Rudd, Ken Marino, David Wain, Timothy Dowling; ***C:*** Russ T. Alsobrook; ***M:*** Craig (Shudder to Think) Wedren.

Roll Along Cowboy **1/2 1937** A vintage sagebrush saga about a cowboy caught by love. Based on Zane Grey's "The Dude Ranger." **55m/B VHS.** Smith Ballew, Cecilia Parker; ***D:*** Gus Meins.

Roll Bounce **2005 (PG-13)** Even if you don't remember the roller-disco craze of the 70s, you'll relive it here. South-side Chicago kid Xavier (Bow Wow) and his buddies find their turf rink closes, so they're forced to go North to the swankier Sweetwater rink where the super-cool Sweetness (Jonathan) holds court. The summer rolls by with skating, flirting, and a growing rivalry until the kids square off in an end-of-summer skate-off. Based on fact, this third film directed by Malcolm Lee (Spike's cousin) is more than worthwhile, rooted in true heart and offering a sweetness that sets it apart. **107m/C DVD.** *US* Bow Wow, Chi McBride, Mike Epps, Wesley Jonathan, Kellita Smith, Meagan Good, Khleo Thomas, Nick Cannon, Rick Gonzalez, Jurnee Smollett, Charlie (Charles Q.) Murphy, Wayne Brady, Marcus T. Paulk, Brandon T. Jackson, Paul Wesley, Darryl "DMC" McDaniels; ***D:*** Malcolm Lee; ***W:*** Norman Vance Jr.; ***C:*** J.(James) Michael Muro; ***M:*** Stanley Clarke.

Roll of Thunder, Hear My Cry **1/2 1978** A black family struggles to survive in Depression-era Mississippi in this inspiring, if somewhat predictable, production. Look for the always impressive Freeman in a supporting role. Based on the novels of Mildred Taylor. **110m/C VHS.** Claudia McNeil, Janet MacLachlan, Morgan Freeman; ***D:*** Jack Smight. **TV**

Roll on Texas Moon **1946** A cowpoke is hired to prevent a feud between the sheep men and the cattle ranchers. **68m/B VHS, DVD.** Roy Rogers, George "Gabby" Hayes, Dale Evans, Dennis Hoey; ***D:*** William Witney.

Roll, Wagons, Roll **1/2 1939** Tex Ritter leads a wagon train to Oregon. **52m/B VHS.** Nelson McDowell, Muriel Evans, Tom London, Reed Howes, Tex Ritter; ***D:*** Al(bert) Herman; ***W:*** Victor Adamson, Edmond Kelso, Roger Merton; ***C:*** Marcel Le Picard.

Roller Blade **1985** In a post-holocaust world a gang of Amazon-style nuns, who worship a "have a nice day" happy face, battle the forces of evil with martial arts and mysticism. Has to be seen to be believed. Extremely low-budget outing. **88m/C VHS.** Suzanne Solari, Jeff Hutchinson, Shaun Mitchelle, Michelle (McClellan) Bauer, Lisa Marie, Barbara Peckinpaugh; ***D:*** Donald G. Jackson; ***M:*** Robert Garrett.

Roller Blade Warriors: Taken By Force **1990** Roller babes battle evil mutant while balancing on big boots with small wheels. **90m/C VHS.** Kathleen Kinmont, Rory Calhoun, Abby Dalton, Elizabeth Kaitan; ***D:*** Donald G. Jackson; ***W:*** Randall Frakes; ***C:*** Donald G. Jackson; ***M:*** Robert Garrett.

Roller Boogie **WOOF! 1979 (PG)** A truly awful film made at the time of the mercifully brief roller-disco craze. Blair runs away from home and winds up helping some friends thwart a businessman looking to close the local roller rink. Everything about this one reeks amateur. **103m/C VHS, DVD.** Linda Blair, Jim Bray, Beverly Garland, Roger Perry, James Van Patten, Kimberly Beck, Mark Goddard, Stoney Jackson, Sean McClory; ***D:*** Mark L. Lester; ***W:*** Barry Schneider; ***C:*** Dean Cundey.

Rollerball ♪♪ 1/2 **1975 (R)** Caan is utterly convincing in this futuristic tale in which a brutal sport assumes alarming importance to a sterile society. Flashy, violent, sometimes exhilirating. **123m/C VHS, DVD.** James Caan, John Houseman, Maud Adams, Moses Gunn, John Beck; ***D:*** Norman Jewison; ***W:*** William Harrison; ***C:*** Douglas Slocombe; ***M:*** Andre Previn.

Rollerball ♪ **2002 (PG-13)** Re-imagination of the 1975 cult classic. The sport of the near-future attracts extreme sports enthusiast Jonathan Cross (Klein), drawn by the big bucks and buddy (LL Cool J), who convinces him to try out. The sport itself, is sort of like pro wrestling on skates and motorcycles. Fleeing the law in the U.S., Jonathan heads to a former Soviet republic where the league is run by ex-KGB agent Petrovich (Reno) who wants to increase the sport's blood and gore factor to gain a stateside cable TV deal. Jonathan finds love with fellow baller Aurora (Romijn-Stamos) whose nearly unnoticeable "deformity" doesn't dissuade her suicidal suitor. Laughable scenarios, seriously ailing editing, corny script, lackluster performances and grave miscasting (the sensitive Klein as a macho macho man) make this one a prime candidate for contraction. **98m/C VHS, DVD.** *US* Chris Klein, LL Cool J, Rebecca Romijn, Jean Reno, Naveen Andrews, Oleg Taktarov, David Hemblen; ***D:*** John McTiernan; ***W:*** Larry Ferguson, John Pogue; ***C:*** Steve Mason; ***M:*** Eric Serra.

Rollercoaster ♪♪ **1977 (PG)** A deranged extortionist threatens to sabotage an amusement park ride. Plucky Segal must stop him. Video renters will be spared the nauseating effects of film's original "Sensurround." **119m/C VHS, DVD.** Helen Hunt, Craig Wasson, Steve Guttenberg, George Segal, Richard Widmark, Timothy Bottoms, Henry Fonda, Susan Strasberg, Harry Guardino; ***D:*** James Goldstone; ***W:*** William Link; ***C:*** David M. Walsh; ***M:*** Lalo Schifrin.

Rollin' Plains ♪ **1938** A Texas Ranger tries to settle a feud between cattlemen and sheepmen over water rights. **60m/B VHS, DVD.** Horace Murphy, Snub Pollard, Hobart Bosworth, Karl Hackett, Jennifer Tisdale, Tex Ritter; ***D:*** Al(bert) Herman; ***W:*** Lindsley Parsons; ***C:*** Edmond Kelso, Gus Peterson.

Rolling Family ♪♪ *Familia Rodante* **2004** Aged matriarch Emilia is invited to be the guest of honor at her grandniece's wedding. So she gathers four squabbling generations of her family and packs them into a worn-out motor home so they can travel cross-country from Buenos Aires to the ceremony. It's hot, there's no air-conditioning, they have repeated motor trouble, and all those smelly people packed into tight quarters leads to some temperamental behavior. Spanish with subtitles. **103m/C DVD.** *AR* Graciana Chironi, Liliana Capuro, Ruth Dobel, Bernardo Forteza, Carlos Resta, Raul Vinoles, Leila Gomez, Laura Glave, Federico Esqurro; ***D:*** Pablo Trapero; ***W:*** Pablo Trapero; ***C:*** Guillermo Nieto; ***M:*** Leon Giecco.

Rolling Home ♪♪ **1948** Tame tale about aging cowpoke, his grandson, and a really swell horse. Saddle up and snooze. **71m/B VHS, DVD.** Jean Parker, Russell Hayden, Pamela Blake, Buss Henry, Raymond Hatton; ***D:*** William Berke; ***W:*** Edwin Westrate; ***C:*** Benjamin (Ben H.) Kline; ***M:*** Kierstin Koppell.

Rolling Thunder ♪♪ 1/2 **1977 (R)** Vietnam vet turns vigilante when he arrives home from POW camp and sees his family slaughtered. Graphically violent, potentially cathartic. Typical of screenwriter Paul Schrader. **99m/C VHS.** William Devane, Tommy Lee Jones, Linda Haynes; ***D:*** John Flynn; ***W:*** Paul Schrader, Heywood Gould; ***C:*** Jordan Cronenweth.

Rolling Vengeance ♪ 1/2 **1987 (R)** Enterprising fellow constructs powerful truck to better facilitate the extermination of gang members who earlier slaughtered his family. Keep on truckin'. **90m/C VHS.** Don Michael Paul, Ned Beatty, Lawrence Dane, Lisa Howard; ***D:*** Steven Hilliard Stern.

Rollover ♪ 1/2 **1981 (R)** Turgid big-budget drama about Arab undermining of American economy. Kristofferson is lifeless, Fonda is humorless. Supporting players Sommer and Cronyn fare better. **117m/C VHS, DVD.** Jane Fonda, Kris Kristofferson, Hume Cronyn, Bob Gunton, Josef Sommer, Martha Plimpton; ***D:*** Alan J. Pakula.

Roman ♪♪ **2006** Alienated Roman (McKee) exists in his own lonely world until he becomes interested in his blonde neighbor (Bell). Too bad he accidentally kills her. Not knowing what to do, Roman starts dismembering the corpse and disposing of it piece by piece. Then death-obsessed Eva (Rose) becomes his new neighbor but maybe Roman should be careful about inviting her to visit. **92m/C DVD.** Lucky McKee, Nectar Rose, Kristen Bell, James Duval, Jesse Hlubik, Ben Boyer; ***D:*** Angela Bettis; ***W:*** Lucky McKee; ***C:*** Kevin Ford; ***M:*** Jaye Barnes Luckett.

Roman de Gare ♪♪ *Crossed Tracks* **2007 (R)** The French title is slang for the type of pulp literature sold in railway stations for waiting travelers to pass the time. In this just-as-pulpy thriller, successful crime novelist Judith (Ardant) is being interrogated about her connection to a serial killer called the Magician, who has escaped from prison. Only it turns out that Judith's books are ghostwritten—possibly by the mysterious Louie (Pinon). And what does Louie want from unhappy hairdresser Huguette (Dana), who's just been abandoned by her boyfriend at a highway service station? Is he looking for a ride, romance, or a new victim? Ah, fate makes fools of us all. French with subtitles. **103m/C DVD.** *FR* Dominique Pinon, Fanny Ardant, Zinedine Soualem, Audrey Dana, Michele Bernier; ***D:*** Claude Lelouch; ***W:*** Claude Lelouch, Pierre Uytterhoeven; ***C:*** Gerard de Battista; ***M:*** Gilbert Becaud, Alex Jaffray.

Roman Holiday ♪♪♪ 1/2 **1953** Hepburn's first starring role is a charmer as a princess bored with her official visit to Rome who slips away and plays at being an "average Jane." A reporter discovers her little charade and decides to cash in with an exclusive story. Before they know it, love calls. Blacklisted screenwriter Trumbo was "fronted" by Ian McLellan Hunter, who accepted screen credit and the Best Story Oscar in Trumbo's stead. The Academy voted to posthumously award Trumbo his own Oscar in 1993. **118m/B VHS, DVD.** Audrey Hepburn, Gregory Peck, Eddie Albert, Tullio Carminati; ***D:*** William Wyler; ***W:*** Dalton Trumbo. Oscars '53: Actress (Hepburn), Costume Des. (B&W), Story; British Acad. '53: Actress (Hepburn); Golden Globes '54: Actress—Drama (Hepburn), Natl. Film Reg. '99;; N.Y. Film Critics '53: Actress (Hepburn).

Roman Polanski: Wanted and Desired ♪♪ 1/2 **2008** Roman Polanski's life is already close to a Hollywood drama, with his parents' death in the Holocaust, his childhood on the streets of Poland, his fame in America as the director of "Chinatown," and the death of his wife and unborn child at the hands of the Manson family. Then in 1977, he was arrested and tried for unlawful sex with a 13-year-old girl. After numerous court mishaps and misunderstandings, Polanski fled to Europe to avoid prison time. Perhaps his tragic background is the motive behind HBO's slightly biased spin, or perhaps because all is apparently forgiven, as Polanski, the accuser, and her family all attended the film's premiere together. **99m/C DVD.** *US* ***D:*** Marina Zenovich; ***W:*** Marina Zenovich, Joe Bini, P.G. Morgan; ***C:*** Tanya Koop; ***M:*** Mar Degli Antoni.

Roman Scandals ♪♪ 1/2 **1933** A penniless young man daydreams himself back to ancient Rome with uproarious results. Lucille Ball appears as one of the Goldwyn Girls. Dance sequences were choreographed by Busby Berkeley. ♫No More Love; Build A Little Home; Keep Young and Beautiful; Rome Wasn't Built in a Day; Put a Tax on Love. **91m/B VHS.** Eddie Cantor, Ruth Etting, Gloria Stuart, Edward Arnold, Lucille Ball, Busby Berkeley; ***D:*** Frank Tuttle; ***C:*** Gregg Toland.

Roman Spring of Mrs. Stone ♪♪♪ *The Widow and the Gigolo* **1961** An aging actress determines to revive her career in Rome but finds romance with a gigolo instead in this adaptation of Tennessee Williams's novella. Leigh and Beatty are compelling, but Lenya nearly steals the show as Leigh's distinctly unappealing confidant. **104m/C VHS, DVD.** Warren Beatty, Vivien Leigh, Lotte Lenya, Bessie Love, Jill St. John, Elspeth March; ***D:*** Jose Quintero; ***W:*** Gavin Lambert.

The Roman Spring of Mrs. Stone ♪♪ 1/2 *Tennessee Williams: The Roman Spring of Mrs. Stone* **2003 (R)** In this slightly revised remake of the 1961 original, older actress Karen Stone (Mirren) becomes infatuated with conniving gigolo Paolo (Martinez) as she tries to rebound from the death of her rich husband while in Italy. **108m/C VHS, DVD.** Helen Mirren, Olivier Martinez, Anne Bancroft, Rodrigo Santoro, Brian Dennehy, Suzanne Bertish, Jane Bertish, Roger Allam, Victor Alfieri, Dona Granata, Aldo Signoretti; ***D:*** Robert Allan Ackerman; ***W:*** Martin Sherman, Tennessee Williams; ***C:*** Ashley Rowe; ***M:*** John Altman. **TV**

Romance ♪♪ **1930** In only her second talkie, Garbo stars as an Italian opera star who seduces a young priest. Poor story and weak acting from everyone with the exception of Garbo. Even she can't save this one. Adapted from the play "Signora Cacllini." **77m/B VHS.** Greta Garbo, Lewis Stone, Gavin Gordon, Elliott Nugent, Florence Lake, Clara Blandick; ***D:*** Clarence Brown; ***C:*** William H. Daniels.

Romance ♪♪ **1999** This journey of erotic self-discovery caused raised eyebrows even among the blase French. Schoolteacher Marie (Ducey) is sexually rejected by her bored male model boyfriend Paul (Stevenin). This so distresses her that Marie flings herself into sexual escapades, including bar-pickup Paolo (Italian porn star Siffredi) and bondage sessions with school principal Robert (Berleand). Very talky, very self-serious, and very explicit. French with subtitles. **93m/C VHS, DVD.** *FR* Caroline Ducey, Sagamore Stevenin, Francois Berleand, Rocco Siffredi; ***D:*** Catherine Breillat; ***W:*** Catherine Breillat; ***C:*** Yorgos Arvanitis; ***M:*** D.J. Valentin, Raphael Tidas.

Romance & Cigarettes ♪♪ **2005 (R)** Although made in 2005, Turturro's musical comedy didn't get much of a release until 2007 although it's not really bad—just, well, odd. Queens ironworker Nick (Gandolfini) is cheating on wife Kitty (Sarandon) with a slinky redhead—lingerie shop owner Tula (a foul-mouthed Winslet). When Kitty finds out, she decides to get even, aided by Cousin Bo (Walken) and the couple's three daughters (Aida Turturro, Parker, Moore). The score is mainly recognizable pop tunes, which the actors either sing or lip-synch to. **106m/C DVD.** James Gandolfini, Susan Sarandon, Kate Winslet, Christopher Walken, Mary-Louise Parker, Aida Turturro, Mandy Moore, Bobby Cannavale, Steve Buscemi, Eddie Izzard, Elaine Stritch; ***D:*** John Turturro; ***W:*** John Turturro; ***C:*** Tom Stern; ***M:*** Paul Chihara.

Romance and Rejection ♪♪ *So This Is Romance?* **1996** Sad-sack Mike (Dinsdale) is looking for love in London. His father tells him to settle for good sex but Mike wants more. Then he meets a woman (Bellar) who may fulfill both parts of the equation. **98m/C VHS, DVD.** *GB* Reece Dinsdale, Clara Bellar, John Hannah, Victoria Smurfit, Frank Finlay, Susannah York, Maryam D'Abo, Rowena King; ***D:*** Kevin W. Smith; ***W:*** Kevin W. Smith; ***C:*** Ian Savage; ***M:*** Howard J. Davidson.

Romance in Manhattan ♪♪ **1934** Recent immigrant to New York struggles to build new life, in spite of unemployment, language barriers, and loneliness. He meets Broadway chorine Rogers and song and dance ensues. America, ain't it a great place? **78m/B VHS.** Ginger Rogers, Francis Lederer, J. Farrell MacDonald; ***D:*** Stephen Roberts; ***M:*** Max Steiner.

Romance of a Horsethief ♪♪ 1/2 **1971 (PG)** Brynner leads this entertaining but slow-paced "Fiddler on the Roof" comedic romp without the music. In 1904 Poland, a Cossack captain takes horses for the Russo-Japanese war. The residents of the town rise up, goaded on by Birkin. **100m/C VHS, DVD.** *YU* Yul Brynner, Eli Wallach, Jane Birkin, Oliver Tobias, Lainie Kazan, David Opatoshu; ***D:*** Abraham Polonsky.

The Romance of Astrea and Celadon ♪♪ *Les Amours d'Astree et de Celadon* **2007** A pastoral romance, set in a mythic 5th-century Gaul, based on the 17th-century novel by Honore d'Urfe. Shepherd Celadon (Gillet) is in love with shepherdess Astrea (Crayencour). But she is led to believe (falsely) that he has been unfaithful and banishes Celadon, who promptly tries to drown himself. He is saved by nymph Galathee (Reymoud), who wants him for herself. Celadon sulks until a druid (Renko) persuades him to dress in drag so he can befriend Astrea. Although the courtly discourse is frequently amusing, the artificial setting and subject will probably be of interest to Rohmer fans only. French with subtitles. **106m/C DVD.** *FR IT SP* Serge Renko, Rodolphe Pauly, Andy Gillet, Stephanie Crayencour, Veronique Reymond, Cecile Cassel, Jocelyn Quivrin; ***D:*** Eric Rohmer; ***W:*** Eric Rohmer; ***C:*** Diane Baratier; ***M:*** Jean-Louis Valero.

Romance on the High Seas ♪♪♪ **1948** A woman is scheduled to take a cruise vacation but skips the boat when she believes her husband is cheating on her. Her husband believes she is taking the cruise to cheat on him and hires a private detective to follow her. Pleasant comedy features the film debut of Doris Day. ♫It's Magic; It's You or No One; The Tourist Trade; Put 'Em in a Box, Tie 'Em with a Ribbon, and Throw 'Em in the Deep Blue Sea; Two Lovers Met in the Night; Run, Run, Run; I'm in Love; Cuban Rhapsody. **99m/C VHS, DVD.** Jack Carson, Janis Paige, Don DeFore, Doris Day, Oscar Levant, S.Z. Sakall, Eric Blore, Franklin Pangborn, Leslie Brooks, William "Billy" Bakewell; ***D:*** Michael Curtiz; ***W:*** Julius J. Epstein.

Romance on the Orient Express ♪ 1/2 **1989** Sparks fly when former lovers meet again on the Orient Express. Don't expect any flesh, though, as this was made for TV. **96m/C VHS.** Cheryl Ladd, Stuart Wilson, John Gielgud; ***D:*** Lawrence Gordon-Clark. **TV**

Romance on the Range ♪ 1/2 **1942** Rogers sets out to trap a gang of fur thieves and finds romance. **60m/B VHS.** Roy Rogers, George "Gabby" Hayes, Sally Payne, Linda Hayes, Harry Woods, Glenn Strange; ***D:*** Joseph Kane; ***W:*** J. Benton Cheney; ***C:*** William Nobles; ***M:*** Tim Spencer, Glenn Spencer.

Romance with a Double Bass ♪♪♪ **1974** When a musician and a princess take a skinny dip in the royal lake and get their clothes stolen, comic complications arise. Reminiscent of Cleese's sojourn as a Monty Python member, with surreal, frequently raunchy humor. **40m/C VHS, DVD.** *GB* John Cleese, Connie Booth, Graham Crowden, Desmond Jones, Freddie Jones, Andrew Sachs; ***D:*** Robert M. Young.

Romancing the Stone ♪♪♪ **1984 (PG)** Uptight romance novelist Joan (Turner) lives out her fantasies after she receives a mysterious map from her murdered brother-in-law and her sister is kidnapped in South America—the ransom being the map. Out to rescue her sister, she's helped and hindered by American soldier of fortune Jack (Douglas) whose main concern is himself and the hidden treasure described in the map. Great chemistry between the stars and loads of clever dialogue in this appealing adventure comedy. First outing with Turner, Douglas, and DeVito. Followed by "The Jewel of the Nile." **106m/C VHS, DVD, Blu-ray Disc.** Mary Ellen Trainor, Michael Douglas, Kathleen Turner, Danny DeVito, Zack Norman, Alfonso Arau, Ron Silver; ***D:*** Robert Zemeckis; ***W:*** Diane Thomas; ***C:*** Dean Cundey; ***M:*** Alan Silvestri. Golden Globes '85: Actress—Mus./Comedy (Turner), Film—Mus./Comedy; L.A. Film Critics '84: Actress (Turner).

Romantic Comedy ♪♪ **1983 (PG)** Writing duo never seem to synchronize their desires for each other in this dull comedy. Engaging stars don't inspire each other much, and supporting cast can't make up the difference. Adapted from the Bernard Slade play. **102m/C VHS, DVD.** Dudley Moore, Mary Steenburgen, Frances Sternhagen, Ron Leibman; ***D:*** Arthur Hiller; ***W:*** Bernard Slade; ***C:*** David M. Walsh; ***M:*** Marvin Hamlisch.

Romantic Englishwoman ♪♪♪ **1975 (R)** Literate comedy-drama about the intertwined lives of several sophisticated and restrained Brits. Caine is a successful novelist with writer's block whose wife falls for another man while on a trip alone. He then invites his wife's lover to stay with them in order to generate ideas for his writing until his jealousy begins to surface. **117m/C VHS.** *GB* Glenda Jackson, Michael Caine, Helmut Berger, Kate Nelligan; ***D:*** Joseph Losey; ***W:*** Tom Stoppard, Thomas Wiseman.

Rome Adventure *Lovers Must Learn* **1962** Spinster librarian Pleshette takes Roman vacation hoping to meet handsome prince. Donahue takes shine to her while girlfriend Dickinson is away, as does suave Roman Brazzi. Soapy, ill-paced romance. **119m/C VHS, DVD.** Pam(ela) Austin, Troy Donahue, Angie Dickinson, Suzanne Pleshette, Rossano Brazzi, Constance Ford, Al Hirt, Chad Everett; ***D:*** Delmer Daves; ***W:*** Delmer Daves; ***M:*** Max Steiner.

Rome '78 ½ **1978** Acclaimed underground film centered around Caligula and the Queen of Sheba in ancient Rome. **60m/C VHS.** Anya Phillips, David McDermott, Eric Mitchell; ***D:*** James Nares.

Romeo and Juliet ½ **1936** One of MGM producer Irving Thalberg's pet projects (and starring Thalberg's wife, Norma Shearer), this Shakespeare classic was given the spare-no-expense MGM treatment. Physically too old to portray teenage lovers, both Howard and Shearer let their acting ability supply all necessary illusions. Also notable is Barrymore's over-the-top portrayal of Mercutio. **126m/B VHS.** Leslie Howard, Norma Shearer, John Barrymore, Basil Rathbone, Edna May Oliver; ***D:*** George Cukor; ***C:*** William H. Daniels.

Romeo and Juliet **1954** Unfulfilling adaptation of Shakespeare's timeless drama of young love cast against family antagonisms. Peculiar supporting cast features both Cabot and ubiquitous master Gielgud. **138m/C VHS.** *IT* Laurence Harvey, Susan Shantall, Aldo Zollo, Sebastian Cabot, Flora Robson, Mervyn Johns, Bill Travers, John Gielgud; ***D:*** Renato Castellani; ***C:*** Robert Krasker. Natl. Bd. of Review '54: Director (Castellani).

Romeo and Juliet ½ **1968 (PG)** Young couple share love despite prohibitive conflict between their families in this adaptation of Shakespeare's classic play. Director Zeffirelli succeeds in casting relative novices Whiting and Hussey in the leads, but is somewhat less proficient in lending air of free-wheeling '60s appeal to entire enterprise. Kudos, however, to cinematographer Pasquale De Santis and composer Nina Rota. Also available in a 45-minute edited version. **138m/C VHS, DVD.** *GB IT* Olivia Hussey, Leonard Whiting, Michael York, Milo O'Shea; ***D:*** Franco Zeffirelli; ***W:*** Franco Zeffirelli, Franco Brusati, Maestro D'Amico; ***C:*** Pasqualino De Santis; ***M:*** Nino Rota; ***Nar:*** Laurence Olivier. Oscars '68: Cinematog., Costume Des.; Golden Globes '69: Foreign Film; Natl. Bd. of Review '68: Director (Zeffirelli).

Romeo Is Bleeding ½ **1993 (R)** Jack (Oldman) is a police detective accepting mobster payoffs from boss Falcone (Scheider) for fingering federally protected witnesses. But the next target proves Jack's undoing—hitwoman Mona (Olin), who's more than a match for any man. Oldman's character is played for a patsy by everyone while Olin's is a kinky psycho-villainess with an enjoyment of violence, red lipstick, and a constant, maniacal laugh. Sciorra is generally wasted as Jack's unhappy wife while Lewis is annoying as his young and vacuous mistress. Part homage, part satire of film noir is overly stylized with intrusive narration but some effective shocks. **110m/C VHS, DVD.** Gary Oldman, Lena Olin, Annabella Sciorra, Juliette Lewis, Roy Scheider, Michael Wincott, David Proval, Paul Butler, Will Patton, Larry Joshua, James Cromwell, Ron Perlman; ***D:*** Peter Medak; ***W:*** Hilary Henkin; ***C:*** Darius Wolski; ***M:*** Mark Isham.

Romeo Must Die ½ **2000 (R)** Romance is decidedly secondary to action in this kung fu/hip hop hybrid. After an over-extended (but flashy) credits sequence, the story kicks in. Black crime lord Isaak O'Day (a magnetic Lindo) and Asian crime boss Ch'u Sing (O) are maintaining an uneasy truce in order to do a mega-business deal. Then Sing's useless younger son is killed and soon O'Day's son bites the dust as well. Into the mix springs good guy/ex-cop Han Sing (Li), who's out to avenge his brother's death, and lovely Trish O'Day (Aaliyah), who wants the same for her brother. (This is the chastest romantic pairing in modern movies.) The action sequences are frequent and frequently amazing and Li has minimal English dialogue to worry about. The supporting players, including Wong and Washington, are also solidly watchable. There's also humor, including Li's introduction to touch football. **115m/C VHS, DVD, UMD.** Jet Li, Aaliyah, Delroy Lindo, Henry O, Isaiah Washington IV, Russell Wong, DMX, DB Woodside, Edoardo Ballerini, Anthony Anderson, Jon Kit Lee, Francoise Yip; ***D:*** Andrzej Bartkowiak; ***W:*** Eric Bernt, John Jarrell; ***C:*** Glen MacPherson; ***M:*** Stanley Clarke, Timbaland.

Romero ½ **1989** Julia is riveting as the Salvadoran archbishop who championed his destitute congregation despite considerable political opposition. A stirring biography financed by the United States Roman Catholic Church. **102m/C VHS, DVD.** Raul Julia, Richard Jordan, Ana Alicia, Eddie Velez, Alejandro Bracho, Tony Plana, Lucy Reina, Harold Gould, Al Ruscio, Robert Viharo; ***D:*** John Duigan; ***W:*** John Sacret Young; ***C:*** Geoff Burton; ***M:*** Gabriel Yared.

Romola ½ **1925** Silent adventure. After Powell and his father are attacked by pirates, Powell escapes. But instead of rescuing his father, he opts for a life of corruption. Dad eventually escapes and returns to exact vengeance. A rather expensive film in its day, troubled by modern-day sights in what was supposed to be old Florence. Gish's drowning scene had to be re-shot because she wouldn't sink. Colman arranged for his then-wife Raye to have a bit part, but they were divorced soon after the film was finished. **120m/B VHS.** Lillian Gish, Dorothy Gish, William Powell, Ronald Colman, Charles Lane, Herbert Grimwood, Bonaventure Ibanez, Frank Puglia, Thelma Raye; ***D:*** Henry King.

Romper Stomper **1992 (R)** Violent confrontations between Australian skinheads and the Vietnamese community mixed in with a disturbed love story. Suburban rich girl Gabe (McKenzie) is drawn to the charasmatic Hando (Crowe), the certifiably loony leader of a group of Melbourne's skinheads. Any romance takes a backseat to the carnage brought by the skinheads' attacks on the local Asian community, who fight back with equal force. Disquieting look at a brutal world which can't be ignored. Film caused a furor upon its Australian release with debates about whether the extreme violence was intended to titilate or explicate the plot. An unrated version at 89 minutes is also available. **85m/C VHS, DVD.** *AU* Alex Scott, Leigh Russell, Daniel Wyllie, James McKenna, Samantha Bladon, Russell Crowe, Jacqueline McKenzie, Daniel Pollock; ***D:*** Geoffrey Wright; ***W:*** Geoffrey Wright; ***C:*** Ron Hagen; ***M:*** John Clifford White. Australian Film Inst. '92: Actor (Crowe), Sound, Score.

Romulus, My Father **2007 (R)** Set in Australia's hard economic struggles of 1961, ten-year old Raimond (Smit-McPhee), a boy with almost divine powers, lives with his eccentric Yugolasvian father Romulus (Bana), both happy and comfortable toiling the days away as the village oddballs. Things begin to spiral out of control once Raimond's German mother, Christina (Potente), appears back at home only to leave just as quickly. Her fierce emotional highs and lows eventually lead Romulus into a mental institution. Told in vignettes, the story spans years in the course of Raimond's life, as he discovers his strengths and fights to keep his father at his side. As melodramatic and often predictable as this coming-of-age tale may be, it's still got guts and an emotional punch. Based on the memoir by German-born, Australian-based philosopher Raimond Gaita. **109m/C DVD.** *AU* Eric Bana, Franka Potente, Russell Dykstra, Marton Csokas, Kodi Smit-McPhee, Jacek Koman; ***D:*** Richard Roxburgh; ***W:*** Nick Drake; ***C:*** Geoffrey Simpson; ***M:*** Basil Hogios.

Romy and Michele's High School Reunion ½ **1997 (R)** Two vacuous ditz queens, Romy (Sorvino) and Michele (Kudrow), best friends and roommates since high school, decide they must impress at their 10-year Tucson high school reunion by passing themselves off as wealthy and successful. Since they're barely bright enough to walk and chew gum at the same time, this proves to be a challenge, especially when the arrival of cynical Heather (Garofalo), who knows the truth, threatens their deception. Music's good, and there are a (very) few funny moments, but you'll concentrate most on trying to ignore those annoying accents. You don't laugh with these would-be babes, you laugh at them. And even then, not all that much. Based on Schiff's play "The Ladies' Room." **91m/C VHS, DVD.** Mira Sorvino, Lisa Kudrow, Janeane Garofalo, Alan Cumming, Julia Campbell, Elaine Hendrix, Jacob Vargas, Camryn Manheim; ***D:*** David Mirkin; ***W:*** Robin Schiff; ***C:*** Reynaldo Villalobos; ***M:*** Steve Bartek.

Ronin ½ **1998 (R)** What a cast! What a director! What a disappointment! Okay, so it's not that bad—the scenery's spectacular (the action takes place between Paris and Nice) and there are some amazing car chases. But, they go on much too long and the story's less than involving. Sam (De Niro) is a world-weary, possibly ex-spy who gets involved with several international players (including Reno, Skarsgard, and Bean) to do a job for tough Irish lass Deirdre (McElhone). She's fronting (for the violent Pryce) a project to retrieve a mysterious suitcase from some Russian bad guys. One of the best things the film's got going for it is the wary buddy relationship that builds between De Niro and Reno. Title refers to a Japanese legend concerning 47 masterless samurai. Richard Weisz is the pseudonym for a rewriting David Mamet. **118m/C VHS, DVD, Blu-ray Disc, UMD.** Robert De Niro, Jean Reno, Stellan Skarsgard, Natascha (Natasha) McElhone, Jonathan Pryce, Skipp (Robert L.) Sudduth, Michael (Michel) Lonsdale, Sean Bean, Jan Triska, Feodor Atkine, Bernard Bloch, Katarina Witt; ***D:*** John Frankenheimer; ***W:*** David Mamet, J.D. Zeik; ***C:*** Robert Fraisse; ***M:*** Elia Cmiral.

Ronin Gai ½ *Ronin-Gai* **1990** Filmed as a tribute to Shozo Makino (regarded as the father of the Japanese Period Drama), this is the fourth version of the original film. It is 1836, and the Samurai are being tossed aside and forgotten. Outside of Edo four former Samurai are drowning their sorrows in sake and prostitutes, until the local whores begin to get cut up by the retainers of the local Shogun. When asked for help, the disgraced Samurai must shrug off their drunkenness for a chance at redemption. **121m/C DVD.** *JP* Yoshio Harada, Kanako Higuchi, Shintaro Katsu; ***D:*** Kazuo Kiroki; ***W:*** Kazuo Kasahara, Itaro Yamagami; ***C:*** Hitoshi Takaiwa; ***M:*** Teizo Matsumura.

Ronnie and Julie ½ **1997 (PG)** Yet another contemporary variation of "Romeo & Juliet" with high-school sweethearts Ronnie (Jackson) and Julie's (Finley) relationship threatened by their respective parents political rivalry in a mayoral campaign. At least this one has a happy ending. **99m/C VHS.** Teri Garr, Joshua Jackson, Margot Finley, Alexandra Purvis, Tom Butler, Garwin Sanford; ***D:*** Philip Spink; ***C:*** Bruce Worrall.

The Roof **1956** Uninteresting outing about a young couple who married against their families' wishes and find that setting up a home of their own is more difficult than they thought. In Italian with English subtitles. **98m/B VHS.** *IT* Gabriella Pallotta, Giorgio Listuzzi; ***D:*** Vittorio De Sica.

Rooftops ½ **1989 (R)** Peculiar but predictable, centering on love between Hispanic girl and white youth who has mastered martial arts dancing. Director Wise is a long way from his earlier "West Side Story." See this one and be the only person you know who has. **108m/C VHS, DVD.** Jason Gedrick, Troy Beyer, Eddie Velez, Tisha Campbell; ***D:*** Robert Wise; ***W:*** Allan Goldstein, Terrence (Terry) Brennan; ***M:*** Michael Kamen.

The Rook ½ **1999 (R)** Freaky yet flat crime thriller with drab Donovan as religious detective out to solve a young woman's murder in a rural community whose residents are as kooky (and not in that "fun to be around" way) as the evidence he uncovers. **85m/C VHS, DVD.** Martin Donovan, John MacKay, Michael Finesilver, Fritz Fox, Karen Abrahams; ***D:*** Eran Palatnik; ***W:*** Richard Lee Purvis; ***C:*** Zack Winestine; ***M:*** Robert Een. **VIDEO**

The Rookie **1990 (R)** Routine cop drama has worldly veteran and wide-eyed newcomer team to crack stolen-car ring managed by Germans. Eastwood and Sheen are reliable, but Hispanics Julia and Braga, though miscast, nonetheless steal this one as the German villains. **121m/C VHS, DVD.** Clint Eastwood, Charlie Sheen, Raul Julia, Sonia Braga, Lara Flynn Boyle, Pepe Serna, Marco Rodriguez, Tom Skerritt, Roberta Vasquez; ***D:*** Clint Eastwood.

The Rookie ½ **2002 (G)** Texas high school teacher and baseball coach Jim Morris (Quaid) challenges his also-ran team by promising to go on a major league tryout if they win the regional championship. The team wins, and the former minor-leaguer keeps his promise and attends a Devil Rays tryout and finds his now-rejuvenated arm can throw a baseball 98 mph. During his journey to the majors, he deals with his relationship with his old man, and life on the other side of 30. If this were't a true story, it'd be one of the hokiest movies ever, but because you know it's real, it's, well...inspiring. It helps that Quaid nails the role, and Jones, as son Hunter, walks off with every scene he's in. One of the producers, Mark Ciardi, is a former teammate of Morris, from his original go-round in the minors. Based on Morris's book "The Oldest Rookie." **127m/C VHS, DVD.** *US* Dennis Quaid, Rachel Griffiths, Angus T. Jones, Brian Cox, Beth Grant, Chad Lindberg, Royce D. Applegate, Jay Hernandez, Russell Richardson, Raynor Scheine, David Blackwell, Edward "Blue" Deckert, Dan Kamin, Trevor Morgan, Rick Gonzalez, Angelo Spizzirri; ***D:*** John Lee Hancock; ***W:*** Mike Rich; ***C:*** John Schwartzman; ***M:*** Carter Burwell.

Rookie of the Year ½ **1993 (PG)** Kid's fluff fantasy come true. Twelve-year-old baseball fanatic Henry has dreams of making it to the big league. He falls, breaks his arm, and when it heals strangely is blessed with a pitching arm so spectacular he finds himself not only playing for the Chicago Cubs, but leading them to the World Series. Enjoyable family outing for first-time director Stern (who also plays a seasoned and very incredulous ballplayer). Keep your eyes peeled for appearances by real-live sluggers Pedro Guerrero, Barry Bonds, and others. **103m/C VHS, DVD.** Thomas Ian Nicholas, Daniel Stern, Gary Busey, Dan Hedaya; ***D:*** Daniel Stern; ***W:*** Sam Harper; ***C:*** Jack N. Green; ***M:*** Bill Conti. Blockbuster '95: Family Movie, V.

The Room **1987** Altman takes on Pinter in this brooding mini-play about two young strangers who try to rent the room already occupied by a disconnected woman and her semi-catatonic husband. **48m/C VHS.** Julian Sands, Linda Hunt, Annie Lennox, David Hemblen, Donald Pleasence; ***D:*** Robert Altman; ***W:*** Harold Pinter; ***C:*** Pierre Mignot; ***M:*** Judith Gruber-Stitzer. **TV**

The Room **WOOF! 2003 (R)** This unintentional laugher/vanity project has become a strange Hollywood cult item among the midnight movie crowd because of its sheer chutzpah and ineptitude. There's a plot in there somewhere (something about love and betrayal) but the Hound is certain that you won't care (and it doesn't make sense anyway). **99m/C DVD.** Greg Sestero, Tommy Wiseau, Juliette Danielle, Philip Haldiman, Carolyn Minnott; ***D:*** Tommy Wiseau; ***W:*** Tommy Wiseau; ***C:*** Todd Barron; ***M:*** Mladen Milicevic.

Room at the Top ½ **1959** Ambitious factory man forsakes true love and marries boss's daughter instead in this grim drama set in industrial northern England. Cast excels, with Harvey and Sears as the worker and his wife. Signoret is also quite compelling as the abandoned woman. Adapted from John Braine's novel and followed by "Life at the Top" and "Man at the Top." **118m/B VHS, DVD.** *GB* Laurence Harvey, Simone Signoret, Heather Sears, Hermione Baddeley, Avril Ungar, Donald Wolfit, Wendy Craig, Allan Cuthbertson, Ian Hendry, Donald Houston, Raymond Huntley, Miriam Karlin, Wilfred Lawson, Richard Pasco, Mary Peach, Prunella Scales, Beatrice Varley, John Westbrook, Delena Kidd; ***D:*** Jack Clayton; ***W:*** Neil Paterson; ***C:*** Freddie Francis; ***M:*** Mario Nascimbene. Oscars '59: Actress (Signoret), Adapt. Screenplay; British Acad. '58: Actress (Signoret), Film; Cannes '59: Actress (Signoret).

Room for One More **1951** Anna Rose (Drake) can't resist taking in strays, which her husband George (Grant) and their three children are used to. Then Anna comes to the rescue of orphaned Jane (Mann), a problem child in need of a foster family, and later to handicapped Jimmy-John (Tatum, Jr.) despite her husband's initial objections. Shameless heart-tugger based on a true story; Grant and Drake were married at the time of filming. **95m/B DVD.** Gary Grant, Betsy Drake, Iris Mann, Clifford Tatum Jr., Lurene Tuttle, Randy Stuart, John Ridgely; ***D:*** Norman Taurog; ***W:*** Jack Rose, Melville Shavelson; ***C:*** Robert Burks; ***M:*** Max Steiner.

Room 43 🦴 1/2 *Passport to Shame* **1958** Campy fable about a British cab driver who falls in love with a French girl, and stumbles onto a white-slavery ring when she falls victim to it. Features a young Caine and future novelist Collins in bit parts. **93m/B VHS.** Diana Dors, Herbert Lom, Eddie Constantine, Michael Caine, Jackie Collins; ***D:*** Alvin Rakoff.

Room Service 🦴🦴 1/2 **1938** The Marx Brothers provide less than the usual mayhem here with Groucho as a penniless theatrical producer determined to remain in his hotel room until he can secure funds for his next play. Ball doesn't help matters much either. Not bad, but certainly not up to the zany Marx clan's usual stuff. **78m/B VHS, DVD.** Groucho Marx, Harpo Marx, Chico Marx, Lucille Ball, Ann Miller, Frank Albertson, Donald MacBride, Charles Halton; ***D:*** William A. Seiter; ***W:*** Morrie Ryskind; ***C:*** J. Roy Hunt; ***M:*** Roy Webb.

Room 314 🦴🦴 **2007** Micro-budget drama, which Knowles adapted from his play, where a hotel room is the scene of five couples' stories. Stacey can't remember her drunken one-nighter with Nick; alcoholic Harry is contemplating suicide, not adultery, when his suspicious wife Gretchen shows up; salesman Jack tries to sell co-worker Kathy on an affair; luckless Matt's pickup Tracey seems to be a psycho; and needy David tries to define his relationship with his moody girlfriend Caly. **100m/C DVD.** Joelle Carter, Michael Laurence, Michael Mosley, Sarah Bennett, Robyn Myhr, Monique Vukovic, Jennifer Marlowe, Matthew Del Negro, Todd Swenson, Michael Knowles; ***D:*** Michael Knowles; ***W:*** Michael Knowles; ***C:*** Michael Knowles, Shawn Regruto.

Room to Let 🦴🦴 **1949** An elderly woman and her daughter take in boarders in Victorian England. They rent a room to a man who claims to be a doctor, but the two women eventually become prisoners of fear, believing the man is actually Jack the Ripper. Will there be a vacancy soon? Somewhat disturbing and suspenseful. **68m/B VHS.** *GB* Jimmy Hanley, Valentine Dyall, Christine Silver, Merle Tottenham, Charles Hawtrey, Connie Smith, Laurence Naismith; ***D:*** Godfrey Grayson.

A Room with a View 🦴🦴🦴🦴 **1986** Engaging adaptation of E.M. Forster's novel of requited love. Lucy Honeychurch (Bonham Carter) is the feisty British idealist who rejects dashing George (Sands) for supercilious Cecil (Day-Lewis), then repents and finds (presumably) eternal passion. A multi-Oscar nominee, with great music (courtesy of Puccini), great scenery (courtesy of Florence), and great performances (courtesy of practically everybody, but supporters Smith, Dench, Callow, and Elliott must be particularly distinguished). Truly romantic, and there's much humor too. **117m/C VHS, DVD, Blu-ray Disc, HD DVD.** *GB* Helena Bonham Carter, Julian Sands, Denholm Elliott, Maggie Smith, Judi Dench, Simon Callow, Daniel Day-Lewis, Rupert Graves, Rosemary Leach; ***D:*** James Ivory; ***W:*** Ruth Prawer Jhabvala; ***C:*** Tony Pierce-Roberts; ***M:*** Richard Robbins. Oscars '86: Adapt. Screenplay, Art Dir./Set Dec., Costume Des.; British Acad. '86: Actress (Smith), Film, Support. Actress (Dench); Golden Globes '87: Support. Actress (Smith); Ind. Spirit '87: Foreign Film; Natl. Bd. of Review '86: Support. Actor (Day-Lewis); N.Y. Film Critics '86: Cinematog., Support. Actor (Day-Lewis); Writers Guild '86: Adapt. Screenplay.

A Room With a View 🦴🦴 **2008** BBC version of E.M. Forster's 1908 novel leaves a bad taste thanks to an unfortunate coda added by writer Davies, allegedly from later material by Forster. Prim (but secretly passionate) Lucy Honeychurch (Cassidy) is touring Italy with her fluttery chaperone Charlotte (Thompson). In Florence they meet garrulous working-class Mr. Emerson and his son George (played by the father/son Spalls) and Lucy is tempted into unexpected romance with the totally unsuitable young man. Lucy's terribly conflicted, weighed down by others' expectations, but will she follow her heart? **86m/C DVD.** *GB* Elaine Cassidy, Rafe Spall, Timothy Spall, Sophie Thompson, Laurence Fox, Mark Williams, Timothy West, Elizabeth McGovern, Sinead Cusack; ***D:*** Nicholas Renton; ***W:*** Andrew Davies; ***C:*** Alan Almond; ***M:*** Gabriel Yared. **TV**

Roommate 1984 A valedictorian churchgoer and a rebellious iconoclast room together at Northwestern University in 1952, with the expected humorous results. Public TV presentation based on a John Updike story. **96m/C VHS.** Lance Guest, Barry Miller, Elaine Wilkes, Melissa Ford, David Bachman; ***D:*** Nell Cox. **TV**

Roommates 🦴🦴 1/2 **1995 (PG)** Rocky Holeczek (Falk) is a cantankerous coot who, at age 75, decides to care for orphaned seven-year-old grandson Michael. Over the 30 years they are together, they fight over Rocky's old school ways and a grown-up Michael's (Sweeney) attempt to have a family of his own. But despite their bickering, Michael soon realizes that his 107-years-old grandfather's words are truly pearls of wisdom when faced with tragedy. Film hits the right sentimental buttons without going overboard with the tissues and Falk's performance, underneath the layers of latex makeup, is charmingly irascible. Based on cowriter Apple's own grandfather. **108m/C VHS, DVD.** Peter Falk, D.B. Sweeney, Julianne Moore, Ellen Burstyn; ***D:*** Peter Yates; ***W:*** Max Apple, Stephen Metcalfe; ***C:*** Mike Southon; ***M:*** Elmer Bernstein.

Rooms for Tourists 🦴🦴 *Habitaciones para Turistas* **2004** Creepy, gory feature (made more so by being filmed in B&W) set in a backwater section of Buenos Aires. Five girls miss their train and find room in a hostel owned by two brothers. Soon they're hunted by a masked killer throughout the dark, decrepit house. Spanish with subtitles. **90m/B DVD.** *AR* Jimena Krouco, Elena Siritto, Mariela Mujica, Brenda Vera, Victoria Witemburg, Rolf Garcia, Alejandro Lise; ***D:*** Adrian Garcia-Bogliano; ***W:*** Adrian Garcia-Bogliano, Ramiro Garcia-Bogliano; ***C:*** Dario Bermeo, Veronica Padron; ***M:*** Rodrigo Franco.

Rooster Cogburn 🦴🦴 1/2 **1975 (PG)** A Bible-thumping schoolmarm joins up with a hard-drinking, hard-fighting marshal in order to capture a gang of outlaws who killed her father. Tired sequel to "True Grit" but the chemistry between Wayne and Hepburn is right on target. **107m/C VHS, DVD.** John Wayne, Katharine Hepburn, Richard Jordan, Anthony Zerbe, John McIntire, Strother Martin, Paul Koslo, Tommy Lee; ***D:*** Stuart Millar; ***W:*** Martin Julien; ***C:*** Harry Stradling Jr.; ***M:*** Laurence Rosenthal.

Rooster: Spurs of Death! WOOF! 1983 (PG) An expose on cock fighting, in which a young idealist tries to stop the thriving sport in a small southern town. Dog of a movie that (not surprisingly) went straight to video. **90m/C VHS.** Vincent Van Patten, Ty Hardin, Kristine DeBell, Ruta Lee; ***D:*** Brice Mack; ***W:*** John Eastman; ***C:*** Eric Saarinen; ***M:*** Robert O. Ragland. **VIDEO**

Roosters 🦴🦴 1/2 **1995 (R)** Gallo Morales (Olmos) is returning home, after serving seven years in prison for manslaughter, anxiously awaited by wife Juana (Braga), 20-year-old rebellious son Hector (Nucci), neglected adolescent daughter Angela (Lassez), and sexy sister Chata (Alonso). Gallo is a noted breeder of fighting cocks, which for him represent machismo and power but, to his resentment, it's Hector who owns a potential prize-winning bird, precipitating some explosive family conflicts. Adapted by Sanchez-Scott from her 1987 play. **93m/C VHS, DVD.** Edward James Olmos, Sonia Braga, Maria Conchita Alonso, Danny Nucci, Sarah Lassez; ***D:*** Robert M. Young; ***W:*** Milcha Sanchez-Scott; ***C:*** Reynaldo Villalobos; ***M:*** David Kitay.

Rootin' Tootin' Rhythm 🦴 *Rhythm on the Ranch* **1938** All's not quiet on the range, but Autry comes along to sing things back to normal. Goofy, clumsy, ubiquitous sidekick Burnette is a symbol for this whole effort. **55m/B VHS.** Gene Autry, Smiley Burnette, Monte Blue; ***D:*** Mack V. Wright.

Roots 🦴🦴🦴🦴 **1977** The complete version of Alex Haley's saga following a black man's search for his heritage, revealing an epic panorama of America's past. Dramatizing the shared heritage of millions of African Americans in an ennobling fashion, this milestone miniseries brought together dozens of black actors to create an accurate, if simplified, picture of several generations in one black family. The story begins with Kunta Kinte (Burton) going through his manhood trials in his Gambian village in Africa, only to be captured by slavers and shipped away to America. **573m/C VHS, DVD.** John Amos, Maya Angelou, Ed Asner, Lloyd Bridges, LeVar Burton, Chuck Connors, Cicely Tyson, Ben Vereen, Sandy Duncan, Tanya Boyd, Lynda Day George, Lorne Greene, Burl Ives, O.J. Simpson, Todd Bridges, Georg Stanford Brown, MacDonald Carey, Olivia Cole, Leslie Uggams, Ossie Davis; ***D:*** David Greene, Marvin J. Chomsky, John Erman, Gilbert Moses; ***W:*** William Blinn, Ernest Kinoy, M. Charles Cohen, James H. Lee; ***C:*** Stevan Larner, Joseph M. Wilcots; ***M:*** Quincy Jones, Gerald Fried. **TV**

Roots of Evil 🦴 1/2 **1991 (R)** This erotic thriller follows a cop on the trail of a murderer who specializes in killing Hollywood's most beautiful prostitutes. Also available in unrated and Spanish-language versions. **95m/C VHS.** Alex Cord, Delia Sheppard, Charles Dierkop, Jillian Kesner; ***D:*** Gary Graver.

Roots: The Gift 🦴🦴 **1988** It's Christmas 1770, and Kunte Kinte (Burton) and Fiddler (Gossett) try to escape slavery via the Underground Railroad. In their attempt, they wind up giving the gift of freedom to several of their fellow slaves. **94m/C VHS.** Louis Gossett Jr., LeVar Burton, Michael Learned, Avery Brooks, Kate Mulgrew, Shaun Cassidy, John McMartin; ***D:*** Kevin Hooks; ***C:*** John A. Alonzo. **TV**

Roots: The Next Generation 🦴🦴🦴 **1979** Sequel to the landmark TV miniseries continuing the story of author Alex Haley's ancestors from the Reconstruction era of the 1880s to 1967, culminating with Haley's visit to West Africa where he is told the story of Kunta Kinte. **685m/C VHS.** Georg Stanford Brown, Lynne Moody, Henry Fonda, Richard Thomas, Marc Singer, Olivia de Havilland, Paul Koslo, Beah Richards, Stan Shaw, Harry (Henry) Morgan, Irene Cara, Dorian Harewood, Ruby Dee, Paul Winfield, James Earl Jones, Debbie Allen; ***Cameos:*** Al Freeman Jr., Marlon Brando; ***D:*** John Erman; ***W:*** Sydney Glass; ***C:*** Joseph M. Wilcots; ***M:*** Gerald Fried. **TV**

Rope 🦴🦴🦴 1/2 **1948 (PG)** In New York City, two gay college students murder a friend for kicks and store the body in a living room trunk. They further insult the dead by using the trunk as the buffet table and inviting his parents to the dinner party in his honor. Very dark humor is the theme in Hitchcock's first color film, which he innovatively shot in uncut ten-minute takes, with the illusion of a continuous scene maintained with tricky camera work. Based on the Patrick Hamilton play and on the Leopold-Loeb murder case. **81m/C VHS, DVD.** James Stewart, John Dall, Farley Granger, Cedric Hardwicke, Constance Collier; ***D:*** Alfred Hitchcock; ***W:*** Arthur Laurents; ***C:*** William V. Skall, Joseph Valentine; ***M:*** David Buttolph.

Rorret 🦴🦴🦴 **1987** "Rorret" is "terror" spelled backwards—a good indication of the psychological and physical terror Mr. Rorret, the owner of the Peeping Tom Cinema, inflicts upon his female patrons. The Cinema is devoted to the horror film and Rorret himself dresses like Peter Lorre in "M"; lives behind the movie screen, watching the films in mirror image; and enjoys the frightened reactions of his female patrons. He enjoys their reactions so much that he later stalks the women for real. Highlighted by recreated sequences from such psycho-terror classics as "Psycho," "Dial M for Murder," "Strangers on a Train," and "Peeping Tom." In Italian with English subtitles. **105m/C VHS.** *IT* Lou Castel, Anna Galiena, Massimo Venturiello; ***D:*** Fulvio Wetzl; ***W:*** Fulvio Wetzl.

Rory O'Shea Was Here 🦴🦴 1/2 *Inside I'm Dancing* **2004 (R)** Rory is the independence-seeking, fun-loving, skirt-chasing new arrival at Carrigmore nursing home. A muscular dystrophy patient, he befriends cerebral palsy sufferer Michael because he seems to be the only one who can understand him. When Rory is denied an independent-living grant because of his recklessness, he persuades Michael to apply, tagging along as his interpreter. They hire Siobhan, a cute supermarket clerk as their helper. Inevitably, they both fall for her. Excellent performances and some genuinely funning and touching scenes help elevate this Irish import above the usual disease-of-the-week fare. **104m/C DVD.** *IR GB FR* Steven Robertson, James McAvoy, Romola Garai, Brenda Fricker, Gerard McSorley, Tom Hickey, Ruth McCabe; ***D:*** Damien O'Donnell; ***W:*** Jeffrey Caine; ***M:*** David Julyan.

Rosa Luxemburg 🦴🦴 **1986** Based on the life of the Jewish political radical, murdered in 1919. Involving herself with the German Social Democratic Party, Luxemburg undergoes numerous imprisonments and maintains a tempestuous personal life. Based primarily on Luxemburg's letters and speeches; charismatic performance by Sukowa. In German with English subtitles. **122m/C VHS.** *GE* Barbara Sukowa, Daniel Olbrychski, Otto Sander, Adelheid Arndt; ***D:*** Margarethe von Trotta; ***W:*** Margarethe von Trotta. Cannes '86: Actress (Sukowa).

The Rosa Parks Story 🦴🦴 1/2 **2002** Rather prosaic bio on Rosa Parks (Bassett) goes into detail on her life (beginning when she was the new girl at a Montgomery school) to her involvement in the N.A.A.C.P. and the Montgomery, Alabama bus boycott sparked by her arrest. **90m/C VHS, DVD.** Angela Bassett, Peter Francis James, Tonea Stewart, Cicely Tyson, Sonny Shroyer; ***D:*** Julie Dash; ***W:*** Paris Qualles. **TV**

Rosalie 🦴🦴 1/2 **1938** A gridiron great from West Point falls for a mysterious beauty from Vassar. He soon learns that her father reigns over a tiny Balkan nation. Expensive, massive, imperfect musical; exotic romantic pairing fails to conceal plot's blah-ness. Oh well, at least Porter's music is good. ♫ I've a Strange New Rhythm in My Heart; Why Should I Care?; Spring Love Is in the Air; Rosalie; It's All Over But the Shouting; Who Knows?; In the Still of the Night; To Love or Not to Love; Close (instrumental). **118m/B VHS.** Nelson Eddy, Eleanor Powell, Frank Morgan, Ray Bolger, Ilona Massey, Reginald Owen, Edna May Oliver, Jerry Colonna; ***D:*** Woodbridge S. Van Dyke; ***M:*** Cole Porter.

Rosalie Goes Shopping 🦴🦴🦴 **1989 (PG-13)** Satire about American consumerism hiding behind slapstick comedy, and it works, most of the time. Misplaced Bavarian (Sagebrecht) moves to Arkansas and begins spending wildly and acquiring "things." Twisty plot carried confidently by confident wackiness from Sagebrecht and supporters. **94m/C VHS.** *GE* Marianne Saegebrecht, Brad Davis, Judge Reinhold, Willie Harlander, Alex Winter, Erika Blumberger, Patricia Zehentmayr; ***D:*** Percy Adlon; ***W:*** Eleonore Adlon, Percy Adlon; ***M:*** Bob Telson.

The Rosary Murders 🦴🦴 **1987 (R)** Based on the William X. Kienzle mystery about a serial killer preying on nuns and priests. Father Koesler (Sutherland) must betray the confessional to stop him. Interesting, though sometimes muddled and too rarely tense. Filmed on location in Detroit. **105m/C VHS.** Donald Sutherland, Charles Durning, Belinda Bauer, Josef Sommer, James Murtaugh, John Danelle, Addison Powell, Kathleen Tolan, Janet Smith; ***D:*** Fred Walton; ***W:*** Fred Walton, Elmore Leonard; ***C:*** David Golia.

The Rose 🦴🦴🦴 **1979 (R)** Modeled after the life of Janis Joplin, Midler plays a young, talented and self-destructive blues/rock singer. Professional triumphs don't stop her lonely restlessness and confused love affairs. The best exhibition of the rock and roll world outside of documentaries. Electrifying film debut for Midler features an incredible collection of songs. ♫ Fire Down Below; I've Written A Letter to Daddy; Let Me Call You Sweetheart; The Rose; Stay With Me; Camellia; Sold My Soul To Rock 'n' Roll; Keep On Rockin'; When A Man Loves a Woman. **134m/C VHS, DVD.** Bette Midler, Alan Bates, Frederic Forrest, Harry Dean Stanton, David Keith; ***D:*** Mark Rydell; ***C:*** Vilmos Zsigmond. Golden Globes '80: Actress—Mus./Comedy (Midler), Song ("The Rose"); Natl. Soc. Film

Critics '79: Support. Actor (Forrest).

The Rose and the Jackal 1990 Fun, intriguing fictionalization about the founder of the Pinkerton detective agency. During the Civil War, bearded, Scottish Reeve tries to persuade a wealthy Southern lady to help save the Union. **94m/C VHS.** Christopher Reeve, Madolyn Smith, Granville Van Dusen, Carrie Snodgress, Kevin McCarthy; ***D:*** Jack Gold. **CABLE**

The Rose Garden 1/2 **1989 (PG-13)** In modern Germany, a Holocaust survivor is put on trial for assaulting an elderly man. The victim, it turns out, was a Nazi guilty of heinous war crimes. Ullmann and Schell lend substance, though treatment of a powerful theme is inadequate. **112m/C VHS.** Liv Ullmann, Maximilian Schell, Peter Fonda, Jan Niklas, Kurt Hubner; ***D:*** Fons Rademakers; ***W:*** Paul Hengge; ***M:*** Egisto Macchi.

Rose Hill 1/2 **1997 (PG)** Adam, Travis, Douglas, and Cole are (unrelated) orphans, living on the streets of 1860s New York City, when they find an abandoned baby girl. They adopt the baby, whom they name Mary Rose, and decide to head west to start a new life as a family. As the years pass the boys build a cattle ranch in Montana they name Rose Hill and over-protect their headstrong teenaged sister, who would like the chance to flirt with some beaus without her brothers hovering around. TV movie based on the Julie Garwood novel "For the Roses." **90m/C VHS, DVD.** Jennifer Garner, Jeffrey D. Sams, Tristan Tait, Zak Orth, Justin Chambers, Casey Siemaszko, David Newcom; ***D:*** Christopher Cain; ***W:*** Earl W. Wallace. **TV**

Rose Marie *Indian Love Call* **1936** An opera star falls in love with the mountie who captured her escaped convict brother. Hollywood legend has it that when a British singer was presented with the first line in "Indian Love Song," which is "When I'm calling you-oo-oo-oo-oo-oo-oo," the confused performer sang, "When I'm calling you, double oh, double oh, double oh..." Maybe true, maybe not, but funny anyway. Classic MacDonald-Eddy operetta. Remade in 1954. ♫Indian Love Call; Pardon Me, Madame; The Mounties; Rose Marie; Totem Tom Tom; Just for You; Tex Yeux; St. Louis Blues; Dinah. **112m/B VHS.** Jeanette MacDonald, Nelson Eddy, James Stewart, Allan Jones, David Niven, Reginald Owen; ***D:*** Woodbridge S. Van Dyke; ***C:*** William H. Daniels; ***M:*** Rudolf Friml.

Rose Marie **1954 (G)** Blyth is a lonely Canadian woman wooed by a mean spirited fur trapper and a gallant mountie. Unremarkable remake of the Eddy/MacDonald musical is saved by specatular technicolor and CinemaScope photography. Choreography by Busby Berkeley. ♫Rose Marie; Indian Love Call; Totem Tom Tom; The Mounties; I Have the Love; The Right Place For A Girl; Free to be Free; The Mountie Who Never Got His Man. **115m/C VHS.** Ann Blyth, Howard Keel, Fernando Lamas, Bert Lahr, Marjorie Main, Joan Taylor, Chief Yowlachie, Abel Fernandez, Al Ferguson, Dabbs Greer, Lumsden Hare; ***D:*** Mervyn LeRoy; ***C:*** Paul Vogel.

Rose of Rio Grande **1938** A western musical about a Mexican gang that avenges the deaths of members of the upper strata. **60m/B VHS.** John Carroll, Movita, Antonio Moreno, Lena Basquette, Duncan Renaldo; ***D:*** William Nigh.

Rose of Washington Square 1/2 **1939** Singer Faye gets involved with the no-account Power, much to the dismay of her friend Jolson. They marry, and she becomes a singing sensation in the Ziegfeld Follies while he becomes an embarassment, eventually winding up on the wrong side of the law. Jolson stole the movie, singing some of his best numbers. This thinly disguised portrait of Fanny Brice caused the performer to sue for defamation of character; she eventually settled out of court. ♫California, Here I Come; My Mammy; Pretty Baby; Toot Toot Tootsie Goodbye; Rock-A-Bye Your Baby with a Dixie Melody; My Man; I'm Just Wild About Harry; I Never Knew Heaven Could Speak; Rose of Washington Square. **86m/B VHS.** Alice Faye, Tyrone Power, Al Jolson, William Frawley, Joyce Compton, Hobart Cavanaugh, Moroni Olsen; ***D:*** Gregory Ratoff; ***W:*** Nunnally Johnson; ***C:*** Karl Freund.

The Rose Tattoo 1/2 **1955** Magnani, in her U.S. screen debut, is just right as a Southern widow who cherishes her husband's memory, but falls for virile trucker Lancaster. Williams wrote this play and screenplay specifically for Magnani, who was never as successful again. Interesting character studies, although Lancaster doesn't seem right as an Italian longshoreman. **117m/B VHS, DVD.** Anna Magnani, Burt Lancaster, Marisa Pavan, Ben Cooper, Virginia Grey, Jo Van Fleet; ***D:*** Daniel Mann; ***W:*** Tennessee Williams, Hal Kanter; ***C:*** James Wong Howe; ***M:*** Alex North. Oscars '55: Actress (Magnani), Art Dir./Set Dec., B&W, B&W Cinematog.; British Acad. '56: Actress (Magnani); Golden Globes '56: Actress—Drama (Magnani), Support. Actress (Pavan); N.Y. Film Critics '55: Actress (Magnani).

Roseanne: An Unauthorized Biography **1994** Boring TV movie about the boorish (ex-)duo of Tom Arnold and Roseanne Barr Pentland Arnold. Recounts her troubled upbringing in Salt Lake City, her stormy marriage, and her long slog toward fame as a "domestic goddess" stand-up comedienne and TV series star. Miscasting of both leads hurts any chance this poor substitute had. **90m/C VHS.** Denny Dillon, David Graf, John Walcutt, John Karlen, Judith Scarpone, Danielle Harris; ***D:*** Paul Schneider; ***W:*** Kam-yuen Szeto; ***C:*** Yuri Neyman; ***M:*** Scott Harper.

Rosebud **1975 (PG)** Embarassingly dull film finds a group of PLO terrorists kidnapping five young women who were vacationing aboard O'Toole's yacht. He's supposedly a journalist but actually works for the CIA. Action ping-pongs between the plight of the victims and what's being done to rescue them but it's so boring you won't care. "Rosebud" is the name of the yacht. Based on a novel by Joan Hemingway and Paul Bonnecarrere. **126m/C VHS.** Peter O'Toole, Richard Attenborough, Kim Cattrall, Brigitte Ariel, Isabelle Huppert, Lalla Ward, Deborah Berger, Cliff Gorman, Claude Dauphin, Peter Lawford, Raf Vallone, Adrienne Corri; ***D:*** Otto Preminger; ***W:*** Eric Lee Preminger, Marjorie Kellogg.

Rosebud Beach Hotel *The Big Lobby; The No-Tell Hotel* **1985 (R)** Wimpy loser tries his hand at managing a run-down hotel in order to please his demanding girlfriend. Camp is okay, but this soft-porn excuse is horrible in every other way. **82m/C VHS, DVD.** Colleen Camp, Peter Scolari, Christopher Lee, Fran Drescher, Eddie Deezen, Chuck McCann, Hank Garrett, Hamilton Camp, Cherie Currie; ***D:*** Harry Hurwitz; ***C:*** Joao Fernandes.

Roseland **1977 (PG)** Three interlocking stories, set at New York's famous old Roseland Ballroom, about lonely people who live to dance. Not fully successful, but strong characters, especially in the second and third stories, make it worth watching, although it lacks energy. **103m/C VHS, DVD.** Christopher Walken, Geraldine Chaplin, Joan Copeland, Teresa Wright, Lou Jacobi; ***D:*** James Ivory; ***W:*** Ruth Prawer Jhabvala.

Rosemary's Baby **1968 (R)** A young woman, innocent and religious, and her husband, ambitious and agnostic, move into a new apartment. Soon the woman is pregnant, but she begins to realize that she has fallen into a coven of witches and warlocks, and that they claim the child as the antichrist. Gripping and powerful, subtle yet utterly horrifying, with luminous performances by all. Polanski's first American film; from Levin's best-seller. **134m/C VHS, DVD.** Mia Farrow, John Cassavetes, Ruth Gordon, Sidney Blackmer, Maurice Evans, Patsy Kelly, Elisha Cook Jr., Ralph Bellamy, Charles Grodin, Hanna Landy, Emmaline Henry, William Castle; ***D:*** Roman Polanski; ***W:*** Roman Polanski; ***C:*** William A. Fraker; ***M:*** Krzysztof Komeda; ***V:*** Tony Curtis. Oscars '68: Support. Actress (Gordon); Golden Globes '69: Support. Actress (Gordon).

Rosencrantz & Guildenstern Are Dead **1990 (PG)** Playwright Stoppard adapted his own absurdist 1967 play to film—which at first look makes as much sense as a "Swan Lake" ballet on radio. Patience is rewarded for those who stick with it. Two tragicomic minor characters in "Hamlet" squabble rhetorically and misperceive Shakespeare's plot tightening fatally around them. Uprooted from the stage environment, it's arcane but hilarious if you're paying attention. Roth and Oldman are superb as the doomed duo. **118m/C VHS, DVD.** *GB* Gary Oldman, Tim Roth, Richard Dreyfuss, Iain Glen, Joanna Roth, Donald (Don) Sumpter, Sven Medvesck, Joanna Miles, Ian Richardson, John Burgess, Vili Matula, Ljubo Zecevic; ***D:*** Tom Stoppard; ***W:*** Tom Stoppard; ***C:*** Peter Biziou; ***M:*** Stanley Myers. Venice Film Fest. '91: Picture.

Rosenstrasse **2003 (PG-13)** Fact-based account of a forgotten incident of heroism in WWII Germany. When remaining Jews of Berlin are rounded up for deportation to death camps in 1943, those married to non-Jewish women, or children of such couples are diverted to temporary prison on Rosenstrasse ("Street of Roses"). Many of the detainees' wives gather outside prison to show support to families inside and demand their release. After several days of quiet courageous protest, prisoners were released and saved from gas chambers. Film tells this story through families directly involved in event. Moving and well-acted retelling of lost piece of history. **136m/C DVD.** *GE NL* Katja Riemann, Maria Schrader, Martin Feifel, Jutta Lampe, Doris Schade, Fedja Van Huet, Carola Regnier, Jan Decleir, Thekla Reuten, Lena Stolze, Isolde Barth, Martin Wuttke, Jurgen Vogel, Svea Lohde, Jutta Wachowiak, Nina Kunzendorf; ***D:*** Margarethe von Trotta; ***W:*** Margarethe von Trotta, Pamela Katz; ***C:*** Jan Betke; ***M:*** Loek Dikker.

Roses Bloom Twice 1/2 **1977** When a middle-aged widow decides to make up for some of the wild living that she missed during her marriage, she shocks her children. **87m/C VHS.** Glynis McNicoll, Michael Craig, Diane Craig, John Allen, Jennifer West; ***D:*** David Stevens.

Rosetta **1999 (R)** Rosetta (Dequenne) is a desperate 17-year-old Belgian who lives in a trailer with her alcoholic mother. Her joyless routine includes caring for her passed-out mom and frantically searching for some kind of employment, even if it means betraying her one friend, Riquet (Rongione), who works at a waffle stand and whose job Rosetta comes to covet. Claustrophobic and depressing. French with subtitles. **95m/C VHS, DVD.** *FR BE* Emilie Dequenne, Fabrizio Rongione, Anne Yernaux, Olivier Gourmet; ***D:*** Jean-Pierre Dardenne, Luc Dardenne; ***W:*** Jean-Pierre Dardenne, Luc Dardenne; ***C:*** Alain Marcoen. Cannes '99: Actress (Dequenne), Film.

Rosewood **1996 (R)** Based on the true story of the well-off African American community of Rosewood, Florida, which was destroyed by a white mob in 1923. Rhames is Mr. Mann, a war vet and Voight a white shopkeeper who, together, try to save innocent people from the tragic massacre that begins when a woman falsely accuses a black man of rape. Accurately shows the tensions present between blacks and whites of the time. Voight's character is not overly romanticized as the great white hope. The real hero is the reticent Rhames, a fictitious blend of real-life characters and Hollywood machismo. Both performances are strong and film succeeds as a detailed visual reminder of country's tragic history. Real-life survivors of the bloodshed finally won reparation from the Florida legislature in 1993. Singleton's location shoots in the Florida swamps caused problems for the crew, one of whom was sent to the hospital after a snake bite. **142m/C VHS, DVD.** Ving Rhames, Jon Voight, Don Cheadle, Michael Rooker, Bruce McGill, Loren Dean, Esther Rolle, Elise Neal, Catherine Kellner, Akosua Busia, Paul Benjamin, Mark Boone Jr., Muse Watson, Badja (Medu) Djola, Kathryn Meisle, Jaimz Woolvett; ***D:*** John Singleton; ***W:*** Gregory Poirier; ***C:*** Johnny E. Jensen; ***M:*** John Williams.

Rosie **1999** Rosie (Coppens) is 13 and is first seen living in an institution for delinquents. Her desperate story is told in flashbacks as the girl grows up in industrial Antwerp in a cramped apartment with her mother, Irene (de Roo), who insists Rosie say they are sisters when men come to visit, which they do frequently. When her moocher Uncle Michel (Vercruyssen) arrives, Rosie is even kicked out of her bedroom. It's no wonder she escapes into a romantic dreamworld she shares with a would-be boyfriend, Jimi (Wijnant), and the dangerous turn her real life takes. Flemish with subtitles. **97m/C VHS.** *BE* Aranka Coppens, Sara de Roo, Joost Wijnant, Frank Vercruyssen; ***D:*** Patrice Toye; ***W:*** Patrice Toye; ***C:*** Richard Van Oosterhout; ***M:*** John Parish.

Rosie: The Rosemary Clooney Story 1/2 **1982** Above average biography of Clooney's up-and-down career. Locke lip-synches Clooney's voice in songs. Orlando doesn't help matters portraying Jose Ferrer. **100m/C VHS.** Sondra Locke, Tony Orlando, Penelope Milford, Katherine Helmond, Kevin McCarthy, John Karlen, Cheryl Anderson, Robert Ridgely, Joey Travolta; ***D:*** Jackie Cooper. **TV**

Roswell: The U.F.O. Cover-Up 1/2 **1994 (PG-13)** Fact-based drama finds intelligence officer Major Jesse Marcel (McLachlan) investigating the wreckage of a craft near his Roswell, New Mexico air base in the summer of 1947. Marcel believes the craft is extraterrestrial—as are the strange bodies recovered from the wreckage. An Air Force press release announces a UFO but is quickly retracted and Marcel's suspicions ridiculed. A 30-year reunion still finds him obsessed and seeking to clear his name but this time Marcel's investigations may finally lead to the truth. Made for TV; based on the book "UFO Crash at Roswell" by Kevin D. Randle and Donald R. Schmitt. **91m/C VHS, DVD.** Kyle MacLachlan, Dwight Yoakam, Kim Greist, Martin Sheen, Xander Berkeley, J.D. Daniels, Doug Wert, John M. Jackson, Peter MacNichol, Bob Gunton, Charles Martin Smith; ***D:*** Jeremy Paul Kagan; ***W:*** Jeremy Paul Kagan, Arthur Kopit, Paul Davids; ***C:*** Steven Poster; ***M:*** Elliot Goldenthal. **TV**

R.O.T.O.R. **1988** R.O.T.O.R. (Robotic Officer of Tactical Operations Research) is a law enforcement robot that is supposed to stop criminals. But watch out! It might go beserk and wreck your town. **90m/C VHS.** Richard Gesswein, Margaret Trigg, Jayne Smith; ***D:*** Cullen Blaine.

The Rough and the Smooth 1/2 *Portrait of a Sinner* **1959** Mike is engaged to heiress Margaret but falls for nympho Ila who proceeds to nearly ruin his life when they have an affair, taunting him about the other men she's also seeing. Based on a novel by Robin Maugham. **96m/B DVD.** *GB* Tony Britton, Nadja Tiller, William Bendix, Natasha Parry, Tony Wright, Norman Wooland, Donald Wolfit, Adrienne Corri; ***D:*** Robert Siodmak; ***W:*** Dudley Leslie, Audrey Erskine-Lindop; ***C:*** Otto Heller; ***M:*** Douglas Gamley.

Rough Cut **1980 (PG)** American diamond thief Reynolds lives in London, pursued by an aging Scotland Yard detective who wants to end his career in a blaze of glory. A beautiful lady is the decoy. Good chemistry; lousy script. **112m/C VHS.** Burt Reynolds, Lesley-Anne Down, David Niven, Timothy West, Joss Ackland, Patrick Magee; ***D:*** Donald Siegel; ***W:*** Larry Gelbart; ***C:*** Frederick A. (Freddie) Young.

Rough Justice 1/2 *La Belva; The Bell; The Beast* **1970** Spaghetti western about a lone gunfighter tracking down three killers. Kinski is a sexually aroused bad guy in this miserable excuse. What could he have been thinking? **95m/C VHS.** *IT* Klaus Kinski, Steven Tedd; ***D:*** Mario Costa; ***W:*** Mario Costa; ***C:*** Luciano Trasatti; ***M:*** Stelvio Cipriani.

Rough Magic *Miss Shumway; Jette un Sort* **1995 (PG-13)** Fantasy-noir-romance-comedy-on-the-road-movie-nostalgia-fest can't decide what it wants to be when it grows up. Fonda is a magician's assistant, with latent powers of her own, who flees to Mexico after witnessing a murder. Her fiance (Moffett) turns out to be the culprit and he hires drifter Crowe to track her down. Along the way, they meet a quack doctor (Broadbent) trying to find a magic Mayan potion, a garage owner who becomes a sausage, and a shaman. Sure, it's confusing, but the performances are good, and you could always play "Name That Genre" afterwards. Adapted from the novel "Miss Shumway Waves a Wand" by James Hadley Chase. **104m/C VHS, DVD.** *GB FR* Bridget Fonda, Russell Crowe, Jim Broadbent, D.W. Moffett, Paul Rodriguez, Euva Anderson; ***D:*** Clare Peploe; ***W:***

Clare Peploe, Robert Mundy, William Brookfield; *C:* John Campbell; *M:* Richard Hartley.

Rough Night in Jericho 🦴 1/2 **1967** Martin plays unredeemable scum in this cliched western. He's an ex-lawman trying to take over the town of Jericho and all that's left to own is the stagecoach line run by Simmons and McIntire. Coming to Simmons aid is Peppard, a former deputy marshall turned gambler. Predicatably violent. **104m/C VHS, DVD.** Dean Martin, Jean Simmons, George Peppard, John McIntire, Slim Pickens, Don Galloway; *D:* Arnold Laven; *W:* Sydney (Sidney) Boehm, Marvin H. Albert; *C:* Russell Metty; *M:* Don Costa.

Rough Riders 🦴🦴 1/2 **1997** Miniseries covering the adventures of the Volunteer Cavalry, led by a pre-presidential Teddy Roosevelt (Berneger), and their travails during the Spanish-American War in 1898. Fighting in Cuba, the Calvary were a mixture of western outlaws and cowboys and eastern bluebloods—all of whom would have to learn to fight together. Filmed on locations in Texas. **240m/C VHS, DVD.** Tom Berenger, Sam Elliott, Gary Busey, Brad Johnson, Christopher Noth, Brian Keith, George Hamilton, R. Lee Ermey, Nicholas Chinlund, Dale Dye, Holt McCallany, Illeana Douglas, Geoffrey Lewis, William Katt, Adam Storke, Dakin Matthews, Francesco Quinn, Titus Welliver, Mark Moses; *D:* John Milius; *W:* John Milius, Hugh Wilson; *C:* Anthony B. Richmond; *M:* Peter Bernstein. **CABLE**

Rough Riders of Cheyenne 🦴 1/2 **1945** Sunset Carson ends the feud between the Carsons and the Sterlings. **54m/B VHS.** Sunset Carson, Peggy Stewart, Mira McKinney, Monte Hale, Wade Crosby, Kenne Duncan, Tom London, Eddy (Eddie, Ed) Waller, Jack Rockwell; *D:* Thomas Carr; *W:* Elizabeth Beecher; *C:* William Bradford.

Rough Riders' Roundup 🦴🦴 **1939** Roy and the boys rid a mining town of its crooked manager. Less yodeling than later Roger's outings; also better all around. **54m/B VHS, DVD.** Roy Rogers, Raymond Hatton, Lynne Roberts, Dorothy Sebastian, Duncan Renaldo, George Montgomery; *D:* Joseph Kane.

Rough Ridin' Rhythm 🦴 1/2 **1937** Wallace is kidnapped to care for the orphaned child of a bandit's sister with Maynard being accused of having murdered the woman. But he's innocent and fights the gang to clear his name. Based on the story "Getting a Start in Life" by James Oliver Curwood. **58m/B VHS.** Kermit Maynard, Beryl Wallace, Ralph Peters, Betty Mack, Curley Dresden; *D:* J(ohn) P(aterson) McGowan.

Rough Riding Ranger 🦴 1/2 *The Secret Stranger* **1935** Threatening letters plague a western ranch family. **57m/B VHS.** Rex Lease, Janet Chandler, Bobby Nelson, Yakima Canutt, George Chesebro, Mabel Strickland, Robert Walker; *D:* Elmer Clifton; *W:* Elmer Clifton, George M. Merrick; *C:* Edward Linden.

Roughly Speaking 🦴🦴 **1945** Sentimental domestic drama based on Randall Pierson's autobiography. Independent-minded Louise (Russell) is taking business classes when she marries conventional Rodney Crane (Woods). They have four kids, but Rodney's a cheat and they get divorced so Louise must support her family any way she can. Then she meets amiable Harold Pierson (Carson) and they marry but their happy family life is frequently plagued by financial difficulties as the story continues through the Depression into World War II. **117m/B DVD.** Rosalind Russell, Jack Carson, Donald Woods, Ann Doran, Alan Hale; *D:* Michael Curtiz; *W:* Louise R. Pierson; *C:* Joseph Walker; *M:* Max Steiner.

Roughnecks 🦴 1/2 **1980** A team of Texas oil drillers attempt to dig the deepest oil well in history and chase women on the side. Too long, and not particularly action-packed or gripping. **240m/C VHS.** Sam Melville, Cathy Lee Crosby, Vera Miles, Harry (Henry) Morgan, Steve Forrest, Stephen McHattie, Wilford Brimley; *D:* Bernard McEveety. **TV**

Round Midnight 🦴🦴🦴 **1986 (R)** An aging, alcoholic black American jazz saxophonist comes to Paris in the late 1950s seeking an escape from his self-destructive existence. A devoted young French fan spurs him to one last burst of creative brilliance. A moody, heartfelt homage to such expatriate bebop musicians as Bud Powell and Lester Young. In English and French with English subtitles. Available in a Spanish-subtitled version. **132m/C VHS, DVD.** *FR* Dexter Gordon, Lonette McKee, Francois Cluzet, Martin Scorsese, Herbie Hancock, Sandra Reaves-Phillips; *D:* Bertrand Tavernier; *W:* Bertrand Tavernier, David Rayfiel; *C:* Bruno de Keyzer. Oscars '86: Orig. Score.

Round Numbers 🦴 1/2 **1991 (R)** Judith Schweitzer believes her husband "Big Al the Muffler King" is having an affair with the gorgeous Muffler Mate of the Month, Mitzi (Playboy Playmate Hope Marie Carlton). Determined to get revenge, Judith books herself into the same health spa that Mitzi attends and the result is pure comedy. **98m/C VHS.** Kate Mulgrew, Samantha Eggar, Marty Ingels, Hope Marie Carlton, Shani Wallis, Natalie Barish, Debra Christofferson; *D:* Nancy Zala; *W:* Nancy Zala.

Round Trip to Heaven 🦴🦴 **1992 (R)** Party guy Larry (Feldman) and his innocent cousin (Galligan) take off in a borrowed Rolls Royce to go meet Larry's dream centerfold in a super model contest. Unfortunately, the Rolls' trunk is loaded with stolen money and Stoneface (Sharkey), the felon who stashed the cash, wants the money back. With Stoneface in pursuit these guys are in for the ride of their lives. For the teen set only. Also available with Spanish subtitles. **97m/C VHS.** Corey Feldman, Zach Galligan, Julie McCullough, Rowanne Brewer, Ray Sharkey; *D:* Alan Roberts.

The Round Up 🦴🦴 1/2 *Szegenylegenyek Nehezeletuck; The Hopeless Ones; The Poor Outlaws* **1966** Brutal tale spins a realistic political web of fear. Set in 1868 in a prison camp, suspected Hungarian subversives, largely peasants and herdsmen, are thrown into jail and tortured. A direct and shocking exploration of life under dehumanizing, totalitarian rule. In Hungarian with English subtitles. **90m/B VHS.** *HU* Janos Gorbe, Tibor Molnar, Andras Kozak; *D:* Miklos Jancso; *W:* Gyula Hernadi.

Round-Up Time in Texas 🦴🦴 **1937** Autry delivers a herd of horses to his diamond-prospector brother in South Africa and has to deal with bandits after the jewels. Typical early Autry entry, with singin' on the side. **54m/B VHS, DVD.** Gene Autry, Smiley Burnette; *D:* Joseph Kane.

The Rounders 🦴🦴 1/2 **1965** Two aging, no-account cowboys (Ford and Fonda) dream of giving up their bronco-busting ways to open a bar in Tahiti where they can watch the world go by. But they have a habit of blowing all their money on women, whiskey, and bad bets. An ornery unbreakable horse may be the key to changing their luck. Mild-mannered comedy with beautiful Arizona scenery. **85m/C VHS, UMD.** Glenn Ford, Henry Fonda, Sue Ane Langdon, Hope Holiday, Chill Wills, Edgar Buchanan, Kathleen Freeman, Joan Freeman, Denver Pyle; *D:* Burt Kennedy; *W:* Burt Kennedy; *C:* Paul Vogel.

Rounders 🦴🦴 1/2 **1998 (R)** Damon plays Mike, a law student who used to be a poker hustler, but is now ready to leave the game and settle down with girlfriend Jo (Mol). His good intentions are undermined by his "friend" Worm (Norton), whose gambling debts are mounting. Mike's return to the table doesn't reduce the debt; instead, he loses money and his reputation. Knowing he must get the money himself, Mike sets up a final showdown with Teddy KGB (Malkovich)—a tense game of Texas Hold 'Em in which Malkovich's drawn-out accent provides the most fun of the movie. Damon holds his own, using some elaborate monologues reminiscent of "Good Will Hunting," while Norton and Malkovich add a lot of spark. It's all style over substance, but that's what makes it (mostly) work. **120m/C VHS, DVD.** Matt Damon, Edward Norton, John Turturro, Gretchen Mol, Famke Janssen, John Malkovich, Martin Landau, Michael Rispoli, Melina Kanakaredes, Josh Mostel, Lenny Clarke, Tom Aldredge, Lenny Venito, Goran Visnjic; *D:* John Dahl; *W:* David Levien, Brian Koppelman; *C:* Jean-Yves Escoffier; *M:* Christopher Young.

Rounding Up the Law 🦴🦴 1/2 **1922** Good guy dupes bad guy while organ plays. **62m/B VHS.** Russell Gordon, Chet Ryan, Patricia Palmer, William (Bill, Billy) McCall, Guinn "Big Boy" Williams; *D:* Charles Seeling.

The Roundup 🦴🦴 **1941** Janet (Morison) is set to marry rancher Steve (Dix) on the rebound after her beloved fiance Greg (Foster) is killed (or so she thinks). But Greg shows up on the wedding day and he's none too happy that Janet's getting hitched to another guy. **90m/B VHS.** Richard Dix, Patricia Morison, Preston Foster, Don Wilson, Betty Brewer; *D:* Lesley Selander; *W:* Harold Shumate, Edmund Day.

Roustabout 🦴🦴 1/2 **1964 (PG)** A roving, reckless drifter joins a carnival and romances the owner's daughter. Elvis rides on good support from Stanwyck et al. Welch has a bit part in her film debut; look for Terri Garr as a dancer. ♫Roustabout; Poison Ivy League; One Track Heart; Little Egypt; Wheels on My Heels; It's a Wonderful World; It's Carnival Time; Hard Knocks; There's a Brand New Day on the Horizon. **101m/C VHS, DVD.** Elvis Presley, Barbara Stanwyck, Joan Freeman, Leif Erickson, Sue Ane Langdon, Pat Buttram, Joan Staley, Dabbs Greer, Steve Brodie, Jack Albertson, Marianna Hill, Beverly Adams, Billy Barty, Richard Kiel, Raquel Welch; *D:* John Rich.

The Rousters 🦴🦴 1/2 **1990 (PG)** Descendants of Wyatt Earp run a carnival in a small Western town. Comic misadventures arise when a modern varmint named Clayton comes looking for action. Cannell (of "The A-Team" and "Riptide" fame) co-wrote and produced—with his usual extraordinary mix of the absurd and the dangerous. Unusual vehicle for Rogers, but she keeps her style and humor. Made for TV. **72m/C VHS.** Jim Varney, Mimi Rogers, Chad Everett, Maxine Stuart, Hoyt Axton; *D:* E.W. Swackhamer; *W:* E.W. Swackhamer, Stephen J. Cannell. **TV**

Route 9 🦴🦴 **1998 (R)** Cliched story has some decent performances. Two smalltown sheriff's deputies (MacLachlan and Williams) discover a couple of dead bodies, drugs, and a stash of cash, which they decide to keep. But their boss (Coyote) gets suspicious and then the feds come investigating. **102m/C VHS, DVD.** Kyle MacLachlan, Wade Andrew Williams, Peter Coyote, Roma Maffia, Amy Locane, Miguel (Michael) Sandoval, Scott Coffey; *D:* David Mackay; *W:* Brendan Broderick, Rob Kerchner; *C:* Brian Sullivan; *M:* Don Davis. **CABLE**

Route 666 🦴🦴 1/2 **2001 (R)** Some very slick stylistic touches are brought to this action/horror that aspires to be another "From Dusk Til Dawn." Marshals Jack (Phillips) and Stephanie (Petty) are escorting a witness to a grand jury in Los Angeles when they become lost on a remote highway. Years ago, a chain gang was murdered there, and they return as inmates of the living dead for revenge. The ultra-violence is silly but some of the visual tricks are pretty cool. **90m/C DVD.** Lou Diamond Phillips, Lori Petty, Steven Williams, Dale Midkiff, Alex McArthur, Mercedes Colon, L.Q. Jones; *D:* William Wesley; *W:* William Wesley, Thomas N. Weber, Scott Fivelson; *C:* Philip Lee; *M:* Terry Plumeri.

Route 30 🦴🦴 **2008** Putch's loosely interconnected stories are set along the Lincoln highway in south-central Pennsylvania. In "Deer Hunters Wives," Civil War tour guide Mandy (Boltt) is obsessed with the story of a female civilian killed at the battle of Gettysburg. "What I Believe" has a man explaining to a Christian Scientist that he injured his back after being chased through the mountains by Bigfoot. And in "Original Bill," writer Bill (DeLuise) buys a farmhouse hoping for quiet and inspiration but discovers his Amish neighbor Martha (Delany) isn't what he expected. **83m/C DVD.** David DeLuise, Dana Delany, Nathalie Boltt, Christine Elise, Curtis Armstrong, Robert Romanus, Kevin Rahm; *D:* John Putch; *W:* John Putch; *C:* Keith J. Duggan; *M:* Alexander Baker.

The Rover 🦴 1/2 *The Adventurer* **1967** Peyrol (Quinn) is involved in counterrevolutionary forces during the Napoleonic War and takes refuge in the home of Caterina (Hayworth), where he falls in love with her shy and mentally slow niece, Arlette (Schiaffino). Very dull adaptation of the Joseph Conrad novel. **103m/C VHS.** *IT* Anthony Quinn, Rosanna Schiaffino, Rita Hayworth, Richard Johnson; *D:* Terence Young; *W:* Luciano Vincenzoni, Jo Eisinger; *C:* Leonida Barboni; *M:* Ennio Morricone.

Rover Dangerfield 🦴🦴 **1991 (G)** Lovable Las Vegas hound Rover Dangerfield searches for respect but finds none. The results are hilarious. Quality animation from a project developed by Rodney Dangerfield and Harold Ramis. **78m/C VHS.** *D:* Jim George; *W:* Harold Ramis; *M:* David Newman; *V:* Rodney Dangerfield.

Row Your Boat 🦴🦴 **1998** Ex-con Jamey (Bon Jovi), who took a burglary rap for his brother (Forsythe), is determined to go straight after his release from prison. He gets a job as a census taker, which is how he meets Asian immigrant single mom Chun Hua (Ling) who will become a part of a scheme by Jamey's no-good brother. **106m/C VHS, DVD.** Jon Bon Jovi, William Forsythe, Bai Ling, Jill(ian) Hennessey, John Ventimiglia; *D:* Sollace Mitchell; *W:* Sollace Mitchell; *C:* Michael Barrow, Zoltan David; *M:* Phil Ramone.

The Rowdy Girls 🦴🦴 **2000** Sharp-shooting Tweed disguises herself as a nun and meets up with bullwhip-wielding wild woman Strain and runaway bride Brooks in order to cross the western frontier. And no amount of scurvy outlaws are going to stop them. Ogle to your heart's content. **88m/C VHS, DVD.** Shannon Tweed, Julie Strain, Deanna Brooks, Laszlo Vargo; *D:* Steve Nevius; *W:* India Allen. **VIDEO**

Rowing Through 🦴🦴 **1996** Tiff Wood (Ferguson) is a top sculler at Harvard who is sacrificing everything in his obsession to win gold at the 1980 Moscow Olympics. And he has the best chance—until the U.S. decides to boycott the games. But Tiff refuses to give up his dream and struggles four more years towards the '84 Olympics—even though it means proving himself against a younger group of competitors. **115m/C VHS, DVD.** *CA JP* Colin Ferguson, Leslie Hope, Peter Murnik, Kenneth Welsh, Michiko Hada, Helen Shaver, James Hyndman, Christopher Jacobs; *D:* Masato Harada; *W:* Masato Harada, Will Aitken; *C:* Sylvain Brault; *M:* Masahiro Kawasaki.

Rowing with the Wind 🦴🦴 *Remando al Viento* **1988 (R)** The story behind Mary Shelley's (McInnerny) writing of "Frankenstein," amidst the decadence of Mary and Percy B.'s (Pelka) 1816 Swiss sojourn with Lord Byron (Grant). Hurley has the relatively small role of Claire, Mary's half-sister and Byron's former lover. **95m/C VHS.** *SP* Lizzy McInnerny, Hugh Grant, Valentine Pelka, Elizabeth Hurley, Jose Luis Gomez, Aitana Sanchez-Gijon; *D:* Gonzalo Suarez; *W:* Gonzalo Suarez; *C:* Carlos Suarez.

Roxanne 🦴🦴🦴 **1987 (PG)** A modern comic retelling of "Cyrano de Bergerac." The romantic triangle between a big nosed, small town fire chief, a shy fireman and the lovely astronomer they both love. Martin gives his most sensitive and believable performance. Don't miss the bar scene where he gets back at a heckler. A wonderful adaptation for the modern age. **107m/C VHS, DVD.** Steve Martin, Daryl Hannah, Rick Rossovich, Shelley Duvall, Michael J. Pollard, Fred Willard, John Kapelos, Max Alexander, Damon Wayans, Matt Lattanzi, Kevin Nealon; *D:* Fred Schepisi; *W:* Steve Martin; *C:* Ian Baker; *M:* Bruce Smeaton. L.A. Film Critics '87: Actor (Martin); Natl. Soc. Film Critics '87: Actor (Martin); Writers Guild '87: Adapt. Screenplay.

Roxie Hart 🦴🦴 1/2 **1942** Sassy '20s Chicago dance hall girl Roxie (Rogers) decides to take the fall when hubby (Chandler) murders a man. (She sees it as a publicity boost to her career). Slick lawyer Billy Flynn (Menjou) knows he can get the tootsie off if she justs flashes the jury her considerable sex appeal. Montgomery's a smitten reporter who catches Roxie's eye. Based on the play "Chicago" by Maurine Watkins and previously filmed in 1927. Bob Fosse later adapted the play for a Broadway musical. **75m/B VHS, DVD.** Ginger Rogers, Adolphe Menjou, George Montgomery, Lynne Overman, Nigel Bruce, Phil Silvers, Sara Allgood, William Frawley, Spring Byington, George Chandler; *D:* William A. Wellman; *W:* Nunnally Johnson; *C:* Leon Shamroy; *M:* Alfred Newman.

The Royal Bed 🦴🦴 1/2 *The Queen's Husband* **1931** King Eric's queen really wears the pants in the family, and when she leaves on a trip, he's left helpless and hapless. A revolution erupts, and his daughter announces she plans to marry a commoner. What's a king to do? **74m/B VHS, DVD.** Lowell Sherman, Nance O'Neil, Mary Astor, Anthony Bushell, Gilbert Emery, Robert Warwick, J. Carrol Naish; ***D:*** Lowell Sherman; ***W:*** J. Walter Ruben; ***C:*** Leo Tover.

Royal Deceit ♪ ½ *Prince of Jutland* **1994 (R)** Young Amled (Bale) is heir to the 6th century kingdom of Jutland. But when his father is murdered by Amled's jealous uncle Fenge (Byrne), the youth feigns insanity to save himself and then begins to plot his revenge. Very familiar story doesn't arouse more than mild interest despite the cast. **85m/C VHS, DVD.** Gabriel Byrne, Helen Mirren, Christian Bale, Brian Cox, Kate Beckinsale, Steven Waddington, Tom Wilkinson, Tony Haygarth, Saskia Wickham, Brian Glover; ***D:*** Gabriel Axel; ***C:*** Henning Kristiansen; ***M:*** Per Norgard.

Royal Flash ♪♪♪ **1975 (PG)** Satirical adventure picture, witty and fast paced, with a few real life period characters thrown in for good measure. Cowardly swashbuckler Flashman, wanting to enter high society, is used to advance a political cause when he is forced to impersonate a Prussian nobleman and marry a duchess. Script by Fraser and based on his series of novels featuring the Flashman character. **98m/C VHS, DVD.** *GB* Malcolm McDowell, Alan Bates, Florinda Bolkan, Oliver Reed, Britt Ekland, Lionel Jeffries, Tom Bell, Alastair Sim, Michael Hordern, Joss Ackland, Christopher Cazenove, Bob Hoskins; ***D:*** Richard Lester; ***W:*** George MacDonald Fraser; ***C:*** Geoffrey Unsworth.

A Royal Scandal ♪♪ ½ **1996** And you thought Chuck and Di made a hash of their marriage. The British should be used to marital scandal as this saga on the disasters befalling Princess Caroline of Brunswick (Lynch) and Prince George (Grant), aptly demonstrates. The extravagant George is forced to marry through political and financial pressure but loathes the unrefined Caroline practically on sight. As soon as a royal heir is on the way, they cease to live together and George goes back to his mistresses. But although Caroline will agree to a settlement, she refuses a divorce and when George becomes King George IV, Caroline fully intends to be Queen. **60m/C VHS.** *GB* Richard E. Grant, Susan Lynch, Frances Barber, Michael Kitchen, Denis Lawson, Oliver Ford Davies, Irene Richards; ***D:*** Sheree Folkson; ***W:*** Stanley Price; ***C:*** John Daly; ***M:*** John Altman; ***Nar:*** Ian Richardson.

The Royal Tenenbaums ♪♪♪ ½ **2001 (R)** Anderson and Wilson's third and most ambitious film concerns a wildly eccentric family of kid geniuses who converge upon their childhood home as unhappy adults, just as their long-estranged father shows up looking for handouts and understanding, and mother is considering remarriage to the family accountant. Book lovers will appreciate the literary allusions—the Tenenbaum house seems lifted from the pages of J.D. Salinger or John Irving—and storybook styling, down to the chapter headings and gruff narration. Inventive script and quirky dialogue carry a story that sometimes becomes cartoonish, as most of the characters are one-dimensional. Some may find the film's overt weirdness a bit much, but there's a heart underneath it all. Hackman's performance as the dastardly, tactless, and yet wholly lovable Royal is a supreme comic feat. Depression has never been so fun. **108m/C VHS, DVD.** *US* Gene Hackman, Anjelica Huston, Gwyneth Paltrow, Ben Stiller, Luke Wilson, Owen Wilson, Bill Murray, Danny Glover, Seymour Cassel, Kumar Pallana, Grant Rosenmeyer, Jonah Meyerson, Stephen Lea Sheppard; ***D:*** Wes Anderson; ***W:*** Owen Wilson, Wes Anderson; ***C:*** Robert Yeoman; ***M:*** Mark Mothersbaugh; ***Nar:*** Alec Baldwin. Golden Globes '02: Actor—Mus./Comedy (Hackman); Natl. Soc. Film Critics '01: Actor (Hackman).

Royal Warriors ♪♪ *In the Line of Duty; Police Assassins; Ultra Force; Huang Jia Zhan Shi* **1986** Watch Michelle kick major butt! Policewoman Yeoh teams up with a retired Japanese cop and an airport security officer to prevent a terrorist highjacking. When the terrorist's associates decide to get even, the three must continue to fight together to save themselves. Chinese with subtitles or dubbed. **85m/C VHS, DVD.** *HK* Michelle Yeoh, Hiroyuki (Henry) Sanada, Michael Wong; ***D:*** David Chung.

Royal Wedding ♪♪♪ *Wedding Bells* **1951** Astaire and Powell play a brother-and-sister dance team who go to London during the royal wedding of Princess Elizabeth, and find their own romances. Notable for the inspired songs and Astaire's incredible dancing on the ceiling and walls; Lerner's first screenplay. The idea came from Adele Astaire's recent marriage to a British Lord. ♫ Too Late Now; Sunday Jumps; How Can You Believe Me When I Said I Love You When You Know I've Been A Liar All My Life?; You're All the World to Me; The Happiest Day of My Life; Open Your Eyes; Ev'ry Night at Seven; I Left My Hat in Haiti; What A Lovely Day For A Wedding. **93m/C VHS, DVD.** Fred Astaire, Jane Powell, Peter Lawford, Keenan Wynn, Sarah Churchill; ***D:*** Stanley Donen; ***W:*** Alan Jay Lerner; ***C:*** Robert Planck; ***M:*** Johnny Green, Burton Lane, Albert Sendrey.

Royce ♪♪ **1993 (R)** After a successful mission, Royce's CIA team is disbanded. But some former agents aren't happy with early retirement and decide to go into business for themselves. **98m/C VHS.** James Belushi, Chelsea Field, Miguel Ferrer, Peter Boyle; ***D:*** Rod Holcomb; ***W:*** Paul Bernbaum.

R.P.M. ♪♪ **1997 (R)** Professional car thief Luke (Arquette) takes up an offer to steal a prototype fuel-less supercar for a very large sum of money. However, he's not the only one after the goods. **91m/C VHS, DVD.** David Arquette, Famke Janssen, Emmanuelle Seigner, Jerry Hall; ***D:*** Ian Sharp; ***C:*** Harvey Harrison; ***M:*** Alan Lisk. **VIDEO**

R.P.M.* (*Revolutions Per Minute) ♪ ½ **1970 (R)** Another chance to relive the '60s. Student activists force the university hierarchy to appoint their favorite radical professor president. Hip prof-turned-prez Quinn is between a rock and a hard place, and allows police to crack down. Could have been intriguing, but loses steam; in any case, the script and direction both stink. **90m/C VHS.** Anthony Quinn, Paul Winfield, Gary Lockwood, Ann-Margret, Rigg Kennedy; ***D:*** Stanley Kramer; ***W:*** Erich Segal; ***M:*** Perry Botkin.

R.S.V.P. ♪ ½ **1984 (R)** Hollywood party honoring a writer turns tragic when a body is found in the guest of honor's pool. Most interesting part is watching the porn stars who make up most of the cast fail at acting while dressed. **87m/C VHS.** Harry (Herbert Streicher) Reems, Lynda Wiesmeier; ***D:*** Lem Amero.

R.S.V.P. ♪ ½ **2002 (R)** Slacker college student Nick (Otto), who has an unhealthy interest in criminology and the Leopold and Loeb case, decides to invite ten friends to a Vegas penthouse for a going away party. His guests start disappearing (as in permanently 'cause they're dead) and the viewers know the killer's identity while the potential victims struggle to figure things out. Steals from master suspenser Hitchcock (see "Rope"), which is good, but is generally obvious and unpleasant, which is bad. **98m/C VHS, DVD.** Rick Otto, Jason Mewes, Majandra Delfino, Glenn Quinn, Grace Zabriskie, Jonathan Banks, Reno Wilson; ***D:*** Mark Anthony Galluzzo; ***W:*** Mark Anthony Galluzzo; ***C:*** Mark Anthony Galluzzo; ***M:*** Michael Muhlfriedel.

Rubberface ♪ **1981 (PG)** Tony Maroni (Carrey) is a very bad but very determined comedian. And he may just catch a break when he teams up with joke writer Janet (Glassbourg). Made for Canadian TV. **48m/C VHS, DVD.** *CA* Jim Carrey, Adah Glassbourg; ***D:*** Glen Salzman, Rebecca Yates. **TV**

Rubber's Lover ♪ ½ **1997** Two scientists are attempting to create psychic powers by hopping up their victims on psychotropic drugs and torturing them with sound waves to create altered mental states. Unfortunately all they do is make people explode or go crazy or commit horrible acts. When the company funding the scientists sends an investigator to find out what they're up to, the loonies decide to rape her and make her a test subject (maybe they've been taking a few drugs themselves). Then everything suddenly goes bad. Highly disturbing and there's lots of screaming, so turn the volume down. **90m/B DVD.** *JP* Nao, Norimizu Ameya, Youta Kawase, Mika Kunihiro, Sosuke Saito; ***D:*** Shozin Fukui; ***W:*** Hiroshi Saito, Shozin Fukui; ***M:*** Tanizaki Tetora.

Rubdown ♪♪ **1993** An ex-baseball player, turned Beverly Hills masseur, finds himself the victim of a frame-up when one of his clients is murdered. **88m/C VHS.** Jack Coleman, Michelle Phillips, Kent Williams, Alan Thicke, Catherine Oxenberg, William Devane; ***D:*** Stuart Cooper; ***W:*** Clyde Allen Hayes; ***M:*** Gerald Gouriet.

Rubin & Ed ♪♪ **1992 (PG-13)** Ed is a real estate groupie who bribes the eccentric Rubin to attend a get-rich-quick seminar. Rubin decides to cash in on the favor by taking Ed on the road in search of the perfect gravesite for Rubin's long-dead feline. If that sounds wacky, just wait—the fun really begins when the duo is stranded in Death Valley and begins to suffer from sunstroke and hallucinations. Those who dream of weirdos bonding in the desert may be enthused but other viewers may thirst for something more. **82m/C VHS.** Crispin Glover, Howard Hesseman, Karen Black, Michael Greene, Brittney Lewis; ***D:*** Trent Harris; ***W:*** Trent Harris; ***C:*** Bryan Duggan.

Ruby ♪♪ **1977 (R)** A young woman, christened in blood and raised in sin, has a love affair with the supernatural and murders up a storm at a drive-in. Confused, uneven horror a step up from most similar flicks. **85m/C VHS, DVD.** Roger Davis, Janit Baldwin, Piper Laurie, Stuart Whitman; ***D:*** Curtis Harrington; ***W:*** Barry Schneider; ***C:*** William Mendenhall; ***M:*** Don Ellis.

Ruby ♪♪ ½ **1992 (R)** Another in the increasing number of Kennedy assassination and conspiracy dramas—this one told from the viewpoint of Jack Ruby, Lee Harvey Oswald's killer. Confusing plot, somewhat redeemed by the performances of Aiello and Fenn. Combines actual footage of Ruby shooting Oswald with black-and-white filmed scenes. Based on the play "Love Field" by Stephen Davis. **111m/C VHS, DVD.** Joe (Johnny) Viterelli, Danny Aiello, Sherilyn Fenn, Arliss Howard, Tobin Bell, David Duchovny, Richard Sarafian, Joe Cortese, Marc Lawrence; ***D:*** John MacKenzie; ***W:*** Stephen Davis; ***C:*** Phil Meheux; ***M:*** John Scott.

Ruby Blue ♪♪ ½ **2007** Grumpy widower Jack has no interest in life until eight-year-old Florrie and her mom move in next door. Soon Jack is looking after Florrie and then, at the instigation of neighbor Stephanie, he offers to help troubled teen Ian train his racing pigeon Ruby Blue. But someone always has to be a busybody and Jack's relationship with the youngsters is subjected to whispers. **112m/C DVD.** *GB* Bob Hoskins, Josiane Balasko, Jody Latham, Jessica Stewart; ***D:*** Jan Dunn; ***W:*** Jan Dunn; ***C:*** Ole Bratt Birkeland; ***M:*** Janette Mason.

Ruby Bridges ♪♪ ½ **1998** On November 14, 1960, six-year-old Ruby Bridges (Monet) became the first black student to integrate the New Orleans public school system. She started her first day of first grade classes at William Frantz Elementary School escorted by four federal marshals, enduring hostile crowds and death threats because of her mother Lucielle's (Rochon) desire for her daughter to get an equal education despite what the Bridges family would endure. **90m/C VHS, DVD.** Michael Beach, Penelope Ann Miller, Lela Rochon, Chaz Monet, Kevin Pollak, Diana Scarwid; ***D:*** Euzhan Palcy; ***W:*** Toni Johnson. **TV**

Ruby Gentry ♪♪ ½ **1952** White-trash girl Jones, cast aside by man-she-loves Heston, marries wealthy Malden to spite him, then seeks revenge. Classic Southern theme of comeuppance, good direction and acting lift it a notch. **82m/B VHS, DVD.** Charlton Heston, Jennifer Jones, Karl Malden; ***D:*** King Vidor.

Ruby in Paradise ♪♪♪ **1993 (R)** Leaving her dead-end life in Tennessee, Gissing (Judd) moves to Panama City, Florida and lands a job selling souvenirs for no-nonsense Mildred Chambers (Lyman). Although pursued by two very different men, Ruby concentrates more on self-exploration, recording her thoughts in a journal. A seemingly effortless portrayal of Ruby Lee by Judd (daughter of Naomi and sister of Wynonna Judd) makes for a pleasurable character study of a young woman on her own. **115m/C VHS.** Ashley Judd, Todd Field, Bentley Mitchum, Allison Dean, Dorothy Lyman, Betsy Dowds; ***D:*** Victor Nunez; ***W:*** Victor Nunez; ***C:*** Alex Vlacos; ***M:*** Charles Engstrom. Ind. Spirit '94: Actress (Judd); Sundance '93: Grand Jury Prize.

Ruby in the Smoke ♪♪ ½ *Sally Lockhart Mysteries: Ruby in the Smoke* **2006** It's 1872 in London and Sally Lockhart has just learned that her father has died while investigating suspicious activity in his shipping business. Spunky Sally is told about the Ruby of Agrapur and her father's part in the gem's disappearance decades before. It seems the cursed stone is leading Sally straight into danger with the city's most ruthless criminals. Based on the mystery by Philip Pullman. **90m/C DVD.** *GB* Julie Walters, J.J. Feild, David Harewood, Hayley Atwell, Billie Piper, Matt Smith, Ramon Tikaram; ***D:*** Brian Percival; ***W:*** Adrian Hodges; ***C:*** Peter Greenhalgh; ***M:*** Martin Phipps; ***V:*** Martin Jarvis. **TV**

Ruby Jean and Joe ♪♪ **1996 (PG-13)** Aging rodeo star Joe Wade (Selleck) doesn't want to leave the circuit even though it's obvious that his body can't take the punishment anymore. Joe gets more depressed until he picks up hitchhiker Ruby Jean (Johnson), a sarcastic teenager in search of a future. The unlikely duo form a friendship that may offer salvation to them both. **100m/C VHS.** Tom Selleck, JoBeth Williams, Rebekah Johnson, Ben Johnson; ***D:*** Geoffrey Sax; ***W:*** James Lee Barrett; ***C:*** James L. Carter; ***M:*** Stephen Graziano. **CABLE**

Ruby's Bucket of Blood ♪♪ ½ **2001 (PG-13)** Life's not easy for Ruby Delacroix (Bassett), the sultry owner of a bayou roadhouse, colorfully called the "Bucket of Blood," especially since she's a black woman in the segregated south of 1960. Neglected by her husband Earl (Mitchell) and constantly battling with her teenaged daughter, Emerald (Smollett), Ruby is feeling vulnerable. Which may be why she allows Johnny (Plummer), the leader of the house band, to hire Billy Dupre (Anderson) as a replacement singer. Billy's white—and married. But Ruby and Billy have an undeniable attraction—and when Earl leaves Ruby, it becomes harder and harder to resist. **96m/C VHS, DVD.** Angela Bassett, Kevin Anderson, Brian Stokes Mitchell, Glenn Plummer, Jurnee Smollett, Angelica Torn; ***D:*** Peter Werner; ***W:*** Julie Hebert. **CABLE**

Ruby's Dream ♪♪ *Dear Mr. Wonderful* **1982** A bowling alley and nightclub owner dreams of making it big in Las Vegas. After his dreams crash to the ground, however, he realizes what is truly important in life. **100m/C VHS, DVD.** Joe Pesci, Ed O'Ross, Evan Handler, Ivy Ray Browning; ***D:*** Peter Lilienthal; ***W:*** Sam Koperwas; ***C:*** Michael Ballhaus; ***M:*** Claus Bantzer.

Ruckus ♪♪ *The Loner* **1981 (PG)** A Vietnam vet uses his training to defend himself when he runs into trouble in a small Alabama town. Less obnoxious than "First Blood," (which came later), but basically the same movie. **91m/C VHS, DVD.** Dirk Benedict, Linda Blair, Ben Johnson, Richard Farnsworth, Matt Clark; ***D:*** Max Kleven; ***W:*** Max Kleven; ***C:*** Don Burgess; ***M:*** Willie Nelson.

Ruddigore ♪♪ **1982** The Lords of Ruddigore have been bound for centuries by a terribly inconvenient curse; they must commit a crime every day or die a horribly painful death. When the Lord of Ruddigore passes his mantle on to the new heir, the young heir loses both his good reputation and his very proper fiancee. A new version of Gilbert and Sullivan's opera. **112m/C VHS, DVD.** *GB* Vincent Price, Keith Michell, Paul Hudson, John Trevelyan, Sandra Dugdale; ***D:*** Barrie Gavin. **TV**

Rude ♪♪ **1996 (R)** Rude (Lewis) is a Jamaican-Canadian pirate-radio DJ in Toronto, who narrates three stories about urban life: window dresser Maxine (Crawford) struggles to recover from an abortion after her lover leaves her; frightened boxer Jordan (Chevolleau) tries to deal with his own homosexuality after participating with friends in a gay bashing; and ex-con Luke (Wint) returns to his wife (now a police officer) and young son. He tries to resist returning to his drug dealing past and cope with a jealous younger brother (Johnson). Debut for director Virgo. **90m/C VHS, DVD.** *CA* Sharon M. Lewis, Richard Chevolleau, Rachael Crawford, Maurice Dean Wint, Stephen Ellen, Clark Johnson, Melanie Nicholls-King, Stephen Shellen; ***D:*** Clement Virgo; ***W:*** Clement Virgo; ***C:*** Barry Stone; ***M:*** Aaron David.

Rude Awakening 1/2 **1981** A real estate agent is tortured by bizarre nightmares which lead to an unusual series of events. Part of the "Thriller Video" series. **60m/C VHS, DVD.** Denholm Elliott, James Laurenson, Pat Heywood; ***D:*** Peter Sasdy.

Rude Awakening **1989 (R)** Hippies Cheech and Roberts (where's Chong?) settled in a South American commune 20 years ago. Now they're back, and don't know what to make of old pals Carradine and Hagerty who have become—that's right—yuppies. Rip Van Winkle-ian farce draws a few yuks, but could have been much funnier. Points for trying. **100m/C VHS.** Eric Roberts, Richard "Cheech" Marin, Julie Hagerty, Robert Carradine, Buck Henry, Louise Lasser, Cindy Williams, Andrea Martin, Cliff DeYoung; ***D:*** Aaron Russo, David Greenwalt; ***W:*** Richard LaGravenese; ***M:*** Jonathan Elias.

Rude Boy: The Jamaican Don **2003 (R)** Wanting to escape his life of crime in Jamaica, DJ Julius instead becomes ensnared with a big-time L.A. drug lord/music producer who promises to make all his rap-reggae dreams come true if Julius serves as his personal hitman. Not much hop when the bullets aren't flying. **92m/C VHS, DVD.** Jimmy Cliff, Mark Danvers, Michael "Bear" Taliferro, John Cornelius, Marcia Griffith, Beenie Man, Ninja Man; ***D:*** Desmond Gumbs. **VIDEO**

Rudo y Cursi 1/2 **2009 (R)** A genially ragged rags-to-riches comedy. Half-brothers Tato (Garcia Bernal) and Beto (Luna) are working on a banana plantation in rural Mexico, dreaming of a better life. Spotted during a pickup soccer game, sly sports agent Batuta (Francella) offers to take them to Mexico City, getting big league positions for Tato as a forward and Beto as a goalie—on rival teams. Of course this leads to sibling rivalry and a showdown at the big game. Title refers to the boys' nicknames: 'Rudo' means tough and 'Cursi' means corny. Spanish with subtitles. **103m/C DVD.** *MX* Gael Garcia Bernal, Diego Luna, Dolores Heredia, Guillermo Francella, Adriana Paz, Jessica Mas; ***D:*** Carlos Cuaron; ***W:*** Carlos Cuaron; ***C:*** Adam Kimmel; ***M:*** Felipe Perez Santiago.

Rudy 1/2 **1993 (PG)** Likeable, true story about a little guy who triumphs over big odds. Daniel "Rudy" Ruettiger (Astin) dreams of playing football for Notre Dame, no matter how farfetched the dream. He's a mediocre student, physically unsuitable for big time college ball, but sheer determination helps him attain his dream. Astin delivers an engaging performance and is backed up by a good supporting cast. Sentimental story stretches the truth with typical shameless Hollywood manipulation, but is still entertaining. From the director and writer of another David beats Goliath sports film, "Hoosiers." **112m/C VHS, DVD, Blu-ray Disc.** Robert J. Steinmiller Jr., Vince Vaughn, Sean Astin, Ned Beatty, Charles S. Dutton, Lili Taylor, Robert Prosky, Jason Miller, Ron Dean, Chelcie Ross, Jon Favreau, Greta Lind, Scott Benjaminson, Christopher Reed; ***D:*** David Anspaugh; ***W:*** Angelo Pizzo; ***C:*** Oliver Wood; ***M:*** Jerry Goldsmith.

Rudy: The Rudy Giulani Story 1/2 **2003** Warts and all bio of former New York mayor Rudy Giuliani (Woods, in an Emmy-nominated performance). The bio begins on September 10, 2001 as the mayor is on his second and last term and what happens during the World Trade Center disaster. Flashbacks highlight Giuliani's political rise as well as his abrasive personality and his controversial private life. **120m/C VHS, DVD.** James Woods, Penelope Ann Miller, Michelle Nolden, John Bourgeois, Kirsten Bishop, Maxim Roy, Michael Woods; ***D:*** Robert Dornhelm; ***W:*** Stanley Weiser; ***C:*** Serge Ladouceur; ***M:*** Harald Kloser. **CABLE**

Rudyard Kipling's The Jungle Book 1/2 *The Jungle Book* **1994 (PG)** Respectable live-action version from Disney of the Rudyard Kipling tale of Mowgli (Lee), the boy who's raised by a wolf pack after getting lost in an Indian jungle. This time around Mowgli gets to grow up—enough to have a romantic interest in the lovely Kitty (Headey), the daughter of British officer, Major Brydon (Neill). His rival is the supercilious Captain Boone (Elwes), who learns Mowgli knows the location of a hidden jungle treasure. Now Mowgli must count on his friends, Grey Brother the wolf, Baloo the bear, and Bagheera the black panther, to defeat the greedy Boone and win Kitty. Filmed in India. **111m/C VHS, DVD.** Jason Scott Lee, Cary Elwes, Sam Neill, Lena Headey, John Cleese; ***D:*** Stephen Sommers; ***W:*** Stephen Sommers.

Rudyard Kipling's the Second Jungle Book: Mowgli and Baloo *Mowgli and Baloo: Jungle Book 2; The Second Jungle Book: Mowgli and Baloo* **1997 (PG)** Actually a prequel to "Rudyard Kipling's The Jungle Book," the story centers on the ten-year-old Mowgli (Williams) and his efforts to stay among his animal friends in the jungle. After he is spotted by a scout for P.T. Barnum's circus (Campbell), he must elude the hastily organized group that's out to capture and exploit him. He must also dodge the Bandars, a group of funky monkeys who want to make Mowgli their unwilling leader. The special effects are nowhere near as good as its predecessor, with matte shots that make some of the animals look like they were added with magic markers. The story is a classic, however, and the performances (especially Williams') are good. **88m/C VHS, DVD.** Jamie Williams, Billy Campbell, Roddy McDowall, Cornelia Hayes O'Herlihy, David Paul Francis, Gulshan Grover, Dyrk Ashton, B.J. Hogg, Amy Robbins, Hal Fowler; ***D:*** Duncan McLachlan; ***W:*** Bayard Johnson, Matthew Horton; ***C:*** Adolfo Bartoli; ***M:*** John Scott.

The Rue Morgue Massacres 1/2 **1973 (R)** A modern reprise of the Poe story with touches of Frankensteinia thrown in; plenty of gore. **90m/C VHS, DVD.** *SP* Paul Naschy, Rossana Yanni, Maria Perschy, Vic Winner, Mary Ellen Arpon; ***D:*** Javier Aguirre.

The Rug Cop 1/2 *Zura Deka; Dura Deka* **2006** An over-the-top parody of Japanese TV cop shows from the seventies, the title character is a detective who can decapitate people by throwing his toupee. Along with his partners Detective Fatty, Detective Big Dick, Old Man, Detective Shorty, and Mr. Handsome he must take on rogue ventriloquist dummies, and terrorists holding a shipment of uranium hostage. Featuring musical numbers on the pains of being bald, men with lightsabers in their pants, and a man who defeats opponents by sweating on them. **79m/C DVD.** *JP* Hideo Nakano, Yusuke Kirishima, Fuyuki Moto; ***D:*** Minoru Kawasaki; ***W:*** Takao Nakano, Minoru Kawasaki.

Ruggles of Red Gap **1935** Classic comedy about an uptight British butler who is "won" by a barbarous American rancher in a poker game. Laughton as the nonplussed manservant is hilarious; supporting cast excellent. Third and far superior filming of Harry Leon Wilson story. One of the all-time great comedies, the film was remade musically with Bob Hope and Lucille Ball as "Fancy Pants" (1950). **90m/B VHS.** Charles Laughton, Mary Boland, Charlie Ruggles, Zasu Pitts, Roland Young, Leila Hyams, James Burke, Maude Eburne; ***D:*** Leo McCarey; ***W:*** Walter DeLeon; ***M:*** Ralph Rainger. N.Y. Film Critics '35: Actor (Laughton).

Rugrats Go Wild! **2003 (PG)** Two Nickelodeon animated series combine in this adventure when the Rugrats, who are vacationing with their parents, get stranded on an island and the Wild Thornberries, on the island to find a rare leopard for their TV show, come to the rescue. It must've seemed like a good idea to combine these two lucrative franchises into one movie, but the sum proved to be less than its parts. Less charming than previous outings for both series, there's just too many characters competing for too little screen time, and the wandering plotlines don't help the situation. Less-discriminating kids may enjoy it on video, but there's nothing for adults or older kids to enjoy. **81m/C VHS, DVD.** *US* ***D:*** Norton Virgien, John Eng; ***W:*** Kate Boutilier; ***M:*** Mark Mothersbaugh; ***V:*** Elizabeth (E.G. Dailey) Daily, Michael Bell, Jodi Carlisle, Nancy Cartwright, Lacey Chabert, Melanie Chartoff, Tim Curry, Cheryl Chase, Flea, Danielle Harris, Tom Kane, Bruce Willis, Chrissie Hynde, Tara Strong, Jack Riley, Kath Soucie, Tress MacNeille, Cree Summer, Dionne Quan, LL Cool J.

Rugrats in Paris: The Movie **2000 (G)** There are enough pop culture references and sly humor for the parents and enough diaper, booger and barf jokes for the kids to make this entertaining viewing for the entire family. Tommy, Chuckie and the rest of the gang from the animated Nickelodeon series return for their second full-length feature, this time trekking off to France as Tommy's inventor dad tries to fix a mechanical dinosaur at a very EuroDisney-style theme park. Also, Chuckie's dad Chas is wooed by the kid-hating park operator Coco La Bouche (voice of Susan Sarandon), who only wants to marry him because she thinks that there's a promotion in it for her. This all leads to a bizarre chase through Paris involving the giant dinosaur and a huge escargot. **80m/C VHS, DVD.** ***D:*** Stig Bergqvist, Paul Demeyer; ***W:*** David N. Weiss, Jill Gorey, Barbara Herndon, Kate Boutilier; ***M:*** Mark Mothersbaugh; ***V:*** Elizabeth (E.G. Dailey) Daily, Christine Cavanaugh, Susan Sarandon, Jack Riley, Michael Bell, Melanie Chartoff, Tara Strong, Kath Soucie, John Lithgow, Debbie Reynolds, Mako, James D. Stern, Cheryl Chase, Julia Kato, Lisa McClowry.

The Rugrats Movie **1998 (G)** Precocious one-year-old Tommy is afraid he'll be forgotten by his parents with the arrival of baby brother Dil, so he and his pals decide to return the infant to the hospital. Boarding a talking wagon named Reptar (invented by Tommy's father), they embark on an adventure that takes them to a scary forest where they run into wolves, a "wizard," and a band of escaped circus monkeys that kidnap Dil in the film's most frightening sequence. While dishing out lessons about responsibility, bravery, friendship, and jealousy, film also contains parodies of and homages to several films, including "Raiders of the Lost Ark." The humor works on many levels, so this one is enjoyable for all ages. **79m/C VHS, DVD.** ***D:*** Norton Virgien, Igor Kovalyov; ***W:*** David N. Weiss, J. David Stem; ***M:*** Mark Mothersbaugh; ***V:*** Elizabeth (E.G. Dailey) Daily, Christine Cavanaugh, Tara Strong, Melanie Chartoff, Jack Riley, Joe Alaskey, Phil(ip) Proctor, Whoopi Goldberg, David Spade, Kath Soucie, Cheryl Case, Cree Summer, Michael Bell, Tress MacNeille, Busta Rhymes.

The Ruins 1/2 **2008 (R)** Rather than being content hanging by the pool at their Mexican seaside resort, Jeff (Tucker), Amy (Malone), Eric (Ashmore), and Stacy (Ramsay) accept the questionable invite of Mathias (Anderson) to visit an archeological dig at a Mayan ruin. The armed locals are very unhappy by these turistas and chase them up the vine-covered pyramid, but it's definitely not to safety. There's a gruesomely creepy twist to what attacks them but otherwise it's horror business as usual. Scott B. Smith adapted his novel. **90m/C DVD.** *US* Jonathan Tucker, Jena Malone, Shawn Ashmore, Laura Ramsey, Joe Anderson, Dimitri Baveas; ***D:*** Carter Smith; ***W:*** Scott B. Smith; ***C:*** Darius Khondji; ***M:*** Graeme Revell.

Rule #3 **1993** "Never believe everything you see." That's the rule con artist Travis West lives by. This time he's got two scams planned—a Las Vegas real estate swindle and a cash ripoff of a former nemesis. Double- and triple-crosses abound. Based on the true story of West, who swindled more than $9 million in 15 years. **93m/C VHS.** Mitchell Cox, Marcia Swayze; ***D:*** Mitchell Cox.

Rulers of the City *I Padroni della Citta; The Big Boss; Blood and Bullets; Mister Scarface* **1976** Young gangster avenges his father's death. **91m/C VHS.** *IT* Gisela Hahn, Vittorio Caprioli, Jack Palance, Edmund Purdom, Al Cliver, Harry Baer; ***D:*** Fernando Di Leo; ***W:*** Fernando Di Leo, Peter Berling; ***C:*** Erico Menczer; ***M:*** Luis Bacalov.

The Rules of Attraction **2002 (R)** Follows a group of shallow, overprivileged, drug-addled college students apparently attending Hedonism University. Drug dealer Sean (Van Der Beek) is in lust with campus goddess Lauren (Sossamon). Lauren's bisexual ex-boyfriend Paul (Somerhalder) has a crush on the straight Sean. Lauren yearns for Victor (Pardue), a coked up vacationing druggie who once slept with Paul. As a result of this turmoil, everyone does drugs and sleeps with everyone else. Avary uses many production tricks and a fluctuating timeline in order to convey the feeling of the Bret Easton Ellis novel on which the movie is based. The technique works, especially the fast-forward view of Victor's trip, but the characters are so unlikable that none of them deserves to get what they want. **104m/C VHS, DVD.** *US* James Van Der Beek, Ian Somerhalder, Shannyn Sossamon, Jessica Biel, Kip Pardue, Thomas Ian Nicholas, Kate (Catherine) Bosworth, Fred Savage, Eric Stoltz, Clifton (Gonzalez) Collins Jr., Faye Dunaway, Swoosie Kurtz, Russell Sams, Matthew Lang; ***D:*** Roger Avary; ***W:*** Roger Avary; ***C:*** Robert Brinkmann; ***M:*** Tomandandy.

Rules of Engagement 1/2 **2000 (R)** Marine Childers (Jackson) is assigned the task of rescuing an ambassador and his family from a hostile area in Yemen. The mission goes terribly wrong and an order is given by Childers, resulting in the death of 83 Yemeni women and children. To keep the US from suffering any terrorist backlash, Childers is charged with mass murder. Effective courtroom drama (which spares us the clichéd surprise witness), although it merely grazes the complex issues of military decision-making due to its skeletal script. Intensity and momentum is sustained by the towering performances of leads Jackson and Jones as Childers's buddy and lawyer. After two weeks as box-office leader, film received some protest over its negative portrayal of Arab-Americans. Based on a story by ex-Secretary of the Navy James Webb. **128m/C VHS, DVD.** Elayne J. Taylor, Samuel L. Jackson, Tommy Lee Jones, Guy Pearce, Bruce Greenwood, Blair Underwood, Philip Baker Hall, Anne Archer, Ben Kingsley, Mark Feuerstein, Dale Dye; ***D:*** William Friedkin; ***W:*** Stephen Gaghan; ***C:*** Nicola Pecorini, William A. Fraker; ***M:*** Mark Isham.

The Rules of the Game *Le Regle du Jeu* **1939** Renoir's masterpiece, in which a group of French aristocrats, gathering for a weekend of decadence and self-indulgence just before WWII, becomes a metaphor for human folly under siege. The film was banned by the French government, pulled from distribution by the Nazis, and not restored to its original form until 1959, when it premiered at the Venice Film Festival. A great, subtle, ominous film landmark. In French with English subtitles. Heavily copied and poorly remade in 1989 as "Scenes from the Class Struggle in Beverly Hills." **110m/B VHS, DVD.** Marcel Dalio, Nora Gregor, Jean Renoir, Mila Parely, Julien Carette, Gaston Modot, Roland Toutain, Paulette Dubost, Odette Talazac; ***D:*** Jean Renoir; ***W:*** Jean Renoir.

The Ruling Class 1/2 **1972 (PG)** The classic cult satire features O'Toole as the unbalanced 14th Earl of Gurney, who believes that he is either Jesus Christ or Jack the Ripper. Tongue-in-cheek look, complete with dance and music, at eccentric upper-class Brits and their institutions. Uneven, chaotic, surreal and noteworthy. **154m/C VHS, DVD.** *GB* Peter O'Toole, Alastair Sim, Arthur Lowe, Harry Andrews, Coral Browne, Nigel Green, Michael Bryant, William Mervyn, Carolyn Seymour, James Villiers; ***D:*** Peter Medak; ***W:*** Peter Barnes; ***C:*** Ken Hodges; ***M:*** John Cameron. Natl. Bd. of Review '72: Actor (O'Toole).

Rumble Fish **1983 (R)** A young street punk worships his gang-leading older brother, the only role model he's known. Crafted by Coppola into an important story of growing up on the wrong side of town, from the novel by S.E. Hinton. Ambitious and experimental, with an atmospheric music score; in black and white. **94m/B VHS, DVD.** Matt Dillon, Mickey Rourke, Dennis Hopper, Diane Lane, Vincent Spano, Nicolas Cage, Diana Scarwid, Christopher Penn, Tom Waits; ***D:*** Francis Ford Coppola; ***W:*** Francis Ford Coppola; ***C:*** Stephen Burum; ***M:*** Stewart Copeland.

Rumble in the Bronx 1/2 **1996 (R)** Singapore action star Chan plays a Hong Kong cop who comes to the South Bronx to attend his uncle's wedding and winds up caught in a crime war between the mob and a vicious motorcycle gang. Living special effect Chan choreographed and performed all of his own stunts, and they are remarkable (pay special attention to the hovercraft scene). Over-the-top cheesy dubbing and streets that are obviously not New York (filmed in Vancouver) add to the cartoonish fun. After several attempts to break into the American market, this is Chan's first release in the United States. **91m/C VHS, DVD.** *HK* Jackie Chan, Anita (Yim-Fong) Mui, Francoise Yip, Bill Tung, Morgan Lam, Marc Akerstream; ***D:*** Stanley Tong; ***W:*** Edward Tang, Fibe Ma; ***C:*** Jingle Ma; ***M:*** J. Peter Robinson.

Rumble in the Streets 1/2 **1996 (R)** Street-smart young Rowe discovers that a psycho cop has decided to clean up the streets of Dallas by hunting down and killing kids like her and she must use her own toughness to survive. **74m/C VHS.** Kimberly Rowe, David Courtemarche, Patrick DeFazio; ***D:*** Bret McCormick.

Rumor Has It... **2005 (PG-13)** Rumor has it... this movie blows. And, unfortunately, that ain't gossip. Rob Reiner continues to explore the latter, significantly crappier stage of his directorial career in this monumental waste of time and talent. It's a nifty concept—at her sister's wedding, the engaged Sarah (Aniston) discovers that her family was the basis for "The Graduate" and finds herself falling for the man (Costner) who seduced both her mother and grandmother (MacLaine)—but everyone involved in the production looks uncomfortable and there are no laughs to be found. Nice job, Meathead. **96m/C DVD, Blu-ray Disc, HD DVD.** *US* Jennifer Aniston, Kevin Costner, Shirley MacLaine, Mark Ruffalo, Richard Jenkins, Christopher McDonald, Mena Suvari, Steve Sandvoss; ***D:*** Rob Reiner; ***W:*** T.M. Griffin; ***C:*** Peter Deming; ***M:*** Marc Shaiman.

The Rumor Mill 1/2 *Malice in Wonderland* **1986** The careers and titanic rivalry of influential Hollywood gossip writer Hedda Hopper and Louella Parsons, played with verve by Taylor and Alexander. Fictionalized script based on the book "Hedda and Louella" by George Eels. **94m/C VHS, DVD.** Elizabeth Taylor, Jane Alexander, Richard Dysart, Joyce Van Patten; ***D:*** Gus Trikonis; ***W:*** Jacqueline Feather, David Seidler; ***M:*** Charles Bernstein. **TV**

A Rumor of Angels **2000 (PG-13)** Cloying coming-of-age tale somewhat redeemed by Redgrave's performance as eccentric recluse Maddy Bennett. 12-year-old James (Morgan) is spending the summer on the Maine coast. His mother died in a car accident, he resents his new stepmom Mary (McCormack), doesn't get along with his neglectful father Nathan (Liotta), and also has his misfit Uncle Charlie (Livingston) to deal with. After James vandalizes Maddy's property, the two become unlikely confidantes and Maddy helps him to deal with his problems. **94m/C VHS, DVD.** Vanessa Redgrave, Trevor Morgan, Ray Liotta, Catherine McCormack, Ron Livingston; ***D:*** Peter O'Fallon; ***W:*** Peter O'Fallon, James Eric, Jamie Horton; ***C:*** Roy Wagner; ***M:*** Tim Simonec.

A Rumor of War 1/2 **1980** The first big Vietnam drama for TV is a triumph, portraying the real-life experience of author Philip Caputo (based on his bestseller), from naive youth to seasoned soldier to bitter murder suspect at court martial. Succeeds where Stone's later, much-ballyhooed "Born on the Fourth of July" fails. Adapted by John Sacret Young. **195m/C VHS.** Brad Davis, Keith Carradine, Michael O'Keefe, Stacy Keach, Steve Forrest, Richard Bradford, Brian Dennehy, John Friedrich, Perry Lang, Chris Mitchum, Dan Shor, Jeff Daniels, Laurence Fishburne, Lane Smith, Gail Youngs, Bobby Ellerbee; ***D:*** Richard T. Heffron; ***W:*** John Sacret Young; ***C:*** Stevan Larner, Jorge Stahl Jr.; ***M:*** Charles Gross.

Rumpelstiltskin **1982** From "Faerie Tale Theatre" comes the story of a woman who can spin straw into gold (Duvall) and the strange man who saves her life (Villechaize). Enjoyable for the whole family. **60m/C VHS, DVD.** Bud Cort, Ned Beatty, Shelley Duvall, Herve Villechaize, Paul Dooley; ***D:*** Emile Ardolino. **CABLE**

Rumpelstiltskin **1986 (G)** Musical retelling of the classic Brother Grimm fairy tale. Irving plays a young girl who says she can spin straw into gold. Barty is a dwarf who helps her. The catch: she must give up her first born to pay him. Lackluster direction and uninspired acting make this version a yawner. Irving's real-life mother (Pointer) and brother have roles too. **84m/C VHS, DVD.** Amy Irving, Billy Barty, Robert Symonds, Priscilla Pointer, Clive Revill, John Moulder-Brown; ***D:*** David Irving.

Rumpelstiltskin WOOF! **1996 (R)** First director Jones inflicts "Leprechaun" upon us and now there's another warped dwarf on the loose. Single L.A. mom Shelly (Johnston-Ulrich) finds a wishing stone in a thrift shop and unwittingly summons up the little demon, who immediately tries to steal her young son. **91m/C VHS, DVD.** Kim Johnston-Ulrich, Tommy Blaze, Max Grodenchik, Allyce Beasley; ***D:*** Mark Jones; ***W:*** Mark Jones; ***C:*** Doug Milsome; ***M:*** Charles Bernstein.

Run 1/2 **1991 (R)** A high energy action cartoon, with little plot but lots of stunts. Dempsey is a super-smart law student hired to drive a car to Atlantic City. A stop on the way starts trouble. Instant romance with a local girl balances mayhem from crime boss. Expect no more than physical feats and you'll be happy with this lightweight fare. **91m/C VHS.** Patrick Dempsey, Kelly Preston, Ken Pogue, Alan C. Peterson, Sean McCann; ***D:*** Geoff Burrowes; ***W:*** Michael Blodgett; ***C:*** Bruce Surtees.

Run, Angel, Run! 1/2 **1969 (R)** Ex-biker Angel is on the run from his former gang after he helps expose them in a magazine article. He settles on a sheep ranch with his girl and then the gang shows up with revenge in mind. Prime drive-in fare with title song sung by none other than Ms. Tammy Wynette. **90m/C VHS, DVD.** William (Bill) Smith, Margaret Markov, Valerie Starrett; ***D:*** Jack Starrett; ***W:*** V.A. Furlong, Jerome Wish; ***C:*** John Stephens; ***M:*** Stu Phillips.

Run, Fatboy, Run 1/2 **2007 (PG-13)** David Schwimmer makes his directorial debut, oddly enough, in British territory, but very much in the vein of a "Friends" episode. Like the bonehead he is, Dennis (Pegg) leaves pregnant Libby (Newton) at the altar for no good reason. Five years later, somehow still friends with Libby and working as a security guard in a lingerie shop, Dennis desperately tries to win her back as she's about to marry Whit (Azaria), a rich American marathon runner. Of course, the way to win her heart is to challenge the fiance to a race. (Despite the fat jokes, Dennis is not fat. Out of shape and lazy, yes, but not fat.) Cute and charming, but never laugh-out-loud funny. **100m/C DVD, Blu-ray Disc.** *GB* Simon Pegg, Thandie Newton, Hank Azaria, Dylan Moran, Harish Patel, India de Beaufort, Matthew Fenton; ***D:*** David Schwimmer; ***W:*** Michael Ian Black, Michael Parker; ***C:*** Richard Greatrex; ***M:*** Alex Wurman.

Run for the Dream: The Gail Devers Story 1/2 **1996 (PG-13)** Inspirational biopic on U.S. track star Devers (Woodard) who won a gold medal in the 100m sprint in the 1992 Olympics. But 17 months before, Devers suffers complications from a debilitating thyroid condition, Graves's Disease, which could not only cost her her career but her life. **99m/C VHS.** Alfre Woodard, Louis Gossett Jr., Robert Guillaume; ***D:*** Neema Barnette; ***W:*** Dianne Houston, Scott Abbott; ***C:*** Edward Pei; ***M:*** Pete Anthony. **CABLE**

Run for the Roses 1/2 *Thoroughbred* **1978 (PG)** "National Velvet" clone about a young Puerto Rican boy and a champion race horse in Kentucky. Cheery family fare. **93m/C VHS.** Lisa Eilbacher, Vera Miles, Stuart Whitman, Sam Groom; ***D:*** Henry Levin.

Run If You Can **1987 (R)** A woman sees a brutal murderer killing his victims on her TV. Will she be next? **92m/C VHS, DVD.** Martin Landau, Yvette Nipar, Jerry Van Dyke; ***D:*** Virginia Lively Stone.

Run Lola Run 1/2 *Lola Rennt* **1998 (R)** Berlin punkette Lola (Potente) receives a frantic phone call from her smalltime criminal boyfriend Manni (Bleibtreu). He's lost a bag of money he was delivering to his boss and has only 20 minutes to make good or he's history. Lola then sprints off in a manic attempt to find the money needed to save her man. The plot comes roaring to a halt, and is then repeated with different outcomes based on small changes in Lola's path, with different styles to match. Writer/director Tom Tykwer's energetic style helps push this creative and technically brilliant thriller across the winner's line. German with subtitles. **81m/C VHS, DVD.** *GE* Franka Potente, Moritz Bleibtreu, Joachim Krol, Herbert Knaup, Armin Rohde; ***D:*** Tom Tykwer; ***W:*** Tom Tykwer; ***C:*** Frank Griebe; ***M:*** Tom Tykwer. Ind. Spirit '00: Foreign Film.

Run of the Arrow *Hot Lead* **1956** Rather than surrender to the North at the end of the Civil War, an ex-Confederate soldier (Steiger) joins the Sioux nation, engaged in war against the white man. Steiger's Irish brogue is weird and distracting, and the intriguing premise fails to satisfy, but the cast is competent and interesting. **85m/C VHS.** Olive Carey, Rod Steiger, Brian Keith, Charles Bronson, Ralph Meeker, Tim McCoy, Sara Montiel, Jay C. Flippen, H.M. Wynant, Neyle Morrow, Frank De Kova, Frank Baker; ***D:*** Samuel Fuller; ***W:*** Samuel Fuller; ***C:*** Joseph Biroc; ***M:*** Victor Young, Max Steiner; ***V:*** Angie Dickinson.

The Run of the Country **1995 (R)** Amid the scenic splendor of a small town south of the North Irish border in County Cavan, Danny (Keeslar) comes of age, sometimes the hard way. His relationship with his bullying dad (Finney), the local Garda officer, begins to crumble after the tragic death of his mum. So he runs away to live with the town malcontent Prunty (Brophy) and falls in love with the beautiful Annagh (Smurfit), who lives north of the border. Life gets even more complicated when Annagh learns she's pregnant. Director Yates, reunited with Finney for the first time since they won Oscars for "The Dresser," sometimes digs too deep into a big crock of standard Irish stew, occasionally delivering Celtic melodrama instead of poignant slice of life. The usual themes of family dysfunction, religious rebellion and moral dilemma are augmented by the occasional appearance of the IRA. As the frustrated, violent father, Finney shines. In their debut, Keeslar and Smurfit are fine, but Brophy's Prunty is the one you'll remember. Adapted by Connaughton (who used similar geography for "The Playboys") from his novel. **109m/C VHS.** Albert Finney, Matt Keeslar, Victoria Smurfit, Anthony Brophy, David Kelly; ***D:*** Peter Yates; ***W:*** Shane Connaughton; ***C:*** Mike Southon; ***M:*** Cynthia Millar.

Run, Rebecca, Run 1/2 **1981** Interesting family adventure yarn for the family about a South American refugee who tries to stop a young girl from leaving from an Australian island where they are both stranded. She eventually befriends him, and attempts to get permission for him to enter the country. **90m/C VHS.** *AU* Simone Buchanan, Henri Szeps; ***D:*** Peter Maxwell.

Run Silent, Run Deep **1958** Submarine commander Gable battles his officers, especially the bitter Lancaster who vied for the same command, while stalking the Japanese destroyer that sunk his former command. Top-notch WWII sub action, scripted from Commander Edward L. Beach's novel. **93m/B VHS, DVD.** Burt Lancaster, Clark Gable, Jack Warden, Don Rickles, Brad Dexter, Nick Cravat, Joe Maross, Mary Laroche, Eddie Foy III, Rudy Bond, H.M. Wynant, Joel Fluellen, Ken Lynch, John Bryant; ***D:*** Robert Wise; ***W:*** John Gay; ***C:*** Russell Harlan; ***M:*** Franz Waxman.

Run, Stranger, Run *Happy Mother's Day, Love, George* **1973 (PG)** The inhabitants of a seaside house in Nova Scotia are paralyzed with fear when a number of brutal murders occur. A couple of sicko slasher scenes, but hard to swallow. **110m/C VHS.** Ron Howard, Patricia Neal, Cloris Leachman, Bobby Darin; ***D:*** Darren McGavin; ***C:*** Walter Lassally.

Runaway 1/2 **1984 (PG-13)** A cop and his sidekick track down a group of killer robots wreaking havoc. Self-serious, sorry sci-fi. Features Simmons of the rock group KISS. **100m/C VHS, DVD.** Tom Selleck, Cynthia Rhodes, Gene Simmons, Stan Shaw, Kirstie Alley; ***D:*** Michael Crichton; ***W:*** Michael Crichton; ***C:*** John A. Alonzo; ***M:*** Jerry Goldsmith.

The Runaway 1/2 **2000** Luke Winter (Newton) and Joshua Monroe (McLaughlin) are best friends growing up in 1940s rural Georgia despite the fact that one is black and one white. While on an adventure, they make a discovery that leads new sheriff Frank Richards (Cain) into reopening the investigation into the unsolved murders of three local black men. The town wants to hush up the whole incident but the sheriff wants justice to prevail. **98m/C VHS, DVD.** Dean Cain, Maya Angelou, Debbi (Deborah) Morgan, Pat Hingle, Kathryn Erbe, Cliff DeYoung, Cody Newton, Duane McLaughlin, Roxanne Hart, Sonny Shroyer; ***D:*** Arthur Allan Seidelman; ***W:*** Ron Raley; ***C:*** Ron Garcia; ***M:*** Ernest Troost. **TV**

Runaway **2005** Michael is hiding out in a rural community, secretly caring for his younger brother Dylan after having run away from their abusive dad. He's working at a gas station where co-worker Carly is romantically interested in him and eventually Michael begins confiding in her. Flashbacks show how bad things were for Michael and it all ends with a dramatic flourish. **80m/C DVD.** Aaron Stanford, Robin Tunney, Zack Savage, Peter Gerety, Melissa Leo, Michael Gaston, Terry Kinney; ***D:*** Tim McCann; ***W:*** Bill True; ***C:*** Frank Barerra.

The Runaway Barge **1975** Tiresomely ordinary TV yarn about three adventurers earning their living on a riverboat. The usual cliches are present, including a gang of bad guys. **78m/C VHS.** Bo Hopkins, Tim Matheson, Jim Davis, Nick Nolte, Devon Ericson, Christina Hart, James Best; ***D:*** Boris Sagal.

Runaway Bride **1999 (PG)** If you don't mind being manipulated by masters (and you really won't), the predictability of this romantic comedy won't bother you either. Hey, if you weren't looking for a happy ending, you wouldn't be watching a romantic comedy. New York columnist Ike Graham (Gere) gets into hot water (as in fired) when his story on Maggie Carpenter (Roberts), the bolting bride (three trips down the aisle and no vows), is filled with errors. So Ike decides to go to Maggie's hometown, where she's on her fourth engagement, and get the real scoop. Of course, he falls for the would-be bride and she for him but things aren't all hearts and flowers. Appealing performances and boy, does Roberts know how to wear a wedding dress. **116m/C VHS, DVD.** Julia Roberts, Richard Gere, Joan Cusack, Hector Elizondo, Christopher Meloni, Rita Wilson, Paul Dooley, Laurie Metcalf, Jean Schertler, Donal Logue, Reg Rogers, Yul Vazquez, Lisa Roberts Gillan, Sela Ward, Tom Mason; ***D:*** Garry Marshall; ***W:*** Josann McGibbon, Sara Parriott; ***C:*** Stuart Dryburgh; ***M:*** James Newton Howard.

The Runaway Bus **1954** Filled with the requisite motley crew of passengers, including a gold-carrying thief and the ever-befuddled Margaret Rutherford, a bus gets lost between airports and ends up in a deserted village. Would-be wacky comedy. **78m/B VHS.** *GB* Frankie Howerd, Margaret Rutherford, Petula Clark, George Coulouris, Belinda Lee, Reginald Beckwith, Terence Alexander, Toke Townley, John Horsley, Anthony Oliver, Stringer Davis, Lisa Gastoni, Frank Phillips; ***D:*** Val Guest; ***W:*** Val Guest; ***C:*** Stanley Pavey; ***M:*** Ronald Binge.

Runaway Daughters **1994 (PG-13)** Part of Showtime's "Rebel Highway" remakes of '50s flicks, in this case the 1956 AIP juvie drama (although the similarities are minimal). Three small town teen babes (Bowen, Lewis, Fields) fake their own kidnappings so they can steal a car and head out on the highway to catch the runaway beau (Young) of one babe who's knocked up. **82m/C DVD.** Julie Bowen, Holly Fields, Jenny Lewis, Paul Rudd, Chris Young, Dick Miller, Fabian, Joe Flaherty, Belinda Balaski, Robert Picardo, Dee Wallace; ***Cameos:*** Cathy Moriarty; ***D:*** Joe Dante; ***W:*** Charles S. Haas; ***C:*** Richard Bowen; ***M:*** Hummie Mann. **CABLE**

Runaway Father 1/2 **1991** Pat Bennett's husband fakes his own death in an attempt to abandon his family. When Bennett discovers he's alive she works to set a legal precedent—17 years worth of back child support. Based on a true story. **94m/C VHS, DVD.** Donna Mills, Jack Scalia, Chris Mulkey, Jenny Lewis; ***D:*** John Nicolella. **TV**

Runaway Jury **2003 (PG-13)** John Grisham-penned legal thriller has the goods. Hot-shot jury consultant Rankin Fitch (Hackman) is hired by a gun manufacturer on trial after an office massacre. The unscrupulous Fitch spies on potential jurors and isn't above using blackmail in his quest to find a totally sympathetic jury. His goal of a totally biased jury is endangered when he's forced to include Nicholas (Cusack), a man with a secret. A-list cast, interesting supports, well-rounded characters, and top-notch direction more than make up for not-quite-fully-realized plot development and a less than satisfying ending. This is the first on-screen pairing of former roommates Hackman and Hoffman, and they make the most of it. **127m/C VHS, DVD.** *US* John Cusack, Gene Hackman, Dustin Hoffman, Rachel Weisz, Bruce Davison, Bruce McGill, Jeremy Piven, Nick Searcy, Stanley Anderson, Clifford Curtis, Nestor Serrano, Leland Orser, Jennifer Beals, Gerry Bamman, Joanna Going, Bill Nunn, Juanita Jennings, Marguerite Moreau, Nora Dunn, Guy Torry, Rusty Schwimmer; ***D:*** Gary Fleder; ***W:*** Brian Koppelman, David Levien, Rick Cleveland, Matthew Chapman; ***C:*** Robert Elswit; ***M:*** Christopher Young.

Runaway Nightmare **1984** Two western worm ranchers are kidnapped by a female gang whose members torture and initiate them, then talk about their plan to steal from organized criminals. Just another typical worm rancher flick. **104m/C VHS.** Michael Cartel, Al Valletta; ***D:*** Michael Cartel.

Runaway Train **1985 (R)** A tough jailbird and his sidekick break out of the hoosegow and find themselves trapped aboard a brakeless freight train heading for certain derailment in northwestern Canada. Harrowing existential action drama based on a screenplay by Akira Kurosawa. Voight is superb. **112m/C VHS, DVD.** Edward (Eddie) Bunker, Jon Voight, Eric Roberts, Rebecca De Mornay, John P. Ryan, T.K. Carter, Kenneth McMillan, John Bloom; ***D:*** Andrei Konchalovsky; ***W:*** Andrei Konchalovsky, Djordje Milicevic, Edward (Eddie) Bunker, Paul Zindel; ***C:*** Alan Hume; ***M:*** Trevor Jones. Golden Globes '86: Actor—Drama (Voight).

Runaways *Fugitive Lovers* **1975** A corrupt politician's wife falls in love with the man who saved her when she attempted suicide. The two try to escape her husband's wrathful vengeance. **95m/C VHS.** Steve Oliver, Sondra Currie, John Russell, Virginia Mayo, Doodles Weaver, Juanita Moore, Frankie Darro, Vincent Barbi; ***D:*** John Carr; ***W:*** John Carr; ***C:*** Michael Mileham; ***M:*** Alex Barnhardt.

The Runaways **1975** A boy runs away from an unhappy foster home situation and becomes friends with a leopard that has escaped from an animal park. Sentimental but well-done family fun. **76m/C VHS.** Dorothy McGuire, John Randolph, Neva Patterson, Josh Albee; ***D:*** Harry Harris.

The Runaways **2010 (R)** This coming-of-age music bio about the '70s all-girl hard rock band "The Runaways" focuses on guitarist Joan Jett (Stewart) and lead singer Cherie Currie (Fanning) while letting the other band members fade into the background. Overall, it's a pretty rockin' tale of the excessive music business of the day. Driven by egomaniacal Svengali Kim Fowley (Shannon), the pre-pubescent girls rise from obscurity to success before the inevitable downward spiral caused by the temptations of rock 'n roll life. Good performances from Fanning and Stewart, who nails Jett's swagger. The script was largely drawn from Currie's memoir "Neon Angel." **109m/C DVD.** *US* Kristen Stewart, Dakota Fanning, Scout Taylor-Compton, Stella Maeve, Alia Shawkat, Hannah Marks, Michael Shannon, Brett Cullen, Tatum O'Neal; ***D:*** Floria Sigismondi; ***W:*** Floria Sigismondi; ***C:*** Benoit Debie.

The Rundown **1/2 2003 (PG-13)** Amusing buddy/action comedy works because of the Rock's self-deprecating charm (and physical abilities) and Scott's insolent exuberance. Bounty hunter Beck (Johnson) takes one last job—that of retrieving the wastrel son of his boss. Travis (Scott) is an archeology student who's in the Amazon seeking a priceless golden artifact, which is also sought by his ex-girlfriend Marianna (Dawson), who wants to use the treasure to free her people from the inhuman working conditions imposed by manic mine owner Hatcher (Walken, who's obviously having a good time playing another crazy bad guy). The action (and there's lots of it) is briskly paced, and Hawaii's rain forests and the San Gabriel Mountains provide appropriate substitutes for the Amazon. Watch for the scene with the Rock and some amorous monkeys. **104m/C VHS, DVD, Blu-ray Disc, UMD, HD DVD.** *US* Dwayne "The Rock" Johnson, Seann William Scott, Rosario Dawson, Christopher Walken, Ewen Bremner, Jon(athan) Gries, William Lucking, Ernie Reyes Jr., Stuart Wilson; ***Cameos:*** Arnold Schwarzenegger; ***D:*** Peter Berg; ***W:*** R.J. Stewart, James Vanderbilt; ***C:*** Tobias Schliessler; ***M:*** Harry Gregson-Williams.

The Runestone **1991 (R)** After the eponymous viking relic is unearthed, an archaeologist's meddling frees a long-imprisoned wolf-beast that terrorizes New York. An adequate horror flick that taps the seldom-explored vein of Norse mythology. Based on a novel by Mark E. Rogers. **105m/C VHS.** Peter Riegert, Joan Severance, William Hickey, Tim Ryan, Chris Young, Alexander Godunov; ***D:*** Willard Carroll; ***W:*** Willard Carroll; ***M:*** David Newman.

The Runner **1999 (R)** Eldard stars as a compulsive Vegas gambler who's so deeply in debt he agrees to his shady uncle's (Mantegna) offer to get him a job with gangster Goodman. Eldard places bets with sports bookies (with mob money) and falls for cocktail waitress Cox, using some of Goodman's money to buy her a diamond ring. The vengeful Goodman doesn't take kindly to this. **95m/C VHS, DVD.** Ron Eldard, John Goodman, Courteney Cox, Joe Mantegna, Bokeem Woodbine; ***D:*** Ron Moler; ***W:*** Anthony E. Zuiker, Dustin Lee Abraham; ***C:*** James Glennon; ***M:*** Anthony Marinelli.

The Runner Stumbles **1/2 1979 (R)** Dated melodrama about a priest who goes on trial for murdering the nun with whom he fell in love in a mining town in the 1920s. Based on a true incident, from the play by Milan Stiff. Van Dyke in an unwanted serious role is miserably grim and wooden. **109m/C VHS.** Dick Van Dyke, Kathleen Quinlan, Maureen Stapleton, Ray Bolger, Beau Bridges, Tammy Grimes; ***D:*** Stanley Kramer; ***M:*** Ernest Gold.

The Runnin' Kind **1/2 1989 (R)** A yuppie expecting to inherit his father's Ohio law firm goes on a wild spree with an all-girl rock band. Sexy drummer Howard shows him the sights of certain parts of L.A. Original, fun comedy. Independent. **89m/C VHS.** David Packer, Pleasant Gehman, Brie Howard, Susan Strasberg; ***D:*** Max Tash.

Running Against Time **1/2 1990 (PG)** A teacher tries to change history (and erase his brother's Vietnam War death) by time-warping back to 1963 and preventing JFK's murder. Cable TV movie takes an offhanded gee-whiz approach to a tantalizing premise, as temporal paradoxes multiply in "Back to the Future" style. No assassination-conspiracy theories, by the way, but Lyndon Johnson fans may not like his portrayal here. Based on the novel "A Time to Remember" by Stanley Shapiro. **93m/C VHS.** Robert Hays, Catherine Hicks, Sam Wanamaker, James DiStefano, Brian Smiar; ***D:*** Bruce Seth Green; ***W:*** Robert Glass. **CABLE**

Running Away **1989 (PG-13)** Bittersweet story of WWII romance, with a twist of adventure. Strong cast creates good chemistry, but somehow the story is not engaging. Loren and Penny are mother and daughter, leaving Rome for the hills and encountering dangers. **101m/C VHS.** Sophia Loren, Sydney Penny, Robert Loggia, Andrea Occhipinti; ***D:*** Dino Risi.

Running Blind **1978** Espionage/adventure thriller has a double agent and a beautiful woman on the run in Iceland. **120m/C VHS.** *GB* George Sewell, Vladek Sheybal, Ian McCulloch, Richard Hurndall, Stuart Wilson, Heidi Steindorsottir; ***D:*** William Brayne; ***W:*** Jack Gerson; ***M:*** Christopher Gunning.

Running Brave **1983 (PG)** The true story of Billy Mills, a South Dakota Sioux Indian who won the Gold Medal in the 10,000 meter run at the 1964 Tokyo Olympics. Not bad, but hokey in the way of many of these plodding true-story flicks. **90m/C VHS, DVD.** Robby Benson, Claudia Cron, Pat Hingle, Denis Lacroix; ***D:*** D.S. Everett; ***W:*** Henry Bean.

Running Cool **1993 (R)** Two easy-going bikers join up with an old friend to protect his wetlands property from a lowlife developer and his stooges. Chicks (there's a romance with a local biker babe), motorcyles, fighting, and saving the environment—what more could you want? **106m/C VHS.** Andrew Divoff, Tracy Sebastian, Dedee Pfeiffer, James Gammon, Paul Gleason, Arlen Dean Snyder, Bubba Baker; ***D:*** Beverly Sebastian, Ferd Sebastian; ***W:*** Beverly Sebastian, Ferd Sebastian.

Running Delilah **1/2 1993** Delilah (Cattrall) is a secret agent who is apparently killed by a vicious arms dealer. Only her fellow agent (Zane) resurrects her and Delilah is transformed into a cybernetic super agent. And her assignment is to go after a terrorist who's building a nuclear weapon with plutonium supplied by Delilah's killer. **85m/C VHS.** Kim Cattrall, Billy Zane, Diana Rigg; ***D:*** Richard Franklin; ***W:*** Ron Koslow; ***C:*** Ellery Ryan; ***M:*** Lee Holdridge.

Running Free **1/2 1994 (PG)** Sullen Garrett joins his naturalist mother in the Alaskan wilderness and establishes a friendship with a wolverine cub (who's smarter than the kid). **90m/C VHS, DVD.** Jesse Montgomery Sythe, Jayme Lee Misfeldt, Michael Pena; ***D:*** Steve Kroschel.

Running Free **1/2 2000 (G)** Inspiring story of the friendship between an orphaned servant boy and an abandoned colt named Lucky who is destined for a life of hard labor. Their quest for freedom from their proscribed lives creates a visually stunning tale about the triumph of the human spirit. **85m/C DVD.** Chase Moore, Jan Decleir, Arie Verveen, Maria Geelbooi, Lukas Haas; ***D:*** Sergei Bodrov; ***W:*** Jeanne Rosenberg; ***C:*** Dan Laustsen; ***M:*** Nicola Piovani.

Running Hot **1/2** *Highway to Hell; Lucky 13* **1983 (R)** Seventeen-year-old convicted murderer Stoltz gets love letter in prison from older woman Carrico. When he escapes, they flee the law together. Quick-paced and entertaining. **88m/C VHS.** Monica Carrico, Eric Stoltz, Stuart Margolin, Virgil Frye, Richard Bradford, Sorrels Pickard, Juliette Cummins; ***D:*** Mark Griffiths; ***W:*** Mark Griffiths.

The Running Man **1/2 1987 (R)** Special-effects-laden adaptation of the Stephen King novel (under his Richard Bachman pseud) about a futuristic TV game show. Convicts are given a chance for pardon—all they have to do is survive a battle with specially trained assassins in the bombed-out sections of Los Angeles. Sci-fi with an attitude. **101m/C VHS, DVD.** Arnold Schwarzenegger, Richard Dawson, Maria Conchita Alonso, Yaphet Kotto, Mick Fleetwood, Dweezil Zappa, Jesse Ventura, Jim Brown, Edward (Eddie) Bunker, Kurt Fuller, Lin Shaye, Toru Tanaka, Erland van Lidth, Gus Rethwisch; ***D:*** Paul Michael Glaser; ***W:*** Steven E. de Souza; ***C:*** Thomas Del Ruth; ***M:*** Harold Faltermeyer.

Running Mates **1986 (PG-13)** Occasionally intriguing drama of two teens who fall in love, but are kept apart by their fathers' local political rivalry. Could have been better, but cardboard characters abound. **90m/C VHS.** Greg Webb, Barbara Howard, J. Don Ferguson, Clara Dunn; ***D:*** Thomas L. Neff.

Running Mates **1992 (PG-13)** Cynically amusing political satire about a bachelor politician and his too intelligent lady love. Harris is Hugh, a U.S. senator looking forward to the presidential primaries when he meets widowed children's novelist Aggie (Keaton). She hates politics and he's Mr. Slick, although decent enough behind the political expediency. Aggie, however, has a potentially damaging secret in her past which causes the scandal-scenting pack of press hounds to bay in salivating anticipation. Will Hugh stick by Aggie and will Aggie overcome her natural political distaste for everything to end happily? A well-played romp. **88m/C VHS, DVD.** Ed Harris, Diane Keaton, Ed Begley Jr., Ben Masters, Robert Harper, Brandon Maggart, Russ Tamblyn; ***D:*** Michael Lindsay-Hogg; ***W:*** A.L. Appling. **CABLE**

Running Mates **1/2 2000** Liberal governor James Pryce (Selleck) is a shoo-in for the presidential nomination at the L.A. Democratic convention. But he still has to choose his veep running mate. And he's got four powerful women giving him opinions, including his wife Jenny (Travis), his campaign manager Lauren (Linney), Hollywood fundraiser Shawna (Hatcher), and boozy socialite Meg (Dunaway), who's the wife of Pryce's mentor (Culp). So will he go with the idealistic senator (Gunton) or the power broker (McGill)? **90m/C VHS, DVD.** Tom Selleck, Laura Linney, Nancy Travis, Teri Hatcher, Bruce McGill, Bob Gunton, Faye Dunaway, Robert Culp, Caroline Aaron, Matt Malloy; ***D:*** Ron Lagomarsino; ***W:*** Claudia Salter; ***C:*** Alan Caso; ***M:*** John Debney. **CABLE**

Running on Empty **1988 (PG-13)** Two 1960s radicals are still on the run in 1988 for a politically motivated Vietnam War-era crime. Though they have managed to stay one step ahead of the law, their son wants a "normal" life, even if it means never seeing his family again. Well-performed, quiet, plausible drama. **116m/C VHS, DVD.** Christine Lahti, River Phoenix, Judd Hirsch, Martha Plimpton, Jonas Arby, Ed Crowley, L.M. Kit Carson, Steven Hill, Augusta Dabney, David Margulies, Sidney Lumet; ***D:*** Sidney Lumet; ***W:*** Naomi Foner; ***C:*** Gerry Fisher; ***M:*** Tony Mottola. Golden Globes '89: Screenplay; L.A. Film Critics '88: Actress (Lahti); Natl. Bd. of Review '88: Support. Actor (Phoenix).

Running on Karma **1/2** *Da zhi lao; Daai chek liu; An Intelligent Muscle Man* **2003** Big (Andy Lau) is a former Buddhist monk who has taken up competitive weight-lifting and stripping despite having gained psychic powers from his former religious vocation after killing a sparrow in a fit of rage. He can see the sins committed in past lives (karma) by those who are about to die. And the perky young female cop who has just arrested him for indecent exposure is one such individual. Knowing that karma can't be opposed, Big decides to help her do so anyway, along with helping her track down a murderer. Buddhist theology, muscle suits, and neat fights abound. **93m/C DVD.** *HK* Andy Lau, Cecilia Cheung, Siu-fai Cheung, Wen Zhong Yu, Lian Sheng Hou, Meng Zhang; ***D:*** Johnny To, Kai-Fai Wai; ***W:*** Kai-Fai Wai, Nai-Hoi Yau, Tin-Shing Yip, Kin-Yee Au; ***C:*** Siu Keung Cheng; ***M:*** Cacine Wong.

Running out of Luck **1/2 1986 (R)** A light, song-packed story about a rock star very much like Jagger who is abandoned in South America and believed dead, until he returns to his world. Features songs from Jagger's solo album "She's the Boss." **88m/C VHS.** Mick Jagger, Dennis Hopper, Jerry Hall, Rae Dawn Chong; ***D:*** Julien Temple.

Running Out of Time *Dias Contados; Numbered Days* **1994** Antonio (Gomez) is a Basque who belongs to a terrorist organization. He's sent to Madrid to carry out an assignment, winds up getting involved with drug-addicted prostitute Charo (Gabriel), and finds that his mission overlaps with his relationship. Spanish with subtitles. **93m/C VHS, DVD.** *SP* Carmelo Gomez, Ruth Gabriel, Javier Bardem, Karra Elejalde, Candela Pena; ***D:*** Imanol Uribe; ***W:*** Imanol Uribe; ***C:*** Javier Aguirresarobe; ***M:*** Jose Nieto.

Running out of Time **1999** Jewel thief Andy (Lau) knows that he has only two weeks to live. He goes ahead and pulls a job that sets him against Sean (Wan), a canny police negotiator. Director Johnny To employs some flashy visuals in this over-achieving crime movie and he got first-rate performances from his leads, particularly Lau Ching Wan, a tremendous character actor. **89m/C DVD.** *HK* Andy Lau, Lau Ching Wan, Waise Lee, Hui Siu Hung, Yoyo Mung; ***D:*** Johnny To; ***W:*** Yau Nai Hoi; ***C:*** Cheng Siu Keung; ***M:*** Wong Ying Wah.

Running Out of Time 2 *Am zin 2; Am zhan 2; Hidden War 2* **2006** Inspector Ho (Lau Ching-Wan) from the original film has been promoted to a desk job, but he inevitably winds up on the streets again when a magician-turned-art thief tries a series of heists. Not as well done as the original, it's often thought of as more of an overly complicated parody of the first film than a sequel to it (proving that even in China, sequels usually suck). **91m/C DVD.** *HK* Ching-Wan Lau, Ekin Cheng, Kelly Lin, Suet Lam, Ruby Wong, Shiu Hung Hui, Yun Shang Ding; ***D:*** Johnny To, Wing-cheong Law; ***W:*** Nai-Hoi Yau, Kin-Yee Au, Laurent Cortiaud, Julien Carbon; ***C:*** Siu Keung Cheng; ***M:*** Raymond Wong.

Running Red **1999 (R)** Gregori was once a member of an elite Soviet commando team. Sickened by the corruption, he quits and eventually sets up a new life for himself in the U.S. But his past comes back when his ex-boss contacts him and threatens to kill his family unless Greg does an assassination job for him. **92m/C VHS, DVD.** Jeff Speakman, Angie Everhart, Stanley Kamel, Elya Baskin, Geoffrey Rivas, DeLane Matthews, Bart Braverman; ***D:*** Jerry P. Jacobs; ***W:*** David Stauffer; ***C:*** Ken Blakey; ***M:*** Jim Halfpenny. **VIDEO**

Running Scared **1979 (PG)** Two young men, returning from military service as stowaways aboard an Army cargo plane, are caught by an intelligence agent and thought to be spies, because Reinhold has unknowingly photographed a secret U.S. base with his stolen Army-issue camera. Not-bad spy thriller with a twist—the "spies" are hapless nobodies, now on the lam. **92m/C VHS.** Ken Wahl, Judge Reinhold, John Saxon, Annie McEnroe, Bradford Dillman, Pat Hingle; ***D:*** Paul Glickler.

Running Scared 1/2 **1986 (R)** Hip, unorthodox Chicago cops Hines and Crystal have to handle an important drug arrest before taking an extended vacation in Key West. Not as relentless as "48 Hrs," but more enjoyable in some ways. Ever wonder what it's like to ride in a car at high speed on the tracks? Find out here. **107m/C VHS, DVD.** Gregory Hines, Billy Crystal, Dan Hedaya, Jimmy Smits, Darlanne Fluegel, Joe Pantoliano, Steven Bauer; ***D:*** Peter Hyams; ***W:*** Gary De Vore; ***C:*** Peter Hyams.

Running Scared 1/2 **2006 (R)** Frenetic actioner has small-time hood Joe (Walker) charged with disposing of a gun for his Mob cronies after a drug deal gone bad. The reason it went bad is that some crooked cops crashed the party and a few of them ended up dead. When a neighbor kid takes the gun and uses it to shoot his Russian mob-affiliated, abusive stepdad, things go sideways for everyone in a big hurry. Joe must race the clock, the cops, his associates, and the Russians to find the kid and the gun, both of which change hands with astonishing regularity over the course of the night. What this one lacks in cohesion and plausibility, it makes up for in pacing (which rarely slackens) and urgency. **122m/C DVD.** *US* Paul Walker, Cameron Bright, Vera Farmiga, Karel Roden, Johnny Messner, Ivana Milicevic, Chazz Palminteri, Alex Neuberger, Michael Cudlitz, Bruce Altman, Elizabeth Mitchell, Arthur J. Nascarelli, John Noble, David Warshofsky, Idalis DeLeon; ***D:*** Wayne Kramer; ***W:*** Wayne Kramer; ***C:*** James Whitaker; ***M:*** Mark Isham.

Running Wild **1927** Early silent comedy starring mustachioed Fields as an eternal coward who suddenly turns into a lion by hypnosis. Odd, often unfunny Fields entry sometimes hits the mark. He's awfully mean, though. **68m/B VHS.** W.C. Fields, Mary Brian, Claud Buchanan; ***D:*** Gregory La Cava; ***M:*** Gaylord Carter.

Running Wild 1/2 **1973 (G)** A free-lance photographer becomes involved in a dispute to save a corral of wild mustang horses. The usual great Colorado scenery enhances a good, family-view story. **102m/C VHS.** Lloyd Bridges, Dina Merrill, Pat Hingle, Gilbert Roland, Morgan Woodward; ***D:*** Robert McCahon; ***W:*** Robert McCahon.

Running Wild **1994 (R)** Beautiful woman abandons her much older fiance to go on a wild road trip with his son that includes sex and crime. **91m/C VHS.** Jennifer Barker, Daniel Dupont, Daniel Spector, Eliott Keener; ***D:*** Philippe Blot.

Running Wild 1/2 **1999** Harrison stars as Maj. Matt Robinson, a retired Air Force pilot who has taken a position with the U.N. to track elephant migrations in Africa. He takes his children Angela (Nevin) and Nicholas (Jones) with him. Once they arrive in Africa, Matt meets a pretty veternarian, Rachel (Hallier) and a guide, Isaac (Kanaventi). They enjoy a great adventure until Matt realizes that there are many elephant-hunting poachers in the area, and when they threaten Angela and Nicholas, Matt and Rachel spring into action to rescue the children. Fun film for the entire family, although a bit too preachy at times concerning the plight of endangered animals. Contains fine performances, as well as breathtaking nature photography. Horror-industry vet Harry Alan Towers executive produced this family film, which was directed by the writer of the slasher classic "Happy Birthday to Me"! **92m/C VHS, DVD.** Gregory Harrison, Lori Hallier, Cody Jones, Brooke Nevin, Munyaradzi Kanaventi; ***D:*** Timothy Bond. **CABLE**

Running with Scissors **2006 (R)** Sex, drugs, and insanity are manifest in the debuting Murphy's adaptation of Augusten Burrough's memoirs of his screwed-up adolescence. Narcissist monster mom Deirdre (Bening) has divorced son Augusten's (Cross) alcoholic father Norman (Baldwin) and is in therapy with bizarre shrink Dr. Finch (Cox). The two adults decide Augusten will live with Finch's family in their ramshackle Victorian house, where he is subjected to such eccentricities as the depressed, kibble-eating Mrs. Finch (Clayburgh) and adoptive son Neil (Fiennes), who seduces the willing teenager. Also ensconced are Bible-reading Hope Finch (Paltrow) and her rebellious younger sister Natalie (Wood), who befriends Augusten. Cross has the least showy role as reactive narrator and the flick is more scenic than coherent. **121m/C DVD.** *US* Joseph Cross, Annette Bening, Brian Cox, Joseph Fiennes, Evan Rachel Wood, Alec Baldwin, Jill Clayburgh, Gwyneth Paltrow, Gabrielle Union, Kristin Chenoweth, Patrick Wilson, Jack Kaeding, Gabriel Guedj; ***D:*** Ryan Murphy; ***W:*** Ryan Murphy; ***C:*** Christopher Baffa; ***M:*** James Levine.

Running Woman **1998 (R)** Emily Russo (Russell) is accused of the mysterious death of her young son and goes on the lam to prove her inncence. With the police on her trail, Emily's quest leads her to a gang that's terrorizing some seedier parts of L.A. **84m/C VHS, DVD.** Theresa Russell, Andrew (Andy) Robinson, Gary (Rand) Graham, Eddie Velez, Anthony Crivello, Robert LaSardo, Chris Pennock; ***D:*** Rachel Samuels; ***W:*** Rachel Samuels; ***C:*** Chris Manley; ***M:*** Christopher Lennertz. **VIDEO**

Rupert's Land 1/2 **1998** British lawyer Rupert is reunited for the first time since childhood with his hard-living half-brother Dale, a British Columbia fisherman, at the funeral of their father. The Canadian side of Rupert's family seems to be more than a little eccentric, including Dale's mother Trudy, the keeper of the family's sordid secrets. Rupert and Dale suffer through a series of misadventures as they try to reunite as brothers and deal with their father's flawed legacy. **95m/C VHS.** *CA* Samuel West, Ian Tracey, George Wendt, Susan Hogan, Gabrielle Miller; ***D:*** Jonathan Tammuz; ***W:*** Graeme Manson; ***C:*** Gregory Middleton; ***M:*** Phil Marshall.

Rush **1984** A post-nuclear world war movie in which a rebel named Rush battles the rulers of a slave colony. **83m/C VHS.** *IT* Conrad Nichols, Gordon Mitchell, Laura Trotter, Rita Furlan; ***D:*** Tonino Ricci.

Rush **1991 (R)** Texas drug culture, circa 1975, is portrayed in this bleak cop drama. Rookie narcotics officer Kristen Cates (Leigh) goes undercover with the experienced Raynor (Patric) to catch a big-time dealer, menancingly played by Allman, and their bosses don't much care how they do it. Cates falls in love with Raynor and is drawn ever deeper into the drug-addicted world they are supposed to destroy. Fine performances and a great blues score by Clapton. The directorial debut of Zanuck. Based on ex-narcotics cop Kim Wozencraft's autobiographical novel. **120m/C VHS, DVD.** Jason Patric, Jennifer Jason Leigh, Gregg Allman, Max Perlich, Sam Elliott, Tony Frank, William Sadler, Special K. McCray; ***D:*** Lili Fini Zanuck; ***W:*** Pete Dexter; ***C:*** Kenneth Macmillan; ***M:*** Eric Clapton.

Rush Hour 1/2 **1998 (PG-13)** Cliched buddy film that's sauced up a bit with the unlikely pairing of loud-mouthed Tucker and swift-footed Chan. Motormouth L.A. detective James Carter (Tucker) is temporarily assigned to the FBI to babysit Hong Kong detective Lee (Chan) and keep him away from a kidnapping case that Lee is anxious to solve for personal reasons. Chan is more subdued stuntwise than in his own pictures but nonetheless a charmer against the abrasive Tucker. The culture clash scenes and some high gloss action moments make for a rousing action-comedy. Film was a surprise boxoffice smash. **98m/C VHS, DVD, UMD.** Jackie Chan, Chris Tucker, Tzi Ma, Julia Hsu, Philip Baker Hall, Rex Linn, Elizabeth Pena, Mark Rolston, Tom Wilkinson; ***D:*** Brett Ratner; ***W:*** Jim Kouf, Ross LaManna; ***C:*** Adam Greenberg; ***M:*** Lalo Schifrin. MTV Movie Awards '99: On-Screen Duo (Chris Tucker/Jackie Chan).

Rush Hour 2 **2001 (PG-13)** Director Ratner and stars Tucker and Chan all reteam for the sequel to their $250 million 1998 comedy. Det. Carter (Tucker) travels to Hong Kong with his new buddy, Det. Lee (Chan), where they get involved in a criminal conspiracy. The jokes aren't as funny or fresh as in the original, and that situation isn't helped by the fact that before the movie's half over you just want Tucker to shut up. Chan does a fine job with his duties, which are to continue to amusingly mangle the English language, and do some more of those great martial-arts stunts. He gets some help in the acrobatic martial-arts department from Ziyi, Lone, and a nice cameo by Cheadle. They should stop now, but they won't. RH3 is almost guaranteed. **91m/C VHS, DVD, UMD.** *US* Chris Tucker, Jackie Chan, Harris Yulin, Zhang Ziyi, John Lone, Alan King, Roselyn Sanchez, Kenneth Tsang, Ernie Reyes Jr., Jeremy Piven, Saul Rubinek, Don Cheadle; ***D:*** Brett Ratner; ***W:*** Jeff Nathanson; ***C:*** Matthew F. Leonetti; ***M:*** Lalo Schifrin, Kathy Nelson.

Rush Hour 3 1/2 **2007 (PG-13)** Third in the franchise brings nothing fresh to the table except a new location, Paris, for Chan and Tucker's wacky culture clash schtick. After the attempted murder of the Chinese ambassador (Ma), the two travel to Paris to track the assassin, protect his daughter, and make a bunch of jokes that constantly refer back to the previous, better entries in the series. Chan and Tucker still have chemistry but director Ratner doesn't give them much to work with. The fight scenes seem slowed-down, shorter, and less fun, and even the standard end-of-movie blooper reel is a yawn. Roman Polanski cameos as a particularly nasty French commissioner. **91m/C DVD, Blu-ray Disc.** *US* Jackie Chan, Chris Tucker, Max von Sydow, Hiroyuki (Henry) Sanada, Yvan Attal, Roselyn Sanchez, Roman Polanski, Noemie Lenoir, Vinnie Jones, Tzi Ma, Julie Depardieu, Youki Kudoh, Dana Ivey, Zhang Jingchu; ***D:*** Brett Ratner; ***W:*** Jeff Nathanson; ***C:*** J.(James) Michael Muro; ***M:*** Lalo Schifrin.

Rush It 1/2 **1977** Scriptwriters ponder possible plots over capucino: "I've got it! 'Bike Messengers in Love'!" "Nah. The title's too obvious. Why don't we call it 'Rush It'?" Much hard work and many months later, the result is forgettable. **78m/C VHS.** Tom Berenger, Jill Eikenberry, John Heard, Christina Pickles; ***D:*** Gary Youngman; ***W:*** Gary Youngman; ***C:*** Don Lenzer; ***M:*** Buzzy Linhart.

Rush Week **1988 (R)** Dead coeds populate campus during frat week. Greg Allman has bit part and the Dickies perform two songs. **93m/C VHS, DVD.** Dean Hamilton, Gregg Allman, Kathleen Kinmont, Roy Thinnes, Pamela Ludwig; ***D:*** Bob Bravler; ***W:*** Michael W. Leighton, Russell V. Manzatt; ***C:*** Jeff Mart.

Rushmore 1/2 **1998 (R)** Fresh and original comedy from Wes Anderson follows 15-year-old Max (Schwartzman), an underachieving yet overconfident student at Rushmore Academy. He has romantic designs on teacher Miss Cross (Williams), and enlists the help of wealthy alum Herman Blume (Murray) in his quest to impress her. Blume also falls for the woman, however, instigating a war of nasty tricks between the two quirky rivals. Murray drops his trademark smirk and gives his best performance to date. Also shining is newcomer Schwartzman, who is the son of Talia Shire. At this rate, the Coppola show biz clan may take over Hollywood by sheer population as well as talent. **93m/C VHS, DVD.** Bill Murray, Jason Schwartzman, Olivia Williams, Seymour Cassel, Brian Cox, Mason Gamble, Sara Tanaka, Connie Nielsen, Kim Terry, Stephen McCole, Ronnie McCawley, Keith McCawley; ***D:*** Wes Anderson; ***W:*** Wes Anderson, Owen Wilson; ***C:*** Robert Yeoman; ***M:*** Mark Mothersbaugh. Ind. Spirit '99: Director (Anderson), Support. Actor (Murray); L.A. Film Critics '98: Support. Actor (Murray); N.Y. Film Critics '98: Support. Actor (Murray); Natl. Soc. Film Critics '98: Support. Actor (Murray).

Ruslan **2009 (R)** Ruslan Drachev (Seagal) is an ex-mobster turned crime writer whose past comes back to bite him when his daughter decides to marry his bitterest rival and his family is threatened. But Ruslan hasn't forgotten how to be a bad guy. **?m/C DVD.** Steven Seagal, Laura Mennell, Mike Dopud, Dan Payne, Holly Eglington, Zak Santiago, Inna Korobkina; ***D:*** Jeff King; ***C:*** Thomas M. Harting; ***M:*** Peter Allen. **VIDEO**

Russell Mulcahy's Tale of the Mummy *Tale of the Mummy; Talos the Mummy* **1999 (R)** Archeologists break open the sealed tomb of an Egyptian prince and are destroyed by the curse of Talos. Fifty years later, Samantha Turkel (Lombard) discovers her grandfather's logbook and decides to retrace the course of his deadly expedition. She recovers a sacred amulet and suddenly the power of Talos threatens again. The film was originally released at 119 minutes under the title "Talos the Mummy." **87m/C VHS, DVD.** Jason Scott Lee, Louise Lombard, Sean Pertwee, Lysette Anthony, Michael Lerner, Jack Davenport, Honor Blackman, Christopher Lee, Shelley Duvall, Jon Polito; ***D:*** Russell Mulcahy; ***W:*** Russell Mulcahy, John Esposito; ***C:*** Gabriel Beristain. **VIDEO**

The Russia House 1/2 **1990 (R)** Russian scientist Brandauer attempts to publish book debunking Soviet Union's claims of military superiority by passing it through ex-lover Pfeiffer to British editor Connery, apparently unaware of impending glasnost. Star-studded spy thriller aspires to heights it never quite reaches. Adapted from John Le Carre's novel, Stoppard's screenplay is very fine, actually making some aspects of the novel work better. **122m/C VHS, DVD.** Sean Connery, Michelle Pfeiffer, Roy Scheider, James Fox, John Mahoney, Klaus Maria Brandauer, Ken Russell, J.T. Walsh, Michael Kitchen, David Threlfall, Ian McNeice, Christopher Lawford; ***D:*** Fred Schepisi; ***W:*** Tom Stoppard; ***C:*** Ian Baker; ***M:*** Jerry Goldsmith.

Russian Dolls 1/2 *Les Poupees Russes* **2005** Set five years after Klapisch's 2002 comedy "L'Auberge Espagnole," the roommates of the Barcelona apartment are older but only a little wiser. Narrator Xavier (Duris) is now 30 and writing for a TV soap in Paris while maintaining a friendship with his exasperating ex Martine (Tautou). His co-writer is Brit Wendy (Reilly), whose brother William (Bishop) is engaged to Russian ballerina Natacha (Obraztsova). The friends are reuniting in St. Petersburg for the wedding. Generally picturesque froth. English, French, Spanish, and Russian with subtitles. **125m/C DVD.** *FR GB* Romain Duris, Audrey Tautou, Cecile de France, Kelly Reilly, Kevin Bishop, Lucy Gordon, Aissa Maiga, Eugenya Obraztsova; ***D:*** Cedric Klapisch; ***W:*** Cedric Klapisch; ***C:*** Dominique Colin; ***M:*** Loik Dury, Laurent Levesque.

Russian Roulette **1975** The Russian premier is visiting Vancouver in 1970, and the Mounties must prevent a dissident KGB terrorist from assassinating him. Unthrilling spy yarn fails to deliver on intriguing premise. **100m/C VHS.** George Segal, Christina Raines, Bo Brundin, Denholm Elliott, Louise Fletcher; ***D:*** Lou Lombardo.

Russian Roulette 1/2 **1993** Routine story about an American woman on vacation in Russia who finds herself in the middle of a plot to locate a hidden Czarist artifact and smuggle it out of the country. Everyone on her tour group is suspect, an American businessman becomes involved, and a killer starts eliminating the number of players. Great location scenery. **89m/C VHS, DVD.** Susan Blakely, Barry Bostwick, E.G. Marshall, Jeff Altman; ***D:*** Greydon Clark.

The Russian Terminator **1990 (R)** An FBI agent is up against a one-man "death squad." **90m/C VHS.** Helena Michaelson, Frederick Offrein, Harley Melin, Tina Tjung; ***D:*** Mats Helge; ***W:*** Mats Helge.

The Russians Are Coming, the Russians Are Coming **1966** Based on the comic novel "The Off-Islanders" by Nathaniel Benchley, this is the story of a Russian sub which accidentally runs aground off the New England coast. The residents falsely believe that the nine-man crew is the beginning of a Soviet invasion, though the men are only looking for help. A memorable set of silly events follows the landing, engineered by a gung-ho police chief and a town filled with overactive imaginations. **126m/C VHS, DVD.** Alan Arkin, Carl Reiner, Theodore Bikel, Eva Marie Saint, Brian Keith, Paul Ford, Jonathan Winters, Ben Blue,

Tessie O'Shea, Doro Merande, John Phillip Law; ***D:*** Norman Jewison; ***C:*** Joseph Biroc. Golden Globes '67: Actor—Mus./Comedy (Arkin), Film—Mus./Comedy.

Russkies ½ **1987 (PG)** A jolly comedy about three adorable American kids who capture, and eventually grow to like, a stranded Russian sailor. Friendly and peace-loving, but dull. **98m/C VHS, DVD.** Joaquin Rafael (Leaf) Phoenix, Whip Hubley, Peter Billingsley, Stefan DeSalle, Susan Walters; ***D:*** Rick Rosenthal; ***M:*** James Newton Howard.

Rustin ½ **2001 (PG-13)** Every cliche possible appears in this cross between an afterschool special and a movie-of-the-week. Billy Stagen (Johnson) is a former pro football player who's becomes the sheriff of his Alabama hometown, Rustin. He slides by on charm and local celebrity until troubled teen Lee (Johnson) shows up, claiming to be his daughter. Now it's time to see if Billy can handle adult responsibilities. Meat Loaf is the current high school coach and Bryan is the latest football player-hero (in case you're wondering why they're featured on the box cover). **100m/C VHS, DVD.** Rick Johnson, Meat Loaf Aday, Ashley Johnson, Zachery Ty Bryan, Michael (Mike) Papajohn, Shawn Weatherly; ***D:*** Rick Johnson; ***W:*** Jon Lucas; ***C:*** Wally Pfister; ***M:*** Jonathan Price.

Rustler's Hideout *Rustler's Roundup* **1944** One of numerous westerns starring Crabbe as cowboy do-gooder Billy Carson, here plodding through standard histrionics against rustlers, a cardsharp, and a business fraud. **60m/C VHS.** Buster Crabbe, Al "Fuzzy" St. John, Charles "Blackie" King, John Merton, Lane Chandler, Hal Price, Edward Cassidy, Bud Osborne; ***D:*** Sam Newfield.

Rustlers of Red Dog ½ **1935** A 12-chapter western serial about Indian wars and cattle rustlers. **235m/B VHS, DVD.** Johnny Mack Brown, Raymond Hatton, Joyce Compton, Walter Miller, Harry Woods, William Desmond, Wally Wales, Chief Thundercloud, Art Mix, Bill(y) (William Patten) Patton, Bud Osborne, Lafe (Lafayette) McKee; ***D:*** Lew Landers.

Rustler's Paradise **1935** Carey seeks revenge on the man who stole his wife and daughter. **59m/B VHS.** Harry Carey Sr., Gertrude Messinger, Edmund Cobb; ***D:*** Harry Fraser.

Rustler's Rhapsody **1985 (PG)** A singing cowboy rides into a small western town and encounters all kinds of desperados in this earnest would-be satire of '40s B-movie westerns. **89m/C VHS, DVD.** Tom Berenger, Patrick Wayne, G.W. Bailey, Andy Griffith, Marilu Henner; ***D:*** Hugh Wilson; ***W:*** Hugh Wilson; ***C:*** Jose Luis Alcaine; ***M:*** Steve Dorff.

Rustler's Roundup ½ **1933** Mix rides to the rescue of Sinclair, whose daddy has been murdered by villains out to steal the ranch. **58m/B VHS.** Tom Mix, Diane Sinclair, Noah Beery Jr., Douglass Dumbrille, Roy Stewart, Nelson McDowell, William Desmond, Frank Lackteen, Pee Wee Holmes, Bud Osborne; ***D:*** Henry MacRae.

Rustler's Valley **1937** Hopalong Cassidy is a ranch foreman who tries to save his employer from the clutches of a crooked lawyer. Pretty fun ordinary range-ridin' saga. **59m/B VHS, DVD.** William Boyd, George "Gabby" Hayes, Lee J. Cobb; ***D:*** Nate Watt.

Rusty's Birthday ½ **1949** Danny searches for the lost Rusty who's been taken in by a family of transient workers. When Danny discovers his pal, he finds the young son of the family doesn't want to give Rusty up. **61m/B VHS.** Ted Donaldson, John Litel, Ann Doran, Jimmy Hunt, Ray Teal; ***D:*** Seymour Friedman; ***W:*** Brenda Weisberg.

The Rutanga Tapes ½ **1990 (R)** Soviet bloc country has representatives in Africa producing deadly chemicals used for war and a dissident has taped evidence of native deaths. Reporter babe Simpson wants an exclusive, Petersen wants the dissident, Libyan agents want the tapes, and you'll want to fast forward to the end. **88m/C VHS.** Henry Cele, Arnold Vosloo, Wilson Dunster, David Dukes, Susan Anspach; ***D:*** David Lister.

The Rutherford County Line **1987** A tough small-town sheriff searches for the killer of his deputies. **98m/C VHS.** Earl Owensby; ***D:*** Thom McIntyre.

The Ruthless Four *Every Man For Himself; Each One For Himself; Sam Cooper's Gold; Each Man For Himself* **1970** Quartet of unlikely mining partners match wills and wits and battle the elements. Not-so-hot spaghetti western, with good lead from Heflin. **97m/C VHS.** *IT* Van Heflin, Klaus Kinski, Gilbert Roland, George Hilton; ***D:*** Giorgio Capitani.

Ruthless People **1986 (R)** DeVito and his mistress spend a romantic evening plotting his obnoxious wife's untimely demise. Before he can put his plan into action, he's delighted to discover she's been kidnapped by some very desperate people—who don't stand a chance with Bette. High farcical entertainment is a variation on the story "The Ransom of Red Chief," by O. Henry. **93m/C VHS, DVD.** Bette Midler, Danny DeVito, Judge Reinhold, Helen Slater, Anita Morris, Bill Pullman; ***D:*** David Zucker, Jim Abrahams, Jerry Zucker; ***W:*** Dale Lanner; ***C:*** Jan De Bont; ***M:*** Michel Colombier.

Ruyblas **1948** Revenge and romance beset the court of Charles II in this tale of mistaken identity (with Marais in a dual role). Based on the novel by Victor Hugo. **90m/B VHS.** *FR* Jean Marais, Danielle Darrieux; ***D:*** Pierre Billon; ***W:*** Jean Cocteau.

RV **2006 (PG)** When Bob Munro (Williams) is forced to cancel a vacation for a business trip to Colorado, he decides it's the perfect opportunity to reconnect with his over-scheduled family. Bob rents a hideously gaudy RV and tricks wife Jamie (Hines), grumpy teen daughter Cassie (Levesque), and macho young son Carl (Hutcherson) into a road trip. Bob is basically clueless, and they run into various calamities (generally involving raw sewage) as well as the goofy, constantly upbeat Gornicke family, who live in their RV and really want to bond with the Munros. Headed by Daniels and Chenoweth, the Gornickes are a really scary/funny bunch. Williams does shtick but at least the schmaltz is minimal. **98m/C DVD, Blu-ray Disc, UMD.** *US* Robin Williams, Jeff Daniels, Cheryl Hines, Kristin Chenoweth, Joanna "JoJo" Levesque, Josh Hutcherson, Will Arnett, Brendan Fletcher, Brian Markinson, Barry Sonnenfeld, Hunter Parrish, Rob LaBelle, Chloe Sonnenfeld, Alex Ferris, Tony Hale, Brian Howe; ***D:*** Barry Sonnenfeld; ***W:*** Geoff Rodkey; ***C:*** Fred Murphy; ***M:*** James Newton Howard.

Rx ½ *Simple Lies* **2006** When his parents face financial ruin, Andrew (Balfour) decides to head south of the border with two friends, Jonny (Hanks) and Melissa (German), to pull off a big-money drug deal. Things take a bad turn for the twentysomethings, however, and their only hope of returning home from Mexico is in the form of a perilous pact with gay German drug dealers—who enjoy partying dressed as Nazis—that also endangers their lives. Predictable but definitely not dull. **86m/C DVD.** Eric Balfour, Colin Hanks, Lauren German, Danny Pino, Lulu Molina; ***D:*** Ariel Vromen; ***W:*** Ariel Vromen, Morgan Land. **VIDEO**

Ryan's Daughter ½ **1970 (PG)** Irish woman (Miles) marries a man she does not love and then falls for a shell-shocked British major who arrives during the 1916 Irish uprising to keep the peace. Not surprisingly, she is accused of betraying the local IRA gunrunners to her British lover. Tasteful melodrama with lots of pretty scenery that goes on a bit too long. **194m/C VHS, DVD.** *GB* Sarah Miles, Robert Mitchum, John Mills, Trevor Howard, Christopher Jones, Leo McKern; ***D:*** David Lean; ***W:*** Robert Bolt; ***C:*** Frederick A. (Freddie) Young; ***M:*** Maurice Jarre. Oscars '70: Cinematog., Support. Actor (Mills); Golden Globes '71: Support. Actor (Mills).

Ryder P.I. **1986 (PG-13)** P.I Ryder and his sidekick fight crime and solve weird cases in the big city. **92m/C VHS, DVD.** Bob Nelson, Dave Hawthorne, John Mulrooney, Howard Stern; ***D:*** Karl Hosch, Chuck Walker; ***W:*** Bob Nelson, Dave Hawthorne, Karl Hosch, Chuck Walker; ***C:*** Phil Arfman; ***M:*** Kevin Kelly.

Ryna **2005** In rural Romania, beautiful teenager Ryna (Petre) is forced to dress as a boy and work as a mechanic by her abusive father (Popescu). But she asserts her independence after a tragedy. Romanian and French with subtitles. **94m/C DVD.** *RO SI* Doroteea Petre, Valentin Popescu, Nicolae Praida, Matthiew Roze; ***D:*** Ruxandra Zenide; ***W:*** Ruxandra Zenide, Marek Epstein; ***C:*** Marius Panduru; ***M:*** Antoine Auberson.

S. Darko: A Donnie Darko Tale **2009 (R)** Tedious repetition and dull characters doom this bad sequel to the cult original. Donnie's younger sister Samantha (Chase) has yet to recover from her brother's death. She and her best pal Corey (Evigan) decide to drive to L.A. but their car breaks down in a small Utah town that's soon hit by a meteor. While Corey is partying with the locals, Samantha starts having end-of-the-world visions. **103m/C DVD.** Daveigh Chase, Briana Evigan, Ed Westwick, James Lafferty, John Hawkes, Elizabeth Berkley, Matthew Davis, Jackson Rathbone, Bret Roberts; ***D:*** Chris Fisher; ***W:*** Nathan Atkins; ***C:*** Marvin V. Rush; ***M:*** Ed Harcourt. **VIDEO**

S21: The Khmer Rouge Killing Machine *S21: La Machine De Mort Khmere Rouge; S21: The Khmer Rouge Death Machine* **2003** From 1975-1979, the Khmer Rouge, led by Pol Pot, instituted a series of murderous purges that took place at S21, a high school turned interrogation and torture center in Phnom Penh where 17,000 prisoners were "processed." Only three lived to tell about it. Vahn Nath, an artist, relates his story of survival by painting flattering portraits of the guards. Journals kept by guards and re-creations describe the painful techniques used on prisoners. Director Rithy Panh (himself an inmate at S21) takes an unvarnished look at the horrors perpetrated in the name of the state. **105m/C DVD.** *FR* ***D:*** Rithy Panh; ***W:*** Rithy Panh; ***C:*** Rithy Panh, Prum Mesar; ***M:*** Mark Marder.

Sabaka *The Hindu* **1955** Adventure set in India about a scary religious cult. Karloff and the cast of stalwart "B" movie performers have fun with this one, and you should, too. **81m/C VHS, DVD.** Boris Karloff, Reginald Denny, Victor Jory, Lisa Howard, Jeanne Bates, Jay Novello, June Foray; ***D:*** Frank Ferrin.

Sabata ½ **1969 (PG-13)** Van Cleef is the man in black as gunslinger Sabata in this exuberant, if confusing, spaghetti western. Sabata enters the town of Daugherty just after a robbery of Union Army funds. Sabata wants the reward but quickly discovers that three of the town's leaders funded the theft so he decides to blackmail them. They send numerous assassins after Sabata with no luck. **111m/C DVD.** *IT* Lee Van Cleef, William Berger, Ignazio Spalla, Frank Ressel, Aldo Canti, Gianni Rizzo, Antonio Gradoli; ***D:*** Gianfranco Parolini; ***W:*** Gianfranco Parolini, Renato Izzo; ***C:*** Sandro Moncori; ***M:*** Marcello Giombini.

Sabotage *A Woman Alone; Hidden Power* **1936** Early Hitchcock thriller based on Conrad's "The Secret Agent." A woman who works at a movie theatre (Sidney) suspects her quiet husband (Homolka) might be the terrorist planting bombs around London. Numerous sly touches of the Master's signature humor. **81m/B VHS, DVD.** Oscar Homolka, Sylvia Sidney, John Loder, Desmond Tester, Joyce Barbour, Matthew Boulton, S.J. Warmington, William Dewhurst, Austin Trevor, Torin Thatcher, Aubrey Mather, Peter Bull, Charles Hawtrey, Martita Hunt, Hal Walters, Frederick Piper; ***D:*** Alfred Hitchcock; ***W:*** Charles Bennett, Ian Hay, Alma Reville, E.V.H. Emmett, Helen Simpson; ***C:*** Bernard Knowles.

Sabotage **1996 (R)** A disgraced ex-Navy counterterrorism operative and bodyguard is on the trail of the man who murdered his boss, along with the FBI agent assigned to the case. Standard-issue shoot-em-up with decent action. **99m/C VHS.** *CA* Mark Dacascos, Carrie-Anne Moss, Tony Todd, Graham Greene, John Neville, James Purcell; ***D:*** Tibor Takacs; ***W:*** Michael Stokes; ***C:*** Curtis Petersen; ***M:*** Guy Zerafa.

Saboteur **1942** A man wrongly accused of sabotaging an American munitions plant during WWII sets out to find the traitor who framed him. Hitchcock uses his locations, including Boulder Dam, Radio City Music Hall, and the Statue of Liberty, to greatly intensify the action. Stunning resolution. **108m/B VHS, DVD.** Priscilla Lane, Robert Cummings, Otto Kruger, Alan Baxter, Norman Lloyd, Charles Halton; ***D:*** Alfred Hitchcock; ***W:*** Alfred Hitchcock, Peter Viertel; ***C:*** Joseph Valentine; ***M:*** Frank Skinner.

Sabre Jet **1953** Run-of-the-mill wartime drama of hubbies flying combat missions in Korea and long-suffering spouses on the home front. **90m/C VHS.** Robert Stack, Amanda Blake, Louis King; ***D:*** Louis King.

Sabretooth WOOF! **2001 (R)** Stupid scientist uses fossil DNA to genetically re-create the sabretooth tiger, loses control of the new beastie, which goes on a killing spree (of campers no less). Supremely dumb, unintentionally humorous, with bad acting (by actors who certainly have done better work), bad special effects...well, if you like cheap horror flicks, this woof is for you. **90m/C VHS, DVD.** David Keith, Vanessa Angel, John Rhys-Davies, Lahmard Tate; ***D:*** James D.R. Hickox; ***W:*** Tom Woolsley; ***C:*** Christopher Pearson. **VIDEO**

Sabrina *Sabrina Fair* **1954** Two wealthy brothers, one an aging businessman (Bogart) and the other a dissolute playboy (Holden), vie for the attention of their chauffeur's daughter (Hepburn), who has just returned from a French cooking school. Typically acerbic, in the Wilder manner, with Bogart and Holden cast interestingly against type (but it's Hepburn's picture anyway). Based on the play "Sabrina Fair" by Samuel Taylor. **113m/B VHS, DVD.** Audrey Hepburn, Humphrey Bogart, William Holden, Walter Hampden, Francis X. Bushman, John Williams, Martha Hyer, Marcel Dalio; ***D:*** Billy Wilder; ***W:*** Billy Wilder, Ernest Lehman; ***C:*** Charles B(ryant) Lang Jr. Oscars '54: Costume Des. (B&W); Directors Guild '54: Director (Wilder); Golden Globes '55: Screenplay; Natl. Bd. of Review '54: Support. Actor (Williams), Natl. Film Reg. '02.

Sabrina ½ **1995 (PG)** Updated version of Billy Wilder's 1954 fairytale that starred a luminous Audrey Hepburn. This time around the pretty Ormond is the chauffeur's daughter who gets closely involved with the wealthy Larrabees. And this time the emphasis is more on workaholic business mogul Linus (Ford), who plays a dangerous game when he decides to transfer Sabrina's affections from his feckless engaged brother David (Kinnear) to himself in order to protect a business merger. Ford's a little too stodgy (you'll wonder why Sabrina bothers except she's probably just too nice to say no) but Kinnear's suitably charming (in his film debut) and Marchand properly matriarchal. **127m/C VHS, DVD.** Harrison Ford, Julia Ormond, Greg Kinnear, Nancy Marchand, John Wood, Richard Crenna, Angie Dickinson, Lauren Holly, Fanny Ardant, Dana Ivey, Patrick Bruel, Miriam Colon, Elizabeth Franz; ***D:*** Sydney Pollack; ***W:*** David Rayfiel, Barbara Benedek; ***C:*** Giuseppe Rotunno; ***M:*** John Williams.

Sabrina the Teenage Witch ½ **1996 (PG)** Based on the Archie Comics, this lighthearted movie finds 16-year-old Sabrina (Hart) being told by her two eccentric aunts, Hilda (Miller) and Zelda (Fernetz), that she is a witch, descended from a long line of good witches and warlocks. Sabrina's having enough trouble fitting in at Riverdale High without this kind of news but she does find that her magical powers have their advantages. Pilot for the TV series. **90m/C VHS, DVD.** Melissa Joan Hart, Charlene Fernetz, Sherry Miller, Michelle Beaudoin, Ryan Reynolds, Tobias Mehler, Lalainia Lindbjerg; ***D:*** Tibor Takacs; ***W:*** Barney Cohen, Kathryn Wallack, Nicholas Factor. **CABLE**

Sacco & Vanzetti *Sacco e Vanzetti* **1971 (PG)** Two Italian immigrants and acknowledged anarchists are caught amidst communist witch-hunts and judicial negligence when they are tried and executed for murder in 1920s America. Based on the true-life case, considered by some a flagrant miscarriage of justice and political martyrdom, by others, honest American judicial-system proceedings. Well-made and acted. Joan Baez sings the title song "The Ballad of Sacco and Vanzetti." **120m/C VHS, DVD.** Gian Marie Volonte, Riccardo Cucciolla, Milo O'Shea, Cyril Cusack, Geoffrey Keen; ***D:*** Guiliano Montaldo; ***M:*** Ennio Morricone. Cannes '71: Actor (Cucciolla).

The Sacketts ½ **1979** Follows the adventures of three Tennessee brothers who migrate to the West after the Civil War. Based on two Louis L'Amour novels. **198m/C VHS, DVD.** Jeffery Osterhage, Tom Selleck, Sam Elliott, Glenn Ford, Ben Johnson, Mercedes McCambridge, Ruth Roman, Jack Elam, Gilbert Roland; ***D:*** Robert Totten. **TV**

The Sacred Family ♂♂ *La Sagrada Familia* **2004** College freshman Marco (Cantillana) takes his new actress girlfriend Sofia (Lopez) home on Easter weekend to meet his parents. Drama-queen Sofia charms his frisky father (Hernandez) but mom Soledad (Guazzini) is rightly concerned as Sofia's manipulative nature causes sexual tension and family friction. Spanish with subtitles. **99m/C DVD.** *CL* Sergio Hernandez, Juan Miranda, Nestor Cantillana, Patricia Lopez, Coca Guazzini, Macarena Teke, Mauricio Diocares; ***D:*** Sebastian Campos; ***W:*** Sebastian Campos; ***C:*** Gabriel Diaz; ***M:*** Javier Parra.

Sacred Ground ♂♂ **1983 (PG)** A trapper and his pregnant Apache wife unknowingly build shelter on the Paiute Indians' sacred burial ground. When the wife dies in childbirth, the pioneer is forced to kidnap a Paiute woman who has just buried her own deceased infant. Average western drama. **100m/C VHS, DVD.** Tim McIntire, Jack Elam, L.Q. Jones, Mindi Miller; ***D:*** Charles B. Pierce; ***W:*** Charles B. Pierce.

The Sacrifice ♂♂♂ **1986 (PG)** Tarkovsky's enigmatic final film, released after his death. Deals with a retired intellectual's spiritually symbolic efforts at self-sacrifice in order to save his family on the eve of a nuclear holocaust. Stunning cinematography by Nykvist. Acclaimed, but sometimes slow going; not everyone will appreciate Tarkovsky's visionary spiritualism. In Swedish and Russian with English subtitles. **145m/C VHS, DVD.** *FR SW* Erland Josephson, Susan Fleetwood, Valerie Mairesse, Allan Edwall, Gudrun Gisladottir, Sven Wollter, Filippa Franzen; ***D:*** Andrei Tarkovsky; ***W:*** Andrei Tarkovsky; ***C:*** Sven Nykvist. British Acad. '87: Foreign Film.

Sacrifice ♂♂ **2000 (R)** Serial killer has murdered the daughter of felon Tyler Pearce, who escapes from prison to get revenge. He hooks up with an ex-prostitute (Luner) but he'll have to avoid an FBI agent who wants to put Tyler back behind bars. **91m/C VHS, DVD.** Michael Madsen, Bokeem Woodbine, Jamie Luner, Joshua Leonard; ***D:*** Mark L. Lester. **VIDEO**

Sacrilege ♂ ½ **1986** A nun and a nobleman engage in a hot love affair that fosters scandal, murder and, revenge. Cynical use of religious theme masks otherwise ordinary sex/romance flick. Controversial Italian-made erotic drama. **104m/C VHS.** *IT* Myriem Roussel, Alessandro Gassman; ***D:*** Luciano Odorisio.

The Sad Sack ♂♂ **1957** A bumbling hero with a photographic memory winds up in Morocco as a member of the French Foreign Legion. Although a success at the box office, Lewis's second movie (without partner Dean Martin) seems jerky and out of sorts today. Based on the comic strip character by George Baker, but not effectively. **98m/B VHS.** Jerry Lewis, Phyllis Kirk, David Wayne, Peter Lorre, Gene Evans, Mary Treen; ***D:*** George Marshall; ***C:*** Loyal Griggs; ***M:*** Burt Bacharach, Hal David.

Sadat ♂♂ ½ **1983 (PG)** Gossett Jr. well plays his title role of Egyptian leader and Nobel Peace Prize-winner Anwar el Sadat. But the controversial life and peace efforts of the president (assassinated in 1981) are given a quick overview in this average drama. **195m/C VHS.** Louis Gossett Jr., John Rhys-Davies, Jeremy Kemp, Nehemiah Persoff, Madolyn Smith, Anne Heywood, Jeffrey Tambor, Barry Morse; ***D:*** Richard Michaels; ***M:*** Charles Bernstein. **TV**

The Saddest Music in the World ♂♂ ½ **2003** Arty but amusing take on the classic musicals and screwball comedies of the 1930s set in Depression-era Winnipeg, Canada. Eccentric plot has legless beer baroness Lady Helen Port-Huntly (Rossellini) proclaiming she will offer a prize of $25,000 and a crown of frozen tears to any nation that comes up with the world's saddest music. Americans Chester Kent (McKinney), a failed Broadway producer and Canadian ex-pat, and Narcissa (de Medeiros), his amnesiac, nymphomanic muse, decide to take a crack at it. Truly stylish, madcap and clever, zaniness nonetheless wears thin by the conclusion. Appropriately eclectic soundtrack. Based on an original screenplay by Kazuo Ishiguro. **99m/B DVD.** *CA* Isabella Rossellini, Mark McKinney, Maria De Medeiros, Ross McMillan, David Fox, Claude Dorge, Darcy Fehr; ***D:*** Guy Maddin; ***W:*** Guy Maddin, George Toles, Kazuo Ishiguro; ***C:*** Luc Montpellier; ***M:*** Christopher Dedrick.

Saddle Aces ♂ ½ **1935** Unjustly convicted, Steve Brandt and his pal Montana are on their way to prison but they jump off the moving train and hide out on June Langston's ranch. Land grabber Pete Sutton is trying to get the property and when the boys help June out, they discover Sutton is the man behind their original conviction. **56m/B DVD.** Rex Bell, Ruth Mix, Buzz Barton, Stanley Blystone, Earl Dwire, John Elliott; ***D:*** Harry Fraser; ***W:*** Harry Fraser.

The Saddle Buster ♂♂ **1932** A rodeo cowboy loses his nerve after being thrown by a tough horse, but gets it back again by the end of the hour. Actual rodeo footage is incorporated into this low-budget bronco saga. **59m/B VHS.** Tom Keene, Helen Foster, Charles Quigley, Marie Quillen, Robert Frazer, Charles "Slim" Whitaker; ***D:*** Fred Allen.

Saddle Mountain Roundup ♂ **1941** The Range Busters are on the trail again as they smoke out a murderer. **61m/B VHS, DVD.** Ray Corrigan, John "Dusty" King, Max Terhune, Lita Conway, George Chesebro, Jack Mulhall, Willie Fung, John Elliott; ***D:*** S. Roy Luby; ***W:*** Earle Snell, John Vlahos; ***C:*** Robert E. Cline.

Saddle the Wind ♂♂ ½ **1958** Taylor's exceptionally good as ex-gunfighter Steve Sinclair who's given up his guns for ranching. His quiet life is upset when his quick-tempered, trigger-happy younger brother Tony (Cassavetes) suddenly returns home with dancehall gal Joan (London), whom he says is his fiance. Soon Tony is getting into scrapes showing off his gun skills, which causes trouble for Steve with big landowner Deneen (Crisp), who likes things peaceful in his town. **84m/C DVD.** Robert Taylor, John Cassavetes, Julie London, Donald Crisp, Royal Dano, Richard Erdman, Douglas Spencer, Ray Teal, Charles McGraw, Robert Parrish; ***D:*** John Cassavetes, Donald Crisp, Robert Parrish; ***W:*** John Cassavetes, Rod Serling; ***C:*** George J. Folsey; ***M:*** Elmer Bernstein.

Saddle Tramp ♂ ½ **1947** Carefee cowpoke Chuck Conner (McCrea) is suddenly saddled with four kids after his best friend (a widower and the boys' father) is killed riding Chuck's horse. He takes a job at a ranch but has to keep the kids on the down-low, which is made more difficult by the addition of Della—a runaway girl from a neighboring ranch. To make matters worse, Chuck finds evidence of cattle rustling and the rustlers don't much like Chuck snooping around. **90m/C DVD.** Joel McCrea, Wanda Hendrix, John Russell, John McIntire, Jeannette Nolan, Russell Simpson, Ed Begley Sr.; ***D:*** Hugo Fregonese; ***W:*** Harold Shumate; ***C:*** Charles P. Boyle; ***M:*** Joseph Gershenson.

Sade ♂♂ **2000** Director Jacquot takes a low-key approach to a short period in the life of the notorious Marquis de Sade (Auteuil). In 1794, the fiftyish Sade (Auteuil), who's depicted as a manipulative bon vivant rather than a sexual libertine, is one of many aristocrats imprisoned at a former convent called Picpus during the Reign of Terror. His relatively luxurious abode is thanks to the machinations of a former mistress he's nicknamed Sensible (Denicourt), which she is since she's now under the protection of Fournier (Colin), one of Robespierre's men. Sade enjoys his situation by staging sexual tableaus and plotting the seduction of virginal teen Emilie (Le Besco) by handsome gardener Augustin (Lespert). (All to save her life of course.) Based on the novel "La Terreur du Boudoir" by Serge Bramly. French with subtitles. **100m/C DVD.** *FR* Daniel Auteuil, Marianne (Cuau) Denicourt, Gregoire Colin, Islid Le Besco, Jeanne Balibar, Jean-Pierre Cassel, Jalil Lespert; ***D:*** Benoit Jacquot; ***W:*** Jacques Fieschi, Bernard Minoret; ***C:*** Benoit Delhomme.

Sadie McKee ♂♂♂ **1934** A melodrama with Crawford as a maid searching for love in the big city. She falls for a self-destructive ne'er-do-well, marries an alcoholic millionaire, and eventually finds true love with the wealthy Tone (who would become Crawford's third husband). Professional acting and directing elevate the story. **90m/B VHS.** Joan Crawford, Franchot Tone, Gene Raymond, Edward Arnold; ***D:*** Clarence Brown.

Sadie Thompson ♂♂♂ **1928** Swanson plays a harlot with a heart of gold, bawdy and good-natured, in the South Seas. A zealot missionary (Barrymore) arrives and falls in love with her. The last eight minutes of footage have been recreated by using stills and the original title cards, to replace the last reel which had decomposed. Remade as "Rain," "Dirty Gertie From Harlem," and "Miss Sadie Thompson." Based on W. Somerset Maugham's "Rain." **97m/B VHS, DVD.** Gloria Swanson, Lionel Barrymore, Raoul Walsh, Blanche Frederici, Charles Lane, James A. Marcus; ***D:*** Raoul Walsh; ***W:*** Raoul Walsh; ***C:*** George Barnes, Robert B. Kurrle, Oliver Marsh.

The Sadist ♂♂ ½ *The Profile of Terror* **1963** Three teachers on their way to Dodger Stadium find themselves stranded at a roadside garage and terrorized by a snivelling lunatic. Tense and plausible. **95m/B VHS, DVD.** Arch Hall Jr., Helen Hovey, Richard Alden, Marilyn Manning; ***D:*** James Landis; ***W:*** James Landis; ***C:*** Vilmos Zsigmond.

Safari 3000 ♂ ½ **1982 (PG)** "Playboy" writer is assigned to do a story on a three-day, 3,000 kilometer car race in Africa. Doesn't take itself too seriously, and neither should we. Dumb, dull, and disjointed. **91m/C VHS.** Stockard Channing, David Carradine, Christopher Lee; ***D:*** Harry Hurwitz; ***M:*** Ernest Gold.

Safe ♂♂♂ **1995 (R)** Surburban California housewife Carol (Moore) literally becomes allergic to her environment and winds up seeking relief in a holistic center in Albuquerque, where director Haynes takes a shot at the New Age and finds a link to the AIDS crisis. Serious, stylistically detached look at a near future riddled with environmental toxins is led by Moore's performance as the sunny suburbanite undone by the unseen. **119m/C VHS, DVD.** Julianne Moore, Peter Friedman, Xander Berkeley, Susan Norman, James LeGros, Mary Carver, Kate McGregor-Stewart, Jessica Harper, Brandon Cruz; ***D:*** Todd Haynes; ***W:*** Todd Haynes; ***C:*** Alex Nepomniaschy; ***M:*** Ed Tomney.

Safe Harbour ♂ ½ *Danielle Steel's Safe Harbour* **2007 (PG-13)** Ophelie's (Gilbert) husband and son are killed in a plane crash and she retreats with 14-year-old daughter Pip (Liberato) to a rented beach house to grieve. While walking the beach, Pip meets artist Matt (Johnson) but Ophelie is horrified that her daughter is talking to strangers until Matt introduces himself. (Naturally, he has family problems of his own to work through.) Her best friend Andrea (Staab) urges Ophelie to have a little fun with Matt but she thinks it's too soon and then she finds out a secret. It's all really nice and stilted and passion-free and Gilbert tries to use a French accent (since the character in Danielle Steel's book was French) but doesn't pull it off. **101m/C DVD.** Melissa Gilbert, Brad Johnson, Rebecca Staab, Edithe Swensen, Liana Liberato, Katie Walder; ***D:*** William Corcoran; ***C:*** Curtis Petersen; ***M:*** Joey Newman. **VIDEO**

Safe House ♂♂ ½ **1999** Comedy-thriller with a terrific lead performance by Stewart. A retiree succumbing to Alzheimer's, Mace Sowell's become increasingly paranoid and taken to carrying a gun and maintaining an elaborate security system around his L.A. home. Mace claims to be an ex-government agent, marked for death by his former boss who's now a presidential candidate. His fears are dismissed by his shrink (Elizondo) and his daughter forces him to get an in-home caregiver, Andi Travers (Williams). But soon Andi begins to think her charge may not be crazy after all. **125m/C VHS, DVD.** Patrick Stewart, Kimberly Williams, Hector Elizondo, Craig Shoemaker; ***D:*** Eric Steven Stahl; ***W:*** Eric Steven Stahl, Sean McLain; ***C:*** Vincent Donohue; ***M:*** Kevin Kiner. **CABLE**

Safe Men ♂♂ **1998 (R)** Goofy, low-budget indie comedy whose pieces don't quite fit together. Set in Providence, R.I., talentless would-be singers Sam (Rockwell) and Eddie (Zahn) are mistaken by the local Jewish mafia for a couple of expert safecrackers. The inept duo are pressured by Big Fat Bernie Gayle (Lerner) and his henchman Veal Chop (Giamatti) to break into the home of Bernie's rival, Good Stuff Leo (Fierstein). Some dumb luck and a lot of coincidence work in the guys favor. But then the real safecracking team turns up. **89m/C VHS, DVD.** Sam Rockwell, Steve Zahn, Paul Giamatti, Michael Lerner, Harvey Fierstein, Mark Ruffalo; ***D:*** John Hamburg; ***W:*** John Hamburg; ***C:*** Michael Barrett; ***M:*** Theodore Shapiro.

Safe Passage ♂♂ **1994 (PG-13)** Grueling family drama with Sarandon and Shepherd portraying an unhappily married couple who are the parents of seven sons, one of whom is missing and presumed dead in the Sinai Desert war. One by one the grown boys arrive home to await any further news. They rehash memories, watch old videos, open old wounds, and generally affirm life. None of the performances, with the exception of Sarandon, are truly believable. She is the only one that brings any depth to her character as the tough matriarch that holds the family together. Feels like a TV movie, albeit one with classier names. Based on the novel by Ellyn Bache. **98m/C VHS, DVD.** Susan Sarandon, Sam Shepard, Robert Sean Leonard, Sean Astin, Marcia Gay Harden, Nick Stahl, Jason London, Philip Bosco, Matt Keeslar; ***D:*** Robert Allan Ackerman; ***W:*** Deena Goldstone; ***C:*** Ralf Bode; ***M:*** Mark Isham.

A Safe Place ♂ **1971** Jaglom makes his directorial debut in this muddled story of Weld regressing to her childhood—the only time she felt safe. Welles' role as the magician refers to a character the child Susan met in Central Park. Most of the pic was filmed in the apartment of Jaglom's parents. **94m/C DVD.** Tuesday Weld, Orson Welles, Jack Nicholson, Phil(ip) Proctor, Gwen Welles; ***D:*** Henry Jaglom; ***W:*** Henry Jaglom.

Safety Last ♂♂♂ **1923** Lloyd silent comedy about an average guy who goes to the big city to become a success, and his misadventures. Hilarious and still awe-inspiring building climbing scene set new standards for movies in sight gags and comedy-thrill stunts, which became Lloyd's trademark. **78m/B VHS, DVD.** Harold Lloyd, Mildred Davis, Bill Strothers, Noah Young; ***D:*** Fred Newmeyer, Sam Taylor; ***W:*** Sam Taylor, Jean C. Havez, Tim Whelan. Natl. Film Reg. '94.

The Safety of Objects ♂♂ ½ **2001 (R)** The lives of four suburban families intersect in Troche's third feature, based on stories by A.M. Homes. Esther Gold (Close) is committed to caring for her comatose son Paul (Jackson), who was the secret lover of divorcee Annette (Clarkson), who makes a pass at lawn & pool guy Randy (Olyphant). Then there's Jim (Mulroney) who doesn't tell wife Susan (Kelly) he's left his job and whose young son is obsessed with his sister's Barbie-like doll. And Esther and Susan get involved in a contest to win an SUV and still the neighborhood's tentacles continue to spread among the inhabitants. **121m/C VHS, DVD.** *US* Glenn Close, Dermot Mulroney, Jessica Campbell, Patricia Clarkson, Joshua Jackson, Moira Kelly, Robert Klein, Timothy Olyphant, Mary Kay Place, Kristen Stewart, Alex House; ***D:*** Rose Troche; ***W:*** Rose Troche; ***C:*** Enrique Chediak.

Safety Patrol ♂♂ ½ **1998** Clumsy 11-year-old Scout (Hall) is determined to join his school's safety patrol team and instead winds up involved with a mother/son team of con artists. **92m/C VHS.** Bug Hall, Leslie Nielsen, Lainie Kazan, Wink Martindale, Ed McMahon, Curtis Armstrong, Charlene Tilton, Alex McKenna, Kurtwood Smith, Stephanie Faracy; ***D:*** Savage Steve Holland. **VIDEO**

Saga of Death Valley ♂♂ ½ **1939** Rogers battles a band of outlaws and discovers that their leader is his own brother. Exciting and likeable early Rogers western. **56m/B VHS, DVD.** Roy Rogers, George "Gabby" Hayes, Donald (Don "Red") Barry, Doris Day; ***D:*** Joseph Kane.

The Saga of the Draculas ♂ *Dracula Saga; Dracula: The Bloodline Continues...; The Saga of Dracula* **1972 (R)** An aging vampire wishes to continue his bloodline and seeks to convert his niece's baby to his bloodsucking ways. **90m/C VHS, DVD.** *SP* Narciso Ibanez Menta, Tina Sainz, Tony Isbert, Maria Koski, Cristina Suriani, Helga Line; ***D:*** Leon Klimovsky.

Saga of the Vagabond ½ *Sengoku Gunto-Den* **1959** Arranged by master director Akira Kurosawa. A band of ruthless outlaws careen across a civil war-torn countryside. With English subtitles. **115m/C VHS.** *JP* Toshiro Mifune, Michiyo Aratama, Misa(ko) Uehara; ***D:*** Toshio Sugie.

Sagebrush Law ½ **1943** Western yarn has Holt playing a young man trying to clear the name of his bank president father. Barclay serves as the love interest and "Ukulele Ike" Edwards provides needed comic and music relief. **56m/B VHS.** Tim Holt, Cliff Edwards, Joan Barclay, Edward Cassidy, Karl Hackett, Roy Barcroft, Ernie Adams; ***D:*** Sam Nelson; ***W:*** Bennett Cohen.

Sagebrush Trail **1933** Wayne's second-ever western, complete with all sorts of tumbleweed and white-hat cliches. Our hero is wrongly accused of killin' a man, and busts out of the hoosegow to clear his name. Interesting plot twists makes for fun, compelling viewing. **53m/B VHS, DVD.** John Wayne, Yakima Canutt, Wally Wales; ***D:*** Armand Schaefer; ***W:*** Lindsley Parsons; ***C:*** Archie Stout.

Sahara **1943** A British-American unit must fight the Germans for their survival in the Libyan desert during WWII. Plenty of action and suspense combined with good performances makes this one a step above the usual war movie. **97m/B VHS, DVD.** Humphrey Bogart, Dan Duryea, Bruce Bennett, Lloyd Bridges, Rex Ingram, J. Carrol Naish, Richard Nugent, Pat O'Moore, Kurt Kreuger, John Wengraf, Carl Harbord, Louis Mercier, Guy Kingsford, Peter Lawford; ***D:*** Zoltan Korda; ***W:*** Zoltan Korda, John Howard Lawson, James O'Hanlon; ***C:*** Rudolph Mate; ***M:*** Miklos Rozsa.

Sahara WOOF! 1983 (PG) Disappointing "Perils of Pauline" type adventure. Shields disguises herself as a man (sure) to complete a race across the desert in honor of her late father, and a sheik captures her. **111m/C VHS.** Brooke Shields, Lambert Wilson, Horst Buchholz, John Rhys-Davies, Ronald Lacey, John Mills, Steve Forrest, Perry Lang, Cliff (Potter) Potts; ***D:*** Andrew V. McLaglen; ***W:*** James R. Silke; ***M:*** Ennio Morricone.

Sahara ½ **2005 (PG-13)** Second attempt to construct a franchise around Clive Cussler's popular Dirk Pitt character (the first was 1980's "Raise the Titanic"). Pitt (McConaughey) and his buddy, Al Giordino (Zahn), are ex-Navy treasure-hunters searching for a lost Civil War battleship off the coast of West Africa. Cruz is a UN doctor who enlists Pitt in helping her find the source of a virulent African plague. The plot reeks of modern-day Indiana Jones and, thankfully, doesn't try to hide it, helped along by McConaughey and Zahn's boisterous chemistry. Eisner wisely chooses to keep things light throughout, which makes the film both charmingly self-aware and easily dismissible. **127m/C DVD, Blu-ray Disc, UMD, HD DVD.** *US* Matthew McConaughey, Steve Zahn, Penelope Cruz, Lambert Wilson, Glynn Turman, William H. Macy, Delroy Lindo, Lennie James, Rainn Wilson, Patrick Malahide; ***D:*** Breck Eisner; ***W:*** John C. Richards, Thomas Dean Donnelly, Joshua Oppenheimer, James V. Hart; ***C:*** Seamus McGarvey; ***M:*** Clint Mansell.

Saigon ½ **1947** In Shanghai after WWII, pilots Larry (Ladd) and Pete (Cassell) are informed that their pal Mike (Dick) doesn't have much time left. Instead of giving Mike the bad news, they intend to spend the rest of Mike's time living it up. To finance the fun, they accept a shady deal and end up crash-landing in the Asian jungle with the financier's secretary and her briefcase full of cash. **93m/B DVD.** Alan Ladd, Veronica Lake, Douglas Dick, Wally Cassell, Luther Adler, Morris Carnovsky; ***D:*** Leslie Fenton; ***W:*** Julian Zimet, Arthur Sheekman; ***M:*** Robert Emmett Dolan.

Saigon Commandos **1988 (R)** Commandos, on the eve of the fall of Saigon in the 1970s, attempt to prevent heroin dealers from toppling the already-shaky government. So-so war/action flick. **84m/C VHS.** Richard Young, P.J. Soles, John Allen Nelson, Jimi B Jr.; ***D:*** Clark Henderson.

Saigon: Year of the Cat **1987** Drama about an American ambassador, a CIA operative, and a British bank clerk who try to leave Saigon in 1974 before the Vietcong enter the city. **106m/C VHS, DVD.** *GB* Frederic Forrest, E.G. Marshall, Judi Dench; ***D:*** Stephen Frears; ***W:*** David Hare; ***M:*** George Fenton. **TV**

Sailing Along **1938** British musical about a young starlet who sacrifices her career for true love. **80m/B VHS.** *GB* Jessie Matthews, Barry Mackay, Jack Whiting, Roland Young, Noel Madison, Athene Seyler, Patrick Barr; ***D:*** Sonnie Hale.

Sailor Beware **1952** Naive Melvin Jones (Lewis) is inducted into the Navy along with lothario singer Al Crowthers (Martin). In this typical slapstick mishmash of comedy and music, Lewis causes havoc aboard a submarine and becomes the judge of the most kissable girl contest in Hawaii while Martin romances singer Calvert (playing herself). Betty Hutton has a cameo as one of Dean's gals during the recruitment scene. **108m/B DVD.** Jerry Lewis, Dean Martin, Marion Marshall, Robert Strauss, Corrine Calvert, Leif Erickson, Don "The Dragon" Wilson, Vince Edwards; ***Cameos:*** Betty Hutton; ***D:*** Hal Walker; ***W:*** Martin Rackin, James Allardice; ***C:*** Daniel F. Fapp; ***M:*** Joseph J. Lilley.

Sailor of the King **1953** A British naval ship is torpedoed in the Pacific during WWII and survivor Andrew Brown (Hunter) is rescued by the German cruiser Essen. The damaged ship pulls into a cove at a Galapagos island to make emergency repairs and Brown escapes (with a rifle), determined to delay their departure until a force of British ships get closer. There's a framing story that involves Rennie and Hiller but it's so much filler. Adapted from the C.S. Forester novel "Brown on Resolution." **85m/B DVD.** *GB* Jeffrey Hunter, Peter Van Eyck, Michael Rennie, Wendy Hiller, Bernard Lee, Victor Maddern; ***D:*** Roy Boulting; ***W:*** Valentine Davies; ***C:*** Gilbert Taylor; ***M:*** Clifton Parker.

The Sailor Who Fell from Grace with the Sea **1976 (R)** Perverse tale of a disillusioned sailor who rejects the sea for the love of a lonely young widow and her troubled son. Graphic sexual scenes. Based on the novel by Yukio Mishima, the film suffers from the transition of Japanese culture to an English setting. **105m/C VHS, DVD.** *GB* Sarah Miles, Kris Kristofferson, Jonathan Kahn, Margo Cunningham; ***D:*** Lewis John Carlino; ***W:*** Lewis John Carlino.

The Saint **1968** Moore is Simon Templar, Leslie Charteris's mysterious British detective/hero in this adventure tale that takes him to Naples. Revival of and improvement on earlier movie series, and based on the very popular British TV show. **98m/C VHS, DVD.** *GB* Roger Moore, Ian Hendry.

The Saint ½ **1997 (PG-13)** The plot makes about as much sense as that of "Mission: Impossible," the villains are average ego-driven bad guys, and Shue's naive scientist/babe is totally unbelieveable (she's like a deer caught in a car's headlights). The only reason the movie works at all is due to the debonair, if angst-ridden, charms of Kilmer as super-thief and master of disguise Simon Templar. He's hired by Russian strongman Ivan Tretiak (Serbedzija) to steal the formula for cold fusion from scientist Emma Russell (Shue) so that Tretiak can save a freezing Moscow by delivering cheap energy and thus make Russia a formidable power once again (with himself as leader, natch). Only problem is Templar, who names all his alter egos after saints, falls for Emma and tries to get them out of harm's way by double-crossing Tretiak. At least the Moscow and Oxford settings are scenic. Templar's exploits are featured in a series of novels by Leslie Charteris, and previously appeared in earlier movies and on TV. **118m/C VHS, DVD.** Val Kilmer, Elisabeth Shue, Rade Serbedzija, Valery (Valeri Nikolayev) Nikolaev, Henry Goodman, Alun Armstrong, Michael Byrne, Eugene (Yevgeny) Lazarev, Charlotte Cornwell, Irina Apeximova, Emily Mortimer; ***D:*** Phillip Noyce; ***W:*** Jonathan Hensleigh, Wesley Strick; ***C:*** Phil Meheux; ***M:*** Graeme Revell.

St. Benny the Dip ½ *Escape If You Can* **1951** Three con-men evade police by posing as clergymen, and end up going straight after a series of adventures in a skid row mission. Funny in parts but extremely predictable. Still, good for a few laughs. **80m/B VHS, DVD.** Dick Haymes, Nina Foch, Roland Young, Lionel Stander, Freddie Bartholomew; ***D:*** Edgar G. Ulmer.

St. Elmo's Fire ½ **1985 (R)** Seven Georgetown graduates confront adult problems during their first post-graduate year. Reminiscent of "The Big Chill," but a weak story wastes lots of talent and time. **110m/C VHS, DVD.** Rob Lowe, Demi Moore, Andrew McCarthy, Judd Nelson, Ally Sheedy, Emilio Estevez, Mare Winningham, Martin Balsam, Jenny Wright, Joyce Van Patten, Andie MacDowell, Anna Maria Horsford; ***D:*** Joel Schumacher; ***W:*** Carl Kurlander, Joel Schumacher; ***C:*** Stephen Burum; ***M:*** David Foster. Golden Raspberries '85: Worst Support. Actor (Lowe).

Saint-Ex: The Story of the Storyteller **1995 (PG)** Ambitious bio based on famous French aviator, and author of the children's classic "The Little Prince," Antoine de Saint-Exupery (Ganz). Flashbacks show his childhood obsession with flying that eventually lead to Saint-Exuprey's perilous North African mail flights during WWII. Beyond his passion for flying is his marriage to Consuelo (Richardson), who comes to resent his frequent absences, and the later, more-supportive love of Genevieve (McTeer). Striking visuals but that's about all. **90m/C VHS.** *GB* Bruno Ganz, Miranda Richardson, Janet McTeer, Ken Stott, Katrin Cartlidge, Eleanor Bron, Brid Brennan, Karl Johnson; ***D:*** Anand Tucker; ***W:*** Frank Cottrell-Boyce; ***C:*** David C(lark) Johnson; ***M:*** Barrington Pheloung.

The St. Francisville Experiment **2000 (PG-13)** Psychic, amateur ghost hunter, history student, and filmmaker fly to Louisiana to investigate a haunted house plagued by the spirit of slaves. **79m/C VHS, DVD.** Tim Baldini, Madison Charap, Ryan Larson, Paul Palmer, Paul James, Paul Salamoff, Troy Taylor; ***D:*** Tim Thompson.

St. Helen's, Killer Volcano ½ **1982** A young man and an old man develop a deep friendship amid the devastation, fear, greed, and panic surrounding the eruption of the Mt. St. Helen's volcano. Based on the true story of Harry Truman (!), who refused to leave his home. Pretty good. **95m/C VHS, DVD.** Art Carney, David Huffman, Cassie Yates, Bill McKinney, Ron O'Neal, Albert Salmi, Cesare Danova; ***D:*** Ernest Pintoff.

The Saint in London **1939** The Saint investigates a gang trying to pass counterfeit banknotes. The third in "The Saint" series. **72m/B VHS.** George Sanders, Sally Gray; ***D:*** Jack Paddy Carstairs.

The Saint in New York **1938** The Saint, Simon Templar, turns Robin Hood to help the Civic Committee clean up a gang of desperados. First of "The Saint" series. **71m/B VHS.** Louis Hayward, Kay Sutton, Jack Carson, Charles Halton; ***D:*** Ben Holmes.

St. Ives **1976 (PG)** Former police reporter Bronson agrees to recover some stolen ledgers and finds himself dealing with betrayal and murder. Bisset is sultry and the tale is slickly told, but dumb. Co-stars Travanti, later of TV's "Hill Street Blues." **94m/C VHS, DVD.** Charles Bronson, Jacqueline Bisset, John Houseman, Harry Guardino, Maximilian Schell, Harris Yulin, Elisha Cook Jr., Daniel J. Travanti; ***D:*** J. Lee Thompson; ***W:*** Barry Beckerman; ***M:*** Lalo Schifrin.

St. Ives ½ *Robert Louis Stevenson's St. Ives; All for Love* **1998 (R)** During the Napoleonic Wars, dashing French officer, Captain Jacques St. Ives (Barr), is captured during battle and sent to a POW camp in the Scottish Highlands that is run by Major Chevening (Grant). St. Ives and the Major become friends but that doesn't mean that he won't try to escape, especially since Jacques has the aid of plucky lassie Flora (Friel). A leisurely paced costume romp. **90m/C VHS, DVD.** *GB* Jean-Marc Barr, Anna Friel, Richard E. Grant, Miranda Richardson, Michael Gough, Jason Isaacs, Tim Dutton, Cecile Pallas; ***D:*** Harry Hook; ***W:*** Allan Cubitt; ***C:*** Robert Alazraki.

Saint Jack **1979 (R)** The story of a small-time pimp with big dreams working the pleasure palaces of late-night Singapore. Engrossing and pleasant. Based on Paul Theroux's novel. **112m/C VHS, DVD.** Ben Gazzara, Denholm Elliott, Joss Ackland, George Lazenby, Peter Bogdanovich; ***D:*** Peter Bogdanovich; ***W:*** Peter Bogdanovich; ***C:*** Robby Muller.

Saint Joan **1957** Film of the George Bernard Shaw play, adapted by Graham Greene, about the French Maid of Orleans at her trial. Otto Preminger went on a nationwide talent hunt for his leading actress and chose the inexperienced Seberg (her screen debut). A good thing for her career, but not for this ill-begotten, overambitious opus. Seberg doesn't fit. Also available colorized. **131m/B VHS.** Jean Seberg, Anton Walbrook, Richard Widmark, John Gielgud, Harry Andrews, Felix Aylmer, Richard Todd; ***D:*** Otto Preminger; ***W:*** Graham Greene; ***C:*** Georges Perinal.

Saint John of Las Vegas **2009 (R)** Did someone lose a bet? How else would a completely unfunny, whimsical roadtrip comedy loosely based on Dante's Inferno get made? Ex-gambler John (Buscemi) falls under the influence of insurance fraud investigator Virgil (Malco) and is lured back to Vegas under the guise of investigating a stripper's injury claim. Along the way they meet a series of wacky characters who don't seem to fit anywhere unless you have a working knowledge of Dante. Appallingly bad and made worse by the disappointing use of its usually dependable cast and involvement of high-profile producers Spike Lee and Stanley Tucci. **85m/C DVD.** *US* Steve Buscemi, Romany Malco, Tim Blake Nelson, Sarah Silverman, Peter Dinklage, John Cho, Emmanuelle Chriqui; ***D:*** Hue Rhodes; ***W:*** Hue Rhodes; ***C:*** Giles Nuttgens; ***M:*** David Torn.

Saint Maybe **1998** Quietly affecting family saga adapted from the novel by Anne Tyler. Heedless Ian Bedloe (McCarthy) is disturbed when his older brother Danny (Nordling) impulsively marries scatty divorcee Lucy (Parker) who has two kids. When Lucy gets pregnant, Ian's interference results in a double tragedy. Seeking to atone for his mistake, Ian discovers the Church of the Second Chance and he decides to raise his brother's three children. **98m/C VHS.** Thomas (Tom) McCarthy, Blythe Danner, Edward Herrmann, Mary-Louise Parker, Jeffrey Nordling, Melina Kanakaredes, Glynnis O'Connor, Amy Hargreaves, Kristoffer Ryan Winters, Denis O'Hare, Rene Augesen, Bethel Leslie; ***D:*** Michael Pressman; ***W:*** Robert W. Lenski; ***C:*** Shelly Johnson; ***M:*** Ernest Troost. **TV**

St. Michael Had a Rooster *San Michele Aveva un Gallo* **1972** In 19th-century Italy, idealist anarchist Giulio Manieri (Brogi) hopes to inspire the local peasantry through armed raids. Imprisoned for his trouble, Manieri learns upon his release after 10 years that his political struggles have been forgotten and he has to make a difficult adjustment to life on the outside. Based on the Leo Tolstoy story "The Divine and the Human." Italian with subtitles. **87m/C VHS, DVD.** *IT* Giulio Brogi, Danielle Dublino, Renato Scarpa; ***D:*** Paolo Taviani, Vittorio Taviani; ***W:*** Paolo Taviani, Vittorio Taviani; ***C:*** Mario Masini.

The Saint of Fort Washington ½ **1993 (R)** Sweetly naive and schizophrenic Matthew (Dillon) is homeless and through government screw-ups is sent to the Fort Washington Armory, which houses more than 700 homeless men. Harassed by others, Matthew is befriended by Jerry, a kindly Vietnam vet, who tries to care for him. Subject is taken seriously but slips into mawkishness; good performances by the leads. **104m/C VHS.** Danny Glover, Matt Dillon, Rick Aviles, Nina Siemaszko, Ving Rhames, Joe Seneca; ***D:*** Tim Hunter; ***W:*** Lyle Kessler; ***C:*** Frederick Elmes; ***M:*** James Newton Howard.

St. Patrick: The Irish Legend ½ **2000** Unfortunately neither the impressive cast, the beautiful scenery, or the special effects can transform this costumer from being bland and boring. Patrick (who allegedly drove all the snakes out of Ireland) was the privileged son of a nobleman in 5th century Britian, who suffered through six years as a slave before finding his religious calling. Over great opposition, he's eventually appointed as the first bishop of Ireland though he must still struggle with his enemies in the Church of England. **120m/C VHS, DVD.** Patrick Bergin, Malcolm McDowell, Alan Bates, Susannah York, Luke Griffin, Eamon Owens, Stephen Brennan, Chris McHallen, Michael Caven; ***D:*** Robert C. Hughes; ***W:*** Robert C. Hughes, Martin Duffy; ***C:*** James Mathers. **CABLE**

St. Patrick's Day **1999 (PG-13)** Widowed Mary McDonaugh (Laurie) is the matriarch of a dysfunctional Irish-American family. Four generations gather at her house for St. Patrick's Day where she announces she has taken the pledge and refuses to allows any whiskey in her home (which is ignored by certain members). As the day progresses, family secrets are revealed, including romantic feelings finally acknowledged, divorcing spouses, extramarital affairs, and other sexual shenanigans. **106m/C VHS, DVD.** Piper Laurie, Joanne Baron, Jim Metzler, Julie Strain, Herta Ware, Redmond M. Gleeson, David Ault, Colleen (Ann) Fitzpatrick, Chris Valenti, Stephen O'Mahoney; ***D:*** Hope Perello; ***W:*** Hope Perello; ***C:*** Denise Brassard; ***M:*** Michael Muhlfriedel.

Saint Ralph **2004 (PG-13)** With his mother in the hospital dying, young Ralph (Adam Butcher) decides that if he can pull off the miracle of winning the Boston Marathon, his mother will benefit from the overflow. Heartfelt story, but lacks grit and emotion, leading to a rather flat end. **98m/C DVD.** Campbell Scott, Gordon Pinsent, Jennifer Tilly, Tamara Hope, Adam Butcher, Shauna Macdonald, Michael Kanev; ***C:*** Rene Ohashi; ***M:*** Andrew Lockington.

The Saint Strikes Back **1939** Sanders debuts as the mysterious Simon Templar in this competent series. On a trip to San Francisco, the Saint aims to clear the name of a murdered man. The second in the series. **67m/B VHS.** George Sanders, Wendy Barrie, Jonathan Hale, Jerome Cowan, Neil Hamilton, Barry Fitzgerald, Edward (Ed) Gargan, Robert Strange; ***D:*** John Farrow.

The Saint Strikes Back: Criminal Court **1946** A suspense double feature: The Saint helps a daughter clear the name of her murdered father, a San Francisco police commissioner in "The Saint Strikes Back," and a young lawyer becomes involved in murder in "Criminal Court." **127m/B VHS.** George Sanders, Wendy Barrie, Barry Fitzgerald, Tom Conway, Steve Brodie; ***D:*** John Farrow.

The Saint Takes Over **1940** More adventures with the British mystery man; this time involving racetrack gambling. An original story that wasn't based on a Leslie Charteris novel as were the others. **69m/B VHS.** George Sanders, Jonathan Hale, Wendy Barrie, Paul Guilfoyle, Morgan Conway, Cy Kendall; ***D:*** Jack B. Hively.

The St. Tammany Miracle 1/2 **1994** Predictable, good-natured sports film about young coach Lootie Pfannder (Luner) who takes a job at a prep school and turns the losing girls basketball team into winners. Her broadcaster boyfriend Carl (Gosselaar) thinks she's crazy but aided by her assistant (Frye), Lootie is determined to prove everyone wrong. **90m/C VHS, DVD.** Jamie Luner, Mark Paul Gosselaar, Soleil Moon Frye, Jeffrey Meek, Julie McCullough; ***Cameos:*** Steve Allen; ***D:*** Jim McCullough Sr.; ***W:*** Jim McCullough Jr.; ***M:*** Jay Weigel.

St. Trinian's **2007 (PG-13)** Britcom based on the Ronald Searle cartoons and the five Ealing studio movies filmed between 1954 and 1980. Shady art dealer Carnaby Fritton (Everett) transfers his daughter Annabelle (Riley) to the girls school run by his flirty sister Camilla (Everett in drag) where chaos (and criminal behavior) rule. With the school in financial straits, minister of education Geoffrey Thwaites (Firth) is planning to close it down and sell the property as a profitable real estate venture. So some of the students decide to steal a painting from London's National Gallery while they're participating in a national quiz program there. Not as anarchical as the originals but pic has its moments. **100m/C DVD.** *GB* Rupert Everett, Colin Firth, Talulah Riley, Lucy Punch, Tamsin Egerton, Aamir Khan, Chloe, Russell Brand, Lena Headey, Anna Chancellor, Celia Emrie, Toby Jones, Mischa Barton, Fenella Woolgar, Gemma Arterton, Juno Temple, Stephen Fry; ***D:*** Oliver Parker, Barnaby Thompson; ***W:*** Piers Ashworth, Nick Moorcraft; ***C:*** Gavin Finney; ***M:*** Charlie Mole.

The St. Valentine's Day Massacre 1/2 **1967** Corman's big studio debut re-creates the events leading to one of the most violent gangland shootouts in modern history: the bloodbath between Chicago's Capone and Moran gangs on February 14, 1929. Uninspired and unremittingly violent. Watch for Jack Nicholson's bit part. **100m/C VHS, DVD.** Jason Robards Jr., Ralph Meeker, Jean Hale, Joseph Campanella, Bruce Dern, Clint Ritchie, Richard Bakalyan, George Segal, Harold J. Stone, Jonathan Haze, Dick Miller, Barboura Morris, Jack Nicholson, Frank Silvera, Milton Frome, Alex Rocco, John Agar, Tom Signorelli; ***D:*** Roger Corman; ***W:*** Howard Browne; ***C:*** Milton Krasner; ***M:*** Lionel Newman.

A Saintly Switch 1/2 **1999** Aging quarterback Grier has just moved his pregnant wife Fox and their kids to a New Orleans. Mom's very unhappy and the kids are worried that their parents are going to split up—at least until they manage to mysteriously swap their parents' bodies. So now dad gets to be pregnant and mom has to learn to score touchdowns. **90m/C VHS, DVD.** David Alan Grier, Vivica A. Fox, Rue McClanahan, Al Waxman; ***D:*** Peter Bogdanovich. **TV**

Saints and Sinners 1/2 **1995 (R)** Street-smart "Pooch" Puccia (Chapa) returns to his 'hood as an undercover cop to set up childhood buddy, drug dealer Big Boy Baynes (Plank), and winds up getting involved with seductive bad girl Eve (Rubin), who's also bedding Baynes. Then Pooch discovers his police contact is in the pay of the mob. Lots of macho posturing (attractive actors). **99m/C VHS.** Damian Chapa, Scott Plank, Jennifer Rubin, Damon Whitaker, Panchito Gomez, William Atherton; ***D:*** Paul Mones; ***W:*** Paul Mones; ***C:*** Michael Bonvillain.

Saints and Soldiers 1/2 **2003 (PG-13)** Ragtag group of G.I.s narrowly escapes a massacre during the Battle of the Bulge, only to find themselves stumbling around and philosophizing in No-Man's-Land. Mormon sponsored WWII film is surprisingly quiet and even-handed in dealing with big metaphysical conundrums, but prowar theme may raise the hackles of some. **90m/C DVD.** Corbin Allred, Petre Asle Holden, Alexander Polinsky, Kirby Heyborne, Larry Bagby, Ethan Vincent; ***D:*** Ryan Little; ***M:*** Bart Hendrickson.

The Saint's Double Trouble **1940** Leslie Charteris' suave detective becomes embroiled in another mystery, this one involving jewel thieves. Sanders plays a dual role as the hero and the crook. The fourth in the series. **68m/B VHS.** George Sanders, Helene Whitney, Jonathan Hale, Bela Lugosi, Donald MacBride, John Hamilton; ***D:*** Jack B. Hively.

Sakharov **1984** The true story of the Russian physicist who designed the H-bomb and then rose to lead the Soviet dissident movement and win the Nobel Peace Prize. Robards is excellent. Topical and powerful. **120m/C VHS.** Glenda Jackson, Jason Robards Jr., Michael Bryant; ***D:*** Jack Gold; ***M:*** Carl Davis. **CABLE**

Salaam Bombay! **1988** A gritty film about a child street beggar in the slums of Bombay trying to raise enough money to return to his mother's house in the country. The boy experiences every variety of gutter life imaginable, from humiliation to love. Moving and searing. Filmed on location, with actual homeless children; Nair's first feature. In Hindi with subtitles. **114m/C VHS, DVD.** *IN GB* Shafiq Syed, Hansa Vithal, Chanda Sharma, Nana Patekar, Aneeta Kanwar, Sarfuddin Quarassi, Raju Barnad, Raghuvir Yadav; ***D:*** Mira Nair; ***W:*** Sooni Taraporevala; ***C:*** Sandi Sissel; ***M:*** L. Subramaniam.

The Salamander 1/2 **1982 (R)** A French detective tries to find the assassin of the leaders of a neo-fascist underground movement in Italy and follows clues that lead back to WWII. Disappointing, overwrought adaptation of a Morris West novel. **101m/C VHS, DVD.** *GB* Franco Nero, Anthony Quinn, Martin Balsam, Sybil Danning, Christopher Lee, Cleavon Little, Paul Smith, Claudia Cardinale, Eli Wallach; ***D:*** Peter Zinner; ***M:*** Jerry Goldsmith.

Salammbo 1/2 **1914** An early silent epic in the grand Italian tradition. Loosely based on Flaubert's novel about ancient Carthage. **49m/B VHS.** *IT* Ernesto Pagani; ***D:*** Giovanni Pastrone.

Salem's Lot 1/2 *Blood Thirst* **1979 (PG)** Based on Stephen King's novel about a sleepy New England village which is infiltrated by evil. A mysterious antiques dealer takes up residence in a forbidding hilltop house—and it becomes apparent that a vampire is on the loose. Generally creepy; Mason is good, but Soul only takes up space in the lead as a novelist returning home. **112m/C VHS, DVD.** David Soul, James Mason, Lance Kerwin, Bonnie Bedelia, Lew Ayres, Ed Flanders, Elisha Cook Jr., Reggie Nalder, Fred Willard, Kenneth McMillan, Marie Windsor; ***D:*** Tobe Hooper; ***W:*** Paul Monash; ***C:*** Jules Brenner; ***M:*** Harry Sukman. **TV**

Salem's Lot **2004** Made-for-TNT remake of the 1979 miniseries based on Stephen King's novel, this time a bit more faithful to the book, but still using the miniseries format. Writer Ben Mears (Lowe) returns to his hometown to exorcise some personal demons, only to find a real-life demon, in the form of vampire Barlow (Hauer) taking over. Resurrects characters and subplots that the original ignored, but the pacing is too rushed to create any real atmosphere or genuine chills. Another in a long line of disappointing King adaptations. **180m/C DVD.** Rob Lowe, Samantha Mathis, Andre Braugher, Donald Sutherland, Robert Mammone, Rutger Hauer, James Cromwell, Julia Blake, Dan Byrd, Andy Anderson, Robert Grubb, Steven Vidler, Elizabeth (Liz) Alexander, Nicholas Hammond, Tara Morice, Penny McNamee; ***D:*** Mikael Salomon; ***W:*** Peter Filardi; ***C:*** Ben Nott; ***M:*** Patrick Cassidy, Lisa Gerrard, Christopher Gordon. **TV**

Sallah **1963** A North African Jew takes his family to Israel in 1949 in hopes of making his fortune. He finds himself in a transit camp and runs up against the local bureaucracy in a quest for permanent housing as well as the European work ethic. Amusing and enjoyable satire. In Hebrew with English subtitles. **105m/B VHS, DVD.** *IS* Chaim Topol, Geula Noni, Gila Almagor, Arik Einstein, Shraga Friedman, Esther Greenberg; ***D:*** Ephraim Kishon; ***C:*** Floyd Crosby. Golden Globes '65: Foreign Film.

Sally 1/2 **1929** Cinderella story finds orphaned Sally (Miller) working as a New York waitress although her dream is to dance on Broadway. Sally meets booking agent Otis Hooper (Barnes), who has her impersonate a famous Russian dancer who eloped, and this leads to Sally getting her own starring gig in the Ziegfeld Follies. The tiny Miller had a lot of natural charisma although the merits of her singing and dancing are still debated; she only made three talkies, preferring her stage career. Includes sequences in two-strip Technicolor. Based on the 1920 musical by Jerome Kern and Guy Bolton in which Miller also starred. **101m/C DVD.** T. Roy Barnes, Joe E. Brown, Pert Kelton, Ford Sterling, Nora Lane, Marilyn Miller, Alexander Gray, Maude Turner Gordon; ***D:*** John Francis Dillon; ***W:*** Waldemar Young; ***C:*** Devereaux Jennings, Charles E. Schoenbaum.

Sally Hemings: An American Scandal 1/2 **2000** Soap opera-ish romance based on the relationship between widowed ambassador (and third President) Thomas Jefferson (Neill) and his young mulatto house slave Sally Hemings (Ejogo)—an affair that lasted for 38 years. (DNA proved Jefferson to be the father of one and possibly all six of Heming's children.) Sally remains dignified through the years as does Jefferson. The most excitement is Sally castigating her lover about his contradictory attitudes towards slavery. **173m/C VHS, DVD.** Carmen Ejogo, Sam Neill, Diahann Carroll, Mare Winningham, Rene Auberjonois, Mario Van Peebles; ***D:*** Charles Haid; ***W:*** Tina Andrews; ***C:*** Donald M. Morgan; ***M:*** Joel McNeely. **TV**

Sally of the Sawdust 1/2 **1925** Fields's first silent feature; he is carnival barker Professor Eustace McGargle who's the guardian of orphaned Sally (Dempster). Then Sally's wealthy grandfather (Alderson), a stern judge, becomes determined to claim her from showbiz lowlifes. Fields gets to demonstrate his talent for juggling, conning customers, and car chasing. Interesting movie caught director Griffith on the decline and Fields on the verge of stardom. Remade as a talkie in 1936 entitled "Poppy." Includes musical score. **113m/B VHS, DVD.** W.C. Fields, Carol Dempster, Erville Alderson; ***D:*** D.W. Griffith; ***W:*** Forrest Halsey; ***C:*** Harry Fischbeck, H. Sintzenich.

Salmonberries 1/2 **1991 (R)** East German Roswitha (Zech) is devastated when her lover is killed trying to scale the Berlin Wall. She manages to escape and finds herself stuck in a remote Eskimo community in Alaska where she becomes involved with Kotzebue (lang in her film debut), who poses as a man to work on the Alaskan pipeline. The title has something to do with preserved berries—don't bother, it makes about as much sense as the entire movie. English and German with English subtitles. **94m/C VHS, DVD.** *GE CA* Rosel Zech, k.d. lang, Chuck Connors, Jane Lind, Oscar Kawagley, Wolfgang Steinberg, Wayne Waterman, Christel Merian; ***D:*** Percy Adlon; ***W:*** Percy Adlon, Felix Adlon; ***C:*** Newton Thomas (Tom) Sigel.

Salo, or the 120 Days of Sodom **1975** Extremely graphic film follows 16 children (eight boys and eight girls) who are kidnapped by a group of men in Fascist Italy. On reaching a secluded villa in the woods, the children are told to follow strict rules and then subjected to incredible acts of sadomasochism, rape, violence, and mutilation. This last film of Pasolini's was taken from a novel by the Marquis de Sade. Viewers are strongly recommended to use their utmost discretion when watching this controversial film. In Italian with English subtitles. **117m/C VHS, DVD.** *IT FR* Caterina Boratto, Giorgio Cataldi, Umberto P. Quintavalle, Paolo Bonacelli; ***D:*** Pier Paolo Pasolini; ***W:*** Pier Paolo Pasolini, Sergio Citti; ***C:*** Tonino Delli Colli; ***M:*** Ennio Morricone.

Salome 1/2 **1922** Garish silent rendition of Oscar Wilde's scandalous tale. **54m/B VHS, DVD.** Alla Nazimova, Madame Rose (Dion) Dione, Mitchell Lewis, Earl Schenck; ***D:*** Charles Bryant. Natl. Film Reg. '00.

Salome **1953** An over-costumed version of Oscar Wilde's Biblical story about King Herod's lascivious stepdaughter who danced her way to stardom and tried to save the life of John the Baptist. Talented cast can't overcome hokey script. **103m/C VHS.** Rita Hayworth, Stewart Granger, Charles Laughton, Judith Anderson, Cedric Hardwicke, Basil Sydney, Maurice Schwartz; ***D:*** William Dieterle; ***C:*** Charles B(ryant) Lang Jr.; ***M:*** George Duning.

Salome 1/2 **1985 (R)** An updated and graphic version of the Oscar Wilde historical fantasy about the temptress Salome who helped topple Herod's Biblical kingdom with her dance of the Seven Veils. Not really a remake of the 1953 film since this is set during the 1940s. **100m/C VHS.** Jo Champa, Tomas Milian, Pamela Salem; ***D:*** Claude D'Anna; ***C:*** Pasqualino De Santis.

Salome, Where She Danced **1945** Set during the Franco-Prussian war. A European dancer helps an American reporter in a spy scheme. She eventually relocates to America and becomes the toast of San Francisco. Somehow, De Carlo managed to spring from this ridiculous camp outing to stardom. **90m/C VHS.** Yvonne De Carlo, Rod Cameron, David Bruce, Walter Slezak; ***D:*** Charles Lamont; ***C:*** William Howard Greene, Hal Mohr.

Salome's Last Dance **1988 (R)** A theatrical, set-surreal adaptation of the Wilde story. Typically flamboyant Russell. **113m/C VHS, DVD.** Glenda Jackson, Stratford Johns, Nickolas Grace, Douglas Hodge, Imogen Millais Scott; ***D:*** Ken Russell; ***W:*** Ken Russell; ***C:*** Harvey Harrison.

The Salon 1/2 **2005 (PG-13)** The release was delayed until 2007, which makes this stereotypical comedy even more dated (Ben Affleck/J.Lo jokes, anyone?). Lame rehash of "Barbershop" and "Beauty Shop" set in Baltimore, with Jenny (Fox) as the owner of the hair salon that's also the local meeting place filled with the usual eccentrics (both workers and customers). The shop's threatened by an urban renewal project but Jenny's determined to fight City Hall. Writer/director/producer Brown, who also produced the "Barbershop" flicks, needs to find a new thematic 'do. **92m/C DVD.** *US* Vivica A. Fox, Kym E. Whitley, Brooke Burns, Darrin Dewitt Henson, Terrence Howard, Dondre T. Whitfield, Garrett Morris, Monica Calhoun, Taral Hicks, Greg Germann, D'Angelo Wilson, Sheila Kutchlow; ***D:*** Mark Brown; ***W:*** Mark Brown; ***C:*** Brandon Trost.

Salsa **1988 (PG)** An auto repairman would rather dance in this "Dirty Dancing" clone. Rosa was formerly a member of the pop group Menudo. **97m/C VHS, DVD.** Robby Rosa, Rodney Harvey, Magali Alvarado, Miranda Garrison, Moon Orona, Kamar De Los Reyes; ***D:*** Boaz Davidson; ***W:*** Boaz Davidson, Tomas Benitez.

Salt **2010** CIA officer Evelyn Salt (Jolie) is accused of being a sleeper agent by a Russian spy so she goes on the run to clear her name. Jolie has many talents but being a dangerous action babe is one of the strongest. **m/C DVD.** *US* Angelina Jolie, Liev Schreiber, Chiwetel Ejiofor, Zoe Lister-Jones; ***D:*** Phillip Noyce; ***W:*** Brian Wimmer, Brian Helgeland; ***C:*** Robert Elswit; ***M:*** James Newton Howard.

Salt & Pepper ½ **1968 (PG-13)** Uninspired spy comedy that's very dated '60s mod. Lawford and Davis Jr. run a London nightclub and are reluctantly recruited as spies thanks to a couple of murders at said club. MI-5 is trying to stop a crazy military officer from hijacking a nuclear sub and overthrowing the British government and think the duo can help. Followed by 1970's "One More Time." **101m/C DVD.** *GB* Sammy Davis Jr., Peter Lawford, John Le Mesurier, Michael Bates, Ernest Clark, Graham Stark, Ilona Rodgers; ***D:*** Richard Donner; ***W:*** Michael Pertwee; ***C:*** Ken Higgins; ***M:*** John Dankworth.

Salt of the Earth ½ **1954** Finally available in this country after being suppressed for 30 years, this controversial film was made by a group of blacklisted filmmakers during the McCarthy era. It was deemed anti-American, communist propaganda. The story deals with the anti-Hispanic racial strife that occurs in a New Mexico zinc mine when union workers organize a strike. **94m/B VHS, DVD.** Rosaura Revueltas, Will Geer, David Wolfe; ***D:*** Herbert Biberman; ***W:*** Michael Wilson; ***C:*** Stanley Meredith, Leonard Stark; ***M:*** Sol Kaplan. Natl. Film Reg. '92.

The Salton Sea **2002 (R)** Feature debut by helmer Caruso is very good at getting down into the sleaze and grime of the world of methedrine addicts, dealers, and victims. Maybe too good. The parade of degradation drowns out everything else; the performances of Kilmer as the nominal hero, and D'Onofrio as kingpin/sadist Pooh-Bear, the time-addled plot that begs for concentration, and any sense that anything good will come from viewing this film. What it does, it does well, the question is, does anyone have the stomach to see it done? **103m/C VHS, DVD.** *US* Val Kilmer, Vincent D'Onofrio, Adam Goldberg, Luis Guzman, Doug Hutchison, Anthony LaPaglia, Glenn Plummer, Peter Sarsgaard, Deborah Kara Unger, Chandra West, B.D. Wong, R. Lee Ermey, Shalom Harlow, Shirley Knight, Meat Loaf Aday, Azura Skye, Danny Trejo, Josh Todd; ***D:*** D.J. Caruso; ***W:*** Tony Gayton; ***C:*** Amir M. Mokri; ***M:*** Thomas Newman.

Salty **1973** A lovable but mischievous sea lion manages to complicate two brothers' lives when they volunteer to help a friend renovate a Florida marina, which is threatened by a mortgage foreclosure. Straightforward and inoffensive tale. **93m/C VHS.** Clint Howard, Mark Slade, Nina Foch; ***D:*** Ricou Browning.

Salty O'Rourke ½ **1945** Salty (Ladd) and Smitty (Demarest) are in desperate need of some quick cash to pay bookie Doc Baxter (Cabot). They get a race horse and disbarred jockey, Johnny Cates (Clements), who fakes his identity in order to race and win the gamblers some cash. But the plan is foiled when Johnny and Salty both fall for the gorgeous Ms. Brooks (Byington), and Johnny decides to throw the race for revenge. **100m/B DVD.** Alan Ladd, Gail Russell, William Demarest, Stanley Clements, Bruce Cabot, Spring Byington; ***D:*** Raoul Walsh; ***W:*** Milton Holmes; ***C:*** Theodor Sparkuhl; ***M:*** Robert Emmett Dolan.

Salut l'Artiste **1974** Two bad actors try to make it in the industry. Delightfully funny with an excellent cast, especially Mastroianni. Snide and irreverent, yet loving and comic look at the world of acting. In French with English subtitles. **96m/C VHS.** *FR* Marcello Mastroianni, Jean Rochefort, Francoise Fabian, Carla Gravina; ***D:*** Yves Robert; ***M:*** Vladimir Cosma.

Salute John Citizen **1942** The life of an average English family during the early days of WWII is depicted, focusing on the deprivation and horror of the Nazi blitzkrieg. Adapted from the novels "Mr. Bunting" and "Mr. Bunting at War" by Robert Greenwood. **74m/B VHS.** *GB* Edward Rigby, Jimmy Hanley, Peggy Cummins, Mabel Constanduros, Eric Micklewood, Dinah Sheridan, Charles Deane, Stanley Holloway, George Robey; ***D:*** Maurice Elvey; ***W:*** Clemence Dane, Elizabeth Baron; ***C:*** James Wilson.

Salvador ½ **1986 (R)** Photo journalist Richard Boyle's unflinching and sordid adventures in war-torn El Salvador. Boyle (Woods) must face the realities of social injustice. Belushi and Woods are hard to like, but excellent. Early critical success for director Stone. **123m/C VHS, DVD.** James Woods, James Belushi, John Savage, Michael Murphy, Elpidia Carrillo, Cynthia Gibb, Tony Plana, Colby Chester, Will MacMillan, Jose Carlos Ruiz, Jorge Luke, Juan Fernandez, Valerie Wildman; ***D:*** Oliver Stone; ***W:*** Oliver Stone, Richard Boyle; ***C:*** Robert Richardson; ***M:*** Georges Delerue. Ind. Spirit '87: Actor (Woods).

Salvation! ½ *Salvation! Have You Said Your Prayers Today?* **1987 (R)** A mean-tempered, timely satire about a money-hungry TV evangelist beset by a family of fervent, equally money-hungry followers, who proceed to cheat, seduce and blackmail him. Occasionally quite funny, but sloppy and predictable. Underground director Beth B's first above-ground film. **80m/C** Stephen McHattie, Exene Cervenka, Dominique Davalos, Viggo Mortensen, Rockets Redglare, Billy Bastiani; ***D:*** Beth B; ***W:*** Beth B.

The Salzburg Connection ½ **1972 (PG)** A list of Nazi collaborators is discovered in Austria. A vacationing American lawyer is caught up in the battle for its possession. Filmed on location, it's still a poor, cheesy adaptation of the Helen MacInnes novel. **94m/C VHS.** Barry Newman, Anna Karina, Klaus Maria Brandauer, Karen Jensen; ***D:*** Lee H. Katzin.

Sam & Janet **2002 (PG-13)** Sam (Brown) goes through a messy divorce and is reluctant to hook up again, until he meets Janet (Ferguson). What follows is a long and tedious courtship in which Janet hides her past, which includes a nasty ex-husband who causes trouble. Most of the movie is devoted to the growing relationship, which is realistic but gets boring. It's basically like seeing your most boring friends' stories about how they met played out on your TV. Should garner a strong following among the Lifetime set. **90m/C VHS, DVD.** Gary Busey, Ryan Brown, Jennifer Ferguson, Anna Beck, Blake Wolney, George Back; ***D:*** Rick Walker; ***W:*** Rick Walker; ***C:*** Byron Werner; ***M:*** David Percefull.

Sam Whiskey ½ **1969 (PG-13)** Charming but uneven western/heist flick has widow Dickinson hire a motley group of misfits, led by Sam Whiskey (Reynolds) to retrieve her late husband's gold from the bottom of a river. Only she wants them to return it to the U.S. Mint from which he stole it. Quirky comedy has a great cast, but doesn't always equal the sum of its parts. **96m/C DVD.** Burt Reynolds, Clint Walker, Ossie Davis, William Schallert, Angie Dickinson, Woodrow Parfrey, Anthony James, Del Reeves, William Boyett; ***D:*** Arnold Laven; ***W:*** William W. Norton Sr.; ***M:*** Herschel Burke Gilbert.

Samantha ½ **1992 (PG)** Twenty-one year-old Samantha discovers she was left on her parents' doorstep in a basket and decides to find out where she came from. Good cast and high charm quotient help this film along. **101m/C VHS, DVD.** Martha Plimpton, Dermot Mulroney, Hector Elizondo, Mary Kay Place, Ione Skye; ***D:*** Steven La Rocque; ***W:*** John Golden, Steven La Rocque.

Samar ½ **1962 (PG)** A liberal penal colony commandant rebels against his superiors by leading his prisoners through the Philippine jungles to freedom. Original action drama with an interesting premise. **89m/C VHS, DVD.** George Montgomery, Gilbert Roland, Joan O'Brien, Ziva Rodann; ***D:*** George Montgomery.

Samaritan Girl *Samaria* **2004 (R)** Yeo-Jin (Ji-min Kwak) pimps out her fellow teen Jae-yeong (Yeo-reum Han) so they can buy tickets to Europe. Jae-yeong ends up in the hospital after jumping out a window and asks her friend to retrieve one of her former clients, who won't go to the hospital unless Yeo-Jin has sex with him. By the time they arrive, Jae-yeong is dead, and Yeo-Jin vows to find all her friends former clients, have sex with them, and return their money. In the meantime her father (a cop) is hunting down and sometimes killing the men sleeping with his daughter. **97m/C DVD.** *KN* Yeo-reum Han, Ji-min Kwak, Eol Lee, In-gi Jung; ***D:*** Ki-Duk Kim; ***W:*** Ki-Duk Kim; ***C:*** Sun Sang-Jae, Sang-jae Seon; ***M:*** Park Ji, Ji-woong Park.

Samaritan: The Mitch Snyder Story **1986** Effective TV drama based upon the true story of Vietnam vet Mitch Snyder (Sheen) who battles various government agencies and ultimately fasts to call national attention to his crusade against homelessness. (Snyder eventually committed suicide.) Tyson appears as a bag lady. **90m/C VHS.** Martin Sheen, Roxanne Hart, Joe Seneca, Stan Shaw, Cicely Tyson; ***D:*** Richard T. Heffron. **TV**

Same Old Song *On Connait la Chanson* **1997** Amusing melodrama that replaces some dialogue with lip-synched popular song lyrics ala Dennis Potter's "Pennies from Heaven" and "The Singing Detective." (Pic is dedicated to Potter). Camille (Jaoui) is helping her sister Odile (Azema) and brother-in-law Claude (Arditti) look for a new Paris apartment, while beginning an affair with real estate broker Marc (Wilson) and ignoring the overtures of love-sick Simon (Dussollier). Meanwhile, Nicolas (Bacri), Odile's now-married ex-flame is also apartment hunting and Odile's vulnerable since Claude doesn't love her anymore. Everybody lies to everybody else (and themselves) and misinterprets all the situations. French with subtitles. **122m/C VHS.** *FR* Agnes Jaoui, Jean-Pierre Bacri, Andre Dussollier, Sabine Azema, Lambert Wilson, Pierre Arditti, Jane Birkin, Jean-Paul Roussillon; ***D:*** Alain Resnais; ***W:*** Agnes Jaoui, Jean-Pierre Bacri; ***C:*** Renato Berta; ***M:*** Bruno Fontaine. Cesar '98: Actor (Dussollier), Film, Film Editing, Sound, Support. Actor (Bacri), Support. Actress (Jaoui), Writing.

Same River Twice ½ **1997** Four men who became friends while working as river rafting guides decide to have a reunion on the same river some 13 years after the death of a friend in a rafting accident. But each man realizes that the years have brought a certain amount of caution and that they are no longer young daredevils. Likewise, their personal quirks must be overcome if they are to successfully negogiate the white water rapids ahead of them. **103m/C VHS, DVD.** John Putch, Dwier Brown, Shea Farrell, Robert Curtis-Brown; ***D:*** Scott Featherstone; ***W:*** Scott Featherstone; ***C:*** Art Wilder; ***M:*** Bradley Smith. **VIDEO**

Same Time, Next Year **1978** A chance meeting between an accountant and a housewife results in a sometimes tragic, always sentimental 25-year affair in which they meet only one weekend each year. Well-cast leads carry warm, touching story based on the Broadway play by Bernard Slade. **119m/C VHS, DVD.** Ellen Burstyn, Alan Alda; ***D:*** Robert Mulligan; ***C:*** Robert L. Surtees; ***M:*** Marvin Hamlisch. Golden Globes '79: Actress—Mus./Comedy (Burstyn).

Sammy & Rosie Get Laid **1987** An unusual social satire about a sexually liberated couple living in London whose lives are thrown into turmoil by the arrival of the man's father—a controversial politician in India. Provides a confusing look at sexual and class collisions. From the makers of "My Beautiful Laundrette." **97m/C VHS.** *GB* Shashi Kapoor, Frances Barber, Claire Bloom, Ayub Khan-Din, Roland Gift, Wendy Gazelle, Meera Syal; ***D:*** Stephen Frears; ***W:*** Hanif Kureishi; ***C:*** Oliver Stapleton; ***M:*** Stanley Myers.

Sammy, the Way-Out Seal **1962** Two young boys bring a mischievous seal to live in their beach house and try to keep it a secret from their parents. Disney in its early '60s phase. **89m/C VHS.** Michael McGreevey, Billy Mumy, Patricia Barry, Robert Culp; ***D:*** Norman Tokar.

Sam's Son **1984 (PG)** Sentimental, autobiographical tale about how a young man's athletic prowess opens the door for an acting career in Hollywood. Good performance by Wallach as the boy's father. Self-indulgent, though entertaining. **107m/C VHS.** Eli Wallach, Anne Jackson, Timothy Patrick Murphy, Hallie Todd, James Karen, Allan Hayes, Joanna Lee, Michael Landon; ***D:*** Michael Landon; ***W:*** Michael Landon.

Samson **1961** Samson attempts to keep wits and hair about him. **90m/C VHS, DVD.** *IT* Brad Harris, Luisella Boni, Alan Steel, Serge Gainsbourg, Mara Berni; ***D:*** Gianfranco Parolini.

Samson Against the Sheik *Maciste Contro lo Sceicco* **1962** Samson survives long enough to battle a sheik in the Middle Ages. **106m/C VHS.** *IT* Ed Fury, Carlo Latimer, Pierro Lulli, Adriano Micantoni; ***D:*** Domenico Paolella; ***W:*** Gian Paolo Callegari, Alessandro Ferrau; ***C:*** Carlo Bellero; ***M:*** Carlo Savina.

Samson and Delilah **1950** The biblical story of the vindictive Delilah, who after being rejected by the mighty Samson, robbed him of his strength by shearing his curls. Delivered in signature DeMille style. Wonderfully fun and engrossing. Mature is excellent. **128m/C VHS, DVD.** Victor Mature, Hedy Lamarr, Angela Lansbury, George Sanders, Henry Wilcoxon, Olive Deering, Fay Holden; ***D:*** Cecil B. DeMille; ***C:*** George Barnes. Oscars '50: Art Dir./Set Dec., Color, Costume Des. (C).

Samson and Delilah **1984** TV version of the biblical romance, semi-based on DeMille's 1950 version. Original Samson (Mature) plays Samson's father. Too long but inoffensive; see the DeMille version instead. **95m/C VHS, DVD.** Antony (Tony) Hamilton, Belinda Bauer, Max von Sydow, Jose Ferrer, Victor Mature, Maria Schell; ***D:*** Lee Philips; ***M:*** Maurice Jarre. **TV**

Samson and Delilah **1996** Another in TNT's biblical retellings, this time with Israelite shepherd Samson (Thal), who also the strongest man alive, falling for beautiful-but-treacherous Philistine Delilah (Hurley). Seems Samson is causing havoc with General Tariq's (Hopper) Philistine army and Delilah is to discover the secret of his strength. **180m/C VHS, DVD.** Eric Thal, Elizabeth Hurley, Dennis Hopper, Michael Gambon, Diana Rigg, Ben Becker, Paul Freeman, Daniel Massey, Pinkas Braun, Debora Caprioglio, Alessandro Gassman, Mark McGann, Jonathan Rhys Meyers; ***D:*** Nicolas Roeg; ***W:*** Allan Scott; ***C:*** Raffaele Mertes; ***M:*** Marco Frisina. **CABLE**

Samson and His Mighty Challenge ½ **1964** In this rarely seen muscle epic, Hercules, Maciste, Samson and Ursus all take part in a battle royale. **94m/C VHS.** *IT* Alan Steel, Red Ross; ***D:*** Giorgio Capitani.

Samson and the 7 Miracles of the World *Maciste Alla Corte Del Gran Khan; Maciste at the Court of the Great Khan; Goliath and the Golden City* **1962** This time the hero known as Maciste (renamed Samson for Americans) is in the 13th century battling brutal Tartar warlords. The very Earth itself shakes when our hero goes into battle! **80m/C VHS, DVD.** *FR IT* Gordon Scott, Yoko Tani, Gabriele Antonini, Leonardo Severini, Valeri Inkizhinov, Helene Chanel; ***D:*** Riccardo Freda; ***M:*** Les Baxter.

Samson in the Wax Museum ½ *Santo en el Museo de Cera; Santo in the Wax Museum* **1963** Masked Mexican wrestling hero Santo (here called Samson) does battle with a scientist who has discovered a way to make wax monsters come to life. **92m/B VHS, DVD.** *MX* Santo, Claudio Brook, Ruben Rojo, Norma Mora, Roxana Bellini; ***D:*** Alfonso Corona Blake.

Samson vs. the Vampire Women ✐ 1/2 **1961** Santo (here called Samson) the masked hero and athlete, battles the forces of darkness as a horde of female vampires attempt to make an unsuspecting girl their next queen. Not bad if you're into the Mexican wrestling genre. **89m/B VHS, DVD.** *MX* Santo, Lorena Lalazquez, Jaime Fernandez, Maria Duval; ***D:*** Alfonso Corona Blake.

Samurai 1: Musashi Miyamoto ✐✐✐ 1/2 **1955** The first installment in the film version of Musashi Miyamoto's life, as he leaves his 17th century village as a warrior in a local civil war only to return beaten and disillusioned. Justly award-winning. In Japanese with English subtitles. **92m/C VHS, DVD.** *JP* Toshiro Mifune, Kaoru Yachigusa, Rentaro Mikuni, Eiko Miyoshi; ***D:*** Hiroshi Inagaki; ***W:*** Hiroshi Inagaki, Tokuhei Wakao; ***C:*** Jun Yasumoto; ***M:*** Ikuma Dan. Oscars '55: Foreign Film.

Samurai 2: Duel at Ichijoji Temple ✐✐✐ 1/2 **1955** Inagaki's second film depicting the life of Musashi Miyamoto, the 17th century warrior, who wandered the disheveled landscape of feudal Japan looking for glory and love. In Japanese with English subtitles. **102m/C VHS, DVD.** *JP* Toshiro Mifune, Akihiko Hirata, Daisuke Kato, Mariko Okada, Sachio Sakai, Kaoru Yachigusa; ***D:*** Hiroshi Inagaki; ***W:*** Hiroshi Inagaki; ***C:*** Jun Yasumoto; ***M:*** Ikuma Dan.

Samurai 3: Duel at Ganryu Island ✐✐✐ 1/2 **1956** The final film of Inagaki's trilogy, in which Musashi Miyamoto confronts his lifelong enemy in a climactic battle. Depicts Miyamoto's spiritual awakening and realization that love and hatred exist in all of us. In Japanese with English subtitles. **102m/C VHS, DVD.** *JP* Toshiro Mifune, Koji Tsurata, Kaoru Yachigusa, Mariko Okada; ***D:*** Hiroshi Inagaki; ***W:*** Hiroshi Inagaki, Tokuhei Wakao; ***C:*** Kazuo Yamada; ***M:*** Ikuma Dan.

Samurai Banners ✐✐ 1/2 *Furin Kazan; Under the Banner of Samurai; Wind-Fire-Forest-Mountain* **1969** In the 16th century, while working to advance the cause of a united Japan, a Samurai warrior and his master both fall in love with the same woman who happens to be the daughter of a slain rival. Handsome production moves along well, balancing a complex story with grand battles and scenes of intimacy. **165m/C VHS, DVD.** *JP* Toshiro Mifune, Yoshiko Sakuma, Kinnosuke Nakamura, Katsuo Nakamura, Masakazu Tamura, Yujiro Ishihara, Mayumi Ozora; ***C:*** Kazuo Yamada; ***M:*** Masaru Sato. **VIDEO**

Samurai Cowboy ✐✐ **1993** Sato (Go) is a successful Japanese businessman who worships the American western ideal so he decides to give up the rat race by moving to Running Moose, Montana, and buying a cattle ranch. Talk about culture shock! Inoffensive fish-out-of-water comedy. Go is a popular singer in his native Japan. **101m/C VHS.** Hiromi Go, Catherine Mary Stewart, Robert Conrad, Conchata Ferrell, Matt McCoy; ***D:*** Michael Keusch; ***W:*** Michael Keusch; ***M:*** Osamu Kitajima.

Samurai Fiction ✐✐✐ *SF: Episode One* **1999** A satiric parody of old samurai films as well as being a tribute to them. Inukai is a young and foolish samurai, and when his family's sword is stolen in a misunderstanding involving a new hire, he and his friends set out to retrieve it from the thief. Said thief is actually a competent swordsman who gives them a sound thrashing. While Inukai is being nursed back to health by a beautiful young woman and her father, the thief becomes a bodyguard for an evil female gambler. Eventually they must meet again, but in the meantime some funny stuff ensues. **111m/B DVD.** *JP* Morio Kazama, Mitsuru Fukikoshi, Mari Natsuki, Taketoshi Naito, Tomoyasu Hotei, Tamaki Ogawa, Hiroshi Kanbe, Ryo Iwamatsu, Kei Tani, Fumiya Fujii, Ken Osawa, Ryoichi Yuki, Akiko Monou, Taro Maruse, Yuji Nakamura, Ramo Nakajima, Shogo Suzuki, Pierre Taki, Diamond Yukai, Utaroku Miyakoya, Yoshiyaki Umegaki, Masahiro Saitoh, Kazuhide Motooka, Norikazu Kobayashi, Nagine Hoshikawa, Yasuhito Hida, Hideaki Yoshioka, Ryuji Takasaki, Masataka Haji, Kenzo Hagiwara, Kenshi Yamamiya, Funezou Yamagata, Hiroya Sugisaka, Takayuki Akaike, Masato Yoshioka, Rie Nonaka, Kayano Komaki, Yoko Yakushijii; ***D:*** Hiroyuki Nakano; ***W:*** Hiroshi Saito, Hiroyuki Nakano; ***C:*** Yujiro Yajima; ***M:*** Tomoyasu Hotei.

Samurai Rebellion ✐✐✐ *Rebellion* **1967** Isaburo (Mifune) is a reknowned swordsman in 18th-century Japan who is the model of loyalty until his overlord demands the return of a former mistress, who is now Isaburo's daughter-in-law. This insult to his family forces Isaburo to take a deadly stand, which turns out to be against his best friend (Nakadai) who's trying to uphold the feudal code. Lots of swordplay. Last in Kobayashi's trilogy following "Harakiri" (1962) and "Kwaidan" (1964). Japanese with subtitles. **121m/B VHS, DVD.** *JP* Toshiro Mifune, Tatsuya Nakadai; ***D:*** Masaki Kobayashi; ***W:*** Shinobu Hashimoto.

Samurai Reincarnation ✐✐ **1981** After the Shogunate government kills 18,000 Christian rioters in the revolt of 1638, and publicly beheads the leader Shiro Amakusa, Shiro reincarnates during a monstrous thunderstorm. Consumed with hatred, he discards the teachings of Jesus Christ and seeks revenge. In Japanese with English subtitles. **122m/C VHS, DVD.** *JP* Sonny Chiba, Kenji Sawada, Akiko Kana, Ken Ogata, Hiroyuki (Henry) Sanada; ***D:*** Kinji Fukasaku; ***W:*** Kinji Fukasaku; ***C:*** Kiyoshi Hasegawa.

San Antonio ✐✐ **1945** A bad girl working in a dance hall turns over a new leaf on meeting the good guy. Trite plot, but good production. **105m/C VHS.** Errol Flynn, Alexis Smith, S.Z. Sakall, Victor Francen, Florence Bates, John Litel, Paul Kelly; ***D:*** David Butler; ***W:*** W.R. Burnett; ***M:*** Max Steiner.

San Demetrio, London ✐✐ 1/2 **1947** Set in 1940, the crew of a crippled tanker endures harrowing situations to reach port. A decent anti-war movie in its time, it's now showing its age. Based on a true story, the plot sags with unbelievable scenes and holes on the plot side. **76m/B VHS.** Walter Fitzgerald, Mervyn Johns, Ralph Michael, Robert Beatty, Charles Victor, Frederick Piper; ***D:*** Charles Frend.

San Fernando Valley ✐✐ *San Fernando* **1944** Another lawman-in-evil-town epic. Rogers received his first on-screen kiss in 1944's biggest western. Fairly typical, pleasant cowboy tale. **54m/B VHS.** Jean Porter, Andrew Tombes, Edward (Ed) Gargan, Roy Rogers, Dale Evans; ***D:*** John English; ***W:*** Dorrell McGowan, Stuart E. McGowan; ***C:*** William Bradford; ***M:*** Gordon Jenkins.

San Francisco ✐✐✐ 1/2 **1936** The San Francisco Earthquake of 1906 serves as the background for a romance between an opera singer and a Barbary Coast saloon owner. Somewhat overdone but gripping tale of passion and adventure in the West. Wonderful special effects. Finale consists of historic earthquake footage. Also available colorized. ♫ San Francisco; A Heart That's Free; Would You?; Air des Bijoux; Sempre Libera. **116m/B VHS, DVD.** Jeanette MacDonald, Clark Gable, Spencer Tracy, Jack Holt, Jessie Ralph, Al Shean, Ted Healy, Shirley Ross, Margaret Irving, Harold Huber, Edgar Kennedy, Kenneth Harlan, Roger Imhof, Russell Simpson, Bert Roach, Warren Hymer; ***D:*** Woodbridge S. Van Dyke; ***W:*** Anita Loos. Oscars '36: Sound.

San Franpsycho ✐ **2006 (R)** Serial killer. Yawn. Two San Francisco detectives, a priest, and a reporter hunt for a serial killer who has been sending the newshound letters after each slaying. **?m/C DVD.** Joe Estevez, Jose Rosette, Todd Bridges, Eleni C. Krimitsos, Chris Angelo, Victor Zaragoza, Elias Castillo; ***D:*** Eduardo Quiroz, Jose Quiroz; ***W:*** Eduardo Quiroz, Jose Quiroz; ***C:*** Rocky Robinson; ***M:*** Eduardo Quiroz. **VIDEO**

San Quentin ✐✐ 1/2 **1937** Former army officer Stephen Jameson (O'Brien) heads to San Q to try some reform work on the rowdy cons, including Red Kennedy (Bogart), who isn't buying his routine. Jameson has it bad for Red's singing sister May (Sheridan), who thinks he's okay for trying to help Red. Only Red, egged on by con Hanson (Sawyer), escapes the road gang to have it out with May. Convinced it's real love, Red surrenders and makes a plea to give Jameson's methods a chance—which Red doesn't get. Much of the melodrama was shot in and around the prison itself. **70m/B DVD.** Pat O'Brien, Humphrey Bogart, Ann Sheridan, Barton MacLane, Joseph (Joe) Sawyer, Veda Ann Borg, Joe King, Gordon Oliver, Emmett Vogan, Garry Owen, Marc Lawrence, George Lloyd; ***D:*** Lloyd Bacon; ***W:*** John Bright, Peter Milne, Robert Tasker; ***C:*** Sid Hickox; ***M:*** Charles Maxwell, David Raksin, Heinz Roemheld.

San Saba ✐ 1/2 **2008** PI Bud (Macfadyen) is discovered unconscious next to the corpse of a corporate bigwig. Bud's the prime suspect though his amnesia about the events makes it a problem for him to find out whodunit. But Bud's first step is contacting old high school classmate Leigh (Rohm), who's related to the dead guy. **?m/C DVD.** Angus MacFadyen, Elisabeth Rohm, Sunny Mabrey, Vivica A. Fox, John Enos, Daniel Zacapa, Benton Jennings, Mehera Blum; ***D:*** Michael Greene; ***W:*** Chris Beams; ***C:*** Jeffrey Smith; ***M:*** Ron Sures. **VIDEO**

Sanctimony **WOOF!** **2001** It's just like "American Psycho"... only much, much worse. Director Uwe Boll, the second worst thing that Germany's ever been responsible for, steals liberally from Bret Easton Ellis and David Fincher's "Se7en" in one of the clumsiest serial killer stories ever put to film. Two cops (Pare and Rubin) suspect that stock broker Tom Merrick (Van Dien) is really the psycho murderer known as the "Monkey Maker." (Worst. Villain. Name. Ever.) So what do they do about it? Not much. Boll's screenplay (He writes too!) is as aimless as friendly fire and just as entertaining. By the time you get to the inexplicable snuff film sequence, you'll be wondering if Boll had a stroke halfway through writing the script. **87m/C VHS, DVD.** *GE US* Casper Van Dien, Eric Roberts, Michael Pare, Jennifer Rubin, Catherine Oxenberg; ***D:*** Uwe Boll; ***W:*** Uwe Boll; ***C:*** Mathias Neumann; ***M:*** Uwe Spies. **VIDEO**

Sanctuary ✐✐ **1998 (R)** A former government agent, Luke Connolly has completely changed his life by becoming a clergyman. However, when his old agency discovers his whereabouts, the deadly skills he's renounced may be all that can save him. **110m/C VHS, DVD.** Mark Dacascos, Kylie Travis, Jaimz Woolvett, Alan Scarfe; ***D:*** Tibor Takacs; ***W:*** Michael Stokes; ***M:*** Norman Orenstein. **VIDEO**

Sanctuary of Fear ✐ 1/2 *Girl in the Park* **1979** A priest in New York City helps an actress subjected to a series of terrorizing incidents. Uninspired would-be TV pilot based on Chesterton's "Father Brown" series. **98m/C VHS.** George Hearn, Barnard Hughes, Kay Lenz, Michael McGuire, Robert Schenkkan, David Rasche, Fred Gwynne, Elizabeth Wilson; ***D:*** John Llewellyn Moxey. **TV**

Sand ✐✐ **2000** Tyler Briggs (Vartan) wants to start over—away from his violent father (Quaid) and brothers. So after his mother's death, he heads to the quiet beach town where his mom grew up. There Tyler falls for Sandy (Wuhrer) and starts to make a peaceful new life but trouble and family follow. **90m/C VHS, DVD.** Michael Vartan, Denis Leary, Randy Quaid, Kari Wuhrer, Marshall Bell, Julie Delpy, Rodney Eastman, Bodhi (Pine) Elfman, Emilio Estevez, John Hawkes, Jon Lovitz, Norman Reedus, Peter Simmons, Harry Dean Stanton; ***D:*** Matt Palmieri; ***W:*** Matt Palmieri; ***C:*** John Skotchdopole.

Sand and Blood ✐✐ 1/2 *Blood and Sand; De Sable et de Sang* **1987** A young matador who wishes to escape poverty and a young, cultivated doctor, who despises bullfighting, meet and eventually become friends. A woman enters the picture and completes the love triangle. Widely praised by critics. Interesting and moving. In French with English subtitles. **101m/C VHS.** *FR* Sami Frey, Andre Dussollier, Clementine Celarie, Patrick Catalifo, Maria Casares, Catherine Rouvel; ***D:*** Jeanne Labrune; ***W:*** Jeanne Labrune.

The Sand Pebbles ✐✐✐ 1/2 **1966** An American expatriate engineer, transferred to a gunboat on the Yangtze River in 1926, falls in love with a missionary teacher. As he becomes aware of the political climate of American imperialism, he finds himself at odds with his command structure; the treatment of this issue can be seen as commentary on the situation in Vietnam at the time of the film's release. Considered one of McQueen's best performances, blending action and romance. **193m/C VHS, DVD, Blu-ray Disc.** Steve McQueen, Richard Crenna, Richard Attenborough, Candice Bergen, Marayat Andriane, Mako, Larry Gates, Gavin MacLeod, Simon Oakland, James Hong, Richard Loo, Barney (Bernard) Phillips, Tommy Lee, Ford Rainey, Walter Reed, Gus Trikonis, Joe Turkel, Glenn Wilder; ***D:*** Robert Wise; ***W:*** Robert Anderson; ***C:*** Joe MacDonald; ***M:*** Jerry Goldsmith. Golden Globes '67: Support. Actor (Attenborough).

Sand Serpents ✐ 1/2 **2009** Basic monsters vs. soldiers flick with a limited cast, cliched plot and dialogue, but decent CGI. A small force of Marines is sent into the Afghan desert but the Taliban are the least of their worries after they encounter giant, hungry prehistoric sand worms with very big teeth. **90m/C DVD.** Jason Gedrick, Michelle Asante, Sebastian Knapp, Tamara Hope, Elias Toufexis, Chris Jarman; ***D:*** Jeff Renfroe; ***W:*** Raul Inglis; ***M:*** Pierpaolo Tiano. **CABLE**

Sand Trap ✐✐ 1/2 **1997 (R)** Wealthy businessman Nelson Yeager (Koepenick) gets pushed over a cliff by his best friend, Jack (James). But when Jack and Nelson's not-so-grieving widow Margo (Morehead) report the accident and the local sheriff (Thompson) goes to find the body, it's not there. Now a murder plot turns into a desire for revenge. Low-budget modern noir. **99m/C VHS.** Elizabeth Morehead, David John James, Brad Koepenick, Bob Thompson; ***D:*** Harris Done; ***W:*** Harris Done; ***C:*** Mark W. Gray. **VIDEO**

Sandakan No. 8 ✐✐✐ *Brothel 8; Sandakan House 8* **1974** A Japanese woman working as a journalist befriends an old woman who was sold into prostitution in Borneo in the early 1900s. Justly acclaimed feminist story dramatizes the role of women in Japanese society. Japanese with English subtitles. **121m/C VHS.** *JP* Kinuyo Tanaka, Yoko Takakashi, Komake Kurihara, Eitaro (Sakae, Saka Ozawa) Ozawa; ***D:*** Kei Kumai. Berlin Intl. Film Fest. '75: Actress.

Sanders of the River ✐✐✐ *Bosambo* **1935** A British officer in colonial Africa must work with the local chief to quell a rebellion. Tale of imperialism. Dated but still interesting and of value. Robeson is very good; superb location cinematography. **80m/B VHS, DVD.** *GB* Paul Robeson, Leslie Banks, Robert Cochran; ***D:*** Zoltan Korda; ***C:*** Georges Perinal.

Sandflow ✐✐ 1/2 **1937** Well-made Western with Jones playing a man whose father has cheated many ranchers. Jones is out to avenge all of his father's misdeeds and build a new life for himself in this above-average oater. **58m/B VHS.** Buck Jones, Lita Chevret, Robert F. (Bob) Kortman, Arthur Aylesworth, Robert Terry, Enrique DeRosas; ***D:*** Lesley Selander.

The Sandlot ✐✐✐ **1993 (PG)** Young Scotty (Guiry) moves to a new neighborhood in California in 1962 and tries to make friends despite not knowing anything about playing baseball. His scrappy teammates include the friendly Benny (Vitar), a chubby loud-mouthed catcher named Ham (Renna), and Squints (Leopardi), a would-be Lothario before his time. Action revolves around Scotty's attempt to get baseball autographed by Babe Ruth out of the clutches of giant killer junkyard dog owned by Jones before dad Leary discovers it's missing. Small wonder is nostalgic without being sentimental, and tells its tale with grace and humor, supported by a period soundtrack. **101m/C VHS, DVD.** Tom Guiry, Mike Vitar, Patrick Renna, Chauncey Leopardi, Marty York, Brandon Adams, Denis Leary, Karen Allen, James Earl Jones, Maury Wills, Art LaFleur, Marley Shelton, Brooke Adams; ***D:*** David Mickey Evans; ***W:*** David Mickey Evans, Robert Gunter; ***C:*** Anthony B. Richmond; ***M:*** David Newman; ***V:*** Arliss Howard.

The Sandlot 2 ✐ 1/2 **2005 (PG)** The original came out in 1993, so this sequel basically features the same plot with a new group of baseball-playing kids. Now set in 1972, the sandlot guys team up with several softball-playing girls to take on some rivals. There's also a subplot about a rocket-loving shrimp who accidentally gets his hands on a NASA prototype and you can figure out what happens next. Innocuous fun but not destined to be a childhood classic. **97m/C DVD.** Brett Kelly, Reece Thompson, James Earl Jones, Teryl Rothery, Greg Germann, Max Lloyd-Jones, Samantha Burton, James Willson, Cole Evan Weiss, Sean Brady, Neilen Benvegnu, Jessica King, Mckenzie Freemantle; ***D:*** David Mickey Evans; ***W:*** David Mickey Evans; ***C:*** David Pelletier; *M:* Laura Karpman. **VIDEO**

The Sandlot 3: Heading Home ☙ ½ **2007 (PG)** More of the same but with a couple of the characters from the 1993 original appearing as grown-ups: Benny Rodriguez (Nucci) is the manager of the L.A. Dodgers and pharmacy owner Squints (Leopardi) sponsors the newest sandlot team. But the story is about arrogant major-leaguer Tommy Santorelli (Perry), who gets beaned on the head and wakes up as a 12-year-old in 1976. Given a do-over, he now has the chance to choose friends and loyalty over selfish gains. **96m/C DVD.** Luke Perry, Danny Nucci, Chauncey Leopardi, Sarah Deakins, Keanu Pires, Brandon Olds, Cole Heppell, Kai James; *D:* William Dear; *W:* Keith Mitchell, Allie Dvorin; *C:* Pascal Jean Provost; *M:* Kendall Marsh. **VIDEO**

The Sandpiper ☙☙ **1965** Free-spirited artist Taylor falls in love with Burton, the married headmaster of her son's boarding school. Muddled melodrama offers little besides starpower. Filmed at Big Sur, California. ♫The Shadow of Your Smile. **117m/C VHS.** Elizabeth Taylor, Richard Burton, Charles Bronson, Eva Marie Saint, Robert Webber, Morgan Mason; *D:* Vincente Minnelli; *C:* Milton Krasner. Oscars '65: Song ("The Shadow of Your Smile").

Sandra of a Thousand Delights ☙☙ *Sandra; Of a Thousand Delights; Vaghe Stelle Dell'Orsa* **1965** Haunting drama with strong women (and weak men). Sandra returns to Italy from her American home in order to attend a ceremony honoring her father—a Jewish scientist who died in a Nazi concentration camp. Back with her family, Sandra tries to deal with her past, including her mother's possible betrayal of her father and her brother's incestuous longings. Italian with subtitles. **100m/B VHS.** *IT* Claudia Cardinale, Jean Sorel, Marie Bell, Michael Craig, Renzo Ricci; *D:* Luchino Visconti; *W:* Luchino Visconti, Suso Cecchi D'Amico.

Sands of Iwo Jima ☙☙☙ ½ **1949** Wayne earned his first Oscar nomination as a tough Marine sergeant, in one of his best roles. He trains a squad of rebellious recruits in New Zealand in 1943. Later they are responsible for the capture of Iwo Jima from the Japanese—one of the most difficult campaigns of the Pacific Theater. Includes striking real war footage. **109m/B VHS, DVD.** John Wayne, Forrest Tucker, John Agar, Richard Jaeckel, Adele Mara, Wally Cassell, James Brown, Richard Webb, Arthur Franz, Julie Bishop, William Murphy, George Tyne, Hal Baylor, John McGuire, Martin Milner, William (Bill) Self, Peter Coe, I. Stanford Jolley, Col. D.M. Shoup, Lt. Col. H.P. Crowe, Capt. Harold G. Shrier, Rene A. Gagnon, Ira H. Hayes, John H. Bradley; *D:* Allan Dwan; *W:* Harry Brown, James Edward Grant; *C:* Reggie Lanning; *M:* Victor Young.

Sands of Sacrifice ☙☙ ½ *Tangled Trails* **1921** Hart, a Northwest Mountie, seeks an unscrupulous promoter who's selling worthless mining stock. **56m/B VHS.** Neal Hart, Violet Palmer, Gladys Hampton, Jules Cowles, Jean Bary, Ed Roseman; *D:* Charles Bartlett.

The Sandy Bottom Orchestra ☙☙ ½ **2000** Sandy Bottom, Wisconsin is a quaint small town that is resistant to change. Big city Ingrid (Headly), a former classical pianist, discovered this when she married local dairy farmer Norman (Irwin). Norman is also having problems—he wants to include a classical concert in the town's annual summer festival rather than the usual marching band and is meeting with opposition. Their daughter Rachel (Zima) also longs to fit in but her musical talent has outgrown the limited resources of the community and decisions must be made. **100m/C VHS, DVD.** Glenne Headly, Tom Irwin, Madeline Zima, Jane Powell, Richard McMillan, Tamara Hope, Roger Dunn, Bradley Reid; *D:* Bradley Wigor; *W:* Joseph Maurer; *C:* Robert Primes; *M:* David Bell. **CABLE**

Sanjuro ☙☙☙ *Tsubaki Sanjuro* **1962** In this offbeat, satiric sequel to "Yojimbo," a talented but lazy samurai comes to the aid of a group of naive young warriors. The conventional ideas of good and evil are quickly tossed aside; much less earnest than other Kurosawa Samurai outings. In Japanese with English subtitles. **96m/B VHS, DVD.** *JP* Toshiro Mifune, Tatsuya Nakadai, Keiju Kobayashi, Yuzo Kayama; *D:* Akira Kurosawa; *W:* Akira Kurosawa, Ryuzo Kikushima, Hideo Oguni; *C:* Fukuzo Koizumi, Takao Saito; *M:* Masaru Sato.

Sans Soleil ☙☙☙ *Sunless* **1982** A female narrator reads and comments on the letters she receives from a friend, a freelance cameraman traveling through Japan, West Africa, and Iceland. The cameraman meditates on the cultural dislocation he feels and the meaning of his work and of life itself. Both narrator and cameraman remain unseen with the visuals being the cameraman's work in progress. **100m/C VHS.** *FR* *D:* Chris Marker; *W:* Chris Marker; *Nar:* Alexandra Stewart.

Sanshiro Sugata ☙☙☙ **1943** Kurosawa's first film. A young man learns discipline in martial arts from a patient master. Climactic fight scene is early signature Kurosawa. In Japanese with English subtitles. **82m/B VHS, DVD.** *JP* Denjiro Okochi, Yukiko Todoroki, Ranko Hanai, Ryonosuke Tsukigata, Sugisaku Aoyama, Kokuten Kodo, Susumo Fusuita, Takashi Shimura; *D:* Akira Kurosawa.

Sansho the Bailiff ☙☙☙☙ *The Bailiff; Sansho Dayu* **1954** A world masterpiece by Mizoguchi about feudal society in 11th century Japan. A woman and her children are sold into prostitution and slavery. As an adult, the son seeks to right the ills of his society. Powerful and tragic, and often more highly esteemed than "Ugetsu." In Japanese with English subtitles. **132m/B VHS.** *JP* Kinuyo Tanaka, Yoshiaki Hanayagi, Kyoko Kagawa, Eitaro Shindo, Ichiro Sugai; *D:* Kenji Mizoguchi; *W:* Yoshikata Yoda; *M:* Fumio Hayasaka.

Santa and Pete ☙☙ **1999** Kind of a weird take on the Santa story. Grandpa Nicholas and grandson Terrence are decorating the Xmas tree and the last two ornaments are of a Santa and a Moor who Gramps says is Santa's sidekick Pete. Seems the legendary St. Nick gets arrested in Spain while making his rounds and gets thrown in jail where he meets a Muslim named Pete. They escape and begin traveling together and little pieces of the Santa legend (reindeer, red suit, etc.) get explained as they make their deliveries. **98m/C DVD.** James Earl Jones, Hume Cronyn, Flex Alexander, Erica Gimpel, Sedrathe Gillespie, Tempestt Bledsoe; *D:* Duwayne Dunham; *W:* Greg Taylor; *C:* John Newby; *M:* Alan Williams. **TV**

Santa Baby ☙☙ ½ **2006 (PG)** Amusing comedy about finding the true spirit of Christmas. Mary (McCarthy) is a successful marketing exec who decides her dad's (Wendt) business needs to run more efficiently. And, of course, dad is Santa Claus. Mary returns to the North Pole when Santa has some heart trouble and tries to whip those elves into shape (too many cookie breaks) while rekindling a romance with ex-beau Luke (Sergei). **89m/C DVD.** Jenny McCarthy, George Wendt, Ivan Sergei, Lynne Griffin; *D:* Ron Underwood; *W:* Garrett Frawley, Brian Turner; *C:* Derick Underschultz; *M:* Misha Segal. **CABLE**

Santa Buddies ☙☙ ½ **2009 (G)** Puppy Paws (the son of Santa Paws) and the Buddies attempt to stop a holiday disaster at the North Pole when the magical Christmas icicle starts melting and everyone forgets the true meaning of the season. **88m/C DVD.** George Wendt, Christopher Lloyd, Danny Woodburn; *D:* Robert Vince; *W:* Robert Vince, Anna McRoberts; *C:* Kamal Derkaoui; *M:* Brahm Wenger; *V:* Zachary Gordon, Field Cate, Josh Flitter, Ty Panitz. **VIDEO**

Santa Claus WOOF! **1959** Santa Claus teams up with Merlin the Magician to fend off an evil spirit who would ruin everyone's Christmas. Mexican camp classic. **94m/C VHS, DVD.** *MX* Jose Elias Moreno, Cesareo Quezada; *D:* Rene Cardona Sr.; *Nar:* Ken Smith.

Santa Claus Conquers the Martians ☙ *Santa Claus Defeats the Aliens* **1964** A Martian spaceship comes to Earth and kidnaps Santa Claus and two children. Martian kids, it seems, are jealous that Earth tykes have Christmas. Features then-child star Pia Zadora. **80m/C VHS, DVD.** John Call, Leonard Hicks, Vincent Beck, Victor Stiles, Donna Conforti, Bill McCutcheon, Christopher Month, Pia Zadora; *D:* Nicholas Webster; *W:* Glenville Mareth; *C:* David Quaid; *M:* Milton Delugg.

Santa Claus: The Movie ☙☙ **1985 (PG)** A big-budgeted spectacle about an elf who falls prey to an evil toy maker and almost ruins Christmas and Santa Claus. Boring, 'tis-the-season fantasy-drama meant to warm our cockles. **112m/C VHS, DVD.** Dudley Moore, John Lithgow, David Huddleston, Judy Cornwell, Burgess Meredith; *D:* Jeannot Szwarc; *W:* David Newman; *C:* Arthur Ibbetson; *M:* Henry Mancini.

The Santa Clause ☙☙ ½ **1994 (PG)** If you like Allen, you'll enjoy this lightweight holiday comedy about divorced workaholic dad Scott Calvin and eight-year-old son Charlie (Lloyd). Seems Santa injures himself falling off the Calvin roof and dad winds up putting on Santa's suit. But as it turns out when you put on Santa's suit, you become Santa, including a noticeable weight gain, a fluffy beard, and all those reindeer and elves to deal with (but where's Mrs. Claus?). **97m/C VHS, DVD.** Tim Allen, Eric Lloyd, Judge Reinhold, Wendy Crewson, David Krumholtz, Mary Gross; *D:* John Pasquin; *W:* Leo Benvenuti, Steve Rudnick; *C:* Walt Lloyd; *M:* Michael Convertino. Blockbuster '95: Male Newcomer, T. (Allen).

The Santa Clause 2 ☙☙ ½ **2002 (G)** Sequel to the 1994 film has Santa (Allen again) facing expulsion if he doesn't find himself a Mrs. Claus. He also has to deal with the fact that his son Charlie (Lloyd) just landed on the "naughty" list. When Santa/Scott heads back to the U.S. to help Charlie, he runs afoul of the school's female principal (can you see where this is going?). Back at the Pole, the clone Santa he left in charge is staging a coup, of sorts. Funnier, with more of an edge than the original, this one gives adults plenty to smirk at while the kids are distracted by all the yuletide yahooey. **95m/C VHS, DVD.** *US* Tim Allen, Elizabeth Mitchell, David Krumholtz, Eric Lloyd, Judge Reinhold, Wendy Crewson, Spencer Breslin, Liliana Mumy, Art LaFleur, Kevin Pollak, Jay Thomas, Michael Dorn, Danielle Woodman, Aisha Tyler; *D:* Michael Lembeck; *W:* Don Rhymer, Cinco Paul, Ken Daurio, Edward Decter, John J. Strauss, Leo Benvenuti; *C:* Adam Greenberg; *M:* George S. Clinton.

The Santa Clause 3: The Escape Clause ☙ ½ **2006 (G)** Tim Allen returns to beat a dead reindeer in this pointless sequel. Reprising his role as Scott/Santa, he's faced with a pregnant Mrs. Claus (Mitchell) and an uprising by Jack Frost (Short), who wants to turn the North Pole into Upper Vegas. Forced to deal with a visit by his in-laws (Arkin, Margret) and toy sabotage by Frost, he contemplates quitting his seasonal job. The anti-commercialism message is a little hypocritical for a movie that could have been called "Beclause We Want More of your Dough." **91m/C DVD, Blu-ray Disc.** *US* Tim Allen, Elizabeth Mitchell, Martin Short, Spencer Breslin, Judge Reinhold, Wendy Crewson, Eric Lloyd, Liliana Mumy, Alan Arkin, Ann Margret; *Cameos:* Kevin Pollak, Jay Thomas, Peter Boyle, Aisha Tyler; *D:* Michael Lembeck; *W:* Edward Decter, John J. Strauss; *C:* Robbie Greenberg; *M:* George S. Clinton.

Santa Fe ☙☙ **1951** Action-packed western with Scott playing a Confederate soldier who heads West to take a job with the Santa Fe Railroad. However, his brothers, with their wounded rebel pride, have different ideas for forgetting the defeat. Refusing to take money from Northern businesses, they become outlaws. Based on a story by Louis Stevens and the novel by James Marshall. **89m/C VHS, DVD.** Randolph Scott, Janis Carter, Jerome Courtland, Peter Thompson, John Archer, Warner Anderson, Roy Roberts, Billy House; *D:* Irving Pichel; *W:* Kenneth Gamet.

Santa Fe ☙☙ ½ **1997 (R)** Muddled romantic drama with an appealing cast. It's taken cop Paul Thomas (Cole) eight months to recover from bullet wounds suffered in a shoot-out with a local cult. In the meantime, wife Leah's (Kelley) distanced herself from the marriage but still urges Paul into group counseling with charismatic Eleanor (Davidovich). Despite Paul's mistrust of her guru-like status, he's naturally drawn to Eleanor (and she to him). There's some tedious subplot stuff but the leads do fine. **97m/C VHS, DVD.** Gary Cole, Lolita (David) Davidovich, Sheila Kelley, Tina Majorino, Jere Burns, Pamela Reed, Phyllis Frelich, Mark Medoff, Tony Plana, Jeffrey Jones; *D:* Andrew Shea; *W:* Andrew Shea, Mark Medoff; *C:* Paul Elliott; *M:* Mark Governor.

Santa Fe Bound ☙☙ **1937** Tyler must work to clear his name when he is falsely accused of having murdered a man. **58m/B VHS.** Tom Tyler, Jeanne Martel, Richard Cramer, Charles "Slim" Whitaker, Edward Cassidy, Lafe (Lafayette) McKee, Dorothy Woods, Charles "Blackie" King; *D:* Harry S. Webb.

Santa Fe Marshal ☙☙ **1940** The 27th Hopalong Cassidy movie, if anyone's counting. In the title job the Hopster goes undercover with a medicine show to smash a criminal gang. A little different than usual, right up to the surprise identity of the crooked mastermind. **66m/B VHS.** William Boyd, Russell Hayden, Marjorie Rambeau, Bernadene Hayes, Earle Hodgins, Kenneth Harlan, Eddie Dean; *D:* Lesley Selander.

Santa Fe Stampede ☙☙ ½ **1938** The Three Mesquiteers join an old prospector in his claim but when he is killed, one of them (Wayne) is framed. The photography makes up for the weak storyline and direction. **58m/B VHS, DVD.** John Wayne, Ray Corrigan, Max Terhune, William Farnum, June Martel, Leroy Mason, Yakima Canutt, Curley Dresden; *D:* George Sherman.

Santa Fe Trail ☙☙ ½ **1940** Historically inaccurate but entertaining tale about the pre-Civil War fight for "bloody Kansas." The action-adventure depicts future Civil War Generals J.E.B. Stuart (Flynn) and George Armstrong Custer (Reagan!) as they begin their military career (although Custer was really just a youth at this time). Good action scenes. Also available colorized. **110m/B VHS, DVD.** Errol Flynn, Olivia de Havilland, Ronald Reagan, Van Heflin, Raymond Massey, Alan Hale; *D:* Michael Curtiz; *W:* Robert Buckner; *C:* Sol Polito; *M:* Max Steiner.

Santa Fe Uprising ☙☙ ½ **1946** Red Ryder has to save Little Beaver from kidnappers. Good first entry for Lane in the "Red Ryder" series. **54m/B VHS, DVD.** Allan "Rocky" Lane, Robert (Bobby) Blake, Martha Wentworth, Barton MacLane, Jack La Rue, Dick Curtis, Pat Michaels, Edythe Elliott, Tom London, Edmund Cobb; *D:* R.G. Springsteen; *W:* Earle Snell; *C:* Bud Thackery.

Santa Sangre ☙☙☙ **1990 (R)** A circus in Mexico City, a temple devoted to a saint without arms, and a son who faithfully dotes upon his armless mother are just a few of the bizarre things in this wildly fantastic film. Fenix acts as his mother's arms, plays the piano for her, and carries out any wish she desires—including murder. Visually intoxicating but strange outing may prove too graphic for some viewers. Not as rigorous as other Jodorowsky outings. Also available in an NC-17 version. **123m/C VHS.** *IT MX* Axel Jodorowsky, Sabrina Dennison, Guy Stockwell, Blanca Guerra, Thelma Tixou, Adan Jodorowsky, Faviola Tapia, Jesus Juarez; *D:* Alejandro Jodorowsky; *W:* Robert Leoni, Claudio Argento, Alejandro Jodorowsky; *C:* Danielle Nannuzzi; *M:* Simon Boswell.

The Santa Trap ☙☙ ½ **2002** Having just moved from snowy New England to the desert Southwest, it just doesn't feel like Christmas to the Emerson family. Young Judy is afraid Santa isn't real, so she sets a trap and captures a jolly intruder, who's arrested and thrown in jail. Now what'll happen to Christmas if Santa can't make his deliveries? And what about those reindeer on the Emersons' roof? **92m/C DVD.** Shelley Long, Robert Hays, Dick Van Patten, Stacy Keach, Sierra Abel, Corbin Bernsen, Amanda Pays, Steve Monroe; *D:* John Shepphird; *W:* John Shepphird; *C:* Neal Brown; *M:* Joseph Conlan. **TV**

Santa with Muscles ☙ ½ **1996 (PG)** Cartoonish holiday-themed comedy finds the Hulkster as Scrooge-like millionaire Blake Thorne. Through a series of stupid circumstances, Thorne winds up in a Santa suit in a shopping mall hiding from the cops. But a blow to the head makes him believe he's the Jolly-Old-Elf himself and he comes to the aid of a local orphanage, whose tykes are about to be evicted. Silly's the kindest thing to say.

97m/C VHS. Hulk Hogan, Don Stark, Ed Begley Jr., Clint Howard, Robin Curtis, Garrett Morris, Adam Wylie; *D:* John Murlowski; *W:* Jonathan Bond, Fred Mata, Dorrie Krum Raymond; *C:* Michael Gfelner; *M:* James Covell.

Santee 🦴🦴 **1973 (PG)** A father-son relationship develops between a bounty hunter and the son of a man he killed. Good, but not great, Western. **93m/C VHS, DVD.** Glenn Ford, Dana Wynter, Jay Silverheels, John Larch, Michael Burns; *D:* Gary Nelson.

Santitos 🦴🦴 **1999 (R)** Esperanza Diaz (Heredia) is a young Mexican widow whose 12-year-old daughter Blanca (Zapata) has supposedly died, although her mother never saw the child's body. When Esperanza's favorite saint, St. Jude the patron of lost causes, starts appearing to her, she begins a search for her lost child that takes her to the La Casa Rosa brothel in Tijuana. But faith and motherly love will help Esperanza survive anything. Disarmingly innocent film based on the novel by Escandon, who also wrote the screenplay. Spanish with subtitles. **99m/C VHS, DVD.** *MX* Dolores Heredia, Fernando Torre Lapham, Juan Duarte, Ana Bertha Espin, Maya Zapata, Roberto Cobo; *D:* Alejandro Springall; *W:* Maria Ampara Escandon; *C:* Xavier Perez Grobet; *M:* Carlo Nicolau, Rosino Serrano.

The Saphead 🦴🦴 ½ **1921** Keaton's first outing as the rich playboy has him playing the none-to-bright son of a Wall Street mogul. Some great moments provide a glimpse of cinematic greatness to come from the budding comedic genius. Based on the play "The New Henrietta" by Winchell Smith and Victor Mapes. Silent. **70m/B VHS, DVD.** William H. Crane, Buster Keaton, Carol Holloway, Edward Connelly, Irving Cummings; *D:* Herbert Blache; *W:* June Mathis; *C:* Harold Wenstrom.

Sapphire 🦴🦴🦴 **1959** Two Scotland Yard detectives seek the killer of a beautiful black woman who was passing for white. Good mystery and topical social comment; remains interesting and engrossing. Superbly acted all around. **92m/C VHS.** *GB* Nigel Patrick, Yvonne Mitchell, Michael Craig, Paul Massie, Bernard Miles; *D:* Basil Dearden. British Acad. '59: Film.

Saps at Sea 🦴🦴 ½ **1940** A doctor advises Ollie to take a rest away from his job at a horn factory. He and Stan rent a boat, which they plan to keep tied to the dock, until an escaped criminal happens by and uses the boys (and their boat) for his getaway. Cramer is a good bad guy; Stan and Ollie cause too much trouble, as always. **57m/B VHS.** Stan Laurel, Oliver Hardy, James Finlayson, Ben Turpin, Richard Cramer; *D:* Gordon Douglas.

Sara Dane 🦴🦴 **1981** A strong young woman in the 18th century rises in the world through marriage and business acumen. Interesting but imperfect and slow. **150m/C VHS.** *AU* Harold Hopkins, Brenton Whittle, Barry Quin, Sean Scully; *D:* Rod Hardy, Gary Conway.

Saraband 🦴🦴🦴 ½ **2003 (R)** Bergman's final film has his "Scenes From a Marriage" (1974) characters reuniting after a 30-year separation. When Marianne (Ullman) visits Johan (Josephson) she finds he is still bitter and full of hatred, which is geared mostly toward his son Henrik (from another marriage) and granddaughter Karin who live in his guest house. When Karin is provided an opportunity to study music in Helsinki, an emotional confrontation comes to a head. Exceptional swan song. **107m/C DVD.** *SW IT GE FI DK AT* Erland Josephson, Liv Ullmann, Borje Ahlstedt, Julia Dufvenius, Gunnel Fred; *D:* Ingmar Bergman; *W:* Ingmar Bergman; *C:* Raymond Wemmenlov, Sofi Stridh, P.O. Lantto.

Sarafina! 🦴🦴🦴 **1992 (PG-13)** Part coming-of-age saga, part political drama, part musical, and all emotionally powerful. Sarafina is a young girl in a township school in Soweto, South Africa in the mid-'70s, gradually coming into a political awakening amid the Soweto riots. Khumalo recreates her stage role as the glowing and defiant Sarafina with both Goldberg and Makeba good in their roles as Sarafina's outspoken and inspirational teacher and her long-suffering mother, respectively. Adapted from Ngema's stage musical. **98m/C VHS, DVD.** Leleti Khumalo, Whoopi Goldberg, Miriam Makeba, John Kani, Mbongeni Ngema; *D:* Darrell Roodt; *W:* Mbongeni Ngema, William Nicholson; *M:* Stanley Myers.

The Saragossa Manuscript 🦴🦴 ½ *Rekopis Znaleziony W Saragossie* **1965** Ambitious fantasy based on the 1813 novel "Sanatorium under the Hourglass" by Bruno Schultz. A romantic Belgian army officer, travelling to Spain, meets two beautiful princesses who send him on a fantastic journey to prove himself worthy of their affections. Polish with subtitles. **174m/B VHS, DVD.** *PL* Zbigniew Cybulski, Iga Cembrzynska, Joanna Jedryka, Slawomir Linder; *D:* Wojciech Has; *W:* Tadeusz Kwiatkowski; *C:* Mieczyslaw Jahoda; *M:* Krzysztof Penderecki.

Sarah, Plain and Tall 🦴🦴🦴 **1991 (G)** New England school teacher (Close) travels to Kansas circa 1910 to care for the family of a widowed farmer who has advertised for a wife. Superior entertainment for the whole family. Adapted from Patricia MacLachlan's novel of the same name by MacLachlan and Carol Sobieski. Nominated for nine Emmy Awards. A "Hallmark Hall of Fame" presentation. **98m/C VHS, DVD.** Glenn Close, Christopher Walken, Lexi (Faith) Randall, Margaret Sophie Stein, Jon (John) DeVries, Christopher Bell; *D:* Glenn Jordan; *W:* Carol Sobieski; *C:* Mike Fash; *M:* David Shire. **TV**

Sarah, Plain and Tall: Skylark 🦴🦴 ½ *Skylark* **1993 (G)** In a sequel to Hallmark Hall of Fame's hugely successful "Sarah, Plain and Tall," the whole Kansas crew shows up for more of their little-farm-on-the-prairie life. After two years in America's squarest state, mail-order bride Sarah (Close) loves Jacob (Walken), but not the scenery and still yearns for the lush greenery of Maine. When drought and fire threaten the farm, Jacob fears for the family's health and safety, and sends them back East for a visit. Close's "tough Yankee" expression grows a bit tiresome in a plot that is a tad predictable, yet the simplistic charm and nostalgia are unresistable and work to propel this quality Hallmark production. **98m/C VHS, DVD.** Glenn Close, Christopher Walken, Lexi (Faith) Randall, Christopher Bell, Tresa Hughes, Lois Smith, Lee Richardson, Elizabeth Wilson, Margaret Sophie Stein, Jon (John) DeVries, James Rebhorn, Woody Watson; *D:* Joseph Sargent; *W:* Patricia MacLachlan; *C:* Mike Fash; *M:* David Shire. **TV**

Sarah, Plain and Tall: Winter's End 🦴🦴🦴 *Winter's End* **1999 (G)** The third installation of the "Sarah" saga is set in 1918. A harsh winter is making life difficult for Sarah (Close), Jacob (Walken), and their three children. Then their lives take a strange turn when Jacob's father, John Witting (Palance), who abandoned his family when Jacob was a boy, suddenly shows up on their farm. A devastating storm proves just as paralyzing as the unresolved feelings between Jacob and John, but Sarah is determined to do what's best for her family. **99m/C VHS, DVD.** Glenn Close, Christopher Walken, Jack Palance, Lexi (Faith) Randall, Christopher Bell, Emily Osment; *D:* Glenn Jordan; *C:* Ralf Bode; *M:* David Shire. **TV**

Sarah Silverman: Jesus Is Magic 🦴🦴 ½ **2005** Stand-up show performed by delightfully potty-mouthed comedian Silverman at North Hollywood's El Portal Theater, with a couple of offstage skits thrown in. Her routine is an equal opportunity offender of race, religion, sex, and current events as Silverman hypes her Jewish American Princess attractiveness and her nice-girl-gone-naughty persona. Best left to her fans. **72m/C DVD.** *US* Sarah Silverman; *D:* Liam Lynch; *C:* Rhet Baer; *M:* Sarah Silverman, Liam Lynch.

Sarah's Child 🦴🦴 ½ **1996 (PG-13)** Sarah LaMere is devastated to learn that she can never have children. While husband Michael tries to accept, Sarah's upbringing has led her to believe that's her only purpose in life and she becomes increasingly unbalanced. Seemingly out of nowhere children's clothes and toys appear in their home and soon a strange young girl named Melissa appears, whom Sarah treats as her own child. When their landlady dies horribly after questioning Melissa, Michael is afraid the line between reality and fantasy has been breached but just how can he fight? **90m/C VHS, DVD.** Mary Parker Williams, Michael Berger, Ruth Hale, Bryce Chamberlain; *D:* Ron Beckstrom; *W:* Muffy Mead Thomas; *C:* Gregg Stouffer; *M:* Jim Ball, Glenn Workman.

Saratoga 🦴🦴 ½ **1937** Gable plays a bookie and Harlow the daughter of an impoverished horse breeder in this romantic comedy centered around the race tracks. This was the final film appearance for Harlow, who died before the film's completion. Mary Dees was chosen as her stand-in and had to finish many of the scenes. "Saratoga" was released just a month after Harlow's death and became one of the biggest moneymakers of the year. **94m/B VHS.** Jean Harlow, Clark Gable, Lionel Barrymore, Walter Pidgeon, Frank Morgan, Una Merkel, Cliff Edwards, George Zucco, Hattie McDaniel, Jonathan Hale; *D:* Jack Conway; *W:* Anita Loos, Robert Hopkins.

Saratoga Trunk 🦴🦴 ½ **1945** Lavish, if slow-moving, version of Edna Ferber's romance novel reteams Cooper and Bergman (who starred in "For Whom the Bell Tolls"). It's 1875 New Orleans and bitter Clio, the half-Creole illegitimate daughter of a local, is determined to marry rich. But first, she gets involved with Texas gambler Clint Maroon (Cooper). He's in a business deal with wealthy Van Steed (Warburton), about the Saratoga railroad line, and Clio decides to go after him. Of course, she really wants Clint and they go through lots of bother before ending up together. Filmed in 1943 but release was delayed because of WWII. **135m/B VHS.** Gary Cooper, Ingrid Bergman, John Warburton, Flora Robson, Florence Bates, Jerry Austin; *D:* Sam Wood; *W:* Casey Robinson; *C:* Ernest Haller; *M:* Max Steiner.

Sardinia Kidnapped 🦴🦴 ½ **1975** A beautiful girl is trapped in a clash between two powerful families while on vacation in Sardinia, where the peasants' custom is to kidnap a member of a rival family and then exchange the victim for land. Former documentary maker Mingozzi creates a realistic and uncompromising look at culture and change. In Italian; dubbed. **95m/C VHS.** *IT* Charlotte Rampling, Franco Nero; *D:* Gianfranco Mingozzi.

Sars Wars: Bangkok Zombie Crisis 🦴🦴 ½ *Khun Krabi Pheerabad; Khun krabii hiiroh; Sars Wars* **2004** The fourth generation of the SARS virus is ravaging the world. It's mutated and now apparently turns people into ravenous zombies. Except in Thailand, until one of its researchers unleashes it while trying to find a cure. Immediately quarantined, the military surrounds it and prepares to invade while a bizarre kidnapping plot ensues inside. Crosses every niche genre known to man (including animation), sometimes seemingly at random. **95m/C DVD.** *TH*

Sartana's Here... Trade Your Pistol for a Coffin 🦴 **1970** A soldier of fortune searches for a missing shipment of gold in the Old West. **92m/C VHS, DVD.** *IT* George Hilton, Charles Southwood, Erika Blanc, Linda Sini; *D:* Giuliano Carnimeo; *W:* Tito Carpi; *C:* Stelvio Massi; *M:* Francesco De Masi.

S.A.S. San Salvador 🦴 **1984** A CIA agent tries to prevent a psychotic from running amok in El Salvador. **95m/C VHS.** *FR GE* Raimund Harmstorf, Anton Diffring, Sybil Danning, Miles O'Keeffe, Dagmar Lassander, Catherine Jarrett; *D:* Raoul Coutard; *W:* Gerard de Villiers; *C:* Georges Liron; *M:* Michel Magne.

Sasquatch **WOOF!** **1976** Purported "documentary" about the mythical creature Bigfoot. Includes pictures of the "actual" monster. For those real stupid moods. **94m/C VHS, DVD.** George Lauris; *D:* Ed Ragozzini.

Sasquatch 🦴🦴 ½ *The Untold* **2002 (R)** Mogul Harlan Knowles (Henriksen) runs a bio-tech company and is frantic when one of the company's planes crashes in the forests of the Pacific Northwest. Not only is his daughter (Parker) aboard but so is the very expensive prototype of a DNA testing machine. So Knowles assembles a rescue team and heads into the woods—only to discover the plane's crew torn to shreds. **86m/C VHS, DVD.** *CA* Lance Henriksen, Andrea Roth, Philip Granger, Russell Ferrier, Jeremy Radick, Erica Durance; *D:* Jonas Quastel; *W:* Jonas Quastel, Chris Lanning; *C:* Shaun Lawless; *M:* Tal Bergman, Larry Seymour. **VIDEO**

The Sasquatch Gang 🦴 *The Sasquatch Dumpling Gang* **2006** Three mild-mannered loser buddies (Sumpter, Palmer, Pinkston) upset their stoner neighbor Zerk (Long) with their sword-and-fantasy fights. So he decides to play a trick by having the trio stumble over a faked Bigfoot site in the woods. Clumsy comedy. **86m/C DVD.** Jeremy Sumpter, Justin Long, Rob Pinkston, Joey Kern, Hubbel Palmer, Addie Land, Carl Weathers, Jon(athan) Gries, Stephen Tobolowsky, Michael Mitchell; *D:* Tim Skousen; *W:* Tim Skousen; *C:* Munn Powell; *M:* John Swihart. **VIDEO**

Satan in High Heels 🦴 ½ **1961** Sordid show-biz tale of a carnival dancer (Myles) who dreams of making it big on Broadway. First she finagles her way into a position as a nightclub singer and the mistress of a convenient millionaire. But she loses it all for love when she falls for the millionaire's misbehaving son. Flamboyant performance by Hall as the lesbian nightclub owner. **90m/B VHS, DVD.** Meg Myles, Grayson Hall, Del Tenney, Mike Keene, Robert Yuro, Sabrina, Earl Hammond, Paul Scott; *D:* Jerald Intrator; *W:* John T. Chapman; *C:* Bernard Herschensen; *M:* Mundell Lowe.

The Satan Killer 🦴 ½ **1993** A vicious serial killer is targeted by two tough police detectives. What makes it personal is Detective Stephen's fiance is one of the killer's victims and he's not going to let justice stand in the way of his revenge. **90m/C VHS.** Steve Sayre, Billy Franklin, James Westbrook, Belinda Creason, Cindy Healy; *D:* Stephen Calamari.

Satan Met a Lady 🦴🦴 ½ **1936** A weak adaptation of Dashiell Hammett's "Maltese Falcon." This version has Davis employing a private detective to track down a mysterious woman. The hunted woman is herself searching for a valuable collectible. **74m/B VHS.** Bette Davis, Warren William, Alison Skipworth, Arthur Treacher, Marie Wilson, Porter Hall, Olin Howlin; *D:* William Dieterle.

The Satanic Rites of Dracula 🦴🦴 *Count Dracula and His Vampire Bride; Dracula Is Dead and Well and Living in London* **1973** Count Dracula is the leader of a satanic cult of prominent scientists and politicians who develop a gruesome plague virus capable of destroying the human race. Preceded by "Dracula A.D. 1972" and followed by "The 7 Brothers Meet Dracula." **88m/C VHS, DVD.** *GB* Christopher Lee, Peter Cushing, Michael Coles, William Franklyn, Freddie Jones, Joanna Lumley, Richard Vernon, Patrick Barr, Barbara Yu Ling; *D:* Alan Gibson; *W:* Don Houghton; *C:* Brian Probyn; *M:* John Cacavas.

Satanik 🦴 **1969 (R)** A hideous old hag is turned into a lovely young woman by a stolen potion, but it doesn't last long and she becomes a monster. **85m/C VHS, DVD.** *IT SP* Magda Konopka, Julio Pena, Luigi Montini, Armando Calvo, Umberto Raho; *D:* Piero Vivarelli.

Satan's Black Wedding 🦴 **1975 (R)** The ghouls arrive at a Monterey monastery in their Sunday best to celebrate devildom's most diabolical ritual, the "Black Wedding." **61m/C VHS, DVD.** Greg Braddock, Ray Miles, Lisa Milano; *D:* Steve Millard; *W:* Steve Millard.

Satan's Blood 🦴 *Escalofrio* **1977** Uncut version of the Spanish horror flick that was condemned upon its release for its sex and sadism (and nudity). A young married couple, visiting friends at their isolated country home, are influenced by occult forces to participate in Satanic rituals. Spanish with subtitles. **82m/C DVD.** *SP* Angel Aranda, Sandra Alberti, Mariana Karr, Jose Maria Guillen; *D:* Carlos Puerto; *W:* Eva Del Castillo; *C:* Andres Berenguer; *M:* Librado Pastor.

Satan's Brew 🦴🦴 *Satansbraten* **1976** Aspiring poet (Raab) murders his mistress and assumes the identity of 19th-century symbolist poet Stefan George, including his idol's homosexual tastes. Fassbinder at his most excessive. German with subtitles. **100m/C VHS, DVD.** *GE* Kurt Raab, Margit Carstensen, Volker Spengler, Ingrid Caven, Helen Vita; *D:* Rainer Werner Fassbinder; *W:* Rainer Werner Fassbinder; *C:* Michael Ballhaus; *M:* Peer Raben.

Satan's Cheerleaders WOOF! **1977 (R)** A demonic high school janitor traps a bevy of buxom cheerleaders at his Satanic altar for sacrificial purposes. The gals use all of their endowments to escape the clutches of the evil sheriff and his fat wife. Is it ever campy! **92m/C VHS, DVD.** John Carradine, John Ireland, Yvonne De Carlo, Kerry Sherman, Jacqulin Cole, Hilary Horan, Alisa Powell, Sherry Marks, Jack Kruschen, Sydney Chaplin; ***D:*** Greydon Clark; ***W:*** Greydon Clark, Alvin L. Fast; ***C:*** Dean Cundey; ***M:*** Gerald Lee.

Satan's Harvest ♪ 1/2 **1965** American detective inherits estate in Johannesburg, only to find the place is being used by drug smugglers. Sidesteps the political climate and shows the beauty of the land. And a good thing: the story is virtually nonexistent. **88m/C VHS.** George Montgomery, Tippi Hedren; ***D:*** Ferde Grofe Jr.

Satan's Little Helper ♪ **2004 (R)** On Halloween, naive Doug befriends a masked serial killer, not realizing that the carnage they leave behind is real, and takes him home to meet his family. His mom (Plummer) and sister (Winnick) must then save the family from the maniac. Terrible genre spoof is cheap, distasteful, and pointless. **99m/C DVD.** Amanda Plummer, Alexander Brickel, Stephen Graham, Dan Ziskie, Katheryn Winnick, Joshua Annex; ***D:*** Jeff Lieberman; ***W:*** Jeff Lieberman; ***C:*** Dejan Georgevich; ***M:*** David Horowitz. **VIDEO**

Satan's Princess ♪ **1990** Satanic cult with a female leader runs amuck. Sloppy and forgettable. **90m/C VHS.** Robert Forster, Caren Kaye, Lydie Denier, Phillip Glasser, Michael (M.K.) Harris, Ellen Geer, Jack Carter; ***D:*** Bert I. Gordon; ***W:*** Stephen Katz.

Satan's Sadists ♪ **1969 (R)** Tamblyn and his biker gang terrorize folks in the Southern California desert, including a retired cop, a Vietnam vet and a trio of vacationing coeds. Violent film will probably be best appreciated by Adamson completists. **88m/C VHS, DVD.** Russ Tamblyn, Regina Carrol, Gary Kent, Jackie Taylor, John Cardos, Kent Taylor, Robert Dix, Scott Brady, Evelyn Frank, Greydon Clark, Bill Bonner, Bobby Clark, Yvonne Stewart, Cheryl Anne, Randee Lynn, Bambi Allen, Breck Warwick; ***D:*** Al Adamson; ***W:*** Dennis Wayne; ***C:*** Gary Graver; ***M:*** Harley Hatcher.

Satan's School for Girls ♪ 1/2 **1973** When a young woman investigates the circumstances that caused her sister's suicide, it leads her to a satanic girl's academy. Dumb and puerile made for TV "horror." **74m/C VHS, DVD.** Pamela Franklin, Roy Thinnes, Kate Jackson, Lloyd Bochner, Jamie Smith-Jackson, Jo Van Fleet, Cheryl Ladd, Gwynne Gilford, Bing (Neil) Russell; ***D:*** David Lowell Rich; ***W:*** Arthur Ross; ***M:*** Laurence Rosenthal. **TV**

Satan's Touch WOOF! **1984 (R)** A simpleton worships the Devil and gets burned for his trouble. **86m/C VHS.** Paul Davies, James Lawless, Shirley Venard; ***D:*** John Goodell; ***W:*** John Goodell.

Satanwar WOOF! **1979** A fictional look at various forms of Satan worship. **95m/C VHS.** Bart LaRue, Sally Schermerhorn, Jimmy Drankovitch; ***D:*** Bart La Rue; ***W:*** Bart La Rue; ***C:*** Laura Andrus; ***M:*** William Eucker.

Satin Rouge ♪♪ 1/2 **2002** Lilia (Abbass) is a very proper widowed seamstress who lives with her in-laws and rebellious teenaged daughter Salma (El Fahem). Salma is taking belly-dancing classes and Lilia suspects the girl is flirting with musician Chokri (Kamoun), so she follows him to a club and is seduced by the exuberance of the dancers. One, Folla (Hichri), invites Lilia in and soon she is leading a double-life—grieving widow by day and costumer and part-time dancer by night. Arabic with subtitles. **95m/C VHS, DVD.** *FR* Hiam Abbass, Hend El Fahem, Maher Kamoun, Monia Hichri; ***D:*** Raja Amari; ***W:*** Raja Amari; ***C:*** Diane Baratier; ***M:*** Nawfel El Manaa.

Satisfaction ♪ **1988 (PG-13)** An all-girl, high school rock band play out the summer before college. The Keatons should have sent Bateman to her room for this stunt. **93m/C VHS, DVD.** Justine Bateman, Trini Alvarado, Britta Phillips, Julia Roberts, Scott Coffey, Liam Neeson, Deborah Harry; ***D:*** Joan Freeman; ***W:*** Charles Purpura; ***M:*** Michel Colombier.

Saturday Night and Sunday Morning ♪♪♪ 1/2 **1960** This "kitchen sink" drama finds the 23-year-old Finney in star form as working-class Arthur Seaton, who's devoted to good times, spending his weekends with boozing, brawling, and willing women. He's having an affair with the older, married Brenda (Roberts) and pursuing the strictly moral Doreen (Field), who refuses to sleep with him without a commitment. Arthur thinks he's falling in love and is (eventually) ready for marriage but not without complications and not before warning Doreen that he's unlikely to completely change his carefree ways. Reisz's first feature film; Sillitoe adapted from his novel. Finney was voted the most promising newcomer at the British Academy's (BAFTA) awards. **98m/B VHS, DVD.** *GB* Albert Finney, Rachel Roberts, Shirley Anne Field, Bryan Pringle, Norman Rossington, Hylda Baker, Robert Cowdra, Elsie Wagstaff, Frank Pettitt; ***D:*** Karel Reisz; ***W:*** Alan Sillitoe; ***C:*** Freddie Francis; ***M:*** John Dankworth. British Acad. '60: Actress (Roberts), Film; Natl. Bd. of Review '61: Actor (Finney).

Saturday Night at the Baths ♪♪ **1975** A no-budget production that's a time capsule for post-Stonewall and pre-AIDS gay life. Desperately needing work, straight Michael gets a job playing piano at NYC's Continental Baths (the kind of place where Bette Midler sang and drag queens and disco boys performed). He complains to girlfriend Tracy that the manager keeps propositioning him, but then Michael stops complaining. Beware the edited version. **86m/C DVD.** Robert Aberdeen, Don Scotti, Ellen Sheppard, Steve Ostrow; ***D:*** David Buckley; ***W:*** David Buckley, Franklin Khedouri; ***C:*** Ralf Bode.

Saturday Night Fever ♪♪ 1/2 **1977 (R)** Brooklyn teenager (Travolta), bored with his daytime job, becomes the nighttime king of the local disco. Based on a story published in "New York Magazine" by Nik Cohn. Acclaimed for its disco dance sequences, memorable soundtrack by the Bee Gees, and carefree yet bleak script; extremely dated, although it made its mark on society in its time. Followed by the sequel "Staying Alive." Also available in a 112-minute "PG" rated version. ♫ Staying Alive; Night Fever; More Than a Woman; How Deep Is Your Love?. **118m/C VHS, DVD.** John Travolta, Karen (Lynn) Gorney, Barry Miller, Donna Pescow, Joseph Cali, Bruce Ornstein, Paul Pape, Fran Drescher; ***D:*** John Badham; ***W:*** Norman Wexler; ***C:*** Ralf Bode; ***M:*** David Shire. Natl. Bd. of Review '77: Actor (Travolta).

Saturday Night Special ♪ 1/2 **1992 (R)** Country singer/songwriter Travis (played by Nashville stalwart Burnette) gets a job fronting the house band of Tennessee tavern owner T.J. (Dean). Travis also takes up with ambitious Darlene (Ford), who happens to be T.J.'s wife. But it's Darlene who has the brains in this unpleasant trio, she decides to get rid of hubby and sets Travis up to take the fall. It's all been done before (and better). **75m/C VHS, DVD.** Billy Burnette, Maria Ford, Rick Dean; ***D:*** Dan Golden; ***W:*** Jonathan Banks; ***M:*** Billy Burnette, Nicholas Rivera.

Saturday the 14th ♪ 1/2 **1981 (PG)** A parody of the popular axe-wielding-maniac genre, about a family inheriting a haunted mansion. Poorly made; not funny or scary. Followed by even worse sequel: "Saturday the 14th Strikes Back." **91m/C VHS, DVD.** Richard Benjamin, Paula Prentiss, Severn Darden, Jeffrey Tambor, Kari Michaelsen, Kevin Brando, Rosemary DeCamp, Stacy Keach; ***D:*** Howard R. Cohen; ***W:*** Howard R. Cohen, Jeff Begun; ***C:*** Daniel Lacambre; ***M:*** Parmer Fuller.

Saturday the 14th Strikes Back ♪ **1988** Continuing the name, but not the story line, cast, or characters of the original, this one concerns the invasion of a birthday party by a vampire (Stonebrook) and her monstrous friends. The monsters decide that the birthday boy (Presson) should be their new leader. Pretty lame, even by the original's standards. **91m/C VHS, DVD.** Ray Walston, Avery Schreiber, Patty McCormack, Julianne McNamara, Rhonda Aldrich, Daniel Will-Harris, Joseph Ruskin, Pamela Stonebrook, Phil Leeds, Jason Presson, Michael Berryman, Victoria Morsell; ***D:*** Howard R. Cohen; ***W:*** Howard R. Cohen; ***C:*** Levie Isaacks; ***M:*** Parmer Fuller.

Saturn in Opposition ♪♪ 1/2 *Saturno Contro* **2007** The title is an astrological term referring to upheaval and change, which is what happens to a group of 30-somethings in this ensemble drama. Davide and his partner Lorenzo have a wonderful life with devoted friends. Then Lorenzo is rushed to the hospital, where he dies; while Davide struggles to cope, his friends' lives fall apart as well. Italian with subtitles. **110m/C DVD.** *IT TU* Pierfrancesco Favino, Stefano Accorsi, Margherita Buy, Serra Yilmaz, Ennio Fantastichini, Luigi Diberti, Isabella Ferrari, Luca Argentero, Ambra Angiolini, Michelangelo Tommaso, Filippo Timi, Lunetta Savino; ***D:*** Ferzan Ozpetek; ***W:*** Ferzan Ozpetek; ***C:*** Gianfilippo Corticelli; ***M:*** Giovanni Pellini.

Saturn 3 ♪ 1/2 **1980 (R)** Two research scientists create a futuristic Garden of Eden in an isolated sector of our solar system, but love story turns to horror story when a killer robot arrives. Sporadically promising, but ultimately lame; dumb ending. For Farrah fans only. **88m/C VHS, DVD.** *GB* Farrah Fawcett, Kirk Douglas, Harvey Keitel, Ed Bishop; ***D:*** Stanley Donen; ***W:*** Martin Amis; ***C:*** Billy Williams; ***M:*** Elmer Bernstein.

Saul and David ♪♪ 1/2 *Saul e David* **1964** Beautifully filmed story of David's life with King Saul, the battle with Goliath, and the tragic end of Saul. From the "Bible" series. **120m/C VHS, DVD.** Norman Wooland, Gianni "John" Garko, Elisa Cegani, Virgilio Teixeira; ***D:*** Marcello Baldi; ***W:*** Tonino Guerra; ***C:*** Juan Ruiz Romero, Marcello Masciocchi; ***M:*** Teo Usuelli.

Sauna ♪ **2008** Disjointed and dull horror from Finland. In 1595, Finland is divided between warring Russia and Sweden. Siblings Eerik (Vertanen) and Knut (Eronen) are part of a group charged with mapping the new borders. Ghosts appear and the brothers discover an uncharted village although it's unclear if the villagers are actually dead. Finnish and Russian with subtitles. **83m/C DVD.** *FI* Ville Vertanen, Tommi Eronen, Viktor Klimenko, Sonja Petajajaravi, Rain Tolk, Kati Outinen, Kari Ketonen; ***D:*** Antti-Jussi Annila; ***W:*** Iiro Kuttner; ***C:*** Henri Blomberg; ***M:*** Panu Aaltio.

Savage! WOOF! *Black Valor* **1973 (R)** A savage foreign mess with ex-baseball star Iglehart killing people with grenades and guns, abetted by an army full of murderous models. **81m/C VHS.** *MX* James Iglehart, Lada Edmund, Carol Speed, Rossana Ortiz, Sally Jordan, Aura Aurea, Vic Diaz; ***D:*** Cirio H. Santiago.

The Savage ♪♪ *Le Sauvage* **1975** Unlikely adventure-comedy starring Deneuve and Montand. In Caracas, Nelly runs away from her would-be fiance Vittorio (Vannucchi), taking a valuable painting with her. She's unexpectedly aided by Vincent, who's fled his own marital and business woes by retreating to a small island. Nelly flirts with Vincent so he'll help her sell the painting. But first the duo have to deal with Vincent's enraged wife (Wynter), who has finally tracked him down, as well as Vittorio and his goons. English and French with subtitles. **110m/C DVD.** *FR* Catherine Deneuve, Yves Montand, Luigi Vannucchi, Dana Wynter, Tony Roberts, Vernon Dobtcheff, Bobo Lewis; ***D:*** Jean-Paul Rappeneau; ***W:*** Jean-Paul Rappeneau, Elisabeth Rappeneau, Jean-Loup Dabadie; ***C:*** Pierre Lhomme; ***M:*** Michel Legrand.

Savage ♪♪ **1996 (R)** Mad scientist discovers the gateway to a future world, which unleashes a powerful guardian known known as the Savage (Gruner). The Savage must prevent the doorway between the worlds from exploding and causing an apocalypse, even as he hunts his nemesis. **103m/C VHS.** Olivier Gruner, Kario Salem, Jennifer Grant, Sam McMurray, Kristin Minter; ***D:*** Avi Nesher; ***W:*** Patrick Highsmith, Peter Sagal; ***C:*** Peter Fernberger; ***M:*** Roger Neill.

Savage Abduction ♪ **1973 (R)** Two girls visiting Los Angeles are kidnapped by a bizarre man. **84m/C VHS, DVD.** Tom Drake, Stephen Oliver, Sean Kenney; ***D:*** John Lawrence.

Savage Attraction ♪ 1/2 *Hostage: The Christine Maresch Story; Hostage* **1983 (R)** True story of a 16-year-old girl forced to marry an ex-Nazi, and her hellish life thereafter. Frustrating because it could have been much better. **93m/C VHS, UMD.** *AU GE* Kerry Mack, Ralph Schicha; ***D:*** Frank Shields.

Savage Beach ♪ **1989 (R)** A pair of well-endowed female federal agents battle assorted buccaneers on a remote Pacific isle over a rediscovered cache of gold from WWII. Exploitative, pornographic, and degrading to watch. Sequel to "Picasso Trigger." **90m/C VHS, DVD.** Dona Speir, Hope Marie Carlton, Bruce Penhall, Rodrigo Obregon, John Aprea, Teri Weigel, Lisa London; ***D:*** Andy Sidaris.

The Savage Bees ♪♪ **1976** A South American ship harbored at New Orleans during Mardi Gras unleashes killer bees into the celebratory crowds. Not bad, relatively exciting, TV thriller. **90m/C VHS.** Ben Johnson, Michael Parks, Paul Hecht, Horst Buchholz, Gretchen Corbett, Bruce French, James Best; ***D:*** Bruce Geller; ***W:*** Guerdon (Gordon) Trueblood; ***C:*** Richard C. Glouner. **TV**

Savage Capitalism ♪♪ *Capitalismo Salvaje* **1993** Melodramatic romance between a reporter and a mining company exec crumbles when the exec's presumed dead wife returns. Meanwhile, the reporter uncovers the truth behind the company's plans to mine in the interior of Brazil, which could cause ecological ruin. Portuguese with subtitles. **86m/C VHS.** *BR* Fernanda Torres, Jose Mayer, Marisa Orth, Marcelo Tass; ***D:*** Andre Klotzel; ***W:*** Andre Klotzel, Djalma Batista.

Savage Dawn ♪ 1/2 **1984 (R)** In yet another desert town, yet another pair of combat-hardened vets are confronted by yet another vicious motorcycle gang. Haven't we seen this one before? **102m/C VHS.** George Kennedy, Karen Black, Richard Lynch, Lance Henriksen, William Forsythe; ***D:*** Simon Nuchtern.

Savage Drums ♪ 1/2 **1951** Sabu returns to his South Seas island to help end tribal warfare there. Dated and dumb, but fun-to-watch melodrama/action. **70m/B VHS.** Sabu, Lita Baron, H.B. Warner, Sid Melton, Steven Geray, Margia Dean, Hugh Beaumont; ***D:*** William Berke; ***W:*** Fenton Earnshaw; ***C:*** Jack Greenhalgh; ***M:*** Darrell Calker.

Savage Fury ♪ *The Call of the Savage* **1935** Feature-length version of the popular movie serial. **80m/B VHS.** Harry Woods, Bryant Washburn, Fred MacKaye, Noah Beery Jr., Dorothy Short; ***D:*** Lew Landers; ***C:*** Richard Fryer, William Sickner.

The Savage Girl ♪ **1932** A hunter journeys through the darkest jungle in search of prey. Instead, he stumbles across a beautiful white jungle girl, falls in love with her and attempts to take her back with him. **64m/B VHS, DVD.** Rochelle Hudson, Walter Byron, Harry C. (Henry) Myers, Ted Adams, Adolph Milar, Floyd Schackleford; ***D:*** Harry Fraser.

Savage Grace ♪ 1/2 **2007** Based on the sordid true crime story of the heirs to the Bakelite plastics fortune. Insecure Brooks Baekeland (Dillane) is soon indifferent to his wife Barbara (Moore), a poseur who craves acceptance within their jet-set society. Pathologically needy for love, Barbara smothers only son Tony (Redmayne) to the point of being incestuous, which exacerbates his mental instability until he murders mommy dearest. Although it covers decades (from the mid-1940s to the early 1970s), Moore never ages, which is just one of the conundrums. **96m/C DVD.** *US FR SP* Julianne Moore, Stephen (Dillon) Dillane, Eddie Redmayne, Hugh Dancy, Elena Anaya; ***D:*** Tom Kalin; ***W:*** Howard A. Rodman; ***C:*** Juanmi Azpiroz; ***M:*** Fernando Velazquez.

Savage Harvest 2: October Blood ♪ 1/2 **2006** Sequel that was 13 years in the making follows low-budget horror film director Tyge Murdock (Gaa) as he returns home to reassess his life after an actor is accidentally killed on one of his sets. But home is where the nightmares are. Reuniting with his high school flame (Haack) brings back remnants of a mass murder that took place ten years earlier and the old gang quickly finds themselves trapped in a demonic gore-spattered nightmare. Script is decent enough but the cast doesn't have the chops to pull it off, Haack being the exception as the deadly-intense Ashley Lomack. **119m/C DVD.** Benjamin Gaa, Emily Haack, Eric

Stanze, David Propst, Jonathan Baker; *D:* Jason Christ; *W:* Jason Christ; *C:* Jason Christ; *M:* Shawn Donoho. **VIDEO**

Savage Hearts ♪ 1/2 **1995** Terminally ill mob hitwoman Beatrice Baxter (D'Abo) has six months left to live and she wants her last days to be spent in style. So she steals $2 million from her mob employer Roger Focely (Harris)—who's determined to get the money back. **90m/C VHS.** Maryam D'Abo, Richard Harris, Myriam Cyr, Jerry Hall; *D:* Mark Ezra.

Savage Hunger ♪ **1984** Ten plane crash survivors struggle to survive in the Baja desert. **90m/C VHS.** Chris Makepeace, Scott Hylands, Anne Lockhart; *D:* Sparky Green.

Savage Instinct ♪♪ *They Call Me Macho Woman* **1989** A woman stumbles across a drug ring and becomes a target when they fear she could expose them. Only Mongo and his crew are even more surprised when she decides to fight back. **95m/C VHS.** Debra Sweaney, Brian Oldfield; *D:* Patrick G. Donahue; *W:* Patrick G. Donahue; *C:* Mike Pierce; *M:* Emilio Kauderer.

Savage Intruder ♪ **1968 (R)** A wandering opportunist worms his way into the heart and home of a rich ex-movie star. She soon discovers that he's a sexual deviant who mutilates and murders for fun. Twisted doings with Hopkins in her final role. **90m/C VHS.** John David Garfield, Miriam Hopkins, Gale Sondergaard, Florence Lake, Joe Besser, Minta Durfee; *D:* Donald Wolfe.

Savage Is Loose **WOOF!** **1974 (R)** Drivel about a scientist, his wife, and their son stranded on a deserted island for 20 years. Not surprisingly, as junior matures he realizes there isn't a woman for him—or is there? Completely lacking in redeeming qualities. Absurd pseudo-Freudian claptrap produced by Scott. **114m/C VHS.** George C. Scott, Trish Van Devere, John David Carson, Lee Montgomery; *D:* George C. Scott.

Savage Island ♪ 1/2 **1985 (R)** Women's prison in the tropics sets the scene for the usual exploitative goings-on. Blair is actually in the film only for a few minutes. Chopped-up, even worse version of "Escape From Hell." **74m/C VHS, DVD.** *SP IT* Nicholas Beardsley, Linda Blair, Anthony Steffen, Ajita Wilson, Christina Lai, Leon Askin; *D:* Edward (Edoardo Mulargia) Muller; *W:* Nicholas Beardsley. Golden Raspberries '85: Worst Actress (Blair).

Savage Island ♪ 1/2 **2003** Wanting to escape their troubled marriage, Steven and Julie seek refuge with their baby at her parents' remote island home. The serenity is squelched when they're held responsible for a horrible accident that claims the life of one of the island's other inhabitants—the rural Savage family—who will stop at nothing to avenge their loss. **90m/C VHS, DVD.** Winston Rekert, Brendan Beiser, Gregg Scott, Don S. Davis, Steven Man, Kristina Copeland, Beverley Breuer, Zoran Vukelic, Nahanni Arntzen; *D:* Jeffrey Scott Lando; *W:* Kevin Mosley; *C:* Geoff Rogers; *M:* Chris Nickel. **VIDEO**

Savage Journey ♪ 1/2 **1983 (PG)** A wagon train of pioneers has difficulty on its westward journey. Simple story with no real appeal. **99m/C VHS, DVD.** Richard Moll, Maurice Grandmaison, Faith Clift; *D:* Tom McGowan.

Savage Justice ♪ **1988** A young woman seeks revenge against leftist rebels (boo, hiss) in a Southeast Asian country who killed her parents and raped her. She hooks up with an ex-Green Beret, and they fight and love their way through the jungle. The usual nudity and violence; derivative and dumb. **90m/C DVD.** Julia Montgomery, Steven Memel, Ken Metcalfe; *D:* Joey Romero.

Savage Land ♪♪ 1/2 **1994 (PG)** Family western finds a young brother and sister travelling by stage to meet up with their father. The stage is robbed by some bumbling bad guys, who then pursue the kids and two other passengers across the frontier. The kids, of course, are smarter than most of the adults, and manage to get the best of the bad hombres. **91m/C VHS, DVD.** Graham Greene, Corbin Bernsen, Vivian Schilling, Mercedes McNab, Corey Carrier, Brion James, Bo Svenson, Charlotte Ross; *D:* Dean Hamilton; *W:* Dean Hamilton; *C:* Roland Smith; *M:* Michael Conway Baker.

Savage Messiah ♪♪♪ **1972 (R)** Bio of young French sculptor Henri Gaudier and his intense, though platonic, affair with a refined Polish woman 20 years his senior. Stylized drama is spared most of director Russell's noted excesses but he manages to believably show their magnetic attraction. Gaudier was killed in WWI at the age of 24. Based on the biography by H.S. Ede. **96m/C VHS.** *GB* Scott Antony, Dorothy Tutin, Helen Mirren, Lindsay Kemp, Peter Vaughan, Michael Gough; *D:* Ken Russell; *W:* Christopher Logue; *C:* Dick Bush.

Savage Messiah ♪♪ *Moise: L'Affaire Roch Theriault* **2002 (R)** Canadian social worker Paula Jackson (Walker) discovers that charismatic Roch Theriault (Picard), who calls himself Moses, maintains a backwoods commune/religious cult consisting of several women who think of themselves as his wives. When Paula tries to intercede on behalf of their children, she finds the women would rather give their kids up to social services than leave their leader despite their abuse at his hands. Based on a true story, which took place in Quebec. English and French with subtitles. **96m/C VHS, DVD.** *CA* Polly Walker, Luc Picard, Isabelle Blais, Isabelle Cyr, Pascale Montpetit, Domini Blythe, Julie La Rochelle, Elizabeth Robertson; *D:* Mario Azzopardi; *W:* Sharon Riis; *C:* Serge Ladouceur; *M:* Frank Ilfman. Genie '02: Actor, Adapt. Score, Support. Actress (Montpetit).

Savage Run ♪♪♪ *Run, Simon, Run* **1970** Reynolds is a Papago Indian framed and imprisoned for his brother's murder. Sprung from the pen, he heads back to the reservation to find the real killers and to avenge his brother's death. Convincing drama. Stevens's last role before her suicide. **73m/C VHS, DVD.** Burt Reynolds, Inger Stevens, James Best, Rodolfo Acosta, Don Dubbins, Joyce Jameson, Barney (Bernard) Phillips, Eddie Little Sky; *D:* George McCowan. **TV**

Savage Sam ♪♪ **1963** Intended as a sequel to "Old Yeller." Sam, the offspring of the heroic dog named Old Yeller, tracks down some children kidnapped by Indians. Fun, but not fully successful. **103m/C VHS, DVD.** Tommy Kirk, Kevin Corcoran, Brian Keith, Dewey Martin, Jeff York, Marta Kristen; *D:* Norman Tokar; *C:* Edward Colman.

The Savage Seven ♪♪ **1968** An underground classic where everyone loses. A motorcycle gang rides into an Indian town which is at the mercy of corrupt businessmen. The gang's leader becomes involved in the Indians' problems but the businessmen and the cops cause trouble for all concerned. Less than memorable. Produced by Dick Clark. **96m/C VHS.** Larry Bishop, Joanna Frank, Adam Roarke, Robert Walker Jr.; *D:* Richard Rush.

Savage Streets ♪ 1/2 **1983 (R)** Blair seeks commando-style revenge on the street gang that raped her deaf sister. Extended rape scene betrays the exploitative intentions, though other bits are entertaining, in a trashy kind of way. **93m/C VHS, DVD.** Linda Blair, John Vernon, Sal Landi, Robert Dryer, Debra Blee, Linnea Quigley; *D:* Danny Steinmann; *M:* John D'Andrea. Golden Raspberries '85: Worst Actress (Blair).

Savage Weekend **WOOF!** *The Killer Behind the Mask; The Upstate Murders* **1980 (R)** A killer behind a ghoulish mask stalks human prey in the boonies, of course. Astoundingly, there is one interesting role—William Sanderson's looney. Otherwise, throw this one no bones. **88m/C VHS, DVD.** Christopher Allport, James Doerr, Marilyn Hamlin, Caitlin (Kathleen Heaney) O'Heaney, David Gale, William Sanderson; *D:* David Paulsen, John Mason Kirby; *W:* David Paulsen.

Savage Wilderness ♪♪ 1/2 *The Last Frontier* **1955** When a trio of fur trappers lose a year's worth of skins to a band of marauding Indians, they decide to take scouting jobs at a cavalry outpost. But they find the new commander (Preston) hasn't gotten his nickname as the "Butcher of Shiloh" without reason. Adapted from the novel "The Gilded Rooster" by Richard Emery Roberts. **98m/C VHS, DVD.** Victor Mature, Robert Preston, Guy Madison, James Whitmore, Anne Bancroft, Russell Collins, Peter Whitney, Pat Hogan, Manuel Donde, Guy Williams; *D:* Anthony Mann; *W:* Philip Yordan, Russell S. Hughes; *M:* Leigh Harline.

The Savage Woman ♪♪ **1991** Marianna escapes from a desperate situation and is found unconscious in the woods by Elysee. He nurses her back to health, learns her terrible secret, and tries to help Marianna decide whether to turn herself into the police or keep running. In French with English subtitles. **100m/C VHS.** *CA* Patricia Tulasne, Matthias Habich; *D:* Lea Pool.

Savages ♪♪ **1972** A group of savages descend on a palatial mansion, and after living there for some time, become refined ladies and gentlemen. The moral savages and "civilized" men are really the same. **106m/C VHS, DVD.** Lewis J. Stadlen, Anne Francine, Thayer David, Salome Jens, Susan Blakely, Kathleen Widdoes, Sam Waterston; *D:* James Ivory; *C:* Walter Lassally.

Savages ♪♪ 1/2 **1975** Griffith as a demented nut-case stalking another man in the desert? That's right, Opie. "The Most Dangerous Game" remade-sort of-for TV. **74m/C VHS, DVD.** Andy Griffith, Sam Bottoms, Noah Beery Jr.; *D:* Lee H. Katzin.

The Savages ♪♪♪ 1/2 **2007 (R)** The Savages are a highly dysfunctional family consisting of middle-aged siblings Wendy (Linney) and Jon (Hoffman) as well as their aging father Lenny (Bosco), who still lives in his recently deceased girlfriend's condo in Sun City, Arizona. After years of estrangement, two phone calls bring to light Lenny's advancing dementia, which reunites the three as they return Lenny to Buffalo. This task is complicated by the predictable but hilarious neuroses of the self-absorbed sibs. Writer/director Tamara Jenkins has taken the pathetic inevitability of midlife and shines a light on all of the ridiculous humor that bubbles up through the cracks. A wholly worthwhile viewing experience. **113m/C DVD.** *US* Laura Linney, Philip Seymour Hoffman, Philip Bosco, Peter Friedman, Cara Seymour; *D:* Tamara Jenkins; *W:* Tamara Jenkins; *C:* W. Mott Hupfel III; *M:* Stephen Trask. Ind. Spirit '08: Actor (Hoffman), Screenplay.

Savages from Hell ♪ *Big Enough and Old Enough* **1968 (R)** Greasy biker dude beats up a young black guy because he was flirting with the biker's woman. The biker also tries to rape a migrant farmworker's daughter because he lusts after her. Trashy exploitation film. **79m/C VHS, DVD.** Bobbie Byers, Cyril Poitier, Diwaldo Myers, Viola Lloyd, William Kelley; *D:* Joseph Prieto; *W:* Joseph Prieto.

Savannah Smiles ♪♪ 1/2 **1982 (PG)** Poor little rich girl Anderson runs away from home, into the clutches of two ham-handed crooks. She melts their hearts, and they change their ways. Decent, sentimental family drama. **104m/C VHS, DVD.** Bridgette Andersen, Mark Miller, Donovan Scott, Peter Graves, Chris Robinson, Michael Parks; *D:* Pierre De Moro.

Save Me ♪♪ **1993 (R)** Jim Stevens' (Hamlin) wife has left him and his boss is involved in some dirty deals that could cost Jim his job. So things couldn't get worse, could they? Well, of course they could—and do. Because Jim meets Ellie (Anthony), a sexual adventuress just destined to bring trouble to a lonely guy. Also available in an unrated version. **89m/C VHS.** Harry Hamlin, Lysette Anthony, Michael Ironside, Olivia Hussey, Bill Nunn, Steve Railsback; *D:* Alan Roberts; *W:* Neil Ronco; *M:* Richard (Rick) Marvin.

Save Me ♪ **2007** Mark (Allen) is a self-destructive, drug-addicted, multi-suicide attempt survivor who just can't come to grips with his sexuality. So he checks into Genesis House to get sexual healing via a steady dose of Christianity and heterosexuality, a promised one-two punch with unquestioned effectiveness. But getting locked in with other sexually broken men might not be the best prescription—a better one might get to his underlying drug abuse and self-hatred issues, perhaps? Anyway, Mark meets fellow 12-stepper Scott (Gant), they dig each other, and the melodrama churns away. **96m/C DVD.** *US* Chad Allen, Robert Gant, Judith Light, Stephen Lang, Robert Baker; *D:* Robert Cary; *W:* Craig Chester, Robert Desiderio, Alan Hines; *C:* Rodney Taylor; *M:* Jeff Cardoni.

Save the Green Planet ♪♪ 1/2 *Jigureul jikyeora* **2003** Not for the faint of heart, this film seesaws wildly between comedy, suspense, and brutal violence. A meth addicted, disgruntled employee comes to believe his boss is an alien hell-bent on paving the way for an invasion, and he convinces his pudgy girlfriend to help him kidnap the evil monster to torture his secrets out of him. Or maybe he just wants an excuse to beat up his employer and live every working man's dream. **116m/C DVD.** *KN* Ha-Kyun Shin, Ju-Bong Gi, Yun-kyun Baek, Jeong-min Hwang, Jae-yong Lee, Ju-hyeon Lee; *D:* Joon-Hwan Jang; *W:* Joon-Hwan Jang; *C:* Kyung-Pyo Hing; *M:* Dong-jun Lee.

Save the Lady ♪♪ **1982** Plucky kids fight city hall to save an old ferry, the Lady Hope, from the scrap heap. Nothing offensive here—just a pleasant family flick. **76m/C VHS.** Matthew Excell, Robert Clarkson, Miranda Cartledge, Kim Clifford; *D:* Leon Thau.

Save the Last Dance ♪♪ 1/2 **2001 (PG-13)** "Fame" (or "Flashdance" or "Saturday Night Fever") meets "Romeo and Juliet" (or "West Side Story" or any trashy talk show) in this clearly not-so-original but solid teen drama. White, middle-class Sara (Stiles) adjusts to life and rediscovers her passion for dance in an all-black, inner-city Chicago high school when she must give up her dreams of attending Juilliard and move in with her down-on-his-luck father (Kinney) on the South Side. There, she befriends Chenille (Washington), who helps her get hip, and falls for her smart, ambitious brother Derek (Thomas), who helps her learn hip-hop. Stiles and Thomas turn in good performances despite somewhat stereotypical cast of characters. **112m/C VHS, DVD.** *US* Julia Stiles, Sean Patrick Thomas, Fredro Starr, Kerry Washington, Terry Kinney, Bianca Lawson, Garland Whitt, Vince Green; *D:* Thomas Carter; *W:* Duane Adler, Cheryl Edwards; *C:* Robbie Greenberg; *M:* Mark Isham.

Save the Tiger ♪♪♪ **1973 (R)** A basically honest middle-aged man sees no way out of his failing business except arson. The insurance settlement will let him pay off his creditors, and save face. David, as the arsonist, and Gilford, as Lemmon's business partner, are superb. Lemmon is also excellent throughout his performance. **100m/C VHS, DVD.** Jack Lemmon, Jack Gilford, Laurie Heineman, Patricia Smith, Norman Burton, Thayer David; *D:* John G. Avildsen; *M:* Marvin Hamlisch. Oscars '73: Actor (Lemmon); Writers Guild '73: Orig. Screenplay.

Saved! ♪♪ 1/2 **2004 (PG-13)** Uneven, subversive satire about teens at a fundamentalist Christian high school hits a lot of standard cliches and makes a plea for tolerance at the same time. Good girl Mary (Malone) finds out boyfriend Dean (Faust) is gay and has a vision of "curing" him through sex. She winds up pregnant, which puts Mary clearly on the side of the sinners as far as the school's self-righteous queen bee Hilary Faye (Moore) is concerned. Of course, the sinners seem to be having more fun. Mary's situation engages the sympathy of sweet believer Patrick (Fugit), the son of the school's zealous principal, Pastor Skip (Donovan). Moore and Malone well play the opposing force of their characters and are ably supported by the rest of the cast. **92m/C DVD.** Jena Malone, Mandy Moore, Macaulay Culkin, Patrick Fugit, Heather Matarazzo, Eva Amurri, Martin Donovan, Mary-Louise Parker, Chad Faust, Elizabeth Thai; ***Cameos:*** Valerie Bertinelli; *D:* Brian Dannelly; *W:* Brian Dannelly, Michael Urban; *C:* Bobby Bukowski; *M:* Christophe Beck.

Saved by the Light ♪♪ 1/2 **1995** On September 17, 1975, ruthless Dannion Brinkley's (Roberts) life was changed forever—he died. Struck by a bolt of lightning, Brinkley was declared dead, only to wake up 28 minutes later in the morgue. A changed man, which some of Brinkley's acquaintances find hard to believe, he becomes a public speaker, telling about his trip to heaven and his belief in love and salvation. TV movie based on Brinkley's book about his near-death experience. **95m/C VHS.** Eric Roberts, Lynette Walden, K. Callan; *D:* Lewis Teague. **TV**

Saving Face ♪♪ 1/2 **2004 (R)** Director/writer Alice Wu's debut effort adeptly explores some familiar, and not so familiar, mother/daughter themes with a Chinese-American backdrop. Ma (Chen) is disappointed that her up-and-coming surgeon daughter, Wilhelmina (Krusiec), or Wil, isn't married yet as Ma is in denial over Wil's lesbianism. Just when Wil begins a hot, new, and still-closeted romance, the 48-year-old Ma (who has lived with her parents since her husband died, as is custom) moves in after being kicked out once her pregnancy by an unnamed man is revealed, which forces the pair to confront their issues. **90m/C DVD.** *US* Michelle Krusiec, Joan Chen, Lynn Chen, Li Zhiyu, Shen Gung Lan, Jessica Hecht, Ato Essandoh; ***D:*** Alice Wu; ***W:*** Alice Wu; ***C:*** Harlan Bosmajian; ***M:*** Anton Sanko.

Saving God 1/2 **2008 (PG-13)** Ex-con Armstrong Cane (Rhames) returns to the 'hood to serve as a minister in his father's old church. As he tries to stay on the right path, Cane counsels young dealer Norris (Murphy) to leave the thug life behind but Norris' boss Blaze (McDermott) isn't happy with the pastor's interference. Strong Christian themes without becoming overbearing. **101m/C DVD.** Ving Rhames, Dwain Murphy, Dean McDermott, Kate Todd, Ricardo Chavira, Genelle Williams; ***D:*** Duane Crichton; ***W:*** Michael Jackson; ***C:*** Rudolf Blahacek; ***M:*** Eric Cadesky, Nick Dyer.

Saving Grace **1986 (PG)** A tale of the fictional youngest Pope of modern times, Pope Leo XIV (Conti). Beset by duty, he decides to shed his robes and get in touch with the world's peasantry. Improbable, but that's okay; the mortal sin is that it's improbable and slow and boring. **112m/C VHS.** Tom Conti, Fernando Rey, Giancarlo Giannini, Erland Josephson, Donald Hewlett, Edward James Olmos; ***D:*** Robert M. Young; ***W:*** David S. Ward; ***M:*** William Goldstein.

Saving Grace 1/2 **2000 (R)** Widowed Blethyn finds out her late hubby has left her deeply in debt and in order to maintain her comfortable lifestyle, her gardener (Ferguson) suggests that she grow pot and sell it. Quaint comedy has the trademark quirky characters and gently bawdy humor you'd expect. Blethyn and Ferguson are fine, and it's all veddy cheerful. Low-key approach lends itself well to the small screen. **93m/C VHS, DVD.** *GB* Brenda Blethyn, Craig Ferguson, Martin Clunes, Tcheky Karyo, Jamie Foreman, Valerie Edmond, Tristan Sturrock; ***D:*** Nigel Cole; ***W:*** Craig Ferguson, Mark Crowdy; ***C:*** John de Borman.

Saving Private Ryan **1998 (R)** Big-budget WWII Spielberg epic finds eight soldiers, led by army captain Hanks, forced to go behind enemy lines in order to rescue downed paratrooper James Ryan (Damon). He's the sole surviving brother of four soldier siblings and the government wants some good PR—the men pulling the duty are less than enthusiastic, however. Pick your favorite reviewer-speak word—gripping, moving, intense, masterpiece—any or all of them will work. The opening 25-minute graphic depiction of Omaha Beach on D-Day is, on its own, Oscar-worthy. Hanks and the rest of the cast (which included a few surprise cameos) are excellent. Spielberg deglamorizes war, without belittling the sacrifices made by those who fought. The actors (except Damon) went through boot camp in England in order to get the proper attitude. **175m/C VHS, DVD.** Tom Hanks, Edward Burns, Tom Sizemore, Jeremy Davies, Giovanni Ribisi, Adam Goldberg, Barry Pepper, Vin Diesel, Matt Damon, Ted Danson, Dale Dye, Dennis Farina, Harve Presnell, Paul Giamatti, Bryan Cranston, David Wohl, Leland Orser, Joerg Stadler, Maximillian Martini, Amanda Boxer, Harrison Young; ***D:*** Steven Spielberg; ***W:*** Robert Rodat, Frank Darabont; ***C:*** Janusz Kaminski; ***M:*** John Williams. Oscars '98: Cinematog., Director (Spielberg), Film Editing, Sound, Sound FX Editing; British Acad. '98: Sound; Directors Guild '98: Director (Spielberg); Golden Globes '99: Director (Spielberg), Film—Drama; L.A. Film Critics '98: Cinematog., Director (Spielberg), Film; N.Y. Film Critics '98: Film; Broadcast Film Critics '98: Director (Spielberg), Film, Score.

Saving Sarah Cain 1/2 **2007 (PG)** Sarah (Pepper) is a struggling Portland newspaper columnist who travels back to her Pennsylvania Amish family for the funeral of her sister. Sarah learns that she is now the guardian of her sister's five children and she moves the kids back to the city with her, using their story as the topic of her columns. But Sarah soon realizes that she must choose between her own ambitions and what's best for the kids. Based on the novel "The Redemption of Sarah Cain" by Beverly Lewis. **103m/C DVD.** Elliott Gould, Tess Harper, Soren Fulton, David Clennon, Lisa Pepper, Abigail Mason; ***D:*** Michael Landon Jr.; ***W:*** Brian Bird, Cindy Kelley; ***C:*** Matthew Williams; ***M:*** Mark McKenzie. **CABLE**

Saving Shiloh 1/2 **2006 (PG)** The last of the trilogy based on the Phyllis Reynolds Naylor novels finds adorable beagle Shiloh and his master, Marty (Dolley), believing that their troubled neighbor Judd (Wilson) is sincere about becoming a better person. Marty continues to stand by Judd even when the man is accused of thievery and worse. But Judd isn't all they have to worry about—there's also a watery rescue and some escaped convicts to deal with. Wholesome without being too sweet. **90m/C DVD.** *US* Scott Wilson, Gerald McRaney, Jason Dolley, Ann Dowd, Jordan Garrett; ***D:*** Sandy Tung; ***W:*** Dale Rosenbloom; ***C:*** Lex du Pont; ***M:*** Adam Gorgoni.

Saving Silverman *Evil Woman* **2001 (PG-13)** Testosterone-driven comedy has three buddies' bond threatened by ball-breaking fiancee of one of the boys. Peet is the whip-wielding control freak Judith Snodgrass-Fessbeggler, out to tame Neil Diamond-loving loser Darren (Biggs) and despised by best buds Wayne (Zahn) and J.D. (Black). The boys scheme to break up the duo by kidnaping Judith and re-acquainting Darren with his first love, now an aspiring nun. Black and Zahn provide much-needed comic relief, as do the scenes with their Diamond cover band. However, over-the-top characters and sophomoric humor mixed with increasingly gross gags ultimately not so much save but sink "Silverman." **90m/C VHS, DVD.** *US* Jason Biggs, Steve Zahn, Jack Black, Amanda Peet, R. Lee Ermey, Amanda Detmer, Neil Diamond; ***D:*** Dennis Dugan; ***W:*** Hank Nelken, Greg DePaul; ***C:*** Arthur Albert; ***M:*** Mike Simpson.

Savior **1998 (R)** After his wife and son are killed in a terrorist bombing, an American officer (Quaid) turns mercenary and assumes a new identity. As Guy, he's a soulless killing machine, working for the Serbs in Bosnia. At a prisoner exchange, he is told to take a pregnant young Serbian woman, Vera (Ninkovic), back to her village. Guy winds up delivering the baby and protecting Vera on their hazardous (and ultimately tragic) journey as he slowly regains flickers of his own humanity. Excellent change-of-pace performance by Quaid in a gut-wrenching film inspired by a true story. **104m/C VHS, DVD.** Dennis Quaid, Natasa Ninkovic, Sergej Trifunovic, Stellan Skarsgard, Nastassja Kinski; ***D:*** Pedrag (Peter) Antonijevic; ***W:*** Robert Orr; ***C:*** Ian Wilson; ***M:*** David Robbins.

Saw **2004 (R)** Splatter film finds a serial killer named Jigsaw playing sadistic games with two men he's kidnapped: doctor Lawrence Gordon (Elwes) and photog Adam (co-writer Whannell). They're chained on opposite corners of a filthy bathroom with a corpse between them, several other items, a couple of hacksaws, and a time limit. They have to collaborate and figure out the clues left them in order to free themselves before the doc's wife and child (who are being held hostage) are killed. Oh, and the saws aren't strong enough to cut through metal but flesh and bone isn't a problem. Glover figures in as an obsessed ex-cop who's had previous dealings with Jigsaw. Lots of gruesome flashbacks and various cheap scares. **100m/C DVD, Blu-ray Disc, UMD.** *US* Leigh Whannell, Cary Elwes, Danny Glover, Ken Leung, Dina Meyer, Shawnee Smith, Monica Potter, Ned Bellamy, Tobin Bell, Makenzie Vega; ***D:*** James Wan; ***W:*** Leigh Whannell; ***C:*** David Armstrong; ***M:*** Charlie Clouser.

Saw 2 **2005 (R)** Since the sequel is just more of the same, if you liked the first one, you'll find this outing equally sadistic, disgusting, and enjoyable. Sicko Jigsaw (Bell) has trapped eight victims in a house with a number of booby traps that will force them to play his life-or-death games. One victim is the teenaged son (Knudsen) of the detective (Wahlberg) who has captured the madman. Of course, the groundwork is laid for more sequels. **93m/C DVD, Blu-ray Disc, UMD.** *US* Tobin Bell, Shawnee Smith, Donnie Wahlberg, Erik Knudsen, Franky G., Glenn Plummer, Beverley Mitchell, Dina Meyer, Emmanuelle Vaugier; ***D:*** Darren Lynn Bousman; ***W:*** Darren Lynn Bousman, Leigh Whannell; ***C:*** David Armstrong; ***M:*** Charlie Clouser.

Saw 3 1/2 **2006 (R)** With death sequences so unnecessarily elaborate, even fans of the franchise may be tiring of the gore. Along with accomplice Amanda (Smith), a dying Jigsaw (Bell) kidnaps surgeon Lynn (Soomekh), with the hope that she can remove his brain tumor. A difficult procedure, especially when you're wearing an explosive neck brace that will detonate if your patient's heart rate flatlines. Distracting flashbacks supposedly offer motivations for the actions but, by now, the franchise lacks the surprise of the original. **107m/C DVD, Blu-ray Disc.** *US* Tobin Bell, Shawnee Smith, Angus MacFadyen, Dina Meyer, Bahar Soomekh, Mpho Koaho, Debra McCabe, Donnie Wahlberg, Barry Flatman, Lyriq Bent, Costas Mandylor, Betsy Russell; ***D:*** Darren Lynn Bousman; ***W:*** Leigh Whannell; ***C:*** David Armstrong; ***M:*** Charlie Clouser.

Saw 4 **WOOF!** **2007 (R)** John/Jigsaw (Bell) is at it again in this bloody mesh of soft-core porn and horror that "Saw" fans have come to expect from director Bousman, this time doling out his special brand of moral murder from the afterlife. At the autopsy, a tape recorder is found in John's stomach echoing the killer's words and setting the scene for the fourth installment as his murder-machines continue all that yucky butchering in his absence. Flashbacks are thrown in between the gore and the (ahem) plot, offering glimpses into just what made this formerly successful and previously normal guy into the film franchise he is today. Pop the corn and settle in if you must, but this "Saw" ends up being about as sharp as a butter knife. **108m/C DVD.** *US* Tobin Bell, Costas Mandylor, Scott Patterson, Betsy Russell, Lyriq Bent, Athena Karkanis, Billy Otis; ***D:*** Darren Lynn Bousman; ***W:*** Patrick Melton, Marcus Dunstan; ***C:*** David Armstrong; ***M:*** Charlie Clouser.

Saw 5 **2008 (R)** Money-making horror franchises have taught us one thing. Even if dead, the killer will always return for a paycheck. Jigsaw (Bell) is back for another post-mortem torture game, this time involving an FBI agent, who, after escaping death, begins to unravel the mystery behind a shady cop who survived the previous sequel. Relentless flashbacks using recycled footage, and disjointed editing makes this just another cheap, confusing notch on the blade. **92m/C DVD, Blu-ray Disc.** *US* Tobin Bell, Shawnee Smith, Costas Mandylor, Julie Benz, Scott Patterson, Meagan Good, Betsy Russell, Carlo Rota; ***D:*** David Hackl; ***W:*** Patrick Melton, Marcus Dunstan; ***C:*** David Armstrong; ***M:*** Charlie Clouser.

Saw 6 **2009 (R)** Hasn't this franchise's blade become dull yet? Because it's certainly lost its edge—even the torture scenes. Agent Strahm is really dead and Hoffman has taken over Jigsaw's (who's seen in flashbacks and recorded messages) legacy. This time the main victims are evil insurance company executives—one of whom denied Jigsaw experimental gene treatment for his cancer. **90m/C DVD.** *US* Costas Mandylor, Mark Rolston, Betsy Russell, Tobin Bell, Shawnee Smith, Peter Outerbridge, Athena Karkanis, George Newbern; ***D:*** Kevin Greutert; ***W:*** Marcus Dunstan, Patrick Melton; ***C:*** David Armstrong; ***M:*** Charlie Clouser.

Sawbones **1995 (R)** Medical school reject Willy Knapp (Harvey) takes out his frustrations by murdering people and then performing gruesome surgeries on the bodies. Cop But Miller (Baldwin) investigates. **78m/C VHS.** Don Harvey, Adam Baldwin, Barbara Carrera, Nina Siemaszko, Nicholas Sadler, Don Stroud; ***D:*** Catherine Cyran; ***C:*** Christopher Baffa. **CABLE**

Sawdust & Tinsel *The Naked Night; Sunset of a Clown; Gycklarnas Afton* **1953** Early Bergman film detailing the grisly, humiliating experiences of a traveling circus rolling across the barren Swedish countryside. Lonely parable of human relationships. In Swedish with English subtitles. **87m/B VHS.** *SW* Harriet Andersson, Ake Gronberg; ***D:*** Ingmar Bergman; ***W:*** Ingmar Bergman.

Say Anything **1989 (PG-13)** A semi-mature, successful teen romance about an offbeat loner Lloyd Dobler (Cusack, in a winning performance), whose interested in the martial arts and going after the beautiful class brain, Diane Court (Skye), of his high school. Things are complicated when her father James (Mahoney) is suspected of embezzling by the IRS. Joan Cusack, John's real-life sister, also plays his sister in the film. Works well on the romantic level without getting too sticky. **100m/C VHS, DVD.** John Cusack, Ione Skye, John Mahoney, Joan Cusack, Lili Taylor, Richard Portnow, Pamela Segall, Jason Gould, Loren Dean, Bebe Neuwirth, Aimee Brooks, Eric Stoltz, Chynna Phillips, Joanna Frank, Jeremy Piven, Don "The Dragon" Wilson; ***D:*** Cameron Crowe; ***W:*** Cameron Crowe; ***C:*** Laszlo Kovacs; ***M:*** Anne Dudley, Richard Gibbs, Nancy Wilson.

Say Goodbye, Maggie Cole 1/2 **1972** A widow goes to work as a doctor in a Chicago street clinic and becomes emotionally involved with a dying child. Hayward's final role in moving made-for-TV drama. **78m/C VHS.** Susan Hayward, Darren McGavin, Michael Constantine, Nichelle Nichols, Dane Clark; ***D:*** Jud Taylor.

Say Hello to Yesterday 1/2 **1971 (PG)** A May-December romance that takes place entirely in one day. An unhappy housewife meets an exciting young traveler while both are in London. Cast and director try hard but fail to get the point across to the audience. **91m/C VHS.** *GB* Jean Simmons, Leonard Whiting, Evelyn Laye; ***D:*** Alvin Rakoff.

Say It Isn't So 1/2 **2001 (R)** The Farrelly brothers produced this tale of boy-meets-girl, boy-gets-girl, boy-finds-out-girl-is-his-sister. They should've kept their money and done it themselves, it might've been a better movie. Klein stars as good-guy orphan Gilly, who meets cute with Jo (Graham), an inept hairdresser with the most screwed-up family this side of the Mansons. Her mom (Field) decides Gilly isn't upwardly mobile enough so she makes everyone think the couple are kin. Gilly sets out to set things right amid Farrelly-approved gross-out gags and humiliations galore. First-time helmer Rogers lacks the Farrelly sense of timing and sentiment, which results in most of the jokes falling flat or not developing at all. **95m/C VHS, DVD.** *US* Chris Klein, Heather Graham, Orlando Jones, Sally Field, Richard Jenkins, John Rothman, Jack Plotnick, Eddie Cibrian, Mark Pellegrino, Richard Riehle, Brent Briscoe, Henry Cho, Suzanne Somers, Brent Hinkley; ***D:*** James B. Rogers; ***W:*** Peter Gaulke, Gerry Swallow; ***C:*** Mark Irwin; ***M:*** Mason Daring.

Say It With Songs 1/2 **1929** Carousing radio singer Joe Lane (Jolson) accidentally kills his boss Arthur (Thomson) after he made a sleazy pass at Joe's neglected missus Katherine (Nixon). While Joe's in prison, Katherine goes back to work as a nurse to support herself and their son (Lee) and surgeon Burnes (Bowers) falls for her. Joe gets paroled but more heartbreak follows. Jolson's first full-length, all-talkie (plus the usual singing) film. **95m/B DVD.** Al Jolson, Davey Lee, Marion (Marian) Nixon, John Bowers, Holmes Herbert, Kenneth Thomson; ***D:*** Lloyd Bacon; ***W:*** Joseph Jackson; ***C:*** Lee Garmes.

Say Nothing **2001 (R)** While on vacation by herself, unhappy Grace (Kinski) has a one-nighter with wealthy Julian (Baldwin) who becomes obsessed and wants to get her away from her unemployed husband Matt (Bochner). He even hires Matt to work at his company—much to Grace's distress. A low-budget "Fatal Attraction" minus the boiled bunny. **94m/C VHS, DVD.** Nastassja Kinski, William Baldwin, Hart Bochner, Michelle Duquet; ***D:*** Allan Moyle; ***W:*** Madeline Sunshine; ***C:*** Walter Bal. **CABLE**

Say Uncle **2005 (R)** Paul (Paige) dotes excessively on his young godson and is devastated when he learns the boy and his family are moving to Japan. So he decides to take his surrogate parenting to the local park where the watchful mothers eye this man-child with suspicion, especially after he admits to mom Maggie (Najimy) that he's gay. Paul's actions may be misconstrued but he behaves stupidly as well, although Maggie is little more than a one-note hysteric. Paige's directorial debut. **91m/C DVD.** Peter Paige,

Kathy Najimy, Anthony Clark, Melanie Lynskey, Gabrielle Union, Lisa Edelstein; *D:* Peter Paige; *W:* Peter Paige; *C:* David Makin; *M:* Kurt Swinghammer.

Say Yes! 🦴 1/2 **1986 (PG-13)** A nutty millionaire (Winters) bets $250 million that his inept nephew cannot get married within 24 hours. Three times the length of usual wacky sitcom, alas. **87m/C VHS.** Jonathan Winters, Art Hindle, Logan Ramsey, Lissa Layng; *D:* Larry Yust.

Sayonara 🦴🦴🦴 **1957** An Army major is assigned to a Japanese airbase during the Korean conflict at the behest of his future father-in-law. Dissatisfied with his impending marriage, he finds himself drawn to a Japanese dancer and becomes involved in the affairs of his buddy who, against official policy, marries a Japanese woman. Tragedy surrounds the themes of bigotry and interracial marriage. Based on the novel by James Michener. **147m/C VHS, DVD.** Marlon Brando, James Garner, Ricardo Montalban, Patricia Owens, Red Buttons, Miyoshi Umeki, Martha Scott, Kent Smith, Miiko Taka; *D:* Joshua Logan; *W:* Paul Osborn; *C:* Ellsworth Fredericks; *M:* Franz Waxman. Oscars '57: Art Dir./Set Dec., Sound, Support. Actor (Buttons), Support. Actress (Umeki); Golden Globes '58: Support. Actor (Buttons).

The Scalawag Bunch 🦴 **1975** Yet another retelling of Robin Hood and his Merry Men and their adventures in Sherwood Forest. **100m/C VHS.** *IT* Mark Damon, Luis Davila, Silvia Dionisio; *D:* George Ferron.

Scalp Merchant 🦴 **1977** Private investigator Cliff Rowan hunts for a missing payroll. Someone would rather see him dead than successful. **108m/C VHS.** Cameron Mitchell, John Waters, Elizabeth (Liz) Alexander, Margaret Nelson; *D:* Howard Rubie.

Scalpel 🦴🦴 *False Face* **1976 (R)** After his daughter's death, a plastic surgeon creates her image on another woman to get an inheritance. Violent and graphic, with a surprise ending. Not too bad; interesting premise. **95m/C VHS.** Robert Lansing, Judith Chapman, Arlen Dean Snyder, Sandy Martin, David Scarroll; *D:* John Grissmer; *W:* John Grissmer.

The Scalphunters 🦴🦴 1/2 **1968** Semi-successful, semi-funny western about an itinerant trapper (Lancaster) who is forced by Indians to trade his pelts for an educated black slave (Davis); many chases and brawls ensue. Good performances. **102m/C VHS, DVD.** Burt Lancaster, Ossie Davis, Telly Savalas, Shelley Winters, Nick Cravat, Dabney Coleman, Paul Picerni; *D:* Sydney Pollack; *W:* William W. Norton Sr.; *M:* Elmer Bernstein.

Scalps 🦴🦴 **1983 (R)** Hunted Indian princess and man whose family was killed by Indians form uneasy alliance in old West. **90m/C VHS, DVD.** Karen Wood, Alberto (Albert Farley) Farnese, Benny Cardosa, Charlie Bravo, Vassili Garis; *D:* Werner Knox.

Scam 🦴🦴 1/2 **1993 (R)** Maggie and her partner Barry are con artists making their living scamming high rollers in Miami Beach. Then Maggie tries to pull a con on the wrong man. Jack Shanks is an ex-FBI agent with a score to settle and he blackmails Maggie into helping him. **102m/C VHS.** Christopher Walken, Lorraine Bracco, Miguel Ferrer; *D:* John Flynn.

The Scamp 🦴 1/2 *Strange Affection* **1957** Neglected 10-year-old Tod is victimized by his drunken father so schoolteacher Stephen Leigh and his wife Barbara try to get him moved somewhere safe. But the situation worsens and, when Tod thinks he's committed a horrible crime, he runs to the Leighs for help. **88m/B DVD.** *GB* Richard Attenborough, Dorothy Allison, Colin Petersen, Terence Morgan, Jill Adams; *D:* Wolf Rilla; *W:* Wolf Rilla; *C:* Freddie Francis; *M:* Francis Chagrin.

Scandal 🦴🦴 *Shuban* **1950** Handsome artist (Mifune) and beautiful concert singer (Yamaguchi) become the victims of a libelous article in a gossip magazine. The artist decides to sue but, being softhearted, chooses a questionable lawyer because the man's young daughter is dying. Then the unethical lawyer accepts a bribe to prejudice the case. Japanese with subtitles. **105m/B VHS.** *JP* Toshiro Mifune, Takashi Shimura, Yoshiko (Shirley) Yamaguchi; *D:* Akira Kurosawa; *W:* Ryuzo Kikushima, Akira Kurosawa; *M:* Fumio Hayasaka.

Scandal 🦴🦴🦴 **1989 (R)** A dramatization of Britain's Profumo government sex scandal of the 1960s. Hurt plays a society doctor who enjoys introducing pretty girls to his wealthy friends. One of the girls, Christine Keeler, takes as lovers both a Russian government official and a British Cabinet Minister. The resulting scandal eventually overturned an entire political party, and led to disgrace, prison, and death for some of those concerned. Also available in an unedited 115-minute version which contains more controversial language and nudity. Top-notch performances make either version well worth watching. **105m/C VHS, DVD.** *GB* John Hurt, Joanne Whalley, Ian McKellen, Bridget Fonda, Jeroen Krabbe, Britt Ekland, Roland Gift, Daniel Massey, Leslie Phillips, Richard Morant; *D:* Michael Caton-Jones; *W:* Michael Thomas; *C:* Mike Molloy; *M:* Carl Davis.

Scandal in a Small Town 🦴🦴 **1988** A cocktail waitress in a small town has to defend herself and her daughter from the town's critical eye and hateful actions. Self-righteous made for TV drama rehashes several earlier plots. **90m/C VHS.** Raquel Welch, Christa Denton, Peter Van Norden, Ronny Cox; *D:* Anthony Page. **TV**

A Scandal in Paris 🦴🦴 1/2 *Thieves Holiday* **1946** Based on the real-life escapades of 19th-century criminal Francois Eugene Vidocq. Vidocq (Sanders) escapes from prison, briefly joins Napoleon's army, and catches the eye of Therese (Hasso), whose father is an important official. Under an assumed name, Vidocq joins the Paris police force in order to perpetrate his biggest crime. Instead, thanks to Therese's love, he goes straight. Sanders does an excellent job. **100m/B VHS, DVD.** George Sanders, Signe Hasso, Akim Tamiroff, Carole Landis, Gene Lockhart, Alan Napier, Vladimir Sokoloff, Alma Kruger; *D:* Douglas Sirk; *W:* Ellis St. Joseph; *C:* Guy Roe; *M:* Hanns Eisler, Heinz Roemheld.

Scandal Man 🦴🦴 1/2 **1967** A French photographer gets in over his head when he snaps the daughter of an American KKK leader embracing a black man in a nightclub. In French with English subtitles. **86m/C VHS.** Josephine Chaplin, Vittorio De Sica, Raymond Pellegrin, Francis Blanche, Maurice Ronet; *D:* Richard Balducci; *W:* Richard Balducci; *M:* Francis Lai.

Scandal Sheet 🦴🦴 1/2 **1952** Crawford is compelling as bullying editor Mark Chapman, who turns a respected New York newspaper into a tabloid and boosts circulation through a series of stunts. Protege reporter McCleary (Derek) thinks it's great but writer gal pal Julie (Reed) finds Chapman a sleaze. Chapman's past comes back to haunt him and he's involved in a murder, which is then investigated by McCleary who turns out to be more tenacious that Chapman gave him credit for. Based on Samuel Fuller's novel "The Dark Page." **82m/B DVD.** Broderick Crawford, John Derek, Donna Reed, Rosemary DeCamp, Henry O'Neill, Harry (Henry) Morgan, James Millican, Jonathan Hale; *D:* Phil Karlson; *W:* Ted Sherdeman, James Poe, Eugene Ling; *C:* Burnett Guffey; *M:* George Duning.

Scandal Sheet 🦴🦴 **1985 (PG)** How low can you go? Writer Helen Grant (Reed) is a broke single mom working in New York, who is lured to la-la land by ruthless Harold Fallan (Lancaster), the publisher of a celebrity scandal rag. Helen learns her employment isn't random; Fallan wants her write a nasty piece on the attempted comeback of fresh-out-of-alcohol-rehab actor Ben Rowan (Urich) since she was the college roomie of his wife, actress Meg (Hutton). Helen tries to take the high road but Fallan puts the pressure on and Helen is soon down in the muck with the rest of the scavengers. **101m/C VHS.** Burt Lancaster, Pamela Reed, Robert Urich, Lauren Hutton, Peter Jurasik; *D:* David Lowell Rich; *W:* Howard Rodman; *C:* Jacques "Jack" Marquette; *M:* Randy Edelman. **TV**

Scandalous 🦴 1/2 **1984 (PG)** A bumbling American TV reporter becomes involved with a gang of British con artists. Starts well but peters out. Look for the scene where Gielgud attends a Bow Wow Wow concert. **93m/C VHS.** Robert Hays, Pamela Stephenson, John Gielgud, Jim Dale, M. Emmet Walsh; *D:* Rob Cohen; *W:* Rob Cohen, Larry Cohen, John Byrum; *C:* Jack Cardiff; *M:* Dave Grusin.

Scandalous 🦴 **1988** A duke and his uncle work together to find a secretary who disappeared after witnessing a murder. **90m/C VHS.** Albert Fortell, Lauren Hutton, Ursula Carven, Capucine; *D:* Robert W. Young.

Scandalous John 🦴🦴 **1971 (G)** Comedy western about a last cattle drive devised by an aging cowboy (Keith) in order to save his ranch. Keith's shrewd acting as the ornery cattle man who won't sell to developers carries this one. **113m/C VHS.** Brian Keith, Alfonso Arau, Michele Carey, Rick Lenz, John Ritter, Harry (Henry) Morgan; *D:* Robert Butler.

Scanner Cop 🦴 1/2 **1994 (R)** When deranged scientist Sigmund Glock escapes from prison, he's determined to take revenge on Peter Harrigan, the cop who put him behind bars. With the aid of an evil assistant and a mind-altering drug, Glock kidnaps and programs innocent citizens into cop-killing maniacs. Harrigan's only weapon is a rookie cop with the Scanner power to read minds—and then destroy them. **94m/C VHS.** Daniel Quinn, Darlanne Fluegel, Richard Lynch, Mark Rolston, Hilary Shepard, Gary Hudson, Cyndi Pass, Luca Bercovici, Brion James; *D:* Pierre David; *W:* John Bryant, George Saunders.

Scanner Cop 2: Volkin's Revenge 🦴🦴 **1994 (R)** Scanner cop Sam Staziak (Quinn) has become curious about his family, asking Carrie Goodart (Haje) to find out what she can. But Carrie's attacked by evil scanner Carl Volkin (Kilpatrick), whom Sam once sent to prison, and left in a coma. Then Sam discovers Volkin is draining the life force of other scanners in order to make himself invincible when he and Sam have their final showdown. **95m/C VHS.** Daniel Quinn, Patrick Kilpatrick, Khrystyne Haje, Robert Forster, Stephen Mendel; *D:* Steve Barnett; *W:* Mark Sevi; *C:* Thomas Jewett.

A Scanner Darkly 🦴🦴 1/2 **2006 (R)** Trippy, faithful adaptation of Philip K. Dick's 1977 novel of the same name forecasts a blurry, drug-fueled world of paranoia in which the government not only listens to phone calls but watches its denizens through ambiguous undercover police whose identities are secret even to their bosses. Fred (Reeves) is one such agent, ordered to spy on his pill-popping friends (Downey Jr., Harrelson, Cochrane, and Ryder) and the owner of the house where they drop in to check out, who happens to be another incarnation of himself. Confusing? That's the point. Director Linklater utilizes a technique known as "interpolated rotoscoping," essentially digitally adding a layer of animation over footage of live actors, which effectively enhances the altered-states feel. **102m/C DVD, Blu-ray Disc, HD DVD.** *US* Keanu Reeves, Winona Ryder, Robert Downey Jr., Woody Harrelson, Rory Cochrane, Melody Chase, Lisa Marie Newmyer; *D:* Richard Linklater; *W:* Richard Linklater; *C:* Shane Kelly; *M:* Graham Reynolds.

Scanners 🦴🦴 1/2 **1981 (R)** "Scanners" are telepaths who can will people to explode. One scanner in particular harbors Hitlerian aspirations for his band of psychic gangsters. Gruesome but effective special effects. **102m/C VHS, DVD.** *CA* Stephen Lack, Jennifer O'Neill, Patrick McGoohan, Lawrence Dane, Michael Ironside, Robert A. Silverman; *D:* David Cronenberg; *W:* David Cronenberg; *C:* Mark Irwin; *M:* Howard Shore.

Scanners 2: The New Order 🦴🦴 1/2 **1991 (R)** This not-bad sequel to the 1981 cult classic finds a power-mad police official out to build a psychic militia of captured Scanners. More story than last time, plus more and better special effects. **104m/C VHS.** *CA* David Hewlett, Deborah Raffin, Yvan Ponton, Isabelle Mejias, Valentin Trujillo, Tom Butler, Vlasta Vrana, Dorothee Berryman, Raoul Trujillo; *D:* Christian Duguay; *W:* B.J. Nelson; *M:* Marty Simon.

Scanners 3: The Takeover 🦴 1/2 **1992 (R)** The third sequel in which Scanner siblings battle for control of the world. Lacks the creativity and storyline of the first two films. **101m/C VHS.** Steve Parrish, Liliana Komorowska, Valerie Valois; *D:* Christian Duguay.

Scanners: The Showdown 🦴 1/2 **1994 (R)** Carl Volkin (Kilpatrick), the "scanner" killer, has escaped jail and is stalking the streets of L.A. His ultimate target is Sam Staziak (Quinn), the scanner cop who sent him away. Since Volkin's powers grow with every kill, Staziak better get to Volkin in a hurry. **95m/C VHS.** Patrick Kilpatrick, Daniel Quinn, Khrystyne Haje, Stephen Mendel, Brenda Swanson, Jewel Shepard, Robert Forster; *D:* Steve Barnett; *W:* Mark Sevi.

The Scar 🦴🦴 1/2 *Hollow Triumph* **1948** A cunning criminal robs the mob, then hides by "stealing" the identity of a lookalike psychologist. But he's overlooked one thing...or two. Farfetched film noir showcases a rare villainous role for Henreid (who also produced). Based on a novel by Murray Forbes. **83m/B VHS, DVD.** Paul Henreid, Joan Bennett, Eduard Franz, Leslie Brooks, John Qualen, Mabel Paige, Herbert Rudley; *D:* Steve Sekely.

Scar of Shame 🦴🦴 **1927** Explores the ill-fated romance between a successful black concert pianist and the lower-class woman he marries. Gives a look at the color caste system and divisions within the black community of the era. **90m/B VHS.** Harry Henderson, Lucia Lynn Moses, Ann Kennedy, Norman Johnstone; *D:* Frank Peregini.

Scaramouche 🦴🦴 **1923** Based on Rafael Sabatini's historical novel. Orphaned Andre-Louis Moreau (Novarro) is an outspoken opponent of the aristocracy during the French Revolution. He must flee the wrath of cruel swordsman, the Marquis de la Tour d'Azyr (Stone), who also desires Alice (Terry), the daughter of Moreau's patron. Moreau joins a traveling acting troupe, disguising himself as roguish clown Scaramouche, while he practices his swordsmanship until the inevitable showdown with the Marquis. **123m/B DVD.** Ramon Novarro, Lewis Stone, Alice Terry, Lloyd Ingraham, Julia Swayne Gordon, George Siegmann; *D:* Rex Ingram; *W:* Willis Goldbeck; *C:* John Seitz.

Scaramouche 🦴🦴🦴 1/2 **1952** Thrilling swashbuckler about a nobleman (Granger, very well cast) searching for his family during the French Revolution. To avenge the death of a friend, he joins a theatre troupe where he learns swordplay and becomes the character "Scaramouche." Features a rousing six-and-a-half-minute sword battle. **111m/C VHS, DVD.** Stewart Granger, Eleanor Parker, Janet Leigh, Mel Ferrer, Henry Wilcoxon, Nina Foch, Richard Anderson, Robert Coote, Lewis Stone, Elisabeth Risdon, Howard Freeman; *D:* George Sidney; *C:* Charles Rosher.

Scarecrow 🦴🦴 1/2 **1973 (R)** Two homeless drifters (Hackman and Pacino) walk across America, heading toward a car wash business they never reach. An oft-neglected example of the early 70s extra-realistic subgenre initiated by "Midnight Cowboy." Engrossing until the end, when it falls flat. Filmed on location in Detroit. **112m/C VHS, DVD.** Gene Hackman, Al Pacino, Ann Wedgeworth, Eileen Brennan, Richard Lynch, Fredric Myrow, Penelope Allen, Dorothy Tristan, Rutanya Alda; *D:* Jerry Schatzberg; *W:* Garry Michael White; *C:* Vilmos Zsigmond. Cannes '73: Film.

Scared Stiff 🦴🦴🦴 **1953** Fleeing a murder charge, Martin and Lewis find gangsters and ghosts on a Caribbean island. Funny and scary, a good remake of "The Ghost Breakers," with cameos by Hope and Crosby. ♫San Domingo; Song of the Enchilada Man; Mama Yo Quiero; You Hit the Spot; I Don't Care If the Sun Don't Shine; I'm Your Pal; When Somebody Thinks You're Wonderful. **108m/B VHS.** Dean Martin, Jerry Lewis, Lizabeth Scott, Carmen Miranda, Dorothy Malone; ***Cameos:*** Bob Hope, Bing Crosby; *D:* George Marshall.

Scared Stiff 🦴 **1987 (R)** Three people move into a mansion once owned by a sadistic slave trader. Once there, they become unwilling victims of a voodoo curse. Bad special effects and script, not redeemed by decent but unoriginal story. **85m/C VHS.** Andrew Stevens, Mary Page Keller; *D:* Richard Friedman; *W:* Richard Friedman, Mark Frost, Daniel F. Bacaner.

Scared to Death 🦴 1/2 **1946** Begins with a woman dying of fright when shown the death mask of the man she framed. Dead woman then proceeds to narrate remainder of the story, which focuses on events leading up to her unfortunate, untimely, and fairly uninteresting demise. Memorable as Lugosi's only color film. DVD version is paired with 1941's "The Devil Bat." **60m/C VHS, DVD.** Bela Lugosi, George Zucco, Douglas Fowley, Nat Pendleton, Joyce Compton; ***D:*** Christy Cabanne.

Scared to Death **1980 (R)** A scientific experiment goes awry as a mutation begins killing off the residents of Los Angeles. **93m/C VHS, DVD.** John Stinson, Diana Davidson, David Moses, Kermit Eller; ***D:*** William Malone; ***M:*** Tom Chase.

Scarface *Scarface: The Shame of a Nation* **1931** The violent rise and fall of 1930s Chicago crime boss Tony Camonte—magnetically played by Muni—and based on the life of notorious gangster Al Capone. Release was held back by censors due to the amount of violence and its suggestion of incest between the title character and his sister (Dvorak). Morley is ice-cold as Tony's moll Poppy. Producer Howard Hughes recut and filmed an alternate ending, without director Hawks' approval, to pacify the censors, and both versions of the film were released at the same time. Almost too violent and intense at the time. Remains brilliant and impressive. Remade in 1983. **93m/B VHS, DVD.** Paul Muni, Ann Dvorak, Karen Morley, Osgood Perkins, George Raft, Boris Karloff, W.R. Burnett, Ben Hecht, John Lee Mahin, Seton I. Miller; ***D:*** Howard Hawks; ***W:*** Fred Pasley, W.R. Burnett; ***C:*** Lee Garmes; ***M:*** Gus Arnheim, Adolph Tandler. Natl. Film Reg. '94.

Scarface **1983 (R)** Al Pacino is a Cuban refugee who becomes powerful in the drug trade until the life gets the better of him. A remake of the 1932 classic gangster film of the same name, although the first film has more plot. Extremely violent, often unpleasant, but not easily forgotten. **170m/C VHS, DVD, UMD.** Al Pacino, Steven Bauer, Michelle Pfeiffer, Robert Loggia, F. Murray Abraham, Mary Elizabeth Mastrantonio, Harris Yulin, Paul Shenar, Oliver Stone, Pepe Serna, Mark Margolis, Richard Belzer, Victor Campos, Gregg Henry; ***D:*** Brian De Palma; ***W:*** Oliver Stone; ***C:*** John A. Alonzo; ***M:*** Giorgio Moroder.

Scarface Mob *Tueur de Ch Icago* **1962** This is the original TV pilot film for the popular series "The Untouchables," about Eliot Ness's band of good guys battling Chicago's crime lord, Al Capone. Still strong stuff. Narrated by Walter Winchell. **120m/B VHS.** Robert Stack, Neville Brand, Barbara Nichols; ***D:*** Phil Karlson; ***W:*** Paul Monash; ***Nar:*** Walter Winchell. **TV**

The Scarlet & the Black 1/2 **1983** A priest clandestinely works within the shield of the Vatican's diplomatic immunity to shelter allied soldiers from the Nazis in occupied Rome. His efforts put him at odds with the Pope and target him for Gestapo assassination. Swashbuckling adventure at its second-best. Based on the nonfiction book "The Scarlet Pimpernel of the Vatican" by J.P. Gallagher. **145m/C VHS, DVD.** Gregory Peck, Christopher Plummer, John Gielgud, Raf Vallone, Angelo Infanti; ***D:*** Jerry London; ***M:*** Ennio Morricone. **TV**

The Scarlet Car **1917** Chaney is a bank cashier who discovers his boss has been embezzling funds. A fight causes Chaney to believe he has killed his employer and he hides out in a remote cabin where guilt preys on his mind. **50m/B VHS.** Lon Chaney Sr., Franklyn Farnum, Edith Johnson, Sam De Grasse; ***D:*** Joseph DeGrasse.

Scarlet Claw *Sherlock Holmes and the Scarlet Claw* **1944** Holmes and Watson solve the bloody murder of an old lady in the creepy Canadian village of Le Mort Rouge. The best and most authentic of the Sherlock Holmes series. **74m/B VHS, DVD.** Basil Rathbone, Nigel Bruce, Miles Mander, Gerald Hamer, Kay Harding; ***D:*** Roy William Neill.

The Scarlet Clue **1945** A better script and faster pacing improved this Monogram entry in the Chan series. Charlie investigates a series of mysterious deaths which lead to a plot to steal secret government radar plans. **65m/B VHS, DVD.** Sidney Toler, Benson Fong, Mantan Moreland, Robert E. Homans, Helen Devereaux; ***D:*** Phil Rosen.

Scarlet Dawn 1/2 **1932** Lavish sets and costumes abound in this romantic drama starring Fairbanks as a Russian aristocrat and Carroll as his maid servant. Together they flee Russia during the Revolution, marry, and settle into the life of the common working class. Restless under his new status, Fairbanks pursues Tashman and tries his hand at swindling. A slow but interesting love story. Adapted from the novel "Revolt" by Mary McCall. **58m/B VHS.** Douglas Fairbanks Jr., Nancy Carroll, Lilyan Tashman, Sheila Terry, Guy Kibbee, Richard Alexander, Frank Reicher; ***D:*** William Dieterle; ***W:*** Douglas Fairbanks Jr., Niven Busch, Erwin Gelsey.

Scarlet Diva **2000** Writer/director/star Argento, daughter of Italian horror director Dario Argento, explores the trappings of fame in her semi-autobiographical debut. As Anna Battista, Argento is an Italian actress tired of her success and looking for love and fulfillment. Anna's mother (Argento's real life mother, Nicolodi), glimpsed in flashbacks, died of a methadone overdose, and her childhood in general has clearly left her damaged. She becomes easy prey for Hollywood vultures like the lascivious producer (Coleman) who wants to cast her in a "Cleopatra" remake opposite Robert De Niro. Back in Rome, Anna's decadent lifestyle is briefly interrupted when she falls in love with an Australian rock star (Shepherd) who promptly leaves her pregnant and devastated. Strangely watchable, but wildly formless style and digital video format matches pic's equally rambling writing and acting. In English, French, and Italian. **91m/C VHS, DVD.** *IT* Asia Argento, Daria Nicolodi, Joe Coleman, Francesca D'Aloja, Jean Shepard, Herbert Fritsch, Gianluca Arcopinto; ***D:*** Asia Argento; ***W:*** Asia Argento; ***C:*** Frederic Fasano.

Scarlet Empress 1/2 **1934** One of Von Sternberg's greatest films tells the story of Catherine the Great and her rise to power. Dietrich stars as the beautiful royal wife who outwits her foolish husband Peter (Jaffe) to become empress of Russia. Incredibly rich decor is a visual feast for the eye, as perfectionist von Sternberg fussed over every detail. Dietrich is excellent as Catherine, and von Sternberg's mastery of lighting and camera work makes for a highly extravagant film. Based on the diary of Catherine the Great. **110m/B VHS, DVD.** Marlene Dietrich, John Lodge, Sam Jaffe, Louise Dresser, Maria Sieber, Sir C. Aubrey Smith, Ruthelma Stevens, Olive Tell; ***D:*** Josef von Sternberg; ***W:*** Manuel Komroff; ***C:*** Bert Glennon.

The Scarlet Letter **1934** Unlikely comic relief provides only measure of redemption for this poorly rendered version of Hawthorne's classic novel about sin and Hester Prynne. **69m/B VHS, DVD.** Colleen Moore, Hardie Albright, Henry B. Walthall, Alan Hale, Cora Sue Collins, Betty Blythe; ***D:*** Robert G. Vignola.

The Scarlet Letter **1973** A studied, thoughtful, international production of the Nathaniel Hawthorne classic about a woman's adultery which incites puritanical violence and hysteria in colonial America. Fine modernization by Wenders. In German with English subtitles. **90m/C VHS, DVD.** *SP GE* Senta Berger, Lou Castel, Yella Rottlaender, William Layton, Yelena Samarina, Hans-Christian Blech; ***D:*** Wim Wenders.

The Scarlet Letter **1979** Faithful yet passionate TV adaptation of Hawthorne's classic novel of 17th-century New England. Hester Prynne (Foster) is condemned by her Puritan fellows for having a child out of wedlock and is forced to wear a scarlet letter A for adultery. Secretly sharing Hester's torment is the Rev. Arthur Dimmesdale (Heard), the baby's father, and Hester's vengeful back-from-the-dead husband, Roger Chillingsworth (Conway). **240m/C VHS, DVD.** Meg Foster, John Heard, Kevin Conway, Josef Sommer; ***D:*** Rick Hauser; ***W:*** Allan Knee, Alvin Sapinsley; ***M:*** John Morris.

The Scarlet Letter **WOOF! 1995 (R)** Ewwwwww—ego-driven stinker of '95 ("Showgirls" not-withstanding). Feisty Hester Prynne (Moore) is condemned to wear the scarlet letter "A" of adultery by her 17th-century Puritan neighbors because she bore a child out of wedlock. Oldman is the lusty Reverend Arthur Dimmesdale (her partner in illicit passion) while Duvall chews scenery as Hester's wronged hubby. This "freely adapted" version of the 1850 American classic should have set author Nathaniel Hawthorne spinning in his grave as his moral saga of sin and redemption meets 20th-century moviemaking by having the passion made explicit and a happy ending tacked on. **135m/C VHS, DVD.** Demi Moore, Gary Oldman, Robert Duvall, Robert Prosky, Edward Hardwicke, Joan Plowright, Roy Dotrice, Dana Ivey, Sheldon Peters Wolfchild, Diane Salinger, Lisa Jolliff-Andoh, Amy Wright, Tim Woodward; ***D:*** Roland Joffe; ***W:*** Douglas Day Stewart; ***C:*** Alex Thomson; ***M:*** John Barry. Golden Raspberries '95: Worst Remake/Sequel.

The Scarlet Pimpernel 1/2 **1934** Sir Percy Blakeney (Howard) is a supposed dandy of the English court who assumes the identity of "The Scarlet Pimpernel" in order to outwit the French Republicans and aid innocent aristocrats during the French Revolution. The frustrated French send sinister ambassador Chauvelin (Massey) to discover the rogue's identity and involve Blakeney's French wife, Marguerite (Oberon) in their plot. Classic rendering of Baroness Orczy's novel, full of exploits, 18th century costumes, intrigue, damsels, etc. Produced by Alexander Korda, who fired the initial director, Rowland Brown. Remade twice for TV. **95m/B VHS, DVD.** *GB* Leslie Howard, Joan Gardner, Merle Oberon, Raymond Massey, Anthony Bushell, Nigel Bruce, Bramwell Fletcher, Walter Rilla, O.B. Clarence, Ernest Milton, Edmund Breon, Melville Cooper, Gibb McLaughlin, Morland Graham, Allan Jeayes; ***D:*** Harold Young; ***W:*** Robert Sherwood, Arthur Wimperis, Lajos Biro; ***C:*** Harold Rosson; ***M:*** Arthur Benjamin.

The Scarlet Pimpernel **1982** Remake of the classic about a British dandy who saved French aristocrats from the Reign of Terror guillotines during the French Revolution. Almost as good as the original 1935 film, with beautiful costumes and sets and good performances from Seymour and Andrews. **142m/C VHS, DVD.** *GB* Anthony Andrews, Jane Seymour, Ian McKellen, James Villiers, Eleanor David; ***D:*** Clive Donner; ***M:*** Nick Bicat. **TV**

The Scarlet Pimpernel 1/2 **1999** Wealthy, foppish English aristocrat, Sir Percy Blakeney (Grant), is not the fool he seems. Indeed, he masquerades as the daring Scarlet Pimpernel, the rescuer of those persecuted by the French Revolution, and the bane of French spy Chauvelin (Shaw). Why Percy has even managed to fool his lovely French wife, Marguerite (McGovern), who was once involved with Chauvelin, and who comes to see her husband in a more heroic light. Based on the novels by Baroness Emmuska Orczy. **120m/C VHS, DVD.** Richard E. Grant, Elizabeth McGovern, Martin Shaw, Anthony Green, Ronan Vibert, Christopher Fairbank, Jonathan Coy, Emilia Fox, Dominic Mafham; ***D:*** Patrick Lau; ***W:*** Richard Carpenter; ***C:*** Simon Kossoff; ***M:*** Michael Pavlicek. **CABLE**

The Scarlet Pimpernel 2: Mademoiselle Guillotine 1/2 **1999** The Scarlet Pimpernel and wife Marguerite head to France to save the daughter of a French nobleman from the clutches of Gabrielle Damiens (Black), AKA Mademoiselle Guillotine, and her band of revolutionaries. The disgraced Chauvelin is also involved and then Marguerite gets captured, so quite a lot of rescuing needs to be done. Based on the books by Baroness Emmuska Orczy. **90m/C VHS, DVD.** Richard E. Grant, Elizabeth McGovern, Martin Shaw, Anthony Green, Ronan Vibert, Christopher Fairbank, Jonathan Coy, Denise Black, James Callis, Peter Jeffrey, Julie Cox; ***D:*** Patrick Lau; ***W:*** Richard Carpenter; ***C:*** Simon Kossoff; ***M:*** Michael Pavlicek. **CABLE**

The Scarlet Pimpernel 3: The Kidnapped King 1/2 **1999** France's 10-year-old Dauphin is under the control of Robespierre when he is captured by a masked figure. As Sir Percy investigates, all clues point to legendary swordsman Chevalier D'Orly. Meanwhile, Marguerite has supposedly left Sir Percy and although Robespierre isn't convinced, Chauvelin is plotting to win back his former love. Based on the books by Baroness Emmuska Orczy. **90m/C VHS.** Richard E. Grant, Elizabeth McGovern, Martin Shaw, Anthony Green, Ronan Vibert, Christopher Fairbank, Jonathan Coy, Suzanne Bertish, Jerome Willis, Bryce Engstrom, Dalibor Sipek; ***D:*** Edward Bennett; ***W:*** Richard Carpenter; ***C:*** John Hooper; ***M:*** Michael Pavlicek. **CABLE**

Scarlet Spear **WOOF! 1954** Filmed in Nairobi National Park in Kenya. A great white hunter convinces a young African chief that the ancient practices of his people are uncivilized. Pathetically stated and culturally offensive by today's standards. **78m/C VHS.** John Bentley, Martha Hyer, Morasi; ***D:*** George Breakston, C. Ray Stahl; ***W:*** George Breakston, C. Ray Stahl; ***M:*** Ivor Slaney.

Scarlet Street **1945** A mild-mannered, middle-aged cashier becomes an embezzler when he gets involved with a predatory, manipulating woman. Lang remake of Jean Renoir's "La Chienne" (1931). Set apart from later attempts on the same theme by excellent direction by Lang and acting. Also available Colorized. **95m/B VHS, DVD.** Edward G. Robinson, Joan Bennett, Dan Duryea, Samuel S. Hinds; ***D:*** Fritz Lang; ***C:*** Milton Krasner.

The Scarlet Tunic 1/2 **1997** Based on the novella "The Melancholy Hussar of the German Legion" by Thomas Hardy. It's 1802 in Hardy's fictional Wessex countryside where a light cavalry regiment of bored Germans, fighting with the British against Napoleon, has an encampment on the land of retired doctor Edward Groves (Shepherd). Groves' pretty daughter Frances (Fielding) is engaged to local businessman Humphrey Gould (Sessions) but, of course, she falls for dashing German hussar Matthaus Singer (Barr). Since this is a Hardy story, don't expect any happy endings. **101m/C VHS.** *GB* Jean-Marc Barr, Emma Fielding, Simon Callow, John Sessions, Jack Shepherd, Andrew Tiernan, Thomas Lockyer; ***D:*** Stuart St. Paul; ***W:*** Stuart St. Paul, Mark Jenkins, Colin Clements; ***C:*** Malcolm McLean; ***M:*** John Scott. **TV**

Scarlett 1/2 **1994 (PG-13)** Well, fiddle-dee-dee. While purists may object to any tampering of "Gone With the Wind," this epic TV miniseries, from the Alexandra Ripley novel, manages to be good if overlong fun for those willing to sit back and relax. Scarlett tries to get back Tara and Rhett (they divorce but still battle continuously); explores her Irish family ties and even moves to Ireland; then gets involved with the wrong man and is accused of murder so Rhett can save her and everything can turn out okay (there's lots more). The big budget is up on-screen with lavish costumes and sets and a big cast—although why two Brits got the leads in this Southern melodrama is anyone's guess (Whalley and Dalton try hard). **360m/C VHS, DVD.** Joanne Whalley, Timothy Dalton, Ann-Margret, Barbara Barrie, Sean Bean, Brian Bedford, Stephen Collins, John Gielgud, Annabeth Gish, George Grizzard, Julie Harris, Tina Kellegher, Melissa Leo, Colm Meaney, Esther Rolle, Jean Smart, Elizabeth Wilson, Paul Winfield, Betsy Blair, Peter Eyre, Pippa Guard, Ronald Pickup, Gary Raymond, Dorothy Tutin; ***D:*** John Erman; ***W:*** William Hanley; ***M:*** John Morris. **TV**

Scarred 1/2 *Street Love; Red on Red* **1984 (R)** Unwed teenage mother becomes prostitute to support baby. Predictable plot and acting pull this one down. **85m/C VHS.** Jennifer Mayo, Jackie Berryman, David Dean; ***D:*** Rosemarie Turko; ***W:*** Rosemarie Turko.

Scarred City **1998 (R)** Cliched and predictable actioner with a decent cast. Trigger-happy cop John Trace (Baldwin) is forced to join an elite crime unit, headed by Laine Devon (Palminteri), which uses any means necessary to get the job done. But Trace soon decides that his fellow cops are basically just fulfilling their own violent impulses. Then Trace saves hooker Candy (Carrere) from a mob hit and his buddies decide they'd be better off without him. **95m/C VHS, DVD.** Chazz Palminteri, Stephen Baldwin, Tia Carrere, Gary Dourdan, Michael Rispoli, Steve Flynn; ***D:*** Ken Sanzel; ***W:*** Ken Sanzel; ***C:*** Michael Slovis; ***M:*** Anthony Marinelli.

The Scars of Dracula 1/2 **1970 (R)** A young couple tangles with Dracula in their search for the man's missing brother. Gory, creepy, violent, sexy tale from the dark side. Don't see it late at night. Preceded by "Taste the Blood of Dracula" and followed by "Dracula A.D. 1972." **96m/C VHS, DVD.** *GB* Christopher Lee, Jenny Hanley, Dennis Waterman, Wendy Hamilton, Patrick Troughton, Michael Gwynn, Anouska (Anoushka) Hempel, Michael Ripper, Christopher Matthews, Delta Lindsay; ***D:*** Roy Ward Baker; ***W:*** John (Anthony Hinds) Elder; ***M:*** James Bernard.

Scary Movie ✓ 1/2 **2000 (R)** If the last few Leslie Nielsen outings didn't convince you that the genre spoof was played out, this parody of "Scream" and all its progeny will. The Wayans brothers go for quantity of jokes and targets, and quality definitely suffers for it. Fart gags and gratuitous cussing (neither of which we often object to, but we have our limits) are substituted for focused satire. If you're looking for well-done genre spoofery, rent "Airplane" and "I'm Gonna Git You Sucka" and leave this one to the discount previously viewed bin. **85m/C VHS, DVD, Blu-ray Disc.** Keenen Ivory Wayans, Marlon Wayans, Shawn Wayans, Carmen Electra, Jon Abrahams, Shannon Elizabeth, Lochlyn Munro, Cheri Oteri, Anna Faris, Regina Hall, Kurt Fuller, David Lander, Dave Sheridan, Dan Joffre; ***D:*** Keenen Ivory Wayans; ***W:*** Marlon Wayans, Shawn Wayans; ***C:*** Francis Kenny; ***M:*** David Kitay.

Scary Movie 2 ✓ **2001 (R)** You knew they were lying when the tagline of the first film declared "No mercy, no shame, no sequel," especially since the spoof brought in more than $144 mil worldwide. The plot, such as it is, consists of a spooky doctor (Curry) convincing the cast from the original to spend the night in a haunted house to study insomnia. Familiar, no? But it's really just an excuse for the Wayans to parody a whole new batch of movies and do a lot (and we mean A LOT) of bodily fluid and sex jokes. Unfortunately, they don't do it any better than they did the first time, and whatever freshness the original had is long gone. **82m/C VHS, DVD.** *US* Anna Faris, Tim Curry, Shawn Wayans, Marlon Wayans, Chris Elliott, Tori Spelling, Christopher K. Masterson, Kathleen Robertson, Regina Hall, James Woods, David Cross, Andy Richter, Natasha Lyonne, Veronica Cartwright, Richard Moll; ***D:*** Keenen Ivory Wayans; ***W:*** Shawn Wayans, Marlon Wayans, Alyson Fouse, Greg Grabianski, Dave Polsky, Michael Anthony Snowden, Craig Wayans; ***C:*** Steven Bernstein; ***V:*** Colleen (Ann) Fitzpatrick.

Scary Movie 3 ✓ 1/2 **2003 (PG-13)** Zucker-directed spoof pushes the limits of parody in this Wayans-created franchise with rehashed gags and strained satire. Mainly a send up of flicks "The Ring" and "Signs." TV reporter Cindy Campbell (Faris), from the previous "Srarys", ends up on the farm of Tom Logan (Sheen) and his little brother George (Rex) while tracking down a mysterious videotape portending doom to whoever watches. Machine-gun fire gags whiz by, missing most of their targets, as Zucker takes the worst of the movies he spoofs and plays them for all they're worth, which isn't very much. Blond moment between Anderson and McCarthy is a highlight, as is Latifah in a "Matrix" spoof. **90m/C VHS, DVD.** *US* Anna Faris, Anthony Anderson, Leslie Nielsen, Camryn Manheim, Simon Rex, George Carlin, Queen Latifah, Eddie Griffin, Denise Richards, Regina Hall, Charlie Sheen, Kevin Hart; ***Cameos:*** Pamela Anderson, Jenny McCarthy, Jeremy Piven, D.L. Hughley, Ja Rule, Master P, Macy Gray, Redman, Raekwon, RZA; ***D:*** Jerry Zucker; ***W:*** Craig Mazin, Pat Proft; ***C:*** Mark Irwin; ***M:*** James L. Venable.

Scary Movie 4 ✓ 1/2 **2006 (PG-13)** Critic-proof spoof has Zucker returning for a second director's stint and the formula staying the same. Nominal story involves Cindy (Faris) being a home care worker for an elderly woman (unbilled Leachman) and falling for divorced dad Tom (Bierko, doing that Cruise couch-jumping thing in front of a fake Oprah). Films spoofed include "Saw" (with Shaq and Dr. Phil), "The Grudge," "The Village," "War of the Worlds," and more. Some jokes hit, more miss, but the franchise made $41 million its opening weekend so it's likely to lead to a fifth go-round. **83m/C DVD, HD DVD.** *US* Anna Faris, Regina Hall, Craig Bierko, Anthony Anderson, Carmen Electra, Chris Elliott, Kevin Hart, Cloris Leachman, Michael Madsen, Leslie Nielsen, Bill Pullman, Simon Rex, Charlie Sheen, Molly Shannon, Shaquille O'Neal, Bryan Callen, Dave Attell, Conchita Campbell, Debra Wilson, Patrice O'Neal; ***D:*** David Zucker; ***W:*** David Zucker, Craig Mazin, Jim Abrahams; ***C:*** Thomas Ackerman; ***M:*** James L. Venable; ***Nar:*** James Earl Jones.

Scavenger Hunt ✓ **1979 (PG)** Action begins when a deceased millionaire's will states that his 15 would-be heirs must compete in a scavenger hunt, and whoever collects all the items first wins the entire fortune. Big cast wanders about aimlessly. **117m/C VHS.** Richard Benjamin, James Coco, Ruth Buzzi, Cloris Leachman, Cleavon Little, Roddy McDowall, Scatman Crothers, Tony Randall, Robert Morley, Richard Mulligan, Dirk Benedict, Willie Aames, Vincent Price; ***D:*** Michael A. Schultz; ***M:*** Billy Goldenberg.

Scavengers ✓ **1987 (PG-13)** A man and a woman become involved in a spy plot and wind up in all sorts of danger. Pathetic excuse for a "thriller." **94m/C VHS.** Kenneth Gilman, Brenda Bakke, Ken Gampu, Norman Anstey, Crispin De Nys; ***D:*** Duncan McLachlan.

Scenario du Film Passion ✓✓✓ **1982** A classically self-analyzing video piece by Godard, in which he recreates on tape the scenario for his film "Passion," resulting in a reflexive, experimental essay on the process of image-making and conceptualizing films, especially Godard's. In French with English subtitles. **54m/C VHS.** ***D:*** Jean-Luc Godard, Anne-Marie Mieville, Barnard Menoud.

Scene of the Crime ✓✓ 1/2 **1985** Three short mysteries, which the audience is asked to solve: "The Newlywed Murder," "Medium Is the Murder," and "Vote for Murder." **74m/C VHS.** Markie Post, Alan Thicke, Ben Piazza; ***D:*** Walter Grauman; ***Nar:*** Orson Welles. **TV**

Scene of the Crime ✓✓✓ **1987** Beautiful widow, trapped in small French town, is sexually awakened by escaped convict hiding out near her home. Acclaimed, but sometimes distracting camera technique and slow pace undermine the film. In French with English subtitles. **90m/C VHS.** *FR* Catherine Deneuve, Danielle Darrieux, Wadeck Stanczak, Victor Lanoux, Nicolas Giraudi, Jean Bousquet, Claire Nebout; ***D:*** Andre Techine; ***W:*** Olivier Assayas.

Scenes from a Mall ✓✓ **1991 (R)** Conspicuous consumers spend 16th wedding anniversary waltzing in mall while marriage unravels with few laughs. Surprisingly superficial comedy given the depth of talent of Allen and Midler. **87m/C VHS, DVD.** Woody Allen, Bette Midler, Bill Irwin, Daren Firestone, Rebecca Nickels; ***Cameos:*** Fabio; ***D:*** Paul Mazursky; ***W:*** Paul Mazursky; ***C:*** Fred Murphy.

Scenes from a Marriage ✓✓✓✓ **1973 (PG)** Originally produced in six one-hour episodes for Swedish TV, this bold and sensitive film excruciatingly portrays the painful, unpleasant, disintegration of a marriage. Ullmann is superb. Realistic and disturbing. Dubbed. **168m/C VHS, DVD.** *SW* Liv Ullmann, Erland Josephson, Bibi Andersson, Jan Malmsjo, Anita Wall; ***D:*** Ingmar Bergman; ***W:*** Ingmar Bergman; ***C:*** Sven Nykvist. Golden Globes '75: Foreign Film; N.Y. Film Critics '74: Actress (Ullmann), Screenplay; Natl. Soc. Film Critics '74: Actress (Ullmann), Film, Screenplay, Support. Actress (Andersson).

Scenes from a Murder ✓ 1/2 **1972** A killer (Savalas) stalks a beautiful actress (Heywood). Dull excuse for a suspense flick. **91m/C VHS.** *IT* Telly Savalas, Anne Heywood, Giorgio Piazza; ***D:*** Alberto De Martino.

Scenes from the Class Struggle in Beverly Hills ✓✓ 1/2 **1989 (R)** Social satire about the wealthy, their servants, and their hangers-on in two Hollywood households. Two chauffeurs spend their spare time lusting after their lovely employers, and bet to see who can accomplish reality first. All kinds of erotic capers result. Usually funny and irreverent; occasionally misfires or takes itself too seriously. Reunites the trio from cult classic "Eating Raoul": Bartel, Woronov, and Beltran. Remake of Renoir's "The Rules of the Game." **103m/C VHS.** Jacqueline Bisset, Ray Sharkey, Mary Woronov, Robert Beltran, Ed Begley Jr., Wallace Shawn, Paul Bartel, Paul Mazursky, Arnetia Walker, Rebecca Schaeffer, Edith Diaz; ***Cameos:*** Little Richard, Michael Feinstein; ***D:*** Paul Bartel; ***W:*** Bruce Wagner; ***C:*** Steven Fierberg; ***M:*** Stanley Myers.

Scenes from the Goldmine ✓ 1/2 **1987 (R)** A young woman joins a rock band and falls in love with its lead singer. Realistic but bland; music not memorable (performed mostly by the actors themselves). **99m/C VHS.** Catherine Mary Stewart, Cameron Dye, Joe Pantoliano, John Ford Coley, Steve Railsback, Timothy B. Schmit, Jewel Shepard, Alex Rocco, Lee Ving, Lesley-Anne Down; ***D:*** Marc Rocco.

Scenes of a Sexual Nature ✓✓ **2006 (R)** All talk and no action, in case you were wondering about that title. The relationships of seven couples are explored during one summer afternoon on London's Hampstead Heath. There's a gay couple, a divorced couple, one on a blind date, one couple arguing and breaking up, and one meeting accidentally years after their romance, among other moments. **92m/C DVD.** *GB* Ewan McGregor, Eileen Atkins, Hugh Bonneville, Holly Aird, Douglas Hodge, Adrian Lester, Andrew Lincoln, Thomas (Tom) Hardy, Gina McKee, Sophie Okonedo, Mark Strong, Catherine Tate, Elgantine Rembauville, Polly Walker, Benjamin Whitrow; ***D:*** Ed Blum; ***W:*** Aschlin Ditta; ***C:*** David Meadows; ***M:*** Dominik Scherrer.

The Scent of a Woman ✓✓ 1/2 *Sweet Smell of Woman; Profumo di Donna* **1975** An acclaimed dark comedy that may be an acquired taste for some. A blinded military officer and his valet take a sensual tour of Italy, the sightless man seducing beautiful women on the way. But at the end of the journey awaits a shock, and the real point of the tale, based on a novel by Giovanni Arpino. In Italian with English subtitles. Remade in 1992 as "Scent of a Woman." **103m/C VHS, DVD.** *IT* Alessandro Momo, Agostina Belli, Moira Orfei, Franco Ricci, Vittorio Gassman; ***D:*** Dino Risi; ***W:*** Ruggero Maccari, Dino Risi; ***C:*** Claudio Civillo; ***M:*** Armando Trovajoli.

Scent of a Woman ✓✓✓ **1992 (R)** Pacino is a powerhouse (verging on caricature) in a story that, with anyone else in the lead, would be your run-of-the-mill, overly sentimental coming of age/redemption flick. Blind, bitter, and semi-alcoholic Pacino is a retired army colonel under the care of his married niece. He's home alone over Thanksgiving, under the watchful eye of local prep school student Charlie (O'Donnell). Pacino's abrasive (though wonderfully intuitive and romantic) colonel makes an impact on viewers that lingers like a woman's scent long after the last tango. O'Donnell is competently understated in key supporting role, while the tango lesson between Pacino and Anwar dances to the tune of "classic." Box-office winner is a remake of 1975 Italian film "Profumo di Donna." **157m/C VHS, DVD, HD DVD.** Al Pacino, Chris O'Donnell, James Rebhorn, Gabrielle Anwar, Philip Seymour Hoffman, Richard Venture, Bradley Whitford, Rochelle Oliver, Margaret Eginton, Tom Riis Farrell, Frances Conroy, Ron Eldard; ***D:*** Martin Brest; ***W:*** Bo Goldman; ***C:*** Donald E. Thorin; ***M:*** Thomas Newman. Oscars '92: Actor (Pacino); Golden Globes '93: Actor—Drama (Pacino), Film—Drama, Screenplay.

The Scent of Green Papaya ✓✓✓ *Mui du du Xanh* **1993** Tranquil film, set in 1951 Vietnam, follows 10-year-old peasant girl Mui as she spends the next 10 years as a servant in a troubled family, gracefully accommodating herself to the small changes in her life. At 20, she finds a fairy-tale romance with her next employer, a young pianist. Presents a romanticized view of the stoicism of Vietnamese women but is visually beautiful. Directorial debut of Hung is based on his childhood memories of Vietnam, which he re-created on a soundstage outside Paris. In Vietnamese with English subtitles. **104m/C VHS, DVD.** *VT* Tran Nu Yen-Khe, Lu Man San, Truong Thi Loc, Vuong Hoa Hoi; ***D:*** Tran Anh Hung; ***W:*** Tran Anh Hung, Patricia Petit; ***C:*** Benoit Delhomme; ***M:*** Ton That Tiet.

Schemes ✓✓ **1995 (R)** Grieving widower Paul Stewart (McCaffrey) becomes interested in Laura Pierce (Hope), a lovely young woman who said she knew his late wife. Then, Paul's business partner Evelyn (Draper) discovers Laura's not on the up and up and is really interested in Paul's substantial insurance payoff. Laura's part of a con job set up by volaile Victor (Glover), but since Evelyn's also in love with Paul, things aren't at all what they seem. **95m/C VHS, DVD.** John Glover, Polly Draper, Leslie Hope, James McCaffrey, John de Lancie, Allison Mackie; ***D:*** Derek Westervelt; ***W:*** Derek Westervelt; ***C:*** Claudio Obregon; ***M:*** Mark Chait.

Schindler's List ✓✓✓✓ **1993 (R)** Spielberg's staggering evocation of the Holocaust finds its voice in Oscar Schindler (Neeson), womanizing German businessman and aspiring war profiteer, who cajoled, bribed, and bullied the Nazis into allowing him to employ Jews in his Polish factories during WWII. By doing so he saved over 1,000 lives. The atrocities are depicted matter of factly as a by-product of sheer Nazi evil. Shot in black and white and powered by splendid performances. Neeson uses his powerful physique as a protective buffer; Kingsley is watchful as his industrious Jewish accountant; and Fiennes personifies evil as Nazi Amon Goeth. Based on the novel by Thomas Keneally, which itself was based on survivor's memories. Filmed on location in Cracow, Poland; due to the sensitive nature of the story, sets of the Auschwitz concentration camp were reconstructed directly outside the camp after protests about filming on the actual site. A tour de force and labor of love for Spielberg, who finally garnered the attention and respect as a filmmaker he deserves. **195m/B VHS, DVD.** Liam Neeson, Ben Kingsley, Ralph Fiennes, Embeth Davidtz, Caroline Goodall, Jonathan Sagalle, Mark Ivanir, Malgoscha Gebel, Shmulik Levy, Beatrice Macola, Andrzej Seweryn, Friedrich von Thun, Norbert Weisser, Michael Schneider, Anna Mucha; ***D:*** Steven Spielberg; ***W:*** Steven Zaillian; ***C:*** Janusz Kaminski; ***M:*** John Williams. Oscars '93: Adapt. Screenplay, Art Dir./Set Dec., Cinematog., Director (Spielberg), Film Editing, Picture, Orig. Score; AFI '98: Top 100; British Acad. '93: Adapt. Screenplay, Director (Spielberg), Film, Support. Actor (Fiennes); Directors Guild '93: Director (Spielberg); Golden Globes '94: Director (Spielberg), Film—Drama, Screenplay; L.A. Film Critics '93: Cinematog., Film; Natl. Bd. of Review '93: Film, Natl. Film Reg. '04;; N.Y. Film Critics '93: Cinematog., Film, Support. Actor (Fiennes); Natl. Soc. Film Critics '93: Cinematog., Director (Spielberg), Film, Support. Actor (Fiennes); Writers Guild '93: Adapt. Screenplay.

Schizo ✓ *Amok; Blood of the Undead* **1977 (R)** Devious intentions abound as a middle-aged man is overcome by weird scenes and revelations, caused by the impending wedding of the figure skater he adores. Confusing tale of insanity, obsession, and skating. **109m/C VHS, DVD.** *GB* Lynne Frederick, John Leyton, Stephanie Beacham, John Fraser, Jack Watson, John McEnery; ***D:*** Pete Walker; ***W:*** John M. Watson Sr.; ***C:*** Peter Jessop.

Schizo ✓✓ *Shiza* **2004** Set amid the dusty and desolate bleakness of rural Kazakhstan, film follows 15 year old Mustafa (Eralibeva), who has been given the nickname Schizo because of an apparent mental disorder. His mother's boyfriend, who he idolized, is a small time gangster whose racket is setting up illegal bare-fisted boxing matches. With little else to do in his dead-end town, Mustafa gets involved by recruiting men looking for a quick buck in the ring. When one combatant dies after an especially brutal fight, Mustafa is obliged to fulfill the man's dying wish to deliver his winnings to his girlfriend. This leads to an unlikely romantic involvement, which has the uneasy feel of Mustafa stepping into another man's shoes. **86m/C DVD.** Olzhas Nusuppaev, Eduard Tabychev, Olga Landina, Bakhytbek Baymukhanbetov, Soukhorukov, Gulnara Jeralieva, Kanagat Nurtay; ***D:*** Gulshad Omarova; ***W:*** Sergei Bodrov, Gulshad Omarova; ***C:*** Khasan Kydyraliyev; ***M:*** Sig.

Schizoid ✓ *Murder by Mail* **1980 (R)** Advice-to-the-lovelorn columnist Hill receives a series of threatening letters causing her to wonder whether psychiatrist Kinski is bumping off his own patients. Boring blood dripper that's difficult to follow. **91m/C VHS.** Klaus Kinski, Marianna Hill, Craig Wasson; ***D:*** David Paulsen.

Schizopolis ✓✓ **1997** Experimental, empty satire on modern spirituality and communication combines a number of weird and wacky devices that are not particularly entertaining. In an interesting premise, Soderburgh takes the lead in a dual role as Fletcher Munson, a manically neurotic employee of a self-help guru and his own lookalike, a ho-hum dentist having an affair with Fletcher's wife. Soderburgh's real-life ex, actress Brantley, plays his wife, who also has a double that shows up at the dentist. Things grow more bizarre for no apparent reason, as secondary cast members speak in other languages or just complete nonsense while strange sound effects confuse, in a film which also lists no credits (the title is shown in film on a character's t-shirt). Soderburgh, who wrote, directed and lensed this surrealist homage, shot on a super-low $250,000 budget as a way of expressing ideas not allowed in bigger budget, conventional films. To most, this just looks like expensive therapy. **96m/C VHS, DVD.** Steven Soderbergh, Betsy Brantley, David Jensen; ***D:*** Steven Soderbergh; ***W:*** Steven Soderbergh; ***C:*** Steven Soderbergh.

Schlock 𝒥𝒥 *The Banana Monster* **1973 (PG)** Accurately titled horror parody is first directorial effort for Landis, who does double duty as a missing link who kills people and falls in love with blind girl. Look for cameo appearance by Forrest J. Ackerman; ape-makeup by Rick Baker. **78m/C VHS, DVD.** John Landis, Saul Kahan, Joseph Piantadosi, Eliza (Simons) Garrett, Emil Hamaty, Eric Allison; ***Cameos:*** Forrest J Ackerman; ***D:*** John Landis; ***W:*** John Landis; ***C:*** Robert E. (Bob) Collins; ***M:*** David Gibson.

Schnelles Geld 𝒥 1/2 **1984** A mild-mannered guy gets involved with a prostitute, and is plunged into a world of crime and drugs. In German with English subtitles. **90m/C VHS.** *GE* Dieter Schidor, Anne Bennent, Hub Martin, Gila von Weitershausen; ***D:*** George Moorse; ***W:*** George Moorse; ***C:*** Wolfgang Dickmann.

School Daze 𝒥𝒥𝒥 **1988 (R)** Director/writer/star Lee's second outing is a rambunctious comedy (with a message, of course) set at an African-American college in the South. Skimpy plot revolves around the college's homecoming weekend and conflict among frats and sororities and African-Americans who would lose their racial identity and others who assert it. Entertaining and thought provoking. A glimpse at Lee's "promise," fulfilled in "Do the Right Thing." **114m/C VHS, DVD.** Spike Lee, Laurence Fishburne, Giancarlo Esposito, Tisha Campbell, Ossie Davis, Joe Seneca, Art Evans, Ellen Holly, Branford Marsalis, Bill Nunn, Kadeem Hardison, Darryl M. Bell, Joie Lee, Tyra Ferrell, Jasmine Guy, Gregg Burge, Kasi Lemmons, Samuel L. Jackson, Phyllis Hyman, James Bond III; ***D:*** Spike Lee; ***W:*** Spike Lee; ***C:*** Ernest R. Dickerson; ***M:*** Bill Lee.

School for Scoundrels 𝒥𝒥𝒥 **1960** Top-notch British satire finds lifelong loser Henry Palfrey (Carmichael) about to have the girl of his dreams fall into the hands of rival Raymond Delauncey (Terry-Thomas). In desperation, Henry enrolls at the College of Lifemanship, learning to one-up his competition. Observed by teacher Potter (Sim), Henry tries turning the tables on those who've taken advantage of him. Vastly preferable to the mean-spirited 2006 remake. **90m/B DVD.** *GB* Ian Carmichael, Alastair Sim, Janette Scott, Dennis Price, Irene Handl, Terry-Thomas; ***D:*** Robert Hamer; ***W:*** Hal E. Chester, Patricia Moyes; ***C:*** Erwin Hillier; ***M:*** John Addison.

School for Scoundrels 𝒥 **2006 (PG-13)** Remake of the 1960 British comedy about a student-teacher battle for the same girl. Wimp Roger (Heder) needs to man up so he signs on for a course on self-esteem taught by arrogant Dr. P (Thornton). Roger gains enough confidence to ask out pretty neighbor Amanda (Barrett), only to discover that the leering doc is after the same babe, who is too good for either of these losers. A comedy that's not at all funny drags itself from mean-spirited to mushy. **101m/C DVD.** *US* Billy Bob Thornton, Jon Heder, Jacinda Barrett, Michael Clarke Duncan, Ben Stiller, Luis Guzman, Horatio Sanz, Sarah Silverman, David Cross, Todd Louiso, Steve Monroe; ***D:*** Todd Phillips; ***W:*** Todd Phillips, Scot Armstrong; ***C:*** Jonathan Brown; ***M:*** Christophe Beck.

School of Life 𝒥𝒥 1/2 **2006 (PG)** Stodgy middle school biology teacher Matt Warner (Paymer) is bent on continuing his late dad's (Astin) "Teacher of the Year" legacy but he feels challenged when a young and hip history teacher, Mr. D (Reynolds), comes along and wows everyone. A little touchy-feely at times, though Reynolds is fun to watch. **100m/C DVD.** David Paymer, Ryan Reynolds, John Astin, Andrew Robb, Kate Vernon; ***D:*** William Dear; ***W:*** Jonathan Kahn; ***C:*** Brian Pearson; ***M:*** Ari Wise. **TV**

School of Rock 𝒥𝒥𝒥 **2003 (PG-13)** Substitute any other actor for Jack Black and this movie becomes a direct-to-video blip, or doesn't get made at all. Black is Dewey Finn, a life-long rocker and true believer who gets tossed by his band and forced to get a job. Dewey snakes a teaching gig from his roomie, ending up at an exclusive elementary school with a stuffy principal (Cusack). There he finds a classroom full of precocious kids with musical talent and an entire spectrum of self-esteem problems. He molds them into a rock band with the intention of entering the Battle of the Bands. Some plot points are treated casually (sometimes to the point of ignoring them), but Black's wild-eyed, fully-committed performance easily carries the day, and he's ably supported by the kids, all of whom can actually play and sing, and by a savvy script that takes the music seriously. **108m/C VHS, DVD.** *US* Jack Black, Joan Cusack, Mike White, Sarah Silverman, Joey Gaydos, Miranda Cosgrove, Kevin Alexander Clark, Rebecca Julia Brown, Robert Tsai, Maryam Hassan, Caitlin Hale, Aleisha Allen, Brian Falduto, Zachary Infante, James Hosey, Angelo Massagli, Cole Hawkins, Nicole Afflerbach, Jordan-Claire Green, Adam Pascal, Chris Stack, Tim Hopper, Nicky Katt, Kate McGregor-Stewart; ***D:*** Richard Linklater; ***W:*** Mike White; ***C:*** Rogier Stoffers; ***M:*** Craig (Shudder to Think) Wedren.

School Spirit 𝒥 **1985 (R)** A hormonally motivated college student is killed during a date. He comes back as a ghost to haunt the campus, disrupt the stuffy president's affair, and fall in love. Forgettable, lame, low-grade teen sex flick. **90m/C VHS, DVD.** Tom Nolan, Elizabeth Foxx, Larry Linville; ***D:*** Allan Holleb; ***W:*** Geoffrey Baere; ***M:*** Tom Bruner.

School Ties 𝒥𝒥𝒥 **1992 (PG-13)** Encino man Fraser does a dramatic turn as a talented 1950s quarterback who gets a scholarship to the elite St. Matthew prep school. To conform with the closed-mindedness of the McCarthy era, both his father and coach suggest that he hide his Jewish religion. Fraser's compliance results in his big-man-on-campus status, until his rival in football and his love interest both find out that he is Jewish, creating an ugly rift in the school. What easily could have been just another teen hunk flick looks at much more than just Fraser's pretty face in successful, unflinching treatment of anti-Semitism. **110m/C VHS, DVD.** Brendan Fraser, Matt Damon, Chris O'Donnell, Randall Batinkoff, Andrew Lowery, Cole Hauser, Ben Affleck, Anthony Rapp, Amy Locane, Peter Donat, Zeljko Ivanek, Kevin Tighe, Michael Higgins, Ed Lauter; ***D:*** Robert Mandel; ***W:*** Darryl Ponicsan, Dick Wolf; ***C:*** Freddie Francis; ***M:*** Maurice Jarre.

School's Out 𝒥𝒥 1/2 *Schrei - denn ich werde dich toten!* **1999 (R)** At a high school graduation party/dance, some of the students wander off to pull pranks in the deserted school on the same night that a homicidal maniac who killed his last victim in the school escapes from an asylum. Bloody mayhem ensues. German import provides some first rate scares. **90m/C VHS, DVD.** *GE* Katharina Wackernagel, Marlene Meyer-Dunker, Nils Nellessen, Niels Bruno Schmidt; ***D:*** Robert Sigl; ***W:*** Kai Meyer; ***C:*** Sven Kirsten.

Schtonk 𝒥𝒥 **1992** Hermann Willie is a down-and-out journalist who thinks he's come upon the find of the century when he's given what are supposedly Hitler's diaries. Based on the 1983 scandal when the German publication "Der Stern" paid $5 million and printed what turned out to be not-very-clever forgeries. Director Dietl mocks the greedy gullibility of the journal, the ingenuity of the forger, as well as the nostalgia of the ex- and neo-Nazis of the modern Germany. The title is a meaningless expletive uttered by Charlie Chaplin in "The Great Dictator." German with subtitles. **115m/C VHS, DVD.** *GE* Goetz George, Uwe Ochsenknecht, Rolf Hoppe; ***D:*** Helmut Dietl; ***W:*** Helmut Dietl. Berlin Intl. Film Fest. '92: Actor (George), Director (Dietl), Film.

Schultze Gets the Blues 𝒥𝒥 1/2 **2003 (PG)** Bittersweet, sentimental comedy finds hefty bachelor salt miner Schultze (Krause) pushed into early retirement and wondering what he's going to do besides play the accordion at his local polka club. One night, Schultze's world changes when he happens to catch a zydeco song on the radio. Amazed at how different an accordion can sound, he sets his familiar polkas to a zydeco beat. Schulze's friends are equally amazed and decide to take up a collection and send him to compete in a music festival in their sister city of Moulton, Texas. Adventure is just the liberating journey that shy Schultze needs. German with subtitles. **114m/C DVD.** Horst Krause, Harald Warmbrunn, Karl-Fred Muller, Hannelore Schubert, Wolfgang Boos, Rosemarie Deibel, Wilhelmine Horschig, Anne V. Angelle, Ursula Schucht, Alozia St. Julien; ***D:*** Michael Schorr; ***W:*** Michael Schorr; ***C:*** Axel Schneppat; ***M:*** Thomas Wittenbecher.

Sci-Fighter 𝒥 1/2 *X-Treme Fighter* **2004** After playing a virtual reality game his grandpa designed, a teenager needs his father to join in to free him from the clutches of a vicious virus that won't let them leave without a fight. **90m/C VHS, DVD.** Don "The Dragon" Wilson, Cynthia Rothrock, Aki Aleong, Lorenzo Lamas, Dan(eya) Mayid, Rebecca Chaney; ***D:*** Art Camacho; ***W:*** Tom Callicoat; ***C:*** Andrea V. Rossotto; ***M:*** Vince DiCola. **VIDEO**

Sci-Fighters 𝒥𝒥 1/2 **1996 (R)** Renegade cop Cameron Grayson (Piper) is tracking rapist Adrian Dunn (Drago) in 2009 Boston and discovers that Dunn has been exposed to a deadly, mutating virus. It's actually changing the bad guy into an alien methane-breathing lifeform that, of course, wants to inhabit the earth. Appropriately gross alien makeup and some decent special effects. **94m/C VHS, DVD.** Roddy Piper, Billy Drago, Jayne Heitmeyer; ***D:*** Peter Svatek; ***W:*** Mark Sevi; ***C:*** Barry Gravelle; ***M:*** Milan Kymlicka.

Science Crazed 𝒥 1/2 **1990** A scientist creates a monster who could conceivably destroy the world. **90m/C VHS.** *CA* Tony Della Ventura, Robin Hartsell, Cameron Klein; ***D:*** Ron Switzer; ***W:*** Ron Switzer; ***C:*** Joe Maagdenberg.

The Science of Sleep 𝒥𝒥 **2006 (R)** Fanciful and surreal effort will appeal most to fans of Gondry's previous work. Immature and hyper-imaginative graphic artist Stephane (Garcia Bernal) has just returned to Paris and his mother (Miou-Miou) after growing up in Mexico with his divorced dad. Maybe he's suffering from culture shock and maybe Stephane is more than a little weird but he's certainly more comfortable living in his own fantasies. Stephane chums up with artist neighbor Stephanie (Gainsbourg) but pulls back from the romantic impulses he can't handle, going back into his dream world. Visually fascinating and sometimes funny, but the perpetual parade of dream sequences never pays off. **105m/C DVD.** *FR IT* Gael Garcia Bernal, Charlotte Gainsbourg, Alain Chabat, Miou-Miou, Pierre Vaneck, Emma de Caunes, Sacha Bourdo, Alain de Noyencourt; ***D:*** Michel Gondry; ***W:*** Michel Gondry; ***C:*** Jean-Louis Bompoint; ***M:*** Jean-Michel Bernard.

Scissors 𝒥 1/2 **1991 (R)** Yes, this Hitchcock imitation needs trimming. An unstable young woman contends with a rapist, devious lookalikes, birds, and a prison-like apartment, not all of which are relevant to the plot. An unsharp stab at suspense from novelist/filmmaker DeFelitta. **105m/C VHS.** Sharon Stone, Steve Railsback, Michelle Phillips, Ronny Cox, Albert "Poppy" Popwell; ***D:*** Frank De Felitta; ***W:*** Frank De Felitta.

Scooby-Doo 𝒥𝒥 **2002 (PG)** Zoinks! Everybody's favorite cartoon Great Dane comes to life in this live action-plus-CGI summer blockbuster. Fred (Prinze) is out to debunk the apparent haunting of theme-park Spooky Island, accompanied by Daphne (Gellar), Velma (Cardellini), Shaggy (Lillard), and Scooby, of course. The plot, which is shaky to begin with, goes against the theme of the cartoon, where there are no ghosts, and meddling kids overcome mean old men in wacky costumes. The movie only takes off when the CGI Scooby (a large reason for the inflated budget) is on screen. Based on the 1969 cartoon, "Scooby-Doo, Where Are You?" **87m/C VHS, DVD, UMD.** *US* Freddie Prinze Jr., Sarah Michelle Gellar, Matthew Lillard, Linda Cardellini, Rowan Atkinson, Miguel A. Nunez Jr., Stephen Grives, Isla Fisher, Sam Greco; ***D:*** Raja Gosnell; ***W:*** James Gunn, Craig Titley; ***C:*** David Eggby; ***M:*** David Newman.

Scooby-Doo 2: Monsters Unleashed 𝒥𝒥 **2004 (PG)** Those meddling kids are at it again! During their enshrinement into the Coolsonian Criminology Museum for all their prior do-good acts, all the ghosts and goblins on display suddenly come back to life and the gang sets out to unmask the culprit responsible. Shaggy (Lillard) and the CGI Scooby do not disappoint but this second act is weighed down with special-effects action sequences that play more violently (cartoonish, but still) than its predecessor. Seth Green is fun to watch as the museum's curator and Velma's love interest. **93m/C DVD.** *US* Freddie Prinze Jr., Sarah Michelle Gellar, Linda Cardellini, Matthew Lillard, Seth Green, Peter Boyle, Tim Blake Nelson, Alicia Silverstone; ***D:*** Raja Gosnell; ***W:*** James Gunn; ***C:*** Oliver Wood; ***M:*** David Newman; ***V:*** Neil Fanning, Ian Abercrombie. Golden Raspberries '04: Worst Remake/Sequel.

Scoop 𝒥𝒥 **2006 (PG-13)** Allen's 35th directorial feature is evidence he should ease up on that yearly quota. This time the kvetching centers around a naive journalism student (Johansson) who is given the scoop of a lifetime by the ghost of a muckraking journalist (McShane), and must investigate with the help of a third-rate magician (Allen) on whose stage the ghost appeared. Feels like a patchwork collection of past Allen flicks with nothing new or interesting, including the requisite abundance of self-centered Judaic jokes. **96m/C DVD.** *US* Woody Allen, Scarlett Johansson, Hugh Jackman, Ian McShane, Charles Dance, Romola Garai, Fenella Woolgar, Julian Glover, Victoria Hamilton, Anthony Head; ***D:*** Woody Allen; ***W:*** Woody Allen; ***C:*** Remi Adefarasin.

Scorched 𝒥𝒥 **2002 (PG-13)** Tepid crime caper finds three disgruntled bank tellers—unbeknownst to each other—deciding to rob their bank branch on the same day. Sheila has just been dumped by bank manager/longtime boyfriend Rick (Leonard) and wants to rob the ATM so he'll lose his job. Milquetoast desert-dwelling Jason (Harrelson) decides to steal the contents of the safety deposit box of evil millionaire Mr. Merchant (Cleese), who's caused him grief. And Stuart (Costanzo) has a Vegas get-rich-quick scheme that he decides to finance by taking the bank's ready cash. **94m/C DVD.** Alicia Silverstone, Woody Harrelson, John Cleese, Paulo Costanzo, Joshua Leonard, Rachael Leigh Cook, David Krumholtz; ***D:*** Gavin Grazer; ***W:*** Joe Wein; ***C:*** Bruce Douglas Johnson; ***M:*** John (Gianni) Frizzell.

Scorcher 𝒥 1/2 **2002 (R)** China sets off a series of underground nuclear explosions that cause tectonic plate shifts, earthquakes, volcanoes, and a rapid rise in global temperature. The only way to save the planet is a nuclear counterstrike—centered beneath L.A. in three days. So the city is evacuated and the usual team of misfits is assembled to do the impossible. At least this flick's fast-paced enough to run right over all those pesky plot holes. **87m/C VHS, DVD.** Mark Dacascos, Rutger Hauer, John Rhys-Davies, Mark Rolston, G.W. Bailey, Rayne Marcus, Tamara Davies; ***D:*** James Seale; ***W:*** Steve Latshaw, Rebecca Morrison; ***C:*** Maximo Munzi; ***M:*** Bill Brown. **VIDEO**

Scorchers 𝒥𝒥 **1992 (R)** Back in the bayou, Splendid (Lloyd), a newlywed who won't sleep with her husband, and her cousin Talbot (Tilly), a preacher's daughter whose husband prefers the town whore Thais (Dunaway), find their lives intertwined because of their marital and sexual problems. A real "scorcher." **81m/C VHS, DVD.** Faye Dunaway, Denholm Elliott, James Earl Jones, Emily Lloyd, Jennifer Tilly, Leland Crooke, James Wilder, Anthony Geary; ***D:*** David Beaird; ***W:*** David Beaird.

Scorchy 𝒥 **1976 (R)** Low-budget female cop action flick about a narcotics agent (Stevens) on the trail of a drug kingpin. Blood and guts, guns, and violence. Poor casting. **100m/C VHS.** Connie Stevens, William (Bill) Smith, Cesare Danova, Marlene Schmidt; ***D:*** Howard (Hikmet) Avedis; ***W:*** Howard (Hikmet) Avedis.

Score 𝒥𝒥 **1972** Swinging marrieds Jack and Elvira turn their attention to a newlywed couple in order to indulge their sexual desires. Campy, culty erotica. **89m/C VHS, DVD.** Calvin Culver, Claire Wilbur, Lynn Lowry, Gerald Grant, Carl Parker; ***D:*** Radley Metzger; ***W:*** Jerry Douglas; ***C:*** Franco Vodopivec.

Score WOOF! 1995 If you've seen "Hard Boiled," "City on Fire," or "Reservoir Dogs," then you can skip this one. Chance (Ozawa) is released from prison and forced to return to work for his old crime boss. Chance recruits three other thieves to rip off a jewelry store. Following the robbery, distrust sets in amongst the crooks and a pair of hitchhikers interfere with their getaway plans. Borrows liberally from the films mentioned above and is never exciting or engaging. Instead, it's morally ambiguous and boring. Also, this film features some of the thinnest and reddest blood ever seen in a movie. **94m/C DVD.** *JP* Hitoshi Ozawa, Osamu Ebara, Ryuuji Minakami, Kazuyoshi Ozawa, Miyuki Takano, Masahiro Yamashita; ***D:*** Atsushi Muroga.

The Score ♂♂ 1/2 2001 (R) Slow-starting crime comedy with De Niro as a semi-retired thief, living a quiet life running a Montreal jazz club, until his fence (Brando) and a wannabe theif (Norton) talk him into pulling another job in Montreal's customs house. Bassett is DeNiro's squeeze (good taste there) who wants him out of the life. Painstaking but realistic in its portrayal of the preparation and events leading to the heist, but when things finally get going, it crackles with tense "will-they-get-caught" moments and double-crosses aplenty. De Niro is solid, as always, but he seems like he may be getting too old for this stuff. Norton gets most of the screen time, and uses it well. Brando is surprisingly understated in an amusing way. **124m/C VHS, DVD.** *US* Robert De Niro, Edward Norton, Marlon Brando, Angela Bassett, Gary Farmer, Paul Soles, Jamie Harrold; ***D:*** Frank Oz; ***W:*** Kario Salem, Scott Marshall Smith, Lem Dobbs; ***C:*** Rob Hahn; ***M:*** Howard Shore.

Scorned ♂♂ 1993 (R) Seductive Patricia Langley loves her husband Truman so much that she'll do anything to help him get that promotion, including seducing another man. Too bad Alex Weston gets the promotion instead. Really too bad, since Patricia decides Alex has ruined her life and she's going to get revenge by ruining his. Also available in an unrated version. **100m/C VHS.** Shannon Tweed, Andrew Stevens, Michael D. Arenz, Kim Morgan Greene, Stephen Young, Daniel McVicar; ***D:*** Andrew Stevens; ***W:*** Barry Avrich.

Scorned 2 ♂ 1/2 1996 (R) Amanda (McClure) seems happily married to psych prof Mark—even if she is having those bad dreams. But when her hubby is tempted by a pretty coed and Amanda finds out—well this is one woman that should never be scorned. **105m/C VHS, DVD.** Tane McClure, Wendy Schumacher, Myles O'Brien, John McCook, Andrew Stevens, Seth Jaffe; ***D:*** Rodney McDonald; ***W:*** Sean McGinley; ***C:*** Gary Graver; ***M:*** Patrick Seymour.

Scorpio ♂♂ 1/2 1973 (PG) Okay cat-and-mouse espionage tale about a wily, veteran CIA agent (Lancaster) who may have turned traitor. He's set-up to be killed by a CIA boss but the assassin, code-name Scorpio (Delon), has some trouble fulfilling his assignment. Cross- and double-cross abound. **114m/C VHS, DVD.** Burt Lancaster, Alain Delon, Paul Scofield, John Colicos, Gayle Hunnicutt, J.D. Cannon, Joanne Linville, Melvin Stewart, James B. Sikking, Vladek Sheybal, William (Bill) Smithers, Celeste Yarnall; ***D:*** Michael Winner; ***W:*** David W. Rintels, Gerald Wilson.

The Scorpio Factor ♂♂ 1990 Murder and mayhem follow microchip heist. **87m/C VHS, DVD.** Attila Bertalan, David Nerman, Wendy Dawn Wilson; ***D:*** Michel Wachniuc; ***W:*** Carole Sauve, June Pinheiro; ***C:*** Bruno Philip; ***M:*** Richard Gresko.

Scorpio One ♂ 1/2 1997 (R) Scientists aboard spacestation Scorpio One have made a discovery that has cost them their lives and may now cause the destruction of earth. **92m/C VHS.** Jeff Speakman, Robert Carradine, Robin Curtis, Steve Kanaly, George Murdock, Judith Chapman; ***D:*** Worth Keeler; ***W:*** Steve Latshaw; ***C:*** Doyle Smith; ***M:*** David Wurst, Eric Wurst.

Scorpion ♂ 1986 (R) A karate-master and anti-terrorist expert defuses a skyjacking and infiltrates international assassination conspiracies. Ex-real life karate champ Tulleners is a ho-hum hero, and the story is warmed over. **98m/C VHS, DVD.** Tonny Tulleners, Allen Williams, Don Murray; ***D:*** William Reed.

The Scorpion King ♂♂ 2002 (PG-13) Billed as a prequel to "The Mummy" series, this actioner is more in the "Sword 'n' Sandals" vein. The Rock is the title star, an assassin hired by a group of beleaguered tribes to defeat the evil warlord Memnon (Brand). The warlord is helped, somewhat unenthusiastically, by a sorceress (Hu) who can foresee the outcome of battles. Yes, it's cheesy, and downright silly at times, but it doesn't really strive for any more than that. The only motivation behind the whole endeavor seems to be to make The Rock a movie star, and if he sticks with action pics, he seems to be on his way. All the men do the requisite amount of killing, and discussing killing, and the women are all scantily clad. The target audience should be overjoyed. **94m/C VHS, DVD, HD DVD.** *US* Dwayne "The Rock" Johnson, Michael Clarke Duncan, Steven Brand, Kelly Hu, Bernard Hill, Grant Heslov, Peter Facinelli, Ralph (Ralf) Moeller, Branscombe Richmond, Roger Rees, Sherri Howard, Conrad Roberts; ***D:*** Chuck Russell; ***W:*** Stephen Sommers, William Osborne, David Hayter; ***C:*** John R. Leonetti; ***M:*** John Debney.

The Scorpion King 2: Rise of a Warrior ♂ 1/2 2008 (PG-13) A prequel to the 2002 prequel that follows the standard how-a-legend-is-born template. Young Mathayus witnesses his father's murder at the hands of evil warlord Sargon (Couture). He hones his body and fighting skills until the adult Mathayus (Copon) can get his revenge on the man, who is now king. There's also a sword-wielding, leather-clad babe (David), who takes up with our hero, and a sorceress hottie (Becker) on the bad guy's side. **109m/C DVD.** Michael Copon, Karen Shenaz David, Randy Couture, Natalie Becker, Simon Quaterman; ***D:*** Russell Mulcahy; ***W:*** Randall McCormick; ***C:*** Glynn Speeckaert; ***M:*** Klaus Badelt. **VIDEO**

Scorpion Spring ♂♂ 1996 (R) Drug runner Astor (Morales) is on the lam through the desert with a beautiful hostage (Aviles) when two unsuspecting travelers (Molina and McGaw) offer the stranded duo a ride. But drug lord El Rojo (McConaughey) wants Astor dead and doesn't care who gets in his way and there's also a border patrol officer (Blades) on their trail as well. **89m/C VHS, DVD.** Esai Morales, Alfred Molina, Patrick McGaw, Matthew McConaughey, Angel Aviles, Ruben Blades, Miguel (Michael) Sandoval, Richard Edson, John Doe; ***D:*** Brian Cox; ***W:*** Brian Cox; ***C:*** Nancy Schreiber; ***M:*** Lalo Schifrin.

Scorpion with Two Tails ♂ 1982 In an underworld of terror, people die grotesque deaths that a woman dreams of. **99m/C VHS.** *IT* Paolo Malco, Claudio Cassinelli, Marilu Tolo, Elvire Audray, John Saxon, Van Johnson; ***D:*** Sergio Martino; ***W:*** Ernesto Gastaldi; ***C:*** Giancarlo Ferrando; ***M:*** Fabio Frizzi.

The Scorpion Woman ♂♂ 1989 A female Viennese judge becomes entwined in an unusual case which partially parallels her own life. Her new young lover turns out to be bisexual. Not gripping. In German with English subtitles. **101m/C VHS.** *GE* Angelica Domrose, Fritz Hammel; ***D:*** Susanne Zanke.

The Scorpion's Tail ♂ 1971 Graphic murder scenes rev up this early thriller by Martino filmed with plot twists and visual games. Dubbed in English. **90m/C VHS, DVD.** *IT SP* Evelyn Stewart, Anita Strindberg, George Hilton, Luigi Pistilli, Janine Reynaud; ***D:*** Sergio Martino; ***W:*** Sauro Scavolini, Ernesto Gastaldi; ***M:*** Bruno Nicolai.

Scotland, PA ♂♂ 1/2 2002 (R) Shakespeare's "Macbeth" meets Mcjobs in director Morrissette's original black comedy set in 1970s rural Pennsylvania. Far from royalty, these McBeths, Slacker Mac (LeGros) and wife Pat (Tierney), are burger flippers at Duncan's, toiling away on minimum wage. At Pat's urging, they off nepotistic restaurant owner Norm Duncan (Rebhorn) after a promotion goes to his two sons. After a fryer "mishap" and a cover-up, the power-hungry couple are then free to have it their way, remodeling the restaurant and changing the name to McBeth's, complete with a (wink-wink) giant "M." However, vegetarian cop McDuff (Walken) is assigned to find Duncan's killer. Falls just short of reaching full potential, but Tierney is especially great and the black humor should prove enjoyable for both Shakespeare and non-Shakespeare fans alike. **102m/C VHS, DVD.** *US* Maura Tierney, James LeGros, Christopher Walken, Kevin Corrigan, James Rebhorn, Tom Guiry, Amy Smart, Andy Dick, Josh Pais, Geoff Dunsworth; ***D:*** Billy Morrissette; ***W:*** Billy Morrissette; ***C:*** Wally Pfister; ***M:*** Anton Sanko.

Scotland Yard Inspector ♂♂ *Lady in the Fog* **1952** An American newspaperman (Romero) in London looks for a killer. Nothing special. **73m/B VHS.** *GB* Cesar Romero, Bernadette O'Farrell, Lois Maxwell, Geoffrey Keen, Campbell Singer; ***D:*** Sam Newfield; ***W:*** Orville H. Hampton; ***C:*** Walter J. (Jimmy W.) Harvey; ***M:*** Ivor Slaney.

Scott of the Antarctic ♂♂ 1/2 1948 Drama of doomed British expedition of 1911 struggling to be the first group to reach the South Pole. Much of the stunning location filming was shot in the Swiss Alps. Story is authentic, but oddly uninvolving, as though seen from afar. **111m/C VHS, DVD.** *GB* John Mills, Christopher Lee, Kenneth More, Derek Bond; ***D:*** Charles Frend; ***C:*** Geoffrey Unsworth.

Scott Pilgrim vs. the World 2010 Twenty-something garage band bass player Scott Pilgrim (Cera) almost has it all, especially when beautiful Ramona Flowers (Winstead) shows up. Too bad she has seven crazy ex-boyfriends who want to eliminate Scott from Ramona's life—permanently. Adapted from Bryan Lee O'Malley's graphic novel. **m/C DVD.** *US* Michael Cera, Mary Elizabeth Winstead, Kieran Culkin, Chris Evans, Anna Kendrick, Alison Pill, Brandon Routh, Jason Schwartzman, Mae Whitman, Brie Larson, Aubrey Plaza; ***D:*** Edgar Wright; ***W:*** Edgar Wright, Michael Bacall; ***C:*** Bill Pope.

Scott Turow's The Burden of Proof ♂♂ 1/2 *The Burden of Proof* **1992** Attorney Alejandro "Sandy" Stern (Elizondo) struggles to discover the reasons behind his wife's baffling suicide and deal with the problems caused by the federal investigation of his brother-in-law's commodities business. The character of Stern was also featured in the film "Presumed Innocent" (played by Raul Julia). TV movie; on two cassettes. **184m/C VHS.** Hector Elizondo, Brian Dennehy, Mel Harris, Stefanie Powers, Victoria Principal, Adrienne Barbeau, Anne Bobby, Gail Strickland, Concetta Tomei, Jeffrey Tambor; ***D:*** Mike Robe; ***C:*** Kees Van Oostrum.

The Scout ♂♂ 1994 (PG-13) Brooks is an about-to-be-canned scout for the New York Yankees who discovers a weird, though genuine, phenom pitcher (Fraser) on a trip to Mexico. He convinces the Yankees to take the phenom on, though he's not sure whether Fraser isn't a few innings shy of a complete game. But with a 100 mph fast ball and a bat that would have made Babe Ruth envious, who cares? Film straddles sports comedy and melodrama territories, satisfying in neither. Fraser plays variation on Encino Man. Brooks rewrote part of the script, adding much needed biting humor, but not enough. Bombastic real-life team owner Steinbrenner plays himself. **101m/C VHS, DVD.** Albert Brooks, Brendan Fraser, Dianne Wiest, Lane Smith, Michael Rapaport, Steve Garvey, Bob Costas, Roy Firestone, Anne Twomey, Tony Bennett; ***D:*** Michael Ritchie; ***W:*** Albert Brooks, Andrew Bergman, Monica Johnson; ***C:*** Laszlo Kovacs; ***M:*** Bill Conti.

Scout's Honor ♂♂ 1980 An orphan (Coleman) is determined to become the best Cub Scout ever when he joins a troop led by an executive who dislikes children. Harmless, enjoyable family tale includes several former child stars as Scout parents. **96m/C VHS.** Gary Coleman, Katherine Helmond, Wilfrid Hyde-White, Pat O'Brien, Joanna Moore, Meeno Peluce, Jay North, Harry (Henry) Morgan, Angela Cartwright; ***D:*** Henry Levin. **TV**

Scream ♂ 1983 (R) Vacationers on a raft trip down the Rio Grande are terrorized by a mysterious murderer. Hopelessly dull. **86m/C VHS.** Pepper Martin, Hank Worden, Alvy Moore, Woody Strode, John Ethan Wayne; ***D:*** Byron Quisenberry.

Scream ♂♂♂ *Scary Movie* **1996 (R)** Director Craven playfully tweaks the cliches of teen slasher pics (which he helped create with "Nightmare on Elm Street") with this tongue-in-cheek thriller. Yep, where there's a mad slasher on the loose, there must be a group of teenagers "just out for a good time." The difference is both the killer and the victims have been raised on '80s splatter movies and, therefore, know all the rules. Sexual activity and/or substance abuse? Start picking out coffins. The stalker uses his cellular phone to terrorize his victims. He also uses it to ask his prey trivia questions or offer critiques of low-grade horror movies. Campbell plays the virginal heroine in the tight sweater, with Ulrich playing opposite as the sexually frustrated boyfriend. More fun than a bucket full of Karo syrup with red dye #3. **111m/C VHS, DVD.** Matthew Lillard, Drew Barrymore, Neve Campbell, Courteney Cox, David Arquette, Skeet Ulrich, Rose McGowan, Henry Winkler, Liev Schreiber, W. Earl Brown, Jamie Kennedy, Lawrence Hecht; ***Cameos:*** Wes Craven, Linda Blair; ***D:*** Wes Craven; ***W:*** Kevin Williamson; ***C:*** Mark Irwin; ***M:*** Marco Beltrami. MTV Movie Awards '97: Film.

Scream 2 ♂♂♂ *Scream Again* **1997 (R)** Sidney (Campbell) trades psychotheraphy for college, only to be harassed by a lunatic willing to duplicate her nightmares from the original. All the cast that survived the first pic are back (and some new faces, with O'Connell as Sidney's new boyfriend) including TV-tabloider Gale Weathers (Cox), who has turned a best-seller about the murders into a movie called "Stab"; lovable, huggable sheriff Dewey (Arquette); and horror film fanatic Randy (Kennedy). Director Craven and writer Williamson add more of the satirical spark that propelled its predecessor into box-office success. By following the rules of sequels, they increase the suspense (everyone is a suspect) and gore to tantalizing fun, making this entry to the popular franchise a hard one to top. **120m/C VHS, DVD.** Courteney Cox, Neve Campbell, Jerry O'Connell, David Arquette, Jada Pinkett Smith, Jamie Kennedy, Liev Schreiber, Sarah Michelle Gellar, Laurie Metcalf, Elise Neal, Lewis Arquette, Duane Martin, Omar Epps, David Warner, Timothy Olyphant, Rebecca Gayheart, Portia de Rossi, Heather Graham; ***Cameos:*** Tori Spelling; ***D:*** Wes Craven; ***W:*** Kevin Williamson; ***C:*** Peter Deming; ***M:*** Marco Beltrami. MTV Movie Awards '98: Female Perf. (Campbell).

Scream 3 ♂♂ 1/2 2000 (R) The filmmakers swear that this series is indeed only a trilogy. Good thing because, while entertaining enough, this third film is showing wear. Sidney is working as a crisis counselor and living in blessed anonymity in northern California. However, the actors involved in "Stab 3" are being offed and it ties in to her mother's mysterious past, so Sid is forced to resurface. Ambitious Gale (Cox Arquette) returns as does dopey Dewey (Arquette) and newcomer LAPD detective Kincaid (Dempsey) tries to figure out if there are any film rules that will help him catch a killer. **116m/C VHS, DVD.** Neve Campbell, David Arquette, Courteney Cox, Patrick Dempsey, Scott Foley, Lance Henriksen, Matt Keeslar, Jenny McCarthy, Emily Mortimer, Parker Posey, Deon Richmond, Patrick Warburton, Liev Schreiber, Heather Matarazzo, Jamie Kennedy, Carrie Fisher, Kevin Smith, Jason Mewes, Roger Corman; ***D:*** Wes Craven; ***W:*** Ehren Kruger; ***C:*** Peter Deming; ***M:*** Marco Beltrami.

Scream and Scream Again ♂♂ 1/2 *Screamer* **1970 (PG)** Price is a sinister doctor who tries to create a super race of people devoid of emotions. Cushing is the mastermind behind the plot. Lee is the agent investigating a series of murders. Three great horror stars, a psychadelic disco, great '60s fashions; it's all here. **95m/C VHS, DVD.** *GB* Vincent Price, Christopher Lee, Peter Cushing, Judy Huxtable, Alfred Marks, Anthony Newlands, Uta Levka, Judi Bloom, Yutte Stensgaard; ***D:*** Gordon Hessler; ***W:*** Christopher Wicking; ***C:*** John Coquillon.

Scream, Baby, Scream ♂ *Nightmare House* **1969** An unsuccessful artist switches from sculpting clay to carving young models' faces into hideous deformed creatures. **86m/C VHS, DVD.** Ross Harris, Eugenie Wingate, Chris Martell, Suzanne Stuart, Larry Swanson, Brad Grinter; ***D:*** Joseph Adler.

Scream Blacula Scream ♂♂ 1973 (R) Blacula returns from his dusty undoing in the original movie to once again suck the blood out of greater Los Angeles. A voodoo priestess (Grier) is the only person with the power to stop him. A weak follow up to the great "Blacula," but worth a look for Marshall and Grier. **96m/C VHS, DVD.** William Marshall, Don Mitchell, Pam Grier, Michael Conrad, Richard Lawson, Lynne Moody, Janee Michelle, Barbara Rhoades, Bernie Hamilton; ***D:*** Bob Kelljan.

Scream Bloody Murder WOOF! 1972 (R) A young boy grinds his father to death with a tractor but mangles his own hand trying to jump off. After receiving a steel claw and being released from a mental institution he continues his murderous ways in and around his home town. Inspiring. **90m/C VHS, DVD.** Fred Holbert, Leigh Mitchell, Robert Knox, Suzette Hamilton; ***D:*** Robert Emery.

Scream Dream 1989 (R) A beautiful rock star uses her supernatural powers to control her fans, turning them into revenge-seeking monsters when she wants to. Heavy on the blood and skin; heavily exploitative. **80m/C VHS.** Melissa Moore, Carole Carr, Nikki Riggins, Jesse Ray; ***D:*** Donald Farmer; ***W:*** Donald Farmer.

Scream for Help 1986 (R) A young girl discovers that her cheating stepfather is plotting to murder her mother, but no one will believe her. Is she paranoid? So bad it's funny; otherwise, it's just bad, and far from suspenseful. **95m/C VHS.** Rachael Kelly, David Allan Brooks, Marie Masters; ***D:*** Michael Winner; ***W:*** Tom Holland.

Scream of Fear *Taste of Fear* **1961** A wheelchair-bound young woman goes to visit her father and new stepmother only to find her father is away on business. But she believes she sees her father's corpse. Is someone trying to drive her mad? Abounds in plot twists and mistaken identities. A truly spooky film, suspenseful, and well-made. **81m/B VHS.** *GB* Susan Strasberg, Ronald Lewis, Ann Todd, Christopher Lee; ***D:*** Seth Holt; ***W:*** Jimmy Sangster.

Scream of the Demon Lover WOOF! 1971 (R) A young biochemist has a busy day as she works for a reclusive Baron. She fantasizes about him, tries to track down a murderer, and eventually discovers a mutant in the cellar. About as bad as they come, but short! **75m/C VHS.** Jennifer Hartley, Jeffrey Chase; ***D:*** Jose Luis Merino.

Scream of the Wolf 1974 Author and ex-hunter John (Graves) is called on to help the police in their investigation of a series of murders that seem to have been caused by a wolf that can walk on two legs. He turns to Byron (Walker), an old friend and obsessive hunter (think Zaroff in "The Most Dangerous Game") for help, but Byron refuses, arguing that the murders are making the people in the community feel more alive than ever. Byron involves John in a battle of brawn and hunting skill that will ultimately reveal the truth behind the killings. Passable TV movie by director Curtis feels like another attempt to create a "Kolchak: The Night Stalker"-type TV series, complete with Graves's flashy red Corvette, and a jazzy '70s "wokka-chikka" soundtrack. **74m/C VHS, DVD.** Peter Graves, Clint Walker, JoAnn Pflug, Phil Carey, James Storm; ***D:*** Dan Curtis; ***W:*** Richard Matheson, David Case; ***C:*** Paul Lohmann; ***M:*** Robert Cobert. **TV**

Screamer 1974 A woman wants revenge after she is viciously attacked and raped. Now every man she sees is her attacker as she becomes more and more unbalanced. **71m/C VHS.** Pamela Franklin, Donal McCann; ***D:*** Shaun O'Riordan; ***W:*** Brian Clemens.

Screamers *L'Isola Degli Uomini Pesce; Island of the Fishmen; Something Waits in the Dark* **1980 (R)** A mad scientist on a desert island gleefully turns escaped convicts into grotesque monstrosities. Gory and gratuitous. **83m/C VHS.** Richard Johnson, Joseph Cotten, Barbara Bach; ***D:*** Dan T. Miller, Sergio Martino.

Screamers 1996 (R) In the year 2078, Colonel Joe Hendricksson (Weller) and a small band of survivors fight a civil war on the radiation contaminated planet Sirius 6B. They run up against the screamers—mechanical creatures with razor-sharp claws, originally designed to protect humans. The screamers are bent on destroying all life in the universe while somehow mutating and breeding on their own. Unfortunately, director Duguay doesn't give any indication how this is taking place. Some fine stunt work and special effects redeem standard action adventure. Based on the novella "Second Variety" by Philip K. Dick ("Blade Runner"). **107m/C VHS, DVD.** Peter Weller, Jennifer Rubin, Andrew Lauer, Charles Powell, Ron White, Michael Caloz; ***D:*** Christian Duguay; ***W:*** Dan O'Bannon, Miguel Tejada-Flores; ***C:*** Rodney Gibbons; ***M:*** Normand Corbeil.

Screamers: The Hunting ½ 2009 (R) It's been 13 years since the robotic screamers destroyed the human colony on Sirius 6B. But when a distress signal is picked up from the supposedly deserted planet it attracts a rescue team. What they discover is that the screamers have evolved into mutant machine/human hybrids still out to destroy the human race. Based on the Philip K. Dick story. **95m/C DVD.** Greg Bryk, Gina Holden, Tim Rozon, Christopher Redman, Lance Henriksen; ***D:*** Sheldon Wilson; ***W:*** Miguel Tejada-Flores; ***C:*** John Tarver; ***M:*** Benoit Grey. **VIDEO**

The Screaming Dead *Dracula vs. Frankenstein* **1972** Monsters rise from the tomb to do battle with planet Earth and each other. Not to be confused with the Al Adamson epic "Dracula vs. Frankenstein." **84m/C VHS, DVD.** *SP* Dennis Price, Howard Vernon, Alberto Dalbes, Mary Francis, Genevieve Deloir, Josianne Gibert, Fernando Bilbao; ***D:*** Jess (Jesus) Franco.

Screaming Dead 2003 (R) Satisfactory exploitation/horror flick has a fetish photographer, his assistant, and some models doing a shoot in an abandoned, possibly haunted hospital where hundreds of patients were tortured and killed in a basement dungeon. Not as much skin or gore as you'd expect from the set-up, and it takes a while to get going, but it's not too bad for fans of the genre. **95m/C DVD.** Misty Mundae, Rob Monkiewicz, Joseph Farrell, Rachael Robbins, Heidi Kristoffer; ***D:*** Bret Piper; ***W:*** Bret Piper; ***M:*** Jon Greathouse. **VIDEO**

The Screaming Skull ½ 1958 Man redecorates house with skulls in attempt to drive already anxious wife insane. **68m/B VHS, DVD.** William (Bill) Hudson, Peggy Webber, Toni Johnson, Russ Conway, Alex Nicol; ***D:*** Alex Nicol; ***M:*** Ernest Gold.

Screams of a Winter Night 1979 (PG) Ghostly tale of an evil monster from the lake and the terror he causes. **92m/C VHS.** Matt Borel, Gil Glasco; ***D:*** Philippe Mora; ***W:*** Philippe Mora.

Screamtime 1983 (R) Two fiendish friends filch a trilogy of horror tapes for home viewing. After the show, real scary things happen. **89m/C VHS.** Jean Anderson, Robin Bailey, Dora Bryan, David Van Day; ***D:*** Al Beresford.

Screen Test WOOF! 1985 (R) Oversexed silly teenagers arrange fake screen tests in order to meet girls. **84m/C VHS.** Michael Allan Bloom, Robert Bundy, Paul Lueken, David Simpatico, Cynthia Kahn, Mari Laskarin, Katherine Sullivan, Monique Gabrielle, Michelle (McClellan) Bauer, Deborah Blaisdell; ***D:*** Sam Auster; ***W:*** Sam Auster; ***C:*** Jeffrey Jur.

Screw Loose *Svitati* **1999 (R)** Bernardo's (Greggio) dying father (Barra) has one last request—he wants a reunion with his American WWII buddy Jake (Brooks). So being a dutiful son, Bernardo comes to America and discovers Jake is in an L.A. mental institution. Nevertheless, he breaks him out and flies Jake back to Italy with him—followed by Jake's doctor, Barbara (Condra). And it turns out maybe Jake isn't the only one with a few loose screws. Slapsticky, with a weak script. **85m/C VHS, DVD.** *IT* Mel Brooks, Ezio Greggio, Gianfranco Barra, Julie Condra, Randi Ingerman; ***D:*** Ezio Greggio; ***W:*** Rudy DeLuca, Steve Haberman; ***C:*** Luca Robecchi.

Screwball Academy ½ 1986 (R) A beautiful female director makes a soft-core film on a secluded island, and gets trouble from thugs, evangelists, horny crew members and others. Former "SCTV" director John Blanchard understandably used a pseudonym to direct this lame effort. **90m/C VHS.** Colleen Camp, Kenneth Welsh, Christine Cattall; ***D:*** Reuben Rose.

Screwballs 1983 (R) Freewheeling group of high school boys stirs up trouble for their snooty and virginal homecoming queen. Another inept teen sex comedy with no subtlety whatsoever. Sequel: "Loose Screws." **80m/C VHS.** Peter Keleghan, Lynda Speciale; ***D:*** Rafal Zielinski; ***W:*** Jim Wynorski.

Screwed WOOF! 2000 (PG-13) Chauffeur MacDonald tries kidnapping his mean boss's dog for ransom but things get screwed up so badly that the boss thinks it's the chauffeur that's been kidnapped. Lame physical and gross-out "comedy" ensues. Just who the title refers to is never made clear, but it seems like it's the producers, who had to pay the actors and writer/directors for this, ahem, dog. DeVito is the only one on screen who seems to know what he's doing, and Alexander and Karaszewski look to be cashing in on some far superior prior screenwriting work. **82m/C VHS, DVD.** Norm MacDonald, Elaine Stritch, Danny DeVito, Dave Chappelle, Daniel Benzali, Sherman Hemsley, Malcolm Stewart; ***D:*** Scott M. Alexander, Larry Karaszewski; ***W:*** Scott M. Alexander, Larry Karaszewski; ***C:*** Robert Brinkmann; ***M:*** Michel Colombier.

Scrooge 1935 On Christmas Eve a miser changes his ways after receiving visits from the ghosts of Christmas past, present, and future. Co-scripter Hicks gives an interesting performance as Ebeneezer Scrooge. Based on the classic novel "A Christmas Carol" by Charles Dickens. **61m/B VHS, DVD.** *GB* Sir Seymour Hicks, Maurice Evans, Robert Cochran, Donald Calthrop, Mary Glynne, Oscar Asche; ***D:*** Henry Edwards; ***W:*** Sir Seymour Hicks; ***C:*** Sydney Blythe, William Luff.

Scrooge ½ 1970 (G) Well done musical version of Charles Dickens' classic "A Christmas Carol," about a miserly old man who is faced with ghosts on Christmas Eve. Finney is memorable in the title role. ♫ The Beautiful Day; Happiness; Thank You Very Much; A Christmas Carol; Christmas Children; I Hate People; Farver Chris'mas; See the Phantoms; December the 25th. **86m/C VHS, DVD.** *GB* Albert Finney, Alec Guinness, Edith Evans, Kenneth More; ***D:*** Ronald Neame; ***W:*** Leslie Bricusse; ***C:*** Oswald Morris; ***M:*** Leslie Bricusse. Golden Globes '71: Actor—Mus./Comedy (Finney).

Scrooged 1988 (PG-13) Somewhat disjointed big-budgeted version of the hallowed classic. A callous TV executive staging "A Christmas Carol" is himself visited by the three ghosts and sees the light. Kane is terrific as one of the ghosts. Film is heavy-handed, Murray too sardonic to be believable. **101m/C VHS, DVD.** Bill Murray, Carol Kane, John Forsythe, David Johansen, Bob(cat) Goldthwait, Karen Allen, Michael J. Pollard, Brian Doyle-Murray, Alfre Woodard, John Glover, Robert Mitchum, Buddy Hackett, Robert Goulet, Jamie Farr, Mary Lou Retton, Lee Majors, Damon Hines, Mary Ellen Trainor, Mabel King, Wendie Malick, Joel Murray, John Houseman, Steve Kahan, Kate McGregor-Stewart; ***D:*** Richard Donner; ***W:*** Mitch Glazer, Michael O'Donoghue; ***C:*** Michael Chapman; ***M:*** Danny Elfman.

Scrubbers 1982 (R) Young girl is sent to reform school where she's forced to survive in a cruel and brutal environment. Low-budget "reform school" movie with no point, but lots of lesbianism. **93m/C VHS.** *GB* Amanda York, Chrissie Cotterill, Elizabeth Edmonds, Kate Ingram, Debbie Bishop, Dana Gillespie; ***D:*** Mai Zetterling.

Scruples ½ 1980 Set in the glamorous, jet-setting world of Beverly Hills, this top-rated miniseries follows the career of Billy Ikehorn (Wagner) as she weds a wealthy industrialist and opens a clothing boutique named "Scruples." She caters to high society's haute couture, and encounters unscrupulous individuals who threaten to dethrone her from her position of power and privilege. Based on the best-selling novel by Judith Krantz. **279m/C VHS.** Lindsay Wagner, Barry Bostwick, Kim Cattrall, Gavin MacLeod, Connie Stevens, Efrem Zimbalist Jr., Gene Tierney; ***M:*** Charles Bernstein.

The Sculptress 1997 Troubled writer Rosalind Leigh (Goodall) prepares to interview convicted killer Olive Martin (Quirke), who five years before was found with the dead bodies of her mother and sister. Nicknamed "The Sculptress" for the gruesome nature of the murders, the equally troubled Olive is also a convincing liar. Although Olive says she's guilty, Roz is certain she's hiding something and becomes determined to discover the truth. Very creepy. Made for British TV; based on the novel by Minette Walters. **180m/C VHS, DVD.** *GB* Caroline Goodall, Pauline Quirke, Christopher Fulford, Dermot Crowley, David Horovitch, Jay Villiers, Lynda Rooke; ***D:*** Stuart Orme; ***W:*** Reg Gadney; ***C:*** Gavin Finney; ***M:*** Colin Towns. **TV**

Scum 1979 Adapted from Roy Minton's acclaimed play, this British production looks at the struggle among three young men in a British Borstal (a prison for young convicts.) Portrays the physical, sexual, and psychological violence committed. Horrifying and powerful. **96m/C VHS, DVD.** *GB* Phil Daniels, Mick Ford, Ray Winstone; ***D:*** Alan Clarke.

Scum of the Earth ½ 1963 Early '60s skin flick about innocent young Kim (Miles), who is cruelly tricked into posing topless for a photographer and is then blackmailed into a downward spiral of sleaze that ends in murder and suicide. The film features much of the cast and crew of director Lewis's "Blood Feast." **73m/B DVD.** Vicki (Allison Louise Downe) Miles, Lawrence Wood, Mal Arnold, Thomas Sweetwood, Sandy Sinclair; ***D:*** Herschell Gordon Lewis; ***W:*** Herschell Gordon Lewis.

The Sea 2002 A "King Lear" variation set in Iceland and concerned with fish. Fierce patriarch Thordur (Eyolfsson) summons his three adult children to discuss the family fishery. The kids are upset because dad never modernized the business and it can't compete with the larger corporations. His unhappy progeny want to sell out, divide the profits, and get on with their lives. Everyone enjoys spreading their own particular misery and angst around. Icelandic with subtitles. **109m/C DVD.** *IC* Gunnar Eyjolfsson, Kristbjorg Kjeld, Hilmir Snaer Gudnason, Gundrun S. Gisladottir, Sigurdur Skulason, Herdis Orvaldsdottir; ***D:*** Baltasar Kormakur; ***W:*** Baltasar Kormakur, Olafur Haukur Simonarson; ***C:*** Jean-Louis Vialard; ***M:*** Jon Asgeirsson.

Sea Beast *Troglodyte* **2008** The CGI is barely adequate but this SciFi Channel flick actually gets bloody and scary. Fisherman Will McKenna (Nemec) has one of his crew snatched by a beastie during a storm. Meanwhile, his teenaged daughter Carly (McDonald) has snuck off to an island cabin with her boyfriend (Wisler). The cabin is located in the beast's (and its babies) territory. So Will teams ups with marine biologist Arden (Sullivan) and local drunk Ben (Stait) to stop the hungry sea critters. **87m/C DVD.** Corin "Corky" Nemec, Camille Sullivan, Miriam McDonald, Brent Stait, Daniel Wisler, Gary Hudson, Gwynyth Walsh; ***D:*** Paul Ziller; ***W:*** Paul Ziller, Gordon Williams; ***C:*** Mahlon Todd Williams; ***M:*** Chuck Cirino. **CABLE**

The Sea Change 1998 Ambitious businessman Rupert Granger has been neglecting his girlfriend Alison at the worst possible time (she's just found out she's pregnant). He goes to Barcelona to close a deal and gets stranded at the airport, which forces Rupert to share a hotel room with relaxed, working-class bloke Chas, who decides Rupert (who's always complaining) needs a personality makeover before he returns home. **92m/C DVD.** *GB* Sean Chapman, Ray Winstone, Maryam D'Abo, Andre Bernard; ***D:*** Michael Bray; ***W:*** Michael Bray, Jill Uden; ***C:*** Josep Civit; ***M:*** Mark Thomas.

Sea Chase ½ 1955 An odd postwar sea adventure, wherein a renegade German freighter captain is pursued by British and German navies as he leaves Australia at the outbreak of WWII. A Prussian Wayne rivaled only by his infamous Genghis Khan in "The Conqueror" for strange character selection. Turner is on board as Wayne's girlfriend. **117m/C VHS, DVD.** John Wayne, Lana Turner, Tab Hunter, James Arness, Lyle Bettger, David Farrar, Richard (Dick) Davalos, Claude Akins, John Qualen; ***D:*** John Farrow; ***C:*** William Clothier.

Sea Devils 1931 Sentenced to prison for a crime he didn't commit, a man escapes and joins a boatload of treasure hunters, but mutiny is afoot. Don't get soaked by this cheapie. **77m/B VHS.** Walter Long, Edmund Burns, Henry Otto, James Donnelly; ***D:*** Joseph Levering.

Sea Devils 🦴🦴 **1937** The tale of a sea captain and his lovely daughter who have differing opinions on whom she should marry. While her father would like her to marry a tame gentlemen under his command, she has her heart set on another beau. Sound predictable? It is, but fun. **88m/B VHS.** Victor McLaglen, Preston Foster, Ida Lupino, Donald Woods, Gordon Jones; ***D:*** Ben Stoloff.

Sea Devils 🦴🦴 **1953** A smuggler and a beautiful spy come together during the Napoleonic Wars in this sea romance filled with intrigue and adventure. **86m/C VHS.** *GB* Rock Hudson, Yvonne De Carlo, Maxwell Reed; ***D:*** Raoul Walsh.

The Sea God 🦴 1/2 **1930** Pink Barker's (Arlen) dive is sabotaged when he searches for treasure off a tropical island that is the scene of a war between rival native groups. The outdoor footage (rare for its time) was shot on Catalina Island. Based on the novel "The Lost God" by John Russell. **75m/B VHS.** Richard Arlen, Fay Wray, Eugene Pallette, Robert Gleckler, Ivan Simpson; ***D:*** George Abbott; ***W:*** George Abbott; ***C:*** Archie Stout.

Sea Gypsies 🦴🦴 **1978 (G)** A sailing crew of five is shipwrecked off the Aleutian Islands. They must escape before winter or learn to survive. Passable family drama. **101m/C VHS.** Robert F. Logan, Mikki Jamison-Olsen, Heather Rattray, Cjon Damitri; ***D:*** Stewart Raffill; ***W:*** Stewart Raffill.

The Sea Hawk 🦴🦴 **1924** Gentleman privateer Sir Oliver Tressilian (Sills) has retired to his Cornish estate and hopes to marry Rosamund Godolphin (Bennett). After Lionel (Hughes), Oliver's half-brother, kills Rosamund's brother in a duel, he blames Oliver and arranges for his kidnapping by Capt. Leigh (Beery Sr.). Leigh's ship is captured by the Spanish and Oliver is chained to the oars until the ship is besieged by Moors and Oliver joins their ranks to become the dreaded Sea Hawk. Lots of swashbuckling and a more faithful adaptation of the Rafael Sabatini novel than the 1940 Errol Flynn remake. **123m/B DVD.** Milton Sills, Enid Bennett, Lloyd Hughes, Wallace Beery, Wallace MacDonald, Frank Currier, William "Buster" Collier Jr.; ***D:*** Frank Lloyd; ***W:*** J.G. Hawks; ***C:*** Norbert Brodine.

The Sea Hawk 🦴🦴🦴 1/2 **1940** An English privateer learns the Spanish are going to invade England with their Armada. After numerous adventures, he is able to aid his queen and help save his country, finding romance along the way. One of Flynn's swashbuckling best. Available colorized. **128m/B VHS, DVD.** Errol Flynn, Claude Rains, Donald Crisp, Alan Hale, Flora Robson, Brenda Marshall, Henry Daniell, Gilbert Roland, James Stephenson, Una O'Connor; ***D:*** Michael Curtiz; ***W:*** Howard Koch.

Sea Hound **1947** A 15-part series set in the late 1940s that charts the voyage of a group of pirates searching for buried treasure. Everything goes well until Crabbe emerges to wreck their hopes. **?m/B VHS.** Buster Crabbe, Jimmy Lloyd, Pamela Blake, Ralph Hodges, Bob (Robert) Barron; ***D:*** Walter B. Eason, Mack V. Wright.

The Sea Inside 🦴🦴🦴 *Mar Adentro* **2004 (PG-13)** Poignant, unsentimental, fact-based drama based on the life of Spanish quadriplegic Ramon Sampedro, who tried for some 30 years for the right to commit assisted suicide. Paralyzed in a diving accident, Ramon (Bardem) becomes a cause celebre as he lies bedridden, cared for by his religious family who are opposed to his decision. He builds his case with the help of his lawyer Julia (Rueda), who suffers herself from a degenerative disease. Ramon also inspires Rosa (Duenas), a neighbor who tries to convince the single-minded man to live and then falls in love with him. Bardem does an amazing job since, except for some brief flashbacks and fantasies, his movement is limited to his neck and head. The real Sampedro wrote poetry and a best-selling memoir, gave numerous interviews, and filmed his assisted suicide (in 1998) so it could be shown on TV. Spanish with subtitles. **125m/C DVD.** Javier Bardem, Celso Bugallo, Jose Maria Pou, Belen Rueda, Lola Duenas, Mabel Rivera, Clara Segura, Joan Dalmau, Alberto Jimenez, Tamar Novas, Francesc Garrido; ***D:*** Alejandro Amenabar; ***W:*** Alejandro Amenabar, Mateo Gil; ***C:*** Javier Aguirresarobe; ***M:*** Alejandro Amenabar. Oscars '04: Foreign Film; Golden Globes '05: Foreign Film; Ind. Spirit '05: Foreign Film.

The Sea is Watching 🦴🦴🦴 *Umi wa miteita; The Sea Witches* **2002 (R)** Akira Kurosawa was working on the screenplay for this film but was prevented from filming it due to his untimely death, and it was turned over to director Kei Kumai to finish. Life for women at the end of the Tokugawa period was hard, and many found prostitution to be the only means they had of putting food on the table. Here are the stories of two of them, O-Shin (Nagiko Tono), who is naive and desperately hopes to wed a man and thus escape her situation, and her more cynical friend Kikuno (Misa Shimizu). **119m/B DVD.** *JP* Misa Shimizu, Masatoshi Nagase, Hidetaka Yoshioka, Eiji Okuda, Renji Ishibashi, Yumiko Nogawa, Yukiya Kitamura, Nagiko Tono, Miho Tsumuki, Michiko Kawai, Tenshi Kamogawa; ***D:*** Kei Kumai; ***W:*** Akira Kurosawa, Shugoro Yamamoto; ***C:*** Kazuo Okuhara; ***M:*** Teizo Matusmura.

The Sea Lion 🦴🦴 **1921** A vicious sea captain, embittered by a past romance, becomes sadistic and intolerable, until the truth emerges. Lots of action, but plodding, rehashed plot. Silent. **50m/B VHS.** Hobart Bosworth, Emory Johnson, Bessie Love, Carol Holloway, Charles Clary, Jack Curtis; ***D:*** Rowland V. Lee; ***W:*** Joseph Poland; ***C:*** J.O. Taylor.

Sea of Dreams 🦴 **1990** Don't expect much in the way of a script from this soft-core production. **80m/C VHS.** Jon Rodgers, Chad Scott, Jacky Peel, Renee O'Neil.

Sea of Love 🦴🦴🦴 1/2 **1989 (R)** A tough, tightly wound thriller about an alcoholic cop with a mid-life crisis. While following the track of a serial killer, he begins a torrid relationship with one of his suspects. Pacino doesn't stand a chance when Barkin heats up the screen. **113m/C VHS, DVD, HD DVD.** Al Pacino, Ellen Barkin, John Goodman, Michael Rooker, William Hickey, Richard Jenkins; ***D:*** Harold Becker; ***W:*** Richard Price; ***C:*** Ronnie Taylor; ***M:*** Trevor Jones.

Sea of Sand 🦴🦴 1/2 *Desert Patrol* **1958** Typical actioner set in WWII finds a British desert patrol's latest mission is to blow up Rommel's fuel supply before the battle of El Alamein. Lots of heroics against the Nazis and stiff upper lips. **97m/B VHS.** *GB* Richard Attenborough, John Gregson, Michael Craig, Vincent Ball, Ray McAnally; ***D:*** Guy Green; ***W:*** Robert Westerby; ***C:*** Wilkie Cooper; ***M:*** Clifton Parker.

Sea People 🦴🦴 **2000** Teen swimmer Amanda (Moss) rescues elderly John McRae (Cronyn) after he leaps from a bridge into the water. But she discovers that John wasn't trying to commit suicide and that he and his wife, Bridget (Gregson), have a very unique relationship with the sea. **92m/C VHS, DVD.** Hume Cronyn, Tegan Moss, Joan Gregson, Ron Lea, Don McKellar, Cedric Smith; ***D:*** Vic Sarin. **CABLE**

Sea Racketeers 🦴 1/2 **1937** Soggy old tribute to the Coast Guard inadvertently makes them look like a bunch of bumblers, as they belatedly uncover a fur-smuggling racket working under their noses from a floating nightclub. **64m/B VHS.** Weldon Heyburn, Jeanne Madden, Warren Hymer, Dorothy McNulty, J. Carrol Naish, Joyce Compton, Charles Trowbridge, Syd Saylor, Lane Chandler, Benny Burt; ***D:*** Hamilton MacFadden.

The Sea Serpent 🦴 1/2 **1985** A young sea captain and a crusty scientist unite to search out a giant sea monster awakened by atomic tests. Not one of Milland's better films. **92m/C VHS.** *SP* Timothy Bottoms, Ray Milland, Jared Martin; ***D:*** Gregory Greens.

The Sea Shall Not Have Them 🦴🦴 1/2 **1955** A British bomber crashes into the North Sea during WWII. Film tells of the survivors' rescue by the Air-Sea Rescue Unit. Decent drama/adventure. **92m/B VHS.** Michael Redgrave, Dirk Bogarde; ***D:*** Lewis Gilbert; ***M:*** Malcolm Arnold.

Sea Wife 🦴🦴 1/2 *Sea Wyf and Biscuit* **1957** Using nicknames and a newspaper's personal column to correspond, Sea Wife, Bulldog, and Biscuit are apparently rehashing a crime committed against a fourth person that's still haunting them. A flashback reveals three men and a woman in a lifeboat after their ship has been torpedoed by the Japanese in 1942. Only three ultimately survive their ordeal. Collins plays a nun of all things, although she keeps her calling a secret from the others. Rather drab adaptation of J.M. Scott's adventure/thriller "Sea-Wyf." **82m/C VHS.** *GB* Richard Burton, Joan Collins, Basil Sydney, Ronald Squire, Cy Grant, Joan Hickson, Lloyd Lamble, Eileen Way; ***D:*** Bob McNaught; ***W:*** George K. Burke; ***C:*** Edward Scaife; ***M:*** Kenneth V. Jones, Leonard Salzedo.

The Sea Wolf 🦴🦴🦴 1/2 **1941** Jack London's adventure novel about brutal, canny Captain Wolf Larsen (Robinson), his rebellious crew, and some unexpected passengers. Knox and Lupino are shipwreck survivors, picked up by Robinson and forced into working aboard his ship, the aptly named "Ghost." Crewman Garfield falls for Lupino and tries to rally his shipmates into resisting the meglomaniacal Robinson. Fine performances by all, especially Robinson as the personification of malevolent ego. Screen debut of Knox. Director Curtiz filmed entirely in studio tanks, sets, and pervasive fog machines. Previously filmed three times; later remade as "Barricade" and "Wolf Larsen." **90m/C VHS.** Edward G. Robinson, Alexander Knox, John Garfield, Ida Lupino, Gene Lockhart, Barry Fitzgerald, Stanley Ridges, Francis McDonald, David Bruce, Howard da Silva, Frank Lackteen, Ralf Harolde; ***D:*** Michael Curtiz; ***W:*** Robert Rossen.

The Sea Wolf 🦴🦴 **1993** Yet another adaptation of Jack London's classic battle of wills tale. Captain Wolf Larsen (Bronson) commands a surly ship of seal hunters through sheer ruthlessness and ego. He rescues snobbish theatre critic Van Weyden (Reeve) and pretty scam artist Flaxen (Stewart) from a capsized ferry. The self-educated captain wants to test out his theories about survival of the fittest by making the rich Van Weyden his cabin boy (Flaxen gets leered at). Lots of teeth-gnashing and bellowing in this turgid TV remake, although Revill has fun as the sniveling Cookie. See the Edward G. Robinson version instead. **120m/C VHS.** Charles Bronson, Christopher Reeve, Catherine Mary Stewart, Clive Revill; ***D:*** Michael Anderson Sr.; ***W:*** Andrew J. Fenady; ***M:*** Charles Bernstein.

Sea Wolves 🦴🦴 1/2 **1981 (PG)** True WWII story about a commando-style operation undertaken by a group of middle-aged, retired British cavalrymen in India in 1943. Decent acting, though Peck's British accent fades in and out, with Moore as Bond. **120m/C VHS, DVD.** *GB* Gregory Peck, Roger Moore, David Niven, Trevor Howard, Patrick Macnee, William Morgan Sheppard; ***D:*** Andrew V. McLaglen; ***W:*** Reginald Rose.

Seabiscuit 🦴🦴🦴 1/2 **2003 (PG-13)** Equine Cinderella story of the legendary Seabiscuit—a funny-looking, ill-tempered thoroughbred—and the men who shaped him into a racing legend: owner Charles Howard (Bridges); partially blind, over-sized, luck-challenged jockey Red Pollard (Maguire); and trainer "Silent" Tom Smith (Cooper) who believed in the underdog horse. The ragtag trio eventually wangles a race with the more-celebrated War Admiral, whose owner had previously refused to share a track with the far inferior Seabiscuit. Writer/director Ross delivers suitably rousing race scenes in this can't miss story of an unlikely champion who brought hope and inspiration to the Depression-era crowds and became a symbol of hope. All three leads are outstanding, as is Macy as an excitable radio announcer. Based on Laura Hillenbrand's best-seller "Seabiscuit: An American Legend." **140m/C VHS, DVD, HD DVD.** *US* Tobey Maguire, Jeff Bridges, Chris Cooper, Elizabeth Banks, William H. Macy, Gary Stevens, Eddie Jones, Ed Lauter, Michael O'Neill, Royce D. Applegate, Annie Corley, Valerie Mahaffey; ***D:*** Gary Ross; ***W:*** Gary Ross; ***C:*** John Schwartzman; ***M:*** Randy Newman; ***Nar:*** David McCullough.

The Seafarers **1953** Promotional documentary, made by 25-year-old Stanley Kubrick, extolling the benefits to sailors in joining the Seafarers International Union. Kubrick's first work in color. **30m/C DVD.** ***D:*** Stanley Kubrick; ***W:*** Will Chasen; ***Nar:*** Don Hollenbeck.

The Seagull 🦴🦴🦴 **1971** A pensive, sensitive adaptation of the famed Chekhov play about the depressed denizens of an isolated country estate. In Russian with English subtitles. **99m/B VHS.** Alla Demidova, Lyudmila Savelyeva, Yuri Yakovlev; ***D:*** Yuri Karasik.

The Seagull 🦴🦴 1/2 **1975** Danner's sensitive performance as Nina, an aspiring actress with fragile emotions, highlights this filmed production of Chekhov's "The Seagull," originally staged by the Williamstown Theatre Festival. **117m/C VHS, DVD.** Blythe Danner, Olympia Dukakis, Lee Grant, Frank Langella, Kevin McCarthy, Marian Mercer, William Swetland, Louis Zorich; ***D:*** John J. Desmond, Nikos Psacharopoulos; ***M:*** Arthur B. Rubinstein. **TV**

Seal Team 🦴 1/2 **2008 (R)** A black ops counterterrorism team is dispatched behind enemy lines in Iraq on a covert mission days before Operation: Desert Shield is to begin. When their mission is compromised, the team must focus on surviving so they can return home. **97m/C DVD.** Zach McGowan, Jeremy Davis, Chris Warner, Kristoffer Garrison, Ken Gamble, Neto DePaula Pimenta; ***D:*** Mark C. Andrews; ***W:*** Mark C. Andrews; ***C:*** Chia-Yu Chen; ***M:*** Matt Gates. **VIDEO**

Seamless **WOOF!** **2000 (R)** Overwrought, silly and senseless story about a group of rave-happy homeless kids who are offered work and a place to live by paternalistic J.B. (charmless Kentaro Seagal, Steven's son). Things don't work out so the kids wind up back on the street, resorting to drug dealing, prostitution and the like to get by, and that's bad but not nearly as bad as this dreck. **91m/C VHS, DVD.** Shannon Elizabeth, Peter Alexander, Melinda Scherwinski, Broc Benedict; ***D:*** Debra Lemattre; ***C:*** Denise Brassard; ***M:*** Mamoru Mochizuki. **VIDEO**

Seance 🦴🦴 *Korei; Ko-Rei* **2000** The police are searching for a small girl kidnapped by a pedophile, and she ends up escaping and hiding in a sound technician's equipment case. His psychic wife finds the girl unconscious and decides that this is her big break, so she concocts a nutty scheme to make the rescue more dramatic and cement her reputation as a medium. But nutty schemes tend to go wrong, sometimes in big ways. **97m/C DVD.** *JP* Koji Yakusho, Jun Fubuki, Tsuyoshi Kusanaga, Daikei Shimizu; ***D:*** Kiyoshi Kurosawa; ***W:*** Kiyoshi Kurosawa, Mark McShane, Tetsuya Onishi; ***C:*** Takahide Shibanushi; ***M:*** Gary Ashiya.

Seance 🦴 **2006 (R)** Typically dumb, low-budget teen slasher/horror flick. College student Lauren (Erickson) gets a nasty surprise when she sees the ghost of a young girl in her dorm room. Stuck on campus over Thanksgiving break, the remaining students decide to hold a séance and see if they can contact Cara, whom Lauren learned died suspiciously in their dorm. Instead, Spence (Paul) appears and they quickly discover that the former janitor was a serial killer who's not done yet. **88m/C DVD.** Adrian Paul, Kandis Erickson, A.J. Lamas, Tori White, Chauntal Lewis, Joel Geist, Bridget Shergalis; ***D:*** Mark Smith; ***W:*** Mark Smith; ***C:*** Geoffrey Schaaf; ***M:*** Vincent Gillioz. **VIDEO**

Seance on a Wet Afternoon 🦴🦴🦴 1/2 **1964** Dark, thoughtful film about a crazed pseudo-psychic who coerces her husband into a kidnapping so she can gain recognition by divining the child's whereabouts. Directed splendidly by Forbes, and superb acting from Stanley and Attenborough, who co-produced with Forbes. **111m/B VHS, DVD.** *GB* Kim Stanley, Richard Attenborough, Margaret Lacey, Maria Kazan, Mark Eden, Patrick Magee; ***D:*** Bryan Forbes; ***M:*** John Barry. British Acad. '64: Actor (Attenborough); Natl. Bd. of Review '64: Actress (Stanley); N.Y. Film Critics '64: Actress (Stanley).

The Search 🦴🦴🦴 1/2 **1948** Clift, an American solider stationed in post-WWII Berlin, befriends a homeless nine-year-old amnesiac boy (Jandl) and tries to find his family. Meanwhile, his mother has been searching the Displaced Persons camps for her son. Although Clift wants to adopt the boy, he steps aside, and mother and son are finally reunited. "The Search" was shot on location in the American Occupied Zone of Germany. Jandl won a special juvenile Oscar in his first (and only) film role. This was also Clift's first screen appearance, although this movie was actually filmed after his debut in "Red River," it was released first. **105m/B VHS.** Montgomery Clift, Aline MacMahon, Ivan Jandl, Jarmila Novotna, Wendell Corey; ***D:*** Fred Zinnemann; ***W:*** Paul Jarrico. Oscars '48: Story; Golden Globes '49: Screenplay.

Search and Destroy 🦴 *Striking Back* **1981 (PG)** Deadly vendetta is begun by a Vietnamese official during the war. It is continued in the U.S. as he hunts down the American soldiers he feels betrayed him. Sub-par, forgettable war/action flick. **93m/C VHS.** Perry King, Don Stroud, Park Jong Soo, George Kennedy, Tisa Farrow; ***D:*** William Fruet.

Search and Destroy 🦴 **1988 (R)** Sci-fi action flick about the capture of a secret biological warfare research station. Lotsa action, that's for sure—where's the plot? **87m/C VHS, DVD.** Stuart Garrison Day, Dan Kuchuck, Peggy Jacobsen; ***D:*** J. Christian Ingvordsen; ***W:*** J. Christian Ingvordsen; ***C:*** Steven Kaman; ***M:*** Chris Burke.

Search and Destroy 🦴🦴 **1994 (R)** Complex story finds bankrupt businessman Martin Mirkheim (Dunne) trying to overcome his financial woes by making a film based on a book by self-help guru, Dr. Luther Waxling (Hopper). Of course, since Martin's broke, he first has to find someone willing to invest in his venture, and the shady duo (Walken and Turturro) he does just leave him with more problems. Tediously stagy adaptation of Howard Korders' play. Directorial debut by artist Salle at least looks great and provides some quirky moments. **91m/C VHS, DVD.** Griffin Dunne, Dennis Hopper, Rosanna Arquette, Christopher Walken, John Turturro, Ileana Douglas, Ethan Hawke; ***Cameos:*** Martin Scorsese; ***D:*** David Salle; ***W:*** Michael Almereyda; ***C:*** Michael Spiller, Bobby Bukowski; ***M:*** Elmer Bernstein.

Search for Beauty 🦴🦴 **1934** American Don (Crabbe) and Brit Barbara (Lupino) are both Olympic medal winners. Being physically fit and attractive, they are offered the chance to help edit a physiques magazine, but discover the publishers are more interested in cheesecake than health and are running a scam contest to attract athletes to pose. **78m/B DVD.** Buster Crabbe, Ida Lupino, Toby Wing, James Gleason, Robert Armstrong, Gertrude Michael; ***D:*** Erle C. Kenton; ***W:*** Frank Butler, Claude Binyon; ***C:*** Harry Fischbeck.

The Search for Bridey Murphy 🦴🦴 **1956** Long before channelers, Ramtha and New-Age profiteers, there was a Colorado housewife who under hypnosis described a previous life as an Irish girl. Her famous claim was never proven—but that didn't stop this well-acted but dull dramatization. Neither sensationalist, nor likely to persuade skeptics. Based on the book by Morey Bernstein, hypnotist in the case. **84m/B VHS.** Teresa Wright, Louis Hayward, Nancy Gates, Kenneth Tobey, Richard Anderson; ***D:*** Noel Langley; ***W:*** Noel Langley.

The Search for John Gissing 🦴🦴 **2001** Skillfully done corporate comedy. American Matthew Barnes (Binder) assumes he's been brought to London to consult on a business merger but he's actually a replacement for his British counterpart, John Gissing (a wonderfully supercilious Rickman). Gissing intends to make every moment of Barnes and his sharp-tongued wife Linda's (Garofalo) stay a nightmare so Matthew will go away. When he finally realizes what's going on, Matthew prepares to get even until he and John realize that they have a lot in common, including protecting themselves from corporate chicanery. **91m/C DVD.** Mike Binder, Alan Rickman, Janeane Garofalo, Juliet Stevenson, Allan Corduner, Sonya Walger, James Lance; ***D:*** Mike Binder; ***W:*** Mike Binder; ***C:*** Sue Gibson; ***M:*** Lawrence Nash Groupe.

The Search for One-Eye Jimmy 🦴🦴 **1996 (R)** Good-natured slice-of-life comedy about lowlife friends in the Brooklyn neighborhood of Red Hook. Film school grad Les (McCallany) returns to his old stomping grounds to make a documentary and decides missing local character Jimmy (Rockwell) will be his topic. Only no one except Jimmy's parents seem really concerned and Les' friends are such dimwits that they couldn't find a hole in the ground anyway. **86m/C VHS, DVD.** Holt McCallany, Nicholas Turturro, Steve Buscemi, Michael Badalucco, Ray "Boom Boom" Mancini, Anne Meara, John Turturro, Samuel L. Jackson, Sam Rockwell; ***D:*** Sam Henry Kass; ***W:*** Sam Henry Kass; ***C:*** Charles Levey; ***M:*** William Bloom.

Search for Signs of Intelligent Life in the Universe 🦴🦴🦴 **1991 (PG-13)** Tomlin's brilliant one-woman show has been expanded into a wonderful film. As Tomlin's cast of 12 female and male characters meet and interact, they show every viewer his/her own humanity. **120m/C VHS, DVD.** Lily Tomlin; ***D:*** John Bailey; ***W:*** Jane Wagner; ***M:*** Jerry Goodman.

Search for the Gods 🦴 1/2 **1975** A dig in the Southwest turns interesting when one of the archeologists comes across an exquisite ancient medallion that could answer questions about alien visitors. Pilot for a TV series that didn't make it. **100m/C VHS.** Kurt Russell, Stephen McHattie, Ralph Bellamy, Victoria Racimo, Raymond St. Jacques; ***D:*** Jud Taylor. **TV**

The Searchers 🦴🦴🦴🦴 **1956** The classic Ford western, starring John Wayne as a hard-hearted frontiersman who spends years doggedly pursuing his niece, who was kidnapped by Indians. A simple western structure supports Ford's most moving, mysterious, complex film. Many feel this is the best western of all time. **119m/C VHS, DVD, Blu-ray Disc, HD DVD.** John Wayne, Jeffrey Hunter, Vera Miles, Natalie Wood, Ward Bond, John Qualen, Harry Carey Jr., Olive Carey, Antonio Moreno, Henry (Kleinbach) Brandon, Hank Worden, Lana Wood, Dorothy Jordan, Patrick Wayne; ***D:*** John Ford; ***W:*** Frank Nugent; ***C:*** Winton C. Hoch; ***M:*** Max Steiner. AFI '98: Top 100, Natl. Film Reg. '89.

Searching for Bobby D 🦴 **2005 (R)** Lame wiseguy/showbiz comedy. Four bit part Brooklyn actors decide to make their own movie and, thanks to family mobster connections, wind up in Pennsylvania. There, Johnny's cousin Leo has lied to a financial backer by saying Robert De Niro is starring in their flick (they bring in a look-alike). Naturally, much stupidity follows. **105m/C DVD.** William DeMeo, James Madio, Tyson Beckford, Louis Vanaria, Daniel Margotta, Tony Darrow, Carmen Electra; ***D:*** Paul Borghese; ***W:*** William DeMeo, Paul Borghese; ***C:*** George Mitas; ***M:*** Neil Berg.

Searching for Bobby Fischer 🦴🦴🦴 1/2 **1993 (PG)** Seven-year-old Josh Waitzkin (Pomeranc, in his debut) shows an amazing gift for chess, stunning his parents, who must then try to strike the delicate balance of developing his abilities while also allowing him a "normal" childhood. Excellent cast features Mantegna and Allen as his parents, Kingsley as demanding chess teacher Pandolfini, and Fishburne as an adept speed-chess hustler. Pomeranc is great, and his knowledge of chess (he's a ranked player) brings authenticity to his role. Title comes from Pandolfini's belief that Josh may equal the abilities of chess whiz Bobby Fischer. Underrated little gem based on a true story and adapted from the book by Waitzkin's father. **111m/C VHS, DVD.** Joe Mantegna, Max Pomeranc, Joan Allen, Ben Kingsley, Laurence Fishburne, Robert Stephens, David Paymer, William H. Macy, Hal Scardino; ***D:*** Steven Zaillian; ***W:*** Steven Zaillian; ***C:*** Conrad L. Hall; ***M:*** James Horner. MTV Movie Awards '94: New Filmmaker (Zaillian).

Searching for Paradise 🦴 1/2 **2002 (R)** Gilda (Pratt) is obsessed with New York actor Michael De Santis (Noth). After her father dies (and she's disillusioned by some family skeletons), Gilda decides to take up her grandmother's offer to visit her in the Big Apple—the better to stalk De Santis. Hopelessly naive and a little unhinged, Gilda eventually poses as a journalist to meet her hero. Underdeveloped drama with little character development or explantion. Writer/director Paci's debut. **88m/C VHS, DVD.** Susan May Pratt, Christopher Noth, Jeremy Davies, Mary Louise Wilson, Josef Sommer, Michele Placido, Laila Robins; ***D:*** Myra Paci; ***W:*** Myra Paci; ***C:*** Teodoro Maniaci; ***M:*** Carter Burwell.

Searching For Wooden Watermelons 🦴🦴 1/2 **2001** A small-town woman with big-time dreams of becoming a television writer battles her trepidations about ditching her hum-drum life for the Hollywood hills in this poignant narrative drawn from star/co-producer/writer English's personal experiences. While the moral might be simplistic and overstated, the players are genuine. **86m/C VHS, DVD.** Wendy English, Chad Safar, Scott M. Rudolph, Dixie Tucker, Victoria Anne LeBlanc; ***D:*** Bryan Goldsworthy; ***W:*** Wendy English; ***C:*** David M. Sammons; ***M:*** Andy Daniels. **VIDEO**

Seas Beneath 🦴🦴 **1931** Commander Bob Kingsley and his men are sent on a secret mission to sink a German U-boat. Maria, whom Kingsley loves, turns out to be a German spy whose brother is the captain of the U-boat. She tries to sabotage Kingsley's mission but is thwarted. Shot off Catalina Island, Ford received naval assistance, including the use of two submarines and a mine sweeper. **90m/B DVD.** George O'Brien, Mona Maris, Henry Victor, John Lodge, Marion Lessing, Steve Pendleton, Larry Kent; ***D:*** John Ford; ***W:*** Dudley Nichols; ***C:*** Joseph August.

Seaside Swingers 🦴 1/2 *Every Day's a Holiday* **1965** A group of teenagers at a seaside resort work to win a talent competition on TV. But where is the talent? Dumb teen romance comedy with accidental plot. ♫All I Want Is You; A Girls Needs a Boy; Second Time Around; Indubitably Me; Love Me, Please; Now, Ain't That Somethin'—Caw Blimey; Romeo Jones; What's Cookin, **94m/C VHS.** *GB* Michael Sarne, Grazina Frame, John Leyton; ***D:*** James Hill.

Season for Assassins 🦴 1/2 **1971** Police commissioner Castroni is the only man who can stop a wave of violence enveloping Rome. **102m/C VHS.** *IT* Magali Noel, Rossano Brazzi, Joe Dallesandro, Martin Balsam; ***D:*** Marcello Andrei; ***W:*** Marcello Andrei; ***C:*** Luciano Trasatti; ***M:*** Alberto Verrecchia.

A Season for Miracles 🦴🦴 1/2 **1999** Because their drug-addict mother, Berry (Dern), is in jail, Alanna (Whitman) and younger brother J.T. (Sabara) are about to be placed in foster care. Instead, they go on the lam with their devoted Aunt Emilie (Gugino), whose car breaks down in the quaint community of Bethlehem (hey, it's a Christmas movie!). The family are taken under the eccentric wing of a diner waitress (Duke) and the trio warily settle in—with Emilie even drawing the romantic interest of handsome cop Nathan (Conrad). Of course, trouble comes calling when their secret is exposed. (It's Christmas—there's a happy ending.) Adapted from the book by Marilyn Papano. **90m/C VHS.** Carla Gugino, David Conrad, Kathy Baker, Laura Dern, Patty Duke, Lynn Redgrave, Mae Whitman, Evan Sabara, Faith Prince, Mary Louise Wilson; ***D:*** Michael Pressman; ***W:*** Maria Nation; ***C:*** Shelly Johnson; ***M:*** Craig Safan. **TV**

Season of Change 🦴 1/2 **1994** Tepid coming of age saga set in rural Montana, circa 1946. Thirteen-year-old Sally Mae (Tom) notices the tensions between her Bible-bound mother (Anderson) and war vet dad (Madsen), who's worried about finding a job to support his family. Sally Mae tries to understand all these adult notions even as she herself becomes attracted to teen mechanic Bobby (Randall). Cliched script and awkward performances don't help. **93m/C VHS, DVD.** Nicholle Tom, Michael Madsen, Jo Anderson, Hoyt Axton, Ethan (Randall) Embry; ***D:*** Robin Murray; ***W:*** Shirley Hillard.

Season of Fear 🦴 1/2 **1989 (R)** A young man visits his estranged father's home. Abandoned as a child, he's embroiled in a murder scheme engineered by his father's beautiful young wife. Intriguing premise, forgettable execution. **89m/C VHS.** Michael Bowen, Clancy Brown, Clare Wren, Ray Wise, Michael J. Pollard; ***D:*** Doug Campbell; ***W:*** Doug Campbell.

Season of the Witch 🦴 1/2 *Hungry Wives; Jack's Wife* **1973 (R)** A frustrated housewife becomes intrigued with a neighboring witch and begins to practice witchcraft herself, through murder and seduction. Meant to be suspenseful, thrilling, and topical, it is none of these. Poorly acted at best. Originally 130 minutes! **89m/C DVD.** Jan White, Ray Laine, Bill Thunhurst, Joedda McClain, Virginia Greenwald, Ann Muffly, Neil Fisher, Esther Lapidus, Dan Mallinger, Ken Peters; ***D:*** George A. Romero; ***W:*** George A. Romero; ***C:*** George A. Romero.

Season of the Witch **2010** Fourteenth-century knights are transporting a girl suspected of spreading the Black Plague through witchcraft. **m/C DVD.** Nicolas Cage, Ron Perlman, Ulrich Thomsen, Claire Foy, Stephan Campbell Moore, Stephen Graham; ***D:*** Dominic Sera; ***W:*** Bragi Schut Jr.; ***C:*** Amir M. Mokri; ***M:*** Atli Ovarsson.

A Season on the Brink 🦴🦴 1/2 **2002 (R)** Indiana University basketball coach Bobby Knight (Dennehy) is determined that the 1985-86 season will be a winning one. But his constant tirades are beginning to negatively affect his players. Dennehy owns this role as the abusive blowhard but since there's nothing sympathetic about Knight, it's hard to get too involved. Based on the book by journalist John Feinstein. **87m/C VHS, DVD.** Brian Dennehy, Al Thompson, James Lafferty, Michael James Johnson, James Kirk; ***D:*** Robert Mandel; ***W:*** David W. Rintels; ***C:*** Claudio Chea; ***M:*** Randy Edelman, Steve Porcaro. **CABLE**

Sebastian 🦴🦴 1/2 *Mr. Sebastian* **1968** Mathematics whiz is employed by the British to decipher codes. He falls in love with York, another code breaker, and becomes involved in international intrigue. A bit too fast-paced and busy, but enjoyable spy drama. Sutherland has a small role. **100m/C VHS.** *GB* Dirk Bogarde, Susannah York, Lilli Palmer, John Gielgud, Margaret Johnston, Nigel Davenport, Donald Sutherland; ***D:*** David Greene; ***M:*** Jerry Goldsmith.

Sebastiane 🦴🦴🦴 **1979** An audacious film version of the legend of St. Sebastian, packed with homoerotic imagery and ravishing visuals. Honest, faithful rendering of the Saint's life and refusal to obey Roman authorities. Jarman's first film, in Latin with English subtitles. **90m/C VHS, DVD.** *GB* Leonardo Treviglio, Barney James, Neil Kennedy, Richard Warwick, Lindsay Kemp; ***D:*** Derek Jarman, Paul Humfress; ***W:*** Derek Jarman, Paul Humfress; ***C:*** Peter Middleton; ***M:*** Brian Eno.

The Second Awakening of Christa Klages 🦴🦴 *Das Zweite Erwachen der Christa Klages* **1978** Young divorced mother Christa (Engel) decides to finance her money-troubled day-care center by robbing a bank with her lover Werner (Muller-Westernhagen). Werner's killed and Christa becomes a fugitive, taking refuge with her friend Ingrid (Reize). German with subtitles. **90m/C VHS, DVD.** *GE* Tina Engel, Sylvia Reize, Marius Muller-Westernhagen, Peter Schneider, Katharina Thalbach; ***D:*** Margarethe von Trotta; ***W:*** Margarethe von Trotta, Luisa Francia; ***C:*** Franz Rath; ***M:*** Klaus Doldinger.

Second Best 🦴🦴🦴 **1994 (PG-13)** Quiet, intimate drama about a lonely Welsh postmaster (Hurt) who decides to adopt a son (Miles). James, the 11-year-old boy he considers adopting, comes from a troubled background and is prone to violent outbursts. Graham, the village postmaster, is dealing with emotional demons of his own, and his problems are interwoven with those of the deprived, temperamental James. Although Hurt seems miscast as a shy, middle-aged Welshman, he turns in one of the best performances of his career. Richly acted and flawlessly directed, Menges has created a convincing and effective father-son drama. Based on David Cook's novel. **105m/C VHS.** *GB* William Hurt, Chris Cleary Miles, Keith Allen, Prunella Scales, Jane Horrocks, Alan Cumming, John Hurt; ***D:*** Chris Menges; ***W:*** David Cook; ***M:*** Simon Boswell.

Second Best 🦴🦴 **2005** In this 'guy flick' Elliot (Pantoliano) is the protagonist, emotionally dwelling a few levels below the incessant whinings of Woody Allen. Fired from a Manhattan publishing house for not producing best sellers, he now spends his days hosting a Web site for downcasts like himself and writing stories he never has the guts to submit to a publisher. When a long-time friend, now a hot shot movie producer

(Gaines), returns home and treats his buddies to some greener pastures, Elliot is forced to seriously reassess his life. Directing is a bit laid back and the buddies' kvetch sessions become somewhat wearing, but it does make poignant observations amidst the wry humor. **86m/C DVD.** *US* Joe Pantoliano, Boyd Gaines, Jennifer Tilly, Peter Gerety, Bronson Pinchot, Polly Draper, Barbara Barrie, James Ryan, Paulina Porizkova, Matthew Arkin, Fiona Gallagher; ***D:*** Eric Weber; ***W:*** Eric Weber; ***C:*** Christopher Norr; ***M:*** Tom O'Brien, Nathan Wilson, John Leccese, Joe Weber.

Second Best Secret Agent in the Whole Wide World ½ *Licensed to Kill* **1965** A klutzy agent attempts to prevent a Swedish anti-gravity formula from falling into Russian hands. Surprisingly good early spoof of the James Bond genre. **93m/C VHS.** *GB* Tom Adams, Veronica Hurst, Peter Bull, Karel Stepanek, John Arnatt; ***D:*** Lindsay Shonteff.

Second Chance ½ **1953** A former prizefighter (Mitchum) travels to Mexico where he protects a gangster's moll (Darnell) targeted for murder. But Palance is on their tail. Originally released theatrically on a wide screen in 3-D. Good melodrama. **82m/C VHS.** Robert Mitchum, Linda Darnell, Jack Palance, Reginald (Reggie, Reggy) Sheffield, Roy Roberts; ***D:*** Rudolph Mate; ***W:*** Robert Presnell Sr., Sydney (Sidney) Boehm, Oscar Millard; ***C:*** William E. Snyder; ***M:*** Roy Webb.

Second Chance **1980** When a woman finds her husband is in love with another, her marital happiness is shattered. She leaves her betrayer and struggles to adapt to life as a single mother. **270m/C VHS.** *GB* Susannah York, Ralph Bates; ***D:*** Gerry Mill, Richard Handford. **TV**

The Second Chance **2006 (PG-13)** Ethan (Smith) is a young pastor preaching the faith from his dad's ministry via a protected world of TV performances to mostly rich white folks. As a lesson, he's sent to work with the troubled members of an urban black church led by Jake (Carr), a move that he initially rebuffs, but eventually Jake makes him see the error of his ways. Fans of popular Christian rock singer Smith will enjoy his first foray into film. **102m/C DVD.** *US* Michael W. Smith, J. Don Ferguson, Lisa Arrindell Anderson, David Alford, Jeff Obafemi Carr, Henry Haggard, Kenda Benward, Jonathan Thomas, Calvin Hobson, Bobby Daniels, Shirley Cody, Peggy Walton Walker, Vilia Steele; ***D:*** Steve Taylor; ***W:*** Steve Taylor, Henry O. Arnold, Ben Pearson; ***C:*** Ben Pearson; ***M:*** Michael W. Smith.

Second Chances ½ **1998** Think a family version of "The Horse Whisperer." 10-year-old Sunny is left unable to walk without crutches after a car accident and becomes emotionally withdrawn. She and her mom move next door to former rodeo champ Ben Taylor and Sunny develops a rapport with both Ben and a crippled horse named Ginger. **107m/C VHS.** Tom Amandes, Kelsey Mulrooney, Isabel Glasser, Stuart Whitman, Theodore Bikel, Terry Moore, Madeline Zima; ***D:*** James Fargo. **VIDEO**

Second Chorus ½ **1940** Rivalry of two trumpet players for a girl and a job with Artie Shaw Orchestra. Music, dance, and romance. Nothing great, but pleasant. ♫Would You Like to Be the Love of My Life?; Poor Mr. Chisholm; (I Ain't Hep to That Step) But I'll Dig It; Swing Concerto; Sweet Sue; I'm Yours. **83m/B VHS, DVD.** Fred Astaire, Paulette Goddard, Burgess Meredith, Artie Shaw, Charles Butterworth; ***D:*** H.C. Potter.

The Second Civil War ½ **1997 (R)** Political satire falls apart at the end but until then manages to provide some dark comedy. In the near future, Idaho Governor Farley (Bridges) closes his state's borders to a planeload of refugee children from a Pakistan-India nuclear war. The President (Hartman), who wants to look tough, gives Farley 72 hours to change his mind and the media, led by executive producer Mel Burgess (Hedaya), goes into a typical frenzy. **105m/C VHS, DVD.** Beau Bridges, Phil Hartman, James Coburn, Dan Hedaya, Elizabeth Pena, Kevin Dunn, Denis Leary, James Earl Jones, Ron Perlman, Joanna Cassidy; ***D:*** Joe Dante; ***W:*** Martyn Burke; ***C:*** Mac Ahlberg; ***M:*** Hummie Mann. **CABLE**

Second Coming of Suzanne ½ **1980** Young actress encounters a hypnotic film director. Her role: to star in a crucifixion—which may be more real than she imagines. Winner of two international film festivals. **90m/C VHS, DVD.** Sondra Locke, Richard Dreyfuss, Gene Barry, Paul Sand, Jared Martin; ***D:*** Michael Barry; ***W:*** Michael Barry; ***C:*** Isidore Mankofsky.

Second Fiddle ½ *Irving Berlin's Second Fiddle* **1939** Power is a studio flack who's hired to mount a huge talent search for a girl to star in a new film epic (very clear parallels to the Scarlett O'Hara "Gone With the Wind" hunt). He's sent to smalltown Minnesota where he meets Henie, who lives with her forbidding aunt (Oliver), who doesn't want her niece to go to wicked Hollywood. Nevertheless, Henie gets the part, becomes a success, and falls for her co-star Vallee. But it's all a publicity stunt on his part and Power is the one who really loves the girl. Henie gets to do some skating. ♫Back to Back; I'm Sorry for Myself; I Poured My Heart Into Song; An Old-Fashioned Tune is Always New; When Winter Comes; Song of the Metronome. **86m/B VHS.** Sonja Henie, Tyrone Power, Rudy Vallee, Edna May Oliver, Mary Healy, Lyle Talbot, Alan Dinehart, Minna Gombell; ***D:*** Sidney Lanfield; ***W:*** Harry Tugend; ***M:*** Irving Berlin.

The Second Front **2005 (R)** American agent Frank Hossom (Sheffer) must make certain that German Jewish scientist Nicky Raus doesn't fall into Nazi or Russian hands. But Frank makes the mistake of getting romantically interested in Nicky's lover, Olga (Metkina), who happens to be a KGB spy. Nonsensical melodrama enlivened by a certain amount of gunfire. **87m/C DVD.** Craig Sheffer, Ron Perlman, Svetlana Metkina; ***D:*** Dmitri Fiks; ***W:*** Cris Sterzhen; ***C:*** Goran Paviceric; ***M:*** Igor Khoroshev.

Second Honeymoon ½ **1937** Vicki's (Young) divorced from playboy Raoul (Power) and married to successful but dull businessman Bob (Talbot). When Vicki's vacationing in Miami, she runs into Raoul and those old sparks start to re-ignite. To smother the embers, Raoul throws a party and introduces Vicki to his new girlfriend, Joy (Weaver). Misunderstandings keep occurring until Vicki decides to follow her heart. **79m/B DVD.** Tyrone Power, Loretta Young, Lyle Talbot, Stuart Erwin, Marjorie Weaver, Claire Trevor, J. Edward Bromberg; ***D:*** Walter Lang; ***W:*** Kathryn Scola, Darrell Ware; ***C:*** Ernest Palmer; ***M:*** David Buttolph.

Second in Command **2005 (R)** Military attache Sam Keenan (Van Damme) is assigned to the American embassy in a small East European country whose government is targeted by rebels. Keenan rescues the country's president and takes him to the embassy, which is now besieged by the rebel militia, leaving Keenan and a few Marines to hold their position. Routine actioner. **95m/C DVD.** *US* Jean-Claude Van Damme, Julie Cox, Velibor Topic, William Tapley, Alan McKenna, Serban Celea; ***D:*** Simon Fellows; ***W:*** David Corley, Jonathan Bowers, Jayson Rothwell; ***C:*** Doug Milsome; ***M:*** Mark Sayfritz. **VIDEO**

Second Sight **1989 (PG)** A detective (Larroquette) and a goofy psychic (Pinchot) set out to find a kidnapped priest. Flick is sidetracked along the way by such peculiarities as a pixieish nun for romantic, not religious, intrigue. Remember this one? No? That's because you blinked when it was released to theatres. Eminently missable. **84m/C VHS.** Dominic Chianese, John Larroquette, Bronson Pinchot, Bess Armstrong, James Tolkan, Christine Estabrook, Cornelia Guest, Stuart Pankin, William Prince, John Schuck; ***D:*** Joel Zwick; ***W:*** Patricia Resnick, Tom Schulman.

Second Sight **1999** Hard-charging Detective Chief Inspector Ross Tanner (Owen) is called to investigate the murder of a college student who was beaten to death within yards of his family's home. But beyond the murder, Tanner has a serious personal problem—a rare eye disease is causing him to go blind. Trying to keep his condition a secret, Tanner is forced to rely on new Detective Inspector Catherine Tully (Skinner), who has her own reasons for keeping quiet. **180m/C VHS, DVD.** *GB* Clive Owen, Claire Skinner, Stuart Wilson, Phoebe Nicholls, Tom Mullion, Louise Atkins, Eddie Marsan, Rebecca Egan, Benjamin Smith; ***D:*** Charles Beeson; ***W:*** Paula Milne; ***C:*** Rex Maidment. **TV**

Second Skin *Segunda Piel* **1999** Self-centered engineer Alberto (Molla) is married to the loving Elena (Gil) but is miserable. He hates his job even though he's successful and is terrified that his wife will discover he's been unfaithful—with doctor Diego (Bardem) who doesn't know Alberto is even married. When Elena does find out, Alberto swears he's broken off the relationship but he's lying and his security continues to crumble since he won't make a choice between either of his lovers. Molla's a diappointment since it's not clear what either lover or wife sees in him but Bardem and Gil make up for his shortcomings. Spanish with subtitles. **104m/C VHS, DVD.** *SP* Javier Bardem, Jordi Molla, Ariadna Gil, Cecilia (Celia) Roth, Javier Albala, Mercedes Sampietro, Adrian Sac; ***D:*** Gerardo Vera; ***W:*** Angeles Gonzalez-Sinde; ***C:*** Julio Madurga; ***M:*** Roque Banos.

Second Skin ½ **2000 (R)** Sam Kane (MacFayden) falls in love with Crystal (Henstridge), who's suffering from amnesia after a car crash. Sam tries to help her out and Crystal remembers that she and Sam have a previous and dangerous connection. **91m/C VHS, DVD.** Angus MacFadyen, Natasha Henstridge, Peter Fonda, Liam Waite; ***D:*** Darrell Roodt.

Second Thoughts **1983 (PG)** Frustrated woman attorney divorces her stuffy husband and takes up with an aging hippie. She comes to regret her decision when it becomes obvious that her new man has his head firmly stuck in the 60s. Comedy-drama lacking real laughs or drama. **109m/C VHS.** Lucie Arnaz, Craig Wasson, Ken Howard, Joe Mantegna; ***D:*** Lawrence Turman; ***W:*** Steve Brown; ***M:*** Henry Mancini.

Second Time Lucky **1984** The devil makes a bet with God that if the world began all over again Adam and Eve would repeat their mistake they made in the Garden of Eden. Bites off a lot, but has no teeth nor laughs. **98m/C VHS, DVD.** *AU NZ* Diane Franklin, Roger Wilson, Robert Morley, Jon Gadsby, Bill Ewens; ***D:*** Michael Anderson Sr.

The Second Track *Das Zweite Gleis* **1962** Brock, a train inspector, witnesses a robbery at the railyard and recognizes one of the thieves from his wartime days, though he hides the fact from the police. But Brock's daughter has become curious about her father's past and her investigation uncovers some Nazi-era secrets that the thief (and her father) want to stay hidden. German with subtitles. **80m/B DVD.** *GE* Walter Richter, Erik S. Klein, Albert Hetterle, Annekathrin Burger, Horst Jonischkan, Helga Goring; ***D:*** Joachim Kunert; ***W:*** Joachim Kunert, Gunter Kunert; ***C:*** Rolf Sohre; ***M:*** Pavol Simai.

Second Victory ½ **1987 (PG)** Major Mark Hanlon has been appointed an Occupation Officer in the winter of 1945. He expects this will be his chance to work for peace but when a good friend is brutally murdered all his thoughts turn to revenge. Based on the novel by Morris West. **95m/C VHS.** Anthony Andrews, Max von Sydow, Renee Soutendijk; ***D:*** Gerald Thomas.

Second Wind **1976 (PG)** Wagner and Naughton are trying to settle into their new life together, but find they must make a variety of difficult choices. **93m/C VHS.** *CA* Ken Pogue, Tedde Moore, Tom Harvey, Lindsay Wagner, James Naughton; ***D:*** Donald Shebib; ***W:*** Hal Ackerman; ***C:*** Reginald Morris; ***M:*** Hagood Hardy.

The Second Woman ½ *Here Lies Love; Twelve Miles Out* **1951** An architect, suffering from blackouts and depression, believes himself responsible for the death of his fiancee. Well-done psychodrama. **91m/B VHS, DVD.** Robert Young, Betsy Drake, John Sutton; ***D:*** James V. Kern; ***W:*** Mort Briskin, Robert Smith; ***C:*** Hal Mohr.

Secondhand Lions **2003 (PG)** Timid Walter (Osment) is left with his eccentric uncles Hub (Duvall) and Garth (Caine) by his husband-seeking flaky mom Mae (Sedgewick). Finding no TV when he arrives, Walter becomes fascinated by the uncles' tales of an adventurous past, which are told in flashback in B-action movie style. Alternately syrupy and quirky, pic tries too much to be everything to everybody, and may not appeal to younger, jaded viewers. Their parents and grandparents, nostalgic for this kind of wholesome family entertainment, will be more receptive. Duvall and Caine make up for many of the flaws, but Osment doesn't register as strongly as hoped in his first post-child star role. **107m/C VHS, DVD, UMD.** *US* Michael Caine, Robert Duvall, Haley Joel Osment, Nicky Katt, Kyra Sedgwick, Emmanuelle Vaugier, Christian Kane, Kevin Michael Haberer, Josh(ua) Lucas, Adrian Pasdar; ***D:*** Tim McCanlies; ***W:*** Tim McCanlies; ***C:*** Jack N. Green; ***M:*** Patrick Doyle.

Seconds **1966 (R)** Aging banker Arthur Hamilton (Randolph) is frantic to escape his dead-end existence and accepts an invitation from a mysterious organization to give him a second chance at life. Through surgery, Arthur's transformed into handsome artist Tony Wilson (Hudson). Uncomfortably living in Malibu, he soons finds out all his new neighbors are also "seconds," who are afraid he'll betray their secrets. Wilson decides he wants out of his new arrangement and back to his former life but it comes at a very high price. Eerie film manages to (mostly) overcome its plot problems, with a fine performance by Hudson. Based on the novel by Donald Ely. **107m/B VHS, DVD.** Rock Hudson, John Randolph, Salome Jens, Will Geer, Jeff Corey, Richard Anderson, Murray Hamilton, Karl Swenson, Khigh (Kaie Deei) Deigh, Frances Reid, Wesley Addy; ***D:*** John Frankenheimer; ***W:*** Lewis John Carlino; ***C:*** James Wong Howe; ***M:*** Jerry Goldsmith.

Secre of the Andes ½ **1998 (PG)** Rebellious Diana (Belle) travels to Argentina with her mother (Allen) to visit her estranged father (Keith). He's an archeologist searching for gold and Diana dabbles in the supernatural to help him out. **102m/C VHS, DVD.** David Keith, Nancy Allen, John Rhys-Davies, Camilla Belle, Jerry Stiller; ***D:*** Alejandro Azzano.

The Secret ½ **1993** Businessman and political candidate Mike Dunsmore (Douglas) comes to terms with his lifelong battle with dyslexia when his grandson begins to show signs of the same affliction. Set in picturesque New England fishing village. **92m/C VHS, DVD.** Kirk Douglas, Bruce Boxleitner, Brock Peters, Laura Harrington; ***D:*** Karen Arthur.

The Secret *Si J'Etais Toi* **2007 (R)** This French remake of Yojiro Takita's 1999 Japanese flick "Himitsu" is not so much horror as just weird. Hannah (Taylor) and 16-year-old daughter Samantha (Thirlby) get into a terrible car accident. Sam lives and Hannah dies but Hannah refuses to actually leave distraught husband Ben (Duchovny), so her consciousness occupies Sam's body while Sam is in some kind of limbo. Ben and Hannah try to act normally, so Sam's body goes back to high school (which is unnerving for Hannah because of the teenaged boys and stuff) but the situation gets quite frustrating (and kinda queasy with a hint of incest). **92m/C DVD.** *FR* David Duchovny, Lili Taylor, Olivia Thirlby, Brendan Sexton III, Corey Servier, Macha Grenon; ***D:*** Vincent Perez; ***W:*** Ann Cherkis; ***C:*** Paul Sarossy; ***M:*** Nathaniel Mechaly.

A Secret **2007** Miller's devastating look at how the past—and its secrets—cast a pall on the present. In 1985, Parisian Francois is informed that his elderly father is missing. This triggers flashbacks to 1955 when the shy, sickly youngster realizes he's a disappointment to his athletic parents Tania and Maxime. Francois invents an imaginary older brother who is better at everything and then discovers a family secret—there was an older half-brother from Maxime's first marriage to Hannah. This leads to more revelations about the family's Jewish heritage, the Nazi invasion of France, and how his family survived the occupation. French with subtitles. **105m/C DVD.** *FR* Mathieu Amalric, Patrick Bruel, Cecile de France, Julie Depardieu, Ludivine Sagnier, Valentin Vigourt, Quentin Dubuis, Orlando Nicoletti; ***D:*** Claude Miller; ***W:*** Claude Miller, Natalie Carter; ***C:*** Gerard de Battista; ***M:*** Zbigniew Preisner.

Secret Admirer **1985 (R)** A teenager's unsigned love letter keeps falling into the wrong hands. Intends to be funny, and sometimes is; too often, though, it surrenders to obviousness and predictability. **98m/C VHS, DVD.** C. Thomas Howell, Cliff DeYoung, Kelly Preston, Dee Wallace, Lori Loughlin, Fred Ward, Casey Siemaszko, Corey Haim, Leigh Taylor-Young; ***D:*** David Greenwalt.

The Secret Agent **1936** Presumed dead, a British intelligence agent (Gielgud) reappears and receives a new assignment. Using his faked death to his advantage, he easily journeys to Switzerland where he is to eliminate an enemy agent. Strange Hitchcockian melange of comedy and intrigue; atypical, but worthy offering from the Master. **83m/B VHS, DVD.** *GB* Madeleine Carroll, Peter Lorre, Robert Young, John Gielgud, Lilli Palmer, Percy Marmont, Charles Carson, Florence Kahn; ***D:*** Alfred Hitchcock; ***W:*** Charles Bennett; ***C:*** Bernard Knowles; ***M:*** Louis Levy.

The Secret Agent *Joseph Conrad's The Secret Agent* **1996 (R)** Rain, rain go away. In this waterlogged adaptation of the Conrad novel, Hoskins plays Adolf Verloc, a cowardly agent provocateur who heads a group of anarchists in soggy Victorian England. His real mission, however, is to report the actions of the expatriates to the Russian government. After he is bullied into a terrorist attack on the Greenwich Observatory by his contact at the Russian embassy, the lives of Verloc, his wife Winnie (Arquette) and her mentally disabled brother Stevie (Bale) are blown to pieces (sometimes literally) by the consequences. The only spark in the otherwise dank and gloomy production is Williams (listed as George Spelvin) as the demented explosives expert known only as the Professor. Alfred Hitchcock also used a loose interpretation of Conrad's novel for "Sabotage." **95m/C VHS, DVD.** *GB* Bob Hoskins, Patricia Arquette, Gerard Depardieu, Robin Williams, Jim Broadbent, Christian Bale, Elizabeth Spriggs, Peter Vaughan, Julian Wadham; ***D:*** Christopher Hampton; ***W:*** Christopher Hampton; ***C:*** Denis Lenoir; ***M:*** Philip Glass.

Secret Agent 00 *Operation Kid Brother* **1967 (R)** A master criminal plans to blackmail the western world and only special Secret Agent 00 can stop him. Bad spy genre ripoff, interesting only as the screen debut of Sean Connery's brother. **97m/C VHS.** *IT* Neil Connery, Daniela Bianchi, Adolfo Celi; ***D:*** Alberto De Martino; ***M:*** Ennio Morricone.

The Secret Agent Club ½ **1996 (PG)** Secret agent Ray Chase (Hogan) steals a laser gun that evil Eve (Down) is determined to sell to the highest bidder. Ray returns home and, under the pretext of his job as a toy store owner, hides the gun in the store where his son Jeremy (McCurley) assumes it's a new toy. Eve's henchmen manage to capture Ray but not before Jeremy gets the gun and plans a rescue mission with his friends. **90m/C VHS, DVD.** Hulk Hogan, Richard Moll, Lesley-Anne Down, Mathew McCurley, Edward Albert, Lyman Ward, James Hong, Barry Bostwick, Jack Nance; ***D:*** John Murlowski; ***W:*** Rory Johnston; ***C:*** S. Douglas Smith.

Secret Agent 00-Soul ½ **1989** International spy decides to fulfill his dream of opening a detective agency in his old neighborhood. Release of this direct-to-video mishmash was delayed until '95. **71m/C VHS.** Billy Dee Williams, Amanda Le Flore, Marjean Holden, Tommy (Tiny) Lister; ***D:*** Julius Le Flore.

Secret Agent Super Dragon *Super Dragon* **1966** The CIA calls in the agent known as "Super Dragon" when it is discovered that a Venezuelan drug czar plans to spike U.S. gum and candy with an LSD-like drug. Less than competent production offers some unintended laughter. Ferroni used the pseudonym Calvin Jackson Padget. **95m/C VHS.** *FR IT GE* Ray Danton, Marisa Mell, Margaret Lee, Jess Hahn, Carlo D'Angelo, Andriana Ambesi; ***D:*** Giorgio Ferroni.

Secret Ballot *Raye Makhfi* **2001 (G)** Iranian road picture/comedy gets laughs and provokes thought as a macho soldier and a liberated female pollster travel around the desert. Brought together when a ballot box parachutes down from the sky and onto the desolate beach that the soldier is guarding, the two are classic opposites. The reluctant, hardened soldier (Ab) is eventually coerced by the hopeful electioneer (Abdi) into driving her to each city on her mission to collect every vote possible for the upcoming election. The journey proves useful to both as they get more than a glimpse of the other's point of view. Their radically different views are fertile soil for the ensuing comedy as well as food for thought. The personalities and culture of Iran are explored through their journey, sometimes whimsically, in the light of democracy. Charming score matches pic's equally winsome vision of the Middle East. **105m/C VHS, DVD.** *IA* Nassim Abdi, Cyrus Abidi; ***D:*** Babak Payami; ***W:*** Babak Payami.

Secret Beyond the Door **1948** A wealthy heiress marries a widower and soon discovers that he murdered his first wife. Understandably, she wonders what plans he might have for her. Capably done chiller, but the plot is hackneyed pseudo-Hitchcock. **99m/B VHS, DVD.** Joan Bennett, Michael Redgrave, Barbara O'Neil, Anne Revere; ***D:*** Fritz Lang; ***M:*** Miklos Rozsa.

Secret Ceremony ½ **1969 (R)** An aging prostitute and a young, aimless waif resemble each other's dead mother and dead daughter, respectively, and the relationship goes on, strangely, from there. This original big-screen version is very good Freudian psycho-drama; 101-minute TV version is unfortunately greatly diluted. **109m/C VHS.** Elizabeth Taylor, Robert Mitchum, Mia Farrow, Pamela Brown, Peggy Ashcroft; ***D:*** Joseph Losey; ***M:*** Richard Rodney Bennett.

The Secret Code **1942** A 15-chapter serial with the Black Commando (Kelly) thwarting the Nazis' attempts at sabotage. After each chapter's cliffhanger ending a new form of secret code is explained and decoded. **315m/B VHS.** Paul Kelly, Anne Nagel, Clancy Cooper, Trevor Bardette, Gregory Gay, Ludwig Donath, Eddie (Ed, Eddy, Edwin) Parker; ***D:*** Spencer Gordon Bennet.

The Secret Diary of Sigmund Freud **1984** Spoofy look at the early years of Sigmund Freud, the father of modern psychoanalysis. Freud (Cort) has an affair with lisping nurse Kane while tending to patient Shawn and answering to mama Baker, who's carrying on with mad doctor Kinski. Talented cast falls asleep on couch. **129m/C VHS.** Bud Cort, Carol Kane, Carroll Baker, Klaus Kinski, Marisa Berenson, Dick Shawn, Ferdinand "Ferdy" Mayne; ***D:*** Danford B. Greene.

Secret File of Hollywood ½ *Secret File: Hollywood* **1962** A down-and-out private eye gets a job taking photos for a sleazy Hollywood scandal sheet and finds himself in the midst of a blackmail plot masterminded by his editor. An often childish potboiler, perhaps inspired by the once-feared Confidential Magazine. **85m/B VHS.** Robert Clarke, Francine York, Syd Mason, Maralou Gray, John Warburton; ***D:*** Ralph Cushman.

The Secret Four *The Four Just Men* **1940** Three young men seek to avenge the death of their friend at the hands of British traitors, and become involved in a plot to sabotage the Suez canal. Poorly adapted from the novel by Edgar Wallace. **79m/B VHS.** *GB* Hugh Sinclair, Griffith Jones, Francis L. Sullivan, Frank Lawton, Anna Lee, Alan Napier, Basil Sydney; ***D:*** Walter Forde.

Secret Games ½ **1992 (R)** An unhappily married woman (Brin) is searching for relief from her restrictive marriage. At the "Afternoon Demitasse," an exclusive brothel where women are paid for fulfilling their ultimate fantasies, she meets a man (Hewitt) who pushes her beyond her sexual limits and threatens to totally possess her. **90m/C VHS, DVD.** Martin Hewitt, Michele Brin, Delia Sheppard, Billy Drago; ***D:*** Alexander Gregory (Gregory Dark) Hippolyte; ***W:*** Georges des Esseintes; ***C:*** Wally Pfister, Thomas Denove; ***M:*** Joseph Smith.

Secret Games 2: The Escort ½ **1993 (R)** A performance artist (Hewitt) learns how to seduce women from a beautiful escort (Rochelle). However, he falls for his trainer despite being a star pupil who could have anyone he wanted. Plot conveniently lends itself to lots of steamy love scenes. Also available in an unrated version. **84m/C VHS.** Martin Hewitt, Amy Rochelle, Sara Suzanne Brown, Marie Leroux; ***D:*** Alexander Gregory (Gregory Dark) Hippolyte; ***W:*** Russell Lavalle; ***M:*** Ashley Irwin.

Secret Games 3 ½ **1994 (R)** A bored doctor's wife gets her kicks by visiting a club catering to women's fantasies. But then she meets a criminal who wants her all to himself. An unrated version is available at 91 minutes. **82m/C VHS, DVD.** Woody Brown, Brenda Swanson, Rochelle Swanson; ***D:*** Alexander Gregory (Gregory Dark) Hippolyte; ***C:*** Wally Pfister; ***M:*** Ashley Irwin.

The Secret Garden **1949** Orphaned Mary Lennox (O'Brien) is sent to live with her cold and uncaring Uncle Archibald Craven (Marshall), who has never recovered from his wife's death. He keeps his crippled son, Colin (Stockwell), a virtual prisoner in the house until Mary discovers his presence and befriends him. She also discovers a neglected hidden garden, once the pride of Mrs. Craven, which Mary secretly begins to tend. Touching tearjerker based on the novel by Frances Hodgson Burnett. O'Brien leads an outstanding cast in one of her final juvenile roles. In black and white, with Technicolor for later garden scenes. **92m/B VHS.** Margaret O'Brien, Herbert Marshall, Dean Stockwell, Gladys Cooper, Elsa Lanchester, Brian Roper; ***D:*** Fred M. Wilcox; ***C:*** Ray June; ***M:*** Bronislau Kaper.

The Secret Garden ½ **1984** Orphaned Mary Lennox is sent to live with her mysterious uncle after her parents die. Mary is willful and spoiled and her uncle's house holds a number of secrets, including a crippled cousin. When Mary discovers a mysteriously abandoned locked garden she makes it her mission to restore the garden to life. Based on the children's classic by Frances Hodsgon Burnett. **107m/C VHS, DVD.** *GB* Sarah Hollis Andrews, David Patterson; ***D:*** Katrina Murray. **TV**

The Secret Garden **1987 (PG)** Lonely orphan Mary Lennox is sent to live with her uncle in England after her parent's deaths. Mary, who has grown up in India, is selfish and unhappy until she discovers two secrets on her uncle's estate. Class production of the children's classic by Frances Hodgson Burnett with wonderful performances; added prologue and afterword showing Mary as an adult are unnecessary, but don't detract either. Made for television as a "Hallmark Hall of Fame" special. **100m/C VHS, DVD.** Gennie James, Barret Oliver, Jadrien Steele, Michael Hordern, Derek Jacobi, Billie Whitelaw, Lucy Gutteridge, Julian Glover, Colin Firth, Alan Grint; ***D:*** Alan Grint; ***W:*** Blanche Hanalis; ***C:*** Robert Paynter; ***M:*** John Cameron. **TV**

The Secret Garden ½ **1993 (G)** Rekindled interest in Frances Hodgon Burnett's classic tale has prompted a Broadway musical, two TV movies, and this latest big screen version. Befitting director Holland's reputation this version is beautiful but dark, with children prey to very adult anxieties. **102m/C VHS, DVD.** Kate Maberly, Maggie Smith, Haydon Prowse, Andrew Knott, John Lynch; ***D:*** Agnieszka Holland; ***W:*** Caroline Thompson; ***C:*** Roger Deakins; ***M:*** Zbigniew Preisner. L.A. Film Critics '93: Score.

Secret Honor *Lords of Treason; Secret Honor: The Last Testament of Richard M. Nixon; Secret Honor: A Political Myth* **1985** Idiosyncratic, single-set, one-man film version adapted by Donald Freed and Arnold Stone from their stage play about Richard Nixon coping with the death of his presidency on the night he's decided to blow his brains out. Made with students at the University of Michigan, and carried by the ranting and raving of Hall as a tragic Shakespearean Nixon with plenty of darkly humorous lines. **90m/C VHS, DVD.** Philip Baker Hall; ***D:*** Robert Altman; ***W:*** Donald Freed, Arnold Stone; ***C:*** Pierre Mignot; ***M:*** George Burt.

The Secret in Their Eyes *El Secreto de Sus Ojos* **2009** Former criminal-court employee Benjamin decides to write a novel based on a 20-year-old rape and murder. He believes the immigrant workers convicted of the crime were forced to confess and Benjamin foolishly decides to hunt for the real killer so the case can be formally reopened. Spanish with subtitles. **127m/C DVD.** *AR* Ricardo Darin, Soledad Villamil, Guillermo Francella, Pablo Rago, Javier Godino; ***D:*** Juan J. Campanella; ***W:*** Juan J. Campanella; ***C:*** Felix Monti; ***M:*** Federico Jusid. Oscars '09: Foreign Film.

Secret Ingredient ½ **1992** A legendary cognac recipe is the secret formula of the monks of St. Celare, whose monastery is located in the mountains of Yugoslavia. A wealthy American sends his flighty heiress daughter to pry the secret recipe from the monks but she runs into more than she bargains for when she falls for a handsome friar and gets caught up with a band of bumbling gypsies and the inept state police. **95m/C VHS.** Rick Rossovich, Catherine Hicks, Gary Kroeger, Jeff Corey, Brad Dexter, Sam Wanamaker; ***D:*** Slobodan Shijan.

The Secret Invasion ½ **1964** In 1943, British intelligence officer Major Richard Mace (Granger) offers pardons to five criminals (Vallone, Rooney, Byrnes, Silva, Campbell) in return for their expertise. Their mission is to rescue an Italian general who has promised that his troops will switch sides and fight for the allies. Said general is imprisoned by the Nazis in Dubrovnik, Yugoslavia. Actioner was well-done by Corman before 1967's "The Dirty Dozen." **95m/C DVD.** Stewart Granger, Raf Vallone, Mickey Rooney, Edd Byrnes, William Campbell, Henry Silva, Spela Rozin, Helmo Kinderman, Enzo Fiermonte, Peter Coe; ***D:*** Roger Corman; ***W:*** Arthur E. Arling; ***C:*** Hugo Friedhofer.

Secret Life of an American Wife **1968** A bored housewife (Jackson) tries to seduce a client of her husband's, with less than hilarious results. Too much dialogue, not enough genuine humor. Disappointing inversion of director Axelrod's "The Seven Year Itch." **97m/C VHS.** Walter Matthau, Anne Jackson, Patrick O'Neal, Edy Williams, John MacKay; ***D:*** George Axelrod; ***W:*** George Axelrod.

The Secret Life of Bees **2008 (PG-13)** Big screen adaptation of the wildly successful 2002 novel by Sue Monk Kidd. In 1964 South Carolina, Lily Owens (Fanning), an idealistic 14-year-old girl with no mother, helps her black housekeeper Rosaleen (Hudson) flee the homegrown racism of a small town that had her arrested for trying to vote. The two journey to Tiburon—a place Lily remembers seeing written on her mother's honey jar label—where they're taken in by beekeeper August (Latifah) and her two sisters, June (Keys) and May (Okonedo), and both Lily and Rosaleen discover the strength of womanhood that had been hidden and suppressed all their lives. Fanning truly finds herself in this role, building from the inherent mistakes in "Hounddog." Heartfelt and well-acted all around, but the book's nuances are lost in a somewhat predictable coming-of-age melodrama. **110m/C DVD.** *US* Queen Latifah, Dakota Fanning, Jennifer Hudson, Sophie Okonedo, Nathaniel Parker, Hilarie Burton, Paul Bettany, Alicia Keyes, Tristan Wilds; ***D:*** Gina Prince-Bythewood; ***W:*** Gina Prince-Bythewood; ***C:*** Rogier Stoffers.

The Secret Life of Girls ½ **1999** Fifteen-year-old Natalie (Delfino) is caught in the midst of family turmoil when her unhappy mother, Ruby (Hamilton), reveals that Natalie's college professor father, Hugh (Levy), has been fooling around with one of his students. Natalie hides out in the university library where she shyly flirts with a cute boy, but the family chaos continues when Hugh suffers the pangs of conscience. **90m/C VHS.** Majandra Delfino, Linda Hamilton, Eugene Levy, Kate Vernon, Meagan Good, Aeryk Egan, Andrew Ducote; ***D:*** Holly Goldberg Sloan.

The Secret Life of Mrs. Beeton ½ **2006** Beginning in the 1850s, Isabelle Beeton writes domestic advice columns for her husband Sam's various London publications. She produces a collection of recipes (though she can't cook) and household management tips that become a best-selling sensation. However, her own marriage is fraught with secrets that include financial difficulties, many personal tragedies, and her own early death at the age of 28. **90m/C DVD.** J.J. Feild, Jim Carter, Anna Chancellor, Anna Madeley, Siobhan Hayes, Joseph Mawle, Andrea Riseboroughe; ***D:*** Jon Jones; ***W:*** Sarah Williams; ***C:*** Ian Moss; ***M:*** Charlie Mole. **TV**

The Secret Life of Walter Mitty **1947** An entertaining adaptation of the James Thurber short story about a meek man (Kaye) who lives an unusual secret fantasy life. Henpecked by his fiancee and mother, oppressed at his job, he imagines himself in the midst of various heroic fantasies. While Thurber always professed to hate Kaye's characterization and the movie, it scored at the boxoffice and today stands as a comedic romp for Kaye. Available with digitally remastered stereo and original movie trailer. **110m/C VHS, DVD.** Danny Kaye, Virginia Mayo, Boris Karloff, Ann Rutherford, Fay Bainter, Florence Bates; ***D:*** Norman Z. McLeod; ***W:*** Everett Freeman, Ken Englund, Philip Rapp; ***C:*** Lee Garmes; ***M:*** Sylvia Fine, David Raksin.

The Secret Lives of Dentists **2002 (R)** Rudolph's funny, dead-on take on married dentists in crisis. Mild-mannered David (Scott) suspects his wife and fellow dentist Dana (Davis) may be having an affair with a member of her community opera troupe when his imagination begins to go wild. His acerbic, misogynist patient (Leary in a no-brainer bit of casting) plays devil's advocate as David begins to see him everywhere, imparting advice on how to handle the situation. As the marriage continues to decay, David's hilarious waking dreams continue unabated and he is forced to deal with the darker side of his milquetoast persona. Refreshingly realistic, original, and well-acted. Based on the novel "The Age of Grief" by Jane Smiley. **104m/B VHS, DVD.** *US* Campbell Scott, Hope Davis, Denis Leary, Robin Tunney, Kevin Carroll; ***D:*** Alan Rudolph; ***W:*** Craig Lucas; ***C:*** Florian Ballhaus; ***M:*** Gary DeMichele. Ind. Spirit '04: Support. Actress (Davis); N.Y. Film Critics '03: Actress (Davis).

Secret Mission 1/2 **1942** Four British intelligence agents are sent into occupied France to assess the strength of Nazi forces. But after discovering the information, their cover is blown and it's a race to get the intelligence into the right hands before the Nazis get to them first. **94m/B VHS.** *GB* James Mason, Hugh Williams, Roland Culver, Michael Wilding, Carla Lehmann, Nancy Price, Percy Walsh, Karel Stepanek, Herbert Lom, Stewart Granger; ***D:*** Harold French; ***W:*** Anatole de Grunwald, Basil Bartlett; ***C:*** Bernard Knowles, Cyril Knowles; ***M:*** Mischa Spoliansky.

Secret Obsession **1988 (PG)** A love triangle among a father, his illegitimate son, and the woman they both love, set in North Africa in 1955. Sounds intriguing, but don't be fooled. Slow, dull, and poorly acted. **82m/C VHS, DVD.** Julie Christie, Ben Gazzara, Patrick Bruel, Jean Carmet; ***D:*** Henri Vart.

The Secret of Dr. Kildare **1939** Badly dated but worth seeing for the era's familiar faces and the difference in medical attitudes. Grumpy Dr. Gillespie (Barrymore) is terminally ill and trying to continue his research into new treatments for pneumonia. He doesn't have time for wealthy Paul Messenger (Atwill) and his apparently neurotic debutante daughter Nancy's (Gilbert) health problems, so he sends young Dr. Kildare (Ayres) to look into the matter. The third in the MGM B-movie series. **84m/B DVD.** Lew Ayres, Lionel Barrymore, Lionel Atwill, Helen Gilbert, Walter Kingford, Samuel S. Hinds, Emma Dunn, Nat Pendleton, Laraine Day; ***D:*** Harold Bucquet; ***W:*** Harry Ruskin, Willis Goldbeck; ***C:*** Alfred Gilks; ***M:*** David Snell.

The Secret of El Zorro 1/2 **1957** Don Diego's friend, Don Ricardo, threatens to unmask Zorro's secret identity when he challenges the legendary swordsman to a duel. **75m/B VHS.** Guy Williams.

The Secret of Kells *Brendan and the Secret of Kells* **2009** Young novice Brendan lives in the abbey of Kells, Ireland in the 9th century where he helps the monks illustrate the gospels. The abbey is in peril from Viking raiders and Brendan is not supposed to go beyond the walls, especially not into the supposedly haunted forest, which he does when certain berries are needed to make ink for the book. **75m/C DVD.** *IR BE FR* ***D:*** Tomm Moore; ***W:*** Fabrice Ziolkowski; ***C:*** Fabienne Alvarez-Giro; ***M:*** Bruno Coulais; ***V:*** Brendan Gleeson, Mick (Michael) Lally, Evan McGuire.

The Secret of My Success **1987 (PG-13)** Country bumpkin Fox goes to the Big Apple to make his mark. He becomes the corporate mailboy who rises meteorically to the top of his company (by impersonating an executive) in order to win the love of an icy woman executive. He spends his days running frantically between his real job in the mailroom and his fantasy position, with various sexual shenanigans with the boss's wife thrown in to keep the viewer alert. Fox is charismatic while working with a cliche-ridden script that ties up everything very neatly at the end. **110m/C VHS, DVD.** Michael J. Fox, Helen Slater, Richard Jordan, Margaret Whitton, Fred Gwynne; ***D:*** Herbert Ross; ***W:*** Jim Cash, Jack Epps Jr., A.J. Carothers; ***C:*** Carlo Di Palma; ***M:*** David Foster.

The Secret of Navajo Cave *Legend of Cougar Canyon* **1976 (G)** Fair family adventure. Two young friends explore the mysterious Navajo cave, where one can be assured that a secret awaits. **84m/C VHS, DVD.** Holger Kasper, Steven Benally Jr., Johnny Guerro; ***D:*** James T. Flocker; ***Nar:*** Rex Allen.

The Secret of NIMH **1982 (G)** Animated tale, produced by a staff of Disney-trained artists led by "American Tail's" Bluth; concerns a newly widowed mouse who discovers a secret agency of superintelligent rats (they've escaped from a science lab) who aid her in protecting her family. As is usually the case with Bluth films, the animation is superb while the socially aware plot struggles to keep pace. That aside, it's still an interesting treat for the youngsters. Adapted from Robert C. O'Brien's "Mrs. Frisby and the Rats of N.I.M.H." **84m/C VHS, DVD.** ***D:*** Don Bluth; ***W:*** Don Bluth; ***M:*** Jerry Goldsmith; ***V:*** John Carradine, Derek Jacobi, Dom DeLuise, Elizabeth Hartman, Peter Strauss, Aldo Ray, Edie McClurg, Wil Wheaton.

The Secret of NIMH 2 1/2 **1998 (G)** Timmy, the youngest son of heroic mouse Jonathan Brisby, is sent from Thorn Valley to study at the university. At school, Timmy meets Jenny McBride, who has escaped from NIMH (National Institute of Mental Health), and seeks Timmy's help in rescuing her family and the other animals imprisoned there. Then Timmy discovers his older brother Martin is also being held prisoner. **68m/C VHS, DVD.** ***D:*** Dick Sebast; ***W:*** Sam Graham, Chris Hubbell; ***M:*** Lee Holdridge; ***V:*** Ralph Macchio, Eric Idle, Dom DeLuise, Harvey Korman, Peter MacNichol, William H. Macy, Andrea Martin, Meshach Taylor. **VIDEO**

The Secret of Roan Inish 1/2 **1994 (PG)** Irish myth comes to life in this fantasy about the importance of family and place, seen through the eyes of 10-year-old Fiona Coneelly (newcomer Courtney) who's sent to live with her grandparents in post-WWII County Donegal. Fiona's drawn to her grandfather's stories about the family's ancestral home on the island of Roan Inish and the loss of her baby brother Jamie, who was carried out to sea. Another family tale is about a Selkie—a beautiful seal/woman captured by a Coneelly fisherman who eventually returned to her ocean home. When Fiona visits Roan Inish she becomes convinced that Jamie is alive and being cared for by the island's seals. Director Sayles keeps a firm grip on the cuteness factor while cinematographer Wexler works his usual magic on the sea, sky, and land of Ireland. Based on the 1957 novel "Secret of the Ron Mor Skerry" by Rosalie K. Fry. **102m/C VHS, DVD.** Jeni Courtney, Mick (Michael) Lally, Eileen Colgan, John Lynch, Richard Sheridan, Susan Lynch, Cillian Byrne; ***D:*** John Sayles; ***W:*** John Sayles; ***C:*** Haskell Wexler; ***M:*** Mason Daring.

The Secret of Santa Vittoria 1/2 **1969 (PG)** Italo Bambolini (Quinn) is an amiable drunk who unexpectedly becomes the mayor of his wine-making village during WWII. Hearing the Nazis are headed toward Santa Vittoria to loot their supply of vintage wines, Italo and his savvy wife, Rosa (Magnani), enlist the villagers to hide most of the bottles in a cave outside of town, leaving a token amount to satisfy suspicious German Commander Von Prum (Kruger), who tries to learn the truth. Overly long but still amusing. Based on the novel by Robert Crichton. **139m/C VHS.** Anthony Quinn, Anna Magnani, Hardy Kruger, Virna Lisi, Renato Rascel, Giancarlo Giannini, Valentina Cortese, Sergio Franchi; ***D:*** Stanley Kramer; ***W:*** William Rose, Ben Maddow; ***C:*** Giuseppe Rotunno; ***M:*** Ernest Gold.

Secret of Stamboul 1/2 *The Spy in White* **1936** British take on Hollywood action films finds two soldiers thrown out of their regiment thanks to a slinky seductress (Hobson) and into a devilish rebel plot to overthrow the Turkish government. **85m/B VHS.** Valerie Hobson, Peter Haddon, Frank Vosper, Kay Walsh, Cecil Ramage, James Mason; ***D:*** Andrew Marton; ***W:*** Laszlo Benedek, George Hill. **VIDEO**

Secret of the Black Trunk 1/2 **1962** Chilling Edgar Wallace story about a series of murders at a famed English hotel. Filmed in Great Britain. **96m/C VHS.** *GE* Joachim Hansen, Senta Berger, Hans Reiser, Leonard Steckel, Peter Carsten; ***D:*** Werner Klingler.

Secret of the Cave **2006 (PG)** Fourteen-year-old American Roy Wallace is spending the summer with his aunt and uncle in the small Irish village where his father grew up. Rumors of ghosts have the villagers in a tizzy and Roy's investigations point to a nearby sea cave. Pretty scenery and a Christian message as the film was sponsored by Southern Adventist University. **89m/C DVD.** Kevin Novotny, Joseph Kelly, Patrick Bergin, Niall O'Brien, Niamh Finn, Noelle Brown; ***D:*** Zach C. Gray; ***W:*** Aaron Adams, Scott Fog; ***C:*** David George; ***M:*** John Carta.

The Secret of the Golden Eagle **1991** A boy and his new adventurer friend are on a quest to find the strange "Golden Statue" that causes people to grow old before their time. They must take it from criminals who are using it for evil purposes. A good adventure/fantasy for the entire family. **90m/C VHS.** Michael Berryman, Brandon McKay; ***D:*** Cole McKay.

Secret of the Ice Cave **1989 (PG-13)** A motley band of explorers, hijackers and mercenaries go after a secret treasure in the remote mountains. **106m/C VHS.** Michael Moriarty, Sally Kellerman, David Mendenhall, Virgil Frye, Gerald Anthony, Norbert Weisser; ***D:*** Radu Gabrea.

The Secret of the Loch 1/2 **1934** Scottish scientist claims to have seen Loch Ness Monster but everyone thinks his bagpipe's blown a reed. **80m/B VHS.** *GB* Sir Seymour Hicks, Nancy O'Neil, Gibson Gowland, Frederick Peisley; ***D:*** Milton Rosmer.

The Secret of the Telegian 1/2 *The Telegian* **1961** Rare Japanese sci-fi flick about a soldier who uses a teleportation device to kill fellow soldiers who tried to kill him. He could find his victims wherever they hid. **85m/C VHS.** *JP* Koji Tsurata, Yumi Shirakawa, Akihiko Hirata, Tadao Nakamura; ***D:*** Jun Fukuda.

Secret of Yolanda *Mute Love; Ahava Ilemeth* **1982 (R)** Steamy romance about a young deaf-mute whose guardian and riding instructor both fall for her. **90m/C VHS.** *IS* Aviva Ger, Asher Tzarfati, Shraga Harpaz; ***D:*** Joel Silberg; ***W:*** Eli Tavor; ***C:*** David Gurfinkel; ***M:*** Kobi Oshrat.

The Secret Passion of Robert Clayton **1992 (R)** When Robert Clayton Jr. (Valentine) returns to his home town to take the position of D.A., he is forced to go head to head in a lurid murder trial with the defense attorney (Mahoney), who also happens to be his own father. **92m/C VHS.** John Mahoney, Scott Valentine, Eve Gordon, Kevin Conroy; ***D:*** E.W. Swackhamer; ***W:*** Brian Ross; ***C:*** Billy Dickson.

Secret Passions 1/2 *Haunted by the Past* **1987** A young couple are haunted by a dark, romance-novel-type secret. **99m/C VHS.** John James, Susan Lucci; ***D:*** Michael Pressman. **TV**

Secret Places 1/2 **1985 (PG)** On the brink of WWII, a German girl in an English school finds friendship with a popular classmate. Touching and involving, but somehow unsatisfying. **98m/C VHS.** *GB* Maria Therese Relin, Tara MacGowran, Claudine Auger, Jenny Agutter; ***D:*** Zelda Barron; ***W:*** Zelda Barron.

The Secret Policeman's Other Ball **1982 (R)** Engaging live performance by most of the Monty Python troupe and guest rock artists, staged for Amnesty International. Follows 1979's "The Secret Policeman's Ball," and followed by 1987's "The Secret Policeman's Third Ball." **101m/C VHS.** *GB* John Cleese, Graham Chapman, Michael Palin, Terry Jones, Pete Townshend, Sting, Billy Connolly, Bob Geldof; ***D:*** Julien Temple; ***W:*** Michael Palin.

Secret Policeman's Private Parts 1/2 **1981** Various sketches and performances from the various Secret Policeman occasions, featuring classic Python sketches including "I'm a Lumberjack and I'm OK." Also featured are performances by Phil Collins, Pete Townshend, Donovan, and Bob Geldof. Thank you very much. **77m/C VHS.** *GB* John Cleese, Michael Palin, Terry Jones, Eric Idle, Graham Chapman, Terry Gilliam, Pete Townshend, Julien Temple, Phil Collins, Peter Cook, Donovan, Bob Geldof; ***D:*** Roger Graef, Julien Temple.

The Secret Rapture **1994 (R)** Two sisters clash in this family drama, adapted by Hare from his 1988 play. The bohemian Isobel (Stevenson) and her estranged sister, the forbidding Marion (Wilton), are brought together by their father's death. While Isobel grieves, Marion seeks to gain advantage in the family business, and both must deal with their young, alcoholic, and volatile stepmother Katherine (Whalley-Kilmer). Emotional intensity with good performances but abrupt shifts in tone. **96m/C VHS.** *GB* Juliet Stevenson, Penelope Wilton, Joanne Whalley, Alan Howard, Neil Pearson, Robert Stephens, Hilton McRae; ***D:*** Howard Davies; ***W:*** David Hare; ***C:*** Ian Wilson; ***M:*** Richard Hartley.

Secret Smile 1/2 **2005** Would have been better if Ashfield wasn't so wooden as the heroine; and the twist ending couldn't be seen from a mile off. Miranda (Ashfield) has a fling with Brendan (Tennant) and thinks it's over when she says so. Then her younger sister Kathy (Goose) is excited to introduce her new boyfriend (guess who). When people she's close to start turning up dead, Miranda has to decide just how far she'll go to prove Brendan is the killer, especially since no one believes her. Based on the novel by Nicci French. **137m/C DVD.** *GB* David Tennant, Kate Ashfield, Claire Goose, John Bowe, Jill Baker, Rory Kinnear, Rob Lowe, Susannah Wise; ***D:*** Christopher Menaul; ***W:*** Kate Brooke; ***C:*** Jake Polonsky; ***M:*** Edmund Butt. **TV**

Secret Society **2000** Pleasingly plump Daisy gets a job in a canning factory and discovers that a group of her fellow buxom female workers are secretly meeting after work to train as Sumo wrestlers. As Daisy becomes more involved with the group, her husband Ken gets suspicious and then intervenes when he witnesses Daisy in a match. He winds up in the hospital and Daisy promises to quit until the women decide to accept the challenge of going public and fighting a group of male Japanese sumo wrestlers. **89m/C VHS, DVD.** *GB* Charlotte Brittain, Lee Ross, Annette Badland, James Wooton; ***D:*** Imogen Kimmel; ***W:*** Imogen Kimmel, Catriona McGowan; ***C:*** Glynn Speeckaert; ***M:*** Paul Heard.

A Secret Space 1/2 **1988** Story of a young man, born of secular parents, searching for the meaning of his Jewish roots as he nears his Bar Mitzvah. He is helped along by a group of Jews who are also searching for this meaning. **80m/C VHS.** Robert Klein, Phyllis Newman, John Matthews, Sam Schacht, Virginia Graham; ***D:*** Roberta Hodes.

The Secret War of Harry Frigg 1/2 **1968 (R)** Non-conformist WWII Private Harry Frigg is promoted to general as part of a scheme to help five Allied generals escape from the custody of the Germans. Rare Newman bomb; dismal comedy. **123m/C VHS.** Paul Newman, Sylva Koscina, John Williams, Tom Bosley, Andrew Duggan; ***D:*** Jack Smight; ***C:*** Russell Metty.

Secret Weapon **1990** An Israeli technician flees his country with atomic secrets and a beautiful government agent is sent to induce him to return. Based on the true case of Mordecai Vanunu. Slow-paced and not very suspenseful. **95m/C VHS.** Griffin Dunne, Karen Allen, Stuart Wilson, Jeroen Krabbe, Brian Cox, John Rhys-Davies, Ian Mitchell; *D:* Ian Sharp. **CABLE**

Secret Weapons 1/2 *Secrets of the Red Bedroom* **1985** Sexy Russian babes are KGB-trained to get any secret from any man. Strains credibility as well as patience. Made for TV. **100m/C VHS, DVD.** Linda Hamilton, Sally Kellerman, Hunt Block, Viveca Lindfors, Christopher Atkins, Geena Davis, James Franciscus; *D:* Don Taylor; *M:* Charles Bernstein. **TV**

Secret Window 1/2 **2004 (PG-13)** Wandering around with a wicked case of bed-head in a ratty old bathrobe and talking incessantly to himself, Johnny Depp cranks this ho-hum psycho-thriller up a notch with a typically quirky and subtly humorous performance as Mort Rainey, an eccentric mystery writer. After catching wife Amy (Bello) in the sack with another man (Hutton) Mort holes up in a remote lake cottage during his traumatic divorce only to be roused from his depression-induced torpor and writers block by Shooter (Turturro) a deranged hayseed in an Amish-looking hat who claims Mort stole his story. Mort, who is increasingly showing signs that he may not be playing with a full deck, is almost sure that isn't true and can prove it if he can only find the back issue of a magazine that published his story years before Shooter claims to have penned his. Adapted from a novella by Stephen King. **95m/C VHS, DVD, Blu-ray Disc.** *US* Johnny Depp, John Turturro, Maria Bello, Timothy Hutton, Charles S. Dutton, Len Cariou, John Dunn-Hill, Vlasta Vrana; *D:* David Koepp; *W:* David Koepp; *C:* Fred Murphy; *M:* Philip Glass.

The Secretary 1/2 **1994 (R)** Another bland variation of "The Temp." Career woman Ellen Bradford (Harris) has a new fast-track job and a highly efficient secretary in Deidre (Kelley). But it turns out Deidre's also lethally efficient in disposing of co-workers through a series of inexplicable accidents and "suicides." So just what's Ellen going to do to show Deidre who's boss? **94m/C VHS.** Mel Harris, Sheila Kelley, Barry Bostwick, James Russo; *D:* Andrew Lane; *C:* Steven Bernstein; *M:* Louis Febre.

Secretary **2002 (R)** Lighter look at S&M conveniently hooks up submissive secretary Lee (Gyllenhaal, in a breakthrough role), with her obsessive perfectionist new boss, Edward. After too many misspelled words (bad secretary!), Lee discovers the dominant Edward is perfect at fulfilling her masochistic fantasies. With a sketchy (at best) romantic history, the plucky heroine tries a normal relationship with an old classmate, Peter (Davies) but still craves her kinky boss's brand of quiet discipline. Alternately poignant and funny, story is original and doesn't fall prey to cliche or pathos. Adapted from a 1988 story by Mary Gaitskill. **104m/C VHS, DVD.** *US* James Spader, Maggie Gyllenhaal, Lesley Ann Warren, Jeremy Davies, Patrick Bauchau, Stephen McHattie, Oz (Osgood) Perkins II, Jessica Tuck, Amy Locane, Michael Mantell; *D:* Steven Shainberg; *W:* Erin Cressida Wilson; *C:* Steven Fierberg; *M:* Angelo Badalamenti.

Secrets 1/2 **1971 (R)** A wife, her husband, and her daughter each have a sexual experience which they must keep secret. Bisset's nude love scene is an eye-opener. Fast forward through the rest of this dull, overwrought drama. **86m/C VHS.** Jacqueline Bisset, Per Oscarsson, Shirley Knight, Robert Powell, Tarka Kings, Martin C. Thurley; *D:* Philip Saville; *M:* Michael Gibbs.

Secrets **1977** An unhappy young bride starts having numerous affairs when her mother dies. Hardly worth the effort. **100m/C VHS.** Susan Blakely, Roy Thinnes, Joanne Linville, John Randolph, Anthony Eisley, Andrew Stevens; *D:* Paul Wendkos. **TV**

Secrets **1982** British drama about the confused life of an innocent schoolgirl who's the victim of a mess of authoritative misunderstandings. One of David Puttnam's "First Love" series. **79m/C VHS.** *GB* Helen Lindsay, Anna Campbell-Jones, Daisy Cockburn; *D:* Gavin Millar.

Secrets 1/2 **1994 (PG-13)** Teenager Anna Berter, growing up in turn-of-the-century Iowa, is told by her snobbish mother Etta (Hamel) not to befriend the help, which include the woman who raised Anna alongside her granddaughter Edwina. When Edwina is seduced by a Berter family friend and left pregnant, Etta decides to adopt her baby daughter—whether Edwina wants to let the baby go or not. All this obsessive behavior leads Anna to discover some very unhappy family secrets surrounding her own birth. Made for TV. **92m/C VHS.** Veronica Hamel, Julie Harris, Richard Kiley, Thomas Gibson, Shae D'Lyn, Jessica Bowman, Reed Edward Diamond; *D:* Jud Taylor. **TV**

The Secrets *Ha-Sodot* **2007 (R)** Israeli Naomi (Bokstein) is raised in an ultra Orthodox community by her strict rabbi father. When her mother dies, Naomi is expected to marry her father's rabbinical prodigy. A gifted student of the Torah, Naomi persuades her father to allow her a year's study at a women's seminary where she is befriended by newly-arrived Frenchwoman, Michelle (Shtamler). Both are assigned to aid the terminally ill and tragic Anouk (Ardant), which results in Naomi and Michelle falling in love. Good performances by the three leads but the plot seems slow and overextended. French and Hebrew with subtitles. **127m/C DVD.** *FR IS* Fanny Ardant, Dana Ivgy, Ania Bokstein, Michal Shtamler, Tali Oren, Adir Miller, Sefi Rivlin, Guri Alfi; *D:* Avi Nesher; *W:* Avi Nesher, Hadar Galron; *C:* Michel Abramowicz; *M:* Daniel Salomon, Eyal Sela.

Secrets and Lies **1995 (R)** Too-long film focusing on family and identity. The adoptive parents of black Yuppie Londoner Hortense (Jean-Baptiste) have just died and she decides it's time to seek out her birth parents. She's warned about the emotional consequences, especially upon discovering her biological mother is white—factory worker Cynthia (Blethyn), who has another daughter, Roxanne (Rushbrook), who doesn't get along with mum. Naturally, when Hortense is introduced to the rest of Cynthia's family, there's lots of dysfunction to explore. Good performances, although Hortense's character is bland, but pacing drags. **142m/C VHS, DVD.** *GB* Brenda Blethyn, Marianne Jean-Baptiste, Timothy Spall, Claire Rushbrook, Phyllis Logan, Lee Ross, Ron Cook, Lesley Manville; ***Cameos:*** Alison Steadman; *D:* Mike Leigh; *W:* Mike Leigh; *C:* Dick Pope; *M:* Andrew Dickson. Australian Film Inst. '97: Foreign Film; British Acad. '96: Actress (Blethyn), Orig. Screenplay; Cannes '96: Actress (Blethyn), Film; Golden Globes '97: Actress—Drama (Blethyn); L.A. Film Critics '96: Actress (Blethyn), Director (Leigh), Film.

Secrets of a Married Man **1984** A married man's philandering ways are his ruination when he falls hard for a beautiful prostitute. Shatner and Shepherd contain their laughter as they make their way through this hyper-earnest family drama. **96m/C VHS, DVD.** William Shatner, Cybill Shepherd, Michelle Phillips, Glynn Turman; *D:* William A. Graham.

Secrets of a Soul 1/2 **1925** A visually impressive presentation of Freudian psychoanalytic theory, in which a professor, wanting a child and jealous of his wife's childhood sweetheart, moves toward madness (we did say Freudian) and is cured through dream interpretation. Great dream sequences bring out the arm-chair psychoanalyst. Silent. **94m/B VHS.** *GE* Werner Krauss, Ruth Weyher, Jack Trevor; *D:* G.W. Pabst.

Secrets of Sweet Sixteen WOOF! **1974 (R)** Gag-fest about budding sexuality in high school. **84m/C VHS, DVD.** *GE* Kristina Lindberg, Sasha Hehn; *D:* Ernest Hofbauer; *W:* Erich Tomek; *C:* Peter Reimer; *M:* Gerhard Heinz.

Secrets of the Heart *Secretos del Corazon* **1997** Javi (Erburu) grows up in a provincial town in Spain in the 1960s. Director Armendariz isn't as flamboyant as Fellini in "Amarcord" but his intentions are similar. **108m/C DVD.** *SP* Carmelo Gomez, Charo Lopez, Andoni Erburu, Silvia Munt, Alvaro Nagore; *D:* Montxo Armendariz; *W:* Montxo Armendariz; *C:* Javier Aguirresarobe.

Secrets of Three Hungry Wives **1978** When a multi-millionaire is killed, the women with whom he was having affairs are suspected. Tacky TV flick. **97m/C VHS.** Jessica Walter, Gretchen Corbett, Eve Plumb, Heather MacRae, James Franciscus, Craig Stevens; *D:* Gordon Hessler. **TV**

Secrets of Women *Kvinnors Vantan; Waiting Women* **1952** A rare Bergman comedy about three sisters-in-law who tell about their affairs and marriages as they await their husbands at a lakeside resort. His first commercial success, though it waited nine years for release (1961). In Swedish with English subtitles. **114m/B VHS, DVD.** *SW* Anita Bjork, Karl Arne Homsten, Eva Dahlbeck, Maj-Britt Nilsson, Jarl Kulle; *D:* Ingmar Bergman; *W:* Ingmar Bergman.

The Secrets of Wu Sin **1932** A suicidal news writer in Chinatown is given a reason to live by a news editor who gives her a job. She starts investigating a ring smuggling Chinese workers, with the trail leading to, of course, Chinatown. Low-budget crime thriller. **65m/B VHS.** Lois Wilson, Grant Withers, Dorothy Revier, Robert Warwick, Toshia Mori; *D:* Richard Thorpe.

Seduce Me: Pamela Principle 2 1/2 *Pamela Principle 2* **1994 (R)** Charles is a bored, married, architectural photographer who decides a change of pace is in order. So he starts shooting lingerie fashion spreads and gets seduced by model Pamela, who likes her men married. The only connection to the 1991 film is the married man/affair angle. **96m/C VHS.** Alina Thompson, Nick Rafter, India Allen; *D:* Edward Holzman.

Seduced **1985** When a rich businessman turns up dead, the ambitious politician who was involved with his wife must find the killer. Not memorable or exceptional, but not boring or offensive either. **100m/C VHS, DVD.** Gregory Harrison, Cybill Shepherd, Jose Ferrer, Adrienne Barbeau, Michael C. Gwynne, Karmin Murcelo, Paul Stewart; *D:* Jerrold Freedman. **TV**

Seduced and Abandoned *Sedotta e Abbandonata* **1964** A lothario seduces his fiancee's young sister. When the girl becomes pregnant, he refuses to marry her. Family complications abound. A comic look at the Italian code of honor. In Italian with English subtitles. **118m/B VHS, DVD.** *IT* Saro Urzi, Stefania Sandrelli, Aldo Puglisi, Leopoldo Trieste; *D:* Pietro Germi; *W:* Pietro Germi. Cannes '64: Actor (Urzi).

Seduced by Evil **1994** A journalist (Somers) is investigating a story in a small Southwest town when she encounters a sorcerer (Vargas) who decides he wants her for himself alone. Even if it means destroying everyone she holds dear. Adapted from the novel "Brujo" by Jann Arrington Wolcott. **88m/C VHS.** Suzanne Somers, John Vargas, Julie Carmen, James B. Sikking, Mindy Spence, Nancy Moonves; *D:* Tony Wharmby; *W:* Bill Svanoe.

Seduced: Pretty When You Cry 1/2 *Pretty When You Cry* **2001 (R)** Albert (Kennedy) is the mild-mannered suspect in the murder of nightclub owner Frank (Cavalieri) because Albert's in love with Frank's wife Sarah (Elizabeth), who happens to be missing. Detective Black (Elliott) is investigating and learns that Frank and Sarah were into some kinky sex scenes that may have gone too far. **90m/C VHS, DVD.** Sam Elliott, Jamie Kennedy, Carlton Elizabeth, Michael Cavalieri, Keith David, Lori Heuring; *D:* Jack N. Green; *W:* Christopher Keller; *C:* Jack N. Green; *M:* Normand Corbeil. **VIDEO**

The Seducer *Some Like It Sexy; Come Back Peter* **1969 (R)** Things get dangerous when a playboy's goals turn from love to death. **72m/C VHS.** *GB* Nicola Pagett, Erika Bergmann, Penny Riley, Mary Collinson, Madeleine Collinson, Christopher Mathews; *D:* Donovan Winter; *W:* Donovan Winter; *C:* Gus Coma, Ian Struthers.

The Seducers **1970** An acid-dropping mother takes her shy, withdrawn son on a Mediterranean cruise and asks along some of her girlfriends in the hopes of stoking his libido. However, she finds it difficult to control her own impulses. The boy gets a chance when the ship runs aground on a remote island and he meets an innocent native girl. His mother, though, has designs of her own. Dubbed from Italian. **84m/C VHS.** *GE* Rosalba Neri, Edwige Fenech, Maud de Belleroche, Maurizio Bonuglia, Ruggero Miti, Ewa Thulin; *D:* Ottavio Alessi.

Seducers *Death Game* **1977 (R)** Wealthy, middle-aged man unsuspectingly allows two young lesbians to use his telephone. A night of bizarre mayhem and brutal murder begins. They tease him, tear apart his house, and generally make him miserable. Why? Good question. **90m/C VHS, DVD.** Sondra Locke, Colleen Camp, Seymour Cassel, Beth Brickell; *D:* Peter S. Traynor.

Seducing Doctor Lewis 1/2 *La Grande Seduction* **2003** Dying Quebec fishing village must find a resident doctor if it is to attract new factory owners. The villagers find a possible pigeon in a young Montreal plastic surgeon (Boutin) who comes for a visit. They pretend to love everything he does, from playing cricket rather than their favored hockey to throwing a beef stroganoff festival because it's his favorite food. Very lightweight but enjoyable comedy in the style of "Waking Ned Devine." **110m/C VHS, DVD.** *CA* David Boutin, Lucie Laurier, Benoit Briere, Bruno Blanchet, Raymond Bouchard, Bruno Blanchet, Pierre Collin, Rita Lafontaine; *D:* Jean-Francois Pouliot; *M:* Jean-Marie Benoit.

Seducing Maarya **1999** Maarya is an East Indian/Canadian working in a Montreal restaurant. She agrees to an arranged marriage with the restaurant owner's son, even though he's gay, and then begins a romance with the sixtysomething dad. No one seems too concerned by the situation until Maarya's violent brother turns up, exposing a family secret, and Maarya announces her pregnancy. Melodramatic. **107m/C VHS, DVD.** *CA* Nandana Sen, Mohan Agashe, Vijay Mehta, Ryan Hollyman, Cas Anvar; *D:* Hunt Hoe; *W:* Hunt Hoe; *C:* Michael Wees; *M:* Dino Giancola, Janet Lumb.

The Seduction **1982 (R)** Superstar TV anchorwoman is harassed by a psychotic male admirer. Usual run of the mill exploitive "B" thriller with no brains behind the camera. **104m/C VHS, DVD.** Morgan Fairchild, Michael Sarrazin, Vince Edwards, Andrew Stevens, Colleen Camp, Kevin Brophy; *D:* David Schmoeller; *W:* David Schmoeller; *C:* Mac Ahlberg; *M:* Lalo Schifrin.

The Seduction of Joe Tynan 1/2 **1979 (R)** Political drama about a young senator (Alda) torn between his family, his political career, and his mistress (Streep). Alda also wrote the thin screenplay, which reportedly is loosely based on the remarkable life of Ted Kennedy. Relatively shallow treatment of the meaty themes of power, hypocrisy, sex, and corruption in our nation's capital. **107m/C VHS.** Alan Alda, Meryl Streep, Melvyn Douglas, Barbara Harris, Rip Torn; *D:* Jerry Schatzberg; *W:* Alan Alda; *M:* Bill Conti. L.A. Film Critics '79: Support. Actor (Douglas), Support. Actress (Streep); Natl. Bd. of Review '79: Support. Actress (Streep); N.Y. Film Critics '79: Support. Actress (Streep); Natl. Soc. Film Critics '79: Support. Actress (Streep).

Seduction of Mimi *Mimi Metallurgico Ferito Nell'Onore* **1972 (R)** Comic farce of politics and seduction about a Sicilian laborer's escapades with the Communists and the local Mafia. Giannini is wonderful as the stubborn immigrant to the big city who finds himself in trouble. One of the funniest love scenes on film. Basis for the later movie "Which Way is Up?" Italian with subtitles. **92m/C VHS, DVD.** *IT* Giancarlo Giannini, Mariangela Melato, Turi Ferro, Agostina Belli, Elena Fiore; *D:* Lina Wertmuller; *W:* Lina Wertmuller; *C:* Dario Di Palma; *M:* Piero Piccioni.

Seduction: The Cruel Woman **1989** A curiously uninvolving look at sexual games and fantasies. Wanda is a dominatrix, who also owns a sado-masochistic gallery where her various friends and current and formers lovers act out their basest desires. Stylized, with some graphic sex. Based on the novel "Venus in Furs" by Leopold Sacher-Masoch. In German with English subtitles. **84m/C VHS, DVD.** *GE* Mechthild Grossmann, Carola Regnier, Udo Kier, Sheila McLaughlin; *D:* Elfi Mikesch, Monika Treut; *W:* Elfi Mikesch, Monika Treut.

The Seductress 1/2 **2000** Beautiful Alexis (O'Brien) is a black widow with a string of murdered wealthy husbands behind her.

Kay Sanders (Hall) is a researcher obsessed with keeping tabs on each of Alexis's new identities, especially when the babe goes after Kay's boyfriend Paul (Smith). But it turns out that Kay and Alexis have a closer connection than that. The R-rated version is a mere 70 minutes. **82m/C VHS, DVD.** Shauna O'Brien, Gabriella Hall, Jonathan Smith; ***D:*** J Edie Martin. **VIDEO**

See How She Runs 1978 Running becomes a central and redefining experience for a 40-year-old divorced schoolteacher (Woodward). Her training culminates with a run in the Boston marathon. Her loved ones, though concerned for her health and sanity, cheer her on. Excellent made for TV drama. Screen daughter Newman is also Woodward's real-life daughter. **92m/C VHS.** Joanne Woodward, John Considine, Lissy Newman, Barbara Manning; ***D:*** Richard T. Heffron. **TV**

See No Evil *Blind Terror* 1971 **(PG)** A blind girl gradually discovers the murdered bodies of her uncle's family. Trapped in the family mansion, she finds herself pursued by the killer. Chilling and well crafted. **90m/C VHS, DVD.** Mia Farrow, Dorothy Allison, Robin Bailey; ***D:*** Richard Fleischer; ***W:*** Brian Clemens; ***M:*** Elmer Bernstein.

See No Evil 2006 **(R)** Wrestling star Kane (7 feet tall and some 400 pounds) plays psycho Jacob Goodnight, who's living in an abandoned hotel. He's pleasantly surprised when his ex-cop nemesis (Vidler) and eight delinquents on a community service detail show up. And he welcomes them one-by-one (keeping eyeballs as souvenirs). Typically gory teen-slasher flick. **84m/C DVD, Blu-ray Disc.** *US* Michael J. Pagan, Christina Vidal, Steven Vidler, Penny McNamee, Glen "Kane" Jacobs, Samantha Noble, Luke Pegler, Rachael Taylor, Craig Horner; ***D:*** Gregory Brown; ***W:*** Dan Madigan; ***C:*** Ben Nott; ***M:*** Tyler Bates.

See No Evil, Hear No Evil 1989 **(R)** Another teaming for Pryor and Wilder, in which they portray a blind man and a deaf man both sought as murder suspects. Pryor and Wilder deserve better. **103m/C VHS, DVD.** Gene Wilder, Richard Pryor, Joan Severance, Anthony Zerbe, Kevin Spacey; ***D:*** Arthur Hiller; ***W:*** Andrew Kurtzman, Eliot Wald, Earl Barret, Arne Sultan, Gene Wilder; ***C:*** Victor Kemper; ***M:*** Stewart Copeland.

See No Evil: The Moors Murders 2006 Released on the 40th anniversary of the 1966 trial of killers Ian Brady (Harris) and Myra Hindley (Peake). In the early 1960s, 3 children and 2 teenagers are kidnapped, tortured, and murdered, with their bodies buried on Saddleworth Moor outside Manchester. When Brady tries to entice his sister's husband, David Smith (McNulty), to participate, Smith goes to the police instead and the duo is finally caught. Made with the cooperation of the victims' families, the reconstruction of trial evidence can be rather gruesome. Also released the same year was "Longford," which featured an older Hindley's attempts to get parole. **180m/C DVD.** *GB* Sean Harris, George Costigan, John Henshaw, Maxine Peake, Matthew McNulty, Joanne Froggatt; ***D:*** Christopher Menaul; ***W:*** Neil McKay; ***C:*** Lukas Strebel; ***M:*** John Lunn. **TV**

See Spot Run WOOF! 2001 **(G)** How can you not like a movie with dogs? Easy, put David Arquette in it. Spot, an FBI-trained dog, has a contract on his life after removing "one of the family jewels" of crime family boss Sonny Talia (Sorvino) and ends up in a doggie witness protection program. He lands in the possession of James (Jones), his mother (Bibb), and babysitter neighbor Gordon (Arquette). One may find the true essence of the movie in the middle of a large pile of Spot's morning business, where Gordon eventually finds himself. More scatological humor and other crass gags send "Spot" to the doghouse. Duncan is the sole high point as the dog's FBI handler. **97m/C VHS, DVD.** *US* David Arquette, Michael Clarke Duncan, Leslie Bibb, Angus T. Jones, Joe (Johnny) Viterelli, Paul Sorvino, Anthony Anderson; ***D:*** John Whitesell; ***W:*** George Gallo, Dan Baron, Chris Faber; ***C:*** John Bartley; ***M:*** John Debney.

See You in the Morning 1/2 1989 **(PG-13)** Ill-conceived romantic comedy-drama about a divorced psychiatrist and a widow, both of whom had unhappy marriages, who meet and marry. They must cope with their respective children, family tragedies, and their own expectations, in order to make this second marriage work. **119m/C VHS.** Jeff Bridges, Alice Krige, Farrah Fawcett, Drew Barrymore, Lukas Haas, Macaulay Culkin, David Dukes, Frances Sternhagen, Theodore Bikel, George Hearn, Linda Lavin; ***D:*** Alan J. Pakula; ***W:*** Alan J. Pakula.

Seed WOOF! 2008 Urban legend maintains that if a criminal can withstand three 15 minute bursts of power in the electric chair and live, he has to be let go. It's complete nonsense, of course, except in the mind of Uwe Boll. Villainous serial killer Sam Seed actually survives the ordeal of electrocution, so worried authorities bury him alive. He subsequently digs himself out to revenge in the goriest, most disturbing ways possible. **90m/C DVD.** Michael Pare, Will Sanderson, Ralph (Ralf) Moeller, Jodelle Ferland, Thea Gill, Andrew Jackson, Brad Turner, Phil Mitchell, Mike Dopud, Tyron Leitso, John Sampson; ***D:*** Uwe Boll; ***W:*** Uwe Boll; ***C:*** Mathias Neumann; ***M:*** Jessica de Rooij. **VIDEO**

Seed of Chucky 1/2 2004 **(R)** The fifth in the "Child's Play" series is filled with the usual camp and carnage, and a movie-within-a-movie premise. Tilly plays herself as an actress filming a "Chucky" movie as well as the voice of Chucky's doll bride, Tiffany. Homicidal dolls Chuck (voiced by Dourif) and Tiff are on-set and are eventually reunited with long-lost offspring Glen (voiced by Boyd), who has a gender crisis due to a lack of anatomical correctness and is sometimes Glenda (a nod to Ed Wood's 1953 masterpiece). Chucky thinks it would be swell if Glen/Glenda could have a sibling, with Tilly as the mom. The actress is nothing if not game for a variety of indignities and snarky one-liners. Waters appears briefly as a pesky paparazzo. **86m/C DVD, HD DVD.** *US* Jennifer Tilly, Hannah Spearritt, John Waters, Jason Flemyng, Keith-Lee Castle, Steve Lawton, Redman, Tony Gardner; ***D:*** Don Mancini; ***W:*** Don Mancini; ***C:*** Vernon Layton; ***M:*** Pino Donaggio; ***V:*** Jennifer Tilly, Brad Dourif, Billy Boyd.

Seedpeople 1/2 1992 Mindless horror flick has bloodthirsty plants inhabiting peaceful Comet Valley after their seeds fall from outer space and germinate. These "seedpeople" possess tremendous powers and soon have the rural residents transformed into zombies. Bears an uncanny resemblance to "Invasion of the Bodysnatchers," and is so bad it's almost good. Also available with Spanish subtitles. **87m/C VHS.** Sam Hennings, Andrea Roth, Dane Witherspoon, David Dunard, Holly Fields, Bernard Kates, Anne Betancourt, Sonny Carl Davis; ***D:*** Peter Manoogian; ***W:*** Jackson Barr; ***M:*** Bob Mithoff.

Seeds of Doubt 1/2 1996 **(R)** Formula thriller finds reporter Jennifer Kingsley (Watson) working to free convicted murderer Crawford (Lando) from prison because she thinks he's innocent (and she's fallen for him). Detective Dexter (Coyote) is unsuccessful in convincing her otherwise but Jennifer begins to have her own doubts when a new series of killings begin after Crawford's release. **94m/C VHS.** Alberta Watson, Peter Coyote, Joe Lando; ***D:*** Peter Foldy.

Seeds of Evil *The Gardener* 1976 **(R)** Warhol alumnus Dallesandro is a strange gardener who grows flowers that can kill. He can also turn himself into a tree and figures to seduce rich and bored housewife Houghton (niece of Katharine Hepburn) after he finishes tending her garden. Strange, quirky horror flick. **97m/C VHS, DVD.** Katharine Houghton, Joe Dallesandro, Rita Gam; ***D:*** James H. Kay.

Seeing Other People 1/2 2004 **(R)** About-to-be-married couple begin seeing other people in this fun, top-notch sex comedy romp. Ed (Mohr) and Alice (Nicholson) decide to sow some wild oats before settling down into marital bliss. Initially exciting for both, the affairs spark their own lagging passion. Soon, however, the two enter more dangerous territory when conquest Donald (Davis) begins obsessing over Alice and Ed meets waitress Sandy (Ritchie) and it is clear no good can come of this hair-brained experiment. Despite a rather worn-out premise, characters have wonderful chemistry and are likeable, unique and well-drawn. Able supports include Graham, as Alice's sister, and Richter as Ed's grounded best friend. **90m/C DVD.** *US* Jay Mohr, Julianne Nicholson, Lauren Graham, Bryan Cranston, Josh Charles, Andy Richter, Matthew Davis, Helen Slater, Jill Ritchie, Alex Borstein, Mimi Rogers, Nicole Marie Lenz, Jonathan Davis, Mike Faiola, Sheeri Rappaport, Liz Phair; ***D:*** M. Wallace Wolodarsky; ***W:*** M. Wallace Wolodarsky, Maya Forbes; ***C:*** Mark Doering-Powell; ***M:*** Alan Elliott.

Seeing Red 1/2 1999 British soap opera star Coral Atkins (Lancashire) is doing a charity event in the 1970s at a children's home where she finds the conditions untenable. Having survived a terrible childhood herself, Coral improbably decides to switch careers and open her own home for abused children, though British social bureaucracy thwarts her every decision. Based on Atkins' 1990 memoir. **100m/C VHS.** *GB* Nicholas Gecks, Sarah Lancashire; ***D:*** Graham Theakston; ***W:*** Christopher Monger. **TV**

The Seeker: The Dark Is Rising 1/2 2007 **(PG)** Fourteen-year-old Will (Ludwig), transplanted from America to England, wakes up one day with magical powers and an important destiny in this all-too-familiar tale that is both a lousy adaptation of a 1973 book and a rip-off of comparable, contemporary stories. McShane, as Will's mentor Merriman, does his best with the poor script, but there's no saving this mess. Needlessly simplifies and Americanizes the original story until there's not much left except a bad "Harry Potter" retread. **94m/C DVD.** *US* Christopher Eccleston, Ian McShane, Frances Conroy, Wendy Crewson, Alexander Ludwig, John Benjamin Hickey, Gregory Edward Smith, James Cosmo, Jim Piddock; ***D:*** David L. Cunningham; ***W:*** John Hodge; ***C:*** Joel Ransom; ***M:*** Christophe Beck.

The Seekers 1979 The story of the Kent family continues, as Abraham Kent, his wife and young son are forced to leave the safety of Boston for the rugged, untamed Pacific Northwest. TV movie based on the novel by John Jakes; preceded by "The Bastard" and "The Rebels." **200m/C VHS.** Randolph Mantooth, Edie Adams, Neville Brand, Delta Burke, John Carradine, George DeLoy, Julie Gregg, Roosevelt "Rosie" Grier, George Hamilton, Alex Hyde-White, Brian Keith, Ross Martin, Gary Merrill, Martin Milner, Vic Morrow, Timothy Patrick Murphy, Hugh O'Brian, Robert Reed, Allan Rich, Barbara Rush, Sarah Rush, Stuart Whitman, Ed Harris, Jeremy Licht, Eric Stoltz; ***D:*** Sidney Hayers.

Seems Like Old Times 1/2 1980 **(PG)** A sweet lawyer (Hawn) finds herself helping her ex-husband (Chase) when two robbers force him to hold up a bank. Grodin is the new spouse threatened by Chase's appearance and by the heavies he's trying to escape. Better-than-average script, with funny and appealing characters. **102m/C VHS, DVD.** Goldie Hawn, Chevy Chase, Charles Grodin, Robert Guillaume, Harold Gould, George Grizzard, T.K. Carter; ***D:*** Jay Sandrich; ***W:*** Neil Simon; ***C:*** David M. Walsh; ***M:*** Marvin Hamlisch.

Seize the Day 1986 A man approaching middle age (Williams) feels that he is a failure. Brilliant performances by all, plus a number of equally fine actors in small roles. Based on the short novel by Saul Bellow. **93m/C VHS, DVD.** Robin Williams, Joseph Wiseman, Jerry Stiller, Glenne Headly, Tony Roberts; ***D:*** Fielder Cook.

Seizure 1974 **(PG)** Three demonic creatures from a writer's dreams come to life and terrorize him and his houseguests at a weekend party. Slick but disjointed; Stone's directorial debut. Interesting cast includes Tattoo from "Fantasy Island." **93m/C VHS, DVD.** *CA* Jonathan Frid, Herve Villechaize, Christina Pickles, Martine Beswick, Joseph Sirola, Troy Donahue, Mary Woronov, Anne Meacham; ***D:*** Oliver Stone; ***W:*** Oliver Stone, Edward Andrew (Santos Alcocer) Mann; ***C:*** Roger Racine.

Seizure: The Story of Kathy Morris 1980 The real-life anguish and struggle of a young music student who must have brain surgery and comes out of it unable to read or count. Workaday dramatization. **104m/C VHS.** Leonard Nimoy, Penelope Milford; ***D:*** Gerald I. Isenberg.

Selena 1/2 1996 **(PG)** Lopez is appealing in the title role of the 23-year-old Tejano superstar singer who was just breaking into international prominence when she was murdered by the president of her fan club in 1995. Flashbacks show dad Abraham's (Olmos) dashed musical aspirations and he serves as a stage father to his children, recognizing his daughter Selena's exceptional voice. Film covers her marriage to guitarist Chris Perez (Seda) and her building success until the final tragedy (which isn't shown). Film concludes with concert footage of the real Selena. **127m/C VHS, DVD.** Jennifer Lopez, Edward James Olmos, Jon Seda, Constance Marie, Jacob Vargas, Lupe Ontiveros, Jackie Guerra, Sal Lopez, Rebecca Lee Mezza; ***D:*** Gregory Nava; ***W:*** Gregory Nava; ***C:*** Edward Lachman; ***M:*** Dave Grusin.

Self-Defense 1/2 1983 **(R)** When a city's police force goes on strike, the citizens band together into vigilante troops. **85m/C VHS.** Tom Nardini, Brenda Bazinet; ***D:*** Paul Donovan; ***W:*** Paul Donovan; ***C:*** Les Krizsan; ***M:*** Peter Jermyn.

A Self-Made Hero *Un Heros Tres Discret; A Very Discreet Hero* 1995 Albert Delhousse (Kassovitz) is a young Frenchman who manages to avoid military service in WWII. His one great talent is his confidence and his ability as a salesman. So, with some help from a true freedom fighter known as the Captain (Dupontel), he sells himself as a hero of the Resistance in 1945 Paris and manages to do so very effectively for the rest of his life. Kassovitz does an excellent job as the assured imposter. Based on the novel by Jean-Francoise Deniau; French with subtitles. **105m/C VHS.** *FR* Mathieu Kassovitz, Anouk Grinberg, Albert Dupontel, Sandrine Kiberlain, Jean-Louis Trintignant, Nadia Barentin; ***D:*** Jacques Audiard; ***W:*** Jacques Audiard, Alain Le Henry; ***C:*** Jean-Marc Fabre; ***M:*** Alexandre Desplat.

Sell Out 1/2 1976 **(PG)** A former spy living in Jerusalem is called out of retirement; his protege, who defected to the Soviets, now wants out. **102m/C VHS, DVD.** Richard Widmark, Oliver Reed, Gayle Hunnicutt, Sam Wanamaker; ***D:*** Peter Collinson; ***W:*** Judson Kinberg, Murray Smith; ***C:*** Arthur Ibbetson; ***M:*** Colin Frichter.

Selma, Lord, Selma 1/2 1999 Civil rights drama focuses on the youngest two participants in a 1965 voting-rights march from Selma to Montgomery. Preteen Sheyann Webb (Smollett) is inspired by Dr. Martin Luther King Jr.'s (Powell) message of nonviolent demonstration and becomes dedicated to the cause, along with her best friend Rachel Nelson (Peyton). Things come to a climax with the March 7th march to the Edmund Pettus Bridge in Selma, a day that became known as "Bloody Sunday" when state troopers attacked the demonstrators. Adapted from the book "Selma, Lord, Selma" by Webb-Christburg, Nelson, and Frank Sikora. **88m/C VHS, DVD.** Jurnee Smollett, Stephanie Zandra Peyton, Clifton Powell, Yolanda King; ***D:*** Charles Burnett; ***W:*** Cynthia Whitcomb. **TV**

Semi-Pro 2008 **(R)** Faced with low fan turnout, the failing ABA of the '70s plans to dissolve the league and incorporate four of its best teams into the NBA. Owner/player Jackie Moon (a fully-froed Ferrell) rises to the occasion, pulling out all the stops to get his lousy Flint Tropics (that's Flint, Michigan, nowhere near anything remotely tropical) on the map and into contention. He recruits aging star Ed Monix (Harrelson) and stages events like bear wrestling to get fans in the door. A funny premise that awkwardly confuses itself with an actual underdog sports drama. As with most of Ferrell's co-stars, Harrelson and Benjamin (as Coffee Black) take a backseat to the SNL alum's outrageous antics, making this little more than a scattering of Will Ferrell sketches. **90m/C DVD, Blu-ray Disc.** *US* Will Ferrell, Woody Harrelson, Andre Benjamin, Maura Tierney, Will Arnett, Andy Richter, David Koechner, Rob Corddry, Matt Walsh, Jackie Earle Haley, Andrew Daly; ***D:*** Kent Alterman; ***W:*** Scot Armstrong; ***C:*** Shane Hurlbut; ***M:*** Theodore Shapiro.

Semi-Tough 1/2 1977 **(R)** Likeable, still current social satire involving a couple of pro-football buddies and their mutual interest in their team owner's daughter. Romantic comedy, satire of the sports world, zany highjinks—it's all here, though not enough of any of these. Pleasant and enjoyable. Based on the novel by Dan Jenkins. **107m/C VHS, DVD.** Burt Reynolds, Kris Kristofferson, Jill Clayburgh, Lotte Lenya, Robert Preston, Bert Convy, Richard Masur, Carl Weathers, Brian Dennehy, John Matuszak, Ron Silver; ***D:*** Michael Ritchie; ***W:*** Walter Bernstein.

Seminole Uprising 🦴 **1955** Stock western on a mini budget tells the familiar story of the cavalry rounding up the Indians. Lieutenant Cam Elliot (Montgomery) is charged with the delivery of terrorizing tribe leader Black Cat, who has just kidnapped Colonel Hannah's daughter and Cam's love interest Susan (Booth) and is about to trade her to renegades in return for guns. Cam's men pursue, forcing a bloody battle in typical western-style. Stock battle footage offers a confusing but not unexpected disjointed feel to this low-budget flick. **74m/C DVD.** George Montgomery, Karin (Karen, Katharine) Booth, William "Bill" Fawcett, Steven Ritch, Ed Hinton, John Pickard, James Maloney, Rory Mallinson, Howard Wright, Rus Conklin; ***D:*** Earl Bellamy; ***W:*** Curt Brandon, Robert E. Kent.

The Senator Was Indiscreet 🦴🦴🦴 *Mr. Ashton was Indiscreet* **1947** A farcical comedy concerning a slightly loony senator with presidential aspirations. He thinks he can win the nomination because he keeps a diary that would prove embarrassing to numerous colleagues. The diary then falls into the hands of a journalist. Powell is wonderful as the daffy politician. Playwright Kaufman's only directorial effort. **75m/B VHS.** William Powell, Ella Raines, Hans Conried; ***D:*** George S. Kaufman; ***C:*** William Mellor. N.Y. Film Critics '47: Actor (Powell).

Send Me No Flowers 🦴🦴🦴 **1964** Vintage Hudson-Day comedy. Hudson plays a hypochondriac who thinks his death is imminent. He decides to provide for his family's future by finding his wife a rich husband. She thinks he's feeling guilty for having an affair. **100m/C VHS, DVD.** Rock Hudson, Doris Day, Tony Randall, Paul Lynde; ***D:*** Norman Jewison; ***W:*** Julius J. Epstein; ***C:*** Daniel F. Fapp.

The Sender 🦴🦴 **1982 (R)** An amnesiac young man is studied by a psychiatrist. She discovers that her patient is a "sender," who can transmit his nightmares to other patients at a hospital. **92m/C VHS.** *GB* Kathryn Harrold, Zeljko Ivanek, Shirley Knight, Paul Freeman, Sean Hewitt, Harry Ditson, Marsha A. Hunt, Al Matthews, Angus MacInnes, Olivier Pierre; ***D:*** Roger Christian; ***W:*** Thomas Baum; ***M:*** Trevor Jones.

The Sender 🦴🦴 ½ **1998 (R)** Naval officer Dallas Grayson (Madsen) and his daughter Lisa are possessed of a mysterious power they may have inherited from Dallas' long-missing father, a Naval pilot shot down in the '60s. Whatever they have, the government wants, and they don't care how they get it. **98m/C VHS, DVD.** Michael Madsen, Dyan Cannon, Robert Vaughn, R. Lee Ermey, Steven Williams, Brian Bloom, Shelli Lether; ***D:*** Richard Pepin; ***W:*** Richard Preston Jr., Nathan Long; ***C:*** Michael Weaver.

Senior Skip Day 🦴 ½ **2008 (R)** Average high school senior Adam (Lundy) is trying to avoid the senior skip day party because he can't stand that his dream girl Cara (Ewell) doesn't know he exists. Then Adam accidentally spills the party location to mean principal Dickwalder (Miller), who's determined to punish anyone not in class. To make amends, Adam promises to hold the bash at his house and uses a classmate's funeral as the excuse for the seniors to be out of school. Yeah, it's over-the-top and kinda offensive but about average for a teen comedy. **81m/C DVD.** Larry Miller, Lea Thompson, Tara Reid, Clint Howard, Norm MacDonald, Gary Lundy, Kayla Ewell; ***D:*** Nick Weiss; ***W:*** Evan Wassserstrom; ***C:*** Michael Negrin; ***M:*** Chris Boardman. **VIDEO**

Senior Trip 🦴 **1981** N.Y.C. will never be the same after a bunch of rowdy Midwestern high school seniors tear up the town on their graduation trip. **96m/C VHS.** James Carroll, Scott Baio, Mickey Rooney, Faye Grant, Vincent Spano, Jane Hoffman; ***D:*** Kenneth Johnson. **TV**

Senior Week **WOOF!** **1988** A batch of girl-hungry teens have a wacky time on their Florida vacation just before graduation. **97m/C VHS.** Michael St. Gerard, Devon Skye, Leesa Bryte; ***D:*** Stuart Goldman.

The Seniors 🦴🦴 **1978 (R)** A group of college students decide to open a phony sex clinic, but the joke is on them when the clinic becomes a success. Better than it sounds. Pretty good acting and much harmless goofiness. **87m/C VHS, DVD.** Dennis Quaid, Priscilla Barnes, Jeffrey Byron, Gary Imhoff; ***D:*** Rod Amateau.

Senora Tentacion 🦴🦴 **1949** Musical melodrama about a composer who fights to leave his mother, sister, and girlfriend in order to flee with Hortensia, a famous singer. In Spanish with English subtitles. **82m/B VHS.** David Silva, Susana Guizar, Ninon Sevilla; ***D:*** Jose Diaz Morales; ***W:*** Jose Diaz Morales; ***C:*** Ezequiel Carrasco; ***M:*** Antonio Diaz Conde.

Sensation 🦴🦴 **1994 (R)** A college co-ed agrees to participate in a professor's paranormal experiments in order to test her psychic abilities. Unfortunately what she senses is her prof involved in the unsolved sex-murder of a former student. **102m/C VHS.** Kari Wuhrer, Eric Roberts, Ron Perlman, Ed Begley Jr., Paul LeMat, Claire Stansfield, Kieran Mulroney, Tracey Needham; ***D:*** Brian Grant; ***W:*** Doug Wallace; ***M:*** Arthur Kempel.

The Sensation of Sight 🦴 ½ **2006 (R)** An awkward and solemn story that slowly reveals its connections via flashbacks. Former English teacher Finn (Strathairn) inexplicably takes to selling encyclopedias door-to-door after some sort of tragedy that involves a loner (Somerhalder), a troubled young man (Gillies), a single mother (Adams), and a widower (Wilson). **134m/C DVD.** David Strathairn, Ian Somerhalder, Daniel Gillies, Jane Adams, Scott Wilson, Ann Cusack, Joseph Mazzello, Elizabeth Waterston; ***D:*** Aaron J. Wiederspahn; ***W:*** Aaron J. Wiederspahn; ***C:*** Christopher Lanzenberg; ***M:*** Rupert A. Thompson.

Sensations 🦴🦴 **1987 (R)** A woman and a man who aren't exceptionally fond of one another share a lottery ticket and win. Vincent is best known as a former director of porno flicks, and he manages to work in sexual overtones. **91m/C VHS.** Krista Lane, Blake Bahner, Jennifer Delora, Rick Savage, Loretta Palma, Frank Stewart; ***D:*** Chuck Vincent.

Sensations of 1945 🦴🦴 ½ *Sensations* **1944** A press agent turns his firm over to one of his clients, a dancer with some wild promotional ideas. Brings together numerous variety and musical acts. W. C. Fields has a cameo in his last film role. Mostly unremarkable, occasionally fun musical. **86m/B VHS.** Eleanor Powell, Dennis O'Keefe, Sir C. Aubrey Smith, Eugene Pallette, Cab Calloway, Sophie Tucker, Woody Herman, Lyle Talbot, Marie Blake; ***Cameos:*** W.C. Fields; ***D:*** Andrew L. Stone.

Sense & Sensibility 🦴🦴 **1985** BBC miniseries adaptation of Jane Austen's first novel concerning two sisters striving for happiness in their well-ordered lives. **174m/C VHS, DVD.** *GB* Irene Richard, Tracey Childs; ***D:*** Rodney Bennett. **TV**

Sense and Sensibility 🦴🦴🦴 ½ **1995 (PG)** Thanks to the machinations of greedy relatives, the impecunious Dashwood family is forced to move to a country cottage when father dies. Sensible Elinor (Thompson) looks after the household while overly romantic Marianne (Winslet) pines for passion—ignoring the noble attentions of middle-aged neighbor Brandon (Rickman) for the far more dashing Willoughby (Wise). Elinor has her own hopes for marriage with boyishly ineffectual Edward (Grant) but all three men have secrets that could crush romantic dreams (at least temporarily). Somewhat slow-paced but witty adaptation (by Thompson) of Jane Austen's first novel, well-acted and beautifully photographed (oh, to be in the English countryside). **135m/C VHS, DVD, Blu-ray Disc.** *GB* Emma Thompson, Kate Winslet, Hugh Grant, Alan Rickman, Greg Wise, Robert Hardy, Elizabeth Spriggs, Emile Francois, Gemma Jones, James Fleet, Harriet Walter, Imogen Stubbs, Imelda Staunton, Hugh Laurie, Richard Lumsden; ***D:*** Ang Lee; ***W:*** Emma Thompson; ***C:*** Michael Coulter; ***M:*** Patrick Doyle. Oscars '95: Adapt. Screenplay; British Acad. '95: Actress (Thompson), Film, Support. Actress (Winslet); Golden Globes '96: Film—Drama, Screenplay; L.A. Film Critics '95: Screenplay; Natl. Bd. of Review '95: Actress (Thompson), Director (Lee), Film; N.Y. Film Critics '95: Director (Lee); Screen Actors Guild '95: Support. Actress (Winslet); Writers Guild '95: Adapt. Screenplay; Broadcast Film Critics '95: Film, Screenplay.

Sense & Sensibility 🦴🦴 ½ **2007** When her husband dies, Mrs. Dashwood (McTeer) is forced to remove herself and her daughters Elinor (Morahan), Marianne (Wakefield), and young Margaret (Boynton) into genteel poverty at a country cottage. Impulsive, romantic Marianne is drawn to charming cad Willoughby (Cooper), despite the more suitable Colonel Brandon (Morrissey) also expressing his interest. Meanwhile, practical Elinor is quietly pining for the unassuming Edward Ferrars (Stevens) who has familial (and other) obligations that prevent him from courting her. So the Dashwood sisters' romantic hopes seem destined to be, well, dashed. Based on the novel by Jane Austen. **180m/C DVD.** *GB* Janet McTeer, Dan Stevens, David Morrissey, Dominic Cooper, Claire Skinner, Mark Gatiss, Jean Marsh, Charity Wakefield, Hattie Morahan, Lucy Boyton; ***D:*** John Alexander; ***W:*** Andrew Davies; ***C:*** Sean Bobbitt; ***M:*** Martin Phipps. **TV**

A Sense of Freedom 🦴🦴🦴 **1978 (R)** A hopeless racketeering criminal is thrust from institution to institution until the Scottish authorities decide on an innovative style of reform. Based on Jimmy Boyle's autobiographical book. Excellent and disturbing. **81m/C VHS.** *GB* David Hayman, Alex Norton, Jake D'Arcy, Sean Scanlan, Fulton Mackay; ***D:*** John MacKenzie.

Senseless 🦴🦴 **1998 (R)** Darryl (Wayans) is a poverty stricken college student trying to work his way through school while still supporting his family back home. He agrees to be a medical test subject for a procedure intended to heighten the senses. Unfortunately, as one sense is amplified, the others are drowned out, and Darryl becomes a flailing buffoon. Meanwhile he is in a competition against smarmy frat boy Scott (Spade, who looks about ten years late for his last Econ class) that would land him a job on Wall Street. After dealing with sounds that are too loud and smells that are too pungent, his body adjusts itself. The slapstick bits are hit and miss, but the likable Wayans and dislikable Spade prop up the movie fairly well. **93m/C VHS, DVD.** Marlon Wayans, David Spade, Matthew Lillard, Rip Torn, Tamara Taylor, Brad Dourif, Ken Lerner, Ernie Lively, Richard McGonagle, Esther Scott, Kenya Moore; ***D:*** Penelope Spheeris; ***W:*** Greg Erb, Craig Mazin; ***C:*** Daryn Okada; ***M:*** Yello.

Senso 🦴🦴🦴 *The Wanton Contessa* **1954** Tragic story of romance and rebellion as Italian patriots battle the Austro-Hungarian empire for independence in 1866. An Italian noblewoman betrays her marriage, and almost her country, to be with a cynical Austrian soldier in this visually stunning piece of cinematography. In Italian with English subtitles or dubbed. **125m/C VHS, DVD.** *IT* Alida Valli, Massimo Girotti, Heinz Moog, Farley Granger; ***D:*** Luchino Visconti; ***C:*** Robert Krasker.

The Sensual Man 🦴 ½ **1974 (R)** Hot-blooded Italian falls in love and gets married only to find out that his wife cannot consummate their marriage. Exploitative, misogynistic, and unfunny. **90m/C VHS.** Giancarlo Giannini, Rossana Podesta, Lionel Stander; ***D:*** Marco Vicario.

Sensual Partners **WOOF!** **1987** Young actresses are lured to Tangier by a fake movie producer and sold as sex slaves. Emphasis on soft-focus, soft-core flesh. **87m/C VHS.** *GE* Josianne Gibert, Esther Studer, Jacques Stany, Gina Jansen, Eric Falk; ***D:*** Jacques Guy; ***W:*** Jacques Guy; ***C:*** Alain Hardy; ***M:*** Walter Baumgartner.

The Sensuous Nurse 🦴🦴 **1976 (R)** Italian comedy about a beautiful nurse hired by the greedy, treacherous relatives of a weak-hearted count in hopes that her voluptuousness will give him a heart attack. It doesn't, and she falls in love. Mindless, but fun and sexy. Dubbed in English. **79m/C VHS, DVD.** *IT* Ursula Andress, Mario Pisu, Dulio Del Prete, Jack Palance; ***D:*** Nello Rosatti.

Sensuous Summer 🦴 ½ **1993 (R)** When Bobby returns home to the town of Elk Lake he finds the family business, run by his brother Nick, is in deep trouble. It seems Alex, an unscrupulous banker, wants to foreclose. But business comes second to pleasure when Bobby is reunited with old flame Jill and Nick takes up again with ex-girlfriend Cindy. **80m/C VHS.** Tom Case, Christina Campbell, Brittany McGrea, Gina Jorand; ***D:*** Boots Rakely; ***W:*** Boots Rakely; ***C:*** Brett Webster; ***M:*** Gene Ober.

The Sensuous Teenager **WOOF!** *Libido; Forbidden Passions* **1970 (R)** Overwhelmingly erotic and uncontrollably seductive, a teenage girl aims to please by releasing all the sensuality within her. **80m/C VHS.** Sandra Julien, Janine Reynaud, Michel Lemoine; ***D:*** Max Pecas.

The Sentinel 🦴🦴 **1976 (R)** A model, who has moved into a New York City brownstone, encounters an aging priest and some unusual neighbors. When she investigates strange noises she finds out that the apartment building houses the doorway to hell—and that she's intended to be the next doorkeeper. Modest suspense film with a good cast and enough shock and special effects to keep the viewer interested. **92m/C VHS, DVD.** Chris Sarandon, Christina Raines, Ava Gardner, Jose Ferrer, Sylvia Miles, John Carradine, Burgess Meredith, Tom Berenger, Beverly D'Angelo, Jeff Goldblum, Arthur Kennedy, Deborah Raffin, Eli Wallach, Christopher Walken; ***D:*** Michael Winner; ***W:*** Michael Winner, Jeffrey Konvitz; ***C:*** Richard Kratina; ***M:*** Gil Melle.

The Sentinel 🦴🦴 ½ **2006 (PG-13)** Veteran Secret Service agent Pete Garrison (Douglas) is in charge of guarding first lady Sarah Ballentine (Basinger), which is really convenient since they're having an affair. It's bad news though when Garrison gets blackmailed and learns that a presidential assassination is planned. Accused of treason and on the run, Garrison is pursued by his former protege-turned-enemy David Breckinridge (a grim Sutherland). Longoria provides supporting eye candy as rookie agent Jill Marin. Much like Harrison Ford, Douglas excels as a strong (ageless) man who can overcome any crisis and take on all his (younger) adversaries. **105m/C DVD, Blu-ray Disc.** *US* Michael Douglas, Kiefer Sutherland, Martin Donovan, Ritchie Coster, Eva Longoria, Kim Basinger, Blair Brown, David Rasche, Kristen Lehman, Raynor Scheine, Chuck Shamata, Paul Calderon, Clark Johnson; ***D:*** Clark Johnson; ***W:*** George Nolfi; ***C:*** Gabriel Beristain; ***M:*** Christophe Beck.

Seoul Raiders 🦴 *Tokyo Raiders 2; Han Cheng Gong Lue* **2005** Silly action-comedy about a Korean counterfeiting ring in possession of plates for forging U.S. currency. Cutrate, freelancing spy Lam and ambitious thief JJ are both after the goods. Lam gets the plates only to be doublecrossed by his contact. The action is less than spectacular and the comedy is lame. Cantonese with subtitles. **99m/C DVD.** *HK* Tony Leung Chiu-wai, Qi Shu, Richie Ren, James Kim, Jeong-jin Lee; ***D:*** Jingle Ma; ***W:*** Jingle Ma, Brian Chung, Eric Lin; ***C:*** Kwok Hung Chan; ***M:*** Tommy Wai.

Separate but Equal 🦴🦴🦴 ½ **1991 (PG)** One of TV's greatest history lessons, a powerful dramatization of the 1954 Brown vs. The Board of Education case that wrung a landmark civil rights decision from the Supreme Court. Great care is taken to humanize all the participants, from the humblest schoolchild to NAACP lawyer Thurgood Marshall (Poitier). On two cassettes. **194m/C VHS, DVD.** Sidney Poitier, Burt Lancaster, Richard Kiley, Cleavon Little, John McMartin, Graham Beckel, Lynne Thigpen, Albert Hall; ***D:*** George Stevens Jr.; ***W:*** George Stevens Jr.

Separate Lives 🦴 ½ **1994 (R)** Psych prof Lauren Porter (Hamilton) is in need of some counseling herself. Seems she has a sexy alter ego calling herself Lena and Lauren fears she may have killed someone in her Lena persona. So she turns to her student Tom (Belushi), who happens to be an ex-cop, for help. Sketchy characters and a tired formula make this one a yawner. **101m/C VHS.** Linda Hamilton, James Belushi, Vera Miles, Elisabeth (Elissabeth, Elizabeth, Liz) Moss, Drew Snyder, Mark Lindsay Chapman, Marc Poppel, Elizabeth Arlen; ***D:*** David Madden; ***W:*** Steven Pressfield; ***M:*** William Olvis.

A Separate Peace 🦴🦴 **1973 (PG)** Two young men in a New England prep school during WWII come to grips with the war, coming of age, and a tragic accident. Cheap rendition of a not-so-great novel by John Knowles. **104m/C VHS.** John Heyl, Parker Stevenson, William Roerick; ***D:*** Larry Peerce; ***M:*** Charles Fox.

A Separate Peace 🦴 1/2 **2004 (R)** Uninspired coming of age story based on the John Knowles novel. In 1942, bookworm Gene (Barton) transfers to the all-male Devon prep school in New England. His roomie is campus jock/rule breaker Finny (Moore), who can't wait to enlist. Finny practices his paratrooper moves by jumping from a tree into the lake below. Gene is the only one who'll jump with him and they forge a bond until a questionable accident affects their friendship. **92m/C DVD.** J Barton, Toby Moore, Jacob Pitts, Aaron Ashmore, Danny Swerdlow, Alison Pill, Sean McCann, Hume Cronyn; ***D:*** Peter Yates; ***W:*** Wendy Kesselman; ***C:*** Checco Varese. **CABLE**

Separate Tables 🦴🦴🦴 1/2 **1958** Adaptation of the Terence Rattigan play about a varied cast of characters living out their personal dramas in a British seaside hotel. Guests include a matriarch and her shy daughter, a divorced couple, a spinster, and a presumed war hero. Their secrets and loves are examined in grand style. Fine acting all around. **98m/B VHS, DVD.** Burt Lancaster, David Niven, Rita Hayworth, Deborah Kerr, Wendy Hiller, Rod Taylor, Gladys Cooper, Felix Aylmer, Cathleen Nesbitt, Audrey Dalton, May Hallatt, Priscilla Morgan, Hilda Plowright; ***D:*** Delbert Mann; ***W:*** John Gay; ***C:*** Charles B(ryant) Lang Jr.; ***M:*** David Raksin. Oscars '58: Actor (Niven), Support. Actress (Hiller); Golden Globes '59: Actor—Drama (Niven); N.Y. Film Critics '58: Actor (Niven).

Separate Tables 🦴🦴 1/2 **1983 (PG)** A remake of the 1958 film adapted from Terence Rattigan's play. Separated into two parts, "Table by the Window" and "Table Number Seven." The lives of the lonely inhabitants of a hotel are dramatized through wonderful acting by Christie and Bates. **50m/C VHS.** Julie Christie, Alan Bates, Claire Bloom, Irene Worth; ***D:*** John Schlesinger. **CABLE**

Separate Vacations 🦴 1/2 **1986 (R)** A married man leaves his wife and kids to take a separate vacation, hoping he'll find exciting sex. Wife and kids end up at a ski resort, where romance comes her way. A lightweight, old story. **91m/C VHS.** David Naughton, Jennifer Dale, Mark Keyloun; ***D:*** Michael Anderson Sr.

Separate Ways 🦴 1/2 **1982 (R)** Unhappily married couple involved in various affairs split up in order to deal with themselves and their marriage. Good cast; bad script wandering down Maudlin Lane. **92m/C VHS.** Karen Black, Tony LoBianco, David Naughton, Sybil Danning; ***D:*** Howard (Hikmet) Avedis; ***C:*** Dean Cundey.

The Separation 🦴🦴 **1994** Emotions (and fine performances) rather than action move along this domestic drama. Anne (Huppert) and Pierre (Auteuil) are living together in Paris with their toddler son when Anne suddenly announces that she's involved with another man. Anne doesn't see why this this should cause any rift in their domestic arrangements but Pierre slowly falls to pieces. Adapted from the novel by Dan Franck; French with subtitles. **85m/C VHS, DVD.** *FR* Isabelle Huppert, Daniel Auteuil, Karin Viard, Jerome Deschamps; ***D:*** Christian Vincent; ***W:*** Christian Vincent, Dan Franck; ***C:*** Denis Lenoir.

Sepia Cinderella 🦴🦴 **1947** A songwriter, who finds himself with a hit, abandons his current life and love to try high society. He finds out it's not what he wants after all. **67m/B VHS.** Sheila Guyse, Rubel Blakely, Freddie Bartholomew, Sid Catlett, Deke Wilson; ***D:*** Arthur Leonard; ***W:*** Vincent Valentini; ***C:*** George Webber; ***M:*** Charlie Shavers.

September 🦴🦴 1/2 **1988 (PG-13)** Woody does Bergman again with a shuttered, claustrophobic drama about six unhappy people trying to verbalize their feelings in a dark summer house in Vermont. Well-acted throughout and interesting at first, but the whining and angst attacks eventually give way to boredom. Of course, the Woodman went on to "Crimes and Misdemeanors," blending his dark and comedic sides masterfully, so the best way to look at this is as a training film. **82m/C VHS, DVD.** Mia Farrow, Dianne Wiest, Denholm Elliott, Sam Waterston, Elaine Stritch, Jack Warden; ***D:*** Woody Allen; ***W:*** Woody Allen; ***C:*** Carlo Di Palma; ***M:*** Art Tatum.

September Affair 🦴🦴 1/2 **1950** A married engineer and a classical pianist miss their plane from Naples. When the plane crashes, they're presumed dead, and they find themselves free to continue their illicit love affair. They find they cannot hide forever and must make peace with their pasts. Features the hit "September Song," recorded by Walter Huston. **104m/B VHS.** Joseph Cotten, Joan Fontaine, Francoise Rosay, Jessica Tandy, Robert Arthur; ***D:*** William Dieterle; ***C:*** Charles B(ryant) Lang Jr. Golden Globes '52: Score.

September Dawn WOOF! **2007 (R)** Take a stock Old West setting, add a theme of religious intolerance, a "Romeo and Juliet" subplot, a ton of gratuitous violence, Jon Voight, and the label "based on a true story," and you have this truish fiasco about a Mormon militia massacring 120 settlers on September 11th, 1857. Bishop Jacob Samuelson (Voight) isn't pleased about a wagon train of non-Mormons and their worldy ways passing through his territory, but when his son (Ford) falls for one of the settlers (Hope), he goes berserk and decides to show them who's religion is right, after all. Mass-murder of the settlers (and the viewer's tolerance) ensues. Voight chews scenery while the movie collapses into a pit of one-dimensional characters, heavy-handed plotting, and made-for-TV level production values. Movie stirred controversy and accusations of anti-Mormon bias because of the implication that Mormon leader Brigham Young authorized the massacre. **110m/C DVD.** *US CA* Jon Voight, Trent Ford, Taylor Handley, Tamara Hope, Jon(athan) Gries, Shaun Johnston, Lolita (David) Davidovich, Dean Cain, Huntley Ritter, Terence Stamp; ***D:*** Christopher Cain; ***W:*** Christopher Cain, Carole Whang Schutter; ***C:*** Juan Ruiz-Anchia; ***M:*** William Ross.

September Gun 🦴🦴 1/2 **1983** A nun hires an aging gunfighter to escort her and a group of Apache children to a church school 200 miles away. Preston is excellent as the ornery varmint in this enjoyable, pleasant western comedy. **94m/C VHS.** Robert Preston, Patty Duke, Christopher Lloyd, Geoffrey Lewis, Sally Kellerman; ***D:*** Don Taylor. **TV**

The September Issue 🦴🦴 **2009 (PG-13)** Meryl Streep's character in "The Devil Wears Prada" is said to be based on Anna Wintour, "Vogue"'s icy, brusque longtime editor-in-chief. Cutler's documentary examines the fashion-publishing icon as she and her team of designers, stylists, and photographers put together "Vogue"'s influential September 2007 issue (which came in at 800 pages). **90m/C DVD.** *US* Sienna Miller, Anna Wintour; ***D:*** R.J. Cutler; ***C:*** Bob Richman; ***M:*** Craig Richey.

September 30, 1955 🦴🦴 1/2 *9/30/55* **1977 (PG)** A college undergrad (Thomas) in a small Arkansas town is devastated when he learns of the death of his idol, James Dean. (The title refers to the day Dean died.) Jimmy gathers a group of friends together for a vigil which turns into a drinking-binge, resulting in police chases and, finally, tragedy. Film debut of Quaid. **107m/C VHS.** Richard Thomas, Lisa Blount, Deborah Benson, Tom Hulce, Dennis Christopher, Dennis Quaid, Susan Tyrrell; ***D:*** James Bridges; ***W:*** James Bridges.

Seraphim Falls 🦴🦴 **2006 (R)** Irishmen Neeson and Brosnan star as a couple of post-Civil War soldiers (film's set in 1868) in an old-fashioned and beautifully filmed tale of brutal revenge. Wounded Yankee Gideon (Brosnan) is being hunted by Confederate Carver (Neeson) and his four hired guns over a wartime horror, but he won't go easily. There are various showdowns as Gideon picks off the thugs while awaiting that inevitable final confrontation. **115m/C DVD.** *US* Liam Neeson, Pierce Brosnan, Anjelica Huston, Michael Wincott, Robert Baker, Ed Lauter, John Robinson, Tom Noonan, Kevin J. O'Connor; ***D:*** David Von Ancken; ***W:*** David Von Ancken, Abby Everett Jaques; ***C:*** John Toll; ***M:*** Harry Gregson-Williams.

Seraphine 🦴🦴🦴 **2008** Vivid biography of French primitive painter Seraphine Louis (Moreau), a middle-aged domestic living in the small town of Senalis in pre-WWI France. Her precious free time is spent painting fruit and flowers with the limited amount of paint she can afford supplemented with animal's blood, dirt, and other substances. German art critic Wilhelm Uhde (Tukur) is shocked by the power of her work after seeing one of her paintings and promptly becomes Seraphine's champion in the art world. They are reunited in the 1920s (Seraphine paints throughout the war) but her mental deterioration leads to an unhappy end. French and German with subtitles. **126m/C DVD.** *BE FR* Yolande Moreau, Ulrich Tukur, Anne Bennent, Genevieve Mnich, Adelaide Leroux, Nico Rogner; ***D:*** Martin Provost; ***W:*** Martin Provost, Marc Abdelnour; ***C:*** Laurent Brunet; ***M:*** Michael Galasso.

Serendipity 🦴🦴 1/2 **2001 (PG-13)** Romance finds Jonathan (Cusack) and Sara (Beckinsale) falling in love one cold New York winter's night but then they part company because Sara believes if it's meant to be, fate will bring them back together. Sara's a twinkling twit. Ten years later both are engaged, but Jon and Sara also become separately convinced that they are destined to be together—if they can find each other again. Lots of near-misses and travel between New York and San Francisco until the inevitable happens. Swoony romanticism and more dippy than serendipitous but done in an expert manner. **87m/C VHS, DVD.** *US* John Cusack, Kate Beckinsale, Molly Shannon, John Corbett, Jeremy Piven, Bridget Moynahan, Eugene Levy; ***D:*** Peter Chelsom; ***W:*** Marc Klein; ***C:*** John de Borman; ***M:*** Alan Silvestri.

Serenity 🦴🦴🦴 **2005 (PG-13)** Failed TV shows usually make pretty crappy movies (remember "Mod Squad?"), but Joss Whedon's big-screen adaptation of his small-screen "Firefly" series is one of the coolest sci fi adventures in recent memory. Captain Mal Reynolds (Fillion) and the crew of his cargo ship, Serenity, attempt to hide River Tam (Glau), a waifishly good-natured super-assassin, from the evil government Alliance that created her. Things hit the fan when the coolly evil Operative (Ejiofor) gets on their trail, but that won't keep Mal from "aiming to misbehave." Imagine a movie based on everything you loved about Han Solo and the Millenium Falcon, and you'll get an idea of why so many fanboys worship at the altar of Whedon. **119m/C DVD, Blu-ray Disc, UMD, HD DVD.** *US* Nathan Fillion, Gina Torres, Alan Tudyk, Adam Baldwin, Sean Maher, Ron Glass, Chiwetel Ejiofor, Morena Baccarin, Jewel Staite, Summer Glau; ***D:*** Joss Whedon; ***W:*** Joss Whedon; ***C:*** Jack N. Green; ***M:*** David Newman.

The Sergeant 🦴🦴 **1968** Master Sgt. Albert Callan (Steiger) is a stern, by-the-book super soldier who is stationed in an Army camp in post-WWII France. His commanding officer (Latimore) is a lush and only too happy to let Callan take over although his undisciplined soldiers resent Callan's strict policies. Then Callan begins eyeing handsome Pvt. Swanson (Law) and all those lonely, repressed sexual urges come bubbling up. Since Callan can't openly express them, he makes Swanson's life and his own miserable until the inevitable final act. **108m/C DVD.** Rod Steiger, John Phillip Law, Ludmila Mikael, Frank Latimore; ***D:*** John Flynn; ***W:*** Dennis Murphy; ***C:*** Henri Persin; ***M:*** Michel Magne.

Sgt. Bilko 🦴 1/2 **1995 (PG)** Popular '50s sitcom doesn't march so much as limp to the big screen with Martin leading the troops as the wise-cracking title character, crafted so brilliantly by Phil Silvers on the small screen. Martin flims and flams with frenetic energy as he tries to save his base from Washington cutbacks and the film from utter disaster. Enter Major Thorn (Hartman), Bilko's old adversary, who's plotting revenge on the con artist sergeant. Aykroyd's Bilko's naive boss, Col. Hall, but has little to do. Director Lynn finds his usual comic flair on leave this time around—too few laughs, spread too thin. Sentimental stroke has Catherine Silvers, Phil's daughter, playing Lt. Monday. **95m/C VHS, DVD.** Steve Martin, Dan Aykroyd, Phil Hartman, Glenne Headly, Daryl (Chill) Mitchell, Max Casella, Brian Leckner, Pamela Segall, Eric Edwards, Dan Ferro, John Marshall Jones, Brian Ortiz, Dale Dye; ***D:*** Jonathan Lynn; ***W:*** Andy Breckman; ***C:*** Peter Sova; ***M:*** Alan Silvestri.

Sgt. Kabukiman N.Y.P.D. WOOF! **1994** When New York cop Harry Griswold (Gianasi) investigates the death of a famous Japanese Kabuki actor, he suddenly finds himself in a kimono, having really bad hair-days, and vested with the powers of "Kabukiman." With the help of his beautiful teacher Lotus (Byun), he learns to channel his command of such amazing weapons as suffocating sushi rolls and lethal chopsticks into crime fighting. Stupid and insulting (deliberately so), all at the same time. A PG-13 version runs 95 minutes. **104m/C VHS, DVD.** Rick Gianasi, Susan Byun, Brick Bronsky, Bill Weeden, Thomas Crnkovich, Larry Robinson, Noble Lee Lester; ***D:*** Lloyd Kaufman, Michael Herz; ***W:*** Lloyd Kaufman, Andrew Osborn; ***C:*** Bob Williams; ***M:*** Bob Mithoff.

Sergeant Matlovich vs. the U.S. Air Force 🦴🦴 1/2 **1978** A serviceman fights to remain in the Air Force after admitting his homosexuality. Compelling theme (from a true story) and good lead performance from Dourif are not enough to carry a rather flat made for TV script. **100m/C VHS.** Brad Dourif, Marc Singer, Frank Converse, William Daniels, Stephen Elliott, David Spielberg, Rue McClanahan, Mitchell Ryan, David Ogden Stiers; ***D:*** Paul Leaf. **TV**

Sgt. Pepper's Lonely Hearts Club Band WOOF! **1978 (PG)** "Rip-off" would be putting it kindly. A classic album by one of the greatest rock bands of all time deserves the respect of not having a star-studded extravaganza "filmization" made of it. Gratuitous, weird casting, bad acting give it a surreal feel. And the Bee Gees? Please. A nadir of '70s popular entertainment. ♫ Sgt. Pepper's Lonely Hearts Club Band; With a Little Help From My Friends; Fixing a Hole; Getting Better; Here Comes the Sun; I Want You (She's So Heavy); Good Morning, Good Morning; Nowhere Man; Polythene Pam. **113m/C VHS, DVD.** Takaaki Yamashita, Maurice Gibb, Peter Frampton, Barry Gibb, Steve Martin, George Burns, Donald Pleasence; ***D:*** Michael A. Schultz.

Sergeant Rutledge 🦴🦴🦴 **1960** The story of a court-martial, told in flashback, about a black cavalry officer on trial for rape and murder. A detailed look at overt and covert racism handled by master director Ford. It is always apparent Strode (as Rutledge) is a heroic, yet human, figure who refuses to be beaten down by circumstances. The courtroom setting is deliberately oppressive but does make the film somewhat static. Based on the novel "Captain Buffalo" by James Warner Bellah. **112m/C VHS, DVD.** Woody Strode, Jeffrey Hunter, Constance Towers, Billie Burke, Juano Hernandez, Carleton Young, Charles Seel, Jan Styne, Mae Marsh; ***D:*** John Ford; ***W:*** Willis Goldbeck, James Warner Bellah; ***M:*** Howard Jackson.

Sergeant Ryker 🦴🦴 1/2 **1968** Confident lead acting from Marvin as a U.S. serviceman accused of treason during the Korean War carries this otherwise blah army/courtroom drama. Remake of 1963 TV film "The Case Against Sergeant Ryker." Dillman is good as Marvin's energetic lawyer. **85m/C VHS.** Lee Marvin, Bradford Dillman, Vera Miles, Peter Graves, Lloyd Nolan, Murray Hamilton; ***D:*** Buzz Kulik; ***M:*** John Williams.

Sergeant York 🦴🦴🦴🦴 **1941** Timely and enduring war movie based on the true story of Alvin York, the country boy from Tennessee drafted during WWI. At first a pacifist, Sergeant York (Cooper, well cast in an Oscar-winning role) finds justification for fighting and becomes one of the war's greatest heros. Gentle scenes of rural life contrast with horrific battlegrounds. York served as a consultant. **134m/B VHS, DVD.** Gary Cooper, Joan Leslie, Walter Brennan, Dickie Moore, Ward Bond, George Tobias, Noah Beery Jr., June Lockhart, Stanley Ridges, Margaret Wycherly, James Anderson, David Bruce, Lane Chandler, Elisha Cook Jr., Erville Alderson, Howard da Silva, Donald "Don" Douglas, Frank Faylen, Pat Flaherty, Joseph Girard, Creighton Hale, Russell Hicks, George Irving, Selmer Jackson, Jack Pennick, Harvey Stephens, Kay Sutton, Clem Bevans, Charles Trowbridge, Guy Wilkerson, Gig Young; ***D:*** Howard Hawks; ***W:*** Abem Finkel, Harry Chandler, Howard Koch, John Huston; ***C:*** Sol Polito; ***M:*** Max Steiner. Oscars '41: Actor (Cooper), Film Editing, Natl. Film Reg. '08;; N.Y. Film Critics '41: Actor (Cooper).

Sergeants 3 🦴 1/2 **1962** A 'Rat Pack' western with Sinatra, Martin, and Lawford as the titular brawling cavalry sergeants (Davis

Jr. is the company bugler) who take on warring Native American chief Mountain Hawk (Silva). There's also a subplot about Lawford's character wanting to leave the military and his buddies for marriage to Lee. It's actually a remake of 1939's "Gunga Din" played for a few laughs and some action. Three of Bing Crosby's sons are cast as soldiers. **113m/C DVD.** Frank Sinatra, Dean Martin, Peter Lawford, Sammy Davis Jr., Joey Bishop, Henry Silva, Ruta Lee, Buddy Lester, Philip Crosby, Lindsay Crosby, Dennis Crosby; ***D:*** John Sturges; ***W:*** W.R. Burnett; ***C:*** Winton C. Hoch; ***M:*** Billy May.

Sergio Lapel's Drawing Blood 🦴 *Drawing Blood* **1999** Artist/vampire Diana (Spinella) fulfills her artistic visions with blood instead of oils or watercolors. Her human slave Edmond (Wilson) supplies a constant flow of "models" until he meets homeless prostitute Dee (Smith) and decides to take control of his life. Edmond also has his hands full keeping his ever-horny dad (Palatta) out of trouble. The Troma label says it all: non-existent production values, mediocre acting, plenty of flowing red stuff, and ample female exposure (although this time there's a genuine narrative logic to all the nudity). **90m/C DVD.** Kirk Wilson, Larry Palatta, Dawn Spinella, Leo Otero, Erin Smith; ***D:*** Sergio Lapel; ***W:*** Noel Anderson; ***C:*** Shawn Lewallen.

Serial 🦴🦴🦴 **1980 (R)** Fun spoof of hyper-trendiness—open marriage, health foods, fad religions, navel-gazing—in Marin County, the really cool place to live across the Golden Gate from San Francisco. Mull in his first lead is the oddly normal guy surrounded by fruits and nuts. Based on Cyra McFadden's novel. **90m/C VHS.** Martin Mull, Sally Kellerman, Tuesday Weld, Tom Smothers, Bill Macy, Peter Bonerz, Barbara Rhoades, Christopher Lee; ***D:*** Bill Persky; ***W:*** Rich Eustis, Michael Elias.

Serial Bomber 🦴🦴 **1996 (R)** A would-be bomber in Seattle targets his ex-girlfriend but his plan is foiled by an FBI agent. So the bomber shifts targets. Based on the novel "Christmas Apocalypse" by Toshiyuki Tajima. **89m/C VHS, DVD.** Jason London, Lori Petty, James LeGros, Yuki Amami; ***D:*** Keoni Waxman.

Serial Killer 🦴🦴 **1995 (R)** Selby Younger (Delaney) is able to think like a killer in order to catch them. That's how the beautiful cop captured serial killer William Lucian Morrano (Bell) who has now escaped—Selby's his ultimate target but first he wants revenge. So he uses her friends as bait and leaves the bodies for Selby to discover. **94m/C VHS, DVD.** Kim Delaney, Gary Hudson, Tobin Bell, Pam Grier, Marco Rodriguez, Lyman Ward, Cyndi Pass, Andrew Prine; ***D:*** Pierre David; ***W:*** Mark Sevi; ***C:*** Thomas Jewett; ***M:*** Louis Febre.

Serial Killing 101 🦴🦴 *Serial Killing 4 Dummys* **2004 (R)** Outcast high-school kid Casey decides that he wants to be a serial killer when he grows up. His suicidal (and presumably equally outcast) girlfriend thinks this is a great idea. At least they won't have to sweat the SATs. When a real serial killer shows up, guess who the cops suspect. Myriad problems (besides the tasteless premise) ensure a small audience for this one. **88m/C VHS, DVD.** Thomas Haden Church, Justin Urich, Lisa Loeb, Rick Overton, George Murdock, Barbara Niven; ***D:*** Trace Slobotkin; ***W:*** Trace Slobotkin; ***C:*** John Tarver; ***M:*** Jeffrey Alan Jones. **VIDEO**

Serial Mom 🦴🦴🦴 **1994 (R)** June Cleaver-like housewife Turner is nearly perfect, except when someone disrupts her orderly life. Didn't rewind your videotape? Chose the white shoes after Labor Day? Uh oh. Stardom reigns after she's caught and the murderer-as-celebrity phenomenon is exploited to the fullest. Darkly funny Waters satire tends toward the mainstream and isn't as perverse as earlier efforts, but still maintains a shocking edge (vital organs are good for an appearance or two). Turner's chameleonic performance as the perfect mom/crazed killer is right on target, recalling "The War of the Roses." Waterston, Lake, and Lillard are terrific as her generic suburban family. **93m/C VHS, DVD.** Kathleen Turner, Sam Waterston, Ricki Lake, Matthew Lillard, Mink Stole, Traci Lords, Suzanne Somers, Joan Rivers, Patty (Patricia Campbell) Hearst, Mary Jo Catlett, Justin Whalin, Susan Lowe, Alan J. Wendl, Mary Vivian Pearce; ***D:*** John Waters; ***W:*** John Waters; ***C:*** Robert M. Stevens; ***M:*** Basil Poledouris; ***V:*** John Waters.

Serial Slayer 🦴 ½ *Claustrophobia* **2003 (R)** A serial killer hunts in the daylight. Three office workers are trapped in a suburban house trying to avoid being the next victims of the Crossbow Killer. Modestly suspenseful, although it can't avoid most of the genre's cliches. At least the three chicks don't run around screaming in their scanties (sorry, guys). **79m/C DVD.** Melanie Lynskey, Sheeri Rappaport, Mary Lynn Rajskub, Judith O'Dea; ***D:*** Mark Tapio Kines; ***W:*** Mark Tapio Kines; ***C:*** Bevan Crothers; ***M:*** Christopher Farrell.

Series 7: The Contenders 🦴🦴 ½ **2001 (R)** Reality TV takes to the big screen in this morbid but insightful portrayal of a fictional show called "The Contenders" in which the participants hunt each other down to their ultimate, televised, demise. Pic is presented in the form of a marathon of the show, which stars eight-months pregnant Dawn (Smith), the champ who takes on five new challengers, including an 18-year-old girl (Wever), a cancer victim and artist who was also, coincidentally, Dawn's first boyfriend (Fitzgerald). Revealing portrayals make all the contestants sympathetic, but Dawn and Jeff's unique plight is the most interesting. A scene where Dawn casually guns people down in a convenience store while bystanders look on is a highlight in this interesting social satire. **86m/C VHS, DVD.** *US* Brooke Smith, Glenn Fitzgerald, Merritt Wever, Michael Kaycheck, Richard Venture, Donna Hanover, Marylouise Burke, Nada Despotovich, Danton Stone, Jennifer Van Dyck, Angelina Phillips, Tanny McDonald; ***D:*** Daniel Minahan; ***W:*** Daniel Minahan; ***C:*** Randy Drummond; ***M:*** Girls Against Boys; ***Nar:*** Will Arnett.

Serious Charge 🦴🦴 ½ **1959** Howard Phillips (Qualyle) is a single clergyman, newly-arrived at his small town parish. The progressive reverend is determined to stem the juvenile delinquent problem but has his work cut out for him, especially with psychotic troublemaker Larry (Ray), who falsely accuses Phillips of indecent assault. His lie is backed up by vindictive spurned spinster Hester (Churchill), but in order to save his reputation, Phillips must get Hester to tell the truth. Cliff Richard (in his film debut) gets to sing. Based on the Philip King play. **99m/B DVD.** *GB* Anthony Quayle, Sarah Churchill, Andrew Ray, Irene Browne, Percy Herbert, Noel Howlett, Cliff Richard; ***D:*** Terence Young; ***W:*** Guy Elmes, Mickey Delamar; ***C:*** Georges Perinal; ***M:*** Leighton Lucas.

A Serious Man 🦴🦴🦴 **2009 (R)** A Coen brothers' film that's personal and an angst-ridden dark comedy. Problems arise for the Jewish Gropnik family in 1967 in an unnamed Minnesota city suburb. Physicist Larry's wife Judith is having an affair with his obnoxious university colleague Sy and wants a divorce. His crazy mathematician brother Larry is unemployable and living with the family, son Danny is buying pot and goes to his bar mitzvah stoned, and daughter Sarah steals money from Larry's wallet to save up for a nose job. Larry is worried he won't get tenure even as a graduate student gives him grief and his beautiful neighbor shakes his libido by sunbathing in the nude. If Larry reminds you of the biblical Job—well that's deliberate. **105m/C DVD.** *US* Michael Stuhlbarg, Richard Kind, Sari Lennick, Fred Melamed, Adam Arkin, Fyvush Finkel, Aaron Wolff, Jessica McManus; ***D:*** Joel Coen, Ethan Coen; ***W:*** Joel Coen, Ethan Coen; ***C:*** Roger Deakins; ***M:*** Carter Burwell. Ind. Spirit '10: Cinematog.

Serious Moonlight 🦴 ½ **2009** High-powered attorney Louise (Ryan) is expecting a romantic weekend getaway with hubby Ian (Hutton) only to find out he's planning on leaving her for a trip to Paris with his much-younger mistress Sara (Bell). Enraged, Louise knocks Ian out and then duct-tapes him to the toilet while haranguing him about making their marriage work. Meanwhile, Sara gets tired of waiting for Ian and shows up on their doorstep and weird gardener Todd (Long) comes along and drunkenly decides to rob the place. Unfortunately shrill marital comedy is the directorial debut for Hines, who acted with late screenwriter Shelly in the 2007 film "Waitress." **84m/C DVD.** ***D:*** Cheryl Hines.

The Serpent and the Rainbow WOOF! **1987 (R)** A good, interesting book (by Harvard ethnobotanist Wade Davis) offering serious speculation on the possible existence and origin of zombies in Haiti was hacked and slashed into a cheap Wes Craven-ized screen semblance of itself. And a shame it is: the result is racist, disrespectful, exploitative, and superficial. **98m/C VHS, DVD.** Paul Guilfoyle, Bill Pullman, Cathy Tyson, Zakes Mokae, Paul Winfield, Conrad Roberts, Badja (Medu) Djola, Theresa Merritt, Brent Jennings, Michael Gough; ***D:*** Wes Craven; ***W:*** Richard Maxwell, A.R. Simoun; ***C:*** John Lindley; ***M:*** Brad Fiedel.

Serpent Island 🦴 ½ **1954** Two seamen fight over a Caribbean woman amid voodoo rituals, sea monsters and buried treasure. **63m/C VHS.** Mary Munday, Don Blackman, Tom Monroe, Rosalind Hayes, Sonny Tufts; ***D:*** Tom Gries; ***C:*** Bert I. Gordon; ***M:*** Domingo Rodrigues.

The Serpent's Egg 🦴 ½ *Das Schlangenei* **1978 (R)** Big disappointment from the great Bergman in his second film in English. Ullmann is not sultry and Carradine is horrible. Big budget matched by big Bergman ego, making a big, bad parody of himself. The plot concerns a pair of Jewish trapeze artists surviving in Berlin during Hitler's rise by working in a grisly and mysterious medical clinic. **119m/C VHS, DVD.** *GE* David Carradine, Liv Ullmann, Gert Frobe, James Whitmore; ***D:*** Ingmar Bergman; ***W:*** Ingmar Bergman; ***C:*** Sven Nykvist.

The Serpent's Kiss 🦴🦴 **1997 (R)** Great cast can't quite overcome the story's predictability. In 1699, young Dutch landscape artist Meneer Chrome (MacGregor) accepts a job at the remote English estate of Thomas Smithers (Postlethwaite) who wants a magnificent garden to present to his bored wife, Julianna (Scacchi). But Chrome is secretly employed by Juliana's scheming cousin, James Fitzmaurice (Grant), to bankrupt Smithers so that James can regain Juliana affections. Of course, Julianna casts her eyes on the handsome gardener instead, and then there's the matter of the Smithers' teenaged daughter, Thea (Chaplin). Rousselot is better known as a cinematographer (this is his first directorial effort) and the film at least looks gorgeous. **110m/C VHS, DVD.** *GB FR* Ewan McGregor, Greta Scacchi, Pete Postlethwaite, Richard E. Grant, Carmen Chaplin, Donal McCann, Charley Boorman; ***D:*** Philippe Rousselot; ***W:*** Tim Rose Price; ***C:*** Jean-Francois Robin; ***M:*** Goran Bregovic.

Serpent's Lair 🦴🦴 **1995 (R)** Tom (Fahey) and Alex (Medway) have just moved into what's supposed to be their dream apartment in L.A. Too bad there's lots of secrets and Tom's soon drawn into the web of sultry beauty Lillith (Lisa B.), who's not just your average femme fatale. **90m/C VHS.** Jeff Fahey, Heather Medway, Lisa Barbuscia, Anthony Palermo, Kathleen Noone, Taylor Nichols, Patrick Bauchau, Jack Kehler; ***D:*** Jeff Reiner; ***W:*** Marc Rosenberg; ***C:*** Feliks Parnell; ***M:*** Vinnie Golia.

Serpico 🦴🦴🦴 **1973 (R)** Based on Peter Maas's book about the true-life exploits of Frank Serpico, a New York undercover policeman who exposed corruption in the police department. Known as much for his nonconformism as for his honesty, the real Serpico eventually retired from the force and moved to Europe. South Bronx-raised Pacino gives the character reality and strength. Excellent New York location photography. **130m/C VHS, DVD.** Al Pacino, John Randolph, Jack Kehoe, Barbara Eda-Young, Cornelia Sharpe, F. Murray Abraham, Tony Roberts; ***D:*** Sidney Lumet; ***W:*** Waldo Salt, Norman Wexler; ***C:*** Arthur Ornitz; ***M:*** Mikis Theodorakis. Golden Globes '74: Actor—Drama (Pacino); Natl. Bd. of Review '73: Actor (Pacino); Writers Guild '73: Adapt. Screenplay.

The Servant 🦴🦴🦴 ½ **1963** A dark, intriguing examination of British class hypocrisy and the master-servant relationship. Wealthy, bored aristocratic playboy Tony (Fox) is ruined by his socially inferior but crafty and ambitious Cockney manservant Hugo (Bogarde). Playwright Harold Pinter wrote the adaptation of Robin Maugham's novel in his first collaboration with expatriate American director Losey. The best kind of British societal navel-gazing. **112m/B VHS, DVD.** *GB* Dirk Bogarde, James Fox, Sarah Miles, Wendy Craig, Catherine Lacey, Richard Vernon; ***D:*** Joseph Losey; ***W:*** Harold Pinter; ***C:*** Douglas Slocombe; ***M:*** John Dankworth. British Acad. '63: Actor (Bogarde); N.Y. Film Critics '64: Screenplay.

Servants of Twilight 🦴🦴 **1991 (R)** Religious zealots target a small boy for assassination because their cult leader says he's the anti-Christ. Adaptation of the Dean R. Koontz novel. Packed with action, its spell on the viewer hinges on a cruel shock ending that undercuts what came before. **95m/C VHS, DVD.** Bruce Greenwood, Belinda Bauer, Grace Zabriskie, Richard Bradford, Jarrett Lennon, Carel Struycken, Jack Kehoe, Kelli Maroney, Dale Dye; ***D:*** Jeffrey Obrow; ***W:*** Stephen Carpenter. **CABLE**

Service De Luxe 🦴🦴 **1938** Glamorous New York businesswoman Helen Murphy (Bennett) caters to a rich clientele by dealing with all the problems they don't wish to. Wealthy Scott Robinson (Ruggles) wants to prevent his country-bred nephew Robert Wade (Price, in his film debut) from bothering him. But Helen finds the rugged inventor a breath of fresh air. **85m/B VHS.** Constance Bennett, Vincent Price, Charlie Ruggles, Helen Broderick, Mischa Auer; ***D:*** Rowland V. Lee; ***W:*** Gertrude Purcell, Leonard Spigelgass; ***C:*** George Robinson.

Serving in Silence: The Margarethe Cammermeyer Story 🦴🦴🦴 **1995** Army nurse Margarethe Cammermeyer (Close) has had a distinguished career for 24 years, a bronze star earned in Vietnam, and obtained the rank of colonel. During a security clearance interview, she admits to the military that she is a lesbian and finds herself reluctantly in the eye of the media storm. The TV film won 3 EMMY awards: Best Actress for Close; Best Supporting Actress for Davis (as Margarethe's lover); and Best Screenplay. **92m/C VHS.** Glenn Close, Judy Davis, Jan Rubes, Wendy Makkena, William Converse-Roberts, Susan Barnes, Colleen Flynn, William Allen Young; ***D:*** Jeff Bleckner; ***W:*** Allison Cross. **TV**

Serving Sara 🦴 **2002 (PG-13)** Unfunny comedy stars Perry as process server Joe Tyler, who is trying to serve divorce papers on flirty Englishwoman Sara Moore (Hurley), who's married to womanizing Texas cattle baron Gordon (Campbell). But Sara turns the tables by bribing Joe to try to serve divorce papers to the elusive Gordon instead. Perry's trip to rehab during filming delayed production but the lack of laughs surely can't be laid solely at his door. **99m/C VHS, DVD.** *US* Matthew Perry, Elizabeth Hurley, Bruce Campbell, Vincent Pastore, Cedric the Entertainer, Amy Adams, Terry Crews, Jerry Stiller, Joe (Johnny) Viterelli; ***D:*** Reginald (Reggie) Hudlin; ***W:*** Jay Scherick, David Ronn; ***C:*** Robert Brinkmann; ***M:*** Marcus Miller.

Sesame Street Presents: Follow That Bird 🦴🦴 ½ *Follow That Bird* **1985 (G)** Possibly the best children's TV show in the history of the medium makes a so-so transition to the big screen. Suffering an identity crisis, a lonely Big Bird allows himself to be adopted by a family of birds. Quickly realizing that his new family is a bunch of do-dos (literally), the big guy heads back to NYC, followed by a vindictive social worker, two scheming carnival owners, and the assorted residents of Sesame Street. There are great moments (mostly involving Super-Grover and Ernie & Bert) and some fun cameos from Waylon Jennings and SCTV alumni, but it never lives up to the potential of the TV show. **92m/C VHS, DVD.** Sandra Bernhard, John Candy, Chevy Chase, Joe Flaherty, Dave Thomas, Waylon Jennings; ***D:*** Ken Kwapis; ***W:*** Judy Freudberg, Tony Geiss; ***C:*** Curtis Clark; ***M:*** Lennie Niehaus; ***V:*** Carroll Spinney, Jim Henson, Frank Oz.

Session 9 🦴🦴 **2001 (R)** Hazardous materials contractor Gordon (Mullan) bids on a job to remove asbestos from a run-down insane asylum. He secures the contract by promising to complete the work in a week, although under ideal circumstances it should take a month. Unfortunately, "ideal circumstances" are not afoot in the creepy booby hatch. The oppressive atmosphere soon gets to Gordon and his crew, who begin turning on each other after the discovery of nine audio tapes confirming rumors of satanic rituals and torture of patients. Somewhat marred by editing that gives away the plot too early, and also by the fact that for workers under a deadline, these guys stand around getting freaked out way too much. Shot using Sony's CineAlta HD digital video cameras instead of film. **100m/C VHS, DVD.** *US* Peter Mullan, David Caruso, Josh(ua) Lucas, Brendan Sexton III, Paul Guilfoyle, Stephen Gevedon; ***D:*** Brad Anderson; ***W:*** Brad Anderson, Stephen Gevedon; ***C:*** Uta Briesewitz; ***M:*** Climax Gold Twins.

A Session with The Committee 🦴🦴 **1968 (PG)** Comedy film of the seminal comedy troupe "The Committee," specialists in short, punchy satire. Dated, but of interest to comedy buffs. **88m/C VHS, DVD.** Wolfman Jack, Howard Hesseman, Barbara Bosson, Peter Bonerz, Garry Goodrow, Carl Gottlieb; ***D:*** Jack Del.

Sessions 🦴🦴 **1983** Mentally exhausted by her roles as sister, single parent, lover, exercise enthusiast, and high-priced prostitute, Leigh Churchill (Hamel) seeks professional counselling. Hamel's first role after "Hill Street Blues" is only average in this made for TV drama. **96m/C VHS.** Veronica Hamel, Jeffrey DeMunn, Jill Eikenberry, David Marshall Grant, George Coe, Henderson Forsythe, Deborah Hedwall; ***D:*** Richard Pearce. **TV**

Set It Off 🦴🦴 ½ **1996 (R)** Lethal "Waiting to Exhale," finds four female friends in Los Angeles pushed over the edge and taking up bank robbery to escape poverty and strike a blow against "the man." The felonious, funky divas of crime include Stony (Pinkett, who seems to be having fun with this role) and Latifah as Cleo, in a powerhouse performance. Butt-kicking action scenes are most entertaining combined with a soundtrack, including Seal, En Vogue, the Fugees and Brandy, to match. Melodramatic sequences, including Stony's romance with Keith (Underwood), drag. **121m/C VHS, DVD.** Jada Pinkett Smith, Queen Latifah, Vivica A. Fox, Kimberly Elise, Blair Underwood, John C. McGinley, Anna Maria Horsford, Ella Joyce, Charles Robinson, Chaz Lamar Shepherd, Vincent Baum, Van Baum, Thomas Jefferson Byrd, Samantha MacLachlan; ***D:*** F. Gary Gray; ***W:*** Kate Lanier, Takashi Bufford; ***C:*** Marc Reshovsky; ***M:*** Christopher Young.

Set Me Free 🦴🦴 ½ *Emporte-Moi* **1999** Thirteen-year-old Hanna is trying to deal with her loneliness in 1963 Montreal. Her Polish immigrant father (Manojivoic) is a frustrated writer who takes his problems out on his family while his depressed wife (Pussieres) slaves in a garment factory to support them. Hanna tries to find solace at the cinema where she becomes enamored of actress Anna Karina, the sultry star of Jean-Luc Godard's "My Life to Live," in which she plays an independent prostitute (not a first-choice role model). Hanna's confusion and unhappiness go unresolved, but then she still has a lot of living to do. French with subtitles. **95m/C VHS.** *CA SI* Karine Vanasse, Miki (Predrag) Manojlovic, Pascale Bussieres, Alexandre Merineau, Charlotte Christeler, Nancy Huston, Monique Mercure; ***D:*** Lea Pool; ***W:*** Lea Pool, Monique H. Messier, Nancy Huston; ***C:*** Jeanne Lapoirie.

The Set-Up 🦴🦴🦴 ½ **1949** Excellent, original if somewhat overwrought morality tale about integrity set in the world of boxing. Filmed as a continuous narrative covering only 72 minutes in the life of aging fighter Stoker Thompson (Ryan). His manager (Tobias) takes a gangster's bribe for Thompson to throw the fight (without informing him), never believing the washed-up boxer has a chance to win. Powerful, with fine performances, especially from Ryan in the lead. Inspired by Joseph Moncure March's narrative poem. **72m/B VHS, DVD.** Robert Ryan, Audrey Totter, George Tobias, Alan Baxter, James Edwards, Wallace Ford; ***D:*** Robert Wise; ***W:*** Art Cohn; ***C:*** Milton Krasner.

The Set Up 🦴🦴 ½ **1995 (R)** Electronic engineer-turned-cat burglar Charlie Thorpe (Zane) is now apparently reformed after a prison stint and works designing and installing security systems. His latest job is for Chairman Jeremiah Cole (Coburn) at Charter Trust bank where he begins romancing the beautiful Gina (Sara). But she becomes the hostage of Charlie's ex-prison buddy Kliff (Russo), who wants Charlie's help in breaking into the bank. However, there's a double-cross (or maybe even a triplecross) that has Charlie scrambling to save his life. Based on the book "My Laugh Comes Last" by James Hadley Chase. **103m/C VHS, DVD.** Billy Zane, Mia Sara, James Coburn, James Russo; ***D:*** Strathford Hamilton; ***W:*** Michael Thoma; ***C:*** David Lewis; ***M:*** Conrad Pope.

The Settlement 🦴🦴 **1999** Con men Jerry and Pat try to make money by buying life insurance policies on the terminally ill. Unfortunately for them, their clients have been living a lot longer than anticipated. Then they meet the seriously ill Barbara and things begin to change. **92m/C VHS, DVD.** Kelly McGillis, John C. Reilly, William Fichtner, Dan Castellaneta, David Rasche; ***D:*** Mark Steilen; ***C:*** Judy Irola; ***M:*** Brian Tyler.

Seven 🦴🦴 ½ **1979 (R)** Freelance desperado Smith takes $7 million of your tax dollars at work from the feds to get rid of Hawaiian gangsters. Might be tongue in cheek, though sometimes it's hard to tell. Fun action pic unfortunately characterized by bad camera work and over-earnest direction. Features the original of a gag made famous in "Raiders of the Lost Ark." **100m/C VHS.** William (Bill) Smith, Barbara Leigh, Guich Koock, Art Metrano, Martin Kove, Richard Le Pore, Susan Kiger, Lenny Montana; ***D:*** Andy Sidaris.

Seven 🦴🦴🦴 *Se7en* **1995 (R)** If this grim thriller can't make you jump, you're dead, and you won't be the only one. Arrogant, ignorant detective David Mills (Pitt) is newly partnered with erudite old-timer William Somerset (Freeman) and they're stuck with the bizarre case of a morbidly obese man who was forced to eat himself to death. The weary Somerset is certain it's just the beginning and he's right—the non-buddy duo are on the trail of a serial killer who uses the seven deadly sins (gluttony, greed, sloth, pride, lust, envy, and wrath) as his modus operandi. Since most of the film is shot in dark, grimy, and unrelentingly rainy circumstances, much of the grotesqueness of the murders is left to the viewer's imagination—which will be in overdrive. **127m/C VHS, DVD.** Brad Pitt, Morgan Freeman, Gwyneth Paltrow, Kevin Spacey, R. Lee Ermey, Richard Roundtree, John C. McGinley, Julie Araskog, Reg E. Cathey, Peter Crombie; ***D:*** David Fincher; ***W:*** Andrew Kevin Walker; ***C:*** Darius Khondji; ***M:*** Howard Shore. MTV Movie Awards '96: Film, Most Desirable Male (Pitt), Villain (Spacey); Natl. Bd. of Review '95: Support. Actor (Spacey); N.Y. Film Critics '95: Support. Actor (Spacey); Broadcast Film Critics '95: Support. Actor (Spacey).

Seven Alone 🦴🦴 ½ *House Without Windows* **1975 (G)** Family adventure tale (based on Monroe Morrow's book "On to Oregon," based in turn on a true story) about seven siblings who undertake a treacherous 2000-mile journey from Missouri to Oregon, after their parents die along the way. Inspiring and all that; good family movie. **85m/C VHS, DVD.** Dewey Martin, Aldo Ray, Anne Collins, Dean Smith, Stewart Petersen; ***D:*** Earl Bellamy.

Seven Beauties 🦴🦴🦴🦴 *Pasqualino Settebellezze; Pasqualino: Seven Beauties* **1976** Very dark war comedy about a small-time Italian crook in Naples with seven ugly sisters to support. He survives a German prison camp and much else; unforgettably, he seduces the ugly commandant of his camp to save his own life. Good acting and tight direction. **116m/C VHS, DVD.** *IT* Giancarlo Giannini, Fernando Rey, Shirley Stoler, Elena Fiore, Enzo Vitale; ***D:*** Lina Wertmuller; ***W:*** Lina Wertmuller; ***C:*** Tonino Delli Colli.

Seven Brides for Seven Brothers 🦴🦴🦴 ½ **1954** The eldest of seven fur-trapping brothers in the Oregon Territory brings home a wife. She begins to civilize the other six, who realize the merits of women and begin to look for romances of their own. Thrilling choreography by Michael Kidd—don't miss "The Barn Raising." Charming performances by Powell and Keel, both in lovely voice. Based on Stephen Vincent Benet's story. Thrills, chills, singin', dancin'—a classic Hollywood good time. ♫When You're In Love; Spring, Spring, Spring; Sobbin' Women; Bless Your Beautiful Hide; Goin' Co'tin; Wonderful, Wonderful Day; June Bride; Lonesome Polecat Lament. **103m/C VHS, DVD.** Howard Keel, Jane Powell, Russ Tamblyn, Julie Newmar, Jeff Richards, Tommy (Thomas) Rall, Virginia Gibson; ***D:*** Stanley Donen; ***W:*** Albert Hackett, Frances Goodrich, Dorothy Kingsley; ***C:*** George J. Folsey. Oscars '54: Scoring/Musical, Natl. Film Reg. '04.

Seven Chances 🦴🦴🦴 ½ **1925** Silent classic that Keaton almost didn't make, believing instead that it should go to Harold Lloyd. Desperate lawyer Jimmie Shannon (Keaton) finds that he can inherit $7 million from his grandfather's estate if he marries by 7:00 p.m. on his 27th birthday, which is that day. After his girlfriend (Dwyer) turns down his botched proposal, chaos breaks loose when Jimmie advertises for someone—anyone—to marry him and make him rich. Suddenly he finds what seems to be hundreds of women willing to make the sacrifice, setting up one of the great film pursuits. Memorable boulder sequence was re-shot after preview audience indicated climax was lacking that certain something. Based on the play by David Belasco and remade with Chris O'Donnell as "The Bachelor" (1990). **60m/B VHS, DVD.** Buster Keaton, T. Roy Barnes, Snitz Edwards, Ruth Dwyer, Frankie Raymond; ***D:*** Buster Keaton; ***W:*** Clyde Bruckman, Jean C. Havez, Joseph A. Mitchell; ***C:*** Byron Houck, Elgin Lessley.

Seven Cities of Gold 🦴🦴 **1955** An expedition of Spanish conquistadors and missionaries descend on 18th-century California, looking for secret Indian caches of gold. Semi-lavish costume epic. **103m/C VHS.** Anthony Quinn, Michael Rennie, Richard Egan, Rita Moreno, Jeffrey Hunter, Eduardo Noriega, John Doucette; ***D:*** Robert D. Webb.

Seven Days Ashore 🦴 ½ **1944** Sailor Dan Arland (Oliver) wants to enjoy his shore leave in San Francisco only he has three girls waiting for him in port. So he pawns Carol (Mayo) and Lucy (Ward) off on his pals Monty (Brown) and Orval (Carney) so he can romance debutante Annabelle (Shepard). Only the girls find out what Dan's done and decide to pay him back. Brown and Carney were a popular comedy duo at the time. **74m/B VHS.** Gordon Oliver, Wally Brown, Alan Carney, Elaine Shepard, Virginia Mayo, Amelita Ward, Marcy McGuire, Dooley Wilson; ***D:*** John H. Auer; ***W:*** Lawrence Kimble, Irving Phillips, Edward Verdier; ***C:*** Russell Metty.

Seven Days in May 🦴🦴🦴 ½ **1964** Topical but still gripping Cold War nuclear-peril thriller. After President Jordan Lyman (March) signs a nuclear disarmament treaty with the Soviets, General James M. Scott (Lancaster), the leader of the Joint Chiefs of Staff, plans a military takeover because he considers the president's pacifism traitorous. Lyman learns of the potential coup and works to expose the plot before it's too late. Highly suspenseful, with a breathtaking climax. Based on a novel by Fletcher Knebel and Charles Waldo Bailey II. **117m/B VHS, DVD.** Burt Lancaster, Kirk Douglas, Edmond O'Brien, Fredric March, Ava Gardner, Martin Balsam, George Macready, Whit Bissell, Hugh Marlowe, Richard Anderson, Andrew Duggan, John Houseman; ***D:*** John Frankenheimer; ***W:*** Rod Serling; ***C:*** Ellsworth Fredericks; ***M:*** Jerry Goldsmith. Golden Globes '65: Support. Actor (O'Brien).

Seven Days' Leave 🦴🦴 **1942** Radio star-crammed musical comedy about a soldier who must marry a certain already betrothed gal (Ball) within a week so he can inherit a fortune. Songs include "Can't Get Out of this Mood," "A Touch of Texas," and "Baby, You Speak My Language." Following the completion of the film, Mature joined the Coast Guard. Lively but not memorable. **87m/B VHS.** Victor Mature, Lucille Ball, Harold (Hal) Peary, Mary Cortes, Ginny Simms, Marcy McGuire, Peter Lind Hayes, Walter Reed, Wallace Ford, Arnold Stang, Buddy Clark, Charles Victor; ***D:*** Tim Whelan.

Seven Days of Grace 🦴 **2006 (PG-13)** Despite the familiar faces in the cast, this looks like a low-budget amateur production. Struggling Hollywood actress Grace (Coyne) has inherited her father's failing Italian eatery. So she joins forces with three female friends in an effort to keep the place going until she can figure out how to duplicate the secret rib recipe he took to his grave. **90m/C DVD.** Stephanie Beacham, Olivia Hussey, Lesley-Anne Down, Gavan O'Herlihy, Peter Evans, Ria Coyne; ***D:*** Don E. Fauntleroy; ***C:*** Don E. Fauntleroy; ***M:*** Michael Werckle. **VIDEO**

Seven Days to Live 🦴🦴 ½ **2001 (R)** Ellen (Plummer) and her hubby Martin Shaw (Pertwee) move to a remote country house to recover from the death of their son. Of course, the house just happens to be built over a graveyard and Ellen is haunted by warnings that she has only, well, the title tells it all. Quite creepy. **96m/C VHS, DVD.** Amanda Plummer, Sean Pertwee, Nick Brimble, Gina Bellman; ***D:*** Sebastian Niemann.

Seven Days to Noon 🦴🦴 ½ **1950** Dated but still powerful story detailing the threat of a nuclear explosion. Unbalanced atomic scientist John Willingdon (Jones) threatens to blow up the center of London unless the Prime Minister (Adam) agrees to stop research into nuclear weapons. And Willingdon can do it, too, since he's stolen an atomic bomb. Scotland Yard has until noon of the following Sunday to find him. **94m/B VHS.** Barry Jones, Andre Morell, Ronald Adam, Olive Sloane, Joan Hickson, Hugh Cross, Sheila Manahan; ***D:*** John Boulting, Roy Boulting; ***W:*** Roy Boulting, Paul Dehn, James Bernard, Frank Harvey; ***C:*** Gilbert Taylor; ***M:*** John Addison.

Seven Deadly Sins 🦴🦴🦴 **1953** A collection of tales concerning destructive emotions and the downfalls they cause. Contains shorts from some of Europe's finest directors (five French and two Italian). Stories and their directors are "Avarice and Anger" (de Filippo), "Sloth" (Dreville), "Lust" (Allegret), "Envy" (Rossellini), "Gluttony" (Rim), "Pride" (Autant-Lara) and "The Eighth Sin" (Lacombe). **127m/B VHS.** *FR IT* Eduardo de Filippo, Isa Miranda, Jacqueline Plessis, Louis de Funes, Paolo Stoppa, Frank Villard, Jean Richard, Francoise Roşay, Jean Debucourt, Louis Seigner; ***D:*** Eduardo de Filippo, Jean Dreville, Yves Allegret, Roberto Rossellini, Carlo Rim, Claude Autant-Lara, Georges Lacombe.

Seven Deaths in the Cat's Eye 🦴🦴 **1972** A ravenous beast slaughters people in a small Scottish village. This flick reveals a little-known fact about felines. **90m/C VHS, DVD.** *IT* Anton Diffring, Jane Birkin; ***D:*** Anthony M. Dawson.

Seven Doors to Death 🦴 **1944** Young architect tries to solve a crime to avoid being placed under suspicion. The suspects are six shop owners in this low-budget attempt at a murder mystery. **70m/B VHS, DVD.** Chick Chandler, June Clyde, George Meeker, Gregory Gay, Edgar Dearing; ***D:*** Elmer Clifton.

7 Faces of Dr. Lao 🦴🦴🦴 **1963** Dr. Lao is the proprietor of a magical circus that changes the lives of the residents of a small western town. Marvelous special effects and makeup (Randall plays seven characters) highlight this charming family film in the Pal tradition. Charles Finney adapted from his novel. **101m/C VHS, DVD.** Tony Randall, Barbara Eden, Arthur O'Connell, Lee Patrick, Noah Beery Jr., John Qualen, John Ericson, Royal Dano; ***D:*** George Pal; ***W:*** Charles Beaumont; ***C:*** Robert J. Bronner; ***M:*** Leigh Harline.

Seven Girlfriends 🦴🦴 **2000 (R)** Melancholy romantic comedy has thirtysomething bachelor Jesse (Daly) so disheartened by his string of failed romances that he seeks out seven ex-girlfriends to find out what went wrong. Good cast. **100m/C VHS, DVD.** Timothy Daly, Laura Leighton, Mimi Rogers, Olivia D'Abo, Jami Gertz, Elizabeth Pena, Melora Hardin, Arye Gross, Katy Selverstone; ***D:*** Paul Lazarus; ***W:*** Paul Lazarus, Stephen Gregg; ***C:*** Don E. Fauntleroy; ***M:*** Christopher Tyng.

The Seven Hills of Rome 🦴🦴 ½ **1958** Quiet story of a TV star (Lanza) who follows his girlfriend (Castle) to Rome after a lovers' quarrel, and there falls in love with Allasio. Fantastic music makes up for a weak plot. Based on a story by Giueseppi Amato. ♫Arrivederci Roma; Seven Hills of Rome; Never Till Now; Earthbound; Come Dance With Me; Lolita; There's Gonna Be a Party Tonight; Italian Calypso; Questa o Quella. **107m/C VHS.** Mario Lanza, Peggy Castle, Renato Rascel, Marisa Allasio, Clelia Matania, Rosella Como; ***D:*** Roy Rowland; ***W:*** Giorgio Prosperi, Art Cohn; ***M:*** Georgie Stoll.

Seven Hours to Judgment 🦴🦴 **1988 (R)** When the punks who murdered his wife go free, a psychotic man (Leibman) decides to take justice into his own hands. He kidnaps the wife of the judge in charge (Bridges, who also directed) and leads him on a wild goose chase. Leibman steals the film as the psycho. Ex-Springsteen spouse

Phillips plays the judge's wife. Ambitious but credulity-stretching revenge/crime drama. Screenplay written by de Souza under the pseudonym Elliot Stephens. **90m/C VHS, DVD.** Beau Bridges, Ron Leibman, Julianne Phillips, Al Freeman Jr., Reggie Johnson; ***D:*** Beau Bridges; ***W:*** Steven E. de Souza, Walter Halsey Davis; ***C:*** Hanania Baer; ***M:*** John Debney.

Seven Keys to Baldpate **1917** Early version of the famous stage play by George M. Cohan in which George Washington Magee accepts a challenge that he can finish a novel in 24 hours while staying at the deserted Baldpate Inn. **66m/B VHS.** Hugh Ford, Anna Q. Nilsson, George M. Cohan, Hedda Hopper, Corene Uzzell, Joseph Smiley, Armand Cortes, C. Warren Cook; ***D:*** Mae Gaston.

Seven Keys to Baldpate 1/2 **1929** Early talkie version of the film which was based on the famous stage play of the same name by George M. Cohan which follows an author into a deserted Baldpate Inn on a bet that he can't finish a novel in 24 hours while in the Inn. **70m/B VHS.** Richard Dix, Miriam Seegar, Crauford Kent, Margaret Livingston, Lucien Littlefield; ***D:*** Reginald Barker.

The Seven Little Foys **1955** Enjoyable musical biography of Eddie Foy (played ebulliantly by Hope) and his famed vaudevillian troupe. Cagney's appearance as George M. Cohan is brief, but long enough for a memorable dance duet with Hope. ♫ Mary's a Grand Old Name; I'm a Yankee Doodle Dandy; I'm the Greatest Father of Them All; Nobody; Comedy Ballet; I'm Tired; Chinatown, My Chinatown. **95m/C VHS, DVD.** Bob Hope, Milly Vitale, George Tobias, Angela (Clark) Clarke, James Cagney; ***D:*** Melville Shavelson; ***W:*** Melville Shavelson, Jack Rose.

Seven Magnificent Gladiators **1984 (PG)** Seven gladiators team up to save a peaceful Roman village from total annihilation. Dismal effort at a remake of "The Seven Samaurai"—see the original instead, please. Ferrigno was "The Incredible Hulk" on TV. **86m/C VHS.** Lou Ferrigno, Sybil Danning, Brad Harris, Dan Vadis, Carla Ferrigno; ***D:*** Bruno Mattei.

Seven Minutes in Heaven **1986 (PG)** Sensitive love story about a 15-year-old girl who invites her platonic male friend to live in her house, and finds it disturbs her boyfriend, as these things will. Ever so tasteful (unlike most other teen comedies), with gentle comedy—but forgettable. **90m/C VHS.** Jennifer Connelly, Byron Thames, Maddie Corman, Lauren Holly; ***D:*** Linda Feferman; ***W:*** Jane Bernstein; ***C:*** Steven Fierberg.

The Seven-Per-Cent Solution **1976 (PG)** Dr. Watson (Duvall) persuades Sherlock Holmes (Nicholson) to meet with Sigmund Freud (Arkin) to cure his cocaine addiction. Holmes and Freud then find themselves teaming up to solve a supposed kidnapping. Adapted by Nicholas Meyer from his own novel. One of the most charming Holmes films; well-cast, intriguing blend of mystery, drama, and fun. Title refers to the solution of cocaine Holmes injects. **113m/C VHS, DVD.** Alan Arkin, Nicol Williamson, Laurence Olivier, Robert Duvall, Vanessa Redgrave, Joel Grey, Samantha Eggar, Jeremy Kemp, Charles Gray, Regine; ***D:*** Herbert Ross; ***W:*** Nicholas Meyer; ***C:*** Oswald Morris; ***M:*** John Addison.

Seven Pounds 1/2 **2008 (PG-13)** A depressed IRS agent, Ben (Smith), kicks things off by calling a 911 operator to report his own suicide. Cue the uncertainty—and flashback scenes—behind what motivates Ben to act as he does, apparently seeking out seven individuals to assist for various reasons as part of a larger plan for his own redemption. However, things get complicated when he falls in love with one of the recipients, Emily (Dawson), who suffers from a congenital heart disorder yet sees beyond her own pain and senses Ben's. Visually bleak reteaming of Smith and director Muccino puts the star back on his superhero-esque pedestal, though he has enough charm to pull it off, as does Dawson who's more than worthy of sharing the screen with him. **123m/C DVD.** *US* Will Smith, Rosario Dawson, Woody Harrelson, Michael Ealy, Barry Pepper, Bill Smitrovich, Elpidia Carrillo, Robine Lee, Tim Kelleher, Gina Hecht, Joseph A. Nunez; ***D:*** Gabriele Muccino; ***W:*** Grant Nieporte; ***C:*** Philippe Le Sourd; ***M:*** Angelo Milli.

Seven Samurai *Shichinin No Samurai; The Magnificent Seven* **1954** Kurosawa's masterpiece, set in 16th-century Japan. A small farming village, beset by marauding bandits, hires seven professional soldiers to rid itself of the scourge. Wanna watch a samaurai movie? This is the one. Sweeping, complex human drama with all the ingredients: action, suspense, comedy. Available in several versions of varying length, all long—and all too short. Splendid acting. In Japanese with English subtitles. **204m/B VHS, DVD.** *JP* Toshiro Mifune, Takashi Shimura, Yoshio Inaba, Kuninori Kodo, Isao (Ko) Kimura, Seiji Miyaguchi, Minoru Chiaki, Daisuke Kato, Bokuzen Hidari, Kamatari (Keita) Fujiwara, Yoshio Kosugi, Yoshio Tsuchiya, Jun Tatara, Sojin, Kichijiro Ueda, Jun Tazaki, Keiji Sakakida, Keiko Tsushima, Gen Shimizu; ***D:*** Akira Kurosawa; ***W:*** Akira Kurosawa, Shinobu Hashimoto, Hideo Oguni; ***C:*** Asakazu Nakai; ***M:*** Fumio Hayasaka. Venice Film Fest. '54: Silver Prize.

Seven Seconds **2005 (R)** Snipes' career isn't helped by this confusing and lackluster actioner. Professional thief Jack Tolliver (Snipes) and his crew are after an armored car when a rival gang shows up to steal a Van Gogh that's also inside. During the melee, Jack gets away with the painting but most of his crew are dead, except for one who has been taken as a hostage. Now he must rescue his partner, aided or hindered by NATO cop Kelly Anders (Outhwaite). **90m/C DVD, UMD.** *US* Wesley Snipes, Pete Lee-Wilson, Dhobi Oparei, Georgina Rylance, Tamzin Outhwaite, Serge Soric; ***D:*** Serge Soric; ***W:*** Simon Fellows; ***C:*** Michael Slovis; ***M:*** Barry Taylor. **VIDEO**

Seven Sinners *Cafe of the Seven Sinners* **1940** A South Seas cabaret singer (Dietrich) attracts sailors like flies, resulting in bar brawls, romance, and intrigue. Manly sailor Wayne falls for her. A good-natured, standard Hollywood adventure. Well cast; performed and directed with gusto. **83m/B VHS.** Marlene Dietrich, John Wayne, Albert Dekker, Broderick Crawford, Mischa Auer, Billy Gilbert, Oscar Homolka; ***D:*** Tay Garnett; ***W:*** John Meehan, Harry Tugend; ***C:*** Rudolph Mate; ***M:*** Frank Skinner.

Seven Thieves **1960** Charming performances and nice direction make this tale of the perfect crime especially watchable. Robinson, getting on in years, wants one last big heist. With the help of Collins and Steiger, he gets his chance. From the Max Catto novel "Lions at the Kill." Surprisingly witty and light-hearted for this subject matter, and good still comes out ahead of evil. **102m/C VHS, DVD.** Joan Collins, Edward G. Robinson, Eli Wallach, Rod Steiger, Alexander Scourby, Michael Dante, Berry Kroeger, Sebastian Cabot, Marcel Hillaire, John Beradino, Jonathan Kidd; ***D:*** Henry Hathaway; ***W:*** Sydney (Sidney) Boehm; ***C:*** Sam Leavitt; ***M:*** Dominic Frontiere.

The Seven-Ups 1/2 **1973 (PG)** An elite group of New York City detectives seeks to avenge the killing of a colleague and to bust crooks whose felonies are punishable by jail terms of seven years or more. Unoriginal premise portends ill; plotless cop action flick full of car chases. Scheider tries hard. Directed by the producer of "The French Connection." **109m/C VHS, DVD.** Roy Scheider, Tony LoBianco, Larry Haines, Jerry Leon; ***D:*** Philip D'Antoni.

7 Virgins 1/2 **2005** Coming-of-age drama has 16-year-old Tano (Ballesta) getting a 48-hour pass from reform school to attend his brother's wedding in Seville. Once home, Tano immediately hooks up with his best friend Richi (Carroza) and the rest of their street gang and they get into all kinds of trouble. Tano finally gets glimmers that his friends are thugs and their lives will never be anything more but can he change his own? Title refers to an Andalusian legend. Spanish with subtitles. **86m/C DVD.** *SP* Juan Jose Ballesta, Jesus Carroza, Alba Rodriguez, Vicente Romero, Julian Villagran; ***D:*** Alberto Rodriguez; ***W:*** Alberto Rodriguez, Rafael Cobos Lopez; ***C:*** Alex Catalan; ***M:*** Julio de la Rosa.

Seven Were Saved 1/2 **1947** Dull effort despite the actual footage of the Air-Sea Rescue Service's operations. A plane goes down in the Pacific Ocean and the survivors are adrift in a life raft, awaiting rescue. Relating to the recently ended WWII: one survivor is a Japanese commander on his way to a war crimes trial and two are former POWs from a Japanese camp. **72m/B DVD.** Richard Denning, Catherine Craig, Russell Hayden, Ann Doran, John Eldridge, Richard Loo, Don Castle; ***D:*** William H. Pine; ***W:*** Maxwell Shane; ***C:*** Jack Greenhalgh; ***M:*** Darrell Calker.

The Seven Year Itch **1955** Classic, sexy Monroe comedy. Stunning blonde model (who else?) moves upstairs just as happily married guy Ewell's wife leaves for a long vacation. Understandably, he gets itchy. Monroe's famous blown skirt scene is here, as well as funny situations and appealing performances. **105m/C VHS, DVD.** Marilyn Monroe, Tom Ewell, Evelyn Keyes, Sonny Tufts, Victor Moore, Doro Merande, Robert Strauss, Oscar Homolka, Carolyn Jones; ***D:*** Billy Wilder; ***W:*** Billy Wilder, George Axelrod; ***C:*** Milton Krasner; ***M:*** Alfred Newman. Golden Globes '56: Actor—Mus./Comedy (Ewell).

Seven Years Bad Luck **1921** French comic Linder has the proverbial seven years' bad luck all in one day (!) after he breaks a mirror. Original and quite funny; full of fetching sophisticated sight gags. Silent with music score. **67m/B VHS, DVD.** Max Linder, Thelma Percy, Alta Allen, Betty Peterson; ***D:*** Max Linder; ***W:*** Max Linder; ***C:*** Charles Van Enger.

Seven Years in Tibet 1/2 **1997 (PG-13)** Big budget epic of a cold-hearted Austrian mountaineer Heinrich Harrer (Pitt) who becomes a WWII POW in a British internment camp in India. When he and fellow climber Peter Aufschnaiter (Thewlis) escape, they travel to Tibet where Harrer bonds with and becomes a tutor to the young Dalai Lama (Wangchuk). Sweeping vistas and snow-capped mountain scenery does little to aid the sluggish and unfocused narrative, which tries to cover too many subplots and doesn't really get going until halfway through. Pitt's screen presence is forceful and his performance capable but hampered by a somewhat labored Austrian accent. Based on Harrer's memoirs, film ran into numerous problems, including the revelation that Harrer had Nazi ties, China's sensitivity to the storyline, and India's refusal to allow filming. Director Annaud wound up substituting the Argentine Andes for the Himalayas. **131m/C VHS, DVD, Blu-ray Disc.** Brad Pitt, David Thewlis, B.D. Wong, Jamyang Jamtsho Wangchuk, Mako, Victor Wong, Ingeborga Dapkounaite; ***D:*** Jean-Jacques Annaud; ***W:*** Becky Johnston; ***C:*** Robert Fraisse; ***M:*** John Williams.

Seventeen Again **2000** Willie (Tahj Mowry) is doing a science project involving an anti-aging formula that accidentally gets mixed into some soap that his divorced grandparents, Cat (Clarke) and Gene (Hooks), wind up using. This turns them both in 17-year-olds (Tamara Mowry as Cat and Taylor as Gene). Cat winds up going to high school with look-alike granddaughter Sydney (Tia Mowry) and has a second chance with the teenaged Gene. Meanwhile, Willie is searching for an antidote since his formula has some potentially serious flaws. That the story is silly isn't the problem—it's also incoherent. **97m/C VHS, DVD.** Tia Mowry, Tamera Mowry, Tahj Mowry, Mark Taylor, Hope Clarke, Robert Hooks; ***D:*** Jeff Byrd; ***W:*** Stewart St. John; ***C:*** John Tarver; ***M:*** Christopher Franke, Shawm Stockman. **CABLE**

17 Again 1/2 **2009 (PG-13)** Mike O'Donnell (Efron) is a star on the high school basketball team with a bright future in his grasp. Instead, he trades it to share his life with his girlfriend Scarlett (Miller) and the baby he just learned they are expecting. Almost 20 years later, Mike's (Perry) glory days are decidedly behind him—he's in a dead-end job, separated from his wife (Mann), and his own teenaged kids think he's a loser—but he's given another chance when he is miraculously transformed back to the age of 17. Unfortunately, Mike may look 17 again, but his thirtysomething outlook is totally uncool with the class of 2009. If the silly premise sounds familiar, it should, as both the original *Freaky Friday* as well as the Lindsey Lohan/Jamie Lee Curtis version are both superior to this, which says a lot. Might appeal to teen girls who simply want to stare at Efron. **102m/C DVD.** *US* Matthew Perry, Zac Efron, Leslie Mann, Thomas Lennon, Michelle Trachtenberg, Sterling Knight; ***D:*** Burr Steers; ***W:*** Jason Filardi; ***C:*** Tim Suhrstedt; ***M:*** Rolfe Kent.

1776 **1972 (G)** Musical comedy about America's first Continental Congress. The delegates battle the English and each other trying to establish a set of laws and the Declaration of Independence. Adapted from the Broadway hit with many members of the original cast. ♫ The Lees of Old Virginia; He Plays the Violin; But, Mr. Adams; Sit Down John; Till Then; Piddle, Twiddle and Resolve; Yours, Yours, Yours; Mama, Look Sharp; The Egg. **141m/C VHS, DVD.** William Daniels, Howard da Silva, Ken Howard, Donald Madden, Blythe Danner, Ronald Holgate, Virginia Vestoff, Stephen Nathan, Ralston Hill; ***D:*** Peter H. Hunt; ***C:*** Harry Stradling Jr.

The Seventeenth Bride **1984** Set in a Czechoslovakian town; a strong-willed young woman is slowly destroyed by the insanity of war and racism. **92m/C VHS, DVD.** Lisa Hartman Black, Rosemary Leach; ***D:*** Israeli Nadav Levitan.

Seventh Cavalry 1/2 **1956** A somewhat different look at Custer's defeat at the Little Big Horn. A soldier who was branded a coward for not taking part in the festivities tries to assuage his guilt by heading up the burial detail. The muddled ending tries to tell us that the Indians were afraid of Custer's horse. **75m/C VHS, DVD.** Randolph Scott, Barbara Hale, Jay C. Flippen, Jeannette Nolan, Frank Faylen, Leo Gordon, Denver Pyle, Harry Carey Jr., Michael Pate, Donald Curtis, Frank Wilcox, Pat Hogan, Russell Hicks; ***D:*** Joseph H. Lewis; ***C:*** Ray Rennahan.

The Seventh Coin 1/2 **1992 (PG-13)** The legendary King Herod minted seven coins bearing his image which have become coin collector Emil Saber's (O'Toole) obsession. (He's a homicidal lunatic who thinks he's the reincarnation of Herod anyway.) Saber has found six of the coins but the seventh has fallen into the unsuspecting hands of Salim (Chowdhry), a pickpocket who has actually snatched it from the equally unsuspecting Ronnie (Powers), an American teenager visiting Jerusalem (good local color). The two become allies when Saber comes after them. They're an appealing couple; O'Toole camps it up shamelessly; and the movie is easygoing escapism. **92m/C VHS.** Alexandra Powers, Navin Chowdhry, Peter O'Toole, John Rhys-Davies, Ally Walker; ***D:*** Dror Soref; ***W:*** Michael Lewis, Dror Soref; ***C:*** Avi (Avraham) Karpik.

The 7th Commandment 1/2 **1961** Unlikely melodrama about a man afflicted with amnesia following an auto accident. He becomes a successful evangelist only to be blackmailed by an old girlfriend. Don't you just hate when that happens? **82m/B VHS.** Jonathan Kidd, Lynn Statten; ***D:*** Irvin Berwick.

The Seventh Cross **1944** Tracy stars as one of seven men who escape from a German concentration camp. When it is discovered they're gone, the commandant nails seven crosses to seven trees, intending them for the seven escapees. Watch for Tandy ("Driving Miss Daisy") in her first screen appearance. Effective war-time drama. From the novel by Anna Seghers. **110m/B VHS.** Spencer Tracy, Signe Hasso, Hume Cronyn, Jessica Tandy, Agnes Moorehead, Herbert Rudley, Felix Bressart, Ray Collins, Alexander Granach, George Macready, Steven Geray, Karen Verne, George Zucco, Katherine Locke, Paul Guilfoyle, Kurt Katch, Konstantin Shayne, John Wengraf, Eily Malyon; ***D:*** Fred Zinnemann; ***W:*** Helen Deutsch; ***C:*** Karl Freund; ***M:*** Roy Webb.

The Seventh Dawn **1964** Cliched adventure romance set in Malaysia in 1945. Guerrilla fighter Ferris (Holden) decides to become a landowner and stay on with mistress Dhana (Capucine) after the war. Ferris's old buddy Ng (Tamba) takes off for Moscow and returns indoctrinated and determined to convert the country to Communism. Ng and his fighters exclude Ferris from their attacks until British governor Trumphrey (Goodliffe) accuses Dhana of treason and threatens to execute her. So Ferris has to get Ng or risk Dhana. The young York plays Candace, the governor's daughter who has a crush on Ferris and helps him out. Based on the novel "The Durian Tree" by Michael

Koen. **123m/C VHS.** *GB US* William Holden, Capucine, Susannah York, Tetsuro Tamba, Michael Goodliffe, Allan Cuthbertson, Maurice Denham, Beulah Quo; *D:* Lewis Gilbert; *W:* Karl Tunberg; *C:* Frederick A. (Freddie) Young; *M:* Riz Ortolani.

The Seventh Floor ✂ 1/2 **1993 (R)** Kate's computer-controlled apartment becomes her prison when a psycho takes charge of the system. **99m/C VHS, DVD.** *AU* Brooke Shields, Masaya Kato, Craig Pearce, Linda Cropper; *D:* Ian Barry.

7th Heaven ✂✂ **1927** Paris sewer worker Chico (Farrell) takes pity on waif Diane (Gaynor), who's been forced into prostitution by her vicious sister (Brockwell), after some gendarmes get suspicious. He declares they are married and lets her stay in his garret. The lug doesn't realize he loves her until he's sent to the front in WWI. Diane's been told he's dead but Chico does return (although he's now blind) and they mutually admit their love. The first romantic pairing (of 12 movies) for Gaynor and Farrell. **115m/B DVD.** Janet Gaynor, Charles Farrell, Ben Bard, David Butler, Gladys Brockwell, Marie Mosquini; *D:* Frank Borzage; *W:* Benjamin Glazer; *C:* Ernest Palmer.

Seventh Heaven ✂✂ **1998** Married Mathilde (Kiberlain) is sunk in a serious depression that only begins to lessen when she meets a mysterious doctor (Berleand) who specializes in hynosis and alternative medicine. He tells her there are seven levels of heaven—the last a sort of self-fulfilled bliss. After a successful session with the doctor, Mathilde is suddenly sexually and emotionally rejuvenated—much to the consternation of her (til then) dominating spouse, Nico (Lindon). The more Mathilde takes control, the less Nico is able to cope with their role reversals. French with subtitles. **91m/C VHS, DVD.** *FR* Sandrine Kiberlain, Vincent Lindon, Francois Berleand; *D:* Benoit Jacquot; *W:* Benoit Jacquot, Jerome Beaujour; *C:* Romain Winding.

Seventh Moon ✂ 1/2 **2008 (R)** Too much shaky-cam does not a scary horror story make. Yul (Chiou) has taken his American bride Melissa (Smart) to honeymoon in China so they can meet his family. They get stranded in a remote village where a Chinese myth that ghosts rise on the seventh lunar moon during a full moon is about to come true. **87m/C DVD.** Tim Chiou, Amy Smart, Dennis Chan; *D:* Eduardo Sanchez; *W:* Eduardo Sanchez; *C:* Wah-Chen Lam; *M:* Tony Cora, Kent Sparling. **VIDEO**

The Seventh Seal ✂✂✂✂ *Det Sjunde Inseglet* **1956** As the plague sweeps through Europe a weary knight convinces "death" to play one game of chess with him. If the knight wins, he and his wife will be spared. The game leads to a discussion of religion and the existence of God. Considered by some Bergman's masterpiece. Von Sydow is stunning as the knight. In Swedish with English subtitles. **96m/B VHS, DVD.** *SW* Gunnar Bjornstrand, Max von Sydow, Bibi Andersson, Bengt Ekerot, Nils Poppe, Gunnel Lindblom; *D:* Ingmar Bergman; *W:* Ingmar Bergman; *C:* Gunnar Fischer; *M:* Erik Nordgren. Cannes '57: Grand Jury Prize.

The Seventh Sign ✂✂ **1988 (R)** A pregnant woman realizes that the mysterious stranger boarding in her house and the bizarre events that accompany him are connected to Biblical prophesy and her unborn child. Tries hard, but it's difficult to get involved in the supernatural goings-on. **105m/C VHS, DVD.** Demi Moore, Jurgen Prochnow, Michael Biehn, John Heard, Peter Friedman, Manny Jacobs, John Taylor, Lee Garlington, Akosua Busia; *D:* Carl Schultz; *W:* W.W. Wicket; *C:* Juan Ruiz-Anchia; *M:* Jack Nitzsche.

The Seventh Stream ✂✂ 1/2 **2001** Filmed on location in the west of Ireland and based on the Celtic legend of the selkies. Owen Quinn (Glenn) is a fisherman whose life is empty since the death of his wife. Then he comes to the rescue of Mairead (Burrows), a beautiful and mysterious woman with strong ties to the sea. Owen opens his heart and home to her but will Mairead vanish as easily as she appeared? **98m/C VHS, DVD.** Scott Glenn, Saffron Burrows, John Lynch, Fiona Shaw, Eamon Morrissey; *D:* John Gray; *W:* John Gray; *C:* Seamus Deasy; *M:* Ernest Troost. **TV**

The Seventh Veil ✂✂✂ 1/2 **1946** A concert pianist loses the use of her hands in a fire, and with it her desire to live. Through the help of her friends and a hypnotizing doctor, she regains her love for life. Superb, dark psycho-drama. Todd as the pianist and Mason as her guardian are both unforgettable. Wonderful music and staging. **91m/B VHS.** *GB* James Mason, Ann Todd, Herbert Lom, Hugh McDermott, Albert Lieven; *D:* Compton Bennett. Oscars '46: Orig. Screenplay.

The Seventh Victim ✂✂✂ **1943** Another Val Lewton-produced low-budget exercise in shadowy suggestion, dealing with a woman searching for her lost sister, who'd gotten involved with Satanists. The Hays Office's squeamishness regarding subject matter makes the film's action a bit cloudy but it remains truly eerie. **71m/B VHS, DVD.** Kim Hunter, Tom Conway, Jean Brooks, Hugh Beaumont, Erford Gage, Isabel Jewell, Evelyn Brent; *D:* Mark Robson; *W:* Charles "Blackie" O'Neal.

The Seventh Voyage of Sinbad ✂✂✂ **1958 (G)** Sinbad seeks to restore his fiancee from the midget size to which an evil magician (Thatcher) has reduced her. Ray Harryhausen works his animation magic around a well-developed plot and engaging performances by the real actors. Great score and fun, fast-moving plot. **94m/C VHS, DVD, Blu-ray Disc.** Kerwin Mathews, Kathryn Grant, Torin Thatcher, Richard Eyer, Alec Mango, Danny Green, Harold Kasket, Alfred Brown; *D:* Nathan "Jerry" Juran; *W:* Kenneth Kolb; *C:* Wilkie Cooper; *M:* Bernard Herrmann. Natl. Film Reg. '08.

The '70s ✂✂ 1/2 **2000** Follows "The '60s" miniseries with the same superficial exploration of the decade seen through the eyes of four friends and lots of music. (Disco rules!) Dexter (Torry), Byron (Rowe), Eileen (Shaw), and Christine (Smart) are all at Kent State on that fateful day with the National Guard and their lives continue through numerous hot-button issues, including Watergate, feminism, drugs, sex, the Black Panthers, the environment, and religious cults. Cast is surprisingly strong. **170m/C VHS, DVD.** Brad Rowe, Guy Torry, Vinessa Shaw, Amy Smart, Kathryn Harrold, Graham Beckel, Tina Lifford, Chandra West, Robert Joy, Jeanetta Arnette, Michael Easton, Peggy Lipton; *D:* Peter Werner; *W:* Mitch Brian, Kevin Willmott; *C:* Neil Roach; *M:* Peter Manning Robinson. **TV**

75 Degrees ✂✂ 1/2 *75 Degrees in July* **2000** A family reunion leads to the reopening of old wounds in this downbeat drama. Letty Anderson (Silas) visits her family's Texas ranch to see her parents and married sister, Kay (Swedberg). Letty is a successful artist with a show at a local gallery and Kay is resentful because their manipulative mother, Jo Beth (Knight), squashed her dreams of becoming a singer. Instead, Kay takes her frustrations out on ranch foreman hubby Jed (Moses), who has his own problems with her family. Jo Beth's husband, Rick (Yulin), is neglectful and callous and treats everyone badly. Not exactly a family you'd want to spend a lot of time with, although the cast is compelling. **98m/C DVD.** Heidi Swedberg, Harris Yulin, Shirley Knight, William R. Moses, Karen Silas; *D:* Hyatt Bass; *W:* Hyatt Bass; *C:* Michael Barrett; *M:* Stephen (Steve) Edwards.

Severance ✂ **1988** An ex-pilot attempts to save his daughter from the world of drugs and violence. **93m/C VHS.** Lou Liotta, Lisa Nicole Wolpe, Linda Christian-Jones; *D:* David Max Steinberg.

Severance ✂✂ **2006 (R)** In a team-building exercise, the sales division of an international arms manufacturer heads for a weekend retreat at a desolate chalet located in a Hungarian forest. But it seems the woods are filled with booby-traps and crazed commandos determined to see them all dead. An extreme example of how team spirit and cooperation will save your life (not to mention your job). **96m/C DVD.** *GE GB* Tim (McInnerny) McInnery, Laura Harris, Toby Stephens, Danny Dyer, Claudie Blakley, Andy Nyman, Babou Ceesay; *D:* Chris Smith; *W:* Chris Smith, James Moran; *C:* Ed Wild; *M:* Christian Henson.

The Severed Arm WOOF! **1973 (R)** Trapped in a cave, five men are compelled to cut off the arm of a companion in order to ward off starvation. Then as luck would have it, they're rescued. Years later, one by one they meet a bloody demise. Is it the one-armed man? **89m/C VHS, DVD.** Deborah Walley, Marvin Kaplan, Paul Carr, John Crawford, David Cannon; *D:* Thomas Alderman.

Severed Ties ✂ 1/2 **1992 (R)** Brilliant genetic scientist experiments with human limb regeneration in order to re-grow his accidentally severed arm. His strange mixture of lizard and serial-killer genes results in a repulsive repitilian limb with a nasty habit of slithering out of his shoulder. His mother discovers his experiments and tries to sell his discovery to the Nazis but her son escapes into a bizarre subterranean society and vows revenge. So bad it's just bad. **95m/C VHS.** Billy Morrissette, Elke Sommer, Oliver Reed, Garrett Morris; *D:* Damon Santostefano.

Severed Ways ✂ **2009** In the 11th-century, two Vikings are the only survivors of a massacre of their North American camp and must struggle to live amidst harsh conditions. Minimal, unconventional narrative with a score comprised of heavy-metal music. **107m/C DVD.** Dave Perry, Tony Stone, Fiore Tedesco, Noelle Bailey, James Fuentes; *D:* Tony Stone; *W:* Tony Stone; *C:* Nathan Corbin, Damien Paris.

Sex ✂✂ 1/2 **1920** Interesting dated relic. Morality play about a Broadway star who uses her charms to destroy a marriage only to dump her lover for richer prospects. The businessman she lands then shamelessly betrays her. What a title, especially for its time! **87m/B VHS.** Adrienne Renault, Louise Glaum, Irving Cummings, Peggy Pearce, Myrtle Stedman; *D:* Fred Niblo.

Sex Adventures of the Three Musketeers WOOF! **1971** Soft-core spoof of the Dumas classic. Dubbed. **79m/C VHS.** *GE* Inga Steeger, Achim Hammer, Peter Graf, Jurg Coray; *D:* Erwin C. Dietrich; *W:* Erwin C. Dietrich; *C:* Peter Baumgartner; *M:* Walter Baumgartner.

Sex and Breakfast ✂ 1/2 **2007 (R)** Having couples troubles, James (Culkin) and Heather (Dziena) and Ellis (Becker) and Renee (Dushku) experiment with group sex while trying to figure out what makes a relationship successful. But jealousy, confusion, and insecurity make things as difficult as you might expect. Not as sexual as you might expect though, despite the title and rating. **81m/C DVD.** Macaulay Culkin, Alexis Dziena, Kuno Becker, Eliza Dushku, Joanna Miles, Eric Lively, Tracie Thoms, Jaime Ray Newman; *D:* Miles Brandman; *W:* Miles Brandman; *C:* Mark Schwartzband.

Sex and Buttered Popcorn **1991 (R)** Stylish and entertaining documentary of the Hollywood sexploitation moguls, and their films, from the 1920s through the 1950s. These films shamelessly catered to audience's prurient interests, but typically delivered saccharin-coated morality messages and stock footage of routine baby births or the horrible effects of sexually transmitted diseases. Hosted by Ned Beatty, and featuring clips from the actual films, plus an interview with the widow of Kroger Babb, the most notorious of the exploiteers. A real hoot. **70m/C VHS, DVD.** David Friedman; *D:* Sam Harrison.

Sex and Death 101 ✂ **2007 (R)** Crude but stupid sex fantasy has Roderick Blank (a miscast Baker, who just comes across as too sweet) receiving an anonymous email that lists the names of the 101 women he will have sex with before he dies. The first 29 are accurate, including his fiance Fiona (Bowen), so Rod dumps her and gets busy. Then there's Ryder, playing a bizarre feminist avenger nicknamed Death Nell, who kills off high-profile sex sleazes. **117m/C DVD, Blu-ray Disc.** Simon Baker, Winona Ryder, Leslie Bibb, Julie Bowen, Mindy Cohn, Robert Wisdom, Patton Oswalt, Frances Fisher, Tanc Sade; *D:* Daniel Waters; *W:* Daniel Waters; *C:* Daryn Okada; *M:* Rolfe Kent.

Sex & Drugs & Rock & Roll **2010** A perhaps-too-stylish bio of colorful '70s British punk rock pioneer Ian Drury (Serkis), who had to deal with childhood polio (which left him partially paralyzed) to fulfill his dreams. The film dwells as much (if not more) on his chaotic family life as his music career. Drury died from cancer in 2000 although the bio ends before that. Title refers to Drury's 1977 hit song. **115m/C DVD.** *GB* Andy Serkis, Ray Winstone, Olivia Williams, Bill Milner, Naomie Harris, Wesley Nelson, Mackenzie Crook, Toby Jones, Tom Hughes, Luke Evans; *D:* Mat Whitecross; *W:* Paul Viragh; *C:* Christopher Ross; *M:* Chaz Jankel.

Sex and Fury ✂✂ *Furyo anego den: Inoshika Ocho* **1973** Ocho (Reiko Ike) is a gambler, thief, and all around butt-kicking machine who has vowed revenge on the murderers of her father. When a fellow gambler is killed, his dying wish is for Ocho to fetch his sister from a brothel she has been sold to. The final scene features Ocho battling an entire gang with swords and sharpened gambling tiles while completely naked. Don't say we didn't warn you. **88m/C DVD.** *JP* Akemi Negisha, Reiko Ike, Ryoko Ema, Yoko Hori, Naomi Oka, Rena Ichinose, Rie Saotome, Jun Midorikawa, Tadashi Naruse, Takashi Shirai; *D:* Norifumi Suzuki; *W:* Norifumi Suzuki, Taro Bonten, Masahiro Kakefuda; *C:* Motoya Washyo; *M:* Ichiro Araki.

Sex & Lies in Sin City: The Ted Binion Scandal ✂✂ **2008** Sleazy true story about a stripper, a Vegas casino heir, murder, and a trial. Stripper Sandy (Suvari) has it made when she shacks up with smitten casino heir/junkie Ted Binion (Modine). Ted is found dead and Sandy becomes the prime suspect, especially after her guy-on-the-side Rick (Schaech) is caught with some of Ted's property. Adapted from the book "Murder in Sin City" by Jeff German. **89m/C DVD.** Mena Suvari, Matthew Modine, Johnathon Schaech, Marcia Gay Harden; *D:* Peter Medak; *W:* Teena Booth; *C:* Anthony B. Richmond; *M:* Ed Shearmur. **CABLE**

Sex and Lucia ✂✂ *Lucia y el Sexo* **2001** Sexually explicit, if confusing, story finds waitress Lucia (Vega) learning that her ex-boyfriend, writer Lorenzo (Ulloa), has supposedly died. So, she decides to revisit the island where they first met. Lucia meets scuba-diver Carlos (Freire) who lives with Elena (Nimri), who has ties to Lorenzo that Lucia never suspected. Elena's brother, Pepe (Camara), happens to be Lorenzo's best friend and introduces nanny Belen (Anaya) into the menage and it all just kinda goes 'round and 'round. Spanish with subtitles. **128m/C DVD.** *SP* Paz Vega, Tristan Ulloa, Najwa Nimri, Daniel Freire, Elena Anaya, Silvia Llanos, Javier Camara; *D:* Julio Medem; *W:* Julio Medem; *C:* Kiko de la Rica; *M:* Alberto Iglesias.

Sex & Mrs. X ✂✂ 1/2 **2000** New York magazine journalist Joanna Scott (Hamilton) thought her marriage was as successful as her career—until husband Dale (Bick) leaves her for a younger woman. So Joanna is happy to go to Paris to interview the notorious Madame Simone (Bisset), but she winds up learning just as much about herself and how to face her new future. **91m/C VHS, DVD.** Linda Hamilton, Jacqueline Bisset, Paolo Seganti, Stewart Bick, Peter MacNeill, Tracy Bregman, Daniel Pilon; *D:* Arthur Allan Seidelman; *W:* Elisa Bell; *C:* Don E. Fauntleroy; *M:* Joseph Conlan. **CABLE**

Sex and the City 2 **2010** Returning writer/director King has tried to keep the sequel's plot on ice but here's what we hear happens. The gal pals are all back in NYC and settled down but not really. Carrie gets pregnant and she and Big have major issues since he doesn't want to be a dad and takes off. Samantha is now the only single, childless female left in the quartet but ex-lover Smith shows up and offers to change one of those two things. Charlotte and Miranda have domestic issues. Rumor has it that a Carrie ex returns to rekindle some sparks since Big is away. **m/C DVD.** *US* Sarah Jessica Parker, Kim Cattrall, Kristin Davis, Cynthia Nixon, Christopher Noth, David Eigenberg, Evan Handler, Jason Lewis, Mario Cantone, Willie Garson, Penelope Cruz; *Cameos:* Liza Minnelli; *D:* Michael Patrick King; *W:* Michael Patrick King; *C:* John Thomas.

Sex and the City: The Movie ✂✂ 1/2 **2008 (R)** What's essentially a supersized episode of the hugely popular HBO series becomes the mother of all chick flicks. The well-heeled galpals, now over forty but still able to spend a ridiculous amount of time together, serve up more of the same as they each ponder the fate of their impossibly fabulous domestic lives. This time it's Carrie's (Parker) non-wedding to Mr. Big (Noth) that anchors the break-ups and make-ups. What the plot lacks in substance (and at times, sense), it makes up for in style. Davis's Charlotte is especially sharp amid the melodrama and silliness, but it's the witty, shameless glee of the collective sisterhood that's the real draw. **135m/C DVD.** *US* Sarah Jessica Parker, Kim Cattrall, Kristin Davis, Cynthia Nixon, Christopher Noth, David Eigenberg, Jason Lewis, Evan Handler, Jennifer Hudson, Willie Garson, Mario Cantone, Lynn Cohen, Candice Bergen, Lynn Cohen; ***D:*** Michael Patrick King; ***W:*** Michael Patrick King; ***C:*** John Thomas; ***M:*** Aaron Zigman.

Sex and the College Girl **1964** Folks talk about their relationship problems while vacationing in Puerto Rico. Tame talkfest providing Grodin with his first role. Included as part of Joe Bob Brigg's "Sleaziest Movies in the History of the World" series, probably just for the title. **100m/C VHS.** Charles Grodin, Richard Arlen, Luana Anders; ***D:*** Joseph Adler.

Sex and the Other Man *Captive* **1995 (R)** Bill's (Eldard) having this little impotence problem, which girlfriend Jessica (Wuhrer) naturally finds frustrating. So much so that she succumbs to the charms of her married boss, Arthur (Tucci). But when Bill catches them together in bed, his reaction is something none of them expected. Based on the play "Captive" by Paul Weitz. **89m/C VHS, DVD.** Ron Eldard, Kari Wuhrer, Stanley Tucci; ***D:*** Karl Slovin; ***W:*** Karl Slovin; ***C:*** Frank Prinzi; ***M:*** Anton Sanko.

Sex and the Single Girl 1/2 **1964** Curtis is a reporter for a trashy magazine who intends to write an expose on "The International Institute of Advanced Marital and Pre-Marital Studies," an organization run by Wood. Curtis poses as a man having marital trouble, using his neighbor's name and marital problems, in order to get close to Wood. Things get sticky when Wood wants to meet Curtis' wife and three women show up claiming to be her. This confusing but amusing tale twists and turns until it reaches a happy ending. Loosely based on the book by Helen Gurley Brown. **114m/C VHS.** Tony Curtis, Natalie Wood, Henry Fonda, Lauren Bacall, Mel Ferrer, Fran Jeffries, Leslie Parrish, Edward Everett Horton, Larry Storch, Count Basie; ***D:*** Richard Quine; ***W:*** David R. Schwartz; ***C:*** Charles B(ryant) Lang Jr.; ***M:*** Neal Hefti.

Sex and the Single Parent 1/2 **1982** St. James and Farrell, both divorced, both with kids, have a relationship. Complications set in—just how does one be a single parent and have a fulfilling sex life in this day and age? **98m/C VHS.** Susan St. James, Mike Farrell, Dori Brenner, Warren Berlinger, Julie Sommars, Barbara Rhoades; ***D:*** Jackie Cooper. **TV**

Sex and Zen **1993** Softcore Hong Kong sex film based on the 17th century novel "Prayer Mat for the Flesh" by Li Yu. Mei Yang (Ng) gets married to beautiful Yuk Heung (Yip) but intends to commit adultery as often as possible. There's lots of bizarre sexual practices and Yuk ends up in a brothel while Mei finds his decadent lifestyle not quite as entertaining as he imagined. Cantonese with subtitles or dubbed. **99m/C VHS, DVD.** *HK* Lawrence Ng, Amy Yip, Kent Cheng, Isabella Chow, Lo Lieh, Carrie Ng; ***D:*** Michael Mak; ***W:*** Lee Ying Kit; ***C:*** Peter Ngor; ***M:*** Chan Wing Leung.

Sex Crimes **1992** A tough female judge is brutally raped and she keeps the attack a secret. However, she does ask a friendly police detective to teach her how to use a gun. He's suspicious of her reasons and decides to trail her as she sets out for revenge on her attacker. Predictable actioner. **90m/C VHS, DVD.** Jeffery Osterhage, Maria Richwine, Fernando Garzon, Craig Alan, Grace Morley; ***D:*** David Garcia.

Sex Drive **2008 (R)** Desperate 18-year-old virgin Ian (Zuckerman), tempted by online chats with "Ms. Tasty," drags his geeky buddy Lance (Clarke) on a road trip in a stolen 1969 GTO from Wisconsin to Tennessee to consummate his cyber-love. Also along for the ride (for no apparent recent other than to be grossed out by the boys' behavior) is female friend Felicia (Crew). Their trip takes them to Amish country during its annual sex orgy, of course, among other non-stop ridiculous, raunchy situations. Despite its obvious attempt to cash in on the horny teen flick revival (first re-launched by "American Pie," then done better years later by "Superbad"), this one lacks the heart of its more successful predecessors. **109m/C DVD, Blu-ray Disc.** *US* Josh Zuckerman, Amanda Crew, Clark Duke, James Marsden, Seth Green, Katrina Bowden, Alice Greczyn; ***D:*** Sean Anders; ***W:*** Sean Anders, John Morris; ***C:*** Tim Orr; ***M:*** Stephen Trask.

Sex, Drugs, and Rock-n-Roll **WOOF!** **1984** Several girls frequent a rock club looking for all the action they can get their hands on. **90m/C VHS.** Jeanne Silver, Sharon Kane, Tish Ambrose, Josey Duval.

Sex, Drugs, Rock & Roll: Eric Bogosian **1991 (R)** Bogosian's 1990 concert performance, taped live at the Wilur Theate in Boston, exhibits the electricity and finely nuanced characters for which he is justly famous. The characters share a depressingly negative side, however, which keeps this film from being strictly belly-laugh territory. **96m/C VHS.** Eric Bogosian; ***D:*** John McNaughton; ***W:*** Eric Bogosian.

Sex is Comedy **2002** Breillat's plot is a fictionalized re-creation of her own difficulties filming the crucial sex scene between a 15-year-old girl (Mesquida, reprising her role) and her older boyfriend (Colin) for her 2001 film "Fat Girl." Breillat's stand-in as director is the neurotic and demanding Jeanne (Parillaud), whose troubles include lousy weather, leads who can't stand each other, and a problematic prosthetic penis. Jeanne irritates her actors and crew (and they her) and only finds a sympathetic ally in her smitten assistant Leo (Wanninger). Actors are always quick to say that filming sex scenes is not erotic and here's the proof. French with subtitles. **92m/C DVD.** Anne Parillaud, Ashley Wanninger, Dominique Colladant; ***D:*** Catherine Breillat; ***W:*** Catherine Breillat; ***C:*** Laurent Machuel.

Sex Is Crazy **1979** A melange from Italian horror director Franco containing some epic, some horror, some sex, some sitcom, and some documentary. Little green aliens touch down and impregnate earth women in one skit. In another, a gambler's girlfriend demands two thugs ravage her for the sheer sexual thrill. And in a third, a severed hand commands a heroine to martyr herself to the great god Cucufat. Spanish with English subtitles. **81m/C VHS.** *SP* Lina Romay, Anthony (Jose, J. Antonio, J.A.) Mayans, Tony Skios; ***D:*** Jess (Jesus) Franco.

sex, lies and videotape **1989 (R)** Acclaimed, popular independent film by first-timer Soderbergh, detailing the complex relations among a childless married couple, the wife's adulterous sister, and a mysterious college friend of the husband's obsessed with videotaping women as they talk about their sex lives. Heavily awarded, including first prize at Cannes. Confidently uses much (too much?) dialogue and slow (too slow?) pace. **101m/C VHS, DVD.** James Spader, Andie MacDowell, Peter Gallagher, Laura San Giacomo, Ron Vawter, Steven Brill; ***D:*** Steven Soderbergh; ***W:*** Steven Soderbergh; ***C:*** Walt Lloyd; ***M:*** Cliff Martinez. Cannes '89: Actor (Spader), Film; Ind. Spirit '90: Actress (MacDowell), Director (Soderbergh), Film, Support. Actress (San Giacomo); L.A. Film Critics '89: Actress (MacDowell), Natl. Film Reg. '06;; Sundance '89: Aud. Award.

Sex, Love and Cold Hard Cash 1/2 **1993 (PG-13)** Sarah (Williams) is a high-priced hooker whose life savings ($20 million in stocks and bonds) have just been stolen. She hires an ex-con (Denison) to help recover the money and the two partners find themselves on the wrong side of some Mob trouble as well. Enough twists to keep a viewer interested as well as the prerequisite amount of shootings and chase scenes. **86m/C VHS.** JoBeth Williams, Anthony John (Tony) Denison, Joel Swetow, Henry Brown, Bradford English, Robert Forster, Eric Pierpoint, Richard Sarafian, Tobin Bell; ***D:*** Harry S. Longstreet; ***W:*** Harry S. Longstreet; ***C:*** Rob Draper; ***M:*** John Keane.

The Sex Machine **WOOF!** *Conviene far Bene L'Amore* **1975 (R)** In the year 2037, a scientist finds two of the world's greatest lovers and unites them so he can transform their reciprocating motion into electricity. It worked on paper. Italian with subtitles. **80m/C VHS.** *IT* Agostina Belli, Elenora Giorgi, Christian de Sica, Gigi Proietti, Adriana Asti; ***D:*** Pasquale Festa Campanile; ***W:*** Pasquale Festa Campanile; ***C:*** Franco Di Giacomo; ***M:*** Fred Borgusto.

The Sex Monster **1999 (R)** Unhappy husband convinces reluctant wife to get involved in a menage-a-trois. Only she's more turned on by the other woman than he is. Not very funny for a comedy, and not very sexy for a flick with the word "sex" in the title. Binder does Woody Allen without the humor, but then, so does Woody lately. **97m/C VHS, DVD.** Mike Binder, Mariel Hemingway, Renee Humphrey, Taylor Nichols, Missy (Melissa) Crider, Stephen Baldwin; ***D:*** Mike Binder; ***W:*** Mike Binder; ***C:*** Keith L. Smith.

Sex on the Run **WOOF!** *Cassanova and Co.; Some Like It Cool* **1978 (R)** Love-starved wife of an oil-rich sheik, stimulated by the idea of having Casanova for her lover, teases her master into delivering him, but Casanova finds peace in the arms of three convent lovelies. Disgusting, amateurish, and offensive. **88m/C VHS, DVD.** Tony Curtis, Marisa Berenson, Britt Ekland; ***D:*** Francosis Legrand.

Sex Positive **2009 (R)** Documentary is a belated portrait of gay activist Richard Berkovitz and his experiences in 1970s New York when he worked as an S&M hustler, giving him a front seat to the burgeoning AIDS epidemic. Berkowitz was early to espouse safe-sex practices (and was frequently discredited by the gay community among others). And, along with activist Michael Callan, he wrote the first safe sex guide although his experiences eventually led to a drug addiction. Wein has interviews with the HIV-positive Berkowitz as well as others in the community and uses various archival video from newscasts as well. **76m/C VHS, DVD.** *US* ***D:*** Daryl Wein; ***C:*** Alex Bergman; ***M:*** Michael Tremante.

Sex Through a Window *Extreme Close-Up* **1972 (R)** TV reporter becomes an obsessive voyeur after filing a report on high tech surveillance equipment. Flimsy premise is a yucky, lame excuse to show skin. **81m/C VHS.** James McMullan, James A. Watson Jr., Kate Woodville, Bara Byrnes, Al Checco, Antony Carbone; ***D:*** Jeannot Szwarc; ***W:*** Michael Crichton.

Sex with a Smile **1976 (R)** Five slapstick episodes by five different directors with lots of sexual satire pointed at religion and politics in Italy. Don't know much about Italy? Then you'll be left out of the joke here. And really, only one episode is funny anyway (the one with Feldman of "Young Frankenstein" fame). **100m/C VHS.** *IT* Marty Feldman, Edwige Fenech, Alex Marino, Enrico Monterrano, Giovanna Ralli; ***D:*** Sergio Martino.

Sexpot **1988 (R)** A voluptuous woman's rich husbands mysteriously keep dying, but not before they leave their fortunes to her. **95m/C VHS.** Ruth (Coreen) Collins, Troy Donahue, Joyce Lyons, Gregory Patrick, Frank Stewart, Jack Carter; ***D:*** Chuck Vincent.

Sextette **WOOF!** **1978 (PG)** Lavish film about an elderly star who is constantly interrupted by former spouses and well-wishers while on a honeymoon with her sixth husband. West unwisely came out of retirement for this last film role, based on her own play. Exquisitely embarrassing to watch. Interesting cast. **91m/C VHS, DVD.** Mae West, Timothy Dalton, Ringo Starr, George Hamilton, Dom DeLuise, Tony Curtis, Alice Cooper, Keith Moon, George Raft, Rona Barrett, Walter Pidgeon, Regis Philbin; ***D:*** Ken Hughes; ***W:*** Herbert Baker; ***C:*** James A. Crabe; ***M:*** Artie Butler.

Sexton Blake and the Hooded Terror **1938** Sexton Blake a British private detective a la Holmes, is after "The Snake," a master criminal, and his gang The Hooded Terror. One of a series of melodramatic adventures interesting chiefly for Slaughter's performance as the gangleader. **70m/B VHS.** *GB* Tod Slaughter, Greta Gynt, George Curzon; ***D:*** George King.

Sexual Intent **1994 (R)** Based on the true story of pathological liar John Walsome, known as "the Sweetheart Scammer," who seduced and robbed more than 40 women. This con artist transformed himself into whatever kind of Mr. Right his victim needed—until he picked on the wrong woman. **88m/C VHS.** Gary Hudson, Michele Brin, Sarah Hill; ***D:*** Kurt MacCarley; ***W:*** Kurt MacCarley.

The Sexual Life of the Belgians 1/2 *La Vie Sexuelle des Belges* **1994** Autobiographical comedy of sexual manners covering 1950 to 1978. Jan Bucquoy (Compere) grows up with a grim mother and immediately takes an interest in sex and beautiful women, which only heightens as he winds up in Brussels during the hedonistic '60s. He has a short, disastrous marriage, lots of affairs, not much sense, and a mocking disregard for Belgian provincialism. French with subtitles. **80m/C VHS.** *BE* Jean-Henri Compere, Isabella Legros, Sophie Schneider, Michele Shor; ***D:*** Jan Bucquoy; ***W:*** Jan Bucquoy; ***C:*** Michel Baudour.

Sexual Malice **1993 (R)** Another erotic thriller finds a bored wife involved in an obsessive affair with a mystery man who has murder on his mind. Also available in an unrated version. **96m/C VHS, DVD.** Diana Barton, John Laughlin, Chad McQueen, Edward Albert, Don Swayze, Kathy Shower, Samantha (Sam) Phillips; ***D:*** Jag Mundhra; ***W:*** Carl Austin; ***C:*** James Mathers.

Sexual Response **1992 (R)** Eve, a radio talk show "sexologist," is ironically unhappy in her marriage but scoffs at her producer's suggestion of an affair. That is until she meets a brash sculptor and they begin a torrid, and increasingly obsessive, romance. Her lover suggests that her husband have an "accident" with his hunting rifle, but Eve refuses and throws him out. The sculptor, however, breaks into the husband's loft to steal the rifle and finds some news clippings about the man's past that could ruin the lives of many. Little more than an excuse for torrid love scenes. Also available in an unrated version. **87m/C VHS.** Shannon Tweed, Catherine Oxenberg, Vernon Wells, Emile Levisetti; ***D:*** Yaky Yosha.

Sexual Roulette **1996 (R)** A distaff and decidedly raunchier "Indecent Proposal." Jed and Sally wind up in money trouble and get in deeper by trying to recoup their loses (and losing bigtime) in a Vegas horse race. Then a rich blonde with some kinky preferences makes Jed an offer he can't afford to refuse. The unrated version is six minutes longer. **90m/C VHS, DVD.** Tane McClure, Tim Abell, Gabriella Hall, Richard Gabai, Myles O'Brien, G. Gordon Baer; ***D:*** Gary Graver; ***W:*** Sean McGinley; ***C:*** Gary Graver.

Sexus 1/2 *Nuit la Plus Longue; Enfer Dans la Peau* **1964** Beautiful Virginia (de Solen) is kidnapped by Blackie (Tissier) and his cohorts and held in an abandoned farmhouse until her father pays her ransom. In the meantime, her looks provoke both jealousy and passion. French with subtitles. **88m/B VHS.** *FR* Willy Braque, Virginia De Soten, Yves Duffaut, Annie Jasse, Alain Tissier; ***D:*** Jose Benazeraf; ***W:*** Jose Benazeraf; ***C:*** Alain Derobe; ***M:*** Chet Baker.

Sexy Beast 1/2 **2000 (R)** This British suspense/thriller is not only tense and caustically funny at times, it also has the guy who played Gandhi as a snarling, bad-ass gangster. Ben Kingsley plays Logan, who's sent to southern Spain to lure retired gangster "Gal" Dove (Winstone) back to England for the standard "one last job." When Gal refuses, Logan threatens non-non-violence on Gal's wife Deedee (Redman) and pals Aitch (Kendall, in his last role) and Jackie (White). Gal is forced into accepting after some unfortunate events, and the plot, masterminded by Logan's boss Teddy (McShane), is carried out. After the caper is done, however, Gal will have a harder time relaxing poolside with the reminders of the "sexy beast" of his criminal life all too close. Kingsley dominates the movie as the profanity-spewing Logan, but the rest of the cast also turn in outstanding performances. **88m/C VHS, DVD.** *GB* Ray Winstone, Ben Kingsley, Ian McShane, Amanda Redman, James Fox, Robert Atiko, Julianne White, Cavan Kendall, Alvaro Monje; ***D:*** Jonathan Glazer; ***W:*** Louis Mellis, David Scinto; ***C:*** Ivan Bird; ***M:*** Roque Banos. Broadcast Film Critics '02: Support. Actor (Kingsley).

S.F.W. **1994 (R)** Get out your cliche-o-meter for another look at Generation X. Suburban teen Cliff Spab (Dorff) unwillingly becomes a media sensation during a terrorist hostage crisis at a convenience store. The phrasemaking teen's apathetic words are adopted by his peers just as he realizes that there is something he actually cares about—fellow hostage Wendy Pfister (Witherspoon), a cheerleader who wouldn't have given him the time of day before. A somewhat heavy-handed commentary on fame in our tabloid-intensive society. Title acronym stands for "So F***ing What." Many reviewers had a similar reaction. Based on the novel by Andrew Wellman. **92m/C VHS, DVD.** Stephen Dorff, Reese Witherspoon, Jake Busey, Joey Lauren Adams, Pamela Gidley, David Barry Gray, Jack Noseworthy, Richard Portnow; ***D:*** Jefery Levy; ***W:*** Jefery Levy, James Foley.

Shack Out on 101 **1955** A waitress (Moore) in an isolated cafe on a busy highway notices suspicious doings among her customers. What could they be up to? Communist subversion, of course. Of-its-era anti-pinko propoganda, but with a twist: Moore uncovers commie plots, pleases her customers, and fends off unwelcome lecherous advances all in 80 minutes, on a single set! **80m/B VHS.** Lee Marvin, Terry Moore, Keenan Wynn, Frank Lovejoy, Whit Bissell, Jess Barker, Donald Murphy, Frank De Kova, Len Lesser, Fred Gabourie; ***D:*** Edward Dein; ***W:*** Edward Dein, Mildred Dein; ***C:*** Floyd Crosby; ***M:*** Paul Dunlap, Louis Prima.

Shackleton **2002** Stirring adventure about the ill-fated expedition of Sir Ernest Shackleton (Branagh) to Antarctica in 1914. His ship, the Endurance, gets trapped in ice and eventually sinks, leaving Shackleton and his crew of 27 to set up camp on a nearby island. Shackleton and two of the crew set out for help to a whaling station on South Georgia Island—an unbelievably difficult journey of survival for those travelling and those left behind. **200m/C VHS, DVD.** Kenneth Branagh, Kevin McNally, Chris Larkin, Mark McGann, Lorcan Cranitch, Nicholas (Nick) Rowe, Pip Torrens, Shaun Dooley, Matt(hew) Day; ***D:*** Charles Sturridge; ***W:*** Charles Sturridge; ***C:*** Henry Braham; ***M:*** Adrian Johnston. **CABLE**

Shade **2003 (R)** Glamorous group of LA card sharks finds it's a very bad idea to scam the mob and need to take on ultimate legend "The Dean" (Stallone) to worm their way out of dire straits. Nieman, in his first directorial feature, shows that you can still flop with a winning hand as he leads the talent of this A-list of actors down the river. **95m/C VHS, DVD.** Sylvester Stallone, Gabriel Byrne, Melanie Griffith, Hal Holbrook, Thandie Newton, Stuart Townsend, Dina Merrill, Bo Hopkins, Jamie Foxx, Patrick Bauchau, Louis Freese, Roger Guenveur Smith, Charles Rocket, Michael Dorn, Jack Conley, Frank Medrano, Glenn Plummer, Damien Nieman; ***D:*** Damien Nieman; ***W:*** Damien Nieman; ***C:*** Anthony B. Richmond; ***M:*** Christopher Young.

Shades of Black **1993** Young, small-town photographer/athlete Kate becomes the romantic obsession of charismatic, older artist Lilly. But Lilly's manipulations also hide the deeper secret of her mental instability, which soon proves dangerous to Kate. **115m/C VHS.** ***D:*** Mary Haverstick.

Shades of Darkness **1/2 2000 (R)** Stephen King sort of story has to do with a woman (Trebilcock) who returns to her small hometown and finds that supernatural forces are at work. **90m/C DVD.** John Maczko, Annie Trebilcock; ***D:*** Christopher Johnson.

Shades of Fear *Great Moments in Aviation* **1993 (R)** Adventurous would-be aviatrix Gabriel Angel (Ayola), who's sailing from Grenada to England, is mistakenly assigned a room with Duncan (Pryce) and decides to pose as his wife to avoid a scandal. But a fellow passenger (Hurt) believes Duncan is also the art forger who ran off with his wife and caused her death. On their last night at sea, there's a final confrontation. **93m/C VHS, DVD.** *GB* Jonathan Pryce, Rakie Ayola, John Hurt, Vanessa Redgrave, Dorothy Tutin; ***D:*** Beeban Kidron. **TV**

Shadey **1/2 1987 (PG-13)** The premise for this oddball comedy came to someone in the wee hours: I've got it! Mild-mannered mechanic can film people's thoughts; wants to use his gift only for good, but needs money for a sex-change operation. Assorted bad guys want to use him for evil purposes. Strange, but not bad; Helmond's character is memorable. **90m/C VHS.** *GB* Anthony Sher, Billie Whitelaw, Patrick Macnee, Katherine Helmond, Leslie Ash, Larry Lamb, Bernard Hepton; ***D:*** Philip Saville; ***W:*** Snoo Wilson; ***C:*** Roger Deakins; ***M:*** Colin Towns.

The Shadow **1/2 1936** Scotland Yard pulls out all the stops to track down a murderous extortionist, enlisting the aid of a novelist in their efforts. Long on talk and short on action. **63m/B VHS, DVD.** *GB* Henry Kendall, Elizabeth Allan, Jeanne Stuart, Felix Aylmer, Cyril Raymond; ***D:*** George Cooper.

Shadow *Cien* **1956** A man is murdered and director Kowalerowicz offers three possible versions of events leading up to the crime. Ran afoul of censorship for its depiction of government corruption and stupidity. Polish with subtitles. **98m/B DVD.** *PL* Ignacy Machowski, Zygmunt Kestowicz, Adolf Chronicki, Michael Mattison, Tadeusz Jurasz; ***D:*** Jerzy Kawalerowicz; ***W:*** Aleksander Scibor-Rylski; ***C:*** Jerzy Lipman; ***M:*** Andrzej Markowski.

The Shadow **1/2 1994 (PG-13)** Who knows what evil lurks in the hearts of men? Why "The Shadow" of course, as is shown in this highly stylized big screen version of the '30s radio show that once starred Orson Welles. Billionaire playboy Lamont Cranston (Baldwin) is a master of illusion and defender of justice thanks to his alter ego. Aided by companion Margo Lane (Miller), da Shadow battles super-criminal Shiwan Khan (Lone), the deadliest descendant of Ghenghis Khan. Numerous and elaborate special effects provide icing on the cake for those in the mood for a journey back to the radio past or a quick superhero fix. **112m/C VHS, DVD.** Sab Shimono, Alec Baldwin, John Lone, Penelope Ann Miller, Peter Boyle, Ian McKellen, Tim Curry, Jonathan Winters, Andre Gregory, James Hong, Joseph Maher, John Kapelos, Max Wright, Aaron Lustig, Ethan Phillips, Larry Joshua, Al Leong, Abraham Benrubi, Armin Shimerman, Steve Hytner, Kate McGregor-Stewart; ***D:*** Russell Mulcahy; ***W:*** David Koepp; ***C:*** Stephen Burum; ***M:*** Jerry Goldsmith.

The Shadow Box **1980** Three terminally ill people at a California hospice confront their destinies. Pulitzer Prize-winning play by Michael Cristofer is actually improved by director Newman and a superb, well-chosen cast. Powerful. **96m/C VHS.** Joanne Woodward, Christopher Plummer, Robert Urich, Valerie Harper, Sylvia Sidney, Melinda Dillon, Ben Masters, John Considine, James Broderick; ***D:*** Paul Newman; ***M:*** Henry Mancini.

The Shadow Conspiracy **1996 (R)** Laughable innocent-on-the-run tale of presidential advisor Bobby Bishop (Sheen), who finds himself smack in the middle of an assassination conspiracy against the Prez (Waterston). Accused of murder, Bishop hooks up with ex-gal pal, reporter Amanda Givens (Hamilton) to get to the truth before the police and the bad guys get to them. Hunting the duo is a pro known as "The Agent" (Lang). Lang's lethal Agent comes off as one of the only believable characters here, perhaps because he has absolutely no dialogue to sabotage him. Sutherland fares better than most as Chief of Staff Conrad Jacob. Ludicrous plot twists and unconvincing performances by leads Sheen and Hamilton. **103m/C VHS, DVD.** Charlie Sheen, Linda Hamilton, Stephen Lang, Donald Sutherland, Sam Waterston, Ben Gazzara, Nicholas Turturro, Charles Cioffi, Theodore Bikel, Stanley Anderson, Dey Young, Gore Vidal, Paul Gleason, Terry O'Quinn; ***D:*** George P. Cosmatos; ***W:*** Rick Gibbs, Wayne Beach; ***C:*** Buzz Feitshans IV; ***M:*** Bruce Broughton.

Shadow Creature **1996 (R)** Detective investigating a series of grisly murders finds a mad scientist and a mysterious formula that could unlock the secrets of immortality. The downside being the entire mutation of all life on earth into monsters. **?m/C VHS.** Shane Minor, Dennis Keefe, Scott Heim; ***D:*** James Gribbins.

Shadow Dancer **1996 (R)** Formulaic Corman exploitation finds L.A. stripper Narita (Hall) under investigation for the murder of two fellow dancers. **89m/C VHS.** Gabriella Hall, Robert Donovan, Kate McNeil, Ron Johnson; ***D:*** Stan Kane. **VIDEO**

Shadow Dancing **1988 (PG)** The proprietor of the auspicious Beaumont Theater of Dance is haunted by one of his former dancers who died unexpectedly during a performance of "Medusa." Now, over 50 years later, Jessica, the pick for the lead in a new production, begins to take on her predecessor's mannerisms and spirit as she faces her impending doom. Surprisingly believable and suspenseful—and scary! **100m/C VHS.** Nadine Van Der Velde, James Kee, John Colicos, Shirley Douglas, Christopher Plummer; ***D:*** John Furey; ***M:*** Jay Gruska.

Shadow Force **1/2 1992** Homicide detective Rick Kelly is investigating the murders of a district attorney and a police sergeant. With the help of Mary, the usual beautiful female journalist, he uncovers a plot to assassinate key law enforcement officers. **80m/C VHS.** Dirk Benedict, Lance LeGault, Lise Cutter, Jack Elam, Glenn Corbett, Bob Hastings; ***D:*** Darrell Davenport.

The Shadow in the North **2007** It's six years after Sally Lockhart's (Piper) first adventure (in "The Ruby in the Smoke") and she has become a financial consultant to her late father's shipping company in 1870s London. A client asks her to look into a mysterious ship sinking since the insurance company won't pay up until the matter is investigated. Meanwhile, beau Frederick Garland (Feild) has become a private detective and has a peculiar case with a magician claiming he's going to be murdered. Naturally, the investigations overlap. Based on the novel by Philip Pullman. **86m/C DVD.** *GB* Billie Piper, J.J. Feild, Matt Smith, Jared Harris, Hayley Atwell, Julian Rhind-Tutt, John Standing, Dona Croll, David Harewood; ***D:*** John Alexander; ***W:*** Adrian Hodges; ***C:*** Adam Suschitzky; ***M:*** John Lunn. **TV**

Shadow Magic **1/2 2000 (PG)** Englishman Raymond Wallace (Harris) turns up in Peking in 1902 with a hand-cranked, black and white, soundless camera and projector, thus bringing the first moving images to China. Local photographer Liu Jinglun (Yu), intrigued by the new technolgy, bridges the cultural barriers between Raymond and the community, causing problems of loyalty with his own family and friends and even jeopardizing his marriage chances. Mandarin with subtitles. **115m/C VHS, DVD.** *GE* Jared Harris, Xia Yu, Peiqi Liu, Liping Lu, Xing Yufei, Wang Jingming, Li Yusheng; ***D:*** Ann Hu; ***W:*** Ann Hu, Huang Dan, Tang Louyi, Kate Raisz, Bob McAndrew; ***C:*** Nancy Schreiber; ***M:*** Zhang Lida.

The Shadow Man *Street of Shadows* **1953** A casino operator in London (Romero) is accused of killing a former girlfriend and works to clear himself. Family conventional action mystery: nothing to write home about. **76m/B VHS.** *GB FR IT* Jacques Champreux, Ugo Pagliali, Cesar Romero, Simone Silva, Kay Kendall, John Penrose, Edward Underdown, Victor Maddern; ***D:*** Richard Vernon, Georges Franju; ***W:*** Richard Vernon, Ugo Pagliali; ***C:*** Phil Grindrod, Guido Bertoni; ***M:*** Eric Spear, Georges Franju.

Shadow Man **1975 (PG)** A mysterious thief, a master of disguise, sets out to steal the Treasure of the Knights Templar and nothing will stand in his way. **89m/C VHS.** Josephine Chaplin, Gert Frobe, Gayle Hunnicutt.

Shadow Man **1/2 2006 (R)** Mediocre adventure from Seagal. Jack Foster is a retired CIA agent who is taking his daughter (Bennett) to visit Bucharest, the home of her late mother. Only she gets kidnapped because the bad guys think Foster is in possession of a bio-weapon that he knows nothing about but rogue CIA agents do. **91m/C DVD.** Steven Seagal, Werner Daehn, Imelda Staunton, Skye Bennett, Garrick Hagon; ***D:*** Michael Keusch; ***W:*** Steven Collins, Joe Halpin; ***C:*** Geoffrey Hall. **VIDEO**

Shadow of a Doubt **1/2 1943** Uncle Charlie has come to visit his relatives in Santa Rosa. Although he is handsome and charming, his young niece slowly comes to realize he is a wanted mass murderer—and he comes to recognize her suspicions. Hitchcock's personal favorite movie; a quietly creepy venture into Middle American menace. Good performances, especially by Cronyn. From the story by Gordon McConnell. **108m/B VHS, DVD.** Teresa Wright, Joseph Cotten, Hume Cronyn, MacDonald Carey, Henry Travers, Wallace Ford; ***D:*** Alfred Hitchcock; ***W:*** Thornton Wilder, Sally Benson, Alma Reville; ***C:*** Joseph Valentine; ***M:*** Dimitri Tiomkin. Natl. Film Reg. '91.

Shadow of a Scream **1997 (R)** Detective Alice Redmond (Massey) goes undercover to investigate a suspected killer (Chokachi) and discovers his rough sexual fantasies appeal to the less staid side of her nature. So much so that she gets a little too up close and personal with this possible murderer. **84m/C VHS.** Athena Massey, David Chokachi, Cyril O'Reilly, Timothy Busfield; ***D:*** Howard McCain.

Shadow of Angels *Schatten der Engel* **1976** Beautiful prostitute Lily Brest's (Caven) latest client, a wealthy real estate investor (Lowitsch), just wants to talk and Lily's a good listener. So good, that more and more of her clients tell her all their darkest secrets and fears, leaving Lily herself falling into such a deep depression that she wonders if she can go on. Based on Fassbinder's play "The Garbage, the City and Death"; Fassbinder himself appears as a pimp. German with subtitles. **103m/C VHS.** *GE* Ingrid Caven, Klaus Lowitsch; ***Cameos:*** Rainer Werner Fassbinder; ***D:*** Daniel Schmid; ***W:*** Rainer Werner Fassbinder, Daniel Schmid.

Shadow of Chikara *Thunder Mountain; The Curse of Demon Mountain* **1977 (PG)** A Confederate Army Captain and an orphan girl encounter unexpected adventures as they search for a fortune in diamonds hidden in a river in northern Arkansas. **96m/C VHS, DVD.** Joe Don Baker, Sondra Locke, Ted Neeley, Slim Pickens; ***D:*** Earl E. Smith; ***W:*** Earl E. Smith; ***C:*** Jim Roberson; ***M:*** Jaime Mendoza-Nava.

Shadow of China **1991 (PG-13)** A young man struggles for power and love in Hong Kong, while an English beauty and an Asian activist hold the keys to his future and a past which could destroy him. Excellent acting, stunning location photography. Exotic and intense. Based on the Japanese bestseller "Snakehead." **100m/C VHS.** John Lone, Sammi Davis, Vivian Wu; ***D:*** Mitsuo Yanagimachi; ***W:*** Mitsuo Yanagimachi, Richard Maxwell.

Shadow of Chinatown **1/2 1936** Mad scientist creates wave of murder and terror in Chinatown. Edited version of a 15-chapter serial. **70m/B VHS, DVD.** Bela Lugosi, Bruce Bennett, Joan Barclay, Luana Walters, Maurice Liu, William Buchanan; ***D:*** Robert F. "Bob" Hill.

Shadow of Doubt **1/2 1998 (R)** L.A. defense attorney Kitt Devereux (Griffiths) likes high-profile cases. And her latest has the added tension of being prosecuted by ex-lover, Asst. D.A. Jack Campioni (Berenger). Kitt works with an investigaotr (Lewis) to prove a rapper (Dominguez) innocent of murder while being threatened by an accused rapist (Sheffer) and a prominent Senator, who's angling for a presidential nomination. How everything ties together is something Kitt will have to figure out if she wants to discover the truth. **103m/C VHS.** Melanie Griffith, Tom Berenger, Craig Sheffer, Huey Lewis, John Ritter, Wade Dominguez; ***D:*** Randal Kleiser; ***W:*** Raymond De Felitta, Myra Byanka.

Shadow of the Eagle **1932** Former wartime flying ace Wayne is accused of being a criminal known as "The Eagle." He's using his flying skills (which include skywriting) to threaten a corporation which has stolen plans for a new invention. But can Wayne really be our villain? 12-chapter serial. **226m/B VHS, DVD.** John Wayne, Dorothy Gulliver, Walter Miller; ***D:*** Ford Beebe.

Shadow of the Thin Man **1941** In the fourth "Thin Man" film, following "Another Thin Man," Nick and Nora stumble onto a murder at the racetrack. The rapport between Powell and Loy is still going strong, providing us with some wonderful entertainment. Followed by "The Thin Man Goes Home." **97m/B VHS, DVD.** William Powell, Myrna Loy, Barry Nelson, Donna Reed, Sam Levene, Alan Baxter, Dickie Hall, Loring Smith,

Joseph Anthony, Henry O'Neill; *D:* Woodbridge S. Van Dyke.

Shadow of the Vampire ☙☙☙ **2000** Behind the scenes look at what possibly went on during the making of the silent vampire classic, 1922's "Nosferatu." Director F.W. Murnau (Malkovich) and his crew head for Czechoslovakia for location shooting on his version of "Dracula" and the first meeting of the dedicated actor who will play the title role—a very eccentric Max Schreck (Dafoe). Only Murnau has struck a devil's bargain with Schreck, who is an actual vampire—the leading man gets leading lady Greta (McCormack) as a reward—and a snack. But it seems Schreck can't wait, as the crew starts to fall mysteriously ill. A little slow going but strangely compelling and the two lead performances are outstanding. **93m/C VHS, DVD.** *GB* John Malkovich, Willem Dafoe, Catherine McCormack, Cary Elwes, Eddie Izzard, Udo Kier, Ronan Vibert, Aden (John) Gillett; *D:* Edmund Elias Merhige; *W:* Steven Katz; *C:* Lou Bogue; *M:* Dan (Daniel) Jones. L.A. Film Critics '00: Support. Actor (Dafoe).

Shadow of the Wolf ☙☙ *Agaguk: Shadow of the Wolf* **1992 (PG-13)** Phillips is Agaguk, the son of the village leader, in this epic saga of survival set against the wilderness of the Arctic. Agaguk decides he cannot accept the white man's intrusion, so he sets out on his own. His father believes his departure to be the ultimate betrayal and casts upon him the "curse of the white wolf." Now Agaguk and his companion (Tilly) must face the harsh tundra alone and struggle to stay alive in the Great White North. Based on the novel "Agaguk" by Yves Theriault. **108m/C VHS.** *CA* Lou Diamond Phillips, Donald Sutherland, Jennifer Tilly, Toshiro Mifune; *D:* Jacques Dorfmann; *W:* Rudy Wurlitzer, Evan Jones. Genie '93: Art Dir./Set Dec., Costume Des.

Shadow on the Sun ☙ 1/2 **1988** The life of Beryl Markham, pioneer female aviator and adventurer of the 1930s. Way too long and boring TV answer to "Out of Africa." **192m/C VHS.** Stefanie Powers, Claire Bloom, Frederic Forrest, James Fox, John Rubinstein, Jack Thompson; *D:* Tony Richardson. **TV**

Shadow Play ☙ 1/2 **1986 (R)** A successful female playwright is haunted by visions of a past lover. Her life slowly falls apart, but not before this film does. **98m/C VHS.** Dee Wallace, Cloris Leachman; *D:* Susan Shadburne; *W:* Susan Shadburne.

Shadow Puppets ☙ **2007** Strangers wake up in some kind of dank medical facility/prison minus both their clothes (they're in their underwear) and their memories. They try to figure out what's going on but something in the shadows is out to get 'em. Generally dopey psycho-thriller. **103m/C DVD.** James Marsters, Jolene Blalock, Tony Todd, Jonathan Hale, Marc Winnick; *D:* Michael Winnick; *W:* Michael Winnick; *M:* Ross Nykiforuk. **VIDEO**

The Shadow Riders ☙☙ *Louis L'Amour's "The Shadow Riders"* **1982 (PG)** Two brothers who fought on opposite sides during the Civil War return home to find their brother's fiancee kidnapped by a renegade Confederate officer who plans to use her as ransom in a prisoner exchange. They set out to rescue the woman. Preceded by "The Sacketts" and based on the works of Louis L'Amour. **96m/C VHS, DVD.** Tom Selleck, Sam Elliott, Ben Johnson, Katharine Ross, Jeffery Osterhage, Gene Evans, R.G. Armstrong, Marshall Teague, Dominique Dunne, Jeanetta Arnette; *D:* Andrew V. McLaglen; *W:* Jim Byrnes; *C:* Jack Whitman; *M:* Jerrold Immel. **TV**

The Shadow Strikes ☙ 1/2 **1937** Adaptation of the radio serial. The sleuth pursues a killer and a gangster. Meanwhile, the police try to pin a robbery on the "Shadow." Who did it? The Shadow knows! **61m/B VHS, DVD.** Rod La Rocque, Lynn Anders, James Blakely, Walter McGrail, Cy Kendall, Kenneth Harlan, John St. Polis, Wilson Benge; *D:* Lynn Shores; *W:* Al Martin; *C:* Marcel Le Picard.

Shadow Warriors ☙ 1/2 **1995 (R)** Greedy security expert Connors (O'Quinn) sells computerized bodyguards that are created from human corpses, aided by doctor Natalie (Graham). Only one of the latest creations has just gone on a killing spree, so they use another "technosapien" (Lurie) to prevent further mayhem. **80m/C VHS, DVD.** Evan Lurie, Terry O'Quinn, Russ Tertyask, Ashley Anne Graham, Timothy Patrick Cavanaugh; *D:* Lamar Card; *C:* M. David Mullen.

Shadow Warriors ☙☙ *Assault on Devil's Island* **1997** Navy SEALS, led by Mike McBride (Hogan), plan an assault on the island hideaway of drug lord Gallindo (Drago). Lending assistance is undercover DEA agent Hunter Wiley (being that the part is played by Tweed she's never really covered, appearing in a variety of lingerie and bikinis while kicking butt). However, when the SEALS get Gallindo, his crew retaliates. **94m/C VHS, DVD.** Hulk Hogan, Carl Weathers, Shannon Tweed, Martin Kove, Billy Drago, Trevor Goddard, Billy Blanks; *D:* Jon Cassar. **CABLE**

Shadow Warriors 2: Hunt for the Death Merchant ☙☙ 1/2 **1997 (R)** The elite commando unit of Hogan, Weathers, and Tweed return—and this time they must rescue a group of American gymnasts who are being held hostage. If you enjoyed the first movie, you'll enjoy this one since it's more of the action-filled same. **95m/C VHS.** Hulk Hogan, Carl Weathers, Shannon Tweed, Martin Kove; *D:* Jon Cassar. **CABLE**

The Shadow Whip ☙ 1/2 *Ying zi shen bian* **1971** Fang Chen-tian (Feng Tien) is a master of the whip, and saves a young girl (Pei-pei Cheng) from bandits. Accused of stealing the jewels the bandits were after, he goes into hiding raising the girl as his daughter and teaching her to use the whip to aid him in his quest to clear his name. Inevitably bad stuff happens. Unique as it's one of the few (maybe only) Kung-Fu movies set in winter. **78m/C DVD.** *HK* Pei Pei Cheng, Hung Kam-Bo, Feng Ku, Wei Lo, Feng Tien, Yua Hueh; *D:* Wei Lo; *W:* Wei Lo, Kuang Ni.

A Shadow You Soon Will Be ☙☙ *Una Sombra Ya Pronto Seras* **1994** An allegory of the emptiness of contemporary Argentinian society, following the end of military rule, and based on a 1990 novel by Soriano, who co-wrote the screenplay. A man known merely as "The Engineer" (Sola) returns from Europe where he's lived in exile during the military dictatorship. Without family or friends, he wanders through the southern pampas, briefly communicating with other eccentric travelers, and non-commitally watching the world go by. Spanish with subtitles. **105m/C VHS, DVD.** *AR* Miguel Angel Sola, Eusebio Poncela, Pepe Soriano, Alicia Bruzzo, Luis Brandoni, Diego Torres, Gloria Carra; *D:* Hector Olivera; *W:* Hector Olivera, Osvaldo Soriano; *C:* Felix Monti; *M:* Osvaldo Montes.

Shadowboxer ☙ 1/2 **2006 (R)** Gratuitous, graphic sex and violence dominate a story about biracial assassins who are not only lovers but stepmother and stepson, played for some reason by the great Mirren and Gooding. Complications arise when a job doesn't go as planned and the odd couple find themselves on the lam with their target and her just-born infant. Add a half bone for somehow landing Oscar-caliber leads. **93m/C DVD.** *US* Cuba Gooding Jr., Helen Mirren, Vanessa Ferlito, Macy Gray, Joseph Gordon-Levitt, Mo'Nique, Stephen Dorff; *D:* Lee Daniels; *W:* William Lipz; *C:* M. David Mullen; *M:* Mario Grigorov.

Shadowheart ☙ 1/2 **2009 (PG-13)** Bounty hunter James Conners (Ament) returns to Legend, New Mexico to avenge his father's death at the hands of Will Tunney (Macfadyen). When James has the chance to reunite with first love Mary Cooper (Alton) he has to decide if revenge is worth giving up his second chance. **114m/C DVD.** Angus MacFadyen, Marnie Alton, William Sadler, Dean Alioto, Justin Ament, Michael Spears; *D:* Dean Alioto; *W:* Dean Alioto; *C:* Andrew Huebscher; *M:* Gregor Narholz. **VIDEO**

Shadowhunter ☙☙ **1993 (R)** Glenn stars as a burned-out big city detective who is sent to a Navajo reservation in Arizona to bring a murder suspect back to Los Angeles. When the alleged killer escapes custody Glenn must track him across forbidding desert territory and face his suspect's unusual mystical powers. **98m/C VHS.** Scott Glenn; *D:* J.S. Cardone; *W:* J.S. Cardone; *C:* Dick Bush.

Shadowlands ☙☙☙ *C.S. Lewis Through the Shadowlands* **1985** A look at the later life of bachelor-scholar C.S. Lewis (also the author of the "Chronicles of Narnia"). A devout proponent of Christianity, the middle-aged Lewis fell in love and married Joy Gresham, a divorced American poet with two young sons. Joy was diagnosed with cancer and her illness provided Lewis with the clearest test of his faith. Wonderful performances by both Ackland and Bloom. **90m/C VHS.** *GB* Joss Ackland, Claire Bloom, Rupert Baderman; *D:* Norman Stone.

Shadowlands ☙☙☙ **1993 (PG)** Touching, tragic story of the late-in-life romance between celebrated author and Christian theologian C.S. Lewis (Hopkins) and brash New York divorcee Joy Gresham (Winger). Attenborough's direction is rather stately and sweeping and Winger is really too young for her role but Hopkins is excellent as (another) repressed man who finds more emotions than he can handle. Critically acclaimed adaptation of Nicholson's play will require lots of kleenex. **130m/C VHS, DVD.** *GB* Anthony Hopkins, Debra Winger, Edward Hardwicke, Joseph Mazzello, Michael Denison, John Wood, Peter Firth, Peter Howell; *D:* Richard Attenborough; *W:* William Nicholson; *C:* Roger Pratt; *M:* George Fenton. British Acad. '93: Film; L.A. Film Critics '93: Actor (Hopkins); Natl. Bd. of Review '93: Actor (Hopkins).

Shadows ☙☙ **1922** A Chinese laundryman (Chaney) lives with a group of his countrymen in a New England seacoast village. All is peaceful until the local minister decides to convert the "heathen" Chinese. Ludicrous but worth seeing for Chaney's fun performance. Silent with music score. **70m/B VHS, DVD.** Lon Chaney Sr., Harrison Ford; *D:* Tom Forman; *W:* Eve Unsell, Hope Loring; *C:* Harry Perry; *M:* Gaylord Carter.

Shadows ☙☙☙ **1960** Director Cassavettes' first indie feature finds jazz player Hugh (Hurd) forced to play dives to support his brother Ben (Carruthers) and sister Lelia (Goldoni). Light-skinned enough to pass for white, Lelia takes on the uptown New York art crowd and gets involved with the white Tony (Ray), who leaves when he finds out her true heritage. Meanwhile, Ben drifts along with his friends who abandon him when trouble finds them. Script was improvised by cast. **87m/B VHS, DVD.** Hugh Hurd, Lelia Goldoni, Ben Carruthers, Anthony Ray, Rupert Crosse, Tom Allen; *D:* John Cassavetes; *C:* Erich Kollmar; *M:* Charles Mingus, Shifi Hadi. Natl. Film Reg. '93.

Shadows ☙ *Senki* **2007** Heavy-handed symbolism and an overextended runtime lessen the otherworldly drama you might expect. Bored young physician Lazar (Nacev) is nearly killed in a car accident and a year later is experiencing hallucinatory sights and sounds. Deciphering the meaning behind these encounters leads to Lazar's overbearing mother (Ajrula-Tozija) and her past. Macedonian with subtitles. **130m/C DVD.** *MA* Borce Nacev, Vesna Stanojevska, Sabina Ajrula-Tozija, Salaetin Bilal, Filareta Atanasova, Ratka Radmanovic; *D:* Milcho Manchevski; *W:* Milcho Manchevski; *C:* Fabio Cianchetti; *M:* Ryan Shore.

The Shadows ☙ 1/2 **2007** Horror writer Stephen Grimes is being pressured by both his editor and his ex-wife to turn out another best-seller ASAP. Driving home one night, Stephen accidentally hits a young man and takes him to the hospital. Emmet just happens to share a last name with Stephen and the two are soon moving from friends to sexual partners. But Emmet isn't really as innocent as he seems and the relationship starts looking like a plot from one of Stephen's novels. **80m/C DVD.** Joe Lia, Emmett Allen; *D:* Guillermo R. Rodriguez; *W:* Guillermo R. Rodriguez; *C:* Gavin Kelly; *M:* Patrick Kirst. **VIDEO**

Shadows and Fog ☙☙ **1992 (PG-13)** Offbeat, unpredictable Allen film that is little more than an exercise in expressionistic visual stylings. The action centers around a haunted, alienated clerk (Allen) who is awakened in the middle of the night to join a vigilante group searching the streets for a killer. Although reminiscent of a silent film, Carlo DiPalma's black-and-white cinematography is stunning. Several stars appear briefly throughout this extremely unfocused comedy. **85m/B VHS, DVD.** Woody Allen, Kathy Bates, John Cusack, Mia Farrow, Jodie Foster, Fred Gwynne, Julie Kavner, Madonna, John Malkovich, Kenneth Mars, Kate Nelligan, Donald Pleasence, Lily Tomlin, Philip Bosco, Robert Joy, Wallace Shawn, Kurtwood Smith, Josef Sommer, David Ogden Stiers, Michael Kirby, Anne Lange; *D:* Woody Allen; *W:* Woody Allen; *C:* Carlo Di Palma.

Shadows in the Storm ☙☙ **1988 (R)** A librarian/poet retreats to a secluded forest after losing his job. There he meets an exotically beautiful young woman who becomes his lover. With her love, she brings blackmail, murder, and mystery. **90m/C VHS.** Ned Beatty, Mia Sara, Michael Madsen; *D:* Terrell Tannen.

Shadows of Death ☙ 1/2 **1945** Crabbe is the hero who must track down a gang of outlaws who kill to grab the land along the path of a new railroad. One of the "Billy Carson" series. **60m/B VHS, DVD.** Buster Crabbe, Al "Fuzzy" St. John, Charles "Blackie" King, Karl Hackett, Edward (Eddie) Hall, Dona Dax; *D:* Sam Newfield; *W:* Fred Myton; *C:* Jack Greenhalgh.

Shadows of Forgotten Ancestors ☙☙☙ *Tini Zabutykh Predkiv; Shadows of Our Ancestors; Shadows of Our Forgotten Ancestors; Wild Horses of Fire* **1964** Set in rural Russia in the early 20th century. Brings to expressive life the story of a man whose entire life has been overtaken by tragedy. Folk drama about a peasant who falls in with the daughter of his father's killer, then marries another woman. Strange, resonant and powerful with distinctive camera work. In Ukrainian with English subtitles. **99m/C VHS.** *RU* Ivan Micholaichuk, Larisa Kadochnikova; *D:* Sergei Paradjanov.

Shadows of the Orient **1937** Two detectives are out to smash a Chinese smuggling ring. **70m/B VHS, DVD.** J. Farrell MacDonald, Oscar Apfel, Sidney Blackmer, Regis Toomey, Esther Ralston; *D:* Burt Lynwood; *W:* Charles Francis Royal; *C:* James S. Brown Jr.

Shadows of Tombstone ☙ 1/2 **1953** There's corruption in the western town of Shadow Rock as the crooked sheriff and saloonkeeper make things miserable for the inhabitants. Rex and Slim try to right the wrongs but take their time about it. **54m/B VHS.** Rex Allen, Slim Pickens, Roy Barcroft, Emory Parnell, Jeanne Cooper; *D:* William Witney; *W:* Gerald Geraghty; *C:* Bud Thackery; *M:* R. Dale Butts.

Shadows on the Sage ☙ 1/2 **1942** A gang keeps killing the sheriffs of a small town and the Mesquiteers plan to put a stop to the murders. Steele plays the dual role of good guy Tucson and bad guy Curly. The 46th film in the series. **58m/B DVD.** Bob Steele, Tom Tyler, Jimmie Dodd, Cheryl Walker, Harry Holman, Freddie Mercer, Bryant Washburn, Griff Barnett, Tom London, Yakima Canutt; *D:* Les(ter) Orlebeck; *W:* J. Benton Cheney; *C:* Edgar Lyons; *M:* Mort Glickman.

Shadows on the Stairs ☙☙ **1941** A creepy boarding house is the scene of a number of mystery-drenched murders. A bizarre assortment of suspects make things even crazier. **63m/B VHS, DVD.** Frieda Inescort, Paul Cavanagh, Heather Angel, Bruce Lester, Miles Mander, Lumsden Hare, Turhan Bey; *D:* David Ross Lederman.

Shadows over Shanghai ☙ 1/2 **1938** This adventure relic was set during the Japanese invasion of China prior to WWII and uses much newsreel footage of that infamy. As for the plot, it's a groaner about good guys and bad skulking around the eponymous port in search of a treasure. **66m/B VHS, DVD.** James Dunn, Ralph Morgan, Robert Barrat, Paul Sutton, Edward (Eddie) Woods; *D:* Charles Lamont.

Shadows Run Black ☙ 1/2 **1984** A police detective must save a college coed from the clutches of a maniac wielding a meat cleaver. Ordinary slash-'em-up. Bet Costner's embarrassed now about this early role—like Stallone's porno role in "The Italian Stallion." **89m/C VHS, DVD.** William J. Kulzer, Elizabeth Trosper, Kevin Costner; *D:* Howard Heard.

Shadowzone ☙☙ **1989 (R)** As a result of NASA experiments in dream travel, an interdimensional monster invades our world in search of victims. Begins well, with slightly interesting premise, but degenerates into typical monster flick. Good special effects. **88m/C VHS, DVD.** Louise Fletcher, David Beecroft, James Hong, Shawn Weatherly, Lu Leonard; ***D:*** J.S. Cardone; ***W:*** J.S. Cardone.

ShadowZone: The Undead Express 🦴🦴 1/2 **1996 (PG-13)** Teenaged Zach (Leopardi) winds up in New York's subway tunnels where he meets the vampire Valentine (Silver) and his fellow bloodsuckers. Based on the book by J.R. Black. **98m/C VHS, DVD.** Chauncey Leopardi, Ron Silver, Natanya Ross, Tony T. Johnson, Ron White; ***Cameos:*** Wes Craven; ***D:*** Stephen Williams; ***W:*** Roy Swallows; ***C:*** Curtis Petersen; ***M:*** Reg Powell. **CABLE**

Shadrach 🦴🦴 1/2 **1998 (PG-13)** The Dabneys run-down Depression Era southern farm was once a rich tobacco plantation and, as they learn, the former home to aged black man Shadrach (Sawyer) who returns in order to die on the land where he grew up. Flawed family patriarch Vernon (Keitel) gives his word to the ex-slave that he can be buried on the land, but learns otherwise from the local sheriff. Still, Vernon tries to fulfill his promise. Director Susanna Styron's lethargic adaptation of her father William's 1978 short story proves that the story should have stayed shorter than 90 minutes. Although the relatively small budget shows, the cast provides good performances. **88m/C VHS, DVD.** Edward (Eddie) Bunker, Harvey Keitel, John Franklin Sawyer, Andie MacDowell, Scott Terra, Monica Bugajski, Darrell Larson, Deborah Hedwall, Daniel Treat; ***D:*** Susanna Styron; ***W:*** Susanna Styron, Bridget Terry; ***C:*** Hiro Narita; ***M:*** Van Dyke Parks.

Shaft 🦴🦴🦴 **1971 (R)** A black private eye (Roundtree) is hired to find a Harlem gangster's (Gunn) kidnapped daughter. Lotsa sex and violence; suspenseful and well directed by notable "Life" photographer Parks. Great ending. Academy Award-winning theme song by Isaac Hayes, the first music award from the Academy to an African American. Adapted from the novel by Ernest Tidyman. Followed by "Shaft's Big Score" and "Shaft in Africa." ♫ Theme From Shaft. **98m/C VHS, DVD.** Richard Roundtree, Moses Gunn, Charles Cioffi, Christopher St. John, Gwen Mitchell, Lawrence Pressman, Victor Arnold, Antonio Fargas, Drew "Bundini" Brown; ***D:*** Gordon Parks; ***W:*** John D.F. Black, Ernest Tidyman; ***C:*** Urs Furrer; ***M:*** Isaac Hayes, J.J. Johnson. Oscars '71: Song ("Theme from Shaft"); Golden Globes '72: Score, Natl. Film Reg. '00.

Shaft 🦴🦴🦴 *Shaft Returns* **2000 (R)** Singleton's updated the 1971 blaxploitation flick with Jackson starring as the nephew of the coolest private dick ever (Roundtree has a cameo in his original role). But Jackson can more than hold his own in the cool department as he tracks down rich-kid murderer Walter Wade Jr. (Bale), who's after the only witness to his crime, a scared waitress (Collette). Wade hires a Latino drug dealer (Wright, in a standout performance almost equal to Jackson's) and a couple of bad cops to find the girl and kill Shaft, setting off much gunfire and snappy dialoque. Jackson has charisma to burn, but other characters, as well as potentially interesting plot points, get short shrift. This is most likely a result of Wright's part being (deservedly) beefed up from the original screenplay (about which Singleton and Jackson were said to be not entirely happy). **98m/C VHS, DVD.** Samuel L. Jackson, Christian Bale, Vanessa L(ynne) Williams, Jeffrey Wright, Philip Bosco, Toni Collette, Angela Pietropinto, Dan Hedaya, Josef Sommer, Richard Roundtree, Ruben Santiago-Hudson, Lynne Thigpen, Pat Hingle, Busta Rhymes, Mekhi Phifer, Zach Grenier, Catherine Kellner, Isaac Hayes, Lee Tergesen, Gloria Reuben, Gordon Parks, Daniel von Bargen; ***D:*** John Singleton; ***W:*** Richard Price; ***C:*** Stuart Dryburgh; ***M:*** Isaac Hayes, David Arnold.

The Shaft 🦴🦴 *Down* **2001 (R)** The express elevators in New York's Millennium Building start to malfunction (as in killing passengers) but no one seems to want mechanic Mark (Marshall) to fix the problem. So Mark decides to investigate, aided by nosy reporter Jennifer (Watts). **109m/C DVD.** *US NL* James Marshall, Naomi Watts, Eric Thal, Michael Ironside, Edward Herrmann, Dan Hedaya, Ron Perlman; ***D:*** Dick Maas; ***W:*** Dick Maas; ***C:*** Marc Felperlaan.

Shaft in Africa 🦴🦴 1/2 **1973 (R)** Violent actioner finds detective Shaft forced into helping an African nation stop some modern-day slave trading. Second sequel, following "Shaft's Big Score." **112m/C VHS, DVD.** Richard Roundtree, Frank Finlay, Vonetta McGee, Neda Arneric, Jacques Marin; ***D:*** John Guillermin; ***W:*** Stirling Silliphant.

Shaft's Big Score 🦴🦴 1/2 **1972 (R)** This first sequel to the extremely sucessful "Shaft" has Roundtree's detective trying to mediate between several mobsters while investigating a friend's murder. Lots of action and an exciting Brooklyn chase scene involving cars, helicopters, and boats but still routine when compared to the original. Followed by "Shaft in Africa." **105m/C VHS, DVD.** Richard Roundtree, Moses Gunn, Joseph Mascolo, Drew "Bundini" Brown, Wally Taylor, Kathy Imrie, Julius W. Harris, Rosalind Miles, Joe Santos; ***D:*** Gordon Parks; ***W:*** Ernest Tidyman; ***M:*** Gordon Parks.

Shag: The Movie 🦴🦴🦴 **1989 (PG)** The time is 1963, the setting Myrtle Beach, South Carolina, the latest craze shaggin' when four friends hit the beach for one last weekend together. Carson (Cates) is getting ready to marry staid Harley (Power); Melaina (Fonda) wants to be discovered in Hollywood; and Pudge (Gish) and Luanne (Hannah) are off to college. They encounter lots of music, boys, and dancing in this delightful film. Not to be confused with other "teen" movies, this one boasts a good script and an above average cast. **96m/C VHS, DVD.** Phoebe Cates, Annabeth Gish, Bridget Fonda, Page Hannah, Scott Coffey, Robert Rusler, Tyrone Power Jr., Jeff Yagher, Carrie Hamilton, Shirley Anne Field, Leilani Sarelle Ferrer; ***D:*** Zelda Barron; ***W:*** Robin Swicord, Lanier Laney, Terry Sweeney; ***C:*** Peter Macdonald.

The Shaggy D.A. 🦴🦴 **1976 (G)** Wilby Daniels is getting a little worried about his canine alter ego as he is about to run for District Attorney. Fun sequel to "The Shaggy Dog." **90m/C VHS, DVD.** Dean Jones, Tim Conway, Suzanne Pleshette, Keenan Wynn, Helene Winston; ***D:*** Robert Stevenson; ***M:*** Buddy (Norman Dale) Baker.

The Shaggy Dog 🦴🦴 1/2 **1959 (G)** When young Wilby Daniels utters some magical words from the inscription of an ancient ring he turns into a shaggy dog, causing havoc for family and neighbors. Disney slapstick is on target at times, though it drags in places. Followed by "The Shaggy D.A." and "Return of the Shaggy Dog." **101m/B VHS, DVD.** Fred MacMurray, Jean Hagen, Tommy Kirk, Annette Funicello, Tim Considine, Kevin Corcoran; ***D:*** Charles T. Barton; ***C:*** Edward Colman.

The Shaggy Dog 🦴🦴 **2006 (PG)** Allen goes from man to dogman after being bitten by a 300-year-old Tibetan collie with magical DNA in this remake of Disney's 1959 live-action blockbuster. Allen plays a district attorney and full-time dad now prone to loads of anthropomorphic shtick—barking, lifting his leg to pee, chasing cats, and, of course, sniffing rear-ends. Often comes across more creepy than goofy. Downey succeeds as the prototypical mad scientist villain. Strictly for the kiddies. **98m/C DVD.** *US* Tim Allen, Robert Downey Jr., Kristin Davis, Spencer Breslin, Joshua Leonard, Danny Glover, Jane Curtin, Zena Grey, Philip Baker Hall, Craig Kilborn, Annabelle Gurwitch, Bess Wohl, Shawn Pyfrom, Laura Kightlinger, Jarrad Paul; ***D:*** Brian Robbins; ***W:*** Cormac Wibberley, Marianne S. Wibberley, Geoff Rodkey, Jack Amiel, Michael Begler; ***C:*** Gabriel Beristain; ***M:*** Alan Menken.

Shaka Zulu 🦴🦴🦴 **1983** British miniseries depicting the career of Shaka, king of the Zulus (Cele). Set in the early 19th century during British ascendency in Africa. Good, absorbing cross-cultural action drama would have been better with more inspired directing by Faure. **300m/C VHS, DVD.** *GB* Edward Fox, Robert Powell, Trevor Howard, Christopher Lee, Fiona Fullerton, Henry Cele; ***D:*** William C. Faure. **TV**

Shake Hands with Murder 🦴🦴 **1944** Three people spend their time bailing criminals out of jail for profit. One is murdered, and the other two become implicated in comedy. **63m/B VHS.** Iris Adrian, Frank Jenks, Douglas Fowley, Jack Raymond, Claire Rochelle, Herbert Rawlinson, Forrest Taylor; ***D:*** Al(bert) Herman.

Shake Hands with the Devil 🦴🦴🦴 **1959** It's the Irish Republican Army against the British Black and Tans as Ireland fights for independence in 1921. Cagney is a teaching surgeon who is secretly a militant, obsessed with the idea of gaining Irish freedom. He urges his students to join with him, which Irish-American Murray does. When Murray learns that Cagney is out to sabotage a peace treaty, he must decide whether to betray Cagney in order to stop further violence. Cagney is excellent as the hard-bitten revolutionary who can't see beyond his own ideals. Filmed on location in Dublin, which further heightens the film's tension. **110m/B VHS.** James Cagney, Don Murray, Dana Wynter, Glynis Johns, Michael Redgrave, Sybil Thorndike, Harry Brogan, Robert Brown; ***D:*** Michael Anderson Sr.; ***W:*** Ivan Goff.

Shake Hands With the Devil: The Journey of Romeo Dallaire 🦴🦴🦴 1/2 **2004** In 1992 Lt. Gen. Romeo Dallaire went to Rwanda to help save their tormented people only to find his pleas for humane intervention from the U.N., the U.S., and other world powers blatantly ignored. He was not given authority to confiscate Hutu weapons and his soldiers dwindled quickly with no replacements being sent, but he chose to remain in country, trying to save as many lives as possible. As the General returns to Rwanda a decade after the civil war slaughter of 800,000 Tutsis and moderate Hutus, his words along with archival footage give a brutal recounting of atrocities that were given but a flash in Western news reports. Deserved winner of the Audience Best Film Documentary award at Sundance. **91m/C DVD.** ***D:*** Peter Raymont; ***C:*** John Westheuser; ***M:*** Mark Korven.

Shake, Rattle and Rock 🦴🦴 1/2 **1957** A deejay wants to open a teen music club playing rock 'n' roll, which has all the conservative parents up in arms. A court case follows (which the kids win). Incidental plot to the great music by Fats Domino, Joe Turner, Annita Ray, and Tommy Charles. Songs include "Ain't It a Shame," "Honey Chile," "I'm in Love Again," "Feelin' Happy," and "Sweet Love on My Mind." **76m/C VHS, DVD.** Mike Connors, Lisa Gaye, Sterling Holloway, Margaret Dumont, Raymond Hatton, Douglass Dumbrille; ***D:*** Edward L. Cahn; ***W:*** Lou Rusoff.

Shake, Rattle & Rock! 🦴🦴 1/2 **1994 (PG-13)** Remake of the 1957 flick. Teenager Susan (Zellweger) scandalizes her uptight mom (Dunn) and the other conservative adults in town because of her love of that evil rock 'n' rock music—and bad boy Lucky (Doe). Made as part of Showtime's "Rebel Highway" series. **83m/C VHS, DVD.** Renee Zellweger, John Doe, Nora Dunn, Howie Mandel, Patricia Childress, Mary Woronov, Max Perlich, Dick Miller, William Schallert, Paul Anka; ***D:*** Allan Arkush; ***W:*** Trish Soodik; ***C:*** Jean De Segonzac; ***M:*** Joseph (Joey) Altruda. **CABLE**

Shakedown 🦴🦴 1/2 *Blue Jean Cop* **1988 (R)** Power-packed action film. An overworked attorney and an undercover cop work together to stop corruption in the N.Y.P.D. Although lacking greatly in logic or plot, the sensational stunts make this an otherwise entertaining action flick. **96m/C VHS, DVD.** Sam Elliott, Peter Weller, Patricia Charbonneau, Antonio Fargas, Blanche Baker, Richard Brooks, Jude Ciccolella, George Loros, Tom Waits, Shirley Stoler, Rockets Redglare, Kathryn Rossetter; ***D:*** James Glickenhaus; ***W:*** James Glickenhaus; ***C:*** John Lindley; ***M:*** Jonathan Elias.

Shakedown 🦴🦴 **2002 (R)** Perlman is the leader of a doomsday cult that plans to steal a biological weapon and unleash it on the population. They take over the L.A. bank where the weapon is stored just at the same time that an earthquake hits, which traps the bad guys. When the military discovers the situation, a general (Dryer) decides to destroy the bank to prevent the virus from escaping. **92m/C VHS, DVD.** Ron Perlman, Erika Eleniak, Fred (John F.) Dryer, Wolf Larson, Matt Westmore; ***D:*** Brian Katkin; ***W:*** Brian Katkin; ***C:*** Yoram Astrakhan; ***M:*** Chris Farrell. **VIDEO**

Shaker Run 🦴 1/2 **1985** A stunt car driver and his mechanic transport a mysterious package. They don't know what to do—they're carrying a deadly virus that every terrorist wants! Car chases galore, and not much else. However, if you like chase scenes... **91m/C VHS, DVD.** *NZ* Leif Garrett, Cliff Robertson, Lisa Harrow; ***D:*** Bruce Morrison.

Shakes the Clown 🦴 **1992 (R)** Chronicles the rise and fall of Shakes, an alcoholic clown wandering through the all-clown town of Palukaville. Framed for the murder of his boss by his archrival, Binky, Shakes takes it on the lam in order to prove his innocence, aided by his waitress girlfriend Judy, who dreams of becoming a professional bowler. Meant as a satire of substance-abuse recovery programs and the supposed tragedies of a performer's life, the film is sometimes zany, but more often merely unpleasant and unamusing. Williams has an uncredited role as a mime. **83m/C VHS, DVD.** Bob(cat) Goldthwait, Julie Brown, Blake Clark, Adam Sandler, Tom Kenny, Sydney Lassick, Paul Dooley, Tim Kazurinsky, Florence Henderson, LaWanda Page; ***Cameos:*** Robin Williams; ***D:*** Bob(cat) Goldthwait; ***W:*** Bob(cat) Goldthwait; ***C:*** Bobby Bukowski, Elliot Davis.

Shakespeare in Love 🦴🦴🦴🦴 **1998 (R)** Lively romantic comedy about a frustrated Elizabethan playwright suffering from writer's block—who just happens to be William Shakespeare (Fiennes). Will owes a comedy to bankrupt theatre manager Henslowe (Rush) but just can't come up with a suitable story. His creative (and other) juices are sparked by wealthy beauty Viola De Lesseps (Paltrow), who so loves the theatre that she disguises herself as a boy in order to act. (Women are forbidden to be seen on the stage.) But their affair is bittersweet since Viola is about to be married. Ah well, at least Will comes up with "Romeo and Juliet." Terrific script, fine performances, spectacular costumes and cinematography, and you don't have to be a Shakespeare scholar to enjoy yourself. **122m/C VHS, DVD.** Joseph Fiennes, Gwyneth Paltrow, Ben Affleck, Geoffrey Rush, Colin Firth, Judi Dench, Simon Callow, Tom Wilkinson, Imelda Staunton, Jim Carter, Rupert Everett, Martin Clunes, Antony Sher, Joe Roberts; ***D:*** John Madden; ***W:*** Marc Norman, Tom Stoppard; ***C:*** Richard Greatrex; ***M:*** Stephen Warbeck. Oscars '98: Actress (Paltrow), Art Dir./Set Dec., Costume Des., Orig. Screenplay, Picture, Support. Actress (Dench), Orig. Mus./Comedy Score; British Acad. '98: Film, Film Editing, Support. Actor (Rush), Support. Actress (Dench); Golden Globes '99: Actress—Mus./Comedy (Paltrow), Film—Mus./Comedy, Screenplay; MTV Movie Awards '99: Kiss (Joseph Fiennes/Gwyneth Paltrow); N.Y. Film Critics '98: Screenplay; Natl. Soc. Film Critics '98: Support. Actress (Dench); Screen Actors Guild '98: Actress (Paltrow), Cast; Writers Guild '98: Orig. Screenplay; Broadcast Film Critics '98: Orig. Screenplay.

Shakespeare Wallah 🦴🦴🦴 1/2 **1965** Tender, plausible drama of romance and postcolonial relations in India. A troupe of threadbare traveling Shakespeareans quixotically tours India trying to make enough money to return to England. Wonderfully acted and exquisitely and sensitively directed by Ivory. Based in part on the real-life experiences of the theatrical Kendal family. **120m/B VHS, DVD.** Felicity Kendal, Shashi Kapoor, Madhur Jaffrey, Geoffrey Kendal, Laura Liddell; ***D:*** James Ivory; ***W:*** James Ivory, Ruth Prawer Jhabvala; ***C:*** Subrata Mitra; ***M:*** Satyajit Ray.

The Shakiest Gun in the West 🦴🦴 1/2 **1968** Remake of Bob Hope's "Paleface" has Philadelphia dentist Jesse W. Heywood (Knotts) heading off for a new practice in the wild west of Big Springs. There he unwittingly takes on bad guys and sultry Penny (Rhoades), an undercover government agent who ropes the nervous dentist into marriage for the sake of her job. **101m/C VHS, DVD.** Helene Winston, Don Knotts, Barbara Rhoades, Jackie Coogan, Donald (Don "Red") Barry, Ruth McDevitt, Dub Taylor, Noriyuki "Pat" Morita; ***D:*** Alan Rafkin; ***W:*** James Fritzell, Everett Greenbaum.

Shaking the Tree 🦴🦴 1/2 **1992 (PG-13)** Group of four high school buddies are still in quest of self-fulfillment ten years after high school as they grapple with problems in the real world of adulthood, seeking distraction in adventure, romance, friendship, and sex. **97m/C VHS, DVD.** Arye Gross, Gale Hansen,

Doug Savant, Steven Wilde, Courteney Cox, Christina Haag, Michael Arabian, Nathan Davis; ***D:*** Duane Clark; ***W:*** Duane Clark; ***M:*** David E. Russo.

Shakma 1/2 **1989** A group of medical researchers involved with experiments on animal and human tendencies toward aggression take a night off to play a quiet game of "Dungeons and Dragons." The horror begins when their main experimental subject comes along and turns things nasty! **101m/C VHS, DVD.** Roddy McDowall, Christopher Atkins, Amanda Wyss, Ari Meyers; ***D:*** Hugh Parks.

Shalako **1968** Connery/Bardot pairing promises something special, but fails to deliver. European aristocrats on a hunting trip in New Mexico, circa 1880, are menaced by Apaches. U.S. Army scout tries to save captured countess Bardot. Strange British attempt at a Euro-western. Poorly directed and pointless. Based on a Louis L'Amour story. **113m/C VHS, DVD.** Brigitte Bardot, Sean Connery, Stephen Boyd, Honor Blackman, Woody Strode, Alexander Knox; ***D:*** Edward Dmytryk; ***W:*** Scot (Scott) Finch, James J. Griffith, Hal Hopper, Clarke Reynolds; ***C:*** Ted Moore; ***M:*** Robert Farnon.

Shall We Dance **1937** And shall we ever! Seventh Astaire-Rogers pairing has a famous ballet dancer and a musical-comedy star embark on a promotional romance and marriage, to boost their careers, only to find themselves truly falling in love. Score by the Gershwins includes memorable songs. Thin, lame plot—but that's okay. For fans of good singing and dancing, and especially of this immortal pair. ♫ Slap That Bass; Beginner's Luck; Let's Call the Whole Thing Off; Walking the Dog; They All Laughed; They Can't Take That Away From Me; Shall We Dance. **116m/B VHS, DVD.** Fred Astaire, Ginger Rogers, Edward Everett Horton, Eric Blore; ***D:*** Mark Sandrich; ***M:*** George Gershwin, Ira Gershwin.

Shall We Dance? *Shall We Dansu?* **1996** A timid Japanese businessman (Yakusyo) is lured to ballroom dancing when he glimpses a beautiful, sad-eyed teacher (Kusakari) through a window. As much commentary on controlled Japanese society as a spirited discovery of learning to live and dance. Well-drawn, quirky characters and good humor amid the observant social commentary should put this one at the top of the anyone's foreign film dance card. In Japanese with subtitles. **118m/C VHS, DVD.** *JP* Koji Yakusho, Tamiyo Kusakari, Naoto Takenaka, Akira (Tsukamoto) Emoto, Eriko Watanabe, Yu Tokui, Hiromasa Taguchi, Reiko Kusamura; ***D:*** Masayuki Suo; ***W:*** Masayuki Suo; ***C:*** Naoke Kayano; ***M:*** Yoshikazu Suo. Natl. Bd. of Review '97: Foreign Film; Broadcast Film Critics '97: Foreign Film.

Shall We Dance? **2004 (PG-13)** Well-to-do, attractive lawyer (Gere) with a beautiful, loving wife (Sarandon) and children suddenly faces a mid-life crisis and decides to ballroom dance his way out. Inoffensive, though forgettable, remake of a much better and more logical 1996 Japanese movie of the same name. Attractive leads are fine, as are the multitude of daffy supporting characters, but it all seem flimsy and one-dimensional. **106m/C VHS, DVD, Blu-ray Disc.** *US* Richard Gere, Jennifer Lopez, Susan Sarandon, Stanley Tucci, Lisa Ann Walter, Richard Jenkins, Bobby Cannavale, Omar Benson Miller, Anita Gillette, Mya, Stark Sands, Tamara Hope, Nick Cannon; ***D:*** Peter Chelsom; ***W:*** Masayuki Suo; ***C:*** John de Borman; ***M:*** Gabriel Yared, John Altman.

Shall We Kiss? *Un Baiser S'il Vous Plait?* **2007** Wry comedy-of-manners with a framing story involving Emilie (Gayet), who refuses to (even casually) kiss new acquaintance Gabriel (Cohen) because she says every kiss can change your life. Then she tells him the story of Nicolas (Mouret) and Judith (Ledoyen), longtime friends who take the step into intimacy (despite Judith's marriage) because sad-sack Nicolas is such a wuss with women and the complications that ensue. French with subtitles. **96m/C DVD.** *FR* Emmanuel Mouret, Virginie Ledoyen, Julie Gayet, Stefano Accorsi, Michael Cohen, Frederique Bel, Frank Mouris, Virginie Ledoyen, Julie Gayet, Michael Cohen, Stefano Accorsi, Frederique Bal; ***D:*** Emmanuel Mouret, Frank Mouris; ***W:*** Emmanuel Mouret, Frank Mouris; ***C:*** Laurent Desmet, Laurent Desmet.

Shall We Kiss **2009** When Gabriel and Emilie meet by chance, he offers her a ride, and they spend the evening talking, laughing and getting along famously. At the end of the night, Emilie declines Gabriel's offer of "a kiss without consequences." Emilie admonishes him that the kiss could have unexpected consequences, and tells him a story, unfolding in flashbacks, about the impossibility of indulging your desires without affecting someone else's life. **96m/C DVD.** Virginie Ledoyen, Julie Gayet, Emmanuel Mouret; ***D:*** Emmanuel Mouret; ***W:*** Emmanuel Mouret.

Shallow Grave 1/2 **1987 (R)** Four coeds en route to Florida witness a murder in rural Georgia and then are pursued relentlessly by the killer, a local sheriff. Decent premise and talented cast could have offered something better, given a meatier script. **90m/C VHS.** Tony March, Lisa Stahl, Tom Law, Carol Cadby; ***D:*** Richard Styles.

Shallow Grave 1/2 **1994 (R)** Juliet (Fox), David (Eccleston), and Alex (McGregor), three completely unlikable housemates, face a moral dilemma when their new roomie, Hugo (Allen), turns up dead of a drug overdose, leaving behind a suitcase stuffed with cash. Their decision to chop up the body, bury the bits, and keep the loot leads to a well-deserved descent into paranoia, betrayal, and dementia. Interesting character study in which the veneer of civility is totally destroyed at the first hint of temptation. Style wins out over substance as the characters are never humanized before they're demonized. **91m/C VHS, DVD.** *GB* Kerry Fox, Christopher Eccleston, Ewan McGregor, Keith Allen, Ken Stott, Colin McCredie, John Hodge; ***D:*** Danny Boyle; ***W:*** John Hodge; ***C:*** Brian Tufano; ***M:*** Simon Boswell.

Shallow Ground **2004 (R)** Unable to catch a serial killer, a small-town yokel sheriff is closing up shop a year later when—this just in!—a major break in the case appears on his doorstep in the form of a muted young man carrying the murder weapon and covered in the red stuff. Script, direction, music, and acting make for one bloody mess. **97m/C DVD.** *CA* Timothy Murphy, Stan Kirsch, Patty McCormack, Natalie Avital, Myron Natwick, John Kapelos, Patty McCormack, Lindsey Stoddart; ***D:*** Sheldon Wilson; ***W:*** Sheldon Wilson; ***C:*** John Tarver; ***M:*** Steve London. **VIDEO**

Shallow Hal **2001 (PG-13)** Dumpy loser Hal (Black), along with buddy Mauricio (Alexander), will only go after supermodel-perfect women (with predictable results), until self-help guru Tony Robbins hypnotizes him into seeing the inner beauty of the women he encounters. This leads him to meet and pursue Rosemary (Paltrow), who he sees as the physical ideal, but the rest of the world knows to be 300 pounds. The Farrellys try to have it both ways, making fat jokes while projecting the message that appearance shouldn't matter. They're only moderately and intermittently successful. Paltrow does a good job of showing Rosemary's wariness and self-acceptance, while Black at times seems to be trying a little too hard. **114m/C VHS, DVD, UMD.** *US* Jack Black, Gwyneth Paltrow, Jason Alexander, Joe (Johnny) Viterelli, Bruce McGill, Susan Ward, Rene Kirby, Tony Robbins, Zen Gesner, Brooke Burns, Rob Moran, Nan Martin; ***D:*** Bobby Farrelly, Peter Farrelly; ***W:*** Bobby Farrelly, Peter Farrelly, Sean Moynihan; ***C:*** Russell Carpenter.

The Shaman 1/2 **1987 (R)** Members of a family succumb to the hypnotic spell of the Shaman as he searches for the perfect one to inherit his powers. **88m/C VHS.** Michael Conforti, Elvind Harum, James Farkas, Lynn Weaver; ***D:*** Michael Yakub.

Shame 1/2 *The Intruder; I Hate Your Guts; The Stranger* **1961** Strangely unsuccessful low-budget Corman effort, starring pre-"Star Trek" Shatner as a freelance bigot who travels around Missouri stirring up opposition to desegregation. Moralistic and topical but still powerful. Adapted from the equally excellent novel by Charles Beaumont. Uses location filming superbly to render a sense of everydayness and authenticity. **84m/B VHS, DVD.** William Shatner, Frank Maxwell, Jeanne Cooper, Robert Emhardt, Leo Gordon, Charles Beaumont, Beverly Lunsford, William F. Nolan, George Clayton Johnson; ***D:*** Roger Corman; ***W:*** Charles Beaumont; ***C:*** Taylor Byars; ***M:*** Herman Stein.

The Shame 1/2 **1968 (R)** A Bergman masterpiece focusing on the struggle for dignity in the midst of war. Married concert musicians Ullmann and von Sydow flee a bloody civil war for a small island off their country's coast. Inevitably, the carnage reaches them and their lives become a struggle to endure and retain a small measure of civilized behavior as chaos overtakes them. Deeply despairing and brilliantly acted. In Swedish with English subtitles. **103m/C VHS, DVD.** *SW* Max von Sydow, Liv Ullmann, Gunnar Bjornstrand, Sigge Furst, Birgitta Valberg, Hans Alfredson, Ingvar Kjellson; ***D:*** Ingmar Bergman; ***W:*** Ingmar Bergman; ***C:*** Sven Nykvist. Natl. Soc. Film Critics '68: Actress (Ullmann), Director (Bergman), Film.

Shame **1987 (R)** Strange Australian revenge drama about a female lawyer/biker who rides into a small town and finds herself avenging the rape of a 16-year-old girl. Is it a genuinely feminist movie about justice and a strong woman taking charge? Or is it exploitative trash using a politically correct theme and "message" as a peg for much—very much—gratuitous violence? Hard to tell. Cultish for sure; made on a B budget. **95m/C VHS.** *AU* Deborra-Lee Furness, Tony Barry, Simone Buchanan, Gillian Jones; ***D:*** Steve Jodrell; ***W:*** Beverly Blakenship, Michael Brindley.

Shame **1992** In a small logging town a group of violent high school thugs get away with rape because the women are too terrified to go to the cops. Then lawyer Diana Cadell (Donohoe) gets stuck in town when her motorcycle breaks down. When she finds out what's been happening, she urges one victim (Balk) to speak out and suddenly they become the targets of both the vicious attackers and a town which would like to hush the entire mess up. Very strong performances by Donohoe and Balk. U.S. version of the same-titled 1987 Australian movie. **91m/C VHS.** Amanda Donohoe, Fairuza Balk, Dean Stockwell, Dan Gauthier; ***D:*** Dan Lerner; ***W:*** Rebecca Soladay. **CABLE**

Shame of the Jungle 1/2 **1975 (R)** Animated spoof of Tarzan featuring the voices of John Belushi, Bill Murray, and Johnny Weissmuller Jr. **73m/C VHS.** *BE FR* ***D:*** Jean-Paul Picha, Boris Szulzinger, Anne Beatts; ***W:*** Jean-Paul Picha, Michael O'Donoghue, Anne Beatts; ***C:*** Raymond Burlet; ***V:*** Johnny Weissmuller Jr., John Belushi, Bill Murray, Brian Doyle-Murray, Christopher Guest, Andrew Duncan.

Shame, Shame on the Bixby Boys 1/2 **1982** Somewhere in the Old West, outside a small town, lives a band of misfits who persist in rustling cattle. The Bixby Boys and their Pa have made a bad habit into a family tradition. **90m/C VHS.** Monte Markham, Sammy Jackson; ***D:*** Anthony Bowers.

Shame, Shame, Shame 1/2 **1998 (R)** Pretty much lives up to its title. A Ph.D candidate working on her thesis asks her subjects to disrobe as part of her interviewing process and discovers as they shed their clothes they shed their secrets and inhibitions as well. **87m/C VHS.** Heidi Schanz, Costas Mandylor, Audie England, Valerie Perrine, Olivia Hussey; ***D:*** Zalman King. **VIDEO**

Shameless *Mad Dogs and Englishmen* **1994 (R)** Wealthy Antonia Dyer (Hurley) is the self-centered, drug addict daughter of aristocrat Sir Harry Dyer (Treves). Her dealer is upper-class Tony Vernon-Smith (Brett), who's involved with Sandy (Delamere), the daughter of corrupt narcotics cop Stringer (Ackland). Stringer discovers the two girls know each other and irrationally blames Antonia for his daughter's heroin habit. Meanwhile, American student Mike (Howell) has been trying to get girlfriend Antonia off the drugs. Hurley's properly snooty and manipulative while Howell seems out-of-place and uncomfortable. **99m/C VHS, DVD.** *GB* Elizabeth Hurley, C. Thomas Howell, Joss Ackland, Jeremy Brett, Frederick Treves, Claire Bloom, Louise Delamere, Chris(topher) Adamson; ***D:*** Henry Cole; ***W:*** Tim Sewell; ***C:*** John Peters; ***M:*** Barrie Guard.

The Shaming 1/2 *The Sin; Good Luck, Miss Wyckoff* **1979 (R)** Puritanical schoolteacher is raped by a janitor, then develops a voracious sexual appetite. Horrible script, offensive premise can't be saved by good cast. Based on a novel by William Inge. **90m/C VHS.** Anne Heywood, Donald Pleasence, Robert Vaughn, Carolyn Jones; ***D:*** Marvin J. Chomsky.

Shampoo 1/2 **1975 (R)** A satire of morals (and lack thereof) set in Southern California, concerning a successful hairdresser (Beatty) and the many women in his life. A notable scene with Julie Christie is set at a 1968 presidential election-night gathering. Fisher's screen debut, only one year before "Star Wars" made her famous. Has a healthy glow in places and a perky bounce, but too many split ends. **112m/C VHS, DVD.** Warren Beatty, Julie Christie, Goldie Hawn, Jack Warden, Lee Grant, Tony Bill, Carrie Fisher, William Castle, Howard Hesseman; ***D:*** Hal Ashby; ***W:*** Warren Beatty, Robert Towne; ***M:*** John Barry. Oscars '75: Support. Actress (Grant); Natl. Soc. Film Critics '75: Screenplay; Writers Guild '75: Orig. Screenplay.

Shamus **1973 (PG)** Private dick Reynolds investigates a smuggling ring, beds a sultry woman, gets in lotsa fights. Classic Burt vehicle meant as a send-up. Unoriginal but fun. **91m/C VHS, DVD.** Burt Reynolds, Dyan Cannon, John P. Ryan; ***D:*** Buzz Kulik; ***W:*** Barry Beckerman; ***M:*** Jerry Goldsmith.

Shane **1953** A retired gunfighter, now a drifter, comes to the aid of a homestead family threatened by a land baron and his hired gun. Ladd is the mystery man who becomes the idol of the family's young son. Classic, flawless Western. Pulitzer prize-winning western novelist A.B. Guthrie Jr. adapted from the novel by Jack Schaefer. Long and stately; worth savoring. **117m/C VHS, DVD.** Alan Ladd, Jean Arthur, Van Heflin, Brandon de Wilde, Jack Palance, Ben Johnson, Elisha Cook Jr., Edgar Buchanan, Emile Meyer; ***D:*** George Stevens; ***W:*** Jack Sher; ***C:*** Loyal Griggs; ***M:*** Victor Young. Oscars '53: Color Cinematog.; AFI '98: Top 100; Natl. Bd. of Review '53: Director (Stevens), Natl. Film Reg. '93.

Shanghai **2009** American expat Paul Soames returns to Japanese-occupied Shanghai four months before Pearl Harbor to investigate the murder of friend. **m/C DVD.** John Cusack, Jeffrey Dean Morgan, Gong Li, Daniel Lapaine, Chow Yun-Fat, Nicholas (Nick) Rowe; ***D:*** Mikael Hafstrom; ***W:*** Hossein Amini; ***C:*** Benoit Delhomme; ***M:*** Gabriel Yared.

The Shanghai Cobra 1/2 **1945** Below-average mystery has Chan hired by the government to investigate several supposed cobra bite murders. All motives lead to stealing a supply of radium. **64m/B VHS, DVD.** Sidney Toler, Benson Fong, Mantan Moreland, Walter Fenner, James B. Cardwell, Joan Barclay, James Flavin; ***D:*** Phil Karlson.

Shanghai Express 1/2 **1932** Dietrich is at her most alluring in this mystical and exotic story that made legends out of both star and director. Dietrich plays Shanghai Lily, a woman of objectionable reputation, who has a reunion of sorts with ex-lover Brook aboard a slow-moving train through China. Remade as "Peking Express." Based on a story by Harry Hervey. **80m/B VHS.** Marlene Dietrich, Clive Brook, Anna May Wong, Warner Oland, Eugene Pallette, Lawrence Grant, Louise Closser Hale; ***D:*** Josef von Sternberg; ***W:*** Jules Furthman; ***C:*** Lee Garmes. Oscars '32: Cinematog.

The Shanghai Gesture 1/2 **1942** A wildly baroque, subversive melodrama. An English financier tries to close a gambling den, only to be blackmailed by the female proprietor—who tells him not only is the man's daughter heavily indebted to her, but that she is the wife he abandoned long ago. Based on a notorious Broadway play. Von Sternberg had to make numerous changes to the script in order to get it past the Hays censors; the director's final Hollywood work, and worthy of his oeuvre, but oddly unsatisfying. **97m/B VHS, DVD.** Walter Huston, Gene Tierney, Victor Mature, Ona Munson, Albert Bassermann, Eric Blore, Maria Ouspenskaya, Phyllis Brooks, Mike Mazurki; ***D:*** Josef von Sternberg; ***W:*** Josef von Sternberg, Jules Furthman, Geza Herczeg, Karl Vollmoller; ***C:*** Paul Ivano; ***M:*** Richard Hageman.

Shanghai Kiss **2007** Twenty-something Liam Liu (Leung) is a struggling Chinese-American actor in L.A. who befriends 16-year-old high school genius Adelaide (Panettiere). Imagine the complications when romance starts lurking, and Liam can't quite forget temptation when he decides to move to Shanghai after inheriting his grandmother's house. **106m/C DVD.** Ken Leung, Hayden Panettiere, Kelly Hu, Joel David Moore, James Hong, Timothy Bottoms; ***D:*** Kern Konwiser, David Ren; ***W:*** David Ren; ***C:*** Alexander Buono; ***M:*** David Kitay. **VIDEO**

Shanghai Knights ♂♂ 1/2 **2003 (PG-13)** Chon Wang (Chan) and Roy (Wilson) team up again when Wang's father is killed while guarding the Imperial Seal. Wang's sister Li (Fann) has witnessed the crime and followed the culprit to London, where the duo also converge. There they find a plot by frustrated royal heirs Rathbone (Gillen) and Wu Chan (Yen) to overthrow the British and Chinese thrones. Chan and Wilson still have their great chemistry, and the script gives them plenty of opportunities to show it. Chan choreographs the fight scenes like numbers in a musical to excellent effect, paying homage to "Singin' in the Rain" as well as some of his influences such as the Keystone Kops, Harold Lloyd, Abbott and Costello, and Charlie Chaplin. Victorian-era cultural references are fun to catalogue as well. **107m/C VHS, DVD.** *US* Jackie Chan, Owen Wilson, Aidan Gillen, Fann Wong, Donnie Yen, Gemma Jones, Kim Chan, Aaron Johnson, Thomas (Tom) Fisher, Oliver Cotton; ***D:*** David Dobkin; ***W:*** Alfred Gough, Miles Millar; ***C:*** Adrian Biddle; ***M:*** Randy Edelman.

Shanghai Noon ♂♂ 1/2 **2000 (PG-13)** Goofy, good-natured, western action/comedy finds Chinese imperial guard Chon Wang (Chan) in trouble for not preventing Princess Pei Pei (Liu) from running off to America (circa 1880) with her American tutor (Connery). But it all turns out to be a kidnapping scheme and Wang winds up in Nevada, helping to deliver the ransom gold. Through some unlikely events, Wang hooks up with talkative, unsuccessful outlaw Roy O'Bannon (Wilson), learns some of the west's wilder ways, and the buds set out to rescue the damsel, who's no shrinking flower herself. Chan and Wilson are both throughly ingratiating and you've got the Chan stunts to look forward to as well. **110m/C VHS, DVD.** Jackie Chan, Lucy Liu, Owen Wilson, Roger Yuan, Xander Berkeley, Jason Connery, Henry O, Walton Goggins, Russ Badger, Rafael Baez, Brandon Merrill; ***D:*** Tom Dey; ***W:*** Alfred Gough, Miles Millar; ***C:*** Dan Mindel; ***M:*** Randy Edelman.

Shanghai Surprise ♂ 1/2 **1986 (PG-13)** Tie salesman Penn and missionary Madonna (yeah, right) are better than you'd think, and the story (of opium smuggling in China in the '30s) is intrepid and wildly fun, but indifferently directed and unsure of itself. Executive producer George Harrison wrote the songs and has a cameo. **90m/C VHS, DVD.** Sean Penn, Madonna, Paul Freeman, Richard Griffiths; ***Cameos:*** George Harrison; ***D:*** Jim Goddard; ***W:*** Robert Bentley; ***M:*** George Harrison, Michael Kamen. Golden Raspberries '86: Worst Actress (Madonna).

Shanghai Triad ♂♂♂ 1/2 *Yao a Yao Yao Dao Waipo Qiao* **1995 (R)** Seventh collaboration of director Yimou and star Li takes place in violent crime dynasty of 1930s Shanghai. Here, eight days are seen through the eyes of a young boy (Cuihua) initiated into the Triad to be the lackey of the mob boss's arrogant mistress (Li). The trio and some trusty associates flee to the country after things heat up with a rival mob. Yimou subtly distinguishes the dichotomy between the jaded criminals and the naive youth with the move from the city to the country and his use of color and tone while avoiding cliche. Plot twists are fresh and technical aspects impeccable. Chinese with subtitles. **108m/C VHS, DVD.** *FR CH* Gong Li, Baotian Li, Xuejian Li, Shun Chun Shusheng, Wang Xiaoxiao Cuihua, Jiang Baoying; ***D:*** Yimou Zhang; ***W:*** Bi Feiyu; ***C:*** Lu Yue; ***M:*** Zhang Guangtain.

Shank ♂ 1/2 **2009** Suffers from inexperience both in front of and behind the camera (it's Pearce's directorial debut) but has some powerful moments. Eighteen-year-old Bristol gang member Cal is immersed in a world of drugs, violence, and anonymous sex as he tries to keep secret the fact that he is gay and deeply attracted to his best mate Jonno. Would-be leader Nessa is suspicious, especially when Cal is disgusted by an attempted gay bashing and allows French exchange student Olivier to escape. Incensed by Cal's betrayal, Nessa goads Jonno into a violent revenge. **89m/C DVD.** *GB* Wayne Virgo, Marc Laurent, Tom Bott, Alice Payne, Garry Summers; ***D:*** Simon Pearce; ***W:*** Christian Martin, Darren Flaxstone; ***C:*** Simon Pearce; ***M:*** Bernaby Taylor.

Shanty Tramp ♂ **1967** Small-town tramp puts the moves on an evangelist, a motorcycle gang, and a young black man, who risks his life trying to save her from her loose morals. Another cheesy flick made for the drive-in crowd. **72m/B VHS, DVD.** Lee Holland, Bill Rogers, Lawrence Tobin; ***D:*** Joseph Prieto. **TV**

Shaolin & Wu Tang ♂♂♂ *Shaolin Wu Tang; Shao Lin yu Wu Dang; Shaolin Temple, Part II* **1981** Often considered an early kung fu classic, the only American version of this film has fairly bad dubbing along with subtitles translated from Chinese that don't match the dubbed dialogue, leading to moments of unintended fun. A Manchu prince sets the Shaolin and Wu Tang clans against one another to learn their secrets, and two friends turn against each other as they belong to opposite sides. Eventually making up, they team up to take on the Prince in revenge. **90m/C DVD.** *HK* Shen Chan, Adam Cheng, Hoi-Shan Kwan, Chia Hui Liu, Elvis Tsui, Lung-Wai Wang, Idy Chan, Hoi San Lee; ***D:*** Chia Hui Liu.

Shaolin Soccer ♂♂ 1/2 *Siulam Chukkau; Siu lam juk kau* **2001 (PG-13)** Wacky action-comedy about Sing (Chow), a kung fu expert and Shaolin monk, playing on a soccer team with other monks vying for Hong Kong's national championship against "Team Evil." Went on to become the highest-grossing film in Hong Kong's history. In Cantonese, with English subtitles. **87m/C DVD, UMD.** Stephen (Chiau) Chow, Man-Tat Ng, Cecilia Cheung, Vicki Zhao, Yin (Patrick) Tse; ***D:*** Stephen (Chiau) Chow; ***W:*** Stephen (Chiau) Chow, Kan-Cheung (Sammy) Tsang; ***C:*** Ting Wo Kwong, Pak-huen Kwen; ***M:*** Lowell Lo, Raymond Wong.

The Shape of Things ♂♂ **2003 (R)** LaBute is back to his own skewed view of the world, taken from his 2001 play. Nebbishy Adam (Rudd) works as a guard at a college art museum. Evelyn (Weisz) is the art student who bedazzles him, and she begins to make him over into someone desirable, which angers his chauvinistic best friend Philip (Weller). But the "new" Adam sparks feelings in Philip's fiancee Jenny (Mol), who was once the object of Adam's unrequited affection. Never subtle, LaBute's intention to leave no cruelty unexplored is blatant and wears quickly. Despite the best efforts of the actors involved, the film's stage origins and LaBute's obvious direction combine to lessen the film's impact. **96m/C VHS, DVD.** *US* Paul Rudd, Rachel Weisz, Gretchen Mol, Frederick Weller; ***D:*** Neil LaBute; ***W:*** Neil LaBute; ***C:*** James L. Carter; ***M:*** Elvis Costello.

Shark! ♂ 1/2 *Man-Eater; Un Arma de Dos Filos* **1968 (PG)** American gun smuggler Reynolds, stranded in a tiny seaport in Africa, joins the crew of a marine biologist's boat. He soon discovers the boat's owner and his wife are trying to retrieve gold bullion that lies deep in shark-infested waters. Typical Reynoldsian action-infested dumbness. Like "Twilight Zone: The Movie," earned notoriety because of on-location tragedy: a stunt diver really was killed by a shark. Edited without the consent of Fuller, who disowned it. **92m/C VHS, DVD.** Burt Reynolds, Barry Sullivan, Arthur Kennedy; ***D:*** Samuel Fuller; ***W:*** Samuel Fuller.

Shark Attack ♂ 1/2 **1999 (R)** A marine biologist investigates a rash of shark attacks terrorizing an African fishing village that have claimed the life of a friend. **95m/C VHS, DVD.** *SA* Casper Van Dien, Ernie Hudson, Bentley Mitchum, Jenny (Jennifer) McShane; ***D:*** Bob Misiorowski; ***W:*** Scott Devine, William Hooke; ***C:*** Lawrence Sher. **VIDEO**

Shark Attack 2 ♂ 1/2 **2000 (R)** Biological experiment on shark goes awry causing a mutant to go on a particularly nasty tear. Yeah, some shark hunters go after the beastie but you know they're just appetizers. **93m/C VHS, DVD.** Nikita Ager, Daniel Alexander, Thorsten Kaye, Danny Kei; ***D:*** David Worth, Yossi Wein; ***W:*** William Hooke, Scott Devine; ***M:*** Mark Morgan. **VIDEO**

Shark Attack 3: Megalodon ♂♂ **2002 (R)** An amusing goof of a killer sea critter flick. A company lying cable on the ocean floor wakes up a prehistoric Megalodon shark that decides to snack on vacationers at a nearby ocean resort. This is bad for business, so resort minion Ben (Barrowman) and paleontologist Cataline (McShane) hunt the beastie down. And then find out they've only killed a baby. And boy is mama mad! **94m/C VHS, DVD.** John Barrowman, Jenny (Jennifer) McShane, Ryan Cutrona, George Stanchev; ***D:*** David Worth; ***W:*** Scott Devine, William Hooke; ***C:*** David Worth; ***M:*** Bill Wandel. **VIDEO**

Shark Hunter ♂ *Guardians of the Deep; Il Cacciatore di Squali* **1979** Shark hunter gets ensnared in the mob's net off the Mexican coast as they race for a cache of sunken millions. The usual garden-variety B-grade adventure. **95m/C VHS.** *IT SP* Franco Nero, Jorge Luke, Mike Forrest, Werner Pochath; ***D:*** Enzo G. Castellari; ***W:*** Tito Carpi; ***C:*** R(aul) P. Cubero; ***M:*** Guido de Angelis, Maurizio de Angelis.

Shark River ♂ 1/2 **1953** A man attempts to get his brother, a Civil War veteran accused of murder, through the Everglades and send him to safety in Cuba. Good photography of the great swamp; disappointing story. **80m/C VHS.** Steve Cochran, Carole Mathews, Warren Stevens; ***D:*** John Rawlins; ***W:*** Lewis Meltzer, Louis Lantz.

Shark Skin Man and Peach Hip Girl ♂♂ 1/2 *Samehada otoko to momojiri onna* **1998 (R)** Toshiko (Shie Koinata) wants to escape the life she leads working at a hotel being molested by her pervert uncle. Kuro (Tadanobu Asano) has just stolen a bunch of money from his Yakuza bosses and is running down the street in his underwear, when Toshiko plows into him. Love is born. They of course end up on the run from Kuro's insane boss, and Toshiko's pervert uncle. Based on the comic by Minetaro Michezuki. **108m/C DVD.** *JP* Tadanobu Asano, Ittoku Kishibe, Kimie Shingyoki, Susumu Terajima, Sie Kohinata, Shingo Tsurumi, Yoji Tanaka, Yoshiyuki Morishita, Kanji Tsuda, Tatsuya Gashuin, Daigaku Sekine, Koh Takasugi, Shingoro Yamada, Hitoshi Kiyokawa, Keisuke Horibe, Youhachi Shimada, Hisaji Yamano; ***D:*** Katushito Ishii; ***W:*** Katushito Ishii, Minetaro Mochizuki; ***C:*** Hiroshi Machida.

Shark Swarm ♂ 1/2 **2008** An over-extended TV mini without enough shark action. Greedy industrialist Hamilton Lux (Assante) has been dumping toxins into the waters of Full Moon Bay in an effort to destroy the local fishing industry so he can buy property cheap for his planned resort. It's discovered that the local shark population of Great Whites have mutated and are even deadlier since they now hunt in packs—killing anything (or anyone) occupying their waters. **164m/C DVD.** John Schneider, Armand Assante, Daryl Hannah, Roark Critchlow, Heather McComb, F. Murray Abraham, John Enos; ***D:*** James A. Contner; ***W:*** David Rosiak, Matthew Chernov; ***C:*** Dane Peterson; ***M:*** Nathan Furst. **TV**

Shark Tale ♂♂ 1/2 **2004 (PG)** This animated underwater comedy has the faint smell of dead fish clinging to it—probably because it tries too hard. Boastful guppy Oscar (Smith) works at the mob-fronted Whale Wash and is in trouble with his boss (Scorsese), who thinks the kid should be taught a lesson. Teaching lessons is also on the mind of shark mob boss Lino (De Niro), who wants son Frankie (Imperioli) to straighten out his younger bro, Lenny (Black), a sweet schnook who's gone vegetarian. Oscar takes the credit when Frankie accidentally gets killed and then must defend his reputation as a sharkslayer, aided by a reluctant Lenny. Longtime collaborators De Niro and Scorsese have a blast spoofing wiseguys but a lot of the humor will only be understood by movie-loving adults and may prove sleep-inducing to the younger set. **92m/C VHS, DVD.** ***D:*** Victoria Jenson, Bibo Bergeron, Rob Letterman; ***W:*** Michael J. Wilson, Rob Letterman; ***M:*** Hans Zimmer; ***V:*** Will Smith, Robert De Niro, Renee Zellweger, Jack Black, Angelina Jolie, Martin Scorsese, Peter Falk, Michael Imperioli, Vincent Pastore, Doug E. Doug, Ziggy Marley, Katie Couric, Jenifer Lewis, Lenny Venito, Phil LaMarr.

Sharks' Treasure ♂ 1/2 **1975 (PG)** A band of escaped convicts commandeer a boat filled with gold. Old fashioned sunken-treasure tale unexceptional except as a virtual one man show by writer/actor/director/producer/fitness nut Wilde. **96m/C VHS.** Cornel Wilde, Yaphet Kotto, John Nellson, Cliff Osmond, David Canary, David Gilliam; ***D:*** Cornel Wilde.

Sharky's Machine ♂♂ 1/2 **1981 (R)** A tough undercover cop (Reynolds) is hot on the trail of a crooked crime czar. Meanwhile he falls for a high-priced hooker. Well done but overdone action, with much violence. Based on the William Diehl novel. **119m/C VHS, DVD.** Burt Reynolds, Rachel Ward, Vittorio Gassman, Brian Keith, Charles Durning, Bernie Casey, Richard Libertini, Henry Silva, John Fiedler, Earl Holliman; ***D:*** Burt Reynolds; ***W:*** Gerald Di Pego; ***C:*** William A. Fraker.

Sharma & Beyond ♂ **1984** A teenage would-be science fiction writer falls in love with the daughter of a famous sci-fi author. **85m/C VHS.** Suzanne Burden, Robert Urquhart, Michael Maloney; ***D:*** Brian Gilbert; ***M:*** Rachel Portman.

Sharon's Secret ♂♂ 1/2 **1995 (R)** When the mutilated bodies of wealthy Richard Harly and his wife are discovered, investigating detective Thomas McGregor (Henry) looks to place the blame on their traumatized 16-year-old daughter Sharon (Cameron), who'll inherit a fortune. Psychiatrist Laurel O'Connor (Harris) is assigned to help Sharon recover and she's defended by family attorney Frank Bowdin (McArthur) but it seems everyone has something to hide. **91m/C VHS.** Candace Cameron, Mel Harris, Gregg Henry, Alex McArthur, Paul Regina, Elaine Kagan, James Pickens Jr.; ***D:*** Michael Scott; ***W:*** Mark Homer. **CABLE**

Sharpe's Battle ♂♂ 1/2 **1994** Sharpe (Bean) must prepare the Royal Irish company, led by Lord Kiely (Durr) and used to only ceremonial duties, for their first battle. Meanwhile, Kiely's wife (Byrne) goes to Sharpe for help with a personal matter and there's more trouble with the French. Based on the novel by Bernard Cornwell; made for British TV. **100m/C VHS, DVD.** *GB* Sean Bean, Daragh O'Malley, Hugh Fraser, Jason Durr, Allie Byrne; ***D:*** Tom Clegg; ***W:*** Russell Lewis. **TV**

Sharpe's Challenge ♂♂ 1/2 **2006** After Waterloo, Richard Sharpe (Bean) is dispatched to India because a local Maharaja is threatening British interests. Things worsen when Sharpe discovers best friend Harper (O'Malley) is missing, a general's daughter (Brown) has been kidnapped, and the beautiful but scheming Madhuvanthi (Lakshmi) wants to use Richard to further her own ambitions. Filmed in Rajasthan, India; based on the Bernard Cornwell novels. The first new TV Sharpe adventure since 1997. **136m/C DVD.** *GB* Sean Bean, Padma Lakshmi, Toby Stephens, Daragh O'Malley, Lucy Brown, Hugh Fraser, Michael Cochrane, Peter Symonds, Karan Panthaky; ***D:*** Tom Clegg; ***W:*** Russell Lewis. **TV**

Sharpe's Company ♂♂ 1/2 **1994** Sharpe (Bean) sets out to rescue Spanish lover Teresa (Serna) and his infant daughter, trapped in the French-held city of Badajoz, which is about to be stormed by British troops. To make matters worse, Sharpe must also deal with the machinations of underhanded madman Sergeant Obadiah Hakeswill (Postlethwaite), an old enemy with a grudge to settle. Based on the novel by Bernard Cornwell; made for British TV. **100m/C VHS, DVD.** *GB* Sean Bean, Assumpta Serna, Daragh O'Malley, Pete Postlethwaite, Hugh Fraser, Clive Francis, Louise Germaine; ***D:*** Tom Clegg; ***W:*** Charles Wood. **TV**

Sharpe's Eagle ♂♂ 1/2 **1993** Sharpe (Bean) and his chosen band of sharpshooters are once again in the thick of battle against Napoleon's troops but this time they have the misfortune to be led by the imbecilic Sir Henry Simmerson (Cochrane). Thanks to Simmerson's cowardice, the regimental colors are captured and a heroic officer Sharpe admires is killed. Setting out for revenge, Sharpe is determined to capture the French mascot, a carved golden eagle carried into battle, and settle some personal scores. Based on the novel by Bernard Cornwell; made for British TV. **100m/C VHS, DVD.** *GB* Sean Bean, Assumpta Serna, Brian Cox, David Troughton, Daragh O'Malley, Michael Cochrane,

Katia Caballero; ***D:*** Tom Clegg; ***W:*** Eoghan Harris; ***C:*** Ivan Strasburg; ***M:*** Dominic Muldowney. **TV**

Sharpe's Enemy 1/2 **1994** Sharpe (Bean) is sent to a mountain stronghold, held by a band of deserters, to ransom Isabella (Hurley), the bride of English colonel, Sir Augustus Farthingdale (Child). But the evil Hakeswill (Postlethwaite) is leading the criminals and he refuses to make things easy for our hero—nor will the French troops leave the English soldiers in peace. Based on the novel by Bernard Cornwell; made for British TV. **100m/C VHS, DVD.** *GB* Sean Bean, Assumpta Serna, Pete Postlethwaite, Daragh O'Malley, Hugh Fraser, Elizabeth Hurley, Michael Byrne, Jeremy Child, Nicholas (Nick) Rowe; ***D:*** Tom Clegg; ***W:*** Eoghan Harris. **TV**

Sharpe's Gold 1/2 **1994** Circa 1813 and Richard Sharpe (Bean) has now been promoted to Major—still leading his band of renegade sharpshooters. This time they're assigned to trade rifles for deserters held by the partisans and search for hidden Aztec gold, as Wellington (Fraser) prepares to push on into France. Sharpe must also protect Wellington's cousin Bess (Linehan) and her daughter Ellie (Ashbourne) as they search for Bess' missing husband. Based on the novel by Bernard Cornwell; made for British TV. **100m/C VHS, DVD.** *GB* Sean Bean, Daragh O'Malley, Hugh Fraser, Rosaleen Linehan, Jayne Ashbourne, Abel Folk, Peter Eyre; ***D:*** Tom Clegg; ***W:*** Nigel Kneale. **TV**

Sharpe's Honour 1/2 **1994** Sharpe (Bean) becomes a pawn of French spy Pierre Ducos when he's forced to cross enemy lines, disguised as a Spanish rebel, in order to defend himself against allegations of dishonor. Sharpe's also unable to resist the attractions of the Marquesa Dorada (Krige), who's also part of Ducos' plan. Based on the novel by Bernard Cornwell; made for British TV. **100m/C VHS, DVD.** *GB* Sean Bean, Daragh O'Malley, Alice Krige, Hugh Fraser, Michael Byrne, Ron Cook; ***D:*** Tom Clegg; ***W:*** Colin MacDonald. **TV**

Sharpe's Justice 1/2 **1997** Having cleared his name, Richard Sharpe (Bean) returns to England and is ordered north where he's to command the local militia. But Sharpe soon has to decide whether to support the local gentry or the working class in a time of social unrest. Based on the novel by Bernard Cornwell. **100m/C VHS, DVD.** *GB* Sean Bean, Daragh O'Malley, Abigail Cruttenden, Alexis Denisof, Douglas Henshall, Caroline Langrishe, Philip Glenister; ***D:*** Tom Clegg. **TV**

Sharpe's Legend 1/2 **1997** Highlights from the British TV series detailing the life, loves, and career of 19th-century British soldier/hero Richard Sharpe (Bean). Narrated by Rifleman Cooper (Mears). **90m/C VHS, DVD.** *GB* Sean Bean, Michael Mears; ***D:*** Paul Wilmshurst. **TV**

Sharpe's Mission 1/2 **1996** Sharpe (Bean) joins with Colonel Brand (Strong) and his men to blow up an ammunition depot as Wellington continues his invasion of France. But Brand arouses Sharpe's suspicions that the supposedly heroic Colonel is actually a French spy. Based on the novel by Bernard Cornwell. **100m/C VHS, DVD.** *GB* Sean Bean, Daragh O'Malley, Hugh Fraser, James Laurenson, Mark Strong, Abigail Cruttenden; ***D:*** Tom Clegg; ***W:*** Eoghan Harris. **TV**

Sharpe's Regiment 1/2 **1996** Wellington prepares for the invasion of France in June, 1813 but the South Essex batallion needs more men. So Sharpe (Bean) and Harper (O'Malley) are sent back to London for recruits and uncover corruption in high places. Based on the novel by Bernard Cornwell. **100m/C VHS, DVD.** *GB* Sean Bean, Daragh O'Malley, Nicholas Farrell, Michael Cochrane, Abigail Cruttenden, Caroline Langrishe, James Laurenson; ***D:*** Tom Clegg; ***W:*** Eoghan Harris. **TV**

Sharpe's Revenge 1/2 **1997** The Penisular War is over but Sharpe (Bean) is accused of stealing Napoleon's treasures by old enemy Ducos. Abandoned by his wife when he's convicted of the crime, Sharpe escapes from prison and crosses postwar France in search of the truth. Based on the novel by Bernard Cornwell. **100m/C VHS, DVD.** *GB* Sean Bean, Daragh O'Malley, Abigail Cruttenden, Feodor Atkine, Alexis Denisof, Cecile Paoli, Philip Whitchurch; ***D:*** Tom Clegg; ***W:*** Eoghan Harris. **TV**

Sharpe's Rifles 1/2 **1993** Swashbuckling heroics dominate as the Duke of Wellington's British soldiers battle Napoleon's French forces in the 1809 Penisular War (fought in Spain and Portugal). Common soldier Richard Sharpe (Bean) has just been promoted and given the unenviable task of leading a group of malcontent sharpshooters on a secret mission to aid Britain's Spanish allies. But it's not all hard times for Sharpe since the Spanish commander happens to be a very lovely woman. Adapted from the novel by Bernard Cornwell; made for British TV. **100m/C VHS, DVD.** *GB* Sean Bean, Assumpta Serna, Brian Cox, David Troughton, Daragh O'Malley, Julian Fellowes, Timothy Bentinck, Simon Andreu, Michael Mears, John Tams, Jason Salkey, Paul Trussell; ***D:*** Tom Clegg; ***W:*** Eoghan Harris; ***C:*** Ivan Strasburg; ***M:*** Dominic Muldowney. **TV**

Sharpe's Siege 1/2 **1996** In the winter of 1813, Napoleon Bonaparte sends his best spy, Major Ducos (Atkine), to find out where Wellington plans to invade France. The newly married Sharpe (Bean) is forced to leave his ill wife, Jane (Cruttenden), and capture a French fort while preventing Ducos' treachery. Based on the novel by Bernard Cornwell. **100m/C VHS, DVD.** *GB* Sean Bean, Daragh O'Malley, Hugh Fraser, Abigail Cruttenden, James Laurenson, Feodor Atkine; ***D:*** Tom Clegg; ***W:*** Eoghan Harris. **TV**

Sharpe's Sword 1/2 **1994** Sharpe's (Bean) sent to protect Wellington's top spy, El Mirador, and finds himself up against Napoleon's top swordsman Colonel Leroux (Fierry). When Sharpe's wounded, it's up to Lass (Mortimer), a young mute convent girl, to save our hero's life. Based on the novel by Bernard Cornwell; made for British TV. **100m/C VHS, DVD.** *GB* Sean Bean, Daragh O'Malley, Patrick Fierry, Emily Mortimer, John Kavanagh; ***D:*** Tom Clegg; ***W:*** Eoghan Harris. **TV**

Sharpe's Waterloo 1/2 **1997** Sharpe's (Bean) making a new life with new love Lucille (Paoli) at their French chateau. But when Napoleon returns from exile, Sharpe returns to the army and the Chosen Men to organize a defense before the battle of Waterloo. Based on the novel by Bernard Cornwell. **100m/C VHS, DVD.** *GB* Sean Bean, Daragh O'Malley, Hugh Fraser, Cecile Paoli, Alexis Denisof, Paul Bettany; ***D:*** Tom Clegg. **TV**

Sharpshooter 1/2 **2007** Remar's really the only reason to watch this by-the-numbers thriller. Special ops sniper Dillon (Remar) is looking forward to a peaceful retirement. Then his government contact Flick (Van Peebles) persuades him to do one last mission—eliminate a terrorist who's plotting mayhem on U.S. soil. But Dillon soon has second thoughts about the validity of his assignment and wonders just who the true target is. **89m/C DVD.** James Remar, Mario Van Peebles, Catherine Mary Stewart, Bruce Boxleitner, Al Sapienza; ***D:*** Armand Mastroianni; ***W:*** Steven H. Berman; ***C:*** Dane Peterson; ***M:*** Stephen Graziano. **TV**

Shattered *Scherben* **1921** Key film in Germany's kammerspiel (chamber play) movement, which emphasized naturalism with a minimum number of characters. A railway worker's daughter is seduced by her father's supervisor. When the man abandons her, the girl's father takes revenge. **62m/B VHS.** *GE* Werner Krauss, Edith Posca, Paul Otto; ***D:*** Lupu Pick; ***W:*** Carl Mayer.

Shattered 1/2 *Something to Hide* **1972 (R)** Finch plays Harry, a man blamed for a failed marriage, held hostage in his home by his own paranoia, and driven to bouts of drinking. Slowly his tenuous grip on sanity slips and at any moment his fragile and crumbling life may be shattered. Tired, overwrought domestic drama. **100m/C VHS.** *GB* Peter Finch, Shelley Winters, Colin Blakely; ***D:*** Alastair Reid.

Shattered **1991 (R)** An architect recovering from a serious automobile accident tries to regain the memory that he has lost. As he begins to put together the pieces of his life, some parts of the puzzle don't quite fit. For example, he recalls his now loving wife's affair as well as his own. He remembers that he hired a private detective to follow his wife and shockingly, he remembers that he once believed his wife had planned to kill him. Are these memories the real thing, or are they all part of some mad, recuperative nightmare? Who knows. **98m/C VHS, DVD.** Tom Berenger, Bob Hoskins, Greta Scacchi, Joanne Whalley, Corbin Bernsen, Theodore Bikel; ***D:*** Wolfgang Petersen; ***W:*** Wolfgang Petersen.

Shattered *Butterfly on a Wheel* **2007 (R)** Neil (Butler) and his wife Abby (Bello) must perform a series of nearly-impossible (and criminal) tasks around Chicago in order to save their young daughter, who's been kidnapped by sociopath Ryan (Brosnan). Implausible and unsubtle (with a twist ending) but that's one cool cast. **95m/C DVD.** *CA* Pierce Brosnan, Gerard Butler, Maria Bello, Claudette Mink, Callum Keith Rennie, Nicholas Lea, Samantha Ferris; ***D:*** Mike Barker; ***W:*** Maila Nurmi; ***C:*** Ashley Rowe; ***M:*** Robert Duncan.

Shattered City: The Halifax Explosion 1/2 **2003** In 1917, the city of Halifax, Nova Scotia, is a particularly bustling port due to WWI. But on December 6th, the French freighter Mont Blanc, carrying thousands of tons of TNT, collides with a Belgian relief ship in the harbor, causing a devastating explosion that nearly destroys the city and results in thousands of deaths and injuries. The city officials eventually look for someone to blame and harbor pilot Mackey may be the fall guy until Capt. Charlie Collins takes over his defense. Based on a true incident. **181m/C DVD.** *CA* Tamara Hope, Shauna Macdonald, Pete Postlethwaite, Paul Doucet, Graham Greene, Richard Donat, Zachary Bennett, Leon Pownall, Vincent Walsh, Ted Dykstra; ***D:*** Bruce Pittman; ***W:*** Keith Ross Leckie; ***C:*** Rene Ohashi; ***M:*** Christopher Dedrick. **TV**

Shattered Dreams 1/2 **1990** TV movie about domestic violence finds Wagner as the battered wife of a prominent, high-profile government official. Based on a true story. **94m/C VHS, DVD.** Georgann Johnson, James Karen, Lindsay Wagner, Michael Nouri; ***D:*** Robert Iscove; ***W:*** David Hill; ***C:*** John Beymer; ***M:*** Michael Convertino.

Shattered Glass **2003 (PG-13)** Christensen loses the Jedi robes to take on a character lured by a less-mystical dark side. Wunderkind Stephen Glass, a young New Republic journalist, is found to have fabricated 27 of the 41 articles he'd published. He also goes to great lengths to give truth to the lies, falsifying phone numbers, creating a bogus website, keeping fake notes. First-time director Ray was in close council with the principals involved in the true tale and does a fabulous job keeping the depiction believable. Background as to what drove him to it is all that's missing in this journalist suspense story. **99m/C VHS, DVD.** *US* Hayden Christensen, Peter Sarsgaard, Chloe Sevigny, Rosario Dawson, Melanie Lynskey, Steve Zahn, Hank Azaria, Luke Kirby, Cas Anvar, Ted Kotcheff, Mark Blum, Simone-Elise Girard, Chad E. Donella; ***D:*** Billy Ray; ***W:*** Billy Ray; ***C:*** Mandy Walker; ***M:*** Mychael Danna. Natl. Soc. Film Critics '03: Support. Actor (Sarsgaard).

Shattered Image 1/2 **1993 (R)** Confusing thriller about the FBI's involvement in the kidnapping of the owner of a model agency, as well as plastic surgery, and a big money scam. **100m/C VHS, DVD.** Bo Derek, Jack Scalia, John Savage, Dorian Harewood, Ramon Franco, Carol Lawrence, Michael (M.K.) Harris, David McCallum; ***D:*** Fritz Kiersch. **CABLE**

Shattered Image 1/2 **1998** Jessie (Parillaud) is either a cold-blooded hit woman dreaming she's a honeymooner, or a newly-wed dreaming she's a psycho assassin. Or both. After whacking a businessman in the men's room at a Seattle restaurant, our heroine goes home to bed, and wakes up a different woman. Literally. On her way to Jamaica with her new husband (Baldwin), Jessie again nods off and she's back in Seattle on her next hit. Each reality features characters from the alternate one, although (like Jessie) each has a different personality. Ruiz fills the screen with stunning homages (Wellesian mirror shots and Hitchcockian split personalities), a truly outrageous ending, and the surrealistic feel of a dream, making for psychotic, if not completely convincing, fun. **102m/C VHS, DVD.** Anne Parillaud, William Baldwin, Lisanne Falk, Graham Greene, Bulle Ogier, Billy Wilmott, O'Neil Peart, Leonie Forbes; ***D:*** Raul Ruiz; ***W:*** Duane Poole; ***C:*** Robby Muller; ***M:*** Jorge Arriagada.

Shattered Silence 1/2 *When Michael Calls* **1971** A woman is tormented by phone calls that seem to be coming from her dead son as her life is torn apart by divorce. Leaves unanswered the question: Will there be any suspense? Made for TV. Worthless and dumb. **73m/C VHS, DVD.** Elizabeth Ashley, Ben Gazzara, Michael Douglas, Karen Pearson; ***D:*** Philip Leacock. **TV**

Shattered Spirits 1/2 **1986 (PG-13)** Quiet family man cracks and goes on a rampage through his normally peaceful suburban neighborhood. Been done before and better. **93m/C VHS, DVD.** Martin Sheen, Melinda Dillon, Matthew Laborteaux, Roxana Zal, Lukas Haas; ***D:*** Robert Greenwald; ***W:*** Gregory Goodell; ***C:*** John R. Jensen; ***M:*** Michael Hoenig.

Shattered Vows **1984** A young nun struggles with her love for a priest and her desire for a child. Bertinelli is convincing as the confused teen in otherwise ordinary TV drama. Adapted from the true story of Dr. Mary Gilligan Wong as told in her book, "Nun: A Memoir." **95m/C VHS.** Valerie Bertinelli, David Morse, Caroline McWilliams, Patricia Neal, Millie Perkins, Leslie Ackerman, Lisa Jane Persky; ***D:*** Jack Bender.

Shaun of the Dead **2004 (R)** Brits Wright and Pegg's flick has been referred to as a "rom zom com" or romantic zombie comedy-certainly a cinematic rarity. Slacker clerk Shaun (Pegg), who lives with dim loser chum Ed (Frost), who is dumped by frustrated girlfriend Liz (Ashfield) and goes to his favorite pub to drown his sorrows. Because of his morning hangover, Shaun is unaware that London is suddenly overrun with the walking dead. It takes a zombie in the garden to get Shaun and Ed to take action—armed with a cricket bat, shovel, and unwanted vinyl discs from their record collection (the better to slice off a zombie's head). But there's an up side: the zombie crisis brings out the best in Shaun as the survivors retreat to the pub for a final stand, and more beer. **99m/C VHS, DVD, UMD, HD DVD.** Kate Ashfield, Penelope Wilton, Bill Nighy, Simon Pegg, Nick Frost, Lucy Davis, Dylan Moran, Nicola Cunningham, Jessica Stevenson; ***D:*** Edgar Wright; ***W:*** Simon Pegg, Edgar Wright; ***C:*** David M. Dunlap; ***M:*** Daniel Mudford, Peter Woodhead.

The Shawshank Redemption 1/2 **1994 (R)** Bank veep Andy (Robbins) is convicted of the murder of his wife and her lover and sentenced to the "toughest prison in the Northeast." While there he forms a friendship with lifer Red (Freeman), experiences the brutality of prison life, adapts, offers financial advice to the guards, and helps the warden (Gunton) cook the prison books...all in a short 19 years. In his theatrical debut, director Darabont avoids belaboring most prison movie cliches while Robbins' talent for playing ambiguous characters is put to good use, and Freeman brings his usual grace to what could have been a thankless role. Adapted from the novella "Rita Hayworth and the Shawshank Redemption" by Stephen King. **142m/C VHS, DVD, Blu-ray Disc.** Tim Robbins, Morgan Freeman, Bob Gunton, William Sadler, Clancy Brown, Mark Rolston, Gil Bellows, James Whitmore; ***D:*** Frank Darabont; ***W:*** Frank Darabont; ***C:*** Roger Deakins; ***M:*** Thomas Newman.

She 1/2 **1925** H. Rider Haggard's famous story about the ageless Queen Ayesha, (Blythe), who renews her life force periodically by walking through a pillar of cold flame. Story and titles by Haggard. Blythe is a stirringly mean queen, and the story remains fresh and fun. Silent film with music score. **69m/B VHS.** Betty Blythe, Carlyle Blackwell, Mary Odette, Tom Reynolds; ***D:*** Leander De Cordova, G(eorge) B(erthold) Samuelson; ***W:*** Walter Summers.

She 1/2 **1935** First sound version of H. Rider Haggard's popular 1887 adventure tale, although the film's location was changed from Africa to the frozen Arctic. Explorers Scott and Bruce are searching for a fire that preserves rather than destroys life. They are captured by a mysterious tribe and discover a living goddess—She-Who-Must-Be-Obeyed (Gahagan)—who bathed in the Flame of Life and is now eternal. She falls for Scott, who doesn't return her love, and there's trouble. Fantastic Art Deco sets and special effects. **95m/B VHS, DVD.** Helen Gahagan, Randolph Scott, Nigel Bruce, Helen Mack, Gustav von Seyffertitz; ***D:*** Irving Pichel, Lansing C. Holden; ***W:*** Dudley Nichols, Ruth Rose; ***C:*** J. Roy Hunt; ***M:*** Max Steiner.

She ♂♂ **1965** Hammer Films' lavish version of the H. Rider Haggard adventure novel. In 1918, Leo Vincey (Richardson) meets slave girl Ustane (Monteras) in Jerusalem and she insists on taking him to her mistress Ayesha (Andress). Ayesha offers Leo a fortune to meet her in the legendary city of Kuma because she's convinced he's the reincarnation of the man she loved (and murdered) centuries before. Followed by 1967's "The Vengeance of She" (with Richardson but minus Andress). **104m/C DVD.** *GB* Ursula Andress, John Richardson, Rosenda Monteros, Peter Cushing, Bernard Cribbins, Christopher Lee; ***D:*** Robert Day; ***W:*** David Chantler, James Bernard; ***C:*** Harry Waxman; ***M:*** James Bernard.

S*H*E ♂♂ **1979** A flashy made for TV spy thriller. The female agent S*H*E (Securities Hazards Expert) must save the world's oil; good locations, nifty plot and looker Sharpe as the she-Bond add up to a reasonably fun time. Scripted by "Bond"-writer Maibaum. **100m/C VHS.** Cornelia Sharpe, Robert Lansing, William Taylor, Isabella Rye, Anita Ekberg; ***Cameos:*** Omar Sharif; ***D:*** Robert Lewis; ***W:*** Richard Maibaum; ***M:*** Michael Kamen. **TV**

She ♂ **1983** A beautiful female warrior rules over the men in a post-holocaust world. She is kidnapped by a wealthy merchant who uses her to fight evil mutants. Utter rubbish vaguely based on the Haggard novel. **90m/C VHS.** Sandahl Bergman, Harrison Muller, Quin Kessler, David Goss; ***D:*** Avi Nesher.

She and He ♂♂ ½ **1963** Hani's look at the oppression of women, marital and spiritual discontent, and class divisions. Naoko is a bored housewife, living in a sterile high-rise apartment with her equally dissatisfied husband, and yearning for something to express her inner feelings. She accidentally meets an old classmate of her husband's who has become a poor ragpicker and tries to aid him. But all her efforts only lead to further tragedies. In Japanese with English subtitles. **110m/C VHS.** *JP* Sachiko Hidari, Eiji Okada, Kikuji Yamashita; ***D:*** Susumu Hani.

The She-Beast ♂ ½ *Il Lago di Satana; The Revenge of the Blood Beast; La Sorella de Satan; The Sister of Satan* **1965** Burned at the stake in 18th-century Transylvania, a witch returns in the body of a beautiful young English woman on her honeymoon (in Transylvania?!), and once again wreaks death and destruction. Caution, Barbara Steele fans: she appears for all of 15 minutes. Sporadically funny. **74m/C VHS, DVD.** *IT YU* Barbara Steele, Ian Ogilvy, Mel Welles, Lucretia Love; ***D:*** Michael Reeves; ***W:*** Michael Reeves; ***M:*** Ralph Ferraro.

She Came on the Bus WOOF! 1969 Young thugs break into a well-kept suburban home and terrorize the housewife through rape and torture. Then they kidnap a bus and pose as the drivers until they can find more victims. Contains scenes of graphic violence which would be considered offensive even by today's standards. **58m/C VHS, DVD.** ***D:*** Harry Vincent.

She Came to the Valley ♂ *Texas in Flames* **1977 (PG)** A tough pioneer woman becomes embroiled in political intrigue during the Spanish-American War. Based on Cleo Dawson's book. **90m/C VHS, DVD.** Ronee Blakley, Dean Stockwell, Scott Glenn, Freddy Fender; ***D:*** Albert Band; ***W:*** Albert Band; ***C:*** Daniel Pearl; ***M:*** Tommy Leonetti.

She Couldn't Say No ♂♂ *Beautiful But Dangerous* **1952** A wealthy oil heiress (Simmons) with good intentions plans to give her money away to those friends who had helped her when she was struggling. Things don't go quite as planned; her philanthropy leads to unexpected mayhem in her Arkansas hometown. Passable, but not memorable comedy. Mitchum as a small-town doctor? **88m/B VHS.** Robert Mitchum, Jean Simmons, Arthur Hunnicutt, Edgar Buchanan, Wallace Ford; ***D:*** Lloyd Bacon.

She Creature ♂♂ ½ *Mermaid Chronicles Part 1: She Creature* **2001 (R)** In 1905, carnival barker Angus Shaw (Lily) is traveling in Ireland with his girlfriend Lily (Gugino) posing as a mermaid in a sideshow attraction. They meet drunken ex-sailor Woolrich (Morris) who takes them to his home where he has his own attraction—a real live mermaid (Kilhstedt). Angus steals the mermaid and sails for America but the mermaid begins attacking crewman and Lily develops a symbiotic relationship with the creature. Very loosely based on the AIP 1956 B-movie of the same title, this was one of a series of cable remakes under the umbrella title "Creature Features." **91m/C VHS, DVD.** Rufus Sewell, Carla Gugino, Rya Kihlstedt, Aubrey Morris, Jim Piddock, Gil Bellows, Reno Wilson; ***D:*** Sebastian Gutierrez; ***W:*** Sebastian Gutierrez; ***C:*** Thomas Callaway; ***M:*** David Reynolds. **CABLE**

She Demons WOOF! 1958 Pleasure craft loaded with babes crashes into a remote island controlled by a mad ex-Nazi scientist who transforms pretty girls into rubber-faced Frankensteins. Incomprehensible, to say the least. **68m/B VHS, DVD.** Irish McCalla, Tod Griffin, Victor Sen Yung, Rudolph Anders, Tod Andrews, Gene Roth, Bill Coontz, Billy Dix; ***D:*** Richard Cunha; ***W:*** Richard Cunha, H.E. Barrie; ***C:*** Meredith Nicholson; ***M:*** Nicholas Carras.

She-Devil ♂♂ ½ **1989 (PG-13)** A comic book version of the acidic Fay Weldon novel "The Life and Loves of a She-Devil"; a fat, dowdy suburban wife (Arnold) becomes a vengeful beast when a smarmy romance novelist steals her husband. Uneven comedic reworking of a distinctly unforgiving feminist fiction. Arnold is given too much to handle (her role requires an actual range of emotions); Streep's role is too slight, though she does great things with it. **100m/C VHS, DVD.** Meryl Streep, Roseanne, Ed Begley Jr., Linda Hunt, Elizabeth Peters, Bryan Larkin, A. Martinez, Sylvia Miles; ***D:*** Susan Seidelman; ***W:*** Mark Burns, Barry Strugatz; ***C:*** Oliver Stapleton; ***M:*** Howard Shore.

She Devils in Chains ♂♂ *American Beauty Hostages; Ebony, Ivory, and Jade; Foxforce* **1976 (PG)** A group of traveling female athletes are kidnapped by a groups of sadists who torture and beat them. In the end, however, the girls get their revenge, and it's bloody. **82m/C VHS, DVD.** Colleen Camp, Rosanne Katon, Sylvia Anderson, Ken Washington, Leo Martinez; ***D:*** Cirio H. Santiago; ***M:*** Eddie Nova.

She-Devils on Wheels WOOF! 1968 Havoc erupts as an outlaw female motorcycle gang, known as "Maneaters on Motorbikes," terrorizes a town—especially the men. Really, really bad biker flick finely honed by Lewis. **83m/C VHS, DVD.** Betty Connell, Christie Wagner, Pat Poston, Nancy Lee Noble, Ruby Tuesday, Roy Collodi, David Harris, Steve White; ***D:*** Herschell Gordon Lewis; ***W:*** Allison Louise Downe; ***C:*** Roy Collodi; ***M:*** Larry Wellington.

She Done Him Wrong ♂♂♂ **1933** Singer Lady Lou (West) fronts an 1890s Bowery saloon for her shady boss, Gus Jordan (Beery Sr.) Gus gives her diamonds but when she gets an eyeful of young Salvation Army Capt. Cummings (Grant), Lou starts to think there's other things in life worth having. West imparts the screen version of her Broadway hit "Diamond Lil" with her usual share of double entendres and racy comments. ♫Silver Threads Among the Gold; Masie, My Pretty Daisy; Easy Rider; I Like a Guy What Takes His Time; Frankie and Johnny. **65m/B VHS.** Mae West, Cary Grant, Owen Moore, Noah Beery Sr., Gilbert Roland, Louise Beavers, Rafaela (Rafael, Raphaella) Ottiano; ***D:*** Lowell Sherman; ***W:*** Harvey Thew, John Bright; ***C:*** Charles B(ryant) Lang Jr.; ***M:*** Ralph Rainger, David Landau. Natl. Film Reg. '96.

She-Freak ♂ *Alley of Nightmares* **1967** Remake of Tod Brownings' "Freaks." A cynical waitress burns everyone in a circus and gets mauled by the resident freaks. Pales beside its unacknowledged, classic original. **87m/C VHS, DVD.** Claire Brennan, Lynn Courtney, Bill McKinney, Lee Raymond, Madame Lee, Claude Smith, Ben Moore; ***D:*** Byron Mabe; ***W:*** David Friedman; ***C:*** William G. Troiano; ***M:*** William Allen Castleman.

She Gods of Shark Reef ♂ *Shark Reef* **1956** Typical no-budget Corman exploitation tale of two brothers shipwrecked on an island inhabited by beautiful pearl-diving women. Filmed in Hawaii. **63m/C VHS, DVD.** Bill Cord, Don Durant, Lisa Montell, Carol Lindsay, Jeanne Gerson; ***D:*** Roger Corman.

She Goes to War ♂♂ **1929** King's first part-sound effort that takes place in the milieu of WWI. Boardman plays a spoiled rich girl who grows up fast when confronted with the horrors of the frontline while working in a canteen. **50m/B VHS.** Eleanor Boardman, Alma Rubens, Al "Fuzzy" St. John; ***D:*** Henry King.

She Hate Me ♂ ½ **2004 (R)** Spike Lee's latest film is about corporate whistleblowers. No wait, it's about the AIDS epidemic. Hold on a second, it's about Watergate and lesbians and fatherhood and the Mafia. Confused? So is this movie. John Henry Armstrong is a vice-president of a drug company. After blowing the whistle and getting fired, Armstrong finds a second career as a stud for lesbians who want to be impregnated. While the movie touches on some very interesting material, Lee randomly jumps from one subject to the next, creating a rather schizophrenic hodge-podge of political rants. **138m/C VHS, DVD.** *US* Anthony Mackie, Kerry Washington, Ellen Barkin, Monica Bellucci, Jim Brown, Ossie Davis, Jamel Debbouze, Brian Dennehy, Woody Harrelson, Bai Ling, Lonette McKee, Paula Jai Parker, Q-Tip, John Turturro, Chiwetel Ejiofor, Dania Ramirez, David Bennett, Isiah Whitlock Jr.; ***D:*** Spike Lee; ***W:*** Spike Lee, Michael Genet; ***C:*** Matthew Libatique; ***M:*** Terence Blanchard.

She Must Be Seeing Things ♂♂ **1987** Filmmaker Jo (Weaver) is making a picture about a 17th-century woman who lived her life as a man. Jo's lover Agatha (Dabney) becomes disturbed when she reads Jo's diary, learns she's been having affairs with men, and begins to fantasize about Jo's unfaithfulness with the men in her film crew. Agatha's insecurities finally lead her to disguising herself as a man in order to spy on Jo—mirroring what's happening in Jo's film. **95m/C VHS.** Sheila Dabney, Lois Weaver, Kyle DiCamp, John Erdman; ***D:*** Sheila McLaughlin; ***W:*** Sheila McLaughlin.

She Shall Have Music ♂ ½ **1936** A magnate hires a dance band to broadcast from a cruise ship. Features music by Jack Hylton and his band, one of Britain's most popular orchestras of the 1930s. **76m/B VHS.** *GB* Jack Hylton, June Clyde, Claude Dampier, Bryan Lawrence, Gwen Farrar; ***D:*** Leslie Hiscott; ***W:*** C. Denier Warren; ***C:*** Sydney Blythe, William Luff.

She Shoulda Said No ♂ *The Devil's Weed; Wild Weed; Marijuana the Devil's Weed* **1949** Funny smelling cigarettes ruin the lives of all who inhale. Viewers' advice: just say no. Leed's actual drug bust with Robert Mitchum got her the lead. **70m/B VHS, DVD.** Lila Leeds, Alan Baxter, Lyle Talbot, Jack Elam, David Gorcey; ***D:*** Sam Newfield.

She Waits ♂♂ **1971** When a newlywed couple moves into an old house, the bride becomes possessed by the spirit of her husband's first wife. Unoriginal and mediocre horror. **74m/C VHS.** Dorothy McGuire, Patty Duke, David McCallum; ***D:*** Delbert Mann. **TV**

She Wolf of London ♂ ½ **1946** In turn of the century London, Phyllis Allenby (Lockhart) learns that people are being murdered by a wolf in a nearby park. Since the Allenby family suffers from a werewolf curse, Phyllis decides that she must be the killer (though she doesn't remember doing anything). But her fiance Harry (Porter) is determined to prove her innocent. **62m/B VHS, DVD.** June Lockhart, Don Porter, Sara Haden, Jan Wiley, Lloyd Corrigan, Dennis Hoey, Martin Kosleck, Eily Malyon, Frederick Worlock; ***D:*** Jean Yarbrough; ***W:*** George Bricker, William Lava; ***C:*** Maury Gertsman.

She Wore a Yellow Ribbon ♂♂♂ ½ **1949** An undermanned cavalry outpost makes a desperate attempt to repel invading Indians. Wayne shines as an officer who shuns retirement in order to help his comrades. Still fun and compelling. The second chapter in director Ford's noted cavalry trilogy, preceded by "Fort Apache" and followed by "Rio Grande." **93m/C VHS, DVD.** John Wayne, Joanne Dru, John Agar, Ben Johnson, Harry Carey Jr., Victor McLaglen, Mildred Natwick, George O'Brien, Arthur Shields, Noble Johnson, Harry Woods, Michael Dugan, Jack Pennick, Paul Fix, Francis Ford, Cliff Lyons, Tom Tyler, Chief John Big Tree; ***D:*** John Ford; ***W:*** Frank Nugent, Laurence Stallings; ***C:*** Winton C. Hoch, Charles P. Boyle; ***M:*** Richard Hageman. Oscars '49: Color Cinematog.

She Wouldn't Say Yes ♂♂ **1945** Shrink Susan Lane (Russell) wants to prove her theory that a person can maintain a healthy mental state by strictly controlling their emotions. Cartoonist Michael Kent (Bowman), who believes in free expression, becomes her guinea pig and they fall in love despite their differences. **87m/B DVD.** Rosalind Russell, Lee Bowman, Adele Jergens, Charles Winninger, Harry Davenport, Percy Kilbride, Sara Haden; ***D:*** Alexander Hall; ***W:*** John Jacoby, Virginia Van Upp, Sarett Tobias; ***C:*** Joseph Walker; ***M:*** Marlin Skiles.

Sheba, Baby ♂♂ **1975 (PG)** A female dick (Grier) heads to Louisville where someone is trying to threaten her rich father and his loan company. Oddly non-violent for action-flick vet Grier; poorly written and directed. **90m/C VHS, DVD.** Pam Grier, Rudy Challenger, Austin Stoker, D'Urville Martin, Charles Kissinger; ***D:*** William Girdler; ***W:*** William Girdler; ***C:*** William Asman; ***M:*** Alex Brown.

Sheena WOOF! 1984 (PG) TV sportscaster aids a jungle queen in defending her kingdom from being overthrown by an evil prince. Horrid bubble-gum "action" fantasy. **117m/C VHS, DVD.** Tanya Roberts, Ted Wass, Donovan Scott, Elizabeth Toro; ***D:*** John Guillermin; ***W:*** David Newman; ***C:*** Pasqualino De Santis.

The Sheep Has Five Legs ♂♂ ½ **1954** Quintuplet brothers return from around the world for a reunion in their small French village. Fernandel plays the father and all five sons; otherwise, comedy is only average-to-good. In French with English subtitles. **96m/B VHS.** *FR* Fernandel, Edouard Delmont, Louis de Funes, Paulette Dubost; ***D:*** Henri Verneuil.

The Sheepman ♂♂ ½ **1958** Western comedy starring a deadpan Ford as gambler/ex-gunslinger Jason Sweet. Sweet wins a flock of sheep in a poker game and decides to graze them on the public land of Powder River. But the town is basically owned by cattle baron Stephen Bedford (Nielsen), who doesn't want any woolies around. Too bad Sweet recognizes Bedford as former rival gunslinger Johnny Bledsoe, who's assumed a new identity to live a new life. **86m/C DVD.** Glenn Ford, Shirley MacLaine, Leslie Nielsen, Mickey Shaughnessy, Edgar Buchanan, Pernell Roberts, Willis Bouchey, Slim Pickens; ***D:*** George Marshall; ***W:*** William Bowers, James Edward Grant; ***C:*** Robert J. Bronner; ***M:*** Jeff Alexander.

Sheer Madness ♂♂♂ **1984** Focuses on the intense friendship between a college professor and a troubled artist, both women. Engrossing and subtle exposition of a relationship. Ambiguous ending underscores film's general excellence. Subtitled. **105m/C VHS, DVD.** *GE FR* Hanna Schygulla, Angela Winkler; ***D:*** Margarethe von Trotta; ***W:*** Margarethe von Trotta; ***C:*** Michael Ballhaus.

The Sheik ♂♂♂ **1921** High camp Valentino has English woman fall hopelessly under the romantic spell of Arab sheik who flares his nostrils. Followed by "Son of the Sheik." **80m/B VHS, DVD.** Agnes Ayres, Rudolph Valentino, Adolphe Menjou, Walter Long, Lucien Littlefield, George Waggner, Patsy Ruth Miller; ***D:*** George Melford.

Sheitan ♂ ½ *Satan* **2006** Beautiful Eve (Mesquida) invites a group of horny, drunken teens she met at the disco to join her at her isolated farmhouse on Christmas Eve.

Strange servant Joseph (Cassel) seems to have something sinister planned. Weird and creepy rather than horror gory. French with subtitles. **94m/C DVD.** *FR* Vincent Cassel, Roxane Mesquida, Olivier Barthelemy, Leila Bekhti, Nico Le Phat Tan, Ladj Ly; ***D:*** Kim Chapiron; ***W:*** Kim Chapiron, Christian Chapiron; ***C:*** Alex Lamarque; ***M:*** Nguyen Le.

She'll Be Wearing Pink Pajamas **1984** Eight women volunteer for a rugged survival course to test their mettle. The intense shared experience gives them all food for thought. Well acted from a pretty thin story. **90m/C VHS.** Julie Walters, Anthony (Corlan) Higgins; ***D:*** John Goldschmidt; ***M:*** John Du Prez.

The Shell Seekers 1/2 **1989 (PG)** The widowed Penelope Keeling (Lansbury) is recovering from a heart attack and her three grown children want her to take things easy. But the scare has convinced Penelope to revisit her past and the happiness she once knew. So she returns to her childhood home in Cornwall to see what she can discover. Fine cast in a heart-tugger (with some lovely scenery from Cornwall, England and the island of Ibiza). Adapted from the novel by Rosamunde Pilcher. A Hallmark Hall of Fame presentation. **94m/C VHS, DVD.** *GB* Angela Lansbury, Sam Wanamaker, Anna Carteret, Michael Gough, Christopher Bowen, Patricia Hodge, Denis Quilley, Sophie Ward, Irene Worth; ***D:*** Waris Hussein; ***W:*** John Pielmeier. **TV**

Shell Shock 1/2 *Betzilo Shel Helem Krav; China Ranch* **1963** Four GI's fight off the Germans and the longings for home during WWII. Hebrew with subtitles. **90m/C VHS, DVD.** *IS* Anat Atzmon, Gili Ben-Uzilo, Stanislav Chaplin, Dan Turgeman, Asher Tzarfati; ***D:*** Yoel Sharon; ***W:*** Yoel Sharon; ***C:*** Yoav Kosh; ***M:*** Edward Reyes, Arik Rudich.

Shelter **1998 (R)** ATF agent Martin Roberts (Allen) is set up by his commanding officer and has a bounty on his head. He takes refuge with a crime lord (Onorati), whom the bad guys feds are also after, and plans how to get even. **92m/C VHS, DVD.** John Allen Nelson, Peter Onorati, Brenda Bakke, Costas Mandylor, Charles Durning, Linden Ashby, Kurtwood Smith; ***D:*** Scott Paulin; ***W:*** Max Strom; ***C:*** Eric Goldstein; ***M:*** David Williams.

Shelter 1/2 **2007 (R)** Zach (Wright) delays his dreams of going to art school to care for his five-year-old nephew Cody (Wurth) since his manipulative single mom sister Jeanne (Holmes) is so irresponsible. Feeling stuck in San Pedro, Zack likes to go surfing and hooks up with Shaun (Rowe), the older brother of his best friend Gabe (Thomas). An L.A.-based writer, Shaun is taking an extended break and is only too happy to spend time with Zach. And he's really happy to help Zach figure out that they can be more than friends. Sweet-natured coming of age, coming out story. **97m/C DVD.** Trevor Wright, Brad Rowe, Tina Holmes, Ross Thomas, Katie Walder, Jackson Wurth; ***D:*** Jonah Markowitz; ***W:*** Jonah Markowitz; ***C:*** Joseph White; ***M:*** J. Peter Robinson. **CABLE**

Shelter Island **2003 (R)** Lou (Sheedy) was living the good life, but a brutal assault makes her and lesbian lover Alex (Kensit) run away to Lou's island digs. One dark and stormy night brings a creepy, uninvited guest (Baldwin) who gets grim with 'em when the lights go out. Familiar cast drifts aimlessly out to sea trying to create a tense erotic thriller. **83m/C VHS, DVD.** Ally Sheedy, Patsy Kensit, Stephen Baldwin, Mimi Langeland, Christopher Penn, Joey Gironda, Kathleen York; ***D:*** Geoffrey Schaaf; ***W:*** Paul Corvino; ***M:*** Jeff Rona. **VIDEO**

The Sheltering Sky **1990 (R)** American couple Winger and Malkovich flee the plasticity of their native land for a trip to the Sahara desert where they hope to renew their spirits and rekindle love. Accompanied by socialite acquaintance Scott with whom Winger soon has an affair, their personalities and belief systems deteriorate as they move through the grave poverty of North Africa in breathtaking heat. Based on the existential novel by American expatriate Paul Bowles who narrates and appears briefly in a bar scene. Overlong but visually stunning, with cinematography by Vittorio Storaro. **139m/C VHS, DVD.** Debra Winger, John Malkovich, Campbell Scott, Jill Bennett, Timothy Spall, Eric Vu-An, Sotigui Koyate, Amina Annabi, Paul Bowles; ***D:*** Bernardo Bertolucci; ***W:*** Mark Peploe, Bernardo Bertolucci; ***C:*** Vittorio Storaro; ***M:*** Ryuichi Sakamoto, Richard Horowitz. Golden Globes '91: Score; N.Y. Film Critics '90: Cinematog.

Shenandoah **1965** A Virginia farmer (Stewart, in a top-notch performance) who has raised six sons and a daughter, tries to remain neutral during the Civil War. War takes its toll as the daughter marries a Confederate soldier and his sons become involved in the fighting. Screen debut for Ross. **105m/C VHS, DVD.** James Stewart, Doug McClure, Glenn Corbett, Patrick Wayne, Rosemary Forsyth, Katharine Ross, George Kennedy, Phillip Alford, James Best, Charles Robinson, James McMullan, Tim McIntire, Eugene Jackson, Paul Fix, Denver Pyle, Harry Carey Jr., Dabbs Greer, Strother Martin, Warren Oates, Kelly Thordsen; ***D:*** Andrew V. McLaglen; ***W:*** James Lee Barrett; ***C:*** William Clothier; ***M:*** Frank Skinner.

Shep Comes Home **1949** Shep the wonder canine accompanies an orphan through the Midwest where he nabs a band of bankrobbers. Sequel to "My Dog Shep." **62m/B VHS.** Robert Lowery, Sheldon Leonard, Billy Kimbley, Margia Dean, Martin Garralaga, Michael Whalen, J. Farrell MacDonald, Lyle Talbot, Frank Jenks, Edna Holland, Matt Willis; ***D:*** Ford Beebe; ***W:*** Ford Beebe; ***C:*** Ernest Miller; ***M:*** Walter Greene.

Shepherd **1999 (R)** Offers plenty of cheap thrills as long as you don't expect the plot to make any sense. You've got your basic futuristic nightmare world—this time ruled by rival religious cults who use guns to extend their power. Howell is a sharpshooting mercenary who decides not to follow orders anymore—and there's hell to pay. **86m/C VHS.** C. Thomas Howell, Roddy Piper, Robert Carradine, Heidi von Palleske; ***D:*** Peter Hayman. **VIDEO**

The Shepherd: Border Patrol **2008 (R)** Van Damme has slowed down a kick or two but he's still got enough moves to make this action flick enjoyable. Jack Robideaux is a border patrol agent in New Mexico who's attempting to stop a rogue American Special Forces unit from smuggling heroin into the U.S. **94m/C DVD.** Jean-Claude Van Damme, Scott Adkins, Stephen Lord, Garry McDonald, Isaac Florentine, Natalie Robb; ***W:*** Joe Gayton, Cade Courley; ***C:*** Douglas Milstone; ***M:*** Mark Sayfritz. **VIDEO**

The Shepherd of the Hills **1941** Young Ozark mountain moonshiner Matt Matthews (Wayne) vows to one day find and kill the unknown father who deserted his family, leading to the early death of Matt's mother. His hatred is so strong that his girlfriend Sammy (Field) refuses to marry him because of it. Then a stranger, Daniel Howitt (Carey Sr.), comes to town and his kind deeds have everyone calling him "The Shepherd." Even Matt warms to the man—until he discovers that Howitt is his father. Based on the novel by Harold Bell Wright. **89m/B VHS, DVD.** John Wayne, Harry Carey Sr., Betty Field, Beulah Bondi, James Barton, Marjorie Main, Ward Bond, Fuzzy Knight; ***D:*** Henry Hathaway; ***W:*** Grover Jones, Stuart Anthony; ***C:*** Charles B(ryant) Lang Jr., William Howard Greene; ***M:*** Gerard Carbonara.

The Sheriff of Fractured Jaw 1/2 **1959** A spoof of the old west with More as a Londoner who inherits a gun company and decides to head to the Wild West to show off his wares. He is tricked into becoming the sheriff of a lawless town but never loses his British stiff-upper-lip. Mansfield is the tough-talking sharpshooter who sets out to get her man. **103m/C VHS, DVD.** *GB* Charles Farrell, Kenneth More, Jayne Mansfield, Henry Hull, William Campbell; ***D:*** Raoul Walsh; ***W:*** Howard Dimsdale; ***C:*** Otto Heller; ***M:*** Robert Farnon.

Sheriff of Tombstone 1/2 **1941** Trouble begins when a "judge" takes a sharpshooter in a poker game. **60m/B VHS, DVD.** Roy Rogers, George "Gabby" Hayes, Elyse Knox, Addison Richards, Sally Payne, Harry Woods, Zeffie Tilbury, Wally Wales, Jay Novello, Jack Ingram; ***D:*** Joseph Kane; ***W:*** Olive Cooper; ***C:*** William Nobles.

Sherlock: Case of Evil 1/2 *Case of Evil* **2002 (R)** A young Sherlock Holmes (D'Arcy) is out to make a name for himself in London where he is hired by drug lord Ben Harrington (Rodger) to discover who is killing the local dealers and introducing a new narcotic—heroin—in an effort to control the market. That will turn out to be Professor Moriarty (D'Onofrio); also in the mix is Mycroft Holmes (Grant), who here is a drug addict, and Dr. Watson (Morlidge), who is not Sherlock's confidante at this time. In fact, Holmes's assistant is actress Rebecca (Anwar), who has her own agenda. **100m/C VHS, DVD.** James D'Arcy, Vincent D'Onofrio, Gabrielle Anwar, Roger Morlidge, Struan Rodger, Nicholas Gecks, Richard E. Grant; ***D:*** Graham Theakston; ***W:*** Piers Ashworth; ***C:*** Lukas Strebel; ***M:*** Mike Moran. **CABLE**

Sherlock Holmes 1/2 **1922** The screenplay is a muddle, probably because the plot was taken from several Conan Doyle stories, and Barrymore makes for a surprisingly dull Holmes. Arch-villain Moriarty is introduced through his connection to a Cambridge student scandal although Holmes and Watson take some time to make an appearance. This silent version was thought lost and the restoration is taken from various prints, although some pieces still seem to be missing. Young and Powell make their screen debuts. **85m/B DVD.** John Barrymore, Roland Young, Gustav von Seyffertitz, William Powell, Carol Dempster, Louis Wolheim, Percy Knight, Hedda Hopper; ***D:*** Albert Parker; ***W:*** Earle Browne, Marion Farifax; ***C:*** J. Roy Hunt.

Sherlock Holmes **2009 (PG-13)** Brit director Ritchie makes Arthur Conan Doyle's Victorian-era detective into an action hero thanks to Downey's vivid (if disheveled) portrayal of a man with a frightening intellect, drug problems, few social boundaries, and fighting skills. Law is exasperated partner/confidante Dr. Watson and there's a hint of romance in McAdams' portrayal of the criminally-minded Irene Adler, although the actress really doesn't have much to do. Naturally, the plot involves a satanic sort of aristo baddie (Strong)—who apparently comes back from the dead—bent on destruction of the British Empire. Ritchie's problem is he can't leave well enough alone and has to overstuff his pic with too much scenery, action, and CGI though it is entertaining in a frenetic way. But both Holmes and Ritchie need to stop and have a soothing cup of tea. **128m/C DVD.** *US* Robert Downey Jr., Jude Law, Rachel McAdams, Mark Strong, Kelly Reilly, Eddie Marsan, James Fox, Hans Matheson, Geraldine James; ***D:*** Guy Ritchie; ***W:*** Guy Ritchie, Michael R. Johnson, Anthony Peckham, Simon Kinberg; ***C:*** Philippe Rousselot; ***M:*** Hans Zimmer. Golden Globes '10: Actor—Mus./Comedy (Downey).

Sherlock Holmes and the Deadly Necklace 1/2 *Sherlock Holmes Und Das Halsband des Todes; Valley of Fear* **1962** Once again, Holmes and Watson are up against their old nemesis Moriarty. This time, Moriarty wants to get his hands on a necklace stolen from Cleopatra's tomb. Not only does Scotland Yard not consider him a suspect, they seek his advice. Enter Holmes and Watson, and the game's afoot. The offbeat casting and direction help make this one of the odder versions of Conan Doyle's work. **84m/B VHS, DVD.** *GE* Christopher Lee, Senta Berger, Hans Sohnker, Hans Nielsen, Ivan Desny, Leon Askin, Thorley Walters; ***D:*** Terence Fisher.

Sherlock Holmes and the Incident at Victoria Falls 1/2 *Incident at Victoria Falls* **1991** A substandard Holmes excursion brings the Baker Street sleuth out of retirement to transport the world's largest diamond from Africa to London. The resulting mystery involves Teddy Roosevelt, the inventor of radio, and poor plotting. **120m/C VHS, DVD.** *GB* Christopher Lee, Patrick Macnee, Jenny Seagrove; ***D:*** Bill Corcoran.

Sherlock Holmes and the Secret Weapon *Secret Weapon* **1942** Based on "The Dancing Men" by Sir Arthur Conan Doyle. Holmes battles the evil Moriarty in an effort to save the British war effort. Good Holmes mystery with gripping wartime setting. Hoey is fun as bumbling Inspector Lestrade. Available colorized. **68m/B VHS, DVD.** Basil Rathbone, Nigel Bruce, Karen Verne, William Post Jr., Dennis Hoey, Holmes Herbert, Mary Gordon, Henry Victor, Philip Van Zandt, George Eldredge, Leslie Denison, James Craven, Paul Fix, Hugh Herbert, Lionel Atwill; ***D:*** Roy William Neill; ***W:*** Scott Darling; ***C:*** Lester White; ***M:*** Frank Skinner.

Sherlock Holmes Faces Death **1943** Dead bodies are accumulating in a mansion where the detecting duo are staying. Underground tunnels, life-size dress boards, and unanswered mysteries... Top-notch Holmes. Peter Lawford appears briefly as a sailor. Also available with "Hound of the Baskervilles" on Laser Disc. **68m/B VHS, DVD.** Basil Rathbone, Nigel Bruce, Hillary Brooke, Milburn Stone, Halliwell Hobbes, Arthur Margetson, Gavin Muir; ***D:*** Roy William Neill.

Sherlock Holmes in Washington 1/2 **1943** A top-secret agent is murdered; seems it's those blasted Nazis again! Holmes and Watson rush off to Washington, D.C. to solve the crime and to save some vitally important microfilm. Heavily flag-waving Rathbone-Bruce episode. Dr. Watson is dumbfounded by bubble gum. **71m/B VHS, DVD.** Basil Rathbone, Nigel Bruce, Henry Daniell, George Zucco, Marjorie Lord, John Archer; ***D:*** Roy William Neill.

Sherlock Holmes: The Voice of Terror 1/2 **1942** Holmes and Watson try to decode German radio messages during WWII. First Rathbone-as-Holmes effort for Universal, and first in which we are asked to believe the Victorian sleuth and his hairdo could have lived in this century. Patriotic and all that—and lots of fun. **65m/B VHS, DVD.** Basil Rathbone, Nigel Bruce, Hillary Brooke, Reginald Denny, Evelyn Ankers, Montagu Love; ***D:*** John Rawlins.

Sherlock, Jr. 1/2 **1924** Keaton stars as a movie projectionist who's learning to be a detective by reading a how-to book. He delivers a box of candy to his girl McGuire only to be upstaged by rival Crane. Back at the movie theatre, Keaton falls asleep during the romantic film and dreams that he and his girl are the on-screen couple, still being beset by his rival, although the situations keep changing. He then dreams that he's the famous detective Sherlock, Jr. who must rescue a damsel from villains. Packs an amazing amount into 44 minutes, which came at a transitional point in Keaton's career when he had moved on from two-reel shorts to longer features. **44m/B VHS, DVD.** Buster Keaton, Kathryn McGuire, Ward Crane, Joe Keaton, Erwin Connelly; ***D:*** Buster Keaton; ***W:*** Clyde Bruckman, Jean C. Havez, Joseph A. Mitchell; ***C:*** Byron Houck, Elgin Lessley. Natl. Film Reg. '91.

Sherlock: Undercover Dog 1/2 **1994 (PG)** Billy (Eroen) arrives on Catalina island to spend the summer with his father, an eccentric inventor. He makes a human friend in Emma (Cameron) and a canine companion in Sherlock, a police dog who's able to talk but naturally only to the two kids. Seems Sherlock's policeman master has been kidnapped by bumbling smugglers and its up to the trio to come to the rescue. **80m/C VHS, DVD.** Benjamin Eroen, Brynne Cameron, Anthony Simmons, Margy Moore, Barry Philips; ***D:*** Richard Harding Gardner; ***W:*** Richard Harding Gardner; ***M:*** Lou Forestieri.

Sherman's March **1986** Director Ross McElwee set out to re-trace Sherman's March through Georgia and document that event's lingering effect on the modern South. Instead, after his girlfriend left him shortly before filming began, he ended up documenting how the various southern women he encountered affected him. McElwee's self-depracating manner and the interesting variety of women he meets keep things enjoyable. **157m/C DVD.** ***Cameos:*** Burt Reynolds; ***D:*** Ross McElwee; ***W:*** Ross McElwee; ***C:*** Ross McElwee.

Sherman's Way 1/2 **2008** Uptight recent law grad Sherman Black (Shulman) finally makes an impulsive decision and goes to visit his girlfriend in Napa Valley, only to witness her reunion with an old boyfriend. When he finds himself stranded, Sherman makes a second impulsive decision and accepts a ride from eccentric Palmer (LeGros), a former Olympic skier who's down on his luck. Naturally free-spirit Palmer intends to loosen up stuffy Sherman. **98m/C DVD.** Michael Shulman, James LeGros, Enrico Colantoni, Brooke Nevin, Donna Murphy, Thomas Ian Nicholas, Lacey Chabert, M. Emmet Walsh; ***D:*** Craig Saavedra; ***W:*** Tom Nance; ***C:*** Joaquin Sedillo; ***M:*** David Michael Frank.

Sherrybaby ✌✌ **2006** Gyllenhaal startles in the title role of this compelling but disturbing drama. Sherry is a needy, emotionally stunted and impulsive ex-heroin addict who has cleaned herself up and has just been paroled from prison. She desperately wants to regain custody of her young daughter Alexis (Simpkins), who's bonded with her surrogate family, Sherry's brother Bobby (Henke) and his wife Lynette (Barkan). They've got a right to be cautious of Sherry's plans since the only way she knows to get what she needs is by using her sexuality, and her temptation to slip back into her druggy ways is still strong. **95m/C DVD.** *US* Maggie Gyllenhaal, Brad William Henke, Danny Trejo, Giancarlo Esposito, Bridget Barkan, Ryan Simpkins, Sam Bottoms; ***D:*** Laurie Collyer; ***W:*** Laurie Collyer; ***C:*** Russell Fine; ***M:*** Jack Livesey.

She's All That ✌✌ **1999 (PG-13)** There are no surprises to be found in this formulaic Pygmalion-via-MTV teen comedy. Zack (Prinze Jr.) is the BMOC in yet another broadly drawn high school pecking order. After he's dumped by girlfriend Taylor (O'Keefe) for vain semi-celebrity Brock (Lillard, in an amusing send-up of MTV's "The Real World"), he accepts a bet from a pal that he can make artsy wallflower Laney (Cook) into a prom queen. The intelligent Laney suspects his motives, but proceeds with the makeover with caution. When Taylor decides she wants her man back, the stage is set for a predictable prom night showdown. **97m/C VHS, DVD.** Rachael Leigh Cook, Freddie Prinze Jr., Matthew Lillard, Paul Walker, Jodi Lyn O'Keefe, Kevin Pollak, Anna Paquin, Kieran Culkin, Elden (Ratliff) Henson, Usher Raymond, Gabrielle Union, Dule Hill, Kimberly (Lil' Kim) Jones, Milo Ventimiglia, Sarah Michelle Gellar, Tamara Mello, Clea DuVall, Tim Matheson, Debbi (Deborah) Morgan, Alexis Arquette, Dave Buzzotta, Katharine Towne, Flex Alexander; ***D:*** Robert Iscove; ***W:*** R. Lee Fleming Jr.; ***C:*** Francis Kenny; ***M:*** Stewart Copeland.

She's Back ✌ ½ **1988 (R)** Murderee Fisher pesters hubby Joy from beyond the grave to avenge her death at the hands of a motorcycle gang. Uneven, but occasionally funny. **89m/C VHS.** Bobby DiCicco, Carrie Fisher, Robert Joy; ***D:*** Tim Kincaid.

She's Dressed to Kill ✌✌ *Someone's Killing the World's Greatest Models* **1979** Beautiful models are turning up dead during a famous designer's comeback attempt at a mountain retreat. Who could be behind these grisly deeds? Suspenseful in a made for TV kind of way, but not memorable. **100m/C VHS.** Eleanor Parker, Jessica Walter, John Rubinstein, Connie Sellecca; ***D:*** Gus Trikonis. **TV**

She's Gotta Have It ✌✌✌ **1986 (R)** Lee wrote, directed, edited, produced and starred in this romantic comedy about an independent-minded black girl in Brooklyn and the three men and one woman who compete for her attention. Full of rough edges, but vigorous, confident, and hip. Filmed entirely in black and white except for one memorable scene. Put Lee on the film-making map. **84m/B VHS.** Tracy C. Johns, Spike Lee, Tommy Redmond Hicks, Raye Dowell, John Canada Terrell, Joie Lee, S. Epatha Merkerson, Bill Lee, Cheryl Burr, Aaron Dugger, Stephanie Covington, Renata Cobbs, Cheryl Singleton, Monty Ross, Lewis Jordan, Erik Todd Dellums, Reginald (Reggie) Hudlin, Eric Payne, Marcus Turner, Gerard Brown, Ernest R. Dickerson; ***D:*** Spike Lee; ***W:*** Spike Lee; ***C:*** Ernest R. Dickerson; ***M:*** Bill Lee. Ind. Spirit '87: First Feature.

She's Having a Baby ✌✌ ½ **1988 (PG-13)** Newlyweds Bacon and McGovern tread the marital waters with some difficulty, when news of an impending baby further complicates their lives. Told from Bacon's viewpoint as the tortured young writer/husband, who wonders if the yuppie life they lead is trapping him. Hughes's first venture into the adult world isn't as satisfying as his teen angst flicks, although the charming leads help. Major drawbacks are the arguably sexist premise and dull resolution. Great soundtrack; observant viewers will notice the beemer's license plate is the title's acronym: "SHAB." **106m/C VHS, DVD.** Kevin Bacon, Elizabeth McGovern, William Windom, Paul Gleason, Alec Baldwin, Cathryn Damon, Holland Taylor, James Ray, Isabel Lorca, Dennis Dugan, Edie McClurg, John Ashton; ***D:*** John Hughes; ***W:*** John Hughes; ***C:*** Don Peterman; ***M:*** Stewart Copeland.

She's in the Army Now ✌ **1981** Farce about military life. Two bubble-headed females undergo basic training. "Private Benjamin" ripoff was meant as a TV pilot. **97m/C VHS.** Jamie Lee Curtis, Kathleen Quinlan, Melanie Griffith, Susan Blanchard, Julie Carmen, Janet MacLachlan; ***D:*** Hy Averback; ***M:*** Artie Butler. **TV**

She's Out of Control ✌ ½ **1989** Dad Danza goes nuts when teen daughter Dolenz (real-life daughter of Monkee Mickey Dolenz) takes the advice of Dad's girlfriend on how to attract boys. Formulaic plot could almost be an episode of "Who's the Boss?" Danza is appealing, but not enough to keep this one afloat. **95m/C VHS, DVD.** Tony Danza, Ami Dolenz, Catherine Hicks, Wallace Shawn, Dick O'Neill, Laura Mooney, Derek McGrath, Matthew Perry, Dana Ashbrook, Todd Bridges, Robbie (Reist) Rist; ***D:*** Stan Dragoti; ***C:*** Don Peterman; ***M:*** Alan Silvestri, Alan Silvestri.

She's Out of My League ✌✌ *Hard 10* **2010 (R)** This is another entry into the "there's no way that odd guy can date that hot girl" formula, and the outcome won't surprise anyone. Geeky airport screener Kirk (Baruchel) and hottie Molly (Eve) meet cute when he saves her from travel hassles. She asks him out, but his trio of close buds warns him against pursuing her. They rate her as a ten, and he is merely a five. Kirk proceeds to embrace his inner ten-ness, and wander through embarrassing and awkward situations with the result never in doubt. It doesn't really break any new ground, but it's pleasant enough. **106m/C DVD.** Jay Baruchel, Alice Eve, T.J. Miller, Nate Torrence, Krysten Ritter, Geoff Stults, Lindsay Sloane; ***D:*** Jim Field Smith; ***W:*** Sean Anders, John Morris; ***C:*** Jim Denault; ***M:*** Michael Andrews.

She's So Lovely ✌✌ ½ *She's De Lovely; Call It Love* **1997 (R)** Troubled young alcoholic Eddie (Penn) disappears for three days on his pregnant wife Maureen (Wright), and returns to discover that she has been brutalized by a neighbor. Retaliation costs him 10 years in a mental institution. Upon his release, Eddie decides to find his now ex-wife and the daughter he's never known. Maureen's moved on—she's happily married to Joey (Travolta), has two daughters by him, and is justifiable worried that Eddie's love (which is as strong as ever) will upset the balance of her new life. Somewhat unevenly directed by Nick Cassavetes from a screenplay written by his late father John, who had already cast Penn and was set to direct when he became ill. Film revels in the style that made the elder Cassavetes famous (or infamous), and is best appreciated as a tribute. Travolta and Penn play well off each other. **97m/C VHS, DVD.** Sean Penn, Robin Wright Penn, John Travolta, Harry Dean Stanton, Debi Mazar, James Gandolfini, Gena Rowlands, Kelsey Mulrooney, David Thornton, Susan Traylor, Chloe Webb, Burt Young; ***D:*** Nick Cassavetes; ***W:*** John Cassavetes; ***C:*** Thierry Arbogast; ***M:*** Joseph Vitarelli. Cannes '97: Actor (Penn).

She's the Man ✌✌ ½ **2006 (PG-13)** Get past the familiar story and the fact that adorable Bynes can in no way pass for a boy, and this light-hearted teen comedy provides an amusing take on Shakespeare's "Twelfth Night." When the girls' soccer team is disbanded at her prep school, star soccer player Viola (Bynes) disguises herself as her twin brother Sebastian (Kirk) and takes his place at his new school. Her first problem (besides the cross-dressing) is falling for handsome roomie/soccer captain Duke (Tatum), who has a crush on Olivia (Ramsey) who's soon crushing on Viola—ah, Sebastian. Confusion follows. **105m/C DVD.** *US* Amanda Bynes, Channing Tatum, Laura Ramsey, Vinnie Jones, Robert Hoffman III, Julie Hagerty, David Cross, Alex Breckinridge, Jonathan Sadowski, Emily Perkins, James Kirk, Clifton McCabe Murray, Brandon Jay McLaren; ***D:*** Andy Fickman; ***W:*** Karen McCullah Lutz, Kirsten Smith, Ewan Leslie; ***C:*** Greg Gardiner; ***M:*** Nathan Wang.

She's the One ✌✌ ½ **1996 (R)** Another Irish family saga from Burns covering lots of the same territory as "The Brothers McMullen." Semi-slacker taxi driver Mickey Fitzpatrick (Burns) impulsively marries passenger Hope (Bahns) and their romance is contrasted with the disintegrating marriage of Mickey's younger brother, buttoned-down stockbroker Francis (McGlone) and his frustrated wife Rene (Aniston). No wonder she's frustrated, Francis is having an affair with slutty Heather (Diaz), who turns out to be Mickey's former flame. Mahoney offers a typically fine performance, along with bad marital advice as the boys' father. Again the blustering men don't have a clue about the usually smarter women. **95m/C VHS, DVD.** Edward Burns, Mike McGlone, Jennifer Aniston, Cameron Diaz, Maxine Bahns, John Mahoney, Leslie Mann, George McCowan, Amanda Peet, Anita Gillette, Frank Vincent; ***D:*** Edward Burns; ***W:*** Edward Burns; ***C:*** Frank Prinzi; ***M:*** Tom Petty.

Shifting Sands **1918** Compelling film tells the tale of a young girl looking to be a successful artist. Her landlord makes constant overtures towards her. She refuses, so he has her thrown in jail for prostitution as an act of revenge. She fears her past may prevent her from obtaining true love. **52m/B VHS.** Gloria Swanson, Joe King, Lillian Langdon; ***D:*** Albert Parker; ***W:*** Charles Dazey; ***C:*** Pliny Horne.

Shiloh ✌✌ ½ **1997 (PG)** Schmaltzy but redeeming story about small town West Virginia 11-year-old Marty (Heron), who seeks to rescue and care for mistreated hunting dog Shiloh, who belongs to mean hermit Judd (Wilson). Goes beyond the typical "boy and his dog" theme with moral and ethical issues that Marty faces when he takes the dog from its owner. Frannie (who plays Shiloh) is a very cute and expressive beagle. Adapted from the Newberry award-winning novel by Phyllis Reynolds Naylor. **93m/C VHS, DVD.** Blake Heron, Michael Moriarty, Scott Wilson, Rod Steiger, Ann Dowd, Bonnie Bartlett; ***D:*** Dale Rosenbloom; ***W:*** Dale Rosenbloom; ***C:*** Frank Byers; ***M:*** Joel Goldsmith.

Shiloh 2: Shiloh Season ✌✌ ½ **1999** Low-key rural drama finds 12-year-old Marty Preston (Browne) claiming responsibility for lovable beagle Shiloh from his hard-drinking owner, Judd Travers (Wilson). But when Travers is injured in an accident, the kid has enough compassion to ask his parents to help him with the ornery cuss. Adapted from the novel by Phyllis Reynolds Naylor. **96m/C VHS, DVD.** Zachary Browne, Scott Wilson, Michael Moriarty, Ann Dowd, Rod Steiger, Bonnie Bartlett, Joe Pichler; ***D:*** Sandy Tung; ***W:*** Dale Rosenbloom; ***C:*** Troy Smith; ***M:*** Joel Goldsmith.

Shin Heike Monogatari ✌✌✌✌ *New Tales of the Taira Clan* **1955** Mizoguchi's second to last film, in which a deposed Japanese emperor in 1137 endeavors to win back the throne from the current despot, who cannot handle the feudal lawlessness. Acclaimed; his second film in color. In Japanese with English subtitles. **106m/C VHS.** *JP* Raizo Ichikawa, Ichijiro Oya, Michiyo Kogure, Eijiro Yanagi, Tatsuya Ishiguro, Yoshiko Kuga; ***D:*** Kenji Mizoguchi.

Shinbone Alley ✌✌ ½ **1970 (G)** Animated musical about Archy, a free-verse poet reincarnated as a cockroach, and Mehitabel, the alley cat with a zest for life. Based on the short stories by Don Marquis. **83m/C VHS, DVD.** ***D:*** John D. Wilson; ***V:*** Carol Channing, Eddie Bracken, John Carradine, Alan Reed.

Shine ✌✌✌ ½ **1995 (PG-13)** Astonishing true portrayal of musical genius and its cost. Teenaged pianist David Helfgott (Taylor) is a prodigy in his native Australia but is pushed to the limit by his authoritarian father Peter (Mueller-Stahl). Eventually defying his father's strictures, David accepts a scholarship to London's Royal College of Music where he triumphs under the tutelege of professor Cecil Parkes (Gielgud), but then collapses from strain. For 15 years, he is confined to psychiatric hospitals, unable to play the piano, until the now-adult David (Rush) has a chance meeting with the loving Gillian (Redgrave), whose support enables him to resume his career. Helfgott himself plays piano for his screen counterparts. **105m/C VHS, DVD.** *AU* Geoffrey Rush, Noah Taylor, Armin Mueller-Stahl, Lynn Redgrave, John Gielgud, Googie Withers, Chris Haywood, Sonia Todd, Alex Rafalowicz, Randall Berger; ***D:*** Scott Hicks; ***W:*** Jan Sardi; ***C:*** Geoffrey Simpson; ***M:*** David Hirschfelder. Oscars '96: Actor (Rush); Australian Film Inst. '96: Actor (Rush), Cinematog., Director (Hicks), Film, Film Editing, Orig. Screenplay, Sound, Support. Actor (Mueller-Stahl), Score; British Acad. '96: Actor (Rush); Golden Globes '97: Actor—Drama (Rush); L.A. Film Critics '96: Actor (Rush); Natl. Bd. of Review '96: Film; N.Y. Film Critics '96: Actor (Rush); Screen Actors Guild '96: Actor (Rush); Broadcast Film Critics '96: Actor (Rush).

Shine a Light ✌✌ ½ **2008 (PG-13)** Scorsese does the Stones. Most of the documentary is devoted to the band's 2006 performance at the Beacon Theater with some pre-performance set-up. The director also primarily focuses on lead showman Jagger (with cutaways to Watts, Wood, and Richards), and the ravages of time over their 40-year career are highlighted with some interspersed interview footage from earlier decades. Performance-wise the Stones live up to the legend, but on screen, it all seems a little forced. Guest performers include Buddy Guy, Christina Aguilera, and Jack White. **122m/C DVD.** *US* ***D:*** Martin Scorsese; ***C:*** Robert Richardson.

Shine on, Harvest Moon ✌✌ **1938** Rogers brings a band of outlaws to justice and clears an old man suspected of being their accomplice. Title bears no relation to story line. **60m/B VHS.** Roy Rogers, Lynne Roberts, Stanley Andrews; ***D:*** Joseph Kane.

Shiner ✌✌ ½ **2000** Caine delivers the goods as a small-time boxing promoter from London's East End on the brink of hitting it big. As Billy "Shiner" Simpson, Caine preps his son Eddie for a high-profile, possibly career-making match against an American. The match has disaster written all over it early on, however, when Billy's daughter interrupts to bring up some past legal problems, Eddie doesn't perform as expected, and murder, betrayal, and doublecrosses rear their ugly heads. A showcase for Caine's talents, unfortunately, the story around him loses it's luster after a solid first half turns disappointing. Borrows liberally from Shakespeare's "King Lear." **99m/C VHS, DVD.** *GB* Michael Caine, Martin Landau, Matthew Marsden, Frances Barber, Frank Harper, Andy Serkis, Claire Rushbrook, Danny (Daniel) Webb, Kenneth Cranham, David Kennedy, Peter Wight, Nicola Walker; ***D:*** John Irvin; ***W:*** Scott Cherry; ***C:*** Mike Molloy; ***M:*** Paul Grabowsky.

The Shining ✌✌ ½ **1980 (R)** Very loose adaptation of the Stephen King horror novel about a writer and his family, snowbound in a huge hotel, who experience various hauntings caused by either the hotel itself or the writer's dementia. Technically stunning, and pretty dang scary, but too long, pretentious and implausible. Nicholson is excellent as the failed writer gone off the deep end. **143m/C VHS, DVD, Blu-ray Disc, HD DVD.** Jack Nicholson, Shelley Duvall, Danny Lloyd, Scatman Crothers, Joe Turkel, Barry Nelson, Philip Stone, Lia Beldam, Billie Gibson, Barry Dennen, David Baxt, Lisa Burns, Alison Coleridge, Kate Phelps, Anne Jackson, Tony Burton; ***D:*** Stanley Kubrick; ***W:*** Stanley Kubrick, Diane Johnson; ***C:*** John Alcott; ***M:*** Walter (Wendy) Carlos, Rachel Elkind.

The Shining Hour ✌✌ ½ **1938** A compelling melodrama in which Crawford portrays a New York night club dancer who is pursued by the rather conservative Douglas. His brother tries to persuade him from marrying Crawford, but then he soon finds himself attracted to her. A devastating fire wipes out all problems of family dissension in this intelligent soap opera. **76m/B VHS.** Joan Crawford, Margaret Sullavan, Melvyn Douglas, Robert Young, Fay Bainter, Allyn Joslyn; ***D:*** Frank Borzage; ***W:*** Ogden Nash, Jane Murfin; ***C:*** George J. Folsey.

A Shining Season ✌✌✌ **1979** Tearjerker about a potential-packed long-distance runner, John Baker, stricken with cancer. He spends his last year training a girls' track team to a championship. Earnest, well-performed and involving. Based on a true story. Made for TV. **100m/C VHS.** Timothy Bottoms, Rip Torn, Allyn Ann McLerie, Ed Begley Jr., Benjamin Bottoms, Mason Adams, Constance Forslund, Ellen Geer; ***D:*** Stuart Margolin; ***M:*** Richard Bellis. **TV**

Shining Star ✌ ½ *That's the Way of the World* **1975 (PG)** A recording company is run by the mob. Potentially interesting film is hampered by quality of sound and photography and general lack of purpose or direction. **100m/C VHS, DVD, HD DVD.** Harvey Keitel, Ed Nelson, Cynthia Bostick, Bert Parks; *D:* Sig Shore.

Shining Through ✂✂ 1/2 **1992 (R)** Baby-voiced Griffith as a spy sent behind enemy lines without training? Douglas as a spy sent behind enemy lines without speaking German? Old-fashioned blend of romance, espionage, and derring-do where noble hero saves spunky heroine from nasty Nazis in WWII Germany works despite thin plot. Series of flash-forwards to an aged Griffith is annoying and tends to stop action cold, but everyone tries hard and period flavor is authentic. Adapted from best-selling Susan Isaacs novel, but bears little resemblance to book. **133m/C VHS, DVD.** Michael Douglas, Melanie Griffith, Liam Neeson, Joely Richardson, John Gielgud, Francis Guinan, Patrick Winczewski, Sylvia Syms; *D:* David Seltzer; *W:* David Seltzer; *C:* Jan De Bont; *M:* Michael Kamen. Golden Raspberries '92: Worst Picture, Worst Actress (Griffith), Worst Director (Seltzer).

Shinobi ✂✂✂ *Shinobi: Heart Under Blade* **2005 (R)** Based on the novel "The Kouga Ninja Scrolls", the Iga and Koga Ninja clans are asked to live in peace after 400 years of war. But eventually the Shogun decides they are a threat to the peace and has his advisor create a plot to have them both killed in a pointless fight. When the heads of the clan die, it is discovered that the new heads are in love with each other. However, their being in love doesn't stop the many magically infused ninja fights. **91m/C DVD.** *JP* Joe Odagiri, Kippei Shiina, Tak Sakaguchi, Houka Kinoshita, Minori Terada, Toshiya Nagasawa, Yutaka Matsushige, Renji Ishibashi, Kazuo Kitamura, Yukie Nakama, Tomoka Kurotani, Erika Sawajiri, Takeshi Masu, Mitsuki Koga, Shun Ito, Riri, Masaki Nishina; *D:* Ten Shimoyama; *W:* Kenya Hirata, Futaro Yamada; *C:* Masasai Chikamori; *M:* Taro Iwashiro.

Shinobi no Mono ✂✂✂ *Ninja 1; The Ninja; Band of Assassins* **1962** Loosely adapted on history, this is the first of eight ninja films made in the 60s, and said to be part of the inspiration for the James Bond film "You Only Live Twice." Tyrannical Lord Oda Nobunaga is waging war on all the Shinobi (ninja) clans, and they are competing to be the ones who kill him first. Considered among the most realistic of ninja films made, possibly in part because two former ninja were said to be technical advisors. **105m/C DVD.** *JP* Raizo Ichikawa, Yunosuke Ito, Shiho Fujimura, Kyoko Kishida, Chitose Maki, Tomisaburo Wakayama, Katsuhiko Kobayashi, Reiko Fujiwara; *D:* Satsuo Yamamoto; *W:* Hajime Taikawa; *C:* Yasukazu Takemura; *M:* Michiaki Watanabe.

Shinobi no Mono 2: Vengeance ✂✂✂ *Zoku shinobi no mono; The Ninja Part II* **1963** The second of the 1960s ninja series, and the last of the eight to have actual ninjas as advisors. The Iga ninja clan has been all but destroyed by Odan Nobunaga, and he is conducting a terror campaign to find the last of them—Goemon (Raizo Ichikawa). He teams up with Hattori Hanzo (Date Saburo) to bring down Nobunaga once and for all. A bit more brutal than the first film, and definitely darker, it shows feudal Japan as a dangerous place to have lived. **93m/C DVD.** *JP* Raizo Ichikawa, Shiho Fujimura, Mikiko Tsubouchi, Tomisaburo Wakayama, Date Saburo; *D:* Satsuo Yamamoto; *W:* Hajime Taikawa, Tomoyoshi Murayama; *C:* Senkichiro Takeda; *M:* Michiaki Watanabe.

Ship Ahoy ✂✂ 1/2 **1942** Songs, comedy, a spy spoof, and some patriotism thrown in for good measure. Powell plays a dancer who works with Tommy Dorsey and his orchestra. They're on their way to Puerto Rico, via ocean liner, along with her pulp fiction writer boyfriend (Skelton). Emery, posing as an FBI man, convinces Powell to smuggle a package for him but he's really a spy and the whole thing's a con which turns out to be based on one of Skelton's potboiler plots. An uncredited Frank Sinatra is the singer with the Dorsey band, along with drummer Buddy Rich and trumpeter Ziggy Elman who provide some great musical solos. ♫Last Call For Love; Poor You; On Moonlight Bay; Tampico; I'll Take Tallulah; Cape Dance; Ship Ahoy. **95m/B VHS.** Eleanor Powell, Red Skelton, Bert Lahr, Virginia O'Brien, John Emery, William Post Jr.; *D:* Edward Buzzell; *W:* Harry Kurnitz, Harry Clork, Irving Brecher.

Ship of Fools ✂✂✂ **1965** A group of passengers sailing to Germany in the '30s find mutual needs and concerns, struggle with early evidence of Nazi racism, and discover love on their voyage. Twisted story and fine acting maintain interest. Appropriate tunes written by Ernest Gold. Based on the Katherine Ann Porter novel. Leigh's last film role; she died two years later. Kramer grapples with civil rights issues in much of his work. **149m/B VHS, DVD.** Vivien Leigh, Simone Signoret, Jose Ferrer, Lee Marvin, Oskar Werner, Michael Dunn, Elizabeth Ashley, George Segal, Jose Greco, Charles Korvin, Heinz Ruhmann; *D:* Stanley Kramer; *W:* Abby Mann; *C:* Ernest Laszlo; *M:* Ernest Gold. Oscars '65: Art Dir./Set Dec., B&W, B&W Cinematog.; Natl. Bd. of Review '65: Actor (Marvin); N.Y. Film Critics '65: Actor (Werner).

Shipmates Forever ✂✂ **1935** To please his Admiral father, Dick (Powell) enters the Naval Academy even though he would rather have a singing career. He's in love with dancer June (Keeler), whose family has a long Navy tradition so she tells him he should make the effort to get through the training. Dick doesn't want to make friends with any of his fellow cadets but circumstances change in a tragic way. **109m/B DVD.** Dick Powell, Ruby Keeler, Lewis Stone, Ross Alexander, John Arledge, Eddie Acuff, Dick Foran; *D:* Frank Borzage; *W:* Delmer Daves; *C:* Sol Polito.

The Shipping News ✂✂ **2001 (R)** Spacey is Quoyle, a middle-aged lifetime loser who returns to his childhood home of Newfoundland with his daughter and aunt (Dench) after his adulterous wife (Blanchett) dies. There, among the absurdly quirky citizenry, he meets Wavey (Moore) a widow who runs the day-care center and may hold the key to changing Quoyle's life around. Those who read the book (and there are many), will be deeply disappointed, and those who haven't may merely be deeply depressed. The desolate landscape is beautifully shot, but Spacey is badly miscast as the sad-sack loser, and subplots that could lead to some drama are dropped inexplicably. Blanchett and Moore distinguish themselves nicely. **120m/C VHS, DVD.** *US* Kevin Spacey, Judi Dench, Cate Blanchett, Julianne Moore, Pete Postlethwaite, Scott Glenn, Rhys Ifans, Gordon Pinsent, Jason Behr, Larry Pine, Jeanetta Arnette, Robert Joy, Alyssa Gainer, Kaitlyn Gainer, Lauren Gainer; *D:* Lasse Hallstrom; *W:* Robert Nelson Jacobs; *C:* Oliver Stapleton; *M:* Christopher Young. Natl. Bd. of Review '01: Support. Actress (Blanchett).

Ships in the Night ✂✂ *Ships of the Night* **1928** Logan is the plucky heroine who is searching for her missing brother who has been captured by pirates. She is aided in her search by handsome hero Mower. **86m/B VHS.** Frank Moran, Jacqueline Logan, Jack Mower, Andy Clyde; *D:* Duke Worne; *W:* Arthur Hoerl; *C:* Hap Depew.

Shipwrecked ✂✂ 1/2 *Haakon Haakonsen* **1990 (PG)** Kiddie swashbuckler based on the 1873 popular novel "Haakon Haakonsen." A cabin boy is marooned on an island where he defends the hidden pirate treasure he finds by boobytrapping the island. **93m/C VHS.** *NO* Gabriel Byrne, Stian Smestad, Louisa Haigh, Trond Munch, Bjorn Sundquist, Eva Von Hanno, Kjell Stormoen; *D:* Nils Gaup; *W:* Nils Gaup, Nick Thiel; *M:* Patrick Doyle.

Shiri ✂✂ *Swiri* **1999 (R)** After a year's disappearance the North Korean super assassin Lee Bang Hee (Yunjin Kim) returns, and is spotted killing an arms dealer. Two agents assigned to capture her discover she and her North Korean spy buddies intend to steal an undetectable new liquid explosive, and blow up a soccer match between North and South Korea that the leaders of both countries will be attending, causing a war. One of the top grossing films in Korea of all time. **125m/C DVD.** *KN* Suk-kyu Han, Min-Sik Choi, Yunjim Kim, Kang-ho Song, Johnny Kim; *D:* Je-gyu Kang; *W:* Je-gyu Kang; *C:* Sung-Bok Kim; *M:* Dong-jun Lee.

Shirley Valentine ✂✂✂ **1989** A lively middle-aged English housewife gets a new lease on life when she travels to Greece without her husband. Collins reprises her London and Broadway stage triumph. The character frequently addresses the audience directly to explain her thoughts and feelings; her energy and spunk carry the day. Good script by Russell from his play. From the people who brought us "Educating Rita." **108m/C VHS, DVD.** *GB* Pauline Collins, Tom Conti, Alison Steadman, Julia McKenzie, Joanna Lumley, Bernard Hill, Sylvia Syms; *D:* Lewis Gilbert; *W:* George Hadjinassios, Willy Russell; *C:* Alan Hume; *M:* Willy Russell. British Acad. '89: Actress (Collins).

Shiver ✂✂ *Eskalofrio* **2008** A young boy's medical condition causes him massive burns (and lengthened incisors) if he's exposed too long to the sun. His mom moves them into a mansion in a forest that doesn't get much sunlight, but pretty soon the boy is being blamed for dead cattle and eventually a dead school kid. It seems like a nice setup, but you'll see every plot twist coming long before it arrives. **91m/C DVD.** *SP* Junio Valverde, Blanca Suarez, Jimmy Barnatan, Mar Sodupe, Francesc Orella; *D:* Isidro Ortiz; *W:* Isidro Ortiz, Hernan Migoya, Jose Gamo, Alejandro Hernandez; *C:* Josep Civit; *M:* Fernando Velasquez. **VIDEO**

The Shock ✂✂ 1/2 **1923** Crippled low-life Chaney becomes restored spiritually by a small-town girl and rebels against his Chinese boss. This causes an unfortunate string of melodramatic tragedies, including the San Francisco earthquake of 1906. Silent. Odd, desultory tale with bad special effects is worth seeing for Chaney's good acting. **96m/B VHS, DVD.** Lon Chaney Sr., Virginia Valli; *D:* Lambert Hillyer.

Shock! ✂✂ **1946** A psychiatrist is called on to treat a woman on the edge of a nervous breakdown. He then discovers she saw him murder his wife, and tries to keep her from remembering it. Interesting premise handled in trite B style. Price's first starring role. **70m/B VHS, DVD.** Vincent Price, Lynn Bari, Frank Latimore, Anabel Shaw; *D:* Alfred Werker.

Shock ✂✂ 1/2 *Beyond the Door 2; Shock (Transfer Suspense Hypnos); Suspense; Al 33 di Via Orologio fa Sempre Freddo* **1979 (R)** Better treatment of the possession theme, but this time the door is to the home of a new family: Colin (from the original) plays a boy possessed by his dead father, who seeks revenge on his widow and her new husband. Director Bava's last feature. **90m/C VHS, DVD.** *IT* John Steiner, Daria Nicolodi, David Colin Jr., Ivan Rassimov, Nicola Salerno; *D:* Mario Bava; *W:* Lamberto Bava, Franco Barbieri, Dardano Sacchetti, Paolo Brigenti; *C:* Alberto Spagnoli.

Shock Corridor ✂✂✂ **1963** A reporter, dreaming of a Pulitzer Prize, fakes mental illness and gets admitted to an asylum, where he hopes to investigate a murder. He is subjected to disturbing experiences, including shock therapy, but does manage to solve the murder. However, he suffers a mental breakdown in the process and is admitted for real. Disturbing and lurid. **101m/B VHS, DVD.** Peter Breck, Constance Towers, Gene Evans, Hari Rhodes, James Best, Philip Ahn, Larry Tucker, Paul Dubov; *D:* Samuel Fuller; *W:* Samuel Fuller; *C:* Stanley Cortez; *M:* Paul Dunlap. Natl. Film Reg. '96.

Shock 'Em Dead ✂✂ **1990 (R)** A devil worshipper trades his life to Lucifer for a chance at rock and roll fame and beautiful Miss Lords. Sexy thriller, with a good share of violence and tension. Ironically, ex porn great Lords is one of the few starlets who doesn't disrobe in the film. **94m/C DVD.** Traci Lords, Aldo Ray, Troy Donahue, Stephen Quadros, Tim Moffett, Gina Parks, Laurel Wiley, Tyger Sodipe, Karen Russell; *D:* Mark Freed; *W:* Mark Freed, Andrew Cross, Dave Tedder; *C:* Ron Chapman.

Shock! Shock! Shock! ✂ **1987** Another low-budget slasher flick, with a homicidal lunatic wielding a butcher knife. Space alien jewel thieves add an element, for what it's worth. Makes one ponder the cosmic question: What's the diff between a bad slasher flick and a spoof of a bad slasher flick? Whichever this one is, it's really bad! **60m/B VHS.** Brad Issac, Cyndy McCrossen, Allen Rickman, Brian Fuorry; *D:* Todd Rutt, Arn McConnell.

A Shock to the System ✂✂✂ **1990 (R)** Business exec. Caine is passed over for a long-deserved promotion in favor of a younger man. When he accidentally pushes a panhandler in front of a subway in a fit of rage, he realizes how easy murder is and thinks it may be the answer to all his problems. Tries to be a satire take on corporate greed, etc., but somehow loses steam. Excellent cast makes the difference; Caine adds class. Based on the novel by Simon Brett. **88m/C VHS.** Michael Caine, Elizabeth McGovern, Peter Riegert, Swoosie Kurtz, Will Patton, Jenny Wright, John McMartin, Barbara Baxley; *D:* Jan Egleson; *W:* Andrew Klavan; *C:* Paul Goldsmith; *M:* Gary Chang.

Shock to the System ✂✂ 1/2 **2006 (R)** In the second Donald Strachey mystery (following "Third Man Out"), the Albany PI (Allen) is suspicious when client Paul Hale allegedly commits suicide. He discovers Paul's homophobic mom (Fairchild) pushed him towards a gay conversion therapy group run by the shady Dr. Cornell (Woods). So Donald decides to go undercover to investigate, which may cost him his own life. Based on the series by Richard Stevenson. **95m/C DVD.** Chad Allen, Sebastian Spence, Michael Woods, Morgan Fairchild, Daryl Shuttleworth, Nelson Wong, Anne Marie Deluise; *D:* Ron Oliver; *W:* Ron McGee; *C:* C. Kim Miles; *M:* Peter Allen. **CABLE**

Shock Treatment ✂ 1/2 *Traitement de Choc* **1981 (PG)** Seldom-seen mediocre semi-sequel to the cult classic, "The Rocky Horror Picture Show" (1975). Brad and Janet, now married and portrayed by different leads, find themselves trapped on a TV gameshow full of weirdos. Same writers, same director, and several original cast members do make an appearance. **94m/C VHS, DVD.** Richard O'Brien, Jessica Harper, Cliff DeYoung, Patricia Quinn, Charles Gray, Ruby Wax, Nell Campbell, Rik Mayall, Barry Humphries, Darlene Johnson, Manning Redwood; *D:* Jim Sharman; *W:* Jim Sharman, Richard O'Brien; *C:* Mike Molloy; *M:* Richard Hartley, Richard O'Brien.

Shock Waves ✂✂ *Death Corps; Almost Human* **1977 (PG)** Group of mutant-underwater-zombie-Nazi-soldiers terrorizes stranded tourists staying at a deserted motel on a small island. Cushing is the mad scientist intent on recreating the Nazi glory days with the seaweed-attired zombies. Odd B-grade, more or less standard horror flick somehow rises (slightly) above badness. Halpin's name was erroneously listed as Halprin—even on the original movie poster! **90m/C VHS, DVD.** Peter Cushing, Brooke Adams, John Carradine, Luke Halpin, Jack Davidson, Fred Buch; *D:* Ken Wiederhorn; *W:* Ken Wiederhorn, John Kent Harrison; *C:* Reuben Trane; *M:* Richard Einhorn.

Shocker ✂✂ 1/2 **1989 (R)** Another Craven gore-fest. A condemned serial killer is transformed into a menacing electrical force after being fried in the chair. Practically a remake of Craven's original "Nightmare on Elm Street." Great special effects, a few enjoyable weird and sick moments. What's Dr. Timothy Leary doing here? **111m/C VHS, DVD.** Michael Murphy, Peter Berg, Camille (Cami) Cooper, Mitch Pileggi, Richard Price, Timothy Leary, Heather Langenkamp, Theodore (Ted) Raimi, Richard Brooks, Sam Scarber; *D:* Wes Craven; *W:* Wes Craven; *C:* Jacques Haitkin; *M:* William Goldstein.

Shockproof ✂✂ **1949** Minor noir. Tough Jenny Marsh (Knight) is paroled on a self-defense rap and parole officer Griff Marat (Wilde) gets her work caring for his blind mother after warning her against meeting up with her bad news ex-beau Harry (Baragrey). Eventually, Jenny and Griff fall for each other and Harry tries to blackmail them. Has a forced, hokey ending that was allegedly written by Deutsch not Fuller. **79m/B DVD.** Cornel Wilde, John Baragrey, Howard St. John, Russell Collins, Patricia Knight, Esther Minciotti, Charles Bates; *D:* Douglas Sirk; *W:* Helen Deutsch, Samuel Fuller; *C:* Charles Lawton Jr.; *M:* George Duning.

The Shoes of the Fisherman ✂ 1/2 **1968 (G)** Morris West's interesting, speculative best seller about Russian Pope brought to the big screen at much expense, but with little care or thought. Siberian prison-camp vet Quinn, elected Pope, tries to arrest nuclear war. Director Anderson wasted the prodigious talents of Olivier, Gielgud, et al. Sloppy use of good cast and promising plot.

160m/C VHS, DVD. Anthony Quinn, Leo McKern, Laurence Olivier, John Gielgud, Vittorio De Sica, Oskar Werner, David Janssen; ***D:*** Michael Anderson Sr.; ***M:*** Alex North. Golden Globes '69: Score; Natl. Bd. of Review '68: Support. Actor (McKern).

Shoeshine 1947 Two shoeshine boys struggling to survive in post-war Italy become involved in the black market and are eventually caught and imprisoned. Prison scenes detail the sense of abandonment and tragedy that destroys their friendship. A rich, sad achievement in neo-realistic drama. In Italian with English subtitles. **90m/B VHS, DVD.** *IT* Franco Interlenghi, Rinaldo Smordoni, Annielo Mele, Bruno Ortensi, Pacifico Astrologo; ***D:*** Vittorio De Sica; ***W:*** Cesare Zavattini, Sergio Amidei, Adolfo Franci, C.G. Viola.

Shogun ½ *James Clavell's Shogun* **1980** Miniseries chronicling the saga of a shipwrecked English navigator who becomes the first Shogun, or Samurai warrior chief, from the Western world. Colorfully adapted from the James Clavell bestseller. Also released in a two-hour version, but this full-length version is infinitely better. **550m/C VHS, DVD.** Richard Chamberlain, Toshiro Mifune, Yoko Shimada, John Rhys-Davies, Damien Thomas, William Morgan Sheppard; ***D:*** Jerry London; ***M:*** Maurice Jarre; ***Nar:*** Orson Welles. **TV**

Shogun Assassin ½ **1980 (R)** Story of a proud samurai named Lone Wolf who served his Shogun master well as the Official Decapitator, until the fateful day when the aging Shogun turned against him. Extremely violent, with record-breaking body counts. Edited from two other movies in a Japanese series called "Sword of Vengeance"; a tour de force of the cutting room. The samurai pushes his son's stroller through much of the film-sets it aside to hack and slash. **89m/C VHS, DVD.** *JP* Tomisaburo Wakayama, Kayo Matsuo, Shin Kishida, Masahiro Tomikawa; ***D:*** Robert Houston; ***W:*** Robert Houston, David Weisman, Kazuo Koike; ***C:*** Chishi Makiura; ***M:*** W. Michael Lewis, Mark Lindsay.

Shogun Assassin 2: Lightning Swords of Death *Kozure Okami: Shinikazeni mukau ubaguruma; Baby Cart; Shogun Assassin 2: Lightning Swords of Death; Lone Wolf and Cub: Baby Cart to Hades* **1973** Few Japanese comics are more iconic than the Lone Wolf and Cub series, about a rogue samurai and his young son facing down an army of assassins. In the seventies they were made into six films, and these were dubbed and re-edited into Shogun Assassins for U.S. release. **89m/C DVD.** *JP* Tomisaburo Wakayama, Yuko Hamada, Isao Yamagata, Akihiro Tomikawa, Jun Hamamura, Go Kato, Michitaro Mizushima; ***D:*** Kenji Misumi; ***W:*** Kazuo Koike, Goseki Kojima; ***C:*** Chishi Makiura; ***M:*** Hiroshi Kamayatsu, Hideaki Sakurai.

Shogun's Ninja ½ **1983** In 16th-century Japan, an age-old rivalry between two ninja clans sparks a search for a dagger which will lead to one clan's hidden gold. Martial arts performed and directed by Sonny Chiba. In Japanese with usual poor English dubbing. **112m/C VHS, DVD.** *JP* Hiroyuki (Henry) Sanada, Etsuko (Sue) Shihomi, Sonny Chiba; ***D:*** Noribumi Suzuki.

Shogun's Samurai—The Yagyu Clan Conspiracy ½ *Yagyu ichizoku no inbo; The Shogun's Samurai; Yagyu Clan Conspiracy* **1978** It is 1624, and the Shogun has died leaving behind two sons— Iemitsu (a disfigured son who should be the successor) and Tadanaga (a younger son who has the backing of the Imperial Court)—neither of which he named as successor. The government tells the brothers to decide, opening the way for them to become rivals. Things get complicated quickly when various factions begin to manipulate events behind the scenes, and Iemitsu's secret is revealed. **130m/C DVD.** *JP* Kinnosuke Nakamura, Sonny Chiba, Hiroki Matsukata, Reiko Ohara, Yoshio Harada, Etsuko (Sue) Shihomi, Hideo Murota, Hiroyuki (Henry) Sanada, Tetsuro Tamba, Etsushi Takahashi, Isao Natsuyagi, Mikio Narita, Sanae Nakahara, Isuzu Yamada, Toshiro Mifune, Teruhiko Saiga, Kentaro Kudo, Jiro Chiba, Mayumi Asano, Ichiro Nakatani, Shinsuke Ashida; ***D:*** Yudai Yamaguchi, Kinji Fukasaku; ***W:*** Kinji Fukasaku, Hiro Matsuda, Tatsuo Nogami; ***C:*** Toru Nakajima; ***M:*** Toshiaki Tsushima.

Shoot **1976 (R)** Five hunting buddies fall prey to a group of crazed killers after one man is shot by accident. What's the message: Anti-gun? Anti-hunting? Silly, unbelievable, irresponsibly moralistic, and gratuitously violent. **98m/C VHS.** *CA* Ernest Borgnine, Cliff Robertson, Henry Silva, Helen Shaver; ***D:*** Harvey Hart; ***W:*** Richard Berg; ***C:*** Zale Magder; ***M:*** Doug Riley.

Shoot **1992 (R)** Photographer Katie Tracy goes undercover to expose an illegal gambling ring fronted by an exotic nightclub. The latest gambling stakes involve the Emperor's pearls, offered in a private auction which could turn deadly, especially when Katie gets involved with the group's handsome ringleader. **90m/C VHS.** Dedee Pfeiffer, Miles O'Keeffe, Christopher Atkins; ***D:*** Hugh Parks.

Shoot 'Em Up ½ **2007 (R)** Mystery man Smith (Owen) sees a pregnant woman being chased by a crew of thugs and decides to step in. The woman dies, but not before Smith delivers the baby and takes it under his protection, recruiting prostitute Donna (Bellucci) to help nurse it. Meanwhile he's got to fight off mercenary Hertz (Giamatti), who's determined to get the baby no matter what it takes. Inevitably, the bodies start to pile up as Smith shows that he's handled a gun or four in his past. Extraordinarily violent with a tongue-in-cheek attitude, owing much to John Woo and other Asian action directors (Davis cites "Hard Boiled" as his inspiration). It doesn't match other big guns/big explosion actioners in quality but it hits fairly often, although Davis doesn't have Woo's knack for story or breaking the tension between onslaughts of extreme violence. **87m/C DVD, Blu-ray Disc.** *US* Clive Owen, Paul Giamatti, Monica Bellucci, Daniel Pilon, Julian Richings; ***D:*** Michael Davis; ***W:*** Michael Davis; ***C:*** Peter Pau; ***M:*** Paul Haslinger.

Shoot It Black, Shoot It Blue ½ **1974** Rogue cop shoots a black purse snatcher and thinks he has gotten away with it. Unknown to him, a witness has filmed the incident and turns the evidence over to a lawyer. **93m/C VHS.** Michael Moriarty, Eric Laneuville, Paul Sorvino, Earl Hindman, Linda Scruggs; ***D:*** Dennis McGuire; ***W:*** Dennis McGuire; ***C:*** Bob Bailin; ***M:*** Terry Stockdale.

Shoot Loud, Louder, I Don't Understand! ½ *Spara Forte, Piu Forte...Non Capisco* **1966** A sculptor who has a hard time separating reality from dreams thinks he witnessed a murder. Shenanigans follow. Meant to be a black comedy, but when not dull, it is confusing. Welch looks good, as usual, but doesn't show acting talent here. In Italian with English subtitles. **101m/C VHS, DVD.** *IT* Marcello Mastroianni, Raquel Welch; ***D:*** Eduardo de Filippo; ***M:*** Nino Rota.

Shoot or Be Shot ½ **2002 (PG-13)** Harvey Wilkes (Shatner) is a movie-lover who bolted from the psych ward with a script of his very own. As luck would have it, he happens upon a film crew shooting in the desert and usurps the production. Shatner is in great comedic form in this otherwise stale mockery of all that is Hollywood. **90m/C VHS, DVD.** William Shatner, Harry Hamlin, Tim Thomerson, James Healy Jr., Scott Rinker; ***D:*** Randy Argue; ***C:*** Ralph Linhardt; ***M:*** Joseph Alfuso. **VIDEO**

Shoot Out ½ *Shootout* **1971** Ham-fisted western based on Will James' novel "The Lone Cowboy" and previously filmed in 1934. Clay Lomax (Peck) gets out a prison and wants revenge on the partner, Sam Foley (Gregory), who doublecrossed him. So Foley hires a young gunslinger (Lyons) to take care of Lomax. In addition, Lomax gets stuck with an orphaned 8-year-old girl, who's the daughter of an ex-lover (and may be Lomax's flesh-and-blood). Peck's just too nice while Lyons chews all the scenery. **94m/C DVD.** Gregory Peck, Robert F. Lyons, Susan Tyrrell, Jeff Corey, James Gregory, Rita Gam, Pepe Serna, John Davis Chandler, Paul Fix, Arthur Hunnicutt, Nicolas Beauvy; ***D:*** Henry Hathaway; ***W:*** Marguerite Roberts; ***C:*** Earl Rath; ***M:*** Dave Grusin.

Shoot the Living, Pray for the Dead *Prega il Morto e Ammazza il Vivo* **1970** While travelling through Mexico, the leader of a band of killers promises his guide half of a share in stolen gold if he can lead them to it. **90m/C VHS.** *IT* Klaus Kinski, Victoria Zinny, Paul Sullivan, Dino Stano; ***D:*** Giuseppe Vari; ***C:*** Franco Villa; ***M:*** Mario Migliardi.

Shoot the Moon ½ **1982 (R)** A successful writer, married and with four children, finds his life unrewarding and leaves his family to take up with a younger woman. The wife must learn to deal with her resentment, the fears of her children, and her own attempt at a new love. Fine acting but a worn-out story. **124m/C VHS.** Diane Keaton, Albert Finney, Karen Allen, Peter Weller, Dana Hill, Viveka Davis, Tracey Gold, Tina Yothers; ***D:*** Alan Parker; ***W:*** Bo Goldman.

Shoot the Piano Player *Tirez sur le Pianiste; Shoot the Pianist* **1962** Former concert pianist (Aznavour, spendidly cast) changes his name and plays piano at a low-class Paris cafe. A convoluted plot ensues; he becomes involved with gangsters, though his girlfriend wants him to try a comeback. Lots of atmosphere, character development, humor, and romance. A Truffaut masterpiece based on a pulp novel by David Goodis. In French with English subtitles. **92m/B VHS, DVD.** *FR* Charles Aznavour, Marie DuBois, Nicole Berger, Michele Mercier, Albert Remy; ***D:*** Francois Truffaut; ***W:*** Marcel Moussey, Francois Truffaut; ***C:*** Raoul Coutard; ***M:*** Georges Delerue.

Shoot the Sun Down ½ **1981 (PG)** Four offbeat characters united in a search for gold turn against each other. "Gilligan's Island"-style assortment of characters (Indian; gunfighter; girl; sea captain) are cast away in a pointless plot from which they never escape. Too bad; talented cast could have done better. **102m/C VHS.** Christopher Walken, Margot Kidder, Geoffrey Lewis, Bo Brundin, Sacheen Little Feather; ***D:*** David Leeds.

Shoot to Kill ½ **1947** B-grade noir-esque mystery about a crooked D.A. and a gangster who bite the dust. Suspenseful, dark, street-level crime drama uncovered by ambitious journalist Ward. **64m/B VHS, DVD.** Russell Wade, Luana Walters, Nestor Paiva, Edmund MacDonald, Vince Barnett, Robert Kent, Charles Trowbridge, Harry Cheshire; ***D:*** William Berke; ***W:*** Edwin Westrate; ***C:*** Benjamin (Ben H.) Kline; ***M:*** Darrell Calker.

Shoot to Kill **1988 (R)** A city cop (Poitier, better than ever after 10 years off the screen) and a mountain guide (Berenger) reluctantly join forces to capture a killer who is part of a hunting party traversing the Pacific Northwest and which is being led by the guide's unsuspecting girlfriend (Alley). Poitier may be a bit old for the role, but he carries the implausible plot on the strength of his performance. Good action. **110m/C VHS, DVD.** Sidney Poitier, Tom Berenger, Kirstie Alley, Clancy Brown, Richard Masur, Andrew (Andy) Robinson, Frederick Coffin, Kevin Scannell; ***D:*** Roger Spottiswoode; ***W:*** Michael Burton, Harv Zimmel, Daniel Petrie Jr.; ***C:*** Michael Chapman; ***M:*** John Scott.

Shoot to Kill *Disparen a Matar* **1990** An innocent young man is murdered during a police round-up while his mother watches helplessly. The police try a white-wash—proclaiming the victim a criminal—but she launches a long campaign for justice. Spanish with subtitles. **90m/C VHS, DVD.** *VZ* Amalia Perez Diaz, Jean Carlo Simancas, Dan Alvarado, Flor Nunez; ***D:*** Carlos Azpurua; ***W:*** David Suarez; ***C:*** Adriano Moreno; ***M:*** Waldemar D'Lima.

The Shooter ½ **1997** The frontier town of Kingston is being terrorized by outlaw Krantz (Smith) and his gang until gunfighter Michael Atherton (Dudikoff) becomes their reluctant defender. Modest budget but lots of action. **93m/C VHS.** Michael Dudikoff, Randy Travis, Andrew Stevens, William (Bill) Smith; ***D:*** Fred Olen Ray. **VIDEO**

Shooter ½ **2007 (R)** Political conspiracy action thriller, based on the novel "Point of Impact" by Stephen Hunter. Former Marine sniper Bob Lee Swagger (Wahlberg, the perfect stoic hero) is living peacefully in a Wyoming cabin when he's approached by retired colonel Isaac Johnson (Glover), who tells Swagger his expertise is needed to prevent a presidential assassination. Naturally, it's all a set-up and Swagger has to go on the run to counteract those government weasels. Pena and Mara serve as allies while Glover, Beatty, Koteas, and Sherbedgia are on the side of evil. **122m/C DVD, Blu-ray Disc, HD DVD.** *US* Mark Wahlberg, Michael Pena, Danny Glover, Kate Mara, Elias Koteas, Rhona Mitra, Rade Serbedzija, Levon Helm, Ned Beatty, Tate Donovan, Justin Louis; ***D:*** Antoine Fuqua; ***W:*** Jonathan Lemkin; ***C:*** Peter Menzies Jr.; ***M:*** Mark Mancina.

Shooters ½ **1989** A wacky platoon of misfits is paired off against a group of vicious killers in a "war game" training session. Not completely unfunny or worthless. **84m/C VHS.** Ben Schick, Robin Sims, Aldo Ray; ***D:*** Peter Yuval; ***W:*** Michael Yuval; ***C:*** Paul Maibaum; ***M:*** Todd Hayen.

Shooters **2000 (R)** South London bad boy Gilly (Dempsey) is out on parole after six years. All he wants is his share from a long-ago heist with violent partner J (Howard) but J wants Gily to help him out on one last job that involves an arms dealer (Dunbar). Naturally, things go very wrong. Typical Cool Britannia crime actioner. **95m/C VHS, DVD.** *GB* Louis Dempsey, Andrew Howard, Adrian Dunbar, Gerard Butler, Jason Hughes, Matthew Rhys, Ioan Gruffudd, Melanie Lynskey; ***D:*** Glenn Dufort, Colin Teague; ***W:*** Louis Dempsey, Andrew Howard; ***C:*** Tom Erisman; ***M:*** Kemal Ultanur.

Shootfighter: Fight to the Death ½ **1993 (R)** Two boys become experts in the martial arts and constant rivals. Now grown-up they take their rivalry to a deadly level in a "shootfight," a game which has no rules and is so brutal it's banned as a sport. Not that this stops them. An unrated version is also available. **94m/C VHS.** Bolo Yeung, Martin Kove, William Zabka, Michael Bernardo, Maryam D'Abo, Edward Albert, Kenn Scott; ***D:*** Patrick Allen; ***W:*** Judd B. Lynn, Larry Feliz Jr., Peter Shaner.

Shootfighter 2: Kill or Be Killed! ½ **1996 (R)** The Miami underworld is placed on alert when a police chief, seeking to avenge the death of his son, joins with a martial arts master to recruit and train a group of fighters. Then they'll infiltrate the illegal spectator games of to-the-death-combat and see what mayhem they can cause. **90m/C VHS.** Bolo Yeung, Michael Bernardo, William Zabka; ***D:*** Paul Ziller; ***W:*** Peter Shaner, Greg Mellott.

The Shooting **1966** A mysterious woman, bent on revenge, persuades a former bounty hunter and his partner to escort her across the desert, with tragic results. Offbeat, small film filled with strong performances by Nicholson and Oates. Filmed concurrently with "Ride in the Whirlwind," with the same cast and director. Bang-up surprise ending. **82m/C VHS, DVD.** Warren Oates, Millie Perkins, Jack Nicholson, Will Hutchins; ***D:*** Monte Hellman; ***W:*** Adrien (Carole Eastman) Joyce; ***C:*** Gregory Sandor; ***M:*** Richard Markowitz.

Shooting **1982** Three boys run away when they think they have killed a man in a hunting accident. **60m/C VHS.** Lynn Redgrave, Lance Kerwin, Barry Primus; ***D:*** Michael Ray Rhodes; ***W:*** Josef Anderson; ***C:*** Terry Meade; ***M:*** John Cacavas.

Shooting Dogs *Beyond the Gates* **2005 (R)** The Ecole Technique Officielle is a secondary school located in Kigali, Rwanda. Young British teacher Joe Connor (Dancy) is getting his feet wet by spending a year at the school, run by steadfast Father Christopher (Hurt). Tensions are building between the Hutu and Tutsi factions and the school eventually becomes an uncertain shelter amidst the genocide. Film comes off as well-intentioned but overly familiar, although Hurt is a highlight. **115m/C DVD.** *GB GE* John Hurt, Hugh Dancy, Dominique Horwitz, Nicola Walker, Louis Mahoney, Steve Toussaint; ***D:*** Michael Caton-Jones; ***W:*** Richard Wolstencroft; ***C:*** Ivan Strasburg; ***M:*** Dario Marianelli.

Shooting Elizabeth ½ **1992 (PG-13)** A fed-up husband decides to shut his loudmouthed wife up—permanently. Only before he can kill her, she disappears. The police don't buy it and want to charge him with murder. Can he find his wife before things really get serious? **96m/C VHS, DVD.** Jeff Goldblum, Mimi Rogers; ***D:*** Baz Taylor.

Shooting Fish 1/2 **1998 (PG)** London con-artists Dylan (Futterman) and Jez (Townsend) hire perky temp Georgie (Beckinsale) to lend an air of authenticity to one of their scams. She charms them both, while figuring out that they're not the legit businessmen they pretend to be. When one of their scams goes awry, landing them in prison, Georgie helps them out. All the whiile, she's trying to figure out a way to save her retarded brother's home from her greedy fiance. Breezy, fun comedy benefits from great chemistry between the likable leads, but suffers from plot overload near the end. **109m/C VHS, DVD.** *GB* Dan Futterman, Stuart Townsend, Kate Beckinsale, Dominic Mafham, Claire Cox, Nickolas Grace, Peter Capaldi, Annette Crosbie, Jane Lapotaire; ***D:*** Stefan Schwartz; ***W:*** Stefan Schwartz, Richard Holmes; ***C:*** Henry Braham; ***M:*** Stanislas Syrewicz.

Shooting Livien **2005** John Livien (Behr), named after John Lennon, is a self-destructive rock singer who is about to blow his band's big chance at success with his behavior, which endears him to no one but groupie Emi (Wynter). As Livien becomes increasingly unstable, he connects ever more dangerously with Lennon's life—and death. **94m/C DVD.** Jason Behr, Sarah Wynter, Dominic Monaghan, Joshua Leonard, Ally Sheedy, Polly Draper, Jay O. Sanders; ***D:*** Rebecca Cook; ***W:*** Rebecca Cook; ***C:*** Harlan Bosmajian.

The Shooting Party 1/2 **1977** Told in flashbacks, a story of a crime of passion, an innocent man, and guilty secrets. A magistrate cannot admit his love for a woodsman's daughter so she falls into a loveless marriage and a decadent affair. In a fit of passion, the magistrate kills her and then decides to prosecute her innocent husband for the crime. Based on a story by Chekhov. In Russian with English subtitles. **105m/C VHS.** *RU* Oleg (Yankovsky) Jankowsky, Galina Belyayeva; ***D:*** Emil Loteanu.

The Shooting Party 1/2 **1985** A group of English aristocrats assemble at a nobleman's house for a bird shoot on the eve of WWI. Splendid cast crowned Mason, in his last role. Fascinating crucible class anxieties, rich with social scheming, personality conflicts, and things left unsaid. Adapted from Isabel Colegate's novel. **97m/C VHS, DVD.** *GB* James Mason, Dorothy Tutin, Edward Fox, John Gielgud, Robert Hardy, Cheryl Campbell, Judi Bowker; ***D:*** Alan Bridges; ***W:*** Julian Bond. L.A. Film Critics '85: Support. Actor (Gielgud); Natl. Soc. Film Critics '85: Support. Actor (Gielgud).

Shooting Stars **1985** Two actors who play private eyes on TV are pushed out of their jobs by a jealous co-star. They take to the streets as "real" crime-fighting dicks. Interesting premise goes nowhere. **96m/C VHS.** Billy Dee Williams, Parker Stevenson, Efrem Zimbalist Jr., Edie Adams; ***D:*** Richard Lang. **TV**

Shooting the Past 1/2 **1999** Christopher Anderson (Cunningham) is a wealthy American developer who has just purchased an old London mansion, which he is intending to convert into a business school. The mansion presently houses the Fallon Photo Library, consisting of some 10 million historical pictures. The indifferent Anderson says the pictures must be sold or destroyed within a week. But Anderson reckons without the library's impervious employees, who will do whatever is necessary to save their library. **180m/C VHS, DVD.** *GB* Liam Cunningham, Lindsay Duncan, Timothy Spall, Emilia Fox; ***D:*** Stephen Poliakoff; ***W:*** Stephen Poliakoff. **TV**

The Shootist 1/2 **1976 (PG)** Wayne, in a supporting last role, plays a legendary gunslinger afflicted with cancer who seeks peace and solace in his final days. Town bad guys Boone and O'Brian aren't about to let him rest and are determined to gun him down to avenge past deeds. One of Wayne's best and most dignified performances about living up to a personal code of honor. Stewart and Bacall head excellent supporting cast. Based on Glendon Swarthout's novel. **100m/C VHS, DVD.** John Wayne, Lauren Bacall, Ron Howard, James Stewart, Richard Boone, Hugh O'Brian, Bill McKinney, Harry (Henry) Morgan, John Carradine, Sheree North, Scatman Crothers; ***D:*** Donald Siegel; ***W:*** Scott Hale, Miles Hood Swarthout; ***C:*** Bruce Surtees; ***M:*** Elmer Bernstein.

Shop Angel **1932** A department store dress designer encounters romance and scandal in this low-budget drama of intrigue and romance. She falls in love with the fiance of her boss's daughter, and schemes to blackmail him (the boss). Competently rendered if unexceptional tale. **66m/B VHS.** Marion Shilling, Holmes Herbert, Creighton Hale; ***D:*** E. Mason Hopper.

The Shop Around the Corner 1/2 **1940** A low-key romantic classic in which Stewart and Sullavan are feuding clerks in a small Budapest shop, who unknowingly fall in love via a lonely hearts club. Charming portrayal of ordinary people in ordinary situations. Adapted from the Nikolaus Laszlo's play "Parfumerie." Later made into a musical called "In the Good Old Summertime" and, on Broadway, "She Loves Me." **99m/B VHS, DVD.** Margaret Sullavan, James Stewart, Frank Morgan, Joseph Schildkraut, Sara Haden, Felix Bressart, Charles Halton; ***D:*** Ernst Lubitsch; ***W:*** Samson Raphaelson; ***C:*** William H. Daniels; ***M:*** Werner R. Heymann. Natl. Film Reg. '99.

The Shop on Main Street *The Shop on High Street; Obch Od Na Korze* **1965** During WWII, a Slovak takes a job as an "Aryan comptroller" for a Jewish-owned button shop. The owner is an old deaf woman; they slowly build a friendship. Tragedy ensues when all of the town's Jews are to be deported. Sensitive and subtle. Surely among the most gutwrenching portrayals of human tragedy ever on screen. Exquisite plotting and direction. In Czechoslovakian with English subtitles. **111m/B VHS, DVD.** *CZ* Ida Kaminska, Josef Kroner, Hana Slivkoua, Frantisek Holly, Martin Gregor; ***D:*** Jan Kadar, Elmar Klos; ***W:*** Jan Kadar, Elmar Klos; ***C:*** Vladimir Novotny; ***M:*** Zdenek Liska. Oscars '65: Foreign Film; N.Y. Film Critics '66: Foreign Film.

Shopgirl **2005 (R)** Writer/actor/director Steve Martin adapts his novella about a rather bland, disconnected and melancholy 20-something glove salesgirl. Mirabelle (Danes) shares an unemotional romance with older rich guy Ray Porter (Martin), then meets Jeremy (Schwartzman), who is perhaps a better (and younger) match. Martin doesn't depart from his previous films, again staying in his beloved LA. Characters are a bit flat, but Martin's flair for words and setting the scene add an artsy, high-brow element that absolutely works. **116m/C DVD.** *US* Steve Martin, Claire Danes, Jason Schwartzman, Bridgette Wilson-Sampras, Sam Bottoms, Frances Conroy, Rebecca Pidgeon, Samantha Shelton, Gina Doctor, Clyde Kusatsu, Romy Rosemont, Anne Marie Howard; ***D:*** Anand Tucker; ***W:*** Steve Martin; ***C:*** Peter Suschitzky; ***M:*** Barrington Pheloung.

Shopping **1993 (R)** A crumbling British industrial city (filmed at London's docklands) is the bleak setting for gangs of aimless youth who steal cars, crash into the windows of various shops, grab whatever comes to hand, and then lead the police on high-speed chases. Adrenaline junkie Billy (Law) is accompanied by thrill-seeking girlfriend Jo (Frost) on one such escapade while fending off rival Tommy (Pertwee), who doesn't like his burgeoning criminal empire disturbed. Tries too hard for that rebel youth feeling. **86m/C VHS, DVD.** *GB* Jude Law, Sadie Frost, Sean Pertwee, Fraser James, Sean Bean, Marianne Faithfull, Jonathan Pryce, Daniel Newman; ***D:*** Paul W.S. Anderson; ***W:*** Paul W.S. Anderson; ***C:*** Tony Imi; ***M:*** Barrington Pheloung.

Shopworn Angel **1938** Weepy melodrama about a sophisticated actress who leads on a naive Texas soldier who's in New York prior to being shipped out for WWI duty. Later, just before she goes on stage, she learns he's been killed at the front. She rallys to sing "Pack Up your Troubles in Your Old Kit Bag and Smile, Smile, Smile." Lots of tears. Adapted from the story "Private Pettigrew's Girl" by Dana Burnet. This remake of the same-titled 1929 film considerably softened the characters. Remade again in 1959 as "That Kind of Woman." **85m/B VHS.** Margaret Sullavan, James Stewart, Walter Pidgeon, Nat Pendleton, Alan Curtis, Sam Levene, Hattie McDaniel, Charley Grapewin, Charles D. Brown; ***D:*** H.C. Potter; ***W:*** Waldo Salt; ***C:*** Joseph Ruttenberg.

Shore Leave **1925** Dressmaker Mackaill isn't getting any younger. Tough-guy sailor Bilge Smith (Barthelmess, in top form) meets her on shore leave; little does he realize her plans for him! She owns a dry-docked ship, you see, and it (and she) will be ready for him when he comes ashore next. Lovely, fun (if rather plodding) romantic comedy. Later made into musicals twice, as "Hit the Deck" and "Follow the Fleet." **74m/B VHS.** Richard Barthelmess, Dorothy Mackaill; ***D:*** John S. Robertson.

Short Circuit **1986 (PG)** A newly developed robot designed for the military is hit by lightning and begins to think it's alive. Sheedy and Guttenberg help it hide from the mean people at the weapons lab who want to take it home. Followed two years later, save Sheedy and Guttenberg, by the lame "Short Circuit 2." **98m/C VHS, DVD, Blu-ray Disc, UMD.** Steve Guttenberg, Ally Sheedy, Austin Pendleton, Fisher Stevens, Brian McNamara; ***D:*** John Badham; ***W:*** S.S. Wilson, Brent Maddock; ***C:*** Nick McLean; ***M:*** David Shire.

Short Circuit 2 1/2 **1988 (PG)** A sequel to the first adorable-robot-outwits-bad-guys tale. The robot, Number Five, makes his way through numerous plot turns without much human assistance or much purpose. Harmless (unless you have to spend time watching it), but pointless and juvenile. Very occasional genuinely funny moments. **95m/C VHS, DVD.** Fisher Stevens, Cynthia Gibb, Michael McKean, Jack Weston, David Hemblen; ***D:*** Kenneth Johnson; ***W:*** Brent Maddock, S.S. Wilson; ***C:*** John McPherson; ***M:*** Charles Fox.

Short Cuts 1/2 **1993 (R)** Multi-storied, fish-eyed look at American culture with some 22 characters intersecting—profoundly or fleetingly—through each other's lives. Running the emotional gamut from disturbing to humorous, Altman's portrait of the contemporary human condition is nevertheless fascinating. Based on nine stories and a prose poem by Raymond Carver. **189m/C VHS, DVD.** Natalie Strong, Annie Ross, Lori Singer, Jennifer Jason Leigh, Tim Robbins, Madeleine Stowe, Frances McDormand, Peter Gallagher, Lily Tomlin, Tom Waits, Bruce Davison, Andie MacDowell, Jack Lemmon, Lyle Lovett, Fred Ward, Buck Henry, Huey Lewis, Matthew Modine, Anne Archer, Julianne Moore, Lili Taylor, Christopher Penn, Robert Downey Jr., Jarrett Lennon, Zane Cassidy; ***D:*** Robert Altman; ***W:*** Frank Barhydt, Robert Altman; ***C:*** Walt Lloyd; ***M:*** Mark Isham. Ind. Spirit '94: Director (Altman), Film, Screenplay; Natl. Soc. Film Critics '93: Support. Actress (Stowe); Venice Film Fest. '93: Film.

Short Eyes 1/2 *The Slammer* **1979 (R)** When a child molester (Davison) enters prison, the inmates act out their own form of revenge against him. Filmed on location at New York City's Men's House of Detention, nicknamed "The Tombs." Script by Manuel Pinero from his excellent play; he also acts in the film. Top-notch performances and respectful direction from Young bring unsparingly realistic prison drama to the screen. Title is prison jargon for child molester. **100m/C VHS, DVD.** Bruce Davison, Miguel Pinero, Nathan George, Donald Blakely, Curtis Mayfield, Jose Perez, Shawn Elliott; ***D:*** Robert M. Young.

Short Fuse 1/2 *Good to Go* **1988 (R)** A Washington, D.C. reporter uncovers the truth behind the rape and murder of a nurse. Interesting "go-go" music from the Washington D.C. ghetto aids an otherwise uninteresting film. **91m/C VHS.** Art Garfunkel, Robert DoQui, Harris Yulin, Richard Brooks, Reginald Daughtry; ***D:*** Blaine Novak.

Short Night of Glass Dolls *Corta Notte delle Bambole di Vetro; Paralyzed; Malastrana* **1971** Journalist Gregory Moore (Sorel) is found dead in a Prague square and taken to the morgue. Only he's not dead but paralyzed—he can't move or communicate but his brain works and through flashbacks he tries to remember what's happened to him. Gregory is investigating the disappearance of his girlfriend Mira (Bach) and learns that she is only one of many girls who have gone missing. The police are no help and Gregory's snooping leads to a sinister club and a secret society. Italian with subtitles. **97m/C DVD.** *IT* Jean Sorel, Ingrid Thulin, Mario Adorf, Barbara Bach, Fabian Sovagovic; ***D:*** Aldo Lado; ***W:*** Aldo Lado; ***C:*** Giuseppe Ruzzolini; ***M:*** Ennio Morricone.

Short Time **1990 (PG-13)** Somewhere between "Tango & Cash" and "Airplane" is where you'll find "Short Time." Non-stop action/comedy stars Dabney Coleman and Teri Garr as partners in crime and humor. Coleman is a cop days from retirement; wrongly told he is dying, he tries hard to get killed so his family will be provided for. Coleman is wonderful. Garr, no longer the long-suffering wife of "Oh, God" and "Close Encounters," is appealing here as the indulgent sidekick. **100m/C VHS.** Dabney Coleman, Teri Garr, Matt Frewer, Barry Corbin, Joe Pantoliano, Xander Berkeley, Rob Roy, Kaj-Erik Eriksen; ***D:*** Gregg Champion; ***W:*** John Blumenthal, Michael Berry; ***M:*** Ira Newborn.

The Shortcut 1/2 **2009 (PG-13)** Kids and dogs disappear near the old Hartley place so no one uses the shortcut through the woods until newcomers Derek and his younger brother Tobey do so on a dare. Then Derek and his new high school friends decide to find out just how weird old weirdo Hartley really is. But sometimes the past should be left alone. More creepy mystery than gory horror. **85m/C DVD.** Andrew Seeley, Shannon Marie Woodward, Dave Franco, Katrina Bowden, Nicholas Elia, Raymond J. Barry; ***D:*** Nicholaus Goossen; ***W:*** Scott Sandler. **VIDEO**

Shorts: The Adventures of the Wishing Rock **2009 (PG)** Zippy (if deliberately disjointed) kid comedy finds 11-year-old bullied misfit Toe Thompson (Bennett) living in the company town of Black Hills where his workaholic parents (Cryer, Mann) ignore him in favor of their jobs at Black Box Industries. So naturally when Toe gets hit in the head by a rainbow-colored rock during a freak storm and said rock turns out to be able to grant wishes, Toe asks for friends. Of course, the wishes don't come true in exactly the fashion that anyone expects causing more than a little trouble. **89m/C DVD.** *US* Jimmy Bennett, Kat Dennings, Trevor Gagnon, Jake Short, Jolie Vanier, Leo Howard, Devon Gearhart, Rebel Rodriguez, Leslie Mann, Jon Cryer, William H. Macy, James Spader; ***D:*** Robert Rodriguez; ***W:*** Robert Rodriguez; ***C:*** Robert Rodriguez; ***M:*** Carl Thiel, George Oldziey.

The Shot 1/2 **1996** Shot in 14 days for $40,000 (and sometimes showing it), this independent release follows out-of-work actors Dern Reel (Bell) and Patrick St. Patrick (Rivkin) as they try to break into the movie business. The foil for the two sensitive artist-types is the shallow but successful director David Egoman. Offended by his brainless action movies, the duo decide to "kidnap" the only print of his latest epic. Although production values are low and the sound is a bit dicey, indie fans will probably like this depiction of Hollywood's shady side. Gained some publicity when ten reels of Kevin Spacey's "Albino Alligator" were swiped from an airport baggage claim shortly after its release. **84m/C VHS.** Dan Bell, Michael Rivkin, Mo Gaffney, Michael DeLuise, Vincent Ward, Jack Kehler, Theodore (Ted) Raimi, Jude Horowitz; ***Cameos:*** Dana Carvey; ***D:*** Dan Bell; ***W:*** Dan Bell; ***C:*** Alan Caudillo; ***M:*** Dan Sonis.

Shot 1/2 *Focus* **2001 (R)** Photographer Robert (Karrer) befriends young Marcus (Gray) when he discovers the inner-city youth has a natural ability behind the lens. Robert gets drawn into the thug life but makes a big mistake when he photographs Marcus's older brother, Keith (Cameron), and his gang murdering undercover cops. **97m/C VHS, DVD.** Brandon Karrer, Gary Gray, Trent Cameron, Jennifer Jostyn, Bruce Weitz; ***D:*** Roger Roth; ***W:*** Roger Roth; ***C:*** Mark Woods; ***M:*** Norman Arnold. **VIDEO**

A Shot at Glory **2000 (R)** So-so Scottish soccer saga starring Duvall as McLeod, the manager of a struggling local football club. Looking to launch the lads into stardom, the team's new American owner Cameron (Keaton) hires former star McQuillan (real-life player McCoist) against the wishes of McLeod. Despite McQuillan's drinking and carousing—which has cost him his marriage to none other than McLeod's daughter Kate (Mitchell)—the Knockies soon find their way into the Scottish Cup finals, where McLeod meets up with his old nemesis Smith (Cox), manager of the opposing Glasgow Rangers. Though thin on drama, well-shot soccer action will appeal to sports fans. Duvall's high profile and manufactured brogue bog down an otherwise solid performance. **115m/C VHS, DVD.** Robert Duvall, Michael Keaton, Brian Cox, Cole Hauser, Ally McCoist, Kirsty Mitchell, Morag Hood, Libby Langdon; ***D:*** Michael Corrente; ***W:*** Dennis O'Neill; ***C:*** Alex Thomson; ***M:*** Mark Knopfler.

A Shot in the Dark 🦴½ **1933** A minister suspects murder when a despised miser is thought to have committed suicide. He takes it on himself to investigate in this routine mystery. **53m/B VHS.** *GB* Dorothy Boyd, O.B. Clarence, Jack Hawkins, Russell Thorndike, Michael Shepley; ***D:*** George Pearson.

A Shot in the Dark 🦴🦴 **1935** When his son is murdered at a New England college, a distraught dad takes it on himself to investigate. Movie cowboy Starrett plays the sleuthing pop in this undistinguished mystery. **69m/B VHS, DVD.** Charles Starrett, Robert Warwick, Edward Van Sloan, Marion Shilling, Doris Lloyd, Helen Jerome Eddy, James Bush; ***D:*** Charles Lamont.

A Shot in the Dark 🦴🦴🦴½ **1964** Second and possibly the best in the classic "Inspector Clouseau-Pink Panther" series of comedies. The bumbling Inspector Clouseau (Sellers, of course) investigates the case of a parlor maid (Sommer) accused of murdering her lover. Clouseau's libido convinces him she's innocent,even though all the clues point to her. Classic gags, wonderful music. After this film, Sellers as Clouseau disappears until 1975's "Return of the Pink Panther" (Alan Arkin played him in "Inspector Clouseau," made in 1968 by different folks). **101m/C VHS, DVD.** Peter Sellers, Elke Sommer, Herbert Lom, George Sanders, Bryan Forbes; ***D:*** Blake Edwards; ***W:*** William Peter Blatty, Blake Edwards; ***C:*** Christopher Challis; ***M:*** Henry Mancini.

Shot in the Heart 🦴🦴🦴 **2001 (R)** In 1977, shortly after the Supreme Court reinstated capital punishment, convicted murderer Gary Gilmore (Koteas) requested execution by a Utah firing squad, becoming the first person executed in a decade. But Gilmore's brothers, Frank Jr. (Tergesen), and his younger brother, writer Mikal (Ribisi), come to Draper Prison to plead with him to change his mind. Alienated for years, the brothers' uneasy reunion brings up lots of twisted family memories. Haunting movie about internal demons and brotherly ties; based on Mikal's 1994 memoir of the same name. **98m/C VHS, DVD.** Giovanni Ribisi, Elias Koteas, Lee Tergesen, Sam Shepard, Amy Madigan, Eric Bogosian; ***D:*** Agnieszka Holland; ***W:*** Frank Pugliese; ***C:*** Jacek Petrycki. **CABLE**

Shot Through the Heart 🦴🦴🦴 **1998 (R)** Based on a true story of the ethnic conflict that tore apart the former Yugoslavia and started a civil war between 1992 and 1995. Serbian Slavko (Perez) and Croat Vlado (Roache), whose wife Maida (William) is a Muslim, are childhood friends and former teammates on the Yugoslavian target-shooting team. Slavko is drafted into the Serbian army and urges his friend to flee Sarajevo. Instead, Vlado and his family are trapped in the city and Vlado is forced to take up his rifle in defense against deadly Serbian snipers. Which leads him to a final confrontation with Slavko. Filmed in Sarajevo and Budapest. **115m/C VHS, DVD.** Linus Roache, Vincent Perez, Lothaire Bluteau, Adam Kotz, Lia Williams, Karianne Henderson; ***D:*** David Attwood; ***W:*** Guy Hibbert; ***M:*** Ed Shearmur. **CABLE**

Shotgun 🦴🦴½ **1955** A sheriff on the trail of a killer is accompanied by a girl he's saved from Indians. Average western cowritten by western actor Rory Calhoun, who had hoped to star in the film, but was turned down by the studio. **81m/C VHS.** Sterling Hayden, Zachary Scott, Yvonne De Carlo; ***D:*** Lesley Selander; ***C:*** Ellsworth Fredericks.

Shotgun Stories 🦴🦴 **2007 (PG-13)** Violence begets violence and a blood feud produces only tragedy. Son, Kid, and Boy Hayes are living hardscrabble lives in a small Arkansas town. Their dad was an abusive drunk, but after leaving the family he eventually cleaned up his act, remarried, and had four more sons who are prospering. His funeral causes a graveside fight between the half-brothers that escalates with some predictable (but watchable) results. **92m/C DVD.** Michael Shannon, Natalie Canerday, Douglas Ligon, Barlow Jacobs, Michael Abbott Jr., Travis Smith, Lynsee Provence, David Rhodes, Glenda Pannell, G. Allen Wilkins; ***D:*** Jeff Nichols; ***W:*** Jeff Nichols; ***C:*** Adam Stone; ***M:*** Ben Nichols, Lucero.

The Shout 🦴🦴🦴 **1978 (R)** From a strange Robert Graves story, an even stranger film. A lunatic befriends a young couple, moves in with them, and gradually takes over their lives. The movie's title refers to the man's ability to kill by shouting, a power he learned from his Australian aboriginal past. **88m/C VHS.** *GB* Alan Bates, Susannah York, John Hurt, Tim Curry; ***D:*** Jerzy Skolimowski; ***W:*** Michael Austin; ***M:*** Tony Banks. Cannes '78: Grand Jury Prize.

Shout 🦴🦴 **1991 (PG-13)** Romance and rebellion set in a sleepy Texas town during the 1950s. Jesse Tucker's (Walters) rebellious ways land him in the Benedict Home for Boys and he seems lost until Jack Cabe (Travolta) enters town. Jack introduces Jesse and the gang to the exciting new sounds of rock 'n' roll. Been done before and better. **93m/C VHS, DVD.** John Travolta, James Walters, Heather Graham, Richard Jordan, Linda Fiorentino, Scott Coffey; ***D:*** Jeffrey Hornaday; ***C:*** Robert Brinkmann; ***M:*** Randy Edelman.

Shout at the Devil 🦴½ **1976 (PG)** English officer Moore and Irish-American adventurer Marvin seek to blow up a German battleship out for repairs in East Africa before the outbreak of WWI. There's also some intrigue about ivory smuggling. From the novel by Wilbur Smith and based on an actual incident, but that doesn't make the comedy adventure any more palatable. Marvin's hamming is ludicrous, Moore is unusually wooden, and the big budget permits any number of fairly pointless action-oriented excursions and explosions. **128m/C VHS.** *GB* Lee Marvin, Roger Moore, Barbara Parkins, Ian Holm; ***D:*** Peter Hunt; ***M:*** Maurice Jarre.

The Show 🦴🦴 **1995 (R)** Choppy and incoherent behind-the-scenes look at the attitude and people who make up the explosive hip-hop and rap scene. Mixes black and white concert footage and interviews with Russell Simmons, LL Cool J and Snoop Doggy Dogg, who discuss their music and fans. Will be a disappointment for those looking for a more in-depth study of the music, as this exercise merely scratches the surface. Includes an abundance of cameos from today's top hip hop artists such as Notorious B.I.G., Naughty by Nature and Wu-Tang Clan. **90m/B VHS, DVD.** Craig Mack, Dr. Dre, Run DMC, Slick Rick, Warren G, Kurtis Blow; ***D:*** Brian Robbins; ***C:*** Larry Banks, Steven Consentino, Ericson Core, John L. (Ndiaga) Demps Jr., Todd A. Dos Reis.

Show Boat 🦴🦴🦴🦴 **1936** The second of three film versions of the Jerome Kern/Oscar Hammerstein musical (based on the Edna Ferber novel), filmed previously in 1929, about a Mississippi showboat and the life and loves of its denizens. Wonderful romance, unforgettable music. Director Whale also brought the world "Frankenstein." The laser edition includes a historical audio essay by Miles Kreuger, excerpts from the 1929 version, Ziegfeld's 1932 stage revival, "Life Aboard a Real Showboat" (a vintage short), radio broadcasts, and a 300-photo essay tracing the history of showboats. Remade 15 years later. ♫ Ol' Man River; Ah Still Suits Me; Bill; Can't Help Lovin' Dat Man; Only Make Believe; I Have the Room Above Her; You Are Love; Gallivantin' Around; Cotton Blossom. **110m/B VHS.** Irene Dunne, Allan Jones, Paul Robeson, Helen Morgan, Hattie McDaniel, Charles Winninger, Donald Cook, Bobs Watson; ***D:*** James Whale; ***W:*** Oscar Hammerstein; ***M:*** Oscar Hammerstein, Jerome Kern. Natl. Film Reg. '96.

Show Boat 🦴🦴½ **1951** Third movie version of the 1927 musical about the life and loves of a Mississippi riverboat theatre troupe. Terrific musical numbers, with fun dance routines from Champion, who went on to great fame as a choreographer. Grayson is somewhat vapid, but lovely to look at and hear. Gardner didn't want to do the part of Julie, although she eventually received fabulous reviews—her singing was dubbed by Annette Warren. The 171-foot "Cotton Blossom" boat was built on the Tarzan lake on the MGM back lot at an astounding cost of $126,468. Warfield's film debut—his "Ole Man River"—was recorded in one take. excerpts from "Broadway," "Silent Film," and radio Version of "Show Boat," a documentary featuring life on a real show boat, and a commentary on the performers, the film, and the history of show boats. ♫ Make Believe; Can't Help Lovin' Dat Man; I Might Fall Back On You; Ol' Man River; You Are Love; Why Do I Love You?; Bill; Life Upon the Wicked Stage; After the Ball. **115m/C VHS, DVD.** Kathryn Grayson, Howard Keel, Ava Gardner, William Warfield, Joe E. Brown, Agnes Moorehead, Gower Champion; ***D:*** George Sidney; ***W:*** George Wells, Jack McGowan; ***C:*** Charles Rosher; ***M:*** Oscar Hammerstein.

Show Business 🦴🦴🦴 **1944** Historically valuable film record of classic vaudeville acts, especially Cantor and Davis. A number of vaudevillians re-create their old acts for director Marin—unforgettable slapstick and songs. All this pegged on a plot that follows Cantor's rise to fame with the Ziegfeld Follies. ♫ Alabamy Bound; I Want a Girl (Just Like the Girl Who Married Dear Old Dad); It Had to Be You; Makin' Whoopee; Why Am I Blue; They're Wearing 'Em Higher in Hawaii; The Curse of an Aching Heart; While Strolling in the Park One Day; You May Not Remember. **92m/B VHS.** Eddie Cantor, Joan Davis, George Murphy; ***D:*** Edwin L. Marin.

Show Girl in Hollywood 🦴🦴½ **1930** Broadway chorine Dixie Dugan (White) is performing in a New York nightclub when shifty Hollywood director Frank Buelow (Miljan) offers her a movie contract. Dixie gets the leading role but then turns diva, which ruins the comeback efforts of fading silent star Donna Harris (Sweet). A desperate act by Donna causes Dixie to question the tawdry tinsel behind the glamour. White also played the same role in 1928's "Show Girl." **77m/C DVD.** Alice White, Jack Mulhall, Blanche Sweet, John Miljan, Ford Sterling, Virginia Sale; ***D:*** Mervyn LeRoy; ***W:*** Harvey Thew, James A. Starr; ***C:*** Sol Polito.

Show Me 🦴½ **2004 (R)** No, please don't. Sarah (Nolden) is carjacked and kidnapped by two homeless teens, Jenna (Isabelle) and Jackson (Turton), who force her to take them to her isolated cabin. Only Sarah decides to turn the tables on her captors and plays some mind games herself. Grubby and unpleasant story although Isabelle is frighteningly feral. **97m/C DVD.** *CA* Michelle Nolden, Katharine Isabelle, Kett Turton, Gabriel Hogan; ***D:*** Cassandra Nicolaou; ***W:*** Cassandra Nicolaou; ***C:*** Patrick Mcgowan; ***M:*** Evelyne Datl.

Show Me Love 🦴🦴 **1999** Sixteen-year-old Agnes (Liljeberg) is the new girl in the boring, small Swedish town of Amal. Agnes isn't cool enough to be with the popular crowd (she's a brainy vegetarian) and she's rumored to be a lesbian as well. Agnes does have a crush on bored beauty, Elin (Dahlstrom), who goes to extremes to get her kicks, even making a bet with her sister Jessica (Carlson) about kissing Agnes. Then, shocked by her own reactions, Elin makes out with convenient Johan (Rust). But Elin's betrayal of self leads to self-discovery—for both girls. Swedish with subtitles. **89m/C VHS, DVD.** *SW* Rebecca Liljeberg, Alexandra Dahlstrom, Mathias Rust, Erica Carlson, Stefan Horberg, Ralph Carlsson, Maria Hedborg; ***D:*** Lukas Moodysson; ***W:*** Lukas Moodysson; ***C:*** Ulf Brantas.

A Show of Force 🦴🦴 **1990 (R)** Reporter Irving investigates the coverup of a murder with political ramifications. Brazilian director Barreto cast (surprise!) his girlfriend in the lead; she doesn't exactly carry the day. Phillips is good, but you'll end up feeling cheated if you expect to see much of highly billed Duvall or Garcia. Based on a real incident of 1978, but hardly believable as political realism or even moralism. **93m/C VHS, DVD.** Erik Estrada, Amy Irving, Andy Garcia, Robert Duvall, Lou Diamond Phillips; ***D:*** Bruno Barreto; ***W:*** Evan Jones; ***M:*** Georges Delerue.

The Show Off 🦴🦴½ **1926** Irresponsible Aubrey Piper's (Sterling) incessant boasting wrecks havoc with his wife Amy (Wilson) and their life together. Brooks has a small role as the girl-next-door. **82m/B VHS, DVD.** Ford Sterling, Lois Wilson, Louise Brooks, Claire McDowell, C.W. Goodrich, Gregory Kelly; ***D:*** Malcolm St. Clair; ***W:*** Pierre Collins; ***C:*** Lee Garmes; ***M:*** Timothy Brock.

The Show-Off 🦴½ **1946** Aubrey Piper (Skelton) has big dreams which far out weigh his modest talents. He tells outlandish tales to impress girlfriend Amy (Maxwell) and schemes to make them come true. Dated material which even gifted comedian Skelton can't rescue. Adapted from a play by George Kelly and previously filmed in 1926, 1929, and 1934. **83m/B VHS.** Red Skelton, Marilyn Maxwell, Marjorie Main, Virginia O'Brien, Eddie Anderson, George Cleveland, Leon Ames, Marshall Thompson, Jacqueline White, Lila Leeds, Emory Parnell; ***D:*** Harry Beaumont; ***W:*** George Wells.

Show People 🦴🦴🦴 **1928** A pretty girl from the boonies tries to make it big in Tinseltown. But as a slapstick star?! She wanted to be a leading lady! Enjoyable, fun silent comedy shows Davies's true talents. Interesting star cameos, including director Vidor at the end. **82m/B VHS.** Marion Davies, William Haines, Dell Henderson, Paul Ralli, William S. Hart, Rod La Rocque; ***Cameos:*** King Vidor; ***D:*** King Vidor. Natl. Film Reg. '03.

Show Them No Mercy 🦴🦴🦴 *Tainted Money* **1935** A couple and their baby out for a drive unwittingly stumble into a kidnapping that doesn't go as planned. Tense gangster drama reincarnated as the Western "Rawhide." **76m/B VHS.** Rochelle Hudson, Cesar Romero, Bruce Cabot, Edward Norris, Edward Brophy, Warren Hymer, Herbert Rawlinson; ***D:*** George Marshall.

The Showdown 🦴🦴 **1940** The title actually refers to a tricky poker game, the highlight of yet another Hopalong Cassidy versus hoss thieves quickie epic. Kermit Maynard is the brother of cowboy hero Ken Maynard. **65m/B VHS, DVD.** William Boyd, Russell Hayden, Britt Wood, Morris Ankrum, Jan Clayton, Roy Barcroft, Kermit Maynard; ***D:*** Howard Bretherton.

The Showdown 🦴🦴½ **1950** Elliott plays trail boss Shad Jones who knows one of his fellow cowhands has murdered his brother. Jones is determined to find out who it is and even the score. Brennan is cast against type as a greedy cattle baron. Elliott's last film for Republic. **86m/B VHS.** William (Wild Bill) Elliott, Walter Brennan, Marie Windsor, Harry (Henry) Morgan, Rhys Williams, Jim Davis, Leif Erickson, Yakima Canutt; ***D:*** Stuart E. McGowan, Dorrell McGowan; ***W:*** Stuart E. McGowan, Dorrell McGowan.

Showdown 🦴🦴½ **1973 (PG)** Billy Massey (Martin) and Chuck Garvis (Hudson) had been friends since childhood, until they fell out over the attentions of the pretty Kate (Clark), whom Chuck married. Chuck became the honest town sheriff while Billy took to train robbing. Now it's up to Chuck to bring Billy to justice. Director Seaton's final film. **99m/C VHS.** Dean Martin, Rock Hudson, Susan Clark, Donald Moffat, John McLiam, Ed Begley Jr.; ***D:*** George Seaton; ***W:*** Theodore Taylor; ***C:*** Ernest Laszlo; ***M:*** David Shire.

Showdown 🦴½ **1993 (R)** A small southern town is taken over by a motorcycle gang whose leader, Kincade, decides to set up his fencing and drug operations there. But the local law enforcement has other ideas, calling in a martial arts expert who wants revenge against Kincade for the death of his partner. **92m/C VHS.** Leo Fong, Werner Hoetzinger, Richard Lynch, Michelle McCormick, Frank Marth, Tom MacDowell, Troy Donahue; ***D:*** Leo Fong; ***W:*** Leo Fong.

Showdown 🦴½ **1993 (R)** Ken, the new kid in a particularly nasty high school, gets picked on by the martial-arts expert school bully. After getting beaten up a lot Ken finds out the school janitor can help turn him into a high-kicking fighter. Lots of fast-paced fight scenes which is all the genre demands. An edited PG-13 version is also available. **90m/C VHS.** Kenn Scott, Billy Blanks, Patrick Kilpatrick, Kenneth McLeod; ***D:*** Robert Radler.

Showdown 🦴🦴 *Lookin' Italian* **1994 (R)** New Yorker Vinny (Acovone) has left the family crime business and moved to California for a quieter life. But when his fast-living nephew Anthony (LeBlanc) moves in, Vinny reluctantly finds himself drawn back into violence. **90m/C VHS, DVD.** Jay Acovone, Matt LeBlanc, Lou Rawls, John Lamotta, Stephanie Richards, Real Andrews; ***D:*** Guy Magar; ***W:*** Guy Magar; ***C:*** Gerry Lively; ***M:*** Jeff Beal.

Showdown at Area 51 *Alien vs. Alien* **2007 (R)** Cheap-looking sci-fi smackdown between two alien races who crash-land on Earth and decide to settle their differences without caring if the locals get in their way. The bad alien is after an obelisk that is capable of wiping out all life on the planet so its resources can be plundered. He's opposed by a reasonably good alien and Jake (London), a human ex-soldier who's not too bright. **96m/C DVD.** Jason London, Christa Campbell, Lee Horsley, Gigi Edgley, Coby Bell, Jahidi White, Brock Roberts; ***D:*** C. Roma; ***W:*** Brooke Durham, Kevin Moore, Ari Graham; ***C:*** Christopher Benson; ***M:*** John Dickson. **CABLE**

Showdown at Boot Hill **1958** A bounty hunter (Bronson) kills a wanted murderer but cannot collect the reward because the townspeople will not identify the victim. Rather ordinary plot is carried by Bronson's performance. **76m/B VHS.** Carole Mathews, Thomas B(rowne). Henry, Charles Bronson, Robert Hutton, John Carradine; ***D:*** Gene Fowler Jr.; ***W:*** Louis Vittes; ***C:*** John M. Nickolaus Jr.

Showdown at Williams Creek 1/2 *Kootenai Brown* **1991 (R)** A graphic Canadian Western set in the old Montana territory, where an outcast settler goes on trial for killing an old man. Testimony recounts a shocking history of greed and betrayal. The dark side of the Gold Rush, generally well-acted. Inspired by an actual incident. **97m/C VHS.** *CA* Tom Burlinson, Donnelly Rhodes, Raymond Burr, Michael Thrush, John Pyper-Ferguson, Alex Bruhanski; ***D:*** Allen Kroeker; ***W:*** John Gray; ***M:*** Michael Conway Baker.

Showdown in Little Tokyo **1991 (R)** Lundgren stars as a martial arts master/L.A. cop who was raised in Japan, and has all the respect in the world for his "ancestors" and heritage. Brandon Lee (son of Bruce) is Lundgren's partner, and he's a bona fide American-made, pop-culture, mall junkie. Together, they go after a crack-smuggling gang of "yakuza" (Japanese thugs). Lots of high-kicking action and the unique angle on stereotypes make this a fun martial arts film. **78m/C VHS, DVD.** Dolph Lundgren, Brandon Lee, Tia Carrere, Cary-Hiroyuki Tagawa; ***D:*** Mark L. Lester; ***W:*** Caliope Brattlestreet; ***C:*** Mark Irwin; ***M:*** David Michael Frank.

Shower *Xizao* **2000 (PG-13)** Da Ming (Xin) is a successful modern businessman who returns to Beijing after receiving alarming news from his retarded younger brother Er Ming (Wu) about their father, Liu (Xu). But the worst thing Liu has to worry about is the closure of the old-fashioned bathhouse he runs, which provides a quiet haven for its denizens. Da Ming slowly begins to reconnect to his family and working class roots but what will happen if the bathhouse really does close? Sentimental comic saga. Chinese with subtitles. **94m/C VHS, DVD.** *CH* Zhu Xu, Jiang Wu, Pu Cun Xin; ***D:*** Yang Zhang; ***W:*** Yang Zhang; ***C:*** Jian Zhang; ***M:*** Ye Xiao Gang.

The Showgirl Murders 1/2 **1995 (R)** Stripper Jessica (Ford) goes into management when she turns a failing Las Vegas bar into a money-maker but this femme fatale wants owner Mitch (Preston) to stop sharing the wealth with his boozy wife Carolyn (Case). Meanwhile, blackmailing DEA agent Ridley (McFarland) and hitman Joey (Alber) cause problems. **84m/C VHS, DVD.** Maria Ford, Matt Preston, Jeff Douglas, D.S. Case, Kevin Alber, Bob McFarland; ***D:*** Gene Hertel; ***W:*** Christopher Wooden.

Showgirls **WOOF!** **1995 (NC-17)** Long on ridiculous dialogue and bad acting and short on costumes, coming-of-age tale follows one young woman as she nakedly climbs the ladder of success as a Vegas showgirl. Oh, the things she must do to be headliner. Berkley makes the jump from TV's "Saved by the Bell" to portray Nomi, the young lap dancer with the gift of pelvic thrust and the will to succeed. Whether cavorting clothed or nude, Berkley is uniformly wooden, a mass of lip gloss and mascara struggling to emote. Gershon, as her sly nemesis, brings some wit and splash to her role as the jaded headliner. Eszterhas script descends below its maker's usual standards, which are not particularly high. Titanic amount of female flesh on display fails to give film even a faint hint of sexuality, proof that there is a hell. Rent it, and be prepared to fast forward (to what, we're not sure, though there is a certain camp element that might have been amusing if not imprisoned here). Also available in "R" and unrated versions. **131m/C VHS, DVD.** Elizabeth Berkley, Gina Gershon, Kyle MacLachlan, Glenn Plummer, Alan Rachins, Robert Davi, Gina Ravera; ***D:*** Paul Verhoeven; ***W:*** Joe Eszterhas; ***C:*** Jost Vacano; ***M:*** David A. Stewart. Golden Raspberries '95: Worst Picture, Worst Actress (Berkley), Worst Director (Verhoeven), Worst Screenplay, Worst Song ("Walk into the Wind"), Worst New Star (Berkley).

Showtime **2002 (PG-13)** Murphy hams and De Niro grimaces as they both plod through this lame buddy cop comedy. The odd couple are the fiery LAPD detective Preston (De Niro), who's forced to star in a reality-based TV cop show with beat cop/frustrated actor Sellars (Murphy) after Preston impulsively shoots out a network camera and must avoid a law suit. Russo is the show's producer and has little to do here. The rest of the action involves tracking down some robbers who are also the owners of a really, really big gun. Shatner briefly injects some life into the lackluster action as he coaches the boys on how to play to the camera. Although the two leads are unarguably cast correctly and easy to watch doing what they do best, the premise lets them, and the audience, down. **95m/C VHS, DVD.** *US* Robert De Niro, Eddie Murphy, Rene Russo, Frankie Faison, Mos Def, William Shatner, Pedro Damian, Nestor Serrano, Drena De Niro, Kadeem Hardison, TJ Cross, Judah Friedlander; ***D:*** Tom Dey; ***W:*** Alfred Gough, Keith Sharon, Miles Millard; ***C:*** Thomas Kloss; ***M:*** Alan Silvestri.

Shredder Orpheus **1989** Rock star Orpheus skateboards through hell to stop deadly TV transmissions and rescue his wife. **93m/C VHS.** Jesse Bernstein, Robert McGinley, Vera McCaughan, Megan Murphy, Carlo Scandiuzzi; ***D:*** Robert McGinley.

Shredderman Rules 1/2 **2007** Amusing teen comedy with a few messages about responsibility snuck in. Nolan Byrd (Wekheiser) is constantly tormented by junior high bully Bubba (Caldwell). When the harassment becomes too much, Byrd uses a school computer assignment to create the Shredderman alter-ego and sets up a website filled with video of Bubba's many transgressions, which becomes a big hit with his fellow students. Then Nolan discovers Bubba's businessman dad (Roebuck) has a plan for dumping sewer waste into the town's pond, but trying to expose the plot lands him in real trouble. **91m/C DVD.** Francia Raisa, Tim Meadows, Daniel Roebuck, Dave Coulier, Clare Carey, Curtis Armstrong, Devon Wekheiser, Andrew Caldwell, Marisa Guterman; ***D:*** Savage Steve Holland; ***W:*** Russell Marcus; ***C:*** William Barber; ***M:*** Paul Doucette. **CABLE**

Shrek 1/2 **2001 (PG)** Animated tale from DreamWorks about a grumpy green ogre, Shrek (Myers), who's upset when some annoying fairy types overrun his swamp. So he makes a deal with the local hotshot, Lord Farquaad (Lithgow), to save his home by rescuing Princess Fiona (Diaz) from a tower that's guarded by your not-so-basic dragon type so Farquaad can marry her. Along as Shrek's unwelcome sidekick is a smart-mouthed donkey (Murphy), who insists on helping the ogre out. This one has some eye-popping visuals as well as inside jokes (and digs at Disney) to keep the adults amused. Based (loosely) on the children's book by William Steig. **89m/C VHS, DVD.** *US* ***D:*** Andrew Adamson, Victoria Jenson; ***W:*** Ted Elliott, Terry Rossio, Roger S.H. Schulman, Joe Stillman; ***M:*** Harry Gregson-Williams, John Powell; ***V:*** Mike Myers, Cameron Diaz, Eddie Murphy, John Lithgow, Vincent Cassel, Kathleen Freeman, Conrad Vernon. Oscars '01: Animated Film; British Acad. '01: Adapt. Screenplay; L.A. Film Critics '01: Animated Film; Broadcast Film Critics '01: Animated Film.

Shrek 2 **2004 (PG)** Sequel picks up with Shrek (Myers) and Princess Fiona (Diaz) returning from their honeymoon. They are invited to visit Fiona's parents in the high-falutin' Kingdom of Far, Far Away and Shrek must deal with something more dangerous than dragons or diminutive evil kings—his in-laws, King Harold (Cleese) and Queen Lillian (Andrews), who don't much care to have an ogre in the family (let alone as a daughter). In fact, there's a plot to eliminate Shrek for Fiona's old beau Prince Charming (Everett). The King hires feline assassin Puss-in-Boots (Banderas, uproariously capitalizing on his Spanish heartthrob/Zorro image). Donkey's (Murphy) along as well. The film tries a little too hard in spots, but ya still gotta love the big guy. **92m/C DVD.** *US* ***D:*** Andrew Adamson, Kelly Asbury, Conrad Vernon; ***W:*** Andrew Adamson, Joe Stillman, J. David Stem, David N. Weiss; ***M:*** Harry Gregson-Williams; ***V:*** Mike Myers, Cameron Diaz, Eddie Murphy, John Cleese, Julie Andrews, Rupert Everett, Antonio Banderas, Jennifer Saunders, Larry King, Conrad Vernon.

Shrek Forever After **2010 (PG)** In this fourth and allegedly final installment, Shrek's bored and feels he's lost his ogre mojo to domesticity. So he strikes a (bad) deal with Rumpelstiltskin and (shades of "It's a Wonderful Life") finds out how life in Far Far Away would be if he never existed. In 3-D. **m/C DVD.** *US* ***D:*** Mike Mitchell; ***W:*** Josh Klausner; ***C:*** Yong Duk Jhun; ***M:*** Harry Gregson-Williams; ***V:*** Mike Myers, Cameron Diaz, Eddie Murphy, Antonio Banderas, Walt Dohrn, Justin Timberlake, Julie Andrews, Maya Rudolph, Eric Idle, Craig Robinson, Jon Hamm, Jane Lynch, Amy Sedaris, Ryan Seacrest, Kathy Griffin, Kirsten Schaal, Larry King, Regis Philbin.

Shrek the Third **2007 (PG)** Third time is not the charm in the latest tale of the cranky ogre. Shrek (Myers), Fiona (Diaz), and Donkey (Murphy) must find an heir by the name of Arthur (Timberlake) to replace Fiona's dying father (Cleese), prevent Prince Charming (Everett) from staging a coup, and deal with the idea of tiny baby ogres and donkey-dragon toddlers. Swashbuckling kitty Puss (Banderas) is along for the ride, as well as the standard host of fairy tale and legendary characters, old and new. Potty gags and in-jokes abound, but don't seem nearly as fresh or fun as in previous efforts. The all-star cast and some of the charm of the first two remains, but all in all the movie spends more time trying to be funny rather than actually being funny and doesn't bring anything fresh or new to the story. **92m/C DVD, Blu-ray Disc, HD DVD.** *US* ***D:*** Chris Miller, Raman Hui; ***W:*** Jeffrey Price, Peter S. Seaman, Jon Zack; ***M:*** Harry Gregson-Williams; ***V:*** Mike Myers, Cameron Diaz, Eddie Murphy, Antonio Banderas, John Cleese, Julie Andrews, Justin Timberlake, Rupert Everett, Amy Sedaris, Maya Rudolph, Cheri Oteri, Amy Poehler, John Krasinski, Ian McShane, Eric Idle, Regis Philbin, Larry King, Conrad Vernon, Cody Cameron, Seth Rogen.

Shriek If You Know What I Did Last Friday the 13th 1/2 **2000 (R)** If you're a member of the no joke is too cheap to laugh at club, you'll like this parody of parodies. There's a killer on the loose and he's targeting a group of friends who go to Bulimia High. The humor may date quickly. **86m/C VHS, DVD.** Harley Cross, Tiffani(-Amber) Thiessen, Coolio, Tom Arnold, Julie Benz, Aimee Graham, Majandra Delfino, Shirley Jones, Rose Marie, Mink Stole, Simon Rex, Danny Strong; ***D:*** John Blanchard; ***W:*** Sue Bailey, Joe Nelms; ***C:*** David J. Miller; ***M:*** Tyler Bates. **CABLE**

Shriek in the Night 1/2 **1933** Two rival reporters (Rogers and Talbot, previously paired in "The Thirteenth Guest") turn detective to solve a string of apartment murders. Made on a proverbial shoestring, but not bad. **66m/B VHS, DVD.** Ginger Rogers, Lyle Talbot, Harvey Clark; ***D:*** Albert Ray.

Shriek of the Mutilated **WOOF!** **1974 (R)** An anthropological expedition on a deserted island turns into a night of horror as a savage beast kills the members of the group one by one. **85m/C VHS, DVD.** Alan Brock, Jennifer Stock, Michael (M.K.) Harris, Tawn Ellis, Darcy Brown; ***D:*** Michael Findlay; ***W:*** Ed Adlum, Ed Kelleher; ***C:*** Roberta Findlay.

Shrieker **1997 (R)** Six college students are squatting in an abandoned hospital that just happens to be the scene of a 50-year-old massacre. So, one gets the bright idea of conjuring up the creature that did the deed after learning that it will only kill five victims—and the sixth will become the creature's master. This one's really lame. **80m/C VHS, DVD.** Tanya Dempsey, Jamie Gannon, Parry Shen; ***D:*** Victoria Sloan; ***W:*** Benjamin Carr.

The Shrieking *Hex* **1973 (PG)** Black magic women hang out with biker types in Nebraska in 1919. **93m/C VHS.** Keith Carradine, Christina Raines, Gary Busey, Robert Walker Jr., Dan Haggerty, John Carradine, Scott Glenn; ***D:*** Leo Garen; ***M:*** Charles Bernstein.

The Shrimp on the Barbie 1/2 **1990 (R)** When daddy refuses to bless her marriage to dim bulb boyfriend, Australian Samms hires L.A. low life Marin to pose as new beau. Another pseudonymous Smithee effort. **86m/C VHS, DVD.** Richard "Cheech" Marin, Emma Samms, Vernon Wells, Bruce Spence, Carole (Raphaelle) Davis; ***D:*** Alan Smithee.

Shrink **2009 (R)** Strained and perhaps overly-insider drama about a celebrity shrink who has more problems than his patients. Depressed Henry Carter (Spacey) is still shaken by his wife's suicide and spends his time in a pot-induced stupor, even during sessions with his Hollywood patients, including an actress (Burrows) dealing with age issues, an obnoxious agent (Roberts) with extreme OCD, and an actor (Williams) who will admit to a sex addiction but not a drinking problem. Most of the characters are sketchy although Spacey and Palmer (as a young pro bono patient) know how to make the most of the scenes they're given. **110m/C DVD.** *US* Kevin Spacey, Robin Williams, Saffron Burrows, Keke Palmer, Dallas Roberts, Pell James, Jack Huston, Mark Webber, Robert Loggia, Laura Ramsey; ***D:*** Jonas Pate; ***W:*** Thomas Moffett; ***C:*** Lukas Ettlin; ***M:*** Ken Andrews, Brian Reitzell.

Shrooms **2007** Slasher flick has five American college students meeting up with their Irish friend Jake to go camping. Jake picks a great spot too—a rural area with an abandoned Catholic reformatory that local legend says is haunted because the children were tortured and murdered by sadistic priests! And then they all snack on psychedelic mushrooms! Because, of course, no one will become paranoid and psycho. **85m/C DVD.** *GB IR* Jack Huston, Max Kasch, Alice Greczyn, Lindsey Haun, Robert Hofman, Maya Hazan; ***D:*** Paddy Breathnach; ***W:*** Pearse Elliott; ***C:*** Nanu Segal; ***M:*** Dario Marianelli.

Shrunken Heads 1/2 **1994 (R)** Inspired by their comic book heroes three boys try to take on neighborhood thugs only to be gunned down. But along comes Mr. Sumatra, a retired voodoo specialist, who revives the three (in a somewhat smaller form) so they can fight the good fight once again. Title theme music by director Richard's brother, Danny Elfman. **86m/C VHS.** Aeryk Egan, Meg Foster, Julius W. Harris, Becky Herbst, A.J. Damato, Bo Sharon, Darris Love, Leigh-Allyn Baker, Troy Fromin; ***D:*** Richard Elfman; ***W:*** Matthew Bright; ***M:*** Richard Band.

Shut Up and Kiss Me **2005** Harmless, unremarkable romantic romp with best buds Ryan (Barnes) and Pete (Rowe) who see their 20s in the rearview mirror when true love finally catches up to them—at the same time. The serious Ryan gets plowed over—literally—by Jessica (Richardson) while Pete is in over his head with Tiara (Allen), whose protective mobster uncle (Young) isn't too keen about the surfer dude. **101m/C DVD.** Christopher Daniel Barnes, Krista Allen, Brad Rowe, Burt Young, Kristin Richardson, John Capodice, Victoria Jackson, Frank Bonner, Yelba Osorio, Kevin Meaney; ***D:*** Gary Brockette; ***W:*** Alden "Steve" Chase, Howard Flamm; ***C:*** Jacques Haitkin; ***M:*** Andrew Gross. **VIDEO**

Shutter *Shutter: They Are Around Us* **2005** This superior Thai horror film is the inspiration of the lackluster U.S. remake of the same name. While driving down a country road late at night, a photographer and his wife run down a woman who appears from nowhere, then flee the scene in a panic. But once in Bangkok the spectral woman starts appearing in the photographer's photos and in his wife's dreams. They return to the scene but discover no report of any accident and no victim to speak of. Going back to Bangkok they watch their friends die one after another while trying to figure out what has happened.

The Thai version includes many things omitted from the American remake because they deal with Thai religious practices. **95m/C DVD.** *TH* Ananda Everingham, Nattaweeranuch Thongmee, Achita Sikamana, Unnop Chanpaibool, Titikarn Tongprasearth, Sivigorn Muttamara, Kachormsak Naruepatr, Panitan Mavichak, Tanapon Chansming, Thamonwan Srinatsomsuk; ***D:*** Banjong Pisantahnakun, Parkpoom Wongpoom; ***W:*** Banjong Pisantahnakun, Parkpoom Wongpoom, Sopon Sukdapisit; ***C:*** Niramon Ross; ***M:*** Chartchai Prongpapapan.

Shutter ½ **2008 (PG-13)** Another watered-down version of Asian horror, this time around the 2004 Thai chiller by the same name gets the Hollywood treatment. New bride Jane (Taylor) joins her photographer husband Benjamin (Jackson) on a business trip to Japan. One foggy night the couple accidentally hit a girl in the road. They assume she's okay and life goes on. However, her ghostly image begins appearing in Benjamin's photographs, tormenting the couple. Tame and tepid compared to the original, recycling the usual scare tactics now common in J-horror remakes. **85m/C DVD.** *US* Joshua Jackson, Rachael Taylor, Megumi Okina, David Denman, John Hensley, Maya Hazen, James Kyson Lee; ***D:*** Masayuki Ochiai; ***W:*** Luke Dawson; ***C:*** Katsumi Yanagijima; ***M:*** Nathan Barr.

Shutter Island **2009 (R)** Scorsese takes on the horror and noir genres in this moody thriller set in 1954. U.S. Marshals Teddy Daniels (DiCaprio) and Chuck Aule (Ruffalo) try to find a murderer who disappeared from a hospital for the criminally insane on remote Shutter Island. The staff, headed by Drs. Cawley (Kingsley) and Naehring (von Sydow), prove to be less than helpful. Sinister conspiracies and haunting flashbacks cause Teddy to understand less the more he discovers. The twist ending proves that nothing is as it seems in this gothic asylum. This film marks the fourth collaboration between Scorsese and DiCaprio. Based on a novel by Dennis Lehane. **148m/C DVD.** *US* Leonardo DiCaprio, Mark Ruffalo, Ben Kingsley, Michelle Williams, Emily Mortimer, Max von Sydow, Jackie Earle Haley, Elias Koteas, Patricia Clarkson; ***D:*** Martin Scorsese; ***W:*** Laeta Kalogridis; ***C:*** Robert Richardson.

Shuttle **2009 (R)** Stranded late on a rainy night at the Boston airport, Mel (List) and Jules (Goodman) flag down exactly the wrong shuttle. Along with three male passengers, the gals soon realize that their driver is a psycho. The psycho's got the upper hand until at least the femmes start fighting back, but even with this undemanding plot there's too much that's just dumb. **106m/C DVD.** Peyton List, Cameron Goodman, Cullen Douglas, Dave Power, James Snyder, Tony Curran; ***D:*** Edward A. Anderson; ***W:*** Edward A. Anderson; ***C:*** Michael Fimognari; ***M:*** Henning Lohner.

Shy People **1987 (R)** An urbanized New York journalist and her spoiled daughter journey to the Louisiana bayou to visit long-lost relatives in order to produce an article for "Cosmopolitan." They find ignorance, madness, and ancestral secrets and are forced to examine their motives, their relationships and issues brought to light in the watery, murky, fantastic land of the bayous. Well-acted melodrama with an outstanding performance by Hershey as the cajun matriarch. **119m/C VHS.** Edward (Eddie) Bunker, Jill Clayburgh, Barbara Hershey, Martha Plimpton, Mare Winningham, Merritt Butrick, John Philbin, Don Swayze, Pruitt Taylor Vince; ***D:*** Andrei Konchalovsky; ***W:*** Gerard Brach, Marjorie David; ***C:*** Chris Menges; ***M:*** Tangerine Dream. Cannes '87: Actress (Hershey).

Siam Sunset ½ **1999** Mild fish-out-of-water comedy finds British chemist Perry (Roache), who works on devising new paint colors, caught up in every conceivable disaster while on an Australian holiday. The recent widower (his wife was crushed by a refrigerator) wins his vacation, which turns out to be a decidedly third-rate bus trip cross-country with a petty tyrant operator (Billing) and a number of Aussie eccentrics. Title refers to a particular shade of red that Perry is trying to develop. **91m/C VHS, DVD.** *AU* Linus Roache, Danielle Cormack, Roy Billing, Alan Brough, Ian Bliss, Victoria Hill, Rebecca Hobbs; ***D:*** John Polson; ***W:*** Max Dann, Andrew Knight; ***C:*** Brian J. Breheny; ***M:*** Paul Grabowsky.

Siberiade **1979** Depicts life in a Siberian village from 1909 to 1969 for a wealthy family and a peasant clan and how Soviet society affects them. Rambling narrative with strong characters. In Russian with subtitles. **190m/C VHS, DVD.** *RU* Vladimir Samoilov, Vitaly Solomin, Nikita Mikhalkov, Ludmila Gurchenko, Nathalia Andretchenko; ***D:*** Andrei Konchalovsky; ***W:*** Valentin Yezhov, Andrei Konchalovsky; ***M:*** Eduard Artemyev. Cannes '79: Grand Jury Prize.

Siberian Lady Macbeth ½ *Fury Is a Woman; Sibirska Ledi Magbet* **1961** A Polish version of Shakespeare's Macbeth which ranks with the greatest film translations of his work. In Czarist Russia the passionate wife of a plantation owner begins an affair with a farm hand, and poisons her father-in-law when he finds them out. As her madness grows, she plots the murder of the husband and other suspicious family members. In Serbian with English subtitles. **93m/B VHS, DVD.** *RU* Olivera Markovic, Ljuba Tadic, Kapitalina Eric; ***D:*** Andrzej Wajda; ***W:*** Sveta Lukic; ***C:*** Aleksandar Sekulovic.

The Sibling *Psycho Sisters; So Evil, My Sister* **1972 (PG)** Two sisters become involved in the accidental murder of a man who was a husband to one woman and lover to the other. Of course, one sister has just been released from the mental rehabilitation clinic. **85m/C VHS, DVD.** Susan Strasberg, Faith Domergue, Sydney Chaplin, Steve Mitchell; ***D:*** Reginald LeBorg.

Sibling Rivalry **1990 (PG-13)** Repressed doctor's wife (redundant) Alley rolls in hay with soon to be stiff stranger upon advice of footloose sister. Stranger expires from heart attack in hay and Alley discovers that the corpse is her long-lost brother-in-law. Slapstick cover-up ensues. **88m/C VHS, DVD.** Kirstie Alley, Bill Pullman, Carrie Fisher, Sam Elliott, Jami Gertz, Ed O'Neill, Scott Bakula, Frances Sternhagen, Bill Macy; ***D:*** Carl Reiner.

Siblings **2004 (R)** Toronto teen Joe (Alex Campbell) and his stepsiblings Margaret (Gadon), Pete (Chalmers), and Danielle (Weinstein) want their evil boozy stepmom (Smits) and evil lascivious stepdad (Nicholas Campbell) dead. And then the gruesome twosome die—kinda semi-accidentally. So now the sibs have to get rid of the bodies, claim their inheritance, and watch out for each other. Polley plays the wacky, helpful girl-next-door whom Joe has a crush on. **85m/C VHS, DVD.** *CA* Alex Campbell, Andrew Chalmers, Sarah Polley, Sonja Smits, Nicholas (Nick) Campbell, Tom McCamus, Martha Burns, Sarah Gadon, Samantha Weinstein; ***D:*** David Weaver; ***W:*** Jackie May; ***C:*** David (Robert) A. Greene; ***M:*** Ron Sures.

The Sicilian ½ **1987** Adapted from the Mario Puzo novel and based on the life of Salvatore Giuliano. Chronicles the exploits of the men who took on the government, the Catholic Church, and the Mafia in an effort to make Sicily secede from Italy and become its own nation in the 1940s. Pretentious, overdone, and confused. This long, uncut version was unseen in America, but hailed by European critics; the 115-minute, R-rated American release is also available, but isn't as good. See "Salvatore Giuliano" (Francesco Rosi, 1962) instead of either version. **146m/C VHS, DVD.** Christopher Lambert, John Turturro, Terence Stamp, Joss Ackland, Barbara Sukowa; ***D:*** Michael Cimino; ***W:*** Steve Shagan; ***C:*** Alex Thomson; ***M:*** David Mansfield.

Sicilian Connection ½ **1972** A narcotics agent poses as a nightclub manager to bust a drug-smuggling organization. **100m/C VHS.** *IT* Ben Gazzara, Silvia Monti, Fausto Tozzi, Jess Hahn; ***D:*** Ferdinando Baldi; ***W:*** Ferdinando Baldi, Duilio Coletti; ***C:*** Aiace Parolini; ***M:*** Guido de Angelis, Maurizio de Angelis.

The Sicilian Connection *The Pizza Connection* **1985 (R)** Two brothers in the mob serve out vendettas and generally create havoc wherever they go. **117m/C VHS.** Michele Placido, Mark Switzer, Simona Cavallari, Luigi Burruano; ***D:*** Damiano Damiani; ***W:*** Damiano Damiani, Ernesto Gastaldi, Franco Marotta, Laura Toscano; ***C:*** Nino Celeste; ***M:*** Carlo Savina.

S.I.C.K. Serial Insane Clown Killer ½ *Grim Weekend* **2003** Five unsympathetic characters travel to a remote cabin for a weekend of ghost stories and fun. Instead they find a decidedly unfunny clown, a high body count, and little dolls. Amateurish effort doesn't really have much to recommend it, unless you like evil clowns. **97m/C VHS, DVD.** Ken Hebert, Amanda Watson, Melissa Bale, Chris Bruck, Hank Fields; ***D:*** Bob Willems; ***W:*** Ken Hebert; ***C:*** Jaroslav Vodehnal. **VIDEO**

Sicko ½ **2007 (PG-13)** Rabble-rousing Moore takes on the profit-driven U.S. health care industry. He showcases various Americans who have suffered (primarily because of being denied insurance coverage and/or claims) and looks at other countries with national health care services, including England, France, Canada—and most controversial—Cuba. It's still personal storytelling but less bombastic than Moore's usual rants, and the greed, double-dealing, and health concerns are easy for most Americans to follow. **113m/C DVD.** *US* ***D:*** Michael Moore; ***W:*** Michael Moore; ***M:*** Erin O'Hara.

Sid & Nancy ½ *Sid & Nancy: Love Kills* **1986 (R)** The tragic, brutal, true love story of The Sex Pistols' Sid Vicious and American groupie Nancy Spungen, from the director of "Repo Man." Remarkable lead performances in a very dark story that manages to be funny at times. Depressing but engrossing; no appreciation of punk music or sympathy for the self-destructive way of life is required. Oldman and Webb are superb. Music by Joe Strummer, the Pogues, and Pray for Rain. **111m/C VHS, DVD.** *GB* Gary Oldman, Chloe Webb, Debbie Bishop, David Hayman, Andrew Schofield, Tony London, Xander Berkeley, Biff Yeager, Courtney Love, Iggy Pop; ***D:*** Alex Cox; ***W:*** Alex Cox, Abbe Wool; ***C:*** Roger Deakins; ***M:*** The Pogues, Pray for Rain, Joe Strummer. Natl. Soc. Film Critics '86: Actress (Webb).

Siddhartha **1972** Siddhartha (Kapoor), a wealthy young Brahmin, decides to become a wandering ascetic and follow holy teachings. But after several years, Siddhartha abandons himself to hedonism and the delights of courtesan Kamala (Garewal) until his ultimate decision to return to his search for inner peace. Based on the novel by Herman Hesse. **85m/C VHS, DVD.** Shashi Kapoor, Simi Garewal; ***D:*** Conrad Rooks; ***W:*** Conrad Rooks; ***C:*** Sven Nykvist; ***M:*** Hemant Kumar.

Side by Side **1988** In the same vein as "Cocoon," three senior citizens who aren't ready to retire decide to start their own business and launch a sportswear company designed for seniors. A witty portrayal of graceful aging that is uneven at times. **100m/C VHS.** Milton Berle, Sid Caesar, Danny Thomas; ***D:*** Jack Bender.

Side Effects ½ **2005 (R)** Shrill comedy about corporate evils. Karly is a sales rep for an unscrupulous drug firm. She falls for fellow rep Zach, who wants to throw over corporate greed for country life. Karly decides to work six more months and suddenly the perks are rolling in, just as she learns about some shady dealings. So will Karly decide to listen to her conscience or her cash flow? **90m/C DVD.** Katherine Heigl, Lucian McAfee, David Durbin, Dorian DeMichele; ***D:*** Kathleen Slattery-Moschkau; ***W:*** Kathleen Slattery-Moschkau; ***C:*** Carl F. Whitney; ***M:*** John Tanner, Ralph Bruner.

Side Out ½ **1990 (PG-13)** The first major film about volleyball!? What a claim! What a bore. Midwestern college guy spends summer in Southern Cal. working for slumlord uncle; instead enters "the ultimate" beach volleyball touring. Bogus. Don't see it, dude. **100m/C VHS, DVD.** C. Thomas Howell, Peter Horton, Kathy Ireland, Sinjin Smith, Randy Stoklos, Courtney Thorne-Smith, Harley Jane Kozak, Christopher Rydell; ***D:*** Peter Israelson.

Side Show **1984** A runaway teen joins the circus, witnesses a murder, and must use his wits to stay out of reach of the killer. Forced "suspense" and "drama" of the bad made for TV ilk. **98m/C VHS.** Lance Kerwin, Red Buttons, Anthony (Tony) Franciosa, Connie Stevens; ***D:*** William Conrad; ***M:*** Ralph Burns.

Side Street **1950** Sweaty noir with young postman Joe Norson (Granger) giving into a momentary weakness and finding a world of hurt. He just wants to provide for pregnant wife Ellen (O'Connell), so when he sees a wad of cash in a lawyer's office, he takes it. But the tainted loot is part of a blackmail payoff tied to murder. Joe tries to return the dough but runs into problems and finds more trouble when the money (and the friend who was holding it for him) disappears. About this time Joe learns the greenbacks belonged to gangster Garsell (Craig). Joe has to go on the lam from Garsell and the cops, who now think the poor stooge is tied into the murder. **83m/B DVD.** Farley Granger, Cathy O'Donnell, James Craig, Paul Kelly, Edmon Ryan, Paul Harvey, Jean Hagen, Charles McGraw, Nick Drumman; ***D:*** Anthony Mann; ***W:*** Sydney (Sidney) Boehm; ***C:*** Joseph Ruttenberg; ***M:*** Lennie Hayton.

Sideburns **1991** The Pushkin Club, a group of reactionaries who try to remove the western influence from Russia, attack first a rock band, then innocent civilians as they act as a social cleaning service. Uses humor to try and warn people against the rising fascism in Russia because of the battle between conservative and reformist forces. In Russian with English subtitles. **110m/C VHS.** *RU* Viktor Sukhorukov, Aleksandr Medvedev, Artur Vakha, Vladlen Biryukov, Aleksandr Lykov; ***D:*** Yuri Mamin; ***W:*** Vyacheslav Leikin; ***C:*** Sergei Nekrasov; ***M:*** Aleksei Zalivalov.

Sidekicks **1993 (PG)** Cutesy ego vehicle for executive producer Norris. (Brandis) is bullied by the kids at school and doesn't find much support at home from his well-meaning but ineffectual dad. He has a severe case of hero-worship for Norris, who appears as himself in a series of daydream karate sequences, saving the good guy and maiming the bad. Director Norris is actor Norris' brother. Predictable and sappy. **100m/C VHS.** Chuck Norris, Jonathan Brandis, Beau Bridges, Mako, Julia Nickson-Soul, Danica McKellar, Richard Moll, Joe Piscopo; ***D:*** Aaron Norris; ***W:*** Donald W. Thompson, Lou Illar; ***C:*** Joao Fernandes; ***M:*** Alan Silvestri, David Shire.

Sidewalks of London *St. Martin's Lane* **1938** Laughton's a sidewalk entertainer who takes in homeless waif Leigh and puts her in his act and in his heart. Harrison steals her away and before long she's a star in the music halls. Meanwhile, Laughton has fallen on hard times. Memorable performances. **86m/B VHS, DVD.** *GB* Charles Laughton, Vivien Leigh, Rex Harrison, Larry Adler, Tyrone Guthrie, Gus McNaughton, Bart Cormack, Edward Lexy, Maire O'Neill, Basil Gill, Claire Greet, David Burns, Cyril Smith, Ronald Ward, Romilly Lunge, Helen Haye, Jerry Verno; ***D:*** Tim Whelan; ***W:*** Clemence Dane; ***C:*** Jules Kruger; ***M:*** Arthur Johnston.

Sidewalks of New York ½ **1931** A hapless New York millionaire (Keaton) falls for tenement gal Page and tries to win her heart by saving her street urchin brother from joining the local gang of toughs. Keaton was a silent screen classic as a comedian but his talkie career was disappointing as he lost creative control and battled alcohol problems. **74m/B VHS.** Buster Keaton, Anita Page, Cliff Edwards, Frank LaRue, Frank Rowan, Norman Phillips Jr.; ***D:*** Jules White, Zion Myers.

Sidewalks of New York **2001 (R)** Burns's lightweight comedy about various New Yorkers looking for sex and/or romance suffered from post-Sept. 11 disdain for anything frivolous. But it also suffers from weak writing, obvious "borrowing" from Woody Allen when he was still funny, and too few characters the audience can connect with. Burns is recently dumped TV producer Tommy, who hooks up with recently divorced teacher Maria (Dawson), whose ex, Ben (Krumholtz), thinks they can reunite, before he meets young waitress Ashley (Murphy), who's having an affair with a dentist (Tucci), who's married to Tommy's real-estate agent (Graham), in whom he naturally becomes interested. They're all being interviewed for a documentary on love and sex in NYC. Even if it doesn't work on many levels, the performances are generally fine, with Tucci standing out in the meatiest role. **107m/C VHS, DVD.** *US* Edward Burns, Heather Graham, Rosario Dawson, Dennis Farina, David Krumholtz, Brittany Murphy, Stanley Tucci, Callie (Calliope) Thorne, Aida Turturro, Nadia Dajani, Michael Leydon Campbell; ***D:*** Edward Burns; ***W:*** Edward Burns; ***C:*** Frank Prinzi.

Sideways ½ **2004 (R)** Open a bottle of pinot noir and enjoy the darkly comedic road trip of two self-absorbed, middle-aged buddies in denial. Divorced English teacher, failed novelist, and oenophile Miles (teddy-bearish Giamatti) decides that his lothario, D-list actor pal Jack (Church) deserves a weeklong send-off in the California wine country before his marriage. Naturally, they meet two women infinitely more self-aware and honest than themselves. For Miles, it's kindly blonde waitress Maya (Madsen) while Jack figures he can indulge in a pre-wedding fling with tart-tongued wine pourer Stephanie (Payne's wife Oh). Payne's film is for adults in the best possible way: it's intelligent, amusing, exasperating, and romantic—much like the characters themselves. Great performances by all; based on the novel by Rex Pickett. **124m/C DVD, Blu-ray Disc.** *US* Paul Giamatti, Thomas Haden Church, Virginia Madsen, Sandra Oh, Marylouise Burke, Jessica Hecht, M.C. Gainey, Missy Doty; ***D:*** Alexander Payne; ***W:*** Alexander Payne; ***C:*** Phedon Papamichael; ***M:*** Rolfe Kent. Oscars '04: Adapt. Screenplay; British Acad. '04: Adapt. Screenplay; Golden Globes '05: Film—Mus./Comedy, Screenplay; Ind. Spirit '05: Actor (Giamatti), Director (Payne), Film, Screenplay, Support. Actor (Church), Support. Actress (Madsen); Screen Actors Guild '04: Cast; Writers Guild '04: Adapt. Screenplay.

Sidewinder One **1977 (PG)** Motocross racing is the setting for a romance between a racer and an heiress. Good racing footage, but where's the plot? If you like cars a whole lot... **97m/C VHS, DVD.** Michael Parks, Marjoe Gortner, Susan Howard, Alex Cord, Charlotte Rae; ***D:*** Earl Bellamy; ***W:*** Nancy Voyles Crawford.

Sidney Sheldon's Bloodline
WOOF! *Bloodline* **1979 (R)** Wealthy businesswoman Hepburn finds she is marked for death by persons unknown. Exquisitely bad trash from another Sheldon bestseller. **116m/C VHS.** Audrey Hepburn, Ben Gazzara, James Mason, Michelle Phillips, Omar Sharif, Irene Papas, Romy Schneider, Gert Frobe, Maurice Ronet, Beatrice Straight; ***D:*** Terence Young; ***C:*** Frederick A. (Freddie) Young; ***M:*** Ennio Morricone.

The Siege 1/2 *Against All Enemies* **1998 (R)** Controversial political suspense/action movie caused quite a ruckus when first released. Although protested by Arab-American groups for alleged negative stereotyping, it actually points the finger at the U.S. military as the bad guys. First half centers on FBI honcho Hubbard (Washington) and his prominently Lebanese-American partner Haddad (Shaloub) as they try to stop terrorist bombings of New York. After the bombings escalate, martial law is declared in Brooklyn. Under semi-fascist Gen. Devereaux, all Constitutional rights are suspended and young Arab-Americans are rounded up and imprisoned. Hubbard forms a shaky alliance with shady CIA lady Elise Kraft to break the terrorist ring and restore freedom. Substitutes cardboard cutouts spouting political platitudes for characters. **116m/C VHS, DVD.** Denzel Washington, Tony Shalhoub, Annette Bening, Bruce Willis, Sami Bouajila, David Proval, Jack Gwaltney, Chip Zien, Victor Slezak, Will Lyman, Dakin Matthews, John Rothman, E. Katherine Kerr, Jimmie Ray Weeks, Lance Reddick, Mark Valley, Liana Pai, Amro Salama; ***D:*** Edward Zwick; ***W:*** Edward Zwick, Menno Meyjes, Lawrence Wright; ***C:*** Roger Deakins; ***M:*** Graeme Revell. Golden Raspberries '98: Worst Actor (Willis).

The Siege of Firebase Gloria 1/2 **1989** Story of the Marines who risked their lives defending an outpost against overwhelming odds during the 1968 Tet offensive in Vietnam. Purportedly patriotic war drama made by an Australian director; lead Hauser is a disgusting sadist, and plot is hopelessly hackneyed. **95m/C VHS.** Wings Hauser, R. Lee Ermey, Mark Neely, Gary Hershberger, Clyde Jones, Margi Gerard, Richard Kuhlman, David Anderson, Robert Arevalo, John Calvin, Albert "Poppy" Popwell; ***D:*** Brian Trenchard-Smith; ***W:*** Tony Johnston, William Nagle; ***C:*** Joe Batac; ***M:*** Paul Schutze.

The Siege of Sidney Street **1960** Set in London's East End in 1911 and based on a true incident. Inspector Mannering (Sinden) goes undercover to look into the activities of a gang of foreign anarchists, led by Peter the Painter (Wyngarde). Mannering befriends Sara (Berger), a lonely Russian girl who's Peter's girlfriend until she learns about their violent activities. When Mannering wants to arrest the anarchists, it turns into an armed siege at their headquarters. **93m/B DVD.** *GB* Donald Sinden, Peter Wyngarde, Kieron Moore, Nicole Berger, T.P. McKenna, Tutte Lemkow, Godfrey Quigley; ***D:*** Robert S. Baker, Monty Berman; ***W:*** Jimmy Sangster; ***C:*** Robert S. Baker, Monty Berman; ***M:*** Stanley Black.

Siegfried *Siegfrieds Tod; Siegfried's Death* **1924** Half of Lang's epic masterpiece "Der Niebelungen," based on German mythology. Title hero bathes in the blood of a dragon he has slain. He marries a princess, but wicked Queen Brumhilde has him killed. Part two, in which Siegfried's widow marries Attila the Hun, is titled "Kriemheld's Revenge." These dark, brooding, archetypal tours de force were patriotic tributes, and were loved by Hitler. Silent with music score. **100m/B VHS, DVD.** *GE* Paul Richter, Margareta Schoen; ***D:*** Fritz Lang.

Siesta 1/2 **1987 (R)** Barkin is a professional stunt woman who leaves her current lover/manager, played by Sheen, and returns to visit her former lover and trainer, Byrne, on the eve of his marriage to another woman. Her trip, marked by flashbacks and flights of seemingly paranoid fantasy, leads to the discovery of murder, but she cannot remember who, when, why, or where. The film distorts time, reality, and perception in a sometimes fascinating, sometimes frustrating psychological mystery. Attractively filmed by video director Lambert. Barkin and Byrne were married in real life a year after the film's release. **97m/C VHS.** Ellen Barkin, Gabriel Byrne, Jodie Foster, Julian Sands, Isabella Rossellini, Martin Sheen, Grace Jones, Alexei Sayle; ***D:*** Mary Lambert; ***W:*** Patricia Louisianna Knop; ***M:*** Miles Davis, Marcus Miller.

The Sign of Four 1/2 **1983** Sherlock Holmes and the ever-faithful Watson are hired by a young woman who has been anonymously sent an enormous diamond. An inept production which looks good but that's all. **97m/C VHS, DVD.** *GB* Ian Richardson, David Healy, Thorley Walters, Cherie Lunghi; ***D:*** Desmond Davis; ***W:*** Charles Edward Pogue; ***C:*** Denis Lewiston; ***M:*** Harry Rabinowitz.

The Sign of Four 1/2 **2001** Holmes (Frewer), Watson (Welsh), and the Baker Street Irregulars are invovled in murder, poison darts, a fortune in Indian jewels, and much suspicious behavior. **120m/C VHS, DVD.** *CA* Matt Frewer, Kenneth Welsh, Marcel Jeannin, Sophie Lorain, Edward Yankie, Michel Perron, Kevin Woodhouse; ***D:*** Rodney Gibbons; ***W:*** Joe Wiesenfeld; ***C:*** Eric Cayla; ***M:*** Marc Ouellette. **CABLE**

The Sign of the Cross 1/2 **1933** Depraved Emperor Nero (Laughton) decides he wants a new city so he burns down Rome—blaming the fire on the Christians he also wants to get rid of (preferably by the lions in the arena). Meanwhile, Marcus (March), the Roman Prefect, has fallen for the virginal Christian Mercia (Landi) and risks his life to save her. Besides Laughton's overwhelmingly hammy performance, Colbert slinks seductively as the emperor's vixenish wife, Poppaea. Again, lots of crowd scenes (DeMille's specialty). Based on the play by Wilson Barrett. **125m/B VHS, DVD.** Fredric March, Elissa Landi, Charles Laughton, Claudette Colbert, Ian Keith, Harry Beresford, Arthur Hohl, Nat Pendleton; ***D:*** Cecil B. DeMille; ***W:*** Waldemar Young, Sidney Buchman; ***M:*** Rudolph Kopp.

The Sign of Zorro **1960** Adventures of the masked swordsman as he champions the cause of the oppressed in early California. Full-length version of the popular late-50s Disney TV series. **89m/C VHS.** Guy Williams, Henry Calvin, Gene Sheldon, Romney Brent, Britt Lomond, George Lewis, Lisa Gaye; ***D:*** Norman Foster, Lewis R. Foster.

Signal 7 **1983** An improvised, neoverite document of a night in the lives of two San Francisco taxi drivers. Nilsson's first major release and a notable example of his unique scriptless, tape-to-film narrative technique. **89m/C VHS, DVD.** Bill Ackridge, Dan Leegant; ***D:*** Rob Nilsson; ***W:*** Rob Nilsson.

Signs **2002 (PG-13)** Shyamalan takes on crop circles in this eerily potent psycho-thriller. Widowed father Gibson, a lapsed minister, lives on a farm with children Culkin and Breslin, along with younger brother Phoenix when things start to get strange. Everything seems normal, but even simple everyday actions are steeped in the brand of moodiness and unspoken dread that Shyamalan does best. By the time mysterious circles appear in the cornfields, it's clear that the question of whether or not aliens are to blame for the crop circles is secondary to how the characters will react. Quiet and intense, what doesn't happen is as important as what does in this top-notch suspenser. Film was shot in the director's native Pennsylvania. **120m/C VHS, DVD, Blu-ray Disc.** *US* Mel Gibson, Joaquin Rafael (Leaf) Phoenix, Rory Culkin, Abigail Breslin, Cherry Jones, Patricia Kalember, M. Night Shyamalan; ***D:*** M. Night Shyamalan; ***W:*** M. Night Shyamalan; ***C:*** Tak Fujimoto; ***M:*** James Newton Howard.

Signs & Wonders **2000** Commodities trader Alec (Skarsgard) has been living in Athens with wife Marjoire (Rampling) and their children. He begins an affair with sultry co-worker Katherine (Unger) and abandons his family to go to the States with her and then changes his mind. However, when he returns to Athens, Alec discovers Marjorie has moved on with her own lover, Andreas (Katalifos). But Alec isn't giving up and the consequences are unexpected. **108m/C VHS, DVD.** *FR* Stellan Skarsgard, Charlotte Rampling, Deborah Kara Unger, Dimitris Katalifos, Ashley Remy, Michael Cook; ***D:*** Jonathan Nossiter; ***W:*** Jonathan Nossiter, James Lasdun; ***C:*** Yorgos Arvanitis; ***M:*** Adrian Utley.

Signs of Life *Lebenszeichen* **1968** German soldier Stroszek (Brogle), injured during the occupation of Crete, is sent to recuperate on the remote island of Kos. With his Greek wife Nora, Stroszek has nothing to do but guard a deserted fortress and a store of abandoned ammunition. But soon the suspicious natives and the isolation begin to drive Stroszek to madness and he decides to blow up the ammunition dump (and the island along with it). German with subtitles. **90m/B VHS, DVD.** *GE* Peter Brogle, Wolfgang Reichmann, Athina Zacharopoulous, Wolfgang Stumpf; ***D:*** Werner Herzog; ***W:*** Werner Herzog; ***C:*** Thomas Mauch; ***M:*** Stavros Xarchakos.

Signs of Life 1/2 *One for Sorrow, Two for Joy* **1989 (PG-13)** A boat-building company in Maine closes its doors after centuries in business; the employees and families whose lives have been defined by it for generations learn to cope. Wonderful performances compensate only partly for a week script. An episode on PBS's "American Playhouse." **95m/C VHS.** Beau Bridges, Arthur Kennedy, Vincent D'Onofrio, Kevin J. O'Connor, Will Patton, Kate Reid, Michael Lewis, Kathy Bates, Mary-Louise Parker, Georgia Engel; ***D:*** John David Coles; ***W:*** Mark Malone; ***C:*** Elliot Davis; ***M:*** Howard Shore.

Silas Marner **1985** Superb adaptation of the 1861 George Eliot classic about an itinerant weaver subjected to criminal accusation, poverty, and exile. Wonderful detail and splendid acting. Shot on location in the Cotswold district of England. **92m/C VHS, DVD.** *GB* Ben Kingsley, Jenny Agutter, Patrick Ryecart, Patsy Kensit; ***D:*** Giles Foster; ***M:*** Carl Davis. **TV**

The Silence *Tystnaden* **1963** A brutal, enigmatic allegory about two sisters, one a nymphomaniac, the other a violently frustrated lesbian, traveling with the former's young son to an unnamed country beset by war. Fascinating and memorable but frustrating and unsatisfying: What is it about? What is it an allegory of? Where is the narrative? The third in Bergman's crisis-of-faith trilogy following "Through a Glass Darkly" and "Winter Light." In Swedish with English subtitles or dubbed. **95m/B VHS, DVD.** *SW* Ingrid Thulin, Gunnel Lindstrom, Birger Malmsten; ***D:*** Ingmar Bergman; ***W:*** Ingmar Bergman; ***C:*** Sven Nykvist.

Silence *Crazy Jack and the Boy* **1973 (G)** An autistic boy gets lost in the wilderness and faces an array of difficulties while his foster parents search for him. **82m/C VHS, DVD.** Will Geer, Ellen Geer, Richard Kelton, Ian Geer Flanders, Craig G. Kelly; ***D:*** John Korty.

The Silence 1/2 **2006** Bland Aussie TV police drama. Detective Richard Treloar (Roxburgh) suffers from post-traumatic stress after an accidental shooting death so he's reassigned to curate a photographic exhibit at the Sydney police museum. While looking at 1960s-era crime scene photos, Richard becomes obsessed with May (Rothwell), a murder victim and decides to reinvestigate the unsolved case. **104m/C DVD.** *AU* Richard Roxburgh, Essie Davis, Emily Barclay, Ellouise Rothwell, Alice McConnell, Damien de Montemas; ***D:*** Cate Shortland; ***W:*** Alice Addison, Mary Walsh; ***C:*** Robert Humphreys; ***M:*** Antony Partos. **TV**

Silence Like Glass 1/2 **1990 (R)** Diagnosed with life-threatening illness, two young women struggle to overcome their anger at their fate. They find friendship and together, search for reasons to live. Fine performances, with pacing that keeps the melodrama to a minimum. **102m/C VHS.** Jami Gertz, Martha Plimpton, George Peppard, Rip Torn, James Remar; ***D:*** Carl Schenkel; ***M:*** Anne Dudley.

The Silence of Neto *Silencio de Neto* **1994** A sheltered young boy comes of age in Guatemala during the early 1950s, a period marked by political upheaval and Cold War paranoia. His relationship with his socialist-leaning uncle causes family friction as it reflects on a repressive society and calls for reform. Spanish with subtitles. **106m/C VHS, DVD.** ***D:*** Luis Argueta; ***W:*** Luis Argueta; ***C:*** Ramon Suarez.

Silence of the Hams 1/2 **1993 (R)** Very feeble parody of "The Silence of the Lambs" and others in the thriller/horror genre. Director/writer Greggio also stars as the murder victim, stabbed in the shower, who narrates the story in flashback. There's an eager FBI recruit, a femme fatale, assorted cameo turns, and DeLuise, chewing more scenery than even Anthony Hopkins could swallow, as nutcase Dr. Animal Cannibal Pizza. **85m/C VHS.** Ezio Greggio, Dom DeLuise, Billy Zane, Joanna Pacula, Charlene Tilton, Martin Balsam, Wilhelm von Homburg; ***Cameos:*** Stuart Pankin, John Astin, Phyllis Diller, Bubba Smith, Larry Storch, Rip Taylor, Shelley Winters, Mel Brooks, John Landis, John Carpenter, Joe Dante; ***D:*** Ezio Greggio; ***W:*** Ezio Greggio; ***C:*** Jacques Haitkin.

Silence of the Heart **1984** Mother copes with aftermath of suicide of teenage son. The teen's best friend also tries to deal with his feelings of guilt. Hartley is captivating in this gripping drama. **100m/C VHS, DVD.** Mariette Hartley, Dana Hill, Howard Hesseman, Chad Lowe, Charlie Sheen, Alexandra Powers, Silvania Gallardo, Elizabeth Berridge, Sherilyn Fenn, Casey Siemaszko, Jaleel White; ***D:*** Richard Michaels; ***W:*** Phil Penningroth; ***M:*** Georges Delerue.

The Silence of the Lambs 1/2 **1991 (R)** Foster is FBI cadet Clarice Starling, a woman with ambition, a cum laude degree in psychology, and a traumatic childhood. When a serial killer begins his ugly rounds, the FBI wants psychological profiles from other serial killers and she's sent to collect a profile from one who's exceptionally clever—psychiatrist Hannibal Lecter, a vicious killer prone to dining on his victims. Brilliant performances from Foster and Hopkins, finely detailed supporting characterizations, and elegant pacing from Demme. Some brutal visual effects. Excellent portrayals of women who refuse to be victims. Based on the Thomas Harris novel. **118m/C VHS, DVD, Blu-ray Disc.** Dan E. Butler, Frankie Faison, Kasi Lemmons, Kathryn Witt, Tracey Walter, Obba Babatunde, Ron Vawter, Brent Hinkley, Daniel von Bargen, Jodie Foster, Anthony Hopkins, Scott Glenn, Ted Levine, Brooke Smith, Charles Napier, Roger Corman, Anthony Heald, Diane Baker, Chris Isaak; ***D:*** Jonathan Demme; ***W:*** Ted Tally; ***C:*** Tak Fujimoto; ***M:*** Howard Shore. Oscars '91: Actor (Hopkins), Actress (Foster), Adapt. Screenplay, Director (Demme), Picture; AFI '98: Top 100; British Acad. '91: Actor (Hopkins), Actress (Foster); Directors Guild '91: Director (Demme); Golden Globes '92: Actress—Drama (Foster); Natl. Bd. of Review '91: Director (Demme), Film, Support. Actor (Hopkins); N.Y. Film Critics '91: Actor (Hopkins), Actress (Foster), Director (Demme), Film; Writers Guild '91: Adapt. Screenplay.

Silence of the North 1/2 **1981 (PG)** A widow (Burstyn) with three children struggles to survive under rugged pioneer conditions on the Canadian frontier. The scenery is, not surprisingly, stunning. Based on a true but generic story. **94m/C VHS.** *CA* Ellen Burstyn, Tom Skerritt; ***D:*** Allan Winton King; ***M:*** Michael Conway Baker.

The Silencer **1992 (R)** Walden stars as Harley-riding Angel who is out to stop a slavery and prostitution ring that abuses young runaways. Video arcades hold the clues, and Angel must learn to kill without a conscience. Every time she kills, Angel seeks comfort in the arms of anonymous lovers. However, what she doesn't know is that her demented ex-boyfriend is watching. **85m/C VHS, DVD.** Lynette Walden, Chris Mulkey, Paul Ganus, Morton Downey Jr.; ***D:*** Amy Goldstein; ***W:*** Amy Goldstein, Scott Kraft.

The Silencer **1999 (R)** FBI agent Jason Wells (Elliott) fakes his own death in order to assume a new identity for a new assignment. Now known as Jason Black, he's an eager would-be assassin who wants to join the terrorist organization Division 5 where he can learn from master marksman Quinn Simmons (Dudikoff). But when Jason learns what's really behind his mission, things aren't so simple after all. **92m/C VHS, DVD.** *CA* Michael Dudikoff, Brennan Elliott, Gabrielle Miller, Terence Kelly, Peter Lacroix; ***D:*** Robert Lee; ***M:*** Peter Allen. **VIDEO**

The Silencers **½ 1966** Rompy spy spoof is the first of Martin's Matt Helm films, made to take advantage of the James Bond craze. Sexy secret agent man Helm must save the American atomic missile system from sabotage by Big O, the organization headed by Tung-Tze (Buono). That is if Matt can stay away from the babes and the booze. Based on the novels "The Silencers" and "Death of a Citizen" by Donald Hamilton. Followed by "Murderer's Row" (1966), "The Ambushers" (1967), and "The Wrecking Crew" (1968). **103m/C VHS, DVD.** Dean Martin, Victor Buono, Stella Stevens, Daliah Lavi, Arthur O'Connell, Robert Webber, James Gregory, Nancy Kovack, Roger C. Carmel, Cyd Charisse; ***D:*** Phil Karlson; ***W:*** Oscar Saul; ***C:*** Burnett Guffey; ***M:*** Elmer Bernstein.

The Silencers **½ 1995 (R)** Secret Service agent Chuck Rafferty (Scalia) discovers that his latest enemies, known as the Men In Black, are actually human-appearing aliens seeking to conquer Earth. Now Rafferty's only hope is to team up with inter-galactic peace officer Condor (Christopher) to defeat this evil. **103m/C VHS, DVD.** Jack Scalia, Dennis Christopher, Clarence Williams III, Carlos Lauchu, Lucinda Weist; ***D:*** Richard Pepin.

The Silences of the Palace *Les Silences du Palais* **1994** Set in 1950s Tunisia at the end of the ruling monarchy. Twenty-five-year-old Alia (Lacroix) returns to the run-down palace where she was born and grew up as the daughter of a lifelong servant, Khedija (Hedhili), who was also the sexual favorite of her master, Prince Sidi Ali (Fazaa). She remembers the limited, repressed existence they endured and realizes that, ten years after leaving the palace, she has traded one form of subjugation for another and has yet to find her own independence. Arabic with subtitles. **116m/C VHS.** *FR* Ghalia Lacroix, Amel Hedhili, Kamel Fazaa, Hend Sabri, Najia Overghi; ***D:*** Moufida Tlatli; ***W:*** Moufida Tlatli, Nouri Bouzid; ***C:*** Youssef Ben Youssef.

Silent Assassins **1988** Fists and bullets fly when a scientist is kidnapped in order to gain secrets to biological warfare. Chong and Rhee, real-life owners of a martial arts studio, produced and choreographed the film. Blair is here, but doesn't figure much. A notch up from most similar martial arts pics. **92m/C VHS.** Sam Jones, Linda Blair, Jun Chong, Phillip Rhee; ***D:*** Scott Thomas, Lee Dooyong.

Silent Code **1935** A Mountie is framed for the murder of a young miner. **55m/B VHS.** Tom Tyler, Blanche Mehaffey, Kane Richmond; ***D:*** Stuart Paton; ***W:*** George Morgan; ***C:*** Roland Price.

The Silent Enemy **½ 1958** The true-life exploits of British frogmen battling Italian foes during WWII. Suspenseful and engrossing; good performances and good rendering of underwater action. Video release snips 20 minutes from the original and adds color. **91m/C VHS, DVD.** *GB* Laurence Harvey, John Clements, Michael Craig, Dawn Addams, Sidney James, Alec McCowen, Nigel Stock; ***D:*** William Fairchild.

Silent Fall **½ 1994 (R)** Grisly double murder of his parents is witnessed by autistic nine-year-old, Tim Warden (Faulkner), and his traumatized over-protective teenaged sister Sylvie (Tyler). Retired psychiatrist Jake Rainier (Dreyfuss) is reluctant to get involved, ever since an autistic child in his care died, but when authoritarian rival Dr. Harlinger (Lithgow) is called instead, Jake changes his mind. Second half of film takes a lurid turn as Jake probes Tim's damaged psyche to discover the killer. Trite, clueless whodunnit that generally wastes the talent involved; Tyler and Faulkner make their film debuts. **101m/C VHS, DVD.** Richard Dreyfuss, Ben Faulkner, John Lithgow, Liv Tyler, Linda Hamilton, J.T. Walsh; ***D:*** Bruce Beresford; ***W:*** Akiva Goldsman; ***C:*** Peter James; ***M:*** Stewart Copeland.

Silent Hill **2006 (R)** Visually arresting but nonsensical adaptation of a videogame. Rose (Mitchell) and husband Christopher (a wasted Bean) find their young daughter Sharon (Ferland) sleepwalking, muttering about "Silent Hill." Rose researches the name and learns it's a West Virginia mining community that's been deserted since 1974 due to a devastating fire. Nevertheless, Rose grabs Sharon and heads for the town, only to become lost in some alternate existence where she runs around looking for the vanished Sharon and encounters various ghostly freaks, creepy religious fanatics, and a helpful motorcycle cop named Cybil (Holden). **127m/C DVD, Blu-ray Disc, UMD.** *CA FR* Radha Mitchell, Sean Bean, Laurie Holden, Deborah Kara Unger, Jodelle Ferland, Alice Krige, Kim Coates, Tanya Allen; ***D:*** Christophe Gans; ***W:*** Roger Avary; ***C:*** Dan Laustsen; ***M:*** Jeff Danna.

Silent Hunter **½ 1994 (R)** Undercover cop Jim Paradine (O'Keeffe) retreats to a remote mountains cabin when his family is killed by a gang of bank robbers. Naturally, the thugs just happen to crash land on Paradine's mountain top with their stolen loot and he goes off to hunt them down. **97m/C VHS.** Miles O'Keeffe, Fred Williamson, Lynne Adams, Peter Colvey, Jason Cavalier, Sabine Karsenti; ***D:*** Fred Williamson.

Silent Madness **1984 (R)** A psychiatrist must stop a deranged killer, escaped from an asylum, from slaughtering helpless college coeds in a sorority house. Meanwhile, hospital execs send orderlies to kill the patient, to conceal their mistake. Ludicrous. **93m/C VHS.** Belinda J. Montgomery, Viveca Lindfors, Sydney Lassick; ***D:*** Simon Nuchtern.

The Silent Mr. Sherlock Holmes **1912** These two silent shorts are a rare treat for Holmes fans. "The Copper Beeches" was produced with the "personal supervision of Arthur Conan Doyle." In "The Man with the Twisted Lip," Holmes is hired to find out whether a banker was murdered. **68m/B VHS.** *GB* Ellie Norwood.

Silent Motive **½ 1991** Laura is a Hollywood screenwriter who's shocked to discover that a killer is using her recent script as an outline for a series of film-industry murders. She's even more unnerved when a detective makes Laura his number one suspect. **90m/C VHS.** Patricia Wettig, Mike Farrell, Ed Asner, Rick Springfield, David Packer; ***D:*** Lee Philips; ***W:*** William Bekkala.

Silent Movie **½ 1976 (PG)** A has-been movie director (Brooks) is determined to make a comeback and save his studio from being taken over by a conglomerate. Hilarious at times but uneven. An original idea; not as successful as it could have been. Has music and sound effects, but only one word of spoken dialogue by famous mime Marceau. **88m/C VHS, DVD.** Mel Brooks, Marty Feldman, Dom DeLuise, Burt Reynolds, Anne Bancroft, James Caan, Liza Minnelli, Paul Newman, Sid Caesar, Bernadette Peters, Harry Ritz, Marcel Marceau; ***D:*** Mel Brooks; ***W:*** Mel Brooks, Ron Clark, Rudy DeLuca, Barry Levinson.

Silent Night, Bloody Night *Night of the Dark Full Moon; Death House* **1973 (R)** An escaped lunatic terrorizes a small New England town, particularly a mansion that was once an insane asylum. Not great, but well done by director Gershuny, with some nail-biting suspense and slick scene changes. **83m/C VHS, DVD.** Patrick O'Neal, John Carradine, Walter Abel, Mary Woronov, Astrid Heeren, Candy Darling; ***D:*** Theodore Gershuny.

Silent Night, Deadly Night **1984 (R)** A psycho ax-murders people while dressed as jolly old St. Nick. Violent and disturbing, to say the least. Caused quite a controversy when it was released to theatres. Santa gimmick sold some tickets at the time, but resist the urge to rent it: it's completely devoid of worth, whatever the killer's outfit. As if one were not enough, we've been blessed with four sequels. **92m/C VHS, DVD.** Lilyan Chauvin, Gilmer McCormick, Toni Nero; ***D:*** Charles E. Sellier; ***M:*** Perry Botkin.

Silent Night, Deadly Night 2 **1987 (R)** The psychotic little brother of the psychotic, Santa Claus-dressed killer from the first film exacts revenge, covering the same bloody ground as before. Almost half this sequel consists of scenes lifted whole from the original. **88m/C VHS, DVD.** Eric Freeman, James Newman, Elizabeth Kaitan, Jean Miller; ***D:*** Lee Harry; ***M:*** Michael Armstrong.

Silent Night, Deadly Night 3: Better Watch Out! **½ 1989 (R)** The now grown-up psycho goes up against a young blind woman. Santa is no longer the bad guy, thank goodness. The least bad of the lot, with black humor—though not enough to make it worth seeing. **90m/C VHS.** Richard Beymer, Bill Moseley, Samantha Scully, Eric (DaRe) Da Re, Laura Elena Harring, Robert Culp; ***D:*** Monte Hellman.

Silent Night, Deadly Night 4: Initiation **1990 (R)** A secret L.A. cult of she-demons use the slasher Ricky for their own ends—making for more mayhem and horror. Has virtually nothing to do with the other "sequels"—which is not to say it's very good. **90m/C VHS.** Maud Adams, Allyce Beasley, Clint Howard, Reggie Bannister; ***D:*** Brian Yuzna.

Silent Night, Deadly Night 5: The Toymaker **1991 (R)** A young boy's Christmas is overrun by murderous Santas and viscious stuffed animals. Definitely for fans of the genre only. **90m/C VHS.** Mickey Rooney, William Thorne, Jane Higginson; ***D:*** Martin Kitrosser; ***W:*** Martin Kitrosser, Brian Yuzna; ***C:*** James Mathers; ***M:*** Matthew Morse.

Silent Night, Lonely Night **1969** Two lonely middle-aged people (Bridges and Jones) begin an affair at Christmas to stem the pain of their separately disintegrating marriages. Poignant but not successfully credible. Based on the play by Robert Anderson. **98m/C VHS.** Lloyd Bridges, Shirley Jones, Jeff Bridges, Cloris Leachman, Carrie Snodgress, Lynn Carlin; ***D:*** Daniel Petrie; ***M:*** Billy Goldenberg. **TV**

The Silent One **½ 1986** Featuring underwater photography by Ron and Valerie Taylor, this is the odd story of a mysterious Polynesian boy who has a nautical relationship with a sea turtle. **96m/C VHS.** *NZ* Telo Malese, George Henare; ***D:*** Yvonne Mackay.

The Silent Partner **1978** A bank teller (Gould) foils a robbery, but manages to take some money for himself. The unbalanced robber (Plummer) knows it and wants the money. Good script and well directed, with emphasis on suspense and detail. Unexpectedly violent at times. Early, non-comedic role for big guy Candy. **103m/C VHS, DVD.** *CA* Elliott Gould, Christopher Plummer, Susannah York, John Candy; ***D:*** Daryl Duke; ***W:*** Curtis Hanson; ***C:*** Billy Williams.

Silent Partner **½ 2005 (R)** CIA desk jockey Gordon Patrick (Moran) is sent to Moscow to look into the suspicious death of a major political figure. He meets hooker Dina (Reid), who is in possession of a briefcase filled with incriminating files, which belonged to the dead man. Pop tart Reid is a natural in her role but this is a familiar story. **96m/C DVD.** *US RU* Nick Moran, Tara Reid, Gregg Henry, Patrick Gallagher, Katrina M. Faessel; ***D:*** James D. Deck; ***W:*** James D. Deck; ***C:*** Mikhail Agranovich; ***M:*** Lawrence Brown. **VIDEO**

The Silent Passenger **½ 1935** Amateur sleuth Lord Peter Wimsey makes cinematic debut investigating murder and blackmail on the British railway. Dorothy Sayer's character later inspired BBC mystery series. **75m/B VHS.** *GB* John Loder, Peter Haddon, Mary Newland, Austin Trevor, Donald Wolfit, Leslie Perrins, Aubrey Mather, Ralph Truman; ***D:*** Reginald Denham.

Silent Predators **1999** SNAKE! Of course, not any any snake but mean hybrid rattlesnakes who slither over a small California desert town when an explosion at a construction site disturbs their home. And it's up to fire chief Hamlin to save the town! If the snakes are half as creepy as the video box art, this is one seriously scary snake movie. **91m/C VHS, DVD.** Harry Hamlin, Shannon Sturges, Patty McCormack, Jack Scalia, David Spielberg, Beau Billingslea; ***D:*** Noel Nosseck; ***W:*** John Carpenter, Matt Dorff; ***C:*** John Stokes; ***M:*** Michael Tavera. **CABLE**

Silent Rage **1982 (R)** Sheriff Norris of a small Texas town must destroy killer Libby who has been made indestructible through genetic engineering. Chuck Norris meets Frankenstein, sort of. Nice try, but still thoroughly stupid and boring. **100m/C VHS, DVD.** Chuck Norris, Ron Silver, Steven Keats, Toni Kalem, Brian Libby, Stephen Furst; ***D:*** Michael Miller; ***W:*** Joseph Fraley; ***C:*** Robert C. Jessup, Neil Roach; ***M:*** Peter Bernstein.

Silent Raiders **1954** A commando unit is sent to France in 1943 to knock out a Nazi communications center. **72m/B VHS.** Richard Bartlett, Earle Lyon, Jeanette Bordeau; ***M:*** Elmer Bernstein.

Silent Rebellion **½** *My Palikari* **1982** A Greek immigrant (Savalas) and his son return to Greece, where they reunite with mother and brother and re-discover their heritage and each other. Cross-cultural misunderstandings abound; could have been interesting, but the story is just too generic and uninspired. **90m/C VHS.** Telly Savalas, Keith Gordon, Michael Constantine, Yula Gavala; ***D:*** Charles S. Dubin; ***W:*** Leon Capetanos, George Kirgo; ***C:*** Ennio Guarnieri; ***M:*** John Cacavas.

Silent Running **1971 (G)** Members of a space station orbiting Saturn care for the last vegetation of a nuclear-devastated earth. When orders come to destroy the vegetation, Dern takes matters into his own hands. Speculative sci-fi at its best. Trumbull's directorial debut; he created special effects for "2001" and "Close Encounters." Strange music enhances the alien atmosphere. **90m/C VHS, DVD.** Bruce Dern, Cliff (Potter) Potts, Ron Rifkin; ***D:*** Douglas Trumbull; ***W:*** Michael Cimino, Deric Washburn, Steven Bochco; ***C:*** Charles F. Wheeler; ***M:*** Prof. Peter Schickele.

Silent Scream **½ 1980 (R)** College kids take up residence with the owners of an eerie mansion complete with obligatory murders. Obvious to the point of being gratuitous—and just plain uninteresting. **87m/C VHS, DVD.** Rebecca Balding, Cameron Mitchell, Avery Schreiber, Barbara Steele, Steve Doubet, Brad Reardon, Yvonne De Carlo; ***D:*** Denny Harris; ***W:*** Wallace C. Bennett, Jim Wheat, Ken Wheat; ***C:*** Michael D. Murphy, David Shore.

Silent Scream **1984** A former Nazi concentration camp commandant collects unusual animals and humans as a hobby. **60m/C VHS, DVD.** *GB* Peter Cushing, Brian Cox, Elaine Donnelly; ***D:*** Alan Gibson.

Silent Tongue **1992 (PG-13)** Weird western finds the crazed Talbot Roe (Phoenix) alone in the wilderness, guarding the tree that is the burial place of his half-breed wife Awbonnie (Tousey). Roe's father (Harris) bought his son's bride from her greedy and abusive father McCree (Bates). In an effort to return Talbot to some semblance of normality, Roe offers to buy McCree's other daughter (Arredondo) for his son. But Talbot is haunted by his wife's angry ghost, who wants her spirit set free by ritual burning, and McCree himself fears the vengeance of his one-time Indian wife Silent Tongue (Cardinal). Messy, over-the-top plot with some poignant performances, especially

Phoenix's. **101m/C VHS.** River Phoenix, Sheila Tousey, Richard Harris, Alan Bates, Jeri Arredondo, Dermot Mulroney, Tantoo Cardinal; ***Cameos:*** Bill Irwin, David Shiner; ***D:*** Sam Shepard; ***W:*** Sam Shepard; ***C:*** Jack Conroy; ***M:*** Patrick O'Hearn.

The Silent Touch ☙☙ 1/2 **1994 (PG-13)** Irascible, aged composer Henry Kesdi (Von Sydow), living in Denmark with his long-suffering wife Helena (Miles), hasn't written a note in 40 years. Music student Stefan (Blutheau) dreams of a composition he believes Henry started but never completed. So Stefan naturally sets out to help Henry finish his symphony by mystically healing his composer's block. Yes, it does sound hokey but the fluff is saved by Von Sydow's buoyantly funny performance. **92m/C VHS.** *PL DK GB* Max von Sydow, Lothaire Bluteau, Sarah Miles, Sofie Grabol, Aleksander Bardini, Peter Hesse Overgaard; ***D:*** Krzysztof Zanussi; ***W:*** Peter Morgan, Mark Wadlow; ***M:*** Wojciech Kilar.

Silent Trigger ☙☙ **1997 (R)** Special Forces commando Shooter (Lundgren) becomes a paid assassin for an undercover agency but an ill-fated mission causes him and partner Spotter (Bellman) to question the agency, who then decide the duo are expendable. Fast-paced with some eye-catching action sequences. **94m/C VHS, DVD.** Dolph Lundgren, Gina Bellman, Conrad Dunn; ***D:*** Russell Mulcahy; ***W:*** Sergio D. Altieri; ***C:*** David Franco; ***M:*** Stefano Mainetti.

Silent Valley ☙ **1935** Adventure of the Old West with American cowboy star Tom Tyler. **60m/B VHS.** Tom Tyler, Alan Bridge, Wally Wales, Charles "Blackie" King, Charles "Slim" Whitaker, Murdock MacQuarrie, Nancy Deshon; ***D:*** Bernard B. Ray; ***W:*** Rose Gordon, Carl Krusada; ***C:*** J. Henry Kruse, Abe Scholtz.

Silent Venom ☙ *Recoil* **2008** Snakes in a sub. James O'Neill (Perry) is being forced into retirement and he's not happy about his last assignment. Using a decommissioned sub, he has to evacuate scientist Andrea Swanson (Allen) and her assistant Jake (Mandylor), plus her cargo of mutant snakes, when the military project she was working on is shut down. The sub is attacked by the Chinese and the snakes get loose and start eating the crew. **86m/C DVD.** Luke Perry, Krista Allen, Louis Mandylor, Tom Berenger, John L. Curtis, Anthony Tyler Quinn; ***D:*** Fred Olen Ray; ***W:*** Mark Sanderson; ***C:*** Theo Angell; ***M:*** Stu Goldberg.

Silent Victim ☙☙ 1/2 **1992 (R)** Greene stars as Bonnie Jackson, a Georgia housewife whose marriage has not only gone wrong but turned violent. She takes a drug overdose in a suicide attempt but it results only in a miscarriage. Her furious husband sues her for the murder of their unborn child while an ambitious district attorney petitions the state to charge Bonnie with committing an illegal abortion. Bonnie's torment soon becomes a media circus as she goes on trial. Based on a true story. **116m/C VHS.** Michele Greene, Kyle Secor, Ely Pouget, Alex Hyde-White, Dori Brenner, Leann Hunley; ***D:*** Menahem Golan; ***W:*** Nelly Adnil, Jonathan Platnick; ***M:*** William T. Stromberg.

Silent Victory: The Kitty O'Neil Story ☙☙☙ **1979** Genuinely stirring real-life-overcoming-adversity story of the deaf woman who became a top stunt woman in Hollywood and holder of the land speed record for women. Channing is very good as O'Neil. Made for television. **96m/C** Stockard Channing, Brian Dennehy, Colleen Dewhurst, Edward Albert, James Farentino; ***D:*** Lou Antonio. **TV**

Silent Waters ☙ 1/2 *Khamosh Pani* **2003** When a young Muslim makes an all-too-quick conversion from his romance-filled life to militant indoctrination, it leads his mother to confront her haunted past. Geared primarily for the Pakistani audience, the story takes for granted that Western viewers have a background understanding of the 1947 partitioning of India and Pakistan. While Kirron Kher delivers a full-dimensional performance as the mother, other characters aren't as fleshed out. Teeters between doc and Bollywood. In Punjabi with subtitles. **95m/C DVD.** Arshad Mahmud, Kiron Kher, Aamir Ali Malik, Salman Shahid, Shilpa Shukla, Sarfaraz Ansari; ***D:*** Sabiha Sumar; ***C:*** Ralph Netzer; ***M:*** Madan Gopal Singh, Arshad Mahmud.

Silent Witness ☙ **1985 (R)** A woman (Bertinelli) witnesses her brother-in-law and his friend rape a young woman. She must decide whether to testify against them or keep the family secret. Exploitative and weakly plotted. Rip-off of the much-discussed Massachusetts barroom rape case. **97m/C VHS, DVD.** Valerie Bertinelli, John Savage, Chris Nash, Melissa Leo, Pat Corley, Steven Williams, Jacqueline Brookes, Alex McArthur, Katie McCombs; ***D:*** Michael Miller. **TV**

Silent Witness ☙☙ 1/2 *Do Not Disturb* **1999 (R)** Walter Richmond (Hurt) and his wife Cathryn (Tilly) are in Amsterdam with their mute daughter Melissa so Walter can close a business deal. But Melissa witnesses a murder and then disappears, leaving her frantic parents to find her before the killers do. This one turns out to be more of a parody of the thriller genre than a serious example. **94m/C VHS, DVD.** William Hurt, Jennifer Tilly, Denis Leary, Francesca Brown, Michael Chiklis, Michael Goorjian; ***D:*** Dick Maas.

Silhouette ☙☙ **1991 (R)** Detained in a small Texas town, a woman witnesses the murder of a local girl—but in silhouette, so the killer's identity takes a feature-length running time to resolve. A fair but contrived thriller that the leading lady co-produced. **89m/C VHS.** Faye Dunaway, David Rasche, John Terry, Carlos Gomez, Ron Campbell, Margaret Blye, Talisa Soto, Ritch Brinkley; ***D:*** Carl Schenkel; ***W:*** Victor Buell. **CABLE**

Silicon Towers ☙ 1/2 **1999 (PG-13)** Charlie Cook (Quint) is suddenly promoted to an executive position at Silicon Towers. But a mysterious e-mail warns him that the corporation is illegally accessing bank accounts worldwide and then Charlie gets accused of embezzling. **95m/C VHS, DVD.** Jonathan Quint, Brian Dennehy, Daniel Baldwin, Robert Guillaume, Brad Dourif; ***D:*** Serge Rodnunsky; ***W:*** Serge Rodnunsky. **VIDEO**

Silk ☙ **1986 (R)** A beautiful and bloodthirsty detective cuts a swath through local heroin rings. **84m/C VHS.** Cec Verrell, Bill McLaughlin, Fred Bailey; ***D:*** Cirio H. Santiago.

Silk ☙ **2007 (R)** Boring historical drama strives for epic romance but lacks appealing characters, convincing plot, or any chemistry between its leads. Herve (Pitt) leaves his wife Helene (Knightley) and their 19th-century French village for Japan to obtain silkworms for his boss (Molina), but ends up falling for a concubine (Ashina) of the warlord who provides the silkworms (Yakusho). Movie skips anything interesting about the historical period in which it's set and opts for tired cliches about love and fate while failing to build any dramatic tension. **109m/C DVD.** *CA IT JP* Michael Pitt, Keira Knightley, Koji Yakusho, Alfred Molina, Kenneth Welsh, Sei Ashina; ***D:*** Francois Girard; ***W:*** Francois Girard, Michael Golding; ***C:*** Alan Dostie; ***M:*** Ryuichi Sakamoto.

Silk 2 ☙ **1989 (R)** A foreign-made sequel, in which a beautiful cop stops crime in Honolulu. Ludicrous plot, bad acting, lots of skin and violence—what more could you want? Dreadful. **85m/C VHS.** Monique Gabrielle, Peter Nelson, Jan Merlin, Maria Clair; ***D:*** Cirio H. Santiago.

Silk Degrees ☙ 1/2 **1994 (R)** Actress witnesses a murder and is targeted for elimination by the killer. She's supposed to be protected by a couple of federal agents but it seems there's a traitor around. **81m/C VHS.** Deborah Shelton, Marc Singer, Mark Hamill, Michael Des Barres, Charles Napier, Gilbert Gottfried, Adrienne Barbeau; ***D:*** Armand Garabidian; ***W:*** Stuart Gibbs, Douglas J. Sloan, Robert Gottlieb; ***M:*** Larry Wolff.

Silk 'n' Sabotage ☙ 1/2 *Wildchild 2* **1994** Serious-minded Jamie comes up with a program for a new computer game. When it's stolen by a con artist, Jamie and her frivolous roommates team up to retrieve it. Since the roomies operate a lingerie business there's lots of pulchritude on display. Also available unrated. **70m/C VHS, DVD.** Cherilyn Shea, Stephanie Champlin, Julie Skiru; ***D:*** Joe Cauley.

The Silk Road ☙☙ 1/2 **1992 (PG-13)** In 11th-century China the ancient trading route leads to Dun Huang, a desert city that is the last Chinese outpost on the road. Zhao, a young scholar, travels in a caravan which is attacked by Chinese mercenaries. His life is spared and when his new home is attacked by a neighboring nation, he hides the city's treasures in nearby caves. Adapted from the novel by Yashushi Inoue, which was based on the Thousand Buddha Caves, where a treasure of Buddhist icons and scrolls were discovered in 1900. Billed as an epic, there's lots of pageantry and some impressive battle scenes but is too stately and overdone to be more than merely interesting. In Japanese with English subtitles. **99m/C VHS.** *CH JP* Koichi Sato, Toshiyuki Nishida, Anna Nakagawa, Tsunehiko Watase, Daijiro Harada, Takahiro Tamura; ***D:*** Junya Sato; ***M:*** Masaru Sato.

Silk Stockings ☙☙☙ **1957** Splendid musical comedy adaptation of "Ninotchka," with Astaire as a charming American movie man, and Charisse as the cold Soviet official whose commie heart he melts. Music and lyrics by Cole Porter highlight this film adapted from George S. Kaufman's hit Broadway play. Director Mamoulian's last film. ♫Too Bad; Paris Loves Lovers; Fated to Be Mated; The Ritz Roll 'n Rock; Silk Stockings; Red Blues; All of You; Stereophonic Sound; Josephine. **117m/C VHS, DVD.** Fred Astaire, Cyd Charisse, Janis Paige, Peter Lorre, George Tobias; ***D:*** Rouben Mamoulian; ***M:*** Andre Previn.

Silkwood ☙☙☙ **1983 (R)** The story of Karen Silkwood, who died in a 1974 car crash under suspicious circumstances. She was a nuclear plant worker and activist who was investigating shoddy practices at the plant. Streep acts up a storm, disappearing completely into her character. Cher surprises with her fine portrayal of a lesbian co-worker, and Russell is also good. Nichols has a tough time since we already know the ending, but he brings top-notch performances from his excellent cast. **131m/C VHS, DVD.** Meryl Streep, Kurt Russell, Cher, Diana Scarwid, Bruce McGill, Fred Ward, David Strathairn, Ron Silver, Josef Sommer, Craig T. Nelson; ***D:*** Mike Nichols; ***W:*** Nora Ephron, Alice Arlen; ***C:*** Miroslav Ondricek; ***M:*** Georges Delerue. Golden Globes '84: Support. Actress (Cher).

Silver Bandit ☙ **1950** A bookkeeper is sent to investigate a mine theft. Along the way he sings country and western songs. **54m/B VHS, DVD.** Bob Gilbert, Virginia Jackson, Gene Gray, Richard Elliott, Spade Cooley; ***D:*** Elmer Clifton; ***W:*** Elmer Clifton; ***C:*** Harvey Hines.

Silver Bears ☙☙ **1978 (PG)** Las Vegas mobster Balsam hires con man Caine and sends him to Switzerland to buy a bank for laundering purposes. Only a bankrupt prince (Jourdan) entices Caine into a scheme to control the world's silver market and he ends up being swindled himself. So-so entry adapted from the novel by Paul Erdman. **114m/C VHS.** Michael Caine, Cybill Shepherd, Louis Jourdan, Stephane Audran, David Warner, Tom Smothers, Martin Balsam, Jay Leno, Charles Gray, Joss Ackland; ***D:*** Ivan Passer; ***M:*** Claude Bolling.

The Silver Bullet ☙☙ **1934** Follows the adventures of Tom, the sheriff of a small gold mining town. **55m/C VHS.** Tom Tyler, Jayne Regan, Lafe (Lafayette) McKee, Charles King, George Chesebro, Charles "Slim" Whitaker, Lew Meehan, Franklyn Farnum, Walt Williams; ***D:*** Bernard B. Ray.

The Silver Bullet ☙ 1/2 **1942** The climatic shootout is the highlight of this oater. "Silver Jim" Donovan comes looking for the man who shot him with a silver bullet and killed his father. Jim knows the man has a jagged scar on his arm and asks the local doctor to keep a lookout. Maybe crooked politician Walter Kincaid knows something too. **56m/B DVD.** Johnny Mack Brown, Fuzzy Knight, Jennifer Holt, William Farnum, Leroy Mason, Slim Whitaker, Claire Whitney, Rex Lease, Grace Leonard; ***D:*** Joseph H. Lewis; ***W:*** Elizabeth Beecher; ***C:*** Charles Van Enger.

Silver Bullet ☙☙ *Stephen King's Silver Bullet* **1985 (R)** Adapted from Stephen King's "Cycle of the Werewolf," about a town whose inhabitants are being brutally murdered. It finally dawns on them the culprit is a werewolf. Action moves along at a good clip and the film has its share of suspense. **94m/C VHS, DVD.** Corey Haim, Gary Busey, Megan Follows, Everett McGill, Robin Groves, Leon Russom, Terry O'Quinn, Bill Smitrovich, Kent Broadhurst, Lawrence Tierney; ***D:*** Daniel Attias; ***W:*** Stephen King; ***C:*** Armando Nannuzzi.

The Silver Chalice ☙ **1954** Newman's career somehow survived his movie debut in this bloated, turgid Biblical epic about the momentous events that befall a young Greek sculptor who fashions a holder for the cup that was used at the Last Supper. Newman later took out an ad in Variety to apologize for the film, in which Greene also made his debut. Based on the novel by Thomas Costain. **135m/C VHS.** Paul Newman, Virginia Mayo, Pier Angeli, Jack Palance, Natalie Wood, Joseph Wiseman, Lorne Greene, E.G. Marshall; ***D:*** Victor Saville; ***M:*** Franz Waxman.

Silver City ☙☙ **1984 (PG)** A saga depicting the plight of Polish refugees in Australia in 1949. A pair of lovers find each other in a crowded refugee camp. He's married to her friend. Too-complex, slow but earnest effort. **110m/C VHS.** *AU* Gosia Dobrowolska, Ivar Kants; ***D:*** Sophia Turkiewicz.

Silver City ☙☙ **2004 (R)** Surprisingly clumsy political drama finds Sayles pushing his ensemble in places they're not comfortable going. Conservative Richard "Dim Dickie" Pilager (Cooper) is the son of a U.S. senator (Murphy) and the current frontrunner in the Colorado governor's race. He's about to film a commercial on a picturesque river when he fishes out a very dead body instead of a trout. Savvy and suspicious campaign manager Chuck Raven (Dreyfuss) hires disgraced journalist-turned-PI Danny O'Brien (Huston) to investigate the three prime suspects: talk show host Castleton (Ferrer), environmental crusader Lyle (Waite), and Dickie's black sheep sister Maddy (Hannah). Disappointing tale of a conspiracy of corruption and all-too easy targets. **129m/C DVD.** *US* Danny Huston, Maria Bello, Billy Zane, Chris Cooper, Richard Dreyfuss, Michael Murphy, Daryl Hannah, Kris Kristofferson, Mary Kay Place, David Clennon, Miguel Ferrer, Ralph Waite, Sal Lopez, James Gammon, Tim Roth, Thora Birch, Luis Saguar, Alma Delfina, Aaron Vieyra, Hugo Carbajal; ***D:*** John Sayles; ***W:*** John Sayles; ***C:*** Haskell Wexler; ***M:*** Mason Daring.

Silver City Bonanza ☙☙ 1/2 **1951** Lots of action in this outrageous oater that includes a haunted ranch and an undersea battle as plot devices. Singing cowboy Allen and sidekick Ebsen use a seeing-eye dog to track down the killer of a blind man. Since Roy Rogers and Republic parted company the year of this film's release, singing star Allen was groomed to become the new "King of the Cowboys." However, by this time, the singing-cowboy craze was almost old hat. **67m/B VHS.** Rex Allen, Buddy Ebsen, Mary Ellen Kay, Billy Kimbley, Alix Ebsen, Bill Kennedy, Gregg Barton, Clem Bevans; ***D:*** George Blair; ***W:*** Bob Williams; ***C:*** John MacBurnie; ***M:*** Stanley Wilson.

Silver City Kid ☙ **1945** Two mine owners learn about a rich mineral vein under a rancher's land, kill him, and then try to steal the property from his sister. So it's up to ranch foreman Jack Adams (Lane) to expose the plot and bring the guilty to justice. **56m/B VHS.** Peggy Stewart, Wally Vernon, Twinkle Watts, Harry Woods, Glenn Strange, Lane Chandler, Frank Jaquet, Allan "Rocky" Lane; ***D:*** John English; ***C:*** Reggie Lanning, Taylor Caven; ***M:*** Joseph Dubin.

Silver Dream Racer ☙ 1/2 **1983 (PG)** An English grease monkey wants to win the World Motorcycle Championship title away from an American biker. He's also after someone else's girlfriend. Boring, stilted, unoriginal "Big Race" flick. **103m/C VHS.** Beau Bridges, David Essex, Christina Raines, Diane Keen, Harry H. Corbett; ***D:*** David Wickes; ***M:*** David Essex.

Silver Hawk ☙☙ *Fei Ying* **2004 (PG-13)** Campy kung fu superhero adventure stars Yeoh as socialite Lulu Wong, who masquerades as silver latex-wearing crimebuster Silver Hawk. Her latest rescue mission is a scientist (Chen), working on an artificial intelligence project, who has been kidnapped by her arch-enemy Wolfe (Goss). Yeoh can kick butt, which may be the best reason to see this flick. English and Cantonese with subtitles. **100m/C DVD.** Michelle Yeoh, Luke Goss, Daoming Chen, Michael Jai White, Richie Ren,

Bingbing Li, Brandon Chang; ***D:*** Jingle Ma; ***W:*** Jingle Ma, Susan Chan; ***C:*** Chi Ying Chan.

The Silver Horde 1/2 **1930** Alaskan salmon fishery owner McCrea battles villainous competitor Gordon for both his livelihood and his ladyfriend—dancehall dame Brent. Arthur's the society gal who briefly catches McCrea's eye. Silent screen star Sweet ended her career with a brief role. Based on a novel by Rex Beach. **80m/B VHS, DVD.** Joel McCrea, Evelyn Brent, Jean Arthur, Gavin Gordon, Louis Wolheim, Raymond Hatton, Blanche Sweet, Purnell Pratt, William B. Davidson; ***D:*** George Archainbaud; ***W:*** Wallace Smith; ***C:*** Leo Tover.

Silver Lode 1/2 **1954** A man accused of murder on his wedding day attempts to clear his name while the law launches an intensive manhunt for him. Ordinary story improved by good, energetic cast. **92m/C VHS, DVD.** John Payne, Dan Duryea, Lizabeth Scott, Stuart Whitman; ***D:*** Allan Dwan.

Silver Queen **1942** A woman finds out her father has gambled away a silver mine and left her with debts. She opens a saloon, only to have her fiance use the money to hunt for more silver. **81m/B VHS, DVD.** Priscilla Lane, George Brent, Bruce Cabot, Eugene Pallette; ***D:*** Lloyd Bacon.

Silver River 1/2 **1948** Average western that marked the final collaboration between director Walsh and star Flynn. It never even comes close to their previous works. Flynn plays a no-good, power-hungry cad who will stop at nothing to get what he wants. He happens to want Sheridan, who is married to Bennett, so Flynn schemes to get rid of him. Overall, Flynn acts as though he really isn't interested in the material and had to make a pact with Walsh that he would stay sober until five in the afternoon while filming. Based on an unpublished novel by Stephen Longstreet. **108m/B VHS.** Errol Flynn, Ann Sheridan, Thomas Mitchell, Bruce Bennett, Tom D'Andrea, Barton MacLane, Monte Blue, Jonathan Hale; ***D:*** Raoul Walsh; ***W:*** Stephen Longstreet, Harriet Frank Jr.; ***M:*** Max Steiner.

Silver Spurs 1/2 **1943** Villain tries to get some oil-rich property by murdering the ranch's owner. Ranch foreman Rogers saves the day. **60m/B VHS, DVD.** Roy Rogers, Jerome Cowan, John Carradine, Phyllis Brooks, Smiley Burnette, Joyce Compton; ***D:*** Joseph Kane.

Silver Stallion 1/2 **1941** Thunder the Wonder Horse plays the title character, who fights rattlesnakes, wild dogs and hoss thieves. Too bad he doesn't give acting lessons to the humans in this frail family western with nice scenery and action scenes. **59m/C VHS.** David Sharpe, Carol Hughes, Leroy Mason, Walter Long; ***D:*** Edward Finney.

The Silver Stallion: King of the Wild Brumbies 1/2 *The Silver Brumby* **1993 (G)** The adolescent Indi is enthralled as her writer-mother relates each new chapter in the saga of Thara, the amazing silver stallion. And she images each adventure as the horse triumphs over evil men, other horses, and the elements to become leader of the herd. Based on the Australian children's novel "The Silver Brumby" by Elyne Mitchell. **93m/C VHS, DVD.** *AU* Caroline Goodall, Ami Daemion, Russell Crowe; ***D:*** John Tatoulis; ***W:*** John Tatoulis, Jon Stephens; ***M:*** Tassos Ioannides.

Silver Star **1955** Man elected sheriff of a western town turns down the job because he is a pacifist. He changes his mind when his defeated opponent hires a trio of killers to come after him. **73m/B VHS, DVD.** Edgar Buchanan, Marie Windsor, Lon Chaney Jr., Earle Lyon, Richard Bartlett, Barton MacLane, Morris Ankrum, Edith Evanson; ***D:*** Richard Bartlett; ***W:*** Richard Bartlett, Ian MacDonald; ***C:*** Guy Roe; ***M:*** Leo Klatzkin.

Silver Strand 1/2 **1995 (R)** Hunky Brian Del Piso (Bellows), a navel cadet in the S.E.A.L. training school, makes the big mistake of falling for sexy Michelle (Sheridan), who just happens to be an officer's wife. As if he didn't have enough challenges, should their affair be exposed Brian might just as well kiss his career goodbye. **104m/C VHS.** Gil Bellows, Nicolette Sheridan; ***D:*** George Miller; ***W:*** Douglas Day Stewart; ***C:*** David Connell; ***M:*** Joseph Conlan.

The Silver Streak **1934** The sickly son of a diesel train designer needs an iron lung—pronto. A rival's super-fast locomotive is the only hope for the boy. Murders, runaway engines, and a crew that would rather walk enliven this race against time. **72m/B VHS, DVD.** Sally Blane, Charles Starrett, Arthur Lake, Edgar Kennedy, William Farnum; ***D:*** Thomas Atkins.

Silver Streak **1976 (PG)** Pooped exec Wilder rides a train from L.A. to Chicago, planning to enjoy a leisurely, relaxing trip. Instead he becomes involved with murder, intrigue, and a beautiful woman. Energetic Hitchcock parody features successful first pairing of Wilder and Pryor. **113m/C VHS, DVD.** Gene Wilder, Richard Pryor, Jill Clayburgh, Patrick McGoohan, Ned Beatty, Ray Walston, Richard Kiel, Scatman Crothers; ***D:*** Arthur Hiller; ***W:*** Colin Higgins; ***M:*** Henry Mancini.

Silver Wolf 1/2 **1998** Jesse (Meier) and his dad head into the mountains on a snow board trip when a sudden storm hits. Jesse's dad is killed and he is injured. But he finds a companion, a wounded young wolf he names Silver. However, when Jesse is rescued, Silver disappears and Jesse is desperate to find him. Jesse gets his chance when he's taken in by his mountain man uncle (Biehn) but their search pits them against a villainous hunter (Scheider). **97m/C VHS, DVD.** Michael Biehn, Roy Scheider, Shane Meier, Kimberly Warnat; ***D:*** Peter Svatek; ***W:*** Michael Amo; ***C:*** Curtis Petersen; ***M:*** Robert Carli. **VIDEO**

Silverado **1985 (PG-13)** Affectionate pastiche of western cliches has everything a viewer could ask for—except Indians. Straightforward plot has four virtuous cowboys rise up against a crooked lawman in a blaze of six guns. No subtlety from the first big Western in quite a while, but plenty of fun and laughs. **132m/C VHS, DVD.** Kevin Kline, Scott Glenn, Kevin Costner, Danny Glover, Brian Dennehy, Linda Hunt, John Cleese, Jeff Goldblum, Rosanna Arquette, Jeff Fahey; ***D:*** Lawrence Kasdan; ***W:*** Lawrence Kasdan; ***C:*** John Bailey; ***M:*** Bruce Broughton.

Simba **1955** A young Englishman arrives at his brother's Kenyan farm to find him murdered in a local skirmish between the Mau Maus and white settlers. Well made, thoughtful look at colonialism, racial animosity, and violence. **98m/C VHS.** *GB* Dirk Bogarde, Donald Sinden, Virginia McKenna, Orlando Martins; ***D:*** Brian Desmond Hurst; ***C:*** Geoffrey Unsworth.

The Simian Line 1/2 **1999** Uneven but affecting look at several couples trying to define their romantic relationships. Middle-aged divorcee Katharine (Redgrave) is jealously in love with her younger live-in lover, Rick (Connick), and very fond of throwing dinner parties. But Katharine's latest soiree not only includes two other couples who are also romantically questionable but an eccentric psychic (Daly), who sees two ghosts in the house (Hurt, Mathis) and makes an ominous prediction. Too many stories clutter the film, particularly since the best performances come from Redgrave and Connick (with Daly offering comedic support). **106m/C VHS, DVD.** Lynn Redgrave, Harry Connick Jr., Jamey Sheridan, Cindy Crawford, Tyne Daly, Monica Keena, Dylan Bruno, Samantha Mathis, William Hurt, Eric Stoltz; ***D:*** Linda Yellen; ***W:*** Gisella Bernice; ***C:*** David Bridges; ***M:*** Patrick Seymour.

Simon 1/2 **1980 (PG)** A group of bored demented scientists brainwash a college professor into believing he is an alien from a distant galaxy, whereupon he begins trying to correct the evil in America. Screwball comedy, or semi-serious satire of some kind? Hard to tell. Some terrific set pieces but the movie as a whole doesn't quite hold together. Directorial debut of Brickman, who previously worked as a scriptwriter with Woody Allen ("Sleeper," etc.). **97m/C VHS.** Alan Arkin, Madeline Kahn, Fred Gwynne, Adolph Green, Wallace Shawn, Austin Pendleton; ***D:*** Marshall Brickman; ***W:*** Marshall Brickman, Thomas Baum.

Simon Birch *A Small Miracle* **1998 (PG)** Young Simon Birch (Smith) believes he's destined to become a hero, and that his disability—dwarfism resulting from Morquio's syndrome—is actually a gift from God to facilitate his destiny. After his best friend Joe's idolized mother dies, the two decide to track down Joe's father, who hasn't been seen for years. The quest leads to the climactic disaster that is the impetus for the heroics Simon has been waiting for. Smith's on-screen presence is the main attraction, as most of the emotion and inspiration in the source material, John Irving's novel "A Prayer for Owen Meany," is absent. Irving demanded both the character name change (Meany to Birch) and a screen credit change—from "based on" to "suggested by." **110m/C VHS, DVD.** Ian Michael Smith, Joseph Mazzello, Ashley Judd, Oliver Platt, David Strathairn, Dana Ivey, Jan Hooks, Beatrice Winde, Ceciley Carroll, Sumela-Rose Keramidopulos, Sam Morton, John Robinson; ***D:*** Mark Steven Johnson; ***W:*** Mark Steven Johnson; ***C:*** Aaron Schneider; ***M:*** Marc Shaiman; ***Nar:*** Jim Carrey.

Simon Bolivar 1/2 **1969** The title character leads the Venezuelan revolution in 1817. **110m/C VHS.** *IT SP VZ* Maximilian Schell, Rosanna Schiaffino; ***D:*** Alessandro Blasetti; ***W:*** Joe Luis Dibildos; ***C:*** Manuel Berenguer; ***M:*** Aldemaro Romero.

Simon, King of the Witches 1/2 **1971 (R)** An L.A. warlock who lives in a sewer drain finds himself the center of attention when his spells actually work. This interesting hippie/witchcraft entry bogs down now and then but Prine's performance is droll and lively. **90m/C VHS.** Andrew Prine, Brenda Scott, George Paulsin, Norman Burton, Ultra Violet; ***D:*** Bruce Kessler; ***W:*** Robert Phippeny; ***C:*** David L. Butler.

Simon of the Desert 1/2 *Simon del Desierto* **1966** Not Bunuel's very best, but worthy of the master satirist. An ascetic stands on a pillar in the desert for several decades—closer to God, farther from temptation. Pinal is a gorgeous devil that tempts Simon. Hilarious, irreverent, sophisticated. What's with the weird ending, though? In Spanish with English subtitles. **46m/B VHS.** Claudio Brook, Silvia Pinal, Enrique Alvarez Felix; ***D:*** Luis Bunuel; ***W:*** Luis Bunuel; ***C:*** Gabriel Figueroa; ***M:*** Raul Lavista.

Simon Says 1/2 **2007 (R)** Typical pic in the evil twins/slasher genre with Glover playing crazy yet again. Five college kids on a road trip pick exactly the wrong camping spot. Don't be fooled by the prominence of Blake Lively's name in the ads; her dad Ernie produced the pic and Blake and sister Lori have only small roles. **90m/C DVD.** Crispin Glover, Greg Cipes, Carrie Finklea, Bruce Glover, Blake Lively, Margo Hershman, Kelly Vutz, Artie Baxter, Lori Lively; ***D:*** William Dear; ***W:*** William Dear; ***C:*** Bryan Greenberg; ***M:*** Ludek Drizhal.

Simon Sez 1/2 **1999 (PG-13)** Convoluted spy thriller stars basketball bad boy Dennis Rodman as Simon, an Interpol agent on the trail of effete illegal arms dealer Ashton (Pradon). He must be posing undercover as a gigantic space-age punk rock coloring book, because the nose rings, tattoos and shock treatment hair don't exactly say "inconspicuous." He is approached for help by his old friend and colleague Nick (Cook), a private eye who's in over his head on a kidnapping case. The two cases just happen to be connected, but the plot is just an excuse to show car chases and shoot 'em up action sequences. Rodman shows some decent acting skills, and he's still as bad as he wants to be. Unfortunately, the movie is a lot worse than he wants it to be. **85m/C VHS, DVD.** Dennis Rodman, Dane Cook, Natalia Cigliuti, Filip Nicolic, John Pinette, Jerome Pradon, Ricky Harris; ***D:*** Kevin Elders; ***W:*** Andrew Miller, Andrew Lowery; ***C:*** Avi (Avraham) Karpik; ***M:*** Brian Tyler. **VIDEO**

Simon the Magician *Simon Magus* **1999** At the behest of the French police, Budapest magician Simon (Andorai) travels to Paris to solve a murder, although it doesn't seem very important to the plot. Instead, Simon falls in love with Jeanne (Delarme) and is challenged by rival Peter (Halasz) to a deadly duel—being buried alive for three days. References the biblical story of Simon Magus and St. Peter. Hungarian and French with subtitles. **100m/B DVD.** *FR HU* Peter Andorai, Hubert Kounde, Julie Delarme, Peter Halasz, Mari Nagy; ***D:*** Ildiko Enyedi; ***W:*** Ildiko Enyedi; ***C:*** Tibor Mathe.

Simone **2002 (PG-13)** Part Hollywood send-up and part child of Hollywood, pic shows pitfalls of using gimmicks to sell movies and uses the same gimmick to sell the movie itself. Perfect Tinseltown logic. Pacino is Viktor, a has-been filmmaker, who becomes a high tech Pygmalian when he creates an actress from scratch after inheriting a mad inventor's computer program. Solving his recent dilemma involving a temperamental star (Ryder), Viktor's digital thesp, Simone (short for simulated one) becomes a smash hit and revives his career in the process. Of course, the rabid tabloid press and public expect to see a real actress, not a synthespian, creating a host of publicity problems. Writer/director/producer Niccol is in familiar techno-wizardry territory here, but doesn't match his previous efforts. **117m/C VHS, DVD.** *US* Al Pacino, Catherine Keener, Jay Mohr, Jason Schwartzman, Pruitt Taylor Vince, Stanley Anderson, Evan Rachel Wood, Daniel von Bargen, Rachel Roberts, Elias Koteas, Rebecca Romijn; ***Cameos:*** Winona Ryder; ***D:*** Andrew Niccol; ***W:*** Andrew Niccol; ***C:*** Edward Lachman; ***M:*** Carter Burwell.

Simone Barbes *Simone Barbes ou la Vertu* **1980** Simone (Bourgoin) ushers at a porn theatre where she likes to embarass the clientele. One Parisian night she visits the seedy nightclub where her lesbian lover performs burlesque and decides to embark on some of her own erotic adventures, which prove dangerous. French with subtitles. **80m/C VHS, DVD.** *FR* Ingrid Bourgoin, Michel Delahaye, Martine Simonet, Pascal Bonitzer; ***D:*** Maire-Claude Treilhou; ***W:*** Maire-Claude Treilhou, Michel Delahaye; ***C:*** Jean-Yves Escoffier.

Simpatico 1/2 **1999 (R)** Excellent performances and a disappointing script mark this adaptation of the Sam Shephard play. Nolte is Vinnie, who has evidence of horse breeder Carter's (Bridges) involvement in a past race fixing and blackmail scheme. Vinnie's been blackmailing Carter for years and summons him to California on the pretense of helping Vinnie out of a sexual misconduct rap. The supposed victim (Keener) of the misconduct is unaware that any took place and agrees to help Carter. Vinnie then steals Carter's I.D, car, and plane ticket and visits their old blackmail victim (Finney), but then Carter's wife Rosie (Stone), who was also in on the con. In a haze of confused motivations and implausible plot macinations, the three try to redeem their past deeds, with Vinnie and Carter seemingly switching places. **106m/C VHS, DVD.** Nick Nolte, Sharon Stone, Jeff Bridges, Catherine Keener, Albert Finney, Shawn Hatosy, Kimberly Williams, Liam Waite; ***D:*** Matthew Warchus; ***W:*** Matthew Warchus, David Nicholls; ***C:*** John Toll; ***M:*** Stewart Copeland.

A Simple Curve **2005** Caleb is trying to keep his custom woodworking shop in business despite the contrariness of his widowed father Jim, an aging hippie and one-time draft dodger who's also his partner. When wealthy American Matthew, a former friend of Jim's, arrives in town to build a luxury lodge, Caleb sees his opportunity and secretly makes a deal, which could cost him more than he realizes. Filmed in the Slocan Valley of British Columbia. **92m/C DVD.** *CA* Kris Lemche, Michael Hogan, Matt Craven, Pascale Hutton, Sara Lind, Kett Turton, Michael Robinson; ***D:*** Aubrey Nealon; ***W:*** Aubrey Nealon; ***C:*** David Geddes; ***M:*** Ohad Benchetrit, Justin Small.

Simple Justice 1/2 **1989 (R)** Mindless, justice-in-own-hands anti-liberal hogwash. Overwrought, smug, and violent story of a young couple beaten by robbers who remain at large. **91m/C VHS, DVD.** Cesar Romero, John Spencer, Doris Roberts, Candy McClain; ***D:*** Deborah Del Prete.

The Simple Life of Noah Dearborn 1/2 **1999 (PG)** Simple morality tale with an affecting performance by Poitier. Noah Dearborn is a 91-year-old carpenter and farmer who refuses to sell his Georgia property to developers. So they try to declare the old man incompetent. **87m/C VHS, DVD.** Sidney Poitier, Mary-Louise Parker, Dianne Wiest, George Newbern; ***D:*** Gregg Champion. **TV**

Simple Men **1992 (R)** Odd-ball brothers Bill (a petty criminal) and Dennis (a shy college student) decide to track down their missing father in this fractured comedy. Dad, a former big-league baseball player who bombed the Pentagon in the '60s, is a long-time fugitive hiding out somewhere in the wilds of Long Island. Their search leads them to two equally opposite women, the wary Kate, whom Bill immediately falls for, and the sexy Elina, who turns out to know dear old dad quite well. Deliberately deadpan and cliched, Hartley's quirky style can either irritate or illuminate via the weird turnings of his characters' lives. **105m/C VHS, DVD.** Robert John Burke, William Sage, Karen Sillas, Elina Lowensohn, Martin Donovan, Mark Bailey, John MacKay, Jeffrey Howard, Holly Marie Combs; ***D:*** Hal Hartley; ***W:*** Hal Hartley; ***C:*** Michael Spiller; ***M:*** Hal Hartley.

A Simple Plan **1998 (R)** Hank (Paxton), his "slow" brother Jacob (Thornton), and Jacob's best bud, alcoholic Lou (Briscoe) find the wreckage of a small plane in the snowy Minnesota woods. The pilot is dead and there's a bag filled with $4 million in cash, which they decide is drug money. The trio decide to keep quiet about the find and keep the money hidden until the plane is discovered by someone else. But having all that loot brings out the greed in everyone and soon nasty things begin to happen to all those involved. Adapted from the 1993 novel by Scott Smith. **121m/C VHS, DVD.** Bill Paxton, Billy Bob Thornton, Brent Briscoe, Bridget Fonda, Gary Cole, Becky Ann Baker, Chelcie Ross, Jack Walsh; ***D:*** Sam Raimi; ***W:*** Scott B. Smith; ***C:*** Alar Kivilo; ***M:*** Danny Elfman. L.A. Film Critics '98: Support. Actor (Thornton); Broadcast Film Critics '98: Adapt. Screenplay, Support. Actor (Thornton).

A Simple Promise **2007** Struggling artist Marcus and aspiring singer Madison get romantically involved and make a promise to help each other with their careers. But when one gets that longed-for big break, it causes a lot of friction and they have to figure out if their love can get them through. **95m/C DVD.** Ella Joyce, Layla Kayleigh, Wallace Demarria, Bobby Reed, Bobby Reed, Selwyn Ward, Glen Mac; ***D:*** Earnest Harris; ***W:*** Max Lucas; ***C:*** Andrew Giannetta, Gigi Malavasi; ***M:*** Matt Hamel.

A Simple Story ***Une Histoire Simple*** **1979** A woman faces her 40th birthday with increasing uneasiness, though her life seems perfect from the outside. She evaluates her chances at love, child-bearing, and friendship, after having an abortion and breaking up with her lover. Schneider's performance is brilliant in this gentle, quiet drama. In French with English subtitles. **110m/C VHS.** *FR* Romy Schneider, Bruno Cremer, Claude Brasseur; ***D:*** Claude Sautet.

A Simple Twist of Fate **1/2 1994 (PG-13)** Comedy drama gives Martin chance to flex serious muscles with this update of George Eliot's "Silas Marner." Adoptive father Michael McMann wants to keep his daughter Mathilda (played by the prerequisite adorable twins) in the face of demands from her biological father (Byrne), who happens to be a local politician. Then revelations brought out at the custody hearing threaten the politician's career. Cuddly dad is hardly Martin's image (in spite of "Parenthood"), though strong cast limits the sugar. **106m/C VHS, DVD.** Steve Martin, Gabriel Byrne, Catherine O'Hara, Stephen Baldwin, Alana Austin, Alyssa Austin, Laura Linney, Anne Heche, Michael Des Barres, Byron Jennings; ***D:*** Gilles Mackinnon; ***W:*** Steve Martin; ***M:*** Cliff Eidelman.

A Simple Wish **1/2 1997 (PG)** Equal employment opportunities now even extend to the fairy godmother realm. Anabel (Wilson) knows her dad (Pastorelli) wants to become a Broadway actor. So she wishes for a fairy godmother—and gets stuck with Murray (Short), the first affirmative-action male practitioner, who's really not very good at spellcasting. Both Anabel and Murray have bigger problems—evil fairy godmother Claudia (Turner) is after all the fairy godmothers' magic wands so she can rule the world's wishes. Short's brand of comic energy plays right into the kid audience, and Wilson lights up every scene she's in. **95m/C VHS, DVD.** Mara Wilson, Martin Short, Kathleen Turner, Robert Pastorelli, Amanda Plummer, Teri Garr, Francis Capra, Jonathan Hadary, Alan Campbell, Ruby Dee; ***D:*** Michael Ritchie; ***W:*** Jeff Rothberg; ***C:*** Ralf Bode; ***M:*** Bruce Broughton.

Simply Irresistible **1999 (PG-13)** Romantic comedy in which failing restaurant owner/chef Amanda Shelton (Gellar) falls for exec Tom Barlett (Flanery). Thanks to the intervention of fairy-godfather O'Reilly (Durang) Amanda suddenly possesses a unique culinary ability—every emotion she's feeling goes into her food and winds up affecting her customers. Tries too hard (this kind of whimsical comedy should be lighter than a souffle) and the leads, appealing as they may be, don't generate any heat when together. The film also sounds like an Americanized version of "Like Water for Chocolate," even if no one's admitting to the notion. **95m/C VHS, DVD.** Sarah Michelle Gellar, Sean Patrick Flanery, Patricia Clarkson, Dylan Baker, Christopher Durang, Larry (Lawrence) Gilliard Jr., Betty Buckley; ***D:*** Mark Tarlov; ***W:*** Judith Roberts; ***C:*** Robert M. Stevens; ***M:*** Gil Goldstein.

The Simpsons Movie **2007 (PG-13)** Best. Movie. Ever. Okay, maybe not, but it's pretty good. Homer's infatuation with a condemned pig sparks a near apocalyptic fate for Springfield and a cross-country trek to Alaska for the Simpson clan in their long-awaited big screen debut. All of the main characters, and many of the minor ones, get their shot in the spotlight, and the show's trademark sly humor, social commentary, and digs at popular culture are, thankfully, intact. Marge provides the voice of reason, and some surprising pathos along the way. **87m/C DVD, Blu-ray Disc.** *US* ***D:*** David Silverman; ***W:*** James L. Brooks, David Mirkin, Matt Groening, Mike Reiss, Al Jean, Ian Maxton-Graham, George Meyer, Mike Scully, Matt Selman, John Swartzwelder, Jon Vitti; ***M:*** Hans Zimmer; ***V:*** Dan Castellaneta, Julie Kavner, Nancy Cartwright, Yeardley Smith, Harry Shearer, Hank Azaria, Albert Brooks, Joe Mantegna, Marcia Wallace, Pamela Hayden, Tom Hanks.

Sin **1/2 2002 (R)** Retired cop Eddie Burns (Rhames) searches for his missing sister Kassie (Washington) and discovers she's part of a twisted plot by crime boss Charlie Strom (Oldman) to get revenge on Burns for their shared past. Too many plot holes and unbelievable situations make this revenge thriller less than scintillating despite the pro work of the leads. (Okay, so Oldman chews the scenery but you expect that.) **107m/C DVD.** Ving Rhames, Gary Oldman, Kerry Washington, Brian Cox, Alicia Coppola, William Sage, Gregg Henry, Arie Verveen, Chris Spencer; ***D:*** Michael Stevens; ***W:*** Tim Willocks; ***C:*** Zoran Popovic; ***M:*** Michael Giacchino.

Sin and Redemption **1994 (PG-13)** Billie (Gibb) is raped by an unknown assailant and gives birth to a daughter from the attack. Several years later, she marries Jim (Grieco). But her daughter has an unusual medical condition that leads Billie to believe her new husband was also her rapist. **94m/C VHS.** Cynthia Gibb, Richard Grieco, Concetta Tomei, Cheryl Pollak, Chapelle Jaffe, Ralph Waite; ***D:*** Neema Barnette; ***W:*** Ellen Weston; ***C:*** Tobias Schliessler; ***M:*** David Bell. **TV**

Sin City ***Frank Miller's Sin City*** **2005 (R)** Rodriguez teamed with comic legend Frank Miller to co-direct this overly literal adaptation of Miller's black-and-white crime noir series. Set in the hellishly corrupt Basin City, the plot bounces between a menagerie of unsavory anti-heroes, including Marv (Rourke), a lovable thug bent on avenging a hooker's murder; Dwight (Owen), a moralistic man-with-a-past; and Hartigan (Willis), a cop who spent eight years in prison to protect a virtuous stripper (Alba). More of a slideshow than a film, you'll marvel at how closely it resembles the comic, though the directors' fundamentalist zeal for their source material tests the audience's patience throughout. Acting and pacing are ignored while Rodriguez uses cheap-looking CGI to slavishly reproduce exact panels of Miller's art. Fanboy fervor gone too far. **124m/B DVD, UMD.** *US* Jessica Alba, Devon Aoki, Alexis Bledel, Rosario Dawson, Benicio Del Toro, Michael Clarke Duncan, Carla Gugino, Josh Hartnett, Rutger Hauer, Jaime (James) King, Michael Madsen, Brittany Murphy, Clive Owen, Mickey Rourke, Nick Stahl, Bruce Willis, Elijah Wood, Marley Shelton, Powers Boothe, Nicky Katt, Makenzie Vega, Arie Verveen, Tommy Nix, Jude Ciccolella, Rick Gomez, Lisa Marie Newmyer, Nick Offerman; ***D:*** Robert Rodriguez, Frank Miller; ***C:*** Robert Rodriguez; ***M:*** Robert Rodriguez, Graeme Revell, John Debney.

Sin Nombre **2009 (R)** Teenager Sayra (Gaitan) lives in Honduras but hungers for a brighter future, leading her to illegally emigrate with her estranged father into Mexico and then the United States. Meanwhile, teenager Casper, a.k.a. Willy (Flores) from Tapachula, Mexico, faces a bleak future as a member of the ultra-violent Mara Salvatrucha gang and joins the family after murdering his gang's leader. A gripping tale of the wretched circumstances that drive people from Central America into the "land of opportunity" in hopes of a better life despite the dangers and sacrifices that accompany such a harrowing journey. An excellent debut from writer/director Fukunaga. **96m/C DVD.** Paulina Gaitan, Gerardo Taracena, Edgar Flores, Diane Garcia, Catalina Lopez; ***D:*** Cary Fukunaga; ***W:*** Cary Fukunaga; ***C:*** Adriano Goldman; ***M:*** Marcelo Zarvos.

Sin of Adam & Eve **1/2** ***El Pecado de Adan y Eva*** **1967 (R)** The story of Adam and Eve in the Garden of Eden and their fall from grace. Voice-over narrator is only sound in this strange dialogue-less story of the Adam and Eve, how they got kicked out of the Garden of Eden, and how they lose and then find each other outside. Ancient plot, to say the least. **72m/C VHS.** Candy Wilson, Jorge (George) Rivero; ***D:*** Michael Zachary.

The Sin of Harold Diddlebock **1/2** ***Mad Wednesday*** **1947** A man gets fired from his job, stumbles around drunk, and wins a fortune gambling. He then buys a circus and uses a lion to frighten investors into backing him. Inventive comedy, but missing the spark and timing of "The Freshman" (1925), of which it is a sequel. The final feature film for Lloyd (who did all his own stunts), made at the urging of director Sturges. **89m/B VHS, DVD.** Harold Lloyd, Margaret Hamilton, Frances Ramsden, Edgar Kennedy, Lionel Stander, Rudy Vallee, Franklin Pangborn; ***D:*** Preston Sturges.

The Sin of Madelon Claudet ***The Lullaby*** **1931** Hayes plays common thief who works her way into upper crust of Parisian society only to tumble back into the street, all in the name of making a better life for her illegitimate son. Very sudsy stuff, with an outstanding performance by Hayes. **74m/B VHS.** Helen Hayes, Lewis Stone, Neil Hamilton, Robert Young, Cliff Edwards, Jean Hersholt, Marie Prevost, Karen Morley, Charles Winninger, Alan Hale; ***D:*** Edgar Selwyn. Oscars '32: Actress (Hayes).

Sin Takes a Holiday **1/2 1930** A woman marries her boss to save him from his girl friend. On a trip to Paris, she is wooed by a refined European gentleman, but finds that she really does love her husband. By today's standards, it doesn't sound like much, but in the '30s, it was pretty sophisticated stuff. **81m/B VHS, DVD.** Constance Bennett, Kenneth MacKenna, Basil Rathbone, Rita La Roy, Zasu Pitts, Fred Walton, Richard Carle, Helen Johnson; ***D:*** Paul Stein.

Sin You Sinners **1963** Aging stripper gets ahold of an amulet that allows her to look youthful and manipulate the lives of others. When she loses the amulet, however, bad things happen. Twisted ending. **73m/B VHS, DVD.** June Colbourne, Dian Lloyd, Derek Murcott, Beverly Nazarow, Charles Clements; ***D:*** Anthony Farrar.

Sinai Commandos **1/2** ***Sinai Commandos: The Story of the Six Day War; Ha'Matarah Tiran*** **1968** The story of a group of commandos in the Israeli Six-Day War in 1967 who are assigned to destroy important Arab radar installations. Includes actual combat footage. **99m/C VHS.** Robert Fuller; ***D:*** Raphael Nussbaum.

Sinatra **1/2 1992** TV biopic chronicles the stormy life of crooner Frank Sinatra. Begins with his childhood in Hoboken, New Jersey and works its way through his big band tours, bobby soxer days, career skids, and triumphant comeback with his Oscar-winning performance in "From Here to Eternity," as well as his three marriages, "Rat Pack" friends, and mob connections. Executive Producer Tina Sinatra, Frank's daughter, doesn't gloss over her father's less savory character points and Casnoff does well with his leading role. Songs are lip-synched to classic Sinatra tunes with a few early recordings redone by actor Tom Burlinson and Frank Sinatra Jr. **245m/C VHS.** Philip Casnoff, Olympia Dukakis, Joe Santos, Gina Gershon, Nina Siemaszko, Marcia Gay Harden, Rod Steiger, Bob Gunton, David Raynr, James F. Kelly, Matthew Posey, Jay Robinson, Robin Gammell, Todd Waring, Joris Stuyck, Danny Gans, Jeff Corey; ***D:*** James Sadwith; ***W:*** William Mastrosimone; ***C:*** Reynaldo Villalobos. **TV**

Sinbad **1971** A sardonic portrait of an aging hedonist as he tries to hold onto the pleasures of drink, sex and gluttony. In Magyar (Hungarian), with English subtitles. **98m/C VHS.** *HU* Zoltan Latonovits, Eva Ruttkai, Eva Leelossy, Marjit Dajka; ***D:*** Zoltan Huszarik; ***W:*** Zoltan Huszarik; ***C:*** Sandor Sara; ***M:*** Zoltan Jeney.

Sinbad and the Eye of the Tiger **1977 (G)** The swashbuckling adventures of Sinbad the Sailor as he encounters the creations of Ray Harryhausen's special effects magic. Don't see this one for the plot, which almost doesn't exist. Otherwise, mildly fun. **113m/C VHS, DVD.** *GB* Patrick Wayne, Jane Seymour, Taryn Power, Margaret Whiting; ***D:*** Sam Wanamaker; ***W:*** Beverley Cross; ***C:*** Ted Moore; ***M:*** Roy Budd.

Sinbad: Legend of the Seven Seas **2003 (PG)** Loose retelling of the "Arabian Nights" tale (so loose that it incorporates Greek and Roman legends and gods) from DreamWorks studio that's a combo of computer generated and hand-drawn animation. Sinbad the sailor/thief (voiced by Pitt) gets in trouble when Eris (Pfeiffer), the goddess of chaos, steals the Book of Peace and frames Sinbad for the crime. His best friend, Proteus (Fiennes) believes in Sinbad's innocence and stakes his life on Sinbad's return with the book. Proteus's fiancee Marina (Zeta-Jones) stows away to make sure Sinbad keeps his promises and to provide him with a foil. Jumbled story and inconsistent animation lead to ho-hum outing that the kids may enjoy, if they've tired of "Finding Nemo" after the umpteenth viewing. **86m/C VHS, DVD.** *US* ***D:*** Tim Johnson, Patrick Gilmore; ***W:*** John Logan; ***M:*** Harry Gregson-Williams; ***V:*** Brad Pitt, Catherine Zeta-Jones, Michelle Pfeiffer, Joseph Fiennes, Dennis Haysbert, Timothy West, Adriano Giannini.

Sinbad of the Seven Seas **1/2 1989** Italian muscle epic based on the ancient legends. Ferrigno isn't green, but he's still a hulk, and he still can't act. It's poorly dubbed, which makes little difference; it would be stupid regardless. **90m/C VHS, DVD.** *IT* Lou Ferrigno, John Steiner, Leo Gullotta, Teagan Clive; ***D:*** Enzo G. Castellari.

Sinbad, the Sailor **1947** Fairbanks fits well in his luminent father's swashbuckling shoes, as he searches for the treasure of Alexander the Great. Self-mocking but hamhanded, and confusing if you seek the hidden plot. Still, it's all in fun, and it is fun. **117m/C VHS.** Douglas Fairbanks Jr., Maureen O'Hara, Anthony Quinn, Walter Slezak, George Tobias, Jane Greer, Mike Mazurki, Sheldon Leonard; ***D:*** Richard Wallace; ***C:*** George Barnes.

Since Otar Left... ***Depuis Qu'Otar est Parti*** **2003** Bittersweet female-centric drama set in a rundown flat in Tblisi, in the former Soviet Republic of Georgia. Domineering matriarch Eka (90-year-old Gorintin) dotes on her son who works illegally in Paris. Meanwhile, her middle-aged daughter Marina (Khomassouridze) resents her mother's obvious preference, and her own daughter, Ada (Droukarova), tries to keep the peace between the two women. When Marina and Ada learn that Otar has been killed, they conspire to keep the truth from Eka through an elaborate ruse with unexpected consequences. Russian, Georgian and French with subtitles. **102m/C VHS, DVD.** *FR* Esther Gorintin, Nino Khomassouridze, Dinara Droukarova, Temour Kalandadze, Roussoudan Bolkvadze, Sacha Sarichvili, Douta Skhirtladze; ***D:*** Jule Bertucelli; ***W:*** Jule Bertucelli, Roger Bohbot, Bernard Renucci; ***C:*** Christophe Pollock.

Since You Went Away **1/2 1944** An American family copes with the tragedy, heartache and shortages of wartime in classic mega-tribute to the home front. Be warned: very long and bring your hankies. Colbert is superb, as is the photography. John Derek unobtrusively made his film debut, as an extra. **172m/B VHS, DVD.** Claudette Colbert, Jennifer Jones, Shirley Temple, Joseph Cotten, Agnes Moorehead, Monty Woolley, Guy Madison, Lionel Barrymore, Robert Walker, Hattie McDaniel, Keenan Wynn, Craig Stevens, Albert Bassermann, Alla Nazimova, Lloyd Corrigan, Terry Moore, Florence Bates, Ruth Roman, Andrew V. McLaglen, Dorothy Dandridge, Rhonda Fleming, Addison Richards, Jackie Moran; ***D:*** John Cromwell; ***W:*** David O. Selznick; ***C:*** Stanley Cortez, Lee Garmes; ***M:*** Max Steiner. Oscars '44: Orig. Dramatic Score.

Since You've Been Gone *Dogwater* **1997 (R)** The Clear View High School class of 1987 has their ten-year reunion and rivalries and romance are rediscovered. Grace (Boyle) has a penchant for nasty practical jokes she's never gotten over while Marie (Hatcher) is a self-important would-be exec who insults her one-time classmates and Rob (Schwimmer) is the still-loathed class president. **95m/C VHS, DVD.** David Schwimmer, Lara Flynn Boyle, Teri Hatcher, Joey Slotnick, Tom (Thomas E.) Hodges, Philip Rayburn Smith, Heidi Stillman, David Catlin, Laura Eason; ***Cameos:*** Marisa Tomei, Jon Stewart, Liev Schreiber, Molly Ringwald, Jennifer Grey; ***D:*** David Schwimmer.

Sincerely Charlotte *Signe Charlotte* **1986** Huppert directs her sister in this film about a beautiful singer framed for her boyfriend's murder. She enlists an old lover to help her flee across the countryside. Love story/thriller is pleasingly odd and absorbing. In French with English subtitles. **92m/C VHS.** *FR* Isabelle Huppert, Niels Arestrup, Christine Pascal; ***D:*** Caroline Huppert; ***C:*** Bruno de Keyzer.

Sincerely Yours WOOF! 1956 Liberace wisely stayed away from acting after inauspiciously debuting in this horrible, maudlin remake of "The Man Who Played God." He plays a pianist who loses his hearing and decides to become a philanthropist to help those less fortunate than himself. Laughably cheesy. Thirty-one musical numbers, including Liberace's inimitable arrangement of "Chopsticks." **116m/C VHS.** Liberace, Joanne Dru, Dorothy Malone, William Demarest; ***D:*** Gordon Douglas; ***W:*** Irving Wallace.

Sinful Intrigue 1995 (R) Handyman is main suspect in a series of attacks on women living in a wealthy neighborhood. **88m/C VHS, DVD.** Bobby Johnston, Beckie Mullen, Mark Zuelzke, Griffin (Griffen) Drew; ***D:*** Edward Holzman; ***W:*** John Nelson; ***C:*** Harris Done; ***M:*** Patrick John Scott.

A Sinful Life **1989 (R)** A strained, offbeat, B-grade comedy about an odd, infantile mother fighting to keep her unusual child from being taken away. Definitely not a must-see; can be irritating and obnoxious, depending on viewer and mood. Morris is at her oddball comedic best as the mother and former show dancer. Adult Tefkin plays her little girl. Based on the play "Just Like the Pom Pom Girls." **112m/C VHS.** Anita Morris, Rick Overton, Dennis Christopher, Blair Tefkin, Mark Rolston, Cynthia Szigeti; ***D:*** William Schreiner.

Sing ½ **1989 (PG-13)** The students in the real-life Brooklyn public school "Sing" program endure the trials of adolescence while putting together a musical revue. Hurtles over the edge into cheesiness from the start, with way too much (cheesy) music. From the creator of "Fame" and "Footloose." **111m/C VHS.** Lorraine Bracco, Peter Dobson, Jessica Steen, Louise Lasser, George DiCenzo, Patti LaBelle; ***D:*** Richard Baskin; ***M:*** Jay Gruska.

Sing and Like It **1934** Goofy farce involving a tone-deaf songbird and a love-struck mobster boss. Annie Snodgrass (Pitts) has a voice that could make dogs howl, but moony-eyed gangster Fenny (Pendleton) hears it differently. He's going to make her a star, even threatening a top music critic at gunpoint to give her a glowing review. **72m/B VHS.** Zasu Pitts, Pert Kelton, Edward Everett Horton, Nat Pendleton, Ned Sparks; ***D:*** William A. Seiter; ***W:*** Marion Dix, Laird Doyle.

Sing, Cowboy, Sing **1937** Decent adventure story about a wagon train heading west that runs into a band of outlaws doing outlaw stuff and must somehow get through. **60m/B VHS, DVD.** Tex Ritter, Louise Stanley, Al "Fuzzy" St. John, Charles "Blackie" King, Karl Hackett, Horace Murphy; ***D:*** Robert North Bradbury; ***W:*** Robert Emmett Tansey; ***C:*** Gus Peterson.

Sing Me a Love Song **1937** Jerry Haines (Melton) takes a job working incognito at his late father's department store to see how things are being run. Music-counter clerk Jean (Ellis) falls for Jerry, especially when he helps her out by crooning the hit parade to her customers. But Jerry keeps getting into trouble (must be all that singing) and also discovers some of the store's executives are up to no good. **75m/B VHS.** Patricia Ellis, Hugh Herbert, Zasu Pitts, Allen Jenkins, Nat Pendleton, Walter Catlett, James Melton; ***D:*** Ray Enright; ***W:*** Sid Herzig, Jerry Wald; ***C:*** Arthur L. Todd.

Sing Sing Nights ½ *Reprieved* **1935** A world-famous journalist is killed with three bullets. Three men have confessed, but only one could have actually done it. A professor sets out to solve the case. **60m/B VHS.** Conway Tearle, Mary Doran, Hardie Albright, Patricia "Boots" Mallory, Ferdinand Gottschalk, Berton Churchill, Jameson Thomas; ***D:*** Lewis D. Collins.

Sing Your Worries Away **1942** Songwriter Ebsen inherits $3 million and finds the money causes him nothing but trouble. Band of crooks cause the requisite wacky complications. Fun, harmless musical comedy. ♫ It Just Happened to Happen; Sally, My Dear Sally; Sing Your Worries Away; Cindy Lou McWilliams; How Do You Fall in Love. **71m/B VHS.** Buddy Ebsen, Bert Lahr, June Havoc, Patsy Kelly, Margaret Dumont; ***D:*** Edward Sutherland.

Singapore ½ **1947** Rather boring romantic drama finds pearl smuggler Matt Gordon (MacMurray) returning to Singapore to resume his illegal trade at the end of WWII. He spots Linda (Gardner), the love of his life, but discovers she's suffering from amnesia and has married another man. Gangsters want Matt's hidden supply of pearls and kidnap Linda to get his cooperation. Remade with equal dullness in 1956 as "Istanbul." **80m/B VHS.** Fred MacMurray, Ava Gardner, Roland Culver, Richard Haydn, Thomas Gomez, Spring Byington, Porter Hall; ***D:*** John Brahm; ***W:*** Seton I. Miller, Robert Thoeren; ***C:*** Maury Gertsman; ***M:*** Daniele Amfitheatrof.

Singin' in the Rain **1952** One of the all-time great movie musicals—an affectionate spoof of the turmoil that afflicted the motion picture industry in the late 1920s during the changeover from silent films to sound. Don Lockwood (Kelly) and Lina Lamont (Hagen) are a popular romantic silent screen team when sound comes along. To continue, temperamental Lina must have her terrible voice dubbed by aspiring actress Kathy Selden (Reynolds), whom Don falls for. O'Connor's an acrobatic marvel as Don's best pal, Cosmo Brown, and of course there's Kelly's classic much-copied title dance. Later a Broadway musical. ♫ All I Do is Dream of You; Should I?; Singin' in the Rain; Wedding of the Painted Doll; Broadway Melody; Would You; I've Got a Feelin' You're Foolin'; You Are My Lucky Star; Broadway Rhythm. **103m/C VHS, DVD.** Gene Kelly, Donald O'Connor, Jean Hagen, Debbie Reynolds, Rita Moreno, King Donovan, Millard Mitchell, Cyd Charisse, Douglas Fowley, Madge Blake, Joi Lansing; ***D:*** Gene Kelly, Stanley Donen; ***W:*** Adolph Green, Betty Comden; ***C:*** Harold Rosson; ***M:*** Nacio Herb Brown, Lennie Hayton. AFI '98: Top 100; Golden Globes '53: Actor—Mus./Comedy (O'Connor), Natl. Film Reg. '89.

The Singing Blacksmith ½ **1938** A relic of American Yiddish cinema, adapting popular 1909 play by David Pinski. A married blacksmith is wooed by another woman and falls victim to alcoholism. Overlong, but Oysher and his rich baritone voice still shine. In Yiddish with English subtitles. **95m/B VHS.** *PL* Miriam Riselle, Florence Weiss, Moishe Oysher; ***D:*** Edgar G. Ulmer.

Singing Buckaroo **1937** Dastardly bandits try to pilfer money from pretty blonde damsel and have to battle with yodelin' cowboy. B-level western good guy Scott belts out a few numbers and saves the day. Innocuously pleasant. **58m/B VHS.** Fred Scott, Victoria Vinton, Cliff Nazarro; ***D:*** Tom Gibson.

The Singing Cowgirl **1939** Band of outlaws murder a ranch owner to get to a gold mine. Heroine Page rides in to save the day but gets shot down by western stereotypes. **60m/B VHS, DVD.** Dorothy Page, Dave O'Brien, Vince Barnett, Stanley Price; ***D:*** Samuel Diege; ***W:*** Arthur Hoerl.

The Singing Detective **1986** A musical/mystery/fantasy British miniseries, based on the work by Dennis Potter. Pulp fiction writer Phillip Marlowe (Gambon) is confined to his hospital bed, unable to move due to extreme psoriasis. In his lucid moments he tries to figure out the cause of his condition, but in his elaborate daydreams he's a detective (and big band singer) who's working to solve a series of murders. Six episodes: "Skin," "Heat," "Lovely Days," "Clues," "Pitter Patter," and "Who Done It." **420m/C VHS, DVD.** *GB* Michael Gambon, Patrick Malahide, Janet Suzman, Joanne Whalley; ***D:*** Jon Amiel. **TV**

The Singing Detective ½ **2003 (R)** Dan Dark (Downey) is a pulp crime novelist who suffers from a painful debilitating disease that leaves him confined to a hospital bed. As Dark drifts in and out of reality, his imagination fuses episodes from his novels with memories of his childhood. In his fantasies, Dark imagines himself as a detective of a '50s film noir. Real personas in his life begin to play characters in his fantasy and his delusions begin to bleed into his real life. Adding to the surreality is the slew of '50s pop songs that the characters sing at the slightest provocation. Visually stunning, and a bit convoluted. Downey delivers a solid performance, as do the supporting cast, including an almost unrecognizable Mel Gibson. Based on the BBC mini-series of the same name. **109m/C VHS, DVD.** *US* Robert Downey Jr., Robin Wright Penn, Mel Gibson, Jeremy Northam, Katie Holmes, Adrien Brody, Jon Polito, Carla Gugino, Saul Rubinek, Alfre Woodard; ***D:*** Keith Gordon; ***W:*** Dennis Potter; ***C:*** Tom Richmond.

The Singing Fool ½ **1928** Al Stone (Jolson) becomes a sensation as a singing waiter/songwriter turned Broadway star until his ambitious wife Molly (Dunn) gets bored, walks out, and takes their son with her to Paris. Al then goes on the skids until cigarette girl Grace (Bronson) gets him back on the right track. However, Molly's return also brings tragic news. **105m/B DVD.** Al Jolson, Betty Bronson, Josephine Dunn, Reed Howes, Arthur Housman, Davey Lee, Edward Martindel; ***D:*** Lloyd Bacon; ***W:*** C. Graham Baker, Joseph Jackson; ***C:*** Byron Haskin.

The Singing Kid ½ **1936** Predictable and rather dull Jolson effort finds musical and radio star Al Jackson losing his voice and fortune. But he recovers both thanks to a Maine rest cure, finding landlady Ruth (Roberts) a romantic tonic. (Although it's charming young Sybil Jason as Ruth's niece who steals every scene.) Then Al returns to Broadway to get back on top. **85m/B DVD.** Al Jolson, Beverly Roberts, Sybil Jason, Edward Everett Horton, Allen Jenkins, Lyle Talbot, William B. Davidson, Claire Dodd; ***D:*** William Keighley; ***W:*** Warren Duff, Pat C. Flick; ***C:*** George Barnes.

The Singing Nun **1966** The true story of a Belgian nun who takes a liking to a motherless little boy. She writes a song for him, and a kind-hearted priest talks to a record producer to see about getting the song to go somewhere. The song soon becomes an international hit, and the nun ends up on the "Ed Sullivan Show." Sentimental and sugary sweet, but a big boxoffice hit. **98m/C VHS.** Debbie Reynolds, Ricardo Montalban, Greer Garson, Agnes Moorehead, Chad Everett, Katharine Ross, Juanita Moore, Ricky Cordell, Michael Pate, Tom Drake; ***D:*** Henry Koster; ***C:*** Milton Krasner.

The Singing Princess ½ *La Rosa di Bagdad; The Rose of Baghdad* **1949 (G)** Arabian Nights inspired animated tale features a pretty princess, a poor-but-honest hero, an evil sultan and a slave of the lamp. Julie Andrews made her film debut in the English released version as the voice of Princess Zeila. **76m/C DVD.** *IT* Howard Marion-Crawford, Julie Andrews; ***D:*** Anton Gino Domenighini; ***W:*** Nina Maguire, Tony Maguire.

Singing the Blues in Red **1987** Dark, pessimistic character study of a protest singer/songwriter who leaves his native East Germany to escape repression and finds his loyalties divided. A moving personal story, as well as insightful, subtle social commentary. In English and German with subtitles. **110m/C VHS.** *GE* Gerulf Pannach, Fabienne Babe, Cristine Rose, Trevor Griffiths; ***D:*** Ken Loach; ***W:*** Trevor Griffiths; ***C:*** Chris Menges.

Single Bars, Single Women ½ **1984** Utterly formulaic made for TV comedy-drama based on Dolly Parton's song is not entirely without merit. Lonely people gather in a local pickup joint and share their miseries and hopes. **96m/C VHS.** Shelley Hack, Christine Lahti, Tony Danza, Mare Winningham, Keith Gordon, Paul Michael Glaser; ***D:*** Harry Winer; ***M:*** Basil Poledouris. **TV**

A Single Girl ½ *La Fille Seule* **1996** Follows, in real time, a young woman as she tells her boyfriend that she's pregnant, (Ledoyen) through her job handling room service at a Paris hotel, then again with her boyfriend after work. French with subtitles. Part sexual hotel fantasy, part observation of an ordinary couple going about daily life. **90m/C VHS, DVD.** *FR* Virginie Ledoyen, Benoit Magimel, Vera Briole, Dominique Valadie; ***D:*** Benoit Jacquot; ***W:*** Benoit Jacquot, Jerome Beaujour; ***C:*** Caroline Champetier; ***M:*** Kvarteto Mesta Prahi.

Single Handed Sanders ½ **1932** Blacksmith Matt Sanders (Tyler) discovers his conniving lawyer brother Phillip (Seiter) is part of an unscrupulous scheme by corrupt state senator Graham (Elliott) that threatens the local homesteaders. **61m/B DVD.** Tom Tyler, John Elliott, Fred "Snowflake" Toones, Gordon De Main, Robert Seiter, Margaret Morris; ***D:*** Lloyd Nosler; ***W:*** Charles A. Post; ***C:*** Archie Stout.

A Single Man **2009 (R)** Former fashion designer Tom Ford's directorial debut is based on a 1964 novel by Christopher Isherwood that's set in L.A. in 1962 over a single day. Middle-aged Brit ex-pat college professor George (Firth) is still devastated months later by the car crash death of his longtime lover Jim (Goode) and, because of the times and his own stiff-upper-lip, George is isolated and can't acknowledge his sexuality, let alone his sorrow. Now George is planning to commit suicide. He follows his usual routine while putting his affairs in order and spends his intended last evening with longtime friend, sophisticated, brittle alcoholic Charley (Moore). Ford offers a sunlit California setting that George can only see as unimaginably bleak while Firth gives a stunningly quiet performance of a man overwhelmed by inexpressible grief. **99m/C DVD.** *US* Colin Firth, Julianne Moore, Nicholas Hoult, Matthew Goode, Jon Kortajarena, Lee Pace, Paulette Lamori, Ryan Simpkins, Ginnifer Goodwin, Paul Butler, Aaron Sanders; ***D:*** Tom Ford; ***W:*** Tom Ford, David Scearce; ***C:*** Eduard Grau; ***M:*** Abel Korzeniowski; ***V:*** Jon Hamm. British Acad. '09: Actor (Firth).

Single Room Furnished ½ **1968** The fall of a buxom blonde from uncorrupted innocence through pregnancies to desperate prostitution. Fails to demonstrate any range of talent in Mansfield, who died before it was completed. Exploitative and pathetic. **93m/C VHS, DVD.** Jayne Mansfield, Dorothy Keller; ***D:*** Matt Cimber, Matteo Ottaviano.

The Single Standard **1929** San Francisco deb Garbo flings with artsy Asther and finds out the Hayes Code is just around the corner. **93m/B VHS.** Greta Garbo, Nils Asther, Johnny Mack Brown, Dorothy Sebastian, Lane Chandler, Zeffie Tilbury; ***D:*** John S. Robertson.

Single White Female ½ **1992 (R)** Psycho thriller casts Fonda as chic Manhattan computer consultant Allison Jones, who advertises for a roommate after a falling out with her boyfriend. Leigh is the frumpy, shy, bookstore clerk Hedra who answers the ad and moves into Allie's great Upper West Side apartment. They hit it off, that is until Allie notices Hedra's beginning to look and sound very familiar. Hmm... Derivative, though bonus points for creative murder implements and interesting performances throughout, including Friedman as Allie's gay upstairs neighbor. Based on the novel "SWF Seeks Same" by John Lutz. **107m/C VHS, DVD.** Jessica Lundy, Bridget Fonda, Jennifer Jason Leigh, Steven Weber, Peter Friedman, Stephen Tobolowsky, Frances Bay, Renee Estevez, Kenneth Tobey; ***D:*** Barbet Schroeder; ***W:*** Don Roos; ***C:*** Luciano Tovoli; ***M:*** Howard Shore. MTV Movie Awards '93: Villain (Leigh).

Single White Female 2: The Psycho WOOF! 2005 (R) So in the first movie she wasn't a psycho? Down-on-her-luck young woman moves into an apartment and soon discovers her new roomie has become fixated on her, later turning killer. Inept rehash of the original with all the thrills (and acting ability) removed. And still it took three writers to come up with this dreck. **93m/C DVD.** Kristen Miller, Allison Lange, Brooke Burns, Todd Babcock, Francois Groday, Rif Hutton; ***D:*** Keith Samples; ***W:*** Andy Hurst, Ross Helford, Glenn Hobart; ***C:*** Thomas M. Harting; ***M:*** Steven Stern. **VIDEO**

Singles 1992 (PG-13) Seattle's music scene is the background for this light-hearted look at single 20-somethings in the '90s. Hits dead on thanks to Crowe's tight script and a talented cast, and speaks straight to its intended audience—the "Generation X" crowd. Real life band Pearl Jam plays alternative band Citizen Dick and sets the tone for a great soundtrack featuring the hot Seattle sounds of Alice in Chains, Soundgarden, and Mudhoney. The video contains six extra minutes of footage after the credits that was thankfully edited out of the final cut. Look for Horton, Stoltz (as a mime), Skerritt, and Burton in cameos. **100m/C VHS, DVD.** Matt Dillon, Bridget Fonda, Campbell Scott, Kyra Sedgwick, Sheila Kelley, Jim True-Frost, Bill Pullman, James LeGros, Ally Walker, Devon Raymond, Camillo Gallardo, Jeremy Piven; ***Cameos:*** Peter Horton, Eric Stoltz, Tim Burton, Tom Skerritt; ***D:*** Cameron Crowe; ***W:*** Cameron Crowe; ***C:*** Ueli Steiger; ***M:*** Paul Westerberg.

Singleton's Pluck *Laughterhouse* **1984** Touching British comedy about a determined farmer who must walk his 500 geese 100 miles to market because of a strike. He becomes a celebrity when the TV stations start covering his odyssey. **89m/C VHS.** *GB* Ian Holm, Penelope Wilton, Bill Owen, Richard Hope; ***D:*** Richard Eyre.

The Sinister Invasion *Alien Terror; The Incredible Invasion; Invasion Siniestra* **1968** A turn-of-the-century scientist (Karloff) discovers a death ray. Aliens, who would like a closer peek at what makes it work, use a sex-fiend's body to do so. One of Karloff's last four films, made simultaneously in Mexico. The great horror master's final offering. Excruciating. **95m/C VHS.** *MX* Boris Karloff, Enrique Guzman, Jack Hill, Yerye Beirut, Maura Monti, Tere Valdez; ***D:*** Juan Ibanez, Jack Hill; ***W:*** Luis Enrique Vergara, Karl Schanzer; ***C:*** Raul Dominguez, Austin McKinney.

The Sinister Urge WOOF! *The Young and the Immortal; Hellborn* **1960** Vice cops Duncan and Moore search for the murderer of three women. Seems the disturbed slayer is unbalanced because he's been looking at pictures of naked ladies. Was this meant to be taken seriously at the time? The last film by camp director Wood, maker of the infamous "Plan 9 from Outer Space." A must see for Wood fans. **82m/B VHS.** Kenne Duncan, Duke Moore, Jean Fontaine, Carl Anthony, Harvey B. Dunn, Dino Fantini, Reed Howes, Conrad Brooks; ***D:*** Edward D. Wood Jr.; ***W:*** Edward D. Wood Jr.; ***C:*** William C. Thompson.

Sink or Swim 1/2 *Hacks* **1997 (R)** TV writer/producer Brian (a suitably hangdog Rea) is suffering from creative burnout and depression. His agent, Danny (Arnold), has just landed Brian a new job writing a TV series that he's dreading. His weekly poker buddies (and fellow writers) offer possible scenarios, amidst their backstabbing, but Brian may have reignited his creative spark after witnessing a romantic encounter between two silhouetted figures in a hotel window. He thinks the woman may be Georgia (Douglas), whom he meets in a bar, and Brian wants her story—at practically any price. **93m/C VHS, DVD.** Stephen Rea, Illeana Douglas, Tom Arnold, John Ritter, Dave Foley, Richard Kind, Ryan O'Neal, Ricky Jay, Jason Priestley, Olivia D'Abo, Bob Odenkirk; ***D:*** Gary Rosen; ***W:*** Gary Rosen; ***C:*** Ralf Bode; ***M:*** Anthony Marinelli.

Sink the Bismarck 1960 British navy sets out to locate and sink infamous German battleship during WWII. Good special effects with battle sequences in this drama based on real incidents. One of the better of the plethora of WWII movies, with stirring naval battles and stylish documentary-style direction. **97m/B VHS, DVD.** *GB* Kenneth More, Dana Wynter, Karel Stepanek, Carl Mohner, Laurence Naismith, Geoffrey Keen, Michael Hordern, Maurice Denham, Esmond Knight, Michael Goodliffe, Jack Watling, Jack (Gwyllam) Gwillim, Mark Dignam, Ernest Clark, John Horsley, Sydney Tafler, John Stuart, Walter Hudd, Sean Barrett, Peter Burton, Edward R. Murrow; ***D:*** Lewis Gilbert; ***W:*** Edmund H. North; ***C:*** Christopher Challis; ***M:*** Clifton Parker.

Sinner 2007 Father Romano's faith has been tested by all the scandals in the church and his own parish is teetering on the edge of bankruptcy. Hooker/grifter Lil arrives at the church with the idea of seducing and blackmailing the priest—a con that has worked before. Instead, Father Romano offers cynical Lil sanctuary and a chance to redeem herself while his own belief is rekindled. Good performances by the leads in a strong story. **88m/C DVD.** Georgina Cates, Nicholas Chinlund, Michael E. Rodgers, Brad Dourif; ***D:*** Marc Benardout; ***W:*** Steven Sills; ***C:*** David Kerr; ***M:*** Pinar Toprak.

Sinners 1989 Outrageous portrait of an Italian family in the Big Apple trying to come to terms with the violence that surrounds their neighborhood. **90m/C VHS, DVD.** Joey Travolta, Robert Gallo, Joe Palese, Lou Calvelli, Angie Daglas, Sabrina Ferrand; ***D:*** Charles Kanganis.

Sinner's Blood WOOF! 1970 (R) Bikers terrorize and torture a small town. **81m/C VHS.** Stephen Jacques, Crusty Beal, Nancy Sheldon, Parker Herriott, Julie Connors; ***D:*** Neil Douglas.

Sinners in Paradise 1938 An assortment of trouble-plagued characters alternately hide and face up to their mysterious pasts when their plane crashes on a deserted island. Interesting "crucible" premise runs out of steam, but plucky, resourceful cast and competent direction keep it going. **64m/B VHS, DVD.** Madge Evans, John Boles, Bruce Cabot, Marion Martin, Gene Lockhart, Dwight Frye, Charlotte Wynters, Nana Bryant, Milburn Stone, Donald (Don "Red") Barry, Morgan Conway; ***D:*** James Whale.

Sinners in the Sun 1/2 1932 Proverbial love dilemma finds Carole Lombard as a New York fashion model caught between two loves, one a rich philanderer and the other a poor garage mechanic who truly has her heart. Film was nothing spectacular but interesting to see Grant in his 'diamond in the rough' days. **70m/B VHS.** Carole Lombard, Cary Grant, Chester Morris, Adrienne Ames; ***D:*** Alexander Hall; ***W:*** Samuel Hoffenstein, Vincent Lawrence, Waldemar Young. **VIDEO**

Sins 1985 On her way up the ladder of success in the fashion industry, Helene has stepped on a few toes. Those rivals and her ever-increasing acquisition of power and money make this film an exciting drama. **336m/C VHS.** Joan Collins, Timothy Dalton, Catherine Mary Stewart, Gene Kelly, James Farentino; ***D:*** Douglas Hickox.

Sins of Desire 1992 Highly erotic thriller with Roberts going undercover as a nurse in a sex therapy clinic. It seems her sister was a former patient at the clinic and has since died a mysterious death. Linking up with private eye Cassavetes, Roberts sets out to investigate the doctors who treated her sister, searching for clues to her untimely death. **90m/C VHS.** Tanya Roberts, Jay Richardson, Delia Sheppard, Nick Cassavetes, Jan-Michael Vincent; ***D:*** Jim Wynorski; ***W:*** Mark Thomas McGee, Peter Paul Liapis.

The Sins of Dorian Gray 1982 (PG) A modernized adaptation of "The Portrait of Dorian Grey" by Oscar Wilde, with Dorian as a beautiful woman who remains young for 30 years, while a video screen test ages, like the original character's mirror image. Might have been intriguing and stylish; instead, only disappointing and incompetent. **95m/C VHS.** Belinda Bauer, Joseph Bottoms, Anthony Perkins; ***D:*** Tony Maylam. **TV**

Sins of Jezebel 1954 Biblical epic about Jezebel, who worships an evil god. She marries the king of Israel and brings the kingdom nothing but trouble. **74m/C VHS, DVD.** Paulette Goddard, George Nader, John Hoyt, Eduard Franz, John Shelton, Margia Dean, Joe Besser, Ludwig Donath; ***D:*** Reginald LeBorg; ***W:*** Richard H. Landau; ***C:*** Gilbert Warrenton; ***M:*** Bert Shefter.

The Sins of Rachel Cade 1961 Rachel Cade (Dickinson) is a missionary nurse working in the Belgian Congo at the start of World War II. She manages to win the trust of the local tribe and is smitten when injured RAF volunteer, Dr. Paul Winton (Moore), literally lands at her feet. Rachel succumbs to Paul's blandishments and discovers she's pregnant after he returns home. Belgian administrator Henri Derode (Finch), who is in love with Rachel, informs Paul and he returns but wants Rachel to lie about their previous relationship. She rejects him and realizes she'd chosen the wrong man all along. **122m/C DVD.** Angie Dickinson, Peter Finch, Roger Moore, Juano Hernandez, Woody Strode, Scatman Crothers, Frederick O'Neal, Mary Wickes, Errol John; ***D:*** Gordon Douglas; ***W:*** Edward Anhalt; ***C:*** J. Peverell Marley; ***M:*** Max Steiner.

Sins of Rome 1954 Spartacus risks it all in a bold attempt to free his fellow slaves. Not nearly the equal of Kirk Douglas's "Spartacus," but much better than later Italian adventure epics. **75m/B VHS, DVD.** *IT* Ludmilla Tcherina, Massimo Girotti, Gianna Maria Canale, Yves Vincent; ***D:*** Riccardo Freda.

Sins of the Father 2001 Thomas Frank Cherry (Sizemore) is a middle-aged Texan who comes to believe that his father, Bobby Frank Cherry (Jenkins), was one of four KKK members who bombed the Sixteenth Street Baptist Church in Birmingham, Alabama, in 1963. Four young black girls were killed in the explosion and the investigation dragged on and off for 38 years. When the investigation is revived once again, Tom decides to give testimony before a grand jury that casts down on his father's original alibi. Cherry was convicted of murder in 2002. **93m/C VHS, DVD.** Tom Sizemore, Ving Rhames, Richard Jenkins, Colm Feore; ***D:*** Robert Dornhelm; ***W:*** John Pielmeier; ***C:*** Derick Underschultz; ***M:*** Harald Kloser. **CABLE**

Sins of the Mind 1997 (R) Michelle (Crider), the 25-year-old daughter of Eve (Clayburgh) and William (Farrell) Widener, awakens from a coma after a car accident and turns out to have psychological damage. Previously a conservative, hard-working artist, she's now a hedonist, given to erratic impulses and sexual compulsions. Michelle's actions threaten her family but her father is convinced he can still get his little girl back. **92m/C VHS.** Missy (Melissa) Crider, Mike Farrell, Jill Clayburgh, Louise Fletcher, Michael Mantell, Robert Pine, Cyia Batten, Grayson McCouch; ***D:*** James Frawley. **CABLE**

Sins of the Night 1993 (R) An ex-con insurance investigator is hired to find a sultry exotic dancer. Also available in an unrated version. **82m/C VHS.** Miles O'Keeffe, Richard Roundtree, Matt Roe, Nick Cassavetes, Deborah Shelton; ***D:*** Gregory Dark; ***W:*** Russell Lavalle; ***C:*** Glenn Kershaw; ***M:*** Ashley Irwin.

Sinthia: The Devil's Doll 1970 A little girl is thought to be possessed by a demon after she has horrible dreams about killing her father. **78m/C VHS, DVD.** Shula Roan, Diane Webber; ***D:*** Ray Dennis Steckler.

Sioux City 1/2 1994 (PG-13) Jesse Rainfeather Goldman (Phillips) is a Lakota Sioux adopted away from the reservation of his birth and raised in Beverly Hills by a Jewish family. Jesse's curious when his birth mother suddenly contacts him, but when he arrives at the Sioux City reservation, he discovers she's suddenly died under mysterious circumstances. So Jesse sticks around to find out what's going on and discovers his heritage along the way. Well-meaning but dull. **102m/C VHS, DVD.** Lou Diamond Phillips, Salli Richardson, Melinda Dillon, Ralph Waite, Adam Roarke, Bill Allen, Gary Farmer; ***D:*** Lou Diamond Phillips; ***W:*** L. Virginia Browne; ***M:*** Christopher Lindsey.

Sioux City Sue 1946 Talent scouts looking to cast a western musical find Autry, then trick him into being the voice of a singing donkey in an animated production. But, the yodelin' cowboy belts out a number or two, and the poobahs give him the lead. Singin' and fancy ridin' abound in Autry's first post-WWII role. **69m/B VHS, DVD.** Gene Autry, Lynne Roberts, Sterling Holloway, Richard Lane, Ralph Sanford, Kenneth Lundy, Pierre Watkin; ***D:*** Frank McDonald; ***W:*** Olive Cooper; ***C:*** Reggie Lanning; ***M:*** R. Dale Butts.

Sir Arthur Conan Doyle's The Lost World 1/2 *The Lost World* **1998 (R)** In the '30s, zoologist George Challenger (Bergin) recruits a team of scientists to help him find a mythic land where dinosaurs and other prehistoric creatures exist. Lots of cliches although the special effects aren't bad. **96m/C VHS.** Patrick Bergin, David Nerman, Jayne Heitmeyer, Julian Casey; ***D:*** Bob Keen; ***W:*** Jean LaFleur; ***C:*** Barry Gravelle; ***M:*** Milan Kymlicka. **VIDEO**

Siren of the Tropics 1/2 *La Sirene des Tropiques* **1927** In love with a French businessman, West Indies native girl Papitou (Baker) sneaks back to Paris with him—despite his engagement to another woman—but finds her true calling in life as a dancer in music halls. Memorable only as the legendary Baker's film debut, showcasing her stunning dancing abilities. Silent with French soundtrack added. **86m/B DVD.** Josephine Baker, Pierre Batcheff, Georges Melchior, Regina Dalthy, Regina Thomas; ***D:*** Mario Nalpas, Henri Etievant; ***W:*** Maurice Dekobra.

Sirens 1/2 1994 (R) Staid minister Anthony Campion (Grant) takes Australian artist Norman Lindsay to task for submitting scandalous works to public exhibitions. Noted by one reviewer as "Enchanted April with nipples," comedy of manners is witty but lacks plot and looks remarkably like a centerfold layout. Ample displays of nudity as the models (including supermodel MacPherson in her acting debut) frolic in the buff. Grant is terrific as the seemingly enlightened but easily shocked minister, but Neill's Lindsay is thinly written and too often takes a back seat to the vamping models. Fictionalized account of a true incident from the 1930s; Lindsay's home and some of his artworks were used. Check out writer/director Duigan as a pompous village minister. **96m/C VHS, DVD.** *AU GB* Hugh Grant, Tara Fitzgerald, Sam Neill, Elle Macpherson, Kate Fischer, Portia de Rossi, Pamela Rabe, Ben Mendelsohn, John Polson, Mark Gerber, Julia Stone, Ellie MacCarthy, Vincent Ball; ***Cameos:*** John Duigan; ***D:*** John Duigan; ***W:*** John Duigan; ***C:*** Geoff Burton; ***M:*** Rachel Portman.

Sirens 1999 (R) The sirens in this case are those attached to police cars. Sally Rawlings (Delany) gets a big promotion and decides to share the good news with her ex-hubby (Curtis Hall). They wind up parked under a bridge, steaming up the windows, when a cop car comes along. Trigger-happy cop (Carradine) winds up shooting the unarmed ex dead and the police try to cover up the bad shooting. Of course, Sally wants justice—no matter what it costs. **102m/C VHS.** Dana Delany, Keith Carradine, Vondie Curtis-Hall, Brian Dennehy, Justin Theroux; ***D:*** John Sacret Young; ***W:*** John Sacret Young; ***C:*** Eagle Egilsson; ***M:*** Brian Tyler. **CABLE**

Sirens 2002 Detective Jay Pearson (Nardini) is investigating a London serial rapist while fending off the unwelcome advances of her boss (Glenister). But soon one of the suspects is leading too close to home—sister Ali's (Parish) shrink boyfriend Oliver (Wise) is on the list. Jay learns the motive is tied to a years-old incident that happened at Oxford and the rapist is out for revenge, which puts her in increasing danger. **180m/C DVD.** *GB* Daniela Nardini, Greg Wise, Robert Glenister, Sarah Parish, Anthony Calf; ***D:*** Nicholas Laughland; ***W:*** Chris Lang; ***C:*** Dominic Clemence; ***M:*** John Lunn. **TV**

Siringo 1/2 1994 U.S. Deputy Marshal Charlie Siringo (Johnson) is out to capture escaped convict Wade Lewis (Macht). The two antagonists share a nasty history as Siringo, along with a young deputy, heads out to the ranch of former prostitute Kaitlin (Bernard) for a final showdown. **90m/C VHS.** Brad Johnson, Stephen Macht, Chad Lowe, Crystal Bernard; ***D:*** Kevin G. Cremin.

Sirocco 1/2 **1951** An American gun-runner (Bogart) stuck in Syria in 1925 matches wits with a French intelligence officer amid civil war and intrigue. About the underbelly of human affairs. **111m/B VHS, DVD.** Humphrey Bogart, Lee J. Cobb, Zero Mostel, Everett Sloane, Gerald Mohr; ***D:*** Curtis Bernhardt; ***C:*** Burnett Guffey.

S.I.S. **2008** Spike TV 'guy' movie with lots of action and minimal plot. The Special Investigation Squad is an elite LAPD unit that goes after habitual violent offenders. They're supposed to be on the QT but their controversial methods have drawn the unwelcome attention of police brass. **82m/C DVD.** Keith David, Peter Stebbings, Christina Cox, Omari Hardwick, Colleen Porch, Matthew Nable; ***D:*** John Herzfeld; ***W:*** John Herzfeld; ***M:*** J. Peter Robinson. **CABLE**

Sister Act 1/2 **1992 (PG)** Surprising boxoffice hit casts Goldberg as a Reno lounge singer, Deloris, who's an inadvertent witness to a mob murder by her boyfriend Vince (Keitel). The cops hide her in a convent—where she's as comfortable in a habit as a fish is out of water. Much to the dismay of the poker-faced Mother Superior (Smith), Deloris takes over the rag-tag choir and molds them into a swinging, religious version of a '60s girls group. Stock characters and situations are deflected by some genuinely funny moments and good performances, especially by Najimy and Makkena. Coached by the very clever Shaiman, Whoopi handles her singing bits with gusto, highlight of which is "My God," sung to the tune of "My Guy." **100m/C VHS, DVD.** Whoopi Goldberg, Maggie Smith, Harvey Keitel, Bill Nunn, Kathy Najimy, Wendy Makkena, Mary Wickes, Robert Miranda, Richard Portnow, Joseph Maher; ***D:*** Emile Ardolino; ***W:*** Joseph Howard; ***C:*** Adam Greenberg; ***M:*** Marc Shaiman.

Sister Act 2: Back in the Habit **1993 (PG)** Mediocre retread finds Goldberg once again donning her nun's habit and getting a choir rocking. Deloris has established her singing career in Vegas, but she's persuaded by her nun friends to whip the incorrigible music students at a troubled inner-city high school into shape for an all-state choral competition. The musical numbers and singing are catchy and well-done but Goldberg seems to have phoned her work in; given her reported $7, 000,000 salary, a little more life is expected. She's still sharp with the one-liners but it's all familiar ground. Geared directly towards young viewers. **107m/C VHS, DVD.** Whoopi Goldberg, Kathy Najimy, James Coburn, Maggie Smith, Wendy Makkena, Barnard Hughes, Mary Wickes, Sheryl Lee Ralph, Michael Jeter, Robert Pastorelli, Thomas Gottschalk, Lauryn Hill, Brad Sullivan, Jennifer Love Hewitt; ***D:*** Bill Duke; ***W:*** James Orr, Jim Cruickshank, Judi Ann Mason; ***C:*** Oliver Wood; ***M:*** Miles Goodman. Blockbuster '95: Comedy Actress, V. (Goldberg).

Sister Aimee: The Aimee Semple McPherson Story **2006 (PG)** Famous L.A. evangelist Aimee Semple McPherson (Michaels), founder of the Foursquare Church, disappears from a beach one day in 1926. She reappears a month later, claiming to have been kidnapped, but her story is suspect and rumors fly that the married McPherson was having a tryst with a lover. Rossi then takes a sympathetic look at McPherson's complicated life, beginning with her growing up on a Canadian farm to her conversion and ministry and her problem-plagued personal life. **110m/C DVD.** Rance Howard, Mimi Michaels, Chad Nadolski, Charles Hoyes, Michael Minor, Etienne Eckert, Richard Rossi; ***D:*** Richard Rossi; ***W:*** Richard Rossi; ***M:*** Richard Rossi. **VIDEO**

Sister Dora 1/2 **1977** An idealistic young woman joins a nursing sisterhood in 19th century England but she questions her vocation when she falls in love. Adapted from a popular romance novel. **147m/C VHS.** *GB* Dorothy Tutin, James Grout, Peter Cellier; ***D:*** Mark Miller.

The Sister-in-Law **1974 (R)** Shady dealings, seduction, and adultery run rampant. Savage (who also wrote and sings the folk score) reluctantly agrees to deliver a package across the Canadian border for his brother. Intriguing. **80m/C VHS, DVD.** John Savage, Anne Saxon, Will MacMillan, Meridith Baer; ***D:*** Joseph Rubin.

The Sister-in-Law 1/2 **1995 (PG-13)** Chilling cable suspenser finds the beautiful and evil Sarah Preston (Vernon) assuming the identity of the woman she's just killed—the widow of wealthy George Richards's (McCarthy) estranged son. George is dying and pathetically eager to accept Sarah at face value as is his vulnerable daughter Madlyn (Reed). But Sarah has not chosen the Richards family at random—she has a longtime grudge and plans to take her revenge slowly—so be prepared for a few more bodies to turn up. **95m/C VHS.** Kate Vernon, Kevin McCarthy, Shanna Reed, Craig Wasson; ***D:*** Noel Nosseck; ***W:*** David Callaway, Megan Marks. **CABLE**

Sister Kenny **1946** Follows the story of a legendary Australian nurse crusading for the treatment of infantile paralysis. Stirring, well-made screen biography. Based on Elizabeth Kenny's memoir, "And They Shall Walk." **116m/B VHS.** Rosalind Russell, Dean Jagger, Alexander Knox, Philip Merivale, Beulah Bondi, Charles Halton; ***D:*** Dudley Nichols; ***C:*** George Barnes. Golden Globes '47: Actress—Drama (Russell).

Sister My Sister **1994 (R)** True crime story that served as the inspiration for Jean Genet's play "The Maids." In a French provincial town lives the authoritarian Madame Danzard (Walters), who stifles daughter Isabelle (Thursfield), and subjects her two maids, sisters Christine (Richardson) and Lea (May), to an equally harsh discipline. The tension between the four women reaches a highstrung crescendo, leading to violence. Claustrophobic character study. **89m/C VHS, DVD.** *GB* Julie Walters, Joely Richardson, Jodhi May, Sophie Thursfield; ***D:*** Nancy Meckler; ***W:*** Wendy Kesselman; ***C:*** Ashley Rowe; ***M:*** Stephen Warbeck.

Sister, Sister **1987 (R)** A Congressional aide on vacation in Louisiana takes a room in an old mansion. He gradually discovers the secret of the house and its resident sisters. Dark Southern gothicism, full of plot surprises, with a twisted ending. **91m/C VHS, DVD.** Eric Stoltz, Judith Ivey, Jennifer Jason Leigh, Dennis Lipscomb, Anne Pitoniak, Natalija Nogulich; ***D:*** Bill Condon; ***W:*** Ginny Cerrella, Bill Condon, Joel Cohen; ***M:*** Richard Einhorn.

Sister Street Fighter **1976** Action star Sonny Chiba takes a rest from his "Street Fighter" series in favor of protege Long, who's determined to deliver her own brand of deadly justice in this martial arts fest. **81m/C VHS, DVD.** Etsuko (Sue) Shihomi, Sonny Chiba; ***D:*** Kazuhiko Yamaguchi.

The Sisterhood **1988 (R)** A pair of amazons fight for women's rights in a post-nuclear future. Cheap feminist theme laid over warmed-over sci-fi plot. **75m/C VHS, UMD.** Rebecca Holden, Chuck Wagner, Lynn-Holly Johnson, Barbara Hooper; ***D:*** Cirio H. Santiago.

Sisterhood of the Traveling Pants 1/2 **2005 (PG)** Before heading their own way one summer, four teenage gal pals stumble upon a rare pair of jeans that fits each of them and they pledge to share the jeans via mail while they're apart. Their separate adventures and resulting life lessons are sincere and lively with just a touch of weepiness. Faithful telling of the popular coming-of-age novel by Ann Brashares is highlighted by appealing young actresses. **119m/C DVD.** *US* America Ferrera, Amber Tamblyn, Alexis Bledel, Jenna Boyd, Blake Lively, Bradley Whitford, Nancy Travis, Rachel Ticotin, Mike Vogel, Kyle Schmid; ***D:*** Ken Kwapis; ***W:*** Delia Ephron, Elizabeth Chandler; ***C:*** John Bailey; ***M:*** Cliff Eidelman.

The Sisterhood of the Traveling Pants 2 1/2 **2008 (PG-13)** Fast forward three years from the original and the four BFFs have finished up their freshman year at college and are again headed off for different summer destinations. The charm inspired by those magical jeans is starting to fade, despite the earnest girl-powered message about relationships and identity and nice turns by the leads. Not bad, just typical sequel letdown. Drawn from several novels of the Ann Brashares series. **111m/C DVD.** *US* Blake Lively, Alexis Bledel, America Ferrera, Amber Tamblyn, Rachel Nichols, Shohreh Aghdashloo, Blythe Danner, Kyle MacLachlan, Jesse Williams, Tom Wisdom, Michael Rady, Ernie Lively; ***D:*** Sanaa Hamri; ***W:*** Elizabeth Chandler; ***C:*** Jim Denault; ***M:*** Rachel Portman.

The Sisters **1938** Lavish film of three sisters and their marital problems in turn of the century San Francisco. Davis gives a great performance as the oldest sister with the most trouble—notably in the form of unreliable sports reporter Flynn. Look for Susan Hayward in a bit role, as well as Bogart's wife, Mayo Methot. Based on the bestselling novel by Myron Brinig. **98m/B VHS.** Bette Davis, Errol Flynn, Anita Louise, Jane Bryan, Ian Hunter, Henry Travers, Beulah Bondi, Donald Crisp, Dick Foran, Patric Knowles; ***D:*** Anatole Litvak; ***M:*** Max Steiner.

Sisters **1973 (R)** Siamese twins are separated surgically, but one doesn't survive the operation. The remaining sister is scarred physically and mentally with her personality split into bad and good. And then things really get crazy. DePalma's first ode to Hitchcock, with great music by Hitchcock's favorite composer, Bernard Herrmann. Scary and suspenseful. **93m/C VHS, DVD.** Margot Kidder, Charles Durning, Barnard Hughes, Jennifer Salt, William Finley, Lisle Wilson, Mary Davenport, Dolph Sweet; ***D:*** Brian De Palma; ***W:*** Brian De Palma, Louisa Rose; ***C:*** Gregory Sandor; ***M:*** Bernard Herrmann.

Sisters **1997 (R)** Sisters Phyllis and Elizabeth are both lonely but have always been jealous and afraid of each other. A look at their lives from childhood to adulthood reveals their fantasies, fears, and failures. **89m/C VHS.** Claudia Christian, Valerie Breiman, Peter Berg, Jeff Conaway, Sydney Lassick; ***Nar:*** Charlie Sheen.

The Sisters 1/2 **2005 (R)** Alfieri adapted his play, which was inspired by Anton Chekhov's "The Three Sisters." In this contemporary update, set in a Manhattan college faculty lounge, sisters Olga (Masterson), Marsha (Bello), and Irene (Christensen) gather with their brother Andrew (Nivola) and various lovers and colleagues, most of whom are an insufferable talky bunch. Irene's birthday seems to be just the right time to bring up family secrets and play psychological roulette. Unlike Chekov, this is overwrought yet boring. **113m/C DVD.** *US* Maria Bello, Mary Stuart Masterson, Erika Christensen, Eric McCormack, Chris O'Donnell, Tony Goldwyn, Steven Culp, Alessandro Nivola, Elizabeth Banks, Rip Torn; ***D:*** Arthur Allan Seidelman; ***W:*** Richard Alfieri; ***C:*** Chuy Chavez; ***M:*** Thomas Morse.

Sisters of Death **1976 (PG)** Five members of a sorority gather together for a reunion in a remote California town. Little do they know, a psychopath is stalking them, one by one. Could it have something to do with the terrible secret they each keep? Good, cheap thrills and some Bicentennial fashions to boot. **87m/C VHS, DVD.** Arthur Franz, Claudia Jennings, Cheri Howell, Sherry Boucher, Paul Carr; ***D:*** Joseph Mazzuca.

Sisters of Satan 1/2 **1975 (R)** The nuns of the infamous convent St. Archangelo choose to survive by trading God for the devil. **91m/C VHS, DVD.** *MX* Claudio Brook, David Silva, Tina Romero, Susana Kamini; ***D:*** Juan Lopez Moctezuma.

Sisters of the Gion *Gion No Shimai* **1936** Story follows two geisha sisters, illuminating the plight of women in Japan. Elder sister Umekichi is traditional and dependent on her patrons while her modern younger sister Omocha exploits her customers as much as possible. But no matter the difference in their attitudes, both remain trapped by circumstances. Adapted from the novel "Yama" by Alexander Ivanovich Kuprin. Japanese with subtitles. **66m/B VHS.** *JP* Isuzu Yamada, Yoko Umemura, Eitaro Shindo, Benkei Shiganoya; ***D:*** Kenji Mizoguchi; ***W:*** Kenji Mizoguchi, Yoshikata Yoda; ***C:*** Minoru Miki.

Sisters, Or the Balance of Happiness *Schwestern Oder die Balance des Glucks* **1979** Orderly Maria (Lampe) runs the household for her resentful, dependent sister Anna (Gabriel). Opposites in temperment, the dysfunctional duo can neither live with or without each other. When Anna commits suicide, Maria tries to make-over young typist Miriam (Fruh) to take her sister's place. German with subtitles. **97m/C VHS, DVD.** *GE* Jutta Lampe, Gudrun Gabriel, Jessica Fruh; ***D:*** Margarethe von Trotta; ***W:*** Margarethe von Trotta; ***C:*** Franz Rath; ***M:*** Konstantin Wecker.

Sitcom **1997** Family dysfunction taken to the extreme. There's a pet rat, a new maid whose African husband seduces the son of the family, a daughter who becomes a paraplegic dominatrix, orgies, incest, and dad, who kills everyone when they throw him a surprise birthday party. Or does he? Or does it matter, anyway? French with subtitles. **80m/C VHS, DVD.** *FR* Evelyne Dandry, Francois Marthouret, Marina de Van, Adrien de Van, Stephane Rideau, Lucia Sanchez, Jules-Emmanuel Eyoum Deido; ***D:*** Francois Ozon; ***W:*** Francois Ozon; ***C:*** Yorick Le Saux; ***M:*** Eric Neveux.

The Sitter *While the Children Sleep* **2007** Predictable Lifetime cable movie about a pretty psycho with a shovel. After Meghan (O'Grady) decides to go back to work, eager Abby (Klaveno) becomes the Eastmans live-in babysitter. Turns out she has an unexpected tie to lawyer dad Carter (Moses) that he apparently doesn't remember. But she is really, really grateful—like "get rid of anybody who causes a problem so she can have Carter to herself" grateful. **88m/C DVD.** William R. Moses, Gail O'Grady, Stacy Haiduk, Mariana Klaveno; ***D:*** Russell Mulcahy; ***W:*** Stephen Niver; ***C:*** Maximo Munzi; ***M:*** Elia Cmiral. **TV**

Sitting Bull **1954** Thanks to Cody acting as an advisor, this take on Little Big Horn was more sympathetic to the plight of the Native Americans than the typical western. Sioux chief Sitting Bull (Naish) calls for patience while Crazy Horse (Cody) wants war against the white interlopers. Maj. Bob Parrish (Robertson) gets court-martialed for siding with the Injuns against bloodthirsty Col. Custer (Kennedy). President Grant (Hamilton) wants Parrish to pow-wow with Sitting Bull but there's more trouble coming. **105m/B DVD.** Dale Robertson, J. Carrol Naish, Iron Eyes Cody, Mary Murphy, Douglas Kennedy, John Litel, Josh Hamilton, Joel Fluellen, William Hopper; ***D:*** Sidney Salkow; ***W:*** Sidney Salkow, Jack DeWitt; ***C:*** Charles Van Enger; ***M:*** Raoul Kraushaar.

Sitting Ducks **1980 (R)** Mild-mannered accountant and lecherous pal rip off and then attempt to outrun the mob—all while swapping songs and confessions. Emil and Norman make it up as they go along; their hilarious repartee is largely improvised. They pick up a gorgeous lady (Townsend) and go about their way. **88m/C VHS, DVD.** Michael Emil, Zack Norman, Patrice Townsend, Richard Romanus, Irene Forrest, Henry Jaglom; ***D:*** Henry Jaglom; ***W:*** Henry Jaglom.

Sitting Pretty **1948** Webb is a delight in his Oscar-nominated role as the prissy Lynn Belvedere, who takes a job as a babysitter to the three hellion sons of Harry (Young) and Tacey (O-Hara) in their typical suburban community. Mr. Belvedere has soon wrangled the family in line but there's more to the man than his superior skills. It seems he's doing research and writing on expose on life in the suburbs, which becomes a best-seller and a local scandal. Followed by "Mr. Belvedere Goes to College" and "Mr. Belvedere Rings the Bell." Based on the novel "Belvedere" by Gwen Davenport. **84m/B VHS.** Clifton Webb, Robert Young, Maureen O'Hara, Richard Haydn, Louise Allbritton, Randy Stuart, Ed Begley Sr.; ***D:*** Walter Lang; ***W:*** F. Hugh Herbert; ***C:*** Norbert Brodine; ***M:*** Alfred Newman.

The Situation 1/2 **2006 (R)** Slack pacing and a colorless romantic triangle doom this Iraqi War story to boredom. Journalist Anna (Nielsen) is working in Baghdad. Her friend with benefits is American intelligence agent Dan (Lewis). Iraqi photographer Zaid (Hamada) is in love with her although he struggles with their cultural differences. When a close contact of Anna's is killed in an apparent political assassination, Anna and Zaid want to break the story but leads are elusive and they find themselves being manipulated by various factions—American and Iraqi. English and Arabic with subtitles. **106m/C DVD.** Damian Lewis, Nasser Memarzia, John Slattery, Connie Neilsen, Mido Hamada, Said Amadia, Driss Roukh; ***D:*** Philip Haas; ***W:*** Wendell Steavenson; ***C:*** Sean Bobbitt; ***M:*** Jeff Beal.

Six Days, Seven Nights 🦴🦴 1/2 **1998 (PG-13)** Brash magazine editor Robin Monroe (Heche) is on a tropical vacation with fiance Frank (Schwimmer) when a deadline crisis forces her to ask gruff cargo pilot Quinn Harris (Ford) for a lift to Tahiti. A plane crash strands the incompatible duo on a remote island and naturally they need each other to survive. This started out as a routine romantic comedy but the action quotient was upped as filming progressed, thanks to a storyline involving modern-day pirates that's a waste of time. Also a waste are scenes involving Frank with Quinn's bodacious babe, Angelica (Obradors). Why does the only other woman with a significant part have to be a coochie-coo Charo impersonator? Thankfully, Ford and Heche do have considerable sass between them. Filmed on location in Kauai. **101m/C VHS, DVD.** Harrison Ford, Anne Heche, David Schwimmer, Temuera Morrison, Jacqueline Obradors, Allison Janney, Danny Trejo; ***D:*** Ivan Reitman; ***W:*** Michael Browning; ***C:*** Michael Chapman; ***M:*** Randy Edelman.

Six Days, Six Nights 🦴🦴 *A la Folie* **1994 (R)** Two French sisters—the older and competitive Elsa (Dalle) and the creative and evasive Alice (Parillaud)—move to New York with Alice's boxer boyfriend (Aurignac). Sex and heartbreak ensues, as it usually does. French with subtitles. **96m/C DVD.** Patrick Aurignac, Anne Parillaud, Beatrice Dalle; ***D:*** Diane Kurys; ***W:*** Diane Kurys, Antoine Lacomblez.

Six Degrees of Separation 🦴🦴 1/2 **1993 (R)** Some believe that any two people, anywhere in the world, are connected by links to only six other people, hence the six degrees of separation. For the upper crust New Yorker Kittredges, Ouisa (Channing) and Flan (Sutherland), this becomes an issue when they encounter a charming young man (Smith) who claims to be Sidney Poitier's son and a friend of their children. The story unfolds as they realize they've been hustled—and don't understand why. Guare adapted his hit play, but what worked well there is almost too talky here. Channing, reprising her stage role, is very good as the stuffy Ouisa, with Sutherland delivering another interesting performance. Incredibly, the play was based on a true story. **112m/C VHS, DVD.** Stockard Channing, Will Smith, Donald Sutherland, Mary Beth Hurt, Bruce Davison, Ian McKellen, Richard Masur, Anthony Michael Hall, Heather Graham, Eric Thal, Anthony Rapp, Oz (Osgood) Perkins II, Kitty Carlisle Hart, Catherine Kellner; ***D:*** Fred Schepisi; ***W:*** John Guare; ***C:*** Ian Baker; ***M:*** Jerry Goldsmith.

Six Gun Gospel 🦴🦴 **1943** Hatton masquerades as a preacher to investigate some shady dealings. Laughs come when the women of the congregation prevail upon him to sing, and he croons a ballad about Jesse James! **59m/B VHS.** Johnny Mack Brown, Raymond Hatton, Inna Gest, Eddie Dew, Roy Barcroft, Kenneth MacDonald, Bud Osborne; ***D:*** Lambert Hillyer.

Six Gun Rhythm 🦴 1/2 **1939** Novelty western plot has football player traveling to Texas to avenge his father's murder. **59m/B VHS.** Tex Fletcher, Joan Barclay, Ralph Peters, Reed Howes, Ted Adams, Malcolm "Bud" McTaggart, Kit Guard; ***D:*** Sam Newfield; ***W:*** Fred Myton; ***C:*** Arthur Reed; ***M:*** Lew Porter, Johnny Lange.

Six Gun Trail 🦴 1/2 **1938** Lightning Bill Carson and his sidekick Magpie are after jewel thieves. So Carson disguises himself as a Chinese smuggler and the thieves agree to sell him their gems but they actually plan a doublecross. **59m/B DVD.** Tim McCoy, Ben (Benny) Corbett, Ted Adams, Nora Lane, Alden Chase, Bob Terry, Donald Gallaher; ***D:*** Sam Newfield; ***W:*** Isadore Bernstein; ***C:*** Marcel Le Picard.

633 Squadron 🦴🦴 1/2 **1964** A skilled R.A.F. pilot attempts to lead his squadron on a mission deep into the fjords of Norway in search of a Nazi fuel plant. Robertson tries hard, as always, but is really not British officer material. Well-made war flick, based on a true story. **102m/C VHS, DVD.** Cliff Robertson, George Chakiris, Maria Perschy, Harry Andrews; ***D:*** Walter Grauman; ***W:*** James Clavell.

Six in Paris 🦴🦴 1/2 *Paris vu Par* **1968** Six short films by acclaimed French New Wave directors, each depicting a different Parisian neighborhood. "Saint-Germain-des-Pres" finds an American girl disillusioned by two French boys. "Gare du Nord" has a woman meeting a handsome stranger who announces he's going to kill himself. A shy dishwasher brings a prostitute to his room in the "Rue Saint-Denis." When a salesman is accosted by a derelict in the "Place de l'Etoile", he hits him with his umbrella and then thinks he's killed the man. "Montparnasse-Levallois" has a woman thinking she's mixed-up her meetings with her two lovers. "La Muette" finds a small boy buying earplugs to shut out the noise of his parents constant arguing. In French with English subtitles. **93m/C VHS.** *FR* Barbara Wilkin, Jean-Francois Chappey, Jean-Pierre Andreani, Nadine Ballot, Barbet Schroeder, Gilles Queant, Micheline Dax, Claude Melki, Jean-Michel Rouziere, Marcel Gallon, Joanna Shimkus, Philippe Hiquilly, Serge Davri, Stephane Audran, Gilles Chusseau, Dinah Saril, Claude Chabrol; ***D:*** Jean Douchet, Jean Rouch, Jean-Daniel Pollet, Eric Rohmer, Jean-Luc Godard, Claude Chabrol; ***W:*** Jean Douchet, George Keller, Jean Rouch, Jean-Daniel Pollet, Eric Rohmer, Jean-Luc Godard, Claude Chabrol; ***C:*** Nestor Almendros.

Six of a Kind 🦴🦴🦴 **1934** When Flora (Boland) and J. Pinkham Whinney (Ruggles) decide to drive to California for a second honeymoon, they advertise for another couple to share expenses. Unfortunately, it's Burns and Allen and their exceptionally large Great Dane that answer the ad. There's numerous complications, including bank clerk Whinney's being suspected of embezzlement, prompting Sheriff "Honest John" Hoxley (Fields) to go after the supposed criminals. Veteran comedy performers make this one a delight. **63m/B VHS, DVD.** Charlie Ruggles, Mary Boland, Gracie Allen, George Burns, W.C. Fields, Alison Skipworth; ***D:*** Leo McCarey; ***W:*** Walter DeLeon, Harry Ruskin; ***C:*** Henry Sharp; ***M:*** Ralph Rainger.

Six Pack 🦴 1/2 **1982 (PG)** The Gambler goes auto racing. Rogers, in his theatrical debut, stars as Brewster Baker, a former stock car driver. He returns to the racing circuit with the help of six larcenous orphans (the six-pack, get it?) adept at stripping cars. Kinda cute if you're in the mood for sugar-powered race car story. **108m/C VHS, DVD.** Kenny Rogers, Diane Lane, Erin Gray, Barry Corbin, Anthony Michael Hall; ***D:*** Daniel Petrie; ***M:*** Charles Fox.

Six Shootin' Sheriff 🦴🦴 **1938** A cowboy framed for bank robbery is released and seeks to rid his town of all evil. And he gets the girl! **59m/B VHS.** Ken Maynard, Marjorie Reynolds, Walter Long; ***D:*** Harry Fraser.

Six-String Samurai 🦴🦴 **1998 (PG-13)** In 1957 the USSR bombs and assumes control of the U.S., and Las Vegas is the only safe haven of freedom. Forty years later, a rock musician/samurai is on an odyssey across the desert to replace the recently deceased Elvis as king of the neon city; challenging his quest is another guitar-slinger, Death (Gauger), and his cronies. Our hero Buddy (played by martial artist Falcon as a cross between Buddy Holly and Yojimbo) and his sidekick The Kid (McGuire) must face all the bad guys we've come to expect in a post-apocalyptic adventure. Filled with campy dialogue and well-staged Hong Kong-style action (directed by Falcon), basically all the makings of a good midnight movie, but it doesn't quite come together. **89m/C VHS, DVD.** Jeffrey Falcon, Justin McGuire, Stephane Gauger, John Sakisian; ***D:*** Lance Mungia; ***W:*** Lance Mungia, Jeffrey Falcon; ***C:*** Kristian Bernier; ***M:*** Brian Tyler.

Six: The Mark Unleashed 🦴 1/2 **2004** Christian-themed flick set in a near-future where religion has been usurped by a cult-like leader who demands all his adherents wear a mark to prove their allegiance. Those that don't are thrown into prison and given a month to change their minds or be executed. Car thieves Brody and Jerry wind up in the slammer alongside Luke, who claims to talk to God, and ex-cop Tom, who has been tortured into agreeing to assassinate a Christian leader after plotting an escape with the thieves. **106m/C DVD.** Kevin Downes, Brad Heller, Amy Moon, David A.R. White, Jeffrey Dean Morgan, Stephen Baldwin, Eric Roberts, Troy Winbush; ***D:*** Kevin Downes; ***W:*** Kevin Downes, Chipper Lowell, David A.R. White; ***C:*** Philip Hurn; ***M:*** Marc Fantini, Steffan Fantini. **VIDEO**

Six Ways to Sunday 🦴🦴 **1999 (R)** Weird mob drama about a hitman and his Oedipal relationship with mom. Passive, repressed teenager, Harry Odum (Reedus), lives with his domineering mother, Kate (Harry), who controls his life. That is, until Harry assists his hoodlum buddy Arnie (Brody) with a job and manages to impress Arnie's boss, Mr. Varga (Adler). Since Harry turns out to have a latent talent for violence, he's soon elevated to hit man—although mom's still a problem. Based on the 1962 novel "Portrait of a Young Man Drowning" by Charles Perry. **97m/C VHS, DVD.** Norman Reedus, Deborah Harry, Adrien Brody, Jerry Adler, Peter Appel, Elina Lowensohn, Isaac Hayes, Anna Thomson, David Ross; ***D:*** Adam Bernstein; ***W:*** Adam Bernstein, Marc Gerald; ***C:*** John Inwood; ***M:*** Theodore Shapiro.

Six Weeks 🦴🦴 **1982 (PG)** A young girl dying of leukemia brings together her work-driven mother and an aspiring married politician. Manipulative hanky-wringer has good acting from both Moores but oddly little substance. **107m/C VHS.** Dudley Moore, Mary Tyler Moore, Katherine Healy; ***D:*** Tony Bill; ***M:*** Dudley Moore.

Six Wives of Henry VIII 🦴🦴🦴 **1971** Michell has been called the definitive Henry VIII, and this BBC Classic (shown as part of "Masterpiece Theatre" on PBS) was perhaps the most praised series on British TV. Henry's wives were: Catherine of Aragon, Anne Boleyn, Jane Seymour, Anne of Cleves, Catherine Howard, and Catherine Parr. Each episode tells of their (sometimes tragic) fates as pawns in Henry's quest for an heir, and his changes from an eager young man to aged, bitter monarch. **540m/C VHS, DVD.** *GB* Keith Michell, Annette Crosbie, Dorothy Tutin, Anne Stallybrass, Elvi Hale, Angela Pleasence, Rosalie Crutchley; ***D:*** John Glenister, Naomi Capon. **TV**

Sixteen 🦴🦴 *Like a Crow on a June Bug* **1972 (R)** A naive country lass is attracted to the glitter and hum of the outside world. Her determination and optimism help her triumph. **84m/C VHS, DVD.** Mercedes McCambridge, Parley Baer, Ford Rainey, Beverly (Hills) Powers, John Lozier, Simone Griffeth, Maidie Norman; ***D:*** Lawrence (Larry) Dobkin.

16 Blocks 🦴🦴🦴 **2006 (PG-13)** Willis lets himself go to seed as alcoholic NYPD detective Jack Moseley, a burnout who's been corrupted by the job and is just waiting to collect his pension. He's assigned to transport motor-mouthed witness Eddie Bunker (Mos Def) to a grand jury hearing 16 blocks from the station. Easy—until someone starts shooting at them. Jack calls for backup only to discover that Eddie is testifying about some bad cops, including Jack's ex-partner Frank Nugent (a menacing Morse), who isn't about to let that happen. Donner directed the "Lethal Weapon" series, so he knows how to keep things moving. **105m/C DVD, Blu-ray Disc, HD DVD.** *US* Bruce Willis, Mos Def, David Morse, Cylk Cozart, Casey Sander, David Zayas, Jenna Stern, Robert Racki; ***D:*** Richard Donner; ***W:*** Richard Wenk; ***C:*** Glen MacPherson; ***M:*** Klaus Badelt.

Sixteen Candles 🦴🦴🦴 **1984 (PG)** Almost 25 years after hitting the theatres, "Sixteen Candles" is still popular—reaching near cult status among generation X-ers. Hilarious comedy of errors features the pouty Ringwald as an awkard teen who's been dreaming of her 16th birthday. But the rush of her sister's wedding causes everyone to forget, turning her birthday into her worst nightmare. Hughes may not be critically acclaimed, but his movies are so popular they nearly take on a life of their own. Ringwald and Hall are especially charming as the angst-ridden teens, encountering one trauma after another. Great soundtrack includes the title song by The Stray Cats. **93m/C VHS, DVD.** Molly Ringwald, Justin Henry, Michael Schoeffling, Haviland (Haylie) Morris, Gedde Watanabe, Anthony Michael Hall, Paul Dooley, Carlin Glynn, Blanche Baker, Edward Andrews, Carole Cook, Max (Casey Adams) Showalter, Liane (Alexandra) Curtis, John Cusack, Joan Cusack, Brian Doyle-Murray, Jami Gertz, Cinnamon Idles, Zelda Rubinstein, Billie Bird; ***D:*** John Hughes; ***W:*** John Hughes; ***C:*** Bobby Byrne; ***M:*** Ira Newborn.

Sixteen Fathoms Deep 🦴🦴 **1934** A sponge fisherman risks it all, including his love, when a mean businessman threatens his operation. Good underwater photography, but otherwise undistinguished. **57m/B VHS.** Lon Chaney Jr., Sally O'Neil, George Regas, Maurice Black, Russell Simpson; ***D:*** Armand Schaefer.

16 Years of Alcohol 🦴🦴 **2003 (R)** Abandoned by his mother as a child and raised by an abusive, alcoholic father, Frankie grows up a drunk who leads a brutal gang in Edinburgh. But when he falls in love he decides to straighten up. Former punk rocker and first-time director Richard Jobson loosely adapts his life story. **96m/C VHS, DVD.** *GB* Kevin McKidd, Ewen Bremner, Laura Fraser, Susan Lynch, Stuart Sinclair Blyth, Lisa May Cooper, Lewis Macleod; ***D:*** Richard Jobson; ***W:*** Richard Jobson; ***C:*** John Rhodes. **VIDEO**

The 6th Day 🦴🦴 1/2 **2000 (PG-13)** Arnold's a family guy in the near-future who finds out a clone has taken over his life. Not only that, but the evil corporation behind the clone doesn't want the original around to muck up their nefarious plans. Typical (although somewhat toned-down) Ah-nuld type mayhem ensues. Schwarzenegger has fun with his image, and the supporting players get some fine moments, too. Thought-provoking questions about human cloning add an interesting dimension, raising this one slightly above the genre-pic/star-vehicle level. **124m/C VHS, DVD.** Arnold Schwarzenegger, Tony Goldwyn, Sarah Wynter, Michael Rooker, Robert Duvall, Michael Rapaport, Wendy Crewson, Rodney Rowland, Ken Pogue, Wanda Cannon, Christopher Lawford, Terry Crews, Colin Cunningham, Taylor Anne Reid, Jennifer Gareis, Don McManus, Steve Bacic; ***D:*** Roger Spottiswoode; ***W:*** Cormac Wibberley, Marianne S. Wibberley; ***C:*** Pierre Mignot; ***M:*** Trevor Rabin.

The Sixth Man 🦴 1/2 **1997 (PG-13)** College basketball star Antoine Tyler (Hardison) dies but returns as a ghost to help his brother (Wayans) lead their team to the NCAA finals. Basketball seems to be the sport of choice for Hollywood lately, so you'd think they'd be able to get one of these movies right. Once again, they blow the layup. The first half features the requisite flashback and tear-jerker death scene, both of which are surprisingly effective. But then the focus turns to "hilarious" on-court hijinks and the all-time sports cliche champion: the second-half rally from an impossible deficit. Hardison and Wayans are the bright spots, displaying fine comic and dramatic chemistry. **107m/C VHS, DVD.** Kadeem Hardison, Marlon Wayans, David Paymer, Michael Michele, Kevin Dunn, Gary Jones, Vladimir Cuk, Chris Spencer, Kirk Baily, Saundra McClain, Lorenzo Orr, Travis Ford, Harold Sylvester; ***D:*** Randall Miller; ***W:*** Christopher Reed, Cynthia Carle; ***C:*** Michael Ozier; ***M:*** Marcus Miller.

The Sixth Sense 🦴🦴🦴 **1999 (PG-13)** Creepy psycho thriller about a traumatized young boy who can communicate with the dead (this is not the film's big surprise). Failed child shrink Malcolm Crowe (Willis in an excellent subdued performance) takes on the case of 9-year-old Cole (a touching Osment, carrying the picture on frail shoulders), who's divorced mom, Lynn (Collette), is worried about her terrified son's nightmares and episodes of acting out. Well, if you saw dead people all the time, you'd be scared too. When Crowe (who's dealing with traumas of his own) finally believes Cole, it leads to a breakthrough and an unexpected twist on what's happened before. **107m/C VHS, DVD, Blu-ray Disc.** Bruce Willis, Haley Joel Osment, Toni Collette, Olivia Williams, Donnie Wahlberg, Glenn Fitzgerald, Trevor Morgan, Mischa Barton, Bruce Norris; ***D:*** M. Night Shyamalan; ***W:*** M. Night Shyamalan; ***C:*** Tak Fujimoto; ***M:*** James Newton Howard. MTV Movie Awards '00: Breakthrough Perf. (Osment); Broadcast Film Critics '99: Breakthrough Perf. (Osment).

The '60s 🦴🦴 1/2 **1999 (PG-13)** A quick trip through the decade of peace, love, and Vietnam, told with all the usual cliches. Film uses the parallel stories of two families to hit the high points—the white, middleclass Herlihy family of Chicago and the black Taylor family of Mississippi. You've got hippies, Black Panthers, civil rights, the war, the anti-war movement, drugs, and rock 'n' roll. The soundtrack may be the best thing the miniseries has going for it. **171m/C VHS, DVD.** Jerry O'Connell, Josh Hamilton, Julia Stiles, Bill Smitrovich, Annie Corley, Leonard Roberts, Charles S. Dutton, Jordana Brewster, David Alan Grier, Jeremy Sisto, Cliff Gorman, Donovan Leitch, Carnie Wilson, Rosanna Arquette; ***D:*** Mark Piznarski; ***W:*** Jeffrey Alladin Fiskin; ***C:*** Michael D. O'Shea. **TV**

61* 𝒶𝒶𝒶 **2001** Crystal's nostalgic and meticulous telling of the 1961 home run race between Mickey Mantle (Jane) and Roger Maris (Pepper) clears the fence. Pepper and Jane are excellent as the "M & M Boys," and the rest of the solid cast is up to the task as well. The fine script mixes the baseball action with the behind the scenes material well. Crystal and writer Steinberg take great pains to show the tremendous pressure and outside distractions with which both players had to contend. With the exception of a few sportswriters (the obligatory villains), most of the characters are fleshed out nicely, instead of becoming a checklist of familiar names. Baseball geeks will find nits to pick, but for the most part, the baseball scenes and historical facts are right on the mark. Crystal's daughter plays Mrs. Maris. **128m/C VHS, DVD.** Thomas Jane, Barry Pepper, Chris Bauer, Christopher McDonald, Anthony Michael Hall, Bob Gunton, Bruce McGill, Richard Masur, Bobby Hosea, Donald Moffat, Renee Taylor, Joe Grifasi, Michael Nouri, Paul Borghese, Jennifer Crystal Foley, Seymour Cassel, Peter Jacobson, Robert Joy, Pat(ricia) Crowley, Robert Costanzo; ***D:*** Billy Crystal; ***W:*** Hank Steinberg; ***C:*** Haskell Wexler; ***M:*** Marc Shaiman. **CABLE**

'68 𝒶 **1987 (R)** A Hungarian family struggles with the generation gap in 1968 America. **99m/C VHS, DVD.** Eric Larson, Terra Vandergaw, Neil Young, Sandor Tecsy; ***D:*** Steven Kovacks; ***C:*** Daniel Lacambre; ***M:*** Shony Alex Braun, John Cipollinam.

6ixtynin9 𝒶𝒶 ½ *Ruang talok 69* **1999 (R)** After losing her job due to downsizing, Tum mopes and pouts until somehow a wad of cash is wrongly delivered to her apartment in a noodle carton. This leads to an outrageous series of events dealing with angry thugs hot on her tail, dead cops, and loads of paranoia. Thai black-comedy revels in its cheeky violence a little too much, and may be a few years behind in an already tired genre. Strictly for fans of bizarre Asian cinema. **118m/C DVD.** *TH* Lalita Panyopas, Sirisin Siripornsmathikul, Prompop Lee, Surapong Mekpongsathorn, Tasanawalai Ongartittichai, Black Phomtong, Sritao, Dylan Fergus; ***D:*** Pen-ek Ratanaruang; ***W:*** Pen-ek Ratanaruang; ***C:*** Chankit Chamnivikaipong.

Sizzle 𝒶𝒶 **1981** When her boyfriend is murdered by the mob, nightclub singer Anderson, newly arrived from Hicksville in Roaring '20s Chicago, stops at nothing to get revenge. Bad-guy gangster Forsythe falls for her charms. Fun but unsophisticated. Made for TV. **100m/C VHS.** Loni Anderson, John Forsythe, Leslie Uggams, Roy Thinnes, Richard Lynch, Michael Goodwin; ***D:*** Don Medford; ***M:*** Artie Butler. **TV**

Sizzle Beach U.S.A. 𝒶 *Malibu Hot Summer* **1974 (R)** Three aspiring young actresses want a shot at becoming famous and travel to Los Angeles where they spend their time at the beach with little budget and no particular purchase. Re-released and renamed in 1986 when Costner (in his film debut) became more well-known. **89m/C VHS, DVD.** Terry Congie, Leslie Brander, Roselyn Royce, Kevin Costner; ***D:*** Richard Brander.

Skag 𝒶𝒶𝒶 **1979** Disabled following a stroke, a Pittsburgh steel worker confronts a change in family roles and long-ignored family problems during his convalescence. Malden is exceptional and believable as a Joe Lunchbucket in this well-written, well-cast TV outing, pilot for the NBC series. **145m/C VHS.** Karl Malden, Piper Laurie, Craig Wasson, Leslie Ackerman, Peter Gallagher, Kathryn Holcomb, Powers Boothe; ***D:*** Frank Perry. **TV**

Skateboard 𝒶 **1977 (PG)** A down-and-out Hollywood agent creates a pro skateboarding team and enters them in a race worth $20,000. Quickie premise executed lamely. **97m/C VHS.** Allen (Goorwitz) Garfield, Kathleen Lloyd, Chad McQueen, Leif Garrett, Richard Van Der Wyk, Tony Alva, Antony Carbone; ***W:*** Dick Wolf.

The Skateboard Kid 𝒶 ½ **1993 (PG)** When an outsider finds a magical talking skateboard, he suddenly becomes the envy of the in-group of skateboarding thrashers. **90m/C VHS, DVD.** Bess Armstrong, Timothy Busfield; ***D:*** Larry Swerdlove; ***W:*** Roger Corman; ***V:*** Dom DeLuise.

The Skateboard Kid 2 𝒶𝒶 **1994 (PG)** Mystery creature helps Sammy build his dream skateboard, which turns out to have a mind of its own. **95m/C VHS, DVD.** Trenton Knight, Dee Wallace, Bruce Davison, Andrew Stevens; ***D:*** Andrew Stevens.

Skeeter 𝒶 ½ **1993 (R)** Yes, it's the attack of the killer mosquito! Not just any mosquito of course, but a new gigantic species bred on toxic waste. They're invading the quiet desert town of Mesquite—and they're out for blood! **95m/C VHS, DVD.** Tracy Griffith, Jim Youngs, Charles Napier, Michael J. Pollard; ***D:*** Clark Brandon; ***W:*** Clark Brandon, Lanny Horn; ***M:*** David Lawrence.

Skeezer 𝒶𝒶 ½ **1982** A dog becomes a key factor in a sympathetic doctor's efforts to communicate with emotionally unstable children. Based on reality, and a good cast makes it believable and moving. Quality family fare. **100m/C VHS.** Karen Valentine, Dee Wallace, Tom Atkins, Mariclare Costello, Leighton Greer, Justine Lord; ***D:*** Peter H. Hunt.

Skeleton Coast 𝒶 *Fair Trade* **1989 (R)** Borgnine plays a retired U.S. Marine colonel who organizes a Magnificent Seven-like group of tough mercenaries to go into eastern Africa to save hostages held by Angolan terrorists. Cliches abound, including a token large-breasted woman, Mulford, getting her t-shirt ripped open. No plot and a bad script. **94m/C VHS, DVD.** Ernest Borgnine, Robert Vaughn, Oliver Reed, Herbert Lom, Daniel Greene, Nancy Mulford, Leon Isaac Kennedy; ***D:*** John Cardos.

Skeleton Crew 𝒶 **2009** Low-budget derivative horror from Finland. In an abandoned mental hospital near the Russian border, a film crew discovers the 1970s-era screening room of a nutzo doctor who used it to stage his own snuff films (the directors incorporate torture porn footage to represent his work). Director Steven, working on his own opus, becomes obsessed and suddenly the crew is falling victim to the same old slaughter. **92m/C DVD.** *FI* Steve Porter, David Yolen, Rita Suomalainen, Anna Alkiomaa; ***D:*** Tommi Lepola, Tero Molin; ***W:*** Tommi Lepola, Tero Molin; ***C:*** Tommi Lepola, Tero Molin; ***M:*** Tuomas Kantelinen. **VIDEO**

The Skeleton Key 𝒶𝒶 **2005 (PG-13)** Caroline Ellis (Hudson) is a live-in nurse for a bayou stroke victim who finds herself creeping around in her underwear at night trying to uncover the hoodoo history of the homestead and save her patient from its curses. Tight plot and just enough suspenseful garnish keep the journey engaging enough. **104m/C DVD.** *US* Kate Hudson, Peter Sarsgaard, Gena Rowlands, John Hurt, Joy Bryant; ***D:*** Iain Softley; ***W:*** Ehren Kruger; ***C:*** Dan Mindel; ***M:*** Ed Shearmur.

Skeleton Key 2: 667, the Neighbor of the Beast 𝒶 **2008** A sequel to a 2006 direct-to-video trash horror/comedy film with the same name is a camcorder-quality parade of vampires, zombies, leprechauns, lesbians, songs about pooping yourself, and giant robots forged from bad CGI. **122m/C DVD.** Conrad Brooks, Monique Dupree, Jay Barber, Chris J. Duncan, John Johnson, John R. Price II, Saint, Johnny Sullivan; ***D:*** John Johnson; ***W:*** John Johnson; ***C:*** John Johnson. **VIDEO**

Skeletons 𝒶𝒶 **1996 (R)** Journalist Peter Crane (Silver) decides to leave New York after suffering a heart attack and moves his family to what he thinks will be the quiet of Saugatuck, Maine. They're settling in when Peter is approached by the mother of a young man, who's standing trial for murder, who claims her son is innocent. When Peter investigates, the townspeople suddenly turn hostile and the man is found hanged in his cell. Turns out this town's skeletons go back 100 years and the secrets are deadly. **91m/C VHS.** Ron Silver, James Coburn, Christopher Plummer, Dee Wallace, Kyle Howard, Thomas Wilson Brown; ***Cameos:*** Paul Bartel; ***D:*** David DeCoteau.

Skeletons in the Closet 𝒶𝒶 ½ **2000 (R)** Seth Reed (Jackson) is more than just a rebellious teenager. A loner, he's given to violent outbursts that have his widowed father, Will (Williams), worried. Especially when a series of murders are committed in their New Hampshire town. But since Will is still suffering from the aftermath of his wife's death in a fire, maybe it's his sanity that's in question. Creepy, if sometimes cliched, thriller. **86m/C VHS, DVD.** Treat Williams, Jonathan Jackson, Linda Hamilton, Schuyler Fisk, Gordon Clapp; ***D:*** Wayne Powers; ***W:*** Wayne Powers, Donna Powers; ***C:*** Michael Barrett; ***M:*** Christopher Stone. **VIDEO**

The Skeptic 𝒶 ½ **2009** Seems more like an old-fashioned TV movie-of-the-week than something intended for the big screen. Lawyer Bryan (Daly) inherits a creepy mansion from his late aunt and moves in to prevent break-ins (and as an excuse to separate from his wife). Soon the skeptic is subjected to spectral visions and other hauntings, leading Bryan to eventually connect things to childhood trauma. So he contacts a psychic researcher (Saldana) to rid the house of spooks. Mild scares. **89m/C DVD.** *US* Timothy Daly, Tom Arnold, Zoe Saldana, Edward Herrmann, Andrea Roth, Bruce Altman, Robert Prosky; ***D:*** Tennyson Blackwell; ***W:*** Tennyson Blackwell; ***C:*** Claudio Rocha; ***M:*** Brett Rosenberg.

Sketch Artist 𝒶𝒶 **1992 (R)** Jack Whitfield (Fahey) is a police sketch artist whose latest rendering of a murder suspect looks suspiciously like his wife. Jack decides to keep this information to himself while he does some quiet investigating but he may not have any time. The police have a new murder suspect in mind—Jack! **89m/C VHS.** Jeff Fahey, Sean Young, Drew Barrymore, Frank McRae, Tcheky Karyo, James Tolkan, Charlotte Lewis; ***D:*** Phedon Papamichael; ***W:*** Michael Angeli. **CABLE**

Sketch Artist 2: Hands That See 𝒶𝒶 ½ **1994** Fahey returns as police artist Jack Whitfield, who's asked to draw a sketch of a serial rapist/murderer. Near-victim Emmy (Cox) just happens to be blind but describes to Jack how the rapist looked as she felt his face. Emmy's hubby Glenn (Silverman) is concerned, especially when the creep warns Emmy about her trip to the cops. Solid characters build to good courtroom climax. **95m/C VHS.** Jeff Fahey, Courteney Cox, Jonathan Silverman, Michael Beach, Brion James, James Tolkan, Leilani Sarelle Ferrer, Michael Nicolosi, Scott Burkholder; ***D:*** Jack Sholder; ***W:*** Michael Angeli; ***M:*** Tim Truman.

Sketches of a Strangler 𝒶 ½ **1978** A psychotic art student sketches, then murders prostitutes. Interesting lead character but hardly chilling—just horrible to watch. Made for TV. **91m/C VHS.** Allen (Goorwitz) Garfield, Meredith MacRae; ***D:*** Paul Leder. **TV**

Ski Bum 𝒶 **1975 (R)** A ski bum discovers corruption and violence at a Colorado Rockies resort. Eminently forgettable trash. Scantily based on a novel by Romain Gary. **94m/C VHS.** Charlotte Rampling, Zalman King, Dimitra Arliss, Anna Karina; ***D:*** Bruce (B.D.) Clark.

Ski Party 𝒶𝒶 **1965** Slight and rather lame comedy. Gal pals Deborah and Yvonne are off on a ski trip to Squaw Valley, leaving behind their clueless would-be boyfriends Frankie and Dwayne. The guys decide to follow and cross-dress, passing themselves off as a couple of English chicks to get a better understanding of the mysteries of women. This causes some confusion when Dwayne falls for their sexy Swedish ski instructor (Shaw) and Frankie gets hit on by the clueless Kincaid. Lesley Gore and James Brown and the Flames perform. **90m/C DVD.** Frankie Avalon, Dwayne Hickman, Deborah Walley, Yvonne Craig, Bobbi Shaw, Aron Kincaid, Robert Q. Lewis; ***D:*** Alan Rafkin; ***W:*** Robert Kaufman; ***C:*** Arthur E. Arling; ***M:*** Gary Usher.

Ski Patrol 𝒶𝒶 **1989 (PG)** Wacky ski groupies try to stop an evil developer. Good ski action in a surprisingly plotful effort from the crazy crew that brought the world "Police Academy." **85m/C VHS.** Roger Rose, Yvette Nipar, T.K. Carter, Leslie Jordan, Ray Walston, Martin Mull; ***D:*** Richard Correll.

Ski School 𝒶 **1991 (R)** Rival ski instructors compete for jobs and babes. Brow lowering. **89m/C VHS.** Ava Fabian, Dean Cameron, Tom Breznahan, Stuart Fratkin; ***D:*** Damian Lee.

Ski School 2 𝒶 ½ **1994 (R)** Former ski instructor Dave finds that both his job and his ex-gal have been acquired by a jerk. So Dave decides to get them both back. **92m/C VHS, DVD.** Dean Cameron, Wendy Hamilton, Heather Campbell, Brent Sheppard, Bill Dwyer; ***D:*** David Mitchell; ***W:*** Jay Naples.

Ski Troop Attack 𝒶𝒶 **1960** During WWII, an American ski patrol is sent behind Nazi lines to blow up a German railway bridge. Unexceptional low-budget Corman outing; not among the greatest of war movies. **61m/B VHS, DVD.** Michael Forest, Frank Wolff, Sheila Carol, Richard Sinatra, Wally Campo; ***D:*** Roger Corman; ***W:*** Charles B. Griffith; ***C:*** Andrew M. Costikyan; ***M:*** Fred Katz.

Skier's Dream **1988** This spectacular action-packed film focuses on a young executive in search of the ultimate run. Shot on the most exotic ski locations in the world; covers freestyle skiing, powder skiing, snowboarding, extreme skiing, cliff jumping, paragliding, and wave riding. **75m/C VHS.** John Eaves, Ian Boyd; ***M:*** Jimi Hendrix, Tom Cochrane.

Skin 𝒶 ½ *Howard Beach: Making the Case for Murder* **1989 (PG-13)** Prosecutor seeks the truth after a black man is chased into highway traffic by a gang of white teenaged thugs from Queens. Based on the true story of the death of a young black man in Howards Beach, Queens. Made for TV. **95m/C VHS.** Daniel J. Travanti, Joe Morton, Dan Lauria, William Daniels; ***C:*** Ron Fortunato. **TV**

Skin Art 𝒶 ½ **1993 (R)** Very offbeat character study focusing on Will, a tormented tattoo artist who specializes in decorating the backs of the young Asian prostitutes who work in a nearby brothel. Haunted by his memories as a Vietnam POW, Will decides to exorcise some demons on his latest female canvas. **90m/C VHS.** Kirk Baltz, Jake Weber, Nora Ariffin; ***D:*** W(illiam) Blake Herron; ***W:*** W(illiam) Blake Herron.

Skin Deep 𝒶 ½ **1989 (R)** A boyish Don Juan tries everything to win back his ex-wife. Ritter whines about his mid-life crisis and seduces women; this substitutes for plot. A few funny slapstick scenes still don't make this worth watching. **102m/C VHS, DVD.** John Ritter, Vincent Gardenia, Julianne Phillips, Alyson Reed, Nina Foch, Chelsea Field, Denise Crosby; ***D:*** Blake Edwards; ***W:*** Blake Edwards; ***M:*** Henry Mancini.

Skin Deep 𝒶𝒶 **1994** Lesbian filmmaker Alex is obsessed with making her first feature, which is about the pleasure and pain associated with body art. She places an ad in a tattoo magazine for an assistant and is intrigued by respondent, Chris, who's still dealing with her transgendered experience. As Alex gets deeper into her movie, she fails to notice Chris' growing infatuation with her until Chris decides to do something desperate to gain Alex's attention. **82m/C VHS.** *CA* Natsuko Ohama, Keram Malicki-Sanchez, Dana Brooks, Melanie Nicholls-King, David Crean; ***D:*** Midi Onodera; ***W:*** Midi Onodera, Barbara O'Kelly.

Skin Game 𝒶 ½ **1931** Two British families feud over land rights. Not thrilling; not characteristic of working with Hitchcock. Way too much talking in excruciating, drawn-out scenes. Adapted from the play of the same name. **87m/B VHS, DVD.** *GB* Phyllis Konstam, Edmund Gwenn, Frank Lawton, C.V. France, Jill Esmond, Helen Haye; ***D:*** Alfred Hitchcock; ***W:*** Alfred Hitchcock; ***C:*** Jack Cox.

Skin Game 𝒶𝒶𝒶 **1971 (PG)** A fast talking con-artist (Garner) and his black partner (Gossett) travel throughout the antebellum South setting up scams—Gossett is sold to a new owner by Garner, who helps him escape. Garner and Gossett make a splendid comedy team in this different kind of buddy flick. All is well until Asner turns the tables on them. Finely acted comedy-drama. **102m/C VHS.** James Garner, Louis Gossett Jr., Susan Clark, Ed Asner, Andrew Duggan; ***D:*** Paul Bogart; ***M:*** David Shire.

Skinheads: The Second Coming of Hate 🦴 **1988 (R)** Neo-fascists run rampant. Exploitative effort from schlock-doyen Clark. **93m/C VHS.** Chuck Connors, Barbara Bain, Brian Brophy, Jason Culp, Elizabeth Sagal; ***D:*** Greydon Clark; ***W:*** Greydon Clark.

Skinned Alive WOOF! 1989 A woman and her children travel cross-country to sell leather goods. When a detective discovers where the leather comes from he's hot on their trail. **90m/C VHS, DVD.** Mary Jackson, Scott Spiegel; ***D:*** Jon Killough; ***W:*** Jon Killough.

Skinned Alive 🦴 **½** *Eat Your Heart Out* **2008 (R)** Lonely, depressed Jeffrey enjoys the company of prostitutes, and he falls for the lovely Pandora, who is into skinning people and eating them alive. Bet that costs extra. **90m/C DVD.** Alan Rowe Kelly, Melissa Bacelar, Jack Dillon, Joshua Nelson, Jeanette Bonner, Greg Depetro, Ed Avila; ***D:*** James Tucker; ***W:*** Joshua Nelson; ***C:*** Brian Fass; ***M:*** Duane Peery. **VIDEO**

Skinner 🦴 **1993 (R)** Psychopath Dennis Skinner (Raimi) more than lives up to his grisly name with his penchant for stalking hookers with carving knives and cleavers. Now he's going after his innocent landlady (Lake) and it's up to Heidi (Lords), a victim who managed to get away, to find him before he can kill again. Lords in lingerie (and nasty scars) and some really disgusting skinning scenes. **89m/C VHS, DVD.** Theodore (Ted) Raimi, Traci Lords, Ricki Lake; ***D:*** Ivan Nagy; ***W:*** Paul Hart-Wilden; ***C:*** Greg Littlewood.

Skinner's Dress Suit 🦴🦴 **½ 1926** Meek, hen-pecked office clerk tells domineering wife he got a raise so she'll get off his back. She quickly insinuates them into upper crusty social circle, where the fib pays off big. Remake of the 1917 version based on Henry Irving Dodge's novel. **79m/B VHS.** Reginald Denny, Laura La Plante, Arthur Lake, Hedda Hopper; ***D:*** William A. Seiter.

Skins 🦴🦴 **½ 2002 (R)** The Pine Ridge Indian Reseration in South Dakota is rife with unemployment, alcoholism, drug abuse, and violence, which native cop Rudy (Schweig) contends with on a daily basis. His older brother Mogie (Greene) is an embittered Vietnam vet and alcoholic who can't be a father to his own teenage son Herbie (Watts). While Rudy seems to have a better handle on life, in fact his frustrations lead to an act of destruction that has unexpected consequences. Based on the 1995 novel by Adrian C. Louis. **90m/C VHS, DVD.** *US* Eric Schweig, Graham Greene, Gary Farmer, Noah Watts, Lois Red Elk, Michelle Thrush, Nathaniel Arcand, Chaske Spencer; ***D:*** Chris Eyre; ***W:*** Jennifer D. Lyne; ***C:*** Stephen Kazmierski; ***M:*** B.C. Smith.

Skinwalker 🦴🦴 **½ 2002** Middle-aged Native American detective Joe Leaphorn has moved from the city to an Arizona Navajo reservation at the behest of his wife Emma (Tousey). He's finding it difficult to adjust, particularly when someone—or something—begins killing the local medicine men. His young partner, Officer Jim Chee (Beach) of the Navajo Tribal Police, thinks a skinwalker—an evil shape-shifting force—is at work but Leaphorn thinks the killer is more human than supernatural. Based on the mystery series by Tony Hillerman. **120m/C VHS, DVD.** Wes Studi, Adam Beach, Sheila Tousey, Alex Rice, RuPaul Charles; ***D:*** Chris Eyre; ***W:*** James Redford. **TV**

Skinwalkers 🦴 **2007 (PG-13)** Timothy (Knight) is about to turn thirteen when he discovers that he, like his dead father, uncle, and extended family, is a werewolf—not a bad werewolf, but a good werewolf that fights bad werewolves. Plus, there's a mysterious prophecy about him, so he and Uncle Jonas (Koteas) must go on the run to avoid bad werewolf Varek (Behr) and his crew of motorcycle-riding henchmen. Embarrassing howler (despite Koteas's decent performance) sanitizes the lycanthropic sex and violence for the adolescent set, and the results are dull and silly. **110m/C DVD.** *US CA GE* Jason Behr, Elias Koteas, Rhona Mitra, Matthew Knight, Kim Coates, Tom Jackson, Barbara Gordon; ***D:*** James Isaac; ***W:*** James DeMonaco, James Roday, Todd Harthan; ***C:*** Adam Kane, David Armstrong; ***M:*** Barbara Carrera, Andrew Lockington.

Skipped Parts 🦴 **½ 2000 (R)** Fourteen-year-old Sam Callahan (Hall) and his bad-girl mom, Lydia (Leigh), have been exiled to Wyoming in 1963 by Lydia's southern big daddy, Caspar (Ermey). Lydia promptly takes up with the wrong guy (Greyeyes) and encourages Sam in sexual experimentation with schoolmate Maurey (Barton), with unfortunate results. Based on Sandlin's coming-of-age trilogy, the film is flat and predictable. **93m/C VHS, DVD.** *US* Jennifer Jason Leigh, Bug Hall, Michael Greyeyes, Mischa Barton, Peggy Lipton, Brad Renfro, R. Lee Ermey, Angela Featherstone, Alison Pill, Drew Barrymore, Gerald Lenton-Young; ***D:*** Tamra Davis; ***W:*** Tim Sandlin; ***C:*** Claudio Rocha; ***M:*** Stewart Copeland.

Skirts Ahoy! 🦴🦴 **1952** Williams, Evans, and Blaine are three WAVES who have their eyes set on three handsome men. To get them, of course, they must sing and dance a lot, and Williams must perform one of her famous water ballets. ♫ Oh By Jingo; Hold Me Close to You; What Makes a WAVE?; What Good is a Gal Without a Guy?; Skirts Ahoy!; Glad to Have You Aboard; The Navy Waltz; I Get a Funny Feeling; We Will Fight. **109m/C VHS.** Esther Williams, Joan Evans, Vivian Blaine, Barry Sullivan, Keefe Brasselle, Billy Eckstine, Debbie Reynolds; ***D:*** Sidney Lanfield.

The Skull 🦴🦴 **1965** Horror abounds when Cushing gets his hands on the skull of the Marquis de Sade that has mysterious, murderous powers. Based on a story by Robert Bloch. **83m/C VHS, DVD.** Peter Cushing, Patrick Wymark, Christopher Lee, Nigel Green, Jill Bennett, Michael Gough, George Coulouris, Patrick Magee, Peter Woodthorpe; ***D:*** Freddie Francis; ***W:*** Milton Subotsky; ***C:*** John Wilcox; ***M:*** Elisabeth Lutyens.

Skull: A Night of Terror 🦴🦴 **1988 (R)** A cop vows not to use guns after a tragic accident, then single-handed and unarmed, takes on terrorists who kidnap his family. **80m/C VHS.** Nadia Capone, Robert Bideman, Robbie Fox, Paul Sanders; ***D:*** Robert Bergman; ***W:*** Robert Bergman, Gerard Ciccoritti.

Skull & Crown 🦴🦴 **1935** Rin Tin Tin Jr. helps the hero break up a group of smugglers. A favorite of Tin fans everywhere. **58m/B VHS, DVD.** Jack Mower, Molly O'Day, Lois January, Regis Toomey, Jack Mulhall, James Murray; ***D:*** Elmer Clifton; ***W:*** Bennett Cohen, Carl Krusada; ***C:*** Pliny Goodfriend.

Skullduggery 🦴 **½ 1970 (PG)** When a peaceful race of blond ape-people are discovered in New Guinea, a courtroom battle ensues to prevent their slaughter at the hands of developers. Interesting premise sadly flops. **105m/C VHS.** Burt Reynolds, Susan Clark, Roger C. Carmel, Chips Rafferty, Edward Fox, Wilfrid Hyde-White, Rhys Williams; ***D:*** Gordon Douglas.

Skullduggery WOOF! *Warlock* **1979 (PG)** Costume-store minion Haverstock carries a curse that makes him kill and mutilate. The usual unspeakable horror ensues for a group of medieval-game players. **95m/C VHS.** Thom Haverstock, Wendy Crewson, David Calderisi; ***D:*** Ota Richter.

The Skulls 🦴 **½ 2000 (PG-13)** Well, you just can't trust those darn secret societies. Teen star Jackson is Luke, an ambitious kid from the wrong side of the tracks at an "unnamed" Ivy League school that starts with "Y." Because he's the captain of the rowing team, he's asked to join the elite secret society the "Skulls." After the requisite hazing and initiation, Luke is showered with money and other perks. Membership has its privileges. But when his best friend Will (Harper) is found dead after snooping in Skull business, Luke supects foul play and the movie goes from laughable to ludicrous. This secret society, led by evil judge Litten Mandrake (Nelson), does a lot of its business, including duels and car chases, out in the open. Another entry using the teen-paranoia-adults-are-bad theme, which should, mercifully, help kill off the genre for a while. **106m/C VHS, DVD.** Joshua Jackson, Paul Walker, Hill Harper, Leslie Bibb, Christopher McDonald, Steve Harris, William L. Petersen, Craig T. Nelson; ***D:*** Rob Cohen; ***W:*** John Pogue; ***C:*** Shane Hurlbut; ***M:*** Randy Edelman.

The Skulls 2 🦴🦴 **2002 (R)** College student Ryan (Dunne) becomes a member of the secret fraternity the Skulls but when he sees a girl fall off the fraternity's roof, the situation turns ugly. **100m/C VHS, DVD.** *CA* Robin Dunne, Aaron Ashmore, Ashley Lyn Cafagna, Christopher Ralph, Nathan West, James Callanders, Lindy Booth; ***D:*** Joe Chappelle; ***W:*** Hans Rodionoff, Michele Colucci-Zieger; ***C:*** Steve Danyluk; ***M:*** Christophe Beck. **VIDEO**

The Sky Above, the Mud Below 🦴🦴🦴 *Le Ciel et le Boue* **1961** An acclaimed documentary following a band of explorers transversing New Guinea in 1959, and their confrontations with native rituals, heretofore unknown cannibal tribes and physical calamities. In HiFi. **90m/C VHS.** ***D:*** Pierre-Dominique Gaisseau. Oscars '61: Feature Doc.

Sky Bandits 🦴 **½ 1940** Mounties uncover the mystery of a disappearing plane carrying gold from a Yukon mine. Last of the "Renfrew of the Mounties" pictures. **56m/B VHS, DVD.** James Newill, Dave O'Brien, Louise Stanley; ***D:*** Ralph Staub; ***W:*** Edward Halperin; ***C:*** Mack Stengler.

Sky Blue 🦴 **½** *Wonderful Days* **2003** South Korean anime is a post-apocalyptic story that finds an environmental disaster has devastated the planet. Ecoban is a failing biosphere, run by a brutal elite dependent on refugee miners who are forced to live outside in the appropriately-named Wasteland. Soldier Jay (Cavadini) discovers her childhood sweetheart Shua (Worden) is leading a workers' rebellion against Ecoban's leaders. Predictable story, bad dialogue, sometimes eye-catching animation. **86m/C DVD.** ***D:*** Moon Sang Kim; ***W:*** Sunmin Park; ***C:*** Sun Kwan Lee; ***M:*** Sam Spiegel; ***V:*** Marc Worden, Catherine Cavadini, David Naughton.

Sky Captain and the World of Tomorrow 🦴🦴 **½ 2004 (PG)** More of a film experiment from first-timer Conran (it looks stunning) than a truly engaging film—notable for being the first studio feature where the actors worked against backgrounds that were entirely created digitally. In a pulp wartime melodrama, a sleek, streamlined New York is under attack from giant robots; it must be saved from destruction by the dashing Joe Sullivan (Law) better known as Sky Captain. Former flame/ace girl reporter Polly Perkins (Paltrow) goes along for the ride as she investigates the disappearance of a number of German scientists. The winsome twosome work together, aided (briefly) by eye-patch-wearing British air ace Franky (Jolie), to uncover the sinister plot of evil Dr. Totenkopf (the long-deceased Olivier creepily resurrected via digitized stock footage). **107m/C DVD, Blu-ray Disc, HD DVD.** *US* Gwyneth Paltrow, Jude Law, Angelina Jolie, Giovanni Ribisi, Michael Gambon, Omid Djalili, Laurence Olivier, Trevor Baxter, Julian Curry; ***D:*** Kerry Conran; ***W:*** Kerry Conran; ***C:*** Eric Adkins; ***M:*** Ed Shearmur.

The Sky Crawlers 🦴🦴 *Sukai kurora* **2008** Mamoru Oshii's films are not for every audience, and this one is no exception. In the future mankind has put an end to war, yet still craves violence. So the rival corporations that look as though they pretty much run the world put on wars for entertainment, using genetically altered humans called Kildren (attractive teens who never age) using WWII equipment. Beautifully animated, subtle, and more cerebral, despite the aerial dogfights in the trailers. **122m/C DVD, Blu-ray Disc.** *JP* Rinko Kikuchi, Chiaki Kuriyama, Shosuke Tanihara; ***D:*** Mamoru Oshii; ***W:*** Hiroshi Mori, Chihiro Itou; ***C:*** Hisashi Ezura; ***M:*** Kenji Kawai; ***V:*** Bryce Hitchcock.

Sky Hei$t 🦴🦴 **1975** Criminals plan robbery of police helicopter carrying fortune in gold bullion. **96m/C VHS.** Stefanie Powers, Joseph Campanella, Don Meredith, Larry Wilcox, Frank Gorshin, Shelley Fabares, Ken Swofford, Ray Vitte, Nancy Belle Fuller, Suzanne Somers; ***D:*** Lee H. Katzin. **TV**

Sky High 🦴🦴 **½ 1922** Mix is an immigration agent after a gang smuggling Chinese laborers across the Mexican border. Thrills involve an airplane and mountaintop battles as well as some terrific location footage from the Grand Canyon. **58m/B VHS.** Tom Mix, Eva Novak, J. Farrell MacDonald, Sid Jordan; ***D:*** Lynn F. Reynolds; ***W:*** Lynn F. Reynolds. Natl. Film Reg. '98.

Sky High 🦴 **1951** A spy at an Air Force base is trying to get hold of the plans to a secret plane. A GI is recruited to catch him. **60m/B VHS.** Sid Melton, Mara Lynn, Douglas Evans, Sam Flint, Fritz Feld, Margia Dean, Paul Bryar; ***D:*** Sam Newfield; ***W:*** Orville H. Hampton; ***C:*** Jack Greenhalgh; ***M:*** Bert Shefter.

Sky High 🦴 **1984** Three college students become immersed in international intrigue when the C.I.A. and the K.G.B. pursue them through Greece looking for a secret Soviet tape. **103m/C VHS, DVD.** Daniel Hirsch, Clayton Norcross, Frank Schultz, Lauren Taylor; ***D:*** Nico Mastorakis.

Sky High 🦴🦴🦴 **2005 (PG)** Will Stronghold (Angarano) is expected to follow in the footsteps of his superhero parents the Commander (Russell) and Jetstream (Preston) by attending Sky High School to learn the tricks of the trade. He is at first deemed a sidekick, which adds to his adolescence miseries, including a showdown against nemesis Warren Peace (Strait). Carries just the right mix of action, humor and gooeyness delivered by a top notch all-ages cast. **100m/C DVD, UMD.** *US* Michael Angarano, Kurt Russell, Kelly Preston, Bruce Campbell, Lynda Carter, Dave Foley, Danielle Panabaker, Mary Elizabeth Winstead, Steven Strait, Kevin Heffernan, Nicholas Braun, Kevin McDonald, Cloris Leachman, Dee-Jay Daniels, Kelly Vitz, Jim Rash, Jake Sandvig, Will Harris, Malika Khadijah; ***D:*** Mike Mitchell; ***W:*** Robert Schooley, Mark McCorkle, Paul Hernandez, Paul Amundson; ***C:*** Shelly Johnson; ***M:*** Michael Giacchino; ***V:*** Patrick Warburton.

The Sky Is Falling 🦴🦴 *Il Cielo Cade* **2000** In 1944, young orphaned sisters Penny (Niccolai) and Baby (Campoli) are sent to the Tuscan countryside to live with their Aunt Katchen (Roselli) and German-Jewish Uncle Wilhelm (Krabbe). Although they have managed to survive the war so far, things worsen as the retreating German Army closes in on their small town and the family is urged to make their way to Switzerland. But Uncle Wilhelm doesn't want to leave his home. Based on the autobiographical novel by Lorenza Mazzetti. Italian with subtitles. **102m/C VHS, DVD.** *IT* Isabella Rossellini, Jeroen Krabbe, Veronica Niccolai, Lara Campoli; ***D:*** Andrea Frazzi; ***W:*** Suso Cecchi D'Amico; ***C:*** Franco Di Giacomo; ***M:*** Luis Bacalov.

Sky Liner 🦴 **1949** An FBI agent is trailing a spy who has taken secret documents aboard a west-bound flight. **62m/B VHS.** Richard Travis, Pamela Blake, Rochelle Hudson, Steven Geray, Greg McClure, Steve Pendleton, Michael Whalen, Ralph Peters; ***D:*** William Berke; ***W:*** Maurice Tombragel; ***C:*** Carl Berger; ***M:*** Raoul Kraushaar.

Sky Parade 🦴 **½ 1936** Three World War I buddies (Gargan, Taylor, Fiske) team up to run a commercial airline but don't realize that enemy spies are checking out their design for a new plane. Allen, at the time a well-known teenaged pilot in his only screen appearance, plays himself and comes to save the day. **70m/B VHS.** William Gargan, Kent Taylor, Robert (Fisk) Fiske, Katherine DeMille, Jimmie Allen, Grant Withers, Syd Saylor, Billie Lee; ***D:*** Otho Lovering; ***W:*** Arthur Beckhard, Robert Burtt; ***C:*** William Mellor, Alfred Gilks.

The Sky Pilot 🦴🦴 **½ 1921** Young clergyman sets up a parish on North Pacific coast and finds he must prove himself to the cowboys. He saves young woman from stampede, but her father blames him for her maimed legs and sets the preacher's church on fire, providing girl with excuse to overcome handicap. **63m/B VHS.** John Bowers, Colleen Moore, David Butler, Donald Ian Macdonald; ***D:*** King Vidor.

Sky Pirates WOOF! 1987 Space epic deals about pieces of ancient stone left by prehistoric extraterrestrials, now lost in a time warp. Bad stunts, bad script and notably bad acting make it a woofer in any era. **88m/C VHS.** *AU* John Hargreaves, Max Phipps, Meredith Phillips; ***D:*** Colin Eggleston.

Sky Riders 🦴🦴 **½ 1976 (PG)** Hang-gliders risk it all to take on a group of political kidnappers. Fine hang-gliding footage and glorious Greek locations make up for garden-variety plot. **93m/C VHS.** James Coburn, Susannah York, Robert Culp, Charles Aznavour, Harry Andrews, John Beck; *D:* Douglas Hickox; *W:* Jack DeWitt, Garry Michael White; *M:* Lalo Schifrin.

Skyline 𝒶𝒶𝒶 *La Linea Del Cielo* **1984 (R)** A Spanish photographer comes to New York City to work for a magazine and tries to adjust to his cultural dislocation. Quietly funny, with a startling ending. Partly in Spanish with English subtitles. **84m/C VHS.** *SP* Antonio Resines, Beatriz Perez-Porro, Jaime Nos, Roy Hoffman; *D:* Fernando Colomo.

The Sky's the Limit 𝒶𝒶 ½ **1943** Astaire spends his leave in Manhattan and falls in love with fetching journalist Leslie. He's in civvies, so little does she know he's a war hero. Nothing-special semi-musical, with Fred-Ginger spark missing. ♫ One For My Baby; My Shining Hour; I've Got a Lot in Common With You. **89m/B VHS, DVD.** Fred Astaire, Joan Leslie, Robert Benchley, Robert Ryan, Elizabeth Patterson; *D:* Edward H. Griffith.

Skyscraper 𝒶 **1995 (R)** Gun-wielding helicopter pilot/heroine Carrie Wink (Smith) must battle villainous mercenaries holding hostages in an LA skyscraper. But she stills manages to find time for lots of steamy showers (to best display the only assets the film has). **96m/C VHS, DVD.** Anna Nicole Smith, Richard Steinmetz; *D:* Raymond Martino; *W:* William Applegate Jr.; *C:* Frank Harris; *M:* Jim Halfpenny.

Skyscraper Souls 𝒶𝒶𝒶 **1932** William stars as David Dwight, a ruthless businessman who manipulates stock prices and double-crosses lovers in order to have complete control of a 100-story office building. He sacrifices everything and everyone in this story of big business. Based on the novel "Skyscraper" by Faith Baldwin. **98m/B VHS.** Warren William, Maureen O'Sullivan, Gregory Ratoff, Anita Page, Verree Teasdale, Norman Foster, Jean Hersholt, Wallace Ford; *D:* Edgar Selwyn.

Slacker 𝒶𝒶𝒶 **1991 (R)** Defines a new generation: Overwhelmed by the world and it's demands, "Slackers" react by retreating into lives of minimal expectations. Filmed as a series of improvisational stories about people living on the fringes of the working world and their reactions (or lack thereof) to the life swirling around them. First feature for writer/director Linklater on a budget of $23,000; filmed on location in Austin, Texas with a cast of primarily non-professional actors. **97m/C VHS, DVD.** Richard Linklater, Rudy Basquez, Jean Caffeine, Jan Hockey, Stephan Hockey, Mark James, Samuel Dietert; *D:* Richard Linklater; *W:* Richard Linklater; *C:* Lee Daniel.

Slackers 𝒶 ½ **2002 (R)** Schwartzman is wasted as Ethan, a social outcast college student with his stalker-like eye on the prize—an intelligent college girl with model good looks (former model King). Nicknaming himself "Cool Ethan," our semi-delusional hero blackmails three of the campus's best and brightest, who have gotten that rep entirely through cheating. Ethan demands the boys use their unique methods of chicanery to get him his dream girl, or he'll get them all expelled. Leader of the gang Dave (Sawa) leads the fix-up charade but ends up falling for the cutie himself. Uninteresting, annoying characters, awkward plotting, and the requisite ton of sophomoric, sexual, and gross-out humor, including a gratuitous septugenarian sponge bath. **86m/C VHS, DVD.** *US* Devon Sawa, Jason Schwartzman, Jaime (James) King, Jason Segel, Michael Maronna, Laura Prepon, Mamie Van Doren, Joe Flaherty, Leigh Taylor-Young, Sam Anderson, Cameron Diaz; *D:* Dewey Nicks; *W:* David H. Steinberg; *C:* James R. Bagdonas; *M:* Joseph (Joey) Altruda.

Slam 𝒶𝒶 **1998 (R)** Documentarian Levin makes his feature film debut with this part-prison, part-ghetto drama. Street-smart, low-level drug dealer Ray (Williams) is living in gang-ridden D.C. when he's busted for possession and suspicion of murdering his supplier. Jail's just as rough as the streets since two local inside gangs each want Ray's allegiance. Ray wants to keep to himself and work on his writing—the poetry he composes about what he sees in life. He manages to get bail and then has a lot of hard decisions to make. **100m/C VHS, DVD.** Saul Williams, Sonja Sohn, Bonz Malone; *D:* Marc Levin; *W:* Marc Levin, Saul Williams, Sonja Sohn, Bonz Malone, Richard Stratton; *C:* Mark Benjamin. Sundance '98: Grand Jury Prize.

Slam Dunk Ernest 𝒶 ½ **1995 (PG-13)** Ernest (Varney) becomes a basketball star in a city league exhibition game when the Basketball Angel (Abdul-Jabbar) loans him his magic shoes. **93m/C VHS, DVD.** Jim Varney, Kareem Abdul-Jabbar, Jay Brazeau; *D:* John R. Cherry III; *W:* John R. Cherry III, Daniel Butler; *M:* Mark Adler.

Slamdance 𝒶 ½ **1987 (R)** A struggling cartoonist is framed for the murder of a beautiful young woman while being victimized by the real killer. A complicated murder mystery with a punk beat and visual flash. But the tale is unoriginal—and where's the slamdancing? **99m/C VHS, DVD.** Tom Hulce, Virginia Madsen, Mary Elizabeth Mastrantonio, Harry Dean Stanton, Adam Ant, John Doe; *D:* Wayne Wang.

Slammer Girls 𝒶 **1987 (R)** In this sex-drenched, unfunny spoof on women's prison films, the inmates of Loch Ness Penitentiary try to break out using their sexual wiles. The actresses are pseudonymous porn stars. **82m/C VHS.** Tally Brittany, Jane (Veronica Hart) Hamilton, Jeff Eagle, Devon Jenkin; *D:* Chuck Vincent.

Slander House 𝒶 ½ **1938** Helene (Ames) owes a posh salon with a society clientele obsessed with gossip. Columnist Terry Kent (Newell), who's involved with shop receptionist Mazie (Kelton), prints the tidbits he hears, causing a lot of trouble. But Helene creates her own problems when a married matron mistakenly thinks Helene has taken up with her adulterous lawyer husband. Actually, Helene is trying to avoid the lawyer's client, dashing Pat Fenton (Reynolds), who's fallen for her. **65m/B DVD.** Adrienne Ames, Craig Reynolds, Esther Ralston, William "Billy" Newell, Pert Kelton, George Meeker, Edward (Ed Kean, Keene) Keane, Dorothy Vaughan; *D:* Charles Lamont; *W:* John Krafft, Gertrude Orr; *C:* M.A. Anderson.

The Slap *La Gifle* **1976 (PG)** French teens learn about love the French way. **103m/C VHS.** *FR* Isabelle Adjani, Lino Ventura; *D:* Claude Pinoteau; *M:* Georges Delerue.

Slap Her, She's French 𝒶𝒶 ½ *She Gets What She Wants* **2002 (PG-13)** Ambitious Starla (McGregor) is her high school's head cheerleader, dates the quarterback, and fully intends to become the beauty queen of the Spendora Beef Pageant. But a supposedly French exchange student named Genevieve (Perabo) is out to steal Starla's crown. **91m/C VHS, DVD.** *US* Piper Perabo, Jane McGregor, Jesse James, Trent Ford, Julie White, Brandon Smith, Nicki Aycox, Michael McKean; *D:* Melanie Mayron; *W:* Robert Lee King; *C:* Charles Minsky; *M:* Christophe Beck, David Michael Frank.

Slap Shot 𝒶𝒶𝒶 **1977 (R)** Profane satire of the world of professional hockey. Over-the-hill player-coach of the third-rate Charlestown Chiefs, Reggie Dunlop (Newman), gathers an odd-ball mixture of has-beens and young players and reluctantly initiates them, using violence on the ice to make his team win. The on-ice striptease by star player Ned Braden (Ontkean) needs to be seen to be believed. Charming in its own bone-crunching way. **123m/C VHS, DVD.** Allan Nicholls, Paul D'Amato, Brad Sullivan, Stephen Mendillo, Kathryn Walker, Paul Dooley, Yvon Barrette, Jeff Carlson, Steve Carlson, Dave Hanson, Ned Dowd, Paul Newman, Michael Ontkean, Jennifer Warren, Lindsay Crouse, Jerry Houser, Melinda Dillon, Strother Martin, Andrew Duncan, M. Emmet Walsh, Nancy Dowd, Swoosie Kurtz; *D:* George Roy Hill; *W:* Nancy Dowd; *C:* Victor Kemper; *M:* Elmer Bernstein.

Slap Shot 2: Breaking the Ice 𝒶𝒶 **2002 (R)** Okay, it took 25 years to make a sequel—is this a record? Rude and crude hockey comedy finds the Charlestown Chiefs being sold to media mogul Busey, who moves the team to Omaha, Nebraska. But the team is not supposed to play "real" hockey; they are only supposed to take the money and serve as comic foils to the game, which upsets the geeky Hanson brothers and team captain Baldwin. **104m/C VHS, DVD.** Stephen Baldwin, Jeff Carlson, Steve Carlson, Dave Hanson, Gary Busey, Callum Keith Rennie, Jessica Steen; *D:* Steve Boyum; *W:* Broderick Miller; *C:* Joel Ransom. **VIDEO**

Slappy and the Stinkers 𝒶𝒶 ½ **1997 (PG)** Five young misfits, known as "The Stinkers," are constantly in trouble with their stuffy school principal Morgan Brinway (Wong). On a class trip to the acquarium, the Stinkers meet Slappy the sea lion and decide to liberate him (they think he looks unhappy), stowing Slappy in Mr. Brinway's hot tub. Then the kids find out that evil animal thief Boccoli (McMurray) wants to steal the critter and sell him to a circus. Just as silly as it sounds but Slappy is really cute. **78m/C VHS, DVD.** B.D. Wong, Bronson Pinchot, Sam McMurray, Joseph Ashton, Travis Tedford, Gary LeRoi Gray, Carl Michael Lindner, Scarlett Pomers, Jennifer Coolidge; *D:* Barnet Kellman; *W:* Michael Scott, Bob Wolterstorff.

Slapstick of Another Kind 𝒶 ½ **1984 (PG)** Lewis and Kahn play dual roles as an alien brother and sister and their adoptive Earth parents, who are being pursued by U.S. agents. Rather miserable rendition of a Kurt Vonnegut novel. **85m/C VHS.** Jerry Lewis, Madeline Kahn, Marty Feldman, Jim Backus, Noriyuki "Pat" Morita, Samuel Fuller, Orson Welles; *D:* Steven Paul.

Slash 𝒶 ½ **1987** Each of four people caught in a political takeover harbors a secret that could harm one of the others. Extremely violent. **90m/C VHS.** Romano Kristoff, Michael Monty, Gwen Hung; *D:* John Gale.

Slashdance WOOF! **1989** A really pathetic thriller follows a lady cop undercover in a chorus line to find out who's been murdering the dancers. The acting is on the level of pro wrestling. Don't be fooled by the naked babes on the cassette box—there's no nudity. **83m/C VHS, DVD.** Cindy Maranne, James Carroll Jordan, Deanna (Dee) Booher, Joel von Ornsteiner, Jay Richardson; *D:* James Shyman; *W:* James Shyman.

Slashed Dreams 𝒶𝒶 *Sunburst* **1974 (R)** Hippie couple travels to California wilderness in search of a friend. A pair of woodsmen assault them and rape the woman, which really messes with their heads. Retitled and packaged as slasher movie. **74m/C VHS.** Peter Hooten, Kathrine Baumann, Ric Carrott, Anne Lockhart, Robert Englund, Rudy Vallee, James Keach, David Pritchard, Peter Brown; *D:* James Polakof; *W:* James Keach, David Pritchard.

The Slasher WOOF! *Rivelazioni di un Maniaco Sessuale al Capo Della Squadra Mobile; Revelations of a Sex Maniac to the Head ot the Criminal Investigation Division; So Naked, So Dead; So Sweet, So Dead; Confessions of a Sex Maniac* **1972 (R)** A policeman must find the madman who has been killing off unfaithful married women. Miserably gory, pointless slasher (hence the title) interesting only as an early example of its kind. **88m/C VHS.** *IT* Farley Granger, Sylva Koscina, Nieves Navarro, Annabella Incontrera, Femi Benussi, Jessica Dublin; *D:* Robert Bianchi Montero; *W:* Robert Bianchi Montero; *C:* Fausto Rossi; *M:* Giorgio Gaslini.

Slate, Wyn & Me 𝒶 **1987 (R)** Two bank-robbing, kidnapping brothers flee cross-country from the law, and fall in love with the girl they've snatched. Pointless, and pointlessly violent and vulgar. **90m/C VHS.** Sigrid Thornton, Simon Burke, Martin Sacks; *D:* Don McLennan; *C:* David Connell.

Slaughter 𝒶 **1972 (R)** After his parents are murdered, a former Green Beret goes after their killers. Plenty of brutality. Followed by "Slaughter's Big Ripoff." **92m/C VHS, DVD.** Jim Brown, Stella Stevens, Rip Torn, Cameron Mitchell, Don Gordon, Marlene Clark, Robert Phillips; *D:* Jack Starrett; *W:* Mark Hanna, Don Williams; *C:* Rosalio Solano; *M:* Luchi De Jesus.

Slaughter High 𝒶 **1986 (R)** A high school nerd is accidentally disfigured by a back-firing prank. Five years later, he returns to exact bloody revenge. Available in an unrated version. **90m/C VHS.** Caroline Munro, Simon Scuddamore, Kelly Baker; *D:* George Dugdale.

Slaughter Hotel 𝒶 *Asylum Erotica; La Bestia Uccide a Sangue Freddo* **1971 (R)** An asylum already inhabited by extremely bizarre characters is plagued by a series of gruesome murders. Lots of skin and lots of blood; Neri shines as a nymphomaniacal lesbian nurse. **72m/C VHS, DVD.** Klaus Kinski, Rosalba Neri, Margaret Lee, John Ely; *D:* Fernando Di Leo.

Slaughter in San Francisco 𝒶 *Chuck Norris vs. the Karate Cop; Yellow Faced Tiger; Karate Cop* **1981 (R)** A Chinese-American cop leads a one-man fight against corruption in the department in Daly City, near San Francisco. Norris is the bad guy; made in 1973 but not released until he had an established following (and he still has only some 18 minutes of film footage). Plenty of kicking and karate chops. **92m/C VHS.** *CH* Chuck Norris, Don Wong; *D:* William Lowe.

Slaughter of the Innocents 𝒶𝒶 **1993 (R)** FBI agent Broderick (Glenn) is sent to Salt Lake City to investigate the murders of two children which are found to be connected to a series of bizarre killings that have occurred around Monument Valley. Unbeknownst to his associates, Broderick often uses his 11-year-old whiz-kid son Jesse's (Cameron-Glickenhaus) computer skills to aid his research. Only this time, his inquisitive son gets too close to a serial killer and unless Dad can figure things out on his own, Jesse will be the next victim. **104m/C VHS, DVD.** Scott Glenn, Jesse Cameron-Glickenhaus, Sheila Tousey, Darlanne Fluegel, Zitto Kazann; *D:* James Glickenhaus; *W:* James Glickenhaus.

The Slaughter of the Vampires WOOF! *Curse of the Blood-Ghouls; Curses of the Ghouls* **1962** Newlyweds meet a bloodthirsty vampire in a Viennese chalet. Real, real bad horror flick, poorly dubbed. **81m/C VHS, DVD.** *IT* Walter Brandi, Dieter Eppler, Graziella Granata; *D:* Robert (Roberto) Mauri; *W:* Robert (Roberto) Mauri.

The Slaughter Rule 𝒶𝒶 ½ **2001** In rural Montana, high schooler Roy Chutney (Gosling) gets cut from the football team days after his estranged dad is killed in a train accident. With his divorced mom (Lynch) unable to cope, Roy finds some unexpected diversion when he joins the six-man football squad coached by eccentric loner Gideon Ferguson (Morse). Gideon has a dark past and a somewhat unsavory local reputation but Roy needs someone he can turn to, whatever the consequences. Performances by Gosling and Morse are the reason to watch since the storytelling is uneven. **115m/C VHS, DVD.** Ryan Gosling, David Morse, Clea DuVall, Kelly Lynch, David Cale, Eddie Spears, Amy Adams; *D:* Alex Smith, Andrew Smith; *W:* Alex Smith, Andrew Smith; *C:* Eric Alan Edwards; *M:* Jay Farrar.

Slaughter Trail 𝒶𝒶 **1951** Rancher-turned-stage robber Young shoots two Indians and cavalry colonel Donlevy has to deal with the fallout. Peace returns when Young dies. Ordinary western with balladeer device helping the plot along, or trying to. **78m/C VHS.** Brian Donlevy, Gig Young, Virginia Grey, Andy Devine, Robert Hutton; *D:* Irving Allen.

Slaughterday 𝒶 ½ **1977 (R)** An innocent woman is caught in the middle of an ex-con's elaborate scheme to commit the largest heist of his life. **87m/C VHS.** Rita Tushingham, William Berger, Frederick Jaeger, Michael Hauserman, Gordon Mitchell; *D:* Peter Patzak.

Slaughterhouse WOOF! **1987 (R)** A rotund, pig-loving country boy kills, maims, and eats numerous victims. Features the requisite dumb teens and plenty of blood. **87m/C VHS, DVD.** Joe Barton, Sherry Bendorf, Don Barrett, Bill Brinsfield; *D:* Rick Roessler; *W:* Rick Roessler; *C:* Richard Benda.

Slaughterhouse Five 𝒶𝒶 **1972 (R)** A suburban optometrist becomes "unstuck" in time and flits randomly through the experiences of his life, from the Dresden bombing to an extraterrestrial zoo. Noticed at Cannes but not at theatres; ambitious failure to adapt Kurt Vonnegut's odd novel. **104m/C VHS, DVD.** Sharon Gans, Roberts Blossom, Michael Sacks, Valerie Perrine, Ron Leibman, Eugene Roche, Perry King; *D:* George Roy Hill; *W:*

Stephen Geller; ***C:*** Miroslav Ondricek; ***M:*** Glenn Gould. Cannes '72: Special Jury Prize.

Slaughterhouse Rock WOOF! **1988 (R)** The ghost of a sexy rock star draws a young man into a confrontation with a sadistic spirit that rules a deserted prison. There's also some cannibalism involved. Music group Devo did the score for this flick. **90m/C VHS.** Nicholas Celozzi, Donna Denton, Toni Basil, Hope Marie Carlton; ***D:*** Dimitri Logothetis.

Slaughter's Big Ripoff ½ **1973 (R)** Slaughter is back battling the Mob with guns, planes and martial arts. This undistinguished sequel features McMahon as a mob boss. **92m/C VHS, DVD.** Jim Brown, Brock Peters, Don Stroud, Ed McMahon, Art Metrano, Gloria Hendry; ***D:*** Gordon Douglas; ***W:*** Charles Johnson; ***C:*** Charles F. Wheeler; ***M:*** James Brown, Fred Wesley.

Slave Girls from Beyond Infinity **1987 (R)** In this B-movie spoof, two beautiful intergalactic slave girls escape their penal colony, land on a mysterious planet, and meet a cannibalistic despot. Fun spoof of '50s "B" sci-fi movies. **80m/C VHS, DVD.** Elizabeth Kaitan, Cindy Beal, Brinke Stevens, Don Scribner, Carl Horner, Kirk Graves, Randolph Roehbling, Bud Graves; ***D:*** Ken Dixon; ***W:*** Ken Dixon; ***C:*** Thomas Callaway, Kenneth Wiatrak; ***M:*** Carl Dante.

A Slave of Love **1978** Poignant love story set in the Crimea as the Bolshevik Revolution rages around a film crew attempting to complete a project. Interesting as ideological cinema but also enjoyable romantic drama. In Russian with English subtitles. **94m/C VHS, DVD.** *RU* Elena Solovei, Rodion Nakhapetov, Alexander Kalyagin; ***D:*** Nikita Mikhalkov; ***M:*** Eduard Artemyev.

Slavers **1977 (R)** Detailed depiction of the 19th century African slave trade with a little romance thrown in. **102m/C VHS.** *GE* Trevor Howard, Britt Ekland, Ron Ely, Cameron Mitchell, Ray Milland; ***D:*** Jurgen Goslar.

Slaves in Bondage **1937** Young country girls are lured into the big city and initiated into a life of ill repute in this exploitation classic. A must for camp fans of the '30s. **70m/C VHS, DVD.** Lona Andre, Wheeler Oakman, Donald Reed, Florence Dudley, John Merton, Richard Cramer; ***D:*** Elmer Clifton; ***W:*** Robert A.(R.A.) Dillon; ***C:*** Edward Linden.

Slaves of Hollywood ½ **1999** Paulette (Morgan) is filming a documentary about five aspiring Hollywood wannabe execs as they work their way up the Tinseltown ladder. Lots of stylish flourishes highlight a familiar tale of the backstabbing, schmoozing movie biz. **80m/C VHS, DVD.** Nicholas Worth, Katherin Morgan, Amy Lyndon, Tim Duquette, Hill Harper, Andre Barron, Rob Hyland, Elliot Markman; ***D:*** Terry Keefe, Michael J. Wechsler; ***W:*** Terry Keefe, Michael J. Wechsler; ***C:*** David Alan Parks; ***M:*** Joseph (Joey) Altruda, Bradford T. Ellis.

Slaves of New York ½ **1989 (R)** Greenwich Village artists worry about life and love in the '80s and being artistic enough for New York. Adapted from the stories of Tama Janowitz, who also wrote the screenplay and appears as Abby. Disastrous adaptation of a popular novel. **115m/C VHS, DVD.** Bernadette Peters, Chris Sarandon, Mary Beth Hurt, Madeleine Potter, Adam Coleman Howard, Jsu Garcia, Mercedes Ruehl, Joe Leeway, Charles McCaughan, John Harkins, Anna (Katerina) Katarina, Tama Janowitz, Michael Schoeffling, Steve Buscemi, Anthony LaPaglia, Stanley Tucci; ***D:*** James Ivory; ***W:*** Tama Janowitz; ***C:*** Tony Pierce-Roberts; ***M:*** Richard Robbins.

Slaves to the Underground ½ **1996 (R)** Love affair between Seattle bandmates Shelly (Gross) and Suzy (Ryan) runs into problems when Shelly's ex-boyfriend Jimmy (Bortz) re-enters the picture and some old feelings are also re-ignited. Mediocre yet abrasive, with that dated postgrunge, Seattle-is-so-over feeling. **90m/C VHS, DVD.** Jason Bortz, Molly Gross, Marisa Ryan; ***D:*** Kristine Peterson; ***W:*** Bill Cody; ***C:*** Zoran Hochstatter; ***M:*** Mike Martt.

The Slayer WOOF! *Nightmare Island* **1982 (R)** It's movies like this that give getting back to nature a bad name. That horrible monster is after those nice young people again! This time it's on an island off the coast of Georgia. **95m/C VHS, DVD.** Alan McRae, Sarah Kendall, Frederick Flynn, Carol Kottenbrook; ***D:*** J.S. Cardone; ***W:*** J.S. Cardone; ***C:*** Karen Grossman; ***M:*** Robert Folk.

Slayer ½ **2006** Deliberately gory schlock redo of vampire myths. Major Hawk (Van Dien) and his Army unit are sent to South America to deal with vicious vamps who can come out during the day. Hawk's ex-wife, scientist Laurie Williams (O'Dell), just happens to be in the area doing research and if she needs rescuing, well, Hawk's up for the mission. Most of the budget seems to have been spent on fake blood. **88m/C DVD.** Casper Van Dien, Danny Trejo, Lynda Carter, Alexis Cruz, Jennifer O'Dell, Kevin Grevioux, Ray Park; ***D:*** Kevin Van Hook; ***W:*** Kevin Van Hook; ***C:*** Matt Steinauer; ***M:*** Ludek Drizhal. **CABLE**

Slayground ½ **1984 (R)** Man, distraught at the accidental death of his daughter, hires a hitman to exact revenge. Excruciating adaptation of the novel by Richard Stark (Donald E. Westlake). **85m/C VHS, DVD.** *GB* Peter Coyote, Mel Smith, Billie Whitelaw, Philip Sayer, Kelli Maroney; ***D:*** Terry Bedford; ***M:*** Colin Towns.

SLC Punk! **1999 (R)** Lillard is Stevo, a punk rocker rebelling against "the establishment" in mid-'80s Salt Lake City, Utah before it's time to head off to Harvard Law. He and his friends wander aimlessly from fights with rednecks and hippies to trashy clubs to various girlfriends. Nothing really funny or particularly dramatic happens in the comedy-drama, which seems like an excuse for director/writer Merendino to relive his carefree college years. **97m/C VHS, DVD.** Matthew Lillard, Michael Goorjian, Annabeth Gish, Jennifer Lien, Christopher McDonald, Devon Sawa, James Duval, Til Schweiger, Kevin Breznahan, Jason Segel, Summer Phoenix, Adam Pascal, Chiara Barzini; ***D:*** James Merendino; ***W:*** James Merendino; ***C:*** Greg Littlewood; ***M:*** Melanie Miller.

The Sleazy Uncle *Lo Zio Indegno* **1989** A successful but bored businessman is energized by an encounter with his vice-ridden uncle, a mooching, womanizing beatnik poet who knows how to enjoy life. An energetic but rather formulaic comedy. In Italian with English subtitles. **104m/C VHS.** *IT* Giancarlo Giannini, Vittorio Gassman, Andrea Ferreol, Stefania Sandrelli; ***D:*** Franco Brusati; ***W:*** Franco Brusati, Leonardo Benvenuti, Piero De Bernardi; ***C:*** Romano Albani.

Sledgehammer WOOF! **1983** A madman is wreaking havoc on a small town, annihilating young women with a sledgehammer. **87m/C VHS.** Ted Prior, Doug Matley, Steven Wright; ***D:*** David A. Prior; ***W:*** David A. Prior.

Sleep Easy, Hutch Rimes **2000** Insurance agent Hutch Rimes (Weber) may be a womanizer but he knows nothing about women. When abused wife (and Hutch's squeeze) Holly (Siemaszko) decides to murder hubby Cotton (Henry), she enlists Hutch's help. The plan is botched, Holly dies, and Cotton goes to prison. Ten years later, Hutch is now seeing Olivia (O'Grady) who wants to get rid of her jealous hubby (Tobolowsky) and wants Hutch to aid her. But he's got bigger problems—Cotton is out of prison and out for revenge. Meanwhile, Hutch's faithful secretary (Kurtz) decides it's time to make her romantic feelings known to her boss. **99m/C VHS, DVD.** Steven Weber, Swoosie Kurtz, Gail O'Grady, Gregg Henry, Gabriel Mann, Nina Siemaszko, Stephen Tobolowsky, Stacey Travis, Bonnie Somerville, Jack Johnson; ***D:*** Matthew Irmas; ***W:*** Michael O'Connell; ***C:*** Jerry Sidell; ***M:*** Alex Wurman. **CABLE**

Sleep of Death ½ **1979** Young Englishman's pursuit of a blue-blooded woman seems to set off a series of bizarre and mysterious murders. A gothic thriller based on Sheridan Le Fanu's short story. **90m/C VHS.** Brendan Price, Marilu Tolo, Patrick Magee, Curt Jurgens, Per Oscarsson; ***D:*** Calvin Floyd.

Sleep with Me ½ **1994 (R)** What happens when love comes between friendship? Sarah (Tilly), Joseph (Stoltz), and Frank (Sheffer) are soon to find out. Sarah and Joseph are about to get married when their best friend Frank realizes he's in love with Sarah. So he sets out to seduce her and when Joseph realizes what's going on, he not only questions Frank's friendship but wonders just what signals Sarah's been giving off (although Joseph's hardly blameless). Six writers each wrote one of the social scenes detailing their triangular troubles, including a party where Tarantino does a hilarious riff on the homoerotic subtext in "Top Gun." Kelly's directorial debut. **117m/C VHS, DVD.** Craig Sheffer, Eric Stoltz, Meg Tilly, Todd Field, Adrienne Shelly, Lewis Arquette, Susan Traylor, Tegan West, Parker Posey, Dean Cameron, Thomas Gibson, June Lockhart, Quentin Tarantino, Joey Lauren Adams; ***D:*** Rory Kelly; ***W:*** Rory Kelly, Roger Hedden, Neal Jimenez, Michael Steinberg, Duane Dell'Amico, Joe Keenan; ***M:*** David Lawrence.

Sleepaway Camp **1983 (R)** Crazed killer hacks away at the inhabitants of a peaceful summer camp in this run-of-the-mill slasher. **88m/C VHS, DVD.** Mike Kellin, Jonathan Tiersten, Felissa Rose, Christopher Collet, Robert Earl Jones; ***D:*** Robert Hiltzik; ***W:*** Robert Hiltzik; ***C:*** Benjamin Davis; ***M:*** Edward Bilous.

Sleepaway Camp 2: Unhappy Campers ½ **1988 (R)** A beautiful camp counselor is actually a blood-thirsty, murdering madwoman. Sequel to the 1983 slasher, "Sleepaway Camp." **82m/C VHS, DVD.** Pamela Springsteen, Renee Estevez, Walter Gotell, Brian Patrick Clarke; ***D:*** Michael A. Simpson.

Sleepaway Camp 3: Teenage Wasteland WOOF! **1989 (R)** This second sequel is as bad as the first two movies. Another disturbed camper hacks up another bevy of teenagers. Better luck at the Motel Six. **80m/C VHS, DVD.** Pamela Springsteen, Tracy Griffith, Michael J. Pollard; ***D:*** Michael A. Simpson.

Sleeper ½ **1973 (PG)** Hapless nerd Allen is revived two hundred years after an operation gone bad. Keaton portrays Allen's love interest in a futuristic land of robots and giant vegetables. He learns of the hitherto unknown health benefits of hot fudge sundaes; discovers the truth about the nation's dictator, known as The Leader; and gets involved with revolutionaries seeking to overthrow the government. Hilarious, fast-moving comedy, full of slapstick and satire. Don't miss the "orgasmatron." **88m/C VHS, DVD.** Woody Allen, Diane Keaton, John Beck, Mary Gregory, Don Keefer, John McLiam; ***D:*** Woody Allen; ***W:*** Marshall Brickman, Woody Allen; ***C:*** David M. Walsh; ***M:*** Woody Allen.

Sleeper Cell ½ **2005** Darwyn (Ealy) is a black Muslim FBI agent posing as a disgruntled ex-con to infiltrate an LA terrorist cell. Seems there's a plot by charismatic leader Farik (Fehr) to attack various city sites. Then Darwyn gets distracted from his work by getting involved with single mom Gayle (Sagemiller). Ten-episode miniseries suffers from a saggy middle and a rather bland lead. **600m/C DVD.** *US* Michael Ealy, Oded Fehr, Grant Heslov, Melissa Sagemiller, Alex Nesic, James LeGros, Henri Lubatti; ***D:*** Clark Johnson; ***W:*** Cyrus Voris, Ethan Reiff; ***C:*** Robert Primes; ***M:*** Paul Haslinger. **CABLE**

Sleepers ½ **1996 (R)** Tense, gritty drama based on Lorenzo Carcaterra's book about four teenaged friends from Hell's Kitchen who get into trouble and wind up being sent to a reform school, where they're brutalized by guards. John (Eldard) and Tommy (Crudup), who grow up to be hit men, recognize their chief abuser (Bacon) years later and kill him. Their trial is prosecuted by Michael (Pitt), another of the gang, who's now the assistant DA. It's supposed to be a true story (the book is published as nonfiction) but doubt has been cast on Carcaterra's veracity (his character is the fourth member, journalist Lorenzo, played by Patric). De Niro and Hoffman excel in relatively minor, but pivotal, roles. **150m/C VHS, DVD.** Brad Pitt, Jason Patric, Ron Eldard, Billy Crudup, Kevin Bacon, Robert De Niro, Dustin Hoffman, Vittorio Gassman, Minnie Driver, Terry Kinney, Brad Renfro, Jonathan Tucker, Joe Perrino, Geoff Wigdor, Bruno Kirby, Aida Turturro, Frank Medrano; ***D:*** Barry Levinson; ***W:*** Barry Levinson; ***C:*** Michael Ballhaus; ***M:*** John Williams.

Sleepers West ½ **1941** Ah, the romance of the sleeper train! Only Shayne's (Nolan) on the job, transporting alcoholic ex-showgirl Helen (Hughes) from Denver to San Francisco so she can give her surprise testimony in a murder trial. Also aboard are Shayne's ex-girlfriend, snoopy reporter Kay Bentley (Bari), and her lawyer fiance (Douglas). Could they have anything to do with the attempts to prevent Helen from arriving safely at the station? **74m/B DVD.** Lloyd Nolan, Lynn Bari, Mary Beth Hughes, Donald "Don" Douglas, Louis Jean Heydt, Edward Brophy, Don Costello, Ben Carter; ***D:*** Eugene Forde; ***W:*** Lou Breslow, Stanley Rauh; ***C:*** J. Peverell Marley; ***M:*** Cyril Mockridge.

Sleeping Beauty **1959 (G)** Classic Walt Disney version of the famous fairy tale is set to the music of Tchaikovsky's ballet. Lavishly produced. With the voices of Mary Costa, Bill Shirley, and Vera Vague. **75m/C VHS, DVD.** ***D:*** Clyde Geronimi, Eric Larson, Wolfgang Reitherman, Les Clark; ***M:*** George Bruns; ***V:*** Mary Costa, Bill (William) Shirley, Barbara Luddy, Taylor Holmes, Verna Felton, Barbara Jo Allen, Pinto Colvig, Marvin Miller.

Sleeping Beauty **1983** Peters is the princess put to sleep by the evil queen. Handsome prince Reeve comes to the rescue in this classy retelling of the Sleeping Beauty legend. Combines live action and animation. From Shelley Duvall's "Faerie Tale Theatre." **60m/C VHS, DVD.** Christopher Reeve, Bernadette Peters, Beverly D'Angelo; ***D:*** Jeremy Paul.

Sleeping Beauty ½ **1989** Live action version of the beloved fairy tale, with Welch in the title role. **92m/C VHS.** Tahnee Welch, Morgan Fairchild, Nicholas Clay, Sylvia Miles, Kenny Baker.

The Sleeping Car **1990** A vindictive ghost haunts a group of people living in an old railway car. Fairly fun, fairly competent horror. **87m/C VHS.** David Naughton, Judie Aronson, Kevin McCarthy, Jeff Conaway, Dani Minnick, John Carl Buechler; ***D:*** Douglas Curtis.

Sleeping Car to Trieste **1945** Conspirators in the theft of a diplomat's diary ride the Orient Express, as a wily detective on board tries to piece together murder clues. Based on the story "Rome Express" by Clifford Grey. **95m/B VHS.** Jean Kent, Albert Lieven, David Tomlinson, Finlay Currie; ***D:*** Jack Paddy Carstairs.

The Sleeping Dictionary ½ **2002 (R)** In the 1930s, young Englishman John Truscott (Dancy) is newly arrived to take up his government post in Sarawak, Malaysia (where the movie was filmed). Governor Henry Bullard (Hoskins) tells Truscott that he will only be able to educate the native Iban population by learning their language and customs, so he arranges for the beautiful half-breed Selima (Alba) to become John's tutor. But John is not suppose to fall in love with the girl. Beautiful but slow-moving and that's a body double in Alba's love scenes. **109m/C VHS, DVD.** Hugh Dancy, Jessica Alba, Bob Hoskins, Brenda Blethyn, Emily Mortimer, Noah Taylor; ***D:*** Guy Jenkins; ***W:*** Guy Jenkins; ***C:*** Martin Fuhrer; ***M:*** Simon Boswell.

Sleeping Dogs ½ **1977** A man in near-future New Zealand finds it hard to remain neutral when he is caught between a repressive government and a violent resistance movement. The first New Zealand film ever to open in the U.S., and a fine debut for director Donaldson. **107m/C VHS, DVD.** *NZ* Sam Neill, Ian Mune, Nevan Rowe, Dona Akersten, Warren Oates; ***D:*** Roger Donaldson.

Sleeping Dogs Lie *Stay* **2006 (R)** Should you be completely honest in any relationship? Goldthwait's answer is a firm "no" in this off-the-wall comedy. When she was a bored college student, Amy (Hamilton) got, uh, very friendly with her dog (it's implied, not shown). When her fiance John (Johnson) asks Amy to tell him her deepest, darkest secret, she does. He's repulsed. Unfortunately, this situation occurs during their meet-the-parents weekend and Amy is left to deal with the consequences. Hamilton's a sweetie and the low-budget indie is subversively engaging. **87m/C DVD.** *US* Bryce Johnson, Geoffrey Pierson, Jack Plotnick, Bonita Friedericy, Melinda Page Hamilton, Colby French; ***D:*** Bob(cat) Goldthwait; ***W:*** Bob(cat) Goldthwait; ***C:*** Ian S. Takahashi; ***M:*** Jerry Brunskill.

The Sleeping Tiger 1/2 **1954** A thief breaks into the home of a psychiatrist, who captures him. In exchange for his freedom, the thief agrees to become a guinea pig for the doctor's rehabilitation theories with ultimately tragic results. Director Losey was originally compelled to release the film under a pseudonym, "Victor Hanbury," because he had been blacklisted by Hollywood during the 1950s red scare. First pairing of Losey and Bogarde, who collaborated on several later films, including "Modesty Blaise" (1966) and "Accident" (1967). **89m/B VHS.** Alexis Smith, Alexander Knox, Dirk Bogarde, Hugh Griffith; ***D:*** Joseph Losey; ***W:*** Harold Buchman, Carl Foreman; ***M:*** Malcolm Arnold.

Sleeping with Strangers 1/2 **1994 (R)** Two hoteliers in a small British Columbia town find their rivalry increasing as one hotel gets a boost when a drunken rock star and his Hollywood starlet arrive with their entourage in tow. Of course, the media follows and so does the comedic hysteria. **103m/C VHS.** Adrienne Shelly, Neil Duncan, Shawn Thompson, Kymberley Huffman, Scott McNeil; ***D:*** William T. Bolson; ***W:*** Joan Carr-Wiggin.

Sleeping with the Enemy 1/2 **1991 (R)** Roberts escapes from abusive husband by faking death, flees to Iowa, falls for drama professor, and, gasp, is found by psycho husband. Occasionally chilling but oft predictable thriller based on novel by Nancy Price. **99m/C VHS, DVD.** Julia Roberts, Kevin Anderson, Patrick Bergin, Elizabeth Lawrence, Kyle Secor, Claudette Nevins; ***D:*** Joseph Ruben; ***W:*** Ronald Bass; ***M:*** Jerry Goldsmith.

Sleepless **2001** Argento, the master of arty gore, returns in a familiar story. Retired inspector von Sydow is called back into service when a series of murders is identical to a prostitute murder spree (committed by a dwarf!) that the inspector solved 17 years earlier. Also back is the only witness (Dionisi) from the earlier crimes. **117m/C VHS, DVD.** *IT* Max von Sydow, Stefano Dionisi, Chiara Caselli; ***D:*** Dario Argento; ***W:*** Dario Argento, Franco Ferrini; ***C:*** Ronnie Taylor; ***M:*** The Goblins. **VIDEO**

Sleepless in Seattle 1/2 **1993 (PG)** Witty, sweet romantic comedy explores the differences between men and women when it comes to love and romance. When widower Sam Bladwin (Hanks) talks about his wife on a national talk show, recently engaged Annie Reed (Ryan) responds. Writer/director Ephron's humorous screenplay is brought to life by a perfectly cast ensemble; it also breathed new life into the classic weepie "An Affair to Remember," comparing it to "The Dirty Dozen" in an unforgettable scene. A movie full of fine detail, from Sven Nykvist's camera work to the graphic layout of the opening credits to the great score. Captured millions at the boxoffice, coming in as the fourth highest grossing movie of 1993. **105m/C VHS, DVD.** Tom Hanks, Meg Ryan, Bill Pullman, Ross Malinger, Rosie O'Donnell, Gaby Hoffman, Victor Garber, Rita Wilson, Barbara Garrick, Carey Lowell, Rob Reiner, Sarah Trigger; ***D:*** Nora Ephron; ***W:*** Jeffrey Arch, Larry Atlas, David S. Ward, Nora Ephron; ***C:*** Sven Nykvist; ***M:*** Marc Shaiman.

Sleepover 1/2 **2004 (PG)** Lightweight teen comedy has outsider Julie (Vega) celebrating her graduation from junior high by hosting a sleepover with friends Hannah (Boorem), Yancy (Childress), and Farah (Taylor-Compton). Julie breaks parental rules and sneaks out when challenged by popular Stacie (Paxton) to a scavenger hunt—the winner gaining social status in high school. Since these girls are about 14, some scenes—involving older men, bars, showers, and barely-there attire—are quease-inducing if not downright sleazy, although the intended audience will no doubt think all the highjinks are great fun. **90m/C VHS, DVD.** Alexa Vega, Mika Boorem, Sam Huntington, Jane Lynch, Scout Taylor-Compton, Kallie Flynn Childress, Jeff Garlin, Sean Faris, Sara Paxton, Eileen April Boylan, Timothy Dowling, Brie Lawson; ***D:*** Joe Nussbaum; ***W:*** Elisa Bell; ***C:*** James L. Carter; ***M:*** Deborah Lurie, Deborah Lurie.

Sleepstalker: The Sandman's Last Rites **1994 (R)** A serial killer known as the Sandman (Harris) is executed but returns as a shape-shifting horror who can strip the flesh off his victims with whirling sand. He haunts the nightmares of a reporter (Underwood), the only survivor of one of the killer's massacres, who teams up with a photographer (Morris) to learn the creature's origins and defeat him. Good special effects. **101m/C VHS, DVD.** Jay Underwood, Michael (M.K.) Harris, Kathryn Morris; ***D:*** Turi Meyer.

Sleepwalk **1988 (R)** Odd independent effort about a bored New York desk worker who is given an ancient text of Chinese fairy tales to translate, and finds they're manifesting themselves in dangerous ways in real life. **78m/C VHS.** Suzanne Fletcher, Ann Magnuson; ***D:*** Sara Driver; ***C:*** Frank Prinzi, Jim Jarmusch.

Sleepwalkers 1/2 *Stephen King's Sleepwalkers* **1992 (R)** When Mary and her son Charles arrive in the small town of Travis, Indiana, ugly things begin to happen. And no wonder, it seems the deadly duo are sleepwalkers—fiendish, cat-like vampire creatures who can only survive by sucking the life force out of unsuspecting virgins. Gory but not without some humor, particularly in Krige's portrayal of the sexy and too-loving mother. Not nearly as good as some of King's other horror classics. **91m/C VHS, DVD.** Brian Krause, Madchen Amick, Alice Krige, Jim Haynie, Cindy Pickett, Lyman Ward, Ron Perlman, Stephen King, Tobe Hooper, Mark Hamill, Glenn Shadix, Joe Dante, Clive Barker, John Landis, Dan Martin; ***D:*** Mick Garris; ***W:*** Stephen King; ***C:*** Rodney Charters; ***M:*** Nicholas Pike.

Sleepwalking 1/2 **2008 (R)** Down-and-out single mom Joleen (Theron) and her tween daughter Tara (Robb) are left homeless after Joleen's boyfriend is busted for drugs. The two drop in to visit Joleen's good-natured brother James (Stahl), but mom splits that night, leaving James stuck with the girl. Soon enough James loses his job and apartment, and Tara is taken away by Social Services. James then steals Tara back and they escape to the family farm house, still occupied by James and Joleen's villainous father (Hopper). A depressing, slow-moving indie flick, appropriately titled. **101m/C DVD, Blu-ray Disc.** *CA US* Charlize Theron, Nick Stahl, AnnaSophia Robb, Dennis Hopper, Woody Harrelson, Deborra-Lee Furness; ***D:*** William Maher; ***W:*** Zac Stanford; ***C:*** Juan Ruiz Anchia; ***M:*** Christopher Young.

Sleepy Eyes of Death: The Chinese Jade **1963** Master swordsman Nemuri Kyoshireo slaughters six would-be ambushers and has the seductive Chisa trying to set him against her master's enemy, Chen Sun, all for the sake of discovering the secret of the Chinese Jade. Adapted from the novel by Shibata Renzaburo. Japanese with subtitles. **82m/C VHS.** *JP* Raizo Ichikawa, Tamao Nakamura, Jo Kenzaburo; ***D:*** Tokuzo Tanaka.

Sleepy Hollow **1999 (R)** Gorgeous and grisly Burtonized version of Washington Irving's tale "The Legend of Sleepy Hollow." In this retelling, Ichabod Crane (Depp) is a New York constable who believes in reason and science, which won't do him much good when he's sent to the upstate hamlet of Sleepy Hollow to investigate a series of decapitation murders. Crane is housed by wealthy Balthus Van Tassel (Gambon), whose somewhat fey daughter Katrina (Ricci) falls for the quaking Crane, who refuses to believe that a ghost is committing mayhem. He's soon confronted by the graphic evidence of his own eyes. (Heads do certainly roll). Landau has a wordless cameo as the second victim. **105m/C VHS, DVD, Blu-ray Disc, UMD.** Johnny Depp, Christina Ricci, Miranda Richardson, Michael Gambon, Christopher Walken, Casper Van Dien, Jeffrey Jones, Richard Griffiths, Ian McDiarmid, Michael Gough, Christopher Lee, Marc Pickering, Lisa Marie, Steven Waddington, Claire Skinner, Alun Armstrong, Mark Spalding, Jessica Oyelowo; ***Cameos:*** Martin Landau; ***D:*** Tim Burton; ***W:*** Andrew Kevin Walker; ***C:*** Emmanuel Lubezki; ***M:*** Danny Elfman. Oscars '99: Art Dir./Set Dec.; British Acad. '99: Art Dir./Set Dec., Costume Des.

The Sleepy Time Gal **2001** Frances (Bisset), in her fifties and suffering from cancer, begins reflecting on her life and the daughter she gave up for adoption. Just about this time, her daughter, Rebecca (Plimpton) has been thinking out the her birth mother. Film follows both stories by showing parallels between Frances youth and Rebecca's life. In a subplot, Frances visits old flame (and Rebecca's father) Bob, and ends up bonding with his writer wife Betty. Pic steers perilously close to TV disease-movie-of-the-week territory, but impressive performance by Bisset helps it get by. Interesting melodrama will do if the cable's out and you can't watch Lifetime. **94m/C VHS, DVD.** *US* Jacqueline Bisset, Martha Plimpton, Nick Stahl, Amy Madigan, Frankie Faison, Carmen Zapata, Seymour Cassel, Peggy Gormley, Kate McGregor-Stewart; ***D:*** Christopher Munch; ***W:*** Christopher Munch; ***C:*** Rob Sweeney.

The Slender Thread **1965** Based on a true story, Poitier plays a college student who volunteers at a crisis center and must keep would-be suicide Bancroft on the phone until the police can find her. Filmed on location in Seattle. First film for director Pollack. **98m/C VHS.** Sidney Poitier, Anne Bancroft, Telly Savalas, Steven Hill; ***D:*** Sydney Pollack; ***W:*** Stirling Silliphant; ***C:*** Loyal Griggs; ***M:*** Quincy Jones.

Sleuth 1/2 **1972 (PG)** Milo (Caine), the owner of a chain of hair salons, is invited to the home of detective novelist Andrew Wyke (Olivier), who reveals that he Milo and Wyke's wife Marguerite are lovers. He persuades Milo to assist him with a fake robbery and an insurance scam that will help them both. Of course, Shaffer's complex plot (taken from his play) results in ever shifting, elaborate, and diabolical plots against each man, complete with red herrings, traps, and tricks. Playful, cerebral mystery thriller from top director Mankiewicz. **138m/C VHS, DVD.** Laurence Olivier, Michael Caine, John Matthews, Alec Cawthorne, Teddy Martin; ***D:*** Joseph L. Mankiewicz; ***W:*** Anthony Shaffer; ***C:*** Oswald Morris; ***M:*** John Addison. N.Y. Film Critics '72: Actor (Olivier).

Sleuth **2007 (R)** You'd think that Law would've learned his lesson after trying to fill Caine's shoes in his "Alfie" remake. But no, here he remakes the 1972 pic, tackling the Caine role while Caine himself steps into Laurence Olivier's part. Working-class upstart Milo Tindle (Law) has been boffing the wife of rich mystery writer Andrew Wyke (Caine). Andrew invites Milo to his ultra-modern manor to discuss the situation and says he'll give his wife a divorce if Milo will stage a jewel robbery so Andrew can claim the insurance. Pinter ups the homoerotic subtext and trims a lot of Anthony Shaffer's original dialogue, but it's all for naught as Branagh seems lost without a crowd to direct. However, Caine is as reliable as ever. **86m/C DVD.** *GB US* Michael Caine, Jude Law; ***D:*** Kenneth Branagh; ***W:*** Harold Pinter; ***C:*** Haris Zambarloukos; ***M:*** Patrick Doyle.

Sliding Doors 1/2 **1997 (R)** The sliding doors are those of a London subway train. If Helen (Paltrow) makes it through before they close, her life (and loves) go one way. If she's left on the platform, they go another, and the audience is let in on both options. She'll either dump or stick with cheating boyfriend Gerry (Lynch), who has been sleeping with ultra-bitchy ex-girlfriend Lydia (Tripplehorn). And she will either strike up a relationship with a charming stranger (Hannah) on the train and become fabulously successful, or end up slinging hash in a diner while pregnant with her scumbag boyfriend's baby. The concept and story of the dual possibilities is pulled off well, although it is a bit too cute at times. Will you like it? Depends on if it's already been rented when you're at the video store. If it's out, be careful what you pick, because apparently the small stuff really does matter. **98m/C VHS, DVD.** Gwyneth Paltrow, John Lynch, John Hannah, Jeanne Tripplehorn, Virginia McKenna, Zara Turner, Douglas McFerran, Paul Brightwell, Nina Young; ***D:*** Peter Howitt; ***W:*** Peter Howitt; ***C:*** Remi Adefarasin; ***M:*** David Hirschfelder.

A Slight Case of Murder 1/2 **1938** Robinson spoofs his own tough-guy image in this screwy comedy. Remy (Robinson) and his gang made a fortune as bootleggers selling lousy beer. Now that Prohibition is over, Remy is nearly bankrupt trying to sell the same rotgut and needs cash fast. To top off the bad news, daughter Mary (Bryan) get engaged to state trooper Dick (Parker). The family heads to their country home so Remy can think but he finds four dead gangsters and loot from a heist littering up the place while shooter Innocence (Downing) is lurking around. Oh, and company is coming. **85m/B DVD.** Edward G. Robinson, Jane Bryan, Allen Jenkins, Ruth Donnelly, Willard Parker, John Litel, Edward Brophy, Harold Huber, Paul Harvey, Bobby Jordan, Margaret Hamilton, George E. Stone, Bert Hanlon, Betty Compson, John Harmon, Harry Tenbrook; ***D:*** Lloyd Bacon; ***W:*** Earl Baldwin, Joseph Schrank; ***C:*** Sid Hickox; ***M:*** Adolph Deutsch, Howard Jackson, Heinz Roemheld.

A Slight Case of Murder 1/2 **1999** Cable TV critic Terry Thorpe (Macy) is in a panic after accidentally killing one of his girlfriends. Instead of confessing, Terry tries to keep the truth from the cops (Arkin, Pickens Jr.) and his surviving gal pal (Huffman). Then along comes a suspicious PI (Cromwell) with a blackmail scheme. Goofy film noir that gets too complicated. Based on the novel "A Travesty" by Donald E. Westlake. **94m/C VHS, DVD.** William H. Macy, Adam Arkin, Felicity Huffman, James Cromwell, James Pickens Jr., Julia Campbell, Paul Mazursky, Vincent Pastore; ***D:*** Steven Schachter; ***W:*** William H. Macy, Steven Schachter; ***C:*** Andre Pienaar. **CABLE**

Slightly Honorable 1/2 **1940** A lawyer gets involved in political scandals and becomes a murder suspect. Snappy comedy-drama with good performances but too many subplots. Based on the novel "Send Another Coffin" by F. G. Presnell. **75m/B VHS, DVD.** Pat O'Brien, Broderick Crawford, Edward Arnold, Eve Arden, Evelyn Keyes, Phyllis Brooks; ***D:*** Tay Garnett.

A Slightly Pregnant Man **1979 (PG)** Comic complications abound as a construction worker becomes the world's first pregnant man. Surprise ending saves this simple and not very exciting film. **92m/C VHS, DVD.** *FR IT* Catherine Deneuve, Marcello Mastroianni, Marisa Pavan, Micheline Presle, Claude Melki, Andre Falcon, Maurice Biraud, Alice Sapritch, Micheline Dax; ***D:*** Jacques Demy; ***W:*** Jacques Demy; ***C:*** Andreas Winding; ***M:*** Michel Legrand.

Slightly Scarlet 1/2 **1956** Small-time hood Payne carries out an assignment from boss DeCorsia to smear a law-and-order politico running for mayor. He falls in love with the candidate's secretary, tries to go straight, and ends up running the mob when DeCorsia flees town. A spiffy, low-budget noir crime drama based on the James M. Cain novel "Love's Lovely Counterfeit." **99m/C VHS, DVD.** Rhonda Fleming, Arlene Dahl, John Payne, Kent Taylor, Ted de Corsia; ***D:*** Allan Dwan; ***W:*** Robert Blees; ***C:*** John Alton; ***M:*** Louis Forbes.

Slightly Terrific 1/2 **1944** A group of theatrical newcomers enlist the help of twin brothers (one a producer and the other a wealthy businessman) to help them put on a show. Mistaken identity and confusion follows. **65m/B VHS.** Leon Errol, Eddie Quillan, Richard Lane, Anne Rooney, Ray Malone, Betty Kean, Lorraine Krueger; ***D:*** Edward F. (Eddie) Cline; ***W:*** Stan Davis, Edward Dein; ***C:*** Paul Ivano.

Slime City **1989** The widow of an alchemist poisons her tenants so they will join her husband in the hereafter. Very low-budget; occasionally funny. **90m/C VHS, DVD.** Robert C. Sabin, Mary Huner, T.J. Merrick, Dick Biel; ***D:*** Gregory Lamberson.

The Slime People **WOOF! 1963** Huge prehistoric monsters are awakened from long hibernation by atomic testing in Los Angeles. They take over the city, creating the fog they need to live. Thank goodness for scientist Burton, who saves the day. Filmed in a butcher shop in Los Angeles. **76m/B VHS, DVD.** Robert Hutton, Robert Burton, Susan Hart, William Boyce, Les Tremayne, John Close, Judee Morton; ***D:*** Robert Hutton; ***W:*** Vance Skarstedt; ***C:*** William G. Troiano.

Sling Blade 1/2 **1996 (R)** Mildly retarded killer Karl Childers (Thornton, making his feature directorial debut) is released from a mental hospital, where he was placed after killing his mother and her lover, after 25 years. Returning to his hometown, he befriends a boy (Black) with problems of his own. His mother is living with a mean, bullying drunkard (Yoakam, in a brilliant performance) who has no use for anyone, least of all mom's openly gay co-worker (Ritter). Thornton's excellent script moves at the slow pace of its hero, providing the superb cast plenty of opportunity to explore the rich characterization and dialogue. Filmed in Thornton's home state of Arkansas. **134m/C VHS, DVD.** Billy Bob Thornton, Dwight Yoakam, John Ritter, Lucas Black, Natalie Canerday, James Hampton, Robert Duvall, J.T. Walsh, Rick Dial, Brent Briscoe, Christy Ward, Col. Bruce Hampton, Vic Chesnutt, Mickey Jones, Jim Jarmusch, Ian Moore; ***D:*** Billy Bob Thornton; ***W:*** Billy Bob Thornton; ***C:*** Barry Markowitz; ***M:*** Daniel Lanois. Oscars '96: Adapt. Screenplay; Ind. Spirit '97: First Feature; Writers Guild '96: Adapt. Screenplay.

Slings & Arrows: Season 2 🦴🦴🦴 **2005** Geoffrey Tennant (Gross) is the reluctant artistic director of the financially troubled New Burbage Theater Festival. This season's star-crossed production is that cursed Scottish play "MacBeth," which has Geoffrey clashing with pompous star Henry Breedlove (Wyn Davies) and still seeing his ghostly mentor, Oliver (Ouimette). Company diva Ellen (Burns) is being audited, pretentious director Darren Nichols (McKellar) is staging "Romeo and Juliet," and the festival's image is being re-branded by a cut-throat ad exec (Feore). 6 episodes. **280m/C DVD.** *CA* Paul Gross, Martha Burns, Stephen Ouimette, Colm Feore, Geraint Wyn Davies, Don McKellar, Matt Fitzgerald, Mark McKinney, Susan Coyne; ***D:*** Peter Wellington; ***W:*** Mark McKinney, Susan Coyne, Bob Martin.

The Slingshot 🦴🦴🦴 **1993 (R)** Quirky coming-of-age tale, set in 1920s Stockholm, finds 12-year-old Roland (Salen) trying to survive childhood dilemmas. His mother (Frydman) is a Russian Jew (who sells condoms illegally) and his father (Skarsgard) is a zealous socialist, so Roland is subjected to unceasing bullying and prejudice. But the resourceful Roland doesn't let society get him down—he uses the contraband condoms in an inventive slingshot design that brings him an unwarranted amount of attention. Based on the novel by Roland Schutt. Swedish with subtitles. **102m/C VHS.** *SW* Jesper Salen, Stellan Skarsgard, Basia Frydman, Niclas Olund, Ernst-Hugo Jaregard, Jacob Leygraf; ***D:*** Ake Sandgren; ***W:*** Bjorn Isfalt, Ake Sandgren.

The Slipper and the Rose 🦴🦴 ½ **1976 (G)** Lavish musical adaptation of the fairy tale "Cinderella." Chamberlain is a very princely prince and the lovely Craven makes a fine and spunky servant girl, whom he can't help falling in love with. Besides the lively musical numbers, viewers will also enjoy the beautiful Austrian scenery. **127m/C VHS, DVD.** *GB* Richard Chamberlain, Gemma Craven, Annette Crosbie, Edith Evans, Christopher Gable, Michael Hordern, Margaret Lockwood, Kenneth More, Julian Orchard, Lally Bowers, Sherrie Hewson, Rosalind Ayres, John Turner, Keith Skinner, Polly Williams, Norman Bird, Roy Barraclough, Peter Graves; ***Cameos:*** Bryan Forbes; ***D:*** Bryan Forbes; ***W:*** Bryan Forbes, Robert B. Sherman, Richard M. Sherman; ***C:*** Tony Imi; ***M:*** Robert B. Sherman, Richard M. Sherman.

Slippery Slope 🦴 ½ **2006** Unbending radical feminist Gillian (Hutchinson) has her documentary accepted at Cannes but she needs 50 thou to get it out of hock at the film lab. Desperate, she accepts a job directing porn she's re-worked from literary classics. However, since she's working out of a Long Island motel, Gillian's browbeaten hubby Hugh (True-Frost) thinks she's having an affair. Has its humorous moments but how Gillian does solve her money woes is a letdown. **81m/C DVD.** Jim True-Frost, Laila Robins, Wes Ramsey, Leslie Lyles, Kelly Hutchinson; ***D:*** Sarah Schenck; ***W:*** Sarah Schenck; ***C:*** Wolfgang Held.

A Slipping Down Life 🦴🦴 **1999 (R)** The often-quirky Taylor gives a quirky performance as meek and depressed Evie, who has a crummy amusement park job in a small town and nothing to look forward to. That is, until she becomes obsessed with a struggling local musician called Drumstrings Casey (laconically played by Pearce). She carves his (last) name on her forehead, which at least gets Drumstrings attention and leads to some much-needed publicity. Evie begins to blossom under his interest and he appreciates her devotion, but is that all there is? You'll also be saying that about this indie (Fans of Anne Tyler, on whose novel, her first, the film is based, may not be happy that the teenagers are now twenty-somethings). After showing at the Sundance Film Festival, litigation kept the film out of circulation for five years. **111m/C VHS, DVD.** *US* Lili Taylor, Guy Pearce, John Hawkes, Sara Rue, Irma P. Hall, Tom Bower, Shawnee Smith, Veronica Cartwright, Marshall Bell, Bruno Kirby; ***D:*** Toni Kalem; ***W:*** Toni Kalem; ***C:*** Michael Barrow; ***M:*** Peter Himmelman.

Slipping into Darkness 🦴 ½ **1988 (R)** Three spoiled, rich college girls are held responsible for a retarded local boy's death. Honest and overwrought. **86m/C VHS.** T.J. McFadden, Michelle Johnson, John DiAquino; ***D:*** Eleanor Gaver; ***W:*** Eleanor Gaver.

Slipstream 🦴🦴 **1973** "Turgid" and "gloomy" are the words for this romantic drama set in remote Alberta. The minor plot concerns a young woman who teaches a lonely disc jockey a lesson about life and love. This film feels like a long Canadian winter. **93m/C VHS.** *CA* Luke Askew, Scott Hylands, Patti Oatman, Eli Rill; ***D:*** David Acomba; ***W:*** William Fruet; ***C:*** Marc Champion; ***M:*** Brian Ahern.

Slipstream 🦴🦴 **1989 (PG-13)** A sci-fi adventure set on a damaged Earthscape where people seek to escape a giant jetstream. While tracking down a bounty hunter gone bad, a futuristic cop follows his quarry into the dangerous river of wind. Ambitious "Blade Runner" clone with big names (Hamill is good) was never released theatrically in the US. **92m/C VHS, DVD.** *GB* Mark Hamill, Bill Paxton, Bob Peck, Eleanor David, Kitty Aldridge, Robbie Coltrane, Ben Kingsley, F. Murray Abraham; ***D:*** Steven Lisberger; ***W:*** Tony Kayden; ***C:*** Frank Tidy; ***M:*** Elmer Bernstein.

Slipstream 🦴 **2007 (R)** Hopkins is the star, writer, director, and composer of this self-indulgent, experimental fantasy. Early scenes turn out to be part of a movie script that is being rewritten by aging screenwriter Felix—a production that is falling apart because its star (Slater) has suddenly died. Characters pop in and out of Felix's imagination offering suggestions and complaints while most viewers will wonder what the heck was going on in Hopkins' head. **96m/C DVD.** Anthony Hopkins, Christian Slater, John Turturro, Michael Clarke Duncan, S. Epatha Merkerson, Fionnula Flanagan, Jeffrey Tambor, Camryn Manheim, Gavin Grazer, Lana Antonova; ***D:*** Anthony Hopkins; ***W:*** Anthony Hopkins; ***C:*** Dante Spinotti; ***M:*** Anthony Hopkins.

Slither 🦴🦴🦴 **1973 (PG)** Caan and Boyle become wrapped up in a scheme to recover $300,000 in cash, stolen seven years previously. Along the way they pick up speed freak Kellerman, who assists them in a variety of loony ways. Frantic chase scenes are the highlight. **97m/C VHS.** James Caan, Peter Boyle, Sally Kellerman, Louise Lasser, Allen (Goorwitz) Garfield, Richard B. Shull, Alex Rocco; ***D:*** Howard Zieff; ***W:*** W.D. Richter.

Slither 🦴🦴🦴 **2006 (R)** Slime and disfiguration abound after a meteorite crashes to Earth, allowing a nasty little alien hitchhiker to burrow into the chest of a prominent businessman. From there, things get ugly. Literally. Picture the Elephant Man covered in snot, hungry for flesh, and stripped of his dashing good looks. Done with style, intelligence, and tongue firmly in cheek, it makes for a good ol' fashioned popcorn n' mutations kind of flick. Tremendous props for ditching CGI and utilizing old-school make-up effects. These creatures pulsate and drip and shock better than any MPEG file. **95m/C DVD, HD DVD.** *US CA* Nathan Fillion, Elizabeth Banks, Gregg Henry, Michael Rooker, Brenda James, Don Thompson, Tania Saulnier, Jenna Fischer; ***D:*** James Gunn; ***W:*** James Gunn; ***C:*** Gregory Middleton; ***M:*** Tyler Bates.

Slithis WOOF! *Spawn of the Slithis* **1978 (PG)** Slithis, the nuclear-waste creature, is the menace of Venice, California. Keep your pets (and yourself) indoors! **86m/C VHS.** Alan Blanchard, Judy Motulsky, Mello Alexandria, Dennis Lee Falt, Win Condict; ***D:*** Stephen Traxler; ***W:*** Stephen Traxler; ***C:*** Robert Caramico; ***M:*** Steve Zuckerman.

Sliver 🦴 ½ **1993 (R)** Another voyeuristic thriller starring Stone. She's Carly Norris, a lonely book editor who moves into one of Manhattan's toothpick thin buildings (the "sliver" of the title). She meets pulp novelist Jack (Berenger), whose libido is as overheated as his prose, but gets involved in a steamy affair with handsome neighbor Zeke (Baldwin), a computer whiz who also owns the building. Oh, by the way, he's installed video cameras in every unit that reveal many intimate secrets. Lots of sex and murders. Murky and underdeveloped and the ending, which was reshot, still leaves much to be desired. Lots of hype, little to recommend. **106m/C VHS, DVD.** Sharon Stone, William Baldwin, Tom Berenger, Martin Landau, Polly Walker, Colleen Camp, CCH Pounder, Nina Foch, Keene Curtis; ***D:*** Phillip Noyce; ***W:*** Joe Eszterhas; ***C:*** Vilmos Zsigmond; ***M:*** Howard Shore. MTV Movie Awards '94: Most Desirable Male (Baldwin).

Sloane WOOF! 1984 Typical sleazy sex and violence flick. For the record: organized crime baddies kidnap good guy Resnick's girlfriend and he seeks revenge. **95m/C VHS.** Robert Resnick, Debra Blee, Paul Aragon; ***D:*** Dan Rosenthal.

Slogan 🦴 ½ **1969** Dated French story of amour fou. Middle-aged commercial director Serge (Gainsbourg), married to the pregnant Francoise (Parisy), begins a torrid affair with British teenager Evelyne (Birkin). Evelyne presses Serge to get a divorce and they move in together, though he's still married. But then the teen's eye is caught by daredevil stuntman Dado (Millinaire). Model Birkin was actually in her early 20s and married to Gainsbourg when they made the film. French with subtitles. **90m/C DVD.** *FR* Serge Gainsbourg, Jane Birkin, Daniel Gelin, Andrea Parisy, Gilles Millinaire; ***D:*** Pierre Grimblat; ***W:*** Pierre Grimblat; ***C:*** Claude Gainsbourg; ***M:*** Serge Gainsbourg.

Slow Burn 🦴🦴 **1986** An ex-reporter tries some detective work in the seamy side of Palm Springs, and becomes embroiled in the standard drug, kidnapping, murder routine. Based on the novel "Castles Burning" by Arthur Lyons. **92m/C VHS.** Eric Roberts, Beverly D'Angelo, Dan Hedaya, Dennis Lipscomb; ***D:*** Matthew Chapman; ***W:*** Matthew Chapman; ***M:*** Loek Dikker. **CABLE**

Slow Burn 🦴 **1990 (R)** The Mafia and Chinese Triads are having troubles and a tired cop attempts to reach a peaceful solution. **90m/C VHS.** William (Bill) Smith, Anthony James, Ivan Rogers; ***D:*** John Eyres; ***W:*** Stephen Lister; ***C:*** Nathaniel Massey; ***M:*** Allan Gray.

Slow Burn 🦴🦴 ½ **2000 (R)** Trina (Driver) is searching for a family heirloom—a box of missing diamonds—that were lost in the Mexican desert when her grandmother died. While she hunts around, the goods have already been discovered by a couple of escaped cons (Spader and Brolin) who take Trina hostage and steal her car. But when her car is disabled, things in the desert start to steam, with Trina trying to play both men against one another so she can make off with the treasure. **97m/C VHS, DVD.** Minnie Driver, James Spader, Josh Brolin, Stuart Wilson; ***D:*** Christian Ford; ***W:*** Christian Ford, Roger Soffer; ***C:*** Mark Vicente; ***M:*** Anthony Marinelli. **VIDEO**

Slow Burn 🦴 **2005 (R)** Filmed in 2003, did the festival circuit in '05, and finally saw a limited release in '07; the aging process didn't improve this confusing crime flick. DA Ford Cole (Liotta) is running for mayor but scandal threatens when ADA Nora Timmer (Blalock)—who's also Ford's occasional lover—is arrested for the death of her alleged rapist. But the case isn't so open-and-shut when Luther (LL Cool J) shows up, claiming Nora deliberately did the deed to cover up some secrets. The convoluted script just gets worse and the characters aren't interesting enough to make you care. **93m/C DVD.** *US* Ray Liotta, Jolene Blalock, LL Cool J, Mekhi Phifer, Bruce McGill, Chiwetel Ejiofor, Taye Diggs; ***D:*** Wayne Beach; ***W:*** Wayne Beach; ***C:*** Wally Pfister; ***M:*** Jeff Rona.

Slow Moves 🦴 ½ **1984** Slow story of slow people who meet slowly, have sluggish affair, and find tragedy eventually. **93m/C VHS.** Marshall Gaddis, Roxanne Rogers; ***D:*** Jon Jost; ***W:*** Jon Jost; ***C:*** Jon Jost; ***M:*** Jon Jost.

The Slugger's Wife 🦴 ½ *Neil Simon's The Slugger's Wife* **1985 (PG-13)** The marriage between an Atlanta Braves outfielder and a rock singer suddenly turns sour when their individual careers force them to make some tough choices. **105m/C VHS, DVD.** Michael O'Keefe, Rebecca De Mornay, Martin Ritt, Randy Quaid, Loudon Wainwright III, Cleavant Derricks, Lynn Whitfield; ***D:*** Hal Ashby; ***W:*** Neil Simon; ***C:*** Caleb Deschanel.

Slugs WOOF! 1987 (R) A health inspector discovers that spilled toxic waste is being helpfully cleaned up by the slug population, saving Uncle Sam countless dollars. But wait! The slugs are mutating into blood-thirsty man-eaters. Is this the answer to military cut-backs? **90m/C VHS, DVD.** Michael Garfield, Kim Terry, Philip Machale, Alicia Moro, Santiago Alvarez, Emilio Linder, Concha Cuetos; ***D:*** J(uan) Piquer Simon; ***W:*** J(uan) Piquer Simon; ***C:*** Julio Bragado; ***M:*** Tim Souster.

Slumber Party '57 🦴 ½ **1976 (R)** At a slumber party, six girls get together and exchange stories of how they lost their virginity. Lots of great music by the Platters, Big Bopper, Jerry Lee Lewis, the Crewcuts, and Paul and Paula but complete schlock otherwise. **89m/C VHS.** Noelle North, Bridget Holloman, Debra Winger, Mary Ann Appleseth, Cheryl "Rainbeaux" Smith, Janet Wood, R.L. Armstrong, Rafael Campos, Larry Gelman, Will Hutchins, Joyce Jillson, Victor Rogers, Joe E. Ross, Bill (Billy) Thurman; ***D:*** William A. Levey; ***M:*** Miles Goodman.

Slumber Party Massacre 🦴 ½ **1982 (R)** A psychotic killer with a power drill terrorizes a high school girls' slumber party. Contrived and forced, but not always unfunny. **84m/C VHS, DVD.** Michele Michaels, Robin Stille, Andre Honore, Michael Villela, Debra Deliso, Gina Mari, Brinke Stevens, Jean Vargas, Rigg Kennedy; ***D:*** Amy Holden Jones; ***W:*** Rita Mae Brown; ***C:*** Stephen Posey; ***M:*** Ralph Jones.

Slumber Party Massacre 2 WOOF! 1987 Drowsy babes in lingerie are drilled to death by a perverse madman. Less than disappointing sequel. **75m/C VHS, DVD.** Crystal Bernard, Kimberly McArthur, Juliette Cummins, Patrick Lowe; ***D:*** Deborah Brock; ***W:*** Deborah Brock; ***C:*** Thomas Callaway; ***M:*** Richard Ian Cox.

Slumber Party Massacre 3 WOOF! 1990 (R) Parents: Don't let your daughters have any slumber parties! Yes, it's a drill—for the third time. **76m/C VHS, DVD.** Keely Christian, Brittain Frye, Michael (M.K.) Harris, David Greenle, Hope Marie Carlton, Maria Ford; ***D:*** Sally Mattison; ***W:*** Catherine Cyran; ***C:*** Jurgen Baum; ***M:*** Jaime Sheriff.

Slumdog Millionaire 🦴🦴🦴 ½ **2008** Poor, orphaned teenager Jamil Malik (Patel), a petty criminal who lives in a squalid slum in Mumbai, gets the opportunity to become a contestant on the Indian version of "Who Wants to Be a Millionaire." He's so successful that the police arrest Jamil just before he tries for the ultimate prize, sure that the street boy must be cheating. But as he relates the story of his life, it becomes clear that each experience leads him to a correct answer on the quiz show. Director Boyle achieves the trifecta: a thought provoking film that is also beautiful and entertaining, capturing the disparity between the haves and have-nots with beauty and grace and not a shred of pity. Excellent Indian cast is universally appealing and wonderfully represents universal dreams and ambitions. **116m/C DVD.** *US GB* Anil Kapoor, Irfan Khan, Dev Patel, Freida Pinto, Madhur Mittal; ***D:*** Danny Boyle; ***W:*** Simon Beaufoy; ***C:*** Anthony Dod Mantle; ***M:*** A.R. Rahman. Oscars '08: Adapt. Screenplay, Cinematog., Director (Boyle), Film, Film Editing, Song ("Jai Ho"), Sound, Orig. Score; British Acad. '08: Adapt. Screenplay, Cinematog., Director (Boyle), Film, Film Editing, Sound, Orig. Score; Directors Guild '08: Director (Boyle); Golden Globes '09: Director (Amann), Film—Drama, Screenplay, Orig. Score; Screen Actors Guild '08: Cast; Writers Guild '08: Adapt. Screenplay.

Slums of Beverly Hills 🦴🦴🦴 ½ **1998 (R)** Every few months, Murray Abromowitz (Arkin) packs up daughter Vivian (Lyonne) and sons Ricky (Marienthal) and Ben (Krumholtz) to sneak out of their current dumpy apartment (without paying the rent) and move on to the next one, always within Beverly Hills so the kids can stay in a good school. When cousin Rita (Tomei) escapes from a rehab center, Murray takes her in. While Murray's main concern is the kids' education, Vivian is more obsessed with the size of her breasts and exploring her adolescent sexuality. Semi-autobiographical first film for Jenkins, who scripted while at the Sundance Institute, has lots of character and charm, and just enough bite. Lyonne has no trouble being the center of attention and injects comedy into the many awkward social situations that a teenage girl must endure. **91m/C VHS, DVD.** Natasha Lyonne, Alan Arkin, Marisa Tomei, Kevin Corrigan, David Krumholtz, Carl Reiner, Eli Marienthal, Jessica Walter, Rita Moreno; ***D:*** Tamara Jenkins; ***W:*** Tamara Jenkins; ***C:*** Tom Richmond; ***M:*** Rolfe Kent.

The Small Back Room 🦴🦴🦴 *Hour of Glory* **1949** A crippled WWII munitions expert leads a tormented existence and laments government bureaucracy. Powerfully presented adult storyline. **106m/B VHS.** David Farrar, Jack Hawkins, Cyril Cusack, Kathleen Byron, Anthony Bushell, Michael Gough, Robert Morley; ***D:*** Michael Powell, Emeric Pressburger.

Small Change 🦴🦴🦴🦴 *L'Argent de Poche* **1976 (PG)** Pudgy, timid Desmouceaux and scruffy, neglected Goldman lead a whole pack of heartwarming tykes. A realistically and tenderly portrayed testament to the great director's belief in childhood as a "state of grace." Criticized for sentimentality, "Small Change" followed Truffaut's gloomy "The Story of Adele H." Steven Spielberg suggested the English translation of "L'Argent de Poche." In French with English subtitles. **104m/C VHS, DVD.** *FR* Geory Desmouceaux, Philippe Goldman, Jean-Francois Stevenin, Chantal Mercier, Claudio Deluca, Frank Deluca, Richard Golfier, Laurent Devlaeminck, Francis Devlaeminck, Sylvie Grezel, Pascale Bruchon, Nicole Felix, Francois Truffaut; ***D:*** Francois Truffaut; ***W:*** Suzanne Schiffman, Francois Truffaut; ***C:*** Pierre William Glenn; ***M:*** Maurice Jaubert.

A Small Circle of Friends 🦴 1/2 **1980 (R)** Three Harvard students struggle through their shifting relationships during their college years in the 1960s. **112m/C VHS, DVD.** Brad Davis, Jameson Parker, Karen Allen, Shelley Long; ***D:*** Rob Cohen.

Small Faces 🦴🦴🦴 **1995 (R)** Semi-autobiographical account of three brothers growing up in a working class, gang-ridden section of Glasgow in 1968. Scottish lad Lex MacLean (Robertson) is at the crucial age of 13 and caught between two completely opposite brothers and two warring gangs. Sensitive brother Alan (McFadden) has the stigma of being an artist in a conscientiously macho society, while older brother Bobby (Duffy) has no such problem, being a gang member and all-around punk. When Lex unfortunately injures the eye of gang leader Malky (McKidd) with an air-gun, he unknowingly sets in motion a dangerous chain of events, forcing him to ally with both brothers. Writer/director MacKinnon makes sure even the most tense situations are offset with dark humor, and stages the violent scenes beautifully. Garnering comparisons with other Scottish youth fables like "Trainspotting," film follows somewhat the same storytelling formula, but is much more low-key. Character and plot are given equal attention and film greatly benefits from an outstanding performance by Robertson. CNT Violence and language. **108m/C VHS.** *GB* Iain Robertson, Clare Higgins, Ian McElhinney, Kevin McKidd, Joseph McFadden, J.S. Duffy, Laura Fraser, Garry Sweeney, Mark McConnochie, Steven Singleton, David Walker; ***D:*** Gilles Mackinnon; ***W:*** Gilles Mackinnon, Billy Mackinnon; ***C:*** John de Borman; ***M:*** John Keane.

Small Hotel 🦴🦴 **1957** After discovering that he is to be replaced as headwaiter by a young woman, Harker plots to save his job through espionage, blackmail and cajolery. Average comedy, adapted from a popular British stage play as a star vehicle for Harker. **59m/B VHS.** Gordon Harker, Marie Lohr, John Loder, Irene Handl, Janet Munro, Billie Whitelaw, Francis Matthews, Dora Bryan; ***D:*** David MacDonald.

Small Kill 🦴 1/2 **1993 (R)** Burghoff leaves his lovable MASH character far behind, testing his acting skills as a psycho who disguises himself as a female fortune teller to rob his victims of their life savings so he can become head druglord of his town (what a goal). Two cops try to stop him/her. **86m/C VHS.** Gary Burghoff, Rebecca Ferratti, Donnie Kehr, Jason Miller, Fred Carpenter; ***D:*** Robert M. Fresco; ***W:*** Fred Carpenter, James McTernan.

A Small Killing 🦴🦴 **1981** An undercover cop and a college professor pose as a wino and a bag lady, when trying to put the tabs on a druglord. Made for TV mystery/romance based on "The Rag Bag Clan" by Richard Barth. **100m/C VHS.** Ed Asner, Jean Simmons, Sylvia Sidney, Andrew Prine, J. Pat O'Malley, Anne Ramsey; ***D:*** Steven Hilliard Stern. **TV**

Small Sacrifices 🦴🦴 1/2 **1989** The true story of Diane Downs, an Oregon woman who may have murdered her own three children in 1983. Fine performance from Fawcett, who seems to like made for TV tales of true-life domestic violence as an antidote to her earlier ditzy persona as a Charlie's Angel. Gripping, with a superb script. **159m/C VHS.** Farrah Fawcett, Ryan O'Neal, John Shea, Emily Perkins, Gordon Clapp; ***D:*** David Greene; ***W:*** Joyce Eliason. **TV**

Small Soldiers 🦴🦴 1/2 **1998 (PG-13)** Why do kids today get all the really cool toys? G.I. Joe with the Kung Fu Grip never held any small Ohio towns under siege, and his fingers eventually fell off. But thanks to former defense supplier turned toy maker Globotech and its chairman Gil Mars (Leary), the residents of Winslow Corners receive a shipment of action figures called the Commando Elite. These toys are designed to interact with their owners. And do they ever—they take on a life of their own and wage war, thanks to being mistakenly implanted with military intelligence chips. Led by Chip Hazard (voice of Jones), these commandoes take on the previously quiet town in their quest to eradicate their toy rivals, the peaceful alien Gorgonites. Led by the gentle Archer (voice of Langella), the Gorgonites enlist the help of teens Alan (Smith) and Christy (Dunst) to battle this miniature menace. Combo of computer animation, Stan Winston's animatronic puppets, and live-action bring the toys to life. **110m/C VHS, DVD.** Gregory Edward Smith, Kirsten Dunst, Phil Hartman, Ann Magnuson, Jay Mohr, Denis Leary, Kevin Dunn, Wendy Schaal, Dick Miller, David Cross, Robert Picardo; ***D:*** Joe Dante; ***W:*** Gavin Scott, Adam Rifkin, Ted Elliott, Terry Rossio; ***C:*** Jamie Anderson; ***M:*** Jerry Goldsmith; ***V:*** Tommy Lee Jones, Frank Langella, Ernest Borgnine, Jim Brown, Bruce Dern, George Kennedy, Clint Walker, Christopher Guest, Michael McKean, Harry Shearer, Sarah Michelle Gellar, Christina Ricci.

Small Time 🦴🦴 **1991** Chronicles the downfall of a young, small-time Harlem thief. Vince knows nothing but the streets and peer pressure, indifference, and police abuse lead him inexorably to a fatal crime. Near documentary style only heightens the tensions. **88m/B VHS.** Richard Barboza, Carolyn Hinebrew, Keith Allen, Scott Ferguson, Jane Williams, Carolyn Smith; ***D:*** Norman Loftis; ***W:*** Norman Loftis; ***M:*** Arnold Bieber.

Small Time Crooks 🦴🦴 1/2 **2000 (PG)** Ex-con dishwasher Allen and his manicurist wife Ullman decide to become rich by robbing a New York City bank. Problem is, they team up with three bumblers (Lovitz, Rapaport, Darrow) to pull off the heist. As a result of the mishaps, the couple accidentally gains fame and fortune only to find it doesn't suit them at all. Grant is a well-bred snob trying to teach the lower classes some couth. Ullman, as usual, is endearing, while Allen is hard to fathom as a blue-collar guy turned crook. Hailed by some as Allen's triumphant return to his comedy stylings of old, the comedy in "Small Time Crooks" actually just seems old and tired. **94m/C VHS, DVD.** Woody Allen, Tracey Ullman, Hugh Grant, Jon Lovitz, Michael Rapaport, Elaine May, Tony Darrow, Elaine Stritch, George Grizzard; ***D:*** Woody Allen; ***W:*** Woody Allen; ***C:*** Fei Zhao. Natl. Soc. Film Critics '00: Support. Actress (May).

Small Town Boy 🦴🦴 **1937** The cast does what they can with the brief, hackneyed story of a guy whose personality changes for the worse when he finds a "fortune" (1000 pre-inflationary dollars). **61m/B VHS.** Stuart Erwin, Joyce Compton, Jed Prouty, Clara Blandick, James Blakely; ***D:*** Glenn Tryon; ***W:*** Glenn Tryon.

Small Town Girl 🦴🦴 1/2 *One Horse Town* **1953** Typical romantic musical of the era, as a city slicker picked up for speeding in a hick town is pursued by the sheriff's daughter. Several Busby Berkeley blockbuster musical numbers are shoehorned incongruously into the rural doings. ♫Take Me To Broadway; I've Got To Hear That Beat; My Flaming Heart; Fine, Fine, Fine; The Fellow I'd Follow; Lullaby of the Lord; Small Towns Are Smile Towns; My Gaucho. **93m/C VHS.** Jane Powell, Farley Granger, Bobby Van, Ann Miller, Billie Burke, Robert Keith, S.Z. Sakall, Fay Wray, Nat King Cole, Chill Wills; ***D:*** Leslie Kardos; ***M:*** Andre Previn.

A Small Town in Texas 🦴🦴 **1976 (PG)** An ex-con returns home looking for the sheriff who framed him on a drug charge, and who has stolen his woman. Not-too-violent, predictable revenge flick. **96m/C VHS.** Timothy Bottoms, Susan George, Bo Hopkins; ***D:*** Jack Starrett; ***W:*** William W. Norton Sr.; ***M:*** Charles Bernstein.

Small Vices: A Spenser Mystery 🦴🦴 1/2 **1999** Robert B. Parker's erudite Boston sleuth, Spenser (Mantegna), makes a return appearance along with his associate, Hawk (Mahmud-Bey), and lover Susan Silverman (Harden). This time Spenser is asked to check out a possible miscarriage of justice—did a streetwise young black man actually rape and murder a white suburban college student, the crime for which he's been convicted. But as things turn increasingly dangerous, it's clear someone doesn't want Spenser snooping around. **100m/C VHS.** Joe Mantegna, Marcia Gay Harden, Shiek Mahmud-Bey, Eugene Lipinski, Wood Harris; ***Cameos:*** Robert B. Parker; ***D:*** Robert Markowitz; ***W:*** Robert B. Parker; ***C:*** Ron Garcia; ***M:*** David Shire. **CABLE**

The Smallest Show on Earth 🦴🦴 **1948** A melodramatic tale about the son of an executed murderer who becomes the object of derision in the small town where he lives. One tormentor finally attacks him, and the young man must make a split-second decision that may affect his own mortality. **90m/B VHS, DVD.** Dane Clark, Gail Russell, Ethel Barrymore, Allyn Joslyn, Harry (Henry) Morgan, Lloyd Bridges, Selena Royle, Rex Ingram, Harry Carey Jr.; ***D:*** Frank Borzage.

The Smallest Show on Earth 🦴🦴🦴 *Big Time Operators* **1957** A couple inherit not only an old movie house, but the three people who work there as well. Very funny and charming, with a wonderful cast. Sellers is delightful as the soused projectionist. **80m/B VHS, DVD.** *GB* Bill Travers, Virginia McKenna, Margaret Rutherford, Peter Sellers, Bernard Miles, Leslie Phillips, Stringer Davis, Francis De Wolff, Sidney James, June Cunningham; ***D:*** Basil Dearden; ***W:*** William Rose, John Eldridge; ***C:*** Douglas Slocombe.

Smalltime 🦴🦴 **1996 (R)** Mobster, The Dutchman, needs to deliver a bag full of drugs to a desolate ranch and then wait for someone to pick up the goods and pay him. He decides to pass the job along to lower-level goon, Ben, who figures his two friends should be in on the caper. They get bored waiting and decide to call some girls to have a party, during which time the drugs get used up. Now, they've got nothing to switch for the money. This is going to make a lot of people unhappy. **96m/C VHS, DVD.** Jeff Fahey, Glenn Plummer, Rae Dawn Chong, Darren McGavin; ***D:*** Jeff Reiner; ***W:*** Jeff Reiner, Pat Cupo; ***C:*** Feliks Parnell; ***M:*** Vinnie Golia.

Smart Alecks 🦴 1/2 **1942** The Bowery Boys get involved with gangsters when Jordan helps capture a crook. The usual wise-cracking from Hall and Gorcey helps keep things moving. **88m/B VHS, DVD.** Leo Gorcey, Huntz Hall, Gabriel Dell, Gale Storm, Roger Pryor Jr., Walter Woolf King, Herbert Rawlinson, Joe (Joseph) Kirk, Marie Windsor; ***D:*** Wallace Fox.

Smart House 🦴🦴 **2000** Ben lives with his widowed dad and his younger sister in a typical suburban house. But Ben likes to enter contests and he actually wins a "Smart House," a house designed to take care of all those pesky daily choices thanks to a computer, for his family and persuades his dad to move in. But Ben's dad falls for the house's creator and the house itself gets jealous and decides to keep the family trapped inside. Although the premise has been used for horror movies, this one is strictly a comedy. **82m/C VHS, DVD.** Ryan Merriman, Kevin Kilner, Jessica Steen, Susan Haskell; ***D:*** LeVar Burton; ***V:*** Katey Sagal. **CABLE**

Smart Money 🦴🦴 1/2 **1931** Nick (Robinson) is a small-town barber who holds a poker game in his back room, helped by his assistant, Jack (Cagney). A consistent winner, Nick is encouraged to try his luck in a big-city game and loses everything, only to realize he's been set-up. So Nick sends for Jack and they work out their own scheme to get back at the crooked gamblers. The only time Robinson and Cagney were paired up onscreen. **90m/B DVD.** Edward G. Robinson, James Cagney, Boris Karloff, Noel Francis, Ben Taggart, Ralf Harolde, Evalyn Knapp; ***D:*** Alfred E. Green; ***W:*** Kubec Glasmon, Lucien Hubbard, John Bright, Joseph Jackson; ***C:*** Robert B. Kurrle.

Smart Money 🦴🦴 1/2 **1988** A wrongly jailed man enlists the help of his oddball pals to get revenge on the real thief who committed the computer fraud that put him behind bars. They get even while padding their pockets. **88m/C VHS, DVD.** Spencer Leigh, Alexandra Pigg, Ken Campbell; ***D:*** Bernard Rose; ***W:*** Matthew Jacobs.

Smart People 🦴🦴 **2008 (R)** Who don't act like it and behave badly. Supercilious Lawrence Wetherhold (Quaid) is a widowed English-lit professor at Carnegie Mellon who's bored and contemptuous of his students. His son James (Holmes) avoids the drama by living in the dorm and teen daughter Vanessa (Page) is following too closely in dad's footsteps. An accident that forbids Lawrence from driving brings doctor (and ex-student) Janet Hartigan (Parker) into Lawrence's life as well as his ne'er-do-well adoptive brother Chuck (Church), who moves in as temporary chauffeur. Church has the most fun with his stoner free spirit while everyone else does well enough by their stereotypes. **95m/C DVD.** *US* Dennis Quaid, Sarah Jessica Parker, Thomas Haden Church, Ellen Page, Ashton Holmes; ***D:*** Noam Murro; ***W:*** Mark Jude Poirier; ***C:*** Toby Irwin.

The Smart Set 🦴🦴 **1928** Typical sports-themed comedy from Haines in which he plays an obnoxious jerk who gets his comeuppance and then wins the day. Wealthy, polo-playing Tommy Van Buren makes the girls swoon—except for Polly (Day) since Tommy took her father's spot on the team. Eventually, Tommy's drunken behavior gets him ousted and now he has to redeem himself to regain his both his team and romantic chances. **80m/B DVD.** William Haines, Alice Day, Jack Holt, Hobart Bosworth, Julia Swayne Gordon, Coy Watson, Paul Nicholson, Constance Howard; ***D:*** Jack Conway; ***W:*** Byron Morgan, Ann Price; ***C:*** Oliver Marsh.

Smart Woman 🦴🦴 **1931** If she's so smart how come she's married to such a louse? Nancy Gibson (Astor) is fed up with being blamed for womanizing hubby Don's (Ames) infidelities so she decides to start a flirtation with Guy (Halliday) only to find herself falling in love. Adapted from the play "Nancy's Private Affair" by Myron C. Fagan. **68m/B VHS.** Mary Astor, Robert Ames, John Halliday, Edward Everett Horton, Noel Francis, Ruth Weston, Gladys Gale; ***D:*** Gregory La Cava; ***W:*** Salisbury Field; ***C:*** Nicholas Musuraca.

Smart Woman 🦴🦴 **1948** Not very! Defense attorney Paula Roger's (Bennett) latest client is racketeer Frank McCoy (Sullivan) who's accused of shooting the district attorney. The special prosecutor is none other than Robert Larrimore (Aherne), who's secretly involved with Paula outside the courtroom. But beside this conflict of interest, Paula has been keeping one big secret that makes for a sensational public revelation, which could jeopardize both her personal and professional lives. **93m/B DVD.** Constance Bennett, Brian Aherne, Barry Sullivan, Michael O'Shea, Otto Kruger, James Gleason; ***D:*** Edward Blatt; ***W:*** Alvah Bessie, Herbert Margolis, Louis Morheim, Adela Rogers St. John; ***C:*** Stanley Cortez; ***M:*** Louis Gruenberg.

Smash Palace 🦴🦴 1/2 **1982** A compelling drama of a marriage jeopardized by his obsession with building a race car and her need for love and affection. Melodramatic, but worth watching. Robson as their young daughter is wonderful. **100m/C VHS, DVD.** *NZ* Bruno Lawrence, Anna Maria Monticelli,

Greer Robson, Keith Aberdein; ***D:*** Roger Donaldson; ***W:*** Bruno Lawrence.

Smash-Up: The Story of a Woman *A Woman Destroyed* **1947** A famous nightclub singer gives up her career for marriage and a family, only to become depressed when her husband's career soars. She turns to alcohol and her life falls apart. When her husband sues for divorce and custody of their child, she fights to recover from alcoholism. Hayward's first major role. **103m/B VHS, DVD.** Susan Hayward, Lee Bowman, Marsha Hunt, Eddie Albert; ***D:*** Stuart Heisler; ***W:*** John Howard Lawson.

Smashing the Rackets ½ **1938** FBI agent Jim Conway (Morris) is shunted into a job in the DA's office. He meets playgirl debutante Letty Lane (Johnson) and falls for her more sedate sister Susan (Mercer). Since Letty has a boyfriend (Cabot) who's involved with the mob, Jim decides to use his new position to go after racketeers. Inspired by the career of New York district attorney Thomas E. Dewey. **69m/B VHS.** Chester Morris, Frances Mercer, Rita Johnson, Bruce Cabot, Ben Welden; ***D:*** Lew Landers; ***W:*** Lionel Houser; ***C:*** Nicholas Musuraca.

Smashing Time WOOF! 1967 Abysmal British comedy was never widely released on this side of the Atlantic and it's easy to see why. The film follows two small-town girls—Brenda (Tushingham), who's mousy and bony, and Yvonne (Redgrave), who's loud and pushy—who come to London at the swinging '60s. Unfortunately, they are two of the most unattractive comic heroines ever to hit the screen, and apparently that's a choice the filmmakers made deliberately. Moreover, their accents are difficult to understand and their voices could blister an elephant's hide. **96m/C VHS, DVD.** *GB* Rita Tushingham, Lynn Redgrave, Michael York, Anna Quayle, Irene Handl, Ian Carmichael; ***D:*** Desmond Davis; ***W:*** George Melly; ***C:*** Manny Wynn; ***M:*** John Addison.

Smile **1975 (PG)** Barbed, merciless send-up of small-town America focusing on a group of naive California girls who compete for the "Young American Miss" crown amid rampant commercialism, exploitation and pure middle-class idiocy. Hilarious neglected '70s-style satire. Early role for Griffith. **113m/C VHS, DVD.** Bruce Dern, Barbara Feldon, Michael Kidd, Nicholas Pryor, Geoffrey Lewis, Colleen Camp, Joan Prather, Annette O'Toole, Melanie Griffith, Denise Nickerson, Titos Vandis; ***D:*** Michael Ritchie; ***W:*** Jerry Belson; ***C:*** Conrad L. Hall; ***M:*** Daniel Osborn, Leroy Holmes.

Smile ½ **2005 (PG-13)** Well-off teenager Katie (Boorem) wants to find more meaning to life beyond her bickering parents and her boyfriend's sexual pressuring so she joins an international reconstructive surgery charity that sends her to China to help Ling (Ding), a girl of the same age whose disfigured face has plagued her entire life. Based on director Kramer's own daughter. Uplifting message is obscured by poor execution. **107m/C VHS, DVD.** Sean Astin, Mika Boorem, Beau Bridges, Yi Ding, Linda Hamilton; ***D:*** Jeffrey Kramer; ***W:*** Jeffrey Kramer. **VIDEO**

Smile, Jenny, You're Dead **1974** Janssen discovers that close friend's son-in-law has been murdered, and falls in love with the daughter, the main suspect. Pilot for Janssen's "Harry-O" detective series. **100m/C VHS.** David Janssen, John Anderson, Howard da Silva, Martin Gabel, Clu Gulager, Zalman King, Jodie Foster, Barbara Leigh; ***D:*** Jerry Thorpe. **TV**

A Smile Like Yours ½ **1996 (R)** Too-cute yuppie couple Danny and Jennifer (Kinnear and Holly) decide to start a family, only to discover that Danny's "boys" can't swim. Many formulaic and predictable gags about masturbation and the possiblilty of infidelity ensue. Unfortunately, laughs do not. Kinnear comes off as amiable enough, while Holly turns in an aggravatingly over-the-top performance. Thomas and Cusack, as the couple's best friends, fare better than anyone, with the possible exception of scene-stealer Meullerleile as the cranky clinic nurse. Writer/director Samples is the former head of now-defuct Rysher Entertainment (flick's producing company). Coincidence? We think not. **99m/C VHS, DVD.** Greg Kinnear, Lauren Holly, Jill(ian) Hennessey, Christopher McDonald, Joan Cusack, Jay Thomas, Donald Moffat, France Nuyen, Marianne Muellerleile; ***Cameos:*** Shirley MacLaine; ***D:*** Keith Samples; ***W:*** Keith Samples, Kevin Meyer; ***C:*** Richard Bowen; ***M:*** William Ross.

Smiles of a Summer Night ½ *Sommarnattens Leende* **1955** The best known of Bergman's rare comedies; sharp satire about eight Swedish aristocrats who become romantically and comically intertwined over a single weekend. Inspired Sondheim's successful Broadway musical "A Little Night Music," and Woody Allen's "A Midsummer Night's Sex Comedy." In Swedish with English subtitles. **110m/B VHS, DVD.** *SW* Gunnar Bjornstrand, Harriet Andersson, Ulla Jacobsson, Eva Dahlbeck, Jarl Kulle, Margit Carlquist; ***D:*** Ingmar Bergman; ***W:*** Ingmar Bergman.

Smiley Face **2007 (R)** Lame reefer comedy. Wannabe actress and chronic stoner Jane (Faris) starts off her day eating some pot-laced cupcakes baked by her roommate and then runs mundane errands like going to an audition, visiting her dentist, and paying off her drug dealer while experiencing life in a very high and happy place. However, it's not a place a viewer will care to experience with her unless they're in the same drug-induced state. **88m/C DVD.** Anna Faris, John Krasinski, Danny Masterson, Adam Brody, Ben Falcone; ***D:*** Gregg Araki; ***W:*** Dylan Haggerty; ***C:*** Shawn Kim; ***M:*** David Kitay.

Smiley's People ½ **1982** George Smiley (Guinness) is once again retired from British Intelligence when he learns that the murder of a former colleague is linked to their Soviet spy rival, Karla (Stewart). Smiley doggedly pursues his information, despite opposition, while Karla seeks to cover his tracks. Based on the novel by John Le Carre; the sequel to "Tinker, Tailor, Soldier, Spy." **324m/C VHS, DVD.** *GB* Alec Guinness, Barry Foster, Patrick Stewart, Bernard Hepton, Eileen Atkins, Anthony Bate, Michael Byrne, Sian Phillips, Beryl Reid, Michael Gough, Curt Jurgens, Rosalie Crutchley; ***D:*** Simon Langton; ***W:*** John Hopkins; ***C:*** Kenneth Macmillan; ***M:*** Patrick Gowers. **TV**

Smilin' Through **1933** First sound version of this melodrama/romance which Franklin had directed as a silent in 1922. Shearer is set to marry Howard when jealous rival March shows up armed at the wedding and accidentally kills the bride. March escapes and Howard spends his years as a recluse until his young niece, the image of his dead fiance (naturally, since she's also played by Shearer) arrives to live with him. She meets a young man who turns out to be March's son (played again by March) and they fall in love. Pure sentiment done with high gloss. Remade in 1941. **97m/B VHS.** Norma Shearer, Fredric March, Leslie Howard, O.P. Heggie, Ralph Forbes, Beryl Mercer, Margaret Seddon; ***D:*** Sidney Franklin; ***C:*** Lee Garmes.

Smilin' Through ½ **1941** Third filming, second with sound, first in color, of a popular melodrama. An embittered man whose wife was murdered on their wedding day raises an orphaned niece, only to have her fall in love with the son of her aunt's murderer. Songs include title tune and "A Little Love, a Little Kiss." **101m/C VHS.** Jeanette MacDonald, Brian Aherne, Gene Raymond, Ian Hunter, Frances Robinson; ***D:*** Frank Borzage.

Smiling Fish & Goat on Fire ½ **1999 (R)** Title refers to the childhood nicknames that Chris Remi (Derick Martini) and his brother Tony (Steven Martini) were given by their Native American/Italian grandma. Accountant Chris and aspiring actor Tony share a house in L.A. and have trouble with women. Their current relationships are falling apart, but new ones are looming, and the confused bros get some sage advice from their elderly friend, Clive (Henderson). Low-budget, wry slice-of-life. **90m/C VHS, DVD.** Steven Martini, Derick Martini, Bill Henderson, Christa Miller, Amy Hathaway, Rosemarie Addeo, Heather Jae Marie, Nicole Rae, Wesley Thompson; ***D:*** Kevin Jordan; ***W:*** Kevin Jordan, Steven Martini, Derick Martini; ***C:*** Fred Iannone; ***M:*** Chris Horvath.

The Smiling Lieutenant ½ **1931** Flirting at the wrong time/wrong place can get a guy into big trouble. Niki (Chevalier), an officer with Vienna's Royal Guards, is romancing violinist Franzi (Colbert). During a visit by King Adolf (Barbier), his plain daughter Princess Anna (Hopkins) mistakes a smile meant for Franzi to mean that Niki is interested in her. Duty-bound, Niki is forced into a royal marriage. So the worldly Franzi decides to help Anna win her reluctant new hubby's love by turning her into a knockout. **102m/B DVD.** Maurice Chevalier, Claudette Colbert, Miriam Hopkins, George Barbier, Charlie Ruggles, Robert Strange, Hugh O'Connell; ***D:*** Ernst Lubitsch; ***W:*** Ernst Lubitsch, Ernest Vajda, Samson Raphaelson; ***C:*** George J. Folsey; ***M:*** Oscar Straus.

Smilla's Sense of Snow **1996 (R)** Thriller starts off well but fails to sustain the suspense of the Peter Hoeg mystery on which it is based. Solitary scientist Smilla Jasperson (Ormond) is a half-Inuit, half-American (Danish in the book) resident of Copenhagen who's an expert on snow and ice. Born and raised in Greenland, Smilla is drawn back to her home when the body of six-year-old Isaiah (Miano), whom she's grudgingly befriended, is discovered at their apartment building. Smilla believes the boy was murdered and when she begins investigating it leads to the Greenland mining company where Isaiah's late father worked and which is run by the suspicious Tork (Harris). Location cinematography is particularly impressive. **121m/C VHS, DVD.** *GE DK SW* Julia Ormond, Gabriel Byrne, Richard Harris, Vanessa Redgrave, Robert Loggia, Jim Broadbent, Mario Adorf, Bob Peck, Tom Wilkinson, Peter Capaldi, Emma Croft, Clipper Miano; ***D:*** Bille August; ***W:*** Ann Biderman; ***C:*** Jorgen Persson; ***M:*** Hans Zimmer, Harry Gregson-Williams.

Smith! ½ **1969 (G)** Naive but well intentioned look at present-day treatment of Native Americans. Rancher Ford becomes embroiled in the trial of murder suspect Ramirez. Based on Paul St. Pierre's novel "Breaking Smith's Quarter Horse." **101m/C VHS.** Glenn Ford, Frank Ramirez, Keenan Wynn; ***D:*** Michael O'Herlihy; ***W:*** Louis Pelletier; ***M:*** Robert F. Brunner.

Smithereens ½ **1982 (R)** Working-class girl leaves home for New York's music scene. Rugged, hip character study. Director Seidleman's first feature. **90m/C VHS, DVD.** Susan Berman, Brad Rijn, Richard Hell, Christopher Noth; ***D:*** Susan Seidelman; ***W:*** Ron Nyswaner, Peter Askin.

Smoke ½ **1970** A young boy nurses a lost German sheperd back to health with the help of his new stepfather, whom he learns to trust. Then he runs away with the dog when the original owners show up. Disney fare starring Opie/Richie (and later successful director) Howard. **89m/C VHS.** Earl Holliman, Ron Howard, Andy Devine, Jacqueline Scott, Shug Fisher, Pamelyn Ferdin, Kelly Thordsen; ***D:*** Vincent McEveety; ***C:*** William E. Snyder; ***M:*** Robert F. Brunner. **TV**

Smoke **1993** Three days in the life of Michael, as he travels between fantasy and reality, past and present, searching for love with the perfect older man. **90m/C VHS, DVD.** Nick Discenza, Barbara Andrews, Mark D'Aruia; ***D:*** Mark D'Aruia; ***M:*** Arnold Bieber.

Smoke **1995 (R)** Brooklyn slice of life centers around the local cigar store run by Auggie Wren (Keitel). An ensemble piece, divided into five chapters, which includes such characters as down-on-his luck novelist Paul (Hurt), troubled black teenager Rashid (Perrineau Jr.), Augie's ex-wife Ruby (Channing) and supposed daughter (Judd), and many more (some of whom get lost in the shuffle). Wonderfully acted but the stories tend to disappear in a wisp of smoke. Based on a story by Auster. Wang and Auster also made an impromptu companion film "Blue in the Face." **112m/C VHS, DVD.** Harvey Keitel, William Hurt, Stockard Channing, Forest Whitaker, Harold Perrineau Jr., Ashley Judd, Mary Ward, Victor Argo, Jared Harris, Giancarlo Esposito, Mel Gorham, Stephen Gevedon, Erica Gimpel, Malik Yoba, Jose Zuniga, RuPaul Charles; ***D:*** Wayne Wang; ***W:*** Paul Auster; ***C:*** Adam Holender; ***M:*** Rachel Portman.

Smoke in the Wind ½ **1975 (PG)** Subpar western about men accused of complicity with the Union in postbellum Arkansas. Minor role for Brennan was his last; also director Kane's last film. **93m/C VHS.** John Ashley, Walter Brennan, John Russell, Myron Healey; ***D:*** Joseph Kane.

Smoke Jumpers ½ *Trial by Fire* **2008** Firefighter Kristen is blamed for a colleague's death and branded as unqualified. To prove her detractors wrong, Kristen is determined to join the dangerous ranks of smoke jumpers. Just after her training, Kristen gets the chance to prove herself when she's sent to assist at a forest fire that's gone out of control. **93m/C DVD.** Brooke Burns, Rick Ravanello, Winston Rekert, Erin Karpluk, Robert Molorey; ***D:*** John Terlesky; ***W:*** Jeff Stephenson; ***C:*** C. Kim Miles. **CABLE**

Smoke Signals **1998 (PG-13)** Serious themes are treated in a deceptively simple and humorous manner, based on stories from Alexie's book "The Lone Ranger and Tonto Fistfight in Heaven." Geeky, orphaned Thomas (Adams) lives on the Coeur d'Alene reservation in Idaho where he's reluctantly looked after by stoic Victor (Beach), whose long-gone father Arnold (Farmer) saved Thomas from the fire that killed his parents. When Victor learns of Arnold's death in Phoenix, Thomas says he'll pay the expenses of the trip if he can accompany Victor. The young men reach an understanding during their travels, while Victor struggles to deal with his complicated feelings about his father and the past. **88m/C VHS, DVD.** Adam Beach, Evan Adams, Irene Bedard, Gary Farmer, Tantoo Cardinal, Michelle St. John, Robert Miano, Molly Cheek, Elaine Miles, Michael Greyeyes, Chief Leonard George, John Trudell, Tom Skerritt, Cody Lightning, Cynthia Geary, Simon Baker; ***D:*** Chris Eyre; ***W:*** Sherman Alexie; ***C:*** Brian Capener; ***M:*** B.C. Smith. Ind. Spirit '99: Debut Perf. (Adams); Sundance '98: Aud. Award, Filmmakers Trophy.

The Smokers **2000 (R)** Bleech—this would-be revenge comedy is guaranteed to leave a bad taste in your mouth with its unappealing characters and storyline. Boarding school friends Jefferson (Swain), Karen (Philipps), and Lisa (Pratt) are sick of boys treating them wrong. So with a stolen gun, they are determined to have the miscreants make amends. **97m/C VHS, DVD.** Dominique Swain, Keri Lynn Pratt, Busy Philipps, Oliver Hudson, Ryan Browning, Joel West, Thora Birch, Nicholas M. Loeb; ***D:*** Christina Peters; ***W:*** Christina Peters, Kenny Golde; ***C:*** J.B. Letchinger; ***M:*** Lawrence Gingold.

Smokescreen ½ **1990 (R)** A young ad exec meets the girl of his dreams, and finds himself working for her gangster boyfriend. Competently made and acted, but phoney ending wrecks it. **91m/C VHS.** Kim Cattrall, Dean Stockwell, Matt Craven, Kim Coates, Brian George, Michael Hogan; ***D:*** Martin Lavut.

Smokey and the Bandit ½ **1977 (PG)** The first and best of the series about bootlegger Reynolds is one long car chase. Reynolds makes a wager that he can deliver a truckload of Coors beer—once unavailable east of Texas—to Atlanta from Texas in 28 hours. Gleason is a riot as the "smokey" who tries to stop him. Field is the hitchhiker Reynolds picks up along the way. Great stunts; director Needham was a top stunt man. **96m/C VHS, DVD.** Susan McIver, John Schneider, Hank Worden, Sonny Shroyer, Burt Reynolds, Sally Field, Jackie Gleason, Jerry Reed, Mike Henry, Paul Williams, Pat McCormick; ***D:*** Hal Needham; ***W:*** Hal Needham, Charles Shyer; ***C:*** Bobby Byrne; ***M:*** Bill Justis, Jerry Reed.

Smokey and the Bandit 2 *Smokey and the Bandit Ride Again* **1980 (PG)** Pathetic sequel to "Smokey and the Bandit" proved a boxoffice winner, grossing $40 million. The Bandit is hired to transport a pregnant elephant from Miami to the Republican convention in Dallas. Sheriff Buford T. Justice and family are in hot pursuit. **101m/C VHS, DVD.** David Huddleston, Burt Reynolds, Sally Field, Jackie Gleason, Jerry Reed, Mike Henry, Dom DeLuise, Pat McCormick, Paul Williams, John Anderson, Brenda Lee, Mel Tillis; ***Cameos:*** Joe "Mean Joe" Greene, Don Williams, Terry Bradshaw; ***D:*** Hal Needham; ***W:*** Jerry Belson, Michael Kane, Brock Yates; ***C:*** Michael C. Butler.

Smokey and the Bandit, Part 3 **1983 (PG)** You thought the second one was bad? Another mega car chase, this time sans

Reynolds and director Needham. **88m/C VHS, DVD.** Jackie Gleason, Jerry Reed, Paul Williams, Pat McCormick, Mike Henry, Colleen Camp; ***Cameos:*** Burt Reynolds; ***D:*** Dick Lowry; ***W:*** Stuart Birnbaum, David Dashev.

Smokey & the Hotwire Gang 🦴 1/2 *Mafia Lady* **1979** A convoy of truckers try to track down a beautiful woman driving a stolen car. **85m/C VHS.** James Keach, Stanley Livingston, Tony Lorea, Alvy Moore, George Barris; ***D:*** Anthony Cardoza; ***W:*** T. Gary Cardoza; ***C:*** Gary Graver.

Smokey & the Judge 🦴 **1980 (PG)** Police officer has his hands full with a trio of lovely ladies. **90m/C VHS.** Gene Price, Wayde Preston, Juanita Curiel, Rory Calhoun; ***D:*** Dan Seeger; ***W:*** Harry Hope, Dan Seeger; ***C:*** Misha (Mikhail) Suslov; ***M:*** Bruce Stewart.

Smokey Bites the Dust 🦴 **1981 (PG)** Car-smashing gag-fest about a sheriff's daughter kidnapped by her smitten beau. Near-plotless and literally unoriginal: lifted footage from several other Corman-produced flicks, a technique that can aptly be called garbage picking. **87m/C VHS.** Janet (Johnson) Julian, Jimmy (James Vincent) McNichol, Patrick Campbell, Kari Lizer, John Drew (Blythe) Barrymore Jr., Kedrick Wolfe, Walter Barnes; ***D:*** Charles B. Griffith; ***W:*** Max Apple; ***C:*** Gary Graver; ***M:*** Bent Myggen.

Smokey Smith 🦴 1/2 **1936** Ubiquitous Hayes and steely Steele hunt down the slayers of an elderly couple. Ordinary oater directed by Steele's father, Bradbury. **59m/B VHS, DVD.** Bob Steele, George "Gabby" Hayes; ***D:*** Robert North Bradbury.

Smokin' Aces 🦴🦴 **2007 (R)** Exhaustingly convoluted guy flick from Carnahan has sleazy nightclub magician Buddy "Aces" Israel (Piven) willing to turn FBI snitch on the Nevada mob. Naturally, the head gangster puts out a hit, attracting all sorts of other violent lowlifes, while the feds ineffectually protect Buddy in a sleazy Lake Tahoe penthouse suite. Lots of flash—lots of violence—no payoff (or maybe one too many). Like its location, it's stylish but empty. **109m/C DVD, HD DVD.** *US* Jeremy Piven, Ben Affleck, Andy Garcia, Ray Liotta, Alicia Keys, Ryan Reynolds, Peter Berg, Taraji P. Henson, Martin Henderson, Chris Pine, Jason Bateman, Joseph Ruskin, Davenia McFadden, Nestor Carbonell, Tommy Flanagan, Alex Rocco, Vladimir Kulich, David Proval, Joel Edgerton, Matthew Fox, Common, Mike Falkow, Kevin Durand, Maury Sterling, Christopher Egan; ***D:*** Joe Carnahan; ***W:*** Joe Carnahan; ***C:*** Mauro Fiore; ***M:*** Clint Mansell.

Smokin' Aces 2: Assassins' Ball 🦴 1/2 **2010 (R)** Direct-to-video sequel with lots of violence and killers but not much else to connect it the 2007 flick. Low-level FBI desk jockey Walter Weed is confused upon discovering he's the target of a group of crazy assassins, thanks to a mystery man who's offered a high bounty for his death. **86m/C DVD.** Tom Berenger, Vinnie Jones, Ernie Hudson, Autumn Reeser, Michael Parks, Tommy Flanagan, Clayne Crawford; ***D:*** P.J. Pesce; ***W:*** P.J. Pesce; ***C:*** David Geddes; ***M:*** Tim Jones. **VIDEO**

Smoking/No Smoking 🦴🦴 **1994** Two linked films director Resnais adapted from writer Alan Ayckbourn's eight-play cycle "Intimate Exchanges" (although the screenwriters have only used six stories). Azema and Arditti plays nine characters in various tableaus on marriage and affairs set at a Yorkshire school. The opening sequence of each episode provides the title tie-in, as faculty wife Celia goes onto the terrace, finds a pack of cigarettes, and decides whether or not to light up. A studio set provides all the frankly fake backdrops. Very slight and very long. French with subtitles. **285m/C VHS.** *FR* Sabine Azema, Pierre Arditti; ***D:*** Alain Resnais; ***W:*** Jean-Pierre Bacri, Agnes Jaoui. Cesar '94: Actor (Arditti), Art Dir./Set Dec., Director (Resnais), Film, Writing.

A Smoky Mountain Christmas 🦴🦴 **1986** Dolly gets away from it all in a secluded cabin that has been appropriated by a gang of orphans, and sings a half dozen songs. Innocuous seasonal country fun. Winkler's TV directing debut. **94m/C VHS.** Dolly Parton, Bo Hopkins, Dan Hedaya, Gennie James, David Ackroyd, Rene Auberjonois, John Ritter, Anita Morris, Lee Majors; ***D:*** Henry Winkler; ***W:*** Dolly Parton. **TV**

Smooth Talk 🦴🦴🦴 **1985 (PG-13)** An innocent, flirtatious teenager catches the eye of a shady character, played by Williams. Disturbing and thought-provoking film that caused some controversy when it opened. Dern gives a brilliant performance as the shy, sheltered girl. Based on the Joyce Carol Oates story "Where Are You Going, Where Have You Been?" Made for PBS' "American Playhouse" series. **92m/C VHS, DVD.** Laura Dern, Treat Williams, Mary Kay Place, Levon Helm, William Ragsdale, Margaret Welsh, Sarah Inglis; ***D:*** Joyce Chopra; ***W:*** Tom Cole; ***C:*** James Glennon. Sundance '86: Grand Jury Prize. **TV**

Smooth Talker **WOOF!** **1990 (R)** A serial killer stalks the women of a 976 party line. Bad acting, bad dialog, not a scare to be found. **89m/C VHS.** Joe Guzaldo, Peter Crombie, Stuart Whitman, Burt Ward, Sydney Lassick, Blair Weickgenant; ***D:*** Tom Milo.

Smother 🦴 1/2 **2008 (PG-13)** Shrill family comedy. Noah's (Shepard) just been fired, his wife (Tyler) is pressing him to have a baby, his wife's weird cousin (White) is sleeping on their couch, and the last thing he needs is his needy, manipulative mother (Keaton) moving in with her five dogs. But that's what happens and naturally mom can't resist interfering. **92m/C DVD.** Dax Shepard, Diane Keaton, Liv Tyler, Mike White, Ken Howard, Selma Stern, Sarah Lancaster, Tim Rasmussen, Donnie Booker; ***D:*** Vince Di Meglio; ***W:*** Vince Di Meglio; ***C:*** Julio Macat; ***M:*** Manish Raval, Tom Wolfe.

Smouldering Fires 🦴🦴 1/2 **1925** A tough businesswoman falls in love with an ambitious young employee, who is 15 years her junior. After they marry, problems arise in the form of the wife's attractive younger sister. Surprisingly subtle melodrama, if that's not an oxymoron. **100m/B VHS.** Pauline Frederick, Laura La Plante, Tully Marshall, Malcolm McGregor, Wanda (Petit) Hawley, Helen Lynch, George Cooper, Bert Roach; ***D:*** Clarence Brown.

Smugglers 🦴 *Lover of the Great Bear* **1975** Opportunistic smugglers take advantage of the Russian Revolution to sack the land and make a bundle. **110m/C VHS.** *IT* Senta Berger, Giuliano Gemma; ***D:*** Valintino Orsini.

Smugglers' Cove 🦴🦴🦴 **1948** Gorcey wrongly believes he has inherited a mansion. He and the Bowery Boys move in, only to stumble across a smuggling ring. Plenty of slapsticks; the boys at their best. **66m/B VHS.** Leo Gorcey, Huntz Hall, Gabriel Dell; ***D:*** William Beaudine.

Snake Eyes 🦴🦴 1/2 **1998 (R)** Stylish thriller with Nick Cage at his wild-eyed best. Cage is corrupt Atlantic City cop Rick Santoro, investigating the bold assassination of Secretary of Defense Kirkland (Fabiani) during a heavyweight boxing match. The first half of the film packs a visual punch, with De Palma's trademark jazzy camera work, but shortly after Santoro partners with his Navy officer pal Kevin Dunne (Sinise), and realizes nothing is what it seems, story is ko'd with a combination of implausibility and a lackluster climax. De Palma's first film since directing the b.o. smash "Mission Impossible." Shot exclusively in a Montreal skating arena. **99m/C VHS, DVD.** Nicolas Cage, Gary Sinise, Carla Gugino, John Heard, Stan Shaw, Kevin Dunn, Michael Rispoli, Joel Fabiani, Luis Guzman, Tamara Tunie; ***D:*** Brian De Palma; ***W:*** David Koepp; ***C:*** Stephen Burum; ***M:*** Ryuichi Sakamoto.

The Snake Hunter Strangler 🦴 **1966** A young girl is rescued after 15 years from an evil cult of snake people. **65m/C VHS.** Guy Madison, Ivan Desny; ***D:*** Luigi Capuano.

A Snake of June 🦴🦴 1/2 *Rokugatsu no hebi* **2002 (R)** Rinko is a suicide hotline counselor who has discovered she has breast cancer. Her husband Shigehiko is an obsessive-compulsive cleaner. Terrified of disease, he finds himself unable to touch her. One day Rinko receives explicit photos of herself from Igushi, a former psychiatric patient determined to change her passionless life. Eventually her outraged husband finds out, and determines to track down Igushi. If it weren't directed by Shinya Tsukamoto (of "Tetsuo the Iron Man" fame), this might be a standard erotic drama/thriller. But once Shigehiko starts to track down Igushi, things turn positively surreal, as Shigehiko gets kidnapped himself and subjected to some pretty weird stuff. Or begins hallucinating like mad. **101m/C DVD.** *JP* Shinya Tsukamoto, Mansaku Fuwa, Tomorowo Taguchi, Susumu Terajima, Asuka Kurosawa, Yuji Kohtari, Tomoko Matsumoto, Shuji Otsuki, Masato Tsujioka; ***D:*** Shinya Tsumamoto; ***W:*** Shinya Tsumamoto; ***C:*** Shinya Tsumamoto; ***M:*** Chu Ishikawa.

The Snake People 🦴 *Isle of the Snake People; Cult of the Dead; La Muerte Viviente; Isle of the Living Dead* **1968** A police captain investigates a small island littered with LSD-experimenting scientists, snake-worshippers, and voodoo. One of the infamous quartet of Karloff's final films, all made in Mexico. **90m/C VHS, DVD.** *MX* Boris Karloff, Julissa, Carlos East; ***D:*** Enrique Vergara.

The Snake Pit 🦴🦴🦴 1/2 **1948** One of the first films to compassionately explore mental illness and its treatment. Following an emotional collapse Virginia (de Havilland) is placed in a mental institution by her husband, Robert (Stevens). The severity of her depression causes her sympathetic doctor (Genn) to try such treatments as electric shock, hydrotherapy, and drugs, along with the psychoanalysis which gradually allows her to accept her fears and make her recovery. Tour-de-force performance by de Havilland. Based on the novel by Mary Jane Ward. **108m/B VHS, DVD.** Olivia de Havilland, Mark Stevens, Leo Genn, Celeste Holm, Glenn Langan, Helen Craig, Leif Erickson, Beulah Bondi; ***D:*** Anatole Litvak; ***W:*** Frank Partos, Millen Brand; ***C:*** Leo Tover; ***M:*** Alfred Newman. Oscars '48: Sound; N.Y. Film Critics '48: Actress (de Havilland).

The Snake Woman 🦴 **1961** A herpetologist working in a small English village during the 1890s is conducting strange experiments to try to cure his wife's madness. He tries injecting his pregnant wife with snake venom and she gives birth to a cold-blooded daughter, who, when she grows up, has the ability to change herself into a deadly snake. She promptly begins killing the local male populace until Scotland Yard is called in to investigate. The curvy Travers is appropriately snakey but this movie is dull. **68m/C VHS, DVD.** *GB* John P. McCarthy, Susan Travers, Arnold Marle; ***D:*** Sidney J. Furie.

Snake Woman's Curse 🦴🦴 1/2 *Kaidan hebi-onna; Ghost Story of the Snake Woman* **1968** Director Nakagawa has been considered the father of the modern Japanese horror film, and this is among his last works. Chobei (Seizaburo kawazu) is a brutal, oppressive landlord who murders a peasant farmer and forces his wife and daughter to become his personal servants. He kills a snake that his victim's wife had been protecting, and begins to lose his grip on sanity as he begins experiencing horrible hallucinations. He also believes that his son's beautiful new bride reminds him disturbingly of the dead snake. **85m/C DVD.** *JP* Junzaburo Ban, Seizaburo Kawazu, Kunio Murai, Hideo Murota, Akemi Negisha, Ko Nishimura, Sachiko Kuwahara, Chiaki Tsukioka, Shingo Yamashiro, Yukie Kagawa; ***D:*** Nobuo Nakagawa; ***W:*** Nobuo Nakagawa; ***C:*** Yoshikazu Yamasawa; ***M:*** Shinsuke Kikuchi.

SnakeEater 🦴 **1989 (R)** Loner cop tracks down swine who killed his parents and kidnapped his sister. "Rambo" rip-off with little plot, but lots of action. Followed by two sequels. **89m/C VHS.** Lorenzo Lamas, Larry Csonka, Ron Palillo; ***D:*** George Erschbamer.

SnakeEater 2: The Drug Buster 🦴 **1989 (R)** A cop goes nuts and kills four drug dealers. As a result he is committed to an institution. Iron bars don't make a prison for this guy though, and he's soon back on the streets fighting crime with his pal "Speedboat." Silly sequel is quite bad; followed by yet another. **93m/C VHS.** Lorenzo Lamas, Larry B. Scott, Michelle Scarabelli, Harvey Atkin, Jack Blum, Kathleen Kinmont; ***D:*** George Erschbamer.

SnakeEater 3: His Law 🦴 **1992 (R)** Tough cop Jack Kelly (Lamas), aka SnakeEater, is out to avenge a woman's beating by a gang of thug bikers. Lots of action and violence, not much plot; based on W. Glenn Duncan's novel "Rafferty's Rules." **109m/C VHS.** Lorenzo Lamas, Minor Mustain, Tracy Cook, Holly Chester, Scott "Bam Bam" Bigelow; ***D:*** George Erschbamer; ***W:*** John Dunning.

Snakehead Terror 🦴 **2004** A small northeastern fishing community had a problem with invasive snakehead fish in the local lake. So they dumped a bunch of chemicals in to kill the fishies but instead they turned them into mutants capable of walking on land and eating the local populace. The finale is remarkably gore-soaked yet campy. A Sci-Fi Channel original. **88m/C DVD.** Bruce Boxleitner, Carol Alt, Chelan Simmons, Juliana Wimbles, Ryan McDonell, William B. Davis; ***D:*** Paul Ziller; ***W:*** A.G. Lawrence; ***C:*** Mark Dobrescu; ***M:*** Ken William. **CABLE**

Snakeman **WOOF!** *The Snake King* **2005** Sci-Fi channel cheesefest with lousy CGI. A group of scientists are tramping through the Amazon jungle and encounter a gigantic, multi-headed snake that sees them as chow and a snake-worshiping tribe that would be happy to sacrifice the interlopers. **96m/C DVD.** Stephen Baldwin, Jayne Heitmeyer, Larry Day, Gary Hudson; ***D:*** Allan Goldstein; ***W:*** Allan Goldstein, Declan O'Brien; ***C:*** Eric Moynier; ***M:*** Claude Doisy. **CABLE**

Snakes on a Plane 🦴🦴 **2006 (R)** And the title says it all. An Internet fan-phenom long before its opening, the studio was so taken by the buzz that they had director Ellis do some re-shoots to make the popcorn flick scarier (more snakes, more gore). FBI agent Neville Flynn (Jackson) is escorting a witness on a commercial flight from Hawaii to L.A. When the plane is halfway over the ocean, some 400 deadly snakes are let loose from a time-release crate into the cabin in an effort to eliminate the witness and apparently everyone else. Unfortunately, the flick doesn't live up to the buzz, failing to supply the gleeful camp and wink that the title suggests, and that the audience expects. **105m/C DVD.** *US* Samuel L. Jackson, Julianna Margulies, Kenan Thompson, Nathan Phillips, Flex Alexander, Bobby Cannavale, David Koechner, Sunny Mabrey, Todd Louiso, Lin Shaye, Terry Chen, Elsa Pataky, Taylor Kitsch, Samantha McLeod, Byron Lawson, Rachel Blanchard; ***D:*** David R. Ellis; ***W:*** Sebastian Gutierrez, John Heffernan; ***C:*** Adam Greenberg; ***M:*** Trevor Rabin.

Snap Decision 🦴🦴 1/2 **2001** Widowed mom Jen (Winningham) allows her friend Carrie (Huffman), a professional photographer, to take candid pictures of her three children when Carrie visits. But the owner of a photo-developing shop gets flustered by what she sees and contacts the police about the "obscene" material. The kids are taken away from Jen and she faces prison time for child pornography in this true story that is every parent's nightmare. **92m/C VHS, DVD.** Mare Winningham, Felicity Huffman, Chelcie Ross, Chuck Shamata, Megan Fahlenbock, Ronn Sarosiak, Robert Bockstael, Don Allison; ***D:*** Alan Metzger; ***W:*** Ara Watson, Sam Blackwell; ***C:*** Rhett Morita; ***M:*** James McVay. **CABLE**

Snapdragon 🦴🦴 **1993 (R)** Police psychologist is led astray by his libido while investigating a luscious amnesiac. His sensible vice cop girlfriend then discovers the sexpot is actually a psycho serial killer calling herself the Snapdragon but will her boyfriend even care? **96m/C VHS, DVD.** Steven Bauer, Pamela Anderson, Chelsea Field; ***D:*** Worth Keeter; ***W:*** Gene Church; ***C:*** James Mathers; ***M:*** Michael Linn.

The Snapper 🦴🦴🦴 1/2 **1993 (R)** Originally made for BBC TV, Frears creates a small comic gem based on the second novel of Doyle's Barrytown trilogy. Set in Dublin, 20-year-old Sharon Curley (Kellegher) finds herself unexpectedly pregnant and refuses to name the father. Family and friends are understanding—until they discover the man's identity. Affecting performances, particularly from Meaney as Sharon's dad who takes a much greater interest in the birth of his grandchild than he ever did with his own children. Cheerful semi-sequel to "The Commitments" serves up domestic upheavals graced with humor and a strong sense of family loyalty. **95m/C VHS, DVD.** *IR* Tina

Kellegher, Colm Meaney, Ruth McCabe, Colm O'Byrne, Pat Laffan, Eanna MacLiam, Ciara Duffy; *D:* Stephen Frears; *W:* Roddy Doyle. **TV**

Snapshot ☆ *Sweeter Song* **1977 (R)** Typical grade Z sex comedy; a free-lance photographer ogles lots of variously dishabilled young women through his lens. **84m/C VHS, DVD.** Jim Henshaw, Susan Petrie; *D:* Allan Eastman; *W:* Allan Eastman; *C:* Robert Brooks.

Snapshots ☆☆ ½ **2002 (R)** Aging Larry (Reynolds) has been an American expatriate in Amsterdam for the last 30 years. He runs a used bookstore and is attracted to young, free-spirited Aisha (Chaplin) when she comes into the shop. Eventually, Larry finds out that the girl is the daughter of his long-lost love Narma (Christie), whom he remembers from his visit to Morocco (shown in flashbacks), when circumstances bring them back together. **93m/C VHS, DVD.** Burt Reynolds, Carmen Chaplin, Julie Christie, Eric Michael Cole, Jemima Rooper; *D:* Rudolf Van Den Berg; *W:* Rudolf Van Den Berg, Michael O'Loughlin; *C:* Gabor Szabo.

Snatch ☆☆☆ **2000 (R)** A la "Lock, Stock and 2 Smoking Barrels," director Ritchie's second film is another well-populated and disorganized crime caper, this time with descriptively named lowlifes trying to heist a stolen 84-carat diamond. Leading the mayhem are Turkish (Statham) and Tommy (Graham), two boxing promoters who sign Mickey (Pitt), an Irish Gypsy, to take a dive. Meanwhile, Franky Four Fingers (Del Toro) transports the red-hot rock to London and his boss Avi (Farina), where it promptly gets lifted. Enter Bullet Tooth Tony (Jones) to find missing Franky and a host of others whose seemingly unrelated subplots eventually meet. Casting, lots of action, and Ritchie's dialogue are spot on. Ritchie's usual use of heavy Cockney accents are upstaged by Pitt's Gypsy pugilist and his much talked about thick-as-Guinness brogue which even the other characters can't decipher. The elaborate and sometimes confusing plotlines are aided by titles and narration and effective use of Ritchie's usual slo-mo, fast cutting, and split-screen. **104m/C VHS, DVD, UMD.** *GB* Benicio Del Toro, Dennis Farina, Brad Pitt, Vinnie Jones, Rade Serbedzija, Jason Statham, Lennie James, Ewen Bremner, Alan Ford, Mike Reid, Robbie Gee, Jason Flemyng, Sorcha Cusack, Stephen Graham; *D:* Guy Ritchie; *W:* Guy Ritchie; *C:* Tim Maurice-Jones; *M:* John Murphy.

Snatched ☆☆ **1972** The wives of three wealthy men are held for ransom, but one man doesn't want to pay, while one of the victims needs insulin. Standard TV fare. **73m/C VHS.** Howard Duff, Leslie Nielsen, Sheree North, Barbara Parkins, Robert Reed, John Saxon, Tisha Sterling; *D:* Sutton Roley; *M:* Randy Edelman. **TV**

Sneakers ☆☆ ½ **1992 (PG-13)** Competent thriller about five computer hackers with questionable pasts and an equally questionable government job. Of course, nothing is as it seems. Rather slow-going considering the talents and suspense involved but includes enough turns to keep a viewer's interest. **125m/C VHS, DVD.** Robert Redford, Sidney Poitier, River Phoenix, Dan Aykroyd, Ben Kingsley, David Strathairn, Mary McDonnell, Timothy Busfield, George Hearn, Eddie Jones, James Earl Jones, Stephen Tobolowsky, Donal Logue; *D:* Phil Alden Robinson; *W:* Lawrence Lasker, Walter F. Parkes, Phil Alden Robinson; *C:* John Lindley; *M:* James Horner, Branford Marsalis.

The Sniper ☆☆ **1952** Interesting time capsule of San Francisco in the early '50s as well as a psychological study of a mentally-ill killer. Miller (Franz) knows he's unstable so he seeks help for his compulsion to kill women. Treated with indifference by the medical community, he takes to a rooftop with a rifle and starts picking off women who've rejected him. Lt. Kafka (Menjou) is assigned the politically hot case and eventually gets a lead into the psychosis compelling Miller to kill. **87m/B DVD.** Adolphe Menjou, Arthur Franz, Gerald Mohr, Richard Kiley, Marie Windsor, Frank Faylen; *D:* Edward Dmytryk; *W:* Harry Brown; *C:* Burnett Guffey; *M:* George Antheil.

Sniper ☆☆☆ *The Deadly Tower* **1975** Suspenseful drama based on true story of Charles Whitman, who shot at University of Texas students from Texas Tower on a summer day in 1966. Disney alumunus Russell breaks type as mass killer, with fine support by Yniguez as a police officer on the scene and Beatty as the passerby who lends a hand. Finely crafted re-creation of disturbing, true event. **85m/C VHS, DVD.** Kurt Russell, Richard Yniguez, John Forsythe, Ned Beatty, Pernell Roberts, Clifton James, Paul Carr, Alan Vint, Pepe Serna; *D:* Jerry Jameson. **TV**

The Sniper ☆ ½ *L'Arma* **1978** A law-abiding citizen becomes a vigilante killer after witnessing a violent crime. **90m/C VHS.** *IT* Stefano Satta Flores, Benedetta Fantoli, Claudia Cardinale; *D:* Pasquale Squitieri; *W:* Pasquale Squitieri; *C:* Giulio Albonico; *M:* Tullio De Piscopo.

Sniper ☆ ½ **1992 (R)** Less than compelling shoot-'em-up set in Panama. Lead characters include Sgt. Beckett (Berenger), a seasoned assassin who gets a rush from killing. Also assigned to the case is Richard Miller (Zane), a newcomer who knows his guns but not his jungles. Together they go in search of their target, a politician planning a coup with the help of a druglord. Action is poorly choreographed and plot is cursory at best. **99m/C VHS, DVD.** Tom Berenger, Billy Zane, J.T. Walsh, Aden Young, Ken Radley, Reinaldo Arenas, Carlos Alvarez, Roy Edmonds, Dale Dye; *D:* Luis Llosa; *W:* Michael Frost Beckner, Crash Leyland; *C:* Bill Butler; *M:* Gary Chang.

Sniper 2 ☆ ½ **2002 (R)** This sequel comes some 10 years after the first "Sniper" and you wonder why anyone would bother with such a familiar story. Marine sniper Beckett (Berenger) is called on for one last mission: to kill a Serbian general who's committing atrocities on the Muslim population. Beckett is teamed with soldier Cole (Woodbine), who's on death row and has a chance to earn his freedom if he survives. **91m/C VHS, DVD.** Tom Berenger, Bokeem Woodbine, Dan E. Butler, Erika Marozsan, Linden Ashby; *D:* Craig R. Baxley; *W:* Ron Mita, Jim McClain; *C:* David Connell; *M:* Gary Chang. **VIDEO**

Sniper 3 ☆ **2004 (R)** An assassin's work is never done, so yet again, Beckett dusts off the old hardware to rub out a supposed terrorist for his new employer, the National Security Agency. Things go haywire, seeing as his prey is an old chum and so his aim turns to tracking down the truth. **90m/C VHS, DVD.** Tom Berenger, Byron Mann, John Doman, Denis Arndt, Troy Winbush, Jeanetta Arnette, William Duffy; *D:* P.J. Pesce; *W:* J.S. Cardone, Ross Helford; *C:* Michael Bonvillain; *M:* Timothy S. (Tim) Jones. **VIDEO**

Snipes ☆☆ ½ **2001 (R)** Snipes are the posters you see plastered to walls and lampposts—in this case they're of up-and-coming Philly rapper Prolifik (Nelly), who's got a gangsta background and a shady record deal. The record label owner, Bobby Starr (Winters), is in hock to local mobster Johnnie Maradino (Vincent). When Prolifik gets kidnapped and the master tape of his recordings is also stolen, Starr, for some unknown reason, thinks that gofer/fan Erik (Jones) is somehow mixed up in the mess. Actually, there's a lot that's unclear since first-timer Murray overstuffs the plot. **113m/C VHS, DVD.** Sam Jones III, Dean Winters, Mpho Koaho, Nelly, Zoe Saldana, Frank Vincent; *D:* Rich Murray; *W:* Rich Murray, Rob Wiser; *C:* Alexander Buono.

Sno-Line ☆ **1985 (R)** A New York gangster moves to Texas and begins to wipe out the competition on his way to building his drug and gambling dynasty. Bo-ring excuse for entertainment. No hope, no redemption, no titillation: just ultra-"realistic" depiction of organized crime, poorly acted. **89m/C VHS.** Vince Edwards, Paul Smith, June Wilkinson; *D:* Douglas F. Oneans.

Snow ☆☆ ½ **2004** Handsome, single Nick Snowden (Cavanagh) is training to take over the family business (as Santa Claus' successor) when, three days before Christmas, his favorite reindeer Buddy is kidnapped by evil hunter Buck (Fabian). Buddy winds up in the zoo in San Ernesto, California, where Nick meets single zookeeper Sandy (Williams), whom he thinks would make a swell Mrs. Claus. So Nick moves into Sandy's boarding house and, with the help of street smart young Hector (Thompson), comes up with a plan to rescue Buddy and get the girl (oh, and save Christmas). ABC Family movie. **90m/C DVD.** Tom Cavanagh, Ashley Williams, Patrick Fabian, Jackie Burroughs, Bobb'e J. Thompson; *D:* Alex Zamm; *W:* Rich Burns; *C:* Jim Westenbrink; *M:* David Lawrence. **CABLE**

Snow 2: Brain Freeze ☆☆ **2008** ABC Family channel sequel to 2004's "Snow." Nick Snowden (Cavanagh) has followed his late father into the family business (he's Santa Claus) but his new wife Sandy (Williams) is still overwhelmed by the intensity of the holiday workload. Then Nick has an accident, develops amnesia, and walks away at the most inopportune time. So Sandy goes looking for Nick and runs into her former beau Buck (Fabian), who's so eager to 'help.' **87m/C DVD.** Tom Cavanagh, Ashley Williams, Patrick Fabian, Alexander Conti, Hal Williams; *D:* Mark Rosman; *W:* Rich Burns; *M:* Kenneth Burgomaster. **CABLE**

Snow Angels ☆☆☆ **2007 (R)** Tragedy tolls with the sound of distant gunfire as a high school marching band rehearses on the football field, stunning the students into silence. Flash back several weeks to a dreary, snowy northwest small town, where newly divorced waitress (Annie) and her on-the-edge ex (Rockwell) navigate a tense relationship and share custody of their four-year-old child. Annie's sleeping with a co-worker's (Sedaris) husband, while another young coworker Arthur (Angarano), who she used to babysit, is in the apprehensive beginning stages of a high school romance with Lila (Thirlby). Director Green likes to dump you into his films and let you figure out your emotions along with the characters, which sometimes makes for uncomfortable viewing, but the tactic works in this study of love and loss in a claustrophobic town. **106m/C DVD.** *US* Kate Beckinsale, Sam Rockwell, Michael Angarano, Jeanetta Arnette, Griffin Dunne, Nicky Katt, Olivia Thirlby, Amy Sedaris, Tom Noonan, Connor Paolo, Hudson Grace; *D:* David Gordon Green; *W:* David Gordon Green; *C:* Tim Orr; *M:* Jeff McIlwain.

Snow Buddies ☆☆ ½ **2008 (G)** Big on the awwwww factor since those "Air Bud" pups are as cute as ever. Budderball gets locked into an ice cream truck and when his four siblings try to rescue him, they all wind up in Alaska. (Right, like the plot should make sense.) They're befriended by a couple of sled dogs and before you know it, our cuties are mushing the trail in an effort to get home. **87m/C DVD.** Molly Shannon, Richard Karn, Cynthia Stevenson; *D:* Robert Vince; *W:* Robert Vince, Anna McRoberts; *M:* Brahm Wenger; *V:* Dylan Sprouse, James Belushi, Kris Kristofferson, Josh Flitter, Jimmy Bennett, Liliana Mumy, Skyler Gisondo, Lothaire Bluteau, Henry Hodges. **VIDEO**

Snow Cake ☆☆ **2006** Middle-aged Brit Alex (Rickman) is driving through Ontario and reluctantly offers a ride to hitchhiking teen Vivienne (Hampshire). She's killed in a crash and uninjured Alex decides he must convey his condolences to her mother, only to discover that Linda (Weaver) is autistic and doesn't process emotions. Alan decides to stay for the funeral and meets Linda's secretive neighbor Maggie (Moss), who offers her own personal brand of sympathy. Moss is best as a small-town femme but Rickman and Weaver are chilly and constricted. **112m/C DVD.** *GB CA* Sigourney Weaver, Alan Rickman, Carrie-Anne Moss, James Allodi, Emily Hampshire; *D:* Marc Evans; *W:* Angela Pell; *C:* Steve Cosens; *M:* Broken Social Scene.

Snow Country ☆☆ ½ **1957** Romantic drama of an unsuccessful, married artist from Tokyo who travels to a mountain resort to find himself. He requests a Geisha for the evening and, when none are available, the beautiful adopted daughter of the local music teacher is sent to him instead. Based on the novel by Nobel Prize winner Yasunari Kawabata. In Japanese with English subtitles. Remade in 1965. **104m/B VHS.** *JP* Ryo Ikebe, Keiko Kishi, Akira Kubo, Kaoru Yachigusa, Hisaya Morishige, Mineko Yorozuyo, Etsuko Ichihara, Noriko Sengoku, Kumeko Urabe, Eiko Miyoshi, Akira Tan, Chieko Naniwa, Daisuke Kato, Haruo Tanaka; *D:* Shiro Toyoda.

The Snow Creature **WOOF!** **1954** Stupid troop of explorers bring back a snow creature from the Himalayas. Critter escapes in L.A. and terrorizes all in its path before blending in with club crowd. Very bad monster epic (the first about a snow monster) that strains credibility frame by frame. Occasionally, depending upon camera angle, light, and viewer mood, monster appears to be something other than guy in bad suit sweating. Directed by Billy Wilder's brother and another argument against genetic consistency. **72m/B VHS, DVD.** Paul Langton, Leslie Denison; *D:* W. Lee Wilder.

Snow Day ☆ ½ **2000 (PG)** Goofy, innocuous family comedy may provide a distraction for the little monsters if you're stuck with a snow day of your own. Tom (Chase) is the hapless weatherman who's as surprised as anyone when the white stuff falls. Meanwhile, the neighborhood kids seek to foil the efforts of the evil Snowplowman (Elliott) who is out to destroy their dream of having more than one day off from school. **89m/C VHS, DVD.** Chevy Chase, Chris Elliott, Mark Webber, Jean Smart, Schuyler Fisk, Iggy Pop, Pam Grier, John Schneider, Emmanuelle Chriqui; *D:* Chris Koch; *W:* Will McRobb, Chris Viscardi; *C:* Robbie Greenberg; *M:* Steve Bartek.

Snow Dogs ☆☆ **2002 (PG)** Gooding leads this kid flick as Ted Brooks, a dentist who only finds out about his adoption after his biological mom's death in Alaska. Aside from a rather dilapidated house, mom's estate included a team of frisky Siberian husky sled dogs. Displaced city boy Ted, who's from Miami, hates the cold and the dogs but stays to take care of the estate, seek out his real father, and get better acquainted with friendly local bar owner Barb (Bacalso). Meanwhile, the grizzled Thunder Jack (Coburn) is on Ted's tail, trying to get him to sell the dogs. The expected Iditarod-type dog race ensues. Gooding mugs amiably and the good natured physical humor and action should amuse the young and undiscrimination. **99m/C VHS, DVD.** *US* Cuba Gooding Jr., James Coburn, Sisqo, Nichelle Nichols, M. Emmet Walsh, Graham Greene, Brian Doyle-Murray, Joanna Bascalso, Michael Bolton; *D:* Brian Levant; *W:* Jim Kouf, Tommy Swerdlow, Michael Goldberg, Mark Gibson, Philip Halprin; *C:* Thomas Ackerman; *M:* John Debney.

Snow Falling on Cedars ☆☆ **1999 (PG-13)** Visually beautiful but remarkably dull adaptation of David Guterson's novel. In 1954, journalist and WWII vet, the portentiously named Ishmael Chambers (Hawke), confronts his past when he's assigned to report on the trial of Japanese-American Kazuo Miyamoto (Yune), who's accused of murdering a fellow fisherman (Thal) in a small community north of Puget Sound. Kazuo just happens to be married to Ishmael's former flame, Hatsue (Kudoh)—their romance having been thwarted by the prejudicial times. Lots of impressionistic flashbacks complicate matters while the story meanders along, not helped by Hawke's blank-faced performance. **128m/C VHS, DVD.** Ethan Hawke, Youki Kudoh, Rick Yune, Sam Shepard, Max von Sydow, James Cromwell, James Rebhorn, Richard Jenkins, Eric Thal, Celia Weston, Max Wright; *D:* Scott Hicks; *W:* Scott Hicks, Ronald Bass; *C:* Robert Richardson; *M:* James Newton Howard.

Snow in August ☆☆ ½ **2001** In the summer of 1947, young Michael Devlin's (Tambakis) friendship with immigrant Czech Rabbi Hirsch (Rea) brings on the wrath of the local Irish street gang. Michael witnesses the beating of a Jewish shopkeeper, loses his friends, and decides to turn to an ancient Jewish text to summon the protection of a Golem. Based on the novel by Pete Hamill. **104m/C VHS, DVD.** Peter Tambakis, Stephen Rea, Lolita (David) Davidovich; *D:* Richard Friedenberg; *W:* Richard Friedenberg. **CABLE**

Snow Kill ☆ ½ **1990** Five city-dwellers travel into the mountains for a fun survival training weekend, but the fun turns deadly when they accidentally come across a murderous drug gang. Pseudo-'30s suspense adventure fails to thrill or surprise. **90m/C VHS.** Terence Knox, Patti D'Arbanville, David Dukes; *D:* Thomas J. Wright; *W:* Harv Zimmel. **CABLE**

The Snow Queen ☆☆ ½ **1983** From "Fairie Tale Theatre" comes this adaptation of the Hans Christian Andersen tale. A boy and girl who grow up together are separated by evil when the boy is held captive in the icy palace of the Snow Queen. The girl sets out to rescue him. **60m/C VHS, DVD.** Lauren Hutton, Linda Manz, David Hemmings, Melissa Gilbert, Lee Remick, Lance Kerwin; ***D:*** Peter Medak. **CABLE**

The Snow Queen 🦴🦴 1/2 **2002** An updated reworking of the Hans Christian Andersen fairytale is visually splendid but overly long. Gerda (Hobbs) lives with her bitter father (Wisden) in a remote hotel in the snowy north country. She's attracted to bellboy Kai (Guilbat), who disappears after a beautiful but sinister guest (Fonda) also leaves. So Gerda decides to track them down and save Kai from the evil Snow Queen. **172m/C VHS, DVD.** Bridget Fonda, Robert Wisden, Jeremy Guilbat, Chelsea Hobbs; ***D:*** David Wu; ***W:*** Simon Moore; ***C:*** Gregory Middleton; ***M:*** Lawrence Shragge. **CABLE**

Snow: The Movie 🦴 **1983** Rates creative zero for title, though there is snow, as well as skiing, growing up, romance, and good times among the young people involved. Filmed in Australia. **83m/C VHS.** David Argue, Lance Curtis; ***D:*** Robert Gibson.

Snow Treasure 🦴 **1967 (G)** With the help of an underground agent, Norwegian children smuggle gold out of the country right under the noses of the Nazis. Based on the novel by Marie McSwigan. **96m/C VHS.** James Franciscus, Paul Anstad; ***D:*** Irving Jacoby.

The Snow Walker 🦴🦴 1/2 **2003 (PG)** A pilot and his Inuit passenger struggle to conquer the elements and their cultural differences after they crash-land in the bitterly cold Canadian Arctic—if they want to survive. Drawn from Farley Mowat's short story "Walk Well My Brother." **109m/C VHS, DVD.** Barry Pepper, Annabella Piugattuk, James Cromwell, Kiersten Warren, Jon(athan) Gries, Robin Dunne, Greg Spottiswood, Samson Jorah, Michael Buble; ***D:*** Charles Martin Smith; ***W:*** Charles Martin Smith; ***C:*** David Connell, Jon Joffin, Paul Sarossy; ***M:*** Mychael Danna. **VIDEO**

Snow White 🦴🦴 **1989** The incomparable Rigg stars in this witty retelling of the beautiful girl and her seven little friends. **85m/C VHS, DVD.** Diana Rigg, Sarah Patterson, Billy Barty; ***D:*** Michael Berz.

Snow White: A Tale of Terror 🦴🦴 1/2 *Snow White in the Black Forest; Grimm Brothers' Snow White* **1997 (R)** This definitely puts the grim in the Grimm Brothers version of the fairy tale. In medieval Austria, beautiful Claudia (Weaver) marries widowed Frederick who, unfortunately, has an even-more beautiful daughter, Lilli (Keena), who's put out by this rival for her father's affections. The stepmom/stepdaughter battle increases when Claudia's own long-awaited baby is still-born and the wrathful and unbalanced Claudia orders Lilli's death. Only she's rescued by seven outcasts (only one of whom is a dwarf) living in the forest. The witchy Claudia does still like to talk to her mirror, however. Filmed in the Czech Republic. **101m/C VHS, DVD.** Sigourney Weaver, Sam Neill, Monica Keena, Gil Bellows, Taryn Davis; ***D:*** Michael Cohn; ***W:*** Thomas Szollosi, Deborah Serra; ***C:*** Mike Southon; ***M:*** John Ottman.

Snow White and the Seven Dwarfs 🦴🦴🦴🦴 **1937 (G)** Classic adaptation of the Grimm Brothers fairy tale about the fairest of them all. Beautiful animation, memorable characters, and wonderful songs mark this as the definitive "Snow White." Set the stage for other animated features after Walt Disney took an unprecedented gamble by attempting the first animated feature-length film, a project which took over two years to create and $1.5 million to make, and made believers out of those who laughed at the concept. Lifelike animation was based on real stars; Margery Belcher (later Champion) posed for Snow, Louis Hightower was the Prince, and Lucille LaVerne gave the Queen her nasty look. ♫Some Day My Prince Will Come; One Song; With a Smile and a Song; Whistle While You Work; Bluddle-Uddle-Um-Dum; The Dwarfs' Yodel Song; Heigh Ho; I'm Wishing; Isn't This a Silly Song?. **83m/C VHS, DVD.** ***D:*** David Hand; ***W:*** Ted Sears, Otto Englander, Earl Hurd, Dorothy Blank, Richard Creedon, Dick Richard, Merrill De Maris, Webb Smith; ***M:*** Frank Churchill, Paul J. Smith, Larry Morey, Leigh Harline; ***V:*** Adriana Caselotti, Harry Stockwell, Lucille LaVerne, Moroni Olsen, Billy Gilbert, Pinto Colvig, Otis Harlan, Scotty Matraw, Roy Atwell, Stuart Buchanan, Marion Darlington, Jim Macdonald. AFI '98: Top 100, Natl. Film Reg. '89.

Snow White and the Seven Dwarfs 🦴🦴🦴 **1983** From "Faerie Tale Theatre" comes the story of a princess who befriends seven little men to protect her from the jealous evil queen. **60m/C VHS, DVD.** Elizabeth McGovern, Rex Smith, Vincent Price, Vanessa Redgrave; ***D:*** Peter Medak. **CABLE**

Snow White and the Three Stooges 🦴 *Snow White and the Three Clowns* **1961** The Stooges fill in for the Seven Dwarfs when they go off prospecting in King Solomon's mines. Alas, see any Stooge movie but this one. **107m/C VHS, DVD.** Moe Howard, Larry Fine, Joe DeRita, Carol Heiss, Patricia Medina, Edson Stroll; ***D:*** Walter Lang; ***W:*** Noel Langley, Elwood Ullman; ***C:*** Leon Shamroy; ***M:*** Lyn Murray.

Snow White: The Fairest of Them All 🦴🦴 **2002** Kreuk certainly looks the title part and Richardson makes a fine wicked stepmother and queen but this version of the fairy tale is lame. Snow's mother dies when she's a baby and her father (Irwin) unwittingly places his daughter under a curse when he marries the witchy Elspeth (Richardson). Oh, and the dwarves are rainbow-colored and named after the days of the week. But Snow still gets stuck in that glass coffin until the prince comes along. **90m/C VHS, DVD.** Kristin Kreuk, Miranda Richardson, Tom Irwin, Vera Farmiga, Vincent Schiavelli, Warwick Davis, Michael J. Anderson, Clancy Brown, Tyron Leitso; ***D:*** Caroline Thompson; ***W:*** Caroline Thompson, Julie Hickson; ***C:*** Jon Joffin; ***M:*** Michael Covertino. **TV**

Snowball Express 🦴🦴 **1972 (G)** When a New York City accountant inherits a hotel in the Rocky Mountains, he decides to move his family west to attempt to make a go of the defunct ski resort, only to find that the place is falling apart. Run-of-the-mill Disney comedy, based on the novel "Chateau Bon Vivant" by Frankie and John O'Rear. **120m/C VHS, DVD.** Dean Jones, Nancy Olson, Harry (Henry) Morgan, Keenan Wynn; ***D:*** Norman Tokar; ***M:*** Robert F. Brunner.

Snowballin' 🦴 *Apres-Ski* **1971** A ski instructor gives private lessons to a bunch of snow bunnies. **90m/C VHS.** *CA* Mariette Levesque, Robert Arcand, Seline Lomez, Daniel Pilon; ***D:*** Roger Cardinal; ***W:*** Roger Cardinal; ***C:*** Roger Racine; ***M:*** Mark Hamilton.

Snowballing 🦴 **1985 (PG)** Part of the polluted wave of teen-sex flicks of the 1980s, this is very mild for the genre but still no prize. Lusty high schoolers at a skiing competition look for action on and off the slopes, end up exposing a resort fraud. **96m/C VHS, DVD.** Mary (Elizabeth) McDonough, Bob Hastings; ***D:*** Charles E. Sellier; ***W:*** Thomas Chapman; ***C:*** Henning Schellerup; ***M:*** Larry Whitley.

Snowbeast 🦴 1/2 **1977** The residents of a ski resort are being terrorized by a half-human, half-animal beast leaving a path of dead bodies in its wake. "Jaws" hits the slopes. Not scary or even funny. Made for TV. **96m/C VHS, DVD.** Bo Svenson, Yvette Mimieux, Sylvia Sidney, Clint Walker, Robert F. Logan; ***D:*** Herb Wallerstein. **TV**

Snowblind 🦴🦴 *Ski Lift to Death* **1978** Two ski gondolas derail, placing the passengers in jeopardy. Among the passengers is a mobster being pursued by an assassin. **98m/C VHS, DVD.** Deborah Raffin, Charles Frank, Howard Duff, Don Galloway, Gail Strickland, Don Johnson, Veronica Hamel, Clu Gulager, Lisa Reeves, Suzy Chaffee; ***D:*** William Wiard.

Snowboard Academy 🦴 1/2 **1996 (PG)** Chris Barry (Haim), the younger son of a ski resort owner, gets into trouble when his crazy snowboarder pals take over the slopes. Chris' older brother challenges him to start a school that will turn the bumblers into racers in just two weeks. Filmed at Le Chantecler resort in the Laurentian Mountains near Montreal. **89m/C VHS, DVD.** Corey Haim, Jim Varney, Brigitte Nielsen, Joe Flaherty, Paul Hopkins; ***D:*** John Shepphird; ***W:*** Rudy Rupak, James Salisko; ***C:*** Bruno Philip; ***M:*** Ross Vannelli.

Snowbound: The Jim and Jennifer Stolpa Story 🦴🦴 1/2 **1994** Based on a true story, this TV drama finds Jim (Harris) Stolpa, his wife Jennifer (Williams), and their 5-month-old baby fighting for survival when they're trapped in the open by a Nevada snowstorm for eight days. **120m/C VHS, DVD.** Neil Patrick Harris, Kelli Williams, Susan Clark, Michael Gross, Richard Cox; ***D:*** Christian Duguay; ***W:*** Jonathan Rintels; ***C:*** Peter Woeste; ***M:*** Lou Natale. **TV**

Snowglobe 🦴🦴 1/2 **2007** Angela (Milian) feels overwhelmed by her family. She lives in the same apartment building, works at the family deli, and her mother Rose (Bracco) picks out the guys she dates. If only Angela could have a perfect Christmas just like the one in the antique snowglobe she inherited from her grandmother. She has a dream about entering that world and discovers how to make her own holidays special. An ABC Family original. **90m/C DVD.** Christina Milian, Lorraine Bracco, Matt Keeslar, Josh Cooke, Ron Canada; ***D:*** Ron Lagomarsino; ***W:*** Garrett Frawley, Brian Turner; ***C:*** Derick Underschultz. **CABLE**

The Snows of Kilimanjaro 🦴🦴🦴 **1952** Called by Hemingway "The Snows of Zanuck," in reference to the great producer, this film is actually an artful pastiche of several Hemingway short stories and novels. The main story, "The Snows of Kilimanjaro," acts as a framing device, in which the life of a successful writer is seen through his fevered flashbacks as he and his rich wife, while on safari, await a doctor to save his gangrenous leg. **117m/C VHS, DVD.** Gregory Peck, Susan Hayward, Ava Gardner, Hildegarde Knef, Leo G. Carroll, Torin Thatcher, Ava Norring, Helene Stanley, Marcel Dalio, Vincente Gomez, Richard Allen, Leonard Carey; ***D:*** Henry King; ***W:*** Casey Robinson; ***C:*** Leon Shamroy; ***M:*** Bernard Herrmann.

Snuffy Smith, Yard Bird 🦴 1/2 *Private Snuffy Smith; Snuffy Smith* **1942** The pint-sized moonshiner finds himself in the Army, clashing with his sergeant. Followed by "Hillbilly Blitzkrieg" later the same year. Duncan is perfect for the part, and Kennedy is right on as his foil. **67m/B VHS.** Bud Duncan, Edgar Kennedy, Sarah Padden, Doris Linden, J. Farrell MacDonald, Frank Austin, Jimmie Dodd; ***D:*** Edward F. (Eddie) Cline.

So Close 🦴🦴 1/2 *Chik yeung tin si* **2002 (R)** Lynn (Qi Shu) and Sue (Wei Zhao) are sisters who have become assassins after their father developed a surveillance device that would let its user see through any video camera in the world. Predictably, after fulfilling a contract their former client tries to have them killed, and an obsessive cop begins tailing them as well. **110m/C DVD.** *HK GB* Qi Shu, Karen Mok, Josie Ho, Tats Lau, Wei Zhao, Seung-heon Song, Michael Wai, Siu-Lun Wan, Sau Sek, Ki Yan Lam, Sheung Mo Lam, May Kwong, So Pik Wong, Ben Lam, Ricardo Mamood-Vega; ***D:*** Corey Yuen; ***W:*** Jeff Lau; ***C:*** Kwok-Man Keung; ***M:*** Sam Kao, Kenji Tan.

So Close to Paradise 🦴🦴 *Biandan, Guniang* **1998** Buddies Dong Zi and Gao Ping are farm workers who migrate to Shanghai for better lives. Dong gets a menial job on the docks while Gao turns to petty crime to survive. When a gang boss cheats Gao, he gets revenge by kidnapping the man's mistress, Vietnamese nighclub singer Ruan Hong. After some violence, Gao and Ruan fall in what passes for love but this story is not about to have a happy ending. A Chinese version of B-movie, Hollywood noir. Mandarin with subtitles. **90m/C VHS, DVD.** *CH* Guo Tao, Tong Wang, Yu Shi, Tao Wu; ***D:*** Xiaoshuai Wang; ***W:*** Xiaoshuai Wang, Pang Ming; ***C:*** Tao Yang; ***M:*** Lin Liu.

So Dear to My Heart 🦴🦴🦴 1/2 **1949** A farm boy and his misfit black sheep wreak havoc at the county fair. Several sequences combine live action with animation. Heartwarming and charming; straightforward and likeable but never sentimental. Wonderful, vintage Disney. ♫Sourwood Mountain; Billy Boy; So Dear To My Heart; County Fair; Stick-To-It-Ivity; Ol' Dan Patch; It's Whatcha Do With Watcha Got; Lavender Blue (Dilly Dilly). **82m/C VHS, DVD.** Bobby Driscoll, Burl Ives, Beulah Bondi, Harry Carey Sr., Luana Patten; ***D:*** Harold Schuster.

So Ends Our Night 🦴🦴🦴 **1941** German scorns Nazi ideology, flees Austria, and meets young Jewish couple seeking asylum. Fine adaptation of Erich Maria Remarque's novel "Flotsam," with splendid performances from Sullavan (on loan from Universal) and young Ford. **117m/B VHS, DVD.** Fredric March, Margaret Sullavan, Frances Dee, Glenn Ford, Anna Sten, Erich von Stroheim; ***D:*** John Cromwell; ***C:*** William H. Daniels.

So Fine 🦴🦴 1/2 **1981 (R)** Absent-minded English professor O'Neal tries to rescue his father's clothing business from going bottom-up. He accidentally invents peek-a-boo bottomed jeans, which become an immediate hit and make him rich. Comedy smorgasbord, setting outing from sometime novelist Bergman, hits and misses. O'Neal is memorable, as is the ubiquitous Warden and his sidekick. **91m/C VHS.** Ryan O'Neal, Jack Warden, Mariangela Melato, Richard Kiel; ***D:*** Andrew Bergman; ***W:*** Andrew Bergman; ***M:*** Ennio Morricone.

So I Married an Axe Murderer 🦴🦴 1/2 **1993 (PG-13)** Combination comedy/romance/thriller. Charlie is a hip bookstore owner with a commitment problem. When he finally falls in love with a butcher, he comes to suspect she's a serial killer and he's in line as her next victim. "Saturday Night Live" star Myers has a dual role: as Charlie and as Scottish dad Stuart, allowing him to be fanatically Scottish as Stuart and somewhat more restrained as the angst-ridden Charlie. One-gag movie counted on Myers' "Wayne's World" popularity, which didn't pan out at the boxoffice. Best appreciated by Myers' fans, this one is better on the small screen. **92m/C VHS, DVD, Blu-ray Disc.** Mike Myers, Nancy Travis, Anthony LaPaglia, Amanda Plummer, Brenda Fricker, Matt Doherty; ***Cameos:*** Charles Grodin, Phil Hartman, Steven Wright, Alan Arkin, Michael Richards; ***D:*** Thomas Schlamme; ***W:*** Robbie Fox, Mike Myers; ***M:*** Bruce Broughton.

So Proudly We Hail 🦴🦴🦴 **1943** True story of the lives of three war-front nurses and their heroism under fire during WWII. Colbert is Lt. Davidson in charge of nine Red Cross Army nurses serving in the Pacific. Lake and Goddard play the other leads. With the popularity of its stars and the patriotic spirit of the film, the picture hit boxoffice gold. Critics praised its authenticity, as the film never fell victim to the usual standards of Hollywood glamour. Fans of Lake beware: she has short hair in this film because the government requested that she not appear as a servicewoman with her famous peek-a-boo hair style because female factory workers were getting their long Lake-inspired hair caught in the machinery. **126m/B VHS, DVD.** Claudette Colbert, Paulette Goddard, Veronica Lake, George Reeves, Barbara Britton, Walter Abel, Sonny Tufts, John Litel, Mary Servoss, Ted Hecht, Mary Treen, Helen Lynd, Adrian Booth, Dorothy Adams, Ann Doran, Jean Willes, Jan Wiley, Lynn Walker, Joan Tours, Kitty Kelly, James Bell, Dick Hogan, Bill Goodwin, James Flavin; ***D:*** Mark Sandrich; ***W:*** Allan Scott; ***C:*** Charles B(ryant) Lang Jr.; ***M:*** Miklos Rozsa.

So This Is Africa 🦴🦴 **1933** Spoof of Hollywood jungle pictures stars the comedy team of Wheeler and Woolsey. Wilbur (Wheeler) and Alexander (Woolsey) are a couple of broke vaudevillians with a lion act when they are hired by a movie producer to take their cats and make a jungle picture in Africa. Alexander becomes the plaything of the film's female director (Muir) while Wilbur is the love slave of the Amazon queen (Torres). The duo dress as women to escape the Amazons only to be captured by a pack of jungle Tarzans. The original release ran 90 minutes but ran afoul of censors and was heavily edited for double entendres and sexual content. **61m/B VHS.** Robert Woolsey, Bert Wheeler, Raquel Torres, Esther Muir, Berton Churchill; ***D:*** Edward F. (Eddie) Cline; ***W:*** Norman Krasna; ***C:*** Leonard Smith.

So This Is Love 🦴 1/2 **1953** Technicolor musical bio of American soprano Grace Moore with an adequate performance by Grayson (a better singer than actress) that demonstrates little of the real Moore's charisma. Heading to New York from her Tennessee hometown, Moore makes ends meet by nightclub singing and Broadway musicals before finding success (and 28 curtain calls) with her Met Opera House performance of Mimi in "La Boheme." Moore was killed in a plane crash in 1947. **100m/C DVD.** Kathryn Grayson, Merv Griffin, Joan Weldon, Walter Abel, Rosemary DeCamp; ***D:*** Gordon Douglas; ***W:*** John Monks Jr.; ***C:*** Robert Burks; ***M:*** Max Steiner.

So This Is Paris **1926** Roguish pre-Hayes Code dancing duo seeks spice through alternative lovemates. Classic sophisticated Lubitsch, with outstanding camera work and a bit of jazz. **68m/B VHS.** Monte Blue, Patsy Ruth Miller, Lilyan Tashman, Andre de Beranger, Myrna Loy; ***D:*** Ernst Lubitsch.

So This Is Washington 1/2 *Remove Lum & Abner* **1943** The comedy team go to Washington with wacky inventions to help the war effort. Turns out there's too entirely too much nonsense going around, and the boys give 'em a piece of their mind. Fun, featherweight wartime comedy. **70m/B VHS, DVD.** Alan Mowbray, Mildred Coles, Chester Lauck, Norris Goff; ***D:*** Ray McCarey; ***W:*** Leonard Praskins, Roswell Rogers; ***C:*** Harry Wild.

Soapdish **1991 (PG-13)** The back stage lives of a daytime soap opera, "The Sun Also Sets," and its cast. When the soap's ratings fall, a character written out of series via decapitation is brought back to give things a lift. While the writer struggles to make the reincarnation believable, the cast juggles old and new romances, and professional jealousies abound. Some genuinely funny moments as film actors spoof the genre that gave many of them a start. **97m/C VHS, DVD.** Sally Field, Kevin Kline, Robert Downey Jr., Cathy Moriarty, Whoopi Goldberg, Elisabeth Shue, Carrie Fisher, Garry Marshall, Teri Hatcher, Paul Johansson, Costas Mandylor, Stephen Nichols, Leeza Gibbons, John Tesh, Kathy Najimy, Sheila Kelley, Finola Hughes; ***D:*** Michael Hoffman; ***W:*** Andrew Bergman, Robert Harling; ***C:*** Ueli Steiger; ***M:*** Alan Silvestri.

S.O.B. 1/2 **1981 (R)** Blake Edwards' bitter farce about Hollywood and the film industry wheelers and dealers who inhabit it. When a multi-million dollar picture bombs at the boxoffice, the director turns suicidal, until he envisions re-shooting it with a steamy, "X"-rated scene starring his wife, a star with a goody-two-shoes image. Edwards used his real-life wife, Julie ("Mary Poppins") Andrews, for the scene in which she bared her breasts. Oft-inspired, but oft-terrible. Zestfully uvengeful. William Holden's last film. **121m/C VHS, DVD.** William Holden, Robert Preston, Richard Mulligan, Julie Andrews, Robert Webber, Shelley Winters, Robert Vaughn, Larry Hagman, Stuart Margolin, Loretta Swit, Craig Stevens, Larry Storch, Jennifer Edwards, Robert Loggia, Rosanna Arquette, Marisa Berenson; ***D:*** Blake Edwards; ***W:*** Blake Edwards; ***C:*** Harry Stradling Jr.; ***M:*** Henry Mancini. Natl. Soc. Film Critics '81: Support. Actor (Preston).

Soccer Dog: The Movie 1/2 **1998 (PG)** Clay Newlin (Foley) discovers the small town he's just moved to doesn't seem very friendly. His joins the local soccer team but isn't having much luck and Clay's only friend is stray dog Lincoln, who likes to watch the games. Then, when the team is short a player and in danger of forfeiting, the coach drafts Lincoln and the team actually wins. If you've watch the "Air Bud" movies, you've seen this before. **98m/C VHS, DVD.** Jeremy Foley, James Marshall, Olivia D'Abo; ***D:*** Tony Giglio; ***W:*** Daniel Forman. **VIDEO**

Soccer Mom **2008** When Becca's (Osment) losing soccer team needs a new coach, her crazy mother Wendy (Pyle) decides to masquerade as a famous (male) Italian player and takes the job. The girls start winning and are on their way to the regional finals but how much longer can Wendy and Becca keep up the unraveling charade? **92m/C DVD.** Emily Osment, Missi Pyle, Dan Cortese, Master P, Victoria Jackson, Kristen Wilson, Cassie Scerbo, Jennifer Sciole; ***D:*** Gregory McClatchy; ***W:*** Frederick Ayeroff; ***C:*** Jeff Venditti; ***M:*** Jerry Brunskill. **VIDEO**

Social Error **1935** A college student gets expelled from college for various missteps and escapades, then becomes involved in the kidnapping of an heiress. Zany stunts highlight this Hollywood romp. **60m/B VHS.** Gertrude Messinger, David Sharpe, Monte Blue, Lloyd Hughes, Sheila Terry, Matty Fain, Ted Adams, Roger Williams, Joseph Girard, Mickey Daniels, Fred "Snowflake" Toones; ***D:*** Harry Fraser; ***W:*** Charles E. Roberts; ***C:*** Arthur Brooks.

Social Intercourse **WOOF! 2001** Waste of celluloid concerning the social reclamation of cyber geek Todd (Taylor, who also edited, produced, directed, and coscripted) at a friend's blow-out bash. If horny hijinks, tough-talking chicks, and a water-balloon sniper constituted good plot elements, then "Social Intercourse" would be the "Citizen Kane" of party films. **88m/C DVD.** Steve Taylor, Lee Abbott, Kim Little, Ashley Davis, Steve Grabowsky; ***D:*** Steve Taylor; ***W:*** Steve Taylor, Roger Kristian Jones; ***C:*** Armand Gazarian.

Social Misfits **2000** Twelve troubled teenagers, including our narrator Skylar (co-writer Tann), are sent to Camp Resurrection outside Fresno for a weekend of "re-education." The film claims to be based on events that took place on March 14, 1997, but this alternative boot-camp seems to consist mostly of unsupervised psycho-drama as each of the kids tells his or her story. The whole thing is produced with more enthusiasm than experience or talent. (Note the visible camera shadows.) Production values are minimal but adequate to the subject matter. **91m/C DVD.** Boris Cabrera, Le'Mark Cruise, Gabriel Damon, Isait de la Fuente, Ryan Francis, Bev Land, Eric Gray, Paul Gleason, Tyronne Tann; ***D:*** Rene Villar-Rios; ***W:*** Le'Mark Cruise, Tyronne Tann; ***C:*** Eric Leach; ***M:*** William Richter.

The Social Secretary 1/2 **1916** Driven from the rat race by lecherous men, Talmadge gets new job as rich woman's secretary, where she down-dresses to avoid further lewd encounters. She falls for her boss's son, but isn't considered marriage material until she proves herself. **56m/B VHS.** Norma Talmadge, Kate Lester, Helen Weir, Gladden James, Herbert Frank; ***D:*** John Emerson.

Society **1992 (R)** A teenager wonders if his visions are real or hallucinations when he believes his family, and everyone else around him, are flesh-eating predators. The puzzle isn't much but wait for the special-effects ladened ending to get your fill of gore. **99m/C VHS, DVD.** Billy Warlock, Devin Devasquez, Evan Richards; ***D:*** Brian Yuzna.

Sodbusters 1/2 **1994 (PG-13)** Western spoof about homesteaders versus a greedy cattle baron and the railroad in 1875 Colorado. A lascivious farmer's wife and a mysterious gunslinger—as well as a couple of gay cowboys—are included for additional fun. **97m/C VHS.** Kris Kristofferson, John Vernon, Fred Willard, Wendel Meldrum, Max Gail, Steve Landesberg, Don Lake, James Pickens Jr., John Hemphill; ***D:*** Eugene Levy; ***W:*** John Hemphill, Eugene Levy. **TV**

Sodom and Gomorrah *Sodome et Gomorrhe; The Last Days of Sodom and Gomorrah* **1962** The Italian-made, internationally produced epic about Lot, the Hebrews and the destruction of the two sinful biblical cities. Moderately entertaining—but ponderous, to say the least, and very long. **154m/C VHS.** *IT* Stewart Granger, Stanley Baker, Pier Angeli, Anouk Aimee, Rossana Podesta; ***D:*** Robert Aldrich; ***M:*** Miklos Rozsa.

Sofie 1/2 **1992** Sweet family melodrama about a late 19th Jewish family in Denmark. Sofie (Mynster) is the unmarried 28-year-old daughter of loving, protective parents. She has fallen in love with a gentile artist (Christensen) but gives him up to marry within her faith. Unsuited, Sofie and Jonas (Zeller) lead melancholy lives, which Sofie redeems through her joy in her son. Self-effacing drama is Ullmann's directorial debut. Adapted from the novel "Mendel Philipsen & Son" by Henri Nathansen. In Swedish with English subtitles. **145m/C VHS, DVD.** *SW* Karen-Lise Mynster, Ghita Norby, Erland Josephson, Jesper Christensen, Henning Moritzen, Torben Zeller, Stig Hoffmeyer, Kirsten Rolffes, Lotte Herman; ***D:*** Liv Ullmann; ***W:*** Liv Ullmann, Peter Poulsen.

Soft and Hard 1/2 **1985** Video by Godard and Mieville intends to address the role of media and television in everyday life via a seemingly informal look at the couple's daily existence and the propensity for image production in it. In French; subtitled. **48m/C VHS.** *FR* ***D:*** Anne-Marie Mieville, Jean-Luc Godard. **TV**

Soft Deceit 1/2 **1994 (R)** Master criminal Trent (Bergin) gets caught in the heist of $16 million in mob money. Then Anne (Vernon) shashays into prison offering Trent a deal—half the cash in exchange for breaking him out. She succeeds but maybe a doublecross is next on the agenda. **95m/C VHS.** Patrick Bergin, Kate Vernon, John Wesley Shipp, Gwynyth Walsh, Nigel Bennett, Damir Andrei; ***D:*** Jorge Montesi; ***W:*** Jorge Montesi.

Soft for Digging 1/2 **2001** Something evil is happening in the Maryland woods. Virgil (Mercier) is a hermit-like old man who believes he sees a man strangle a young girl (Ingerson) in the forest. Of course, when the cops arrive there's no body and nothing to indicate a crime happened. But Virgil knows it did—since the little girl is haunting him, demanding justice. Film is nearly without dialogue and title cards divide the scenes. It's an interesting but generally amateurish experiment. **78m/C DVD.** Edmond Mercier, Sarah Ingerson, Andrew Hewitt, David Husko, Joshua Billings; ***D:*** J.T. Petty; ***W:*** J.T. Petty; ***C:*** Patrick McGraw; ***M:*** James L. Wolcott.

Soft Fruit 1/2 **1999 (R)** Patsy (Drynan) is dying of cancer and, though her grumpy husband (Haft) isn't happy about it, her four children show up to care for her—the first time in 15 years that all the family has been together. The three sisters (Lemon, Horler, Talbot) have a long-standing case of sibling rivalry and son Bo (Dykstra) is only out on a prison parole because of his mother's condition. But Patsy has some definite ideas about how she wants to spend her last days, whatever her family thinks. **101m/C VHS.** *AU* Jeanie Drynan, Genevieve Lemon, Sacha Horler, Linal Haft, Alicia Talbot, Russell Dykstra; ***D:*** Christina Andreef; ***W:*** Christina Andreef; ***C:*** Laszlo Baranyai; ***M:*** Antony Partos. Australian Film Inst. '99: Actor (Dykstra), Support. Actress (Horler).

The Soft Kill **1994 (R)** LA private eye Jack Ramsey (Bernsen) becomes the prime murder suspect when his girlfriend is strangled. Can he prove his innocence before more bodies pile up and the cops catch him? **95m/C VHS, DVD.** Corbin Bernsen, Brion James, Matt McCoy, Michael (M.K.) Harris, Kim Morgan Greene, Carrie-Anne Moss; ***D:*** Eli Cohen.

The Soft Skin *Le Peau Douce; Silken Skin* **1964** A classic portrayal of marital infidelity by the master director. A writer and lecturer has an affair with a stewardess. After the affair ends, his wife confronts him, with tragic results. Cliche plot is forgivable; acted and directed to perfection. Frequent Truffaut star Jean-Pierre Leaud served here as an apprentice director. In French with English subtitles. **120m/B VHS, DVD.** *FR* Jean Desailly, Nelly Benedetti, Francoise Dorleac, Daniel Ceccaldi; ***D:*** Francois Truffaut; ***W:*** Francois Truffaut, Jean-Louis Richard; ***C:*** Raoul Coutard; ***M:*** Georges Delerue.

Soggy Bottom U.S.A. **1984 (PG)** A sheriff has his hands full trying to keep the law enforced in a small Southern town. Quite-good cast keeps the plot from disappearing altogether. **90m/C VHS, DVD.** Don Johnson, Ben Johnson, Dub Taylor, Ann Wedgeworth, Lois Nettleton, Anthony Zerbe; ***D:*** Theodore J. Flicker.

Soho Square 1/2 **2000 (R)** Meandering, low-budget, first-time effort from Rafn. A nameless detective (Biggs) is assigned to a serial killer case where the killer preys on young women in London's Soho district, setting them on fire. This detective may not have been the best choice since he's drinking too much and seeing visions of his dead wife. Then he meets Julia (Davenport), a woman who could be his dead wife's doppelganger, and she may be the big break in the case. **90m/C DVD.** *GB* Lucy Davenport, Anthony Biggs, Livy Armstrong, Emma Poole, Sasha Lowenthal, Amanda Haberland, William Wilde; ***D:*** Jamie Rafn; ***W:*** Jamie Rafn; ***C:*** Brendan McGinty; ***M:*** Chris Read.

Sois Belle et Tais-Toi 1/2 *Look Beautiful and Shut Up; Be Beautiful but Shut Up; Be Beautiful and Shut Up; Blonde for Danger* **1958** A police detective tracks jewel thieves and falls in love with a young waif. Several interesting and later famous actors have small parts. Light-hearted adventure. Subtitled in English. **110m/B VHS.** *FR* Henri Vidal, Mylene Demongeot, Jean-Paul Belmondo, Alain Delon, Hugh Brooks, Roger Hanin; ***D:*** Marc Allegret; ***W:*** Roger Vadim, Odette Joyeux, William Benjamin, Jean Marsan, Gabriel Arout; ***C:*** Armand Thirard.

Sol Goode 1/2 **2001 (R)** Sol Goode (Getty) is a familiar character—a 20something wannabe actor who uses his looks and charm to bed the babes. But his best pal Chloe (Towne) knows there's a decent guy lurking somewhere underneath the hipster facade. When a series of minor misfortunes find Sol examining his life, he realizes that Chloe is the woman of his dreams—now he just has to convince her that he's sincere. **100m/C VHS, DVD.** Balthazar Getty, Katharine Towne, Jamie Kennedy, Natasha Gregson Wagner, Tori Spelling, Cheri Oteri, Robert Wagner, Danny Comden, Carmen Electra, Johnathon Schaech, Christina Pickles, Max Perlich, Jason Bateman, China Chow; ***D:*** Danny Comden; ***W:*** Danny Comden; ***C:*** Chris Walling.

Solar Crisis 1/2 **1992 (PG-13)** Eye-popping special effects highlight this Earth-on-the-edge-of-destruction sci-fier. In 2050 the sun has gone on self-destruct and begins throwing off giant solar flares which turn the Earth extra-crispy. A space team is sent to divert the flares but the mission may become a victim of sabotage. Director Sarafian actually forgoes credit for the standard Smithee pseudonym. **111m/C VHS, DVD.** Tim Matheson, Charlton Heston, Peter Boyle, Annabel Schofield, Jack Palance, Corin "Corky" Nemec; ***D:*** Richard Sarafian, Alan Smithee; ***W:*** Joe Gannon, Tedi Sarafian; ***C:*** Russell Carpenter; ***M:*** Maurice Jarre.

Solar Force **1994 (R)** Cop (Pare), stationed on the moon, is sent to earth to find a stolen chemical that is capable of restoring a destroyed environment. But there are secrets behind the assignment which could cost him his life. **91m/C VHS, DVD.** Michael Pare, Billy Drago, Walker Brandt; ***D:*** Boaz Davidson; ***W:*** Terrence Pare; ***C:*** Avi (Avraham) Karpik; ***M:*** Don Peake.

Solarbabies **1986 (PG-13)** Roller-skating youths in a drought-stricken future vie for a mysterious power that will replenish the Earth's water. Shades of every sci-fi movie you've ever seen, from "Mad Max" to "Ice Pirates." Pathetic. **95m/C VHS, DVD.** Richard Jordan, Sarah Douglas, Charles Durning, Lukas Haas, Jami Gertz, Jason Patric; ***D:*** Alan Johnson; ***W:*** Walon Green; ***M:*** Maurice Jarre.

Solaris *Solyaris* **1972** With this the USSR tried to eclipse "2001: A Space Odyssey" in terms of cerebral science-fiction. Some critics thought they succeeded. You may disagree now that the lumbering effort is available on tape. Adapted from a Stanislaw Lem novel, it depicts a dilapidated space lab orbiting the planet Solaris, whose ocean, a vast fluid "brain," materializes the stir-crazy cosmonauts' obsessions—usually morose ex-girlfriends. Talk, talk, talk, minimal special effects. In Russian with English subtitles. In a two-cassette package, with a letterbox format preserving Tarkovsky's widescreen compositions. **167m/C VHS, DVD.** *RU* Donatas Banionis, Natalya Bondarchuk, Juri Jarvet, Vladislav Dvorzhetsky, Nikolai Grinko, Anatoli (Otto) Solonitzin, Sos Sarkisyan; ***D:*** Andrei Tarkovsky; ***W:*** Andrei Tarkovsky; ***C:*** Vadim Yusov; ***M:*** Eduard Artemyev. Cannes '72: Grand Jury Prize.

Solaris 1/2 **2002 (R)** In the midst of grieving over his dead wife Rheya (McElhone), psychologist Chris Kelvin (Clooney) is summoned to help bring back the survivors of a failed mission aboard a space station orbiting the planet Solaris. Once there, he finds the commander dead and the remaining crewmembers in the grip of some planet-induced paranoia. He also finds his supposedly-dead wife in bed with him the next morning. Soderburgh's moody, claustrophobic, deliberately-paced space oddity offers up existential dread, regret, and search for redemption as the main foes for his characters, rather than some malevolent outside force. This will definitely put off those looking for "Star Wars/Alien" type thrills, but will satisfy those looking for a more cerebral exercise. **99m/C VHS, DVD.** *US* George Clooney, Natascha (Natasha) McElhone, Jeremy Davies, Viola Davis, Ulrich Tukur, Morgan Rusler; ***D:*** Steven Soderbergh; ***W:*** Steven Soderbergh; ***C:*** Steven Soderbergh; ***M:*** Cliff Martinez.

Solas 1/2 *Alone* **1999 (R)** Hard-drinking, embittered Maria (Fernandez) moves into an apartment in a run-down Seville neighborhood and gets a job cleaning offices. Her abusive father (De Osca) is in a nearby hospital and Maria's patient mother Rosa (Galiana) temporarily moves in with her resentful daughter. Rosa has always made the best of what life has given her and she soon befriends Maria's courtly neighbor (Alvarez-Novoa) while Maria continues to get involved with the wrong men and make bad choices. Spanish with subtitles. **98m/C VHS, DVD.** *SP* Maria Galiana, Ana Fernandez, Carlos Alvarez-Novoa, Paco De Osca; ***D:*** Benito Zambrano; ***W:*** Benito Zambrano; ***C:*** Tote Trenas; ***M:*** Antonio Meliveo.

Sold for Marriage **1916** A weak romantic drama worth watching for Gish. Russian peasant Marfa (Gish) lives with her avaricious aunt and uncle who are constantly trying to marry her off to ugly-but-wealthy suitors. She loves poor-but-handsome Jan (Bennett) and discovers he's onboard the same ship when they emigrate to America but things don't get any easier for the couple. **54m/B DVD.** Lillian Gish, Frank Bennett, Allan Sears, Pearl Elmore, William Brian Lowery, Walter Long; ***D:*** Christy Cabanne; ***C:*** William Fildew.

Soldat Duroc... Ca Va Etre Ta Fete! *Soldier Duroc* **1975** Days after the 1944 liberation of Paris, a French soldier crosses back over the French lines to see his lover, and is caught as a German sympathizer by American troops. **105m/C VHS.** *FR* Pierre Tornade, Robert Webber, Michel Galabru, Roger Carel; ***D:*** Michel Gerard.

The Soldier *Codename: The Soldier* **1982 (R)** The Russians are holding the world at ransom with a pile of stolen plutonium, and a soldier finds himself in the position to carry out an unauthorized and dangerous plan to preserve the balance of world power. Wildly implausible, gratuitously violent spy trash. **90m/C VHS.** Ken Wahl, Klaus Kinski, William Prince, Alberta Watson; ***D:*** James Glickenhaus.

Soldier **1998 (R)** Steals trite scenes from other post-apolyptic sci-fi shoot-'em-ups just to prove that 47-year-old Kurt Russell had been working out. Genetically engineered soldier Russell is discarded as obsolete on a garbage dump planet inhabited by a freedom-loving survivalist (Pertwee) and his band of human flotsam. When a force led by next-generation soldier Jason Scott Lee invades the planet, Russell helps save the skanky-looking group of squatters. Robbed of his Snake Plissken smirk, Russell delivers a hollow character who is hard to like. The garbage planet set recycles props used in "Demolition Man," "Executive Decision," and "Event Horizon." The movie recycles ideas from every other sci-fi flick. **99m/C VHS, DVD.** Kurt Russell, Jason Scott Lee, Gary Busey, Michael Chiklis, Sean Pertwee, Jason Isaacs, Connie Nielsen, Brenda Wehle, Mark Bringleson, K.K. Dodds; ***D:*** Paul W.S. Anderson; ***W:*** David Peoples; ***C:*** David Tattersall; ***M:*** Joel McNeely.

Soldier Blue **1970 (R)** Two survivors of an Indian attack make their way back to an army outpost. The cavalry then seeks revenge on the Cheyenne tribe accused of the attack. Gratuitously violent Vietnam-era western hits hard on racial themes. Based on the novel "Arrow in the Sun" by Theodore V. Olsen on the Sand Creek Indian massacre. **109m/C VHS, DVD.** Candice Bergen, Peter Strauss, Donald Pleasence, Dana Elcar, Jorge (George) Rivero; ***D:*** Ralph Nelson; ***W:*** John Gay; ***C:*** Robert B. Hauser.

Soldier Boyz 1/2 **1995 (R)** Ex-Marine Major Howard Tolliver (Dudikoff), who now runs a high-security prison for youthful offenders, is called on to rescue a United Nations worker who's being held hostage by a group of revolutionaries in Vietnam. For help, he takes along six of his toughest prisoners. A variation of "The Dirty Dozen." **91m/C VHS.** Michael Dudikoff, Cary-Hiroyuki Tagawa, Tyrin Turner, David Barry Gray, Channon Roe, Cedrick Terrell, Demetrius Navarro, Jacqueline Obradors; ***D:*** Louis Morneau; ***W:*** Darryl Quarles.

Soldier in Love **1967** Teleplay from "George Schaefer's Showcase Theatre" is based on the life of John Churchill, first Duke of Marlborough, and his wife Sarah. The ambitious young couple held the favor of Queen Anne for a time, until political intrigue brought about their downfall. **76m/C VHS.** Jean Simmons, Claire Bloom, Keith Michell; ***D:*** George Schaefer. **TV**

Soldier in the Rain 1/2 **1963** An unusual friendship develops between career sergeant Gleason and wheeler-dealer McQueen. Gleason is in good form, but McQueen is listless, and the story (set in a Southern army camp) is unsatisfying. Weld is the comely teen who makes for an intriguing love triangle. From the novel by William Goldman. **88m/B VHS.** Steve McQueen, Jackie Gleason, Tuesday Weld, Tony Bill, Tom Poston, Ed Nelson; ***D:*** Ralph Nelson; ***W:*** Blake Edwards; ***M:*** Henry Mancini.

Soldier of Fortune 1/2 **1955** A woman (Hayward) enlists mercenaries to help find her lost husband in Red China. Late Gable vehicle with the formula beginning to feel the post-war strain and the star looking a trifle long in the tooth. Still, a fun adventure from a top star. Hayward had been among the myriad starlets vying for the Scarlett O'Hara roles nearly two decades earlier. **96m/C VHS, DVD.** Clark Gable, Susan Hayward, Gene Barry, Alexander D'Arcy, Michael Rennie, Tom Tully, Anna Sten, Russell Collins, Leo Gordon, Jack Kruschen, Robert Quarry; ***D:*** Edward Dmytryk; ***W:*** Ernest K. Gann; ***C:*** Leo Tover; ***M:*** Hugo Friedhofer.

Soldier of Fortune Inc. **1997 (R)** Retired Major Matt Shepherd (Johnson) is recruited by Washington insider Xavier Trout (Selby), who works for a mystery organization that handles covert operations, to extract American POWs from Iraq. Matt puts together a specialized and secret unit in order to accomplish his mission. Action-packed TV pilot of the syndicated series. **98m/C VHS.** Brad Johnson, David Selby, Melinda (Mindy) Clarke, Tim Abell, Real Andrews, Mark Sheppard, Brian Cousins; ***D:*** Robert Radler. **TV**

Soldier of Orange *Soldaat van Oranje* **1978** The lives of six Dutch students are forever changed by the WWII invasion of Holland by the Nazis. Based on the true-life exploits of Dutch resistance leader Erik Hazelhoff. Exciting and suspenseful; cerebral; carefully made and well acted. Made Rutger Hauer an international star. **144m/C VHS, DVD.** *NL* Derek de Lint, Rutger Hauer, Jeroen Krabbe, Edward Fox, Susan Penhaligon; ***D:*** Paul Verhoeven; ***W:*** Paul Verhoeven, Gerard Soeteman, Kees Holierhoek; ***C:*** Jan De Bont; ***M:*** Roger van Otterloo. L.A. Film Critics '79: Foreign Film.

Soldier of the Night 1/2 **1984** Toy-store worker by day, vigilante killer by night. Israeli thriller set in Tel Aviv lacks vim and is badly dubbed. **89m/C VHS.** Yehuda Efroni, Iris Kraner, Sari Raz, Yftach Kataur; ***D:*** Dan Wolman; ***W:*** Dan Wolman; ***C:*** Yossi Wein; ***M:*** Alex Cagan.

A Soldier's Daughter Never Cries 1/2 **1998 (R)** American novelist and WWII vet Bill Willis (Kristofferson) lives in 1960s Paris with his sexy, freethinking and -drinking wife Marcella (Hershey), their adopted French son Billy (Gruen), and teenage daughter Channe, the center of the story. Her relationships with her brother and a rude (yet likable) classmate (Costanzo) provide much of the film's emotional punch. Bill develops heart problems and takes the family home to the States. Against the backdrop of social and political turmoil, Bill's core values help the family through their own challenges. Ivory and Merchant make an admirable leap into the 20th century. Unfortunately, the film's episodic jumps are too confusing to make it a complete success. Based on the 1990 book by Kaylie Jones, daughter of novelist James Jones. **128m/C VHS.** Kris Kristofferson, Barbara Hershey, Leelee Sobieski, Jesse Bradford, Anthony Roth Costanzo, Dominique Blanc, Jane Birkin, Virginie Ledoyen, Isaach de Bankole, Samuel Gruen, Luisa Conlon; ***D:*** James Ivory; ***W:*** James Ivory, Ruth Prawer Jhabvala; ***C:*** Jean-Marc Fabre; ***M:*** Richard Robbins.

Soldier's Fortune 1/2 **1991 (R)** A traveling gun for hire leaves the combat of Central America for the jungles of Los Angeles, only to find out that his daughter had been taken hostage. That's the last thing these kidnappers will ever do when they are found by this tough guy looking for his child. **96m/C VHS.** Gil Gerard, Charles Napier, Dan Haggerty, P.J. Soles, Barbara Bingham, Janus Blythe; ***D:*** Arthur N. Mele.

Soldier's Girl **2003** First-rate drama takes some time to find its pace but boasts superior performances and a strong final act. Unsophisticated Army Pvt. Barry Winchell (Garity) is dragged as a joke to a gay bar in Nashville where he sees Calpernia Addams (Pace), a transgendered nightclub performer, who is taken with Barry's gentlemanly manners. They begin a tentative courtship that progresses from curiosity to love, which threatens the relationship between Barry and his unstable roommate Fisher (Hatosy), who begins spreading rumors about a gay soldier on base. The manipulative Fisher engineers a confrontation between Barry and a young Oklahoma redneck recruit that explodes into stunning violence. Based on the 1999 murder of a G.I. at a Kentucky military base. **112m/C VHS, DVD.** Troy Garity, Lee Pace, Andre Braugher, Shawn Hatosy, Philip Eddolls; ***D:*** Frank Pierson; ***W:*** Ron Nyswaner; ***C:*** Paul Sarossy; ***M:*** Jan A.P. Kaczmarek. **CABLE**

Soldiers of Change *The Painting* **2006 (PG-13)** Follows the life of a young white man, Randy (Freeman), who grows up during the social turmoil that was 1960s America. He falls for a young black woman, Hallie (Dash), faces criticism from both families prior to heading off to the Vietnam War, and endures the struggles of a novice soldier. Bland, though subject matter is treated with respect by the able cast. **95m/C DVD.** Clifton Davis, Charles Shaughnessy, Stacey Dash, Heath Freeman; ***D:*** Peter Manoogian, Joshua D. Rose; ***W:*** J. Marina Muhlfriedel. **VIDEO**

Soldier's Revenge *Vengeance of a Soldier* **1984** A Vietnam vet has a hard time adjusting to life at home. **92m/C VHS, DVD.** Maria Socas, Paul Lambert, Edgardo Moreira, Francisco Cano, John Savage; ***D:*** David Worth; ***W:*** David Worth, Lee Stull; ***C:*** Leonardo Solis; ***M:*** Gary Reast.

A Soldier's Story **1984 (PG)** A black army attorney is sent to a Southern base to investigate the murder of an unpopular sergeant. Features WWII, Louisiana, jazz and blues, and racism in and outside the corps. From the Pulitzer-prize winning play by Charles Fuller, with most of the Broadway cast. Fine performances from Washington and Caesar. **101m/C VHS, DVD.** Howard E. Rollins Jr., Adolph Caesar, Denzel Washington, Patti LaBelle, Robert Kevin Townsend, Scott Paulin, Wings Hauser, Art Evans, Larry Riley, David Alan Grier; ***D:*** Norman Jewison; ***W:*** Charles Fuller; ***C:*** Russell Boyd; ***M:*** Herbie Hancock. L.A. Film Critics '84: Support. Actor (Caesar).

A Soldier's Sweetheart 1/2 **1998 (R)** Bored Vietnam soldier, Rat (Sutherland), narrates the unlikely story of Marianne (Gates). Her high school boyfriend, Fossie (Ulrich), is a lonely medic who manages to bring Marianne over to join him. All the guys in the squad fall for her, but Marianne falls in love with the excitement/uncertainty/terror of war. Adapted from the story "Sweetheart of the Song Tra Bong" by Tim O'Brien. **111m/C VHS.** Kiefer Sutherland, Skeet Ulrich, Georgina Cates, Daniel London, Larry (Lawrence) Gilliard Jr., Christopher Birt, Louis Vanaria; ***D:*** Thomas Michael Donnelly; ***W:*** Thomas Michael Donnelly; ***C:*** Jacek Laskus; ***M:*** Gary Chang. **CABLE**

A Soldier's Tale **1991 (R)** During WWII, a menage-a-trois develops that can only lead to tragedy, yet the participants find themselves unable to resist. **96m/C VHS, DVD.** Gabriel Byrne, Marianne Basler, Judge Reinhold, Paul Wyett; ***D:*** Larry Parr; ***W:*** Larry Parr; ***C:*** Alun Bollinger; ***M:*** John Charles.

Sole Survivor 1/2 **1984 (R)** A group of zombies are searching for a beautiful advertising executive who was the sole survivor of a plane crash. **85m/C VHS.** Anita Skinner, Kurt Johnson, Caren Larkey, Brinke Stevens, Leon Robinson; ***D:*** Thom Eberhardt; ***C:*** Russell Carpenter.

Solid Gold Cadillac **1956** Holliday is a winning lead as Laura Patridge, an idealistic, small-time stockholder who discovers that the corporate board of directors are crooked. She makes waves at a stockholders meeting, gets noticed by the press, finds romance with former CEO Edward McKeever (Douglas), and works to oust the scalawags from power. The title comes from Laura's fervent desire to own a—you guessed it—solid gold cadillac. Based on the Broadway play by George S. Kaufman and Howard Teichmann. **99m/B VHS, DVD.** Judy Holliday, Paul Douglas, Fred Clark, Neva Patterson, Arthur O'Connell, Ray Collins; ***D:*** Richard Quine; ***W:*** Abe Burrows; ***C:*** Charles B(ryant) Lang Jr.; ***M:*** Cyril Mockridge; ***Nar:*** George Burns. Oscars '56: Costume Des. (B&W).

Solitaire for 2 1/2 **1994 (R)** Sweet-natured romantic comedy about a rogue and a psychic. Handsome Daniel Becker (Frankel) is a behavioral psychologist who specializes in interpreting body language and using his expertise to bed as many beautiful women as happen his way. Uptight paleontologist Katie (Pays) has a problem with men—she can literally read their minds and gets angry at their lewd thoughts. So the path to true commitment is going to get a bit bumpy. **105m/C VHS.** *GB* Mark Frankel, Amanda Pays, Roshan Seth, Maryam D'Abo, Jason Isaacs, Annette Crosbie; ***D:*** Gary Sinyor; ***W:*** Gary Sinyor; ***C:*** Henry Braham; ***M:*** David A. Hughes, John Murphy.

The Solitary Man **1982** Glum look at a family breakup, from the husband's point of view. Holliman is good, but the exercise at large is regularly blues-inducing, and not especially inspiring or artful. **96m/C VHS.** Earl Holliman, Carrie Snodgress, Lara Parker, Lane Smith, Nicolas Coster, Michelle Pfeiffer; ***D:*** John Llewellyn Moxey. **TV**

Solitary Man **2010 (R)** Business and romantic indiscretions cause personal and professional problems for Ben (Douglas), the former owner of a car dealership chain. **90m/C DVD.** *US* Michael Douglas, Susan Sarandon, Danny DeVito, Mary-Louise Parker, Jesse Eisenberg, Richard Schiff, Jenna Fischer; ***D:*** Brian Koppelman; ***W:*** Brian Koppelman, David Levien; ***C:*** Alwin Kuchler; ***M:*** Michael Penn.

Solo **1977 (PG)** Young hitchhiker Peers enters the lives of fire patrol pilot Gil and his teenage son. A plotless friendship develops, headed nowhere—like this movie. Great New Zealand scenery might be worth the price of rental. **90m/C VHS.** Vincent (Vince Gill) Gil, Perry Armstrong, Martyn Sanderson, Lisa Peers; ***D:*** Tony Williams.

Solo **1996 (PG-13)** Fast-paced actioner stars Van Peebles as Solo, an android assassin with a heart of gold. It seems the muscle-bound, computerized killer is programmed with not only amazing fighting skills but the ability to think and learn. Solo who, being naughty in the sight of one-dimensional government bigwigs, is scheduled for replacement by a fighting machine that won't be so fickle when it comes to pulling the trigger. The chase is on when Solo learns of their plot and takes to the jungles of Central America, where together with the local peasants, the rebellious robot fights to preserve his humanity and his life. Poor man's "Terminator" is sprinkled with the kind of glib one-liners usually reserved for Schwarzenegger, although Van Peebles' performance hikes this rehashed premise up a notch. Adapted from Robert Mason's novel "Weapon." **106m/C VHS, DVD.** Mario Van Peebles, William Sadler, Seidy Lopez, Barry Corbin, Adrien Brody, Abraham Verduzo, Jaime Gomez, Damian Bechir, Joaquin Garrido; ***D:*** Norberto Barba; ***W:*** David Corley; ***C:*** Chris Walling; ***M:*** Christopher Franke.

Solo **2006** World-weary Sydney killer Jack Barrett (Friels) is a 30-year man in the mob and he wants to retire. While selling his gun collection at a pawn shop, he meets university student Billie (Novakovic), who's writing her thesis on local criminals. Jack talks just enough to make his bosses nervous and they decide that his last hit will be Billie. Good performance by Friels brings this crime story up a notch. **96m/C DVD.** *AU* Colin Friels, Bojana Novakovic, Linal Haft, Angie Milliken, Vince Colosimo, Bruce Spence, Tony Barry, Chris Heywood; ***D:*** Morgan O'Neill; ***W:*** Morgan O'Neill; ***C:*** Hugh Miller; ***M:*** Martyn Love, Damian DeBoos-Smith.

Solo Sunny **1980** Pop singer Sunny (Krossner) is constantly on the road with a mediocre band, trying to make a living. When she's kicked out of the group for consistently resisting the leader's sexual advances, she tries her hand at a solo career in Berlin. But things don't work out well, and Sunny is getting increasingly desperate. German with subtitles. **102m/C VHS.** *GE* Renate Krossner, Alexander Lang, Dieter Montag, Heide Kipp, Klaus Brasch; ***D:*** Konrad Wolf; ***W:*** Wolfgang Kohlhaase; ***C:*** Eberhard Geick; ***M:*** Gunther Fischer.

Solo Voyage: The Revenge **1990** A Russian "Rambo" goes on a murderous rampage, the likes of which humanity has not yet seen. **91m/C VHS.** *RU* Mikhail Nojkine, Alexandre Fatiouchine; ***D:*** Mikhail Toumanichulli.

The Soloist 1/2 **2009 (PG-13)** Downey Jr. and Foxx do right by their characters in this compassionate, albeit romanticized, version of a true story. Los Angeles Times columnist Steve Lopez is researching a story when he hears homeless Nathaniel Ayers playing violin on the streets. He learns that the classically-trained musical prodigy's life fell apart when he became schizophrenic and vows to help him. Steve learns the hardest lesson when he realizes that he can only do so much for Nathaniel and that there is no conventional happy ending for his situation. **105m/C DVD.** *US* Robert Downey Jr., Jamie Foxx, Stephen (Steve) Root, Tom Holland, Lisa Gay Hamilton, Catherine Keener, Lorraine Toussaint; ***D:*** Joe Wright; ***W:*** Susannah Grant; ***C:*** Seamus McGarvey; ***M:*** Dario Marianelli.

Solomon 1/2 **1998** Solomon is crowned King of Israel and vows to build a temple to house the Ark of the Covenant. In return, he is granted the gift of widom, which he doesn't seem to make much use of. He falls deeply in love with the Queen of Sheba but when she is forced to return to her homeland, Solomon falls into such a depression that he neglects his kingdom and allows corruption to spread. **172m/C VHS, DVD.** Ben Cross, Vivica A. Fox, Anouk Aimee, Max von Sydow, Maria Grazia Cucinotta, Stefania Rocca, David Suchet, Richard Dillane; ***D:*** Roger Young. **CABLE**

Solomon and Gaenor **1998 (R)** Around 1911, a young Jewish peddler named Solomon (Gruffudd) meets Gaenor (Roberts), the daughter of Welsh mineworkers. Hiding his Orthodox Jewish origins, Solomon calls himself Sam and the young duo are soon in love. Gaenor winds up pregnant and her family wants to send her away and force her to give up the baby. She finally tracks down Solomon's family but they are equally upset that their son is involved with a gentile. Amidst all this family turmoil, is a violent dispute between the workers and the mine owners. Conventional tear-stained period piece. **103m/C VHS, DVD.** *GB* Ioan Gruffudd, Nia Roberts, Mark Lewis Jones, William Thomas, Maureen Lipman, David Horovitch; ***D:*** Paul Morrison; ***W:*** Paul Morrison; ***C:*** Nina Kellgren; ***M:*** Ilona Sekacz.

Solomon and Sheba **1959** King Solomon's brother and the Egyptian Pharaoh send the Queen of Sheba to Israel to seduce King Solomon so they may gain his throne. Tyrone Power had filmed most of the lead role in this silly, overwrought epic when he died of a heart attack. The role was reshot, with Brynner (with a full head of hair) replacing him. Director Vidor's unfortunate last film. Shot on location in Spain. **139m/C VHS.** Yul Brynner, Gina Lollobrigida, Marisa Pavan, George Sanders, Alejandro Rey; ***D:*** King Vidor; ***C:*** Frederick A. (Freddie) Young; ***M:*** Malcolm Arnold.

The Sombrero Kid **1942** The Kid unwittingly gets involved in a murder and is nearly hanged before his friends help him discover the real culprits. Plenty of action in this straight forward, fun western. **54m/B VHS.** Donald (Don "Red") Barry, Lynn Merrick, Rand Brooks; ***D:*** George Sherman.

Some Call It Loving **1973 (R)** Bad, pretentious modern version of Sleeping Beauty, set in L.A. King buys the sleeping girl (Farrow) from a carnival show, but she doesn't live up to his ideal. **103m/C VHS.** Zalman King, Carol White, Tisa Farrow, Richard Pryor, Pat Priest; ***D:*** James B. Harris.

Some Came Running **1958** James Jones's follow-up novel to "From Here to Eternity" does not translate nearly as well to the screen. Overlong and with little plot, the action centers around a would-be writer, his floozy girl friend, and the holier-than-thou characters which populate the town in which he grew up and to which he has now returned. Strong performances by all. **136m/C VHS, DVD.** Frank Sinatra, Dean Martin, Shirley MacLaine, Martha Hyer, Arthur Kennedy, Nancy Gates; ***D:*** Vincente Minnelli; ***C:*** William H. Daniels; ***M:*** Elmer Bernstein.

Some Folks Call It a Sling Blade **1994** The short film that became 1996's critically acclaimed "Sling Blade." This stark black-and-white short, penned by Billy Bob Thornton and directed by George Hickenlooper ("Hearts of Darkness: A Filmmaker's Apocalypse"), premiered at Sundance. The original version only involves a young reporter's (Ringwald) interview with Karl Childers (Thorton), in which he recalls the events that led him to be in the institution. Also includes "The Making of 'Some Folks Call It a Sling Blade'" (color, 13 minutes) which comprises interviews the stars, director, and producer. **29m/B VHS, DVD.** Billy Bob Thornton, Molly Ringwald, J.T. Walsh, Jefferson Mays, Suzanne Cryer; ***D:*** George Hickenlooper; ***W:*** Billy Bob Thornton; ***C:*** Kent Wakeford; ***M:*** Bill Boll.

Some Girls 1/2 *Sisters* **1988 (R)** A man goes to Quebec to see his college girlfriend who informs him that she is not in love with him anymore. But she has two sisters ready to comfort him! Strange black comedy; Gregory as the girl's father elevates so-so story. **104m/C VHS.** Patrick Dempsey, Andre Gregory, Lila Kedrova, Florinda Bolkan, Jennifer Connelly, Sheila Kelley; ***D:*** Michael Hoffman; ***M:*** James Newton Howard.

Some Kind of Hero **1982 (R)** A Vietnam prisoner of war returns home to a changed world. Pryor tries hard, but can't get above this poorly written, unevenly directed film. **97m/C VHS, DVD.** Richard Pryor, Margot Kidder, Ray Sharkey, Ronny Cox, Lynne Moody, Olivia Cole, Paul Benjamin, Peter Jason, Tim Thomerson; ***D:*** Michael Pressman; ***W:*** Robert Boris; ***C:*** King Baggot; ***M:*** Patrick Williams.

Some Kind of Wonderful **1987 (PG-13)** A high-school tomboy has a crush on a guy who also happens to be her best friend. Her feelings go unrequited as he falls for a rich girl with snobbish friends. In the end, true love wins out. Deutch also directed (and John Hughes also produced) the teen flick "Pretty in Pink," which had much the same plot, with the rich/outcast characters reversed by gender. OK, but completely predictable. **93m/C VHS, DVD.** Eric Stoltz, Lea Thompson, Mary Stuart Masterson, Craig Sheffer, John Ashton, Elias Koteas, Molly Hagan; ***D:*** Howard Deutch; ***W:*** John Hughes.

Some Like It Hot **1959** Two unemployed musicians witness the St. Valentine's Day massacre in Chicago. They disguise themselves as women and join an all-girl band headed for Miami to escape the gangsters' retaliation. Flawless cast includes a fetching Monroe at her best; hilarious script. Curtis does his Cary Grant impression. Classic scenes between Lemmon in drag and Joe E. Brown as a smitten suitor. Brown also has the film's famous closing punchline. Monroe sings "I Wanna Be Loved By You," "Running Wild," and "I'm Through With Love." One of the very funniest movies of all time. **120m/B VHS, DVD.** Marilyn Monroe, Tony Curtis, Jack Lemmon, George Raft, Pat O'Brien, Nehemiah Persoff, Joe E. Brown, Joan Shawlee, Mike Mazurki; ***D:*** Billy Wilder; ***W:*** Billy Wilder, I.A.L. Diamond; ***C:*** Charles B(ryant) Lang Jr.; ***M:*** Adolph Deutsch. Oscars '59: Costume Des. (B&W); AFI '98: Top 100; British Acad. '59: Actor (Lemmon); Golden Globes '60: Actor—Mus./Comedy (Lemmon), Actress—Mus./Comedy (Monroe), Film—Mus./Comedy, Natl. Film Reg. '89.

Some Mother's Son *Sons and Warriors* **1996 (R)** Young IRA members Gerard Quigley (Gillen) and Frank Higgins (O'Hara) are sentenced to long prison terms after an attack on the British army. Tough, politically active Annie Higgins (Flanagan) has already lost one son to "The Troubles" and is willing to support Frank in whatever he does. But her son Gerard's involvement takes apolitical schoolteacher Kathleen (Mirren) completely by surprise. When their sons join in a prison hunger strike, the two mothers must face the choice of supporting their sons' possible deaths by starvation or allowing the prison's officials to force-feed them. The leads give tough, terrific performances in a heartwrenching story. **112m/C VHS.** *IR GB* Helen Mirren, Fionnula Flanagan, Aidan Gillen, David O'Hara, John Lynch, Tim Woodward, Ciaran Hinds, Gerard McSorley, Geraldine O'Rawe; ***D:*** Terry George; ***W:*** Jim Sheridan, Terry George; ***C:*** Geoffrey Simpson; ***M:*** Bill Whelan.

Some Prefer Cake **1997** Best friends Kira (Fontaine) and Sydney (Howley) are also roomies in San Francisco. Kira's stage fright prevents her from pursuing a career as a stand-up comedian and she's resentful when the material she wrote for her sister (Gonzalez) makes her a success. Kira's also got problems with a one-night stand turned stalker (Saito). Meanwhile, Syd is insisting everything is fine but she has career and boyfriend problems. Both women struggle with their co-dependency until realizing that the only way to move forward is to do it without clinging to each other. **95m/C DVD.** Kathleen Fantaine, Tara Howley, Mimi Gonzalez, Machiko Saito, Desi del Valle, Leon Acord; ***D:*** Heidi Arnesen; ***W:*** Jeannie Kahaney; ***C:*** Matt Siegel.

Somebody Has to Shoot the Picture **1990 (R)** Photographer Scheider is hired by a convicted man to take a picture of his execution. Hours before the event, Scheider uncovers evidence that leads him to believe the man is innocent. He then embarks in a race against time to save him. Adapted by Doug Magee from his book "Slow Coming Dark." Unpretentious, tough drama. **104m/C VHS, DVD.** Roy Scheider, Bonnie Bedelia, Robert Carradine, Andre Braugher, Arliss Howard; ***D:*** Frank Pierson; ***W:*** Doug Magee; ***C:*** Bojan Bazelli; ***M:*** James Newton Howard. **CABLE**

Somebody Is Waiting 1/2 **1996 (R)** Charlotte Ellis (Kinski) tries to be the best mom she can to her five kids after her abusive, drunken husband Roger (Byrne) finally abandons them. Eighteen-year-old Leon (Whitworth) seems to be headed down the same dark road after being arrested for drunk driving. Charlotte agrees to set up a bank account for Leon, if he'll move out, and is then killed in a robbery, where Leon is injured. Roger then shows up to look after his shattered family but it's only a matter of time before things get even worse. Pros Bryne and Kinski do what they can but the script is certainly no help. **90m/C VHS.** Gabriel Byrne, Nastassja Kinski, Johnny Whitworth, Rebecca Gayheart, Shirley Knight, Brian Donovan; ***D:*** Martin Donovan; ***W:*** Martin Donovan; ***C:*** Greg Gardiner; ***M:*** Elia Cmiral.

Somebody to Love 1/2 **1994 (R)** Spunky taxi dancer Mercedes (Perez) wants to be an actress despite the bad luck actor/boyfriend Harry (a subdued Keitel) has. One of her clients is the bumpious Ernesto (De Lorenzo), who quickly becomes infatuated by Mercedes and, to impress her, takes a job with local racketeer Emillio (Quinn). Ernesto even decides to take a contract hit to get the money Mercedes needs to help out Harry, leading to tragedy. Confusing look at the fringes of the L.A. showbiz scene, with lots of missed chances though Perez gets some flashy diva scenes. **103m/C VHS, DVD.** Edward (Eddie) Bunker, Rosie Perez, Harvey Keitel, Michael Delorenzo, Anthony Quinn, Steve Buscemi, Stanley Tucci, Gerardo Mejia, Paul Herman; ***Cameos:*** Angel Aviles, Quentin Tarantino; ***D:*** Alexandre Rockwell; ***W:*** Alexandre Rockwell, Sergei Bodrov.

Somebody Up There Likes Me **1956** Story of Rocky Graziano's (Newman) gritty battle from his poor, street-wise childhood to his prison term (where he developed his boxing skills) and his eventual success as the middleweight boxing champion of the world. Adapted from Graziano's autobiography. Superior performance by Newman (in his third screen role, after the miserable "The Silver Chalice" and forgettable "The Rack"); screen debuts for McQueen and Loggia. **113m/B VHS, DVD.** Paul Newman, Pier Angeli, Everett Sloane, Eileen Heckart, Sal Mineo, Robert Loggia, Steve McQueen; ***D:*** Robert Wise; ***W:*** Ernest Lehman; ***C:*** Joseph Ruttenberg; ***M:*** Bronislau Kaper. Oscars '56: Art Dir./Set Dec., B&W, B&W Cinematog.

Someone at the Door **1950** Reporter Medwin arranges to be suspected of killing his sister, thus providing him with a good story and advancing his career. His plan almost backfires, when he is almost executed. Remake of a 1936 film of the same name. **65m/B VHS.** *GB* Michael Medwin, Garry Marsh, Yvonne Owen, Hugh Latimer; ***D:*** Francis Searle.

Someone Behind the Door 1/2 *Two Minds for Murder; Quelqu' Un Derriere la Porte* **1971 (PG)** Evil brain surgeon Perkins implants murderous suggestions into psychopathic amnesia victim Bronson's mind, then instructs him to kill the surgeon's wife and her lover. **97m/C VHS, DVD.** Charles Bronson, Anthony Perkins, Jill Ireland, Henri Garcin; ***D:*** Nicolas Gessner; ***W:*** Nicolas Gessner, Marc Behm; ***C:*** Pierre Lhomme; ***M:*** Georges Garvarentz.

Someone Else's America **1996 (R)** Euro-"Grumpy Old Men" explores friendship and the modern immigrant experience in Brooklyn. Bayo (Manojlovic) is a comical, sad-sack Serb who works at the bar of Alonso (Conti), a Spaniard who immigrated with his blind mother (Casares). Story follows Bayo's family as they illegally immigrate to chase the American dream and adapt to life once they arrive. Touchingly funny highlight involves a scheme by the men which enables Alonso's homesick mother to revisit her village in Spain. Filmed in Germany with sets built to resemble Brooklyn, picture has an appealingly unreal quality. Cast and crew together formed its own melting pot, with over 20 nationalities contributing. English and Serbo-Croatian with subtitles. **116m/C VHS.** *FR GB GE* Tom Conti, Miki (Predrag) Manojlovic, Maria Casares, Zorka Manojlovic, Sergej Trifunovic, Chia-ching Niu, Andjela Stojkovic, Ananda Ellis; ***D:*** Goran Paskalyevic; ***W:*** Gordan Mihic; ***C:*** Yorgos Arvanitis; ***M:*** Andrew Dickson.

Someone I Touched 1/2 **1975** Way-overdone melodrama starring Leachman as a finally pregnant woman who learns her husband and a teenager he slept with have venereal disease. **74m/C VHS.** Cloris Leachman, James Olson, Glynnis O'Connor, Andrew (Andy) Robinson, Allyn Ann McLerie; ***D:*** Lou Antonio.

Someone Like You 1/2 **2001 (PG-13)** New Yorker Jane (Judd) is a talk-show talent booker who falls for the program's new exec, Ray (Kinnear), who seems to be very serious about her too. In fact, Jane gives up her apartment expecting to move in with Ray, then is suddenly dumped. Homeless, Jane agrees to temporarily share the loft of co-worker Eddie (Jackman), a one-night only stud. Well, it does give Jane a chance to test her theory comparing men to bulls, who aren't interested in a cow (or girlfriend) they've had before. Gets by because the cast is so darn cute. Based on the novel "Animal Husbandry" by Laura Zigman. **97m/C VHS, DVD.** *US* Ashley Judd, Hugh Jackman, Greg Kinnear, Marisa Tomei, Ellen Barkin, Peter Friedman, Catherine Dent, Laura Regan; ***D:*** Tony Goldwyn; ***W:*** Elizabeth Chandler; ***C:*** Anthony B. Richmond; ***M:*** Rolfe Kent.

Someone to Die For **1995 (R)** Accused murderer (and cop) Bernsen is out to prove his innocence but learns that the real killer may be very close to home. **98m/C VHS.** Corbin Bernsen, Ally Walker, Robert Stewart; ***D:*** Clay Borris.

Someone to Love **1987 (R)** Rootless filmmaker gathers all his single friends together and interviews them about their failed love lives. Welles's last film as an actor. Wildly uneven, interesting experiment. **110m/C VHS, DVD.** Henry Jaglom, Orson Welles, Sally Kellerman, Andrea Marcovicci, Michael Emil, Oja Kodar, Stephen Bishop, Ronee Blakley, Kathryn Harrold, Monte Hellman; ***D:*** Henry Jaglom; ***W:*** Henry Jaglom; ***C:*** Hanania Baer.

Someone to Watch Over Me **1987 (R)** After witnessing the murder of a close friend, beautiful and very wealthy

Claire Gregory (Rogers) must be protected from the killer. Working-class New York detective Mike Keegan (Berenger), who's assigned the duty, is more than taken with her, despite the fact that he has both a wife (a knowing Bracco) and son at home. A highly watchable, stylish romantic crime thriller. **106m/C VHS, DVD.** Tom Berenger, Mimi Rogers, Lorraine Bracco, Jerry Orbach, Andreas Katsulas, Tony DiBenedetto, James Moriarty, John Rubinstein; *D:* Ridley Scott; *W:* Howard Franklin; *C:* Steven Poster; *M:* Michael Kamen.

Somersault ♪♪ **2004** Troubled Heidi (Cornish) is a luscious, 16-year-old blonde testing her sexuality on her mother's boyfriend, which gets her kicked out of the house. She travels to the ski resort town of Jindabyne, where she casually trades sex for a place to stay. Eventually Heidi lands a job at a convenience store and persuades motel owner Irene (Curran) to rent her a room. She also finds sparks with 20-something Joe (Worthington), the son of a wealthy local farmer, but he's got problems too, and her neediness frightens him off. Debut feature for Shortland skimps on the character details but Cornish is a real heartbreaker. **106m/C DVD.** *AU* Sam Worthington, Lynette Curran, Leah Purcell, Nathaniel Dean, Abbie Cornish, Erik Thomson, Hollie Andrew, Olivia Pigeot, Blake Pittman; *D:* Cate Shortland; *W:* Cate Shortland; *C:* Robert Humpherys.

Something About Sex ♪♪ *Denial* **1998 (R)** Acerbic bachelor Art (Alexander) broaches the subject of marital fidelity with three couples at a dinner party. All the couples publicly denounce flings while privately not practicing what they preach. **92m/C VHS, DVD.** Patrick Dempsey, Jonathan Silverman, Christine Taylor, Amy Yasbeck, Jason Alexander, Leah Lail, Ryan Alosio, Jessica Lundy, Charles Shaughnessy, Angie Everhart, Hudson (Heidi) Leick, Nicholas Worth, Jessica Capshaw, Steve Schirripa; *Cameos:* Adam Rifkin; *D:* Adam Rifkin; *W:* Adam Rifkin; *C:* Francis Kenny.

Something Beneath ♪ **2007** Something beneath dumb and awful actually. In this Sci-Fi Channel original, biologist Dr. Walter Connelly (Beiser) warns that a new resort/conference center is built on toxic ground. An oily black slime starts oozing everywhere and is discovered to be an intelligent organism that causes hallucinations of the nightmarish kind (well, more the hokey kind). Sorbo is the heroic Episcopalian priest who saves the day (and he still gets to flirt with the pretty girl). **93m/C DVD.** Kevin Sorbo, Brendan Beiser, Peter MacNeill, Gordon Tanner, Natalie Brown, Brittany Scobie; *D:* David Winning; *W:* Mark Mullin, Ethlie Ann Vare; *C:* Brenton Spencer; *M:* Michael Richard Plowman. **CABLE**

Something for Everyone ♪♪ 1/2 *The Rook; Black Flowers for the Bride* **1970 (R)** A corrupt footman uses sex and murder in an attempt to take over the estate of an aristocratic Bavarian family in post-WWII Germany. He nearly succeeds in marrying the countess (Lansbury), but someone has been keeping tabs on him. Funny, ambitious black comedy. From the novel "The Code" by Harry Kressing. **112m/C VHS.** Angela Lansbury, Michael York, Anthony (Corlan) Higgins, Heidelinde Weis; *D:* Harold Prince; *C:* Walter Lassally.

Something for the Boys ♪♪ **1944** Chiquita (Miranda), Blossom (Blaine), and Harry (Silvers) are distant cousins who inherit a run-down southern plantation. Army Sgt. Rocky Fulton (O'Shea), who's stationed nearby, convinces them to turn the place into a hotel for military wives and to raise the money needed for restoration, they decide to put on a show. Como's debut as a singing soldier. **87m/C DVD.** Carmen Miranda, Vivian Blaine, Phil Silvers, Michael O'Shea, Sheila Ryan, Perry Como, Glenn Langan, Thurston Hall, Clarence (C. William) Kolb; *D:* Lewis Seiler; *W:* Robert Ellis, Helen Logan, Frank Gabrielson, Frank Gabrielson; *C:* Ernest Palmer; *M:* Jimmy McHugh.

Something in Common ♪♪ 1/2 **1986** A woman discovers her 22-year-old son is having an affair with a woman her own age. Nicely done comedy; Burstyn and Weld both make good use of a solid script. Made for TV. **94m/C VHS.** Ellen Burstyn, Tuesday Weld, Don Murray, Patrick Cassidy, Eli Wallach; *D:* Glenn Jordan; *W:* Susan Rice; *M:* John Addison. **TV**

Something in the Wind ♪♪ 1/2 **1947** Mary Collins (Durbin) is a DJ having a sort of romance with Donald Read (Dall), who gets the mistaken idea that she was once his wealthy Uncle Chester's (Winninger) mistress and is still after the family money. O'Connor gets to steal the show as Durbin's ally, Charlie. ♫Something in the Wind; Turntable Song; It's Only Love; You Wanna Keep Your Baby Lookin' Right; Happy Go Lucky and Free. **89m/B VHS, DVD.** Deanna Durbin, Donald O'Connor, John Dall, Charles Winninger, Helena Carter, Margaret Wycherly; *D:* Irving Pichel; *W:* William Bowers, Harry Kurnitz; *C:* Milton Krasner; *M:* Johnny Green.

Something Like Happiness ♪♪ *Stesti* **2005** Monika, Tonik, and Dasha have been friends since childhood but their adult lives are less than fulfilled. Monika's boyfriend Jiri is finding his fortune in America without her; Tonik has left his conservative family to live with his eccentric aunt in a ramshackle farmhouse; and Dasha, a single mother of two boys, has a married lover and mental problems. When Dasha winds up institutionalized, Monika looks after her children and Tonik offers them all a place to stay at the farmhouse. Czech with subtitles. **102m/C DVD.** Pavel Liska, Anna Geislerova, Marek Daniel, Tatiana Vilhelmova, Zuzana Kronerova, David Dolnik; *D:* Bohdan Slama; *W:* Bohdan Slama; *C:* Divis Marek; *M:* Leonid Soybelman.

Something More ♪♪ **1999 (R)** Sam (Gooojian), the romantic loser, and best bud Jim (Lovgren), the obnoxious womanizer, both fall for Kelly (West). The usual romantic complications abound as do all the usual romantic cliches. Cute cast. **97m/C VHS, DVD.** Michael Goorjian, Chandra West, David Lovgren, Jennifer Beals, Tom Cavanagh; *D:* Rob King; *W:* Peter Bryant; *C:* Jon Kranhouse; *M:* Rob Bryanton.

Something New ♪♪ 1/2 **2006 (PG-13)** Interracial romance with two completely delectable leads. Kenya (Lathan) is a successful African-American accountant who's too busy for romance. She does agree to a blind date, only to discover it's with the very white Brian (Baker), an affable landscape architect. She rejects him as boyfriend material but hires him to redo her pathetic backyard. Kenya then tries to resist his wooing, especially when her upscale family and friends don't approve. Then IBM (Ideal Black Man) Mark (Underwood) enters the picture and Kenya must decide if she can get past her own prejudices and find that happy ending. **100m/C DVD.** *US* Sanaa Lathan, Simon Baker, Mike Epps, Donald Adeosun Faison, Blair Underwood, Wendy Raquel Robinson, Golden Brooks, Taraji P. Henson, Earl Billings, Katharine Towne, Alfre Woodard; *D:* Sanaa Hamri; *W:* Kristopher Turner; *C:* Shane Hurlbut; *M:* Wendy Melvoin, Lisa Coleman, Paul Anthony Stewart.

Something of Value ♪♪♪ **1957** Good ensemble performances in a serious colonial story about the Mau Mau rebellion in Kenya. Hudson and Poitier are torn between their friendship and their opposing loyalties. Drama solidly grounded in fact from the book by Robert Ruark. **113m/B VHS.** Rock Hudson, Sidney Poitier, Wendy Hiller, Dana Wynter, Juano Hernandez; *D:* Richard Brooks; *W:* Richard Brooks; *M:* Miklos Rozsa.

Something Short of Paradise ♪ 1/2 **1979 (PG)** The owner of a Manhattan movie theatre has an on again/off again romance with a magazine writer. Would-be Allenesque romantic comedy is too talky and pretentious. **87m/C VHS, DVD.** David Steinberg, Susan Sarandon, Jean-Pierre Aumont, Marilyn Sokol; *D:* David Helpern; *W:* Fred Barron.

Something Special ♪♪ 1/2 *Willy Milly; I Was a Teenage Boy* **1986 (PG-13)** A 14-year-old girl has her wish come true when she is turned into a boy. Charming, original fantasy-comedy is fun for young and old. **93m/C VHS.** Pamela Segall, Patty Duke, Eric Gurry, John Glover, Seth Green; *D:* Paul Schneider; *W:* Walter Carbone.

Something to Sing About ♪♪ *Battling Hoofer* **1936** Musical melodrama about a New York bandleader's attempt to make it big in Hollywood. Allows Cagney the opportunity to demonstrate his dancing talents; he also sings. Rereleased in 1947. Also available colorized. Frawley was Fred on "I Love Lucy." ♫Any Old Love; Right or Wrong; Loving You; Out of the Blue; Something to Sing About. **84m/B VHS, DVD.** James Cagney, William Frawley, Evelyn Daw, Gene Lockhart; *D:* Victor Schertzinger.

Something to Talk About ♪♪ 1/2 *Grace Under Pressure* **1995 (R)** Romantic comedy/drama finds Grace (Roberts) running her overbearing father Wyly's (Duvall) horsebreeding operation and learning that her husband Eddie (the ever-charming Quaid) is tomcatting around. So Grace tosses him out and makes a temporary move with daughter Caroline (Aull) back home. Tart-tongued sister Emma Rae (Sedgwick) is sympathetic but long-suffering mama Georgia (Rowlands) thinks Grace should make the best of things (the way she's done). Naturally, Eddie wants his family back but the frazzled Grace is just coming to terms with what she wants out of life. Star appeal from both leads lends this familiar plot some spark. **106m/C VHS, DVD.** Julia Roberts, Dennis Quaid, Robert Duvall, Gena Rowlands, Kyra Sedgwick, Brett Cullen, Haley Aull, Muse Watson, Anne Shropshire; *D:* Lasse Hallstrom; *W:* Callie Khouri; *C:* Sven Nykvist; *M:* Hans Zimmer.

Something Weird **WOOF!** **1968** McCabe is disfigured horribly in an electrical accident. A seemingly beautiful witch fixes his face, on condition that he be her lover. The accident also gave him ESP—and it gets cheesier from there. **80m/C VHS, DVD.** Tony McCabe, Elizabeth Lee, William Brooker, Mudite Arums, Taed Heil, Lawrence Wood, Larry Wellington, Roy Collodi, Jeffrey Allen, Stan Dale, Richard Nilsson, Carolyn Smith, Norm Lenet, Louis Newman, Dick Gaffield, Janet Charlton, Lee Ahsmann, Roger Papsch, Daniel Carrington; *D:* Herschell Gordon Lewis; *W:* James F. Hurley; *C:* Herschell Gordon Lewis, Andy Romanoff.

Something Wicked This Way Comes ♪♪ **1983 (PG)** Two young boys discover the evil secret of a mysterious traveling carnival that visits their town. Bradbury wrote the screenplay for this much-anticipated, expensive adaptation of his own novel. Good special effects, but disappointing. **94m/C VHS, DVD.** Jason Robards Jr., Jonathan Pryce, Diane Ladd, Pam Grier, Richard (Dick) Davalos, James Stacy, Royal Dano, Vidal Peterson, Shawn Carson; *D:* Jack Clayton; *W:* Ray Bradbury; *C:* Stephen Burum; *M:* James Horner.

Something Wild ♪♪ 1/2 **1986 (R)** Mild-mannered business exec Daniels is picked up by an impossibly free-living vamp with a Louise Brooks hairdo, and taken for the ride of his up-till-then staid life, eventually leading to explosive violence. A sharp-edged comedy with numerous changes of pace. Too-happy ending wrecks it, but it's great until then. Look for cameos from filmmakers John Waters and John Sayles. **113m/C VHS, DVD.** Jeff Daniels, Melanie Griffith, Ray Liotta, Margaret Colin, Tracey Walter, Dana Peru, Jack Gilpin, Su Tissue, Kenneth Utt, Sister Carol East, John Sayles, John Waters, Charles Napier; *D:* Jonathan Demme; *W:* E. Max Frye; *C:* Tak Fujimoto; *M:* Rosemary Paul, John Cale, Laurie Anderson, David Byrne.

Something's Gotta Give ♪♪♪ **2003 (PG-13)** The title's bland but the film is anything but (particularly for the woman of a certain age). Harry Sanborn (Nicholson) is a legendary womanizer. Now 60-something, he's notorious for dating only much-younger chicks. Harry's current squeeze is Marin (Peet), who takes Harry to her mom's Hamptons beach house to consummate the relationship. Turns out mom, successful (if neurotic) divorced playwright Erica Barry (Keaton), and her sister, feminist professor Zoe (McDormand), are there as well. Harry has a mild heart attack and his doctor, Julian Mercer (Reeves), says Harry can't travel, leading to changing ideas, beds, and relationships. It's Keaton's film all the way (she's a natural wonder) and even scene-stealer Nicholson concedes to her charm; McDormand provides some droll asides and Reeves is relaxed. **124m/C DVD.** *US* Diane Keaton, Jack Nicholson, Keanu Reeves, Amanda Peet, Frances McDormand, Rachel Ticotin, Paul Michael Glaser, Jon Favreau, KaDee Strickland; *D:* Nancy Meyers; *W:* Nancy Meyers; *C:* Michael Ballhaus; *M:* Hans Zimmer. Golden Globes '04: Actress—Mus./Comedy (Keaton); Natl. Bd. of Review '03: Actress (Keaton).

Sometimes a Great Notion ♪♪♪ *Never Give an Inch* **1971 (PG)** Trouble erupts in a small Oregon town when a family of loggers decide to honor a contract when the other loggers go on strike. Newman's second stint in the director's chair; Fonda's first role as an old man. Based on the novel by Ken Kesey. **115m/C VHS.** Paul Newman, Henry Fonda, Lee Remick, Richard Jaeckel, Michael Sarrazin; *D:* Paul Newman; *W:* John Gay; *M:* Henry Mancini.

Sometimes in April ♪♪♪ **2005** In 1994 almost one million citizens of Rwanda were massacred in 100 days. Focusing on two brothers, one a Rwandan Army officer and one a broadcaster at an extremist radio station, the film gives the country's genocide perspective and human faces. In the same vein as "Hotel Rwanda," filmed in Rwanda using the locals as extras. Paints a powerful picture of a genocide that may have otherwise gone unnoticed by most of the Western world. **140m/C DVD.** Idris Elba, Debra Winger, Noah Emmerich, Oris Erhuero, Carole Karemara, Pamela Nomvete; *D:* Raoul Peck; *W:* Raoul Peck; *C:* Eric Gurchard; *M:* Bruno Coulais. **TV**

Sometimes They Come Back ♪♪ **1991 (R)** Another Stephen King tale of terror. Matheson plays a man haunted by the tragedy in his past. A witness to his brother's death, he also witnesses the fiery crash of his brother's killers. Only now the killers have returned from the dead, to take their revenge on him. **97m/C VHS, DVD.** Tim Matheson, Brooke Adams, Robert Rusler, William Sanderson; *D:* Tom McLoughlin; *W:* Mark Rosenthal, Larry Konner; *C:* Bryan England; *M:* Terry Plumeri. **TV**

Sometimes They Come Back... Again ♪ 1/2 **1996 (R)** Psychologist John Porter (Gross) and his teenaged daughter (Swank) return to Porter's hometown after his mother's mysterious death. He should know you can never go home again since they're both soon threatened by a young man (Arquette) involved in the ritualistic murder of Porter's sister years before. Gruesome special effects are the highlight. **98m/C VHS, DVD.** Michael Gross, Hilary Swank, Alexis Arquette, Jennifer Elise Cox, William Morgan Sheppard; *D:* Adam Grossman; *W:* Adam Grossman; *C:* Christopher Baffa; *M:* Peter Manning Robinson.

Sometimes They Come Back... For More ♪♪ **1999 (R)** Two military officers investigate the disappearances of crew members at a government outpost in Antarctica. **89m/C VHS, DVD.** Clayton Rohner, Chase Masterson, Faith Ford, Max Perlich, Damian Chapa; *D:* Daniel Berk.

Somewhere I'll Find You ♪♪♪ **1942** Clark and Turner heat up the screen as correspondents running all over the war-torn world in their second film together. ("Honky Tonk" was their first.) Notable mainly because Gable's beloved wife, Carole Lombard, was killed in a plane crash only three days into production. Gable forced himself to finish the film and it became one of the studio's biggest hits. Although critics applauded his determination to complete the film, many felt his performance was subdued and strained. Film debut of Wynn. Based on a story by Charles Hoffman. **108m/B VHS.** Clark Gable, Lana Turner, Robert Sterling, Reginald Owen, Lee Patrick, Charles Dingle, Tamara Shayne, Leonid Kinskey, Diana Lewis, Molly Lamont, Patricia Dane, Sara Haden, Keenan Wynn; *D:* Wesley Ruggles; *W:* Walter Reisch, Marguerite Roberts.

Somewhere in Sonora ♪♪ **1933** Early Wayne Western set in Old Mexico. Wayne plays a rodeo performer who joins an outlaw gang to save a friend and a silver mine. Like most of the other films of the series, this was a remake of a Ken Maynard silent. Based on a story and the novel "Somewhere South in Sonora" by Will Levington Comfort. **59m/B VHS, DVD.** John Wayne, Henry B. Walthall, Shirley Palmer, J(ohn) P(aterson) McGowan, Frank Rice, Billy Franey, Paul Fix, Ralph Lewis; *D:* Mack V. Wright; *W:* Joe Roach.

Somewhere in the City ♪♪ 1/2 **1997** Covers the screwy lives of six tenants of a Lower East Side New York apartment building. Betty (a subdued Bernhard) is an unlucky-in-love therapist who's still neurotically trying. She agrees to help out Chinese exchange student Lu Lu (Ling) who's desperately seeking a green card marriage. Then there's unhappy wife Marta (Muti), whose upstairs lover, Frankie (Burke), is a completely incompetent crook. There's also gay actor Graham (Stormare), who's disappointed personally and professionally, and basement-dwelling Che (Stewart), a trust-fund baby who wants to be a radical revolutionary. Sporadically amusing with a talented cast. **93m/C VHS, DVD.** Sandra Bernhard, Bai Ling, Ornella Muti, Robert John Burke, Peter Stormare, Paul Anthony Stewart, Bulle Ogier; ***Cameos:*** Edward I. Koch; ***D:*** Ramin Niami; ***W:*** Ramin Niami, Patrick Dillon; ***C:*** Igor Sunara; ***M:*** John Cale.

Somewhere in the Night 🦴🦴 **1946** Marine George Taylor (Hodiak) wakes up in a hospital with a reconstructed face and amnesia, and the only clues to his past are a Dear John letter and an L.A. address. This leads him to a letter of credit signed by someone named Larry Cravat, nightclub owner Mel Phillips (Conte), and songbird Christy Smith (Guild). Is Taylor actually Cravat, who's not only a murder suspect but involved in laundering Nazi cash? Detective Kendall (Nolan) is sure Taylor will figure things out. Noir with convoluted subplots and weak leads, especially debuting starlet Guild. **108m/B DVD.** John Hodiak, Nancy Guild, Lloyd Nolan, Richard Conte, Fritz Kortner, Margo Woode, Josephine Hutchinson, Sheldon Leonard, Houseley Stevenson; ***D:*** Joseph L. Mankiewicz; ***W:*** Joseph L. Mankiewicz, Howard Dimsdale; ***C:*** Norbert Brodine; ***M:*** David Buttolph.

Somewhere in Time 🦴 ½ **1980 (PG)** Playwright Reeve (in his first post-Clark Kent role) falls in love with a beautiful woman in an old portrait. Through self-hypnosis he goes back in time to 1912 to discover what their relationship might have been. The film made a star of the Grand Hotel, located on Mackinac Island in Michigan, where it was shot. Drippy rip-off of the brilliant novel "Time and Again" by Jack Finney. Reeve is horrible; Seymour is underused. All in all, rather wretched. **103m/C VHS, DVD.** Christopher Reeve, Jane Seymour, Christopher Plummer, Teresa Wright; ***D:*** Jeannot Szwarc; ***W:*** Richard Matheson; ***C:*** Isidore Mankofsky; ***M:*** John Barry.

Somewhere Tomorrow 🦴🦴 ½ **1985 (PG)** A lonely, fatherless teenage girl is befriended by the ghost of a young man killed in a plane crash. Charming and moving, if not perfect. **91m/C VHS, DVD.** Sarah Jessica Parker, Nancy Addison, Tom Shea; ***D:*** Robert Wiemer.

Sommersby 🦴🦴 ½ **1993 (PG-13)** A too-good-to-be-true period romance based on the film "The Return of Martin Guerre." A Civil War veteran (Gere) returns to his wife's (Foster) less-than-open arms. She soon warms up to his kind, sensitive and caring manner, but can't quite believe the change that the war has wrought. Neither can the neighbors, especially the one (Pullman) who had his own eye on Laurel Sommersby. So is he really Jack Sommersby or an all too clever imposter? Lots of hankies needed for the tender-hearted. Strong performance by Foster. Filmed in Virginia (passing for the state of Tennessee.) **114m/C VHS, DVD.** Richard Gere, Jodie Foster, Bill Pullman, James Earl Jones, William Windom, Brett Kelley, Richard Hamilton, Maury Chaykin, Lanny Flaherty, Frankie Faison, Wendell Wellman, Clarice Taylor, R. Lee Ermey; ***D:*** Jon Amiel; ***W:*** Nicholas Meyer, Sarah Kernochan; ***C:*** Philippe Rousselot; ***M:*** Danny Elfman.

Son-in-Law 🦴 ½ **1993 (PG-13)** Surfer-dude comic Shore's a laconic fish out of water as a city-boy rock 'n' roller who falls in love with a country beauty, marries her, and visits the family farm to meet the new in-laws. Once there, he weirds out family and neighbors before showing everyone how to live, Pauly style. Silly entertainment best appreciated by Shore fans. **95m/C VHS, DVD.** Pauly Shore, Carla Gugino, Lane Smith, Cindy Pickett, Mason Adams, Patrick Renna, Dennis Burkley, Dan Gauthier, Tiffani(-Amber) Thiessen; ***D:*** Steve Rash; ***W:*** Adam Small, Shawn Schepps, Fax Bahr; ***C:*** Peter Deming; ***M:*** Richard Gibbs.

Son of a Gun 🦴 ½ **1919** A loveable but ornery cowboy gets banished from the county for disturbing the peace. However, he wins the favor of the townspeople when he stands up to a gang of gambling swindlers. Silent. **68m/B VHS.** "Broncho" Billy Anderson, Fred Church, Frank Whitson, Joy Lewis; ***D:*** "Broncho" Billy Anderson; ***W:*** "Broncho" Billy Anderson.

Son of Ali Baba 🦴🦴 **1952** Kashma Baba, son of Ali Baba, enters the military academy to learn to withstand adversity. He has other ideas however, until he must suddenly fill his father's shoes and fight the evil Caliph. He fights bravely with the help of his childhood friend, a beautiful princess, in this swashbuckler. **85m/C VHS.** Tony Curtis, Piper Laurie, Susan Cabot, Victor Jory, Hugh O'Brian, William Reynolds, Gerald Mohr; ***D:*** Ross Hunter.

Son of Captain Blood 🦴 ½ *Il Figlio del Capitano Blood* **1962 (G)** The son of the famous pirate meets up with his father's enemies on the high seas. The son of the famous actor Errol Flynn—Sean—plays the son of the character the elder Flynn played in "Captain Blood." Let's just say the gimmick didn't work. **90m/C VHS.** *IT SP* Sean Flynn, Ann Todd; ***D:*** Tulio Demicheli.

Son of Dracula 🦴🦴🦴 *Young Dracula* **1943** In this late-coming sequel to the Universal classic, a stranger named Alucard is invited to America by a Southern belle obsessed with eternal life. It is actually Dracula himself, not his son, who wreaks havoc in this spine-tingling chiller. **80m/B VHS, DVD.** Lon Chaney Jr., Evelyn Ankers, Frank Craven, Robert Paige, Louise Allbritton, J. Edward Bromberg, Samuel S. Hinds; ***D:*** Robert Siodmak; ***W:*** Eric Taylor; ***C:*** George Robinson.

Son of Flubber 🦴🦴 ½ **1963** Sequel to "The Absent Minded Professor" finds Fred MacMurray still toying with his prodigious invention, Flubber, now in the form of Flubbergas, which causes those who inhale it to float away. Disney's first-ever sequel is high family wackiness. **96m/C VHS, DVD.** Fred MacMurray, Nancy Olson, Tommy Kirk, Leon Ames, Joanna Moore, Keenan Wynn, Charlie Ruggles, Paul Lynde; ***D:*** Robert Stevenson; ***C:*** Edward Colman; ***M:*** George Bruns.

Son of Frankenstein 🦴🦴🦴 **1939** The second sequel (after "The Bride of Frankenstein") to the 1931 version of the horror classic. The good doctor's skeptical son returns to the family manse and becomes obsessed with his father's work and with reviving the creature. Full of memorable characters and brooding ambience. Karloff's last appearance as the monster. **99m/C VHS, DVD.** Basil Rathbone, Bela Lugosi, Boris Karloff, Lionel Atwill, Josephine Hutchinson, Donnie Dunagan, Emma Dunn, Edgar Norton, Lawrence Grant, Lionel Belmore; ***D:*** Rowland V. Lee; ***W:*** Willis Cooper; ***C:*** George Robinson.

Son of Fury 🦴🦴🦴 **1942** Dashing Ben Blake (Power) is left penniless when his sinister uncle (Sanders) wrongfully takes the family fortune. Ben escapes to sea and then to an island paradise—all the while plotting his revenge. But he still finds time to fall for the beautous Tierney. Fine 18th-century costumer done in grand style. Based on the novel "Benjamin Blake" by Edison Marshall. **98m/C VHS, DVD.** Tyrone Power, Gene Tierney, George Sanders, Frances Farmer, Roddy McDowall, John Carradine, Elsa Lanchester, Harry Davenport, Kay Johnson, Dudley Digges, Halliwell Hobbes, Marten Lamont, Arthur Hohl, Pedro de Cordoba, Dennis Hoey, Heather Thatcher; ***D:*** John Cromwell; ***W:*** Philip Dunne; ***M:*** Alfred Newman.

Son of Gascogne 🦴🦴 ½ *Les Fils de Gascogne* **1995** Offbeat comedy about identity, romance, and wish fullfillment. Gawky Harvey (Colin) is serving as a travel guide to a group of Georgian folksingers who are giving concerts in Paris. Harvey falls for their pretty teenaged interpreter, Dinara (Droukarova), who reciprocates. The duo meet Marco (Dreyfus), a chauffeur/con man, who insists that Harvey is the son of the late legendary director Gascogne (Harvey doesn't know who his father is) and insists on introducing him to his dad's cinematic colleagues (thus supplying cameos of numerous French cinema greats). French with subtitles. **106m/C VHS, DVD.** *FR* Gregoire Colin, Jean-Claude Dreyfus, Dinara Drukarova, Bernadette LaFont, Alexandra Stewart, Stephane Audran, Jean-Claude Brialy, Bulle Ogier, Marie-France Pisier, Anemone, Patrice Leconte, Marina Vlady; ***D:*** Pascal Aubier; ***W:*** Pascal Aubier, Patrick Modiano; ***C:*** Jean-Jacques Flori; ***M:*** Angelo Zurzulo.

Son of God's Country 🦴 ½ **1948** Utterly hackneyed, near-comic attempt at a western. Good-guy U.S. Marshal poses as a crook to get the lowdown on the varmints. **60m/B VHS.** Monte Hale, Pamela Blake, Adrian Booth; ***D:*** R.G. Springsteen; ***W:*** Paul Gangelin; ***C:*** John MacBurnie; ***M:*** R. Dale Butts.

Son of Godzilla 🦴🦴 *Gojira no Musuko; Monster Island's Decisive Battle: Godzilla's Son* **1966** Dad and junior protect beauty Maeda from giant spiders on a remote island ruled by a mad scientist. Fun monster flick with decent special effects. **86m/C VHS, DVD.** *JP* Akira Kubo, Beverly (Bibari) Maeda, Tadao Takashima, Akihiko Hirata, Kenji Sahara; ***D:*** Jun Fukuda; ***W:*** Shinichi Sekizawa, Kazue Shiba; ***C:*** Kazuo Yamada; ***M:*** Masaru Sato.

Son of Hercules in the Land of Darkness 🦴 **1963** Argolis (Vadis) must rescue prisoners trapped in an underground city. **74m/B VHS, DVD.** *IT* Dan Vadis, Carol Brown, Spela Rozin; ***D:*** Alvaro Mancori; ***W:*** Alvaro Mancori; ***C:*** Claude Haroy; ***M:*** Francesco De Masi.

Son of Ingagi 🦴 ½ **1940** Lonely ape-man kidnaps woman in search of romance. Early all-black horror film stars Williams of "Amos 'n' Andy." **70m/B VHS, DVD.** Zack Williams, Laura Bowman, Alfred Grant, Spencer Williams Jr., Daisy Bufford, Arthur Ray; ***D:*** Richard C. Kahn; ***W:*** Spencer Williams Jr.; ***C:*** Roland Price, Herman Schopp.

Son of Kong 🦴🦴 ½ **1933** King Kong's descendant is discovered on an island amid prehistoric creatures in this often humorous sequel to RKO's immensely popular "King Kong." Hoping to capitalize on the enormous success of its predecessor, director Schoedsack quickly threw this together. As a result, its success at the boxoffice did not match the original's, and didn't deserve to, but it's fun. Nifty special effects from Willis O'Brien, the man who brought them to us the first time. **70m/B VHS, DVD.** Robert Armstrong, Helen Mack; ***D:*** Ernest B. Schoedsack; ***M:*** Max Steiner.

Son of Lassie 🦴🦴 ½ **1945 (G)** It seems that Lassie's son Laddie just isn't quite as smart as his mother. After the dog sneaks onto his master's plane during WWII, the plane gets shot down, and Lawford parachutes out with Laddie in his arms. The dog goes to get help because Lawford is hurt, but he brings back two Nazis! A sequel to "Lassie Come Home." **102m/C VHS, DVD.** Peter Lawford, Donald Crisp, June Lockhart, Nigel Bruce, William Severn, Leon Ames, Donald Curtis, Nils Asther, Robert Lewis; ***D:*** S. Sylvan Simon.

The Son of Monte Cristo 🦴🦴 ½ **1940** Illegitimate offspring of the great swashbuckler with Robert Donat proves they made pathetic, pointless sequels even back then. **102m/B VHS, DVD.** Louis Hayward, Joan Bennett, George Sanders, Florence Bates, Montagu Love, Ralph Byrd, Clayton Moore; ***D:*** Rowland V. Lee; ***W:*** George Bruce; ***C:*** George Robinson; ***M:*** Edward Ward.

Son of Paleface 🦴🦴🦴 ½ **1952** Hilarious sequel to the original Hope gag-fest, with the Harvard-educated son of the original character (again played by Hope) heading west to claim an inheritance. Hope runs away with every cowboy cliche and even manages to wind up with the girl. Songs include "Buttons and Bows" (reprised from the original), "There's a Cloud in My Valley of Sunshine," and "Four-legged Friend." **95m/C VHS, DVD.** Bob Hope, Jane Russell, Roy Rogers, Douglass Dumbrille, Iron Eyes Cody, Bill Williams, Harry von Zell; ***D:*** Frank Tashlin; ***W:*** Frank Tashlin, Joseph Quillan, Robert L. Welch; ***C:*** Harry Wild.

Son of Rambow 🦴🦴 ½ **2007 (PG-13)** Quirky coming-of-age flick centering around two young boys away at summer camp in early '80s England. Sheltered from the corrupt influence of television, movies, and pop music, scrawny little Will Proudfoot spends most of his time inside his imagination, sketching and doodling. Soon, he strikes up an unlikely friendship with school bully Lee, who's got a video camera and a passion for making movies. Will's tiny world suddenly gets much bigger after Lee introduces him to "First Blood," and the two set out to shoot their own Rambo adventure. Its offbeat flair owes just as much to Wes Anderson as it does Jon Hughes. Unfortunately, a massive wave of sappy sentimentality takes over the second half when a French foreign exchange student is introduced and spoils the fun. **96m/C DVD.** *GB* Jessica Stevenson, Neil Dudgeon, Bill Milner, Will Poulter, Jules Sitruk, Ed Westwick; ***D:*** Garth Jennings; ***W:*** Garth Jennings; ***C:*** Jess Hall; ***M:*** Joby Talbot.

Son of Rusty 🦴🦴 ½ **1947** Danny and his friends are warned to stay away from the farm of suspicious Jed Barlow. But Rusty keeps running away to see Jed's dog Barb and Danny gets to know Jed. Then Danny must stand by his new friend when word of Jed's past turns folks against him. (Rusty and Barb have puppies too.) **70m/B VHS.** Steve (Stephen) Dunne, Tom Powers, Ann Doran, Thurston Hall, Ted Donaldson; ***D:*** Lew Landers; ***W:*** Malcolm Stuart Boylan; ***C:*** Henry Freulich; ***M:*** Clarence Wheeler.

Son of Sam 🦴 **2008 (R)** German horror director Lommel tackles another serial killer story in this boring low-budget retelling. Via flashbacks after his arrest in 1977, David Berkowitz (Joshi) blames a satanic cult and the voices he hears for making him kill people. **80m/C DVD.** Elissa Dowling, Yogi Joshi, Jamie Bernadette; ***D:*** Ulli Lommel; ***W:*** Ulli Lommel; ***C:*** Bianco Pacelli; ***M:*** Green River Band.
VIDEO

Son of Samson 🦴 ½ *Le Geant de la Vallee Das Rois* **1962** Man with large pectoral muscles puts an end to the evil Queen of Egypt's reign of terror **89m/C VHS, DVD.** *FR IT YU* Mark Forest, Chelo Alonso, Angelo Zanolli, Vira (Vera) Silenti, Frederica Ranchi; ***D:*** Carlo Campogalliani.

Son of Sinbad 🦴🦴 *Nights in a Harem* **1955** Sinbad, captured by the Khalif of Baghdad, must bring him the secret of Greek fire to gain his freedom and free the city from the forces of mighty Tamerlane. About three dozen nubile young women wear very little and gambol with our hero herein; much-anticipated skinfest caused a scandal, nurtured by Howard Hughes for profit. **88m/C VHS.** Dale Robertson, Sally Forrest, Vincent Price, Lili St. Cyr, Mari Blanchard, Joi Lansing; ***D:*** Ted Tetzlaff.

The Son of the Bride 🦴🦴 ½ *El Hijo de la Novia* **2001 (R)** Middle-aged Rafael Belvedere (Darin) manages the Buenos Aires restaurant started by his father Nino (Alterio) and mother Norma (Aleandro). Rafael's workaholic behavior has cost him his marriage and estranged him from his daughter and his girlfriend Naty (Verbeke). After suffering a mild heart attack, Rafael is forced to slow down and take more of an interest in domestic matters, including Nino's decision to remarry his wife in the church service they never had, even though Norma is living in a nursing home because she suffers from Alzheimer's and is frequently unaware of what is going on around her. Spanish with subtitles. **123m/C DVD.** *AR* Ricardo Darin, Hector Alterio, Norma Aleandro, Natalia Verbeke, Eduardo Blanco, Gimena Nobile, Claudia Fontan; ***D:*** Juan J. Campanella; ***W:*** Juan J. Campanella, Fernando Castets; ***C:*** Daniel Shulman; ***M:*** Angel Illaramendi.

Son of the Mask 🦴 **2005 (PG)** Ill-conceived sequel has Tim Avery (Kennedy), a low-level cartoonist who yearns to advance beyond his current position at an animation company, finding the magical mask in time for his company's Halloween party. Of course he puts it on and gets transformed. Before the night is over, Avery gets a promotion and impregnates his wife (how's that for multi-tasking?). Soon after their son Alvey is born they realize that he's not like other kids. He has mask-like powers and the ability to warp into a freakish tornado of cartoon characters. Flick wilts under the weight of the digital effects, which on a baby seem creepily misplaced. **86m/C DVD.** *US* Jamie Kennedy, Alan Cumming, Traylor Howard, Steven Wright, Liam Falconer, Ryan Falconer, Kal Penn, Bob Hoskins; ***D:*** Lawrence (Larry) Guterman; ***W:*** Lance Khazei; ***C:*** Greg Gardiner; ***M:*** Randy Edelman. Golden Raspberries '05: Worst Remake/Sequel.

Son of the Morning Star 🦴🦴🦴 **1991 (PG-13)** Lavish made for TV retelling of Custer's famed-butt kicking. Complex characterizations and unusual points of view, based on the book by Evan S. Connell. **186m/C VHS.** Gary Cole, Rosanna Arquette, Dean Stockwell, Rodney A. Grant, Terry O'Quinn, David Strathairn, Stanley Anderson, George American Horse; ***D:*** Mike Robe. **TV**

Son of the Pink Panther 🦴 1/2 *Blake Edwards' Son of the Pink Panther* **1993 (PG)** Lame leftover from the formerly popular comedy series. Director Edwards has chosen not to resurrect Inspector Clouseau, instead opting for his son (Benigni), who turns out to be just as much of a bumbling idiot as his father. Commissioner Dreyfus (Lom), the twitching, mouth-foaming former supervisor of the original Clouseau is looking for a kidnapped princess (Farentino) along with Clouseau, Jr., who himself does not know he is the illegitimate son of his partner's dead nemesis. Many of the sketches have been recycled from previous series entrants. Rather than being funny, they seem used and shopworn like a threadbare rug. **115m/C VHS, DVD.** Roberto Benigni, Herbert Lom, Robert Davi, Debrah Farentino, Claudia Cardinale, Burt Kwouk, Shabana Azmi; ***D:*** Blake Edwards; ***W:*** Blake Edwards; ***C:*** Dick Bush; ***M:*** Henry Mancini.

The Son of the Shark 🦴🦴 *Le Fils du Requin* **1993** Simon (Da Silva) and Martin Vanderhoes (Vandendaele) have been abandoned by their mother and prefer to live as homeless delinquents rather than with their drunken father. The boys commit petty crimes and vandalism to survive (always escaping from foster homes and institutions) while Martin dreams of running away to his true home in the ocean—proclaiming himself to be "the son of a female shark." Depressing and casually cruel; based on a true story. French with subtitles. **88m/C VHS.** *FR* Ludovic Vandendaele, Erick Da Silva, Sandrine Blancke, Maxime LeRoux; ***D:*** Agnes Merlet; ***W:*** Agnes Merlet; ***C:*** Gerard Simon; ***M:*** Bruno Coulais.

Son of the Sheik 🦴🦴🦴 **1926** This sequel to Valentino's star-making "The Sheik" (1921) also turned out to be his last film. Ahmed (Valentino) falls in love with dancing girl Yasmin (Banky). He gets kidnapped by Ghabah (Love), the leader of a group of thieves, who tells the sheik's son that Yasmin has betrayed him. After his escape, Ahmed takes revenge by kidnapping Yasmin. Eventually, all the misunderstandings are resolved. Based on the novel by E.M. Hull. **62m/B VHS, DVD.** Rudolph Valentino, Vilma Banky, Montagu Love, George Fawcett, Karl (Daen) Dane, Agnes Ayres; ***D:*** George Fitzmaurice; ***W:*** Frances Marion; ***C:*** George Barnes. Natl. Film Reg. '03.

Son of Zorro 🦴🦴 **1947** Zorro takes the law into his own hands to protect ranchers from bandits. A serial in 13 chapters. **164m/B VHS.** George Turner, Peggy Stewart, Roy Barcroft, Edward Cassidy, Ernie Adams, Stanley Price, Edmund Cobb, Ken Terrell; ***D:*** Spencer Gordon Bennet, Fred Brannon; ***W:*** Frank (Franklyn) Adreon, Basil Dickey, Jesse Duffy; ***C:*** Bud Thackery.

Sonatine 🦴🦴🦴 **1996 (R)** Middle-age Yakuza mobster Murakama (director Kitano, using his screen name Beat Takeshi) wishes to retire but is instead sent to mediate a low-level gang war. Upon arrival, an attempt is made on his life, so he and his men hole up at a beach house. The young punks of the gang engage in horseplay and antics that indicate their violent natures and signal that all will not remain calm for long. Kitano's performance, writing, and direction are superb, understating the violence while not glamorizing it, and showing the effect it has on the man who carries it out. The relatively tranquil setting of the hideout allows some humor and character development, as well as preventing the cliches that usually pop up in this type of movie. Ever on the prowl for Far East gangster chic, Tarantino's Rolling Thunder brought this one to U.S. shores. Japanese with subtitles. **93m/C VHS, DVD.** *JP* Takeshi "Beat" Kitano, Aya Kokumai, Tetsu Watanabe, Masanobu Katsumura, Susumu Terashima, Ren Osugi, Tonbo Zushi, Eiji Minakata, Kenichi Yajima; ***D:*** Takeshi "Beat" Kitano; ***W:*** Takeshi "Beat" Kitano; ***C:*** Katsumi Yanagishima; ***M:*** Jo Hasaishi.

A Song for Martin 🦴🦴 1/2 *En Sang for Martin* **2001 (PG-13)** Love found and lost but not in the usual way. Martin (Wolter) is a famous conductor/composer and Barbara (Seldahl) is his first violinist. Both are past middle-age and married but that doesn't stop them from falling deliriously in love, divorcing their spouses, and marrying each other. But Martin's memory soon begins to give him trouble and he is diagnosed with Alzheimer's, which causes him to push Barbara away. Swedish with subtitles. **118m/C VHS, DVD.** *DK SW* Sven Wollter, Viveka Seldahl, Reine Brynolfsson, Linda Kallgren, Lisa Werlinder; ***D:*** Bille August; ***W:*** Bille August; ***C:*** Jorgen Persson; ***M:*** Stefan Nilsson.

A Song Is Born 🦴🦴🦴 **1948** A group of music professors try to trace the history of music. Kaye is in charge of a U.S. music foundation whose research has led him up to ragtime. He is soon, however, thrust into the sometimes seedy world of jazz joints and night spots, all in the name of research. Enter love interest Mayo, a woman on the run from her gangster boyfriend who hides out at the foundation. Not one of Kaye's funniest or best, but if you enjoy big band music, you'll love this. Includes music by Louis Armstrong and his orchestra, Tommy Dorsey and his orchestra, and Charlie Barnet and his orchestra. This was Kaye's last film for Goldwyn. ♫ A Song is Born; Bach Boogie; Anitra's Dance; I'm Getting Sentimental Over You; Blind Barnabas; Mockin' Bird; Redskin Rhumba; The Goldwyn Stomp; Daddy-O. **113m/B VHS.** Danny Kaye, Virginia Mayo, Benny Goodman, Hugh Herbert, Steve Cochran, J. Edward Bromberg, Felix Bressart; ***D:*** Howard Hawks; ***C:*** Gregg Toland.

Song o' My Heart 🦴🦴🦴 **1929** An early musical starring popular Irish tenor McCormack as a singer forced to abandon his career when he marries a woman he does not love. A tour de force for the lead in his movie debut. ♫ Little Boy Blue; Paddy Me Lad; I Hear You Calling Me; A Fair Story by the Fireside; Just For a Day; Kitty My Love; The Rose of Tralee; A Pair of Blue Eyes; I Feel You Near Me. **91m/B VHS.** John McCormack, Maureen O'Sullivan, John Garrick, J.M. Kerrigan, Tommy Clifford, Alice Joyce; ***D:*** Frank Borzage.

Song o' My Heart 🦴🦴 **1930** Not so much a movie as an excuse for popular Irish tenor McCormack to perform some 11 songs. The singer makes his film debut as Sean O'Callaghan, who's in love with Mary (Joyce), a young lass forced into marriage with a wastrel who eventually leaves her with two kiddies. Sean unselfishly steps in to help out and then raises the tykes after Mary dies. **85m/B DVD.** John McCormack, Alice Joyce, Maureen O'Sullivan, Tommy Clifford, John Garrick, J.M. Kerrigan, J. Farrell MacDonald; ***D:*** Frank Borzage; ***W:*** Sonya Levien; ***C:*** J.O. Taylor, Chester Lyons, Al Brick.

Song of Arizona 🦴🦴 **1946** Rogers and the Sons of the Pioneers arrive to aid their pal Hayes against a gang of bank robbers in this modern-day oater. Eight songs perpetually punctuate the perfunctory plot, particularly "Will Ya Be My Darling," "Half-a-Chance Ranch," and the title tune. **54m/B VHS, DVD.** Roy Rogers, Dale Evans, George "Gabby" Hayes, Lyle Talbot, Bob Nolan; ***D:*** Frank McDonald.

The Song of Bernadette 🦴🦴🦴 **1943** Depicts the true story of a peasant girl who sees a vision of the Virgin Mary in a grotto at Lourdes in 1858. The girl is directed to dig at the grotto for water that will heal those who believe in its powers, much to the astonishment and concern of the townspeople. Based on Franz Werfel's novel. Directed with tenderness and carefully cast, and appealing to religious and sentimental susceptibilities, it was a boxoffice smash. **156m/B VHS, DVD.** Charles Bickford, Lee J. Cobb, Jennifer Jones, Vincent Price, Anne Revere, Gladys Cooper; ***D:*** Henry King; ***C:*** Arthur C. Miller; ***M:*** Alfred Newman. Oscars '43: Actress (Jones), B&W Cinematog., Orig. Dramatic Score; Golden Globes '44: Actress—Drama (Jones), Director (King), Film—Drama.

Song of Freedom 🦴🦴 1/2 **1936** John Zinga (Robeson) is a British-born black dockworker whose voal gifts are discovered by an opera impresario. After realizing a career as a concert performer, Zinga ventures to Africa to investigate his ancestry and finds he has royal roots, and that his tribe have fallen under the grip of corrupt spiritualists. Robeson turns in a fine performance in what is otherwise an average film. ♫ Sleepy River; Lonely Road; Song of Freedom; The Black Emperor. **80m/B VHS, DVD.** *GB* Paul Robeson, Elisabeth Welch, George Mozart; ***D:*** J. Elder Wills; ***W:*** Ingram D'Abbes, Fenn Sherie; ***C:*** Eric Cross, Harry Rose.

A Song of Innocence 🦴🦴 *La Ravisseuse* **2005** In 1877, ambitious architect Julien (Colin) hires peasant girl Angele-Marie (Le Besco) to come to his country chateau as the wet nurse to his newborn daughter. His convent-bred wife Charlotte (Dequenne) is happy to forgo child-rearing and sex with her husband who wants a son and heir as soon as possible. Bored Charlotte, a teenager like Angele-Marie, soon begins to bond with her supposed servant, much to Julien's displeasure. French with subtitles. **90m/C DVD.** *FR* Gregoire Colin, Islid Le Besco, Emilie Dequenne, Anemone, Frederic Pierrot, Bernard Blancan; ***D:*** Antoine Santana; ***W:*** Antoine Santana; ***C:*** Giorgos Arvanitis; ***M:*** Louis Sclavis.

Song of Love 🦴🦴🦴 *A Love Story* **1947** Hepburn gracefully depicts the gifted 19th-century concert pianist Clara Wieck Schumann, who set aside her talents to be the wife of composer Robert Schumann and care for their seven children, which she did by herself after his untimely death in a mental facility. Clara shunned a marriage proposal from her deceased husband's star pupil, Johannes Brahms, who had long been infatuated with her, in order to dedicate her life to performing Schumann's works. **121m/B VHS, DVD.** Katharine Hepburn, Paul Henreid, Robert Walker, Henry Daniell, Leo G. Carroll, Gigi Perreau, Ann Carter, Jimmy Hunt, Elsa (Else) Janssen, Janine Perreau, Eilene Janssen, Roman Bohnen, Ludwig Stossel, Tala Birell, Konstantin Shayne, Henry Stephenson; ***D:*** Clarence Brown; ***W:*** Robert Ardrey, Ivan Tors, Allen Vincent; ***C:*** Harry Stradling Sr.

Song of Nevada 🦴🦴 1/2 **1944** Rogers woos the high-society daughter (Evans, of course) of a rancher (Hall). Quintessential Roy-n-Dale. ♫ It's Love, Love, Love; New Moon Over Nevada; Hi Ho Little Dogies; The Harum Scarum Baron of the Harmonium; What Are We Going to Do?; A Cowboy Has to Yodel in the Morning. **60m/B VHS, DVD.** Roy Rogers, Dale Evans, Thurston Hall; ***D:*** Joseph Kane.

Song of Norway 🦴🦴 **1970 (G)** A dramatization of the early life of the beloved Norwegian Romantic composer Edvard Grieg. Filmed against the beautiful mountains, waterfalls, and forests of Norway and based on the popular '40s stage production. The scenery is the best thing because Grieg's life was dull—even with cinematic liberties taken. ♫ Strange Music; The Song of Norway; The Little House; Be a Boy Again; Three There Were; A Rhyme and a Reason; Wrong to Dream; I Love You; The Solitary Wanderer. **143m/C VHS.** Toralv Maurstad, Florence Henderson, Edward G. Robinson, Christina Schollin, Frank Porretta, Oscar Homolka, Robert Morley, Harry Secombe; ***D:*** Andrew L. Stone.

Song of Old Wyoming 🦴 1/2 **1945** Three of those songs are presented in the course of an ordinary western about a spunky widow driving badmen out of Wyoming territory. La Rue plays the villainous Cheyanne Kid; this was before he got his own series as the heroic "Lash" La Rue. **65m/C VHS.** Eddie Dean, Sarah Padden, Lash LaRue, Jennifer Holt, Emmett Lynn, John Carpenter, Ian Keith, Bob (Robert) Barron; ***D:*** Robert Emmett Tansey.

Song of Scheherazade 🦴🦴 **1947** Superficial musical bio of Russian composer Rimsky-Korsakov (Aumont) and his romance with dancer Cara de Talavera (De Carlo), who inspires him to write the "Song of Scheherazade." **106m/C VHS.** Jean-Pierre Aumont, Yvonne De Carlo, Brian Donlevy, Eve Arden, Philip Reed, John Qualen; ***D:*** Walter Reisch; ***W:*** Walter Reisch; ***C:*** Hal Mohr, William V. Skall.

The Song of Songs 🦴🦴 1/2 **1933** Orphaned Lily (Dietrich) is living with her elderly Aunt Rasmussen (Skipworth) in Berlin and falling for sculptor, Richard (Aherne). He wants her to pose for a nude statue, based on the Song of Solomon, after getting a gander at Lily's legs. However, wealthy Baron von Merzbach (Atwill), who's Richard's art patron, eventually persuades both Aunt and Richard that Lily needs a better life than either can offer. Their marriage has the Baron making Lily over, so she'll socially be a worthy Baroness, but these situations never work out as anticipated. Based on the novel by Hermann Sudermann and the play by Edward Sheldon. **89m/B VHS.** Marlene Dietrich, Brian Aherne, Lionel Atwill, Alison Skipworth, Hardie Albright, Helen Freeman; ***D:*** Rouben Mamoulian; ***W:*** Samuel Hoffenstein, Leo Birinski; ***C:*** Victor Milner; ***M:*** Karl Hajos, Milan Roder.

Song of Texas 🦴 1/2 **1943** When a young woman journeys west to visit her father at "his" ranch, Roy and his pals must keep the father's secret that he is just another hired hand. Whenever possible, everyone breaks into song. **54m/B VHS, DVD.** Roy Rogers, Harry Shannon, Pat Brady, Barton MacLane, Arline Judge; ***D:*** Joseph Kane.

Song of the Exile 🦴🦴 1/2 **1990** A Chinese/Japanese student living in London in the early 1970s faces racial discrimination and decides to return to her native Hong Kong. But on the home front, she and her family clash emotionally until daughter and mother come to a gradual understanding of how the past affects the present. In Cantonese and Japanese with with English subtitles. **100m/C VHS.** *CH* Maggie Cheung, Shwu-Fen Chang; ***D:*** Ann Hui.

Song of the Gringo 🦴🦴 *The Old Corral* **1936** Tex Ritter stars in his first singing western as a sheriff going after a gang of claim jumpers. **57m/B VHS, DVD.** Tex Ritter, Monte Blue, Joan Woodbury, Fuzzy Knight, Richard Adams, Warner Richmond; ***D:*** John P. McCarthy.

Song of the Islands 🦴🦴 1/2 **1942** Landing families in Hawaii feud over a beach, while the son of one (Mature) and the daughter of the other (Grable) fall in love. Plenty of songs, and dancing to display Grable's legs. Of course happiness and concord reign at the end. Songs include "O'Brien Has Gone Hawaiian," "Sing Me a Song of the Islands," and "What's Buzzin', Cousin?" **75m/C VHS.** Betty Grable, Victor Mature, Jack Oakie, Thomas Mitchell, Billy Gilbert; ***D:*** Walter Lang.

The Song of the Lark 🦴🦴 1/2 **2001** Thea Kronborg (Elliott) is a minister's daughter in 1890s Colorado who is encouraged by local doctor Howard Archie (Howard) to pursue her musical dreams. At first, Thea travels to Chicago to study piano but her teacher (Hules) realizes that Thea's true gift is her voice. Handsome brewery heir Fred Ottenburg (Goldwyn) offers to sponsor her career but their romance is rocky and Thea must eventually make her own way. Based on the novel by Willa Cather. **120m/C VHS, DVD.** Alison Elliott, Arliss Howard, Tony Goldwyn, Maximilian Schell, Norman Lloyd, Robert Floyd, Endre Hules, Nan Martin, Christian Meoli; ***D:*** Karen Arthur; ***W:*** Joseph Maurer; ***M:*** Charles Fox. **TV**

Song of the Thin Man 🦴🦴 1/2 **1947** The sixth and final "Thin Man" mystery. This time Nick and Nora Charles (Powell and Loy) investigate the murder of a bandleader. Somewhat more sophisticated than its predecessor, due in part to its setting in the jazz music world. Sequel to "The Thin Man Goes Home." **86m/B VHS, DVD.** William Powell, Myrna Loy, Keenan Wynn, Dean Stockwell, Philip Reed, Patricia Morison, Gloria Grahame, Jayne Meadows, Don Taylor, Leon Ames, Ralph Morgan, Warner Anderson; ***D:*** Edward Buzzell; ***C:*** Charles Rosher.

Song of the Trail 🦴 1/2 **1936** Our hero saves an old man hornswoggled at cards. **65m/B VHS.** Kermit Maynard, George "Gabby" Hayes, Fuzzy Knight, Wheeler Oakman, Evelyn Brent, Andrea Leeds; ***D:*** Russell Hopton.

Song Spinner 🦴🦴 1/2 **1995 (G)** In a mysterious land, a stranger gives a young girl the power of music, which she hopes to share with the king. But first she must get past the kingdom's noise police. **95m/C VHS.** Meredith Henderson, Patti LuPone, John Neville; ***D:*** Randy Bradshaw.

A Song to Remember 🦴🦴🦴 **1945** With music performed by Jose Iturbi, this film depicts the last years of the great pianist and composer Frederic Chopin, including his affair with famous author George Sand, the most renowned French woman of her day. Typically mangled film biography. ♫ Valse in D Flat (Minute Waltz); Mazurka In B Flat, Opus 7, No. 1; Fantasie Impromptu, Opus 66; Etude In A Flat, Opus 25, No. 1 (partial); Polonaise In A Flat, Opus 53 (partial); Scherzo In B Flat Minor; Etude In C Minor, Opus 10, No. 12; Nocturne In C Minor, Opus 48, No. 1; Nocturn In E Flat, Opus 9, No. 2. **112m/C VHS.** Cornel Wilde, Paul Muni, Merle Oberon, Nina Foch, George Coulouris; ***D:*** Charles Vidor; ***C:*** Gaetano Antonio "Tony" Gaudio; ***M:*** Miklos Rozsa.

Song Without End 🦴🦴 ½ **1960** This musical biography of 19th century Hungarian pianist/composer Franz Lizst is given the Hollywood treatment. The lavish production emphasizes Liszt's scandalous exploits with married women and his life among the royal courts of Europe rather than his musical talents. Features music from several composers including Handel, Beethoven, Bach and Schumann. This film marked the debut of Capucine. Director Vidor died during filming and Cukor stepped in, so there is a noticeable change in style. Although there is much to criticize in the story, the music is beautiful. ♫ Mephisto Waltz; Spozalizio; Sonata In B Minor; Un Sospiro; Fantasy on Themes From "Rigoletto"; Consolation in D Flat; Liebestraum; Les Preludes; Piano Concerto No. 1. **130m/C VHS, DVD.** Dirk Bogarde, Capucine, Genevieve Page, Patricia Morison, Ivan Desny, Martita Hunt, Lou Jacobi; ***D:*** Charles Vidor, George Cukor; ***C:*** James Wong Howe; ***M:*** Morris Stoloff, Harry Sukman. Oscars '60: Scoring/Musical; Golden Globes '61: Film—Mus./Comedy.

Songcatcher 🦴🦴🦴 **1999** Turn-of-the-century musicologist Dr. Lily Penleric (McTeer) heads for Appalachia in a huff after the all-male review board of the East Coast university where she teaches refuses to grant her tenure. She begins teaching at her sister Elna's (Adams) mountain school, harboring a superior attitude toward the rubes she's teaching. She discovers to her amazement that the songs the rustic people sing, dance and live to are barely altered from the time they were brought over from Europe. She rushes to record the native folk music, but meets resistance from local Tom (Quinn) who feels that if the hillbillies have something civilized folk want, they should be payed for it. Excellent performances and visuals throughout. **113m/C VHS, DVD.** Janet McTeer, Aidan Quinn, Pat Carroll, Jane Adams, Emmy Rossum, Mike Harding, Iris DeMent, Greg Cook, David Patrick Kelly, E. Katherine Kerr, Taj Mahal, Muse Watson, Stephanie Ross; ***D:*** Maggie Greenwald; ***W:*** Maggie Greenwald; ***C:*** Enrique Chediak; ***M:*** David Mansfield.

Songs and Bullets 🦴 ½ **1938** Simple zen-like title sums it up. The songs total five in number, the bullets somewhat more as hero cowboys battle rustlers in routine fashion. One of a handful of films (westerns and comedies) produced by funnyman Stan Laurel. **57m/B VHS.** Fred Scott, Al "Fuzzy" St. John, Alice Ardell, Charles "Blackie" King, Karl Hackett, Frank LaRue, Budd Buster; ***D:*** Sam Newfield.

Songwriter 🦴🦴 ½ **1984 (R)** A high-falutin' look at the lives and music of two popular country singers with, aptly, plenty of country tunes written and performed by the stars. Singer-businessman Nelson needs Kristofferson's help keeping a greedy investor at bay. Never mind the plot; plenty of good music. ♫ How Do You Feel About Foolin' Around?; Songwriter; Who'll Buy My Memories; Write Your Own Songs; Nobody Said It Was Going To Be Easy; Good Times; Eye of the Storm; Crossing the Border; Down to Her Socks. **94m/C VHS, DVD.** Willie Nelson, Kris Kristofferson, Rip Torn, Melinda Dillon, Lesley Ann Warren; ***D:*** Alan Rudolph.

Sonic Impact 🦴 ½ **1999 (R)** Nutjob hijacks an airliner and threatens to crash it into the nearest large city. So a group of commandoes led by Nick Halton (Russo) makes plans to stop him. **94m/C VHS, DVD.** James Russo, Ice-T, Mel Harris; ***D:*** Rodney McDonald. **VIDEO**

Sonny 🦴🦴 **2002 (R)** Cage's directorial debut is about one man's frustrated attempts at leaving a life of crime. In 1981 New Orleans, Sonny (Franco) is fresh out of the Army and hopeful about working in his buddy's Texas bookstore. His corrupt pimp mother Jewel (Blethyn) would rather him reenter the family business and attempts to fix him up with Carol (Suvari), one of her new "girls." The two fall in love and, after a disastrous encounter with the "straight" world, Sonny descends back into the life he once dreamed of leaving for good. Stanton is in his element, underplaying the good-hearted, drunk boyfriend of Jewel while Cage makes an amusing appearance as Acid Yellow, a gay pimp. Heavy handed and overly emotional (the hysterical Blethyn is practically unwatchable), with an uneven rhythm and not a lot of explanation. Cage falls victim to first-time indulgence, but respectable narrative manages to make its point. **105m/C VHS, DVD.** *US* James Franco, Mena Suvari, Brenda Blethyn, Harry Dean Stanton, Nicolas Cage, Seymour Cassel, Brenda Vaccaro, Scott Caan; ***D:*** Nicolas Cage; ***W:*** John Carlen; ***C:*** Barry Markowitz; ***M:*** Clint Mansell.

Sonny and Jed 🦴 *La Banda J.&S. Cronaca Criminale del Far West* **1973 (R)** An escaped convict and a free-spirited woman travel across Mexico pillaging freely, followed determinedly by shiny-headed lawman Savalas. Lame rip-off of the Bonnie and Clyde legend. **85m/C VHS, DVD.** *IT* Tomas Milian, Telly Savalas, Susan George, Rosanna Janni, Laura Betti; ***D:*** Sergio Corbucci; ***M:*** Ennio Morricone.

Sonny Boy WOOF! 1987 (R) A transvestite and a psychopath adopt a young boy, training him to do their bidding, which includes murder. **96m/C VHS.** *IT* David Carradine, Paul Smith, Brad Dourif, Conrad Janis, Sydney Lassick, Savina Gersak, Alexandra Powers, Steve Carlisle, Michael Griffin; ***D:*** Robert Martin Carroll; ***W:*** Graeme Whifler; ***C:*** Roberto D'Ettorre Piazzoli; ***M:*** Carlo Maria Cordio.

Sonora Stagecoach 🦴🦴 **1944** Okay sagebrush saga with an interesting lineup; two cowboys, a heroic Indian, and a tough gal pilot escort a murder suspect in the title conveyance and manage to clear him when the real bad guys attack. **61m/B VHS.** Hoot Gibson, Bob Steele, Chief Thundercloud, Rocky Camron, Betty Miles, Glenn Strange, George Eldredge, Karl Hackett; ***D:*** Robert Emmett Tansey.

Sons 🦴🦴 **1989** Three sons decide to honor their father's last wish by taking him back to Normandy where he left behind a French girlfriend during WWII. He's hoping to see her again while his sons experience their own adventures in Paris. **88m/C VHS.** Stephane Audran, Jennifer Beals, Steve Axelrod, Elizabeth Bracco, William Forsythe, Bernard Fresson, Samuel Fuller, Judith Godreche, William Hickey, Robert Miranda, Shirley Stoler, D.B. Sweeney; ***D:*** Alexandre Rockwell; ***W:*** Brandon Cole, Alexandre Rockwell; ***C:*** Stefan Czapsky; ***M:*** Mader.

Sons of Katie Elder 🦴🦴🦴 **1965** After their mother's death, four brothers are reunited. Wayne is a gunman; Anderson is a college graduate; silent Holliman is a killer; and Martin is a gambler. When they learn that her death might have been linked to their father's murder, they come together to devise a way to seek revenge on the killer. The town bullies complicate matters; the sheriff tells them to lay off. Especially strong screen presence by Wayne, in his first role following cancer surgery. One of the Duke's most popular movies of the '60s. **122m/C VHS, DVD.** John Wayne, Dean Martin, Earl Holliman, Michael Anderson Jr., Martha Hyer, George Kennedy, Dennis Hopper, Paul Fix, James Gregory; ***D:*** Henry Hathaway; ***W:*** Harry Essex, Allan Weiss, William Wright; ***C:*** Lucien Ballard; ***M:*** Elmer Bernstein.

Sons of Steel 🦴🦴 **1935** Two brothers, owners of a steel mill, lead vastly different lives. They raise their sons in their own images, causing problems. **65m/B VHS.** Charles Starrett, Polly Ann Young, William "Billy" Bakewell, Walter Walker, Aileen Pringle, Holmes Herbert, Florence Roberts, Richard Carlyle, Lloyd Ingraham; ***D:*** Charles Lamont.

Sons of the Desert 🦴🦴🦴 *Sons of the Legion; Convention City; Fraternally Yours* **1933** Laurel and Hardy in their best-written film. The boys try to fool their wives by pretending to go to Hawaii to cure Ollie of a bad cold when in fact, they are attending their lodge convention in Chicago. Also includes a 1935 Thelma Todd/Patsy Kelly short, "Top Flat." **73m/B VHS, DVD.** Stan Laurel, Oliver Hardy, Mae Busch, Charley Chase, Dorothy Christy; ***D:*** William A. Seiter; ***W:*** Frank Craven; ***C:*** Kenneth Peach Sr.

Sons of the Pioneers 🦴🦴 **1942** Small town sheriff Hayes hires cowboy Roy to rid town of outlaws. **61m/B VHS, DVD.** Roy Rogers, George "Gabby" Hayes, Maris Wrixon, Forrest Taylor; ***D:*** Joseph Kane.

Sons of Trinity 🦴 **1995 (PG)** The two sons, Bambino (Neubert) and Trinity (Kizzier), of legendary cowpokes first meet when Bambino is about to be hung for horse thieving in the town of San Clementino. When Trinity gets his new friend off, they wind up as sheriff and deputy of the same town. Lots of physical comedy. **90m/C VHS, DVD.** Heath Kizzier, Keith Neubert, Ronald Nitschke, Siegfried Rauch; ***D:*** E.B. (Enzo Barboni) Clucher; ***C:*** Juan Amoros; ***M:*** Stefano Mainetti.

The Son's Room 🦴🦴🦴 *La Stanza del Figlio* **2000** Giovanni (Moretti) is a psychiatrist in a provincial seaside town, with a wife, Paola (Morante), and two teenage children—Irene (Trinca) and Andrea (Sanfelice). Their average lives are suddenly shattered when Andrea dies in a diving accident. The family falls apart and begins to distance themselves from each other and their grief. By accident, Arianna (Vigliar), a casual girlfriend of Andrea's who doesn't know about his death, contacts the family and surprisingly becomes a link to help heal. Italian with subtitles. **99m/C VHS, DVD.** *IT FR* Nanni Moretti, Laura Morante, Giuseppe Sanfelice, Jasmine Trinca, Stefano Accorsi, Sofia Vigliar, Silvio Orlando, Claudia Della Seta; ***D:*** Nanni Moretti; ***W:*** Nanni Moretti, Linda Ferri, Heidrun Schleef; ***C:*** Giuseppe Lanci; ***M:*** Nicola Piovani. Cannes '01: Film.

Sooner or Later 🦴 ½ **1978** 13-year-old girl passes herself off as 16 with a local rock idol and must decide whether to go all the way. **100m/C VHS, DVD.** Rex Smith, Judd Hirsch, Denise Miller, Morey Amsterdam, Lynn Redgrave; ***D:*** Bruce Hart. **TV**

Sophia Loren: Her Own Story 🦴🦴 **1980** Bio of Sophia Loren, watching her grow from a spindly child in working-class Naples to a world-renowned movie star, beauty queen, and mother. Loren plays herself and her mother in this tedious account. Based on the biography by A.E. Hotchner. **150m/C VHS.** Sophia Loren, Armand Assante, Ed Flanders, John Gavin; ***D:*** Mel Stuart; ***W:*** Joanna Crawford. **TV**

Sophie Scholl: The Final Days 🦴🦴🦴 *Sophie Scholl: Die Letzten Tage* **2005** Documentary traces the five days prior to the killing of University of Munich students Sophie Scholl (Jentsch) and her brother Hans (Hinrichs) in 1943 by German Nazis for their rebellious behavior in distributing anti-war literature at the school. Powerful interrogation scenes between Sophie and General Alexander Held (Mohr), as her quiet determination affects the general. Whatever empathy he feels can't change her inevitable fate. **117m/C DVD.** Julia Jentsch, Alexander Held, Fabian Hinrichs, Joanna Gastdorf, Andre Hennicke, Florian Stetter; ***D:*** Marc Rothemund; ***W:*** Fred Breinersdorfer; ***C:*** Martin Langer; ***M:*** Johnny Klimek, Reinhold Heil.

Sophie's Choice 🦴🦴🦴 ½ **1982 (R)** A haunting modern tragedy about Sophie Zawistowska, a beautiful Polish Auschwitz survivor settled in Brooklyn after WWII. She has intense relationships with a schizophrenic genius and an aspiring Southern writer. An artful, immaculately performed and resonant drama, with an astonishing, commanding performance by the versatile Streep; a chilling portrayal of the banality of evil. From the best-selling, autobiographical novel by William Styron. **157m/C VHS, DVD.** Meryl Streep, Kevin Kline, Peter MacNichol, Rita Karin, Stephen D. Newman, Josh Mostel; ***D:*** Alan J. Pakula; ***W:*** Alan J. Pakula; ***C:*** Nestor Almendros; ***M:*** Marvin Hamlisch. Oscars '82: Actress (Streep); Golden Globes '83: Actress—Drama (Streep); L.A. Film Critics '82: Actress (Streep); Natl. Bd. of Review '82: Actress (Streep); N.Y. Film Critics '82: Actress (Streep), Cinematog.; Natl. Soc. Film Critics '82: Actress (Streep).

Sophisticated Gents 🦴🦴🦴 **1981** Nine boyhood friends, members of a black athletic club, reunite after 25 years to honor their old coach and see how each of their lives has been affected by being black men in American society. Based on the novel "The Junior Bachelor Society" by John A. Williams. **200m/C VHS.** Paul Winfield, Roosevelt "Rosie" Grier, Bernie Casey, Raymond St. Jacques, Thalmus Rasulala, Dick Anthony Williams, Ron O'Neal, Rosalind Cash, Denise Nicholas, Alfre Woodard, Melvin Van Peebles, Robert Earl Jones, Robert Hooks, Ja'net DuBois, Joanna Miles, Janet MacLachlan, Bibi Besch, Beah Richards, Albert Hall, Harry Guardino, John Zaremba, Al Fann, Matthew "Stymie" Beard, Mario Van Peebles; ***D:*** Harry Falk; ***W:*** Melvin Van Peebles. **TV**

Sorcerer 🦴🦴 ½ *Wages of Fear* **1977 (PG)** To put out an oil fire, four men on the run in South America agree to try to buy their freedom by driving trucks loaded with nitroglycerin over dangerous terrain—with many natural and man-made obstacles to get in their way. Remake of "The Wages of Fear" is nowhere as good as the classic original, but has exciting moments. Puzzlingly retitled, which may have contributed to the boxoffice failure, and the near demise of Friedkin's directing career. **121m/C VHS, DVD.** Roy Scheider, Bruno Cremer, Francisco Rabal, Soudad Amidou, Ramon Bieri; ***D:*** William Friedkin; ***W:*** Walon Green; ***C:*** Dick Bush, John Stephens; ***M:*** Tangerine Dream.

The Sorcerer's Apprentice 2010 In this Walt Disney pic that must at least be inspired by the Mickey Mouse "Fantasia" segment, modern-day master sorcerer Balthazar Blake (Cage) is trying to defend Manhattan from arch-enemy Maxim Horvath (Molina). He recruits hapless and reluctant Dave Stutler (Baruchel) to become his apprentice and gives him a crash course in magic. **m/C DVD.** *US* Nicolas Cage, Jay Baruchel, Alfred Molina, Monica Bellucci, Toby Kebbell; ***D:*** Jon Turteltaub; ***W:*** Matt Lopez, Doug Miro, Carlo Bernard; ***C:*** Bojan Bazelli; ***M:*** Trevor Rabin.

Sorceress WOOF! 1982 (R) The Harris girls are sisters who use their powers of sorcery and fighting skills to battle demons, dragons, and evil. Yeah, sure. Really, they're just a pair of babes parading for the camera. **83m/C VHS.** Leigh Anne Harris, Lynette Harris, Bob Nelson, David Millbern, Bruno Rey, Anna De Sade; ***D:*** Brian Stuart; ***W:*** Jim Wynorski.

Sorceress 🦴🦴🦴 *Le Moine et la Sorciere* **1988** A friar in medieval Europe feels insecure in his religious beliefs after encountering a woman who heals through ancient practices. Historically authentic and interestingly moody. Written, produced, and directed by two women: an art history professor and a collaborator of Francois Truffaut's. In French with English subtitles or dubbed. **98m/C VHS.** *FR* Tcheky Karyo, Christine Boisson, Jean Carmet, Raoul Billerey, Catherine Frot, Feodor Atkine; ***D:*** Suzanne Schiffman; ***W:*** Pamela Berger, Suzanne Schiffman; ***C:*** Patrick Blossier.

Sorceress 🦴 ½ **1994 (R)** Larry Barnes (Poindexter) is on his way to a partnership at his law firm, especially since his wife Erica (Strain) eliminates his competition—permanently. But Erica goes after the wrong guy when she comes up against Howard Reynolds (Albert). Seems Howard's loving spouse Amelia (Blair) happens to be a witch and she has her own evil spells to cast. **93m/C VHS, DVD.** Julie Strain, Larry Poindexter, Linda Blair, Edward Albert; ***D:*** Jim Wynorski; ***W:*** Mark Thomas McGee; ***C:*** Gary Graver; ***M:*** Chuck Cirino, Darryl Way.

Sordid Lives 🦴🦴 **2000** Shores adapted his play but the comedy goes flat before the finale. Texas matriarch Peggy dies (under scandalous circumstances) and her dysfunctional family goes into hyperdrive. There's proper daughter Latrelle (Bedelia) who can't accept that her actor son Ty (Geiger) is gay, probably because her own brother—known only as Brother Boy (Jordan)—is a drag queen confined to a mental institution. But brassy sister LaVonda (Walker) still thinks he should come to the funeral. And there's Aunt Sissy (Grant) and G.W. (Bridges), who was having an affair with Peggy, and his wife Noleta (Burke), who's LaVonda's best friend and...it just kinda goes on and on. **111m/C VHS, DVD.** Bonnie Bedelia, Beth Grant, Delta Burke, Ann Walker, Leslie Jordan, Beau Bridges, Kirk Giger, Rosemary Alexander, Olivia Newton-John; ***D:*** Del Shores; ***W:*** Del Shores; ***C:*** Max CiVon; ***M:*** George S. Clinton.

Sorority Babes in the Slimeball Bowl-A-Rama 🦴🦴 *The Imp* **1987 (R)** An ancient gremlin-type creature is released from a bowling alley, and the great-looking sorority babes have to battle it at the mall, with the help of a wacky crew of nerds. Horrible horror spoof shows plenty of skin. **80m/C DVD.** Linnea Quigley, Brinke Stevens, Andras Jones, John Wildman, Robin Rochelle, Michelle (McClellan) Bauer, George "Buck" Flower; ***D:*** David DeCoteau; ***W:*** Sergei Hasenecz; ***C:*** Scott Ressler, Stephen Blake; ***M:*** Guy Moon; ***V:*** Michael Sonye.

Sorority Boys 🦴 **2002 (R)** Three frat boys (Williams, Rosenbaum and Watson) become bosom buddies when they don girlish garb to pass as sorority sisters in this contrived campus comedy. After being accused of a theft in their frat house, the badly disguised trio head to the notorious loser Delta Omega Gamma (DOG) house to stay in school. The boys teeter in their high heels, can't find dresses big enough for their ample "cabooses," and generally begin to understand the drag of being a gal while the film continues to serve up a kegful of gross-out and misogynist humor. Another in a string of misguided homages to "Animal House," with alums Daughton, Metcalf, Furst, and Vernon showing up for paychecks. Although Williams is considered to be the best of the three leads, all are terrible. Tepid romantic subplot with DOG house president doesn't help matters any. **93m/C VHS, DVD.** *US* Barry Watson, Michael Rosenbaum, Harland Williams, Melissa Sagemiller, Tony Denman, Brad Beyer, Heather Matarazzo, Kathryn Stockwood, Yvonne Scio; ***D:*** M. Wallace Wolodarsky; ***W:*** Joe Jarvis, Greg Coolidge; ***C:*** Michael D. O'Shea; ***M:*** Mark Mothersbaugh.

Sorority Girl 🦴 ½ **1957** Camp classic in which beautiful co-ed Cabot is presented as a malicious rich kid involved in everything from petty fights to blackmail. Cheap production from the Corman factory. **60m/B VHS.** Susan Cabot, Dick Miller, Barbara Crane, June Kenney, Fay Baker, Jeane Wood, Barboura Morris; ***D:*** Roger Corman; ***W:*** Leo Lieberman, Ed Waters; ***C:*** Monroe Askins; ***M:*** Ronald Stein.

Sorority House Massacre WOOF! 1986 (R) A knife-wielding maniac stalks a sorority girl while her more elite sisters are away for the weekend. Yawn—haven't we seen this one before? Unfortunately for us we'll see it again because this one's followed by a sequel. **74m/C VHS, DVD.** Angela O'Neill, Wendy Martel, Pamela Ross, Nicole Rio; ***D:*** Carol Frank; ***W:*** Carol Frank; ***C:*** Marc Reshovsky; ***M:*** Michael Wetherwax.

Sorority House Massacre 2: Nighty Nightmare WOOF! 1992 Another no-brainer with a different cast and director. This time around three lingerie-clad lovelies are subjected to the terrors of a killer their first night in their new sorority house. College just keeps getting tougher all the time. **80m/C VHS, DVD.** Melissa Moore, Robin Harris, Stacia Zhivago, Dana Bentley, Shannon Wilsey; ***D:*** Jim Wynorski; ***W:*** James B. Rogers, Bob Sheridan; ***M:*** Chuck Cirino.

Sorority House Party 🦴 **1992 (R)** A famous rock guitarist is held against his will at the sexiest sorority house on campus. He definitely has mixed feelings about the experience considering the inhabitants saunter around in bikinis and "force" him to party with them. Anders and Attila are transplants from the modeling circuit. **95m/C VHS.** Attila, April Lerman, Kim Little, Avalon Anders, Joe Mundi, Rachel Latt, Mark Stulce, Michael Xavier; ***D:*** David Michael Latt; ***W:*** John Murdy, Steve Taylor.

Sorority House Vampires 🦴 ½ **1995** Sexy college coed Buffy fights to save her man and her sorority from Natalia, Queen of Darkness, and Count Vlad. **90m/C VHS, DVD.** Eugenie Bondurant, Robert Bucholz, Kathy Presgrave; ***D:*** Geoffrey De Vallois. **VIDEO**

Sorority Row 🦴 *The House on Sorority Row* **2009 (R)** A group of Theta Pi seniors try to teach their sister Megan's (Partridge) cheating boyfriend (Lanter) a lesson during pledge week through an elaborate hoax in which Megan's death is staged. Naturally the hoax goes horribly wrong when the freaked out boyfriend plunges a tire iron into her chest. Now with a body to deal with, frosty head sister Jessica (Pipes) invokes the sorority value of secrecy. But eight months later as graduation nears, one by one the sisters are dealt retribution for their ghastly scheme. Carrie Fisher as housemother Mrs. Crenshaw is a treat, but this remake of the 1983 slasher falls short, wobbling between gags and horrors. In the end it seems the boobs were on both sides of the camera. **101m/C DVD.** *US* Briana Evigan, Rumer Willis, Julian Morris, Leah Pipes, Margo Harshman, Jamie Chung, Audrina Patridge, Carrie Fisher; ***D:*** Stewart Hendler; ***W:*** Peter Goldfinger, Josh Stolberg, Mark Rosman; ***C:*** Ken Seng; ***M:*** Lucian Piane.

Sorrento Beach 🦴🦴 *Hotel Sorrento* **1995 (R)** A beachside community outside Melbourne, Australia, Sorrento is home to the Moynihans. The three Moynihan sisters—Meg (Goodall), Hillary (Gillmer), and Pippa (Morice)—are reunited after 10 years by their father's sudden death. Lots of tensions, rivalries, and jealousies come to the surface as well as old secrets regarding a family tragedy. Talky film hasn't quite cast off its stage origins (it's adapted from a play by Hannie Rayson) but the performances are noteworthy. **112m/C VHS.** *AU* Caroline Goodall, Caroline Gillmer, Tara Morice, Joan Plowright, John Hargreaves, Ray Barrett, Ben Thomas, Nicholas Bell; ***D:*** Richard Franklin; ***W:*** Richard Franklin, Peter Fitzpatrick, Hannie Rayson; ***C:*** Geoff Burton; ***M:*** Nerida Tyson-Chew. Australian Film Inst. '95: Adapt. Screenplay, Support. Actor (Barrett).

The Sorrow and the Pity 🦴🦴🦴 ½ **1971** A classic documentary depicting the life of a small French town and its resistance during the Nazi occupation. Lengthy, but totally compelling. A great documentary that brings home the atrocities of war. In French with English narration. **265m/B VHS, DVD.** *FR* Pierre Mendes-France, Sir Anthony Eden, Dr. Claude Levy, Denis Rake, Louis Grave, Maurice Chevalier; ***D:*** Marcel Ophuls; ***C:*** Mandre Gazut, Jurgen Thieme.

Sorrowful Jones 🦴🦴 **1949** A "Little Miss Marker" remake, in which bookie Hope inherits a little girl as collateral for an unpaid bet. Good for a few yuks, but the original is much better. **88m/B VHS, DVD.** Bob Hope, Lucille Ball, William Demarest, Bruce Cabot, Thomas Gomez, Mary Jane Saunders; ***D:*** Sidney Lanfield; ***W:*** Jack Rose, Melville Shavelson; ***C:*** Daniel F. Fapp.

Sorrows of Gin 🦴🦴 ½ **1979** Eight-year-old girl searches for a sense of family amid her parents' lives. Her efforts to deal with alienation and emotional isolation lead her to run away from home. From a short story by John Cheever. **60m/C VHS, DVD.** Edward Herrmann, Sigourney Weaver, Mara Hobel, Eileen Heckart, Rachel Roberts; ***D:*** Jack Hofsiss; ***W:*** Wendy Wasserstein. **TV**

The Sorrows of Satan 🦴🦴🦴 **1926** Dempster and Cortez star as writers in love with each other, but Cortez can't take his poverty and the rejection of publishers. As he is about to end it all, the devil appears to him in disguise and makes an offer he can hardly refuse. He is introduced to London society and winds up marrying a fortune hunter. When he discovers this he goes back to Dempster, who still loves him, and vows to give up everything for her. Menjou then reveals himself to be the devil but Dempster's faith is so strong that the evil is vanquished. **111m/B VHS.** Adolphe Menjou, Carol Dempster, Ricardo Cortez, Lya de Putti; ***D:*** D.W. Griffith.

Sorry, Haters 🦴🦴 **2005** Behaving erratically, New York cable TV executive Phoebe (Wright Penn) hops into a cab driven by Ashade (Kechiche) to head to her ex-husband's house in Jersey seeking to get even with him for remarrying and taking everything. A chemist in his homeland, Ashade is suffering too, as the Syrian Muslim's brother is being unjustly held at Guantanamo, unable to enter the country. But his compassion for her and belief that she could help him are horribly misguided. Wright Penn and Kechiche are solid in this uneven look at post-9/11 culture and attitudes. **83m/C DVD.** *US* Robin Wright Penn, Abdellatif Kechiche, Sandra Oh, Elodie Bouchez, Aasif Mandvi, Remy K. Selma, Fred Durst; ***D:*** Jeff Stanzler; ***W:*** Jeff Stanzler; ***C:*** Mauricio Rubinstein; ***M:*** Raz Mesinai.

Sorry, Wrong Number 🦴🦴🦴 ½ **1948** A wealthy, bedridden wife overhears two men plotting a murder on a crossed telephone line, and begins to suspect that one of the voices is her husband's. A classic tale of paranoia and suspense. Based on a radio drama by Louise Fletcher, who also wrote the screenplay. Remade for TV in 1989. **89m/B VHS, DVD.** Barbara Stanwyck, Burt Lancaster, Ann Richards, Wendell Corey, Harold Vermilyea, Ed Begley Sr.; ***D:*** Anatole Litvak; ***W:*** Lucille Fletcher; ***C:*** Sol Polito; ***M:*** Franz Waxman.

Sorry, Wrong Number 🦴 ½ **1989** Cable remake of the 1948 Barbara Stanwyck thriller about a bed-ridden woman trying to get help after she realizes she's being stalked by a killer. Offers a new twist (drug dealing), but doesn't even approach the Stanwyck original. From the story by Lucille Fletcher. **90m/C VHS.** Loni Anderson, Hal Holbrook, Patrick Macnee, Miguel Fernandes, Carl Weintraub; ***D:*** Tony Wharmby; ***W:*** Ann Louise Bardach; ***M:*** Bruce Broughton. **CABLE**

Sorted 🦴 ½ **2004** Compelled by his brother's odd drowning death in London, Carl noses around only to become consumed with the same wild party scene that could lead him to a similar demise. **105m/C VHS, DVD.** Matthew Rhys, Sienna Guillory, Fay Masterson, Tim Curry, Jason Donovan, Stephen Marcus; ***D:*** Alexander Jovy; ***W:*** Malcolm Campbell, Alexander Jovy, Christian Spurrier, Nick Villiers; ***C:*** Mike Southon; ***M:*** Guy Farley. **VIDEO**

Sorum 🦴🦴 *Soreum* **2001 (R)** Yong-hyun (Kim Myung-min) is a cab driver who needs a new place to live, and all that's available is a run-down apartment building home to a bunch of whacky eccentrics who waste no time telling him his apartment is cheap because it's haunted by a former tenant. One of Yong-hyun's attractive (and murderous) neighbors asks him to help her dispose of her husband's body. He agrees, and the two get busy. Not a good idea. **112m/C DVD.** *KN* Jin-Young Jang, Myeong-min Kim; ***D:*** Jong-chan Yun; ***W:*** Jong-chan Yun; ***C:*** Seo-Shik Hwang.

S.O.S. Coast Guard 🦴🦴 ½ **1937** A fiendish scientist creates a disintegrating gas and the U.S. Coast Guard must stop him from turning it over to unfriendly foreigners. Loads of action in this 12-part serial. **224m/B VHS, DVD.** Ralph Byrd, Bela Lugosi, Maxine Doyle, Richard Alexander, Lawrence Grant, Thomas Carr, Lee Ford, John Picorri, George Chesebro; ***D:*** Alan James, William Whitney; ***W:*** Frank (Franklyn) Adreon, Winston Miller, Barry Shipman; ***C:*** William Nobles.

S.O.S. Pacific 🦴🦴 **1960** A seaplane crashes on a nuclear-test island and the survivors find that they have only five hours before they get nuked. Even though there is plenty of the usual action one would expect from such a film, the story really revolves around the characters. The British and U.S. versions have different endings. **91m/B VHS.** *GB* Eddie Constantine, Pier Angeli, Richard Attenborough, John Gregson, Eva Bartok; ***D:*** Guy Green.

S.O.S. Titanic 🦴🦴 ½ **1979** The story of the Titanic disaster, recounted in flashback, in docu-drama style. James Costigan's teleplay of the familiar story focuses on the courage that accompanied the horror and tragedy. Thoroughly professional, absorbing TV drama. **102m/C VHS, DVD.** *GB* Beverly Ross, David Janssen, Cloris Leachman, Susan St. James, David Warner, Ian Holm, Helen Mirren, Harry Andrews, David Battley, Ed Bishop, Peter Bourke, Shevaun Briars, Nick Brimble, Jacob Brooke, Catherine Byrne, Tony Caunter, Warren Clarke, Nicholas Davies, Deborah Fallender; ***D:*** William (Billy) Hale; ***W:*** James Costigan; ***C:*** Christopher Challis; ***M:*** Howard Blake. **TV**

Sotto, Sotto 🦴🦴 ½ **1985 (R)** A minor Wertmuller comedy about an Italian businessman who is constantly suspicious of his wife's fidelity. As it happens, she's attracted to another woman (de Santis). Massimo Wertmuller is Lina's nephew. Entertaining. In Italian with English subtitles. **104m/C VHS.** *IT* Enrico Montesano, Veronica Lario, Massimo Wertmuller, Luisa de Santis; ***D:*** Lina Wertmuller; ***W:*** Lina Wertmuller.

Soul Assassin 🦴🦴 **2001 (R)** Kevin Burke (Ulrich) works for the security branch of an international investment bank in Rotterdam. He's been mentored by the bank's managing director, Karl Jorgensen (de Lint), much to the disgust of Jorgensen own son, Karl, Jr. (Kamerling). When Kevin's fiancee Rosalind (Lang) is assassinated, Kevin discovers he didn't know her as well as he thought. Seems she was involved in money laundering and corporate espionage. While Kevin seeks the truth, mystery woman Tessa (Swanson) is shadowing him—is she friend or foe? **97m/C VHS, DVD.** *NL* Skeet Ulrich, Kristy Swanson, Derek de Lint, Antoine Kamerling, Rena Owen, Serge-Henri Valcke, Thom Hoffman, Katherine Lang, Pierre Allard; ***D:*** Laurence Malkin; ***W:*** Laurence Malkin, Chad Thurman; ***C:*** Lex Wertwijn; ***M:*** Alan Williams.

Soul-Fire 🦴🦴 **1925** South Pacific high seas induce Cupid's arrow. Silent. **100m/B VHS.** Richard Barthelmess, Bessie Love, Walter Long, Arthur Metcalfe; ***D:*** John S. Robertson.

Soul Food 🦴🦴 ½ **1997 (R)** In between the mouth watering servings of fried-chicken, collard greens and catfish unfolds the lives of sisters Williams, Fox, and Long. They struggle to hold their family together by keeping up their mother's Sunday dinner tradition after she becomes ill. As mom's health deteriorates, so do the sisters' relationships with their significant others, turning things a bit soapy and predictable. Unfulfilling appetizer for those looking for a stark urban drama, but with an attractive ensemble cast which brings to life truthful characters, it's a hearty feast for those hungry for a heartwarming, contemporary tale. Warmth and humor won over audiences across color lines. Boasts many promising debuts, including director/writer Tillman and young narrator Hammond. Produced by music producer Kenneth (Babyface) Edmonds. **114m/C VHS, DVD.** Vanessa L(ynne) Williams, Vivica A. Fox, Nia Long, Michael Beach, Mekhi Phifer, Irma P. Hall, Jeffrey D. Sams, Gina Ravera, Brandon Hammond, Carl Wright, Mel Jackson, Morgan Michelle Smith, John M. Watson Sr.; ***D:*** George Tillman Jr.; ***W:*** George Tillman Jr.; ***C:*** Paul Elliott; ***M:*** Wendy Melvoin, Lisa Coleman.

The Soul Guardians 🦴 ½ *Toemarok* **1998** In a bizarre religious mix from Korea, a satanic cult commits suicide during a raid while one of their members gives birth to a girl before dying. The girl grows up to be a telepathic car mechanic before being told she was intended to be possessed by Satan who needs her body to successfully reincarnate. Defending her are a fallen priest, a video-gamer with magical powers, and a warrior whose knife has a mind of its own. Not quite as bad as it sounds but no classic of the genre. **96m/C DVD.** *KN* Hyeon-jun Shin, Sang-mi Choo, Sung-kee Ahn, Hyun-chul Oh; ***D:*** Kwang-chun Park; ***W:*** K.C. Park, Kwang-chun Park, Woo-hyouk Lee; ***C:*** Hyeon-cheol Park; ***M:*** Dong-jun Lee.

Soul Hustler WOOF! 1976 (PG) A con man becomes rich and famous as a tent-show evangelist. Pathetic drivel. **81m/C VHS.** Fabian, Casey Kasem, Larry Bishop, Nai Bonet; ***D:*** Burt Topper.

Soul Kitchen 2009 Zinos (Bousdoukos) owns and runs a working-class restaurant in a suburb of Hamburg. When he decides to upgrade the place by hiring a temperamental chef, Zinos alienates his regular clientele while getting into trouble with a health officer, a tax inspector, and an aggressive real estate agent while also dealing with his criminally-minded brother Illias (Bleibtreu). German with subtitles. **98m/C DVD.** *GE* Adam Bousdoukos, Moritz Bleibtreu, Pheline Roggan, Birol Unel, Anna Bederke, Dorka Gryllus, Catrin Striebeck, Jan Fedder, Wotan Wilke Moehring; ***D:*** Fatih Akin; ***W:*** Fatih Akin; ***C:*** Rainer Klausmann.

Soul Man 🦴🦴 **1986 (PG-13)** Denied the funds he expected for his Harvard tuition, a young white student (Howell) masquerades as a black in order to get a minority scholarship. As a black student at Harvard, Howell learns about racism and bigotry. Pleasant lightweight comedy with romance thrown in

(Chong is the black girl he falls for), and with pretensions to social satire that it never achieves. **112m/C VHS, DVD.** C. Thomas Howell, Rae Dawn Chong, James Earl Jones, Leslie Nielsen, Arye Gross; ***D:*** Steve Miner; ***W:*** Carol Black; ***C:*** Jeffrey Jur; ***M:*** Tom Scott.

Soul Men 1/2 **2008 (R)** Louis Hinds (Jackson) and Floyd Henderson (Mac) are former backup singers for a 1970s soul act whose lead singer left them for a solo career. Fast-forward to present and their former bandmate has just died, prompting a tribute concert. Louis and Floyd agree to drive cross-country to participate in the concert after more than 20 years of estrangement, which might have something to do with a stolen girlfriend. Basically on a road trip, the two stop to perform along the way as they alternately blow-up and make-up. Much of the plot and gags are pure formula, but Jackson and Mac rise above the predictability to deliver memorable performances. Not the best movie but worth a viewing to see the much-missed Bernie Mac in a performance filmed just months before his untimely death. **100m/C DVD.** *US* Samuel L. Jackson, Bernie Mac, Isaac Hayes, Sharon Leal, Adam Herschman, Sean P. Hayes, Johnny (Martin Margulies) Legend, Jennifer Coolidge, Mike Epps, Affion Crockett; ***D:*** Malcolm Lee; ***W:*** Robert Ramsey, Matthew Stone; ***C:*** Matthew F. Leonetti; ***M:*** Stanley Clarke.

Soul of the Beast 1/2 **1923** An elephant repeatedly saves Bellamy from the villainous Beery. Silent with original organ score. **77m/B VHS.** Madge Bellamy, Cullen Landis, Noah Beery Sr.; ***D:*** John Griffith Wray, John Griffith Wray; ***W:*** Ralph Dixon; ***C:*** Henry Sharp.

Soul of the Game **1996 (PG-13)** Cable movie follows the lives of three talented players in the Negro League during the 1945 season as they await the potential integration of baseball. Brooklyn Dodgers general manager Branch Rickey (Herrmann) has his scouts focusing on three men in particular: flashy, aging pitcher Satchel Paige (Lindo), mentally unstable catcher Josh Gibson (Williamson), and the young, college-educated Jackie Robinson (Underwood). Manages to resist melodrama through terrific performances. **105m/C VHS, DVD.** Delroy Lindo, Mykelti Williamson, Blair Underwood, Edward Herrmann, R. Lee Ermey, Gina Ravera, Salli Richardson, Obba Babatunde, Brent Jennings, Edwin Morrow, Richard Riehle; ***D:*** Kevin Rodney Sullivan; ***W:*** David Himmelstein; ***C:*** Sandi Sissel; ***M:*** Lee Holdridge. **CABLE**

Soul Patrol **1980 (R)** Black newspaper reporter clashes with the all-white police department in a racist city. **90m/C VHS, DVD.** Nigel Davenport, Ken Gampu, Peter Dyneley; ***D:*** Christopher Rowley.

Soul Plane **2004 (R)** Nashawn Wade (Hart) wins a $100 million settlement after a near-disastrous flight and promptly creates a new airline for the "urban traveler." With a pimped out plane, lusty security officer (Mo'Nique) and a pilot (Snoop Dogg) who likes to get high, this one's doomed before the plane even takes off. What it lacks in entertainment, it more than makes up for in raunchiness, over-the-top stereotypes and sleazy sex jokes, making it a sure-fire cable and late-night Comedy Central hit. Tom Arnold also makes an appearance as the token white guy. **86m/C VHS, DVD.** *US* Kevin Hart, Tom Arnold, Method Man, Snoop Dogg, K.D. Aubert, Brian Hooks, D.L. Hughley, Mo'Nique, Godfrey, Arielle Kebbel, Loni Love, Missi Pyle, Stacey Travis; ***D:*** Jessy Terrero; ***W:*** Bo Zenga, Chuck Wilson; ***C:*** Jonathan Sela; ***M:*** RZA.

Soul Power **2008 (PG-13)** Levy-Hinte, who worked on the 1995 documentary "When We Were Kings" about the 1974 Muhammad Ali-George Foreman fight in Kinshasa, Zaire, gathered unedited backstage and concert performances to put together footage of the three-day concert that preceded the boxing match. Includes on-site preparations, interviews, and some 14 musical numbers from James Brown, The Spinners, Celia Cruz, and others. **93m/C DVD.** *US* James Brown, Celia Cruz, Miriam Makeba, Don King, B.B. King, Muhammad Ali, George Plimpton; ***D:*** Jeffrey Levy-Hinte; ***C:*** Paul Goldsmith, Kevin Keating, Albert Maysles, Roderick Young.

Soul Survivor 1/2 **1995 (PG-13)** Set in Toronto's Jamaican community, this urban drama focuses on twentysomething Tyrone (Williams) who's stuck in a custodial job and looking to make some easy money. He goes to work making collections for local gangster Winston (Harris), who tries to reassure his protege that money buys respect. But when Tyrone falls for straight-living social worker Annie (Scott), he begins to see the potholes in the path he's on. **89m/C VHS, DVD.** *CA* Peter Williams, George Harris, Judith Scott, Clark Johnson, David Smith; ***D:*** Stephen Williams; ***W:*** Stephen Williams; ***C:*** David Franco; ***M:*** John McCarthy.

Soul Survivors **WOOF! 2001 (R)** Perhaps the worst slash and burn editing job in the history of film was used to chop this muddled horror flick from an R to a PG-13 rating. Cassie (Sagemiller) and her boyfriend Sean (Affleck) go to one last party with their friends Annabel (Dushku) and Matt (Bentley). The party is a nasty Goth rave held in a cathedral, seemingly run by juvenile delinquent vampires. Sean gets upset when he misinterprets an innocent kiss between Cassie and Matt, who is also her ex. On the way home, a distracted Cassie crashes the car while trying to iron things out with Sean, killing him. Or not, as the case may be, because Cassie keeps seeing her dead boyfriend wherever she goes. Also, she keeps being chased by creepy Goth skanks. So is Cassie crazy? Is Sean alive? Frankly, you won't care even if you make it to the end of this contorted mess. **85m/C VHS, DVD.** *US* Melissa Sagemiller, Wes Bentley, Casey Affleck, Eliza Dushku, Luke Wilson; ***D:*** Stephen Carpenter; ***W:*** Stephen Carpenter; ***C:*** Fred Murphy; ***M:*** Daniel Licht.

Soul Vengeance *Welcome Home Brother Charles* **1975** Black man is jailed and brutalized for crime he didn't commit and wants revenge when he's released. Many afros and platform shoes. Vintage blaxploitation. **91m/C VHS, DVD.** Marlo Monte, Reatha Grey, Stan Kamber, Tiffany Peters, Ven Bigelow, Jake Carter; ***D:*** Jamaa Fanaka; ***W:*** Jamaa Fanaka.

The Souler Opposite **1997 (R)** Buddies Barry (Meloni) and Robert (Busfield) haven't grown up—especially where women are concerned. Most of struggling comic Barry's material is about his failed relationships while complacent, married Robert learns that his wife has decided she's a lesbian. Then sexist Barry meets feminist Thea (Moloney) and sparks fly—but can "souler" opposites really come together? First-time writer/director Kalmenson knows the territory since he's a stand-up comedian himself. **104m/C VHS, DVD.** Christopher Meloni, Timothy Busfield, Janel Moloney, Allison Mackie, John Putch, Rutanya Alda, Steve Landesberg; ***D:*** Bill Kalmenson; ***W:*** Bill Kalmenson; ***C:*** Amit Bhattacharya; ***M:*** Peter Himmelman.

Souls at Sea 1/2 **1937** Good buddy work by Cooper and Raft highlight this complicated seafaring yarn. In the 1840s sailor and abolitionist Nuggin Taylor (Cooper) is secretly sabotaging slave ships, working undercover for the British Navy. With loyal friend Powdah (Raft), Taylor tries to gather evidence against British officer Tarryton (Wilcoxon) even though he's fallen for Tarryton's sister Margaret (Dee). But after a sea disaster, Taylor's accused of murder and brought to trial. Will the truth come out in time to save him? **93m/B VHS.** Gary Cooper, George Raft, Henry Wilcoxon, Frances Dee, Olympe Bradna, George Zucco, Harry Carey Sr., Robert Cummings, Porter Hall, Joseph Schildkraut; ***D:*** Henry Hathaway; ***W:*** Grover Jones, Dale Van Every; ***C:*** Charles B(ryant) Lang Jr.

Souls for Sale **1923** Offers a fascinating glimpse into the world of silent filmmaking with cameos by a number of stars and directors of the era. Remember 'Mem' Steddon (Boardman) impulsively marries Owen Scudder (Cody), who turns out to be a wife-murdering con man. On their honeymoon train trip, Mem gets suspicious and hops off at a water stop in the middle of the California desert. She stumbles onto a movie location shoot where she's befriended by director Frank Claymore (Dix). Mem eventually goes to Hollywood, studies acting, and Frank makes her a star. But her success brings Scudder back into Mem's life. **89m/B DVD.** Eleanor Boardman, Lew Cody, Richard Dix, Frank Mayo, Barbara La Marr, Mae Busch, William Haines, Snitz Edwards, Forrest Robinson; ***D:*** Rupert Hughes; ***W:*** Rupert Hughes.

Soul's Midnight 1/2 **2006 (R)** So how do you feel about bloody cults in Texas? Charles (Floyd) and his pregnant wife Alicia (Bennett) have come home for his dad's funeral. The town is big on celebrating the feast of St. George and the defeat of that pesky dragon, which was fond of human sacrifices. Charles is supposed to be a descendant of St. George and Alicia has weird dreams that hotel owner Simon (Assante) wants their unborn child to carry on the sacrificial ritual. **87m/C DVD.** Armand Assante, Robert Floyd, Elizabeth Bennett, Miguel Perez, Lucila Sola, Joe Nipote; ***D:*** Harry Basil; ***W:*** Brian Cleveland, Jason Cleveland; ***C:*** Keith J. Duggan; ***M:*** Cieri Torjussen. **VIDEO**

Soultaker 1/2 **1990 (R)** The title spirit is after a young couple's souls, and they have just an hour to reunite with their bodies after a car crash. Meanwhile, they're in limbo (literally) between heaven and earth. The ending's OK, if you can make it that far. **94m/C VHS, DVD.** Joe Estevez, Vivian Schilling, Gregg Thomsen, David "Shark" Fralick, Jean Reiner, Chuck Williams, Robert Z'Dar; ***D:*** Michael Rissi; ***W:*** Vivian Schilling; ***C:*** James Rosenthal; ***M:*** Jon McCallum.

The Sound and the Silence 1/2 **1993** Bio of inventor Alexander Graham Bell (Bach). The Scottish Bell's father was a speech specialist and his beloved mother Eliza (Fricker) was severely hearing impaired. Bell himself trained to work with the deaf in Boston and experimented with transmitting speech electronically—a project which only grew when Bell married the deaf Mable Hubbard (Quinn). Bell's lifelong devotion lead to his development of the telephone as well as numerous other inventions (and his founding of "National Geographic" magazine). Bell was hardly a lively character but this TV drama is lavishly done. In two parts. **93m/C VHS.** John Bach, Elizabeth Quinn, Brenda Fricker, Ian Bannen; ***D:*** John Kent Harrison; ***W:*** Tony Foster, William Schmidt, John Kent Harrison; ***M:*** John Charles. **TV**

The Sound Barrier 1/2 **1952** RAF pilot Tony Garthwaite (Patrick) marries Sue (Todd), the daughter of wealthy airplane designer John Ridgefield (Richardson). Ridgefield is obsessed with designing a jet that can break the sound barrier and Sue is worried about her father's reckless disregard for the lives of the test pilots, which soon include her husband. Film ignores the fact that American test pilot Chuck Yeager had already accomplished the goal, with Lean filming in a semi-documentary style complete with aerial footage of actual jets. **110m/B DVD.** *GB* Ralph Richardson, Ann Todd, Nigel Patrick, John Justin, Dinah Sheridan, Joseph Tomelty, Denholm Elliott; ***D:*** Nigel Patrick, David Lean; ***W:*** Terence Rattigan; ***C:*** Jack Hildyard; ***M:*** Malcolm Arnold.

Sound of Horror 1/2 *El Sonido de la Muerte; Sound From a Million Years Ago; The Prehistoric Sound* **1964** The Hound usually admires creative efforts to keep budgets down, but this is too much (or too little). A dinosaur egg hatches, and out lashes an invisible predator. Yes, you'll have to use your imagination as archaeologists are slashed to bits by the no-show terror. **85m/B VHS, DVD.** *SP* James Philbrook, Arturo Fernandez, Soledad Miranda, Ingrid Pitt; ***D:*** Jose Antonio Nieves-Conde.

Sound of Love **1978** The mutual attraction between a deaf female hustler and a deaf race car driver leads to a deep relationship where they both learn about their own fears and desires. **74m/C VHS.** Celia de Burgh, John Jarratt, George Ogilvie; ***D:*** John Power; ***W:*** John Power; ***C:*** Geoff Burton; ***M:*** Peter Best.

Sound of Murder **1982** A successful children's book writer wants to exact revenge on his adulterous wife, but is himself murdered before he can "execute" his plan. **114m/C VHS.** Pippa Scott, Leonard Frey, David Ackroyd, Michael Moriarty, Joanna Miles; ***D:*** Michael Lindsay-Hogg; ***W:*** William Fairchild.

The Sound of Music **1965** The classic film version of the Rodgers and Hammerstein musical based on the true story of the singing von Trapp family of Austria and their escape from the Nazis just before WWII. Beautiful Salzburg, Austria location photography and an excellent cast. Andrews, fresh from her Oscar for "Mary Poppins," is effervescent, in beautiful voice, but occasionally too good to be true. Not Rodgers & Hammerstein's most innovative score, but lovely to hear and see. Plummer's singing was dubbed by Bill Lee. Marni Nixon, behind-the-scenes songstress for "West Side Story" and "My Fair Lady," makes her onscreen debut as one of the nuns. ♫ I Have Confidence In Me; Something Good; The Sound of Music; Preludium; Morning Hymn; Alleluia; How Do You Solve A Problem Like Maria?; Sixteen, Going on Seventeen; My Favorite Things. **174m/C VHS, DVD.** Julie Andrews, Christopher Plummer, Eleanor Parker, Peggy Wood, Charmian Carr, Heather Menzies, Marni Nixon, Richard Haydn, Anna Lee, Norma Varden, Nicholas Hammond, Angela Cartwright, Portia Nelson, Duane Chase, Debbie Turner, Kym Karath; ***D:*** Robert Wise; ***W:*** Ernest Lehman; ***C:*** Ted D. McCord. Oscars '65: Adapt. Score, Director (Wise), Film Editing, Picture, Sound; AFI '98: Top 100; Directors Guild '65: Director (Wise); Golden Globes '66: Actress—Mus./Comedy (Andrews), Film—Mus./Comedy, Natl. Film Reg. '01.

A Sound of Thunder **2005 (PG-13)** Not much more needs to be said other than this is a summer flick, a time-traveling adventure, very loosely based on a Ray Bradbury story. The setting is 2055 Chicago, where folks with deep pockets get the opportunity to run with (okay, hunt) the dinosaurs, courtesy of a greedy entrepreneur (Kingsley). A snafu threatens to change the future, reverting Chicago (and the rest of the planet) back to prehistoric times. Loads and loads of special effects and, well, that's about it. "The Simpsons" fleshed out this premise with more success a few years ago. **102m/C DVD.** *GE US CZ* Edward Burns, Catherine McCormack, Ben Kingsley, Jemima Rooper, August Zirner, Corey Johnson, David Oyelowo, Wilfried Hochholdinger; ***D:*** Peter Hyams; ***W:*** Thomas Dean Donnelly, Joshua Oppenheimer, Gregory Poirier; ***C:*** Peter Hyams; ***M:*** Nick Glennie-Smith.

Sounder **1972 (G)** The struggles of a family of black sharecroppers in rural Louisiana during the Depression. When the father is sentenced to jail for stealing in order to feed his family, they must pull together even more, and one son finds education to be his way out of poverty. Tyson brings strength and style to her role, with fine help from Winfield. Moving and well made, with little sentimentality and superb acting from a great cast. Adapted from the novel by William Armstrong. **105m/C VHS, DVD.** Paul Winfield, Cicely Tyson, Kevin Hooks, Taj Mahal, Carmen Mathews, James Best, Janet MacLachlan; ***D:*** Martin Ritt; ***W:*** Lonnie Elder III; ***C:*** John A. Alonzo; ***M:*** Taj Mahal. Natl. Bd. of Review '72: Actress (Tyson); Natl. Soc. Film Critics '72: Actress (Tyson).

Soundman 1/2 **1999** Very black showbiz comedy about obsessive sound engineer Igby Walters (Pere) who manages to piss off anyone with any clout on his current movie job. As his life just gets worse, Igby's behavior becomes increasingly violent, including his arranging a musical audition for his violin-playing next-door neighbor (Chappuis)—at gunpoint. **105m/C VHS, DVD.** Wayne Pere, William Forsythe, Wes Studi, Eliane Chappuis, Nick Stahl, Tamlyn Tomita, Danny Trejo, John Koyama; ***D:*** Steven Ho; ***W:*** Steven Ho; ***C:*** David Aubrey.

Sounds of Silence **1991** A young deaf boy fears that a killer arsonist may be at large—but can he prove it? One of a number of obscure oddities featuring former youth idol Donahue. **108m/C VHS.** Kristen Jensen, Dennis Castillo, Troy Donahue, Peter Nelson; ***D:*** Peter Borg; ***W:*** Peter Borg; ***C:*** Mats Hallesjo; ***M:*** Martin Brandqvist.

Soup for One 1/2 **1982 (R)** Writer-director Kaufer's first film is a solid entry in the Woody Allen-esque Manhattanite's angst genre. Young Jewish guy Rubinek pines for the woman of his dreams, finds her, is rejected, persists, gets her, wonders if she's what he wants after all. If you like Woody Allen, this is worth seeing. **84m/C VHS.** Saul Rubinek, Marcia Strassman, Gerrit Graham, Richard Libertini, Andrea Martin; ***D:*** Jonathan Kaufer.

Sour Grapes 🦴🦴 **1998 (R)** "Seinfeld" co-creator David's feature directorial debut has cousins Evan and Richie (Weber and Bierko) feuding over an Atlantic City slot machine jackpot. Evan, a successful neurosurgeon lends Richie, an extroverted loser, two quarters for one last pull on the slots. Of course, Richie wins $400,000. Escalating revenge schemes, petty greed, and quirky small talk scream sitcom episode, as do the TV quality production values, and lighting. The dialogue is biting and clever, but on the whole there's not enough here to justify 90 minutes of screen time. Robyn Peterman, the real-life daughter of J. Peterman, plays Richie's girlfriend. If you liked "Seinfeld," this flick's for you. **91m/C VHS, DVD.** Jack Kehler, Steven Weber, Craig Bierko, Karen Sillas, Matt Keeslar, Robyn Peterman, Jennifer Leigh Warren, Richard Gant, James MacDonald, Philip Baker Hall, Ann Guilbert; ***D:*** Larry David; ***W:*** Larry David; ***C:*** Victor Hammer.

Sourdough 🦴🦴 **1977** Fur trapper Perry escapes the hustle and bustle of modern life by fleeing to the Alaskan wilderness. Near-plotless travelog depends heavily on scenery—and there's plenty of that, for sure. **94m/C VHS.** Gil Perry, Charles Brock, Slim Carlson, Carl Clark; ***D:*** Martin J. Spinelli.

Sous Sol 🦴🦴 *Not Me* **1996** In 1967 Montreal, overly sensitive 11-year-old Rene (Moffatt) spies on his parents while they make love and the next morning learns his father has died. Rene becomes certain that sex leads to death, which puts a crimp in his budding sexuality. As a matter of fact he literally refuses to grow up, remaining in his pre-adolescent state for several years while Mom Reine (Portal) eventually hooks up with a new boyfriend Roch (Godin), who moves in. This causes a few more problems for Rene. French with subtitles. **90m/C VHS.** *CA* Louise Portal, Richard Moffatt, Isabelle Pasco, Patrice Godin; ***D:*** Pierre Gang; ***W:*** Pierre Gang; ***C:*** Pierre Mignot; ***M:*** Anne Bourne, Ken Myhr. Genie '96: Orig. Screenplay.

South Beach 🦴🦴 **1992 (R)** Two ex-football players turned private eyes are living the good life and partying it up in Miami Beach. However, their leisurely lifestyles are soon disrupted when they accept a mysterious challenge from the beautiful Vanity. **93m/C VHS, DVD.** Fred Williamson, Gary Busey, Vanity, Peter Fonda; ***D:*** Fred Williamson; ***W:*** Mark Montgomery; ***M:*** Joe Renzetti.

South Beach Academy 🦴 **1996 (R)** Eye candy focusing on a beach school that specializes in surfing, swimming, and volleyball rather than the usual academics. Maybe that's why the school's about to close—unless the lightly clad student body can come up with a plan to save their alma mater. **91m/C VHS.** Corey Feldman, Al Lewis, James Hong, Elizabeth Kaitan; ***D:*** Joe Esposito.

South Bronx Heroes 🦴 **1/2** *The Runaways; Revenge of the Innocents* **1985 (R)** A police officer helps two children when they discover their foster home is the headquarters for a pornography ring. **105m/C VHS, DVD.** Brendan Ward, Mario Van Peebles, Megan Van Peebles, Melissa Esposito, Martin Zurla, Jordan Abeles; ***D:*** William Szarka; ***W:*** William Szarka, Don Shiffrin; ***C:*** Eric Schmitz; ***M:*** Al Zima.

South Central 🦴🦴 **1992 (R)** A low-budget urban drama set in a gang-infested L.A. neighborhood. Bobby is a young black man, and former gang leader, who has spent ten years in prison for murder. His wife has become a drug addict and his young son Jimmie has begun running with his dad's old gang. Now paroled, Bobby hopes to re-establish the bond with his son—enough to protect him from following in his nowhere-to-go-but-down footsteps. Worthy effort with an emotional ending. Feature debut of director Anderson. Based on the novel "Crips" by Donald Bakeer. **99m/C VHS, DVD.** Glenn Plummer, Carl Lumbly, Christian Coleman, LaRita Shelby, Byron Keith Minns; ***D:*** Steve (Stephen M.) Anderson; ***W:*** Steve (Stephen M.) Anderson; ***C:*** Charlie Lieberman; ***M:*** Tim Truman.

South of Heaven, West of Hell 🦴 **1/2 2000 (R)** A marshal (Yoakam), who once ran with an outlaw clan, must deal with his past when the bandits show up to terrorize the Arizona town he's sworn to protect. Yoakam's not much of a leading man and there's a lot of brutal violence to contend with. **133m/C VHS, DVD.** Dwight Yoakam, Bridget Fonda, Vince Vaughn, Billy Bob Thornton, Peter Fonda, Bud Cort, Michael Jeter, Paul (Pee-wee Herman) Reubens; ***D:*** Dwight Yoakam; ***W:*** Dwight Yoakam; ***C:*** James Glennon; ***M:*** Dwight Yoakam.

South of Hell Mountain 🦴 **1/2 1970 (R)** On the run from a gold mine robbery where they left 20 dead, the McHenry brothers meet a mother-daughter team that slows them down. **87m/C VHS.** Ann Stewart, Sam Hall, Nicol Britton; ***D:*** William Sachs, Louis Leahman.

South of Monterey 🦴 **1/2 1947** Western adventure with the Cisco kid. **63m/B VHS.** Gilbert Roland, Martin Garralaga, Frank Yaconelli, Marjorie (Reardon) Riordan; ***D:*** William Nigh.

South of Pago Pago 🦴🦴 **1/2 1940** The unsuspecting natives of a tropical isle are exploited by a gang of pirates searching for a seabed of rare pearls. A notch up from most similar adventure outings, with great violent action and excellent cinematography. Leading lady Farmer was thought to be a rising star, but retired at 29 in 1942 because of alcoholism and spent some time in mental institutions. "Frances" (1982), with Jessica Lange, is based on her life. **98m/B VHS.** Victor McLaglen, Jon Hall, Frances Farmer, Gene Lockhart; ***D:*** Alfred E. Green.

South of Pico 🦴🦴 **2007 (R)** Ensemble drama. The lives of a chauffeur, waitress, doctor, and teenaged boy all change when they witness the same tragedy on L.A.'s Pico Boulevard, and their disparate characters bond over their shared moment. **106m/C DVD.** Kip Pardue, Henry Simmons, Gina Torres, Soren Fulton, Paul Hipp, Jimmy Bennett, Christina Hendricks; ***D:*** Ernst Gossner; ***W:*** Ernst Gossner; ***C:*** Richard Marcus; ***M:*** John Swihart.

South of Reno 🦴🦴 **1/2 1987 (R)** A man living a secluded life in the desert dreams of moving to Reno and learns his wife is cheating on him. Odd, minimal plot. Impressive first feature for Polish diretor Rezyka, who cut his teeth on music videos. **98m/C VHS.** Jeffery Osterhage, Lisa Blount, Joe Estevez, Lewis Van Bergen, Julia Montgomery, Brandis Kemp, Danitza Kingsley, Mary Grace Canfield, Bert Remsen; ***D:*** Mark Rezyka; ***M:*** Nigel Holton.

South of St. Louis 🦴🦴 **1/2 1948** A peaceful cattle rancher turns renegade gunrunner during the Civil War when his stock is destroyed by Union guerrillas. Overplotted but exciting and action-packed western, with Smith dazzling in a plethora of costumes. **88m/C VHS.** Joel McCrea, Zachary Scott, Victor Jory, Douglas Kennedy, Alexis Smith, Alan Hale, Dorothy Malone; ***D:*** Ray Enright; ***C:*** Karl Freund; ***M:*** Max Steiner.

South of Santa Fe 🦴🦴 **1932** Mexican rebels give the hero a hard time in this standard Western. **60m/B VHS.** Bob Steele, Janis Elliott, Chris-Pin (Ethier Crispin Martini) Martin, Jack Clifford, Eddie Dunn, Robert Burns, Hank Bell, Allan Garcia; ***D:*** Bert Glennon.

South of Santa Fe 🦴🦴 **1942** Rogers and friends take on the mob—yes, the mob, armed with machine guns and airplanes—after they are falsely implicated in a crime. In lulls between the rootin' tootin' gunfights, Rogers belts out "We're Headin' for the Home Corral," "Down the Trail," and "Open Range Ahead." **60m/B VHS.** Roy Rogers, George "Gabby" Hayes, Linda Hayes, Paul Fix, Judy Clark; ***D:*** Joseph Kane.

South of the Border 🦴🦴 **1939** Autry and Burnette are government agents sent to Mexico to investigate a possible revolution instigated by foreign agents. Propaganda-heavy singing western appeared just before the U.S. entered WWII; did well at the box-office and boosted Autry's career. **70m/B VHS, DVD.** Gene Autry, Smiley Burnette, June Storey, Lupita Tovar, Mary Lee, Duncan Renaldo, William Farnum, Frank Reicher; ***D:*** George Sherman; ***W:*** Betty Burbridge, Gerald Geraghty; ***C:*** William Nobles.

South of the Rio Grande 🦴 **1/2 1945** The Cisco Kid rides again as he comes to the aid of a rancher whose horses were stolen. Garden-variety law-and-order western. **60m/B VHS.** Duncan Renaldo; ***D:*** Lambert Hillyer.

South Pacific 🦴🦴🦴 **1/2 1958** A young American Navy nurse and a Frenchman fall in love during WWII. Expensive production included much location shooting in Hawaii. Based on Rodgers and Hammerstein's musical; not as good as the play, but pretty darn good still. The play in turn was based on James Michener's novel "Tales of the South Pacific." ♫ My Girl Back Home; Dites-Moi; Bali Ha'i; Happy Talk; A Cockeyed Optimist; Soliloquies; Some Enchanted Evening; Bloody Mary; I'm Gonna Wash That Man Right Out of My Hair. **167m/C VHS, DVD.** Mitzi Gaynor, Rossano Brazzi, Ray Walston, France Nuyen, John Kerr, Juanita Hall, Tom Laughlin; ***D:*** Joshua Logan; ***W:*** Paul Osborn; ***C:*** Leon Shamroy; ***M:*** Richard Rodgers, Oscar Hammerstein; ***V:*** Giorgio Tozzi. Oscars '58: Sound.

South Park: Bigger, Longer and Uncut 🦴🦴 **1/2 1999 (R)** The most unlikely critical darling of the summer of 1999 caught everyone's attention with it's MPAA-baiting language and sexual subject matter, and made audiences laugh—a lot—along the way. Stan, Kenny, Cartman, and Kyle sneak into an R-rated movie and shock their families with what they learn. So, concerned South Park parents form a censorship board to take on Canada (which results in a war, with enough bloody violence to make Sam Peckinpah sick, but didn't faze the MPAA), and the kids decide to fight back. Like most TV shows adapted for the big screen, this one flags at times, but has enough inspired comic moments to (mostly) justify the hype. The easily offended should definitely pass. **80m/C VHS, DVD.** ***D:*** Trey Parker; ***W:*** Trey Parker, Matt Stone, Pam Brady; ***M:*** Marc Shaiman, Trey Parker; ***V:*** Trey Parker, Matt Stone, Isaac Hayes, George Clooney, Minnie Driver, Mike Judge, Eric Idle, Mary Kay Bergman, Brent Spiner, Nick Rhodes, Stewart Copeland.

South Riding 🦴🦴 **1/2 1937** Estate owner Robert Carne (Richardson) lives with teenaged daughter Midge (Johns) and has money woes from keeping ill wife Madge (Todd) in a mental hospital. A city councilman as well, Carne's drawn into a plan that will supposedly built decent housing for the lower classes but is actually a scam (which he discovers). Adapted from the novel by Winifred Holtby. **85m/B VHS.** *GB* Ralph Richardson, John Clements, Edna Best, Glynis Johns, Ann Todd, Edmund Gwenn, Marie Lohr, Milton Rosmer; ***D:*** Victor Saville; ***W:*** Ian Dalrymple; ***C:*** Harry Stradling Sr.; ***M:*** Richard Addinsell.

South Sea Sinner 🦴🦴 **1/2 1950** Jake Davis (Carey) is wandering the South Seas after being framed on a gun-smuggling charge and comes across the bar of Coral (Winters), a gorgeous singer men can't keep their eyes off of. Coral is forced by her boss to spy on Jake but the more time the two spend together the higher the flame grows and the more dangerous the game becomes. Respectable remake of Marlene Dietrich and John Wayne's "Seven Sinners." Features Liberace in his film debut as 'Maestro.' **88m/B VHS.** MacDonald Carey, Shelley Winters, Luther Adler, Frank Lovejoy; ***D:*** H. Bruce Humberstone; ***W:*** Oscar Brodney. **VIDEO**

South Sea Woman 🦴🦴 **1/2 1953** Nightclub tootsie Ginger Martin (Mayo) testifies at the court-martial of Marine Sgt. James O'Hearn (Lancaster). Seems he and buddy Pvt. Davy White (Connors) met the stranded Ginger in Shanghai just before Pearl Harbor. O'Hearn tries to prevent the impulsive White from marrying her and the trio wind up on the Vichy French island of Namou, where O'Hearn discovers some Nazis plotting evil. There's derring-do and various heroics but O'Hearn doesn't make it back to his unit in time and gets accused of desertion—hence the trial. Good action and a light touch—there's more comedy than angst. **99m/B DVD.** Burt Lancaster, Virginia Mayo, Chuck Connors, Barry Kelley, Hayden Rorke, Bob Sweeney, Leon Askin; ***D:*** Arthur Lubin; ***W:*** Earl Baldwin, Edwin Blum, Stanley Shapiro; ***C:*** Ted D. McCord; ***M:*** David Buttolph.

South Seas Massacre **WOOF!** *South Seas* **1974** A cop and a prisoner, shackled together, try to survive modern-day pirates, natives, and each other. They may make it through, but viewers may wish they didn't. **60m/C VHS.** *PH* Dania Ramirez, Juneo Jennings, Vic Vargas, Troy Donahue; ***D:*** Pablo Santiago; ***W:*** Leo Martinez; ***C:*** Joe Batac.

Southern Belles 🦴🦴 **2005 (R)** Hare-brained-but-likeable trailer park chicks Bell (Breckenridge) and Belle (Faris) want to escape their dull lives in rural Georgia to start anew in the "big city" of Atlanta. But they need some quick cash to get there so they concoct a half-baked plan that is interrupted by Bell's affections toward a policeman named Rhett Butler (Chambers). **90m/C DVD.** Anna Faris, Justin Chambers, Frederick Weller, Heather Goldenhersch, Laura Breckenridge; ***D:*** Paul S. Myers, Brennan Shroff; ***W:*** Paul S. Myers, Brennan Shroff. **VIDEO**

Southern Comfort 🦴🦴🦴 **1981 (R)** A group of National Guardsmen are on weekend maneuvers in the swamps of Louisiana. They run afoul of some of the local Cajuns, and are marked for death in this exciting and disturbing thriller. Boothe is excellent in a rare exploration of a little-understood way of life. Lots of blood. If you belong to the National Guard, this could make you queasy. **106m/C VHS, DVD.** Powers Boothe, Keith Carradine, Fred Ward, Franklyn Seales, Brion James, T.K. Carter, Peter Coyote, Ned Dowd, Lewis Smith, Les Lannom, Alan Autry, Sonny Landham; ***D:*** Walter Hill; ***W:*** Walter Hill, David Giler, Michael Kane; ***C:*** Andrew Laszlo; ***M:*** Ry Cooder.

Southern Man 🦴🦴 **1999** Turgid, undernourished drama revolves around an actor (Withers) who goes back to Nashville from Los Angeles to work out childhood problems involving sexual abuse. **104m/C DVD.** Mark Withers, Ellia Vierling, Jesse Head, Leigh Rose, Jack Betts; ***D:*** Rick Rosenberg; ***W:*** Rick Rosenberg, Robert Northup; ***C:*** Ken Glassing; ***M:*** Matthew Ferrado.

A Southern Yankee 🦴🦴 **1/2** *My Hero* **1948** Skelton plays a bumbling bellboy who ends up as a Union spy during the Civil War. Enjoyable comedy, thanks largely to the off-screen input of Buster Keaton. **90m/B VHS.** Red Skelton, Brian Donlevy, Arlene Dahl, George Coulouris, Lloyd Gough, John Ireland, Minor Watson, Charles Dingle, Art Baker, Reed Hadley, Arthur Space, Addison Richards, Joyce Compton, Paul Harvey, Jeff Corey; ***D:*** Edward Sedgwick.

The Southerner 🦴🦴🦴🦴 **1945** A man used to working for others is given some land by an uncle and decides to pack up his family and try farming for himself. They find hardships as they struggle to support themselves. A superb, naturalistic celebration of a family's fight to survive amid all the elements. From the story "Hold Autumn in Your Hand," by George Sessions Perry. Novelist Faulkner had an uncredited hand in the script. He thought Renoir the best contemporary director, and later said "The Southerner" gave him more pleasure than any of his other Hollywood work (though this is faint praise; Faulkner is said to have hated Hollywood). **91m/B VHS, DVD.** Zachary Scott, Betty Field, Beulah Bondi, Norman Lloyd, Bunny Sunshine, Jay Gilpin, Estelle Taylor, Blanche Yurka, Percy Kilbride, J. Carrol Naish; ***D:*** Jean Renoir; ***W:*** Jean Renoir, Hugo Butler, William Faulkner; ***C:*** Lucien N. Andriot; ***M:*** Werner Janssen. Natl. Bd. of Review '45: Director (Renoir); Venice Film Fest. '46: Film.

Southie 🦴🦴 **1998 (R)** Another return of the native son drama offers some decent performances but nothing much that is new. Danny Quinn (Wahlberg) is a South Boston bad boy returning to home turf after a sojourn in New York. Danny's pals are tied up with one Irish gangster crew while his own family is involved with oldtimer Colie (Tierney) and Danny himself has a score to settle with longtime rival, Joey (Cummings). **95m/C VHS, DVD.** Donnie Wahlberg, Rose McGowan, Lawrence Tierney, James (Jimmy) Cummings, Anne Meara, Amanda Peet, John Shea; ***D:*** John Shea; ***W:*** James (Jimmy) Cummings, John Shea, Dave McLaughlin; ***C:*** Allen Baker; ***M:*** Wayne Sharp.

Southland Tales 🦴 **1/2 2006 (R)** The U.S. is now monitored by a Big Brother-esque agency called US-IDENT, but revolutionaries in World War III-era Los Angeles are plotting to turn popular opinion against the government. Meanwhile, right-wing action star Boxer Santaros (Johnson) has lost his memory and has started an affair with porn actress-turned-talk show host Krysta Now (Gellar), which is somehow connected to the anti-government plot and the presidential election, in which his father-in-law (Osborne) is the Republican vice presidential candidate. Oh, and Justin Timberlake guards a pier against terrorist invaders while (mis)quoting T.S. Eliot and Revelations. Kelly's twisted, convoluted sci-fi black comedy is, at best, difficult to follow, with far more questions than it answers. When the movie works, it's an entertaining, absurdist post-9/11 farce; when it doesn't, it verges on incomprehensible. Kelly trimmed 19 minutes after the film was booed at Cannes. **144m/C DVD.** *US* Dwayne "The Rock" Johnson, Sarah Michelle Gellar, Seann William Scott, Curtis Armstrong, Nora Dunn, Wood Harris, John Larroquette, Mandy Moore, Holmes Osborne, Miranda Richardson, Justin Timberlake; ***D:*** Richard Kelly; ***W:*** Richard Kelly; ***C:*** Steven Poster; ***M:*** Moby.

Southward Ho! 𝒮𝒮 **1939** In the first western to team Rogers with sidekick Gabby Hayes, they portray ranchers investigating bloodshed in their valley, Roy meanwhile yodelin' four tunes. Fun outing. **56m/B VHS, DVD.** Roy Rogers, George "Gabby" Hayes, Lynne Roberts, Wade Boteler, Arthur Loft, Lane Chandler, Tom London; ***D:*** Joseph Kane; ***W:*** Gerald Geraghty; ***C:*** Jack Marta.

Souvenir 𝒮𝒮 **1988 (R)** A German soldier returns to France after WWII to find the woman he left behind and the daughter he never saw. Might have been good, but too melodramatic and overwrought, with lukewarm acting. **93m/C VHS, DVD.** Christopher Plummer, Catherine Hicks, Christopher Cazenove, Michael (Michel) Lonsdale; ***D:*** Geoffrey Reeve.

Soylent Green 𝒮𝒮 ½ **1973 (PG)** In the 21st Century, hard-boiled police detective Heston investigates a murder and discovers what soylent green—the people's principal food—is made of. Robinson's final film is a disappointing end to a great career. Its view of the future and of human nature is relentlessly dark. Don't watch it with kids. **95m/C VHS, DVD.** Charlton Heston, Leigh Taylor-Young, Chuck Connors, Joseph Cotten, Brock Peters, Paula Kelly, Edward G. Robinson, Stephen Young, Whit Bissell, Dick Van Patten; ***D:*** Richard Fleischer; ***W:*** Stanley R. Greenberg; ***C:*** Richard H. Kline; ***M:*** Fredric Myrow.

Space Buddies 𝒮𝒮 **2008 (G)** The never-ending franchise now finds those awww-so-cute golden retriever pups stuck aboard a spaceship and they're smart enough to realize that something about the mission isn't quite right. **84m/C DVD, Blu-ray Disc.** Diedrich Bader, Kevin Weisman; ***D:*** Robert Vince; ***W:*** Robert Vince, Anna McRoberts; ***C:*** Kamal Derkaoui; ***M:*** Brahm Wenger; ***V:*** Jason Earles, Bill Fagerbakke, Ali Hillis, Lochlyn Munro, Field Cate. **VIDEO**

Space Chimps 𝒮 ½ **2008 (G)** Circus chimp and slacker Ham III (Samberg)—grandson of first chimp in space, Ham I—is unwittingly recruited to retrieve a space probe that's gone AWOL. Accompanied by "real" astro-chimps Luna (Hines) and commander Titan (Warburton), the trio land on alien Zartog's (Daniels) planet looking to retrieve their probe, but that's not going to be so easy since Zartog has found a rather unique use for it. The trio embark on all sorts of madcap adventures on the alien planet, even while back on Earth there's talk of disbanding the space program entirely. The CGI chimps are kinda creepy, and the gags are just plain cheap. Even so, it's a relatively benign 81 minutes that at least the kiddies will enjoy. **81m/C DVD.** *US* ***D:*** Kirk De Micco; ***W:*** Kirk De Micco, Rob Moreland; ***C:*** Jerrica Cleland; ***M:*** David A. Stewart, Chris P. Bacon; ***V:*** Andy Samberg, Cheryl Hines, Patrick Warburton, Jeff Daniels, Stanley Tucci, Kristin Chenoweth, Kenan Thompson, Omid Abtahi, Patrick Breen, Kath Soucie, Jane Lynch, Zack Shada.

Space Cowboys 𝒮𝒮𝒮 **2000 (PG-13)** Eastwood, starring and directing again, plays a retired Air Force pilot who was passed over for the astronaut training program in the late 1950s. However, now NASA needs his expertise when an ailing 1960s satellite poses a threat if it crashes to Earth. He agrees to go into space and repair it only if he can bring his equally codgerly buddies, Sutherland, Jones, and Garner, to assist. Hey, if John Glenn can go back into space at age 77, why not Eastwood? Fun ensemble piece that successfully weaves some action and thrills into the final act. **123m/C VHS, DVD, Blu-ray Disc, HD DVD.** Clint Eastwood, Tommy Lee Jones, James Garner, James Cromwell, Donald Sutherland, Marcia Gay Harden, Loren Dean, William Devane, Rade Serbedzija, Courtney B. Vance, Barbara Babcock, Blair Brown; ***D:*** Clint Eastwood; ***W:*** Ken Kaufman, Howard Klausner; ***C:*** Jack N. Green; ***M:*** Lennie Niehaus.

Space Jam 𝒮𝒮 ½ **1996 (PG)** Expensive live action-animation combo finds basketball great Jordan forced to play ball against evil intergalatic invaders who are out to capture Bugs Bunny and the rest of the Looney Tunes characters. It's all fairly silly but the kids will enjoy it. **87m/C VHS, DVD.** Michael Jordan, Bill Murray, Wayne Knight, Theresa Randle; ***D:*** Joe Pytka; ***W:*** Leo Benvenuti; ***C:*** Michael Chapman; ***M:*** James Newton Howard; ***V:*** Danny DeVito.

Space Marines 𝒮 ½ **1996 (R)** Cheesy cable thriller finds intergalactic marines battling 21st century space pirates who've stolen a nuclear cargo and taken hostages. **93m/C VHS.** Billy Wirth, John Pyper-Ferguson, Meg Foster, Edward Albert, James Shigeta, Cady Huffman; ***D:*** John Weidner; ***C:*** Garett Griffin. **CABLE**

Space Master X-7 𝒮𝒮 *Blood Rust* **1958** Space satellite "Space Master X-7" returns to earth carrying a Martian fungus, which, in a lab mishap, reveals a creepy penchant for human blood. Tasting human blood and tissue, the "space rust" grows into a blubbery glob of oozing slime, claiming a lab scientist as its first victim just after the scientist and his ex have a nasty confrontation. On her way home to Honolulu, the ex sees a headline announcing the scientist's death—now she's on the lam, but she's also unwittingly spreading the deadly rust. **71m/B DVD.** Bill Williams, Lyn Thomas, Robert Ellis, Paul Frees; ***D:*** Edward L. Bernds; ***W:*** George Worthing Yates, Daniel Mainwaring; ***C:*** Brydon Baker; ***M:*** Josef Zimanich.

Space Monster WOOF! *First Woman into Space; Voyage beyond the Sun* **1964** Really bad, low-budget flick with a rubber monster and a climactic crash into a "sea of monsters" which is really a fish tank full of crabs. Ultra cheap production with handed down cast and props. **80m/B VHS.** Russ Bender, Francine York, James Brown, Baynes Barron; ***D:*** Marlin Skiles; ***W:*** Marlin Skiles; ***C:*** Leonard Katzman; ***M:*** Robert Tobey.

Space Mutiny 𝒮 **1988 (PG)** Spaceship falls under the attack of the mutinous Kalgan. To keep everyone from being sold into slavery, a small band of loyal passengers strike back. Will they be successful in thwarting the attack? Who cares? **93m/C VHS, DVD.** Reb Brown, James Ryan, John Phillip Law, Cameron Mitchell; ***D:*** David Winters; ***W:*** Maria Dante.

Space: 1999—Alien Attack 𝒮𝒮𝒮 **1979** After an explosion on the moon, Moonbase Alpha loses contact with Earth forever. Pilot episode of the popular British sci-fi series. **109m/C VHS.** *GB* Martin Landau, Barbara Bain, Barry Morse, Nick (Nicholas) Tate, Roy Dotrice, Philip Madoc, Lou Satton, Eric Carte; ***D:*** Lee H. Katzin.

Space Rage 𝒮 *Trackers* **1986 (R)** A criminal sentenced to life on a prison planet leads a revolt of the inmates. Lame, formula western set in outer space. **78m/C VHS.** Michael Pare, Richard Farnsworth, John Laughlin, Lee Purcell; ***D:*** Conrad Palmisano.

Space Raiders 𝒮𝒮 *Star Child* **1983 (PG)** A plucky 10-year-old blasts off into a futuristic world of intergalactic desperados, crafty alien mercenaries, starship battles and cliff-hanging dangers. Recycled special effects (from producer Corman's movie factory) and plot (lifted near-whole from "Star Wars"). **84m/C VHS.** Vince Edwards, David Mendenhall; ***D:*** Howard R. Cohen; ***W:*** Howard R. Cohen.

Space Riders WOOF! **1983 (PG)** Action-adventure about the world's championship motorcycle race, with a rock soundtrack featuring Duran Duran, Simple Minds and Melba Moore. **93m/C VHS.** Barry Sheene, Gavan O'Herlihy, Toshiya Ito, Stephanie McLean, Sayo Inaba; ***D:*** Joe Massot.

Space Soldiers Conquer the Universe 𝒮𝒮 **1940** Edited version of the Flash Gordon serial "Flash Gordon Conquers the Universe." The evil Emperor Ming introduces a horrible plague from outer space called "The Purple Death." Dr. Zarkov, Dale, and Flash Gordon travel from the frozen wastes of Frigia to the palaces of Mongo and must take risk after risk. Twelve chapters at 20 minutes each. **240m/B VHS.** Buster Crabbe, Charles Middleton, Carol Hughes; ***D:*** Ford Beebe, Ray Taylor; ***W:*** George Plympton, Basil Dickey, Barry Shipman; ***C:*** Jerome Ash, William Sickner.

Space Truckers 𝒮𝒮 **1997 (PG-13)** Sci-fi spoof about space haulage-truckers in the 21st century. Veteran hauler John Canyon (Hopper) accepts a dangerous assignment when he agrees to transport some sealed containers to Earth—no questions asked. Canyon, girlfriend Cindy (Mazar), and newbie driver Mike (Dorff) have their ship boarded by space pirates, led by Capt. Macaunudo (Dance), who's part-machine. The cargo turns out to be murderous androids, sent to conquer Earth. Canyon and his crew must perform various heroics to save the planet! Lots of campy bad taste. **97m/C VHS, DVD.** *IR* Dennis Hopper, Stephen Dorff, Charles Dance, Debi Mazar, George Wendt, Shane Rimmer, Vernon Wells, Barbara Crampton; ***D:*** Stuart Gordon; ***W:*** Ted Mann; ***C:*** Mac Ahlberg; ***M:*** Colin Towns.

Spaceballs 𝒮𝒮 ½ **1987 (PG)** A humorous Brooks parody of recent science fiction pictures, mostly notably "Star Wars," with references to "Alien," the "Star Trek series," and "The Planet of the Apes." Disappointingly tame and tentative, but chuckle-laden enough for Brooks fans. The great man himself appears in two roles, including puny wise man/wise guy Yogurt. **96m/C VHS, DVD.** Mel Brooks, Rick Moranis, John Candy, Bill Pullman, Daphne Zuniga, Dick Van Patten, John Hurt, George Wyner, Joan Rivers, Lorene Yarnell, Sal Viscuso, Stephen Tobolowsky, Dom DeLuise, Michael Winslow; ***D:*** Mel Brooks; ***W:*** Mel Brooks, Ronny Graham, Thomas Meehan; ***M:*** John Morris.

SpaceCamp 𝒮𝒮 **1986 (PG)** Gang o'teens and their instructor at the U.S. Space Camp are accidentally launched on a space shuttle, and then must find a way to return to Earth. Hokey plot, subpar special effects; why bother? Well, it is "inspirational." **115m/C VHS, DVD.** Kate Capshaw, Tate Donovan, Joaquin Rafael (Leaf) Phoenix, Kelly Preston, Larry B. Scott, Tom Skerritt, Lea Thompson, Terry O'Quinn; ***D:*** Harry Winer; ***M:*** John Williams.

Spaced Invaders 𝒮 ½ **1990 (PG)** Five ultra-cool aliens crash-land in a small midwestern town at Halloween. Local denizens mistake them for trick-or-treaters. Poorly made and a waste of time. **102m/C VHS, DVD.** Douglas Barr, Royal Dano, Ariana Richards, Kevin Thompson, Jimmy Briscoe, Tony Cox, Debbie Lee Carrington, Tommy Madden; ***D:*** Patrick Read Johnson; ***W:*** Scott Lawrence Alexander; ***C:*** James L. Carter.

Spaced Out WOOF! *Outer Reach* **1980 (R)** Naughty sci-fi sex comedy that parodies everything from "Star Wars" to "2001," though not very well. The sultry female aliens are visually pleasing, though. Watch this one with the sound turned off. **85m/C VHS, DVD.** Barry Stokes, Glory Annen; ***D:*** Norman J. Warren.

Spacehunter: Adventures in the Forbidden Zone 𝒮 ½ **1983 (PG)** Galactic bounty hunter agrees to rescue three damsels held captive by a cyborg. Strauss ain't no Harrison Ford. Filmed in 3-D, but who cares? **90m/C VHS, DVD.** *CA* Peter Strauss, Molly Ringwald, Michael Ironside, Ernie Hudson, Andrea Marcovicci; ***D:*** Lamont Johnson; ***W:*** Len Blum; ***C:*** Frank Tidy; ***M:*** Elmer Bernstein.

Spacejacked 𝒮 ½ **1998 (R)** In the future, the wealthy take pleasure trips to the Moon. Only greedy Barnes (Bernsen) sabotages the ship in order to extort money from the passengers—promising them a safe passage home in the escape pod. Of course, Barnes tries to double-cross everyone. Filled with low-budget cliches. **89m/C VHS, DVD.** Corbin Bernsen, Amanda Pays, Steve Bond; ***D:*** Jeremiah Cullinane; ***W:*** Brendan Broderick, Daniella Purcell; ***C:*** Laurence Manly; ***M:*** Siobhan Cleary.

Spaceship 𝒮 ½ *The Creature Wasn't Nice; Naked Space* **1981 (PG)** Misguided attempt to spoof creature-features. Mad scientist tries to protect kindly monster from crazed crew. Not very funny, with the exception of the song-and-dance routine by the monster. **88m/C VHS, DVD.** Cindy Williams, Bruce Kimmel, Leslie Nielsen, Gerrit Graham, Patrick Macnee, Ron Kurowski; ***D:*** Bruce Kimmel.

Spaceways 𝒮 ½ **1953** Scientist Duff is beset by all sorts of troubles: his experimental rockets explode, his wife has an affair with an ambitious scientist, and when they disappear together, he's accused of killing them and placing their bodies in the exploded rocket. All in all, a pretty bad (and long) day for our hero. Why should we suffer through it with him? **76m/B VHS, DVD.** Howard Duff, Eva Bartok, Ceclie Cheyreau, Andrew Osborn; ***D:*** Terence Fisher; ***W:*** Richard H. Landau, Paul Tabori; ***C:*** Reg Wyer; ***M:*** Ivor Stanley.

Spaghetti House 𝒮 ½ **1982** A handful of waiters are held hostage by ruthless killers in this innocuous but worthless Italian comedy. Dubbed. **103m/C VHS.** *IT* Nino Manfredi, Rita Tushingham; ***D:*** Giullo Paradisi.

Spaghetti Western 𝒮 ½ *Cipolla Colt* **1975 (PG)** A farmer and a publisher take on the vile oil baron who is taking over the town. A parody—or is it?—of Eastwoodian B-grade spaghetti westerns. No director credited. **92m/C VHS.** *IT SP* Franco Nero, Martin Balsam, Sterling Hayden, Dick Butkus, Leo Anchoriz, Romano Puppo, Emma Cohen; ***D:*** Enzo G. Castellari; ***W:*** Sergio Donati, Luciano Vincenzoni; ***C:*** Alejandro Ulloa; ***M:*** Guido de Angelis, Maurizio de Angelis.

Spalding Gray: Terrors of Pleasure 𝒮𝒮𝒮 **1988** The ultra-cool Gray tells the story of one man's dream to own land in his own inimitable way. HBO comedy special. **60m/C VHS.** Spalding Gray; ***D:*** Thomas Schlamme.

Spangles 𝒮 **1926** Silent circus drama. **58m/B VHS.** Marion (Marian) Nixon, Hobart Bosworth, Pat O'Malley, Gladys Brockwell; ***D:*** Frank O'Connor.

Spanglish 𝒮 ½ **2004 (PG-13)** Sandler plays a sweetheart of a hubby in Brooks's problematic social comedy. As celebrity chef John Clasky, he's loving and supportive despite the complete self-absorption of his disturbingly unpleasant wife, Deborah (Leoni). Even Deborah's live-in lush of a mother (Leachman) knows what a horror her daughter is. Into this unhappy household comes lovely Flor (Vega), a Mexican illegal (who doesn't yet speak English) who takes the job as housekeeper because it will offer a better life for her own daughter, Cristina (Bruce). Given John's marital circumstances, is it any wonder that he and Flor become increasingly simpatico? Sandler's sincere and Leoni is nothing if not gutsy but it hardly seems worth the effort. **129m/C VHS, DVD.** *US* Adam Sandler, Tea Leoni, Paz Vega, Cloris Leachman, Thomas Haden Church, Shelbie Bruce, Sarah Steele, Ian Hyland, Victoria Luna; ***D:*** James L. Brooks; ***W:*** James L. Brooks; ***C:*** John Seale; ***M:*** Hans Zimmer.

The Spaniard's Curse 𝒮𝒮 ½ **1958** When a man is convicted for a murder he did not commit, he puts a curse on the judge and jury responsible. Mysteriously, the marked people begin dying. Is he responsible? Then he dies and the mystery thickens. Intriguing but sloppy murder mystery. **80m/B VHS.** *GB* Tony Wright, Lee Patterson, Michael Hordern, Ralph Truman, Henry Oscar; ***D:*** Ralph Kemplen.

The Spanish Gardener 𝒮𝒮𝒮 **1957** A boy in a prominent family spends more time with the gentle gardner than with the domineering father, so dad arranges for his rival to be framed and sent to prison. An affecting British adaptation of the A.J. Cronin novel, turned into a showcase for Bogarde in the title role. **95m/C VHS.** Dirk Bogarde, Jon Whiteley, Michael Hordern, Cyril Cusack, Maureen Swanson, Lyndon Brook, Josephine Griffin, Bernard Lee; ***D:*** Philip Leacock.

Spanish Judges 𝒮 ½ **1999 (R)** Boring crime drama set in L.A. finds three criminals—muscle Max (D'Onofrio), brains Jack

(Lillard), and vamp Jamie (Golino)—looking to steal a couple of valuable Spanish pistols. Yes, it does sound roughly like the plot to "The Mexican" but this film is much worse. **98m/C VHS, DVD.** Vincent D'Onofrio, Matthew Lillard, Valeria Golino, Sam Hiona; ***D:*** Oz Scott; ***W:*** William Rehor; ***C:*** Stephen McNutt.

The Spanish Main 1/2 **1945** Typical, gusto-laden swashbuckler, RKO's first in Technicolor. Evil Spanish governor Slezak captures Dutch crew led by Henreid. They escape and kidnap his fiancee (O'Hara) off a ship coming from Mexico. Henreid forces her to marry him, but his crew uses the might of the armada and returns O'Hara to Slezak behind Henreid's back. Wow! **100m/C** Paul Henreid, Maureen O'Hara, Walter Slezak, Binnie Barnes, John Emery, Barton MacLane; ***D:*** Frank Borzage; ***C:*** George Barnes.

The Spanish Prisoner **1997 (PG)** Playwright-filmmaker Mamet goes Hitchcockian in thriller involving an elaborate con game. Naive inventor Joe Ross (Scott) develops a formula for something called "the Process" and soon finds himself a victim of industrial espionage. In a bit of stunt casting that works, Martin plays a sinister, wealthy businessman who befriends Joe and advises him about his coroprate employers. No one is what they appear to be (if they were, it wouldn't be much of a thriller) in this unpredictable and seductive puzzle. Although the staccato dialogue is grating at times, and the emotional payoff is slight, there's enough twists throughout to keep you intrigued. Title comes from an old scam that feeds on the greed and lust of the mark. **112m/C VHS, DVD.** Campbell Scott, Steve Martin, Rebecca Pidgeon, Ben Gazzara, Ricky Jay, Felicity Huffman, Ed O'Neill; ***D:*** David Mamet; ***W:*** David Mamet; ***C:*** Gabriel Beristain; ***M:*** Carter Burwell.

Spanking the Monkey **1994 (R)** "What'd ya do on your summer vacation?" Ray Aibelli (Davies) has an interesting answer in this dark comedy about family dysfunction, sexual politics, incest and masturbation, topics which guarantee it a special place on the video shelf. Returning from his freshman year at M.I.T., Ray learns he must give up a prestigious internship to care for his bedridden mother (Watson) while Dad goes on an extended "business" trip. Much sexual and emotional confusion follows. Mom, it seems, is rather attractive, controlling, and in need of hands-on assistance. Black comedy is understated and sensitive, focusing attention on the story and characters rather than the delicate subject matter, but you'll be aware of the delicate subject matter, nonetheless. Sharp directorial debut by Russell features fine performances by mostly unknown cast, elevating low-budget feel. See it with a relative. **99m/C VHS, DVD.** Jeremy Davies, Alberta Watson, Benjamin Hendrickson, Carla Gallo, Matthew Puckett; ***D:*** David O. Russell; ***W:*** David O. Russell; ***C:*** Mike Mayers. Ind. Spirit '95: First Feature, First Screenplay; Sundance '94: Aud. Award.

Spare Me 1/2 **1992** Family and personal dysfunction mark the long-awaited home video debut of Harrison's cult fave "bowling noir" film. Theo (Paseka) is put on suspension from the Pro Bowler's Tour for attacking an opponent with his bowling ball. He searches out his bowling-legend father, Buzz (Alfred), who might be able to help him out. Along the way he meets and falls for a pyromaniac waitress (MacFayden), whose father is evil bowling kingpin Miles Kastle, and her brother is escaped psycho patient Junior. When Theo finds Pop, he's in cahoots with Miles, helping him run an illegal midget bowling circuit. Harrison's excellent low-budget direction, and a hilarious, if completely twisted script, enables this one to pick up the difficult 7-10 split of cinematic success. **85m/C VHS.** Mark Alfred, Christopher Cooke, Lawton Paseka, Christopher Grimm, Christie MacFadyen, Richard W. Sears Jr., Bill Christ, Sean Haggerty; ***D:*** Matthew Harrison; ***W:*** Christopher Grimm; ***C:*** Mike Mayers; ***M:*** Danny Brenner.

Spare Parts WOOF! 1979 Guests at a remote hotel discover that it is run by black marketeers who kill guests and sell the body parts. Of course, they don't bother signing out. **108m/C VHS.** *GE* Judith Speidel, Wolf Roth; ***D:*** Rainer Erler; ***W:*** Rainer Erler; ***C:*** Wolfgang Grasshoff; ***M:*** Eugen Thomass.

Spark 1/2 **1998** Quarreling lovers Byron and Nina are stranded when their car breaks down in nowheresville. Stuck in a redneck dump while their ride is being fixed, the couple learns too many ugly local secrets. **102m/C DVD.** Terrence Howard, Nicole Ari Parker, Brendan Sexton III, Sandra Ellis Lafferty, Timothy McNeil; ***D:*** Garret Williams; ***W:*** Garret Williams; ***C:*** Samuel Ameen; ***M:*** Marc Anthony Thompson.

Sparkle 1/2 **1976 (PG)** The saga of three singing sisters struggling to rise to the top of the charts in the 1950s. Sound familiar? Well done but cliched fictional version of the Supremes' career. McKee shines. Alcohol, drugs, and mobsters get in the way. Excellent musical score. **98m/C VHS, DVD.** Irene Cara, Lonette McKee, Dwan Smith, Philip Michael Thomas, Mary Alice, Dorian Harewood, Tony King; ***D:*** Sam O'Steen; ***W:*** Joel Schumacher; ***M:*** Curtis Mayfield.

Sparkler 1/2 **1999 (R)** Effervescemt Melba May (Overall) is a trailer-park wife, living just off the highway to Vegas. She leaves husband, Flint (Harvey), for cheating on her and eventually winds up in Vegas with three young men she just met and her old high-school buddy Dottie (Cartwright), who's now a stripper. And everybody gets an education of sorts. Doesn't have a consistent tone, with Overall and Cartwright providing the best performances. **96m/C VHS, DVD.** Park Overall, Veronica Cartwright, Jamie Kennedy, Steven Petrarca, Freddie Prinze Jr., Don Harvey, Grace Zabriskie, Sandy Martin; ***D:*** Darren Stein; ***W:*** Darren Stein, Catherine Eads; ***C:*** Rodney Taylor; ***M:*** David E. Russo.

Sparrows **1926** Hidden in a southern swamp, the evil Grimes (von Seyffertz) runs a baby farm, where unwanted children are sent and used a slave labor. The eldest, nicknamed Mama Mollie (Pickford), tries to protect the others from Grimes's cruelty. They eventually plan their escape but must cross treacherous quicksand with Grimes in pursuit. Silent melodrama features a notable performance by Pickford. **109m/B VHS, DVD.** Mary Pickford, Gustav von Seyffertitz, Charlotte Mineau, Roy Stewart, Mary Louise Miller, "Spec" (Walter) O'Donnell, Mary Frances McLean, Camilla Johnson, Seesel Ann Johnson; ***D:*** William Beaudine; ***W:*** C. Gardner Sullivan, Winifred Dunn; ***C:*** Charles Rosher, Karl Struss, Hal Mohr; ***M:*** William Perry.

Spartacus **1960 (PG-13)** The true story of a gladiator who leads other slaves in a rebellion against the power of Rome in 73 B.C. The rebellion is put down and the rebels are crucified. Douglas, whose political leanings are amply on display herein, also served as executive producer, surrounding himself with the best talent available. Magnificent climactic battle scene features 8,000 real, live Spanish soldiers to stunning effect. A version featuring Kubrick's "director's cut" is also available, featuring a restored, controversial homoerotic bath scene with Olivier and Curtis. Anthony Mann is uncredited as co-director. A boxoffice triumph that gave Kubrick much-desired financial independence. **196m/C VHS, DVD, HD DVD.** Vinton (Hayworth) Haworth, Kirk Douglas, Laurence Olivier, Jean Simmons, Tony Curtis, Charles Laughton, Herbert Lom, Nina Foch, Woody Strode, Peter Ustinov, John Gavin, John Ireland, Charles McGraw, Joanna Barnes; ***D:*** Stanley Kubrick; ***W:*** Dalton Trumbo; ***C:*** Russell Metty; ***M:*** Alex North. Oscars '60: Art Dir./Set Dec., Color, Color Cinematog., Costume Des. (C), Support. Actor (Ustinov); Golden Globes '61: Film—Drama.

Spartan **2004 (R)** The president's daughter has been kidnapped—possibly by a Middle Eastern group of woman slave traders—and cagey special ops agent Robert Scott (Kilmer) is entrusted with the task of bringing her home. But, as with any Mamet venture, what seems to be the reality might not be and the deeper Scott gets into the job the less he can be certain of. His dilemma and the questions that swirl around make for high-octane action-thriller fun...until it sadly runs out of gas toward the end. Kilmer seizes the character along with the fundamentals of the smart, fast-paced language; Luke has a good turn (as Scott's trainee) as do perpetual Mamet performers Macy and O'Neill. **107m/C DVD.** *US* Val Kilmer, Derek Luke, Tia Texada, Kristen Bell, Johnny Messner, Lionel Mark Smith, Tony Mamet, Clark Gregg, Steven Culp, Aaron Stanford, Geoffrey Pierson, William H. Macy, Ed O'Neill, Andrew Davoli, Said Taghmaoui, Matt Malloy, Kick (Christopher) Gurry, David Paymer; ***D:*** David Mamet; ***W:*** David Mamet; ***C:*** Juan Ruiz-Anchia; ***M:*** Mark Isham.

Spasms WOOF! *Death Bite* **1982 (R)** Reed is the unfortunate big game hunter who encounters The Demon Serpent, known as N'Gana Simbu, the deadliest snake in the world. Lame-brained horror fantasy; the producers should have released the nifty Tangerine Dream soundtrack and chucked the movie. Based on the novel "Death Bite" by Michael Maryk and Brent Monahan. **92m/C VHS.** *CA* Peter Fonda, Oliver Reed, Kerrie Keane, Al Waxman, Miguel Fernandes, Marilyn Lightstone, Laurie Brown, Gerard Parkes; ***D:*** William Fruet; ***W:*** Don Enright.

Spawn **1997 (PG-13)** Government agent Al Simmons (White) returns to earth, six years after being murdered, in the form of Spawn, a hell-born creature with supernatural powers. He wants to avenge his death and also save his loved ones from the evil Violator (Leguizamo). With green eyes and a friendship with Satan, Spawn's more of a lethal weapon and way more sinister looking than the villain. An unrecognizable Leguizamo and sleazy Sheen team up as adequate adversaries. Extravagant special effects, and a complex, dark story put a unique spin on the over-exposed superhero premise. Adapted from the best-selling comic book. An R-rated director's cut, which includes a "making of" feature and an interview with Todd McFarlane, is also available. **97m/C VHS, DVD.** Michael (Mike) Papajohn, Michael Jai White, John Leguizamo, Martin Sheen, Theresa Randle, D.B. Sweeney, Nicol Williamson, Melinda (Mindy) Clarke, Miko Hughes; ***D:*** Mark Dippe; ***W:*** Alan B. McElroy; ***C:*** Guillermo Navarro; ***M:*** Graeme Revell.

Spawn of the North 1/2 **1938** Alaska's the final frontier in the early 1900s as fisherman Jim Kimmerlee (Fonda) tries to earn an honest buck. But former friend Tyler Dawson (Raft) has joined a group of Russian pirates who plunder the nets of others and the two men are forced into a deadly confrontation. Solid cast, weak script, and a special Oscar for photographic and sound effects (a glacier's involved). Based on the novel by Barrett Willoughby; remade in 1954 as "Alaska Seas." **110m/B VHS.** Henry Fonda, George Raft, Dorothy Lamour, John Barrymore, Akim Tamiroff, Louise Platt, Fuzzy Knight, Duncan Renaldo; ***D:*** Henry Hathaway; ***W:*** Jules Furthman, Talbot Jennings; ***C:*** Charles B(ryant) Lang Jr.; ***M:*** Dimitri Tiomkin.

Speak **2004 (PG-13)** Stewart gives an amazingly touching performance as Melinda Sordino, a high school freshman who has retreated into selective mutism after being raped at a summer party. Having called the cops on a popular senior, Melinda is now a social pariah, with her parents (Perkins, Sweeney) too preoccupied to recognize her anguish. But over the school year, her unconventional art teacher, Mr. Freeman (Zahn), shows Melinda that expressing herself is a way to confront her experience. Based on the novel by Laurie Halse Anderson. **93m/C DVD.** Kristen Stewart, Steve Zahn, Elizabeth Perkins, D.B. Sweeney, Hallee Hirsh, Eric Lively, Michael Angarano, Robert John Burke, Allison Siko; ***D:*** Jessica Sharzer; ***W:*** Jessica Sharzer, Annie Young; ***C:*** Andrij Parekh. **CABLE**

Speak Easily 1/2 **1932** Keaton is bored with his dull life as a college professor. Durante tries to spice things up with a phony inheritance letter, and Keaton decides to spend his supposed money backing a stage show. Keaton is the star, but Durante steals the show. Great supporting cast. **82m/B VHS, DVD.** Buster Keaton, Jimmy Durante, Ruth Selwyn, Thelma Todd, Hedda Hopper, Sidney Toler, Lawrence Grant, Henry Armetta, Edward Brophy; ***D:*** Edward Sedgwick.

Speak of the Devil **1990** A New Orleans evangelist who seduces his followers moves to Los Angeles and strikes a bargain with Satan. Exploitative, unthinking spoof of Swaggart/Bakker scandals of recent years. **99m/C VHS.** Gil Bottcher, Robert Elarton, Jean Miller, Bernice Tamara Goor, Louise Sherill, Walter Kay, Shawn Patrick Greenfield; ***D:*** Raphael Nussbaum; ***W:*** Raphael Nussbaum; ***C:*** Chuck Colwell.

Speak Up! It's So Dark *Tala! Det ar sa Morkt* **1993** Soren (Norrthon) is a skinhead who gets beaten up at a neo-Nazi rally. He meets Jewish shrink Jacob (Glaser) on a train and Jacob offers to tend to Soren's wounds. Although Soren continually parrots hateful doctrine, Jacob (whose family died at Auschwitz) tries to help him and Soren slowly begins to see he's wrong. Swedish with subtitles. **83m/C VHS.** *SW* Etienne Glaser, Simon Norrthon; ***D:*** Suzanne Osten; ***W:*** Niklas Radstrom; ***C:*** Peter Mokrosinski.

Speaking Parts **1989** VCR-obsessed laundry worker and another woman battle for the attention of bit-part actor McManus who works in ritzy hotel. A telling picture of the inextricable nature of modern technology. **92m/C VHS, DVD.** *CA* Michael McManus, Arsinee Khanjian, David Hemblen, Gabrielle Rose, Tony Nardi, Patricia Collins, Gerard Parkes; ***D:*** Atom Egoyan; ***W:*** Atom Egoyan; ***C:*** Paul Sarossy; ***M:*** Mychael Danna.

Special 1/2 **2006 (R)** Comic book fan Les (Rapaport) is a completely average L.A. working guy. He's accepted into an experimental drug program designed to overcome depression but the side effects have Les believing he's turned into a vigilante superhero. Now delusional, Les is not only a danger to himself but to others. **82m/C DVD.** Michael Rapaport, Paul Blackthorne, Josh Peck, Robert Baker, Jack Kehoe, Alexandra Holden, Ian Bohen; ***D:*** Hal Haberman, Jeremy Passmore; ***W:*** Hal Haberman, Jeremy Passmore; ***C:*** Nelson Craig; ***M:*** Tom Wolfe, Manish Raval.

Special Bulletin **1983** A pacifistic terrorist threatens to blow up Charleston, South Carolina, with a nuclear warhead. Done quite well in docu-drama style as a TV news bulletin. Interesting examination of the media's treatment of dramatic events. Top-notch made-for-TV fare. **105m/C VHS.** Ed Flanders, Christopher Allport, Kathryn Walker, Roxanne Hart; ***D:*** Edward Zwick; ***W:*** Marshall Herskovitz, Edward Zwick. **TV**

A Special Day *Una Giornata Speciale; The Great Day* **1977** The day of a huge rally celebrating Hitler's visit to Rome in 1939 serves as the backdrop for an affair between weary housewife Loren and lonely, unhappy homosexual radio announcer Mastroianni. Good performances from two thorough pros make a depressing film well worth watching. In Italian with English subtitles or dubbed. **105m/C VHS, DVD.** *IT* Sophia Loren, Marcello Mastroianni, John Vernon, Francoise Berd; ***D:*** Ettore Scola; ***W:*** Ettore Scola, Ruggero Maccari, Maurizio Costanzo; ***C:*** Pasqualino De Santis; ***M:*** Armando Trovajoli. Golden Globes '78: Foreign Film.

Special Delivery 1/2 **1976 (PG)** Three unemployed Vietnam veterans decide to rob a bank but their getaway plans go awry. Svenson, the only robber who escapes, stashes the cash in a mailbox only to have it discovered by nutty artist, Shepherd, and crooked barkeep Gwynne. **99m/C VHS.** Bo Svenson, Cybill Shepherd, Vic Tayback, Michael C. Gwynne, Tom Atkins, Sorrell Booke, Deidre Hall, Gerrit Graham, Jeff Goldblum; ***D:*** Paul Wendkos; ***C:*** Harry Stradling Jr.; ***M:*** Lalo Schifrin.

Special Effects **1985 (R)** A desperate movie director murders a young actress, then makes a movie about her death. Solid, creepy premise sinks in the mire of flawed execution; a good film about Hollywood ego trips and obsession is lurking inside overdone script. **103m/C VHS, DVD.** *GB* Zoe Tamerlis, Eric Bogosian, Kevin J. O'Connor, Brad Rijn, Bill Oland, Richard Greene; ***D:*** Larry Cohen; ***W:*** Larry Cohen.

Special Forces *Hell in Normandy* **1968** Eight specially trained soldiers drop behind enemy lines to rescue prisoners of war in WWII. **90m/C VHS, DVD.** *IT* Peter Lee Lawrence, Guy Madison, Erika Blanc, Tony Norton; ***D:*** Alfonso Brescia; ***W:*** Maurice De Vries, Lorenzo Gicca Palli; ***C:*** Fausto Rossi; ***M:*** Italo Fischetti.

Special Forces 1/2 **2003 (R)** American photojournalist Wendy Teller (Deutscher) stumbles across war crimes in a fictitious Eastern European country and is held hostage. A team of Army commandos is sent in to rescue her and their leader (Teague) happens to have a past with the head bad guy

(Danker). **96m/C DVD.** Marshall Teague, Tim Abell, Eli Danker, Scott Adkins, Daniella Deutscher, Danny Lee Clark; ***D:*** Isaac Florentine; ***W:*** David N. White; ***C:*** Gideon Porath; ***M:*** Stephen (Steve) Edwards. **VIDEO**

Special Investigator ✂✂ 1/2 **1936** Dix is a criminal attorney who specializes in getting his mob clients freed. Then his FBI brother gets killed by the same criminals he's been defending. So Dix becomes a special agent and sets out to get the mob boss responsible for his brother's murder. Climax is the big shootout at the gang's hideaway. Based on the novel by Earle Stanley Gardner. **60m/B VHS.** Richard Dix, J. Carroll Naish, Margaret Callahan, Erik Rhodes, Owen Davis Jr., Ray Mayer, Joseph (Joe) Sawyer; ***D:*** Louis King.

Special Olympics **1978** A father attempts to care for his three sons, one of whom is mentally retarded, following the death of his wife. **104m/C VHS.** Charles Durning, Philip Brown, George Parry, Irene Tedrow, Mare Winningham, Herb Edelman, Debra Winger, Constance McCashin; ***D:*** Lee Philips. **TV**

Special Police ✂✂ 1/2 **1985** Police inspector protecting old friend's murder-witnessing sister learns that important politicians are involved with a seedy underground political movement. French thriller also available dubbed. **92m/C VHS.** *FR* Richard Berry, Carole Bouquet, Fanny Cottencon; ***D:*** Michael Vianey; ***W:*** Michael Vianey.

Special Unit 2002 ✂✂ *2002* **2001** Chiu (Nicholas Tse) is a psychic battling ghosts for the Hong Kong Police Department with the aid of a ghostly partner. Since it's time for his friend to reincarnate, Chiu gets a new partner—who everyone loathes to tell is doomed to be killed and become a ghost himself. Fortunately for Chiu his new partner is distracted by a vengeful water spirit out to murder them both. A mix of comedy, CGI effects, and wire-fu should be entertaining for most HK fans. **91m/C DVD.** *HK* Nicholas Tse, Stephen Fung, Kar-Ying Law, Rain Li, Sam Lee, Danielle Graham, Anya, Lik-Sun Fong; ***D:*** Wilson (Wai-Shun) Yip; ***W:*** Wilson (Wai-Shun) Yip, Vincent Kok, Chi-kin Kwok, Kam-yuen Szeto; ***C:*** Hang-Seng Poon; ***M:*** Tommy Wai.

The Specialist ✂ 1/2 **1975 (R)** Lawyer West thinks he has seduced stunning Capri, but she has lured him into her clutches—she's been hired to kill him. Campy crud. It's old home week for '60s TV alums: West was Batman; bailiff Moore was Mr. Kimbell on Green Acres. **93m/C VHS, DVD.** Adam West, John Anderson, Ahna Capri, Alvy Moore; ***D:*** Howard (Hikmet) Avedis; ***W:*** Howard (Hikmet) Avedis, Marlene Schmidt, Ralph B. Potts; ***C:*** Massoud Joseph; ***M:*** Shorty Rogers.

The Specialist ✂ 1/2 **1994 (R)** Buffed bods do not a movie make—at least not in this mechanical actioner featuring Stone as the revenge-minded May Munro. Seems May's parents were killed by Cuban gangsters, led by father/son thugs Joe (Steiger) and Tomas Leon (Roberts), and she decides ex-CIA bomb specialist Ray Quick (Stallone) is just the man she needs to settle the score. But Quick has his own reasons for accepting—his ex-partner is nutball Ned Trent (Woods), who's now working for the Leons. Things blow up a lot, the two leads show off their toned flesh (but not much acting), and Woods gets to steal the movie with his amusing scenery chewing. **110m/C VHS, DVD.** Sylvester Stallone, Sharon Stone, James Woods, Eric Roberts, Rod Steiger; ***D:*** Luis Llosa; ***W:*** Alexandra Seros; ***C:*** Jeffrey L. Kimball; ***M:*** John Barry. Golden Raspberries '94: Worst Actress (Stone).

The Specials ✂✂✂ **2000** This is the movie that "Mystery Men" wanted to be. It's a smart comic book spoof that depends on good acting and well-written characters. The Specials are the sixth or seventh greatest team of superheroes in the business. Headquarters is a suburban house in Silver Lake. Their immediate goal—if they can quit bickering among themselves—it to get a line of action figures on the market. **89m/C DVD.** Rob Lowe, Jamie Kennedy, Thomas Haden Church, Paget Brewster, Judy Greer, James Gunn, Sean Gunn, Jordan Ladd, Kelly Coffield; ***D:*** Craig Mazin; ***W:*** James Gunn; ***C:*** Eliot Rockett; ***M:*** Brian Langsbard, Spring Aspers.

Species ✂✂ 1/2 **1995 (R)** A "friendly" galactic message containing a recipe on how to combine extraterrestrial DNA with human DNA is sent to scientists on Earth. The scientists, led by Fitch (Kingsley), whip up a batch of genetic material resulting in a sexy half alien, half human procreating/killing machine named Sil (model Henstridge's film debut). Naturally, Sil escapes from the lab, leaving the scientists with the unenviable task of catching her/it. All-star special effects team, including "Alien" designer H. R. Giger, create over-the-top, stomach-churning thrills. Dips liberally into the tricks of many sci-fi classics. For avid gore-meisters only. **108m/C VHS, DVD, Blu-ray Disc, UMD.** Ben Kingsley, Michael Madsen, Alfred Molina, Forest Whitaker, Marg Helgenberger, Natasha Henstridge, Michelle Williams; ***D:*** Roger Donaldson; ***W:*** Dennis Feldman; ***C:*** Andrzej Bartkowiak; ***M:*** Christopher Young. MTV Movie Awards '96: Kiss (Natasha Henstridge/Anthony Guidera).

Species 2 ✂ 1/2 **1998 (R)** Genetic scientists, in their quest to see an actual babe who will talk to genetic scientists, create a clone named Eve (Henstridge) from the monster in the original movie. Meanwhile, the U.S. has managed to successfully put an underwear model who can't act on Mars. Astronaut Patrick Ross (Lazard) has been infected with spores of alien DNA. Soon Ross' urge to procreate takes over and nasty alien babies are exploding out of screaming women all over town Government assassin Press Lennox (Madsen) and Dr. Laura Baker (Helgenberger) are once again called in to help track down the new species, with the help of Eve. Can they stop Ross and his brood before they mature? Can they stop Eve and Ross from making the beast with several scaly slimy multi-appendaged backs? Can they please stop making this movie again? **95m/C VHS, DVD.** Natasha Henstridge, Justin Lazard, Michael Madsen, Marg Helgenberger, Mykelti Williamson, George Dzundza, James Cromwell, Myriam Cyr, Baxter Harris; ***D:*** Peter Medak; ***W:*** Chris Brancato; ***C:*** Matthew F. Leonetti; ***M:*** Ed Shearmur.

Species 3 ✂✂ **2004 (R)** Eve has a daughter as she's dying and that girl, Sara (Mabrey), a genetically superior specimen, is out to mate with humans to propogate her species. She is pursued by a military team, a group of half-breed aliens with a fatal defect, and the professor who wants to experiment on her DNA. Lots of female nudity is supposed to make up for an extremely low budget and convoluted story. Surprisingly, it doesn't. **112m/C DVD.** Natasha Henstridge, Sunny Mabrey, Robert Knepper, Robin Dunne, Amelia Cooke, Michael Warren, Christopher Neame, John Paul (J.P.) Pitoc. **VIDEO**

Species 4: The Awakening ✂ **2007** Same old, same old. Miranda (Mattsson) discovers she's been cloned from both human and alien DNA. She awakens from a blackout and learns she's probably a murderer after her alien side goes on the hunt for a mate. **103m/C DVD.** Ben Cross, Dominic Keating, Helena Mattsson, Marco Bacuzzi; ***D:*** Nick Lyon; ***W:*** Ben Ripley; ***C:*** Jaime Reynoso; ***M:*** Paul Cristo, Kevin Haskins. **VIDEO**

Specimen ✂✂ 1/2 **1997 (R)** Twenty-four years ago, aliens impregnated Carol Hillary and she gave birth to a son, Mark. Now, the aliens have returned to claim him, only he doesn't want to go. **85m/C VHS, DVD.** *CA* Mark Paul Gosselaar, Doug O'Keefe, Michelle Johnson, Andrew Jackson; ***D:*** John Bradshaw; ***W:*** Damian Lee, Sheldon Inkol; ***C:*** Gerald R. Goozie; ***M:*** Terence Gowan.

The Speckled Band ✂✂✂ **1931** Set in 1930, this early talkie is a Sherlock Holmes adventure wherein the great detective must solve the mysterious death of a young woman. Massey makes his screen debut as Holmes, making the sleuth cynical, unhappy and pessimistic. Interesting prototypical Holmes case, faithful to the like-titled Conan Doyle story. **84m/B VHS, DVD.** Raymond Massey, Lyn Harding, Athole Stewart, Angela Baddeley, Nancy Price; ***D:*** Jack Raymond; ***C:*** Frederick A. (Freddie) Young.

Spectacular ✂✂ **2009 (G)** In this Nickelodeon teen musical, rebellious rocker Nikko (Funk) needs cash to make a demo. So he agrees to partner with uptight high school singer Courtney (Sursok) who leads a choir that is trying to win the $10,000 first prize in a singing contest. Squeaky-clean similarities to Disney's "High School Musical" franchise are, no doubt, intentional. **93m/C DVD.** Tammin Sursok, Greg Germann, Brittney Irvin, Nolan Gerard Funk, Victoria Justice; ***D:*** Robert Iscove; ***W:*** James Krieg; ***C:*** David Moxness. **CABLE**

The Spectator ✂✂ *La Spettatrice* **2004** Lonely 20-something Valeria (Bobulova), a translator in Turin, becomes obsessed with her middle-aged neighbor Massimo (Renzi), a doctor whose work she translates. When he moves to Rome, Valeria follows, only to discover he has a companion, Flavia (Catillon). After befriending Flavia, Valeria discovers that Massimo is now also interested in her. Romantic tribulations ensue. Italian with subtitles. **98m/C DVD.** *IT* Barbara Bobulova, Andrea Renzi, Brigitte Catillon; ***D:*** Paolo Franchi; ***W:*** Paolo Franchi; ***C:*** Giuseppe Lanci, Stefano Paradiso; ***M:*** Carlo Crivelli.

Specters ✂ *Spettri* **1987** Archaeologists excavating the Roman catacombs break open the gates of hell. Hellishly confused plot is unoriginal, to boot; decent production values hardly compensate. **95m/C VHS.** *IT* Donald Pleasence, John Pepper, Erna Schurer, Katrine Michelsen; ***D:*** Marcello Avallone; ***W:*** Marcello Avallone, Andrea Purgatori, Dardano Sacchetti, Maurizio Tedesco.

Spectre ✂✂ *House of the Damned; Roger Corman Presents: House of the Damned* **1996 (R)** Maura South (Paul) is the heiress to a old mansion in Ireland and when she, husband Will (Evigan), and their young daughter Aubrey (played by Evigan's daughter Briana) move in they discover it's haunted by the vengeful spirit of a young girl. When they discover the girl's body, the family hope a proper burial will set her spirit to rest but the ghost has other ideas. Filmed in Ireland. **82m/C VHS.** Greg Evigan, Alexandra Paul, Briana Evigan, Eamon Draper, Dick Donaghue; ***D:*** Scott Levy; ***W:*** Brendan Broderick; ***C:*** Christopher Baffa; ***M:*** Christopher Lennertz. **CABLE**

The Spectre of Edgar Allen Poe ✂ 1/2 **1973** The horridly fictionalized writer of horror fiction visits the asylum where his love Lenore is being held, and discovers murder and torture. Based very loosely on Poe's own torments. Dorky, rip-off horror. **87m/C VHS.** Cesar Romero, Robert Walker Jr., Tom Drake; ***D:*** Mohy Quandour.

Spectre of the Rose ✂✂ 1/2 **1946** Strange film set in the world of ballet. An impressario contends with an over-the-hill ballerina and a young male dancer with a deadly affinity for knives. **90m/B VHS.** Judith Anderson, Michael Chekhov, Ivan Kirov, Viola Essen, Lionel Stander; ***D:*** Ben Hecht; ***W:*** Ben Hecht.

Speechless ✂✂ 1/2 **1994 (PG-13)** Cute romantic comedy about sparring speechwriters who fall in love, and then briefly turn enemies when they discover they're working at professional odds. Davis is the idealistic liberal working for senatorial candidate Wannamaker, while Keaton is a TV sitcom writer doing a one-shot deal for a millionaire businessman, Republican Garvin. Both stars do a likable job; the supporting cast fares better with Reeve as an egotistical TV reporter, as well as Davis's fiance, and Bedelia as Keaton's ex-wife/campaign press secretary. Although the film parallels the real-life romance of rival Bush-Clinton spin doctors Mary Matalin and James Carville, it was written prior to the last presidential race. **99m/C VHS, DVD.** Michael Keaton, Geena Davis, Christopher Reeve, Bonnie Bedelia, Ernie Hudson, Charles Martin Smith, Gailard Sartain, Ray Baker, Mitchell Ryan; ***D:*** Ron Underwood; ***W:*** Robert King; ***C:*** Don Peterman; ***M:*** Marc Shaiman.

Speed ✂✂✂ 1/2 **1994 (R)** Excellent dude Reeves has grown up (and bulked up) as Los Angeles SWAT cop Jack Traven, up against bomb expert Howard Payne (Hopper, more maniacal than usual), who's after major ransom money. First it's a rigged elevator in a very tall building. Then it's a rigged bus—if it slows, it will blow, bad enough any day, but a nightmare in LA traffic. And that's still not the end. Terrific directorial debut for cinematographer De Bont, who certainly knows how to keep the adrenaline pumping. Fine support work by Daniels, Bullock, and Morton and enough wit in Yost's script to keep you chuckling. Great nonstop actioner from the "Die Hard" school. **115m/C VHS, DVD, Blu-ray Disc, UMD.** Keanu Reeves, Dennis Hopper, Sandra Bullock, Joe Morton, Jeff Daniels, Alan Ruck, Glenn Plummer, Richard Lineback, Beth Grant, Hawthorne James, David Kriegel, Carlos Carrasco, Natsuko Ohama, Daniel Villarreal; ***D:*** Jan De Bont; ***W:*** Graham Yost; ***C:*** Andrzej Bartkowiak; ***M:*** Mark Mancina. Oscars '94: Sound; MTV Movie Awards '95: Female Perf. (Bullock), Most Desirable Female (Bullock), On-Screen Duo (Keanu Reeves/Sandra Bullock), Villain (Hopper), Action Seq.; Blockbuster '95: Movie, V., Action Actress, V. (Bullock), Action Actress, T. (Bullock).

Speed 2: Cruise Control ✂ **1997 (PG-13)** Bigger's certainly not better in this lame sequel. Annie's (Bullock) got a new beau, hot-headed cop Alex (Patric), and the twosome decide to go on a Caribbean cruise for a little romance. Annie's luck with transportation holds as the ship is taken over by villainous computer geek-with-a-grudge John Giger (a particularly wild-eyed Dafoe), who sends the liner on a collision course with an oil tanker. Since Alex is off performing heroics, there's not much togetherness and Annie's left to get taken hostage (again). De Bont spent $25 mil on the ship's endless crash into a Caribbean island, which still manages to look fake and only elicits "you've got to be kidding me" disappointment. Bullock's feisty but powerless to save the flick. Patric's bland, and Dafoe is never menancing enough to create any thrills. This sea disaster crashes against the rocks of high expectations and poor execution. **123m/C VHS, DVD.** Richard Speight Jr., Joe Morton, Enrique Murciano, Sandra Bullock, Jason Patric, Willem Dafoe, Temuera Morrison, Brian McCardie, Glenn Plummer, Royale Watkins, Colleen Camp, Lois Chiles, Michael G. (Mike) Hagerty, Kimmy Robertson, Christine Firkins, Bo Svenson, Patrika Darbo; ***Cameos:*** Tim Conway; ***D:*** Jan De Bont; ***W:*** Jan De Bont, Jeff Nathanson, Randall McCormick; ***C:*** Jack N. Green; ***M:*** Mark Mancina. Golden Raspberries '97: Worst Remake/Sequel.

Speed Dating ✂ 1/2 **2007 (R)** Uneven Irish romcom finds wealthy, lonesome loser James (O'Conor) deciding to try speed dating to find the woman of his dreams. He becomes attracted to a mysterious femme in a bar, gets caught up in a murder mystery, winds up with amnesia, and is cared for by pretty nurse Emma (King). **85m/C DVD.** *IR* Hugh O'Conor, Emma Choy, Don Wycherley, Luke Griffin, David Hayman, Paul Ronan, Charlotte Bradley, Gerry O'Brien; ***D:*** Tony Herbert; ***W:*** Tony Herbert; ***C:*** John Conroy.

The Speed Lovers ✂ **1968** Stock car driver Lorenzen plays himself as an inspiration to a young man to join the auto racing circuit. More of a pat on the industry's back than a serious drama. Features footage from a number of race tracks around the country although shot principally in Atlanta. ♫ Speed Lovers. **102m/C VHS, DVD.** Fred Lorenzen, William F. McGaha, Peggy O'Hara, David Marcus, Carol Street, Glenda Brunson; ***D:*** William F. McGaha; ***W:*** William F. McGaha, Elaine Wilkerson, Fred Tuch.

Speed of Life ✂ 1/2 *Saturn* **1999 (R)** Although Drew (Caan) loves his father (Burmester), he would prefer to be doing anything else instead of having the emotional and physical burden of caring for the terminally-ill man. Meeting drug-addicted Sarah (Kirshner) only heightens his desire to flee. Slow-moving and shallow. **95m/C VHS, DVD.** Scott Caan, Mia Kirshner, Leo Burmester, Anthony Michael Ruivivar; ***D:*** Rob Schmidt; ***W:*** Rob Schmidt; ***C:*** Matthew Libatique; ***M:*** Ryeland Allison. **VIDEO**

Speed Racer ✂✂ 1/2 **2008 (PG)** It's a dizzying FX retro ride with Speed Racer (Hirsch) and his racing family, including Pops (Godman), Mom (Sarandon), Spritle (Litt), and pet chimp Chim-Chim as they fight against corporate overlord Royalton's nasty plan for world domination, with a little help from the mysterious Racer X (Fox), who might just be Rex, Speed's older brother thought to have bought it in a crash. Also on hand is Trixie (Ricci), the girlfriend Speed might have if he weren't so busy righting wrongs behind the wheel of his car, the Mach 5. The story is flat, moody, and weird, but the racing is wild and the visuals are wilder—kids will dig it, as will fans of the original Japanese anime rendering. **129m/C DVD, Blu-ray**

Disc. *US* Emile Hirsch, Christina Ricci, Matthew Fox, John Goodman, Susan Sarandon, Roger Allam, Hiroyuki (Henry) Sanada, Richard Roundtree, Paulie (Litowsky) Litt, Benno Furmann, Scott Porter, Christian Oliver, Kick (Christopher) Gurry, Moritz Bleibtreu, John Benfield, Rain; ***D:*** Andy Wachowski, Larry Wachowski; ***W:*** Andy Wachowski, Larry Wachowski; ***C:*** David Tattersall; ***M:*** Michael Giacchino.

Speed Reporter 🦴 **1936** Talmadge is the intrepid reporter investigating a phony reform movement that's really a front for a gang of criminals. Mediocre drama with Talmadge's thick German accent a hindrance. **56m/B VHS, DVD.** Richard Talmadge, Luana Walters, Richard Cramer; ***D:*** Bernard B. Ray.

The Speed Spook 🦴 **1924** Silent ghost races car and steals documents. **85m/B VHS.** Johnny Hines, Warner Richmond; ***D:*** Charles Hines.

Speed Zone 🦴 **1988 (PG)** Comic celebrities take over a high speed auto race when a redneck cop locks up the real drivers. Unfunny sequel to "Cannonball Run." **96m/C VHS.** Melody Anderson, Peter Boyle, Tim Matheson, Donna Dixon, John Candy, Eugene Levy, Joe Flaherty, Matt Frewer, Shari Belafonte, Tom Smothers, Dick Smothers, Brooke Shields, Lee Van Cleef, Jamie Farr, John Schneider, Michael Spinks; ***D:*** Jim Drake. Golden Raspberries '89: Worst Support. Actress (Shields).

Speeding Up Time 🦴 **1971 (R)** An angry man wants to ice the dudes who torched his mother's tenement. **90m/C VHS.** Winston Thrash, Pamela Donegan; ***D:*** John Evans; ***W:*** John Evans.

Speedtrap 🦴🦴 **1978 (PG)** Typical chase scenes and cross-gender sparring characterize this tale of a private detective and a police officer pursuing car thieves. Good cast and fun chemistry between the leads; weak, typical script. **101m/C VHS.** Joe Don Baker, Tyne Daly, Richard Jaeckel, Robert Loggia, Morgan Woodward, Timothy Carey; ***D:*** Earl Bellamy.

Speedway 🦴🦴 **1929** Brash mechanic Bill (Haines) is seemingly happy working for old racecar driver Jim MacDonald (Torrence) although he takes more than his fair share of credit for their success. He tries to impress Patricia (Page) but has no luck until he rescues her from a plane crash, which gets him publicity. Lee Renny (Miljan) offers Bill the chance to drive in the Indy 500 but it's all a ploy to get Bill to fine-tune his racecar so Renny can then dump Bill and drive a winner. **82m/B DVD.** William Haines, Anita Page, Ernest Torrence, John Miljan, Eugenie Besserer, Karl (Daen) Dane; ***D:*** Harry Beaumont; ***W:*** Joe Farnham; ***C:*** Henry Sharp.

Speedway 🦴🦴 **1968 (G)** Elvis the stock car driver finds himself being chased by Nancy the IRS agent during an important race. Will Sinatra keep to the business at hand? Or will the King melt her heart? Some cameos by real-life auto racers. Watch for a young Garr. Movie number 27 for Elvis. ♫Speedway; He's Your Uncle, Not Your Dad; There Ain't Nothing Like a Song. **90m/C VHS, DVD.** Elvis Presley, Nancy Sinatra, Bill Bixby, Gale Gordon, William Schallert, Carl Ballantine, Ross Hagen; ***Cameos:*** Richard Petty, Cale Yarborough, Teri Garr; ***D:*** Norman Taurog; ***C:*** Joseph Ruttenberg.

Speedway Junky 🦴🦴 ½ **1999** Army brat Johnny (Bradford) dreams of being an auto racing champion. So he runs away from his home in California determined to make it to North Carolina and get a job with driver Richard Petty's crew. At a stop in Vegas, naive Johnny gets robbed and comes to the attention of seasoned hustler Eric (Brower) who offers to teach Johnny the ropes. Johnny agrees but will only deal with women clients—while the gay Eric falls in love with the new kid in town. **105m/C VHS, DVD.** Jesse Bradford, Jordan Brower, Jonathan Taylor Thomas, Daryl Hannah, Patsy Kensit, Tiffani(-Amber) Thiessen; ***D:*** Nickolas Perry; ***W:*** Nickolas Perry; ***C:*** Steve Adcock; ***M:*** Stan Ridgway.

Speedy 🦴🦴🦴 **1928** Lloyd comes to the rescue when the last horse car in NYC, operated by his fiance's grandfather, is stolen by a gang. Thoroughly phoney, fun pursuit/action comedy shot on location. Look for a brief appearance by Babe Ruth. **72m/B VHS, DVD.** Harold Lloyd, Bert Woodruff, Ann Christy; ***D:*** Ted Wilde.

Speedy Death 🦴🦴🦴 *The Mrs. Bradley Mysteries: Speedy Death* **1999** Gladys Mitchell wrote some 66 mysteries starring the witty and clever Mrs. Adela Bradley (Rigg). A wealthy divorcee, Mrs. Bradley has a knack for investigations and a helpful chauffeur, George Moody (Dudgeon). In 1929, Adela is invited to the country estate of friends to celebrate Eleanor Bing's (Fielding) engagement. Only her fiance is murdered and then doesn't turn out to be what he seemed. But then, neither does anyone else. **90m/C VHS, DVD.** *GB* Diana Rigg, Neil Dudgeon, John Alderton, Emma Fielding, Tristan Gemmill, Tom Butcher, Sue Devaney, John Conroy, Michael Troughton; ***D:*** Audrey Cooke; ***W:*** Simon Booker. **TV**

The Spell 🦴🦴 **1977** An obese 15-year-old girl has the power to inflict illness and death on the people she hates. Necessarily mean-spirited, if we're being asked to sympathize with the main character. Therein lies the rub. Made for TV. **86m/C VHS.** Lee Grant, James Olson, Susan Myers, Barbara Bostock, Lelia Goldoni, Helen Hunt; ***D:*** Lee Philips. **TV**

The Spellbinder 🦴 ½ **1988 (R)** L.A. lawyer Daly falls in love with a woman he saves from an attacker, then discovers she's a fugitive from a satanic cult that wants her back. Unoriginal, but slickly made. **96m/C VHS.** Timothy Daly, Kelly Preston, Rick Rossovich, Audra Lindley; ***D:*** Janet Greek; ***W:*** Tracy Torme; ***M:*** Basil Poledouris.

Spellbound 🦴🦴 *The Spell of Amy Nugent* **1941** Broken-hearted over dead girlfriend, young college student attempts to contact her through spiritualism, succeeds, and suffers nervous breakdown. **75m/B VHS, DVD.** *GB* Derek Farr, Vera Lindsay, Frederick Leister, Hay Petrie, Felix Aylmer; ***D:*** John Harlow.

Spellbound 🦴🦴🦴 ½ **1945** Peck plays an amnesia victim accused of murder. Bergman plays the psychiatrist who uncovers his past through Freudian analysis and ends up falling in love with him. One of Hitchcock's finest films of the 1940s, with a riveting dream sequence designed by Salvador Dali. Full of classic Hitchcock plot twists and Freudian imagery. Based on Francis Beeding's novel "The House of Dr. Edwardes." **111m/B VHS, DVD.** Ingrid Bergman, Gregory Peck, Leo G. Carroll, Michael Chekhov, Wallace Ford, Rhonda Fleming, Regis Toomey; ***D:*** Alfred Hitchcock; ***W:*** Ben Hecht; ***C:*** George Barnes; ***M:*** Miklos Rozsa. Oscars '45: Orig. Dramatic Score; N.Y. Film Critics '45: Actress (Bergman).

Spellbound 🦴🦴🦴 **2002 (G)** Excellent documentary follows a group of teenagers and their families as they compete in the 1999 National Spelling Bee. Shows the preparation and competition the students go through to make it to the Nationals. **97m/C VHS, DVD.** ***D:*** Jeffrey Blitz; ***C:*** Jeffrey Blitz; ***M:*** Daniel Hulsizer.

Spellbreaker: Secret of the Leprechauns 🦴🦴 ½ **1996 (G)** Youngster Mike Dennehy (Smith) is on summer vacation in Fairyhill, Ireland where he meets, what else, a band of leprechauns. He finds out the wee folk are battling sinister sorceress Nula, Queen of the Dead, who wants to seize the leprechauns power and destroy them. But not if Mike can stop her! **85m/C VHS.** Gregory Edward Smith, Madeleine Potter, Godfrey James, Tina Martin, Sylvester McCoy, James Ellis; ***D:*** Ted Nicolaou; ***W:*** Ted Nicolaou; ***C:*** Adolfo Bartoli; ***M:*** Richard Kosinski.

Spellcaster 🦴 **1991 (R)** An evil wizard invites a DJ and a band of rock 'n' roll fanatics to his 1000-year-old Italian castle for an evil and bloodcurdling treasure hunt. **83m/C VHS.** Richard Blade, Gail O'Grady, Harold P. Pruett, Bunty Bailey, Rafal Zielinski, Adam Ant; ***D:*** Rafal Zielinski.

Spencer's Mountain 🦴🦴 ½ **1963** Fonda plays the larger-then-life patriarch of nine (with O'Hara as his wife), who's inherited the Wyoming mountain land claimed by his father. Fonda's dream is to build a new house large enough to contain his brood but something always gets in his way. This time it's eldest son MacArthur's dream of a college education. Sentimental family fare based on a novel by Earl Hamner Jr., which also became the basis for the TV series "The Waltons." **118m/C VHS, DVD.** Henry Fonda, Maureen O'Hara, James MacArthur, Donald Crisp, Wally Cox, Mimsy Farmer, Virginia Gregg, Lillian Bronson, Whit Bissell, Hayden Rorke, Dub Taylor, Victor French, Veronica Cartwright; ***D:*** Delmer Daves; ***W:*** Delmer Daves; ***M:*** Max Steiner.

Spenser: A Savage Place 🦴🦴 ½ **1994** PI Spenser (Urich) is lured to Toronto by an old flame who wants him to help her expose a racketeering scam in the city's film industry. **91m/C VHS, DVD.** Robert Urich, Cynthia Dale, Avery Brooks, Ross Petty, Wendy Crewson; ***D:*** Joseph L. Scanlan; ***W:*** Donald Martin; ***C:*** Vic Sarin; ***M:*** Brad MacDonald.

Spenser: Ceremony 🦴🦴 ½ **1993** Urich resumes his role as Robert B. Parker's Boston PI, which he played in the TV series "Spenser: For Hire." This time around Spenser is searching for a troubled runaway who's gotten involved in prostitution. But her suburban dad, who has political aspirations, seems reluctant to have her found. Brooks returns as Spenser's menacing associate Hawk. Toronto stands in for Boston. Based on Parker's novel "Ceremony." **95m/C VHS, DVD.** Robert Urich, Avery Brooks, Barbara Williams, Tanya Allen, David Nichols, Lynne Cormack; ***D:*** Paul Lynch; ***W:*** Joan H. Parker, Robert B. Parker. **CABLE**

Spenser: Pale Kings & Princes 🦴🦴 ½ **1994** Spenser's (Urich) new case involves the murder of a reporter who was investigating a drug-ridden small New England town. But was the journalist killed for what he found out about a Colombian cocaine connection or did his womanizing have deadly consequences? Adapted from Robert B. Parker's novel. **95m/C VHS, DVD.** Robert Urich, Avery Brooks, Barbara Williams; ***D:*** Vic Sarin; ***W:*** Joan H. Parker, Robert P. Parker; ***C:*** Vic Sarin; ***M:*** Paul Zaza. **CABLE**

Spenser: The Judas Goat 🦴🦴 ½ **1994** Boston PI Spenser (Urich) is hired by billionaire mining exec Hugh Dixon (Pownall) and sent to Ottawa, Canada to investigate the deadly car bombing that killed his wife and children. Seems black African political leader Boyko (Bess) was the true target and the assassin hasn't given up. Adapted from the Robert B. Parker novel; made for cable TV. **95m/C VHS, DVD.** Robert Urich, Avery Brooks, Leon Pownall, Ardon Bess, Geordie Johnson, Natalie Radford, Wendy Crewson; ***D:*** Joseph L. Scanlan. **CABLE**

Spent 🦴🦴 ½ **2000** Gambling addict/occassional actor Max (London) has a girlfriend, Brigette (Spradling), who has a drinking problem, and a roommate, Grant (Park), who won't admit he's gay although his crush on Max seems pretty obvious. In fact, any communication is a big problem, since no one really wants to see their lives for what they are. Film coasts along without much happening. **90m/C VHS, DVD.** Jason London, Charlie Spradling, James Parks, Phill Lewis, Richmond Arquette, Barbara Barrie, Gilbert Cates, Rain Phoenix, Margaret Cho; ***D:*** Gil Cates Jr.; ***W:*** Gil Cates Jr.; ***C:*** Robert D. Tomer; ***M:*** Stan Ridgway.

Spetters 🦴🦴 ½ **1980 (R)** Four Dutch teenagers follow the motorcycle racing circuit and motocross champ Hauer. Misdirected youth film with a spicy performance from Soutendijk. Plenty of violence, sex, and gripping photography. Verhoeven went on to direct "Robocop" and "Total Recall." **108m/C VHS, DVD.** *NL* Rutger Hauer, Renee Soutendijk; ***D:*** Paul Verhoeven; ***C:*** Jan De Bont.

Sphere 🦴 ½ **1997 (PG-13)** It must've looked good on paper, but bringing Michael Crichton's decade-old novel to the screen turned out to be a big mistake for all involved. Hoffman, Jackson, and Stone are a team of researchers sent underwater to investigate a mysterious 300-year-old space ship. After realizing the ship has American origins, they stumble across a huge liquid metal sphere that can make their deepest fears come true, in the form of huge squids and sea snakes. Never lives up to the promising premise or high-class looks. Despite three mega-stars and an A-list director, it's a hollow excursion low on thrills and originality, but there's plenty of existential ramblings about the power of the mind. **152m/C VHS, DVD.** Dustin Hoffman, Sharon Stone, Samuel L. Jackson, Peter Coyote, Queen Latifah, Liev Schreiber; ***D:*** Barry Levinson; ***W:*** Paul Attanasio, Stephen Hauser; ***C:*** Adam Greenberg; ***M:*** Elliot Goldenthal.

The Sphinx 🦴🦴 ½ **1933** A murderer causes havoc for his deaf-mute twin (Atwill, good in a dual role) when he frames him for his own crimes. Remade as "The Phantom Killer." **63m/B VHS, DVD.** Lionel Atwill, Theodore Newton, Sheila Terry, Paul Hurst, Luis Alberni, George "Gabby" Hayes; ***D:*** Phil Rosen.

Sphinx WOOF! **1981 (PG)** Woman archaeologist searches for hidden riches in the tomb of an Egyptian king. The scenery is impressive, but otherwise, don't bother. Based on the novel by Robin Cook. **117m/C VHS, DVD.** Lesley-Anne Down, Frank Langella, John Gielgud, Maurice Ronet, John Rhys-Davies; ***D:*** Franklin J. Schaffner; ***W:*** John Byrum.

Spice World: The Movie 🦴 ½ **1997 (PG)** Clear some space on the video rack next to "Cool as Ice," the Spice Girls made a movie! Stretching their acting ability, the pop group plays a band of marginally talented singers who are inexplicably thrown to the top of the charts by a bitter twist of pop culture fate. What passes for the plot is stolen from "A Hard Day's Night," by the Beatles, depicting five days before a sellout concert at Albert Hall. The courageous champions of girl power do battle with the hassles of fame, bossy managers, and the media in their quest to get to the show. They find the time to visit a pregnant ex-Spice, change their clothes a kajillion times, and generally poke fun at themselves along the way. Unfortunately (at least for those over 13) they're not poked with anything really sharp. Loads of celebrity cameos (Elton John, Elvis Costello, Bob Hoskins), some of whom run off screen faster than if they were on fire. **92m/C VHS, DVD.** *GB* Emma (Baby Spice) Bunton, Geri (Ginger Spice) Halliwell, Victoria (Posh Spice) Beckham, Melanie (Sporty Spice) Chisholm, Melanie (Scary Spice) Brown, Richard E. Grant, Alan Cumming, George Wendt, Claire Rushbrook, Mark McKinney, Richard O'Brien, Roger Moore, Barry Humphries, Jason Flemyng, Meat Loaf Aday, Bill Paterson, Stephen Fry, Richard Briers, Michael Barrymore, Naoki Mori, Hugh Laurie, Jennifer Saunders; ***Cameos:*** Elvis Costello, Bob Geldof, Bob Hoskins, Elton John; ***D:*** Bob Spiers; ***W:*** Kim Fuller, Jamie Curtis; ***C:*** Clive Tickner; ***M:*** Paul Newcastle. Golden Raspberries '98: Worst Actress (Bunton), Worst Actress (Halliwell, Beckham, Chisholm, Brown).

Spices 🦴🦴🦴 **1986** Poor woman Sonbai revolts against the sexist mores of rural colonial India in the 1940s. Features actress Patil in her final role. In Hindi with English subtitles. **98m/C VHS.** *IN* Naseeruddin Shah, Om Puri, Sureh Oberoi, Deepti Naval, Smita Patil; ***D:*** Ketan Mehta; ***W:*** Ketan Mehta; ***M:*** Rajat Dholakia.

Spider 🦴🦴🦴🦴 **2002 (R)** Gripping and well-directed psychodrama tells the story of Spider, a paranoid-schizophrenic, as he tries to resolve his convoluted memories and emotions. After being released from a mental hospital, Spider (Ralph Fiennes) lives in an eerie halfway house for mental patients. There he recounts the events of his life that led to his tortured state of mind. Yet, since the film is told entirely from Spider's perspective it's impossible to distinguish between reality and the blurred fiction of a madman, making the entire film both illusionary and fascinatingly real. Stellar performances from Fiennes, Miranda Richardson, Gabriel Byrne, and Bradley Hall in an amazing turn as the young Spider. Cronenberg's most polished drama to date shows that he's successfully outgrown the moniker of Canada's "baron of blood." **98m/C VHS, DVD.** *CA GB* Ralph Fiennes, Miranda Richardson, Gabriel Byrne, Bradley Hall, Lynn Redgrave, John Neville, Gary Reineke, Sara Stockbridge, Philip Craig; ***D:*** David Cronenberg; ***W:*** Patrick McGrath; ***C:*** Peter Suschitzky; ***M:*** Howard Shore. Genie '02: Director (Cronenberg).

The Spider and the Fly 🦴🦴 **1949** A quilting of catch and catch-can, have and have-not stitches together this WWI romantic drama involving a clever French detective and a more clever thief who is loved by the official's woman. **87m/B VHS.** Eric Portman, Guy Rolfe, Nadia Gray, George Cole, John Carol; *D:* Robert Hamer; *W:* Robert Westerby. **VIDEO**

The Spider and the Fly 1/2 **1994 (PG-13)** Mystery writer Dianna Taylor (Harris) and her friends like to play a murder mystery charade known as "The Game." Their latest unsuspecting patsy is crime writer Michael Moore (Shackelford)—who falls for Dianna bigtime. Then their publisher is killed—in the same sort of murder scenario one of them devised. **87m/C VHS.** Mel Harris, Ted Shackleford, Kim Coates, Colm Feore, Frankie Faison, Cynthia Belliveau, Kenneth Welsh, Peggy Lipton; *D:* Michael Katleman; *W:* Robert Pucci, Alanna Hamill; *M:* Richard Bellis. **CABLE**

Spider Baby *The Liver Eaters; Spider Baby, or the Maddest Story Ever Told; Cannibal Orgy, or the Maddest Story Ever Told* **1964** A tasteless horror-comedy about a chauffeur who takes care of a psychotic family. Theme song sung by Lon Chaney. **86m/B VHS, DVD.** Lon Chaney Jr., Mantan Moreland, Carol Ohmart, Sid Haig, Beverly Washburn, Jill Banner, Quinn (K.) Redeker, Mary Mitchell; *D:* Jack Hill; *W:* Jack Hill; *C:* Alfred Taylor; *M:* Ronald Stein.

Spider Forest 1/2 *Gomi Sup; Geomi Sup* **2004 (R)** Kang Min (Gam Wooseong) wakes up in the middle of the forest with a head injury. Spotting a cabin, he enters it and finds a man dead, and his own girlfriend dying. He chases what he presumes is the killer but is struck unconscious. He awakes in a tunnel, and gets knocked out after being struck again, this time by an SUV. Waking up in a hospital, he finds out he's under suspicion for murder. Obviously Kang has had better days—or maybe not, because flashbacks reveal that his wife is dead, too. **120m/C DVD.** *KN* Byeong-ho Son, Woo-seong Kam, Jung Suh, Kyeong-heon Kang, Hyeongseong Jang; *D:* Il-gon Song; *W:* Il-gon Song; *C:* Cheol-ju Kim; *M:* Min-hwa Yun.

Spider Lilies 1/2 *Ci Qing; Tattoo* **2006** Teenaged Jade (Yang) gives private webcam sex shows to support herself and her granny without knowing that her activities are being investigated by a smitten cyber cop. Jade impulsively decides she wants a spider lily tattoo just like Taipei tattoo artist Takeko (Leong), whom she realizes she knew as a child. However there's something tragic about their past connection that makes Takeko reluctant to get involved with her. Though attractive, the leads are also amateurish. Chinese with subtitles. **98m/C DVD.** *TW* Isabella Leong, Rainie Yang, Yuen-chieh Shih, Jian-Hung (John) Shen; *D:* Zero (Mei-ling) Chou; *W:* Zero (Mei-ling) Chou, Singing Chen; *C:* Hoho Liu; *M:* Chien-hsun Huang, Chien-yu Chang.

Spider-Man **2002 (PG-13)** Raimi does a little 21st-century updating of the Marvel comic hero, who first made his appearance back in 1962, but remembers to keep the heart along with the action. Peter Parker (Maguire) is a nerdy teenager who gets tongue-tied every time he's around the babe of his dreams—Mary Jane Watson (Dunst). His life changes—not necessarily for the better—when he gets bitten by a genetically altered spider and takes on weird arachnid traits, such as strength, agility, wall crawling, web shooting, and swinging. After a family tragedy, the newly monickered Spider-Man becomes a crime fighter. His nemesis is, of course, the Green Goblin (Dafoe), who himself has a dual identity. **121m/C VHS, DVD, Blu-ray Disc.** *US* Tobey Maguire, Willem Dafoe, Kirsten Dunst, James Franco, Cliff Robertson, Rosemary Harris, J.K. Simmons, Gerry Becker, Bill Nunn, Jack Betts, Joe Manganiello, Stanley Anderson, Ron Perkins, Theodore (Ted) Raimi, Larry Joshua, Michael (Mike) Papajohn, Joseph (Joe) D'Onofrio; ***Cameos:*** Bruce Campbell, Lucy Lawless; *D:* Sam Raimi; *W:* David Koepp; *C:* Don Burgess; *M:* Danny Elfman.

Spider-Man 2 1/2 **2004 (PG-13)** Spidey's back, with more to worry about than ever. Mary Jane's engaged, Harry Osborne is out to avenge the death of his father (Green Goblin), and there's a new villain in town: Doctor Octopus (Molina). Raimi's first installment was the best comic book adaptation in a while, and he's managed to top it here. Peter Parker's angst over Spidey's affect on his life, romantic conflict over MJ, and guilt over his uncle's death provide more depth than any comic book character has previously been granted on screen. Even Doc Ock is three dimensional and somewhat sympathetic, in no small part because of Molina's portrayal. The effects are again top-notch and non-intrusive. Raimi shows enough humor to remind everybody why they're called comic books. **127m/C DVD, UMD.** Tobey Maguire, Kirsten Dunst, Alfred Molina, James Franco, Elizabeth Banks, Rosemary Harris, J.K. Simmons, Vanessa Ferlito, Bill Nunn, Theodore (Ted) Raimi, Dylan Baker, Donna Murphy, Bruce Campbell, Aasif Mandvi, Willem Dafoe, Cliff Robertson, Daniel Gillies; *D:* Sam Raimi; *W:* Alvin Sargent, Alfred Gough, Miles Millar, Michael Chabon; *C:* Bill Pope; *M:* Danny Elfman. Oscars '04: Visual FX.

Spider-Man 3 1/2 **2007 (PG-13)** Raimi's sublime superhero series falters in this third chapter, thanks largely to the director's cheeseball sensibilities. Spider-Man (Maguire) is enjoying a brief period of popularity, which only makes things worse with his fading star girlfriend MJ (Dunst) and his vengeance-minded pal Harry (Franco). Adding to the mix is a nasty rival photographer (Grace), the powerful ex-con Sandman (Church), and Venom, an evil alien parasite that gives Spidey a black suit and makes him act like a jerk. There's a lot of blockbuster fun, but you'll spend half the movie rolling your eyes at the unconvincing love quadrangle and Raimi's attempts to turn Spidey into the messiah of New York. Still, much better than the third chapters of the X-Men, Superman, or Batman franchises. **139m/C DVD, Blu-ray Disc.** *US* Tobey Maguire, Kirsten Dunst, James Franco, Thomas Haden Church, Topher Grace, Bryce Dallas Howard, James Cromwell, Rosemary Harris, J.K. Simmons, Dylan Baker, Bill Nunn, Theresa Russell, Theodore (Ted) Raimi, Cliff Robertson, Elizabeth Banks, Perla Haney-Jardine, Michael (Mike) Papajohn, Joe Manganiello, Lucy Gordon, Bruce Campbell, Daniel Gillies; *D:* Sam Raimi; *W:* Sam Raimi, Alvin Sargent, Ivan Raimi; *C:* Bill Pope; *M:* Christopher Young.

The Spider Returns 1/2 **1941** Number 14 of the 15-part serial, The Spider Returns offers the typical good-guy sleuth versus criminal mastermind and his band of witless henchmen. The Spider (Hull) routinely undercuts Police Commissioner Kirk (Girard) as he squares off against master criminal "the Gargoyle." The plot is a little thin but the action is where it's at. **300m/B DVD.** Warren Hull, Mary Ainslee, Dave O'Brien, Joseph Girard, Kenne Duncan, Corbet Morris, Bryant Washburn, Charles F. Miller, Anthony Warde, Harry Harvey; *D:* James W. Horne; *W:* Morgan Cox, Lawrence Taylor.

Spider Woman *Sherlock Holmes and the Spider Woman* **1944** A modernized Holmes and Watson adventure as the duo track down a woman responsible for a series of murders. His adversary uses poisonous spiders to do her work. Zestful, superior Holmes. **62m/B VHS, DVD.** Basil Rathbone, Nigel Bruce, Gale Sondergaard, Dennis Hoey; *D:* Roy William Neill.

Spiderman: The Deadly Dust **1978** A live-action episode of Spiderman, from the TV seies, as he attempts to prevent a city-destroying plutonium accident. **93m/C VHS.** Nicholas Hammond, Robert F. Simon, Chip Fields; *D:* Ron Satlof. **TV**

Spiders **1918** One of the earliest surviving films by director Lang, and predates Indiana Jones by almost 60 years. In these first two chapters ("The Golden Lake" and "The Diamond Ship") of an unfinished 4-part thriller, Carl deVogt battles with the evil Spider cult for a mystically powerful Incan diamond. Restored version has original color-tinted scenes. Silent with organ score. **137m/B VHS, DVD.** *GE* Lil Dagover; *D:* Fritz Lang; *M:* Gaylord Carter.

Spiders 1/2 **2000 (R)** Throwback to the "big bug" sci-fi horrors of the 1950s also borrows heavily from "The X-Files." College reporter Marci (Parrilla) and a couple of her pals sneak into a desert military base in time to witness the secret landing of a space shuttle. On board is a spider that has been injected with alien DNA and is doing absolutely disgusting things. It all ends with an arachnid attack on Phoenix! Can the city be saved? **93m/C VHS, DVD.** David Carpenter, Lana Parrilla; *D:* Gary Jones. **VIDEO**

Spiders 2: Breeding Ground 1/2 **2001 (R)** Alexandra (Niznik) and hubby Jason (Cromer) are enjoying a boating holiday when a storm capsizes their craft and they are rescued by freighter captain Bigelow (Quinn). The ship's doctor, Gabac (Moll), gives Jason a shot of "antibiotics," which give him hallucinations about giant spiders that incubate in human bodies. Alex thinks this is nuts until she finds some spiders and realizes that Jason has been infected. She then proceeds to kicks butt 'cause nobody messes with her man! **96m/C VHS, DVD.** Stephanie Niznik, Daniel Quinn, Richard Moll, Greg Cromer; *D:* Sam Firstenberg; *W:* Stephen Brooks; *C:* Peter Belcher, Plamen Somov; *M:* Serge Colbert. **VIDEO**

The Spider's Stratagem **1970** Thirty years after his father's murder by the facists, a young man returns to a small Italian town to learn why his father was killed. The locals resist his efforts, and he is trapped in a mysterious web where history and lies exert a stranglehold on the truth. Intriguing, high literate thriller; outrageously lovely color photography. Based on a short story by Jorge Luis Borges. In Italian with English subtitles. **97m/C VHS.** *IT* Giulio Brogi, Alida Valli; *D:* Bernardo Bertolucci; *W:* Bernardo Bertolucci.

The Spider's Web 1/2 **1938** Crime-fighting Spider (Hull) leads his loyal men including Blinky McQuade (Hull) and Ram Singh (Duncan) against the villainous masked underlord Octopus, who is bent on global destruction. Shootouts galore help this story click along with energy to spare showing the class of the serial genre. **300m/B DVD.** Warren Hull, Iris Meredith, Richard Fiske, Kenne Duncan, Forbes Murray, Donald "Don" Douglas, Marc Lawrence, Charles C. Wilson; *D:* James W. Horne, Ray Taylor; *W:* Robert E. Kent, George Plympton; *C:* Allen Siegler.

Spider's Web **2001 (R)** Investment banker Baldwin is seduced into stealing $40 million from his politically connected father but betrayal follows. **87m/C VHS, DVD.** Stephen Baldwin, Kari Wuhrer, Michael Gregory, George Lazenby, Benjamin King, Scott Williamson, George Murdock; *D:* Paul Levine; *W:* D. Alvelo, David Lloyd, Robert Stift; *M:* Michael Cohen. **VIDEO**

The Spiderwick Chronicles **2008 (PG)** Jared (Highmore), his twin Simon, and sister Mallory (Bolger) move into a rural mansion with their mom (Parker) and discover that their new home is a gateway into a world of magical creatures, some of which aren't so nice. Evil Mulgarath (Nolte) wants a magic book written by Jared's ancestor, and it's up to Jared to protect it while convincing his siblings that the charmed world outside their door is real. Well-written, ably directed adaptation of the bestselling children's series. **97m/C DVD, Blu-ray Disc.** *US* Freddie Highmore, Sarah Bolger, Mary-Louise Parker, David Strathairn, Joan Plowright, Andrew McCarthy; *D:* Mark S. Waters; *W:* Karey Kirkpatrick, David Berenbaum, John Sayles; *C:* Caleb Deschanel; *M:* James Horner; *V:* Nick Nolte, Seth Rogen, Martin Short.

Spies 1/2 *Spione* **1928** A sly criminal poses as a famous banker to steal government information and create chaos in the world in this silent Lang masterpiece. Excellent entertainment, tight plotting and pacing, fine performances. Absolutely relentless intrigue and tension. **88m/B VHS, DVD.** *GE* Rudolf Klein-Rogge, Lupu Pick, Fritz Rasp, Gerda Maurus, Willy Fritsch; *D:* Fritz Lang.

Spies, Lies and Naked Thighs 1/2 **1991** A pair of crackpot CIA agents find themselves in a whirlpool of comedic madness when they are assigned to track down a deadly assassin. The problem? The assassin happens to be the ex-wife of one of the guys. Can he go another round with her and this time come out on top? Who cares? **90m/C VHS, DVD.** Harry Anderson, Ed Begley Jr., Rachel Ticotin, Linda Purl, Wendy Crewson; *D:* James Frawley.

Spies Like Us 1/2 **1985 (PG)** Chase and Aykroyd meet while taking the CIA entry exam. Caught cheating on the test, they seem the perfect pair for a special mission. Pursued by the Soviet government, they nearly start WWIII. Silly, fun homage to the Bing Crosby-Bob Hope "Road" movies that doesn't capture those classics' quota of guffaws, but comes moderately close. Look for several cameos by film directors. **103m/C VHS, DVD.** Chevy Chase, Dan Aykroyd, Steve Forrest, Bruce Davison, William Prince, Bernie Casey, Tom Hatton, Donna Dixon, Frank Oz, Michael Apted, Constantin Costa-Gavras, Terry Gilliam, Ray Harryhausen, Joel Coen, Martin Brest, Bob Swaim; *D:* John Landis; *W:* Lowell Ganz, Babaloo Mandel, Dan Aykroyd; *C:* Robert Paynter; *M:* Elmer Bernstein.

Spike of Bensonhurst 1/2 **1988 (R)** A Brooklyn street kid dreams of becoming a championship boxer. He tries to gain the mob's help by courting the local Don's daughter. Hip-but-stereotyped Morrissey effort is helped by great cast. **101m/C VHS.** Sasha Mitchell, Ernest Borgnine, Maria Pitillo, Talisa Soto, Sylvia Miles, Anne DeSalvo, Geraldine Smith, Rick Aviles, Antonia Rey; *D:* Paul Morrissey; *W:* Paul Morrissey, Alan Bowne; *C:* Steven Fierberg; *M:* Coati Mundi.

Spin **2004 (PG-13)** Orphaned by his parents' deaths, young Eddie's cold uncle passes him off to one of his Hispanic ranch hands and his wife who, despite their best efforts, have difficulty keeping the teenager on the right track. Based on Donald Everett Axinn's novel. **107m/C VHS, DVD.** Ryan Merriman, Stanley Tucci, Dana Delany, Paula Garces, Ruben Blades; *D:* James Redford; *W:* James Redford; *C:* Paul Ryan; *M:* Todd Boekelheide. **VIDEO**

Spin the Bottle **1997** Jonah (Graham) invites four childhood friends, whom he hasn't seen in 10 years, for a weekend reunion at his Vermont lakefront summer house, which leads to sexual hijinks and sweet revenge. Yerkes's debut feature. **83m/C VHS, DVD.** Holter Graham, Jessica Faller, Mitchell Riggs, Kim Winter, Heather Goldenhersch; *D:* Jamie Yerkes; *W:* Amy Sohn; *C:* Harlan Bosmajian.

Spinout *California Holiday* **1966** A pouty traveling singer decides to drive an experimental race car in a rally. Usual Elvis fare with the King being pursued by an assortment of beauties. ♫Adam and Eve; Stop, Look, Listen; All That I Am; Am I Ready; Smorgasbord; Never Say Yes; Beach Shack; I'll Be Back; Spinout. **93m/C VHS, DVD.** Elvis Presley, Shelley Fabares, Carl Betz, Diane McBain, Cecil Kellaway, Jack Mullaney, Deborah Walley, Una Merkel, Warren Berlinger, Will Hutchins, Dodie Marshall; *D:* Norman Taurog.

Spiral **2007** Pathologically shy and delusional, artist Mason (Moore) gets a job at an insurance company, thanks to his only friend Berkeley (Levi). Fellow new employee Amber (Tamblyn) bonds with Mason over their work and she agrees to pose for a portrait. And then the trouble really begins. **91m/C DVD.** Joel David Moore, Amber Tamblyn, Zachary Levi, Tricia Helfer, David Muller, Annie Neal; *D:* Joel David Moore, Adam Green; *W:* Joel David Moore, Jeremy Danial Boreing; *C:* Will Barratt; *M:* Todd Baldwell, Michael "Fish" Herring.

The Spiral Staircase **1946** A mute servant, working in a creepy Gothic mansion, may be the next victim of a murderer preying on women afflicted with deformities, especially when the next murder occurs in the mansion itself. Great performance by McGuire as the terrified victim. Remade for TV in 1975. **83m/B VHS, DVD.** Dorothy McGuire, George Brent, Ethel Barrymore, Kent Smith, Rhonda Fleming, Gordon Oliver, Elsa Lanchester, Sara Allgood; *D:* Robert Siodmak; *W:* Mel Dinelli; *C:* Nicholas Musuraca; *M:* Roy Webb.

Spiral Staircase 1/2 **1975** Mild TV remake of the 1946 classic about a mute servant who is menaced by a psychopathic killer. Why didn't they just show the original? **99m/C VHS.** *GB* Jacqueline Bisset, Christopher Plummer, John Phillip Law, Mildred Dunnock, Sam Wanamaker, Gayle Hunnicutt; *D:* Peter Collinson; *W:* Allan Scott, Chris Bryant.

The Spirit WOOF! **2008 (PG-13)** A rookie cop is murdered but comes back to life as The Spirit (Macht), an immortal crime-fighting sort of superhero, who (naturally) is stalked by an obligatory nemesis, The Octopus (Jackson). The so-called story is drawn from Will Eisner's comic book series though unfortunately none of his ironic wit makes it to the screen. Toss in a couple of poorly named vixens that alternate between lover and assailant and, well, there you have it. The essential lesson here is that not every graphic novel can become a worthwhile feature film, even with eye candy like Mendes and Johansson. If you can't pass on style over substance or off-the-chart camp, go ahead and indulge in this guilty pleasure, but don't say The Hound didn't warn you. **102m/C DVD.** *US* Gabriel Macht, Samuel L. Jackson, Scarlett Johansson, Eva Mendes, Jaime (James) King, Paz Vega, Sarah Paulson, Stana Katic, Eric Balfour, Dan Lauria; ***D:*** Frank Miller; ***W:*** Frank Miller; ***C:*** Bill Pope; ***M:*** David Newman.

Spirit Lost 🦴🦴 **1996 (R)** John (Leon) and wife Willy (Taylor) move to an old seaside home, where he hopes to find artistic inpiration. Instead, he finds an attractive ghost, Arabella (Williams), who has been hanging around for 200 years after her lover's betrayal. And the jealous Arabella wants to get her new lover's wife out of the way. Yes, ghosts CAN do it. Based on the book by Nancy Thayer. **90m/C VHS, DVD.** Leon, Regina Taylor, Cynda Williams, James Avery, Juanita Jennings; ***D:*** Neema Barnette; ***W:*** Joyce Renee Lewis; ***C:*** Yuri Neyman; ***M:*** Lionel Cole.

Spirit of St. Louis 🦴🦴🦴 **1957** A lavish Hollywood biography of famous aviator Charles Lindbergh and his historic transatlantic flight from New York to Paris in 1927, based on his autobiography. Intelligent; Stewart shines as the intrepid airman. Inexplicably, it flopped at the boxoffice. **137m/C VHS, DVD.** James Stewart, Patricia Smith, Murray Hamilton, Marc Connelly; ***D:*** Billy Wilder; ***W:*** Billy Wilder, Wendell Mayes; ***C:*** Robert Burks; ***M:*** Franz Waxman.

Spirit of '76 🦴 1/2 **1991 (PG-13)** In the 22nd century, the Earth faces certain disaster as a magnetic storm wipes out all of American culture. Now time travellers must return to 1776 to reacquire the Constitution to fix things up. But when their computer goes on the blink, the do-gooders land, not in 1776, but in 1976 at the beginning of disco fever! **82m/C VHS, DVD.** David Cassidy, Olivia D'Abo, Leif Garrett, Geoff Hoyle, Jeff (Jeffrey) McDonald, Steve McDonald, Liam O'Brien, Barbara Bain, Julie Brown, Thomas Chong, Iron Eyes Cody, Don Novello, Carl Reiner, Rob Reiner, Moon Zappa, Mark Mothersbaugh, Lucas Reiner; ***D:*** Lucas Reiner; ***W:*** Lucas Reiner; ***C:*** Stephen Lighthill; ***M:*** David Nichtern.

Spirit of the Beehive 🦴🦴🦴 *El Espiritu de la Colmena* **1973** An acclaimed and haunting film about a young Spanish girl enthralled by the 1931 "Frankenstein," embarking on a journey to find the creature in the Spanish countryside. One of the best films about children's inner life; in Spanish with subtitles. **95m/C VHS, DVD.** *SP* Fernando Fernan-Gomez, Teresa Gimpera, Ana Torrent, Isabel Telleria, Laly Soldevilla; ***D:*** Victor Erice; ***W:*** Victor Erice; ***C:*** Luis Cuadrado; ***M:*** Luis De Pablo.

Spirit of the Eagle 🦴🦴 **1990 (PG)** Man and young son wander in mountains and make friends with feathered creature. Then boy is kidnapped, creating problems for dad. Somnolent family fare. **93m/C VHS, DVD.** Dan Haggerty, William (Bill) Smith, Don Shanks, Jeri Arredondo, Trever Yarrish; ***D:*** Boon Collins; ***W:*** Boon Collins; ***C:*** Lew V. Adams; ***M:*** Parmer Fuller.

Spirit of the West 🦴 1/2 **1932** Rodeo star Gibson and his ranch foreman brother work together to save a fair damsel's land from a gang of rustlers. Routine western of its era. **61m/B VHS.** Hoot Gibson, Hooper Atchley; ***D:*** Otto Brower.

The Spirit of West Point 🦴 1/2 **1947** The true story of West Point's two All-American football greats, Doc Blanchard and Glenn Davis (who play themselves), while on leave after graduation from the title school. **77m/B VHS.** Felix "Doc" Blanchard, Glenn Davis, Tom Harmon, Alan Hale Jr., Anne Nagel, Robert Shayne; ***D:*** Ralph Murphy.

The Spirit of Youth 🦴🦴 **1937** Joe Louis supports his family with menial jobs until he shows his knack as a fighter. When he's knocked down, his gal appears at ringside to inspire him, and does. **70m/B VHS, DVD.** Joe Louis, Mantan Moreland, Clarence Muse, Edna Mae Harris, Mae Turner, Cleo Desmond, Jewel Smith, Jesse Lee Brooks; ***D:*** Harry Fraser; ***W:*** Arthur Hoerl; ***C:*** Robert E. Cline; ***M:*** Clarence Muse, Elliot Carpenter.

Spirit Rider 🦴🦴🦴 **1993** Jesse Threebears is a sullen 16-year-old Ojibway who has been shuttled from foster homes since the age of six. Repatriated to his family's Canadian reservation, he's left in the care of his grandfather, Joe Moon. The entire community works to make Jesse's return successful but there are Jesse's resentments and some family tragedies to be overcome first. Based on the novel "Winners" by Mary-Ellen Lang Collura. **120m/C VHS, DVD.** *CA* Herbie Barnes, Adam Beach, Graham Greene, Tantoo Cardinal, Gordon Tootoosis, Tom Jackson, Michelle St. John; ***D:*** Michael Scott; ***W:*** Jean Stawarz.

Spirit: Stallion of the Cimarron 🦴🦴 **2002 (G)** Spirit is a wild stallion and leader of his herd, who is captured and treated badly by a Cavalry Colonel (Cromwell) until he escapes with the help of a young Lakota brave, Little Creek (Studi). Action sequences are impressive, even breathtaking, but the simplistic story and constant musical clues to the moods expressed on screen wear quickly. Combination of traditional 2-D and computer-generated 3-D elements doesn't always work, either. On the other hand, the animals don't speak (except for some of Spirit's thoughts in a voiceover provided by Damon), and there are no wacky sidekicks to clutter what is a pretty serious story for an animated feature. **85m/C VHS, DVD.** *US* ***D:*** Kelly Asbury, Lorna Cook; ***W:*** John Fusco; ***M:*** Hans Zimmer, Bryan Adams; ***V:*** Matt Damon, James Cromwell, Daniel Studi.

Spirited Away 🦴🦴 1/2 *Miyazaki's Spirited Away; Sen to Chihiro—No Kamikakushi* **2001 (PG)** Bratty 10-year-old Chihiro (voiced by Chase) is upset that her family is moving. What's worse is when they get lost and discover what appears to be an abandoned Japanese theme park. Her greedy parents get turned into pigs and Chihiro is trapped inside the park's palace. She learns that it is a resting place for millions of spirits and is run by a sorceress who makes Chihiro work for her and wants the girl to renounce her identity and never return to the human world. Also available in the original Japanese language version. **124m/C VHS, DVD.** *JP* ***D:*** Hayao Miyazaki; ***W:*** Hayao Miyazaki; ***M:*** Joe Hisaishi; ***V:*** Daveigh Chase, Suzanne Pleshette, Jason Marsden, Susan Egan, David Ogden Stiers, Lauren Holly, Michael Chiklis, John Ratzenberger, Tara Strong. Oscars '02: Animated Film.

Spiritism 🦴🦴 *Espiritismo* **1961** Mother uses one of her three wishes to bring back her dead son. Adapted from the "Monkey's Paw." **85m/B VHS.** *MX* Nora Veryan, Jose Luis Jimenez, Jorge Mondragon, Rene Cardona Jr.; ***D:*** Benito Alazraki.

Spirits 🦴 1/2 **1990 (R)** A priest tormented by his lust-filled dreams breaks his vows of chastity with a woman who turns out to be a murderer. Bad luck. **88m/C VHS.** Erik Estrada, Carol Lynley, Robert Quarry, Brinke Stevens, Oliver Darrow, Kathrin Lautner; ***D:*** Fred Olen Ray.

Spirits of the Dead 🦴🦴🦴 *Histoires Extraordinaires; Tre Passi nel Delirio; Tales of Mystery; Tales of Mystery and Imagination; Trois Histoires Extraordinaires d'Edgar Poe* **1968 (R)** Three Edgar Allan Poe stories adapted for the screen and directed by three of Europe's finest. "Metzengerstein," directed by Roger Vadim stars the Fonda siblings in a tale of incestuous lust. "William Wilson" finds Louis Malle directing Delon and Bardot in the story of a vicious Austrian army officer haunted by a murder victim. Finally, Fellini directs "Never Bet the Devil Your Head" or "Toby Dammit" in which Stamp plays a drunken British film star who has a gruesome date with destiny. Although Fellini's segment is generally considered the best (and was released on its own) all three provide an interesting, atmospheric vision of Poe. French and Italian with subtitles. **117m/C VHS, DVD.** *IT FR* Jane Fonda, Peter Fonda, Carla Marlier, Francoise Prevost, James Robertson Justice, Brigitte Bardot, Alain Delon, Katia Christine, Terence Stamp, Salvo Randone; ***D:*** Roger Vadim, Louis Malle, Federico Fellini; ***W:*** Roger Vadim, Louis Malle, Federico Fellini, Daniel Boulanger, Barnardino Zapponi; ***C:*** Tonino Delli Colli, Claude Renoir, Giuseppe Rotunno; ***M:*** Nino Rota, Diego Masson; ***Nar:*** Vincent Price, Clement Biddle Wood.

Spite Marriage 🦴🦴🦴 **1929** When Sebastian's lover dumps her like yesterday's garbage, she marries Keaton out of spite. Much postnuptual levity follows. Keaton's final silent. **82m/B VHS, DVD.** Buster Keaton, Dorothy Sebastian, Edward Earle, Leila Hyams, William Bechtel, Hank Mann; ***D:*** Edward Sedgwick.

Spitfire 🦴🦴🦴 **1934** Sentimental comedy-drama starring Hepburn as a hillbilly faith healer from the Ozarks who falls into a love triangle. One in a string of early boxoffice flops for Hepburn. She wanted to play a role other than patrician Eastern Seaboard, and did, but audiences didn't buy it. **90m/B VHS.** Katharine Hepburn, Robert Young, Ralph Bellamy, Sidney Toler, Martha Sleeper, Sara Haden, Virginia Howell, Will Geer; ***D:*** John Cromwell; ***W:*** Jane Murfin; ***C:*** William Cronjager; ***M:*** Max Steiner.

Spitfire 🦴🦴🦴 *The First of the Few* **1942** True story of Reginald J. Mitchell, who designed "The Spitfire" fighter plane, which greatly assisted the Allies during WWII. Howard's last film. Heavily propagandist but enjoyable and uncomplicated biography, with a splendid score. **88m/B VHS, DVD.** *GB* Leslie Howard, David Niven, Rosamund John, Roland Culver, David Horne, J.H. Roberts, Patricia Medina; ***D:*** Leslie Howard; ***C:*** Georges Perinal; ***M:*** William Walton.

Spitfire 🦴 1/2 **1994 (R)** Feisty gymnast Charlie Case (Phillips) has some super secret info slipped to her by her secret agent father (Henrikson) that is desired by evil Carla Davis (Douglas). With the help of reporter Rex Beacham (Thomerson), Charlie's gonna save the day. **95m/C VHS.** Kristie Phillips, Sarah Douglas, Lance Henriksen, Tim Thomerson; ***D:*** Albert Pyun; ***W:*** Albert Pyun; ***C:*** George Mooradian; ***M:*** Tony Riparetti.

The Spitfire Grill 🦴🦴 1/2 *Care of the Spitfire Grill* **1995 (PG-13)** Newly released from prison, Perry Talbott (Elliott) moves to smalltown Gilead, Maine, and gets a waitressing job at the Spitfire Grill, run by the cranky Hannah (Burstyn). Perry's upfront about her jail time, which doesn't endear her to the suspicious locals. Particularly censorious is businessman Nahum Goddard (Patton), who sends his downtrodden wife Shelby (Harden) to keep an eye on Perry. There are a number of personal dilemmas that take their toll in this familiar setting—redeemed by strong performances. **117m/C VHS, DVD.** Alison Elliott, Ellen Burstyn, Marcia Gay Harden, Will Patton, Kieran Mulroney, Gailard Sartain, Louise De Cormier, John M. Jackson; ***D:*** Lee David Zlotoff; ***W:*** Lee David Zlotoff; ***C:*** Rob Draper; ***M:*** James Horner. Sundance '96: Aud. Award.

Spittin' Image 🦴 **1983** After falling from her mean-spirited father's wagon, a young girl befriends a kind mountain man. She learns the ways of the wilderness and tobacco spitting. **92m/C VHS.** Lloyd "Sunshine" Parker, Trudi Cooper, Sharon Barr, Karen Barr; ***D:*** Russell Kern.

Splash 🦴🦴 1/2 **1984 (PG)** A beautiful mermaid ventures into New York City in search of a man she's rescued twice when he's fallen overboard. Now it's her turn to fall—in love. Charming performances by Hanks and Hannah. Well-paced direction from Howard, with just enough slapstick. Don't miss the lobster scene. **109m/C VHS, DVD.** Tom Hanks, Daryl Hannah, Eugene Levy, John Candy, Dody Goodman, Shecky Greene, Richard B. Shull, Bobby DiCicco, Howard Morris; ***D:*** Ron Howard; ***W:*** Babaloo Mandel, Lowell Ganz; ***C:*** Don Peterman; ***M:*** Lee Holdridge. Natl. Soc. Film Critics '84: Screenplay.

Splatter University **WOOF!** **1984** A deranged killer escapes from an asylum and begins to slaughter and mutilate comely coeds at a local college. Abysmally motiveless killing and gratuitous sex. Also available in a 78-minute "R" rated version. **79m/C VHS, DVD.** Francine Forbes, Dick Biel, Cathy Lacommaro, Ric Randing, Dan Eaton, Denise Texeira, Mary Ellen David, Joanna Mihalakis; ***D:*** Richard W. Haines; ***W:*** Richard W. Haines, John Michaels, Michael Cunningham; ***M:*** Chris Burke.

Splendor 🦴🦴 1/2 **1935** Typical romantic weepie finds beautiful-but-poor Phyllis (Hopkins) marrying into the snobby clan of Brighton Lorrimore (McCrea). His family (whose fortunes are sliding) want to break the duo up and push Phyllis towards an affair with wealthy broker Martin (Cavanagh). There's a scandal and the Lorrimore's separate but true love conquers all, as you expect. **77m/B VHS.** Miriam Hopkins, Joel McCrea, Paul Cavanagh, Helen Westley, Billie Burke, Katherine Alexander, David Niven, Arthur Treacher; ***D:*** Elliott Nugent; ***W:*** Rachel Crothers; ***C:*** Gregg Toland.

Splendor 🦴🦴 1/2 **1999 (R)** A '90s screwball comedy about an unconventional sexual arrangement. Veronica (Robertson) is an aspiring L.A. actress who enjoys her sexual exploits and who falls for two men on the opposite ends of the romantic spectrum. Abel (Schaech) is a freelance music critic who's intelligent and handsome while punk rock drummer Zed (Keeslar) is dumb but really sexy. Veronica refuses to choose between the two, so both move in with her (and prove to be more immature than the lady herself). Then Veronica meets successful and wealthy TV director, Ernest (Mabius), and wonders if it's time for a real adult relationsip. Surprisingly sweet and stylish fluff from Araki. **93m/C VHS, DVD.** Kathleen Robertson, Johnathon Schaech, Matt Keeslar, Eric Mabius, Kelly Macdonald; ***D:*** Gregg Araki; ***W:*** Gregg Araki; ***C:*** Jim Fealy; ***M:*** Daniel Licht.

Splendor in the Grass 🦴🦴🦴 **1961** A drama set in rural Kansas in 1925, concerning a teenage couple who try to keep their love on a strictly intellectual plane and the sexual and family pressures that tear them apart. After suffering a mental breakdown and being institutionalized, the girl returns years later in order to settle her life. Film debuts of Beatty, Dennis, and Diller. Inge wrote the screenplay specifically with Beatty in mind, after the actor appeared in one of Inge's stage plays. Filmed not in Kansas, but on Staten Island and in upstate New York. **124m/C VHS, DVD.** Natalie Wood, Warren Beatty, Audrey Christie, Barbara Loden, Zohra Lampert, Phyllis Diller, Sandy Dennis; ***D:*** Elia Kazan; ***W:*** William Inge; ***C:*** Charles Durnham; ***M:*** David Amram. Oscars '61: Story & Screenplay.

Splice **2009** Clive and Elsa are superstar genetic engineers who splice together the DNA from different animals to create new hybrids. They conduct secret experiments by splicing in human DNA and come up with Dren, a creature both amazing and dangerous. **m/C DVD.** *US* Adrien Brody, Sarah Polley, David Hewlett, Delphine Chaneac; ***D:*** Vincenzo Natali; ***W:*** Vincenzo Natali, Doug Taylor, Antoinette Terry Bryant; ***C:*** Tetsuo Nagata.

Spliced 🦴🦴 1/2 **2003 (R)** Slick slasher that may be derivative but still manages some shudders. High school senior Mary Ryan (Balaban) is obsessed with horror movies and much too suggestible. She becomes convinced that the mad slasher character in one of her faves is not only real but offing her classmates. School doctor Morgan Campbell (Silver) first thinks Mary is merely crazy but then comes to change his mind. **86m/C VHS, DVD.** Liane Balaban, Ron Silver, Sin Baruc, Drew Lachey; ***D:*** Gavin Wilding; ***W:*** Ellen Cook. **VIDEO**

Splinter 🦴🦴 **2006 (R)** L.A. gangbanger brothers Dreamer (Almeida) and Dusty (Gugliemi) are looking for their older brother's killer. Someone is also torturing and killing fellow gang members, which brings in rookie detective Gramm (Atis), who's teamed up with corrupt, unstable veteran Cunningham (Sizemore, perhaps typecast). Maybe someone just wants to expand their turf or maybe a serial killer is targeting the gangs. Olmos plays a police captain and yeah, that's his kid helming this familiar pic. **90m/C DVD.** Tom Sizemore, Edward James Olmos, Noel Guglielmi, Resmine Atis, Enrique Almeida, Dallas Page; ***D:*** Michael D. Olmos; ***W:*** Michael D. Olmos; ***C:*** Bridger Nielson; ***M:*** Jae Chong. **VIDEO**

Split 🦴 **1990** Humanoids from another

dimension manipulate earth activity. **85m/C VHS.** John Flynn, Timothy Dwight, Chris Shaw, Joan Bechtel; ***D:*** Chris Shaw.

Split Decisions 1988 (R) An Irish family of boxers, dad and his two sons, slug it out emotionally and physically, as they come to terms with career choices and each other. Good scenes in the ring but the drama leans toward melodrama. Decent family drama, but somewhat of a "Rocky" rip-off. **95m/C VHS, DVD.** Gene Hackman, Craig Sheffer, Jeff Fahey, Jennifer Beals, John McLiam, Eddie Velez, Carmine Caridi, James Tolkan; ***D:*** David Drury; ***W:*** David Fallon; ***M:*** Basil Poledouris.

Split Image 1982 (R) An all-American boy comes under the spell of a cult. His parents then hire a deprogrammer to bring the boy back to reality. Exceptional performances by Dennehy and Woods. This is a worthwhile film that spent far too little time in theatres. **113m/C VHS.** Michael O'Keefe, Karen Allen, Peter Fonda, Brian Dennehy, James Woods; ***D:*** Ted Kotcheff; ***W:*** Robert Mark Kamen; ***M:*** Bill Conti.

Split Second 1/2 1953 An escaped prisoner holds hostages in a Nevada atomic bomb testing area. McNally's excellent performance as the kidnapper, in addition to strong supporting performances, enhance a solid plot. Powell's directorial debut. **85m/B VHS.** Paul Kelly, Richard Egan, Jan Sterling, Alexis Smith, Stephen McNally; ***D:*** Dick Powell; ***W:*** William Bowers, Irving Wallace.

Split Second 1/2 1992 (R) Hauer is a futuristic cop tracking down a vicious alien serial killer in London in the year 2008. The monster rips out the hearts of his victims and then eats them in what appears to be a satanic ritual in this blood-soaked thriller wanna-be. Hauer gives a listless performance and overall, the action is quite dull. The music soundtrack also manages to annoy with the Moody Blues song "Nights in White Satin" playing at the most inappropriate times. A British/American co-production. **91m/C VHS, DVD.** *GB* Rutger Hauer, Kim Cattrall, Neil Duncan, Michael J. Pollard, Alun Armstrong, Pete Postlethwaite, Ian Dury, Roberta Eaton; ***D:*** Tony Maylam; ***W:*** Gary Scott Thompson; ***C:*** Clive Tickner; ***M:*** Francis Haines, Stephen Parsons.

Split Second 1999 Corporate lawyer Michael Anderson (Owen) is fed up with both his work and home lives. A road rage incident leaves a cyclist dead and Michael fleeing the scene. He tries to repress the incident but it only leads to further angst and anger. Owen is a champion brooder but this is a routine diversion. **90m/C DVD.** *GB* Clive Owen, Helen McCrory, John Bowe, James Cosmo, Tony Curran; ***D:*** David Blair. **TV**

Splitting Heirs 1/2 1993 (PG-13) Idle stars as the offspring of titled parents who is accidentally abandoned in a restaurant as an infant and raised by poor Pakistanis. (His mother winds up claiming the wrong abandoned baby.) When he discovers he's actually the 15th Duke of Bournemouth he plots, ineffectually, to kill off the present unknowing imposter, a nitwit American (Moranis). Cleese pops in as a shabby lawyer hired by Idle to help him claim the title with Hershey as Idle's real mother, the addle-brained and sex-starved Duchess. Convoluted plot, bland comedy. **87m/C VHS, DVD.** Eric Idle, Rick Moranis, Barbara Hershey, John Cleese, Catherine Zeta-Jones, Sadie Frost, Stratford Johns, Brenda Bruce, William Franklyn, Jeremy Clyde, David Ross; ***D:*** Robert M. Young; ***W:*** Eric Idle; ***M:*** Michael Kamen.

Splitz WOOF! 1984 (PG-13) An all-girl rock band agrees to help out a sorority house by participating in a series of sporting events. **89m/C VHS, DVD.** Robin Johnson, Patti Lee, Shirley Stoler, Raymond Serra; ***D:*** Domonic Paris.

Spoiled Children 1/2 *Les Enfants Gates* 1977 A famous film director (Piccoli) tries to work on his new script at home but is too distracted by his family life. So he rents a high-rise apartment for peace and quiet but winds up involved in a tenant/landlord dispute and with a girl half his age. In French with English subtitles. **113m/B VHS.** *FR* Michel Piccoli, Christine Pascal, Michel Aumont, Gerard Jugnot, Arlette Bonnard; ***D:*** Bertrand Tavernier; ***W:*** Christine Pascal, Charlotte Dubreuil, Bertrand Tavernier; ***M:*** Philippe Sarde.

Spoiler 1/2 1998 Wrongly convicted Daniels is stuck in a sadistic 21st-century prison with just one aim—to escape and reunite with his young daughter. **100m/C VHS, DVD.** Gary Daniels, Meg Foster, Bryan Genesse, Jeffrey Combs, Arye Gross, Duane Whitaker, David Groh; ***D:*** Carmen Von Daacke; ***W:*** Michael Kalesniko; ***C:*** Philip Lee. **VIDEO**

The Spoilers 1/2 1914 Virtually unstaged account of gold hunting in the Alaskan wilderness enhanced by gritty film quality. Was a gold mine when released. **110m/B VHS.** William Farnum, Thomas Santschi, Kathlyn Williams, Bessie Eyton, Frank Clark, Wheeler Oakman; ***D:*** Colin Campbell.

The Spoilers 1942 Two adventurers in the Yukon are swindled out of their gold mine and set out to even the score. A trademark scene of all versions of the movie (and there are many) is the climactic fistfight, in this case between hero Wayne and bad-guy Scott. One of the better films adapted from the novel by Rex Beach. William Farnum, who starred in both the 1914 and the 1930 versions, has a small part. **88m/B VHS, DVD.** John Wayne, Randolph Scott, Marlene Dietrich, Margaret Lindsay, Harry Carey Sr., Richard Barthelmess, Charles Halton; ***D:*** Ray Enright; ***C:*** Milton Krasner.

Spoilers of the North 1947 Conniving Alaska salmon fisherman Matt Garraway persuades girlfriend Laura to put up the money for his cannery. Then he dumps her to take up with half-breed Jane so she'll persuade her Native American friends to do some illegal fishing for him. Jane's brother Pete realizes Matt is no good and decides to bring him down. Made cringe-worthy by the blatantly racist attitudes of the day. **66m/B DVD.** Paul Kelly, Evelyn Ankers, Lorna Gray, Francis McDonald, James Millican, Roy Barcroft; ***D:*** Richard Sale; ***W:*** Milton Raison; ***C:*** Alfred S. Keller.

The SpongeBob SquarePants Movie 1/2 2004 (PG) Nickelodeon's animated series (equally popular with kiddies, college students, and wannabe hipsters) makes its debut on the big screen with all its bright colored frivolity intact. Our peppy yellow sea sponge and his dim-witted best pal, starfish Patrick, must save their home of Bikini Bottom from the evil Plankton, who steals the crown of King Neptune. You weren't honestly expecting more of a plot, were you? Hasselhoff appears in all his "Baywatch" glory to save our watery heroes from a desperate dry land fate. **90m/C VHS, DVD, UMD.** *US* ***Cameos:*** David Hasselhoff; ***D:*** Stephen Hillenburg; ***W:*** Derek Drymon, Tim Hill, Stephen Hillenburg, Paul Tibbett; ***C:*** Jerzy Zielinski; ***M:*** Gregor Nabholz; ***V:*** Tom Kenny, Bill Fagerbakke, Clancy Brown, Rodger Bumpass, Alec Baldwin, Scarlett Johansson, Jeffrey Tambor, Carolyn Lawrence, Mary Jo Catlett, Mr. Lawrence, Jill Talley.

Spontaneous Combustion 1989 (R) A grisly horror film detailing the travails of a hapless guy who has the power to inflict the title phenomenon on other people. **97m/C VHS, DVD.** Brad Dourif, Jon Cypher, Melinda Dillon, Cynthia Bain, William Prince, Dey Young, Dick Butkus, John Landis, Dale Dye; ***D:*** Tobe Hooper; ***W:*** Tobe Hooper, Howard Goldberg; ***C:*** Levie Isaacks; ***M:*** Graeme Revell.

Spook Busters 1/2 1948 The Bowery Boys take jobs as exterminators, only to find themselves assigned the unenviable task of ridding a haunted house of ghosts. To make matters worse, the resident mad scientist wants to transplant Sach's brain into a gorilla. Essential viewing for anyone who thought "Ghostbusters" was an original story. **68m/B VHS.** Leo Gorcey, Huntz Hall, Douglass Dumbrille, Bobby Jordan, Gabriel Dell, William Benedict, David Gorcey, Bernard Gorcey, Tanis Chandler, Maurice Cass, Charles Middleton; ***D:*** William Beaudine.

Spook Warfare *Yokai Daisenso; Yokai Monsters 1: Spook Warfare; Ghosts on Parade; Big Monster War* 1968 If Sid and Marty Krofft went to Japan to make a horror film with puppets and rubber suits, this would be that movie. Not quite a true horror film, not quite a children's movie, but definitely unique. Arab tomb raiders awaken a vampire who flies to Japan and possesses the local magistrate of a town. He then begins a bloodsucking spree, and a Kappa (along with several kids) asks the Yokai monsters to help fight him. Fans of Japanese mythology will like the humorous take on monsters from traditional folklore, even if they aren't blood-thirsty killers as they are in the myths. **90m/C DVD.** *JP* Yoshihiko Aoyama, Hideki Hanamura, Chikara Hashimoto, Hiromi Inoue, Mari Kanda, Takashi Kanda, Akane Kawasaki, Gen Kuroki, Ikuko Mori, Osamu Okawa, Tokio Oki, Tomoo Uchida, Yukiyasu Watanabe, Keiko Yukitomo; ***D:*** Yoshiyuki Kuroda; ***W:*** Tetsuro Yoshida; ***C:*** Hiroshi Imai; ***M:*** Sei Ikeno.

The Spook Who Sat by the Door 1/2 1973 (PG) A black CIA agent organizes an army of inner-city youths and launches a revolution. Based on the novel by Sam Greenlee. **95m/C VHS, DVD.** Lawrence Cook, Paula Kelly, J.A. Preston; ***D:*** Ivan Dixon; ***M:*** Herbie Hancock.

Spookies WOOF! 1985 (R) An old master sorcerer who lives in a run-down haunted house sacrifices humans to give eternal life to his unconscious bride. He needs only a few more victims when a group of teenagers come along to explore the house. **85m/C VHS.** Felix Ward, Dan Scott, Maria Pechukas, Brendan Faulkner, Eugine Joseph; ***D:*** Thomas Doran.

Spooks Run Wild 1/2 1941 The East Side Kids seek refuge in a spooky mansion owned by the eerie Lugosi. A fun horror-comedy with the Kids' antics playing off Lugosi's scariness quite well. Co-scripter Carl Foreman later co-wrote "High-Noon," "The Bridge on the River Kwai," and "The Guns of Navarone." Not the same movie as "Ghosts on the Loose" which followed in '43 and also featured Lugosi and the Kids. **64m/B VHS, DVD.** Huntz Hall, Leo Gorcey, Bobby Jordan, Sammy (Earnest) Morrison, Dave O'Brien, Dennis Moore, Bela Lugosi; ***D:*** Phil Rosen; ***W:*** Carl Foreman.

Spooky Encounters 1/2 *Encounters of the Spooky Kind* 1980 Writer/director/star Samo Hung is Cheung, a simple-minded braggart who takes a bet to spend one night in a haunted temple. But it's a set-up. His unfaithful wife's lover hires an evil sorcerer to raise the dead. The film covers practically the entire palette of Chinese horror, including hopping vampires and flesh-eating zombies, along with flying undead and plenty of black magic. Samo pulls the film off easily, using his trademark humor to soften the horrific edge. **94m/C DVD.** *HK* Sammo Hung, Chung Fat; ***D:*** Sammo Hung; ***W:*** Sammo Hung.

The Sporting Club WOOF! 1972 (R) A semi-gothic melodrama about a strict all men's club which, during a 100th anniversary party, reverts to savagery and primitive rites. **104m/C VHS.** Robert Fields, Margaret Blye, Nicolas Coster, Ralph Waite, Jack Warden, Linda Blair; ***D:*** Larry Peerce.

Spotlight Scandals *Spotlight Revue; Spotlight on Scandal* 1943 A barber and a vaudevillian team up and endure the ups and downs of showbiz life in this low-budget musical from prolific B-movie director Beaudine. ♫ The Restless Age; Goodnight Now; The Lilac Tree; Tempo of the Trail; Oh Johnny. **79m/B VHS.** Billy Gilbert, Frank Fay, Bonnie Baker; ***D:*** William Beaudine, William Beaudine; ***W:*** Beryl Sachs, William Beaudine; ***C:*** Mack Stengler.

Spraggue 1984 A Boston professor and his eccentric aunt put the moves on a doctor who may have committed murder. Served as a TV pilot for a series that never materialized. **78m/C VHS.** Michael Nouri, Glynis Johns, James Cromwell, Mark Herrier, Patrick O'Neal, Andrea Marcovicci; ***D:*** Larry Elikann. **TV**

Spread 1/2 2009 (R) Just a gigolo? Kutcher stars as Nicki, a handsome, probably as dumb-as-he-appears Hollywood hustler who specializes in being the kept boy toy of a successful older woman. His latest mark is well-toned, 40-something lawyer Samantha (Heche) who's all about the continuous sex. When she's in New York for a few days, he throws a party at her fabulous home and gets involved with Heather (Levieva), the distaff version of himself. Actually, Heather is a lot better at the sex game since Nicki doesn't have anything tangible to show for his efforts and he can't keep his eye on the prize when he begins suddenly suffering from some vague moral qualms. **97m/C DVD.** *US* Ashton Kutcher, Anne Heche, Margarita Levieva, Sebastian Stan, Rachel Blanchard, Maria Conchita Alonso, Hart Bochner; ***D:*** David Mackenzie; ***W:*** Jason Dean Hall; ***C:*** Steven Poster; ***M:*** John Swihart.

The Spree 1/2 1996 Cliched crime thriller with wooden dialogue has cat burglar Xinia (Beals) luring cop Hatcher (Boothe) into the nasty side of life. **98m/C VHS.** Jennifer Beals, Powers Boothe, Garry Chalk, John Cassini, Nathaniel DeVeaux, Rita Moreno; ***D:*** Tommy Lee Wallace; ***W:*** Livia Linden, Percy Angress; ***C:*** Richard Leiterman; ***M:*** Peter Manning Robinson. **CABLE**

Spriggan 1/2 1998 (R) Based on the comic of the same name, and directed by Katsuhiro Otomo ("Akira"), it's "Raiders of the Lost Ark" on steroids. A super-secret group called Arkam is attempting to find Noah's Ark in order to protect humanity from its power, but a rival American organization wants to use it to rule the world. So the Americans send a team of superhuman assassins code-named Fatman and Little Boy (subtle!) to off the protagonist before he can find the Ark himself. Beautifully animated and lots of action, but the plot is muddled by trying to squeeze several years of comic storyline into an hour and a half. **90m/C DVD.** *JP* ***D:*** Hirotsugu Kawasaki; ***W:*** Hirotsugu Kawasaki, Yasutaka Ito; ***M:*** Kuniaki Haishima; ***V:*** Chris Patton, Kevin Corn, Ted Pfister, Andy McAvin, Kelly Manison, Mike Kleinhenz, Spike Spencer, John Paul Shephard, John Swasey.

The Spring 1/2 1989 Two archaeologists search Florida for the fountain of youth after they find new clues to its whereabouts. However, a greedy industrialist and an evil priest are both on their trail, fighting to keep the secret for themselves at any cost. **110m/C VHS.** Dack Rambo, Gedde Watanabe, Shari Shattuck, Steven Keats; ***D:*** John D. Patterson.

The Spring 1/2 2000 (PG-13) Widower Dennis Conway (MacLachlan) and his son Nick (Cross) stop in the small town of Springville when travelling and Nick has an accident. The kid has to spend some time in the hospital where Dennis becomes involved with his son's doctor, Sophie Weston (Eastwood). But the town hides a secret—the local spring is a modern-day fountain of youth, the residents are much older than they appear, and none can ever leave. Based on the novel by Clifford Irving. **90m/C VHS, DVD.** Kyle MacLachlan, Alison Eastwood, Joseph Cross, George Eads, Zachary Ansley, Aaron Pearl; ***D:*** David Jackson; ***W:*** J.B. White. **TV**

Spring Break 1983 (R) Four college students go to Fort Lauderdale on their spring vacation and have a wilder time that they bargained for, though viewer is deprived of excitement. **101m/C VHS.** Perry Lang, David Knell, Steve Bassett, Paul Land, Jayne Modean, Corinne Alphen; ***D:*** Sean S. Cunningham.

Spring Breakdown 2008 (R) Three 40ish women, who have been friends since their staid college days, vacation on South Padre Island in Texas, which is known as a spring break haven for co-eds. Becky (Posey) has been sent by her senator boss (Lynch) to secretly keep an eye on her daughter Ashley (Tamblyn) while Gayle (Poehler) and Judi (Dratch) decide to indulge in everything they didn't do in their youth, including drunken debauchery with frat boys. **84m/C DVD.** Parker Posey, Amy Poehler, Rachel Dratch, Amber Tamblyn, Seth Meyers, Sophie Monk, Jonathan Sadowski, Missi Pyle, Jane Lynch, Mae Whitman; ***D:*** Ryan Shiraki; ***W:*** Ryan Shiraki; ***C:*** Frank DeMarco; ***M:*** Deborah Lurie.

Spring Fever 1927 Jack Kelly (Haines) may be a lowly shipping clerk but he is a natural golfer who, in return for helping boss Mr. Waters (Fawcett) with his swing, is given a two-week membership to a fancy country club. There he meets (and falls for) wealthy Allie Monte (Crawford) as well as becoming the club's representative in a championship tournament. But will Allie still love him when she discovers Jack's poor? Adapted from a play by Vincent Lawrence. Remade as 1930's "Love in the Rough." **78m/B DVD.** William Haines, Joan Crawford, George Fawcett, Eileen (Elaine Persey) Percy, Bert Woodruff, George K. Arthur; ***D:*** Edward Sedgwick; ***W:*** Frank Davis, Albert Lewin; ***C:*** Ira Morgan.

Spring Fever 1/2 **1981** Heartaches of the junior tennis circuit are brought to the screen in this sports comedy. Previews promised a lot more than this film could ever hope to deliver. Even tennis fans will be disappointed. **93m/C VHS.** *CA* Susan Anton, Frank Converse, Jessica Walter, Stephen Young; ***D:*** Joseph L. Scanlan; ***W:*** Stuart Gillard; ***C:*** Donald Wilder; ***M:*** Fred Mollin.

Spring Fever *Chunfeng Chenzuide Yewan* **2009** A literal translation of the Chinese title is "A Night Deeply Drunk on the Spring Breeze," while the uncertain spring weather matches the ever-changing emotions of the central characters. Married Wang Ping has a male lover but doesn't know his suspicious wife Lin Xue has hired Luo Haitao to follow him, only to have Luo fall for Wang's boyfriend. Banned Chinese filmmaker Ye shot his pic clandestinely in Nanjing, China. Mandarin and Cantonese with subtitles. **116m/C DVD.** *HK FR* Wu Wei, Qin Hao, Chen Sicheng, Jiang Jiaqi, Tan Zhuo, Mei Feng; ***D:*** Lou Ye; ***M:*** Peyman Yazdanian.

Spring Forward 1/2 **1999 (R)** Playwright and director Gilroy's debut stays close to his stage roots in this fastidious character drama involving the budding relationship of two men who work for the parks department in a small New England town. Regular joes Murph (Beatty), a world-weary senior close to retirement, and Paul (Schreiber), a feisty ex-con who wants a second chance, are seeming opposites who bond over the course of numerous events on the job, ranging from the death of Murph's gay son to a chance encounter with a vixen with the hots for Paul. Dead-on dialogue and restrained style, along with pitch perfect performances shine even when drama gets stagnant. Filmed mostly sequentially over the course of a year, seasons and character changes are laudably real. **111m/C VHS, DVD.** Ned Beatty, Liev Schreiber, Campbell Scott, Ian Hart, Peri Gilpin, Bill Raymond, Catherine Kellner, Hallee Hirsh; ***D:*** Tom Gilroy; ***W:*** Tom Gilroy; ***C:*** Terry Stacey; ***M:*** Hahn Rowe.

Spring Parade 1/2 **1940** Typically lighthearted musical starring Durbin in a Viennese setting. Ilona (Durbin) goes to a fair and buys a card from a gypsy fortune teller promising she'll meet someone important and have a happy marriage. She gets a job as a baker's assistant and meets army drummer Harry (Cummings), who secretly composes music. Ilona includes sheet music for one of Harry's waltzes in the pastry order going to the Austrian Emperor and it paves the way for the gypsy's predictions to come true. **89m/B DVD.** Deanna Durbin, Robert Cummings, Mischa Auer, Henry Stephenson, S.Z. Sakall, Edward (Ed) Gargan, Anne Gwynne, Peggy Moran, Reginald Denny, Franklin Pangborn, Allyn Joslyn; ***D:*** Henry Koster; ***W:*** Felix Jackson, Bruce Manning; ***C:*** Joseph Valentine; ***M:*** Charles Previn.

Spring, Summer, Fall, Winter... and Spring *Bom Yeorum Gaeul Gyeoul Geurigo...Bom* **2003 (R)** Telling his tale in five segments as the title suggests, writer-director-actor Ki-Duk departs from his typically violent fare and poignantly walks through the life of a young Buddhist monk—from his beginnings as a mischievous boy to a troubled adult running from the law and his demons—and his relationship with an older monk serving as his mentor. All scenes take place in a floating monastery (created specifically for the film) in a breathtaking Korean lake that truly reflects the drama's elegance and stark simplicity. In Korean, with English subtitles. **102m/C VHS, DVD.** *KN* Oh Young Soo, Kim Ki Duk, Kim Young Min, Seo Jae Kyung, Ha Yeo Jin, Kim Jong Ho, Kim Jung Young, Ji Dae Han, Choi Min, Park Ji A, Song Min Young; ***D:*** Kim Ki Duk, Kim Ki Duk; ***C:*** Baek Dong Hyun; ***M:*** Bark Jee Wong.

Spring Symphony 1/2 *Fruhlingssinfonie* **1986 (PG-13)** A moody, fairy-tale biography of composer Robert Schumann, concentrating on his rhapsodic love affair with pianist Clara Weick. Kinski is very good as the rebellious daughter, while the music is even better. Reasonably accurate in terms of history; dubbed. **102m/C VHS, DVD.** *GE* Nastassja Kinski, Rolf Hoppe, Herbert Gronemeyer; ***D:*** Peter Schamoni; ***W:*** Peter Schamoni; ***C:*** Gerard Vandenburg.

Springfield Rifle 1/2 **1952** Based on the real-life story of Major Les Kearney, who joined forces with outlaws to catch the thief stealing government weapons. Average. **93m/C VHS, DVD.** Gary Cooper, Phyllis Thaxter, David Brian, Lon Chaney Jr., Paul Kelly, Phil Carey, Guinn "Big Boy" Williams; ***D:*** Andre de Toth; ***M:*** Max Steiner.

Springtime in the Rockies **1937** Autry is a cattle-ranch foreman whose employer decides to try raising sheep. This doesn't set well with the other ranchers, but Autry manages to save the day and sing a little too. **60m/B VHS, DVD.** Gene Autry, Polly Rowles, Smiley Burnette; ***D:*** Joseph Kane.

Springtime in the Rockies 1/2 **1942** A Broadway duo Vicky (Grable) and Dan (Payne) just can't get along despite being in love with each other. So Vicky decides to partner up with Victor (Romero) while Dan tries to make Vicky jealous by dating his Brazilian secretary Rosita (Miranda). Top-notch musical, with a touch of romantic tension and comedy. Beautifully filmed in the Canadian Rockies. ♫ I Had the Craziest Dream; Run Little Rainrop Run; A Poem Set to Music; Pan American Jubilee; I Like to Be Love by You; Chattanooga Choo Choo; Tic Tac Do Meu Coracao. **91m/C VHS.** Betty Grable, John Payne, Carmen Miranda, Cesar Romero, Charlotte Greenwood, Edward Everett Horton, Jackie Gleason; ***D:*** Irving Cummings; ***W:*** Ken Englund, Walter Bullock; ***C:*** Ernest Palmer.

Springtime in the Sierras 1/2 *Song of the Sierra* **1947** Rogers and Devine band together to fight a gang of poachers who prey on the wildlife of a game preserve. Features a number of songs by Rogers and The Sons of the Pioneers. **54m/B VHS, DVD.** Roy Rogers, Andy Devine, Jane Frazee, Stephanie Bachelor; ***D:*** William Witney.

The Sprinter 1/2 **1984** A young homosexual, while trying to submerge his confusion in professional track and field, gets to know a homely shot-putter and is seduced by her. In German with English subtitles. **90m/C VHS.** *GE* Dieter Eppler, Jurgen Mikol, Renate Muri; ***D:*** Christoph Boll; ***W:*** Christoph Boll; ***C:*** Peter Gauhe.

Sprung **1996 (R)** The dating scene among four young African Americans is examined in this well-intended, yet unfocused romantic comedy. Couple A are Brandy (Campbell) and Montel (Cundieff) who realize that they have a chance at true love. Couple B are their friends Adina (Parker) and Clyde (Torry) who try to sabatoge Brandy and Montel's happiness in order to save them from being "sprung" (in love) with each other. The camaraderie between the couples is funny, some of the time, but the humor often turns from vulgar to juvenile and scenes drag on a bit. Cundieff and Campbell are too bland to carry over the used plot but Torry is a comedic find who makes the film tolerable. **105m/C VHS, DVD.** Tisha Campbell, Paula Jai Parker, Rusty Cundieff, Joe Torry, John Witherspoon, Clarence Williams III; ***D:*** Rusty Cundieff; ***W:*** Darin Scott, Rusty Cundieff; ***C:*** Joao Fernandes; ***M:*** Stanley Clarke.

Spun **2002** A bleached-out, grunge look at meth heads. Ross (Schwartzman) is on a three-day crystal binge, thanks to hooking up with dealer Spider Mike (Leguizamo). Film lurches along from supplier to dealer to addict and from one disgusting scene to another. Who cares. **96m/C VHS, DVD.** Jason Schwartzman, John Leguizamo, Mena Suvari, Patrick Fugit, Brittany Murphy, Mickey Rourke, Peter Stormare, Alexis Arquette, Eric Roberts; ***D:*** Jonas Akerlund; ***W:*** Will De Los Santos, Creighton Vero; ***C:*** Eric Broms; ***M:*** Billy Corgan.

Spurs **1930** A rodeo star takes on a whole gang of rustlers and their imposing machine gun. This transitional western was made both with and without sound. **60m/B VHS.** Hoot Gibson, Robert E. Homans; ***D:*** B. Reeves Eason.

Sputnik *A Dog, a Mouse, and a Sputnik* **1961** A Frenchman, amnesiac after a car crash, comes up against Russian scientists, space-bound dogs, and weightlessness. Pleasant and charming family fun though clearly dated. Another fine performance from Auer. Dubbed. **80m/B VHS.** *FR* Noelia Noel, Mischa Auer, Denise Grey; ***D:*** Jean Dreville.

Spy **1989** A former spy who knows too much becomes the target of a renegade agency. **88m/C VHS.** Ned Beatty, Tim Choate, Bruce Greenwood, Catherine Hicks, Jameson Parker, Michael Tucker; ***D:*** Philip Frank Messina. **TV**

Spy Game 1/2 **2001 (R)** It's 1991, and cagey veteran spy Nathan Muir (Redford) is on the verge of retirement, when he discovers that former protege Tom Bishop (Pitt) is to be executed in a Chinese prison for espionage. Muir has 24 hours to rescue Bishop, and to do it, he must first outwit his CIA superiors, who would rather lose the rogue agent than risk damaging an international trade agreement. Story's core is implausible but script is dense with information and drama, and the ultra-brisk editing leaves little time to consider the inadequacies. The use of geopolitical atrocities to add weight to a romantic subplot between Bishop and a British foreign-aid worker (McCormack) feels forced and, at times, insensitive. But Redford's cool and sarcastic performance, recalling his role in "Three Days of the Condor," makes up for some deficiencies and anchors the film nicely. **127m/C VHS, DVD, HD DVD.** *US* Robert Redford, Brad Pitt, Catherine McCormack, Stephen (Dillon) Dillane, Larry Bryggman, Michael Paul Chan, Marianne Jean-Baptiste, David Hemmings, Matthew Marsh, Todd Boyce, Charlotte Rampling; ***D:*** Tony Scott; ***W:*** Michael Frost Beckner, David Arata; ***C:*** Dan Mindel; ***M:*** Harry Gregson-Williams.

Spy Games 1/2 *History is Made at Night* **1999** CIA agent Harry (Pullman) and Russian SVR agent Natasha (Jacob) dash around Helsinki chasing a videotape that contains U.S. satellite codes and spatting romantically. Old-fashioned and lame. **94m/C VHS, DVD.** *GB* Bill Pullman, Irene Jacob, Bruno Kirby, Glenn Plummer, Udo Kier, Andre Oumansky, Feodor Atkine; ***D:*** Ilkka Jarvilaturi; ***W:*** Patrick Amos; ***C:*** Michel Amathieu; ***M:*** Courtney Pine.

Spy Hard **1996 (PG-13)** Nielsen does yet another genre spoof—this time a combo of "Die Hard" meets James Bond. Agent Dick Steele aka WD40 (Nielsen) is brought out of retirement to thwart the plans of crazed General Rancor (Griffith) for world domination. Not much else plotwise, which ropes Nielsen along in domino fashion through the myriad of unimaginative spoofs on such films as "Speed" and "Pulp Fiction." Minus the charm and pace of parody pioneers Zucker/Abrahams/Zucker, this latest entry should retire the whole genre. Directorial debut of Friedberg. **80m/C VHS, DVD.** Leslie Nielsen, Nicolette Sheridan, Andy Griffith, Charles Durning, Marcia Gay Harden, Barry Bostwick; ***D:*** Rick Friedberg; ***W:*** Rick Friedberg, Dick Chudnow, Jason Friedberg, Aaron Seltzer; ***C:*** John R. Leonetti; ***M:*** Bill Conti.

Spy in Black *U-Boat 29* **1939** A German submarine captain returns from duty at sea during WWI and is assigned to infiltrate one of the Orkney Islands and obtain confidential British information. Known in the U.S. as "U-Boat 29," this film is based on a J. Storer Clouston novel. This was the first teaming of director Powell and writer Pressburger, who followed with "Contraband" in 1940. **82m/B VHS.** *GB* Conrad Veidt, Valerie Hobson, Sebastian Shaw, Marius Goring, June Duprez, Helen Haye, Cyril Raymond, Hay Petrie; ***D:*** Michael Powell; ***M:*** Miklos Rozsa.

Spy Kids **2001 (PG)** Rare live-action kid's movie that doesn't talk down to its target audience has pre-teens Carmen (Vega)and Juni Cortez (Sabara) bemoaning their boring life and dealing with troublesome bullies until their parents disappear. It seems that Mom (Gugino) and Dad (Banderas) are retired superspies who get kidnapped while on one last mission. It's up to the kids, along with perennial sidekick Marin, to save their folks (and the world) from evil kid-show host Fegan Floop (Cumming, bidding for the title of world's busiest screen villian) and Minion (Shalhoub). Director/writer/editor/composer Rodriquez makes a concerted effort to provide family entertainment with zero objectionable material but plenty of gee-whiz gadgetry, fanciful set design, and exciting action. He said he wanted to make a movie that he'd be proud to show his children and his parents. He has succeeded. **88m/C VHS, DVD.** *US* Alexa Vega, Daryl Sabara, Antonio Banderas, Carla Gugino, Alan Cumming, Tony Shalhoub, Teri Hatcher, Richard "Cheech" Marin, Robert Patrick, Danny Trejo, George Clooney; ***D:*** Robert Rodriguez; ***W:*** Robert Rodriguez; ***C:*** Guillermo Navarro; ***M:*** Robert Rodriguez, Danny Elfman, John Debney.

Spy Kids 2: The Island of Lost Dreams **2002 (PG)** Worthy sequel finds Carmen (Vega) and Juni (Sabara) fighting rival spy kids when they take on a mystery man and his creatures on a distant island. Vexing blond siblings Gary and Gerti Giggles (O'Leary and Osment) take credit for the Cortez's super-sleuthing at every turn. Meanwhile Cortez patriarch Gregorio (Banderas) has his own problems with the Giggles' dad Donnagon (Judge), as they battle for OSS leadership. Life in a spy family isn't always easy. All that aside, the newly minted Junior OSS agents must do their thing and save the day, traveling to the mutant-animal-populated island of mad scientist Buscemi. Nearly as good as the original. Montalban and Taylor as mom Ingrid's disapproving folks are a highlight. **86m/C VHS, DVD.** *US* Antonio Banderas, Carla Gugino, Alexa Vega, Daryl Sabara, Mike Judge, Steve Buscemi, Danny Trejo, Richard "Cheech" Marin, Ricardo Montalban, Holland Taylor, Matt O'Leary, Emily Osment; ***D:*** Robert Rodriguez; ***W:*** Robert Rodriguez; ***C:*** Robert Rodriguez; ***M:*** John Debney, Robert Rodriguez.

Spy Kids 3-D: Game Over **2003 (PG)** Yes, in order to watch the film, you need the funny glasses. Despite that bit of amusing nostalgia, George Clooney as the President of the United States and Sylvester Stallone in four different roles, this third and latest addition to director Rodriguez's "Spy Kids" franchise still doesn't manage to make much of an impression. The evil villain Toymaker (Stallone) and his three quirky alter ego henchmen (also Stallone) make a dangerous virtual reality video game which traps returning adolescent super-spies Juni (Sabara) and Carmen (Vega) inside. So it's parents (Banderas, Gugino) and grandpa (Montalban) to the rescue. With a tired plot, lackluster pacing, unimaginative visuals, and wooden acting, even the plethora of high-profile cameos can't save this chapter from virtual obscurity. **85m/C VHS, DVD.** *US* Antonio Banderas, Carla Gugino, Daryl Sabara, Alexa Vega, Ricardo Montalban, Sylvester Stallone, Holland Taylor, Danny Trejo, Mike Judge, Emily Osment, Matt O'Leary, Salma Hayek, Richard "Cheech" Marin, Bobby Edner, Courtney Jines, Alan Cumming, Tony Shalhoub, Steve Buscemi, Bill Paxton, George Clooney, Elijah Wood; ***D:*** Robert Rodriguez; ***W:*** Robert Rodriguez; ***C:*** Robert Rodriguez; ***M:*** Robert Rodriguez. Golden Raspberries '03: Worst Support. Actor (Stallone).

The Spy Next Door 1/2 **2010 (PG)** Chop-socky legend Chan must have been suffering from post-concussion syndrome when he agreed to star in this formulaic action/comedy for the kiddies. He plays Bob Ho, a mild mannered salesman who also happens to be an international super-spy. After retiring, all he wants to do is settle down with sweetheart-next-door Gillian (Valetta) and her three children, all of whom think Bob is a bore. After a plot device sends their mom out of town, the kids are foisted on Bob with alleged domestic hilarity ensuing. When geeky son Ian accidentally downloads classified material to his iPod, a pair of cartoonish Russian spies come after him. It's up to Bob to save the day and win the admiration of the children. Okay for young kids or fans of Chan's stunts, but predictable for everyone else. **m/C DVD.** Jackie Chan, Madeline Carroll, Alina Foley, Will Shadley, George Lopez, Billy Ray Cyrus, Amber Valletta, Katherine Boecher; ***D:*** Brian Levant; ***W:*** Jonathan Bernstein, James Greer; ***C:*** Dean Cundey; ***M:*** David Newman.

Spy of Napoleon **1936** A French aristocrat agrees to marry the illegitimate daughter of Emperor Napoleon III and finds himself working to uncover traitors to the throne. Based on Baroness Orczy's novel. **77m/B VHS.** *GB* Richard Barthelmess, Dolly Haas, Francis L. Sullivan, Frank Vosper, Joyce Bland, Lyn Harding, Henry Oscar, Marjorie Mars; *D:* Maurice Elvey; *W:* Fred V. Merrick; *C:* Curt Courant.

The Spy Ring *International Spy; Somewhere in Paris* **1938** Captain Todd Hayden (Hall) is the top player on an army-camp polo team. What he doesn't know might kill him—some of the players are evil spies, looking to steal plans for a new anti-aircraft gun. Will Hayden have to throw the big polo match to catch the bad guys? **61m/B VHS.** William Hall, Jane Wyman, Esther Ralston, Robert Warwick, Leon Ames; *D:* Joseph H. Lewis; *W:* George Waggner, Francis Van Wyck Mason.

Spy School *Doubting Thomas* **2008 (PG)** Thomas has been caught telling too many tall tales so no one believes him when he says there's a plot to kidnap the president's daughter. So Thomas is forced to come up with a plan to save her himself. **88m/C DVD.** Forrest Landis, AnnaSophia Robb, Rider Strong, Lea Thompson, D.L. Hughley, Roger Bart; *D:* Mark Blutman; *W:* Mark Blutman, David BuBos; *C:* Paul Elliott. **VIDEO**

Spy Smasher **1942** A war reporter uses his supposed death (and a covenient twin brother) to go underground and fight Nazi counterfeiters trying to wreck the economy. 12-episode serial. "Spy Smasher Returns" is actually a condensed-version not a sequel. **185m/B VHS.** Kane Richmond, Marguerite Chapman, Sam Flint, Hans Schumm, Tristram Coffin; *D:* William Witney.

Spy Smasher Returns ½ **1942** The exciting 12-part serial "Spy Smasher" was cut and edited into feature length and released under this title. The masked marvel and his twin brother battle enemy agents during WWII. This new version is just as exciting as the original cliffhanger. **185m/B VHS.** Kane Richmond, Marguerite Chapman, Sam Flint, Hans Schumm, Tristram Coffin; *D:* William Witney.

Spy Train ½ *Time Bomb* **1943** War correspondent Bruce Grant (Travis) gets mixed up in two stories on a speeding train ride. One is the story of famous-rich-girl-gone-missing, Jane Thornwall (Craig). The other is enemy agents, a mysterious travel bag, and a Nazi bomb that's set to go off at 10:22 p.m. **61m/B DVD.** Richard Travis, Catherine Craig, Chick Chandler, Thelma White, Evelyn Brent; *D:* Harold Young; *W:* Scott Littlefield, Leslie Swabacker; *C:* Mack Stengler.

Spy Trap ½ *Zits* **1988** Four junior-high school friends concoct bogus military plans using futuristic toys for blueprints. The "secret" plans get sold to the Russians and the kids find themselves chased by the unhappy KGB and the CIA. Family adventure. **96m/C VHS.** Elya Baskin, Danielle Du Clos, Jason Kristofer, Cameron Johann, Devin Ratray, Kimble Joyner; *D:* Arthur Sherman; *W:* Robert Littell; *C:* John Stanier; *M:* Jonathan Sheffer.

The Spy Who Came in from the Cold ½ **1965** The acclaimed adaptation of the John Le Carre novel about an aging British spy who attempts to infiltrate the East German agency. Prototypical Cold War thriller, with emphasis on de-glamorizing espionage. Gritty and superbly realistic with a documentary style which hampered it at the boxoffice. **110m/B VHS, DVD.** Richard Burton, Oskar Werner, Claire Bloom, Sam Wanamaker, Peter Van Eyck, Cyril Cusack, Rupert Davies, Michael Hordern; *D:* Martin Ritt; *W:* Paul Dehn, Guy Trosper; *C:* Oswald Morris; *M:* Sol Kaplan. British Acad. '66: Film; Golden Globes '66: Support. Actor (Werner).

The Spy Who Loved Me **1977 (PG)** James Bond teams up with female Russian Agent XXX to squash a villain's plan to use captured American and Russian atomic submarines in a plot to destroy the world. The villain's henchman, 7'2" Kiel, is the steel-toothed Jaws. Carly Simon sings the memorable, Marvin Hamlisch theme song, "Nobody Does It Better." **136m/C VHS, DVD.** *GB* Roger Moore, Barbara Bach, Curt Jurgens, Richard Kiel, Caroline Munro, Walter Gotell, Geoffrey Keen, Valerie Leon, Bernard Lee, Lois Maxwell, Desmond Llewelyn; *D:* Lewis Gilbert; *W:* Christopher Wood, Richard Maibaum; *C:* Claude Renoir, Lamar Boren; *M:* Marvin Hamlisch, Paul Buckmaster.

Spy with a Cold Nose **1966** A sporadically funny spy spoof about a bugged dog passed between British and Soviet intelligence. Hard-working cast keeps it from collapsing. **93m/C VHS.** *GB* Laurence Harvey, Daliah Lavi, Lionel Jeffries; *D:* Daniel Petrie.

The Spy Within *Flight of the Dove* **1994 (R)** Spy Alex (Russell) is working undercover as a call girl and Will (Glenn) is an explosives expert on the run from his past. The two share more than a mutual attraction since a covert organization wants them both dead. Confusing plot but fast-paced action. Railsback's directorial debut. **92m/C VHS, DVD.** Theresa Russell, Scott Glenn, Lane Smith, Terence Knox, Katherine Helmond, Alex Rocco, Joe Pantoliano, Rudy Ramos; *D:* Steve Railsback; *W:* Lewis Green.

Spymaker: The Secret Life of Ian Fleming ½ *Spymaker* **1990** Fictionalized account of the creator of the ultimate spy, James Bond, and his early days in the British Secret Service. Fans of the Bond movies will appreciate the numerous inside jokes. Connery is the son of Sean. **96m/C VHS.** *GB* Jason Connery, Kristin Scott Thomas, Joss Ackland, Patricia Hodge, David Warner, Fiona Fullerton, Richard Johnson; *D:* Ferdinand Fairfax. **TV**

S*P*Y*S **1974 (PG)** An attempt to cash in on the success of "M*A*S*H," this unfunny spy spoof details the adventures of two bumbling CIA men who botch a Russian defection, and get both sides after them. Usually competent director Kershner had a bad day. **87m/C VHS, DVD.** Donald Sutherland, Elliott Gould, Joss Ackland, Zouzou, Shane Rimmer, Vladek Sheybal, Nigel Hawthorne; *D:* Irvin Kershner; *W:* Malcolm Marmorstein, Lawrence J. Cohen; *M:* Jerry Goldsmith.

Squanto: A Warrior's Tale **1994 (PG)** Family adventure fare about 17th-century Massachusetts brave Squanto (Beach), who's captured by English traders and taken to Plymouth, England for display as a "savage." He manages to escape, eventually hiding aboard a trading vessel bound for America, and on returning home even brings about a peace between fearful Pilgrims and a neighboring tribe (which culminates in the first Thanksgiving feast). It may be history lite but it's also a thoughtful, adventurous saga with good performances, and fine location filming in Nova Scotia and Cape Breton, Canada. **101m/C VHS, DVD.** Adam Beach, Mandy Patinkin, Michael Gambon, Nathaniel Parker, Eric Schweig, Donal Donnelly, Stuart Pankin, Alex Norton, Irene Bedard; *D:* Xavier Koller; *W:* Darlene Craviotto; *M:* Joel McNeely.

Square Dance ½ *Home is Where the Heart Is* **1987 (PG-13)** A Texas teenager leaves the farm where she's been raised by her grandfather to live in the city with her promiscuous mother (Alexander, cast against type) where she befriends a retarded young man (yes, it's Lowe, also cast against type). Too slow, but helped by good acting. **118m/C VHS, DVD.** Jane Alexander, Jason Robards Jr., Rob Lowe, Winona Ryder, Deborah Richter, Guich Koock, Elbert Lewis; *D:* Daniel Petrie; *W:* Alan Hines; *M:* Bruce Broughton.

Square Dance Jubilee ½ **1951** TV scouts hit Prairie City in search of cowboy stars, and stumble onto cattle rustlers; 21 C&W tunes support a near-invisible plot, suitable for fridge runs. **78m/B VHS.** Mary Beth Hughes, Donald (Don "Red") Barry, Wally Vernon, John Eldridge; *D:* Paul Landres; *W:* William Nolte, Ron Ormond, Daniel Ullman; *C:* Ernest Miller; *M:* Walter Greene.

The Square Peg **1958** Norman Pitkin (Wisdom) is a civilian worker during WWII who causes continual problems by digging up a road outside an army barracks. Fed-up, the commander has Norman and his colleague Grimsdale (Chapman) conscripted and sent to repair roads in France. Grimsdale is captured by German soldiers and Norman comes to the attention of the French Resistance because he just happens to look exactly like a Nazi general, and they wish to put his presence to good use. Much mistaken bumbling ensues as Norman tries to free British prisoners without getting caught himself. **88m/B DVD.** *GB* Norman Wisdom, Edward Chapman, Honor Blackman, Campbell Singer, Hattie Jacques, Brian Worth, Terence Alexander; *D:* Jack Paddy Carstairs; *W:* Henry Blyth, Jack Davies, Eddie Leslie; *C:* Jack Cox; *M:* Philip Green.

Square Shooter ½ **1935** Tim Baxter was framed and served time; returning home he seeks to reclaim the ranch left to him by his Uncle Cameron. A forged will has given the ranch to varmint Jed Miller and crooked banker Ezra Root. Tim hides out until he can prove what's going on but is betrayed by the last person he expects. **57m/B DVD.** Tim McCoy, Charles Middleton, Julie Bishop, Erville Alderson, John Darrow, J. Farrell MacDonald, William V. Mong; *D:* David Selman; *W:* Harold Shumate; *C:* George Meehan Jr.

Square Shoulders ½ **1929** Adventures of young military school student with geometric anatomy (Coghlan). **58m/B VHS.** Frank "Junior" Coghlan, Louis Wolheim, Anita Louise, C. Montague Shaw; *D:* E. Mason Hopper.

The Squeaker ½ *Murder on Diamond Row* **1937** Good Edgar Wallace mystery about a disgraced inspector trying to clear his name. **77m/C VHS.** Edmund Lowe, Sebastian Shaw; *M:* Miklos Rozsa.

The Squeaker ½ **1965** Complicated but interesting thriller about the underworld goings-on after a big-time diamond heist. German remake of an early (1930) British talkie, also done in 1937, based on the Edgar Wallace novel. **95m/B VHS.** *GE* Heinz Drache, Eddi Arent, Klaus Kinski, Barbara Rutting; *D:* Alfred Vohrer.

The Squeeze **1977 (R)** Scotland Yard detective Keach, fired for drunkeness, gets a chance to reinstate himself when his ex-wife is caught up in a brutal kidnapping scheme. Slim script gives good cast uphill work. Ordinary thriller. Available with Spanish subtitles. **106m/C VHS, DVD.** Stacy Keach, Carol White, David Hemmings, Edward Fox, Stephen Boyd, Angelo Infanti; *D:* Michael Apted.

The Squeeze ½ *Diamond Thieves; The Heist; Rip-Off* **1980** An aging safecracker is hired for a final job, but learns that his cohorts plan to kill him when the heist is finished. Blah revenge thriller. **93m/C VHS, DVD.** *IT* Lee Van Cleef, Karen Black, Edward Albert, Lionel Stander, Robert Alda; *D:* Anthony M. Dawson; *W:* Paul Costello; *C:* Sergio d'Offizi; *M:* Paolo Vasile.

The Squeeze WOOF! **1987 (PG-13)** Keaton is wasted in this attempt at a comedy about a small-time con artist who discovers a Mafia plan to fix a lottery electromagnetically. **101m/C VHS, DVD.** Michael Keaton, Rae Dawn Chong, John Davidson, Ric Abernathy, Bobby Bass, Joe Pantoliano, Meat Loaf Aday, Paul Herman; *D:* Roger Young; *C:* Arthur Albert; *M:* Miles Goodman.

Squeeze **1997 (R)** Self-conscious but not unappealing first effort made on a shoestring budget, with a director who teaches acting at a Boston youth center and who wrote his script based on the lives of his three teenaged lead actors. Tyson (Burton), Hector (Cutanda) and Boa (Duong) lead aimless lives on Boston's meaner streets where trouble finds them despite their efforts to stay (more-or-less) clear. **96m/C VHS, DVD.** Tyrone Burton, Eddie Cutanda, Phuong Duong, Geoffrey Rhue, Russell Jones, Leigh Williams; *D:* Robert Patton-Spruill; *W:* Robert Patton-Spruill; *C:* Richard Moos; *M:* Bruce Flowers.

Squeeze Play WOOF! **1979** Group of young women start a softball team and challenge the boyfriends to a game. Standard battle of the sexes takes places, with a wet T-shirt contest thrown in for good measure. Cheap, plotless, offensive trash from Troma. **92m/C VHS, DVD.** Al Corley, Jennifer Hetrick, Jim Metzler, Jim Harris, Rick Gitlin, Helen Campitelli, Rick Kahn, Diana Valentien; *D:* Lloyd Kaufman; *W:* Charles Kaufman, Haim Pekelis; *C:* Lloyd Kaufman.

The Squid and the Whale **2005 (R)** Writer-director Baumbach's semi-autobiographical tale of two adolescent brothers struggling to cope with their self-centered parents' divorce. Set in Brooklyn in 1986, Walt (Eisenberg) and Frank (Kline) are the progeny of pompous writer Bernard (Daniels), whose career is faltering, and unfaithful writer Joan (Linney), whose career is on the rise. The title refers to a popular exhibit at the Natural History Museum and its significance gradually becomes clear. Expert acting by all concerned; newcomer Kline is the son of actors Kevin Kline and Phoebe Cates. **88m/C DVD.** *US* Jeff Daniels, Laura Linney, Jesse Eisenberg, Owen Kline, Anna Paquin, William Baldwin, Halley Feiffer, David Benger; *D:* Noah Baumbach; *W:* Noah Baumbach; *C:* Robert Yeoman; *M:* Britta Phillips, Dean Wareham. L.A. Film Critics '05: Screenplay; Natl. Bd. of Review '05: Screenplay; N.Y. Film Critics '05: Screenplay; Natl. Soc. Film Critics '05: Screenplay.

Squirm **1976 (R)** Storm disrupts a highly charged power cable, electrifying a host of garden-variety worms. The worms then turn themselves into giant monsters that terrorize a small town in Georgia. The opening credits claim it's based on an actual 1975 incident. Yeah, right. Okay entry in the giant worm genre. **92m/C VHS, DVD.** Don Scardino, Patricia Pearcy, Jean Sullivan; *D:* Jeff Lieberman; *W:* Jeff Lieberman.

Squizzy Taylor **1984** The rise and fall of real-life Australian mob boss Squizzy Taylor in the 1920s. Colorful period gangster drama loses steam about halfway through. **82m/C VHS.** *AU* Jacki Weaver, Alan Cassell, David Atkins; *D:* Kevin James Dobson; *C:* Dan Burstall.

SS Girls WOOF! *Casa Privata per le SS; Private House of the SS* **1977** After the assassination attempt of July 1944, Hitler does not trust the Wehrmacht and extends the power of the SS over Germany. General Berger entrusts Hans Schillemberg to recruit a specially chosen group of prostitutes who must test the fighting spirit and loyalty of the generals. Seedy exploitation. **82m/C VHS, DVD.** *IT* Gabriele Carrara, Marina Daunia, Vassilli Karis, Macha Magal, Thomas Rudy, Lucic Bogoljub Benny, Ivano Staccioli; *D:* Bruno Mattei; *W:* Bruno Mattei; *C:* Emilio Giannini; *M:* Gianni Marchetti.

Sssssss ½ **1973 (PG-13)** Campy, creepy story of snake expert Carl Stoner (Strother Martin) who's developed a serum from cobra venom that just happens to turn human beings into snakes. His latest unwitting guinea pig is reasearch assistant David Blake (Benedict). Cool makeup effects. **99m/C VHS, DVD.** Strother Martin, Dirk Benedict, Heather Menzies, Richard B. Shull, Tim O'Connor, Jack Ging; *D:* Bernard L. Kowalski; *W:* Hal Dresner; *C:* Gerald Perry Finnerman; *M:* Patrick Williams.

Stacey ½ *Stacey and Her Gangbusters* **1973 (R)** Ex-Playmate Randall stars as Stacey Hansen, a beautiful, implausibly talented private detective. Hyper-convoluted plot, too much sex and violence detract from a potentially not-wretched whodunit. **87m/C VHS.** Anne Randall, Marjorie Bennett, Anitra Ford, Alan Landers, James Westmoreland, Christina Raines; *D:* Andy Sidaris.

Stacking *Season of Dreams* **1987 (PG)** In the 1950s, a Montana family is threatened with losing their farm. Typical, boring '80s farmland tragedy with coming of age tale. **95m/C VHS.** Christine Lahti, Megan Follows, Frederic Forrest, Peter Coyote, Jason Gedrick; *D:* Martin Rosen; *W:* Victoria Jenkins; *C:* Richard Bowen, Paul Elliott; *M:* Patrick Gleeson.

Stacy's Knights *Double Down* **1983 (PG)** A seemingly shy girl happens to have an uncanny knack for blackjack. With the odds against her and an unlikely group of "knights" to aid her, she sets up an implausible "sting" operation. Blah TV fodder for the big screen. **95m/C VHS, DVD.** Kevin Costner, Andra Millian; *D:* Jim Wilson; *W:* Michael Blake.

Stag **1997 (R)** Bachelor party goes out of control and it's every guy for himself. Best man Michael (Van Peebles) surprises groom-to-be Victor (Stockwell) by inviting guys to his bachelor party that he hasn't seen in years—for good reason—such as drug dealer Pete (McCarthy). But when stripper Kelly (McShane) is accidentally killed, Pete's the only one to keep his cool and lay out their options. And this group is a lot more interested in self-preservation than in doing the right thing. **92m/C VHS, DVD.** Mario Van Peebles, Andrew McCarthy, John Stockwell, Kevin Dillon, Taylor Dane, William McNamara, Jerry Stiller, Ben Gazzara, John Henson, Jenny (Jennifer) McShane; ***D:*** Gavin Wilding; ***W:*** Evan Tylor; ***C:*** Maryse Alberti; ***M:*** Paul Zaza.

Stage Beauty 1/2 **2004 (R)** Set in London during the 1660s, this entertaining but sometimes stiff drama centers on gender identity. Actor Ned Kynaston (Crudup) is renowned for his female roles (his Desdemona is legendary) at a time when women were banned from the stage. But that does not stop his devoted dresser Maria (Danes) from appearing in the same part in an illegal production that comes to the attention of flamboyant King Charles II (Everett), who is then persuaded that only women should now play female parts. This turn of events makes Ned's life a misery since he doesn't know how to play the man—either on or off the stage. Danes is somewhat mediocre playing a mediocre actress but Crudup is eye-catching as he plays vain, charming, desperate, and, finally, resilient. Adapted by Hatcher from his play "Compleat Female Stage Beauty." **105m/C DVD.** *GE GB US* Billy Crudup, Claire Danes, Rupert Everett, Tom Wilkinson, Ben Chaplin, Edward Fox, Zoe Tapper; ***D:*** Richard Eyre; ***W:*** Jeffrey Hatcher; ***C:*** Andrew Dunn; ***M:*** George Fenton.

Stage Door 1/2 **1937** An energetic ensemble peek at the women of the theatre. A boarding house for potential actresses houses a wide variety of talents and dreams. Patrician Hepburn and wisecracking Rogers make a good team in a talent-packed ensemble. Realistic look at the sub-world of Broadway aspirations includes dialogue taken from idle chat among the actresses between takes. Based on the play by Edna Ferber and George S. Kaufman, who suggested in jest a title change to "Screen Door," since so much had been changed. Watch for young stars-to-be like Ball, Arden, and Miller. **92m/B VHS, DVD.** Katharine Hepburn, Ginger Rogers, Lucille Ball, Eve Arden, Andrea Leeds, Jack Carson, Adolphe Menjou, Gail Patrick; ***D:*** Gregory La Cava. N.Y. Film Critics '37: Director (La Cava).

Stage Door Canteen 1/2 **1943** The Stage Door Canteens were operated by the American Theatre Wing during WWII for servicemen on leave. They were staffed by some of the biggest stars of the day, 65 of whom are featured here. The slight, hokey plot concerns three soldiers who fall for canteen workers while on furlough in NYC. Many musical numbers, cameos, and walk-ons by a plethora of stars. ♫ We Mustn't Say Goodbye; Bombshell From Brooklyn; The Machine Gun Song; Sleep, Baby, Sleep in Your Jeep; Quick Sands; You're Pretty Terrific Yourself; Don't Worry Island; We Meet in the Funniest Places; A Rookie and His Rhythm. **135m/B VHS, DVD.** Cheryl Walker, William Terry, Marjorie (Reardon) Riordan, Lon (Bud) McCallister, Sunset Carson, Tallulah Bankhead, Merle Oberon, Katharine Hepburn, Paul Muni, Ethel Waters, Judith Anderson, Ray Bolger, Helen Hayes, Harpo Marx, Gertrude Lawrence, Ethel Merman, Edgar Bergen, George Raft, Benny Goodman, Peggy Lee, Count Basie, Kay Kyser, Guy Lombardo, Xavier Cugat, Johnny Weissmuller; ***D:*** Frank Borzage; ***W:*** Delmer Daves; ***C:*** Harry Wild; ***M:*** Al Dubin, Freddie Rich.

Stage Fright **1950** Wyman will stop at nothing to clear her old boyfriend, who has been accused of murdering the husband of his mistress, an actress (Dietrich). Disguised as a maid, she falls in love with the investigating detective. Dietrich sings "The Laziest Gal in Town." The Master's last film made in England until "Frenzy" (1971). **110m/B VHS, DVD.** *GB* Jane Wyman, Marlene Dietrich, Alastair Sim, Sybil Thorndike, Michael Wilding, Kay Walsh; ***D:*** Alfred Hitchcock.

Stage Fright **1983** Bashful actress is transformed into a homicidal killer after a latent psychosis in her becomes active. **82m/C VHS.** Jenny Neumann, Gary Sweet; ***M:*** Brian May.

Stage Struck 1/2 **1936** Broadway show dance director George Randall (Powell) gets stuck working with no-talent star Peggy Revere (Blondell), who's only cast because her deep pockets are backing the whole show. George and Peggy are constantly butting heads, but show producer Fred Harris (Williams) smoothes things out by telling Peggy that George is secretly in love with her-and telling George that Peggy is secretly in love with her! **91m/B VHS.** Dick Powell, Joan Blondell, Frank McHugh, Charles Adler; ***D:*** Busby Berkeley; ***W:*** Robert Lord, Tom Buckingham.

Stage Struck 1/2 **1957** Strasberg reprises the role made famous by Katharine Hepburn as a determined, would-be actress in this mediocre remake of "Morning Glory" (1933). Christopher Plummer's screen debut shows little of his later talent. **95m/B VHS.** Henry Fonda, Susan Strasberg, Christopher Plummer, Herbert Marshall, Joan Greenwood; ***D:*** Sidney Lumet; ***M:*** Alex North.

Stage to Mesa City **1948** Marshal LaRue must find out who is behind the pesky attacks on the stage line to Mesa City. Chesebro, as usual, is a good bad guy. A few chuckles between fist fights and shoot-em-ups. **52m/B VHS, DVD.** Lash LaRue, Al "Fuzzy" St. John, George Chesebro, Jennifer Holt, Russell Arms; ***D:*** Ray Taylor.

Stagecoach **1939** Varied group of characters with nothing in common are stuck together inside a coach besieged by bandits and Indians. Considered structurally perfect, with excellent direction by Ford, it's the film that made Wayne a star as the Ringo Kid, an outlaw looking to avenge the murder of his brother and father. The first pairing of Ford and Wayne changed the course of the modern western. Stunning photography by Bert Glennon and Ray Binger captured the mythical air of Monument Valley, a site that Ford was often to revisit. Based on the story "Stage to Lordsburg" by Ernest Haycox. Remade miserably with in 1966 and again—why?—as a TV movie in 1986. **100m/B VHS, DVD.** John Wayne, Claire Trevor, Thomas Mitchell, George Bancroft, John Carradine, Andy Devine, Donald Meek, Louise Platt, Berton Churchill, Tim Holt, Tom Tyler, Chris-Pin (Ethier Crispin Martini) Martin, Francis Ford, Jack Pennick; ***D:*** John Ford; ***W:*** Dudley Nichols; ***C:*** Bert Glennon, Ray Binger. Oscars '39: Support. Actor (Mitchell), Score; AFI '98: Top 100, Natl. Film Reg. '95;; N.Y. Film Critics '39: Director (Ford).

Stagecoach **1986** A forgettable remake of the classic 1939 western about a motley crew of characters in a cross-country coach beset by thieves and Indians. **95m/C VHS, DVD.** Willie Nelson, Waylon Jennings, Johnny Cash, Kris Kristofferson, John Schneider, Elizabeth Ashley, Mary Crosby, Anthony Newley, Anthony (Tony) Franciosa; ***D:*** Ted Post; ***M:*** Willie Nelson. **TV**

Stagecoach Buckaroo 1/2 **1942** Cowboy Steve Hardin is saved from a lynching by Molly Denton and in gratitude signs on with Molly's father as a stagecoach guard. Just in time too since some outlaws are after a gold shipment. **58m/B DVD.** Johnny Mack Brown, Fuzzy Knight, Nell O'Day, Herbert Rawlinson, Anne Nagel, Henry Hall, Ernie Adams, Glenn Strange; ***D:*** Ray Taylor; ***W:*** Al Martin; ***C:*** Jerome Ash.

Stagecoach to Denver **1946** Lane as Red Ryder investigates a stagecoach wreck and uncovers a land-grabbing plot led by-who else?—the pillar of the community (Barcroft). Well-directed "Red Ryder" episode. **53m/B VHS, DVD.** Allan "Rocky" Lane, Roy Barcroft, Robert (Bobby) Blake, Peggy Stewart, Martha Wentworth; ***D:*** R.G. Springsteen.

Stagefright **1987** A maniacal serial killer tries to cover his trail by joining the cast of a play about mass murder. The other actors soon have more to worry about than remembering their lines. Typical low-grade horror. **95m/C VHS, DVD.** David Brandon, Barbara Cupisti, Robert Gligorov; ***D:*** Michele (Michael) Soavi; ***W:*** Luigi Montefiore.

Stairway to Heaven 1/2 *A Matter of Life and Death* **1946 (PG)** Wonderful romantic fantasy features Niven as RAF pilot Peter D. Carter, who falls in love with American WAC June (Hunter). Forced to bail out during a mission, Peter is rescued and must undergo a risky operation. What's riskier is an angel (Goring) has made a mistake and realizes that Peter should have died. While on the operating table, Peter's spirit travels to Heaven and pleads his case for life against a harsh prosecutor (Massey) and a group of judges. Terrific work by cinematographer Cardiff. **104m/C VHS, DVD.** *GB* David Niven, Kim Hunter, Marius Goring, Raymond Massey, Roger Livesey, Robert Coote, Kathleen Byron, Richard Attenborough; ***D:*** Michael Powell, Emeric Pressburger; ***W:*** Michael Powell, Emeric Pressburger; ***C:*** Jack Cardiff; ***M:*** Allan Gray.

Stakeout **1962** An ex-con tries to start life anew, but every time he finds a good job, his past catches up with him. A return to the life of crime looks tempting. Predictable and familiar plot, but performances are sincere. **81m/B VHS.** Bing (Neil) Russell, Billy Hughes, Bill Hale, Jack Harris, Eve Brent; ***D:*** James Landis; ***W:*** James Landis.

Stakeout 1/2 **1987 (R)** A sometimes violent comedy-thriller about a pair of detectives who stake out a beautiful woman's apartment, hoping for a clue to the whereabouts of her psycho boyfriend who has broken out of prison. One of them (Dreyfuss) then begins to fall in love with her. Natural charm among Estevez, Dreyfuss, and Stowe that adds to the proceedings, which are palpably implausible and silly. Slapstick sequel "Another Stakeout" followed in 1993. **117m/C VHS, DVD.** Richard Dreyfuss, Emilio Estevez, Madeleine Stowe, Aidan Quinn, Forest Whitaker, Dan Lauria, Earl Billings; ***D:*** John Badham; ***W:*** Jim Kouf; ***M:*** Arthur B. Rubinstein.

Stalag 17 **1953** A group of American G.I.s in a German POW camp during WWII suspects the opportunistic Sefton (Holden) of being the spy in their midst. One of the very best American movies of the 1950s, adapted from the play by Donald Bevan and Edmund Trzcinski. Wilder, so good at comedy, proved himself equally adept at drama, and brought a top-drawer performance out of Holden. Features superb photography from Ernest Laszlo, and a wonderful score. **120m/B VHS, DVD.** William Holden, Don Taylor, Peter Graves, Otto Preminger, Harvey Lembeck, Robert Strauss, Sig Rumann, Richard Erdman, Neville Brand, Gil Stratton, Robinson Stone, Robert Shawley, Jay Lawrence; ***D:*** Billy Wilder; ***W:*** Billy Wilder, Edwin Blum; ***C:*** Ernest Laszlo; ***M:*** Franz Waxman. Oscars '53: Actor (Holden).

Stalag Luft **1993** Senior British officer James Forrester (Fry) is regarded by fellow POWs as a first-class idiot, since he has a record 23 escapes and re-captures. But he's determined to break all 327 prisoners out of their Nazi camp while the nervous German Kommandant keeps one eye on the advancing Allied army and the other on his prisoners. **103m/C VHS.** *GB* Stephen Fry, Geoffrey Palmer, Nicholas Lyndhurst, David Bamber, Hugh Bonneville; ***D:*** Adrian Shergold. **TV**

Stalin 1/2 **1992** The story of the leader of the Soviet Union who ruled with an iron fist from 1924-53. One of the most feared men of the 20th century, he wrenched the largest country in the world singlehandedly from a backward, pastoral farmland to an industrial landscape. He was also responsible for the feared purges of the late 1930s where more than a million people were executed. Also explored is the dictator's relationships with his family, including how marriage to a cunning, sadistic, paranoid tyrant affected his wife. Filmed at actual historical locations in Russia. **173m/C VHS.** Robert Duvall, Julia Ormond, Jeroen Krabbe, Joan Plowright, Maximilian Schell, Frank Finlay, Roshan Seth, Daniel Massey, Miriam Margolyes, Jim Carter, Joanna Roth, Andras Balint; ***D:*** Ivan Passer; ***W:*** Paul Monash; ***C:*** Vilmos Zsigmond. **CABLE**

Stalingrad **1994** Group of German stormtroopers fall victim to the brutal war of attrition over Stalingrad in 1942 and 1943. Realistic depiction of war is not for the fainthearted. Originally a TV miniseries; German with subtitles. **150m/C VHS, DVD.** *GE* Dominique Horwitz, Thomas Kretschmann, Jochen Nickel; ***D:*** Joseph Vilsmaier; ***W:*** Joseph Vilsmaier; ***C:*** Joseph Vilsmaier; ***M:*** Norbert J. Schneider.

Stalk the Wild Child 1/2 **1976** Well-intentioned but unconvincing American remake of Truffaut's "The Wild Child," about a child psychologist's efforts to rehabilitate a boy raised by wolves. TV pilot inspired "Lucan," a short-lived series. **78m/C VHS.** David Janssen, Trish Van Devere, Benjamin Bottoms, Joseph Bottoms; ***D:*** William (Billy) Hale. **TV**

Stalked 1/2 **1994 (R)** Daryl Gleeson (Underwood) saves the life of the widowed Brooke's (D'Abo) young son (Fennell). Naturally, she's grateful—only Daryl takes her gratitude for something more intimate and becomes fixated on her every move. **95m/C VHS.** Maryam D'Abo, Jay Underwood, Tod Fennell, Lisa Blount, Alex Karzis, Karen Robinson, Vivian Reis; ***D:*** Douglas Jackson.

Stalked WOOF! **1999** Macedonian transplant Aleksandr (Ognenovski) wakes up to an American nightmare, finding himself the target of a small town's wrath when framed for murder. Mayhem ensues, but not without those forced moments of pathos, romance, and testosterone-infused male bonding. Writer/director/star Ognenovski retreads the formula from early Stallone, Schwarzenegger, and Van Damme films: an outsider trapped in a hostile environment with only his wits and a few hundred rounds to protect him. Here, the cliches pile up faster than the body count. Add abysmal dialog, casting misfires (like the actor with a thick Russian accent playing the mayor of a small American town), and fight scenes rife with punches that don't connect, and we are in the presence of a potential Ed Wood for the action crowd. Sublime schlock, any way you slice it. **93m/C DVD.** Jorgo Ognenovski, Meto Jovanovski, Lisa Marie Wilson; ***D:*** Jorgo Ognenovski; ***W:*** Jorgo Ognenovski, Mary Quijano; ***C:*** Ricardo Jacques Gale.

Stalker **1979** A meteorite, crashing to Earth, has caused a wasteland area known as the Zone. The Zone is forbidden to anyone except special guides called Stalkers. Three Stalkers enter the region searching for its center, which contains a room that supposedly reveals fantasies. From the Soviet team that made "Solaris." Filmed with both color and black-and-white sequences. Suspenseful atmosphere due to the director's use of long takes, movement, and color. In Russian with English subtitles. **160m/C VHS, DVD.** *RU* Alexander Kaidanovsky, Nikolai Grinko, Anatoli (Otto) Solonitzin, Alice Freindlikh; ***D:*** Andrei Tarkovsky; ***M:*** Eduard Artemyev.

Stalker 1/2 *Fatal Affair* **1998 (R)** And what a very dumb, psychopathic stalker he is too. Family man Mack Maddox (Howell) is selected for jury duty and realizes that the murder victim is a woman with whom he had an affair. What's worse is the accused killer (Underwood) finds out that Maddox is involved with his wife and begins, well, stalking him and his family, even though Maddox has confessed his involvement to his wife and the cops. The plot never does make any sense and the flat performances don't help either. **93m/C VHS, DVD.** *CA* C. Thomas Howell, Jay Underwood, Mark Camacho, Maxim Roy, Bryn McAuley; ***D:*** Marc S. Grenier; ***W:*** Michael Rauch; ***C:*** Georges Archambault; ***M:*** Normand Corbeil. **VIDEO**

Stalking Danger 1/2 *C.A.T. Squad* **1986 (PG)** A secret government group must terminate an assassination plot by a terrorist organization. **97m/C VHS.** Joe Cortese, Steve James, Patricia Charbonneau, Jack Youngblood; ***D:*** William Friedkin; ***M:*** Ennio Morricone.

Stalking Laura 1/2 *I Can Make You Love Me* **1993** Laura Black (Shields) has just landed her first job at a California engineering firm where she meets co-worker Richard Farley (Thomas). He asks her out—she turns him down—he starts harassing her. Laura reports it to the company, who eventually fire Farley, and obtains a restraining order. He goes on a murderous rampage. Fact-based TV movie with Thomas effective as the dangerous obsessive. **90m/C VHS, DVD.** Brooke Shields, Richard Thomas, Viveka Davis, William Allen Young, Richard Yniguez, Scott Bryce; ***D:*** Michael Switzer; ***W:*** Frank Abatemarco; ***C:*** Rob Draper, Sylvester Levay.

The Stalking Moon 1/2 **1969 (G)** Indian scout Peck, ready to retire, meets a woman and her half-breed son who have been captives of the Apaches for 10 years. He agrees to help them escape but learns that the woman's Indian husband is hunting them down. Skeletal plot with little meat on it; great scenery but you wouldn't know it.

109m/C VHS. Gregory Peck, Eva Marie Saint, Robert Forster, Noland Clay; ***D:*** Robert Mulligan; ***W:*** Alvin Sargent.

Stamp of a Killer **1987 (PG)** A tough cop tries to decipher the pattern of a rampaging serial killer. **95m/C VHS.** Jimmy Smits, Judith Light, Audra Lindley, Michael Parks, Rhea Perlman; ***D:*** Larry Elikann. **TV**

Stan Helsing **2009 (R)** Inept and unfunny parody of horror cliches. On Halloween, video store clerk Stan Helsing and three friends are on their way to a Halloween party when they detour into a ghost town inhabited by such familiar icons as Freddy Kreuger, Pinhead, Leatherface, and Jason. And a cross-dressing Leslie Nielsen. **90m/C DVD.** Steve Howey, Diora Baird, Kenan Thompson, Desi Lydic, Leslie Nielsen; ***D:*** Bo Zenga; ***W:*** Bo Zenga; ***C:*** Robert New; ***M:*** Ryan Shore. **VIDEO**

Stand Alone **1985 (R)** WWII vet Durning battles local dope dealers in his New York neighborhood. Self-serious anti-drug flick miscasts Durning (overweight and looking silly in fight scenes) and Grier. **94m/C VHS.** Charles Durning, Pam Grier, James Keach; ***D:*** Alan Beattie; ***W:*** Roy Carlson.

Stand and Deliver **1928** War vet joins Greek ranks for the smell of gunpowder in the morning and meets woman of his dreams. Kidnapped by infamous outlaws, he pledges allegiance to them before turning them over to the authorities, and he's free to live happily ever after with heartthrob. **57m/B VHS.** Rod La Rocque, Lupe Velez, Warner Oland, James Dime, Frank Lanning, Donald Crisp; ***D:*** Donald Crisp.

Stand and Deliver **1988 (PG)** A tough teacher inspires students in an East L.A. barrio to take the Advanced Placement Test in calculus. A superb, inspirational true story, with a wonderful performance from Olmos. **105m/C VHS, DVD.** Edward James Olmos, Lou Diamond Phillips, Rosanna Desoto, Andy Garcia, Will Gotay, Ingrid Oliu, Virginia Paris, Mark Eliot, Eugene Robert Glazer; ***D:*** Ramon Menendez; ***W:*** Ramon Menendez, Tom Musca; ***C:*** Tom Richmond; ***M:*** Craig Safan. Ind. Spirit '89: Actor (Olmos), Director (Menendez), Film, Screenplay, Support. Actor (Phillips), Support. Actress (Desoto).

Stand by Me **1986 (R)** A sentimental, observant adaptation of the Stephen King novella "The Body." Four 12-year-olds trek into the Oregon wilderness to find the body of a missing boy, learning about death and personal courage. Told as a reminiscence by narrator "author" Dreyfuss with solid performances from all four child actors. Too much gratuitous obscenity, but a very good, gratifying film from can't-miss director Reiner. **87m/C VHS, DVD.** River Phoenix, Wil Wheaton, Jerry O'Connell, Corey Feldman, Kiefer Sutherland, Richard Dreyfuss, Casey Siemaszko, John Cusack; ***D:*** Rob Reiner; ***W:*** Raynold Gideon; ***C:*** Thomas Del Ruth; ***M:*** Jack Nitzsche.

Stand-In **1937** When a Hollywood studio is threatened with bankruptcy, the bank sends in timid efficiency expert Howard to save it. Satire of studio executives and big-budget movie making. Bogart is interestingly cast and effective in his first comedy role, playing a drunken producer in love with star Shelton. **91m/B VHS, DVD.** Humphrey Bogart, Joan Blondell, Leslie Howard, Alan Mowbray, Marla Shelton, Jack Carson; ***D:*** Tay Garnett.

Stand-In **1985** A strange comedy-action film that takes a behind-the-scenes look at sleaze films and organized crime. **87m/C VHS.** Danny Glover; ***D:*** Robert Zagone.

Stand-Ins **1/2 1997** Would-be actresses in pre-WWII Hollywood find themselves looking for fame and unwillingly settling for stand-in status. The girls all hang out at Jack's (Mandylor) bar, where Greta Garbo-double, druggie Shirley (Zuniga), battles with cynical Bette Davis stand-in, Monica (Ladd), as they celebrate the birthday of Jean Harlowish Martha Anne (Davis), along with Mae West clone Peggy (Chatton) and Marlene Dietrich stand-in Rhonda (Crider). This desperate gang are bitchy and frustrated and, of course, theatrical. Based on Kelleher's one-act play. **89m/C VHS, DVD.** Daphne Zuniga, Jordan Ladd, Sammi Davis, Missy (Melissa) Crider, Charlotte Chatton, Costas Mandylor, Katherine Heigl; ***D:*** Harvey Keith; ***W:*** Harvey Keith, Ed Kelleher; ***C:*** Andrzej Sekula; ***M:*** Bill Elliott.

Stand Off **1/2 1989** Two young hoodlums with guns take 18 girls hostage in a dormitory. In Hungarian with English subtitles. **97m/C VHS.** *HU* Ary Beri, Gabor Svidrony, Zbigniew Zapasiewicz, Istvan Szabo; ***D:*** Gyula Gazdag.

Stand Off **1/2** *April One* **1993 (PG-13)** Dramatization of a 14-hour hostage incident that took place at the Bahamanian High Commission in Ottawa on April Fools Day in 1986. Ex-con David Maltby (Shellen) politely demands that an empty firehall become a shelter for women by taking the High Commissioner for the Bahamas, Jane Briscoe (Sears), as a hostage. Somewhat flawed but psychologically interesting. **90m/C VHS.** *CA* Stephen Shellen, Djanet Sears, David Strathairn, Gordon Clapp, Pierre Curzi, Wayne Robson; ***D:*** Murray Battle; ***W:*** Murray Battle; ***M:*** Jonathan Goldsmith.

Stand Up and Cheer **1/2 1934 (PG)** The new federal Secretary of Entertainment organizes a huge show to raise the country's depressed spirits. Near-invisible plot, fantastic premise are an excuse for lots of imagery, dancing, and comedy, including four-year-old Temple singing "Baby Take a Bow." Also available colorized. ♫ I'm Laughing; We're Out of the Red; Broadway's Gone Hillbilly; Baby Take a Bow; This Is Our Last Night Together; She's Way Up Thar; Stand Up and Cheer. **80m/B VHS.** Shirley Temple, Warner Baxter, Madge Evans, Nigel Bruce, Stepin Fetchit, Frank Melton, Lila Lee, James Dunn, John Boles, Scotty Beckett; ***D:*** Hamilton MacFadden; ***W:*** Will Rogers, Ralph Spence; ***C:*** Ernest Palmer.

Standard Operating Procedure **1/2 2008 (R)** Morris's extremely disturbing and morose documentary examines the story behind the infamous photographs out of Abu Ghraib, which portrayed U.S. guards torturing and degrading Iraqi prisoners by posing them in humiliating sexual positions, dressing them up in costumes, and inflicting other indignities. Descriptions by members of the prison's MP squad and reenactments serve to reveal the motivation behind these bizarre acts, which play out as chillingly as any contemporary thriller. **116m/C DVD.** *US* ***D:*** Errol Morris; ***W:*** Errol Morris; ***C:*** Robert Chappell, Robert Richardson; ***M:*** Danny Elfman.

Stander **1/2 2003 (R)** Set in 1976 in South Africa, the volatile antihero of the title (played with bravado by Jane) is the youngest police captain in Johannesburg and is in charge of the riot patrol during a Soweto protest march that quickly turns violent. Guilt-stricken after killing an unarmed black youth, Andre Stander realizes that the police are so busy enforcing apartheid that a white criminal can get away with anything. To test his theory, he robs a bank, and then another bank, and then more. Eventually arrested, Stander, along with mates McCall (Fletcher) and Heyl (O'Hara), breaks out of prison and goes on another bank-robbing spree and into the annals of folk hero notoriety. Loosely based on a true story. **111m/C DVD.** *GB CA SA GE* Thomas Jane, Dexter Fletcher, Deborah Kara Unger, Marius Weyers, David O'Hara, Ashley Taylor; ***D:*** Bronwen Hughes; ***W:*** Bronwen Hughes, Bima Stagg; ***C:*** Jess Hall; ***M:*** David Holmes, Steve Hilton.

Standing in the Shadows of Motown **2002 (PG)** Director Justman and writer Slutsky (who wrote the book of the same name) reveal the behind-the-scenes story of the "Funk Brothers," the musicians who backed-up Motown's best and were unknown to anyone but their peers and music fanatics. There's archival footage, interviews with the remaining "Brothers," and a concert performance with contemporary singers doing the Motown standards accompanied by these living legends. **108m/C VHS, DVD.** *US* ***D:*** Paul Justman; ***W:*** Ntozake Shange, Walter Dallas; ***C:*** Doug Milsome, Lon Stratton. N.Y. Film Critics '02: Feature Doc.

Standing on Fishes **1999 (R)** With their relationship already on the rocks, Caleb, an aspiring sculptor, pushes Erica's feminist ideals to the limit by taking an odd job of designing a fake vagina for a film. So when an adoring kindred soul makes moves on him, he's more than tempted. Writing/directing team Tatum and Scott Lynn also star in the lead roles. **89m/C VHS, DVD.** Bradford Tatum, Meredith Scott Lynn, Jason Priestley, Lauren Fox, Kelsey Grammer, Pamela Reed, James Black; ***D:*** Bradford Tatum, Meredith Scott Lynn; ***W:*** Bradford Tatum; ***C:*** Mark Mervis; ***M:*** Juliet Prater. **VIDEO**

Standing Still **2005 (R)** Talented cast is wasted in an all-too-familiar story about a post-collegiate reunion of 20-somethings who find adulthood a generally bewildering trial. Los Angeles couple Michael (Garcia) and Elise (Adams) gather their friends together for their wedding. Among them are best man Rich (Stanford) and his girlfriend Samantha (Sagemiller), sarcastic Lana (Suvari) and oddball Pockets (Abrahams), movie star Simon (Van Der Beek), agent Quentin (Hanks), and outspoken lesbian Jennifer (German), who has issues with the bride, who's not the only one keeping secrets. **90m/C DVD.** *US* Adam Garcia, Amy Adams, Aaron Stanford, Melissa Sagemiller, Mena Suvari, Jon Abrahams, Xander Berkeley, Lauren German, Colin Hanks, Roger Avary, Ethan (Randall) Embry, James Van Der Beek; ***D:*** Michael Cole Weiss; ***W:*** Timm Sharp, Matthew Perniciaro; ***C:*** Robert Brinkmann; ***M:*** B.C. Smith.

Standing Tall **1978** A small-time cattle rancher takes on a high-class land baron in this average, made-for-TV western set during the Depression. Playing a "half-breed," Forster carries an otherwise mediocre effort. **100m/C VHS.** Robert Forster, Linda Evans, Will Sampson, L.Q. Jones; ***D:*** Harvey Hart.

Standoff **1/2 1997 (R)** A botched FBI raid on a Texas cult stronghold lead the four fed survivors to seek shelter in an abandoned farmhouse. Surrounded by gunfire, they're soon not any safer inside, especially when they capture two of the cult's female recruits. **91m/C VHS.** Robert Sean Leonard, Natasha Henstridge, Dennis Haysbert, Keith Carradine, Tricia Vessey; ***D:*** Andrew Chapman; ***W:*** Andrew Chapman.

Stanley **1/2 1972 (PG)** Seminole Vietnam veteran Robinson uses rattlesnakes as his personal weapon of revenge against most of mankind. Thoroughly wretched effort in the gross-pets vein of "Willard" and "Ben." **108m/C VHS, DVD.** Chris Robinson, Alex Rocco, Susan Carroll; ***D:*** William Grefe.

Stanley and Iris **1/2 1990 (PG-13)** Blue collar recent widow Fonda meets coworker De Niro, whose illiteracy she helps remedy. Romance follows, inevitably but excruciatingly. Leads' strong presence helps along a very slow, underdeveloped plot. **107m/C VHS, DVD.** Jane Fonda, Robert De Niro, Swoosie Kurtz, Martha Plimpton, Harley Cross, Jamey Sheridan, Feodor Chaliapin Jr., Zohra Lampert, Loretta Devine, Julie Garfield; ***D:*** Martin Ritt; ***W:*** Harriet Frank Jr., Irving Ravetch; ***M:*** John Williams.

Stanley and Livingstone **1939** The classic Hollywood kitsch version of the Victorian legend-based-on-fact. American journalist Tracy sets out into darkest Africa to locate a long lost Brisith explorer. Lavish, dramatically solid fictionalized history. (The real Stanley did not become a missionary—but hey, this is the movies). Tracy is excellent, as usual, and low-key. **101m/B VHS.** Spencer Tracy, Cedric Hardwicke, Nancy Kelly, Walter Brennan, Richard Greene, Charles Coburn, Henry Hull, Henry Travers, Miles Mander, Holmes Herbert, Paul Stanton, Brandon Hurst, Joseph Crehan, Russell Hicks; ***D:*** Henry King; ***C:*** George Barnes; ***M:*** Alfred Newman.

The Star **1952** A washed-up and self-destructive former Hollywood star (Davis, who allegedly took the role to lampoon rival Joan Crawford) gets, and blows, one last chance at a comeback and finds love with a former protege (Hayden) who gave up stardom for the simple life. To the chagrin of both him and her daughter (Wood), she can't quite give up the siren song of her past glory and continues to sabotage what could be a happy life. Gut-wrenching and squirmy for the scenes in which Davis's character, for which she received an Oscar nomination, debases herself personally and professionally. **89m/B VHS, DVD.** Bette Davis, Sterling Hayden, Natalie Wood, Warner Anderson, Minor Watson, June Travis, Paul Frees, Robert Warwick, Barbara Lawrence, Fay Baker, Herb Vigran, Stuart Heisler; ***W:*** Katherine Albert, Dale Eunson; ***C:*** Ernest Laszlo; ***M:*** Victor Young.

Star! *Those Were the Happy Times* **1968** Campy showbiz extravaganza based on the life of famed musical comedy performer Gertrude Lawrence (Andrews), star of the London and Broadway stage. Film follows Lawrence's adventures from the British music halls to her fateful meeting with Noel Coward (Massey), who would not only become her dearest friend but perform with and write for her as well. A tumultuous private life is also on display. 17 lavishly staged musical numbers helped boost the cost of the film to $14 million—big bucks in '68. Movie was a colossal flop on opening and was recut, deleting 50 minutes, but still didn't recoup its losses. Has gained a cult following. ♫ Down at the Old Bull and Bush; Piccadilly; Star!; Oh, It's a Lovely War; In My Garden of Joy; Forbidden Fruit; Parisian Pierrot; Someday I'll Find You; Has Anybody Seen Our Ship?. **172m/C VHS, DVD.** Julie Andrews, Daniel Massey, Richard Crenna, Michael Craig, Robert Reed, Bruce Forsyth, Beryl Reid, John Collin, Alan Oppenheimer, Anthony Eisley, Jenny Agutter, J. Pat O'Malley, Richard Karlan, Lynley Laurence, Harvey Jason, Elizabeth St. Clair; ***D:*** Robert Wise; ***W:*** William Fairchild; ***C:*** Ernest Laszlo.

The Star Chamber **1983 (R)** A conscientious judge (Douglas) sees criminals freed on legal technicalities and wonders if he should take justice into his own hands. He finds a secret society that administers justice extra-legally. Implausible yet predictable. **109m/C VHS, DVD.** Michael Douglas, Hal Holbrook, Yaphet Kotto, Sharon Gless, James B. Sikking; ***D:*** Peter Hyams; ***W:*** Peter Hyams, Roderick Taylor.

Star Crash **1/2** *Stella Star* **1978 (PG)** Trio of adventurers (woman, man, and robot) sent by emperor Plummer square off against interstellar evil (Spinell) by using their wits and technological wizardry. Semi-funny and cheesy sci-fi, done with style beyond its limited budget. **92m/C VHS, DVD.** *IT* Caroline Munro, Marjoe Gortner, Christopher Plummer, David Hasselhoff, Robert Tessier, Joe Spinell, Nadia Cassini, Judd Hamilton; ***D:*** Lewis (Luigi Cozzi) Coates; ***W:*** Lewis (Luigi Cozzi) Coates; ***M:*** John Barry.

Star Crystal **1985 (R)** Aboard a spaceship, an indestructible alien hunts down the human crew. Cheap imitation of "Alien." **93m/C VHS, DVD.** C. Jutson Campbell, Faye Bolt, John W. Smith; ***D:*** Lance Lindsay.

Star 80 **1/2 1983 (R)** Based on the true-life tragedy of Playmate of the Year Dorothy Stratten and her manager-husband Paul Snider as they battle for control of her body, her mind, and her money, with gruesome results. Roberts is overpowering as the vile Snider, but the movie is generally unpleasant. Fosse's last film. **104m/C VHS, DVD.** Mariel Hemingway, Eric Roberts, Cliff Robertson, David Clennon, Josh Mostel, Roger Rees, Carroll Baker; ***D:*** Bob Fosse; ***W:*** Bob Fosse; ***C:*** Sven Nykvist; ***M:*** Ralph Burns.

Star Hunter **1/2 1995 (R)** When a bus filled with football players and cheerleaders takes a wrong turn, it winds up in an intergalatic hunting ground where the humans become the prey. Lots of lame chase and would-be action scenes. **80m/C VHS, DVD.** Roddy McDowall, Stella Stevens, Ken Stott, Zack (Zach) Ward, Wendy Schumacher; ***D:*** Cole McKay.

A Star Is Born **1/2 1937** A movie star declining in popularity marries a shy girl and helps her become a star. Her fame eclipses his and tragic consequences follow. Shows Hollywood-behind-the-scenes machinations. Stunning ending is based on the real-life tragedy of silent film star Wallace Reid, who died of a morphine overdose in 1923 at age 31. Remade twice, in 1954 and 1976. **111m/C VHS, DVD.** Janet Gaynor, Fredric March, Adolphe Menjou, May Robson, Andy Devine, Lionel Stander, Franklin Pangborn; ***D:*** William A. Wellman; ***W:*** William A. Wellman, David O. Selznick, Dorothy Parker; ***C:*** William

Howard Greene; ***M:*** Max Steiner. Oscars '37: Story.

A Star Is Born 🦴🦴🦴½ **1954 (PG)** Aging actor helps a young actress to fame. She becomes his wife, but alcoholism and failure are too much for him. She honors his memory. Remake of the 1937 classic was Garland's triumph, a superb and varied performance. Newly restored version reinstates over 20 minutes of long-missing footage, including three Garland musical numbers. ♫ I'll Get By; You Took Advantage of Me; Black Bottom; Peanut Vendor; My Melancholy Baby; Swanee; It's a New World; Gotta Have Me Go with You; Somewhere There's Someone. **175m/C VHS, DVD.** Judy Garland, James Mason, Jack Carson, Tommy Noonan, Charles Bickford, Emerson Treacy, Charles Halton; ***D:*** George Cukor; ***W:*** Moss Hart; ***C:*** Sam Leavitt; ***M:*** Harold Arlen, Ira Gershwin. Golden Globes '55: Actor—Mus./Comedy (Mason), Actress—Mus./Comedy (Garland), Natl. Film Reg. '00.

A Star Is Born 🦴🦴 **1976 (R)** Miserable update of the 1937 and 1954 classics permitting Ms. Streisand to showcase her hit song "Evergreen." The tragic story of one rock star (the relentlessly un-hip Streisand) on her way to the top and another (good old boy Kristofferson) whose career is in decline. Kristofferson is miscast, Streisand eventually numbing, but film may interest those looking into big-budget, big-star misfires. ♫ Watch Closely Now; Spanish Lies; Hellacious Acres; With One More Look At You; Woman in the Moon; Queen Bee; Everything; Crippled Cow; I Believe in Love. **140m/C VHS, DVD.** Barbra Streisand, Kris Kristofferson, Paul Mazursky, Gary Busey, Sally Kirkland, Oliver Clark, Marta Heflin, Robert Englund; ***D:*** Frank Pierson; ***W:*** Frank Pierson, Joan Didion, John Gregory Dunne; ***C:*** Robert L. Surtees; ***M:*** Paul Williams. Oscars '76: Song ("Evergreen"); Golden Globes '77: Actor—Mus./Comedy (Kristofferson), Actress—Mus./Comedy (Streisand), Film—Mus./Comedy, Song ("Evergreen"), Score.

Star Kid 🦴🦴🦴 *The Warrior of Waverly Street* **1997 (PG)** Twelve-year-old Spencer Griffith (Mazzello) is the new wimp in town, with a face that immediately attracts the fists of the biggest bully around, Turbo Bradley (Simmrin). On the run from Turbo, Spencer encounters Cy, an experimental cyber-battlesuit built by cutesy good aliens to save themselves from reptilian bad aliens. After inserting himself into Cy, and solving a few problems common to boy-inside-alien relationships, Spencer takes his first awkward steps, gets some humorous revenge on Turbo, and learns some lessons about confronting one's fears and accepting responsibility. Film delivers enough action and effects to keep everyone happy. **101m/C VHS, DVD.** Joseph Mazzello, Alex Daniels, Richard Gilliland, Joey Simmrin, Brian Simpson, Danny Masterson, Corinne Bohrer, Arthur Burghardt, Ashlee Levitch, Heidi Lotito; ***D:*** Manny Coto; ***W:*** Manny Coto; ***C:*** Ronn Schmidt; ***M:*** Nicholas Pike.

Star Knight 🦴 *Starknight* **1985 (PG-13)** Weird combo of sci fi and medieval romance. A spaceship lands near a European castle and the local princess falls for one of the visitors—much to her daddy's dismay. Very silly. **92m/C VHS, DVD.** *SP* Harvey Keitel, Klaus Kinski, Fernando Rey; ***D:*** Fernando Colomo.

The Star Maker 🦴🦴 *The Star Man; L'Uomo delle Stelle* **1995 (R)** Con man Joe Morelli (Castellitto) travels through the villages of 1950s Sicily claiming to be a movie talent scout. For a fee, he offers the locals a chance to shoot a screen test, which reveals various bits and pieces of their lives. There's a brief romance and Joe's scam eventually comes to light but the story's more nostalgia than narrative. Italian with subtitles. **107m/C VHS, DVD.** *IT* Sergio Castellitto, Tiziana Lodato; ***D:*** Giuseppe Tornatore; ***W:*** Giuseppe Tornatore, Fabio Rinaudo; ***C:*** Dante Spinotti; ***M:*** Ennio Morricone.

Star Maps 🦴🦴 **1997 (R)** Ambitious and ambiguous effort from first-time director Arteta has boyish Carlos (Spain) chase his dreams of movie stardom on the streets of Hollywood. Pimped by his manipulative and brutal father Pepe (Figueroa), Carlos sells "maps of the stars' homes" as a cover for his real job, male prostitute. Dad's hooker mistress (Murphy) mentors him in the family business. Add in a mother (Velez) "recovering" from a nervous breakdown by talking to long-dead Mexican comedy star Cantinflas, and a brother (Chandler) who acts out scenes from Mexican wrestling movies, and it's a wonder he doesn't make his screen debut on Jerry Springer. Despite fine performances and a solid debut effort from Arteta, the tragic elements don't fit well with the attempted comic tone of the rest of the movie. **80m/C VHS.** Douglas Spain, Efrain Figueroa, Lysa Flores, Kandeyce Jensen, Martha Velez, Annette Murphy, Vincent Chandler, Al Vincente, Herbert Siguenza, Robin Thomas, Jeff Michalski; ***D:*** Miguel Arteta; ***W:*** Miguel Arteta; ***C:*** Chuy Chavez; ***M:*** Lysa Flores.

Star of Midnight 🦴🦴 **1935** A lawyer/detective becomes involved in the disappearance of the leading lady in a Broadway show and the murder of a columnist. Powell and Rogers take on characters similar to Nick and Nora Charles, but the pizazz of the "Thin Man" series is missing. **90m/B VHS.** Ginger Rogers, William Powell, Paul Kelly; ***D:*** Stephen Roberts.

The Star Packer 🦴🦴 **1934** Wayne puts on a marshal's badge, straightens out a gang of crooks, and still finds time for romance. Implausible and kind of dull early Wayne vehicle. **53m/B VHS, DVD.** John Wayne, George "Gabby" Hayes, Earl Dwire, Yakima Canutt; ***D:*** Robert North Bradbury; ***W:*** Robert North Bradbury; ***C:*** Archie Stout.

Star Portal 🦴🦴 **1997 (R)** Alien Rena (Massey) comes to Earth seeking blood to help her dying race. Assuming the form of a babe, she falls in love with a hematologist (Bauer), and must battle a law-enforcer from her own planet. **83m/C VHS.** Athena Massey, Steven Bauer, Stephen Davies, Anthony Crivello; ***D:*** Jon Purdy. **VIDEO**

Star Quest 🦴 *Beyond the Rising Moon; Space 2074* **1989** A genetically engineered woman fights for freedom from her corporate creators. Mediocre effects and some pointless action; done much better by Ridley Scott in "Blade Runner." **90m/C VHS.** Tracy Davis, Hans Bachman, Michael Mack; ***D:*** Phillip Cook.

Star Quest 🦴🦴 ½ **1994 (R)** Eight astronauts, suspended in a cryogenic sleep for nearly 100 years, awaken to find the human race has been destroyed by a nuclear holocaust. **95m/C VHS, DVD.** Steven Bauer, Emma Samms, Alan Rachins, Brenda Bakke, Ming Na, Gregory McKinney, Cliff DeYoung; ***D:*** Rick Jacobson.

Star Reporter 🦴 ½ **1939** A son takes over his father's newspaper when dad is killed by gangsters. The son uses the paper in an attempt to destroy the underworld, but stumbles on some startling personal information that could drastically backfire on him. Generally interesting plot, but has some implausibility and too-broad characterization. **62m/B VHS, DVD.** Warren Hull, Marsha Hunt, Morgan Wallace, Clay Clement, Wallis (Clarke) Clark, Virginia Howell, Paul Fix, Joseph Crehan; ***D:*** Howard Bretherton.

Star Slammer 🦴 ½ **1987 (R)** A beautiful woman is unjustly sentenced to a brutal intergalactic prison ship. She leads the convicts to escape amid zany situations. Unevenly funny sci-fi comedy. **85m/C VHS, DVD.** Ross Hagen, John Carradine, Sandy Brooke, Aldo Ray; ***D:*** Fred Olen Ray; ***W:*** Michael Sonye; ***C:*** Paul Elliot; ***M:*** Anthony Harris.

Star Spangled Girl 🦴 ½ **1971 (G)** One of Neil Simon's lesser plays, one of his least movies. A pert, patriotic young lady captures the hearts of two left-wing alternative-newspaperguys next door; their political conflicts never rise above bland sitcom level. **94m/C VHS, DVD.** Sandy Duncan, Tony Roberts, Todd Susman, Elizabeth Allen; ***D:*** Jerry Paris; ***W:*** Neil Simon; ***C:*** Sam Leavitt; ***M:*** Charles Fox.

Star Spangled Rhythm 🦴🦴🦴 **1942** Movie studio guard (Moore) has told his son (Bracken), a sailor, that he's actually the head of the studio in this WW2 musical/comedy. When he learns his son and his pals are coming for a visit, he enlists the aid of a friendly studio switchboard operator (Hutton) to pull a fast one. (Luckily, the real studio boss is out of town). Plot doesn't matter anyway since its just an excuse for a lot of studio stars to show up and perform. ♫ A Sweater, a Sarong and a Peek-a-Boo Bang; That Old Black Magic; Hit the Road to Dreamland; Old Glory; On the Swing Shift; Doing It for Defense; Sharp as a Tack; He Loved Me Till the All-Clear Came. **99m/B VHS, DVD.** Betty Hutton, Eddie Bracken, Victor Moore, Bing Crosby, Ray Milland, Bob Hope, Veronica Lake, Dorothy Lamour, Susan Hayward, Dick Powell, Mary Martin, Alan Ladd, Paulette Goddard, Cecil B. DeMille, Arthur Treacher, Preston Sturges, Eddie Anderson, William Bendix; ***D:*** George Marshall; ***W:*** Melvin Frank, George S. Kaufman, Norman Panama, Arthur Ross, Harry Tugend; ***C:*** Theodor Sparkuhl, Leo Tover.

Star Time 🦴 ½ **1992** Henry is a mentally ill loser who wants to be as happy and famous as his favorite TV stars. Deciding to kill himself, Henry is stopped by the mysterious Sam Bones, who offers him TV stardom—at a steep price. Henry achieves his 15 minutes of fame as a serial killer and his only link to reality is a female social worker. **85m/C VHS.** Michael St. Gerard, John P. Ryan, Maureen Teefy; ***D:*** Alexander Cassini; ***W:*** Alexander Cassini; ***C:*** Fernando Arguelles.

Star Trek 🦴🦴🦴 *Star Trek: The IMAX Experience; Star Trek: The Future Begins* **2009 (PG-13)** Director Abrams boldly takes the Starfleet crew where it hasn't been in a long time—on a lively, eventful, action-charged voyage that introduces the old familiar gang literally from the beginning, in James T. Kirk's (Pine) case when he is born amidst amazingly vibrant and explosive chaos. Spock's Vulcan race becomes the target of baffling vengeance by an angry Romulan, Nero (Bana), and of course the Enterprise and every Federation planet are threatened by association. The new set of actors each holds some fantastical similarity to the original '60s cast but each makes it their own without lampooning. Pine has just the right amount of bravado playing well off of Urban's Bones as well as Quinto's Spock. Adding to the nostalgia is Nimoy's return as elder Spock, who makes a meaningful space-time-continuum appearance. No doubt the crew will live long and prosper—in a sequel or two. **127m/C DVD.** *US* Chris Pine, Zachary Quinto, Simon Pegg, Karl Urban, John Cho, Zoe Saldana, Anton Yelchin, Eric Bana, Winona Ryder, Bruce Greenwood, Ben Cross, Leonard Nimoy, Jenny (Jennifer) Morrison, Rachel Nichols, Tyler Perry, Clifton (Gonzalez) Collins Jr., Faran Tahir, Deep Roy, Chris Hemsworth; ***D:*** J.J. (Jeffrey) Abrams; ***W:*** Roberto Orci, Alex Kurtzman; ***C:*** Dan Mindel; ***M:*** Michael Giacchino; ***V:*** Greg Grunberg, Majel Barrett. Oscars '09: Makeup.

Star Trek: The Motion Picture 🦴🦴 ½ **1979 (PG)** The Enterprise fights a strange alien force that threatens Earth in this first film adaptation of the famous TV series. Shatner's Kirk has been promoted to admiral and is called to take command of the vessel. He gets his old crew to tag along as well. Underrated at its theatrical release, but has benefitted from time, re-evaluation, and a director's cut. **136m/C VHS, DVD.** William Shatner, Leonard Nimoy, DeForest Kelley, James Doohan, Stephen Collins, Persis Khambatta, Nichelle Nichols, Walter Koenig, George Takei, Majel Barrett, Mark Lenard, Grace Lee Whitney; ***D:*** Robert Wise; ***W:*** Harold Livingston; ***C:*** Richard H. Kline; ***M:*** Jerry Goldsmith.

Star Trek 2: The Wrath of Khan 🦴🦴🦴 **1982 (PG)** Picking up from the 1967 Star Trek episode "Space Seed," Admiral James T. Kirk and the crew of the Enterprise must battle Khan, an old foe out for revenge. Warm and comradly in the nostalgic mode of its successors. Introduced Kirk's former lover and unknown son to the series plot, as well as Mr. Spock's "death," which led to the next sequel (1984's "The Search for Spock"). **113m/C VHS, DVD.** William Shatner, Leonard Nimoy, Ricardo Montalban, DeForest Kelley, Nichelle Nichols, James Doohan, George Takei, Walter Koenig, Kirstie Alley, Merritt Butrick, Paul Winfield, Bibi Besch; ***D:*** Nicholas Meyer; ***W:*** Jack Sowards; ***C:*** Gayne Rescher; ***M:*** James Horner.

Star Trek 3: The Search for Spock 🦴🦴 ½ **1984 (PG)** Captain Kirk hijacks the USS Enterprise and commands the aging crew to go on a mission to the Genesis Planet to discover whether Mr. Spock still lives (supposedly he died in the last movie). Klingons threaten, as usual. Somewhat slow and humorless, but intriguing. Third in the series. **105m/C VHS, DVD.** William Shatner, Leonard Nimoy, DeForest Kelley, James Doohan, George Takei, Walter Koenig, Mark Lenard, Robin Curtis, Merritt Butrick, Christopher Lloyd, Judith Anderson, John Larroquette, James B. Sikking, Nichelle Nichols, Cathie Shirriff, Miguel Ferrer, Grace Lee Whitney; ***D:*** Leonard Nimoy; ***W:*** Harve Bennett; ***C:*** Charles Correll; ***M:*** James Horner.

Star Trek 4: The Voyage Home 🦴🦴🦴 **1986 (PG)** Kirk and the gang go back in time (to the 1980s, conveniently) to save the Earth of the future from destruction. Filled with hilarious moments and exhilarating action; great special effects enhance the timely conservation theme. Watch for the stunning going-back-in-time sequence. Spock is particularly funny as he tries to fit in and learn the '80s lingo! Also available as part of Paramount's "director's series," in which Nimoy discusses various special effects aspects in the making of the film. One of the best in the series. **119m/C VHS, DVD.** William Shatner, DeForest Kelley, Catherine Hicks, James Doohan, Nichelle Nichols, George Takei, Walter Koenig, Mark Lenard, Leonard Nimoy, Michael Berryman, Majel Barrett, Brock Peters, John Schuck, Jane Wyatt; ***D:*** Leonard Nimoy; ***W:*** Nicholas Meyer, Harve Bennett, Peter Krikes, Steve Meerson; ***C:*** Don Peterman; ***M:*** Leonard Rosenman.

Star Trek 5: The Final Frontier 🦴 ½ **1989 (PG)** A renegade Vulcan kidnaps the Enterprise and takes it on a journey to the mythic center of the universe. Shatner's big-action directorial debut (he also co-wrote the script) is a poor follow-up to the Nimoy-directed fourth entry in the series. Heavy-handed and pretentiously pseudo-theological. **107m/C VHS, DVD.** William Shatner, Leonard Nimoy, DeForest Kelley, James Doohan, Laurence Luckinbill, Walter Koenig, George Takei, Nichelle Nichols, David Warner, Melanie Shatner, Harve Bennett; ***D:*** William Shatner; ***W:*** David Loughery, William Shatner; ***C:*** Andrew Laszlo; ***M:*** Jerry Goldsmith. Golden Raspberries '89: Worst Picture, Worst Actor (Shatner), Worst Director (Shatner).

Star Trek 6: The Undiscovered Country 🦴🦴 ½ **1991 (PG)** The final chapter in the long running Star Trek series to feature the original crew of the Enterprise. The Federation and the Klingon Empire are preparing a much-needed peace summit but Captain Kirk has his doubts about the true intentions of the Federation's longtime enemies. When a Klingon ship is attacked, Kirk and the crew of the Enterprise, who are accused of the misdeed, must try to find the real perpetrator. Has an exciting, climactic ending. As is typical of the series, the film highlights current events—glasnost—in its plotlines. Meyer also directed th e second Star Trek movie ("The Wrath of Khan") and wrote the screenplay for the fourth ("The Voyage Home"). **110m/C VHS, DVD.** William Shatner, Leonard Nimoy, DeForest Kelley, James Doohan, George Takei, Walter Koenig, Nichelle Nichols, Christopher Plummer, Kim Cattrall, Iman, David Warner, Mark Lenard, Grace Lee Whitney, Brock Peters, Kurtwood Smith, Rosanna Desoto, John Schuck, Michael Dorn, Christian Slater; ***D:*** Nicholas Meyer; ***W:*** Nicholas Meyer, Denny Martin Flinn; ***C:*** Hiro Narita; ***M:*** Cliff Eidelman.

Star Trek: First Contact 🦴🦴🦴 **1996 (PG-13)** The eighth big-screen Trek saga is firmly in the hands of the "Next Generation" cast as Picard and the Enterprise cross paths with the Borg and their sinister Queen. It's hard to tell whether the cry "Resistance is Futile" is coming from the Borg, or the Trek franchise itself, as this installment may well bring in new "Trekkers" with its "less techobabble, more action" approach and the fact that this crew can act. The Borg attempt to change history by travelling back in time (to 2063) to prevent scientist Cromwell from inventing warp drive. While the less-interesting members of the crew stay on Earth to help out with the launch, the battle for the Enterprise rages on up in space. Trademark effects, humor, and idealism are in abundant supply and should please the long-time fan as well as the neophyte. **111m/C VHS, DVD.** Patrick Stewart, Jonathan Frakes, Brent Spiner,

LeVar Burton, Michael Dorn, Marina Sirtis, Gates (Cheryl) McFadden, Alfre Woodard, James Cromwell, Alice Krige, Neal McDonough, Robert Picardo, Dwight Schultz; *D:* Jonathan Frakes; *W:* Brannon Braga, Ronald D. Moore; *C:* Matthew F. Leonetti; *M:* Jerry Goldsmith.

Star Trek: Generations ☙☙☙ **1994 (PG)** The sci-fi phenomena continues with the first film spun off from the recently departed "Star Trek: The Next Generation" TV series and the seventh following the adventures of the Enterprise crew. Captain Kirk is propelled into the future thanks to an explosion and manages to hook up with current starship captain, Picard. Of course, just in time to save the galaxy from the latest space loon, the villainous Dr. Soren (McDowell), renegade Klingons, and your basic mysterious space entity. For comic relief, android Data gets an emotion chip. Terrific special effects (courtesy of Industrial Light and Magic) and yes, the heroic Kirk receives his mandatory grandiose death scene. Other original characters making a brief appearance are Scotty and Chekov. An entertaining romp through time and space. **117m/C VHS, DVD.** William Shatner, Patrick Stewart, Malcolm McDowell, Whoopi Goldberg, Jonathan Frakes, Brent Spiner, LeVar Burton, Michael Dorn, Gates (Cheryl) McFadden, Marina Sirtis, James Doohan, Walter Koenig, Alan Ruck; *D:* David Carson; *W:* Ronald D. Moore, Brannon Braga; *C:* John A. Alonzo; *M:* Dennis McCarthy; *V:* Majel Barrett.

Star Trek: Insurrection ☙☙ **1/2 1990 (PG)** In the ninth film, Captain Picard (Stewart) goes to Data's (Spiner) rescue when the android seemingly goes berserk while on a scientific mission to investigate the non-techno culture of the peaceful Ba'ku. What Picard discovers is a planet that's virtually a fountain of youth and a dastardly plan by the Federation and the evil Son'a, led by bitter Ru'afro (Abraham), to gain the secret even though it means destroying the planet to do so. More humor and romance than usual done in the typical professional manner of the franchise. **100m/C VHS, DVD.** Patrick Stewart, Brent Spiner, Donna Murphy, F. Murray Abraham, Jonathan Frakes, LeVar Burton, Michael Dorn, Anthony Zerbe, Gates (Cheryl) McFadden, Marina Sirtis, Gregg Henry, Daniel Hugh-Kelly, Claudette Nevins; *D:* Jonathan Frakes; *W:* Michael Piller; *C:* Matthew F. Leonetti; *M:* Jerry Goldsmith.

Star Trek: Nemesis ☙☙ **2002 (PG-13)** The venerable (some may say dusty) franchise ends(?) its "Next Generation" incarnation with this disappointing outing. After crew members Riker and Troi get hitched, the Enterprise heads to her homeworld for a celebration, but is sidetracked by the discovery of a dismantled prototype of Data. Picard then receives word of the Romulans' intention to negotiate a peace with the Federation. He smells a rat, and he's right. The leader of the Romulans is actually from Romulus's sister planet Remus, he's a clone of Picard, and he's mad. MAD, I TELL YOU!! Stewart brings his usual gravitas to the role of Picard, even he can't save this snooze-fest that even tried the patience of hard-core Trekkers. **116m/C VHS, DVD, UMD.** *US* Patrick Stewart, Jonathan Frakes, Brent Spiner, LeVar Burton, Michael Dorn, Marina Sirtis, Gates (Cheryl) McFadden, Thomas (Tom) Hardy, Ron Perlman, Shannon Cochran, Dina Meyer, Jude Ciccolella, Kate Mulgrew, Wil Wheaton; *D:* Stuart Baird; *W:* John Logan; *C:* Jeffrey L. Kimball; *M:* Jerry Goldsmith; *V:* Majel Barrett.

Star Wars ☙☙☙☙ *Star Wars: Episode 4—A New Hope* **1977 (PG)** First entry in Lucas's "Star Wars" trilogy proved to be one of the biggest boxoffice hits of all time. A young hero, a captured princess, a hot-shot pilot, cute robots, a vile villain, and a heroic and mysterious Jedi knight blend together with marvelous special effects in a fantasy tale about rebel forces engaged in a life or death struggle with the tyrant leaders of the Galactic Empire. Set a new cinematic standard for realistic special effects, making many pre-"Star Wars" effects seem almost laughable in retrospect. Followed by "The Empire Strikes Back" (1980) and "Return of the Jedi" (1983). **121m/C VHS, DVD.** Mark Hamill, Carrie Fisher, Harrison Ford, Alec Guinness, Peter Cushing, Kenny Baker, James Earl Jones, David Prowse, Anthony Daniels, Peter Mayhew; *D:* George Lucas; *W:* George Lucas; *C:* Gilbert Taylor; *M:* John Williams. Oscars '77: Art Dir./Set Dec., Costume Des., Film Editing, Sound, Visual FX, Orig. Score; AFI '98: Top 100; Golden Globes '78: Score; L.A. Film Critics '77: Film, Natl. Film Reg. '89.

Star Wars: Episode 1—The Phantom Menace ☙☙☙ **1999 (PG)** Lucas's first "Star Wars" film in 16 years is also the beginning of his prequel trilogy. Jedi Master Qui-Gon Jinn (Neeson) and rebellious apprentice Obi-Wan Kenobi (McGregor) are sent to the peaceful planet Naboo to aid young Queen Amidala (Portman), who is being forced to sign a Trade Federation treaty. When the Jedis escape to Tatooine with Amidala, they encounter a slave boy, Anakin (Lloyd), whom Jinn realizes is empowered by the Force, and are pursued by the Federation and evil Dark Lord, Darth Maul (Park). The special effects are all they're cracked up to be (practically the whole thing is computer generated, but doesn't look it), and the action scenes have the zip and excitement you'd expect. The characters and story may aim a little more at kids than some would like, but those kids will be the teenagers that flock to see the next two. Some plot holes, but that's to be expected in the first installment of a trilogy. **130m/C VHS, DVD.** Liam Neeson, Ewan McGregor, Natalie Portman, Jake Lloyd, Ian McDiarmid, Samuel L. Jackson, Ray Park, Pernilla August, Terence Stamp, Brian Blessed, Oliver Ford Davies, Hugh Quarshie, Ralph Brown, Sofia Coppola; *D:* George Lucas; *W:* George Lucas; *C:* David Tattersall; *M:* John Williams; *V:* Ahmed Best, Frank Oz. MTV Movie Awards '00: Action Seq.

Star Wars: Episode 2—Attack of the Clones ☙☙☙ **2002 (PG)** Ambitious Jedi knight Anakin (Christensen) goes further on his journey to the dark side while Obi-Wan (McGregor) tries to rein him in. He and Amidala (Portman), who's now a senator, have a forbidden romance, and the Republic continues to be plagued by enemies from within and without. The romance angle, so touted in the pre-release hype, seems forced due to a lack of chemistry (and some ridiculous dialogue) between the two leads, but everything else is spectacular. The exposition is handled much better that in Episode 1, (and really whets the appetite for Episode 3) and the action set pieces are (as expected) well done, and superbly choreographed. Christensen shows brief flashes of the personality changes to come in Anakin, but his performance is uneven. Jackson finally gets to show what he's got as the baddest Jedi this side of Yoda. **124m/C VHS, DVD.** *US* Ewan McGregor, Hayden Christensen, Natalie Portman, Ian McDiarmid, Temuera Morrison, Samuel L. Jackson, Christopher Lee, Pernilla August, Jimmy Smits, Jack Thompson, Rose Byrne, Oliver Ford Davies, Leanna (Leeanna) Walsman, Anthony Daniels, Kenny Baker, Ronald Falk; *D:* George Lucas; *W:* George Lucas, Jonathan Hales; *C:* David Tattersall; *M:* John Williams; *V:* Frank Oz, Ahmed Best, Andrew Secombe. Golden Raspberries '02: Worst Support. Actor (Christensen).

Star Wars: Episode 3—Revenge of the Sith ☙☙☙ **2005 (PG-13)** After three years of fighting, the Clone Wars are finally ending; the Jedi dispatch Obi-Wan (McGregor) to bring General Grievous to justice; Supreme Chancellor Palpatine (McDiarmid) seeks to consolidate power and bring Anakin Skywalker (Christensen) to the dark side (thus turning him into Darth Vader); the Republic is transformed into the Galactic Empire and the last of the Jedi go into hiding. The end chapter of Lucas' prequel trilogy is appropriately dark, with Lucas's trademark great battle scenes (especially Anakin and Obi-Wan going at it) and at times laughable dialogue and direction. Wraps some elements up neatly, but leaves some major logic holes as well. **140m/C DVD.** *US* Ewan McGregor, Hayden Christensen, Natalie Portman, Samuel L. Jackson, Ian McDiarmid, Peter Mayhew, Jimmy Smits, Kenny Baker, Anthony Daniels, Christopher Lee, Ahmed Best, Oliver Ford Davies, Temuera Morrison, Keisha Castle-Hughes, Bruce Spence, Silas Carson, Jay Laga'aia, Wayne Pygram, David Bowers; *D:* George Lucas; *W:* George Lucas; *C:* David Tattersall; *M:* John Williams; *V:* Frank Oz, James Earl Jones, Matthew Wood. Golden Raspberries '05: Worst Support. Actor (Christensen).

Star Wars: The Clone Wars ☙ **1/2 2008 (PG)** Fairly unnecessary computer-animated "Star Wars" spin-off, bridging the gap between "The Clone Wars" and "Revenge of the Sith." During the epic Clone War between the Republic and Separatists, the Jedi are blamed for the kidnapping of Jabba the Hutt's baby (no joke). Anakin Skywalker and his new Padawan learner Ahsoka Tano are sent off to rescue the Huttlet and clear the Jedi name, while Obi-Wan and Yoda hang back to fight the war. George Lucas is only partly to blame for this stinker, as he places his once-imaginative vision in the hands of video game and cartoon veterans, allowing the franchise to slowly degenerate into tame Saturday morning bantha fodder. **98m/C DVD.** *US D:* Dave Filoni; *W:* Henry Gilroy, Steven Melching, Scott Murphy; *M:* Kevin Kiner; *V:* Matt Lanter, Tom Kane, Ian Abercrombie, Kevin M. Richardson, Ashley Eckstein, James Arnold Taylor, Samuel L. Jackson, Anthony Daniels, Christopher Lee, Corey Burton.

Starbird and Sweet William ☙☙ **1973 (G)** On a solo plane flight, a young Native American crashes in the wilderness. He must fight for survival in the harsh woods with his only friend, a bear cub. Good family fare. **95m/C VHS.** A. Martinez, Louise Fitch, Dan Haggerty, Skip Homeier; *D:* Jack B. Hively.

Starchaser: The Legend of Orin ☙☙ **1/2 1985 (PG)** Animated fantasy about a boy who must save the world of the future from malevolent hordes. **107m/C VHS, DVD.** *D:* Steven Hahn; *W:* Jeffrey Scott; *M:* Andrew Belling; *V:* Joe Colligan, Carmen Argenziano, Anthony DeLongis, Tyke Caravelli, Dennis Alwood, Daryl Bartley.

Stardom ☙☙ **1/2 2000 (R)** Price of fame, media-obsessed drama set in the world of modeling. Sultry teen Tina (Pare) is playing on a women's hockey team in smalltown Ontario when she's discovered. French photog Philippe (Berling) puts her on the road to stardom, American manager Renny (Gibson) moves her career forward, but her success causes trouble for the older man she becomes involved with—celebrity restauranteur Barry Levine (Aykroyd) until Tina moves on. All the while she's part of the disposable, instant celeb culture but you're never too sure who's doing the manipulating and how much Tina is complicit in her own exploitation. **102m/C VHS, DVD.** *FR CA* Jessica Pare, Dan Aykroyd, Thomas Gibson, Charles Berling, Frank Langella, Robert Lepage; *D:* Denys Arcand; *W:* Denys Arcand, Jacob Potashnik; *C:* Guy Dufaux; *M:* Francois Dompierre.

Stardust ☙☙☙ **2007 (PG-13)** Tristan (Cox) wants to win the love of cold-hearted Victoria (Miller) by promising that he'll retrieve a star that's fallen into the magical realm bordering their village. But he discovers that the star has transformed into the lovely Yvaine (Danes)—and Tristan isn't the only one who wants the prize. Among the others are Lamia the witch (Pfeiffer) and cross-dressing pirate Shakespeare (De Niro). The mix of epic magical fable, swashbuckling adventure, romance, and "Princess Bride"-style irreverence doesn't always mesh, but eventually settles into an involving and satisfying tale. Based on the novel by Neil Gaiman. **128m/C DVD, HD DVD.** *GB US* Charlie Cox, Claire Danes, Robert De Niro, Sienna Miller, Michelle Pfeiffer, Peter O'Toole, Jason Flemyng, Rupert Everett, Mark Strong, Henry Cavill, Ricky Gervais, Nathaniel Parker, David Walliams, Kate Magowan, David Kelly, Sarah Alexander; *D:* Matthew Vaughn; *W:* Matthew Vaughn, Jane Goldman; *C:* Benjamin Davis; *M:* Ilan Eshkeri; *Nar:* Ian McKellen.

Stardust Memories ☙☙ **1/2 1980 (PG)** Allen's "8 1/2." A comic filmmaker is plagued with creative blocks, relationships, modern fears and fanatical fans. The last film in Allen's varying self-analysis, with explicit references to Fellini and Antonioni. **88m/B VHS, DVD.** Woody Allen, Charlotte Rampling, Jessica Harper, Marie-Christine Barrault, Tony Roberts, Helen Hanft, Cynthia Gibb, Amy Wright, Daniel Stern; *D:* Woody Allen; *W:* Woody Allen; *C:* Gordon Willis.

The Starfighters ☙ **1/2 1963** Air Force Lieutenant Dornan must prove his courage to his disapproving war hero Congressman father. Dornan flies his F-104 through a dangerous storm, thereby earning his father's respect, which leads them to form a bond. **84m/C VHS.** Robert Dornan, Richard Jordahl, Shirley Olmstead; *D:* Will Zens; *W:* Will Zens; *C:* Leif Rise.

Starflight One ☙☙ *Starflight: the Plane that Couldn't Land* **1983** A space shuttle is called on to save the world's first hypersonic airliner trapped in an orbit above earth. The film features good special effects, but also a predictable "rescue-mission" plot. **155m/C VHS.** Ray Milland, Lee Majors, Hal Linden, Lauren Hutton, Robert Webber, Terry Kiser; *D:* Jerry Jameson.

Stargate ☙☙ **1994 (PG-13)** U.S. military probe of a ring-shaped ancient Egyptian artifact (your tax dollars at work) sends he-man colonel Russell and geeky Egyptologist Spader into a parallel universe. There they meet the builders of the pyramids who are enslaved by an evil despot (Davidson) posing as a sun god. Ambitious premise zapped from prepubescent imagninations gets an A for effort, but a silly plot that jumbles biblical epic panoramas and space odyssey special effects with otherworldly mysticism and needless emotional hang-ups trade shlock for style. Spader's shaggy scholar is neurotically fun, Russell's jarhead a bore, and Davidson's vampy villain an unintended hoot. **119m/C VHS, DVD, Blu-ray Disc, UMD.** Kurt Russell, James Spader, Jaye Davidson, Viveca Lindfors, Alexis Cruz, Leon Rippy, John Diehl, Erik Avari, Mili Avital; *D:* Roland Emmerich; *W:* Dean Devlin, Roland Emmerich; *C:* Jeff Okun; *M:* David Arnold.

Stargate: Continuum ☙☙ **2008** In this stand-alone DTV effort from the "Stargate:SG-1" TV series, the team—plus Jack O'Neill (Anderson)—are offworld to witness the execution of the evil Ba'al (Simon). Of course the bad guy has a plan to survive that involves time-travelling back to 1939 Earth to prevent the Stargate project from ever getting started so that he can eventually conquer the planet. This changes the timeline and makes for sticky situations for Mitchell (Browder), Carter (Tapping), and Jackson (Shanks). The plot jumps around a lot (there's even an Arctic adventure) but if you liked the series, this is like catching up with old friends. **98m/C DVD, Blu-ray Disc.** Ben Browder, Michael Shanks, Amanda Topping, Richard Dean Anderson, Christopher Judge, Beau Bridges, Claudia Black, William Devane, Cliff Simon, Dona S. Davis; *D:* Martin Wood; *W:* Brad Wright; *C:* Peter Woeste; *M:* Joel Goldsmith. **VIDEO**

Stargate: The Ark of Truth ☙☙ **1/2 2008** Direct-to-video movie finishes off most of the story left dangling when "Stargate: SG-1" ended its 10th TV season. In this adventure (think "Raiders of the Lost Ark" with some "Terminator" thrown in), Daniel Jackson, Teal'c, and Vala are continuing their planetary search for the Merlin weapon that will defeat the fanatical Ori before they have a chance to attack Earth. Meanwhile, Mitchell and Sam are aboard the Odyssey dealing with a double-crossing official, Ori motherships, and a lot of replicators. A nice bonus for fans of the series. **102m/C DVD, Blu-ray Disc.** Ben Browder, Amanda Topping, Christopher Judge, Michael Shanks, Claudia Black, Beau Bridges, Currie Graham, Tim Guinee, Morena Baccarin, Sarah Strange, Julian Sands, Michael Beach, Spencer Maybee; *D:* Robert Cooper; *W:* Robert Cooper; *C:* Peter Woeste; *M:* Jeff Goldsmith. **VIDEO**

Starhops ☙ **1/2 1978 (R)** A trio of buxom young women attract business to their drive-in restaurant by wearing skimpy outfits. Surprisingly inoffensive for an "R" rating. **92m/C VHS.** Dorothy Buhrman, Sterling Frazier, Jillian Kesner, Peter Paul Liapis, Paul Ryan, Anthony Mannino, Dick Miller; *D:* Barbara Peeters; *W:* Stephanie Rothman.

Stark ☙ **1/2 1985** Wichita detective journeys to Las Vegas in an effort to locate his missing sister. During his search, he finds himself taking on the mob. Pilot for a TV series that never happened, and Tidyman's last screenplay. A sequel, "Stark: Mirror Image," was made in 1986. **94m/C VHS.** Nicolas Surovy, Dennis Hopper, Marilu Henner, Seth Jaffe; *D:* Rod Holcomb; *W:* Ernest Tidyman. **TV**

Stark Raving Mad ☙☙ **1/2 2002 (R)** Likeable hood Ben (Scott) inherits a big debt to gangster Mr. Gregory (Phillips) after his brother is murdered. His chance to clear it is by stealing a valuable statue from a bank vault located next to a Chinese nightclub that will be hosting a loud and crowded rave. Of course there's all kinds of complicatons, including a potential double-cross, a local Triad member who wants the statue for himself, and a couple of feds working a drug operation on the club. Scott maintains his goofy charm and adds some physical action to the mix but there's nothing new about this tired plot. **98m/C DVD.** Seann William Scott, Lou Diamond Phillips, Patrick Breen, Terry Chen, Monet Mazur, Suzy Nakamura, Timm Sharp, John Crye, Adam Arkin, Dave Foley, Kavan Smith; ***D:*** David Schneider, Drew Drywalt; ***W:*** David Schneider, Drew Drywalt; ***C:*** Chuck Cohen; ***M:*** John Digweed, Nick Muir.

Starkweather ½ **2004 (R)** Humdrum retelling of 19-year-old Charlie Starkweather's (Taylor) 1958 murder spree across Nebraska in the company of his 14-year-old sweetie Caril-Ann Fugate (Lucio). See "Badlands" instead. **90m/C DVD.** Lance Henriksen, Jerry Kroll, Brent Taylor, Shannon Lucio; ***D:*** Byron Werner; ***W:*** Stephen Johnston; ***C:*** Byron Werner. **VIDEO**

Starlift **1951** Basically a variety showcase for Warner Bros. stars that was intended as a patriotic salute to Korean War GIs. The flimsy plot finds starlet Nell (Rule) visiting the troops at San Francisco's Travis Air Force Base and soldier Rick (Hagerthy) falling for her. Doris Day, Gordon MacRae, Virginia Mayo, and James Cagney are among those making an appearance (to a greater or lesser extent). **103m/B DVD.** Janice Rule, Ron Hagerthy, Dick Wessel, Richard Webb, Doris Day, Gordon MacRae; ***D:*** Roy Del Ruth; ***W:*** John Klorer; ***C:*** Ted D. McCord.

Starlight ½ **1997** Alien envoy searches for a genetic component (found in a half-alien/half-human hybrid) that will allow her people to live in a post-apocalytic Earth's polluted atmosphere. **100m/C VHS.** Rae Dawn Chong, Willie Nelson, Billy Wirth, Jim Byrnes, Deborah Wakeham; ***D:*** Jonathan Kay.

Starlight Hotel ½ **1990 (PG)** An unhappy teenage girl sets off to find her father, with the help of a shellshocked veteran wrongly accused of a crime. Set in New Zealand during the Depression. Lovely scenery and good acting highlight nice story of odd friendship. **90m/C VHS.** *NZ* Greer Robson, Peter Phelps, Marshall Napier, Pat Smythe, Alice Fraser; ***D:*** Sam Pillsbury.

Starman **1984 (PG)** An alien from an advanced civilization lands in Wisconsin. He hides beneath the guise of a grieving young widow's recently deceased husband. He then makes her drive him across country to rendezvous with his spacecraft so he can return home. Well-acted, interesting twist on the "Stranger in a Strange Land" theme. Bridges is fun as the likeable starman; Allen is lovely and earthy in her worthy follow-up to "Raiders of the Lost Ark." **115m/C VHS, DVD.** Jeff Bridges, Karen Allen, Charles Martin Smith, Richard Jaeckel, Dirk Blocker, M.C. Gainey; ***D:*** John Carpenter; ***W:*** Bruce A. Evans, Raynold Gideon; ***C:*** Donald M. Morgan; ***M:*** Jack Nitzsche.

Starry Night ½ **1999 (PG-13)** So what would artist Vincent Van Gogh do if he suddenly found himself alive (a century after his death) in modern-day Los Angeles and discovered that his paintings, which were considered ugly and worthless in his lifetime, were collected by the wealthy and worth a fortune? Well, he might decide to steal them back, sell them himself, and give the money to other struggling artists. And he might also find himself falling in love with a pretty art student who inspires him to paint new masterpieces. **98m/C VHS, DVD.** Abbott Alexander, Lisa Waltz, Sally Kirkland, Lou Wagner; ***D:*** Paul Davids; ***W:*** Paul Davids; ***C:*** David W. Smith; ***M:*** Brad Warnaar.

Stars and Bars **1988 (R)** O'Connor misfire strands Day-Lewis in the midst of hillbillies. A stuffy English art expert travels from New York to Georgia to price a Renoir, and happens on a bizarre backwoods family marginally run by Stanton. Stereotypical pursuit of humor teeters precariously on the edge of black comedy without actually being funny. Stinky script dooms fine cast to just acting weird in a "Deliverance" sort of way. Based on the novel by William Boyd. **95m/C VHS.** Daniel Day-Lewis, Harry Dean Stanton, John Cusack, Joan Cusack, Spalding Gray, Will Patton, Martha Plimpton, Glenne Headly, Laurie Metcalf, Maury Chaykin; ***D:*** Pat O'Connor; ***W:*** William Boyd.

Stars and Stripes Forever *Marching Along* **1952** Sumptious, Hollywoodized bio of composer John Phillip Sousa, based on his memoir "Marching Along," but more concerned with the romantic endeavors of young protege Wagner. Accuracy aside, it's solid entertainment even if you're not mad about march music. ♫ Stars and Stripes Forever; El Capitan; Washington Post; King Cotton; The Battle Hymn of the Republic; Dixie; Light Cavalry; Turkey in the Straw; Hail to the Chief. **89m/C VHS.** Clifton Webb, Debra Paget, Robert Wagner, Ruth Hussey, Finlay Currie; ***D:*** Henry Koster.

The Stars Fell on Henrietta ½ **1994 (PG)** Down-on-his-luck wildcatter Mr. Cox (Duvall) searches for oil and redemption. He's looking for it on the failing farm of couple Don and Cora Day (Quinn and Fisher) in the middle of the 1930s Texas dustbowl with the reluctant backing of more successful oil man (Dennehy). Quiet character study of an obsessed wheeler-dealer playing with his last poker chip verges on the romantic in its quest for black gold, true to its message about never giving up hope. Directorial debut for Keach is led by typically excellent portrayals by Duvall and Dennehy, but Quinn and Fisher are given little to work with. Marks the first movie Clint Eastwood's Malpaso company has produced in which he didn't star or direct since "Ratboy." **110m/C VHS.** Robert Duvall, Aidan Quinn, Frances Fisher, Brian Dennehy, Lexi (Faith) Randall, Kaytlyn Knowles, Francesca Ruth Eastwood; ***D:*** James Keach; ***W:*** Philip Railsback; ***C:*** Bruce Surtees; ***M:*** David Benoit.

Stars in My Crown **1950** McCrea provides a moving performance as the pistol-wielding preacher who helps the residents of a 19th-century small town battle a typhoid epidemic and KKK terrorism. Adapted from the novel by Joe David Brown. **89m/B VHS.** Joel McCrea, Ellen Drew, Dean Stockwell, Alan Hale, Lewis Stone, Amanda Blake, Juano Hernandez, Charles Kemper, Connie Gilchrist, Ed Begley Sr., James Arness, Jack Lambert, Arthur Hunnicutt; ***D:*** Jacques Tourneur; ***W:*** Margaret Fitts; ***M:*** Adolph Deutsch; ***Nar:*** Marshall Thompson.

The Stars Look Down **1939** A mine owner forces miners to work in unsafe conditions in a Welsh town and disaster strikes. Redgrave is a miner's son running for office, hoping to improve conditions, and to escape the hard life. Forceful, well-directed effort suffered at the boxoffice, in competition with John Ford's similar classic "How Green Was My Valley." From the novel by A.J. Cronin. The original British version was released at 110 minutes. **96m/B VHS, DVD.** *GB* Michael Redgrave, Margaret Lockwood, Emlyn Williams, Cecil Parker; ***D:*** Carol Reed.

Starship *Lorca and the Outlaws* **1987 (PG)** British sci-fi seems to be an oxymoron. To wit, this lame "Star Wars" ripoff is about human slaves on a planet run by evil robots. **91m/C VHS.** *GB* John Tarrant, Cassandra Webb, Donough Rees, Deep Roy, Ralph Cotterill; ***D:*** Roger Christian.

Starship Invasions **1977 (PG)** Lee leads a group of bad aliens seeking to take over the Earth. He's thwarted by UFO expert Vaughn, who is aided by a group of good aliens. Cheesy special effects have this one looking like a bad sci-fi serial from the '40s. **89m/C VHS.** *CA* Christopher Lee, Robert Vaughn, Daniel Pilon, Helen Shaver, Henry Ramer, Victoria (Vicki) Johnson; ***D:*** Ed(ward) Hunt; ***W:*** Ed(ward) Hunt.

Starship Troopers **1997 (R)** As Bugs Bunny would say, "Of course you know, this means war!" Giant arachnids prove to be an invincible opponent with zero tolerance for things with less than four legs in Verhoeven's comic-book styled, epic slaughter fest. The futuristic, fascist, co-ed Moblie Infantry, led by renegade Commander Rasczak (Ironside), does battle with the sinister arthropods, usually resulting in much human bloodshed. The high body count includes many young actors, but unlike Verhoeven's "Showgirls," their careers should remain relatively unscathed. The acting is straight out of a Mattel toy factory, but the action and confrontations with the enemy insects are a thrill thanks to computer animated special effects. Cheesy, bloody good fun, if you can ignore the fact that fascists are portrayed as the good guys. Based on the 1959 novel by Robert A. Heinlein. **129m/C VHS, DVD, UMD.** Casper Van Dien, Michael Ironside, Neil Patrick Harris, Clancy Brown, Denise Richards, Dina Meyer, Jake Busey, Patrick Muldoon, Seth Gilliam, Rue McClanahan, Marshall Bell, Eric Bruskotter, Blake Lindsley, Anthony Michael Ruivivar, Dean Norris, Dale Dye, Amy Smart; ***D:*** Paul Verhoeven; ***W:*** Edward Neumeier; ***C:*** Jost Vacano; ***M:*** Basil Poledouris.

Starship Troopers 2: Hero of the Federation **WOOF! 2004 (R)** You'll really want the bugs to win in this would-be sequel that's all kinds of bad. A platoon of Federation soldiers are stranded on a bug-infested planet and take refuge in an abandoned outpost while they await rescue. Three stray soldiers show up and soon the grunts are acting weird because a new breed of bugs now uses human hosts. Tippett is an award-winning special effects guy making his directorial debut but he needs to rethink the career move. **92m/C DVD.** Richard Burgi, Colleen Porch, Ed Lauter, Edward Quinn, Brenda Strong, Kelly Carlson, Lawrence Monson; ***D:*** Phil Tippett; ***W:*** Edward Neumeier; ***C:*** Christian Sebaldt; ***M:*** William T. Stromberg, John Morgan. **VIDEO**

Starship Troopers 3: Marauder ½ **2008 (R)** Well anything would be an improvement over the first sequel and at least Van Dien is back (from the original) to save the day. After a Federation ship crash lands on planet OM-1, Johnny Rico (Van Dien), who's in the brig at the time, is released so he can lead a rescue mission. His unit is armed with the latest advanced weapon, called the Marauder, but the low-budget means you really don't get to see it in action that much. Neumeier, who wrote the first two space adventures, takes on directorial duties this time as well. **105m/C DVD.** Casper Van Dien, Jolene Blalock, Amanda Donohoe, Boris Kodjoe, Stephen Hogan; ***D:*** Edward Neumeier; ***W:*** Edward Neumeier; ***C:*** Lorenzo Senatore; ***M:*** Klaus Badelt. **VIDEO**

Starsky & Hutch ½ **2004 (PG-13)** The big-screen adaptation with Ben Stiller (as Starsky) and Owen Wilson (as Hutch) spoofs everything the TV show took so seriously, and to good effect. In this outing, we find out how the duo became partners, and why. It seems both are misfits, with the opposing personality traits of the originals exaggerated to an almost-impossible level, giving them a very high-energy odd-couple buddy vibe as they chase aspiring drug kingpin Reese Feldman (Vaughn). Of course, Huggy Bear is there to assist (in the person of Snoop Dogg, who is spot-on). Stiller and Wilson have this act down, and they never linger on a gag too long. One of the better '70s show spoofs (which may seem like damning with faint praise). Paul Michael Glaser and David Soul have a quick cameo near the end. **97m/C VHS, DVD.** *US* Ben Stiller, Owen Wilson, Snoop Dogg, Fred Williamson, Vince Vaughn, Juliette Lewis, Amy Smart, Carmen Electra, Jason Bateman, Will Ferrell, Christopher Penn, Richard Edson, George Kee Cheung, Jeffrey Lorenzo, Molly Sims, Patton Oswalt; ***Cameos:*** Paul Michael Glaser, David Soul; ***D:*** Todd Phillips; ***W:*** Todd Phillips, John O'Brien, Scot Armstrong; ***C:*** Barry Peterson; ***M:*** Theodore Shapiro.

Starstruck ½ **1982 (PG)** Fun-loving folly about a teen who tries to help his talented cousin make it as a singer. Playfully tweeks Hollywood musicals. Enjoyable and fun. **95m/C VHS, DVD.** *AU* Jo Kennedy, Ross O'Donovan, Pat Evison; ***D:*** Gillian Armstrong; ***C:*** Russell Boyd.

Start the Revolution without Me **1970 (PG)** Hilarious, Moliere-esque farce about two sets of identical twins (Wilder and Sutherland) separated at birth, who meet 30 years later, just before the French Revolution. About as hammy as they come; Wilder is unforgettable. Neglected when released, but now deservedly a cult favorite. **91m/C VHS, DVD.** Gene Wilder, Donald Sutherland, Orson Welles, Hugh Griffith, Jack MacGowran, Billie Whitelaw, Victor Spinetti, Ewa Aulin, Denise Coffey, Helen Fraser, Murray Melvin; ***D:*** Bud Yorkin; ***W:*** Lawrence J. Cohen, Fred Freeman; ***C:*** Jean Tournier; ***M:*** John Addison.

Starter for Ten ½ **2006 (PG-13)** Title refers to the number of points given for starter questions on popular Brit TV quiz show "University Challenge." In 1985, working-class Brian (McAvoy) crosses the social barrier when he's accepted at Bristol University and meets posh blonde Alice (Eve) while trying out for the quiz team. Appealingly geeky, Brian is too starry-eyed to realize he's better suited to firebrand Rebecca (Hall) as he tries to reconcile his past with the potential of his future. **96m/C DVD.** *US GB* James McAvoy, Rebecca Hall, Dominic Cooper, Charles Dance, Alice Eve, Catherine Tate, Benedict Cumberbatch, Mark Gatiss, Lindsay Duncan; ***D:*** Tom Vaughan; ***W:*** David Nicholls; ***C:*** Ashley Rowe; ***M:*** Blake Neely.

The Starter Wife ½ **2007** Hollywood wife Molly Kagan (Messing) gets discarded by her studio honcho louse of a hubby, Kenny (Jacobson), for an ambitious younger bimbo. Her status suddenly gone, Molly is given the loan of boozy buddy Joan's (Davis) beach house where she can lick her wounds and plan for her future. Which may just include suave but depressed movie mogul Lou (Mantegna) or hunky, secretive beach bum Sam (Moyer). Showbiz fluff based on the insider novel by Gigi Levangie Grazer. **276m/C DVD.** Debra Messing, Judy Davis, Stephen Moyer, Peter Jacobson, Lou Mantegna, Miranda Otto, Anika Noni Rose, Aden Young, Chris Diamantopoulos; ***D:*** Jon Avnet; ***W:*** Josann McGibbon, Sara Parriott; ***C:*** Geoffrey Simpson; ***M:*** Ed Shearmur. **CABLE**

Starting Out in the Evening ½ **2007 (PG-13)** Leonard Schiller (Langella) is a 70-year-old, still-respected writer whose books are out of print and who has been working on his latest novel for more than 10 years. Ambitious grad student Heather Wolfe (Ambrose) insists on making Leonard the subject of her master's thesis and also hopes to inspire him to complete his book. She wants to shake up his life; he insists on maintaining his dignity. Meanwhile, Ambrose tries to hold her own against a riveting performance by Langella. **111m/C DVD.** Frank Langella, Lauren Ambrose, Lili Taylor, Adrian Lester, Jessica Hecht; ***D:*** Andrew Wagner; ***W:*** Andrew Wagner, Fred Parnes; ***C:*** Harlan Bosmajian; ***M:*** Adam Gorgoni.

Starting Over **1979 (R)** His life racked by divorce, Phil Potter learns what it's like to be single, self-sufficient, and lonely once again. When a blind date grows into a serious affair, the romance is temporarily halted by his hang-up for his ex-wife. Enjoyable love-triangle comedy loses direction after a while, but Reynolds is subtle and charming, and Bergen good as his ex, a very bad songwriter. Based on a novel by Dan Wakefield. **106m/C VHS, DVD.** Burt Reynolds, Jill Clayburgh, Candice Bergen, Frances Sternhagen, Austin Pendleton, Mary Kay Place, Kevin Bacon, Daniel Stern; ***D:*** Alan J. Pakula; ***W:*** James L. Brooks; ***C:*** Sven Nykvist; ***M:*** Marvin Hamlisch.

Starved **1997** Monica (Beaman) thinks she's found a terrific guy in Scott Dawson (Adams). He gives her flowers, writes her romantic notes, and offers her candle lit dinners. So naturally, Monica falls in love. Too bad, Scott's a sociopath. He takes her prisoner, keeps her in his basement, and uses mind games and starvation to try and break Monica's will. Monica's best friend Jane (Zobel) continues to search for her, even after the police have let the case go. But can she find her in time? Based on a true story. **90m/C VHS, DVD.** Lee Ann Beaman, Hal Adams, Toni Zobel; ***D:*** Guy Crawford, Yvette Hoffman.

State and Main **2000 (R)** Hollywood filmmakers descend on a small New England town, which promptly becomes dazzled by all the showbiz glitter. Much of the story rotates around Hoffman, who plays the down-to-earth writer forced to rewrite his script entitled "The Old Mill" after the crew discovers the town's mill burned down years ago. Meanwhile, he becomes concerned when he realizes the film's star (Baldwin) has become involved with a local teenaged girl. Macy and LuPone, Mamet regulars, also enliven the cast. Entertaining, satirical look at Hollywood egos bumping up against middle America. Not too many guffaws, but nice to see Mamet lighten things up with a comedy. **90m/C VHS, DVD.** Alec Baldwin, Philip Seymour Hoffman, William H. Macy, Julia Stiles, David Paymer, Rebecca Pidgeon, Sarah Jessica Parker, Charles Durning, Patti LuPone; ***D:*** David

Mamet; *W:* David Mamet; *C:* Oliver Stapleton; *M:* Theodore Shapiro.

State Department File 649 1/2 **1949** Insipid spy drama set in northern China. Mongolian rebels hold U.S. agent Lundigan captive; he hopes to capture a Chinese warlord. **87m/C VHS, DVD.** Virginia Bruce, William Lundigan; *D:* Sam Newfield.

State Fair *It Happened One Summer* **1945** The second version of the glossy slice of Americana about a family at the Iowa State Fair, featuring plenty of great songs by Rodgers and Hammerstein. Adapted from the 1933 screen version of Phil Stong's novel. Remade again in 1962. ♫ It Might as Well Be Spring; It's a Grand Night for Singing; That's For Me; Isn't It Kinda Fun?; All I Owe Iowa; Our State Fair. **100m/C VHS, DVD.** Charles Winninger, Jeanne Crain, Dana Andrews, Vivian Blaine, Dick Haymes, Fay Bainter, Frank McHugh, Percy Kilbride, Donald Meek, William Marshall, Harry (Henry) Morgan; *D:* Walter Lang; *W:* Oscar Hammerstein; *C:* Leon Shamroy; *M:* Richard Rodgers, Oscar Hammerstein. Oscars '45: Song ("It Might as Well Be Spring").

State Fair **1962** The third film version of the story of a farm family who travel to their yearly state fair and experience life. The original songs are still there, but otherwise this is a letdown. Texas setting required dropping the song "All I Owe Iowa." ♫ Our State Fair; It's a Grand Night for Singing; That's for Me; It Might as Well Be Spring; Isn't It Kinda Fun?; More Than Just a Friend; It's the Little Things in Texas; Willing and Eager; This Isn't Heaven. **118m/C VHS.** Pat Boone, Ann-Margret, Bobby Darin, Tom Ewell, Alice Faye, Pamela Tiffin, Wally Cox; *D:* Jose Ferrer; *C:* William Mellor.

State of Emergency 1/2 **1994 (R)** John Novelli (Mantegna) is a cynical, overworked emergency-room doctor for an overcrowded, underequipped big-city hospital. His latest casualty is a head trauma case the hospital is ill-prepared to handle and as the patient's condition worsens both doctor and hospital are put at risk. **97m/C VHS, DVD.** Joe Mantegna, Lynn Whitfield, Paul Dooley; *D:* Leslie Linka Glatter; *W:* Susan Black, Lance Gentile. **TV**

State of Grace **1990 (R)** Irish hood Penn returns to old NYC neighborhood as undercover cop and becomes involved with an Irish Westies mob in a fight for survival as urban renewal encroaches on their Hell's Kitchen turf. Shrinking client base for shakedown schemes and protection rackets forces them to become contract killers for the Italian mafia. Fine performances, with Penn tense but restrained, gang honcho Harris intense, and Oldman chewing up gritty urban scenery as psycho brother of Harris, but the story is long and meandering. Well-choreographed violence. **134m/C VHS, DVD.** Joe (Johnny) Viterelli, Sean Penn, Ed Harris, Gary Oldman, Robin Wright Penn, John Turturro, Burgess Meredith, John C. Reilly; *D:* Phil Joanou; *W:* Dennis McIntyre; *C:* Jordan Cronenweth; *M:* Ennio Morricone.

State of Play **2003** Ambitious MP Stephen Collins (Morrissey) learns that his research assistant Sonia has died in a suspicious accident. Could her death be in any way connected to the execution-style murder of a teenaged thief and drug dealer? Newspaper editor Cameron Foster (Nighy) assigns reporters Cal (Simm), Della (Macdonald), and Dan (MacAvoy) to chase leads and soon dirty secrets, political and private, start spilling out. Complex miniseries with notable performances. **350m/C DVD.** *GB* David Morrissey, Bill Nighy, Kelly Macdonald, James McAvoy, John Simm, Polly Walker, Amelia Bullmore, Philip Glenister, Marc Warren, Benedict Wong; *D:* David Yates; *W:* Paul Abbott; *C:* Chris Seager; *M:* Nicholas Hooper. **TV**

State of Play **2009 (PG-13)** A rising congressman, Stephen Collins (Affleck), and a D.C. investigative journalist, Cal McCaffrey (Crowe) are old friends who become embroiled in a case of seemingly unrelated, brutal murders. When Stephen's research assistant (and secret mistress) is killed, Cal and his partner Della (McAdams) are assigned by their ruthless boss (Mirren) to get the story. An engrossing political conspiracy thriller/murder mystery, even if it lacks a bit in character development. Also serves as a commentary on the limitations of journalism in the face of the D.C. political machine. Adapted from the complicated 2003 BBC miniseries, which was better-suited to explore plot twists and the players involved. **127m/C DVD.** *US* Russell Crowe, Ben Affleck, Rachel McAdams, Helen Mirren, Jason Bateman, Robin Wright Penn, Viola Davis, Jeff Daniels, Katy Mixon; *D:* Kevin MacDonald; *W:* Matthew Carnahan, Tony Gilroy, Billy Ray; *C:* Rodrigo Prieto; *M:* Alex Heffes.

State of Siege *Etat de Siege* **1973** Third pairing of Montand and Costa-Gavras, about the real-life death of USAID employee Daniel Mitrione, suspected to be involved in torture and murder in Uruguay in the '60s. Quietly suspenseful, with snazzy editing; conspiracy-theory premise is similar to Stone's "JFK," and similarly disturbing, whether you believe it or not. Dubbed. **119m/C VHS.** *FR* Yves Montand, Renato Salvatori, O.E. Hasse, Jacques Perrin; *D:* Constantin Costa-Gavras.

State of the Union 1/2 *The World and His Wife* **1948** Liberal multimillionaire Tracy is seeking the Republican presidential nomination. His estranged wife (Hepburn) is asked to return so they can masquerade as a loving couple for the sake of his political career. Hepburn tries to help Tracy, as the backstage political machinations erode his personal convictions. Adapted from a highly successful, topical Broadway play; the writers changed dialogue constantly to reflect the news. Capra and his partners at Liberty Pictures originally hoped to cast Gary Cooper and Claudette Colbert. Hepburn and Menjou were at odds politically (over communist witch hunts in Hollywood) but are fine together onscreen. **124m/B VHS, DVD.** Spencer Tracy, Katharine Hepburn, Angela Lansbury, Van Johnson, Adolphe Menjou, Lewis Stone, Howard Smith; *D:* Frank Capra; *C:* George J. Folsey.

State of Things **1982** Ostensibly a mystery involving a film crew trying to remake a B-movie, "The Most Dangerous Man On Earth," but also an in-depth look at the process of filmmaking, a scathing look at nuclear warfare and an homage to Roger Corman and Hollywood at large. An enigmatic, complex film from Wenders prior to his American years. In German with English subtitles; some dialogue in English. **120m/B VHS.** *GE* Patrick Bauchau, Allen (Goorwitz) Garfield, Isabelle Weingarten, Viva, Samuel Fuller, Paul Getty III, Roger Corman; *D:* Wim Wenders. Venice Film Fest. '82: Film.

State Property 2 **WOOF!** **2005 (R)** Rappers who think they can act glamorize their world of drugs and violence in a most reprehensible way. Jail time, scores to settle, double- and triple-crossing, homicidal fantasies and plenty of actual death. Everything you don't want your kids to see. Come to think of it, you probably don't want to see it either. **94m/C DVD.** Beanie Sigel, Michael Bentt, Victor NORE Santiago, Damon Dash, Omillio Sparks, Oschino; *D:* Damon Dash; *W:* Adam Moreno; *C:* Tom Houghton; *M:* Kerry Muzzey.

The State Within 1/2 **2006** A very complicated political conspiracy entangles British ambassador to the U.S., Sir Mark Brydon (Isaacs), with terrorists, corporate hijinks, and the tough-talking U.S. secretary of defense (Gless). When a British airliner is blown up over D.C., the bomb is traced to a British Muslim suicide bomber with apparent ties to a Central Asian nation in political turmoil. Then there's British national Luke Gardner (James), who's on Florida's death row, and is tied into the players in unexpected ways. Isaacs and Gless are outstanding, but the story has too many shadowy characters and subplots for its own good. **360m/C DVD.** *GB* Jason Isaacs, Sharon Gless, Ben Daniels, Eva Birthistle, Lennie James, Neil Pearson, Alex Jennings, Noam Jenkins, Genevieve O'Reilly, Nigel Bennett; *D:* Daniel Percival; *W:* Daniel Percival, Elizabeth (Lizzie) Mickery; *C:* David Perrault; *M:* Jennie Muskett. **CABLE**

Stateline Motel 1/2 *Last Chance For a Born Loser* **1975 (R)** Cheap Italian ripoff of "The Postman Always Rings Twice," with a surprise ending but little of great interest. **86m/C VHS, DVD.** *IT* Eli Wallach, Ursula Andress, Fabio Testi, Barbara Bach; *D:* Maurizio Lucidi.

The Statement **2003 (R)** Michael Caine plays Pierre Brossard, a Frenchman who helped the Nazis in the execution of several Jews during World War II. As a wanted war criminal, Brossard has been eluding authorities for years with the help of arch-conservative extremists within the Catholic church. While an interesting story, the movie is schizophrenic and leaves a lot of questions unanswered. Adapted from the novel by Brian Moore, it is actually based on the true story of Paul Touvier. **120m/C VHS, DVD.** *CA GB FR* Michael Caine, Tilda Swinton, Jeremy Northam, Alan Bates, Charlotte Rampling, John Neville, Ciaran Hinds, Frank Finlay, William Hutt, Matt Craven, Noam Jenkins, Peter Wight, Colin Salmon, David de Keyser; *D:* Norman Jewison; *W:* Ronald Harwood; *C:* Kevin Jewison; *M:* Normand Corbeil.

State's Attorney 1/2 *Cardigan's Last Case* **1931** Mob attorney Barrymore finds trouble after his boss sets him up as District Attorney and he decides to go after his old cronies. His ex-prostitute lover gets caught in the middle after he dumps her for a powerful politico's daughter. Contrived, improbable story succumbs to star-quality lead acting from Barrymore. Remade in 1937 with Lee Tracy as "Criminal Lawyer." **79m/B VHS.** John Barrymore, Jill Esmond, William "Stage" Boyd, Helen Twelvetrees, Mary Duncan, Ralph Ince, Albert Conti, C. Henry Gordon, Leon Ames; *D:* George Archainbaud; *W:* Gene Fowler Sr., Rowland Brown; *C:* Leo Tover; *M:* Max Steiner.

States of Control 1/2 **1998** Penetrating, disturbing character study follows Lisa (Van Dyck) as she transforms herself from secure Manhattan wife into something much different and difficult to define. **84m/C DVD.** Jennifer Van Dyck, Stephen Bogardus, John Cunningham, Ellen Greene, Jennie Moreau, Nancy Giles; *D:* Zack Winestine; *W:* Zack Winestine; *C:* Susan Starr; *M:* Richard Termini.

Stateside **2004 (R)** Romantic soap opera that writer/director Anselmo says is based on a true story. The movie starts in 1984 with hospitalized Marine Mark (Tucker) flashing back to 1980. While drunk, high schooler Mark gets into a serious car accident that his wealthy dad (Mantegna) fixes by having Mark enlist in the Corps rather than doing jail time. On leave, Mark visits gal pal Sue (Bruckner) in a mental hospital and meets her schizophrenic ex-actress/singer roomie Dori (Cook). They immediately fall for each other and the drama ensues. Tucker fares best as his character matures from boy to man under Kilmer's tough drill instructor, while Cook is playing standard Hollywood-crazy. Movie might have benefited from a longer run time since the overstuffed plot doesn't have time to develop. Penny Marshall has an uncredited cameo as a nurse. **96m/C VHS, DVD.** *US GE* Rachael Leigh Cook, Jonathan Tucker, Agnes Bruckner, Val Kilmer, Joe Mantegna, Carrie Fisher, Diane Venora, Ed Begley Jr., Michael Goduti, Daniel Franzese, Penny Marshall; *D:* Reverge Anselmo; *W:* Reverge Anselmo; *C:* Adam Holender; *M:* Joel McNeely.

Static 1/2 **1987 (PG-13)** A strange, disquieting independent film about an eccentric youth who claims to have built a machine through which one can see heaven. Uneven, with some dull stretches. **89m/C VHS.** Keith Gordon, Amanda Plummer, Bob Gunton, Jane Hoffman, Barton Heyman, Lily Knight; *D:* Mark Romanek; *W:* Keith Gordon, Mark Romanek.

Station 1/2 **1981** A Japanese detective's love affair is corrupted by his ruthless search for a bloodthirsty cop killer. With English subtitles. **130m/C VHS.** *JP* Ken Takakura, Chieko Baisho; *D:* Yasuo Furuhata.

The Station **1992** A sophisticated woman, who has just abandoned her fiancee, waits in a tiny station for an early train. The only person around is the young and ordinary stationmaster. Gradually the two are drawn together in a number of charming and comic romantic fantasies. In Italian with English subtitles. **92m/C VHS.** *IT* Margherita Buy, Ennio Fantastichini; *D:* Sergio Rubini; *W:* Sergio Rubini.

The Station Agent **2003 (R)** Reclusive train enthusiast dwarf, Fibar McBride (Dinklage) takes up residence in an abandoned rural New Jersey train station he inherited in writer/director McCarthy's funny and poignant first film. Finbar's seemingly happy solitude is intruded upon by incurably outgoing local coffee cart owner Joe (Cannavale) who is fascinated by the strange newcomer. Among the other lonely locals is the downtrodden Olivia (Clarkson) who is dealing with the death of her child and a divorce. Finbar's passion for trains soon takes a back seat to some regular human contact. Dinklage is a standout in the title role, while Clarkson, Williams and Cannavale are equally excellent in this well-crafted dramedy. **88m/C VHS, DVD.** *US* Peter Dinklage, Patricia Clarkson, Bobby Cannavale, Raven Goodwin, Paul Benjamin, Michelle Williams; *D:* Thomas (Tom) McCarthy; *W:* Thomas (Tom) McCarthy; *C:* Oliver Bokelberg; *M:* Stephen Trask. British Acad. '03: Orig. Screenplay; Ind. Spirit '04: First Screenplay; Natl. Bd. of Review '03: Support. Actress (Clarkson); Natl. Soc. Film Critics '03: Support. Actress (Clarkson).

Station Jim 1/2 **2001** In the 1890s, a performing circus dog escapes its abusive master and is found by railway station porter Bob (Creed-Miles), who names the terrier Jim. Jim becomes a favorite of the kiddies at the local orphanage, especially young Henry (Sangster). Jim and Bob soon find themselves in a battle to save the orphanage from closure, even as the pooch helps Bob with romancing schoolteacher Harriet (Fraser) and thwarts a plot to kill Queen Victoria. **87m/C DVD.** *GB* Charlie Creed-Miles, George Cole, Laura Fraser, Thomas Sangster, Frank Finlay, David Haig, Celia Imrie, Prunella Scales, Timothy West, David Ross; *D:* John Roberts; *W:* Mark Wallington; *C:* Vernon Layton. **TV**

Station West **1948** A disguised Army officer is sent to uncover a mystery of hijackers and murderers. Along the way, he meets up with and falls for a beautiful woman who may be involved in the treachery. Good, solid western with a fine cast and plenty of fun action shot against the requisite beautiful western landscapes. Based on the Luke Short story. Also available colorized. **92m/B VHS.** Dick Powell, Jane Greer, Agnes Moorehead, Burl Ives, Tom Powers, Raymond Burr; *D:* Sidney Lanfield.

The Stationmaster's Wife 1/2 **1977** In Germay's Weimar Republic a provincial stationmaster's wife expresses her boredom with her pleasant ineffectual husband by having numerous meaningless affairs. Meant to invoke postwar German dread and the fake bourgeois morality which covered political and social resentments. Originally shown as a 200-minute miniseries for German TV; subtitled. **111m/C VHS, DVD.** *GE* Elisabeth Trissenaar, Kurt Raab, Gustal Bayrhammer, Bernard Helfrich, Udo Kier, Volker Spengler; *D:* Rainer Werner Fassbinder; *W:* Rainer Werner Fassbinder; *C:* Michael Ballhaus; *M:* Peer Raben. **TV**

The Statue **1971 (R)** Famed sculptress unveils a nude rendering of her Nobel Prize-winning husband. Much hilarity in the British vein is meant to ensue, but doesn't. Niven is OK, but this empty, plotless farce should have been much shorter. **84m/C VHS.** *GB* David Niven, Virna Lisi, Robert Vaughn, Ann Bell, John Cleese; *D:* Rod Amateau.

Stavisky **1974** Sumptuously lensed story of Serge Stavisky, a con-artist and bon-vivant whose machinations almost brought down the French government when his corruption was exposed in 1934. Belmondo makes as charismatic an antihero as you could find. Excellent score complements the visuals. In French with English subtitles. **117m/C VHS, DVD.** Jean-Paul Belmondo, Anny (Annie Legras) Duperey, Charles Boyer, Francois Perier, Gerard Depardieu; *D:* Alain Resnais; *W:* Jorge Semprun; *C:* Sacha Vierny; *M:* Stephen Sondheim. N.Y. Film Critics '74: Support. Actor (Boyer).

Stay 1/2 **2005 (R)** Confusing psychological thriller finds compassionate shrink Sam Foster (McGregor) trying to prevent his patient Henry (Gosling) from committing suicide. Distracting and oblique things happen and Sam begins to question whether what he sees is real or part of a nightmare. ou probably won't be able to understand what you're seeing either. Good cast, good director, but too artsy by far. **99m/C DVD.** *US* Ewan McGregor, Naomi Watts, Ryan Gosling, Janeane

Garofalo, B.D. Wong, Bob Hoskins, Kate Burton, Michael Gaston, Mark Margolis, Elizabeth Reaser, Sherriff Kennelly; *D:* Marc Forster; *W:* David Benioff; *C:* Roberto Schaefer; *M:* Asche & Spencer.

Stay Alive 🦴 **2006 (PG-13)** Hackneyed horror. The title refers to a videogame that was being tested by players who subsequently died. The game is then passed on to Hutch (Foster). When he and his fellow gamers play, more teens die and Hutch finally realizes that when a player dies in the game, they die exactly the same way in real life. Their nemesis (for no good reason) turns out to be sadistic, blood-bathing 16th-century Hungarian countess Elizabeth Bathory, who is now occupying a Louisiana plantation. Apparently the deaths keep her young and beautiful. Makes about as much sense as it sounds like it would. **85m/C DVD.** *US* Jon Foster, Samaire Armstrong, Frankie Muniz, Jimmi Simpson, Wendell Pierce, Sophia Bush, Adam Goldberg; *D:* William Brent Bell; *W:* William Brent Bell, Matthew Peterman; *C:* Alejandro Martinez; *M:* John (Gianni) Frizzell.

Stay As You Are 🦴 ½ **1978** Aging French architect Mastroianni has designs on a teenager who may be his illegitimate daughter from an earlier affair. **95m/C VHS.** *FR* Marcello Mastroianni, Nastassja Kinski, Francisco Rabal; *D:* Alberto Lattuada.

Stay Awake 🦴 **1987 (R)** A demon stalks, haunts and tortures eight young girls sleeping together at a secluded Catholic school. Title might be addressed to the viewer, who will be tempted to snooze. **90m/C VHS, DVD.** *SA* Shirley Jane Harris, Tanya Gordon, Jayne Hutton, Heath Porter; *D:* John Bernard.

Stay Away, Joe 🦴 **1968 (PG)** The King is a singing half-breed rodeo star who returns to his reservation where he finds love and trouble. Utterly cliche, embarrassing, and stupid even by Elvis-movie standards. **98m/C VHS, DVD.** Elvis Presley, Burgess Meredith, Joan Blondell, Thomas Gomez, L.Q. Jones, Katy Jurado, Henry Jones; *D:* Peter Tewkesbury.

Stay Hungry 🦴🦴🦴 **1976 (R)** A wealthy southerner (Bridges) is involved in a real estate deal which depends on the sale of a gym where a number of body builders hang out. He becomes immersed in their world and finds himself in love with the working-class Field. Big Arnold's first speaking role in his own inimitable accent (his first role in "Hercules in New York" was dubbed.) Offbeat and occasionally uneven comedy-drama based on a novel by Charles Gaines is a sleeper. **102m/C VHS, DVD.** Jeff Bridges, Sally Field, Arnold Schwarzenegger, Robert Englund, Scatman Crothers; *D:* Bob Rafelson; *W:* Bob Rafelson.

Stay Tuned 🦴 **1992 (PG-13)** Suburban yuppie couple buys a large-screen TV and satellite dish from Hellvision salesman, are sucked into their dish, and wind up starring in hellish TV shows such as "Wayne's Underworld," "Northern Overexposure," "Sadistic Home Videos," and "My Three Sons of Bitches." If they can survive for 24 hours, they'll be able to return to their normal lives. Clever idea for a film is wasted as this one never really gets off the ground; viewers may not want to stay tuned to the low comedy and frantic yucks. **90m/C VHS, DVD.** John Ritter, Pam Dawber, Jeffrey Jones, Eugene Levy, David Tom, Heather McComb; *D:* Peter Hyams; *W:* Tom S. Parker; *C:* Peter Hyams; *M:* Bruce Broughton.

Stay Tuned for Murder 🦴 ½ **1988** A sexy news reporter gets caught in a web of financial wrongdoings and corruption. The financiers, lawyers, and other sinister types she's investigating decide to give her a story she will never forget—if she ever gets the chance to tell it! **92m/C VHS.** Terry Reeves Wolf, Christopher Ginnaven; *D:* Gary Jones.

Staying Alive 🦴 ½ **1983 (PG)** "Saturday Night Fever" was the ultimate cheesy '70s musical, hence likeable in a dorky way. This pathetic sequel (directed by Stallone from a Rocky-esque script about beating the odds, etc.) is utterly predictable and forgettable. Set six years after the first film, the sequel finds Tony Manero (Travolta) working as a waiter while trying to break into the big lights of Broadway. Music mostly by Frank Stallone, the great heir to Rodgers and Hammerstein. ♫ The Woman In You; I Love You Too Much; Breakout; Someone Belonging to Someone; Life Goes On; Far From Over; Devils and Seducers; (We Dance) So Close to the Fire; Hope We Never Change. **96m/C VHS, DVD.** John Travolta, Cynthia Rhodes, Finola Hughes, Norma Donaldson; *D:* Sylvester Stallone; *W:* Sylvester Stallone; *M:* Frank Stallone.

Staying On 🦴🦴 ½ **1980** Based on the Paul Scott novel, this English drama follows the life of a post-colonial British colonel and his wife who chose to remain in India. **87m/C VHS, DVD.** *GB* Trevor Howard, Celia Johnson; *D:* Irene Shubik.

Staying Together 🦴 ½ **1989 (R)** Three midwestern brothers go into a panic when their father decides to sell the restaurant they've worked at all their adult lives. Somehow they manage the transition and learn about life. Sloppy comedy-drama with way too many unresolved subplots. **91m/C VHS, DVD.** Dermot Mulroney, Tim Quill, Sean Astin, Stockard Channing, Melinda Dillon, Daphne Zuniga; *D:* Lee Grant; *W:* Monte Merrick; *C:* Dick Bush; *M:* Miles Goodman.

The Steagle 🦴 **1971 (R)** The threat of the Cuban missile crisis lets a fantasizing professor loose to enact his wildest dreams. Odd Mitty-esque fantasy comedy might have worked, but ends up confusing and frustrating. **101m/C VHS.** Richard Benjamin, Cloris Leachman; *D:* Paul Sylbert.

Steal Big, Steal Little 🦴🦴 **1995 (PG-13)** Twins Robby and Reuben Martinez (Garcia) battle over the California ranch land left to Reuben by their mother. Evil, manipulative Robby, all fancy suits and slicked-back hair, wants to build condos while gentle, less-fashionable Reuben must fight to fulfill his dream of building a home for the migrant workers he employs. Yawn. Writer/director Davis' flashy action movie technique doesn't fit into the dramatic social commentary—it's too fast and forced to work. Garcia's radical character changes are impressive though. Arkin provides comic relief as the good-hearted used-car dealer who tries to save the day, if not the film. **130m/C VHS, DVD.** Andy Garcia, Alan Arkin, Rachel Ticotin, Joe Pantoliano, David Ogden Stiers, Charles Rocket, Holland Taylor; *D:* Andrew Davis; *W:* Lee Blessing, Jeanne Blake, Terry Kahn, Andrew Davis; *C:* Frank Tidy; *M:* William Olvis.

Steal the Sky 🦴🦴 **1988** Israeli agent Hemingway seduces Iraqi pilot Cross and persuades him to steal a Soviet MIG jet and defect to Israel. Unlikely plot but swell flying scenes. Hemingway is poorly cast, as she often is. **110m/C VHS, DVD.** Mariel Hemingway, Ben Cross, Etta Ankri; *D:* John Hancock. **CABLE**

Steal This Movie! 🦴🦴 *Abbie* **2000 (R)** Bio of anti-war activist and Yippie founder Abbie Hoffman tries to explore the counterculture of the 60s but bites off more than it can chew. Film's fragmented by its structure of using the flashback recollections of Abbie's (D'Onofrio) first wife Anita (Garofalo) and lawyer Gerry Lefcourt (Pollak) to explain the manic and charismatic Hoffman, who wound up spending most of the 70s an underground fugitive and who died a suicide. Garity, who's the son of Tom Hayden and Jane Fonda, plays his activist dad. **111m/C VHS, DVD.** Vincent D'Onofrio, Janeane Garofalo, Jeanne Tripplehorn, Donal Logue, Kevin Pollak, Kevin Corrigan, Troy Garity, Alan Van Sprang; *D:* Robert Greenwald; *W:* Bruce Graham; *C:* Denis Lenoir; *M:* Mader.

Stealing Beauty 🦴🦴 ½ **1996 (R)** The film's main asset, besides the beautiful Tuscan scenery, is the coltish charm of Tyler, who stars as virginal teenager Lucy Harmon. An innocent abroad, she's spending the summer with family friends after her mother's suicide. Ostensibly artist Ian Grayson (McCann) is doing her portrait but Lucy's more interested in finding romance with neighbor lad Niccolo (Zibetti), who bestowed her first kiss on a previous visit. Lucy's sunny appeal doesn't go unnoticed by the villa's other inhabitants, including dying playwright Alex (Irons), but it seems Lucy's growing up won't be easy on anyone (not even herself). **118m/C VHS, DVD.** *IT GB FR* Liv Tyler, Jeremy Irons, Donal McCann, Sinead Cusack, Jean Marais, D.W. Moffett, Stefania Sandrelli, Carlo Cecchi, Roberto Zibetti, Joseph Fiennes, Jason Flemyng, Leonardo Treviglio, Rachel Weisz; *D:* Bernardo Bertolucci; *W:* Bernardo Bertolucci, Susan Minot; *C:* Darius Khondji; *M:* Richard Hartley.

Stealing Candy 🦴🦴 **2004 (R)** Two ex-cons and a computer whiz team up to kidnap a movie star Candi (Lano) so they can stage a pay-per-view internet sex session with her. Predictable thriller piles on the nonstop action and plays on the promise of sex. **83m/C VHS, DVD.** Jenya Lano, Daniel Baldwin, Coolio, Alex McArthur, Julie St. Claire; *D:* Mark L. Lester; *W:* C. Courtney Joyner. **VIDEO**

Stealing Harvard 🦴 **2002 (PG-13)** Prince of low-brow Green adds another tarnished jewel to his crown with this tired, inane crime caper comedy. As Duff, Green is teamed with Jason Lee as John, who needs to raise $30,000 to finance the Harvard education he promised his neice. That should take care of her first semester. His fiancee (Mann), also wants John to bankroll their future together, and won't marry him until he has the exact amount in the bank. What follows are the disastrous duo's clumsy attempts to steal the money. Largely unfunny, with small chunks of mild humor. **83m/C VHS, DVD.** *US* Tom Green, Jason Lee, Leslie Mann, Megan Mullally, Dennis Farina, Richard Jenkins, John C. McGinley, Christopher Penn, Tammy Blanchard, Seymour Cassel, Bruce McCulloch; *D:* Bruce McCulloch; *W:* Peter Tolan; *C:* Ueli Steiger; *M:* Christophe Beck.

Stealing Heaven 🦴🦴 ½ **1988 (R)** Based on the lives of Abelard and Heloise. In 12th-century Paris, a theologian and teacher falls in love with a beautiful young woman, and the two must defend their bond from all comers, including her righteous uncle. Steamy; trimmed to 108 minutes after threatened X rating. Attractive and cerebral. Available in a 115 minute-uncut, unrated version. **108m/C VHS.** *GB YU* Derek de Lint, Kim Thomson, Denholm Elliott, Mark Jax, Bernard Hepton, Kenneth Cranham, Angela Pleasence, Rachel Kempson; *D:* Clive Donner; *W:* Chris Bryant; *M:* Nick Bicat.

Stealing Home 🦴🦴 ½ **1988 (PG-13)** A washed-up baseball player learns his former babysitter (who was also his first love and inspiration), has committed suicide. Their bittersweet relationship is told through flashbacks. Foster's superb performance steals the show in this quiet sleeper. **98m/C VHS, DVD.** Mark Harmon, Jodie Foster, William McNamara, Blair Brown, Harold Ramis, Jonathan Silverman, John Shea, Helen Hunt, Richard Jenkins, Ted Ross, Thatcher Goodwin, Yvette Croskey; *D:* Steven Kampmann, Will Aldis; *W:* Steven Kampmann, Will Aldis; *C:* Bobby Byrne; *M:* David Foster.

Stealing Sinatra 🦴🦴 ½ **2004 (R)** Telling of the screwy but true details behind the 1963 botched kidnapping of Frank Sinatra, Jr. by three amateurs trying to score some quick dough from his renowned father. **95m/C VHS, DVD.** David Arquette, William H. Macy, Ryan Browning, Sam McMurray, Thomas Ian Nicholas, Gillian Barber, Colin Cunningham, Brandy Heidrick, Catherine Barroll, Matthew Bennett, Johnathan Brownlee, Ron Chartier, Michael Coristine; *D:* Ron Underwood; *W:* Howard Korder; *C:* Brian Pearson; *M:* John Powell, James McKee Smith. **TV**

Stealth 🦴 ½ **2005 (PG-13)** Dumb, loud, special effects-heavy action flick falls into the mindless entertainment category. Three elite Navy pilots (Lucas, Biel, Foxx)—who all look really good in their dress whites—are chosen to test the latest stealth aircraft, with a fourth jet as wingman. This is a pilot-less craft controlled by an artificial intelligence known as EDI. Naturally, EDI goes haywire and must be stopped by those puny humans. Director Cohen likes action, and the actors are just along for the ride. **121m/C DVD, Blu-ray Disc, UMD.** *US* Josh(ua) Lucas, Jamie Foxx, Jessica Biel, Sam Shepard, Joe Morton, Richard Roxburgh, Ian Bliss, Nicholas Hammond; *D:* Rob Cohen; *W:* W.D. Richter; *C:* Dean Semler; *M:* BT (Brian Transeau); *V:* Wentworth Miller.

Stealth 🦴 ½ *Comme des Voleurs* **2006** Narcissistic story about family ties. Lionel seems happy with his life and his lover Serge. Then he learns that his paternal grandfather was a Polish emigre to Switzerland and suddenly Lionel goes overboard discovering his roots, to the point of deciding to marry a Polish immigrant facing deportation. This drives Lionel's older sister Lucie over the edge and she drags him on a road trip to Warsaw to get to the truth about their family. Misadventures abound. French and Polish with subtitles. **112m/C DVD.** *SI* Alicja Bachleda-Curus, Lionel Baier, Natacha Koutchoumov, Stephane Rentznik, Michal Rudnicki; *D:* Lionel Baier; *W:* Lionel Baier; *C:* Severine Barde; *M:* Dominique Dalcan.

Stealth Fighter 🦴 ½ **1999 (R)** Naval pilot Owen Turner (Ice-T) fakes his own death and goes to work for the bad guys in South America. Then he steals a stealth fighter from a U.S. military base and starts bombing foreign military installations. So naval officer Ryan Mitchell (Mandylor) is sent to stop him. Wynorski directed under the pseudonym "Jay Andrews." **87m/C VHS, DVD.** Ice-T, Costas Mandylor, Ernie Hudson, Erika Eleniak, Andrew Divoff, John Enos, Steve Eastin; *D:* Jim Wynorski; *W:* Lenny Juliano; *C:* J.E. Bash; *M:* K. Alexander (Alex) Wilkinson. **VIDEO**

Steam: A Turkish Bath 🦴🦴🦴 *Hamam: Il Bagno Turco* **1996** Francesco (Gassman) is a young Italian businessman married to the equally busy Marta (d'Aloja) and living a fashionable life in Rome. When he learns an aunt has left him a building in Istanbul, he leaves to check out his inheritance. What Francesco discovers is that he now possesses a traditional Turkish bath and that the family his aunt lived with and employed is eager for him to stay. Mysterious Istanbul begins to work its magic as does Francesco's unexpected (and mutual) growing attraction to the family's son, Mehmet (Gunsur). Of course, Marta does eventually show up. Italian and Turkish with subtitles. **96m/C VHS, DVD.** *TU IT SP* Alessandro Gassman, Francesca D'Aloja, Carlo Cecchi, Mehmet Gunsur, Serif Sezer, Basak Koklukaya, Halil Ergun, Alberto Molinari; *D:* Ferzan Ozpetek; *W:* Ferzan Ozpetek, Stefano Tummolini; *C:* Pasquale Mari; *M:* Aldo De Scalzi.

Steamboat Bill, Jr. 🦴🦴🦴 ½ **1928** City-educated student returns to his small home-town and his father's Mississippi river boat, where he's an embarrassment to dad. But bond they do, to ward off the owner of a rival riverboat, whose daughter Keaton falls for. Engaging look at small-town life and the usual wonderful Keaton antics, including braving the big tornado. **75m/B VHS, DVD.** Buster Keaton, Ernest Torrence, Marion Byron, Tom Lewis; *D:* Charles Reisner; *W:* Carl Harbaugh; *C:* Bert Haines, Devereaux Jennings.

Steamboat Round the Bend 🦴🦴 ½ **1935** Snake oil salesman Dr. John Pearly (Rogers) is traveling to meet his nephew Duke (McGuire) so they can go into the riverboat business together. But Duke has been falsely convicted of murder and will hang unless Pearly and Duke's girlfriend Fleety Belle (Shirley) can find the only witness to the crime. A big steamboat race is part of the plot. The last film that Rogers shot, although "In Old Kentucky" was released after. **81m/B DVD.** Will Rogers, Anne Shirley, John McGuire, Eugene Pallette, Berton Churchill, Stepin Fetchit, Francis Ford, Irvin S. Cobb, Roger Imhof, Hobart Bosworth, Raymond Hatton; *D:* John Ford; *W:* Lamar Trotti, Dudley Nicholas; *C:* George Schneiderman; *M:* Samuel Kaylin.

Steamboy 🦴🦴 **2005 (PG-13)** Generational conflict explodes into epic machine war above the streets of an alternate Victorian London. It all revolves around something called the steamball, a dangerous revolutionary new form of power created by a father-son pair of mad scientists (Stewart and Molina) who battle for the loyalty of a grandson (Paquin) and the proper use of their invention. Overwrought, over-thought anime spectacle with some absolutely mind-blowing visuals from the mind of "Akira" creator Otomo. Could have benefited from some wise surgical editing. Original and English language versions available. **126m/C DVD, Blu-ray Disc, UMD.** *D:* Katsuhiro Otomo; *W:* Katsuhiro Otomo, Sadayuki Murai; *M:* Steve Jablonsky; *V:* Anne Suzuki, Masane Tsukayama, Katsuo Nakamura, Manami Konishi, Kiyoshi Kodama, Ikki Sawamura, Susumu Terajima, Anna Paquin, Alfred Molina, Patrick Stewart, Kari Wahlgren, Robin Atkin Downes, David Lee.

Steaming 1986 (R) Six women get together in a London bathhouse and review their various troubles with men. Unfortunate adaptation of the good play by Nell Dunn. Where are the laughs—and what happened to the dramatic tension? The last film of Dors and director Losey. **102m/C VHS.** *GB* Vanessa Redgrave, Sarah Miles, Diana Dors; ***D:*** Joseph Losey.

Steel *Look Down and Die; Men of Steel* **1980 (R)** Construction workers on a mammoth skyscraper face insurmountable odds and strong opposition. Will they finish their building? Worth watching, if you don't have anything else to do. **100m/C VHS.** Lee Majors, Jennifer O'Neill, Art Carney, George Kennedy, Harris Yulin, Terry Kiser, Richard Lynch, Roger E. Mosley, Albert Salmi, R.G. Armstrong; ***D:*** Steve Carver; ***W:*** Leigh Chapman; ***M:*** Michel Colombier.

Steel ½ **1997 (PG-13)** Metal specialist John Henry Irons (O'Neal) has designed a top-secret military weapon that falls into the hands of a street gang. Donning a suit of armor he designed, he become super hero Steel and sets out to end the reign of terror of former colleague turned super villian Burke (Nelson). Adaptation of popular DC comic keeps target audience in mind with lots of action and plenty of humor. Shaq proves once again that as an actor he's a pretty good basketball player. **97m/C VHS.** Shaquille O'Neal, Judd Nelson, Annabeth Gish, Richard Roundtree, Irma P. Hall, Charles Napier, Kerrie Keane, Hill Harper, Thom Barry; ***D:*** Kenneth Johnson; ***W:*** Kenneth Johnson; ***C:*** Mark Irwin; ***M:*** Mervyn Warren.

Steel and Lace ½ **1990 (R)** Davison is the scientist brother of a classical pianist who commits suicide after being raped. He revives her as a cyborg, which promptly sets out to enact its revenge. Depressing, morbid sci-fi. **92m/C VHS.** Bruce Davison, Clare Wren, Stacy Haiduk, David Naughton, David Lander; ***D:*** Ernest Farino; ***W:*** Joseph Dougherty, Dave Edison; ***C:*** Thomas Callaway.

Steel Arena **1972 (PG)** Several real life stunt-car drivers appear in this action-packed film, crammed with spins, jumps, explosions and world-record-breaking, life risking stunts. **99m/C VHS.** Dusty Russell, Gene Drew, Buddy Love; ***D:*** Mark L. Lester.

Steel City **2006 (R)** Blue-collar angst and family dysfunction in a low-key drama. Alcoholic Carl (Heard) abandoned his family long ago and is presently jailed for vehicular homicide. Younger son PJ (Guiry) is trying to man up but he's scared and confused and tends to make bad choices while his repentant father offers advice during prison visits and conceals a secret. Debut feature from Jun was shot in his Alton, Illinois, hometown. **95m/C DVD.** John Heard, Tom Guiry, America Ferrera, Clayne Crawford, James McDaniel, Laurie Metcalf, Heather McComb, Raymond J. Barry; ***D:*** Brian Jun; ***W:*** Brian Jun; ***C:*** Ryan Samul; ***M:*** Mark Geary.

The Steel Claw **1961** One-handed ex-Marine Montgomery organizes guerilla forces against the Japanese in the Philippines in WWII. Good location shooting and plenty of action. **95m/C VHS.** George Montgomery, Charito Luna, Mario Barri; ***D:*** George Montgomery.

Steel Cowboy **1978** With his marriage, sanity, and livelihood on the line, an independent trucker agrees to haul a hot herd of stolen steers. Passable made-for-TV macho adventure. **100m/C VHS.** James Brolin, Rip Torn, Jennifer Warren, Strother Martin, Melanie Griffith, Lou Frizzell; ***D:*** Harvey Laidman; ***M:*** Charles Bernstein.

Steel Dawn ½ **1987 (R)** Another "Mad Max" clone: A leather-clad warrior wields his sword over lots of presumably post-apocalyptic desert terrain. Swayze stars with his real-life wife Niemi in unfortunate follow-up to "Dirty Dancing." **90m/C VHS, DVD.** Arnold Vosloo, Patrick Swayze, Lisa Niemi, Christopher Neame, Brett Hool, Brion James, Anthony Zerbe; ***D:*** Lance Hool; ***W:*** Doug Lefler; ***C:*** Jiri (George) Tirl; ***M:*** Brian May.

Steel Frontier ½ **1994 (R)** Post-apocalypse actioner finds a group of survivors trying to make a new life in a town they call New Hope. But then a group of bandit soldiers take over—until a lone hero comes along to save the day. **94m/C VHS, DVD.** Joe Lara, Brion James, Bo Svenson, Stacie Foster; ***D:*** Paul G. Volk, Jacobsen Hart; ***W:*** Jacobsen Hart.

The Steel Helmet ½ **1951** Hurriedly made Korean War drama stands as a top-notch war film. Brooding and dark, GIs don't save the world for democracy or rescue POWs; they simply do their best to survive a horrifying situation. Pointless death, confused loyalties and cynicism abound in writer-director Fuller's scathing comment on the madness of war. **84m/B VHS, DVD.** Gene Evans, Robert Hutton, Steve Brodie, William Chun, James Edwards, Richard Loo, Harold Fong, Neyle Morrow, Sid Melton, Richard Monahan, Lynn Stalmaster; ***D:*** Samuel Fuller; ***W:*** Samuel Fuller; ***C:*** Ernest Miller; ***M:*** Paul Dunlap.

Steel Magnolias **1989 (PG)** Shelby Eatenton (Roberts) is a young woman stricken with severe diabetes who chooses to live her life to the fullest despite her bad health. Much of the action centers around a Louisiana beauty shop (run by Parton) where the women get together to discuss the goings-on of their lives. Screenplay by R. Harling, based on his partially autobiographical play. Sweet, poignant, and often hilarious, yet just as often overwrought. MacLaine is funny as a bitter divorcee; Parton is sexy and fun as the hairdresser; but Field and Roberts (as mother and daughter) go off the deep end and make it all entirely too weepy. **118m/C VHS, DVD.** Sally Field, Dolly Parton, Shirley MacLaine, Daryl Hannah, Olympia Dukakis, Julia Roberts, Tom Skerritt, Sam Shepard, Dylan McDermott, Kevin J. O'Connor, Bill McCutcheon, Ann Wedgeworth, Janine Turner; ***D:*** Herbert Ross; ***W:*** Robert Harling; ***C:*** John A. Alonzo; ***M:*** Georges Delerue. Golden Globes '90: Support. Actress (Roberts).

Steel Sharks **1997 (R)** A military coup in Iran finds chemical weapons expert Dr. Van Tasset (Livingston) kidnapped by revolutionaries. Members of an elite squad of Navy SEALs are sent to rescue him, aided by a U.S. sub. But the good guys wind up prisoners on an Iranian sub and a deadly game of underwater hide-and-seek follows. **94m/C VHS, DVD.** Billy Dee Williams, Gary Busey, Tim Lounibos, Barry Livingston, Billy Warlock, Larry Poindexter, Tim Abell, Robert Miranda, David Roberson, Matthew St. Patrick; ***D:*** Rodney McDonald; ***W:*** Rodney McDonald, William Martell; ***C:*** Bryan Greenberg; ***M:*** David Lawrence. **VIDEO**

Steel Toes **2006 (R)** Jewish liberal lawyer Danny Dunkleman (Straithairn) becomes the court-appointed attorney for skinhead Michael Downey (Walker), who's confessed to murdering an East Indian immigrant in a Montreal alley. Danny is trying to find Michael a defense and make him confront what he has done, without much cooperation. Lots of jailhouse talk; gets an extra half a bone for Straithairn's compelling performance. **90m/C DVD.** *CA* Marina Orsini, David Straithairn, Andrew W. Walker, Ivan Smith; ***D:*** David Gow, Mark Adam; ***W:*** David Gow; ***C:*** Mark Adam; ***M:*** Benoit Groulx.

Steele Justice **1987 (R)** A tough 'Nam vet takes on the whole Vietnamese Mafia in Southern California after his friend is murdered. One of those head-scratchers: Should I laugh, or be offended? **96m/C VHS.** Martin Kove, Sela Ward, Ronny Cox, Bernie Casey, Joseph Campanella, Sarah Douglas; ***D:*** Robert Boris; ***W:*** Robert Boris.

Steele's Law **1991 (R)** A loner cop is forced to take the law into his own hands in order to track down an insane international assassin. **90m/C VHS, DVD.** Fred Williamson, Bo Svenson, Doran Ingham, Phyllis Cicero; ***D:*** Fred Williamson; ***W:*** Charles Eric Johnson; ***C:*** David Blood; ***M:*** Mike Logan.

Steelyard Blues ½ *The Final Crash* **1973 (PG)** A motley-crew comedy about a wacky gang that tries to steal an abandoned WW II airplane. Zany pranks abound. Technically flawed direction from Myerson mars a potentially hilarious story. **93m/C VHS, DVD.** Jane Fonda, Donald Sutherland, Peter Boyle, Howard Hesseman, John Savage, Garry Goodrow; ***D:*** Alan Myerson; ***W:*** David S. Ward; ***M:*** David Shire.

Stella ½ **1955** Mercouri's film debut has her as a free-spirited bar singer who gets involved in a tragic romantic triangle with a middle-class writer and a local football hero. Melodramatic but Mercouri's earthy joie de vivre is already apparent. In Greek with English subtitles. **94m/B VHS, DVD.** *GR* Melina Mercouri, Yiorgo Fountas, Aiekos Alexandrikis, Sophia Vembo; ***D:*** Michael Cacoyannis; ***W:*** Michael Cacoyannis; ***C:*** Costa Theodorides; ***M:*** Manos Hadjidakis.

Stella ½ **1989 (PG-13)** Anachronistic remake update of "Stella Dallas" casts Midler as a single mother who sacrifices everything to give her daughter a better life. Barbara Stanwyck did it much better in 1937. Based on Olive Higgins Prouty's novel. **109m/C VHS, DVD.** Bette Midler, John Goodman, Stephen Collins, Eileen Brennan, Ben Stiller, Trini Alvarado, Marsha Mason; ***D:*** John Erman; ***W:*** Robert Getchell; ***C:*** Billy Williams.

Stella Dallas **1937** Uneducated Stella (Stanwyck) lets go of the daughter (Shirley) she loves when she realizes her ex-husband (Boles) can give the girl more advantages. What could be sentimental turns out believable and worthwhile under Vidor's steady hand. Stanwyck never makes a wrong step. From a 1923 novel by Olive Higgins Prouty. Remade in 1989 as "Stella," starring Bette Midler. **106m/B VHS, DVD.** Barbara O'Neil, Tim Holt, Barbara Stanwyck, Anne Shirley, John Boles, Alan Hale, Marjorie Main; ***D:*** King Vidor; ***W:*** Sarah Y. Mason, Victor Heerman; ***C:*** Rudolph Mate; ***M:*** Alfred Newman.

Stella Does Tricks **1996** Stella (Macdonald) is a teen runaway, working as a prostitute in London for pimp Mr. Peters (Bolam). She was abused by her dad (Stewart) and has revenge fantasies—some of which she takes out on clients, which leads to punishment by her boss. She briefly gets free of Peters and gets a legit job, but Stella has also become involved with junkie Eddie (Matheson) and his drug needs have him betraying Stella. No Cinderella stories here—Stella's life is bleak and violent, with Macdonald giving a powerhouse performance. **97m/C VHS, DVD.** *GB* Kelly Macdonald, James Bolam, Ewan Stewart, Hans Matheson, Andy Serkis, Paul Chahidi; ***D:*** Coky Giedroyc; ***W:*** A.L. Kennedy; ***C:*** Barry Ackroyd; ***M:*** Nick Bicat.

Stella Maris **1918** Pickford inspiringly plays two difficult roles. As Stella Maris, she's a wealthy orphaned cripple who's in love with the married John Risca (Tearle), whose wife, Louise (Ankewich), is an abusive alcoholic. John eventually leaves her and Louise takes out her anger on homely servant Unity Blake (Pickford's second role). When Unity is eventually rescued by John, she also falls in love with him. Brimming with the tragic consequences of love. **100m/B VHS, DVD.** Mary Pickford, Conway Tearle, Camille Ankewich, Ida Waterman, Herbert Standing; ***D:*** Marshall Neilan; ***W:*** Frances Marion; ***C:*** Walter Stradling.

The Stendahl Syndrome *La Sindrome di Stendhal* **1995** Psycho serial-killer thriller about a Rome police detective, Anna (Argento), who has an extreme hallucinatory reaction to artwork (the title syndrome). While visiting an art gallery, she collapses and is assisted by Alfredo (Kretschmann), who turns out to be the very rapist-killer whom she's hunting. Anna escapes from him once (after being tortured) but is captured again. However, she manages to fight back in ways squeamish viewers may want to avoid watching. Inspired by Graziella Magherini's novel "La Sindrome di Stendhal." **118m/C VHS, DVD, Blu-ray Disc.** *IT* Asia Argento, Thomas Kretschmann, Marco Leonardi, Luigi Diberti, Paolo Bonacelli, John Quentin; ***D:*** Dario Argento; ***W:*** Dario Argento; ***C:*** Giuseppe Rotunno; ***M:*** Ennio Morricone.

Step Brothers **2008 (R)** When Brennan's (Ferrell) mom Nancy (Steenburgen) and Dale's (Reilly) dad Robert (Jenkins) get married, the 40ish living-at-home losers find themselves sharing a bedroom, making for some serious sibling rivalry until the men/boys bond over their shared John Stamos crushes and their contempt for Brennan's brother Derek (Scott), an egotistical corporate suit. Ferrell and Reilly masterfully channel their inner brats while maxing out their knack for getting laughs from gross-out gags (like it or not) all the way up to the happy sappy ending. **95m/C DVD, Blu-ray Disc.** *US* Will Ferrell, John C. Reilly, Mary Steenburgen, Richard Jenkins, Adam Scott, Kathryn Hahn, Andrea Savage; ***D:*** Adam McKay; ***W:*** Will Ferrell, Adam McKay; ***C:*** Oliver Wood; ***M:*** Jon Brion.

Step Into Liquid **2003** Brown is the son of surf-documentary pioneer Bruce "Endless Summer" Brown, so he knows his way around visuals. Brown takes on the positive energy of surfing around the world with the sport's top competitors, including Laird Hamilton, Kelly Slater, and Taj Burrow, as well as a number of ordinary folks who just like to catch the wave. **87m/C DVD, Blu-ray Disc.** *US* ***D:*** Dana Brown; ***W:*** Dana Brown; ***C:*** John-Paul Beeghly; ***M:*** Richard Gibbs; ***Nar:*** Dana Brown.

Step Lively ½ **1944** A convoluted plot doesn't slow down the enjoyment of this musical comedy. Naive Glen (Sinatra) writes a dramatic play and sends it—along with his life savings—to slick NY producer Miller (Murphy). When he shows up to see how things are progressing, Glen learns that Miller has used his dough to help finance a new musical, so Miller has showgirl Christine (DeHaven) keep Glen occupied. But the show is in trouble without a male lead—and then Miller hears Glen sing. And the rest is showbiz, folks. ♫ Some Other Time; As Long As There's Been Music; Where Does Love Begin?; Come Out, Come Out, Wherever You Are; Why Must There Be an Opening Song; And Then You Kissed Me; Ask the Madame. **88m/B DVD.** Frank Sinatra, George Murphy, Adolphe Menjou, Walter Slezak, Anne Jeffreys, Eugene Pallette, Gloria DeHaven; ***D:*** Tim Whelan; ***W:*** Peter Milne, Warren Duff; ***C:*** Robert De Grasse.

Step Up ½ **2006 (PG-13)** Tyler Gage (Tatum) is from the wrong side of the Baltimore line. He's assigned to do community service at the elite Maryland School of the Arts after he helps trash their auditorium. Beautiful ballet dancer Nora (Dewan) needs a partner for an important recital and, with her encouragement, Ty discovers his inner Fred Astaire. Dance sequences are excellent, and the cast is appopriately beautiful, but you've seen the rest of the plot before, especially if you've seen writer Adler's "Save the Last Dance." **98m/C DVD.** *US* Channing Tatum, Rachel Griffiths, Damaine Radcliff, Jenna Dewan, Dwight "Heavy D" Myers, De'Shawn Washington, Josh Henderson, Deirdre Lovejoy; ***D:*** Anne Fletcher; ***W:*** Duane Adler, Melissa Rosenberg; ***C:*** Michael Seresin; ***M:*** Aaron Zigman.

Step Up 3D **2010** In this third franchise effort, a tight-knit group of New York street dancers team up with college freshman Moose in a high-stakes showdown against the best breakdancers worldwide. **m/C DVD.** *US* Adam G. Sevani, Rick Malambri, Sharni Vinson, Harry Shum Jr., Ally Maki; ***D:*** John M. Chu; ***W:*** Amy Andelson, Emily Meyer; ***C:*** Ken Seng.

Step Up 2 the Streets **2008 (PG-13)** Andie (Evigan) is kicked out of her crew of street dancers when she's admitted to the prestigious Maryland School of the Arts. She responds by starting her own crew with classmate Chase and demands a chance to compete in a dance contest at a local club. Weak plot is undercut further by movie's fumbling of the race and class issues it raises with its fake-inspirational message, which seems to be, "We're all equal when we dance, especially the white kids who go to the nice high school." **98m/C DVD, Blu-ray Disc.** *US* Briana Evigan, Robert Hoffman, Will(iam) Kemp, Sonja Sohn, Channing Tatum, Adam G. Sevani, Cassie Ventura; ***D:*** John M. Chu; ***W:*** Toni Johnson, Karen Barna; ***C:*** Max Malkin; ***M:*** Aaron Zigman.

The Stepdaughter ½ **2000 (R)** After years of abuse in foster homes, Susan (Roth) wants to strike back at the birth mother who abandoned her. She tracks down the now happily married woman (Pickett), gets a job on the ranch where she lives, and plans her next deadly move. **92m/C VHS, DVD.** Andrea Roth, Lisa Dean Ryan, Jaimz Woolvett, Cindy Pickett, Gary Hudson, Gil Gerard, Matt Farnsworth, Lee Dawson; ***D:*** Peter Paul Liapis; ***W:*** Richard Dana; ***C:*** Maximo Munzi. **VIDEO**

The Stepfather 1987 **(R)** Creepy thriller about a seemingly ordinary stepfather who is actually a homicidal maniac searching for the "perfect family." An independently produced sleeper tightly directed and well written. Followed by two inferior sequels. **89m/C VHS.** Terry O'Quinn, Shelley Hack, Jill Schoelen, Stephen Shellen, Charles Lanyer, Stephen E. Miller; ***D:*** Joseph Ruben; ***W:*** Donald E. Westlake; ***C:*** John Lindley; ***M:*** Patrick Moraz.

The Stepfather 1/2 **2009 (PG-13)** Lazy, clumsy remake of the 1987 flick (based on a screenplay by Donald E. Westlake) that starred Terry O'Quinn in the title role. This time it's Walsh as the psycho whose new wife (Ward) and stepsons don't live up to his perfect family ideals. So he decides to kill them and try again even as troubled teenager Michael (Badgley) gets very suspicious. Walsh plays his character as a smug creep no one with any brains would trust, so the premise is a loser from the beginning. However, Badgley and Heard (as his girlfriend) do provide eye candy with Heard frequently shown scantily clad. **101m/C DVD.** *US* Dylan Walsh, Sela Ward, Penn Badgley, Amber Heard, Jon Tenney, Sherry Stringfield, Jason Wiles; ***D:*** Nelson McCormick; ***W:*** J.S. Cardone; ***C:*** Patrick Cady; ***M:*** Charlie Clouser.

Stepfather 2: Make Room for Daddy 1/2 **1989 (R)** A poor sequel to the suspenseful sleeper, wherein the psychotic family man escapes from an asylum and woos another suburban family, murdering anyone who may suspect his true identity. Followed by yet another sequel. **93m/C VHS, DVD.** Terry O'Quinn, Meg Foster, Caroline Williams, Jonathan Brandis, Henry Brown, Mitchell Laurance; ***D:*** Jeff Burr; ***W:*** John P. Auerbach; ***C:*** Jacek Laskus.

Stepfather 3: Father's Day **1992 (R)** The father from Hell is back! Escaping from the loony bin with a surgically altered face, the stepfather settles in a small town and gets a job at a nursery (the plant kind, not the children kind). His favorite gardening tool fast becomes the mulch machine, and soon locals are fertilizing the garden. Well below the original, but it may please fans of this genre. **110m/C VHS.** Robert Wightman, Priscilla Barnes, Season Hubley; ***D:*** Guy Magar; ***C:*** Alan Caso.

The Stepford Wives **1975** Joanna (Ross) and husband Walter (Masterson) move from bustling Manhattan to the supposedly idyllic Connecticut town of Stepford. Joanna gets suspicious when she notices all the wives are strangely content and subservient and when she meets fellow newcomer, Bobby (Prentiss), they decide to investigate. Creepy adaptation of the Ira Levin novel. **115m/C VHS, DVD.** Katharine Ross, Paula Prentiss, Peter Masterson, Nanette Newman, Patrick O'Neal, Tina Louise, Dee Wallace, William Prince, Mary Stuart Masterson, Carol Rossen; ***D:*** Bryan Forbes; ***W:*** William Goldman; ***C:*** Owen Roizman; ***M:*** Michael Small.

The Stepford Wives 1/2 **2004 (PG-13)** Remake of the spooky 70's classic. Joanna Eberhart (Kidman) is a successful television network executive fired after a reality show disaster. Joanna, her husband Walter (Broderick) and their family move to the seemingly perfect Connecticut town of Stepford. Strangely enough, the impeccably perfect bombshell women of Stepford have no other interests than housecleaning and making their rather nerdy-looking husbands happy. Trades eerie suspense of the original for campy comedy. While there are some well placed barbs and one-liners, plot holds no surprises and loses the satirical edge of the source material. Walker, as the community leader who holds the secret to Stepford, and Midler as a fellow outsider, do well in their respective roles. **93m/C DVD.** *US* Nicole Kidman, Matthew Broderick, Christopher Walken, Glenn Close, Bette Midler, Jon Lovitz, Roger Bart, David Marshall Grant, Faith Hill; ***D:*** Frank Oz; ***W:*** Paul Rudnick; ***C:*** Rob Hahn; ***M:*** David Arnold.

Stephanie Daley **2006 (R)** Disturbing talky drama with flashbacks depicting what happened to a pregnant teen. 16-year-old Stephanie (Tamblyn) gives birth on a school ski trip and is brought up on criminal charges when the baby is found dead. She claims not to have known she was pregnant and that the infant was stillborn. Forensic psychologist Lydie Crane (Swinton) is called in to examine Stephanie, but the situation may be too close for Lydie to be objective. She is pregnant again after suffering a stillbirth herself and both Lydie and Stephanie have a lot of unresolved feelings. Strong performances by both leads in a story with no easy answers. **91m/C DVD.** *US* Amber Tamblyn, Tilda Swinton, Timothy Hutton, Denis O'Hare, Jim Gaffigan, Deirdre O'Connell, Melissa Leo, Halley Feiffer, Kel O'Neill; ***D:*** Hilary Brougher; ***W:*** Hilary Brougher; ***C:*** David Rush Morrison; ***M:*** David Mansfield.

Stephano Quantestorie **1993** Walter Mitty-ish story about daydreaming cop Stephano (Nichetti) who falls for the prime suspect in a robbery he's investigating. He escapes his conflicting feelings by imagining himself living other lives—as a math professor, airline pilot, saxophone player, and thief, but soon all these alter ego are intruding into his work. Italian with subtitles. **90m/C VHS.** *IT* Maurizio Nichetti; ***D:*** Maurizio Nichetti; ***W:*** Maurizio Nichetti.

Stephen King's Golden Years 1/2 *Golden Years* **1991** Stephen King creates a chilling vision of scientific progress gone awry in this shocking techno-thriller. After being accidentally exposed to exotic chemicals in a lab explosion, an aging janitor undergoes an extraordinary transformation and the government will sacrifice anything to learn more about it. **232m/C VHS, DVD.** Keith Szarabajka, Frances Sternhagen, Ed Lauter, R.D. Call, Stephen King, Felicity Huffman, Stephen (Steve) Root; ***D:*** Kenneth Fink, Stephen Tolkin, Allen Coulter, Michael G. Gerrick; ***W:*** Stephen King, Josef Anderson. **TV**

Stephen King's It 1/2 **1990** A group of small town children, who were terrorized by an evil force in their youth, are traumatized again some 30 years later, when they learn a new series of child murders occurred in their Eastern home town. The adults, who now all have successful and diverse careers, must come to terms with the terrible secret they share, as "IT" has returned to wreak havoc in their New England home town. Based on horror master King's bestselling novel of the same name. **193m/C VHS, DVD.** Tim Reid, Richard Thomas, John Ritter, Annette O'Toole, Richard Masur, Dennis Christopher, Harry Anderson, Olivia Hussey, Tim Curry, Jonathan Brandis, Michael Cole; ***D:*** Tommy Lee Wallace; ***W:*** Stephen King; ***M:*** Richard Bellis. **TV**

Stephen King's Rose Red *Rose Red* **2002 (PG-13)** The fictional memoir "The Diary of Ellen Rimbauer" was released shortly before the miniseries aired, rather than the movie being based on an already successful novel. The "Diary's" editor, Dr. Joyce Reardon (Travis), is a college professor looking for the supernatural inside Rose Red, a decaying mansion known for its strange history. She gathers together various paranormals, including autistic teenager Annie (Brown) who has strong telekinetic powers. The house begins to feed off Annie's energy and all hell breaks loose. Last role for Dukes (as Joyce's nemesis Professor Miller) who died during filming. **254m/C VHS, DVD.** Nancy Travis, Kimberly J. Brown, Matt Keeslar, David Dukes, Julian Sands, Judith Ivey, Melanie Lynskey, Matt Ross, Kevin Tighe, Julia Campbell, Jimmi Simpson; ***D:*** Craig R. Baxley; ***W:*** Stephen King; ***C:*** David Connell; ***M:*** Gary Chang. **TV**

Stephen King's The Langoliers 1/2 *The Langoliers* **1995 (PG-13)** Bloated variation of "Ten Little Indians" finds 10 airline passengers dozing off on their L.A.-to-Boston flight and awakening to find their fellow passengers and the crew have vanished. Of course, one passenger (Morse) is a pilot and he gets them to Bangor, Maine (where the miniseries was filmed), only to discover the airport is deserted and very weird things are going on. Oh yeah, the "langoliers" look like flying cannonballs with piranha teeth and have something to do with neurotic Pinchot's character. Not that you'll care much. **180m/C VHS, DVD.** David Morse, Bronson Pinchot, Patricia Wettig, Dean Stockwell, Kate Maberly, Christopher Collet, Kimber Riddle, Mark Lindsay Chapman, Frankie Faison, Baxter Harris, Stephen King, Tom Holland; ***D:*** Tom Holland; ***W:*** Tom Holland; ***C:*** Paul Maibaum; ***M:*** Vladimir Horunzhy. **TV**

Stephen King's The Night Flier *The Night Flier* **1996 (R)** Portrays blood-sucking beings that prey upon the weakness of mortal men in order to survive. And besides tabloid journalists, there's vampires in it, too! Richard Dees (Ferrer) is a reporter/photographer for a National Enquirer-like paper who is not above staging lurid photos to grab Page One. His editor pits him in a contest with rookie papparazzo Katherine (Entwistle) for a story about a murderer who wears a black cape and tricorn hat, flies into small airports in a sinister black plane and drains his victims' blood. Dees follows the killer's trail in his own plane, stopping to ruthlessly grill survivors and doctor up a few pictures. Genuinely spooky showdown will leave only one monster standing. Who is it? Inquiring minds want to know. **97m/C VHS, DVD.** Michael H. Moss, Miguel Ferrer, Julie Entwisle, Dan Monahan, John Bennes, Beverly Skinner, Rob Wilds, Richard Olsen, Elizabeth McCormick; ***D:*** Mark Pavia; ***W:*** Mark Pavia, Jack O'Donnell; ***C:*** David Connell; ***M:*** Brian Keane. **CABLE**

Stephen King's The Stand 1/2 *The Stand* **1994** Ghoulish made for TV adaptation of the King novel about a superflu/plague that decimates the U.S. population. The few survivors are soon divided into two camps—those dreaming of a godly old black woman known as Mother Abigail and others of the satanic Randall Flagg, the Walkin' Dude. Boulder, Colorado (where King was living when he wrote the novel) serves as headquarters for Abigail's brood while Las Vegas (where else) is Flagg territory. It all comes down to a battle of good vs. evil, with the future of mankind at stake. Religious allegory can get tedious but it's a varied cast with some scenes not for those with queasy stomachs. On four cassettes. **360m/C VHS, DVD.** Jamey Sheridan, Ruby Dee, Gary Sinise, Molly Ringwald, Miguel Ferrer, Laura San Giacomo, Rob Lowe, Adam Storke, Matt Frewer, Corin "Corky" Nemec, Ray Walston, Bill Fagerbakke, Ossie Davis, Shawnee Smith, Rick Aviles, John (Joe Bob Briggs) Bloom, Michael (Mike) Lookinland, Ed Harris, Kathy Bates, Kareem Abdul-Jabbar, Stephen King, Sam Raimi; ***D:*** Mick Garris; ***W:*** Stephen King; ***C:*** Edward Pei; ***M:*** W.G. Snuffy Walden. **TV**

Stephen King's The Storm of the Century 1/2 *Storm of the Century* **1999 (PG-13)** Little Tall Island, Maine, is under siege—and not just from the most ferocious storm the island has seen in years. No, there's madness and murder afoot in the form of demonic stranger Andre Linoge (Feore). He seems to know everyone's secrets but what he wants is anybody's guess. Now it's up to amiable constable Michael Anderson (Daly) to control the rising hysteria and come up with a solution. **247m/C VHS, DVD.** Colm Feore, Timothy Daly, Debrah Farentino, Casey Siemaszko, Jeffrey DeMunn, Richard Blackburn; ***D:*** Craig R. Baxley; ***W:*** Stephen King; ***C:*** David Connell; ***M:*** Gary Chang. **TV**

Stephen King's The Tommyknockers 1/2 *The Tommyknockers* **1993 (R)** Another of King's creepy tales, adapted for TV. Bobbi (Helgenberger) and Gard (Smits) live in the small town of Haven, Maine (actually filmed on New Zealand's North Island). She's an aspiring writer; he's a fading poet with a drinking problem and a metal plate in his head (this is important). Walking in the woods, Bobbi stumbles over a long-buried spaceship which begins to take possession of the townspeople—their eyes shine green, their teeth fall out, and they act out their (often violent) fantasies—all but Gard. The whole thing's more silly than scary. The title comes from an old children's rhyme. **120m/C VHS, DVD.** Jimmy Smits, Marg Helgenberger, Joanna Cassidy, E.G. Marshall, Traci Lords, John Ashton, Allyce Beasley, Cliff DeYoung, Robert Carradine, Leon Woods, Paul McIver; ***D:*** John Power; ***W:*** Lawrence D. Cohen; ***M:*** Christopher Franke. **TV**

Stephen King's Thinner *Thinner* **1996 (R)** Holland takes all the meat out of this supernatural horror by turning it into a formulaic pursuit-of-justice bore. Porcine lawyer Billy Halleck (Burke) accidentally hits a gypsy with his car and is cursed with a case of perpetual weight loss. Conveniently for Billy, the client he has just gotten an acquittal for is local mobster Richie "The Hammer" Ginelli (Mantegna) who is now determined to save him. Ponderous plot and lackluster-looking latex is redeemed by decent acting. King makes his requisite cameo as Dr. Bangor (get it, Maine?) Originally published in 1984 under King's pseudonym Richard Bachman. **92m/C VHS, DVD.** Robert John Burke, Joe Mantegna, Lucinda Jenney, Michael Constantine, Kari Wuhrer, John Horton, Sam Freed, Daniel von Bargen, Elizabeth Franz, Joy Lentz, Jeff Ware; ***Cameos:*** Stephen King; ***D:*** Tom Holland; ***W:*** Michael McDowell, Tom Holland; ***C:*** Kees Van Oostrum; ***M:*** Daniel Licht.

Stepmom **1998 (PG-13)** The opening scenes make it look like a comedic catfight-filled ride. Harris is a divorced dad with two kids, a supermom ex-wife (Sarandon), and a glamorous new girlfriend (Roberts), whose career seems more important than the kids. Jibes and glares are traded by the two women until mom is stricken with some form of untreatable terminal cancer. This changes the story from broad comedy to emotional drama as Sarandon must train the younger woman to be the new mom. Columbus seems comfortable with the shift, and manages to keep everything upbeat. The script, penned by five writers, becomes more cliched as the film goes on, but stays just this side of chick-flick. **124m/C VHS, DVD.** Julia Roberts, Susan Sarandon, Ed Harris, Jena Malone, Liam Aiken, Lynn Whitfield, Darrell Larson, Mary Louise Wilson; ***D:*** Chris Columbus; ***W:*** Jessie Nelson, Steven Rogers, Ronald Bass, Gigi Levangie, Karen Leigh Hopkins; ***C:*** Donald McAlpine; ***M:*** John Williams. Natl. Bd. of Review '98: Support. Actor (Harris).

Stepmonster 1/2 **1992 (PG-13)** A boy tries to convince his father that his new stepmother is a monster—literally. Doesn't work any better than "My Stepmother Is an Alien." **85m/C VHS, DVD.** Alan Thicke, Robin Riker, Corey Feldman, John Astin, Ami Dolenz, George Gaynes; ***D:*** Jeremy Stanford.

The Stepmother 1/2 **1971** Yet another Hitchcock ripoff story involving an evil stepmother. Rey is passable, but there's not much else to recommend this dredge. **100m/C VHS.** Alejandro Rey, John Anderson, Katherine Justice, John David Garfield, Marlene Schmidt, Claudia Jennings, Larry Linville; ***D:*** Howard (Hikmet) Avedis.

Steppenwolf 1/2 **1974 (PG)** Static, enigmatic film version of the famous Herman Hesse novel about a brooding writer searching for meaning and self-worth. Interesting to watch, but the offbeat novel doesn't translate to the screen; leaves you flat. **105m/C VHS, DVD.** *SI* Max von Sydow, Dominique Sanda, Pierre Clementi, Carla Romanelli, Roy Bosier; ***D:*** Fred Haines; ***W:*** Fred Haines; ***C:*** Tomislav Pinter; ***M:*** George Gruntz.

Stepping Out **1991 (PG)** Minnelli stars as a would-be Broadway dancer who gives tap dancing lessons in an old church to an assortment of offbeat and interesting characters. When the troupe is asked to perform for a local charity, they make the most of their opportunity. A warm and touching ensemble piece that avoids over-sentimentalizing and utilizes its cast to best advantage. **113m/C VHS.** Liza Minnelli, Shelley Winters, Bill Irwin, Ellen Greene, Julie Walters, Robyn Stevan, Jane Krakowski, Sheila McCarthy, Andrea Martin, Carol Woods, Nora Dunn, Eugene Robert Glazer; ***D:*** Lewis Gilbert; ***W:*** Richard Harris; ***M:*** Peter Matz.

Steps from Hell **1992** Vald Tempest is an evil immortal in control of a cult of zombie women. He's stolen a sacred map that will lead to a gateway which, when opened, will unleash a supreme evil on the world. Unless the heroic John Clark can find a way to prevent it, of course. **90m/C VHS.** Bernardo Rosa, Rocky Tucker, Ron Odell, Philip Cable, Liz Stoeckel, Steve Quimby, Lisa Lund; ***D:*** James Tucker; ***W:*** James Tucker.

The Stepsister **1997 (PG-13)** Pediatrician Donna Canfield is lured to her death by one of her young patients. When daughter Darcy (Sofer) comes home to console her dad, Dr. Derek (Rachins), she finds her place usurped by the widowed Joan (Evans) and her sexpot daughter, Melinda (Wilson). Married in unseemly haste, the wealthy Derek dies equally quickly, leaving Darcy suspicious of her new stepfamily. **91m/C VHS.** Rena Sofer, Bridgette Wilson-

Sampras, Linda Evans, Alan Rachins; *D:* Matt Dorff; *W:* Matt Dorff; *C:* Laszlo George; *M:* Peter Manning Robinson. **CABLE**

Stepsisters **WOOF!** *Hands of Blood; Texas Hill Killings* **1974** Murderous double-crosses occur among a pilot, his wife, and her sister. **75m/C VHS.** Hal Fletcher, Sharyn Talbert, Bond Gideon; *D:* Perry Tong; *W:* Perry Tong; *M:* Sandy Pinkard.

The Sterile Cuckoo *Pookie* **1969 (PG)** An aggressive co-ed pursues a shy freshman who seems to embody her romantic ideal. Minnelli's performance is outstanding; Burton as the naive young man is also fine. Pakula's splendid first directing job. **108m/C VHS.** Liza Minnelli, Wendell Burton, Tim McIntire; *D:* Alan J. Pakula; *W:* Alvin Sargent; *C:* Milton Krasner.

Stevie **1978** Jackson brings her flawless skill to the role of British poet Stevie Smith. Excellent performance from Washbourne as Stevie's spinster aunt. Wooden, lifeless screen rendition for the Hugh Whitemore stage play is helped greatly by good performances, but is too talky and, frankly, rather dull and self-absorbed. **102m/C VHS.** *GB* Glenda Jackson, Mona Washbourne, Alec McCowen, Trevor Howard; *D:* Robert Enders; *C:* Frederick A. (Freddie) Young. L.A. Film Critics '78: Support. Actress (Washbourne); Montreal World Film Fest. '78: Actress (Jackson); N.Y. Film Critics '78: Support. Actress (Washbourne).

Stewardess School **WOOF!** **1986 (R)** Airline spoof aims at wackiness, but misses the runway. Generic title betrays probable badness which turns out to be all too real. An utter woofer. **84m/C VHS.** Sandahl Bergman, Wendie Jo Sperber, Judy Landers, Julia Montgomery, Corinne Bohrer; *D:* Ken Blancato; *W:* Ken Blancato; *M:* Robert Folk.

Stick 1/2 **1985 (R)** Ex-con Stick (Reynolds, directing himself) wants to start a new life for himself in Miami. Lots of drug dealers and guns don't help the interest level in this dull underworld tale. Based upon the Elmore Leonard novel. **109m/C VHS.** Burt Reynolds, Candice Bergen, George Segal, Charles Durning, Dar Robinson; *D:* Burt Reynolds; *W:* Elmore Leonard; *M:* Steve Dorff.

Stick It **2006 (PG-13)** Teenager Haley (Peregrym) walked away from a promising gymnastics career and into trouble. Thanks to her latest run-in with the law, Haley is sentenced to attend a gymnastics academy run by gruff coach Burt Vickerman (Bridges). The other girls dislike her attitude, but training and competition bring them closer as Haley foments rebellion against the sport's conformity and nitpicky rules. Writer/director Bendinger did the similarly girl-powered cheerleading comedy "Bring It On." **105m/C DVD.** *US* Missy Peregrym, Jeff Bridges, Vanessa Lengies, John Patrick Amedori, Nikki SooHoo, Maddy Curley, Kellan Lutz, Svetlana Efremova, Mio Dzakula, Jon(athan) Gries, Gia Carides, Polly Holliday, Julie Warner, John Kapelos, Tarah Paige; *Cameos:* Bart Conner; *D:* Jessica Bendinger; *W:* Jessica Bendinger; *C:* Daryn Okada; *M:* Mike Simpson.

The Stick-Up *Mud* **1977** In 1935, a young American traveling in Great Britain is introduced to some rather illegal fun. Rather sorry attempt at romance/comedy/adventure. **101m/C VHS.** David Soul, Pamela McMyler; *D:* Jeffrey Bloom; *W:* Jeffrey Bloom.

Stickfighter **1989 (PG)** The oppressive reign of an evil Spanish ruler of the Philippines is challenged by the world's best stickfighter. **102m/C VHS.** *PH* Dean Stockwell, Nancy Kwan, Alejandro Rey, Roland Dantes; *D:* Luis Nepomuceno.

Stickmen 1/2 **2001** Bar owner Dave talks three regulars into entering a pool tournament to get him out of debt. The three pals are more than willing, but their relationship problems keep popping up. Not especially original concept is helped by the chemistry of the buddies and some amusingly quirky subplots. **94m/C VHS, DVD.** *NZ* Paolo Rotondo, Robbie Magasiva, Scott Wills, Anne Nordhaus, John Leigh, Simone Kessell, Emma Nooyen, Luann Gordon, Kirk Torrance; *D:* Hamish Rothwell; *W:* Nick Ward; *C:* Nigel Bluck.

Sticks **1998 (R)** Who knew cigars could cause so much trouble? Lenny (Brancato) discovers that an illicit shipment of Cuban cigars, the special private label of Castro himself, have been stolen. Maria (Machado) wants to swap the cigars for weapons to help liberate Cuba while her boyfriend Mark (Brunsmann) just wants some cold hard cash by selling the merchandise to a private Hollywood club frequented by high rollers. And Lenny sees a chance to make his own score. Too bad the mob and the feds have their own ideas. **94m/C VHS, DVD.** Lillo Brancato, Leo Rossi, Justina Machado, Keith Brunsmann; *D:* Brett Mayer; *W:* Brett Mayer; *C:* Nils Erickson; *M:* Bill Elliott. **VIDEO**

Sticks and Stones **1996 (PG-13)** Three high school friends are harassed by the local bully and the situation gets tragically out of control. **96m/C VHS.** Kirstie Alley, Gary Busey, Justin Isfeld, Max Goldblatt, Chauncey Leopardi; *D:* Neil Tolkin; *W:* Neil Tolkin; *C:* Avi (Avraham) Karpik; *M:* Hummie Mann. **VIDEO**

Sticks and Stones 1/2 **2008 (PG)** During a visit to Canada shortly after the start of the Iraq War, a youth hockey team from Boston is booed by anti-war protestors. Appalled by such behavior, the coach of the opposing team organizes a rematch to make amends and demonstrate good sportsmanship. **90m/C DVD.** *CA* David Sutcliffe, Alexander De Jordy, Daniel Magder, John Robinson, Richard Fitzpatrick, Debra McCabe; *D:* George Mihalka; *W:* Sharon Buckingham, Andrew Wreggitt; *C:* Daniel Vincelette. **TV**

The Stickup **2001 (R)** Burned-out cop Parker (Spader) travels to a small resort town and promptly gets involved with the wrong woman (Stefanson), a bank robbery, and the feds. This one is trickier than it seems at first. **97m/C VHS, DVD.** James Spader, Leslie Stefanson, David Keith, John Livingston, Robert Miano, Alf Humphreys; *D:* Rowdy Herrington; *W:* Rowdy Herrington; *C:* Chris Manley; *M:* David Kitay. **VIDEO**

Sticky Fingers **1988 (PG-13)** Two female musicians, asked to watch nearly a million bucks in drug money, go on a mega shopping spree. Completely incredible, unlikeable and mean-spirited attempt at zany comedy. **89m/C VHS.** Melanie Mayron, Helen Slater, Eileen Brennan, Carol Kane, Christopher Guest, Danitra Vance, Gwen Welles, Stephen McHattie, Shirley Stoler; *D:* Catlin Adams; *W:* Catlin Adams, Melanie Mayron; *C:* Gary Thieltges; *M:* Gary Chang.

The Sticky Fingers of Time **1997** New York writer Tucker (Matthews) is not having your average day. She goes out for coffee in 1953 and winds up in 1997 (thanks to some kind of atom-bomb mutation in her DNA). Turns out she's not the only time traveller, according to fellow freak, Isaac (Urbaniak). In fact, Isaac was responsible for bringing Tucker into the future so she wouldn't be murdered. Tucker (who's a pulp novelist) takes everything that happens with chain-smoking aplomb. **81m/B VHS, DVD.** Terumi Matthews, James Urbaniak, Belinda Becker, Nicole Zaray, Samantha Buck; *D:* Hilary Brougher; *W:* Hilary Brougher; *C:* Ethan Mass; *M:* Miki Navazio.

Stiff Upper Lips 1/2 **1996** Spoof of all the upper-crusty British costume dramas replete with sexual innuendoes and enlightening travel to hot climes. Twitish Edward (West) tries to pair off best chum Cedric (Portal) with his virgin sister, Emily (Cates). Only Emily prefers hearty servant, George (Pertwee). Snooty Aunt Agnes (Scales) decides everyone should take a restorative trip to Italy and later to India, where Aunt Agnes herself is subjected to a leering tea-planter, Horace (Ustinov). Meanwhile, Edward and Cedric are exploring their own "strange feelings" for one another. As with any film in this genre some gags work better than others. **85m/C VHS, DVD.** *GB* Samuel West, Robert Portal, Georgina Cates, Sean Pertwee, Prunella Scales, Peter Ustinov, Brian Glover, Frank Finlay; *D:* Gary Sinyor; *W:* Gary Sinyor, Paul Simpkin; *C:* Simon Archer; *M:* David A. Hughes, John Murphy.

Stigma 1/2 **1973** "Miami Vice" star Thomas (then 23; later to restore his middle name, Michael) is a young doctor who treats a syphilis epidemic in a small town. He's indistinguishable, but better than anything else here. Ever seen close-ups of advanced syphilis? Here's your chance—but it's not pretty. **93m/C DVD.** Philip Michael Thomas, Harlan Cary Poe; *D:* David E. Durston.

Stigmata 1/2 **1999 (R)** Disappointing horror flick that's campy instead of creepy. Airhead Pittsburgh beautician Frankie (Arquette) doesn't even believe in God, so why is she suddenly afflicted with visions and seizures that leave her with Christ-like wounds? Could it have anything to do with the rosary her vacationing mom sent her from Brazil? When the media picks up the story, the Vatican decides to send Father Kiernan (Byrne, who makes a very sexy priest) to check things out. Lots of hokey mumbo-jumbo ensues. **103m/C VHS, DVD.** Patricia Arquette, Gabriel Byrne, Jonathan Pryce, Portia de Rossi, Patrick Muldoon, Nia Long, Thomas Kopache, Rade Serbedzija, Enrico Colantoni, Dick Latessa, Ann Cusack; *D:* Rupert Wainwright; *W:* Rick Ramage, Tom Lazarus; *C:* Jeffrey L. Kimball; *M:* Elia Cmiral.

Stiletto 1/2 **1969 (R)** Good cast is wasted in this mediocre depiction of the trouble encountered by a contract Mafia assassin when he decides to change careers. Based on the usual pulp cheese by Harold Robbins. **101m/C VHS.** Alex Cord, Britt Ekland, Patrick O'Neal, Joseph Wiseman, Barbara McNair, Roy Scheider, M. Emmet Walsh, Raul Julia; *D:* Bernard L. Kowalski; *W:* W.R. Burnett; *C:* Jack Priestley.

Stiletto **2008 (R)** Decent cast although the story is nothing special. Femme assassin Raina (Katic) is out to destroy the criminal organization of mobster Virgil Vadalos (Berenger) despite the fact that she used to be his gal. (Her reasons take awhile to surface.) When Virgil discovers who's after him, he hires crooked detective Beck (Sloan) to take care of Raina first. **99m/C DVD.** Stana Katic, Tom Berenger, Michael Biehn, William Forsythe, Paul Sloan, James Russo, Tom Sizemore, Diane Venora, Kelly Hu, Amanda Brooks, Dominique Swain, D.B. Sweeney; *D:* Nick Vallelonga; *C:* Jeffrey Mygatt; *M:* Cliff Martinez.

Stiletto Dance 1/2 **2001 (R)** Anton (Doyle) is the head of the Russian mob in Buffalo, NY, who plans to sell a nuclear device to the Albanians. Undercover cop Kit Adrian (Roberts) has other ideas—before he makes the mistake of falling for a mob enforcer's wife (Laurier). **97m/C VHS, DVD.** Eric Roberts, Shawn Doyle, Brett Porter, Romano Orzari, Lucie Laurier, Yaphet Kotto, Mark Camacho, Justin Louis; *D:* Mario Azzopardi; *W:* Alfonse Ruggiero; *C:* Pierre Jodoin. **CABLE**

Still Breathing 1/2 **1997 (PG-13)** Romance with elements of the fantastical. Fletcher (Fraser) is an eccentric street performer in San Antonio, who dreams of a woman he knows will become his wife (it's a family thing). This turns out to be tough L.A. con woman Rosalyn (Going), whose next sting just happens to involve a Texan. When Fletcher flies to L.A. to find his would-be lady love, they meet cute and have a lot of mistaken assumptions before things come out right. Fraser's character may be wide-eyed but he's no fool and Going displays a needed touch of vulnerability for her manipulative bad girl. **109m/C VHS, DVD.** Brendan Fraser, Joanna Going, Ann Magnuson, Celeste Holm, Lou Rawls, Angus MacFadyen, Paolo Seganti; *D:* James F. Robinson; *W:* James F. Robinson; *C:* John Thomas; *M:* Paul Mills.

Still Crazy 1/2 **1998 (R)** Twenty years after the breakup of his band Strange Fruit, Tony (Rea) is ready to give it a go again. With the Wisbech rock festival beckoning, he rounds up the others: lead singer Ray (Nighy), still a musician living in a mansion; drummer Beano (Spall), a gardener on the run from the tax collector; and singer-bassist Les (Nail), who runs a roofing business. One glitch: lead guitarist Brian (Robinson), the most popular band member, is supposedly dead. Luckily, love of the music (and money) forces the band to get it together. Inspired by a reunion tour of the Animals, but has more "Full Monty" fun and heart than "Spinal Tap" parody to it. The cast is superb and the actual concert makes you want to stand up and cheer, when you're done laughing. **96m/C VHS, DVD.** *GB* Stephen Rea, Billy Connolly, Jimmy Nail, Timothy Spall, Bill Nighy, Juliet Aubrey, Helena Bergstrom, Bruce Robinson, Hans Matheson, Rachael Stirling, Phil Daniels, Frances Barber, Philip Davis; *D:* Brian Gibson; *W:* Dick Clement, Ian La Frenais; *C:* Ashley Rowe; *M:* Clive Langer.

Still Green **2007** Ten teens rent a Florida beach house for a week before separating for college but sun and surf doesn't lessen their need for their emotional baggage to come spilling out, including various family traumas, sexual attractions, and insecurities. **87m/C DVD.** Sarah Jones, Ryan Kelley, Douglas Spain, Noah Segan, Paul Costa, Brandon Meyer, Ashleigh Snyder, Michael Strynkowski, Nicole Komendat, Gricel Castineira; *D:* Jon Artigo; *W:* Georgia Menides; *C:* Brian Crane.

Still Life **1992 (PG-13)** The press has dubbed him "the Art Killer," a serial murderer who makes scupltures out of his victims. He's a sensation—and not ready to stop. This sicko's next "Still Life" may just be a struggling young musician. **83m/C VHS.** Jason Gedrick, Jessica Steen, Stephen Shellen; *D:* Graeme Campbell; *M:* Mychael Danna.

The Still Life **2007** Julian Lamont (Barry) is a reclusive, alcoholic artist who developed a new art genre called destructionism that brings surprising commercial success, which he has not handled well. Struggling to regain his identity, once past the self-loathing and deep-rooted inner-hatred, he comes to realize taking responsibility for his actions is the first step. Too much angst, not enough substance. **155m/C DVD.** Jason Barry, Rachel Miner, Terry Moore, Don S. Davis, Robert Miano; *D:* Joel Miller; *W:* Joel Miller; *C:* Richard Barbadillo.

Still Not Quite Human **1992** Teenage android Chip must do battle with unscrupulous industrialists and their robot weapon Spartacus to rescue his inventor father from their deadly clutches. **84m/C VHS.** Alan Thicke, Christopher Neame, Betsy Palmer, Adam Philipson, Rosa Nevin, Ken Pogue, Jay Underwood; *D:* Eric Luke; *W:* Eric Luke.

Still of the Night **1982 (PG)** A Hitchcock-style thriller about a psychiatrist infatuated with a mysterious woman who may or may not be a killer. **91m/C VHS.** Meryl Streep, Roy Scheider, Jessica Tandy, Joe Grifasi, Sara Botsford, Josef Sommer; *D:* Robert Benton; *W:* Robert Benton, David Newman; *C:* Nestor Almendros.

Still Waiting **2008 (R)** Lame-o sequel to 2005's equally crude "Waiting." The Shenaniganz restaurant is in trouble because of competition from Ta-Ta's Wing Shack next door. The waitresses have left because skimpier uniforms mean bigger tips and the customers are following. But Shenaniganz isn't going down with a (food) fight. **88m/C DVD.** Justin Long, John Michael Higgins, Steve Howey, Andy Milonakis, Rob Benedict, Alanna Ubach, Danneel Harris, Luis Guzman, Vanessa Lengies, Tania Raymonde; *D:* Jeff Balis; *W:* Rob McKittrick; *C:* Thomas Callaway. **VIDEO**

The Stilts **1984** From modern Spanish cinema's preeminent director, this is a study of sexual dynamics revolving around a doomed love triangle. Aging professor Gomez wants young Del Sol to commit to him, but she won't; she has another, younger lover. Overwrought at times, but well acted. In Spanish with English subtitles. **95m/C VHS.** *SP* Laura Del Sol, Francisco Rabal, Fernando Fernan-Gomez; *D:* Carlos Saura.

The Sting 1/2 **1973 (PG)** Newman and Redford together again in this sparkling story of a pair of con artists in 1930s Chicago. They set out to fleece a big-time racketeer, pitting brain against brawn and pistol. Very inventive, excellent acting, Scott Joplin's wonderful ragtime music adapted by Marvin Hamlisch. The same directorial and acting team from "Butch Cassidy and the Sundance Kid" triumphs again. **129m/C VHS, DVD, HD DVD.** Paul Newman, Robert Redford, Robert Shaw, Charles Durning, Eileen Brennan, Harold Gould, Ray Walston, Dana Elcar, Jack Kehoe, Dimitra Arliss, Robert Earl Jones, Sally Kirkland; *D:* George Roy Hill; *W:* David S. Ward; *C:* Robert L. Surtees; *M:* Marvin Hamlisch. Oscars '73: Art Dir./Set Dec., Costume Des., Director (Hill), Film Editing, Picture, Story & Screenplay, Orig. Song Score and/or Adapt.; Directors Guild '73: Director (Hill), Natl. Film Reg. '05.

The Sting 2 1/2 **1983 (PG)** Complicated comic plot concludes with the final con game, involving a fixed boxing match where the stakes top $1 million and the payoff could be murder. Lame sequel to "The Sting" (1973). **102m/C VHS, DVD.** Jackie Gleason, Mac Davis, Teri Garr, Karl Malden, Oliver Reed, Tony Giorgio; *D:* Jeremy Paul Kagan; *W:* David S. Ward; *C:* Bill Butler; *M:* Lalo Schifrin.

Sting of the West ♪ *Te Deum; Father Jackleg* **1972 (PG)** Journeyman con artist swindles his way across the Wild West. **90m/C VHS.** *IT SP* Jack Palance, Giancarlo Prete, Lionel Stander, Renzo Palmer, Eduardo Fajardo; *D:* Enzo G. Castellari; *W:* Tito Carpi; *M:* Guido de Angelis, Maurizio de Angelis.

Stingaree ♪ 1/2 **1934** A strange musical western. Australian bandit Stingaree (Dix) likes to steal for fun and writes songs in his spare time. He's enamored of would-be opera singer Hilda (Dunne) and kidnaps her, though Hilda doesn't protest too much. Stingaree winds up in jail and she goes to Europe with composer Julian Kent (Tearle) to further her career but the lovers will meet again. Based on the novel by E.W. Hornung. **76m/B DVD.** Richard Dix, Irene Dunne, Conway Tearle, Mary Boland, Henry Stephenson, Andy Devine, Una O'Connor; *D:* William A. Wellman; *W:* Becky Gardiner; *C:* James Van Trees.

Stingray ♪ 1/2 **1978 (PG)** Two guys buy a Corvette, not knowing it's loaded with stolen heroin. Gangsters with an interest in the dope come after them, and the chase is on. Very violent and not all that funny. **105m/C VHS, DVD.** Chris Mitchum, Sherry Jackson, Les Lannom; *D:* Richard Taylor.

Stir ♪ **1998** Scientist about to reveal a medical discovery is murdered in his hotel room. Months later, his wife and young son return to the hotel and the son, while sleeping, sees the night of the murder through his father's eyes. **100m/C VHS.** Tony Todd, Traci Lords, Daniel Roebuck, Seth Adkins, Karen Black, Michael J. Pollard, Andrew Heckler; *D:* Rodion Nakhapetov; *W:* Rodion Nakhapetov; *C:* Darko Suvak; *M:* Keith Bilderbeck. **VIDEO**

Stir Crazy ♪♪ 1/2 **1980 (R)** Two down-on-their luck losers find themselves convicted of a robbery they didn't commit and sentenced to 120 years behind bars with a mean assortment of inmates. Wilder and Pryor's second teaming isn't quite as successful as the first go-round, but still provides plenty of laughs. **111m/C VHS, DVD.** Richard Pryor, Gene Wilder, Nicolas Coster, Lee Purcell, Craig T. Nelson, JoBeth Williams, Erland van Lidth, Georg Stanford Brown, Barry Corbin, Charles Weldon, Grand L. Bush; *D:* Sidney Poitier; *W:* Bruce Jay Friedman; *C:* Fred Schuler; *M:* Tom Scott, Michael Masser.

Stir of Echoes ♪♪ 1/2 **1999 (R)** The kid in "The Sixth Sense" isn't the only one seeing dead people, although blue-collar Tom Witzky (Bacon) really doesn't have a clue as to what's happening to him. After being hypnotized at a party by his witchy sister-in-law, Lisa (Douglas), Tom winds up with some very scary clairvoyant abilities, which link him to a neighborhood teenaged girl who's presumed missing but has, in fact, been murdered. Naturally, Tom's visions and obsessions lead to some problems with his family and friends. Based on the novel by Richard Matheson. **110m/C VHS, DVD, Blu-ray Disc.** Kevin Bacon, Illeana Douglas, Kathryn Erbe, Liza Weil, Kevin Dunn, Conor O'Farrell, Zachary David Cope, Jenny (Jennifer) Morrison, Eddie Bo Smith Jr.; *D:* David Koepp; *W:* David Koepp; *C:* Fred Murphy; *M:* James Newton Howard.

Stir of Echoes 2: The Homecoming ♪ 1/2 **2007 (R)** Another of those mostly-in-name-only sequels. Army Captain Ted Cogan (Lowe) and his unit erroneously fire upon a van of civilians (who die) in Iraq, which leads to an insurgent attack that wounds Cogan. After coming out of his coma, Cogan is discharged and returns home to Chicago, where his wife and kid are having their own problems. Cogan starts suffering disturbing flashbacks that include ghosts who seemingly are trying to communicate with him. **89m/C DVD.** Rob Lowe, Marnie McPhail, Katya Gardner, Zachary Bennett, Ben Lewis; *D:* Ernie Barbarash; *W:* Ernie Barbarash; *C:* Francois Dagenais; *M:* Norman Orenstein. **CABLE**

Stitches ♪ **1985 (R)** Adolescent comedy about med students playing practical jokes on the dean using laboratory specimens. So bad the director (actually Rod Holcomb) allegedly did not want his name associated with it. **92m/C VHS.** Eddie Albert, Parker Stevenson, Geoffrey Lewis, Brian Tochi; *D:* Alan Smithee; *W:* Michael Choquette.

Stolen Childhoods ♪♪ **2005** Presents footage shot over seven years in eight different countries of the deplorable conditions and horrific practices under which youths are forced to work. Castigates governments for not enforcing child labor laws, blames the rising frenzy for cheap consumer goods in the Western markets, and praises programs that rehabilitate children and save them from servitude. Well-intentioned premise feels unfocused, losing much of its punch. **83m/C** *US D:* Len Morris; *W:* Georgia Morris; *C:* U. Roberto Romano; *M:* Miriam Cutler.

The Stolen Children ♪♪♪ 1/2 *Il Ladro di Bambini* **1992** Highly acclaimed Italian neo-realist film that tells the story of a shy carabiniere and two children who have been placed in his care. They are an emotionally battered 11-year-old girl who was forced into prostitution by her mother and her sullen 9-year-old brother. As they journey from Milan to Sicily and gradually get to know each other, all three of the characters undergo a slight transformation. Gracefully executed, this haunting masterpiece explores the overriding themes of guilt and innocence and keeps you thinking about them long after the movie's over. Italian with subtitles. **108m/C VHS.** *IT* Enrico Lo Verso, Valentina Scalici, Giuseppe Ieracitano, Florence Darel, Marina Golovine, Fabio Alessandrini; *D:* Gianni Amelio; *W:* Gianni Amelio, Sandro Petraglia, Stefano Rulli; *M:* Franco Piersanti. Cannes '92: Grand Jury Prize.

A Stolen Face ♪♪ **1952** Creepy, implausible drama of a plastic surgeon, spurned by a beautiful concert pianist, who transforms a female convict to look just like her. The convict runs away, but perhaps there's hope in the future with the pianist. **71m/B VHS, DVD.** *GB* Paul Henreid, Lizabeth Scott, Andre Morell, Susan Stephen, Everley Gregg, Cyril Smith; *D:* Terence Fisher; *W:* Martin Berkeley, Richard H. Landau; *C:* Walter J. (Jimmy W.) Harvey; *M:* Malcolm Arnold.

Stolen Hearts ♪ *Two If By Sea* **1995 (R)** Instead of reporting con man Brandon Keyes (Finiani) to the cops after he takes her money, bar owner Dana Andrews (Aletonis) hires PI Justin Gibbons (Dale) to get back her savings. Justin happens to work with a psychic, Tess (Hall), and the twosome have a mutual attraction. They find the sleaze and get back the dough. Very boring. **82m/C VHS, DVD.** Landon Hall, Vincent Dale, Jim Finiani, Paula Aletonis; *D:* Ralph Portillo.

Stolen Hours ♪♪ 1/2 **1963** Inferior remake of Bette Davis's "Dark Victory" casts Hayward as an oil-rich heiress who learns she has a fatal illness. Bring the tissues for this tearjerker. Based on the play "Dark Victory" by George Emerson Brewer Jr. and Bertram Block. **100m/C VHS.** Susan Hayward, Michael Craig, Diane Baker, Edward Judd, Paul Rogers; *D:* Daniel Petrie; *W:* Jessamyn West, Joseph Hayes.

Stolen Identity ♪ 1/2 **1953** A Viennese cabbie sees his American dream dashed for lack of the proper papers. When an American businessman is murdered in his cab he is quick to seize the moment...and the dead man's identity. In no time at all he finds himself involved with the widow, entangled with the murderer and under suspicion for the killing. Predictable and sluggish, the story inches its way to the foregone conclusion. **81m/B VHS.** Francis Lederer, Donald Buka, Joan Camden, Adrienne Gessner; *D:* Gunther Fritsch.

Stolen Kisses ♪♪♪ 1/2 *Baisers Voles* **1968** Sequel to "The 400 Blows," the story of Antoine Doinel: his unsuccessful career prospects as a detective in Paris, and his initially awkward but finally successful adventures with women. Made during Truffaut's involvement in a political crisis involving the sack of Cinematique Francais director Henri Langlois. Truffaut dedicated the film to Langlois and the Cinematique, but it is a thoroughly apolitical, small-scale, charming (some say too charming) romantic comedy, Truffaut-style. Followed by "Bed and Board." **90m/C VHS, DVD.** *FR* Jean-Pierre Leaud, Delphine Seyrig, Michael (Michel) Lonsdale, Claude Jade; *D:* Francois Truffaut; *W:* Francois Truffaut, Claude de Givray; *C:* Denys Clerval; *M:* Antoine Duhamel. Natl. Soc. Film Critics '69: Director (Truffaut).

A Stolen Life ♪♪ **1946** Remake of 1939 film of the same title starring Elisabeth Bergner. Oddly, Davis chose this as her first and last producing effort. Implausible tale of an evil twin (Davis) who takes her sister's (Davis) place so she can have the man they both love. Davis pulls it off as both twins; Ford is good as the hapless hubby. **107m/B VHS.** Bette Davis, Glenn Ford, Dane Clark, Walter Brennan, Charlie Ruggles, Bruce Bennett, Esther Dale, Peggy Knudsen; *D:* Curtis Bernhardt; *M:* Max Steiner.

Stolen Summer ♪♪ *Project Greenlight's Stolen Summer* **2002 (PG)** The background of the film (first-timer Jones won a national competition sponsored by Ben Affleck and Matt Damon) may be more interesting than this decidedly old-fashioned story. It's a Chicago summer in 1976 with young Irish Catholic Pete O'Malley (Stein) deciding that, in order to get to heaven, he needs to convert his Jewish friend Danny Jacobsen (Weinberg). Danny's father (Pollak), who happens to be a rabbi, takes the news benignly while Pete's dad, Joe (Quinn), has some trouble believing that his family is not being condescended to. The performances are appealing and there's a good lesson about the acceptance of another's religion. **95m/C VHS, DVD.** *US* Adi Stein, Mike Weinberg, Aidan Quinn, Kevin Pollak, Bonnie Hunt, Eddie Kaye Thomas, Brian Dennehy; *D:* Pete Jones; *W:* Pete Jones; *C:* Pete Biagi; *M:* Danny Lux.

Stomp the Yard ♪♪ 1/2 **2007 (PG-13)** The yard in question would be a highly competitive step dancing war between two rival black fraternities. L.A. teen DJ (Short) gets into a major beef and is shipped off to his Uncle Nate (Lennix) in Atlanta to be enrolled at historic Truth University. The brash freshman immediately pisses off Mu Gamma Xi hotshot Grant (Henson), but his street moves win DJ a place at rival frat Theta Nu Theta. They want to win that national championship (yes, there's a dance-off). Oh so predictable plot but the dancing is impressive. **114m/C DVD.** *US* Columbus Short, Meagan Good, Brian White, Laz Alonso, Ne-Yo, Yun Qu, Valarie Pettiford, Harry J. Lennix, Allan Louis; *D:* Sylvain White; *W:* Robert Adetuyi; *C:* Scott Kevan; *M:* Sam Retzer, Tim Boland.

The Stone Angel ♪♪ **2007 (R)** Adaptation of Margaret Laurence's 1964 novel. Hagar Shipley (Burstyn) may be 90 but she has no intention of letting her son Marvin (Baker) shuffle her into a nursing home. At least not until she can travel through Manitoba to revisit some of her old haunts and relive her past, including her difficult marriage to reckless Bram. **115m/C DVD.** Ellen Burstyn, Wings Hauser, Cole Hauser, Dylan Baker, Christine Horne, Kevin Zegers, Sheila McCarthy, Ellen Page, Aaron Ashmore, Ted Atherton, Luke Kirby; *D:* Keri Skogland; *C:* Bobby Bukowski; *M:* John McCarthy.

The Stone Boy ♪♪♪ 1/2 **1984 (PG)** A boy accidentally kills his older brother on their family's Montana farm. The family is torn apart by sadness and guilt. Sensitive look at variety of reactions during a crisis, with an excellent cast led by Duvall's crystal-clear performance. **93m/C VHS, DVD.** Mary Ellen Trainor, Glenn Close, Robert Duvall, Jason Presson, Frederic Forrest, Wilford Brimley, Linda Hamilton; *D:* Christopher Cain; *W:* Gina Berriault; *C:* Juan Ruiz-Anchia; *M:* James Horner, John Beal.

Stone Cold WOOF! **1991 (R)** Flamboyant footballer Bosworth made his acting debut in this sensitive human document, playing the usual musclebound, one-punk-army terminator cop, out to infiltrate a sadistic band of fascist biker barbarians engaged in drug running and priest shooting. Profane, lewd, gory, self-deifying; a crash course (accent on crashes) in everything despicable about modern action pics. **91m/C VHS, DVD.** Brian Bosworth, Lance Henriksen, William Forsythe, Arabella Holzbog, Sam McMurray; *D:* Craig R. Baxley; *W:* Walter Doniger; *C:* Alexander Grusynski; *M:* Sylvester Levay.

Stone Cold Dead ♪ 1/2 **1980 (R)** Rugged cop Crenna battles crime lord Williams (Paul Williams? Yeah, sure) over a prostitution ring. Meanwhile, a sniper starts killing hookers. Unoriginal and thoroughly dull would-be thriller. **100m/C VHS.** Richard Crenna, Paul Williams, Linda Sorensen, Belinda J. Montgomery; *D:* George Mendeluk; *W:* George Mendeluk.

Stone Fox ♪♪ **1987** Heartwarming family drama in which a young man must win a dogsled race to save the family farm. Based on John Reynolds Gardiner's popular children's book. **96m/C VHS.** Buddy Ebsen, Joey Cramer, Belinda J. Montgomery, Gordon Tootoosis; *D:* Harvey Hart.

The Stone Killer ♪♪ 1/2 **1973 (R)** Bronson stars as a tough plainclothes cop in this action-packed drama about a Mafia plot to use Vietnam vets in a mass killing. Violent but tense and action-packed revenge adventure set in the underworlds of New York and Los Angeles. **95m/C VHS.** Charles Bronson, Martin Balsam, Norman Fell, Ralph Waite, John Ritter; *D:* Michael Winner.

The Stone Merchant ♪ 1/2 *Il Mercante di Pietre* **2006** Unhappy Leda (March) works for Alitalia airlines and is married to Alceo (Molla), who is a paraplegic because of a terrorist attack. She falls for gemstone merchant Ludivico (Keitel), a convert to Islam, who turns out to be an Al-Qaeda operative who is planning to use Leda to transport some bomb-making material. Grim and obvious. **122m/C DVD.** *GB IT* Harvey Keitel, Jane March, Jordi Molla, F. Murray Abraham; *D:* Renzo Martinelli; *W:* Renzo Martinelli, Fabio Campus; *C:* Blasco Giurato; *M:* Aldo de Scalzi Pivio.

Stone of Silver Creek ♪♪ **1935** The owner of the Bonanza saloon, T. William Stone (Jones), discovers some of his unsavory patrons are planning to rob him. After a friend is shot trying to help him, Stone decides to even the score. Chapter 3 of "Gordon of Ghost City" finds Mary and Gordon entering a mine owned by Mary's grandfather, which turns out to be rich in gold. A figure sets an explosion and Mary and Gordon get trapped in the mine! **87m/B VHS.** Buck Jones, Noel Francis, Niles Welch, Marion Shilling, Peggy Campbell, Harry Semels, Madge Bellamy, Walter Miller; *D:* Nick Grinde, Ray Taylor.

Stone Reader ♪♪♪ **2002 (PG-13)** Mark Moskowitz searches for "The Stones of Summer" author Dow Mossman. He also interviews critic Leslie Fiedler and editor Robert Gottleib, who edited "Catch 22." **128m/C VHS, DVD.** *US D:* Mark Moskowitz; *W:* Mark Moskowitz; *C:* Mark Moskowitz, Joseph Vandergast, Jeffrey Confer; *M:* Michael Mandrell.

Stonebrook ♪♪ **1998 (PG-13)** Two college roommates at a private university gamble to make their tuition money and wind up drawing the attention of a detective who wants to use their illegal activities to incriminate the mob. **90m/C VHS, DVD.** Seth Green, Brad Rowe, Zoe McLellan, William Mesnik, Stanley Kamel; *D:* Byron W. Thompson; *W:* Steven Robert Morris; *C:* John Tarver; *M:* Dean Grinsfelder.

Stoned ♪♪ **2005** A muddled and unenlightening account of the final months of drug addicted Rolling Stones guitarist Brian Jones (Gregory), who was found dead in his swimming pool in 1969. Although "death by misadventure" is the official cause, a 1994 deathbed confession by Jones' contractor/whipping boy Frank Thorogood (Considine) allegedly reveals that Frank admitted drowning Jones. Flashbacks linger on the guitarist's hedonistic lifestyle while, before his death, Jones lethargically stirs himself to torment those around him. Woolley's directorial debut. **102m/C DVD.** *GB* Leo Gregory, Paddy Considine, David Morrissey, Ben Whishaw, Amelia Warner, Monet Mazur, David Walliams, Tuva Novotny, Luke De Woolfson, Melanie Ramsay, Ruediger Rudolph; *D:* Stephen Woolley; *W:* Robert Wade, Neal Purvis; *C:* John Mathieson; *M:* David Arnold.

The Stoned Age ♪ **1994 (R)** Buddies look to get wasted and find some chicks. Set in the '70s. **90m/C VHS, DVD.** Michael Kopelow, China Kantner, Renee Griffen; *D:* James Melkonian.

Stones of Death 1988 (R) An aboriginal curse is invoked when a subdivision is built too close to an ancient burial site. Teenagers begin having all-too-real nightmares about death. **90m/C VHS.** Tom Jennings, Natalie McCurry, Zoe Carides, Eric Oldfield; ***D:*** James Bagle.

Stonewall 1995 (R) Fictional account of the June, 1969 police raid on Greenwich Village gay bar the Stonewall Inn, which is considered to have launched the modern gay rights movement. White-bread, midwestern activist Matty Dean (Weller) arrives in New York and gets thrown in jail for defending streetwise drag queen LaMiranda (Diaz) from harassing cops. They become lovers but Matty is also involved with conservative prepster Ethan (Corbalis), who thinks the flamboyant queens give the gay movement a bad name. Meanwhile, the drag queens at the mob-backed Stonewall are getting fed up with police raids and brutal treatment. Adapted from Martin Duberman's social history "Stonewall." Director Finch died during the final editing stages of the film. **93m/C VHS, DVD.** Frederick Weller, Guillermo Diaz, Brendan Corbalis, Bruce MacVittie, Duane Boutte, Peter Ratray, Luis Guzman; ***D:*** Nigel Finch; ***W:*** Rikki Beadle Blair; ***C:*** Chris Seager; ***M:*** Michael Kamen.

The Stoning of Soraya M. 2008 (R) Blunt and brutal drama (based on a true story) that takes place in flashbacks. French-Iranian journalist Feredoune Sahebjam's (Caviezel) car breaks down in an Iranian village. While he waits for it to be fixed, distraught Zahra (Aghdashloo) tells him about the murder of her niece, Soraya (Marno). Unhappy in an arranged marriage, she refuses to divorce her husband because he is her only means of support. Because he wants to marry a more-compliant teenager, he accuses Soraya of adultery and persuades the local mullah to issue the ultimate medieval punishment—death by stoning. English and Farsi with subtitles. **114m/C DVD.** Shohreh Aghdashloo, James (Jim) Caviezel, Mozhan Marno, Navid Negahban, Vida Ghahremani, David Diaan, Ali Pourtash, Parviz Sayyad; ***D:*** Cyrus Nowrasteh; ***W:*** Cyrus Nowrasteh, Betsy Giffen Nowrasteh; ***C:*** Joel Ransom; ***M:*** John Debney.

The Stooge 1/2 1951 Singer Bill Miller (Martin) asks the antic Ted Rogers (Lewis) to join him in his vaudeville act, where Rogers' clowning has them on the road to success. But then Miller decides he wants to go solo. Sounds more than a little autobiographical. ♫ A Girl Named Mary and a Boy Named Bill; Who's Your Little Whozis?; Just One More Chance; With My Eyes Wide Open I'm Dreaming; Louise; I'm Yours. **100m/B VHS, DVD.** Dean Martin, Jerry Lewis, Polly Bergen, Marion Marshall, Eddie Mayehoff, Richard Erdman, Frances Bavier; ***D:*** Norman Taurog; ***W:*** Martin Rackin, Fred Finklehoffe, Elwood Ullman; ***C:*** Daniel F. Fapp.

Stoogemania 1985 A nerd becomes so obsessed with the Three Stooges that they begin to take over his life and ruin it. Harmless except as a waste of time. Includes actual Stooge footage including some colorized—but see an old Stooges movie instead. **95m/C VHS.** Josh Mostel, Melanie Chartoff, Sid Caesar, Mark Holton, Patrick DeSantis, Armin Shimerman, Thom Sharp, Joshua John Miller, Victoria Jackson, Ron House, Alan Shearman, Diz White; ***D:*** Chuck Workman; ***W:*** Chuck Workman, Jim Geoghan; ***C:*** Christopher Tufty; ***M:*** Hummie Mann, Gary Tigerman.

Stop-Loss 1/2 2008 (R) Fresh from duty in Iraq, Sgt. Brandon King (Phillippe) and his buddy Sgt. Steve Shriver (Tatum) return home to Texas only to struggle with assimilation and strained relationships due to the war experiences. Suddenly, Brandon is ordered to return to Iraq (the title refers to the military term for extending a soldier's enlistment contract without consent or even a heads-up), setting off a bomb of emotion and leading to an AWOL escape that puts him, his friends, and his family in jeopardy. Director and co-writer Kimberly Pierce, whose brother had been stop-lossed by the army, brings honesty and humanity to a subject close to her heart, and the lead performances are grippingly spot-on. **112m/C DVD.** *US* Ryan Phillippe, Abbie Cornish, Channing Tatum, Joseph Gordon-Levitt, Ciaran Hinds, Timothy Olyphant, Josef Sommer, Victor Rasuk, Rob Brown, Mamie Gummer; ***D:*** Kimberly Peirce; ***W:*** Kimberly Peirce, Mark Richard; ***C:*** Chris Menges; ***M:*** John Powell.

Stop Making Sense 1/2 1984 The Talking Heads perform 18 of their best songs in this concert filmed in Los Angeles. Considered by many to be the best concert movie ever made. The band plays with incredible energy and imagination, and Demme's direction and camera work is appropriately frenzied and original. Features such Talking Heads songs as "Burning Down the House," "Psycho Killer," and "Once in a Lifetime." Band member Tina Weymouth's Tom Tom Club also performs for the audience. **99m/C VHS, DVD.** ***D:*** Jonathan Demme; ***C:*** Jordan Cronenweth.

Stop! or My Mom Will Shoot 1992 (PG-13) Getty is an overbearing mother paying a visit to her cop son (Stallone) in Los Angeles. When mom witnesses a crime she has to stay in town longer than intended, which gives her time to meddle in her son's work and romantic lives. If Stallone wants to change his image this so-called comedy isn't the way to do it—because the joke is only on him. Viewers who rent this may find the joke is on them. **87m/C VHS, DVD.** Sylvester Stallone, Estelle Getty, JoBeth Williams, Roger Rees, Martin Ferrero, Gailard Sartain, Dennis Burkley; ***D:*** Roger Spottiswoode; ***W:*** William Osborne, William Davies, Blake Snyder; ***M:*** Alan Silvestri. Golden Raspberries '92: Worst Actor (Stallone), Worst Support. Actress (Getty), Worst Screenplay.

Stop That Cab 1/2 1951 Sloppy crooks accidentally leave precious jewels in the back seat of a taxi, and pursue and torture the cabby who found and hid them. Rather mean-spirited, uninteresting comedy. **56m/B VHS.** Sid Melton, Iris Adrian, Tom Neal, Marjorie Lord, Greg McClure; ***C:*** Carl Berger.

Stopover Tokyo 1957 An American intelligence agent uncovers a plot to assassinate the American ambassador while on leave in Japan. Nice location shooting and scenery; limp story and characters. Based on a novel by John P. Marquand. **100m/C VHS, DVD.** Robert Wagner, Joan Collins, Edmond O'Brien, Ken Scott, Larry Keating, Sarah Selby, Reiko Oyama, Solly Nakamura, H. Okhawa, K.J. Seijto, Denmei Suzuki; ***D:*** Richard L. Breen; ***W:*** Richard L. Breen, Walter Reisch, Charles G. Clarke; ***M:*** Paul Sawtell.

The Stork Club 1945 A little song, a little dance, will Betty Hutton find romance? The actors manage to rise above the script in this silly, overdone fable. Hutton stars as the poor but spunky hatcheck girl who unwittingly saves the life of a cynical billionaire. His expressions of gratitude are less than appreciated by her G.I. beau. Done mainly as a vehicle for Hutton's promotion, so Betty's die-hard fans may find it to their liking. ♫ Doctor, Lawyer, Indian Chief; Baltimore Oriole; I'm a Square in the Social Circle; If I Had a Dozen Hearts; Love Me; China Boy; In the Shade of the Old Apple Tree. **98m/B VHS, DVD.** Betty Hutton, Barry Fitzgerald, Don DeFore, Robert Benchley, Bill Goodwin, Iris Adrian, Noel Neill, Andy Russell; ***D:*** Hal Walker.

Storm 1/2 1987 (PG-13) Uneven thriller finds college students on a camping trip who must fight for their lives when they are confronted by killer thieves. Somewhat contrived, but interesting ending to this low-budget outing. **99m/C VHS.** *CA* David Palffy, Stan Kane, Harry Freedman, Lawrence Elion, Tom Schioler; ***D:*** David Winning; ***M:*** Amin Bhatia.

Storm and Sorrow 1990 Molly Higgins is known as the "Spiderwoman of the Rockies" for her legendary mountain climbing abilities. Then she joins a team looking to scale the 24,000-foot peaks of Russia's Pamir Mountains. The group meets deadly hazards—both natural and those caused by the ego-driven rivalries of the group's members. A fact-based drama based on the novel by Richard Craig. **96m/C VHS, DVD.** Lori Singer, Todd Allen, Steve (Stephen M.) Anderson, Jay Baker; ***W:*** Leigh Chapman.

Storm Catcher 1999 (R) Air Force pilot Jack Holloway (Lundgren) is falsely convicted of stealing a prototype military aircraft. He manages to escape in order to find the real culprits, which also puts Hollway's family in danger. **95m/C VHS, DVD.** Dolph Lundgren, Mystro Clark, Yvonne Zima, Kylie Bax; ***D:*** Anthony Hickox; ***W:*** Bill Gucwa, Ed Masterson. **VIDEO**

Storm Cell 1/2 2008 (PG-13) After an Oklahoma twister kills her parents, April Saunders (Rogers) grows up to study and track tornadoes. While visiting her brother (Moloney) in Seattle with her surly teen daughter Dana (Levesque), April realizes a supercell is building that could destroy the city. Combo of disaster flick and family drama courtesy of the Lifetime channel. **92m/C DVD.** Mimi Rogers, Robert Moloney, Andrew Airlie, Michael Ironside, Ryan Kennedy, Elyse Levesque; ***D:*** Stephen R. Monroe; ***W:*** Graham Ludlow, Michael Konyves; ***C:*** C. Kim Miles; ***M:*** Corey A. Jackson. **CABLE**

Storm Chasers: Revenge of the Twister 1/2 1998 Having lost her husband in a plane crash, "storm chaser" Jaime (McGillis) throws herself into her work. Sent to Colorado to investigate a tornado, she hooks up with hunky FEMA coordinator, Will (Larson). There are some severe disturbances in the atmosphere causing problems—and disturbances on a more personal level as well. Dull and dumb. **96m/C VHS, DVD.** Kelly McGillis, Wolf Larson, Liz Torres, Adrian Zmed, James MacArthur; ***D:*** Mark Sobel. **VIDEO**

Storm in a Teacup 1/2 1937 A reporter starts a campaign to save a sheepdog that the town magistrate has ordered killed because the owner, an old woman, is unable to pay the license tax. As the dog's fate hangs in the balance, this often humorous film provides an interesting look at British society of the 1930s. **80m/B VHS, DVD.** *GB* Vivien Leigh, Rex Harrison, Cecil Parker, Sara Allgood; ***D:*** Victor Saville.

Storm over Asia *The Heir to Genghis Khan* 1928 A Mongolian trapper is discovered to be descended from Genghis Khan and is made puppet emperor of a Soviet province. Beautiful and evocative. Silent masterpiece. **70m/B VHS, DVD.** *RU* I. Inkizhinov, Valeri Inkizhinov, Alexandr Chistyakov, A. Dedinstev, V. Tzoppi, Paulina Belinskaya; ***D:*** Vsevolod Pudovkin; ***C:*** Anatoli Golovnya.

Storm over Wyoming 1950 The old sheep-and-cattle battle again; Holt and Martin find themselves haplessly embroiled in a Wyoming range war. Action-packed but thin, ordinary western. **60m/B VHS.** Tim Holt, Richard Martin, Noreen Nash, Tom Keene, Bill Kennedy, Kenneth MacDonald, Holly (Mike Ragan) Bane; ***D:*** Lesley Selander; ***W:*** Ed Earl Repp; ***C:*** J. Roy Hunt; ***M:*** Paul Sawtell.

Storm Rider 1957 A gunman hired to protect a group of ranchers from a powerful rancher falls in love with a local widow. After his job is done, however, he leaves her behind. Typical western fare. **70m/B VHS, DVD.** Scott Brady, Mala Powers, Bill Williams, Olin Howlin, William "Bill" Fawcett, John Goddard; ***D:*** Edward L. Bernds; ***W:*** Edward L. Bernds; ***M:*** Les Baxter.

Storm Tracker 1/2 *Storm* 1999 (PG-13) Meteorologist Ron Young (Perry) develops a method of manipulating the path of deadly storms and is recruited by General Roberts (Sheen) to perfect his storm-tracking system for government use. Naturally, this isn't altruistic, the General wants to turn the violent storms on his enemies. **90m/C VHS, DVD.** Luke Perry, Martin Sheen, Alexandra Powers, David Moses, Renee Estevez; ***D:*** Harris Done. **CABLE**

Storm Trooper 1/2 1998 Abused wife Grace Tolson (Alt) is just cleaning up after killing her husband when the mysterious Stark (Laughlin) shows up at her back door. Closely following are a group of armed men who manage to wound the stranger, exposing wires and circuitry. Stark the cyborg gets Grace into a lot of danger but she's got a gun and she's not gonna take it anymore. **89m/C VHS.** Carol Alt, John Laughlin, Zach Galligan, Corey Feldman, Richard (Rick) Hill, Kool Moe Dee; ***D:*** Jim Wynorski; ***W:*** T.L. Lankford; ***C:*** J.E. Bash; ***M:*** Terry Plumeri. **VIDEO**

Storm Warning 1951 New York model Martha (Rogers) visits her sister Lucy (Day, in a non-singing role), who's living in a small southern town. She's barely off the bus before Martha witnesses a murder committed by the KKK. She's hiding and sees two men's faces and when she does get to Lucy's, Martha sees that her brutish brother-in-law Hank (Cochran) was one of the killers and the other is his boss, Charlie (Sanders). When prosecutor Burt Rainey (Reagan) learns that Martha was a witness, he tries to get her to testify but she clams up. But her silence doesn't do her any good. Hard-hitting for its time although there are no black characters in the story; the dead man is a white reporter writing an expose. Film was shot in Corona, California and an occasional palm tree incongruously appears. **93m/B DVD.** Ronald Reagan, Ginger Rogers, Doris Day, Steve Cochran, Hugh Sanders, Raymond Greenleaf, Lloyd Gough; ***D:*** Stuart Heisler; ***W:*** Richard Brooks, Daniel Fuchs; ***C:*** Carl Guthrie; ***M:*** Daniele Amfitheatrof.

The Storm Within 1/2 *Les Parents Terribles* 1948 Based on Cocteau's play, many consider this domestic drama of a troubled family's tortured existence to be his finest work. De Bray plays the domineering mother, Marais plays the son, and Day is the woman he (and his father) love in this complex story of sexuality, parental rivalry and jealousy. With the film set in only two locations, Cocteau creates a claustrophobic intimacy within the walls of de Bray's family apartment and Day's apartment. An inferior remake, "Intimate Relations" was released in Britain in 1953. In French with English subtitles. **98m/B VHS.** *FR* Jean Marais, Yvonne de Bray, Gabrielle Dorziat, Marcel Andre, Josette Day; ***D:*** Jean Cocteau; ***W:*** Jean Cocteau; ***Nar:*** Jean Cocteau.

Stormquest WOOF! 1987 Deep in the jungle, a band of women warriors live without men. When it is discovered that one of the group has a male lover, she is sentenced to death. Her man tries to rescue her, and it turns into a war of the sexes—literally. In Spanish with subtitles. **90m/C VHS.** *SP* Kai Baker, Brent Huff; ***D:*** Alex Sessa.

Stormswept 1/2 1995 Actress Brianna (Hughes) rents a haunted Louisiana mansion housing the spirit of a slave master. When a storm strands Brianna and friends, the spirit causes everyone to get up to all sorts of sexual escapades. **94m/C VHS, DVD.** Julie Hughes, Melissa Moore, Kathleen Kinmont, Justin Carroll, Lorissa McComas, Ed Wasser, Kim Kopf, Hunt Scarritt; ***D:*** David Marsh; ***W:*** David Marsh.

Stormy Monday 1/2 1988 (R) An American developer conspires to strike it rich in Newcastle, England real estate by resorting to violence and political manipulations. Sting plays the jazz club owner who opposes him. Slow plot, but acted and directed well; interesting photography. **108m/C VHS, DVD.** *GB* Melanie Griffith, Tommy Lee Jones, Sting, Sean Bean, James Cosmo, Mark Long, Brian Lewis; ***D:*** Mike Figgis; ***W:*** Mike Figgis; ***C:*** Roger Deakins; ***M:*** Mike Figgis.

Stormy Nights 1/2 1997 (R) Femme fatale Nicole (Spaulding) worms her way into the lives of Jennifer McCormick (Tweed) and her weak-willed hubby (Clark), leading to seduction and betrayal. **90m/C VHS.** Shannon Tweed, Tracy Spaulding, Brett (Baxter) Clark; ***D:*** Alberto Vidaurri; ***W:*** Michael Meyer; ***C:*** S. Douglas Smith; ***M:*** Jay Bolton.

Stormy Trails 1936 Bell battles bellicose bad guys who are after his property. At least all the gunfights should keep a viewer awake! **59m/B VHS, DVD.** Rex Bell, Bob Terry, Lois Wilde, Lane Chandler, Earl Dwire, Lloyd Ingraham, Karl Hackett, Murdock MacQuarrie, Jimmy Aubrey, Roger Williams; ***D:*** Sam Newfield; ***W:*** Phil Dunham; ***C:*** Robert E. Cline.

Stormy Waters 1/2 *Remorques* 1941 A romantic French drama about a sea captain falling in love with a woman he rescues from a storm. He goes back to his wife, however, when she becomes critically ill. Director Gremillon insisted on realistic footage of storms at sea; production was delayed because of the difficulties of the German occupation. Dubbed. **75m/B VHS.** *FR* Jean Gabin, Michele Morgan, Madeleine Renaud; ***D:*** Jean Gremillon.

Stormy Weather 1/2 1943 In this cavalcade of black entertainment, the plot takes a back seat to the nearly non-stop array of musical numbers, showcasing this stellar cast at their performing peak. ♫ There's No Two Ways About Love; Stormy Weather; Ain't Misbehavin'; Rhythm Cocktail; Rang Tang Tang; Dat, Dot, Dah; That Ain't Right; I Can't Give You Anything But Love, Baby; Digga Digga Doo. **77m/B VHS, DVD.** Lena Horne, Bill Robinson, Fats Waller, Dooley Wilson, Cab Calloway; ***D:*** Andrew L. Stone; ***C:*** Leon Shamroy. Natl. Film Reg. '01.

The Story Lady 🦴🦴 ½ **1993** A retiree uses her story-telling abilities as a hostess on a public-access children's program. She becomes so popular that two network execs want to exploit her as a spokesperson for a toy company. Only a young girl can help her find a way to resist going commercial. **120m/C VHS, DVD.** Jessica Tandy, Lisa Jakub, Ed Begley Jr., Charles Durning, Stephanie Zimbalist; ***D:*** Larry Elikann; ***M:*** Lee Holdridge. **TV**

The Story of a Cheat 🦴🦴🦴 **1936** The hero of the film discovers at an early age that dishonesty is probably the best policy and he sets out to put his theory into use. Director/writer Guitry also turns in a great performance as the central character. Guitry was a major influence on such different directors as Welles, Resnais and Truffaut. Based on Guitry's novel "Memoires d'Un Tricheur." In French with English subtitles. **83m/B VHS.** *FR* Sacha Guitry; ***D:*** Sacha Guitry; ***W:*** Sacha Guitry.

Story of a Cowboy Angel 🦴 *Christmas Mountains* **1981** On the Christmas Mountain Ranch, a cowboy angel descends to Earth to bestow various beneficences. **90m/C VHS.** Fran Ryan, Mark Miller, Barbara Stanger, Brian Poelman, Slim Pickens; ***D:*** Pierre De Moro; ***W:*** Mark Miller.

Story of a Love Affair 🦴🦴 *Cronaca di un Amore* **1950** Paola (Bose) is the young wife of wealthy industrialist Enrico (Sarmi), who swiftly married her during the war. Now curious about her unknown past, Enrico hires a detective (Rossi) to investigate. This results in reuniting Paola with her ex-lover Guido (Girotti). Both are afraid that questions will be raised about the suspicious death of Guido's fiancee and, as the two rekindle their involvement, they consider getting rid of Enrico to preserve their secrets. Antonioni's first dramatic feature; Italian with subtitles. **98m/B DVD.** *IT* Lucia Bose, Massimo Girotti, Gino Rossi; ***D:*** Michelangelo Antonioni; ***W:*** Michelangelo Antonioni, Francesco Maselli, Daniele D'Anza, Silvio Giovannetti; ***C:*** Enzo Serafin; ***M:*** Giovanni Fusco.

The Story of a Love Story 🦴🦴 ½ *Impossible Object* **1973** Bates plays a writer whose imagination gets the better of him when he attempts an extra-marital affair. Was he with her or not? Unusual concept doesn't stand up in the long run. Fine cast is underutilized. **110m/C VHS.** *FR* Alan Bates, Dominique Sanda, Evans Evans, Lea Massari, Michel Auclair, Laurence De Monaghan; ***D:*** John Frankenheimer; ***W:*** Alan Bates.

Story of a Prostitute 🦴🦴 *Joy Girls; Shunpuden* **1965** Lurid film adapted from a novel by Taijiro Tamura. A betrayed woman volunteers to become a prostitute for a garrison of soldiers stationed on the Manchurian front in WWII. Soon, the commander takes the woman as his sole property, though she has fallen for one of his junior officers. Japanese with subtitles. **86m/B VHS.** *JP* Yumiko Nogawa, Tamio Kawaji, Isao Tamagawa; ***D:*** Seijun Suzuki.

The Story of a Three Day Pass 🦴🦴 ½ *La Permission* **1968** A black American GI falls in love with a white French girl he meets in peacetime Paris. Based on Van Peebles book "La Permission." With English subtitles. Made on a low budget and flawed, but poignant and impressive. **87m/B VHS, DVD.** Harry Baird, Nicole Berger, Pierre Doris; ***D:*** Melvin Van Peebles; ***W:*** Melvin Van Peebles.

The Story of Adele H. 🦴🦴🦴 *L'Histoire d'Adele H* **1975 (PG)** The story of Adele Hugo, daughter of Victor Hugo, whose love for an English soldier leads to obsession and finally to madness after he rejects her. Sensitive and gentle unfolding of characters and story. Beautiful photography. In French with English subtitles. **97m/C VHS, DVD.** *FR* Isabelle Adjani, Bruce Robinson, Sylvia Marriott; ***D:*** Francois Truffaut; ***W:*** Suzanne Schiffman, Jean Gruault; ***C:*** Nestor Almendros; ***M:*** Maurice Jaubert. Natl. Bd. of Review '75: Actress (Adjani); N.Y. Film Critics '75: Actress (Adjani), Screenplay; Natl. Soc. Film Critics '75: Actress (Adjani).

The Story of Alexander Graham Bell 🦴🦴🦴 **1939** Lavish Fox biography on the inventor of the telephone provided Ameche with his most popular role. He's a serious Scot who comes to Boston to teach speech to the deaf and falls in love with the rich, beautiful and hearing impaired Young (whose three sisters, Georgianna, Polly Ann, and Sally are also in the film). Thanks to Young's rich daddy (Coburn), Bell gets the money to work on his invention, aided by enthusiastic assistant Watson (Fonda). No, it's not an entirely accurate retelling but it's well-done. **97m/B VHS.** Don Ameche, Loretta Young, Henry Fonda, Charles Coburn, Spring Byington, Gene Lockhart, Sally Blane, Polly Ann Young, Georgianna Young, Bobs Watson, Jonathan Hale, Harry Davenport; ***D:*** Irving Cummings; ***W:*** Lamar Trotti; ***C:*** Leon Shamroy.

The Story of an African Farm 🦴🦴 ½ *Bustin' Bonaparte: The Story of an African Farm* **2004 (PG)** Grant stars as a gleeful villain named Bonaparte Benkins, who invades the lives of young cousins Em (Weidemann) and Lydall (Kropinski). It's 1870, and the two orphaned girls are stuck on the remote African farm of their strict Aunt Sannie (Van der Laag), whom drifter Bonaparte proceeds to charm into letting him stay. The children are plucky and the adults are generally foolish but the experience is only mildly entertaining. Based on the 1883 children's book by South African Olive Schreiner. **97m/C DVD.** *SA* Richard E. Grant, Armin Mueller-Stahl, Kasha Kropinski, Anneke Weidemann, Karin van der Laag, Luke Gallant; ***D:*** David Lister; ***W:*** Bonnie Rodini, Thandi Brewer, Peter Tischhauser; ***M:*** J.B. Arthur.

The Story of Boys & Girls 🦴🦴🦴 *Storia de Ragazzi e di Ragazze* **1991** Two very different families come together for the wedding feast of their children, during which family secrets are revealed and we come to know and care for everyone present. A 20-course meal rivals the food scenes in "Babette's Feast" and is guaranteed to make your mouth water. Fine ensemble of actors, well directed, with a vivid evocation of 1930s Italy. In Italian with English subtitles. **92m/C VHS.** *IT* Lucrezia Lante della Rovere, Massimo Bonetti, Davide Bechini, Enrica Maria Modugno, Valeria Bruni Tadeschi, Lina Bernardi, Anna Bonaiuto, Alessandro Haber; ***D:*** Pupi Avati; ***W:*** Pupi Avati; ***M:*** Riz Ortolani.

The Story of David 🦴🦴🦴 **1976 (PG)** Well-done Old Testament Bible drama about the shepherd boy who slew Goliath, overcame the Philistines, and united Israel. Then, as King David, he winds up involved in an illicit love affair with Bathsheba that threatens to destroy his kingdom. Fine acting and a literate script highlight this TV production. **192m/C VHS.** Timothy Bottoms, Anthony Quayle, Jane Seymour, Keith Michell, Susan Hampshire; ***D:*** Alex Segal; ***W:*** Ernest Kinoy. **TV**

The Story of Dr. Wassell 🦴🦴 ½ **1944** Courageous true story of Corydon M. Wassell (Cooper), who won the Navy Cross for humanitarianism in WWII. Stationed in Java when the Japanese overrun the island, Wassell's placed in charge of evacuating the wounded. When he learns that stretcher cases must be left behind, he disobeys orders to rescue some badly wounded soldiers and get them to safety. (Naturally, there has to be some romance, so Cooper's paired with Day as a Red Cross nurse). Based on the book by James Hilton. **137m/C VHS.** Gary Cooper, Laraine Day, Signe Hasso, Dennis O'Keefe, Carol Thurston, Carl Esmond, Stanley Ridges, Paul Kelly, Elliott Reid, Philip Ahn, Barbara Britton; ***D:*** Cecil B. DeMille; ***W:*** Charles Bennett, Alan LeMay; ***C:*** Victor Milner; ***M:*** Victor Young.

The Story of Esther Costello 🦴🦴 ½ *Golden Virgin* **1957** Rich American Margaret Landi (Crawford) is visiting her Irish homeland when she meets Esther (Sears), a young girl rendered deaf, mute, and blind by a childhood trauma. The childless Margaret is persuaded to take Esther in as a surrogate daughter and the waif gradually begins to respond to her care, sparking a media frenzy over the inspirational saga. This brings Carlo (Brazzi), Margaret's estranged and money-grubbing husband, out of the woodwork, with some get-rich-quick schemes. Well-done melodrama adapted from the book by Nicholas Monsarrat. **102m/B VHS.** *GB* Joan Crawford, Heather Sears, Rossano Brazzi, Lee Patterson, Ron Randell, Fay Compton, John Loder, Denis O'Dea; ***D:*** David Miller; ***W:*** Charles A. Kaufman; ***C:*** Robert Krasker; ***M:*** Georges Auric.

The Story of Fausta 🦴🦴 ½ *Romance da Empregada* **1988 (R)** An unhappily married cleaning woman in the slums of Rio entices all the money and gifts she can out of an elderly widower. Decidely grim comedy-drama, well-done but unsparing in its depiction of overwhelming greed. In Portuguese with English subtitles. **90m/C VHS.** *BR* Betty Faria, Daniel Filho, Brandao Filho; ***D:*** Bruno Barreto; ***M:*** Ruben Blades.

The Story of G.I. Joe 🦴🦴🦴 ½ **1945** Grunt's-eye-view of the European theatre in WWII, based on the columns of war correspondent Ernie Pyle. Follows an infantry unit through Italy and concentrates on the everyday experiences of the soldiers, registering genuine emotion and realism. Mitchum's breakthrough role. Most of the actual unit played themselves. Pyle was killed by a sniper shortly before the film's release. **109m/B VHS, DVD.** Burgess Meredith, Robert Mitchum, Wally Cassell, William Benedict, William Murphy, Jimmy Lloyd, Freddie (Fred) Steele, William (Bill) Self, Jack Reilly, Tito Renaldo, Hal Boyle, Chris Cunningham, Jack Foisie, George Lah, Bob Landry, Clete Roberts, Robert Rueben, Don Whitehead; ***D:*** William A. Wellman; ***W:*** Leopold Atlas, Guy Endore, Philip Stevenson, Ernie Pyle; ***C:*** Russell Metty; ***M:*** Louis Applebaum, Ann Ronell. Natl. Film Reg. '09.

The Story of Jacob & Joseph 🦴🦴🦴 **1974 (R)** Fine biblical drama finds brothers Jacob and Esau fighting over their birthright, tearing apart their family for 20 years. When the brothers finally reconcile, it's only to cast an envious eye on youngest brother Joseph, whom they sell into slavery. Taken to Egypt Joseph uses his talents to become the Pharoah's chief advisor but he can never forget his family or what was done to him. All-around good acting, directing, and writing. **96m/C VHS, DVD.** Keith Michell, Tony LoBianco, Julian Glover, Colleen Dewhurst, Herschel Bernardi, Harry Andrews; ***D:*** Michael Cacoyannis; ***W:*** Ernest Kinoy; ***M:*** Mikis Theodorakis; ***Nar:*** Alan Bates. **TV**

The Story of Louis Pasteur 🦴🦴🦴 **1936** Formulaic Hollywood biopic raised a notch or two by Muni's superb portrayal of the famous scientist and his career leading up to his most famous discoveries. Acclaimed in its time; excellent despite low budget. **85m/B VHS.** Paul Muni, Josephine Hutchinson, Anita Louise, Fritz Leiber, Donald Woods, Porter Hall, Akim Tamiroff, Walter Kingsford; ***D:*** William Dieterle; ***C:*** Gaetano Antonio "Tony" Gaudio. Oscars '36: Actor (Muni), Story.

The Story of Marie and Julien 🦴🦴 *Histoire de Marie et Julien* **2003** Moody clockmaker Julien (Radziwilowicz) indulges his memories of a brief affair with Marie (Beart), who suddenly re-enters his life. She immediately moves in with him, begging Julien not to ask about her past, but he can't resist. Something supernatural is apparently going on but the entire situation is confusing rather than intriguing and solemn rather than enlightening. Beart's beauty is at least one reason to watch. French with subtitles. **150m/C DVD.** *FR* Emmanuelle Beart, Jerzy Radziwilowicz, Anne Brochet; ***D:*** Jacques Rivette; ***W:*** Jacques Rivette, Christine Laurent, Pascal Bonitzer; ***C:*** William Lubtchansky.

The Story of O 🦴🦴 **1975 (NC-17)** A young woman's love for one man moves her to surrender herself to many men, in order to please him. Soft-core porn with bondage and S&M beautified by camera work. Based on the classic Freudian-erotic novel by Pauline Reage. **105m/C VHS, DVD.** Corinne Clery, Anthony Steel, Udo Kier, Jean Gaven, Christiane Minazzoli, Martine Kelly, Nadine Perles; ***D:*** Just Jaeckin; ***W:*** Sebastien Japrisot; ***C:*** Robert Fraisse, Yves Rodallec; ***M:*** Pierre Bachelet.

The Story of O, Part 2 🦴 **1987** A sort-of sequel to the erotic classic, in which the somewhat soiled vixen takes over an American conglomerate by seducing everyone in it. **107m/C DVD.** *FR* Sandra Wey, Carole James; ***D:*** Eric Rochat; ***W:*** Eric Rochat; ***C:*** Andres Berenguer; ***M:*** Hans Zimmer.

The Story of Qiu Ju 🦴🦴🦴 *Qiu Ju Da Guansi* **1991 (PG)** A simple story, beautifully directed and acted, about a peasant woman's search for justice. The pregnant Qiu Ju's husband is assaulted and injured by the head of their village. Outraged, Qui Ju slowly climbs the Chinese administrative ladder from official to higher official as she insistently seeks redress. Presents a close observance of daily life and customs with a strong female lead. Adapted from the novel "The Wan Family's Lawsuit" by Chen Yuan Bin. In Mandarin Chinese with English subtitles. **100m/C VHS, DVD.** *CH* Gong Li, Lei Lao Sheng, Liu Pei Qu, Ge Zhi Jun, Ye Jun, Yang Liu Xia, Zhu Qanging, Cui Luowen, Yank Huiquin, Wang Jianfa, Lin Zi; ***D:*** Yimou Zhang; ***W:*** Liu Heng; ***C:*** Chi Xiaonin, Yu Xaioqun; ***M:*** Jiping Zhao. Natl. Soc. Film Critics '93: Foreign Film; Venice Film Fest. '92: Actress (Li), Film.

The Story of Robin Hood & His Merrie Men 🦴🦴🦴 *The Story of Robin Hood* **1952** Well-made swashbuckler based on the English legend was Disney's second live action feature. Almost, but not quite, as memorable as the 1938 Michael Curtiz "Adventures of Robin Hood." Curtiz's version had Errol Flynn, after all. **83m/C VHS.** Richard Todd, Joan Rice, Peter Finch, Martita Hunt; ***D:*** Ken Annakin.

The Story of Ruth 🦴🦴 **1960** Biblical saga of adventures of Ruth as she denounces her pagan gods and flees to Israel. Typically "epic" with overwrought performances. Alternately not too bad to downright boring. **132m/C VHS, DVD.** Elana Eden, Viveca Lindfors, Peggy Wood, Tom Tryon, Stuart Whitman, Jeff Morrow, Thayer David, Eduard Franz; ***D:*** Henry Koster.

The Story of Seabiscuit 🦴🦴 ½ *Pride of Kentucky* **1949** The famous racing winner Seabiscuit is featured in a fluffy story of a racetrack romance. Temple is in love with a jockey (McCallister) but wants him to give up racing. Her uncle (Fitzgerald), who is Seabiscuit's trainer, has other things in mind. **93m/C VHS, DVD.** Shirley Temple, Barry Fitzgerald, Lon (Bud) McCallister, Rosemary DeCamp; ***D:*** David Butler.

The Story of the Late Chrysanthemum 🦴🦴🦴 ½ **1939** Classic drama about the son of a Kabuki actor who falls in love with a servant girl against his father's wishes. Their doomed affair is the center of the plot. Acclaimed and sensitive drama, in Japanese with English subtitles. **115m/B VHS.** *JP* Shotaro Hanayagi, Kakuo Mori, Kokichi Takada, Gonjuro Kawarazaki, Yoko Umemura; ***D:*** Kenji Mizoguchi.

The Story of the Weeping Camel 🦴🦴🦴 *Die Geschichte vom Weinenden Kamel* **2003 (PG)** Tale of animal estrangement and reconciliation combining reality sequences with re-creations of authentic situations. Follows a family tribe of shepherds through the camel's birthing season, a way of life that is slowly being eliminated. When one camel mother rejects her white calf, a musician from the village is sent to perform a musical ceremony using a two-stringed, boxlike violin and soothing, hypnotic, melodies to reunite calf and mother. Some may argue the re-created sequences are out of balance or perhaps unnecessary but the story is presented in a thoughtful, honest manner. In Mongolian with English subtitles. **90m/C DVD.** *GE* Odgerel Ayush, Ikhbayar Amgaabazar, Enkhbulgan Ikhbayar, Uuganbaadar Ikhbayar, Chimed Ohin, Janchiv Ayurzana, Amgaabazar Gonzon, Zeveljamz Nyam, Guntbaatar Ikhbayar, Munkhbayar, Ariun'jargal Adiya, Dago Roljav, Chuluunzezeg Gur; ***D:*** Byambasuren Davaa, Luigi Falorni; ***W:*** Byambasuren Davaa, Luigi Falorni; ***C:*** Luigi Falorni; ***M:*** Marcel Leniz. Directors Guild '04: Feature Doc.

The Story of Three Loves 🦴🦴 ½ **1953** Three passengers aboard an ocean liner dwell on romance. Ballet impresario

Charles Coudray (Mason) is enchanted seeing ballerina Paula Woodward (Shearer) privately perform one of his dances and insists on making a new ballet for her, which leads to tragedy. French governess Mademoiselle (Caron) is exasperated by her young American charge Tommy (Nelson), who asks witch Mrs. Pennicott (Barrymore) to make him older. But like Cinderella his wish—which turns him into the adult Thomas (Granger)—has a strict time limit. Daredevil trapeze artist Pierre Narval (Douglas) retired after his female partner died in an accident. After saving guilt-ridden Nina (Angelia) from a suicide attempt, Pierre decides to train her for a new act but when they fall in love, he worries history will repeat itself. **122m/C DVD.** James Mason, Moira Shearer, Agnes Moorehead, Leslie Caron, Ethel Barrymore, Farley Granger, Ricky Nelson, Kirk Douglas, Pier Angeli, Richard Anderson; ***D:*** Gottfried Reinhardt, Vincente Minnelli; ***W:*** George Froeschel, Jan Lustig; ***C:*** Charles Rosher, Harold Rosson; ***M:*** Miklos Rozsa.

The Story of Us 1/2 **1999 (R)** Hey attraction is easy but sustaining a relationship is hard—particularly after 15 years in a marriage of opposites. Crossword puzzle editor Katie (Pfeiffer) is a planner and organizer while hubby Ben (Willis), a TV comedy writer, is a spontaneous free-spirit. The kids are away at summer camp when the constantly bickering duo decide on a trial separation as they wonder what went wrong. Appealing leads but story is repetitive and sentimental. **98m/C VHS, DVD.** Bruce Willis, Michelle Pfeiffer, Rita Wilson, Paul Reiser, Rob Reiner, Tim Matheson, Julie Hagerty, Jayne Meadows, Tom Poston, Betty White, Red Buttons; ***D:*** Rob Reiner; ***W:*** Alan Zweibel, Jessie Nelson; ***C:*** Michael Chapman; ***M:*** Eric Clapton, Marc Shaiman.

The Story of Vernon and Irene Castle **1939** In this, their last film together for RKO, Astaire and Rogers portray the internationally successful ballroom dancers who achieved popularity in the early 1900s. Irene Castle served as technical advisor for the film and exasperated everyone on the set by insisting that Rogers be a brunette. Still fun, vintage Fred and Ginger. ♫ Only When You're In My Arms; Missouri Waltz; Oh, You Beautiful Doll; Nights of Gladness; By the Beautiful Sea; Glow, Little Glow Worm; Destiny Waltz; Row, Row, Row; The Yama Yama Man. **93m/B VHS, DVD.** Fred Astaire, Ginger Rogers, Edna May Oliver, Lew Fields, Jack Perrin, Walter Brennan; ***D:*** H.C. Potter.

The Story of Women *Une Affaire de Femmes* **1988** Riveting factual account of a woman (Huppert) who was guillotined for performing abortions in Nazi-occupied France. In French with English subtitles. **110m/C VHS.** *FR* Isabelle Huppert, Francois Cluzet, Marie Trintignant, Nils (Niels) Tavernier, Louis Ducreux; ***D:*** Claude Chabrol; ***W:*** Claude Chabrol, Colo Tavernier O'Hagan; ***C:*** Jean Rabier; ***M:*** Matthieu Chabrol. L.A. Film Critics '89: Foreign Film; N.Y. Film Critics '89: Foreign Film; Venice Film Fest. '88: Actress (Huppert).

The Story of Xinghua **1993** Obedient wife Xinghua (Wenli) endures the cruelty of her greedy husband (Guoli) in a northern Chinese village, built within the shadow of the Great Wall. Working in the fields alongside handsome farmer Tulin (Shaojun), Xinghua is drawn to his gentleness and the two become lovers. When her husband hears that gold may be buried beneath one of the wall's watchtowers, he persuades his fellow villagers to help him dig beneath the stones—a decision that leads to tragedy. Mandarin with subtitles. **89m/C VHS.** *CH* Jiang Wehli, Zhang Guoli, Tian Shaoujun; ***D:*** Yin Li.

Storybook 1/2 **1995 (G)** Eight-year-old Brandon finds a magic storybook and enters into a realm of fantasy. He discovers the only way to return home from Storyland is to save the kingdom from the rule of Queen Evilia and along with Woody the Woodsman, Pouch the Boxing Kangaroo, and Hoot the Wise Owl, Brandon just may succeed. **88m/C VHS, DVD.** Sean Fitzgerald, William McNamara, Swoosie Kurtz, Robert Costanzo, James Doohan, Brenda Epperson, Gary Morgan, Richard Moll, Jack Scalia, Milton Berle; ***D:*** Lorenzo Doumani; ***W:*** Lorenzo Doumani, Susan Bowen.

Storytelling **2001 (R)** Anthology explores the roles that sex and dysfunction play in creativity. First story, "Fiction" explores the complex relationship of writing student Vi (Blair) and her boyfriend Marcus (Fitzpatrick), who has cerebral palsy. The two are using each other for different ends, most notably to read each other's writing. Vi moves on to an intense one-night stand with her formidable black writing professor (Wisdom). Shaken, Vi weaves the graphic, brutal, but fascinating encounter into a story of her own. In "Nonfiction," feature documentarian Toby (Giamatti) goes to the burbs to document the life of a teen, his extremely dysfunctional family, and their Salvadoran maid. Solondz's characteristic black humor and social satire offers a range of hot topics, including homosexuality, political correctness, social stereotypes, the Holocaust, race, poverty, and the disabled. **87m/C VHS, DVD.** *US* Selma Blair, Leo Fitzpatrick, Aleksa Palladino, Robert Wisdom, Noah Fleiss, Paul Giamatti, John Goodman, Julie Hagerty, Lupe Ontiveros, Franka Potente, Mike Schank, Mark Webber, Jonathan Osser; ***D:*** Todd Solondz; ***W:*** Todd Solondz; ***M:*** Belle & Sebastian, Nathan Larson.

Storyville 1/2 **1974 (PG)** Love and music overcome prostitution and poverty in this turn-of-the-century New Orleans jazz drama, but tragedy prevails. **96m/C VHS.** Tim Rooney, Jeannie Wilson, Butch Benit, Wayne Mack, Bond Gideon, Oley Sassone; ***D:*** Jack Weis.

Storyville **1992 (R)** Southern Gothic tale set in New Orleans about a feckless young lawyer running for a local congressional seat. Neither Cray nor his family are strong candidates for the family values vote. Cray is separated from his wife and willingly indulges in an affair with a beautiful and mysterious young woman. This leads to a blackmail plot when he finds out his lover has been videotaping their antics. There's also a murder investigation and a host of family skeletons rattling around. Robards is fine as the crafty uncle but Spader's low-key attitude works against the story. Directorial debut of Frost. **112m/C VHS, DVD.** James Spader, Joanne Whalley, Jason Robards Jr., Charlotte Lewis, Michael Warren, Piper Laurie, Michael Parks, Chuck McCann, Woody Strode, Charles Haid; ***D:*** Mark Frost; ***W:*** Mark Frost, Lee Reynolds; ***M:*** Carter Burwell.

Stowaway **1936 (G)** After her missionary parents are killed in a Chinese revolution, Shirley stows away on a San Francisco-bound liner and plays cupid to a bickering couple who adopt her. ♫ Good Night, My Love; One Never Knows, Does One; You Gotta S-M-I-L-E to Be H-A-P-P-Y; I Wanna Go To the Zoo; That's What I Want For Christmas. **86m/B VHS.** Shirley Temple, Robert Young, Alice Faye, Eugene Pallette, Helen Westley, Arthur Treacher, Astrid Allwyn; ***D:*** William A. Seiter; ***C:*** Arthur C. Miller.

Straight for the Heart *A Corps Perdu* **1988** Photojournalist Pierre returns to Montreal after a harrowing assignment in Nicaragua. His homecoming is less than happy when he discovers both his lovers, David and Sarah, have deserted him. Pierre takes to wandering the Montreal streets, taking pictures, hoping they will help him make some sense of his life and help him reestablish a connection with beauty and humanity. In French with English subtitles. **92m/C VHS.** *CA* Matthias Habich, Johanne-Marie Tremblay; ***D:*** Lea Pool.

Straight into Darkness 1/2 **2004 (R)** Privates Losey (Francis) and Deming (MacDonald) go AWOL in Nazi-occupied France, eventually finding shelter at an abandoned hotel. The hotel also houses Deacon (Warner), Maria (Thorson), and a brood of orphans who have been trained to fight. The numerous flashbacks are confusing and the fate of the child soldiers is disturbing. **94m/C DVD.** Ryan Francis, Scott MacDonald, David Warner, Linda Thorson, James LeGros, Daniel Roebuck; ***D:*** Jeff Burr; ***W:*** Jeff Burr; ***C:*** Viorel Sergovici Jr.; ***M:*** Michael Convertino.

Straight Line **1988** T.S. Turner is a private investigator who goes after street gangs in order to prevent further violence in this action-packed story. **95m/C VHS.** Mr. T, Sean Roberge, Ron Ryan, Ken Walsh; ***D:*** George Mihalka.

Straight out of Brooklyn **1991 (R)** A bleak, nearly hopeless look at a struggling black family in a Brooklyn housing project. The son seeks escape through crime, his father in booze. An up-close and raw look at part of society seldom shown in mainstream film, its undeniable power is sapped by ragged production values and a loose narrative prone to melodrama. Rich (seen in a supporting role) was only 19 years old when he completed this, funded partly by PBS-TV's "American Playhouse." **91m/C VHS, DVD.** George T. Odom, Ann D. Sanders, Larry (Lawrence) Gilliard Jr., Mark Malone, Reana E. Drummond, Barbara Sanon, Matty Rich; ***D:*** Matty Rich; ***W:*** Matty Rich; ***C:*** John Rosnell; ***M:*** Harold Wheeler. Ind. Spirit '92: First Feature; Sundance '91: Special Jury Prize.

Straight out of Compton 1/2 **1999** Stereotype-riddled saga of a tough Compton local, Henry "Hen" Alabaster, and his plan to score some big time cash and start his own record company. He targets a racist politician named Drake Norelli who's made a fortune laundering mob money. The whole thing seems to want to deliver the meaningful message that "you can't escape your past," but it's lost amidst a mess of cliches and offensive stereotypes. **?m/C DVD.** Ryan Combs, Johnny DeaRenzo, Jules Dupree, Sean Epps; ***D:*** Ryan Combs; ***W:*** Ryan Combs; ***C:*** Eric Green.

Straight Shooter **1999 (R)** Former Foreign Legionnaire Volker Bretz (Ferch) seeks revenge for his daughter's death by killing the politicians he thinks are responsible. Frank Hector (Hopper), his former trainer, may be the only one who can stop him but will he? Hopper's the only English-speaking actor in this German thriller—the other actors are dubbed. **98m/C VHS, DVD.** *GE* Dennis Hopper, Heino Ferch, Ulrich Muhe; ***D:*** Thomas Bohn.

Straight Shootin' 1/2 **1917** Ford's first major effort launched both Carey and Gibson to national fame. Prototypical western; great action, great scenery. Silent. **53m/B VHS.** Harry Carey Sr., Hoot Gibson, Mollie Malone; ***D:*** John Ford.

The Straight Story 1/2 **1999 (G)** Surprisingly sweet true story from the generally eccentric Lynch. Septugenarian Alvin Straight (Farnsworth), who lives in Iowa, is determined to visit his ailing, estranged brother Lyle (Stanton) even though he can no longer drive a car. So, he hitches a small trailer to his riding mower and heads off at a stately 6 miles per hour—to Wisconsin (a 300 mile trip). Alvin realizes this is his last chance at both freedom and family and he's determined to make the most of it. Farnsworth plays Straight as a gruff, straight-talking old geezer and there's little or no sentimentality involved. **111m/C VHS, DVD.** Richard Farnsworth, Harry Dean Stanton, Sissy Spacek; ***D:*** David Lynch; ***W:*** John Roach; ***C:*** Freddie Francis; ***M:*** Angelo Badalamenti. Ind. Spirit '00: Actor (Farnsworth); N.Y. Film Critics '99: Actor (Farnsworth), Cinematog.

Straight Talk 1/2 **1992 (PG)** Shirlee (Parton), a down-home gal from Arkansas, heads for Chicago to start life anew. She finds a job as a receptionist at WNDY radio, but is mistaken for the new radio psychologist. Her homespun advice ("Get off the cross. Somebody needs the wood.") becomes hugely popular and soon "Dr." Shirlee is the toast of the town. Parton's advice is the funniest part of this flimsy movie, but she is helped immensely by Dunne and Orbach. Woods, however, is not in his element in a romantic comedy, and holds the movie down. **91m/C VHS, DVD.** Dolly Parton, James Woods, Griffin Dunne, Michael Madsen, Deirdre O'Connell, John Sayles, Teri Hatcher, Spalding Gray, Jerry Orbach, Philip Bosco, Charles Fleischer, Jay Thomas; ***D:*** Barnet Kellman; ***W:*** Craig Bolotin, Patricia Resnick; ***M:*** Brad Fiedel.

Straight Time **1978 (R)** Ex-con Hoffman hits the streets for the first time in six years and finds himself again falling into a life of crime. Well-told, sobering story flopped at the boxoffice and has never received the recognition it deserved. Convincing, realistic portrayal of a criminal. Hoffman was the original director, but gave the reins to Grosbard. Based on the novel "No Beast So Fierce" by Edward Bunker. **114m/C VHS, DVD.** Dustin Hoffman, Harry Dean Stanton, Gary Busey, Theresa Russell, M. Emmet Walsh, Kathy Bates, Edward (Eddie) Bunker; ***D:*** Ulu Grosbard; ***W:*** Jeffrey Boam, Alvin Sargent, Edward (Eddie) Bunker; ***C:*** Owen Roizman; ***M:*** David Shire.

Straight to Hell 1/2 **1987 (R)** A wildly senseless, anachronistic western spoof about a motley, inept gang of frontier thieves. An overplayed, indiscriminating punk spaghetti oat-opera. **86m/C VHS, DVD.** Dennis Hopper, Joe Strummer, Elvis Costello, Grace Jones, Jim Jarmusch, Dick Rude, Courtney Love, Sy Richardson, Biff Yeager, Xander Berkeley, Shane McGowan; ***D:*** Alex Cox; ***W:*** Alex Cox, Dick Rude; ***C:*** Tom Richmond; ***M:*** The Pogues, Pray for Rain.

Straight Up 1/2 **1990** A musical f/x-ridden attempts to warn MTV-era children about drugs, but visual gimmicks often overwhelm the message. Gossett sings nicely as a cosmic sage of abstinence, who cautions a boy against substance abuse. The smartest segment lambasts cigarette and alcohol ads. **75m/C VHS.** Chad Allen, Louis Gossett Jr.

Strait-Jacket 1/2 **1964** After Crawford is released from an insane asylum where she was sent 20 years for axing her husband and his mistress, mysterious axe murders begin to occur in the neighborhood. Coincidence? Aging axist Crawford is the prime suspect, and even she cannot say for sure who's doing it. Daughter Baker is there to help her adjust. Moderately creepy grade B+ slasher is lifted somewhat by Crawford. Written by Robert Bloch ("Psycho"). Never one to miss a gimmick, director Castle arranged for the distribution of cardboard "bloody axes" to all theatre patrons attending the movie. **89m/B VHS, DVD.** Joan Crawford, Leif Erickson, Diane Baker, George Kennedy, Howard St. John, Rochelle Hudson, Edith Atwater, Lee Majors, John Anthony Hayes, Mitchell Cox, Lee Yeary, Patricia Krest; ***D:*** William Castle; ***W:*** Robert Bloch; ***C:*** Arthur E. Arling; ***M:*** Van Alexander.

Stranded **1987 (PG-13)** A group of aliens escaping interplanetary persecution land on Earth and enlist the aid of an Earth family. Solid characters make it more than sci-fi; sort of a parable of intolerance, human (and alien) goodness, etc. **80m/C VHS.** Maureen O'Sullivan, Ione Skye, Cameron Dye; ***D:*** Tex Fuller; ***W:*** Alan Castle.

The Strange Affair of Uncle Harry 1/2 *Uncle Harry* **1945** Small-town gothic with fine acting by Sanders, an aging bachelor who plots murder when his romance is threatened by a jealous sister. A title card asks you not to reveal the 'surprise' ending—a hackneyed twist that appeased the censors but made producer Joan Harrison resign in protest. Based on a play by Robert Job. Tape suffers from poor film-video transfer. **80m/B VHS.** George Sanders, Geraldine Fitzgerald, Ella Raines, Sara Allgood, Moyna MacGill, Samuel S. Hinds, Harry von Zell; ***D:*** Robert Siodmak.

A Strange and Deadly Occurrence 1/2 **1974** Strange things start to happen to a family when they move to a house in a remote area. **74m/C VHS.** Robert Stack, Vera Miles, L.Q. Jones, Herb Edelman; ***D:*** John Llewellyn Moxey. **TV**

Strange Awakening **1958** Traveling in France while recuperating from amnesia, Barker is trapped in a plot of fraud and theft. Confused and contrived. **75m/B VHS.** *GB* Lex Barker, Carole Mathews, Nora Swinburne, Richard Molinos, Peter Dyneley; ***D:*** Montgomery Tully.

Strange Bedfellows 1/2 **1965** Within 24 hours of Carter Hudson (Hudson) arriving to work in London, he's met and married eccentric Italian Toni Vincenti (Lollobrigida). Complete opposites, the marriage is soon over and Carter returns to the States. Seven years later, he's back in London, ready to officially divorce Toni but learns from company PR whiz Dick Bramwell (Young) that his big promotion is contingent on his happy marriage. Carter courts Toni again, and tries to support her liberal causes and friends, but it turns out her latest stunt is aimed at his firm. Supposedly a check of the closing credits shows the film was shot on a Universal back lot and not on location. **104m/C VHS, DVD.** Rock Hudson, Gina Lollobrigida, Gig Young, Edward Judd, Howard St. John, Nancy Kulp, Bernard Fox, Terry-Thomas; ***D:*** Melvin Frank; ***W:*** Melvin Frank, Michael Pertwee; ***C:*** Leo Tover; ***M:*** Leigh Harline.

Strange Bedfellows 1/2 **2004 (R)** Because of financial problems, lifelong buddies Vince (Hogan) and Ralph (Caton) pose as a gay couple to get a newly-enacted tax break. But suspicious auditor Russell McKenzie (Postlethwaite) comes to their small town to check out their story. Surprisingly charming, though predictable, comedy plays up the outrageous aspects of the deception while still maintaining its heart. **100m/C VHS, DVD.** *AU* Paul Hogan, Michael Caton, Pete Postlethwaite, Alan Cassell, Kestie Morassi, Roy Billing, Glynn Nicholas, Amanda Monroe, Stewart Faichney; ***D:*** Dean Murphy; ***W:*** Dean Murphy, Stewart Faichney; ***C:*** Roger Lanser; ***M:*** Dale Cornelius.

Strange Behavior *Dead Kids; Small Town Massacre* **1981 (R)** In a small Midwestern town, the police chief follows the clues from a series of murders to the experimental lab of the local college. Seems there's a mad scientist involved. Grisly and creepy, but unduly ballyhooed when it appeared. Shot on location in New Zealand. **105m/C VHS, DVD.** Michael Murphy, Louise Fletcher, Dan Shor, Fiona Lewis, Arthur Dignam, Marc McClure, Scott Brady, Dey Young, Charles Lane; ***D:*** Michael Laughlin; ***W:*** Michael Laughlin, Bill Condon; ***C:*** Louis Horvath.

Strange Brew 1/2 **1983 (PG)** The screen debut of the SCTV alumni's characters Doug & Bob MacKenzie, the Great White North duo. They do battle with a powerful, megalomaniacal brew master over—what else?—a case of beer. Dumb, but what did you expect? Watch it, or be a hoser. **91m/C VHS, DVD.** *CA* Rick Moranis, Dave Thomas, Max von Sydow, Paul Dooley, Lynne Griffin, Angus MacInnes; ***D:*** Rick Moranis, Dave Thomas; ***W:*** Steve DeJarnatt, Rick Moranis, Dave Thomas; ***C:*** Steven Poster; ***M:*** Charles Fox; ***V:*** Mel Blanc.

Strange Cargo 1/2 **1940** Convicts escaping from Devil's Island are mystically entranced by a Christ-like fugitive en route to freedom. An odd, pretentious Hollywood fable waiting for a cult following. Gable and Crawford's eighth and final pairing. Adapted by Anita Loos from the book "Not Too Narrow...Not Too Deep" by Richard Sale. **105m/B VHS.** Clark Gable, Joan Crawford, Ian Hunter, Peter Lorre, Paul Lukas, Albert Dekker, J. Edward Bromberg, Eduardo Ciannelli, Frederick Worlock; ***D:*** Frank Borzage; ***W:*** Lesser Samuels; ***C:*** Robert Planck; ***M:*** Franz Waxman.

Strange Case of Dr. Jekyll & Mr. Hyde **1968** An adaptation of the classic Robert Louis Stevenson book about a scientist who conducts experiments on himself to separate good from evil. Palance is oddly but appealingly cast; Jarrott's bad direction wrecks it. Made for TV. **128m/C VHS, DVD.** Jack Palance, Leo Genn, Oscar Homolka, Billie Whitelaw, Denholm Elliott; ***D:*** Charles Jarrott; ***M:*** Robert Cobert. **TV**

Strange Case of Dr. Jekyll & Mr. Hyde 1/2 **1989** The Robert Louis Stevenson classic, with Hyde portrayed as an icy, well-dressed sociopath. An entry in Shelley Duvall's "Nightmare Classics" series. More psychological than special effect-y. **60m/C VHS.** Anthony Andrews, Laura Dern, George Murdock, Nicholas Guest; ***D:*** Michael Lindsay-Hogg. **CABLE**

The Strange Case of Dr. Jekyll and Mr. Hyde **2006 (R)** The umpteenth adaptation of the Robert Louis Stevenson story is an illogical and uninteresting waste of time. In this modern update, Dr. Jekyll (Todd) works at a big lab studying heart problems. He injects himself with a serum intended to cure his own heart defect and unleashes Edward Hyde, a hairy guy with fangs everyone at work not only sees but treats like a new and unpleasant employee. Edward likes to go out and eviscerate college coeds and Jekyll finally figures out what he's become. **79m/C DVD.** Tony Todd, Tracy Scoggins, Vernon Wells, Tim Thomerson, Peter Jason, Stephen Wastell; ***D:*** John Carl Buechler; ***W:*** John Carl Buechler; ***C:*** James M. LeGoy; ***M:*** Andrew Garfield.

The Strange Case of Dr. Rx **1942** What's strange is how boring this Universal flick truly is, probably because it focuses on the dull PI and his personal life more than the crimes. A killer kills killers who were acquitted thanks to a crooked lawyer, leaving a label with the Rx symbol on his victims. PI Jerry Church (Knowles) investigates and thinks his best suspect is sinister Dr. Fish (Atwill with a very brief screen time). And yep, that's "Three Stooges" Howard offering some comic relief. **66m/B DVD.** Patric Knowles, Anne Gwynne, Lionel Atwill, Samuel S. Hinds, Mona Barrie, Shemp Howard, Edmund MacDonald, Mantan Moreland, Paul Cavanagh; ***D:*** William Nigh; ***W:*** Clarence Upson Young; ***C:*** Elwood "Woody" Bredell.

The Strange Case of the End of Civilization As We Know It 1/2 **1993** Cleese stars as the detective grandson of Sherlock Holmes, who also has a reputation for making a mockery of police investigations. Nevertheless, the police commissioner summons him to capture that diabolical criminal Professor Moriarty. **55m/C VHS, DVD.** *GB* Ron Moody, Joss Ackland, Holly Palance, John Cleese, Stratford Johns, Connie Booth, Arthur Lowe; ***D:*** Joseph McGrath; ***W:*** Joseph McGrath, John Cleese; ***C:*** Kenneth Higgins; ***M:*** Ivor Slaney.

Strange Confession **1945** Contains one of the truly rare Inner Sanctum Mysteries from Universal. A scientist working for an unscrupulous pharmaceutical company takes revenge on his boss when the premature release of an untested flu medicine results in the death of his son. **62m/C VHS.** Lon Chaney Jr., Brenda Joyce, J. Carrol Naish, Milburn Stone, Lloyd Bridges; ***D:*** John Hoffman; ***W:*** M. Coates Webster.

The Strange Countess **1961** A girl is almost murdered and no apparent motive can be found until a 20-year-old murder is uncovered in this Edgar Wallace story. **96m/C VHS.** *GE* Joachim Fuchsberger, Lil Dagover, Marianne Hoppe, Brigitte Grothum; ***D:*** Josef von Baky.

Strange Days **1995 (R)** It's 1999 in volatile L.A. and vice cop-turned-street-hustler Lenny Nero (Fiennes) is plying his SQUID trade—discs that offer the wearer the chance to experience any vice. The seedily likeable Lenny draws the line at peddling snuff clips until one capturing the murder of his friend, hooker Iris (Bako), shows up. Lenny's in way over his head and turns to self-sufficient security agent Mace (Bassett) to save him. The phenomenal Bassett heats up the screen (and kicks major butt) while the generally cerebral Fiennes shows why someone could care about his desperate lowlife. Bigelow's an action expert and struts on the film's dark visuals while offering some emotional impact with her society-on-the-eve-of-destruction saga. **145m/C VHS, DVD.** Kelly Hu, Michael Jace, Ralph Fiennes, Angela Bassett, Juliette Lewis, Tom Sizemore, Michael Wincott, Brigitte Bako, Vincent D'Onofrio, William Fichtner, Richard Edson, Glenn Plummer, Josef Sommer; ***D:*** Kathryn Bigelow; ***W:*** James Cameron, Jay Cocks; ***C:*** Matthew F. Leonetti; ***M:*** Graeme Revell.

The Strange Door 1/2 **1951** Laughton hams it up as the evil Alan de Maletroit (Laughton), who's imprisoned his brother Edmond (Cavanagh) for the crime of marrying Alan's one love. Now Maletroit wants to destroy his niece Blanche (Forrest) as well. But Edmond's faithful retainer Voltan (Karloff) is determined to stop the evil. Low-budget hokum adapted from the Robert Louis Stevenson story "The Sire de Maletroits's Door." **81m/B VHS, DVD.** Charles Laughton, Boris Karloff, Paul Cavanagh, Sally Forrest, Richard Stapley, Michael Pate, Alan Napier; ***D:*** Joseph Pevney; ***W:*** Jerry Sackheim; ***C:*** Irving Glassberg.

Strange Fits of Passion 1/2 **1999** Low-budget comedy/drama is McCredie's directorial debut. A nameless overly romantic young woman (Noonan) is convinced that she has just let the perfect man (Finsterer) slip away and she becomes obsessive about finding him again. Her search does not stop her, however, from having some alternative romantic prospects in mind. **83m/C VHS, DVD.** *AU* Michela Noonan, Mitchell Butel, Samuel Johnson, Steve Adams, Anni Finsterer, Jack Finsterer; ***D:*** Elise McCredie; ***W:*** Elise McCredie; ***C:*** Jaems Grant; ***M:*** Cezary Skubiszewski.

Strange Frequency 2 **2001 (R)** Anthology consisting of four episodes from the title TV series: "Soul Man," "Instant Karma," "Cold Turkey," and "Don't Stop Believing." They each have a musical premise and a frequently supernatural twist about the price of fame and success. **84m/C DVD.** Roger Daltrey, Jason Gedrick, Patsy Kensit, Wendie Malick, James Marsters, Peter Strauss; ***D:*** Jeff Woolnough. **TV**

Strange Fruit **2004** Intriguing premise is done in by a sluggish production (although the performances are generally strong). Gay black lawyer William Boyals (Faulcon) reluctantly leaves New York to return to the Louisiana bayou town he left years before after an old friend is found lynched. He needs to conduct his own investigation since the local sheriff (Jones) is a homophobic bigot. **115m/C DVD.** Sam Jones, Cecile Johnson, Kent Faulcon, Berlinda Tolbert, David Raibon; ***D:*** Kyle Schickner; ***W:*** Kyle Schickner; ***C:*** David Oye; ***M:*** Sidney James.

Strange Illusion 1/2 *Out of the Night* **1945** Unbalanced teen Lydon believes his mother, about to remarry, was responsible for his father's death. He feigns insanity in a plan to catch her, but is sent to an asylum, where he nearly goes insane for real. Slow and implausible, but creepy enough to hold your interest. **87m/B VHS, DVD.** Jimmy Lydon, Warren William, Sally Eilers, Regis Toomey, Charles Arnt, George Reed, Jayne Hazard; ***D:*** Edgar G. Ulmer; ***W:*** Adele Comandini; ***C:*** Philip Tannura; ***M:*** Leo Erdody.

Strange Impersonation 1/2 **1946** Dreamy noir has chemist Nora Goodrich (Marshall) injecting herself in order to test a new anesthetic she's developing. (This is never a good idea.) Then her life goes nuts when she can't separate reality from her dreams. **68m/B VHS, DVD.** Brenda Marshall, William Gargan, Hillary Brooke, George Chandler, Ruth Ford, H.B. Warner, Lyle Talbot, Mary Treen; ***D:*** Anthony Mann; ***W:*** Mindret Lord; ***C:*** Robert Pittack.

Strange Interlude *Strange Interval* **1932** Shearer is at her best in screen adaptation of talky Eugene O'Neill play in which she portrays a young wife who wants a child, but discovers that insanity runs in her husband's family. Doing the only sensible thing, she decides to have a child by another man (Gable). Interesting because the characters' thoughts are revealed to the audience through voice-overs. **110m/B VHS.** Norma Shearer, Clark Gable, May Robson, Ralph Morgan, Robert Young, Mary Alden, Maureen O'Sullivan, Henry B. Walthall; ***D:*** Robert Z. Leonard; ***C:*** Lee Garmes.

Strange Interlude 1/2 **1990** Slow PBS production of Eugene O'Neill's famous drama covering two decades of the lives and loves of an upper-class family. Excellent performances help to make up for talkiness. On two cassettes. **190m/C VHS.** Glenda Jackson, Jose Ferrer, David Dukes, Ken Howard, Edward Petherbridge; ***D:*** Herbert Wise.

Strange Invaders **1983 (PG)** Body-snatchers-from-space sci-fi with an attitude—fun spoof of '50s alien flicks. Space folks had taken over a midwestern town in the '50s, assuming the locals' appearance and attire before returning to their ship. Seems one of them married an earthling—but divorced and moved with her half-breed daughter to New York City. So the hicksters from space arrive in Gotham wearing overalls... **94m/C VHS, DVD.** Jack Kehler, Paul LeMat, Nancy Allen, Diana Scarwid, Michael Lerner, Louise Fletcher, Wallace Shawn, Fiona Lewis, Kenneth Tobey, June Lockhart, Charles Lane, Dey Young, Mark Goddard; ***D:*** Michael Laughlin; ***W:*** Bill Condon; ***C:*** Louis Horvath; ***M:*** John Addison.

Strange Justice: The Clarence Thomas and Anita Hill Story 1/2 **1999 (R)** Someone must have lied at the 1991 confirmation hearings for Supreme Court Justice Clarence Thomas (Lindo) and this cable drama takes a look at playing hardball politics. Lobbyist Kenneth Duberstein (Patinkin) is assigned by the Bush White House to get Thomas appointed. But he doesn't anticipate the testimony of Anita Hill (Taylor) and her claims that her former boss sexually harassed her. Based on the nonfiction account by Jane Mayer and Jill Abramson. **111m/C VHS.** Delroy Lindo, Regina Taylor, Mandy Patinkin, Paul Winfield, Louis Gossett Jr.; ***D:*** Ernest R. Dickerson; ***W:*** Jacob Epstein. **CABLE**

The Strange Love of Martha Ivers **1946** Douglas is good in his screen debut as the wimpy spouse of unscrupulous Stanwyck. Stanwyck shines as the woman who must stay with Douglas because of a crime she committed long ago... Tough, dark melodrama; classic film noir. **117m/B VHS, DVD.** Barbara Stanwyck, Van Heflin, Kirk Douglas, Lizabeth Scott, Judith Anderson; ***D:*** Lewis Milestone; ***W:*** Robert Rossen; ***C:*** Victor Milner; ***M:*** Miklos Rozsa.

The Strange Love of Molly Louvain 1/2 *Molly Louvain* **1932** Unwed mother Dvorak finds herself in hiding after her criminal beau fatally shoots a police officer. She falls in love with the unsuspecting newsman (Tracy) hot on her trail. Good performance from Dvorak but the film in general lacks sparkle. Adapted from the play "Tinsel Girl" by Maurine Watkins. **70m/B VHS.** Ann Dvorak, Lee Tracy, Richard Cromwell, Guy Kibbee, Leslie Fenton, Frank McHugh, Evalyn Knapp, Charles Middleton, Mary Doran, C. Henry Gordon; ***D:*** Michael Curtiz; ***W:*** Erwin Gelsey, Brown Holmes.

The Strange Mrs. Crane 1/2 **1948** Gina Crane (Lord) tries to outrun her past life of crime and settles into a comfortable existence as the wife of a politician. When her former partner shows up with blackmail on his mind, she has no choice but to murder him. Innocent Barbara (Brady) gets blamed for the murder, and Gina is selected to serve on the jury. **62m/B DVD.** Marjorie Lord, Robert Shayne, Pierre Watkin, James Seay, Ruth Brady; ***D:*** Sam Newfield; ***W:*** Frank Burt, Robert Libott; ***C:*** Jack Greenhalgh; ***M:*** Paul J. Smith.

Strange New World 1/2 **1975** Three astronauts awake from 188 years in the fridge to find cloning has arrived. Made for TV as a pilot for a hoped-for series that might have been even worse. **100m/C VHS.** John Saxon, Kathleen Miller, Keene Curtis, Martine Beswick, James Olson, Catherine Bach, Richard Farnsworth, Ford Rainey; ***D:*** Robert Butler. **TV**

The Strange One 1/2 **1957** Appropriate title for this dank drama based on Willingham's novel and play "End As a Man." Jacko De Paris (Gazzara) is the student leader at a Southern military school, who uses his power to intimidate and brutalize fellow cadets, aided by minions Knoble (Hingle) and Gatt (Olson). Finally a group of younger students, led by Marquales (Peppard, in his film debut) go after the tyrant. Also filmed as 1957's "Sorority Girl." **100m/B VHS.** Ben Gazzara, Pat Hingle, James Olson, George Peppard, Peter Mark Richman, Larry Gates, Clifton James, Arthur Storch; ***D:*** Jack Garfein; ***W:*** Calder Willingham; ***C:*** Burnett Guffey; ***M:*** Kenyon Hopkins.

Strange Planet 1/2 **1999** Romantic comedy that follows six characters (three young women who share a house and three male buddies) from one New Year's Eve to the next. They have affairs, fall in love, break-up, and get together with different partners over the span of time. It's not new but it's sweet and Watts, Karvan, and Williamson are standouts. **95m/C VHS, DVD.** *AU* Claudia Karvan, Naomi Watts, Alice Garner, Tom Long, Hugo Weaving, Marshall Napier, Aaron Jeffrey, Felix Williamson; ***D:*** Emma-Kate Croghan; ***W:*** Emma-Kate Croghan, Stavros Kazantzidis; ***C:*** Justin Brickle.

Strange Relations **2002** New York shrink Jerry Lipman (Reiser) is diagnosed with leukemia and needs a bone marrow transplant. His mother Esther (Dukakis) finally confesses that Jerry was adopted in England and he heads to Liverpool to find his biological mother. That would be tough-talking, working class Sheila (Walters), who has a soft heart and is eager to welcome Jerry into the family. Jerry keeps his cancer a secret—not wanting to admit that's why he sought out his new relatives, especially as he gets closer to them. Walters is the one to watch but Reiser's sarcasm does help to keep the sentiment at bay. **107m/C VHS, DVD.** Paul Reiser, Julie Walters, George Wendt, Olympia Dukakis, Amy Robbins, Tony Maudsley, Suzanne Hitchmough, Ian Puleston-Davies; ***D:*** Paul Seed; ***W:*** Tim Kazurinsky; ***C:*** Lawrence Jones; ***M:*** Rupert Gregson-Williams. **CABLE**

Strange Shadows in an Empty Room *Blazing Magnums; Shadows in an Empty Room* **1976 (R)** Sleuth Whitman wants answers about the murder of his kid sis. He beats lots of people up, and the viewer leaves the empty living room to look at the inside of the fridge, which is more interesting. De Martino used the pseudonym Martin Herbert. **97m/C VHS.** Stuart Whitman, John Saxon, Martin Landau, Tisa Farrow, Carole Laure, Gayle Hunnicutt; ***D:*** Alberto De Martino.

Strange Wilderness **2008 (R)** Peter Gaulke (Zahn) takes over as host of his dead father's popular wildlife show, but his inept stoner on-air persona pushes it to the brink of cancellation. Desperate, Peter and his loyal soundman Fred Wolf (Covert; note that the writers named the two main characters after themselves) hatch a plan to showcase their search for Bigfoot in Ecuador, with their merry band of dudes in tow. Lots of herbally enhanced gags and goof-ups ensue, none of them particularly amusing (unless you're equally medicated). Given the funny-guy cast, what could have been a clever send-up of nature documentaries is all but wasted (in more ways than one) by the dopey script. **85m/C DVD.** *US* Steve Zahn, Allen Covert, Jonah Hill, Kevin Heffernan, Ashley Scott, Justin Long, Peter Dante, Harry Hamlin, Robert Patrick, Joe Don Baker, Jeff Garlin, Ernest Borgnine; ***D:*** Fred Wolf; ***W:*** Fred Wolf, Peter Gaulke; ***C:*** David Hennings; ***M:*** Waddy Wachtel.

The Strange Woman **1946** Uneventful Hollywood costume drama. Lamarr stalks man after man, but never creates much excitement in spite of Ulmer's fancy camera work and intense pace. **100m/B VHS, DVD.** Hedy Lamarr, George Sanders, Louis Hayward, Gene Lockhart, Hillary Brooke, June Storey; ***D:*** Edgar G. Ulmer; ***W:*** Herb Meadow; ***C:*** Lucien N. Andriot; ***M:*** Carmen Dragon.

Strange World of Coffin Joe *O Estranho Mundo de Ze do Caixao* **1968** A collection of three shocking horror episodes about a truly disgusting dollmaker who becomes tempted by his human-like creations, a balloon seller's repulsive necrophiliac impulses, and a doctor (the disguised Coffin Joe) with a sadistic gift for excruciating torture. In Portugese with English subtitles. **80m/B VHS.** *BR* Jose Mojica Marins; ***D:*** Jose Mojica Marins; ***W:*** Jose Mojica Marins.

The Strangeness **WOOF! 1985** Miners in search of gold release a "strange" creature from far beneath the earth—eek! Made on a negative budget. **90m/C VHS.** Dan Lunham, Terri Berland; ***D:*** David Michael Hillman.

The Stranger 1/2 **1946** Notably conventional for Welles, but swell entertainment nonetheless. War crimes tribunal sets Nazi thug Shayne free hoping he'll lead them to his superior, Welles. Robinson trails Shayne through Europe and South America to a small town in Connecticut. Tight suspense made on a tight budget saved Welles's directorial career. **95m/B VHS, DVD.** Edward G. Robinson, Loretta Young, Martha Wentworth, Konstantin Shayne, Richard Long, Orson Welles; ***D:*** Orson Welles; ***W:*** Victor Trivas; ***C:*** Russell Metty; ***M:*** Bronislau Kaper.

The Stranger 1/2 **1973** Corbett crash-lands on a planet an awful lot like Earth—and must stay on the run. Uneven fugitive thriller in sci-fi drag. Made for TV. **100m/C VHS.** Cameron Mitchell, Glenn Corbett, Sharon Acker, Lew Ayres, George Coulouris, Dean Jagger; ***D:*** Lee H. Katzin. **TV**

The Stranger **1987 (R)** Amnesiac car-wreck victim Bedelia begins regaining her memory, and realizes she witnessed several grisly murders. Is her shrink (Riegert) helping her remember, or keeping something from her? Good, neglected thriller. **93m/C VHS.** *AR* Bonnie Bedelia, Peter Riegert, Barry Primus, David Spielberg, Julio de Grazia, Cecilia (Celia) Roth, Marcus Woinski; ***D:*** Adolfo Aristarain; ***W:*** Dan Gurskis; ***M:*** Craig Safan.

The Stranger 1/2 **1992** Quiet comedy about family loyalties and devalued traditions. The upper-middle-class life of Sudhindra Bose is disturbed by the arrival of his wife Anila's long-lost uncle Manomohan. Although their young son is excited by the visit of this mysterious relative, Anila is bewildered and her husband suspicious—he thinks the man may be an imposter after their money. The independent Manomohan realizes the family's discomfort and slowly turns the tables on all their questions. Ray's last film. In Bengali with English subtitles. **100m/C VHS.** *IN* Deepankar De, Mamata Shankar, Bikram Bhattacharya, Utpal Dutt, Dhritiman Chatterji, Rabi Ghosh, Subrata Chatterji; ***D:*** Satyajit Ray; ***W:*** Satyajit Ray.

The Stranger **1995 (R)** Mystery woman (Long) rides into small town and rids it of a vicious motorcycle gang. Femme version of the lone hero saga. **98m/C VHS.** Kathy Long, Andrew Divoff, Eric Pierpoint, Robin Lynn Heath; ***D:*** Fritz Kiersch; ***W:*** Gregory Poirier.

A Stranger Among Us **1992 (PG-13)** A missing jeweler turns up dead and more than $1 million in diamonds has disappeared. NYPD Detective Emily Eden (Griffith) is called in to solve the case, and she decides she must go undercover in a community of Hasidic Jews to find the perpetrator. She not only finds the criminal, but she also falls in love with one of the group's most devout residents. Griffith is out of her element as a tough cop with her baby voice and cutesy style, but other actors, including Thal (in his movie debut) and Sara, perform splendidly, even though they're held back by a cumbersome script with many similarities to "Witness." **109m/C VHS, DVD.** James Gandolfini, Melanie Griffith, Eric Thal, John Pankow, Tracy Pollan, Lee Richardson, Mia Sara, Jamey Sheridan; ***D:*** Sidney Lumet; ***W:*** Robert J. Avrech; ***C:*** Andrzej Bartkowiak; ***M:*** Jerry Bock. Golden Raspberries '92: Worst Actress (Griffith).

The Stranger and the Gunfighter **1976** The baddest spaghetti western of all time—or is it a kung fu movie? Alcoholic cowpoke Van Cleef and kung fu master Lieh pair up to find hidden treasure. There is a map, but parts are printed on the assorted fannies of various women. **106m/C VHS.** *IT* Patty (Patti) Shepard, Lee Van Cleef, Lo Lieh; ***D:*** Anthony M. Dawson.

Stranger by Night **1994 (R)** Detective Bobby Corcoran and his partner are hunting a mutilating serial killer. Since Corcoran suffers from black-outs and fits of rage the evidence begins pointing very close to home. **96m/C VHS, DVD.** Steven Bauer, William Katt, Jennifer Rubin, Michael Parks, Michele Greene, J.J. Johnston; ***D:*** Gregory Brown; ***W:*** Daryl Haney; ***C:*** Wally Pfister; ***M:*** Ashley Irwin.

The Stranger from Arizona 1/2 **1938** Buck Weylan (Jones) and his pal Skeeter (Worden) get a job as cow hands on Ann's (Fay) ranch in order to investigate cattle rustling. Seems once the cattle are loaded onto boxcars at the rail station, the cows and the boxcars disappear! **54m/B DVD.** Buck Jones, Dorothy Fay, Hank Worden, Hank Mann, Roy Barcroft, Bob Terry, Horace Murphy; ***D:*** Elmer Clifton; ***W:*** Monroe Shaff; ***C:*** Edward Linden.

The Stranger from Pecos **1945** Brown fights a cheater who swindles people at poker and then uses the money to buy their mortgages. Meanwhile, his pal Hatton finds a novel way to help a robbery victim buy back his property. **55m/B VHS.** Johnny Mack Brown, Raymond Hatton, Kirby Grant, Christine McIntyre, Steve Clark, Kermit Maynard; ***D:*** Lambert Hillyer.

The Stranger from Venus **WOOF!** *Immediate Disaster; The Venusian* **1954** "The Day the Earth Stood Still" warmed over. Venusian Dantine tells earth lady Neal he's worried about the future of her planet. Real low budget. Includes previews of coming attractions from classic sci-fi. **78m/B VHS, DVD.** Patricia Neal, Helmut Dantine, Derek Bond; ***D:*** Bob Balaban; ***W:*** Hans Jacoby; ***C:*** Ken Talbot; ***M:*** Eric Spear.

Stranger in Paso Bravo **1968** A distraught drifter returns to a strange Italian town to avenge the murders of his wife and daughter years before. Dubbed. **92m/C VHS.** *IT* Anthony Steffen, Giulia Rubini, Eduardo Fajardo, Andriana Ambesi; ***D:*** Salvatore Rosso; ***W:*** Lucio Battistrada; ***C:*** Alfonso Nieva; ***M:*** Angelo Francesco Lavagnino.

Stranger in the House **1997 (R)** Jack (Railsback) hid a diamond necklace in an old house after his heist went bad. When he gets out of prison and goes to retrieve his loot, he discovers the house is now occupied by Joanna (Greene) and Dan (Dinsmore). Turns out Dan wants to kill Joanna for her money, and Jack's being pursued by an insurance adjuster (Vrana) after the necklace. **94m/C VHS.** Michele Greene, Steve Railsback, Bruce Dinsmore, Vlasta Vrana; ***D:*** Rodney Gibbons; ***W:*** Peter Paul Liapis, Steve Pesce; ***M:*** Marty Simon. **VIDEO**

A Stranger in the Kingdom **1998 (R)** Walt Andrews (Hudson) has been hired sight unseen to be the new minister in a small Vermont community in the '50s. The unseen part is a problem since the townspeople are shocked when Walt turns out to be black. Then Walt gets arrested for the murder of a young housekeeper, Claire (Bayne), whom he was sheltering from her abusive employer and the town seems determined to make him the scapegoat. Based on a Howard Frank Mosher novel. **111m/C VHS, DVD.** Ernie Hudson, David Lansbury, Jean (Louisa) Kelly, Martin Sheen, Sean Nelson, Jordan Bayne, Bill Raymond, Henry Gibson, Larry Pine, Tom Aldredge, Carrie Snodgress; ***D:*** Jay Craven; ***W:*** Jay Craven, Don Bredes; ***C:*** Philip Holahan.

Stranger in Town **1957** A young journalist looks into the murder of an American composer in a sleepy English village. He discovers blackmail and intrigue. So-so thriller. Based on the novel "The Uninvited" by Frank Chittenden. **73m/B VHS.** *GB* Alex Nicol, Ann Page, Mary Laura Wood, Mona Washbourne, Charles Lloyd-Pack; ***D:*** George Pollock.

A Stranger in Town 1/2 **1995** Single mom Kay Tarses (Smart) has relocated to a small, quiet town with her infant son. But her peace is disturbed by menacing Barnes (Hines), a stranger who seems to know Kay has been lying about her past—and her child. When he seems determined to take her child, Kay has to decide whether to run, accept her fate, or fight. **93m/C VHS, DVD.** Jean Smart, Gregory Hines, Jeffrey Nordling, Lucinda Jenney, Richard Riehle; ***D:*** Peter Levin; ***M:*** Mark Snow. **TV**

A Stranger Is Watching 1/2 **1982 (R)** Rapist-murderer Torn holds his victim's 10-year-old daughter hostage, along with a New York TV anchorwoman. Complicated and distasteful. **92m/C VHS, DVD.** Rip Torn, Kate Mulgrew, James Naughton; ***D:*** Sean S. Cunningham. **TV**

The Stranger: Kabloonak 1/2 *Kabloonak* **1995** Pioneering filmmaker Robert Flaherty (Dance) premieres his documentary "Nanook of the North" in 1922 and recalls (in flashback) his difficulties in making the film. History has been tweaked but the cinematography is gorgeous and Dance's lead performance is strong. **105m/C VHS.** *CA FR* Charles Dance; ***D:*** Claude Massot; ***W:*** Claude Massot; ***C:*** Jacques Loiseleux, François Protat, Sebastian Regnier.

Stranger on Horseback **1955** Circuit Court Judge Richard Thorne (McCrea) is determined to bring suspected killer Tom Bannerman (McCarthy) to trial even though Bannerman's cattle baron father (McIntire) controls the town. But the judge isn't above using his six-shooters to make that happen. Based on a story by Louis L'Amour. **66m/C DVD.** Joel McCrea, Kevin McCarthy, John McIntire, Miroslava Stern, John Carradine, Nancy Gates, Emile Meyer; ***D:*** Jacques Tourneur; ***W:*** Don Martin, Herb Meadow; ***C:*** Ray Rennahan; ***M:*** Paul Dunlap.

Stranger on the Third Floor **1940** Reporter McGuire's testimony helped convict cabbie Cook of murder, but he begins to have doubts. Odd, shadowy psycho-thriller considered by some the first film noir. The reporter comes to be suspected of the crime...and his fiancee pounds the pavement to prove him innocent. Average acting, but great camera work gives the whole a deliciously menacing feel. **64m/B VHS.** Peter Lorre, John McGuire, Elisha Cook Jr., Margaret Tallichet, Charles Halton; ***D:*** Boris Ingster.

Stranger than Fiction 1/2 **1999 (R)** Would-be horror thriller wastes its talented cast. Jared (Astin) arrives, hysterical and bloody, at the home of his best friend, Austin (Field), with some confusing tale about a murder in his apartment. Austin, Jared and their friends Emma (Meyer) and Violet (Wagner) return to the scene of the crime, only to discover that Jared has been less than honest with them. **100m/C VHS, DVD.** MacKenzie Astin, Todd Field, Dina Meyer, Natasha Gregson Wagner; ***D:*** Eric Bross; ***W:*** Tim Garrick, Scott Russell; ***C:*** Horacio Marquinez; ***M:*** Larry Seymour.

Stranger Than Fiction 1/2 **2006 (PG-13)** Ferrell stars as milquetoast everyman Harold Crick, a Chicago IRS agent living a tiny little life, which he suddenly starts hearing his life narrated by a British-accented woman. Harold appears to be a character in writer Kay Eiffel's (Thompson) latest book in which that character is supposed to die. Except neurotic Kay has terrible writer's block and can't think of an appropriate way to kill him. Harold, real or imaginary, doesn't want to die and seeks the services of literature professor Jules Hilbert (Hoffman), who advises Harold to do what he's always wanted to do, prompting Harold to turn to feisty baker Ana (Gyllenhaal). Good move, Harold. Cast is first-rate but, remember, Ferrell is supposed to be low-key. **113m/C DVD, Blu-ray Disc.** *US* Will Ferrell, Maggie Gyllenhaal, Dustin Hoffman, Emma Thompson, Queen Latifah, Tony Hale, Tom Hulce, Linda Hunt; ***D:*** Marc Forster; ***W:*** Zach Helm; ***C:*** Roberto Schaefer; ***M:*** Brian Reitzell, Britt Daniel.

Stranger than Paradise **1984 (R)** Would-be New York hipster Willie (Lurie) is a Hungarian emigre who is asked to look after his newly arrived teenaged cousin Eva (Balint). They develop a weird affectionate relationship before Eva heads to Cleveland to live with an aunt (Stark). When Willie realizes he misses her, he and buddy Eddie (Edson) drive to visit her and the threesome then decide to head to Florida for some fun in the sun. The thinking person's mindless flick. Inventive, independent comedy made on quite a low budget was acclaimed at Cannes. **90m/B VHS, DVD.** *GE* John Lurie, Eszter Balint, Richard Edson, Sara Driver, Cecillia Stark, Danny Rosen; ***D:*** Jim Jarmusch; ***W:*** Jim Jarmusch; ***C:*** Tom DiCillo; ***M:*** John Lurie. Natl. Film Reg. '02;; Natl. Soc. Film Critics '84: Film.

The Stranger Who Looks Like Me **1974** Adoptees Baxter and Bridges set out to find their real parents. Not-bad TV fare. Blake is Baxter's real-life mom. Look for a young Patrick Duffy. **74m/C VHS.** Meredith Baxter, Beau Bridges, Whitney Blake; ***D:*** Larry Peerce.

The Stranger Within 1/2 **1974** Made-for-TV "Rosemary's Baby" rip-off. Eden is in a family way, though hubby Grizzard is impotent. The stranger within begins commanding her to do its bidding, just as if she were a genie. **74m/C VHS.** Barbara Eden, George Grizzard, Joyce Van Patten, Nehemiah Persoff; ***D:*** Lee Philips; ***M:*** Charles Fox. **TV**

The Stranger Wore a Gun **1953** Hoping to remove a black mark against his name, Jeff Travis (Scott) goes to Arizona and ends up foiling a stagecoach robbery. Features a great action sequence in a burning saloon. Originally shot in 3-D, this is based on the novel "Yankee Gold" by John M. Cunningham. **83m/C VHS, DVD.** Randolph Scott, Claire Trevor, Joan Weldon, George Macready, Alfonso Bedoya, Lee Marvin, Ernest Borgnine, Pierre Watkin, Joseph (Joe) Vitale; ***D:*** Andre de Toth.

Strangers **1990** Australian horror film revolves around a man in a troubled marriage who fools around with another woman, only to realize she is dead set on mating for life. When he hesitates, she vows to murder his wife. Very similar to the smash hit "Fatal Attraction." **83m/C VHS.** *AU* James Healey, Anne Looby; ***D:*** Craig Lahiff.

Strangers **1991 (R)** Features three provocative vignettes that take place far from home. Fiorentino, Chen, and Hutton each star in an erotic story played out in a foreign land. **85m/C VHS.** Linda Fiorentino, Joan Chen, Timothy Hutton; ***D:*** Joan Tewkesbury.

The Strangers 🦴 **1998** Seems Trent doesn't know as much about his lover Jade as he thinks—until she turns him into a werewolf. He gets away and hides out in the small town of Pine Fork, even beginning to fall in love. Then Jade shows up with her new boyfriend—looking for revenge and fresh meat. **90m/C VHS, DVD.** Richard Bent, Shanna Betz, Victoria Hunter, Jennifer Marks, Matt Martin, Jimmy Lord, J.J. Denton, Joe Durrenberger; ***D:*** Charles Solomon Jr., Peter Cohl; ***W:*** Charles Solomon Jr., Peter Cohl, Steven Weller; ***C:*** Anthony Moncado. **VIDEO**

The Strangers 🦴🦴 **2008 (R)** Young couple James (Speedman) and Kristen (Tyler) retreat to the family cabin after attending an emotionally draining wedding, but they soon discover that they're not alone. A trio of creepy masked psychos quietly stalk the cabin, eventually inflicting utter horror upon the couple. Nearly every slasher flick convention is on display, as expected, but without the cheese, thanks to the patient and skillful execution of rookie director Bertino, who winds the suspense and fear into what we see as well as what we don't. Nevertheless, it still borders on snuff. **90m/C DVD, Blu-ray Disc.** *US* Liv Tyler, Scott Speedman, Glenn Howerton, Gemma Ward, Kip Weeks, Laura Margolis; ***D:*** Bryan Bertino; ***W:*** Bryan Bertino; ***C:*** Peter Sova; ***M:*** Tomandandy.

A Stranger's Heart 🦴 **1/2 2007** A sappy yet faintly disturbing story. Callie's (Mathis) parents died when she was a child and she was raised by relatives. She's always been sickly and now needs a new heart. She meets fellow patient Jasper (Dobson) in the hospital and both receive successful transplants. As their feelings for each other grow stronger during their recoveries, the two are also drawn to young Cricket (Mouser), who turns out to be the now-orphaned daughter of their donors. **85m/C DVD.** Samantha Mathis, Peter Dobson, Kevin Kilner, June Squibb, Thomas Kopache, Raynor Scheine, Marilyn Matilyn Mouser, Gina Hecht; ***D:*** Andy Wolk; ***W:*** Kelli Pryor; ***C:*** Maximo Munzi; ***M:*** Lawrence Shragge. **CABLE**

Strangers in Good Company 🦴🦴🦴 *The Company of Strangers* **1991 (PG)** A loving metaphor to growing older. Director Scott uses non-actors for every role in this quiet little film about a bus-load of elderly women lost in the Canadian wilderness. They wait for rescue without hystrionics, using the opportunity instead to get to know each other and nature. Beautifully made, intelligent, uncommon and worthwhile. **101m/C VHS, DVD.** *CA* Alice Diabo, Mary Meigs, Cissy Meddings, Beth Webber, Winifred Holden, Constance Garneau, Catherine Roche, Michelle Sweeney; ***D:*** Cynthia Scott; ***W:*** Cynthia Scott, David Wilson, Gloria Demers, Sally Bochner; ***M:*** Marie Bernard.

Strangers in Love 🦴 **1/2 1932** Routine melodrama. Evil twin (March) cheats his brother out of his share of their father's inheritance by faking the will. But when he suddenly dies, nice bro assumes his identity, makes amends for his wickedness, and gets the girl (Francis). **76m/B VHS.** Fredric March, Kay Francis, Stuart Erwin, Sidney Toler, Juliette Compton, George Barbier; ***D:*** Lothar Mendes; ***W:*** Grover Jones, William Slavens McNutt; ***C:*** Henry Sharp.

Strangers in Paradise 🦴 **1/2 1984** A scientist who had cryogenically frozen himself to escape the Nazis is thawed out in the present, and his powers are used by a delinquent-obsessed sociopath. **81m/C VHS.** Ulli Lommel, Ken Letner, Geoffrey Barker, Thom Jones; ***D:*** Ulli Lommel; ***W:*** Ulli Lommel; ***M:*** William Pettyjohn.

Strangers in the City 🦴🦴 **1962** Puerto Ricans newly arrived in New York try to make their way. Serious but slightly overwrought immigrant-family melodrama. **80m/B VHS.** Robert Gentile, Camilo Delgado, Rosita De Triana; ***D:*** Rick Carrier.

Strangers Kiss 🦴🦴 **1/2 1983 (R)** Circa 1955: Hollywood director encourages his two leads to have an off-screen romance to bring reality to his film. Conflict arises when the leading lady's boyfriend, the film's financier, gets wind of the scheme. Intriguing, fun, slightly off-center. Based on Stanley Kubrick's film "Killer Kiss." **93m/C VHS.** Peter Coyote, Victoria Tennant, Blaine Novak, Dan Shor, Richard Romanus, Linda Kerridge, Carlos Palomino; ***D:*** Matthew Chapman; ***W:*** Blaine Novak, Matthew Chapman; ***M:*** Gato Barbieri.

Strangers of the Evening 🦴🦴 **1932** In its day this dark comedy/mystery caught flak for its gruesomeness. There's been a mixup at the undertaker's, and the wrong body was buried—possibly alive. Good photography and acting make the humor work, intentionally or not. Based on the novel "The Illustrious Corpse," by Tiffany Thayer. **70m/B VHS.** Zasu Pitts, Eugene Pallette, Lucien Littlefield, Tully Marshall, Miriam Seegar, Theodore von Eltz; ***D:*** H. Bruce Humberstone.

Strangers on a Train 🦴🦴🦴🦴 **1951** Long before there was "Throw Momma from the Train," there was this Hitchcock superthriller about two passengers who accidentally meet and plan to "trade" murders. Amoral Walker wants the exchange and the money he'll inherit by his father's death; Granger would love to end his stifling marriage and wed Roman, a senator's daughter, but finds the idea ultimately sickening. What happens is pure Hitchcock. Screenplay cowritten by murder-mystery great Chandler. Patricia Hitchcock, the director's only child, plays Roman's sister. The concluding "carousel" scene is a masterpiece. From the novel by Patricia Highsmith. **101m/B VHS, DVD.** Farley Granger, Robert Walker, Ruth Roman, Leo G. Carroll, Patricia Hitchcock, Marion Lorne; ***D:*** Alfred Hitchcock; ***W:*** Raymond Chandler; ***C:*** Robert Burks; ***M:*** Dimitri Tiomkin.

Strangers: The Story of a Mother and Daughter 🦴🦴🦴 **1979** Rowlands is the long-estranged daughter of Davis, who won an Emmy for her portrayal of the embittered widow. The great actress truly is at her recent best in this made-for-TV tearjerker, and Rowlands keeps pace. **88m/C VHS.** Bette Davis, Gena Rowlands, Ford Rainey, Donald Moffat; ***D:*** Milton Katselas.

Strangers When We Meet 🦴🦴 **1/2 1960** A married architect and his equally married neighbor begin an affair. Their lives become a series of deceptions. Lavish but uninvolving soaper. Written by Evan Hunter and based on his novel. **117m/B VHS, DVD.** Kirk Douglas, Kim Novak, Ernie Kovacs, Walter Matthau, Barbara Rush, Virginia Bruce, Kent Smith; ***D:*** Richard Quine; ***C:*** Charles B(ryant) Lang Jr.

Strangers with Candy 🦴🦴 **2006 (R)** Sedaris takes her Comedy Central series to the big screen with all its crude tackiness on display. Jerri is a middle-aged ex-junkie, exhooker, ex-con who goes back to high school and wants to win the science fair to make her comatose dad proud. Calling her dim-witted would be kind. But she's in good company because mostly everyone around her falls into freak territory. It's one over-extended sketch with a lead you don't really want to spend time with unless you're already a fan. **97m/C DVD.** *US* Amy Sedaris, Paul Dinello, Stephen Colbert, Deborah Rush, Greg Hollimon, Dan Hedaya, Allison Janney, Philip Seymour Hoffman, Kristen Johnston, Justin Theroux, Matthew Broderick, Sarah Jessica Parker, Ian Holm, Carlo Alban, Maria Thayer, Elisabeth Harnois, Chris Pratt, Elisabeth Harnois, Joseph Cross, David Pasquesi, Alicia Ashley, Ryan Donowho; ***D:*** Paul Dinello; ***W:*** Amy Sedaris, Paul Dinello, Stephen Colbert; ***C:*** Oliver Bokelberg.

Stranglehold 🦴 **1/2 1994 (R)** Cooper (Trimble) is the executive assistant of Congresswoman Fillmore (McWhirter), who becomes the hostage of a nerve gas holding nutcase (Wells). Cooper manages to evade the nutcase's thugs while using his martial arts prowess to rescue his boss. **73m/C VHS, DVD.** *AU* Jerry Trimble, Jillian McWhirter, Vernon Wells; ***D:*** Cirio H. Santiago.

The Strangler 🦴 **1/2 1964** A confused, mother-fixated psychopath strangles young women. Made at the time the Boston Strangler was terrorizing Beantown. The film slayer strangles ten lasses before his love of dolls gives him away. **89m/B VHS, DVD.** Victor Buono, David McLean, Diane Sayer, Ellen Corby, Jeanne Bates, James B. Sikking; ***D:*** Burt Topper.

Strangler of Blackmoor Castle 🦴🦴 **1963** Someone is murdering people at an old English castle and Scotland Yard sends an investigator to track down the killer. **87m/B VHS, DVD.** *GE* Karin Dor, Ingmar Zeisberg, Harry Riebauer, Rudolf Fernau, Hans Nielsen, Dieter Eppler; ***D:*** Harald Reinl; ***W:*** Ladislas Fodor; ***C:*** Ernst W. Kalinke; ***M:*** Oskar Sala.

Strangler of the Swamp 🦴 **1/2 1946** The ghost of an innocent man wrongly hanged for murder returns to terrorize the village where he was lynched. Decidedly B-grade horror features an out-of-focus ghost and Edwards—on the other side of the camera—as one of his would-be victims. **60m/B VHS, DVD.** Rosemary La Planche, Blake Edwards, Charles Middleton, Robert Barrat; ***D:*** Frank Wisbar; ***W:*** Frank Wisbar; ***C:*** James S. Brown Jr.

The Stranglers of Bombay 🦴🦴 **1960** Lurid low-budget Hammer production. Captain Lewis (Rolfe) works for the East India Company in the 1820s. His superiors refuse to listen when he tells them about all the people who have gone missing in the area so he continues his investigation on his own. Lewis discovers that followers of Kali, a blood-thirsty cult known as the Stranglers, are behind the mayhem and he resolves to put a stop to their terror. **80m/B DVD.** *GB* Guy Rolfe, Allan Cuthbertson, George Pastell, Marne Maitland, Jan Holden, John Harvey, Andrew Cruickshank, Paul Stassino, Michael Nightngale; ***D:*** Terence Fisher; ***W:*** David Zelag Goodman, James Bernard; ***C:*** Arthur Grant; ***M:*** James Bernard.

Strapless 🦴🦴 **1/2 1990 (R)** Just-turned-40 American doctor Brown lives and works in London. She has just ended a long-term romance, and takes up with suave foreigner Ganz. Her young sister Fonda, arrives for a visit. Good, interesting if sometimes plodding story of adult relationships. **99m/C VHS, DVD.** *GB* Blair Brown, Bridget Fonda, Bruno Ganz, Alan Howard, Michael Gough, Hugh Laurie, Suzanne Burden, Camille Coduri, Alexandra Pigg, Billy Roch, Gary O'Brien; ***D:*** David Hare; ***W:*** David Hare; ***C:*** Andrew Dunn; ***M:*** Nick Bicat.

Strapped 🦴🦴 **1/2 1993** Earnest urban drama about a young man who needs quick cash and turns to selling guns to get it. ("Strapped" in street lingo means both carrying a gun and needing money.) Diquan's (Woodbine) pregnant girlfriend is in jail for selling crack and he doesn't have the bail money. So he and a partner begin selling guns but it turns out Diquan has also cut a deal with the cops and the deal doesn't stay a secret for long. Whitaker's directorial debut. **102m/C VHS, DVD.** Bokeem Woodbine, Kia Joy Goodwin, Fred "Fredro" Scruggs, Michael Biehn, Craig Wasson; ***D:*** Forest Whitaker; ***W:*** Dena Kleiman. **CABLE**

Strategic Air Command 🦴🦴 **1/2 1955** A classic post-WWII chunk of Air Force patriotism. Veteran third baseman Stewart is recalled to flight duty at the hint of a nuclear war. He's already put in his time in the Big One and thinks he's being singled out now, but he answers his Uncle Sam's call. Allyson plays Stewart's wife for the third time. **114m/C VHS.** James Stewart, June Allyson, Frank Lovejoy, Barry Sullivan; ***D:*** Anthony Mann; ***C:*** William H. Daniels.

The Stratton Story 🦴🦴🦴 **1949** Stewart and Allyson teamed up for the first of the three pictures they'd make together in this true story of Monty Stratton, the Chicago White Sox pitcher. A baseball phenom, Stratton suffers a devastating hunting accident which leads to the amputation of one leg. Learning to walk with an artificial limb, Stratton also struggles to resume his baseball career. Stewart's fine as always, with Allyson lending noble support as the loving wife. Chisox manager Jimmy Dykes played himself as did pitcher Gene Bearden, lending further authenticity to an excellent production. **106m/B VHS, DVD.** James Stewart, June Allyson, Frank Morgan, Agnes Moorehead, Bill Williams, Bruce Cowling; ***D:*** Sam Wood; ***W:*** Guy Trosper, Douglas S. Morrow. Oscars '49: Story.

The Strauss Family 🦴🦴 **1/2 1973** British miniseries covers the drama and scandal surrounding 85 years in the lives of the musical Strauss family of 19th-century Vienna. Woolfe is patriarch Johann Strauss, whose son Schanni (Wilson) will exclipse his egotistical father's talents. Music performed by the London Symphony Orchestra. On 4 cassettes. **390m/C VHS, DVD.** *GB* Eric Woolfe, Stuart Wilson, Anne Stallybrass, Derek Jacobi, Jane Seymour; ***D:*** David Giles, Peter Potter, David Reid; ***W:*** David Butler, David Reid, Anthony Skene. **TV**

Straw Dogs 🦴🦴🦴 **1972 (R)** An American mathematician, disturbed by the predominance of violence in American society, moves with his wife to an isolated Cornish village. He finds that primitive savagery exists beneath the most peaceful surface. After his wife is raped, Hoffman's character seeks revenge. Hoffman is good, a little too wimpy at times. A violent, frightening film reaction to the violence of the 1960s. **118m/C VHS, DVD.** *GB* Sally Thomsett, Colin Welland, Peter Arne, Dustin Hoffman, Susan George, Peter Vaughan, T.P. McKenna, David Warner; ***D:*** Sam Peckinpah; ***W:*** Sam Peckinpah, David Zelag Goodman; ***C:*** John Coquillon; ***M:*** Jerry Fielding.

Strawberry and Chocolate 🦴🦴🦴 *Fresa y Chocolate* **1993 (R)** Sex, politics, and friendship set in 1979 Havana. University student David (Cruz) is sitting morosely in a cafe eating chocolate ice cream when he's spotted by older, educated, gay, strawberry-eating Diego (Perugorria), who manages to persuade David to visit him at his apartment. Resolutely hetero (and communist), David is appalled not only by Diego's sexuality but by his subversive politics. But gradually David's seduced by Diego's ideas and friendship into questioning the regime's harsh policies (and homophobia). Satiric and sympathetic—not only to the characters but to Cuba itself. Ill with cancer, Gutierrez Alea finished the film with the aid of Tabio. From the short story "The Wolf, the Forest and the New Man" by sceenwriter Paz. Spanish with subtitles. **110m/C VHS, DVD.** *CU* Jorge Perugorria, Vladimir Cruz, Mirta Ibarra, Francisco Gattorno, Jorge Angelino, Marilyn Solaya; ***D:*** Tomas Gutierrez Alea, Juan Carlos Tabio; ***W:*** Tomas Gutierrez Alea, Senel Paz; ***C:*** Mario Garcia Joya; ***M:*** Jose Maria Vitier.

Strawberry Blonde 🦴🦴🦴 **1941** A romantic comedy set in the 1890s, with Cagney as a would-be dentist infatuated with money-grubbing Hayworth (the strawberry blonde of the title), who wonders years later whether he married the right woman (chestnut brunette de Havilland). Attractive period piece remade from 1933's "One Sunday Afternoon," and revived yet again in 1948 by Raoul Walsh. **100m/B VHS.** James Cagney, Olivia de Havilland, Rita Hayworth, Alan Hale, George Tobias, Jack Carson, Una O'Connor, George Reeves; ***D:*** Raoul Walsh; ***W:*** Julius J. Epstein, Philip G. Epstein; ***C:*** James Wong Howe.

Strawberry Fields 🦴🦴 **1997** Rebellious teenaged Japanese-American Irene (Nakamura) takes off on a road trip of self-discovery with her boyfriend, whom she soon dumps to spend quality time alone in the Arizona desert figuring out life. **86m/C VHS, DVD.** Suzy Nakamura, James Sie, Chris Tashima, Marilyn Tokuda, Reiko Mathieu, Peter Yoshida, Heather Yoshimura, Takayo Fischer; ***D:*** Rea Tajiri; ***W:*** Rea Tajiri, Kerri Sakamoto; ***C:*** Zack Winestine; ***M:*** Bundy Brown.

Strawberry Roan 🦴🦴 **1933** Maynard plays a stubborn rodeo cowboy, out to prove he ain't whipped yet. One of Maynard's most popular films. Gene Autry bought the story to help him out in later years; the 1948 Autry "remake" uses only the title. **59m/B VHS.** Ken Maynard, Ruth Hall; ***D:*** Ken Maynard.

The Strawberry Statement 🦴🦴 **1970 (R)** Dated message film about a campus radical who persuades a college student to take part in the student strikes on campus during the '60s. Ambitious anti-violence message is lost in too many subplots. Soundtrack features songs by Crosby, Stills, Nash and Young and John Lennon. **109m/C VHS.** Kim Darby, Bruce Davison, Bud Cort, James Coco, Kristina Holland, Bob Balaban, David Dukes, Jeannie Berlin; ***D:*** Stuart Hagmann; ***W:*** Israel Horovitz. Cannes '70: Special Jury Prize.

The Stray 🦴🦴 **2000 (R)** When Vonna Grayson (Everhart) accidentally hits a homeless man (Lysenko) when she's driving home, she insists on having him recover at her ranch. Soon the relationship becomes romantic, but her "stray" has a hidden agenda and Vonna winds up in danger. **98m/C VHS, DVD.** Angie Everhart, Stefan Lysenko, Michael Madsen, Frank Zagarino, Seidy Lopez; ***D:*** Kevin Mock; ***W:*** Terry Cunningham; ***C:*** Ken Blakey; ***M:*** John Sponsler. **VIDEO**

Stray Bullet 𝒮 **1998 (R)** Attorney John Burnside (Carradine) mistakenly picks up the luggage of fellow traveler Stella Crosby (Staab), who invites him to her home for a party. But John gets kidnapped from the party by some thugs who are owed money by Stella's husband, who they have mistaken John for. Instead of setting things straight, Stella persuades John to pose as her husband until she can works things out. John agrees because he has the hots for Stella. John's very dumb. **86m/C VHS.** Robert Carradine, Rebecca Staab, Fred (John F.) Dryer, Ian Beattie; ***D:*** Robert Spera; ***W:*** Christopher Wood; ***C:*** Jules Labarthe; ***M:*** Arthur Kempel. **VIDEO**

Stray Dog 𝒮𝒮𝒮 **1949** A tense, early genre piece by Kurosawa, about a police detective who has his revolver picked from his pocket on a bus, and realizes soon after it's being used in a series of murders. Technically somewhat flawed, but tense and intense. Mifune's pursuit of the criminal with his gun becomes metaphorically compelling. In Japanese with English subtitles. **122m/B VHS, DVD.** *JP* Toshiro Mifune, Takashi Shimura, Isao Kimura; ***D:*** Akira Kurosawa.

Stray Dog 𝒮𝒮 *Stray Dogs; Stray Dog: Kerberos Panzer Cops; Jigoku no banken: kerubersu* **1991** Second film in Mamoru Oshii's Kerberos Panzer Corps saga is the prequel of "The Red Spectacles," and the sequel to the last film "Jin-Roh." Begins with the Kerberos armored police unit making a last stand against the military after being told to disband. Three of them flee via helicopter, and the lone witness is imprisoned for three years, until he is sprung by a group seeking the escaped Kerberos, so he goes off to find his former coworkers. **95m/C DVD.** Shigeru Chiba, Takashi Matsuyama, Yoshikazu Fujiki, Eaching Sue; ***D:*** Mamoru Oshii; ***W:*** Mamoru Oshii; ***C:*** Yousuke Mamiya; ***M:*** Kenji Kawai.

Strayed 𝒮𝒮𝒮 *Les Egares* **2003** Set in the chaotic summer of 1940, when the Germans invaded France. Film follows the flight of recently widowed schoolteacher Odile (Beart) and her children, 13-year-old Philippe (Leprince-Ringuet) and 7-year-old Cathy (Meyer), out of Paris. Part of a stream of refugees heading south, the family is forced into the countryside when German planes strafe the roads; there they meet 17-year-old Yvan (Ulliel), who's illiterate but skilled at survival. Stumbling across an abandoned villa, the foursome set aside their uncertainties to manage a precarious semblance of family life as the sexual tension between Odile and Yvan grows. Since Techine specializes in character studies, this is a story about conflict and desire, civilization versus savagery. Based on the 1983 novel, "The Boy With Grey Eyes," by Gilles Perrault; French with subtitles. **95m/C VHS, DVD.** *FR* Emmanuelle Beart, Samuel Labarthe, Gaspard Ulliel, Gregoire Leprince-Ringuet, Clemence Meyer, Jean Fornerod; ***D:*** Andre Techine; ***W:*** Andre Techine, Gilles Taurand; ***C:*** Agnes Godard; ***M:*** Philippe Sarde.

Strays 𝒮𝒮 **1991 (R)** Here kitty kitty! A young couple move into their dream home, convinced it is the perfect place to raise their daughter. What they don't know is that the area is populated by a pack of wild cats. Before they can get rid of the kitties, one has marked their bedroom as his territory and they find themselves battling a swarm of mean kitties during a bad storm. **83m/C VHS.** Kathleen Quinlan, Timothy Busfield, Claudia Christian; ***D:*** John McPherson; ***W:*** Shaun Cassidy.

Streamers 𝒮𝒮 **1983 (R)** Six young soldiers in a claustrophobic army barracks tensely await the orders that will send them to Vietnam. Written by Rabe from his play. Well acted but downbeat and drawn out. **118m/C VHS.** Bill Allen, Matthew Modine, Michael Wright, Mitchell Lichtenstein, George Dzundza; ***D:*** Robert Altman; ***W:*** David Rabe.

The Street 𝒮𝒮 **½ 1923** A dark classic of German Kammerspiel film, notable for its expressionist treatment of Paris street life. A middle-aged man decides to abandon his wife and job to see what excitement he can find. He is duped by a prostitute, accused of murder, imprisoned, and nearly commits suicide before being rescued. Silent. **87m/B VHS.** *GE* Max Schreck, Anton Edthofer, Leonhard Haskel; ***D:*** Karl Grune; ***W:*** Karl Grune; ***C:*** Karl Hasselmann.

Street Angel 𝒮𝒮 **1928** Silent melodrama. Neapolitan waif Angela (Gaynor) makes an unsuccessful attempt at street walking (hence the title) and then stealing to get money for her sick mama. Hiding out from the cops, Angela meets artist Gino (Farrell), who paints a portrait of her as the Madonna. She's finally caught and jailed, but on her release reunites with Gino, who's been struggling to get over Angela's checkered past. **102m/B DVD.** Janet Gaynor, Charles Farrell, Henry Armetta, Guido Conti, Louis Liggett; ***D:*** Frank Borzage; ***W:*** Marion Orth, Philip Klein, Robert Symonds; ***C:*** Ernest Palmer.

Street Asylum 𝒮 **1990 (R)** Real-life Watergate spook Liddy is pathetically bad as an evil genius who cooks up a scheme to rid the streets of deadbeats and scumbags by implanting cops with a gizmo that makes them kill. Also available in a 94-minute unrated version. **94m/C VHS.** Wings Hauser, Alex Cord, Roberta Vasquez, G. Gordon Liddy, Marie Chambers, Sy Richardson, Jesse Doran, Jesse Aragon, Brion James; ***D:*** Gregory Brown.

Street Corner Justice 𝒮𝒮 **1996** Typical vigilante action movie features ex-cop Mike Justus (Singer), who's possessed of a short fuse and a strong sense of justice. He inherits a house in a crime-ridden L.A. neighborhood and finds himself coming to the aid of merchants who are being terrorized by the local drug-dealing gangs. **102m/C VHS, DVD.** Marc Singer, Steve Railsback, Kim Lankford, Willie Gee; ***D:*** Charles "Chuck" Bail; ***W:*** Charles "Chuck" Bail, Gary Kent, Stan Berkowitz; ***C:*** Doug O'Neons, David Golia; ***M:*** K. Alexander (Alex) Wilkinson.

Street Crimes 𝒮𝒮 **1992 (R)** A street-wise cop convinces gang members to put down their weapons and settle their grudges in the boxing ring. But when a gang leader starts shooting down the police and civilians, the cop and his young partner must work together to keep the neighborhood safe. **93m/C VHS, DVD.** Dennis Farina, Max Gail, Mike Worth; ***D:*** Stephen Smoke; ***W:*** Stephen Smoke; ***M:*** John Gonzalez.

The Street Fighter 𝒮 **½** *Satsujim-ken* **1974** Fast-paced martial arts action finds freelance fighter Terry Tsuguri (Chiba) hired to spring a convicted killer from prison. But after he succeeds, his employers renege on their payment. Big mistake. Dubbed from Japanese. Three sequels: "Return of the Street Fighter," "The Street Fighter's Last Revenge," and "Sister Street Fighter." **91m/C VHS, DVD.** *JP* Sonny Chiba, Gerald (Waichi) Yamada, Tony Cetera, Doris (Yutaka) Nakajima; ***D:*** Shigehiro (Sakae) Ozawa; ***W:*** Motohiro Torii, Koji Takada; ***C:*** Ken Tsukakoshi; ***M:*** Toshiaki Tsushima.

Street Fighter 𝒮 **½ 1994 (PG-13)** Yes, it's a movie based on a popular video game (guess no one worried about the colossal flop of "Super Mario Bros"). Van Damme is action-minded Colonel Guile who is assigned to defeat crazed dictator General Bison (Julia in one of his last roles) in order to rescue kidnapped relief workers. Yes, there's lots of cartoon action but the game's more exciting (and even makes more sense). Shot on location in Australia and Bangkok. **101m/C VHS, DVD, Blu-ray Disc.** Jean-Claude Van Damme, Raul Julia, Wes Studi, Ming Na, Damian Chapa, Simon Callow, Roshan Seth, Kylie Minogue, Byron Mann; ***D:*** Steven E. de Souza; ***W:*** Steven E. de Souza; ***C:*** William A. Fraker; ***M:*** Graeme Revell.

Street Fighter: The Legend of Chun-Li 2009 Female fighter Chun Li (Kreuk) embarks on a quest for justice. Based on the videogame. **m/C DVD.** Kristin Kreuk, Michael Clarke Duncan, Neal McDonough, Moon Bloodgood, Chris Klein, Robin Shou, Josie Ho, Taboo; ***D:*** Andrzej Bartkowiak; ***W:*** Justin Marks; ***C:*** Geoff Boyle; ***M:*** Stephen Endelman.

The Street Fighter's Last Revenge 𝒮 *Revenge! The Killing Fist; Street Fighter Counterattacks* **1974** Third in the martial arts series finds Terry Tsuguri (Chiba) hired by a mob boss to do some dirty work and then getting doublecrossed—resulting in the death of Terry's girl. So, Terry hunts the miscreants down one by one. Lots of action, not much acting. Followed by "Sister Street Fighter." **79m/C VHS, DVD.** *JP* Sonny Chiba, Etsuko (Sue) Shihomi; ***D:*** Teru Ishii.

Street Girls 𝒮 **1975 (R)** A father enters the world of urban drugs and prostitution to find his runaway daughter. **77m/C VHS.** Carol Case, Christine Souder, Paul Pompian; ***D:*** Michael Miller.

Street Gun 𝒮 **1996** Small-time hood Joe Webster (Pagel) pines for some sense of accomplishment in his life. A tip from his hustler-friend lands Joe in the good graces of the local crime boss. As he ingratiates himself into his new malevolent world, the shadows yield betrayal, murder, and no place to hide. Potentially interesting premise is botched, with cowriter/director Milloy aping John Woo gun pyrotechnics and "Reservoir Dogs" attitude (a Woo rip-off once removed). There is also the thorny dilemma of rooting for a hero who aspires to be an exceptional thug. **92m/C DVD.** Justin Pagel, Scott Cooke, Michael Egan; ***D:*** Travis Milloy; ***W:*** Travis Milloy, Timothy Lee; ***C:*** Joel King.

Street Heart 𝒮𝒮 *Le Coeur au Poing* **1998** Louise has structured a very sheltered, controlled (if lonely) world for herself that gradually comes undone as both her sister and her lover abandon her. Feeling the need to reconnect with life, Louise goes about making contact in a dangerous manner. She begins to stop strangers on the street and offers to do whatever they would like for one hour. French with subtitles. **100m/C VHS.** *CA* Pascale Montpetit, Anne-Marie Cadieux, Guy Nadon, Guylaine Tremblay; ***D:*** Charles Biname; ***W:*** Monique Proulx, Charles Biname; ***C:*** Pierre Gill; ***M:*** Richard Gregoire, Yves Desrosiers.

Street Hero WOOF! **1984** A young thug is torn between familial common sense and Mafia connections. **102m/C VHS.** Vince Colosimo, Sigrid Thornton, Sandy Gore; ***D:*** Michael Pattinson; ***W:*** Jan Sardi; ***C:*** Vincent Monton.

Street Hitz 𝒮 **½ 1992** Two brothers in the South Bronx find their family loyalties tested. Joey wants to finish college and get away from the violence in the streets while his brother Junior turns to the gangs to survive. **92m/C VHS.** Angelo Lopez, Melvin Muza, Lyota Ramirez; ***D:*** Joseph B. Vasquez.

Street Hunter WOOF! **1990 (R)** Former cop turned freelance fighter quit the force when his integrity was questioned, but he still helps out now and then. Scumbag drug dealers line up a thug to waste him; epic kung fu battle ensues. **120m/C VHS.** Steve James, Reb Brown, John Leguizamo, Valarie Pettiford, Frank Vincent, Richie Havens; ***D:*** John A. Gallagher; ***C:*** Phil Parmet.

Street Justice 𝒮 **½ 1989 (R)** Overcomplex tale of a CIA agent on the lam. Returning from years of Russian imprisonment, Ontkean finds his wife remarried, his daughter grown and both battling the corrupt town government. Good performances can't help the confusion of too many characters too flatly developed. **94m/C VHS.** Michael Ontkean, Joanna Kerns, Catherine Bach, J.D. Cannon, Jeannette Nolan, Richard Cox, William Windom; ***D:*** Richard Sarafian.

The Street King 𝒮 **½** *King Rikki* **2002 (R)** Rikki Ortega (Seda) wants to be top dog on the gang-ravaged streets of East L.A. And the one man to oppose him is his childhood buddy turned cop, Juan Vallejo (Lopez). It's alleged to be a modern reworking of Shakespeare's "Richard III." **90m/C VHS, DVD.** Jon Seda, Mario Lopez, Timothy Paul Perez, Jill-Michele Melean; ***D:*** James Gavin Bedford; ***W:*** Jesse Graham; ***C:*** Rob Sweeney.

Street Kings 𝒮𝒮 **2008 (R)** Ellroy had a hand in the script (adapted from his novel) but this over-the-top violent melodrama more closely resembles what director Ayers did as a writer with the equally preposterous "Training Day." Widowed vice cop Tom Ludlow (Reeves) drinks on the job and is possibly more violent than the L.A. criminals he's after. Ludlow's commanding officer Wander (Whitaker, practically pop-eyed and frothing) seems to have his back until Tom's ex-partner Washington (Crews) is gunned down after he talks to Internal Affairs, which puts a bullseye on Ludlow's back. **109m/C DVD.** *US* Keanu Reeves, Forest Whitaker, Hugh Laurie, Chris Evans, Jay Mohr, John Corbett, Amaury Nolasco, Cedric the Entertainer, Terry Crews, Naomie Harris, Common, The Game, Martha Higareda; ***D:*** David Ayer, James Moss; ***W:*** Kurt Wimmer, James Ellroy; ***C:*** Gabriel Beristain; ***M:*** Graeme Revell.

Street Knight 𝒮𝒮 **1993 (R)** Gang warfare in L.A. in a routine actioner. Jake is an ex-cop who gets drawn into a battle between two rival gangs when their truce is broken by mysterious murders on both sides. Seems there's an unsuspected third party involved—a para-military band of professional killers that want the gang violence to divert police interest from their own nefarious operations. **88m/C VHS.** Jeff Speakman, Christopher Neame, Lewis Van Bergen, Bernie Casey, Jennifer Gatti, Richard Coca; ***D:*** Albert Magnoli.

Street Law 𝒮 *The Citizen Rebels; Il Cittadino si Ribella* **1974 (R)** Vivid and violent study of one man's frustrated war on crime. **77m/C VHS, DVD.** *IT* Franco Nero, Barbara Bach, Renzo Palmer, Giancarlo Prete; ***D:*** Enzo G. Castellari; ***W:*** Massimo De Rita, Arduino (Dino) Maiuri; ***C:*** Carlo Carlini; ***M:*** Guido de Angelis, Maurizio de Angelis.

Street Law 𝒮𝒮 **1995 (R)** John Ryan (Wincott) is a down-on-his-luck trial lawyer whose childhood buddy Luis Calderone (Prieto) is willing to lend a helping hand. Too bad Luis is an ex-con who hasn't left his dangerous street ways behind him and now John is caught up in some unsavory action. **98m/C VHS, DVD.** Jeff Wincott, Paco Christian Prieto, Christina Cox; ***D:*** Damian Lee; ***W:*** Damian Lee; ***C:*** Gerald R. Goozie; ***M:*** Ronald J. Weiss.

Street Music 𝒮𝒮 **½ 1981** The elderly people living in an old hotel join forces with a young couple to organize a protest that may save their building. Well-directed urban comedy-drama; good location shooting in San Francisco's Tenderloin. **88m/C VHS.** Larry Breeding, Elizabeth (E.G. Dailey) Daily, Ned Glass, Marjorie Eaton, D'Alan Moss, David Parr; ***D:*** Jenny (H. Anne Riley) Bowen; ***W:*** Jenny (H. Anne Riley) Bowen; ***C:*** Richard Bowen. Sundance '82: Grand Jury Prize.

Street of Forgotten Women 𝒮 **1925** Hollywood, in one of its periodic morality binges, came up with this purported expose on prostitution. An innocent girl is seduced and brutalized by a theatrical agent and eventually finds herself walking the pavement for less than moral purposes. Lots of shots of scantily clad showgirls and our heroine in her undies. **55m/B VHS.**

Street of Shame 𝒮𝒮𝒮 **½** *Red-Light District; Akasen Chitai* **1956** A portrayal of the abused lives of six Tokyo prostitutes. Typically sensitive to the roles and needs of women and critical of the society that exploits them, Mizoguchi creates a quiet, inclusive coda to his life's work in world cinema. Kyo is splendid as a hardened hooker and has a memorable scene with her father. Kogure is also good. The great director's last finished work was instrumental in the outlawing of prostitution in Japan. In Japanese with English subtitles. **88m/B VHS.** *JP* Machiko Kyo, Aiko Mimasu, Michiyo Kogure; ***D:*** Kenji Mizoguchi.

Street People WOOF! **1976 (R)** Gratuitous car chases and violence do not a movie make, as in this case in point. Utter woofer has Brit Moore cast as a mafiosa. Yeah, right. **92m/C VHS.** Roger Moore, Stacy Keach, Ivo Garrani, Ettore Manni; ***D:*** Maurizio Lucidi.

Street Scene 𝒮𝒮𝒮 **1931** Life in a grimy New York tenement district, circa 1930. Audiences nationwide ate it up when Elmer Rice adapted his own Pulitzer Prize-winning play and top helmsman Vidor gave it direction. **80m/B VHS, DVD.** Sylvia Sidney, William "Buster" Collier Jr., Estelle Taylor, Beulah Bondi, David Landau; ***D:*** King Vidor; ***W:*** Elmer Rice; ***C:*** George Barnes; ***M:*** Alfred Newman.

Street Smart 𝒮𝒮 **½ 1987 (R)** Reeve was blah as Superman (let's be frank), and he's blah here as a desperate New York freelance writer who fakes a dramatic story about prostitution. When his deception returns to haunt him, he's in trouble with pimps and murderers, as well as the D.A. Freeman and Baker are both superb. Based on screenwriter David Freeman's own experience with "New York" magazine. **97m/C VHS, DVD.** Christopher Reeve, Morgan Freeman, Kathy Baker, Mimi Rogers, Andre Gregory, Jay Patterson, Anna Maria Horsford; ***D:*** Jerry Schatzberg; ***W:*** David Freeman; ***C:*** Adam Holender; ***M:*** Miles Davis. Ind. Spirit '88: Support. Actor (Freeman); L.A. Film Critics '87: Support. Actor (Freeman); N.Y. Film Critics '87: Support. Actor (Freeman); Natl. Soc. Film Critics '87: Support. Actor (Freeman), Support. Actress (Baker).

Street Soldiers 1/2 **1991 (R)** Martial artists are out to take back the streets from the punks and scum who now rule them. **98m/C VHS.** Jun Chong, Jeff Rector, David Homb, Jonathan Gorman, Joon Kim, Katherine Armstrong, Joel Weiss; ***D:*** Lee Harry.

Street Trash WOOF! 1987 In Brooklyn, a strange poisonous liquor is being sold cheap to bums, making them melt and explode. A gross, cheap, tongue-in-cheek shocker. **91m/C VHS, DVD.** Vic Noto, Mike Lackey, Bill Chepil, R.L. Ryan, James Lorinz, Miriam Zucker; ***D:*** J.(James) Michael Muro; ***W:*** Roy Frumkes; ***C:*** David Sperling.

Street Vengeance WOOF! 1995 Drug lord seeks vengeance against cop for death of brother. No-budget shot-on-video flick is atrocious in every way. **85m/C DVD.** Mari Blackwell, Michael Eugene; ***D:*** Rene Migliaccio; ***W:*** Michael Farakash.

Street War *Paura in citta* **1976** A cop pursues the Mob in the name of revenge as well as duty. **90m/C VHS, DVD.** *IT* Maurizio Merli, Silvia Dionisio, Fausto Tozzi, James Mason, Cyril Cusack, Raymond Pellegrin; ***D:*** Giuseppe Rosati; ***W:*** Giuseppe Rosati, Giuseppe Pulieri; ***C:*** Giuseppe Bernardini; ***M:*** Gianpaolo Chiti.

Street Warriors WOOF! *Perros Callejeros* **1977** Ostensibly "serious" look at juvenile crime. Actually miserable, exploitative, offensive junk. **105m/C VHS.** *SP* Christa Leem, Nadia Windell, Victor Petit, Francisco (Frank) Brana; ***D:*** Jose Antonio De La Loma; ***W:*** Jose Antonio De La Loma; ***M:*** Cam Espana.

Street Warriors, Part 2 WOOF! *Perros Callejeros II* **1979** Even worse than its predecessor, and that's saying something. Horrible dubbing from Spanish would be laughable, if the rapes weren't so graphic. **105m/C VHS.** *MX SP* Angel Luis Fernandez, Paul Ramirez, Teresa Giminez, Veronica Miriel, Conrad Tortosa; ***D:*** Jose Antonio De La Loma; ***W:*** Jose Antonio De La Loma; ***C:*** Juan Gelpi.

Street Wars 1/2 **1991 (R)** Violent low-budgeter about 17-year-old Sugarpop, who takes over older brother Frank's Los Angeles drug operation, after Frank is murdered, and finds himself battling a rival gang. **90m/C VHS, DVD.** Alan Joseph, Bryan O'Dell, Clifford Shegog, Jean Pace, Vaughn Cromwell, Cardella Demilo; ***D:*** Jamaa Fanaka; ***W:*** Jamaa Fanaka; ***C:*** John L. (Ndiaga) Demps Jr.; ***M:*** Michael Dunlap, Yves Chicha.

The Street with No Name
1948 In his follow-up to "Kiss of Death," Widmark confirms his rep as one disturbed guy playing psychotic career criminal whose life is a grisly trail of murder and brutality. **93m/B VHS, DVD.** Mark Stevens, Richard Widmark, Lloyd Nolan, Barbara Lawrence, Ed Begley Sr., Donald Buka, Joseph Pevney; ***D:*** William Keighley.

A Streetcar Named Desire
1951 (PG) Powerful film version of Tennessee Williams' play about a neurotic southern belle with a hidden past who comes to visit her sister and is abused and driven mad by her brutal brother-in-law. Grim New Orleans setting for terrific performances by all, with Malden, Leigh, and Hunter winning Oscars, and Brando making highest impact on audiences. Brando disliked the role, despite the great impact it had on his career. **122m/B VHS, DVD.** Vivien Leigh, Marlon Brando, Kim Hunter, Karl Malden; ***D:*** Elia Kazan; ***W:*** Tennessee Williams; ***C:*** Harry Stradling Sr.; ***M:*** Alex North. Oscars '51: Actress (Leigh), Art Dir./Set Dec., B&W, Support. Actor (Malden), Support. Actress (Hunter); AFI '98: Top 100; British Acad. '52: Actress (Leigh); Golden Globes '52: Support. Actress (Hunter), Natl. Film Reg. '99;; N.Y. Film Critics '51: Actress (Leigh), Director (Kazan), Film.

A Streetcar Named Desire
1984 Excellent TV adaptation of the Tennessee Williams drama about fading southern belle Blanche du Bois (Ann-Margret in a terrific performance). D'Angelo is her plain sister Stella who lives with brutish husband Stanley (Williams) in the seamy French Quarter of New Orleans. Can't surpass the original but this version does have the advantage of not having to soft-pedal the drama for the '50s censors. **94m/C VHS.** Ann-Margret, Beverly D'Angelo, Treat Williams, Randy Quaid, Rafael Campos, Erica Yohn; ***D:*** John Erman; ***C:*** Bill Butler; ***M:*** Marvin Hamlisch. **TV**

A Streetcar Named Desire 1/2
1995 Baldwin and Lange recreate their 1992 stage roles of brutal Stanley Kowalski and fragile Southern belle Blanche DuBois from the Broadway revival of Tennessee Williams 1947 Pulitzer Prize-winning play. This TV version is truer to the dialogue and situations of the original production than the censored '51 film. **156m/C VHS.** Jessica Lange, Alec Baldwin, Diane Lane, John Goodman, Frederick Coffin; ***D:*** Glenn Jordan; ***C:*** Ralf Bode; ***M:*** David Mansfield.

Streetfight 1/2 *Coonskin* **1975 (R)** Semi-animated racist exploitation from the creator of "Fritz the Cat." Features some superb animation. **89m/C VHS.** Philip Michael Thomas, Scatman Crothers, Barry White, Charles Gordone; ***D:*** Ralph Bakshi; ***W:*** Ralph Bakshi; ***C:*** William A. Fraker; ***M:*** Chico Hamilton.

Streets **1990 (R)** Applegate (of Fox TV's "Married...With Children") is believable as an illiterate runaway teen. Good drama set in Venice, California about life on the streets is flawed by near-gratuitous pairing with story of a crazy prostitute-killing cop. **90m/C VHS.** Christina Applegate, David Mendenhall, Eb Lottimer; ***D:*** Katt Shea, Andy Ruben; ***W:*** Andy Ruben.

Streets of Blood 1/2 **2009 (R)** Six months after Hurricane Katrina, veteran detective Andy Devereaux (Kilmer) comes to suspect that his late partner didn't drown in the disaster but was murdered. And it seems his new partner Stan (Jackson) is also hiding something while police shrink Nina (Stone) knows more than she's telling too. **95m/C DVD.** Val Kilmer, Curtis "50 Cent" Jackson, Sharon Stone, Michael Biehn, Shirly Brener, Jose Pablo Cantillo; ***D:*** Charles Winkler; ***W:*** Eugene Hess; ***C:*** Roy Wagner; ***M:*** Stephen Endelman. **VIDEO**

Streets of Fire 1/2 **1984** A soldier of fortune rescues his ex-girlfriend, now a famous rock singer, after she's been kidnapped by a malicious motorcycle gang. Violently energetic in its insistent barrage of imagery. Director Hill's never-never land establishes a retro-futuristic feel and is beautifully photographed, however vacuous the ending may be. **93m/C VHS, DVD, HD DVD.** Michael Pare, Diane Lane, Rick Moranis, Amy Madigan, Willem Dafoe, Deborah Van Valkenburgh, Richard Lawson, Rick Rossovich, Bill Paxton, Lee Ving, Stoney Jackson, Robert Kevin Townsend, Grand L. Bush, Mykelti Williamson, Elizabeth (E.G. Dailey) Daily, Lynne Thigpen, Marine Jahan, Ed Begley Jr., John Dennis Johnston, Olivia Brown; ***D:*** Walter Hill; ***W:*** Walter Hill, Larry Gross; ***C:*** Andrew Laszlo; ***M:*** Ry Cooder.

Streets of Gold 1/2 **1986 (R)** Brandauer is good as a Soviet boxer who defected and now washes dishes in Brooklyn. He trains a pair of street youngsters in the hope of beating his old coach in the Olympics. "Rocky"-like in the boxing, and in the rags-to-riches optimism. **94m/C VHS.** Klaus Maria Brandauer, Adrian Pasdar, Wesley Snipes; ***D:*** Joe Roth; ***W:*** Richard Price, Heywood Gould, Tom Cole; ***C:*** Arthur Albert; ***M:*** Jack Nitzsche.

The Streets of L.A. 1/2 **1979** A frustrated middle-aged woman teaches some punks from an L.A. barrio a thing or two about pride and motivation when she demands reimbursement for the tires they slashed. Without thoroughly professional Woodward to carry it, there would not be much of a movie. Woodward's character is resourceful, and so is the actress. Made for TV. **94m/C VHS.** Joanne Woodward, Robert Webber, Michael C. Gwynne; ***D:*** Jerrold Freedman; ***C:*** Allen Daviau. **TV**

The Streets of San Francisco **1972** The pilot that spawned the popular TV series. A streetwise old cop and his young college-boy partner (who else but Malden and Douglas as Stone and Keller) investigate the murder of a young woman. Adapted from "Poor, Poor Ophelia" by Carolyn Weston. **120m/C VHS.** Karl Malden, Robert Wagner, Michael Douglas, Andrew Duggan, Tom Bosley, Kim Darby, Mako; ***D:*** Walter Grauman. **TV**

Streets of Sin 1/2 *Not Wanted* **1949** Written and produced by movie star Lupino (who also took over directing when credited director Clifton became ill), this morality play tells the story of a naive girl's tribulations when she becomes infatuated with a musician and then becomes pregnant by him. Shunned by the musician, she enters a home for unwed mothers to sort out her life and feelings for a crippled veteran who wants to marry her. **91m/B VHS.** Sally Forrest, Keefe Brasselle, Leonard Penn, Dorothy Adams, Rita Lupino; ***D:*** Elmer Clifton; ***W:*** Ida Lupino.

Streetwalkin' **1985 (R)** Life in the Big Apple isn't always rosy for a brother and sister who must contend with prostitutes, drug dealers, and tough cops. She turns to prostitution to get by. Miserable, exploitative trash. **86m/C VHS.** Melissa Leo, Dale Midkiff, Leon Robinson, Julie Newmar, Randall Batinkoff, Annie Golden, Antonio Fargas; ***D:*** Joan Freeman; ***W:*** Joan Freeman, Robert Alden; ***C:*** Steven Fierberg.

Streetwise 1/2 **1984** Eye-opening and candid documentary inspired by a "Life" magazine article. Frank and honest look at homeless children making a living on the streets. Seattle provides the backdrop to the story as the filmmakers hang around with the kids, earning their trust, and receive the truth from them. Cruel, funny, enraging, but always sobering look into a population of homeless in America. A deservedly acclaimed, terrifying vision of urban America. **92m/C VHS.** ***D:*** Martin Bell; ***W:*** Cheryl McCall; ***M:*** Tom Waits.

Stricken **1998 (R)** Six college buddies become obesessed with practical jokes that becomes more and more vicious—all of which are orchestrated by Guffy (Gunn). The butt of most of the gags, Banyon (Kennedy), has certainly had enough and helps play one last joke on Guffy that leads to his accidental death. Everyone but Banyon begins to panic and turn on each other but Banyon sees his chance to get back at everyone who humiliated him. Offers low-budget tension. **90m/C VHS, DVD.** Jamie Kennedy, Sean Gunn, Judy Green, Tait Smith, Kevin Patrick Walls; ***D:*** Paul Chilsen; ***W:*** William W. Vought; ***C:*** Maida Sussman; ***M:*** Todd Scales.

Strictly Ballroom 1/2 **1992 (PG)** Offbeat, cheerfully tacky dance/romance amusingly turns every movie cliche slightly askew. Scott (Mercurio) has been in training for the Pan-Pacific ballroom championships since the age of six. While talented, he also refuses to follow convention and scandalizes the stuffy dance establishment with his new steps. When his longtime partner leaves him, Scott takes up with a love-struck beginner (Morice), with some surprises of her own. Ballet dancer Mercurio (in his film debut) is appropriately arrogant yet vulnerable, with Morice as the plain Jane turned steel butterfly. Wonderful supporting cast; great debut for director Luhrmann. **94m/C VHS, DVD.** *AU* Paul Mercurio, Tara Morice, Bill Hunter, Pat Thomsen, Barry Otto, Gia Carides, Peter Whitford, John Hannan, Sonia Kruger-Tayler, Kris McQuade, Pip Mushin, Leonie Page, Antonio Vargas, Armonia Benedito; ***D:*** Baz Luhrmann; ***W:*** Baz Luhrmann, Craig Pearce; ***C:*** Steve Mason; ***M:*** David Hirschfelder. Australian Film Inst. '92: Costume Des., Director (Luhrmann), Film, Film Editing, Screenplay, Support. Actor (Otto), Support. Actress (Thomsen).

Strictly Business 1/2 **1991 (PG-13)** An upwardly mobile black broker has his career aspirations in order until he meets a beautiful club promoter who finds him square and boring. Wanting to impress her he asks the advice of a young man who works in the mail room for the proper way to dress and talk. A low-rent Pygmalion story. **83m/C VHS.** Halle Berry, Tommy Davidson, Joseph C. Phillips; ***D:*** Kevin Hooks; ***M:*** Michel Colombier.

Strictly G.I. 1/2 **1944** A collection of war-time patriotic shorts, including "All Star Bond Rally." The support and perception of WWII is historically intriguing. **45m/B VHS.** Bing Crosby, Frank Sinatra, Betty Grable, Judy Garland, Harpo Marx, Harry James, Bob Hope, Jerry Colonna.

Strictly Sexual **2008 (R)** Donna and her best friend Christi Ann are bored trying to find relationships in L.A. and decide to go for straight sex. They meet Stanny and Joe at a bar and think they're hustlers so they take them home for the night. The gals discover the guys are actually unemployed construction workers looking for jobs so they make them an offer: they can stay in the pool house in exchange for no-strings booty calls. Naturally, things don't work out that way. **99m/C DVD.** Amber Benson, Kristen Kerr, Johann Urb, Steve Long; ***D:*** Joel Viertel; ***C:*** Andreas Burgess; ***M:*** H. Scott Salinas.

Strictly Sinatra 1/2 *Cocozza's Way* **2001 (R)** Sinatra cover song act Toni Cocozza (Hart) plys his trade in the local pubs of Glasgow, dreaming about making it as big as Old Blue Eyes himself. The Scottish-Italian crooner's tiny faction of fans under 65 includes some local mobsters. When one claims he met Sinatra himself in Vegas, Toni, who's only truly comfortable on-stage, finds himself intrigued and drawn in to their gang, who shower him with the attention and respect he craves. Underworld mayhem complicates a potentially interesting comedy/thriller that doesn't fully live up to either. Technically adroit, with top-notch songs and arrangements and a stunning performance by Hart. **97m/C VHS, DVD.** *GB* Ian Hart, Kelly Macdonald, Brian Cox, Alun Armstrong, Tommy Flanagan, Iain Cuthbertson, Jimmy Chisholm, Jimmy Yuill; ***Cameos:*** Richard E. Grant; ***D:*** Peter Capaldi; ***W:*** Peter Capaldi; ***C:*** Stephen Blackman; ***M:*** Stanislas Syrewicz.

Strike 1/2 **1924** Eisenstein's debut, and a silent classic. Stirring look at a 1912 clash between striking factory workers and Czarist troops. **94m/B VHS, DVD.** *RU* Alexander Antonov, Yudif Glizer, Ivan Klyukvin, Grigori Aleksandrov; ***D:*** Sergei Eisenstein; ***W:*** Grigori Aleksandrov, Sergei Eisenstein; ***C:*** Eduard Tisse.

Strike WOOF! *7-10 Split* **2007** Raunchy, witless smarm with an utterly terrible performance by lead actor/writer Patterson. Struggling actor Ross takes out his frustrations at the bowling alley where he's spotted by PBA recruiter Buddy (Wise), who offers him a chance at a pro career. Packing up his balls, best bud (Crawford), and girlfriend (Reid), Ross travels cross-country working on his game before challenging top bowler Jerry (Huebel) but soon Ross' ego is landing him in the gutter. And yes, that is Tara's brother who's nominally directing. **90m/C DVD.** Ross Patterson, Tara Reid, Clayne Crawford, Ray Wise, Rob Huebel, Vinnie Jones, Robin (Robyn) Lively, Rachel Hunter; ***D:*** Tommy Reid; ***W:*** Ross Patterson; ***C:*** Massimo Zeri; ***M:*** Greg Morgenstein.

Strike a Pose 1/2 **1993 (R)** Erotic thriller finds international model-turned-fashion photographer Miranda Cross, her boyfriend LAPD detective Nick Carter, and Miranda's model friends stalked by a revenge-minded killer. Also available in an unrated version. **75m/C VHS, DVD.** Margie Peterson, Robert Eastwick, Michelle LaMothe; ***D:*** Dean Hamilton.

Strike Back **1980** A convict escapes from prison to find the girl he loves, and is hounded by the police and the mob. **89m/C VHS.** Dave Balko, Brigette Wollner; ***D:*** Carl Schenkel.

Strike Commando WOOF! 1987 (R) Cheap, exploitative ripoff of the expensive, exploitative mega-action thriller "Rambo." Sleepwalking actors; horrible, overwrought script. Mattei used the pseudonym Vincent Dawn. **92m/C VHS.** Reb Brown, Christopher Connelly, Locs Kamme; ***D:*** Bruno Mattei.

Strike Force *Crack* **1975** A New York City cop, a Federal agent and a state trooper work together to battle a large drug ring. Failed made-for-TV pilot. Early Gere appearance; not related to later Robert Stack film with the same title. **74m/C VHS, DVD.** Cliff Gorman, Richard Gere, Donald Blakely; *D:* Barry Shear. **TV**

Strike Force 1981 The jurors on an embezzlement case turn up bloody and headless around town, so a special criminal strike force is brought in to solve the murders. Why do the murders happen only on Tuesdays? Made for TV. **90m/C VHS.** Robert Stack, Dorian Harewood, Herb Edelman; *D:* Richard Lang. **TV**

Strike It Rich ½ *Loser Take All* **1990 (PG)** A honeymooning couple find themselves resorting to the Monte Carlo gambling tables in order to raise money for the ride home. Lightweight fluff unfortunately adapted from Graham Greene's short novel "Loser Takes All." Only for hard-core Gielgudites. **86m/C VHS, DVD.** Molly Ringwald, Robert Lindsay, John Gielgud, Max Wall, Simon de la Brosse; *D:* James Scott; *W:* James Scott; *C:* Robert Paynter; *M:* Cliff Eidelman.

Strike Me Pink 1936 Shy Eddie Pink (Cantor) decides to change his ways after reading a self-help book and takes on the management of the local amusement park. Then some crooks want to muscle in on the action and Eddie must prove his mettle. Merman as girlfriend Joyce gets to belt out a few songs. ♫ The Lady Dances; Shake It Off with Rhythm; You Have Me High, You Have Me Low; Calabash Pipe. **100m/B VHS.** Eddie Cantor, Ethel Merman, Sally Eilers, William Frawley, Parkyakarkus (Harry Einstein), Brian Donlevy, Jack La Rue; *D:* Norman Taurog; *W:* Frank Butler, Walter DeLeon, Francis Martin; *C:* Gregg Toland, Merritt B. Gerstad; *M:* Harold Arlen.

Strike Up the Band ½ **1940** A high school band turns to hot swing music and enters a national radio contest. Rooney and Garland display their usual charm in this high-energy stroll down memory lane. ♫ Over the Waves; The Light Cavalry Overture; Walkin Down Broadway; Five Foot Two, Eyes of Blue; After the Ball; Nobody; Strike Up the Band. **120m/B VHS.** Judy Garland, Mickey Rooney, Paul Whiteman, William Tracy, June Preisser; *D:* Busby Berkeley. Oscars '40: Sound.

Striker **1988 (R)** Mercenary John "Striker" Slade is sent to Nicaragua to free a captured American journalist, not knowing his superiors have betrayed him to the Contras and the Sandinistas. He battles it out with both groups while seeking revenge on the businessmen who set him up. **90m/C VHS.** Frank Zagarino, Melanie Rogers, Paul Werner; *D:* Stephen M. Andrews.

Striker's Mountain ½ **1987** Story of a sports enthusiast who creates heliskiing and builds it into a business. Great ski scenes, but skip the rest. **99m/C VHS.** Bruce Greenwood, Mimi Kuzyk, Leslie Nielsen, August Schellenberg, Jessica Steen; *D:* Allen Simmonds.

Striking Distance ½ **1993 (R)** Tom Hardy (Willis) is a hard-nosed fifth-generation Pittsburgh homicide cop whose police detective father (Mahoney) is killed, apparently by a serial killer. Hardy insists the perp was really a fellow cop and winds up on the River Rescue squad (at least his partner is the fetching Parker). When the serial killer starts striking at women with some connection to Hardy, he finds scant support from his fellow cops. High action quotient backed by a fine cast, but the killer's identity won't be any surprise. **101m/C VHS, DVD.** Bruce Willis, Sarah Jessica Parker, Dennis Farina, Tom Sizemore, Brion James, Robert Pastorelli, Timothy Busfield, John Mahoney, Andre Braugher; *D:* Rowdy Herrington; *W:* Marty Kaplan, Rowdy Herrington; *C:* Mac Ahlberg; *M:* Brad Fiedel.

Striking Point ½ **1994 (R)** Police detectives are determined to stop ex-KGB commandoes from smuggling high-tech weapons into the country. **96m/C VHS.** Chris Mitchum, Tracy Spaulding; *D:* Thomas Fenton; *W:* Thomas Fenton; *C:* Tony Brownrigg; *M:* Laura Porter.

Strip Search ½ **1997 (R)** Police detective Robby (Pare) gets seduced by easy money and sex when he gets involved with sex clubs and underworld gangs. **90m/C VHS, DVD.** *CA* Michael Pare, Pam Grier, Caroline Neron, Lucie Laurier, Maury Chaykin, Heidi von Palleske, MacKenzie Gray; *D:* Rod Hewitt.

Stripes ½ **1981 (R)** Feeling like losers and looking to straighten out their lives, two friends enlist in the Army under the mistaken impression that military life is something like a summer camp for grown-ups. A boxoffice success (despite a weak script) due in large part to Murray's charm and his verbal and sometimes physical sparring with Oates, who is good as the gruff-tempered platoon sergeant. Features humorous stints from various "Second City" players, including Candy, whom Murray turns into a "lean, mean fighting machine." **105m/C VHS, DVD, UMD.** Bill Murray, Harold Ramis, P.J. Soles, Warren Oates, John Candy, John Larroquette, Judge Reinhold, Sean Young, Dave Thomas, Joe Flaherty, Lance LeGault; *D:* Ivan Reitman; *W:* Len Blum, Harold Ramis; *C:* Bill Butler; *M:* Elmer Bernstein.

Stripped to Kill **1987 (R)** A female cop goes undercover to lure a psycho killing strippers. Not-bad entry from Corman and cohorts. Followed by—you guessed it—"Stripped to Kill II." **88m/C VHS, DVD.** Kay Lenz, Greg Evigan, Norman Fell, Pia Kamakahi, Tracy Crowder, Deborah Ann Nassar, Lucia Nagy Lexington, Carlye Byron, Athena Worthy, Michelle Foreman, Diana Bellamy; *D:* Katt Shea; *W:* Katt Shea, Andy Ruben; *C:* John LeBlanc; *M:* John O'Kennedy.

Stripped to Kill II: Live Girls **1989** A young woman with extra-sensory powers dreams of murders which she discovers are all too real. A weak sequel, despite the interesting premise. **83m/C VHS, DVD.** Maria Ford, Eb Lottimer, Karen Mayo-Chandler, Marjean Holden, Birke Tan, Debra Lamb; *D:* Katt Shea; *W:* Katt Shea.

The Stripper ½ *Woman of Summer* **1963** A middle-aged stripper in a traveling show returns to the small Kansas town of her youth. Left stranded, she moves in with an old friend whose teenage son promptly falls in love with her. Based on the play "A Loss of Roses" by William Inge. **95m/B VHS.** Joanne Woodward, Richard Beymer, Claire Trevor, Carol Lynley, Robert Webber, Gypsy Rose Lee; *D:* Franklin J. Schaffner; *M:* Jerry Goldsmith.

Stripper ½ **1986 (R)** A good under-the-covers glimpse of the life and work of several real-life strippers, culminating in the First Annual Stripper's Convention in 1984. **90m/C VHS.** Janette Boyd, Sara Costa, Kimberly Holcomb; *D:* Jerome Gary; *M:* Jack Nitzsche.

Stripshow **1995 (R)** Veteran Vegas stripper shows the ropes to newcomer and then must vie with the upstart for her boyfriend's interest. **96m/C VHS, DVD.** Monique Parent, Tane McClure, Steven Tietsort; *D:* Gary Orona; *W:* Gary Orona.

Striptease ½ **1996 (R)** Single mom Erin Grant (Moore) loses custody of her daughter Angela (Moore's real-life offspring, Rumer) to her lowlife ex, Darrell (Patrick). In order to raise the money for an appeal, she dances at a Miami strip club, where she runs across politician David Dilbeck (Reynolds), who has a thing for both vaseline and Erin. Unlike "Showgirls," this one's intentionally funny and features some fine script work and performances, which got overlooked amidst all the hype, including Moore's record-setting (for an actress) $12 million paycheck, 4 mil of which reportedly was for agreeing to dance nude. Based on the novel by Carl Hiaasen. **115m/C VHS, DVD.** Demi Moore, Armand Assante, Ving Rhames, Robert Patrick, Burt Reynolds, Rumer Willis, Paul Guilfoyle, Dina Spybey; *D:* Andrew Bergman; *W:* Andrew Bergman; *C:* Stephen Goldblatt; *M:* Howard Shore. Golden Raspberries '96: Worst Picture, Worst Actress (Moore), Worst Director (Bergman), Worst Screenplay, Worst Song ("Pussy, Pussy, Pussy (Whose Kitty Cat Are You?)").

Stripteaser ½ **1995 (R)** Sicko psycho Dean holds dancers and patrons hostage in an L.A. strip joint where he provides various humiliations for his captives. Ford's the beautiful ecdysiast whose been the object of the fellow's secret obsessions. Also available unrated. **82m/C VHS, DVD.** Rick Dean, Maria Ford, Lance August; *D:* Dan Golden.

Stroke of Midnight ½ **1990 (PG)** Souped-up Cinderella with Lowe as egotistic high fashion designer, Grey as struggling shoe designer and a pumpkin-colored VW Bug. **102m/C VHS.** Rob Lowe, Jennifer Grey, Andrea Ferreol; *D:* Tom Clegg.

Stroker Ace WOOF! **1983 (PG)** Flamboyant stock car driver tries to break an iron-clad promotional contract signed with a greedy fried-chicken magnate. Off duty, he ogles blondes as dopey as he is. One of the worst from Reynolds—and that's saying something. **96m/C VHS, DVD.** Burt Reynolds, Ned Beatty, Jim Nabors, Parker Stevenson, Loni Anderson, Bubba Smith; *D:* Hal Needham; *W:* Hal Needham, Hugh Wilson; *C:* Nick McLean; *M:* Al Capps. Golden Raspberries '83: Worst Support. Actor (Nabors).

Stromboli ½ **1950** Bergman is a Czech refugee who marries an Italian fisherman in order to escape from her displaced persons camp. He brings her to his home island of Stromboli where she finds the life bleak and isolated and her marriage a trial. In Italian with English subtitles. The melodrama was even greater off-screen than on; this is the movie which introduced Bergman and Rossellini and began their (then) scandalous affair. **107m/B VHS.** *IT* Ingrid Bergman, Mario Vitale, Renzo Cesana; *D:* Roberto Rossellini.

Strong Man **1926** A WWI veteran, passing himself off as an unlikely circus strongman, searches an American city for the girl whose letters gave him hope during the war. Perhaps Langdon's best full-length film. **78m/B VHS, DVD.** Harry Langdon, Gertrude Astor, Tay Garnett; *D:* Frank Capra. Natl. Film Reg. '07.

Strong Medicine ½ **1984** Strange, avant-garde film about a strange, off-written young woman. Cleverly directed experiment that's not for everyone. **84m/C VHS.** Carol Kane, Raul Julia, Wallace Shawn, Kate Manheim, David Warrilow; *D:* Guy Green.

The Strongest Man in the World ½ **1975 (G)** Another crazy mix-up involves Dexter Riley (Russell) and his friends at Medfield College in wacky adventures. One of their experiment gets mixed up with one of the students' breakfast cereal and turns out to give humans super-strength for a short time. The dean makes a deal with the local cereal company, and crooks hired by a rival company try to steal the formula. Typically enjoyable Disney live-action fare from the '70s may provide fun for the young 'uns, and will definitely bring back fond memories for their parents. **92m/C VHS, DVD.** Kurt Russell, Joe Flynn, Eve Arden, Cesar Romero, Phil Silvers, Dick Van Patten, Harold Gould, Richard Bakalyan, Michael McGreevey, William Schallert, Benson Fong, James Gregory, Don Carter, John Debney, Fritz Feld, Roy Roberts, Kathleen Freeman; *W:* Joseph L. McEveety, Herman Groves; *C:* Andrew Jackson; *M:* Robert F. Brunner.

Stroszek **1977** Three German misfits—a singer, a prostitute and an old man—tour the U.S. in search of their dreams. Touching, hilarious comedy-drama with a difference and an attitude. One of Herzog's easiest and also best films. In English and German with English subtitles. **108m/C VHS, DVD.** *GE* Wilhelm von Homburg, Eva Mattes, Bruno S, Clemens Scheitz; *D:* Werner Herzog; *W:* Werner Herzog; *C:* Thomas Mauch; *M:* Chet Atkins, Tom Paxton.

The Structure of Crystals ½ *Struktura Krysztalu* **1969** A member of the scientific elite meets with an old friend who has moved to a remote meteorological station and tries to persuade him to return to the city and resume his work. Zanussi's cerebral first feature was also the first of a series of films to explore the scientific community. In Polish with English subtitles. **76m/B VHS.** *PL* Andrzej Zarnecki, Jan Myslowicz, Barbara Wrzesinska, Wladyslaw Jarema, Daniel Olbrychski; *D:* Krzysztof Zanussi; *W:* Edward Zebrowski, Krzysztof Zanussi.

Struggle **1931** Unfortunately, Griffith's final directorial effort is a ludicrous melodrama about the evils of alcohol. Because of Prohibition, working man Jimmie Wilson (Skelly) takes to illegal hootch, which turns out to be tainted, causing Jimmie to abuse his wife and daughter and destroy their formerly happy home. **87m/B VHS.** Hal Skelly, Zita Johann, Evelyn Baldwin, Charlotte Wynters, Helen Mack, Kate Bruce, Jackson Halliday, Edna Hagan, Claude Cooper, Arthur Lipson, Charles Richman, Scott Moore, Dave Manley; *D:* D.W. Griffith; *W:* D.W. Griffith, Anita Loos, John Emerson; *C:* Joseph Ruttenberg; *M:* D.W. Griffith, Philip A. Scheib.

Stryker WOOF! **1983 (R)** The ever-lovin' nuclear holocaust has occurred, and good guys and bad guys battle it out for scarce water. If you liked "Mad Max," go see it again; don't watch this miserable effort. **86m/C VHS.** *PH* Steve Sandor, Andria Fabio; *D:* Cirio H. Santiago; *W:* Howard R. Cohen.

Stryker ½ **2004** Just your typical Canadian gangster and transvestite flick. Stryker is a speechless 14-year-old boy on the lam after burning down a church near his Indian reservation. He hops a train and finds himself a blank observer, wandering the seedy underbelly Winnipeg. After witnessing a mob throwdown between the warring Indian Posse and the Asian Bomb Squad, he finds protection in a home of transvestite prostitutes and then under the wing of the police. Low budget flair that tries to be quirky and fresh, but suffers from stiff performances and amateur theatrics. Fans of early John Waters may be amused. **93m/C DVD.** Kyle Henry, Ryan Black, Deena Fontaine, Joseph Mesiano, Nick Oullette, Nancy Sanderson; *D:* Noam Gonick; *W:* Noam Gonick, David MacIntosh; *C:* Edward Lachman; *M:* Karmen Omeosoos.

Stuart Bliss **1998** Curious little comedy mixes elements of "The X-Files" and "The Truman Show." Stuart Bliss (Zelnicker) is an ordinary guy who slowly succumbs to paranoia and apocalyptic religious visions. Of course, the question is: Is he crazy or well-informed? **88m/C VHS, DVD.** Michael Zelniker, Dea Lawrence, Derek McGrath, Ania Suli, Mark Fite; *D:* Neil Grieve; *W:* Michael Zelniker, Neil Grieve; *C:* Jens Sturup.

Stuart Little ½ **1999 (PG)** This bigscreen adaptation of E.B. White's 1945 children's classic is hardly faithful but has its own charms. Mr. (Laurie) and Mrs. (Davis) Little decide to expand their family through adoption and wind up with a tiny, talking, clothes-wearing white mouse named Stuart (Fox). Their son George (Lipnicki) has a hard time thinking of a mouse as his little brother and family cat Snowbell (Lane) thinks the rodent is snack food. When his attempt to eat Stuart fails, Snowbell turns to kidnapping. The array of digital effects is amazing. **92m/C VHS, DVD, UMD.** Geena Davis, Hugh Laurie, Jonathan Lipnicki, Brian Doyle-Murray, Estelle Getty, Julia Sweeney, Dabney Coleman; *D:* Rob Minkoff; *W:* M. Night Shyamalan, Greg Booker; *C:* Guillermo Navarro; *M:* Alan Silvestri; *V:* Michael J. Fox, Nathan Lane, Chazz Palminteri, Steve Zahn, Bruno Kirby, Jennifer Tilly, David Alan Grier, Jim Doughan.

Stuart Little 2 **2002 (PG-13)** Amazingly good sequel finds Stuart tooling around Manhattan in his miniature red sport car with a new, similar-sized friend: a cute, yellow bird named Margalo (Griffith). Stuart is smitten with his fine-feathered friend, taking her on a very PG date to a drive-in movie (his car parked in front of the TV set). Unbeknownst to Stuart, Margalo is actually in cahoots with a scheming Falcon (Woods) which sets off numerous adventures out in the big city for Stuart and a reluctant and even snarkier Snowbell (Lane). New York looks just as idyllic and the animation blended with live-action is even better than the original. More faithful adaptation of E.B. White's 1945 children's classic, on which both films were based. **78m/C VHS, DVD, UMD.** *US* Geena Davis, Hugh Laurie, Jonathan Lipnicki, Brad Garrett; *D:* Rob Minkoff; *W:* Bruce Joel Rubin; *C:* Steven Poster; *M:* Alan Silvestri; *V:* Michael J. Fox, Nathan Lane, Melanie Griffith, James Woods, Steve Zahn.

Stuart Saves His Family **1994 (PG-13)** Fired from his self-help TV show on a Chicago public-access station, New-Age advice guru Smalley (Franken) returns home to help his pathetically dysfunctional family sort out their problems and an inheritance, a nonplot that gives Smalley a chance to do his 12-step shtick. And that's..O.K. A tolerable installment in the endless parade of mediocre "Saturday Night Live" sketches stretched for the big screen that takes a few surprisingly maudlin turns. Based on Franken's book of Smalley's "daily affirmations," "I'm Good Enough, I'm Smart Enough, and Doggone It, People Like Me!" **97m/C VHS, DVD.** Al Franken, Laura San Giacomo, Vincent D'Onofrio, Shirley Knight, Harris Yulin, Julia Sweeney, Aaron Lustig, Darrell Larson, Camille Saviola, Gerrit Graham, Theodore (Ted) Raimi, Joe Flaherty; ***D:*** Harold Ramis; ***W:*** Al Franken; ***C:*** Lauro Escorel; ***M:*** Marc Shaiman.

Stuck 𝄞𝄞 **2007 (R)** Sardonic black comedy disturbingly based on a true story. Tom (Rea) has lost his job and become homeless but his life gets infinitely worse when hard-partying Brandi (Suvari) slams into him and Tom is stuck in her windshield. She drives home, parks in the garage, and leaves him there—apparently not realizing (or maybe caring) that he's alive. Next day, Brandi asks her drug-dealing boyfriend Rashid (Hornsby) to dispose of the body. Except Tom's still not dead, but now he's mondo ticked, struggling to get free, and out for payback. **94m/C DVD, Blu-ray Disc.** Mena Suvari, Stephen Rea, Russell Hornsby; ***D:*** Stuart Gordon; ***W:*** John Strysik; ***C:*** Denis Maloney; ***M:*** Bobby Johnson.

Stuck on You 𝄞 **1984 (R)** Couple engaged in a palimony suit takes their case to a judge to work out their differences. Wing-clipped angel Gabriel (Corey) comes to earth to help them patch it up. Never mind. **90m/C VHS, DVD.** Prof. Irwin Corey, Virginia Penta, Mark Mikulski; ***D:*** Lloyd Kaufman, Michael Herz; ***W:*** Lloyd Kaufman, Michael Herz; ***C:*** Lloyd Kaufman.

Stuck On You 𝄞𝄞 ½ **2003 (PG-13)** Surprisingly sentimental movie for the Farrelly brothers. Damon and Kinnear play conjoined twins Bob and Walt Tenor who've adapted to their rather unusual living arrangement with ease. Walt, however, has caught the acting bug and wants to make it big in Hollywood. As fate would have it, Walt becomes an unlikely star. While the movie borders on being a one-joke premise, it does have its sincere moments. **118m/C VHS, DVD.** *US* Matt Damon, Greg Kinnear, Eva Mendes, Wen Yann Shih, Pat Crawford Brown, Jean-Pierre Cassel, Cher, Ray "Rocket" Valliere; ***Cameos:*** Jay Leno; ***D:*** Bobby Farrelly, Peter Farrelly; ***W:*** Bobby Farrelly, Peter Farrelly; ***C:*** Dan Mindel.

Stuckey's Last Stand 𝄞 **1980 (PG)** A group of camp counselors prepare to take 22 children on a nature hike they will never forget. Mindless teen fodder. **95m/C VHS.** Whit Reichert, Tom Murray, Rich Casentino; ***D:*** Lawrence Goldfarb; ***W:*** Lawrence Goldfarb; ***C:*** Arthur J. Fitzsimmons III; ***M:*** Carson Whitsett.

The Stud WOOF! **1978 (R)** Owner of a fashionable "after hours" dance spot hires a young, handsome stud to manage the club and attend to her personal needs. Low-budget look and seemingly scriptless. Faithfully adapted by sister Jackie Collins from her novel. **90m/C VHS, DVD.** *GB* Joan Collins, Oliver Tobias; ***D:*** Quentin Masters; ***W:*** Jackie Collins.

The Student Affair 𝄞 *The Lay of the Land* **1997 (R)** Lame would-be comedy based on Shapiro's stage play, which also starred Kellerman. She's college prof M.J. Dankworth, who suspects hubby Harvey (Begley Jr.) is tossing their tired marriage aside to shtupp his well-endowed grad student Muriel (Taylor). So she hires a P.I. (Margolin) to snoop but he's more interested in his client. Then the marrieds seek out (different) psychiatrists for help and M.J. indulges her rage in silly fantasy scenes. Don't waste your time. **94m/C VHS.** *CA* Sally Kellerman, Ed Begley Jr., Sandra Taylor, Stuart Margolin, Tyne Daly, Rance Howard, Avery Schreiber; ***D:*** Larry Arrick; ***W:*** Mel Shapiro; ***C:*** Frederic Goodich; ***M:*** Jeff Lass.

Student Affairs WOOF! **1988 (R)** A bunch of highschool misfits vie for roles in a movie about a bunch of high school misfits. **92m/C VHS.** Louie Bonanno, Jim Abele, Alan Fisler, Deborah Blaisdell; ***D:*** Chuck Vincent.

Student Bodies WOOF! **1981 (R)** A "Halloween"-style spoof of high-school horror films, except it's not funny. And what's so funny about bloody murder anyway? When the on-the-set problems and strife arose (which they did), why didn't everyone just cut their losses and go home? **86m/C VHS, DVD.** Kristen Riter, Matthew Goldsby, Richard Belzer, Joe Flood, Joe Talarowski, Mimi Weddell; ***D:*** Mickey Rose; ***W:*** Mickey Rose.

Student Confidential 𝄞 **1987 (R)** A Troma-produced spoof of seedy high school youth movies, new and old, involving four students who are led into the world of adult vices by a mysterious millionaire. Badly made and dull. Douglas and Jackson both have brothers named Michael. **99m/C VHS, DVD.** Eric Douglas, Marlon Jackson, Susie Scott, Ronee Blakley, Elizabeth Singer; ***D:*** Richard Horian.

The Student Nurses 𝄞𝄞 **1970 (R)** The adventures, amourous and otherwise, of four last-year nursing students. Followed by four sequels: "Private Duty Nurses," "Night Call Nurses," "The Young Nurses," and "Candy Stripe Nurses." Better than average exploitation fare. First release from Roger Corman's New World studios; it goes down hill from there. **89m/C VHS, DVD.** Elaine Giftos, Karen Carlson, Brioni Farrell, Barbara Leigh, Reni Santoni, Richard Rust, Lawrence Casey, Darrell Larson, Paul Camen, Richard Stahl, Scottie MacGregor, Pepe Serna; ***D:*** Stephanie Rothman; ***W:*** Don Spencer; ***C:*** Stevan Larner.

Student of Prague 𝄞𝄞𝄞 **1913** Early silent classic based on the German Faust legend: a student makes a pact with the devil to win a beautiful woman. Poor fellow. With either German or English title cards. Music track. **60m/B VHS, DVD.** *GE* Lothar Koemer, Grete Berger, Paul Wegener; ***D:*** Paul Wegener, Stellan Rye.

The Student Prince 𝄞𝄞 **1954** Delightful rendition of Sigmund Romberg's famous operetta in which Purdom stars as the Prince of Heidelberg who falls for barmaid Blyth. Lanza recorded the soundtrack, but could not star in this film because of his weight problem. Previously filmed in 1919 and 1927 without music. ♫ Golden Days; Serenade; Deep in My Heart; To the Inn We're Marching; Drink, Drink, Drink; Come Boys, Let's All Be Gay, Boys; Summertime in Heidelberg; Beloved; I Walk With God. **107m/C VHS, DVD.** Ann Blyth, Edmund Purdom, John Ericson, Louis Calhern, Edmund Gwenn, S.Z. Sakall, Betta St. John; ***D:*** Richard Thorpe; ***C:*** Paul Vogel.

The Student Prince in Old Heidelberg 𝄞𝄞 ½ *Old Heidelberg* **1927** Prince Karl Heinrich silently falls in love with lowly barmaid. **102m/B VHS.** Ramon Novarro, Norma Shearer; ***D:*** Ernst Lubitsch.

The Student Teachers 𝄞 ½ **1973** Yet another soft-core Corman product. Three student teachers sleep around, on screen. **79m/C VHS.** Susan Damante-Shaw, Brooke Mills, Bob Harris, John Cramer, Chuck Norris; ***D:*** Jonathan Kaplan.

Studs Lonigan 𝄞𝄞 **1960** Drifting, too artsy rendering a James T. Farrell's trilogy about an Irish drifter growing up in Chicago in the '20s. Good period detail, but oddly off-kilter and implausible as history. **96m/B VHS, DVD.** Christopher Knight, Frank Gorshin, Jack Nicholson, Jay C. Flippen, Katherine Squire, Dick Foran, Carolyn Craig; ***D:*** Irving Lerner; ***W:*** Philip Yordan; ***C:*** Haskell Wexler; ***M:*** Jerry Goldsmith.

A Study in Scarlet 𝄞𝄞 **1933** Owen played Watson the previous year in "Sherlock Holmes"; here he's miscast as Holmes, and the plot differs from the Doyle story of the same title. **77m/B VHS, DVD.** Reginald Owen, Alan Mowbray, Anna May Wong, June Clyde, Alan Dinehart; ***D:*** Edwin L. Marin; ***W:*** Reginald Owen.

A Study in Terror 𝄞𝄞𝄞 *Sherlock Holmes Grosster Fall; Fog* **1966** A well-appointed Sherlock Holmes thriller, and the second one in color. Premise has a young, athletic Holmes in pursuit of an educated Jack the Ripper in 1880s London. **94m/C VHS.** *GE GB* John Neville, Donald Houston, Judi Dench, Anthony Quayle, Robert Morley, Frank Finlay, Cecil Parker; ***D:*** James Hill.

The Stuff 𝄞 ½ **1985 (R)** Surreal horror semi-spoof about an ice cream mogul and a hamburger king who discover that the new, fast-selling confection in town zombifies its partakers. Forced, lame satire from producer/director/writer Cohen. **93m/C VHS, DVD.** Michael Moriarty, Andrea Marcovicci, Garrett Morris, Paul Sorvino, Danny Aiello, Brooke Adams, Patrick O'Neal, Alexander Scourby, Scott Bloom, James Dixon, Tammy Grimes, Clara Peller, Abe Vigoda; ***D:*** Larry Cohen; ***W:*** Larry Cohen; ***C:*** Paul Glickman; ***M:*** Anthony Guefen.

Stuff Stephanie in the Incinerator 𝄞 *In Deadly Heat* **1989 (PG-13)** A Troma gagfest about wealthy cretins who torture and kill young women. "Funny" title betrays utter, exploitive mindlessness. **97m/C VHS, DVD.** Catherine Dee, William Dame, M.R. Murphy, Dennis Cunningham; ***D:*** Don Nardo.

The Stunt Man 𝄞𝄞𝄞𝄞 **1980 (R)** A marvelous and unique exercise in meta-cinematic manipulation. O'Toole, in one of his very best roles, is a power-crazed movie director; Railsback is a fugitive sheltered by him from sherrif Rocco. When a stunt man is killed in an accident, O'Toole prevails on Railsback to replace him, leading Railsback to wonder if O'Toole wants him dead. A labor of love for director-producer Rush, who spent nine years working on it, and waited two years to see it released, by Fox. Based on the novel by Paul Brodeur. **129m/C VHS, DVD.** Peter O'Toole, Steve Railsback, Barbara Hershey, Charles "Chuck" Bail, Alex Rocco, Allen (Goorwitz) Garfield, Adam Roarke, Sharon Farrell, Philip Bruns; ***D:*** Richard Rush; ***W:*** Richard Rush, Lawrence B. Marcus; ***C:*** Mario Tosi; ***M:*** Dominic Frontiere. Golden Globes '81: Score; Montreal World Film Fest. '80: Film; Natl. Soc. Film Critics '80: Actor (O'Toole).

Stunt Pilot 𝄞𝄞 **1939** A young man takes a job at a film studio as a stunt pilot and finds mayhem and romance on and off the ground. One in the "Tailspin Tommy" series. Well-paced and fun to watch. **61m/C VHS.** John Trent, Marjorie Reynolds, Milburn Stone, Jason Robards Sr., Pat O'Malley; ***D:*** George Waggner; ***W:*** George Waggner, Scott Darling; ***C:*** Fred H. Jackman Jr.; ***M:*** Frank Sanucci.

Stuntmen 𝄞 ½ **2009 (R)** A crazy documentary filmmaker reignites the rivalry between the two leading stuntmen in the industry, who have both been nominated for the Stuntman of the Year award. When Steve tries to uncover what's behind the riff, he learns some secrets that could ruin the stunt community. **90m/C DVD.** Marc Blucas, Ross Patterson, Chris Tarantino, Brandon Routh, Dominique Swain, Carly Pope, Zachary Levi, Ray Wise; ***D:*** Eric Amadio; ***W:*** Eric Amadio; ***C:*** Todd Hickey. **VIDEO**

Stunts 𝄞𝄞 *Who Is Killing the Stuntman* **1977 (PG)** See "The Stunt Man" instead. OK script hides near-invisible plot; stunt man engages in derring-do. **90m/C VHS, DVD.** Robert Forster, Fiona Lewis, Joanna Cassidy, Darrell Fetty, Bruce Glover, James Luisi; ***D:*** Mark L. Lester; ***M:*** Michael Kamen.

Stuntwoman 𝄞 ½ **1981** Welch plays a stuntwoman whose death-defying job interferes with her love life. What ever shall she do? **95m/C VHS.** Raquel Welch, Jean-Paul Belmondo; ***D:*** Claude Zidi.

The Stupids 𝄞 ½ **1995 (PG)** In the tradition of "Dumb and Dumber," the aptly named Stupids—dad Stanley (Arnold), mom Joan (Lundy), brother Buster (Hall), and sis Petunia (McKenna)—blunder unwittingly into and out of dangerous adventures involving their garbage. Landing Arnold for the lead seems like the casting coup of the decade but the movie itself is shaky and uninspired. Based on the children's best-selling books. Keep a lookout for Captain Kangaroo (Keeshan) and numerous other cameos. **93m/C VHS, DVD.** Tom Arnold, Jessica Lundy, Bug Hall, Alex McKenna, Mark Metcalf, Matt Keeslar, Frankie Faison, Christopher Lee, Bob Keeshan; ***Cameos:*** Robert Wise, Norman Jewison, Constantin Costa-Gavras, David Cronenberg, Atom Egoyan, Gillo Pontecorvo; ***D:*** John Landis; ***W:*** Brent Forrester; ***C:*** Manfred Guthe; ***M:*** Christopher Stone. Golden Raspberries '96: Worst Actor (Arnold).

Styx 𝄞𝄞 ½ **2000 (R)** Nelson (Weller) decides to get out of the safecracking trade after his brother Mike (MacFadyen) rescues him from a botched bank heist that leaves several accomplices unaccounted for. Nelson tries to go straight but Mike is a losing gambler with a big debt to some loan sharks. Nelson agrees to do a diamond heist only to learn that his not-so-missing partner Art (Brown) is the mastermind and Art just may be holding a grudge. Pro cast and fast-paced action take this above the usual heist flicks. **94m/C VHS, DVD.** Peter Weller, Bryan Brown, Angus MacFadyen, Adrienne Pierce, Anthony Bishop, Nan Hamilton, Shane Howarth, Gerard Rudolf; ***D:*** Alexander Wright; ***W:*** George Ferris; ***C:*** Russell Lyster; ***M:*** Roy Hay.

Sub Down 𝄞 **1997 (PG-13)** Silly underwater saga about a submarine trapped under the polar ice cap in the Bering Strait. Scientists Baldwin, Conti, and Anwar are aboard the USS Portland when it manages to collide with a Russian sub and sink. So they're running out of air and have to figure out a way to survive. Director Gregg Champion took his name off, so be warned. **91m/C VHS, DVD.** Stephen Baldwin, Gabrielle Anwar, Tom Conti, Chris Mulkey, Tony Plana, Joel Thomas Traywick, Doug McKeon; ***D:*** Alan Smithee; ***W:*** Howard Chesley; ***C:*** Hiro Narita; ***M:*** Stefano Mainetti. **CABLE**

Subhuman 𝄞 *Shelf Life* **2004 (R)** Psycho bounty hunter Martin (McDonald) is going around decapitating people when he's accidentally run over by Ben (McLaughlin) and Julie (Kramer). He convinces them not to take him to a hospital; instead they take him to their home (because they're really stupid). Martin tells them he's hunting blood-sucking parasites that can only be destroyed by decapitating the host, which turns out to be true as the couple soon finds out. **90m/C DVD.** *CA* William McDonald, Earl Pastko, Bryce McLaughlin, Courtney Kramer; ***D:*** Mark Tuit; ***W:*** Mark Tuit; ***C:*** Craig Powell; ***M:*** Stephen Bukat, Jeff Tymoschuk.

Subject Two 𝄞 ½ **2006 (R)** A claustrophobic "Frankenstein" variation. In a remote Rocky Mountain cabin, scientist Dr. Vick (Stapleton) uses his new assistant, Adam (Oliver), as a guinea pig in his controversial research on death and resurrection. He kills Adam and revives him, over and over again. **93m/C DVD.** *US* Dean Stapleton, Christian Oliver, Courtney Mace, Jurgen Jones; ***D:*** Philip Chidel; ***W:*** Philip Chidel; ***C:*** Rich Confalone; ***M:*** Erik Godal.

The Subject Was Roses 𝄞𝄞𝄞 ½ **1968** Outstanding story of family dysfunction and love based on Gilroy's Pulitzer Prize-winning play. Timmy Cleary (Sheen) returns from WWII to find that his parents' marriage has disintegrated into open hostility. Formerly mom Nettie's (Neal) fave, Timmy finally starts to learn about blustery dad John (Albertson) and attempts to moderate between the rancorous duo. But he quickly discovers that each of his parents will use him against the other and Timmy decides the best thing for everyone would be if he strikes out on his own. First film for Neal after her recovery from a series of strokes. **107m/C VHS.** Martin Sheen, Patricia Neal, Jack Albertson; ***D:*** Ulu Grosbard; ***W:*** Frank D. Gilroy; ***C:*** Jack Priestley; ***M:*** Lee Pockriss. Oscars '68: Support. Actor (Albertson).

Sublime 𝄞 ½ **2007 (R)** George Grieves (Cavanagh) goes to the hospital for a routine procedure and doctors mistakenly perform a different surgery that results in George contracting a flesh-eating bacteria. This results in more surgeries and a series of flashbacks concerning George's anxieties, including his health care concerns (guess he was right about that). **113m/C DVD.** Tom Cavanagh, Kathleen York, Lawrence-Hilton Jacobs, Kyle Gallner, Katherine Cunningham-Eves, Paget Brewster, Shanna Collins; ***D:*** Tony Krantz; ***W:*** Erik Jendresen; ***C:*** Dermott Downs; ***M:*** Peter Golub. **VIDEO**

Subliminal Seduction 𝄞 *Roger Corman Presents: Subliminal Seduction; The Corporation* **1996 (R)** Videogame designer Ziering realizes that mind-control messages have been coded into CD-ROMS. **81m/C VHS.** Ian Ziering, Dee Wallace, Kin Shriner, Stella Stevens, Katherine Kelly Lang, Larry Manetti, Andrew Stevens; ***D:*** Andrew Stevens. **CABLE**

Submarine Attack 𝄞𝄞 *Torpedo Zone; The Great Hope; La Grande Speranza* **1954** Unconventional war story posits an Italian submarine captain (Baldini) who decides to rescue the survivors of a Danish freighter that he has sunk. **92m/B VHS, DVD.** *IT* Renato Baldini, Lois Maxwell, Folco Lulli, Carlo Bellini, Earl Cameron; ***D:*** Duilio Coletti; ***C:*** Leonida Barboni; ***M:*** Nino Rota.

Submarine Seahawk ✂✂ **1959** When a group of Japanese warships mysteriously disappear, allied intelligence suspect a big battle is brewing. An inexperienced commander who has been tracking the movement of the Japanese ships is put in charge of the submarine Seahawk, even though the crew lacks faith in his command abilities. His own men may prove a bigger obstacle than any of the Japanese. Lots of action and stock WWII footage. **83m/B VHS.** John Bentley, Brett Halsey, Wayne Heffley, Steve Mitchell, Henry McCann, Frank Gerstle; ***D:*** Spencer Gordon Bennet.

Submerged ✂✂ **2000 (R)** Terrorists hijack a commerical airliner carrying a computer decoder that controls a national defense satellite capable of launching nuclear weapons. The hijackers deliberately plunge the plane into the Pacific Ocean and while the passengers struggle to survive, a team of Nacy SEALS attempt a rescue mission and a strike against the bad guys. **95m/C VHS, DVD.** Coolio, Nicole Eggert, Fred Williamson, Dennis Weaver, Maxwell Caulfield, Brent Huff, Tim Thomerson, Stacey Travis, Yvette Nipar; ***D:*** Fred Olen Ray; ***W:*** Steve Latshaw; ***C:*** Thomas Callaway. **VIDEO**

Submerged ✂ **2005 (R)** Cookie-cutter Steven Seagal action flick has the fading star as a notorious "freelance" anti-terrorist agent sprung from prison to help end a US government conspiracy and fight terrorists aboard a nuclear sub. **96m/C DVD.** Steven Seagal, Vinnie Jones, Nick Brimble, William Hope, Christine Adams; ***D:*** Anthony Hickox; ***W:*** Anthony Hickox, Paul DeSouza; ***C:*** David Bridges; ***M:*** Guy Farley. **VIDEO**

Submission ✂ 1/2 **1977 (R)** A pharmacist's sensuality is reawakened when she has a provocative affair with a clerk in her shop. **107m/C VHS.** *IT* Franco Nero, Lisa Gastoni; ***D:*** Salvatore Samperi.

Subspecies ✂ 1/2 **1990 (R)** New improved vampire demons descend on earth. The first full-length feature film shot on location in Transylvania. For horror buffs only. **90m/C VHS, DVD.** Laura Tate, Michael Watson, Anders (Tofting) Hove, Michelle McBride, Irina Movila, Angus Scrimm; ***D:*** Ted Nicolaou.

The Substance of Fire ✂✂ **1996 (R)** Publisher Isaac Geldhart (Rifkin) is an autocrat in both his business and his personal life, which may be why he's having so much trouble with both. A Holocaust survivor, Geldhart's obsessive about publishing a lavish four-volume history of Nazi medical experiments that will bankrupt the family firm. So his children wind up ousting him from the company and Isaac slowly slips over the edge into madness. Very King Lear, with an astonishing performance by Rifkin who also played the character in Baitz's 1991 Off-Broadway play. **100m/C VHS, DVD.** Ron Rifkin, Tony Goldwyn, Timothy Hutton, Sarah Jessica Parker, Ronny Graham, Elizabeth Franz, Gil Bellows; ***D:*** Daniel Sullivan; ***W:*** Jon Robin Baitz; ***C:*** Robert Yeoman; ***M:*** Joseph Vitarelli.

The Substitute ✂✂ **1993 (R)** Donohue plays a sexy high-school substitute teacher who turns out to have homicidal tendencies, which she decides to take out on her students. Film debut for rapper/underwear model Mark. **86m/C VHS.** Amanda Donohoe, Dalton James, Natasha Gregson Wagner, Eugene Robert Glazer, Mark Wahlberg; ***D:*** Martin Donovan; ***W:*** Cynthia Verlaine; ***M:*** Gerald Gouriet.

The Substitute ✂ **1996 (R)** Berenger plays a Vietnam vet mercenary who poses as a substitute teacher to uncover a drug ring after his girlfriend (Venora) is roughed up by the gang. At one point, he displays his unique teaching style by throwing some unruly students out of the second floor window. Hmm...wonder if that was on the test. Being a concerned teacher, he decides to uncover the kingpin of the unruly drug gang. Being an unruly drug gang, they decide to shoot at him...a lot. Unless you're a fan of heavy weaponry, banal one liners or yelling at the screen in frustration, substitute another movie for this one. **114m/C VHS, DVD.** Tom Berenger, Ernie Hudson, Diane Venora, Marc Anthony, Glenn Plummer, Cliff DeYoung, William Forsythe, Raymond Cruz, Sharron Corley, Richard Brooks, Rodney A. Grant, Luis Guzman; ***D:*** Robert Mandel; ***W:*** Alan Ormsby, Roy Frumkes, Rocco Simonelli; ***C:*** Bruce Surtees; ***M:*** Gary Chang.

The Substitute 2: School's Out ✂✂ **1997 (R)** Mercenary Carl Thomasson (Williams) poses as a high school substitute teacher to hunt down the New York gang bangers who murdered his brother during a carjacking. But his plans for revenge put innocent schoolchildren at risk as well. **90m/C VHS, DVD.** Treat Williams, B.D. Wong, Angel David, Michael Michele, Larry (Lawrence) Gilliard Jr.; ***D:*** Steven Pearl; ***W:*** Roy Frumkes, Rocco Simonelli; ***C:*** Larry Banks; ***M:*** Joe Delia. **VIDEO**

The Substitute 3: Winner Takes All ✂✂ 1/2 **1999 (R)** Mercenary Karl Thomasson (Williams) visits Nicole, the daughter of a dead friend who's a teacher at an eastern college. After Nicole is badly beaten, Karl takes over as a substitute and has his fellow mercenaries investigate. They discover members of the football team are on steroids, thanks to an in with the son of the local crime boss, so Karl and his buddies decide to clean things up. **90m/C VHS, DVD.** Treat Williams, Rebecca Staab, Claudia Christian, James Black, Richard Portnow; ***D:*** Robert Radler; ***W:*** Roy Frumkes, Rocco Simonelli; ***C:*** Barry M. Wilson; ***M:*** Tor Hyams. **VIDEO**

The Substitute 4: Failure is Not an Option ✂ 1/2 **2000 (R)** Undercover cop Karl Thomaason (Williams) poses as a teacher at a military academy and discovers a group of neo-Nazi cadets whose aims are supported by members of the staff. The more sequels, the less steam this series has—this one is definitely running on low. **91m/C VHS, DVD.** Treat Williams, Angie Everhart, Bill Nunn, Tim Abell, Simon Rhee, Patrick Kilpatrick, Michael Weatherly, Grayson Fricke; ***D:*** Robert Radler; ***W:*** Dan Gurskis; ***C:*** Richard M. Rawlings Jr.; ***M:*** Stephen (Steve) Edwards. **VIDEO**

The Substitute Wife ✂✂ 1/2 **1994 (PG-13)** Dying Nebraska frontier woman Amy Hightower (Thompson) decides to find her husband Martin (Weller) a new wife to help on the farm and look after their four children. But women are so scarce (and the farm is so isolated) that the only one willing to give it a try is prostitute Pearl (Fawcett), who's fed up with her profession but isn't exactly the motherly type (at least not at first). Amusing relationships develop between the two women and the bewildered husband. Made for TV. **92m/C VHS, DVD.** Farrah Fawcett, Lea Thompson, Peter Weller; ***D:*** Peter Werner; ***W:*** Stan Daniels; ***C:*** Neil Roach; ***M:*** Mark Snow. **TV**

Subterano ✂ **2001 (R)** The low-budget defeats this sci-fier. In a totalitarian future society (yawn), rebel leader Conrad (Dimitriades) and fellow dissdent Stone (Walton) get chased by the feds into an underground parking garage. But they (and others trapped with them) have bigger problems—a crazy videogame designer uses the garage as a set-up for the life-size version of his virtual reality game Subterano and they've just become his new players. **95m/C VHS, DVD.** *AU* Alex Dimitriades, Tasma Walton, Alison Whyte, Kate Sherman, Jason Stojanovski; ***D:*** Esben Storm; ***W:*** Esben Storm; ***C:*** Graeme Wood.

Subterfuge ✂✂ **1968** When a special American security agent goes to England for a "vacation," his presence causes speculation and poses several serious questions for both British Intelligence and the underworld. Nothing special, with the occasional suspenseful moment. **89m/C VHS.** *GB* Tom Adams, Joan Collins, Gene Barry, Richard Todd; ***D:*** Peter Graham Scott.

Subterfuge ✂✂ **1998 (R)** When a plane explodes over the Black Sea, the CIA, Russian spies, and drug runners are all after the black box. **95m/C VHS, DVD.** Matt McColm, Amanda Pays, Glynn Turman, Jason Gould, Richard Brake, Ben Hammer; ***D:*** Herb Freed; ***W:*** Marion Segal; ***C:*** Irek Hartowicz; ***M:*** Jim Halfpenny.

Suburban Commando ✂✂ **1991 (PG)** A goofy, muscular alien mistakenly lands on Earth while on vacation. He does his best to remain inconspicuous, resulting in numerous hilarious situations. Eventually he is forced to confront his arch, interstellar nemesis in order to defend the family who befriended him. A harmless, sometimes cute vehicle for wrestler Hogan, which will certainly entertain his younger fans. **88m/C VHS, DVD.** Hulk Hogan, Christopher Lloyd, Shelley Duvall, Larry Miller, William Ball, JoAnn Dearing, Jack Elam, Roy Dotrice, Christopher Neame, Tony Longo; ***D:*** Burt Kennedy; ***W:*** Frank Cappello.

Suburban Girl ✂✂ **2007 (PG-13)** Naive NYC associate book editor Brett (Gellar) is overwhelmed by her new job. Then she meets lecherous star publisher Archie Knox (Baldwin), who offers to show her how to fit in. The mismatched love affair works kinda well, basically because Baldwin knows how to sell his somewhat smarmy charm. Gellar seems a little out of her depth. Based on two stories from "The Girls' Guide to Hunting and Fishing" by Melissa Grant. **97m/C DVD, Blu-ray Disc.** Sarah Michelle Gellar, Alec Baldwin, James Naughton, Maggie Grace, Chris Carmack; ***D:*** Marc Klein; ***W:*** Marc Klein; ***C:*** Steven Fierberg; ***M:*** Hector Pereira.

Suburban Roulette ✂ **1967** "Adults only" feature from splattermaster Lewis caters to the prurient. Groovy themes like wife swapping and other very daring subjects. Totally '60s. Presented as part of Joe Bob Brigg's "Sleaziest Movies in the History of the World" series. **91m/C VHS.** Elizabeth Wilkinson, Ben Moore, Tony McCabe, Debbie Grant; ***D:*** Herschell Gordon Lewis; ***W:*** Herschell Gordon Lewis; ***C:*** Roy Collodi.

The Suburbans ✂ 1/2 **1999 (R)** Bland and not very funny ensemble comedy. The Suburbans were an '80s one-hit wonder band who reunite 18 years later at member Gil's (Ferrell) wedding. Their impromptu reunion draws the attention of unlikely record company talent scout Kate (Hewitt), who decides she wants to resurrect their would-be music careers. The music satire is funny but the domestic angst is boring. **81m/C VHS, DVD.** Jennifer Love Hewitt, Will Ferrell, Donal Lardner Ward, Craig Bierko, Amy Brenneman, Bridgette Wilson-Sampras, Tony Guma, Robert Loggia, Antonio Fargas, Ben Stiller, Jerry Stiller; ***D:*** Donal Lardner Ward; ***W:*** Donal Lardner Ward, Tony Guma; ***C:*** Michael Barrett; ***M:*** Robbie Kondor.

Suburbia ✂ *The Wild Side* **1983 (R)** When a group of punk rockers move into a condemned suburban development, they become the targets of a vigilante group. Low budget, needless violent remake of anyone of many '50s rebellion flicks that tries to have a "message." **99m/C VHS, DVD.** Chris Pederson, Bill Coyne, Jennifer Clay, Timothy Eric O'Brien, Andrew Pece, Don Allen; ***D:*** Penelope Spheeris; ***W:*** Penelope Spheeris; ***C:*** Tim Suhrstedt; ***M:*** Alex Gibson.

subUrbia ✂✂ **1996 (R)** Ensemble piece featuring three aimless post-high school friends, Jeff (Ribisi), Buff (Zahn), and Tim (Katt) who spend their time hanging out in the parking lot of a convenience store. What's different about this night is that they're joined by Jeff's girlfriend Sooze (Carey) and her friend Bee-Bee (Spybey), and they actually have a purpose for waiting around. The guys are expecting a visit from their old buddy Pony (Bartok), a rock musician just finding success. But when Pony does appear, the fact that he has done something to get out and succeed turns the meeting hostile. Based on the play by Eric Bogosian. **118m/C VHS.** Giovanni Ribisi, Steve Zahn, Nicky Katt, Jayce Bartok, Amie Carey, Dina Spybey, Parker Posey, Ajay Naidu, Samia Shoaib; ***D:*** Richard Linklater; ***W:*** Eric Bogosian; ***C:*** Lee Daniel.

Subway ✂ 1/2 **1985 (R)** Surreal, MTV-esque vision of French fringe life from the director of "Le Dernier Combat." A spike-haired renegade escapes the law by plunging into the Parisian subway system. Once there, he encounters a bizarre subculture living under the city. Plenty of angry-youth attitude, but where's the point? And frankly, too much bad New Wave music. **103m/C VHS, DVD.** *FR* Christopher Lambert, Isabelle Adjani, Jean-Hugues Anglade, Jean Reno, Richard Bohringer, Michel Galabru, Eric Serra, Arthur Simms; ***D:*** Luc Besson; ***W:*** Luc Besson, Pierre Jolivet, Alain Le Henry, Marc Perrier, Sophie Schmit; ***C:*** Carlo Varini; ***M:*** Rickie Lee Jones, Eric Serra. Cesar '86: Actor (Lambert), Art Dir./Set Dec., Sound.

Subway Stories ✂✂ **1997 (R)** Ten short films based on actual experiences on the New York subway system featuring such topics as harassment, flirtation, sex, food, and money. **82m/C VHS.** Bill Irwin, Kris Parker, Denis Leary, Christine Lahti, Steve Zahn, Jerry Stiller, Bonnie Hunt, Lili Taylor, Michael Rapaport, Mercedes Ruehl, Sarita Choudhury, Taral Hicks, Danny Hoch, Mike McGlone, Rosie Perez, Gregory Hines, Anne Heche; ***D:*** Ted (Edward) Demme, Abel Ferrara, Jonathan Demme, Julie Dash, Seth Zvi Rosenfeld, Bob Balaban, Alison Maclean, Lucas Platt, Patricia Benoit, Craig McKay; ***W:*** Danny Hoch, John Guare, Adam Brooks, Julie Dash, Lynn Grossman, Marla Hanson, Seth Zvi Rosenfeld, Joe Viola, Albert Innaurato, Angela Todd; ***C:*** Ken Kelsch, Adam Kimmel, Tom Hurwitz, Anthony C. "Tony" Jannelli.

Subway to the Stars ✂✂ 1/2 *Un Trem Para as Estrelas* **1987** Young saxophonist Fontes searches the back streets of Rio for his missing girlfriend. Realistic and sometimes depressing, if aimless at times. Overall, an intriguing "underworld" flick from Brazil. Portuguese with subtitles. **103m/C VHS.** *BR* Guilherme Fontes, Milton Goncalves, Taumaturgo Ferreira, Ze Trindade, Ana Beatriz Wiltgen; ***D:*** Carlos Diegues.

Success Is the Best Revenge ✂✂ **1984 (R)** Ambitious Polish stage director Alex Rodak (York) and his family are living in exile in London because of Poland's martial law. He's working on a stage production about the subject and turns to a questionable businessman (Hurt) for financing, which displeases his unhappy wife. Also disillusioned is Rodak's teen son Adam (Lyndon), who has made his own arrangements to return to Warsaw. **88m/C DVD.** *GB FR* Michael York, Michael Lyndon, John Hurt, Anouk Aimee, Janna Szerzerbic, Jerry Skal; ***D:*** Jerzy Skolimowski; ***W:*** Jerzy Skolimowski; ***C:*** Mike Fash; ***M:*** Stanley Myers, Hans Zimmer.

Such a Long Journey ✂✂✂ **1998** Bank clerk Gustad Noble has a modest life that is beginning to fall apart. First his young daughter becomes very ill and then his son defies Gustad's ambitions for him. Finally, he receives a letter from an old friend asking for his help and Gustad finds himself caught up in unexpected danger and deception. Set in Bombay in 1971, as India prepares for war, and based on the novel by Rohinton Mistry. **110m/C VHS.** *CA GB* Roshan Seth, Om Puri, Kurush Deboo, Naseeruddin Shah, Ranjit Chowdhari; ***D:*** Sturla Gunnarsson; ***W:*** Sooni Taraporevala; ***C:*** Jan Kiesser. Genie '98: Actor (Seth), Film Editing.

Suck **2009** Joey's (Stefaniuk) 10-year-old indie band is still going nowhere when bassist Jen (Pare) goes home with a weird fan and gets turned into a vampire. She converts the other members and they can suddenly mesmerize their audiences while also being pursued by vamp hunter Eddie Van Helsing (McDowell). **90m/C DVD.** *CA* Rob Stefaniuk, Jessica Pare, Malcolm McDowell, Paul Anthony, Mike Lobel, Chris Ratz, Dave Foley, Henry Rollins, Iggy Pop, Alice Cooper, Alex Lifeson; ***D:*** Rob Stefaniuk; ***W:*** Rob Stefaniuk, Dave Foley; ***C:*** D. Gregor Hagey; ***M:*** John Kastner.

The Sucker ✂✂ *Le Corniauds* **1965** Antoine Marecchal (Bouvril) is on his way to an Italian vacation when his car is wrecked in an accident. The businessman who smashed his car offers Antoine a Cadillac to drive but this turns him into a smuggler. However, Antoine isn't as dumb as he may appear and he makes the most of his unusual situation. French with subtitles. **90m/C VHS.** *FR* Andre Bourvil, Louis de Funes; ***D:*** Gerard Oury.

Sucker Free City ✂✂✂ **2005** Three young men of different ethnicities turn to crime as the answer to surviving their rough lives in San Francisco—Nick (Crowley) steals credit card data at his office mailroom job; K-Luv (Mackie) is part of a black gang but wants out; and Chinese mafia member Lincoln (Leung) is moving up the ranks. Eventually tensions arise and an explosive showdown unfolds. Showtime original movie was directed by Spike Lee as a series pilot, though it wasn't picked up. **116m/C DVD.**

Ken Leung, Anthony Mackie, Darris Love, Laura Allen, Ben Crowley, Kathy Baker; *D:* Spike Lee; *W:* Alex Tse. **CABLE**

Sucker Money ♂ 1/2 *Victims of the Beyond* **1934** Newspaper reporter works to expose phony spiritualist. Good title; little else. Boring. **59m/B VHS.** Mischa Auer, Phyllis Barrington, Earl McCarthy, Ralph Lewis, Mae Busch, Alan Bridge, J. Frank Glendon, Harry Todd; *D:* Dorothy Davenport Reid, Melville Shyer; *W:* Willis Kent; *C:* James Diamond, William Nobles.

Suckerfish ♂♂ **1999** Veteran pet supply salesmen Alan (Donovan) and Dick (Orr) resent that a retiring colleague's lucrative territory is being given to ambitious newbie Ken (Bodden). So they set out to sabotage him. When Ken finds out why he's not making any sales, he plans revenge—starting with the knowledge that Dick's wife Elizabeth (Lawlor) is having an affair with Alan. **88m/C VHS, DVD.** Dan Donovan, Tim Orr, Kurt Bodden, Gerri Lawler; *D:* Brien Burroughs; *C:* Christopher Braun; *M:* Joshua Raoul Brody.

Sudden Death ♂ *Fast on the Draw* **1950** Shamrock and Lucky are back as cowboys posing as hired gunmen in order to foil a wealthy, homesteader-hating land baron. **55m/B VHS.** James Ellison, Russell Hayden, Fuzzy Knight, Raymond Hatton, Julie Adams, Tom Tyler, John Cason, Stanley Price; *D:* Thomas Carr; *W:* Ron Ormond, Maurice Tombragel; *C:* Ernest Miller.

Sudden Death ♂ **1977 (R)** Two professional violence merchants put themselves up for hire. **84m/C VHS, DVD.** Robert Conrad, Felton Perry, Don Stroud, Bill Raymond, Ron Vawter, Harry Roskolenko; *D:* Richard Foreman.

Sudden Death ♂ **1985 (R)** A beautiful businesswoman decides to kill every rapist she can find after she herself has been attacked. Exploitative in its own fashion; fueled and felled by rage. **95m/C VHS.** Denise Coward, Frank Runyeon, Jamie Tirelli; *D:* Sig Shore.

Sudden Death ♂♂ **1995 (R)** Terrorists invade a hockey arena where the Vice President and 17,000 fans, including Fire Marshal Jean-Claude and his kids, are watching the seventh game of the Stanley Cup Finals. The latest in the "Die Hard in a..." genre covers the territory with the now-standard lack of characterization, family member in peril, and ever-increasing body count. Boothe (playing Alan Rickman playing a bad guy) does most of the talking while Van Damme kicks people in the head and plays goalie. Producer Howard Baldwin owns the Pittsburgh Penguins, coincidentally one of the teams on the ice for the second pairing of "Timecop" vets Hyams and Van Damme. **110m/C VHS, DVD.** Jean-Claude Van Damme, Powers Boothe, Ross Malinger, Whittni Wright, Raymond J. Barry, Dorian Harewood, Kate McNeil, Audra Lindley; *D:* Peter Hyams; *W:* Gene Quintano; *C:* Peter Hyams; *M:* John Debney.

Sudden Fear ♂♂♂ **1952** Successful playwright/heiress Myra Hudson (Crawford) has a whirlwind romance, leading to marriage, with oh-so-charming actor Lester Blaine (Palance). But Les is more interested in Myra's money and gets together with former flame Irene (always the bad girl Grahame) to get rid of his new bride and inherit her fortune. But Myra finds out about the plot and puts her writing talent to work in coming up with a new scenario. Good suspenser with fine performances. Adapted from the book by Edna Sherry. **111m/B VHS, DVD.** Joan Crawford, Jack Palance, Gloria Grahame, Bruce Bennett, Virginia Huston, Mike Connors; *D:* David Miller; *W:* Lenore Coffee, Robert Smith; *C:* Charles B(ryant) Lang Jr.; *M:* Elmer Bernstein.

Sudden Impact ♂♂ 1/2 **1983 (R)** Eastwood directs himself in this formula thriller, the fourth "Dirty Harry" entry. This time "Dirty Harry" Callahan tracks down a revenge-obsessed murderess and finds he has more in common with her than he expected. Meanwhile, local mobsters come gunning for him. This is the one where he says, "Go ahead. Make my day." Followed by "The Dead Pool." **117m/C VHS, DVD, Blu-ray Disc.** Clint Eastwood, Sondra Locke, Pat Hingle, Bradford Dillman, Albert "Poppy" Popwell, Jack Thibeau, Michael Currie, Kevyn Major Howard, Bette Ford, Nancy Parsons, Michael V. Gazzo, Camryn Manheim; *D:* Clint Eastwood; *W:* Joseph C. Stinson; *C:* Bruce Surtees; *M:* Lalo Schifrin.

Sudden Manhattan ♂♂ **1996** Unemployed single Donna (Shelly) thinks she witnesses a murder—over and over again. Of course, no one believes her and she tries to figure out the truth. Shelly's directorial debut. **80m/C VHS, DVD.** Adrienne Shelly, Tim Guinee, Roger Rees, Louise Lasser, Hynden Walch; *D:* Adrienne Shelly; *W:* Adrienne Shelly; *C:* Jim Denault; *M:* Pat Irwin.

Suddenly ♂♂♂ 1/2 **1954** Crazed gunman John Baron (Sinatra) holds a family hostage in the hick town of Suddenly, California, as part of a plot to kill the president, who's stopping at the local train station. As things begin to go wrong, Baron begins to unravel. Tense thriller is a good display for Sinatra's acting talent. Unfortunately hard to find because Sinatra forced United Artists to take it out of distribution after hearing that Kennedy assassin Lee Harvey Oswald had watched "Suddenly" only days before November 22, 1963. Really, Ol' Blue Eyes should have stuck with making top-notch thrillers like this one, instead of degenerating into the world's greatest lounge singer. **75m/B VHS, DVD.** Frank Sinatra, Sterling Hayden, James Gleason, Nancy Gates, Paul Frees, Willis Bouchey, Kim Charney, Christopher Dark; *D:* Lewis Allen; *W:* Richard Sale; *C:* Charles G. Clarke; *M:* David Raksin.

Suddenly, Last Summer ♂♂♂ 1/2 **1959** Brain surgeon is summoned to the mansion of a rich New Orleans matron who wishes him to perform a lobotomy on her niece, supposedly suffering from a mental breakdown. Based on the play by Tennessee Williams. Softened for the censors, though the themes of homosexuality, insanity, and murder, characterizations of evil, and unusual settings presage many movies of the next two decades. Extremely fine performances from Hepburn and Taylor. Clift never completely recovered from his auto accident two years before and does not come across with the strength of purpose really necessary in his character. Still, fine viewing. **114m/B VHS, DVD.** Elizabeth Taylor, Katharine Hepburn, Montgomery Clift, Mercedes McCambridge, Albert Dekker; *D:* Joseph L. Mankiewicz; *W:* Gore Vidal; *C:* Jack Hildyard; *M:* Malcolm Arnold. Golden Globes '60: Actress—Drama (Taylor).

Sudie & Simpson ♂♂♂ **1990** Heart-tugging tale of friendship set in rural 1940s Georgia. Twelve-year-old white Sudie's forbidden friendship with the adult black Simpson provides a lot of talk in their small town. Racial barriers finally cause Simpson to be accused of child molestation and the odds of his survival, despite his innocence, don't seem great. Based on Sara Flanigan Carter's autobiographical novel. **95m/C VHS, DVD.** Sara Gilbert, Louis Gossett Jr., Frances Fisher, John M. Jackson, Paige Danahy, Ken Strong; *D:* Joan Tewkesbury; *W:* Sara Flanigan Carter, Ken Koser; *C:* Mario DiLeo; *M:* Michel Colombier. **CABLE**

Suds ♂♂ 1/2 **1920** Pickford is tragic laundress with major crush on a guy who left his shirt at the laundry. **75m/B VHS, DVD.** Mary Pickford, William Austin, Harold Goodwin, Madame Rose (Dion) Dione, Theodore Roberts; *D:* John Francis Dillon.

Sueno ♂♂ **2005 (PG-13)** Simple rags-to-riches musical saga follows Antonio (Leguizamo), a Mexican-born singer-musician who moves to LA to find success in the city's Latino music scene. He's got big dreams that may come true if he can overcome some predictable hardships. Pena is a delightful surprise as Mirabela, a recently divorced mother who regains her confidence when she begins singing with Antonio. **108m/C DVD.** John Leguizamo, Ana Claudia Talancon, Elizabeth Pena, Nestor Serrano, Jsu Garcia, Jose Maria Yazpik; *D:* Renee Chabria; *W:* Renee Chabria; *C:* Eric Moynier; *M:* Joselo Rangel.

Suffering Bastards ♂♂ 1/2 **1990** Buddy and Al have never worked a day in their lives—Mom's nightclub always gave them something to do and a regular paycheck. But when Mom's swindled out of the family business, they decide it's time to take charge. Soon they're caught between bullets, babes, and belly laughs in this action-filled comedy. **95m/C VHS.** Eric Bogosian, John C. McGinley, David Warshofsky; *D:* Bernard McWilliams; *W:* Bernard McWilliams; *C:* Neil Hodges; *M:* Danny Di Paola.

Sugar ♂♂♂ 1/2 **2009 (R)** Miguel 'Sugar' Santos (Soto) is a hot-shot pitching phenom from the baseball hotbed of San Pedro de Macoris, Dominican Republic. Once summoned to the American minor leagues, he experiences isolation, loneliness, bigotry, and a career-threatening injury, as well as the pressure of other talented prospects coming up behind him. He also has to deal with the expectations of his family. Complex drama surprises those expecting a by-the-book, "underdog-beats-the-odds" story by finding bigger ideas, and smaller, more personal moments. **120m/C DVD.** *US* Algenis Perez Soto, Rayniel Rufino, Andre Holland, Ann Whitney, Ellary Porterfield, Jamie Tirelli, Michael Gaston, Richard Bull; *D:* Anna Boden, Ryan Fleck; *W:* Anna Boden, Ryan Fleck; *C:* Andrij Parekh; *M:* Michael Brook.

Sugar & Spice ♂♂♂ **2001 (PG-13)** If there is such a thing as a smart cheerleader teen pic, this is it. Satire of offbeat pep squadders who cheer by day and rob banks by night includes Suvari's rebellious Kansas and Shelton's permanently upbeat Diane. Diane meets Jack (Marsden), and two American kids do the best they can when they learn Diane is pregnant. They decide to marry, move into a seedy apartment, and take up work at a local fast food joint. After losing said employment, the motivation becomes clear for the girls' ensuing illegal capers. Littered with pop culture references: the girls rent "Reservoir Dogs" to prepare for the heist, rob the banks in "Betty" masks, and deal with one of the girls' hots for Conan O'Brien. **81m/C VHS, DVD.** *US* Marley Shelton, James Marsden, Mena Suvari, Marla Sokoloff, Rachel Blanchard, Melissa George, Alexandra Holden, Sara Marsh, Sean Young; *D:* Francine McDougall; *W:* Mandy Nelson; *C:* Robert Brinkmann; *M:* Mark Mothersbaugh.

Sugar Cane Alley ♂♂♂ *Rue Cases Negres* **1983 (PG)** After the loss of his parents, an 11-year-old orphan boy goes to work with his grandmother on a sugar plantation. She realizes that her young ward's only hope is an education. Set in Martinique in the 1930s among black workers. Poignant and memorable. French with subtitles. **106m/C VHS, DVD.** *FR* Garry Cadenat, Darling Legitimus, Douta Seck; *D:* Euzhan Palcy; *W:* Euzhan Palcy; *C:* Dominique Chapuis.

Sugar Cookies **WOOF!** **1977 (R)** Erotic horror story in which young women are the pawns as a satanic satyr and an impassioned lesbian play out a bizarre game of vengeance, love, and death. **89m/C VHS, DVD.** Mary Woronov, Lynn Lowry, Monique Van Vooren; *D:* Michael Herz.

Sugar Hill ♂♂ **1994 (R)** Two brothers (Wright & Snipes) are heroin dealers who have built their own crime empire in the Sugar Hill section of Harlem. Snipes is moved to reconsider his career options when he falls for an aspiring actress (Randle). Jarring editing sequence recaps the seminal event in the brothers' upbringing and serves to explain how the wide-eyed boys became cold-blooded pushers. Good performances by all, but formulaic plot will leave viewers asking themselves if they haven't seen it before and why it was they saw it then. **123m/C VHS, DVD.** Wesley Snipes, Michael Wright, Theresa Randle, Clarence Williams III, Abe Vigoda, Ernie Hudson, Larry Joshua, Leslie Uggams, Khandi Alexander, Raymond Serra, Joe Dallesandro, Vondie Curtis-Hall, Steve Harris, Kimberly Russell, Dule Hill, Donald Adeosun Faison, Nick(y) Corello; *D:* Leon Ichaso; *W:* Barry Michael Cooper; *C:* Bojan Bazelli; *M:* Terence Blanchard.

Sugar Sweet ♂♂ 1/2 **2002** Amusing, if slight, Japanese lesbian romantic comedy. Struggling filmmaker Naomi is trying to pay the bills by shooting lesbian porn but the producers protest that she's being too "arty." Frazzled, Naomi confides her troubles to an online friend named Sugar. Then, Naomi gets the chance to direct a girl-meets-girl matchmaking TV show and casts her pal Azusa and an exotic dancer named Miki to play the romantic couple. Azusa is willing but Miki turns out to be more interest in romancing Naomi. Japanese with subtitles. **67m/C VHS, DVD.** *JP* Saori Kitagawa, Saki, C Snatch Z; *D:* Desiree Lim; *W:* Desiree Lim, Carole Hisasue; *C:* Natsuyo Nakamura; *M:* Masan Tahara, Katsuharu Imano.

Sugar Town ♂♂ **1999 (R)** Ambitions collide in this saga of the L.A. music scene. Savvy and unscrupulous young singer Gwen (Gordon) is determined to land a recording contract while a group of middle age rock stars (Taylor, Des Barres, and Kemp) want to recapture their fame—with music producer Burt (Klein) as their catalyst. There's also struggling studio musician Carl (Doe) and his woes with Latina singer, Rosio (Cavazos) and various other subplots—none of which hang together terribly well. **92m/C VHS.** Michael Des Barres, Jade Gordon, John Taylor, Martin Kemp, Larry Klein, John Doe, Lumi Cavazos, Lucinda Jenney, Rosanna Arquette, Ally Sheedy, Beverly D'Angelo, Richmond Arquette, Jeff (Jeffrey) McDonald, Vincent Berry, Polly Platt, Chris Mulkey; *D:* Allison Anders, Kurt Voss; *W:* Allison Anders, Kurt Voss; *C:* Kristian Bernier; *M:* Larry Klein.

Sugarbaby ♂♂♂ *Zuckerbaby* **1985 (R)** An acclaimed German film about a fat mortuary attendant living in Munich who transforms herself (but doesn't lose weight) in order to seduce a young, handsome subway conductor. Touching and warm film that introduced Sagebrecht to American audiences. A bit too cutting-edge cinematographically. In German with English subtitles. Remade as "Babycakes." Sagebrecht and director Adlon team up again for "Bagdad Cafe" and "Rosalie Goes Shopping." **103m/C VHS.** *GE* Marianne Saegebrecht, Eisi Gulp, Toni Berger, Will Spendler, Manuela Denz; *D:* Percy Adlon; *W:* Percy Adlon.

Sugarhouse ♂ 1/2 **2007 (R)** Middle-class London accountant Tom (Mackintosh) wants to kill his wife's lover so he purchases a gun from crackhead D (Walters). Unfortunately, the gun was stolen from psychotic drug lord Hoodwink (Serkis) who wants it back because it ties him to a murder. Violent, but not much more. Based on the 2003 play "Collision" by Dominic Leyton, who also wrote the screenplay. **94m/C DVD.** *GB* Steven Mackintosh, Ashley Walters, Andy Serkis, Tolga Safer; *D:* Gary Love; *W:* Dominic Leyton; *C:* Michael Price, Dan Bronks.

The Sugarland Express ♂♂♂ **1974 (PG)** To save her son from adoption, a young woman helps her husband break out of prison. In their flight to freedom, they hijack a police car, holding the policeman hostage. Speilberg's first feature film is a moving portrait of a couple's desperation. Based on a true story, adapted by Hal Barwood and Matthew Robbins. **109m/C VHS, DVD.** Goldie Hawn, Ben Johnson, Michael Sacks, William Atherton; *D:* Steven Spielberg; *W:* Steven Spielberg, Matthew Robbins, Hal Barwood; *C:* Vilmos Zsigmond; *M:* John Williams.

Sugartime ♂♂ 1/2 **1995 (R)** Based on the true-life romance of '60s Chicago mobster Sam Giacana (Turturro) and song bird Phyllis Maguire (Parker), one of the wholesome Maguire Sisters. Naturally, getting involved with a crime boss did little for her image and Maguire's career hit the skids while Giacana's volatile jealousy brought unwanted attention from both fellow gangsters and the feds. (He was murdered in 1975 but had broken off with Phyllis before that). The real Maguire denounced the inaccuracy of the TV production. Suggested by William F. Roemer, Jr.'s book "Roemer: Man Against the Mob." **108m/C VHS, DVD.** John Turturro, Mary-Louise Parker, Elias Koteas, Maury Chaykin, Louis Del Grande, Christopher Barry, Richard Blackburn; *D:* John N. Smith; *W:* Martyn Burke; *C:* Pierre Letarte.

Suicide Club ♂♂ *Jisatsu Sakuru* **2002** Fifty-four high school girls join hands and leap to their deaths from a subway platform into the path of an oncoming train. Police detective Kuroda (Ishibashi) receives a message from a mystery girl who informs him of a website that predicts the deaths even before they happen. With a continuing rash of suicides in Tokyo, the police are baffled—are the jumpers part of a cult and does a teen-girl pop group have some strange influence? Very bloody, very surreal, and a wicked social critique of disaffected Japanese youth. Japanese with subtitles. **92m/C VHS, DVD.** *JP* Ryo Ishibashi, Takashi Nomura, Masatoshi Na-gas, Tamao Sato, Mai Housyou; ***D:*** Sono Sion; ***W:*** Sono Sion; ***C:*** Kazuto Sato.

Suicide Fleet **1931** When three playboy sailors aren't fighting German U-boats aboard a decoy ship they're fighting to win the affections of a young woman (Rogers) working on the Coney Island midway. Some great shots of WWI vessels but a poor overall effort. **87m/B VHS.** William Boyd, Robert Armstrong, James Gleason, Ginger Rogers; ***D:*** Albert Rogell; ***W:*** Herbert A. Jones, Lew Lipton. **VIDEO**

Suicide Kings **1997 (R)** When the sister of one of four prep school friends is kidnapped, the guys decide to take retired mobster Charlie Barrett (Walken) hostage so he'll help them. The wanna-be "Reservoir Pups" lose control almost as soon as the caper begins, and the savvy Barrett takes advantage to turn his captors against each other with news that the girl's abduction may have been an inside job. Maze of a plot, which wanders into "Usual Suspects" is-this-all-real? territory, does nothing to help any of the young actors, who are clearly overmatched by Walken. Not much here for anyone except fans of Walken's patented Gangster Cool. **106m/C VHS, DVD.** Henry Thomas, Sean Patrick Flanery, Jay Mohr, Christopher Walken, Denis Leary, Jeremy Sisto, Johnny Galecki, Cliff DeYoung, Laura San Giacomo, Laura Harris, Louis Lombardi, Brad Garrett, Nina Siemaszko, Frank Medrano, Lisanne Falk, Sean M. Whalen; ***D:*** Peter O'Fallon; ***W:*** Josh McKinney, Gina Goldman, Wayne Rice; ***C:*** Christopher Baffa; ***M:*** Graeme Revell, Tim Simonec.

Suicide Ride **1997** Action-movie junkie Barney's (Quill) life is going nowhere, so looking for some real adventure he decides to hire a hitman (Hues) to off him. Only the hitman wants to retire and instead offers Barney his job, which he takes. This causes him lots of trouble. Quirky low-budgeter. **86m/C VHS.** Tim Quill, Matthias Hues, Frank Adonis; ***D:*** Samer Daboul, Trevor Sands.

Suicide Squad **1/2 1935** Braggart Larry Barker gets a job with the fire rescue squad because his girlfriend Mary is the daughter of the local fire captain. Larry's exploits get press but he can't take orders and nearly gets a fellow firefighter killed. Larry resigns rather than face disciplinary action but gets a second chance when Mary is trapped in a fire. **58m/B DVD.** Norman Foster, Joyce Compton, Robert E. Homans, Aggie Herring, Phil Kramer, Peter Warren; ***D:*** Bernard B. Ray; ***W:*** Homer King Gordon; ***C:*** James Diamond.

Suite 16 **1994 (R)** A penthouse suite in a French Riviera hotel is occupied by rich, manipulative, wheelchair-bound Glover (Postlethwaite). Young gigolo/thief Chris (Kamerling), who believes he's killed his latest trick, is given refuge by Glover in exchange for allowing the aging voyeur to watch Chris (via camera) perform with a succession of prostitutes. Finally, Chris wants to leave but Glover offers him a huge amount of money for one final vicarious—and deadly—thrill. Eurotrash, with corny dialogue, but Postlethwaite's chillingly creepy. Also available in an R-rated version. **93m/C VHS, DVD.** *BE GB* Pete Postlethwaite, Antoine Kamerling, Geraldine Pailhas, Thom Jansen; ***D:*** Dominique Deruddere; ***W:*** Charles Higson, Lise Mayer; ***C:*** Jean-Francois Robin; ***M:*** Walter Hus.

The Suitors **1988** When a group of Iranians decide to sacrifice a lamb in their apartment, the New York police send in SWAT team assuming they're terrorists. First time effort by Ebrahimian, in Farsi with English subtitles. **106m/C VHS, DVD.** Pouran Esrafily, Assurbanipal Babila, Shahab Navab, Ali Azizian; ***D:*** Ghasem Ebrahimian; ***W:*** Ghasem Ebrahimian; ***C:*** Manfred Reiff.

Sukiyaki Western Django **1/2 2008 (R)** Best appreciated by fans of director Miike or those who don't mind a genre homage in this Japanese combo samurai/spaghetti western. In the late 1880s, two clans battle over a fortune hidden in a desolate mountain town. A nameless gunman rides in and plans to pick over what's left until he joins in a saloon gal's revenge plot. Subtitled, heavily-accented English dialogue sounds like it was learned phonetically. **121m/C DVD.** *JP* Hideaki Ito, Yoshino Kimura, Koichi Sato, Masanobu Ando, Yusuke Iseya, Takaaki Ishibashi, Kaori Momoi, Teruyuki Kagawa, Ruka Uchida, Quentin Tarantino; ***D:*** Takashi Miike; ***W:*** Takashi Miike, Masaru Nakamura; ***C:*** Toyomichi Kurita; ***M:*** Koji Endo.

Sullivan's Travels **1941** Sturges' masterpiece is a sardonic, whip-quick romp about a Hollywood director tired of making comedies who decides to make a serious, socially responsible film and hits the road masquerading as a hobo in order to know hardship and poverty. Beautifully sustained, inspired satire that mercilessly mocked the ambitions of Depression-era social cinema. Gets a little over-dark near the end before the happy ending; Sturges insisted on 20-year-old Lake as The Girl; her pregnancy forced him to rewrite scenes and design new costumes for her. As ever, she is stunning. **90m/B VHS, DVD.** Joel McCrea, Veronica Lake, William Demarest, Robert Warwick, Franklin Pangborn, Porter Hall, Eric Blore, Byron Foulger, Robert Greig, Torben Meyer, Jimmy Conlin, Margaret (Maggie) Hayes, Chester Conklin, Alan Bridge; ***D:*** Preston Sturges; ***W:*** Preston Sturges; ***C:*** John Seitz; ***M:*** Leo Shuken. Natl. Film Reg. '90.

The Sum of All Fears **1/2 2002 (PG-13)** Affleck takes over as Jack Ryan, who is now just an analyst, and has a girlfriend (Moynihan) who's a young doctor (hmmm...), but the film is still set in the present-day. That's just the first confusing element of this complicated spy thriller. The first half is spent on set pieces that seem to have no connection, until a climactic event (which takes place an hour in). Ryan is trying to prevent a nuclear war between the U.S. and Russia. Neo-Nazis are the baddies who put the world on the brink, and give the audience a safe, cartoony villian to make up for the now all-too-possible nuclear scenario. Affleck shows signs of growing into the role if the franchise continues, but he's not there yet. Pic is at its best when in the conference rooms of the White House and Kremlin, with each leader's advisors pressing their agendas. **118m/C VHS, DVD.** *US* Ben Affleck, Morgan Freeman, James Cromwell, Bridget Moynahan, Liev Schreiber, Ron Rifkin, Alan Bates, Ciaran Hinds, Philip Baker Hall, Bruce McGill, Colm Feore, Josef Sommer, Ken Jenkins, Michael Byrne, John Beasley, Jamie Harrold, Richard Marner, Lee Garlington, Eugene (Yevgeny) Lazarev, Sven-Ole Thorsen, Lisa Gay Hamilton, Lisa Bronwyn Moore; ***D:*** Phil Alden Robinson; ***W:*** Paul Attanasio, Daniel Pyne; ***C:*** John Lindley; ***M:*** Jerry Goldsmith.

The Sum of Us **1994 (R)** Sweet and faithful adaptation of David Stevens' stage play about a father and his gay son. Widowed Harry Mitchell (Thompson) shares his house with son Jeff (Crowe), who's never made a secret of his sexual orientation. Affable Harry only wants what's best for his boy, including his over-enthusiastic welcome to Jeff's potential new boyfriend (Polson). Too bad Harry's not so lucky in love—his new woman friend Joyce (Kennedy) has problems with Jeff's sexuality. Well, she just has to adjust. Pervasive feel-good message may leave less well-adjusted viewer addled. Sensitive performances, though the film's antecedents as a play are highlighted by having the main characters talk directly to the camera. Aussie slang provides a challenge. **99m/C VHS, DVD.** *AU* Jack Thompson, Russell Crowe, John Polson, Deborah Kennedy, Mitch Mathews, Julie Herbert, Joss Moroney, Rebekah Elmaloglou; ***D:*** Kevin Dowling, Geoff Burton; ***W:*** David Stevens; ***C:*** Geoff Burton; ***M:*** Dave Faulkner. Australian Film Inst. '94: Adapt. Screenplay; Montreal World Film Fest. '94: Screenplay.

Summer **1/2** *Le Rayon Vert; The Green Ray* **1986 (R)** The fifth and among the best of Rohmer's "Comedies and Proverbs" series. A romantic but glum young French girl finds herself stuck in Paris during the tourist season searching for true romantic love. Takes time and patience to seize the viewer; moving ending makes it all worthwile. In French with English subtitles. **98m/C VHS, DVD.** *FR* Marie Riviere, Lisa Heredia, Beatrice Romand, Eric Hamm, Rosette, Isabelle Riviere; ***D:*** Eric Rohmer; ***W:*** Eric Rohmer; ***C:*** Sophie Maintigneux; ***M:*** Jean-Louis Valero.

Summer Affair **1/2** *Sole Nella Pelle* **1971** Two young lovers run away from their bickering parents and get shipwrecked on a desert island. **90m/C VHS.** *IT* Ornella Muti, Alessio Orano; ***D:*** George S. Casorati; ***W:*** George S. Casorati; ***C:*** Sergio d'Offizi; ***M:*** Gianni Marchetti.

Summer and Smoke **1/2 1961** Repressed, unhappy Page falls for handsome doctor Harvey. A tour de force for Page, but that's all; adapted clumsily from the overwrought Tennessee Williams play. **118m/C VHS.** Laurence Harvey, Geraldine Page, Rita Moreno, Una Merkel, John McIntire, Thomas Gomez, Pamela Tiffin, Lee Patrick, Max (Casey Adams) Showalter, Earl Holliman, Harry Shannon, Pattee Chapman; ***D:*** Peter Glenville; ***C:*** Charles B(ryant) Lang Jr.; ***M:*** Elmer Bernstein. Golden Globes '62: Actress—Drama (Page); Natl. Bd. of Review '61: Actress (Page).

Summer Camp Nightmare **1/2** *The Butterfly Revolution* **1986 (PG-13)** See "Lord of the Flies" instead. A young fascist incites children at two summer camps to overthrow and imprison the adults. Barbarism rears its ugly head. Self-serious and anticlimatic. Based on the novel "The Butterfly Revolution" by William Butler. **89m/C VHS.** Chuck Connors, Charles Stratton, Harold P. Pruett, Tom Fridley, Adam Carl; ***D:*** Bert L. Dragin; ***C:*** Don Burgess.

Summer Catch **1/2 2001 (PG-13)** Freddie Prinze, Jr. is really gonna have to learn to shake off some of the signs his agent is giving him. In this rip-off of every baseball movie of the last decade, Prinze plays underdog pitcher Ryan, on his last chance in his hometown Cape Cod league. Complicating matters are his flamboyant rival Eric (Pearson) and upperclass babe Tenley (Biel), who he falls for while cutting lawns for his irascible father (Ward). Can Ryan make it to the big leagues with help from grizzled manager Schiffner (Dennehy)? Will he win the bodacious babe despite protests from her blue-blood father (Davison)? Will Lillard make another appearance in a Freddie Prinze, Jr. movie? If you don't know the answers to those questions, you deserve to watch this bush-league flick. **108m/C VHS, DVD.** *US* Freddie Prinze Jr., Jessica Biel, Matthew Lillard, Brian Dennehy, Fred Ward, Jason Gedrick, Brittany Murphy, Marc Blucas, Bruce Davison, Wilmer Valderrama, Christian Kane, Gabriel Mann, Cedric Pendleton, Zena Grey, Corey Pearson; ***D:*** Mike Tollin; ***W:*** Kevin Falls, John Gatins; ***C:*** Tim Suhrstedt; ***M:*** George Fenton.

Summer City **1/2** *Coast of Terror* **1977** Fun-and-sun surfing movie complete with romance, hot rods, murder and great shots of the sea features Gibson in his debut. Ever wonder what Australian surf bums do on weekends? The same as their California counterparts—except they talk funny. **83m/C VHS, DVD.** *AU* Mel Gibson, Phillip Avalon, John Jarratt, Christopher Fraser; ***D:*** Christopher Fraser; ***W:*** Phillip Avalon; ***C:*** Jerry Marek; ***M:*** Phil Butkis.

Summer Fantasy **1984** Mindless TV surf saga about a curvy teen who would rather watch the beach hunks then go to medical school. **96m/C VHS.** Julianne Phillips, Ted Shackleford, Michael Gross, Dorothy Lyman; ***D:*** Noel Nosseck; ***M:*** Peter Bernstein.

Summer Heat **1/2 1987 (R)** In rural, mid-Depression North Carolina, a young, lonely wife and mother is seduced by a drifter and together they plot murder. Her husband neglects her, and you should neglect to see this utter yawner. Based on a Louise Shivers novel. **80m/C VHS.** Lori Singer, Anthony Edwards, Bruce Abbott, Kathy Bates; ***D:*** Michie Gleason; ***C:*** Elliot Davis.

Summer Holiday **1/2 1948** Rooney comes of age with a vengeance during summer vacation in musical rendition of "Ah, Wilderness." Undistinguished musical numbers, inferior to the original, but jazzy Technicolor cinematography. Ended up in the red by over $1.5 million, lotsa money back then. ♫ It's Our Home Town; Afraid to Fall in Love; All Hail, Danville High; The Stanley Steamer; It's Independence Day; I Think You're the Sweetest Kid I've Ever Known; Weary Blues. **92m/C VHS.** Mickey Rooney, Gloria De Haven, Walter Huston, Frank Morgan, Jackie "Butch" Jenkins, Marilyn Maxwell, Agnes Moorehead, Selena Royle, Anne Francis; ***D:*** Rouben Mamoulian.

Summer Hours **1/2** *L'Heure d'Ete* **2008** Assayas' not-too-nostalgic look at the family ties that bind and how to handle a legacy in the present. Helene Berthier (Scob) is celebrating her 75th birthday at her country house with her two sons Frederic (Bering) and Jeremie (Renier), their wives and kids, and her daughter Adrienne (Binoche). They rarely get together (everyone's SO busy) so Helene takes the opportunity to discreetly tell responsible Frederic how she would like everything handled after she's gone. The house is filled with priceless art collected by Helene's Uncle Paul and she would like the collection kept intact for a museum but doesn't want the house and its other contents turned into a shrine. Complicating matters is the fact that Adrienne lives in New York, Jeremie is moving to Shanghai, and Frederic is the only one who wants to keep the past preserved. English and French with subtitles. **103m/C DVD.** *FR* Juliette Binoche, Charles Berling, Jeremie Renier, Edith Scob, Dominique Reymond, Valerie Bonneton, Isabelle Sadoyan; ***D:*** Olivier Assayas; ***W:*** Olivier Assayas; ***C:*** Eric Gautier.

The Summer House **1/2 1994** Comedy of manners set in 1959 England about the manipulations of three middle-aged women (Moreau, Plowright, Walters) over the impending marriage of one's dreamy young daughter (Headey) to a dolt (Threlfall). Moreau stirs things up as the spirited and skeptical friend of Walters, the deluded bride's mother whom she must interrupt from her busy nuptial preparations and somehow communicate the obvious. Plowright is perfectly cast as the gimlet-eyed groom's mother, well aware of her son's flaws, who achieves an odd alliance with polar opposite Moreau. Strong performances from all the veterans carry the day. Based on the novel by Alice Thomas Ellis. **85m/C VHS.** *GB* Jeanne Moreau, Joan Plowright, Julie Walters, Lena Headey, David Threlfall, Padraig Casey, Britta Smith, John Wood; ***D:*** Waris Hussein; ***W:*** Martin Sherman; ***M:*** Stanley Myers.

Summer Interlude **1/2** *Illicit Interlude; Summerplay; Sommarlek* **1950** A ballerina recalls a romantic summer spent with an innocent boy, who was later tragically killed. Contains many earmarks and visual ideas of later Bergman masterpieces. In Swedish with English subtitles. **95m/B VHS, DVD.** *SW* Maj-Britt Nilsson, Birger Malmsten, Alf Kjellin; ***D:*** Ingmar Bergman; ***W:*** Ingmar Bergman.

Summer Lovers **1982 (R)** Summer vacation finds young couple traveling to the exotic Greek island of Santorini. They meet up with a fun-loving woman and discover three-way sexual tension, but little in the way of plot, dialogue, or acting. From the director of "Grease" and "Blue Lagoon" and best watched late at night while half conscious. **98m/C VHS, DVD.** Peter Gallagher, Daryl Hannah, Valerie Quennessen; ***D:*** Randal Kleiser; ***M:*** Basil Poledouris.

Summer Magic **1963** An impecunious recent widow is forced to leave Boston and settle her family in a small town in Maine. Typical, forgettable Disney drama; early Mills vehicle. A remake of "Mother Carey's Chickens." **116m/C VHS, DVD.** Hayley Mills, Burl Ives, Dorothy McGuire, Deborah Walley, Una Merkel, Eddie Hodges; ***D:*** James Neilson; ***M:*** Buddy (Norman Dale) Baker.

Summer Night with Greek Profile, Almond Eyes & Scent of Basil **1987 (R)** A wealthy woman tycoon hires an ex-CIA man to kidnap a high-priced, professional terrorist and hold him for ransom. An ironic battle of the sexes follows. In Italian with English subtitles. **94m/C VHS, DVD.** *IT* Mariangela Melato, Michele Placido, Roberto Herlitzka, Massimo Wertmuller; ***D:*** Lina Wertmuller; ***W:*** Lina Wertmuller.

Summer of '04 **1/2** *Sommer '04* **2006** Considering the subject matter, this is a frequently dull affair. Forty-year-old Miriam (Gedeck) spends summer vacation at a country house with her husband Andre (Davor), 15-year-old son Niels (Kotaranin), and his younger girlfriend Livia (Lohde), who's testing her sexual boundaries. Niels lets Livia go sailing alone with 30-something neighbor Bill (Seeliger), which worries Miriam. She confronts Bill about what might be happening, only to be drawn unexpectedly into a torrid affair. An end twist is unsatisfying. German with subtitles. **97m/C DVD.** *GE* Martina Gedeck, Svea Lohde, Robert Seeliger, Peter Davor, Lucas Kotaranin; *D:* Stefan Krohmer; *W:* Daniel Nocke; *C:* Patrick Orth; *M:* Ellen McIlwaine.

The Summer of Aviya ☊☊ *Kayitz Shel Aviya* **1988** Ten-year-old Aviya has spent most of her life in orphanges as her partisan Jewish mother fought the Nazis. Now, Aviya faces the prospect of returning to a home and woman she doesn't really know, one who is also balanced on the edge of madness. Based on the memoirs of Almagor. Hebrew with subtitles. Followed by "Under the Domim Tree." **95m/C VHS.** *IS* Kaipo Cohen, Gila Almagor; *D:* Eli Cohen; *W:* Eli Cohen, Gila Almagor.

The Summer of Ben Tyler ☊☊ ½ **1996 (PG)** Temple Rayburn (Woods) is an up-and-coming lawyer in a small southern town in 1942 and the protege of influential Spencer Maitland (Cariou). Before his family's black housekeeper dies, Rayburn agrees to take in her mentally handicapped teenaged son, Ben (Mattocks), to the dismay of the white community. Then Maitland insists Rayburn defend his son Junius (Isola) against a drunk driving charge where a woman was killed. TV movie. **134m/C VHS.** James Woods, Len Cariou, Elizabeth McGovern, Charles Mattocks, Kevin Isola, Julia McIlvaine, Clifton James; *D:* Arthur Allan Seidelman; *W:* Robert Inman; *C:* Neil Roach; *M:* Van Dyke Parks; *Nar:* Judith Ivey. **TV**

Summer of Fear ☊☊ *Stranger in Our House* **1978** A happy young woman (Blair) must overcome evil forces when her cousin (a teenage witch not akin to Sabrina) comes to live with—and control—her family. Based on a novel by Lois Duncan, who also wrote the source novel for 1997's "I Know What You Did Last Summer." Pretty scary if ordinary, made-for-TV horror from later-famous Craven. **94m/C VHS, DVD.** Linda Blair, Lee Purcell, Jeremy Slate, Carol Lawrence, MacDonald Carey, Jeff McCracken, Jeff East, Fran Drescher; *D:* Wes Craven; *M:* Tom D'Andrea. **TV**

Summer of '42 ☊☊☊ **1971 (R)** Touching if sentimental story about 15-year-old Hermie's (Grimes) sexual coming of age during his summer vacation on an island off New England. While his friends are fumbling with girls their own age, he falls in love with a beautiful 22-year-old woman (O'Neill) whose husband is off fighting in the war. **102m/C VHS, DVD.** Jennifer O'Neill, Gary Grimes, Jerry Houser, Oliver Conant; *D:* Robert Mulligan; *W:* Herman Raucher; *C:* Robert L. Surtees; *M:* Michel Legrand; *Nar:* Robert Mulligan. Oscars '71: Orig. Dramatic Score.

The Summer of Miss Forbes ☊☊ *El Verano de la Senora Forbes* **1988** A governess rules over two young boys with an iron hand by day and cavorts nude and drunk by night. The boys fantasize about her murder, but fate has different plans. In Spanish with English subtitles. **85m/C VHS.** *SP* Hanna Schygulla, Alexis Castanares, Victor Cesar Villalobos, Guadalupe Sandoval, Fernando Balzaretti, Yuriria Munguia; *D:* Jaime Humberto Hermosillo.

The Summer of My German Soldier ☊☊☊ **1978** A young Jewish girl befriends an escaped German prisoner of war in a small town in Georgia during WWII. Occasionally sentimental but more often genuinely moving TV drama. Rolle won a deserved Emmy as the housekeeper. Adapted from Bette Green's novel. **98m/C VHS.** Kristy McNichol, Esther Rolle, Bruce Davison; *D:* Michael Tuchner. **TV**

Summer of Sam ☊☊ ½ **1999 (R)** Spike Lee's take on the summer of 1977, when serial killer Son of Sam traumatized New York City. The plot does not center on the actual crimes of David Berkowitz, but on the repercussions they had in the neighborhoods of New York. Leguizamo and Sorvino play a married Bronx couple who grow to question pal Ritchie (Brody), a newly converted punk rocker who leads a double life as a gay dancer. As the killer's attacks continue, fear begins to rise along with the temperature, and the neighborhood begins to tear itself apart. Lee's film drew highly publicized protests from the families of Berkowitz's victims. **142m/C VHS, DVD.** Adrien Brody, John Leguizamo, Spike Lee, Mira Sorvino, Jennifer Esposito, Michael Badalucco, Anthony LaPaglia, Patti LuPone, Ben Gazzara, Bebe Neuwirth, John Savage, Roger Guenveur Smith, Michael Rispoli; *D:* Spike Lee; *W:* Spike Lee; *C:* Ellen Kuras; *M:* Terence Blanchard.

Summer of the Monkeys ☊☊ ½ **1998 (G)** Fairly sappy family pic set in rural America. John Lee (Ontkean) is a hardworking farmer with a caring wife, Sara (Hope), precocious son Jay Berry (Sevier), and a crippled daughter, Daisy (Stuart). Gramps (Brimley) runs the local general store and Jay works there, hoping to save money to buy Daisy a pony. When a nearby train wreck leads to the escape of a foursome of circus monkeys, Jay aims to find them first and get the reward for their return. **101m/C VHS.** *CA* Michael Ontkean, Leslie Hope, Corey Sevier, Katie Stuart, Wilford Brimley, Don Francks, B.J. McLellan; *D:* Michael Anderson Sr.; *W:* Greg Taylor, Jim Strain; *C:* Michael Storey; *M:* George Blondheim.

Summer Palace ☊☊☊ *Yihe Yuan* **2006** The lives of Yu Hong (Hao) and her lover Zhou Wei (Guo)are traced from their enrollment in Bejing University in 1988 and subsequently involvement in the demonstrations in Tiananmen Square, into adulthood, which never seems to match the promise of their youth. Frank and explicit in both its sexuality and its examination of the changes China has undergone since 1989. Director Ye was banned from filmmaking for five years by the Chinese government after showing this at Cannes without permission. **140m/C DVD.** *CH FR* Lei Hao, Xiaodong Guo, Ling Hu, Xianmin Zhang; *D:* Ye Lou; *W:* Ye Lou, Mei Feng, The Range Busters; *C:* Qing Hua; *M:* Peyman Yazdanian.

A Summer Place ☊☊ **1959** Melodrama about summer liaisons amid the young and middle-aged rich on an island off the coast of Maine. Too slick; romantic drama is little more than skin-deep, and dialogue is excruciating. Donahue's first starring role. Based on the novel by Sloan Wilson. Featuring "Theme from a Summer Place," which was a number-one hit in 1959. **130m/C VHS, DVD.** Troy Donahue, Richard Egan, Sandra Dee, Dorothy McGuire, Arthur Kennedy, Constance Ford, Beulah Bondi; *D:* Delmer Daves; *W:* Delmer Daves; *C:* Harry Stradling Sr.; *M:* Max Steiner.

Summer Rental ☊☊ **1985 (PG)** That John Candy just can't win, can he? Here, as a hopeless, harried air traffic controller, he tries to have a few days to relax in sunny Florida. Enter mean rich guy Crenna. Candy can add something hefty to the limpest of plots, and does so here. Watch the first hour for yuks, then rewind. **87m/C VHS, DVD.** John Candy, Rip Torn, Richard Crenna, Karen Austin, Kerri Green, John Larroquette, Pierrino Mascarino; *D:* Carl Reiner; *W:* Mark Reisman, Jeremy Stevens; *C:* Ric Waite; *M:* Alan Silvestri.

Summer School ☊ **1977 (R)** A teenaged boy's girlfriend will stop at nothing to prevent him from going out with the pretty new girl in town. **80m/C VHS.** John McLaughlin, Steve Rose, Phoebe Schmidt; *D:* Bethel Buckalew; *W:* Bethel Buckalew; *C:* William E. Hines; *M:* Bill Schereck.

Summer School ☊☊ ½ **1987 (PG-13)** A high-school teacher's vacation plans are ruined when he gets stuck teaching remedial English in summer school. It seems all these students are interested in is re-enacting scenes from "The Texas Chainsaw Massacre," learning to drive, and surfing. Actually, one of the better films of this genre, thanks mostly to Harmon's likeability. **98m/C VHS, DVD.** Mark Harmon, Kirstie Alley, Courtney Thorne-Smith, Shawnee Smith, Robin Thomas, Dean Cameron, Gary Riley, Kelly Jo Minter, Fabiana Udenio, Beau Starr, Ken Olandt, Lucy Lee Flippin, Nels Van Patten; *Cameos:* Carl Reiner; *D:* Carl Reiner; *W:* Jeff Franklin; *C:* David M. Walsh; *M:* Danny Elfman.

Summer School Teachers WOOF! **1975 (R)** Three sultry femmes bounce about Los Angeles high school and make the collective student body happy. Typical Corman doings; sequel to "The Students Teachers." **87m/C VHS.** Candice Rialson, Pat Anderson, Rhonda Leigh Hopkins, Christopher Wales; *D:* Barbara Peeters.

Summer Snow ☊☊ *Nuiyan, Seisap; Woman, Forty* **1994** Broad comedy mixed (not always successfully) with family drama. May (Siao) is forced to take in her father-in-law Sun (Chiao) after his wife dies. The old man immediately causes chaos with his habit of wandering off and bizarre behavior, which is finally diagnosed as being Alzheimer's disease. Working mother May tries to find a practical way to deal with her dilemmas but the strains are beginning to crack the family apart. Cantonese with subtitles. **106m/C VHS.** *HK* Josephine Siao, Roy Chiao, Law Kar-ying, Allen Ting; *D:* Ann Hui; *W:* Chan Mankeung; *C:* Mark Lee Ping-Bin; *M:* Yoshihide Otomo. Berlin Intl. Film Fest. '94: Actress (Siao).

Summer Solstice ☊☊ ½ **1981** Fonda and Loy are splendid as a couple married half a century who revisit the beach where they first met. Fonda especially shines, as a crusty old artist. Yes, it is an awful lot like "On Golden Pond." **75m/C VHS, DVD.** Henry Fonda, Myrna Loy, Lindsay Crouse, Stephen Collins; *D:* Ralph Rosenblum. **TV**

Summer Stock ☊☊☊ *If You Feel Like Singing* **1950** Garland plays farm owner Jane Falbury whose sister, Abigail (DeHaven) arrives with a summer stock troupe, led by Joe Ross (Kelly), to rehearse a show in the family barn. Jane agrees, if the troupe will help her with the farm's harvest. When Abigail decamps for New York, leaving the leading lady role open, guess who steps into the breach. Slim plot papered over with many fun song-and-dance numbers. Also features Garland's first MGM short, "Every Sunday," made in 1936 with Deanna Durbin. ♫ Friendly Star; Mem'ry Island; Dig-Dig-Dig For Your Dinner; If You Feel Like Singing, Sing; Howdy Neighbor; Blue Jean Polka; Portland Fancy; You, Wonderful You; Get Happy. **109m/C VHS, DVD.** Judy Garland, Gene Kelly, Gloria De Haven, Carleton Carpenter, Eddie Bracken, Phil Silvers, Hans Conried, Marjorie Main, Ray Collins; *D:* Charles Walters; *W:* George Wells, Sy Gomberg.

Summer Storm ☊☊ ½ **1944** Based on the Anton Chekhov story "The Shooting Party." In 1912, beautiful and ambitious Russian peasant Olga (Darnell) marries farmer Anton Urbenin (Haas) but is soon having a series of affairs with wealthy men. This includes cynical, aristocratic judge Fedor Petroff (Sanders), who becomes obsessed with Olga, leading to deadly consequences. Not quite as over-the-top as Sirk's best work but still quite the melodrama. **106m/B DVD.** Linda Darnell, George Sanders, Hugo Haas, Anna Lee, Edward Everett Horton, Sig Rumann, Lori Lahner; *D:* Gregg Tallas; *W:* Robert Thoeren, Rowland Leigh; *C:* Eugene Schuftan, Archie Stout; *M:* Karl Hajos.

A Summer Story ☊☊☊ **1988 (PG-13)** Superbly acted, typically British period drama about beautiful farm girl Stubbs and city lawyer Wilby, who fall in love. But can they overcome difference of social class? From the story "The Apple Tree" by John Galsworthy. **97m/C VHS.** *GB* James Wilby, Imogen Stubbs, Susannah York, Sophie Ward, Kenneth Colley, Jerome Flynn; *D:* Piers Haggard; *W:* Penelope Mortimer; *M:* Georges Delerue.

A Summer to Remember ☊☊☊ *Seryozha* **1961** A five-year-old boy spends a summer with his stepfather on a Soviet collective farm. The two become deeply attached. Scenes of collective life will be of more interest to Westerners than the near-sentimental story. Star Bondarchuk later directed the epic, award-winning "War and Peace." **80m/B VHS, DVD.** *RU* Borya Barkhazov, Sergei Bondarchuk, Irana Skobtseva; *D:* Igor Talankin, Georgi Daneliya; *W:* Igor Talankin, Georgi Daneliya; *C:* Anatoli Nitochkin; *M:* Boris Chaikovsky.

A Summer to Remember ☊☊ ½ **1984 (PG)** A deaf boy (played by Gerlis, himself deaf since birth) develops a friendship with an orangutan through sign language. Bad guys abduct the friendly ape—but all is right in the end. Nice, innocuous family viewing. Based on a story by Scott Swanton and Robert Lloyd Lewis. **93m/C VHS, DVD.** Tess Harper, James Farentino, Burt Young, Louise Fletcher, Sean Gerlis, Bridgette Andersen; *D:* Robert Lewis; *C:* Stephen W. Gray; *M:* Charles Fox. **TV**

Summer Vacation: 1999 ☊☊ *1999—Nen No Natsu Yasumi* **1988** Four boys are left behind at boarding school during their summer vacation. They experience all the early pangs of adolescence from love to jealousy. Their summer is then disturbed by the arrival of another boy who appears to be the reincarnation of a dead friend. Romantic look at youth caught between innocence and awareness. In Japanese with English subtitles. **90m/C VHS.** *JP* Eri Miyagima, Miyuki Nakano, Tomoko Otakra, Rie Mizuhara; *D:* Shusuke (Shu) Kaneko.

Summer Wishes, Winter Dreams ☊☊ **1973 (PG)** Woodward and Balsam are a materially prosperous middle-aged couple with little but tedium in their lives—a tedium accurately replicated, in what feels like real life, in this slow, dull film. The two leads and Sidney—in her first screen role in 17 years—are all excellent, but the story of regret and present unhappiness wears the viewer down. **95m/C VHS.** Joanne Woodward, Martin Balsam, Sylvia Sidney, Dori Brenner, Ron Richards; *D:* Gilbert Cates; *W:* Stewart Stern. British Acad. '74: Actress (Woodward); Natl. Bd. of Review '73: Support. Actress (Sidney); N.Y. Film Critics '73: Actress (Woodward).

Summerdog ☊☊ **1978 (G)** Harmless family tale about vacationers who rescue a cheerful, lovable mutt named Hobo. And a good thing they found him: He saves them from many perils. Thanks, Hobo! **90m/C VHS.** James Congdon, Elizabeth Eisenman, Oliver Zabriskie, Tavia Zabriskie; *D:* John Clayton.

Summer's Children ☊ **1979** Man who suffers from amnesia as a result of a car crash becomes the target of a mysterious killer. Forget about it. **83m/C VHS.** *CA* Tom Haoff, Paully Jardine, Kate Lynch, Don Francks, Kate Lynch, Ken James, Patricia Collins, Wayne Best; *D:* Julius Kohanyi; *W:* Jim Osborne; *C:* Josef Seckeresh; *M:* Chris Stone.

Summer's End ☊☊ ½ **1999** In 1983, physician William Blakely (Jones) decides to retire to the small Georgia town where he grew up. But the lakeside community is lily-white and hostile (Blakely's family was originally driven out by racial violence). However, fatherless 12-year-old Jamie (LeDoux) and the doc become friends, despite pressures on the boy to toe the racist line. **101m/C VHS, DVD.** James Earl Jones, Wendy Crewson, Brendan Fletcher, Jake LeDoux; *D:* Helen Shaver. **CABLE**

A Summer's Tale ☊☊ ½ *Conte d'Ete* **1996** Talky and slow-moving vacation comedy is the third in Rohmer's "Tales of the Four Seasons" series. Young Gaspard (Poupaud) is spending a month in a borrowed flat in the seaside resort of Dinard. He becomes friendly with waitress Margot (Langlet) while he waits for his girlfriend Lena (Nolin) to join him, but is also introduced to Margot's friend Solene (Simon), who's interested in a quick fling with Gaspard. When all three women agree to accompany him on a sightseeing trip, he's got more a than a little maneuvering to do. French with subtitles. **133m/C VHS, DVD.** *FR* Melvil Poupaud, Amanda Langlet, Aurelia Nolin, Gwenaelle Simon; *D:* Eric Rohmer; *W:* Eric Rohmer; *C:* Diane Baratier; *M:* Sebastien Erms, Philippe Eidel.

Summertime ☊☊☊ ½ *Summer Madness* **1955** Spinster Hepburn vacations in Venice and falls in love with Brazzi. She is hurt when inadvertently she learns he is married, but her life has been so bleak she is not about to end her one great romance. Moving, funny, richly photographed in a beautiful Old World city. From Arthur Laurents' play "The Time of the Cuckoo." **98m/C VHS, DVD.** Katharine Hepburn, Rossano Brazzi, Isa Miranda, Darren McGavin, Mari Aldon, MacDonald Parke, Jeremy Spenser; *D:* David Lean; *W:* David Lean, H.E. Bates; *C:* Jack Hildyard; *M:* Alessandro Cicognini. N.Y. Film Critics '55: Director (Lean).

Summertree ☊☊ **1971 (PG)** Douglas stars as a young musician in the 1960s trying to avoid the draft and the wrath of his parents. Contrived and heavy-handed. Produced by Douglas pere, Kirk. Adapted from the play by Ron Cower. **88m/C VHS.** Michael Douglas, Jack Warden, Brenda Vaccaro, Barbara Bel Geddes, Kirk Calloway, Bill Vint; *D:* Anthony

Newley; *M:* David Shire.

The Summit 1/2 **2008** Maria Puerto (Maestro) watches her son die from a tainted vaccine and loses her lawsuit against the international pharmaceutical company who made it. Carrying a vial of her son's poisoned blood, Maria travels from Colombia to the G8 summit to protest but the drug company wants her stopped at all costs. However, when people start dying, Maria joins with bio-terrorism expert Thom Lightstone (Purefoy) to find an antidote even while the government ministers deny everything. **180m/C DVD.** *CA* Mia Maestro, James Purefoy, Bruce Greenwood, Christopher Plummer, Rachelle Lefevre, Stephen McHattie, Wendy Crewson, Nigel Bennett; *D:* Nick Copus; *W:* John Krizanc; *C:* Alwyn Kumst; *M:* Tom Third. **TV**

The Sun Comes Up **1949** MacDonald, in her last screen appearance, plays a bitter widow whose life is changed by an orphan's love for a collie. Songbird MacDonald manages to sing a number of songs, some of them backed by a chorus of "orphans." Based on short stories by Marjorie Kinnan Rawlings. **93m/C VHS.** Jeanette MacDonald, Lloyd Nolan, Claude Jarman Jr., Lewis Stone, Dwayne Hickman; *D:* Richard Thorpe; *W:* William Ludwig; *M:* Andre Previn.

Sun Ra & His Intergalactic Solar Arkestra: Space Is the Place **1974** Space age flick starring most appropriately Sun Ra, space-age prophet/jazz musician. Sun Ra returns from a space odyssey and embarks on saving black youth from the world's oppressive control by bringing them back into space with him. The shaman's philosophy on film. ♫ Watusi; Outer Spaceways Inc.; The Satellites are Spinning. **63m/C VHS, DVD.** *D:* John Coney; *W:* Joshua Smith.

The Sun Sets at Dawn 1/2 **1950** Oddball, low-rent allegory with religious overtones. A young man on death row will be the first to die in the state's new electric chair so the story is drawing a lot of attention. Reporters are hanging out at a nearby greasy spoon, speculating about the convict who's still proclaiming his innocence. Various threads come together that lend credence to his claims, but will they be enough to stop the execution? Most of the characters are nameless and what's that supposed to be about? **71m/B DVD.** Patrick Waltz, Walter Reed, Howard St. John, Sally Parr, Houseley Stevenson, Lee Frederick; *D:* Paul Sloane; *W:* Paul Sloane; *C:* Lionel Lindon; *M:* Leith Stevens.

The Sun Shines Bright **1953** Heavily stereotyped, contrived tale of a Southern judge with a heart of gold who does so many good deeds (defending a black man accused of rape; helping a desperate prostitute) that he jeopardizes his re-election. Set during Reconstruction. An unfortunate remake of Ford's own 1934 "Judge Priest," starring Will Rogers. **92m/B VHS.** Charles Winninger, Arleen Whelan, John Russell, Stepin Fetchit, Milburn Stone, Russell Simpson; *D:* John Ford; *C:* Archie Stout.

Sun Valley Serenade 1/2 **1941** Wartime musical fluff about a band that adopts a Norwegian refugee waif as a publicity stunt. She turns out to be a full-grown man-chaser who stirs up things at a ski resort. Fun, but it ends abruptly—because, they say, Henie fell during the huge skating finale, and Darryl Zanuck wouldn't greenlight a reshoot. One of only two feature appearances by Glenn Miller and his Orchestra (the other was "Orchestra Wives"), on video with a soundtrack restored from original dual-track recordings. ♫ Chattanooga Choo Choo; I Know Why and So Do You; It Happened In Sun Valley; The Kiss Polka; In the Mood. **86m/C VHS.** Sonja Henie, John Payne, Glenn Miller, Milton Berle, Lynn Bari, Joan Davis, Dorothy Dandridge; *D:* H. Bruce Humberstone.

Sunburn 1/2 **1979 (PG)** Insurance investigator Grodin hires model Fawcett to pretend to be his wife to get the scoop on a suicide/murder case of a rich guy in Acapulco. Made-for-TV drivel. **110m/C VHS.** Farrah Fawcett, Charles Grodin, Joan Collins, Art Carney, William Daniels; *D:* Richard Sarafian; *W:* James Booth. **TV**

Sunchaser 1/2 **1996 (R)** Mishmash of medicine and mysticism focuses on yuppie UCLA oncologist Dr. Michael Reynolds (Harrelson) who's kidnapped by 16-year-old patient, Brandon "Blue" Monroe (Seda). Blue is a half-Navajo gangbanger whose cancer is inoperable and he needs the doc to drive him to a reservation in Arizona where he feels a medicine man and the waters of a supposedly magical lake can cure him. Reynolds naturally discovers some humanity on the trip and decides to help his truculent patient. Leads give sincere performances but film is half-baked at best. **123m/C VHS.** Woody Harrelson, Jon Seda, Anne Bancroft, Alexandra Tydings, Matt Mulhern, Talisa Soto, Lawrence Pressman, Michael O'Neill, Harry Carey Jr.; *D:* Michael Cimino; *W:* Charles Leavitt; *C:* Doug Milsome; *M:* Maurice Jarre.

Sundance and the Kid *Sundance Cassidy and Butch the Kid; Vivi O, Prefeibilmente, Morti* **1969 (PG)** Slapstick spaghetti western has two estranged brothers trying to collect an inheritance by living together for six months. Hilarity fails to ensue. **84m/C VHS.** *IT* Giuliano Gemma, Sydne Rome, Nino Benvenuti; *D:* Duccio Tessari; *W:* Ennio Flaiano; *C:* Cesare Allione; *M:* Gianni Ferrio.

Sunday **1996** Basically a two-character study of mistaken identity among lonely, middleaged people. On a winter's Sunday morning in Queens, depressed Oliver (Suchet) is greeted by failing British actress Madeleine (Harrow), who mistakes him for a director she once met. She invites him to lunch and Oliver, who's actually a homeless former accountant, struggles to maintain the charade. The unstable Madeleine's bitter when she discovers his deception but is also unwillingly to let the connection between them die. **93m/C VHS, DVD.** David Suchet, Lisa Harrow, Larry Pine, Jared Harris, Joe Grifasi; *D:* Jonathan Nossiter; *W:* Jonathan Nossiter, James Lasdun; *C:* Michael Barrow, John Foster; *M:* Jonathan Nossiter. Sundance '97: Screenplay, Grand Jury Prize.

Sunday, Bloody Sunday **1971 (R)** Adult drama centers around the intertwined love affairs of the homosexual Finch, the heterosexual Jackson, and self-centered bisexual artist Head, desired by both. Fully drawn characters brought to life by excellent acting make this difficult story well worth watching—though Head's central character is sadly rather dull. Day-Lewis makes his first (brief) screen appearance as a car vandalizing teenager. Powerful, sincere, and sensitive. **110m/C VHS, DVD.** *GB* Glenda Jackson, Peter Finch, Murray Head, Peggy Ashcroft, Tony Britton, Maurice Denham, Vivian Pickles, Bessie Love, Daniel Day-Lewis; *D:* John Schlesinger; *W:* Penelope Gilliatt; *C:* Billy Williams; *M:* Ron Geesin. British Acad. '71: Actor (Finch), Actress (Jackson), Director (Schlesinger), Film; Golden Globes '72: Foreign Film; N.Y. Film Critics '71: Screenplay; Natl. Soc. Film Critics '71: Actor (Finch), Screenplay; Writers Guild '71: Orig. Screenplay.

Sunday Daughters **1980** A teenage girl kept in a detention home constantly tries to escape and find some kind of familial love. Stronge performances mix with keen direction. In Hungarian with English subtitles. **100m/C VHS.** *HU* Julianna Nyako; *D:* Janosz Rozsa.

Sunday in New York 1/2 **1963** Distraught Eileen (Fonda) heads to New York to seek counsel from her airline pilot brother Adam (Robertson) after she breaks up with fiance Russ (Wilson). Adam is in the middle of setting up a much-interrupted date with sometime-girlfriend Mona, so Eileen wanders around NYC. Soon she meets cute with suave fella Mike on the bus. Romantic comedy complications follow as Russ comes back into the picture. Amusing look at the changing sexual mores of the time must've seemed mildly shocking then, but now seems quaint. Robertson stands out among great cast. **105m/C VHS, DVD.** Rod Taylor, Jane Fonda, Cliff Robertson, Robert Culp, Jo Morrow, Jim Backus, Rayford Barnes, Jim Hutton; ***Cameos:*** Peter Nero; *D:* Peter Tewkesbury; *W:* Norman Krasna; *C:* Leo Tover; *M:* Peter Nero.

A Sunday in the Country 1/2 *Un Dimanche a la Campagne* **1984 (G)** A lush, distinctively French affirmation of nature and family life. This character study with a minimal plot takes place during a single summer day in 1910 France. An elderly impressionist painter-patriarch is visited at his country home by his family. Highly acclaimed, though the pace may be too slow for some. Beautiful location photography. In French with English subtitles. **94m/C VHS, DVD.** *FR* Louis Ducreux, Sabine Azema, Michel Aumont; *D:* Bertrand Tavernier; *W:* Bertrand Tavernier, Colo Tavernier O'Hagan; *C:* Bruno de Keyzer. Cannes '84: Director (Tavernier); Cesar '85: Actress (Azema), Cinematog., Writing; Natl. Bd. of Review '84: Support. Actress (Azema); N.Y. Film Critics '84: Foreign Film.

Sunday in the Park with George **1986** Taped theatrical performance of the Tony, Grammy, and Pulitzer Prize-winning musical play, which is based upon impressionist Georges Seurat's painting "A Sunday Afternoon on the Island of Grande Jatte." Features a celebrated music score by Sondheim. **120m/C VHS, DVD.** Mandy Patinkin, Bernadette Peters, Barbara Byrne, Charles Kimbrough; *D:* James Lapine; *M:* Stephen Sondheim.

Sunday Too Far Away **1974** The rivalries between Australian sheep shearers and graziers leads to an ugly strike at a remote outback area in 1955. An uncomplicated story and a joy to watch. **100m/C VHS.** *AU* Max Cullen, Robert Bruning, Jerry Thomas, Jack Thompson; *D:* Ken Hannam; *W:* John Dingwall; *C:* Geoff Burton; *M:* Patrick Flynn. Australian Film Inst. '74: Actor (Thompson), Film.

Sundays & Cybele 1/2 *Les Dimanches de Ville d'Arvay; Cybele* **1962** A ragged war veteran and an orphaned girl develop a strong emotional relationship, which is frowned upon by the townspeople. Warm and touching. In French with English subtitles. Also available in a letterboxed edition. **110m/B VHS.** *FR* Hardy Kruger, Nicole Courcel; *D:* Serge Bourguignon; *M:* Maurice Jarre. Oscars '62: Foreign Film.

Sunday's Children 1/2 **1994** Lyrical exploration of childhood continues trilogy that includes "Fanny and Alexander" and "Best Intentions." Wistful childhood memoir takes up the story of Ingmar Bergman's family eight years after the director was born. Many of the same familial issues surface, but story soon narrows its focus to the relationship between little Ingmar, whom everyone calls Pu, and his stern father Henrik. Deeply emotional and intense, film represents the steps toward forgiveness that the elder Bergman is finally able to take regarding the painful relationship he had with his own father. Father-son theme made more poignant with Ingmar's son Daniel making his feature debut as director. **118m/C VHS.** *SW* Thommy Berggren, Lena Endre, Henrik Linnros, Jacob Leygraf, Maria Bolme, Borje Ahlstedt, Per Myrberg; *D:* Daniel Bergman; *W:* Ingmar Bergman.

Sundown 1/2 **1941** In Africa at the beginning of WWII, a local girl aids the British against a German plot to run guns to the natives and start a rebellion. Engaging performances and efficient direction keep it above the usual cliches. Also available in a colorized version. **91m/B VHS, DVD.** Gene Tierney, Bruce Cabot, George Sanders, Harry Carey Sr., Cedric Hardwicke, Joseph Calleia, Dorothy Dandridge, Reginald Gardiner; *D:* Henry Hathaway; *C:* Charles B(ryant) Lang Jr.; *M:* Miklos Rozsa.

Sundown 1/2 **1991 (R)** An ambitious shot at a vampire western fails because it drains almost all vampire lore and winds up resembling a standard oater. Carradine plays a reformed vampire king (guess who) running a desert clinic that weans bloodsuckers away from preying on humans. But undead renegades attack using sixguns and wooden bullets. The climax may outrage horror purists. **104m/C VHS.** David Carradine, Bruce Campbell, Deborah Foreman, Maxwell Caulfield, Morgan Brittany; *D:* Anthony Hickox.

Sundown Fury *Jesse James, Jr* **1942** Young cowboy fights against a group of bandits to hold a telegraph office. **56m/B VHS.** Donald (Don "Red") Barry, Lynn Merrick, Al "Fuzzy" St. John, Douglas Walton, Karl Hackett, Lee Shumway, Stanley Blystone, Frank Brownlee, George Chesebro; *D:* George Sherman; *W:* Doris Schroeder, Richard Murphy; *C:* John MacBurnie; *M:* Cy Feuer.

Sundown Kid 1/2 **1943** A Pinkerton agent goes undercover to break up a counterfeiting operation. Routine western. **55m/B VHS.** Ian Keith, Helen MacKellar, Emmett Lynn, Linda Leighton, Donald (Don "Red") Barry; *D:* Elmer Clifton; *W:* Norman S. Hall; *C:* Ernest Miller; *M:* Mort Glickman.

Sundown Riders **1948** Cowhands are victimized by noose-happy outlaws. Filmed in just over a week on a $30,000 budget and originally shot on 16mm to make it accessible to hospitals and schools with basic viewing equipment. The lesson here: it takes time and money to make a good western. **56m/B VHS.** Russell Wade, Andy Clyde, Jay Kirby; *D:* Lambert Hillyer.

Sundown Saunders **1936** A standard oater about a cowboy whose prize for winning a horse race is a ranch. Trouble is, an outlaw wants the homestead as well. **64m/B VHS.** Bob Steele; *D:* Robert North Bradbury.

Sundown: The Vampire in Retreat **2008 (R)** A group of vampires live the quiet life in a small western town, drinking synthetic blood made at a nearby factory. When the factory begins to malfunction, a scientist is brought in to fix it, and some of the vampires who want to go back to preying on people for the real thing decide to stage a coup. They have guns with wooden bullets and they aren't afraid to use them. Notable for starring Campbell as a descendant of Van Helsing whose devotion to killing vampires goes out the window the second he meets a hot blonde dead girl. **104m/C DVD.** David Carradine, Morgan Brittany, Bruce Campbell, Jim Metzler, Maxwell Caulfield, Deborah Foreman, M. Emmet Walsh, John Ireland Jr., Dana Ashbrook, John Hancock, Dabbs Greer, Bert Remsen, Marion Eaton, Elizabeth (Ward) Gracen, Christopher Bradley, George "Buck" Flower, Sunshine Parker, Helena Carroll, Kathy MacQuarrie Martin, Jack Eiseman, Brendan Hughes, Gerardo Mejia, Erin Gourlay, Vanessa Pierson, Mike Najjar, Phillip Simon, Chris Caputo, Phillip Esposito; *D:* Anthony Hickox; *W:* Anthony Hickox, John Burgess; *C:* Levie Isaacks; *M:* Richard Stone. **VIDEO**

The Sundowners 1/2 **1960** Slow, beautiful, and often moving epic drama about a family of Irish sheepherders in Australia during the 1920s who must continually uproot themselves and migrate. They struggle to save enough money to buy their own farm and wind up training a horse they hope will be a money-winner in racing. Well-acted by all, with Johns and Ustinov providing some humorous moments. Adapted from the novel by Jon Cleary. Filmed in Australia and London studios. **133m/C VHS, DVD.** Deborah Kerr, Robert Mitchum, Peter Ustinov, Glynis Johns, Dina Merrill, Chips Rafferty, Michael Anderson Jr., Lola Brooks, Wylie Watson; *D:* Fred Zinnemann; *C:* Jack Hildyard; *M:* Dimitri Tiomkin. Natl. Bd. of Review '60: Actor (Mitchum); N.Y. Film Critics '60: Actress (Kerr).

Sunny **1941** Another glossed-over, love-conquers-all musical with Neagle as a circus star who falls for a wealthy car maker's son. Dad and crew disapprove, putting a damper on the romance. In spite of the weak storyline and flat direction, Kerns' music and Bolger's dancing make it enjoyable. ♫ Who?; D'ya Love Me?; Sunny; Two Little Bluebirds. **98m/B VHS.** Anna Neagle, Ray Bolger, John Carroll, Edward Everett Horton, Frieda Inescort, Helen Westley, Benny Rubin, Richard Lane, Martha Tilton; *D:* Herbert Wilcox.

Sunny Side Up 1/2 **1928** As stress of pickle factory work takes toll on woman's friend, she makes heroic effort to help her to the country to recover. **66m/B VHS.** Vera Reynolds, Zasu Pitts, Edmund Burns, Sally Rand; *D:* Donald Crisp.

Sunny Skies **1930** Bargain-basement retread has Lease donating a pint of blood. ♫ Sunny Days; I Must Have You; Wanna Find a Boy; Must Be Love. **75m/B VHS.** Benny Rubin, Marceline Day, Rex Lease, Marjorie "Babe" Kane, Wesley Barry; *D:* Norman Taurog.

Sunnyside WOOF! **1979 (R)** Travolta plays a street kid trying to bring an end to the local gang warfare so he can move to Manhattan. Features a host of pop tunes in an attempt to ride the coattails of brother John's successful "Saturday Night Fever." Laughably bad. **100m/C VHS.** Joey Travolta, John Lansing, Stacey Pickren, Andrew Rubin, Michael Tucci, Talia Balsam, Joan Darling; ***D:*** Timothy Galfas.

Sunrise *Sunrise—A Song of Two Humans* **1927** Magnificent silent story of a simple country boy who, prodded by an alluring city woman, tries to murder his wife. Production values wear their age well. Gaynor won an Oscar for her stunning performance. Remade in Germany as "The Journey to Tilsit." Based on a story by Hermann Suderman. **110m/B VHS, DVD.** George O'Brien, Janet Gaynor, Bodil Rosing, Margaret Livingston, J. Farrell MacDonald, Carl Mayer; ***D:*** F.W. Murnau; ***C:*** Charles Rosher, Karl Struss. Oscars '28: Actress (Gaynor), Cinematog., Natl. Film Reg. '89.

Sunrise at Campobello **1960** A successful adaptation of the Tony award-winning play by Schary, who wrote the screenplay and also produced the film. In 1921, the Roosevelt family is vacationing at Campobello when Franklin (Bellamy, re-creating his stage role) becomes ill with what turns out to be polio. His formidable mother Sara (Shoemaker) wants her paralyzed son to give up his political aspirations but politico pal Louis Howe (Cronyn) insists Franklin get on with living, aided by the strength of wife Eleanor (an excellent performance by Garson). **143m/C VHS.** Ralph Bellamy, Greer Garson, Hume Cronyn, Jean Hagen, Jack Perrin, Lyle Talbot, Ann Shoemaker, Tim Considine, Zena Bethune, Pat Close; ***D:*** Vincent J. Donehue; ***W:*** Dore Schary; ***C:*** Russell Harlan; ***M:*** Franz Waxman. Golden Globes '61: Actress—Drama (Garson); Natl. Bd. of Review '60: Actress (Garson).

Sunrise Trail ½ **1931** Lots of action with Steele working undercover for the sheriff, trying to stop a rustler. He also finds the time to fall for barmaid Mehaffey. **65m/B VHS.** Bob Steele, Blanche Mehaffey, Jack Clifford, Eddie Dunn; ***D:*** John P. McCarthy.

The Sun's Burial **1960** Oshima's stylized and violent drama depicts life in Osaka's worst slum—a teeming underworld populated by teen gangs, prostitutes, and criminals. All want control of the area's most profitable business, an illegal blood-selling operation. In Japanese with English subtitles. **87m/C VHS.** *JP* Kayoko Honoo, Koji Nakahara, Masahiko Tsugawa, Fumio Watanabe; ***D:*** Nagisa Oshima.

Sunset **1988 (R)** Edwards wanders the range in this soft-centered farce about a couple of Western legends out to solve a mystery. On the backlots of Hollywood, silent screen star Tom Mix (Willis) meets aging marshal Wyatt Earp (Garner) and participates in a time-warp western circa 1927. They encounter a series of misadventures while trying to finger a murderer. Garner ambles enjoyably, lifting him a level above the rest of the cast. **101m/C VHS, DVD.** Bruce Willis, James Garner, Mariel Hemingway, Darren McGavin, Jennifer Edwards, Malcolm McDowell, Kathleen Quinlan, M. Emmet Walsh, Patricia Hodge, Richard Bradford, Joe Dallesandro, Dermot Mulroney; ***D:*** Blake Edwards; ***W:*** Blake Edwards, Rod Amateau; ***C:*** Anthony B. Richmond; ***M:*** Henry Mancini. Golden Raspberries '88: Worst Director (Edwards).

Sunset Boulevard ½ **1950** Famed tale of Norma Desmond (Swanson), aging silent film queen, who refuses to accept that stardom has ended for her and hires young down-on-his-luck screenwriter Joe Gillis (Holden) to help engineer her movie comeback. The screenwriter, who becomes the actress' kept man, assumes he can manipulate her, but finds out otherwise. Reality was almost too close for comfort, as Swanson, von Stroheim (as her major domo Max), and others very nearly play themselves. A darkly humorous look at the legacy and loss of fame with witty dialog, stellar performances, and some now-classic scenes. Based on the story "A Can of Beans" by Brackett and Wilder. **100m/B VHS, DVD.** Gloria Swanson, William Holden, Erich von Stroheim, Nancy Olson, Buster Keaton, Jack Webb, Cecil B. DeMille, Fred Clark; ***D:*** Billy Wilder; ***W:*** Billy Wilder, Charles Brackett, D.M. Marshman Jr.; ***C:*** John Seitz; ***M:*** Franz Waxman. Oscars '50: Art Dir./Set Dec., B&W, Story & Screenplay, Orig. Dramatic Score; AFI '98: Top 100; Golden Globes '51: Actress—Drama (Swanson), Director (Wilder), Film—Drama, Score, Natl. Film Reg. '89.

Sunset Grill **1992 (R)** While investigating his wife's murder, detective Ryder Hart (Weller) discovers a pattern of grisly killings. Sexy singer Loren Duquesne (Singer) leads him south of the border to her boss and his bloody money-making scheme. Unrated version also available. **103m/C VHS, DVD.** Peter Weller, Lori Singer, Alexandra Paul, John Rhys-Davies, Michael Anderson Jr., Stacy Keach; ***D:*** Kevin Connor.

Sunset Heat *Midnight Heat* **1992 (R)** Former drug dealer (Pare) returns to his home in Los Angeles with a legit job as a photojournalist. He stays with an old friend who turns out to be involved with the obsessed drug czar that Pare used to work for. Trouble comes along when the drug lord is robbed and blames Pare for the crime. Action-packed, with some good plot twists. An unrated version contains two additional minutes of footage. **94m/C VHS.** Michael Pare, Dennis Hopper, Adam Ant, Daphne Ashbrook, Charlie Schlatter; ***D:*** John Nicolella.

Sunset in El Dorado ½ **1945** Roy and Dale thwart a villainous scheme to defraud farmers of their land. **56m/B VHS, DVD.** Roy Rogers, Dale Evans, George "Gabby" Hayes, Hardie Albright, Roy Barcroft, Tom London, Edmund Cobb; ***D:*** Frank McDonald.

Sunset in the West **1950** Deputy sheriff Rogers figures out that local gunrunners are using the railroad to help them move their merchandise and he sets out to stop them. **67m/C VHS.** Roy Rogers, Gordon Jones, Penny Edwards, Estelita Rodriguez; ***D:*** William Witney; ***W:*** Gerald Geraghty; ***C:*** Jack Marta.

Sunset Limousine ½ **1983** An out-of-work stand-up comic gets thrown out by his girlfriend, then takes a job as a chauffeur. Standard vehicle with occasional bursts of speed. **92m/C VHS, DVD.** Charles Lane, John Ritter, Martin Short, Susan Dey, Paul Reiser, Audrie Neehan, Lainie Kazan; ***D:*** Terry Hughes.

The Sunset Murder Case ½ **1938** Showgirl Kathy O'Connor (infamous fan dancer Rand) goes to work at a nightclub to investigate her detective dad's murder and then wants revenge on the mobsters behind the rub-out. Not nearly as risque as originally intended, although lawsuits did hold up the release until 1941. **59m/B DVD.** Sally Rand, Dennis Moore, Paul Sutton, Frank O'Connor, Reed Hadley, Katherine Kane; ***D:*** Louis Gasnier; ***W:*** Paul Franklin, Arthur Hoerl; ***C:*** Mack Stengler.

Sunset on the Desert ½ **1942** Rogers gets to wear a white hat and a black hat as both the leader of a gang of outlaws and the hero who brings them to justice. A poor man's Western omelette. **53m/B VHS, DVD.** Roy Rogers, George "Gabby" Hayes, Lynne Carver, Frank M. Thomas Sr., Bob Nolan, Beryl Wallace, Glenn Strange, Douglas Fowley, Roy Barcroft, Pat Brady; ***D:*** Joseph Kane.

Sunset Park **1996 (R)** Brooklyn phys ed teacher Phyllis Saroka (Perlman) becomes the coach of a high school basketball team that, despite her total lack of knowledge about the game, makes it to the city championships. The cast's excellent performances hold interest, even though the predictable storyline gives away all of its moves before it gets near the hoop. Starr (of the rap group Onyx) is outstanding as the most talented (and most troubled) member of the team. **100m/C VHS, DVD.** Rhea Perlman, Carol Kane, Terrence Howard, Camille Saviola, Fredro Starr, James Harris, Antwon Tanner, Shawn Michael Howard, De'Aundre Bonds; ***D:*** Steve Gomer; ***W:*** Seth Zvi Rosenfeld, Kathleen McGhee-Anderson; ***C:*** Robbie Greenberg; ***M:*** Kay Gee, Miles Goodman.

Sunset Range ½ **1935** The "World's All-Around Champion Cowboy" of 1912 stars in this chaps-slappin', bit-chompin', dust-raisin' saga of the plains. **59m/B VHS, DVD.** Hoot Gibson, Mary Doran, Walter McGrail, James Eagles, John Elliott, Ralph Lewis; ***D:*** Ray McCarey; ***W:*** Paul Schofield; ***C:*** Gilbert Warrenton.

Sunset Serenade **1942** Roy and Gabby outwit murderous duo who plan to eliminate the new heir to a ranch. **60m/B VHS, DVD.** Roy Rogers, George "Gabby" Hayes, Helen Parrish; ***D:*** Joseph Kane.

Sunset Strip **1985** A photographer investigates a friend's murder, and enters the seamy world of drugs and rock and roll in L.A. **83m/C VHS.** Tom Elpin, Cheri Cameron Newell, John Mayall; ***D:*** William Webb; ***W:*** William Webb; ***C:*** Erich Anderson.

Sunset Strip **WOOF!** **1991 (R)** A young dancer finds a job in a strip club and competes against the other women there to find the man of her dreams. The women take their jobs very seriously—even attending ballet classes to improve their performances. However, the viewer probably won't take this movie very seriously since it is just another excuse to show women in as little clothing as possible. **95m/C VHS, DVD.** Jeff Conaway, Michelle Foreman, Shelley Michelle; ***D:*** Paul G. Volk; ***M:*** John Gonzalez.

Sunset Strip **1999 (R)** Slice of L.A. music biz life looks at the infamous eponymous strip in the '70s. Several music-industry wannabes try to make it in the industry and with each other in an interconnected storyline and intertwined lives kind of way. Good cast is wasted on a slight script that tries to cover too much ground and seems derivative of better rock and roll movies. **90m/C VHS, DVD.** Jared Leto, Adam Goldberg, Anna Friel, Nick Stahl, Simon Baker, Rory Cochrane, Tommy Flanagan, Darren E. Burrows, John Randolph, Stephanie Romanov, Mary Lynn Rajskub, Krista Allen, Judy Greer; ***D:*** Adam Collis; ***W:*** Russell DeGrazier, J. Randall Johnson; ***C:*** Ron Fortunato; ***M:*** Stewart Copeland.

Sunset Trail **1932** Routine Maynard sagebrush saga with the hero protecting a woman rancher from outlaws. **60m/B VHS.** Ruth Hiatt, Frank Rice, Philo (Philip, P.H., P.M.) McCullough, Buddy Hunter, Ken Maynard; ***D:*** B. Reeves Eason; ***W:*** Bennett Cohen; ***C:*** Arthur Reed.

Sunshine **1999 (R)** Sprawling look at four generations of an assimilated Hungarian-Jewish family covers a lot of time at the expense of cohesiveness and character. Title refers to the health tonic that makes the family fortune and is a pun on the family's original name, Sonnenschein. Fiennes turns up in three roles as the family prospers in Budapest by changing their name to avoid the anti-Semitic society—eventually converting to Catholicism. It will not protect them, however, from the Nazi holocaust and the turbulent postwar period that leads to the Hungarian Revolution of 1956. **180m/C VHS, DVD.** *CA HU* Ralph Fiennes, Rosemary Harris, Rachel Weisz, Jennifer Ehle, Molly Parker, Deborah Kara Unger, James Frain, William Hurt, John Neville, Miriam Margolyes, Mark Strong; ***D:*** Istvan Szabo; ***W:*** Istvan Szabo, Israel Horovitz; ***C:*** Lajos Koltai; ***M:*** Maurice Jarre. Genie '99: Film.

Sunshine ½ **2007 (R)** The year is 2057, and the sun is dying. A previous mission to reignite it has failed, and the pluckiest, prettiest crew of scientists ever assembled is sent with a massive nuclear bomb to do the job, and of course, technical and human calamities seemingly cobbled from other big-screen space odysseys ensue. Stunning visuals and lots of claustrophobic suspense mix with metaphysical ookiness, and the cast is crank, but even sci-fi fans who can forgive the deja vu will be tested by the "what-planet-are-you-on?" ending. **107m/C DVD, Blu-ray Disc.** *GB US* Cillian Murphy, Chris Evans, Rose Byrne, Michelle Yeoh, Hiroyuki (Henry) Sanada, Clifford Curtis, Troy Garity, Benedict Wong, Mark Strong; ***D:*** Danny Boyle; ***W:*** Alex Garland; ***C:*** Alwin Kuchler; ***M:*** John Murphy.

The Sunshine Boys **1975 (PG)** Two veteran vaudeville partners, who have shared a love-hate relationship for decades, reunite for a TV special. Adapted by Neil Simon from his play. Matthau was a replacement for Jack Benny, who died before the start of filming. Burns, for his first starring role since "Honolulu" in 1939, won an Oscar. **111m/C VHS, DVD.** George Burns, Walter Matthau, Richard Benjamin, Lee Meredith, F. Murray Abraham, Carol Arthur, Howard Hesseman; ***D:*** Herbert Ross; ***W:*** Neil Simon. Oscars '75: Support. Actor (Burns); Golden Globes '76: Actor—Mus./Comedy (Matthau), Film—Mus./Comedy, Support. Actor (Benjamin); Writers Guild '75: Adapt. Screenplay.

The Sunshine Boys **1995** TV version of the Neil Simon play about two old vaudevillians is updated, not necessarily for the better. The feuding duo are a formerly popular 50s TV comedy team whose breakup was not amicable (Think Lewis and Martin. Go ask your folks, we'll wait). They are persuaded to reunite for a special appearance, but the old grudges come back. Suffers by comparison to the original, with Allen and Falk unable to duplicate the chemistry of Burns and Matthau. **90m/C VHS, DVD.** Woody Allen, Peter Falk, Sarah Jessica Parker, Michael McKean, Liev Schreiber, Edie Falco, Kirk Acevedo, Michael Badalucco, Jennifer Esposito, Whoopi Goldberg; ***D:*** John Erman; ***W:*** Neil Simon. **TV**

Sunshine Cleaning ½ **2009 (R)** Single mom Rose (Adams) wants a better life for herself and her troubled 7-year-old son Oscar (Spevack) but poor choices, lousy circumstances, and lousier wages have kept her stuck. That is, till cop Mac (Zhan)—her son's father, now married, and with whom she's having a secret affair—tips her off to the profitability of cleaning up murder and suicide investigation scenes. Rose opens Sunshine Cleaning, enlisting her hapless sister Norah (Blunt) as her partner in not the sunniest of new adventures. They make the most of it while addressing the untidy aspects of their own lives as they scrub up the unspeakable messes. Their father Joe (Arkin) lightens the mood with familiar crusty old man wisecracks, while the quirky interplay between Rose and Norah almost distracts from the gruesome nature of their work. **102m/C DVD.** *US* Amy Adams, Emily Blunt, Alan Arkin, Jason Spevack, Steve Zahn, Mary Lynn Rajskub, Clifton (Gonzalez) Collins Jr., Eric Christian Olsen, Kevin Chapman; ***D:*** Christine Jeffs; ***W:*** Megan Holly; ***C:*** John Toon; ***M:*** Michael Penn.

Sunshine Run ½ *Black Rage* **1979 (PG)** Two escaped slaves and a young widow search for Spanish treasure in the Everglades. **102m/C VHS.** Chris Robinson, Ted Cassidy, David Legge, Phyllis Robinson; ***D:*** Chris Robinson.

Sunshine State **2002 (PG-13)** Sayles returns with a tale of developers invading a northern Florida resort island and the effect on the locals. Of the excellent ensemble, a superb Falco is the unsatisfied Marly, who runs a fleabag motel/restaurant, inherited from her blind, retired father (Waite). The Sea-Vue was her parents' dream but not hers. With a few failed relationships and many shots of tequila under her belt, Marly meets architect Jack (Hutton), one of the pack of real estate sharks after her property. Bassett is Desiree, who returns to her neighboring hometown in an attempt to reconcile with her mother (Alice), whose own island dream home was a nightmare for Desiree growing up. Not so much big biz vs. the little people as a coming to terms with life, family and the past. **141m/C VHS, DVD.** *US* Edie Falco, Angela Bassett, Timothy Hutton, James McDaniel, Mary Steenburgen, Marc Blucas, Jane Alexander, Ralph Waite, Mary Alice, Bill Cobbs, Alex Lewis, Gordon Clapp, Richard Edson, Tom Wright, Perry Lang, Miguel Ferrer, Michael Greyeyes, Alan King, Charlaine Woodard; ***D:*** John Sayles; ***W:*** John Sayles; ***C:*** Patrick Cady; ***M:*** Mason Daring. L.A. Film Critics '02: Support. Actress (Falco).

Sunstorm **2001** Four sisters who've never met unite to find out who killed their father (Keach), who was an important general. When the same people come after the sisters, the stage is set for a ridiculously confused plot and plenty of fight scenes between the sisters and numerous henchmen. Sets out as exploitation, but plays it too seriously and even disappoints in the eye candy department. **94m/C VHS, DVD.** Stacy Keach, Bo Derek, Geoffrey Lewis, Margaret Scarborough, Ray Raglin, Ron Hale, Rebecca Stauber, Michael Manasseri; ***D:*** Mike Marvin; ***C:*** Steve (Steven) Shaw. **VIDEO**

Sunstroke **1992 (R)** Seymour plays a desperate mother searching for her kidnapped child through the Arizona desert. Framed for murder, she cannot contact the police but must track the kidnappers herself, until she meets a drifter with secrets of his own. **91m/C VHS.** Jane Seymour, Stephen Meadows, Steve Railsback, Ray Wise, Don Ameche; ***D:*** James Keach; ***W:*** Duane Poole.

The Super 🦴 1/2 **1991 (R)** Pesci stars as a slumlord who faces a prison sentence thanks to his terminal neglect. The option given to him is to live in his own rat hole until he provides reasonable living conditions. This he does, and predictably learns a thing or two about his own greed and the people who suffer as a result of it. Pesci as always gives an animated performance but poor scripting laden with stereotypes and cliches successfully restricts effort. **86m/C VHS, DVD.** Joe Pesci, Vincent Gardenia, Madolyn Smith, Ruben Blades, Stacey Travis; ***D:*** Rod Daniel; ***C:*** Bruce Surtees.

Super Bitch 🦴 1/2 *Mafia Junction* **1973** Nasty, cold, and uncaring woman uses men to keep up her expensive habits, then ruthlessly tosses them aside when she is done. She purposely entangles them in her drug trade and thinks nothing of their deaths. Proving once again that you get what you pay for. **90m/C VHS.** Stephanie Beacham, Patricia Hayes, Gareth Thomas; ***D:*** Massimo Dallamano.

Super Brother 🦴 *Black Jesus* **1968 (R)** The feared and respected leader of an oppressed people is imprisoned, much to everyone's regret. **90m/C VHS.** *IT* Jean Servais, Franco Citti, Pier Paolo Capponi, Woody Strode; ***D:*** Valerio Zurlini; ***W:*** Valerio Zurlini; ***C:*** Aiace Parolini; ***M:*** Ivan Vandor.

Super Capers WOOF! 2009 (PG) Excruciatingly juvenile spoof of superhero flicks. Deluded Ed Gruberman is sentenced to a halfway house/training academy for dysfunctional minor superheroes. An evil plot is discovered (it may involve the script) and the wannabes go to work. **98m/C DVD.** Justin Whalin, Danielle Harris, Michael Rooker, Christine Lakin, Adam West, Ryan McPartlin, Samuel Lloyd, Ray Griggs; ***C:*** Martin Rodenberg; ***M:*** Nathan Lanier.

Super Force 🦴🦴 **1990** When astronaut Zach Stone (Olandt) returns from an assignment on Mars he finds his policeman brother has been murdered. He quits NASA and joins the force to get revenge, battling evil crime boss Tao Satori (Liddy). Stone also moonlights as a vigilante, complete with motorcycle and high-tech armoured suit. It's dumb but there's lots of action. **92m/C VHS.** Ken Olandt, G. Gordon Liddy, Larry B. Scott, Lisa Niemi, Marshall Teague; ***Cameos:*** Patrick Macnee; ***D:*** Richard Compton.

Super Fuzz 🦴 1/2 *Supersnooper* **1981 (PG)** Rookie policeman develops super powers after being accidentally exposed to radiation. Somewhat ineptly, he uses his abilities to combat crime. Somewhat ineptly acted, written, and directed as well. **97m/C VHS, DVD.** Terence Hill, Joanne Dru, Ernest Borgnine; ***D:*** Sergio Corbucci; ***W:*** Sergio Corbucci.

Super Inframan WOOF! *Infra-Man; The Super Inframan; Zong guo chhao ren; Chinese Superman* **1976 (PG)** Ten-million-year-old Princess Dragon Mon awakens and proceeds to conquer the world with an army of goofy costumed monsters. In response a professor turns a young man into an equally goofy bionic superhero. If you like over-the-top 1970s martial arts films, unintentionally funny dialogue, outdated effects, and guys in monster costumes, there's no reason to miss this. **90m/C DVD.** *HK* Danny Lee, Terry Liu, Bruce Le, Hsieh Wang, Man-Tzu Yuan, Wen-wei Lin; ***D:*** Shan Hua; ***W:*** Kuang Ni; ***C:*** Tadashi Nishimoto; ***M:*** Yung-Yu Chen.

Super Mario Bros. 🦴🦴 1/2 **1993 (PG)** $42 million adventure fantasy based on the popular Nintendo video game. The brothers are in hot pursuit of the Princess Daisy who's been kidnapped by evil slimebucket Hopper and taken to Dinohattan, a fungi-infested, garbage-strewn, rat-hole version of Manhattan. Hopper will amuse the adults, doing a gleeful reptilian version of Frank Booth from "Blue Velvet." Hoskins and Leguizamo act gamely in broad Nintendo style, enthusiastically partaking in high-tech wizardry and the many gags. Hits bullseye of target audience—elementary and junior high kids—with frenetic pace, gaudy special effects, oversized sets, and animatronic monsters. **104m/C VHS, DVD.** Bob Hoskins, John Leguizamo, Samantha Mathis, Fisher Stevens, Richard Edson, Dana Kaminsky, Dennis Hopper, Fiona Shaw, Mojo Nixon, Lance Henriksen; ***D:*** Rocky Morton, Annabel Jankel; ***W:*** Edward Solomon, Parker Bennett, Terry Runte; ***M:*** Alan Silvestri.

Super Seal 🦴 **1977 (G)** An injured seal pup disrupts a family's normal existence after the young daughter adopts him. **95m/C VHS.** Foster Brooks, Sterling Holloway, Sarah Brown; ***D:*** Michael Dugan.

Super Size Me 🦴🦴🦴 **2004** Director Spurlock becomes a human guinea pig in his cautionary tale/experiment into the apparently very dangerous world of fast food. Vowing to eat three meals a day at McDonald's for a full 30 days, Spurlock also had a strict "always say yes" policy when asked by a Mickey D's employee if he wanted to super size. The result was a 30-pound weight gain, severely declining health, and a film so controversial it caused McDonald's to stop their super size promotion months after the film debuted at the Sundance Film Festival. Gross-out doc mixes comedy with concern. Watching this one might even have die hard fast food freaks munching salad. Includes interviews with ice cream heir John Robbins, former surgeon general David Sacher, and Subway poster-boy Jared. **98m/C DVD.** ***D:*** Morgan Spurlock; ***W:*** Morgan Spurlock; ***C:*** Scott Ambrozy; ***M:*** Steve Horowitz, Michael Parrish.

Super Sucker 🦴🦴 **2003 (R)** Daniels wrote, directed, and starred in this sometimes sleazy and intermittently funny comedy. Fred Barlow (Daniels) works for Johnson City Super Sucker Vacuums as a salesman, only his career is in trouble. The company has launched a sales contest to see (essentially) who will remain employed and who will get the boot. Fred is despondent until he discovers his wife using one of the vacuum's attachments for personal satisfaction that has nothing to do with household cleaning. Suddenly Fred has the proper gimmick to sell the vacuum to the city's lonely housewives. **95m/C VHS, DVD.** Jeff Daniels, Matt Letscher, Harve Presnell, Guy Sanville, Sandra Birch, John Seibert, Kate Peckham, Dawn Wells; ***D:*** Jeff Daniels; ***W:*** Jeff Daniels; ***C:*** Richard Brauer.

Super Troopers 🦴🦴 1/2 *Broken Lizard's Super Troopers* **2001 (R)** Vermont is the setting for this snobs vs. slobs comedy that pits wacky state troopers facing a budget-forced shutdown against the local cops, who curry favor with the politicians. Plot involving a jurisdictional fight over a murder and a drug bust only occassionally interferes with the drug, sex, and gross-out humor that carries the pic to a satisfying conclusion. Cox is hilarious as the barely-in-control commander of the station, while Von Bargen does a great job as his nemesis. **100m/C VHS, DVD, Blu-ray Disc, UMD.** Jay Chandrasekhar, Kevin Heffernan, Steve Lemme, Paul Soter, Erik Stolhanske, Brian Cox, Daniel von Bargen, Marisa Coughlan, Michael Weaver, Jim Gaffigan, John Bedford Lloyd, Lynda Carter; ***D:*** Jay Chandrasekhar; ***W:*** Jay Chandrasekhar, Kevin Heffernan, Steve Lemme, Paul Soter, Erik Stolhanske; ***C:*** Joaquin Baca-Asay.

Superargo 🦴🦴 *Il Re Dei Criminali; Superargo the Giant; The King of Criminals* **1967** A wrestler becomes a superhero with psychic powers and a bulletproof leotard, fighting a madman who is turning athletes into robots. Successful Italian hero who wouldn't last two minutes in the ring with Batman. **95m/C VHS.** *IT SP* Guy Madison, Ken Wood, Liz Barrett, Diana Loris; ***D:*** Paul Maxwell.

Superbabies: Baby Geniuses 2 WOOF! 2004 (PG) A super stupid waste of time. The who cares follow-up to the 1999 release pits evil German media mogul Biscane (Oscar-winner Voight, who once had a real career) against four toddlers who have a super ability to communicate with each other via really bad dubbing and Kahuna (the Fitzgerald triplets), who only looks like a 7-year-old (don't ask). Biscane's diabolical plan is to control the minds of children by brainwashing them via subliminal messages through the TV. Wait, hasn't that already been done? Baio and Angel pop in as the owners of an L.A. daycare center. **90m/C VHS, DVD.** *GE GB* Jon Voight, Scott Baio, Vanessa Angel, Peter Wingfield, Justin Chatwin, Gerry Fitzgerald, Leo Fitzgerald, Myles Fitzgerald, Skyler Shaye, Max Iles, Michael Iles, Jared Scheideman, Jordan Scheideman, Maia Bastidas, Keana Bastidas, Joshua Lockhart, Maxwell Lockhart; ***D:*** Bob (Benjamin) Clark; ***W:*** Gregory Poppen; ***C:*** Maher Maleh; ***M:*** Paul Zaza, Helmut Zerlett.

Superbad 🦴🦴🦴 1/2 **2007 (R)** Seth (Hill) and Evan (Cera) are crude, socially inept, and sex-obsessed, like most teenage boys. When the girls they have crushes on ask them to buy booze for a graduation party, Seth sees this as their last chance to woo their beloveds the best way he knows how—by getting them drunk. Roping their fake-ID wielding friend Fogell (Mintz-Plasse) into Seth's scheme, their night becomes an odyssey of cops, robbers, crazed bums, cokeheads, violent thugs, party-crashing losers, vomit, and facing fears about their futures. Unapologetically teems with both raunch and heart. Hill and Cera shine as the hapless leads (named after writers Rogan and Goldberg, who penned the original version of the project while in junior high), but newcomer Mintz-Plasse steals every scene as the hopeless geek who re-names himself "McLovin." **112m/C DVD, Blu-ray Disc.** *US* Jonah Hill, Michael Cera, Bill Hader, Seth Rogen, Christopher Mintz-Plasse, Aviva, Stacy Edwards, Kevin Corrigan, Emma Stone, Martha MacIsaac; ***D:*** Greg Mottola; ***W:*** Seth Rogen, Greg Mottola, Evan Goldberg; ***C:*** Russ T. Alsobrook; ***M:*** Lyle Workman.

Superbug Super Agent 🦴 1/2 **1976** Dodo, the wonder car puts the brakes on crime in this silly action-adventure tale. A lemon in a lot full of Herbies. **90m/C VHS.** *GE* Robert Mark, Heidi Hansen, George Goodman; ***D:*** Rudolf Zehetgruber; ***W:*** Rudolf Zehetgruber; ***C:*** Hannes Staudinger; ***M:*** Jurgen Elert.

Superchick WOOF! 1971 (R) Mild-mannered stewardess by day, sexy blonde with karate blackbelt by night. In addition to stopping a skyjacking she regularly makes love to men around the world. A superbomb that never gets off the ground. **94m/C VHS, DVD.** Joyce Jillson, Louis Quinn, Thomas Reardon, Uschi Digart; ***D:*** Ed Forsyth; ***W:*** Gary Crutcher; ***C:*** Paul Hipp; ***M:*** Allan Alper.

Supercop 🦴🦴 1/2 *Police Story 3: Supercop* **1992 (R)** Super Hong Kong cop Kevin Chan (Chan) heads to China to assist the authorities in cracking an international drug ring. He's partnered with disciplined-but-beautiful Director Yang (Yeoh), who's also a terrific fighter, and the duo go undercover (as a married couple) to infilitrate the operation, which takes them to a Malaysian resort. Then Chan's girlfriend shows up, blowing their cover. Lots of action-packed fighting and wild chases. The 1996 American release loses about a half-hour of run time from the original. Dubbed from Cantonese. **93m/C VHS, DVD.** *HK* Jackie Chan, Michelle Yeoh, Maggie Cheung, Kenneth Tsang, Yuen Wah; ***D:*** Stanley Tong; ***W:*** Edward Tang, Fibe Ma, Lee Wai Yee; ***C:*** Ardy Lam; ***M:*** Joel McNeely.

Supercop 2 🦴🦴 *Police Story 3, Part 2* **1993 (R)** Rising star Inspector Jessica Yang (Yeoh) has her life disrupted when her boyfriend David is dishonorably discharged from the police force and leaves town. Several months later, Jessica is assigned to stop a crime ring that turns out to be headed by David. Chan has a brief cameo (in drag). **94m/C VHS, DVD.** *HK* Michelle Yeoh, Yukari Oshima, Eric Tsang, Rongguang Yu, Athene Chu, Siu-wong Fan, Jackie Chan, Emile Chau, Chu Yan; ***D:*** Stanley Tong; ***W:*** Stanley Tong, Mok Tang Han, Sui Lai Kang.

Supercross: The Movie 🦴 1/2 **2005 (PG-13)** In case you are unaware, supercross is an offshoot of motocross racing but is held on indoor tracks equipped with gravity-defying jumps. Brothers KC (Howey) and Trip (Vogel) want to become champs but, for now, they are underdogs. KC has to play second bike to corporate sponsor star Rowdy (Tatum), so Trip decides he'd be better off going it alone and gets his own sponsor, Earl Cole (Patrick, the only one with actual acting ability). Richardson and Bush are the chicks the brothers get involved with. The plot may be clunky but director Boyum cranks up the racing thrills and noise level. **98m/C DVD.** *US* Mike Vogel, Channing Tatum, J.D. Pardo, Robert Carradine, Steve Howey, Cameron Richardson, Sophia Buh, Aaron Carter, Carolina Garcia, Ryan Locke; ***D:*** Steve Boyum; ***W:*** Ken Solarz, Bart Baker; ***C:*** William Wages.

Superdad 🦴 **1973 (G)** A middle-aged parent is determined to bridge the generation gap by trying his hand at various teenage activities. Disney family fare that's about as complicated as a TV commercial. The adolescents are two-dimensional throwbacks to the fun-loving '50s. **94m/C VHS.** Bob Crane, Kurt Russell, Joe Flynn, Barbara Rush, Kathleen (Kathy) Cody, Dick Van Patten; ***D:*** Vincent McEveety; ***M:*** Buddy (Norman Dale) Baker.

SuperFire 🦴 1/2 **2002 (PG-13)** Hackneyed heroes story. Jim Merrick (Sweeney) is a disgraced fire-fighter tanker pilot whose mistakes cost the lives of 12 smokejumpers. So no one is ready to listen when Jim says an enormous superfire is forming that will obliterate the local community. Then the wildfire gets out of control and it's up to Jim to save the day. **99m/C VHS, DVD.** D.B. Sweeney, Wes Studi, Chad E. Donella, Diane Farr, Ellen Muth, Katrina Hobbs; ***D:*** Steven Quale; ***W:*** Michael Vickerman; ***C:*** William Wages. **TV**

Superfly 🦴🦴 1/2 **1972 (R)** Controversial upon release, pioneering blaxploitation has Harlem dope dealer finding trouble with gangs and police as he attempts to establish retirement fund from one last deal. Excellent period tunes by Curtis Mayfield. Two lesser sequels. **98m/C VHS, DVD.** Ron O'Neal, Carl Lee, Sheila Frazier, Julius W. Harris, Charles McGregor; ***D:*** Gordon Parks Jr.; ***W:*** Phillip Fenty; ***C:*** James Signorelli; ***M:*** Curtis Mayfield.

Superfly T.N.T. WOOF! *Super Fly T.N.T* **1973 (R)** This confusing sequel to "Superfly" finds O'Neal returning as Youngblood Priest. The now ex-drug dealer has retired with his girlfriend to Rome where he is approached by an African gun-runner (Browne) for help in a revolution against an oppressive government. Cheap exploitation. **87m/C VHS.** Ron O'Neal, Roscoe Lee Browne, Sheila Frazier, Robert Guillaume, Jacques Sernas, William Berger; ***D:*** Ron O'Neal; ***W:*** Alex Haley.

Supergirl 🦴 1/2 **1984 (PG)** Big-budget bomb in which Slater made her debut and nearly killed her career, with the help of Kryptonite. Unexciting and unsophisticated story of a young woman, cousin to Superman, with super powers, based on the comic book series. She's in pursuit of a magic paperweight, but an evil sorceress wants it too. Dunaway is a terrifically vile villainess with awesome black magic powers. Slater is great to look at, but is much better in almost any other film. **114m/C VHS, DVD.** *GB* Faye Dunaway, Helen Slater, Peter O'Toole, Mia Farrow, Brenda Vaccaro, Marc McClure, Simon Ward, Hart Bochner, Maureen Teefy, David Healy, Matt Frewer; ***D:*** Jeannot Szwarc; ***W:*** David Odell; ***C:*** Alan Hume; ***M:*** Jerry Goldsmith.

Supergrass 🦴🦴 **1987 (R)** A low-brow British farce about a nebbish who poses as a drug smuggler to impress his girlfriend, and is then mistaken for a real one by the authorities. **105m/C VHS.** *GB* Adrian Edmondson, Peter Richardson, Nigel Planer, Jennifer Saunders, Ronald Allen, Dawn French; ***D:*** Peter Richardson.

SuperGuy: Behind the Cape 🦴 1/2 **2002** Leaping into a thin plot with a single bound, this comic-book farce exposes the increasingly mortal superhero SuperGuy who fights having his super-image tarnished as humanlike weaknesses are revealed and his once-adoring fans afford him no pity. **74m/C VHS, DVD.** Charles Dierkop, Katherine Victor, Mark Teague, Jan Garrett, Christopher Fey, Elizabeth Jaeger-Rydall, Marcello Paz-Pulliam, Tim Peyton, Peter Stacker, David Anthony Hernandez; ***D:*** Bill Lae; ***C:*** Mike Ziemkowski. **VIDEO**

Superhero Movie 🦴 **2008 (PG-13)** Holy send-up, Batman! In this swing at blockbuster superhero flicks, weakling Rick Riker (likable teen dream Bell) is bitten by a genetically altered dragonfly and transforms into a dragonfly superhero, possessing all manner of super powers—except he can't fly. Dragonfly then has a showdown with power-crazed CEO-turned-villainous-arch enemy Hourglass (McDonald). Strings together the usual lazy jabs at pop-culture targets and D-list cameos, the irony of which will be lost on the target teenybopper audience. Another waste of time and effort. **86m/C DVD, Blu-ray Disc.** *US* Drake Bell, Marion Ross, Sara Paxton, Christopher McDonald, Leslie Nielsen, Ryan Hansen; ***C:*** Thomas Ackerman; ***M:*** James L. Venable.

Superheroes 🦴🦴 **2007** Suffering from post-traumatic stress disorder, Iraqi War vet Ben Patchett (Mihok) can no longer cope with his family and self-medicates as he struggles to get through each day. Young and earnest videographer Nick Jones (Clark) is taping a VA outpatient group Ben is attending. They form a tentative friendship and Nick agrees to accompany Ben on a change-of-pace country retreat the vet hopes will offer him a little peace. **87m/C DVD.** Dash Mihok, Spencer (Treat) Clark, Nancy Giles, Margo Martindale, Kelly McAndrew; ***D:*** Alan Brown; ***W:*** Alan Brown; ***C:*** Derek McKane; ***M:*** Paul Cantelon.

Superman: The Movie ♪♪♪ 1/2 **1978 (PG)** The DC Comics legend comes alive in this wonderfully entertaining saga of Superman's life from a baby on the doomed planet Krypton (with Brando as Supe's dad) to Earth's own Man of Steel (a chiseled Reeve). Hackman and Beatty pair marvelously as super criminal Lex Luthor and his bumbling sidekick Otis, while Kidder is an intelligent Lois Lane. Award-winning special effects and a script that doesn't take itself too seriously make this great fun. Followed by three sequels. **152m/C VHS, DVD, Blu-ray Disc, HD DVD.** Christopher Reeve, Margot Kidder, Marlon Brando, Gene Hackman, Glenn Ford, Susannah York, Ned Beatty, Valerie Perrine, Jackie Cooper, Marc McClure, Trevor Howard, Sarah Douglas, Terence Stamp, Jack O'Halloran, Phyllis Thaxter; ***D:*** Richard Donner; ***W:*** Mario Puzo, Robert Benton, David Newman; ***C:*** Geoffrey Unsworth; ***M:*** John Williams. Oscars '78: Visual FX.

Superman 2 ♪♪♪ **1980 (PG)** The sequel to "the movie" about the Man of Steel. This time, he has his hands full with three super-powered villains from his home planet of Krypton. The romance between reporter Lois Lane and our superhero is made believable and the story line has more pace to it than the original. A sequel that often equals the first film—leave it to Superman to pull off the impossible. **128m/C VHS, DVD, Blu-ray Disc, HD DVD.** Christopher Reeve, Margot Kidder, Gene Hackman, Ned Beatty, Jackie Cooper, Sarah Douglas, Jack O'Halloran, Susannah York, Marc McClure, Terence Stamp, Valerie Perrine, E.G. Marshall; ***D:*** Richard Lester; ***W:*** Mario Puzo, David Newman; ***C:*** Robert Paynter; ***M:*** John Williams.

Superman 3 ♪♪ **1983 (PG)** Villainous businessman Ross Webster (Vaughn) tries to conquer Superman (Reeve) via the expertise of bumbling computer expert Gus Gorman (Pryor) and the judicious use of an artificial form of Kryptonite. Superman explores his darker side after undergoing transformation into sleaze ball. Promising satiric start ultimately defeated by uneven story and direction and boring physical comedy. Notable is the absence of Lois Lane as a main character, instead the big guy takes up with former flame Lana Lang (O'Toole). Followed by "Superman 4." **123m/C VHS, DVD.** Christopher Reeve, Richard Pryor, Annette O'Toole, Jackie Cooper, Margot Kidder, Marc McClure, Annie Ross, Robert Vaughn; ***D:*** Richard Lester; ***W:*** David Newman; ***C:*** Robert Paynter; ***M:*** John Williams.

Superman 4: The Quest for Peace ♪♪ **1987 (PG)** The third sequel, in which the Man of Steel endeavors to rid the world of nuclear weapons, thereby pitting himself against nuclear-entrepreneur Lex Luthor and his superpowered creation, Nuclear Man. Special effects are dime-store quality and it appears that someone may have walked off with parts of the plot. Reeve deserves credit for remaining true to character through four films. **90m/C VHS, DVD.** Christopher Reeve, Gene Hackman, Jon Cryer, Marc McClure, Margot Kidder, Mariel Hemingway, Sam Wanamaker; ***D:*** Sidney J. Furie; ***W:*** Mark Rosenthal; ***M:*** John Williams; ***V:*** Susannah York.

Superman & the Mole Men ♪♪ 1/2 *Superman and the Strange People* **1951** The cast of the popular 1950s' TV show made this rarely seen feature as a pilot for the series. Superman faces the danger threatened by the invasion of radioactive mole-men who make their way to the surface world from the bowels of the earth through an oil-well shaft. Simple fun. **58m/C VHS.** George Reeves, Phyllis Coates, Jeff Corey; ***D:*** Lee Sholem. **TV**

Superman Returns ♪♪ 1/2 **2006 (PG-13)** Over-hyped and overlong return of the Man of Steel, last seen on the big screen in 1987's "Superman IV." Christopher Reeve look-alike Routh fills out the spandex but lacks a certain superhero charm as Supes returns to Earth five years after the events of "Superman 2" (like everyone else, they pretend that "III" and "IV" never happened). Clark Kent heads back to the "Daily Planet" where he discovers that Lois (a shallow Bosworth) is on an anti-Superman rant and also has a son and a fiance. Lex Luthor (Spacey) wants to take over the world—again. Superman comes to the rescue—again. Singer plays the story straight and there's not a lot of gee-whiz joy to be found. **140m/C DVD, Blu-ray Disc, HD DVD.** *US* Brandon Routh, Kate (Catherine) Bosworth, Kevin Spacey, James Marsden, Eva Marie Saint, Parker Posey, Frank Langella, Sam Huntington, Kal Penn, Noel Neill, Jack Larson, Marlon Brando, Tristan Lake Leabu, David Fabrizio; ***D:*** Bryan Singer; ***W:*** Bryan Singer, Michael Dougherty, Daniel P. "Dan" Harris; ***C:*** Newton Thomas (Tom) Sigel; ***M:*** John Ottman.

Supernatural ♪♪ 1/2 **1933** Roma (Lombard) falls prey to a phony medium (Dinehart) who promises to call up the spirit of her recently murdered twin brother. At the same moment of the seance a murderess dies in the electric chair and her body is used in Dr. Houston's (Warner) life-after-death experiment. Too bad Roma becomes possessed by the woman's evil spirit. Now the doctor and Roma's fiance (Scott) must undo the curse. A hokey B-grade movie disliked by Lombard. **78m/B VHS.** Carole Lombard, Randolph Scott, H.B. Warner, Alan Dinehart, Vivienne Osborne, Beryl Mercer, William Farnum, Willard Robertson; ***D:*** Victor Halperin; ***W:*** Harvey Thew, Brian Marlow; ***C:*** Arthur Martinelli.

The Supernaturals ♪ 1/2 **1986 (R)** Confederate Civil War-era ghosts, bent on avenging their deaths, haunt a wooded area in which modern Yankee army maneuvers are practiced. Antebellum boredom. **85m/C VHS.** Bobby DiCicco, Maxwell Caulfield, LeVar Burton, Nichelle Nichols; ***D:*** Armand Mastroianni; ***C:*** Peter Lyons Collister.

Supernova ♪ 1/2 **1999 (PG-13)** This one got stuck on the studio shelf for awhile and didn't improve with age. In fact, director Walter Hill was so incensed over studio re-editing that he removed his name, leaving the pseud. "Thomas Lee" to grace this space mishmash. Nick Vanzant (Spader) is stuck piloting a 22nd-century medical vessel after the captain (Forster) is killed. The craft receives a distress call and makes the mistake of rescuing Karl (Facinelli), an odd duck who proves to be very dangerous. You'll wonder what got left on the cutting-room floor. **91m/C VHS, DVD.** James Spader, Angela Bassett, Robin Tunney, Peter Facinelli, Lou Diamond Phillips, Wilson Cruz, Robert Forster; ***D:*** Walter Hill; ***W:*** David Campbell Wilson; ***C:*** Lloyd Ahern II; ***M:*** David Williams.

Supernova WOOF! *2012 : Supernova* **2009** You don't really expect scientific accuracy in a cheesy sci-fi flick, but c'mon! Fires in the vacuum of outer space?! And that's just some of the egregious crapola foisted on unsuspecting viewers in this cheapie that suffers from lame plot, acting, and CGI. An exploding star is going to destroy the Earth unless an astrophysicist and two fellow scientists can come up with a way to save the planet. **90m/C DVD.** Brian Krause, Heather McComb, Najarra Townsend, Londale Theus; ***D:*** Anthony Fankhauser; ***W:*** Anthony Fankhauser, Jon Macy; ***C:*** Mark Atkins; ***M:*** Chris Ridenhour. **VIDEO**

Supersonic Man WOOF! **1978 (PG)** Incoherent shoestring-budget Superman spoof with a masked hero fighting to save the world from the evil intentions of a mad scientist. **85m/C VHS.** *SP* Michael Coby, Cameron Mitchell, Diana Polakov; ***D:*** J(uan) Piquer Simon.

Superstar ♪♪ **1999 (PG-13)** Yet another SNL skit tries to stretch to feature film length and remain funny. Don't these people ever give up?! What's next? "Weekend Update: The Movie?" This time producer Lorne Michaels showcases klutzy Catholic schoolgirl Mary Katherine Gallagher (Shannon) as she tries to win a school talent contest and a kiss from the campus hunk (Ferrell). Of course, it's really about her strange armpit sniffing technique and panty-flashing behavior. The material doesn't translate well to movie length (shocking!), and the "teenagers" look like they're about 20 years late for homeroom. There are some funny bits, however, and if you like the character on the show you'll probably like the movie. Warning: There are scenes where Ms. Gallagher french kisses a tree, which sounds a lot funnier than it actually is. **82m/C VHS, DVD.** Molly Shannon, Will Ferrell, Elaine Hendrix, Glynis Johns, Mark McKinney, Harland Williams, Emmy Laybourne; ***D:*** Bruce McCulloch; ***W:*** Steve Koren; ***C:*** Walt Lloyd; ***M:*** Michael Gore.

Superstar: The Life and Times of Andy Warhol ♪♪♪ **1990** Even if you didn't grok Andy's 'pop' artwork and self-created celebrity persona, this ironic, kinetic, oft-rollicking documentary paints a vivid picture of the wild era he inspired and exploited. Interviewees range from Warhol cohorts like Dennis Hopper to proud executives at the Campbell Soup plant. One highlight: a Warhol guest shot on "The Love Boat." **87m/C VHS, DVD.** Tom Wolfe, Sylvia Miles, David Hockney, Taylor Mead, Dennis Hopper, Viva, Allen Ginsberg, Ultra Violet, Paul Morrissey, Sally Kirkland, Fran Lebowitz, Lou Reed, Shelley Winters, Holly Woodlawn; ***D:*** Chuck Workman; ***W:*** Chuck Workman; ***C:*** Burleigh Wartes.

Superstition ♪ 1/2 *The Witch* **1982** A reverend and his family move into a vacant house despite warnings about a curse from the townsfolk. Some people never learn. **85m/C VHS, DVD.** James Houghton, Albert Salmi, Lynn Carlin; ***D:*** James Robertson.

Supervixens ♪♪ *Russ Meyer's SuperVixens; SuperVixens Eruption; Vixens* **1975** True to Meyer's low-rent exploitation film canon, this wild tale is filled with characteristic Amazons, sex and violence. A gas station attendant is framed for the grisly murder of his girlfriend and hustles out of town, meeting a succession of well-endowed women during his travels. As if it needed further problems, it's hampered by a tasteless storyline and incoherent writing. **105m/C VHS, DVD.** Shari Eubank, Charles Napier, Uschi Digart, Charles Pitts, Henry Rowland, Sharon Kelly, Haji; ***D:*** Russ Meyer; ***W:*** Russ Meyer; ***C:*** Russ Meyer; ***M:*** William Loose.

Support Your Local Gunfighter ♪♪♪ **1971 (G)** Garner plays a western con man with his tongue firmly in his cheek. He comes to the small town of Purgatory and is thought to be a notorious gunfighter. He decides to go with the mistaken identity and use it to his profitable advantage. Elam is his bumbling sidekick and Pleshette the love interest. A delightful, deliberately cliche-filled western. A follow-up, not a sequel, to "Support Your Local Sheriff" (1969). **92m/C VHS, DVD.** James Garner, Jack Elam, Suzanne Pleshette, Harry (Henry) Morgan, Dub Taylor, John Dehner, Joan Blondell, Ellen Corby, Henry Jones; ***D:*** Burt Kennedy; ***W:*** James Edward Grant; ***C:*** Harry Stradling Jr.; ***M:*** Jack Elliott, Allyn Ferguson.

Support Your Local Sheriff ♪♪♪ 1/2 **1969 (G)** Amiable, irreverent western spoof with more than its fair share of laughs. When a stranger stumbles into a gold rush town, he winds up becoming sheriff. Garner is perfect as the deadpan sheriff, particularly in the scene where he convinces Dern to remain in jail, in spite of the lack of bars. Neatly subverts every western cliche it encounters, yet keeps respect for formula western. Followed by "Support Your Local Gunfighter." **92m/C VHS, DVD.** James Garner, Joan Hackett, Walter Brennan, Bruce Dern, Jack Elam, Harry (Henry) Morgan; ***D:*** Burt Kennedy; ***W:*** William Bowers; ***C:*** Harry Stradling Jr.

Suppose They Gave a War and Nobody Came? ♪♪ 1/2 *War Games* **1970 (G)** A small Southern town battles with a local army base in this entertaining but wandering satire. The different acting styles used as the producers wavered on making this a comedy or drama were more at war with one another than the characters involved. **113m/C VHS, DVD.** Tony Curtis, Brian Keith, Ernest Borgnine, Suzanne Pleshette, Ivan Dixon, Bradford Dillman, Don Ameche; ***D:*** Hy Averback; ***W:*** Don McGuire.

Supreme Sanction ♪♪ **1999 (R)** An assassin (Swanson) working for a covert government agency decides not to kill the journalist who's threatening to expose the corrupt organization that trained her. This doesn't please her bosses and they mark her for death. **95m/C VHS, DVD.** Michael Madsen, Kristy Swanson, David Dukes, Donald Adeosun Faison, Tommy (Tiny) Lister, Ron Perlman; ***D:*** John Terlesky; ***W:*** John Terlesky. **VIDEO**

Surabaya Conspiracy ♪ 1/2 **1975** Mystery and intrigue surround a quest for gold in Africa. **90m/C VHS.** Michael Rennie, Richard Jaeckel, Barbara Bouchet, Mike (Michael) Preston; ***D:*** Roy Davis.

Sure Fire ♪♪ **1990** Wes (Blair) is a mercurial entrepreneur who thinks he has found the financial ticket to paradise with his vacation home scheme. Much to the chagrin of his wife Ellen (Dezina), he refuses to let anything stand in the way of his sure-fire fortune, even his family. Wes develops a little self-control as he realizes he's beginning to flake out, but it may be too late. Director Jost has put together a surprisingly unpretentious film with a virtually no-name cast, its plot speaking volumes on the American condition while unfolding in the bleak Utah desert. **86m/C VHS, DVD.** Tom Blair, Kristi Hager, Robert Ernst, Kate Dezina, Phillip R. Brown; ***D:*** Jon Jost; ***W:*** Jon Jost.

The Sure Thing ♪♪♪ **1985 (PG-13)** College students who don't like each other end up travelling to California together, and of course, falling in love. Charming performances make up for predictability. Can't-miss director (and ex-Meathead) Reiner's second direct hit at the boxoffice. **94m/C VHS, DVD.** John Cusack, Daphne Zuniga, Anthony Edwards, Boyd Gaines, Lisa Jane Persky, Viveca Lindfors, Nicolette Sheridan, Tim Robbins; ***D:*** Rob Reiner; ***W:*** Jonathan Roberts, Steven L. Bloom; ***C:*** Robert Elswit; ***M:*** Tom Scott.

Surf Nazis Must Die ♪ **1987** A piece of deliberate camp in the Troma mold, about a group of psychotic neo-Nazi surfers taking over the beaches of California in the wake of a devastating earthquake. Tongue-in-cheek, tasteless and cheap, but intentionally so. **83m/C VHS, DVD.** Barry Brenner, Gail Neely, Michael Sonye, Dawn Wildsmith, Tom Shell, Bobbie Bresee; ***D:*** Peter George; ***W:*** John Ayre; ***C:*** Rolf Kestermann; ***M:*** Jon McCallum.

Surf Ninjas ♪♪ 1/2 *Surf Warriors* **1993 (PG)** Action comedy for the kiddies finds two young surfer dudes who are actually the long-lost crown princes of the obscure nation of Patu San. The country's incompetent (what a surprise, it's Nielsen) warlord wants the boys to stay lost. Lame jokes and tame martial arts sequences. **87m/C VHS, DVD.** Kelly Hu, Ernie Reyes Jr., Nick Cowen, Leslie Nielsen, Tone Loc, Rob Schneider, John Karlen, Ernie Reyes Sr.; ***D:*** Neal Israel; ***W:*** Dan Gordon; ***C:*** Arthur Albert; ***M:*** David Kitay.

Surf Party ♪ 1/2 **1964** Romance among the sands of Malibu with Vinton as the owner of a surf shop. Risque in 1964; utterly campy today. ♫If I Were an Artist; That's What Love Is; Pearly Shells. **68m/C VHS.** Bobby Vinton, Jackie DeShannon, Patricia Morrow, Kenny (Ken) Miller; ***D:*** Maury Dexter.

Surf 2 WOOF! *Surf 2: The End of the Trilogy* **1984 (R)** A most excellent group of surfers get sick from drinking tainted Buzz Cola concocted by demented chemist Deezen in most heinous effort to obliterate surfer population from Southern California. Bogus, dude. No, you didn't miss "Surf 1" (there's not one), the title is the sort of in-joke this exercise in mental meltdown perpetuates as comedy. Ha. **91m/C VHS.** Morgan Paull, Cleavon Little, Lyle Waggoner, Ruth Buzzi, Linda Kerridge, Carol Wayne, Eddie Deezen, Eric Stoltz, Brandis Kemp, Terry Kiser; ***D:*** Randall Badat; ***W:*** Randall Badat; ***M:*** Peter Bernstein.

Surface to Air ♪♪ **1998 (R)** Naval pilot Steven Madison (McQueen) is estranged from half-brother Zach (Madsen), who's in the Marines. But both wind up in Persian Gulf. Steve and fellow pilot Lori (Shatner) are captured by Iraqi terrorists and face certain death—unless Zach can come to the rescue. **93m/C VHS.** Michael Madsen, Chad McQueen, Melanie Shatner, Larry Thomas; ***D:*** Rodney McDonald. **VIDEO**

Surfacing WOOF! **1984** A girl braves the hostile northern wilderness to search for her missing father. This pseudo-psychological, sex-driven suspense flick makes little sense.

90m/C VHS. Joseph Bottoms, Kathleen Beller, R.H. Thomson, Margaret Dragu; *D:* Claude Jutra.

Surfer, Dude 2008 (R) Seems to be a very lame excuse to get McConaughey shirtless and frolicking in the Malibu surf and sun. He nominally stars as long-board surfer Steve Addington, who returns from his travels happy but broke. A slick endorsement sponsor wants Steve to participate in a reality TV show while Steve is more worried about the lack of wave action. Although babes and weed are a lot easier to find. **88m/C DVD, Blu-ray Disc.** Matthew McConaughey, Jeffrey Nordling, Woody Harrelson, Ramon Rodriguez, Willie Nelson, Alexie Gilmore; *D:* S. R. Bindler; *W:* S. R. Bindler, Cory Van Dyke, George Mays, Mark Gustawes; *C:* Elliot Davis; *M:* Matthew McConaughey, Blake Neely, Xavier Rudd.

Surf's Up 1/2 2007 (PG) Dude! Penguins march, tap dance, and now they surf. Young Cody Maverick (LaBeouf) is an outcast among his peers with his surfer dreams. He follows a scout to the tropical Pen Gu Island, the home of a championship contest, and finds a mentor in laid-back legend Big Z (Bridges). Cody even gets a much more competent potential love interest in lifeguard Lani (Deschanel). Sidekick Chicken Joe (Heder) provides some diversion. Not groundbreaking in the animation department (although the look of the waves is impressive), but the story is fun and the vocal work just right. **85m/C DVD, HD DVD.** *US D:* Chris Buck, Ash Brannon; *W:* Lisa Addario, Joe Syracuse, Christian Darren, Don Rhymer; *M:* Mychael Danna; *V:* Shia LaBeouf, Jeff Bridges, Zooey Deschanel, Jon Heder, James Woods, Diedrich Bader, Mario Cantone, Jane Krakowski, Brian Benben, Michael McKean, Dana Belben.

Surfwise 2007 (R) Less a surfing documentary, and more a glimpse into the world of the nomadic Paskowitz family, dubbed "the first family of surfing." After graduating from Stanford's med school, Dorian "Doc" Paskowitz, twice-divorced, sold all his possession and traveled the world, introducing the sport of surfing to Israel and meeting his soon-to-be-wife, Juliette, along the way. The two raised eight children in a 24-foot camper, cruising the coasts, substituting a standard education for a crash course in the zen of the wave, creating a gap that some of the children grew to resent. At 85, the surfing bohemian and his wife reunite with their children to hash out the family differences. Insightful and unbiased, always allowing its subjects to tell the story. **93m/C DVD.** *US D:* Doug Pray; *C:* Dave Homcy; *M:* Joh Dragonetti.

The Surgeon *Exquisite Tenderness* 1994 (R) Routine hospital horror finds Dr. Theresa McCann (Glasser) caught up in murder when patients and doctors become poison victims. Aided by toxicologist Benjamin Hendricks (Remar), McCann finds a lollipop left behind and realizes the killer is ex-boyfriend/doctor Julian Matar (Haberle), whose unlawful experiments in tissue regeneration got him suspended. Now he's hiding out in the hospital and killing to get the pituitary glands necessary for his miracle serum. Film's original title "Exquisite Tenderness" is a term for the point when pain becomes so extreme it turns to pleasure—the film merely turns grisly. **100m/C VHS, DVD.** *GE* Isabel Glasser, James Remar, Sean Haberle, Charles Dance, Peter Boyle, Malcolm McDowell, Charles Bailey-Gates, Gregory West, Mother Love; *D:* Carl Schenkel; *W:* Patrick Cirillo; *C:* Thomas Burstyn; *M:* Christopher Franke.

Surprise Attack 1970 The Spanish Civil War forms the backdrop for this action opus. **124m/C VHS.** Simon Andreu, Dan (Daniel, Danny) Martin, Patty (Patti) Shepard; *D:* Jose Antonio De La Loma.

Surrender 1/2 1987 (PG) A struggling woman artist and a divorced author fall in love but won't admit it for fear of being hurt again. Jumbled plot, unfortunate casting. Available in a Spanish-subtitled version. **95m/C VHS.** Michael Caine, Sally Field, Steve Guttenberg, Peter Boyle, Jackie Cooper, Julie Kavner, Louise Lasser, Iman; *D:* Jerry Belson; *W:* Jerry Belson; *C:* Juan Ruiz-Anchia; *M:* Michel Colombier.

Surrender Dorothy 1/2 1998 Weird psychosexual drama focuses on 26-year-old sexually confused Trevor (Pryor), who's afraid of women. He offers drugs and a place to crash to heroin addict Lahn (Di Novis) but their arrangement soons turn bizarre when Trevor desires Lahn to cross-dress as Dorothy, his concept of the ideal girlfriend, and then wants to take his obsession even farther. **97m/B VHS, DVD.** Kevin Di Novis, Peter Pryor, Jason Centeno, Elizabeth Casey; *D:* Kevin Di Novis; *W:* Kevin Di Novis; *C:* Jonathan Kovel; *M:* Christopher Matarazzo.

Surrogate 1988 A young couple fights to keep their marriage afloat by turning to a sex surrogate. Strong cast helps carry odd, confusing script, with plenty of (you guessed it) sex, and a mystery to solve. **100m/C VHS.** *CA* Art Hindle, Shannon Tweed, Carole Laure, Michael Ironside, Marilyn Lightstone; *D:* Don Carmody.

Surrogates 2009 (PG-13) In the near future, humans live isolated and safe in their homes while lookalike robotic surrogates manage their lives outside. After a series of murders, Agent Greer (Willis) discovers he'll actually have to leave his house for the first time in years if he expects to solve the crimes. His investigation leads him to an underground band of rebel humans, called The Dreads, revolting against the robotic surrogate world, lead by The Prophet (Rhames). What could've been an intriguing allegorical sci-fi mystery quickly turns into a cut-and-paste action flick. Based on the graphic novel series. **88m/C DVD.** *US* Bruce Willis, Radha Mitchell, Rosamund Pike, Boris Kodjoe, James Francis Ginty, James Cromwell, Ving Rhames, Jack Noseworthy, Michael Cudlitz, Devin Ratray, Helena Mattsson, Jeffrey De Serrano; *D:* Jonathan Mostow; *W:* Michael Ferris, John Brancato; *C:* Oliver Wood; *M:* Richard (Rick) Marvin.

Surveillance 2008 (R) What on earth would draw actors the caliber of Ormond and Pullman (who both overact to compensate) to this graphically tasteless mediocrity? Two masked serial killers attack a married couple in a desert community. Then there's a mass highway shooting that brings in FBI agents Anderson (Ormond) and Hallaway (Pullman) and some unprofessional (and lying) cops interrogating witnesses. **97m/C DVD.** Julia Ormond, Bill Pullman, Pell James, Ryan Simpkins, Cheri Oteri, Hugh Dillon, Michael Ironside, French Stewart, Gill Gayle, Kent Harper; *W:* Kent Harper; *M:* Todd Bryanton.

Surveillance 24/7 2007 Low-budget thriller that doesn't quite hang together. Gay teacher Adam heads off to London to party and get laid. He picks up Jake and his life goes to hell, especially when Jake turns up dead. Why? Well, although Adam was unaware, Jake gave him some evidence that a British royal is involved in a gay affair and no one wants the truth to come out. **87m/C DVD.** *GB* Simon Callow, Tom Harper, Dawn Steele, Sean Brosnan; *D:* Paul Oremland; *W:* Kevin Sampson; *C:* Alistair Cameron; *M:* Helen Jane Long.

Survival Game 1987 A young combat expert (Chuck Norris's son) gets involved with some ex-hippies in search of a $2 million cache. High-kickin' action. **91m/C VHS.** Mike Norris, Deborah Goodrich, Seymour Cassel; *D:* Herb Freed.

Survival Island *Demon Island; The Pinata: Survival Island* 2002 (R) Kinda cheesy horror fun. Group of college students are on a Cinco de Mayo treasure hunt on a tropical island when something evil turns up—a killer pinata! Actually, it's a demon hidden inside the pinata that starts picking off the clueless one by gory one. What a way to get voted off the island. **90m/C VHS, DVD.** Nicholas Brendon, Jaime Pressly, Garrett Wang, Eugene Byrd, Daphne Lynn Duplaix; *D:* David Hillenbrand, Scott Hillenbrand; *W:* David Hillenbrand, Scott Hillenbrand; *C:* Philip D. Schwartz; *M:* David Hillenbrand. **VIDEO**

Survival of the Dead *George A. Romero's Survival of the Dead* 2009 In this sixth installment, zombies are causing havoc on Plum Island, off the Delaware Coast, and the two main island families are at odds over how to deal with the problem. **88m/C DVD.** *CA* Alan Van Spang, Eric Woolfe, Kenneth Welsh, Richard Fitzpatrick, Kathleen Munroe, Stefano di Matteo, Joris Jarsky; *D:* George A. Romero; *W:* George A. Romero; *C:* Adam Swica; *M:* Robert Carli.

Survival Quest 1/2 1989 (R) Students in a Rocky Mountain survival course cross paths with a band of bloodthirsty mercenaries-in-training. A battle to the death ensues; you'll wish they'd all put each other out of their misery a lot sooner. **90m/C VHS, DVD.** Lance Henriksen, Dermot Mulroney, Mark Rolston, Steve Antin, Paul Provenza, Ben Hammer, Traci Lind, Catherine Keener, Reggie Bannister; *D:* Don A. Coscarelli; *W:* Don A. Coscarelli.

Survival Run 1980 (R) Six California teenagers become stranded in the Mexican desert, where they witness Graves and Milland making a shady deal. The chase is on, the story is lame, the gory parts aren't gory—so why bother? **90m/C VHS.** Peter Graves, Ray Milland, Vincent Van Patten; *D:* Larry Spiegel; *W:* Gerard M. Cahill.

Survival Zone WOOF! 1984 (R) Nuclear holocaust survivors battle a violent band of marauding motorcyclists on the barren ranches of the 21st century. Advice to director Rubens and cohorts: Next time, find a plot that's not growing mold. **90m/C VHS.** Gary Lockwood, Morgan Stevens, Camilla Sparv; *D:* Percival Rubens.

The Survivalist 1987 (R) An arms-ready survivalist nut defends his family and supplies against a panicked society awaiting nuclear war. Poorly acted, little tension, and ineffective plotting make boredom seem a more critical issue than survival. **96m/C VHS.** Steve Railsback, Susan Blakely, Marjoe Gortner, David Wayne, Cliff DeYoung; *D:* Sig Shore; *W:* Robert Dillon.

Surviving Christmas 2004 (PG-13) Affleck finds himself stuck in another boxoffice disaster as wealthy yuppie Drew, who gets dumped by snooty girlfriend Missy (Morrison) right before the holidays. Following some bad advice from his shrink, Drew decides to reconnect with his past by visiting his boyhood home. The house is now occupied by working-class grump Tom Valcos (Gandolfini), his frustrated wife Christine (O'Hara), their porn-obsessed teen son Brian (Zuckerman) and serious daughter Alicia (Applegate). For $250,000, the Valcos agree to be Drew's rented relatives and indulge his Christmas dreams. Comedic embarrassment follows resulting in a few, brief, reluctant chuckles. **92m/C VHS, DVD.** *US* Ben Affleck, James Gandolfini, Christina Applegate, Catherine O'Hara, Josh Zuckerman, Bill Macy, Jenny (Jennifer) Morrison, Stephen (Steve) Root; *D:* Mike Mitchell; *W:* Deborah Kaplan, Harry Elfont, Jeffrey Ventimilia, Joshua Sternin; *C:* Peter Collinson, Tom Priestley; *M:* Randy Edelman.

Surviving Desire 1991 Donovan plays Jude, a neurotic, romantic English professor who falls madly in love with an independently minded student, Sophie. Unfortunately, Sophie is more interested in how the seduction will advance her writing than how it will affect her life. The lovers explore their brief affair by analyzing every emotion and motive in a series of quirky conversations. Intelligent, amusing, and stylized film from director Hartley. The tape also includes two Hartley shorts: "Theory of Achievement" and "Ambition." **86m/C VHS, DVD.** Martin Donovan, Mary B. Ward, Matt Malloy, Rebecca Nelson; *D:* Hal Hartley; *C:* Michael Spiller.

Surviving Picasso 1/2 1996 (R) Merchant-Ivory team takes time off from bodice-rippers to tear into the personal life of the Cubist legend, Pablo Picasso. Takes an unglamourous look at the mythically famous artist, focusing on the rocky ten-year affair with Francoise Gilot (newcomer McElhone), who met the artist in Nazi-occupied Paris when she was 22 and he was 62. Hopkins is well-cast as the insufferable senior and adds a strong dose of charm to soften his portrayal. Scores high tech credits, especially picture's sumptuous look, compliments of production designer and frequent collaborator Luciana Arrighi. Unfortunately adapted from the decidedly one-sided biography "Picasso: Creator and Destroyer" by controversial author Arianna Huffington. Denied use of the artist's works by his estate, the filmmakers settled for some "work in progress" replicas. **126m/C VHS.** Anthony Hopkins, Natascha (Natasha) McElhone, Julianne Moore, Joss Ackland, Joan Plowright, Diane Venora, Peter Eyre, Jane Lapotaire, Joseph Maher, Bob Peck; *D:* James Ivory; *W:* Ruth Prawer Jhabvala; *C:* Tony Pierce-Roberts; *M:* Richard Robbins.

Surviving the Game 1994 (R) Poorly made hunt-the-human story. Homeless Ice-T is hired by a group of men to assist them on their annual hunt. But wait, he's the prey. Unbelievable premise pits the streetwise, down and out Ice-T against the savvy and weapons rich group—and he beats them at their own game. Few high-impact action sequences. The violence, although there isn't as much as might be expected, is graphic. **94m/C VHS, DVD.** Rutger Hauer, Ice-T, F. Murray Abraham, Gary Busey, Charles S. Dutton, John C. McGinley, William McNamara, Jeff Corey; *D:* Ernest R. Dickerson; *W:* Eric Bernt; *C:* Bojan Bazelli; *M:* Stewart Copeland.

Survivor 1980 A jetliner crashes, leaving but one survivor, the pilot, who is then plagued by visions, tragedies, and ghosts of dead passengers. Viewers also suffer. **91m/C VHS, DVD.** *AU* Robert Powell, Jenny Agutter, Joseph Cotten, Angela Punch McGregor; *D:* David Hemmings; *W:* David Ambrose; *M:* Brian May.

Survivor 1987 A lone warrior on a post-nuclear holocaust wasteland battles a megalomaniac ruler. Moll as the evil villian is watchable, but overall the film is a wasteland, too. **92m/C VHS.** Chip (Christopher) Mayer, Richard Moll, Sue Kiel; *D:* Michael Shackleton.

The Survivor 1998 (R) Yet another sci-fier where Earth is a mess—this time it's a rainforest-covered penal colony run by the violent Kyla (Moll) and his vicious minions. When the president's (Herd) spaceship crashes, convicted murderer Tarkin (Declie) tries to save him from Kyla. Not bad special effects and lots of action. **95m/C VHS.** Richard Moll, Xavier DeClie, Richard Herd; *D:* Nick Davis. **VIDEO**

Survivors 1983 (R) Two unemployed men find themselves the target of a hit man, whom they have identified in a robbery attempt. One of the men goes gun-crazy protecting himself. Uneven comedy with wild Williams and laid-back Matthau. **102m/C VHS, DVD.** Robin Williams, Walter Matthau, Jerry Reed, John Goodman, James Wainwright, Kristen Vigard; *D:* Michael Ritchie; *W:* Michael Leeson; *C:* Billy Williams; *M:* Paul Chihara.

Susan and God *The Gay Mrs. Trexel* 1940 A selfish socialite returns from Europe and starts practicing a new religion, much to the dismay of her friends and family. Despite her preaching, her own domestic life is falling apart and she realizes that her preoccupation and selfish ways have caused a strain on her marriage and her relationship with her daughter. An excellent script and a fine performance from Crawford make this a highly satisfying film. **115m/B VHS.** Joan Crawford, Fredric March, Ruth Hussey, John Carroll, Rita Hayworth, Nigel Bruce, Bruce Cabot, Rose Hobart, Rita Quigley, Marjorie Main, Gloria De Haven; *D:* George Cukor; *W:* Anita Loos.

Susan Lenox: Her Fall and Rise 1/2 *The Rise of Helga; Rising to Fame* 1931 Garbo, the daughter of an abusive farmer, falls into the arms of the handsome Gable to escape an arranged marriage. Both stars are miscast, but the well-paced direction keeps the melodrama moving. **84m/B VHS.** Greta Garbo, Clark Gable, Jean Hersholt, John Miljan, Alan Hale, Hale Hamilton; *D:* Robert Z. Leonard; *C:* William H. Daniels.

Susan Slade 1/2 1961 A glossy soap with pretty leads. Teenaged Susan (Stevens) gets pregnant by her boyfriend who inconveniently dies. An extended trip out of the country has mom Leah (McGuire) deciding they can pass off the baby as her own after they return. Susan eventually gets marriage proposals from wealthy but dull Wells Corbett (Convy) and sullen would-be writer Hoyt Brecker (Donahue). But when Susan's "little brother" is injured in a fire, the truth comes out and only one of the two guys is willing to stand by her. **116m/C DVD.** Connie Stevens, Troy Donahue, Dorothy McGuire, Lloyd Nolan, Bert Convy, Brian Aherne, Natalie Schafer, Grant Williams; *D:* Delmer Daves; *W:* Delmer Daves; *C:* Lucien Ballard; *M:* Max Steiner.

Susan Slept Here 1/2 1954 While researching a movie on juvenile delinquents, a Hollywood script writer (Powell) is given custody of a spunky 17-year-old delinquent girl (Reynolds) during the Christmas holidays. Cute sex comedy. Based on the play "Susan," by Alex Gottlieb and Steve Fisher. **98m/C VHS.** Dick Powell, Debbie Reynolds, Anne Francis; *D:* Frank Tashlin.

Susana 🦴🦴🦴 **1951** Minor though still interesting Bunuel, in which a sexy delinquent young girl is rescued from vagrancy by a Spanish family, and how she subsequently undermines the family's structure through sexual allurement and intimidation. In Spanish with English subtitles. **87m/B VHS.** *MX* Rosita Quintana, Fernando Soler, Victor Manuel Mendoza, Matilde Palou; *D:* Luis Bunuel.

Susanna Pass 🦴🦴 **1949** Oil deposits underneath a fish hatchery lake attract bad guys. They set off explosions to destroy the fishery, but game warden Rogers investigates. Minor outing for Roy. **67m/C VHS, DVD.** Roy Rogers, Dale Evans, Estelita Rodriguez, Martin Garralaga, Robert Emmett Keane, Lucien Littlefield, Douglas Fowley; *D:* William Witney.

Susannah of the Mounties 🦴🦴 ½ **1939 (PG)** An adorable young girl is left orphaned after a wagon train massacre and is adopted by a Mountie. An Indian squabble gives Shirley a chance to play little peacemaker and teach Scott how to tap dance, too. Could she be any cuter? Available colorized. **78m/B VHS.** Shirley Temple, Randolph Scott, Margaret Lockwood, J. Farrell MacDonald, Moroni Olsen, Victor Jory; *D:* William A. Seiter; *C:* Arthur C. Miller.

Suspect 🦴🦴 ½ **1987 (R)** An overworked Washington, DC, public defender (Cher) is assigned to a controversial murder case in which her client is a deaf-mute, skid-row bum. A cynical lobbyist on the jury illegally researches the case himself. They work together to uncover a far-reaching conspiracy. Unrealistic plot, helped along by good performances and tight direction. **101m/C VHS, DVD.** Dennis Quaid, Cher, Liam Neeson, E. Katherine Kerr, Joe Mantegna, John Mahoney, Philip Bosco; *D:* Peter Yates; *W:* Eric Roth; *C:* Billy Williams; *M:* Michael Kamen.

Suspect Device 🦴 ½ *Roger Corman Presents: Suspect Device* **1995 (R)** Nonsensical cable thriller finds government computer researcher Dan (Howell) mistakenly accessing a secret file and becoming an immediate assassination target. Then Dan discovers he isn't even human—he's really a genetically engineered cross between a robot and a nuclear bomb! Part "Terminator," part "Three Days of the Condor," and all silliness. **90m/C VHS.** C. Thomas Howell, Stacey Travis, Jed Allan, John Beck, Marcus Aurelius, Jonathan Fuller; *D:* Rick Jacobson; *W:* Alex Simon; *C:* John Aronson; *M:* Christopher Lennertz. **CABLE**

Suspect Zero 🦴 ½ **2004 (R)** Maverick FBI agent Thomas Mackelway (Eckhart) has been demoted to a backwater bureau just in time to discover a serial killer whose M.O. is that he kills other serial killers and likes to taunt the fed via fax. Soon, Mackelway is joined by no-nonsense former partner/lover Fran Kulok (Moss in a thankless role). Eckhart's generally wasted as the standard troubled good guy (he works better in edgier roles) while Kingsley does what a professional does—make the most of an absurd movie sociopath. Merhige apparently prefers to set an artistic moodiness rather than worry about pace, plot, or coherence. **99m/C DVD.** *US* Aaron Eckhart, Ben Kingsley, Carrie-Anne Moss, Harry J. Lennix, William Mapother, Ellen Blake, Chloe Russell, Kevin Chamberlin; *D:* Edmund Elias Merhige; *W:* Zak Penn, Billy Ray; *C:* Michael Chapman; *M:* Clint Mansell.

Suspended Alibi 🦴 ½ *Suspected Alibi* **1956** British crime-drama about an adulterous man unjustly accused when his alibi is murdered. Overlook the convenient coincidence. **64m/B VHS.** *GB* Patrick Holt, Honor Blackman, Andrew Keir, Valentine Dyall; *D:* Alfred Shaughnessy.

Suspended Animation 🦴🦴 **2002** Animator Thomas Kempton (McArthur) takes a break from his work to go snowmobiling with some buddies. He gets separated from the group and taken captive by a couple of crazy sisters who have a hatred of men and a love of cannibalism. Menacing and engaging script mixes the "Misery" with comic spatterings. Hancock goes old-school but fails to overcome structural flaws. **114m/C DVD.** *US* Alex McArthur, Sage Allen, Rebecca Harrell, Laura Esterman, Maria Cina; *D:* John Hancock; *W:* Dorothy Tristan; *C:* Misha (Mikhail) Suslov; *M:* Angelo Badalamenti.

Suspicion 🦴🦴🦴 ½ **1941** Alfred Hitchcock's suspense thriller about a woman who gradually realizes she is married to a killer and may be next on his list. An excellent production unravels at the end due to RKO's insistence that Grant retain his "attractive" image. This forced the writers to leave his guilt or innocence undetermined. Available colorized. **99m/B VHS, DVD.** Cary Grant, Joan Fontaine, Cedric Hardwicke, Nigel Bruce, May Whitty, Leo G. Carroll, Heather Angel; *D:* Alfred Hitchcock; *C:* Harry Stradling Sr.; *M:* Franz Waxman. Oscars '41: Actress (Fontaine); N.Y. Film Critics '41: Actress (Fontaine).

Suspicion 🦴🦴 **1987** Remake of the chilling Hitchcock tale. Newlywed bride is consumed with fears about her wealthy new husband. The suspense builds as she comes to suspect that she is married to a cold-blooded killer. Curtin in way over her head. **97m/C VHS.** Jane Curtin, Anthony Andrews, Jeremy Northam, Ron Pember, Betsy Blair, Michael Hordern, Vivian Pickles, Jo Anderson; *D:* Andrew Grieve.

Suspicion 🦴🦴 **2003** Carol Finnegan (Redman) is celebrating her 20th wedding anniversary to husband Mark (Dunbar) when she begins receiving a series of anonymous emails accusing Mark of having an affair with his secretary. She tells Mark, who dismisses them as the work of a disgruntled ex-employee, but Carol's suspicions grow. Then the secretary is murdered and it's Carol who is accused of the crime. **150m/C DVD.** *GB* Amanda Redman, Adrian Dunbar, Saskia Reeves, Adam Kotz; *D:* Jamie Payne; *W:* Peter Whalley; *C:* Chris Seager; *M:* Nick Bicat. **TV**

Suspicious Agenda 🦴🦴 ½ **1994 (R)** Cop with a past is assigned to a task force that's hunting down a sadistic vigilante. **97m/C VHS.** Richard Grieco, Nick Mancuso, Jim Byrnes; *D:* Clay Borris; *W:* Kevin Rock.

Suspicious Minds 🦴🦴 ½ **1996 (R)** PI Jack Ramsey (Bergin) is hired to get the goods on Isabelle's (Heitmeyer) alleged infidelities. But Jack winds up in an affair with the femme, whose other lover has just been murdered. **97m/C VHS.** Patrick Bergin, Jayne Heitmeyer, Gary Busey, Daniel Pilon; *D:* Alain Zaloum.

Suspicious River 🦴 **2000** Leila's answer to a stale marriage and the small-town blues? Start hooking with guests at her seedy motel job of course! And wait for that very special lunatic to come along and steal her heart and beat her up a time or two. **92m/C VHS, DVD.** Molly Parker, Callum Keith Rennie, Mary Kate Welsh, Joel Bissonnette, Deanna Milligan, Sarah Jane Redmond, Norman Armour, Byron Lucas, Michael Shanks, Don S. Davis, Jay Brazeau, Gillian Barber, Paul Jarrett, Bruno Verdoni, Ingrid Tesch, Bill Dow; *D:* Lynne Stopkewich; *W:* Lynne Stopkewich; *C:* Gregory Middleton; *M:* Don MacDonald. **VIDEO**

Suspiria 🦴🦴🦴 **1977 (R)** An American dancer enters a weird European ballet academy and finds they teach more than movement as bodies begin piling up. Sometimes weak plot is aided by great-but-gory special effects, fine photography, good music, and a chilling opening sequence. Also available in unrated version. **99m/C VHS, DVD.** *IT* Jessica Harper, Joan Bennett, Alida Valli, Udo Kier, Stefania Casini, Flavio Bucci, Barbara Magnolfi, Rudolf Schuendler; *D:* Dario Argento; *W:* Dario Argento, Daria Nicolodi; *C:* Luciano Tovoli; *M:* Dario Argento, The Goblins.

Suture 🦴🦴 **1993** Quirky thriller is a homage to late '50s melodramas with its strange tale of mistaken identity. Vincent wants to hide his unsavory past by assuming the identity of his estranged half-brother, Clay, which should be difficult since Vincent is white and Clay is black but the movie's premise is that everyone confuses the two. Vincent tries to kill Clay in an explosion but he survives—with amnesia and with everyone in the hospital assuming he's Vincent. Shifting points of view as he struggles to piece together his memory offer disorientation not just for Clay but the viewer as well. Feature film debut for the directors. **96m/B VHS, DVD.** Dennis Haysbert, Sab Shimono, Mel Harris, Michael (M.K.) Harris, Dina Merrill, David Graf, Fran Ryan; *D:* Scott McGehee, David Siegel; *W:* Scott McGehee, David Siegel; *C:* Greg Gardiner; *M:* Cary Berger. Sundance '94: Cinematog.

Suzanne 🦴 ½ **1980 (R)** Set in 1950s Quebec, the story of a good woman whose criminal boyfriend leaves her pregnant when he is sent to prison. Ten years later, he returns, threatening her happy marriage. Confused script can't be saved by valiant cast. **103m/C VHS.** *CA* Jennifer Dale, Gabriel Arcand, Winston Rekert, Ken Pogue; *D:* Robin Spry; *W:* Robin Spry; *C:* Miklos Lente; *M:* Francois Cousineau.

Suzy 🦴🦴 ½ **1936** Harlow's fourth film and her only one with Grant is a mixture of romance, action, and comedy set during WWI. Grant plays a French flier who falls in love with Harlow, although she is married to Tone. Excellent air footage and some good funny scenes keep this film moving right along. Even has Grant singing hit song, "Did I Remember?" **99m/B VHS.** Jean Harlow, Franchot Tone, Cary Grant, Benita Hume, Lewis Stone, Inez Courtney; *D:* George Fitzmaurice.

Svengali 🦴🦴🦴 **1931** A music teacher uses his hypnotic abilities to manipulate one of his singing students and make her a star. Soon the young woman is singing for sell-out crowds, but only if her teacher is present. Barrymore in a hypnotic performance. Adapted from "Trilby" by George Du Maurier. Remade in 1955 and 1983. **76m/B VHS, DVD.** John Barrymore, Marian Marsh, Donald Crisp; *D:* Archie Mayo; *W:* J. Grubb Alexander; *C:* Barney McGill.

Svengali 🦴🦴 ½ **1955** Limp remake of the 1931 film about Trilby, an artist's model, falling under the mesmerizing spell of the title character, who is determined to make her into a famous singer. Chiefly notable for its visuals which were based on the illustrations from the original novel "Trilby" by George du Maurier. **82m/C VHS.** *GB* Hildegarde Knef, Donald Wolfit, Terence Morgan, Derek Bond, Paul Rogers, David Kossoff; *D:* Noel Langley; *W:* Noel Langley.

Svengali 🦴🦴 ½ **1983** Flamboyant but faded music star O'Toole mentors Foster, a young pop singer looking for stardom. Boring remake of the Barrymore classic. **96m/C VHS, DVD.** Peter O'Toole, Jodie Foster, Elizabeth Ashley, Larry Joshua, Pamela Blair, Barbara Byrne, Holly Hunter; *D:* Anthony Harvey; *M:* John Barry. **TV**

Swamp Devil 🦴 ½ **2008** SciFi Channel creation where the twists are obvious and the only reason to watch is Dern. Sheriff turned swamp hermit Howard Blaime (Dern) is accused of murdering a teenaged girl, which brings his estranged daughter Melanie (Sampson) back to their small town. A local walking compost pile (the titular devil) is apparently the real culprit. **90m/C DVD.** Bruce Dern, Cindy Sampson, Nicholas Wright, Robert Higden, Allison Graham, James Kidnie; *D:* David Winning; *W:* Gary Dauberman, Ethlie Ann Vare; *C:* Daniel Vincelette; *M:* James Gelfand. **CABLE**

Swamp Fire 🦴 ½ **1946** Mississippi riverboat captain Weissmuller, wrestles alligators and battles with Crabbe for the woman he loves in this turgid drama. Look for Janssen in an early screen performance. **69m/B VHS, DVD.** Johnny Weissmuller, Virginia Grey, Buster Crabbe, Carol Thurston, Edwin Maxwell, Pedro de Cordoba, Pierre Watkin, David Janssen; *D:* William H. Pine; *W:* Daniel Mainwaring; *C:* Fred H. Jackman Jr.; *M:* Rudolph (Rudy) Schrager.

Swamp of the Lost Monster 🦴 **1965** An incredible Mexican horror/western/musical that features a mouse-like monster that'll scare the cheese out of you. **88m/B VHS.** *MX* Gaston Santos, Sarah Cabrera, Manuel Donde; *D:* Rafael Baledon Sr.

Swamp Thing 🦴🦴 ½ **1982 (PG)** Overlooked camp drama about scientist accidentally turned into tragic half-vegetable, half-man swamp creature, with government agent Barbeau caught in the middle, occasionally while topless. A vegetarian nightmare or ecology propaganda? You be the judge. Adapted from the comic book by Craven. **91m/C VHS, DVD.** Adrienne Barbeau, Louis Jourdan, Ray Wise, Dick Durock; *D:* Wes Craven; *W:* Wes Craven; *C:* Robbie Greenberg; *M:* Harry Manfredini.

Swamp Women 🦴 *Swamp Diamonds; Cruel Swamp* **1955** Four escaped women convicts, known as the "Nardo Gang," chase after a stash of diamonds in this super cheap, super bad action adventure from cult director Corman. **73m/C VHS, DVD.** Mike Connors, Marie Windsor, Beverly Garland, Carole Mathews, Susan Cummings, Jonathan Haze, Jill Jarmyn, Ed Nelson, Lou Place; *D:* Roger Corman; *W:* David Stern; *M:* Bill Holman.

The Swan 🦴🦴 ½ **1925** Princess' arranged marriage with a prince is complicated by a poor man also in love with her. Classic romantic comedy of the silent era. Remade in 1956. Based on a play by Ferenc Molnar. **50m/B VHS.** Adolphe Menjou, Ricardo Cortez, Frances Howard; *D:* Dimitri Buchowetzki.

The Swan 🦴🦴🦴 **1956** A twist on the Cinderella story with Kelly (in her last film before her marriage) as the charming beauty waiting for her prince. Both Guinness, as the crown prince, and Jourdan, as her poor tutor, want her hand (and the rest of her). Attractive cast, but story gets slow from time to time. Remake of a 1925 silent film. **112m/C VHS.** Grace Kelly, Louis Jourdan, Alec Guinness, Jessie Royce Landis, Brian Aherne, Estelle Winwood; *D:* Charles Vidor; *C:* Joseph Ruttenberg, Robert L. Surtees.

The Swan Princess 🦴🦴 ½ **1994 (G)** Formulaic prince-and-princess love story based loosely on "Swan Lake" takes a modern twist: Princess Odette, offended by the emphasis her intended, Prince Derek, places on her beauty, flees the kingdom. She's kidnapped by the evil Rothbart, an enchanter who turns her into a swan able to take human form only when touched by moonlight. A snappy trio of animal characters eventually helps Odette reunite with her newly P.C. love, with lots of zesty musical numbers and various Disney-inspired plot points along the way. Adults may yawn, but kiddies will be charmed just the same. **90m/C VHS, DVD.** *D:* Richard Rich; *W:* Richard Rich, Brian Nissen; *M:* Lex de Azevedo; *V:* Jack Palance, Michelle Nicastro, Howard McGillin, Liz Callaway, John Cleese, Steven Wright, Steve Vinovich, Dakin Matthews, Sandy Duncan, Mark Harelik, James Arrington, Davis Gaines, Joel McKinnon Miller.

The Swan Princess 2: Escape from Castle Mountain 🦴🦴 ½ **1997 (G)** Heroine Odette changes back into a swan to help husband Derek defeat evil magician Clavius. Some humor, some action, some nice tunes, and decent animation should keep the kids happy. ♫That's What You Do for a Friend; The Magic of Love; You Gotta Love It. **75m/C VHS.** *D:* Richard Rich; *W:* Brian Nissen; *M:* Lex de Azevedo; *V:* Michelle Nicastro, Douglas Sills, Jake Williamson, Christy Landers.

Swann 🦴 ½ **1996** Too many loose ends and weak direction from Benson Gyles (in her feature film debut) waste the efforts of a talented cast. Chicago-based writer Sarah Maloney (Richardson) is doing a biography of Mary Swann, wife/murder victim of a backwater Ontario farmer, who secretly wrote poetry (and gets compared to Emily Dickinson). Sarah heads to Nadeau to meet with Mary's friend Rose (Fricker) and discovers she may have altered some of the published poetry but there's not much there to really care about. Based on a novel by Carol Shields. **98m/C VHS.** *GB CA* Miranda Richardson, Brenda Fricker, Michael Ontkean, Sean McCann, John Neville, Sean Hewitt, Kyra Harper, David Cubitt, Geny Walter; *D:* Anna Benson Gyles; *W:* David Young; *C:* Gerald Packer; *M:* Richard Rodney Bennett.

Swann in Love 🦴🦴 ½ *Un Amour De Swann* **1984 (R)** A handsome, wealthy French aristocrat makes a fool of himself over a beautiful courtesan who cares nothing for him. Elegant production lacks spark. Based upon a section of Marcel Proust's "Remembrance of Things Past." In French with English subtitles or an English language version. **110m/C VHS, DVD.** *FR GE* Jeremy Irons, Ornella Muti, Alain Delon, Fanny Ardant, Marie-Christine Barrault; *D:* Volker Schlondorff; *W:* Peter Brook, Jean-Claude Carriere; *C:* Sven

Nykvist. Cesar '85: Art Dir./Set Dec., Costume Des.

The Swap ♪ 1/2 *Sam's Song* **1971 (R)** Ex-con searches for his brother's killer. Muddled story uses clips from early De Niro film "Sam's Song." **120m/C VHS, DVD.** Robert De Niro, Jered Mickey, Jennifer Warren, Terrayne Crawford, Martin Kelley; ***D:*** Jordan Leondopoulos; ***C:*** Alex Phillips Jr.; ***M:*** Gershon Kingsley.

Swap Meet ♪ **1979 (R)** Wacky teen sex comedy about shenanigans at a small town swap meet. Strictly bargain basement. **86m/C VHS.** Ruth Cox, Deborah Richter, Danny Goldman, Cheryl Rixon, Jon(athan) Gries; ***D:*** Brice Mack.

The Swarm ♪ **1978 (PG)** Low-brow insect contest as scientist Caine fends off a swarm of killer bees when they attack metro Houston. The bees are really just black spots painted on the film. And the acting is terrible. "B" movie on bees, but it's still better than "The Bees." **116m/C VHS, DVD.** Michael Caine, Katharine Ross, Richard Widmark, Lee Grant, Richard Chamberlain, Olivia de Havilland, Henry Fonda, Fred MacMurray, Patty Duke, Ben Johnson, Jose Ferrer, Slim Pickens, Bradford Dillman, Cameron Mitchell; ***D:*** Irwin Allen; ***W:*** Stirling Silliphant; ***C:*** Fred W. Koenekamp; ***M:*** Jerry Goldsmith, John Williams.

Swashbuckler ♪ *Scarlet Buccaneer* **1976 (PG)** Jaunty pirate returns from sea to find his friends held captive by dastardly dictator for their political views. He rescues them, and helps them overthrow the erstwhile despot. **101m/C VHS, DVD.** Robert Shaw, James Earl Jones, Peter Boyle, Genevieve Bujold, Beau Bridges, Geoffrey Holder; ***D:*** James Goldstone; ***W:*** Jeffrey Bloom; ***C:*** Philip Lathrop; ***M:*** John Addison.

Swashbuckler ♪ 1/2 *The Scarlet Buccaneer* **1984** Eighteenth-century pirate fracas that can't compete with Errol Flynn. **100m/C VHS.** *FR* Jean-Paul Belmondo, Marlene Jobert, Laura Antonelli, Michel Auclair, Julien Guiomar; ***D:*** Jean-Paul Rappeneau.

S.W.A.T. ♪♪ 1/2 **2003 (PG-13)** Hondo (Jackson) is the leader of the elite LAPD Special Weapons and Tactics unit. He and his crew have to guard captured drug lord Alex (Martinez) and move him into federal custody. Only Alex has an open offer of $100 mil to anyone who can free him. Above-average big screen version of the mid-seventies TV series provides the correct summer blockbuster mix of action, stunts, and humor, with just enough character development to make you care about the outcome, but not so much that you get bored. **111m/C VHS, DVD, Blu-ray Disc, UMD.** *US* Samuel L. Jackson, Colin Farrell, LL Cool J, Josh Charles, Michelle Rodriguez, Olivier Martinez, Jeremy Renner, Brian Van Holt, Reg E. Cathey, Larry Poindexter, Domenick Lombardozzi, Lucinda Jenney, Reed Edward Diamond; ***Cameos:*** Clark Johnson, Steve Forrest; ***D:*** Clark Johnson; ***W:*** David Ayer, David McKenna; ***C:*** Gabriel Beristain; ***M:*** Elliot Goldenthal.

Sweater Girls WOOF! **1978 (R)** Sex comedy about two girls starting their own club called the "Sweater Girls." Terrible teen exploitaiton film. **90m/C VHS.** Charlene Tilton, Harry Moses, Meegan King, Noelle North, Kate Sarchet, Carol Seflinger, Tamara Barkley, Julie Parsons; ***D:*** Donald M. Jones.

Swedenhielms ♪♪ 1/2 **1935** A poor Swedish scientist struggles to support his family while hoping to win a Nobel prize, while his two sons get involved in a money-lending scandal. Bergman is the rich fiance of one son, to whom poverty is a puzzlement. Fine performances by Ekman and the 20-year-old Bergman (in her third film). In Swedish with English subtitles. **92m/B VHS.** *SW* Gosta Ekman, Karin Swanstrom, Bjorn Berglund, Hakan Westergren, Tutta Rolf, Ingrid Bergman, Sigurd Wallen; ***D:*** Gustaf Molander.

Sweeney Todd: The Demon Barber of Fleet Street ♪♪ 1/2 **1984** A filmed performance of Sondheim's Tony-winning Broadway musical. Creepy thriller about a demon barber, his razor, and his wife's meatpies. **139m/C VHS, DVD.** *GB* Angela Lansbury, George Hearn; ***D:*** Harold Prince; ***M:*** Stephen Sondheim.

Sweeney Todd: The Demon Barber of Fleet Street ♪♪ **2007 (R)** Some critics seemed to think that this adaptation of the Stephen Sondheim Broadway musical was too gory. Well, it's true, it's a lot harder to deal with buckets of blood onstage than in the movies, and Burton does seem to revel in his subject matter, which happens to be a singing, throat-slitting serial killer whose victims get turned into meat pies in dank, 19th-century London. A real toe-tapper that is. Sweeney (Depp) was unfairly transported to Australia when corrupt judge Turpin (Rickman) coveted his wife and daughter. Now years later, barber Sweeney has returned (unrecognizable) to exact his revenge, partnered in crime by his equally corpse-like (and ever-loving) landlady Mrs. Lovett (Bonham Carter). Not a direct adaptation (Burton omits and abridges songs and does some reshaping) and neither Depp nor Bonham Carter are singers, but you have to admire the sheer chutzpah. **117m/C DVD.** *US* Johnny Depp, Helena Bonham Carter, Alan Rickman, Timothy Spall, Sacha Baron Cohen, Jayne Wisner, Jamie Campbell Bower, Edward Sanders; ***D:*** Tim Burton; ***W:*** John Logan; ***C:*** Darius Wolski; ***M:*** Stephen Sondheim. Oscars '07: Art Dir./Set Dec.; Golden Globes '08: Actor—Mus./Comedy (Depp), Film—Mus./Comedy.

The Sweeper ♪♪ 1/2 **1995 (R)** LA cop Mark Goddard (Howell) has a problem—his suspects have a bad habit of dying in his custody. Then he's recruited by a secret police organization whose aim is to dispense their own brand of deadly justice and Mark discovers a key to his troubled past and the murder of his cop father (Fahey). **101m/C VHS, DVD.** C. Thomas Howell, Ed Lauter, Cynda Williams, Jeff Fahey; ***D:*** Joseph Merhi; ***W:*** William Applegate Jr.; ***C:*** Ken Blakey; ***M:*** K. Alexander (Alex) Wilkinson.

Sweepers ♪♪ **1999 (R)** Former land mine sweeper Christian Erickson (Lundgren) is called out of retirement to help bomb expert Michelle Flynn (Stansfield) uncover a terrorist plan to plant landmines in the U.S. **96m/C VHS, DVD.** Dolph Lundgren, Claire Stansfield, Bruce Payne; ***D:*** Darby Black; ***W:*** Darby Black, Kevin Bernhardt; ***C:*** Yossi Wein. **VIDEO**

Sweet Adeline ♪♪ **1926** Smalltime hayseed makes it big in the music business while brother steals his girl back home. Not easily put off, young songster perseveres. **60m/B VHS.** Charles Ray, Gertrude (Olmstead) Olmsted, Jack Clifford, Ida Lewis; ***D:*** Jerome Storm.

Sweet Adeline ♪♪ 1/2 **1935** Dunne attracts all the men in her father's Hoboken beer garden but Woods plays the songwriter with whom she finds real love. Wonderful score. ♫ Play Us a Polka, Dot; Here Am I; We Were So Young; Why Was I Born?; Mollie O'Donahue; Lonely Feet; 'Twas Not So Long Ago; Don't Ever Leave Me. **87m/B VHS.** Irene Dunne, Donald Woods, Hugh Herbert, Ned Sparks, Joseph Cawthorn, Louis Calhern; ***D:*** Mervyn LeRoy; ***M:*** Jerome Kern, Oscar Hammerstein.

Sweet and Lowdown ♪♪ 1/2 **1999 (PG-13)** Slight jazzy comedy, set in the '30s, traces the up-and-down career of fictional musician Emmet Ray (Penn), who's haunted by the fact that he's the second-best jazz guitarist in the world (Django Reinhardt is the first). However talented Emmet is musically, he's scum as a human being, abandoning Hattie (Morton), the mute laundress who turns out to be the love of his life in favor of wealthy writer Blanche (Thurman). Fine cast, good look, great music. **95m/C VHS, DVD.** Sean Penn, Samantha Morton, Uma Thurman, Brian Markinson, Anthony LaPaglia, Gretchen Mol, Vincent Guastaferro, John Waters, James Urbaniak, Constance Shulman, Kellie Overbey, Michael Sprague, Woody Allen; ***D:*** Woody Allen; ***W:*** Woody Allen; ***C:*** Fei Zhao; ***M:*** Dick Hyman.

Sweet Beat ♪ *The Amorous Sex* **1959** A young woman gets a chance to become a singer when she reaches the finals of a British beauty contest. Pedestrian story enlivened by music from popular British bands of the time. **66m/B VHS.** *GB* Julie Amber, Sheldon Lawrence, Irv Bauer, Billy Myles; ***D:*** Ronnie Albert; ***C:*** S.D. Onions.

Sweet Bird of Youth ♪♪♪ **1962** An acclaimed adaptation of the Tennessee Williams play about Chance Wayne, a handsome drifter who travels with an aging movie queen to his small Florida hometown, hoping she'll get him started in a movie career. However, coming home turns into a big mistake, as the town boss wants revenge on Chance for seducing his daughter, Heavenly. Williams's original stage ending was cleaned up, providing a conventional "happy" movie ending for the censors. Remade for TV in 1989 with Elizabeth Taylor and Mark Harmon in the lead roles. **120m/C VHS, DVD.** Paul Newman, Geraldine Page, Ed Begley Sr., Mildred Dunnock, Rip Torn, Shirley Knight, Madeline Sherwood, Kelly Thordsen; ***D:*** Richard Brooks; ***W:*** Richard Brooks; ***C:*** Milton Krasner. Oscars '62: Support. Actor (Begley); Golden Globes '63: Actress—Drama (Page).

Sweet Bird of Youth ♪♪ **1989 (R)** TV remake of the Tennessee Williams's play, which was filmed for the big screen in 1962, with Harmon and Taylor having the unenviable task of following in the roles played by Paul Newman and Geraldine Page. She is an egotistical, has-been movie star and he is her ambitious gigolo who wants a movie career of his own. Unfortunately, the trouble that drove him from his Florida hometown is still there when he reappears, actress in tow. Things don't bode well. The TV production uses Williams's original ending, which was cleaned up for a "happier" version in the '62 film. **95m/C VHS, DVD.** Elizabeth Taylor, Mark Harmon, Rip Torn, Valerie Perrine, Ruta Lee, Seymour Cassel, Kevin Geer, Michael Wilding Jr.; ***D:*** Nicolas Roeg; ***W:*** Gavin Lambert; ***M:*** Ralph Burns. **TV**

Sweet Charity ♪♪♪ **1969** An ever-optimistic dime-a-dance girl has a hard time finding a classy guy to marry. MacLaine is appealing in this big-budget version of the popular Broadway musical by Neil Simon (derived from Fellini's "Notti di Cabiria"). Fosse's debut as film director. Watch for Cort as a flower child. ♫ My Personal Property; It's a Nice Face; Hey, Big Spender; Rich Man's Frug; If My Friends Could See Me Now; There's Gotta Be Something Better Than This; Rhythm of Life; Sweet Charity; I'm a Brass Band. **148m/C VHS, DVD.** Shirley MacLaine, Chita Rivera, John McMartin, Paula Kelly, Sammy Davis Jr., Ricardo Montalban, Bud Cort; ***D:*** Bob Fosse; ***C:*** Robert L. Surtees; ***M:*** Cy Coleman.

Sweet Country ♪ 1/2 **1987 (R)** During the overthrow of the Allende government in Chile, the lives of a Chilean family and an American couple intertwine. Heavy-going propaganda is a cross between tragedy and unintentional comedy. Made by the director of "Zorba the Greek." **147m/C VHS.** Jane Alexander, John Cullum, Carole Laure, Franco Nero, Joanna Pettet, Randy Quaid, Irene Papas, Jean-Pierre Aumont, Pierre Vaneck, Katia Dandoulaki; ***D:*** Michael Cacoyannis.

Sweet Country Road ♪ 1/2 **1983** A rock singer journeys to Nashville to try to cross over into country music. **95m/C VHS.** Buddy Knox, Kary Lynn, Gordy Trapp, Johnny Paycheck, Jeanne Pruett; ***D:*** Jack McCallum; ***W:*** Gordy Trapp; ***C:*** Cyrus Black.

Sweet Creek County War ♪ **1979 (PG)** Retired sheriff must leave his quiet ranch to battle a greedy businessman. **90m/C VHS.** Richard Egan, Albert Salmi, Nita Talbot, Slim Pickens; ***D:*** J. Frank James; ***W:*** J. Frank James; ***C:*** Gregory von Berblinger; ***M:*** Richard Bowden.

Sweet Dreams ♪♪ 1/2 **1985 (PG-13)** Biography of country singer Patsy Cline (Lange), who is struggling until her recording of "Walking After Midnight" becomes a hit. Her second marriage to fan Charlie Dick (Harris) begin to unravel as his drinking and her success both increase and Charlie turns abusive. Patsy's rise to stardom ended in an early death. Fine performances thoughout, with Lange lip-synching to Cline's original recordings. ♫ Walking After Midnight; Crazy; Sweet Dreams; San Antonio Rose; Blue Moon of Kentucky; Lovesick Blues; Seven Lonely Days; Foolin' Around; Your Cheatin' Heart. **115m/C VHS, DVD.** Jessica Lange, Ed Harris, Ann Wedgeworth, David Clennon, John Goodman, James Staley, Gary Basaraba, P.J. Soles; ***D:*** Karel Reisz; ***W:*** Robert Getchell; ***C:*** Robbie Greenberg; ***M:*** Charles Gross.

Sweet Ecstasy ♪ 1/2 *Douce Violence; Sweet Violence* **1962** Wealthy shenanigans on the French Riviera. Olivier (Pezy) is the upright young man who can't sleep with anyone unless he's in love, much to sex bomb Elke's (Sommer) dismay. **75m/B VHS, DVD.** *FR* Elke Sommer, Pierre Brice, Christian Pezy, Claire Maurier; ***D:*** Max Pecas; ***M:*** Charles Aznavour.

Sweet Evil ♪ 1/2 **1995 (R)** Naomi and Mike seek the help of a surrogate after a number of failed fertility treatments. Jenny seems to be perfect but after she moves into their home, they learn Jenny's got a nasty secret. **92m/C VHS, DVD.** Bridgette Wilson-Sampras, Peter Boyle, Scott Cohen, Eiko Matsuda, Claudette Nevins; ***D:*** Rene Eram. **VIDEO**

Sweet Evil ♪ **1998** Anthony Thurman is the owner of a club that specializes in exotic dancers and sometimes the married Anthony gets a little too involved with the entertainment. His wife knows about his habits and doesn't mind until one of Anthony's affairs uncovers an old secret that was better left hidden. **87m/C VHS, DVD.** Al Sapienza, Andrea Riave, Douglas De Marco; ***D:*** Michael Paul Girard; ***W:*** Michael Paul Girard; ***C:*** Luis Escobar; ***M:*** Michael Paul Girard. **VIDEO**

Sweet 15 **1990** A young Hispanic girl learns that there is more to growing up than parties when she learns her father is an illegal alien. Originally aired on PBS as part of the "Wonderworks" family movie series. **120m/C VHS, DVD.** Karla Montana, Panchito Gomez, Tony Plana, Jenny Gago, Susan Ruttan; ***D:*** Victoria Hochberg.

Sweet Georgia ♪ **1972** Soft-core star Jordan is a lusty wife whose husband is an alcoholic, so she has a roll in the hay with almost every other cast member. Lots of action, too, including a pitchfork fight. Ride 'em cowboy. **80m/C VHS, DVD.** Marsha Jordan, Barbara Mills, Gene Drew, Chuck Lawson; ***D:*** Edward Boles; ***W:*** Ron Hennessy; ***M:*** Hal Southern.

Sweet Hearts Dance ♪♪ **1988 (R)** Parallel love stories follow two long-time friends, one just falling in love, the other struggling to keep his marriage together. Charming performances from all, but a slow pace undermines the film. **95m/C VHS, DVD.** Don Johnson, Jeff Daniels, Susan Sarandon, Elizabeth Perkins, Justin Henry, Holly Marie Combs; ***D:*** Robert Greenwald; ***W:*** Ernest Thompson; ***C:*** Tak Fujimoto; ***M:*** Richard Gibbs.

The Sweet Hereafter ♪♪♪ 1/2 **1996 (R)** A schoolbus crash kills 14 children in the small town of Sam Dent, British Columbia. Big city lawyer Mitchell Stephens (Holm) arrives to persuade the townspeople to begin a class-action suit targeting city authorities and the bus manufacturer, while struggling to deal with his drug-addicted daughter Zoe (Banks). Paralyzed teenaged survivor Nicole Burnell (Polley) tries to cope with the aftermath of the tragedy as does widower Billy Ansell (Greenwood), whose two children died in the crash. But the case soon begins to tear the reeling town apart as everyone struggles with loss and fate. Egoyan's intimate, lyrical adaptation of the novel by Russell Banks, is filled with wonderful performances, particularly by Polley. **110m/C VHS, DVD.** *CA* Ian Holm, Sarah Polley, Bruce Greenwood, Tom McCamus, Arsinee Khanjian, Alberta Watson, Gabrielle Rose, Maury Chaykin, David Hemblen, Earl Pastko, Peter Donaldson, Caerthan Banks, Brook Johnson, Stephanie Morgenstern; ***D:*** Atom Egoyan; ***W:*** Atom Egoyan; ***C:*** Paul Sarossy; ***M:*** Mychael Danna. Cannes '97: Grand Jury Prize; Genie '97: Actor (Holm), Cinematog., Director (Egoyan), Film, Film Editing, Sound, Score; Ind. Spirit '98: Foreign Film; Toronto-City '97: Canadian Feature Film.

Sweet Home Alabama ♪♪ 1/2 **2002 (PG-13)** Rich hot city guy or hot poor country guy? That's the choice NYC fashion designer Melanie (Witherspoon) has to make in this amiable romantic comedy. The dueling beaus are Andrew (Dempsey), son of NYC mayor Bergen, and Jake (Lucas), Melanie's high school sweetheart (and current husband) back home in Alabama who still has the hots for her. When Andrew pops the question in high style, Melanie accepts and then races off to Alabama to finish matters with Jake, who hasn't given her a divorce. Complications abound when sparks fly with Jake and Mel's snooty city friends discover her well-hidden, trailer-trash upbringing.

Witherspoon plays her trademark plucky act well, elevating a so-so vehicle. **105m/C VHS, DVD.** *US* Reese Witherspoon, Josh(ua) Lucas, Patrick Dempsey, Candice Bergen, Mary Kay Place, Fred Ward, Jean Smart, Ethan (Randall) Embry, Melanie Lynskey, Courtney Gains, Rhona Mitra, Mary Lynn Rajskub, Nathan Lee Graham, Dakota Fanning, Michelle Krusiec; ***D:*** Andy Tennant; ***W:*** C. Jay Cox; ***C:*** Andrew Dunn; ***M:*** George Fenton.

Sweet Hostage 𝄞𝄞 1/2 **1975** Escaped mental patient kidnaps uneducated farm girl and holds her captive in a remote cabin. Blair and Sheen turn in good performances. Adaptation of Nathaniel Benchley's "Welcome to Xanadu." **93m/C VHS.** Linda Blair, Martin Sheen, Jeanne Cooper, Lee DeBroux, Dehl Berti, Bert Remsen; ***D:*** Lee Philips. **TV**

Sweet Insanity WOOF! 2006 (R) Despite being troubled by nightmares (no doubt caused by a series of local murders), high schooler Stacey (Hoyle) invites strange transfer student Christina (Firgens) to her party when her parents go out of town for the weekend. Boring and stupid even by teen slasher standards. **87m/C DVD.** *US* Rebekah Hoyle, MacKenzie Firgens, David Fine, Josh McRae; ***D:*** Daniel Hess; ***W:*** Daniel Hess, Adam Weis; ***C:*** Kenn Ferro, Virgil Harper; ***M:*** Jesper Kyd.

Sweet Jane 𝄞𝄞 1/2 **1998** Teenaged Tony (Gordon-Levitt) has AIDS and no family. He becomes infatuated with HIV-positive heroin addict Jane (Mathis), whom he sees in the hospital, and follows her into a dangerous street life. Although Jane treats him badly, Tony sticks around to "protect" her and they slowly establish a mutally dependent relastionship that offers surrogate family ties and solace for them both. **83m/C VHS, DVD.** Samantha Mathis, Joseph Gordon-Levitt, Bud Cort, William McNamara, Mary Woronov; ***D:*** Joe Gayton; ***W:*** Joe Gayton; ***C:*** Greg Littlewood; ***M:*** Walter Werzowa.

Sweet Justice 𝄞 1/2 **1992 (R)** This time its the women who get to be commandos, have all the adventures, and get revenge on various scum. The nominal plotline has Sunny Justice (Carter) and her group of gal-warriors avenging the sadistic murder of a friend. Martial arts, weapons, and action galore. **92m/C VHS, DVD.** Finn Carter, Kathleen Kinmont, Marc Singer, Frank Gorshin, Mickey Rooney; ***D:*** Allen Plone; ***W:*** Allen Plone, Jim Tabilio.

Sweet Killing 𝄞𝄞 **1993 (R)** A banker murders his shrewish wife to be with another woman. He thinks he has the perfect alibi, but then his fictitious excuse comes to life when a mysterious stranger begins stalking him. Based on the novel "Qualthrough" by Agnes Hall. **87m/C VHS, DVD.** Anthony (Corlan) Higgins, F. Murray Abraham, Leslie Hope, Michael Ironside, Andrea Ferreol; ***D:*** Eddy Matalon; ***W:*** Eddy Matalon.

Sweet Land 𝄞𝄞 1/2 **2005 (PG)** Inge Ottenberg (Reaser) becomes a mail-order bride for Norwegian-American farmer Olaf (Guinee) in Minnesota just after WWI. But the fact that she is German (and knows minimal English) causes strong feelings within the community and the local minister (Heard) refuses to marry them. Olaf moves into the barn to preserve decorum while Inge tries to settle in and they fall in love. Sweet story, told in flashbacks. **110m/C DVD.** Elizabeth Reaser, Tim Guinee, Alan Cumming, John Heard, Alex Kingston, Ned Beatty, Lois Smith, Paul Sand; ***D:*** Ali Selim; ***W:*** Ali Selim; ***C:*** David Tumblety; ***M:*** Mark Orton.

Sweet Liberty 𝄞𝄞 **1986 (PG)** Alda's hometown is overwhelmed by Hollywood chaos during the filming of a movie version of his novel about the American Revolution. Pleasant but predictable. **107m/C VHS, DVD.** Alan Alda, Michael Caine, Michelle Pfeiffer, Bob Hoskins, Lillian Gish; ***D:*** Alan Alda; ***W:*** Alan Alda; ***M:*** Bruce Broughton.

Sweet Lies 𝄞 1/2 **1988 (R)** An insurance investigator tracking a scam artist in Paris is preyed upon by a group of single women betting one another that any man can be seduced. Slow comedy. **86m/C VHS.** Treat Williams, Joanna Pacula, Julianne Phillips, Laura Manszky, Norbert Weisser, Marilyn Dodds Frank; ***D:*** Nathalie Delon; ***M:*** Trevor Jones.

Sweet Light in a Dark Room 𝄞𝄞𝄞 *Romeo, Julia a Tma; Romeo, Juliet and Darkness* **1960** A student in Prague during the Nazi Occupation hides a Jewish girl. He falls in love with her but becomes the suspect in the murder of a Nazi officer. Directed by the great Czech filmmaker Weiss who was himself forced to leave his country during Nazi occupation. In Czech with English subtitles. **93m/B VHS.** *CZ* Ivan Mistrik, Dana Smutna; ***D:*** Jiri Weiss.

Sweet Lorraine 𝄞𝄞𝄞 **1987 (PG-13)** A bittersweet, nostalgic comedy about the staff and clientele of a deteriorating Catskills hotel on the eve of its closing. **91m/C VHS, DVD.** Maureen Stapleton, Lee Richardson, Trini Alvarado, Freddie Roman, John Bedford Lloyd, Giancarlo Esposito, Edie Falco, Todd Graff, Evan Handler; ***D:*** Steve Gomer; ***W:*** Michael Zettler, Shelly Altman; ***M:*** Richard Robbins.

Sweet Love, Bitter 𝄞𝄞 1/2 *It Won't Rub Off, Baby; Black Love, White Love* **1967** The downfall of a black jazz saxophonist in the 1950s. The character is loosely based on the life of legendary musician Charlie "Bird" Parker. Alto sax man Charles McPherson dubs Gregory's solos. Adapted from the novel "Night Song" by John A. Williams. **92m/C VHS.** Dick Gregory, Don Murray, Diane Varsi, Robert Hooks; ***D:*** Herbert Danska; ***W:*** Lewis Jacobs, Herbert Danska; ***M:*** Mal Waldron.

Sweet Movie 𝄞𝄞 **1975** A provocative cult classic concerning a South African tycoon who purchases a virgin bride and then exploits her sexually. In English and French with subtitles. **120m/C VHS, DVD.** *CA FR GE* Carole Laure, Pierre Clementi, Sami Frey, Anna Prucnal, Jane Mallet, John Vernon; ***D:*** Dusan Makavejev; ***W:*** Dusan Makavejev; ***C:*** Pierre Lhomme; ***M:*** Manos Hadjidakis.

Sweet Murder WOOF! 1993 (R) "Single White Female" rip-off features Udy allowing Davidtz to share her apartment—with nasty consequences. **101m/C VHS.** Helene Udy, Embeth Davidtz, Russell Todd; ***D:*** Percival Rubens.

Sweet Nothing 𝄞𝄞𝄞 **1996 (R)** Wall Street up-and-comer Angel (Imperioli) is given some crack by a buddy (Calderon) to celebrate the birth of his child. This starts a downward spiral into addiction and dealing. At first, his wife Monika (Sorvino) goes along, but as Angel deteriorates, she learns not to trust him. Excellent performances by Imperioli and Sorvino avoid over-the-top theatrics. Script provides a realistic look at how addiction affects real people, and steers clear of obvious cliches. Based on diaries found in a Bronx apartment building. Film's producers tracked down the author and paid for his rehab. **89m/C VHS.** Michael Imperioli, Mira Sorvino, Paul Calderon, Billie Neal; ***D:*** Gary Winick; ***W:*** Lee Drysdale.

Sweet Nothing in My Ear 𝄞𝄞 **2008** This Hallmark Hall of Fame production leaves itself with an unresolved ending after an often dramatic and contentious situation. Dan (Daniels), who can hear, is married to Laura (Matlin), who is deaf. Their eight-year-old son Adam (Valencia) lost his own hearing at age five and a doctor is now recommending Adam as a candidate for cochlear implants that could restore some of his hearing. This alarms Laura and irritates her activist deaf parents, who don't think their grandson needs to be fixed. The situation gets so bad that the Millers separate and begin a custody battle for Adam. Voiceovers are used to translate the sign language. Adapted by Sachs from his play. **98m/C DVD.** Jeff Daniels, Marlee Matlin, Sonya Walger, Phyllis Frelich, David Oyelowo, Rosemary Forsyth, Bradford English, Noah Valencia, Ed Waterstreet; ***D:*** Joseph Sargent; ***W:*** Stephen Sachs; ***C:*** Donald M. Morgan; ***M:*** Charles Bernstein. **TV**

Sweet November 𝄞𝄞 **1968** Tearjerker stars Dennis as Sara Deever, a terminally ill woman who shares her apartment with a different lover each month. She helps the guy with his particular hang-up and he helps her, well, live. That is until Mr. November (Newley) refuses to leave when his month is up because he's fallen in love. Remade in 2001. **113m/C VHS.** Sandy Dennis, Anthony Newley, Theodore Bikel, Burr de Benning, Sandy Baron, Marj Dusay, Martin West, Virginia Vincent, King Moody; ***D:*** Robert Ellis Miller; ***W:*** Herman Raucher; ***C:*** Daniel F. Fapp; ***M:*** Michel Legrand.

Sweet November 𝄞 1/2 **2001 (PG-13)** Stale and contrived remake of the 1968 film stars Theron as a kooky, carefree boho looking to rehabilitate uptight businessmen one month at a time, until her inevitable demise from a mysterious illness. Nelson Moss (Reeves) is Mr. November, who is invited to live with Sara in exchange for losing his cell phone, monkeysuit, and too-tense attitude for a day at the beach (literally). As the November holiday looms and Sara's secret is sappily revealed, we can give thanks that the movie is almost over. Improbable story with decent performance by Theron, while Reeves's is less so, shocking no one. **114m/C VHS, DVD.** *US* Keanu Reeves, Charlize Theron, Jason Isaacs, Greg Germann, Liam Aiken, Lauren Graham, Michael Rosenbaum, Robert Joy, Jason Kravits, Frank Langella; ***D:*** Pat O'Connor; ***W:*** Kurt Voelker; ***C:*** Edward Lachman; ***M:*** Christopher Young.

Sweet Perfection 𝄞𝄞 *The Perfect Model* **1990 (R)** Jackson plans a big promotion for her beauty contest. Who will be voted the "Perfect Woman?" Tired premise, but it has its moments. **90m/C VHS, DVD.** Stoney Jackson, Anthony Norman McKay, Catero Colbert, Liza Crusat, Reggie Theus, Tatiana Tumbtzen; ***D:*** Daryll Roberts; ***C:*** Sam Sako.

Sweet Poison 𝄞𝄞 **1991 (R)** Bobby Stiles is a ruthless criminal who has just broken out of prison. He wants to get home and settle the score with his brother, who actually committed the crime Bobby was imprisoned for. Henry and Charlene Odell are traveling cross-country when Bobby crosses their path and forces them to drive him home. Bobby's not too busy eluding the police to notice that his captives' marriage is a little shaky—and that Charlene is attractive and sexy. As Bobby and Charlene get closer husband Henry just becomes another problem. **101m/C VHS.** Steven Bauer, Patricia Healy, Edward Herrmann; ***D:*** Brian Grant.

Sweet Revenge 𝄞𝄞 **1987 (R)** TV journalist kidnapped by a white slavery ring in the Asian jungles. After escaping, she returns for vegeance. Meek drama. **79m/C VHS.** Ted Shackleford, Nancy Allen, Martin Landau; ***D:*** Mark Sobel.

Sweet Revenge 𝄞𝄞 **1990** When a judge tells a divorced couple that the woman must pay the man alimony, she hires an actress to marry her ex. The tables are turned in this way-out marriage flick, reminiscent of the screwball comedies of the 1940s. **89m/C VHS.** Rosanna Arquette, Carrie Fisher, John Sessions; ***D:*** Charlotte Brandstrom; ***W:*** Janet Brownell; ***M:*** Hubert Bougis.

Sweet Revenge 𝄞 1/2 *The Revengers' Comedies* **1998** Even this professional cast can't rescue this predictable black comedy that is condensed from two 1991 Alan Ayckbourn plays, "The Revengers' Comedies." After saving each other from committing suicide, depressed businessman Henry Bell (Neill) and orphaned aristocrat Karen Knightly (Bonham Carter) agree on reciprocal revenge plots. Karen will punish the guy (Coogan) who stole Henry's job while Henry will destroy the neurotic wife (Scott Thomas) whose husband was once Karen's lover. Then Henry discovers Karen hasn't been telling him the truth. Too much seems to be lost from the original source. **82m/C VHS, DVD.** *GB FR* Sam Neill, Helena Bonham Carter, Kristin Scott Thomas, Martin Clunes, Rupert Graves, Steve Coogan, John Wood, Liz Smith, Charlotte Coleman; ***D:*** Malcolm Mowbray; ***W:*** Malcolm Mowbray; ***C:*** Romain Winding; ***M:*** Alexandre Desplat. **CABLE**

Sweet Rosie O'Grady 𝄞𝄞 1/2 **1943** Musical-comedy star Grable has returned to New York after success in England, where she caught the eye of nobleman Gardiner. Ex-boyfriend Young is a tabloid reporter who's expected by editor Menjou to get the scoop on her past. Seems she used to perform in Bowery saloons although that's not what Grable's been telling everyone. Slight story, charming performers, and lots of songs. Remade in 1948 as "That Wonderful Urge." ♫My Heart Tells Me; My Sam; Oh Where is the Groom?; The Wishing Waltz; Going to the Country Fair; Get Your Police Gazette; Battle Cry; Sweet Rosie O'Grady; Two Little Girls in Blue. **74m/C VHS.** Betty Grable, Robert Young, Adolphe Menjou, Reginald Gardiner, Virginia Grey, Phil Regan, Sig Rumann, Alan Dinehart; ***D:*** Irving Cummings; ***C:*** Ernest Palmer.

Sweet 16 𝄞𝄞 **1981 (R)** Serial killings in Texas town begin to set off muffled alarms in big head of sheriff Hopkins. Sixteen-year-old Melissa has recently moved into town. She's beautiful, mysterious, and promiscuous, and she has a big problem—all her boyfriends end up dead. No real puzzle. **90m/C VHS.** Susan Strasberg, Bo Hopkins, Don Stroud, Dana Kimmell, Patrick Macnee, Larry Storch; ***D:*** Jim Sotos.

Sweet Sixteen 𝄞𝄞𝄞 **2002 (R)** Compston is exceptional in his debut role of teenaged Liam, who lives in Greenock, Scotland where unemployment and violence are rampant. Liam's one wish is to buy a trailer he can move his mother Jean (Coulter) into when she's released from prison in time for his 16th birthday. In order to get the money, petty criminal Martin and his friend Pinball (Ruane) steal the heroin stash of Jean's dealer boyfriend Stan (McCormack). Selling it puts the boys in opposition to local gangster Tony (McCardie), who decides to hire Martin himself. Then things go from bad to worse. Film is melancholy, humorous, tender, and subtitled because of the thick Scottish accents. **106m/C VHS, DVD.** *GB GE SP* Martin Compston, William Ruane, Annmarie Fulton, Michelle Coulter, Gary McCormack, Martin McCardie, Michelle Abercromby, Tommy McKee; ***D:*** Ken Loach; ***W:*** Paul Laverty; ***C:*** Barry Ackroyd; ***M:*** George Fenton. Cannes '03: Screenplay.

Sweet Smell of Success 𝄞𝄞𝄞 1/2 **1957** Powerful and ruthless New York City gossip columnist J.J. Hunsecker (Lancaster) writes a syndicated newspaper column that pandering press agent Sidney Falco (Curtis) is desperate to have his clients be a part of. Hunsecker only cares about the welfare of his younger sister, Susan (Harrison), and is outraged over her budding romance with jazz musician Steve Dalls (Milner). So he strong arms Falco into breaking up the relationship, with unexpected consequences. Engrossing performances, great dialogue. **96m/C VHS, DVD.** Burt Lancaster, Tony Curtis, Martin Milner, Barbara Nichols, Sam Levene, Susan Harrison; ***D:*** Alexander MacKendrick; ***W:*** Ernest Lehman, Clifford Odets; ***C:*** James Wong Howe; ***M:*** Elmer Bernstein. Natl. Film Reg. '93.

Sweet Spirits WOOF! *The Red Headed Corpse* **1971** Soft-sell European fluff about a modern mannequin having a raucous affair with an artist. **87m/C VHS.** *IT* Erika Blanc, Farley Granger; ***D:*** Renzo Russo; ***W:*** Renzo Russo.

Sweet Sugar 𝄞 1/2 *Chaingang Girls; Captive Women 3: Sweet Sugar* **1972 (R)** Slave girls try to escape from a Costa Rican sugar cane plantation and its cruel owner. Needless to say, vulgar exploitation runs hither and yon in this film. **90m/C VHS.** Phyllis E. Davis, Ella Edwards, Pamela Collins, Cliff Osmond, Timothy Brown; ***D:*** Michel Levesque.

Sweet Sweetback's Baadasssss Song 𝄞𝄞𝄞 **1971** A black pimp kills two policemen who beat up a black militant. He uses his street-wise survival skills to elude his pursuers and escape to Mexico. A thriller, but racist, sexist, and violent. **97m/C VHS, DVD.** Melvin Van Peebles, Simon Chuckster, Hubert Scales, John Dullaghan, Rhetta Hughes, John Amos, West Gale, Niva Rochelle, Nick Ferrari, Mario Van Peebles, Megan Van Peebles; ***D:*** Melvin Van Peebles; ***W:*** Melvin Van Peebles; ***C:*** Robert Maxwell; ***M:*** Melvin Van Peebles.

Sweet Talker 𝄞𝄞 1/2 **1991 (PG)** Following his release from prison, a charming con man shows up in a small coastal village, thinking the townsfolk will be ripe for the picking. What he doesn't know is they can do some sweet talking of their own, and he soon finds himself caring for a pretty widow and her son. Enjoyable light comedy works thanks to likable leads. **91m/C VHS, DVD.** *AU* Bryan Brown, Karen Allen, Chris Haywood, Bill Kerr, Bruce Spence, Bruce Myles, Paul Chubb, Peter Hehir, Justin Rosniak; ***D:*** Michael Jenkins; ***W:*** Tony Morphett; ***C:*** Russell Boyd; ***M:*** Richard Thompson, Peter Filleul.

Sweet Thing ✓✓✓ **2000 (R)** Well-constructed tale concerning a troubled young artist, Sean Fields (Fox), who begins a potentially meteoric rise with a series of controversial paintings. His abusive stepfather, Ray Fields (Lunning), a district judge, has announced his intention to run for U.S. Congress and his campaign success is mirrored by the growing popularity of Sean's work, although the graphic nature of the paintings sparks a warped media frenzy. **115m/C DVD.** Jeremy Fox, Amalia Stifter, Ev Lunning Jr.; ***D:*** Mark David; ***W:*** Mark David, Mark Spacek; ***C:*** Mark David, Levy Castleberry, Marc Wiskemann.

Sweet Trash **WOOF!** **1970 (R)** A vice cop, having an affair with a 17-year-old prostitute, is blackmailed by an underworld figure. Lives up to its name. **80m/C VHS.** Anthony (Tony) Vorno, Sharon Matt, Luke Perry, Bonnie Clark, Gene Blackey; ***D:*** John Hayes.

Sweet William ✓✓✓ **1979 (R)** A philandering and seemingly irresistible young man finds that one sensitive woman hasn't the patience or time for his escapades. Adult comedy concerned with sex without displaying any on the screen. **88m/C VHS.** *GB* Sam Waterston, Jenny Agutter, Anna Massey, Arthur Lowe; ***D:*** Claude Whatham; ***W:*** Beryl Bainbridge.

Sweet Young Thing *Monique and Julie* **1979** Young students at a French girls' school receive all sorts of attention from the male staff. **83m/C VHS.** *FR* Germaine Dhont, Hugette Parmain, Rudy Lenoir, Jean-Louis Cabula, Jean Tolzac, Bernard Musson; ***D:*** Alain Payet; ***W:*** Alain Payet; ***C:*** Maurice Fellous; ***M:*** Philippe Brejean.

The Sweetest Gift ✓✓ ½ **1998** Two Florida neighbors (Carroll and Shaver) turn out to have many of the same problems—they're both single parents trying to raise their kids as best they can while dealing with poverty and prejudice. And despite the racial differences, their kids become friends. **90m/C VHS.** Helen Shaver, Diahann Carroll, Tisha Campbell; ***D:*** Stuart Margolin; ***W:*** Rosa Jordan; ***C:*** Ron Stannett; ***M:*** Lawrence Shragge. **CABLE**

The Sweetest Thing ✓✓ **2002 (R)** Girls can be just as sex-obsessed and disgusting as boys as this raunchy comedy sets out to prove. San Francisco party girl Christina Walters (Diaz) isn't looking for Mr. Right—just Mr. Right Now. And she thinks she's met him when Christina and gal pal Courtney (Applegate) take the third of their Musketeer trio—the just-dumped Jane (Blair)—out to a dance club to drink and flirt. Christina meets cute with Peter (Jane) but doesn't follow through. After getting ragged on by Courtney, the babe duo decide to track him down at the oh-so-genteel wedding he's attending. Havoc ensues. Film's both giddy and sleazy but if you like Diaz at her daffiest, you'll sit through the tacky situations. **84m/C VHS, DVD.** *US* Cameron Diaz, Christina Applegate, Thomas Jane, Selma Blair, Jason Bateman, Parker Posey; ***D:*** Roger Kumble; ***W:*** Nancy M. Pimenthal; ***C:*** Anthony B. Richmond; ***M:*** Ed Shearmur.

Sweetheart of the Navy ✓ ½ **1937** Sailors help a cafe singer out of a jam, with one of them almost giving up his career for her. Standard fare, but Parker is well worth listening to. **63m/B VHS.** Eric Linden, Cecilia Parker, Roger Imhof, Bernadene Hayes, Jason Robards Sr., Don Barclay; ***D:*** Duncan Mansfield.

Sweethearts ✓✓✓ **1938** MacDonald and Eddy star as married stage actors trying to get some time off from their hectic schedule in this show-within-a-show. Trouble ensues when their conniving producer begs, pleads and tricks them into staying. Lots of well-staged musical numbers. ♫Wooden Shoes; Every Lover Must Meet His Fate; Sweethearts; Pretty as a Picture; Summer Serenade; On Parade. **114m/C VHS.** Jeanette MacDonald, Nelson Eddy, Frank Morgan, Florence Rice, Ray Bolger, Mischa Auer; ***D:*** Woodbridge S. Van Dyke.

Sweethearts ✓✓ ½ **1997 (R)** Manic-depressive Jasmine (Garofalo) responds to a personal ad placed by Arliss (Rouse), so she'll have a date for her 31st birthday. When the experience goes badly, Jasmine prevents Arliss from leaving by pulling a gun on him. Offbeat and downbeat. **85m/C VHS.** Janeane Garofalo, Mitch Rouse, Margaret Cho, Bob(cat) Goldthwait; ***D:*** Aleks Horvat; ***W:*** Aleks Horvat; ***C:*** John Peters; ***M:*** Carl Schurtz.

Sweetie ✓✓✓ **1989 (R)** Bizarre, expressive Australian tragicomedy about a pair of sisters—one a withdrawn, paranoid Plain Jane, the other a dangerously extroverted, overweight sociopath who re-enters her family's life and turns it upside down. Campion's first feature. **97m/C VHS, DVD.** *AU* Genevieve Lemon, Karen Colston, Tom Lycos, Jon Darling, Dorothy Barry, Michael Lake, Andre Pataczek; ***D:*** Jane Campion; ***W:*** Gerard Lee, Jane Campion; ***M:*** Martin Armiger.

Sweetwater: A True Rock Story ✓✓ ½ **1999 (PG-13)** TV music journalist Cami Carlson (Williams) gets out of drug rehab and learns her new assignment is a "where are they now" story about '60s band Sweetwater, the opening act at Woodstock. Teenaged singer Nansi Nevins (Johnson) disappeared after the festival and the band soon broke up. Cami tracks down ex-band members and flashbacks show how the band started and what caused Nansi to take off. **95m/C VHS.** Kelli Williams, Amy Jo Johnson, Kurt Max Runte, Robert Moloney, Frederic Forrest, Michelle Phillips, Terry David Mulligan, Nancy Warren; ***D:*** Lorraine Senna; ***W:*** Victoria Wozniak; ***C:*** Bernard Couture. **CABLE**

Swept Away... ✓✓✓ *Swept Away...By an Unusual Destiny in the Blue Sea of August* **1975 (R)** A rich and beautiful Milanese woman is shipwrecked on a desolate island with a swarthy Sicilian deck hand, who also happens to be a dedicated communist. Isolated, the two switch roles, with the wealthy woman dominated by the crude proletarian. Sexy and provocative. Italian with subtitles. **116m/C VHS, DVD.** *IT* Giancarlo Giannini, Mariangela Melato; ***D:*** Lina Wertmuller; ***W:*** Lina Wertmuller; ***C:*** Julio Battiferri; ***M:*** Piero Piccioni.

Swept Away ✓ **2002 (R)** Guy Ritchie directs his wife Madonna in this ill-advised remake of Lina Wertmuller's politically charged romantic comedy. Amber (Madonna) arrives with her husband (Greenwood) as part of a group of ugly Americans taking a tour of the Greek islands on a yacht. A demanding prima (Ma)donna, she is especially rude to first mate Giuseppe (Giannini), whom she calls either "Guido" or "Pee Pee." Amber demands that Guiseppe take her out in the dinghy and they run out of gas and are forced to drift. They end up on a deserted island where Giuseppe now has the upper hand and begins to dominate Amber. Despite the fact that these actors fail at chemistry worse than remedial students, we're supposed to believe that they fall in love. "Gilligan's Island" is more believable, with more romantic sparks. Adriano Giannini reprises the role his father Giancarlo played in the original. **93m/C VHS, DVD.** *US* Madonna, Adriano Giannini, Jeanne Tripplehorn, Bruce Greenwood, David Thornton, Yorgo Voyagis, Elizabeth Banks, Michael Beattie; ***D:*** Guy Ritchie; ***W:*** Guy Ritchie; ***C:*** Alex Barber; ***M:*** Michel Colombier. Golden Raspberries '02: Worst Picture, Worst Actress (Madonna), Worst Director (Ritchie).

Swept from the Sea ✓✓ ½ *Amy Foster* **1997 (PG-13)** Shipwrecked foreigner (Perez) and ostracized servant girl (Weisz) are star-crossed lovers in 19th century Cornwall. Told in flashback by Dr. Kennedy (McKellen) to Kathy Bates' invalid Miss Swaffer, he recalls how the native Ukrainian Yanko, who could speak no English, was thought to be an idiot by all in town, except the kind and gentle Amy, who found him washed up on the shore. Kennedy and Yanko bond through a game of chess, and the kindly doctor teaches him English. Armed with the native words of love, Yanko goes a'courtin' Miss Amy. Definitely for die-hard romantics, the films throws in all the melodrama it can muster and then some, but performances are worthy (especially McKellen's). Based on a short story by Joseph Conrad. **115m/C VHS, DVD.** *GB* Vincent Perez, Rachel Weisz, Kathy Bates, Ian McKellen, Joss Ackland, Tom Bell, Zoe Wanamaker, Tony Haygarth, Fiona Victory; ***D:*** Beeban Kidron; ***W:*** Tim Willocks; ***C:*** Dick Pope; ***M:*** John Barry.

Swift Justice ✓✓ **1988** Mayor of a small town thinks he's gotten away with murder after leaving a young girl for dead in a junk yard. However, the mayor and his violent pals are soon hunted by an ex-Green Beret with a penchant for justice. **90m/C VHS.** Jon Greene, Cindy Rome, Cameron Mitchell, Aldo Ray, Chuck "Porky" Mitchell, Wilson Dunster, Ted Leplat; ***D:*** Harry Hope.

Swifty ✓ ½ **1935** A cowpoke is accused of murder but escapes to track down the real culprit and win the hand of the girl he loves. **60m/B VHS.** Hoot Gibson, June Gale, George "Gabby" Hayes, Ralph Lewis, Lafe (Lafayette) McKee, Robert F. (Bob) Kortman, William (Bill) Gould, Wally Wales; ***D:*** Alan James; ***W:*** Roger Allman, Walter Farrar; ***C:*** Arthur Reed.

Swim Team ✓ **1979** New coach for a terminally inept school swimming team whips them into shape. Doesn't hold much water. **81m/C VHS.** Stephen Furst, James Daughton, Jenny Neumann, Kim Day, Buster Crabbe; ***D:*** James Polakof.

Swimfan ✓ ½ **2002 (PG-13)** Watered down, teen "Fatal Attraction." Ben Cronin (Bradford) is a suburban NYC high school swimming star, and Madison Bell (Christensen) a new girl in town who hooks the studly jock and reels him in. Otherwise involved, the promising athlete allows Madison to seduce him in the pool on one occasion, which automatically sets off her crazy mechanism. She immediately begins to run the well-worn stalker playbook. Ben's life begins to unravel due to Madison's devious designs and after a face-off with his psycho one-night-stand, he's forced to fight back with the help of her cousin, the class nerd. Mildly thrilling pic suffers from editing and continuity gaffes. **93m/C VHS, DVD.** *US* Erika Christensen, Jesse Bradford, Shiri Appleby, Kate Burton, Clayne Crawford, Jason Ritter, Kia Joy Goodwin, Dan Hedaya, Michael Higgins, Nick Sandow, James DeBello, Pamela Isaacs, Phyllis Somerville; ***D:*** John Polson; ***W:*** Charles F. Bohl, Phillip Schneider; ***C:*** Giles Nuttgens; ***M:*** Louis Febre.

The Swimmer ✓✓✓ ½ **1968 (PG)** A lonely suburbanite swims an existential swath through the pools of his neighborhood landscape in an effort at self-discovery. A surreal, strangely compelling work based on a story by John Cheever. **94m/C VHS, DVD.** Burt Lancaster, Janice Rule, Janet Landgard, Marge Champion, Kim Hunter, Rose Gregorio, John David Garfield; ***D:*** Frank Perry; ***M:*** Marvin Hamlisch.

Swimming ✓✓ ½ **2000** Teenaged tomboy Frankie (Ambrose) works in the family diner in the resort town of Myrtle Beach, S.C., alongside her older brother Neil (Pais). Her best friend is extroverted body piercer Nicola (Dundas Lowe), who is somewhat overprotective of the inexperienced Frankie. This shows when Neil hires slinky, confident Josee (Carter) as a waitress and Josee makes a pass at Frankie, who doesn't know how to react. Frankie also catches the eye of newcomer Heath (Harrold) to whom she is drawn, although he makes her no romantic promises. Coming-of-ager with an appealing performance by Ambrose. **98m/C VHS, DVD.** Lauren Ambrose, Joelle Carter, Jennifer (Jennie) Dundas Lowe, Jamie Harrold, Josh Pais, Anthony Michael Ruivivar; ***D:*** Robert Siegel; ***W:*** Robert Siegel, Liza Bazadona, Grace Woodard; ***C:*** John Leuba; ***M:*** Mark Wike.

Swimming Pool ✓✓ ½ **1970 (PG)** Two men and two women spend a weekend in a villa on the French Riviera, manipulating each other, playing sexual games, and changing partners. Their escapades end in murder. Romantic melodrama is sensuous if slow-moving. French film dubbed in English. **85m/C VHS.** *FR* Romy Schneider, Alain Delon, Maurice Ronet, Jane Birkin; ***D:*** Jacques Deray.

Swimming Pool ✓✓✓ **2003 (R)** Sophisticated, tricky thriller stars Rampling as successful British crime writer Sarah Morton—who's suffering from writer's block. Sarah complains to her publisher, John (Dance), and he offers her his summer house in the South of France. She accepts, thinking a change of scene will be inspiring and hoping John will visit. Instead, Sarah's quiet vacation is rudely interrupted by the arrival of John's uninhibited French daughter from his first marriage, Julie (Sagnier). The neglected teen moves in, flaunts her sexuality (and body) in front of the repressed Englishwoman, and brings home a series of one-night stands. Sarah surreptitiously watches Julie and begins a novel about her. Then, when one of Julie's lovers disappears, Sarah fantasizes that something deadly has occurred. A surprise denouncement may leave viewers frustrated but there's an uneasy seduction to the the film, with both actresses giving their roles edge and vulnerability. **102m/C VHS, DVD.** *FR GB* Charlotte Rampling, Ludivine Sagnier, Charles Dance, Marc Fayolle, Jean-Marie Lamour; ***D:*** Francois Ozon; ***W:*** Francois Ozon, Emmanuele Bernheim; ***C:*** Yorick Le Saux; ***M:*** Philippe Rombi.

Swimming to Cambodia ✓✓✓ **1987** Gray tells the story of his bit part in "The Killing Fields," filmed in Cambodia, and makes ironic observations about modern life. It works. **87m/C VHS.** Spalding Gray; ***D:*** Jonathan Demme; ***C:*** John Bailey; ***M:*** Laurie Anderson.

Swimming Upstream ✓✓ **2003 (PG-13)** Dysfunctional family drama with a sports twist based on a true story. Screenwriter/exec producer Anthony Fingleton fictionalizes his own story of competitive swimming during the 50s and 60s in Brisbane, Australia. His career did not reach true heights due to an overbearing and increasingly violent alcoholic father. Perhaps this poorly executed film had a more cathartic effect on the creator than it does on an audience. **113m/C DVD.** Geoffrey Rush, Judy Davis, Jesse Spencer, Deborah Kennedy, Mark Hembrow, Melissa Thomas, Tim Draxl, David Hoflin, Craig Horner, Brittany Byrnes, Mitchell Dellevergin, Thomas Davidson, Kain O'Keefe, Robert Quinn, Keeara Byrnes, Des Drury, Dawn Fraser, Remi Broadway, Murray Rose; ***D:*** Russell Mulcahy; ***W:*** Anthony Fingleton; ***C:*** Martin McGrath; ***M:*** Reinhold Heil, Johnny Klimek.

Swimming with Sharks ✓✓✓ *The Buddy Factor* **1994 (R)** Budding screenwriter Guy (Whaley) goes to work for notoriously insulting movie producer Buddy (Spacey). Soon, Guy grows tired of his boss's demeaning treatment and cruel means of communication and devises a scheme which would even the score. Hollywood satire has more bite than "The Player," and a devious cilmax, but it's mostly an opportunity for Spacey to hang his hams, which he does with glee. Debut for director Huang, who based his script on his experience as a production assistant. See it with your boss. **93m/C VHS, DVD.** Kevin Spacey, Frank Whaley, Michelle Forbes, Benicio Del Toro; ***D:*** George Huang; ***W:*** George Huang; ***C:*** Steven Finestone; ***M:*** Tom Heil. N.Y. Film Critics '95: Support. Actor (Spacey).

Swimsuit ✓ ½ **1989** A young ad executive decides to revitalize a swimsuit company's failing business by sponsoring a contest for the perfect swimsuit model in this TV fluff. **100m/C VHS, DVD.** William Katt, Catherine Oxenberg, Cyd Charisse, Nia Peeples, Tom Villard, Cheryl Pollak, Billy Warlock, Jack Wagner; ***D:*** Chris Thomson; ***W:*** Robert Schiff; ***C:*** Laszlo George; ***M:*** John D'Andrea. **TV**

Swindle ✓ **1992** Two life-long friends set up scam after scam in their quest for sex and money. Their latest con involves a phony marriage broker business, which provides the opportunity to meet a lot of lovely ladies. Only it turns out the hustlers may be the ones getting hustled. **85m/C VHS.** Robby West, Britt Houston, Elaina Dunn, Samantha Fong, Bobby Tess, Donna Thomas; ***D:*** Jason Holt.

The Swindle ✓✓ *Rien ne va plus* **1997** Chabrol's 50th film deals with femme fatale con woman Betty (Huppert) and her older partner, Victor (Serrault). Their modus operandi is for Betty to pick up a businessman, go to his hotel room, and after he passes out from the mickey she's put in his drink, Betty and Victor steal just enough to make it worth their time without raising immediate suspicions. But Betty wants to go for higher stakes and works her own scam with shady Maurice (Cluzet), which has unexpected consequences for the trio. French with subtitles. **105m/C VHS, DVD.** *FR* Isabelle Huppert, Michel Serrault, Francois Cluzet, Jean-Francois Balmer; ***D:*** Claude Chabrol; ***W:*** Claude Chabrol; ***C:*** Eduardo Serra; ***M:*** Matthieu Chabrol.

Swindle ✓ ½ **2002 (R)** One-dimensional heist flick. Seth George (Sizemore) is a New York undercover cop who's maybe been undercover a little too long. He's investigating a crime syndicate run by nightclub owner Sophie (Fenn), who's planning a bank heist using Seth as muscle. Since his superiors decide Seth is untrustworthy, they try to shut down his operation, but, having fallen for Sophie, Seth is determined to see her plans through. **93m/C VHS, DVD.** Tom Sizemore, Sherilyn Fenn, Dave Foley, Conrad Pla; ***D:*** K.C. Bascombe; ***W:*** K.C. Bascombe; ***C:*** Bruce Chun.

Swindled 🦴🦴 *Incautos* **2004** Young con man Ernesto (Altiero) partners up with older Manco (Alexandre) and the fabled Federico (Luppi) for a potentially lucrative real estate swindle. However, they need the help of sexy Pilar (Abril), a former lover of Federico's who has double-crossed him before. Can they trust each other enough to work together? Or will the temptation of the con be too much for the shady partners? Spanish with subtitles. **107m/C DVD.** *SP* Ernesto Alterio, Victoria Abril, Federico Luppi, Manuel Alexandre; ***D:*** Miguel Bardem; ***W:*** Miguel Bardem, Carlos Martin; ***C:*** Thierry Arbogast; ***M:*** Juan Bardem.

Swing 🦴🦴 ½ **1998 (R)** Martin Luxford (Speer) is out on parole, having learned to play the sax in the slammer from his cellmate Jack (Clemons, who does the sax solos). So he decides to put together a neo-'40s swing band in Liverpool with his sultry ex-girlfriend, singer Joan (Stansfield), who's now married to jealous cop, Andy (McCall). Martin has to recruit musicians, get them gigs, and manage to avoid getting into trouble that could land him back in jail (and win back Joan). It's an amusing "let's put on a show" Brit style. **98m/C VHS.** *GB* Hugo Speer, Lisa Stansfield, Tom Bell, Rita Tushingham, Paul Usher, Alexei Sayle, Danny McCall, Clarence Clemons, James Hicks, Scot Williams, Tom Georgeson; ***D:*** Nick Mead; ***W:*** Nick Mead; ***C:*** Ian Wilson.

Swing High, Swing Low 🦴🦴 ½ **1937** A trumpet player fights the bottle and the dice to become a hit in the jazz world and marry the woman he loves. Solid drama. From the stage play "Burlesque." Made first as "The Dance of Life," then as "When My Baby Smiles At Me." **95m/B VHS, DVD.** Carole Lombard, Fred MacMurray, Charles Butterworth, Dorothy Lamour; ***D:*** Mitchell Leisen.

Swing It, Professor 🦴🦴 ½ *Swing it Buddy* **1937** A stodgy music professor refuses to recognize jazz as a valid musical form and subsequently loses his job. During his unemployment, he wanders into a nightclub and discovers jazz isn't so bad after all. Nice camera work. ♫ I'm Sorta Kinda Glad I Met You; An Old-Fashioned Melody; Richer Than A Millionaire. **62m/B VHS.** Pinky Tomlin, Paula Stone, Mary Kornman, Milburn Stone, Pat Gleason; ***D:*** Marshall Neilan.

Swing It, Sailor! 🦴🦴 **1937** Two footloose sailors go after the same woman while on shore leave. Decent screwball comedy. **61m/B VHS, DVD.** Wallace Ford, Ray Mayer, Isabel Jewell, Mary Treen; ***D:*** Raymond Cannon.

Swing Kids 🦴🦴 **1993 (PG-13)** In 1939 in Germany, big band or "swing" music is the instrument used by a group of young people to rebel against the conformity demanded by Hitler. Highlights the politics of the era, but concentrates mainly on three teenagers and the strains that Nazi power put on their friendship. Although the premise is based in historic fact, there is still something disturbingly silly about the entire production. Dance sequences are lively and well-choreographed. Branagh (in an uncredited role) plays a smooth-talking Gestapo chief. Filmed on location in Prague, Czechoslovakia (as a substitute for Hamburg, Germany). **114m/C VHS, DVD.** Robert Sean Leonard, Christian Bale, Frank Whaley, Barbara Hershey, Tushka Bergen, David Tom, Kenneth Branagh, Noah Wyle; ***D:*** Thomas Carter; ***W:*** Jonathan Marc Feldman; ***C:*** Jerzy Zielinski; ***M:*** James Horner.

Swing Parade of 1946 🦴 ½ **1946** One of the multitude of 1940s musicals. Young songwriter falls in love with club owner. Highlights include an appearance by the Three Stooges. ♫ Stormy Weather; Just a Little Fond Affection; Don't Worry About the Mule; A Tender Word Will Mend It All; On the Sunny Side of the Street; Oh, Brother; After All This Time; Caledonia. **74m/B VHS.** Gale Storm, Phil Regan, Moe Howard, Edward Brophy, Connee Boswell; ***D:*** Phil Karlson.

Swing Shift 🦴🦴 ½ **1984 (PG)** When Hawn takes a job at an aircraft plant after her husband goes off to war, she learns more than riveting. Lahti steals the film as her friend and co-worker. A detailed reminiscence of the American home front during WWII that never seems to gel. Produced by Hawn. **100m/C VHS, DVD.** Goldie Hawn, Kurt Russell, Ed Harris, Christine Lahti, Holly Hunter, Chris Lemmon, Belinda Carlisle, Fred Ward, Roger Corman, Lisa Pelikan; ***D:*** Jonathan Demme; ***W:*** Ron Nyswaner, Bo Goldman; ***C:*** Tak Fujimoto. N.Y. Film Critics '84: Support. Actress (Lahti).

Swing Time 🦴🦴🦴 **1936** Astaire, a dancer who can't resist gambling, is engaged to marry another woman, until he meets Ginger. One of the team's best efforts. ♫ The Way You Look Tonight; Waltz in Swing Time; Never Gonna Dance; Pick Yourself Up; A Fine Romance; Bojangles of Harlem. **103m/B VHS, DVD.** Fred Astaire, Ginger Rogers, Helen Broderick, Betty Furness, Eric Blore, Victor Moore; ***D:*** George Stevens; ***M:*** Jerome Kern, Dorothy Fields. Oscars '36: Song ("The Way You Look Tonight"), Natl. Film Reg. '04.

Swing Vote 🦴🦴 ½ **2008 (PG-13)** Panicked, butt-kissing presidential campaigns swarm to a New Mexico trailer park when news breaks that the results of the election rest in the hands of one man's final vote. Bud Johnson (Costner), a hung-over lovable-loser and affectionate father, turns out to be the lucky voter who's whisked away by both Republican (Grammer) and Democratic (Hopper) candidates in hopes of winning his vote. A Capra-esque human comedy that pits the Everyday Guy up against The Man, and somehow almost spins the entire far-fetched scenario into something logical. **119m/C DVD, Blu-ray Disc.** *US* Kevin Costner, Madeline Carroll, Paula Patton, Kelsey Grammer, Dennis Hopper, Nathan Lane, Stanley Tucci, George Lopez, Judge Reinhold, Mare Winningham, Nana Visitor, Mark Moses, Floyd "Red Crow" Westerman; ***D:*** Joshua Michael Stern; ***W:*** Joshua Michael Stern, Jason Richman; ***C:*** Shane Hurlbut; ***M:*** John Debney.

Swingers 🦴🦴🦴 **1996 (R)** Hip, hilarious, and highly entertaining low-budget comedy features five young showbiz wanna-bes on the prowl for career breaks and beautiful "babies" in the Hollywood retro club scene. Mike (screenwriter Favreau) is a struggling actor/comedian from New York who's having trouble getting over his ex. His slick, handsome friend Trent (Vaughn, in a star-making turn) and the rest of his neo-Rat Pack buddies try to get him back in the game with nightly parties and lounge-hopping. Witty script and clever camera work make this one "money, baby, money!" **96m/C VHS, DVD, UMD.** Jon Favreau, Vince Vaughn, Ron Livingston, Patrick Van Horn, Alex Desert, Brooke Langton, Heather Graham, Deena Martin, Katherine Kendall, Blake Lindsley; ***D:*** Doug Liman; ***W:*** Jon Favreau; ***C:*** Doug Liman; ***M:*** Justin Reinhardt. MTV Movie Awards '97: New Filmmaker (Liman).

A Swingin' Summer 🦴 ½ **1965** A bunch of groovy guys and gals go-go to the beach for a vacation of fun and sun and end up starting a rock 'n' roll concert series. Everybody gets part of the action...even the bespectacled Welch, who gets a chance to sing. Performances from the Righteous Brothers and rock semi-legends Donnie Brooks, Gary Lewis and the Playboys, and the Rip Chords. ♫ Red Hot Roadster; Justine; Penny the Fool; Out to Lunch; Nitro; Ready to Groove. **81m/C VHS.** James Stacy, William Wellman Jr., Quinn O'Hara, Martin West, Mary Mitchell, Allan Jones, Raquel Welch; ***D:*** Robert Sparr; ***W:*** Leigh Chapman.

The Swinging Cheerleaders 🦴🦴 ½ **1974 (PG)** A group of amorous cheerleaders turn on the entire campus in this typical sexploiter. **90m/C VHS, DVD.** Cheryl "Rainbeaux" Smith, Colleen Camp, Rosanne Katon, Jo Johnston, Mae Mercer, Bob Minor, George D. Wallace; ***D:*** Jack Hill; ***W:*** Betty Conklin; ***C:*** Alfred Taylor; ***M:*** William Allen Castleman, William Loose.

Swingtime Johnny 🦴🦴 **1943** Typical wartime musical fare. The Andrews Sisters forgo their showbiz careers to help out the war effort by taking factory work making artillery shells. But they still find time to harmonize. **61m/B VHS.** The Andrews Sisters, Harriet Hilliard Nelson, Peter Cookson, John Hamilton, Herbert Heywood; ***D:*** Edward F. (Eddie) Cline; ***W:*** Clyde Bruckman; ***C:*** Jerome Ash.

Swiss Conspiracy 🦴🦴 *Per Saldo Mord* **1977 (PG)** Against the opulent background of the world's richest financial capital and playground of the wealthy, one man battles to stop a daring and sophisticated blackmailer preying on the secret bank account set. Fast-paced, if sometimes confusing. **92m/C VHS, DVD.** *GE* David Janssen, Senta Berger, John Saxon, Ray Milland, Elke Sommer; ***D:*** Jack Arnold; ***W:*** Norman Klenman, Philip Saltzman, Michael Stanley; ***M:*** Klaus Doldinger.

The Swiss Family Robinson 🦴🦴🦴 **1960** A family, seeking to escape Napoleon's war in Europe, sets sail for New Guinea, but shipwrecks on a deserted tropical island. There they build an idyllic life, only to be confronted by a band of pirates. Lots of adventure for family viewing. Filmed on location on the island of Tobago. Based on the novel by Johann Wyss. **126m/C VHS, DVD.** John Mills, Dorothy McGuire, James MacArthur, Tommy Kirk, Janet Munro, Sessue Hayakawa, Kevin Corcoran; ***D:*** Ken Annakin; ***W:*** Lowell S. Hawley; ***C:*** Harry Waxman; ***M:*** William Alwyn.

Swiss Miss 🦴🦴 ½ **1938** Stan and Ollie are mousetrap salesmen on the job in Switzerland. Highlights include Stan's tuba serenade and the gorilla-on-the-bridge episode. Also included on this tape is a 1935 Thelma Todd/Patsy Kelly short, "Hot Money." **97m/B VHS.** Stan Laurel, Oliver Hardy, Della Lind, Walter Woolf King, Eric Blore, Patsy Kelly; ***D:*** John Blystone.

The Switch 🦴🦴 *The Con Artists; Bluff Storia di Truffe e di Imbroglioni* **1976 (R)** An escaped convict takes the place of a talented conman and chaos ensues. **105m/C VHS, DVD.** *IT* Anthony Quinn, Adriano Celentano, Capucine, Corinne Clery; ***D:*** Sergio Corbucci; ***W:*** Massimo De Rita; ***C:*** Marcello Gatti; ***M:*** Lelio Luttazzi.

Switch 🦴🦴🦴 **1991 (R)** A chauvinist louse, slain by the girlfriends he misused, is sent back to Earth as an alluring female to learn the other side's point of view. The plot may lack urgency, but this is a sparkling adult comedy that scores as it pursues the gimmicky concept to a logical, outrageous and touching conclusion. Barkin's act as swaggering male stuck in a woman's body is a masterwork of physical humor. **104m/C VHS, DVD.** Ellen Barkin, Jimmy Smits, JoBeth Williams, Lorraine Bracco, Perry King, Bruce Payne, Tony Roberts; ***D:*** Blake Edwards; ***W:*** Blake Edwards; ***C:*** Dick Bush; ***M:*** Henry Mancini.

The Switch *The Baster* **2010 (PG-13)** Neurotic Wally (Bateman) learns his best friend Kassie (Aniston) is using artificial insemination to have a baby. So he secretly substitutes his own swimmers for the original donor's and then must live with the secret of his fatherhood. Adapted from the Jeffrey Eugenides' short story. **m/C DVD.** *US* Jennifer Aniston, Jason Bateman, Patrick Wilson, Scott Elrod, Juliette Lewis, Jeff Goldblum, Todd Louiso; ***D:*** Will Speck, Josh Gordon; ***W:*** Allan Loeb; ***C:*** Jess Hall; ***M:*** Alex Wurman.

Switchback 🦴🦴 *Going West in America* **1997 (R)** FBI agent Frank Lacrosse (Quaid) pursues the serial killer who kidnapped his son. Against the backdrop of a Texas sheriff's election and a Colorado snowstorm, the killer, who may or may not be a former rail worker (Glover) or the hitchhicking ex-doctor (Leto) he picked up, leads Lacrosse on a convoluted cat-and-mouse game with no apparent logic or motive. First-time director Stuart, who wrote "Die Hard" and "The Fugitive," wrote this one in film school, and it shows. Connect-the-dots set pieces and plot twists only provide Quaid more time to perfect his Harrison Ford impression and Glover more scenery and dialogue to chew. Ermey is impressive as the put-upon small-town sheriff. Stunt work is well done and the Colorado countryside looks great. **120m/C VHS, DVD.** Dennis Quaid, Danny Glover, Jared Leto, R. Lee Ermey, William Fichtner, Ted Levine, Leo Burmester, Merle Kennedy, Julio Oscar Mechoso; ***D:*** Jeb Stuart; ***W:*** Jeb Stuart; ***C:*** Oliver Wood; ***M:*** Basil Poledouris.

Switchblade Sisters WOOF! *The Jezebels; Playgirl Gang* **1975** Crime gang of female ex-cons wreaks pseudo-feminist havoc. Bruce is Lenny Bruce's daughter. **91m/C VHS, DVD.** Robbie Lee, Joanne Nail, Monica Gayle, Kitty Bruce, Asher Brauner, Chase Newhart, Marlene Clark, Janice Karman, Don Stark, Kate Murtagh, Bill Adler; ***D:*** Jack Hill; ***W:*** F.X. Maier; ***C:*** Stephen M. Katz; ***M:*** Les Baxter, Medusa, Chuck Day, Richard Person.

Switched at Birth 🦴🦴 ½ **1991 (PG)** A fact-based drama about two girls, switched in a hospital nursery at birth. Only when one girl dies, a decade later, do her parents discover that she could not have been their biological child. Their search for their daughter leads to an emotional conflict between the girl, the man that raised her, and the biological parents who seek to claim her. Beware of the sappy Hollywood ending; five years later the story of Kimberly Mays was still going through the U.S. judicial system. **200m/C VHS.** Bonnie Bedelia, Brian Kerwin, Ed Asner, Caroline McWilliams, John M. Jackson, Lois Smith, Eve Gordon, Judith Hoag, Ariana Richards; ***D:*** Waris Hussein. **TV**

Switching Channels 🦴🦴 ½ **1988 (PG)** A modernized remake of "His Girl Friday," and therefore the fourth version of "The Front Page." Beautiful TV anchorwoman (Turner) wants to marry handsome tycoon (Reeve), but her scheming ex-husband (Reynolds) gets in the way. Weak performances from everyone but Beatty and lackluster direction render this off-told story less funny than usual. **108m/C VHS.** Burt Reynolds, Kathleen Turner, Christopher Reeve, Ned Beatty, Henry Gibson, George Newbern, Al Waxman, Ken James, Joe Silver, Charles Kimbrough, Tony Rosato; ***D:*** Ted Kotcheff; ***W:*** Jonathan Reynolds; ***M:*** Michel Legrand.

Swoon 🦴🦴🦴 **1991** Kalin's directorial debut is a stylish rendering of the sensational 1924 kidnapping and murder of Bobby Franks by Richard Loeb and Nathan Leopold Jr. and their subsequent trial and imprisonment. Core elements of the case remain but Kalin imposes contemporary styles and morals on the past, particularly his protest against the homophobic attitudes influencing the trial while acknowledging the jaded and dispassionate behavior of the two young men. Previous cinematic versions of the murder case include "Rope" and "Compulsion" but Kalin graphically portrays the characters homosexuality, which was only hinted at in the earlier films. **95m/B VHS, DVD.** Daniel Schlachet, Craig Chester, Ron Vawter, Michael Kirby, Michael Stumm, Valda Z. Drabla, Natalie Stanford; ***D:*** Tom Kalin; ***W:*** Tom Kalin; ***C:*** Ellen Kuras; ***M:*** James Bennett. Sundance '92: Cinematog.

The Sword and the Cross 🦴 ½ **1958** A grade-B adventure about the life of Mary Magdelene. **93m/B VHS.** Yvonne De Carlo, Jorge Mistral; ***D:*** Carlo L. Bragaglia.

Sword & the Dragon 🦴🦴 *Ilya Mourometz* **1956** A young warrior must battle any number of giant mythical creatures. **81m/C VHS, DVD.** *RU* Boris Andreyer, Andrei Abrikosov; ***D:*** Alexander Ptushko.

The Sword & the Rose 🦴🦴 ½ *When Knighthood Was in Flower* **1953** Mary Tudor, sister of King Henry VIII, shuns the advances of a nobleman for the love of a commoner. Johns is an obstinate princess; Justice, a fine king. Based on the book "When Knighthood Was in Flower." **91m/C VHS.** Richard Todd, Glynis Johns, Michael Gough, Jane Barrett, James Robertson Justice; ***D:*** Ken Annakin; ***C:*** Geoffrey Unsworth.

Sword & the Sorcerer 🦴 ½ **1982 (R)** Young prince strives to regain control of his kingdom, now ruled by an evil knight and a powerful magician. Mediocre script and acting is enhanced by decent special effects. **100m/C VHS, DVD.** Lee Horsley, Kathleen Beller, George Maharis, Simon MacCorkindale, Richard Lynch, Richard Moll, Robert Tessier, Nina Van Pallandt, Anna Bjorn, Jeff Corey; ***D:*** Albert Pyun; ***W:*** Albert Pyun; ***C:*** Joseph Mangine; ***M:*** David Whitaker.

The Sword in the Stone 🦴🦴🦴 **1963 (G)** The Disney version of the first volume of T.H. White's "The Once and Future King" wherein King Arthur, as a boy, is instructed in the ways of the world by Merlin and Archimedes the owl. Although not in the Disney masterpiece fold, boasts the usual superior animation and a gripping mythological tale. **79m/C VHS, DVD.** ***D:*** Wolfgang Reitherman; ***W:*** Bill Peet; ***M:*** George Bruns; ***V:*** Ricky Sorenson, Sebastián Cabot, Karl Swenson, Junius Matthews, Alan Napier, Norman Alden, Martha Wentworth, Barbara Jo Allen.

Sword Masters: Brothers Five 🦴 1/2 *Wu hu tu long; Ng fu tiu lung; Brothers Five* **1970** Yen Hsing-Kung (Pei-pei Ching) has vowed revenge on the usual all powerful villain, and is on a quest to unite the five brothers of the Gao family to aid her. Like most revenge martial arts films, it's a little light on story and heavy on fights. In this case more so than usual as at least two thirds of the film is fight scenes—though at least they are pretty well done. **90m/C DVD.** *HK* Pei Pei Cheng, Han Chin, Yi Chang, Yuen Kao, Hua Yueh, Lieh Lo, Feng Tien, Feng Ku; ***D:*** Wei Lo; ***W:*** Wei Lo, Kuang Ni; ***C:*** Cho-Hua Wu; ***M:*** Fu-ling Wang.

Sword Masters: The Battle Wizard 🦴🦴 *Tian long ba bu; Tin lung bat bou; Battle Wizard* **1977** Less a martial arts film than a bizarre fantasy movie, loosely based on an old Chinese novel. Tuan Yu (Danny Lee) is a scholar pursuing the magical red python, which can grant superhuman strength and power. Standing in his way are a kung fu gorilla and a fire breathing wizard with metal chicken legs. **73m/C DVD.** *HK* Danny Lee, Ni Tien, Chen Chi Lin; ***D:*** Hsueh Li Pao; ***W:*** Louis Cha, Kuang Ni; ***C:*** Ting Pan Yuan; ***M:*** Yung-Yu Chen.

Sword Masters: Two Champions of Shaolin 🦴🦴 *Shao Lin yu Wu Dang; Two Champions of Shaolin; Two Champions of Death* **1980** Tung Chien-Chen (Meng Lo) is accepted into the Shaolin temple despite being a despised Manchu because his family has been murdered by the Manchu. Upon ending his apprenticeship in Kung Fu, he is told to keep his head low as the Manchurians and the Wu Tang clan are after the Shaolin temple, and while he tries to hide his rage it's inevitable he gets into a fight with a knife fighter from the Wu Tang looking for revenge on the Shaolin for an act of revenge they committed earlier. Basically everyone wants revenge on someone else. **105m/C DVD.** *HK* Tat-wah Cho, Yu Hsiao, Chung Kwan, Chien Sun, Siu-hou Chin, Ying Tan, Hsueh-erh Wen, Ching-Ching Yeung, Tai Ping Yu; ***D:*** Cheh Chang; ***W:*** Kuang Ni; ***C:*** Hui-chi Tsao.

Sword of Doom 🦴🦴🦴 *Daibosatsu Toge* **1967** A rousing samurai epic detailing the training of an impulsive, bloodlusting warrior by an elder expert. In Japanese with English subtitles. **120m/B VHS, DVD.** *JP* Tatsuya Nakadai, Toshiro Mifune; ***D:*** Kihachi Okamoto.

The Sword of El Cid 🦴 1/2 *La Spada del Cid* **1962** Not much dash and very little daring-do in this poorly plotted, overly dramatic saga of good vs. evil, Spanish style. Rightful heir to the crown threatens, challenges and enevitably crosses swords with the pretender to his throne. Costume mavens may find something to hold their interest. **86m/C VHS.** *SP IT* Roland Carey, Sandro Moretti, Chantal Deberg, Iliana Grimaldi, Jose Luis Pellicena, Daniela Bianchi; ***D:*** Miguel Iglesias.

Sword of Gideon 🦴🦴 1/2 **1986** An action-packed and suspenseful TV film about an elite commando group who set out to avenge the Munich Olympic killings of 1972. Adapted from "Vengeance" by George Jonas. **148m/C VHS, DVD.** Steven Bauer, Michael York, Rod Steiger, Colleen Dewhurst, Robert Joy, Laurent Malet, Lino Ventura, Leslie Hope; ***D:*** Michael Anderson Sr.; ***W:*** Chris Bryant; ***M:*** Georges Delerue. **TV**

Sword of Honor 🦴 1/2 **1994 (R)** Undercover cop and martial arts expert Johnny Lee (Leigh) investigates his partner's mysterious death amidst the tawdry glamor of Vegas. **97m/C VHS, DVD.** Steven Leigh, Sophia Crawford, Angelo Tiffe, Jerry Tiffe, Jeff Pruitt, Debbie Scofield; ***D:*** Robert Tiffe; ***W:*** Robert Tiffe, Clay Ayers; ***M:*** David Rubinstein. **VIDEO**

Sword of Honour 🦴🦴 **2001** After a divorce, 35-year-old Guy Crouchback (Craig) finds new resolve by joining up (although his unit is composed of misfits) and battling the Nazis—until the absurdities of war cause cracks in his idealism. Based on Evelyn Waugh's WWII trilogy. **200m/C DVD.** *GB* Daniel Craig, Katrin Cartlidge, Megan Dodds, Robert Pugh, Guy Henry, Nicholas Boulton; ***D:*** Bill Anderson; ***W:*** William Boyd; ***C:*** Daf Hobson; ***M:*** Nina Humphreys. **TV**

Sword of Lancelot 🦴🦴 1/2 *Lancelot and Guinevere* **1963** A costume version of the Arthur-Lancelot-Guinevere triangle, with plenty of swordplay and a sincere respect for the old legend. **115m/C VHS, DVD.** *GB* Cornel Wilde, Jean Wallace, Brian Aherne, George Baker; ***D:*** Cornel Wilde.

Sword of Monte Cristo 🦴 1/2 **1951** Masked female avenger, seeking the liberty of the French people, discovers a valuable sword that holds the key to a vast fortune. But the sword is also desired by an evil government minister. **80m/C VHS.** George Montgomery, Rita (Paula) Corday; ***D:*** Maurice Geraghty.

Sword of Sherwood Forest 🦴🦴 1/2 **1960** The Earl of Newark plots the murder of the Archbishop of Canterbury in yet another rendition of the Robin Hood legend. Cushing is truly evil as the villain. **80m/C VHS.** *GB* Richard Greene, Peter Cushing, Niall MacGinnis, Richard Pasco, Jack (Gwyllam) Gwillim, Sarah Branch, Nigel Green, Oliver Reed; ***D:*** Terence Fisher.

Sword of the Valiant 🦴🦴 **1983 (PG)** The Green Knight arrives in Camelot to challenge Gawain. Remake of "Gawain And The Green Knight." Connery adds zest to a minor epic. **102m/C VHS, DVD.** *GB* Sean Connery, Miles O'Keeffe, Cyrielle Claire, Leigh Lawson, Trevor Howard, Peter Cushing, Wilfrid Brambell, Lila Kedrova, John Rhys-Davies; ***D:*** Stephen Weeks; ***W:*** Philip M. Breen; ***C:*** Frederick A. (Freddie) Young.

Sword of Venus 🦴 *Island of Monte Cristo* **1953** Uninspired production finds the son of the Count of Monte Cristo the victim in a scheme to deprive him of his wealth. **73m/B VHS, DVD.** Robert Clarke, Catherine McLeod, Dan O'Herlihy, William Schallert; ***D:*** Harold Daniels.

Swordfish 🦴🦴 **2001 (R)** CIA operative Gabriel Shear (Travolta) uses associate Ginger (Berry) to coerce a computer hacker (Jackman), who's just been released from prison, to steal nine billion dollars from a DEA slush fund. In return, the hacker gets a fresh start with his wife and daughter. The plot goes on from there, but it's too convoluted and pointless to bother with. As is usually the case with anything directed by Sena or produced by Joel Silver, the emphasis is on flash, high-energy action set pieces, and collateral damage, all of which is well done, if eventually repetitive, here. Travolta is an expert at playing the smirking supervillain, but it does wear. Jackman and Cheadle give better performances than the flick deserves, and Berry has fun with her obligatory femme fatale role. **99m/C VHS, DVD, Blu-ray Disc, UMD, HD DVD.** *US* John Travolta, Hugh Jackman, Halle Berry, Don Cheadle, Vinnie Jones, Sam Shepard, Zach Grenier, Camryn Grimes, Rudolf Martin, Drea De Matteo; ***D:*** Dominic Sena; ***W:*** Skip Woods; ***C:*** Paul Cameron; ***M:*** Christopher Young.

Swords of Death 🦴🦴 **1971** Final film by Uchida, released posthumously, deals with the adventurous period exploits of the irrepressible Miyamoto Musashi. With English subtitles. **76m/C VHS.** *JP* Kinnosuke Nakamura, Rentaro Mikuni; ***D:*** Tomu Uchida.

The Swordsman 🦴🦴 1/2 **1992 (R)** The quest to return the stolen sword of the legendary Alexander the Great to a museum is muscular detective Lamas' assignment. Turns out the detective and his evil millionaire antagonist have been chasing each other through time in their endless quest for revenge and power. **98m/C VHS, DVD.** Lorenzo Lamas, Claire Stansfield, Michael Champion; ***D:*** Michael Kennedy; ***W:*** Michael Kennedy.

Swordsmen in Double Flag Town 🦴 1/2 **1991** Stylized martial arts flick best-appreciated by aficionados. Young Hei Ge (Gao) enters the village of Double Flag Town to claim his promised bride. He kills a man trying to rape his intended and provokes the wrath of the man's brother, a well-known killer called the Lethal Swordsman. Naturally, there's the Chinese equivalent of a showdown at high noon. Mandarin with subtitles. **90m/C DVD.** *CH* Wei Gao, Mana Zhao, Jiang Chang, Haiying Sun, Gang Wang; ***D:*** Ping He; ***W:*** Ping He, Zhangguang Yang; ***C:*** Deling Ma; ***M:*** Long Tao.

Sworn Enemies 🦴🦴 1/2 **1996 (R)** Clifton Santier (Greene) goes on a killing spree in a small town where the local sheriff turns out to be his ex-partner, Pershing Quinn (Pare). Now the two enemies decide that only death will settle their old (and new) scores. **101m/C VHS, DVD.** *CA* Peter Greene, Michael Pare, Macha Grenon; ***D:*** Shimon Dotan; ***W:*** Rod Hewitt; ***C:*** Sylvain Brault; ***M:*** Walter Christian Rothe, Richard Anthony Boast.

Sworn to Justice 🦴 1/2 **1997 (R)** Psychologist Jana Dane (Rothrock) wakes up with psychic powers after sustaining a serious head injury from the burglars who killed her sister and nephew. Jana then decides to put her new abilities to work for her by becoming a night time avenger. **90m/C VHS, DVD.** Cynthia Rothrock, Kurt McKinney, Tony LoBianco, Brad Dourif, Mako, Kenn Scott; ***D:*** Paul Maslak; ***W:*** Robert Easter; ***C:*** Richard Benda; ***M:*** John Coda.

Sybil 🦴🦴🦴 **1976** Fact-based story of a woman who developed 16 distinct personalities, and the supportive psychiatrist who helped her put the pieces of her ego together. Excellent production featuring Field's Emmy-winning performance. **122m/C VHS, DVD.** Sally Field, Joanne Woodward, Brad Davis, Martine Bartlett, Jane Hoffman; ***D:*** Daniel Petrie. **TV**

Sydney White 🦴🦴 **2007 (PG-13)** Hi ho, hi ho, it's off to college we go. Shut out of her dead mother's sorority, Sydney (Bynes) ends up living with seven, ahem, dorks and must find a way to defeat "fairest-of-them-all" sorority president Rachel (Paxton), win the heart of dreamy Tyler Prince (Long), and teach the entire campus to appreciate the diverse assortment of nerds she calls sidekicks. Bynes has ample charm and talent, but that can't overcome the failings of this modern-day retelling of the Snow White story, whose message is undercut by the fact that it mocks a lot of the characters as much as it uplifts them. **105m/C DVD.** *US* Amanda Bynes, Matt Long, Sara Paxton, John Schneider, Crystal Hunt, Jack Carpenter, Jeremy Howard; ***D:*** Joe Nussbaum; ***W:*** Chad Gomez Creasy; ***C:*** Mark Irwin; ***M:*** Deborah Lurie.

Sylvester 🦴🦴 **1985 (PG)** A 16-year-old girl and a cranky stockyard boss team up to train a battered horse named Sylvester for the National Equestrian trials. Nice riding sequences and good performances can't overcome familiar plot, but the kids will enjoy this one. **104m/C VHS, DVD.** Melissa Gilbert, Richard Farnsworth, Michael Schoeffling, Constance Towers; ***D:*** Tim Hunter.

Sylvia 🦴🦴 1/2 **1986 (PG)** Biography of author/educator Sylvia Ashton-Warner, and her efforts to teach Maori children in New Zealand to read via unorthodox methods. David is a marvel. Based on Ashton-Warner's books "Teacher" and "I Passed This Way." **99m/C VHS.** *NZ* Eleanor David, Tom Wilkinson, Nigel Terry, Mary Regan; ***D:*** Michael Firth.

Sylvia 🦴🦴 1/2 **2003 (R)** Paltrow gamely takes on the life of the talented but tortured American poet Sylvia Plath in Jeff's bummer biopic. Following Plath's seven-year marriage to English poet Ted Hughes (Craig) until her 1963 suicide in London at 30, pic deals impartially with the details of the affair that caused Plath to jettison Hughes. Also explores her mental illness and long-time grief over her father's death, as well as her conflicted feelings over the dueling roles of artist and wife/mother, and icon for budding feminist issues. Thoughtfully directed, although Paltrow doesn't quite get her teeth into the challenging role. **110m/C VHS, DVD.** *GB* Gwyneth Paltrow, Daniel Craig, Jared Harris, Amira Casar, Andrew Havill, Sam Troughton, Anthony Strachan, Lucy Davenport, Blythe Danner, Michael Gambon, David Birkin, Michael Mears; ***D:*** Christine Jeffs; ***W:*** John Brownlow; ***C:*** John Toon; ***M:*** Gabriel Yared.

Sylvia and the Phantom 🦴🦴🦴 *Sylvia and the Ghost* **1945** A charming French comedy about a lonely young girl who is befriended by the ghost of a man killed decades earlier in a duel over the girl's grandmother. Based on the play by Alfred Adam. In French with English subtitles. **88m/B VHS.** *FR* Odette Joyeux, Jacques Tati, Francois Perier; ***D:*** Claude Autant-Lara.

Sylvia Scarlett 🦴🦴 1/2 **1935** An odd comedy/drama about a woman who masquerades as a boy while on the run with her father, who causes all kinds of instinctive confusion in the men she meets. **94m/B VHS, DVD.** Katharine Hepburn, Cary Grant, Brian Aherne, Edmund Gwenn, Natalie Paley, Dennie Moore, Lennox Pawle, Daisy Belmore, Nola Luxford; ***D:*** George Cukor; ***W:*** John Collier, Gladys Unger, Mortimer Offner; ***C:*** Russell Metty.

Sympathy for Mr. Vengeance 🦴🦴🦴 *Boksuneun naui geot* **2002 (R)** The first and most brutal of director Park Chan-wook's Vengeance trilogy. A young deaf-mute works in a factory to gain money for his ailing sister's kidney transplant. After being laid off he manages to get a $10k loan from a bank to buy her a kidney from the black market. Instead he is beaten unconscious and robbed, and one of his kidneys is removed, sparking an increasingly disturbing cycle of retribution and violence, which manages to actually further the story (as opposed to being merely gratuitous). **121m/C DVD.** *JP* Kang-ho Song, Du-na Bae, Dae-yeon Lee, Ha-Kyun Shin, Bo-bae Han; ***D:*** Chan-wook Park; ***W:*** Chan-wook Park, Jae-sun Lee, Mu-yeong Lee, Yong-jong Lee; ***C:*** Byeong-il Kim.

Sympathy for the Devil 🦴🦴 *One Plus One* **1970** Rolling Stones provide music for confused, revolutionary documentary. Episodic jumble is odd, sometimes fascinating. **110m/C VHS.** *FR* Mick Jagger, Rolling Stones; ***D:*** Jean-Luc Godard.

Sympathy for the Underdog 🦴🦴 1/2 *Bakuto Gaijin Butai; Gamblers in Okinawa* **1971** Old-fashioned yakuza Masuo Gunji (Tsuruta) is released after a 10-year prison stint and discovers that all the dock action has been commandeered by the Daitokai crime syndicate. So he gets his former crew together and tells them he wants to muscle in on the black market in Okinawa instead. This doesn't prove to be so easy. There's a suitably bloody final showdown between the criminal gangs. Japanese with subtitles. **93m/C DVD.** *JP* Koji Tsurata, Tomisaburo Wakayama, Tsunehiko Watase, Noboru Ando, Kenji Imai, Akiko Kudo; ***D:*** Kinji Fukasaku; ***W:*** Kinji Fukasaku, Hiro Matsuda, Fumio Konami; ***C:*** Hanjiro Nakazawa; ***M:*** Takeo Yamashita.

Synapse 🦴🦴 **1995 (R)** Black-marketeer Andre (Makepeace) is doublecrossed by a partner and arrested by Life Corp., which runs this futuristic civilization. As an experimental punishment, his mind is implanted into the body of Celeste (Duffy), who manages to escape and join up with a band of revolutionaries determined to destroy the evil corporation. Fast-paced story and good special effects. **89m/C VHS, DVD.** Karen Duffy, Saul Rubinek, Matt McCoy, Chris Makepeace; ***D:*** Allan Goldstein.

Synecdoche, New York 🦴🦴🦴 **2008 (R)** A genius in his own mind, stage director Caden Cotard (Hoffman), who suffers from a variety of ailments, goes off the deep end to conceive his grand opus: a replication of Manhattan in a warehouse and a re-enactment of his life-is-art philosophy. Oscar-winning writer Kaufmann shows he has as much talent behind the camera in his directorial debut. Hoffman delivers another Oscar-worthy performance and anchors the occasionally meandering, existential script, which showcases Kaufmann's unique voice and ability to portray melancholy with such depth and wit as to avoid his material being utterly depressing. **124m/C DVD.** *US* Philip Seymour Hoffman, Samantha Morton, Michelle Williams, Catherine Keener, Emily Watson, Dianne Wiest, Jennifer Jason Leigh, Hope Davis, Tom Noonan; ***D:*** Charlie Kaufman; ***W:*** Charlie Kaufman; ***C:*** Fred Elmes; ***M:*** Jon Brion. Ind. Spirit '09: First Feature.

Syngenor 🦴 1/2 **1990 (R)** Syngenor stands for Synthesized Genetic Organism, to differentiate it from all other organisms. Created by science, it escapes, and a crack team of scientists and gung-ho military types are mobilized to track it down. **98m/C VHS, DVD.** Starr Andreeff, Mitchell Laurance, David Gale, Charles Lucia, Riva Spier, Jeff Doucette, Bill Gratton, Lewis Arquette, Jon Korkes, Melanie Shatner; ***D:*** George Elanjian Jr.; ***M:*** Tom Chase, Steve Rucker.

The Syrian Bride 🦴🦴 **2004** Mona (Khoury) isn't thrilled about her arranged marriage to her Syrian cousin since it means she can't return to visit her family in the Golan Heights because of the political situation. But Mona, accompanied by her older sister Amal (Abbass), prepares to fulfill her family's wishes despite endless red tape at the border crossing. Arabic and Hebrew with subtitles. **97m/C DVD.** *IS FR GE* Hiam Abbass, Ashraf Barhoum, Clara Khoury, Eyad Sheety, Derar Sliman; ***D:*** Eran Riklis; ***W:*** Eran Riklis, Suha Arraf; ***C:*** Michael Wiesweg; ***M:*** Cyril Morin.

Syriana 🦴🦴🦴 ½ **2005 (R)** Gaghan once again uses multiple storylines to tackle a major social issue (after his excellent "Traffic"). This time he studies the interactions of foreign and U.S. governments, Wall Street, the CIA, energy companies, ordinary workers, and lawyers that control the flow of oil to consumers. Dense narrative follows a displaced oil field worker, corporate troubleshooting lawyer (Wright), an energy analyst (Damon) who suffers a tragic loss, a betrayed CIA operative (Clooney), an oil-rich prince (Siddiq), and a behind-the-scenes power broker (Plummer) as they maneuver to, intentionally or not, affect who controls the energy market, through backroom deals, terrorism (or the threat of it), and even less-pleasant methods. Well-done, if confusing film will generate discussion and reflection. **126m/C DVD, Blu-ray Disc, HD DVD.** *US* George Clooney, Matt Damon, Jeffrey Wright, Chris Cooper, William Hurt, Tim Blake Nelson, Amanda Peet, Christopher Plummer, Alexander Siddig, Akbar Kurtha, Max Minghella, David Clennon, Robert Foxworth, Mark Strong, Mazhar Munir, Khan Shadid Ahmed, William C. Mitchell, Dadral Sonnell; ***D:*** Stephen Gaghan; ***W:*** Stephen Gaghan; ***C:*** Robert Elswit; ***M:*** Alexandre Desplat, Cynthia Weil. Oscars '05: Support. Actor (Clooney); Golden Globes '06: Support. Actor (Clooney); Natl. Bd. of Review '05: Adapt. Screenplay.

T-Bird Gang 🦴 ½ **1959** A high school student goes undercover to infiltrate a teen gang. When his cover is blown, things get hairy. Laughable sleazebag production. **75m/B VHS, DVD.** Ed Nelson, John Brinkley, Pat George, Beach Dickerson, Tony Miller; ***D:*** Richard Harbinger; ***M:*** Shelley Manne.

T Bone N Weasel 🦴🦴 **1992 (PG-13)** Hines and Lloyd play not-so-ex-cons who steal a car and try to lead a life of ease. Crime doesn't pay. **94m/C VHS.** Gregory Hines, Christopher Lloyd, Ned Beatty, Larry Hankin, Graham Jarvis, Rusty Schwimmer, Rip Torn, Sam Whipple; ***D:*** Lewis Teague; ***C:*** Thomas Del Ruth; ***M:*** Steve Tyrell. **CABLE**

T-Force 🦴🦴 ½ **1994 (R)** T-Force is a successful cybernetic law enforcement team set up in the year 2007. But when innocent people get caught in the T-Force crossfire, a team shutdown is ordered, causing the members to turn renegade and fight for their survival instead. The plot rarely gets in the way of the hard-hitting action. **101m/C VHS, DVD.** Jack Scalia, Erin Gray, Evan Lurie, Daron McBee; ***D:*** Richard Pepin.

T-Men 🦴🦴🦴 **1947** Treasury Department agents Dennis O'Brien (O'Keefe) and Tony Genaro (Ryder) infiltrate a mob counterfeiting gang. Filmed in semi-documentary style, exciting tale serves also as an effective commentary on the similarities between the agents and those they pursue. Mann and cinematographer Alton do especially fine work here. **96m/B VHS, DVD.** Alfred Ryder, Dennis O'Keefe, June Lockhart, Mary Meade, Wallace Ford, Charles McGraw; ***D:*** Anthony Mann; ***W:*** John C. Higgins; ***C:*** John Alton; ***M:*** Paul Sawtell.

Table for Five 🦴🦴 ½ **1983 (PG)** A divorced father takes his children on a Mediterranean cruise and while sailing, he learns that his ex-wife has died. The father and his ex-wife's husband struggle over who should raise the children. Sentimental and well-acted. **120m/C VHS, DVD.** Jon Voight, Millie Perkins, Richard Crenna, Robbie Kiger, Roxana Zal, Son Hoang Bui, Marie-Christine Barrault, Kevin Costner; ***D:*** Robert Lieberman; ***W:*** David Seltzer; ***M:*** Miles Goodman.

Table for Three 🦴🦴 **2009 (R)** After Scott's (Routh) girlfriend dumps him and his roommate moves away, he meets seemingly perfect couple Mary (Bush) and Ryan (Bradford) and they move in. Without any concept of personal boundaries, the duo are soon taking over Scott's life, which becomes a big problem when he falls for Leslie (Morrison). Mary and Ryan don't want any interference in their perfect arrangement, which complements their dysfunctional relationship, and try to sabotage the romance (in a funny, not horrific way). **93m/C DVD.** Brandon Routh, Sophia Bush, Jesse Bradford, Jenny (Jennifer) Morrison, Johnny Galecki; ***D:*** Michael Samonek; ***W:*** Michael Samonek; ***C:*** Matthew Irving; ***M:*** Philip Griffin.

Table One 🦴 ½ **2000 (R)** Mildly amusing but too familiar comedy finds Norman (Herman) and his buddies deciding to open a restaurant/bar in Manhattan so they can meet chicks. But they can't quite raise enough money, so Norman gets a local mobster to become a partner, only the mobster sends along his right-hand man Jimmy (Baldwin) to keep an eye on his investment. **84m/C VHS, DVD.** David Herman, Stephen Baldwin, Michael Rooker, Luis Guzman, Burt Young, Ben Shenkman; ***D:*** Michael Scott Bregman; ***W:*** Michael Scott Bregman.

Table Settings 🦴🦴 **1984** A taped performance of James Lapines' comedy about the lives of three generations of a Jewish family. **90m/C VHS.** Robert Klein, Stockard Channing, Dinah Manoff, Eileen Heckart; ***D:*** Trevor Evans; ***W:*** James Lapine.

Tabloid! 🦴 ½ **1988** Unorthodox woman prints and sells racy trash for enquiring minds. **99m/C VHS.** Scott Davis, Glen Coburn; ***D:*** Bret McCormick, Matt Shaffen.

Taboo 🦴🦴 *Gohatto* **1999** In 1865 in Kyoto, the Shogunate is crumbling and Japanese politics are turbulent. Two new recruits join a strict samurai academy—the rugged Tashiro (Asano) and a delicate teenager named Kano (Matsuda). Kano soon proves his worth to the militia commander, Kondo (Sai), and Captain Hijikata (Kitano) but his androgynous beauty begins to cause dissension—leading Kondo to forbid any relations between his men. Japanese with subtitles. **100m/C VHS, DVD.** *JP* Takeshi "Beat" Kitano, Ryuhei Matsuda, Shinji Takeda, Tadanobu Asano; ***D:*** Nagisa Oshima; ***W:*** Nagisa Oshima; ***C:*** Toyomichi Kurita; ***M:*** Ryuichi Sakamoto.

Taboo 🦴 **2002 (R)** Mish-mash horror/psycho-thriller flick. Six college friends gather at a remote mansion to play a provocative game of "Taboo" involving a sex question. The following New Year's Eve they gather again and each receives an anonymous note condemning their previous answer. Then the killings start. **80m/C VHS, DVD.** Nick Stahl, Eddie Kaye Thomas, January Jones, Lori Heuring, Derek Hamilton, Amber Benson; ***D:*** Max Makowski; ***W:*** Chris Fisher; ***M:*** Ryan Beveridge.

Tabu: A Story of the South Seas 🦴🦴🦴 ½ **1931** Fascinating docudrama about a young pearl diver's ill-fated romance. The gods have declared the young woman he desires "taboo" to all men. Filmed on location in Tahiti. Authored and produced by Murnau and Flaherty. Flaherty left in mid-production due to artistic differences with Murnau, who was later killed in an auto accident one week before the premiere of film. **81m/B VHS, DVD.** ***D:*** Robert Flaherty, F.W. Murnau; ***C:*** Floyd Crosby. Oscars '31: Cinematog., Natl. Film Reg. '94.

Tactical Assault 🦴🦴 ½ **1999 (R)** During the Gulf War, Air Force pilot John Holiday (Hauer) loses it under pressure and nearly shoots down an unarmed passenger jet. Pilot Lee Banning (Patrick) is forced to shoot down Holiday's plane instead to save the situation. But Holiday doesn't see things that way and decides to get revenge on Lee. Good action in what's really a revenge thriller. **89m/C VHS, DVD.** Rutger Hauer, Robert Patrick, Isabel Glasser, Ken Howard; ***D:*** Mark Griffiths. **VIDEO**

Tadpole 🦴🦴 ½ **2002 (PG-13)** You know you've hit a chord when your movie's title has been adopted as a verb (tadpoling) for the trend of older women cruising younger men. Precocious, prep-schooler Oscar Grubman (Stanford) comes home to Manhattan to spend the holidays with his remarried dad (Ritter) and his new stepmom (Weaver), on whom he promptly develops a crush. Soon the unrequited love for his new mum, the aptly named Eve, is soothed instead by her cradle-robbing best friend (a show-stealing Neuwirth). Stanford shines, even through the drab digital camerawork, in this witty, new millennium "Graduate." **77m/C VHS, DVD.** *US* Aaron Stanford, Sigourney Weaver, John Ritter, Bebe Neuwirth, Robert Iler, Peter Appel, Adam LeFevre; ***D:*** Gary Winick; ***W:*** Heather McGowan, Niels Mueller; ***C:*** Hubert Taczanowski.

Tae Guk Gi: The Brotherhood of War 🦴🦴🦴 **2004 (R)** Two brothers are dragged into the ugly chaos of the Korean War when they're conscripted into the South Korean army after North Korea invades. Elder brother Jin-tae does what he can to protect his promising younger brother Jin-seok from the conflict, but both are swept up in the carnage and blood lust. Graphic and powerful anti-war film that puts the viewer in the center of what for most Americans is a historical footnote. Dizzyingly violent battle scenes may make some queasy. **140m/C DVD.** *KN* Dong-Kun Jang, Won Bin, Lee Eun-joo; ***D:*** Kang Je-gyu; ***W:*** Kang Je-gyu; ***C:*** Hong Kyung-Pyo; ***M:*** Lee Dong-Jun.

Taffin 🦴 ½ **1988 (R)** An Irish bill collector battles a group of corrupt businessmen who want to replace the local soccer field with a hazardous chemical plant. Pretty dull fare, overall, with Brosnan much less charismatic than usual. **96m/C VHS, DVD.** *GB* Pierce Brosnan, Ray McAnally, Alison Doody, Patrick Bergin; ***D:*** Francis Megahy; ***W:*** David Ambrose.

Tag: The Assassination Game 🦴 ½ **1982 (PG)** An exciting new game has been discovered by a group of university students. Players act as spies and assassins, "killing" each other to make points. But a school newspaper sportswriter finds the game has become more real than make-believe. Timely topic in the early '80s when Dungeons and Dragons and other "war" games were popular on college campuses across the nation. **92m/C VHS.** Robert Carradine, Linda Hamilton, Michael Winslow, Kristine DeBell, Perry Lang; ***D:*** Nick Castle; ***W:*** Nick Castle.

Tagget 🦴 **1990 (PG-13)** A former CIA operative who has erased his nightmarish stint in Vietnam gradually begins to recall his past. When pieces of the puzzle begin to come together, he remembers a few things that the government would prefer he forget. Soon, CIA men are on his trail and their mission is to see that he forgets his past—permanently. **89m/C VHS.** Daniel J. Travanti, William Sadler, Roxanne Hart, Stephen Tobolowsky, Peter Michael Goetz, Sarah Douglas, Noel Harrison; ***D:*** Richard T. Heffron. **CABLE**

Tai-Pan 🦴 ½ **1986 (R)** A 19th century Scottish trader and his beautiful Chinese mistress are the main characters in this confusing attempt to dramatize the story of Hong Kong's development into a thriving trading port. Too many subplots and characters are introduced in a short time to do justice to James Clavell's novel of the same name, the basis for the movie. The first American production completely filmed in China. **130m/C VHS, DVD.** Bryan Brown, Joan Chen, John Stanton, Kyra Sedgwick, Tim Guinee, Russell Wong, Bert Remsen; ***D:*** Daryl Duke; ***W:*** John Briley; ***C:*** Jack Cardiff; ***M:*** Maurice Jarre.

Tail Lights Fade 🦴🦴 **1999 (R)** Angie (Allen) is living in Toronto when she learns her marijuana-dealing brother has been busted. So she convinces boyfriend Cole (Meyer) that they should drive to Vancouver in order to destroy his greenhouse crop before the cops discover it. And for some reason, Cole decides this would be a perfect opportunity to convince their friends Bruce (Busey) and Wendy (Richards) that they should indulge in a cross-country relay race. Dumb. Title comes from a Buffalo Tom song. **87m/C VHS, DVD.** *CA* Tanya Allen, Breckin Meyer, Jake Busey, Denise Richards, Lisa Marie, Elizabeth Berkley, Jaimz Woolvett; ***D:*** Malcolm Ingram; ***W:*** Matthew Gissing; ***C:*** Brian Pearson.

The Tailor of Panama 🦴🦴🦴 ½ **2000 (R)** British spy Andrew Osnard (Brosnan) threatens to expose the shady past of society tailor Harry Pendel (Rush) unless Harry passes on information about the political situation in Panama. But since Harry doesn't really know anything, he just makes up plausible lies. Le Carre and Boorman create a smart, cynical film from Le Carre's 1996 novel, utilizing Brosnan to treak his famous alter-ego and expose the corruption of post-Cold War espionage and Western foreign affairs. Well-written, with believable characterizations and subtle, consistent plotting, and as an added bonus, the performances match the high standards of the writing. **109m/C VHS, DVD.** *US IR* Pierce Brosnan, Geoffrey Rush, Jamie Lee Curtis, Brendan Gleeson, Catherine McCormack, Leonor Varela, Harold Pinter, Daniel Radcliffe, David Hayman, Mark Margolis, Martin Ferrero, John Fortune; ***D:*** John Boorman; ***W:*** John Boorman, Andrew Davies, John Le Carre; ***C:*** Philippe Rousselot; ***M:*** Shaun Davey.

Tails You Live, Heads You're Dead 🦴🦴 **1995 (R)** Cable thriller features Bernsen as psycho Neil Jones, who kills at random—and tells a stranger, Jeff Quint (McGinley), whom he met at a bar that the man is his next victim. After several unsuccessful attempts on his life, Quint turns to private detective McKinley (Matheson) for help. Based on the short story "Liar's Dice" by Bill Pronzini. **91m/C VHS.** Corbin Bernsen, Ted McGinley, Tim Matheson, Maria Del Mar; ***D:*** Tim Matheson; ***W:*** Miguel Tejada-Flores; ***C:*** Francois Protat; ***M:*** David Michael Frank. **CABLE**

Tailspin: Behind the Korean Airline Tragedy 🦴🦴 **1989** Made-for-TV docudrama on the 1983 downing of Korean Aire flight 007 in Soviet airspace. Purports to show the U.S. government's reaction to what became a major international incident. **82m/C VHS.** Michael Moriarty, Michael Murphy, Chris Sarandon, Harris Yulin, Gavan O'Herlihy, Ed O'Ross; ***D:*** David Darlow; ***M:*** David Ferguson.

Tailspin Tommy 🦴🦴 **1934** Features 12 chapters of the great action serial. Intrepid pilot helps a small airline win a mail contract then must battle an unscrupulous rival to keep it. **248m/B VHS.** Maurice Murphy, Noah Beery Jr., Walter Miller, Patricia Farr, Grant Withers, John Davidson, William Desmond, Charles A. Browne; ***D:*** Lew Landers.

Tainted 🦴 ½ **1988** Small-town woman tries to endure after being raped. Both her husband and the attacker are killed, and she is forced to conceal their deaths. Poorly scripted. **90m/C VHS.** Shari Shattuck, Park Overall, Gene Tootle, Magilla Schaus, Blaque Fowler; ***D:*** Orestes Matacena.

Tainted 🦴🦴 ½ **1998** Ever wonder what would happen if the guys from "Clerks" fell in with a bunch of vampires? Well, lucky you. Now you can find out. Video clerks Ryan and J.T. hitch a ride to the midnight movie with their new co-worker Alex, who just happens to be a vampire whose ex is shacking up with the new vamp in town, who wants to taint the city's blood supply with undead blood. Script has many laughs, lots of attitude, and plenty of pop-culture knowledge, but gets a bit windy at times. Sometimes the actors seem to to trying a little too hard, but it doesn't detract from the story. Filmed in Detroit with lots of excellent local product placement. **106m/C VHS.** Dusan "Dean" Cechvala, Greg James, Sean Farley, Jason Brouwer, Tina Kapousis, Edward Zeimis, Robert St. Mary, Brian Evans; ***D:*** Brian Evans; ***W:*** Sean Farley; ***C:*** Brian Evans; ***M:*** Jessie McClear. **VIDEO**

Tainted Blood 🦴🦴 **1993 (R)** Welch stars as an investigative reporter whose latest story has her attempting to find the teenage twin of a psychotic killer. **86m/C VHS.** Raquel Welch, Alley Mills, Kerri Green, Natasha Gregson Wagner, Joan Van Ark; ***D:*** Matthew Patrick; ***W:*** Kathleen Rowell, Ginny Cerrella; ***C:*** Billy Dickson.

Tainted Image 🦴🦴 **1991** Artist woman starts to lose sanity with help of boyfriend, psycho neighbor and rash of bizarre deaths. She turns to canvas for solace and decides she needs secret ingredient that can't be found in art supply store to complete masterpiece. **95m/C VHS.** Tom Saunders, Sandra Frances, Annetta Arpin, Ken La Mothe, Heidi Emerich, Steve Kornacki; ***D:*** Steve Kornacki.

The Take 🦴🦴 **1990 (R)** Recovering alcoholic cop faces wrath of drug lord and marriage on the rocks. **91m/C VHS.** Ray Sharkey, R. Lee Ermey, Lisa Hartman Black, Larry Manetti, Joe Lala; ***D:*** Leon Ichaso; ***W:*** Edward Anhalt, Handel Glassberg; ***M:*** David Beal.

The Take ½ **2007 (R)** Armored car driver Felix (Leguizamo) works hard to support his wife Marina (Perez) and their kids in L.A.'s tough Boyle Heights neighborhood. Felix barely survives a hijacking, carried out by vicious Adell Baldwin (Gibson). Shot in the head, Felix struggles with memory loss and anger issues and then learns the bad guys are trying to frame him for their crimes, but not if he gets to them first. **91m/C DVD.** John Leguizamo, Rosie Perez, Tyrese Gibson, Bobby Cannavale, Yul Vazquez, Carlos Sanz, Roger Guenveur Smith, Matthew Hatchette, Jake Muxworthy; ***D:*** Brad Furman; ***W:*** Jonas Pate, Josh Pate; ***C:*** Lukas Ettlin; ***M:*** Chris Hajian. **VIDEO**

Take a Hard Ride ½ **1975 (R)** Dull spaghetti western about a cowboy transporting money to Mexico, evading bandits and bounty hunters. **103m/C VHS, DVD.** *IT* Jim Brown, Lee Van Cleef, Fred Williamson, Jim Kelly, Barry Sullivan; ***D:*** Anthony M. Dawson; ***M:*** Jerry Goldsmith.

Take Care of My Cat ½ *Goyangileul butaghae* **2001** Five girlfriends graduate from a port city in Korea and try to make lives for themselves after high school, with varying degrees of success. The girls try to arrange for reunions to remain together despite their distance. Uses the same bleaching method as "Seven" to achieve a kind of odd color palette for the film. **112m/C DVD.** *KN* Du-na Bae, Yu-won Lee, Ji-young Ok, Eung-sil Lee; ***D:*** Jae-eun Jeong; ***W:*** Jae-eun Jeong; ***C:*** Yeong-hwon Choi.

Take Down **1979 (PG)** Hermann is charming as a high school English teacher turned reluctant wrestling coach. **96m/C VHS.** Lorenzo Lamas, Kathleen Lloyd, Maureen McCormick, Edward Herrmann, Nicolas Beauvy, Stephen Furst, Kevin Hooks; ***D:*** Keith Merrill.

Take Down ½ *Deliver Them from Evil: The Taking of Alta View* **1992 (PG-13)** Rick Worthington (Hamlin) takes hostages in a Utah hospital maternity ward, seeking revenge on the doctors who sterilized his wife. He threatens to detonate a bomb even as a hostage negogiator (O'Quinn) tries to defuse the situation. **96m/C VHS, DVD.** Harry Hamlin, Teri Garr, Terry O'Quinn, Gary Frank, Keith Coulouris; ***D:*** Peter Levin; ***W:*** John Miglis; ***C:*** Ronald Orieux; ***M:*** Mark Snow. **TV**

Take It Big ½ **1944** Uninspired B-musical starring the Tin Man from the "Wizard of Oz." Haley is an impoverished actor who inherits a ranch and saves it by—surprise—putting on a show. ♫ Sunday, Monday, and Always; Love and Learn; Life Can Be Beautiful; Take It Big; I'm a Big Success with You. **75m/B VHS.** Jack Haley, Harriet Hilliard Nelson, Mary Beth Hughes, Arline Judge, Nils T. Granlund, Fuzzy Knight, Ozzie Nelson; ***D:*** Frank McDonald; ***W:*** Howard J. Green; ***C:*** Fred H. Jackman Jr.

Take It to the Limit ½ **2000** Troubled teen Rick (Fitzpatrick) is sent to stay with his uncle (Marlo) in hopes that it'll straighten him out. But that happens when Jill (Roenfeldt), a cute girl, introduces him to rock climbing. This is a pretty good movie for kids. It's a bit obvious, but it treats the characters seriously. **87m/C DVD.** Leo Fitzpatrick, John Marlo, Gretel Roenfeldt, Jason Bortz, Christin Couto; ***D:*** Sam Kieth; ***W:*** Arthur Jeon; ***C:*** Michael Anderson; ***M:*** Louis Gabriel Cowan.

Take Me ½ **2001** Jack and Kay Chambers move to a new community in hopes of saving their marriage but all their neighbors are wife-swappers and the Chambers' are soon joining in. Then there's a problem with a murder and the dull overextended sexcapades turn into a dull overextended thriller. **300m/C DVD.** *GB* Robson Green, Beth Goddard, Danny (Daniel) Webb, Keith Barron, Olga Sosnovska; ***D:*** Alex Pillai; ***W:*** Caleb Ranson; ***C:*** Simon Maggs; ***M:*** John Harle. **TV**

Take Me Back to Oklahoma **1940** Musical western with comedy. **64m/B VHS, DVD.** Tex Ritter, Terry Walker, Karl Hackett, George Eldredge; ***D:*** Al(bert) Herman.

Take Me Home: The John Denver Story **2000** Biopic of the 70s country-folk crooner hits the high points and explores the lows, but it's typical TV movie fare, made quickly after Denver's death in a plane crash. Although he bares no physical resemblance to the the singer, Lowe does a fine job. Based on the autobiography Denver co-wrote with Arthur Tobier. **90m/C VHS, DVD.** Chad Lowe, Kristin Davis, Gerald McRaney, Brian Markinson, Susan Hogan, Garry Chalk; ***D:*** Jerry London; ***W:*** Stephen Harrigan; ***C:*** Mike Fash; ***M:*** Lee Holdridge. **TV**

Take Me Out to the Ball Game ½ *Everybody's Cheering* **1949** Williams manages a baseball team, locks horns with players Sinatra and Kelly, and wins them over with song. Naturally, there's a water ballet scene. Contrived and forced, but enjoyable. ♫ Take Me Out to the Ball Game; The Hat My Father Wore on St. Patrick's Day; O'Brien to Ryan to Goldberg; The Right Girl for Me; It's Fate, Baby, It's Fate; Yes, Indeedy; Strictly U.S.A. **93m/C VHS, DVD.** Frank Sinatra, Gene Kelly, Esther Williams, Jules Munshin, Betty Garrett, Edward Arnold, Tom Dugan, Richard Lane; ***D:*** Busby Berkeley; ***W:*** Harry Tugend, George Wells; ***C:*** George J. Folsey; ***M:*** Roger Edens.

Take My Eyes *Te Day Mis Ojos* **2003** Pilar takes her young son Juan and hides out at her sister Ana's to escape violent husband Antonio. He, of course, can't understand what he did wrong and insists Pilar come back, but Ana has gotten her a job that gives her a little independence and self-esteem. When Antonio goes into counseling, Pilar reluctantly agrees to return but things are soon back to their nasty routine. Spanish with subtitles. **106m/C DVD.** *SP* Laia Marull, Luis Tosar, Candela Pena, Rosa Maria Sarda, Sergi Calleja; ***D:*** Iciar Bollain; ***W:*** Iciar Bollain, Alicia Luna; ***C:*** Carlos Gusi; ***M:*** Alberto Iglesias.

Take the Lead ½ **2006 (PG-13)** Charming Banderas dances with happy feet in this cliched, inspirational saga based on a true story. The instructor/owner of a Manhattan ballroom dance academy, Pierre Dulaine offers his services to Principal James (Woodard) in an effort to teach her South Bronx high school detention students some discipline and manners. The kids are reluctantly impressed by a smoldering tango, and Dulaine is equally intrigued when they add their hip-hop moves to his formal steps. Everyone is gradually won over and, yes, it all leads up to a big "I've had the time of my life" dance competition. **117m/C DVD.** *US* Antonio Banderas, Alfre Woodard, Jenna Dewan, Dante Basco, Rob Brown, Yaya DaCosta, Lauren Collins, John Ortiz, Brandon D. Andrews; ***D:*** Liz Friedlander; ***W:*** Dianne Houston; ***C:*** Alex Nepomniaschy; ***M:*** Aaron Zigman.

Take the Money and Run **1969 (PG)** Allen's directing debut; he also co-wrote and starred. "Documentary" follows a timid, would-be bank robber who can't get his career off the ground and keeps landing in jail. Little plot, but who cares? Nonstop one-liners and slapstick. **85m/C VHS, DVD.** Woody Allen, Janet Margolin, Marcel Hillaire, Louise Lasser, Jacquelyn Hyde, Lonny (Lonnie) Chapman, Jan Merlin, James Anderson, Jackson Beck, Howard Storm; ***D:*** Woody Allen; ***W:*** Mickey Rose, Woody Allen; ***C:*** Lester Shorr; ***M:*** Marvin Hamlisch.

Take This Job & Shove It **1981 (PG)** The Johnny Paycheck song inspired this story of a hot-shot efficiency expert who returns to his hometown to streamline the local brewery. Encounters with old pals inspire self-questioning. Alternately inspired and hackneyed. Cameos by Paycheck and other country stars. **100m/C VHS, DVD.** Robert Hays, Art Carney, Barbara Hershey, David Keith, Martin Mull, Eddie Albert, Penelope Milford; ***Cameos:*** Johnny Paycheck, David Allan Coe, Charlie Rich, Lacy J. Dalton; ***D:*** Gus Trikonis; ***W:*** Barry Schneider.

Take Two **1987 (R)** A woman has an affair with her husband's twin brother. Interesting metaphysically: Are you my husband or my lover? But is an adultery/murder drama with Frank Stallone worth 101 minutes of your time? **101m/C VHS.** Grant Goodeve, Robin Mattson, Frank Stallone, Warren Berlinger, Darwyn Swalve, Nita Talbot; ***D:*** Peter Rowe.

Take Your Best Shot ½ **1982** Standard TV comedy about an out-of-work actor struggling with his low self-esteem and his failing marriage. **96m/C VHS.** Robert Urich, Meredith Baxter, Jeffrey Tambor, Jack Bannon, Claudette Nevins; ***D:*** David Greene. **TV**

Taken ½ **1999 (R)** Businessman Coleman gets kidnapped only both his wife and business partners see a financial opportunity and decide not to pay the ransom. When he realizes this, Coleman thinks it prudent to befriend kidnapper Boutsikaris and hope that something can be worked out. **96m/C VHS, DVD.** *CA* Dabney Coleman, Dennis Boutsikaris, Linda Smith, Dorothee Berryman, Carl Alacchi; ***D:*** Max Fischer; ***W:*** Pierre Lapointe.

Taken ½ *Steven Spielberg Presents: Taken* **2002** There was nothing "mini" about this 10-part series shown on the Sci Fi Channel. It's a classic saga of alien abductions over 60 years and three generations, beginning in 1947. Series is narrated by 10-year-old Allie Keys (Fanning), the granddaughter of WWII fighter pilot Russell (Burton), who is taken by mysterious blue lights. There's also that Roswell incident and contact with aliens and strange powers and, well, a lot. **900m/C DVD.** Steve (Stephen) Burton, Julie Benz, Joel Gretsch, Michael Moriarty, Tina Holmes, Catherine Dent, Eric Close, Ryan Hurst, Chad Morgan, Willie Garson, Matt Frewer, James McDaniel, Emily Bergl, Dakota Fanning; ***D:*** Tobe Hooper, Bryan Spicer, Felix Alcala, Thomas J. Wright, Jeremy Paul Kagan, Jeff Woolnough, John Fawcett, Breck Eisner, Sergio Mimica-Gezzan, Michael Kattleman; ***W:*** Leslie Bohem; ***C:*** Jonathan Freeman, Joel Ransom; ***M:*** Laura Karpman; ***Nar:*** Dakota Fanning. **CABLE**

Taken ½ **2008 (PG-13)** Ex-spy and estranged dad Bryan Mills (Neeson) moves to L.A. to be nearer 17-year-old daughter Kim, his ex-wife (Janssen), and her moneyed second husband to atone for his years of absence—but Kim's off to Paris for the summer. His concerns for her safety dismissed, Kim goes and is almost immediately abducted, although she makes one desperate phone call to dad who sets retirement aside and springs into action. With help from former colleagues and a lifetime of experience facing bad guys, Mills has mere hours to sort out ruthless Albanian kidnappers, perverse Arab sheiks, and assorted nasty evildoers to spare Kim from a violent career as a sex slave. Typical action thriller, but Neeson is imposing in the midst of a pretty implausible narrative. **93m/C DVD.** *FR* Liam Neeson, Maggie Grace, Famke Janssen, Xander Berkeley, Katie Cassidy, Olivier Rabourdin, Leland Orser, Jon(athan) Gries, Gerard Watkins, Arben Bajraktaraj; ***D:*** Pierre Morel; ***W:*** Luc Besson, Robert Mark Kamen; ***C:*** Michel Abramowicz; ***M:*** Nathaniel Mechaly.

Taken Alive ½ **1995 (PG-13)** Secret agent working for the U.S. government winds up in Italy to help a presidential candidate whose mistress has been kidnapped. In a case of mistaken identity, she hires a local sculptor (whom she believes is a professional assassin) to help her out. **92m/C VHS.** Franco (Columbo) Columbu, Barbara Niven, Frank Stallone, Robert Ginty, William (Bill) Smith; ***D:*** Christopher Holmes; ***W:*** Franco (Columbo) Columbu.

Taken Away ½ **1989** Struggling young divorcee Stephanie Monroe waits tables during the day and studies to be a computer tech at night in order to provide her eight-year-old daughter Abby with a better life. Unable to afford child care, Stephanie leaves Abby alone in the afternoon until she can get home from work. But when the welfare system finds out Stephanie is accused of child neglect and must fight a bureaucratic nightmare in order to get her child back. **94m/C VHS.** Valerie Bertinelli, Kevin Dunn, Joshua Maurer, Anna Maria Horsford, Juliet Sorcey, Nada Despotovich, Matthew Faison, James Arone; ***D:*** John D. Patterson; ***W:*** Robert Freedman, Selma Thomson. **TV**

The Takeover ½ **1994 (R)** East coast crime boss Danny Stein (Drago) decides to take over the L.A. operations of rival Tony Valachi (Mancuso). Lots of mayhem ensues. **91m/C VHS.** Billy Drago, Nick Mancuso, John Savage, Eric (DaRe) Da Re, Cali Timmins, David Amos, Gene Mitchell; ***D:*** Troy Cook; ***W:*** Gene Mitchell; ***M:*** Jimmy Lifton.

Takers **2010** A gang of criminals pull off a series of perfectly-executed bank robberies and then lay low between jobs. When they attempt one last high stakes heist, an obsessed New York police detective is determined to finally bring them down. **m/C DVD.** Matt Dillon, Paul Walker, Idris Elba, Jay Hernandez, Tip "T.I." Harris, Michael Ealy, Chris Brown, Johnathon Schaech, Hayden Christensen, Zoe Saldana; ***D:*** John Luessenhop; ***W:*** John Luessenhop, Peter Allen, Gabriel Casseus, Avery Duff; ***C:*** Michael Barrett; ***M:*** Paul Haslinger.

Taking Care of Business ½ *Filofax* **1990 (R)** Too familiar tale of switched identity has crazed Cubs fan Belushi find Grodin's Filofax, allowing him to pose as businessman. Old jokes and a story full of holes. **108m/C VHS, DVD.** James Belushi, Charles Grodin, Anne DeSalvo, Loryn Locklin, Veronica Hamel, Hector Elizondo, Mako, Gates (Cheryl) McFadden, Stephen Elliott; ***D:*** Arthur Hiller; ***W:*** J.J. (Jeffrey) Abrams; ***C:*** David M. Walsh; ***M:*** Stewart Copeland.

Taking Chance ½ **2009** Based on the experiences of Lt. Col. Michael Strobl (an overly stoic Bacon), a Desert Storm vet, who volunteers to accompany the body of an Iraq War soldier back to his Wyoming hometown. The film details the lengths the military goes to in honoring its dead through the ritual of military escort and Strobl's random encounters with ordinary citizens on his journey. **77m/C DVD.** Kevin Bacon, Tom Wopat, Ann Dowd, Paige Turco; ***D:*** Ross Katz; ***W:*** Ross Katz, Michael Strobl; ***C:*** Alar Kivilo; ***M:*** Marcelo Zarvos. **CABLE**

Taking Chances **2009 (R)** Geeky Chase Revere (Long) joins with babe Lucy Shanks (Chriqui) when he learns an Indian casino is going to be built on their small town's ignored Revolutionary War-era battlefield. Since the community needs the income and jobs the casino will offer, no one else is happy about their interference. **99m/C DVD.** Justin Long, Emmanuelle Chriqui, Keir O'Donnell, Rob Corddry, Missi Pyle, Nick Offerman, David Jensen, Phil Reeves, Robert Beltran; ***D:*** Talmage Cooley; ***W:*** Annie Nocenti; ***C:*** Steve Gainer; ***M:*** Scott Glasgow. **VIDEO**

Taking Lives **2004 (R)** Illeana Scott (Jolie), a sexy FBI profiler with an affinity for the macabre, is called in by the Montreal police to use her "special" skills to track down a serial killer who assumes the identity of his victims. Since the heroine cannot be without a love interest, along comes art gallery owner James Costa (Hawke) who, naturally, is a witness...no, wait, he's a suspect...oh, now he's a target. Keep your scorecards handy, folks. Caruso strives to craftily overwhelm his audience with loads of gruesome gore, and perhaps if the plot weren't as mangled as the victims it would have succeeded. Sutherland does little more than play the convenient scapegoat while Rowlands masters the role of the alleged slayer's surly mother. Adapted from Michael Pye's novel where, interestingly, Jolie's character didn't exist. **103m/C VHS, DVD.** *US* Angelina Jolie, Ethan Hawke, Kiefer Sutherland, Gena Rowlands, Olivier Martinez, Tcheky Karyo, Jean-Hugues Anglade, Paul Franklin Dano, Justin Chatwin; ***D:*** D.J. Caruso; ***W:*** Jon Bokenkamp; ***C:*** Amir M. Mokri; ***M:*** Philip Glass.

The Taking of Beverly Hills ½ **1991 (R)** Deranged billionaire Bat Masterson designs a bogus toxic spill that leaves the wealth of Beverly Hills his for the taking. Football hero Boomer Hayes teams up with renegade cop Ed Kelvin to try and stop Masterson and save the city of Beverly Hills. **96m/C VHS.** Ken Wahl, Matt Frewer, Robert Davi, Harley Jane Kozak, Lee James, Branscombe Richmond, Lyman Ward, Michael Bowen, William Prince, Ken Swofford, George Wyner; ***D:*** Sidney J. Furie; ***W:*** Sidney J. Furie, David Burke.

The Taking of Flight 847: The Uli Derickson Story *The Flight* **1988** Wagner plays the stewardess who acted as a go-between for the passengers during a 1985 terrorist hijacking, saving all but one life. True-story drama is suspenseful and entertaining, nominated for several Emmys. **100m/C VHS.** Laurie Walters, Sandy McPeak, Ray Wise, Leslie Easterbrook, Lindsay Wagner, Eli Danker, Joseph Nasser; ***D:*** Paul Wendkos; ***W:*** Norman Merrill. **TV**

The Taking of Pelham One Two Three **1974 (R)** A hijack team, lead by the ruthless Shaw, seizes a NYC subway car and holds the 17 passengers for $1 million ransom. Fine pacing keeps things on the edge. New cinematic techniques used by cameraman Owen Roizman defines shadowy areas like never before. **105m/C VHS, DVD.** Robert Shaw, Walter Matthau, Martin Balsam, Hector Elizondo, James Broderick, Earl Hindman, Dick O'Neill, Jerry Stiller, Tony Roberts, Doris Roberts, Kenneth McMillan, Julius W. Harris, Sal Viscuso; ***D:*** Joseph Sargent; ***W:*** Peter Stone; ***C:*** Owen Roizman; ***M:*** David Shire.

The Taking of Pelham 123 🦴🦴 1/2 **2009 (R)** New York subway dispatcher Walter Garber's (Washington) shift isn't starting well after a subway train is hijacked by homicidal nutjob Ryder (Travolta) and his armed crew. They threaten to execute passengers one-by-one until a large ransom is paid, but how exactly do they then plan to escape? Remake of the 1974 thriller (that starred Walter Matthau and Robert Shaw) is filled with Scott's swooping, fast-paced images; Washington's workmanlike, compromised, reluctant hero; Travolta's over-the-top, tattooed baddie; and a visually interesting comparison of a post 9/11 Big Apple vs. the grungy city of the 1970s. **106m/C DVD.** *US* Denzel Washington, John Travolta, Luis Guzman, John Turturro, James Gandolfini, Michael Rispoli; ***D:*** Tony Scott; ***W:*** Brian Helgeland; ***C:*** Tobias Schliessler; ***M:*** Harry Gregson-Williams.

Taking Sides 🦴🦴🦴 1/2 *Der Fall Furtwangler* **2001** Szabo again looks at Nazi-era Germany, this time in the story of famed conductor Wilhelm Furtwangler, who stayed in Germany as conductor of the Berlin Philharmonic under the Nazis. The film concentrates on Furtwangler's (Skaarsgaard) pretrial interrogation by American Denazification Committee officer Steve Arnold (Keitel), whose aides, both of German and Jewish decscent, have some sympathy for Furtwangler. Arnold is caustic and unrelenting in his mission to get to the bottom of the conductor's collaboration, while Furtwangler refuses to believe he has anything to apologize for, invoking his allegiance to his art, and his professed belief that he was making a difference. Both performances are magnificent and aid greatly in Szabo and Harwood's ability to let you know where they stand, yet be balanced in their portrayal of both views of the man. **105m/C DVD.** *FR GE GB AT* Harvey Keitel, Stellan Skarsgard, Moritz Bleibtreu, Birgit Minichmayr, Oleg Tabakov, Ulrich Tukur, Hanns Zischler, August Zirner, R. Lee Ermey, Robin Renucci; ***D:*** Istvan Szabo; ***W:*** Ronald Harwood; ***C:*** Lajos Koltai.

Taking the Heat 🦴🦴 1/2 **1993 (R)** When mobster Arkin kills a sporting-goods dealer with a golf club the murder is witnessed by yuppie Goldwyn. Whitfield is the ambitious cop who wants Goldwyn to testify against the gangster—if she can keep him alive long enough to get him to court. One long chase scene. **91m/C VHS.** Lynn Whitfield, Tony Goldwyn, Alan Arkin, George Segal, Peter Boyle; ***D:*** Tom Mankiewicz; ***W:*** Dan Gordon. **CABLE**

Taking Woodstock **2009 (R)** Adaptation of Elliot Tiber's memoir of the festival where he became its unexpected host while trying to drum up business for his family's failing motel, which was located nearby. **m/C DVD.** *US* Imelda Staunton, Liev Schreiber, Eugene Levy, Emile Hirsch, Kelli Garner, Paul Franklin Daho, Jeffrey Dean Morgan, Demetri Martin, Dan Fogler, Henry Goodman, Mamie Gummer, Jonathan Groff; ***D:*** Ang Lee; ***W:*** James Schamus; ***C:*** Eric Gautier; ***M:*** Danny Elfman.

Tale of a Vampire 🦴🦴 1/2 **1992 (R)** In present day London, ageless vampire Alex (Sands) still mourns his long-lost vampiric love, Virginia, when he meets Anne (Hamilton) (who resembles Virginia). Alex doesn't know he's being stalked by Virginia's husband, Edgar (Cranham), also a vampire. Edgar decides to use Anne (with whom Alex has fallen in love) as bait, in a revenge plot. A tiny budget and slow pacing mar the film's fine visual style and good work by the two male leads. Film debut for director Sato. **93m/C VHS.** *GB* Julian Sands, Kenneth Cranham, Suzanna Hamilton; ***D:*** Shimako Sato; ***W:*** Jane Corbett, Shimako Sato; ***M:*** Julian Joseph.

The Tale of Despereaux 🦴 1/2 **2008 (G)** Universal's computer-animated feature is less of a hip, frantic, wise-cracking modern legacy Pixar and more of a somber older Disney cartoon. Castle mouse Despereaux (Broderick), a misfit rodent content with reading books, dreams of adventures outside the dreary castle walls. Desperaeux's tale mixes with the stories of two other unhappy residents—grumpy rat Roscuro (Hoffman) and frumpy girl Miggery Sow (Ullman), who believes she's destined to be a princess. Based on Kate DiCamillo's Newberry Award-winning children's book, the uneven script may be too slow and confusing for most kids. **93m/C DVD.** *US* ***D:*** Sam Fell, Robert Stevenhagen; ***W:*** Gary Ross; ***C:*** Brad Blackbourn; ***M:*** William Ross; ***V:*** Matthew Broderick, Dustin Hoffman, Emma Watson, Tracey Ullman, Christopher Lloyd, Kevin Kline, William H. Macy, Stanley Tucci, Robbie Coltrane, Ciaran Hinds, Tony Hale, Frances Conroy, Richard Jenkins, Frank Langella, Charles Shaughnessy; ***Nar:*** Sigourney Weaver.

The Tale of Ruby Rose 🦴🦴🦴 **1987 (PG)** Living in the mountains of Tasmania, Ruby Rose, her husband Henry, and their adopted son Gem, struggle to survive the '30s depression by hunting and trapping. Having spent all her life in the mountains, Ruby Rose has a very superstitious view of life and a terror of nightfall. But after an argument with her husband, Ruby Rose sets out on a cross-country journey to find her grandmother and discover the secrets of her past. **101m/C VHS.** *AU* Melita Jurisic, Chris Haywood; ***D:*** Roger Sholes; ***W:*** Roger Sholes; ***M:*** Paul Schutze.

A Tale of Springtime 🦴🦴 1/2 **1989 (PG)** Comedy-romance is the first film in Rohmer's planned new series, the "Tales of the Four Seasons," not to be confused with his "Six Moral Tales" or his "Comedies and Proverbs." Centers around Jeanne, a high school philosophy teacher; Natacha, a young student; and Igor, Natacha's father. As characteristic of Rohmer films, texture and character largely overshadow linear plots and social messages. However, the efficiency and directness of his camera work make it a pleasure to watch. **107m/C VHS, DVD.** *FR* Anne Teyssedre, Hugues Quester, Florence Darel, Eloise Bennett, Sophie Robin; ***D:*** Eric Rohmer; ***W:*** Eric Rohmer; ***C:*** Luc Pages; ***M:*** Robert Schumann.

The Tale of the Frog Prince 🦴🦴🦴 1/2 **1983** Superb edition of Shelley Duvall's "Faerie Tale Theatre" finds Williams the victim of an angry fairy godmother's spell. Garr to the rescue as the self-centered princess who saves him with a kiss. Directed and written by Idle of Monty Python fame. **60m/C VHS, DVD.** Robin Williams, Teri Garr; ***D:*** Eric Idle; ***W:*** Eric Idle.

A Tale of Two Cities 🦴🦴🦴🦴 **1936** Lavish production of the Dickens' classic set during the French Revolution, about two men who bear a remarkable resemblance to each other, both in love with the same girl. Carefree lawyer Sydney Carton (Colman) roused to responsibility, makes the ultimate sacrifice. A memorable Madame DeFarge from stage star Yurka in her film debut, with assistance from other Dickens' film stars Rathbone, Oliver, and Walthall. **128m/B VHS, DVD.** Ronald Colman, Elizabeth Allan, Edna May Oliver, Reginald Owen, Isabel Jewell, Walter Catlett, H.B. Warner, Donald Woods, Basil Rathbone, Blanche Yurka, Henry B. Walthall; ***D:*** Jack Conway; ***W:*** W.P. Lipscomb, S.N. Behrman; ***M:*** Herbert Stothart.

A Tale of Two Cities 🦴🦴🦴 **1958** A well-done British version of the Dickens' classic about a lawyer who sacrifices himself to save another man from the guillotine during the French Reign of Terror. The sixth remake of the tale. **117m/B VHS, DVD.** *GB* Dirk Bogarde, Dorothy Tutin, Christopher Lee, Donald Pleasence, Ian Bannen, Cecil Parker; ***D:*** Ralph Thomas.

A Tale of Two Cities 🦴🦴 1/2 **1980** Impressive looking but bloodless adaptation of the Dickens novel set in the French Revolution. Saradon takes on the dual role of sacrificing English lawyer Carton and French nobleman Darnay, with Krige as the lovely woman caught between the two. **156m/C VHS.** Chris Sarandon, Alice Krige, Peter Cushing, Kenneth More, Barry Morse, Flora Robson, Billie Whitelaw; ***D:*** Jim Goddard; ***W:*** John Gay. **TV**

A Tale of Two Cities 🦴🦴🦴 **1989** Masterpiece Theatre production of the classic Dickens tale. The French revolution was a time of revenge and brutality, but also provided the proving ground for a love greater than life. Terrific cast and perfectly detailed production. **240m/C VHS, DVD.** James Wilby, Serena Gordon, John Mills, Jean-Pierre Aumont, Anna Massey; ***D:*** Philippe Monnier; ***W:*** Arthur Hopcraft; ***M:*** Serge Franklin.

A Tale of Two Pizzas 🦴 1/2 **2003 (PG)** Predictable family comedy with some charm. Rival Yonkers pizzeria owners Vito (Pastore) and Frank (Vincent) are constantly at odds over whose secret recipe is best. However, their kids, Angela (Paul) and Tony (Dubin), have more than sauce and crust on their minds. **82m/C DVD.** Vincent Pastore, Frank Vincent, Conor Dubin, Patti D'Arbanville, Robin Paul, Angela Pietropinto, Louis Guss; ***D:*** Vincent Sassone; ***W:*** Vincent Sassone; ***C:*** Peter Nelson; ***M:*** Peter Fish.

Tale of Two Sisters 🦴🦴 1/2 **1989** Sheen narrates sensual drama about two beautiful, ambitious sisters. **90m/C VHS, DVD.** Valerie Breiman, Claudia Christian, Sydney Lassick, Jeff Conaway, Peter Berg; ***D:*** Adam Rifkin; ***W:*** Charlie Sheen; ***C:*** John Parenteau; ***M:*** Marc David Decker; ***Nar:*** Charlie Sheen.

A Tale of Two Sisters 🦴🦴🦴 *Janghwa, Hongryeon* **2003** Two sisters return home after a mysterious absence to the cold attentions of a near-psychotic stepmother and emotionally impotent father. A horrid tragedy occurred in this house, revealed piece by piece: sometimes slowly and indirectly, sometimes shockingly and brutally. Creepy Korean horror film works its way under the skin, sometimes borrowing the style of recent Japanese shockers. Actually reaches level of Greek tragedy through powerful ending. **115m/C DVD.** *KN* Jung-ah Yum, Su-jeong Lim, Geun-yeong Mum, Kap-su Kim; ***D:*** Ji-woon Kim; ***W:*** Ji-woon Kim; ***C:*** Mo-gae Lee; ***M:*** Byung-woo Lee.

A Tale of Winter 🦴🦴 1/2 *Conte D'Hiver* **1992** Portrays the romantic trials of a young French woman who cannot choose between her two smitten lovers and her one true love, the long disappeared father of her child. Felicie (Very) hopelessly loves Charles (Van Den Driessche), whom she met five years before, but mistakenly gave the wrong address. Rohmer's trademark conversation-filled scenes find her brooding over her predicament, running from one lover and back again, until a revelation during a viewing of Shakespeare's "The Winter's Tale." A charming cast carries the story to a surprise twist of an ending. Second in the series "Tales of the Four Seasons." In French with English subtitles. **114m/C VHS.** *FR* Charlotte Very, Frederic Van Dren Driessche, Michel Voletti, Herve Furic, Ava Loraschi, Jean-Luc Revol, Haydee Caillot, Jean-Claude Biette, Rosette, Marie Riviere; ***D:*** Eric Rohmer; ***W:*** Eric Rohmer; ***C:*** Luc Pages; ***M:*** Sebastien Erms.

Talent for the Game 🦴🦴 1/2 **1991 (PG)** A slight but handsomely produced baseball pleasantry about a talent scout who recruits a phenomenonal young pitcher, then sees the kid exploited by the team owner. More like an anecdote than a story, with an ending that aims a little too hard to please. Good for sports fans and family audiences. **91m/C VHS, DVD.** Edward James Olmos, Lorraine Bracco, Jeff Corbett, Jamey Sheridan, Terry Kinney; ***D:*** Robert M. Young; ***W:*** David Himmelstein, Thomas Michael Donnelly, Larry Ferguson; ***M:*** David Newman.

The Talent Given Us 🦴🦴🦴 **2004** Writer/director/producer Andrew Wagner gives this road trip story a quasi-reality twist by casting his father Allen, mother Judy and sisters Emily and Maggie as, well, themselves. The Wagners have not seen their elusive son Andrew (Wagner) in several years, and embark on a cross-country drive from Manhattan to Los Angeles to catch up with him, picking up family friend Bumby (Dixon) en route. The miles are filled with unfiltered and sometimes unflattering discussion of everything from driving habits to sex to prescription drugs to thoughts of infidelity. The unnerving fascination with the line between real life and fantasy is a major draw. **97m/C DVD.** *US* Billy Wirth, Judy Wagner, Allen Wagner, Emily Wagner, Maggie Wagner, Judy Dixon; ***D:*** Andrew Wagner; ***W:*** Andrew Wagner; ***C:*** Andrew Wagner; ***M:*** David Dyas.

The Talented Mr. Ripley 🦴🦴 1/2 **1999 (R)** Beautiful but ultimately hollow adaptation of Patricia Highsmith's chiller, which was previously filmed as 1960's "Purple Noon." This time around Damon takes on the title role as a poor nobody who is sent to Italy in 1958 to persuade rich playboy, Dickie Greenleaf (Law), to return to the bosom of his family in New York. Only the more the emotionally needy Ripley sees of Dickie's sybaritic lifestyle—the more he wants it for himself, even if it means killing Dickie and literally assuming his identity. Law is the draw and the movie suffers a letdown after his death. **139m/C VHS, DVD.** Matt Damon, Jude Law, Gwyneth Paltrow, Cate Blanchett, Philip Seymour Hoffman, Jack Davenport, James Rebhorn, Sergio Rubini, Philip Baker Hall, Lisa Eichhorn, Stefania Rocca; ***D:*** Anthony Minghella; ***W:*** Anthony Minghella; ***C:*** John Seale; ***M:*** Gabriel Yared. British Acad. '99: Support. Actor (Law); Natl. Bd. of Review '99: Director (Minghella), Support. Actor (Hoffman).

Tales from a Parallel Universe: Eating Pattern 🦴🦴 *Eating Pattern* **1997 (R)** The Lexx space cruiser is part machine and part organic matter, so it needs nourishment, as does its crew. But Zev and Stanley make a big mistake stopping for food at the planet Klaagya. Seems the inhabitants are controlled by parasitic worms that feed on their brains and they're always interested in a fresh meal. Now it's up to Kai to come to the rescue. Third episode in the series. **93m/C VHS.** Brian Downey, Eva Habermann, Michael McManus, Rutger Hauer; ***D:*** Rainer Matsutani; ***W:*** Paul Donovan; ***C:*** Les Krizsan; ***M:*** Marty Simon. **CABLE**

Tales from a Parallel Universe: Giga Shadow 🦴🦴 *Giga Shadow* **1997 (R)** The Lexx crew must make a dangerous attempt to replenish Kai's supply of proto-blood, which brings them perilously near their arch-enemy, His Shadow. The fourth (and last) film of the series. **93m/C VHS.** Brian Downey, Eva Habermann, Michael McManus, Malcolm McDowell; ***D:*** Robert Sigl; ***W:*** Paul Donovan; ***C:*** Les Krizsan; ***M:*** Marty Simon. **CABLE**

Tales from a Parallel Universe: I Worship His Shadow 🦴🦴 *I Worship His Shadow* **1997 (R)** Space rebels try to unseat a tyrannical ruler known as His Shadow, in this first of a four-part series. A prophecy states that the ruler will be defeated by a dying race and aiding that prediction are rebel leader Thodin (Bostwick), cowardly Stanley Tweedle (Downey), warrior Kai (McManus), and Zev (Habermann), His Shadow's unwilling love slave. Followed by the "Super Nova" episode. **95m/C VHS.** Brian Downey, Eva Habermann, Michael McManus, Barry Bostwick, Ellen Dubin; ***D:*** Paul Donovan; ***W:*** Paul Donovan; ***C:*** Les Krizsan; ***M:*** Marty Simon. **CABLE**

Tales from a Parallel Universe: Super Nova 🦴🦴 *Super Nova* **1997 (R)** A continuation of the "I Worship His Shadow" episode, which finds the rebels in possession of the mile-long spacecraft known as The Lexx, which also happens to be the most destructive weapon in the universe. But they don't want to destroy the craft, instead they use the Lexx to visit the lost planet of Brunnis in hopes of restoring their lost leader to life. Only the rebels get captured by the Poet Man (Curry), and their deaths could lead to the total annihilation of the universe. **93m/C VHS.** Brian Downey, Eva Habermann, Michael McManus, Ellen Dubin, Tim Curry; ***D:*** Ron Oliver; ***W:*** Paul Donovan; ***C:*** Les Krizsan; ***M:*** Marty Simon. **CABLE**

Tales from the Crypt 🦴🦴🦴 **1972 (PG)** A collection of five scary stories from the classic EC comics that bear the movie's title. Richardson tells the future to each of five people gathered in a cave, each tale involving misfortune and, of course, gore. **92m/C VHS.** *GB* Ralph Richardson, Joan Collins, Peter Cushing, Richard Greene, Ian Hendry; ***D:*** Freddie Francis.

Tales from the Crypt **1989** Three contemporary tales of the macabre, "The Man Who Was Death," "'Twas the Night Before," and "Dig That Cat...He's Real Gone," linked together by a special-effects host. Ry Cooder provides the musical score for the second episode. Based on stories published by William M. Gaines in EC Comics. **81m/C VHS.** William Sadler, Mary Ellen Trainor, Larry Drake, Joe Pantoliano, Robert Wuhl, Gustav Vintas; ***D:*** Richard Donner, Walter Hill, Robert Zemeckis; ***M:*** Ry Cooder, Alan Silvestri. **CABLE**

Tales from the Crypt Presents Bordello of Blood *Bordello of Blood* **1996 (R)** Detective Rafe Guttman (Miller) is on the case of a Bible thumper's (Eleniak) missing brother (Feldman). The trail leads him to a unique establishment, a brothel presided over by vampire queen Lilith (Everhart), whose clients all wind up dead (but probably with smiles on their faces), and the strange Reverend Current (Sarandon, who made a fine vampire himself in "Fright Night"). Crypt Keeper's second big screen outing showcases Miller's slant on the leading man gig and serves up campy fun with the blood. **87m/C VHS, DVD.** Dennis Miller, Angie Everhart, Chris Sarandon, Corey Feldman, Erika Eleniak; ***D:*** Gilbert Adler; ***W:*** Gilbert Adler, A.L. Katz; ***C:*** Tom Priestley; ***M:*** Chris Boardman.

Tales from the Crypt Presents Demon Knight *Demon Knight; Demon Keeper* **1994 (R)** Gruesomely garish big-screen version of the TV series that was inspired by the lurid 1950s E.C. comics. Horrormeister Crypt Keeper offers his usual pun-filled introduction to a tale set in a seedy boarding-house. Brayker (Sadler) is the guardian of an ancient key that keeps the forces of darkness from overwhelming mankind, a key desired by the charismatic Collector (Zane), who unleashes a disgusting mix of demons against the house's inhabitants. Curious hybrid of spoof/splatter pic that doesn't quite work in either genre. **93m/C VHS, DVD.** Billy Zane, William Sadler, Jada Pinkett Smith, Brenda Bakke, CCH Pounder, Dick Miller, Thomas Haden Church, John Schuck, Gary Farmer, Charles Fleischer; ***D:*** Ernest R. Dickerson; ***W:*** Ethan Reiff, Cyrus Voris, Mark Bishop; ***C:*** Rick Bota; ***M:*** Ed Shearmur; ***V:*** John Kassir.

Tales from the Darkside: The Movie **1990 (R)** Three short stories in the tradition of the ghoulish TV show are brought to the big screen, with mixed results. The plot centers around a boy who is being held captive by a cannibal. In order to prolong his life, he tells her horror stories. The tales were written by Sir Arthur Conan Doyle, Stephen King, and Michael McDowell. **93m/C VHS, DVD.** Deborah Harry, Christian Slater, David Johansen, William Hickey, James Remar, Rae Dawn Chong, Julianne Moore, Robert Klein, Steve Buscemi, Matthew Lawrence; ***D:*** John Harrison; ***W:*** George A. Romero, Michael McDowell; ***C:*** Rob Draper.

Tales from the Gimli Hospital **1988** A smallpox outbreak at the turn of the century finds Einar and Gunnar sharing a hospital room. They begin telling each other increasingly bizarre personal secrets and develop a serious rivalry. Sharp dialogue with some equally grotesque imagery. Director Maddin's first feature film. **68m/B VHS, DVD.** *CA* Kyle McCulloch, Michael Gottli, Angela Heck, Margaret Anne McLeod; ***D:*** Guy Maddin; ***W:*** Guy Maddin; ***C:*** Guy Maddin.

Tales from the Hood **1995 (R)** Horror anthology with that urban twist. Three young thugs search for lost drugs inside a funeral parlor run by creepy Mr. Simms (Williams III) and instead walk into a world of four chilling and funny stories of fright dealing with racism and black on black crime. Tales aren't very original and are often too preachy for true enjoyment, but its nice to see someone attempt to breath life into an old and familiar genre. Williams III, with his pop-eyed stares and Don King coif, is fitting as the eerie storyteller. **97m/C VHS, DVD.** Lamont Bentley, De'Aundre Bonds, Tom Wright, Michael Massee, Duane Whitaker, Brandon Hammond, Paula Jai Parker, Roger Guenveur Smith, Art Evans, Clarence Williams III, Corbin Bernsen, David Alan Grier, Wings Hauser, Rosalind Cash, Rusty Cundieff, Joe Torry, Anthony Griffith, Darin Scott; ***D:*** Rusty Cundieff; ***W:*** Rusty Cundieff, Darin Scott; ***C:*** Anthony B. Richmond; ***M:*** Christopher Young.

Tales of Beatrix Potter 1/2 *Peter Rabbit and Tales of Beatrix Potter* **1971 (G)** The Royal Ballet Company of England performs in this adaptation of the adventures of Beatrix Potter's colorful and memorable creatures. Beautifully done. **90m/C VHS, DVD.** *GB* ***D:*** Reginald Mills.

Tales of Erotica *Die Erotische Geschichten* **1993 (R)** Four stories made for German TV. "The Dutch Master" finds New Yorker Teresa (Sorvino) becoming obsessed with a Vermeer-style painting at a museum. She begins to dress like the lively characters and eventually disappears into the picture itself. "The Insatiable Mrs. Kirsch" finds a vacationing writer (Shepherd) becoming fascinated by a fellow guest (Baynes), who seems to be hiding something. In "Vroom Vroom Vroom" luckless Leroy (Barboza) asks a voodoo doctor for help with the girls and winds up with a motorcycle that transforms itself into a beautiful woman when ridden. "Wet" has bathroom-fixture salesman Bruce (Howard) enticed by persistent customer Davida (Williams), who insists they both try out the showroom hot tub before she'll consider buying. **104m/C VHS, DVD.** *GE* Mira Sorvino, Aida Turturro, Simon Shepherd, Hetty Baynes, Ken Russell, Richard Barboza, Arliss Howard, Cynda Williams; ***D:*** Ken Russell, Susan Seidelman, Melvin Van Peebles, Bob Rafelson; ***W:*** Susan Seidelman, Melvin Van Peebles, Bob Rafelson, Jonathan Brett; ***C:*** Maryse Alberti, Hong Manley, Igor Sunara; ***M:*** Melvin Van Peebles, Wendy Blackstone, David McHugh. **TV**

The Tales of Hoffmann 1/2 **1951** A ballet-opera consisting of three stories by Jacques Offenbach covering romance, magic and mystery arising out of a poet's misadventures in love. Lavishly designed and highly stylized. **138m/C VHS, DVD.** Robert Rounseville, Robert Helpmann, Moira Shearer; ***D:*** Michael Powell, Emeric Pressburger.

Tales of Manhattan **1942** Star-studded anthology about a tailor who curses a tailcoat that then travels, with varying degrees of good and bad fortune, from owner to owner. There's a love triangle, a love match, a concert appearance, a down-on-his-luck lawyer, a swanky party, a crook, and a windfall for some sharecroppers. Fields' party episode (he wears the coat to give a lecture and winds up wreaking havoc) was cut out of the original theatrical release. **118m/C VHS.** Charles Boyer, Rita Hayworth, Thomas Mitchell, Ginger Rogers, Henry Fonda, Cesar Romero, Elsa Lanchester, Charles Laughton, Edward G. Robinson, George Sanders, James Gleason, J. Carrol Naish, Paul Robeson, Ethel Waters, Eddie Anderson, W.C. Fields, Margaret Dumont; ***D:*** Julien Duvivier; ***W:*** Ben Hecht, Donald Ogden Stewart, Samuel Hoffenstein, Ferenc Molnar, Alan Campbell; ***C:*** Joseph Walker; ***M:*** Sol Kaplan.

Tales of Ordinary Madness **1983** Gazzara as a poet who drinks and sleeps with assorted women. Based on the stories of Charles Bukowski. Pretentious and dull. **107m/C VHS, DVD.** Ben Gazzara, Ornella Muti, Susan Tyrrell, Tanya Lopert, Roy Brocksmith, Katya Berger; ***D:*** Marco Ferreri; ***W:*** Marco Ferreri, Sergio Amidei, Anthony Foutz; ***C:*** Tonino Delli Colli; ***M:*** Philippe Sarde.

Tales of Robin Hood 1/2 **1952** A low-budget depiction of the Robin Hood legend. **59m/B VHS.** Robert Clarke, Mary Hatcher, Paul Cavanagh, Wade Crosby, Whit Bissell, Ben Welden, Robert Bice, Bruce Lester, Margia Dean, Lester Matthews; ***D:*** James Tinling; ***W:*** George Robinson.

Tales of Terror *Poe's Tales of Terror* **1962** Three tales of terror based on stories by Edgar Allan Poe: "Morella," "The Black Cat," and "The Case of M. Valdemar." Price stars in all three segments and is excellent as the bitter and resentful husband in "Morella." **90m/C VHS, DVD.** Vincent Price, Peter Lorre, Basil Rathbone, Debra Paget, Joyce Jameson, Maggie Pierce, Leona Gage, Edmund Cobb; ***D:*** Roger Corman; ***W:*** Richard Matheson; ***C:*** Floyd Crosby; ***M:*** Les Baxter.

Tales of the Kama Sutra 2: Monsoon **1998** Naval officer Kenneth Blake (Tyson) and his fiancee Sally (McShane) travel to the island of Goa, off the coast of India, to enjoy a resort vacation. But Blake is drawn into an affair with Leela (Brodie), who tells him that they are the reincarnation of legendary lovers who leaped to their death from the island's lighthouse 500 years before. It's one way to get a man interested. **96m/C VHS, DVD.** Richard Tyson, Helen Brodie, Jenny (Jennifer) McShane, Matt McCoy, Doug Jeffery, Gulshan Grover; ***D:*** Jag Mundhra. **VIDEO**

Tales of the Kama Sutra: The Perfumed Garden *The Perfumed Garden* **1998 (R)** Not particularly erotic story centers on Americans Michael and Lisa, who have a rocky romantic relationship. Lisa follows Michael to India where he is helping to restore the erotic sculptures of Khajuraho. However, Michael's lust is aroused by a mysterious Indian woman (Kumar), who happens to resemble the statue he's repairing, which leads to a retelling of one Kama Sutra story about a royal courtesan set 1000 years earlier. **104m/C VHS, DVD.** Pravesh Kumar, Ivan Baccarat, Amy Lindsey, Rajeshwari Sachdev, Bhupinder Singh, Nasser; ***D:*** Jag Mundhra.

Tales of the Klondike: In a Far Country **1987** An adaptation of Jack London's story exploring the fears, dangers, and joys experienced by prospectors in the harsh wilderness of northwest Canadian gold country. **60m/C VHS.** Robert Carradine, Scott Hylands; ***D:*** Janine Manatis; ***Nar:*** Orson Welles. **TV**

Tales of the Klondike: Race for Number One **1987** Two men compete in a highly contested dog-sled race—the goal of which is to be the first to reach a tract of gold-laden land. Adapted from a story by Jack London. **60m/C VHS.** David Ferry, John Ireland; ***D:*** David Cobham; ***Nar:*** Orson Welles. **TV**

Tales of the Klondike: The Scorn of Women **1987** An available man is enthusiastically courted by every single woman in Dawson City, Alaska. From a story by Jack London. **60m/C VHS.** Tom Butler, Eva Gabor; ***D:*** Claude Fournier; ***Nar:*** Orson Welles. **TV**

Tales of the Klondike: The Unexpected **1987** Five gold prospectors grow rich, but lose all that is most valuable through overwhelming greed. Adapted from a story by Jack London. **60m/C VHS.** John Candy, Cherie Lunghi; ***D:*** Peter Pearson; ***Nar:*** Orson Welles. **TV**

Tales of the Unexpected 1/2 **1991** Four tales designed to startle the senses and provoke the imagination. Episodes include "People Don't Do Such Things," about a marriage gone awry, "Youth from Vienna," about a weird fountain of youth, "Skeleton in the Cupboard," which tells of a man desperately trying to hide some strange secret and finally, "Bird of Prey," in which a pet parrot leaves its owners an enormous egg before dying. **101m/C VHS.** Arthur Hill, Samantha Eggar, Don Johnson, Dick Smothers, Sharon Gless, James Carroll Jordan, Charles Dance, Zoe Wanamaker, Sondra Locke, Frank Converse; ***D:*** Gordon Hessler, Norman Lloyd, Paul Annett, Ray Danton.

Tales That Witness Madness 1/2 **1973 (R)** An asylum is the setting for four tales of horror, as a doctor tells a visitor how four patients ended up in his clinic. Stories are "Mr. Tiger," "Penny Farthing," "Mel" and "Luau." At the time this was Novak's first film appearance in four years. **90m/C VHS, DVD.** *GB* Jack Hawkins, Donald Pleasence, Suzy Kendall, Joan Collins, Kim Novak, Mary Tamm, Georgia Brown, Donald Houston, David Wood, Peter McEnery; ***D:*** Freddie Francis.

Talion *An Eye for an Eye* **1966 (PG)** A western revenge movie that features two disabled men, a rancher and a bounty hunter, who team up to find the gang that slaughtered the rancher's family. **92m/C VHS.** Robert Lansing, Slim Pickens, Patrick Wayne; ***D:*** Michael D. Moore.

Talisman 1/2 **1998 (R)** Theriel, the Black Angel, has been fused to an ancient Talisman for centuries. Summoned from his rest, he must offer seven human sacrifices to complete an evil ritual that will open the gates of hell and usher in the end of the world. Two teenagers are chosen to help Theriel but they've got other things in mind. Director DeCoteau used the pseud "Victoria Sloan" for this venture. **90m/C VHS.** Walter Jones, Jason Adelman, Billy Parish, Ilinca Goia; ***D:*** David DeCoteau; ***W:*** Benjamin Carr. **VIDEO**

Talk **1994** Sharp conversation between two thirtysomething women as they wander around the streets of Sydney. Stephanie (Milliken) and Julia (Longley) are collaborators on graphic novels—Stephanie's single and adventurous while Julia is seemingly settled in the country with her lover and child. As they talk, the women learn that both their lives have conflicts. Fantasy sequences, which slow the story down, find the women stepping into their own comic-book adventures. **86m/C VHS.** *AU* Victoria Longley, Angie Milliken, Richard Roxburgh, Jacqueline McKenzie, John Jarratt; ***D:*** Susan Lambert; ***W:*** Jan Cornall; ***C:*** Ron Hagen; ***M:*** John Clifford White.

Talk of Angels **1996 (PG-13)** Young Irish aristocrat Mary (Walker) leaves her homeland for Spain to serve as governess for a wealthy family, just as the country is about to erupt into civil war. She ignites passion in everyone she encounters, especially her married employer and his married son. This forbidden relationship serves as the crux of the story. Unfortunately, good looks alone (which both stars have) don't create chemistry, and Walker and Perez simply fizzle on screen. The film and its leads are certainly nice to look at, but there's something missing: an interesting story. With several obvious thefts from the ultimate wartime love story, "Gone With the Wind" (including a blatant rip-off of the famous scene where Scarlett walks among the sea of dead soldiers), the story is hardly original. **97m/C VHS, DVD.** Polly Walker, Vincent Perez, Frances McDormand, Franco Nero, Marisa Paredes, Penelope Cruz, Ruth McCabe, Francisco Rabal, Ariadna Gil, Rossy de Palma; ***D:*** Nick Hamm; ***W:*** Ann Guedes, Frank McGuinness; ***C:*** Alexei Rodionov; ***M:*** Trevor Jones.

Talk of the Town **1942** A brilliantly cast, strange mixture of screwball comedy and lynch-mob melodramatics. An accused arsonist, a Supreme Court judge and the girl they both love try to clear the former's name and evade the cops. **118m/B VHS, DVD.** Ronald Colman, Cary Grant, Jean Arthur, Edgar Buchanan, Glenda Farrell, Rex Ingram, Emma Dunn; ***D:*** George Stevens.

Talk Radio **1988 (R)** Riveting Stone adaptation of Bogosian's one-man play. An acidic talk radio host confronts America's evil side and his own past over the airwaves. The main character is loosely based on the life of Alan Berg, a Denver talk show host who was murdered by white supremacists. **110m/C VHS, DVD.** Eric Bogosian, Alec Baldwin, Ellen Greene, John Pankow, John C. McGinley, Michael Wincott, Leslie Hope; ***D:*** Oliver Stone; ***W:*** Eric Bogosian, Oliver Stone; ***C:*** Robert Richardson; ***M:*** Stewart Copeland.

Talk to Her 1/2 *Hable con Ella* **2002 (R)** Powerful entry from director Almodovar about the bond of two men caring for comatose women. Marco (Grandinetti), a travel writer, in the early stages of dating Spain's most famous female bullfighter Lydia (Flores), finds himself looking after her after she is gored by a bull. Benigno (Camara) is a male nurse who looks after the comatose Alicia (Watling), a ballerina he has only seen from afar but loves. The two men meet in the hospital and, sharing similar experiences, come to know one another in their grief. While both men are truly caring during their bedside vigils, a slightly disturbing, kinky undercurrent is also at work, and strange and shocking events will occur before film fully unspools. Refusing to judge these actions, however, Almodovar artfully offers some alternate motivations for his characters' seemingly antisocial behaviors and takes material that could have easily been a soap opera in lesser hands, and elevates it to a new level. Silent fantasy sequence depicts director's signature sexual exploration. **112m/C VHS, DVD.** *SP* Javier Camara, Dario Grandinetti, Rosario Flores, Leonor Watling, Geraldine Chaplin; ***D:*** Pedro Almodovar; ***W:*** Pedro Almodovar; ***C:*** Javier Aguirresarobe; ***M:*** Alberto Iglesias. Oscars '02: Orig. Screenplay; British Acad. '02: Foreign Film, Orig. Screenplay; Golden Globes '03: Foreign Film; L.A. Film Critics '02: Director (Almodovar); Natl. Bd. of Review '02: Foreign Film.

Talk to Me 1/2 **1984** A successful New York accountant checks into the Hollins Communication Institute to cure his stuttering. While there, he meets and falls in love with a squirrel-hunting stuttering woman from Arkansas. **90m/C VHS.** Austin Pendleton, Michael Murphy, Louise Fletcher, Brian Backer, Clifton James; ***D:*** Julius Potocsny; ***W:*** Nelson Breen; ***C:*** Julius Potocsny; ***M:*** Coleridge-Taylor Perkinson.

Talk to Me 1/2 **2007 (R)** Back when radio personalities had, well, personality, ex-con turned DJ Ralph Waldo "Petey" Greene Jr. (Cheadle) used his outlandish on- and off-air presence to lend a voice to the simmering racial and social unrest in 1960s Washington DC. Cheadle is magnetic as Greene battles both his uptight station director (the excellent Ejifor) and his own personal demons during his tumultuous flash of fame. Director Lemmons explores both the hilarity and gravity of Greene's complex story, resisting the need to tie it up with a neat, triumphant bow. **118m/C DVD, HD DVD.** *US* Don Cheadle, Chiwetel Ejiofor, Martin Sheen, Taraji P. Henson, Cedric the Entertainer, Elle Downs, Mike Epps, Vondie Curtis-Hall; ***D:*** Kasi Lemmons; ***W:*** Michael Genet, Rick Famuyiwa; ***C:*** Stephane Fontaine; ***M:*** Terence Blanchard. Ind. Spirit '08: Support. Actor (Ejiofor).

Talkin' Dirty after Dark **1991 (R)** Sexy comedy starring Lawrence as a suave comedian who will do anything to get a late-night spot at Dukie's comedy club. **89m/C VHS, DVD.** Martin Lawrence, Jedda Jones, Phyllis Stickney, Darryl Sivad; ***D:*** Topper Carew; ***W:*** Topper Carew.

Talking about Sex 1/2 **1994** Publishing party for a shrink's self-help manual sparks many conversations about sex and romance among a group of fashionable Los Angelenos. The breezy party chatter is broken up by B&W pseudo-documentary interludes of women exchanging confidences. **83m/C VHS.** Kim Wayans, Marcy Walker, Daniel Beer, Randy Powell, Kerry Ruff, Joe Richards, Daria Lynn; ***D:*** Aaron Speiser; ***W:*** Aaron Speiser, Carl Nelson; ***M:*** Tim Landers.

Talking Head 1/2 *Mamoru Oshii's - Talking Head* **1992** During the making of Talking Head the anime, which is set to debut in two months, the director vanishes. So a ringer is brought in to finish the project when he encounters a ghost, the staff being murdered one by one, and the anime bleeding into reality. **105m/C DVD.** *JP* Yoshikazu Fujiki, Keishi Hunt, Masaya Kato, Takashi Matsuyama, Shin'Ichi Ishihara, Hisayoshi Izaki, Kujira, Eri Mayama, Zenchu Mitsui, Sho Nobushi, Natsumi Sasaki, Mayumi Tanaka; ***D:*** Mamoru Oshii; ***W:*** Mamoru Oshii; ***C:*** Yousuke Mamiya; ***M:*** Kenji Kawai.

Talking Walls 1/2 *Motel Vacancy* **1985** A college sociology student uses high-tech surveillance equipment to spy on the clients of a seedy motel, in order to complete his thesis on human sexuality. **85m/C VHS.** Stephen Shellen, Marie Laurin, Barry Primus, Sally Kirkland; ***D:*** Stephen Verona.

The Tall Blond Man with One Black Shoe *Le Grand Blond avec une Chassure Noire* **1972 (PG)** A violinist is completely unaware that rival spies mistakenly think he is also a spy, and that he is the center of a plot to booby-trap an overly ambitious agent at the French Secret Service. A sequel followed called "Return of the Tall Blond Man with One Black Shoe" which was followed by a disappointing American remake, "The Man with One Red Shoe." In French with English subtitles or dubbed. **90m/C VHS.** *FR* Pierre Richard, Bernard Blier, Jean Rochefort, Mireille Darc, Jean Carmet; ***D:*** Yves Robert; ***W:*** Francis Veber; ***M:*** Vladimir Cosma.

Tall, Dark and Deadly 1/2 **1995 (R)** Roy (Scalia) romances Maggie (Delaney), a young woman he's met in a bar. The viewer's already clued in that Roy's a bad 'un (seein' as how he's killed one woman) and when he chains Maggie to a sink, she picks up on the idea that he's a wacko. Basic damsel-in-distress with a cast that manages to keep straight faces in the most preposterous of circumstances. **88m/C VHS.** Jack Scalia, Kim Delaney, Todd Allen, Gina Mastrogiacomo, Ely Pouget; ***D:*** Kenneth Fink; ***W:*** MaryAnne Kasica, Michael Scheff; ***M:*** Joseph Vitarelli. **CABLE**

The Tall Guy **1989 (R)** Goldblum is a too-tall actor who tries the scene in London and lands the lead in a musical version of 'The Elephant Man,' becoming an overnight success. Not consistently funny, but good British comedy, including an interesting sex scene. **92m/C VHS, DVD.** Jeff Goldblum, Emma Thompson, Rowan Atkinson, Geraldine James, Kim Thomson, Anna Massey; ***D:*** Mel Smith; ***W:*** Richard Curtis; ***C:*** Adrian Biddle; ***M:*** Peter Brewis.

Tall in the Saddle 1/2 **1944** A misogynist foreman (Wayne) finds himself accused of murder. Meanwhile, he falls in love with his female boss's niece. An inoffensive and memorable western. **79m/B VHS, DVD.** John Wayne, Ella Raines, George "Gabby" Hayes, Ward Bond; ***D:*** Edwin L. Marin.

Tall Lie *For Men Only* **1953** A student quits a fraternity hazing exercise. He's pursued by a psychotic bunch of his fraternity brothers and is killed in a smash-up. A local doctor goes onto an anti-hazing campaign in the aftermath. **93m/B VHS.** Paul Henreid, Robert Sherman; ***D:*** Paul Henreid.

The Tall Men **1955** Standard western features frontier hands on a rough cattle drive confronting Indians, outlaws, and the wilderness while vying with each other for the love of Russell. **122m/C VHS.** Clark Gable, Jane Russell, Robert Ryan, Cameron Mitchell, Mae Marsh; ***D:*** Raoul Walsh; ***W:*** Sydney (Sidney) Boehm, Frank Nugent; ***C:*** Leo Tover; ***M:*** Victor Young.

Tall Story **1960** Perkins is a star basketball player who must pass a crucial test in order to continue to play the game. In addition to the pressure of the exam, he is being pressured by gamblers to throw a game against the Russians. Fonda makes her screen debut as a cheerleader who is so awe-struck by Perkins that she takes the same classes just to be close to him. Based on the play by Howard Lindsay and Russel Crouse, and the novel "The Homecoming Game" by Howard Nemerov. **91m/C VHS.** Anthony Perkins, Jane Fonda, Ray Walston, Marc Connelly, Anne Jackson, Tom Laughlin, Gary Lockwood, Elizabeth Patterson, Barbara Darrow; ***D:*** Joshua Logan; ***W:*** Julius J. Epstein; ***C:*** Ellsworth Fredericks; ***M:*** Cyril Mockridge.

The Tall T 1/2 **1957** A veteran rancher (Pat) stumbles onto big trouble when by chance he catches a stage coach that is eventually overrun by an evil band of cutthroats. After killing everyone on the coach except Pat and the daughter of a wealthy copper mine owner (Doretta), the renegades decide to leave the scene with the unfortunate two as hostages. Pat and Doretta, although in dire straits, find time to fall in love and devise an intricate plan for their escape. Regarded in certain western-lover circles as a cult classic. **77m/B VHS.** Randolph Scott, Richard Boone, Maureen O'Sullivan, Arthur Hunnicutt, Skip Homeier, Henry Silva, Robert Burton, Robert Anderson; ***D:*** Budd Boetticher; ***W:*** Burt Kennedy. Natl. Film Reg. '00.

Tall Tale: The Unbelievable Adventures of Pecos Bill **1995 (PG)** Having trouble with greedy land owners out for his pa's land, Daniel Hackett (Stahl) summons the help of three Old West legends: Pecos Bill (Swayze), John Henry (Brown), and Paul Bunyan (Platt) to face off with the evil industrialist J.P. Stiles (Glenn). Disney's variation on the "Wizard of Oz" is riddled with cartoonish characters and sleep-inducing dialogue. It would truly be a tall tale if it were said that this movie was any good. **98m/C VHS.** Patrick Swayze, Oliver Platt, Roger Aaron Brown, Nick Stahl, Scott Glenn, Stephen Lang, Jared Harris, Catherine O'Hara; ***D:*** Jeremiah S. Chechik; ***W:*** Steven L. Bloom, Robert Rodat; ***C:*** Janusz Kaminski.

Tall, Tan and Terrific **1946** Things really go crazy when the owner of a nightclub in Harlem is accused of murder. **40m/C VHS.** Mantan Moreland, Monte Hawley, Francine Everett, Dots Johnson; ***D:*** Bud Pollard.

Tall Texan 1/2 **1953** A motley crew seeks gold in an Indian burial ground in the desert. Flawed but interesting and suspenseful. Greed, lust, Indians and desert heat. **82m/B VHS, DVD.** Lloyd Bridges, Lee J. Cobb, Marie Windsor, George Steele; ***D:*** Elmo Williams; ***C:*** Joseph Biroc.

Talladega Nights: The Ballad of Ricky Bobby **2006 (PG-13)** It's a no-brainer concept—Will Ferrell as a NASCAR driver—but Ferrell's talented enough that he could probably make "Will Ferrell as a stamp collector" pretty entertaining. Race car legend Ricky Bobby is the oblivious king of his racing circuit until French Formula-1 driver Jean Girard (Baron Cohen) bests him and ruins Ricky's confidence. There are lots of laughs as Ricky claws his way back on top, but the scenario is so similar to Ferrell and director Adam McKay's previous effort, "Anchorman", that the whole affair has a "been there, done that" vibe. McKay's inability to ever yell "cut" during Ferrell's increasingly tedious tangents doesn't help either. **108m/C DVD, Blu-ray Disc, UMD.** *US* Will Ferrell, John C. Reilly, Sacha Baron Cohen, Michael Clarke Duncan, Leslie Bibb, Amy Adams, Gary Cole, Molly Shannon, Jane Lynch, Andy Richter, Houston Tumlin, Grayson Russell; ***D:*** Adam McKay; ***W:*** Will Ferrell, Adam McKay; ***C:*** Oliver Wood; ***M:*** Alex Wurman.

Talons of the Eagle **1992 (R)** Martial arts adventure centers around three undercover agents who go up against crimelord Mr. Li (Hong). To impress Li, martial arts champion Tyler Wilson (Blanks) and vice detective Michael Reeds (Merhi) enter a deadly martial arts tournament. They later hook up with beautiful agent Cassandra Hubbard (Barnes), who has already investigated Li's drug, gambling, and prostitution rings. Features the most advanced fighting techniques ever filmed. **96m/C VHS, DVD.** Billy Blanks, Jalal Merhi, James Hong, Priscilla Barnes, Matthias Hues; ***D:*** Michael Kennedy; ***W:*** J. Stephen Maunder.

Tamango **1959** A confusing drama set on a slave ship travelling from Africa to Cuba in 1830. Jurgens is the ship's captain who takes the black Dandridge as his mistress. Meanwhile, the slaves are plotting a revolt, with Dandridge as a conspirator. The interracial romance does takes a secondary role to the racial conflicts. The title refers to the leader of the slave revolt, played by Cressan. Filmed in both English- and French-language versions. **98m/C VHS.** *FR* Curt Jurgens, Dorothy Dandridge, Jean Servais, Alex Cressan; ***D:*** John Berry.

The Tamarind Seed 1/2 **1974** Andrews and Sharif are star-crossed lovers kept apart by Cold War espionage. Dated, dull and desultory. **123m/C VHS.** Julie Andrews, Omar Sharif, Anthony Quayle, Dan O'Herlihy, Sylvia Syms; ***D:*** Blake Edwards; ***W:*** Blake Edwards; ***C:*** Frederick A. (Freddie) Young; ***M:*** John Barry.

The T.A.M.I. Show 1/2 **1964** The Santa Monica Civic Auditorium was the site, the Teenage Awards Music International was the show featuring Rock and R&B performances by such greats as Smokey Robinson and the Miracles, Jan and Dean, Marvin Gaye, Chuck Berry, the Supremes and the Rolling Stones. Young Teri Garr is a go-go dancer. Legendary show was a long time in coming to DVD. **100m/B DVD.** ***D:*** Steve Binder; ***W:*** Steve Binder. Natl. Film Reg. '06.

The Taming of the Shrew 1/2 **1929** Historically interesting early talkie featuring sole (if perhaps unfortunate) pairing of Pickford and Fairbanks. Features the legendary credit line "By William Shakespeare, with additional dialogue by Sam Taylor." Re-edited in 1966; 1967 Zeffirelli remake featured Taylor and Burton. **66m/B VHS, DVD.** Mary Pickford, Douglas Fairbanks Sr., Edwin Maxwell, Joseph Cawthorn; ***D:*** Sam Taylor; ***C:*** Karl Struss.

The Taming of the Shrew 1/2 **1967** A lavish screen version of the classic Shakespearean comedy. Burton and Taylor are violently physical and perfectly cast as the battling Katherine and Petruchio. At the time the film was made, Burton and Taylor were having their own marital problems, which not only added an inner fire to their performances, but sent the interested moviegoers to the theatres in droves. **122m/C VHS, DVD.** *IT* Elizabeth Taylor, Richard Burton, Michael York, Michael Hordern, Cyril Cusack; ***D:*** Franco Zeffirelli; ***W:*** Franco Zeffirelli; ***C:*** Oswald Morris; ***M:*** Nino Rota.

Tammy and the Bachelor 1/2 **1957** A backwoods Southern girl becomes involved with a romantic pilot and his snobbish family. They don't quite know what to make of her but she wins them over with her down-home philosophy. Features the hit tune, "Tammy." Charming performance by Reynolds. **89m/C VHS.** Debbie Reynolds, Leslie Nielsen, Walter Brennan, Fay Wray, Sidney Blackmer, Mildred Natwick, Louise Beavers; ***D:*** Joseph Pevney; ***W:*** Oscar Brodney.

Tammy and the Doctor **1963** Sandra Dee reprises Debbie Reynolds's backwoods gal ("Tammy and the Bachelor"). Dee becomes a nurse's aide and is wooed by doctor Fonda, in his film debut. **88m/C VHS.** Sandra Dee, Peter Fonda, MacDonald Carey; ***D:*** Harry Keller; ***W:*** Oscar Brodney.

Tammy and the T-Rex 1/2 **1994 (PG-13)** All Michael (Walker) wanted was a date with the lovely Denise (Richards)—he didn't expect to almost die for her. Nor did he expect a mad scientist to transplant his brain into a mechanical three-ton dinosaur. Part teen angst—part camp horror—all good-natured hooey. **82m/C VHS.** Paul Walker, Denise Richards, Terry Kiser, John Franklin; ***D:*** Stewart Raffill.

Tampopo *Dandelion* **1986** A hilarious, episodic Japanese comedy. Young restaurant hostess Tampopo (Miyamoto) is coached by 10 gallon-hatted stranger Goro (Yamazaki) in how to make the perfect noodle so she can open her own successful shop. There's also a food-loving gangster (Yakusho) who serves as an occasional narrator and gourmet. Popular, free-form hit that established Itami in the West. Japanese with subtitles. **114m/C VHS, DVD.** *JP* Ken(saku) Watanabe, Tsutomu Yamazaki, Nobuko Miyamoto, Koji Yakusho, Rikiya Yasuoka, Kinzo Sakura, Hideji Otaki; ***D:*** Juzo Itami; ***W:*** Juzo Itami; ***C:*** Masaki Tamura; ***M:*** Kunihiko Murai.

Tangiers **1983** The disappearance of a British intelligence agent in Gibraltar sets off a chain-reaction of violent incidents. **82m/C VHS.** Billie Whitelaw, Glynis Barber, Oscar Quitak, Ronald Lacy, Ronny Cox; ***D:*** Michael E. Briant; ***W:*** Michael Russell; ***C:*** Ernest Vincze; ***M:*** Paul Reade.

Tangled 1/2 **2001 (R)** After being found on a country road badly beaten, David (Hatosy) struggles to remember and explain what happened to a detective (Bracco) who is also investigating the disappearance of David's friend Jenny (Cook). Jenny was swept off her feet by David's old roommate Alan (Rhys-Meyers), who was strictly bad news. When Alan gets into trouble for drug posession, he blames David and Jenny and is determined to get revenge. Too tangled for its own good. **89m/C VHS, DVD.** Shawn Hatosy, Rachael Leigh Cook, Jonathan Rhys Meyers, Lorraine Bracco, Estella Warren; ***D:*** Jay Lowi; ***W:*** Jeffrey Lieber; ***C:*** Bobby Bukowski; ***M:*** Reinhold Heil, Johnny Klimek.

Tangled Destinies 1/2 **1932** Old dark house thriller involving a deserted mansion, murder, and faux diamonds. Good acting and a decent storyline make it one of the few successful independently made films of its time. **64m/B VHS, DVD.** Lloyd Whitlock, Glenn Tryon, Vera Reynolds, Doris Hill, Sidney Bracy; ***D:*** Frank Strayer; ***W:*** Edward T. Lowe.

Tango 1/2 **1936** An early melodrama follows the ups and down of a chorus girl and the guy who sticks with her through thick and thin and poorly filmed dance routines. Based on a novel by Vida Hurst. **66m/B VHS.** Marion (Marian) Nixon, Chick Chandler, Matty Kemp, Marie Prevost, Warren Hymer, Herman Bing, Franklin Pangborn, George Meeker; ***D:*** Phil Rosen.

Tango **1998 (PG-13)** There's not much plot and it's not really needed when cinematographer Storaro so stunningly lenses Saura's semi-documentary look at Argentina's national dance. Middleaged Buenos Aires director Mario Suarez (Sola) is depressed after being abandoned by his wife, Laura (Narova), and decides to throw himself into making a movie about the tango. The film's shady investor, Angelo Larroca

(Galiardo), insists Mario hire his young dancer mistress, Elena (Maestro), with whom Mario unwisely starts to fall in love. Spanish with subtitles. **115m/C VHS, DVD.** *SP* Miguel Angel Sola, Juan Luis Galiardo, Mia Maestro, Cecilia Narova; ***D:*** Carlos Saura; ***W:*** Carlos Saura; ***C:*** Vittorio Storaro; ***M:*** Lalo Schifrin.

Tango and Cash **1989 (R)** Stallone and Russell are L.A. cops with something in common: they both think they are the best in the city. Forced to work together to beat drug lord Palance, they flex their muscles a lot. Directing completed by Albert Magnoli, after Andrei Konchalovsky left in a huff. **104m/C VHS, DVD.** Sylvester Stallone, Kurt Russell, Jack Palance, Brion James, Teri Hatcher, Michael J. Pollard, James Hong, Marc Alaimo, Robert Z'Dar, Edward (Eddie) Bunker, Clint Howard, Lewis Arquette, Michael Jeter, Glenn Morshower, Geoffrey Lewis; ***D:*** Andrei Konchalovsky; ***W:*** Randy Feldman; ***C:*** Donald E. Thorin; ***M:*** Harold Faltermeyer.

Tango Bar **1/2 1988** A romantic triangle between a tango dancer who leaves Argentina during a time of political unrest, his former partner, and his wife, who both stay behind. They are reunited after years of separation. Gives the viewer a detailed vision of the historical and cultural significance of the tango. Charming, interesting and very watchable. In Spanish with English subtitles. **90m/C VHS.** *AR* Raul Julia, Valeria Lynch, Ruben Juarez; ***D:*** Marcos Zurinaga.

The Tango Lesson **1/2 1997 (PG)** Semiautobiographical tale of director/star/writer and former dancer Potter ("Orlando" director), as Sally, who finds love and the meaning of life in the tango while living in Paris. While penning a noncommercial script called "Rage" about a paraplegic designer who stalks leggy models, Sally meets a tango instructor (Pablo) without a partner, and soon the two are doing more than just the tango. Sally grooms Pablo to star in her upcoming pic as long as he allows the headstrong director to take the lead while they dance. Occasionally departs from the story to the "Rage" script, played out in color. While light on their toes, performances by the real-life director and real-life tango instructor are as heavy and stilted as some of the dialogue. Using dance as the metaphor for control and power in relationships, Potter falls flat in a pretentious "Lesson." **101m/B VHS.** *GB* Sally Potter, Pablo Veron, Gustavo Naveira, Fabian Salas, David Toole, Carolina Iotti, Carlos Copello, Peter Eyre, Heathcote Williams; ***D:*** Sally Potter; ***W:*** Sally Potter; ***C:*** Robby Muller; ***M:*** Fred Frith, Sally Potter.

Tank **1/2 1983 (PG)** Retired Army officer Garner's son is thrown into jail on a trumped-up charge by a small town sheriff. Dad comes to the rescue with his restored Sherman tank. Trite and unrealistic portrayal of good versus bad made palatable by Garner's performance. **113m/C VHS, DVD.** James Garner, Shirley Jones, C. Thomas Howell, Mark Herrier, Sandy Ward, Jenilee Harrison, Dorian Harewood, G.D. Spradlin; ***D:*** Marvin J. Chomsky; ***W:*** Dan Gordon; ***C:*** Donald Birnkrant; ***M:*** Lalo Schifrin.

Tank Commando **1/2 1959** Mediocre WWII actioner, set in Italy, about a demolition squad of battle-hardened Americans trying to locate a secret German crossing point. It turns out to be an underwater bridge and an Italian orphan is the only one, besides the Germans, to know its location. Can the Americans persuade the kid to talk? **79m/B VHS.** Bob (Robert) Barron, Wally Campo, Maggie Lawrence, Donato Farretta, Leo V. Metranga, Jack Sowards, Anthony Rich, Larry Hudson; ***D:*** Burt Topper; ***W:*** Burt Topper.

Tank Girl **1/2 1994 (R)** Big-budget adaption of the underground British comic book about a brash punker chick (Petty), her mutant friends, and the evil establishment in the post-apocalyptic future. The heavily armed pixie battles the tyrannical Department of Water and Power, run by evil Dr. Kesslee (McDowell), for control of the world's water supply in the year 2033. Straying a bit too far from the source comic, the plot (such as it is) is crammed into a rigid action-movie structure that lacks excitement. Plays like a cheap Gen-X marketing ploy with its bizarre mixture of pop culture references and a hipper-than-thou soundtrack coordinated by Courtney Love. **104m/C VHS, DVD.** Lori Petty, Malcolm McDowell, Ice-T, Naomi Watts, Jeff Kober, Reg E. Cathey, Scott Coffey, Ann Cusack, Don Harvey, Brian Wimmer, Stacey Linn Ramsower, Iggy Pop, Ann Magnuson; ***D:*** Rachel Talalay; ***W:*** Tedi Sarafian; ***C:*** Gale Tattersall; ***M:*** Graeme Revell.

Tanks a Million **1941** Despite the title, tanks aren't even mentioned in this. Tracy stars as a wacky genius who gets drafted. His excellent memory keeps getting him into one predicament after another. Though he gets promoted quickly, he shows himself no leader. Lots of time-worn gags, but they still work. **50m/B VHS.** William Tracy, James Gleason, Noah Beery Jr., Joseph (Joe) Sawyer, Elyse Knox, Douglas Fowley, Frank Faylen, Dick Wessel, Frank Melton, Harold Goodwin, William (Bill) Gould, Norman Kerry; ***D:*** Fred Guiol.

Tanner '88 *Tanner: A Political Fable* **1988** Murphy is excellent as a longshot politician on the trail of the Democratic presidential nomination. Precise political satire from a story by Gary "Doonesbury" Trudeau. **120m/C VHS, DVD.** Michael Murphy, Pamela Reed, Cynthia Nixon; ***D:*** Robert Altman. **CABLE**

Tanner on Tanner **2004** Trudeau's Tanner (Murphy) returns sixteen years later with Alex (Nixon) struggling to make a documentary of her dad's dashed presidential dreams while her own life is unraveling. Meanwhile, he's busily inflating his prominence within the party during the national convention. **120m/C VHS, DVD.** Michael Murphy, Cynthia Nixon, Pamela Reed, Matt Malloy, Ilana Levine, Jim Fyfe, Avery Clyde; ***Cameos:*** Tom Brokaw, Steve Buscemi, Mario Cuomo, Howard Dean, Michael Dukakis; ***D:*** Robert Altman; ***W:*** Garry Trudeau; ***C:*** Robert Altman, Tom Richmond. **TV**

Tanya's Island **1/2 1981 (R)** Abused girlfriend fantasizes about life on deserted island and romance with an ape. Vanity billed as D.D. Winters. **100m/C VHS, DVD.** Vanity, Dick Sargent, Mariette Levesque, Don McCleod; ***D:*** Alfred Sole.

The Tao of Steve **2000 (R)** Overweight, intelligent kindergarten teacher Dex (Logue) is a hit with the ladies, but feels a vague sense of wanting something more. The title of the film comes from Dex's personal philosophy of cool, which he takes from the images of such icons as Steve McQueen, Steve McGarrett, and Steve Austin—but is also tossed with equal parts Kierkegaard and Aquinas. He's ripe for some growing up, and only needs to find the perfect mate, who comes along in the form of Syd (played by Greer Goodman, sister of the director and one of the film's three screenwriters), one of Dex's one-night stands. A sweet romantic comedy that can thank Logue for much of its charm. **87m/C VHS, DVD.** Donal Logue, Greer Goodman, Kimo Wills, Ayelet Kaznelson, David Aaron Baker, Nina Jaroslaw; ***D:*** Jenniphr Goodman; ***W:*** Greer Goodman, Jenniphr Goodman, Duncan North; ***C:*** Teodoro Maniaci; ***M:*** Joe Delia.

Tap **1/2 1989 (PG-13)** The son of a famous tap dancer, a dancer himself, decides to try to get away from his former life of crime by helping an aging hoofer revitalize the art of tap dancing. Fun to watch for the wonderful dancing scenes. Davis' last big screen appearance. Hines is sincere in this old-fashioned story, and dances up a storm. Captures some never-before-filmed old hoofers. **106m/C VHS, DVD.** Gregory Hines, Sammy Davis Jr., Suzzanne Douglass, Joe Morton, Terrance McNally, Steve Condos, Jimmy Slyde, Harold Nicholas, Etta James, Savion Glover, Dick Anthony Williams, Howard "Sandman" Sims, Bunny Briggs, Pat Rico, Arthur Duncan; ***D:*** Nick Castle; ***W:*** Nick Castle; ***M:*** James Newton Howard.

Tape **2001 (R)** Director Linklater makes digital technology an asset in this intriguing, claustrophobic character study based on a play by Stephen Belber. Johnny (Leonard) pays a visit to high school chum Vince (Hawke), who's working as a low-level drug dealer. Their casual conversation becomes increasingly hostile as Vince begins making accusations involving Johnny and his first love, Amy (Thurman), who soon pays a visit herself. Despite a tiny cast and only one location, story stays stimulating throughout, as the script deftly shifts viewer allegiance between characters and explores interesting themes of memory, subjectivity and ownership of one's past. Linklater's use of high-definition video gives the film a vitality and spontaneous feel that suits the material. **86m/C VHS, DVD.** *US* Ethan Hawke, Robert Sean Leonard, Uma Thurman; ***D:*** Richard Linklater; ***W:*** Stephen Belber; ***C:*** Maryse Alberti.

Tapeheads **1/2 1989 (R)** Silly, sophomoric, sexy comedy starring Cusack and Robbins as young wanna-be rock-video producers who get mixed up with perverted politicos, conniving music-industry types, and asinine bands looking for MTV stardom before they eventually strike it big helping their childhood idols, The Swanky Modes. Many big-name music industry cameos and a great soundtrack help keep things lively when the plot goes out of control. Sam Moore and Junior Walker are the Sam & Dave-esque Modes. **93m/C VHS, DVD.** Courtney Love, Ebbe Roe Smith, Lee Arenberg, Rocky Giordani, John Marshall Jones, John Durbin, Milton Selzer, Zander Schloss, Jo Harvey Allen, Sy Richardson, Coati Mundi, John Fleck, John Cusack, Tim Robbins, Mary Crosby, Connie Stevens, Susan Tyrrell, Lyle Alzado, Don Cornelius, Katy Boyer, Doug McClure, Clu Gulager, Jessica Walter, Stiv Bators, Sam Moore, Junior Walker, Martha Quinn, Ted Nugent, Weird Al Yankovic, Bob(cat) Goldthwait, Michael Nesmith, Xander Berkeley, Bojan Bazelli; ***D:*** Bill Fishman; ***W:*** Bill Fishman, Peter McCarthy; ***C:*** Bojan Bazelli.

Taps **1/2 1981 (PG)** Military academy students led by Hutton are so true to their school they lay siege to it to keep it from being closed. An antiwar morality play about excesses of zeal and patriotism. Predictable but impressive. **126m/C VHS, DVD.** Timothy Hutton, George C. Scott, Ronny Cox, Sean Penn, Tom Cruise, Giancarlo Esposito, Evan Handler, Brendan Ward, John P. Navin Jr., Earl Hindman; ***D:*** Harold Becker; ***W:*** Darryl Ponicsan, Robert Mark Kamen; ***C:*** Owen Roizman; ***M:*** Maurice Jarre.

Tar **1997** Female cop Prescott and crook Thigpen were high school sweethearts who went their separate ways. But they're reunited when Thigpen hijacks a squad car that just happens to be driven by guess who. There's also a story involving a group of black nationalists who kidnap white businessman and cover them in—you guessed it—tar. Likeable leads, improbable characters. **90m/C VHS, DVD.** Kevin Thigpen, Nicole Prescott, Seth Gilliam, Ron Brice, Frank Minucci; ***D:*** Goetz Grossmann; ***W:*** Goetz Grossmann; ***C:*** Lloyd Handwerker; ***M:*** John Hill.

Tara Road **1/2 2005 (PG)** American Marilyn's (MacDowell) son dies in an accident and she can't recover from her grief, while Irish Ria (Williams) is told by her husband (Glen) that he's leaving her to marry his pregnant girlfriend. Through a series of coincidences, the unhappy women decide to switch houses for two months and see if it will change their lives. Bland adaptation of the novel by Maeve Binchy. **97m/C DVD.** *IR* Andie MacDowell, Olivia Williams, Iain Glen, Stephen Rea, Brenda Fricker, Jean-Marc Barr; ***D:*** Gilles Mackinnon; ***W:*** Shane Connaughton; ***C:*** John de Borman; ***M:*** John Keane.

Tarantella **1/2 1995** Aspiring New York photographer Diane DiSorella (Sorvino) gets a shock when her mother dies suddenly. After returning to the New Jersey home and Italian-American community she rejected, Diane is given a journal her mother secretly kept by old family friend Pina (Gregorio). Small-scale story with Diane's big change being learning to accept where she came from. **84m/C VHS, DVD.** Mira Sorvino, Rose Gregorio, Stephen Spinella, Matthew Lillard, Antonia Rey, Frank Pellegrino; ***D:*** Helen DeMichiel; ***W:*** Helen DeMichiel, Richard Hoblock; ***C:*** Teodoro Maniaci; ***M:*** Norman Moll.

Tarantula **1955** If you're into gigantic killer insect movies this is one of the best with nifty special effects and some good action. Carroll plays a scientist working on a growth formula which he's testing on a spider when it accidentally gets loose. This eight-legged horror grows to 100 feet high and causes havoc in the Arizona desert until the Air Force napalms the sucker. Look for Eastwood in the final sequence as an Air Force pilot. **81m/B VHS, DVD.** Leo G. Carroll, John Agar, Mara Corday, Nestor Paiva, Ross Elliott, Clint Eastwood; ***D:*** Jack Arnold; ***W:*** Robert M. Fresco, Martin Berkeley, Jack Arnold.

Tarantulas: The Deadly Cargo **1977** Eek! Hairy spiders terrorizing our sleepy town and destroying our orange crop! Made-for-TV cheapie not creepy; will make you sleepy. **100m/C VHS, DVD.** Claude Akins, Charles Frank, Deborah Winters, Pat Hingle, Sandy McPeak, Bert Remsen, Howard Hesseman, Tom Atkins, Charles Siebert, Matthew Laborteaux, Pepe Serna; ***D:*** Stuart Hagmann; ***W:*** Guerdon (Gordon) Trueblood; ***C:*** Robert L. Morrison; ***M:*** Mundell Lowe. **TV**

Taras Bulba **1/2 1962** Well-photographed costume epic on the 16th century Polish revolution. Brynner as the fabled Cossack; Curtis plays his vengeful son. Good score. Shot on location in Argentina. Based on the novel by Nikolai Gogol. **122m/C VHS.** Tony Curtis, Yul Brynner, Christine Kaufmann, Sam Wanamaker, George Macready, Vladimir Sokoloff, Perry Lopez; ***D:*** J. Lee Thompson.

Target **1985 (R)** Normal dad/hubby Hackman slips into a figurative phone booth and emerges as former CIA when his better half is kidnapped in Paris. Good action scenes, but poorly scripted and too long. **117m/C VHS, DVD.** Gene Hackman, Matt Dillon, Gayle Hunnicutt, Josef Sommer; ***D:*** Arthur Penn; ***W:*** Howard Berk.

The Target **1/2** *The Piano Player* **2002 (R)** Mercenary Alex Laney (Lambert) goes to South Africa to protect wealthy businessman Robert Nile (Hopper) from the crime boss (Majiba) who's now in jail thanks to Nile's promised testimony. But those who attempt to testify soon wind up dead, so after some near-misses, Niles, his daughter (Kruger), and Laney wind up in a small town with the bad guy (freed from prison) still on their trail. Typical "B" movie action. **94m/C VHS, DVD.** Christopher Lambert, Dennis Hopper, James Faulkner, Diane Kruger, Simon Majiba; ***D:*** Jean-Pierre Roux; ***W:*** Brad Mirman; ***C:*** Larry Smith.

Target Eagle **1984** Spanish police chief von Sydow hires mercenary Rivero to infiltrate drug ring. Good performances; ho-hum story. **99m/C VHS.** *SP MX* Max von Sydow, George Peppard, Maud Adams, Chuck Connors, Jorge (George) Rivero, Susana Dosamantes; ***D:*** Jose Antonio De La Loma.

Target: Favorite Son **1987 (R)** An attractive, ammunition-laden woman sharp-shoots her way to power in this made-for-TV movie. **115m/C VHS.** Linda Kozlowski, Harry Hamlin, Robert Loggia, Ronny Cox, James Whitmore; ***D:*** Jeff Bleckner; ***W:*** Steve Sohmer; ***C:*** Bradford May; ***M:*** John Morris.

Target for Killing **1966** Mediocre thriller about a secret agent who must protect a young heiress from a Lebanese syndicate that's out to kill her. **93m/C VHS.** Stewart Granger, Curt Jurgens, Molly Peters, Adolfo Celi, Klaus Kinski, Rupert Davies; ***D:*** Manfred Kohler.

Target of Opportunity **1/2 2004 (R)** Rousing action tale hits the mark. Jim Jacobs (Cochran) is a former CIA guy who heads to Eastern Europe to rescue childhood buddy Nick Carlton (Jensen), an agent jailed for being on the wrong side of some spy games. But in the process Jim finds himself on his old employer's most wanted list. **91m/C VHS, DVD.** Todd Jensen, Hristo Naumov Shopov, Dean Cochran, Nadia Konakchieva, Bashar Rahal; ***D:*** Dan Lerner; ***W:*** Les Weldon. **VIDEO**

Targets **1968 (PG)** Bogdanovich's suspenseful directorial debut. An aging horror film star plans his retirement, convinced that real life is too scary for his films to have an audience. A mad sniper at a drive-in movie seems to prove he's right. Some prints still have anti-gun prologue, which was added after Robert Kennedy's assassination. **90m/C VHS, DVD.** Boris Karloff, James Brown, Tim O'Kelly, Peter Bogdanovich, Mary Jackson, Sandy Baron, Monte Landis, Mike Farrell, Nancy Hsueh, Arthur Peterson, Tanya Morgan, Randy Quaid; ***D:*** Peter Bogdanovich; ***W:*** Peter Bogdanovich; ***C:*** Laszlo Kovacs.

Tarnation **1/2 2003** Feature debut of Caouette is an experimental documentary constructed from home movies, photographs, letters, phone messages, and created video footage that Caouette edited on his home computer and layered with appropriate songs. It follows the emotional journey of Caouette and his mentally ill mother from a Texas childhood legacy of abuse, neglect, and an escape into a self-created fantasy world, to their lives 20-odd years later. **88m/C DVD.** *D:* Jonathan Caouette; *W:* Jonathan Caouette; *C:* Jonathan Caouette; *M:* John Califra, Max Lichtenstein.

Tarnished Angels 🦴🦴🦴 **1957** Reporter Burke Devlin (Hudson) is writing a story for the local New Orleans paper about a tormented trio of air circus barmstormers. A former WWI ace, Roger Shumann (Stack) cares more about flying than he does his sizzling wife Laverne (Malone), who's loved-from-afar by loyal mechanic Jiggs (Carson). When Roger's plane cracks up, he uses his wife to obtain use of an experimental aircraft in order to win a race—and brings disaster crashing around them all. Good action, fine cast. Based on William Faulkner's 1930 novel "Pylon." **91m/B VHS.** Rock Hudson, Robert Stack, Dorothy Malone, Jack Carson, Robert Middleton, Troy Donahue, Alan Reed, Robert J. Wilke, William Schallert; *D:* Douglas Sirk; *W:* George Zuckerman; *C:* Irving Glassberg; *M:* Frank Skinner.

Tart 🦴🦴 **2001 (R)** Cat Storm (Swain) is desperate to belong to the in-crowd at her New York prep school even if it means dumping her best friend, Delilah (Phillips). But privilege has its price. **94m/C VHS, DVD.** Dominique Swain, Brad Renfro, Bijou Phillips, Mischa Barton, Lacey Chabert, Alberta Watson, Myles Jeffrey, Scott Thompson, Melanie Griffith; *D:* Christina Wayne; *W:* Christina Wayne; *C:* Stephen Kazmierski; *M:* Jeehun Hwang.

Tartuffe 🦴🦴 *Herr Tartuff* **1925** Murnau's film-within-a-film adaptation of Moliere's play. A greedy housekeeper (Valetti) wants to profit from her elderly employer's (Picha) will so she tells him that his actor grandson (Mattoni) is a wastrel. The grandson disguises himself as a traveling film projectionist and shows his grandfather the film about Tartuffe (Jannings), which parallels their own story of greed and hypocrisy. **74m/B DVD.** *GE* Emil Jannings, Lil Dagover, Werner Krauss, Rosa Valetti, Andre Mattoni, Hermann Picha; *D:* F.W. Murnau; *W:* Carl Mayer; *C:* Karl Freund.

Tartuffe 🦴🦴 ½ **1984** Popular French leading man Depardieu makes directorial debut with Moliere classic about religious hypocrisy and an imposter taking advantage of a wealthy merchant and his family. In French with English subtitles. **140m/C VHS.** *FR* Gerard Depardieu, Francois Perier, Elisabeth Depardieu; *D:* Gerard Depardieu.

Tartuffe 🦴🦴 ½ **1990** Moliere's famous comedy has Tartuffe posing as a holy man who has attracted the incredulous merchant Orgon. Orgon is willing to give Tartuffe anything—money, social position, even his daughter—and Tartuffe is more than happy to accept. **110m/C VHS.** Anthony Sher, Nigel Hawthorne, Alison Steadman; *D:* Bill Alexander.

Tarzan 🦴🦴🦴 **1999 (G)** Disney animated film finds baby Tarzan lost in the jungle and raised by a gorilla family—patriarch Kerchak (Henriksen), nurturing mom Kala (Close), and bossy big sister Terk (O'Donnell). But, years later, a now grownup Tarzan's (Goldwyn) life is thrown into chaos when he first encounters humans—and realizes he is one. Eccentric gorilla scientist Professor Porter (Hawthorne) and his lovely daughter Jane (Driver) are willing to help, but jungle guide Clayton (Blessed) is the villain on the scene. Disney's animation is even more amazing than usual thanks to some new computer software that gives the jungle background unbelievable depth and Tarzan glides, surfs, and jumps in a wow! look! manner. **88m/C VHS, DVD.** *D:* Kevin Lima, Chris Buck; *W:* Tab Murphy, Bob Tzudiker, Noni White; *M:* Phil Collins; *V:* Tony Goldwyn, Minnie Driver, Rosie O'Donnell, Glenn Close, Lance Henriksen, Wayne Knight, Brian Blessed, Nigel Hawthorne, Alex D. Linz. Oscars '99: Song ("You'll Be In My Heart"); Golden Globes '00: Song ("You'll Be In My Heart").

Tarzan 2 🦴🦴 ½ **2005** Animated prequel to the 2004 Disney flick finds young Tarzan (Chad) upset that he's not as strong or as fast as his ape foster family. When his human weakness puts his mom's (Close) life in danger, Tarzan leaves the tribe and seeks out a cranky, old hermit ape (Carlin) for advice. Lots of fun for the pee-wee set (and their parents will enjoy the Carlin humor). **72m/C DVD.** *D:* Brian J. Smith; *W:* Bob Tzudiker, Noni White; *M:* Mark Mancina; *V:* Harrison Chad, Glenn Close, George Carlin, Brad Garrett, Lance Henriksen, Ron Perlman, Estelle Harris. **VIDEO**

Tarzan and His Mate 🦴🦴🦴 **1934** Second entry in the lavishly produced MGM Tarzan series. Weissmuller and O'Sullivan cohabit in unmarried bliss before the Hays Code moved them to a tree house with twin beds. Many angry elephants, nasty white hunters, and hungry lions. **93m/B VHS, DVD.** Johnny Weissmuller, Maureen O'Sullivan, Neil Hamilton, Paul Cavanagh; *D:* Jack Conway; *W:* Leon Gordon, James Kevin McGuinness, Howard Emmett Rogers; *C:* Clyde De Vinna, Charles G. Clarke; *M:* William Axt. Natl. Film Reg. '03.

Tarzan and the Green Goddess 🦴 ½ *New Adventures of Tarzan* **1938** Tarzan searches for a statue that could prove dangerous if in the wrong hands. **72m/B VHS, DVD.** Bruce Bennett, Ula Holt, Frank Baker; *D:* Edward Kull.

Tarzan and the Lost City 🦴🦴 ½ *Tarzan and Jane; Greystoke 2: Tarzan and Jane* **1998 (PG)** Gorgeous locations in South Africa are a decided plus in this routine hero/adventure story. Lord Greystoke, AKA Tarzan (Van Dien), returns to Africa from England in order to save his home from mercenaries hunting the lost city of Opar. Spunky fiance Jane (March) heads to the jungle after her Ape Man and gets into (and out of) trouble with bad guy Nigel Ravens (Waddington). Not very convincing special effects but Van Dien looks good in his loincloth and has the action moves down cold. **84m/C VHS, DVD.** Casper Van Dien, Jane March, Steven Waddington, Winston Ntshona, Rapulana Seiphemo, Ian Roberts; *D:* Carl Schenkel; *W:* Bayard Johnson, J. Anderson Black; *C:* Paul Gilpin; *M:* Christopher Franke.

Tarzan and the Lost Safari 🦴 ½ **1957** Scott's second film as Tarzan has him leading the survivors of a plane crash to safety. But hunter Tusker Hawkins (Beatty) has made a deal with the natives to give the survivors to them as human sacrifices in return for lots of ivory. Shot in CinemaScope on location in Africa. **84m/C DVD.** *GB* Gordon Scott, Robert Beatty, Yolande Donlan, Betta St. John, Peter Arne, Wilfrid Hyde-White, George Coulouris; *D:* H. Bruce Humberstone; *W:* Montgomery Pittman, Lillie Hayward; *C:* C.M. Pennington-Richards, Miki Carter; *M:* Clifton Parker.

Tarzan and the She-Devil 🦴 ½ **1953** Barker makes his fifth and final appearance as Tarzan in the RKO series. Greedy Lyra (Van Vooren) and her minions are ivory-poachers, which means killing elephants. Lyra imprisons Tarzan, who doesn't try hard to escape since he thinks they've killed Jane. When he realizes that Jane is alive, he calls his elephants to stampede. **76m/B DVD.** Lex Barker, Monique Van Vooren, Raymond Burr, Tom Conway, Joyce MacKenzie, Michael Granger; *D:* Kurt Neumann; *W:* Karl Kamb, Carroll Young; *C:* Karl Struss; *M:* Paul Sawtell.

Tarzan and the Slave Girl 🦴 ½ **1950** Or would-be slave girls anyway as Jane (Brown) and nurse Lola (Darcel) are kidnapped by a lion-worshipping tribe dying from a mysterious plague. Their ruler thinks they need some new blood to repopulate his people but it's Tarzan (Barker's second appearance) to the rescue. **74m/B DVD.** Lex Barker, Vanessa Brown, Hurd Hatfield, Denise Darcel, Robert Alda, Robert Warwick, Arthur Shields; *D:* Lee Sholem; *W:* Arnold Belgard, Hans Jacoby; *C:* Russell Harlan; *M:* Paul Sawtell.

Tarzan and the Trappers 🦴 ½ **1958** Bad-guy trappers and would-be treasure-seekers wish they hadn't messed with the ape man. **70m/B VHS, DVD.** Gordon Scott, Eve Brent, Ricky Sorenson, Maurice Marsac; *D:* Charles F. Haas, H. Bruce Humberstone, Sandy Howard.

Tarzan Escapes 🦴🦴🦴 **1936** Jane is tricked by evil hunters into abandoning her fairy tale life with Tarzan, so the Ape Man sets out to reunite with his one true love. The third entry in MGM's Weissmuller/O'Sullivan series is still among the better Tarzan movies thanks to the leads, but the Hays Office made sure Jane was wearing a lot more clothes this time around. **95m/B VHS, DVD.** Johnny Weissmuller, Maureen O'Sullivan, John Buckler, Benita Hume, William Henry; *D:* Richard Thorpe.

Tarzan Finds a Son 🦴🦴🦴 **1939** Weissmuller and O'Sullivan returned to their roles after three years with the addition of the five-year-old Sheffield as Boy. He's an orphan whose awful relatives hope he stays lost so they can collect an inheritance. Jane and Tarzan fight to adopt the tyke and when the new family are captured by a wicked tribe only an elephant stampede can save them! **90m/B VHS, DVD.** Johnny Weissmuller, Maureen O'Sullivan, John(ny) Sheffield, Ian Hunter, Henry Stephenson, Frieda Inescort, Henry Wilcoxon; *D:* Richard Thorpe.

Tarzan of the Apes 🦴🦴 **1917** Brawny Lincoln is the original screen Tarzan. Silent film well done and more faithful to the book than later versions. **63m/B VHS, DVD.** Elmo Lincoln, Enid Markey; *D:* Scott Sidney.

Tarzan, the Ape Man 🦴🦴🦴 **1932** The definitive Tarzan movie; the first Tarzan talkie; the original of the long series starring Weissmuller. Dubiously faithful to the Edgar Rice Burroughs story, but recent attempts to remake, update or improve it (notably the pretentious 1984 Greystoke) have failed to near the original's entertainment value or even its technical quality. O'Sullivan as Jane and Weissmuller bring style and wit to their classic roles. **99m/B VHS, DVD.** Johnny Weissmuller, Maureen O'Sullivan, Neil Hamilton; *D:* Woodbridge S. Van Dyke; *C:* Clyde De Vinna.

Tarzan, the Ape Man WOOF! **1981 (R)** Plodding, perverted excuse to see Derek cavort nude in jungle. So bad not even hard-core Tarzan fans should bother. **112m/C VHS, DVD.** Bo Derek, Richard Harris, John Phillip Law, Miles O'Keeffe, Wilfrid Hyde-White, Akushula Selayah, Steven Strong, Laurie Main, Harold Ayer; *D:* John Derek; *W:* Gary Goddard; *C:* John Derek; *M:* Perry Botkin. Golden Raspberries '81: Worst Actress (Derek).

Tarzan the Fearless 🦴 ½ **1933** Tarzan (Crabbe) helps a young girl find her missing father. **84m/B VHS, DVD.** Buster Crabbe, Julie Bishop, E. Alyn (Fred) Warren, Edward (Eddie) Woods, Philo (Philip, P.H., P.M.) McCullough, Matthew Betz; *D:* Robert F. "Bob" Hill; *W:* Walter Anthony; *C:* Joseph Brotherton, Harry Neumann.

Tarzan the Magnificent 🦴 ½ **1960** Scott's sixth and final Tarzan movie was a cheap, dull effort that had the loinclothed hero leading criminal Coy Banton (Mahoney) through the jungle to the authorities with various problems accompanying them. Mahoney would succeed Scott in the Tarzan role while Scott himself went to Italy to make Hercules flicks. **82m/C DVD.** *GB* Gordon Scott, Jock Mahoney, John Carradine, Betta St. John, Lionel Jeffries, Alexandra Stewart; *D:* Robert Day; *W:* Robert Day, Berne Giler; *C:* Edward Scaife; *M:* Ken Jones.

Tarzan the Tiger **1929** Series of 15 chapters is loosely based on the Edgar Rice Burroughs novel entitled "Tarzan and the Jewels of Opar." These chapters were filmed as silent pieces, and were later released with a musical score and synchronized sound effects. Here Merrill is the first to sound the cry of the bull ape, Tarzan's trademark. **?m/B VHS, DVD.** Frank Merrill, Natalie Kingston, Lilian Worth, Al Ferguson; *D:* Henry MacRae.

Tarzana, the Wild Girl 🦴 **1969** Jungle cheapie about an expedition that finds a beautiful, scantily clad girl living wildly in the jungle. **87m/C VHS.** Ken Clark, Franca Polesello, Frank Ressel, Andrew Ray, James Reed; *W:* Philip Shaw.

Tarzan's Fight for Life 🦴 ½ **1958** Jane (Brent) finally shows up in Scott's third outing, which finds our jungle man trying to convince a superstitious tribe to give Dr. Sturdy's (Reid) modern methods a try over their witch doctor Futa's (Edwards) efforts. This results in Tarzan's being captured since Futa wants to use his heart in a tribal ceremony. **86m/C DVD.** Gordon Scott, Eve Brent, Jill Jarmyn, Carl Benton Reid, James Edwards, Ricky Sorenson, Woody Strode, Harry Lauter; *D:* H. Bruce Humberstone; *W:* Thomas Hal Phillips; *C:* William E. Snyder, Mike Carter; *M:* Ernest Gold.

Tarzan's Greatest Adventure 🦴🦴 **1959** Scott's fifth outing is a surprisingly violent (and well-done) revenge story. Ruthless diamond smuggler Slade (Quayle) is more interested in killing Tarzan (who once put him in jail) than his ill-gotten goods. Tarzan has other ideas. **88m/C DVD.** *GB* Gordon Scott, Anthony Quayle, Sara Shane, Sean Connery, Niall MacGinnis, Al Mulock, Scilla Gabel; *D:* John Guillermin; *W:* John Guillermin, Berne Giler; *C:* Edward Scaife; *M:* Douglas Gamley.

Tarzan's Hidden Jungle 🦴 ½ **1955** Beefcake Scott's first (of six) Tarzan films was the last made in black and white and the last from the RKO studio. Tarzan and his elephants go after evil hunters who have involved a local doctor and nurse in a plot that upsets the natives. **73m/B DVD.** Gordon Scott, Robert Beatty, Yolande Donlan, Betta St. John, Peter Arne, Wilfrid Hyde-White, George Coulouris; *D:* H. Bruce Humberstone; *W:* Montgomery Pittman, Lillie Hayward; *C:* C.M. Pennington-Richards, Miki Carter; *M:* Clifton Parker.

Tarzan's Magic Fountain 🦴 ½ **1948** Barker takes over from Weissmuller in the first of his five appearances as Tarzan in this RKO series. Jane (Joyce) is an aviatrix who crashes in the jungle and finds the fountain of youth in a hidden valley. Tarzan eventually comes along to lead her back to civilization but not before some nosy hunters try to find the valley themselves. **73m/B DVD.** Lex Barker, Brenda Joyce, Evelyn Ankers, Alan Napier, Albert Dekker, Charles Drake; *D:* Lee Sholem; *W:* Curt Siodmak, Harry Chandlee; *C:* Karl Struss; *M:* Alexander Laszlo.

Tarzan's New York Adventure 🦴🦴 ½ **1942** O'Sullivan's final appearance as Jane is a so-so adventure with some humorous moments when Tarzan meets the big city. When Boy is kidnapped by an evil circus owner, Tarzan, Jane, and Cheta head out to rescue him. Tarzan shows off his jungle prowess by climbing skyscrapers and diving off the Brooklyn Bridge into the East River. Lincoln, the screen's first Tarzan, has a cameo. **70m/B VHS, DVD.** Johnny Weissmuller, Maureen O'Sullivan, John(ny) Sheffield, Virginia Grey, Charles Bickford, Paul Kelly, Chill Wills, Russell Hicks, Cy Kendall; ***Cameos:*** Elmo Lincoln; *D:* Richard Thorpe.

Tarzan's Peril 🦴 ½ **1951** Gunrunners are willing to trade for jewels with King Bulam (O'Neal) so that his Yorango tribe can attack the peaceful Ashubas, led by Queen Melmendi (Dandridge). (The King is peeved that the Queen rejected him.) But Tarzan (Barker) isn't going to stand for that. Barker's third appearance in the title role. **79m/B DVD.** Virginia Huston, Frederick O'Neal, Dorothy Dandridge, Douglas Fowley, Lex Barker, George Macready, Glenn Anders, Alan Napier; *D:* Byron Haskin; *W:* Francis Swann, Samuel Newman; *C:* Karl Struss; *M:* Michel Michelet.

Tarzan's Revenge 🦴 **1938** Morris is a better Olympic runner than actor; Holm is horrible. Only for serious Tarzan fans. **70m/B VHS, DVD.** Glenn Morris, Eleanor Holm, Hedda Hopper; *D:* David Ross Lederman.

Tarzan's Savage Fury 🦴 ½ **1952** Tarzan (Barker in No. 4) is approached by two British agents who need a guide into the diamond-rich Wazuri region. But imagine his fury when Tarzan discovers he's been duped and the men are thieves! **79m/B DVD.** Lex Barker, Dorothy Hart, Patric Knowles, Charles Korvin, Tommy Carlton; *D:* Cy Enfield; *W:* Hans Jacoby, Cyril Hume, Shirley White; *C:* Karl Struss; *M:* Paul Sawtell.

Tarzan's Secret Treasure 🦴🦴 ½ **1941** Tarzan saves an expedition from a savage tribe only to be repaid by having the greedy hunters hold Jane and Boy hostage. They want Tarzan's help in finding a secret cache of gold. But Tarzan doesn't take kindly to threats to his family and teaches those evil-doers a lesson! **81m/B VHS, DVD.** Johnny Weissmuller, Maureen O'Sullivan, John(ny) Sheffield, Reginald Owen, Barry Fitzgerald, Tom Conway, Philip Dorn; *D:* Richard Thorpe.

Task Force ⅋⅋ 1/2 **1949** History of naval aviation and the development of the aircraft carrier highlighted by actual WWII combat footage (in color). Cooper and his naval buddies try to convince the brass that planes can be landed on the decks of ships. Slowly the Navy goes ahead and when Pearl Harbor is attacked, Cooper is given command of his own aircraft carrier. The use of the carriers proved very effective in Pacific battles and Cooper is finally vindicated. **116m/B VHS.** Gary Cooper, Jane Wyatt, Wayne Morris, Walter Brennan, Julie London, Bruce Bennett, Jack Holt, Stanley Ridges, John Ridgely, Richard Rober, Art Baker, Moroni Olsen; ***D:*** Delmer Daves; ***W:*** Delmer Daves.

A Taste for Flesh and Blood ⅋⅋ **1990 (R)** A monster from outer space comes to earth and is delighted with the easy pickings for his insatiable appetite. A brave boy and girl, and a NASA commander must join forces to take the alien out. This one is billed as a campy salute to '50s B movies. **84m/C VHS.** Rubin Santiago, Lori Karz, Tim Ferrante; ***D:*** Warren F. Disbrow.

A Taste for Killing ⅋⅋ **1992 (R)** Two boys, both from well-to-do families, decide to take summer jobs on an offshore Texas oil rig. The best friends think a summer of adventure awaits them; however, their lives are made miserable by their blue-collar boss, who is resentful of their high society background. Then they meet Bo Landry, who befriends them and helps them survive. Unfortunately, Bo turns out to be anything but a friend as he reveals himself as a deadly con-artist in this intense psychological thriller. **87m/C VHS.** Jason Bateman, Henry Thomas, Michael Biehn, Edward "Blue" Deckert, Helen Cates; ***D:*** Lou Antonio; ***W:*** Dan Bronson.

A Taste of Blood ⅋ 1/2 **1967** Gore-meister Lewis's vampire film is actually fairly restrained when compared to "2000 Maniacs" and "Blood Feast." When John Stone (Rogers) drinks brandy containing the blood of Count Dracula, he turns into a green-faced killer bent on revenge against the ancestors of...oh, never mind. **118m/C DVD.** Bill Rogers, Elizabeth Wilkinson, William Kerwin, Lawrence Tobin; ***D:*** Herschell Gordon Lewis; ***W:*** Donald Stanford; ***C:*** Andy Romanoff.

The Taste of Cherry ⅋⅋ *Ta'm e Guilass; Taste of Cherries* **1996** Despairing, middle-aged Mr. Badii (Ershadi) is contemplating suicide and looking for someone who will bury his corpse discreetly. (He's already dug his own shallow grave in the countryside.) He drives through the streets and picks up several different men—all of whom remind him that suicide goes against the teachings of Islam. Finally, one old Turkish man relates his own story of attempted suicide and seemingly persuades Badii to rethink his actions. **95m/C VHS, DVD.** *IA* Homayon Ershadi, Abdolrahma Bagheri, Afshin Bakhtiari; ***D:*** Abbas Kiarostami; ***W:*** Abbas Kiarostami; ***C:*** Homayun Payvar. Cannes '97: Film; Natl. Soc. Film Critics '98: Foreign Film.

Taste of Death ⅋ *Quanto Costa Morire; Cost of Dying* **1968** A youth discovers his courage within when he stands up to the bandits invading his village. **90m/C VHS, DVD.** *IT* Raymond Pellegrin, Bruno Corazzari, Andrea Giordana, John Ireland; ***D:*** Sergio Merolle; ***W:*** Biagio Proietti; ***C:*** Benito Frattari; ***M:*** Francesco De Masi.

A Taste of Hell ⅋ **1973 (PG)** Two American soldiers fight a guerilla outfit in the Pacific during WWII. A low-budget film with few redeeming characteristics. **90m/C VHS.** Liza Lorena, William (Bill) Smith, John Garwood; ***D:*** Neil Yarema; ***W:*** Neil Yarema; ***C:*** Fred Conde; ***M:*** Nestor Robles.

A Taste of Honey ⅋⅋⅋ **1961** A plain working-class girl falls in love with a black sailor. When she becomes pregnant, a homosexual friend helps her out. A moving film with strong, powerful performances. Based on the London and Broadway hit play by Shelagh Delaney. **100m/B VHS.** *GB* Rita Tushingham, Robert Stephens, Dora Bryan, Murray Melvin, Paul Danquah; ***D:*** Tony Richardson; ***W:*** Tony Richardson, Shelagh Delaney; ***C:*** Walter Lassally; ***M:*** John Addison. British Acad. '61: Film, Support. Actress (Bryan); British Acad. '62: Screenplay; Cannes '62: Actor (Melvin), Actress (Tushingham).

The Taste of Others ⅋⅋⅋ *Le Gout des Autres* **2000** This classy import is a hard sell to American audiences; first, it's in French, and second, it begins as if the first reel is missing—the low-key action opens with two banal conversations at separate tables. Actress/writer Jaoui, in her directorial debut, takes time in sorting out relationships. Eventually it becomes clear that married, boorish businessman Castella (Bacri) is falling for 40-year-old actress Clara (Alvaro), who's fretting about aging and her uncertain prospects, and who has been hired to teach Castella English. He pursues, she resists—at first. Meanwhile, Castella's tough bodyguard Moreno (Lanvin) is involved with Clara's friend, free-spirited barmaid Manie (Jaoui). For fans of Rohmer, it works. The characters are engagingly different and interesting. The film looks as sharp and polished as a comparable Hollywood ensemble comedy. French with subtitles. **112m/C DVD.** *FR* Jean-Pierre Bacri, Christiane Millet, Agnes Jaoui, Anne Alvaro, Gerard Lanvin, Wladimir Yordanoff, Brigitte Catillon, Xavier De Guillebon, Alain Chabat, Raphael Defour; ***D:*** Agnes Jaoui; ***W:*** Jean-Pierre Bacri, Agnes Jaoui; ***C:*** Laurent Dailland; ***M:*** Jean-Charles Jarrell.

The Taste of Tea ⅋⅋⅋ *Cha no aji* **2004** The Father of the Haruno family is a hypnotherapist who experiments on his own family while Mom wants to draw anime. Their daughter is haunted by a giant version of herself who looks like she's always ticked off. Grandpa lives life in his own personal world and the son merely has trouble controlling his hormones. All is (surprisingly) well with them until their Uncle visits to confront the family. **143m/C DVD.** *JP* Tadanobu Asano, Tatsuya Gashuin, Tomoko Nakajima, Tomokazu Miura, Anna Tsuchiya, Maya Banno, Takahiro Sato, Satomi Tezuka; ***D:*** Katushito Ishii; ***W:*** Katushito Ishii; ***C:*** Kotsuke Matsushima; ***M:*** Tempo Little.

Taste the Blood of Dracula ⅋⅋ 1/2 **1970 (PG)** Lee's Dracula only makes a brief appearance in this Hammer horror film which has three children taking over from the bloodsucker. Three Victorian dandies have killed the wizard who revived Dracula and he seeks their deaths by using their own children as the means of his revenge. Not enough Lee but still creepy. Preceded by "Dracula Has Risen from the Grave" and followed by "Scars of Dracula." **91m/C VHS, DVD.** *GB* Christopher Lee, Ralph Bates, Geoffrey Keen, Gwen Watford, Linda Hayden, John Carson, Peter Sallis, Isla Blair, Martin Jarvis, Roy Kinnear, Anthony (Corlan) Higgins, Michael Ripper; ***D:*** Peter Sasdy; ***W:*** John (Anthony Hinds) Elder; ***C:*** Arthur Grant; ***M:*** James Bernard.

Tatie Danielle ⅋⅋⅋ **1991** Pitch-black comedy from the director of "Life Is a Long Quiet River" sees a bitter, elderly widow moving in with her young nephew and making his life a hell. In French with yellow English subtitles. **114m/C VHS.** *FR* Tsilla Chelton, Catherine Jacob, Isabelle Nanty, Neige Dolsky, Eric Prat, Laurence Fevrier; ***D:*** Etienne Chatiliez; ***W:*** Etienne Chatiliez.

The Tattered Web ⅋⅋ **1971** A police sergeant confronts and accidently kills the woman with whom his son-in-law has been cheating. He's then assigned the case. When he tries to frame a wino for the murder, things get more and more messy. Fine performances. **74m/C VHS, DVD.** Lloyd Bridges, Frank Converse, Broderick Crawford, Murray Hamilton, Sallie Shockley; ***D:*** Paul Wendkos; ***M:*** Robert Jackson Drasnin. **TV**

Tattle Tale ⅋ 1/2 **1992 (PG)** Vindictive ex-wife writes book accusing her actor ex of abusing her and he loses out on his career-breaking role. So he decides to disguise himself and seduce her into telling the truth. Even dumber than it sounds. **96m/C VHS.** C. Thomas Howell, Ally Sheedy; ***D:*** Baz Taylor.

Tattoo ⅋⅋ **1981 (R)** A model becomes the object of obsession for a crazy tattoo artist. He relentlessly pursues her, leaving behind all his other more illustrated clients. Starts out fine, but deteriorates rapidly. Controversial love scene between Dern and Adams. **103m/C VHS.** Bruce Dern, Maud Adams, Leonard Frey, Rikke Borge, John Getz; ***D:*** Bob Brooks; ***W:*** Joyce Bunuel.

Tattoo, a Love Story ⅋⅋ 1/2 **2002** Sara's perfectly planned future crumbles when she's dumped by her groom-to-be, but the elementary school teacher lets loose after "not-her-type" tattoo artist Virgil pops in for show-and-tell. Predictable yet pleasing indie romance. **95m/C VHS, DVD.** Megan Edwards, Stephen Davies, India Allen, Virgil Mignanelli, Benjamin Burdick, Kathryn Cherasaro, Gordon Reinhart, Stitch Marker, Stacey Bean, Nick Garcia, Tom Willmorth, Ben Larned, Tyler Maier, Christina Lang, E.J. Pettinger, Travis Swartz, Sara Bruner, Gene Bickley, Amy Krengal, Jim Agenbroad, Eryn Spaeth, Ariel Spaeth, Gus Pollio, Phil Atlakson, Flint Weisser, Mark Salow, Kate Gorney, Jacelyn Anderson, Michelle Waddell, Grant Lawley, Jessyca Harrold, Angie Lachapelle, Nick Halfrich, Curtis Stigers, Dave Yasuda, Carlie Powell, Walker Ragan, Jordan Gore, Joel Hawkins; ***D:*** Richard W. Bean; ***W:*** Richard W. Bean, Gregg Sacon; ***C:*** David Klein; ***M:*** Pete Droge, Pete Droge. **VIDEO**

The Tattooist ⅋ **2007 (R)** Tedious horror. American tattooist Jake Sawyer (Behr) goes to Singapore for an exhibition and meets New Zealand native Sina (Blake) while exploring a display of Samoan cultural tattooing. Jake steals one of the traditional tools (cutting himself in the process) and then decides to head for Auckland to learn Samoan tattooing. Too bad that Jake's stolen tool contains a now-released evil spirit and when he starts using it, the tattoos he inks take over their wearers' bodies and kill them. Sina's in a lot of trouble unless Jake can find a solution. **91m/C DVD.** *NZ* Jason Behr, Robbie Magasiva, Michael Hurst, Mia Blake, David Fane, Caroline Cheong; ***D:*** Peter Burger; ***W:*** Jonathan King, Matthew Grainger; ***C:*** Leon Narbey; ***M:*** Peter Scholes. **VIDEO**

The Tavern ⅋⅋ **2000** Ronnie (Dye) is a bartender who wants to buy a Manhattan watering hole from its alleged Florida-bound owner, Kevin (Zittel). He borrows the money from a number of people, including his best friend Dave (Geer), who becomes his partner. But they're underfinanced and beset by competition and numerous other problems soon surface threatening their business survival. Unsentimental and downbeat. **88m/C VHS, DVD.** Cameron Dye, Kevin Geer, Margaret Cho, Greg Zittel, Nancy Ticotin, Steven Marcus, Carlo Alban, Kym Austin, Gary Perez; ***D:*** Walter Foote; ***W:*** Walter Foote; ***C:*** Kurt Lennig; ***M:*** Bill Lacey, Loren Toolajian.

Tax Season ⅋⅋ **1990 (PG-13)** A small-time businessman buys a Hollywood tax service sight-unseen, and finds it employing a hooker, a bookie and a variety of other unconventional types. **93m/C VHS.** Fritz Bronner, James Hong, Jana Grant, Toru Tanaka, Dorie Krum, Kathryn Knotts, Arte Johnson, Rob Slyker; ***D:*** Tom Law.

Taxi ⅋ 1/2 **2004 (PG-13)** Nowhere comedy loosely based on director Luc Besson's 1998 French film. Stripped of his driver's license, inept New York cop Andy Washburn (Fallon, a negligible screen presence) enlists the aid of dynamo cabbie Belle Williams (Queen Latifah) to drive him to the scene of a bank robbery. The heist turns out to have been committed by a quartet of gorgeous Brazilian gals who are also supermodels (led by Bundchen in her, um, acting debut). Ann-Margaret lends support in a wincing comic turn as Andy's lush of a mother. The Queen, as always, is an irrepressible delight and the only reason to spend any time with this hack. **97m/C VHS, DVD.** *US* Jimmy Fallon, Jennifer Esposito, Ann-Margret, Henry Simmons, Christian Kane, Queen Latifah, Gisele Bundchen, Ana Christine de Oliveira, Ingrid Vandebosch, Magali Amadei; ***D:*** Tim Story; ***W:*** Ben Garant, Thomas Lennon, Jim Kouf; ***C:*** Vance Burberry; ***M:*** Christophe Beck.

Taxi Blues ⅋⅋⅋ 1/2 **1990** A political allegory with the two protagonists representing the new and old Soviet Union. A hard-working, narrow-minded cabdriver keeps the saxophone of a westernized, Jewish, jazz-loving musician who doesn't have his fare. The two strike up a wary friendship as each tries to explain his view of life to the other. Good look at the street life of Moscow populated by drunks, punks, and black marketeers. Directorial debut of Lounguine. In Russian with English subtitles. **110m/C VHS.** *RU* Piotr Mamonov, Piotr Zaitchenko, Natalia Koliakanova, Vladimir Kachpour; ***D:*** Pavel (Lungin) Lounguine; ***W:*** Pavel (Lungin) Lounguine. Cannes '90: Director (Lounguine).

Taxi Dancers ⅋ 1/2 **1993** Smalltown Billie arrives in Hollywood with dreams of becoming an actress. Naturally, her dreams turn to despair and she resorts to "dancing" at the Shark Club where she becomes involved with a gambler who owes money to the wrong people. **97m/C VHS.** Sonny Landham, Robert Miano, Brittany McCrena, Tina Fite, Mirage Micheaux, Michele Hess, Randall Irwin; ***D:*** Norman Thaddeus Vane; ***W:*** Norman Thaddeus Vane; ***M:*** Larry Blank.

Taxi Driver ⅋⅋⅋ **1976 (R)** A psychotic NYC taxi driver tries to save a child prostitute and becomes infatuated with an educated political campaigner. He goes on a violent rampage when his dreams don't work out. Repellant, frightening vision of alienation. On-target performances from Foster and De Niro. **112m/C VHS, DVD.** Robert De Niro, Jodie Foster, Harvey Keitel, Cybill Shepherd, Peter Boyle, Albert Brooks, Leonard Harris, Joe Spinell, Martin Scorsese; ***D:*** Martin Scorsese; ***W:*** Paul Schrader; ***C:*** Michael Chapman; ***M:*** Bernard Herrmann. AFI '98: Top 100; British Acad. '76: Support. Actress (Foster); Cannes '76: Film; L.A. Film Critics '76: Actor (De Niro), Natl. Film Reg. '94;; N.Y. Film Critics '76: Actor (De Niro); Natl. Soc. Film Critics '76: Actor (De Niro), Director (Scorsese), Support. Actress (Foster).

The Taxi Mystery ⅋ **1926** Guy saves Broadway starlet from band of ne'er-do-wells thanks to deserted taxi, then tries to figure out who she is, unaware that her sinister understudy plans to do her in. **50m/B VHS.** Edith Roberts, Robert Agnew, Virginia Pearson, Phillips Smalley; ***D:*** Fred Windermere.

Taxi to the Dark Side ⅋⅋⅋ 1/2 **2007 (R)** Grim, disturbing documentary about government-sanctioned torture in the war on terror. The film centers around the brutal treatment and murder of a taxi driver named Dilawar in Afghanistan while in American custody, but does not limit itself to the one incident. Instead, it uses that as a foundation for the examination of U.S. torture policies and the changing attitudes towards torture since 9/11. Director Gibney occasionally indulges in some gimmickry but overall presents a doggedly investigated film that asks hard questions and doesn't back down from brutal answers, including those provided through interviews with the men who killed Dilawar. **106m/C DVD.** *US* ***D:*** Alex Gibney; ***W:*** Alex Gibney; ***C:*** Maryse Alberti, Greg Andracke; ***M:*** Ivor Guest, Robert Logan; ***Nar:*** Alex Gibney. Oscars '07: Feature Doc.

Taxi zum Klo ⅋⅋⅋ **1981** An autobiographical semi-documentary about the filmmaker's aimless existence and attempts at homosexual affairs after being fired from his job as a teacher. Explicit. In German with English subtitles. Sordid sexual situations. **98m/C VHS, DVD.** *GE* Bernd Broaderup, Frank Ripploh; ***D:*** Frank Ripploh.

A Taxing Woman ⅋⅋⅋ 1/2 *Marusa No Onna* **1987** Satiric Japanese comedy about a woman tax collector in pursuit of a crafty millionaire tax cheater. Followed by the equally hilarious "A Taxing Woman's Return." In Japanese with English subtitles. **127m/C VHS, DVD.** *JP* Nobuko Miyamoto, Tsutomu Yamazaki, Hideo Murota, Shuji Otaki; ***D:*** Juzo Itami; ***W:*** Juzo Itami; ***C:*** Yonezo Maeda; ***M:*** Toshiyuki Honda.

A Taxing Woman's Return ⅋⅋⅋ *Marusa No Onna II* **1988** Funny, sophisticated, action-packed. Miyamoto returns as the dedicated tax investigator to fight industrialists, politicians, and other big swindlers, who have contrived to inflate Tokyo's real estate values. Sequel to "A Taxing Woman." In Japanese with English subtitles. **127m/C VHS.** *JP* Nobuko Miyamoto, Rentaro Mikuni, Masahiko Tsugawa, Tetsuro Tamba, Toru Masuoka, Takeya Nakamura, Hosei Komatsu, Mihoko Shibata; ***D:*** Juzo Itami; ***W:*** Juzo Itami.

The Taxman ⅋⅋ **1998 (R)** Al Benjamin (Pantoliano) is an obsessive New York State tax investigator who stumbles across six dead bodies in a Brighton Beach gasoline company while on the job. He teams up with a pain-in-the-butt cop, Joseph Romero (Dominguez), who's proficient in Russian—a necessity in the immigrant community. Their sleuthing leads them to the Russian mob, a scam involving gasoline taxes, and a lot of violence. **95m/C VHS, DVD.** Joe Pantoliano, Wade Dominguez, Elizabeth Berkley, Michael Chiklis, Robert Kevin Townsend; ***D:*** Avi Nesher;

W: Avi Nesher, Roger Berger; ***C:*** Jim Denault; ***M:*** Roger Neill.

TC 2000 🦴 1/2 **1993 (R)** Jason Storm and Zoey Kinsella are cops working for The Controller, who has the unenviable task of protecting the community from roving gangs of vicious punks. When Zoey is killed, The Controller converts her into a super-cybernetic killing machine unleashed on the gangs. Meanwhile Jason is considered a liability and must battle the gangs, The Controller, and cyber-Zoey to save himself. Oh, there's also something about saving the Earth's atmosphere from nuclear destruction. Lots of action. **92m/C VHS.** Billy Blanks, Bobbie Phillips, Jalal Merhi, Bolo Yeung, Matthias Hues; ***D:*** T.J. Scott; ***W:*** T.J. Scott.

Tchaikovsky 🦴🦴 1/2 **1971** The glorious music is all that saves this pedestrian biography of the 19th century Russian composer, which ignores his homosexuality and glosses over the dissolution of his marriage. Lead performance by Smoktunovsky does manage to rise above the moribund script. Originally released at 191 minutes. In Russian with English subtitles. **153m/C VHS, DVD.** *RU* Innokenti Smoktunovsky, Antonina Shuranova, Yevgeny Leonov, Maya Plisetskaya, Vladislav Strzeltchik, Alla Demidova, Kirill Lavrov; ***D:*** Igor Talankin; ***W:*** Igor Talankin, Yuri Nagibin, Budimir Metalnikov; ***C:*** Margarita Pilikhina.

Tchao Pantin 🦴🦴🦴 **1984** An acclaimed French film noir about an ex-cop being drawn into drug smuggling underground via a young Arab. English subtitles. Finely drawn characters skillfully portrayed make this a winner. **100m/C VHS.** *FR* Coluche, Richard Anconina, Agnes Soral; ***D:*** Claude Berri. Cesar '84: Actor (Coluche), Cinematog., Sound, Support. Actor (Anconina).

Tea and Sympathy 🦴🦴🦴 **1956** A young prep school student, confused about his sexuality, has an affair with an older woman, his teacher's wife. The three leads recreate their Broadway roles in this tame adaption of the Robert Anderson play which dealt more openly with the story's homosexual elements. **122m/C VHS.** Deborah Kerr, John Kerr, Leif Erickson, Edward Andrews, Darryl Hickman, Norma Crane, Dean Jones; ***D:*** Vincente Minnelli; ***W:*** Robert Anderson; ***C:*** John Alton.

Tea for Three 🦴🦴 **1984 (R)** Sexual trio develops and seeks therapy after a fledgling doctor has been having sexual relationships with two women, and the females finally meet. **89m/C VHS.** Iris Berben, Mascha Gonska, Heinz Marecek; ***D:*** Gerhard Janda.

Tea for Two 🦴🦴🦴 **1950** This take-off on the Broadway play "No, No, Nanette" features Day as an actress who takes a bet that she can answer "no" to every question for 24 hours (life was less complex back then). If she can, she gets to finance and star in her own Broadway musical. ♫ I Know That You Know; Crazy Rhythm; Charleston; I Only Have Eyes For You; Tea For Two; I Want to be Happy; Oh Me, Oh My; The Call of the Sea; Do Do Do. **98m/C VHS.** Doris Day, Gordon MacRae, Gene Nelson, Patrice Wymore, Eve Arden, Billy DeWolfe, S.Z. Sakall, Bill Goodwin, Virginia Gibson, Crauford Kent, Harry Harvey; ***D:*** David Butler.

Tea with Mussolini 🦴🦴 **1999 (PG)** Semiautobiographical account of director Zeffirelli's own childhood in fascist Italy. In 1935, young Luca (Lucas) is abandoned by his mother and his neglectful father is happy when the boy is taken in by a group of middleaged, eccentric Englishwomen, including Mary (Plowright), Lady Hester (Smith), and Arabella (Dench). Soon, their group is joined by flamboyantly wealthy (and Jewish) American Elsa (Cher). But as Mussolini consolidates his power and WWII begins, Luca is sent away to school, and the women find themselves unwelcome foreigners. **116m/C VHS, DVD.** *IT GB* Joan Plowright, Maggie Smith, Judi Dench, Cher, Baird Wallace, Charlie Lucas, Lily Tomlin, Paolo Seganti, Massimo Ghini, Claudio Spadaro; ***D:*** Franco Zeffirelli; ***W:*** Franco Zeffirelli, John Mortimer; ***C:*** David Watkin; ***M:*** Alessio Vlad, Stefano Arnaldi. British Acad. '99: Support. Actress (Smith).

Teach Me 🦴 **1997 (R)** Erotic romance novelist Sara Kane gets a story idea from observing a troubled couple at a restaurant. Janine's got some sexual fears that are causing problems in her marriage but Sara's willing to intercede and help ease her tensions. **90m/C VHS.** Shannon Leahy, Raasa Leela Shields, Greg Provance; ***D:*** Gary Delfiner. **VIDEO**

The Teacher 🦴🦴 *The Seductress* **1974 (R)** TV's "Dennis the Menace" (North) has an affair with his high school teacher; the pair is menaced by a deranged killer. Cheap but enjoyable. **97m/C VHS, DVD.** Angel Tompkins, Jay North, Anthony James; ***D:*** Howard (Hikmet) Avedis.

Teachers 🦴🦴 **1984 (R)** A lawsuit is brought against a high school for awarding a diploma to an illiterate student. Comedy-drama starts slowly and seems to condemn the school system, never picking up strength or resolving any issues, though Nolte is fairly intense. Shot in Columbus, Ohio. **106m/C VHS.** Nick Nolte, JoBeth Williams, Lee Grant, Judd Hirsch, Ralph Macchio, Richard Mulligan, Royal Dano, Morgan Freeman, Laura Dern, Crispin Glover, Madeline Sherwood, Zohra Lampert; ***D:*** Arthur Hiller.

Teacher's Pet 🦴🦴🦴 **1958** Cynical newspaper editor Jim Gannon (Gable) enrolls in a night college journalism course, believing that it won't teach anything of substance. But that's before he gets an eyeful of teacher Erica Stone (Day). Gannon decides to continue to pose as a student but watch the sparks fly when Erica finds out about his deception. Charming comedy with a well-written script and a superb comic performance by Young as Day's lovelorn suitor. **120m/B VHS, DVD.** Clark Gable, Doris Day, Mamie Van Doren, Gig Young, Nick Adams, Marion Ross, Jack Albertson, Charles Lane; ***D:*** George Seaton; ***W:*** Fay Kanin, Michael Kanin; ***C:*** Haskell Boggs; ***M:*** Roy Webb.

Teaching Mrs. Tingle 🦴🦴 *Killing Mrs. Tingle* **1999 (PG-13)** Williamson delivers a disappointing directorial debut in this teen horror/comedy adapted from one of his first scripts. Wrong-side-of-the-tracks Leigh Ann (Holmes) is anticipating being high school valedictorian until her sadistic English teacher Mrs. Tingle (Mirren) mistakenly accuses her of cheating. Leigh Ann and friends Jo Lynn (Coughlan) and Luke (Watson) go to Mrs. Tingle's house to plead their case and beg for mercy, but the heartless old hag refuses to listen to them. During an argument, Mrs. Tingle is knocked unconscious and the teens decide to tie her up and exact their revenge. **96m/C VHS, DVD.** Katie Holmes, Helen Mirren, Liz Stauber, Barry Watson, Jeffrey Tambor, Vivica A. Fox, Marisa Coughlan, Molly Ringwald, Michael McKean; ***D:*** Kevin Williamson; ***W:*** Kevin Williamson; ***C:*** Jerzy Zielinski; ***M:*** John (Gianni) Frizzell.

The Teahouse of the August Moon 🦴🦴 1/2 **1956** An adaptation of the John Patrick play. Post-war American troops are assigned to bring civilization to a small village in Okinawa and instead fall for Okinawan culture and romance. Lively cast keeps it generally working, but assessments of Brando's comedic performance vary widely. **123m/C VHS.** Glenn Ford, Marlon Brando, Eddie Albert, Paul Ford, Machiko Kyo, Harry (Henry) Morgan; ***D:*** Daniel Mann; ***C:*** John Alton.

Team America: World Police 🦴🦴🦴 **2004 (R)** The guys behind "South Park" take on Osama Bin Laden, Kim Jong Il, America's "bull-in-a-china-shop" foreign relations, the Hollywood Left, the Far Right, Jerry Bruckheimer movies, and especially the MPAA with-...puppets (marionettes, to be exact). With a truly heroic commitment to over-the-top satire, they tell the story of America's elite anti-terrorist force, the World Police, a gung-ho, if collateral damage-intensive band of action flick archetypes. New member Gary is recruited for his acting ability and goes through the usual conflicts before battling terrorists, the aforementioned North Korean dictator, and actor/activists such as Alec Baldwin. It's all pretty ridiculous, but that's the point. Add or subtract bones depending on your tolerance for puppet sex, vomit, and intentionally horrible dialogue. **98m/C DVD, UMD.** *US* ***D:*** Trey Parker; ***W:*** Trey Parker, Matt Stone, Pam Brady; ***C:*** Bill Pope; ***M:*** Harry Gregson-Williams; ***V:*** Trey Parker, Matt Stone, Masasa, Maurice LaMarche, Kristen Miller, Daran Norris, Phil Hendrie.

Teamster Boss: The Jackie Presser Story 🦴🦴🦴 **1992 (R)** Well-done cable movie powered by a riveting performance by Dennehy. Presser followed Jimmy Hoffa as president of the Teamsters and was equally caught between the mob and the government as he tried to do what he considered best for the union. **111m/C VHS, DVD.** Brian Dennehy, Jeff Daniels, Maria Conchita Alonso, Eli Wallach, Robert Prosky, Donald Moffat, Tony LoBianco, Kate Reid, Henderson Forsythe, Al Waxman; ***D:*** Alastair Reid. **CABLE**

Tearaway 🦴 1/2 **1987 (R)** Australian story of a street punk with an alcoholic father. Story has potential, but ends up going nowhere. **100m/C VHS.** *NZ AU* Matthew Hunter, Mark Pilisi, Peter Bland, Kim Willoughby, Rebecca Saunders; ***D:*** Bruce Morrison.

Tears in the Rain 🦴🦴 **1988** Casey Cantrell (Stone) travels to London to deliver a deathbed letter from her mother to Lord Richard Bredon. While in England, she is pursued by two men, an heir to the Bredon fortune, and his wealthy friend. After she finds a love which is forbidden, she makes a bizarre discovery that changes her life forever. **100m/C VHS, DVD.** *GB* Sharon Stone, Christopher Cazenove, Leigh Lawson, Paul Daneman; ***D:*** Don Sharp. **TV**

Tears of the Black Tiger 🦴🦴 *Fah talai jone* **2000** A modern alternate universe western set in Thailand, mixing the staples of Thai folk tales with the similar themes of American Westerns. It's a cliche boy meets girl/loses girl/vies to regain girl story with pretty, brightly colored visuals (everything looks like it comes from a painting). The cartoonish (if excessive) violent plays more as parody or satire than as gory. The genre-hopping limits the appeal, but still lovely to watch. **113m/C DVD.** *TH* Supakorn Kitsuwon, Sombat Metanee, Chartchai Ngamsan, Suwinit Panjamawat, Stella Malucchi, Arawat Ruangvuth, Pairoj Jaisingha, Kanchit Kwanpracha, Chamloen Sridang; ***D:*** Wisit Sasanatieng; ***W:*** Wisit Sasanatieng; ***C:*** Nattawut Kittikhun.

Tears of the Sun 🦴🦴 1/2 **2003 (R)** Navy SEAL team, led by Lt. Waters (Willis), is sent into the middle of a Nigerian civil war to rescue Americans at a missionary hospital. When they get there, the doctor (Bellucci) refuses to go without the people she's been treating, who will surely be slaughtered by the rebels in the area. Waters defies orders to lead them all on a hazerdous journey out of the country. Fuqua follows up "Training Day" with this visually stunning, almost thoughtful battle picture. Until the film degenerates into standard action fare at the end, it aspires to answer questions about the difficulty of America's role as world cop and what makes a hero. Fuqua is aided immensely by Willis's stoic performance and the work of editor Conrad Bluff. **121m/C VHS, DVD, Blu-ray Disc.** *US* Bruce Willis, Monica Bellucci, Cole Hauser, Tom Skerritt, Eamonn Walker, Nicholas Chinlund, Fionnula Flanagan, Malick Bowens, Paul Francis, Johnny Messner, Akosua Busia, Peter Mensah, Chad Smith, Charles Ingram; ***D:*** Antoine Fuqua; ***W:*** Alex Lasker, Patrick Cirillo; ***C:*** Mauro Fiore; ***M:*** Hans Zimmer.

Tecumseh: The Last Warrior 🦴🦴 1/2 **1995** Oh-so-noble TV biography of the Shawnee leader (1768-1813) and his refusal to give up the battle against white settlement of the Indiana Territory. North Carolina substitutes for Ohio and Indiana. Based on the book "Panther in the Sky" by James Alexander Thom. **90m/C VHS.** Jesse Borrego, David Clennon, Tantoo Cardinal, David Morse, Holt McCallany, August Schellenberg, Jimmie F. Skaggs, Jeri Arredondo; ***D:*** Larry Elikann; ***W:*** Paul F. Edwards; ***M:*** David Shire.

Ted & Venus 🦴🦴 1/2 **1993 (R)** Cort plays Ted, an oddball cult poet in love with Linda, a beach beauty who finds him repulsive. The more she rejects him, the more obsessed about her Ted gets, especially when his equally oddball friends offer him romantic advice. **100m/C VHS, DVD.** Bud Cort, Kim Adams, Rhea Perlman, James Brolin, Carol Kane; ***Cameos:*** Gena Rowlands, Martin Mull, Woody Harrelson, Andrea Martin, Timothy Leary, Cassandra Peterson; ***D:*** Bud Cort; ***W:*** Bud Cort, Paul Ciotti.

Teddy at the Throttle 🦴🦴 **1916** Teddy, the Great Dane, must rescue Gloria Swanson from a villain who has tied up her boyfriend. Silent. **20m/B VHS, DVD.** Bobby Vernon, Gloria Swanson, Wallace Beery; ***D:*** Clarence Badger.

Teen Alien 🦴 *The Varrow Mission* **1978 (PG)** On Halloween, a young boy and his friends run into a hostile alien. It could happen. **88m/C VHS.** Michael Dunn, Keith Nelson, Dan Harville, Vern Adix; ***D:*** Peter Senelka; ***W:*** Peter Senelka.

Teen Vamp 🦴 **1988** Dorky high schooler is bitten by a prostitute; becomes a cool vampire. Mindless "comedy." **87m/C VHS.** Clu Gulager, Karen Carlson, Angela Brown; ***D:*** Samuel Bradford.

Teen Witch 🦴🦴 **1989 (PG-13)** A demure high schooler uses black magic to woo the most popular guy in school. **94m/C VHS, DVD.** Robin (Robyn) Lively, Zelda Rubinstein, Dan Gauthier, Joshua John Miller, Dick Sargent; ***D:*** Dorian Walker; ***W:*** Robin Menken.

Teen Wolf 🦴🦴 1/2 **1985 (PG)** A nice, average teenage basketball player begins to show werewolf tendencies which suddenly make him popular at school when he leads the team to victory. The underlying message is to be yourself, regardless of how much hair you have on your body. Lighthearted comedy carried by the Fox charm; followed by subpar "Teen Wolf Too." **92m/C VHS, DVD.** Michael J. Fox, James Hampton, Scott Paulin, Susan Ursitti; ***D:*** Rod Daniel; ***M:*** Miles Goodman.

Teen Wolf Too 🦴🦴 **1987 (PG)** The sequel to "Teen Wolf" in which the Teen Wolf's cousin goes to college on a boxing scholarship. More evidence that the sequel is rarely as good as the original. **95m/C VHS, DVD.** Jason Bateman, Kim Darby, John Astin, Paul Sand; ***D:*** Christopher Leitch; ***W:*** Timothy King.

Teenage 🦴 **1944** Low budget juvenile schlock film that tries to figure out what's wrong with modern youth. Pure camp. **55m/B VHS.** Herbert (Hayes) Heyes, Wheeler Oakman, Florence Dudley, Vera Steadman; ***D:*** Richard L'Estrange; ***W:*** Elmer Clifton, J.D. Kendis.

Teenage Bad Girl 🦴🦴 1/2 *Bad Girl; My Teenage Daughter* **1959** A woman who edits a magazine for teenagers can't control her own daughter. The kid does time in the pen after staying out all night and generally running around with the wrong crowd. Syms first lead performance is memorable in an otherwise routine teensploitation flick. **100m/B VHS.** Anna Neagle, Sylvia Syms, Norman Wooland, Wilfrid Hyde-White, Kenneth Haigh, Julia Lockwood; ***D:*** Herbert Wilcox.

Teenage Bonnie & Klepto Clyde 🦴 1/2 **1993 (R)** Like their '30s namesakes, Clyde Barrow and Bonnie Parker are just two high-spirited kids who let their need for excitement get in the way of their better judgment (ha!). Bonnie and Clyde meet in a fast-food joint, become shoplifting buddies, fall in love, graduate to armed robbery, try to run for the border, and die. **90m/C VHS.** Bentley Mitchum, Tom Bower, Maureen Flannigan, Scott Wolf; ***Cameos:*** Don Novello; ***D:*** John Shepphird; ***W:*** John Shepphird; ***C:*** Neal Brown; ***M:*** Terry Plumeri.

Teenage Catgirls in Heat 🦴🦴 **2000** On their lighthearted commentary track, the filmmakers admit that they had originally titled this Texas-produced horror simply "Catgirls." It was the good folks at Troma who came up with the modifiers that turns it into an inspired piece of exploitation. If the film doesn't quite live up (or down) to it, that's not too surprising. It is a nice, silly little horror and nobody involved takes it very seriously. **90m/C DVD.** Gary Graves, Carrie Vanston, Dave Cox; ***D:*** Scott Perry; ***W:*** Scott Perry, Grace Smith; ***C:*** Thad Halci; ***M:*** Randy Buck, Nenad Vugrinec.

Teenage Caveman 🦴🦴 *Out of the Darkness; Prehistoric World* **1958** A teenage boy living in a post-apocalypse yet prehistoric world journeys across the river, even though he was warned against it, and finds an old man who owns a book about past civilizations in the 20th Century. Schlocky, and one of the better bad films around. The dinosaur shots were picked up from the film

"One Million B.C." **66m/B VHS.** Robert Vaughn, Darrah Marshall, Leslie Bradley, Frank De Kova, Jonathan Haze, Beach Dickerson, Marshall Bradford, Robert Shayne, Joseph H. Hamilton, June Jocelyn, Charles P. Thompson; ***D:*** Roger Corman; ***W:*** Robert W(right) Campbell; ***C:*** Floyd Crosby; ***M:*** Albert Glasser.

Teenage Caveman **2001 (R)** Post-apocalyptic nightmare world has a small group of cave dwellers, led by elders who ban sex to keep the population down. But teenage hormones will out and David leads girlfriend Sarah and a group of friends into the wilderness where they meet Neil and Judith, who are the result of genetic experimentation that has some unpleasant side effects for our little band of survivors (think sex). A "Creature Features" remake of the 1958 movie. **100m/C VHS, DVD.** Andrew Keegan, Tara Subkoff, Richard Hillman, Shan Elliot, Tiffany Limos, Stephen Jasso, Crystal Grant, Hayley Keenan, Paul Hipp; ***D:*** Larry Clark; ***W:*** Christos N. Gage; ***C:*** Steve Gainer; ***M:*** Zoe Poledouris. **CABLE**

Teenage Crime Wave **1955** Route 66 provides thrills for a couple of teen punks, but things get out of hand when they blow a sheriff's head off. They scoop up a couple of babes and hightail it with the police close behind, ultimately confronting their destiny at a mountain top observatory. **77m/B VHS.** Tommy Cook, Mollie McCart, Sue England, Frank Griffin, James Bell, Kay Riehl; ***D:*** Fred F. Sears.

Teenage Devil Dolls **1953** A cheap exploitation teenage flick wherein an innocent girl is turned on to reefer and goofballs, and eventually ends up on the street. **70m/C VHS, DVD.** Barbara Marks, Bramlef L. Price Jr.; ***D:*** B. Lawrence Price.

Teenage Doll **1957** Good old Corman teen exploitation pic features a good girl who's tired of being good and gets mixed up with some street punks. She even manages to set off a gang war by accidentally kiling a beat girl from a rival group. **71m/B VHS, DVD.** Fay Spain, John Brinkley, June Kenney, Collette Jackson, Barbara Wilson, Ed Nelson, Richard Devon, Ziva Rodann, Barboura Morris, Bruno VeSota; ***D:*** Roger Corman; ***W:*** Charles B. Griffith; ***C:*** Floyd Crosby; ***M:*** Walter Greene.

Teenage Exorcist **½ 1993** Tired horror spoof finds the prim Diane (Stevens) renting a creepy house from an equally creepy real estate agent (Berryman). After she moves in, Diane begins having horrible nightmares and calls her family for help. When they arrive Diane has turned into a chainsaw-wielding seductress. The family is so distressed that they misdial the phone and wind up with a pizza delivery geek (Deezen) instead of the exorcist they need. **90m/C VHS, DVD.** Brinke Stevens, Eddie Deezen, Michael Berryman, Robert Quarry, Jay Richardson, Tom Shell, Elena Sahagun; ***D:*** Grant Austin Waldman; ***W:*** Brinke Stevens.

Teenage Frankenstein **½ 1958** A descendent of Dr. Frankenstein makes his own scramble-faced monster out of a teenage boy. Lurid '50s drive-in fare (companion to "I Was a Teenage Werewolf") is campy fun in small doses only. **72m/B VHS.** Whit Bissell, Phyllis Coates, Robert Burton, Gary Conway, George Lynn, John Cliff; ***D:*** Herbert L. Strock.

Teenage Gang Debs **1966** These chicks throw a sleazy coming out party the likes of which defy description. Simply the most important social function of 1966. **77m/B VHS, DVD.** Diana Conti, Linda Gale, Eileen Scott, Sandra Kane, Robin Nolan, Linda Cambi, Sue McManus, Geri Tyler, Joey Naudic, John Batis, Tom Yourk, Thomas Andrisano, George Winship, Doug Mitchell, Tom Eldred, Frank Spinella, Alec Primrose, Gene Marrin, Lyn Kennedy, Janet Banzet; ***D:*** Sande N. Johnsen; ***W:*** Hy Cahl; ***C:*** Harry Petricek; ***M:*** Steve Karmen.

Teenage Monster **WOOF!** *Meteor Monster* **1957** A young boy is hit by a meteor and is somehow transformed into a raving, slime-covered maniac. **65m/B VHS, DVD.** Gilbert Perkins, Stephen Parker, Anne Gwynne, Stuart Wade, Gloria Castillo, Chuck Courtney; ***D:*** Jacques "Jack" Marquette; ***W:*** Ray Buffum; ***C:*** Taylor Byars.

Teenage Mother **WOOF!** **1967** A Swedish sex education teacher comes to town and poisons the minds of the local high school kids. Naturally one becomes pregnant and has to try to trick the father into marrying her. More awful stuff from the director of "Girl On a Chain Gang." **78m/C VHS.** Arlene Sue Farber, Frederick Riccio, Julie Ange, Howard Le May, George Peters; ***D:*** Jerry Gross; ***W:*** Jerry Gross; ***C:*** Richard Brooks; ***M:*** Steve Karmen.

Teenage Mutant Ninja Turtles: The Movie **½ 1990 (PG)** Four sewer-dwelling turtles that have turned into warrior ninja mutants due to radiation exposure take it upon themselves to rid the city of crime and pizza. Aided by a television reporter and their ninja master, Splinter the Rat, the turtles encounter several obstacles, including the evil warlord Shredder. A most excellent live-action version of the popular comic book characters which will hold the kids' interest. Much head-kicking and rib-crunching action as Leonardo, Donatello, Raphael, and Michelangelo fight for the rights of pre-adolescents everywhere. Combines real actors with Jim Henson creatures. **95m/C VHS, DVD.** Judith Hoag, Elias Koteas; ***D:*** Steven Barron; ***W:*** Todd W. Langen; ***C:*** John Fenner; ***M:*** John Du Prez; ***V:*** Robbie (Reist) Rist, Corey Feldman, Brian Tochi, Kevin Clash, David McCharen.

Teenage Mutant Ninja Turtles 2: The Secret of the Ooze **1991 (PG)** Amphibious pizza-devouring mutants search for the toxic waste that turned them into marketable martial artist ecologically correct kid idols. Same formula as the first go-round with some new characters tossed in. Animatronic characters from the laboratory of Jim Henson, first screen appearance by rapper Vanilla Ice. Marked end of pre-teen turtle craze. **88m/C VHS, DVD.** Francois Chau, David Warner, Paige Turco, Ernie Reyes Jr., Vanilla Ice; ***D:*** Michael Pressman.

Teenage Mutant Ninja Turtles 3 **1993 (PG)** Check it out dudes; the Teenage Mutant Ninja Turtles hit 17th century Japan to rescue loyal friend, reporter April O'Neil. Plenty of smoothly executed, blood-free martial arts moves keep the pace rolling, while the turtles battle an evil lord and English pirates. Seeing the TMNT's use a little more of their reptilian grey matter, and snarf a little less pizza should contribute to a relatively high adult tolerance level (considering the genre), and loads of good clean fun for the kiddies. **95m/C VHS.** Elias Koteas, Paige Turco, Stuart Wilson, Sab Shimono, Vivian Wu; ***D:*** Stuart Gillard; ***W:*** Stuart Gillard; ***M:*** John Du Prez; ***V:*** Randi Mayem Singer, Matt Hill, Jim Raposa, David Fraser.

Teenage Strangler **WOOF!** **1964** A homicidal teen terrorizes his school. Cheap film features drag races, rumbles, dances, babes, rock 'n' roll and more. One for the "bad enough to be fun" category. **61m/C VHS, DVD.** Bill A. Bloom, Jo Canterbury, John Ensign, Jim Asp, Johnny Haymer, Bill Mills, Ron Ormond; ***D:*** Bill Posner; ***W:*** Clark Davis; ***C:*** Fred Singer; ***M:*** Danny Dean.

Teenage Wolfpack **½ 1957** Boring film about German juvenile delinquents, robbery, violence, and murder. **90m/C VHS, DVD.** *GE* Horst Buchholz, Karin Baal, Christian Doermer; ***D:*** Georg Tressler.

Teenage Zombies **WOOF!** **1958** Mad scientist on remote island kidnaps teenagers and uses her secret chemical formula to turn them into zombies as part of her plan to enslave the world. Not as good as it sounds. **71m/B VHS, DVD.** Don Sullivan, Katherine Victor, Chuck Niles; ***D:*** Jerry Warren; ***W:*** Jerry Warren; ***C:*** Allen Chandler.

Teenager **1974 (R)** Three desperate, reckless individuals, all caught up in making a low budget movie, interact and eventually self-destruct. **91m/C VHS.** Andrea Cagan, Reid Smith, Susan Bernard; ***D:*** Gerald Seth Sindell.

Teenagers from Outer Space **WOOF!** *The Gargon Terror* **1959** Low-budget sci-fi effort finds extraterrestrial youngsters visiting earth to conquer it and find food for their "monstrous pets" (they're really lobster shadows.) So cheaply made and melodramatic that it just may be good for a laugh. **86m/B VHS, DVD.** Tom Graeff, Dawn Anderson, Harvey B. Dunn, Bryant Grant, Thomas Lockyer, King Moody, Bob Williams; ***D:*** Tom Graeff; ***W:*** Tom Graeff; ***C:*** Tom Graeff; ***M:*** Tom Graeff.

Teeth **½ 2007 (R)** A darkly comic horror take on vagina dentate. Good girl Dawn (Weixler) preaches abstinence to her classmates in her little town next to a nuclear power plant, but when her boyfriend (Appleman) decides he's going to lose his virginity no matter what, she discovers that something strange is going on down there, and it's chomping off anything that tries to get inside. Weixler's Sundance-winning performance stands out in this biting satire whose main joke too soon runs its course, as Dawn leaves a trail of severed male body parts in her wake. **88m/C DVD.** *US* Jess Weixler, John Hensley, Josh Pais, Lenny Von Dohlen, Hale Appleman, Vivienne Benesch; ***D:*** Mitchell Lichtenstein; ***W:*** Mitchell Lichtenstein; ***C:*** Wolfgang Held; ***M:*** Robert Miller.

TekWar **½ 1994** It's 2044 and society is plagued by "Tek," an illegal, addictive drug-like computer disk that creates powerful but destructive virtual-reality fantasies. Jake Cardigan (Evigan) is an cop framed on drug and murder charges, fresh out of prison, who's trying to both clear his name and find out what happened to his now ex-wife and son. Shatner, who wrote the Tek novels, guests as Walter Bascom, the head of a detective agency who promises to help Cardigan if Jake helps find a missing scientist. Made for TV. **92m/C VHS.** Greg Evigan, Eugene Clark, Torri Higginson, William Shatner; ***D:*** William Shatner. **TV**

Telefon **1977 (PG)** Suspenseful, slick spy tale. Soviet agents battle a lunatic comrade who tries to use hypnotized Americans to commit sabotage. Daly, later of TV's "Cagney and Lacey," is memorable. **102m/C VHS.** Charles Bronson, Lee Remick, Donald Pleasence, Tyne Daly, Patrick Magee, Sheree North; ***D:*** Donald Siegel; ***W:*** Stirling Silliphant, Peter Hyams; ***M:*** Lalo Schifrin.

Telegraph Trail **½ 1933** Weak Wayne entry about an Army scout who helps some workers complete the first transcontinental wire line. Of course, Wayne ends up getting tough with some Indians. Cheaply made, with most of the action footage lifted from the 1926 silent, "The Red Raiders." **60m/B VHS, DVD.** John Wayne, Marceline Day, Frank McHugh, Otis Harlan, Yakima Canutt, Lafe (Lafayette) McKee; ***D:*** Tenny Wright; ***W:*** Kurt Kempler.

The Telephone **WOOF!** **1987 (R)** A neurotic out-of-work actress begins a comedic chain of events via a few prank phone calls. Goldberg has managed to salvage some bad material with the strength of her comedic performances, but not so here. In fact, she sued to prevent this version from ever seeing the light of day. Too bad she didn't have a better lawyer. Torn's directorial debut. **96m/C VHS.** Whoopi Goldberg, Elliott Gould, John Heard, Amy Wright; ***D:*** Rip Torn; ***W:*** Terry Southern.

Tell It to the Judge **½ 1949** Russell plays the exuberant ex-wife of lawyer Cummings. They repeatedly try reconciling but ditzy blonde McDonald always manages to catch Cummings' eye. Fed up Russell takes off for a holiday in the mountains where she meets Young. When her ex-hubby follows her, she decides to try and make him jealous using Young as the bait. **87m/B VHS.** Rosalind Russell, Robert Cummings, Gig Young, Marie McDonald, Harry Davenport, Louise Beavers; ***D:*** Norman Foster.

Tell Me a Riddle **½ 1980 (PG)** A dying woman attempts to reconcile with her family in this poignant drama about an elderly couple rediscovering their mutual love after 47 years of marriage. Fine acting; Grant's directorial debut. **94m/C VHS.** Melvyn Douglas, Lila Kedrova, Brooke Adams, Peter Coyote; ***D:*** Lee Grant; ***W:*** Joyce Eliason.

Tell Me That You Love Me **½ 1984 (R)** A tear-jerking portrait of a disintegrating modern marriage. **88m/C VHS.** Nick Mancuso, Barbara Williams, Belinda J. Montgomery; ***D:*** Tzipi Trope.

Tell Me Where It Hurts **1974** A middle-aged housewife changes her life when she forms a women's consciousness-raising group with her friends. The script won an Emmy. Stapleton's performance is redeeming in this otherwise slow movie. **78m/C VHS.** Maureen Stapleton, Paul Sorvino; ***D:*** Paul Bogart; ***M:*** David Shire. **TV**

Tell No One **½** *Ne le Dis a Personne* **2006** Pediatrician Alexandre Beck (Cluzet) struggles to piece together the events of a mysterious day at the lake eight years earlier when his wife was murdered and he was struck on the head, rendering the details fuzzy. When two more bodies are found buried at the murder site, police once again suspect Beck and inquire about possible evidence that turns up in his apartment. The airtight plot spirals out of control when Beck begins receiving cryptic emails regarding the day in question and he is forced to flee the cops. A perplexing thriller that will reward only those willing to trust the material and not second-guess the outcome. **125m/C DVD.** *CA* Francois Cluzet, Andre Dussollier, Marie Josee Croze, Kristin Scott Thomas, Nathalie Baye, Francois Berleand, Jean Rochefort, Marina Hands, Guillaume Canet, Gilles Lellouche; ***D:*** Guillaume Canet; ***W:*** Guillaume Canet, Philippe Lefebvre; ***C:*** Christophe Offenstein; ***M:*** Mathieu Chedid.

The Tell-Tale Heart **½** *The Hidden Room of 1,000 Horrors* **1960** Daydreaming author fantasizes about falling for major babe and killing his best friend for her. Adapted Poe tale. **78m/B VHS, DVD.** *GB* Laurence Payne, Adrienne Corri, Dermot Walsh, Selma Vaz Dias, John Scott, John Martin, Annette Carell, David Lander; ***D:*** Ernest Morris; ***W:*** Brian Clemens.

Tell Them Who You Are **2005 (R)** Mark Wexler's documentary about his cinematographer father Haskell Wexler is not so much about the man's award-winning movie work as it is an expose of their father-son relationship. Acknowledged for his work and political endeavors, Haskell is undeniably witty, egotistical and outspokenly blunt. "I don't think there's a movie that I've been on that I wasn't sure I could direct better," he says at one point, and that includes his son's. **95m/C DVD.** *US* ***D:*** Mark S. Wexler; ***W:*** Mark S. Wexler, Robert DeMaio; ***C:*** Mark S. Wexler.

Tell Them Willie Boy Is Here **1969 (PG)** Western drama set in 1909 California about a Paiute Indian named Willie Boy and his white bride. They become the objects of a manhunt (led by the reluctant local sheriff, Redford) after Willie kills his wife's father in self-defense. This was once-blacklisted Polonsky's first film in 21 years. **98m/C VHS.** Robert Redford, Katharine Ross, Robert (Bobby) Blake, Susan Clark, Barry Sullivan, John Vernon, Charles McGraw; ***D:*** Abraham Polonsky; ***W:*** Abraham Polonsky; ***C:*** Conrad L. Hall; ***M:*** Dave Grusin.

Telling Lies **2006 (R)** Troubled Faith (Harrison) returns to her private school to discover her boyfriend Derek (Di Angelo) is hooking up with her BFF Portia (Lipskis). Faith starts acting out and gets more self-destructive after meeting bad girl Eve (Stables), who convinces Faith to invent a boyfriend (they call him Vincent) to make Derek jealous. Only a real Vincent is murdered and evidence points to Faith's involvement, especially since Eve has mysteriously vanished. However, Det. Maggie Thomas (Brown) doesn't think the case against Faith is so cut-and-dried. **81m/C DVD.** *GB* Kelly Stables, Melanie (Scary Spice) Brown, Jason Flemyng, Jenna Harrison, Matt Di Angelo, Algina Lipskis; ***D:*** Antara Bhardwai; ***W:*** Carl Austin, Michael Kramer; ***C:*** Ravi Yadav; ***M:*** Pravin Mani.

Telling Lies in America **1996 (PG-13)** Semiautobiographical Esterhaus-penned coming-of-ager allies a star-struck and naive Hungarian immigrant teen with dirty deejay on the take in early 60s Cleveland. Karchy Jones (Renfro) worships the slick polyester prince of the airwaves Billy Magic (Bacon), and through a contest at school, wins a chance to become his eager-beaver lackey. The twisted rock-n-roll mentor shows Karchy his own, highly cynical version of attaining the American Dream which, naturally, leads to trouble. Universally acclaimed performance by Bacon, who takes a one-dimensional persona and runs with it. Flockhart plays the "it" girl of Karchy's dreams. Smoothly told story suffers from a few of the usual cliches, but makes up for in heart.

101m/C VHS, DVD. Kevin Bacon, Brad Renfro, Maximilian Schell, Calista Flockhart, Paul Dooley, Jonathan Rhys Meyers, Luke Wilson; ***D:*** Guy Ferland; ***W:*** Joe Eszterhas; ***C:*** Reynaldo Villalobos; ***M:*** Nicholas Pike.

Telling You 1/2 **1998 (R)** Buddies Phil (Facinelli) and Dennis (Mihok) work at the local pizzeria and try to score but don't have much success since they're, basically, amiable losers. Fluff and Hewitt's role is small as Phil's ex-girlfriend. **94m/C VHS, DVD.** Peter Facinelli, Dash Mihok, Matthew Lillard, Jennifer Love Hewitt, Richard Libertini, Robert DeFranco, Frank Medrano, Jennifer Jostyn, Rick Rossovich, Jennie Garth; ***D:*** Robert DeFranco; ***W:*** Robert DeFranco, Marc Palmieri; ***C:*** Mark Doering-Powell; ***M:*** Russ Landau.

The Temp WOOF! **1993 (R)** Unbelievably bad attempt at office horror. Beautiful, mysterious Kris temps for Hutton, a junior exec at the Mrs. Appleby baked goods company. She's almost too good to be true with unbelievable organizational skills and her dead serious ambition to climb the corporate ladder. Pyscho-drama has pyscho, but lacks drama, direction, plot development, intelligent dialogue, and anything resembling motive. While Hutton is tolerable, we nominate ex-Twin Peaker Boyle for the bad acting hall of shame as the conniving psycho. **99m/C VHS, DVD.** Timothy Hutton, Lara Flynn Boyle, Faye Dunaway, Dwight Schultz, Oliver Platt, Steven Weber, Scott Coffey, Colleen Flynn, Dakin Matthews, Maura Tierney; ***D:*** Tom Holland; ***W:*** Kevin Falls; ***C:*** Steve Yaconelli; ***M:*** Frederic Talgorn. Golden Raspberries '93: Worst Support. Actress (Dunaway).

Tempest **1928** This must have been particularly intriguing at the time since the events it depicts were still so historically fresh. Russian peasant Markov (Barrymore) rises in the ranks of the Czar's army although his lowly birth causes him to be insulted by Princess Tamara (Horn). It's because of her that Markov is imprisoned, although the Russian Revolution frees him and he then switches sides to become a rising Party member. Tamara is now jailed and threatened with execution but Markov (who loves her) tries to come to her rescue. **111m/B DVD.** John Barrymore, Camilla Horn, Louis Wolheim, George Fawcett, Boris DeFas, Ullrich Haupt; ***D:*** Sam Taylor; ***W:*** C. Gardner Sullivan; ***C:*** Charles Rosher.

The Tempest 1/2 **1963** Shakespeare's classic tale of the fantasy world of spirits, sorcerers, maidens, monsters, and scheming noblemen is brought to life in George Schaefer's ethereal production. **76m/C VHS.** Maurice Evans, Richard Burton, Roddy McDowall, Lee Remick, Tom Poston; ***D:*** George Schaefer. **TV**

The Tempest **1982 (PG)** New York architect Phillip (Cassavettes), fed up with city living, chucks it all and brings his daughter Miranda (Ringwald in her screen debut), and singer Aretha (Sarandon) to live with him on a barren Greek island where they encounter a hermit named Kalibanos (Julia). Then, thanks to a shipwreck, all the other people in Phillip's life, including his unfaithful wife Antonia (Rowland), show up to complicate his midlife crisis. Loosley based on the Shakespeare play of the same name. Well-written, thoughtfully acted, and beautifully filmed. **140m/C VHS, DVD.** John Cassavetes, Gena Rowlands, Susan Sarandon, Vittorio Gassman, Molly Ringwald, Paul Stewart, Sam Robards, Raul Julia; ***D:*** Paul Mazursky; ***W:*** Paul Mazursky, Leon Capetanos; ***C:*** Donald McAlpine; ***M:*** Stomu Yamashta.

The Tempest 1/2 **1999 (PG-13)** This time around the Shakespeare fantasy is transported to a Civil War-era Mississippi bayou, which is where magic-studying Gideon Prosper (Fonda) is living with his daughter, Miranda (Heigl), and a runaway slave, Ariel (Perrineau). Into this secluded world stumbles young Union soldier, Frederick Allen (Mills), with whom the lonely Miranda immediately falls in love, while Gideon is finally forced to reckon with the world in the form of his unscrupulous brother, Anthony (Glover). **90m/C VHS.** Peter Fonda, John Glover, Harold Perrineau Jr., Katherine Heigl, Eddie Mills, John Pyper-Ferguson, Dennis Redfield; ***D:*** Jack Bender; ***W:*** James Henerson; ***C:*** Steve (Steven) Shaw. **TV**

Temptation **1994 (R)** Ex-con Eddie (Fahey) gets hired to work on a luxury yacht, which helps him keep track of his double-crossing former partner. Too bad for Eddie that the guy's wife is such a distraction. **91m/C VHS.** Jeff Fahey, Alison Doody, Philip Casnoff, David Keith, Patricia Durham, W. Paul Bodie; ***D:*** Strathford Hamilton.

Temptation of a Monk **1994** Costume drama about China's 7th-century Tang Dynasty finds General Shi (Hsin-kuo) duped into an assassination plot against the crown prince. After a massacre, the General flees and finds sanctuary with a group of Buddhist monks at a remote temple. There's also the General's sometime lover and a mystery woman (both played by Chen). Sometimes slow-moving and confusing but with exotic visuals. Based on a novel by Lilian Lee; Mandarin with subtitles. **118m/C VHS, DVD.** *CH* Wu Hsin-kuo, Joan Chen, Fengyi Zhang, Michael Lee; ***D:*** Clara Law; ***W:*** Eddie Ling-Ching Fong; ***C:*** Andrew Lesnie; ***M:*** Tats Lau.

The Temptations 1/2 **1998** Miniseries bio of the Motown group from its high school beginnings in 1958 (under various names) through a meeting with Motown founder Berry Gordy (Babatunde) and major success in the '60s. Told from the viewpoint of the last original Temp, Otis Williams (Whitfield), as he and buddies Melvin Franklin (Woodside) and Paul Williams (Payton) hook up with first lead singer Eddie Kendricks (Brooks). When Kendricks goes solo it's the turn of David Ruffin (Leon) but the group suffers various ego traumas and tragedies. Naturally, the music's the real highlight. **150m/C VHS, DVD.** Charles Malik Whitfield, DB Woodside, Terron Brooks, Christian Payton, Leon, Alan Rosenberg, Obba Babatunde, Charles Ley, Tina Lifford, Gina Ravera, Vanessa Bell Calloway, Chaz Lamar Shepherd; ***D:*** Allan Arkush; ***W:*** Kevin Arkadie, Robert P. Johnson; ***C:*** Jamie Anderson. **TV**

Tempted **2001 (R)** Wealthy builder Charlie LeBlanc (Reynolds) hires college student Jimmy Mulante (Facinelli) to do some carpentry work—and test the fidelity of his beautiful young wife Lilly (Burrows). Charlie heads out of town after offering Jimmy mucho bucks to seduce Lilly but Jimmy confesses the scheme to her instead and she decides to use the stud for her own purposes. **95m/C VHS, DVD.** Burt Reynolds, Peter Facinelli, Saffron Burrows, Mike Starr, George DiCenzo, Eric Mabius; ***D:*** Bill Bennett; ***W:*** Bill Bennett; ***C:*** Tony Clark; ***M:*** David Bridie.

The Tempter *L'Anticristo; The Antichrist* **1974 (R)** Mirrors the gruesomeness of "The Exorcist," with story following an invalid's adventures with witchcraft, bestiality, and Satanism. **96m/C VHS, DVD.** *IT* Mel Ferrer, Carla Gravina, Arthur Kennedy, Alida Valli, Anita Strindberg, George Coulouris; ***D:*** Alberto De Martino; ***M:*** Ennio Morricone.

The Temptress **1926** Garbo plays a femme fatale, who is the cause of her own unhappiness. Parisian Elena falls in love with Argentine engineer Manuel and neglects to tell him she's married to his friend the Marquis (he finds out). The couple visit Manuel in Argentina where Elena vamps every man around, including bandit Duras, which leads to a shocking bullwhip duel between the two men. **90m/B DVD.** Greta Garbo, Antonio Moreno, Roy D'Arcy, Marc McDermott, Armand Kaliz, Lionel Barrymore, Robert Anderson; ***D:*** Fred Niblo; ***W:*** Dorothy Farnum; ***C:*** William H. Daniels, Gaetano Antonio "Tony" Gaudio.

The Temptress 1/2 **1949** A doctor attempting to find a cure for polio is coerced by an irresistible woman into murder and blackmail. Well-told story, if somewhat grim. **85m/B VHS.** *GB* Joan Maude, Arnold Bell, Don Stannard, Shirley Quentin, John Stuart, Ferdinand "Ferdy" Mayne; ***D:*** Oswald Mitchell.

Temptress **1995 (R)** Photographer Karin Swann (Delaney) returns from a spiritual retreat in India obsessed with the deadly goddess Kali. Karin's new overtly sexual personality startles lover Matthew (Sarandon) while her work has also undergone some changes. When a friend is murdered, Matthew begins to wonder if Kali's evil powers have overtaken Karin. **93m/C VHS.** Kim Delaney, Chris Sarandon, Corbin Bernsen, Dee Wallace, Jessica Walter, Ben Cross; ***D:*** Lawrence Lanoff; ***W:*** Melissa Mitchell; ***M:*** Michael Stearns.

Temptress Moon *Feng Yue* **1996 (R)** 1920s Shanghai is displayed in all its decadence with opium-addicted Ruyi (Li) forced to officially head the Pang family after the death of her father. Power actually lies with distant male cousin Duanwen (Lin), who manages the household and is drawn to his cold relative. Ruyi's childhood playmate and fellow addict, Zhongliang (Cheung), is now a professional gigolo and blackmailer, working for a gangster (Tian) who wants him to seduce Ruyi and steal the Pang fortune. What happens is an obsessive affair between two beautiful manipulators. Chilly high-style soap opera. Mandarin with subtitles. **113m/C VHS, DVD.** *HK* Gong Li, Leslie Cheung, Kevin Lin, Xie Tian, Zhou Jie, Saifei He; ***D:*** Chen Kaige; ***W:*** Shu Kei; ***C:*** Christopher Doyle; ***M:*** Jiping Zhao.

10 1/2 **1979 (R)** A successful songwriter who has everything finds his life is incomplete without the woman of his dreams, the 10 on his girl-watching scale. His pursuit brings surprising results. Also popularizes Ravel's "Bolero." **121m/C VHS, DVD.** Dudley Moore, Julie Andrews, Bo Derek, Dee Wallace, Brian Dennehy, Robert Webber; ***D:*** Blake Edwards; ***W:*** Blake Edwards; ***C:*** Frank Stanley; ***M:*** Henry Mancini.

The Ten **2007 (R)** Number eleven must be "thou shalt be funny," because the lack of laughs in this collection of ten irreverent sketch-style short films based on the Ten Commandments is surely a sin of omission. Rudd plays the tablet-toting narrator who introduces each vignette, played out by a bevy of Hollywood B-listers. Yeah, a "thou shalt not steal" tale starring Winona Ryder is kinda clever, but the rest of the warped jokes have narrow appeal—some hit, others miss, and most are too smug to gauge when a gag has gone on too long. **93m/C DVD.** *US* Paul Rudd, Jessica Alba, Adam Brody, Bobby Cannavale, Famke Janssen, Gretchen Mol, Justin Theroux, Winona Ryder, Rob Corddry, Oliver Platt, Ron Silver, Ken Marino; ***D:*** David Wain; ***W:*** Ken Marino, David Wain; ***C:*** Yaron Orbach; ***M:*** Craig (Shudder to Think) Wedren.

Ten Benny *Nothing to Lose* **1998 (R)** Frustrated New Jersey shoe salesman Ray (Brody) borrows $10,000 from a local wiseguy in order to win enough money at the track to set himself up in business. Bad idea. As his luck continues a downward spiral, he abuses his wife (Temchen) into the arms of his buddy (Gallagher) and becomes more desparate to climb out of the hole he's dug for himself. First-time director Bross has obviously studied the Scorsese school of filmmaking, but must've skipped the classes on originality, subtlety, and characterization. Not much going on here that hasn't been done (better) somewhere else, but Brody turns in a fine performance. **98m/C VHS, DVD.** Adrien Brody, Sybil Temchen, Michael Gallagher, Tony Gillan, James Moriarty, Frank Vincent; ***D:*** Eric Bross; ***W:*** Eric Bross, Tom Cudworth; ***C:*** Horacio Marquinez; ***M:*** Chris Hajian.

The Ten Commandments 1/2 **1923** The silent epic that established DeMille as a popular directorial force and which he remade 35 years later as an even bigger epic with sound. Follows Moses' adventures in Egypt, plus a modern story of brotherly love and corruption. Features a new musical score by Gaylord Carter. Remade in 1956. **146m/B VHS, DVD.** Theodore Roberts, Richard Dix, Rod La Rocque, Edythe Chapman, Nita Naldi; ***D:*** Cecil B. DeMille; ***C:*** Archie Stout; ***M:*** Gaylord Carter.

The Ten Commandments **1956 (G)** DeMille's remake of his 1923 silent classic (and his last film) is a lavish Biblical epic that tells the life story of Moses, who turned his back on a privileged life to lead his people to freedom outside of Egypt. Exceptional cast, with Fraser Heston (son of Charlton) as the baby Moses. Parting of Red Sea rivals any modern special effects. A 35th Anniversary Collector's Edition is available uncut at 245 minutes, in widescreen format and Dolby Surround stereo, and 1,000 copies of an Autographed Limited Edition that includes an engraved bronze plaque and an imprinted card written and personally signed by Charlton Heston are also available. **219m/C VHS, DVD.** Charlton Heston, Yul Brynner, Anne Baxter, Yvonne De Carlo, Nina Foch, John Derek, H.B. Warner, Henry Wilcoxon, Judith Anderson, John Carradine, Douglass Dumbrille, Cedric Hardwicke, Martha Scott, Vincent Price, Debra Paget; ***D:*** Cecil B. DeMille; ***W:*** Aeneas MacKenzie, Jesse Lasky Jr., Frederic M. Frank, Jack Gariss; ***C:*** Loyal Griggs; ***M:*** Elmer Bernstein. Natl. Film Reg. '99.

Ten Days That Shook the World 1/2 *October; Oktyabr* **1927** Silent masterpiece based on American author John Reed's book of the same name. Eisenstein, commissioned by the Soviet government, spared no expense to chronicle the Bolshevik Revolution of 1917 (in a flattering Communist light, of course). He was later forced to cut his portrayal of Leon Trotsky, who was then an enemy of the state. Includes rare footage of the Czar's Winter Palace in Leningrad. Haunting score, combined with some of Eisenstein's most striking work. See Warren Beatty's "Reds" for a fictional look at Reed and the Russian Revolution. **104m/B VHS, DVD.** *RU* Nikandrov, N. Popov, Boris Livanov; ***D:*** Sergei Eisenstein, Grigori Alexandrov; ***W:*** Sergei Eisenstein, Grigori Alexandrov; ***C:*** Vladimir Popov, Eduard Tisse; ***M:*** Edmund Meisel.

Ten Days Wonder 1/2 *La Decade Prodigieuse* **1972 (PG)** Mystery/drama focuses on the patriarch of a wealthy family (Welles), his young wife, and his adopted son (Perkins), who is having an affair with his stepmother. It also turns out that Perkins is certifiable and is trying to break all of the Ten Commandments, which he succeeds in doing before killing himself (gruesomely). Based on the mystery novel by Ellery Queen. **101m/C VHS, DVD.** *FR* Orson Welles, Anthony Perkins, Marlene Jobert, Michel Piccoli, Guido Alberti; ***D:*** Claude Chabrol.

10 Items or Less **2006 (R)** Minimalist flick that focuses on a nameless big-time actor (Freeman) venturing into method territory. He travels outside LA in order to spend time at a local downscale grocery store to study how his store-manager character would behave, but instead observes all-business checkout clerk Scarlet (Vega) at work. When he's left stranded, Scarlet agrees to drive him home and he offers to help her prepare for a secretarial job interview the way he would prep for an audition. You can't deny the warmth of either Freeman or Vega but even for an indie this is slight material. **81m/C DVD.** *US* Morgan Freeman, Paz Vega, Bobby Cannavale, Anne Dudek, Jonah Hill, Danny DeVito, Rhea Perlman; ***D:*** Brad Silberling; ***W:*** Brad Silberling; ***C:*** Phedon Papamichael; ***M:*** Antonio Pinto.

Ten Little Indians 1/2 *And Then There Were None* **1975 (PG)** Ten people are gathered in an isolated inn under mysterious circumstances. One by one they are murdered, each according to a verse from a children's nursery rhyme. British adaptation of the novel and stage play by Agatha Christie. **98m/C VHS, DVD.** *GB* Herbert Lom, Richard Attenborough, Oliver Reed, Elke Sommer, Charles Aznavour, Stephane Audran, Gert Frobe, Adolfo Celi, Orson Welles; ***D:*** Peter Collinson.

Ten Little Indians *Agatha Christie's Ten Little Indians* **1989 (PG)** A group of prize-winning vacationers find themselves embarking on an African adventure. They all wind up at the same camp, and realize that they are being murdered one by one. Based on the work of Agatha Christie. **100m/C VHS.** Donald Pleasence, Brenda Vaccaro, Frank Stallone, Herbert Lom, Sarah Maur-Thorp; ***D:*** Alan Birkinshaw.

The Ten Million Dollar Getaway **1991 (PG-13)** True story of the 1978 Lufthansa robbery at Kennedy Airport in which the criminals were forced to leave 10 of their $20 million heist behind when a pick-up van didn't show. Standard cable fare produced to cash in on the same scenario played out in "Goodfellas." **93m/C VHS.** John Mahoney, Karen Young, Tony LoBianco, Gerry Bamman, Joseph Carberry, Terrence Mann, Kenneth John McGregor, Christopher Murney; ***D:*** James A. Contner; ***W:*** Christopher Canaan. **CABLE**

Ten Nights in a Bar-Room **1931** A turn-of-the-century mill owner succumbs to alcoholism and ruins his life and family. Later, he sees the error of his ways and gives up drinking. This was one of many films made during this era that chronicled the evils of alcohol and fanned the flames of the prohibition debate. Remake of the 1913 silent film. **60m/B VHS.** William Farnum, Thomas Santschi, John Darrow, Robert Frazer; ***D:*** William A. O'Connor.

Ten Nights in a Barroom 🦴🦴 **1913** The evils of alcohol are dramatized when they ruin a man's life. One of many propaganda films about alcohol and the problems that it caused that were made during the prohibition era. Silent, with a musical score. Remade in 1931. **68m/B VHS.** Robert Lawrence, Marie Trado, Gladys Egan, Violet Horner, Jack Regan; ***D:*** Lee Beggs; ***W:*** Lee Beggs.

Ten North Frederick 🦴🦴 **1/2 1958** A shrewish wife (Fitzgerald) forces her gentle lawyer husband (Cooper) into cut-throat politics. He consoles himself in the arms of a much younger woman. Good performances, hokey script, based on the John O'Hara novel. **102m/B VHS.** Gary Cooper, Diane Varsi, Suzy Parker, Geraldine Fitzgerald, Tom Tully, Stuart Whitman; ***D:*** Philip Dunne; ***W:*** Philip Dunne.

10 Rillington Place 🦴🦴🦴 **1971 (PG)** A grimy, upsetting British film about the famed serial killer John Christie and the man wrongly hanged for his crimes, the incident that led to the end of capital punishment in England. Impeccably acted. One of Hurt's earliest films. **111m/C VHS.** *GB* Richard Attenborough, John Hurt, Judy Geeson, Gabrielle Daye, Andre Morell, Bernard Lee, Isobel Black, Pat Heywood; ***D:*** Richard Fleischer; ***W:*** Clive Exton; ***C:*** Denys Coop; ***M:*** John Dankworth.

Ten Speed 🦴🦴 **1976** Two advertising executives compete in a 400-mile bicycle race from San Francisco to Malibu. **89m/C VHS.** William Woodbridge, Patricia Hume, David Clover; ***D:*** Steven A. Hull.

Ten Things I Hate about You 🦴🦴🦴 **1999 (PG-13)** This Bill Shakespeare guy must be raking in the royalties, dude! The Bard is once again adapted for teens in this update of his very un-PC comedy "The Taming of the Shrew." Obstetrician and single dad Walter (Miller) has seen enough teen pregnancies to fear all adolescent boys who show up with flowers. He decrees that his ultra-popular daughter Bianca (Oleynik) cannot date before her man-hating sister Kat (Stiles) does. Two lovesick suitors, vain Joey (Keegan) and sensitive guy Cameron (Gordon-Levitt), bribe new-kid-in-town Patrick (Ledger) to make advances on Kat in order to play "jumpeth the maiden" with Bianca. Kat and Patrick then engage in a duel of verbal thrusts and parries, gradually falling for each other. Incorporates some of Shakespeare's dialogue, but glosses over the more chauvinistic elements of his play. **97m/C VHS, DVD.** Julia Stiles, Heath Ledger, Larisa Oleynik, Joseph Gordon-Levitt, Andrew Keegan, David Krumholtz, Larry Miller, Susan May Pratt, Daryl (Chill) Mitchell, Allison Janney, David Leisure, Gabrielle Union; ***D:*** Gil Junger; ***W:*** Karen McCullah Lutz, Kirsten Smith; ***C:*** Mark Irwin; ***M:*** Richard Gibbs. MTV Movie Awards '00: Breakthrough Perf. (Stiles).

10,000 A.D.: The Legend of the Black Pearl 🦴 **2008 (PG-13)** A few thousand years after WWIII, humanity is represented by two warring tribes who complain through the movie about the horrifying drought conditions caused by the war while standing in a forest next to a river. A mysterious Evil known as the Sinasu begins hunting both tribes, and the hunt is on for the one man who can stop it. Massively cliched and full of plot holes, it is quite beautifully filmed for an indie. **86m/C DVD.** *IT* Raul Gasteazoro, Julian Perez, Russ Russo, Lilly Husbands, Chyna Layne, Joaquin Perez, Loukas Papas, Nevin Millan, Edgar Feliciano, Nina Carney, Celina Murk; ***D:*** Raul Gasteazoro, Giovanni Messner; ***W:*** Raul Gasteazoro; ***C:*** Giovanni Messner; ***M:*** Jed Smith.

10,000 B.C. 🦴 **2008 (PG-13)** In some prior "mythical age" on earth, tribal peoples (who all speak different languages; lucky for us, one of them is English) live on a land ruled by nature and spirits. D'Leh (Strait), a young hunter, and Evolet (Belle), the blue-eyed beauty, are lovers in a remote mountain tribe. Evolet is kidnapped by a band of raiders and D'Leh heads out to save her. D'Leh and his small crew meet up with other civilizations along the way and soon there's an army behind him. Good thing, as it turns out that his mission isn't just to save Evolet, but civilization, too. All of which sounds okay in theory, but on screen it falls especially flat in all its cheesy computer-generated glory. The special effects are cheap, the supposedly prehistoric actors too gorgeous, and the whole thing doesn't even try to make sense, with woolly mammoths trotting about at the same time pyramids are being erected. Stick with "The Flintstones." **109m/C DVD, Blu-ray Disc.** *US* Steven Strait, Camilla Belle, Clifford Curtis, Joel Virgel, Ben Badra; ***D:*** Roland Emmerich; ***W:*** Roland Emmerich, Harald Kloser; ***C:*** Ueli Steiger; ***M:*** Harald Kloser, Thomas Wander; ***Nar:*** Omar Sharif.

Ten Thousand Bedrooms 🦴 **1/2 1957** After splitting with partner Lewis, this dull MGM musical nearly ended Martin's solo film career. Hotel magnate Ray Hunter heads to Rome to check on his latest investment and gets entangled with the four marriageable daughters of Vittorio Martelli (Slezak). **114m/C DVD.** Dean Martin, Anna Maria Alberghetti, Eva Bartok, Dewey Martin, Walter Slezak, Lisa Montell, Lisa Gaye, Jules Munshin, Paul Henreid; ***D:*** Richard Thorpe; ***W:*** Leonard Spigelgass, Art Cohn, Laszlo Vadnay, William Ludwig; ***C:*** Robert J. Bronner.

Ten 'Til Noon 🦴🦴 **2006 (R)** Low-budget but ingenious thriller that shows a ten-minute period (11:50 to noon) from several different viewpoints. Tech tycoon Larry Taylor (Wasserman) is rudely awakened by hitman Mr. Jay (Freeman) and his associate (Lano), who announce his murder. Maybe his unfaithful wife (Guest) has something to do with it, maybe it's the ruthless Mr. Duke (Kopache), or maybe someone else is pulling the strings. **88m/C DVD.** Jenya Lano, Dylan Kussman, Thomas Kopache, Daniel Nathan Spector, Rick D. Wasserman, Alfonso Freeman, Rayne Guest, Jason Hamer, Daniel Hagen, George Williams; ***D:*** Scott Storm; ***W:*** Paul Osborne; ***C:*** Alice Brooks; ***M:*** Joe Kraemer.

Ten to Midnight 🦴🦴 **1983 (R)** Vigilante Bronson is on the prowl again, this time as a police officer after a kinky serial murderer. The psychotic killer stalks his daughter and Dad's gonna stop him at any cost. **101m/C VHS, DVD.** Charles Bronson, Wilford Brimley, Lisa Eilbacher, Andrew Stevens; ***D:*** J. Lee Thompson; ***W:*** William Roberts.

10 Violent Women WOOF! **1979 (R)** Ten women who take part in a million dollar jewelry heist are tossed into a women's prison where brutal lesbian guards subject them to degradation and brutality. **97m/C VHS, DVD.** Sherri Vernon, Dixie Lauren, Sally Gamble; ***D:*** Ted V. Mikels; ***W:*** Ted V. Mikels; ***C:*** Yuval Shousterman; ***M:*** Nicholas Carras.

Ten Wanted Men 🦴 **1954** A successful cattle baron is confronted by a pistol-wielding landowner determined to ruin him. Standard fare, with better than average performances from Scott and Boone. **80m/C VHS, DVD.** Randolph Scott, Jocelyn Brando, Richard Boone, Skip Homeier, Leo Gordon, Jack Perrin, Donna (Dona Martel) Martell; ***D:*** H. Bruce Humberstone; ***W:*** Harriet Frank Jr., Irving Ravetch.

Ten Who Dared 🦴🦴 **1960** Ten Civil War heroes brave the Colorado River in an effort to chart its course. Although it's based on an actual historic event, the film is poorly paced and lacks suspense. **92m/C VHS.** Brian Keith, John Beal, James Drury; ***D:*** William Beaudine.

Tenacious D in the Pick of Destiny 🦴🦴 **1/2 2006 (R)** Big screen story of one guitar pick, two rockers and quite a bit of mind-altering substances. JB (Black) and KG (Gass) are Tenacious D, the hard-rockin' duo that simultaneously pays tribute to and pokes fun at the cliches of the world of hard rock. This hit-and-miss comedy traces the origins of the band and their experiences with talking Dio posters, Sasquatch and a musical duel with the Devil (Grohl). A must-see for fans of the band (however, it does not have powers comparable to Wonderboy), it is also entertaining for others. Raise your Goblet of Rock and lower your cognitive capacity for this one. **93m/C DVD.** *US* Jack Black, Kyle Gass, Troy Gentile, Ben Stiller, Jason (JR) Reed, Tim Robbins, Meat Loaf Aday, Amy Poehler, Paul F. Tompkins, David Grohl, Colin Hanks, Amy Adams, David Krumholtz, John C. Reilly, Fred Armisen, Ned Bellamy; ***D:*** Liam Lynch; ***W:*** Jack Black, Kyle Gass, Liam Lynch; ***C:*** Robert Brinkmann; ***M:*** Tenacious D.

The Tenant 🦴🦴🦴 **1/2** *Le Locataire* **1976 (R)** Disturbing story of a hapless office worker who moves into a spooky Paris apartment house. Once lodged inside its walls, he becomes obsessed with the previous occupant, who committed suicide, and the belief that his neighbors are trying to kill him. Based on a novel by Roland Topor. **126m/C VHS, DVD.** *FR* Lila Kedrova, Claude Dauphin, Michel Blanc, Roman Polanski, Isabelle Adjani, Melvyn Douglas, Jo Van Fleet, Bernard Fresson, Shelley Winters; ***D:*** Roman Polanski; ***W:*** Gerard Brach, Roman Polanski; ***C:*** Sven Nykvist; ***M:*** Philippe Sarde.

The Tenant of Wildfell Hall 🦴🦴 **1/2 1996** Anne Bronte gets her turn in the spotlight with this TV adaptation of her 1848 novel. When the mysterious Helen Graham (Fitzgerald) and her young son become the new tenants of decaying Wildfell Hall, they naturally elicit lots of gossip in their rural community. Then young farmer Gilbert Markham (Stephens) becomes romantically interested in Helen and she's eventually forced to reveal her secret—she's run away from her alcoholic and abusive husband Arthur Huntingdon (Graves), who has now kidnapped their son to force Helen to return. **180m/C VHS.** *GB CA* Tara Fitzgerald, Toby Stephens, Rupert Graves, Beatie Edney, James Purefoy, Jonathan Cake, Kenneth Cranham, Janet Dale; ***D:*** Mike Barker; ***W:*** Janet Barron, David Nokes; ***C:*** Daf Hobson; ***M:*** Richard G. Mitchell. **TV**

The Tenants 🦴 **1/2 2006 (R)** Adaptation of Bernard Malamud's 1972 novel, helmed by first-time director Green, is a small, grim drama about the failure to bridge racial and ethnic divides. Landlord Levenspiel (Cassel) is trying to force Harry (McDermott), his last legal tenant, to vacate his crumbling Brooklyn tenement so it can be torn down. But the obsessive writer refuses to go until he can finish his third novel; squatter Willie (Snoop Dogg) is an unpublished writer also working on his opus. The two meet, but racial tensions and mistrust eventually erupt. Snoop is convincing (in a stereotypical role) but the movie isn't. **97m/C DVD.** *US* Dylan McDermott, Snoop Dogg, Rose Byrne, Seymour Cassel, Niki J. Crawford, Laz Alonso; ***D:*** Danny Green; ***W:*** David Diamond, Danny Green; ***C:*** David W. Dubois; ***M:*** Leigh Gorman.

The Tender Age 🦴🦴 *The Little Sister* **1984** Troubled 18-year-old girl gets out of a detention home and is put on probation. She captivates her idealistic probation officer, whose interest may extend beyond professional concern. Fine idea, but under-played. **103m/C VHS.** John Savage, Tracy Pollan, Roxanne Hart, Richard Jenkins; ***D:*** Jan Egleson; ***W:*** Jan Egleson.

Tender Comrade 🦴🦴 **1943** Flag-waving violin-accompanied tearjerker about five women who live together to make ends meet while their men do manly things during WWII. Intended to puff your heart up with patriotic gusto. Ironically, thanks to the girls' communal living arrangement, director Dmytryk was later accused of un-American activities. **101m/B VHS.** Ginger Rogers, Robert Ryan, Ruth Hussey, Patricia Collinge, Mady Christians, Kim Hunter, Jane Darwell, Mary Forbes, Richard Martin; ***D:*** Edward Dmytryk.

Tender Flesh WOOF! **1997** Unashamed exercise in sleaze from the prolific Jess Franco is worth noting for only one scene wherein a woman urinates on camera. Beyond that dubious distinction, it's yet another unfocused variation on "The Most Dangerous Game." **90m/C DVD.** *SP* Lina Romay, Amber Newman, Monique Parent; ***D:*** Jess (Jesus) Franco; ***W:*** Jess (Jesus) Franco; ***M:*** Jess (Jesus) Franco.

Tender Is the Night 🦴🦴 **1/2 1955** A TV adaptation of the F. Scott Fitzgerald classic, set in the roaring '20s, in which a psychiatrist marries one of his patients and then heads down the road to ruin, driven by his marriage and the times in which he lives. An entry from the "Front Row Center" series. **60m/B VHS.** Mercedes McCambridge, James Daly. **TV**

Tender Loving Care 🦴 **1973** Three nurses dispense hefty doses of T.L.C. in their hospital, and the patients aren't the only ones on the receiving end. **72m/C VHS, DVD.** Donna Desmond, Leah Simon, Anita King; ***D:*** Don Edmonds.

Tender Mercies 🦴🦴🦴 **1983 (PG)** Down-and-out country singer Mac Sledge (Duvall) gets roaring drunk after breaking up with his wife Dixie (Buckley) andfinds himself waking up at a motel/gas station run by religious widow, Rosa Lee (Harper). mac sticks arounds and finds his life redeemed by the love of a good woman and he also decides to attempt a comeback. Aided by Horton Foote's script, Duvall, Harper, and Barkin (as Mac's daughter Sue Anne) keep this from being simplistic and sentimental. Duvall wrote as well as performed the songs in his Oscar-winning performance. Wonderful, life-affirming flick. **88m/C VHS, DVD.** Robert Duvall, Tess Harper, Betty Buckley, Ellen Barkin, Wilford Brimley, Lenny Von Dohlen, Allan Hubbard; ***D:*** Bruce Beresford; ***W:*** Horton Foote; ***C:*** Russell Boyd; ***M:*** George Dreyfus. Oscars '83: Actor (Duvall), Orig. Screenplay; Golden Globes '83: Actor—Drama (Duvall); L.A. Film Critics '83: Actor (Duvall); N.Y. Film Critics '83: Actor (Duvall); Writers Guild '83: Orig. Screenplay.

The Tender Trap 🦴🦴 **1/2 1955** Charlie Reader (Sinatra) is a bachelor not content with the many women in his life. He meets the innocent Julie Gillis (Reynolds) and falls head over heels for her. He then torments himself over a marriage proposal, unwilling to let go of his freedom. **111m/C VHS.** Frank Sinatra, Debbie Reynolds, Celeste Holm, David Wayne, Carolyn Jones, Lola Albright, Tom Helmore, Howard St. John, Willard Sage, James Drury, Benny Rubin, Frank Sully, David White; ***D:*** Charles Walters; ***W:*** Julius J. Epstein; ***C:*** Paul Vogel.

The Tender Warrior 🦴🦴 **1971 (G)** A beautifully photographed animal adventure with Haggerty as the woodsman. **85m/C VHS.** Dan Haggerty, Charles Lee, Liston Elkins; ***D:*** Stewart Raffill.

The Tender Years 🦴🦴 **1947** Sentimental drama of a minister trying to outlaw dog fighting, spurred on by his son's fondness for a particular dog. **81m/B VHS.** Joe E. Brown, Richard Lyon, Noreen Nash, Charles Drake, Josephine Hutchinson; ***D:*** Harold Schuster.

Tenderness 🦴 **1/2 2008 (R)** Despite the cast, this is a static crime drama with no particular payoff. Eighteen-year-old Eric Poole (Foster) moves in with his aunt (Dern) after being released from a juvenile detention center where he was incarcerated for murdering his parents. Troubled teen Lori (Traub) is obsessed with the crime and ingratiates herself into Eric's life. Eric is also being tracked by Detective Cristofuoro (Crowe) who doesn't believe Eric has been rehabilitated at all. Based on the Robert Cormier novel. **101m/C DVD.** *AU* Jon Foster, Russell Crowe, Sophie Traub, Laura Dern, Alexis Dziena; ***D:*** John Polson; ***W:*** Emil Stern; ***C:*** Tom Stern; ***M:*** Jonathan Goldsmith.

Tenderness of the Wolves 🦴🦴 *Die Zartlichkeit der Wolfe* **1973** Inspired by Fritz Lang's film "M" but sticking closer to its source material, the case of real-life mass murderer Peter Kurten, known as the Dusseldorf Vampire. Lommel's film is also given the "Fassbinder" spin (he's in the cast as well as the producer and editor). In 1925, black marketeer Fritz Haarmann (Raab) lures young runaway boys with the promise of a job, only to seduce and murder them—and sell their remains as meat. Raab rather resembles the Peter Lorre character but his Hartmann is all surface quiet and seething madness underneath. Very chilling. German with subtitles. **86m/C VHS, DVD.** *GE* Kurt Raab, Jeff Roden, Margit Carstensen, Rainer Werner Fassbinder, Wolfgang Schenck, Brigitte Mira, Ingrid Caven, Jurgen Prochnow; ***D:*** Ulli Lommel; ***W:*** Kurt Raab; ***C:*** Jurgen Jurges; ***M:*** Peer Raben.

Tennessee 🦴🦴 **2008 (R)** Familiar brotherly love, road trip story. Years ago, Carter Armstrong (Rothenberg) left home with his younger brother Ellis to escape their abusive, alcoholic father Roy (Sage). Carter himself has turned into a bitter, hard-drinking cab driver still looking after the sweet-natured Ellis (Peck). Ellis has been diagnosed with leukemia, so Carter reluctantly agrees to return to Tennessee to see if Roy is a bone-marrow match. When their car breaks down, waitress Krystal (Carey), who's in an abusive marriage to state trooper Frank (Reddick), helps them out and then runs away to join them on the road, with Frank in pursuit. Then the movie really gets sentimental. Rothenberg offers the strongest performance although Carey has a modest appeal. **99m/C DVD.** *US* Adam Rothenberg, Mariah Carey, Lance Reddick, Bill Sage, Michelle Harris, Ethan Peck; *D:* Aaron Woodley; *W:* Russell Schaumburg; *C:* David (Robert) A. Greene; *M:* Mario Grigorov.

Tennessee Stallion ♂ **1978** A low-class horse-trainer breaks into the world of aristocratic thoroughbred racing. **87m/C VHS.** Audrey Landers, Judy Landers, James Van Patten; *D:* Don Hulette; *W:* Don Hulette.

Tennessee's Partner ♂♂ **1955** Enjoyable, unexceptional buddy Western. Reagan intervenes in an argument and becomes Payne's pal. Adapted from a story by Bret Harte. **87m/C VHS, DVD.** Ronald Reagan, Rhonda Fleming, John Payne; *D:* Allan Dwan; *W:* D.D. Beauchamp, Milton Krims, Teddi Sherman, G. Graham Baker; *C:* John Alton; *M:* Louis Forbes.

Tension ♂♂ **1950** Nice guy Warren Quimby (Basehart) has modest ambitions: a steady job, a house, and a loving wife. Well, two out of three...seems sultry Mrs. Q (Totter) is bored, so she finds a wealthy beachboy brute (Gough) to satisfy her itch. When Warren finds out, he plots to assume a new identity, kill the interloper, and get the missus back. But things don't work out as intended—putting Warren in the crosshairs of cynical detective Bonnabel (Sullivan). **95m/B DVD.** Richard Basehart, Audrey Totter, Barry Sullivan, Cyd Charisse, Lloyd Gough, William Conrad; *D:* John Berry; *W:* Allen Rivkin; *C:* Harry Stradling Sr.; *M:* Andre Previn.

Tension at Table Rock ♂♂ **1956** Accused of cowardice, a lone gunman must prove he killed in self-defense. Well-cast serious Western. **93m/C VHS.** Richard Egan, Dorothy Malone, Cameron Mitchell; *D:* Charles Marquis Warren.

Tentacles WOOF! *Tentacoli* **1977 (PG)** Cheesy Italian version of "Jaws" lacking only the suspense and cogent storytelling. Huston slums as the investigator charged with finding the octopus gone mad, while Fonda collects check and makes a quick exit. Hopkins is in charge of the killer whales that save the day. You'll cheer when Winters is devoured by sea pest. From the director of an "Exorcist" rip-off, "Beyond the Door" (that's not a recommendation). **90m/C VHS, DVD.** *IT* John Huston, Shelley Winters, Bo Hopkins, Henry Fonda, Cesare Danova, Delia Boccardo, Alan Boyd, Claude Akins; *D:* Ovidio G. Assonitis; *W:* Steven W. Carabatsos, Tito Carpi, Sonia Molteni; *C:* Roberto D'Ettorre Piazzoli; *M:* Stelvio Cipriani.

Tentacles of the North ♂♂ ½ **1926** Two ships are trapped in the ice of the Arctic with the only survivor of one ship being a fearful young girl. Tinted print. **54m/B VHS.** Gaston Glass, Alice Calhoun, Al Ferguson, Joseph Girard; *D:* Louis Chaudet.

10th & Wolf ♂♂ **2006 (R)** In 1991, ex-Marine Tommy Santoro (Marsden) returns to his Pittsburgh 'hood, and finds out that his cousin Joey (Ribisi) and younger bro Vincent (Renfro) are heavily involved in the family's mob business. Tommy cuts a deal with FBI agent Horvath (Dennehy) to wear a wire and get the goods on the deal between Joey and the drug lord who's moving into their territory. Lots of gangland cliches. **107m/C DVD.** James Marsden, Giovanni Ribisi, Brad Renfro, Brian Dennehy, Piper Perabo, Lesley Ann Warren, Dash Mihok, Dennis Hopper, Francesco Salvi, Tommy Lee, Val Kilmer; *D:* Robert Moresco; *W:* Robert Moresco; *C:* Alex Nepomniaschy; *M:* Aaron Zigman.

The Tenth Circle ♂♂ **2008** Lifetime cable movie based on the Jodi Picoult novel, the title of which refers to Dante's circles of hell. College lit professor Laura Stone (Preston) and her husband Daniel (Eldard) are caught in a nightmare when their lovesick 14-year-old daughter Trixie (Robertson) gets jilted by her boyfriend (Johnston). She then says that he date raped her—with her accusation throwing their small town and all their lives into chaos. **89m/C DVD.** Kelly Preston, Ron Eldard, Brittany Robertson, Michael Riley, Jamie Johnston; *D:* Peter Markle; *W:* Maria Nation; *C:* Joel Ransom; *M:* Velton Ray Bunch. **CABLE**

The 10th Kingdom ♂♂ ½ **2000** Overly long but visually impressive fairytale extravganza. New Yorkers Virginia (Williams) and her father Tony (Larroquette) find themselves magically transported into an alternate universe that consists of nine kingdoms filled with trolls, evil queens, human/beast hybrids, and all sorts of adventures. Their quest to return home (to what they learn is their own tenth kingdom) is consistently thwarted until they clear up a little good vs. evil battle that's raging. **350m/C VHS, DVD.** Kimberly Williams, John Larroquette, Scott Cohen, Ann-Margret, Rutger Hauer, Camryn Manheim, Ed O'Neill, Dianne Wiest, Daniel Lapaine, Dawnn Lewis, Jimmy Nail, Warwick Davis, Timothy Bateson, Robert Hardy, Aden (John) Gillett, Moira Lister; *D:* David Carson, Herbert Wise; *C:* Lawrence Jones, Chris Howard; *M:* Anne Dudley. **TV**

The Tenth Man ♂♂ ½ **1988** Hopkins stars as a wealthy French lawyer, captured by the Nazis and sentenced to death. He discovers a fellow prisoner who is willing to take his place in exchange for Hopkins's wealth going to support the man's family. After his release, Hopkins returns to his old home, now occupied by the dead man's family, but doesn't reveal his true identity. When an imposter appears, claiming to be Hopkins, another twist is added. Slow-going but the usual excellent performances by Hopkins and Jacobi. Based on a novella by Graham Greene. **99m/C VHS.** Anthony Hopkins, Kristin Scott Thomas, Derek Jacobi, Cyril Cusack, Brenda Bruce, Paul Rogers; *D:* Jack Gold. **TV**

Tenth Month ♂♂ **1979** Carol Burnett plays a divorced, middle-aged woman who becomes pregnant by a married man. She refuses help, choosing instead to live alone and keep an ever-hopeful vigil for the birth of her child. Sappy but touching TV drama. **123m/C VHS.** Carol Burnett, Keith Michell, Dina Merrill; *D:* Joan Tewkesbury.

10th Victim ♂♂♂ *La Decima Vittima; La Dixieme Victime* **1965** Sci-fi cult film set in the 21st century has Mastroianni and Andress pursuing one another in a futuristic society where legalized murder is used as the means of population control. Intriguing movie where Andress kills with a double-barreled bra, the characters hang out at the Club Masoch, and comic books are considered literature. Based on "The Seventh Victim" by Robert Sheckley. **92m/C VHS, DVD.** *IT* Ursula Andress, Marcello Mastroianni, Elsa Martinelli, Salvo Randone, Massimo Serato; *D:* Elio Petri; *W:* Elio Petri, Tonino Guerra, Ennio Flaiano, Giorgio Salvioni; *C:* Gianni Di Venanzo; *M:* Piero Piccioni.

Teorema ♂♂ **1968** Scathing condemnation of bourgeois complacency. Stamp, either a devil or a god, mysteriously appears and enters into the life of a well-to-do Milanese family and raises each member's spirituality by sleeping with them. Ultimately, the experience leads to tragedy. In Italian with English subtitles. **98m/C VHS, DVD.** *IT* Terence Stamp, Silvana Mangano, Massimo Girotti, Anna Wiazemsky, Laura Betti, Andres Jose Cruz; *D:* Pier Paolo Pasolini; *M:* Ennio Morricone.

Tequila Body Shots ♂ **1999 (R)** Low-budget nightmare is suffered not just by the portentously named main character, Johnny Orpheus (Lawrence). Johnny is convinced by some buddies to attend a Day of the Dead party held on a Mexican beach where he imbibes some whacked Tequila that enables him to read women's thoughts and experience some afterlife horrors, courtesy of evil spirit Hector (Moreno). Turns out Hector is after his reincarnated wife who just happens to be the girl (Mouser) that Johnny is interested in. Oh yeah, and its all played for laughs (but you won't be). **94m/C VHS, DVD.** Joey Lawrence, Dru Mouser, Rene L. Moreno, Nathan Anderson, Josh Marchette, Jennifer Lyons, Henry Darrow; *D:* Tony Shyu; *W:* Tony Shyu; *C:* Lawrence Schweich; *M:* Shayne Fair, Larry Herbstritt.

Tequila Sunrise ♂♂ ½ **1988 (R)** Towne's twisting film about two lifelong friends and a beautiful woman. Gibson is a (supposedly) retired drug dealer afraid of losing custody of his son to his nagging ex-wife. Russell is the cop and old friend who's trying to get the lowdown on a drug shipment coming in from Mexico. Pfeiffer runs the poshest restaurant on the coast and is actively pursued by both men. Questions cloud the plot and confuse the viewer; loaded with double-crosses, intrigue and surprises around every corner, still the photogenic leads are pleasant to watch. Steamy love scene between Pfeiffer and Gibson. **116m/C VHS, DVD.** Mel Gibson, Kurt Russell, Michelle Pfeiffer, Raul Julia, Arliss Howard, Arye Gross, J.T. Walsh, Ann Magnuson; *D:* Robert Towne; *W:* Robert Towne; *C:* Conrad L. Hall; *M:* Dave Grusin.

Teresa Venerdi ♂♂♂ *Doctor Beware* **1941** An unusual Italian comedy about a man and his financial difficulties. His mistress, his fiance and a young girl make his troubles more confusing. Unusually sweet and humorous DeSica. **90m/B VHS.** *IT* Vittorio De Sica, Irasema Dilian, Anna Magnani, Adriana Benetti, Arturo Bragaglia, Olga Vittoria Gentilli; *D:* Vittorio De Sica; *W:* Vittorio De Sica; *C:* Vincenzo Seratrice; *M:* Renzo Rossellini.

Teresa's Tattoo ♂ **1994** A bimbo (Shelly) with a Chinese dragon tattoo somehow obtains a pair of earrings containing details of the U.S. space program. She's kidnapped by inept thugs and dies in a freak accident. Now the kidnappers need a look-alike for their extortion scheme so they kidnap another girl (Shelly again) and drug and tattoo her. Naturally, when she wakes up she manages to escape. Thin farce striving too hard to be madcap and whimsical. **88m/C VHS.** Adrienne Shelly, C. Thomas Howell, Nancy McKeon, Lou Diamond Phillips, Casey Siemaszko, Jonathan Silverman, Diedrich Bader; *Cameos:* Majel Barrett, Anthony Clark, Nanette Fabray, Tippi Hedren, k.d. lang, Joe Pantoliano, Mary Kay Place, Mare Winningham, Kiefer Sutherland, Melissa Etheridge; *D:* Julie Cypher; *W:* Georgie Huntington; *C:* Sven Kirsten; *M:* Melissa Etheridge.

Tereza ♂♂♂ **1961** In politically chaotic Czechoslovakia, a female police detective tries to solve an intricate murder mystery. In Czech with English subtitles. **91m/B VHS.** *CZ* Jirina Svorcova; *D:* Pavel Blumenfeld.

Term of Trial ♂♂ **1963** Typical '60s Brit 'kitchen sink' drama stars a miscast Olivier who is too dynamic an actor to convincingly play a milquetoast character. Alcoholic schoolteacher Graham Weir is married to contemptuous Anna (Signoret), who constantly taunts him for his lack of backbone. He teaches at a tough inner-city school in Northern England where he's harassed by school tough Mitchell (Stamp) and teenaged student Shirley (Miles) has a crush on him. Humiliated when Graham rejects her advances, Shirley tells her parents Graham assaulted her and he goes to trial. Miles and Stamp make their film debuts. **113m/B DVD.** *GB* Laurence Olivier, Simone Signoret, Sarah Miles, Hugh Griffith, Terence Stamp, Roland Culver, Thora Hird, Norman Bird, Dudley Foster; *D:* Peter Glenville; *W:* Peter Glenville, James Barlow, Oswald Morris; *M:* Jean-Michel Demase.

The Terminal ♂♂ **2004 (PG-13)** Viktor Navorski (Hanks), traveling to New York, must stay in the airport's international zone because his home country has fallen into civil war and technically no longer exists. With plucky resolve Navorski creates a makeshift life for himself while winning allies among the terminal's workforce. Central players are good: Tucci as cruel airport overseer; Zeta-Jones as love interest; and Hanks always appealing as the confused but intrepid traveler. Often clever, but basically cotton candy: sweet, but way too fluffy. Based on the true story of an Iranian immigrant who got stuck in Charles de Gaulle Airport in Paris. **128m/C VHS, DVD.** *US* Tom Hanks, Catherine Zeta-Jones, Stanley Tucci, Chi McBride, Diego Luna, Barry (Shabaka) Henley, Zoe Saldana, Eddie Jones, Michael Nouri, Kumar Pallana, Jude Ciccolella, Corey Reynolds, Guillermo Diaz, Rini Bell, Stephen Mendel, Valery (Valeri Nikolayev) Nikolaev; *D:* Steven Spielberg; *W:* Andrew Niccol, Jeff Nathanson, Sacha Gervasi; *C:* Janusz Kaminski; *M:* John Williams.

Terminal Bliss ♂ ½ **1991 (R)** Teen heartthrob Perry stars as a spoiled rich druggie in this "Less Than Zero" knock-off. Perry and childhood pal Owen grow up sharing everything—lacrosse, girlfriends, and drugs. However, their friendship is really put to the test when a beautiful new girl (Chandler) moves to town just before graduation. Release was delayed, but obviously wants to capitalize on Perry's popularity. **94m/C VHS.** Luke Perry, Timothy Owen, Estee Chandler, Sonia Curtis, Micah Grant, Alexis Arquette; *D:* Jordan Alan; *W:* Jordan Alan; *C:* Greg Smith; *M:* Frank Becker.

Terminal Choice ♂ ½ **1985 (R)** Staff at a hospital conduct a betting pool on patients' life expectancies. Someone decides he should win more often and uses a computer to help hedge his bets. Wasted cast on this unsuspenseful and bloody film. **98m/C VHS.** Joe Spano, Diane Venora, David McCallum, Ellen Barkin; *D:* Sheldon Larry; *W:* Neal Bell.

Terminal Entry ♂ ½ **1987 (R)** Teen computer geeks accidentally find a terrorist online network, and inadvertently begin transmitting instructions to destroy U.S. targets. The premise is intriguing but poorly done. **95m/C VHS.** Edward Albert, Yaphet Kotto, Kabir Bedi; *D:* John Kincade; *C:* James L. Carter.

Terminal Error ♂ *Peace Virus* **2002 (PG-13)** Disgruntled businessman cripples his old company with a computer virus to settle the score but the bug happens to spill out into the city and spells doom unless the CEO and his smarty-pants son can stop it. **90m/C VHS, DVD.** Robert Casey, Marina Sirtis, Michael Nouri, Timothy Busfield; *D:* John Murlowski; *C:* Philip Lee; *M:* James T. Sales. **VIDEO**

Terminal Exposure ♂♂ **1989 (R)** Predictable but likeable comedy-mystery. A pair of Venice, CA, beach denizens capture a murder on film and try to solve it. **105m/C VHS.** Steve Donmyer, John Vernon, Ted Lange, Joe Estevez, Hope Marie Carlton, Mark Hennessy, Scott King; *D:* Nico Mastorakis.

Terminal Force ♂ *Rescue Force* **1988 (R)** Stupid, poorly executed story of kidnapping and the mob. So bad it never saw the inside of a theatre; went straight to video. **83m/C VHS, DVD.** Troy Donahue, Richard Harrison, Dawn Wildsmith; *D:* Fred Olen Ray. **VIDEO**

Terminal Impact ♂♂ **1995 (R)** Bounty hunters Saint (Zagarino) and Max (Genesse) agree to a high-paying assignment at Delta Tech Labs without asking any questions. They discover that the lab's chairman Sheen (Roberts) is messing around with DNA and has been implanting insect DNA into unwilling human subjects, which turns them into killer cyborgs as well. **94m/C VHS.** Bryan Genesse, Frank Zagarino, Jenny (Jennifer) McShane, Ian Roberts; *D:* Yossi Wein; *W:* Jeff Albert, Dennis Dimster-Denk; *C:* Rod Stewart.

Terminal Invasion ♂♂ **2002 (R)** Cheeseball fun courtesy of the Sci-Fi Channel and Bruce Campbell, who doesn't take himself or the material seriously. Anxious passengers are stuck at a rural airport with no outside communications because of a blizzard. Then two guards show up with convicted murderer Jack Edwards (Campbell) after their transport van is in an accident. But the real problem is that some of the passengers aren't really what they seem (as in human). **84m/C DVD.** Bruce Campbell, Chase Masterson, C. David Johnson, Sarah Lafleur, Andrew Tarbet, Kedar Brown; *D:* Sean S. Cunningham; *W:* Lewis Abernathy, John Jarrell; *C:* Rudolf Blahacek; *M:* Harry Mandredini. **CABLE**

Terminal Island ♂ ½ **1973 (R)** Tough southern California penal colony is crowded with inmates from death row. When prison becomes coed, violence breaks out. Exploitative and unappealing. **88m/C VHS, DVD.** Phyllis E. Davis, Tom Selleck, Don Marshall, Ena Hartman, Marta Kristen; *D:* Stephanie Rothman.

Terminal Justice: Cybertech P.D. 🦴 ½ **1995 (R)** Cop Bobby Chase (Lamas) is assigned to protect VR sex babe, Pamela Travis (Wuhrer). Turns out wealthy VR game manufacturer, Reginald Matthews (Sarandon) has teamed up with sicko doctor, Deacon (Vivyan), to clone beautiful women so they can be used in snuff films. And Matthews wants Pam's DNA to begin the process. **95m/C VHS, DVD.** Lorenzo Lamas, Chris Sarandon, Kari Wuhrer, Peter Coyote; ***D:*** Rick King; ***W:*** Frederick Bailey; ***C:*** Chris Holmes Jr.; ***M:*** Michael Hoenig. **VIDEO**

The Terminal Man 🦴🦴 ½ **1974 (R)** A slick, visually compelling adaptation of the Michael Crichton novel. A scientist plagued by violent mental disorders has a computer-controlled regulator implanted in his brain. The computer malfunctions and he starts a murdering spree. Futuristic vision of man-machine symbiosis gone awry. Well acted, but still falls short of the novel. **107m/C VHS.** George Segal, Joan Hackett, Jill Clayburgh, Richard Dysart, James B. Sikking, Norman Burton; ***D:*** Mike Hodges; ***W:*** Mike Hodges.

Terminal Rush 🦴🦴 **1996 (R)** Army Ranger Johnny Price (Wilson) is thrown out of the service after being framed for a crime. But when terrorists (led by Piper) take over Hoover Dam, Price is the one person with the necessary skills to thwart this vindictive madman. **94m/C VHS, DVD.** Don "The Dragon" Wilson, Roddy Piper; ***D:*** Damian Lee. **VIDEO**

Terminal Velocity 🦴🦴 **1994 (PG-13)** Skydiving instructor Ditch Brodie (Sheen) thinks he sees student Chris Morrow (Kinski) plummet to her death, only it turns out she's not dead and certainly not a beginner. Upon further investigation, he finds the usual web of international intrigue descending upon him, and that the KGB definitely wants him to mind his own business. Still, he pushes on. Another no-brainer actioner with few surprises satisfies the guilty pleasures of action addicts only. **132m/C VHS, DVD.** Charlie Sheen, Nastassja Kinski, James Gandolfini, Christopher McDonald, Melvin Van Peebles; ***D:*** Deran Sarafian; ***W:*** David N. Twohy; ***C:*** Oliver Wood; ***M:*** Joel McNeely.

Terminal Virus 🦴🦴 **1996 (R)** A deadly sexually trasmitted disease has made reproduction impossible, so humanity is on the verge of extinction. It's up to an outlaw and a scientist to convince a suspicious population that a new serum is the cure everyone's been waiting for. **74m/C VHS.** James Brolin, Richard Lynch, Bryan Genesse; ***D:*** Dan Golden.

Termination Man 🦴🦴 **1997 (R)** Serbian terrorist blackmails NATO and the United Nations with a nerve gas threat and genetically enhanced agent Dylan Pope (Railsback), who may be immune to the gas, must lead a covert squad to save the day. Action by the numbers. **92m/C VHS, DVD.** Steve Railsback, Athena Massey, James Farentino, Eb Lottimer; ***D:*** Fred Gallo; ***W:*** Fred Gallo, Charles Philip Moore; ***C:*** Eugeny Guslinsky; ***M:*** Deddy Tzur. **VIDEO**

Termination Point 🦴🦴 **2007 (PG-13)** The military has been working on a secret time travel project but head scientist Dr. Daniel Winter (Phillips) becomes convinced the technology is too dangerous to entrust to them. So he steals it, and Special Agent Caleb Smith (Priestley) is set to track him down before Winter can alter the course of history. **89m/C DVD.** Jason Priestley, Lou Diamond Phillips, Garwin Sanford, Gary Hudson, Stefanie von Pfetten, Michael Eklund; ***D:*** Jason Bourque; ***W:*** Peter Sullivan; ***C:*** C. Kim Miles; ***M:*** Kyle Kenneth Batter, Gregory Tripi. **VIDEO**

The Terminator 🦴🦴🦴 **1984 (R)** Futuristic cyborg (Schwarzenegger, suitably robotic and menacing) is sent to present-day Earth. His job: kill the woman, Sarah Connor (Hamilton), who will conceive the child destined to become the great liberator and arch-enemy of the Earth's future rulers. The cyborg is also pursued by another futuristic visitor, Kyle Reese (Biehn), who falls in love with the intended victim. Cameron's pacing is just right in this exhilarating, explosive thriller which displays Arnie as one cold-blooded villain who utters a now famous line: "I'll be back." Followed by "Terminator 2: Judgment Day." **108m/C VHS, VHS, DVD, Blu-ray Disc.** Arnold Schwarzenegger, Michael Biehn, Linda Hamilton, Paul Winfield, Lance Henriksen, Bill Paxton, Rick Rossovich, Dick Miller, Earl Boen; ***D:*** James Cameron; ***W:*** James Cameron; ***M:*** Brad Fiedel. Natl. Film Reg. '08.

Terminator 2: Judgment Day 🦴🦴🦴 ½ **1991 (R)** He said he'd be back and he is, programmed to protect the boy who will be mankind's post-nuke resistance leader. But the T-1000, a shape-changing, ultimate killing machine, is also on the boy's trail. Twice the mayhem, five times the special effects, ten times the budget of the first, but without Arnold it'd be half the movie. The word hasn't been invented to describe the special effects, particularly THE scariest nuclear holocaust scene yet. Worldwide megahit, but the $100 million budget nearly ruined the studio; Arnold accepted his $12 million in the form of a jet. **139m/C VHS, DVD, Blu-ray Disc.** Arnold Schwarzenegger, Linda Hamilton, Edward Furlong, Robert Patrick, Earl Boen, Joe Morton; ***D:*** James Cameron; ***W:*** James Cameron; ***C:*** Adam Greenberg; ***M:*** Brad Fiedel. Oscars '91: Makeup, Sound, Sound FX Editing, Visual FX; MTV Movie Awards '92: Film, Male Perf. (Schwarzenegger), Female Perf. (Hamilton), Breakthrough Perf. (Furlong), Most Desirable Female (Hamilton), Action Seq.

Terminator 3: Rise of the Machines 🦴🦴🦴 **2003 (R)** Satisfying third chapter does not suffer from the absence of James Cameron or Linda Hamilton. This time around, the new bad Terminator is the female T-X (Loken) but the job is the same—kill future resistance leader John Connor (Stahl). Arnold's again sent back to protect him, as well as future cohort Kate (Danes). Solid script provides plenty of action, some inside humor, and (perhaps most importantly) a logical progression from the first two movies. Stahl does a good job as Connor, and Arnold proves he's still got the goods after a few disappointing outings. The special effects are, thankfully, seamless enough not to distract from the action at hand. **110m/C VHS, DVD, Blu-ray Disc, UMD, HD DVD.** *US* Arnold Schwarzenegger, Nick Stahl, Claire Danes, Kristanna Loken, David Andrews, Mark Famiglietti; ***D:*** Jonathan Mostow; ***W:*** John Brancato, Michael Ferris; ***C:*** Don Burgess; ***M:*** Marco Beltrami.

Terminator Salvation 🦴🦴 **2009 (PG-13)** Yeah, we know that a PG-13 rating is more 'family' accessible but the studio should have gone for an 'R' and really made this 4th installment a Terminator movie. Bale goes from brooding Batman to brooding John Connor and is once again upstaged by a supporting performer. In this case, it's Worthington. Set in a post-apocalyptic 2018, Skynet has just about completed its quest to get rid of the human population. Connor has to make sure to protect Kyle Reese (Yelchin)—well if you don't already know who and how things fit together, this isn't the time for explanations. Director McG manages that metallic rubble look and can stage the prerequisite chases, crashes, and explosions with intensity. **115m/C DVD.** *US* Christian Bale, Sam Worthington, Anton Yelchin, Bryce Dallas Howard, Moon Bloodgood, Common, Helena Bonham Carter, Michael Ironside, Jane Alexander, Jadagrace; ***D:*** McG; ***W:*** Michael Ferris, John Brancato; ***C:*** Shane Hurlbut; ***M:*** Danny Elfman.

Termini Station 🦴🦴 ½ **1989** Dewhurst gives an excellent performance as the alcoholic matriarch of a small-town Canadian family. She drinks all day and dreams of traveling to Italy, while her children work and believe there is something more to life than their mundane existence. When they finally do leave, they discover an intriguing new world. Dewhurst and Follows also appear together in "Anne of Green Gables" and "Anne of Avonlea." **105m/C VHS.** *CA* Colleen Dewhurst, Megan Follows, Gordon Clapp, Hannah Lee, Leon Pownall, Debra McGrath, Elliott Smith, Norma Dell'Agnese; ***D:*** Allen King; ***M:*** Mychael Danna.

Terms of Endearment 🦴🦴🦴 **1983 (PG)** A weeper following the changing relationship between a young woman and her mother, over a 30-year period. Beginning as a comedy, turning serious as the years go by, this was Brooks' debut as screenwriter and director. Superb supporting cast headed by Nicholson's slyly charming neighbor/astronaut, with stunning performances by Winger and MacLaine as the two women who often know and love each other too well. Adapted from Larry McMurtry's novel. **132m/C VHS, DVD.** Shirley MacLaine, Jack Nicholson, Debra Winger, John Lithgow, Jeff Daniels, Danny DeVito; ***D:*** James L. Brooks; ***W:*** James L. Brooks; ***C:*** Andrzej Bartkowiak; ***M:*** Michael Gore. Oscars '83: Actress (MacLaine), Adapt. Screenplay, Director (Brooks), Picture, Support. Actor (Nicholson); Directors Guild '83: Director (Brooks); Golden Globes '84: Actress—Drama (MacLaine), Film—Drama, Screenplay, Support. Actor (Nicholson); L.A. Film Critics '83: Actress (MacLaine), Director (Brooks), Film, Screenplay, Support. Actor (Nicholson); Natl. Bd. of Review '83: Actress (MacLaine), Director (Brooks), Support. Actor (Nicholson); N.Y. Film Critics '83: Actress (MacLaine), Film, Support. Actor (Nicholson); Natl. Soc. Film Critics '83: Actress (Winger), Support. Actor (Nicholson); Writers Guild '83: Adapt. Screenplay.

Terraces 🦴🦴 ½ **1977** TV series pilot about high-rise tenants whose balconies are their only common ground. Good performances. **90m/C VHS.** Lloyd Bochner, Eliza (Simons) Garrett, Julie Newmar, Tim Thomerson; ***D:*** Lila Garrett. **TV**

Terranova 🦴🦴 **1991** Six characters in search of themselves, with the profound changes in their lives coming through an unlikely friendship. Rosetta is the poor matriarch of an Italian immigrant family while wealthy Noemi is an artistocratic landowner. But they share similiar frustrations and the desire to change their lives. Set in a rural Venezuelan town in the 1950s; Spanish with subtitles. **96m/C VHS.** *IT* Marisa Laurito, Mimi Lazo, Antonio Banderas, Patrick Bauchau, Massimo Bonetti, Nathalia Martinez; ***D:*** Calogero Salvo.

Terrified 🦴🦴 ½ **1994 (R)** Erotic thriller about a nympho being stalked by a mystery assailant. Genuinely creepy. **90m/C VHS, DVD.** Heather Graham, Lisa Zane, Rustam Branaman, Tom Breznahan, Max Perlich, Balthazar Getty, Richard Lynch, Don Calfa; ***D:*** James Merendino; ***W:*** James Merendino, Megan Heath.

The Terror 🦴🦴 **1938** A hostelry is the scene of a number of brutal murders. Remake of a 1928 film and based on a play by Edgar Wallace. Good story, but weak version of it. **63m/B VHS, DVD.** *GB* Wilfred Lawson, Bernard Lee, Arthur Wontner, Linden Travers, Henry Oscar, Alastair Sim; ***D:*** Richard Bird.

The Terror 🦴🦴 *Lady of the Shadows* **1963** A lieutenant in Napoleon's army chases a lovely maiden and finds himself trapped in a creepy castle by a mad baron. Movie legend has it Corman directed the movie in three days as the sets (from his previous movie "The Raven") were being torn down around them. **81m/C VHS, DVD.** Boris Karloff, Jack Nicholson, Sandra Knight, Dick Miller, Dorothy Neumann, Jonathan Haze; ***D:*** Roger Corman, Jack Hill, Francis Ford Coppola, Monte Hellman, Dennis Jacob, Jack Nicholson; ***W:*** Roger Corman, Leo Gordon, Jack Hill; ***C:*** John M. Nickolaus Jr.; ***M:*** Ronald Stein.

The Terror WOOF! 1979 (R) After 100 years, a man reveals in a film that his family killed a witch. Friends who see the film are attacked by supernatural forces. Originally double-billed with "Dracula's Dog." **86m/C VHS, DVD.** John Nolan, Carolyn Courage, James Aubrey, Glynis Barber, Sarah Keller, Tricia Walsh; ***D:*** Norman J. Warren; ***W:*** Lester Young, David McGillivray; ***C:*** Lester Young; ***M:*** Ivor Slaney.

Terror at London Bridge 🦴🦴 *Bridge Across Time; Arizona Ripper* **1985** London Bridge is transported brick by brick to Arizona. It carries its history with it, including the havoc-wreaking spirit of Jack the Ripper. Campy made-for-TV effort. **96m/C VHS.** David Hasselhoff, Stephanie Kramer, Adrienne Barbeau, Randolph Mantooth; ***D:*** E.W. Swackhamer; ***C:*** Gil Hubbs.

Terror at Red Wolf Inn 🦴🦴 *Club Dead; Terror House; The Folks at Red Wolf Inn* **1972 (R)** Young woman wins a vacation; finds she's been invited for dinner, so to speak. Not campy enough to overcome stupidity. **90m/C VHS.** Linda Gillin, Arthur Space, John Neilson, Mary Jackson, Janet Wood, Margaret Avery; ***D:*** Bud Townsend; ***W:*** Allen Actor.

Terror at Tenkiller 🦴 **1986** Two girls vacationing in the mountains are seemingly surrounded by a rash of mysterious murders. **87m/C VHS, DVD.** Mike Wiles, Stacey Logan; ***D:*** Ken Meyer; ***W:*** Claudia Meyer; ***C:*** Steven Wacks; ***M:*** Robert Farrar. **VIDEO**

Terror Beach 🦴 *Night of the Seagulls; La Noche de las Gaviotas* **1975** A doctor and his bride move to a coastal village, only to find it enmeshed in witchcraft and devil worship. **90m/C VHS.** *SP* Jose Calvo, Victor Petit, Julie James, Maria Costi, Sandra Mozar; ***D:*** Armando de Ossorio; ***W:*** Armando de Ossorio; ***C:*** Francisco Sanchez; ***M:*** Anton Abril.

Terror Beneath the Sea 🦴🦴 ½ *Kaitei Daisenso; Water Cyborgs* **1966** A mad scientist wants to rule the world with his cyborgs. American and Japanese scientists unite to fight him. Fine special effects, especially the transformation from human to monster. **85m/C VHS, DVD.** *JP* Sonny Chiba, Peggy Neal, Franz Gruber, Gunther Braun, Andrew Hughes, Mike Daneen; ***D:*** Hajime Sato.

Terror by Night 🦴🦴 ½ **1946** Holmes and Watson attempt to solve the murder of the owner of a gigantic, beautiful jewel. Their investigation must be completed before their train arrives at its destination, where the murderer can escape. **60m/B VHS, DVD.** Basil Rathbone, Nigel Bruce, Alan Mowbray, Dennis Hoey, Renee Godfrey; ***D:*** Roy William Neill; ***W:*** Frank Gruber; ***C:*** Maury Gertsman.

Terror Creatures from the Grave 🦴 **1966** Husband summons medieval plague victims to rise from the grave to drop in on his unfaithful wife. Should've been better. **85m/C VHS, DVD.** *IT* Barbara Steele, Riccardo Garrone, Walter Brandi; ***D:*** Ralph Zucker.

Terror Eyes 🦴 ½ **1987 (PG-13)** Spoof-thriller revolves around an "agent from Hell," sent to Earth to recruit writers for a horror film. **90m/C VHS.** Daniel Roebuck, Vivian Schilling, Dan Bell, Lance August; ***D:*** Eric Parkinson, Stephen Sommers, Michael Rissi; ***W:*** Eric Parkinson, Vivian Schilling; ***C:*** Robert Grant, Mark Irwin; ***M:*** Jon McCallum.

Terror House WOOF! 1997 There's this creepy house, see, that's got an ugly family secret—in this case it's half-human and lives on warm blood. So these three college students think they have a chance at some big money if they can stay in the house, and they have visions of this beautiful woman, and night's coming, and the thing in the basement is hungry. You get the idea. **80m/C VHS, DVD.** Jon McBride, Mark Alan Polonia, Bob Daniels, Clyde Burroughs, Holly Harrington; ***D:*** Jon McBride, Mark Alan Polonia, John Polonia; ***W:*** Mark Alan Polonia; ***C:*** Arthur Daniels.

Terror in a Texas Town 🦴🦴 ½ **1958** George Hansen (Hayden) is a Swedish seaman who returns home to discover his farmer father has been gunned down by the greedy Johnny Crale (Young), who's after the land so he can drill for oil. So Hansen's out for revenge. There's a final showdown that not only includes six-shooters but a harpoon. **120m/B VHS, DVD.** Sterling Hayden, Nedrick Young, Sebastian Cabot, Victor Millan; ***D:*** Joseph H. Lewis; ***W:*** Dalton Trumbo; ***C:*** Ray Rennahan; ***M:*** Gerald Fried.

Terror in Beverly Hills WOOF! 1990 When the President's daughter is kidnapped, it's up to an ex-marine to save her. The trouble is, the head terrorist hates the marine's guts as he blames him for the deaths of his wife and children. So incredibly bad it's campy and fun. **88m/C VHS.** Frank Stallone, Cameron Mitchell, William (Bill) Smith; ***D:*** John Myhers; ***W:*** John Myhers.

Terror in Paradise 🦴 ½ **1990 (R)** Jason and Vickie think they're going to have a romantic holiday on a beautiful island paradise. But they've picked the wrong spot to vacation. It seems the island harbors a terrorist group and when they see more than they should the lovers become the next targets. **93m/C VHS.** Joanna Pettet, Gary Lockwood, David Anthony Smith, Leslie Ryan; ***D:*** Peer J. Oppenheimer.

Terror in the Haunted House 🦴🦴 ½ *My World Dies Screaming* **1958** Newlyweds move into an old house. The bride remembers it from her nightmares. First release featured the first use of Psychorama, a technique in which scary words or advertising messages were flashed on the screen for a fraction of a second—just long enough to cause subliminal response. The technique was banned later in the year. **90m/C VHS, DVD.** Gerald Mohr, Cathy O'Donnell, William Ching, John Qualen, Barry Bernard; ***D:*** Harold Daniels; ***W:*** Robert C. Dennis; ***C:*** Frederick E. West; ***M:*** Darrell Calker.

Terror in the Jungle **1968 (PG)** Plane crashes in Peruvian wilds and young boy survivor meets Jivaro Indians who think he's a god. Much struggling to survive and battling with horrible script. **95m/C VHS.** Jimmy Angle, Fawn Silver; ***D:*** Tom De Simone; ***M:*** Les Baxter.

Terror in the Swamp **1985 (PG)** When not hanging out in the local murky waters, a swamp creature terrorizes the residents of a small town. **89m/C VHS.** Billy Holliday; ***D:*** Joe Catalanotto.

Terror in the Wax Museum **WOOF! 1973 (PG)** The owner of a wax museum is killed while mulling over the sale of the museum. The new owner has little better luck as the bodies continue to pile up. Production uses every out-of-work horror film actor of the time. The most suspenseful part of this low-budget flick is waiting to see how long the "wax dummies" can hold their breath. **94m/C VHS.** Ray Milland, Broderick Crawford, Elsa Lanchester, Louis Hayward, Maurice Evans, John Carradine; ***D:*** Georg Fenady; ***W:*** Jameson Brewer; ***M:*** George Duning.

Terror Is a Man *Blood Creature* **1959** A mad scientist attempts to turn a panther into a man on a secluded island. Early Filipino horror attempt inspired by H.G. Wells' "The Island of Doctor Moreau." **89m/B VHS, DVD.** *PH* Francis Lederer, Greta Thyssen, Richard Derr, Oscar Keesee; ***D:*** Gerardo (Gerry) De Leon; ***W:*** Harry Paul Harber; ***C:*** Emmanuel I. Rojas; ***M:*** Ariston Auelino.

Terror of Mechagodzilla 1/2 *Monsters from the Unknown Planet; The Escape of Megagodzilla; Mekagojira No Gyakushu* **1978 (G)** It's monster vs. machine in the heavyweight battle of the universe as a huge mechanical Godzilla built by aliens is pitted against the real thing. The last Godzilla movie made until "Godzilla 1985." **79m/C VHS, DVD.** *JP* Katsuhiko Sasakai, Tomoko Al; ***D:*** Inoshiro Honda; ***W:*** Yukiko Takayama; ***C:*** Mototaka Tomioka; ***M:*** Akira Ifukube.

Terror of Rome Against the Son of Hercules **1964** Muscle-bound gladiators battle it out in this low-budget Italian action flick. Dubbed. **100m/C VHS.** *FR IT* Mark Forest, Marilu Tolo; ***D:*** Mario Caiano.

Terror of the Bloodhunters **1962** A French author is sentenced to Devil's Island for a crime he didn't commit. The warden's daughter takes a liking to him and arranges for him and a friend to escape, but numerous perils await them in the jungle. **60m/B VHS, DVD.** Robert Clarke, Steve Conte, Dorothy Haney; ***D:*** Jerry Warren; ***W:*** Jerry Warren.

Terror of the Steppes **1964** Yet another sword and sandal extravaganza in which a musclebound hero conquers all. **97m/C VHS.** *IT* Kirk Morris, Moira Orfei, Daniele Vargas, Furio Meniconi, Ombretta Colli; ***D:*** Tanio Boccia; ***W:*** Tanio Boccia; ***C:*** Aldo Giordani; ***M:*** Carlo Rustichelli.

The Terror of the Tongs *Terror of the Hatchet Men* **1961** Chung King (Lee) is the leader of Hong Kong's Red Dragon Tong, a band of drug and slave traders. When Captain Jackson Sale (Toone) tries to stop them, they murder his daughter and want to publicly execute him as a warning to others not to defy them. But Sale teams up with former slave Lee (Monlaur) to incite a riot to destroy the tong. **80m/C DVD.** *GB* Christopher Lee, Geoffrey Toone, Yvonne Monlaur, Marne Maitland, Brian Worth, Barbara Brown, Richard Leech, Charles Lloyd-Pack, Burt Kwouk, Ewen Solon, Marie Burke; ***D:*** Anthony Bushnell; ***W:*** Jimmy Sangster; ***C:*** Arthur Grant; ***M:*** James Bernard.

Terror of Tiny Town **1938** Main characteristic of this musical/western is its entire midget cast, all members of Jed Buell's Midgets. Otherwise the plot is fairly average and features a bad guy and the good guy who finally teaches him a lesson. Newfield plays up the cast's short stature—they walk under saloon doors and ride Shetland ponies. **63m/B VHS, DVD.** Billy Curtis, Yvonne Moray, "Little Billy" Rhodes, Billy Platt, John Bambury, Charles Becker; ***D:*** Sam Newfield; ***W:*** Fred Myton, Clarence Marks; ***C:*** Mack Stengler.

Terror on Alcatraz **1986** The only prisoner to successfully escape from Alcatraz Island returns to retrieve the safety deposit box key he needs to get his stolen loot. And anyone who gets in his way is in for trouble. **96m/C VHS.** Veronica Porsche Ali, Sandy Brooke, Aldo Ray, Scott Ryder; ***D:*** Philip Marcus.

Terror on the 40th Floor **1974** Seven people make an attempt to escape from the 40th floor of an inflamed skyscraper. Poorly done re-hash of "Towering Inferno." Uninspired. **98m/C VHS, DVD.** John Forsythe, Anjanette Comer, Don Meredith, Joseph Campanella; ***D:*** Jerry Jameson.

Terror on Tour **WOOF! 1983** The Clowns, a rock group on their way up, center their stage performance around sadistic, mutilating theatrics. When real murders begin, they become prime suspects. Exploitive, bloody, disgusting. **90m/C VHS.** Dave Galluzzo, Richard Styles, Rick Pemberton; ***D:*** Don Edmonds.

Terror Out of the Sky 1/2 *Revenge of the Savage Bees* **1978** A scientist must disguise himself as one of the insects to divert the attention of a horde of killing bees from a busload of elementary children. Subpar sequel to "The Savage Bees." **95m/C VHS, DVD.** Efrem Zimbalist Jr., Dan Haggerty, Tovah Feldshuh, Lonny (Lonnie) Chapman, Ike Eisenmann, Steve Franken, Bruce French, Richard Herd, Philip Baker Hall; ***D:*** Lee H. Katzin; ***W:*** Guerdon (Gordon) Trueblood; ***C:*** Michael Hugo; ***M:*** William Goldstein, William Goldstein. **TV**

Terror Ship **1954** Three people find an abandoned yacht which they believe was used for smuggling. While searching it, they find that it was used to transport stolen uranium. Before the police can arrive, the thieves show up. Not a very good handling of what was actually an interesting idea. Released as "Dangerous Voyage" in Great Britain. **72m/B VHS.** *GB* William Lundigan, Naomi Chance, Vincent Ball, Jean Lodge, Richard Stewart; ***D:*** Vernon Sewell.

Terror Squad **1987** An unsuspecting high school population is put under siege by Libyan terrorists. The students get a hands-on lesson in revolution and guerrilla war tactics. **95m/C VHS.** Kerry Brennan, Bill Calvert, Chuck Connors, Greer Brodie; ***D:*** Peter Maris.

Terror Stalks the Class Reunion 1/2 **1993 (PG-13)** Kay (Nelligan) is a teacher who disappears at a class reunion. Police dismiss the case as a runaway wife, except for Virginia, a young detective (Beals) who doesn't accept that theory. And she's right—Kay is held hostage in a remote cabin by an obsessed former student (Davies). Kay needs all her wits to fend off her deranged and possibly deadly suitor while Virginia races to find her. Based on the novel by Mary Higgins Clark. **95m/C VHS.** Kate Nelligan, Jennifer Beals, Geraint Wyn Davies; ***D:*** Clive Donner; ***W:*** Marc Princi; ***C:*** Gernot Roll; ***M:*** Carlo Siliotto.

Terror Street *36 Hours* **1954** An Air Force pilot's wife is murdered. He has 36 hours to clear his name and find the killer. **84m/B VHS, DVD.** Dan Duryea, Elsy Albiin, Ann Gudrun, Eric Pohlmann, Marianne Stone; ***D:*** Montgomery Tully; ***W:*** Steve Fisher; ***C:*** Walter J. (Jimmy W.) Harvey; ***M:*** Ivor Slaney.

Terror Taxi *Gongpo Taxi; Ghost Taxi; Taxi of Terror* **2004** Gil-nam (Seo-jin Lee) is a taxi driver who was run down before he could propose to his girlfriend. Suddenly he discovers that he does in the afterlife what he did in life: drive a taxi. Except ghost taxis run on blood, and one of their drivers, the mysterious Mantis, is a murdering fiend who may be responsible for Gil-nam's death and may now be pursuing his loved ones. Apparently all the professional editors in Korea were busy when this incoherent flick came around. **91m/C DVD.** *KN* Jae-yeong Jeong, Seo-Jin Lee, Ho Lim, Yu-Jeong Choi, Hae-gyu Jeong; ***D:*** Seung-Jun Heo; ***C:*** Gil-woong Ji.

Terror Tract **2000 (R)** Real estate agent Bob (Ritter) takes newlyweds Allen (DeLuise) and Mary Ann (Smith) to each of three homes he has for sale. But each home was the site of some horrible evil: in one a wife kills her abusive husband, only to fear he's not really dead; in the second, a father tries to stop the mischief caused by his daughter's evil pet monkey; and in the third house, a teenager finds himself psychically linked to a killer who blames the teen for his crimes. Comfortably scary fun. **97m/C VHS, DVD.** John Ritter, Marcus Bagwell, Bryan Cranston, Will Estes, Brenda Strong, Rachel York, Allison Smith, Carmine D. Giovinazzo, David DeLuise, Wade Andrew Williams, Frederic Lehne; ***D:*** Geoffrey Wright, Lance Dreesen, Clint Hutchison; ***W:*** Clint Hutchison; ***C:*** Ken Blakey; ***M:*** Brian Tyler. **VIDEO**

Terror Trail 1/2 **1933** As usual, Mix uses guns and fists to bring bad guys to justice, and gets the girl in the bargain. **62m/B VHS.** Tom Mix, Naomi Judge, Arthur (L.) Rankin, Raymond Hatton, Francis McDonald, Robert F. (Bob) Kortman, John St. Polis, Lafe (Lafayette) McKee, Buffalo Bill Jr.; ***D:*** Armand Schaefer.

Terror Train *Train of Terror* **1980 (R)** A masquerade party is held on a chartered train. But someone has more than mask-wearing in mind as a series of dead bodies begin to appear. Copperfield provides magic, Curtis provides screams in this semi-scary slasher movie. **97m/C VHS, DVD.** Jamie Lee Curtis, Ben Johnson, Hart Bochner, David Copperfield, Vanity, Howard Busgang, Michael Shanks, Amanda Tapping, Troy Kennedy-Martin, Anthony Sherwood, Timothy Webber; ***D:*** Roger Spottiswoode; ***W:*** Alec Curtis; ***C:*** John Alcott.

Terror 2000 1/2 *Intensivstation Deutschland* **1992** Satire/exploitation/slapstick and gross-out humor converge in a story about a husband and wife detective team sent to a German refugee camp to investigate the disappearance of a Polish family seeking asylum. The detectives discover the family has been kidnapped by a group of neo-Nazis. German with subtitles. **79m/C VHS.** *GE* Margit Carstensen, Alfred Edel, Udo Kier, Peter Kern, Gary Indiana; ***D:*** Christoph Schlingensief; ***W:*** Christoph Schlingensief.

The Terror Within **1988 (R)** Reptilian mutants hit the streets searching for human women to breed with. Have the Teenage Mutant Ninja Turtles grown up? **90m/C VHS, DVD.** George Kennedy, Andrew Stevens, Starr Andreeff, Terri Treas; ***D:*** Thierry Notz; ***W:*** Thomas McKelvey Cleaver; ***C:*** Ronn Schmidt; ***M:*** Rick Conrad.

The Terror Within 2 1/2 **1991 (R)** In a world destroyed by biological warfare, a warrior and the woman he rescued traverse the badlands occupied by hideous mutants. What they don't know is that the real terror comes from within. How can they possibly survive? Not without decent dialogue, that's for sure. **90m/C VHS.** Andrew Stevens, Stella Stevens, Chick Vennera, R. Lee Ermey; ***D:*** Andrew Stevens.

Terrorgram **1990 (R)** Not a very special delivery. An offscreen James Earl Jones introduces three lesser tales of terror. Best seg: a sleazy filmmaker gets trapped in the world of his own exploitation scripts. The other two are bloody but negligible revenge-from-the-grave yarns. All start off with the receipt of a sinister package, hence a postal motif. **88m/C VHS.** Michael Hartson, J.T. Wallace; ***D:*** Stephen Kienzle; ***W:*** Stephen Kienzle; ***C:*** Gregory Irwin; ***M:*** Roy J. Ravio; ***Nar:*** James Earl Jones.

The Terrorist *Malli* **1998** Malli (Dharkar) is a 19-year-old terrorist trained to kill from an early age and to die if necessary. She lives with her fellow militants in a camp and is chosen to kill a politician by detonating a bomb that will be strapped to her waist. But when Malli is forced to wait in the city for her victim, she begins to question her mission and her cause. Inspired by the 1991 assassination of Indian prime minister Rajiv Gandhi although the film itself never mentions country, group, or politics specifically. **95m/C VHS, DVD.** *IN* Ayesha Dharker; ***D:*** Santosh Sivan; ***W:*** Santosh Sivan; ***C:*** Santosh Sivan; ***M:*** Sonu Sisupal.

The Terrorist Next Door **2008 (PG-13)** Canadian telepic tells the true crime story of Muslim extremist Ahmed Ressam (Hundal) who smuggled a bomb into the U.S. with the intention of blowing up the L.A. International Airport on New Year's Eve in 1999. Director Ciccoritti does a good job maintaining suspense, especially since you know the plot failed. **92m/C DVD.** *CA* Chenier Hundal, Kathleen Robertson, Chris William Martin, Michael Ironside, Reda Gureinik, Paul Doucet, Joseph Antaki; ***D:*** Jerry Ciccoritti; ***W:*** Suzette Couture; ***C:*** Norayr Kasper; ***M:*** Robert Carli. **TV**

The Terrorists 1/2 **1974 (PG)** Just as later he was a Scottish Lithuanian sub-commander in "The Hunt for Red October" (1990), here Connery is a Scottish Norwegian security chief. Good cinematography and premise are wasted; generic title betrays sloppy execution. **89m/C VHS, DVD.** Sean Connery, Ian McShane, John Quentin; ***D:*** Casper Wrede; ***M:*** Jerry Goldsmith.

Terrorists **1988** An Army investigator discovers a plot to assassinate the President. It's up to him to move quickly enough to stop it. Brutal action. **81m/C VHS.** Nick Millard, Marland Proctor, Irmgard Millard; ***D:*** Nick Millard; ***W:*** Nick Millard.

The Terrornauts **WOOF! 1967** When man begins space exploration, Earth is attacked by aliens. The defenders are taken to an out-dated fortress where they learn that their forebears were similarly attacked. Juvenile, lackluster, contrived, and really dumb. **77m/C VHS.** *GB* Simon Oates, Zena Marshall, Charles Hawtrey, Stanley Meadows; ***D:*** Montgomery Tully.

Terrorvision **WOOF! 1986 (R)** OUR TV GAVE BIRTH TO SPACE ALIENS! It's amazing what modern technology can do: Suburban family buys a fancy satellite dish; bad black comedy and gory special effects result. **84m/C VHS.** Gerrit Graham, Mary Woronov, Diane Franklin, Bert Remsen, Alejandro Rey; ***D:*** Ted Nicolaou; ***W:*** Ted Nicolaou; ***M:*** Richard Band.

The Terry Fox Story **1983** In the spring of 1980, a young man who had lost his right leg to cancer dipped his artificial limb into the Atlantic Ocean and set off on a fund-raising "Marathon of Hope" across Canada, drawing national attention. Inspiring true story is well-scripted and avoids corniness. Good acting from real-life amputee Fryer and, as usual, from Duvall. **96m/C VHS.** Eric Fryer, Robert Duvall, Chris Makepeace, Michael Zelniker, Rosalind Chao; ***D:*** Ralph L. (R.L.) Thomas; ***M:*** Bill Conti. Genie '84: Actor (Fryer), Film, Support. Actor (Zelniker). **TV**

Tess **1979 (PG)** Sumptuous adaptation of the Thomas Hardy novel "Tess of the D'Ubervilles." Kinski is wonderful as an innocent farm girl who is seduced by the young aristocrat she works for and then finds marriage to a man of her own class only brings more grief. Polanski's direction is faithful and artful. Nearly three hours long, but worth every minute. **170m/C VHS, DVD.** *GB FR* Nastassja Kinski, Peter Firth, Leigh Lawson, John Collin; ***D:*** Roman Polanski; ***W:*** Roman Polanski, Gerard Brach; ***C:*** Ghislan Cloquet, Geoffrey Unsworth. Oscars '80: Art Dir./Set Dec., Cinematog., Costume Des.; Cesar '80: Cinematog., Director (Polanski), Film; Golden Globes '81: Foreign Film; L.A. Film Critics '80: Cinematog., Director (Polanski); N.Y. Film Critics '80: Cinematog.

Tess of the D'Urbervilles 1/2 **1998** Thomas Hardy's rural Victorian England is the setting for romantic tragedy. Tess Durbeyfield (Waddell) is a poor, naive 16-year-old who's unwillingly sent to work for the wealthy D'Urbervilles, whom her family believes are distant relatives. There, Tess becomes the target of wastrel Alec's (Flemyng) desires and he takes advantage of her. Several years later, Tess is now working as a dairymaid and falls in true love with Angel Clare (Milburn), but he can't accept her soiled past even though they've married. Heartbroken Tess falls deeper into hardship until Alec suddenly reappears in her life—and so does Angel. **180m/C VHS.** *GB* Justine Waddell, Jason Flemyng, Oliver Milburn, John

McEnery, Lesley Dunlop, Gerald James, Debbie Chazen; *D:* Ian Sharp; *W:* Ted Whitehead; *C:* Richard Greatrex; *M:* Alan Lisk. **TV**

Tess of the D'Urbervilles **2008** Typically tragic (and drawn-out) retelling of Thomas Hardy's 1891 novel. Innocent teenager Tess Durbeyfield (Arterton) is dispatched by her hardscrabble family to claim kin with the wealthier D'Urbervilles and is soon seduced by her 'cousin' Alec (Matheson). A disgraced Tess flees and eventually takes a job on a farm where she meets the priggishly noble Angel Clare (Redmayne). Things go from bad to worse for poor Tess when Angel abandons the lovelorn girl after discovering her sordid past and an obsessed Alec finds her again. **240m/C DVD.** *GB* Gemma Arterton, Eddie Redmayne, Hans Matheson, Anna Massey, Christopher Fairbank, Jodie Whittaker, Kenneth Cranham, Ian Puleston-Davies, Ruth Jones, Rebekah Station, Jo Woodcock; *D:* David Blair; *W:* David Nicholls; *C:* Wojciech Szepel; *M:* Robert (Rob) Lane. **TV**

Tess of the Storm Country 1/2 **1922** Pickford remade her own 1914 film for the better, starring as poor Tessibel Skinner, who takes in her lover Frederick Graves' (Hughes) pregnant sister, Teola (Hope), and then says the child is hers to protect the unwed mom from her ruthless father (Torrence). Tessibel temporarily loses Frederick until the truth comes out. **120m/B VHS, DVD.** Mary Pickford, Lloyd Hughes, David Torrence, Gloria Hope, Jean Hersholt; *D:* John S. Robertson; *W:* Elmer Harris; *C:* Charles Rosher, Paul Eagler; *M:* Jeffrey Mark Silverman.

The Tesseract 1/2 **2003 (R)** The lives of four folks—a psychologist, drug gopher, female assassin, and bellboy—each of whom has their own thing going on, collide at the same ratty Bangkok hotel. Wanders around in a "hopefully hip" kind of way. Based on Alex Garland's novel. **96m/C VHS, DVD.** Jonathan Rhys Meyers, Saskia Reeves, Carlo Monni, Alexander Rendel, Lene Christensen, Veradis Vinyarath; *D:* Oxide Pang Chun; *W:* Alex Garland, Oxide Pang Chun; *C:* Decha Srimantra. **VIDEO**

Test of Donald Norton 1/2 **1926** Good early Western. A young man raised by Indians finds work with the Hudson's Bay Company and does well, but is haunted by suspicions that he is a half-breed. **68m/B VHS.** George Walsh, Tyrone Power Sr., Eugenia Gilbert, Robert Graves, Virginia True Boardman; *D:* B. Reeves Eason.

A Test of Love *Annie's Coming Out* **1984 (PG)** Incorrectly diagnosed as retarded, a young woman with cerebral palsy struggles to adjust to life outside an institution. Predictable but touching and well-acted. **93m/C VHS.** *AU* Angela Punch McGregor, Drew Forsythe, Tina Arhondis; *D:* Gil Brealey; *W:* Chris Borthwick. Australian Film Inst. '84: Film.

Test Pilot 1/2 **1938** Gable and Spencer star as daring test pilot and devoted mechanic respectively. When Gable has to land his experimental craft in a Kansas cornfield, he meets and falls in love with farm girl Loy. The two marry and raise a family, all the while she worries over his dangerous profession. When the Air Force asks him to test their new B-17 bomber, she refuses to watch, thinking the test will end in tragedy. Superb aviation drama featuring excellent cast. **118m/B VHS.** Clark Gable, Myrna Loy, Spencer Tracy, Lionel Barrymore, Samuel S. Hinds; *D:* Victor Fleming.

Test Tube Babies WOOF! *Sins of Love; The Pill* **1948** A married couple's morals begin to deteriorate as they mourn the fact they can't have a child. The day is saved, however, when they learn about the new artificial insemination process. Amusing, campy propaganda in the vein of "Reefer Madness." Rereleased in 1967 as "The Pill" with extra scenes featuring Monica Davis and John Maitland. **83m/B VHS, DVD.** Dorothy Dube, Timothy Farrell, William Thomason; *D:* W. Merle Connell; *W:* Richard McMahan.

Test Tube Teens from the Year 2000 *Virgin Hunters* **1993 (R)** When sex is banned in the year 2000, horny teenagers are left with no choice but to travel through time for some action. **74m/C VHS.** Morgan Fairchild, Ian Abercrombie, Brian Bremer, Christopher Wolf, Michelle Matheson, Sara Suzanne Brown, Don Dowe, Chuck Borden, Robin Joi Brown, Conrad Brooks; *D:* David DeCoteau; *W:* Kenneth J. Hall; *M:* Reg Powell.

Testament **1983 (PG)** Well-made and thought-provoking story of the residents of a small California town struggling to survive after a nuclear bombing. Focuses on one family who tries to accept the reality of post-holocaust life. We see the devastation but it never sinks into sensationalism. An exceptional performance from Alexander. **90m/C VHS, DVD.** Jane Alexander, William Devane, Rossie (Ross) Harris, Roxana Zal, Kevin Costner, Rebecca De Mornay, Lukas Haas, Mako, Philip Anglim, Lilia Skala, Leon Ames, Lurene Tuttle; *D:* Lynne Littman; *W:* John Sacret Young; *M:* James Horner.

The Testament of Dr. Cordelier *Testament in Evil; Le Testament du Docteur Cordelier* **1959** A strange, experimental fantasy about a Jekyll and Hyde-type lunatic stalking the streets and alleys of Paris. Originally conceived as a TV play, Renoir attempted to create a new mise-en-scene, using multiple cameras covering the sequences as they were performed whole. French with English subtitles. **95m/C VHS.** *FR* Jean-Louis Barrault, Michel Vitold, Teddy Billis, Jean Topart, Micheline Gary; *D:* Jean Renoir; *W:* Jean Renoir; *C:* Georges Leclerc; *M:* Joseph Kosma.

Testament of Dr. Mabuse 1/2 *The Crimes of Dr. Mabuse; The Last Will of Dr. Mabuse* **1962** The director of an asylum is controlled by the evil genius, Dr. Mabuse, who hypnotizes him in this well-done remake of Lang's 1933 classic. **88m/B VHS, DVD.** Gert Frobe, Wolfgang Preiss, Senta Berger; *D:* Werner Klingler; *W:* Ladislas Fodor, Robert A. Stemmle; *C:* Albert Benitz; *M:* Raimund Rosenberger.

The Testament of Orpheus 1/2 *Le Testament D'Orphee* **1959** Superb, personal surrealism; writer-director Cocteau's last film. Hallucinogenic, autobiographical dream-journey through time. Difficult to follow, but rewarding final installment in a trilogy including "The Blood of the Poet" and "Orpheus." In French with English subtitles. **80m/B VHS, DVD.** *FR* Jean Cocteau, Edouard Dermithe, Maria Casares, Francois Perier, Yul Brynner, Jean-Pierre Leaud, Daniel Gelin, Jean Marais, Pablo Picasso, Charles Aznavour; *D:* Jean Cocteau; *W:* Jean Cocteau; *C:* Roland Pointoizeau; *M:* Georges Auric.

Testament of Youth 1/2 **1979** Based on the autobiography of British feminist, author, and pacifist Vera Brittain (Campbell). Vera is enjoying herself at Oxford University in 1913 until war is declared. Vera then becomes a nurse on the frontlines in France and her experiences eventually shatter her, leading her to painfully change her life. **200m/C VHS, DVD.** *GB* Cheryl Campbell, Rupert Frazer, Emrys James, Rosalie Crutchley, Joanna McCallum, Michael Troughton, Peter Woodward; *D:* Moira Armstrong; *W:* Elaine Morgan. **TV**

Testosterone **2003** Lurid black comedy about unrequited love, obsession, and revenge. When Pablo (Sabato) leaves Dean (Sutcliffe) without explanation after a torrid affair, Dean follows him to Argentina. There he gets mixed up with Pablo's intense circle of family and admirers. Some help, some hinder Dean in his attempt to confront his errant lover. Wicked take on gay romance with some tasty over-the-top performances, especially Braga as Pablo's mother. **105m/C DVD.** *US AR* David Sutcliffe, Jennifer Coolidge, Sonia Braga, Celia Font, Antonio Sabato Jr., Leonardo Brezicki, Dario Dukah; *D:* David Moreton; *W:* David Moreton, Dennis Hensley; *C:* Ken Kelsch; *M:* Marco d'Ambrosio.

Tetro **2009** Coppola's visually striking B&W (with some color flashbacks) family drama about fathers, sons, and brothers. Teenaged Bennie (Ehrenreich) works a cruise ship to Buenos Aires to track down the much-older brother (Gallo) he idolized as a child but hasn't seen in years. The self-named Tetro is a failed writer and malcontent, seemingly overwhelmed by resentment towards their successful father (Brandauer), an internationally-successful conductor and terrible human being. Tetro's generous girlfriend Miranda (Verdu) welcomes Bennie as family secrets are gradually revealed, although the revelations won't be much of a surprise. Gallo's acting isn't much of a surprise either; fortunately newcomer Ehrenreich is the one to watch. **127m/B DVD.** *US AR IT SP* Vincent Gallo, Maribel Verdu, Klaus Maria Brandauer, Carmen Maura, Alden Ehrenreich; *D:* Francis Ford Coppola; *W:* Francis Ford Coppola; *C:* Mihai Malaimare Jr.; *M:* Osvaldo Golijoy.

Tetsujin 28 1/2 *Tetsujin niju-hachigo* **2004** Originally a comic strip from the 1950s that spawned a classic anime TV series (the first featuring a giant robot, released as "Gigantor" in the states), a modern remake of the old anime, and this live action film mixed with cgi. Post-WWII Tokyo is being devastated by a giant robot called Black Ox. Japan's only hope is another giant robot named Tetsujin 28, remotely controlled by a young elementary student. But the live-action film unfortunately has none of the depth shown in the previous series it's based on. **114m/C DVD.** *JP* Yu Aoi, Naoyuki Morita; *D:* Hiroshi Saito; *W:* Hiroshi Saito, Kota Yamada, Mitsuteru Yokoyama.

Tetsuo: The Iron Man *The Ironman* **1992** A weird live-action science-fiction cartoon about a white-collar Japanese worker who finds himself being gradually transformed into a walking metal collection of cables, drills, wires, and gears. The newly formed metal creature then faces off with an equally bizarre metals fetishist (played by the director). In Japanese with English subtitles. **67m/B VHS, DVD.** *JP* Tomorowo Taguchi, Kei Fujiwara, Shinya Tsukamoto; *D:* Shinya Tsukamoto; *W:* Shinya Tsukamoto; *C:* Shinya Tsukamoto; *M:* Chu Ishikawa.

Tetsuo 2: Body Hammer **1997** Taniguchi (Yaguchi) strikes back at the cyborgs who kidnapped and killed his young son by transforming himself into a killer robotic machine man. Japanese with subtitles. **83m/C VHS, DVD.** *JP* Tomorowo Taguchi; *D:* Shinya Tsukamoto; *W:* Shinya Tsukamoto; *C:* Shinya Tsukamoto.

Tevye 1/2 *Teyve der Milkhiker* **1939** Sholom Aleichem's story of Jewish family life, intermarriage, and turmoil in Poland. When Khave, the daughter of Tevye the dairyman, seeks to marry a Ukrainian peasant, Tevye must come to terms with his love for his daughter and his faith and loyalty to tradition. Also the basis for the musical "Fiddler on the Roof." In Yiddish with English subtitles. **96m/B VHS.** Maurice Schwartz, Miriam Riselle; *D:* Maurice Schwartz. Natl. Film Reg. '91.

Tex 1/2 **1982 (PG)** Fatherless brothers in Oklahoma come of age. Dillon is excellent. Based on the novel by S.E. Hinton. **103m/C VHS, DVD.** Matt Dillon, Jim Metzler, Meg Tilly, Bill McKinney, Frances Lee McCain, Ben Johnson, Emilio Estevez, Charles S. Haas; *D:* Tim Hunter; *W:* Tim Hunter, Charles S. Haas; *C:* Ric Waite; *M:* Pino Donaggio.

Tex Rides with the Boy Scouts 1/2 **1937** Scouts aid Ritter in capturing gold bandits with a little bit of singing thrown in for good measure. **60m/B VHS.** Tex Ritter, Marjorie Reynolds, Horace Murphy, Charles "Blackie" King, Snub Pollard, Tommy Bupp, Karl Hackett, Forrest Taylor; *D:* Ray Taylor; *W:* Edmond Kelso; *C:* Gus Peterson.

The Texans 1/2 **1938** Ex-Confederate soldier Kirk Jordan (Scott) struggles to make a new life for himself as a trail boss, aiming to get 10,000 head of cattle to the railroad in Abilene. But there's temptation in the form of Ivy Preston (Bennett) and a scheme to reignite the war. Remake of 1924 silent "North of '36." **93m/B VHS, DVD.** Randolph Scott, Joan Bennett, Walter Brennan, May Robson, Robert Cummings, Raymond Hatton, Robert Barrat, Harvey Stephens, Chris-Pin (Ethier Crispin Martini) Martin, Francis Ford; *D:* James Hogan; *W:* Bertram Millhauser, Paul Sloane, William Wister Haines.

Texas **1941** Two friends wander through the West after the Civil War getting into scrapes with the law and eventually drifting apart. Ford takes a job on a cattle ranch run by Trevor and discovers Holden has joined a gang of rustlers aiming to steal her herd. The two men vie for Trevor's affections. Although friends, a professional rivalry also existed between the two leading actors and they competed against each other, doing their own stunts during filming. Well-acted, funny, and enthusiastic Western. **94m/B VHS, DVD.** William Holden, Glenn Ford, Claire Trevor, Edgar Buchanan, George Bancroft; *D:* George Marshall.

Texas 1/2 *James A. Michener's Texas* **1994** Stephen Austin (Duffy) sets up a colony in 1821 Texas, with Mexican law requiring the settlers to become Mexican citizens. Eventually, calls for statehood begin and Austin's initial resistance is overturned by rebellion and prodding from Sam Houston (Keach) and Jim Bowie (Keith). Lots of action amidst the history, including the battle for the Alamo, but it's a routine extravaganza. Made for TV miniseries adapted from Michener's novel. Filmed on location in Del Rio, Texas. **180m/C VHS, DVD.** Patrick Duffy, Stacy Keach, David Keith, Maria Conchita Alonso, Anthony Michael Hall, Rick Schroder, Benjamin Bratt, Chelsea Field, John Schneider, Grant Show, Randy Travis, Woody Watson; *D:* Richard Lang; *W:* Sean Meredith; *M:* Lee Holdridge. **TV**

Texas Across the River 1/2 **1966** Sam Hollis (Martin) is a wise-cracking gun runner who, along with Indian sidekick Kronk (Bishop), is recruiting men to help him ship guns through hostile Comanche territory. Don Andrea, a Spanish nobleman (played by Frenchman Delon) wrongly accused of murder, joins up and much comic misadventure ensues. **101m/C VHS.** Dean Martin, Alain Delon, Joey Bishop, Rosemary Forsyth, Tina Aumont, Peter Graves, Michael Ansara, Linden Chiles, Andrew Prine, Richard Farnsworth, Kelly Thordsen; *D:* Michael Gordon; *W:* Ben Starr, Wells Root, Harold Greene; *C:* Russell Metty.

Texas, Adios 1/2 *The Avenger* **1966** Curious spaghetti western stars Franco Nero as a sheriff who goes to Texas with his kid brother Jim (Dell'Acqua) to get the man who murdered their father. The action has all of the affectations of this rarified branch of the genre, and that makes it lots of fun for fans and virtually unwatchable for everyone else. **92m/C DVD.** *IT* Franco Nero, Alberto Dell'Acqua, Cole Kitosch, Elisa Montes, Jose Suarez; *D:* Ferdinando Baldi; *W:* Ferdinando Baldi; *C:* Enzo Barboni.

Texas Bad Man 1/2 **1932** Sheriff Mix goes undercover to get in with Kohler's gang of outlaws and bring them to justice. **60m/B VHS.** Tom Mix, Fred Kohler Sr., Lucille Powers, Ed LeSaint, Richard Alexander; *D:* Edward Laemmle.

Texas Buddies 1/2 **1932** Steele plays a former military pilot who uses his trusty monoplane to round up outlaws. Interesting twist on standard oater, but suffers from poor execution. **57m/B VHS, DVD.** Bob Steele, Nancy Drexel, George "Gabby" Hayes, Francis McDonald, Harry Semels; *D:* Robert North Bradbury; *W:* Robert North Bradbury.

Texas Carnival **1951** Williams and Skelton star as carnival performers who operate the dunk tank. When Skelton is mistaken for an oil tycoon, he lives high on the hog until the mistake is discovered. Believe it or not, this musical has only one water ballet sequence. Songs include "It's Dynamite," "Whoa! Emma," and "Young Folks Should Get Married." **77m/C VHS.** Esther Williams, Red Skelton, Howard Keel, Ann Miller, Paula Raymond, Keenan Wynn, Tom Tully; *D:* Charles Walters.

The Texas Chainsaw Massacre 1/2 **1974 (R)** The movie that put the "power" in power tools. An idyllic summer afternoon drive becomes a nightmare for a group of young people pursued by a chainsaw-wielding maniac. Made with tongue firmly in cheek, this is nevertheless a mesmerizing saga of gore, flesh, mayhem, and violence. **86m/C VHS, DVD, Blu-ray Disc.** Marilyn Burns, Allen Danzinger, Paul A. Partain, William Vail, Teri McMinn, Edwin Neal, Jim Siedow, Gunnar Hansen, John Dugan, Jerry Lorenz; *D:* Tobe Hooper; *W:* Tobe Hooper, Kim Henkel; *C:* Daniel Pearl; *M:* Tobe Hooper, Wayne Bell; *Nar:* John Larroquette.

The Texas Chainsaw Massacre **2003 (R)** Rancid remake of Hooper's 1974 classic horror original stars Biel and much more blood and gore than actual chills. Once again, five teenagers take a journey across Texas and pick up a mysterious hitchhiker who blows her brains out in their van after uttering a prophetic warning that they will all die. Enter Leatherface (Bryniarski) and his famously phallic chainsaw hacking up the horny teens to his evil heart's delight. Gruesome highlight as Leatherface has a literal face-off with Biel. Director Nispel, weaned on music videos, has a slicker looking product than the micro-budget original but far less of the palpable tension and shocking originality of its predecessor. **98m/C VHS, DVD, UMD.** *US* Jessica Biel, Jonathan Tucker, Erica Leerhsen, Mike Vogel, Andrew Bryniarski, R. Lee Ermey, David Dorfman, Eric Balfour, Terrence Evans; *D:* Marcus Nispel; *W:* Scott Kosar; *C:* Daniel Pearl; *M:* Steve Jablonsky; *Nar:* John Larroquette.

The Texas Chainsaw Massacre 2 WOOF! **1986 (R)** A tasteless, magnified sequel to the notorious blood-bucket extravaganza, about a certain family in southern Texas who kill and eat passing travelers. Followed by "Leatherface: The Texas Chainsaw Massacre 3." **90m/C VHS, DVD.** Dennis Hopper, Caroline Williams, Bill Johnson, Jim Siedow, Bill Moseley, Lou Perry, John (Joe Bob Briggs) Bloom; *D:* Tobe Hooper; *W:* L.M. Kit Carson; *C:* Richard Kooris; *M:* Tobe Hooper.

The Texas Chainsaw Massacre 4: The Next Generation 𝒥𝒥 *Return of the Texas Chainsaw Massacre* **1995 (R)** Heroine Jenny (Zellweger) and her three friends take a wrong turn down a dark country road and wind up in the nightmare clutches of homicidal tow-truck driver Vilmer (McConaughey), his accomplice Darla (Perenski), and the infamous Leatherface (Jacks). No restraint here—as the borderline sadism and tension builds to, unfortunately, something of a letdown. Feature debut for Henkel, who co-wrote Tobe Hooper's 1977 horror classic. Film finally got a release in 1997 after both McConaughey and Zellweger became stars in more mainstream films. Pay attention to "Love Theme from Texas Chainsaw Massacre," sung by Debbie Harry and Leatherface himself. **94m/C VHS, DVD.** Renee Zellweger, Matthew McConaughey, Robert Jacks, Tony Perenski, Lisa Marie Newmyer, John Dugan, Marilyn Burns; *D:* Kim Henkel; *W:* Kim Henkel; *C:* Levie Isaacks; *M:* Wayne Bell.

The Texas Chainsaw Massacre: The Beginning WOOF! **2006 (R)** Ugly is okay, ugly and dull is not. Contrary to what the title suggests, this is a prequel to the 2003 remake, although it provides flashbacks to Leatherface's origins, which include being born, hideously deformed, in a slaughterhouse. Ermey reprises his role as psycho cop/cannibal Hoyt, who becomes proud papa to his newly adopted gutter-child. As usual, a group of over-sexed teens are offered up for bloody sacrifice. With its unrelenting gore and sadism, flick's not for the squeamish. **84m/C DVD.** *US* Jordana Brewster, R. Lee Ermey, Andrew Bryniarski, Diora Baird, Taylor Handley, Matt Bomer, Lee Tergesen, Lew Temple; *D:* Jonathan Liebesman; *W:* Sheldon Turner; *C:* Lukas Ettlin; *M:* Steve Jablonsky.

Texas Cyclone 𝒥𝒥 **1932** A stranger rides into a town that turns out to be incredibly friendly. Later he realizes the entire town thinks he is a prominent citizen who disappeared years ago. **58m/B VHS, DVD.** Tim McCoy, Wheeler Oakman, Shirley Grey, Walter Brennan, John Wayne, Wallace MacDonald, Vernon Dent, Mary Gordon; *D:* David Ross Lederman.

Texas Detour 𝒥 **1977** On a trip across country, a trio of young Californians have their van stolen. They decide to take the law into their own hands when the redneck sheriff gives them no help. Dull, undistinguished "action" flick. **90m/C VHS.** Cameron Mitchell, Priscilla Barnes, Patrick Wayne, Mitch Vogel, Lindsay Bloom, R.G. Armstrong; *D:* Howard (Hikmet) Avedis.

A Texas Funeral 𝒥𝒥 **1999 (R)** Sheen is a Texas patriarch, seen only in flashbacks since it's his funeral that's being attended by his crazy family, which has a long tradition of dysfunction. Set in the late-'60s. **98m/C VHS, DVD.** Martin Sheen, Robert Patrick, Jane Adams, Christopher Noth, Isaiah Washington IV, Joanne Whalley, Grace Zabriskie, Olivia D'Abo, Quinton Jones; *D:* W(illiam) Blake Herron; *W:* W(illiam) Blake Herron; *C:* Michael Bonvillain; *M:* James Legg.

Texas Gunfighter 𝒥𝒥 **1932** Your basic western from the Maynard series, with everything a western could have. **60m/B VHS.** Sheila Bromley, Lloyd Ingraham, Harry Woods, Jim Mason, Ken Maynard; *D:* Phil Rosen; *W:* Bennett Cohen; *C:* Jackson Rose.

Texas Guns 𝒥𝒥 *Once Upon a Texas Train* **1990 (PG)** A gritty western about an old-time gunman (Nelson) and his quest for one last robbery, killing those who stand in his way and some just for fun. Also watch for Cassidy's comeback. **96m/C VHS, DVD.** Willie Nelson, Richard Widmark, Shaun Cassidy, Angie Dickinson, Kevin McCarthy, Royal Dano, Chuck Connors, Ken Curtis, Dub Taylor; *D:* Burt Kennedy; *W:* Burt Kennedy; *C:* Ken Lamkin; *M:* Arthur B. Rubinstein.

Texas Jack 𝒥 ½ **1935** The head of a medicine show tries to trace the disappearance of his sister. **55m/B VHS.** Jack Perrin, Jayne Regan, Nelson McDowell, Budd Buster, Lew Meehan; *D:* Bernard B. Ray.

Texas John Slaughter: Geronimo's Revenge 𝒥𝒥 **1960** An Indian-loving rancher frets and fights when Geronimo attacks innocent settlers. Compiled from Disney TV episodes. **77m/C VHS.** Tom Tryon, Darryl Hickman, Betty Lynn; *D:* Harry Keller. **TV**

Texas John Slaughter: Stampede at Bitter Creek 𝒥𝒥 **1962** Good guy Texas John Slaughter meets a variety of threatening obstacles when he tries to move his cattle herd into New Mexico. Originally from the "Walt Disney Presents" TV series. **90m/C VHS.** Tom Tryon; *D:* Harry Keller. **TV**

Texas Justice 𝒥 ½ **1942** The "Lone Rider" cavorts around in the desert, dispensing justice in the guise of a monk. **60m/B VHS.** George Houston, Al "Fuzzy" St. John, Dennis Moore, Wanda McKay, Claire Rochelle; *D:* Sam Newfield.

Texas Kid 𝒥 ½ **1943** A typical western. Hero helps a vengeance-minded kid catch the robber-gang who robbed and killed his father. Yee-Haw. **53m/B VHS.** Johnny Mack Brown, Kermit Maynard, Raymond Hatton, Shirley Patterson, Edmund Cobb, Charles "Blackie" King; *D:* Lambert Hillyer.

Texas Lady 𝒥𝒥 **1956** When a woman wins $50,000 gambling, she buys a Texas newspaper on the stipulation that she can edit it in this standard fare western. Good vehicle for Colbert to look beautiful, but the plot and script are average and uninspired. **86m/C VHS.** Claudette Colbert, Barry Sullivan, Gregory Walcott; *D:* Tim Whelan.

Texas Legionnaires 𝒥𝒥 *Man from Music Mountain* **1943** Roy comes back to his home town and gets caught between feuding cattle and sheep herders. **71m/B VHS, DVD.** Roy Rogers, Ruth Terry, Paul Kelly, Ann Gillis, George Cleveland, Pat Brady; *D:* Joseph Kane, Joseph Kane; *W:* Betty Burbridge, Lucille Ward; *C:* Jack Marta.

Texas Lightning 𝒥 ½ **1981 (R)** Innocuous B-grade touching movie about a father and son and their family woes. **93m/C VHS, DVD.** Cameron Mitchell, Channing Mitchell, Maureen McCormick, Peter Jason; *D:* Gary Graver; *W:* Gary Graver; *C:* Gary Graver; *M:* Tommy Vig.

Texas Masquerade 𝒥𝒥 **1944** Standard good cowboys versus land-grabbers action filler. William Boyd plays Hopalong Cassidy. Andy Clyde plays California Carson. Jimmy Rogers plays...Jimmy Rogers. **59m/B VHS, DVD.** William Boyd, Andy Clyde, Jimmy Rogers, Mady Correll, Don Costello, Russell Simpson, Nelson Leigh, Francis McDonald, J. Farrell MacDonald; *D:* George Archainbaud.

Texas Payback 𝒥𝒥 **1995 (R)** Convicted killer Cody Giles (Hudson) busts out of prison in order to get revenge on the now-retired-and-working-in-Vegas Texas Ranger Louis Gentry (Jones) who put him away. **96m/C VHS.** Sam Jones, Gary Hudson, Kathleen Kinmont, Bo Hopkins; *D:* Richard W. Munchkin; *W:* Brian Page; *C:* Mark Morris; *M:* Jim Halfpenny.

Texas Pioneers 𝒥 ½ *The Blood Brother* **1932** A frontier scout is sent to an outpost town besieged by crooks. **54m/B VHS.** Bill Cody, Sheila (Manors) Mannors, Frank Lackteen, Iron Eyes Cody; *D:* Harry Fraser; *W:* Harry Fraser, Wellyn Totman; *C:* Faxon M. Dean.

The Texas Rangers 𝒥𝒥 ½ **1936** Banditos Jim Hawkins (MacMurray) and Wahoo Jones (Oakie) roam the Texas frontier until the Rangers come in, establishing order. So, they switch over to the good guys but are then told to bring in their old partner-in-crime Sam McGee (Nolan). Lots of confronting villains and battling varmints. Based on the book by Walter Prescott Webb. Followed by "The Texas Rangers Ride Again" and remade as "The Streets of Laredo" (1949). **99m/B VHS, DVD.** Fred MacMurray, Jack Oakie, Lloyd Nolan, Jean Parker, Edward Ellis, Fred Kohler Sr., George "Gabby" Hayes; *D:* King Vidor; *W:* Louis Stevens.

The Texas Rangers 𝒥𝒥 **1951** A prisoner is given the opportunity to capture the notorious Sam Bass gang in exchange for freedom. Good B Western; lotsa shootin'. **68m/C VHS.** George Montgomery, Gale Storm, Jerome Courtland, Noah Beery Jr.; *D:* Phil Karlson.

Texas Rangers 𝒥𝒥 **2001 (PG-13)** Western featuring Van Der Beek and Kucher (they're dreamy!) as greenhorns who volunteer to fight bandits along the Rio Grande in 1875 Texas. McDermott's Ranger McNelly of the famous Texas Rangers is their demanding mentor who teaches them a'ropin' and a'shootin'. All are robbed of their families by the bad guys, and there's a passel o' gunfights, but taming the West takes a backseat to the real drama centered mostly around the ailing McNelly's fate in this revenge actioner. Cast is good but hindered by a weak script and direction. After sitting on the shelf for two years, yella-bellied studio execs denied the stale oater an advance screening, well aware of its weak appeal. **90m/C VHS, DVD.** *US* James Van Der Beek, Dylan McDermott, Ashton Kutcher, Usher Raymond, Robert Patrick, Rachael Leigh Cook, Leonor Varela, Randy Travis, Jon Abrahams, Matt Keeslar, Vincent Spano, Marco Leonardi, Oded Fehr, Joe Spano, Tom Skerritt, Alfred Molina; *D:* Steve Miner; *W:* Scott Busby, Martin Copeland; *C:* Daryn Okada; *M:* Trevor Rabin.

The Texas Rangers Ride Again 𝒥𝒥 ½ **1940** When cattle keep disappearing from the Dangerfield ranch, owner Robson secretly calls in the Texas Rangers to find out what's going on. Howard and Crawford work undercover to root out the criminals while Howard also finds the time to make goo-goo eyes at Robson's granddaughter Drew. **68m/B VHS.** John Howard, Broderick Crawford, May Robson, Ellen Drew, Anthony Quinn, Akim Tamiroff, Charley Grapewin, Harvey Stephens; *D:* James Hogan; *W:* William R. Lipman, Horace McCoy.

Texas Terror 𝒥𝒥 **1935** Young Wayne resigns his badge when he mistakenly believes he has shot and killed his friend. He later rescues his friend's sister, learns the truth, and (naturally) finds true love. **50m/B VHS, DVD.** John Wayne, George "Gabby" Hayes, Lucille Browne, Leroy Mason, Fern Emmett; *D:* Robert North Bradbury; *W:* Robert North Bradbury; *C:* William (Bill) Hyer.

Texas to Bataan 𝒥 ½ **1942** The Range Busters ship horses to the Philippines and encounter enemy spies. Part of the "Range Busters" series. **56m/B VHS, DVD.** John "Dusty" King, David Sharpe, Max Terhune; *D:* Robert Emmett Tansey.

Texas Trouble 𝒥 ½ *Billy the Kid's Range War* **1941** Hackett is out to stop Barclay's road building by using a Billy the Kid imposter to halt construction. But the real Billy is ticked off and comes to the rescue. **57m/B VHS.** Bob Steele, Al "Fuzzy" St. John, Carleton Young, Joan Barclay, Karl Hackett, Rex Lease; *D:* Sam Newfield; *W:* William Lively; *C:* Jack Greenhalgh; *M:* Lew Porter.

Texas Wildcats 𝒥 ½ **1939** A cowboy helps make sure that sinister adversaries are brought to justice on the American Frontier. **60m/B VHS.** Joan Barclay, Ben (Benny) Corbett, Forrest Taylor, Ted Adams, Tim McCoy; *D:* Sam Newfield; *W:* George Plympton.

Texasville 𝒥𝒥 ½ **1990 (R)** Sequel to "The Last Picture Show" finds the characters still struggling after 30 years, with financial woes from the energy crisis, mental illness inspired by the Korean War, and various personal tragedies. Lacks the melancholy sensitivity of its predecessor, but has some of the wit and wisdom that comes with age. Based again on a Larry McMurtry novel. Not well received during its theatrical release. **120m/C VHS, DVD.** Timothy Bottoms, Jeff Bridges, Annie Potts, Cloris Leachman, Eileen Brennan, Randy Quaid, Cybill Shepherd, William McNamara; *D:* Peter Bogdanovich; *W:* Peter Bogdanovich.

The Texican 𝒥 ½ **1966** Former sheriff Jess Carlin (Murphy) is living in Mexico but must return to the Texas town of Rim Rock when his newspaperman brother is murdered. Town boss Luke Starr (Crawford) is behind the crime but the townspeople are too scared to help Carlin out—except for saloon gal Kit (Lorys). **86m/C VHS, DVD.** Audie Murphy, Broderick Crawford, Diana Lorys, Aldo Sambrel, Antonio Casas; *D:* Lesley Selander; *W:* John C. Champion; *C:* Francis Marin.

Thank God It's Friday 𝒥 ½ **1978 (PG)** Episodic and desultory disco-dancing vehicle which won the Best Song Oscar for Donna Summer's rendition. Life is irony. Co-produced by Motown. ♫ Last Dance; After Dark; Find My Way; It's Serious; Let's Make A Deal; Romeo and Juliet; You're the Reason I Feel Like Dancing; From Here to Eternity; Dance All Night. **100m/C VHS, DVD.** Valerie Landsburg, Teri Nunn, Chick Vennera, Jeff Goldblum, Debra Winger; *D:* Robert Klane; *W:* Armyan Bernstein. Oscars '78: Song ("Last Dance").

Thank You & Good Night 𝒥𝒥 ½ **1991** Director Oxenberg gathers members of her own family around a purple armchair of grandma's to talk about life, love, and family memories, including grandma's illness and recent death. **81m/C VHS.** *D:* Jan Oxenberg; *W:* Jan Oxenberg; *C:* Claudia Raschke.

Thank You for Smoking 𝒥𝒥 ½ **2006 (R)** Smooth satire, based on the novel by Christopher Buckley, where no one onscreen is actually shown smoking. But if they wanted to, they have that right, which is what slick tobacco lobbyist Nick Naylor (Eckhart) is all about. No surprise that his friends are fellow "Merchants of Death," alcohol lobbyist Polly Bailey (Bello) and firearms lobbyist Bobby Jay Bliss (Koechner). Divorced Nick would like to be a good guy—he tries hard to be a concerned dad—but the game is just too enticing, even when it means bribing former cowboy icon (think Marlboro Man) Lorne Lutch (Elliott), who's dying of lung cancer, to stop attacking cigarette smoking. His opponents don't stand a chance and Eckhart plays Nick with outlandish, glib charm and confidence. **92m/C DVD.** *US* Aaron Eckhart, Maria Bello, Cameron Bright, Adam Brody, Sam Elliott, David Koechner, Katie Holmes, Rob Lowe, William H. Macy, J.K. Simmons, Robert Duvall, Kim Dickens, Connie Ray, Todd Louiso; *D:* Jason Reitman; *W:* Jason Reitman; *C:* James Whitaker; *M:* Rolfe Kent. Ind. Spirit '07: Screenplay.

Thank you, Mr. Moto 𝒥𝒥 **1937** A series of Chinese scrolls reveal the hidden location of the treasure-laden tomb of Genghis Khan. Mr. Moto (Lorre) and his friend, Prince Chung (Ahn), are determined to protect the tomb from treasure hunters. 2nd in the series. **67m/B DVD.** Peter Lorre, Thomas Beck, Philip Ahn, Pauline Frederick, Jayne Regan, Sidney Blackmer, John Carradine, Sig Rumann; *D:* Norman Foster; *W:* Norman Foster, Willis Cooper; *C:* Virgil Miller; *M:* Samuel Kaylin.

Thank Your Lucky Stars 𝒥𝒥𝒥 **1943** A lavish, slap-dash wartime musical that emptied out the Warner's lot for an array of uncharacteristic celebrity turns. Features Shore in her movie debut. ♫ They're Either Too Young or Too Old; Blues in the Night; Hotcha Cornia; Ridin' For A Fall; We're Staying Home Tonight; Goin' North; Love Isn't Born, It's Made; No You, No Me; Ice Cold Katie. **127m/B VHS.** Eddie Cantor, Dinah Shore, Joan Leslie, Errol Flynn, Bette Davis, Edward Everett Horton, Humphrey Bogart, John Garfield, Alan Hale, Ann Sheridan, Ida Lupino, Jack Carson, Dennis Morgan, Olivia de Havilland; ***D:*** David Butler; ***W:*** Norman Panama.

Thanks for Everything 1/2 **1938** Promoters Harcourt (Menjou) and Bates (Oakie) set up a radio contest to find the average American to use in their ads. The contest is won by grocery clerk Henry Smith (Haley) who is promptly put to work as a spokesman. Henry falls for small-town Madge (Whelan), who upsets everybody's plans when she realizes that Henry is being exploited. **70m/B VHS.** Adolphe Menjou, Jack Oakie, Jack Haley, Arleen Whelan, Tony Martin, Binnie Barnes, George Barbier; ***D:*** William A. Seiter; ***W:*** Curtis Kenyon, Harry Tugend; ***C:*** Lucien N. Andriot; ***M:*** Louis Silvers.

Thanks for the Memory **1938** After Hope and Ross sang "Thanks for the Memory" in "The Big Boradcast of 1938," Paramount decided to capitalize on its popularity in this lame comedy. Steve Merrick (Hope) tends to the house while trying to write a novel. Meanwhile, wife Anne (Ross) is working as a model to support the couple. Steve rebels against being a "kept man" and their marriage enters shaky ground until they come to their senses. **79m/B VHS.** Bob Hope, Shirley Ross, Charles Butterworth, Otto Kruger, Hedda Hopper, Laura Hope Crews, Eddie Anderson; ***D:*** George Archainbaud; ***W:*** Lynn Starling; ***C:*** Karl Struss.

Tharus Son of Attila *Thar Figlio di Attila* **1962** A couple of sword-wielding barbarians battle each other and an evil emperor. **89m/C VHS.** *IT* Jerome Courtland, Rik van Nutter, Lisa Gastoni; ***D:*** Robert Bianchi Montero.

That Beautiful Somewhere 1/2 **2006 (R)** Two lost souls bond in this dreary thriller. Troubled Ontario police detective Conk Adams (Dupuis) gets help from equally unhappy forensic archeologist Catherine Nyland (McGregor) when a body is found in a bog. Catherine must determine if the corpse is new or old but the bog is thought to have special curative properties by members of the local native tribe, and they don't want it disturbed. **93m/C DVD.** *CA* Roy Dupuis, Jane McGregor, Gordon Tootoosis, David Fox; ***D:*** Robert Budreau; ***W:*** Robert Budreau; ***C:*** Andrew Watt; ***M:*** Steve London.

That Brennan Girl 1/2 **1946** A maudlin soap opera about how a girl's upbringing by an inconsiderate mother makes her a devious little wench. Fortunately her second husband had a better mom, and redemption is at hand. **95m/B VHS.** James Dunn, Mona Freeman, William Marshall, June Duprez, Frank Jenks, Charles Arnt; ***D:*** Alfred Santell.

That Certain Age 1/2 **1938** Alice (Durbin) is charmed by her newspaper-owning father's houseguest, older and sophisticated journalist Vincent Bullitt (Douglas). She gets a big crush and dumps boyfriend Ken (Cooper), causing much consternation to all. ♫ That Certain Age; You're as Pretty as a Picture; Be a Good Scout; Has Anybody Ever Told You Before?; My Own. **101m/B VHS, DVD.** Deanna Durbin, Melvyn Douglas, Jackie Cooper, John Halliday, Irene Rich, Nancy Carroll, Jackie Searl, Charles Coleman; ***D:*** Edward Ludwig; ***W:*** Bruce Manning; ***C:*** Joseph Valentine.

That Certain Thing 1/2 **1928** Very early silent Capra comedy about a bachelor with a silver spoon in his mouth who loses his inheritance when he marries for love. It's got that certain Capra screwball feeling. **65m/B VHS.** Viola Dana, Ralph Graves, Burr McIntosh, Aggie Herring, Syd Crossley; ***D:*** Frank Capra.

That Certain Woman 1/2 **1937** Sentimental drama with Davis portraying a gangster's widow who wants to make a new life for herself. Fonda plays the rich playboy with whom she falls in love. Because of Davis' star power, she demanded that Fonda play opposite her. It seems Davis had a real life crush on him when they were both players in a stock company several years earlier. Remake of Goulding's "The Trespasser" which starred Gloria Swanson. **91m/B VHS.** Bette Davis, Henry Fonda, Ian Hunter, Anita Louise, Donald Crisp, Katherine Alexander, Minor Watson; ***D:*** Edmund Goulding; ***W:*** Edmund Goulding; ***M:*** Max Steiner.

That Championship Season **1982 (R)** Long-dormant animosities surface at the reunion of a championship basketball team. Unfortunate remake of Miller's Pulitzer-prize winning play, with none of the fire which made it a Broadway hit. **110m/C VHS, DVD.** Martin Sheen, Bruce Dern, Stacy Keach, Robert Mitchum, Paul Sorvino, Jason Miller; ***D:*** Jason Miller; ***C:*** John Bailey; ***M:*** Bill Conti.

That Championship Season **1999 (R)** Tom Daley (Sinise) returns to his hometown for the 20th anniversary of his high-school basketball team's championship victory. A night of nostalgia with Daley, his brother (Kinney), some friends (Shalhoub, D'Onofrio), and their coach (Sorvino, who directed this remake), turns into a drunken rehash of old grievances and the airing of some dirty laundry. Miller adapted his 1973 Pulitzer Prize-winning play, which he also directed for the big screen in 1982. **126m/C VHS.** Gary Sinise, Terry Kinney, Vincent D'Onofrio, Tony Shalhoub, Paul Sorvino; ***D:*** Paul Sorvino; ***W:*** Jason Miller; ***C:*** Bruce Surtees; ***M:*** Larry Blank. **CABLE**

That Cold Day in the Park 1/2 **1969 (R)** Early Altman. An unhappy woman takes in a homeless young man from the park near her home. The woman (Dennis) is obsessive and odd; so is the film. Dennis is excellent. Reminiscent of "The Collector." **91m/C VHS.** Sandy Dennis, Michael Burns, Susanne Benton, Michael Murphy, John David Garfield; ***D:*** Robert Altman.

That Darn Cat 1/2 **1965 (G)** Vintage Disney comedy about a Siamese cat that helps FBI Agent Jones thwart kidnappers. Could be shorter, but suspenseful and funny with characteristic Disney slapstick. Based on the book "Undercover Cat" by The Gordons. **115m/C VHS, DVD.** Hayley Mills, Dean Jones, Dorothy Provine, Neville Brand, Elsa Lanchester, Frank Gorshin, Roddy McDowall; ***D:*** Robert Stevenson; ***C:*** Edward Colman; ***M:*** Robert F. Brunner.

That Darn Cat 1/2 **1996 (PG)** Innocuous Disney remake of the 1965 Disney comedy falls into the "why bother" category. Bored 16-year-old Patti (Ricci) finds some unexpected excitement when her alley-wandering cat D.C. (for Darned Cat) returns home from a prowl with a wristwatch around his neck. Turns out it's a clue in a bungled kidnapping and Patti manages to convince rookie FBI agent Zeke (Doug) to investigate. Jones, who played the FBI agent in the original, is the wealthy husband of would-be kidnap victim Cannon. Ricci's appealing as the sarcastic teen and Elvis the cat has a certain scrappy charm as well. Based on the novel "Undercover Cat" by Mildred and Gordon Gordon. **89m/C VHS, DVD.** Christina Ricci, Doug E. Doug, Dean Jones, George Dzundza, Peter Boyle, Michael McKean, Bess Armstrong, Dyan Cannon, John Ratzenberger, Estelle Parsons, Rebecca Schull, Thomas F. Wilson, Brian Haley, Mark Christopher Lawrence; ***D:*** Bob Spiers; ***W:*** Scott M. Alexander, Larry Karaszewski; ***C:*** Jerzy Zielinski; ***M:*** Richard Gibbs.

That Darn Sorceress **1988** A child witch has grown up, and so has her power. To keep her disciples, she must perform increasingly horrible feats. **89m/C VHS.** Pauline Adams, Bettie (Betty) Page; ***D:*** Whitney Bain.

That Evening Sun **2009 (PG-13)** Stubborn, cantankerous 80-year-old widowed Tennessee farmer Abner Meecham (Holbrook) has walked away from the retirement home his lawyer son Paul (Goggins) stuck him in. Abner returns homes to discover that the place has been rented to redneck ne'er-do-well Lonzo Choat (McKinnon) and his family. The old man knows that Choat (whom he calls 'white trash') won't be able to afford the purchase option so he moves into the farm's tenant shack prepared to wait Choat out—going mano-a-mano with the increasingly desperate and violent younger man. Choat's despicable (he's a drunk who beats his teenaged daughter) but McKinnon also makes him understandable and Holbrook's unsentimental performance is simply superb. Filmed in and around Knoxville, Tennessee. Adapted from William Gay's short story "I Hate to See the Evening Sun Go Down." **110m/C DVD.** *US* Hal Holbrook, Ray McKinnon, Mia Wasikowska, Walton Goggins, Carrie Preston, Barry Corbin, Dixie Carter; ***D:*** Scott Teems; ***W:*** Scott Teems; ***C:*** Rodney Taylor; ***M:*** Michael Penn.

That Eye, the Sky **1994** Alice (Harrow) and Sam (Fairall) Flack live on a small farm with their two children and senile grandmother. Sam's in a serious car crash and is eventually returned home still in a deep coma. Alice, who's having trouble coping, is grateful when wandering evangelist Harry Warburton (Coyote) shows up on her doorstep offering his help. But is this mystery man offering a miracle or more heartache? Based on the book by Tim Winton. **105m/C VHS.** *AU* Lisa Harrow, Peter Coyote, Mark Fairall, Jamie Croft, Amanda Douge, Alethea McGrath; ***D:*** John Ruane; ***W:*** John Ruane, Jim Barton; ***C:*** Ellery Ryan; ***M:*** David Bridie. Australian Film Inst. '95: Support. Actress (Douge).

That Forsyte Woman *The Forsyte Saga* **1950** Based on the novel "A Man of Property" by John Galsworthy, a married Victorian woman falls for an architect engaged to be wed. Remade later (and better) for BBC-TV as "The Forsythe Saga." **112m/C VHS, DVD.** Errol Flynn, Greer Garson, Walter Pidgeon, Robert Young, Janet Leigh, Harry Davenport, Stanley Logan, Lumsden Hare, Aubrey Mather, Matt Moore; ***D:*** Compton Bennett; ***C:*** Joseph Ruttenberg.

That Funny Feeling **1965** Lightweight romantic comedy has freelance maid Joan (Dee) meeting and falling for businessman Tom (Darin). Instead of bringing him to her small apartment, which she shares with a roommate, she takes him to a client's place, unaware that it's Tom's. He goes along since he wants to get to know her better. Humor ensues as she tries to keep up appearances by keeping the place clean. **93m/C DVD.** Sandra Dee, Bobby Darin, Donald O'Connor, Nita Talbot, Larry Storch, Leo G. Carroll, James Westerfield, Robert Strauss, Arte Johnson, Kathleen Freeman, Ben Lessy; ***D:*** Richard Thorpe; ***W:*** David R. Schwartz; ***C:*** Clifford Stine; ***M:*** Bobby Darin.

That Gang of Mine **1940** "East Side Kids" episode about gang member Mugg's ambition to be a jockey. Good racing scenes. **62m/B VHS, DVD.** Bobby Jordan, Leo Gorcey, Clarence Muse, Dave O'Brien; ***D:*** Joseph H. Lewis.

That Girl from Paris 1/2 **1936** An opera singer from Paris stows away on an ocean liner to be near the swing bandleader she has fallen in love with. An entertaining film with many songs; remade as "Four Jacks and a Jill." ♫ Una Voce Poco Fa; The Blue Danube; Love and Learn; The Call to Arms; Seal It With A Kiss; My Nephew From Nice; Moon Face; Tarantella. **105m/B VHS.** Lily Pons, Gene Raymond, Jack Oakie, Herman Bing, Lucille Ball, Mischa Auer, Frank Jenks; ***D:*** Leigh Jason.

That Hamilton Woman *Lady Hamilton* **1941** Screen biography of the tragic 18th-century love affair between British naval hero Lord Nelson and Lady Hamilton. Korda exaggerated the film's historical distortions in order to pass the censor's production code about adultery. Winston Churchill's favorite film which paralleled Britain's heroic struggles in WWII. **125m/B VHS.** Laurence Olivier, Vivien Leigh, Gladys Cooper, Alan Mowbray, Sara Allgood, Henry Wilcoxon; ***D:*** Alexander Korda; ***M:*** Miklos Rozsa. Oscars '41: Sound.

That Long Night in '43 1/2 *The Long Night of '43; La Lunga Notte del '43* **1960** Young married woman has an affair with an Army deserter during WWII while the local fascist leader makes a power grab by executing his opposition, including the deserter's father. Italian with subtitles. **110m/B VHS.** *IT* Belinda Lee, Gabriele Ferzetti, Enrico Maria Salerno; ***D:*** Florestano Vancini; ***W:*** Florestano Vancini, Ennio de Concini, Pier Paolo Pasolini; ***C:*** Carlo Di Palma; ***M:*** Carlo Rustichelli.

That Lucky Touch **1975** York is a reporter covering NATO games; Moore is Bond warmed over as an arms dealer. Sexual and professional tension becomes unlikely romance. Slight and dull. Cobb's last film. **92m/C VHS.** Roger Moore, Susannah York, Shelley Winters, Lee J. Cobb, Jean-Pierre Cassel, Raf Vallone, Sydne Rome; ***D:*** Christopher Miles; ***W:*** John Briley.

That Man Bolt **1973** Jefferson Bolt (Williamson) is a kung fu expert who agrees to carry $1 million from Hong Kong to Mexico City while being pursued by a government agent. Typical blaxpoitation feature. **102m/C VHS, DVD.** Fred Williamson, Teresa Graves, Byron Webster, Miko Mayama, Satoshi Nakamura, Jack Ging, Vassili Lambrinos, John Orchard; ***D:*** Henry Levin, David Lowell Rich; ***W:*** Quentin Werty; ***C:*** Gerald Perry Finnerman; ***M:*** Charles Bernstein.

That Man from Rio 1/2 *L'Homme de Rio; L'Uomo di Rio* **1964** Engaging adventure spoof with Belmondo as a pilot whose girlfriend (Dorleac) has just been kidnapped. Her father led an expedition to South America in search of an Amazon treasure and the kidnappers think she knows how to find it. So of course Belmondo does some international adventuring in order to rescue her. In French with English subtitles. **114m/C VHS.** *FR IT* Jean-Paul Belmondo, Francoise Dorleac, Jean Servais, Simone Renant; ***D:*** Philippe de Broca; ***W:*** Philippe de Broca, Jean-Paul Rappeneau; ***M:*** Georges Delerue. N.Y. Film Critics '64: Foreign Film.

That Midnight Kiss 1/2 **1949** Glossy production of a musical romance featuring Lanza in his film debut. Thin plot has Lanza starring as a singing truck driver who is discovered by opera diva Grayson. ♫ They Didn't Believe Me; I Know, I Know, I Know; Three O'Clock in the Morning; Santa Lucia; Down Among the Sheltering Palms; Revolutionary Etude; Cara Nome; Celeste Aida; Una Furtiva Lacrima. **96m/C VHS.** Kathryn Grayson, Jose Iturbi, Ethel Barrymore, Mario Lanza, Keenan Wynn, J. Carrol Naish, Jules Munshin; ***D:*** Norman Taurog; ***C:*** Robert L. Surtees.

That Naughty Girl **1958** The bored daughter of a nightclub owner decides to experience all life has to offer. **77m/C VHS, DVD.** *FR* Brigitte Bardot, Jean Bretonniere, Francoise Fabian; ***D:*** Michel Boisrond.

That Night 1/2 **1993 (PG-13)** A view of romance through the eyes of a young girl, circa 1961. Ten-year-old Alice (Dushku) is the confidant of rebellious 17-year-old neighbor Cheryl (Lewis), who enlists the young girl's aid as a go-between with her wrong-side-of-the tracks boyfriend Rick (Howell). 21 soundtrack oldies are featured. Directorial debut for screenwriter Bolotin. Based on a novel by Alice McDermott. **89m/C VHS.** C. Thomas Howell, Juliette Lewis, Eliza Dushku, Helen Shaver, John Dossett; ***D:*** Craig Bolotin; ***W:*** Craig Bolotin.

That Night in Rio 1/2 **1941** Ameche plays a dual role as entertainer Larry Martin and wealthy Baron Duarte, who's in financial trouble because of his failing airline. Needing to discreetly leave town to take care of business, the Baron asks Larry to step in, but he can't fool Duarte's wife, Cecilia (Faye), while Larry's singer girlfriend Carmen (Miranda) doesn't know what's going on. Remake of 1935's "Folies Bergere." **91m/C DVD.** Don Ameche, Alice Faye, Carmen Miranda, S.Z. Sakall, J. Carrol Naish, Curt Bois, Leonid Kinskey; ***D:*** Irving Cummings; ***W:*** Bess Meredyth, George Seaton, Hal Long; ***C:*** Ray Rennahan, Leon Shamroy; ***M:*** Mack Gordon, Harry Warren.

That Obscure Object of Desire 1/2 *Cet Obscur Objet du Desir* **1977 (R)** Bunuel's last film, a comic nightmare of sexual frustration. A rich Spaniard obtains a beautiful girlfriend who, while changing physical identities, refuses to sleep with him. Based on a novel by Pierre Louys, which has been used as the premise for several other films, including "The Devil is a Woman," "La Femme et le Pantin," and "The Female." Available with subtitles or dubbed. **100m/C VHS, DVD.** *SP* Fernando Rey, Carole Bouquet, Angela Molina, Julien Bertheau; ***D:*** Luis Bunuel; ***W:*** Luis Bunuel, Jean-Claude Carriere; ***C:*** Edmond Richard. L.A. Film Critics '77: Foreign Film; Natl. Bd. of Review '77: Director (Bunuel); Natl. Soc. Film Critics '77: Director (Bunuel).

That Old Feeling **1996 (PG-13)** Bitter ex-spouses Lilly (Midler) and Dan (Farina) are reunited at the wedding of their daughter and things turn ugly. They cause a scene and are sent out of the reception to cool down. Instead, their old passion flares up and they're found reeling in that old feeling in the back seat of a Porshe. After leaving to see where their whirlwind of romance takes them, they are trailed by their daughter (Marshall), her weenie husband (Denton), and their respective current spousal units Rowena (O'Grady) and Alan (Rasche). Fluffy romantic comedy carried mostly by the performances of Midler and Farina. **105m/C VHS, DVD.** Bette Midler, Dennis Farina, Danny Nucci, Paula Marshall, Gail O'Grady, David Rasche, Jayne (Jane) Eastwood; ***D:*** Carl Reiner; ***W:*** Leslie Dixon; ***C:*** Steve Mason; ***M:*** Patrick Williams.

That Russell Girl 𝒮𝒮 **2008** Sarah Russell (Tamblyn) left her hometown and loved ones behind after a tragedy for which she still blames herself. Having been diagnosed with leukemia, Sarah decides to return home to tell her family, only to find that the past will not leave her alone when she gets an antagonistic reception from depressed neighbor Lorraine (Ehle). Instead of making the story about Sarah's illness, the TV pic focuses on her past trauma and how to forgive, with mixed results. **98m/C DVD.** Amber Tamblyn, Jennifer Ehle, Mary Elizabeth Mastrantonio, Tim DeKay, Henry Czerny, Paul Wesley, Max Morrow, Daniel Clark, Richard Leacock, Ben Lewis; ***D:*** Jeff Bleckner; ***W:*** Jill Blotevogel; ***C:*** Charles Minsky; ***M:*** Jeff Beal. **TV**

That Sinking Feeling 𝒮𝒮𝒮 **1979 (PG)** A group of bored Scot teenagers decide to steal 90 sinks from a plumber's warehouse. Well received early film from Forsyth is genuinely funny as the boys try to get rid of the sinks and turn a profit. **82m/C VHS.** *GB* Robert Buchanan, John Hughes, Billy Greenlees, Alan Love; ***D:*** Bill Forsyth; ***W:*** Bill Forsyth; ***C:*** Michael Coulter.

That Summer of White Roses 𝒮𝒮 **1/2 1990 (R)** Compelling action drama about a lifeguard working at a resort in Nazi-occupied Yugoslavia and his love for a woman resistance fighter and her child. **98m/C VHS.** Tom Conti, Susan George, Rod Steiger; ***D:*** Rajko Grlic.

That Thing You Do! 𝒮𝒮𝒮 **1996 (PG)** The Wonders, a small-town foursome, hit the big time in 1964 after a substitute drummer (like that could ever happen) adds some kick to the band's new song and sets the local kids a-fruggin'. Developed by freshman director/screenwriter Hanks (who also plays the band's Svengali-like record exec) as a diversion from Oscar hype, it's nostalgic and uncomplicated to a fault, but engaging nonetheless. Hanks clone Scott puts the beat into the charmingly wholesome quartet, while the underused Tyler is disarming as the put-upon girlfriend. Look quick or you'll miss bosom buddy Scolari as a TV host. Can't-get-it-out-of-your-head title track (played 11 times in the film) was selected from over 300 submissions after Hanks put out the call to music publishers. **110m/C VHS, DVD.** Johnathon Schaech, Tom Hanks, Liv Tyler, Tom Everett Scott, Steve Zahn, Ethan (Randall) Embry, Obba Babatunde, Charlize Theron, Peter Scolari, Alex Rocco, Bill Cobbs, Rita Wilson, Chris Isaak, Kevin Pollak, Giovanni Ribisi, Bryan Cranston, Holmes Osborne, Dawn Maxey, Sean M. Whalen, Clint Howard, Kathleen Kinmont, Barry Sobel, Gedde Watanabe, Jonathan Demme, Marc McClure, Colin Hanks; ***D:*** Tom Hanks; ***W:*** Tom Hanks; ***C:*** Tak Fujimoto; ***M:*** Howard Shore.

That Touch of Mink 𝒮𝒮 **1/2 1962** In New York City, an unemployed secretary finds herself involved with a business tycoon. On a trip to Bermuda, both parties get an education as they play their game of "cat and mouse." Enjoyable romantic comedy. **99m/C VHS, DVD.** Cary Grant, Doris Day, Gig Young, Audrey Meadows, John Astin, Dick Sargent; ***D:*** Delbert Mann; ***W:*** Stanley Shapiro, Nate Monaster; ***C:*** Russell Metty; ***M:*** George Duning. Golden Globes '63: Film—Mus./Comedy.

That Uncertain Feeling 𝒮𝒮 **1/2 1941** Light comedy about a couple's marital problems increasing when she develops the hiccups and a friendship with a flaky piano player. A remake of the earlier Lubitsch silent film, "Kiss Me Again." Available colorized. **86m/B VHS, DVD.** Merle Oberon, Melvyn Douglas, Burgess Meredith, Alan Mowbray, Eve Arden, Sig Rumann, Harry Davenport; ***D:*** Ernst Lubitsch; ***W:*** Donald Ogden Stewart, Walter Reisch; ***C:*** George Barnes; ***M:*** Werner R. Heymann.

That Was Then... This Is Now 𝒮𝒮 **1985 (R)** Lame adaptation of S.E. Hinton teen novel about a surly kid who is attached to his adoptive brother and becomes jealous when the brother gets a girlfriend. **102m/C VHS, DVD.** Emilio Estevez, Craig Sheffer, Kim Delaney, Jill Schoelen, Barbara Babcock, Frank Howard, Larry B. Scott, Morgan Freeman; ***D:*** Christopher Cain; ***W:*** Emilio Estevez.

That Wonderful Urge 𝒮𝒮 **1948** Powers remade his own 1937 film "Love Is News," although some of the sparkle is gone. He's again a newspaperman writing about a scandal-plagued heiress (Tierney instead of Loretta Young). Sara finds out Tom has been deceiving her and kicks him to the curb—but not before ruining his career. They both try to one-up each other by pretending to be married but that really gets them into trouble. A more mature Power plays a more mature character and the beautiful Tierney turns out to be a sprightly comedienne. **82m/B DVD.** Tyrone Power, Gene Tierney, Gene Lockhart, Lucile Watson, Reginald Gardner, Arleen Wheelan, Lloyd Gough, Chill Wills; ***D:*** Robert B. Sinclair; ***W:*** Jay Dratler; ***C:*** Charles G. Clarke; ***M:*** Cyril Mockridge.

That'll Be the Day 𝒮𝒮 **1/2 1973 (PG)** The early rock 'n' roll of the 1950s is the only outlet for a frustrated young working-class Brit. Prequel to "Stardust." Good, meticulous realism; engrossing story. **91m/C VHS, DVD.** Ringo Starr, Keith Moon, David Essex, Rosemary Leach, James Booth, Billy Fury, Rosalind Ayres, Robert Lindsay, Brenda Bruce, Verna Harvey, James Ottaway, Deborah Watling, Beth Morris, Daphne Oxenford, Kim Braden, Ron Hackett, Johnny Shannon, Susan Holderness, The Debonairs; ***D:*** Claude Whatham; ***W:*** Ray Connolly; ***C:*** Peter Suschitzky.

That's Adequate 𝒮𝒮 **1990 (R)** Mock documentary about a fictional film studio. Lampoons just about every movie made in the last 60 years. Premise might have been adequate for a sketch, but hardly for a feature-length film. Zaniness gets old quickly. **82m/C VHS.** Tony Randall, Robert Downey, Rocky Aoki, Bruce Willis, Robert Kevin Townsend, James Coco, Jerry Stiller, Peter Riegert, Susan Dey, Richard Lewis, Robert Vaughn, Renee Taylor, Stuart Pankin, Brother Theodore, Anne Bloom, Chuck McCann, Anne Meara; ***D:*** Harry Hurwitz; ***W:*** Harry Hurwitz.

That's Dancing! 𝒮𝒮𝒮 **1985 (G)** This anthology features some of film's finest moments in dance from classical ballet to breakdancing. **104m/C VHS, DVD.** Fred Astaire, Ginger Rogers, Ruby Keeler, Cyd Charisse, Gene Kelly, Shirley MacLaine, Liza Minnelli, Sammy Davis Jr., Mikhail Baryshnikov, Ray Bolger, Jennifer Beals, Dean Martin; ***D:*** Jack Haley Jr.; ***M:*** Henry Mancini.

That's Entertainment 𝒮𝒮𝒮 **1974 (G)** A compilation of scenes from the classic MGM musicals beginning with "The Broadway Melody" (1929) and ending with "Gigi" (1958). Great fun, especially for movie buffs. **132m/C VHS, DVD.** Judy Garland, Fred Astaire, Frank Sinatra, Gene Kelly, Esther Williams, Bing Crosby; ***D:*** Jack Haley Jr.; ***M:*** Henry Mancini.

That's Entertainment, Part 2 𝒮𝒮 **1/2 1976 (G)** A cavalcade of great musical and comedy sequences from MGM movies of the past. Also stars Jeanette MacDonald, Nelson Eddy, the Marx Brothers, Laurel and Hardy, Jack Buchanan, Ann Miller, Mickey Rooney, Louis Armstrong, Oscar Levant, Cyd Charisse, Elizabeth Taylor, Maurice Chevalier, Bing Crosby, Jimmy Durante, Clark Gable, and the Barrymores. Not as unified as its predecessor, but priceless nonetheless. **129m/C VHS, DVD.** ***D:*** Gene Kelly; ***W:*** Leonard Gershe; ***C:*** George J. Folsey; ***M:*** Nelson Riddle; ***Nar:*** Fred Astaire, Gene Kelly.

That's Entertainment, Part 3 𝒮𝒮 **1993 (G)** Third volume contains 62 MGM musical numbers from over 100 films, hosted by nine of the original stars, and is based on outtakes and unfinished numbers from studio archives. One new technique used here is a split-screen showing both the actual film with a behind-the-scenes shot that includes cameramen, set designers, and dancers scurrying around. Although it has its moments, TE3 doesn't generate the same reverence for Hollywood's Golden Age that its predecessors managed to do. That 18-year gap between sequels may say something about what the studio execs thought of their film vault's remainders. **113m/C VHS, DVD.** ***D:*** Bud Friedgen, Michael J. Sheridan; ***W:*** Bud Friedgen, Michael J. Sheridan; ***M:*** Marc Shaiman.

That's Life! 𝒮𝒮 **1986 (PG-13)** A lackluster semi-home movie starring Edwards' family and friends. A single weekend in the lives of a writer who's turning 60, his singer wife who has been diagnosed with cancer, and their family. **102m/C VHS, DVD.** Jack Lemmon, Julie Andrews, Sally Kellerman, Chris Lemmon, Emma Walton, Robert Knepper, Robert Loggia, Jennifer Edwards; ***D:*** Blake Edwards; ***W:*** Blake Edwards; ***M:*** Henry Mancini.

That's My Baby! 𝒮𝒮 **1/2 1944** A number of (then-)popular musical performers (Peppy and Peanuts, Gene Rodgers, Mitchell & Lytell) as well as animated cartoons from Dave Fleisher pop up in this oddball combo of music and drama from Republic Pictures. Betty Moody (Drew) and her boyfriend Tim (Arlen) try to snap her wealthy father R.P. (Watson) out of his melancholia by having every performer they know from the clubs do their act and make him smile. Nothing works until Mrs. Moody remembers that R.P. once wanted to be a cartoonist, which brings in Fleischer's efforts. Doesn't make any sense but it's nostalgic fun. **68m/B DVD.** Richard Arlen, Ellen Drew, Minor Watson, Leonid Kinskey, Richard Bailey, Madeline Grey, Marjorie Manners; ***D:*** William Berke; ***W:*** William Tunberg, Nicholas T. Barrows; ***C:*** Robert Pittack.

That's My Baby! 𝒮 **1988 (PG-13)** A man wants his girlfriend to have their baby, but the only thing she wants is a career. War between the sexes poorly done. **97m/C VHS.** Sonja Smits, Timothy Webber; ***D:*** Edie Yolles, John Bradshaw.

That's the Way I Like It 𝒮𝒮 **1/2 1999 (PG-13)** Homage to disco but set in the East rather than the West. It's 1977 and Sinapore clerk Hock (Pang) wants to win a disco tournament so he can buy a motorcycle. He drops his usual partner (Tang) for the flashier Julie (Francis) and the rivalry between the dance teams gets intense. But Hock just happens to have the spirit of the legendary "Saturday Night Fever" studster himself, Tony Manero (Pace), to give him that extra dance fever. **92m/C VHS, DVD.** Adrian Pang, Anna Belle Francis, Dominic Pace, Madeline Tang, Caleb Goh; ***D:*** Glen Goei; ***W:*** Glen Goei; ***C:*** Brian J. Breheny; ***M:*** Guy Gross.

The Thaw 𝒮𝒮 **2009 (R)** Environmentalist David Kruipen chooses three college students to work at his Arctic base where they are joined by Kruipen's bitter daughter Evelyn. The station contains a decaying wooly mammoth infested by a parasite that bites several of the newcomers, causing a violent reaction. An eco-doomsday scenario that's both moderately gross and suspenseful. **94m/C DVD.** Val Kilmer, Martha MacIsaac, Kyle Schmid, Steph Song, Aaron Ashmore, Anne Marie Deluise, William B. Davis; ***D:*** Mark Lewis; ***W:*** Mark Lewis; ***C:*** Jan Kiesser; ***M:*** Michael Neilson. **VIDEO**

Theatre of Blood 𝒮𝒮𝒮 *Much Ado about Murder* **1973 (R)** Shakespearean ham actor Edward Lionheart (Price) committed suicide after losing an award and being ridiculed by the critics. Now those same critics are being murdered in bizarre ways—in fact, their deaths parallel those in the plays of the Bard. Well, it's no big surprise to discover that Lionheart is indeed alive and committing the inventive crimes with the assistance of his lovely daughter, Edwina (Rigg). Top drawer comedy noir with a great supporting cast of Britain's best (and quite a bit of gore). **104m/C VHS, DVD.** *GB* Vincent Price, Diana Rigg, Ian Hendry, Robert Morley, Dennis Price, Diana Dors, Milo O'Shea, Harry Andrews, Coral Browne, Robert Coote, Jack Hawkins, Michael Hordern, Arthur Lowe; ***D:*** Douglas Hickox; ***W:*** Anthony Greville-Bell; ***C:*** Wolfgang Suschitzky; ***M:*** Michael Lewis.

Theatre of Death 𝒮𝒮 **1/2** *Blood Fiend; Female Fiend* **1967** Horror master Lee is back, this time as a theatre director in Paris. Meanwhile, police are baffled by a series of mysterious murders, each bearing a trace of vampirism. Well-plotted suspense. A racy voodoo dance sequence, often cut, is available on some video versions. **90m/C VHS, DVD.** Christopher Lee, Lelia Goldoni, Julian Glover, Evelyn Laye, Jenny Till, Ivor Dean; ***D:*** Samuel Gallu; ***W:*** Ellis Kadison, Roger Marshall; ***C:*** Gilbert Taylor.

Thelma & Louise 𝒮𝒮𝒮 **1991 (R)** Hailed as the first "feminist-buddy" movie, Sarandon and Davis bust out as best friends who head directly into one of the better movies of the year. Davis is the ditzy Thelma, a housewife rebelling against her dominating, unfaithful, abusive husband (who, rather than being disturbing, provides some of the best comic relief in the film). Sarandon is Louise, a hardened and world-weary waitress in the midst of an unsatisfactory relationship. They hit the road for a respite from their mundane lives, only to find violence and a part of themselves they never knew existed. Outstanding performances from Davis and especially Sarandon, with Pitt notable as the stud who gets Davis' motor revved. Director Scott has a fine eye for set details. **130m/C VHS, DVD.** Susan Sarandon, Geena Davis, Harvey Keitel, Christopher McDonald, Michael Madsen, Brad Pitt, Timothy Carhart, Stephen Tobolowsky, Lucinda Jenney; ***D:*** Ridley Scott; ***W:*** Callie Khouri; ***C:*** Adrian Biddle; ***M:*** Hans Zimmer. Oscars '91: Orig. Screenplay; Natl. Bd. of Review '91: Actress (Sarandon), Actress (Davis); Natl. Soc. Film Critics '91: Support. Actor (Keitel); Writers Guild '91: Orig. Screenplay.

Them! 𝒮𝒮𝒮 **1954** A group of mutated giant ants wreak havoc on a southwestern town. The first of the big-bug movies, and far surpassing the rest, this is a classic fun flick. See how many names you can spot among the supporting cast. **93m/B VHS, DVD.** James Whitmore, Edmund Gwenn, Fess Parker, James Arness, Onslow Stevens, Jack Perrin, Joan Weldon, Sean McClory, Sandy Descher, Dub Taylor, William Schallert, Leonard Nimoy, Richard Deacon; ***D:*** Gordon Douglas; ***W:*** Ted Sherdeman; ***C:*** Sid Hickox; ***M:*** Bronislau Kaper.

The Theme 𝒮𝒮𝒮 *Tema* **1979** Esenin is a mediocre middle-aged playwright who knows his success comes from kow-towing to the party line. Trying to find inspiration he visits his native village where he meets the young Sasa, an artist who has refused to compromise. Although Esenin falls for her, Sasa has only contempt for his lack of principles and stays with her poet/lover, who is reduced to digging graves and has decided to emigrate to Israel. The film went unreleased for eight years because of its themes of artistic freedom and emigration. In Russian with English subtitles. **100m/C VHS.** *RU* Mikhail Ulyanov, Inna Churikova, Stanislav Lyubshin, Evgeny Vesnik, Sergei Nikonenko, Natalya Selezneva; ***D:*** Gleb Panfilov. Berlin Intl. Film Fest. '79: Golden Berlin Bear.

Then Came Bronson 𝒮𝒮 **1/2 1968** Pilot TV movie for the 1969-70 TV series. Parks stars as ambitious journalist James Bronson who hits the road on his Harley Roadster after his best friend (Sheen) commits suicide. Bronson travels up and down the California coast finding adventure, including a runaway bride and a hippie campsite. **90m/C DVD.** Michael Parks, Bonnie Bedelia, Akim Tamiroff, Gary Merrill, Sheree North, Martin Sheen, Bert Freed; ***D:*** William A. Graham; ***W:*** Denne Petticlerc; ***C:*** Ray Flin; ***M:*** George Duning. **TV**

Then She Found Me 𝒮𝒮 **2007 (R)** In her directorial debut, Hunt (who also co-scripted) lets all actress vanity fall by the wayside as the tense, frazzled lead. Schoolteacher April is stunned by the sudden end to her brief marriage to mama's boy Ben (Broderick). This is on top of caring for her ill adoptive mother Trudy (Cohen) and finding out her birth mother is the brassy, self-absorbed Bernice (Midler). Recently divorced Frank (Firth), the father of one of April's pupils, offers advice and a manly shoulder although he's not too stable himself. Oh, and April finds out she's pregnant from her marital break-up sex. Self-deprecating comedy that's a little too anxious—much like April herself. Based on the novel by Elinor Lipman. **100m/C DVD, Blu-ray Disc.** *US* Helen Hunt, Colin Firth, Bette Midler, Matthew Broderick, Ben Shenkman, Lynn Cohen, Salman Rushdie, John Benjamin; ***D:*** Helen Hunt; ***W:*** Helen Hunt, Alice Arlen, Victor Levin; ***C:*** Peter Donahue; ***M:*** David Mansfield.

Theodora Goes Wild 𝒮𝒮𝒮 **1936** Tiny, priggish Lynnfield, Connecticut is shocked to discover that a scandalous best seller about smalltown life has been written pseudonymously by their very own Theodora Lynn (Dunne). When Theodora gets a chance to meet sophisticated New Yorker Michael Grant (Douglas), who did the illustrations for her book, she falls for him. But both must throw aside their own (and everyone else's) expectations and limitations for them to be happy. Dunne's first comedic lead role. **94m/B VHS.** Irene Dunne, Melvyn Douglas, Thomas Mitchell, Thurston Hall, Rosalind Keith, Spring Byington, Elisabeth Risdon, Margaret McWade; ***D:*** Richard Boleslawski; ***W:*** Sidney Buchman; ***C:*** Joseph Walker; ***M:*** Morris Stoloff.

Theodore Rex ½ **1995 (PG)** Futuristic comedy finds cynical, seasoned cop Katie Coltrane (Goldberg) furious at being teamed with Teddy, who just happens to be an eight-foot-tall, three-ton, returned-from-extinction Tyrannosaurus Rex (who has a taste for cookies). And Teddy's not exactly the brightest dinosaur on the block, which makes Katie's job all the harder when they stumble across a major crime caper. **92m/C VHS, DVD.** Whoopi Goldberg, Armin Mueller-Stahl, Richard Roundtree, Juliet Landau; ***D:*** Jonathan Betuel; ***W:*** Jonathan Betuel; ***C:*** David Tattersall; ***M:*** Robert Folk.

The Theory of Flight **1998 (R)** Awkward film reflects the relationship between Jane Hatchard (Bonham Carter), a wheelchair-bound woman suffering from a motor-neurological disease, and her eccentric, reluctant caregiver, Richard (Branagh). Richard is an artist who dreams of human flight, and one of his attempts gets him assigned to community service and to the independent, dying Jane. Her one wish is to lose her virginity but Richard won't oblige, although he's willing to set her up with a gigolo (Stevenson). Flirts with bad taste and is generally worth watching because of Bonham Carter's fierce performance. **98m/C VHS.** *GB* Helena Bonham Carter, Kenneth Branagh, Gemma Jones, Holly Aird, Ray Stevenson; ***D:*** Paul Greengrass; ***W:*** Richard Hawkins; ***C:*** Ivan Strasburg; ***M:*** Rolfe Kent.

The Theory of the Leisure Class **2001** Kids on a field trip discover the murdered bodies of some children, missing from a small western community. City reporter Callie (Knight) shows up and begins snooping around, uncovering the town's secrets. Based on a true story. **108m/C VHS, DVD.** Tuesday Knight, Michael Massee, Christopher McDonald, Brad Renfro; ***D:*** Gabriel Bologna; ***W:*** Amber Benson, Gabriel Bologna; ***C:*** Christopher Tufty; ***M:*** Howard Drossin.

There Goes Barder *Ca Va Barder* **1954** Constantine plays a con-man who's hired by a crooked ship owner to be a security agent. **90m/B VHS.** *FR* Eddie Constantine, May Britt, Jean Carmet, Jean Danet, Monique Van Vooren; ***D:*** John Berry; ***W:*** John Berry; ***C:*** Jacques Lemare.

There Goes Kelly ½ **1945** Moran and Miller are page boys at a radio station who try to get the station receptionist a singing job. When the vocalist on a popular show is murdered, the duo not only get their protege a break but get themselves a mystery to solve as well. **62m/B VHS.** Jackie Moran, Sidney Miller, Wanda McKay, Ralph Sanford, Jan Wiley, Anthony Warde; ***D:*** Phil Karlson.

There Goes My Baby ½ **1992 (R)** Eight California high school grads confront their futures on two nights in '65 (as the Watts riots ignite). There are Vietnam protests, flower children, would-be rock stars, friendships, and romantic complications. Yes, it sounds a lot like "American Graffiti" but the cast are winning and there's a good deal of affection without sinking to mawkishness. **99m/C VHS, DVD.** Dermot Mulroney, Rick Schroder, Kelli Williams, Jill Schoelen, Noah Wyle, Kristin Minter, Lucy Deakins, Kenny Ransom, Seymour Cassel, Paul Gleason, Frederick Coffin, Andrew (Andy) Robinson, Shon Greenblatt, J.E. Freeman; ***D:*** Floyd Mutrux; ***W:*** Floyd Mutrux.

There Goes the Neighborhood ½ **1992 (PG-13)** A dying convict tells prison psychiatrist Daniels where he has buried $8.5 million—under the home of neighbor O'Hara. Daniels and O'Hara try to discreetly dig up the fortune but when the neighborhood finds out everyone wants a chance at the cash. **88m/C VHS.** Jeff Daniels, Catherine O'Hara, Dabney Coleman, Hector Elizondo, Judith Ivey, Rhea Perlman, Harris Yulin, Jonathan Banks, Chazz Palminteri, Mary Gross; ***D:*** Bill Phillips; ***M:*** David Bell.

There Was a Crooked Man ½ **1970 (R)** An Arizona town gets some new ideas about law and order when an incorruptible and innovative warden takes over the town's prison. The warden finds he's got his hands full with one inmate determined to escape. Offbeat western black comedy supported by an excellent and entertaining production, with fine acting all around. **123m/C VHS, DVD.** Kirk Douglas, Henry Fonda, Warren Oates, Hume Cronyn, Burgess Meredith, John Randolph, Arthur O'Connell, Alan Hale Jr., Lee Grant; ***D:*** Joseph L. Mankiewicz; ***W:*** Robert Benton, David Newman; ***C:*** Harry Stradling Jr.

There Will Be Blood ½ **2007 (R)** Director Anderson ventures from the contemporary to a saga that covers some 30 years (from 1898 to the 1920s) following the fortunes of silver prospector turned oil magnate Daniel Planview (Day-Lewis). Misanthrope Planview wheels, deals, and cheats his way to a fortune, dogged by evangelical preacher Eli Sunday (Dano), whose family Plainview took advantage of to get his oil derricks gushing. Plainview's one human contact is the orphan H.W. (Freasier), whom he adopts (and later dismisses) in his obsessive quest for power and wealth. Foreboding, with a powerful performance from Day-Lewis as an egotist driven mad by his ambitions. Loosely based on Upton Sinclair's 1927 novel, "Oil!" **158m/C DVD, Blu-ray Disc.** *US* Daniel Day-Lewis, Paul Franklin Dano, Kevin J. O'Connor, Ciaran Hinds, Dave Willis, Dillon Freasier, Russell Harvard, Sydney McCallister, Colleen Foy; ***D:*** Paul Thomas Anderson; ***W:*** Paul Thomas Anderson; ***C:*** Robert Elswit; ***M:*** Johnny Greenwood. Oscars '07: Actor (Day-Lewis), Cinematog.; British Acad. '07: Actor (Day-Lewis); Golden Globes '08: Actor—Drama (Day-Lewis); Screen Actors Guild '07: Actor (Day-Lewis).

Theremin: An Electronic Odyssey **1995 (PG)** Profiles the life of Russian scientist Leon Theremin (who died in 1993), founder of electronic music, and his revolutionary musical invention, the Theremin. Martin located the 95-year-old Theremin in Moscow in 1991, interviewed him on camera, then brought him back to the U.S. to film reunions with friends and colleages he hadn't seen in 50 years. Martin's focus is on the impact of the Theremin on Hollywood movie scores heard in '50s sci-fi and thriller classics ("The Day the Earth Stood Still") and in popular music (The Beach Boys' "Good Vibrations" is commented on by Brian Wilson). Theremin's life proves as curious as his instrument, with his controversial interracial marriage to a ballet star, abduction by Russian agents, and imprisonment in a Soviet mental hospital. "Theremin" provides a fascinating and heartfelt tribute to the man's work and life. **84m/C VHS, DVD.** ***D:*** Steven M. Martin; ***W:*** Steven M. Martin; ***C:*** Robert Stone, Edward Lachman, Chris Lombardi; ***M:*** Hal Willner.

There's a Girl in My Soup **1970 (R)** Sellers is a gourmet who moonlights as a self-styled Casanova. Early post "Laugh-In" Hawn is the young girl who takes refuge at his London love nest when her boyfriend dumps her. Lust ensues. Has its funny parts, but not a highlight of anyone's career. Based on the hit play. **95m/C VHS, DVD.** *GB* Peter Sellers, Goldie Hawn, Diana Dors; ***D:*** Roy Boulting.

There's No Business Like Show Business **1954** A top husband and wife vaudevillian act make it a family affair. Filmed in CinemaScope, allowing for full and lavish musical numbers. Good performances and Berlin's music make this an enjoyable film. ♫ When the Midnight Choo-Choo Leaves for Alabam; Let's Have Another Cup of Coffee; Play a Simple Melody; After You Get What You Want You Don't Want It; You'd Be Surprised; A Sailor's Not a Sailor; A Pretty Girl is Like a Melody; If You Believe Me; A Man Chases a Girl Until She Catches Him. **117m/C VHS, DVD.** Charlotte Austin, Ethel Merman, Donald O'Connor, Marilyn Monroe, Dan Dailey, Johnny Ray, Mitzi Gaynor, Frank McHugh, Hugh O'Brian; ***D:*** Walter Lang; ***W:*** Phoebe Ephron, Henry Ephron; ***C:*** Leon Shamroy; ***M:*** Irving Berlin, Lionel Newman, Alfred Newman.

There's Nothing out There **1990** A group of seven teenagers spends Spring Break at a secluded mountain cabin. It sounds wonderful, but one of the boys (who claims to have seen every horror movie on video) knows the signs of a horror movie just waiting to happen. **91m/C VHS, DVD.** Craig Peck, Wendy Bednarz, Mark Collver, Bonnie Bowers, John Carhart III, Claudia Flores, Jeff Dachis, Lisa Grant; ***D:*** Rolfe Kanefsky; ***W:*** Rolfe Kanefsky; ***C:*** Ed Hershberger; ***M:*** Christopher Thomas.

There's Something about Mary **1998 (R)** Outrageously funny comedy that only veers from the gutter when it feels like taking a dip in the sewer. Set in 1985, the prologue introduces us to geeky Ted (Stiller), who gets a prom date with class knockout Mary (Diaz) after sticking up for her retarded brother Warren (Brown). The big date is not to be, however, for a vicious tuxedo zipper to the privates incapacitate Ted. Thirteen years later, Ted is still depressed over the incident, and still carries a torch for Mary. He hires Pat (Dillon), an oily detective with enormous choppers, to find her. Unfortunately for Ted, Pat is instantly smitten with Mary and lies. Ted learns the truth and heads to Miami to find her himself. Merely looking at the plot does not do justice to this lowbrow masterpiece. **118m/C VHS, DVD, UMD.** Ben Stiller, Matt Dillon, Cameron Diaz, Chris Elliott, Lee Evans, Lin Shaye, Jeffrey Tambor, Markie Post, Keith David, Jonathan Richman, W. Earl Brown, Khandi Alexander, Richard Tyson, Rob Moran, Lenny Clarke, Zen Gesner, Harland Williams, Richard Jenkins; ***Cameos:*** Brett Favre; ***D:*** Bobby Farrelly, Peter Farrelly; ***W:*** Bobby Farrelly, Peter Farrelly, Edward Decter, John J. Strauss; ***C:*** Mark Irwin; ***M:*** Jonathan Richman. MTV Movie Awards '99: Film, Female Perf. (Diaz), Villain (Dillon), Fight; N.Y. Film Critics '98: Actress (Diaz).

Therese **1986** Stylish biography of a young French nun and her devotion to Christ bordering on romantic love. Explores convent life. Real-life Therese died of TB and was made a saint. A directorial tour de force for Cavalier. In French with English subtitles. **90m/C VHS, DVD.** *FR* Catherine Mouchet, Aurore Prieto, Sylvie Habault, Ghislaine Mona; ***D:*** Alain Cavalier; ***W:*** Alain Cavalier; ***C:*** Isabelle Dedieu. Cannes '86: Special Jury Prize; Cesar '87: Cinematog., Director (Cavalier), Film, Writing.

Therese & Isabelle ½ **1967** Story of growing love and physical attraction between two French schoolgirls. On holiday together, they confront their mutual desires. Richly photographed soft porn based on the novel by Violet Leduc. Not vulgar, but certainly for adults. French with subtitles. **118m/B VHS, DVD.** Essy Persson, Anna Gael, Barbara Laage, Anne Vernon; ***D:*** Radley Metzger; ***W:*** Jesse Vogel; ***C:*** Hans Jura; ***M:*** Georges Auric.

Therese Raquin ½ **1980** Therese Raquin (Nelligan)is a young woman unhappily married to mama's boy Camille (Cranham). She has an affair with Laurent (Cox) and the lovers do away with the inconvenient spouse. But their guilt turns to loathing for each other and haunts them into further acts of betrayal and violence. Based on the novel by Emile Zola. **173m/C VHS, DVD.** *GB* Kate Nelligan, Brian Cox, Mona Washbourne, Kenneth Cranham, Alan Rickman, Richard Pearson; ***D:*** Simon Langton; ***W:*** Philip Mackie; ***M:*** Patrick Gowers. **TV**

Therese: The Story of Saint Therese of Lisieux **2004** Therese is born into a privileged French family but begs to follow her older sister into a Carmelite convent though she has self-doubts, which she describes in her journals. She becomes more and more of an ascetic, following a life of simplicity, humility, and compassion, which is revealed when her writings are published after her early death. **90m/C DVD.** Linda Hayden, Lindsay Younce, Samantha Kramer, Judith Kaplan, Leonardo Defilippis; ***D:*** Leonardo Defilippis; ***W:*** Patti Defilippis; ***C:*** Lourdes Ambrose; ***M:*** Sister Marie Therese Sokol.

These Foolish Things ½ **2006** A sentimental and predictable wisp of a melodrama set in 1930s London. The orphaned daughter of a stage star, Diana (Tapper) decides to follow her mother's profession. She falls in love with ambitious playwright Robin (Leon), whose new play stars Douglas (Umbers), who wants to personally work with Robin offstage as well. Stamp's an all-knowing butler, Huston's the American financing the play, and Bacall plays another star. Based on the novel by Noel Langley. **107m/C DVD.** Zoe Tapper, David Leon, Mark Umbers, Lauren Bacall, Anjelica Huston, Terence Stamp, Joss Ackland, Andrew Lincoln, Julia McKenzie; ***D:*** Julia Taylor-Stanley; ***W:*** Julia Taylor-Stanley; ***C:*** Gavin Finney; ***M:*** Ian Lynn.

These Girls **2005 (R)** Best teen friends Keira (Dhavernas), Lisa (Lewis), and Glory (Walsh) all have a crush on married 30-year-old pot dealer Keith (Boreanaz). After discovering that Glory is already having a fling with Keith, her gal pals decide they should share the unwilling stud equally, using blackmail about Glory's underage tryst as leverage. Since none of the attractive actresses can remotely pass for teenagers, this slight comedy is already at a disadvantage. Based on a play by Vivienne Laxdal. **92m/C DVD.** *CA* Caroline Dhavernas, David Boreanaz, Holly Lewis, Amanda Walsh; ***D:*** John Hazlett; ***W:*** John Hazlett; ***C:*** Alex Vendler; ***M:*** Ned Bouhalassa. **VIDEO**

These Old Broads ½ **2001** Three actresses—Addie Holden (Collins), Kate Westbourne (MacLaine), and Piper Grayson (Reynolds)—starred in a '60s musical that over the years has become a cult hit. A TV exec (Carbonell) wants to engineer a TV reunion special but the trio hate each other. Maybe the agent (Taylor) they all share can persuade them. **95m/C VHS.** Debbie Reynolds, Joan Collins, Shirley MacLaine, Elizabeth Taylor, Jonathan Silverman, Peter Graves, Gene Barry, Pat Harrington; ***D:*** Matthew Diamond; ***W:*** Carrie Fisher, Elaine Pope; ***C:*** Eric Van Haren Noman; ***M:*** Guy Moon, Steve Tyrell. **TV**

These Three ½ **1936** A teenaged girl ruins the lives of two teachers by telling a malicious lie. Excellent cast. Script by Lillian Hellman, based on her play "The Children's Hour." Remade by the same director as "The Children's Hour" in 1961. **92m/B VHS.** Miriam Hopkins, Merle Oberon, Joel McCrea, Bonita Granville, Marcia Mae Jones, Walter Brennan, Margaret Hamilton, Catherine Doucet, Alma Kruger, Carmencita Johnson, Mary Ann Durkin, Frank McGlynn; ***D:*** William Wyler; ***W:*** Lillian Hellman; ***C:*** Gregg Toland; ***M:*** Alfred Newman.

Thesis *Tesis; Snuff* **1996 (R)** Angela (Torrent) is a university student writing her thesis on violence in the media. She comes across a snuff film that shows a girl being tortured to death. While trying to discover if the film is real, Angela finds out that the girl was a university student and that the film was actually shot on campus. Now it's Angela's life in danger. Suspenseful with a shocker ending. Spanish with subtitles. **121m/C VHS, DVD.** *SP* Ana Torrent, Fele Martinez, Eduardo Noriega; ***D:*** Alejandro Amenabar; ***W:*** Alejandro Amenabar, Mateo Gil; ***C:*** Hans Burman; ***M:*** Alejandro Amenabar, Mariano Marin.

They *Invasion from Inner Earth; Hell Fire* **1977** Beings from beneath the earth's crust take their first trip to the surface. **88m/C VHS, DVD.** Paul Dentzer, Debbie Pick, Nick Holt; ***D:*** Ito Rebane.

They All Kissed the Bride ½ **1942** Tough cookie Margaret Drew (Crawford) must take over the family's trucking business when dad dies and support her ditzy mother (Burke) and younger sister Vivian (Parrish). Crusading newspaperman Michael Holmes (Douglas) blasts Margaret's business practices in print but when they finally meet, the sparks fly. Crawford manages the physical comedy well and Douglas is suitably charming. **87m/B VHS.** Joan Crawford, Melvyn Douglas, Billie Burke, Helen Parrish, Roland Young, Allen Jenkins, Emory Parnell; ***D:*** Alexander Hall; ***W:*** Andrew Solt, P.J. Wolfson; ***C:*** Joseph Walker; ***M:*** Werner R. Heymann.

They All Laughed **1981 (PG)** Three detectives become romantically involved with the women they were hired to investigate. Essentially light-hearted fluff with little or no script. Further undermined by the real-life murder of Stratten before the film's release. **115m/C VHS, DVD.** Ben Gazzara, John Ritter, Audrey Hepburn, Colleen Camp, Patti Hansen, Dorothy Stratten, Elizabeth Pena; ***D:*** Peter Bogdanovich; ***W:*** Peter Bogdanovich.

They Bite WOOF! 1995 (R) A pornographic filmmaker's latest epic about lustful gill-men is filming at the same Florida beach where a zoologist is investigating reports of man-like fish monsters killing swimmers. Just a coincidence? Ultra- (and deliberately) cheesy; an unrated version is also available. **96m/C VHS.** Donna Frotscher, Nick Baldasare, Charlie Barnett, Ron Jeremy; ***D:*** Bret Piper; ***W:*** Bret Piper.

They Call It Murder **1971** D.A. Doug Selby (Hutton) investigates the matter of a corpse found floating in a swimming pool. The characters are based on Erle Stanley Gardner. **120m/C DVD.** Jim Hutton, Lloyd Bochner, Jessica Walter, Leslie Nielsen, JoAnn Pflug, Nita Talbot, William (Bill) Elliott, Vic Tayback; ***D:*** Walter Grauman; ***W:*** Sam Rolfe; ***M:*** Robert Jackson Drasnin. **TV**

They Call It Sin *The Way of Life* **1932** Often told story of a young country girl heading to the Big Apple in search of her big break and "Mr. Right." Young is a chorus line girl romantically involved with her married producer (Calhern) while faithful admirer Brent waits nearby. Predictable plot adapted from the novel by Alberta Stedman Eagan. **68m/B VHS, DVD.** Loretta Young, George Brent, David Manners, Louis Calhern, Una Merkel, Joseph Cawthorn, Helen Vinson; ***D:*** Thornton Freeland; ***W:*** Lillie Hayward, Howard J. Green.

They Call Me Bruce? *A Fist Full of Chopsticks* **1982 (PG)** A bumbling Bruce Lee look-alike meets a karate-chopping Mafia moll in this farce. Silly premise creates lots of laughs. Followed by a sequel, "They Still Call Me Bruce." **88m/C VHS, DVD.** Johnny Yune, Margaux Hemingway; ***D:*** Elliot Hong; ***W:*** Tim Clawson.

They Call Me Mr. Tibbs! **1970 (R)** Lieutenant Virgil Tibbs (Poitier) investigates the murder of a prostitute. The prime suspect is his friend, the Reverend Logan Sharpe (Landau). He is torn between his duty as a policeman, his concern for the reverend, and the turmoil of his domestic life. Less tense, less compelling sequel to "In the Heat of the Night." **108m/C VHS, DVD.** Sidney Poitier, Barbara McNair, Martin Landau, Juano Hernandez, Anthony Zerbe, Ed Asner, Norma Crane, Jeff Corey; ***D:*** Gordon Douglas; ***W:*** Alan R. Trustman; ***C:*** Gerald Perry Finnerman; ***M:*** Quincy Jones.

They Call Me Sirr **1/2 2000** Based on the true story of Sirr Parker (Scott), a talented but poverty-stricken high school football player in South Central L.A. After Sirr and his younger brother are abandoned by their mother, Sirr struggles to look after his family (including an ailing grandmother) while keeping his place on the team. But the teen is finally forced to turn to his coach (Duncan) for help. **97m/C VHS, DVD.** Kente Scott, Michael Clarke Duncan; ***D:*** Robert Munic; ***W:*** Robert Munic; ***C:*** David Perrault; ***M:*** Sharon Farber. **CABLE**

They Call Me Trinity **1/2** *Lo Chiamavano Trinita* **1972 (G)** Lazy drifter-gunslinger and his outlaw brother join forces with Mormon farmers to rout bullying outlaws. Spoofs every western cliche with relentless comedy, parodying "The Magnificent Seven" and gibing the spaghetti western. Followed by "Trinity is Still My Name." Dubbed. **110m/C VHS, DVD.** *IT* Terence Hill, Bud Spencer, Farley Granger, Steffen Zacharias; ***D:*** E.B. (Enzo Barboni) Clucher.

They Came Back **1/2** *Les Revenants* **2004** Warning: this is not your normal zombie-eats-people movie. Instead, thousands of the dead have shuffled back to their small French village to just live their dull old lives. Sort of. As the living must work to deal with the sudden population explosion, the now-dimwitted undead have been holding secret nightly meetings. First-time director Campillo goes for a quiet look at society's reaction to the walking dead's return rather than a gorefest, a la George Romero. In French with English subtitles. **102m/C VHS, DVD.** *FR* Geraldine Pailhas, Jonathan Zaccai, Frederic Pierrot, Victor Garrivier, Catherine Samie; ***D:*** Robin Campillo; ***W:*** Robin Campillo, Brigitte Tijou; ***C:*** Jeanne Lapoirie; ***M:*** Martin Wheeler. **VIDEO**

They Came from Beyond Space **1967** Aliens invade the earth and possess the brains of humans. They only want a few slaves to help them repair their ship which crashed on the moon. The only person able to stop them is a scientist with a steel plate in his head. Silly and forgettable. **86m/C VHS, DVD.** *GB* Robert Hutton, Michael Gough; ***D:*** Freddie Francis.

They Came from Within **1/2** *Shivers; The Parasite Murders; Frissons* **1975 (R)** The occupants of a high-rise building go on a sex and violence spree when stricken by an aphrodisiac parasite. Queasy, sleazy, and weird. First major film by Cronenberg. **87m/C VHS, DVD.** *CA* Paul Hampton, Joe Silver, Lynn Lowry, Barbara Steele, Susan Petrie, Allan Migicovsky, Ronald Mlodzik; ***D:*** David Cronenberg; ***W:*** David Cronenberg; ***C:*** Robert Saad; ***M:*** Ivan Reitman.

They Came to Cordura **1/2** **1959** Mexico, 1916: a woman and six American soldiers—five heroes and one who has been branded a coward—begin a journey to the military headquarters in Cordura. Slow journey brings out personalities. Look for "Bewitched" hubby Dick York. Based on Glendon Swarthout's best-seller. **123m/C VHS, DVD.** Gary Cooper, Rita Hayworth, Van Heflin, Tab Hunter, Dick York, Richard Conte; ***D:*** Robert Rossen; ***W:*** Ivan Moffat.

They Crawl *Crawlers* **2001 (R)** More complicated than usual for the creepy crawlie genre. Ted Gage (Cosgrove) learns his biophysicist brother has been electrocuted and all his organs removed. Ted teams up with cop Gina (Davies) to figure out what's going on and finds connections between the murder, a homicidal cult, and lethal cockroaches linked to a government surveillance project. Everybody looks convinced that this makes some kind of sense. **93m/C VHS, DVD.** Daniel Cosgrove, Dennis Boutsikaris, Tim Thomerson, Tamara Davis, Tone Loc, Mickey Rourke, Grace Zabriskie; ***D:*** John Allardice; ***W:*** Curtis Joseph, David Mason; ***C:*** Maximo Munzi; ***M:*** Neal Acree. **VIDEO**

They Died with Their Boots On **1941** The Battle of Little Big Horn is re-created Hollywood style. Takes liberties with historical fact, but still an exciting portrayal of General Custer's last stand. The movie also marks the last time de Havilland worked with Flynn. Also available colorized. **141m/B VHS, DVD.** Errol Flynn, Sydney Greenstreet, Anthony Quinn, Hattie McDaniel, Arthur Kennedy, Gene Lockhart, Regis Toomey, Olivia de Havilland, Charley Grapewin, G.P. (Tim) Huntley Jr., Frank Wilcox, Joseph (Joe) Sawyer, Eddie Acuff, Minor Watson, Tod Andrews, Stanley Ridges, John Litel, Walter Hampden, Joseph Crehan, Selmer Jackson, Gig Young, Dick Wessel; ***D:*** Raoul Walsh; ***W:*** Aeneas MacKenzie; ***C:*** Bert Glennon; ***M:*** Max Steiner.

They Drive by Night **1/2** *The Road to Frisco* **1940** Two truck-driving brothers break away from a large company and begin independent operations. After an accident to Bogart, Raft is forced to go back to the company where Lupino, the boss's wife, becomes obsessed with him and kills her husband to gain the company and win Raft. When he rejects her, she accuses him of the murder. Well-plotted film with great dialogue. Excellent cast gives it their all. **97m/B VHS, DVD.** Humphrey Bogart, Ann Sheridan, George Raft, Ida Lupino, Alan Hale, Gale Page, Roscoe Karns, Charles Halton; ***D:*** Raoul Walsh.

They Got Me Covered **1943** Two WWII-era journalists get involved in a comic web of murder, kidnapping and romance. Hope is very funny and carries the rest of the cast. Look for Doris Day in a bit part and listen for Bing Crosby singing whenever Hope opens his cigarette case. **95m/B VHS, DVD.** Doris Day, Bob Hope, Dorothy Lamour, Otto Preminger, Eduardo Ciannelli, Donald Meek, Walter Catlett; ***D:*** David Butler; ***W:*** Harry Kurnitz; ***C:*** Rudolph Mate; ***M:*** Leigh Harline; ***V:*** Bing Crosby.

They Had to See Paris **1929** The first sound film to feature humorist Rogers. Pike Peters (Rogers) is a simple Oklahoman who becomes rich when oil is discovered on his property. His wife Idy (Rich) insists the family go to Paris for some culture and they rent a chateau where Idy is happy to indulge herself in society. But Pike would much rather be at home. **96m/B DVD.** Will Rogers, Irene Rich, Marguerite Churchill, Owen Davis Jr., Fifi d'Orsay, Ivan Lebedeff, Rex Bell, Marcelle Corday; ***D:*** Frank Borzage; ***W:*** Sonya Levien, Owen Davis Jr.; ***C:*** Chester Lyons.

They Knew What They Wanted **1940** A lonely San Francisco waitress begins a correspondence romance with a grape grower and agrees to marry him after he sends her a photo which shows him as being young and handsome. She arrives to discover Laughton had sent her a picture of another man. An accident, an affair, and a pregnancy provide further complications before a satisfactory ending is suggested. Flawed adaptation of Sidney Howard's play still has strong performances from Lombard and Laughton. **96m/B VHS.** Charles Laughton, Carole Lombard, Harry Carey Sr., Karl Malden, William Gargan; ***D:*** Garson Kanin; ***C:*** Harry Stradling Sr.

They Live **1/2** *Creepers* **1988 (R)** A semi-serious science-fiction spoof about a drifter who discovers an alien conspiracy. They're taking over the country under the guise of Reaganism, capitalism and yuppiedom. Screenplay written by Carpenter under a pseudonym. Starts out fun, deteriorates into cliches and bad special effects makeup. **88m/C VHS, DVD.** Roddy Piper, Keith David, Meg Foster, George "Buck" Flower, Peter Jason, Raymond St. Jacques, John Lawrence, Sy Richardson, Jason Robards III, Larry Franco, Wendy Brainard, Dana Bratton; ***D:*** John Carpenter; ***W:*** John Carpenter, Frank Armitage; ***C:*** Gary B. Kibbe; ***M:*** John Carpenter, Alan Howarth.

They Live by Night **1/2** *The Twisted Road; Your Red Wagon* **1949** Bowie (Granger) is a naive young criminal who joins a prison break with hardened cons Chickamaw (da Silva) and T-Dub (Flippen) who then use him as an extra pair of hands in a bank heist. Bowie tries to go straight by marrying young Keechie (O'Donnell) but gets sucked back in by his criminal compatriots and winds up a fugitive with no hope. Classic film noir was Ray's first attempt at directing. Based on Edward Anderson's novel "Thieves Like Us," under which title it was remade in 1974. Compelling and suspenseful. **95m/B VHS, DVD.** Cathy O'Donnell, Farley Granger, Howard da Silva, Jay C. Flippen, Helen Craig, Will Wright; ***D:*** Nicholas Ray; ***W:*** Nicholas Ray, Charles Schnee; ***C:*** George E. Diskant; ***M:*** Leigh Harline.

They Made Me a Criminal **1/2** *I Became a Criminal; They Made Me a Fugitive* **1939** A champion prizefighter, believing he murdered a man in a drunken brawl, runs away. He finds refuge in the West with the Dead End Kids. Remake of "The Life of Jimmy Dolan." Berkeley was best-known for directing and choreographing musicals and surprisingly did very well with this movie. **92m/B VHS, DVD.** John Garfield, Ann Sheridan, Claude Rains, Leo Gorcey, Huntz Hall, Gabriel Dell, Bobby Jordan, Billy Halop; ***D:*** Busby Berkeley; ***W:*** Sid Herzig; ***C:*** James Wong Howe; ***M:*** Max Steiner.

They Made Me a Fugitive **1/2** *I Became a Criminal; They Made Me a Criminal* **1947** Former RAF officer Clem Morgan (Howard) gets drawn into the excitement of the black market after the war but then is framed by his gang boss Narcey (Jones) when Morgan won't deal drugs. After he gets out of jail, Morgan heads back to Soho to get his revenge. Based on the novel "A Convict Has Escaped" by Jackson Budd. **96m/B VHS, DVD.** *GB* Trevor Howard, Griffith Jones, Sally Gray, Rene Ray, Mary Merrall, Vida Hope, Charles Farrell, Ballard Berkeley; ***D:*** Alberto Cavalcanti; ***W:*** Noel Langley; ***C:*** Otto Heller; ***M:*** Marius Francois Gaillard.

They Meet Again **1941** The final segment of the Dr. Christian series. The country doctor sets out to prove the innocence of a man who has been wrongly accused of stealing money. Slow moving and not particularly exciting. **68m/B VHS, DVD.** Jean Hersholt, Dorothy Lovett; ***D:*** Erle C. Kenton.

They Met in a Taxi **1936** A young woman (Wray) gets involved in a jewelry heist after modeling some wedding dresses at the home of an aristocrat. She convinces her taxi driver to protect her from the law and hide her from her rich father as they uncover the truth behind the theft. A classic in cuteness. **70m/B VHS.** Chester Morris, Fay Wray, Lionel Stander, Raymond Walburn; ***D:*** Alfred E. Green; ***W:*** Howard J. Green, Octavus Roy Cohen. **VIDEO**

They Met in Bombay **1/2 1941** Two jewel thieves team up in this romantic action-comedy, complete with exotic locations and two big boxoffice stars. A Japanese invasion makes Russell reconsider her life of crime and gives Gable a chance to play hero. Look for Alan Ladd in a bit part in his pre-"This Gun for Hire" days. Based on a story by John Kafka. **86m/B VHS.** Clark Gable, Rosalind Russell, Peter Lorre, Jessie Ralph, Reginald Owen, Eduardo Ciannelli, Alan Ladd; ***D:*** Clarence Brown; ***W:*** Anita Loos, Edwin Justus Mayer, Leon Gordon.

They Might Be Giants **1971 (G)** Woodward is a woman shrink named Watson who treats retired judge Scott for delusions that he is Sherlock Holmes. Scott's brother wants him committed so the family loot will come to him. Very funny in places; Woodward and Scott highlight a solid cast. **98m/C VHS, DVD.** George C. Scott, Joanne Woodward, Jack Gilford, Eugene Roche, Kitty Winn, F. Murray Abraham, M. Emmet Walsh; ***D:*** Anthony Harvey; ***W:*** James Goldman; ***C:*** Victor Kemper; ***M:*** John Barry.

They Never Come Back **1/2 1932** A boxer breaks his arm in the ring, retires to a job as a bouncer in a sleazy nightclub, and meets a dancer in distress. This all leads him back into the ring. **62m/B VHS.** Regis Toomey, Dorothy Sebastian, Edward (Eddie) Woods, Greta Granstedt, Earle Foxe, Gertrude Astor, Jack (H.) Richardson; ***D:*** Fred Newmeyer; ***W:*** Arthur Hoerl, Sherman Lowe; ***C:*** James Diamond.

They Only Kill Their Masters **1/2** **1972 (PG)** Garner plays a California police chief investigating the death of a wild beach town resident, supposedly killed by her doberman pinscher. He discovers the woman was actually drowned and there are any number of secrets to uncover. Mild whodunit. **98m/C VHS.** James Garner, Katharine Ross, June Allyson, Hal Holbrook, Harry Guardino, Christopher Connelly, Tom Ewell, Peter Lawford, Edmond O'Brien, Arthur O'Connell, Ann Rutherford, Art Metrano; ***D:*** James Goldstone; ***M:*** Perry Botkin.

They Paid with Bullets: Chicago 1929 **1/2** *Tempo di Charleston - Chicago 1929* **1969** The story of one man's rise to power, and eventual downfall as a Mafia consigliatore. **88m/C VHS.** *SP* Peter Lee Lawrence, Ingrid Schoeller, William Bogart; ***D:*** Julio Diamante; ***W:*** Odoardo Fiory; ***C:*** Emilio Foriscot; ***M:*** Enrico Simonetti.

They Saved Hitler's Brain WOOF! *Madmen of Mandoras; The Return of Mr. H* **1964** Fanatical survivors of the Nazi holocaust gave eternal life to the brain of their leader in the last hours of the war. Now it's on a Caribbean island giving orders again. One of the truly great "bad" movies. Shot in pieces in the U.S., the Philippines, and elsewhere, with chunks of other films stuck in to hold the "story" together. **91m/B VHS, DVD.** Walter Stocker, Audrey Caire, Nestor Paiva, Carlos Rivas, Dani Lynn, Bill Freed, John Holland, Scott Peters, Marshall Reed; ***D:*** David Bradley; ***W:*** Richard Miles, Steve Bennett; ***C:*** Stanley Cortez; ***M:*** Don Hulette.

They Shall Have Music *Melody of Youth; Ragged Angels* **1939** A poverty-stricken child hears a concert by violinist Heifetz and decides to become a musician. He joins Brennan's nearly bankrupt music school and persuades Heifetz to play at a benefit concert. Hokey but enjoyable Goldwyn effort to bring classical music to the big screen. ♫ Rondo Capriccioso; Hora Staccato; Estrellita; Melody; Concerto in E Minor for Violin and Orchestra; Waltz in D Flat, Opus 64, No. 1; Cara Nome; Casta Diva. **101m/B VHS.** Walter Brennan, Joel McCrea, Gene Reynolds, Jascha Heifetz, Marjorie Main, Porter Hall, Andrea Leeds, Terence (Terry) Kilburn; *D:* Archie Mayo; *W:* Robert Presnell Sr.; *C:* Gregg Toland; *M:* Alfred Newman.

They Shoot Horses, Don't They? ☙☙☙ 1/2 **1969 (R)** Powerful period piece depicting the desperation of the Depression Era. Contestants enter a dance marathon in the hopes of winning a cash prize, not realizing that they will be driven to exhaustion. Fascinating and tragic. **121m/C VHS, DVD.** Jane Fonda, Michael Sarrazin, Susannah York, Gig Young, Red Buttons, Bonnie Bedelia, Bruce Dern, Allyn Ann McLerie, Severn Darden, Al Lewis, Michael Conrad; *D:* Sydney Pollack; *W:* James Poe; *C:* Philip Lathrop; *M:* Johnny Green. Oscars '69: Support. Actor (Young); British Acad. '70: Support. Actress (York); Golden Globes '70: Support. Actor (Young); N.Y. Film Critics '69: Actress (Fonda).

They Still Call Me Bruce ☙ **1986 (PG)** A Korean searches for the American who saved his life when he was young and instead becomes big brother to an orphan. Supposedly a sequel to "They Call Me Bruce," but has little in common with it. Poorly done and not particularly entertaining. **91m/C VHS.** Johnny Yune, Robert Guillaume, Pat Paulsen; *D:* Johnny Yune.

They Watch ☙☙ 1/2 *They* **1993 (PG-13)** Workaholic Bergin neglects his family and suffers the consequences when his young daughter dies in an auto accident. In fact, he's so distressed that he relies on blind psychic Redgrave to get in touch with his little girl's spirit. Based on the story "They" by Rudyard Kipling. **100m/C VHS.** Patrick Bergin, Vanessa Redgrave, Valerie Mahaffey; *D:* John Korty; *W:* Edithe Swensen; *M:* Gerald Gouriet. **TV**

They Went That-a-Way & That-a-Way **WOOF! 1978 (PG)** Two bumbling deputies pose as convicts in this madcap prison caper. Terrible re-hash of Laurel-and-Hardy has nothing going for it. **96m/C VHS, DVD.** Tim Conway, Richard Kiel, Chuck McCann, Sonny Shroyer, Lenny Montana; *D:* Edward Montagne; *W:* Tim Conway.

They Were Expendable ☙☙☙ 1/2 **1945** Two American captains pit their PT boats against the Japanese fleet. Based on the true story of a PT boat squadron based in the Philippines during the early days of WWII. One of the best (and most underrated) WWII films. Also available in a colorized version. **135m/B VHS, DVD.** Robert Montgomery, John Wayne, Donna Reed, Jack Holt, Ward Bond, Cameron Mitchell, Leon Ames, Marshall Thompson, Paul Langton, Donald Curtis, Jeff York, Murray Alper, Jack Pennick, Alex Havier, Charles Trowbridge, Robert Barrat, Bruce Kellogg, Louis Jean Heydt, Russell Simpson, Philip Ahn, Betty Blythe, William B. Davidson, Pedro de Cordoba, Arthur Walsh, Harry Tenbrook, Tim Murdock, Vernon Steele; *D:* John Ford; *W:* Frank Wead; *C:* Joseph August; *M:* Herbert Stothart, Eric Zeisl.

They Were So Young ☙☙ 1/2 **1955** European models become the pawns of wealthy Brazilian magnates when they are sent to South America. They are threatened with death if they do not cooperate. The scenes were shot in Italy and Berlin. Well acted and believable, although rather grim story. **78m/B VHS, DVD.** *GE* Scott Brady, Johanna (Hannerl) Matz, Raymond Burr; *D:* Kurt Neumann.

They Were Ten ☙☙ 1/2 **1961** Ten Soviet Jews make Palestine their home in the 1800s despite Arab and Turkish persecution and pressures among themselves. In Hebrew with English subtitles. **105m/B VHS.** *IS* Ninette, Oded Teomi, Leo Filer, Yosef Safra; *D:* Baruch Dienar.

They Won't Believe Me ☙☙☙ **1947** A man plots to kill his wife, but before he does, she commits suicide. He ends up on trial for her "murder." Interesting acting by Young and Hayward against type. Surprising, ironic ending. **95m/B VHS.** Robert Young, Susan Hayward, Rita Johnson, Jane Greer; *D:* Irving Pichel.

They Won't Forget ☙☙☙ 1/2 **1937** When a young girl is murdered in a southern town, personal interests take precedence over justice. Turner is excellent in her first billed role, as are the other actors. Superb script, and expert direction by LeRoy pulls it all together. Based on Ward Greene's "Death in the Deep South." **95m/B VHS.** Claude Rains, Otto Kruger, Lana Turner, Allyn Joslyn, Elisha Cook Jr., Edward Norris; *D:* Mervyn LeRoy; *W:* Robert Rossen, Aben Kandel.

They're Playing with Fire **WOOF! 1984 (R)** An English teacher seduces a student and gets him involved in a murder plot to gain an inheritance. Turns out someone else is beating them to the punch. Sleazy semi-pornographic slasher. **96m/C VHS, DVD.** Sybil Danning, Eric Brown, Andrew Prine, Paul Clemens, K.T. Stevens, Alvy Moore; *D:* Howard (Hikmet) Avedis; *W:* Howard (Hikmet) Avedis.

Thick as Thieves ☙☙ 1/2 **1999 (R)** Master thief Mackin (Baldwin) likes to get the job done and then return to his quietly sophisticated private life. Pointy (White) is the arrogant up-and-comer, with mob ties, who wants to eliminate the competition by setting Mackin up for a crime. The dual between the duo upsets mob boss Sal Capetti (Byrd) and has police officer Petrone (DeMornay) also very interested. **93m/C VHS, DVD.** Alec Baldwin, Michael Jai White, Rebecca De Mornay, Andre Braugher, Bruce Greenwood, David Byrd, Richard Edson, Khandi Alexander, Robert Miano, Janeane Garofalo, Julia Sweeney, Ricky Harris, Michael Jace; *D:* Scott Sanders; *W:* Scott Sanders, Arthur Krystal; *C:* Chris Walling; *M:* Christophe Beck. **CABLE**

Thicker Than Water ☙☙ **1993** Eerie psychological thriller exploring the relationship between identical twins. Sam Crawford (Pryce) is a successful doctor, happily married to Jo (Russell), whose sister Debbie (Russell again) is completely different in temperament. The two share a strong psychic bond, however, and when Jo dies in a suspicious hit-and-run accident Debbie feels compelled to make Sam her own. Based on the novel by Dylan Jones. **150m/C VHS, DVD.** *GB* Theresa Russell, Jonathan Pryce, Robert Pugh; *D:* Marc Evans; *W:* Trevor Preston.

Thicker than Water ☙ 1/2 **1999 (R)** Typical urban gangsta flick. Two rival LA gang leaders, DJ and Lonzo, want to get into the music biz. They decide to put their rivalries aside and get the money for their venture by organizing their homeboys and pushing product for drug kingpin Gator. But just when the money starts rolling in, Gator pulls a doublecross and the gang rivalries explode again. **90m/C DVD.** Mack-10, Fat Joe, Ice Cube, Kidada Jones, CJ Mac, MC Eight, Louis Freese, Flesh N Bone, Big Pun; *D:* Richard Cummings Jr.; *W:* Ernest Nyle Brown; *C:* Robert Benavides; *M:* Tyler Bates, Quincey Jones III.

The Thief ☙☙ **1952** An American commits treason and is overcome by guilt. Novel because there is not one word of dialogue, though the gimmmick can't sustain the ordinary story. A product of the Communist scare of the 1950s, it tends to be pretentious and melodramatic. **84m/B VHS, DVD.** Ray Milland, Rita Gam, Martin Gabel, Harry Bronson, John McKutcheon; *D:* Russell Rouse; *W:* Russell Rouse, Clarence Greene; *C:* Sam Leavitt; *M:* Herschel Burke Gilbert.

Thief ☙☙ 1/2 **1971** A successful businessman (Crenna) attempts to put his criminal past behind him. He's trapped when looking for a quick way to get some money to pay off a gambling debt. Well-written and -directed drama with tepid acting. **74m/C VHS.** Richard Crenna, Angie Dickinson, Cameron Mitchell, Hurd Hatfield, Robert Webber; *D:* William A. Graham. **TV**

Thief ☙☙☙ *Violent Streets* **1981 (R)** A big-time professional thief likes working solo, but decides to sign up with the mob in order to make one more big score and retire. He finds out it's not that easy. Taut and atmospheric thriller is director Mann's feature film debut. **126m/C VHS, DVD.** James Caan, Tuesday Weld, Willie Nelson, James Belushi, Elizabeth Pena, Robert Prosky, Dennis Farina; *D:* Michael Mann; *W:* Michael Mann; *C:* Donald E. Thorin; *M:* Tangerine Dream.

The Thief ☙☙ *Vor* **1997 (R)** Postwar Russian drama set in 1952. Katya (Rednikova) is a young widow with a six year-old-son, Sanya (Philipchuk). She's traveling by train when a soldier named Tolyan (Mashkov) enters their compartment. But the end of the trip, Katya's decided to go off with Tolyan and the threesome become a family. But Tolyan harbors a violent streak and Katya also discovers that Tolyan is an imposter—he's not a soldier but a thief. Still, she loves him and soon becomes his accomplice. Russian with subtitles. **92m/C VHS, DVD.** *RU* Vladimir Mashkov, Yekaterina Rednikova, Misha Philipchuk; *D:* Pavel Chukhrai; *W:* Pavel Chukhrai; *C:* Vladimir Klimov; *M:* Vladimir Dashkevich.

The Thief and the Cobbler ☙☙☙ 1/2 **1996 (G)** Musically animated fairy tale about Tack, a humble cobbler (Broderick) who aids the clever and beautiful Princess Yum Yum (Beals) when their town's golden treasures are stolen. Legendary villain Price lends his voice as the evil Zig Zag. Three time Oscar winning director Williams (of "Who Framed Roger Rabbit?" fame), and a team of animators led by Harris (part of the team that created Bugs Bunny) created sophisticated optical illusions that the team dubbed "two and a half dimensional." Incorporating intricate lighting, shadows and smooth motion, the project took almost three decades to complete. Soundtrack performed by the London Symphony Orchestra. **72m/C VHS, DVD.** *D:* Richard Williams; *W:* Richard Williams; *C:* John Leatherbarrow; *M:* Robert Folk; *V:* Vincent Price, Matthew Broderick, Jennifer Beals, Eric Bogosian, Toni Collette, Jonathan Winters, Clive Revill, Kenneth Williams, Clinton Sundberg, Thick Wilson.

The Thief Lord ☙☙ **2006 (PG)** Fantasy is based on a popular children's book by Cornelia Fulke, and the Venice setting is gorgeous, but it's best seen by undemanding kiddies who won't mind its contrivances. Orphaned brothers Prosper and Bo are befriended by teenaged Scipio, the self-proclaimed Thief Lord, who cares for a group of child thieves living in an abandoned cinema. Scipio is hired by a greedy dealer to find a mysterious antique that can allegedly reverse time and the brothers get caught up in the adventure. **98m/C DVD.** *GB GE LU* Aaron Johnson, Rollo Weeks, Jim Carter, Caroline Goodall, Jasper Harris, Alexei Sayle, Richard Bathurst; *D:* Richard Claus; *W:* Richard Claus, Daniel Musgrave; *C:* David Slama; *M:* Nigel Clarke, Michael Csanyi-Wills.

The Thief of Bagdad ☙☙☙ 1/2 **1940** A wily young thief enlists the aid of a powerful genie to outwit the Grand Vizier of Baghdad. An Arabian Nights spectacular with lush photography, fine special effects, and striking score. Outstanding performance by Ingram as the genie. **106m/C VHS, DVD.** *GB* Sabu, Conrad Veidt, June Duprez, Rex Ingram, John Justin, Miles Malleson, Morton Selten, Mary Morris; *D:* Tim Whelan, Michael Powell, Ludwig Berger, Alexander Korda, Zoltan Korda, William Cameron Menzies; *W:* Lajos Biro, Miles Malleson; *C:* Georges Perinal; *M:* Miklos Rozsa. Oscars '40: Color Cinematog.

The Thief of Baghdad ☙☙☙ **1924** The classic silent crowd-pleaser, about a roguish thief who uses a genie's magic to outwit Baghdad's evil Caliph. With famous special effects in a newly struck print, and a new score by Davis based on Rimsky-Korsakov's "Scheherezade." Remade many times. **153m/B VHS, DVD.** Douglas Fairbanks Sr., Snitz Edwards, Charles Belcher, Anna May Wong, Etta Lee, Brandon Hurst, Sojin, Julanne Johnston; *D:* Raoul Walsh; *M:* Carl Davis. Natl. Film Reg. '96.

Thief of Baghdad ☙☙ *Il Ladro Di Bagdad; Le Voleur De Bagdad* **1961** An Arabian Nights fantasy about a thief in love with a Sultan's daughter who has been poisoned. He seeks out the magical blue rose which is the antidote. Not as lavish as the previous two productions by this title, nor as much fun. **89m/C VHS.** *IT* Georgia Moll, Steve Reeves; *D:* Arthur Lubin.

The Thief of Baghdad ☙☙ 1/2 **1978 (G)** A fantasy-adventure about a genie, a prince, beautiful maidens, a happy-go-lucky thief, and magic. Easy to take, but not an extraordinary version of this oft-told tale. Ustinov is fun as he tries to marry off his daughter. **101m/C VHS.** Peter Ustinov, Roddy McDowall, Terence Stamp, Frank Finlay, Ian Holm; *D:* Clive Donner. **TV**

Thief of Hearts ☙☙ **1984 (R)** A thief steals a woman's diary when he's ransacking her house. He then pursues the woman, using his secret knowledge. Slick, but too creepy. Re-edited with soft porn scenes in some video versions. Stewart's first film. **101m/C VHS, DVD.** Steven Bauer, Barbara Williams, John Getz, Christine Ebersole, George Wendt; *D:* Douglas Day Stewart; *W:* Douglas Day Stewart; *C:* Andrew Laszlo; *M:* Harold Faltermeyer.

The Thief of Paris ☙☙☙ 1/2 *Le Voleur* **1967** Gentle study of a 19th-century burglar, Georges (Belmondo), who enters his profession out of necessity but stays because of obsession, is one of the most unjustly overlooked films of Louis Malle's career. There are many light moments, but at heart it's a gloomy and melancholy tale of a man lost in the details of his job—his work means everything to him, and he's willing to give everything up for it. The downbeat tone didn't go over in the U.S. Visually stunning, delicate, and surprisingly affecting. **120m/C DVD.** *FR* Jean-Paul Belmondo, Genevieve Bujold, Marie DuBois, Julien Guiomar, Francoise Fabian, Marlene Jobert, Bernadette LaFont, Martine Sarcey, Roger Crouzet, Charles Denner, Paul Le Person, Christian Lude; *D:* Louis Malle; *W:* Louis Malle, Jean-Claude Carriere, Georges Darien; *C:* Henri Decae.

A Thief of Time ☙☙ 1/2 **2004** Navaho tribal policemen Joe Leaphorn and Jim Chee suspect a missing anthropologist was selling Anasazi pottery on the black market. This leads them to rival colleagues, poachers, and shady collectors, as well as dead bodies. Based on the novel by Tony Hillerman. **95m/C DVD.** Wes Studi, Adam Beach, Gary Farmer, Graham Greene, Sheila Toussey, Peter Fonda, Lee Tergesen, James Pollard; *D:* Chris Eyre; *W:* Alice Arden; *C:* Roy Wagner; *M:* B.C. Smith. **TV**

The Thief Who Came to Dinner ☙☙ **1973 (PG)** A computer analyst and a wealthy socialite team up to become jewel thieves and turn the tables on Houston's high society set. Comedy plot gets complex, though O'Neal and Bisset are likeable. Early Clayburgh role as O'Neal's ex. Based on a novel by Terence Lore Smith. **103m/C VHS.** Ryan O'Neal, Jacqueline Bisset, Warren Oates, Jill Clayburgh, Ned Beatty, Gregory Sierra, Michael Murphy, Austin Pendleton, John Hillerman, Charles Cioffi; *D:* Bud Yorkin; *W:* Walter Hill; *M:* Henry Mancini.

Thieves Like Us ☙☙☙ 1/2 **1974 (R)** Story of doomed lovers during the Depression is thoughtfully told by Altman. Older criminals Remsen and Schuck escape from jail with young killer Carradine. They only know one way to make a living—robbing banks—and it isn't long before they're once more working at their trade. They get a lot of press but they have a distinct problem. They're not really very good at what they do. Cops on their trail, the gang tries, unsuccessfully, to survive. Fletcher's film debut as Remsen's sister-in-law. Good period atmosphere and strong characters. Based on the novel by Edward Anderson and previously filmed as "They Live by Night." **123m/C VHS, DVD.** Keith Carradine, Shelley Duvall, Bert Remsen, John Schuck, Louise Fletcher, Anne Latham, Tom Skerritt; *D:* Robert Altman; *W:* Joan Tewkesbury, Calder Willingham, Robert Altman.

Thieves of Fortune **WOOF! 1989 (R)** Former Miss Universe stars as a contestant in a high stakes fortune hunt that spans half the globe. She meets with more than her share of action-packed encounters among the ruffians who compete for the $28 million purse. Implausible; horrible script; cliched. **100m/C VHS, DVD.** Michael Nouri, Lee Van Cleef, Shawn Weatherly; *D:* Michael Maccarone; *W:* Michael Maccarone; *C:* James Robb.

Thin Air ☙☙ *Robert B. Parker's Thin Air* **2000** Frank Belson (Ferry) didn't know much about his pretty new wife Lisa (Butler) before he married her. So when she suddenly disappears, he hires Spenser (Mantegna) to locate her and the PI also uncovers some secrets from her past. Based on the novel by Robert B. Parker. **90m/C DVD.** Joe Mantegna, Marcia Gay Harden, David Ferry, Yancy Butler, Luis Guzman, Jon Seda, Miguel (Michael) Sandoval; *D:* Robert Mandel; *W:* Robert B. Parker; *C:* Robert L. Surtees; *M:* David Shire. **CABLE**

The Thin Blue Lie ☙☙ 1/2 **2000 (R)** Based on a real-life police corruption scandal that took place in the '70s in Philadelphia.

Jonathan Neumann (Morrow) takes over the court beat for the Philadelphia Examiner and is soon wallowing in cases of police abuse, which he promptly documents in print. He's soon threatened by the cops and gets on the bad side of blustery mayor, Frank Rizzo (Sorvino). Docudrama's kinda blustery itself. **97m/C VHS, DVD.** Rob Morrow, Randy Quaid, Paul Sorvino, Cynthia (Cyndy, Cindy) Preston, G.W. Bailey, Al Waxman, Beau Starr, Chuck Shamata; ***D:*** Roger Young; ***W:*** Daniel Helfgott; ***C:*** Donald M. Morgan; ***M:*** Patrick Williams. **CABLE**

The Thin Blue Line 1/2 **1988** The acclaimed docudrama about the 1977 shooting of a cop in Dallas County, and the incorrect conviction of Randall Adams for the crime. A riveting, spellbinding experience. Due to the film's impact and continued lobbying by Morris, Adams is now free. **101m/C VHS, DVD.** ***D:*** Errol Morris; ***W:*** Errol Morris; ***C:*** Robert Chappell, Stefan Czapsky; ***M:*** Philip Glass. Natl. Film Reg. '01.

Thin Ice **1937** Successful musical romance featuring European prince Power falling for commoner Henie. A fine score, solid script, and Henie's excellent ice skating routines make this her best film. Based on the play "Der Komet" by Attila Obok. ♫ I'm Olga from the Volga; My Swiss Hillbilly; My Secret Love Affair; Over Night. **78m/B VHS.** Sonja Henie, Tyrone Power, Arthur Treacher, Raymond Walburn, Joan Davis, Alan Hale, Sig Rumann, Melville Cooper, Maurice Cass, George Givot, Torben Meyer; ***D:*** Sidney Lanfield; ***W:*** Boris Ingster, Milton Sperling.

A Thin Line Between Love and Hate **1996 (R)** Writer/director/star Lawrence shows that there's no line between a crude, foulmouthed ego trip and an unfunny, unsuspenseful film. Darnell Wright is a smooth talker constantly on the lookout for women to conquer and discard. Eventually, he meets the wrong lady (Whitfield), a classic movie psycho who turns his life upside down. Drawing heavily from "Fatal Attraction," this halfhearted effort offers bad pacing, a weak script, and totally unsympathetic characters, which could almost be overlooked if it was at all funny. Whitfield holds the flick's only redeeming value as the femme fatale. **106m/C VHS, DVD.** Tracy Morgan, Martin Lawrence, Lynn Whitfield, Regina King, Bobby Brown, Della Reese, Roger E. Mosley, Malinda Williams, Daryl (Chill) Mitchell, Simbi Khali; ***D:*** Martin Lawrence; ***W:*** Martin Lawrence, Bentley Kyle Evans, Kenny Buford, Kim Bass; ***C:*** Francis Kenny; ***M:*** Roger Troutman.

The Thin Man 1/2 **1934** Married sleuths Nick (Powell) and Nora (Loy) Charles investigate the mysterious disappearance of a wealthy inventor. Charming and sophisticated, this was the model for all husband-and-wife detective teams that followed. Don't miss Asta, their wire-hair terrier. Based on the novel by Dashiell Hammett. Its enormous popularity triggered five sequels, starting with "After the Thin Man." **90m/B VHS, DVD.** William Powell, Myrna Loy, Maureen O'Sullivan, Cesar Romero, Porter Hall, Nat Pendleton, Minna Gombell, Natalie Moorhead, Edward Ellis; ***D:*** Woodbridge S. Van Dyke; ***W:*** Albert Hackett, Frances Goodrich; ***C:*** James Wong Howe. Natl. Film Reg. '97.

The Thin Man Goes Home 1/2 **1944** Married sleuths Nick and Nora Charles solve a mystery with Nick's disapproving parents looking on in the fifth film from the "Thin Man" series. Despite a three-year gap and slightly less chemistry between Powell and Loy, audiences welcomed the skinny guy. Sequel to "Shadow of the Thin Man"; followed by "Song of the Thin Man." **100m/B VHS, DVD.** William Powell, Myrna Loy, Lucile Watson, Gloria De Haven, Anne Revere, Harry Davenport, Helen Vinson, Lloyd Corrigan, Donald Meek, Edward Brophy, Charles Halton; ***D:*** Richard Thorpe.

The Thin Red Line 1/2 **1964** First adaptation of the James Jones novel about the fight for Guadalcanal focuses on the relationship between Sgt. Welsh (Warden) and Pvt. Doll (Dullea). As battle experience hardens Doll, the mutual hatred the two have changes to a grudging respect. Effectively portrays the dehumanizing psychological effects of war. **99m/B VHS, DVD.** Keir Dullea, Jack Warden, James Philbrook, Kieron Moore, Ray Daley, Merlyn Yordan, Bob Kanter, Stephen Levy; ***D:*** Andrew Marton; ***W:*** Bernard Gordon; ***C:*** Manuel Berenguer; ***M:*** Malcolm Arnold.

The Thin Red Line **1998 (R)** After a long hiatus, director Malick returns in this epic WWII saga about a rifle company fighting at Guadalcanal. Visually stunning and focused on the inner thoughts, feelings, and philosophical leanings of the soldiers, the film sacrifices plot and continuity to study the questions of Man vs. Nature and the Origin of Evil. Plot difficulties are highlighted by the physical similarities of relative newcomers Chaplin and Caviezel. Combat scenes are, naturally, beautifully shot and effective, while the relationship between Penn and Caviezel makes the biggest impression among the many subplots (some of which go nowhere) and the star-laden, large cast. Based on the 1962 novel by James Jones. **170m/C VHS, DVD.** Kirk Acevedo, Miranda Otto, Nick Stahl, James (Jim) Caviezel, Adrien Brody, Sean Penn, Nick Nolte, John Cusack, George Clooney, Woody Harrelson, Ben Chaplin, Elias Koteas, Jared Leto, John Travolta, Tim Blake Nelson, John C. Reilly, John Savage, Arie Verveen, David Harrod, Thomas Jane, Paul Gleason, Penelope Allen, Don Harvey, Shawn Hatosy, Donal Logue, Dash Mihok, Larry Romano; ***D:*** Terrence Malick; ***W:*** Terrence Malick; ***C:*** John Toll; ***M:*** Hans Zimmer. N.Y. Film Critics '98: Director (Malick); Natl. Soc. Film Critics '98: Cinematog.

The Thing 1/2 *The Thing from Another World* **1951** One of the best of the Cold War allegories and a potent lesson to those who won't eat their vegetables. Sci fi classic about an alien craft and creature (Arness in monster drag), discovered by an Arctic research team. The critter is accidentally thawed and then wreaks havoc, sucking the blood from sled dog and scientist alike. It's a giant seed-dispersing vegetable run amuck, unaffected by missing body parts, bullets, or cold. In other words, Big Trouble. Excellent direction, assisted substantially by producer Hawks, and supported by strong performances. Available colorized; remade in 1982. Loosely based on "Who Goes There?" by John Campbell. **87m/B VHS, DVD.** James Arness, Kenneth Tobey, Margaret Sheridan, Dewey Martin, Robert Cornthwaite, Douglas Spencer, James L. Young, Robert Nichols, William (Bill) Self, Eduard Franz, Sally Creighton, John Dierkes, George Fenneman; ***D:*** Christian Nyby, Howard Hawks; ***W:*** Charles Lederer, Ben Hecht; ***C:*** Russell Harlan; ***M:*** Dimitri Tiomkin. Natl. Film Reg. '01.

The Thing 1/2 **1982 (R)** A team of scientists at a remote Antarctic outpost discover a buried spaceship with an unwelcome alien survivor still alive. Bombastic special effects overwhelm the suspense and the solid cast. Less a remake of the 1951 science fiction classic than a more faithful version of John Campbell's short story "Who Goes There?," since the seeds/spores take on human shapes. **109m/C VHS, DVD, HD DVD.** Kurt Russell, Wilford Brimley, T.K. Carter, Richard Masur, Keith David, Richard Dysart, David Clennon, Donald Moffat, Thomas G. Waites, Charles Hallahan; ***D:*** John Carpenter; ***W:*** Bill Lancaster; ***C:*** Dean Cundey; ***M:*** Ennio Morricone.

The Thing About My Folks 1/2 **2005 (PG-13)** What happens when an old man on the brink of a divorce drops into his adult son's life? You get a vehicle for Peter Falk's patented crusty lovability. Sam Kleinman (Falk), after a lifetime spent buried in his work, is alone and unfulfilled after his wife Muriel (Dukakis) walks out. Son Ben (Reiser), a successful New York professional who is happily married to Rachel (Perkins), is considering a move to the country. Ben takes his father to inspect a property and the two are plunged into an adventure which includes a classic car, a billiard hall and a fishing trip, all of which serve as a framework for unraveling the meaning of life. Totally worth seeing Falk's magic. **96m/C DVD.** *US* Paul Reiser, Peter Falk, Olympia Dukakis, Elizabeth Perkins, Mackenzie Connolly, Lydia Grace Jordan, Ann Dowd, Claire Beckman, Mimi Lieber; ***D:*** Raymond De Felitta; ***W:*** Paul Reiser; ***C:*** Dan Gillham; ***M:*** Steven Argila.

The Thing Called Love 1/2 **1993 (PG-13)** Take last year's surprise hit "Singles" and replace grunge rock and Seattle with Country/Western and Nashville for this unsentimental tale of four 20-something singles trying to make their mark in the world of country music. The idea for the plot comes from the real-life Bluebird Cafe—the place where all aspiring singers and songwriters want to perform. Phoenix, Mathis, Mulroney, and Bullock did their own singing; look for Oslin as the Cafe owner. Phoenix's last completed film role. **116m/C VHS, DVD.** River Phoenix, Samantha Mathis, Sandra Bullock, Dermot Mulroney, K.T. Oslin, Anthony Clark, Webb Wilder; ***Cameos:*** Trisha Yearwood; ***D:*** Peter Bogdanovich; ***W:*** Allan Moyle, Carol Heikkinen; ***C:*** Peter James.

The Thing with Two Heads 1/2 **1972 (PG)** The inspired box copy says it all: "They share the same body...but hate each other's guts!" Max Kirshner (Milland), a white racist surgeon, plans to cheat death by having his head attached to another body. Imagine his surprise when he finds his noggin stitched onto black Jack Moss (Grier), right next to the original head. Nobody involved is taking the material too seriously. **93m/C DVD.** Ray Milland, Roosevelt "Rosie" Grier, Don Marshall, Roger Perry, Kathrine Baumann, Lee Frost, Wes Bishop, Rick Baker; ***D:*** Lee Frost; ***W:*** James Gordon White; ***C:*** Jack Steely; ***M:*** Robert O. Ragland.

Things **1989** A man creates a monster during his freakish experiments with artificial insemination. The monster returns to his house seeking revenge, and the man's visiting brother and a friend disappear, probably a clever move given their lackluster circumstances. **90m/C VHS.** Barry Gillis, Amber Lynn, Doug Bunston, Bruce Roach; ***D:*** Andrew Jordan; ***W:*** Andrew Jordan; ***C:*** Dan Riggs; ***M:*** Jack Procher.

Things 1/2 **1993** Two horror tales told by a jilted wife who's holding her husband's mistress hostage. "The Box" finds evil Mayor Black (Delama) incensed about a newly opened brothel in his hick Nevada town. So he decides to teach the hookers a lesson with the help of a bizarre, boxed creature that's with him at all times. "Thing in a Jar" finds an abusive husband and his mistress plotting to kill his mousy wife. Only the murder victim comes back to haunt the deadly duo—at least parts of her do. Nicely grotesque special effects courtesy of Mike Tristano. **85m/C VHS.** Neil Delama, Trey Howard, Debra Stevens, Courtney Lercara, Kinder Hunt; ***Cameos:*** Jeff Burr; ***D:*** Dennis Devine, Jay Woelfel; ***W:*** Dennis Devine, Steve Jarvis, Mike Bowler.

Things 2 1/2 **1997** Sequel to 1993's "Things." When a pizza delivery girl gets stranded at the creepy home of a strange horror novelist he entertains her with two tales of terror. Oh yes, if the girl can solve the mysteries within the stories, she gets to live. If not, well... The first has a cheating wife plotting to rid herself of hubby by using the ferocious small creature (with big teeth) she's trained to kill on her command. But the creature has other ideas. The second story finds a fashion photographer suspecting that a serial killer stalking her neighborhood may not be human. **85m/C VHS.** Angela Eads, David Hussey, Rich Ward, Margie Rey; ***D:*** Steve Jarvis, Dennis Devine, Mike Bowler; ***W:*** Steve Jarvis, Dennis Devine, Mike Bowler; ***C:*** Craig Incardone; ***M:*** Adam Karpel.

Things Behind the Sun 1/2 **2001 (R)** Writer/director Anders partially takes on her own traumatic past to tell a story of rape and its long aftermath. Troubled singer-songwriter Sherry McGrale (Dickens) has a radio hit with a song about being raped as a girl in her Florida hometown. Music reporter Owen (Mann) gets the assignment to interview Sherry after revealing that he and Sherry were friends in school and he knows who raped her. When Owen finally meets Sherry again, the circumstances of the past are revealed to them both. **117m/C VHS, DVD.** Kim Dickens, Gabriel Mann, Don Cheadle, Eric Stoltz, Elizabeth Pena, Rosanna Arquette, Alison Folland, Patsy Kensit, CCH Pounder; ***D:*** Allison Anders; ***W:*** Allison Anders, Kurt Voss; ***C:*** Terry Stacey.

Things Change **1988 (PG)** An old Italian shoeshine guy agrees, for a fee, to be a fall guy for the Mafia. A lower-echelon mob hood, assigned to watch over him, decides to give the old guy a weekend of fun in Vegas before going to jail. Director Mamet co-wrote the screenplay with Silverstein, best-known for his children's books ("Where the Sidewalk Ends," "The Giving Tree"). Combines charm and menace with terrific performances, especially from Ameche and Mantegna. **114m/C VHS, DVD.** Joe Mantegna, Don Ameche, Robert Prosky, J.J. Johnston, Ricky Jay, Mike Nussbaum, Jack Wallace, Dan Conway, J.T. Walsh, William H. Macy; ***D:*** David Mamet; ***W:*** David Mamet, Shel Silverstein; ***M:*** Alaric Jans. Venice Film Fest. '80: Actor (Ameche); Venice Film Fest. '88: Actor (Mantegna).

Things Happen at Night **1948** Scientist and insurance investigator determine that friendly ghost has possessed a family's youngest daughter. Not much happens. **79m/B VHS.** *GB* Gordon Harker, Alfred Drayton, Robertson Hare, Olga Lindo, Wylie Watson; ***D:*** Francis Searle.

Things I Never Told You **1996** Over-educated clerk Ann's (Taylor) just been dumped long-distance by her boyfriend. After a half-hearted suicide attempt, she calls a hot line and is connected to Don (McCarthy), who's equally depressed about the way his life is going. He discovers who Ann is and tentatively begins to court her, without revealing his true identity. The entire movie is tentative (including most of the performances). **93m/C VHS, DVD.** Lili Taylor, Andrew McCarthy, Debi Mazar, Alexis Arquette, Leslie Mann, Richard Edson, Seymour Cassel; ***D:*** Isabel Coixet; ***W:*** Isabel Coixet; ***C:*** Teresa Medina; ***M:*** Alfonso Vilallonga.

Things in Their Season 1/2 **1974** Melodrama about the imminent death of the mother of a Wisconsin farm family who makes those around her realize the value of happiness. Neal is excellent, rest of cast better than average in a well-told and sincere film. **79m/C VHS.** Patricia Neal, Ed Flanders, Marc Singer, Meg Foster; ***D:*** James Goldstone. **TV**

The Things of Life *Les Choses De La Vie* **1970** A car crash makes a man re-evaluate his life, goals, and loves. In the end he must choose the course of his future and decide between his wife and mistress. In French with English subtitles. **90m/C VHS.** *FR* Romy Schneider, Michel Piccoli, Lea Massari; ***D:*** Claude Sautet.

Things to Come 1/2 **1936** Using technology, scientists aim to rebuild the world after a lengthy war, followed by a plague and other unfortunate events. Massey and Scott each play two roles, in different generations. Startling picture of the world to come, with fine sets and good acting. Based on an H.G. Wells story, "The Shape of Things to Come." **92m/B VHS, DVD.** *GB* Raymond Massey, Margaretta Scott, Ralph Richardson, Cedric Hardwicke, Derrick DeMarney, Maurice Braddell; ***D:*** William Cameron Menzies; ***W:*** H.G. Wells; ***C:*** Georges Perinal; ***M:*** Arthur Bliss.

Things to Do **2006** Dissatisfied 25-year-old Adam (Stansko) quits his office job and moves back home for the summer. He comes up with a list of things he's always wanted to do and decides to see what he can accomplish before ultimately returning to adult responsibility. He enlists eccentric high-school buddy Mac (Wilson) to help him out. Of course, things don't always work out as expected. **85m/C DVD.** *CA* Daniel Wilson, Michael Stansko, Amy Ballantyne, Pat McManus, Joanne Oke, Santo D'Asaro; ***D:*** Theodore Bezaire; ***W:*** Michael Stansko, Theodore Bezaire; ***C:*** Eric Schiller; ***M:*** Michael Stansko.

Things to Do in Denver When You're Dead **1995 (R)** Jimmy the Saint (Garcia) is an ex-mobster gone straight who is called upon by his former boss, the Man With the Plan (Walken), to do one last easy-money job. Jimmy agrees and rounds up his old gang, a colorfully off-color group which includes Pieces (Lloyd), a porn movie projectionist and Critical Bill (Williams), a hair-trigger psycho who works in a funeral parlor. The job goes awry and the group becomes a target of hitman Mr. Shhh (Buscemi). Hipster dialogue, crime-gone-wrong formula, and the presence of Buscemi instantly scream Tarantino rip-off, but the performances make it a worthwhile genre entry. **115m/C VHS, DVD.** Andy Garcia, Christopher Lloyd, William Forsythe, Bill Nunn, Treat Williams, Jack Warden, Steve Buscemi, Fairuza

Balk, Gabrielle Anwar, Christopher Walken, Glenn Plummer, Don Cheadle, Bill Cobbs, Josh Charles, Michael Nicolosi, Marshall Bell, Sarah Trigger, Jenny McCarthy, Tommy (Tiny) Lister; ***D:*** Gary Fleder; ***W:*** Scott Rosenberg; ***C:*** Elliot Davis; ***M:*** Michael Convertino.

Things We Lost in the Fire 🦴🦴 ½ **2007 (R)** Audrey Burke (Berry) is the widow of murdered husband Brian (Duchovny—who, for a dead character has a lot of screen time). Although she's left financially sound, she is now a grieving single mother to two young children. Audrey invites Brian's best friend, heroin addict Jerry Sunborne (Del Toro), to the funeral and something makes the two of them put aside their obvious and seemingly overwhelming differences to cling together in their grief. What works is the emotional interplay between the two, as Jerry struggles to kick his habit and Audrey struggles to rebuild a new life for herself and her children; both Del Toro and Berry shine. What doesn't is that too many elements—the differing ethnic backgrounds, Jerry's addiction, Audrey's acceptance of Jerry—simply beg questions, and at times the study of grief overpowers and feels manufactured. **118m/C DVD.** *US* Halle Berry, Benicio Del Toro, David Duchovny, Alison Lohman, Omar Benson Miller, John Carroll Lynch, Robin Weigert, Alexis Llewellyn, Micah Berry, Paula Newsome; ***D:*** Suzanne (Susanne) Bier; ***W:*** Allan Loeb; ***C:*** Tom Stern; ***M:*** Johan Soderqvist.

Things You Can Tell Just by Looking at Her 🦴🦴 ½ **2000 (PG-13)** Ensemble female cast tells five stories that intersect in odd ways. Dr. Keener (Close) gets unhappy romantic news from tarot card reader Christine (Flockhart), whose own lover, Lilly (Golino), is terminally ill. Meanwhile, Rebecca (Hunter) has an abortion (performed by Dr. Keener) and then has an emotional breakdown. Then there's single mother Rose (Baker), who becomes intrigued by her new neighbor—a dwarf (Woodburn), and finally staid Kathy (Brenneman) and her exhuberantly sexy blind sister Carol (Diaz). **106m/C VHS, DVD.** Cameron Diaz, Glenn Close, Calista Flockhart, Holly Hunter, Amy Brenneman, Kathy Baker, Valeria Golino, Matt Craven, Gregory Hines, Noah Fleiss, Miguel (Michael) Sandoval, Danny Woodburn, Roma Maffia; ***D:*** Rodrigo Garcia; ***W:*** Rodrigo Garcia; ***C:*** Emmanuel Lubezki; ***M:*** Ed Shearmur.

Think Big 🦴🦴 ½ **1990 (PG-13)** Former professional wrestlers, the Pauls are truck drivers in this silly, enjoyable comedy. They pick up a brilliant teenager running from bad guys. Mayhem ensues. **86m/C VHS.** Peter Paul, David Paul, Martin Mull, Ari Meyers, Richard Kiel, David Carradine, Richard Moll, Peter Lupus; ***W:*** Jim Wynorski, R.J. Robertson.

Think Dirty 🦴🦴 *Every Home Should Have One* **1970 (R)** Lascivious comedy about ad exec Feldman's attempt to develop a series of sexy commercials to sell cereal. At the same time his wife forms a "clean up TV" group. Not very interesting or funny. **93m/C VHS.** *GB* Marty Feldman, Judy Cornwell, Shelley Berman; ***D:*** Jim Clark.

Think Fast, Mr. Moto 🦴🦴 ½ **1937** Japanese sleuth Mr. Moto (Lorre) is trailing diamond smugglers and boards a ship bound for Shanghai. He befriends Robert Hitchings (Beck), the son of the ship's owner. Robert has fallen for singer Gloria (Field) who's tied in with the smugglers and, upon their arrival, Moto must sort out the criminals from the patsies. More action-packed than the Charlie Chan mysteries although Mr. Moto is equally inscrutable. Based on the J.P. Marquand novels. First in the series. **66m/B DVD.** Peter Lorre, Thomas Beck, Virginia Field, Lee Phelps, Sig Rumann, John Rogers, Murray Kinnell; ***D:*** Norman Foster; ***W:*** Norman Foster, Charles Kenyon, Howard E. Smith; ***C:*** Harry Jackson; ***M:*** Samuel Kaylin.

Think Tank 🦴 ½ **2006 (PG)** Four 20-something uber-nerds are horrified when their favorite hang-out—the local pool hall—is in danger of closing. So they use their smarts to come up with a solution. Goofy and gross-free dumb comedy. **90m/C DVD.** Tina Majorino, Eric Artell, Keith Paugh, Greg Neil, Michael Miranda, Gordon Goodman, Brian Petersen; ***D:*** Brian Petersen; ***W:*** Brian Petersen; ***C:*** Michael Fimognari; ***M:*** John Swihart. **VIDEO**

Thinkin' Big 🦴 **1987 (R)** Guys and gals cavort on the Texas coast, except for one lonely fat guy who tries to increase his sexual prowess. The usual teen sex frenzy. **96m/C VHS.** Bruce Anderson, Kenny Sargent, Randy Jandt, Nancy Buechler, Darla Ralston; ***D:*** S.F. Brownrigg.

The Third 🦴🦴 *Der Dritte; Her Third* **1972** Margit (Hoffmann) has two children and two divorces after marrying men who wanted her more than she wanted them. So when Margit decides to take a third chance on love, she resolves to do the choosing. She picks unsuspecting colleague Hrdlistchka (Ludwig) and is determined to get him to say yes. German with subtitles. **107m/C VHS.** *GE* Jutta Hoffmann, Rolf Ludwig, Armin Mueller-Stahl, Peter Kohnke, Barbara Dittus; ***D:*** Egon Gunther; ***W:*** Gunther Rucker; ***C:*** Erich Gusko; ***M:*** Karl-Ernst Sasse.

The Third 🦴 ½ *Trzeci* **2004** A 30-something married couple goes yachting off the Polish coast, hoping a vacation will reignite some romantic sparks. They collide with a smaller boat—nearly drowning its carefree, older occupant. Is he a danger or the salvation that will shake up their boring lives? Polish with subtitles. **96m/C DVD.** *PL* Jacek Poniedzalek, Marek Kondrat, Magdalena Cielecka; ***D:*** Jan Hryniak; ***W:*** Wojciech Ziminsk; ***C:*** Marek Rajca; ***M:*** Wojciech Waglewski.

Third Degree Burn 🦴🦴 **1989** Mystery about a small-time detective hired by a businessman to follow a woman, only to become a suspect when the woman's real husband is killed. **97m/C VHS.** Treat Williams, Virginia Madsen, Richard Masur; ***D:*** Roger Spottiswoode. **CABLE**

The Third Key 🦴🦴 ½ *The Long Arm* **1957** A solid British crime drama follows a dogged detective as he probes serial safecrackings, with a climax set at London's Festival Hall. Based on the book by Robert Barr, who co-scripted. **96m/B VHS.** Jack Hawkins, Dorothy Allison, Geoffrey Keen, Richard Leech, Ian Bannen; ***D:*** Charles Frend.

The Third Man 🦴🦴🦴🦴 **1949** An American writer of pulp westerns (Cotten) arrives in post-war Vienna to take a job with an old friend, but discovers he has been murdered. Or has he? Based on Graham Greene's mystery, this classic film noir thriller plays on national loyalties during the Cold War. Welles is top-notch as the manipulative Harry Lime, blackmarket drug dealer extraordinare. The underground sewer sequence is not to be missed. With a haunting (sometimes irritating) theme by Anton Karas on unaccompanied zither. **104m/B VHS, DVD, Blu-ray Disc.** *GB* Joseph Cotten, Orson Welles, Alida Valli, Trevor Howard, Bernard Lee, Wilfrid Hyde-White, Ernst Deutsch, Erich Ponto, Siegfried Breuer, Hedwig Bleibtreu, Paul Hoerbiger, Herbert Halbik, Frederick Schreicker, Jenny Werner, Nelly Arno, Alexis Chesnakov, Leo Bieber, Paul Hardtmuth, Geoffrey Keen, Annie Rosar; ***D:*** Carol Reed; ***W:*** Graham Greene; ***C:*** Robert Krasker; ***M:*** Anton Karas. Oscars '50: B&W Cinematog.; AFI '98: Top 100; British Acad. '49: Film; Cannes '49: Film; Directors Guild '49: Director (Reed).

Third Man on the Mountain 🦴🦴 ½ *Banner in the Sky* **1959 (G)** A family epic about mountain climbing, shot in Switzerland and based on James Ramsey Ullman's "Banner in the Sky." A young man is determined to climb the "Citadel" as his ancestors have. He finds there's more to climbing than he imagined. Look for Helen Hayes (MacArthur's mother) in a cameo. Standard Disney adventure drama. **106m/C VHS, DVD.** James MacArthur, Michael Rennie, Janet Munro, James Donald, Herbert Lom, Laurence Naismith; ***Cameos:*** Helen Hayes; ***D:*** Ken Annakin.

Third Man Out: A Donald Strachey Mystery 🦴🦴 ½ **2005** Donald Stachey (Allen) is a semi-successful gay PI who works in Albany, New York and lives with his politico lover, Tim Callahan (Spence). Donald reluctantly takes the case of hectoring gay activist John Rutka (Wetherall), whose tabloid outings have made him a target for violence. When Rutka winds up dead, Donald has a long list of suspects but things aren't always what they appear to be. Adapted from Richard Stevenson's 1992 mystery. **98m/C DVD.** *US* Chad Allen, Sebastian Spence, Jack Wetherall, Sean Young, Woody Jeffreys; ***D:*** Ron Oliver; ***W:*** Mark Saltzman. **CABLE**

The Third Miracle 🦴🦴 ½ **1999 (R)** Harris makes for one sexy and dynamic priest. He's Father Frank Shore who is struggling with his faith and is in a kind of voluntary retirement. However, he's summoned by power player, Bishop Cahill (Haid), to investigate the purported miracles of the late Helen O'Regan (Sukowa). A cult is growing up around her memory and the mention of sainthood (which requires three proven miracles) has the church wary. Film is set in Chicago in 1979 and based on the book by Richard Vetere. **119m/C VHS, DVD.** Ed Harris, Anne Heche, Charles Haid, Armin Mueller-Stahl, Michael Rispoli, Jean-Louis Roux, Ken James, James Gallanders, Barbara Sukowa; ***D:*** Agnieszka Holland; ***W:*** John Romano, Richard Vetere; ***C:*** Jerzy Zielinski; ***M:*** Jan A.P. Kaczmarek.

The Third Sex 🦴🦴 *Anders Als du und Ich* **1957** One of the first films to deal with homosexuality in which parents try to "straighten out" their gay son. German with subtitles. **90m/C VHS.** *GE* Paul Dahlke, Paula Wesley, Hans Nielsen, Christian Wolff, Friedrich Joloff, Hilde Korber, Gunther Theil; ***D:*** Veit Harlan; ***W:*** Felix Lutzkendorff; ***C:*** Kurt Grigoleit; ***M:*** Erwin Halletz.

Third Solution 🦴🦴 *Russicum* **1989 (R)** An Italian-made film about the discovery of a secret pact made between the Kremlin and the Vatican that may start WWIII. Well-cast, but poorly conceived spook drama, with music by Vangelis. **93m/C VHS.** *IT* Treat Williams, F. Murray Abraham, Danny Aiello, Nigel Court, Rita Rusic, Rossano Brazzi; ***D:*** Pasquale Squitieri; ***M:*** Vangelis.

Third Walker 🦴🦴🦴 **1979** A desperate woman sacrifices her marriage to immerse herself in efforts to reunite her twin sons, who were inadvertently separated at birth. An original and intriguing directorial debut by McLuhan. **85m/C VHS.** William Shatner, Colleen Dewhurst, Marshall McLuhan, Monique Mercure, Andree Pelletier; ***D:*** Teri McLuhan; ***W:*** Teri McLuhan, Robert Thom.

The Third Wheel 🦴🦴 **2002 (PG-13)** Shy businessman Stanley finally gets up the nerve to ask out coworker Diana (Richards) after pining for her for a year. The night of the date, he hits a homeless guy Phil (screenwriter Lacopo) with his car, so Phil tags along. Stan also has to deal with a bunch of co-workers who've wagered on the outcome of the date, and are secretly monitoring the proceedings. Damon and Affleck's planned follow-up to "Good Will Hunting" sat on a shelf at Miramax for over two years, probably because of the inconsistent laughs and direction. Good cast does what it can with what it has to work with. **90m/C DVD.** Luke Wilson, Denise Richards, Ben Affleck, Jay Lacopo, Matt Damon, Meredith Salenger, Bobby Slayton, Lauren Graham, Nicole Sullivan; ***D:*** Jordan Brady; ***W:*** Jay Lacopo; ***C:*** Jonathan Brown; ***M:*** Lisa Coleman, Wendy Melvoin. **VIDEO**

Third World Cop 🦴🦴 **1999 (R)** Detective Capone (Campbell) returns to his childhood home in Kingston and discovers that his best bud Ratty (Danvers) is the right-hand man for local crime boss One Hand (Bradshaw). Their friendship leaves the gangsters suspicious that Ratty is a police informer but even when he finally agrees to help Capone, things go wrong. Straight-ahead crime story does have the advantage of the Jamaican settings to take it out of the norm. **98m/C VHS, DVD.** *JM* Paul Campbell, Carl Bradshaw, Mark Danvers, Audrey Reid; ***D:*** Christopher Browne; ***W:*** Christopher Browne, Suzanne Fenn, Chris Salewicz; ***C:*** Richard Lannaman; ***M:*** Sly Dunbar, Robbie Shakespeare.

Thirst 🦴🦴 **1979 (R)** A girl is abducted by a secret society that wants her to become their new leader. There is just one catch: she has to learn to like the taste of human blood. Chilling but weakly plotted. **96m/C VHS, DVD.** David Hemmings, Henry Silva, Chantal Contouri; ***D:*** Rod Hardy.

The Thirst 🦴 ½ **2006** Since Lisa (Kramer) has terminal cancer, she doesn't ask a lot of questions when Mariel (Scott Thomas) offers a chance at life—even if it's the undead kind. Naturally, ex-beau Maxx (Keeslar) is confused to see her out clubbing, but Lisa soon turns him and they join Eurotrash Darius (Sisto and his wandering accent) and his blood crew. Eventually the reunited lovebirds find out they don't really enjoy swilling human red. **88m/C DVD.** Matt Keeslar, Clare Kramer, Jeremy Sisto, Serena Scott Thomas, Neil Jackson, Adam Baldwin, Erik Palladino, Charlotte Ayanna; ***D:*** Jeremy Kasten; ***W:*** Jeremy Kasten; ***C:*** Raymond N. Stella; ***M:*** Joe Kraemer. **VIDEO**

Thirst 🦴🦴🦴 *Bakjwi* **2009 (R)** Long, operatic, and carnal horror melodrama from South Korea. A priest becomes a volunteer in a hospital project to discover a vaccine for an emerging virus. Instead, a tainted blood transfusion leads to Sang-hyeon (Song) becoming a vampire with a lot of lust (and not just for blood). He begins an affair with bored housewife Tae-ju (Kim), the wife of his childhood friend, which soon turns very deadly. Korean with subtitles. **133m/C DVD.** *US KN* Kang-ho Song, Ok-vin Kim, Ha-Kyun Shin, Haesook Kim; ***D:*** Chan-wook Park; ***W:*** Chan-wook Park, Seo-gyeong Jeong; ***C:*** Jeong-hun Jeong; ***M:*** Yeong-wook Jo.

The Thirsty Dead **WOOF!** *The Blood Cult of Shangri-La; Blood Hunt* **1974 (PG)** Maybe they could learn to like Gatorade. An eternally young jungle king is looking for a wife. She can be young forever too, if she's not above vampirism and sacrificing virgins. In spite of the jungle vampire slant, this Filipino-made movie is a woofer. **90m/C VHS, DVD.** *PH* John Considine, Jennifer Billingsley, Judith McConnell, Fredricka Meyers, Tani Phelps Guthrie; ***D:*** Terry Becker.

Thirteen 🦴🦴🦴 **2003 (R)** Genuinely original indie probes the transformation of Tracy (Wood) a well-behaved, slightly nerdy, L.A. teen who, practically overnight, becomes a ragingly rebellious, boy-crazy shoplifter, thanks to psychologically scarred but savvy schoolmate Evie (co-writer Reed), who invites Tracy into her world of popularity, piercings, and partying. As Tracy's mom Melanie, a recovering alcoholic, frets over Tracy's disturbing personality makeover, Evie begins to bond with her. Performances are uniformly sparkling. Spot-on characters and all-too-real details come from director/co-writer Hardwicke's collaboration with the then 13-year-old Reed—whom she met while dating Reed's father—the real-life good girl of the story. **95m/C VHS, DVD.** *US* Evan Rachel Wood, Nikki Reed, Holly Hunter, Jeremy Sisto, Deborah Kara Unger, Kip Pardue, Brady Corbet, Sarah Clarke, D.W. Moffett, Vanessa Anne Hudgens; ***D:*** Catherine Hardwicke; ***W:*** Nikki Reed, Catherine Hardwicke; ***C:*** Elliot Davis; ***M:*** Mark Mothersbaugh. Ind. Spirit '04: Debut Perf. (Reed); Sundance '03: Director (Hardwicke).

XIII 🦴🦴 **2008 (R)** Convoluted political conspiracies reign when the U.S. president is assassinated and an amnesiac agent—known as XIII (Dorff) because of his tattoo—is blamed for the crime. He's hunted by a lot of unsavory types who want him dead so he can take the fall without the truth becoming known. Based on a series of French-Belgian comic books. Originally shown as an NBC miniseries; the DVD is the unedited release. **180m/C DVD.** *CA FR* Val Kilmer, Stephen McHattie, Jessalyn Gilsig, Ted Atherton, Stephen Dorff, John Bourgeois, Lucinda Davis, Caterina Murino, Mimi Suzyk, Greg Bryk; ***D:*** Duane Clark; ***W:*** David Wolkove, Philippe Lyon; ***C:*** David Greene; ***M:*** Nicolas Errera. **TV**

Thirteen Conversations About One Thing 🦴🦴🦴 ½ **2001 (R)** "We plan, God laughs," as the saying goes. Smart, literary indie offers a fresh take on the familiar theme of destiny and the forms it takes. Focuses on the intersecting lives of five New Yorkers: college physics professor Turturro wants to change his boring life; housewife Irving confronts her hubby about his infidelity; lawyer McConaughey's life suddenly takes a wrong turn; housekeeper DuVall waits for something wonderful to happen; and cynical businessman Arkin is disturbed by his relentlessly upbeat coworker. Director Jill Sprecher and her sister, cowriter Karen, illustrates (in 13 sections), how even the smallest actions can have enormous consequences. Detailed omens arise everywhere, foreshadowing events to come in this karma chameleon of a movie. Well acted, deftly directed and smartly written. **104m/C VHS, DVD.** *US* Matthew McConaughey, Alan Arkin, John Turturro, Clea

DuVall, Amy Irving, Barbara Sukowa, Tia Texada, Frankie Faison, William Wise, Shawn Elliott, David Connolly, Alex Burns; *D:* Jill Sprecher; *W:* Jill Sprecher, Karen Sprecher; *C:* Dick Pope; *M:* Alex Wurman.

Thirteen Days 1/2 **2000 (PG-13)** The Cuban Missile Crisis seen through the eyes of President JFK, Attorney General Robert Kennedy, and presidential aide Kenny O'Donnell (Costner). Director Donaldson wisely opts not to over-dramatize what was clearly a suspenseful story to begin with (and realizes, as well, that we know the outcome). The few sacrifices of historical accuracy made in the name of dramatic license are basically harmless. Greenwood and Culp ably handle the often difficult task of portraying the brothers Kennedy, and Costner is solid as the brothers' trusted confidante. Donaldson and Costner notably worked together on 1987's "No Way Out." **145m/C VHS, DVD.** Kevin Costner, Bruce Greenwood, Steven Culp, Dylan Baker, Michael Fairman, Kevin Conway, Tim Kelleher, Len Cariou, Bill Smitrovich, Dakin Matthews, Madison Mason, Christopher Lawford, Ed Lauter, Elya Baskin, Boris Krutonog, Peter White, James Karen, Tim Jerome, Olek Krupa, Lucinda Jenney, Henry Strozier, Frank Wood, Stephanie Romanov; *D:* Roger Donaldson; *W:* David Self; *C:* Andrzej Bartkowiak; *M:* Trevor Jones.

13 Ghosts 1/2 **1960** A dozen ghosts need another member to round out their ranks. They have four likely candidates to choose from when a family moves into the house inhabited by the ghoulish group. Originally viewed with "Illusion-O," a technology much like 3-D, which allowed the viewing of the ghosts only through a special pair of glasses. **88m/C VHS, DVD.** Charles Herbert, Jo Morrow, Martin Milner, Rosemary DeCamp, Donald Woods, Margaret Hamilton, John van Dreelen; *D:* William Castle; *W:* Robb White; *C:* Joseph Biroc; *M:* Von Dexter.

13 Ghosts **2001 (R)** Another attempt to meld humor and horror in a William Castle remake ala "House on Haunted Hill" misfires in this flashy screamfest. Arthur (Shalhoub) inherits a weird glass mansion from his shadowy Uncle Cyrus (Abraham). He moves into the house with his kids Kathy (Elizabeth) and Bobby (Roberts) and their nanny Maggie (Digga). Along for kicks is spastic psychic Rafkin (Lillard), which is good, because the mansion ends up being a gigantic infernal contraption powered by ghosts complete with whirling gears and sliding glass panels that attack the inhabitants. It seems that crazy Uncle Cyrus built the house to open the Eye of Hell and it's up to Arthur to stop it. The special effects are above average, but the plot is clearly not. **91m/C VHS, DVD.** *US* Tony Shalhoub, Embeth Davidtz, Matthew Lillard, Shannon Elizabeth, Alec Roberts, Rah Digga, J.R. Bourne, F. Murray Abraham; *D:* Steve Beck; *W:* Richard D'Ovidio, Neal Marshall Stevens; *C:* Gale Tattersall; *M:* John (Gianni) Frizzell.

13 Going on 30 1/2 **2004 (PG-13)** Broadly appealing Garner makes the successful leap to bona fide big screen lead in this harmless body-switch comedy. Jenna (Allen) is an insecure 13-year-old who magically becomes the "30, flirty, and thriving" fashion magazine editor played by Garner. Comedy ensues when she is forced to deal with adult concerns foreign to a 13-year-old, including work at the magazine; her new, mature body; and her hockey player boyfriend, all of which she does with an endearing childlike zeal. Along with the perks, Jenna's transformation has also alienated her former best friend Matt (Marquette), once a chubby nerd who is now, 17 years later, a handsome and engaged hunk (Ruffalo). Of course, Jenna would like to get reacquainted. Garner and Ruffalo elevate a so-so vehicle into an appealing romantic comedy. **97m/C DVD, Blu-ray Disc.** *US* Jennifer Garner, Mark Ruffalo, Judy Greer, Andy Serkis, Christa B. Allen, Kathy Baker, Phil Reeves, Joe Grifasi, Courtney Chase, Maz Jobrani, Robine Lee, Jim Gaffigan, Sean Marquette, Alex Black, Alexandra Kyle, Renee Olstead; *D:* Gary Winick; *W:* Josh Goldsmith, Cathy Yuspa; *C:* Don Burgess; *M:* Theodore Shapiro.

13 Moons **2002 (R)** Only a full moon in Los Angeles could pull together several intertwining yet divergent storylines to tell what really is a simple tale of a man, Mo (Proval), whose son, Timmy (Wolff), will die without a kidney transplant. Problem is the donor is a drug addict who flees the hospital. Along with a rag-tag group of otherwise-afflicted folks (including a fired TV clown, a stripper, and a rap executive), Mo must find him...and fast! While the performances evoke a sense of sincerity, the backbone is too weak to support them. **94m/C VHS, DVD.** Steve Buscemi, Karyn Parsons, Peter Dinklage, David Proval, Austin Wolff, Daryl (Chill) Mitchell, Rose Rollins, Peter Stormare, Pruitt Taylor Vince, Gareth Williams, Francesco Messina, Jennifer Beals, Elizabeth Bracco, Matthew Sussman, Michael Badalucco, Danny Trejo; *D:* Alexandre Rockwell; *W:* Alexandre Rockwell; *C:* Phil Parmet; *M:* Brian Kelly, Kevin Salem. **VIDEO**

13 Rue Madeleine **1946** Cagney plays a WWII spy who infiltrates Gestapo headquarters in Paris in order to find the location of a German missile site. Actual OSS footage is used in this fast-paced early postwar espionage propaganda piece. Rex Harrison rejected the part taken by Cagney. **95m/B VHS, DVD.** James Cagney, Annabella, Richard Conte, Frank Latimore, Walter Abel, Sam Jaffe, Melville Cooper, E.G. Marshall, Karl Malden, Red Buttons, Blanche Yurka, Peter Von Zerneck, Marcel Rousseau, Dick Gordon, Alfred Linder; *D:* Henry Hathaway; *W:* Sy Bartlett, John Monks Jr.; *C:* Norbert Brodine; *M:* David Buttolph.

Thirteenth Day of Christmas **1985** A psychotic boy is left alone by his parents on Christmas night. **60m/C VHS.** *GB* Patrick Allen, Elizabeth Spriggs; *D:* Patrick Lau. **TV**

The 13th Floor 1/2 **1988 (R)** A young girl fuses with the spirit of a young boy her father ruthlessly killed years before, and together they wreak havoc. **86m/C VHS, DVD.** Lisa Hensley, Tim McKenzie, Miranda Otto; *D:* Chris Roach.

The Thirteenth Floor 1/2 **1999 (R)** Silly sci-fier with a confusing virtual-reality plot and a lot of visual effects. An investigation into the mysterious death of tycoon Hannon Fuller (Mueller-Stahl) leads to the realization that he lived in parallel worlds—one in the present and one in 1937. Exec Douglas Hall (Bierko) stands to inherit, which raises the suspicious of cop McBain (Haysbert), while mysterious femme Jane (Mol) shows up, claiming to be Fuller's daughter. And then there's Hall's colleague Whitney (D'Onofrio), who also exists in the 1937 as a barkeep with a very important letter. Not that any of this turns out to be particularly interesting. **100m/C VHS, DVD.** Craig Bierko, Vincent D'Onofrio, Armin Mueller-Stahl, Gretchen Mol, Dennis Haysbert, Steven Schub, Jeremy Roberts, Tia Texada, Alison Lohman; *D:* Josef Rusnak; *W:* Josef Rusnak; *C:* Wedigo von Schultzendorff; *M:* Harald Kloser.

13th Guest *Lady Beware* **1932** Two people try to solve a murder that occurred at a dinner party. An incredibly creaky early talkie melodrama that created some of the cliches of the genre. **70m/B VHS, DVD.** Ginger Rogers, Lyle Talbot, J. Farrell MacDonald, Paul Hurst; *D:* Albert Ray.

The Thirteenth Man 1/2 **1937** When a journalist investigating the murder of a district attorney is also killed, the paper's gossip columnist takes the case. Entertaining, fast-paced mystery. **70m/B VHS.** Weldon Heyburn, Inez Courtney, Selmer Jackson, Milburn Stone, Matty Fain; *D:* William Nigh.

The 13th Mission 1/2 **1991** A low-budget overseas combat adventure, no better than the first 12. **95m/C VHS.** Robert Marius, Jeff Griffith, Michael Monty, David Morisson, Paul Home, John Falch, Albert Bronski, Chantal Manz; *D:* Antonio Perez.

Thirteenth Reunion **1981** A newspaperwoman uncovers a bizarre secret society when she does a routine story on a health spa. **60m/C VHS, DVD.** Julia Foster, Dinah Sheridan, Richard Pearson; *D:* Peter Sasdy.

The 13th Warrior *Eaters of the Dead* **1999 (R)** Banderas stars as Ahmed Ibn Fahdlan, a sophisticated Arabian poet and lover-turned-reluctant-warrior, who gets exiled from his homeland and caught up in a quest with a bunch of uncouth, slaughter-loving Vikings. Based on the 1976 book by Michael Crichton, this one has been sitting on the shelf a while after a rocky filming history. However, if you like bloody, action-packed epics it will satisfy your cravings. **103m/C VHS, DVD.** Antonio Banderas, Vladimir Kulich, Clive Russell, Omar Sharif, Diane Venora, Sven Wollter, Dennis Storhoi, Anders T. Anderson, Richard Bremmer, Neil Maffin, Tony Curran, Mischa Hausserman, Asbjorn Riis, Daniel Southern, Oliver Sveinall, Albie Woodington; *D:* Michael Crichton, John McTiernan; *W:* Michael Crichton; *C:* Peter Menzies Jr.; *M:* Jerry Goldsmith.

Thirty Day Princess 1/2 **1934** Princess Catterina (Sidney) comes to New York, immediately gets sick, and is unable to fulfill her royal obligations. Banker Richard Gresham (Arnolds), who has a lot financially invested in the visit, finds a double in struggling actress Nancy (Sidney again). But newspaper publisher Porter Madison (Grant) gets suspicious, despite falling for the dame. There are a few more comedic plot points but Sidney and Grant carry through the familiarity with loads of charm. **74m/B DVD.** Cary Grant, Sylvia Sidney, Edward Arnold, Vince Barnett, Henry Stephenson, Edgar Norton; *D:* Marion Gering; *W:* Preston Sturges, Frank Partos, Sam Hellman, Edwin Justus Mayer; *C:* Leon Shamroy.

30 Days of Night 1/2 **2007 (R)** Vampires have discovered that Barrow, Alaska, offers the perfect combination of human flesh and 30-day absence of sunlight, so they descend upon the town like the darkness they require, devouring all but a small number of survivors, among them two sheriffs, Eban Oleson (Hartnett) and his estranged wife Stella (George). The story, based on a graphic novel series, unfolds as a horrible game of hide-and-seek, with the town's surviving inhabitants eventually discovering how to rid themselves of the bloodthirsty pestilence. The biggest problem is the predictability and repetition of the storyline, but with no shortage of stylized violent horror for those with an unquenchable thirst for such things. A great twist on the classic vampire story not to be missed by admirers of the genre. **113m/C DVD.** *US* Josh Hartnett, Melissa George, Danny Huston, Ben Foster, Mark Boone Jr., Mark Rendall; *D:* David Slade; *W:* Stuart Beattie, Steve Niles, Brian Nelson; *C:* Jo Willems; *M:* Brian Reitzell.

The 30-Foot Bride of Candy Rock **1959** A junk dealer invents a robot, catapults into space and causes his girlfriend to grow to 30 feet in height. Lightweight, whimsical fantasy was Costello's only solo starring film, and his last before his untimely death. **73m/B VHS.** Lou Costello, Dorothy Provine, Gale Gordon; *D:* Sidney Miller.

30 Is a Dangerous Age, Cynthia 1/2 **1968** Dudley Moore stars as a nightclub pianist who spends a lot of his time daydreaming about being rich, famous, and married to a beautiful woman. Moore determines to attain all these dreams before his 30th birthday, which is only six weeks away. **85m/C VHS.** *GB* Dudley Moore, Suzy Kendall, Eddie Foy Jr.; *D:* Joseph McGrath; *W:* Dudley Moore; *M:* Dudley Moore.

Thirty Seconds Over Tokyo **1944** Dated but still interesting classic wartime flagwaver details the conception and execution of the first bombing raids on Tokyo by Lt. Col. James Doolittle and his men. Look for Blake Edwards, as well as Steve Brodie in his first screen appearance. Based on a true story. **138m/B VHS, DVD.** Spencer Tracy, Van Johnson, Robert Walker, Robert Mitchum, Phyllis Thaxter, Scott McKay, Stephen McNally, Louis Jean Heydt, Leon Ames, Paul Langton, Don DeFore, Tim Murdock, Alan Napier, Dorothy Morris, Jacqueline White, Selena Royle, Bill Phillips, Donald Curtis, Gordon McDonald, John R. Reilly, Douglas Cowan, Ann Shoemaker, Steve Brodie; *D:* Mervyn LeRoy; *W:* Dalton Trumbo; *C:* Robert L. Surtees, Harold Rosson; *M:* Herbert Stothart.

30 Years to Life **2001 (R)** Six friends try to cope with the reality of turning 30, and the re-evaluation of their lives that the milestone brings. Natalie, a Wall Street success, pretends to be domesticated to attract a conservative doctor. Commitment-averse Leland is forced to propose to his live-in girl Joy because of a jewelry shop mix-up; Troy, a stand-up comedian wonders if he'll get that big break; Stephanie has liposuction to change her outlook and prospects; and Malik quits his job to become a model. It all has a very sitcomy feel, but the writing is good enough to make the various lessons learned more palatable. **110m/C VHS, DVD.** Erika Alexander, Melissa De Sousa, Tracy Morgan, Kadeem Hardison, Paula Jai Parker, Allen Payne, T.E. Russell, Eddie Brill, Janet Hubert-Whitten, Jim Gaffigan; *D:* Vanessa Middleton; *W:* Vanessa Middleton; *C:* Cliff Charles; *M:* Timbaland. **VIDEO**

32 Short Films about Glenn Gould **1993** Perceptive docudrama about the iconoclastic Canadian classical pianist who secluded himself in the studio, forsaking live performances for much of his career. A combination of dramatic recreation, archival material, and interviews depict the biographical details of the driven artist who died at the age of 50. Feore is memorable in the title role, especially since he's never actually shown playing the piano. Title and film structure refer to Bach's "Goldberg" Variations, a recording which made Gould's reputation. **94m/C VHS, DVD.** *CA* Colm Feore, Gale Garnett, David Hughes, Katya Ladan, Gerry Quigley, Carlo Rota, Peter Millard, Yehudi Menuhin, Bruno Monsaingeon; *D:* Francois Girard; *W:* Don McKellar, Francois Girard; *C:* Alan Dostie. Genie '93: Cinematog., Director (Girard), Film, Film Editing.

35 Shots of Rum 1/2 *35 Rhums* **2008** Warm family drama from Denis about letting go of restrictive-but-loving familial ties finds college student Josephine (Diop) devotedly living with her widowed, train conductor father Lionel (Descas). Happy in their routine, change still comes when Lionel's long-time colleague Rene (Toussaint) retires, leaving the middle-aged man feeling adrift. But Dad isn't too self-absorbed to notice that family friend Noe's (Colin) attraction to Josephine is not only mutual but heating up. French with subtitles. **99m/C DVD.** *FR GE* Alex Descas, Gregoire Colin, Mati Diop, Nicole Dogue, Julieth Mars Toussaint; *D:* Claire Denis; *W:* Claire Denis, Jean-Pol Fargeau; *C:* Agnes Godard; *M:* Tindersticks.

36 Fillete **1988** Lili, an intellectually precocious 14-year-old French girl who's literally bursting out of her children's dress size 36 fillete, discovers her sexuality. So while on vacation with her family she becomes determined to see if she can seduce a middle-aged playboy. In French with English subtitles. **88m/C VHS, DVD.** *FR* Delphine Zentout, Etienne Chicot, Oliver Parniere, Jean-Pierre Leaud; *D:* Catherine Breillat; *W:* Catherine Breillat, Roger Salloch; *C:* Laurent Dailland.

36 Hours **1964** Maj. Pike (Garner) is a high-ranking WWII Army officer with knowledge of top secret invasion plans who wakes up in an Army hospital with amnesia, a wife (Saint) he didn't know he had, and a shrink telling him that the war's been over for some time. But Pike's not sure what's real and what isn't, especially when the doc asks him to explain, in great detail, what happened just before he lost his memory. Are they telling the truth, or is this an elaborate hoax? Tight, suspenseful plot, and fine performances all around make this an enjoyable thriller even after that question is answered. Remade for TV in 1989 with Corbin Bernsen in the Garner role. **115m/B VHS, DVD.** James Garner, Eva Marie Saint, Rod Taylor, Werner Peters, John Banner, Russ Thorson, Alan Napier, Oscar Beregi, Edmund Gilbert, Sig Rumann, Celia Lovsky, Karl Held, Marjorie Bennett, Martin Kosleck, Henry Rowland, Hilda Plowright, Joseph Mell, Rudolph Anders, James Doohan; *D:* George Seaton; *W:* George Seaton, Roald Dahl, Carl K. Hittleman; *C:* Philip Lathrop; *M:* Dimitri Tiomkin.

Thirty-Six Hours of Hell 1/2 **1977** A troop of Marines battle Japanese forces in the South Pacific during WWII. Dubbed. **95m/C VHS.** Richard Harrison, Pamela Tudor; *D:* Roberto Marrtero.

36 Hours to Die 1/2 **1999** Noah Stone (Williams) is a brewery owner recovering from heart bypass surgery. As if he doesn't have enough to worry about, a crime syndicate wants to use his business as a front in an extortion scam and he's got a day-and-a-half to make up his mind (hence the title). Stone's wife (Cattrall), her ex-cop uncle (O'Connor), and even Stone's bowling team unite to take on the bad guys. **96m/C VHS.** Treat Williams, Saul Rubinek, Kim Cattrall, Carroll O'Connor, George Touliatos, Scott Hylands; ***D:*** Yves Simoneau; ***W:*** Robert Rodat. **CABLE**

The 36th Chamber of Shaolin ♪♪♪ 1/2 *Shao Lin shan shi liu fang; Shaolin Master Killer; 36th Chamber; The Master Killer* **1978 (R)** Often called "the greatest Kung Fu movie of all time" (aren't there several movies that say that?), this Shaw Brothers film from the 1970s is definitely one of the most recognizable. Liu (Gordon Lau) is an ethics scholar whose friends and family are murdered by the Manchu government. Vowing revenge, he travels to the Shaolin temple to learn kung fu. After a bad start he proves to be the temple's best student, mastering in a mere five years what takes most a lifetime. Cast out for wanting to teach kung fu to the masses, he assembles a team of fighters and goes after the general responsible for the massacre of his town. **109m/C DVD.** *HK* Chia Hui Liu, Lieh Lo, Norman Chu, Chia Yung Liu; ***D:*** Chia-Liang Liu; ***W:*** Kuang Ni; ***C:*** Yeh-tai Huang, Arthur Wong; ***M:*** Yung-Yu Chen.

'38: Vienna before the Fall ♪♪ 1/2 **1988** Wartime Vienna explodes with love and politics. Academy Award nominee for Best Foreign Language Film. In German with English subtitles. **97m/C VHS.** *GE* Tobias Engel, Sunnyi Melles; ***D:*** Wolfgang Gluck.

39 Pounds of Love ♪♪ 1/2 **2005** Ami Ankilewitz, now living in Israel and working as a computer animator, celebrates his 34th birthday by traveling back to the hometown of his youth in Texas where at 18 months old he was diagnosed with spinal muscular atrophy, a condition, which was expected to shorten his life to no more than 6 years. Ami wishes to confront the doctor who predicted his early death, reconnect with his estranged brother Oscar and ride a Harley. Intercut with scenes from Ankilewitz's animated work, which provides insight into much of his inner thinking—a good portion of which revolves around the unrequited love he holds for his former caregiver Christina. **70m/C DVD.** *US* ***D:*** Dani Menkin; ***M:*** Chris Gubisch.

The 39 Steps ♪♪♪♪ **1935** The classic Hitchcock mistaken-man-caught-in-intrigue thriller, featuring some of his most often copied set-pieces and the surest visual flair of his pre-war British period. Remade twice, in 1959 and 1979. **81m/B VHS, DVD.** *GB* Robert Donat, Madeleine Carroll, Godfrey Tearle, Lucie Mannheim, Peggy Ashcroft, John Laurie, Wylie Watson, Helen Haye, Frank Cellier, Gus McNaughton, Jerry Verno, Peggy Simpson, Hilda Trevelyan, John Turnbull, Elizabeth Inglis, Wilfrid Brambell; ***D:*** Alfred Hitchcock; ***W:*** Charles Bennett, Alma Reville, Ian Hay; ***C:*** Bernard Knowles; ***M:*** Louis Levy.

The Thirty-Nine Steps ♪♪ 1/2 **1979** Hitchcock remake is a visually interesting, but mostly uninvolving, mystery. Powell is the man suspected of stealing plans to begin WWI. Above average, but not by much. **98m/C VHS, DVD.** *GB* Robert Powell, David Warner, Eric Porter, Karen Dotrice, John Mills, Andrew Keir; ***D:*** Don Sharp.

This Above All ♪♪ **1942** Her distinguished family is upset when Prudence Cathaway (Fontaine) decides to join the WAAFs as a private and learn from the bottom up. She agrees to a blind date with troubled Clive Briggs (Power), a working-class man wounded at Dunkirk. He's bitterly opposed to the British aristocracy so Prudence keeps their class differences a secret until she learns that Clive has decided to go AWOL. Degenerates into flag-waving propaganda (hardly surprising since it's a wartime film), but Fontaine is lovely and sincere and Power does well in an early serious role. **110m/B DVD.** Tyrone Power, Joan Fontaine, Philip Merivale, Thomas Mitchell, Henry Stephenson, Nigel Bruce, Gladys Cooper; ***D:*** Anatole Litvak; ***W:*** R.C. Sherriff; ***C:*** Arthur C. Miller; ***M:*** Alfred Newman. Oscars '43: Art Dir./Set Dec., B&W.

This Boy's Life ♪♪♪ **1993 (R)** In 1957, Carolyn (Barkin) and her teenage son Toby (DiCaprio) are in search of a new life, far from her abusive ex-boyfriend. In the town of Concrete, just outside Seattle, she meets ex-military man Dwight (De Niro), a slick but none too suave mechanic who might be the answer to her dreams, but then again, he might not. Nicely crafted performances from all, but keep your eye on DiCaprio (great in his first major role) as the confused and abused teen divided between dreams of prep school and the allure of the going-nowhere crowd. Based on the memoirs of Tobias Wolff; director Caton-Jones sensitively illustrates the skewed understanding of masculinity in the 1950s. Vintage soundtrack takes you back. **115m/C VHS, DVD.** Robert De Niro, Ellen Barkin, Leonardo DiCaprio, Jonah Blechman, Eliza Dushku, Chris Cooper, Carla Gugino, Zachary Ansley, Tracey Ellis, Kathy Kinney, Gerrit Graham; ***D:*** Michael Caton-Jones; ***W:*** Robert Getchell; ***C:*** David Watkin; ***M:*** Carter Burwell.

This Christmas ♪♪ **2007 (PG-13)** After several years apart, the Whitfields are reunited for the holidays at the solidly upper-middle-class family home in L.A. Ma'Dere (Devine) is the matriarch of this African American family whose members include the military son Claude (Short), the musician son Quentin (Elba), oldest daughter Lisa (King), workaholic Kelli (Leal), college student Mel (London), and Baby (Brown), who announces his plan to follow their long-absent father into the jazz world. His is not the only bombshell to fall as everyone has a turn having his or her buttons pushed. Ma'Dere's long-time boyfriend Joe (Lindo) does a great job of holding everyone together long enough for them to realize what a treasure they have in each other. A tad overdone and over the top but still a fun holiday romp. **117m/C DVD.** *US* Delroy Lindo, Idris Elba, Loretta Devine, Sharon Leal, Lauren London, Reina King, Chris Brown, Keith D. Robinson, Laz Alonso, Columbus Short, Mekhi Phifer; ***D:*** Preston A. Whitmore II; ***W:*** Preston A. Whitmore II; ***C:*** Alexander Grusynski.

This Could Be the Night ♪♪ 1/2 **1957** Rocco and Tony are two small-fry gangsters who run a nightclub. Anne is a prim schoolteacher who takes a part-time job as their secretary. She falls for the handsome Tony much to the dismay of Rocco who knows his partner's less-than-sterling character. Sweet but minor comedy. Franciosa's first film. ♫This Could Be The Night; Hustlin' News Gal; I Got It Bad; I'm Gonna Live Till I Die; Taking a Chance on Love; Trumpet Boogie; Mamba Combo; Blue Moon; Dream Dancing. **105m/B VHS.** Jean Simmons, Paul Douglas, Anthony (Tony) Franciosa, Joan Blondell, Julie Wilson, Neile Adams, J. Carrol Naish, Rafael Campos, Zasu Pitts, Tom Helmore; ***D:*** Robert Wise.

This England ♪ 1/2 **1942** Patriotic morale booster is a rather dull jog through Britain's fight for freedom as an American journalist, visiting England, learns a village's history from a country squire, including surviving the Norman conquest, Spanish Armada, Napoleonic Wars, WWI, and the 1940 air attacks. **84m/B VHS.** *GB* Emlyn Williams, John Clements, Constance Cummings; ***D:*** David MacDonald.

This Film Is Not Yet Rated ♪♪ **2006** Veteran filmmaker Kirby Dick tackles the secrecy surrounding the MPAA ratings board, with Dick out to illustrate their nonsensical approach to the process. Created in 1968, its anonymous panel (which Dick aims to identify) is frequently accused of being lenient towards violence and uptight about sex. Filmmakers generally have no way of knowing just what the board objects to since they don't offer specific criticism because that would be censorship. Kirby uses some questionable methods to get board members on camera and he has no particular suggestions about reform, but if you're interested in filmmaking, the documentary and its revealing interviews makes for compelling viewing. **97m/C DVD.** *US* ***D:*** Kirby Dick; ***C:*** Shana Hagan, Kirsten Johnson, Amy Vincent.

This Girl's Life ♪♪ **2003 (R)** Moon (knockout Marquis in her film debut) is a forthright beauty who likes sex and makes her living in the porn industry. Film is matter-of-fact about her life, which includes caring for her Pops (Woods), who has Parkinson's, worrying about an AIDS scare, and wondering about a budding relationship with a non-industry boyfriend (Pardue). Kudos to director/writer Ash for making a flick that's compelling without being violent or exploitative despite its subject matter. **101m/C DVD.** James Woods, Kip Pardue, Tomas Arana, Michael Rapaport, Juliette Marquis, Rosario Dawson, Ioan Gruffudd, Isaiah Washington IV, Cheyenne Silver, Kam Heskin, Natalie Taylor; ***D:*** Ash; ***W:*** Ash; ***C:*** Alessandro Zezza; ***M:*** Agartha Halou.

This Gun for Hire ♪♪♪ 1/2 **1942** In his first major film role, Ladd plays a hired gun seeking retribution from a client who betrays him. Preston is the cop pursuing him and hostage Lake. Ladd's performance as the cold-blooded killer with a soft spot for cats is stunning; his train-yard scene is an emotional powerhouse. Based on Graham Greene's novel "A Gun for Sale." Remade as "Short Cut to Hell." The first of several films using the Ladd-Lake team, but the only one in which Ladd played a villain. **81m/B VHS, DVD.** Alan Ladd, Veronica Lake, Robert Preston, Laird Cregar, Tully Marshall, Marc Lawrence, Yvonne De Carlo; ***D:*** Frank Tuttle; ***W:*** Albert (John B. Sherry) Maltz, W.R. Burnett; ***C:*** John Seitz; ***M:*** David Buttolph.

This Gun for Hire ♪♪ **1990 (R)** A professional assassin finds that he has been duped into killing a powerful political figure, whom he was told was a New Orleans mobster. Now on the run, he takes a nightclub performer hostage, unaware that she is the fiance of the FBI agent who is after him. All odds are against him, but the special relationship he forms with the woman may just be his ticket out. Adapted from novel by Graham Greene. **89m/C VHS.** Robert Wagner, Nancy Everhard, Frederic Lehne, John Harkins; ***D:*** Lou Antonio.

This Happy Breed ♪♪♪ 1/2 **1947** A celebrated film version of Noel Coward's classic play depicts the changing fortunes of a large family in England between the world wars. Happiness, hardships, triumph and tragedy mix a series of memorable episodes, including some of the most cherished moments in popular British cinema, though its appeal is universal. **114m/C VHS.** *GB* Robert Newton, Celia Johnson, John Mills, Kay Walsh, Stanley Holloway, Amy Veness, Alison Leggatt, Eileen Erskine, John Blythe, Guy Verney, Betty Fleetwood, Merle Tottenham; ***D:*** David Lean; ***W:*** David Lean, Noel Coward, Ronald Neame; ***C:*** Ronald Neame; ***M:*** Noel Coward, Muir Mathieson; ***Nar:*** Laurence Olivier.

This Happy Feeling ♪♪ 1/2 **1958** Reynolds is a young woman who is romantically attracted to both Jurgens, a sophisticated retired actor, and Saxon, a younger suitor who is Jurgens' neighbor. Good acting all around. Charming telling of old tale. **83m/C VHS.** Curt Jurgens, Debbie Reynolds, John Saxon, Alexis Smith, Mary Astor, Estelle Winwood; ***D:*** Blake Edwards; ***W:*** Blake Edwards.

This Is a Hijack ♪ **1973 (PG)** Gambler hijacks the plane carrying his wealthy boss to help pay his debts. What it lacks in suspense, it lacks in performance and direction as well. **90m/C VHS.** Adam Roarke, Neville Brand, Jay Robinson, Lynn Borden, Dub Taylor; ***D:*** Barry Pollack; ***C:*** Bruce Logan; ***M:*** Charles Alden.

This Is Elvis ♪♪ **1981 (PG)** The life of Elvis, combining documentary footage with dramatizations of events in his life. Includes more than three dozen songs. Generally seen as an attempt to cash in on the myth, but was well-received by his fans. **144m/C VHS.** Elvis Presley; ***D:*** Malcolm Leo, Andrew Solt; ***W:*** Malcolm Leo, Andrew Solt; ***C:*** Gil Hubbs.

This Is England ♪♪ **2006** Meadows' autobiographical film about a lonely 12-year-old who is befriended by local skinheads in 1983 Britain. Shaun (non-pro Turgoose), whose soldier dad was killed in the Falklands, lives with his mum in a rundown community. He stands up to the teasing of the (essentially harmless) neighborhood gang and earns the respect of young leader Woody (Gilgun). Things change when older Combo (Graham) gets out of prison. A supporter of the National Front, Combo's racist rhetoric causes a split, but Shaun sticks with him since he sees Combo as a surrogate dad. **98m/C DVD.** *GB* Stephen Graham, Thomas Turgoose, Joe Gilgun, Vicky McClure, Andrew Shim, Jo Hartley; ***D:*** Shane Meadows; ***W:*** Shane Meadows; ***C:*** Danny Cohen; ***M:*** Ludovico Einaudi.

This Is My Father ♪♪ 1/2 **1999 (R)** Teacher Kieran Johnson (Caan) decides to research his Irish roots after discovering a photo of his mother with a mystery man who may have been his father. Told in flashback, it portraits the class differences in rural Ireland in the '30s and the doomed romance between wealthy, teenaged Fiona Flynn (Farrelly) and Kieran O'Dea (Quinn), a poor tenant farmer who works for the Flynn family. Affecting role for Aidan Quinn, who worked with brothers Paul and Declan. Script is based on a story Theresa Quinn told her children. **120m/C VHS, DVD.** Aidan Quinn, James Caan, Stephen Rea, Moya Farrelly, John Cusack, Jacob Tierney, Colm Meaney, Donal Donnelly, Brendan Gleeson; ***D:*** Paul Quinn; ***W:*** Paul Quinn; ***C:*** Declan Quinn; ***M:*** Donal Lunny.

This Is My Life ♪♪ **1992 (PG-13)** The story of a working mother torn between her skyrocketing career as a stand-up comic and her two daughters. Kavner plays the divorced mom who is determined to chuck her cosmetic sales job for comic success. Her career starts to really take off; she hires an agent and makes appearances on talk shows. As offers pour in, she eventually realizes that her girls are suffering as a result of her success. Good performances highlight an otherwise average drama. **105m/C VHS.** Julie Kavner, Samantha Mathis, Carrie Fisher, Dan Aykroyd, Gaby Hoffman; ***D:*** Nora Ephron; ***W:*** Nora Ephron, Delia Ephron.

This Is Not a Love Song ♪♪ **2002** Petty criminal Heaton (Glenaan) has just picked up his pal Spike (Colgan) who was doing a short stint in a Glasgow prison. When their car runs out of gas on a lonely country road, they hike to the nearest farm in search of help. Too bad the farmer thinks these ruffians are there to rob the place. In the ensuing confusion, Spike accidentally shoots and kills the farmer's daughter. Now the two friends take off across the moors—pursued not only by the police but by a vigilante group of locals. Title is taken from the Public Image Ltd. song that is heard in various versions. **92m/C VHS, DVD.** *GB* Michael Colgan, Kenny Glenaan, David Bradley, John Henshaw; ***D:*** Bille Eltringham; ***W:*** Simon Beaufoy; ***C:*** Robbie Ryan; ***M:*** Adrian Johnston, Mark Rutherford.

This Is Not a Test ♪♪ **1962** When news comes of an impending nuclear attack, a state trooper at a roadblock offers sanctuary to passing travellers. The effectiveness of the film's social commentary is hindered by its small budget. **72m/B VHS, DVD.** Seamon Glass, Mary Morlass, Thayer Roberts, Aubrey Martin; ***D:*** Frederic Gadette; ***W:*** Frederic Gadette, Peter Abenheim, Betty Laskey; ***C:*** Brick Marquard; ***M:*** Greig McRitchie.

This Is Spinal Tap ♪♪♪ 1/2 *Spinal Tap* **1984 (R)** Pseudo-rockumentary about heavy-metal band Spinal Tap, profiling their career from "England's loudest band" to an entry in the "where are they now file." Hilarious satire, featuring music performed by Guest, McKean, Shearer, and others. Included are Spinal Tap's music video "Hell Hole," and an ad for their greatest hits album, "Heavy Metal Memories." Features great cameos, particularly David Letterman's Paul Shaffer as a record promoter and Billy Crystal as a surly mime. First feature for Reiner (Meathead on "All in the Family"). Followed by "The Return of Spinal Tap." **82m/C VHS, DVD, Blu-ray Disc.** Michael McKean, Christopher Guest, Harry Shearer, Tony Hendra, Bruno Kirby, Rob Reiner, June Chadwick, Howard Hesseman, Billy Crystal, Dana Carvey, Ed Begley Jr., Patrick Macnee, Fran Drescher, Paul Shaffer, Anjelica Huston, Fred Willard, Paul Benedict, Archie Hahn; ***D:*** Rob Reiner; ***W:*** Michael McKean, Christopher Guest, Harry Shearer, Rob Reiner; ***C:*** Peter Smokler; ***M:*** Michael McKean, Christopher Guest, Harry Shearer, Rob Reiner. Natl. Film Reg. '02.

This Is the Army ♪♪ 1/2 **1943** A robust tribute to the American soldier of WWII based on the hit play by Irving Berlin. Murphy, who later was a senator from California, played Reagan's father. ♫Your Country and My Country; My Sweetie; Poor Little Me, I'm on K.P.; We're On Our Way to France; What Does He Look Like?; This is the Army, Mr. Jones; I'm Gettin' Tired So I Can Sleep; Mandy; Ladies of the Chorus. **105m/C VHS, DVD.** George Murphy, Joan Leslie, Ronald Reagan, Alan Hale, Kate Smith, George Tobias, Irving Berlin, Joe Louis; ***D:*** Michael Curtiz; ***M:*** Max Steiner. Oscars '43: Scoring/Musical.

This Is the Sea ♪♪ 1/2 **1996 (R)** Belfast Protestant teenager Hazel Stokes (Morton) falls in love with Catholic boy, Malachy

McAliskey (McDade), with trouble sure to follow. Interesting cast but the film winds up being simplistic and cliched. Director McGuckian also appears as Cathy, Padhar McAliskey's girlfriend, who is played by McGuckian's husband, Lynch. Title comes from a 1985 Waterboys song. **104m/C VHS.** *IR* Mary McGuckian, Samantha Morton, Ross McDade, Richard Harris, John Lynch, Gabriel Byrne, Marc O'Shea, Des McAleer; ***D:*** Mary McGuckian; ***W:*** Mary McGuckian; ***C:*** Des Whelan.

This Island Earth 𝒮𝒮 1/2 **1955** The planet Metaluna is in desperate need of uranium to power its defense against enemy invaders. A nuclear scientist and a nuclear fission expert from Earth are kidnapped to help out. The first serious movie about interplanetary escapades. Bud Westmore created pulsating cranium special effects makeup. **86m/C VHS, DVD.** Jeff Morrow, Faith Domergue, Rex Reason, Russell Johnson; ***D:*** Joseph M. Newman; ***M:*** Herman Stein.

This Land Is Mine 𝒮𝒮𝒮 **1943** A timid French schoolteacher gathers enough courage to defy the Nazis when they attempt to occupy his town. Laughton's characterization is effective as the meek fellow who discovers the hero within himself in this patriotic wartime flick. **103m/B VHS.** Charles Laughton, Maureen O'Hara, George Sanders, Walter Slezak, George Coulouris, Una O'Connor; ***D:*** Jean Renoir. Oscars '43: Sound.

This Lightning Always Strikes Twice **1985** An elegant murder mystery made for British television. **60m/C VHS.** *GB* Amanda Root, Julia Goodman, Claire Bloom, Trevor Howard, Charles Dance; ***D:*** David Carson; ***W:*** Michael Robson. **TV**

This Man Must Die 𝒮𝒮𝒮 1/2 *Que La Bete Meure; Uccidero Un Uomo; Killer!* **1970 (PG)** A man searches relentlessly for the driver who killed his young son in a hit-and-run. When found, the driver engages him in a complex cat-and-mouse chase. Another stunning crime and punishment tale from Chabrol. **112m/C VHS, DVD.** *FR* Michel Duchaussoy, Caroline Cellier, Jean Yanne, Anouk Ferjac, Maurice Pialat; ***D:*** Claude Chabrol; ***W:*** Paul Gegauff; ***C:*** Jean Rabier.

This Matter of Marriage 𝒮 1/2 **1998** Hallie Mitchell (Hope) and Donnalee Crawford (Miller) are best friends and struggling business partners who have sacrificed their personal lives for their careers as architects. Guy-next-door Steve (Peters) is interested in Hallie but she thinks he's a lunkhead. She'll change her mind. From the Harlequin Romance Series; adapted from the Debbie Macomber novel. **95m/C DVD.** *CA* Leslie Hope, Rick Peters, Sherry Miller, Michael Nouri, Karl Pruner, Carl Marotte, Natasha Greenblatt; ***D:*** Brad Turner; ***W:*** Peter Lauterman; ***C:*** John Berrie; ***M:*** Christopher Dedrick. **TV**

This Property Is Condemned 𝒮𝒮 **1966** It's a hot time down south once again in this adaptation of the Tennessee Williams play. Wood is the overly flirtatious southern charmer who takes a shine to the latest tenant of her loathsome mama's boardinghouse. And since it's Redford, who can blame her. Things steam up when he returns her interest but there's trouble a'brewin'. Both leads are lovely but the film itself is overly southern-fried. Williams was reportedly unhappy with the script and wanted his name removed from the film. **109m/C VHS, DVD.** Robert Redford, Natalie Wood, Charles Bronson, Kate Reid, Mary Badham, Jon(athan) Provost, Robert (Bobby) Blake, John Harding; ***D:*** Sydney Pollack; ***W:*** Francis Ford Coppola, Edith Sommer, Fred Coe.

This Revolution 𝒮𝒮 **2005** An action-addict network TV reporter (Crooker) covers the street protests that preceded the NYC-GOP convention. The blending of real footage with fictional is most effective and difficult to distinguish. Gives a relatively interesting twist on a topic covered in documentaries like "Fahrenheit 9/11" and "Bush's Brain." Movie became part of the story when Dawson was arrested at one of the rallies being filmed. **95m/C DVD.** *US* Nathan Crooker, Rosario Dawson, Amy Redford, Brendan Sexton III, Brett DelBuono; ***D:*** Stephen Marshall; ***W:*** Stephen Marshall; ***C:*** Brian Jackson.

This Special Friendship 𝒮𝒮 1/2 *Les Amities Particulieres* **1967** Powerful, if overdone French drama about an emotionally sensitive young man at a Catholic boarding school. His sexual relationship with another boy leads to tragedy. Based on the novel by Roger Peyrefitte. **99m/B VHS.** *FR* Francis Lacombrade, Didier Haudepin, Lucien Nat, Louis Seigner, Michel Bouquet, Francois Leccia; ***D:*** Jean Delannoy.

This Sporting Life 𝒮𝒮𝒮 **1963** A gritty, depressing portrait of former coal miner Frank Machin (Harris), who breaks into the violent world of professional rugby, and whose inability to handle social differences causes problems. He begins an affair with widow Mrs. Hammond (Roberts), from whom he rents a room, but finds they are capable of only a physical attachment. One of the best of the British early '60s working-class angry young man melodramas. **134m/B VHS, DVD.** *GB* Richard Harris, Rachel Roberts, Alan Badel, William Hartnell, Colin Blakely, Vanda Godsell, Arthur Lowe; ***D:*** Lindsay Anderson; ***W:*** David Storey; ***C:*** Denys Coop; ***M:*** Roberto Gerhard. British Acad. '63: Actress (Roberts); Cannes '63: Actor (Harris).

This Stuff'll Kill Ya! **WOOF!** **1971 (PG)** A backwoods preacher who believes in free love and moonshining runs into trouble with the locals when a series of gruesome religious murders are committed. Southern drive-in material from one of the genre's masters. Holt's last film. **100m/C VHS, DVD.** Jeffrey Allen, Tim Holt, Gloria King, Ray Sager, Eric Bradly, Terence McCarthy, Larry Drake; ***D:*** Herschell Gordon Lewis; ***W:*** Herschell Gordon Lewis; ***C:*** Alex Ameri; ***M:*** Herschell Gordon Lewis.

This Sweet Sickness 𝒮𝒮 1/2 *Dites-Lui Que Je L'Aime* **1977** Destructive passion and sexual delusion is explored in this adaptation of the Patricia Highsmith novel. David seems to be a hardworking loner who is loved by the sweet Juliette. Rejected by him, Juliette then discovers that David has built a remote mountain chalet for the woman he does love, Lise, who's married and unaware of David's obsessional devotions. Extravagant emotions lead to tragedy. In French with English subtitles. **107m/C VHS.** *FR* Gerard Depardieu, Miou-Miou, Dominique Laffin, Claude Pieplu, Christian Clavier, Jacques Denis, Josiane Balasko, Veronique Silver, Jacqueline Jeanne, Michel Such; ***D:*** Claude Miller; ***W:*** Claude Miller, Luc Beraud; ***C:*** Pierre Lhomme.

This Thing of Ours 𝒮 **2003** Lame wiseguy movie hits all the cliches as broadly as possible. Ambitious hood Nick Santini (Provenzano) wants to impress the old New Jersey mobsters so he schemes with some pals to use computers to siphon off money from bank accounts worldwide and stash the cash offshore. Provenzano went to prison for tax evasion and racketeering so you'd think his experience would make the flick more compelling—no dice. **100m/C DVD.** *US* Christian Maelen, Louis Vanaria, Frank Vincent, James Caan, Danny Provenzano, Vincent Pastore; ***D:*** Danny Provenzano; ***W:*** Danny Provenzano, Tewd A. Bohus.

This Time I'll Make You Rich 𝒮 **1975 (PG)** Two American hoodlums work out a drug-ring heist in the Far East. Parolini used the pseudonym Frank Kramer. **97m/C VHS.** Antonio (Tony) Sabato, Robin McDavid; ***D:*** Gianfranco Parolini.

This Woman Is Dangerous 𝒮𝒮 1/2 **1952** Crawford's last role under her Warner Bros.' contract finds her portraying a gangster's moll with a criminal record of her own. Beth Austin is loved by jealous killer Matt Jackson (Brian). After another heist, Beth learns she's going blind and goes into the hospital for eye surgery, performed by Dr. Ben Halleck (Morgan). The two fall in love while Matt is in hiding and the FBI is tracking them down. When Matt learns his gal loves another, he decides to eliminate the competition. **97m/B DVD.** Joan Crawford, Dennis Morgan, David Brian, Richard Webb, Mari Aldon, Phil Carey, Ian MacDonald; ***D:*** Felix Feist; ***W:*** Daniel Mainwaring, George Worthing Yates; ***C:*** Ted D. McCord; ***M:*** David Buttolph.

This World, Then the Fireworks 𝒮𝒮 1/2 **1997 (R)** Long on style but short on substance, overwrought neo-noir tells the tragic tale of traumatized twins living a totally debauched life. After seeing their father murdered in a romantic triangle, which left their mother (McClanahan) with physical and emotional scars, brother Marty (Zane) and sister Carol (Gershon) cling to each other as they grow up and engage in an implied incestuous relationship. The duo winds up grifters, murdering and pillaging their way through a small coastal town in the 1950s. Lee plays a messed-up cop who, tragically, becomes an easy mark for Marty. Based on a 1955 short story by Jim Thompson, director Oblowitz's debut gets too caught up in the excesses of pulp and focuses on slick visuals and dramatic score over a coherent story. Well-cast performances are universally solid and engaging. **100m/C VHS.** Billy Zane, Gina Gershon, Sheryl Lee, Rue McClanahan, Seymour Cassel, Will Patton, Richard Edson, William Hootkins; ***D:*** Michael Oblowitz; ***W:*** Larry Gross; ***C:*** Tom Priestley; ***M:*** Pete Rugolo.

Thomas and the Magic Railroad 𝒮𝒮 **2000 (G)** Thomas, a spunky blue steam engine, is bullied by big bad engine, Diesel, and aided by Mr. Conductor (Baldwin), as well as young Lily (Wilson) and her train-loving grandad (Fonda) who also come to Thomas' rescue. Part live-action, part animation adaptation of the British children's series will be fine for the kidlets but parents will overdose on the whimsy factor. **84m/C VHS, DVD.** Mara Wilson, Alec Baldwin, Peter Fonda, Didi Conn; ***D:*** Britt Allcroft; ***W:*** Britt Allcroft; ***C:*** Paul Ryan; ***M:*** Hummie Mann.

The Thomas Crown Affair 𝒮𝒮𝒮 *Thomas Crown and Company; The Crown Caper* **1968 (R)** A multimillionaire (McQueen) decides to plot and execute the perfect theft, a daring daylight robbery of a bank. Dunaway is the gorgeous and efficient insurance investigator determined to nab him. One of the best visual scenes is the chess match between the two as they begin to fall in love. Strong production with Oscar-winning theme "The Windmills of Your Mind." ♫ The Windmills of Your Mind. **102m/C VHS, DVD.** Steve McQueen, Faye Dunaway, Jack Weston, Yaphet Kotto, Gordon Pinsent; ***D:*** Norman Jewison; ***W:*** Alan R. Trustman; ***C:*** Haskell Wexler. Oscars '68: Song ("The Windmills of Your Mind"); Golden Globes '69: Song ("The Windmills of Your Mind").

The Thomas Crown Affair 𝒮𝒮𝒮 **1999 (R)** Slick, lavish, updated, and loose adaptation of the 1968 Steve McQueen/Faye Dunaway caper. Thomas Crown (Brosnan) is a self-made New York billionaire, who just can't resist pulling off the perfect crime by stealing a Monet from the Metropolitan Museum of Art. Catherine Banning (Russo) is the gorgeous insurance investigator on his trail, who can't help falling for the very charming criminal. The fortysomething duo sizzle (how fantastic to see two age-appropriate lovers for a change) and if the ending has a tacked-on feel, it doesn't really matter. Dunaway makes a cameo appearance as Crown's therapist. **111m/C VHS, DVD.** Pierce Brosnan, Rene Russo, Denis Leary, Frankie Faison, Ben Gazzara, Fritz Weaver, Charles Keating, Mark Margolis, Faye Dunaway, Esther Canadas; ***D:*** John McTiernan; ***W:*** Leslie Dixon, Kurt Wimmer; ***C:*** Tom Priestley; ***M:*** Bill Conti.

Thomas Graal's Best Film 𝒮𝒮𝒮 **1917** The famous comical adventures of a film scriptwriter wooing his secretary, followed by "Thomas Graal's First Child." Silent. **70m/B VHS.** *SW* Victor Sjostrom, Karin Molander; ***D:*** Mauritz Stiller.

Thomas Graal's First Child 𝒮𝒮𝒮 **1918** The sequel to "Thomas Graal's Best Film." The comical screenwriter and actress couple attempt to raise a baby. Silent. **70m/B VHS.** Victor Sjostrom, Karin Molander; ***D:*** Mauritz Stiller.

Thomas in Love 𝒮𝒮 *Thomas Est Amoureux* **2001** Oddball Belgian drama set slightly in the future where agoraphobic Thomas (Verhaert) spends all his time on his computer—living his life through its screen. In fact, the viewer never sees Thomas, just hears his voice and sees what he sees, including his arrangements for therapy and cybersex. French with subtitles. **97m/C VHS, DVD.** *BE* Benoit Verhaert, Aylin Yay, Magali Pinglault, Micheline Hardy, Alexandre von Sivers, Frederic Topart, Serge Lariviere; ***D:*** Pierre-Paul Renderss; ***W:*** Philippe Blasband; ***C:*** Virginie Saint-Martin; ***M:*** Igor Sterpin.

Thompson's Last Run 𝒮 1/2 **1990** Boyhood friends grow up on either side of the law. They come face-to-face, though, when one is assigned to transport the other to prison. **95m/C VHS, DVD.** Robert Mitchum, Wilford Brimley, Kathleen York, Susan Tyrrell; ***D:*** Jerrold Freedman; ***M:*** Miles Goodman. **TV**

Thor and the Amazon Women 𝒮 *Women Gladiators* **1960** The mighty Thor leads his enslaved men on an attack against the evil Queen Nera and her female-dominated Amazon society. **85m/C VHS, DVD.** *IT* Harry Baird, Maria Fiore, Claudia Capone, Alberto Cerenini, Antonio Leonviola, Jannin Hendy, Joe Robinson, Susy Andersen; ***W:*** Fabio Piccioni; ***C:*** Guglielmo Mancori; ***M:*** Roberto Nicolosi.

The Thorn 𝒮 1/2 **1974 (R)** The Virgin Mary and Joseph try to raise Jesus Christ in the modern world. **90m/C VHS.** Bette Midler, John Bassberger; ***D:*** Peter Alexander.

The Thorn Birds 𝒮𝒮𝒮 **1983** Pioneers find danger and romance in the Australian outback as they struggle to begin a dynasty. Charismatic priest sometimes hurts, sometimes helps them. One of Stanwyck's last performances; Ward's American TV debut. Originally a ten-hour TV miniseries based on Colleen McCullough novel. Emmy nominations for actor Chamberlain, supporting actors Brown and Plummer, supporting actress Laurie, direction, photography, music, costume design, and editing. **486m/C VHS, DVD.** Rachel Ward, Richard Chamberlain, Jean Simmons, Ken Howard, Mare Winningham, Richard Kiley, Piper Laurie, Bryan Brown, Christopher Plummer, Barbara Stanwyck; ***D:*** Daryl Duke; ***C:*** Bill Butler; ***M:*** Henry Mancini. **TV**

The Thorn Birds: The Missing Years 𝒮𝒮𝒮 **1996** Follow-up to the critically acclaimed miniseries "The Thorn Birds." Fills in the 19-year gap since the original romantic melodrama aired. **178m/C DVD.** Richard Chamberlain, Amanda Donohoe, Julia Blake, Olivia Burnette, Michael Caton, Zach English, Peter Ford, Jonathan Hardy, Ingrid Mason, Maximilian Schell, Jack Thompson, Simon Westaway, Paul Bertram, Rob Doran, Christopher Gabardi, Adam Grossetti, John Heywood, Phillip Hinton, Enrico Mammarella, Marijke Mann, Todd Schulberg; ***D:*** Kevin James Dobson; ***W:*** David Stevens, Colleen McCullough; ***C:*** Ross Berryman; ***M:*** Garry McDonald, Lawrence Stone. **TV**

Thoroughbreds Don't Cry 𝒮𝒮 1/2 **1937** Rooney plays a jockey who throws a race so his no-good father can win enough money to pay for his supposed medical problems. The owner of the horse then drops dead from a heart attack. Rooney feels guilty, so he asks his father to loan the owner's grandson $1,000 to run in another race. His father says no, so Rooney steals the money from him, and when the father finds out he tells the track officials that Rooney threw the race. Garland is Rooney's best friend and moral support, and she sings a few songs too! A fairly good horse racing story. **80m/B VHS.** Judy Garland, Mickey Rooney, Sophie Tucker, Sir C. Aubrey Smith, Ronald Sinclair, Forrester Harvey; ***D:*** Alfred E. Green.

Thoroughly Modern Millie 𝒮𝒮 1/2 **1967 (G)** Andrews is a young woman who comes to New York in the early 1920s where she meets another newcomer, the innocent Moore. Andrews decides to upgrade her image to that of a "modern" woman, a flapper, and sets out to realize her ambition, to become a stenographer and marry the boss. Meanwhile, Moore has become an object of interest to Lillie, who just happens to run a white-slavery ring. Lots of frantic moments and big production numbers in this campy film. Channing and Lillie are exceptional fun. ♫ Thoroughly Modern Millie; The Tapioca; Jimmy; The Jewish Wedding Song; Baby Face; Do It Again; Poor Butterfly; Rose of Washington Square; I Can't Believe That You're In Love With Me. **138m/C VHS, DVD.** Julie Andrews, Carol Channing, Mary Tyler Moore, John Gavin, Beatrice Lillie, James Fox, Noriyuki "Pat" Morita; ***D:*** George Roy Hill; ***W:*** Richard Morris; ***C:*** Russell Metty; ***M:*** Elmer Bernstein. Oscars '67: Orig. Score; Golden Globes '68: Support. Actress (Channing).

Those Calloways 𝒥𝒥 1/2 **1965 (PG)** A small town family attempts to establish a sanctuary for the flocks of wild geese who fly over the woods of Swiftwater, Maine. Fine Disney family fare, with good cast. Based on Paul Annixter's novel "Swiftwater." **131m/C VHS, DVD.** Brian Keith, Vera Miles, Brandon de Wilde, Walter Brennan, Ed Wynn, John Qualen, Linda Evans; ***D:*** Norman Tokar; ***W:*** Louis Pelletier; ***C:*** Edward Colman; ***M:*** Max Steiner.

Those Daring Young Men in Their Jaunty Jalopies 𝒥𝒥 *Monte Carlo or Bust; Quei Temerari Sulle Loro Pazze, Scatenate, Scalcinate Carriole* **1969 (G)** Daring young men in noisy slow cars trek 1500 miles across country in the 1920s and call it a race. **125m/C VHS, DVD.** *GB* Tony Curtis, Susan Hampshire, Terry-Thomas, Eric Sykes, Gert Frobe, Peter Cook, Dudley Moore, Jack Hawkins; ***D:*** Ken Annakin; ***W:*** Ken Annakin, Jack Davies; ***C:*** Gabor Pogany; ***M:*** Ronald Goodwin.

Those Endearing Young Charms 𝒥𝒥 **1945** Romance develops between a young Air Corps mechanic and a salesgirl. Complications arise when another man enters the scene. Light romantic comedy. Based on the play by Edward Chodorov. **82m/B VHS.** Robert Young, Laraine Day, Anne Jeffreys, Lawrence Tierney; ***D:*** Lewis Allen.

Those Fantastic Flying Fools 𝒥𝒥 1/2 *Blast-Off; Jules Verne's Rocket to the Moon* **1967** A mad race to be the first on the moon brings hilarious results. Loosely based on a Jules Verne story. **95m/C VHS, DVD.** *GB* Burl Ives, Troy Donahue, Gert Frobe, Terry-Thomas, Hermione Gingold, Daliah Lavi, Lionel Jeffries; ***D:*** Don Sharp.

Those Glory, Glory Days 𝒥 1/2 **1983** An English woman, secure in her position as an outstanding sports journalist, reminisces about the days when she and her friends idolized the boys on the soccer team. Nothing extraordinary, but nicely made. **92m/C VHS, DVD.** *GB* Zoe Nathenson, Liz Campion, Cathy Murphy; ***D:*** Philip Saville; ***M:*** Trevor Jones.

Those Lips, Those Eyes 𝒥𝒥 1/2 **1980 (R)** A pre-med student takes a job as a prop boy in a summer stock company and winds up falling in love with the company's lead dancer. Sub-plot about aging actor is more interesting, better played by Langella. O'Connor is appropriately lovely. Nicely made, charming sleeper of a film. **106m/C VHS.** Frank Langella, Tom Hulce, Glynnis O'Connor, Jerry Stiller, Kevin McCarthy; ***D:*** Michael Pressman.

Those Magnificent Men in Their Flying Machines 𝒥𝒥𝒥 **1965** In 1910, a wealthy British newspaper publisher is persuaded to sponsor an air race from London to Paris. Contestants come from all over the world and shenanigans, hijinks, double-crosses, and romance are found along the route. Skelton has fun in prologue, while Terry-Thomas is great as the villain. Fun from start to finish. **138m/C VHS, DVD.** *GB* Stuart Whitman, Sarah Miles, Robert Morley, Alberto Sordi, James Fox, Gert Frobe, Jean-Pierre Cassel, Flora Robson, Sam Wanamaker, Terry-Thomas, Irina Demick, Benny Hill, Gordon Jackson, Millicent Martin, Red Skelton; ***D:*** Ken Annakin; ***W:*** Ken Annakin, Jack Davies.

Those People Next Door 𝒥 1/2 **1952** Class-conscious family drama, based on the play by Zelda Davees, remains static and stagebound. Working-class Anne Twigg (Cufts) falls in love with WWII RAF officer Victor Stevens (Forbes-Robertson) to the dismay of both sets of parents. However, when Victor goes missing in action after being shot down, it brings everyone together. **77m/B DVD.** *GB* Patricia Cufts, Peter Forbes-Robertson, Jack Warner, Marjorie Rhodes, Garry Marsh, Anthony Newley, Gladys Henson, Charles Victor; ***D:*** Anthony Newley, John Harlow; ***W:*** John Harlow; ***C:*** Roy Fogwell.

Those Who Love Me Can Take the Train 𝒥𝒥 *Ceux Qui M'Aiment Predront le Train* **1998** Bisexual artist Jean-Baptiste Emmerich (Trintignant) has died in Paris but wished to be buried in his hometown of Limoges—a four-hour train trip for his motley group of mourners, which include friends, relatives, and former lovers of both sexes. Things don't calm down at the cemetery where yet more relatives await, including the artist's estranged twin brother. Rather than bonding in grief, the trip and funeral succeed in bringing out old hurts and rivalries and causing the shakeup of more than one relationship. French with subtitles. **122m/C VHS, DVD.** *FR* Jean-Louis Trintignant, Pascal Greggory, Charles Berling, Bruno Todeschini, Valeria Bruni-Tedeschi, Vincent Perez, Dominique Blanc, Sylvain Jacques, Marie Daems; ***D:*** Patrice Chereau; ***W:*** Patrice Chereau, Daniele Thompson, Pierre Trividic; ***C:*** Eric Gautier. Cesar '99: Cinematog., Director (Chereau), Support. Actress (Blanc).

Thou Shalt Not Kill...Except 𝒥 *Stryker's War* **1987** A Vietnam vet seeks revenge on the violent cult who kidnapped his girlfriend. **84m/C VHS, DVD.** Brian Schulz, Robert Rickman, John Manfredi, Tim Quill, Cheryl Hansen, Sam Raimi, Perry Mallette, Theodore (Ted) Raimi, Glenn Barr, Scott Spiegel, Bruce Campbell, Paul Grabke; ***D:*** Josh Becker; ***W:*** Josh Becker, Scott Spiegel; ***C:*** Josh Becker; ***M:*** Joseph LoDuca.

Though None Go With Me 𝒥𝒥 **2006** While Elizabeth (Grabow) is growing up during the 1950s, she devotes herself to a life of service to God. But over the years, the many hardships that follow have her questioning her faith even when she's courted by both Ben (Rowe) and Will (Narona). Ladd plays the older Elizabeth who recounts her story to her granddaughter. Based on the inspirational novel by Jerry B. Jenkins. **100m/C DVD.** Cheryl Ladd, Brad Rowe, Denise Grayson, Christopher Allport, Amy Grabow, David Narona; ***D:*** Armand Mastroianni; ***W:*** Pamela Wallace; ***C:*** Amit Bhattacharya; ***M:*** Nathan Furst. **CABLE**

Thoughts Are Free 𝒥𝒥𝒥 1/2 **1984 (PG)** A young soldier, wounded in WWII, escapes from the train that is transporting him and his comrades to a Soviet labor camp and rejoins his family. Under the repressive communist regime, he plots his family's escape to the West but his plans are thwarted when the Berlin Wall is erected, leaving him in the West and his wife and daughter in the East. As the years go by, they can get together only by outwitting the bureaucrats. The film's title is taken from an old German folk song "Die Gedanken sind frei." **93m/C VHS.** Herbert Ludwig, Kathrin Kratzer; ***D:*** Josef Sommer.

A Thousand Acres 𝒥𝒥 **1997 (R)** Based on Jane Smiley's Pulitzer Prize-winning novel, it's "King Lear" set on an Iowa farm. Sisters (Pfeiffer, Lange, and Leigh) discover that their father has decided to divide the family's thousand-acre farm amongst the three of them. Then stranger Firth comes to town and divides Pfeiffer and Lange even further by showing an interest in both of them. Melodramatic and contrived, with every hot-button women's issue imaginable thrown into the mix. Director Moorhouse purportedly considered removing her name from the picture. **105m/C VHS, DVD.** Jessica Lange, Michelle Pfeiffer, Jennifer Jason Leigh, Colin Firth, Jason Robards Jr., Keith Carradine, Pat Hingle, Kevin Anderson, John Carroll Lynch, Anne Pitoniak, Vyto Ruginis, Michelle Williams, Elisabeth (Elissabeth, Elizabeth, Liz) Moss; ***D:*** Jocelyn Moorhouse; ***W:*** Laura Jones; ***C:*** Tak Fujimoto; ***M:*** Richard Hartley.

A Thousand and One Nights 𝒥𝒥 1/2 **1945** Handsome Aladdin (Wilde) falls in love with beautiful Princess Armina (Jergens) but fate steps in and Aladdin and sidekick Abdullah (Silvers) are off in search of a magic lamp. This time around the genie is a beautiful woman (Keyes), who falls for Aladdin herself and tries to thwart his would-be romance. Clever fun. **92m/C VHS.** Cornel Wilde, Evelyn Keyes, Adele Jergens, Phil Silvers, Rex Ingram, Dennis Hoey, Philip Van Zandt, Gus Schilling; ***D:*** Alfred E. Green; ***W:*** Jack Henley, Richard English; ***C:*** Ray Rennahan; ***M:*** Marlin Skiles.

A Thousand Clowns 𝒥𝒥𝒥 **1965** A nonconformist has resigned from his job as chief writer for an obnoxious kiddie show in order to enjoy life. But his independence comes under fire when he becomes guardian for his young nephew and social workers take a dim view of his lifestyle. Balsam won an Oscar for his role as Robard's agent brother. Adapted from Herb Gardner's Broadway comedy. **118m/B VHS.** Jason Robards Jr., Barry J. Gordon, William Daniels, Barbara Harris, Gene Saks, Martin Balsam; ***D:*** Fred Coe; ***W:*** Herb Gardner; ***C:*** Arthur Ornitz. Oscars '65: Support. Actor (Balsam).

The Thousand Eyes of Dr. Mabuse 𝒥𝒥 1/2 *The Secret of Dr. Mabuse; The Diabolical Dr. Mabuse; The Shadow Versus the Thousand Eyes of Dr. Mabuse; Die Tausend Augen des Dr. Mabuse* **1960** Lang's last film is a return to his pre-war German character, the evil Dr. Mabuse. A series of strange murders occur in a Berlin hotel and police believe the killer thinks he's a reincarnation of the doctor. Disorienting chiller. German with subtitles. **103m/B VHS, DVD.** *GE* Dawn Addams, Peter Van Eyck, Gert Frobe, Wolfgang Preiss; ***D:*** Fritz Lang; ***W:*** Fritz Lang, Jan Fethke, Heinz Oskar Wuttig; ***C:*** Karl Lob; ***M:*** Gerhard Becker, Bert Grund.

A Thousand Heroes 𝒥𝒥 1/2 *Crash Landing: The Rescue of Flight 232* **1992 (PG)** Based on the true story of United Airlines Flight 232 which took off on a flight from Denver to Chicago and then suffered engine explosions over Iowa. The jumbo jet crashed in a fiery explosion but some 200 people survived. **95m/C VHS.** Leon Russom, John M. Jackson, Tom O'Brien, Philip Baker Hall, Richard Thomas, Charlton Heston, James Coburn; ***D:*** Lamont Johnson; ***W:*** Harve Bennett; ***C:*** William Wages; ***M:*** Charles Fox.

Thousand Pieces of Gold 𝒥𝒥𝒥 **1991 (PG-13)** A young Chinese woman is sold by her father to a marriage broker, but instead of a respectable marriage she is shipped to America and expected to work as a prostitute in an Idaho mining town. Instead she works taking in laundry as she tries to make her way in a man's world, finding a sweet romance of opposites along the way. Based on a true story. Excellent performances by Chao and Cooper. **105m/C VHS.** Rosalind Chao, Dennis Dun, Michael Paul Chan, Chris Cooper, Jimmie F. Skaggs, William Oldham, David Hayward, Beth Broderick; ***D:*** Nancy Kelly; ***W:*** Anne Makepeace; ***C:*** Bobby Bukowski; ***M:*** Gary Remal Malkin.

A Thousand Years of Good Prayers 𝒥𝒥 **2007** After his wife dies, Mr. Shi decides to travel to America and visit his estranged daughter Yilan in Spokane. However, Yilan barely acknowledges his presence as she continues to go on with her usual pursuits. Despite cultural shock and his limited English, Mr. Shi walks around the city, striking up conversations with strangers while struggling at home to reconnect with Yilan. English and Chinese with subtitles. **83m/C DVD.** Henry O, Feihong Yu, Vida Ghahremani, Pavel Lychnikoff; ***D:*** Wayne Wang; ***W:*** Yiyun Lee; ***C:*** Patrick Lindenmaier; ***M:*** Lesley Barber.

Thousands Cheer 𝒥𝒥 1/2 **1943** A flag-waving wartime musical about a tap-dancing Army private who falls in love with the colonel's daughter, culminating with an all-star (MGM) USO show. Songs include "Honeysuckle Rose," sung by Horne, and "The Joint Is Really Jumping Down at Carnegie Hall," sung by Garland. **126m/C VHS, DVD.** Gene Kelly, Kathryn Grayson, Judy Garland, Mickey Rooney, Mary Astor, John Boles, Lucille Ball, Eleanor Powell, Virginia O'Brien, Margaret O'Brien, Red Skelton, Lionel Barrymore, June Allyson, Frank Morgan, Kay Kyser, Bob Crosby, Lena Horne, Donna Reed; ***D:*** George Sidney; ***W:*** Paul Jarrico; ***C:*** George J. Folsey.

Thrashin' 𝒥 **1986 (PG-13)** A new-to-L.A. teen must prove himself to a tough gang on skateboards by skateboarding a certain treacherous race. For skateboarding fans only. **93m/C VHS, DVD.** Josh Brolin, Pamela Gidley, Robert Rusler, Chuck McCann; ***D:*** David Winters; ***W:*** Paul Bown; ***M:*** Barry Goldberg.

Threads 𝒥𝒥𝒥 **1985** The famed dramatic re-creation of the effects of nuclear war on a British city and two of its families. A disturbing, uncompromising, and somewhat plausible drama. **110m/C VHS.** *GB* Karen Meagher, Rita May, David Brierly, Reece Dinsdale, Harry Beety; ***D:*** Mick Jackson. **TV**

Threat 𝒥𝒥 1/2 **1949** A killer escapes from jail and returns to settle the score with those who convicted him. Tense, fast-moving thriller. **66m/B VHS.** Michael O'Shea, Virginia Grey, Charles McGraw; ***D:*** Felix Feist.

Threat of Exposure 𝒥 1/2 **2002 (R)** Hypnotherapist Dr. Daryl Sheleigh (Young) is having a problem with her patients—they keep disappearing. Cop Badger Welldon (Schaub) goes undercover as a patient to investigate since one of the missing is his younger brother. But disturbing secrets emerge from Badger's past, including an abusive childhood and his own violent nature, and evidence begins to point to Daryl as the prime suspect. It's all too easy to see where this wannabe thriller is headed. **90m/C DVD.** *US* Sean Young, William Devane, Will Schaub, D. Paul Thomas, Sara Crawford; ***D:*** Tom Whitus; ***W:*** Frederick Bailey, Jeno Hodl; ***C:*** Fred Paddock; ***M:*** Jamie Howarth, Kinny Landrum. **VIDEO**

Thr3e 𝒥 1/2 **2007 (PG-13)** Plodding Christian psycho-thriller features Seattle seminary student Kevin Parsons (Blucas) being targeted by a serial bomber known as the Riddle Killer. He calls his victims, accuses them of getting away with a crime, and then threatens to set off a bomb unless they confess. Except RK doesn't even play by his own rules. Adapted from the book by Ted Dekker. **101m/C DVD.** *US* Marc Blucas, Justine Waddell, Max Ryan, Priscilla Barnes, Laura Jordan, Tom Bower, Bill Moseley, Jeff Hollis, Philip Dunbar; ***D:*** Robby Henson; ***W:*** Alan B. McElroy; ***C:*** Sebastian Milaszewski; ***M:*** David Bergeaud.

Three Ages 𝒥𝒥𝒥 **1923** A parody of D.W. Griffith's 1916 film "Intolerance." Keaton's first feature film casts him in prehistoric days, ancient Rome, and in modern times. Silent with musical score. **59m/B VHS, DVD.** Wallace Beery, Oliver Hardy, Buster Keaton; ***D:*** Buster Keaton, Edward F. (Eddie) Cline.

3 A.M. 𝒥𝒥𝒥 **2001** Slice-of-life ensemble drama traces the doings of NYC cabbies over 36 hours. The struggling cab company, run by the owner's daughter Box (Choudhury), is on the verge of bankruptcy and her drivers are spooked by a serial killer targeting cabbies. Meawhile, Hershey (Glover) is stretching the patience of girlfriend George (Grier); Latina Salgado (Rodriguez) is tired of being sexually harassed; Bosian refugee Rasha (Tifunovic) is on the brink of being fired; and ambitious Jose (Cannavale) finds a briefcase of stolen money. **92m/C VHS, DVD.** Danny Glover, Pam Grier, Michelle Rodriguez, Sarita Choudhury, Sergej Trifunovic, Bobby Cannavale, Isaach de Bankole, Mike Starr, Paul Calderon; ***D:*** Lee Davis; ***W:*** Lee Davis; ***C:*** Enrique Chediak; ***M:*** Branford Marsalis. **CABLE**

Three Amigos 𝒥𝒥 **1986 (PG)** Three out-of-work silent screen stars are asked to defend a Mexican town from bandits; they think it's a public appearance stint. Spoof of Three Stooges and Mexican bandito movies that at times falls short, given the enormous amount of comedic talent involved. Generally enjoyable with some very funny scenes. Co-written by former "Saturday Night Live" producer Michaels. Short's first major film appearance. **105m/C VHS, DVD.** Chevy Chase, Steve Martin, Martin Short, Joe Mantegna, Patrice Martinez, Jon Lovitz, Phil Hartman, Randy Newman, Alfonso Arau; ***D:*** John Landis; ***W:*** Lorne Michaels, Steve Martin, Randy Newman; ***C:*** Ronald W. Browne; ***M:*** Elmer Bernstein.

The Three Avengers 𝒥𝒥 1/2 *Enter Three Dragons* **1980 (R)** Hung Tack (Lee) is the master of a kung fu school in a town plagued by two evil businessmen, who force Hung to take on the local gangs. During a fight, he's spotted by a talent scout and starts a career in the movies but is around to rescue a friend who's gotten into trouble. Hey, the fighting's the important part anyway. **93m/C VHS.** *HK* Dragon Lee, Bolo Yeung, Bruce Li, Bruce Lee; ***D:*** Wah Kay Wong; ***W:*** Wah Kay Wong; ***C:*** Chin Chiang Ma; ***M:*** Chao Wah Li.

Three Bad Men 𝒥 **2005 (PG-13)** Dull, incompetent western. Three bank robbers are heading for the Colorado border when they come across a dying man whose wife has been kidnapped. He begs them to rescue his missus and the outlaws must decide whether to risk their own lives or keep on riding. **118m/C DVD.** Mike Moroff, George Kennedy, Peter Brown, John Dixon, Chris Gann;

D: Jeff Hathcock; *W:* Jeff Hathcock; *M:* Tom Crosby.

Three Blind Mice 1/2 **2002 (R)** Hacker Thomas Cross (Furlong) is obsessed with Internet webcam sites. One night, he witnesses a grisly murder at his favorite website, but when he contacts the police, Thomas realizes he doesn't know the victim's real name or address. He's soon involved in the investigation by cop Claire (Fox). Mild and implausible thriller wannabe. **92m/C VHS, DVD.** *FR GB* Edward Furlong, Emilia Fox, Chiwetel Ejiofor, Ben Miles, Elsa Zylberstein, James Laurenson; *D:* Mathias Ledoux; *W:* Mikael Ollivier; *C:* Stephane Le Parc; *M:* Eric Neveux.

Three Blondes in His Life
1961 Looks like a pulp detective novel brought to big-screen life. Insurance investigator Duke Wallace (Mahoney) is looking into the disappearance of a fellow agent who's implicated in a jewel theft. The agent (who's been murdered) had affairs with three married blondes whom Wallace now has to question. It's a tough job. **81m/B DVD.** Jock Mahoney, Greta Thyssen, Anthony Dexter, Jesse White, Elaine Edwards, Valerie Porter; *D:* Leon Chooluck; *W:* George Moskov; *C:* Ernest Haller.

Three Broadway Girls *The Greeks Had a Word for Them* **1932** Three gold-diggers go husband-hunting. Well-paced, very funny telling of this old story. Remade many times, including "How to Marry a Millionaire," "Three Blind Mice," "Moon Over Miami," and "Three Little Girls in Blue." **78m/B VHS, DVD.** Joan Blondell, Ina Claire, Madge Evans, David Manners, Lowell Sherman; *D:* Lowell Sherman.

Three Brothers *Tre Fratelli* **1980 (PG)** An acclaimed Italian film by veteran Rosi about three brothers summoned to their small Italian village by a telegram saying their mother is dead. Sensitive and compassionate. In Italian with English subtitles. Adapted from Platonov's story "The Third Son." **113m/C VHS, DVD.** *IT* Philippe Noiret, Charles Vanel, Michele Placido, Vittorio Mezzogiorno, Andrea Ferreol, Simonetta Stefanelli; *D:* Francesco Rosi; *W:* Francesco Rosi; *C:* Pasqualino De Santis; *M:* Piero Piccioni.

Three Bullets for a Long Gun 1/2 **1973 (PG)** Two prairie renegades battle bandits as they search for an inherited gold mine. **89m/C VHS.** Keith Van Der Wat, Patrick Munhardt; *D:* Peter Henkel; *W:* Keith Van Der Wat.

The Three Burials of Melquiades Estrada **2005 (R)** Powerful meditation on the brutality of the U.S.-Mexico border region. Rancher Pete Perkins (Jones) forces Mike Norton (Pepper) to carry the body of Pete's friend Melquiades Estrada (Cedillo) from their dusty Texas border town to the dead man's home in Mexico for burial in his family cemetery. But the bigger story is how their journey acts as a metaphor for the all-too human boundaries of wealth, sex, race, and religion. Norton, a racist patrol officer (and Estrada's murderer) is transformed from a thug with a badge into a man who must seek redemption after his eyes are opened to the weight of his actions. Amazing performances are buoyed by Arriaga's knowing script. **120m/C DVD.** Tommy Lee Jones, Barry Pepper, Dwight Yoakam, January Jones, Melissa Leo, Levon Helm, Vanessa Bauche, Julio Cesar Cedillo, Mel Rodriguez, Cecilia Suarez, Ignacio Guadalupe; *D:* Tommy Lee Jones; *W:* Guillermo Arriaga; *C:* Chris Menges; *M:* Marco Beltrami.

Three by Hitchcock **1928** Condensed versions of three of Hitchcock's early films (1927-28). Consists of "The Ring," "Champagne," and "The Manxman," his last silent film. **90m/B VHS.** *D:* Alfred Hitchcock.

The Three Caballeros 1/2 **1945 (G)** Donald Duck stars in this journey through Latin America. Full of music, variety, and live-action/animation segments. Stories include "Pablo the Penguin," "Little Gauchito," and adventures with Joe Carioca, who was first introduced in Disney's "Saludos Amigos." Today this film stands as one of the very best pieces of animation ever created. Great family fare. ♫The Three Caballeros; Baia. **71m/C VHS, DVD.** *D:* Norman Ferguson; *V:* Sterling Holloway, Aurora Miranda.

Three Came Home **1950** Colbert is an American married to a British administrator in the Far East during WWII. Conquering Japanese throw the whole family into a brutal POW concentration camp, and their confinement is recounted in harrowing and unsparing detail. Superior drama, also laudable for a fairly even-handed portrayal of the enemy captors. Based on an autobiographical book by Agnes Newton-Keith. **106m/B VHS, DVD.** Claudette Colbert, Patric Knowles, Sessue Hayakawa, Florence Desmond, Sylvia Andrew, Mark Keuning, Phyllis Morris, Howard Chuman; *D:* Jean Negulesco; *W:* Nunnally Johnson; *C:* William H. Daniels, Milton Krasner; *M:* Hugo Friedhofer.

Three Can Play That Game 1/2 **2007 (R)** In this sequel to "Two Can Play That Game," relationship expert Shante (Fox) moves to Atlanta and continues to offer advice on how to bring your man to heel. Byron's (George) the winner of a TV game show offering a job opportunity with manager Carla (Smith), who promptly makes a play for the looker. Of course this is witnessed by Byron's girlfriend Tiffany (Lewis), who won't believe that nothing happened. She turns to Shante for some questionable help while Byron's best friend Gizzard (Rock) offers his own opinions. The women are manipulative shrews, which isn't very appealing (though they are attractive). **91m/C DVD.** Vivica A. Fox, Jason Winston George, Jazsmin Lewis, Tony Rock, Kellita Smith, Terri J. Vaughn, Melyssa Ford, Rashin Ali; *D:* Mody Mod; *W:* Mark Brown; *C:* Tommy Maddox-Upshaw; *M:* Kenyatta Beasley.

Three Cases of Murder **1955** Three fast-paced tales of mayhem. "In the Picture" features a deranged taxidermist, a creepy house, and a hapless museum guide. From a story by Roderick Wilkinson. Two friends are in love with the same girl in "You Killed Elizabeth" and when she turns up dead it's clear one of them is guilty. From a story by Brett Halliday. The best features Welles as "Lord Mountdrago," who destroys the career of a fellow Parliament Member and is haunted by fears of retaliation. Based on a story by W. Somerset Maugham. **99m/B VHS.** *GB* Alan Badel, John Gregson, Orson Welles, Elizabeth Sellars, Hugh Pryse, Jack Lambert; *D:* Wendy Toye, David Eady, George More O'Ferrall; *W:* Donald Wilson, Sidney Carroll, Ian Dalrymple; *C:* Georges Perinal; *M:* Doreen Carwithen.

Three Charlies and One Phoney!
1918 Three of Charlie Chaplin's best comedy shorts, plus one featuring his best-known imitator—Billy West. Included are "Recreation" ("Fun is Fun") ("Spring Fever"), "His Musical Career" ("The Piano Movers") ("Musical Tramps"), "The Bond" (featuring Charlie in a Liberty Bond appeal) and "His Day Out" with Billy West imitating Chaplin. All but "His Day Out" were written and directed by Chaplin. **69m/B VHS.** Charlie Chaplin, Mack Swain, Charley Chase, Edna Purviance, Sydney Chaplin, Albert Austin; *D:* Charlie Chaplin; *W:* Charlie Chaplin.

Three Coins in the Fountain 1/2 **1954** Three women throw money into fountain and get romantically involved with Italian men. Outstanding CinemaScope photography captures beauty of Italian setting. Sammy Cahn theme song sung by Frank Sinatra. ♫Three Coins in the Fountain. **102m/C VHS, DVD.** Clifton Webb, Dorothy McGuire, Jean Peters, Louis Jourdan, Maggie McNamara, Rossano Brazzi; *D:* Jean Negulesco; *C:* Milton Krasner. Oscars '54: Color Cinematog., Song ("Three Coins in the Fountain").

Three Comrades **1938** Taylor, Tone, and Young are three friends, reunited in bleak, post-WWI Germany, who meet and befriend Sullavan, a tubercular beauty. Reluctant to marry because of her health, she's finally persuaded to wed Taylor, amidst the country's increasing unrest. Tragedy strikes Sullavan and the politicized Young and the two remaining comrades face an uncertain future. Bleak but forceful and passionate drama. Sullavan's performance is superb. Based on the novel by Erich Maria Remarque. Fitzgerald's script was heavily rewritten because both Sullavan and producer Mankiewicz found his approach too literary with unspeakable dialogue. **99m/B VHS.** Robert Taylor, Margaret Sullavan, Robert Young, Franchot Tone, Lionel Atwill, Guy Kibbee, Henry Hull, George Zucco, Monty Woolley, Charley Grapewin, Spencer Charters, Sarah Padden; *D:* Frank Borzage; *W:* F. Scott Fitzgerald, Edward Paramore; *C:* Joseph Ruttenberg; *M:* Franz Waxman. N.Y. Film Critics '38: Actress (Sullavan).

Three Daring Daughters 1/2
1948 When her husband leaves her and she almost misses her daughter's graduation due to a fainting spell, MacDonald takes hiatus on a cruise ship where she meets and marries pianist Iturbi. Unknowing, the three daughters at home conspire to get Dad back in the family. Enraged when Mom returns with new-found hubby, the threesome do all in their power to make the newlyweds as miserable as possible. Happily ended musical-comedy is chock full of memorable tunes. Based on the play "The Bees and the Flowers" by Kohner and Albert Manning. ♫Route 66; The Dickey Bird Song; Alma Mater; Fleurette; Passepied; Where There's Love; Ritual Fire Dance; You Made Me Love You; Happy Birthday. **115m/C VHS.** Jeanette MacDonald, Jose Iturbi, Jane Powell, Edward Arnold, Harry Davenport, Moyna MacGill, Elinor Donahue, Ann E. Todd; *D:* Fred M. Wilcox; *W:* Sonya Levien, John Meehan, Albert Mannheimer, Frederick Kohner.

Three Days of Rain 1/2 **2002** Based on six loosely-connected short stories by Chekov, and set in Cleveland under a brooding rain. Director Michael Meredith attempts to highlight the small ways in which people reveal both cruelty and kindness. A wife's indifference toward a homeless person's hunger triggers a man's reevaluation of his life. A taxi driver has just lost his son, but his passenger (Danner) cannot muster an ounce of sympathy. The other stories are equally troubling, with a boozing father who takes advantage of everyone including his son, and a supervisor plotting to eliminate a mentally challenged janitor. Unfortunately these stories are no different than what you can see most days by walking out your own front door. **94m/C DVD.** *US* Peter Falk, Don Meredith, Merle Kennedy, Erik Avari, Maggie Walker, Joy Bilow, Michael Santoro, Penny Allen, Heather Kafka, Bill Stockton; *D:* Michael Meredith; *C:* Cynthia Pusheck; *M:* Bob Belden.

Three Days of the Condor
1975 (R) CIA researcher Joe Turner (Redford) leaves the office to get some lunch and returns to find all his colleagues murdered. He calls for help but learns his own organization is responsible for the slaughter. So Joe goes on the run until he can expose the conspiracy. Good performance by Dunaway as photographer Kathy Hale, who is forced by Joe to help him but then becomes a willing accomplice. A post-Watergate tale of paranoia and suspense. Based on "Six Days of the Condor" by James Grady. **118m/C VHS, DVD.** Robert Redford, Faye Dunaway, Cliff Robertson, Max von Sydow, John Houseman; *D:* Sydney Pollack; *W:* David Rayfiel; *C:* Owen Roizman; *M:* Dave Grusin.

Three Days to a Kill **1991 (R)** Calvin Sims is a mercenary hired to rescue a kidnapped ambassador—by any means necessary. **90m/C VHS.** Fred Williamson, Bo Svenson, Henry Silva, Chuck Connors, Van Johnson, Sonny Landham; *D:* Fred Williamson.

Three Days to Vegas **2007 (PG-13)** Old pros having fun. Gus (Falk) is enjoying his Florida retirement, swapping stories with golf buddies Joe (Torn), Marvin (Cobbs), and Dominic (Segal). Gus's daughter Elizabeth (Young) announces she's rushing off to Vegas to marry her foreign friend Laurent (Diamantopoulos) because he has visa problems. Gus disapproves and hauls his friends and Elizabeth's ex-beau Billy (Burke) aboard a luxury tour bus for a cross-country jaunt to stop the nuptials. 'Cause flying would mean they couldn't get into silly situations along the way. **120m/C DVD.** Peter Falk, Rip Torn, Bill Cobbs, George Segal, Billy Burke, Chris Diamantopoulos, Coolio, Mario Cantone, Taylor Negron, Nancy Young; *D:* Charlie Picerni; *W:* Charlie Picerni; *C:* Tom Priestley. **VIDEO**

Three Desperate Men **1950** Three brothers accused of murder become outlaws. Not innovative, but satisfactory tale of the Old West. **71m/B VHS.** Preston Foster, Virginia Grey, Jim Davis; *D:* Sam Newfield.

Three ... Extremes **2004 (R)** Twisted horror trilogy from Hong Kong, Korea, and Japan. Chan's truncated "Dumplings" (also a 90-minute feature) finds a vain former actress (Yeung), desperate to keep her looks and husband, partaking of the titular food prepared by Mei (Ling) with a secret ingredient and serious side effects. Park's "Cut" centers on the revenge taken on horror director Ryu (Lee) and his wife (Gang) by a resentful extra (Lim). Miikie's "Box" has successful novelist Kyoko (Hasegawa) haunted by the death of her twin sister in childhood and forced to continually relive her part in the tragedy. Japanese, Cantonese, and Korean with subtitles. **126m/C DVD.** Bai Ling, Tony Leung Ka-Fai, Pauline Lau, Meme Tian, Miraim Yeung Chin Wah, Sum-Yeung Wong, Wai-Man Wu, Chak-Man Ho, Miki Yeung, So-Fun Wong, Kai-Piu Yau, Kam-Mui Fung, Byung-hun Lee, Won-hie Lim, Hye-jeong Kang, Jung-ah Yum, Dae-yeon Lee, Gene Woo Park, Mi Mi Lee, Gyu-sik Kim, Kyoko Hasegawa, Atsuro Watabe, Mai Suzuki, Yuu Suzuki, Mitsuru Akashobi; *D:* Fruit Chan, Takashi Miike, Chan-wook Park; *W:* Chan-wook Park, Lilian Lee, Haruko Fukushima, Bun Saikou; *C:* Christopher Doyle, Jeong-hun Jeong, Koichi Kawakami; *M:* Kwong Wing Chan, Koji Endo.

3 Extremes 2 1/2 *Saam Gaang* **2002 (R)** Released as the sequel to "3 Extremes" in the U.S., "3 Extremes II" was actually the first set of films to be done in Asia. In "Memories" a woman disappears from her home, and somehow ends up in a futuristic city with no idea how she got there. Meanwhile her husband doesn't know why she left. "The Wheel" is a story of a young puppeteer who tries to prevent a traditional dance troupe from using cursed puppets in a performance. The last, and best, film is "Coming Home." A father searches for his missing son in their creepy new apartment building, and is abducted by an insane neighbor who believes his dead wife will wake up one day. **129m/C DVD.** *HK KN TH* Leon Lai, Eric Tsang, Eugenia Yuan, Jung-Hee Moon, Hye-su Kim, Bo-seok Jeong, Suwinit Pangamawat, Ting-Fung Li, Kanyavae Chatiawaipreacha, Jeong-won Choi, Pornchai Chuvanon, Anusak Intasorn, Pattama Jangjarut, Jung-Won Jang, Sung-keun Jee, Savika Kanchanamas, Tsz-Wing Lau, Manop Meejamarat, Hee-soon Park, Tinnapob Seeweesriruth, John Sham, Camy Ting, Tak-Ming Ting, Vinn Vasinanon, Pongsanart Vinsiri, Heng Wong, Komgrich Yuttiyong; *D:* Peter Chan, Ji-woon Kim, Nonzee Nimibutr; *W:* Ji-woon Kim, Matt Chow, Jojo Hui, Nonzee Nimibutr, Teddy Chan, Ek Leumchuen, Nitas Singhamat, Chao-Bin Su; *C:* Christopher Doyle, Nattawut Kittihun, Kyung-Pyo Hong; *M:* Peter Kam, Byung-woo Lee, Sung-woo Jo, Sinnapa Sarasas, Apisit Wongshoti.

The Three Faces of Eve 1/2
1957 Emotionally disturbed Eve (Woodward) seeks the help of psychiatrist Dr. Luther (Cobb), who eventually discovers she has three distinct personalities: a downtrodden housewife, a party girl, and a well-educated, well-balanced woman. So Luther decides to integrate all three into one Eve. Although Woodward gives a powerful performance, the film has dated badly, particularly the narration by Cooke, which gives the film a now-stilted air. Although the film is fact-based, the story was deemed too implausible for the public to believe at the time without the assurances of the narrator. **91m/B VHS, DVD.** Joanne Woodward, David Wayne, Lee J. Cobb, Nancy Kulp, Edwin Jerome, Vince Edwards; *D:* Nunnally Johnson; *W:* Nunnally Johnson; *C:* Stanley Cortez; *M:* Robert Emmett Dolan; *Nar:* Alistair Cooke. Oscars '57: Actress (Woodward); Golden Globes '58: Actress—Drama (Woodward).

Three Faces West *The Refugee* **1940** A dust bowl community is helped by a Viennese doctor who left Europe to avoid Nazi capture. He's aided by the Duke in this odd combination of Western frontier saga and anti-Nazi propaganda. Works only part of the time. **79m/B VHS, DVD.** John Wayne, Charles Coburn, Sigrid Gurie, Sonny Bupp, Russell Simpson; *D:* Bernard Vorhaus.

3:15—The Moment of Truth
1986 (R) A vicious high school gang is confronted by an angry ex-member in this so-so teen delinquent film. **86m/C VHS.** Adam Baldwin, Deborah Foreman, Rene Auberjonois, Danny De La Paz; *D:* Larry Gross; *W:* Sam Bernard; *M:* Gary Chang.

357 Magnum **1979** Jonathan Hightower, the CIA's special investigator in the Far East, speaks softly and carries a very big gun. **85m/C VHS.** *MX* Mario Almada, Ferdinando Almada, Ursula Prats, James Whitworth; *D:* Ruben Galindo.

Three for Bedroom C 1952 A movie star and a scientist make romance on a train bound for Los Angeles. Swanson's follow-up to "Sunset Boulevard." **74m/C VHS.** Gloria Swanson, Fred Clark, Steve Brodie, Hans Conried, Margaret Dumont; *D:* Milton Bren.

Three for the Road **1987 (PG)** A young aspiring political aide and his roommate must escort a Senator's ill-mannered and spoiled daughter to a reform institution. On the road, they run into more than a few obstacles. Good performances elevate a bland script. Sheen made this movie before his riveting performance as a young GI in "Platoon." **98m/C** Charlie Sheen, Kerri Green, Alan Ruck, Sally Kellerman; *D:* Bill W.L. Norton; *W:* Tim Metcalfe; *M:* Barry Goldberg.

Three for the Show ½ **1955** Julie (Grable) is a song-and-dance queen whose husband, Marty (Lemmon), was presumed dead in WWII. After she marries his songwriting partner, Vernon (Champion), Marty naturally shows up. Because she loves both men, Julie decides to set-up a household threesome until she can make up her mind. Champion's real-life spouse and dance partner, Marge, plays Grable's best friend. Some good dance numbers don't make up for the weak script. Based on the W. Somerset Maugham play "Too Many Husbands" and filmed under that title in 1940. ♫ Someone to Watch Over Me; WHich One?; Down Boy!; I've Been Kissed Before; I've Got a Crush on You; How Come You Like Me Like You Do?; Three for the Show. **93m/C VHS.** Betty Grable, Jack Lemmon, Gower Champion, Marge Champion, Myron McCormick, Paul Harvey; *D:* H.C. Potter; *W:* Leonard Stern, Edward Hope; *C:* Arthur E. Arling; *M:* George Duning.

Three Fugitives **1989 (PG-13)** An ex-con holdup man (Nolte) determined to go straight is taken hostage by a bungling first-time bank robber, who is only attempting the holdup in order to support his withdrawn young daughter. Nolte winds up on the lam with the would-be robber and his daughter. The comedy is fun, the sentimental moments too sweet and slow. Remake of French "Les Fugitifs." **96m/C VHS, DVD.** Nick Nolte, Martin Short, James Earl Jones, Kenneth McMillan, Sarah Rowland Doroff, Alan Ruck, Bruce McGill, Sy Richardson, Larry Miller, Lee Garlington, John Aylward, Kathy Kinney; *D:* Francis Veber; *W:* Francis Veber; *C:* Haskell Wexler; *M:* David McHugh.

Three Godfathers **1948** A sweet and sentimental western has three half-hearted outlaws on the run, taking with them an infant they find in the desert. Dedicated to western star and Ford alumni Harry Carey Sr. (whose son is one of the outlaws in the film), who died of cancer the year before. Ford had first filmed the tale with Carey Sr. as "Marked Men" in 1919. **82m/C VHS, DVD.** John Wayne, Pedro Armendariz Sr., Harry Carey Jr., Ward Bond, Mae Marsh, Jane Darwell, Ben Johnson, Mildred Natwick, Guy Kibbee; *D:* John Ford; *C:* Winton C. Hoch.

Three Guys Named Mike **1951** Wyman plays an overly enthusiastic airline stewardess who finds herself the object of affection from three guys named Mike, including an airline pilot, an advertising man, and a scientist. A cute comedy. **89m/B VHS, DVD.** Jane Wyman, Van Johnson, Barry Sullivan, Howard Keel, Phyllis Kirk, Jeff Donnell; *D:* Charles Walters; *W:* Sidney Sheldon.

300 **2007 (R)** Blood, brutality, and buff bodies with the stylized action all done against bluescreen. Adaptation of Frank Miller's graphic novel follows the historical Battle of Thermopylae in 480 B.C. Sparta's King Leonidas (Butler) refuses to bow to the rule of the Persians and takes 300 of his best warriors to battle bejeweled and multi-pierced Xerxes (Santoro) and his hordes. Meanwhile, back at Sparta, the unfortunately-named Queen Gorgo (Headey) is battling sniveling politicos to get her hubby some reinforcements. This time Internet fanboy enthusiasm translated into blockbuster boxoffice bucks. **116m/C DVD, Blu-ray Disc, HD DVD.** *US* Gerard Butler, Lena Headey, Dominic West, David Wenham, Rodrigo Santoro, Andrew Tiernan, Tom Wisdom, Vincent Regan, Michael Fassbender, Stephen McHattie; *D:* Zack Snyder; *W:* Zack Snyder, Kurt Johnstad, Michael B. Gordon; *C:* Larry Fong; *M:* Tyler Bates.

301/302 *301, 302* **1995** The woman living in apartment 302 is obsessed with cooking, sex, and eating to the point of neurosis. Her neighbor in 301 is an anorexic/bulimic who can't stand anything entering her body (even food) as a result of being repeatedly violated by her father as a child. So 302 makes it her life's mission to fatten 301 up. Eventually 301 disappears and detectives come asking why. Warning: eating while watching this film is not advised. **99m/C DVD.** *KN* Eun-Jin Bang, Sin-Hye Hwang, Eun-Jin Bang, Sin-Hye Hwang; *D:* Chul-Soo Park, Chul-Soo Park; *W:* Suh-Goon Lee, Sun Ryong Byun, Suh-Goon Lee, Sun Ryong Byun; *C:* Eun-ju Lee, Eun-ju Lee.

365 Nights in Hollywood **1934** With stars in her eyes, Alice (Faye) comes to Hollywood to work in the movies but is snookered into attending a fraudulent acting school run by Delmar (Mitchell) and his partner Almont (Bradford). Delmar persuades wealthy Frank Young (Medford) to bankroll a film starring Alice, intending to sabotage the production and pocket the cash. Only desperate director Jimmy Dale (Dunn) is determined to make the most of his last opportunity and make Alice a star. **86m/B DVD.** Alice Faye, James Dunn, Grant Mitchell, Frank Mitchell, John Bradford, Frank Melton, Jack Durant, John Qualen; *D:* George Marshall; *W:* William Conselman, Harry Jackson, Henry Johnson; *M:* Samuel Kaylin.

The 300 Spartans ½ **1962** Typical sword-and-sandal epic (surprisingly not of the Italian muscleman variety) that's big on battles and small on character development. Sparta's King Leonidis (Egan) and his band of 300 warriors defend the mountain pass at Thermopylae against the much larger force of effete Persian king Xerxes (Farrar) in 480 B.C. Richardson is dignified as an Athenian military advisor but Egan is as stiff as the brush in that Spartan helmet. **108m/C DVD.** Richard Egan, Ralph Richardson, David Farrar, Barry Coe, Diane Baker, Kieron Moore, Donald Houston; *D:* Rudolph Mate; *C:* Geoffrey Unsworth; *M:* Manos Hadjidakis.

The 300 Year Weekend ½ **1971** Ten people gather for a weekend-long group therapy session, led by Dr. Marshall (Tolan), that reveals what troubles them. You won't be interested. **123m/C VHS.** Michael (Lawrence) Tolan, William Devane, Gabriel Dell, Dorothy Lyman, James Congdon, Sharon Laughlin, Roy Cooper, M'el Dowd, Bernard Ward, Carole Demas; *D:* Victor Stoloff; *W:* William Devane, Victor Stoloff; *C:* Joseph Brun; *M:* Gilber Fuller.

The 317th Platoon **1965** An emotionally gripping war drama of the French-Vietnemese War in which the 317th Platoon of the French Army, consisting of four French commanders and 41 Laotians, is ordered to leave Luong Ba, Cambodia and retreat to Tao Tsai. The men begin their march and slowly succumb to the elements and ambushes. Days later, when what is left of the platoon finally reaches Tao Tsai, the camp is in enemy hands and the remnants of the 317th Platoon are killed in cold blood. Director Shoendoerffer portrays this struggle, conflict, and the quiet haunting tension of war with great skill. In French with English subtitles. **100m/B VHS.** *FR* Jacques Perrin, Bruno Cremer, Pierre Fabre, Manuel Zarzo; *D:* Pierre Schoendoerffer; *W:* Pierre Schoendoerffer; *C:* Raoul Coutard; *M:* Gregorio Garcia Segura, Pierre Jansen.

Three Husbands ½ **1950** A deceased playboy leaves letters for the title characters incriminating their wives in extramarital affairs. The men's reactions are pure farce—even though this same concept was played straight with a sex change in the earlier "A Letter to Three Wives." **79m/B VHS, DVD.** Eve Arden, Ruth Warrick, Vanessa Brown, Howard da Silva, Shepperd Strudwick, Jane Darwell; *D:* Irving Reis.

Three in the Attic ½ **1968 (R)** A college student juggles three girlfriends at the same time. When the girls find out they are being two-timed, they lock their boyfriend in an attic and exhaust him with forced sexual escapades. Then they talk. Limited trashy and foolish appeal. **92m/C VHS.** Christopher Jones, Yvette Mimieux, John Beck; *D:* Richard Wilson.

Three in the Cellar *Up in the Cellar* **1970 (R)** A disgruntled college student seeks revenge on the school president by seducing his wife, daughter and mistress. Good screenplay helps carry it off. **92m/C VHS.** Wes Stern, Joan Collins, Larry Hagman, Judy Pace; *D:* Theodore J. Flicker.

Three in the Saddle ½ **1945** Ritter and the Texas Rangers fight for law and order. **61m/B VHS, DVD.** Tex Ritter, Dave O'Brien, Charles "Blackie" King; *D:* Harry Fraser; *C:* Robert E. Cline.

Three Kinds of Heat **1987 (R)** Three Interpol agents track down a warring Asian crime lord. Alternately tongue-in-cheek and silly. Never released in theatres—it found it's home on video. Stevens created "The Outer Limits" for TV. **88m/C VHS.** Robert Ginty, Victoria Barrett, Shakti; *D:* Leslie Stevens. **VIDEO**

Three Kings **1999 (R)** Director Russell turns the war movie genre on its ear with his subversive, chaotic, and ultimately satisfying studio film debut. At the end of the Gulf War, Special Forces Major Gates (Clooney) recruits three Army reservists to join him on an illegal mission to steal gold bullion which Hussein's troops had stolen from Kuwait. They wind up learning too much about U.S. policies and broken promises in the Middle East. Clooney is perfect as the pragmatic Gates, and Russell supplies the right mix of cynicism, dark humor, and action-movie heroism. **115m/C VHS, DVD.** George Clooney, Mark Wahlberg, Ice Cube, Spike Jonze, Nora Dunn, Jamie Kennedy, Mykelti Williamson, Clifford Curtis, Said Taghmaoui, Judy Greer, Liz Stauber, Holt McCallany; *D:* David O. Russell; *W:* David O. Russell; *C:* Newton Thomas (Tom) Sigel; *M:* Carter Burwell. Broadcast Film Critics '99: Breakthrough Perf. (Jonze).

Three Legionnaires ½ *Three Crazy Legionnaires* **1937** Three Allied soldiers in post-WWI Russia become involved in the Russian Revolution when they fall in love with a White Russian princess in a small village. **67m/B VHS.** Robert Armstrong, Lyle Talbot, Fifi d'Orsay, Anne Nagel, Donald Meek, Lyle Talbot, Stanley Fields, Maurice Black, Man Mountain Dean; *D:* Hamilton MacFadden; *W:* Carl Harbaugh, George Wagner; *C:* Ira Morgan.

The Three Little Pigs ½ **1984** From "Faerie Tale Theatre" comes the story of three little pigs, the houses they lived in and the wolf that tried to do them in. **60m/C VHS, DVD.** Billy Crystal, Jeff Goldblum, Valerie Perrine; *D:* Howard Storm. **CABLE**

Three Little Words ½ **1950** A musical biography of songwriting team Harry Ruby and Bert Kalmar, filled with Kalmar-Ruby numbers. Helen Kane (famous for her boop-boop-de-boops) dubbed "I Wanna Be Loved By You" for Reynolds. A musical in the best MGM tradition. ♫ I Wanna Be Loved By You; Who's Sorry Now?; Three Little Words; I Love You So Much; She's Mine, All Mine; So-Long, Oo-Long; Hooray for Captain Spaulding; Up In The Clouds; All Alone Monday. **102m/C VHS, DVD.** Fred Astaire, Red Skelton, Vera-Ellen, Arlene Dahl, Keenan Wynn, Gloria De Haven, Debbie Reynolds, Gale Robbins; *D:* Richard Thorpe; *M:* Andre Previn. Golden Globes '51: Actor—Mus./Comedy (Astaire).

Three Lives and Only One Death ½ *Trois Vies et Une Seule Mort* **1996** Surrealist film features Mastroianni in four roles. Salesman Mateo Strano walks out on his wife Maria (Paredes) and doesn't see her for 20 years. When he finally returns, Mateo wants her back, although Maria's got a new husband, Andre (Atkine). Then there's Georges Vickers, negative anthropology professor-turned street tramp who takes up with hooker Tania (Galiena), who also has another identity. Then he's a butler who's trying to murder a young couple and steal their child and finally, Mastroianni's a rich industrialist who seems to be suffering from multiple personalities. And yes, somehow all the stories do tie together. French with subtitles. **124m/C VHS.** *FR* Marcello Mastroianni, Anna Galiena, Marisa Paredes, Melvil Poupaud, Chiara Mastroianni, Arielle Dombasle, Feodor Atkine, Jean-Yves Gautier, Pierre Bellemare, Lou Castel, Jacques Pieller; *D:* Raul Ruiz; *W:* Raul Ruiz, Pascal Bonitzer; *C:* Laurent Machuel; *M:* Jorge Arriagada.

The Three Lives of Karen ½ **1997 (PG-13)** Thriller finds Karen Winthrop (O'Grady) engaged to state trooper Matt (Guinee) and seemingly happy until Paul Riggs (Boutsikaris) shows up. He has proof that Karen is actually his wife Emily who disappeared four years before, abandoning him and their daughter Jessica (Bugajski). So the confused Karen returns with Paul to try and remember what happened to her. She learns that she's actually disappeared twice before and the flashbacks Karen has of her past are terrifying. **89m/C VHS.** Gail O'Grady, Dennis Boutsikaris, Tim Guinee, Monica Bugajski; *D:* David Burton Morris; *W:* David Chisholm; *C:* John L. (Ndiaga) Demps Jr. **CABLE**

The Three Lives of Thomasina **1963 (PG)** In turn-of-the-century Scotland, a veterinarian orders his daughter's beloved cat destroyed when the pet is diagnosed with tetanus. After the cat's death (with scenes of kitty heaven), a beautiful and mysterious healer from the woods is able to bring the animal back to life and restore the animal to the little girl. Lovely Disney fairy tale with good performances by all. **95m/C VHS, DVD.** Patrick McGoohan, Susan Hampshire, Karen Dotrice, Matthew Garber; *D:* Don Chaffey; *V:* Elspeth March.

The 3 Marias ½ *As Tres Marias* **2003** Three decades after Filomena (Severo) dumped Guerra (Vereza) and married his rival, Guerra murders her husband and sons in cold blood. Things get messy when Filomena conspires with her three daughters—all named Maria—to avenge the deaths. Common bloody revenge tale includes bits of dark humor. In Portuguese, with English subtitles. **90m/C VHS, DVD.** *PT* Maria Luisa Mendonca, Marieta Severo, Julia Lemmertz, Luiza Mariani, Carlos Vereza; *D:* Aluisio Abranches; *W:* Heitor Dhalia, Wilson Friere; *C:* Marcelo Durst. **VIDEO**

Three Men and a Baby **1987 (PG)** The arrival of a young baby forever changes the lives of three sworn bachelors living in New York. Well-paced, charming and fun, with good acting from all. A remake of the French movie "Three Men and a Cradle." **102m/C VHS, DVD.** Tom Selleck, Steve Guttenberg, Ted Danson, Margaret Colin, Nancy Travis, Philip Bosco, Celeste Holm, Derek de Lint, Cynthia Harris, Lisa Blair, Michelle Blair, Paul Guilfoyle; *D:* Leonard Nimoy; *W:* James Orr, Jim Cruickshank; *C:* Adam Greenberg; *M:* Marvin Hamlisch.

Three Men and a Cradle ½ *Trois Hommes et un Couffin* **1985 (PG-13)** Three carefree bachelors, Jacques (Dussollier), Pierre (Giraud), and Michel (Boujenah), find a baby girl in a basket outside the door of the home they share. One is the father—although none of the men are sure which one it is. After the initial shock of learning how to take care of a child, they fall in love with her and won't let her go. There's a strange subplot about Jacques hiding heroin in the baby's diapers that gets them all involved with drug dealers. Still, everything is played for laughs and the film has heaps of charm. French with subtitles. Remade in 1987 as "Three Men and a Baby." **100m/C VHS, DVD.** *FR* Roland Giraud, Michel Boujenah, Andre Dussollier, Phillippe LeRoy, Marthe Villalonga, Dominique Lavanant; *D:* Coline Serreau; *W:* Coline Serreau; *C:* Jean-Yves Escoffier. Cesar '86: Film, Support. Actor (Boujenah), Writing.

Three Men and a Little Lady ½ **1990 (PG)** In this sequel to "Three Men and a Baby," the mother of the once abandoned infant decides that her child needs a father. Although she wants Selleck, he doesn't get the message and so she chooses a snooty British director. The rest of the movie features various semi-comic attempts to rectify the situation. **100m/C VHS, DVD.** Tom Selleck, Steve Guttenberg, Ted Danson, Nancy Travis, Robin Weisman, Christopher Cazenove, Fiona Shaw, Sheila Hancock, John Boswall, Jonathan Lynn, Sydney Walsh; *D:* Emile Ardolino; *W:* Charlie Peters, Sara Parriott, Josann McGibbon; *C:* Adam

Greenberg; *M:* James Newton Howard.

Three Men in a Boat ♂♂ **1956** Harris, J, and George decide to escape daily drudgery and romantic complications by taking a boating trip up the Thames to Oxford. But their male bonding is interrupted when they cross paths with the lovely Sophie, Primrose, and Bluebell, and the trip ends in chaos at a cricket match. Victorian-era comic nostalgia based on the Jerome K. Jerome novel. **84m/C DVD.** *GB* Jimmy Edwards, Laurence Harvey, David Tomlinson, Shirley Eaton, Lisa Gastoni, Jill Ireland, Adrienne Corri, Martita Hunt; *D:* Ken Annakin; *W:* Vernon Harris, Hubert Gregg; *C:* Eric Cross; *M:* John Addison.

Three Men on a Horse ♂♂♂ **1936** Comedy classic about mild-mannered McHugh's ability to predict horse races and the bettors that try to take advantage of him. Blondell is great as the Brooklynese girlfriend of one of the bettors. Lots of laughs, but don't watch for the horse-racing scenes, because there aren't many. **88m/B VHS.** Frank McHugh, Joan Blondell, Carol Hughes, Allen Jenkins, Guy Kibbee, Sam Levene; *D:* Mervyn LeRoy.

The Three Mesquiteers ♂♂ **1936** When New Mexico territory is opened by the government to homesteaders, a group of WWI vets and their families stake their claims. When the Mesquiteers (vets themselves) learn the local cattle barons are threatening the nesters, they come to their aid. Features a climatic gun battle that includes hand grenades. The first of the 51 films in the Republic series. **61m/B DVD.** Robert "Bob" Livingston, Ray Corrigan, Syd Saylor, Kay Hughes, J(ohn) P(aterson) McGowan, Alan Bridge, Bob Bryant; *D:* Ray Taylor; *W:* Jack Natteford; *C:* William Nobles.

Three Monkeys ♂♂ **2008** Politician Servet accidentally kills a pedestrian while driving. Panicked, he calls his usual driver Eyup who agrees to take the rap, though it means a year in prison, in return for a big payoff when he gets out as well as his usual salary to support his wife and teenage son. Title refers to the monkey trio of see, hear, and speak no evil. Turkish with subtitles. **109m/C DVD.** *TU* Yavuz Bingol, Hatice Aslan, Ahmet Rifat Sungar, Ercan Kesal, Cafer Kose; *D:* Nuri Bilge Ceylan; *W:* Ercan Kesal, Ebru Ceylan; *C:* Gokhan Tiryaki.

The Three Musketeers ♂♂ *D'Artagnan* **1916** One of the many movie adaptation of Alexandre Dumas' adventure, but this one comes from the hand of famed movie pioneer Ince. D'Artagnan joins the title characters in saving France's Queen Anne from a nefarious plot. Silent with the original organ score. **74m/B VHS.** Orin Johnson, Dorothy Dalton, Louise Glaum, Walt Whitman; *D:* Charles Swickard.

The Three Musketeers ♂♂♂ 1/2 **1921** D'Artagnan swashbuckles silently amid stylish sets, scores of extras and exquisite costumes. Relatively faithful adaptation of Alexandre Dumas novel, slightly altered in favor of D'Artagnan's lover. Classic Fairbanks, who also produced. **120m/B VHS, DVD.** Douglas Fairbanks Sr., Leon Bary, George Siegmann, Eugene Pallette, Boyd Irwin, Thomas Holding, Sidney Franklin, Charles Stevens, Nigel de Brulier, Willis Robards, Mary MacLaren; *D:* Fred Niblo; *W:* Lotta Woods, Douglas Fairbanks Sr.; *C:* Arthur Edeson; *M:* Louis F. Gottschalk.

The Three Musketeers ♂ 1/2 **1933** Modern adaptation of the classic tale by Alexander Dumas depicts the three friends as members of the Foreign Legion. Weakest of Wayne serials, in 12 parts. **215m/B VHS, DVD.** Jack Mulhall, Raymond Hatton, Lon Chaney Jr., John Wayne, Francis X. Bushman, Ruth Hall, Noah Beery Jr., Al Ferguson; *D:* Colbert Clark, Armand Schaefer; *W:* Colbert Clark, Bennett Cohen, Wyndham Gittens, Norman S. Hall; *C:* Tom Galligan, Ernest Miller.

The Three Musketeers ♂♂ **1935** Three swordsmen, loyal to each other, must battle the corrupt Cardinal Richelieu. Generally regarded as the least exciting adaptation of Alexander Dumas' classic tale. The first talking version. **95m/B VHS.** Walter Abel, Paul Lukas, Moroni Olsen, Ian Keith, Margot Grahame, Heather Angel, Onslow Stevens, Miles Mander; *D:* Rowland V. Lee; *M:* Max Steiner.

The Three Musketeers ♂♂ 1/2 *The Singing Musketeer* **1939** Musical-comedy version of the famed Alexandre Dumas swashbuckling saga. Ameche is a singing D'Artagnan and the three Ritz brothers are the inept and cowardly Musketeers (who turn out to be phonies, after all). Silly fun. ♫ My Lady; Song of the Musketeers; Voila; Chicken Soup. **73m/B VHS, DVD.** Don Ameche, Al Ritz, Harry Ritz, Jimmy Ritz, Binnie Barnes, Lionel Atwill, Miles Mander, Gloria Stuart, Pauline Moore, Joseph Schildkraut, John Carradine, Douglass Dumbrille; *D:* Allan Dwan; *W:* M.M. Musselman, William A. Drake, Sam Hellman.

The Three Musketeers ♂♂ 1/2 **1948** The three musketeers who are "all for one and one for all" join forces with D'Artagnan to battle the evil Cardinal Richelieu in this rambunctious adaptation of the classic tale by Alexander Dumas. Good performances by the cast, who combined drama and comedy well. Turner's first color film. **126m/C VHS, DVD.** Lana Turner, Gene Kelly, June Allyson, Gig Young, Angela Lansbury, Van Heflin, Keenan Wynn, Robert Coote, Reginald Owen, Frank Morgan, Vincent Price, Patricia Medina; *D:* George Sidney.

The Three Musketeers ♂♂♂ 1/2 **1974 (PG)** Extravagant and funny version of the Dumas classic. Three swashbucklers (Reed, Chamberlain, Finlay) and their country cohort (York), who wishes to join the Musketeers, set out to save the honor of the French Queen (Chaplin). To do so they must oppose the evil cardinal (Heston) who has his eyes on the power behind the throne and who is aided by cohort Milady (Dunaway). Welch is amusing as clumsy lady-in-waiting Constance. A strong cast leads this winning combination of slapstick and high adventure. Followed by "The Four Musketeers" and "The Return of the Musketeers." **105m/C VHS, DVD.** Richard Chamberlain, Oliver Reed, Michael York, Raquel Welch, Frank Finlay, Christopher Lee, Faye Dunaway, Charlton Heston, Geraldine Chaplin, Simon Ward, Jean-Pierre Cassel, William Hobbs; *D:* Richard Lester; *W:* George MacDonald Fraser; *C:* David Watkin; *M:* Michel Legrand. Golden Globes '75: Actress—Mus./Comedy (Welch).

The Three Musketeers ♂♂ 1/2 **1993 (PG)** Yet another version of the classic swashbuckler with Porthos, Athos, Aramis, and the innocent D'Artanan banding together against the evil Cardinal Richelieu and the tempting Milady DeWinter to save France. Cute stars, a little swordplay, a few jokes, and cartoon bad guys. Okay for the younger crowd. **105m/C VHS, DVD.** Kiefer Sutherland, Charlie Sheen, Chris O'Donnell, Oliver Platt, Rebecca De Mornay, Tim Curry, Gabrielle Anwar, Julie Delpy, Michael Wincott; *D:* Stephen Herek; *W:* David Loughery; *C:* Dean Semler; *M:* Michael Kamen.

3 Ninjas ♂♂ 1/2 **1992 (PG)** Lively kid's actioner about three brothers who are trained as ninjas by their grandpa. When a group of bad guys tries to kidnap the boys, they're in for trouble. Sort of a cross between "The Karate Kid" and "Home Alone" that is suitable for family viewing. Followed by "3 Ninjas Kick Back." **84m/C VHS, DVD.** Victor Wong, Michael Treanor, Max Elliott Slade, Chad Power, Rand Kingsley, Alan McRae, Margarita Franco, Toru Tanaka, Patrick Laborteaux; *D:* Jon Turteltaub; *W:* Edward Emanuel; *M:* Richard (Rick) Marvin.

3 Ninjas: High Noon at Mega Mountain ♂♂ *Three Ninjas: Showdown at Mega Mountain* **1997 (PG)** Fourth installment of the kid-fantasy franchise finds brothers Rocky (Botuchis), Colt (O'Laskey), and Tum-Tum (Roeske) in the middle of a takeover at an amusement park. The ninja trained brothers, along with a computer-whiz neighbor (Earlywine) and retiring action hero Dave Dragon (Hogan) must save the day when Medusa (Anderson) and her henchmen ransom the park and its guests. Typically, the adults are incompetent when they're not busy being nasty. Pre-pubescent kids are the only ones likely to find this entertaining—if they're not too discriminating. The "action" is somewhere between cartoon and pro wrestling. Varney stands out as Medusa's lead henchman. **93m/C VHS, DVD.** Hulk Hogan, Loni Anderson, Jim Varney, Victor Wong, Mathew Botuchis, Michael J. O'Laskey II, J.P. Roeske II, Chelsey Earlywine, Alan McRae, Margarita Franco, Kirk Baily; *D:* Sean McNamara; *W:* Sean McNamara, Jeff Phillips; *C:* Blake T. Evans; *M:* John Coda.

3 Ninjas Kick Back ♂♂ 1/2 **1994 (PG)** Sequel to the popular "3 Ninjas." Three brothers help their grandfather protect a ceremonial knife won in a ninja tournament in Japan 50 years earlier. Gramps' ancient adversary in that tournament, now an evil tycoon, wants the sword back and he's willing to enlist the aid of his three American grandchildren, members of garage band Teenage Vomit, to get it. The showdown eventually heads to Japan, where "Kick Back," unlike predecessors, dispenses with the Japan-bashing. High-spirited action fare that kids will enjoy. **95m/C VHS, DVD.** Victor Wong, Max Elliott Slade, Sean Fox, Evan Bonifant, Sab Shimono, Dustin Nguyen, Jason Schombing, Caroline Junko King, Angelo Tiffe; *D:* Charles Kanganis; *W:* Mark Saltzman; *C:* Christopher Faloona; *M:* Richard (Rick) Marvin.

3 Ninjas Knuckle Up ♂♂ 1/2 **1995 (PG-13)** Brothers Rocky (Treanor), Tum Tum (Power), and Colt (Slade) spend their summer vacation with ever-wise Grandpa Mori (Wong) and get to practice their martial arts skills on a variety of villains. Seems a waste management company has been illegally dumping toxins onto the nearby Indian reservation where the boys' friend Jo (Lightning) lives and have even kidnapped her dad (Shanks) to keep him silent. So it's our pint-sized heroes to the rescue. Filmed in '92 but released after "3 Ninjas Kick Back," which explains why Treanor and Power are missing from the second film. **94m/C VHS, DVD.** Victor Wong, Michael Treanor, Chad Power, Max Elliott Slade, Crystle Lightning, Patrick Kilpatrick, Don Shanks, Charles Napier, Nick Ramus, Vincent Schiavelli; *D:* Simon S. Sheen; *W:* Alex S. Kim; *C:* Eugene Shlugleit; *M:* Gary Stevan Scott.

Three Nuts in Search of a Bolt ♂ 1/2 **1964 (R)** Three neurotics send a surrogate to a comely psychiatrist for help, but the shrink thinks the surrogate's a three-way multiple personality. Raunchy monkey-shines ensue. Includes Van Doren's infamous beer bath scene. **78m/C VHS, DVD.** Mamie Van Doren, Tommy Noonan, Paul Gilbert, Alvy Moore; *D:* Tommy Noonan.

301, 302 ♂ **1994** Confusing horror story told in flashbacks focuses on two women in neighboring high-rise apartments. A young policeman is investigating the disappearance of the woman from apartment 302 (Hwang). He questions the tenant across the hall in 301 (Pang), an obsessive cook who tries to share her culinary results with Hwang, who happens to be an anorexic writer. Both have dark secrets in their pasts, which they share, leading to a grotesque resolution of their friendship. **99m/C VHS, DVD.** *KN* Eun-Jin Bang, Sin-Hye Hwang, Chu-Ryun Kim; *D:* Chul-Soo Park; *W:* Suh-Goon Lee.

Three o'Clock High ♂♂ 1/2 **1987 (PG)** A nerdy high school journalist is assigned a profile of the new kid in school, who turns out to be the biggest bully, too. He approaches his task with great unease. Silly teenage farce is given souped-up direction by Spielberg protege Joanou. Features decent work by the young cast. **97m/C VHS, DVD.** Casey Siemaszko, Anne Ryan, Stacey Glick, Jonathan Wise, Richard Tyson, Jeffrey Tambor, Philip Baker Hall, John P. Ryan; *D:* Phil Joanou; *W:* Richard Christian Matheson, Thomas Szollosi; *M:* Tangerine Dream.

Three of Hearts ♂ 1/2 **1993 (R)** Slick look at love in contemporary downtown New York. The triangle consists of Connie (Lynch), just dumped by bisexual girlfriend Ellen (Fenn), who is in turn seduced by hired escort Joe (Baldwin), who will break her heart, causing her to turn back to the sympathetic Connie. But guess what happens. Hiply superficial plot is transparent although the three leads are likeable, especially Lynch as the lanky lovelorn Connie. Don't read further if you don't want to know what happens since the film was shot with two endings. The U.S. release pairs Joe and Ellen for a typically American happy ending; the European release doesn't. **102m/C VHS, DVD.** Kelly Lynch, William Baldwin, Sherilyn Fenn, Joe Pantoliano, Gail Strickland, Cec Verrell, Claire Callaway, Tony Amendola; *D:* Yurek Bogayevicz; *W:* Adam Greenman; *M:* Richard Gibbs.

Three on a Match ♂♂♂ **1932** An actress, a stenographer and a society woman get together for a tenth year reunion. They become embroiled in a world of crime when Blondell's gangster boyfriend takes a liking to Dvorak. She leaves her husband and takes up with the crook. The results are tragic. Bogart's first gangster role. **64m/B VHS.** Joan Blondell, Warren William, Ann Dvorak, Bette Davis, Lyle Talbot, Humphrey Bogart, Patricia Ellis, Grant Mitchell; *D:* Mervyn LeRoy.

Three on a Meathook WOOF! 1972 When a young man and his father living on an isolated farm receive female visitors, bloodshed is quick to follow. Essentially a remake of "Psycho," and very loosely based on the crimes of Ed Gein. Filmed in Louisville, Kentucky. **85m/C VHS, DVD.** Charles Kissinger, James Pickett, Sherry Steiner, Carolyn Thompson; *D:* William Girdler; *W:* William Girdler; *C:* William Asman; *M:* William Girdler.

Three on a Ticket ♂ 1/2 **1947** A private detective stumbles into Michael Shayne's (Beaumont) office, apparently shot, and drops dead before he can tell Shayne what has happened. Shayne's only clue is a torn-up baggage claim ticket clutched in the dead man's hand, which leads to a bag off stolen loot. Now Shayne has to find the crooks and the rightful owners of the cash. **64m/B DVD.** Hugh Beaumont, Cheryl Walker, Paul Bryar, Ralph Dunn, Louise Currie; *D:* Sam Newfield; *W:* Brett Halliday, Fred Myton; *C:* Jack Greenhalgh; *M:* Emil Cadkin.

Three on the Trail ♂♂♂ **1936** This fifth entry in the "Hopalong Cassidy" series is one of the more ambitious. The fast-moving plot concerns Hoppy's (Boyd) efforts to help young schoolmarm Mary Stevens (Evans) from the clutches of an evil saloon keeper. **65m/B DVD.** William Boyd, James Ellison, George "Gabby" Hayes, Onslow Stevens, Mary Evans, Claude King, William Duncan; *D:* Howard Bretherton; *W:* Doris Schroeder, Harrison Jacobs; *C:* Archie Stout.

The Three Penny Opera ♂♂ *Die Dreigroschenoper* **1962** Mack the Knife presides over an exciting world of thieves, murderers, beggars, prostitutes and corrupt officials in a seedy section of London. Based on the opera by Kurt Weill and Bertold Brecht, which was based on "The Beggar's Opera" by John Gay. Remake of "The Threepenny Opera" (1931). **124m/B VHS.** *GE* Curt Jurgens, Hildegarde Knef, Gert Frobe, June Ritchie, Lino Ventura, Sammy Davis Jr.; *D:* Wolfgang Staudte; *W:* Wolfgang Staudte; *C:* Roger Fellous; *M:* Kurt Weill.

Three Priests ♂ 1/2 **2008** Jacob Sands (Parks) has a ranch in Montana that he runs with his wife Rachel (Hussey) and dutiful son Joe (Duffey). His other son, Dustin (Martin), is a troublemaker who follows the rodeo circuit and has an eye for the ladies. When Dustin comes home for a visit, sibling rivalry breaks out when he starts eyeing local beauty Abby (Jones) whom Joe is sweet on. **90m/C DVD.** Michael Parks, Olivia Hussey, Julia Jones, Wes Studi, Alexander Martin, Aaron Duffey; *D:* Jim Comas Cole; *W:* Jim Comas Cole; *C:* Guy Pieres; *M:* Daniel Cole. **VIDEO**

Three Sailors and a Girl ♂♂ 1/2 **1953** Good tunes (by Sammy Fain and Sammy Cahn), usual silly musical plot (that's supposedly based on the George S. Kaufman play "The Butter and Egg Man"). Three submarine sailors (MacRae, Nelson, Leonard) dock in New York and are introduced to struggling singer Penny (Powell). They agree to invest in shady producer Joe Woods' (Levene) show with Penny as the lead and manage to turn the previous flop into a hit. **95m/C DVD.** Jane Powell, Gordon MacRae, Gene Nelson, Jack E. Leonard, Sam Levene, George Givot, Veda Ann Borg, Burt Lancaster; *D:* Roy Del Ruth; *W:* Roland Kibbee, Devery Freeman; *C:* Carl Guthrie.

Three Seasons ♂♂ **1998 (PG-13)** First American indie production to be shot in Vietnam with native-speaking actors since the war (by Vietnam-born, U.S.-raised director Bui in his feature debut) has a number of beautiful shots but not much story to back it up. Bustling Ho Chi Minh City (Saigon) sets the stage for the intertwining fortunes of five characters: young flower seller Kien An (Hiep), street kid Woody (Duoc), cyclo driver

Hai (Duong), prostitute Lan (Bui), and ex-Marine Hager (Keitel), who's searching for his Amer-Asian daughter. **110m/C VHS.** Harvey Keitel, Don Duong, Nguyen Ngoc Hiep, Zoe Bui, Nguyen Huu Duoc, Tran Manh Cuong; ***D:*** Tony Bui; ***W:*** Tony Bui, Timothy Linh Bui; ***C:*** Lisa Rinzler; ***M:*** Richard Horowitz. Ind. Spirit '00: Cinematog.; Sundance '99: Cinematog., Aud. Award, Grand Jury Prize.

Three Secrets ✗✗ 1/2 **1950** A plane crashes and the only survivor is a five-year-old boy. Three women, each with a secret, seek to claim him as the child each gave up for adoption five years before. Tearjerker with good cast. **98m/B VHS.** Eleanor Parker, Patricia Neal, Ruth Roman, Frank Lovejoy, Leif Erickson; ***D:*** Robert Wise.

The Three Sisters ✗✗ 1/2 **1965** A stage production from the Actor's Studio of Chekhov's play about unhappy siblings in turn-of-the-century Russia. The three sisters believe all their problems are caused by living in the provinces and would be solved if they could return to their childhood home in Moscow. **167m/B VHS.** Shelley Winters, Sandy Dennis, Geraldine Page, Kevin McCarthy, Kim Stanley, Luther Adler, Robert Loggia, James Olson, Gerald Hiken; ***D:*** Paul Bogart.

Three Smart Girls ✗✗✗ 1/2 **1936** Fast-moving musical features three high-spirited sisters who attempt to bring their divorced parents back together. Their plan is thwarted when they learn of their father's plan to marry a gold digger. 15-year-old singing sensation Durbin made her debut in this film. Based on a story by Commandini. Followed by "Three Smart Girls Grow Up." ♫ My Heart is Singing; Someone to Care for Me. **84m/B VHS, DVD.** Deanna Durbin, Binnie Barnes, Alice Brady, Ray Milland, Charles Winninger, Mischa Auer, Nan Grey, Barbara Read; ***D:*** Henry Koster; ***W:*** Adele Comandini, Austin Parker; ***C:*** Joseph Valentine.

Three Smart Girls Grow Up ✗✗✗ **1939** Durbin once again plays matchmaker, this time for her two older sisters and their fellas. A delightful mix of comedy and song, this lighthearted sequel turned out to be one of the top-grossing films of the year. Durbin sings "Because," which became one of her biggest hits. **88m/B VHS.** Deanna Durbin, Charles Winninger, Nan Grey, Helen Parrish, Robert Cummings, William Lundigan, Ernest Cossart; ***D:*** Henry Koster; ***W:*** Felix Jackson, Bruce Manning.

Three Sovereigns for Sarah ✗✗ 1/2 **1985** Witch-hunters tortured and toasted Sarah's two sisters for practicing witchcraft in the past. Now, accused of witchery herself, she struggles to prove the family's innocence. Excellent, made-for-PBS. Fine performances from all, especially Redgrave. **152m/C VHS, DVD.** Vanessa Redgrave, Phyllis Thaxter, Patrick McGoohan; ***D:*** Philip Leacock.

Three Stooges in Orbit ✗✗ 1/2 **1962** Three TV performers (you know who) looking for a shtick and a place to live, encounter a crazy scientist with a rocket-like invention. In a shocking plot twist, the boys accidently launch the rocket and must battle Martians to save the world and their TV career. **87m/B VHS, DVD.** Moe Howard, Larry Fine, Joe DeRita, Emil Sitka, Carol Christensen, Edson Stroll; ***D:*** Edward L. Bernds.

The Three Stooges Meet Hercules ✗✗ 1/2 **1961** The Three Stooges are transported back to ancient Ithaca by a time machine with a young scientist and his girlfriend. When the girl is captured, they enlist the help of Hercules to rescue her. **80m/B VHS, DVD.** Moe Howard, Larry Fine, Joe DeRita, Vicki Trickett, Quinn (K.) Redeker, Samson Burke, Lewis Charles, Marlin McKeever, Michael McKeever, John Cliff, George Neise; ***D:*** Edward L. Bernds; ***W:*** Elwood Ullman; ***C:*** Charles S. Welbourne; ***M:*** Paul Dunlap.

Three Stops to Murder ✗ *Blood Orange* **1953** An FBI agent investigates the murder of a beautiful model in this early, unspectacular Hammer production. **76m/B VHS.** *GB* Tom Conway, Mila Parely, Naomi Chance, Eric Pohlmann, Andrew Osborn, Richard Wattis, Eileen Way, Delphi Lawrence; ***D:*** Terence Fisher; ***W:*** Jan Read; ***C:*** Walter J. (Jimmy W.) Harvey; ***M:*** Ivor Slaney.

Three Strange Loves ✗✗✗ *Thirst* **1949** Men and women struggle with loneliness, old age, and sterility. Sometimes disjointed, but for the most part, well-made. Finely acted. In Swedish with English subtitles. **88m/B VHS.** *SW* Eva Henning, Brigit Tengroth, Birger Malmsten; ***D:*** Ingmar Bergman.

Three Strikes WOOF! **2000 (R)** Two-time loser Rob is released from jail determined to stay straight and thus avoid the harsh sentencing of California's "Three Strikes" law. But as luck, and a lame script filled with fart jokes and little esle would have it, his buddy picks him up from jail in a stolen car and promptly gets in a gunfight with the cops. On the run from the police and gang members, Rob tries to find a way to clear himself and get home. There's not much to redeem this disaster of a flick, unless you find embarrassingly stereotypical characters and "In Living Color" refect jokes amusing. **83m/C VHS, DVD.** Brian Hooks, N'Bushe Wright, Faizon Love, Starletta DuPois, David Alan Grier, Dean Norris, Meagan Good, De'Aundre Bonds, Antonio Fargas, Vincent Schiavelli, David Leisure, Gerald S. O'Loughlin, George Wallace, E40, Barima McNight, Mo'Nique, Shawn Fonteno; ***D:*** DJ Pooh; ***W:*** DJ Pooh; ***C:*** Johnny (John W.) Simmons; ***M:*** Aaron Anderson, Andrew Slack.

3:10 to Yuma ✗✗✗ 1/2 **1957** In order to collect $200 he desperately needs, a poor cattle rancher (Heflin) has to hold a dangerous killer at bay while waiting to turn the outlaw (Ford) over to the authorities arriving on the 3:10 train to Yuma. Stuck in a hotel room with the outlaw's gang gathering outside, the question arises as to who is the prisoner. Heflin is continually worked on by the outlaw Ford, in a movie with more than its share of great dialogue. The two leads are exceptional, with Ford making the most of his character's cunning charm. Suspenseful, well-made action western adapted from an Elmore Leonard story. **92m/B VHS, DVD.** Glenn Ford, Van Heflin, Felicia Farr, Richard Jaeckel, Leora Dana, Robert Emhardt, Henry Jones, Ford Rainey; ***D:*** Delmer Daves; ***W:*** Halsted Welles; ***C:*** Charles Lawton Jr.; ***M:*** George Duning.

3:10 to Yuma ✗✗✗ 1/2 **2007 (R)** Remake of the 1957 classic western pits legendary outlaw Ben Wade (Crowe) against rancher Dan Evans (Bale) in a battle that's as much about psychology as it is gunplay. Crippled by war injury and battling a drought, Evans struggles to keep his ranch and the respect of his wife (Mol) and son (Lerman). When Wade is captured mid-crime spree, Evans joins the posse that will transport him to the titular train. Wade quickly recognizes the weaknesses of the men guarding him and turns them to his advantage, leaving Evans to defend himself and his son against Wade's madman second-in command Charlie Prince (Foster, in a career-making role). Masterfully explores the grey area between good and bad, and Mangold infuses the genre with a level of energy and excitement that hasn't been seen in a western in a while. **120m/C DVD, Blu-ray Disc.** *US* Russell Crowe, Christian Bale, Ben Foster, Logan Lerman, Peter Fonda, Gretchen Mol, Dallas Roberts, Alan Tudyk, Vinessa Shaw, Kevin Durand, Johnny Whitworth; ***D:*** James Mangold; ***W:*** Halsted Welles, Michael Brandt, Derek Haas; ***C:*** Phedon Papamichael; ***M:*** Marco Beltrami.

Three Texas Steers ✗ 1/2 *Danger Rides the Range* **1939** A circus owner inherits some land that the government wants for a water project and her manager tries to get it for himself. Enter the terrific trio to set things right. Last of the series for Terhune. The scenes of the circus fire were taken from "Circus Girl" (1937). **59m/B VHS.** John Wayne, Ray Corrigan, Max Terhune, Carole Landis, Ralph Graves, Roscoe Ates; ***D:*** George Sherman.

Three the Hard Way ✗✗ 1/2 **1974 (R)** An insane white supremacist has a plan to eliminate blacks by contaminating water supplies. A big blaxploitation money maker and the first to team Brown, Williamson, and Kelly, who would go on to make several more pictures together. **93m/C VHS.** Jim Brown, Fred Williamson, Jim Kelly, Sheila Frazier, Jay Robinson, Alex Rocco; ***D:*** Gordon Parks.

3000 Miles to Graceland ✗ 1/2 **2001 (R)** Shockingly original pic sets Elvis impersonators in Vegas, only these Presleys wanna rob, not rock. Ex-cellmates Russell and Costner are the lead Kings, Michael and Murphy, who team up with Arquette, Slater, and Woodbine, and head to the quaint desert burg to relieve its wagering establishments of some extra cash. After a strong opening segment, only moments of comic relief are scattered throughout, highlighted by the Elvii strutting through town in a "Reservoir Dogs" homage. Gratuitous violence and cliched action doesn't help movie's one-note appeal but the look is slick and the boys drive cool cars. **125m/C VHS, DVD.** *US* Kevin Costner, Kurt Russell, Christian Slater, Bokeem Woodbine, David Arquette, Courteney Cox, Kevin Pollak, Jon Lovitz, Howie Long, Thomas Haden Church, Ice-T, David Kaye, Louis Lombardi; ***D:*** Demian Lichtenstein; ***W:*** Demian Lichtenstein, Richard Recco; ***C:*** David Franco; ***M:*** George S. Clinton.

Three Times ✗✗ *Zuihaode Shiguang* **2005** A trio of linked stories (about romantic longing) set in three time periods with Qi Shu and Chen Chang playing the leads. "A Time for Love" (1966) has a young soldier romancing a pool-hall hostess. "A Time for Freedom" (1911) is a silent drama with a courtesan in a brothel hoping a client will purchase her freedom. "A Time for Youth" (2005) finds a bisexual singer in Taipei drifting into an affair with a photographer. Mandarin and Taiwanese with subtitles. **139m/C DVD.** *TW* Shu Qi, Chang Chen; ***D:*** Hou Hsiao-Hsien; ***W:*** Chu Tien-Wen; ***C:*** Mark Lee Ping-Bin.

Three to Tango ✗ 1/2 **1999 (PG-13)** Dopey would-be romantic comedy only demonstrates that actors who make it big in TV series should think about sticking to the small screen. (Or being more careful about their big screen choices.) Married tycoon Charles Newman (McDermott) has it in his power to award a lucrative contract to struggling architect Oscar Novak (Perry) and his partner, Peter Steinberg (Peter). Somehow, Newman gets the impression that Oscar is gay and would be the perfect guy to spy on Newman's young mistress, Amy (Campbell), whom he fears is about to wander. Naturally, Oscar falls for the girl and then must work around all the mistaken assumptions. Yawn. **98m/C VHS, DVD.** Dylan McDermott, Neve Campbell, Matthew Perry, Oliver Platt, Cylk Cozart, John C. McGinley, Bob Balaban, Kelly Rowan, Deborah Rush, Patrick Van Horn; ***D:*** Damon Santostefano; ***W:*** Rodney Vaccaro, Aline Brosh McKenna; ***C:*** Walt Lloyd; ***M:*** Graeme Revell.

Three Violent People ✗✗ **1957** Family feud set in post-Civil War Old West features Heston and Baxter impulsively marrying and returning to run the family ranch. Heston's brother (Tryon) wants to sell the ranch in order to get his share of the inheritance and then Heston finds out Baxter was once a prostitute. In this case family squabbles don't make for an exciting film. **100m/C VHS, DVD.** Charlton Heston, Anne Baxter, Gilbert Roland, Tom Tryon, Forrest Tucker, Elaine Stritch, Bruce Bennett, Barton MacLane; ***D:*** Rudolph Mate; ***W:*** James Edward Grant; ***C:*** Loyal Griggs; ***M:*** Walter Scharf.

Three Warriors ✗ 1/2 **1977** Young Native American boy is forced to leave the city and return to the reservation, where his contempt for the traditions of his ancestors slowly turns to appreciation and love. **100m/C VHS.** Charles White Eagle, Lois Red Elk, McKee "Kiko" Red Wing, Randy Quaid, Christopher Lloyd, Trey Wilson; ***D:*** Keith Merrill; ***W:*** Sy Gomberg; ***C:*** Bruce Surtees; ***M:*** Merrill Jenson.

3-Way ✗✗ *Three Way Split* **2004 (R)** Sure it can be fun to watch the pretty people double-cross each other in this adaptation of Gil Brewer's 1963 novel "Wild to Possess" but even that wears thin. A philandering hubby and his girlfriend plot to kidnap his rich wife (Gershon) then bump her off after they get the ransom. Enter Lew (Purcell)—a troubled soul (with a heart)—who overhears the scheme and sees an easy score; however a blackmailer (Yoakam) arrives just in time to foul things up. Too few degrees of separation among the players make for far-fetched scenarios that deflate potentially intriguing plot twists. **88m/C VHS, DVD.** Joy Bryant, Gina Gershon, Dwight Yoakam, Desmond Harrington, Ali Larter, Dominic Purcell; ***D:*** Scott Ziehl; ***W:*** Russell P. Marleau; ***C:*** Antonio Calvache; ***M:*** Christopher Hoag. **VIDEO**

Three Way Weekend ✗ **1981 (R)** Two young girls set off on a back-packing trip through the mountains of Southern California to enjoy camping and romance. **78m/C VHS.** Dan Diego, Jody Lee Olhava, Richard Blye, Blake Parrish; ***D:*** Emmett Alston.

The Three Weird Sisters ✗✗ **1948** The three weird sisters from "Macbeth" strive to maintain their life of luxury by plotting to kill their half-brother for the inheritance. Not a bad effort for Birt's first time out as director; script co-written by his wife, Louise and poet Thomas. **82m/B VHS.** *GB* Nancy Price, Mary Clare; ***D:*** Daniel Birt; ***W:*** Dylan Thomas, Louise Birt.

Three Wishes ✗✗ **1995 (PG)** Mysterious—and perhaps mystical—stranger Jack (Swayze) moves into the lives of a 1950s suburban widow (Mastrantonio) and her kids (Mazzello and Mumy) after she hits him with her car. Jack proceeds to use Zen philosophy, stories of a genie disguised as a dog, and nude sunbathing to help the kids' Little League team, make a boy fly, and scandalize the neighborhood. Adults will recognize the beatnik, Kerouac-influenced philosophy of nonconformity. They'll also recognize the sellout of that ideal with the sickeningly sappy ending. Mumy is the son of former "Lost in Space" child star Billy Mumy. **115m/C VHS, DVD.** Patrick Swayze, Mary Elizabeth Mastrantonio, Joseph Mazzello, David Marshall Grant, Michael O'Keefe, John Diehl, Jay O. Sanders, Diane Venora, Seth Mumy; ***D:*** Martha Coolidge; ***W:*** Elizabeth Anderson; ***C:*** Johnny E. Jensen; ***M:*** Cynthia Millar.

3 Women ✗✗✗ **1977 (PG)** Altman creates a surreal, dreamlike, sometimes creepy tale of women's relationships with each other. Shy reserved Pinky (Spacek) gets a job in a senior care center where she meets Millie (Duvall), a therapist who doesn't seem to acknowledge her invisibility. She immediately idolizes and moves in with Millie, following in Millie's wannabe modern woman footsteps, and slowly begins to take over her life. The two are friends with Willie (Rule), the morose, pregnant artist wife of their landlord who paints frightening figures in the bottom of the building's pool. Admittedly influenced by Ingmar Bergman, Altman deftly handles tragedy, questions of identity, and our dreams' relationship to our waking lives. **124m/C DVD.** Shelley Duvall, Sissy Spacek, Janice Rule, Robert Fortier, Ruth Nelson, John Cromwell, Sierra Pecheur, Craig Richard Nelson, Maysie Hoy, Dennis Christopher; ***D:*** Robert Altman; ***W:*** Robert Altman, Patricia Resnick; ***C:*** Charles Rosher Jr.

Three Word Brand ✗✗ **1921** Hart plays three roles in this film, a homesteader who is killed by Indians and his twin sons, who are separated after their father's death and reunited many years later. Silent with musical score. **75m/B VHS.** William S. Hart, Jane Novak, S.J. Bingham; ***D:*** Lambert Hillyer.

The Three Worlds of Gulliver ✗✗ 1/2 *The Worlds of Gulliver* **1959** A colorful family version of the Jonathan Swift classic about an Englishman who discovers a fantasy land of small and giant people. Visual effects by Ray Harryhausen. **100m/C VHS, DVD.** Kerwin Mathews, Jo Morrow, Basil Sydney, Mary Ellis; ***D:*** Jack Sher; ***W:*** Jack Sher, Arthur Ross; ***C:*** Wilkie Cooper; ***M:*** Bernard Herrmann.

The Threepenny Opera ✗✗ *Die Dreigroschenoper; L'Opera De Quat'Sous; Beggars' Opera* **1931** A musical about the exploits of gangster Mack the Knife. Adapted from Bertolt Brecht's play and John Gay's "The Beggar's Opera." In German with English subtitles. **107m/B VHS.** Rudolph Forster, Lotte Lenya, Carola Neher, Reinhold Schunzel, Fritz Rasp, Valeska Gert, Ernst Busch; ***D:*** G.W. Pabst; ***W:*** Ladislao Vajda, Bela Balazs, Leo Lania; ***C:*** Fritz Arno Wagner; ***M:*** Kurt Weill.

Three's Trouble ✗✗ **1985** A middle-class family erupts when a young male babysitter enters to care for its three mischievous sons. **93m/C VHS.** *AU* John Waters, Jacki Weaver, Steven Vidler; ***D:*** Chris Thomson.

Threesome WOOF! **1994 (R)** Another Generation X movie that tries hard to be hip, but fails miserably. Due to a college administrative error, Alex (Boyle) winds up sharing a suite with two male roommates, Eddy (Charles) and Stuart (Baldwin). Despite having completely different personalities, they soon become best friends and form one cozy little group, with cozy being the key word. Sexual tension abounds—Alex wants Eddy who wants Stuart who wants Alex. Filled with pathetic dialogue (most of it relating to bodily functions and body parts) and shallow, obnoxious characters, this menage a trois film is a flop. **93m/C VHS, DVD.** Lara Flynn Boyle, Stephen Baldwin, Josh Charles, Alexis Arquette, Mark Arnold, Martha Gehman, Michelle Matheson; ***D:*** Andrew Fleming; ***W:*** Andrew Fleming; ***C:*** Alexander Grusynski; ***M:*** Thomas Newman.

Threshold 🦴🦴 1/2 **1983 (PG)** An internationally acclaimed research biologist is frustrated by his inability to save a dying 20-year-old woman born with a defective heart. She becomes the recipient of the first artificial heart. Solid performances. **97m/C VHS.** ***CA*** Donald Sutherland, Jeff Goldblum, John Marley, Mare Winningham; ***D:*** Richard Pearce. Genie '83: Actor (Sutherland).

Threshold 🦴 **2003** A Sci-Fi Channel original, which means it's low-budget and bad in numerous ways. Space shuttle Oklahoma suffered meteorite damage on its last mission and an astronaut turns out to have been infected with insectoid-like aliens that need new hosts for each stage of their development. Drs. Horne and Bailey have been given 48 hours to find a way to stop the critters or Houston will be destroyed to contain the outbreak. **85m/C DVD.** Nicholas Lea, Jamie Luner, Stephen J. Cannell, Steve Bacic, David Lipper, Teryl Rothery, Karl Pruner; ***D:*** Chuck Bowman; ***W:*** Kim LeMasters; ***C:*** Richard Wincent; ***M:*** Richard John Baker. **CABLE**

The Thrill Killers WOOF! *The Monsters Are Loose; The Maniacs Are Loose* **1965** Young murderous thugs rampage through Los Angeles suburbs, killing indiscriminately. Pretentious and exploitative. Sometimes shown with Hallucinogenic Hypo-Vision—a prologue announcing the special effect would be shown before the film, and on cue, hooded ushers would run through the theatre with cardboard axes. Weird. **82m/C VHS, DVD.** Ray Dennis Steckler, Liz Renay, Brick Bardo, Ron Haydock, Atlas King, Gary Kent, Carolyn Brandt, Herb Robins, Ron Burr, George Morgan, Arch (Archie) Hall Sr.; ***D:*** Ray Dennis Steckler; ***W:*** Gene Pollock, Ray Dennis Steckler; ***C:*** Joseph Mascelli; ***M:*** Andre Brummer.

Thrill of a Romance 🦴🦴 **1945** Johnson, an Army hero, meets Williams, a swimming instructor of all things, at a resort in the Sierra Nevadas. The only problem is that she's married. Typical swim-romance vehicle. ♫ Don't Say No, Say Maybe; I Should Care; Lonely Night; Vive L'Amour; Schubert's Serenade; The Thrill of a Romance. **105m/C VHS.** Esther Williams, Van Johnson, Frances Gifford, Henry Travers, Spring Byington, Lauritz Melchior; ***D:*** Richard Thorpe.

The Thrill of It All! 🦴🦴 1/2 **1963** An average housewife becomes a star of TV commercials, to the dismay of her chauvinist husband, a gynecologist. Fast and funny, with numerous acidic jokes about television sponsors and programs. **108m/C VHS, DVD.** James Garner, Doris Day, Arlene Francis, Edward Andrews, Carl Reiner, Elliott Reid, Reginald Owen, Zasu Pitts; ***D:*** Norman Jewison; ***W:*** Carl Reiner; ***C:*** Russell Metty.

Thrill Seekers 🦴🦴 1/2 *The Timeshifters* **1999 (PG-13)** Fast-pace helps overcome the plot holes in this sci-fi thriller. Merrick (Van Dien) is a tabloid reporter who is researching great past catastrophes. He discovers that aliens are traveling back in time (to earth's present) to take part in disasters of their own contrivance. Trying to prevent an arena fire, Merrick teams up with another reporter, Elizabeth (Bell), and they run into a couple of alien assassins (Saldana, Outerbridge). **92m/C VHS, DVD.** Casper Van Dien, Catherine Bell, Peter Outerbridge, Theresa Saldana, Martin Sheen, Mimi Kuzyk, Lawrence Dane, Catherine Van Dien; ***D:*** Mario Azzopardi; ***W:*** Kurt Inderbitzin, Gay Walch; ***C:*** Derick Underschultz; ***M:*** Fred Mollin. **CABLE**

Thrilled to Death 🦴 1/2 **1988 (R)** An utterly naive husband and wife get caught in the middle of a lethal game when they befriend a scheming couple. **90m/C VHS.** Blake Bahner, Krista Lane, Richard Maris, Christine Moore; ***D:*** Chuck Vincent.

Thrillkill 🦴 **1984** A young girl is enmeshed in a multi-million-dollar burglary scheme after her computer-whiz/embezzler sister disappears. **88m/C VHS.** Robin Ward, Gina Massey, Anthony Kramroither; ***D:*** Anthony D'Andrea.

Throne of Blood 🦴🦴🦴🦴 *Kumonosujo, Kumonosu-djo; Cobweb Castle; The Castle of the Spider's Web* **1957** Kurosawa's masterful adaptation of "Macbeth" transports the story to medieval Japan and the world of the samurai. Mifune and Chiaki are warriors who have put down a rebellion and are to be rewarded by their overlord. On their way to his castle they meet a mysterious old woman who prophesizes that Mifune will soon rule—but his reign will be short. She is dismissed as crazy but her prophesies come to pass. So steeped in Japanese style that it bears little resemblance to the Shakespearean original, this film is an incredibly detailed vision in its own right. In Japanese with English subtitles. **105m/B VHS, DVD.** ***JP*** Toshiro Mifune, Isuzu Yamada, Takashi Shimura, Minoru Chiaki, Akira Kubo; ***D:*** Akira Kurosawa; ***W:*** Hideo Oguni, Shinobu Hashimoto, Ryuzo Kikushima, Akira Kurosawa; ***C:*** Asakazu Nakai; ***M:*** Masaru Sato.

Throne of Fire WOOF! 1982 A mighty hero battles the forces of evil to gain control of the powerful Throne of Fire. Dubbed. **91m/C VHS.** ***IT*** Peter McCoy, Sabrina Siani; ***D:*** Franco Prosperi.

Through a Glass Darkly 🦴🦴🦴 *Sasom I En Spegel* **1961** Oppressive interactions within a family sharing a holiday on a secluded island: a woman recovering from schizophrenia, her husband, younger brother, and her psychologist father. One of Bergman's most mysterious, upsetting and powerful films. In Swedish with English subtitles. Part of Bergman's Silence-of-God trilogy followed by "Winter Light" and "The Silence." **91m/B VHS, DVD.** ***SW*** Harriet Andersson, Max von Sydow, Gunnar Bjornstrand, Lars Passgard; ***D:*** Ingmar Bergman; ***W:*** Ingmar Bergman; ***C:*** Sven Nykvist. Oscars '61: Foreign Film.

Through Naked Eyes 🦴🦴 1/2 **1987** Thriller about two people who spy on each other. They witness a murder and realize that someone else is watching them. What a coincidence. **91m/C VHS.** David Soul, Pam Dawber; ***D:*** John Llewellyn Moxey. **TV**

Through the Breakers 🦴 1/2 **1928** Heartbroken woman suffers silently on South Pacific isle. **55m/B VHS.** Margaret Livingston, Holmes Herbert, Clyde Cook, Natalie Joyce; ***D:*** Deborah Schwartz; ***W:*** Harold Shumate; ***C:*** Ray June.

Through the Eyes of a Killer 🦴🦴 1/2 **1992 (R)** Laurie Fisher (Helgenberger) has dumped cheating boyfriend Jerry (Pantoliano) and has declared her independence by finding a spacious but crummy New York apartment in desperate need of renovation. Enter handsome handyman Ray Bellano (Anderson), who's happy to work on the apartment—and Laurie as well. But where Laurie sees a fling, Ray sees true love, and since brooding Ray's got the prerequisite mystery past, you know Laurie's in for the shock of her life. Long-time nice guy Anderson does a credible turn as an obsessive psycho. Based on the short story "The Master Builder" by Christopher Fowler; made for TV. **94m/C VHS.** Richard Dean Anderson, Marg Helgenberger, Joe Pantoliano, David Marshall Grant, Melinda Culea, Tippi Hedren; ***D:*** Peter Markle; ***W:*** John Pielmeier; ***M:*** George S. Clinton. **TV**

Through the Fire 🦴🦴🦴 **2005** In a sort of mini-"Hoop Dreams," director Hock engagingly follows 18-year-old basketball player Sebastian Telfair during his senior year at Coney Island's Lincoln High School. A surprisingly level-headed Telfair debates whether to play college ball or risk jumping into the uncertainties of the NBA draft as his brother unsuccessfully did a few years before. But his path becomes clear when violence erupts at his family's projects and their chance to escape rests on him. **103m/C DVD.** ***US D:*** Jonathan Hock; ***C:*** Alastair Christopher; ***M:*** Duncan Sheik, Pete Miser.

Through the Olive Trees 🦴🦴🦴 *Under the Olive Trees; Zire Darakhtan Zeyton* **1994 (G)** Film-within-a-film is the last of a trilogy concerned with Persian village life, following "Where Is My Friend's House?" and "And Life Goes On." Director, filming in an earthquake-ravaged village, discovers that the young bricklayer playing the bridegroom in his film is actually in love with the local girl who's playing the bride. However, she's turned down his real-life marriage proposal, feeling that the uneducated man is beneath her. Farsi with subtitles. It may be rated G but considering the subject matter and the fact that the film is subtitled, don't consider this one for the kiddies. **104m/C VHS.** ***IA*** Hossein Rezai, Mohamad Ali Keshavarz, Taherek Ladania, Zarifeh Shivah; ***D:*** Abbas Kiarostami; ***W:*** Abbas Kiarostami; ***C:*** Hossein Jafarian, Farhad Saba.

Throw Down 🦴 **2000** Ex-Marine martial artist Max Finister (Wingster) comes home to find that drug pushers have taken over the neighborhood. The rest of the story follows the familiar formula. This is an unusually inept action picture. The fights (directed by Wingster) tend to be slow and director Cyrus Beyzavi tends to cut people's heads off. **90m/C DVD.** La'Mard J. Wingster, Mark G. Young, Maribel Velez, Wendy Fajardo, John "Kato" Hollis, Patrick "Gun" Ryan; ***D:*** Cyrus Beyzavi; ***C:*** Mike Dolgetta.

Throw Momma from the Train 🦴🦴🦴 **1987 (PG-13)** DeVito plays a man, henpecked by his horrific mother, who tries to persuade his writing professor (Crystal) to exchange murders. DeVito will kill Crystal's ex-wife and Crystal will kill DeVito's mother. Only mama isn't going to be that easy to get rid of. Fast-paced and entertaining black comedy. Ramsey steals the film. Inspired by Hitchcock's "Strangers on a Train." **88m/C VHS, DVD.** Danny DeVito, Billy Crystal, Anne Ramsey, Kate Mulgrew, Kim Greist, Branford Marsalis, Rob Reiner, Bruce Kirby; ***D:*** Danny DeVito; ***W:*** Stu Silver; ***C:*** Barry Sonnenfeld; ***M:*** David Newman.

The Throwback 🦴 1/2 **1935** When Jones was a lad the townspeople accused his father of cattle rustling. When he returns as an adult he sets out to clear his father's name. **61m/B VHS.** Buck Jones, Muriel Evans, Eddie (Edward) Phillips, George "Gabby" Hayes, Bryant Washburn, Paul Fix, Frank LaRue; ***D:*** Ray Taylor.

Thumb Tripping 🦴🦴 **1972 (R)** A dated '60s/hippie film. Two flower children hitchhike and encounter all kinds of other strange people in their travels on the far-out roads. **94m/C VHS.** Meg Foster, Michael Burns, Bruce Dern, Marianna Hill, Michael Conrad, Joyce Van Patten; ***D:*** Quentin Masters.

Thumbelina 🦴🦴🦴 **1982** From "Faerie Tale Theatre" comes the story of a tiny girl who gets kidnapped by a toad and a mole, but meets the man of her dreams in the nick of time. Adapted from the classic tale by Hans Christian Andersen. **60m/C VHS, DVD.** Carrie Fisher, William Katt, Burgess Meredith; ***D:*** Michael Lindsay-Hogg. **CABLE**

Thumbelina 🦴🦴 1/2 *Hans Christian Andersen's Thumbelina* **1994 (G)** Ornery little girl named Mia gets magically sucked into the pages of the "Thumbelina" storybook she's reading and finds all sorts of adventures. Loose adaptation of Hans Christian Andersen fairy tale from Bluth is lackluster, with acceptable songs. Not up to the level of recent Disney animated features, but pleasant enough for the kids. **86m/C VHS, DVD.** ***D:*** Don Bluth, Gary Goldman; ***W:*** Don Bluth; ***M:*** William Ross, Barry Manilow, Barry Manilow, Jack Feldman, Bruce Sussman; ***V:*** Jodi Benson, Gary Imhoff, Charo, Gilbert Gottfried, Carol Channing, John Hurt, Will Ryan, June Foray, Kenneth Mars. Golden Raspberries '94: Worst Song ("Marry the Mole").

Thumbsucker 🦴🦴🦴 **2005 (R)** Seventeen year old Justin's (Pucci) underachieving, unfulfilled parents Mike (D'Onofrio) and Audrey (Swinton), saddled with their own baggage, are incapable of dealing with their son's embarrassing thumb-sucking habit. Justin's habit lands him in the office of the orthodontist/new-age guru Dr. Perry Lyman (Reeves), who uses hypnosis to break Justin's habit. But now without a coping mechanism Justin suffers from ADD. Newly armed with Ritalin and a pharmaceutically enhanced self-confidence, he becomes an arrogant, bullying monster. The beauty of this film is in the way Justin relates to the adults around him—all of whom range from eccentric to obscure and are played to perfection. **97m/C DVD.** ***US*** Lou Taylor Pucci, Tilda Swinton, Vince Vaughn, Vincent D'Onofrio, Keanu Reeves, Benjamin Bratt, Kelli Garner, Chase Offerle; ***D:*** Mike Mills; ***W:*** Mike Mills; ***C:*** Joaquin Baca-Asay.

Thunder Alley 🦴🦴 1/2 **1967** Annette teams up with Fabian again in this AIP stock car story. Daytona driver Fabian has a blackout during a race and causes a fatal crash. He and girlfriend McBain go on a thrill driving circuit, run by Murray. Annette is Murray's daughter and a swell stunt driver herself. To ingratiate himself with Annette, Fabian agrees to teach her boyfriend (Berlinger) how to be a pro racer and they become rivals. Annette's last role for AIP was a bit more mature than what she'd previously done and the flick overall is geared more towards action than boy/girl fun in the sun. **90m/C DVD.** Fabian, Annette Funicello, Diane McBain, Warren Berlinger, Jan Murray, Stanley Adams; ***D:*** Richard Rush; ***W:*** Sy Salkowitz; ***C:*** Monroe Askins; ***M:*** Michael Curb.

Thunder Alley 🦴 1/2 **1985** In middle America, two friends and their rock group struggle for success. One of the friends dies after an accidental overdose and the other's grief propels him to stardom. ♫ Can't Look Back; Just Another Pretty Boy; Sometimes in the Night; Heart to Heart; Can You Feel My Heart Beat; Do You Feel Alright?; Danger, Danger; Surrender; Gimme Back My Heart. **102m/C VHS.** Roger Wilson, Leif Garrett, Jill Schoelen, Clancy Brown, Scott McGinnis, Cynthia Eilbacher, Phil Brock; ***D:*** J.S. Cardone; ***W:*** J.S. Cardone.

Thunder and Lightning 🦴🦴 **1977 (PG)** A mismatched young couple chase a truckload of poisoned moonshine. Action-packed chases ensue. Nice chemistry between Carradine and Jackson. **94m/C VHS, DVD.** David Carradine, Kate Jackson, Roger C. Carmel, Sterling Holloway, Eddie Barth; ***D:*** Corey Allen.

Thunder & Mud 1989 Female mud wrestlers battle over their favorite rock band. Hahn's attempt to cash in on her notoriety after the Bakker scandal. **90m/C VHS.** Jessica Hahn; ***D:*** Penelope Spheeris.

Thunder Bay 🦴🦴🦴 **1953** Stewart and Duryea are a pair of Louisiana wildcat oil drillers who believe there is oil at the bottom of the Gulf of Mexico off the coast of the town of Port Felicity. They decide to construct an oil platform which the shrimp fisherman of the town believe will interfere with their livelihoods. Tensions rise between the two groups and violence seems likely. Action packed, with timely storyline as modern oil drillers fight to drill in waters that have historically been off-limits. **82m/C VHS.** James Stewart, Joanne Dru, Dan Duryea, Gilbert Roland, Marcia Henderson; ***D:*** Anthony Mann; ***W:*** John Michael Hayes; ***C:*** William H. Daniels.

Thunder Birds 🦴🦴 1/2 **1942** Combat flight instructor Steve Britt (Foster) trains Brit cadet Stackhouse (Sutton) to become an ace fighter pilot in spite of the fact that they love the same women (Tierney). Fine performances and an intersting story keep this from being just another WW2-era flag-waver. **78m/C DVD.** Gene Tierney, Preston Foster, John Sutton, Jack Holt, May Whitty, George Barbier, Richard Haydn, Reginald Denny, Ted North, C. Montague Shaw, Peter Lawford; ***D:*** William A. Wellman; ***W:*** Lamar Trotti; ***C:*** Ernest Palmer; ***M:*** David Buttolph.

Thunder County 🦴 1/2 *Cell Block Girls; Swamp Fever* **1974** Federal agents and drug runners are after a group of four convicts who have just escaped from prison. **78m/C VHS, DVD.** Mickey Rooney, Ted Cassidy, Chris Robinson, Carol Locatell, Anya Ormsby, Phyllis Robinson; ***D:*** Chris Robinson; ***C:*** Jack Beckett; ***M:*** Jaime Mendoza-Nava.

Thunder in God's Country 🦴 **1951** A dishonest gambler eyes a peaceful western town as the next Vegas-like gambling capital.

Before this occurs he is exposed as a cheat. **67m/B VHS.** Buddy Ebsen, Ian MacDonald, Paul Harvey, Harry Lauter, Rex Allen, Mary Ellen Kay; ***D:*** George Blair; ***W:*** Arthur Orloff; ***C:*** John MacBurnie; ***M:*** Stanley Wilson.

Thunder in Paradise ♪♪ 1/2 **1993 (PG-13)** R.J. Hurricane Spencer (Hogan) is a soldier of fortune who heads into Cuba to help a woman and child escape political imprisonment, using his high-tech, weapon-filled speedboat. He has to fight off a small army and manages to find a buried treasure as well. Simple-minded TV pilot. **104m/C VHS.** Hulk Hogan, Robin Weisman, Chris Lemmon, Carol Alt, Patrick Macnee, Sam Jones, Charlotte Rae; ***D:*** Douglas Schwartz. **TV**

Thunder in Paradise 2 ♪ 1/2 **1994 (PG)** Damsel sends up a distress signal and it's the Hulkster and his pal to the rescue. Unfortunately, their commando raid fails and now they need an escape plan. From the syndicated TV series. **90m/C VHS, DVD.** Hulk Hogan, Chris Lemmon, Carol Alt, Patrick Macnee; ***D:*** Douglas Schwartz.

Thunder in Paradise 3 ♪ 1/2 **1994 (PG-13)** Hogan is on a top secret mission to capture a drug lord who's holding his daughter hostage. **88m/C VHS, DVD.** Chris Lemmon, Carol Alt, Ashley Gorrell, Hulk Hogan; ***D:*** Douglas Schwartz; ***W:*** Deborah Schwartz.

Thunder in the City ♪♪♪ **1937** Robinson is an intense American promoter in the sales game who is sent to London by his employers to learn a more subdued way of doing business. Instead, he meets a pair of down-on-their-luck artistocrats whose only asset is an apparently worthless Rhodesian mine. Robinson, however, comes up with a way to promote the mine and get enough capital together to make it profitable. Good satire with Robinson well cast. Robinson wasn't taken with the script in its original form and persuaded his friend, playwright Robert Sherwood, to re-write it. **85m/B VHS, DVD.** *GB* Edward G. Robinson, Nigel Bruce, Ralph Richardson, Constance Collier; ***D:*** Marion Gering; ***M:*** Miklos Rozsa.

Thunder in the Desert ♪ **1938** A cowhand joins an outlaw gang in order to catch his uncle's killer. **56m/C VHS, DVD.** Bob Steele, Louise Stanley, Don Barclay, Charles "Blackie" King, Lew Meehan, Budd Buster; ***D:*** Sam Newfield.

Thunder in the Pines ♪ **1949** Two lumberjack buddies send for the same French girl to marry, unbeknownst to each other. When she arrives, the dismayed men agree to a contest to see who will marry her. Meanwhile the French girl falls for the local saloon owner and his jilted girlfriend vows to get even. She does, with the help of the lumberjacks. **61m/B VHS, DVD.** Denise Darcel, George Reeves, Ralph Byrd, Lyle Talbot, Michael Whalen, Roscoe Ates, Vince Barnett; ***D:*** Robert Edwards.

Thunder Mountain ♪ 1/2 **1935** Zane Grey's novel about two prospectors who are bushwhacked on their way to file a claim comes to life on the screen. **56m/B VHS.** George O'Brien, Frances Grant, Morgan Wallace, Barbara Fritchie, William Bailey, Dean Benton, George "Gabby" Hayes, Ed LeSaint; ***D:*** David Howard; ***W:*** Daniel Jarrett, Don Swift; ***C:*** Frank B. Good.

Thunder Over Texas ♪ **1934** The cowboy hero gets embroiled in a railroad scandal that involves a kidnapping. Directed by Edgar G. Ulmer, who used the alias John Warner because he was moonlighting. His first western; previously he was best known for "The Black Cat." **52m/B VHS.** Marion Shilling, Helen Westcott, Victor Potel, Tiny Skelton; ***D:*** Edgar G. Ulmer.

Thunder Pass ♪♪ **1937** Gold and greed are the motives for murder as two young brothers become separated when their wagon train is attacked and their family is slaughtered. One brother searches for the other and finds him several years later. Based on the novel "Arizona Ames" by Zane Grey. Also released as "Thunder Trail." **58m/B VHS.** Charles Bickford, Marsha Hunt, Gilbert Roland, Monte Blue; ***D:*** Charles T. Barton.

Thunder Pass ♪♪ **1954** Routine story about a wagon train threatened by hostile Indians and the Army officer who leads them to safety. Based on a story by George Van Marter. **76m/B VHS.** Dane Clark, Dorothy Patrick, Andy Devine, Raymond Burr, John Carradine, Mary Ellen Kay; ***D:*** Frank McDonald; ***W:*** Tom Hubbard, Fred Eggers.

Thunder River Feud ♪♪ **1942** The Rangebusters help two ranchers avoid a range war. Part of "The Rangebusters" series. **58m/B VHS.** Ray Corrigan, John "Dusty" King, Max Terhune, Jan Wiley, Carleton Young, George Chesebro, Budd Buster, Jack Holmes, Rick Anderson; ***D:*** S. Roy Luby; ***W:*** Earle Snell, John Vlahos; ***C:*** Robert E. Cline; ***M:*** Jean George.

Thunder Road ♪♪♪ **1958 (PG)** Luke Doolin (Mitchum) comes home to Tennessee from Korea and takes over the family moonshine business, fighting both mobsters and federal agents. An exciting chase between Luke and the feds ends the movie with the appropriate bang. Robert Mitchum not only produced, wrote and starred in this best of the moonshine-running films, but also wrote the theme song "Whippoorwill" (which later became a radio hit). Mitchum's teenaged son, James, made his film debut as brother Robin Doolin and later starred in a similar movie "Moonrunners." A cult favorite. **92m/B VHS, DVD.** Robert Mitchum, Jacques Aubuchon, Gene Barry, Keely Smith, Trevor Bardette, Sandra Knight, Jim Mitchum, Betsy Holt, Frances Koon, Mitchell Ryan, Peter Breck; ***D:*** Arthur Ripley; ***W:*** Walter Wise, Robert Mitchum; ***C:*** Alan Stensvold; ***M:*** Jack Marshall.

Thunder Run ♪ **1986 (PG-13)** When a load of uranium needs to be transferred across Nevada, a retired trucker takes on the job. The trip is made more difficult since terrorists are trying to hijack the shipment to use for a bomb. **84m/C VHS.** Forrest Tucker, John Ireland, John Shepherd, Jill Whitlow, Wallace (Wally) Langham, Cheryl Lynn; ***D:*** Gary Hudson; ***W:*** Charles Davis.

Thunder Trail ♪♪ **1937** Set of twins, separated by a wagon trail massacre, meet up years later on opposite sides of the law. **58m/C VHS.** Gilbert Roland, Charles Bickford, Marsha Hunt, J. Carrol Naish, James Craig, Monte Blue; ***D:*** Charles T. Barton.

Thunder Warrior ♪ *Thunder* **1985 (R)** A young Indian turns into a one-man army determined to punish the local authorities who are abusing his fellow tribe members. De Angelis used the pseudonym Larry Ludman. **84m/C VHS.** Raimund Harmstorf, Bo Svenson, Mark Gregory; ***D:*** Fabrizio de Angelis.

Thunder Warrior 2 ♪ **1985 (PG-13)** A tough Native American is provoked to violence by small-town prejudice. De Angelis used the pseudonym Larry Ludman. **114m/C VHS.** *IT* Mark Gregory, Karen Reel, Bo Svenson; ***D:*** Fabrizio de Angelis.

Thunder Warrior 3 ♪ **1988** The Indian Thunder has vowed to live in peace, but forswears the oath when his wife is kidnapped and family is terrorized. Revenge is the top priority as he torments the bad guys. De Angelis used the pseudonym Larry Ludman. **90m/C VHS.** Mark Gregory, John Phillip Law, Ingrid Lawrence, Werner Pochath, Horts Schon; ***D:*** Fabrizio de Angelis.

Thunderball ♪♪ 1/2 **1965 (PG)** The fourth installment in Ian Fleming's James Bond series finds 007 on a mission to thwart SPECTRE, which has threatened to blow up Miami by atomic bomb if 100 million pounds in ransom is not paid. One of the more tedious Bond entries but a big boxoffice success. Tom Jones sang the title song. Remade as "Never Say Never Again" in 1983 with Connery reprising his role as Bond after a 12-year absence. **125m/C VHS, DVD, Blu-ray Disc.** *GB* Sean Connery, Claudine Auger, Adolfo Celi, Luciana Paluzzi, Rik van Nutter, Martine Beswick, Molly Peters, Guy Doleman, Bernard Lee, Lois Maxwell, Desmond Llewelyn; ***D:*** Terence Young; ***W:*** John Hopkins, Richard Maibaum; ***C:*** Ted Moore; ***M:*** John Barry. Oscars '65: Visual FX.

Thunderbirds ♪ 1/2 **2004 (PG)** Thunderbirds are go! Nobody's really sure why, since it's a 40-year-old British TV show about creepy puppets (remember "Supermarionation"?) rescuing other, equally creepy puppets. This version is live-action but it's still wooden. Billionaire ex-astronaut Jeff Tracy (Paxton) lives on an island in the South Pacific with his five sons (all named after astronauts) and five specially designed aircraft. He uses the Thunderbirds to run International Rescue. Telekinetic evil guy, The Hood (Kingsley), is bent on world domination (what else?) and strands Dad and the four older boys on their orbiting space station, leaving youngest wannabe Thunderbird Alan (Corbett) and a couple of his pals to save the day. The 10-and-under crowd may be persuaded to sit through this harmless but lackluster adventure. **94m/C DVD.** *US* Bill Paxton, Brady Corbet, Ben Kingsley, Anthony Edwards, Sophia Myles, Ron Cook, Genie Francis, Lou Hirsch, Nicola Walker, Johannes Zadrozny, Soren Fulton, Vanessa Anne Hudgens, Philip Winchester, Dhobi Oparei, Kyle Herbert, Dominic Colenso, Ben Torgersen, Lex Shrapnel; ***D:*** Jonathan Frakes; ***W:*** Peter Hewitt, William Osborne, Michael McCullers; ***C:*** Brendan Galvin; ***M:*** Hans Zimmer.

Thunderbolt & Lightfoot ♪♪♪ **1974 (R)** Eastwood is an ex-thief on the run from his former partners (Kennedy and Lewis) who believe he's made off with the loot from their last job, the robbery of a government vault. He joins up with drifter Bridges, who helps him to escape. Later, Eastwood manages to convince Kennedy he doesn't know where the money is. Bridges then persuades the men that they should plan the same heist and rob the same government vault all over again, which they do. But their getaway doesn't go exactly as planned. All-around fine acting; notable is Bridges' scene dressed in drag. First film for director Cimino. **115m/C VHS, DVD.** Clint Eastwood, Jeff Bridges, George Kennedy, Geoffrey Lewis, Gary Busey; ***D:*** Michael Cimino; ***W:*** Michael Cimino; ***C:*** Frank Stanley; ***M:*** Dee Barton.

Thunderground ♪ **1989 (R)** A beautiful con artist teams with a fighter and together they travel to New Orleans to arrange a bout with the king of bare-knuckled fighting. **92m/C VHS.** Paul Coufos, Margaret Langrick, Jesse Ventura, M. Emmet Walsh; ***D:*** David Mitchell.

Thunderheart ♪♪♪ **1992 (R)** Young FBI agent Kilmer is sent to an Oglala Sioux reservation to investigate a murder. He is himself part Sioux, but resents being chosen for the assignment because of it. Aided by a veteran partner (Shepard), Ray learns, professionally and personally, from a shrewd tribal police officer (well played by Greene). Set in the late '70s, the film is loosely based on actual events plaguing the violence-torn Native American community at that time. Great cinematography by Roger Deakins. Filmed on the Pine Ridge Reservation in South Dakota. Director Apted deals with the actual incidents this film is based on in his documentary about Leonard Peltier, "Incident at Oglala." **118m/C VHS, DVD.** Val Kilmer, Sam Shepard, Graham Greene, Fred Ward, Fred Dalton Thompson, Sheila Tousey, Chief Ted Thin Elk, John Trudell, Dennis Banks, David Crosby; ***D:*** Michael Apted; ***W:*** John Fusco; ***C:*** Roger Deakins; ***M:*** James Horner.

Thundering Forest ♪♪ **1941** Australian actioneer pitting loggers against saboteurs. **?m/C VHS.** *AU* Frank Leighton.

Thundering Gunslingers ♪ **1944** A group of gunmen terrorizing townspeople finally meet their match in this Western. **91m/B VHS.** Al "Fuzzy" St. John, Frances Gladwin, Charles "Blackie" King, Jack Ingram, Kermit Maynard, Karl Hackett, Buster Crabbe; ***D:*** Sam Newfield; ***W:*** Fred Myton; ***C:*** Robert Cline.

Thundering Trail ♪ *Thunder on the Trail* **1951** Two cowboys encounter plenty of trouble before they take the President's newly appointed territorial governor to his office. **55m/B VHS.** Lash LaRue, Al "Fuzzy" St. John, Sally Anglim, Archie Twitchell, Ray Bennett; ***D:*** Ron Ormond; ***W:*** Ira Webb; ***C:*** Ernest Miller; ***M:*** Walter Greene.

Thundersquad ♪ **1985** Mercenaries help a South American rebel leader rescue his kidnapped son. **90m/C VHS.** *IT* Sal Borgese, Julia Fursich, Antonio (Tony) Sabato; ***D:*** Umberto Lenzi; ***W:*** Robert Leoni; ***C:*** Giancarlo Ferrando; ***M:*** Stelvio Cipriani.

Thursday ♪♪ 1/2 **1998 (R)** Familiarity does breed something close to contempt in this comic crime thriller. Ex-drug dealer Casey Wells (Jane) has left L.A. for the straight and narrow life of a married Houston architect. That is until his lowlife ex-partner Nick (Eckhart) turns up one Thursday with a briefcase full of dope and some gangster problems. A succession of other nasty characters then proceeds to darken Casey's doorway and his efforts to get his life back just cause things to spin further out of control. The leads do a good job but it's nothing you haven't seen before. Also available in an unrated version. **82m/C VHS.** Thomas Jane, Aaron Eckhart, Paulina Porizkova, James LeGros, Paula Marshall, Michael Jeter, Glenn Plummer, Mickey Rourke; ***D:*** Skip Woods; ***W:*** Skip Woods; ***C:*** Denis Lenoir.

Thursday's Child ♪♪ **1943** A child's success in films causes trouble for her family. Melodramatic and sappy, but Howes, as the kid, is excellent. One of Granger's early supporting roles. **95m/B VHS.** *GB* Stewart Granger, Sally Ann Howes, Wilfred Lawson, Kathleen O'Regan, Eileen Bennett, Marianne Davis, Gerhard Kempinski, Felix Aylmer, Margaret Yarde, Vera Bogetti, Percy Walsh, Ronald Shiner; ***D:*** Rodney Ackland; ***W:*** Rodney Ackland, Donald Macardle; ***C:*** Desmond Dickinson.

Thursday's Game ♪♪♪ **1974 (PG)** Two crisis-besieged businessmen meet every Thursday, using poker as a ruse to work on their business and marital problems. Wonderful cast; intelligently written. **99m/C VHS.** Gene Wilder, Ellen Burstyn, Bob Newhart, Cloris Leachman, Nancy Walker, Valerie Harper, Rob Reiner; ***D:*** James L. Brooks; ***W:*** James L. Brooks. **TV**

THX 1138 ♪♪♪ **1971 (PG)** In the dehumanized world of the future, people live in underground cities run by computer, are force-fed drugs to keep them passive, and no longer have names—just letter/number combinations (Duvall is THX 1138). Emotion is also outlawed and when the computer-matched couple THX 1138 and LUH 3417 discover love, they must battle the computer system to escape. George Lucas' first film, which was inspired by a student film he did at USC. **88m/C VHS, DVD.** Robert Duvall, Donald Pleasence, Maggie McOmie; ***D:*** George Lucas; ***W:*** George Lucas; ***M:*** Lalo Schifrin.

Tiara Tahiti ♪♪ **1962** Intrigue, double-cross, romance, and violence ensue when two old army acquaintances clash in Tahiti. Very fine performances from the two leading men. **100m/C VHS.** James Mason, John Mills, Claude Dauphin, Rosenda Monteros, Herbert Lom; ***D:*** Ted Kotcheff.

The Tic Code ♪♪ 1/2 **1999 (R)** Twelve-year-old Miles (Marquette) aspires to be a jazz pianist but must practice at the local bar because his single mom Laura (Draper) can't afford a piano. But Miles has a bigger problem—he suffers from the misunderstood Tourette's syndrome, which brings him close to his idol, sax player Tyrone (Hines), who is similarly afflicted. Soon Tyrone is also playing some sweet music with Laura but the trio are on shaky ground since Tyrone can't deal with his illness. **91m/C VHS, DVD.** Gregory Hines, Polly Draper, James McCaffrey, Christopher Marquette, Carol Kane, Bill Nunn, Tony Shalhoub, Desmond Robertson, Fisher Stevens, Camryn Manheim, David Johansen; ***D:*** Gary Winick; ***W:*** Polly Draper; ***C:*** Wolfgang Held; ***M:*** Michael Wolff.

Tick Tock ♪♪♪ **2000 (R)** In Bakersfield, California, trophy wife Rachel (Ward) and her pal Carla (Minter) plot to get rid of wealthy hubby (Dukes). That's only the beginning of a plot that stacks trick upon trick, double-cross upon double-cross. Think "Blood Simple" lite. It's a delightful guilty pleasure made all the more enjoyable by polished production values. **93m/C DVD.** Megan Ward, Kristin Minter, Linden Ashby, John Ratzenberger, David Dukes; ***D:*** Kevin S. Tenney; ***W:*** Kevin S. Tenney; ***C:*** Jack Conroy; ***M:*** Dennis Michael Tenney.

Tick Tock Lullaby ♪♪ **2007** Sasha (Gornick) and her girlfriend Maya (Cassidy) are serious about having a baby but they want to conceive the old-fashioned way, which means one of them has to find a heterosexual sex partner. But their problems aren't much different from those of their straight friends as the road to parenthood is paved with obstacles and questionable intentions. The brief run-time keeps the plot moving. **73m/C DVD.** *GB* Lisa Gornick, Raquel

Cassidy, Sarah Patterson, Joanna Bending, William Bowry; *D:* Lisa Gornick; *W:* Lisa Gornick; *C:* Inge Blackman; *M:* Mat Davidson.

Ticker 🦴 1/2 **2001 (R)** San Francisco detective Sizemore is tracking mad bomber Hopper (reprising his "Speed" role to little effect) aided by bomb squad leader Seagal. Nothing that hasn't been done a zillion times before (and much better). **92m/C VHS, DVD.** Tom Sizemore, Steven Seagal, Nas, Jaime Pressly, Dennis Hopper, Chilli, Peter Greene; ***Cameos:*** Ice-T; *D:* Albert Pyun; *W:* Paul B. Margolis. **VIDEO**

The Ticket 🦴🦴 **1997 (PG-13)** Keith Reicker (Marshall) works as a pilot for a financially ailing charter company. His marriage to CeCe (Doherty) is rocky but when Keith wins a lottery worth $123 million, he's certain his life has finally turned around. He persuades CeCe and their 13-year-old son to fly with him and collect the money but the plane is sabotaged. Now they must not only survive the wilderness but whoever is out to steal the ticket and make certain the Reickers don't get out alive. **88m/C VHS.** James Marshall, Shannen Doherty, Heidi Swedberg, Al Mancini, John Tench; *D:* Stuart Cooper; *W:* David Alexander; *C:* Curtis Petersen; *M:* Charles Bernstein. **CABLE**

Ticket of Leave Man 🦴🦴 **1937** London's most dangerous killer fronts a charitable organization designed to help reform criminals. It actually steers them into a crime syndicate that cheats philanthropists out of their fortunes. **71m/B VHS.** *GB* Tod Slaughter, John Warwick, Marjorie Taylor, Robert Adair, Peter Gawthorne, Jenny Lynn, Norman Pierce; *D:* George King; *W:* H.F. Maltby, A.R. Rawlinson; *C:* Hone Glendinning; *M:* Jack Beaver.

Ticket to a Crime 🦴 1/2 **1934** Ex-cop turned PI Holt (Graves) gets into friendly competition with old friend/local cop McGinnis (Burke) over a theft and murder at the local country club. But it's Holt and secretary Peggy (Lane) who find the clue that breaks the case. **64m/B DVD.** Ralph Graves, James Burke, Lola Lane, Lois Wilson, Edward Earle, Charles Ray; *D:* Lewis D. Collins; *W:* John Thomas "Jack" Neville, Charles Logue; *C:* Gilbert Warrenton.

Ticket to Heaven 🦴🦴🦴 **1981 (PG)** A young man, trying to deal with the painful breakup of a love affair, falls under the spell of a quasi-religious order. His friends and family, worried about the cult's influence, have him kidnapped in order for him to be de-programmed. Mancuso is excellent, as are his supporting players Rubinek and Thomson. **109m/C VHS, DVD.** *CA* Nick Mancuso, Meg Foster, Kim Cattrall, Saul Rubinek, R.H. Thomson, Jennifer Dale, Guy Boyd, Paul Soles; *D:* Ralph L. (R.L.) Thomas; *W:* Anne Cameron; *C:* Richard Leiterman; *M:* Micky Erbe. Genie '82: Actor (Mancuso), Film, Support. Actor (Rubinek).

Ticket to Tomahawk 🦴🦴 1/2 **1950** A gunslinger is hired by a stagecoach company to sabotage a railroad. Look for Marilyn Monroe as a chorus girl in a musical number. **90m/C VHS.** Dan Dailey, Anne Baxter, Rory Calhoun, Walter Brennan, Charles Kemper, Connie Gilchrist, Arthur Hunnicutt, Victor Sen Yung, Marilyn Monroe, Jack Elam; *D:* Richard Sale; *W:* Richard Sale, Mary Loos; *C:* Harry Jackson; *M:* Cyril Mockridge.

Tickle Me 🦴 1/2 **1965** An unemployed rodeo star finds work at an all-girl health spa and dude ranch. He falls in love with a young lady who has a treasure map and keeps her safe from the evil men who want her fortune. For die-hard Elvis fans only. ♫ (It's a) Long, Lonely Highway; Night Rider; It Feels So Right; Dirty, Dirty Feeling; (Such an) Easy Question; Put the Blame on Me; I'm Yours; I Feel That I've Known You Forever; Slowly but Surely. **90m/C VHS, DVD.** Elvis Presley, Julie Adams, Jack Mullaney; *D:* Norman Taurog.

Ticks 🦴 1/2 *Infested* **1993 (R)** Mammoth mutant killer insects terrorize a Northern California campground! The predatory woodticks are the victims of steroids dumped in the water supply and a group of unwary teen campers fall prey to their deadly venom! And if that's not bad enough, a forest fire breaks out, trapping the teens! **85m/C VHS.** Ami Dolenz, Rosalind Allen, Alfonso Ribeiro, Peter Scolari; *D:* Tony Randel.

Tidal Wave 🦴 1/2 *Nippon Chiubotsu; The Submersion of Japan; Japan Sinks* **1975 (PG)** Scientists discover that Japan is slowly sinking and order the island to be evacuated. Originally a popular Japanese production, the American version is a poorly dubbed, re-edited mess. **82m/C VHS.** *JP* Lorne Greene, Keiju Kobayashi, Rhonda Leigh Hopkins, Hiroshi Fujioka, Shiro Moriana; *D:* Andrew Meyer.

Tideland 🦴 **2005 (R)** First 10-year-old Jeliza-Rose's (Ferland) junkie mom (Tilly) overdoses in L.A., prompting her junkie dad (Bridges) to drag her to a middle-of-nowhere Texas farmhouse where he, of course, overdoses, leaving the girl to retreat into a not-so-pleasant fantasy world with dear-old-dead-dad's corpse nearby. When not conversing with her headless dolls, she wanders the grassy fields near the train tracks, where she runs into some odd neighbors—a taxidermist who, um, helps Jeliza-Rose with the dead dad problem, and the woman's brother, a mentally-challenged man-child whose relationship with the young Jeliza-Rose gets a little creepy. Ferland's excellent performance stands out in what is otherwise an unredeemable mess. Based on Mitch Cullin's 2005 novel. **122m/C DVD.** *CA GB* Jodelle Ferland, Janet McTeer, Brendan Fletcher, Jeff Bridges, Jennifer Tilly; *D:* Terry Gilliam; *W:* Terry Gilliam, Tony Grisoni; *C:* Nicola Pecorini; *M:* Mychael Danna, Jeff Danna.

Tides of War 🦴🦴 **1990** In the twilight of WWII, a German officer begins to question his role in a proposed missile attack on Washington in light of the S.S. brutality he witnesses. **90m/C VHS.** Yvette Heyden, Rodrigo Obregon, David Soul, Bo Svenson; *D:* Neil Rossati.

Tidy Endings 🦴 1/2 **1988** A man who died from AIDS leaves behind his male lover and his ex-wife. The two form a friendship as they both try to cope with the man's death. Based on the play by Fierstein. **54m/C VHS.** Harvey Fierstein, Stockard Channing; *D:* Gavin Millar; *W:* Harvey Fierstein.

Tie Me Up! Tie Me Down! 🦴🦴 1/2 *Atame!* **1990 (NC-17)** A young psychiatric patient kidnaps a former porno actress he has always had a crush on, and holds her captive, certain that he can convince her to love him. Black comedy features a fine cast and is well directed. At least one fairly explicit sex scene and the bondage theme caused the film to be X-rated, although it was originally released unrated by the distributor. In Spanish with English subtitles. **105m/C VHS, DVD.** *SP* Victoria Abril, Antonio Banderas, Loles Leon, Francisco Rabal, Julieta Serrano, Maria Barranco, Rossy de Palma; *D:* Pedro Almodovar; *W:* Pedro Almodovar; *C:* Jose Luis Alcaine; *M:* Ennio Morricone.

The Tie That Binds 🦴 **1995 (R)** Insipid thriller is a cheap imitation of its cousin, "The Hand that Rocks the Cradle" (made by the same producers), but what the former movie did to the nanny business, this flick does to a whole genre. Leanne and John Netherwood (Hannah and Carradine) are psycho parents out to reclaim their daughter from the lame-brain yuppie couple (Spano and Kelly) who adopted her. Out of all the children there, they choose the one who likes to sleep with a butcher knife under her pillow. Duh! Every "family in danger from psychotic" cliche is employed in a vain attempt to build suspense for the silly conclusion. Dismal directorial debut of screenwriter Strick. **98m/C VHS, DVD.** Daryl Hannah, Keith Carradine, Moira Kelly, Vincent Spano, Julia Devin, Ray Reinhardt, Cynda Williams; *D:* Wesley Strick; *W:* Michael Auerbach; *C:* Bobby Bukowski; *M:* Graeme Revell.

Tiefland 🦴🦴 1/2 **1944** Melodrama based on the libretto for D'Abert's opera about a gypsy dancer and her loves. Unreleased until 1954, this film is the last of Riefenstahl's career; she subsequently turned to still photography. In German with English subtitles. **98m/B VHS, DVD.** *GE* Leni Riefenstahl, Franz Eichberger, Bernard Minetti, Maria Koppenhofer, Luise Rainer; *D:* Leni Riefenstahl.

Tierra 🦴🦴 *Earth* **1995** Metaphysical messiness. Mystery exterminator Angel (Gomez) comes to Aragon, a land of red soil and lightning strikes, to fumigate the woodlice infesting the vineyards. He recruits some locals and gypsies to help him out while becoming involved with a couple of women—shy Angela (Suarez) and hot Mari (Klein). But Angel is also literally haunted by an alter ego—a situation that no doubt has some deep meaning that is never very clear. But neither is the rest of the movie. Spanish with subtitles. **122m/C VHS, DVD.** *SP* Carmelo Gomez, Emma Suarez, Silke Klein, Karra Elejalde, Nancho Novo, Txema Blasco; *D:* Julio Medem; *W:* Julio Medem; *C:* Javier Aguirresarobe; *M:* Alberto Iglesias.

Tieta of Agreste 🦴🦴 **1996** After many years, wealthy Tieta (Braga) returns to her village with her stepdaughter and immediately causes havoc for her greedy family. Based on a novel by Jorge Amado. Portuguese with subtitles. **140m/C VHS, DVD.** *BR* Sonia Braga, Marilia Pera, Zeze Motta, Jorge Amado; *D:* Carlos Diegues; *W:* Carlos Diegues; *C:* Edgar Moura; *M:* Caetano Veloso.

Tiffany Jones 🦴 **1975 (R)** Tiffany Jones is a secret agent who has information that presidents and revolutionaries are willing to kill for. **90m/C VHS.** Anouska (Anoushka) Hempel, Ray Brooks, Eric Pohlmann, Martin Benson, Susan Sneers; *D:* Pete Walker.

Tiger and the Pussycat 🦴🦴 1/2 *Il Tigre* **1967 (R)** A successful Italian businessman's infatuation with an attractive American art student leads him to marital and financial woes. **110m/C VHS, DVD.** Ann-Margret, Vittorio Gassman, Eleanor Parker; *D:* Dino Risi.

The Tiger and the Snow 🦴 1/2 *La Tigre e la Neve* **2005** First it was the Holocaust and now Benigni uses the backdrop of the war in Iraq, circa 2003, for his absurdist tragicomedy romance. Exuberant Roman poet Attilio (Benigni) passes himself off as an aid worker and heads to Baghdad when he discovers Vittoria (Brachi), the woman he loves, has been seriously injured in a bombing. Italian with subtitles. **110m/C DVD.** *IT* Roberto Benigni, Nicoletta Braschi, Jean Reno, Tom Waits, Emilia Fox; *D:* Roberto Benigni; *W:* Roberto Benigni, Vincenzo Cerami; *C:* Fabio Cianchetti; *M:* Nicola Povani.

Tiger Bay 🦴🦴🦴 **1959** A young Polish sailor, on leave in Cardiff, murders his unfaithful girlfriend. Lonely ten-year-old Gillie sees the crime and takes the murder weapon, thinking it will make her more popular with her peers. Confronted by a police detective, she convincingly lies but eventually the sailor finds Gillie and kidnaps her, hoping to keep her quiet until he can get aboard his ship. A delicate relationship evolves between the child and the killer as she tries to help him escape and the police close in. Marks Hayley Mills' first major role and one of her finest performances. **107m/B VHS, DVD.** *GB* John Mills, Horst Buchholz, Hayley Mills, Yvonne Mitchell, Megs Jenkins, Anthony Dawson, Kenneth Griffith, Michael Anderson Jr.; *D:* J. Lee Thompson; *W:* John Hawkesworth; *C:* John Hawkesworth; *M:* Laurie Johnson.

Tiger Claws 🦴 1/2 **1991 (R)** The pretty, petite Rothrock has been called the female Bruce Lee. Perhaps, but at least he got a good script every once in a while. This time Rothrock's a kung-fu cop investigating the strange ritual-murders of martial-arts champions. **93m/C VHS, DVD.** Cynthia Rothrock, Bolo Yeung, Jalal Merhi; *D:* Kelly Markin; *W:* J. Stephen Maunder; *C:* Curtis Petersen, Mark Willis.

Tiger Fangs 🦴 1/2 **1943** When Nazis threaten the Far East rubber production with man-eating tigers, real-life big game hunter Frank Buck comes to the rescue. **57m/B VHS, DVD.** Frank Buck, June Duprez, Duncan Renaldo; *D:* Sam Newfield.

Tiger Heart 🦴🦴 1/2 **1996 (PG-13)** Teenaged karate champ Eric Chase (Roberts) is looking forward to a lazy summer with girlfriend Stephanie (Lyons) before heading off to college. But when his neighborhood comes under attack from an unscrupulous developer and Stephanie runs afoul of his goons, Eric decides to take action. **90m/C VHS, DVD.** Ted Jan Roberts, Jennifer Lyons, Robert LaSardo, Carol Potter, Timothy Williams; *D:* Georges Chamchoum; *W:* William Applegate Jr.; *M:* John Gonzalez.

Tiger Joe 🦴 **1985** There's trouble in Southeast Asia, and the U.S. military confuses things even more. **96m/C VHS.** Alan Collins, David Warbeck; *D:* Anthony M. Dawson.

Tiger of Eschnapur 🦴🦴 1/2 *Der Tiger von Eschnapur* **1959** Architect Harald Berger (Hubschmid) travels to Eschnapur to build schools and hospitals for Chandra (Reyer), the district's all-powerful Maharaja. Along the way he falls in love with temple dancer Seetha (Paget), not knowing that Chandra has asked her to Eschnapur with the intention of making her his new Maharani. Seetha and Berger become pawns in a plan by Chandra's brother Prince Ramigani (Deltgen) to seize the throne. The tone is somewhere between "The Thief of Bagdad" and "The Wind and the Lion," minus massive battle scenes. There's nothing outright fantastical about the movie, but every scene has the feel of its exotic, alien locations. **101m/C DVD.** *GE* Debra Paget, Paul (Christian) Hubschmid, Walter Reyer, Claus Holm, Luciana Paluzzi; *D:* Fritz Lang; *W:* Werner Jorg Luddecke; *C:* Richard Angst; *M:* Michel Michelet.

Tiger of the Seven Seas 🦴🦴 **1962** A female pirate takes over her father's command and embarks on adventures on the high seas. Generous portions of action, intrigue, and romance. Sequel to "Queen of the Pirates." **90m/C VHS.** *IT FR* Gianna Maria Canale, Anthony Steel, Maria Grazia Spina, Ernesto Calindri; *D:* Luigi Capuano.

Tiger Shark 🦴🦴 **1932** San Diego tuna fisherman Mike (Robinson) saves best pal Pipes (Arlen) but loses his hand to a shark and it's replaced by a hook. When another friend is killed at sea, Mike asks the man's impoverished daughter Quita (Johann) to marry him (though she doesn't love him) so he can look after her. Quita and Pipes find themselves attracted to each other and Mike gets jealous and vengeful. But Mike has really bad luck with sharks. **80m/B DVD.** Edward G. Robinson, Richard Arlen, Zita Johann, J. Carrol Naish, Leila Bennett, William Ricciardi; *D:* Howard Hawks; *W:* Wells Root; *C:* Gaetano Antonio "Tony" Gaudio.

Tiger Town 🦴🦴 1/2 **1983 (G)** A baseball player, ending an illustrious career with the Detroit Tigers, sees his chance of winning a pennant slipping away. A young fan, however, proves helpful in chasing that elusive championship. **76m/C VHS.** Roy Scheider, Justin Henry, Ron McLarty, Bethany Carpenter, Noah Moazezi; *D:* Alan Shapiro; *C:* Robert Elswit. **CABLE**

A Tiger Walks 🦴🦴 1/2 **1964** A savage tiger escapes from a circus and local children start a nationwide campaign to save its life. Notable for its unflattering portrayal of America's heartland and small town dynamics. Radical departure from most Disney films of the period. **88m/C VHS.** Sabu, Pamela Franklin, Brian Keith, Vera Miles, Kevin Corcoran, Peter Brown, Una Merkel, Frank McHugh, Edward Andrews; *D:* Norman Tokar; *M:* Buddy (Norman Dale) Baker.

Tiger Warsaw 🦴 1/2 *The Tiger* **1987 (R)** A young man returns to the town where he once lived, before he shot his father. He hopes to sort out his life and repair family problems. Muddled and sappy. **92m/C VHS, DVD.** Patrick Swayze, Barbara Williams, Piper Laurie, Bobby DiCicco, Kaye Ballard, Lee Richardson, Mary McDonnell; *D:* Amin Qamar Chaudhri.

The Tiger Woman 🦴 1/2 **1945** Nightclub singer Sharon Winslow (Mara)—billed as "The Tiger Woman"—is a tough broad who knocks off her husband for the insurance money, then knocks off the lover who helped her kill her husband. Detective Jerry Devery (Richmond) investigates, but finds himself falling for The Tiger Woman's charms. **57m/B DVD.** Adele Mara, Kane Richmond, Richard Fraser, Peggy Stewart; *D:* Philip Ford; *W:* George Carleton Brown, John Dunkel; *C:* Ernest Miller.

The Tiger Woods Story 🦴🦴 1/2 **1998 (PG-13)** Kain stars as the young man who, at 21, became the youngest player ever to win the Masters Golf Tournament. Based on the book "Tiger" by John Strege. **103m/C VHS.** Khalil Kain, Keith David, Freda Foh Shen; *D:* LeVar Burton; *W:* Takashi Bufford. **CABLE**

Tigerland 🦴🦴🦴 **2000 (R)** Irish newcomer Farrell made a big (and deserved) splash as Army draftee Roland Bozz, one of a group of grunts at the final stage of infantry training at Fort Polk, Louisiana in 1971. The title refers to the wilderness area designed for jungle combat simulation before the newbies are shipped out to Nam. But the rebellious, cynical Bozz gets away with defying every rule thrown at him to the disbelief of the others in the platoon. Familiar story but the ensemble cast is right on the mark and director Schumacher keeps tight control in this old-fashioned low-budget drama. **101m/C VHS, DVD.** *US* Colin Farrell, Matthew Davis, Clifton (Gonzalez) Collins Jr., Tom Guiry, Russell Richardson, Cole Hauser, Shea Whigham; ***D:*** Joel Schumacher; ***W:*** Ross Klaven, Michael McGruther; ***C:*** Matthew Libatique; ***M:*** Nathan Larson.

Tigers in Lipstick 1/2 *Wild Beds* **1980 (R)** Seven short vignettes featuring the beautiful actresses as aggressive women and the men that they influence. **88m/C VHS.** *IT* Laura Antonelli, Monica Vitti, Ursula Andress, Sylvia Kristel; ***D:*** Luigi Zampa.

A Tiger's Tale 1/2 **1987 (R)** A middle-aged divorced nurse begins an affair with her daughters's ex-boyfriend. **97m/C VHS.** Ann-Margret, C. Thomas Howell, Charles Durning, Kelly Preston, Ann Wedgeworth, Tim Thomerson, Steven Kampmann, Traci Lind, Angel Tompkins, William Zabka; ***D:*** Peter Douglas; ***C:*** Tony Pierce-Roberts.

The Tiger's Tale **2006 (R)** Liam O'Leary (Gleeson) has risen from humble beginnings to become a wealthy property owner in Dublin with a big house, a trophy wife (Cattrall), and a rebellious teen son (played by Gleeson's own son). Liam starts seeing a sinister doppelganger (though no one believes him) who takes over his life. Liam winds up at a homeless shelter while the double comes up against the realities of a bankrupt business. The answers to the mystery turn out to be mundane. Title refers to the 'celtic tiger' term coined to describe Ireland's economic boom. **107m/C DVD.** *IR* Brendan Gleeson, Kim Cattrall, Sinead Cusack, Ciaran Hinds, Briain Gleeson 1, Sean McGinley; ***D:*** John Boorman; ***W:*** John Boorman; ***C:*** Seamus Deasy; ***M:*** Stephen McKeon.

Tigershark **1987 (R)** A martial arts expert goes to Southeast Asia to rescue his girlfriend, who has been kidnapped by communist forces and held captive for arms and ammunition. Strictly for fans of the martial arts. **97m/C VHS.** Mike Stone, John Quade, Pamela Bryant; ***D:*** Emmett Alston; ***W:*** Ivan Rogers.

Tight Spot **1955** Been-around-the-block model Sherry Conley (Rogers) is serving time for a crime she didn't commit when she's offered a deal by U.S. attorney Lloyd Hallett (Robinson) if she'll testify against mob boss Benjamin Costain (Greene). But since no other potential witness lived to the trial date, Sherry's against cooperating. However, Hallett puts her up in a hotel with bodyguard Vince Striker (Keith) in hopes she'll change her mind. But Costain has a lot of clout and is determined to get to Sherry. Rogers gives an excellent performance in a dramatic role with fine support from the rest of the cast. **97m/B VHS.** Ginger Rogers, Edward G. Robinson, Brian Keith, Lorne Greene, Katherine Anderson; ***D:*** Phil Karlson; ***W:*** William Bowers; ***C:*** Burnett Guffey; ***M:*** George Duning.

Tightrope **1984 (R)** Police inspector Wes Block pursues a killer of prostitutes in New Orleans' French Quarter. The film is notable both as a thriller and as a fascinating vehicle for Eastwood, who experiments with a disturbing portrait of a cop with some peculiarities of his own. **115m/C VHS, DVD.** Clint Eastwood, Genevieve Bujold, Dan Hedaya, Jennifer Beck, Alison Eastwood, Randi Brooks, Regina Richardson, Jamie Rose; ***D:*** Richard Tuggle; ***C:*** Bruce Surtees; ***M:*** Lennie Niehaus.

The Tigress 1/2 **1993 (R)** In 1920s Berlin two con artists set out to scam a rich American using sex as a lure. Things don't go as planned. Also available in an unrated version. **89m/C VHS, DVD.** *GE* Valentina Vargas, James Remar, George Peppard; ***D:*** Karin Howard; ***W:*** Karin Howard.

Til There Was You 1/2 **1996 (PG-13)** You know what most great romance movies have in common? The couples actually meet each other before the end of the movie. Not here. That's one of the reasons this one isn't even good. Ghostwriter Gwen (Tripplehorn) and architect Nick (McDermott), although seemingly destined for one another, have more near-misses than a drunken, nearsighted airline pilot. They're shown in the same room, in adjoining rooms, leaving a room as soon as the other enters, etc., etc. Meanwhile, minor characters appear, speak some ham-fisted dialogue and then disappear. This happens for 20 years. Then they meet and the movie is (thankfully) over. Parker, however, does an excellent job as a rehab-addicted former child star who has ties to both characters. Feature directorial debut for Winant. **113m/C VHS, DVD.** Dylan McDermott, Sarah Jessica Parker, Jeanne Tripplehorn, Jennifer Aniston, Ken Olin, Craig Bierko, Nina Foch, Alice Drummond, Christine Ebersole, Michael Tucker, Patrick Malahide, Kasi Lemmons, Karen Allen; ***D:*** Scott Winant; ***W:*** Winnie Holzman; ***C:*** Bobby Bukowski; ***M:*** Miles Goodman, Terence Blanchard.

Tilai *The Law* **1990** When Saga returns to his African village after a long absence, it's to discover that his young fiancee, Nogma, has been forced into marriage with his own father. According to his tribe's code of honor Saga can do nothing but love won't be denied and they begin an affair, which is deemed incestuous by the village. So Saga and Nogma flee, hoping to live out of the reach of tribal law. **81m/C VHS.** Rasmane Ouedraogo, Ina Cisse, Roukietou Barry; ***D:*** Idrissa Ouedraogo; ***W:*** Idrissa Ouedraogo; ***C:*** Pierre-Laurent Chenieux, Jean Monsigny; ***M:*** Abdullah Ibrahim. Cannes '90: Grand Jury Prize.

Till Death Do Us Part 1/2 **1972 (PG)** Three married couples spend a weekend at a counseling retreat, unaware that the proprietor is a murderous maniac. **77m/C VHS.** James Keach, Claude Jutra, Matt Craven; ***D:*** Timothy Brand.

Till Death Do Us Part **1992 (R)** An ex-cop turns into an evil killer who seduces unsuspecting women and murders them for their insurance money. Contains footage not seen in the TV movie. Based on a true story and the book by Vincent Bugliosi. **93m/C VHS.** Treat Williams, Arliss Howard, Rebecca Jenkins; ***D:*** Yves Simoneau.

Till Human Voices Wake Us 1/2 **2002 (R)** Confusing romantic drama about memory. Psych professor Sam Franks (Pearce) is going home for his dad's funeral. He has an odd encounter with Ruby (Bonham Carter), rescues her from a suicide leap off a bridge, and discovers she has amnesia. Efforts to unlock Ruby's memories help Sam with his own teenaged tragedy that revolves around his girlfriend drowning. However, the story never does make much sense. **97m/C VHS, DVD.** *AU* Guy Pearce, Helena Bonham Carter, Frank Gallacher, Lindley Joyner, Brooke Harman, Peter Curtin, Margot Knight, Anthony Martin, Dawn Klingberg; ***D:*** Michael Petroni; ***W:*** Michael Petroni; ***C:*** Roger Lanser; ***M:*** Dale Cornelius.

Till Marriage Do Us Part 1/2 *Dio Mio, Come Sono Caduta in Basso; How Long Can You Fall?* **1974 (R)** An innocent couple discovers on their wedding night that they are really brother and sister. Since they can't in good conscience get a divorce or consummate their marriage, they must seek sexual gratification elsewhere. Antonelli is deliciously tantalizing in this silly satire. In Italian with English subtitles. **97m/C VHS.** *IT* Laura Antonelli, Alberto Lionello, Jean Rochefort, Michele Placido, Karin Schubert; ***D:*** Luigi Comencini.

Till Murder Do Us Part 1/2 *A Woman Scorned: The Betty Broderick Story* **1992 (PG-13)** Based on the true story of Betty Broderick, an obsessively devoted wife and mother whose husband leaves her for another woman. Even after a bitter divorce, Betty refuses to let go. Until she commits murder. **95m/C VHS, DVD.** Meredith Baxter, Stephen Collins, Michelle Johnson, Kelli Williams, Stephen (Steve) Root; ***D:*** Dick Lowry. **TV**

Till the Clouds Roll By 1/2 **1946** An all-star, high-gloss musical biography of songwriter Jerome Kern, that, in typical Hollywood fashion, bears little resemblance to the composer's life. Filled with wonderful songs from his Broadway hit. ♫ Showboat Medley; Till the Clouds Roll By; Howja Like to Spoon with Me?; The Last Time I Saw Paris; They Didn't Believe Me; I Won't Dance; Why Was I Born?; Who?; Sunny. **137m/C VHS, DVD.** Robert Walker, Van Heflin, Judy Garland, Frank Sinatra, Lucille Bremer, Kathryn Grayson, June Allyson, Dinah Shore, Lena Horne, Virginia O'Brien, Tony Martin; ***D:*** Richard Whorf; ***W:*** Myles Connolly, Jean Holloway; ***C:*** Harry Stradling Sr.; ***M:*** Conrad Salinger, Roger Edens, Lennie Hayton.

Till the End of the Night 1/2 **1994 (R)** D'arcy (Enos) is an ex-con who will do anything to get back his ex-wife Diana Davenport (Lang) and it doesn't matter that she has a new husband, John (Valentine) and two kids. D'arcy manages to kidnap Diana and it's up to John to save his wife. **90m/C VHS.** John Enos, Katherine Kelly Lang, Scott Valentine, David Keith; ***D:*** Larry Brand; ***W:*** Larry Brand.

Till the End of Time 1/2 **1946** Three GIs have trouble adjusting to civilian life in their home town after WWII. Fine performances and excellent pacing. Popular title song. Adapted from "They Dream of Home" by Niven Busch. **105m/C VHS.** Robert Mitchum, Guy Madison, Bill Williams, Dorothy McGuire, William Gargan, Tom Tully; ***D:*** Edward Dmytryk.

Till There Was You **1991 (PG-13)** A struggling musician travels to a faraway tropical isle to solve the mystery of his brother's death. **94m/C VHS.** Mark Harmon, Deborah Kara Unger, Jeroen Krabbe, Shane Briant; ***D:*** John Seale; ***M:*** Graeme Revell.

Tillie Wakes Up 1/2 **1917** Third in the Tillie series, following "Tillie's Punctured Romance" and "Tillie's Tomato Surprise." Tillie (Dressler) decides she needs a little fun in her life so she asks her hen-pecked nieghbor Mr. Pipkin (Hines) to spend the day with her on Coney Island. **48m/B VHS.** Marie Dressler, Johnny Hines, Frank Beamish, Ruby de Remer; ***D:*** Harry Davenport; ***W:*** Frances Marion.

Tillie's Punctured Romance **1914** The silent comedy which established Chaplin and Dressler as comedians. Chaplin, out of his Tramp character, is the city slicker trying to put one over on farm girl Dressler, who pursues revenge. First feature length comedy film. Followed by "Tillie's Tomato Surprise" and "Tillie Wakes Up," which starred Dressler but not Chaplin. **73m/B VHS, DVD.** Charlie Chaplin, Marie Dressler, Mabel Normand, Mack Swain, Chester Conklin; ***D:*** Mack Sennett; ***W:*** Hampton Del Ruth; ***C:*** Frank D. Williams.

The Tillman Story **2010** Explores the public lies and cover-ups surrounding the death of Pat Tillman in Afghanistan. The football pro left his career after 9/11 to join the Army Rangers and was killed on his second tour of duty. His family became suspicious of the Army's official explanation of his death, eventually leading to an investigation and a Congressional hearing. **94m/C DVD.** *US* ***D:*** Amir Bar-Lev; ***W:*** Amir Bar-Lev, Mark Monroe, Joe Bini; ***C:*** Sean Kirby, Igor Martinovic; ***M:*** Philip Sheppard; ***Nar:*** Josh Brolin.

Tilt **1978 (PG)** Flimsy storyline concerns a young runaway's adventures with an aspiring rock star. Shields' pinball expertise eventually leads her to a match against pinball champ Durning. **111m/C VHS.** Charles Durning, Ken Marshall, Brooke Shields, Geoffrey Lewis; ***D:*** Rudy Durand; ***W:*** Rudy Durand, Donald Cammell.

Tim 1/2 **1979** Follows the relationship between a handsome, mentally retarded young man and an attractive older businesswoman. Sappy story line is redeemed by Gibson's fine performance in one of his first roles. Based on Colleen McCullough's first novel. **94m/C VHS, DVD.** *AU* Mel Gibson, Piper Laurie, Peter Gwynne, Alwyn Kurts, Pat Evison; ***D:*** Michael Pate; ***W:*** Michael Pate; ***C:*** Paul Onorato; ***M:*** Eric Jupp. Australian Film Inst. '79: Actor (Gibson).

Tim Burton's Corpse Bride *Corpse Bride* **2005 (PG)** The magnificent visual aesthetic of Burton's animation and a lead character voiced by Johnny Depp. What more could you want? Well what you get is a sweet story of love lost with a nether-worldly twist or two. Victor Van Dort (Depp) is set to marry Victoria Everglat (Watson) in a parentally-arranged union. Nervous and awkward, Victor retreats to the nearby graveyard, practicing the vows he has struggled to memorize, where he accidentally slips the ring on the finger (which he takes for a twig) of the long dead Corpse Bride (Carter). She comes to life and insists she is now his wife, and he is then plunged into the much brighter world of the dead. **75m/C DVD, Blu-ray Disc, HD DVD.** *GB US* ***D:*** Michael Johnson, Tim Burton; ***W:*** John August, Caroline Thompson, Pamela Pettler; ***C:*** Pete Kozachik; ***M:*** Danny Elfman; ***V:*** Johnny Depp, Helena Bonham Carter, Emily Watson, Tracey Ullman, Joanna Lumley, Albert Finney, Richard E. Grant, Michael Gough, Christopher Lee, Jane Horrocks, Deep Roy, Danny Elfman, Paul Whitehouse, Enn Reitel, Stephen Ballantyne, Lisa Kay. Natl. Bd. of Review '05: Animated Film.

Tim Tyler's Luck **1937** Lost but not forgotten serial in its 12-chapter entirety. The fearless Tim Tyler uses whatever he can to do battle with the sinister Spider Web gang. **235m/B VHS, DVD.** Frankie Thomas Jr., Frances Robinson, Al Shean, Norman Willis, Earl Douglas, Jack Mulhall, Frank Mayo, Pat J. O'Brien; ***D:*** Ford Beebe, Wyndham Gittens.

Timber! 1/2 **1942** Pals Arizona (Devine) and Quebec (Carrillo) are trying to keep the Crowley Lumber Company's lumber camp and mill running, but operations are threatened by a series of suspicious accidents. U.S. Forestry Service troubleshooter Kansas (Dailey) arrives to help out, and finds out that some employees are in the business of sabotage. The three friends need to get to the ringleader before it's too late. **60m/B DVD.** Leo Carrillo, Andy Devine, Dan Dailey, Marjorie Lord, Edmund MacDonald; ***D:*** Christy Cabanne; ***W:*** Larry Rhine, Ben Chapman; ***C:*** Jack MacKenzie; ***M:*** Hans J. Salter.

Timber Queen **1944** A WWII flier comes home and aids his best friend's widow, who must make a quota of timber or lose her sawmill to gangsters. Old-fashioned. **66m/B VHS.** Richard Arlen, Mary Beth Hughes, June Havoc, Sheldon Leonard, George E. Stone, Dick Purcell; ***D:*** Frank McDonald.

Time *Shi gan* **2006** After two years, pathologically jealous She-hee believes her lover Ji-woo no longer finds her attractive, so she disappears for six months. After undergoing extensive plastic surgery, she returns with a new identity to woo him again, only to find she's competing with the memory of herself. Korean with subtitles. **97m/C DVD.** *JP KN* Heyon-a Seong, Jung-woo Ha, Ji-yeon Park; ***D:*** Ki-Duk Kim; ***W:*** Ki-Duk Kim; ***C:*** Jong-mu Seong; ***M:*** Hyeong-woo Noh.

Time After Time **1979 (PG)** In Victorian London, circa 1893, H.G. Wells is experimenting with his time machine. He discovers the machine has been used by an associate, who turns out to be Jack the Ripper, to travel to San Francisco in 1979. Wells follows to stop any further murders and the ensuing battle of wits is both entertaining and imaginative. McDowell is charming as Wells and Steenburgen is equally fine as Well's modern American love interest. **112m/C VHS, DVD.** Malcolm McDowell, David Warner, Mary Steenburgen, Patti D'Arbanville, Charles Cioffi; ***D:*** Nicholas Meyer; ***W:*** Nicholas Meyer; ***M:*** Miklos Rozsa.

Time and Tide *Seunlau Ngaklau* **2000 (R)** Non-stop action from Hark with the usual convoluted plot. Tyler (Tse) is working as a bodyguard for a client who turns out to be a Triad boss. Tyler's friend Jack (Bai) is an ex-mercenary whose pregnant wife, Hui (Lo), is the criminal's estranged daughter. And then Jack's former South American colleagues show up in Hong Kong with a plan to assassinate the Triad boss, among other gun battles. Oh, and Tyler is also about to become a father, courtesy of a one-night stand who doesn't want anything to do with him. Chinese with subtitles. **113m/C VHS, DVD.** *HK* Nicholas Tse, Wu Bai, Anthony Wong, Candy Lo, Cathy Chui, Joventino Couto Remotigue; ***D:*** Tsui Hark; ***W:*** Tsui Hark, Koan Hui; ***C:*** Herman Yau, Ko Chiu-lam; ***M:*** Tommy Wai.

Time at the Top 1/2 **1999** Fourteen-year-old Susan Shawson travels back in time (via her apartment's elevator) from the Philadelphia of the present to the same city in 1881. There Susan befriends Victoria Walker and her younger brother Robert, who need help with their family troubles. The trio manage to time travel back and forth and the change both the past and the present. Based on the book by Edward Ormondroyd. **96m/C VHS.** Timothy Busfield, Elisha Cuthbert, Gabrielle Boni, Matthew Harbour, Lynne Adams, Denys Chapdelaine; ***D:*** Jim Kaufman; ***W:*** Linda Brookover; ***C:*** Francois Protat; ***M:*** Simon Carpentier. **CABLE**

Time Bandits 1/2 **1981 (PG)** A group of dwarves help a young boy to travel through time and space with the likes of Robin Hood, Napoleon, Agamemnon, and other time-warp playmates. Epic fantasy from Monty Python alumni. **110m/C VHS, DVD, UMD.** *GB* John Cleese, Sean Connery, Shelley Duvall, Katherine Helmond, Ian Holm, Michael Palin, Ralph Richardson, Kenny Baker, Peter Vaughan, David Warner, Craig Warnock; ***D:*** Terry Gilliam; ***W:*** Terry Gilliam, Michael Palin; ***C:*** Peter Biziou; ***M:*** Mike Moran, George Harrison.

Time Bomb 1/2 **2008** Iraq vet Jason Philby (Busey) is deeply troubled by his battlefield experience and the death of his young son. The images haunting his dreams spill over into his daytime hours until he doesn't know what's real. But when Jason learns he may have been infected with a virus designed to create soldier/suicide bombers, he's determined to find out if the military done him wrong. **87m/C DVD.** Jake Busey, Robert Bockstael, Deborah Odell, Daniel Cook, David Haydn-Jones; ***D:*** Erin Berry; ***W:*** Erin Berry, David Plusauskas; ***C:*** Simon Shohet; ***M:*** Alphonse Lanza. **VIDEO**

Time Chasers **1995** Nick Miller (Burch) invents a device that permits his airplane to travel through time. But, after selling his invention, he soon discovers that it has turned the future into a desolate wasteland. Now Nick must try to regain control and put things back to normal. **90m/C VHS.** Matthew Burch, Bonnie Pritchard, Peter Harrington; ***D:*** David Giancola.

Time Code *Timecode* **2000 (R)** Figgis shot his film in one day, using four digital video cameras and 28 actors to tell four separate (though inter-connected) stories that were shown simultaneously onscreen in four rectangular quadrants. The stories center around a film production company headed by producer Alex Green (Skarsgard), whose wife Emma (Burrows) plans to leave him because he is having an affair with actress Rose (Hayek), whose own relationship with Lauren (Tripplehorn) is falling apart. Then there's various producers, directors, and actors pitching ideas or auditioning for parts. It's not as confusing as might be imagined although how it will play on video is a challenge. **97m/C VHS, DVD.** Stellan Skarsgard, Saffron Burrows, Salma Hayek, Jeanne Tripplehorn, Richard Edson, Julian Sands, Xander Berkeley, Glenne Headly, Holly Hunter, Danny Huston, Kyle MacLachlan, Alessandro Nivola, Steven Weber, Viveka Davis, Aimee Graham, Andrew Heckler, Daphna Kastner, Leslie Mann, Mia Maestro; ***D:*** Mike Figgis; ***W:*** Mike Figgis; ***C:*** Patrick Alexander Stewart; ***M:*** Mike Figgis, Anthony Marinelli.

A Time for Dancing **2000 (PG-13)** Jules and Sam grew up best friends and shared a love for dancing that was to lead the girls to Juilliard College. When Jules learns that she has late-stage cancer, their life plans take a tragic shift. **94m/C VHS, DVD.** Larisa Oleynik, Shiri Appleby, Peter Coyote, Amy Madigan, Shane West, Lynn Whitfield, Patricia Kalember, Anton Yelchin; ***D:*** Peter Gilbert; ***W:*** Kara Lindstrom; ***C:*** Alex Nepomniaschy. **TV**

A Time for Miracles 1/2 **1980** Dramatic biography of the first native-born American saint, Elizabeth Bayley Seton, who was canonized in 1975. **97m/C VHS.** Kate Mulgrew, Lorne Greene, Rossano Brazzi, John Forsythe, Jean-Pierre Aumont, Milo O'Shea; ***D:*** Michael O'Herlihy. **TV**

Time for Revenge 1/2 **1982** A demolitions worker attempts to blackmail his corrupt employer by claiming a workplace explosion made him speechless. He finds himself in a contest of silence and wits. In Spanish with English subtitles. **112m/C VHS.** *AR* Federico Luppi, Haydee Padilla, Julio de Grazia, Ulises Dumont; ***D:*** Adolfo Aristarain. Montreal World Film Fest. '82: Film.

The Time Guardian 1/2 **1987 (PG)** Time-travelers of the future arrive in the Australian desert in 1988, intent on warning the local populace of the impending arrival of killer cyborgs from the 40th century. Muddled and confusing. **89m/C VHS.** Tom Burlinson, Carrie Fisher, Dean Stockwell, Nikki Coghill; ***D:*** Brian Hannant; ***W:*** Brian Hannant, John Baxter; ***C:*** Geoff Burton.

Time Indefinite **1993** Cinema verite effort once again follows filmmaker McElwee who returns to his Southern roots to confront personal tragedy by recording every moment on film. It is an emotional journey in which he discovers that his camera may not be enough to protect him from his own feelings. Moving, with occasional lapses into self-absorption. Companion film to McElwee's "Sherman's March." **117m/C VHS, DVD.** ***D:*** Ross McElwee; ***W:*** Ross McElwee.

Time Lapse **2001 (PG-13)** Agent Clay Pierce (McNamara) is a member of a U.S. antiterrorist unit who unknowingly prevents an attempt to sell a nuclear device to the Iraquis. Too bad Clay is the only one who makes it back alive (more or less). He's got a lot of questions for his boss LaNova (Scheider), who turns out to be a double-dealer. And he deals with Clay by giving him an experimental drug that causes amnesia—so Clay is really confused about why people keep trying to kill him. **88m/C VHS, DVD.** Roy Scheider, William McNamara, Dina Meyer, Henry Rollins; ***D:*** David Worth. **VIDEO**

Time Lock **1957** An expert safe-cracker races against time to save a child who is trapped inside a bank's pre-set time-locked vault. Canada is the setting, although the film was actually made in England. Based on a play by Arthur Hailey. **73m/B VHS.** *GB* Robert Beatty, Betty McDowall, Vincent Winter, Lee Patterson, Sandra Francis, Alan Gifford, Robert Ayres, Victor Wood, Jack Cunningham, Peter Mannering, Gordon Tanner, Larry Cross, Sean Connery; ***D:*** Gerald Thomas; ***W:*** Peter Rogers; ***C:*** Peter Hennessy; ***M:*** Stanley Black.

The Time Machine **1960** English scientist living near the end of the 19th century invents time travel machine and uses it to travel into various periods of the future. Rollicking version of H.G. Wells' classic cautionary tale boasts Oscar-winning special effects. Remade in 1978. **103m/C VHS, DVD.** Rod Taylor, Yvette Mimieux, Whit Bissell, Sebastian Cabot, Alan Young, Paul Frees, Bob Barran, Doris Lloyd; ***D:*** George Pal; ***W:*** David Duncan; ***C:*** Paul Vogel; ***M:*** Russell Garcia.

Time Machine 1/2 **1978 (G)** Yet another adaptation of H.G. Wells' classic novel about a scientist who invents a machine that enables him to travel through time. Inferior remake of the 1960 version. **99m/C VHS.** John Beck, Priscilla Barnes, Andrew Duggan; ***D:*** Henning Schellerup.

The Time Machine **2002 (PG-13)** Well, the special effects are pretty cool but this sci-fi adventure has little to do with H.G. Wells' 1894 novel. Eccentric scientist Alexander Hartdegen (an anorexic-looking Pearce) lives in New York, circa 1900. He's devastated when his fiance Emma (Guillory) is killed and is determined to change fate by building a time machine. But going back in time changes nothing so Hartdegen goes forward to discover why he can't change things. He accidentally winds up in 800,000 when the Earth is once again pastoral and its inhabitants are divided into the gentle surface-dwelling Elois and the monstrous, cannibalistic subterranean Morlocks. Irish singer Mumba debuts as Mara, whom Hartdegen falls for, and a heavily made-up Irons is the Uber-Morlock. Unfortunately, the story is dull rather than what it should be—rousing in a who-cares-about-logic, B-movie way. **96m/C VHS, DVD.** *US* Guy Pearce, Samantha Mumba, Mark Addy, Sienna Guillory, Omera Mumba, Jeremy Irons, Orlando Jones, Phyllida Law, Yancey Arias; ***Cameos:*** Alan Young; ***D:*** Simon Wells; ***W:*** John Logan; ***C:*** Donald McAlpine; ***M:*** Klaus Badelt.

A Time of Destiny **1988 (PG-13)** During WWII, an American soldier vows to kill his brother-in-law, who he believes caused his father's death. Meanwhile, the two men have become good friends in the army, never realizing their connection. A strange, overblown family saga from the director of "El Norte." Beautiful photography, terrific editing. **118m/C VHS.** William Hurt, Timothy Hutton, Melissa Leo, Stockard Channing, Megan Follows, Francisco Rabal; ***D:*** Gregory Nava; ***W:*** Gregory Nava, Anna Thomas; ***M:*** Ennio Morricone.

Time of Favor **2000** Military commander Meanchem (Avni) and best friend Pini (Alterman) have a falling out over Michal (Tinkerbell), the disillusioned daughter of radical Orthodox Rabbi Meltzer (Dayan), whom the men follow. But when Pini is rejected, he decides to channel his frustrations by committing an act of terrorism. Hebrew with subtitles. **98m/C DVD.** *IS* Aki Avni, Tinkerbell, Edan Alterman, Assi Dayan, Micha Selektar, Amnon Volf; ***D:*** Joseph Cedar; ***W:*** Joseph Cedar; ***C:*** Ofer Inov; ***M:*** Jonathan Bar-Girora.

The Time of His Life 1/2 **1955** Bumbling Charles Pastry (Hearne) is an ex-con who has been released into the care of his snooty socialite daughter Lady Florence (Pollock). She is so embarrassed by him that she first tries to have him emigrate to Australia (that doesn't work) and then locks him in the attic so he won't ruin his granddaughter's birthday party. He gets loose of course, causing well-meant havoc. **74m/B DVD.** *GB* Richard Hearne, Ellen Pollock, Frederick Leister, Richard Wattis, Robert Moreton; ***D:*** Leslie Hiscott; ***W:*** Leslie Hiscott; ***C:*** Ken Talbot.

Time of Indifference *Gli Indifferenti; Les Deux Rivales* **1964** Based on the novel by Alberto Moravia. Tale of the disintegration of values in 1920s Italy is unable to take full advantage of its fine cast or potentially thought-provoking themes. **84m/B VHS.** *IT* Rod Steiger, Shelley Winters, Claudia Cardinale, Paulette Goddard, Tomas Milian; ***D:*** Francesco Maselli.

Time of the Gypsies *Dom Za Vesanje* **1990 (R)** Acclaimed Yugoslavian saga about a homely, unlucky Gypsy boy who sets out to steal his way to a dowry large enough to marry the girl of his dreams. Beautifully filmed, magical, and very long. In the Gypsy language, Romany, it's the first feature film made in the Gypsy tongue. **136m/C VHS.** *YU* Davor Dujmovic, Sinolicka Trpkova, Ljubica Adzovic, Hunsija Hasimovic, Bora Todorovic; ***D:*** Emir Kusturica. Cannes '89: Director (Kusturica).

Time of the Wolf *Le Temps du Loup* **2003 (R)** City family on a weekend outing to their country home discover it occupied by squatters after an unspecified widespread disaster. Dad (Duval) tries to dispel any potential violence but is shot dead for his trouble, with the rest of the family escaping to find a suddenly very different, very dangerous outside world. They set out on a nightmarish journey across desolate and unfamiliar landscape where survival is never certain. Harsh apocalyptic vision is reminiscent of "Night of the Living Dead" and Godard's "Weekend." Austrian director Haneke is great at creating a very realistic and claustrophobic atmosphere. **113m/C DVD.** *FR AT GE* Isabelle Huppert, Maurice Benichou, Lucas Biscombe, Patrice Chereau, Beatrice Dalle, Daniel Duval, Olivier Gourmet, Rona Hartner, Anais Demoustier, Maryline Even, Brigitte Rouan, Florence Loiret-Caille; ***D:*** Michael Haneke; ***W:*** Michael Haneke; ***C:*** Jurgen Jurges.

The Time of Their Lives 1/2 *The Ghost Steps Out* **1946** A pair of Revolutionary War-era ghosts haunt a modern country estate. One of the best A & C comedies. **82m/B VHS, DVD.** Bud Abbott, Lou Costello, Marjorie Reynolds, Binnie Barnes, Gale Sondergaard, John Shelton; ***D:*** Charles T. Barton.

The Time of Your Life 1/2 **1948** The only Cagney film that ever lost money. A simple but engaging story of people trying to live their dreams. Cagney is delightful as a barroom philosopher who controls the world around him from his seat in the tavern. Although it was not very popular with audiences at the time, the critics hailed it as an artistic achievement. Based on William Saroyan's play. **109m/B VHS, DVD.** James Cagney, William Bendix, Jeanne Cagney, Broderick Crawford, Ward Bond, James Barton, Paul Draper, Natalie Schafer; ***D:*** H.C. Potter.

Time Out *L'Emploi du Temps* **2001 (PG-13)** Vincent (Recoing) can't admit to his family and friends that he's lost his job so he fabricates a new position working for the U.N. in Switzerland and takes to the road, driving aimlessly in his car. He uses an investment scam in order to pay his bills and then tries working for a trafficker in bogus designer goods, all the while sinking deeper into his life of lies. Very loosely based on a true story. French with subtitles. **132m/C VHS, DVD.** *FR* Aurelien Recoing, Karin Viard, Serge Livrozet, Nicolas Kalsch, Jean-Pierre Mangeot, Monique Mangeot, Maxime Sassier; ***D:*** Laurent Cantet; ***W:*** Laurent Cantet, Robin Campillo; ***C:*** Pierre Milon; ***M:*** Jocelyn Pook.

Time Out for Love 1/2 *Les Grandes Personnes; The Five Day Lover* **1961** An American girl travels to Paris in search of romance, but discovers more than she bargained for. In French with English subtitles. **91m/B VHS.** *IT FR* Jean Seberg, Micheline Presle, Maurice Ronet, Francoise Prevost, Annibale Ninchi, Nando (Fernando) Bruno; ***D:*** Jean Valere; ***M:*** Georges Delerue.

Time Regained 1/2 *Le Temps Retrouve* **1999 (R)** Based on Marcel Proust's final volume of "Remembrance of Things Past," this ambitious adaptation is a sweeping and sometimes surreal saga of an elderly man's life and memories. Concentrating on turn of the century Paris, period piece time travels around the world inhabited by Marcel (Mazzarella), based on the author himself, who mingles with the wealthy and beautiful. Legendary French beauties litter the screen in supporting roles, including Deneuve, as Odette, who used her looks to get ahead and Beart, as Gilberte, her stepdaughter trapped in an unhappy marriage. Greggory is Saint-Loup, Gilberte's philandering, bisexual husband who cheats on her with Zylberstein and Perez, while Malkovich does a turn as his even more depraved uncle. Worthy performance from Proust look-alike Mazzarella. In French with subtitles. **165m/C VHS, DVD.** *FR IT* Marcello Mazzarello, Catherine Deneuve, Emmanuelle Beart, Vincent Perez, John Malkovich, Pascal Greggory, Marie-France Pisier, Chiara Mastroianni, Arielle Dombasle, Edith Scob, Elsa Zylberstein, Philippe Morier-Genoud, Melvil Poupaud, Mathilde Seigner, Jacques Pieller, Laurence Fevrier, Jean-Francois Balmer, Jerome Prieur; ***D:*** Raul Ruiz; ***W:*** Raul Ruiz, Gilles Taurand; ***C:*** Ricardo Aronovich; ***M:*** Jorge Arriagada; ***V:*** Patrice Chereau.

Time Runner **1992 (R)** It's 2022 and the Earth is being used as target practice by alien invaders. Space captain Hamill manages to find a hole in time and slip back to 1992 where he can battle the first of the alien infiltrators and maybe change Earth's destiny. The time-travel theme (including Hamill watching his own birth) is fun and the special effects are well done. **90m/C VHS.** Mark Hamill, Brion James, Rae Dawn Chong; ***D:*** Michael Mazo.

Time Served 1/2 **1999 (R)** Typically sleazy women-in-prison movie. Sarah McKinney (Oxenberg) is wrongly convicted by a psycho judge and sent to the slammer where she faces a crooked warden and lecherous guards. Sarah also discovers that the prison's work release program means stripping at an underground sex club frequented by the judge and his cronies. Sarah wants to expose more than just herself and tries to get the truth out. **94m/C VHS.** Catherine Oxenberg, Louise Fletcher, Jeff Fahey, Bo Hopkins, James Handy; ***D:*** Glen Pitre. **CABLE**

Time Stands Still *Megall Az Ido* **1982** Two brothers experience troubled youth in Budapest. Artful, somberly executed, with American pop soundtrack. Subtitled in English. **99m/C VHS.** *HU* Istvan Znamenak, Henrik Pauer, Aniko Ivan, Sander Soth, Peter Galfy; ***D:*** Peter Gothar; ***W:*** Peter Gothar; ***C:*** Lajos Koltai; ***M:*** Gyorgy Selmeczi. N.Y. Film Critics '82: Foreign Film.

Time to Die 1/2 *Seven Graves for Rogan* **1983 (R)** WWII victim of heinous war crimes, obsessed with revenge, stalks his prey for a final confrontation, while eluding U.S. intelligence. Disappointing despite good cast working with Mario Puzo story. **89m/C VHS, DVD.** Edward Albert, Rex Harrison, Rod Taylor, Raf Vallone; ***D:*** Matt Cimber; ***M:*** Ennio Morricone.

A Time to Die ½ **1991 (R)** Lords plays a police photographer who, well, photographs the police. But her camera catches one in the act of murder. Routine crime thriller. **93m/C VHS, DVD.** Traci Lords, Jeff Conaway, Richard Roundtree, Bradford Bancroft, Nitchie Barrett; ***D:*** Charles Kanganis; ***W:*** Charles Kanganis; ***M:*** Ennio Morricone.

Time to Kill ½ **1942** Private eye Michael Shayne (Nolan) is hired to retrieve a valuable antique coin, stolen from its owner by her son and daughter-in-law who've got some blackmailers on their tail. But the case isn't so simple, as murder, more blackmail, and family secrets abound. **61m/B DVD.** Lloyd Nolan, Heather Angel, Doris Merrick, Ralph Byrd, Richard Lane; ***D:*** Herbert I. Leeds; ***W:*** Raymond Chandler, Brett Halliday; ***C:*** Charles G. Clarke; ***M:*** Emil Newman.

Time to Kill *Tempo di Uccidere* **1989 (R)** A young soldier in Africa wanders away from his camp and meets a woman whom he rapes and kills. But when he returns to his outfit he finds he can't escape his tormenting conscience. **110m/C VHS, DVD.** Nicolas Cage, Giancarlo Giannini, Robert Liensol; ***D:*** Guiliano Montaldo; ***W:*** Furio Scarpelli; ***M:*** Ennio Morricone.

A Time to Kill ½ **1996 (R)** Powerful story of revenge, racism, and the question of justice in the "new south." John Grisham had a lot of clout when he finally sold his first and favorite novel to the movies, including veto power over the leading man—director Schumacher was for Woody Harrelson, Grisham was opposed but both finally agreed on newcomer McConaughey. He's outstanding as idealistic smalltown Mississippi lawyer Jake Brigance, called to defend anguished father Carl Lee Hailey (Jackson), who's accused of killing the rednecks who raped his young daughter. Jake's assisted by former mentor Lucien Wilbanks (Sutherland) and ambitious northern law student Ellen Roark (Bullock) against ruthless prosecutor Rufus Buckley (Spacey). Is it emotionally manipulative? You betcha. But Grisham's done well on screen and Schumacher (who also did "The Client") knows how to get the most from his cast and script. **150m/C VHS, DVD, Blu-ray Disc.** Matthew McConaughey, Samuel L. Jackson, Sandra Bullock, Kevin Spacey, Donald Sutherland, Brenda Fricker, Oliver Platt, Charles S. Dutton, Kiefer Sutherland, Chris Cooper, Ashley Judd, Patrick McGoohan, Rae'ven (Alyia Larrymore) Kelly, John Diehl, Tonea Stewart, M. Emmet Walsh, Anthony Heald, Kurtwood Smith; ***D:*** Joel Schumacher; ***W:*** Akiva Goldsman; ***C:*** Peter Menzies Jr.; ***M:*** Elliot Goldenthal. MTV Movie Awards '97: Breakthrough Perf. (McConaughey).

Time to Leave *Les Temps Qui Reste* **2005** French flick takes an unflinching look at death and dying from the perspective of a narcissistic young photographer who learns that he has terminal cancer and reacts in a very realistic, un-Hollywood way. First he has sex with his live-in lover and then immediately kicks him out; he insults and further alienates his single-mother sister during a family dinner while telling no one about his illness except for his outcast grandmother "because you're like me, you'll be dying soon," he bluntly tells her. An absence of melodrama and an interesting subplot involving a childless waitress followed by a genuinely moving end makes for a fine French import. **85m/C DVD.** *FR* Melvil Poupaud, Jeanne Moreau, Valeria Bruni-Tedeschi, Daniel Duval, Marie Riviere, Christian Sengewald, Louise-Anne Hippeau, Walter Pagano, Ugo Soussan Trabelsi; ***D:*** Francois Ozon; ***W:*** Francois Ozon; ***C:*** Jeanne Lapoirie.

A Time to Live ½ **1985** Adaptation of Mary Lou Weisman's "Intensive Care" about a family's adjustment to a young boy's fight with Muscular Dystrophy. Minnelli's first appearance in a TV movie. **97m/C** Liza Minnelli, Jeffrey DeMunn, Swoosie Kurtz, Corey Haim, Scott Schwartz; ***D:*** Rick Wallace; ***M:*** Georges Delerue. **TV**

A Time to Live and a Time to Die *Tong Nien Wang Shi* **1985** Family from southern mainland China emigrate to Taiwan in the '40s to escape from hardship and are unable to return after the communist takeover. They find themselves cut off from their cultural heritage, and though the years pass, everyone still thinks of the mainland as home. Taiwanese with subtitles. **137m/C VHS.** *CH* Yu-Yuen Yang, Feng Tien, Shufen Xin, Ann-Shuin Yiu, Mei Feng; ***D:*** Hsiao-Hsien Hou; ***C:*** Pin Bing Lee.

A Time to Love & a Time to Die ½ **1958** Lush adaptation of Erich Maria Remarque novel about WWII German soldier who falls in love with a young girl during furlough. The two are married, only to be separated when he is forced to return to the Russian front. Sympathetic treatment of Germans opposed to Hitler's policies. Hutton's first film, credited to his real name, Dana J. Hutton. **133m/C VHS.** John Gavin, Lilo (Liselotte) Pulver, Jock Mahoney, Keenan Wynn, Klaus Kinski, Don DeFore, Thayer David, Dieter Borsche, Erich Maria Remarque, Barbara Rutting, Charles Regnier, Dorothea Wieck, Kurt Meisel, Clancy Cooper, John van Dreelen, Dana J. Hutton; ***D:*** Douglas Sirk; ***W:*** Orin Jannings; ***C:*** Russell Metty; ***M:*** Miklos Rozsa.

A Time to Remember ½ **1987** Sticky with sentiment, this family film tells of a boy with a gift for singing, encouraged by a priest, discouraged by his father. At one point the kid loses his voice—he probably choked on the pathos. **90m/C VHS.** Ruben Gomez, Raymond Serra, Donald O'Connor, Morgana King; ***D:*** Thomas Travers; ***W:*** Thomas Travers; ***C:*** Riche Lee; ***M:*** Bill Grabowski.

A Time to Remember ½ **2003** Maggie (Roberts) has been diagnosed with Alzheimer's. A family Thanksgiving reunites her with her very different daughters, Valetta (Gallagher) and Brit (Delaney), who must learn to forgive old hurts in order to deal with the present. **88m/C DVD.** Doris Roberts, Megan Gallagher, Louise Fletcher, Rosemary Forsyth, Dana Delaney; ***D:*** John Putch; ***W:*** William Sims Myers; ***C:*** James W. Wrenn; ***M:*** Joe Kraemer. **CABLE**

Time Tracers ½ **1997** A group of scientists, detectives, and a reporter time travel back to the Civil War and the Jurassic period to correct a glitch that could alter earth's future. El tacky production reminiscent of Saturday matinee filler that uses stock footage for its monsters. **93m/C VHS.** Jeffrey Combs, Rocky Patterson, T.J. Myers, Tyler Mason; ***D:*** Bret McCormick.

Time Trackers **1988 (PG)** A Roger Corman cheapie about a race through time, from present-day New York to medieval England, to recover a time machine before it alters the course of history. **87m/C VHS.** Kathleen Beller, Ned Beatty, Will Shriner, Parley Baer, Robert Cornthwaite, Bridget Hoffman, Alex Hyde-White; ***D:*** Howard R. Cohen; ***W:*** Howard R. Cohen; ***C:*** Ronn Schmidt; ***M:*** Parmer Fuller.

The Time Travelers *Time Trap* **1964** Scientists discover and pass through a porthole leading to earth's post-armageddon future where they encounter unfriendly mutants. Frightened, they make a serious effort to return to the past. Remade as "Journey to the Center of Time." **82m/C VHS.** Preston Foster, Phil Carey, Merry Anders, John Hoyt, Joan Woodbury, Dolores Wells, Dennis Patrick; ***D:*** Ib Melchior.

The Time Traveler's Wife ½ **2009 (PG-13)** Wistful romantic fantasy adapted from Audrey Niffenegger's 2004 novel. A rare genetic anomaly causes Henry DeTamble (Bana) to time travel uncontrollably through the past, present, and future of his own life, which includes Henry's perennial romance with Clare (McAdams). The two aren't always in sync so a (naked) adult Henry confronting a six-year-old Clare about their friendship is only one unsettling circumstance. And, as you might imagine, the plot gets rather confusing. Fortunately, Bana and McAdams make you believe. **107m/C DVD.** *US* Eric Bana, Rachel McAdams, Ron Livingston, Stephen Tobolowsky, Arliss Howard, Michelle Nolden; ***D:*** Robert Schwentke; ***W:*** Bruce Joel Rubin; ***C:*** Florian Ballhaus; ***M:*** Mychael Danna.

Time Troopers *Morgen Grauen; Morning Terror* **1989 (R)** In another post-nuke society, special police must execute anyone who has misused their allotted "energy clips" for illicit behavior. Dime-store budget sci-fi. **90m/C VHS.** *AT* Albert Fortell, Hannelore Elsner; ***D:*** L.E. Neiman.

Time Walker **1982 (PG)** An archaeologist unearths King Tut's coffin in California. An alien living inside is unleashed and terrorizes the public. **86m/C VHS.** Ben Murphy, Nina Axelrod, Kevin Brophy, James Karen, Austin Stoker; ***D:*** Tom Kennedy; ***W:*** Tom Friedman, Karen Levitt; ***M:*** Richard Band.

Time Without Pity ½ **1957** Anti-capital punishment plea finds desperate alcoholic David Graham (Redgrave) discovering that his son Alec (McCowen) is about to be executed for murder. But David doesn't believe in the boy's guilt and has 24 hours to find the real killer. The audience knows Alec is innocent from the get-go, making for a certain suspense. Based on the play "Someone Waiting" by Emlyn Williams. **88m/B VHS, DVD.** *GB* Michael Redgrave, Alec McCowen, Ann Todd, Leo McKern, Peter Cushing, Renee Houston, Paul Daneman, Lois Maxwell, Richard Wordsworth, George Devine, Joan Plowright; ***D:*** Joseph Losey; ***W:*** Ben Barzman; ***C:*** Freddie Francis; ***M:*** Tristram Cary.

Timebomb ½ **1991 (R)** When someone attempts to kill Biehn, he turns to a beautiful psychiatrist for help. She triggers flashbacks that send her hunted patient on a dangerous, perhaps deadly, journey into his past. **96m/C VHS.** Michael Biehn, Patsy Kensit, Tracy Scoggins, Robert Culp, Richard Jordan, Raymond St. Jacques, Jim Maniaci, Billy Blanks, Ray "Boom Boom" Mancini, Steven J. Oliver; ***D:*** Avi Nesher; ***W:*** Avi Nesher; ***M:*** Patrick Leonard.

Timecop ½ **1994 (R)** "Terminator" rip-off is fodder for Van Damme followers with lots of action and special effects (you weren't expecting acting too). 2004 policeman Max Walker (Van Damme) must travel back in time to prevent corrupt politician Aaron McComb (Silver) from altering history for personal gain. It's also Walker's chance to alter his personal history since his wife Melissa (Sara) was killed in an explosion he can now prevent. Futuristic thriller based on a Dark Horse comic. **98m/C VHS, DVD.** Jean-Claude Van Damme, Ron Silver, Mia Sara, Bruce McGill, Scott Lawrence, Kenneth Welsh, Gabrielle Rose, Duncan Fraser, Ian Tracey, Gloria Reuben, Scott Bellis, Jason Schombing, Kevin McNulty, Sean O'Byrne, Malcolm Stewart, Alfonso Quijada, Glen Roald, Theodore Thomas; ***D:*** Peter Hyams; ***W:*** Mark Verheiden, Gary De Vore; ***C:*** Peter Hyams; ***M:*** Mark Isham.

Timecop 2: The Berlin Decision ½ **2003 (R)** Convoluted, confusing actioner. Timecop Ryan Chang (Lee) is sent to 1940s Germany where colleague Miller Branson (Griffith) is about to alter history by killing Hitler. While stopping Branson, Chang inadvertently kills Branson's wife, which means the guy wants revenge. Branson keeps on hopping through time trying to change situations for his own benefit and Chang keeps following him to fix things. You won't really care—best to stick with the Van Damme original if you like this sort of thing. **81m/C VHS, DVD.** Jason Scott Lee, Thomas Ian Griffith, Mary Page Keller, John Beck, Tava Smiley; ***D:*** Steve Boyum; ***W:*** Gary Scott Thompson; ***C:*** Crescenzo G.P. Notarile; ***M:*** Andy Gray. **VIDEO**

Timecrimes ½ *Los Cronocrimenes* **2007 (R)** Low-budget smoke-and-mirrors that is done effectively. Everyman Hector (Elejalde) is staying in the country with his girlfriend (Fernandez). He goes to investigate the presence of a mysterious naked girl he spots in the woods, is attacked, and ends up in a research lab where a scientist (played by writer/director Vigalondo) uses Hector in his time experiments so that every incidence is shown again from a different point of view. Hector seems more interested in not missing dinner. Spanish with subtitles. **88m/C DVD.** *SP* Karra Elejalde, Candela Fernandez, Barbara Goenaga, Nacho Vigalondo; ***D:*** Nacho Vigalondo; ***W:*** Nacho Vigalondo; ***C:*** Flavio Labiano; ***M:*** Chucky Namanera.

Timeless ½ **1996** Hart's experimental feature debut uses Super-8, 16mm, and 35mm formats to tell a familiar story. Eighteen-year-old Terry (Bryne) hangs out on the streets of Queens doing various odd jobs for a variety of small-time gamblers, dealers, and mobsters. He falls for Lyrica (Duge) and gets her away from her abusive lover and the teen twosome head out of town, hoping for a better life. **90m/C VHS, DVD.** Peter Byrne, Michael Griffiths, Melissa Duge; ***D:*** Chris Hart; ***W:*** Chris Hart.

Timeline ½ **2003 (PG-13)** Weak big screen adaption of Michael Cricton's novel of the same name. Archaeologists travel back in time to medieval France to rescue a colleague. Features some of the most wooden performances since Pinnochio. While it's easy to blame the actors for their lackluster performance, a decent script would have helped them out a lot. **116m/C VHS, DVD.** *US* Paul Walker, Frances O'Connor, Gerard Butler, Billy Connolly, David Thewlis, Anna Friel, Neal McDonough, Matt Craven, Ethan (Randall) Embry, Michael Sheen, Lambert Wilson, Marton Csokas; ***D:*** Richard Donner; ***W:*** Jeff Maguire, George Nolfi; ***C:*** Caleb Deschanel; ***M:*** Brian Tyler.

Timelock **1999** In the 23rd century, asteroid Alpha 4 serves as a maximum security prison for the most dangerous criminals. However, the inmates have now gained controlled and its up to the reluctant heroics of a petty thief and a shuttle pilot to get the bad guys back in their cages. **100m/C VHS, DVD.** Maryam D'Abo, Arye Gross, Jeff Speakman, Jeffrey Meek, Martin Kove; ***D:*** Robert Munic; ***W:*** Joseph John Barmettler Jr.; ***C:*** Steve Adcock. **VIDEO**

Timemaster ½ **1995 (PG-13)** The orphaned 12-year-old Jesse (Cameron-Glickenhaus) dreams his parents are alive in another time, so he asks inventor Isaiah (Morita) for help. The duo discover Jesse's parents are being held hostage by a galactic dictator (Dorn), who's using them in sinister virtual-reality games and Jesse must time-travel to rescue them. **100m/C VHS, DVD.** Jesse Cameron-Glickenhaus, Noriyuki "Pat" Morita, Joanna Pacula, Michael Dorn, Duncan Regehr, Michelle Williams; ***D:*** James Glickenhaus; ***W:*** James Glickenhaus.

Timerider ½ *The Adventure of Lyle Swan* **1983 (PG)** Motorcyclist riding through the California desert is accidentally thrown back in time to 1877, the result of a scientific experiment that went awry. There he finds no gas stations and lots of cowboys. Co-written and co-produced by Michael Nesmith, best known for his days with the rock group "The Monkees." **93m/C VHS, DVD.** Fred Ward, Belinda Bauer, Peter Coyote, Richard Masur, Ed Lauter, L.Q. Jones, Tracey Walter; ***D:*** William Dear; ***W:*** Michael Nesmith, William Dear; ***C:*** Larry Pizer; ***M:*** Michael Nesmith.

Times Have Been Better ½ *La Ciel Sur la Tete* **2006** Successful Jeremy is his parents' golden first-born, much to the dismay of younger brother Robin, who's the only one to know that Jeremy is gay. That changes when Jeremy announces that he's moved in with his boyfriend. Seems his mom and dad aren't as liberal or progressive as they imagined when they decide to figure out what when "wrong" with their son. French with subtitles. **90m/C DVD.** *FR* Bernard Le Coq, Amaud Binard, Olivier Gueritee, Charlotte de Truckheim, Stephane Boucher, Thierry Desroses, Pierre Deny; ***D:*** Regis Musset; ***W:*** Nicolas Mercier. **TV**

Times of Harvey Milk ½ **1983** A powerful and moving documentary about the life and career of San Francisco supervisor and gay activist Harvey Milk. The film documents the assassination of Milk and Mayor George Moscone by Milk's fellow supervisor, Dan White. Highly acclaimed by both critics and audiences, the film gives an honest and direct look at the murder and people's reactions. News footage of the murders and White's trial is included. **90m/C VHS, DVD.** ***D:*** Robert Epstein. Oscars '83: Feature Doc.

Times Square ½ **1980 (R)** A 13-year-old girl learns about life on her own when she teams up with a defiant, anti-social child of the streets. Unappealing and unrealistic, the film features a New Wave music score. **111m/C VHS, DVD.** Tim Curry, Trini Alvarado, Robin Johnson, Peter Coffield, Elizabeth Pena, Anna Maria Horsford; ***D:*** Allan Moyle; ***W:*** Jacob Brackman; ***C:*** James A. Contner.

Times to Come *Lo Que Vendra* **1981** Taut thriller reminiscent of bleak futuristic movies like "Clockwork Orange." Three people try to survive in a desolate, aggressive, and unstable future. In Spanish with English subtitles. **98m/C VHS.** *AR* Hugo Soto, Juan Leyrado, Charly Garcia; ***D:*** Gustavo Mosquera.

Timestalkers 1/2 **1987** A college professor's infatuation with a young woman is complicated by their pursuit of a criminal from the 26th century into the past. Mildly entertaining adventure. Tucker's last film. **100m/C VHS.** William Devane, Lauren Hutton, Klaus Kinski, John Ratzenberger, Forrest Tucker, Gail Youngs; ***D:*** Michael A. Schultz. **TV**

Tin Cup **1996 (R)** You've got your romantic triangle, you've got your sports, you've got Costner reteamed with Shelton—"Bull Durham" on a golf course? Can lightening strike twice? Ron "Tin Cup" McAvoy (Costner) is a West Texas golf hustler who has the ability but not the steadiness to be on the pro tour. When McAvoy decides on a last-ditch effort to qualify for the U.S. Open, he turns to psychologist Dr. Molly Griswold (Russo) to get his game together. And the fact that Molly is the girlfriend of McAvoy's longtime rival—and successful PGA player—Don Simms (Johnson), well Tin Cup isn't adverse to playing for the lady's affections either. The U.S. Open scenes were filmed at Houston's Kingwood Country Club and the actors do hit their own shots. **133m/C VHS, DVD.** Kevin Costner, Don Johnson, Rene Russo, Richard "Cheech" Marin, Linda Hart, Dennis Burkley, Rex Linn, Lou Myers, Richard Lineback, Mickey Jones; ***D:*** Ron Shelton; ***W:*** Ron Shelton, John Norville; ***C:*** Russell Boyd; ***M:*** William Ross.

The Tin Drum *Die Blechtrommel* **1979 (R)** German child in the 1920s wills himself to stop growing in response to the increasing Nazi presence in Germany. He communicates his anger and fear by pounding on a tin drum. Memorable scenes, excellent cast. In German with English subtitles. Adapted from the novel by Gunter Grass. **141m/C VHS, DVD.** *GE* David Bennent, Mario Adorf, Angela Winkler, Daniel Olbrychski, Katharina Thalbach, Heinz Bennent, Andrea Ferreol, Charles Aznavour; ***D:*** Volker Schlondorff; ***W:*** Jean-Claude Carriere, Volker Schlondorff; ***C:*** Igor Luther; ***M:*** Maurice Jarre. Oscars '79: Foreign Film; Cannes '79: Film; L.A. Film Critics '80: Foreign Film.

Tin Man 1/2 **1983** Garage mechanic born totally deaf designs and builds a computer that can both hear and speak for him. His world is complicated, however, when a young speech therapist introduces him to new and wonderful sounds and unscrupulous and exploitative computer salesmen. Interesting premise and nice performances. **95m/C VHS, DVD.** Timothy Bottoms, Deana Jurgens, Troy Donahue, Will MacMillan; ***D:*** John G. Thomas.

Tin Man **2007** Surreal use of L. Frank Baum's "The Wizard of Oz" that can't really offer much in the way of heart or brain. The Outer Zone (or O.Z.) is an alternative universe ruled by evil sorceress Azkadellia (Robertson) and her heaving bosom. Our Dorothy is glowering tomboy D.G. (Deschanel), who still arrives by tornado, and meets her posse: Glitch (Cumming), whose brain has been removed; psychic beastie Raw (Trujillo); shape-shifting Toto (Mankuma); and grieving Wyatt Cain (McDonough), who's called a "tin man" because he was a cop. And they have to find some emerald that will free O.Z. from Azkadellia's rule. And yes, there's a sorta druggie wizard/magician (Drefuss). A Sci-Fi Channel miniseries. **360m/C DVD.** Zooey Deschanel, Neal McDonough, Kathleen Robertson, Alan Cumming, Raoul Trujillo, Blu Mankuma, Richard Dreyfuss, Callum Keith Rennie, Nick Willing, Anna Galvin; ***W:*** Steve Mitchell, Craig W. Van Sickle; ***C:*** Thomas Burstyn; ***M:*** Simon Boswell.

Tin Men 1/2 **1987 (R)** Set in Baltimore in the 1960s, this bitter comedy begins with two aluminum-siding salesmen colliding in a minor car accident. They play increasingly savage pranks on each other until one seduces the wife of the other, ruining his marriage. Like "Diner," the movie is full of Levinson's idiosyncratic local Baltimore color. **112m/C VHS, DVD.** Richard Dreyfuss, Danny DeVito, Barbara Hershey, John Mahoney, Jackie Gayle, Stan Brock, Seymour Cassel, Bruno Kirby, J.T. Walsh, Michael Tucker; ***D:*** Barry Levinson; ***W:*** Barry Levinson; ***C:*** Peter Sova; ***M:*** David Steele.

Tin Pan Alley 1/2 **1940** Tin Pan Alley songwriters Oakie and Payne meet singing sisters Faye and Grable, who agree to plug their material. At first their music business thrives but when the women head off to sing in a hit London show, the business goes downhill. Since WWI has been declared, the boys enlist and wind up in England, where they get a second chance to see their gals. The first teaming of Faye and Payne, who would star together in three more films. Remade as "I'll Get By." ♫ The Sheik of Araby; You Say the Sweetest Things, Baby; America I Love You; Goodbye Broadway, Hello France; K-K-K-Katy; Moonlight Bay; Honeysuckle Rose; Moonlight and Roses. **92m/B VHS.** Alice Faye, John Payne, Betty Grable, Jack Oakie, Allen Jenkins, Esther Ralston, John Loder, Elisha Cook Jr., Fred Keating, Billy Gilbert; ***D:*** Walter Lang; ***W:*** Robert Ellis, Helen Logan; ***C:*** Leon Shamroy; ***M:*** Alfred Newman. Oscars '40: Score.

The Tin Soldier 1/2 **1995 (PG)** Updated version of the Hans Christian Andersen story finds 12-year-old Billy (Knight) moving with his widowed mom (Sheedy) to a tough L.A. neighborhood. He's intimidated by the school bully to join a gang and smitten by a pretty girl who doesn't like his new friends. What's a guy to do? Why meet a mysterious toy shop owner (DeLuise), who gives Billy a tin soldier that magically transforms into a very real medieval knight named Yarik (Voight). Good intentions—no subtlety. Voight's directorial debut. **99m/C VHS.** Trenton Knight, Ally Sheedy, Dom DeLuise, Jon Voight; ***D:*** Jon Voight. **CABLE**

The Tin Star **1957** Perkins is the young sheriff who persuades veteran bounty hunter Fonda to help him rid the town of outlaws. Excellent Mann western balances humor and suspense. **93m/B VHS, DVD.** Henry Fonda, Anthony Perkins, Betsy Palmer, Neville Brand, Lee Van Cleef, John McIntire, Michel Ray; ***D:*** Anthony Mann; ***C:*** Loyal Griggs; ***M:*** Elmer Bernstein.

The Tingler **1959** Coroner Price discovers that a creepy creature is capable of growing on the human spine and increasing in size through fear. The only way to get rid of it is through constant screaming. Price takes what is probably the screen's first LSD trip and a partial color sequence fights nice red blood pouring from a faucet. One of Castle's cheesy best that originally wowed movie audiences in "Percepto" format, which consisted of installing electric buzzers under the seats for that true tingling sensation. **82m/B VHS, DVD.** Vincent Price, Darryl Hickman, Judith Evelyn, Philip Coolidge, Patricia Cutts, Pamela Lincoln; ***D:*** William Castle; ***W:*** Robb White; ***C:*** Wilfred M. Kline; ***M:*** Von Dexter.

Tinker, Tailor, Soldier, Spy **1980** Guinness is brilliant as world-weary spy master George Smiley, who has been somewhat forcibly retired from British Intelligence, better known as "The Circus," after a change at the top. But when a mole is discovered operating at the very highest levels, Smiley is approached on the quiet to root him out without giving the game away. Complex and sometimes confusing espionage drama based on the novel by John Le Carre. Followed by "Smiley's People." **324m/C VHS, DVD.** *GB* Alec Guinness, Michael Aldridge, Ian Bannen, Bernard Hepton, Ian Richardson, Terence Rigby, Anthony Bate, Hywel Bennett, Michael Jayston, Joss Ackland, Warren Clarke, Beryl Reid, Sian Phillips, Patrick Stewart; ***D:*** John Irvin; ***W:*** Arthur Hopcraft; ***C:*** Tony Pierce-Roberts; ***M:*** Geoffrey Burgon. **TV**

Tinseltown **1997 (R)** Two broke screenwriters, who are living in a self-storage facility, suspect that the man who rents the space next to them is an infamous L.A. serial killer. Naturally, the desperate duo are inspired by his deeds to write a screenplay, which could make them his next victims. Based on the play "Self-storage" by Tony Spiridakis and Shem Bitterman. **84m/C VHS.** Arye Gross, Joe Pantoliano, Ron Perlman, Tom Wood, Kristy Swanson, Rebecca Gray, John Considine, David Dukes; ***D:*** Tony Spiridakis; ***W:*** Tony Spiridakis.

Tintorera... Tiger Shark **WOOF!** *Tintorera; Tintorera...Bloody Waters* **1978 (R)** Three shark hunters attempt to discover why buxom swimmers are disappearing. Phony takeoff of "Jaws." **91m/C VHS, DVD.** *GB MX* Susan George, Fiona Lewis, Jennifer Ashley; ***D:*** Rene Cardona Jr.

Tiny Toon Adventures: How I Spent My Vacation **1991** How the tiny toons of Acme Acres spend their summer vacation in this animated adventure that spoofs several popular films and amusements. Plucky Duck and Hampton Pig journey to "Happy World Land" (a takeoff on Walt Disney World), Babs and Buster Bunny's water adventure parodies "Deliverance," there's a spoof of "The Little Mermaid," and the Road Runner even makes a cameo appearance. Parents will be equally entertained by the level of humor and the fast-paced action. Based on the Steven Spielberg TV cartoon series, this is the first made-for-home-video animated feature ever released in the United States. **80m/C VHS.** ***D:*** Rich Arons; ***V:*** Charles Adler, Tress MacNeille, Joe Alaskey, Donald E. Messick, Jonathan Winters, Edie McClurg.

The Tioga Kid 1/2 **1948** Dean takes on two roles here, that of a Texas Ranger and an outlaw who goes by the name of "The Tioga Kid." Andy Parker and the Plainsmen provide the cowboy tunes. **54m/B VHS, DVD.** Eddie Dean, Roscoe Ates, Jennifer Holt, Dennis Moore, William "Bill" Fawcett; ***D:*** Ray Taylor; ***W:*** Ed Earl Repp.

The Tip-Off 1/2 **1931** Lovable boxer (Armstrong) and vivacious girlfriend (Rogers) save less-than-bright friend from getting involved with mean mobster's girlfriend. Major chemistry between Rogers and Armstrong. **75m/B VHS.** Eddie Quillan, Robert Armstrong, Ginger Rogers, Joan Peers, Ernie Adams; ***D:*** Albert Rogell.

Tipping the Velvet 1/2 **2002** Provocative miniseries based on the Sarah Waters novel. Set in the 1890s, it takes a look at the unconventional life of male impersonator and music hall star Nan Astley (Stirling), who takes up her profession after becoming infatuated with cross-dressing performer Kitty Butler (Hawes). Hired as Kitty's assistant, Nan eventually reveals her love and the duo become partners on and off the London stage. But Nan's life takes a turn for the dark side when she turns to prostitution, gets involved with dominating aristocrat, Diana (Chancellor), and seeks help from potential new love, Florence (May). **180m/C DVD.** *GB* Rachael Stirling, Keeley Hawes, Anna Chancellor, Jodhi May, Hugh Bonneville, Alexei Sayle, John Bowe, Sally Hawkins; ***D:*** Geoffrey Sax; ***W:*** Andrew Davies; ***C:*** Cinders Forshaw; ***M:*** Adrian Johnston. **TV**

Tiptoes **2003 (R)** Rolfe (Oldman) and Steven (McConaughey) are brothers. Rolfe is a dwarf, and Steven isn't, which causes some worry for Steven's girlfriend Carol (Beckinsale) when she becomes pregnant and worries that her child will get the dwarf gene. In a twist, she falls for Rolfe, and comedy, drama, and romance ensues. Director Bright had a falling out with the producers and was fired during the shoot, resulting in an uneven film and Bright issuing a scathing monologue against the producers at the film's debut at the Sundance Film Festival. Performances are good but can't save film from falling flat. **90m/C DVD.** Gary Oldman, Matthew McConaughey, Kate Beckinsale, Peter Dinklage, Patricia Arquette, Debbie Lee Carrington; ***W:*** Bill Weiner; ***C:*** Sonja Rom. **VIDEO**

'Tis a Pity She's a Whore 1/2 *Addio, Fratello, Crudele* **1973 (R)** A brother and sister engage in an incestuous affair. She becomes pregnant and is married off. Her husband, however, becomes infuriated when he learns of his wife's pregnancy. Photography is by Vittorio Storaro in this highly stylized drama set in Renaissance Italy. **102m/C VHS, DVD.** *IT* Charlotte Rampling, Oliver Tobias, Fabio Testi, Antonio Falsi, Rick (Rik) Battaglia, Angela Luce, Rino Imperio; ***D:*** Giuseppe Patroni-Griffi; ***M:*** Ennio Morricone.

Titan A.E. 1/2 **2000 (PG)** Animated adventure set after Earth is destroyed by aliens. Young Cale begins a journey through space to find a legendary lost ship—The Titan—that holds the secret to mankind's salvation. Visuals—both computer-generated and traditionally drawn—are breathtaking, but the script is earthbound. Dialogue too often falls flat, and the story, aimed at teen boys, never lives up to the epic visual dazzle. **95m/C VHS, DVD.** ***D:*** Don Bluth, Gary Goldman; ***W:*** Ben Edlund, John August, Joss Whedon; ***M:*** Graeme Revell; ***V:*** Matt Damon, Drew Barrymore, Bill Pullman, Nathan Lane, Janeane Garofalo, John Leguizamo, Tone Loc, Ron Perlman, Alex D. Linz, Jim Breuer.

Titanic **1953** Hollywoodized version of the 1912 sinking of the famous luxury liner sets the scene for the personal drama of a mother (Stanwyck) who wants to flee her husband (Webb) for a new life in America. Story gets a little too melodramatic, but it's not a bad retelling of the sea tragedy. Film is quite effective in conveying the panic and the calm of the actual sinking. A 20-foot-long model of the ship was built for the re-creation of that fateful moment when the "Titanic" hit the inevitable iceberg. **98m/B VHS, DVD.** Clifton Webb, Barbara Stanwyck, Robert Wagner, Richard Basehart, Audrey Dalton, Thelma Ritter, Brian Aherne; ***D:*** Jean Negulesco; ***W:*** Charles Brackett, Walter Reisch, Richard L. Breen. Oscars '53: Story & Screenplay.

Titanic 1/2 **1996 (PG-13)** Dull and draggy TV version of the 1912 tragedy between the luxury liner and an iceberg that resulted in the deaths of more than 1000 passengers. There are the usual romantic subplots, villains, and heroes, and Scott is properly noble as the veteran captain making his last voyage before retirement. Otherwise you've seen this many times before. **165m/C VHS, DVD.** George C. Scott, Peter Gallagher, Catherine Zeta-Jones, Eva Marie Saint, Tim Curry, Roger Rees, Harley Jane Kozak, Marilu Henner, Felicity Waterman, Scott Hylands, Kevin McNulty, Malcolm Stewart; ***D:*** Robert Lieberman; ***W:*** Ross LaManna, Joyce Eliason; ***C:*** David Hennings; ***M:*** Lennie Niehaus.

Titanic **1997 (PG-13)** Skipper Cameron's mega-budget three-hour tour had its own brushes with disaster with a mammoth budget and delays. A love story that happens to have the sinking of the historic ship as a backdrop, real and fictional characters are blended for a detailed re-enactment of the luxury liner's only voyage. The two lovebirds, Jack Dawson (DiCaprio) and debutante Rose Bukater (Winslet) are from different ends of the economic and social ladder. DiCaprio and Winslet are dynamic and make the running time less of a chore. The special effects are impressive, with a life-size version of the ship built just for this film. Cameron's prowess as a storyteller keeps the outcome of the ship suspenseful and tense even though the ending is no secret. **197m/C VHS, DVD.** Kate Winslet, Leonardo DiCaprio, Billy Zane, Kathy Bates, Frances Fisher, Gloria Stuart, Jonathan Hyde, Danny Nucci, David Warner, Bill Paxton, Bernard Hill, Victor Garber, Suzy Amis, Bernard Fox; ***D:*** James Cameron; ***W:*** James Cameron; ***C:*** Russell Carpenter; ***M:*** James Horner. Oscars '97: Art Dir./Set Dec., Cinematog., Costume Des., Director (Cameron), Film Editing, Picture, Song ("My Heart Will Go On"), Sound, Sound FX Editing, Visual FX, Orig. Score; Directors Guild '97: Director (Cameron); Golden Globes '98: Director (Cameron), Film—Drama, Song ("My Heart Will Go On"), Score; MTV Movie Awards '98: Film, Male Perf. (DiCaprio); Screen Actors Guild '97: Support. Actress (Stuart); Broadcast Film Critics '97: Director (Cameron).

Title Shot **1981 (R)** A crafty manager convinces a millionaire to bet heavily on the guaranteed loss of his heavyweight contender in an upcoming fight. He doesn't realize the boxer is too stupid to throw the fight. **88m/C VHS.** Tony Curtis, Richard Gabourie, Susan Hogan, Robert Delbert; ***D:*** Les Rose.

Tito and Me *Tito i Ja; Tito and I* **1992** Ten-year-old Zoran lives in 1954 Belgrade and is fascinated by Yugoslavian leader Marshall Tito. Crowded into a flat with his extended family, Zoran learns about volatility firsthand. Then there's romance—he has a crush on a classmate who breaks up with him when she is chosen as one of Tito's Young Pioneers, which means a two-week trip to the country. Political indoctrination means nothing but love—ahh. Debut role for the young Vojnov, who carries the weight of the movie with perfect aplomb. In Serbo-Croation with English subtitles. **104m/C VHS, DVD.** *YU* Dimitrie Vojnov, Lazar Ristovski,

Anica Dobra, Miki (Predrag) Manojlovic, Olivera Markovic; *D:* Goran Markovic; *W:* Goran Markovic; *C:* Radoslav Vladic; *M:* Zoran Simjanovic.

Titus 𝒮𝒮 **1999 (R)** Flashy version of a lesser-known early Shakespeare play, the gory "Titus Andronicus." Theatrical driector Taymor makes her film debut with verve and a wild mixture of styles. Victorius Roman general Titus (Hopkins) has just defeated the Goths and has captured Tamora (Lange), the Goth Queen and her sons, one of whom Titus promptly sacrifices to appease the gods. Decadent Emperor Saturninus (Cumming) claims Tamora for his queen; her daughter Lavinia (Fraser) suffers a fate worse than death; Tamora wants revenge; Titus wants revenge; there's a villainous Moor, Aaron (Lennix); and a lot of campy fantasy and blood. **162m/C VHS, DVD.** Anthony Hopkins, Jessica Lange, Alan Cumming, Harry J. Lennix, Colm Feore, Laura Fraser, James Frain, Angus MacFadyen, Jonathan Rhys Meyers, Geraldine McEwan, Matthew Rhys, Bruno Bilotta; *D:* Julie Taymor; *W:* Julie Taymor; *C:* Luciano Tovoli; *M:* Elliot Goldenthal.

TMNT (Teenage Mutant Ninja Turtles) 𝒮𝒮 **2007 (PG)** Our hard-shelled heroes haven't hit the big screen since 1993; maybe the producers are hoping to entice a new generation with improved CGI and (basically) the same old story. Well, not quite, since bad guy Shredder isn't around and the turtle quartet spend more time squabbling among themselves than being a team. That is until evil cosmic forces align to destroy mankind, like they do. There's a few jokes and a few fights and not enough pizza. **86m/C DVD, HD DVD.** *US HK D:* Kevin Munroe; *W:* Kevin Munroe; *C:* Steve Lumley; *M:* Klaus Badelt; *V:* Mitchell Whitfield, James Taylor, Mako, Patrick Stewart, Mikey Kelley, Nolan North, Chris Evans, Sarah Michelle Gellar.

T.N.T. 𝒮𝒮 **1998 (R)** Gruner's managed to extricate himself from a covert fighting force but now they're threatening his family unless he does what he's told. **87m/C VHS, DVD.** Olivier Gruner, Eric Roberts, Randy Travis, Sam Jones, Rebecca Staab; *D:* Robert Radler; *C:* Bryan Duggan; *M:* Stephen (Steve) Edwards. **VIDEO**

TNT Jackson WOOF! 1975 (R) A kung fu mama searches for her brother while everyone in Hong Kong tries to kick her out of town. **73m/C VHS, DVD.** Stan Shaw, Pat Anderson, Ken Metcalfe, Jeannie Bell; *D:* Cirio H. Santiago; *W:* Ken Metcalfe, Dick Miller; *C:* Felipe Sacdalan.

To All a Goodnight WOOF! 1980 (R) Five young girls and their boyfriends are planning an exciting Christmas holiday until a mad Santa Claus puts a damper on things. Total gorefest, with few, if any, redeeming virtues. **90m/C VHS.** Jennifer Runyon, Forrest Swanson, Linda Gentile, William Lover; *D:* David A(lexander) Hess.

To All My Friends on Shore 𝒮𝒮𝒮 **1971** Drama about a father dealing with his young son's sickle cell anemia. Fine performances, realistic script make this an excellent outing. **74m/C VHS, DVD.** Bill Cosby, Gloria Foster, Dennis Hines; *D:* Gilbert Cates. **TV**

To Be or Not to Be 𝒮𝒮𝒮 ½ **1942** Sophisticated black comedy set in wartime Poland. Lombard and Benny are Maria and Josef Tura, the Barrymores of the Polish stage, who use the talents of their acting troupe to protect the Warsaw Resistance against the invading Nazis. The opening sequence is regarded as a cinema classic. One of Benny's finest film performances, the movie marks Lombard's final screen appearance—she was killed in a plane crash druing a war bond drive shortly after completing the film. Classic Lubitsch. Remade in 1983 with Mel Brooks and Anne Bancroft. **102m/B VHS, DVD.** Carole Lombard, Jack Benny, Robert Stack, Sig Rumann, Lionel Atwill, Felix Bressart, Helmut Dantine, Tom Dugan, Charles Halton, Stanley Ridges, George Lynn, Halliwell Hobbes, Miles Mander, Henry Victor, Leslie Denison, Frank Reicher, John Kellogg, James Finlayson, Roland Varno; *D:* Ernst Lubitsch; *W:* Ernst Lubitsch, Edwin Justus Mayer, Melchior Lengyel; *C:* Rudolph Mate; *M:* Werner R. Heymann, Miklos Rozsa. Natl. Film Reg. '96.

To Be or Not to Be 𝒮𝒮 ½ **1983 (PG)** In this remake of the 1942 film, Bancroft and Brooks are actors in Poland during WWII. They accidently become involved with the Polish Resistance and work to thwart the Nazis. Lots of laughs, although at times there's a little too much slapstick. **108m/C VHS, DVD.** Mel Brooks, Anne Bancroft, Charles Durning, Jose Ferrer, Tim Matheson, Christopher Lloyd; *D:* Alan Johnson; *W:* Ronny Graham.

To Be the Best 𝒮 ½ **1993 (R)** Eric, a member of the U.S. Kickboxing Team, lets his love for the beautiful Cheryl and his hot temper get the best of him. When a ruthless gambler threatens to kill Cheryl if Eric doesn't throw his big match, he joins with his family, fellow teammates, and most feared opponent, to set things right. **99m/C VHS, DVD.** Mike Worth, Martin Kove, Phillip Troy, Brittney Powell, Alex Cord, Steven Leigh; *D:* Joseph Merhi; *W:* Michael January.

To Catch a Killer 𝒮𝒮𝒮 **1992** A chilling performance by Dennehy highlights this true-crime tale of a detective's relentless pursuit of serial killer John Wayne Gacy, who preyed on young men and hid the bodies in his home. Made for television. **95m/C VHS, DVD.** Brian Dennehy, Michael Riley, Margot Kidder, Meg Foster; *D:* Eric Till; *W:* Judson Kinberg; *C:* Rene Ohashi; *M:* Paul Zaza. **TV**

To Catch a King 𝒮𝒮 **1984** Garr is a singer working in Wagner's nightclub in 1940s' Lisbon. The pair becomes involved in trying to foil the Nazi plot to kidnap the vacationing Duke and Duchess of Windsor. Average cable fare. **120m/C VHS, DVD.** Robert Wagner, Teri Garr, Horst Janson, Barbara Parkins, John Standing; *D:* Clive Donner; *M:* Nick Bicat. **CABLE**

To Catch a Thief 𝒮𝒮𝒮 **1955** On the French Riviera, a reformed jewel thief falls for a wealthy American woman, who suspects he's up to his old tricks when a rash of jewel thefts occur. Oscar-winning photography by Robert Burks, a notable fireworks scene, and snappy dialogue. A change of pace for Hitchcock, this charming comedy-thriller proved to be as popular as his other efforts. Based on the novel by David Dodge. Kelly met future husband Prince Rainier during a photo shoot while she was attending the Cannes Film Festival. **103m/C VHS, DVD.** Cary Grant, Grace Kelly, Jessie Royce Landis, John Williams, Charles Vanel, Brigitte Auber; *D:* Alfred Hitchcock; *W:* John Michael Hayes; *C:* Robert Burks. Oscars '55: Color Cinematog.

To Catch a Yeti 𝒮 ½ **1995 (PG)** Big game hunter Meat Loaf is all set for a trip to the Himalayas when the Yeti winds up being spotted in the canyons of Manhattan (and it turns out to be very tiny). **88m/C VHS.** Chantellese Kent, Jim Gordon, Richard Howland, Meat Loaf Aday; *D:* Bob Keen; *W:* Paul Adam; *C:* David Perrault.

To Cross the Rubicon 𝒮𝒮 ½ **1991** Romantic comedy finds Kendall (Royce) getting dumped by David (Souther), her boyfriend of eight years, who then reconciles with former flame, Claire (Devon). Meanwhile, Kendall involves herself with James (Burke), a young musician, and becomes new best friends with—you guessed it—Claire. But will David and Kendall's previous relationship cause friction? **120m/C VHS, DVD.** Patricia Royce, J.D. Souther, Lorraine Devon, Billy Burke; *D:* Barry Caillier; *W:* Patricia Royce, Lorraine Devon; *C:* Christopher Tufty; *M:* Paul Speer, David Lanz.

To Dance with the White Dog 𝒮𝒮𝒮 **1993 (PG)** Robert Samuel Peek (Cronyn) is a pecan-tree grower from rural Georgia who has been married to Cora (Tandy) for 57 years. Then she dies and their fussing daughters (Baranski and Wright) wonder how their father will survive. But Sam's increasing loneliness is checked when he befriends a stray white dog that it seems no one else can see. Based on the novel by Terry Kay. **98m/C VHS, DVD.** Hume Cronyn, Jessica Tandy, Christine Baranski, Amy Wright, Esther Rolle, Harley Cross, Frank Whaley, Terry Beaver, Dan Albright, David Dwyer; *D:* Glenn Jordan; *W:* Susan Cooper; *C:* Neil Roach. **TV**

To Die For 𝒮 ½ *Dracula: The Love Story* **1989 (R)** A vampire stalks, woos, and snacks on a young real estate woman. **99m/C VHS, DVD.** Brendan Hughes, Scott Jacoby, Duane Jones, Steve Bond, Sydney Walsh, Amanda Wyss, Ava Fabian; *D:* Deran Sarafian; *W:* Leslie King; *C:* Jacques Haitkin; *M:* Cliff Eidelman.

To Die For 𝒮𝒮𝒮 **1995 (R)** Beauteous, manipulative Suzanne Stone (Kidman) wants to be somebody—preferably a big TV personality—and nothing will stop her. She recruits a scruffy threesome to help her ice sweet-but-dim hubby, Larry (Dillon), even if it does means seducing aimless teenager Jimmy (Phoenix). Black comedy, loosely based on the Pamela Smart murder case and adapted from the novel by Joyce Maynard, takes on the media-obsessed culture with a wicked grin. Van Sant retains his fresh and hip storytelling in his first film for a major studio. Backed by Henry's zesty script, all the actors shine—with standout performances from Kidman as the monstrous Suzanne and Phoenix (River's younger brother) as the lost/horny Jimmy. Shot entirely in Canada. **103m/C VHS, DVD.** Nicole Kidman, Matt Dillon, Joaquin Rafael (Leaf) Phoenix, Casey Affleck, Alison Folland, Illeana Douglas, Dan Hedaya, Wayne Knight, Kurtwood Smith, Holland Taylor, Maria Tucci, Susan Traylor; ***Cameos:*** George Segal, Buck Henry; *D:* Gus Van Sant; *W:* Buck Henry, Johnny Burne; *C:* Eric Alan Edwards; *M:* Danny Elfman. Golden Globes '96: Actress—Mus./Comedy (Kidman); Broadcast Film Critics '95: Actress (Kidman).

To Die For 2: Son of Darkness 𝒮 ½ *Son of Darkness: To Die For 2* **1991 (R)** This far outclasses part one in terms of acting and production values, but the plot still isn't back from the grave. Strange, because all the vampires are, despite their fiery deaths last time they flock around the adoptive mother of a baby secretly sired by a bloodsucker. **95m/C VHS.** Rosalind Allen, Steve Bond, Scott Jacoby, Michael Praed, Jay Underwood, Amanda Wyss, Remy O'Neill, Vince Edwards; *D:* David F. Price.

To Die (Or Not) 𝒮 ½ *Morir (O No)* **1999** It begins with a director and his wife arguing about his new film, then seven short stories that result in the death of the main character in various ways are shown. The wife rejects these depressing endings so the stories are then retold with her suggestions. Spanish with subtitles. **92m/C DVD.** *SP* Roger Coma, Carmen Elias, Ana Azcona, Lluis Hmar, Carlotta Bantula; *D:* Ventura Pons; *W:* Ventura Pons; *C:* Jesus Escosa; *M:* Carles Cases.

To Die Standing 𝒮 ½ **1991 (R)** Two mavericks team up to do what the D.E.A. and cops simply cannot... capture a dangerous international drug lord. High action. **87m/C VHS.** Cliff DeYoung, Robert Beltran, Jamie Rose, Gerald Anthony, Orlando Sacha, Michael Ford; *D:* Louis Morneau; *W:* Ross Bell, Daryl Haney.

To Each His Own 𝒮𝒮𝒮 **1946** Top-notch melodrama finds middle-aged businesswoman Josephine Norris (de Havilland) recalling her past as she carries on through London's blitz. As a young woman, Josephine fell in love with a dashing WWI pilot (Lund), became pregnant, and had her lover killed in action. To avoid scandal, she gives the baby up for adoption, although she stays in touch with his adoptive mother (Anderson) and befriends the boy. When Gregory (Lund again) grows up, he too becomes a pilot and visits Josephine—who's still longing to tell him the truth. Lund's film debut. **100m/B VHS.** Olivia de Havilland, John Lund, Mary Anderson, Roland Culver, Virginia Welles, Bill Goodwin, Phillip Terry; *D:* Mitchell Leisen; *W:* Charles Brackett, Jacques Thery; *C:* Daniel F. Fapp; *M:* Victor Young. Oscars '46: Actress (de Havilland).

To End All Wars 𝒮𝒮 **2001 (R)** Based on Ernest Gordon's autobiographical 1962 novel "Through the Valley of the Kwai," bares the horrors that a group of WWII Allied soldiers suffered at the hands of their Japanese captors who torture the POWs during the erecting of the so-called "Railway of Death" in the nasty Burmese jungle. Related to events depicted in "The Bridge of the River Kwai" but not nearly so well imitated. **117m/C VHS, DVD.** Robert Carlyle, Kiefer Sutherland, Ciaran McMenamin, Mark Strong, Masayuki Yui, James Cosmo, John Gregg, Pip Torrens, Sakae Kimura, Shu Nakajima, Yugo Saso, Greg Ellis, Adam Sinclair, Winton Nicholson, James McCarthy, Brendan Cowell, Duff Armour, Sergio Jones, Christopher White, Jeremy Pippin, Robert Jobe; ***Cameos:*** Ernest Gordon, Takashi Nagase; *C:* Greg Gardiner; *M:* John Cameron, Maire Brennan. **VIDEO**

To Forget Venice 𝒮𝒮 ½ **1979** Portrays the sensitive relationships among four homosexuals, and their shared fears of growing older. Dubbed in English. **90m/C VHS.** *IT* Erland Josephson, Mariangela Melato, David Pontremoli, Elenora Giorgi; *D:* Franco Brusati.

To Gillian on Her 37th Birthday 𝒮𝒮 **1996 (PG-13)** Overly sentimental weeper explores the effects of a mother's death on the ones she's left behind. Gillian's been dead for two years but widower David Lewis (Gallagher) hasn't been able to let her spirit go and daughter Rachel (Danes) is having trouble growing up with a father who spends more time on the beach with his dead wife's ghost than with her. Enter nosy sister-in-law Esther (Baker) and annoying husband (Altman) who try to set him up on the anniversary of Gillian's death and you've got a mental family breakdown coming. Pfeiffer appears as Gillian in this script by husband Kelley, based on the play by Michael Brady. **92m/C VHS, DVD.** Peter Gallagher, Claire Danes, Kathy Baker, Wendy Crewson, Bruce Altman, Michelle Pfeiffer, Freddie Prinze Jr.; *D:* Michael Pressman; *W:* David E. Kelley; *C:* Tim Suhrstedt; *M:* James Horner.

To Grandmother's House We Go 𝒮𝒮 ½ **1994** The Olsen twins want to give mom a restful Christmas vacation so they decide to visit Grandma (on their own) and wind up in the hands of a pair of bumbling kidnappers. Made for TV movie. **89m/C VHS, DVD.** Ashley (Fuller) Olsen, Mary-Kate Olsen, Cynthia Geary, Rhea Perlman, J. Eddie Peck, Stuart Margolin; ***Cameos:*** Bob Saget, Lori Loughlin; *D:* Jeff Franklin; *W:* Jeff Franklin. **TV**

To Have & Have Not 𝒮𝒮𝒮 ½ **1944** Martinique charter boat operator gets mixed up with beautiful woman and French resistance fighters during WWII. Top-notch production in every respect. Classic dialogue and fiery romantic bouts between Bogart and Bacall. Bacall's first film. Based on a story by Ernest Hemingway. Remade in 1950 as "The Breaking Point" and in 1958 as "The Gun Runners." **100m/B VHS, DVD.** Humphrey Bogart, Lauren Bacall, Walter Brennan, Hoagy Carmichael, Marcel Dalio, Dolores Moran, Sheldon Leonard, Dan Seymour; *D:* Howard Hawks; *W:* Jules Furthman, William Faulkner.

To Heal a Nation 𝒮𝒮 ½ **1988** The story of veteran Jan Scruggs, who spearheaded the movement to build the Vietnam Veterans memorial. The then little-known Ross Perot provided major financial support for Scruggs' dream. **100m/C VHS.** Eric Roberts, Conrad Bachmann, Glynnis O'Connor, Marshall Colt, Scott Paulin, Lee Purcell, Laurence Luckinbill, Linden Chiles, Brock Peters; *D:* Michael Pressman; *W:* Lionel Chetwynd. **TV**

To Hell and Back 𝒮𝒮 ½ **1955** Adaptation of Audie Murphy's autobiography. Murphy plays himself, from his upbringing as the son of Texas sharecroppers to his Army career in WWII, where he was the most-decorated American soldier. Murphy won more than 20 medals, including the Congressional Medal of Honor. Features realistic battle sequences punctuated with grand heroics. **106m/C VHS, DVD.** Audie Murphy, Marshall Thompson, Jack Kelly, Charles Drake, Gregg (Hunter) Palmer, Paul Picerni, David Janssen, Bruce Cowling, Paul Langton, Art Aragon, Felix Noriego, Denver Pyle, Brett Halsey, Susan Kohner, Anabel Shaw, Mary Field, Gordon Gebert, Rand Brooks, Richard Castle, Gen. Walter Bedell Smith; *D:* Jesse Hibbs; *W:* Gil Doud; *C:* Maury Gertsman; *M:* Henry Mancini.

To Joy 𝒮𝒮𝒮 *Till Gladje* **1950** The rocky marriage of a violinist and his wife illuminate the problems of the young in Swedish society. Early Bergman. In Swedish with English subtitles or dubbed. **90m/B VHS, DVD.** *SW* Maj-Britt Nilsson, Birger Malmsten, Margit Carlquist, Stig Olin, John Ekman, Victor Sjostrom; *D:* Ingmar Bergman; *W:* Ingmar Bergman; *C:* Gunnar Fischer.

To Kill a Clown 𝒮𝒮 **1972 (R)** Painter and his wife working to save their marriage are trapped on an isolated island and terrorized by a crazed Vietnam veteran. This helps pull them together. Some holes in the plot, but generally effective. **82m/C VHS.** Alan Alda, Blythe Danner, Heath Lamberts; ***D:*** George Bloomfield.

To Kill a King ☙☙ 1/2 **2003** Historical drama set during Britain's 17th-century civil war. Sir Thomas Fairfax (Scott) joins with his friend, General Oliver Cromwell (Roth), to dethrone (and eventually behead) King Charles I (Everett). But the two allies are soon at odds as Cromwell is resentful of Fairfax's aristocratic background and public popularity and Fairfax is increasingly disturbed by Cromwell's puritanical ruthlessness. **102m/C DVD.** *GB* Dougray Scott, Tim Roth, Rupert Everett, Olivia Williams, James Bolam, Corin Redgrave, Finbar Lynch, Julian Rhind-Tutt; ***D:*** Mike Barker; ***W:*** Jenny Mayhew; ***C:*** Eigil Bryld; ***M:*** Richard G. Mitchell.

To Kill a Mockingbird ☙☙☙☙ **1962** Faithful adaptation of powerful Harper Lee novel, both an evocative portrayal of childhood innocence and a denunciation of bigotry. Peck's performance as southern lawyer Atticus Finch defending black Tom Robinson (Peters), who's accused of raping a white woman, is flawless. Duvall debuted as the dim-witted Boo Radley. Lee based her characterization of "Dill," the Finch children's "goin' on seven" friend, on Truman Capote, her own childhood friend. **129m/B VHS, DVD.** Gregory Peck, Brock Peters, Phillip Alford, Mary Badham, Robert Duvall, Rosemary Murphy, William Windom, Alice Ghostley, John Megna, Frank Overton, Paul Fix, Collin Wilcox-Paxton; ***D:*** Robert Mulligan; ***W:*** Horton Foote; ***C:*** Russell Harlan; ***M:*** Elmer Bernstein; ***Nar:*** Kim Stanley. Oscars '62: Actor (Peck), Adapt. Screenplay, Art Dir./Set Dec., B&W; AFI '98: Top 100; Golden Globes '63: Actor—Drama (Peck), Score, Natl. Film Reg. '95.

To Kill a Priest ☙☙ **1989 (R)** Based on the true story of Father Jerzy Popieluszko, a young priest in 1984 Poland who defies his church and speaks out publicly on Solidarity. He is killed by the government as a result. Harris is good as the menacing police official. **110m/C VHS.** Christopher Lambert, Ed Harris, David Suchet, Tim Roth, Joanne Whalley, Pete Postlethwaite, Cherie Lunghi, Joss Ackland; ***D:*** Agnieszka Holland; ***W:*** Agnieszka Holland; ***C:*** Adam Holender; ***M:*** Georges Delerue.

To Kill a Stranger ☙☙ **1984** A beautiful pop singer is stranded in a storm, and then victimized by a mad rapist/murderer. **100m/C VHS, DVD.** *MX* Donald Pleasence, Dean Stockwell, Angelica Maria, Aldo Ray, Sergio Aragones; ***D:*** Juan Lopez Moctezuma; ***W:*** Juan Lopez Moctezuma; ***C:*** Alex Phillips Jr.; ***M:*** Mort Garson.

To Live ☙☙☙☙ *Huozhe* **1994** Superb drama follows the lives of one family—weak but adaptable Fugui (You), his strong-willed wife Jiazhen (Li), and their young daughter and son—from prerevolutionary China in the 1940s through the '60s Cultural Revolution. Fugui loses the family fortune in the gambling houses, actually a blessing when the Communists come to power, and the family must struggle to survive financial and increasingly difficult political changes, where fate can change on a whim. Subtle saga about ordinary human lives reacting to terrifying conditions boasts extraordinary performances and evocative imagery. Adapted from the novel "Lifetimes" by Yu Hua. Chinese with subtitles. **130m/C VHS, DVD.** *CH* Ge You, Gong Li, Niu Ben, Guo Tao, Jiang Wu; ***D:*** Yimou Zhang; ***W:*** Lu Wei, Yu Hua; ***C:*** Lu Yue; ***M:*** Jiping Zhao. British Acad. '94: Foreign Film; Cannes '94: Actor (You), Grand Jury Prize.

To Live and Die in Hong Kong ☙ 1/2 **1989** Two sailors arrive in Hong Kong for a little R & R, until they are mistaken for spies by both the Hong Kong police and the Chinese mob. Action-packed tale. **98m/C VHS.** Rowena Cortes, Lawrence Jan, Mike Kelly, Laurens C. Postma; ***D:*** Lau Shing Hon.

To Live & Die in L.A. ☙☙ **1985 (R)** Fast-paced, morally ambivalent tale of cops and counterfeiters in L.A. After his partner is killed shortly before his retirement, a secret service agent sets out to track down his ruthless killer. Lots of violence; some nudity. Notable both for a riveting car chase and its dearth of sympathetic characters. **114m/C VHS, DVD, UMD.** William L. Petersen, Willem Dafoe, John Pankow, Dean Stockwell, Debra Feuer, John Turturro, Darlanne Fluegel, Robert Downey; ***D:*** William Friedkin; ***W:*** William Friedkin.

To Love Again ☙ 1/2 **1980** A middle-aged love story about a reclusive college professor and the campus handyman. **96m/C VHS.** Lynn Redgrave, Brian Dennehy, Conchata Ferrell; ***D:*** Joseph Hardy.

To Paris with Love ☙☙ 1/2 **1955** A British man and his son fall in love with a shop girl and her boss while on vacation in Paris. Charming and humorous, with a witty performance from Guinness. **75m/C VHS.** Alec Guinness, Odile Versois, Vernon Gray; ***D:*** Robert Hamer; ***M:*** Edwin Astley.

To Play or to Die ☙☙ **1991** The introverted Kees attends an all-boy school where powerful bullies and sadomasochistic games are the rule. Kees is fascinated by the handsome Charel, the bullies leader. He invites Charel to his home, intending to turn the tables on his tormentor, but nothing goes as planned. Intense and controversial look at gay teens. Directorial debut of Krom. In Dutch with English subtitles. **150m/C VHS, DVD.** *NL* Geert Hunaerts, Tjebbo Gerritsma; ***D:*** Frank Krom; ***W:*** Anne Van De Putte, Frank Krom; ***C:*** Nils Post; ***M:*** Kim Hayworth, Ferdinand Bakker.

To Play the King ☙☙☙ **1993** Sequel to "The House of Cards" finds Francis Urquhart (Richardson), having murdered his way to the Prime Ministery, now bored with his political situation. But things may be changing—the Queen has been succeeded by her liberal son (Kitchen) and Francis, goaded by his equally vicious wife (Fletcher), plots treachery to bring down the monarchy. Followed by "The Final Cut"; adapted from the novel by Michael Dobbs. **212m/C VHS, DVD.** *GB* Ian Richardson, Michael Kitchen, Diane Fletcher, Kitty Aldridge, Bernice Stegers, Colin Jeavons, Rowena King, Erika Hoffman, Nicholas Farrell; ***D:*** Paul Seed; ***W:*** Andrew Davies.

To Please a Lady ☙☙ 1/2 *Red Hot Wheels* **1950** Romantic comedy-drama about race car driver Gable and reporter Stanwyck. Although leads do their best with the script, they're unable to generate any sparks. However, race track scenes are excellent. Filmed at the Indianapolis Speedway, the spectacular racing footage makes up for overall average film. **91m/B VHS.** Clark Gable, Barbara Stanwyck, Adolphe Menjou, Will Geer, Roland Winters; ***D:*** Clarence Brown; ***W:*** Barre Lyndon, Marge Decker.

To Protect and Serve ☙☙ **1992 (R)** When crooked cops start getting killed, two young cops are assigned to investigate. Suspicion points to a rookie (Howell), who just may have decided to clean things up his own way. **93m/C VHS.** C. Thomas Howell, Lezlie (Dean) Deane, Richard Romanus, Joe Cortese; ***D:*** Eric Weston.

To Race the Wind ☙☙ **1980** Blind man wants to be treated like a normal person as he struggles through Harvard Law School. Based upon Harold Krents's autobiography "Butterflies Are Free." **97m/C VHS.** Steve Guttenberg, Lisa Eilbacher, Randy Quaid, Barbara Barrie; ***D:*** Walter Grauman. **TV**

To Save a Life ☙ 1/2 *How to Save a Life* **2010 (PG-13)** In this unsubtle, religious teen drama, all-star athlete Jake Taylor (Wayne) is shaken by the gun suicide of his childhood friend and decides he must change his own life to save the lives of others. It's too bad his spiritual quest comes straight from political talking points, as Jake must endure rejection from his Christianity-hating peers and prevent his girlfriend from getting an abortion. Movie toys with hard questions but all it serves up is easy answers as it devolves into a poorly camouflaged after-school special for evangelical youth groups. Panders to believers and won't convert anyone who isn't. **120m/C DVD.** *US* Randy Wayne, Sean Michael Afable, Robert Bailey Jr., Deja Kreutzberg, Kim Hidalgo, Joshua Weigel, Steve Crowder, Bubba Lewis; ***D:*** Brian Baugh; ***W:*** Jim Britts; ***C:*** C. Clifford Jones; ***M:*** Christopher Lennertz.

To See Paris and Die ☙☙ *Uvidet Parizh i Umeret* **1993** Elena Orekhova (Vasilyeva) is a Russian stage mother who will do absolutely anything to ensure pianist son Yuri gets chosen for a prestigious competition in Paris—even though she knows secrets from her past could place a blight on his career. Russian with subtitles. **110m/C VHS.** *RU* Tatyana Vasilyeva, Dimitry Malikov, Stanislav Lyubshin, Vladimir Steklov, Nina Usatova; ***D:*** Alexander Proshkin; ***W:*** Georgi Branev; ***C:*** Boris Brozhovsky.

To Sir, with Love ☙☙ 1/2 **1967** Teacher in London's tough East End tosses books in the wastebasket and proceeds to teach his class about life. Skillful and warm performance by Poitier as idealistic teacher; supporting cast also performs nicely. Based on the novel by E.R. Braithwaite. LuLu's title song was a big hit in 1967-68. **105m/C VHS, DVD.** *GB* Sidney Poitier, Lulu, Judy Geeson, Christian Roberts, Suzy Kendall, Faith Brook; ***D:*** James Clavell; ***W:*** James Clavell; ***C:*** Paul Beeson; ***M:*** Ron Grainer.

To Sleep with a Vampire ☙☙ **1992 (R)** A Los Angeles bloodsucker is tired of his violent existence and craves the one thing he can't have—daylight. As he stalks his latest victim, a stripper, he decides to take her home and have her tell him about living in daytime. When she realizes what's going on, the intended victim decides to fight for her life. Action and eroticism raises this one above the norm. Remake of "Dance of the Damned." **90m/C VHS, DVD.** Scott Valentine, Charlie Spradling, Richard Zobel, Ingrid Vold, Stephanie Hardy; ***D:*** Adam Friedman; ***W:*** Patricia Harrington.

To Sleep with Anger ☙☙☙ 1/2 **1990 (PG)** At first a comic, introspective look at a black middle-class family going about their business in the heart of Los Angeles. Sly charmer Glover shows up and enthralls the entire family with his slightly sinister storytelling and a gnawing doom gradually permeates the household. Insightful look into the conflicting values of Black America. Glover's best performance. **105m/C VHS.** Danny Glover, Mary Alice, Paul Butler, Richard Brooks, Carl Lumbly, Vonetta McGee, Sheryl Lee Ralph; ***D:*** Charles Burnett; ***W:*** Charles Burnett; ***C:*** Walt Lloyd. Ind. Spirit '91: Actor (Glover), Director (Burnett), Screenplay, Support. Actress (Ralph); Natl. Soc. Film Critics '90: Screenplay; Sundance '90: Special Jury Prize.

To the Death ☙ 1/2 **1993 (R)** A kickboxer wants to retire from the boxing tournaments but the corrupt promoters refuse to let him go unless he manages to kill his rivals in the ring. **90m/C VHS.** John Barrett, Michael Quissi; ***D:*** Darrell Roodt.

To the Devil, a Daughter ☙☙ *Child of Satan* **1976 (R)** A nun is put under a spell by a priest who has been possessed by Satan. She is to bear his child. A writer on the occult intervenes. Based on the novel by Dennis Wheatley. One of Kinski's early films. **93m/C VHS, DVD.** Richard Widmark, Christopher Lee, Nastassja Kinski, Honor Blackman, Denholm Elliott, Michael Goodliffe; ***D:*** Peter Sykes; ***W:*** Christopher Wicking; ***C:*** David Watkin.

To the Last Man ☙ **1933** An early Scott sagebrush epic, about two feuding families. Temple is seen in a small role. Based on Zane Grey's novel of the same name. **70m/B VHS, DVD.** Randolph Scott, Esther Ralston, Jack La Rue, Noah Beery Sr., Buster Crabbe, Gail Patrick, Barton MacLane, Fuzzy Knight, John Carradine, Jay Ward, Shirley Temple; ***D:*** Henry Hathaway.

To the Lighthouse ☙☙ **1983** The Ramsay family's annual proper British holiday at their Cornwall home turns into a summer of disillusionment in this adaptation of the Virginia Woolf novel. Made for British TV. **115m/C VHS, DVD.** Rosemary Harris, Michael Gough, Suzanne Bertish, Lynsey Baxter, T.P. McKenna, Kenneth Branagh; ***D:*** Colin Gregg. **TV**

To the Limit ☙ **1995 (R)** Actioner finds the pulchritudinous Colette (Smith) revealing to mobster Frank (Travolta) that she's a CIA agent (and if you believe that I have a bridge in Brooklyn to sell you) and that they are the targets of a rogue agent (Richmond). No, Smith can't act but since she takes lots of showers and is supported by some professionals who can, this gets by on trash value alone. **96m/C VHS, DVD.** Anna Nicole Smith, Joey Travolta, Michael Nouri, Branscombe Richmond, John Aprea, Kathy Shower, Rebecca Ferratti, David Proval; ***D:*** Raymond Martino; ***W:*** Raymond Martino, Joey Travolta; ***C:*** Henryk Cymerman; ***M:*** Jim Halfpenny.

To the Shores of Hell ☙☙ **1965** Leaving his sweetheart behind, Major Greg Donahue attacks Da Nang and plots to rescue his brother from the Viet Cong. **82m/C VHS.** Marshall Thompson, Richard Arlen, Richard Jordahl, Kiva Lawrence; ***D:*** Will Zens; ***W:*** Will Zens; ***C:*** Leif Rise; ***M:*** Will(iam) Schaefer.

To the Shores of Tripoli ☙☙ **1942** Wartime propaganda in the guise of drama, in which a smarmy playboy is transformed into a Marine in boot camp. **82m/C VHS, DVD.** John Payne, Maureen O'Hara, Randolph Scott, Nancy Kelly, Harry (Henry) Morgan, Maxie "Slapsie" Rosenbloom, William Tracy, Minor Watson, Alan Hale Jr., Hugh Beaumont, Hillary Brooke; ***D:*** H. Bruce Humberstone.

To Walk with Lions ☙☙ 1/2 **1999 (PG)** Continues the story of lion expert George Adamson, told previously in "Born Free" and "Living Free." Tony Fitzjohn (Michie) takes what he thinks will be a temporary job with Adamson (Harris) and his brother Terence (Bannen) in Kenya in the 1980s. The brothers are running a private wildlife preserve that rehabilitates zoo lions for life in the wild. Tony is naturally wary of his new employment and his curmudgeonly new employers but comes to value them all, even falling in love with anthropologist Lucy (Fox) who's working with the local tribes. Has some disturbing violence (both animal and human). **108m/C VHS, DVD.** *CA GB* Richard Harris, Ian Bannen, Kerry Fox, John Michie, Hugh Quarshie, Honor Blackman, Geraldine Chaplin; ***D:*** Carl Schultz; ***W:*** Keith Ross Leckie; ***C:*** Jean Lepine; ***M:*** Alan Reeves.

To Wong Foo, Thanks for Everything, Julie Newmar ☙☙ 1/2 **1995 (PG-13)** Hot on the high heels of "The Adventures of Priscilla, Queen of the Desert," comes the sanitized for your protection Yankee version. And its all about hanging on to your dreams and how we're all the same inside, with politically correct gay drag queens doing the sermonizing. Yes, this is the feel-good drag road movie for the 90s. Den mother Vida (Swayze), tough beauty queen Noxeema (Snipes), and hot-blooded Chi Chi (Leguizamo doing his best Rosie Perez) head to Hollywood in a 1967 Cadillac convertible that inconveniently breaks down in a tiny Nebraska town. The "girls" work their magic, and presumably the people of this uncultured, anachronistic backwater will never be the same. One-dimensional characters, flat direction, and inconsistent script undercut exceptional efforts by Swayze and Leguizamo. **108m/C VHS, DVD.** Wesley Snipes, Patrick Swayze, John Leguizamo, Stockard Channing, Blythe Danner, Melinda Dillon, Arliss Howard, Jason London, Christopher Penn, RuPaul Charles; ***Cameos:*** Julie Newmar, Robin Williams; ***D:*** Beeban Kidron; ***W:*** Douglas Carter Beane; ***M:*** Rachel Portman.

The Toast of New Orleans ☙☙ 1/2 **1950** A poor fisherman rises to stardom as an opera singer. Likable, though fluffy production features a plethora of musical numbers. ♫ Be My Love; Tina Lina; I'll Never Love You; The Toast of New Orleans; Song of the Bayou; Boom Biddy Boom Boom. **97m/C VHS.** Kathryn Grayson, Mario Lanza, David Niven, Rita Moreno, J. Carrol Naish; ***D:*** Norman Taurog.

Toast of New York ☙☙☙ **1937** Arnold plays Jim Fisk, a New England peddler who rises to become one of the first Wall Street giants of industry. Atypical Grant performance. **109m/B VHS.** Edward Arnold, Cary Grant, Frances Farmer, Jack Oakie, Donald Meek, Billy Gilbert; ***D:*** Rowland V. Lee.

Tobor the Great ☙ 1/2 **1954** Sentimental and poorly executed, this film tells the tale of a boy, his grandfather, and Tobor the robot. Villainous communists attempt to make evil use of Tobor, only to be thwarted in the end. **77m/B VHS.** Charles Drake, Billy Chapin, Karin (Karen, Katharine) Booth, Taylor Holmes, Joan Gerber, Steven Geray, Helen Winston; ***D:*** Lee Sholem.

Tobruk 🦴🦴 **1966** American GI's endeavor to knock out the guns of Tobruk, to clear the way for a bombing attack on German fuel supply depots of North Africa in this WWII actioner. **110m/C VHS.** Rock Hudson, George Peppard, Guy Stockwell, Nigel Green; ***D:*** Arthur Hiller.

Toby McTeague 🦴🦴 **1987 (PG)** A story about an Alaskan family that breeds Siberian Huskies. When his father is injured, the youngest son tries to replace him in the regional dog-sled race. **94m/C VHS, DVD.** Winston Rekert, Wannick Bisson, Timothy Webber; ***D:*** Jean-Claude Lord; ***W:*** Djordje Milicevic, Jamie Brown.

Toby Tyler 🦴🦴🦴 **1959 (G)** A boy runs off to join the circus, and teams up with a chimpanzee. A timeless and enjoyable Disney film that still appeals to youngsters. Good family-fare. **93m/C VHS, DVD.** Kevin Corcoran, Henry Calvin, Gene Sheldon, Bob Sweeney; ***D:*** Charles T. Barton.

Today I Hang 🦴🦴 **1942** A man is framed for murder and sentenced to hang. His buddies on the outside do their best to prove his innocence. Meanwhile, in prison, the accused encounters any number of interesting characters. **67m/B VHS.** Walter Woolf King, Mona Barrie, William Farnum, Harry Woods, James Craven; ***D:*** Oliver Drake.

Today We Kill, Tomorrow We Die 🦴 **1971 (PG)** A rancher is unjustly sent to prison; when his sentence is over he hires a gang to relentlessly track down the culprit who framed him. **95m/C VHS, DVD.** Montgomery Ford, Bud Spencer, William Berger, Tatsuya Nakadai, Wayde Preston; ***D:*** Tonino Cervi.

Today We Live 🦴🦴 1/2 **1933** Triangle love story set in WWI. Crawford is a hedonistic Brit having a fling with her naval brother's (Tone) friend (Young). When American flyer Cooper appears she sets her sights on him but soon he's off to combat in France where he's reported killed. Crawford returns to Young but, naturally, reports of Cooper's death have been greatly exaggerated and the two eventually reunite. Faulkner coscripted from his story "Turn About" which had no female character and concerned the rivalry between naval officers and fly boys. **113m/B VHS.** Gary Cooper, Joan Crawford, Franchot Tone, Robert Young, Roscoe Karns, Louise Closser Hale; ***D:*** Howard Hawks; ***W:*** Dwight Taylor, William Faulkner, Edith Fitzgerald.

The Todd Killings 🦴 1/2 *A Dangerous Friend; Skipper* **1971 (R)** A psychotic young man commits a series of murders involving young women. Sleazy, forgettable picture wastes a talented cast. **93m/C VHS.** Robert F. Lyons, Richard Thomas, Barbara Bel Geddes, Ed Asner, Sherry Miles, Gloria Grahame, Belinda J. Montgomery; ***D:*** Barry Shear; ***W:*** Joel Oliansky.

Todd McFarlane's Spawn 🦴🦴🦴 *Spawn* **1997** McFarlane's comic book creation makes his cable TV animated debut. Hellspawn was once human CIA assassin Al Simmons, murdered in the line of duty, who sold his soul to see his wife one last time. When he comes back from the grave with superhuman powers it's again as a killer with attitude, who leaves a high body count. A PG-13 version clocks in at 90 minutes. **147m/C VHS, DVD, UMD.** ***D:*** Eric Radomski; ***W:*** Alan B. McElroy, Gary Hardwick; ***V:*** Keith David, Richard Dysart, Ronny Cox. **CABLE**

Toga Party 🦴 *Pelvis; Disco Madness* **1977 (R)** Fraternity house throws a wild toga party in this raunchy low-rent depiction of college life. **82m/C VHS, DVD.** Luther Bud Whaney, Mary Mitchell; ***D:*** Robert T. Megginson; ***W:*** Straw Weisman; ***C:*** Lloyd Freidus.

Together? 🦴 1/2 **1979 (R)** Divorced woman and a male chauvinist test the limits of their sexual liberation as well as viewer patience. **91m/C VHS.** *IT* Maximilian Schell, Jacqueline Bisset, Terence Stamp, Monica Guerritore; ***D:*** Armenia Balducci; ***M:*** Burt Bacharach.

Together 🦴🦴 1/2 *He Ni Zaiyiqi* **2002 (PG)** Sentimental story about a musical prodigy, his dad, and the "new" China. With many of the restrictions of the Cultural Revolution a thing of the past, Western classical music is once more taught and performed. Violin prodigy Liu Xiaochun (Tang, who does his own playing) is 13 and his father Li Cheng (Liu) is determined to make the most of the boy's talents though the family is poor. Cheng and Xiaochun head to Beijing for an important musical competition and the boy makes an impressive showing. So much so, that his father is able to persuade a crancky but talent teacher (Wang) to mentor Xiaochun. While in the big city, the lad also becomes infatuated with beautiful new neighbor Lili (Chen), a model with a consumer-oriented lifestyle from whom he receives important lessons about sacrifice and friendship. Mandarin with subtitles. **116m/C VHS, DVD.** *CH KN* Yun Tang, Peiqi Liu, Zhiwen Wang, Hong Chen, Chen Kaige; ***D:*** Chen Kaige; ***W:*** Chen Kaige, Xiaolu Xue; ***C:*** Hyung-koo Kim; ***M:*** Lin Zhao.

Together Again 🦴🦴 1/2 **1943** Anne Crandall (Dunne) inherited the position of mayor of a small Vermont town after her husband's death. Father-in-law Jonathan (Coburn) wants Anne to remarry and when a statue of Anne's husband is damaged, he sends her to New York to meet with sculptor Corday (Boyer), who mistakes Anne for his new (nude) model. Further mistaken impressions and romantic complications ensue when Corday follows Anne back to Vermont. **93m/B DVD.** Irene Dunne, Charles Boyer, Charles Coburn, Mona Freeman, Jerome Courtland; ***D:*** King Vidor; ***W:*** F. Hugh Herbert, Virginia Van Upp; ***C:*** Joseph Walker; ***M:*** Werner R. Heymann.

Together Again for the First Time 🦴 1/2 **2008** The Wolders-Frobisher clan are a reluctantly blended family who haven't spent any time together since their parents' marriage seven years before. Now circumstances have reunited them on Christmas Eve, which results in them struggling to get along and exposing some family secrets. **85m/C DVD.** David Ogden Stiers, Julia Duffy, Larisa Oleynik, Joey Lawrence, Kirby Heyborne, Blake Bashoff, Kelly Stables, Lauren Storm, Michelle Page; ***D:*** Jeff Parkin; ***W:*** Jeff Parkin, Reed McColm; ***C:*** Brandon Christensen; ***M:*** Michael Cohen. **VIDEO**

Togetherness 🦴 1/2 **1970** Two wealthy, good-for-nothing playboys chase after the same blonde, a Communist, in Greece. **101m/C VHS.** George Hamilton, Peter Lawford, Olinka (Schoberova) Berova, John Banner, Jesse White; ***D:*** Arthur Marks.

The Toilers and the Wayfarers 🦴🦴 **1997** New Ulm, Minnesota is an ultraconservative German-American community where the teenaged Dieter (Klemp) is the object of affection for best friend Phillip (Woodhouse). Although Dieter thinks he might be gay, he rejects Phillip, who soon takes off for Minneapolis. This leaves Dieter open to the attentions of slightly older, free-spirited Udo (Schirg). Dieter's father strongly disapproves and the young man leaves to join Phillip in the big bad city, with Udo in tow. But since none of the boys have any money, they're soon working the streets to survive. English and German with subtitles. **85m/C VHS, DVD.** Matt Klemp, Ralf Schirg, Andrew Woodhouse; ***D:*** Keith Froelich; ***W:*** Keith Froelich; ***C:*** Jim Tittle; ***M:*** Chan Poling.

Tokyo! 🦴🦴 **2009** Directors Gondry, Carax, and Bong tell three separate stories set in Japan's capitol city of Tokyo. Instead of a love letter type tribute to the metropolis' hustle and bustle, a la "New York Stories," the setting is more of a convenience for its title. Gondry's segment features a couple feeling lost and isolated as they move to Tokyo with "Eraserhead"-esque filmmaking dreams. Bong's story is about a shut-in who hordes pizza boxes and eventually falls in love with a pizza delivery girl. Finally, Carax brings a sewer-dwelling gnome out into sunlit Tokyo for an urban adventure. Strange, but uneven and mismatched short films that say little about anything, and unfortunately aren't as engaging as they may sound. Japanese and French with subtitles. **112m/C DVD.** *JP FR* Ayako Fujitani, Ryo Kase, Ayumi Ito, Jean-Francois Balmer, Denis Levant, Yu Aoi, Teruyuki Kagaway; ***D:*** Michel Gondry, Leos Carax, Joon-ho Bong; ***W:*** Michel Gondry, Leos Carax, Joon-ho Bong, Gabrielle Bell; ***C:*** Caroline Champetier, Jun Fukumoto, Masami Inomoto; ***M:*** Etienne Charry, Lee Byung Woo.

Tokyo Cowboy 🦴🦴 **1994** Tokyo burger flipper No Ogawa (Ida) dreams of the wild west and becoming a cowboy, inspired by the letters of his childhood pen pal, Kate (Hirt). So he decides to head for Kate's small Canadian hometown and realize his fantasies. Kate's meddling mom makes him welcome but Kate herself, only recently returned home, is hiding the fact that her friend Shelly (Mortil) is also her lover. Both have some unrealistic expectations to overcome in their quest for happiness. **94m/C VHS, DVD.** Hiromoto Ida, Christianne Hirt, Janne Mortil, Anna Ferguson, Michael Ironside; ***D:*** Kathy Garneau; ***W:*** Caroline Adderson; ***C:*** Kenneth Hewlett; ***M:*** Ari Wise.

Tokyo Decadence 🦴 1/2 **1991 (NC-17)** Ai is a high-paid prostitute working in Tokyo for an agency that specializes in sado-masochism. Film follows her various sexual escapades in humiliating detail as well as her drug-addled search for a client Ai thinks she's in love with. Since Ai remains a cipher, the film also remains unfocused except for its creepy and explicit sex scenes. Adaptation of director Murakami's novel "Topaz." In Japanese with English subtitles or dubbed. **92m/C VHS, DVD.** *JP* Miho Nikaido, Tenmei Kano, Yayoi Kusama, Sayoko Amano; ***D:*** Ryu Murakami; ***W:*** Ryu Murakami; ***C:*** Tadashi Aoki; ***M:*** Ryuichi Sakamoto.

Tokyo Drifter 🦴🦴 *Tokyo Nagaremono* **1966** Surreal yakuza film follows an honorable gangster hunted by both his own bosses and a rival mob, who chase him across Japan. Lots of camera trickery. Japanese with subtitles. **83m/C VHS, DVD.** *JP* Eiji Go, Chieko Matsubara, Tetsuya Watari, Tamio Kawaji, Hideaki Nitani, Ryuji Kita; ***D:*** Seijun Suzuki; ***W:*** Yasunori Kawauchi; ***C:*** Shigeyoshi Mine; ***M:*** So Kaburagi.

Tokyo-Ga 🦴🦴🦴 1/2 **1985** Impelled by his love for the films of Yasujiro Ozu, Wenders traveled to Tokyo and fashioned a caring document of both the city and of Ozu's career, using images that recall and comment on Ozu's visual motifs. **92m/C VHS, DVD.** ***D:*** Wim Wenders; ***W:*** Wim Wenders.

Tokyo Gore Police 🦴🦴 *Tokyo zankoku keisatsu* **2008** In the future, private corporations run the Tokyo cops, and suicide and self-mutilation are fads among teens. A madman called "Key Man" has unleashed genetically modified superhumans called Engineers that can fuse weapons into their injuries, making them walking nightmares. Ruka (Eihi Shiina) is the police force's top Engineer killer, slicing her way through monsters while searching for the truth of her father's murder. **110m/C DVD.** *JP* Eihi Shiina, Itsuji Itao, Jiji Bu; ***D:*** Yoshihiro Nishimura; ***W:*** Kengo Kaji, Sayako Nakoshi, Yoshihiro Nishimura; ***C:*** Shu G. Momose; ***M:*** Kou Nakagawa.

Tokyo Joe 🦴 1/2 **1949** A war hero/nightclub owner returns to Tokyo and becomes ensnared in blackmail and smuggling while searching for his missing wife and child. Slow-moving tale has never been considered one of Bogart's better movies. **88m/B VHS, DVD.** Humphrey Bogart, Florence Marly, Alexander Knox, Sessue Hayakawa, Jerome Courtland, Lore Lee Michel; ***D:*** Stuart Heisler.

Tokyo Olympiad 🦴🦴🦴 **1966** A monumental sports documentary about the 1964 Olympic Games in its entirety. Never before available for home viewing. Letterboxed with digital sound. In Japanese with English subtitles. **170m/C VHS, DVD.** *JP* ***D:*** Kon Ichikawa; ***W:*** Kon Ichikawa; ***C:*** Kazuo Miyagawa.

Tokyo Pop 🦴🦴 1/2 **1988 (R)** A punk rocker travels to Japan to find stardom and experiences a series of misadventures. Enjoyable in its own lightweight way. Hamilton is the daughter of Carol Burnett. **99m/C VHS.** Carrie Hamilton, Yutaka Tadokoro, Tetsuro Tamba, Taiji Tonoyama, Masumi Harukawa; ***D:*** Fran Rubel Kuzui; ***W:*** Lynn Grossman, Fran Rubel Kuzui; ***M:*** Alan Brewer.

Tokyo Raiders 🦴🦴🦴 **2000 (PG-13)** Remarkably stylish Hong Kong action flick. Director Jingle Ma brings a music video sensibility to the proceedings. The plot concerns a detective (Tony Leung) and his hunt for a gangster, but that's a negligible excuse for a series of cleverly choreographed action scenes. The physical violence is carefully modulated for a young audience, and many gadgets are employed. **100m/C DVD.** *HK* Tony Leung Chiu-Wai, Ekin Cheng, Toru Nakamura, Hiroshi Abe, Kelly Chen, Kumiko Endo, Minami Shirakawa, Majyu Ozawa, Cecilia Cheung; ***D:*** Jingle Ma; ***W:*** Susan Chan, Felix Chong; ***C:*** Jingle Ma, Chan Chi Ying; ***M:*** Peter Kam.

Tokyo Sonata 🦴🦴🦴 1/2 **2009 (PG-13)** A Japanese businessman, husband, and father of two unexpectedly loses his job. Unable to break the news to his devoted wife, he dresses up every morning and pretends to go to work, instead wasting the days away with a former classmate who is also unemployed. Although unaware, his family begins to disobey him—his teenage son enlists in the Army to fight for the United States, while his adolescent son goes behind his back to take piano lessons. Known for creepy neo-horror flicks, director Kurosawa (not *that* Kurosawa) effectively portrays the horror of a disintegrating family in the wake of a global recession that translates to any culture, with just enough well-timed humor to keep it from being morose. **119m/C DVD.** *JP HK* Teruyuki Kagawa, Kyoko Koizumi, Yukimi Koyanagi, Kanji Tsuda, Koji Yakusho, Inowaki Kai, Haruka Igawa, Kazuya Kojima; ***D:*** Kiyoshi Kurosawa; ***W:*** Kiyoshi Kurosawa, Max Mannix, Sachiko Tanaka; ***C:*** Akiko Ahsizawa; ***M:*** Kazumasa Hashimoto.

Tokyo Story 🦴🦴🦴🦴 *Tokyo Monogatari* **1953** Poignant story of elderly couple's journey to Tokyo where they receive little time and less respect from their grown children. Masterful cinematography, and sensitive treatment of universally appealing story. In Japanese with English subtitles. **134m/B VHS, DVD.** *JP* Chishu Ryu, Chieko Higashiyama, So Yamamura, Haruko Sugimura, Setsuko Hara; ***D:*** Yasujiro Ozu; ***W:*** Yasujiro Ozu; ***C:*** Yuuharu Atsuta; ***M:*** Kojun Saito.

Tol'able David 🦴🦴 **1921** A simple tale of mountain folk, done in the tradition of Mark Twain stories. A family of hillbillies is embroiled in a feud with a clan of outlaws. When the community's mail is stolen by the troublesome ruffians, the family's youngest member, who harbors dreams of becoming a mail driver, comes to the rescue. Silent film. **91m/B VHS, DVD.** Richard Barthelmess, Gladys Hulette, Ernest Torrence; ***D:*** Henry King; ***W:*** Henry King, Edmund Goulding; ***C:*** Henry Cronjager. Natl. Film Reg. '07.

The Toll Gate 🦴🦴 1/2 **1920** Quick on the draw outlaw Black Deering (Hart) is betrayed by one of his own men but manages to escape the authorities. He heads into the wilderness and finds shelter with an abandoned young mother (Nilsson). But the law is on his trail. **73m/B VHS, DVD.** William S. Hart, Anna Q. Nilsson, Jack (H.) Richardson, Joseph Singleton; ***D:*** Lambert Hillyer; ***W:*** Lambert Hillyer; ***C:*** Joseph August.

Toll of the Desert 🦴 **1935** A lawman learns that his father is a ruthless, backstabbing renegade. Now he must try and catch him. **58m/B VHS.** Roger Williams, Ted Adams, Edward Cassidy, Tom London, John Elliott, Earl Dwire, Betty Mack, Fred Kohler Jr.; ***D:*** William Berke.

Tollbooth 🦴🦴 **1994 (R)** Romantic dreamer Jack (Von Dohlen) mans a tollbooth on a stretch of Florida Keys highway while his equally longing honey Doris (Balk) works at a nearby gas station and has a thing going on the side with bait salesman Dash (Patton). The return of Doris' long-gone daddy Leon (Cassel) causes some family problems while Jack's new associate Vic (Wilder) has a scam that's drawing interest from the state police. Thin plot but lots of charm from the two leads helps hold interest in Breziner's first film. **108m/C VHS.** Fairuza Balk, Lenny Von Dohlen, Will Patton, Seymour Cassel, James Wilder, Louise Fletcher, William Katt; ***D:*** Salome Breziner; ***W:*** Salome Breziner; ***C:*** Henry Vargas; ***M:*** Adam Gorgoni.

The Tollbooth 🦴🦴 **2004** Ernest, cliched comedy follows 22-year-old Sarabeth Cohen (Sokoloff) as she tries to escape what she sees as her smothering Brooklyn Jewish family for the life of a rebellious artist in Manhattan. She even gets a sweet goy boyfriend, Simon (McElhenney), but familial problems interfere while Sarabeth decides where her life should truly be going. **85m/C DVD.** *US* Marla Sokoloff, Liz Stauber, Rob McElhenney, Idina Menzel, Jayce Bartok, Ronald Guttman, Tovah Feldshuh; ***D:*** Debra Kirschner; ***W:*** Debra Kirschner; ***C:*** Stefan Forbes; ***M:*** David Shire.

Tom and Francie 🦴🦴🦴 ½ **2005** Spinal Tap meets Sesame Street in this fabulous spoof on low-budget TV kids' shows. Twelve years after Tom and Francie's children show "The Flower Shop" is cancelled, they plan a comeback with their new show "Accepting Everyone Through Music." They are joined by a prop master who expresses his hostility through his puppets and a lawyer who smells a post-Barney gravy train. Apple-cheeked Golden is a standout as kid-show trouper Francie. **85m/C DVD.** Annie Golden, Chris Fields, Steven Skybell, Tara O'Boyle; ***D:*** Patrick Michael Denny; ***W:*** Patrick Michael Denny; ***C:*** Patrick Michael Denny; ***M:*** Annie Golden, Chris Fields, Patrick Michael Denny. **VIDEO**

Tom and Huck 🦴🦴🦴 **1995 (PG)** Tom Sawyer and pal Huck Finn are the only witnesses to a murder. Tom's friend Muff is framed for the crime and the boys are being tracked by the real killer, Injun Joe. They must decide to come forward, expose the true fiend, and risk their own hides or run away and let an innocent man hang. True to the Twain story, Thomas plays a mischievious Tom to Renfro's troublemaking Huck. Film was shot in Mooresville, Alabama, population 69, just down the road a piece from the Hannibal, Missouri of Twain fame. **91m/C VHS, DVD.** Jonathan Taylor Thomas, Brad Renfro, Eric Schweig, Charles Rocket, Amy Wright, Michael McShane, Marian Seldes, Rachael Leigh Cook, Lanny Flaherty, Courtland Mead, Peter M. MacKenzie, Heath Lamberts; ***D:*** Peter Hewitt; ***W:*** Stephen Sommers, David Loughery; ***C:*** Bobby Bukowski; ***M:*** Stephen Endelman.

Tom and Jerry: The Movie 🦴🦴 **1993 (G)** Everybody's favorite animated cat/mouse duo (who began life in a 1940 MGM short "Puss Gets the Boot") hit the big screen, this time talking (unlike their animated shorts). Rather than cartoon mayhem our two protagonists are goody-two-shoes (with songs yet!) but still retain their charm. Kids will like it, but true "Tom and Jerry" fans should probably stick to the original cartoons. **84m/C VHS, DVD.** ***D:*** Phil Roman; ***W:*** Dennis Marks; ***M:*** Henry Mancini, Leslie Bricusse; ***V:*** Richard Kind, Dana Hill, Charlotte Rae, Henry Gibson, Rip Taylor, Howard Morris, Edmund Gilbert, David Lander.

Tom & Viv 🦴🦴🦴 **1994 (PG-13)** American T.S. Eliot (Dafoe) is an Oxford student in 1914 when he meets the moody, monied Vivien Haigh-Wood (Richardson). After a whirlwind courtship, they marry—disastrously. Eliot begins to establish himself as a poet, while Vivien serves as muse/typist and unsuccessfully battles her misdiagnosed illnesses with too much drinking and drugs, as well as embarrassing public scenes. As Eliot gains success, he increasingly distances himself from the unhappy Viv, until finally committing her to an asylum. Dafoe is fine as the chilly, withdrawn poet but Richardson steals the film as his flamboyant, lost wife. Based on the play by Michael Hastings, who co-wrote the screenplay. **115m/C VHS, DVD.** *GB* Willem Dafoe, Miranda Richardson, Rosemary Harris, Tim Dutton, Nickolas Grace, Philip Locke, Clare Holman, Joanna McCallum; ***D:*** Brian Gilbert; ***W:*** Michael Hastings, Adrian Hodges; ***M:*** Debbie Wiseman. Natl. Bd. of Review '94: Actress (Richardson), Support. Actress (Harris).

Tom Brown's School Days 🦴🦴 ½ *Adventures at Rugby* **1940** Depicts life among the boys in an English school during the Victorian era. Based on the classic novel by Thomas Hughes. Remade in 1951. **86m/B VHS, DVD.** *GB* Cedric Hardwicke, Jimmy Lydon, Freddie Bartholomew; ***D:*** Robert Stevenson.

Tom Brown's School Days 🦴🦴🦴 **1951** Tom enrolls at Rugby and is beset by bullies in classic tale of English school life. British remake of the 1940 version. Based on the novel by Thomas Hughes. **93m/B VHS.** *GB* Robert Newton, John (Howard) Davies, James Hayter; ***D:*** Gordon Parry.

Tom Clancy's Netforce 🦴🦴 *Netforce* **1998 (R)** In 2005, technology has become so advanced that a special unit of the FBI, known as Netforce, has been established to police the Internet. Alex Michaels (Bakula) heads the unit after the murder of predecessor Steve Day (Kristofferson), leading Michaels to believe that criminals are trying to cause a global computer crash. Michael's two prime suspects are computer mogul Will Stiles (Reinhold) and crime boss Leong Cheng (Tagawa). Based on a story co-written by Clancy. **90m/C VHS, DVD.** Scott Bakula, Joanna Going, Brian Dennehy, Kris Kristofferson, Judge Reinhold, Cary-Hiroyuki Tagawa, CCH Pounder, Paul Hewitt, Chelsea Field, Frank Vincent, Alexa Vega, Victor Raider-Wexler; ***D:*** Robert Lieberman; ***W:*** Lionel Chetwynd; ***C:*** David Hennings; ***M:*** Jeff Rona. **TV**

Tom, Dick, and Harry 🦴🦴 ½ **1941** Dreamy girl is engaged to three men and unable to decide which to marry. It all depends on a kiss. Remade as "The Girl Most Likely." **86m/B VHS.** Ginger Rogers, George Murphy, Burgess Meredith, Alan Marshal, Phil Silvers; ***D:*** Garson Kanin; ***W:*** Paul Jarrico.

Tom Horn 🦴🦴 **1980 (R)** The final days of one of the Old West's legends, Gunman Tom Horn, hired by Wyoming ranchers to stop cattle rustlers, goes about his job with a zeal that soon proves embarrassing to his employers. Beautifully photographed and authentic in its attention to details of the period, the film nonetheless takes liberties with the facts of Horn's life and is lacking in other aspects of production. **98m/C VHS, DVD.** Steve McQueen, Linda Evans, Richard Farnsworth, Billy Green Bush, Slim Pickens; ***D:*** William Wiard; ***W:*** Thomas McGuane; ***C:*** John A. Alonzo; ***M:*** Ernest Gold.

Tom Jones 🦴🦴🦴🦴 **1963** Bawdy comedy based on Henry Fielding's novel about a rustic playboy's wild life in 18th century England. Hilarious and clever with a grand performance by Finney. One of the sexiest eating scenes ever. Redgrave's debut. Theatrically released at 129 minutes, the film was recut by the director, who decided it needed tightening before its 1992 re-release on video. **121m/C VHS, DVD.** *GB* Albert Finney, Susannah York, Hugh Griffith, Edith Evans, Joan Greenwood, Diane Cilento, George Devine, David Tomlinson, Joyce Redman, Lynn Redgrave, Julian Glover, Peter Bull, David Warner; ***D:*** Tony Richardson; ***W:*** John Osborne; ***C:*** Walter Lassally; ***M:*** John Addison. Oscars '63: Adapt. Screenplay, Director (Richardson), Picture, Orig. Score; British Acad. '63: Film, Screenplay; Directors Guild '63: Director (Richardson); Golden Globes '64: Film—Mus./Comedy, Foreign Film; Natl. Bd. of Review '63: Director (Richardson); N.Y. Film Critics '63: Actor (Finney), Director (Richardson), Film.

Tom Jones 🦴🦴🦴 **1998** Miniseries based on the Henry Fielding novel goes further than the hit 1963 movie by including Fielding (Sessions) as the narrator of Tom's bawdy adventures. Tom (Beesley) is an 18th-century orphan with a heart of gold, an affinity for trouble, and an eye for the ladies. His true love is Sophie (Morton), the daughter of the boisterous Squire Western (Blessed). But of course, the path of true love never runs smooth. Lavish adaptation and lots of fun. **300m/C VHS, DVD.** *GB* Max Beesley, Samantha Morton, Brian Blessed, John Sessions, Benjamin Whitrow, Frances de la Tour; ***D:*** Metin Huseyin; ***W:*** Simon Burke. **CABLE**

Tom Sawyer 🦴🦴🦴 **1930** Winning adaptation of Mark Twain's oft told tale of boyhood in Hannibal, Missouri. Cast reprised their roles the following year in "Huckleberry Finn." **86m/B VHS.** Jackie Coogan, Mitzie Green, Lucien Littlefield, Tully Marshall; ***D:*** John Cromwell; ***C:*** Charles B(ryant) Lang Jr.

Tom Sawyer 🦴🦴 ½ **1973 (G)** Musical version of the Mark Twain tale of the boisterous Tom, his friend Becky Thatcher, and various adventures, including the fence whitewashing. Amusing kid fare shot on location in Missouri. ♫River Song; Gratification; Tom Sawyer; Freebootin'; Aunt Polly's Soliloquy; If'n I Was God; A Man's Gotta Be What He's Born To Be; How Come?; Hannibal, Mo. **104m/C VHS, DVD.** Johnny Whitaker, Jodie Foster, Celeste Holm, Warren Oates, Jeff East; ***D:*** Don Taylor; ***M:*** John Williams.

Tom Thumb 🦴🦴🦴 **1958** Diminutive boy saves village treasury from bad guys. Adapted from classic Grimm fairy tale. Special effects combine live actors, animation, and puppets. **92m/C VHS, DVD.** *GB* Russ Tamblyn, Peter Sellers, Terry-Thomas; ***D:*** George Pal; ***W:*** Ladislas Fodor; ***C:*** Georges Perinal; ***M:*** Douglas Gamley.

Tomahawk 🦴🦴 ½ **1951** Indian sympathizer Jim Bridger (Heflin) is a local scout who anticipates trouble when the government decides to build a wagon route straight through Sioux hunting grounds in order to reach Montana's gold mines. The touchy situation is made worse by cavalry officer Dancy (Nicol) who thinks the only good Indian is a dead one. **82m/C VHS.** Van Heflin, Preston Foster, Yvonne De Carlo, Alex Nicol, Jack Oakie, Tom Tully, Rock Hudson, Ann Doran; ***D:*** George Sherman; ***W:*** Maurice Geraghty, Silvia Richards; ***C:*** Charles P. Boyle; ***M:*** Hans J. Salter.

Tomb 🦴🦴 **1986** Fortune seekers disturb the slumber of a magical, sadistic princess much to their everlasting regret. Adapted from a Bram Stoker novel. **106m/C VHS.** Cameron Mitchell, John Carradine, Sybil Danning, Richard Hench, Michelle (McClellan) Bauer, Susan Stokey, David Pearson, Francesca "Kitten" Natividad; ***D:*** Fred Olen Ray; ***C:*** Paul Elliott.

Tomb of Ligeia 🦴🦴🦴 *Tomb of the Cat* **1964** The ghost of a man's first wife expresses her displeasure when groom and new little missus return to manor. One of the better Corman adaptations of Poe. Also available with "The Conqueror Worm" on Laser Disc. **82m/C VHS, DVD.** *GB* Vincent Price, Elizabeth Shepherd, John Westbrook, Oliver Johnston, Richard Johnson, Derek Francis, Richard Vernon, Ronald Adam, Frank Thornton, Penelope Lee, Denis Gilmore; ***D:*** Roger Corman; ***W:*** Robert Towne; ***C:*** Arthur Grant; ***M:*** Kenneth V. Jones.

Tomb of the Undead 🦴 ½ **1972** The sadistic guards of a prison camp are rudely awakened by the prisoners they tortured to death when they return as flesh-eating zombies looking to settle the score. **60m/C VHS.** *GB* Duncan McLeod, Lee Frost, John Dennis; ***D:*** John Hayes.

Tomb of Torture WOOF! *Metempsycose* **1965** Murdered countess is reincarnated in the body of a newspaperman's mistress. Together they investigate monster reports in a murder-ridden castle. The butler may have something to do with it. Filmed in Sepiatone and dubbed. **88m/B VHS, DVD.** Annie Albert, Thony Maky, Mark Marian; ***D:*** William Grace.

The Tomboy 🦴 ½ **1924** A young woman behaves boyishly in Colonial America. **64m/B VHS.** Dorothy Devore, Lotta Williams, Herbert Rawlinson, Harry Gribbon, Lee Moran; ***D:*** David Kirkland.

Tomboy 🦴 **1940** Shy country boy and a not-so-shy city girl meet, fall in love, and overcome obstacles that stand in their path. **70m/B VHS.** Jackie Moran, Marcia Mae Jones, Grant Withers, Charlotte Wynters, George Cleveland, Clara Blandick; ***D:*** Robert McGowan; ***W:*** Dorothy Davenport Reid, Marion Orth; ***C:*** Harry Neumann; ***M:*** Edward Kay.

Tomboy WOOF! **1985 (R)** A pretty auto mechanic is determined to win not only the race but the love and respect of a superstar auto racer. **91m/C VHS, DVD.** Betsy Russell, Eric Douglas, Jerry Dinome, Kristi Somers, Richard Erdman, Toby Iland; ***D:*** Herb Freed.

Tomboy & the Champ 🦴🦴 **1958** Despite many obstacles, a music-loving calf becomes a prize winner with the help of its loving owner. Kids will love it, but adults will find this one a little sugary. **82m/C VHS.** Candy Moore, Ben Johnson, Jesse White; ***D:*** Francis D. Lyon.

Tombs of the Blind Dead 🦴🦴 ½ *The Blind Dead; La Noche dell Terror Ciego; La Noche de la Muerta Ciega; Crypt of the Blind Dead; Night of the Blind Dead* **1972 (PG)** Blinded by crows for using human sacrifice in the 13th century, zombies rise from the grave to wreak havoc upon 20th-century Spaniards. Atmospheric chiller was extremely popular in Europe and spawned three sequels. The sequels, also on video, are "Return of the Evil Dead" and "Horror of the Zombies." **102m/C VHS, DVD.** *SP PT* Caesar Burner, Lone Fleming, Helen Harp, Joseph Thelman, Rufino Ingles, Maria Silva; ***D:*** Armando de Ossorio; ***W:*** Armando de Ossorio; ***C:*** Pablo Ripoll; ***M:*** Anton Abril.

Tombstone 🦴🦴🦴 **1993 (R)** Saga of Wyatt Earp and his band of law-abiding large moustaches beat the Kasdan/Costner vehicle to the big screen by several months. Legendary lawman Wyatt (Russell) moves to Tombstone, Arizona, aiming to start a new life with his brothers, but alas, that's not to be. The infamous gunfight at the OK Corral is here, and so is best buddy Doc Holliday, gunslinger and philosopher, a role designed for scenery chewing (Kilmer excels). Romance is supplied by actress Josephine, though Delany lacks the necessary romantic spark. Russell spends a lot of time looking troubled by the violence while adding to the body count. Too self-conscious, suffers from '90s western revisionism, but blessed with a high energy level thanks to despicable villains Lang, Biehn, and Boothe. **130m/C VHS, DVD.** Kurt Russell, Val Kilmer, Michael Biehn, Sam Elliott, Dana Delany, Bill Paxton, Powers Boothe, Stephen Lang, Jason Priestley, Dana Wheeler-Nicholson, Billy Zane, Thomas Haden Church, Joanna Pacula, Michael Rooker, Harry Carey Jr., Billy Bob Thornton, Charlton Heston, Robert John Burke, John Corbett, Buck Taylor, Terry O'Quinn, Pedro Armendariz Jr., Chris Mitchum, Jon Tenney; ***D:*** George P. Cosmatos; ***W:*** Kevin Jarre; ***C:*** William A. Fraker; ***M:*** Bruce Broughton; ***Nar:*** Robert Mitchum.

Tombstone Canyon 🦴 ½ **1932** Death rides the range until Maynard and his horse Tarzan put a halt to it. **60m/B VHS, DVD.** Ken Maynard, Sheldon Lewis, Cecilia Parker, Lafe (Lafayette) McKee, Frank Brownlee; ***D:*** Alan James; ***W:*** Earle Snell, Claude Rister; ***C:*** Ted D. McCord.

Tombstone Terror 🦴 **1934** A cowboy is beleaguered by a case of mistaken identity. **55m/B VHS.** George "Gabby" Hayes, Earl Dwire, Kay McCoy, Bob Steele; ***D:*** Robert North Bradbury; ***W:*** Robert North Bradbury; ***C:*** Harry Forbes.

Tomcat: Dangerous Desires 🦴🦴 **1993 (R)** Tom (Grieco) suffers from a rare degenerative condition and agrees to become a guinea pig in a secret, genetic imprinting experiment that has him injected with feline RNA. Tom's health is restored but the side effects give him the predatory instincts of a cat and the need to kill to stay alive. **96m/C VHS.** Richard Grieco, Maryam D'Abo, Natalie Radford; ***D:*** Paul Donovan; ***W:*** Paul Donovan; ***C:*** Peter Wunstorf; ***M:*** Graeme Cleman.

Tomcats WOOF! **2001 (R)** Writer/director Pourier takes a half-step down from his previous occupation of porn screenwriter with this steaming pile of misogyny. Michael (O'Connell) is a basically decent guy up to his ethics in gambling debt. The only way out is to marry off his last single friend, Kyle (Busey), in order to win a bet made with their other buddies. He tracks down Natalie (Elizabeth), the only one of Kyle's conquests that he regrets dumping, who agrees, for half the dough and a measure of revenge, but soon the plotters fall in love. Every woman here is depicted as some form of evil, and humiliated accordingly. This isn't new, but it wouuld help if something was at least chuckle-worthy. There's no such relief here, unless you find renegade cancerous sex organs amusing. **92m/C VHS, DVD, UMD.** *US* Jerry O'Connell, Shannon Elizabeth, Jake Busey, Jaime Pressly, Bernie Casey, David Ogden Stiers, Travis Fine, Heather Stephens, Horatio Sanz, Julia Schultz; ***D:*** Gregory Poirier; ***W:*** Gregory Poirier; ***C:*** Charles Minsky; ***M:*** David Kitay.

Tomie 🦴 ½ **1999** Originally an episodic manga by Japanese horror writer Junji Ito, later made into a series of films generally regarded as not quite as scary as the comics they were based on (though to be blunt the comics are so violent it's doubtful they could be released as a film if they were absolutely true to the source material). All of the stories feature an immortal high school girl named Tomie. She inspires jealous rage and obsession in all the men (and some women) around her, causing them to commit acts of violence in brief bursts of rage. Inevitably she is always killed, but regenerates regardless of what is done to her. **95m/C DVD.** *JP* Miho Kanno, Tomorowo Taguchi, Rumi, Ikko Suzuki, Mami Nakamura, Yoriko Douguchi, Kouta Kusano, Kenji Mizhuhashi; ***D:*** Ataru Oikawa; ***W:***

Ataru Oikawa, Junji Ito; ***C:*** Akira Sakoh, Kazuhiro Suzuki.

Tommy 🦴🦴 *The Who's Tommy* **1975 (PG)** Peter Townsend's rock opera as visualized in the usual hyper-Russell style about the deaf, dumb, and blind boy who becomes a celebrity due to his amazing skill at the pinball machines. A parade of rock musicians perform throughout the affair, with varying degrees of success. Despite some good moments, the film ultimately falls prey to ill-conceived production concepts and miscasting. ♫ Underture; Captain Walker Didn't Come Home; It's a Boy; '51 Is Going to Be a Good Year; What About the Boy?; The Amazing Journey; Christmas; See Me, Feel Me; Eyesight to the Blind. **108m/C VHS, DVD.** *GB* Ann-Margret, Elton John, Oliver Reed, Tina Turner, Roger Daltrey, Eric Clapton, Keith Moon, Pete Townshend, Jack Nicholson, Robert Powell, Paul Nicholas, Barry Winch, Victoria Russell, Ben Aris, Mary Holland, Jennifer Baker, Susan Baker, Arthur Brown, John Entwhistle; ***D:*** Ken Russell; ***W:*** Ken Russell, Keith Moon, John Entwhistle; ***C:*** Ronnie Taylor, Dick Bush; ***M:*** Pete Townshend, John Entwhistle. Golden Globes '76: Actress—Mus./Comedy (Ann-Margret).

Tommy Boy 🦴🦴 **1995 (PG-13)** Not-too-bright rich kid Tommy (Farley) teams up with snide, officious accountant Richard (Spade) to save the family auto parts business after dad (Dennehy) buys the farm. Tommy and Richard must deal with a conniving stepmom and stepbrother (Derek and Lowe), a ruthless rival (Aykroyd), and a road trip from hell to drum up some new business. Not as bad as it sounds, but inconsistent direction and too-familiar characters offset the amusing chemistry between Farley and Spade. **98m/C VHS, DVD.** Chris Farley, David Spade, Brian Dennehy, Bo Derek, Dan Aykroyd, Julie Warner, Rob Lowe; ***D:*** Peter Segal; ***W:*** Bonnie Turner, Terry Turner; ***C:*** Victor Kemper; ***M:*** David Newman. MTV Movie Awards '96: On-Screen Duo (Chris Farley/David Spade).

Tomorrow 🦴🦴🦴 **1972 (PG)** Powerful tale of the love of two lonely people. Outstanding performance by Duvall as lumber mill worker who falls for a pregnant woman. Based on the neglected Faulkner story. **102m/B VHS, DVD.** Robert Duvall, Olga Bellin, Sudie Bond; ***D:*** Joseph Anthony; ***W:*** Horton Foote.

Tomorrow at Seven 🦴🦴 ½ **1933** A mystery writer is determined to discover the identity of the Ace of Spades, a killer who always warns his intended victim, then leaves an ace of spades on the corpse as his calling card. **62m/B VHS, DVD.** Chester Morris, Vivienne Osborne, Frank McHugh, Allen Jenkins, Henry Stephenson; ***D:*** Ray Enright.

Tomorrow Is Forever 🦴🦴 ½ **1946** Welles and Colbert marry shortly before he goes off to fight in WWI. Badly wounded and disfigured, he decides to stay in Europe while Colbert, believing Welles dead, eventually marries Brent. Fast forward to WWII when Brent, a chemical manufacturer, hires a new scientist to work for him in the war effort (guess who). This slow-moving melodrama wastes a good cast. Six-year-old Wood debuts as Welles' adopted daughter. **105m/B VHS.** Claudette Colbert, Orson Welles, George Brent, Lucile Watson, Richard Long, Natalie Wood; ***D:*** Irving Pichel; ***C:*** Joseph Valentine; ***M:*** Max Steiner.

The Tomorrow Man 🦴🦴 **2001 (R)** Just go with the flow, cause this time travel adventure yarn doesn't make a whole lot of sense. Larry Mackey (Bernsen) is your average joe, living an average life in the 1970s with his son Bryon. Then Mackey's son is kidnapped by notorious criminal Mac (Rusler) who happens to have time-traveled from 30 years in the future. Larry gets together with a time cop (Kennedy) to get the kid back and discovers that Byron actually grows up to be Mac—and dad needs to figure out why. **95m/C VHS, DVD.** Corbin Bernsen, Zach Galligan, Beth Kennedy, Morgan Rusler, Adam Sutton; ***D:*** Doug Campbell. **VIDEO**

Tomorrow Never Comes 🦴 ½ **1977** When he discovers his girlfriend has been unfaithful, a guy goes berserk and eventually finds himself in a stand-off with the police. Violent. **109m/C VHS.** Oliver Reed, Susan George, Raymond Burr, John Ireland, Stephen McHattie, Donald Pleasence; ***D:*** Peter Collinson.

Tomorrow Never Dies 🦴🦴 **1997 (PG-13)** 18th installment of the James Bond series is all style and little else packaged in a tedious action adventure. Our villain is a media mogul (Pryce) who plans to start WWIII in order to increase his newspaper revenues. (Rupert Murdoch, start your lawyers!) In between the blantant product placements (from Heineken to Visa), our secret agent Bond (Brosnan, who seems bored with the role in his second appearance) sets out to foil the nutty plans. Bond gets help from Hong Kong action queen Yeoh as a Chinese agent, and a bevy of toys from the antiquated Q, including a BMW controlled by remote. Direction and flow is on autopilot after the opening scene and despite Yeoh's energetic high-kicks and the sleek techno toys, it can't revitalize what has become a third-class imitator of its predecessors. **119m/C VHS, DVD.** Pierce Brosnan, Jonathan Pryce, Michelle Yeoh, Teri Hatcher, Judi Dench, Colin Salmon, Samantha Bond, Desmond Llewelyn, Joe Don Baker, Ricky Jay, Vincent Schiavelli, Geoffrey Palmer; ***D:*** Roger Spottiswoode; ***W:*** Bruce Feirstein; ***C:*** Robert Elswit; ***M:*** David Arnold.

Tomorrow the World 🦴🦴 **1944** This bizarre little wartime drama is dated in almost every respect. Emil Bruckner (Homeier) is a Hitler Youth who's sent to live with his uncle (March) in America. The conflict between a fascist mindset and liberal tolerance is painted with very broad strokes. Both acting and writing have an extravagant quality that contemporary audiences will have trouble accepting. **86m/B DVD.** Fredric March, Betty Field, Agnes Moorehead, Skip Homeier, Joan Carroll, Boots Brown, Edit Angold, Rudy Wiesler, Marvin Davis, Patsy Ann Thompson, Mary Newton, Tom Fadden; ***D:*** Leslie Fenton; ***W:*** Ring Lardner Jr., Leopold Atlas; ***C:*** Henry Sharp.

Tomorrow's Child 🦴🦴 **1982** TV drama about in vitro fertilization (test-tube babies) and surrogate motherhood. **100m/C VHS.** Stephanie Zimbalist, William Atherton, Bruce Davison, Ed Flanders, Salome Jens, James Shigeta, Susan Oliver, Arthur Hill; ***D:*** Joseph Sargent. **TV**

Tomorrow's Children 🦴 **1934** An alarmist melodrama warning against the threat of government-induced female sterilization asks the question: if a woman's family is weird, should her tubes be tied? **55m/B VHS, DVD.** Sterling Holloway, Diana Sinclair, Sarah Padden, Donald "Don" Douglas; ***D:*** Crane Wilbur.

The Tong Man 🦴🦴 ½ **1919** Robbins owes the tong money and Hayakawa, as the tong's executioner, is sent to kill him when he won't pay up. Only it turns out Hayakawa is in love with Eddy, Robbins daughter, and refuses. Then the tong decide to kill him for disobeying their orders. **58m/B VHS.** Sessue Hayakawa, Helen Jerome Eddy, Marc Robbins, Toyo Fujita; ***D:*** William Worthington.

Tongs: An American Nightmare 🦴 **1988 (R)** Chinese-American street gangs in Chinatown battle over turf and drug shipments. **80m/C VHS.** Ian Anthony Leung, Christopher O'Conner, Simon Yam; ***D:*** Philip Chan.

Toni 🦴🦴🦴 ½ **1934** An Italian worker falls for his landlady and they make plans to marry. A grim turn of events, however, brings tragic consequences. Based on the lives of several townsfolk in the village of Les Martiques, the film was shot in the town and members of the local populace were used as characters. In French with English subtitles. **90m/B VHS.** *FR* Charles Blavette, Jenny Helia, Edouard Delmont, Celia Montalvan; ***D:*** Jean Renoir; ***W:*** Jean Renoir; ***C:*** Claude Renoir; ***M:*** Paul Bozzi.

Tonight and Every Night 🦴🦴 ½ **1945** Cabaret singer and RAF pilot fall in love during WWII. Her music hall post puts her in the midst of Nazi bombing, and her dedication to her song and dance career puts a strain on the romance. Imaginative production numbers outweigh pedestrian storyline. ♫ Cry and You Cry Alone; What Does an English Girl Think of a Yank; Anywhere; The Boy I Left Behind; You Excite Me; Tonight and Every Night. **92m/C VHS.** Rita Hayworth, Lee Bowman, Janet Blair, Marc Platt, Leslie Brooks; ***D:*** Victor Saville.

Tonight for Sure 🦴 ½ **1961** Coppola made this nudie, his first film, as a student at UCLA. Two men, one who spies on women and the other who imagines nude women everywhere, plan an escapade. **66m/B VHS.** ***D:*** Francis Ford Coppola; ***W:*** Francis Ford Coppola; ***M:*** Carmine Coppola.

Tonight or Never 🦴🦴 **1931** Nella (Swanson) is a young opera singer whose Venice debut is criticized for her lack of passion. So she spends the night with a nameless handsome admirer (Douglas), which does the trick. Nella is suddenly offered a contract with the Metropolitan Opera and learns that her new lover is a talent scout who arranged the whole thing and everything works out just peachy. Film is adapted from a play by Lili Hatvany, in which Douglas also starred. **80m/B VHS, DVD.** Gloria Swanson, Melvyn Douglas, Ferdinand Gottschalk, Alison Skipworth, Boris Karloff, Robert Greig; ***D:*** Mervyn LeRoy; ***W:*** Ernest Vajda, Frederic Hatton, Fanny Hatton; ***C:*** Gregg Toland; ***M:*** Alfred Newman.

Tonio Kroger 🦴🦴 **1965** A young writer travels through Europe in search of intellectual and sensual relationships and a home that will suit him. He must balance freedom and responsibility. Works best if one is familiar with the Thomas Mann novel on which film is based. In German with English subtitles. **92m/B VHS.** *GE* Jean-Claude Brialy, Nadja Tiller, Gert Frobe; ***D:*** Rolf Thiele.

Tonka 🦴🦴 ½ *A Horse Named Comanche* **1958** A children's story about a wild horse tamed by a young Indian, only to have it recruited for the Battle of Little Bighorn. Mineo is fine as the Indian brave determined to be reunited with his steed. The film also makes a laudable effort to portray the Indians as a dignified race. The movie, however, stumbles at its conclusion and is contrived throughout. **97m/C VHS.** Sal Mineo, Phil Carey, Jerome Courtland; ***D:*** Lewis R. Foster.

Tonto Basin Outlaws 🦴🦴 **1941** The Range Busters team up with Teddy Roosevelt's Rough Riders in order to stop a gang of cattle rustlers. Standard oater material. Based on the story by Earle Snell. **60m/B VHS, DVD.** Ray Corrigan, John "Dusty" King, Max Terhune, Jan Wiley, Tristram Coffin, Edmund Cobb; ***D:*** S. Roy Luby; ***W:*** John Vlahos.

The Tonto Kid 🦴 **1935** Action-packed western featuring Rex Bell. **56m/B VHS.** Rex Bell, Ruth Mix, Buzz Barton, Joseph Girard, Jack Rockwell, Murdock MacQuarrie; ***D:*** Harry Fraser.

Tony Draws a Horse 🦴🦴 ½ **1951** An eight-year-old draws an anatomically correct horse on the door of his father's office, leading to a rift between the parents as they argue how to handle the heartbreak of precociousness. Somewhat uneven but engaging comedy, based on a play by Lesley Storm. **90m/B VHS.** Cecil Parker, Anne Crawford, Derek Bond, Barbara Murray, Mervyn Johns, Barbara Everest, David Hurst; ***D:*** Jack Paddy Carstairs.

Tony n' Tina's Wedding 🦴 ½ **2007 (R)** Adaptation of the long-running off-Broadway comedy (and filmed in 2004) hits every broad cliche possible. Tony (McIntyre) and Tina (Kunis) are a young Italian-American couple from Queens whose wedding and reception prove to be tests of their love. Obstacles include her mother (Lopez) and his father (Fiore), who hate each other and refuse to stop fighting; Tina's drunken ex-boyfriend (Grenier), who causes trouble; the flamboyant videographer (Diaz); Tony's pot-smoking groomsmen; and general tackiness and mayhem. **105m/C DVD.** Mila Kunis, Adrian Grenier, Priscilla Lopez, John Fiore, Guillermo Diaz, Krista Allen, Dean Edwards, Kim Director, Richard Portnow; ***D:*** Roger Paradiso; ***W:*** Roger Paradiso; ***C:*** Giselle Chamma.

Tony Rome 🦴🦴 ½ **1967** Tony Rome (Sinatra) is a P.I. living the good life on his boat in Miami. He's hired by wealthy builder Rudolph Kosterman (Oakland) to keep an eye on his erratic daughter, Diana (Lyons). Turns out there's organized crime and blackmail involved as well—oh, and a babe named Ann (St. John). An entertaining diversion based on the novel "Miami Mayhem" by Marvin H. Albert. Followed by "The Lady in Cement" (1968). **110m/C VHS, DVD.** Frank Sinatra, Jill St. John, Simon Oakland, Gena Rowlands, Richard Conte, Lloyd Bochner, Jeffrey Lynn, Sue Lyon; ***D:*** Gordon Douglas; ***W:*** Richard L. Breen; ***C:*** Joseph Biroc; ***M:*** Billy May.

Too Bad She's Bad 🦴🦴 ½ *Peccato Che Sia una Canaglia* **1954** Wide-eyed cab driver Paolo (Mastroianni) can't help but desire sexy Lina (Loren with a blonde 'do) despite her attempt to swipe his ride. Later he realizes that thievery is her family's business and believes marrying her will turn her around. First of thirteen films starring the Italian acting legends. In Italian, with subtitles. **96m/B VHS, DVD.** Vittorio De Sica, Sophia Loren, Marcello Mastroianni, Memmo Carotenuto, Giorgio Sanna, Michael Simone, Margherita Bagni, Wanda Benedetti, Maria Britneva, Manlio Busoni, Giulio Cali, Carloni Pietro, Giullo Paradisi, Cella Marga, Pasquale Cennamo, Nino Dal Fabbro, Giacomo Furia, Enrico Leurini, Marcella Melnati, Amalia Pellegrini, Giuseppe Ricagno, Giulio Tomasini, John Stacy, Walter Bartoletti, Mauro Sacripante; ***D:*** Alessandro Blasetti; ***W:*** Suso Cecchi D'Amico, Alessandro Continenza, Ennio Flaiano, Alberto Moravia; ***C:*** Aldo Giordani; ***M:*** Alessandro Cicognini.

Too Beautiful for You 🦴🦴 *Trop Belle pour Toi* **1988 (R)** A successful car salesman, married for years to an extraordinarily beautiful woman, finds himself head over heels for his frumpy secretary. Depardieu plays the regular guy who finds he's never believed in the love and fidelity of a woman he thinks is too beautiful for him. In French with English subtitles. **91m/C VHS, DVD.** *FR* Gerard Depardieu, Josiane Balasko, Carole Bouquet, Roland Blanche, Francois Cluzet; ***D:*** Bertrand Blier; ***W:*** Bertrand Blier; ***C:*** Philippe Rousselot. Cannes '89: Grand Jury Prize; Cesar '90: Actress (Bouquet), Director (Blier), Film, Writing.

Too Busy to Work 🦴🦴 ½ **1932** Hobo Jubilo (Rogers) has been searching for the man who ran off with his wife and daughter long ago. He becomes a reluctant handyman at Judge Hardy's (Burton) and discovers his daughter Rose (Nixon) is happy and living the good life and that his wife has died. Jublio decides to keep his identity a secret and encourages Rose's romance with Dan (Powell). Rogers remade his 1919 silent "Jubilo." **70m/B DVD.** Will Rogers, Marion (Marian) Nixon, Dick Powell, Frederick Burton, Daniel Cosgrove, Louise Beavers, Charles Middleton, Bert Hanlon, Constantine Romanoff; ***D:*** John Blystone; ***W:*** Barry Connors, Philip Klein; ***C:*** Charles G. Clarke.

Too Cool for Christmas 🦴🦴 *A Very Cool Christmas* **2004** Forbidden to go on a ski trip with her friends, disdainful 16-year-old Lindsay (Nevin) doesn't want to hang with her family so she heads to the mall. Santa Claus (Hamilton) wants a makeover to impress Mrs. Claus (Mills) and rewards Lindsay's efforts by taking her along on his Christmas Eve run, which brings home the true meaning of the holidays. In this version, Lindsay has two dads; in the alternate "A Very Cool Christmas," they were replaced by a mom/dad combo. **91m/C DVD.** Brooke Nevin, George Hamilton, Donna Mills, Barclay Hope, Adam Harrington, Jodelle Ferland; ***D:*** Sam Irvin; ***W:*** Michael Gelbart; ***C:*** Anthony C. Metchie; ***M:*** Peter Allen. **CABLE**

Too Far to Go 🦴🦴🦴 **1979** Terrific TV adaptation of a series of John Updike stories focusing on the rocky longtime marriage of not-so-proper New Englanders Danner and Moriarty. **98m/C VHS, DVD.** Blythe Danner, Michael Moriarty, Glenn Close, Ken Kercheval; ***W:*** William Hanley.

Too Fast, Too Young 🦴 **1996 (R)** L.A. police captain Floyd Anderson (Ironside) finds himself shouldering the blame when violent offender Dalton (Tiller) escapes from prison and goes on a cop-killing spree. **90m/C VHS.** Michael Ironside, Patrick Tiller, James Wellington, Kasia (Katarzyna) Figura, Marshall Bell; ***D:*** Tim Everitt; ***W:*** Tim Everitt.

Too Good to Be True 🦴 ½ **1998** Jamie, Tina, and Silvia head to the beach at spring break for the usual ritual of sun, surf, and guys. First they attract nerds, then hoods, then hot guy Rick hits it off with Jamie and things seem to be going just swell. But the film isn't called "Too Good to Be True" for nuthin'. **91m/C VHS.** John O'Brien, Carole Bardwell, Spence Decker, Lisa Reissman, Angie Janu, Isaac Allan; ***D:*** Eric Swelstad; ***W:*** Cliff Hollingsworth; ***C:*** Scott Spears. **VIDEO**

Too Hot to Handle 🦴🦴🦴 **1938** Two rival photographers searching for a beautiful lady-pilot's missing brother wind up in Brazil, where they encounter a dangerous tribe of voodoo types. Amusing, if exaggerated, picture of the lengths to which reporters will go to for a story. Classic Gable. **105m/B VHS.** Clark Gable, Myrna Loy, Walter Pidgeon, Walter Connolly, Leo Carrillo, Virginia Weidler; ***D:*** Jack Conway.

Too Hot to Handle **1976** Voluptuous lady contract killer fights against the mob with all the weapons at her disposal. Filmed on location in Manila. **88m/C VHS.** Cheri Caffaro, Aharon Ipale, Corinne Calvet, John van Dreelen, Vic Diaz, Jordan Rosengarten, Butz Aquino, Subas Herrero; ***D:*** Don Schain; ***W:*** J. Michael Sherman, Albert (Don) Buday; ***C:*** Fred Conde; ***M:*** Hugo Montenegro.

Too Late for Tears *Killer Bait* **1949** An honest husband and his not so honest wife stumble on a load of mob-stolen cash and become entangled in a web of deceit and murder as the wife resorts to increasingly desperate measures to keep her newfound fortune. Atmospheric and entertaining film noir albeit sometimes confusing. **99m/B VHS, DVD.** Lizabeth Scott, Don DeFore, Dan Duryea, Arthur Kennedy, Kristine Miller, Barry Kelley, Denver Pyle, Jimmy Ames, Billy Halop, Jimmie Dodd; ***D:*** Byron Haskin; ***W:*** Roy Huggins; ***C:*** William Mellor; ***M:*** R. Dale Butts.

Too Late the Hero *Suicide Run* **1970 (PG)** Unlikely band of allied soldiers battle Japanese force entrenched in the Pacific during WWII. Rousing adventure, fine cast. **133m/C VHS, DVD.** Michael Caine, Cliff Robertson, Henry Fonda, Ian Bannen, Harry Andrews, Denholm Elliott, William Beckley, Ronald Fraser, Percy Herbert, Patrick Jordan, Harvey Jason, Sam Kydd, Ken Takakura; ***D:*** Robert Aldrich; ***W:*** Robert Aldrich, Lois Heller; ***C:*** Joseph Biroc; ***M:*** Gerald Fried.

Too Many Crooks **1959** A British spoof of crime syndicate films. Crooks try to extort, but bungle the job. Terry-Thomas is fun, as always. **85m/B VHS.** *GB* Terry-Thomas, Brenda de Banzie, George Cole; ***D:*** Mario Zampi.

Too Many Girls 1/2 **1940** Beautiful heiress goes to a small New Mexico college to escape from a cadre of gold-digging suitors. Passable adaptation of the successful Rodgers and Hart Broadway show, with many original cast members and the original stage director. Lucy and Desi met while making this film, and married shortly after. ♫ Spic and Spanish; Heroes in the Fall; Pottawatomie; 'Cause We All Got Cake; Love Never Went to College; Look Out; I Didn't Know What Time It Was; The Conga; You're Nearer. **85m/B VHS, DVD.** Lucille Ball, Richard Carlson, Eddie Bracken, Ann Miller, Desi Arnaz Sr., Hal LeRoy, Libby Bennett, Frances Langford, Van Johnson; ***D:*** George Abbott; ***M:*** George Bassman, Richard Rodgers, Lorenz Hart.

Too Many Husbands **1940** Vicky (Arthur) is told that adventurer husband Bill (MacMurray) drowned during a shipwreck so eventually she marries Henry (Douglas), Bill's best friend and business partner. Then Bill is rescued from an island and returns to his wife—who isn't anymore. The men vie for Vicky's affections and she likes the attention since both neglected her the first go-round. However, they get tired of her indecision. **84m/B DVD.** Jean Arthur, Fred MacMurray, Melvyn Douglas, Harry Davenport, Dorothy Peterson, Melville Cooper, Edgar Buchanan, Dorothy Peterson; ***D:*** Wesley Ruggles; ***W:*** Claude Binyon; ***C:*** Joseph Walker; ***M:*** Frederick "Friedrich" Hollander.

Too Many Winners 1/2 *Michael Shayne* **1947** Michael Shayne (Beaumont) takes on a gang of pari-mutuel race ticket counterfeiters while his secretary, Phyllis (Marshall), smells trouble and tries to get him to vacation with her instead. When the trail of bodies starts adding up, Shayne jumps into action to find the killer. **61m/B DVD.** Hugh Beaumont, Trudy Marshall, Ralph Dunn, Claire Carleton, Charles Mitchell, John Hamilton, Grandon Rhodes; ***D:*** William Beaudine; ***W:*** Brett Halliday, Fred Myton; ***C:*** Jack Greenhalgh; ***M:*** Alvin Levin.

Too Much Sun 1/2 **1990 (R)** A dying man can prevent his fortune from falling into the hands of a corrupt priest simply by having one of his two children produce an heir. The problem is, they're both gay! **97m/C VHS.** Robert Downey Jr., Ralph Macchio, Eric Idle, Andrea Martin, Laura Ernst, Jim Haynie; ***D:*** Robert Downey.

Too Pretty to Be Honest *Trop Jolie pour Etre Honette* **1972** Four women sharing an apartment witness a robbery and begin to suspect that their neighbor is the culprit. So they decide to steal the money from him. In French with subtitles. **95m/C VHS.** *FR* Jane Birkin, Bernadette LaFont, Serge Gainsbourg; ***D:*** Richard Balducci; ***M:*** Serge Gainsbourg.

Too Scared to Scream 1/2 **1985 (R)** Policeman and an undercover agent team up to solve a bizarre series of murders at a Manhattan apartment house. **104m/C VHS.** Mike Connors, Anne Archer, Leon Isaac Kennedy, John Heard, Ian McShane, Maureen O'Sullivan, Murray Hamilton; ***D:*** Tony LoBianco; ***W:*** Neal Barbera.

Too Shy to Try *Je Suis Timide* **1978 (PG)** An incredibly shy man meets his dream girl, and enrolls in a psychology course to overcome his ineptitude. A ribald, slapstick French comedy. **89m/C VHS.** *FR* Pierre Richard, Aldo Maccione, Jacques Francois, Mimi Coutelier; ***D:*** Pierre Richard; ***W:*** Pierre Richard; ***C:*** Claude Agostini; ***M:*** Vladimir Cosma.

Too Smooth *Hairshirt* **1998 (R)** Danny (Paras) is a smooth-talking actor wannabe who lies to every woman he knows—until he meets naive Corey (Wright), whom he thinks is the girl of his dreams. But when his vindictive starlet ex (Campbell) learns about Corey's new romance, she becomes determined to expose him for the lying dog she's sure he remains. **91m/C VHS, DVD.** Dean Paras, Neve Campbell, Katie Wright, Rebecca Gayheart, Christian Campbell, David DeLuise, Stefan Brogren, Adam Carolla, Marley Shelton; ***D:*** Dean Paras; ***W:*** Dean Paras; ***M:*** Nathan Barr.

Too Wise Wives **1921** A story of would-be marital infidelity and misunderstandings. Silent. **90m/C VHS.** Louis Calhern, Claire Windsor; ***D:*** Lois Weber.

Too Young to Die **1990 (R)** Teenager Amanda (Lewis) hooks up with the wrong guy in sleazy Billy (Pitt), who hooks her on drugs and turns her into a prostitute. She meets nice guy Mike (O'Keefe), who briefly takes her away from the life but when their relationship falls apart, Amanda goes back to Billy. Billy eggs her on to get revenge for being dumped and Amanda winds up on trial for murder. Fact-based TV movie. **92m/C VHS, DVD.** Juliette Lewis, Brad Pitt, Michael Tucker, Michael O'Keefe, Emily Longstreth, Alan Fudge; ***D:*** Robert Markowitz; ***W:*** David Hill; ***C:*** Eric Van Haren Noman; ***M:*** Charles Bernstein.

The Toolbox Murders **1978 (R)** Unknown psychotic murderer brutally claims victims one at a time, leaving police mystified and townsfolk terrified. Sick and exploitative, with predictably poor production values. **93m/C VHS, DVD.** Cameron Mitchell, Pamelyn Ferdin, Wesley Eure, Nicolas Beauvy, Aneta Corsaut, Tim Donnelly, Evelyn Guerrero; ***D:*** Dennis Donnelly; ***W:*** Robert Easter, Ann Kindberg; ***C:*** Gary Graver.

Tooth and Nail **2007 (R)** You've got your post-apocalyptic world, you've got your struggle to survive, you've got cannibals, and it's still boring. Civilization collapses and chaos rules when the world runs out of oil. One struggling group has taken over an abandoned hospital, working together to stay alive, which is hard enough—and it only gets worse when a gang of marauding cannibals comes along, looking for their next meal. **94m/C DVD.** Rachel Miner, Rider Strong, Michael Kelly, Robert Carradine, Vinnie Jones, Michael Madsen, Gregg Easterbrook; ***D:*** Mark Young; ***W:*** Mark Young; ***C:*** Elia Cmiral.

The Tooth Fairy **2006** Peter (Munro) is renovating an old house, and his girlfriend Darcy (West) and her 12-year-old daughter Pamela (Munoz) come to help out. While looking around, Pam meets young Emma (Ballard), who tells her that the house was owned by an old woman named Elizabeth Craven (Konoval), who lured neighborhood kids inside with the promise of presents if they would give her their baby teeth. Instead, she killed them. Apparently, renovating the house has stirred up "The Tooth Fairy" and when Pam's last baby tooth happens to fall out, the horrors begin again. Silly rather than scary. **89m/C DVD.** Lochlyn Munro, Chandra West, Karin Konoval, P.J. Soles, Steve Bacic, Nicole Munoz, Jianna Ballard; ***D:*** Chuck Bowman; ***W:*** Stephen J. Cannell, Corey Strode, Cookie Rae Brown; ***C:*** David Pelletier; ***M:*** Richard John Baker, Jon Lee. **VIDEO**

Tooth Fairy **2010 (PG)** Minor league hockey player Derek Thompson (Johnson) has earned his nickname because his opponents have lost a lot of their teeth in games. When Derek tells his girlfriend Carly's (Judd) six-year-old Tess (Whitlock) that the tooth fairy isn't real, the angry tooth fairy shows up and makes Derek substitute for him for two weeks—complete with tutu, wings, and magic wand. Also strained, in typical fashion, is his relationship with Carly's teenage son Randy (Ellison). And, naturally, just as things seem to turn around for Derek he whiffs on his shot, literally. Despite the cliches, a likeable Johnson is entertaining for kids of all ages and the rest of the cast—including Lily, the tooth fairy godmother (Andrews), and Jerry, the fairy gadget guy (Crystal)—helps an otherwise lackluster flick take flight. **101m/C DVD.** Dwayne "The Rock" Johnson, Julie Andrews, Destiny Whitlock, Stephen Merchant, Ryan Sheckler, Ashley Judd, Billy Crystal, Seth MacFarlane, Chase Ellison; ***D:*** Michael Lembeck; ***W:*** Lowell Ganz, Babaloo Mandell, Joshua Sternin, Jeffrey Ventimilia; ***C:*** David Tattersall; ***M:*** George S. Clinton.

Toothless 1/2 **1997** Katherine Lewis (Alley) is a work-obsessed dentist who is struck by a car and wakes up in Limbo Land (yes, she's dead). The supervisor, Ms. Rogers (Redgrave), informs Katherine that because she had no emotional connections in life her entry into heaven will have to wait—and she's going to do her time as the Tooth Fairy. Katherine is not supposed to intervene with her charges but this sarcastic lady, who doesn't much care for her princess-like Tooth Fairy attire, does get involved with 12-year-old Bobby (Mallinger) and his widowed dad (Midkiff). **85m/C VHS, DVD.** Kirstie Alley, Ross Malinger, Dale Midkiff, Lynn Redgrave, Daryl (Chill) Mitchell, Melanie Mayron, Kimberly Scott, Helen Slater; ***W:*** Mark S. Kaufman. **TV**

Tootsie **1982 (PG)** Stubborn, unemployed actor Michael Dorsey (Hoffman) disguises himself as a woman named Dorothy Michaels to secure a part on a soap opera. As his popularity on TV mounts, his love life becomes increasingly soap operatic. Hoffman is delightful, as is the rest of the stellar cast, especially Lange as the cast member he falls in love with. Debut of Davis; Murray's performance was unbilled. Director Pollack plays Michael's put-upon agent, George Fields. **110m/C VHS, DVD.** Dustin Hoffman, Jessica Lange, Teri Garr, Dabney Coleman, Bill Murray, Charles Durning, Geena Davis, George Gaynes, Estelle Getty, Christine Ebersole, Sydney Pollack; ***D:*** Sydney Pollack; ***W:*** Larry Gelbart, Murray Schisgal, Don McGuire; ***C:*** Owen Roizman; ***M:*** Dave Grusin. Oscars '82: Support. Actress (Lange); AFI '98: Top 100; British Acad. '83: Actor (Hoffman); Golden Globes '83: Actor—Mus./Comedy (Hoffman), Film—Mus./Comedy, Support. Actress (Lange); L.A. Film Critics '82: Screenplay, Natl. Film Reg. '98;; N.Y. Film Critics '82: Director (Pollack), Screenplay, Support. Actress (Lange); Natl. Soc. Film Critics '82: Actor (Hoffman), Film, Screenplay, Support. Actress (Lange); Writers Guild '82: Orig. Screenplay.

Top Dog 1/2 **1995 (PG-13)** Another cop-and-dog-team-up-to-get-the-bad-guys flick. This one, however, is meant to appeal to the kids who liked "Sidekicks." That raises a problem with the unfortunately topical right-wing-hate group-bombing plot. Jake Wilder (Norris), a beer-swillin' karate-choppin' loner cop, teams up with canine Reno, whose ex-partner was killed by the neo-Nazi terrorists. Weak script and erratic storyline can't find a comfortable balance between the too-cute pooch scenes and the (admittedly toned-down) violence. Reno steals every scene he's in, and provides the flick's few redeeming moments. **93m/C VHS, DVD.** Chuck Norris, Clyde Kusatsu, Michele Lamar Richards, Carmine Caridi, Peter Savard Moore, Erik von Detten, Herta Ware, Kai Wulff, Francesco Quinn, Timothy Bottoms; ***D:*** Aaron Norris; ***W:*** Ron Swanson; ***C:*** Joao Fernandes.

Top Gun 1/2 **1986 (PG)** Young Navy pilots compete against one another on the ground and in the air at the elite Fighter Weapons School. Cruise isn't bad as a maverick who comes of age in Ray Bans, but Edwards shines as his buddy. Awesome aerial photography and high-cal beefcake divert from the contrived plot and stock characters. The Navy subsequently noticed an increased interest in fighter pilots. Features Berlin's Oscar-winning song "Take My Breath Away." ♫ Take My Breath Away; Danger Zone; Destination Unknown; Heaven in Your Eyes; Hot Summer Nights; Mighty Wings; Playing with the Boys; Through the Fire; Top Gun Anthem. **109m/C VHS, DVD, HD DVD.** Tom Cruise, Kelly McGillis, Val Kilmer, Tom Skerritt, Anthony Edwards, Meg Ryan, Rick Rossovich, Michael Ironside, Barry Tubb, Whip Hubley, John Stockwell, Tim Robbins, Adrian Pasdar; ***D:*** Tony Scott; ***W:*** Jim Cash, Jack Epps Jr.; ***C:*** Jeffrey L. Kimball; ***M:*** Harold Faltermeyer. Oscars '86: Song ("Take My Breath Away"); Golden Globes '87: Song ("Take My Breath Away").

Top Hat **1935** Ginger isn't impressed by Fred's amorous attentions since she's mistaken him for a friend's other half. Many believe it to be the duo's best film together. Choreography by Astaire and score by Berlin makes this one a classic Hollywood musical. Look for a young Lucille Ball as a clerk in a flower shop. ♫ Cheek to Cheek; Top Hat, White Tie and Tails; Isn't This A Lovely Day; The Piccolino; No Strings. **97m/B VHS, DVD.** Fred Astaire, Ginger Rogers, Erik Rhodes, Helen Broderick, Edward Everett Horton, Eric Blore, Lucille Ball; ***D:*** Mark Sandrich; ***W:*** Dwight Taylor, Allan Scott; ***M:*** Irving Berlin, Max Steiner. Natl. Film Reg. '90.

Top of the Heap **1972 (R)** A cop is denied a promotion and gets angry. Deciding to chuck the laws of due process, he goes on a criminal-killing rampage. **91m/C VHS.** Christopher St. John, Paula Kelly, Patrick McVey; ***D:*** Christopher St. John.

Top of the World 1/2 **1997 (R)** Newly released con Ray Mercer (Weller) travels to Vegas with his estranged wife, Rebecca (Carrere), who wants a quickie divorce. She's got a new boyfriend, casino manager Steve Atlas (Hopper). But Ray just happens to get caught in the middle of a heist planned by Atlas to cover up his embezzling at the casino. Sounds like it should be entertaining but it's not. **98m/C VHS, DVD.** Peter Weller, Tia Carrere, Dennis Hopper, Joe Pantoliano, Martin Kove, Peter Coyote, David Alan Grier, Cary-Hiroyuki Tagawa; ***D:*** Sidney J. Furie; ***W:*** Bart Madison; ***C:*** Alan Caso; ***M:*** Robert O. Ragland.

Top Secret! **1984 (PG)** Unlikely musical farce parodies spy movies and Elvis Presley films. Young American rock star Nick Rivers goes to Europe on goodwill tour and becomes involved with Nazis, the French Resistance, an American refugee, and more. Sophisticated it isn't. From the creators of "Airplane!" **90m/C VHS, DVD.** Val Kilmer, Lucy Gutteridge, Christopher Villiers, Omar Sharif, Peter Cushing, Jeremy Kemp, Michael Gough, Billy Mitchell; ***D:*** Jim Abrahams, Jerry Zucker, David Zucker; ***W:*** Jim Abrahams, Jerry Zucker, David Zucker, Martyn Burke; ***C:*** Christopher Challis; ***M:*** Maurice Jarre.

Top Secret Affair 1/2 **1957** Dottie Peale (Hayward), who runs a publishing empire, supports a civilian for an important diplomatic post. She's incensed when Army Major General Melville Goodwin (Douglas) gets the job instead and is determined to discredit him. Of course they fall in love but misunderstandings lead Dottie to print an unflattering article that lands Melville in front of a Senate committee. Based on the novel by John P. Marquand. **100m/B DVD.** Kirk Douglas, Susan Hayward, Paul Stewart, Jim Backus, John Cromwell, Roland Winters; ***D:*** H.C. Potter; ***W:*** Allan Scott, Roland Kibbee; ***C:*** Stanley Cortez; ***M:*** Roy Webb.

Topaz **1969 (PG)** American CIA agent and French intelligence agent combine forces to find information about Russian espionage in Cuba. Cerebral and intriguing, but not classic Hitchcock. Based on the novel by Leon Uris. **126m/C VHS, DVD.** John Forsythe, Frederick Stafford, Philippe Noiret, Karin Dor,

Michel Piccoli; *D:* Alfred Hitchcock; *W:* Samuel A. Taylor; *C:* Jack Hildyard; *M:* Maurice Jarre. Natl. Bd. of Review '69: Director (Hitchcock), Support. Actor (Noiret).

Topaze **1933** A shy, depressed teacher is fired from his job at a private school and takes a new job, unaware that his boss is using him in a business scam. From the French play by Marcel Pagnol. An American version was also filmed in 1933; Pagnol produced his own version in '51. In French with English subtitles. **92m/B VHS.** *FR* Louis Jouvet, Edwige Feuillere, Marcel Vallee; *D:* Louis Gasnier; *W:* Marcel Pagnol; *M:* Max Steiner.

Topaze **1933** American adaptation of the Marcel Pagnol play, about an innocent, doltish schoolmaster who becomes the unknowing front for a baron's illegal business scam. Remade in two French versions, in 1933, and in 1951 by Pagnol. **127m/B VHS.** John Barrymore, Myrna Loy, Jobyna Howland, Jackie Searl; *D:* Harry D'Abbadie D'Arrast.

Topaze 1/2 **1951** After losing his job, a pathetic school teacher gets involved with the mob and winds up a powerful businessman. Remake of two earlier versions, one French and one American. Based on the play by director Pagnol. In French with English subtitles. **95m/B VHS.** *FR* Fernandel, Helen Perdriere, Pierre Larquey; *D:* Marcel Pagnol.

The Topeka Terror **1945** Lane stars as a federal agent who joins forces with a frontier lawyer to stop greedy land-grabber Barcroft from ripping off a group of homesteaders. Based on a story by Patricia Harper. **55m/B VHS.** Allan "Rocky" Lane, Linda Stirling, Roy Barcroft, Earle Hodgins, Bud Geary; *D:* Howard Bretherton; *W:* Patricia Harper, Norman S. Hall.

Topkapi **1964** An international bevy of thieves can't resist the treasures of the famed Topkapi Palace Museum, an impregnable fortress filled with wealth and splendor. Comic thriller based on Eric Ambler's "The Light of Day." **122m/C VHS, DVD.** Melina Mercouri, Maximilian Schell, Peter Ustinov, Robert Morley, Akim Tamiroff, Jess Hahn, Gilles Segal; *D:* Jules Dassin; *W:* Monja Danischewsky; *C:* Henri Alekan; *M:* Manos Hadjidakis. Oscars '64: Support. Actor (Ustinov).

Topper 1/2 **1937** Wealthy, madcap George (Grant) and Marion (Bennett) Kerby return as ghosts after a fatal car accident, determined to assist their morose banker pal Cosmo Topper (Young) to enjoy life. Of course, since Cosmo is the only one who can see the ghostly Kerbys his life becomes very complicated. Immensely popular at the box-office; followed by "Topper Takes a Trip" (1939) and "Topper Returns" (1941). The series uses trick photography and special effects to complement the comedic scripts. Based on Thorne Smith's novel, "The Jovial Ghosts." Inspired a TV series and remade in 1979 as TV movie. **97m/B VHS, DVD.** Cary Grant, Roland Young, Constance Bennett, Billie Burke, Eugene Pallette, Hoagy Carmichael; *D:* Norman Z. McLeod.

Topper Returns **1941** Cosmo Topper helps ghost find the man who mistakenly murdered her and warns her friend, the intended victim. Humorous conclusion to the trilogy preceded by "Topper" and "Topper Takes a Trip." Followed by a TV series. **87m/B VHS, DVD.** Roland Young, Joan Blondell, Dennis O'Keefe, Carole Landis, Eddie Anderson, H.B. Warner, Billie Burke; *D:* Roy Del Ruth; *W:* Gordon Douglas, Jonathan Latimer; *C:* Norbert Brodine.

Topper Takes a Trip **1939** Cosmo Topper and his wife are having falling out and ghosts Kerby help them get back together. The special effects sequences are especially funny. Followed by "Topper Returns." Also available colorized. **85m/B VHS.** Constance Bennett, Roland Young, Billie Burke, Franklin Pangborn, Alan Mowbray; *D:* Norman Z. McLeod.

Topsy Turvy 1/2 **1984 (R)** A comedy about reckless romance and not much else. **90m/C VHS.** Lisbet Dahl, Ebbe Rode; *D:* Edward Fleming.

Topsy Turvy 1/2 **1999 (R)** The very contemporary Leigh takes a pass at Victorian England for his very long and chatty look at life in the theatre. His focus is on the comic-opera partnership of irascible lyricist W.S. Gilbert (Broadbent) and pleasure-loving composer, Sir Arthur Sullivan (Corduner). Their latest creation (after 10 hits) is a flop, causing a serious rift but Gilbert, after a visit to a Japanese art exhibit, is inspired to write "The Mikado" and pulls Sullivan back in. The film then follows the production of the opera from rehearsal to the 1885 premiere with all its difficulties and triumphs. **160m/C VHS, DVD.** *GB* Jim Broadbent, Allan Corduner, Lesley Manville, Eleanor David, Ron Cook, Timothy Spall, Kevin McKidd, Mark Benton, Shirley Henderson, Martin Savage, Jessie Bond; *D:* Mike Leigh; *W:* Mike Leigh; *C:* Dick Pope; *M:* Carl Davis. Oscars '99: Costume Des., Makeup; British Acad. '99: Makeup; N.Y. Film Critics '99: Director (Leigh), Film; Natl. Soc. Film Critics '99: Director (Leigh), Film.

Tor 1/2 **1964** Medieval barbarian endeavors to free an enslaved village from a band of murderous hoodlums. **94m/C VHS.** Joe Robinson, Bella Cortez, Harry Baird; *D:* Antonio Leonviola.

Tora! Tora! Tora! **1970 (G)** The story of events leading up to December 7, 1941, is retold by three directors from both Japanese and American viewpoints in this tense, large-scale production. Well-documented and realistic treatment of the Japanese attack on Pearl Harbor that brought the U.S. into WWII; notable for its good photography but lacks a story line equal to its epic intentions. **144m/C VHS, DVD.** Martin Balsam, So Yamamura, Joseph Cotten, E.G. Marshall, Tatsuya Mihashi, Wesley Addy, Jason Robards Jr., James Whitmore, Leon Ames, George Macready, Takahiro Tamura, Eijiro Tono, Shogo Shimada, Koreya Senda, Jun Usami, Richard Anderson, Kazuo Kitamura, Keith Andes, Edward Andrews, Neville Brand, Leora Dana, Walter Brooke, Norman Alden, Ron Masak, Edmon Ryan, Asao Uchida, Frank Aletter, Jerry Fogel; *D:* Richard Fleischer, Toshio Masuda, Kinji Fukasaku; *W:* Ryuzo Kikushima, Hideo Oguni, Larry Forrester; *C:* Sinsaku Himeda, Charles F. Wheeler, Osamu Furuya; *M:* Jerry Goldsmith. Oscars '70: Visual FX.

The Torch 1/2 **1950** Mexican revolutionary restores law and order when he captures a small town but then finds himself in turmoil as he falls for an aristocratic young woman. **90m/C VHS, DVD.** *MX* Gilbert Roland, Paulette Goddard, Pedro Armendariz Sr., Walter Reed; *D:* Emilio Fernandez.

Torch Singer **1933** Sally Trent (Colbert) discovers she's preggers after beau Michael (Manners) leaves for China to make his fortune. Unable to support herself and the baby, Sally gives her daughter up for adoption and changes her name to Mimi Benton, becoming a successful nightclub singer. When she unexpectedly gets a part hosting a kiddie radio show, Sally/Mimi figures she might be able to find her tyke again using her on-air success. Meanwhile, Michael has returned and is trying to find Sally. **70m/B DVD.** Claudette Colbert, David Manners, Ricardo Cortez, Lyda Roberti, Florence Roberts, Charley Grapewin; *D:* Alexander Hall, George Somnes; *W:* Lenore Coffee, Lynn Starling; *C:* Karl Stuss.

Torch Song **1953** In this muddled melodrama, a tough, demanding Broadway actress meets her match when she is offered true love by a blind pianist. Contains a couple of notoriously inept musical numbers. Made to show off Crawford's figure at age 50. Crawford's singing in the movie is dubbed. **90m/C VHS.** Joan Crawford, Michael Wilding, Marjorie Rambeau, Gig Young, Harry (Henry) Morgan, Dorothy Patrick, Benny Rubin, Nancy Gates; *D:* Charles Walters.

Torch Song Trilogy 1/2 **1988 (R)** Adapted from Fierstein's hit Broadway play about a gay man who "just wants to be loved." Still effective, but the rewritten material loses something in the translation to the screen. Bancroft heads a strong cast with a finely shaded performance as Fierstein's mother. **126m/C VHS, DVD.** Anne Bancroft, Matthew Broderick, Harvey Fierstein, Brian Kerwin, Karen Young, Charles Pierce; *D:* Paul Bogart; *W:* Harvey Fierstein; *C:* Mikael Salomon; *M:* Peter Matz.

Torchlight **1985 (R)** A young couple's life begins to crumble when a wealthy art dealer teaches them how to free base cocaine. Heavy-handed treatment of a subject that's been tackled with more skill elsewhere. **90m/C VHS, DVD.** Pamela Sue Martin, Steve Railsback, Ian McShane, Al Corley, Rita Taggart; *D:* Thomas J. Wright.

Torero *Bullfighter* **1956** A young man becomes a bullfighter to overcome his fear of bulls. **89m/B VHS.** *MX* Luis Procuna, Manolete, Dolores Del Rio, Carlos Arruza; *D:* Carlos Velo; *W:* Carlos Velo, Hugo Butler.

Torment *Hets; Frenzy* **1944** Tragic triangle has young woman in love with fellow student and murdered by sadistic teacher. Atmospheric tale hailed by many as Sjoberg's finest film. Ingmar Bergman's first filmed script. In Swedish with English subtitles. **90m/B VHS, DVD.** *SW* Alf Kjellin, Mai Zetterling, Stig Jarrel, Olof Winnerstrand, Gunnar Bjornstrand; *D:* Alf Sjoberg; *W:* Ingmar Bergman; *C:* Martin Bodin; *M:* Hilding Rosenberg.

Torment **1985 (R)** A mild-mannered fellow is secretly a mass murderer specializing in young lovers. He struggles to hide his secret as his daughter approaches dating age and a relentless detective gets closer to the truth. A low-budget slasher. **85m/C VHS.** Taylor Gilbert, William Witt, Eve Brenner; *D:* Samson Aslanian, John Hopkins; *W:* Samson Aslanian, John Hopkins.

Tormented 1/2 **1960** Man pushes his mistress out of a lighthouse, killing her. Her ethereal body parts return to haunt him. **75m/B VHS, DVD.** Richard Carlson, Susan Gordon, Juli Reding; *D:* Bert I. Gordon; *W:* Bert I. Gordon, George Worthing Yates; *C:* Ernest Laszlo; *M:* Albert Glasser, Calvin Jackson.

The Tormentors WOOF! **1971 (R)** Vaguely neo-Nazi gangs rape and murder a man's family, and he kills them all in revenge. **78m/C VHS, DVD.** James Craig, Anthony Eisley, Chris Noel, William Dooley, Bruce Kemp, Inga Wede, James Gordon White; *D:* Boris Eagle; *W:* James Gordon White.

Torn Apart **1989 (R)** Traditional Middle East hatreds undermine the love affair between two young people. Excellent performances from the principals highlight this drama. Adapted from the Chayin Zeldis novel "A Forbidden Love." **95m/C VHS.** Adrian Pasdar, Cecilia Peck, Machram Huri, Arnon Zadok, Barry Primus; *D:* Jack Fisher; *M:* Peter Arnow.

Torn Between Two Lovers **1979** A beautiful married woman has an affair with an architect while on a trip. Remick is enjoyable to watch, but it's a fairly predictable yarn. **100m/C VHS, DVD.** Lee Remick, Joseph Bologna, George Peppard, Giorgio Tozzi; *D:* Delbert Mann. **TV**

Torn Curtain 1/2 **1966** American scientist poses as a defector to East Germany in order to uncover details of the Soviet missile program. He and his fiancee, who follows him behind the Iron Curtain, attempt to escape to freedom. Derivative and uninvolving. **125m/C VHS, DVD.** Paul Newman, Julie Andrews, Lila Kedrova, David Opatoshu; *D:* Alfred Hitchcock; *W:* Brian Moore; *C:* John F. Warren; *M:* John Addison.

Tornado **1983** An army sergeant revolts against his superiors and the enemy when his captain leaves him stranded in Vietnam. **90m/C VHS.** Giancarlo Prete, Tony Marsina, Alan Collins; *D:* Anthony M. Dawson.

Tornado! 1/2 **1996 (PG)** TV movie with cheesy special effects chronicles a week with tornado chaser Campbell, meteorologist Hudson, and government accountant Sturges who wants to stop funding for Hudson's new storm-warning device. Lame attempt to capture some of the "Twister" audience fails miserably. **90m/C VHS, DVD.** Bruce Campbell, Ernie Hudson, Shannon Sturges, L.Q. Jones, Bo Eason; *D:* Noel Nosseck; *W:* John Logan; *C:* Paul Maibaum; *M:* Garry Schyman.

Torpedo Alley **1953** A guilt-ridden WWII Navy pilot feels responsible for the deaths of his crew. After the war, he joins a submarine crew and gradually learns to deal with his guilt. Average drama with plenty of submarine footage. **84m/B VHS.** Dorothy Malone, Mark Stevens, Charles Winninger, Bill Williams; *D:* Lew Landers.

Torpedo Attack **1972** Greek sailors, in an outdated submarine, bravely but hopelessly attack Mussolini's Italy during WWII. **88m/C VHS.** *GR* John Ferris, Sidney Kazan; *D:* George Law.

Torpedo Run **1958** Standard submarine melodramatics, about a U.S. sub that must torpedo a Japanese aircraft carrier which holds some of the crew's family members. Sometimes slow, generally worthwhile. **98m/C VHS.** Glenn Ford, Ernest Borgnine, Dean Jones, Diane Brewster, L.Q. Jones; *D:* Joseph Pevney; *C:* George J. Folsey.

Torque **2004 (PG-13)** "The Fast and the Furious" on crotch rockets. Cary Ford (Henderson) is a tough-guy rider who's looking to patch things up with his girlfriend (Mazur) while trying to dodge the wrath of local gang leader Trey Wallace (Ice Cube). Turns out, Cary's been framed for the murder of Trey's brother by evil crimelord Henry James (Schulze), who's mad at Cary over the loss of a couple bikes full of crystal meth. Sounds confusing? Doesn't matter. Music video director Joseph Kahn's first feature is jam-packed with videogame action and lots of CGI effects, but the screenplay is mostly brainless with only occasional funny moments (like Ice Cube quoting his own song) to break up what's basically an 81 minute chase scene. **81m/C DVD.** *US* Martin Henderson, Ice Cube, Monet Mazur, Adam Scott, Matt Schulze, Jaime Pressly, Jay Hernandez, Will Yun Lee, Fredro Starr, Justina Machado, John Doe, Faizon Love; *D:* Joseph Kahn; *W:* Matt Johnson; *C:* Peter Levy; *M:* Trevor Rabin.

Torremolinos 73 1/2 **2003** Alfredo (Camara) is a struggling encyclopedia salesman in Spain during the waning days of Franco's puritanical regime. Desperate for money, he and his wife Carmen (Pena) are initially reluctant partners in his boss, Don Carlos' (Diego), latest scheme: producing "educational" Super-8 sex films for the Scandinavian market. They turn out to be naturals, with Alfredo directing and Carmen starring. Then Alfredo gets ambitious and decides he wants to be the new Ingmar Bergman, writing a script (the movie's title) and persuading a disillusioned Carmen to go along with his idea. Spanish and Danish with subtitles. **91m/C DVD.** Javier Camara, Candela Pena, Juan Diego, Malena Alterio, Fernando Tejero; *D:* Pablo Berger; *W:* Pablo Berger; *C:* Kiko de la Rica.

Torrents of Spring **1990 (PG-13)** Based on an Ivan Turgenev story, this lavishly filmed and costumed drama concerns a young Russian aristocrat circa 1840 who is torn between two women. Predictably, one is a good-hearted innocent, the other a scheming seductress. **102m/C VHS, DVD.** Timothy Hutton, Nastassja Kinski, Valeria Golino, William Forsythe, Urbano Barberini, Francesca De Sapio, Jacques Herlin; *D:* Jerzy Skolimowski.

Torrid Zone **1940** Nick (Cagney) is the former manager of a Central America banana plantation (set up on Warner's back lot) who's about to head for Chicago and a new job. But owner Steve Case (O'Brien) is in a bind since he thinks new manager Anderson (Cowan) is incompetent and a local revolutionary (Tobias) wants to take back the plantation's land. Throw in saloon singer Lee (Sheridan), who clashes with Nick, and Anderson's hot to trot wife Gloria (Vinson), and Nick's got his fair share of trouble. Sounds kinda like 1932's "Red Dust." **88m/B DVD.** James Cagney, Ann Sheridan, Pat O'Brien, Helen Vinson, Andy Devine, Jerome Cowan, George Reeves, George Tobias; *D:* William Keighley; *W:* Richard Macaulay, Jerry Wald; *C:* James Wong Howe; *M:* Adolph Deutsch.

Torso WOOF! *I Corpi Presentano Tracce Di Violenza Carnale; Bodres Bear Traces of Carnal Violence* **1973 (R)** Crazed psychosexual killer stalks beautiful women and dismembers them. Fairly bloodless and uninteresting, in spite of lovely Kendall. Italian title translates: The Bodies Showed Signs of Carnal Violence—quite an understatement for people missing arms and legs. **91m/C VHS, DVD.** *IT* Suzy Kendall, Tina Aumont, John Richardson; *D:* Sergio Martino; *W:* Sergio Martino, Ernesto Gastaldi; *C:* Giancarlo Ferrando; *M:* Maurizio de Angelis, Guido de Angelis.

Torso 1/2 **2001 (R)** In the small Canadian town of Hamilton, Ontario, a butchered torso is discovered in 1946. Soon, femme fatale Evelyn Dick (Robertson) is accused of the brutal murder of her streetcar conductor husband. Evelyn admits to numerous affairs with wealthy and powerful men and a desire to lead the good life but did she really commit murder? **90m/C VHS, DVD.** Kathleen Robertson, Victor Garber, Callum Keith Rennie, Brenda Fricker, Jonathan Potts, John Henry Canavan; ***D:*** Alex Chapelle; ***W:*** Dennis Foon; ***C:*** Nikos Evdemon; ***M:*** Christopher Dedrick.

Tortilla Flat **1942** Based on the John Steinbeck novel of the same name, two buddies, Tracy and Garfield, struggle to make their way on the wrong side of the tracks in California. Garfield gets a break by inheriting a couple of houses, Tracy schemes to rip-off a rich, but eccentric, dog owner. In the meantime, both fall for the same girl, Lamarr, in perhaps the finest role of her career. Great performances from all, especially Morgan. **105m/B VHS.** Spencer Tracy, Hedy Lamarr, John Garfield, Frank Morgan, Akim Tamiroff, Sheldon Leonard, John Qualen, Donald Meek, Connie Gilchrist; ***D:*** Victor Fleming; ***C:*** Karl Freund.

Tortilla Heaven **2007 (PG-13)** A tiny border town in New Mexico is propelled into the national spotlight when the face of Jesus appears on a tortilla at Isidor's modest restaurant. Soon worshippers are appearing from all over and Isidor is making a tidy profit charging admission. But city-slicker Gil Garcia tells Isidor he could be making a lot more by capitalizing on his notoriety and soon greed divides the community. **97m/C DVD.** Jose Zuniga, Miguel (Michael) Sandoval, Olivia Hussey, George Lopez, Marcelo Tubert, Irene Bedard, Lupe Ontiveros, Alexis Cruz, Ana Ortiz; ***D:*** Judy Hecht Dumontet; ***W:*** Judy Hecht Dumontet, Julius Robinson; ***C:*** John Bedford Lloyd; ***M:*** Christopher Lennertz.

Tortilla Soup **½ 2001 (PG-13)** Widower Martin Naranjo (Elizondo) is a Mexican-American patriarch trying to control the lives of his three grown daughters. Schoolteacher Leticia (Pena) fears love has passed her by; successful Carmen (Obradors) questions her career choice; and Maribel (Mello) has graduated from high school and is just eager to leave home. Meanwhile, Martin is a chef who's lost his sense of taste and smell and is being pursued by divorced Hortensia (Welch). Food and family dinners bring the various crises out in the open. And yes, the film is the American version of the 1994 Taiwanese film "Eat, Drink, Man, Woman" with an equally engaging cast. **102m/C VHS, DVD.** *US* Hector Elizondo, Jacqueline Obradors, Elizabeth Pena, Tamara Mello, Nikolai Kinski, Raquel Welch, Paul Rodriguez, Joel Joan, Constance Marie; ***D:*** Maria Ripoli; ***W:*** Tom Musca, Ramon Menendez, Vera Blasi; ***C:*** Xavier Perez Grobet; ***M:*** Bill Conti.

Torture Chamber of Baron Blood **½** *Baron Blood; Gli Orrori del Castello di Norimberga; The Blood Baron; Chamber of Tortures; The Thirst of Baron Blood* **1972 (PG)** Baron with gorgeous thirst for the red stuff is reanimated and lots of innocent bystanders meet a grisly fate in this spaghetti gorefest. Familiar story has that certain Bava feel. **90m/C VHS, DVD.** *IT* Joseph Cotten, Elke Sommer, Massimo Girotti, Rada Rassimov, Antonio Cantafora; ***D:*** Mario Bava; ***W:*** Vincent Fotre, William Bairn; ***M:*** Les Baxter.

The Torture Chamber of Dr. Sadism **½** *Blood Demon; Castle of the Walking Dead; Die Schlangengrube und das Pendel* **1969** Decapitated and drawn and quartered for sacrificing 12 virgins, the evil Count Regula is pieced together 40 years later to continue his wicked ways. Great fun, terrific art direction. Very loosely based on Poe's "The Pit and the Pendulum." Beware of the heavily edited video version. **120m/C VHS, DVD.** *GE* Christopher Lee, Karin Dor, Lex Barker, Carl Lange, Vladimir Medar, Christiane Rucker, Dieter Eppler; ***D:*** Harald Reinl.

Torture Dungeon **1970 (R)** Director Milligan tortures audience with more mindless medieval pain infliction from Staten Island. **80m/C VHS.** Jeremy Brooks, Susan Cassidy; ***D:*** Andy Milligan.

Torture Garden **1967** A sinister man presides over an unusual sideshow where people can see what is in store if they allow the evil side of their personalities to take over. Written by Bloch ("Psycho") and based on four of his short stories. **93m/C VHS, DVD.** *GB* Jack Palance, Burgess Meredith, Peter Cushing, Beverly Adams; ***D:*** Freddie Francis; ***W:*** Robert Bloch; ***M:*** Don Banks, James Bernard.

The Torture of Silence **½** *Mater Dolorosa* **1917** A simple little drama about a doctor's neglected wife seeking out the doctor's best friend for love, remade by Gance in 1932. **55m/B VHS.** *FR* Emmy Lynn, Firmin Gemier, Armand Tallier, Anthony Gildes, Paul Vermoyal; ***D:*** Abel Gance; ***W:*** Abel Gance; ***C:*** Leonce-Henri Burel.

Torture Ship **½ 1939** Director Halperin, who earlier made the minor horror classic "White Zombie," was all at sea in this becalmed thriller about a mad doctor who uses convicts for glandular experiment in his shipboard laboratory. Based on the short story "A Thousand Deaths" by Jack London. **57m/B VHS, DVD.** Lyle Talbot, Irving Pichel, Julie Bishop, Sheila (Manors) Mannors; ***D:*** Victor Halperin.

Torture Train **½** *Night Train Murders* **1975 (R)** Mayhem, murder, and knife-wielding psychosis occurs on board a train. **78m/C VHS, DVD.** *IT* Marina Berti, Irene Miracle, Laura D'Angelo, Macha Meril, Enrico Maria Salerno, Flavio Bucci, Gianfranco de Grassi; ***D:*** Aldo Lado; ***W:*** Aldo Lado; ***C:*** Gabor Pogany; ***M:*** Ennio Morricone.

Tortured **2008 (R)** Hauser is an FBI agent who has gone undercover in a major organized crime syndicate, spending his time performing minor errands for an unseen person known only as Ziggy, who he intends to bring down. He is asked to spend a week torturing an accountant for information on $10 million dollars of Ziggy's money that's gone missing, and the feds tell him to go ahead with it rather than break cover. Somewhere in all the harm he does, he begins to notice events are taking a certain pattern, and he begins to realize all is not as it seems. **107m/C DVD.** Cole Hauser, Laurence Fishburne, James Cromwell, Emmanuelle Chriqui, Jon Cryer, James Denton; ***D:*** Nolan Lebovitz; ***W:*** Nolan Lebovitz; ***C:*** Steven Bernstein; ***M:*** Nathan Barr. **VIDEO**

Total Eclipse **1995 (R)** Unfortunate look at the mutually destructive relationship between 19th-century French poets Arthur Rimbaud (DiCaprio) and Paul Verlaine (Thewlis). Rimbaud was a 16-year-old Parisian sensation for his iconoclastic work but what's presented is an obnoxious showoff, while the older, married Verlaine is a drunken lout who abuses his teenaged wife Mathilde (Bohringer). There's lots of dissolute, violent behavior and absolutely no insight into their work (which is the only reason to care). Ugly film wastes a lot of talent. **111m/C VHS, DVD.** Leonardo DiCaprio, David Thewlis, Romane Bohringer, Dominique Blanc; ***D:*** Agnieszka Holland; ***W:*** Christopher Hampton; ***C:*** Yorgos Arvanitis; ***M:*** Jan A.P. Kaczmarek.

Total Exposure **1991 (R)** Total idiocy involving unclad babes and hormonally imbalanced men in blackmail and murder. 1990 Playboy Playmate Deborah Driggs proves there is life of sorts after playmatedom. **96m/C VHS.** Michael Nouri, Season Hubley, Christian Bocher, Robert Prentiss, Deborah Driggs, Jeff Conaway; ***D:*** John Quinn.

Total Force **1998** Two men team up to destroy a weapon that uses satellite technology to turn ordinary citizens into killers. **100m/C VHS.** Timothy Bottoms, Frank Stallone, Richard Lynch; ***D:*** Steven Kaman; ***M:*** Barry Coffing. **VIDEO**

Total Reality **½ 1997 (R)** In order to escape execution, disgraced soldier Anthony Rand (Bradley) undertakes to follow renegade general Tunis (Kretschmann) back through time and prevent the destruction of the universe. **97m/C VHS, DVD.** David Bradley, Thomas Kretschmann, Ely Pouget, Bill Shaw, Misa Koprova; ***D:*** Phillip J. Roth; ***W:*** Phillip J. Roth, Robert Tossberg; ***C:*** Andres Garreton. **VIDEO**

Total Recall **1990 (R)** Mind-bending sci-fi movie set in the 21st century. Construction worker Quaid (Schwarzenegger) dreams every night about the colonization of Mars, so he decides to visit a travel service that specializes in implanting vacation memories into its clients' brains and buy a memory trip to the planet. Only during the implant, Quaid discovers his memories have been artificially altered and he must find out just what's real and what's not. Intriguing plot and spectacular special effects. Laced with graphic violence. Based on Phillip K. Dick's "We Can Remember It for You Wholesale." **113m/C VHS, DVD, UMD.** Arnold Schwarzenegger, Rachel Ticotin, Sharon Stone, Michael Ironside, Ronny Cox, Roy Brocksmith, Marshall Bell, Mel Johnson Jr.; ***D:*** Paul Verhoeven; ***W:*** Gary Goldman, Dan O'Bannon; ***C:*** Jan De Bont; ***M:*** Jerry Goldsmith. Oscars '90: Visual FX.

Total Recall 2070: Machine Dreams **1999 (R)** Pilot movie for the brief series that had only a tentative connection to the Ah-nuld movie and the short stories of Philip K. Dick. David Hume (Easton) is a 21st century cop who is supposed to keep an eye on the Consortium, the group of private companies that unofficially now run the world. They create mayhem and he tries to clean it up. Hume must battle rogue androids and solve the murders that occurred at the virtual reality vacation agency, Total Rekall. **83m/C VHS, DVD.** Michael Easton, Karl Pruner, Cynthia (Cyndy, Cindy) Preston, Judith Krant, Nick Mancuso; ***D:*** Mario Azzopardi; ***C:*** Peter Wunstorf. **CABLE**

Total Western **2000** Rochant's homage to the spaghetti western set in modern-day France. Gerard agrees to help his boss' nephew carry out a drug deal with associates of mobster Ludo Daes. Unfortunately there's a shootout and only Gerard gets out alive—with a bag of Daes' money. He hides out on a farm where a group of juvenile delinquents are participating in a reform school program, but Daes' thugs come after him. So Gerard and the teenaged toughs come up with a plan. French with subtitles. **84m/C DVD.** *FR* Samuel Le Bihan, Jean-Pierre Kalfon, Jean-Francois Stevenin, Kahena Saighi; ***D:*** Eric Rochant; ***W:*** Eric Rochant, Laurent Chalumeau; ***C:*** Vincenzo Marano, Yves Agostini; ***M:*** Marco Prince.

Totally Blonde **2001 (PG-13)** Brunette Meg (Allen) is having trouble finding Mr. Right, so she decides to hit the peroxide bottle and see if blondes really do have more fun. Of course, club owner Van (Buble) already thinks Meg is hot but she's been looking at him as just a friend. Instead, Meg hooks up with mister hot (and rich) body Brad (Hutzler). Funny thing, Meg gets green-eyed when her pal Liv (Quinlan) decides to go after Van for herself. **98m/C VHS, DVD.** Krista Allen, Maeve Quinlan, Michael Buble, Brody Hutzler, Mindy Sterling, Charlene Tilton; ***D:*** Andrew Van Slee; ***W:*** Andrew Van Slee; ***C:*** Jim Orr; ***M:*** Andrew Van Slee, Miles Hill, Ian Putz. **VIDEO**

Totally F*ed Up** **1994** The first of director Araki's teen trilogy, followed by "The Doom Generation" and "Nowhere," concerns itself with the teen angst experienced by a loose group of friends—four gays and a lesbian couple. In short chapters, they meet, talk, and wander through a soulless L.A. as one of their group, film school student Steven (Luna), makes a video documentary about their situation (footage of which in intercut throughout the film). **80m/C VHS, DVD.** James Duval, Gilbert Luna, Lance May, Roko Belic, Susan Behshid, Jenee Gill, Alan Boyce; ***D:*** Gregg Araki; ***W:*** Gregg Araki; ***C:*** Gregg Araki.

Toto le Heros *Toto the Hero* **1991 (PG-13)** Bitter old man, who as a child fantasized that he was a secret agent named Toto, harbors deep resentment over not living the life he's convinced he should have had. He maintains a childhood fantasy that he and his rich neighbor were switched at birth in the confusion of a fire at the hospital. Series of flashbacks and fast forwards show glimpses of his life, not necessarily as it was, but how he perceived it. Sounds complex, but it's actually very clear and fluid. Mix of comedy and tragedy, with lots of ironic twists, and precise visuals. In French with English subtitles. **90m/C VHS, DVD.** *FR* Michel Bouquet, Jo De Backer, Thomas Godet, Mireille Perrier, Sandrine Blancke, Didier Ferney, Hugo Harold Harrisson, Gisela Uhlen, Peter Bohlke; ***D:*** Jaco Van Dormael; ***W:*** Jaco Van Dormael; ***C:*** Walther Vanden Ende; ***M:*** Pierre Van Dormael. Cesar '91: Foreign Film.

The Touch **½** *Be Roringen* **1971 (R)** Straightforward story of a woman who is satisfied with her husband until the arrival of a stranger. The stranger soon has her yearning for a life she has never known. Bergman's first English film lacks the sophistication of his earlier work. **112m/C VHS.** *SW* Bibi Andersson, Elliott Gould, Max von Sydow; ***D:*** Ingmar Bergman; ***W:*** Ingmar Bergman; ***C:*** Sven Nykvist.

Touch **½ 1996 (R)** Sleazebags, fundamentalists, and a maybe saint would seem to make for a surefire success in this easygoing adaptation of the offbeat Elmore Leonard novel. And while individual scenes and performances shine, the film doesn't completely hang together. Young Juvenal (Ulrich) is a former monk, now working at an L.A. alcohol rehab center, who possesses the stigmata and seems to have an authentic gift for healing. Naturally, this brings the crazies and the scammers out of the woodwork, including former preacher Bill Hill (Walken), whose partner (Fonda) falls for the lad, and paramilitary religious fanatic August Murray (Arnold). **96m/C VHS.** Skeet Ulrich, Bridget Fonda, Christopher Walken, Tom Arnold, Gina Gershon, Lolita (David) Davidovich, Paul Mazursky, Janeane Garofalo, John Doe, Conchata Ferrell, Mason Adams, Breckin Meyer, Anthony Zerbe; ***D:*** Paul Schrader; ***W:*** Paul Schrader; ***C:*** Edward Lachman; ***M:*** David Grohl.

Touch & Go **1980 (PG)** Three beautiful women commit grand larceny in order to raise funds for underprivileged children. **92m/C VHS.** *AU* Wendy Hughes; ***D:*** Peter Maxwell; ***W:*** Alan Ormsby.

Touch and Go **½ 1986 (R)** Sentimental drama about a self-interested hockey pro who learns about love and giving through a young delinquent and his attractive mother. **101m/C VHS.** Michael Keaton, Maria Conchita Alonso, Ajay Naidu, Maria Tucci, Max Wright, John C. Reilly; ***D:*** Robert Mandel; ***W:*** Harry Colomby.

Touch Me Not *The Hunted* **1974 (PG)** A neurotic secretary is used by an industrial spy to gain information on her boss. Weak thriller. **84m/C VHS, DVD.** *GB* Lee Remick, Michael Hinz, Ivan Desny, Ingrid Garbo; ***D:*** Douglas Fifthian.

A Touch of Class **1973 (PG)** Married American insurance adjustor working in London plans quick and uncommitted affair but finds his heart doesn't obey the rules. Jackson and Segal create sparkling record of a growing relationship. **105m/C VHS, DVD.** George Segal, Glenda Jackson, Paul Sorvino, Hildegard(e) Neil, K. Callan, Mary Barclay, Cec Linder; ***D:*** Melvin Frank; ***W:*** Jack Rose; ***C:*** Austin Dempster; ***M:*** John Cameron. Oscars '73: Actress (Jackson); Golden Globes '74: Actor—Mus./Comedy (Segal), Actress—Mus./Comedy (Jackson); Writers Guild '73: Orig. Screenplay.

Touch of Evil **1958 (PG-13)** Stark, perverse story of murder, kidnapping, and police corruption in Mexican border town. Welles portrays a police chief who invents evidence to convict the guilty. Filled with innovative photography reminiscent of "Citizen Kane," as filmed by Russell Metty. In 1998, Walter Murch restored the film working from Welles's notes, re-editing the work to what Welles had originally envisioned before studio intervention; this version is 101 minutes and is unrated. **108m/B VHS, DVD.** Charlton Heston, Orson Welles, Janet Leigh, Joseph Calleia, Akim Tamiroff, Marlene Dietrich, Valentin de Vargas, Dennis Weaver, Joanna Moore, Mort Mills, Victor Millan, Ray Collins; ***Cameos:*** Joi Lansing, Zsa Zsa Gabor, Mercedes McCambridge, Joseph Cotten; ***D:*** Orson Welles; ***W:*** Orson Welles; ***C:*** Russell Metty; ***M:*** Henry Mancini. Natl. Film Reg. '93.

Touch of Pink **2004 (R)** Kyle MacLachlan plays the ghost of Cary Grant as he advises Alim (Mistry), a gay Pakistani film studio photographer. It seems Alim needs the advice, as his conservative mother (Mathew), whom he has yet to tell of his sexual orientation, is coming to visit him. Of course, Alim, who lives with his British lover Giles (Holden-Ried), decides to hide the fact with a fake fiancee. The usual hijinx occur.

Mostly unremarkable except for a great performance by MacLachlan. **92m/C VHS, DVD.** Jimi Mistry, Kyle MacLachlan, Kris Holden-Ried, Brian George, Lisa Repo Martell, Suleka Mathew, Veena Sood, Raoul Bhaneja; ***D:*** Ian Iqbal Rashid; ***W:*** Ian Iqbal Rashid; ***C:*** David Makin; ***M:*** Andrew Lockington.

The Touch of Satan *The Touch of Melissa; Night of the Demon; Curse of Melissa* **1970 (PG)** Lost on the road, a young man meets a lovely young woman and is persuaded to stay at her nearby farmhouse. Things there are not as they seem, including the young woman—who turns out to be a very old witch. **90m/C VHS, DVD.** Michael Berry, Emby Mallay, Lee Amber, Yvonne Wilson, Jeanne Gerson; ***D:*** Don Henderson.

Touch the Top of the World 1/2 **2006** Well-done inspirational pic based on the autobiography of Erik Weihenmayer. As a child, Erik (Facinelli) is diagnosed with a rare eye disease that leads to blindness. His parents (Campbell, Greenhouse) challenge him to make any dream a reality and Erik becomes an expert ice and rock climber with the ultimate goal of being the first blind person to reach the top of Mount Everest. **89m/C DVD.** Peter Facinelli, Bruce Campbell, Kate Greenhouse, Sarah Manninen, Robert Moloney, Saxon DeCocq; ***D:*** Peter Winther; ***W:*** Peter Silverman; ***C:*** Attila Szalay; ***M:*** Joseph LoDuca. **CABLE**

Touchdown 1/2 **1931** College football coach Dan Curtis (Arlen) is a win-at-all-costs kind of guy, that is until one of players is seriously injured after Curtis pushes him too hard. Things come to a head when the team is set to play their arch-rival, and Curtis has to decide which is more important—his team or the win? **m/B VHS.** Richard Arlen, Peggy Shannon, Jack Oakie, Regis Toomey, George Barbier, J. Farrell MacDonald, George Irving; ***D:*** Norman Z. McLeod; ***W:*** Grover Jones, William Slavens McNutt.

Touched **1982 (R)** Two young people struggle with the outside world after their escape from a mental institution. Although melodramatic and poorly scripted, the film is saved by fine performances by Hays and Beller. **89m/C VHS.** Robert Hays, Kathleen Beller, Ned Beatty, Gilbert Lewis; ***D:*** John Flynn.

Touched **2005 (R)** A terrible car accident claims the life of Scott Davis' (Batinkoff) young son and leaves Scott in a coma for two years. He awakens in a long-term care facility under the supervision of nurse Angela Martin (Elfman). Scott's wealthy parents (Venora, Davidson) decide to bring him home but since it appears that Scott has lost his sense of touch and is suffering hallucinations, they hire Angela as a live-in nurse. Scott and Angela fall in love. It's not quite as sappy as it sounds and it's refreshing to see the sunny Elfman try her talents in a drama. **90m/C DVD.** Jenna Elfman, Randall Batinkoff, Samantha Mathis, Diane Venora, Frederick Koehler, Mina (Badiyi) Badie, Bruce Davidson; ***D:*** Timothy Scott Bogart; ***W:*** Timothy Scott Bogart; ***C:*** Irv Goodnoff. **VIDEO**

Touched by Love 1/2 *To Elvis, With Love* **1980 (PG)** The true story of a handicapped child who begins to communicate when her teacher suggests she write to Elvis Presley. Sincere and well performed. **95m/C VHS.** Deborah Raffin, Diane Lane, Christina Raines, Clu Gulager, John Amos; ***D:*** Gus Trikonis; ***W:*** Hesper Anderson; ***M:*** John Barry.

Touching Evil **1997** London police detective Dave Creegan (Green) and his fellow cops at the (fictional) Organized and Serial Crime Unit investigate three creepy cases in this three-tape series. The first concerns the kidnapping of three small boys; the second involves patients being drugged and killed while in hospital; and the third involves corpses, university students, and the Internet. The detectives are a fine, flawed unit and make for some interesting company. Followed by two sequels. **360m/C VHS.** *GB* Robson Green, Ian McDiarmid, Nicola Walker, Michael Feast, Adam Kotz, Kenneth MacDonald, Antony Byrne, Shaun Dingwall; ***D:*** Julian Jarrold, Marc Munden; ***W:*** Paul Abbott, Russell T. Davies; ***C:*** David Odd; ***M:*** Adrian Johnston. **TV**

Touching the Void **2003** Documentarian Macdonald turns to reenactments to provide a dramatic narrative for this saga of two British climbers whose adventure in the Peruvian Andes in 1985 goes horribly wrong. Simpson (Mackey) and Yates (Aaron), both in their early twenties, decide to test their abilities on the previously unclimbed west face of Siula Grande. They make it to the top but are beset by a storm during their descent when Simpson breaks his leg. Yates attempts to lower his partner down the mountain but Simpson goes into a crevasse. Uncertain if Simpson is still alive, Yates must then decide whether to cut the rope binding them together and make his way alone back to base camp or risk dying himself. How they both survive constitutes the rest of this harrowing story of survival. Simpson and Yates provide their own narration; based on the book by Simpson. **106m/C VHS, DVD.** Brendan Mackey, Nicholas Aaron; ***D:*** Kevin MacDonald; ***C:*** Mike Eley; ***M:*** Alex Heffes.

Tough and Deadly 1/2 **1994 (R)** CIA agent teams up with bounty hunter to stop a drug ring. **92m/C VHS.** Richard Norton, James Karen, Charles Kahlenberg, Billy Blanks, Roddy Piper; ***D:*** Steve Cohen; ***W:*** Steve Cohen; ***C:*** James Roberson; ***M:*** William Kidd.

Tough Assignment **1949** A reporter in the West discovers and infiltrates a gang of organized rustlers who are forcing butchers to buy inferior meat. **64m/B VHS, DVD.** Donald (Don "Red") Barry, Marjorie Steele, Steve Brodie, Marc Lawrence, Ben Welden, Sid Melton, John Cason, Fred Kohler Jr., Michael Whalen, Stanley Price, Leander De Cordova, William Beaudine; ***W:*** Carl K. Hittleman; ***C:*** Benjamin (Ben H.) Kline; ***M:*** Albert Glasser.

Tough Enough **1983 (PG)** A country-western singer and songwriter decides to finance his fledgling singing career by entering amateur boxing matches. Insipid and predictable, with fine cast wasted. **107m/C VHS, DVD.** Dennis Quaid, Charlene Watkins, Warren Oates, Pam Grier, Stan Shaw, Bruce McGill, Wilford Brimley, Bob Watson; ***D:*** Richard Fleischer.

Tough Guy **1953** Based on the play by Bruce Walker, a London hood carouses, mugs, breaks hearts and personifies his generation's anxiety. **73m/B VHS.** *GB* James Kenney, Hermione Gingold, Joan Collins; ***D:*** Lewis Gilbert.

Tough Guy *Kung Fu: The Head Crusher* **1970** Two undercover policemen battle local gangsters in a bid to smash their crime ring. **90m/C VHS, DVD.** Chen Ying, Charlie Chiang; ***D:*** Chieng Hung.

Tough Guys 1/2 **1986 (PG)** Two aging ex-cons, who staged America's last train robbery in 1961, try to come to terms with modern life after many years in prison. Amazed and hurt by the treatment of the elderly in the 1980s, frustrated with their inability to find something worthwhile to do, they begin to plan one last heist. Tailor-made for Lancaster and Douglas, who are wonderful. Script becomes cliched at end. **103m/C VHS.** Burt Lancaster, Kirk Douglas, Charles Durning, Eli Wallach, Jake Steinfeld, Dana Carvey, Alexis Smith, Darlanne Fluegel, Billy Barty, Monty Ash; ***D:*** Jeff Kanew; ***W:*** James Orr, Jim Cruickshank; ***M:*** James Newton Howard.

Tough Guys Don't Dance 1/2 **1987 (R)** Mailer directed this self-satiric mystery thriller from his own novel. A writer may have committed murder—but he can't remember. So he searches for the truth among various friends, enemies, lovers, and cohorts. **110m/C VHS, DVD.** Ryan O'Neal, Isabella Rossellini, Wings Hauser, Debra Sandlund, John Bedford Lloyd, Lawrence Tierney, Clarence Williams III, Penn Jillette, Frances Fisher; ***D:*** Norman Mailer; ***W:*** Norman Mailer; ***C:*** John Bailey; ***M:*** Angelo Badalamenti. Golden Raspberries '87: Worst Director (Mailer).

Tough Kid **1939** A bad kid with gang connections attempts to shield his boxer brother from corruption at the hands of the same gang. Poor production all around. **61m/B VHS.** Frankie Darro, Dick Purcell, Judith Allen, Lillian Elliot; ***D:*** Howard Bretherton.

Tough to Handle 1/2 **1937** ...And no picnic to watch, either. A reporter cracks a criminal racket that rips off lottery sweepstakes winners. A laughably inept production. **58m/B VHS.** Frankie Darro, Kane Richmond, Phyllis Fraser, Harry Worth; ***D:*** S. Roy Luby.

Tougher Than Leather **1988 (R)** The rap triumvirate battles criminals, vigilante-style, in their home neighborhood. Poorly executed and exploitative fare. **92m/C VHS.** Run DMC, The Beastie Boys, Slick Rick, Richard Edson, Jenny Lumet; ***D:*** Rick Rubin.

Toughlove **1985** The parents of a juvenile delinquent organize a tough parental philosophy and a support group for other parents having a difficult time with their teens. **100m/C VHS.** Lee Remick, Bruce Dern, Piper Laurie, Louise Latham, Dana Elcar, Jason Patric, Eric Schiff, Dedee Pfeiffer; ***D:*** Glenn Jordan. **TV**

Touki Bouki *Journey of the Hyena* **1973** Feeling alienated from their African society, Mory and Anta see freedom in the flashy consumerism of European culture and embark on a quest to meet happiness in Paris. A Bonnie & Clyde-like story symbolizing Africa's advancement toward a technological civilization. In Wolof with English subtitles. **85m/C VHS, DVD.** *SE* Magaye Niange, Mareme Niange, Aminata Fall, Ousseynou Diop; ***D:*** Djibril Diop Mambety; ***W:*** Djibril Diop Mambety; ***C:*** Georges Bracher.

Tour of Duty 1/2 **1987** Follows the trials that the members of an American platoon face daily during the Vietnam war. Pilot for the TV series. **93m/C VHS, DVD.** Terence Knox, Stephen Caffrey, Joshua Maurer, Ramon Franco; ***D:*** Bill W.L. Norton. **TV**

Tourist Trap **1979 (PG)** While traveling through the desert, a couple's car has a flat. A woman's voice lures the man into an abandoned gas station, where he discovers that the voice belongs to a mannequin. Or is it? Not very interesting or suspenseful. **90m/C VHS, DVD.** Tanya Roberts, Chuck Connors, Robin Sherwood, Jocelyn Jones, Jon Van Ness, Dawn Jeffory, Keith McDermott; ***D:*** David Schmoeller; ***W:*** David Schmoeller; ***C:*** Nicholas Josef von Sternberg; ***M:*** Pino Donaggio.

Tourist Trap 1/2 **1998** Frustrated banker George Piper (Stern) decides his family needs "together" time. So he buys an RV and shanghais his workaholic wife (Hagerty) and rebellious kids into a vacation. George decides to retrace the footsteps of his famous ancestor Jeremiah Piper and leads his brood into all kinds of comic misadventures. **89m/C VHS.** Daniel Stern, Julie Hagerty, Margot Finley, Blair Slater, Paul Giamatti, David Rasche, Ken Tremblett; ***D:*** Richard Benjamin. **VIDEO**

Tournament 1/2 *Le Tournoi dans la Cite* **1929** Renoir's second-to-last silent film, in which Protestants and Catholics joust out their differences in era of Catherine de Medici. **90m/B VHS.** *FR* Enrique Rivero, Suzanne Despress, Blanche Bernis, Gerard Mack, Jackie Monnier, Aldo Nadi; ***D:*** Jean Renoir; ***W:*** Jean Renoir.

The Tournament **2009 (R)** Every 10 years, 30 of the world's best killers face off in a winner-take-all contest where the last assassin standing gets a very big payoff. This time the killing field is a small Scottish town and the local clergyman (Carlyle) may not be exactly what he seems. Meanwhile, gamblers watch and bet on the outcome via closed-circuit TV. Offers undemanding, fast-paced action. **95m/C DVD.** *GB* Ving Rhames, Robert Carlyle, Kelly Hu, Ian Somerhalder, Scott Adkins, Liam Cunningham; ***D:*** Scott Mann; ***W:*** Jonathan Frank, Nick Rowntree, Nick Rowntree; ***C:*** Gary Young; ***M:*** Emil Topuzov, Laura Karpman. **VIDEO**

Tous les Matins du Monde *All the Mornings of the World* **1992** Haunting tale of two 17th century French baroque composers and their relationship with each other and their music. Gerard Depardieu plays Marin Marais who eventually becomes a court composer at Versailles. As a young man, he studies under Sainte Colombe, a private and soulful musician, about whom little is known even today. Depardieu's son Guillaume (in his film debut) plays the young Marais, who startles the quiet Sainte Colombe home and has an affair with one of his daughters (Brochet). Filmmaker Corneau lends a quiet austere tone which parallels the life and music of Sainte Colombe. In French with English subtitles. **114m/C VHS, DVD.** *FR* Gerard Depardieu, Guillaume Depardieu, Jean-Pierre Marielle, Anne Brochet, Caroline Sihol, Carole Richert, Violaine Lacroix, Nadege Teron, Miriam Boyer, Michel Bouquet; ***D:*** Alain Corneau; ***W:*** Pascal Quignard, Alain Corneau; ***C:*** Yves Angelo; ***M:*** Jordi Savall. Cesar '92: Cinematog., Director (Corneau), Film, Support. Actress (Brochet), Score.

Toute Une Nuit *All Night Long* **1982** Assorted people stumble melodramatically in and out of one another's lives on steamy summer night in Brussels. Fine combination of avant-garde technique and narrative. In French with English subtitles. **90m/C VHS.** *BE FR* Aurore Clement, Tcheky Karyo, Veronique Silver, Angelo Abazoglou, Natalia Ackerman; ***D:*** Chantal Akerman; ***W:*** Andra Akers.

Toward the Terra **1980** In the distant future mankind is forced to evacuate Earth and settles on the planet Atarakusha. Society ruthlessly suppresses anything which could destabalize it in an effort to prevent the mistakes which destroyed the Earth. The most destablizing presence is the MU, a new race with incredible mental powers, who are ruthlessly hunted and eliminated. But the leader of the MU reaches out to a human with his own inexplicable powers to aid in establishing a new world. In Japanese with subtitles. **112m/C VHS.** *JP* ***D:*** Hideo Onchi; ***W:*** Hideo Onchi; ***M:*** Masaru Sato; ***V:*** Toru Furuya, Yasuo Hisamatsu, Taro Shigaki, Masako Ikeda.

Towards Darkness *Hacia la Oscuridad* **2007 (R)** Jose Gutierrez has just returned home to Colombia when he's kidnapped. Since kidnapping is a big business in the country, the Gutierrez family thought they were prepared but their insurance won't pay the ransom after all. With the kidnappers getting impatient, the family brings in a team of hostage negotiators but time is running out. Colombian-born Negret knows the situation but he overstuffs his story with a number of subplots that lessen the tension. English and Spanish with subtitles. **92m/C DVD.** Tony Plana, David Sutcliffe, William Atherton, America Ferrera, Cameron Daddo, Carlos Valencia, Alonso Arias, Fernando Solorzano, Roberto Urbina; ***D:*** Jose Antonio Negret; ***W:*** Jose Antonio Negret; ***C:*** John Ealer; ***M:*** Chris Westlake.

Towelhead *Nothing is Private* **2007 (R)** Jasira (Bishil), a 13-year-old Lebanese-American girl living with her mother in Syracuse, New York, obsesses over her newly discovered sexuality to the point that her mother fears for the girl's safety and ships her off to live with her father in Houston. Dad seems nice, but explodes with rage, violence, and even racism when confronting Jasira's womanhood—slapping her for wearing a t-shirt, forbidding her to use tampons, and keeping her away from the black teenage boy next door. Good thing he doesn't know about the father of the kid she babysits, who takes a sick liking to the girl. An overtly melodramatic button-pusher from experienced suburban nightmare writer Ball ("American Beauty"), who lays it on too thick. Based on the 2005 novel by Alicia Erian. **124m/C DVD.** *US* Summer Bishil, Aaron Eckhart, Maria Bello, Toni Collette, Peter Macdissi, Matt Letscher, Chris Messina, Carrie Preston, Chase Ellison, Shari Headley, Lynn Collins, Gemmenne de la Pena, Eugene Jones III; ***D:*** Alan Ball; ***W:*** Alan Ball; ***C:*** Newton Thomas (Tom) Sigel; ***M:*** Thomas Newman.

Tower of Evil WOOF! *Horror on Snape Island; Beyond the Fog* **1972 (R)** Anthropologists and treasure hunters unite in search of Phoenician hoard on Snape Island. Suddenly, inanimate bodies materialize. Seems the island's single inhabitant liked it quiet. Cult favorite despite uneven performances. So bad it's not bad. **86m/C VHS, DVD.** *GB* Bryant Haliday, Jill Haworth, Jack Watson, Mark Edwards, George Coulouris; ***D:*** James O'Connolly; ***W:*** James O'Connolly; ***C:*** Desmond Dickinson; ***M:*** Kenneth V. Jones.

The Tower of London 1/2 **1939** Tells the story of Richard III (Rathbone), the English monarch who brutally executed the people who tried to get in his way to the throne. This melodrama was considered extremely graphic for its time, and some of the torture scenes had to be cut before it was released. **93m/B VHS.** Basil Rathbone, Boris Karloff, Barbara O'Neil, Ian Hunter, Vincent Price, Nan Grey, John Sutton, Leo G. Carroll, Miles Mander; ***D:*** Rowland V. Lee; ***W:*** Robert N. Lee; ***C:*** George Robinson; ***M:*** Hans J. Salter, Frank Skinner.

Tower of London **1962** A deranged lord (Price) murdering his way to the throne of England is eventually crowned Richard III. Sophisticated and well-made Poe-like thriller. More interesting as historic melodrama than as horror film. A remake of the 1939 version starring Basil Rathbone, in which Price played a supporting role. **79m/B VHS, DVD.** Vincent Price, Michael Pate, Joan Freeman, Robert Brown, Sandra Knight, Justice Watson; ***D:*** Roger Corman; ***W:*** Leo Gordon, F. Amos Powell, James B. Gordon; ***C:*** Arch R. Dalzell; ***M:*** Michael Anderson.

Tower of Screaming Virgins
1968 The Queen of France maintains a tower in which she has her lovers killed—after she makes love to them. An extremely loose adaptation of a Dumas novel; with English subtitles. **89m/C VHS.** *GE* Uschi Glas, Marie-Ange Anies, Terry Torday, Jean Piat; ***D:*** Franz Antel; ***W:*** Kurt Nachmann; ***C:*** Oberdan Troiani; ***M:*** Mario Migliardi.

Tower of Terror 1/2 **1942 (NC-17)** Woman escapes from a German concentration camp and takes refuge in a lighthouse. The proprietor sees in her an uncanny resemblance to his late wife, whom he killed, and soon plots to do away with her. Story hampered by poor acting. **62m/B VHS.** *GB* Wilfred Lawson, Movita, Michael Rennie, Morland Graham, John Longden, George Woodbridge; ***D:*** Lawrence Huntington.

Tower of Terror 1/2 **1997** This Disney TV movie really isn't very scary and is related to the thrill ride located at Disney World. Disgraced reporter Buzzy (Guttenberg) and his niece (Dunst) investigate the 60-year-old murder of the family of a popular 1930s child star in a supposedly haunted hotel. **89m/C VHS, DVD.** Steve Guttenberg, Kirsten Dunst, Nia Peeples; ***D:*** D.J. MacHale. **TV**

Tower of the Firstborn *I Guardiani del Cielo* **1998 (PG-13)** Archeologist Diane goes searching the Sahara desert for her missing father, whom she believes discovered the legendary ancient tower of the title, which contains vast knowledge of the universe. Or something like that because this tedious production never makes much sense. Originally broadcast as a miniseries on Italian TV. **180m/C DVD.** *IT* Ione Skye, Peter Weller, Ben Cross, Guy Lankester, Heino Ferch, Marco Bonini; ***D:*** Alberto Negrin; ***W:*** Alberto Negrin, George Eastman; ***M:*** Ennio Morricone. **TV**

The Towering Inferno **1974 (PG)** Raging blaze engulfs the world's tallest skyscraper on the night of its glamorous dedication ceremonies. Allen had invented the disaster du jour genre two years earlier with "The Poseidon Adventure." Features a new but equally noteworthy cast. ♫We May Never Love Like This Again. **165m/C VHS, DVD.** Steve McQueen, Paul Newman, William Holden, Faye Dunaway, Fred Astaire, Jennifer Jones, Richard Chamberlain, Susan Blakely, O.J. Simpson, Robert Vaughn, Robert Wagner; ***D:*** John Guillermin, Irwin Allen; ***W:*** Stirling Silliphant; ***C:*** Joseph Biroc, Fred W. Koenekamp; ***M:*** John Williams. Oscars '74: Cinematog., Film Editing, Song ("We May Never Love Like This Again"); British Acad. '75: Support. Actor (Astaire); Golden Globes '75: Support. Actor (Astaire).

Town and Country **2001 (R)** Yep, it's as bad as you've heard. The oft-delayed and much-discussed romantic-comedy features characters you don't care about (rich Manhattanites with more money than they need) in situations that've been done to death (bed-hopping amidst middle age angst and closet-hiding). Shandling and Beatty are the cad husbands who decide to risk 25-year marriages in the name of fighting boredom. Keaton and Hawn are the revenge-fueled wives. All are upstaged by Heston and Seldes as the gun-toting, foul-mouthed parents of one of Beatty's dalliances (McDowell). **104m/C VHS, DVD.** *US* Warren Beatty, Diane Keaton, Goldie Hawn, Andie MacDowell, Jenna Elfman, Garry Shandling, Charlton Heston, Marian Seldes, Tricia Vessey, Josh Hartnett, Nastassja Kinski, Katharine Towne, Buck Henry; ***D:*** Peter Chelsom; ***W:*** Buck Henry, Michael Laughlin; ***C:*** William A. Fraker; ***M:*** Rolfe Kent.

A Town Called Hell *A Town Called Bastard* **1972 (R)** Two men hold an entire town hostage while looking for "Aguila," the Mexican revolutionary. Greed, evil, and violence take over. Shot in Spain. Whatever you call it, just stay out of it. **95m/C VHS, DVD.** *GB SP* Robert Shaw, Stella Stevens, Martin Landau, Telly Savalas, Fernando Rey; ***D:*** Robert Parrish.

A Town Has Turned to Dust 1/2
1998 Lame remake of a 1958 Rod Serling script for "Playhouse 90." Serling's story was set in the old west; this version goes for sci-fi and a futuristic desert town called Carbon run by mob boss Perlman who controls the water supply and the main industry, which is mining. But when Perlman hangs an innocent man, he finally provoking drunken sheriff Lang to take action. **91m/C VHS, DVD.** Ron Perlman, Stephen Lang, Gabriel Olds, Judy Collins; ***W:*** Rod Serling. **CABLE**

The Town Is Quiet 1/2 *La Ville Est Tranquille* **2000** This town isn't quiet at all. Michele (Ascaride) works in a Marseilles fish market and then returns to her dingy apartment to care for her junkie prostitute daughter Fiona (Parmetier), the latter's baby daughter, and her own alcoholic husband (Banderet). Taxi driver Paul (Darroussin) pays Michele for sex so she can buy drugs for her daughter from her former lover Gerard (Meylan). There's several subplots, murders, and a suicide. Don't watch if you're prone to depression. French with subtitles. **132m/C VHS, DVD.** *FR* Ariane Ascaride, Gerard Meylan, Julie-Marie Parmentier, Pierre Banderet, Jean-Pierre Darroussin, Jacques Boudet, Pascale Roberts, Jacques Pieller, Christine Brucher, Alexandre Ogou; ***D:*** Robert Guediguian; ***W:*** Robert Guediguian, Jean-Louis Milesi; ***C:*** Bernard Cavalie.

A Town Like Alice 1/2 **1985** An Australian miniseries based on a novel by Nevil Shute. The story follows women prisoners of war during WWII. Jean Paget is a British prisoner in the camps of Malaya when she meets and falls in love with a fellow prisoner, the rugged Australian, Joe. Separated by their captors, they reunite years later and try to see if their love has survived. Remake of a 1951 film of the same name that is also known as "Rape of Malaya." **301m/C VHS.** *AU* Bryan Brown, Helen Morse, Gordon Jackson; ***D:*** David Stevens. **TV**

The Town That Banned Christmas 1/2 *A Merry Little Christmas* **2006** Christmas is banned in Greenlawn when the town's annual decorating contest turns ruthless, all because of new resident Norbert Bridges (McCoy). Bridges is writing a book on human behavior and goads his neighbors into a must-win mentality so he can study what happens. But when he realizes he's ruined the holiday, Bridges tries to restore the true Christmas spirit. **85m/C DVD.** Matt McCoy, Jane Sibbett, Adam Ferrara, Carol Alt, Christa B. Allen, Anne Ramsay; ***D:*** John Dowling Jr.; ***W:*** P. J. McIlvaine; ***C:*** Robe Haley; ***M:*** Jeff Denlea, Peter Mazzeo.

Town That Dreaded Sundown 1/2 **1976 (R)** A mad killer is on the loose in a small Arkansas town. Based on a true story, this famous 1946 murder spree remains an unsolved mystery. **90m/C VHS.** Ben Johnson, Andrew Prine, Dawn Wells, Jimmy Clem, Charles B. Pierce; ***D:*** Charles B. Pierce; ***W:*** Earl E. Smith; ***C:*** Jim Roberson.

Town without Pity 1/2 *Stadt ohne Mitleid* **1961** Though the subject of this courtroom drama remains far too timely, its treatment is dated in some key scenes. Of course, being 40 years old will do that to a movie. In 1960, four American GIs (Blake, Jaeckel, Sutton, Sondock) stationed in Germany are accused of raping a local girl, Karin (Kaufmann). Lawyer Steve Garrett (Douglas) is brought in to defend them and elects to put the young woman on trial and on the stand. Gripping courtroom tale never fails to deliver dramatic punch. Based on the Manfred Gregor novel "The Verdict." Gene Pitney had his biggest hit with the Academy Award-nominated title song. **103m/B VHS, DVD.** *GE* Kirk Douglas, E.G. Marshall, Robert (Bobby) Blake, Richard Jaeckel, Frank Sutton, Alan Gifford, Barbara Rutting, Christine Kaufmann, Mal Sondock; ***D:*** Gottfried Reinhardt; ***W:*** Silvia Reinhardt, Georg Hurdalek; ***C:*** Kurt Hasse; ***M:*** Dimitri Tiomkin. Golden Globes '61: Song ("Town without Pity").

The Toxic Avenger 1/2 **1986 (R)** Tongue-in-cheek, cult fave has 98-pound weakling Melvin (Torgl) fall into barrel of toxic waste to emerge as Toxie (Cohen), a lumbering, bloodthirsty hulk of sludge and mire. He falls for blind babe Sara (Maranda) and sets out to do good (and get revenge). Set in the legendary city of TromaVille. Billed as "The first Super-Hero from New Jersey." Followed by: "The Toxic Avenger, Part 2;" "The Toxic Avenger, Part 3: The Last Temptation of Toxie;" and "Citizen Toxie: The Toxic Avenger, Part 4." **90m/C VHS, DVD, UMD.** Mitchell Cohen, Andree Maranda, Jennifer Baptist, Robert Prichard, Cindy Manion, Mark Torgl, David Weiss; ***D:*** Michael Herz, Lloyd Kaufman; ***W:*** Joe Ritter; ***C:*** James London.

The Toxic Avenger, Part 2 1/2 **1989 (R)** Sequel to "Toxic Avenger." Hulky slimer targets Japanese corporations that built toxic chemical dump in Tromaville. Followed by "The Toxic Avenger, Part 3: The Last Temptation of Toxie." **90m/C VHS, DVD.** Ron Fazio, Phoebe Legere, Rick Collins, John Altamura, Rikiya Yasuoka, Lisa Gaye, Mayako Katsuragi; ***D:*** Michael Herz, Lloyd Kaufman; ***W:*** Lloyd Kaufman, Gay Partington Terry; ***C:*** James London; ***M:*** Barrie Guard.

The Toxic Avenger, Part 3: The Last Temptation of Toxie 1/2
1989 (R) Unemployed superhero is tempted to sell out to greedy capitalists when his cutie Claire needs an eye operation. Also available in an unrated version. **102m/C VHS, DVD.** Ron Fazio, Phoebe Legere, John Altamura, Rick Collins, Lisa Gaye, Jessica Dublin; ***D:*** Michael Herz, Lloyd Kaufman; ***W:*** Gay Partington Terry, Lloyd Kaufman; ***C:*** James London; ***M:*** Christopher De Marco.

The Toy 1/2 **1982 (PG)** Penniless reporter finds himself the new "toy" of the spoiled son of a multimillionaire oil man. Unfortunate casting of Pryor as the toy owned by Gleason, with heavy-handed lecturing about earning friends. Slow and terrible remake of the Pierre Richard comedy "Le Jouet." **102m/C VHS, DVD.** Richard Pryor, Jackie Gleason, Ned Beatty, Wilfrid Hyde-White, Scott Schwartz; ***D:*** Richard Donner; ***W:*** Carol Sobieski; ***C:*** Laszlo Kovacs; ***M:*** Patrick Williams.

Toy Soldiers 1/2 **1984 (R)** A group of college students are held for ransom in a war-torn Central American country. When they escape, they join forces with a seasoned mercenary who leads them as a vigilante force. **85m/C VHS, DVD.** Cleavon Little, Jason Miller, Tim Robbins, Tracy Scoggins; ***D:*** David Fisher.

Toy Soldiers **1991 (R)** This unlikely action tale stops short of being laughable but still has a fair share of silliness. South American narco-terrorists seize an exclusive boys' school. The mischievous students turn their talent for practical jokes to resistance-fighting. Orbach has an uncredited cameo. Based on a novel by William P. Kennedy. **104m/C VHS, DVD.** Sean Astin, Wil Wheaton, Keith Coogan, Andrew Divoff, Denholm Elliott, Louis Gossett Jr., Shawn (Michael) Phelan; ***Cameos:*** Jerry Orbach; ***D:*** Daniel Petrie Jr.; ***W:*** Daniel Petrie Jr.; ***C:*** Thomas Burstyn; ***M:*** Robert Folk.

Toy Story **1995 (G)** First feature length, wholly computer animated film confirms what we suspected all along—toys do have lives of their own when we're not around. Pull-string cowboy Woody (Hanks), as favorite toy, presides over his fellow playthings in Andy's room. Enter new toy on the block, Buzz Lightyear (Allen), a space ranger action figure who thinks he's real. Jealous Woody and his delusional, high-tech companion soon find themselves in the outside world, where they must join forces to survive. Funny, intelligent script and voice characterizations that rival many live-action movies in depth and emotion. All this, and Don Rickles berating an actual hockey puck. **84m/C VHS, DVD, UMD.** ***D:*** John Lasseter; ***W:*** Joss Whedon, Joel Cohen, Alec Sokolow; ***M:*** Randy Newman; ***V:*** Tom Hanks, Tim Allen, Annie Potts, John Ratzenberger, Wallace Shawn, Jim Varney, Don Rickles, John Morris, R. Lee Ermey, Laurie Metcalf, Erik von Detten. Natl. Film Reg. '05.

Toy Story 2 **1999 (G)** Woody is kidnapped by a greedy toy collector and finds out that he was the star of a popular '50s children's show (think Howdy Doody) with a posse of his own. Buzz and the other denizens of Andy's room set out to save him, and in the process meet up with Buzz's archnemesis Emperor Zurg. All of the original cast members return to their now-classic characters, and the plentiful new characters, in-jokes, and tributes to other movies keep this installment just as entertaining for kids and adults as the original. This one actually has more depth than the first, dealing with issues such as mortality and the meaning of (a toy's) life. Watch for the outtakes reel while the final credits roll. **92m/C VHS, DVD.** ***D:*** John Lasseter, Lee Unkrich, Ash Bannon; ***W:*** Ash Bannon, Rita Hsiao, Doug Chamberlin, Chris Webb, Andrew Stanton; ***M:*** Randy Newman; ***V:*** Tom Hanks, Tim Allen, Joan Cusack, Don Rickles, John Ratzenberger, Annie Potts, Wayne Knight, Laurie Metcalf, Jim Varney, Estelle Harris, Kelsey Grammer, Wallace Shawn, John Morris, R. Lee Ermey, Jodi Benson, Jonathan Harris, Joe Ranft, Andrew Stanton, Robert Goulet. Golden Globes '00: Film—Mus./Comedy.

Toy Story 3 **2010** Andy is college-bound so Buzz, Woody and the rest of the toy box crowd wonder what will happen to them. After a room-cleaning, they're donated to a daycare center and realize they may be a bit too settled down for all those new little sticky fingers. In 3-D. **m/C DVD.** *US* ***D:*** Lee Unkrich; ***W:*** Michael Arndt; ***M:*** Randy Newman; ***V:*** Tom Hanks, Tim Allen, Joan Cusack, Wallace Shawn, John Ratzenberger, Don Rickles, Estelle Harris, Blake Clark, R. Lee Ermey, Michael Keaton, Jodi Benson, Ned Beatty, Timothy Dalton, Laurie Metcalf, John Morris, Bonnie Hunt, Jeff Garlin, Kirsten Schaal, Lou Romano, Richard "Cheech" Marin, Whoopi Goldberg, Frank Welker, Beatrice Miller, Lee Unkrich.

Toys 1/2 **1992 (PG-13)** Diappointingly earnest comedy about Leslie (Williams), the whimsical son of a toy manufacturer who must fight to keep the playful spirit of the factory alive after it passes into the hands of his deranged uncle (Gambon). This uncle is a general who attempts to transform the factory into an armaments plant. Leslie receives assistance in this battle from his sister Alsatia (Cusack) and his cousin Patrick (L.L. Cool J). Flat characters; generally falls short by trying too hard to send a message to viewers about the folly of war. Does have extremely vivid and intriguing visuals and special effects. **121m/C VHS, DVD.** Robin Williams, Joan Cusack, Michael Gambon, LL Cool J, Robin Wright Penn, Donald O'Connor; ***D:*** Barry Levinson; ***W:*** Valerie Curtin, Barry Levinson; ***C:*** Adam Greenberg.

Toys in the Attic 1/2 **1963** A man returns to his home in New Orleans with his child bride, where they will live with his two impoverished, spinster sisters. Toned-down version of the Lillian Hellman play. **88m/B VHS.** Dean Martin, Geraldine Page, Yvette Mimieux, Wendy Hiller, Gene Tierney, Nan Martin, Larry Gates, Frank Silvera; ***D:*** George Roy Hill; ***W:*** James Poe; ***C:*** Joseph Biroc.

Trace of Stones *Spur der Steine* **1966** Building construction foreman Hannes Balla benevolently rules over a mammoth building site where he's supported by his workers because things run smoothly. Until, that is, a young female engineer, Kati Klee, and the new Party Secretary Werner Horrath show up. Balla soon isn't the top man anymore and, what's worse, he finds himself in a romantic triangle with Kati and Horrath. Based on the novel by Erik Neutsch. German with subtitles. **138m/B VHS.** *GE* Manfred Krug, Krystyna Stypulkowska, Eberhard Esche; ***D:*** Frank Beyer; ***W:*** Karl-Georg Egel; ***C:*** Gunter Marczinkowski.

Traces of Red **1992 (R)** Set in affluent Palm Beach, and filled with dead bodies, colorful suspects, and red herrings. The complex plot, often so serious it's funny, leads viewers through a convoluted series of events. Cop Jack Dobson (Belushi) is found dead in the opening scene; in homage to

"Sunset Boulevard," his corpse acts as the narrator, a vehicle which unfortunately doesn't work as well here. He promises to recount the events leading up to his death which circle around a series of murders, and the people in his life who are possible suspects. Although Belushi's performance is average, Goldwyn, as Dobson's partner, shows off the talent he displayed in "Ghost." **105m/C VHS, DVD.** James Belushi, Lorraine Bracco, Tony Goldwyn, William Russ, Michelle Joyner, Joe Lisi, Jim Piddock; ***D:*** Andy Wolk; ***W:*** Jim Piddock; ***C:*** Tim Suhrstedt; ***M:*** Graeme Revell.

The Tracey Fragments 1/2 **2007** McDonald uses a number of visual tricks (including split screens) to take us into the teen angst of 15-year-old Tracey Berkowitz (Page), but his disjointed storytelling proves more annoying than enlightening. Tracey uses fantasy to deal with the loneliness and frustration of her dysfunctional world. But her reality takes a hit when Tracey's young brother Sonny (Souwand) disappears while in her care and Tracey has to find him. Medved adapted from her novel. **77m/C DVD.** *CA* Ellen Page, Ari Cohen, Julian Richings, Zie Souwand, Erin McMurtry, Max Maccabe-Lokos; ***D:*** Bruce McDonald; ***W:*** Maureen Medved; ***C:*** Steve Cosens; ***M:*** Broken Social Scene.

Track of the Moonbeast **1976** An American Indian uses mythology to capture the Moonbeast, a lizard-like creature that is roaming the deserts of New Mexico. **90m/C VHS, DVD.** Chase Cordell, Donna Leigh Drake; ***D:*** Richard Ashe.

Track of the Vampire 1/2 *Blood Bath* **1966** Half an hour of leftover footage from a Yugoslavian vampire movie stuck into the story of a California painter who kills his models. Gripping and atmospheric, but disjointed. **80m/B VHS, DVD.** *YU* William Campbell, Jonathan Haze, Sid Haig, Marissa Mathes, Lori Saunders, Sandra Knight; ***D:*** Stephanie Rothman, Jack Hill.

Track 16 1/2 **2002** Paul, the lead singer of a small-town rock band, gets mistakenly mixed up in the investigation of a murdered woman. Now the real killer is out for Paul's blood. Not cool, especially when he's got a gig the next night! Dopey rock soundtrack goes great with a lot of dopey action, reaching its embarrassing (ahem) climax with a song called "Sex with Someone You Love," during, yup, a sex scene. Mini-budget thriller that looks and sounds more like a demo tape. **90m/C DVD.** Billy Frank, Bobbi Ashton, Alan Pratt; ***D:*** Michael (Mick) McCleery; ***W:*** Michael (Mick) McCleery; ***C:*** Michael (Mick) McCleery; ***M:*** Billy Frank. **VIDEO**

Track 29 1/2 **1988 (R)** A confusing black comedy about a lonely woman, her husband who has a model train fetish, and a stranger who claims to be her son. Filmed in North Carolina. **90m/C VHS.** Theresa Russell, Gary Oldman, Christopher Lloyd, Colleen Camp, Sandra Bernhard, Seymour Cassel, Leon Rippy, Vance Colvig; ***D:*** Nicolas Roeg; ***W:*** Dennis Potter.

Tracked *Dogboys* **1998** Prisoner Julian Taylor (Cain) is sent to the patrol-dog training detail and discovers that the twisted department head (Brown) "rents" out his dogs and prisoners to hunters who want human prey. Carrere is the beautiful D.A. who investigates the rash of inmate deaths and discovers Julian is the next quarry. **92m/C VHS.** Bryan Brown, Dean Cain, Tia Carrere, Ken James, Von Flores, Richard Chevolleau, Sean McCann; ***D:*** Ken Russell; ***W:*** David Taylor; ***C:*** Jamie Thompson; ***M:*** John Altman. **CABLE**

The Tracker 1/2 *Dead or Alive* **1988** HBO western about a retired gunman/tracker who must again take up arms. His college-educated son joins him as he searches for a murdering religious fanatic. Fairly decent for the genre. **102m/C VHS, DVD.** Kris Kristofferson, Scott Wilson, Mark Moses, David Huddleston, John Quade, Don Swayze, Brynn Thayer; ***D:*** John Guillermin; ***M:*** Sylvester Levay. **CABLE**

The Trackers 1/2 **1971** A frontier man searches for the people who kidnapped his daughter and killed his son. He is joined by a cocky black tracker. Borgnine brings strength to his character as the rancher seeking revenge. **73m/C VHS.** Sammy Davis Jr., Ernest Borgnine, Julie Adams, Connie Kreski, Jim Davis; ***D:*** Earl Bellamy. **TV**

Tracks 1/2 **1976 (R)** Vietnam veteran accompanies the body of a buddy on a long train ride home. He starts suffering flashbacks from the war and begins to think some of the passengers are out to get him. **90m/C VHS, DVD.** Dennis Hopper, Dean Stockwell, Taryn Power, Zack Norman, Michael Emil, Barbara Flood; ***D:*** Henry Jaglom; ***W:*** Henry Jaglom; ***C:*** Paul Glickman.

Tracks 1/2 **2005 (R)** Dull prison flick based on a true story. Fifteen-year-old Peter Madigan and his buds get wasted along some New Jersey train tracks and come up with a dumb prank that results in the derailing of a commuter train, killing the conductor. Peter and his pals become the first juveniles in New Jersey history to be sentenced to an adult maximum security facility. Follows Peter's adjustment to prison life as corrections officer Clark (Ice-T) takes a concerned interest in the young man, although Peter stays a pretty unsympathetic character. **92m/C DVD.** Ice-T, John Heard, Chris Gunn, Barbara Christie; ***D:*** Peter Wade; ***W:*** Peter Wade; ***C:*** Jesse Weathington. **CABLE**

Tracks of a Killer **1995 (R)** David (Brolin) and Clair (LeBrock) Hawker are vacationing at their isolated winter retreat with corporate climber Patrick (Larsen) and his wife Bella (Taylor). When Bella is killed on David's snowmobile in an accident-that's-no-accident, it turns out Patrick is after David's company in the worst possible way. **100m/C VHS.** Kelly Le Brock, James Brolin, Wolf Larson, Courtney Taylor, George Touliatos; ***D:*** Harvey Frost; ***W:*** Michael Cooney; ***C:*** Bruce Worrall; ***M:*** Barron Abramovitch.

Trade **2007 (R)** Truth-based expose of human slave trafficking is more lurid and sleazy than illuminating. Thirteen-year-old Adriana (Gaitan) is kidnapped and taken from Mexico to New Jersey to be sold into sex slavery on the internet. Her brother Jorge (Ramos) and investigator Ray (Kline) pursue, then infiltrate the operation. Director Kreuzpaintner cranks up every sleazy detail, dwelling extensively on the abuse heaped on Adriana and her fellow victims by cruel captor Manuelo (Perez). The result is more sensational than condemning, however, and it's topped off with a cop-out happy ending to make you feel less icky for watching it. **119m/C DVD.** *US* Kevin Kline, Cesar Ramos, Alicja Bachleda-Curus, Paulina Gaitan, Marco Perez; ***D:*** Marco Kreuzpaintner; ***W:*** Jose Rivera; ***C:*** Daniel Gottschalk; ***M:*** Jacobo Lieberman, Leonardo Heiblum.

Trade Off **1995 (R)** Beautiful, unhappily married Jackie (Russell) seduces equally miserable married businessman Thomas (Baldwin) and jokes about getting rid of their respective spouses. Then Thomas' wife is killed in a car crash and Thomas learns Jackie caused the "accident." He should have watched "Strangers on a Train" to see where trading murders can get you. **92m/C VHS.** Theresa Russell, Adam Baldwin, Megan Gallagher, Barry Primus, Pat Skipper; ***D:*** Andrew Lane.

Trade Secrets *Flagrant Desir* **1986** Special investigator Jerry Morrison is assigned to probe the mysterious death of an heiress to a wine fortune. His investigation leads to the secrets and private fantasies of the woman's family and friends. **91m/C VHS.** Sam Waterston, Marisa Berenson, Lauren Hutton, Arielle Dombasle, Anne Roussel; ***D:*** Claude Faraldo; ***W:*** Claude Faraldo; ***C:*** Willy Kurant; ***M:*** Gabriel Yared. **TV**

Trader Horn 1/2 **1931** Early talkie was the first Hollywood picture to be filmed in Africa. Carey and Renaldo are traders who tangle with a native tribe while searching for the long-lost daughter of a missionary, who turns out to be a tribal goddess. Based on a novel by Alfred Aloysius Horn and Ethelreda Lewis. Boring remake in 1973. **105m/B VHS.** Harry Carey Sr., Duncan Renaldo, Edwina Booth, Sir C. Aubrey Smith, Mutia Omoolu, Olive Carey; ***D:*** Woodbridge S. Van Dyke; ***W:*** Cyril Hume, Richard Schayer, Dale Van Every, John Thomas "Jack" Neville; ***C:*** Clyde De Vinna.

Trader Tom of the China Seas **1954** A young island trader and a shipwrecked beauty get involved in espionage while helping the UN to safeguard the Asian corridor. A 12-part serial on two cassettes. **167m/B VHS.** Harry Lauter, Aline Towne, Lyle Talbot, Fred Graham; ***D:*** Frank (Franklyn) Adreon; ***W:*** Ronald Davidson; ***C:*** Bud Thackery; ***M:*** R. Dale Butts.

Trading Favors **1997 (R)** Seductress Alex (Arquette) talks eager high-school student Lincoln (Gummersall) into giving her a ride, not knowing she's trying to escape from her violent boyfriend (Greene). But that's only the beginning of the trouble. **103m/C VHS.** Rosanna Arquette, Devon Gummersall, George Dzundza, Peter Greene, Julie Ariola, Alanna Ubach, Jason Hervey, Craig Nigh, Mary Jo Catlett, Lin Shaye, Richard Riehle, William Frankfather, Frances Fisher, Chad Lowe; ***D:*** Sondra Locke; ***W:*** Timothy Albaugh, Tag Mendillo; ***C:*** Jerry Sidell; ***M:*** Jeff Rona.

Trading Hearts **1987 (PG)** Over-the-hill baseball player falls for an unsuccessful singer and single mom at a Florida training camp set in the 1950s. **88m/C VHS.** Beverly D'Angelo, Raul Julia, Jenny Lewis, Parris Buckner, Robert Gwaltney; ***D:*** Neil Leifer; ***W:*** Frank Deford.

Trading Mom 1/2 **1994 (PG)** Harried single parent Spacek is erased from the lives of her three kids, who decide they want a parent who's more fun. So, thanks to some magic, they head off to the Mommy Mart to try out a trio of bizarre choices. This gives Spacek a chance at three more roles before the kids come to their senses. Based on "The Mommy Market" by Nancy Brelis; directorial debut for daughter Tia. **82m/C VHS.** Sissy Spacek, Anna Chlumsky, Aaron Michael Metchik, Asher Metchik, Maureen Stapleton; ***D:*** Tia Brelis; ***W:*** Tia Brelis; ***M:*** David Kitay.

Trading Places 1/2 **1983 (R)** Two elderly businessmen wager that environment is more important than heredity in creating a successful life, using a rich nephew and an unemployed street hustler as guinea pigs. Curtis is winning as a hooker-with-a-heart-of-gold who helps the hapless Aykroyd. Oft-told tale succeeds thanks to strong cast. Murphy's second screen appearance. **118m/C VHS, DVD, Blu-ray Disc.** Eddie Murphy, Dan Aykroyd, Jamie Lee Curtis, Ralph Bellamy, Don Ameche, Denholm Elliott, Paul Gleason, James Belushi, Al Franken, Tom Davis, Giancarlo Esposito, Kristin Holby, Stephen Stucker, Nicholas Guest, Robert Earl Jones, Bill Cobbs; ***D:*** John Landis; ***W:*** Herschel Weingrod, Timothy Harris; ***M:*** Elmer Bernstein. British Acad. '83: Support. Actor (Elliott), Support. Actress (Curtis).

Traffic 1/2 **1971** Eccentric auto designer Monsieur Hulot tries to transport his latest contraption from Paris to Amsterdam for an international auto show. As usual, everything goes wrong. Tati's last feature film and his fifth to feature Hulot. French with subtitles. **89m/C VHS.** *FR* Jacques Tati, Maria Kimberly, Marcel Fraval; ***D:*** Jacques Tati; ***W:*** Jacques Lagrange, Jacques Tati; ***C:*** Eddy van der Enden, Marcel Weiss; ***M:*** Charles Dumont.

Traffic 1/2 **2000 (R)** Based on the 1990 British miniseries "Traffik," Soderbergh's film has three loosely intertwined stories about the drug trade: Supreme Court Justice Douglas is appointed as head of the National Drug Task Force but learns his own daughter is a heroin addict; San Diego socialite wife Zeta-Jones learns the drug trade when her drug lord hubby gets busted; and Mexican border cop Del Toro works on his power base. Soderbergh takes on a large, complex subject with a large, complex film populated by a large, uniformly excellent cast. The outcomes of the various storylines may not end happily or neatly (just like in real life), but the characters and ideas explored along the way are compelling. **147m/C VHS, DVD, HD DVD.** Michael Douglas, Catherine Zeta-Jones, Benicio Del Toro, Dennis Quaid, Benjamin Bratt, Albert Finney, Amy Irving, Don Cheadle, Luis Guzman, Steven Bauer, James Brolin, Erika Christensen, Clifton (Gonzalez) Collins Jr., Miguel Ferrer, Tomas Milian, D.W. Moffett, Marisol Padilla Sanchez, Peter Riegert, Jacob Vargas, Rena Sofer, Stacey Travis, Salma Hayek, Topher Grace, Beau Holden, Enrique Murciano, Jsu Garcia; ***D:*** Steven Soderbergh; ***W:*** Stephen Gaghan; ***C:*** Steven Soderbergh; ***M:*** Cliff Martinez. Oscars '00: Adapt. Screenplay, Director (Soderbergh), Film Editing, Support. Actor (Del Toro); British Acad. '00: Adapt. Screenplay, Support. Actor (Del Toro); Golden Globes '01: Screenplay, Support. Actor (Del Toro); L.A. Film Critics '00: Director (Soderbergh); Natl. Bd. of Review '00: Director (Soderbergh); N.Y. Film Critics '00: Director (Soderbergh), Film, Support. Actor (Del Toro); Natl. Soc. Film Critics '00: Director (Soderbergh), Support. Actor (Del Toro); Screen Actors Guild '00: Actor (Del Toro), Cast; Writers Guild '00: Adapt. Screenplay; Broadcast Film Critics '00: Adapt. Screenplay, Director (Soderbergh).

Traffic in Souls **1913** Silent melodrama dealing with white slavery. Immigrants and gullible country girls are lured into brothels where they are trapped with no hope of escape until, in a hail of bullets, the police raid the dens of vice and rescue them. **74m/B VHS.** Matt Moore, Jane Gail, William Welsh; ***D:*** George Tucker. Natl. Film Reg. '06.

Traffic Jam 1/2 *Jutai* **1991** A light comedy about a Japanese family's attempt to travel on a holiday weekend. Tokyo couple and their two young children decide to visit the husband's family who happen to live on a distant island. Naturally, traffic's horrendous, they have very little time, and things continuously go wrong. Japanese with subtitles. **108m/C VHS.** *JP* Kenichi Hagiwara, Hitomi Kuroki, Ayako Takarada, Shingo Yazawa, Eiji Okada; ***D:*** Mitsuo Kurotsuchi.

Traffik **1990** A tense, unnerving look at the international world of heroin smuggling. The British drama follows the lives of three men involved in the drug trade: a farmer in the poppy fields of Pakistan, a drug smuggler in Hamburg, and a Tory cabinet minister who heads his government's anti-drug cabinet and then comes to realize his own daughter is an addict. The basis for Steven Soderbergh's much-lauded 2000 film "Traffic." **360m/C VHS, DVD.** *GB* Lindsay Duncan, Bill Paterson, Jamal Shah, Talat Hussain, Fritz Muller-Scherz, Julia Ormond, Knut Hinz, Feryal Gauhar Shah, Peter Lakenmacher, Vincenzo Benestante; ***D:*** Alastair Reid; ***W:*** Simon Moore; ***C:*** Clive Tickner; ***M:*** Tim Souster. **TV**

The Tragedy of a Ridiculous Man *La Tragedia di un Uomo Ridicolo* **1981 (PG)** The missing son of an Italian cheese manufacturer may or may not have been kidnapped by terrorists. Lesser Bertolucci effort may or may not have a point. In Italian with English subtitles. **116m/C VHS.** *IT* Ugo Tognazzi, Anouk Aimee, Victor Cavallo, Ricky Tognazzi, Laura Morante; ***D:*** Bernardo Bertolucci; ***W:*** Bernardo Bertolucci; ***C:*** Carlo Di Palma; ***M:*** Ennio Morricone. Cannes '81: Actor (Tognazzi).

Tragedy of Flight 103: The Inside Story **1991 (PG)** Dramatization of the events surrounding the destruction of Pan Am flight 103 over Lockerbie, Scotland, due to a terrorist-planted bomb. **89m/C VHS.** Ned Beatty, Peter Boyle, Vincent Gardenia, Timothy West, Michael Wincott, Harry Ditson, Aharon Ipale, John Shrapnel; ***D:*** Leslie Woodhead.

Trahir *Betrayal* **1993** In 1948 Romania journalist George Vlaicu (Leysen) writes a controversial article on the death of democracy in his country and is imprisoned for 11 years. In 1959 he's offered a deal, go free as long as he talks weekly to a police inspector (Repan). He begins a new career as a poet and marries his former typist, Laura (Perrier), but after a tragedy learns that his meetings with the inspector aren't as innocuous as they've seemed. Excellent performances and a cold look at how a police state is able to control its artists and writers. Filmed primarily in Romania. Director Mihaileanu's first feature film. French with subtitles. **104m/C VHS.** *FR SI SP RO* Johan Leysen, Mireille Perrier, Alexandru Repan, Razvan Vasilescu, Maia Morgenstern, Radu Beligan; ***D:*** Radu Mihaileanu; ***W:*** Laurent Moussard, Radu Mihaileanu; ***M:*** Temistocle Popa. Montreal World Film Fest. '93: Actor (Leysen), Film.

Trail Beyond 1/2 **1934** A cowboy and his sidekick go on the trek to the northwest to find a girl and a gold mine. **57m/B VHS, DVD.** John Wayne, Noah Beery Sr., Verna Hillie, Noah Beery Jr.; ***D:*** Robert North Bradbury; ***W:*** Lindsley Parsons; ***C:*** Archie Stout.

Trail Drive **1933** Adventures of a cowboy during a big cattle drive. **63m/B VHS.** Ken Maynard, Cecilia Parker, Jack Rockwell,

Lafe (Lafayette) McKee, Frank Rice, Robert F. (Bob) Kortman, Fern Emmett; *D:* Alan James; *W:* Alan James, Nate Gatzert; *C:* Ted D. McCord.

The Trail of '98 ⚘⚘ **1928** During the Klondike gold rush, a motley assortment of would-be fortune hunters is traveling by ship from San Francisco to Skagway. Among them are hired help Berna (Del Rio) and would-be prospector Larry (Forbes), who fall in love. The hard trip to the gold fields of Dawson City involves blizzards, fires, starvation, claim jumpers, and many other trials. **90m/B DVD.** Delores Del Rio, Ralph Forbes, Harry Carey Sr., Karl (Daen) Dane, Tully Marshall, George Cooper, Tenen Holtz, Emily Fitzroy; *D:* Clarence Brown; *W:* Benjamin Glazer; *C:* John Seitz.

Trail of a Serial Killer ⚘⚘ **1998 (R)** FBI agent Jason Enola (Penn) and detective Brad Abraham (Madsen) team up to find a serial killer leaving a trail of dismembered corpses. **95m/C VHS, DVD.** Christopher Penn, Michael Madsen, Jennifer Dale, Chad McQueen; *D:* Damian Lee. **VIDEO**

Trail of Robin Hood ⚘⚘ ½ **1950** Rogers sees to it that poor families get Christmas trees, in spite of the fact that a big business wants to raise the prices. Features a number of western stars, including Holt playing himself. **67m/C VHS, DVD.** Roy Rogers, Penny Edwards, Gordon Jones, Jack Holt, Emory Parnell, Rex Allen, Allan "Rocky" Lane, Clifton Young, Monte Hale, Kermit Maynard, Tom Keene, Ray Corrigan, William Farnum; *D:* William Witney.

Trail of Terror ⚘ **1935** G-Man poses as an escaped convict to get the goods on a gang. **60m/B VHS, DVD.** Bob Steele, Beth Marion, Forrest Taylor, Charles "Blackie" King, Lloyd Ingraham, Charles French; *D:* Robert North Bradbury.

Trail of the Hawk ⚘ **1937** Saga of frontier justice and love on the plains. **50m/B VHS.** Yancey Lane, Betty Jordan, Dick(ie) Jones; *D:* Edward Dmytryk.

The Trail of the Lonesome Pine ⚘⚘⚘ **1936** The first outdoor film to be shot in three-color Technicolor. Two backwoods Kentucky clans, the Tolliver and the Falins, have been feuding so long no one remembers what started the fuss. But young engineer Jack Hale (MacMurray) gets stuck in the middle when he comes to build a railroad through the Blue Ridge Mountains. Hale saves the life of Dave Tolliver (Fonda) but Dave's not happy when the city slicker starts mooning over Dave's sister, June (Sidney). And the Falins aren't happy about the railroad, which leads to even more fighting. Based on the novel by John Fox Jr. and previously filmed in 1916 and 1923. **102m/C VHS.** Henry Fonda, Fred MacMurray, Sylvia Sidney, Robert Barrat, Fred Stone, Nigel Bruce, Beulah Bondi, George "Spanky" McFarland, Fuzzy Knight; *D:* Henry Hathaway; *W:* Grover Jones, Horace McCoy, Harvey Thew; *C:* William Howard Greene, Robert C. Bruce.

Trail of the Mounties ⚘ **1947** A Mountie gallops smack into a murdering slew of fur thieves, which includes his ne'er-do-well twin brother. **41m/B VHS.** Russell Hayden, Emmett Lynn, Terry Frost, Harry Cording, Jennifer Holt; *D:* Howard Bretherton; *W:* Betty Burbridge; *C:* Benjamin (Ben H.) Kline.

Trail of the Pink Panther ⚘⚘ **1982 (PG)** The sixth in Sellers' "Pink Panther" series. Inspector Clouseau disappears while he is searching for the diamond known as the Pink Panther. Notable because it was released after Sellers' death, using clips from previous movies to fill in gaps. Followed by "Curse of the Pink Panther." **97m/C VHS, DVD.** Peter Sellers, David Niven, Herbert Lom, Capucine, Burt Kwouk, Robert Wagner, Robert Loggia; *D:* Blake Edwards; *W:* Blake Edwards, Frank Waldman; *C:* Dick Bush; *M:* Henry Mancini.

Trail of the Silver Spurs ⚘ ½ **1941** A lone man remaining in a ghost town discovers gold and becomes rich. Part of the "Range Busters" series. **57m/B VHS.** Ray Corrigan, John "Dusty" King, Max Terhune, I. Stanford Jolley, Dorothy Short; *D:* S. Roy Luby.

Trail Riders ⚘ ½ **1942** The Range Busters set a trap to capture a gang of outlaws who killed the son of the town marshal during a bank robbery. Part of the "Range Busters" series. **55m/B VHS, DVD.** John "Dusty" King, David Sharpe, Max Terhune, Evelyn Finley, Forrest Taylor, Charles "Blackie" King, Kermit Maynard; *D:* Robert Emmett Tansey; *W:* Frances Kavanaugh; *C:* Robert E. Cline.

Trail Street ⚘ ½ **1947** Scott is Bat Masterson, the western hero. He aids the struggle of Kansans as they conquer the land and local ranchers. **84m/B VHS.** Randolph Scott, Robert Ryan, Anne Jeffreys, George "Gabby" Hayes, Madge Meredith, Jason Robards Sr.; *D:* Ray Enright.

Trail to San Antone ⚘ ½ **1947** Gene trades the prairie for the racetrack when he helps out an injured jockey, whom Autry wants to ride for him in the big race. **67m/B VHS.** Gene Autry, Peggy Stewart, Sterling Holloway, William Henry; *D:* John English; *W:* Jack Natteford; *C:* William Bradford.

Trailer, the Movie ⚘⚘ **1999** Goofy experimental comedy combines elements of "Last Action Hero" and "Purple Rose of Cairo." In a black-and-white introduction, two lonely guys (McCrudden and Pope) sneak into a theatre one night and fall in love with two actresses (Hicks and Crigler) they see in a trailer. After the guys are tossed out, they wish their way into a color world where the rules of movies apply. Unfortunately, this well-meaning independent production lacks the wit to make full use of the engaging premise. **101m/C DVD.** Ian McCrudden, Will Pope, Miranda Hicks, Marjorie Crigler; *D:* Ian McCrudden; *C:* Matthew Uhry.

Trailin' ⚘⚘ ½ **1921** Mix stars as a cowboy in search of his parentage. Based on the Max Brand story. **58m/B VHS.** Tom Mix, Eva Novak, James Gordon; *D:* Lynn F. Reynolds.

Trailing Double Trouble ⚘ ½ **1940** A corrupt attorney murders a rancher to pursue a business scheme. Three ranch hands kidnap the rancher's orphaned baby to keep her safe from the attorney. The second entry in the "Range Busters" series. **56m/B VHS.** Ray Corrigan, John "Dusty" King, Max Terhune; *D:* S. Roy Luby; *W:* Oliver Drake; *C:* Edward Linden.

Trailing Trouble ⚘ ½ **1930** Gibson is a cowpoke who gets robbed of the money he received for a cattle sale. When he rescues a Chinese girl from danger she helps him recover the money. He also has to battle a rival for his girlfriend's affections. He should have battled for a better script. **58m/B VHS.** Hoot Gibson, Margaret Quimby, Pete Morrison, Olive Young, William (Bill, Billy) McCall; *D:* Arthur Rosson.

Trailing Trouble ⚘ ½ **1937** Slow-moving western. Good guy Friendly Fields (Maynard) is mistaken for gunslinger Blackie. He uses his new reputation to get a job as foreman at Patience Blair's (Andre) ranch and settles a water rights dispute, which makes Patience look kindly on the cowpoke. But then the real Blackie shows up, none too happy. **58m/B DVD.** Ken Maynard, Lona Andre, Roger Williams, Phil Dunham, Grace Wood, Fred Burns; *D:* Arthur Rosson; *W:* Phil Dunham, Philip Graham White; *C:* Tom Galligan.

Trails of the Wild ⚘ ½ **1935** Mounties Jim McKenna and Windy Cameron encounter trouble on Ghost Mountain when they look for a missing mining engineer. Then they stumble across the hideout of an outlaw gang as well. **61m/B DVD.** Ken Maynard, Billie Seward, Monte Blue, Theodore von Eltz, Fuzzy Knight, Matthew Betz, Wheeler Oakman, Robert Frazer, John Elliott; *D:* Sam Newfield; *W:* Joseph O'Donnell; *C:* Jack Greenhalgh.

The Train ⚘⚘⚘⚘ *Le Train; Il Treno* **1965** During the German occupation of Paris in 1944, a German colonel (Scofield) is ordered to ransack the city of its art treasures and put them on a train bound for Germany. Word gets to the French Resistance who then persuade the train inspector (Lancaster) to sabotage the train. A battle of wills ensues between Scofield and Lancaster as each becomes increasingly obsessed in outwitting the other—though the cost to all turns out to be as irreplaceable as the art itself. Filmed on location in France. Frankenheimer used real locomotives, rather than models, throughout the film, even in the spectacular crash sequences. **133m/C VHS, DVD.** *FR IT* Burt Lancaster, Paul Scofield, Jeanne Moreau, Michel Simon, Suzanne Flon, Wolfgang Preiss, Albert Remy, Charles Millot, Jacques Marin, Donald O'Brien, Jean-Pierre Zola, Arthur Brauss, Howard Vernon, Richard Munch, Paul Bonifas, Jean-Claude Bercq; *D:* John Frankenheimer; *W:* Frank Davis, Walter Bernstein, Franklin Coen; *C:* Jean Tournier, Walter Wottitz; *M:* Maurice Jarre.

The Train Killer ⚘ **1983** A mad Hungarian is bent on destroying the Orient Express. **90m/C VHS.** Michael Sarrazin; *D:* Sandor Simo.

Train Man: Densha Otoko ⚘⚘ ½ **2005** Few things are more stereotypical about Japanese society than Otaku (think super geeks) and perverts who grope women on the subway. In this case the former rescues a pretty girl from the latter. She's so grateful she asks for his address in order to return his kindness. Being an Otaku he has no idea how to socially interact with a woman, and asks advice from his friends on the Internet. Things do not go well. Supposedly a true story that has been made into a book, four comics, a theatrical play, this film, and a TV series. **102m/C DVD.** *JP* Miki Nakatani, Takayuki Yamada, Ryoko Kuninaka, Eita, Kuranosuke Sasaki, Tae Kimura, Yoshinori Okada; *D:* Shosuke Murakami; *W:* Hitori Nakano, Arisa Kaneko; *C:* Shigeki Murano; *M:* Takayuki Hattori.

Train of Events ⚘⚘ ½ **1949** An interesting look at lives affected by a train wreck just outside London, taking the form of four short episodes. Three are frankly somber, depressing tales of the ill-fated train driver, a murderer and an escaped prisoner-of-war. The fourth segment is a refreshingly lighthearted piece about romantic jealousies in a traveling orchestra. A precursor to the later swarm of crass disaster movies, except here emphasis is on character over special effects. **89m/B VHS.** Jack Warner, Gladys Henson, Susan Shaw, Patric Doonan, Miles Malleson, Leslie Phillips, Joan Dowling, Laurence Payne, Valerie Hobson, John Clements, Peter Finch, Mary Morris, Laurence Naismith, Michael Hordern; *D:* Sidney Cole, Basil Dearden, Charles Crichton.

Train of Life ⚘⚘ *Train de Vie* **1998 (R)** Theatrical fable set in 1941 in a mountainous village shtetl near the Russian border. Schlomo the fool (Abelanski) tells the village elders that the Nazis are on their way. So the Rabbi (Harari) and the villagers decide to construct their own mock deportation train and make their way to Palestine. Mordechai (Rufus) plays the role of the Nazi commandant (a little too well), while the others delegate various roles and the train begins to roll out, with any number of problems along the way. French with subtitles. **103m/C VHS.** *FR* Rufus, Clement Harari, Agathe de la Fontaine, Lionel Abelanski, Michel Muller; *D:* Radu Mihaileanu; *W:* Radu Mihaileanu; *C:* Yorgos Arvanitis, Laurent Dailland; *M:* Goran Bregovic.

Train Robbers ⚘⚘ **1973 (PG)** A widow employs the services of three cowboys to help her recover some stolen gold in order to clear her late husband's name. At least that's what she says. **92m/C VHS, DVD.** John Wayne, Ann-Margret, Rod Taylor, Ben Johnson, Christopher George, Ricardo Montalban, Bobby Vinton, Jerry Gatlin; *D:* Burt Kennedy; *W:* Burt Kennedy; *C:* William Clothier.

Train Station Pickups ⚘ **1979** Trashy film about young girls who hook at a local train depot, until something goes wrong. **96m/C VHS.** Marco Knoger, Katja Carrol, Ingeborg Steinbach, Benjamin Carwath; *D:* Walter Boos.

Train to Hollywood ⚘⚘⚘ **1986** Marilyn Monroe-obsessed young Polish girl daydreams incessantly as she works on dining car. Funny and surreal. Polish dialogue with English subtitles. **96m/C VHS.** *PL* Kasia (Katarzyna) Figura, Piotr Siwkiewicz, Rafal Wegrzyniak, Grazyna Krukowna; *D:* Radoslaw Piwowarski; *W:* Radoslaw Piwowarski; *C:* Witold Adamek; *M:* Jerzy Matula.

Train to Tombstone ⚘ **1950** A train running from Albuquerque to Tombstone carries a motley mob of the usual characters. **60m/B VHS.** Donald (Don "Red") Barry, Judith Allen, Robert Lowery, Tom Neal; *D:* Charles Reisner.

Trained to Kill ⚘ ½ **1988** Two brothers seek revenge on the mean streets of L.A. **94m/C VHS.** Frank Zagarino, Glen Eaton, Lisa Aliff, Marshall Teague, Robert Z'Dar, Henry Silva, Arlene Golonka, Ron O'Neal, Harold Diamond, Chuck Connors; *D:* H. Kaye Dyal; *W:* H. Kaye Dyal, Arthur Webb.

Trained to Kill, U.S.A. ⚘ ½ *The No Mercy Man* **1975 (R)** Vietnam veteran relives his war experiences when a gang of terrorists threaten his hometown. **88m/C VHS, DVD.** Stephen Sander, Heidi Vaughn, Rockne Tarkington, Richard X. Slattery; *D:* Daniel Vance; *W:* Daniel Vance; *C:* Dean Cundey.

Training Day ⚘⚘ ½ **2001 (R)** Until the script finally goes completely off the rails, this cop corruption tale is worth watching for the ferocious performance of Washington alone. He's veteran undercover narc Alonzo Harris, who's been the big dog on the L.A. streets for so long, he's become morally bankrupt and works on the might makes right theory of justice. Opposing him is rookie Jake Hoyt (Hawke), who first wants to be a part of Harris's team and then learns just what it will cost him. Fuqua shot on location so you can definitely feel the grit. **120m/C VHS, DVD, Blu-ray Disc, UMD, HD DVD.** *US* Denzel Washington, Ethan Hawke, Scott Glenn, Clifford Curtis, Dr. Dre, Snoop Dogg, Tom Berenger, Harris Yulin, Raymond J. Barry, Charlotte Ayanna, Macy Gray, Eva Mendes, Nicholas Chinlund, Jaime Gomez, Raymond Cruz; *D:* Antoine Fuqua; *W:* David Ayer; *C:* Mauro Fiore; *M:* Mark Mancina. Oscars '01: Actor (Washington); L.A. Film Critics '01: Actor (Washington).

Trainspotting ⚘⚘⚘ **1995 (R)** From the same team who offered the violently comedic "Shallow Grave," comes an equally destructive look at a group of Edinburgh junkies and losers. Heroin-user Mark Renton (McGregor) once again decides to get off junk but to do so he has to get away from his friends: knife-wielding psycho Begbie (Carlyle), Sick Boy (Miller), Spud (Bremner), and Tommy (McKidd). He heads for a semi-respectable life in London but Begbie and Spud wind up involving him in a serious money drug deal that spells trouble. Strong fantasy visuals depict drug highs and lows while heavy Scottish accents (and humor) may prove difficult. Based on the 1993 cult novel by Irvine Welsh. Film drew much controversy for supposingly being pro-heroin but the junkie's life is hardly portrayed as being attractive in any way. **94m/C VHS, DVD.** *GB* Ewan McGregor, Ewen Bremner, Jonny Lee Miller, Robert Carlyle, Kevin McKidd, Kelly Macdonald, Shirley Henderson, Pauline Lynch; *D:* Danny Boyle; *W:* John Hodge; *C:* Brian Tufano. British Acad. '95: Adapt. Screenplay.

The Traitor ⚘ ½ **1936** Undercover man joins a gang of bandits. **57m/B VHS, DVD.** Frances Grant, Frank Melton, Karl Hackett, Pedro Regas, Tim McCoy; *D:* Sam Newfield; *W:* Joseph O'Donnell; *C:* Jack Greenhalgh.

Traitor ⚘⚘ ½ **2008 (PG-13)** Worthy entry in the post-9/11 espionage thriller subgenre puts a fairly interesting spin on an otherwise formulaic plot, showcasing the always solid Cheadle as Samir Horn, a Sudanese-American who is either a spy working for the U.S. or a converted terrorist who has embraced Muslim extremism. Pic keeps the secret well as Cheadle deftly plays both sides, and is further enhanced by strong performances by Pearce as an open-minded FBI agent and an underutilized Daniels as an intelligence bureaucrat who seems to know the truth. Stereotypes and convoluted manufactured plot twists bog things down a bit, but ultimately it's Cheadle's subtle and nuanced performance, which never tips his character's hand, that makes it worthwhile. **113m/C DVD, Blu-ray Disc.** *US* Don Cheadle, Guy Pearce, Neal McDonough, Said Taghmaoui, Archie Panjabi, Jeff Daniels, Mozhan Marno; *D:* Jeffrey Nachmanoff; *W:* Jeffrey Nachmanoff; *C:* J.(James) Michael Muro; *M:* Mark Kilian.

Tramp at the Door ⚘⚘ ½ **1987** Delightful drama about a wandering, magical man who enters the lives of an embittered family. He helps them sort the skeletons in their closets, and works wonders on their relationships. **81m/C VHS.** Ed McNamara, August Schellenberg, Monique Mercure, Eric Peterson; *D:* Allen Kroeker.

Tramp, Tramp, Tramp ⚘⚘ ½ **1926** Langdon's first feature-length comedy, produced by his own company, features the silent star as the hapless son of a shoemaker who is facing bankruptcy. Wealthy shoe manufacturer John Burton (Davis) has offered substantial prize money for a coast-to-coast walking race and Harry is persuaded to enter the contest in order to save the family business. Naturally, there are many obstacles to overcome—he almost falls from a precipice, must escape from a chain gang, and is nearly killed by a cyclone. The plot is merely a series of sketches but Langdon is cheery and fearless; Crawford has an early role as his girlfriend. Langdon used numerous (uncredited) gag men for his film, including Frank Capra. The DVD also includes the Langdon short, "All Night Long." **84m/B VHS, DVD.** Harry Langdon, Joan Crawford, Alec B. Francis, Edwards Davis; ***D:*** Harry Edwards; ***C:*** Elgin Lessley.

Tramplers **1966** A rebel father and son split over the hanging of a Yankee during the Civil War. Italian made spaghetti western without much plot and lots of gratuitous gunplay. **103m/C VHS.** *IT* Joseph Cotten, Gordon Scott; ***D:*** Albert Band, Mario Sequi.

Trancers *Future Cop* **1984 (PG-13)** A time-traveling cult from the future goes back in time to 1985 to meddle with fate. Only Jack Deth, defender of justice, can save mankind. Low-budget "Blade Runner." Followed by two sequels. **76m/C VHS, DVD.** Tim Thomerson, Michael Stefoni, Helen Hunt, Art LaFleur, Telma Hopkins; ***D:*** Charles Band; ***W:*** Danny Bilson.

Trancers 2: The Return of Jack Deth **1990 (R)** Retro cop is back from the future again, but seems to have lost his wit and nerve in between sequels. Ward is miscast and the pacing undermines whatever suspense that might have been. **85m/C VHS.** Tim Thomerson, Helen Hunt, Megan Ward, Biff Manard, Martine Beswick, Jeffrey Combs, Barbara Crampton, Richard Lynch; ***D:*** Charles Band.

Trancers 3: Deth Lives ½ **1992 (R)** In the third film of the "Trancers" series, time-traveling cop Jack Deth fights the deadliest form of government-sponsored Trancer yet—it has a brain. **83m/C VHS.** Tim Thomerson, Melanie Smith, Andrew (Andy) Robinson, Tony Pierce, Dawn Ann Billings, Helen Hunt, Megan Ward, Stephen Macht, Telma Hopkins; ***D:*** C. Courtney Joyner; ***W:*** C. Courtney Joyner; ***M:*** Richard Band.

Trancers 4: Jack of Swords ½ **1993 (R)** Time-traveling cop Jack Deth finds himself in a mystical new dimension where the bloodsucking Trancers have enslaved the local population as feeders. If Jack expects to conquer he'll first need to survive an ancient wizard's prophecy of death. Filmed on location in Romania. **74m/C VHS.** Tim Thomerson, Stacie Randall, Ty Miller, Terri Ivens, Mark Arnold, Clabe Hartley, Alan Oppenheimer, Stephen Macht, David Nutter; ***W:*** Peter David; ***M:*** Gary Fry.

Trancers 5: Sudden Deth ½ **1994 (R)** Irreverant time-travelling cop Jack Deth (Thomerson) returns to help the Tunnel Rats occupy the castle of Caliban. But the evil Lord Caliban is resurrected and his only desire is to destroy Jack. This is supposedly the final chapter of Deth's saga. **73m/C VHS.** Tim Thomerson, Stacie Randall, Ty Miller, Terri Ivens, Mark Arnold, Clabe Hartley, Alan Oppenheimer, Jeff Moldovan, Lochlyn Munro, Stephen Macht; ***D:*** David Nutter; ***W:*** Peter David; ***M:*** Gary Fry.

Transamerica **2005 (R)** Bree (Huffman) is a transsexual formerly known as Stanley on the brink of completing her male to female transformation through gender reassignment surgery. (S)he lives in Los Angeles, but just prior to her long-awaited surgery she receives a call from New York street hustler Toby (Zegers). Toby is looking for Stanley, who, as a result of a brief affair with his late mother, he believes to be his father. Because her therapist insists she must come to terms with this before her surgery, Bree heads to New York. From this point the film becomes a funny and touching road trip flick, as Bree and Toby drive back to L.A. learning about each other. **104m/C DVD.** *US* Felicity Huffman, Kevin Zegers, Fionnula Flanagan, Elizabeth Pena, Graham Greene, Burt Young, Carrie Preston; ***D:*** Duncan Tucker; ***W:*** Duncan Tucker; ***C:*** Stephen Kazmierski; ***M:*** David Mansfield. Golden Globes '06: Actress—Drama (Huffman); Ind. Spirit '06: Actress (Huffman), First Screenplay; Natl. Bd. of Review '05: Actress (Huffman).

Transatlantic Merry-Go-Round **1934** An early semi-musical mystery about an eclectic assortment of passengers aboard a luxury liner. ♫ It Was Sweet of You; Rock and Roll; Moon Over Monte Carlo; Oh Leo, It's Love; If I Had a Million Dollars. **90m/B VHS.** Jack Benny, Gene Raymond, Nancy Carroll, Boswell Sisters, Ralph Morgan, Sidney Blackmer; ***D:*** Ben Stoloff.

Transatlantic Tunnel ½ *The Tunnel* **1935** An undersea tunnel from England to America is attempted, despite financial trickery and undersea disasters. Made with futuristic sets which were advanced for their time. **94m/B VHS.** *GB* Richard Dix, Leslie Banks, Madge Evans, Helen Vinson, Sir C. Aubrey Smith, George Arliss, Walter Huston; ***D:*** Maurice Elvey.

Transfixed ½ *Bad Genres; Mauvais Genres* **2001** A whodunnit set in the seamy side of Brussels. Cross-dressing Bo (Stevenin) sees police inspector Paul Huysmans (Bohringer) arrest his father for pedophilia. Does this crime tie into a serial killer who's going after the local tranvestites and prostitutes? Muddled wannabe Hitchcock, although Stevenin gives a stellar performance. Based on the novel "Transfixions" by Brigitte Aubert. French with subtitles. **109m/C DVD.** *BE FR* Robinson Stevenin, Richard Bohringer, Micheline Presle, Stephane Metzger; ***D:*** Francis Girod; ***W:*** Francis Girod, Philippe Cougrand; ***C:*** Thierry Jault; ***M:*** Alexandre Desplat.

Transformations ½ **1988 (R)** An interplanetary pilot battles a deadly virus that threatens life throughout the universe. Obscure space jetsam. **84m/C VHS.** Rex Smith, Patrick Macnee, Lisa Langlois, Christopher Neame; ***D:*** Jay Kamen; ***W:*** Mitch Brian.

Transformers **2007 (PG-13)** The Autobots wage their battle to destroy the evil forces of... heck, if you were alive during the 1980s, you know how the song goes. Bombast specialist Bay brings the successful toy/TV show franchise to the big screen, with this tale of transforming robots from outer space whom travel to Earth in search of the mythical Allspark cube. There's lots of rock 'em-sock-'em action, but the whole movie isn't nearly as big, dumb, or fun as it should be, though LaBeouf's "boy and his robot" storyline is the best of the multiple plotlines. **140m/C DVD, Blu-ray Disc, HD DVD.** *US* Shia LaBeouf, Megan Fox, Josh Duhamel, Tyrese Gibson, Anthony Anderson, John Turturro, Jon Voight, Rachael Taylor, Glenn Morshower, Bernie Mac, Amaury Nolasco, Kevin Dunn, Zack (Zach) Ward, Michael O'Neill, Julie White, Travis Van Winkle, Peter Jacobson, William Morgan Sheppard, John Robinson, Chris Ellis, Samantha Smith, Rick Gomez; ***D:*** Michael Bay; ***W:*** Alex Kurtzman, Roberto Orci; ***C:*** Mitchell Amundsen; ***M:*** Steve Jablonsky; ***V:*** Peter Cullen, Hugo Weaving, Keith David, Robert Foxworth, Reno Wilson, Darius McCrary, Mark Ryan.

Transformers: Revenge of the Fallen **2009 (PG-13)** In part both prequel and sequel, tells of when mankind actually first met the Transformers and of their current status quo on Earth. In this second chapter the Autobots are working with the government to track down any remaining Decepticons, and their human liaison Sam (LaBeouf) is off to college trying to live a normal life. With the discovery of a piece of the Allspark, an ancient map, and the return of Megatron aided by a new foe, the heroes are again brought together to save mankind and possibly the universe itself. Raunchier and darker than the original but with the same heart-pounding CGI action. **147m/C DVD.** *US* Megan Fox, John Turturro, Josh Duhamel, Tyrese Gibson, Shia LeBeouf, Kevin Dunn, Shia LaBeouf; ***D:*** Michael Bay; ***W:*** Ehren Kruger, Alex Kurtzman, Roberto Orci; ***C:*** Ben Seresin; ***M:*** Steve Jablonsky; ***V:*** Charles Adler, Peter Cullen. Golden Raspberries '09: Worst Picture, Worst Director (Bay), Worst Screenplay.

Transformers: The Movie **1986 (G)** A full-length animated film featuring the universe-defending robots fighting the powers of evil. These robots began life as real toys, so there's some marketing going on. **85m/C VHS, DVD.** ***D:*** Nelson Shin; ***M:*** Vince DiCola; ***V:*** Orson Welles, Eric Idle, Judd Nelson, Leonard Nimoy, Robert Stack.

Transmutations *Underworld* **1985 (R)** Mad scientist Elliott develops a mind-altering drug which is tested by a group of young people. They find out too late that the drug causes horrible facial disfigurement, as well as leaving them hopelessly addicted, and they hide out underground, plotting their revenge. Cowper, a young hooker in the group, turns out to be immune to the side effects and works with her ex-mobster boss to get help. Confusing. Barker co-scripted from one of his stories but later disowned the film. **103m/C VHS.** *GB* Denholm Elliott, Steven Berkoff, Miranda Richardson, Nicola Cowper, Larry Lamb, Art Malik, Ingrid Pitt, Irina Brook, Paul Bown; ***D:*** George Pavlou; ***W:*** Clive Barker, James Caplin; ***C:*** Syd Macartney.

Transport from Paradise ½ *Transport Z Raje* **1965** Follows the story of Jewish life in the Terezin ghetto before the inhabitants are imprisoned and shipped off to Auschwitz as part of Hitler's final solution. Based on a novel by Arnold Lustig. In Czech with English subtitles. **93m/B VHS.** *CZ* Zdenek Stepanek, Ilja Prachar, Jiri Vrstala, Cestmir Randa; ***D:*** Zbynek Brynych; ***W:*** Zbynek Brynych; ***C:*** Jan Curik; ***M:*** Jiri Sternwald.

The Transporter **2002 (PG-13)** Short on plot but long on action, this product of the Luc Besson action factory is yet another of the producer's efforts to bring kung-fu fightin' to France. Mercenary "delivery man" Frank Martin (Statham) lives by three simple rules: Never change the deal, never exchange names and never look in the package. When one of his packages starts squirming, however, he breaks one of his rules. He opens a duffel bag and discovers beautiful Taiwanese girl Lai (Qi Shu), who reveals a plot involving smuggled Asians used as slave labor. This angers the bad guys, an evil American known as Wall Street (Schulze) and Lai's creepy father Kwai (Young). They send countless henchmen after the heroes, and Martin delivers large amounts of bullets and kicks to the head without once asking anyone to sign for them. Directed by veteran Hong Kong fight choreographer Corey Yuen. **92m/C VHS, DVD, Blu-ray Disc, UMD.** Jason Statham, Shu Qi, Francois Berleand, Matt Schulze, Ric Young; ***D:*** Corey Yuen; ***W:*** Luc Besson, Robert Mark Kamen; ***C:*** Pierre Morel; ***M:*** Stanley Clarke.

Transporter 2 ½ **2005 (PG-13)** Second in what appears will be a series. This time Frank (Statham) is in Miami, working as a driver for one very wealthy family's young son, Jack (Clary). Jack is kidnapped in a sinister plot to bilk his parents out of beaucoup bucks. Powerful dad (Modine) and distraught mom (Vallotta) are really just along for the ride. Even hard-core action fans might balk at some of the implausible scenes (one involving a jet ski on a highway is particularly goofy), though the commitment to jam-packing action into the film is impressive. Plot is eerily similar to "Man on Fire" although the execution is not. **88m/C DVD, Blu-ray Disc, UMD.** *US FR* Jason Statham, Alessandro Gassman, Amber Valletta, Matthew Modine, Jason Flemyng, Keith David, Kate Nauta, Francois Berleand, Jeffrey Chase, Hunter Clary; ***D:*** Louis Leterrier; ***W:*** Luc Besson, Robert Mark Kamen; ***C:*** Mitchell Amundsen; ***M:*** Alexandre Azaria.

Transporter 3 ½ **2008 (PG-13)** Frank Martin has relocated to Paris to continue his business of delivering high-risk packages on time and with no questions asked. This time the "package" is the beautiful daughter of a criminal kingpin and Frank doesn't have a choice in the matter, as he is rigged with explosives set to detonate if he fails to deliver. The third try at what started out promisingly as Besson's working-man's James Bond has become a parody of itself, simply rehashing the same impossible, over-the-top action and fight sequences and jazzing them up with copious amounts of explosions and Statham's bare, chiseled torso. More of the same mindless indulgence, just not as good as its own predecessors. **105m/C DVD.** *FR* Jason Statham, Francois Berleand, Robert Knepper, Jeroen Krabbe, Natalya Rudakova, David Atrakchi; ***D:*** Olivier Megaton; ***W:*** Luc Besson, Robert Mark Kamen; ***C:*** Giovanni Fiore Coltellacci; ***M:*** Alexandre Azaria.

Transsiberian **2008 (R)** After wrapping up their Christian-based work in China, married Americans Roy (Harrelson) and Jessie (a dynamic Mortimer) embark on a week-long train ride from Beijing to Moscow, where they are joined by Spaniard Carlos (Noriega) and his younger American girlfriend Abby (Mara). The chance encounter proves disastrous after Roy is separated from the group and Carlos' pursuit of the once-troubled Jessie—unnoticed by the naive Roy—takes a tragic turn that leaves Jessie the unknowing possessor of illegal drugs. Enter possibly-suspect Russian detective Grinko (the reliable Kingsley) whose suspicions are piqued. Murder-mystery tumbles into an action-mishap. **111m/C DVD.** *SP GE GB LI* Emily Mortimer, Woody Harrelson, Ben Kingsley, Kate Mara, Eduardo Noriega, Thomas Kretschmann; ***D:*** Brad Anderson; ***W:*** Will Conroy; ***C:*** Xavi Gimenez; ***M:*** Alfonso de Villalonga.

Transylmania **2009 (R)** Crude and obvious spoof of dumb American college students who get entangled with vampires. Rusty (Skoog) convinces his friends to join him in a study-abroad trip to Romania where the college is located in a castle allegedly belonging to his lookalike—vampire Radu. There's a crazy, Frankenstein-like doctor, a vampire huntress, various bloodsuckers, and a sorceress whose spirit possesses student Lynne (Lyons). This is actually the third installment of the Hillenbrand brothers' previously direct-to-DVD "National Lampoon's Dorm Daze" series. **95m/C DVD.** *US* Paul H. Kim, Oren Skoog, Irena A. Hoffman, Natalie Garza, Nicole Garza, Patrick Cavanaugh, James DeBello, Tony Denman, Jennifer Lyons, David Steinberg, Musetta Vander; ***D:*** David Hillenbrand, Scott Hillenbrand; ***W:*** Patrick Casey, Worm Miller; ***C:*** Viorel Sergovici Jr.

Transylvania 6-5000 **1985 (PG)** Agreeably stupid horror spoof about two klutzy reporters who stumble into modern-day Transylvania and encounter an array of comedic creatures. Shot in Yugoslavia. **93m/C VHS, DVD.** Jeff Goldblum, Joseph Bologna, Ed Begley Jr., Carol Kane, John Byner, Geena Davis, Jeffrey Jones, Norman Fell, Michael Richards; ***D:*** Rudy DeLuca; ***W:*** Rudy DeLuca; ***C:*** Tomislav Pinter; ***M:*** Lee Holdridge.

Transylvania Twist ½ **1989 (PG-13)** Moronic comedy about vampires, teenage vampire hunters and half-naked babes. **90m/C VHS, DVD.** Robert Vaughn, Teri Copley, Steve Altman, Ace Mask, Angus Scrimm, Jay Robinson, Brinke Stevens; ***D:*** Jim Wynorski; ***W:*** R.J. Robertson.

The Trap **1922** Chaney kidnaps the son of a man he's sent to prison on false charges. Rather than give up the kid when the man is released, he plans a trap. **?m/B VHS.** Lon Chaney Sr., Alan Hale, Irene Rich; ***D:*** Robert Thornby; ***W:*** George C. Hall; ***C:*** Virgil Miller.

The Trap ½ *The Baited Trap* **1959** In trying to escape justice, a ruthless crime syndicate boss holds a small desert town in a grip of fear. **84m/C VHS.** Richard Widmark, Tina Louise, Lee J. Cobb, Earl Holliman, Lorne Greene, Carl Benton Reid; ***D:*** Norman Panama; ***W:*** Norman Panama.

Trap *L'Aventure Sauvage* **1966** A trapper buys a mute girl as his wife. Together they try to make a life for themselves in the Canadian wilderness. Fine telling of interesting western tale. Unusual and realistic. **106m/C VHS.** *GB CA* Rita Tushingham, Oliver Reed, Rex Sevenoaks; ***D:*** Sidney Hayers; ***C:*** Robert Krasker.

Trap on Cougar Mountain **1972 (G)** A young boy begins a crusade to save his animal friends from the traps and bullets of hunters. **97m/C VHS.** Eric Larsen, Keith Larsen, Karen Steele; ***D:*** Keith Larsen.

Trap Them & Kill Them *Emanuelle and the Last Cannibals; Emanuelle's Amazon Adaventure; Emanuelle e Gli Ultimi Cannibali* **1977** American group traveling through the Amazon jungle encounter a terrifying aborigine tribe. Point of trip undergoes considerable reexamination. **90m/C VHS, DVD.** *IT* Laura Gemser, Gabriele Tinti, Nieves Navarro,

Donald O'Brien, Monica Zanchi; ***D:*** Joe D'Amato; ***W:*** Joe D'Amato; ***C:*** Joe D'Amato; ***M:*** Nico Fidenco.

Trapeze ☘☘☘ **1956** Lancaster is a former trapeze artist, now lame from a triple somersault accident. Curtis, the son of an old friend, wants Lancaster to teach him the routine. Lollobrigida, an aerial acrobat, is interested in both men. Exquisite European locations, fine camera work. The actors perform their own stunts. **105m/C VHS.** Burt Lancaster, Tony Curtis, Gina Lollobrigida, Katy Jurado, Thomas Gomez; ***D:*** Carol Reed; ***C:*** Robert Krasker; ***M:*** Malcolm Arnold.

Trapped ☘☘ **1/2 1949** Semi-documentary crime drama shows in semi-documentary style how the feds hunt down a gang of counterfeiters by springing one of their comrades from prison. Well-paced, suspenseful and believable. **78m/B VHS, DVD.** Lloyd Bridges, Barbara Payton, John Hoyt, James Todd; ***D:*** Richard Fleischer.

Trapped ☘ **1/2 1989 (R)** A woman working late in her high-rise office is stalked by a killer and must rely on her ingenuity to outwit him. **93m/C VHS.** Kathleen Quinlan, Bruce Abbott, Katy Boyer, Ben Loggins; ***D:*** Fred Walton; ***W:*** Fred Walton. **CABLE**

Trapped ☘ **1/2** *24 Hours* **2002 (R)** Heavy on torture, light on revenge thriller tears a perfect family's lives apart when serial kidnappers snatch their only child. Trapped in different cities at the time, parents Will (Townsend) and Karen (Theron) Jennings are at the mercy of extortionists Bacon, Love and Vince. Vince babysits the child; Love takes on the out-of-town Townsend; while Bacon terrorizes mom at their picturesque seaside home. To make matters worse, it is revealed the child is a severe asthmatic. Bacon's efforts to seduce Theron don't help matters. Overly sadistic, pointless, and painfully unwatchable despite slick production values and creepily winning performance by vet Bacon. Based upon Iles's novel "24 Hours." **105m/C VHS, DVD.** *US* Stuart Townsend, Charlize Theron, Kevin Bacon, Courtney Love, Pruitt Taylor Vince, Dakota Fanning, Colleen Camp; ***D:*** Luis Mandoki; ***W:*** Greg Iles; ***C:*** Frederick Elmes, Piotr Sobocinski; ***M:*** John Ottman.

Trapped ☘ *Dangerous Isolation* **2006** Lame thriller with eyeball-rolling acting. Internet security expert Samantha (Paul) is struggling to have a love life and raise her bratty 16-year-old daughter Gwen (Maslany). Mom and daughter are kidnapped by Adrien (Christopher), who wants Sam to hack into the FBI's database and find the whereabouts of a woman in the Witness Protection Program or Gwen is a goner. **88m/C DVD.** Alexandra Paul, Dennis Christopher, Nicholas Turturro, Tatiana Maslany, Barbara Bain, Michelle Wolf; ***D:*** Rex Piano; ***W:*** Peter Sullivan, Jason Preston; ***C:*** Mark Melville; ***M:*** Chris Anderson. **CABLE**

Trapped Alive ☘ **1/2 1993** Robin and Monica are abducted by three escaped convicts who want their car as a getaway vehicle. Trying to avoid a police roadblock the car crashes through the cover of a long-abandoned mine. When the group try to find their way out of the maze of tunnels they realize they're not down there alone. **92m/C VHS.** Alex Kubik, Elizabeth Kent, Michael Nash, Randolph Powell, Mark Witsken, Sullivan Hester, Laura Kallison, Cameron Mitchell; ***D:*** Leszek Burzynski; ***W:*** Leszek Burzynski.

Trapped by the Mormons ☘☘ *The Mormon Peril* **1922** Mormons seduce innocent young girls to add to their harems. An interesting piece of paranoid propaganda. Silent with original organ music. **97m/B VHS.** Olive Sloane, Ward McAllister, Olaf Hytten, George Wynn, Evelyn Brent, Lewis Willoughby; ***D:*** H.B. Parkinson; ***W:*** Frank Miller.

Trapped in Paradise ☘ **1/2 1994 (PG-13)** Three bungling brothers make off with a bundle of cash from the Paradise—the town, not the afterlife—bank on Christmas Eve. The locals, naive refugees from a Rockwell painting, don't recognize the buffoons as criminals, and reward their crime with hospitality that would make Frank Capra proud. Chase scenes and subplots abound as the boys spend what seems an eternity trying to make their getaway. Routine, humdrum comedy is hampered by an obvious plot. Watchable only because of Carvey, Lovitz, and Cage. **111m/C VHS, DVD.** Nicolas Cage, Jon Lovitz, Dana Carvey, John Ashton, Madchen Amick, Donald Moffat, Richard Jenkins, Florence Stanley, Angela Paton, Vic Manni, Frank Pesce, Sean McCann, Kathryn Witt, Richard B. Shull; ***D:*** George Gallo; ***W:*** George Gallo; ***M:*** Robert Folk.

Trapped in Silence ☘☘ **1986** Young Sutherland, abused since childhood, stops speaking to protect himself mentally and physically. Psychologist Mason is determined to break down the walls to help him confront his pain. Interesting cameo by Silver as a gay counselor forced out of his job when his sexual preference is discovered. Mildly melodramatic made-for-TV message drama. **94m/C VHS, DVD.** Marsha Mason, Kiefer Sutherland, John Mahoney, Amy Wright; ***Cameos:*** Ron Silver; ***D:*** Michael Tuchner.

Trapped in Space ☘☘ **1/2 1994 (PG-13)** On a mission to Venus a space shuttle is damaged by a meteor strike, leaving only enough oxygen for one person. So, what's everyone else suppose to do? Based on a short story by Arthur C. Clarke. **87m/C VHS.** Jack Wagner, Jack Coleman, Craig Wasson, Sigrid Thornton, Kay Lenz; ***D:*** Arthur Allan Seidelman; ***W:*** John Vincent Curtis, Melinda M. Snodgrass; ***M:*** Jay Gruska.

Trapper County War ☘ **1989 (R)** A city boy and a Vietnam vet band together to rescue a young woman held captive by a backwoods clan. **98m/C VHS, DVD.** Robert Estes, Bo Hopkins, Ernie Hudson, Betsy Russell, Don Swayze, Noah Blake; ***D:*** Worth Keeter; ***W:*** Russell V. Manzatt; ***C:*** Irl Dixon; ***M:*** Shuki Levy.

Traps ☘☘ **1/2 1993 (R)** Australian journalist Michael Duffield (Reynolds) and his English photographer wife Louise (Reeves) arrive for an assignment in 1950 French Indochina. Michael is to write about life on a French-owned rubber plantation, managed by Daniel (Frey), who lives with his rather peculiar daughter Viola (McKenzie). The plantation is troubled by the increasingly militant Viet-Minh rebels and it becomes clear that the four characters all have their own emotional difficulties to deal with, as well. Loosely adapted from the novel "Dreamhouse" by Kate Grenville. Feature film directing debut for Chan. **95m/C VHS.** *AU* Saskia Reeves, Robert Reynolds, Sami Frey, Jacqueline McKenzie; ***D:*** Pauline Chan; ***W:*** Pauline Chan, Robert Carter; ***C:*** Kevin Hayward; ***M:*** Douglas Stephen Rae.

Trash ☘☘ **1970** Andy Warhol's profile of a depraved couple (Warhol-veteran Dallesandro and female impersonater Woodlawn) living in a lower east side basement and scouting the streets for food and drugs. Not for those easily offended by nymphomaniacs, junkies, lice, and the like; a must for fans of underground film and the cinema verite style. **110m/C VHS, DVD.** Joe Dallesandro, Holly Woodlawn, Jane Forth, Michael Sklar, Geri Miller, Bruce Pecheur, Andrea Feldman; ***D:*** Paul Morrissey; ***W:*** Paul Morrissey; ***C:*** Paul Morrissey.

Trauma ☘ **1/2 1962** A girl suffers amnesia after the trauma of witnessing her aunt's murder. She returns to the mansion years later to piece together what happened. A sometimes tedious psychological thriller. **93m/C VHS, DVD.** John Conte, Lynn Bari, Lorrie Richards, David Garner, Warren Kemmerling, William Bissell, Bond Blackman, William Justine; ***D:*** Robert M. Young.

Trauma ☘ **1/2 2004 (R)** Style trumps plot. Londoner Ben (Firth) awakens from a coma and learns his wife Elisa (Harris) was killed in the same car accident that injured him. Devastated and trying to make a fresh start, Ben moves into a new place and is befriended by neighbor Charlotte (Suvari). Things aren't going so well though since Ben keeps having visions of his dead wife and a police detective (Cranham) also suspects him of involvement in the murder of a pop singer. **96m/C DVD.** *GB* Colin Firth, Mena Suvari, Naomie Harris, Kenneth Cranham, Tommy Flanagan, Sean Harris, Brenda Fricker; ***D:*** Marc Evans; ***W:*** Richard Curson Smith; ***C:*** John Mathieson; ***M:*** Alex Heffes.

Traveling Companion ☘☘ *Compagna di Viaggio* **1996** Cora (Argento) is a somewhat unstable teenager who makes a living with a variety of jobs, including dog-walking. One of her clients, Ada (Cohen), hires Cora to follow Ada's elderly father, Cosimo (Piccoli). A retired professor, Cosimo has become forgetful and gets lost while wandering around Rome. When Cosimo gets on a train, Cora follows and embarks on a series of encounters that lead to a journey of self-discovery. Italian with subtitles. **104m/C VHS, DVD.** *IT* Asia Argento, Michel Piccoli, Lino Capolicchio, Silvia Cohen, Max Malatesta; ***D:*** Peter Del Monte; ***W:*** Gloria Malatesta, Peter Del Monte, Claudia Sbarigia; ***C:*** Giuseppe Lanci; ***M:*** Dario Lucantoni.

Traveling Man ☘☘ **1989** Drama about a veteran traveling salesman who's assigned an eager young apprentice when his sales go down. Lithgow gives a great performance as the burnt-out traveling salesman. **105m/C VHS, DVD.** John Lithgow, Jonathan Silverman, Margaret Colin, John Glover; ***D:*** Irvin Kershner; ***M:*** Miles Goodman. **CABLE**

The Traveling Saleswoman ☘ **1/2 1950** Western comedy in which Mabel (Davis) becomes a traveling saleswoman for King Soap to help her father save the company from bankruptcy. But Mabel manages to get herself in trouble with rustlers and gunfights. **75m/B VHS.** Joan Davis, Andy Devine, Adele Jergens, Joseph (Joe) Sawyer, Dean Reisner, John Cason; ***D:*** Charles Reisner; ***W:*** Howard Dimsdale; ***C:*** George E. Diskant.

Traveller ☘☘☘ **1996 (R)** Deriving its name from the real-life group of wily Irish-American con men who prowl the Southeast, this view into the lives and clannish ways of its members may have you checking that brand-spankin' new driveway sealant. Their basic philosophy is: if you're not one of us, we're allowed to take all of your money. Bokky (Paxton) is the jack-of-all-tricks who takes the younger Pat (Wahlberg) under his wing after the boy is shunned by the rest of the group. Pat's father married outside the clan, and that's not allowed. Bokky falls into the same trap, however, when a beautiful bartender (Margulies), who he has just fleeced, steals his heart. Rather violent ending dims the good feeling that builds and may leave you feeling...well, cheated. Directorial debut of long-time Clint Eastwood cinematographer Jack Green, who also shot "Twister" with Paxton. **100m/C VHS, DVD.** Bill Paxton, Mark Wahlberg, Julianna Margulies, James Gammon, Luke Askew, Michael Shaner, Nikki Deloach, Danielle Wiener; ***D:*** Jack N. Green; ***W:*** Jim McGlynn; ***C:*** Jack N. Green; ***M:*** Andy Paley.

Travelling North ☘☘ **1987 (PG-13)** A belligerent retiree falls in love with a divorcee and they move together to a rustic retreat. They have an idyllic existence until the man discovers he has a serious heart condition. Adaptation of David Williamson's play has fine performances. **97m/C VHS.** *AU* Leo McKern, Julia Blake; ***D:*** Carl Schultz; ***W:*** David Williamson. Australian Film Inst. '87: Actor (McKern); Montreal World Film Fest. '87: Actor (McKern).

The Travelling Players ☘☘ *O Thiassos* **1975** Slow-going for those unfamiliar with Greek myths and modern Greek history as the country is continually oppressed and betrayed. A travelling company of provicial actors ply their trade over some 16 years (1936-1952) while their country experiences the upheavals of a fascist dictatorship, WWII, occupation, civil war, and repression by the right-wing regime. The focus is on ordinary people in ordinary surroundings (with Angelopoulous leaning towards the communist sensibility). Greek with subtitles. **230m/C VHS.** *GR* Eva Kotamanidou, Maria Vassilou, Petros Zarkadis, Aliki Georgouli, Stratos Pahis; ***D:*** Theo Angelopoulos; ***W:*** Theo Angelopoulos; ***C:*** Yorgos Arvanitis; ***M:*** Loukianos Kilaidonis.

Travels with My Aunt ☘☘ **1/2 1972 (PG)** A banker leading a mundane life is taken on a wild, whirlwind tour of Europe by an eccentric woman claiming to be his aunt. Based on Graham Greene's best-selling novel. **109m/C** Maggie Smith, Alec McCowen, Louis Gossett Jr., Robert Stephens, Cindy Williams; ***D:*** George Cukor; ***W:*** Jay Presson Allen. Oscars '72: Costume Des.

Traxx ☘ **1987 (R)** Satire about an ex-cop soldier of fortune. Not surprisingly, Stevens doesn't do much with this lame script. **84m/C VHS.** Shadoe Stevens, Priscilla Barnes, Willard Pugh, John Hancock, Robert Davi, Rick Overton; ***D:*** Jerome Gary; ***W:*** Gary De Vore; ***M:*** Jay Gruska.

Treacherous Beauties ☘☘ **1994** Photojournalist Anne Marie Kerr's (Samms) brother Alan (Rutledge) has supposedly been killed in a hunting accident. Suspicious, Anne Marie assumes a new identity and gets a job at Hollister Farms to investigate. She realizes the horse farm has big financial problems and someone doesn't want Anne Marie snooping around either. From the Harlequin Romance Series; adapted from the Cheryl Emerson novel. **91m/C DVD.** *CA* Emma Samms, Mark Humphrey, Bruce Greenwood, Tippi Hedren, Catherine Oxenberg, Ron White, Paul Rutledge; ***D:*** Charles Jarrott; ***W:*** Jim Henshaw, Naomi Janzen; ***C:*** Malcolm Cross; ***M:*** Jack Lenz. **TV**

Treacherous Crossing ☘☘ **1992 (PG)** When her husband disappears on their honeymoon cruise heiress Wagner tries to get the ship's crew to help her. They think she's crazy, but aided by new friend Dickinson, Wagner intends to find out just what's going on. Based on the radio play "Cabin B-13" by John Dickson Carr. **88m/C VHS.** Lindsay Wagner, Angie Dickinson, Grant Show, Joseph Bottoms, Karen Medak, Charles Napier, Jeffrey DeMunn, Erik Avari; ***D:*** Tony Wharmby; ***W:*** Elisa Bell; ***C:*** Brian West; ***M:*** Curt Sobel.

Tread Softly Stranger ☘☘ **1/2 1958** British blonde bombshell Dors is the catalyst for trouble in this crime drama. Gambler Johnny Mansell (Baker) flees his London debts to return to his Rawborough hometown. He moves in with his clerk brother Dave (Morgan), who has a girlfriend, nightclub dancer Calico (Dors), with expensive tastes. Dave has turned to embezzlement to buy her presents and Johnny tries to win money at the track before Dave's light fingers are discovered. Urged on by Calico, Dave goes ahead with a plan to rob the payroll office, but things go wrong. **90m/B DVD.** *GB* George Baker, Terence Morgan, Diana Dors, Patrick Allen, Jane Griffiths, Maureen Delaney; ***D:*** Gordon Parry; ***W:*** George Minter, Denis O'Dell; ***C:*** Douglas Slocombe; ***M:*** Tristram Cary.

Treason ☘☘ **1933** Confederate sympathizer Joan Randall has established her own republic in southern Kansas and the government has put a price on her head. Army scout Jeff Connors infiltrates her troops and falls in love with Joan so he hopes to obtain a pardon for her but there's more trouble to come. **63m/B DVD.** Buck Jones, Shirley Grey, Robert Ellis, Ed LeSaint, Frank Lackteen, Ivor McFadden, Charles Hill Mailes; ***D:*** George B. Seitz; ***W:*** George Battle; ***C:*** John Boyle.

Treasure Island ☘☘☘ **1/2 1934** Fleming's adaptation of Robert Louis Stevenson's 18th-century English pirate tale of Long John Silver is a classic. Beery is great as the pirate; Cooper has trouble playing the boy. Also available colorized. Multitudinous remakes. **102m/B VHS, DVD.** Wallace Beery, Jackie Cooper, Lionel Barrymore, Lewis Stone, Otto Kruger, Douglass Dumbrille, Charles "Chic" Sale, Nigel Bruce; ***D:*** Victor Fleming; ***C:*** Clyde De Vinna.

Treasure Island ☘☘☘ **1/2 1950 (PG)** Spine-tingling Robert Louis Stevenson tale of pirates and buried treasure, in which young cabin boy Jim Hawkins matches wits with Long John Silver. Some editions excise extra violence. Stevenson's ending is revised. Full Disney treatment, excellent casting. **96m/C VHS, DVD.** Bobby Driscoll, Robert Newton, Basil Sydney, Walter Fitzgerald, Denis O'Dea, Ralph Truman, Finlay Currie; ***D:*** Byron Haskin; ***C:*** Frederick A. (Freddie) Young.

Treasure Island ☘☘ *La Isla Del Tersoro* **1972 (G)** Unexceptional British reheat of familiar pirate tale. Welles' interpretation of Long John Silver may be truer to Stevenson, but it's one heckuva blustering binge. **94m/C VHS.** *GB* Orson Welles, Kim Burfield, Walter Slezak, Lionel Stander; ***D:*** John Hough; ***W:*** Orson Welles.

Treasure Island ☘☘ **1/2 1989** Excellent cable version of the classic Robert Louis Stevenson pirate tale with Heston as Long John Silver. Written, produced, and directed by Fraser Heston, son of Charlton. **131m/C VHS.** Charlton Heston, Christian Bale, Julian Glover, Richard Johnson, Oliver Reed, Christopher Lee, Clive Wood, Nicholas Amer, Michael Halsey; ***D:*** Fraser Heston; ***W:*** Fraser Heston. **CABLE**

Treasure Island 1/2 **1999** Near the end of WWII, two officers of the fictional intelligence compound called "Treasure Island" are given a dead body and a covert assignment: construct a fake "backstory." When dumped in the ocean, it is hoped that the false information will send the Japanese in the wrong direction. The two officers find themselves consumed by visions of the body, which seems to show up everywhere. Challenging and ambitious puzzle of a film which is filled with coded messages, encrypted dialogue, and implied meanings. Certainly not for all audiences, but a funny and fascinating exercise in style and cinematic invention. **83m/B DVD.** Lance Baker, Nick Offerman, Jonah Blechman; ***D:*** Scott King; ***W:*** Scott King; ***C:*** Scott King, Phillip Glau; ***M:*** Chris Anderson.

Treasure Island 1/2 **1999 (PG)** Appropriately adventurous version of Robert L. Stevenson's often-filmed tale of young Jim Hawkins, who has a treasure map and a boatload of pirates eager for the riches hidden on Treasure Island! Palance is notably snarly as peg-legged Long John Silver. **95m/C VHS, DVD.** *CA* Jack Palance, Kevin Zegers, Patrick Bergin; ***D:*** Peter Rowe; ***W:*** Peter Rowe; ***C:*** Marc Charlebois.

Treasure of Arne 1/2 **1919** A 16th century Scottish mercenary kills and loots the estate of rich, well-to-do property owner Sir Arne. Famous early Swedish silent that established Stiller as a director. **78m/B VHS, DVD.** *SW* Erik Stocklassa, Bror Berger, Richard Lund, Axel Nilsson, Hjalmar Selander; ***D:*** Mauritz Stiller; ***W:*** Gustaf Molander, Mauritz Stiller; ***C:*** Julius Jaenzon.

The Treasure of Bengal 1/2 **1953** Sabu attempts to stop his chief from trading the village's precious gem (the largest ruby in the world) for firearms. **72m/C VHS.** *IT* Brigitte Corey, Luigi Tosi, Sabu; ***D:*** Gianni Vernuccio; ***W:*** Gian Paolo Callegari; ***C:*** Renato Del Frate; ***M:*** Italo Delle Case.

Treasure of Fear 1/2 *Scared Stiff* **1945** A bungling newspaper reporter gets involved with four jade chessmen once owned by Kubla Khan. A few laughs in this contrived haunted house story. **66m/B VHS, DVD.** Jack Haley, Barton MacLane, Ann Savage, Veda Ann Borg, Arthur Aylesworth, Lucien Littlefield, George E. Stone, Paul Hurst, Robert Emmett Keane, Eily Malyon; ***D:*** Frank McDonald; ***W:*** Maxwell Shane, Daniel Mainwaring; ***C:*** Fred H. Jackman Jr.

The Treasure of Jamaica Reef 1/2 **1974 (PG)** Adventurers battle sharks and other nasty fish as they seek a sunken Spanish galleon and its cache of golden treasure. **96m/C VHS, DVD.** Cheryl Ladd, Stephen Boyd, Roosevelt "Rosie" Grier, David Ladd, Darby Hinton; ***D:*** Virginia Lively Stone.

The Treasure of Matecumbe **1976 (G)** A motley crew of adventurers led by a young boy search for buried treasure as they are pursued by Indians and other foes. Filmed in the Florida Key Islands. **107m/C VHS.** Billy Attmore, Robert Foxworth, Joan Hackett, Peter Ustinov, Vic Morrow; ***D:*** Vincent McEveety; ***M:*** Buddy (Norman Dale) Baker.

Treasure of Monte Cristo **1950** A woman marries a seaman said to be an ancestor of the Count for his inheritance. Instead, she finds love and mystery. **78m/B VHS, DVD.** *GB* Adele Jergens, Steve Brodie, Glenn Langan; ***D:*** William Berke.

Treasure of Pancho Villa 1/2 **1955** An American adventurer plots a gold heist to help Villa's revolution. He encounters every obstacle in the West while on his way to help the Mexican rebel. **96m/C VHS.** Rory Calhoun, Shelley Winters, Gilbert Roland; ***D:*** George Sherman.

The Treasure of the Amazon 1/2 *El Tesoro del Amazones* **1984** Three fortune hunters embark on a perilous search for wealth in the South American jungles. Silly and unnecessarily violent. **105m/C VHS, DVD.** *MX* Stuart Whitman, Donald Pleasence, Ann Sydney, Bradford Dillman, John Ireland; ***D:*** Rene Cardona Jr.

Treasure of the Four Crowns **1982 (PG)** Aging history professor hires a team of tough commandos to recover four legendary crowns containing the source of mystical powers. The crowns are being held under heavy guard by a crazed cult leader. **97m/C VHS.** *SP* Tony Anthony, Anna (Ana Garcia) Obregon, Gene Quintano; ***D:*** Ferdinando Baldi; ***W:*** Lloyd Battista, James Bryce; ***M:*** Ennio Morricone.

Treasure of the Golden Condor 1/2 **1953** A swashbuckler heads to the jungles of 18th-century Guatemala in search of ancient treasure. Contains interesting footage of Mayan ruins, but otherwise ordinary. A remake of "Son of Fury." **93m/C VHS.** Cornel Wilde, Connie Smith, Fay Wray, Anne Bancroft, Leo G. Carroll, Robert (Bobby) Blake; ***D:*** Delmer Daves.

Treasure of the Lost Desert 1/2 **1983** A Green Beret crushes a terrorist operation in the Middle East. **93m/C VHS.** Bruce Miller, Susan West, Larry Finch; ***D:*** Tony Zarindast.

Treasure of the Moon Goddess **WOOF! 1988 (R)** A dizzy nightclub singer is mistaken by Central American pirates and natives for the earthly manifestation of their Moon Goddess. **90m/C VHS.** Don Calfa, Joann Ayres, Asher Brauner; ***D:*** Joseph Louis Agraz.

Treasure of the Sierra Madre **1948** Three prospectors in search of gold in Mexico find suspicion, treachery and greed. Bogart is superbly believable as the paranoid, and ultimately homicidal, Fred C. Dobbs. Huston directed his father and wrote the screenplay, based on a B. Traven story. **126m/B VHS, DVD.** Humphrey Bogart, Walter Huston, Tim Holt, Bruce Bennett, Barton MacLane, Robert (Bobby) Blake, Alfonso Bedoya; ***D:*** John Huston; ***W:*** John Huston; ***C:*** Ted D. McCord; ***M:*** Max Steiner. Oscars '48: Director (Huston), Screenplay, Support. Actor (Huston); AFI '98: Top 100; Golden Globes '49: Director (Huston), Film—Drama, Support. Actor (Huston); Natl. Bd. of Review '48: Actor (Huston), Natl. Film Reg. '90;; N.Y. Film Critics '48: Director (Huston), Film.

Treasure of the Yankee Zephyr *Race for the Yankee Zephyr* **1983 (PG)** Trio joins in the quest for a plane that has been missing for 40 years...with a cargo of $50 million. They have competition in the form of Peppard and cronies. Decent cast muddles through the predictable plotting. **108m/C VHS, DVD.** *AU NZ* Ken Wahl, George Peppard, Donald Pleasence, Lesley Ann Warren, Bruno Lawrence, Grant Tilly; ***D:*** David Hemmings; ***M:*** Brian May.

Treasure Planet 1/2 **2002 (PG)** Futuristic fairy tale has pirate ships in space gracing this awkwardly mod animated update of Robert Louis Stevenson's classic "Treasure Island." Jim Hawkins (voiced by Gordon-Levitt, with singing voice of Rzeznik), the troubled teen hero, and a trio of irritating sidekicks take to the skies in their souped-up space galleon to find buried treasure on (where else?) Treasure Planet. Mutiny and other problems, including a looming black hole and space storms just as scary as the ones at sea, show up to threaten the mission. Innovative mix of hand drawn and computer animation is visually rich, even magical, at times but fails to fully delight. **95m/C VHS, DVD.** *US* ***D:*** John Musker, Ron Clements; ***W:*** John Musker, Ron Clements, Rob Edwards; ***M:*** James Newton Howard; ***V:*** Joseph Gordon-Levitt, Brian Murray, Emma Thompson, David Hyde Pierce, Michael Wincott, Martin Short, Laurie Metcalf, Patrick McGoohan, Roscoe Lee Browne, Corey Burton, Michael McShane, Dane A. Davis, Austin Majors; ***Nar:*** Tony Jay.

The Treasure Seekers **1979** Four rival divers set off on a perilous Caribbean expedition in search of the legendary treasure of Morgan the Pirate. **88m/C VHS.** Rod Taylor, Stuart Whitman, Elke Sommer, Keenan Wynn, Jeremy Kemp; ***D:*** Henry Levin; ***W:*** Rod Taylor; ***C:*** Joe Jackman, Richard A. Kelley; ***M:*** Byron Lee.

The Treat **1998 (R)** Smalltown prostitutes get invited to work the mayor's birthday party where a disaster leaves them struggling to get out alive. **87m/C VHS, DVD.** Julie Delpy, Georgina Cates, Pamela Gidley, Daniel Baldwin, Patrick Dempsey, Seymour Cassel, Vincent Perez, Alfred Molina, Michael York, Yancy Butler, Mark Boone Jr., Richmond Arquette, Larry Drake; ***D:*** Jonathan Gems; ***W:*** Jonathan Gems; ***C:*** Joey Forsyte; ***M:*** Stephen Croes.

The Treatment 1/2 **2006** Slight romantic comedy set mainly in New York's Upper West Side finds angst-ridden English teacher Jake (Eigeman) trying to deal with his romantic travails in his weekly sessions with demanding Freudian shrink, Dr. Morales (Holm). When Jake becomes interested in wealthy and recently widowed Allegra (Janssen), Morales encourages a fling but no deep involvement, advice Jake promptly ignores. A generally smart take on NY neuroses, with performances and a script to match. Adapted from Daniel Menaker's 1998 novel. **86m/C DVD.** *US* Christopher Eigeman, Famke Janssen, Harris Yulin, Stephanie March, Blair Brown, Roger Rees, Stephen Lang; ***D:*** Oren Rudavsky; ***W:*** Oren Rudavsky, Daniel Housman; ***C:*** Andrij Parekh; ***M:*** John Zorn.

A Tree Grows in Brooklyn 1/2 **1945 (PG)** Sensitive young Irish lass growing up in turn-of-the-century Brooklyn tries to rise above her tenement existence. Based on the novel by Betty Smith. Kazan's directorial debut. **128m/B VHS, DVD.** Peggy Ann Garner, James Dunn, Dorothy McGuire, Joan Blondell, Lloyd Nolan, Ted Donaldson, James Gleason, John Alexander, Charles Halton; ***D:*** Elia Kazan; ***C:*** Leon Shamroy; ***M:*** Alfred Newman. Oscars '45: Support. Actor (Dunn).

The Tree of Wooden Clogs 1/2 *L'Albero Degli Zoccoli* **1978** Epic view of the lives of four peasant families working on an estate in turn of the century Northern Italy. The title comes from the shoes the peasants wear. When a young boy breaks a shoe, his father risks punishment by cutting down one of his landlord's trees to make a new pair of clogs. Slow moving and beautiful, from former industrial filmmaker Olmi. In Italian with English subtitles. **185m/C VHS, DVD.** *IT* Luigi Ornaghi, Francesca Moriggi, Omar Brignoll, Antonio Ferrari; ***D:*** Ermanno Olmi; ***W:*** Ermanno Olmi; ***C:*** Ermanno Olmi. Cannes '78: Film; N.Y. Film Critics '79: Foreign Film.

Treehouse Hostage 1/2 **1999 (PG)** Timmy needs a real current-events project if he doesn't want to get stuck in summer school. Fortunately, he and some friends manage to capture an escaped counterfeiter, Banks (Varney), and turn him in for a grade. Only it turns out that the school principal is actually the head of the counterfeiting ring. **90m/C VHS, DVD.** Jim Varney, Joey Zimmerman, Richard Kline, Todd Bosley, Mark Moses, Debbie Boone, Jack McGee, Aria Noelle Curzon, Vincent Schiavelli; ***D:*** Sean McNamara; ***W:*** Jeff Phillips; ***C:*** Mark Doering-Powell; ***M:*** John Coda.

Treeless Mountain **2008** Desperate Seoul mom dumps her two young daughters on her alcoholic sister-in-law when she decides to look for her absent husband. The young girls are bewildered and their aunt is indifferent to them so the sisters' plight can only get better when they are later sent on to their grandparents farm in the country. Korean with subtitles. **89m/C DVD.** *KN* Heo-yeon Kim, Song-hee Kim, Soo-ah Lee, Mi-hyang Kim, Park-boon Tak; ***D:*** So-yong Kim; ***W:*** So-yong Kim; ***C:*** Anne Misawa; ***M:*** Asobi Seksu.

Tree's Lounge 1/2 **1996 (R)** First time director/writer Buscemi takes a look at the downward-spiraling life of Tommy Basilio (Buscemi), a working-class misfit who loses his job and then spends most of his time hanging out at the dreary local bar. He finally winds up driving an ice cream truck, only leading to more trouble when his teenaged helper, Debbie (Sevigny), develops a crush on him—a situation her hot-headed father Jerry (Baldwin) takes exception to. And the irresponsible Tommy is finally forced to realize that his ill-concerned actions have consequences. **94m/C VHS, DVD.** Steve Buscemi, Chloe Sevigny, Daniel Baldwin, Elizabeth Bracco, Anthony LaPaglia, Debi Mazar, Carol Kane, Seymour Cassel, Mark Boone Jr., Eszter Balint, Mimi Rogers, Kevin Corrigan, Samuel L. Jackson; ***D:*** Steve Buscemi; ***W:*** Steve Buscemi; ***C:*** Lisa Rinzler; ***M:*** Evan Lurie.

Tremors 1/2 **1989 (PG-13)** A tiny desert town is attacked by giant man-eating worm-creatures. Bacon and Ward are the handymen trying to save the town. Amusing, with good special effects. **96m/C VHS, DVD, HD DVD.** Kevin Bacon, Fred Ward, Finn Carter, Michael Gross, Reba McEntire, Bibi Besch, Bobby Jacoby, Charlotte Stewart, Victor Wong, Tony Genaros, Ariana Richards; ***D:*** Ron Underwood; ***W:*** S.S. Wilson, Brent Maddock; ***C:*** Alexander Grusynski; ***M:*** Ernest Troost.

Tremors 2: Aftershocks 1/2 **1996 (PG-13)** They're baaaaack! The Graboids have resurfaced to eat their way through Mexican oil fields and it's up to tough guys Earl Bassett (Ward) and Burt Gummer (Gross) to get rid of the toothy worms once and for all. Same mix of tongue-in-cheek humor and special effects as the first film. **100m/C VHS, DVD.** Fred Ward, Michael Gross, Helen Shaver, Christopher Gartin, Marcelo Tubert; ***D:*** S.S. Wilson; ***W:*** S.S. Wilson, Brent Maddock; ***C:*** Virgil Harper; ***M:*** Jay Ferguson.

Tremors 3: Back to Perfection **2001 (PG-13)** Gross returns to his hometown of Perfection, Nevada, and sees a cheesy theme park based on the Graboids has opened. Then real Graboids return to wreck havoc again. **104m/C VHS, DVD.** Michael Gross, Charlotte Stewart, Shawn Christian, Ariana Richards, Susan Chung, Helen Shaver, Christopher Gartin; ***D:*** Brent Maddock; ***W:*** John Whelpley; ***C:*** Virgil Harper; ***M:*** Kevin Kiner. **VIDEO**

The Trench 1/2 **1999** A sober look at the two-day buildup to the catastrophic Battle of the Somme in 1916 from the point of view of teenaged British Army soldier Billy Macfarlane (Nicholls). His tough sargeant, Telford Winter (Craig), tries to prepare the raw recruits for battle as they hunker down in their damp, vermin-infested trench but nothing can prepare them for the senseless carnage to come. Familiar cliches abound but the performances are strong. **90m/C VHS, DVD.** *GB* Paul Nicholls, Daniel Craig, Julian Rhind-Tutt, Danny Dyer, James D'Arcy, Ciaran McMenamin, Tam Williams, Anthony Strachan; ***D:*** William Boyd; ***W:*** William Boyd; ***C:*** Tony Pierce-Roberts; ***M:*** Evelyn Glennie, Greg Malcangi.

Trenchcoat 1/2 **1983** Aspiring mystery writer travels to Malta to research her new novel and is drawn into a real-life conspiracy. Silly and contrived spoof of the detective genre. **95m/C VHS.** Margot Kidder, Robert Hays; ***D:*** Michael Tuchner; ***W:*** Jeffrey Price, Peter S. Seaman; ***M:*** Charles Fox.

Trespass *Looters* **1992 (R)** Violent crime tale set in East St. Louis, Illinois. Two redneck firemen learn about stolen gold artifacts supposedly hidden in an abandoned building and go on a treasure hunt. When they witness a murder they also get involved in a battle between two crime lords—who want these interlopers dead. What follows is a deadly game of cat-and-mouse. Lots of action but it's all fairly routine. Original release date of summer 1992 was delayed until the winter because of unfortunate similarities to the L.A. riots. **104m/C VHS, DVD.** Ice Cube, Ice-T, William Sadler, Bill Paxton, Art Evans; ***D:*** Walter Hill; ***W:*** Robert Zemeckis, Bob Gale; ***C:*** Lloyd Ahern II; ***M:*** Ry Cooder.

Trespasser **1981** A painter has an affair with a young woman. He comes to regret destroying his family and their life together. Based on a D.H. Lawrence novel. **90m/C VHS.** *GB* Alan Bates, Dinah Stabb, Pauline Morgan, Margaret Whiting; ***D:*** Colin Gregg; ***W:*** Hugh Stoddart; ***C:*** John Metcalfe; ***M:*** Julian Dawson-Lyell.

Trespasses **1986 (R)** Couple of drifters wander into a Texas town where they rape a local woman and kill a local rancher's son. So the fathers of the victims decide to get revenge. Brutal and tedious. **90m/C VHS.** Lou Diamond Phillips, Robert Kuhn, Ben Johnson, Adam Roarke, Mary Pillot, Van Brooks; ***D:*** Adam Roarke, Lauren Bivens; ***W:*** Lou Diamond Phillips.

The Trial *Le Proces; Der Prozess; Il Processo* **1963** Expressionistic Welles adaptation of classic Kafka novella about an innocent man accused, tried, and convicted of an unknown crime in an unnamed exaggeratedly bureaucratic country. Another Welles project that met with constant disaster in production, with many lapses in continuity. **118m/B VHS, DVD.** *FR* Anthony Perkins, Jeanne Moreau, Orson Welles, Romy Schneider, Akim Tamiroff, Elsa Martinelli; ***D:*** Orson Welles; ***W:*** Orson Welles; ***C:*** Edmond Richard; ***M:*** Jean Ledrut.

The Trial **1993** Spare adaptation of Franz Kafka's novel finds Prague bank clerk Joseph K (MacLachlan) arrested on unknown charges. His increasing guilt and paranoia fit well into a world where the most illogical things happen in the most matter of fact way. Good visuals. **120m/C VHS, DVD.** Kyle MacLachlan, Anthony Hopkins, Jason Robards Jr., Polly Walker, Juliet Stevenson, Alfred Molina; ***D:*** David Hugh Jones; ***W:*** Harold Pinter; ***C:*** Phil Meheux; ***M:*** Carl Davis.

Trial & Error ½ *The Dock Brief* **1962** Comedic satire, based on the play by John Mortimer, finds hapless lawyer Morgenhall (Sellers) thinking he's finally got his big chance when he defends wife murderer Fowle (Attenborough). Fowle wants to plead guilty but Morgenhall dreams of being a court star and insists on pleading his client innocent. It's a disaster just waiting to happen. **78m/B VHS, DVD.** *GB* Peter Sellers, Richard Attenborough, Beryl Reid, David Lodge, Frank Pettingell, Eric Woodburn; ***D:*** James Hill; ***W:*** Pierre Rouve; ***C:*** Edward Scaife; ***M:*** Ron Grainer.

Trial and Error ½ **1992** Peter Hudson (Matheson) is an overly zealous prosecutor who successfully convicts a small time criminal of murder, sending him to death row. This launches Hudson's political career and five years later he's about to be nominated for Lieutenant Governor, just as the felon's execution draws near. Suddenly, new evidence points to the man's innocence, but if Hudson investigates it could ruin his political future. But he's got a bigger problem—the real killer decides to make Hudson's wife his next victim. **91m/C VHS.** Tim Matheson, Helen Shaver, Sean McCann, Eugene Clark; ***D:*** Mark Sobel.

Trial and Error ½ **1996 (PG-13)** Courtroom comedy may remind you of another law oriented movie. No, not "Kramer vs. Kramer." It's "My Cousin Vinny," also directed by Lynn. Both feature fake lawyers defending hopeless clients in small towns. In this case, lawyer Charles Tuttle (Daniels) is too messed up from his bachelor party to make it to court for a case in which the defendent Benny (Torn), a relative of Chuck's big-wig future father-in-law, is accused of selling mail-order "commemorative copper Lincoln engravings" which are actually pennies. His best bud Richard (Richards), an actor, decides to stand in for him, and the legal slip-and-pratfalls ensue. Richards as the physical comedian and Daniels as the white bread straight man have great comic chemistry, but the plot won't surprise you much. **98m/C VHS, DVD.** Michael Richards, Jeff Daniels, Rip Torn, Charlize Theron, Jessica Steen, Austin Pendleton, Alexandra Wentworth, Lawrence Pressman, Dale Dye, Max Casella, Jennifer Coolidge; ***D:*** Jonathan Lynn; ***W:*** Sarah Bernstein, Gregory Bernstein; ***C:*** Gabriel Beristain; ***M:*** Phil Marshall.

Trial by Jury ½ **1994 (R)** Strong cast, lame script. Idealistic single mother Valerie Alston (Whalley-Kilmer) winds up on the jury trying notorious mobster Rusty Pirone (Assante). Rusty's henchman, Tommy Vesey (Hurt), lets Valerie know that her son is in mortal danger if she doesn't find his boss innocent. Of course DA Daniel Graham (Byrne) is equally adamant about a conviction and is willing to use Valerie any way he has to. **107m/C VHS, DVD.** Joanne Whalley, William Hurt, Gabriel Byrne, Armand Assante, Kathleen Quinlan, Stuart Whitman, Margaret Whitton, Ed Lauter, Joe Santos, Richard Portnow, Beau Starr, Mike Starr, John Capodice, Lisa Arrindell Anderson; ***D:*** Heywood Gould; ***W:*** Heywood Gould, Jordan Katz; ***C:*** Frederick Elmes; ***M:*** Terence Blanchard.

Trial by Media ½ *An American Daughter* **2000** Lyssa Dent Hughes (Lahti) is a prominent D.C. doctor (and senator's daughter) who has been nominated to become surgeon general. But thanks to media scrutiny, and some careless remarks, she becomes a target and her nomination is in jeopardy. Wasserstein scripted from her 1997 play "American Daughter." **92m/C VHS, DVD.** Christine Lahti, Tom Skerritt, Jay Thomas, Mark Feuerstein, Lynne Thigpen, Stanley Anderson, Blake Lindsley; ***D:*** Sheldon Larry; ***W:*** Wendy Wasserstein; ***C:*** Albert J. Dunk; ***M:*** Phil Marshall. **CABLE**

The Trial of Billy Jack **WOOF!** **1974 (PG)** Billy Jack takes on the feds and beats the hell out of a lot of people to prove that the world can live in peace. Awful, pretentious film. **175m/C VHS, DVD.** Tom Laughlin, Delores Taylor, Victor Izay, Teresa Laughlin, William Wellman Jr., Russell Lane, Michelle Wilson, Geo Ann Sosa, George Aguilar, Sacheen Little Feather; ***D:*** Frank Laughlin, Tom Laughlin; ***W:*** Tom Laughlin, Delores Taylor; ***C:*** Jack Marta; ***M:*** Elmer Bernstein.

The Trial of Lee Harvey Oswald **1977** What would've happened if Jack Ruby had not shot Oswald. Oswald's trial and its likely results are painstakingly created. **192m/C VHS, DVD.** Ben Gazzara, Lorne Greene, John Pleshette, Lawrence Pressman; ***D:*** Gordon Davidson. **TV**

The Trial of Old Drum ½ **2000 (PG)** Set in 1955 and based on a true story. 11-year-old Charlie (Edner) lives in a small farming community with his widowed father Charles (Perlman). His best friend is his golden retriever Drum, who was trained by his late mother to protect the boy. The duo's problems lie with his surly maternal Uncle Lon (Schuck), who dislikes the dog and says Drum is a sheep-killer. Lon shoots the dog for being on his property and the sheriff sends poor Drum to the pound before his case goes to court. Charlie and his father enlist the services of lawyer George Graham Vest (Bakula) and Drum's trial is both humorous and touching. **88m/C VHS, DVD.** Bobby Edner, Ron Perlman, John Schuck, Scott Bakula, Randy Travis, David Graf, Dick Martin, Alia Shawkat; ***D:*** Sean McNamara; ***W:*** Ralph Gaby Wilson; ***C:*** Mark Doering-Powell.

Trial of the Catonsville Nine ½ **1972 (PG)** Riveting political drama that focuses on the trial of nine anti-war activists, including Father Daniel Berrigan, during the Vietnam War days of the late 1960s. Imperfect, but involving. **85m/C VHS.** Ed Flanders, Douglas Watson, William Schallert, Peter Strauss, Richard Jordan; ***D:*** Gordon Davidson.

The Trial of the Incredible Hulk **1989** The Hulk returns to battle organized crime and is aided by his blind superhero/lawyer friend Daredevil. Followed by "The Death of the Incredible Hulk." **96m/C VHS, DVD.** Bill Bixby, Lou Ferrigno, Rex Smith, John Rhys-Davies, Marta DuBois, Nancy Everhard, Nicholas Hormann; ***D:*** Bill Bixby. **TV**

The Trials of Oscar Wilde *The Man with the Green Carnation; The Green Carnation* **1960** Finch is the highlight as playwright/wit Wilde, who ill-advisedly sues the Marquis of Queensbury (Jeffries) for libel when the peer accuses him of being a sodomite. Wilde is, in fact, having an affair with the Marquis' son, Lord Alfred Douglas (Fraser), which eventually leads to Wilde's imprisonment and the destruction of his life. Based on the play "The Stringed Lute" by John Furnell and the book "The Trials of Oscar Wilde" by Montgomery Hyde. **123m/C VHS.** *GB* Peter Finch, John Fraser, Lionel Jeffries, Nigel Patrick, James Mason, Yvonne Mitchell, Maxine Audley, James Booth, Paul Rogers, Ian Fleming, Laurence Naismith; ***D:*** Ken Hughes; ***W:*** Ken Hughes; ***C:*** Ted Moore; ***M:*** Ronald Goodwin.

The Triangle **2001** This triangle is the Bermuda kind as friends charter a boat for their annual Caribbean fishing trip and instead discover the Queen of Scots, a ghostly luxury liner that has been missing for 60 years. Boarding the ship turns out to be a big mistake since the tragedy that overtook the lives of the passengers and crew lingers and begins to affect the present. **92m/C VHS, DVD.** Luke Perry, Dan Cortese, Olivia D'Abo, Dorian Harewood, Polly Shannon, David Hewlett; ***D:*** Lewis Teague; ***W:*** Ted Humphrey; ***C:*** Ric Waite; ***M:*** Lawrence Shragge. **CABLE**

The Triangle Factory Fire Scandal **1979** Based on the true-life Triangle factory fire at the turn of the century. The fire killed 145 garment workers and drastically changed industrial fire and safety codes. **100m/C VHS, DVD.** Tom Bosley, David Dukes, Tovah Feldshuh, Janet Margolin, Stephanie Zimbalist, Lauren Front, Stacey Nelkin, Ted Wass, Charlotte Rae, Milton Selzer, Valerie Landsburg; ***D:*** Mel Stuart. **TV**

Tribes ½ *The Soldier Who Declared Peace* **1970** When a hippie is drafted into the Marines, despite the furious efforts of his drill sergeant, he refuses to conform to military life. Soon his boot-camp mates are trying his methods of defiance and survival. Well-made mix of comedy and social commentary. **90m/C VHS.** Jan-Michael Vincent, Darren McGavin, Earl Holliman; ***D:*** Joseph Sargent. **TV**

Tribulation **2000** Police detective Tom Canboro (Busey) goes up against the evil Messiah (Mancuso) in another entry in the "Left Behind" series of adventures based on the Book of Revelation. **97m/C DVD.** Gary Busey, Howie Mandel, Margot Kidder, Nick Mancuso, Sherry Miller, Leigh Lewis; ***D:*** Andre Van Heerden; ***W:*** Peter LaLonde, Paul LaLonde; ***C:*** Jiri (George) Tirl.

Tribute **1980 (PG)** A dying man is determined to achieve a reconciliation with his estranged son. Adapted by Bernard Slade from his play. **125m/C VHS.** *CA* Jack Lemmon, Robby Benson, Lee Remick, Kim Cattrall; ***D:*** Bob (Benjamin) Clark.

Tribute **2009** Former child star Cilla McGowan (Murphy) now restores houses and has bought her late grandmother's neglected Virginia farmhouse. Janet Hardy, a famous actress, allegedly died of an overdose in the house 30 years before and there's still a lot of bad blood within the community because Janet was supposedly having an affair with a married man. Neighbor Ford Sawyer (Lewis) is happy to help Cilla out when old family secrets turn into present-day nightmares. Romantic suspense from Lifetime that's based on the book by Nora Roberts. **90m/C DVD.** Brittany Murphy, Jason Lewis, Tippi Hedren, Diana Scarwid, Christian Oliver, Tiffany Morgan, Wallace Merck; ***D:*** Martha Coolidge; ***W:*** Gary Tieche; ***C:*** Gary Tieche, Johnny E. Jensen. **CABLE**

Tribute to a Bad Man **1956** Hard-nosed rancher Cagney will stop at nothing to retain his worldly possessions in this 1870s Colorado territory western. His ruthless behavior drives girlfriend Papas into the arms of hired hand Dubbins. Spencer Tracy and Grace Kelly were originally cast for the roles of Jeremy Rodock and Jocasta Constantine, but Kelly backed out and Tracy was fired due to differences with director Wise. Based on the short story by Jack Schaefer. **95m/C VHS.** James Cagney, Don Dubbins, Stephen McNally, Irene Papas, Vic Morrow, Royal Dano, Lee Van Cleef, James J. Griffith, Onslow Stevens, James Bell, Jeannette Nolan, Bud Osborne, Tom London, Dennis Moore, Buddy Roosevelt, Carl Pitti; ***D:*** Robert Wise; ***W:*** Michael Blankfort; ***M:*** Miklos Rozsa.

Tricheurs *Cheaters* **1984** Scam artists hit largest casino in the world and look forward to golden years of retirement. From the director of "Reversal of Fortune." In French with English subtitles. **95m/C VHS.** *FR* Jacques Dutronc, Bulle Ogier, Kurt Raab, Virgilio Teixeira, Steve Baes; ***D:*** Barbet Schroeder.

Trick **1999 (R)** Cheery gay romantic comedy. Quiet Gabriel (Campbell) is a struggling Broadway composer with a horn-dog straight roommate (Beyer) who is constantly taking over their apartment for his one-nighters (and locking Gabe out). Which leaves Gabriel in a dilemma when he meets hunky go-go boy, Mark (Pitok), and the duo can't find a place to be alone. But as the night wears on, they discover that lust may be taking a backseat to some deeper feelings. **90m/C VHS, DVD.** Missi Pyle, Christian Campbell, John Paul (J.P.) Pitoc, Tori Spelling, Brad Beyer, Clinton Leupp, Lorri Bagley, Steve Hayes; ***D:*** Jim Fall; ***W:*** Jason Schafer; ***C:*** Terry Stacey; ***M:*** David Friedman.

Trick or Treat ½ **1986 (R)** A high school student is helped to exact violent revenge against his bullying contemporaries. His helper is the spirit of a violent heavy metal rock star who he raises from the dead. Sometimes clever, not terribly scary. **97m/C VHS, DVD.** Tony Fields, Marc Price, Ozzy Osbourne, Gene Simmons, Elaine Joyce, Glenn Morgan, Lisa Orgolini, Doug Savant; ***D:*** Charles Martin Smith; ***W:*** Joel Soisson, Michael S. Murphy, Rhet Topham; ***C:*** Robert Elswit.

Trick or Treats **WOOF!** **1982 (R)** Young boy's pranks on his terrified babysitter backfire on Halloween night. His deranged father, escaped from an asylum, shows up to help him "scare" her. Giroux doesn't look very frightened in this extremely tedious film from Welles' best camera man. **90m/C VHS.** Carrie Snodgress, David Carradine, Jackie Giroux, Steve Railsback, Chris Graver, Peter Jason, Jillian Kesner, Paul Bartel; ***D:*** Gary Graver.

Trick 'r Treat **2008 (R)** Good old-fashioned fright fest. This Halloween anthology is set in a small Ohio town that celebrates in a big way with various characters recurring over the stories. School principal Steven takes extreme measures to rid himself of trick-or-treaters while a crusty old codger learns tricking rather than treating has dire consequences. A Little Red Riding Hood costume worn by college virgin Laurie attracts some predatory attention; a married couple breaks the Jack o' Lantern holiday rule; and a group of teens use an urban legend to play a trick that backfires on them. **82m/C DVD.** Dylan Baker, Anna Paquin, Lauren Lee Smith, Brian Cox, Leslie Bibb, Tahmoh Penikett, Quinn Lord; ***D:*** Michael Dougherty; ***C:*** Glen MacPherson; ***M:*** Douglas Pipes. **VIDEO**

Tricks **1997 (R)** Once a Las Vegas showgirl, Jackie (Rogers) is now a gift shop clerk in Reno, making some extra dough by turning tricks at night. After being beaten by a john, Jackie loses her job and has trouble finding work. Her roommate Sarah (Daly) introduces her to old-time gangster Big Sam (Walston), who offers to help her get even with the guy who beat her but it's not that easy. **96m/C VHS.** Mimi Rogers, Tyne Daly, Ray Walston, Callum Keith Rennie, Kevin McNulty; ***D:*** Kenneth Fink; ***W:*** Deborah Amelon; ***C:*** John Bartley; ***M:*** Patrick Seymour. **CABLE**

Tricks of the Trade **1988 (R)** Goody-two-shoe housewife and hooker accomplice search for husband's murderer. Racy TV fodder. **100m/C VHS.** Cindy Williams, Markie Post, Chris Mulkey, James Whitmore Jr., Scott Paulin, John Ritter, Apollonia; ***D:*** Jack Bender. **TV**

Trident Force **1988** International counter-terrorism team is ordered to destroy the Palestinian Revolutionary Legion by any means possible. **90m/C VHS.** Anthony Alonzo, Mark Gil, Nanna Anderson, Steve Rogers, Eddie M. Gaerlan; ***D:*** Richard Smith.

The Trigger Effect ½ **1996 (R)** Nightmare in yuppiedom when a suspicious electromagnetic pulse knocks out all electrical power, telephone, and broadcast signals for hundreds of miles around a tranquil southern California community, which becomes increasingly unsettled. Matt (MacLachlan), wife Annie (Shue), and friend Joe (Mulroney) hang out together during the mystery power outage with lots of mounting tension both within and without. Film, however dread-producing, doesn't really make that much sense. **103m/C VHS, DVD.** Kyle MacLachlan, Elisabeth Shue, Dermot Mulroney, Michael Rooker, Richard T. Jones, Bill Smitrovich, William Lucking, Molly Morgan, Richard Schiff; ***D:*** David Koepp; ***W:*** David Koepp; ***C:*** Newton Thomas (Tom) Sigel; ***M:*** James Newton Howard.

Trigger Happy ½ *Mad Dog Time* **1996 (R)** Director Bishop (son of Rat-Packer Joey, who's in the film) tells a tale of crime lord Vic (Dreyfuss) and various gangsters in what should be a knowingly cool story but isn't. Vic's about to get out of the loony bin and has informed his enforcer, Ben London (Byrne), to get rid of his rivals and disloyal fellow mobsters in time for his return. Meanwhile, his chief of staff, Mickey (Goldblum), has been romancing both Vic's gal Grace (Lane) and her jealous older sister, Rita (Barkin). This situation does not make Vic happy. The movie won't make you happy either. **93m/C VHS, DVD.** Richard Dreyfuss, Gabriel Byrne, Jeff Goldblum, Diane Lane, Ellen Barkin, Gregory Hines, Kyle MacLachlan, Larry

Bishop, Burt Reynolds, Henry Silva; ***Cameos:*** Joey Bishop, Angie Everhart, Michael J. Pollard, Richard Pryor, Rob Reiner, Billy Idol; ***D:*** Larry Bishop; ***W:*** Larry Bishop; ***C:*** Frank Byers; ***M:*** Earl Rose.

Trigger, Jr. 1/2 **1950** Rogers and his Western Show find themselves in the middle of a dispute between intimidated ranchers and an evil local range patrol office. When Trigger is injured by a killer stallion, Roy turns to two unlikely allies—a 10-year-old boy who's scared of horses and frisky Trigger Jr. **67m/B VHS, DVD.** Roy Rogers, Dale Evans, Grant Withers, Pat Brady, Gordon Jones, Peter Miles, George Cleveland; ***D:*** William Witney; ***W:*** Gerald Geraghty.

Trigger Men 1/2 *Billy the Kid's Fighting Pals* **1941** Steele, Young, and St. John find a dying U.S. marshal who has been ambushed by the villainous Peil. Seems Peil and his gang have taken over a small border town in order to set up a smuggling operation with Mexico. So the trio avenge the marshal by putting a stop to the nefarious doings. Newfield directed under the pseudonym Sherman Scott. **59m/B VHS.** Bob Steele, Al "Fuzzy" St. John, Carleton Young, Edward Peil Sr., Phyllis Adair, Charles "Blackie" King, Curley Dresden, Hal Price, George Chesebro, Forrest Taylor, Budd Buster; ***D:*** Sam Newfield.

Trigger Pals 1/2 **1939** Jarrett stars in this basic oater about bringing a gang of rustlers to justice. Besides the usual gunplay, he also attempts to sing a few songs. **58m/B VHS.** Art Jarrett, Lee Powell, Al "Fuzzy" St. John, Dorothy Fay, Charles "Blackie" King, Frank LaRue; ***D:*** Sam Newfield.

Trigger Tricks 1/2 **1930** Gibson's brother becomes the victim of a vicious cattleman and Hoot is out for revenge. **60m/B VHS.** Hoot Gibson, Sally Eilers, Neal Hart, Monte Montague, Pete Morrison, Robert E. Homans, Jack (H.) Richardson; ***D:*** B. Reeves Eason.

The Trigger Trio 1/2 **1937** Rancher with diseased cattle kills a ranch inspector. The Three Mesquiteers are called in to crack the case. **54m/B VHS.** Ray Corrigan, Max Terhune, Ralph Byrd, Robert Warwick, Cornelius Keefe, Wally Wales; ***D:*** William Witney.

Triggermen **2002 (R)** Two inept con men hit the jackpot after slipping off with a cash-packed suitcase—problem is it's an advance to two hit men to snuff out a mob boss. Naturally they don't split the scene right away and the hit men catch up to them, but the hoopla doesn't end there in this mildly amusing farce. **96m/C VHS, DVD.** Pete Postlethwaite, Neil Morrissey, Donnie Wahlberg, Adrian Dunbar, Michael Rapaport, Claire Forlani, Amanda Plummer, Saul Rubinek; ***D:*** John Bradshaw; ***W:*** Tony Johnston; ***C:*** Barry Stone; ***M:*** Terence Gowan, Blair Packham. **VIDEO**

Trilby **1917** Original screen production of Du Maurier's classic tale of Svengali. **59m/B VHS.** Clara Kimball Young, Wilton Lackaye, Chester Barnett; ***D:*** Maurice Tourneur.

Trilogy of Terror 1/2 **1975** Black shows her versatility as she plays a tempting seductress, a mousy schoolteacher, and the terrified victim of an African Zuni fetish doll in three horror shorts. **78m/C VHS, DVD.** Karen Black, Robert (Skip) Burton, John Karlen, Gregory Harrison, George Gaynes, James Storm, Kathryn Reynolds, Tracy Curtis; ***D:*** Dan Curtis; ***W:*** Richard Matheson; ***C:*** Paul Lohmann; ***M:*** Robert Cobert. **TV**

Trilogy of Terror 2 **1996 (R)** Curtis follows up his 1975 TV movie with an okay sequel headed by Anthony. "Graveyard Rats" features flesh-eating, cemetery-dwelling rodents and a greedy wife who bumped off her wealthy husband, a mother strikes a fiendish bargain to bring her drowned son back to life in "Bobby," and the deadly African Zuni fetish doll returns in "He Who Kills." **90m/C VHS, DVD.** Lysette Anthony, Richard Fitzpatrick, Geraint Wyn Davies, Matt Clark, Geoffrey Lewis, Blake Heron; ***D:*** Dan Curtis; ***W:*** Dan Curtis, William F. Nolan, Richard Matheson; ***C:*** Elemer Ragalyi; ***M:*** Robert Cobert. **CABLE**

Trinity Is Still My Name 1/2 *Continuavamo A Chiamarlo Trinita* **1975 (G)** Sequel to "They Call Me Trinity." Insouciant bumbling brothers Trinity and Bambino, oblivious to danger and hopeless odds, endure mishaps and adventures as they try to right wrongs. A funny parody of Western cliches that never becomes stale. **117m/C VHS, DVD.** *IT* Bud Spencer, Terence Hill, Harry Carey Jr.; ***D:*** E.B. (Enzo Barboni) Clucher.

Trio **1950** Sequel to "Quartet," featuring the W. Somerset Maugham stories "The Verger," "Mr. Knowall," and "Sanatorium Acclaimed." **88m/B VHS.** Jean Simmons, Michael Rennie, Bill Travers, James Hayter, Kathleen Harrison, Felix Aylmer, Nigel Patrick, Finlay Currie, John Laurie; ***D:*** Ken Annakin, Harold French; ***C:*** Geoffrey Unsworth, Reg Wyer.

The Trio **1997** Unconvincing German sex comedy finds gay middle-aged Zobel (George) and his daughter Lizzie (Hain) constantly on the move as they exercise their pickpocketing profession, along with Zobel's lover Karl (Redl). After Karl dies in an auto accident, Lizzie recruits hunky drifter Rudolf (Eitner) to take his place. Which Rudolf does in more ways than one, since he soon becomes the lover of both father and daughter. German with subtitles. **97m/C VHS, DVD.** *GE* Goetz George, Jeanette Hain, Felix Eitner, Christian Redl; ***D:*** Hermine Huntgeburth; ***W:*** Hermine Huntgeburth, Horst Sczerba, Volker Einrauch; ***C:*** Martin Kukula; ***M:*** Niki Reiser.

The Trip **1967** A psychedelic journey to the world of inner consciousness, via drugs. A TV director, unsure where his life is going, decides to try a "trip" to expand his understanding. Hopper is the drug salesman, Dern, the tour guide for Fonda's trip through sex, witches, torture chambers, and more. Great period music. **85m/C VHS, DVD.** Peter Fonda, Susan Strasberg, Bruce Dern, Dennis Hopper, Salli Sachse, Barboura Morris, Judith Lang, Luana Anders, Beach Dickerson, Dick Miller, Michael Nader, Michael Blodgett, Caren Bernsen, Katherine Walsh, Peter Bogdanovich, Tom Signorelli; ***D:*** Roger Corman; ***W:*** Jack Nicholson; ***C:*** Arch R. Dalzell; ***M:*** Barry Goldberg.

The Trip **2002 (R)** In 1973 Los Angeles, young Republican Alan Oakley (Sullivan) is working for an establishment newspaper and denying the fact that he's gay. In fact, Alan's writing a book that's a conservative attack on gay rights. When Alan meets gay rights activist Tommy (Braun), things change personally and professionally. Too bad Alan's manuscript gets published anonymously by envious wannabe lover, Peter (Baker). Film eventually makes its way to 1984 when Alan learns ex-lover Tommy is dying of AIDS in Mexico but would like to see Alan one more time. Not quite as sappy as you may think, since writer/director Swain is certainly sincere, but it's also basic melodrama. **93m/C VHS, DVD.** Larry Sullivan, Steve Braun, Ray Baker, Art Hindle, Jill St. John, Alexis Arquette; ***D:*** Miles Swain; ***W:*** Miles Swain; ***C:*** Charles L. Barbee, Scott Kevan; ***M:*** Steven Chesne.

The Trip to Bountiful **1985 (PG)** An elderly widow, unhappy living in her son's fancy modern home, makes a pilgrimage back to her childhood home in Bountiful, Texas. Based on the Horton Foote play. Fine acting with Oscar-winning performance from Page. **102m/C VHS, DVD.** Geraldine Page, Rebecca De Mornay, John Heard, Carlin Glynn, Richard Bradford; ***D:*** Peter Masterson; ***W:*** Horton Foote; ***C:*** Fred Murphy. Oscars '85: Actress (Page); Ind. Spirit '86: Actress (Page), Screenplay.

TripFall 1/2 **2000 (R)** Tom Williams (Ritter) decides he, wife Gina (Hunter), and their kids need some family time, so they head off on vacation. And run into the nightmare of Eddie (Roberts) and his gang of kidnappers. With his wife and kids in Eddie's slimy hands, Tom has one day to get more than a million bucks together if he wants them back alive. **95m/C VHS, DVD.** John Ritter, Eric Roberts, Rachel Hunter; ***D:*** Serge Rodnunsky; ***W:*** Serge Rodnunsky; ***C:*** Greg Patterson; ***M:*** Evan Evans. **VIDEO**

Triple Agent **2004** Rohmer enters murky political territory in his moral spy yarn based on a true crime. In 1936, Tsarist sympathizer Fiodor Voronin (Renko) is living in exile in Paris with his Greek-born wife Arsinoe (Didaskalou). His frequent business trips arouse Arsinoe's suspicions, but Fiodor is not having an affair: he's a spy playing the White Russians against the communists and the fascists in a dangerous and increasingly complicated triple-cross. French, Russian, and German with subtitles. **115m/C DVD.** *FR IT GR RU SP* Serge Renko, Amanda Langlet, Emmanuel Salinger, Katerina Didaskalou, Cyrielle Clair, Grigori Manoukov; ***D:*** Eric Rohmer; ***W:*** Eric Rohmer; ***C:*** Diane Baratier.

Triple Cross **1967** Plummer is a British safecracker imprisoned on the channel islands at the outbreak of WWII. When the Germans move in, he offers to work for them if they set him free. The Germans buy his story and send him to England, but once there he offers his services to the British as a double agent. Based on the exploits of Eddie Chapman, adapted from his book, "The Eddie Chapman Story." **91m/C VHS.** *FR GB* Christopher Plummer, Romy Schneider, Trevor Howard, Gert Frobe, Yul Brynner, Claudine Auger, Georges Lycan, Jess Hahn, Howard Vernon; ***D:*** Terence Young.

Triple Echo 1/2 *Soldier in Skirts* **1977 (R)** A young woman falls for an army deserter who is hiding from the military police by dressing as a woman. Mistrust and deception get the best of some of the involved parties. **90m/C VHS.** *GB* Glenda Jackson, Oliver Reed, Brian Deacon; ***D:*** Michael Apted; ***W:*** Robin Chapman.

Triple Impact **1992** Hall, Cook, and Riley are three martial-arts experts who join forces against illegal gambling syndicates who are staging full-contact bloodmatches. Their alliance leads them to Asia where the prize is death—or a fortune in gold. **97m/C VHS.** Dale "Apollo" Cook, Ron Hall, Bridgett "Baby Doll" Riley, Robert Marius, Steve Rogers, Nick Nicholson, Ned Hourani, Mike "Cobra" Cole; ***D:*** David Hunt; ***W:*** Steve Rogers.

TripleCross 1/2 **1985** Three former cops strike it rich and although they love the money, they miss the game, so they get involved in a murder case. These wealthy detectives encounter high-level gangsters, a baseball scandal, and a hit man in their race to solve the perfect crime. **97m/C VHS.** Ted Wass, Markie Post, Gary Swanson; ***D:*** David Greene.

Triplecross 1/2 **1995 (R)** Jewel thief Jimmy Ray (Bergin) is after a fortune in diamonds and obsessive FBI agent Oscar (Williams) is looking to bring him down. Oscar decides to use Jimmy Ray's ex-cell mate Teddy (Pare) but Teddy gets involved with J.R.'s girlfriend Julia (Laurence) instead of tending to business. Wooden crime caper. **95m/C VHS, DVD.** Patrick Bergin, Billy Dee Williams, Michael Pare, Ashley Laurence; ***D:*** Jeno Hodi. **CABLE**

The Triplets of Belleville *Les Triplettes de Belleville; Belleville Rendez-Vous* **2002 (PG-13)** Surreal French animated tale of a joyless bicycle racer and his eccentric grandmother charms, surprises, and confounds with flights of fancy and wonderfully imaginative scenarios. Champion is a sad little boy who doesn't respond to anything until his grandmother buys him a tricycle. This leads him to become a top-level bike racer who is eventually kidnapped by French mobsters. His stalwart grandma stops at nothing to rescue him. **91m/C DVD.** *FR BE CA* ***D:*** Sylvain Chomet; ***W:*** Sylvain Chomet; ***M:*** Benoit Charest. L.A. Film Critics '03: Animated Film, Score.

Tripods: The White Mountains 1/2 **1984** Sci-fi thriller about the takeover of earth by alien tripods. The conquerors start controlling human minds, but not until after they are 16 years old. Two boys seek to end the terror. **150m/C VHS.** John Shackley, Jim Baker, Cari Seel; ***D:*** Graham Theakston.

The Tripper **2006 (R)** Arquette's directorial debut is a lame horror satire that makes you wonder if everyone on set was maybe tripping. Three hippie couples are driving through a North Carolina forest when they're attacked by a psycho wearing a Ronald Reagan mask and fondling sharp and deadly inplements. **93m/C DVD.** Thomas Jane, Jaime (James) King, Richmond Arquette, Paz de la Huerta, Balthazar Getty, Lukas Haas, Jason Mewes, Paul (Pee-wee Herman) Reubens, David Arquette; ***D:*** David Arquette; ***W:*** David Arquette, Joe Harris; ***C:*** Bobby Bukowski; ***M:*** Jimmy Haun, Dave Wittman.

Trippin' **1999 (R)** Gregory (Richmond) is a daydreamer who can't keep his mind on his studies until he finds out that the prom queen, Cinny (Campbell), goes for the brainy type. Between fantasies of fame, fortune, and exotic locales, Gregory, with the help of his ne'er-do-well buddies Fish (Torry) and June (Faison), tries to improve his grades and get her to the prom. Likeable cast and a nice message about the importance of getting an education balance out a gratuitous subplot about a local crime boss recruiting June. Lightweight but amusing. **92m/C VHS, DVD.** Deon Richmond, Maia Campbell, Donald Adeosun Faison, Guy Torry, Harold Sylvester, Stoney Jackson, Michael Warren, Aloma Wright, Bill Henderson; ***D:*** David Raynr; ***W:*** Gary Hardwick; ***C:*** John Aronson.

Tripwire 1/2 **1989 (R)** A vengeance-crazed government agent tracks down the terrorist who murdered his wife. **120m/C VHS.** Terence Knox, David Warner, Charlotte Lewis, Isabella Hofmann, Yaphet Kotto, Thomas Chong, Meg Foster; ***D:*** James (Momel) Lemmo.

Tristan & Isolde 1/2 **2006 (PG-13)** Pretty actors play tragic lovers in a romantic drama based on a Celtic legend. Dark Ages Irish princess Isolde (Myles) is the marriageable bargaining chip for her scheming father (O'Hara), whose aim is to rule the squabbling English tribes. Isolde rescues, and falls in love with, injured warrior Tristan (Franco), who happens to be the champion of powerful Briton Lord Marke (Sewell). Unbeknownst to the lovers, Isolde has been promised to Marke; they try to do the right thing. It's appropriately swoony and teary and noble. **125m/C DVD.** *GB GE US* James Franco, Sophia Myles, Rufus Sewell, David O'Hara, Mark Strong, Henry Cavill, Bronagh Gallagher, Ronan Vibert, Lucy Russell, Thomas Sangster, JB Blanc, Graham Mulins; ***D:*** Kevin Reynolds; ***W:*** Dean Georgaris; ***C:*** Arthur Reinhart; ***M:*** Anne Dudley.

Tristana **1970 (PG)** Allegorical tale of a beautiful girl (Deneuve) who moves in with a hypocritical benefactor following the death of her mother. She is quickly exploited and seduced by the one who would protect her, but runs away with an artist in pursuit of love. Searing in its commentary on Catholicism, death, lust, and the woebegone place of humanity in the world, the movie is also widely seen as a depiction of fascist Spain's attempt to find its place in the 20th century. Based on the novel by Benito Perez Galdos. In Spanish with English subtitles. **98m/C VHS.** *SP IT FR* Catherine Deneuve, Fernando Rey, Franco Nero, Lola Gaos, Antonio Casas, Jesus Fernandez, Vincent Solder; ***D:*** Luis Bunuel; ***W:*** Julio Alejandro, Luis Bunuel; ***C:*** Jose F. Aguayo.

Tristram Shandy: A Cock and Bull Story **2005 (R)** Peculiar film-within-a-film follows Brit comedian Coogan playing an exaggerated version of "Steve Coogan" as he takes the title role in the filming of the eccentric 18th-century novel "The Life and Opinions of Tristram Shandy." Insecure and vain, Coogan annoys the director (Northam) and screenwriter (Hart), while childishly sparring with his primary co-star (Brydon) and ignoring his visiting girlfriend (Macdonald) and their baby. Best for Coogan fans or those interested in movie minutia. **91m/C DVD.** Steve Coogan, Rob Brydon, Keeley Hawes, Shirley Henderson, Dylan Moran, Jeremy Northam, Naomie Harris, Kelly Macdonald, Elizabeth Berrington, Mark Williams, James Fleet, Ian Hart, Kieran O'Brien, Stephen Fry, Gillian Anderson, David Walliams, Anthony H. Wilson; ***D:*** Michael Winterbottom; ***W:*** Martin Hardy; ***C:*** Marcel Zyskind; ***M:*** Michael Nyman, Edward Nogria.

The Triumph of Hercules *Il Trionfo di Ercole; Hercules and the Ten Avengers; Hercules vs. the Giant Warriors* **1966** Hercules gets stripped of his powers by a peeved Zeus and must try to battle a sorceress and 10 giant bronze warriors without them, until Zeus reconsiders. **94m/C VHS, DVD.** *IT FR* Dan Vadis, Moira Orfei, Pierre Cressoy, Marilu Tolo, Pierro Lulli; ***D:*** Alberto De Martino; ***W:*** Robert Gianviti; ***C:*** Pier Ludovico Pavoni; ***M:*** Francesco De Masi.

The Triumph of Love **2001 (PG-13)** Not much of a triumph but not a complete waste of time either. Adapted from Pierre

Marivaux's 18th-century play, Sorvino plays Princess Leonide, who knows that her family usurped their throne and she is determined to see its rightful owner, Prince Agis (Rodan), returned to power. Of course, he's a handsome prince and the princess has fallen in love but there are complications that involve her disguising herself as a male philosophy student and insinuating herself into his guardians' (Kingsley, Shaw) austere lives. Deceptions abound. **107m/C VHS, DVD.** *IT GB* Mira Sorvino, Ben Kingsley, Fiona Shaw, Jay Rodan, Rachael Stirling, Ignazio Oliva; ***D:*** Clare Peploe; ***W:*** Clare Peploe, Bernardo Bertolucci, Marilyn Goldin; ***C:*** Fabio Cianchetti; ***M:*** Jason Osborn.

The Triumph of Sherlock Holmes ✓✓ 1/2 **1935** Wontner and Fleming teamed for an early series of Holmesian romps. In one of their best outings, Sherlock Holmes comes out of retirement as a series of bizarre murders of Pennsylvania coal miners lure him back into action. From "The Valley of Fear" by Sir Arthur Conan Doyle. **84m/B VHS, DVD.** *GB* Arthur Wontner, Ian Fleming; ***D:*** Leslie Hiscott.

Triumph of the Spirit ✓✓✓ **1989 (R)** Gritty account of boxer Salamo Arouch's experiences in Auschwitz. The boxer became champion in matches between prisoners conducted for the amusement of Nazi officers. Filmed on location in Auschwitz. **115m/C VHS, DVD.** Willem Dafoe, Robert Loggia, Edward James Olmos, Wendy Gazelle, Kelly Wolf, Costas Mandylor, Kario Salem; ***D:*** Robert M. Young; ***W:*** Robert M. Young, Shimon Arama, Andrzej Krakowski, Laurence Heath, Arthur Coburn, Millard Lampell; ***M:*** Cliff Eidelman.

Triumph of the Will ✓✓✓ 1/2 *Triumph des Willens* **1934** Director Riefenstahl's formidable, stunning film, documenting Hitler and the Sixth Nazi Party Congress in 1934 in Nuernberg, Germany. The greatest and most artful propaganda piece ever produced. German dialogue. Includes English translation of the speeches. **115m/B VHS, DVD.** *GE* ***D:*** Leni Riefenstahl; ***W:*** Leni Riefenstahl; ***C:*** Sepp Allgeier; ***M:*** Herbert Windt.

Triumphs of a Man Called Horse ✓✓ **1983 (R)** An Indian must save his people from prospectors in order to keep his title as Peace, Chief of the Yellow Hand Sioux. Inadequate sequel to two previous films: "A Man Called Horse" and "The Return of a Man Called Horse." **91m/C VHS.** *MX* Richard Harris; ***D:*** John Hough; ***W:*** Carlos Aured, Jack DeWitt, Ken Blackwell.

Trixie ✓✓ **2000 (R)** Performances by a fine ensemble cast are mangled almost as badly as the English language in this wandering comedy-mystery. Trixie (Watson) is a malaprop-spouting security guard at a resort casino who wants to be a detective. She stumbles onto a murder mystery involving bombastic Senator Avery (Nolte) and decides that if she solves the crime, a career as a detective will surely follow. Many false leads are chased, and the theme that not everyone is as they appear is hammered home time and time again. Among the list of usual suspects are a golddigging barfly (Murphy), a washed-up lounge singer (Warren), a two-bit ladies man (Mulroney) and an impressionist/singer with a shady past (Lane). **117m/C VHS, DVD.** Emily Watson, Nick Nolte, Dermot Mulroney, Nathan Lane, Brittany Murphy, Lesley Ann Warren, Will Patton, Stephen Lang; ***D:*** Alan Rudolph; ***W:*** Alan Rudolph; ***C:*** Jan Kiesser; ***M:*** Mark Isham, Roger Neill.

Trois Couleurs: Blanc ✓✓✓ *White; Three Colors: White* **1994 (R)** Bittersweet comedic rags-to-riches tale spiced with revenge and lasting love. "White" focuses on equality and begins when a bewildered Polish hairdresser is divorced by his disdainful French wife, who takes him for everything he has. Returning to his family in Poland, Karol doggedly works his way into wealth. Then he decides to fake his death and leave his fortune to the ex he still loves—or does he? In Polish and French with English subtitles. Part 2 of Kieslowski's trilogy, following "Trois Couleurs: Bleu" and followed by "Trois Couleurs: Rouge." **92m/C VHS, DVD.** *FR SI PL* Zbigniew Zamachowski, Julie Delpy, Janusz Gajos, Jerzy Stuhr, Aleksander Bardini, Grzegorz Warchol, Cezary Harasimowicz, Jerzy Nowak, Jerzy Trela, Cezary Pazura, Michel Lisowski, Philippe Morier-Genoud; ***Cameos:*** Juliette Binoche, Florence Pernel; ***D:*** Krzysztof Kieslowski; ***W:*** Krzysztof Kieslowski, Krzysztof Piesiewicz; ***C:*** Edward Klosinski; ***M:*** Zbigniew Preisner. Berlin Intl. Film Fest. '94: Director (Kieslowski).

Trois Couleurs: Bleu ✓✓✓ *Three Colors: Blue; Blue* **1993 (R)** First installment of director Kieslowski's trilogy inspired by the French tricolor flag. "Blue" stands for liberty—here freedom is based on tragedy as Julie (Binoche) reshapes her life after surviving an accident which killed her famous composer husband and their young daughter. Excellent performance by Binoche, which relies on the internalized grief and brief emotion which flits across her face rather than overwhelming displays for expression. In French with English subtitles. **98m/C VHS, DVD.** *FR* Juliette Binoche, Benoit Regent, Florence Pernel, Charlotte Very, Helene Vincent, Philippe Volter, Claude Duneton, Hugues Quester, Florence Vignon, Isabelle Sadoyan, Yann Tregouet, Jacek Ostaszewski; ***Cameos:*** Emmanuelle Riva; ***D:*** Krzysztof Kieslowski; ***W:*** Krzysztof Kieslowski, Krzysztof Piesiewicz, Slawomir Idziak, Agnieszka Holland, Edward Zebrowski; ***C:*** Slawomir Idziak; ***M:*** Zbigniew Preisner. Cesar '94: Actress (Binoche), Film Editing, Sound; L.A. Film Critics '93: Score; Venice Film Fest. '93: Actress (Binoche), Film.

Trois Couleurs: Rouge ✓✓✓ 1/2 *Three Colors: Red; Red* **1994 (R)** "Red" is for fraternity in the French tricolor flag and, in director Kieslowski's last film in his trilogy, emotional connections are made between unlikely couples. There's law student Auguste and his girlfriend Karin, young fashion model Valentine, and a nameless retired judge, brought together by circumstance and destined to change each other's lives. Subtle details make for careful viewing but it's a rewarding watch and a visual treat (keep an eye on cinematographer Sobocinski's use of the color red). Binoche and Delpy, who starred in the earlier films, also make an appearance, as Kieslowski uses the finale to tie up loose ends. In French with English subtitles. **99m/C VHS, DVD.** *FR PL SI* Irene Jacob, Jean-Louis Trintignant, Frederique Feder, Jean-Pierre Lorit, Samuel Le Bihan, Marion Stalens, Teco Celio, Bernard Escalon, Jean Schlegel, Elzbieta Jasinska; ***Cameos:*** Juliette Binoche, Julie Delpy, Benoit Regent, Zbigniew Zamachowski; ***D:*** Krzysztof Kieslowski; ***W:*** Krzysztof Kieslowski, Krzysztof Piesiewicz; ***C:*** Piotr Sobocinski; ***M:*** Zbigniew Preisner. Cesar '94: Score; Ind. Spirit '95: Foreign Film; L.A. Film Critics '94: Foreign Film; N.Y. Film Critics '94: Foreign Film; Natl. Soc. Film Critics '94: Foreign Film.

Trojan Eddie ✓✓✓ **1996** Stephen Rea puts his perpetual hangdog mug to good use as the hapless Trojan Eddie, so named for the make of the van in which he transports and sells stolen goods. He is married to the shrewish town tramp, who helps little in raising their two girls and makes fun of his dream of opening his own business. His boss is John Power (Harris), leader of a group of clannish con men. He is teamed with Power's nephew Dermot (Townsend), who's secretly romancing his uncle's much younger wife-to-be. The young lovers take off with the cache of wedding loot on the night of the nuptials, and Power involves Eddie in an all-out search for the couple. After they're caught and pardoned by Power, however, the spiral of betrayal and violence spins faster than ever, with Eddie always eyeing the chance to escape. Excellent rapport between Rea and Harris as their fortunes shift and reverse. **103m/C VHS, DVD.** Stephen Rea, Richard Harris, Brendan Gleeson, Sean McGinley, Angeline Ball, Brid Brennan, Stuart Townsend, Aislin McGuckin; ***D:*** Gilles Mackinnon; ***W:*** Billy Roche; ***C:*** John de Borman; ***M:*** John Keane.

The Trojan Horse ✓✓ 1/2 *The Trojan War; The Mighty Warrior* **1962** Greek warrior Aeneas (Reeves), under the command of Ulysses (Barrymore), gets to hide out in the Trojan horse with his fellow fighters and then get those Trojans when they take the wooden beast into their city. When they're successful, Aeneas takes his guys and decides to go off and found the city of Rome. You were maybe expecting historical or mythological accuracy? **105m/C VHS, DVD.** *IT FR* Steve Reeves, John Drew (Blythe) Barrymore Jr., Juliette Mayniel, Edy Vessel, Lidia Alfonsi, Luciana Angiolillo, Arturo Dominici, Mimmo Palmara, Carlo Tamberlani, Nando Tamberlani; ***D:*** Giorgio Ferroni; ***W:*** Ugo Liberatore; ***C:*** Rino Filippini; ***M:*** Giovanni Fusco.

The Trojan Horse ✓✓ 1/2 **2008 (R)** Complicated Canadian thriller that's a sequel to the 2004 miniseries "H2O." Former Prime Minister Tom McLaughlin (Gross) watches in disgust as his countrymen vote for a union with the U.S.A., and Canada is divided into six new states. Tom, secretly backed by a European cartel, runs as an independent candidate for the presidency with his ex-wife, Texas Governor Mary Miller (Burns), as his veep choice. Veteran British journalist Helen Madigan (Scacchi) uncovers a plan to commit voter fraud and her knowledge turns out to be very, very dangerous. **180m/C DVD.** *CA* Paul Gross, Martha Burns, Greta Scacchi, Tom Skerritt, William Hutt, Clark Johnson, Saul Rubinek, Stephen McHattie, Heino Ferch, Kenneth Welsh, Jean Pearson; ***D:*** Charles Biname; ***C:*** Derick Underschultz. **TV**

Trojan War ✓✓ 1/2 **1997 (PG-13)** Yes, the title does refer to the condom brand. High schooler Brad Kimble (Friedle) has finally convinced dream girl Brooke (Shelton) to get romantic—if he has the proper protection, of course. But as his search is continually thwarted, this gives his best gal pal Lea (Hewitt)—who would like to be something more—the chance to show who really loves him. Harmless, although sexually overt, teen fluff. **90m/C VHS.** Lee Majors, Wendie Malick, David Patrick Kelly, Anthony Michael Hall, Jennifer Love Hewitt, Will Friedle, Marley Shelton; ***D:*** George Huang; ***W:*** Andy Burg, Scott Myers; ***C:*** Dean Semler; ***M:*** George S. Clinton.

Trojan Women ✓✓ **1971 (G)** Euripides' tragedy on the fate of the women of Troy after the Greeks storm the famous city. The play does not translate well to the screen, in spite of tour-de-force acting. **105m/C VHS, DVD.** Katharine Hepburn, Vanessa Redgrave, Irene Papas, Genevieve Bujold, Brian Blessed, Patrick Magee; ***D:*** Michael Cacoyannis. Natl. Bd. of Review '71: Actress (Papas).

Troll ✓ 1/2 **1986 (PG-13)** A malevolent troll haunts an apartment building and possesses a young girl in hopes of turning all humans into trolls. Sometimes imaginative, sometimes embarrassing. Followed by a sequel. **86m/C VHS, DVD.** Noah Hathaway, Gary Sandy, Anne Lockhart, Sonny Bono, Shelley Hack, June Lockhart, Michael Moriarty, Jennifer Beck, Phil Fondacaro, Brad Hall, Julia Louis-Dreyfus, Albert Band, Charles Band; ***D:*** John Carl Buechler; ***W:*** Ed Naha; ***C:*** Romano Albani; ***M:*** Richard Band.

Troll 2 ✓ 1/2 **1992 (PG-13)** A young boy can only rely on his faith in himself when no one believes his warnings about an evil coming to destroy his family. Entering into a nightmare world, Joshua must battle witches' spells and the evil trolls who carry out their bidding. **95m/C VHS, DVD.** Michael Stephenson, Connie McFarland, Gavin Reed; ***D:*** Drago Floyd; ***W:*** Clyde (Claudio Fragasso) Anderson.

A Troll in Central Park ✓✓ 1/2 **1994 (G)** Animated fantasy about Stanley the troll, who is cast out of his kingdom (because he's a good guy) and winds up in New York's Central Park. There, Stanley brings happiness to a little girl and her skeptical brother, all the while battling the evil troll queen. Strictly average family fare. **76m/C VHS, DVD.** ***D:*** Don Bluth, Gary Goldman; ***W:*** Stu Krieger; ***M:*** Robert Folk; ***V:*** Dom DeLuise, Cloris Leachman, Jonathan Pryce, Hayley Mills, Charles Nelson Reilly, Phillip Glasser, Robert Morley, Sy Goraleb, Tawney Sunshine Glover, Jordan Metzner.

Troma's War WOOF! **1988 (R)** The survivors of an air crash find themselves amid a tropical terrorist-run civil war. Also available in a 105-minute, unrated version. Devotees of trash films shouldn't miss this one. **90m/C VHS, DVD.** Carolyn Beauchamp, Sean Bowen, Michael Ryder, Jessica Dublin, Steven Crossley, Lorayn Lane DeLuca, Charles Kay Hune, Ara Romanoff, Alex Cserhart, Aleida Harris; ***D:*** Michael Herz, Lloyd Kaufman; ***W:*** Lloyd Kaufman, Mitchell Dana, Eric Hattler, Thomas Martinek; ***C:*** James London; ***M:*** Christopher De Marco.

Tromba, the Tiger Man ✓ 1/2 *Tromba* **1952** A circus tiger tamer uses a special drug that hypnotizes the critters into obeying his every whim. When he tries the same drug on women, things get out of hand. **62m/B VHS.** *GE* Rene Deltgen, Angelika Hauff, Gustav Knuth, Hilde Weissner, Grethe Weiser, Gardy Granass, Adrian Hoven; ***D:*** Helmut Weiss.

Tromeo & Juliet ✓✓ **1995 (R)** There've been many versions of Shakespeare, but the Bard may never recover from being "Tromatized." On the outskirts of New York City, teenaged Tromeo Que (Keenan) falls in lust with babe Juliet Capulet (Jensen), but the family feud is still around to cause major disharmony. There's lots of profanity, perversity, and gore to keep your interest. As the movie's tagline says, "Body Piercing. Kinky Sex. Dismemberment. The things that made Shakespeare great." The unrated version is 105 minutes. **95m/C VHS, DVD.** Will Keenan, Jane Jensen, Debbie Rochon, Lemmy, Valentine Miele, Sean Gunn; ***D:*** Lloyd Kaufman; ***W:*** James Gunn; ***C:*** Brendan Flynt; ***M:*** Willie Wisely.

Tron ✓✓ **1982 (PG)** A video game designer enters into his computer, where he battles the computer games he created and seeks revenge on other designers who have stolen his creations. Sounds better than it plays. Terrific special effects, with lots of computer-created graphics. **96m/C VHS, DVD, UMD.** Jeff Bridges, Bruce Boxleitner, David Warner, Cindy Morgan, Barnard Hughes, Dan Shor, Peter Jurasik, Tony Stephano; ***D:*** Steven Lisberger; ***W:*** Steven Lisberger; ***C:*** Bruce Logan; ***M:*** Walter (Wendy) Carlos.

Troop Beverly Hills ✓ **1989 (PG)** Spoiled housewife Long isn't really spoiled, just misunderstood. She takes over leadership of her daughter's Wilderness Girls troop and finds the opportunity to redeem herself by offering her own unique survival tips to the uncooperative little brats who make up the troop. Everyone learns meaningful life lessons, Long is finally understood, and everyone lives happily ever after in posh Beverly Hills. Sheer silliness makes this one almost painful to watch, a shame since it boasts a good cast whose talent is totally wasted. **105m/C VHS, DVD.** Shelley Long, Craig T. Nelson, Betty Thomas, Mary Gross, Stephanie Beacham, Audra Lindley, Edd Byrnes, Ami Foster, Jenny Lewis, Kellie Martin; ***D:*** Jeff Kanew; ***W:*** Pamela Norris, Margaret Grieco Oberman; ***M:*** Randy Edelman.

Tropic of Cancer ✓✓✓ **1970 (NC-17)** Based on Henry Miller's once-banned, now classic novel, this film portrays the sexual escapades of the expatriate author living in 1920s Paris. Torn stars as the carefree, loose-living writer and Burstyn plays his disgusted wife. **87m/C VHS.** Rip Torn, James Callahan, Ellen Burstyn, David Bauer, Phil Brown; ***D:*** Joseph Strick.

Tropic Thunder ✓✓✓ **2008 (R)** Dead-on parody of Hollywood self-absorption and egotism has five actors on location in Vietnam filming a war movie with things constantly going wrong. They wind up alone on a remote jungle location where they are mistaken for DEA agents by the local drug lords. Stiller's the vacuous action star, Black's a druggie comedian, and Downey Jr. brilliantly plays an Oscar-winning Method actor who dyes his skin black when he discovers that his grunt character was supposed to be African-American. This and other bits caused some protests from people who didn't get that Stiller was making fun of the film industry's insular cluelessness. Tom Cruise hilariously cameos in a fat suit as a foul-mouthed studio exec. **106m/C DVD, Blu-ray Disc.** *US* Ben Stiller, Robert Downey Jr., Jack Black, Jay Baruchel, Danny McBride, Bill Hader, Steve Coogan, Nick Nolte, Brandon T. Jackson, Tom Cruise, Matthew McConaughey, Justin Theroux, Christine Taylor, Amy Stiller, Brandon Soo Hoo; ***Cameos:*** Tobey Maguire, Jon Voight, Tyra Banks, Jennifer Love Hewitt; ***D:*** Ben Stiller; ***W:*** Ben Stiller, Justin Theroux, Etan Cohen; ***C:*** John Toll; ***M:*** Theodore Shapiro.

Tropical Heat ✓✓ **1993 (R)** When the Maharajah is killed on safari, his grieving widow (D'Abo) files a $5 million insurance claim before returning to India. She's followed by an investigator (Rossovich) who becomes infatuated with the lovely D'Abo. Through palaces, primitive villages, and ancient jungle temples, they are drawn into a mystery involving blackmail and murder. Based on a story by Jag Mundhra, Michael

W. Potts, and Simon Levy. **86m/C VHS.** Rick Rossovich, Maryam D'Abo, Lee Ann Beaman, Asha Siewkumar; ***D:*** Jag Mundhra; ***W:*** Michel W. Potts; ***M:*** Del Casher.

Tropical Malady 1/2 *Sud pralad* **2004** Maybe it makes more sense to a Thai audience. In present-day Thailand, soldier Keng (Lamnoi) meets country boy Tong (Kaewbuadee) and the two fall in love. Then we go from the natural to the supernatural world and something involving a Thai legend about a shaman who can transform himself into animals. Keng encounters a tiger in the jungle or maybe it's just a spirit tiger and Tong disappears except maybe he's the animal—or maybe not. And there's a talking monkey and the spirit of a dead cow. Thai with subtitles. **120m/C DVD.** *TH* Banlop Lomnoi, Sakda Kaewbuadee; ***D:*** Apichatpong Weerasethakul; ***W:*** Apichatpong Weerasethakul; ***C:*** Jean-Louis Vialard, Vichet Tanapanitch, Jarin Pengpanitch.

Tropical Snow **1988 (R)** A pair of lovers living poorly in Colombia decide to enter the drug trade in exchange for passage to the U.S. offered to them by drug kingpin Carradine. Unfortunately, they get more than they bargained for. Shot on location. **87m/C VHS.** David Carradine, Madeleine Stowe, Jsu Garcia, Argermiro Catiblanco; ***D:*** Ciro Duran.

Tropix 1/2 **2002** Poor Corrine thinks her hubby whisked her to Costa Rica to salvage their wreck of a marriage only to realize that the no-good cad actually has crooked business dealings on the agenda. When things go haywire she's kidnapped and spends most of her time struggling to cut loose from her captors in the jungle. **98m/C VHS, DVD.** Keith Brunsmann, Ryan Barton-Grimley, Danielle Bisutti, Michelle Jones, Thomas Scott-Stanton; ***D:*** Percy Angress, Livia Linden; ***W:*** Livia Linden; ***C:*** Luc G. Nicknair. **VIDEO**

Trouble along the Way 1/2 **1953** Wayne is a once big-time college football coach who takes a coaching job at a small, financially strapped Catholic college in an effort to retain custody of his young daughter. His underhanded recruiting methods result in his firing—and the probable loss of his daughter. Unusual and sentimental role for Wayne proves he can handle comedy as well as action. **110m/B VHS, DVD.** John Wayne, Donna Reed, Charles Coburn, Tom Tully, Sherry Jackson, Marie Windsor, Tom Helmore, Dabbs Greer, Leif Erickson, Douglas Spencer; ***D:*** Michael Curtiz; ***W:*** Jack Rose, Melville Shavelson; ***M:*** Max Steiner.

Trouble Bound **1992 (R)** Madsen is Harry, a guy just out of prison, on his way to Nevada with trouble dogging him every step. He's got a dead body in the car trunk, drug dealers after him, and when he offers a lift to a pretty cocktail waitress (Arquette) his luck only gets worse. She plans to kill a Mob boss and it's no secret. Chases and violence. **90m/C VHS, DVD.** Michael Madsen, Patricia Arquette, Florence Stanley, Seymour Cassel, Sal Jenco; ***D:*** Jeff Reiner; ***W:*** Darrell Fetty, Francis Delia; ***M:*** Vinnie Golia.

Trouble Busters **1933** Troubled locals worry about who to call when oil is discovered in their town, bringing evil profiteers with it. The Trouble Busters come into town to set things straight. **51m/B VHS.** Jack Hoxie, Lane Chandler; ***D:*** Lewis D. Collins.

Trouble Chasers 1/2 **1945** Two crooks screw up the heist of a valuable necklace and frame an innocent man for the crime. Then, they get involved in the fight game, where they discover a link between a boxer and their patsy. **63m/B VHS.** Billy Gilbert, Maxie "Slapsie" Rosenbloom, Shemp Howard, Gloria Marlen; ***D:*** Lew Landers; ***W:*** Ande Lamb, George Plympton; ***C:*** Marcel Le Picard.

Trouble in Mind **1986 (R)** Stylized romance is set in the near future in a rundown diner. Kristofferson is an ex-cop who gets involved in the lives of a young couple looking for a better life. Look for Divine in one of her/his rare appearances outside of John Waters' works. **111m/C VHS.** Allan Nicholls, Kris Kristofferson, Keith Carradine, Genevieve Bujold, Lori Singer, Divine, Joe Morton, George Kirby, John Considine, Dirk Blocker, Gailard Sartain, Tracy Kristofferson; ***D:*** Alan Rudolph; ***W:*** Alan Rudolph; ***C:*** Toyomichi Kurita; ***M:*** Mark Isham. Ind. Spirit '86: Cinematog.

Trouble in Paradise **1932** Oh-so-assured sophisticated comedy finds gentleman jewel thief Gaston (Marshall) meeting his match in upscale pickpocket Lily (Hopkins). Even though they team up, their personal relationship doesn't get in the way of their professional ambitions. Gaston cons his way into the graces of wealthy widow Mariette Colet (Francis), who's well-aware she'd being used but is more amused than outraged. The same can't be said of her two devoted and dull suitors (Ruggles, Horton), who don't like the competition. And maybe Gaston is getting a little too interested in Mariette for even Lily's piece of mind. Both leading actresses are flirty and lovely and Marshall is suave and gallant. Because this is a pre-Production Code film, there's lots of sexual innuendo (both visual and verbal) and crime without punishment. **83m/B VHS, DVD.** Herbert Marshall, Miriam Hopkins, Kay Francis, Charlie Ruggles, Edward Everett Horton, Sir C. Aubrey Smith, Robert Greig; ***D:*** Ernst Lubitsch; ***W:*** Grover Jones, Samson Raphaelson; ***C:*** Victor Milner; ***M:*** W. Franke Harling.

Trouble in Paradise **1988** Welch stars as a widow stranded in a tropical island paradise with an Australian sailor. The two must struggle as they are stalked by a gang of drug smugglers, hence the title. **92m/C VHS, DVD.** Raquel Welch, Jack Thompson, Nicholas Hammond, John Gregg; ***D:*** Di Drew. **TV**

Trouble in Store 1/2 **1953** A bumbling department store employee stumbles on a gangster's plot. Fun gags and a good cast. **85m/B VHS.** *GB* Margaret Rutherford, Norman Wisdom, Moira Lister, Megs Jenkins; ***D:*** Jack Paddy Carstairs.

Trouble in Texas **1937** Outlaws go to a rodeo and try to steal the prize money. Tex wants to find out who killed his brother and in his spare time, sings and tries to stop the crooks. Notable because it is the last film Hayworth made under her original stage name (Rita Cansino). **65m/B VHS, DVD.** Tex Ritter, Rita Hayworth, Earl Dwire, Yakima Canutt; ***D:*** Robert North Bradbury.

Trouble in the Glen 1/2 **1954** A Scottish-American soldier returns to his ancestral home and becomes involved in a dispute between the town residents and a lord over a closed road. Uneven script undermines comic idea. **91m/C VHS.** *GB* Orson Welles, Victor McLaglen, Forrest Tucker, Margaret Lockwood; ***D:*** Herbert Wilcox.

The Trouble with Angels 1/2 **1966 (PG)** Two young girls turn a convent upside down with their endless practical jokes. Russell is everything a Mother Superior should be: understanding, wise, and beautiful. **112m/C VHS, DVD.** Hayley Mills, June Harding, Rosalind Russell, Gypsy Rose Lee, Binnie Barnes; ***D:*** Ida Lupino; ***C:*** Lionel Lindon; ***M:*** Jerry Goldsmith.

The Trouble with Dick **1988 (R)** An ambitious young science fiction writer's personal troubles begin to appear in his writing. Although the box cover displays a "Festival Winner" announcement, don't be fooled! Story becomes tedious after first five minutes. **86m/C VHS.** Tom Villard, Susan Dey, Elizabeth Gorcey, David Clennon, Marianne Muellerleile; ***D:*** Gary Walkow; ***W:*** Gary Walkow; ***C:*** Elaine Giftos, Daryl Studebaker; ***M:*** Roger Bourland. Sundance '87: Grand Jury Prize.

The Trouble with Girls (and How to Get into It) *The Chautauqua* **1969 (G)** A 1920s traveling show manager tries to solve a local murder. Not as much singing as his earlier films, but good attention is paid to details. This is definitely one of the better Elvis vehicles. ♫Almost; Clean Up Your Own Back Yard. **99m/C VHS, DVD.** Elvis Presley, Marlyn Mason, Nicole Jaffe, Sheree North, Edward Andrews, John Carradine, Vincent Price, Joyce Van Patten, Dabney Coleman, John Rubinstein, Anthony Teague, Helene Winston; ***D:*** Peter Tewkesbury.

The Trouble with Harry **1955 (PG)** When a little boy finds a dead body in a Vermont town, it causes all kinds of problems for the community. No one is sure who killed Harry and what to do with the body. MacLaine's film debut and Herrmann's first musical score for Hitchcock. **90m/C VHS, DVD.** John Forsythe, Shirley MacLaine, Edmund Gwenn, Jerry Mathers, Mildred Dunnock, Mildred Natwick, Royal Dano; ***D:*** Alfred Hitchcock; ***W:*** John Michael Hayes; ***C:*** Robert Burks; ***M:*** Bernard Herrmann.

The Trouble with Spies **1987 (PG-13)** A bumbling British spy goes to Ibizia to locate a Russian agent, makes a million mistakes and wins anyway. A loser of a film, wasted a fine cast. Made in 1984; no one bothered to release it for three years. **91m/C VHS.** Donald Sutherland, Malcolm Morley, Lucy Gutteridge, Ruth Gordon, Ned Beatty, Michael Hordern, Robert Morley; ***D:*** Burt Kennedy; ***W:*** Burt Kennedy.

Troublemakers 1/2 **1994 (PG)** Travis (Hill) is the fastest gun in the west—but his brother Moses (Spencer) is the country's meanest bounty hunter. But their mother loves them, and wants both her boys home for Christmas. So she leaves it up to Travis to lure Moses back to the homestead. **98m/C VHS, DVD.** Terence Hill, Bud Spencer, Anne Kasprik, Ruth Buzzi, Ron Carey; ***D:*** Terence Hill; ***W:*** Jess Hill; ***C:*** Carlo Tafani; ***M:*** Pino Donaggio.

Troubles 1/2 **1988** In 1919, Major Brendan Archer arrives on the coast of Wicklow, Ireland to be reunited with his fiancee, Angela Spencer, at the family hotel, the decaying Majestic. Brendan is puzzled by the changes in both the hotel and Angela and begins to turn his interests to her friend, Sarah Devlin, who is a passionate Irish nationalist. But volatile Irish politics puts the romance in danger. Based on the 1970 novel by J.G. Farrell. **208m/C VHS, DVD.** *GB* Ian Charleson, Ian Richardson, Sean Bean, Emer Gillespie, Susannah Harker; ***D:*** Christopher Morahan; ***W:*** Charles Sturridge. **TV**

The Troubles We've Seen 1/2 *Veillees d'armes* **1994** Footage of old and recent war coverage and journalist Marcel Ophuls' own work while in Sarajevo is woven together with interviews of various war correspondents to provide an insider's view of the ethical and philosophical difficulties of covering the insanity of war while clinging to one's own precarious grip on sanity. This in-depth documentary explores topics as diverse as a reporter revealing his own opposition to the war he's covering to the dark truth that, as one subject puts it, "the more horrible the situation, the more successful we become." **224m/C DVD.** ***D:*** Marcel Ophuls; ***W:*** Marcel Ophuls; ***C:*** Pierre Milon, Pierre Boffety.

Troy 1/2 **2004 (R)** Petersen's epic telling of the Trojan War finally hit the screen after many delays (including Pitt injuring his Achilles tendon, oh the irony!) and budget-busting incidents. Merely inspired by Homer's "The Iliad," it dispenses with all those pesky Greek gods and makes it all about the warriors. When beautiful Helen (Kruger) flees her Spartan husband Menaleus (Gleeson) with pretty-boy lover Paris (Bloom), her greedy brother-in-law Agamemnon (Cox) decides Troy's wealth is worth a little fighting. Arrogant Achilles (Pitt) is persuaded to join in, and while Paris is no fighter, big brother Hector (Bana) is. Naturally, Achilles and Hector will have to go mano-a-mano (in one of the film's best scenes). Also around to show those youngsters what acting's all about is O'Toole as aging King Priam. It's all handled professionally but it's just not terribly compelling. **162m/C DVD, Blu-ray Disc, HD DVD.** *GB* Brad Pitt, Orlando Bloom, Eric Bana, Peter O'Toole, Diane Kruger, Brendan Gleeson, Brian Cox, Sean Bean, Julian Glover, Julie Christie, Saffron Burrows, John Shrapnel, James Cosmo, Rose Byrne, Garrett Hedlund, Nathan Jones, Vincent Regan, Trevor Eve, Tyler Mane; ***D:*** Wolfgang Petersen; ***W:*** David Benioff; ***C:*** Roger Pratt; ***M:*** James Horner.

The Truce *La Tregua* **1996** Adaptation of the novel by Primo Levi, based on his true account of traveling home across Europe after the liberation of Auschwitz at the end of WWII. Tells the story of Levi's arduous journey home to Turin through Eastern Europe, as well as his slow rediscovery of life and hope. Has the trappings of a grand historical epic, but works best as a quiet introspective look at a man trying to reclaim his humanity after experiencing unimaginable horror. Flashback scenes in the camp are appropriately harrowing, but the film loses focus when joining Levi and his ragtag compadres on the road home, sometimes slipping into banal sentimentality or outright melodrama, two things a story this powerful doesn't need. Turturro, who committed to the project several years ago, gives the performance of his career, understated and convincing. Levi committed suicide in 1987, shortly after giving Rosi's adaptation his blessing. **117m/C VHS, DVD.** *IT FR GE SI* John Turturro, Rade Serbedzija, Massimo Ghini, Stefano Dionisi, Teco Celio, Claudio Bisio, Roberto Citran, Andy Luotto, Agnieszka Wagner; ***D:*** Francesco Rosi; ***W:*** Stefano Rulli, Sandro Petraglia, Tonino Guerra, Francesco Rosi; ***C:*** Pasqualino De Santis, Marco Pontecorvo; ***M:*** Luis Bacalov.

Truck Stop *L'Amour Chez les Poids Lourds* **1978** This truck stop has all a trucker needs—including the owner, voluptuous Pamela. **80m/C VHS.** *FR* Georges Gueret, Nikki Gentile, Elizabeth Turner, Jean Marie Pallardy; ***D:*** Jean Marie Pallardy; ***W:*** Jean Marie Pallardy; ***C:*** Guy Maria; ***M:*** Georges Bacri.

Truck Stop Women **1974 (R)** Female truckers become involved in smuggling and prostitution at a truck stop. The mob wants a cut of the business and will do anything to get their way. Better than it sounds. **88m/C VHS.** Claudia Jennings, Lieux Dressler, John Martino, Dennis Fimple, Dolores Dorn, Gene Drew, Paul Carr, Jennifer Burton; ***D:*** Mark L. Lester.

Truck Turner 1/2 **1974 (R)** He's a bounty hunter, he's black and he's up against a threadbare plot. Hayes methodically eliminates everyone involved with his partner's murder while providing groovy soundtrack. Quintessential blaxploitation. **91m/C VHS, DVD.** Isaac Hayes, Yaphet Kotto, Annazette Chase, Nichelle Nichols, Scatman Crothers, Dick Miller; ***D:*** Jonathan Kaplan; ***W:*** Leigh Chapman; ***C:*** Charles F. Wheeler; ***M:*** Isaac Hayes.

Trucker **2008 (R)** Diane Ford (Monaghan) is a foul-mouthed, independent loner who works as a long-haul trucker. She unexpectedly (and unwillingly) needs to change her life when her estranged 11-year-old son Peter (Bennett) comes to live with her because his dad Leonard (Bratt) is in the hospital with cancer. Peter is as profane and angry at the situation as his birth mother, who hasn't willingly seen him in years, so the kid has abandonment issues as well. They learn to tolerate each other but don't expect any big bonding, touchy-feely scenes. **90m/C DVD.** *US* Michelle Monaghan, Jimmy Bennett, Benjamin Bratt, Nathan Fillion, Joey Lauren Adams, Bryce Johnson; ***D:*** James Mottern; ***W:*** James Mottern; ***C:*** Lawrence Sher; ***M:*** Mychael Danna.

Trucker's Woman **1975 (R)** Man takes a job driving an 18-wheel truck in order to find the murderers of his father. **90m/C VHS, DVD.** Michael Hawkins, Mary Cannon; ***D:*** Will Zens.

Trucks **1997 (R)** A group of residents are terrorized by driverless trucks going on a rampage through their small town, which happens to be located in Area 51. Based on the short story by Stephen King and previously filmed as 1986's "Maximum Overdrive." **99m/C VHS, DVD.** Timothy Busfield, Brenda Bakke, Brendan Fletcher, Jay Brazeau, Amy Stewart; ***D:*** Chris Thomson; ***W:*** Brian Taggert; ***C:*** Rob Draper, Keith Holland; ***M:*** Michael Richard Plowman. **CABLE**

The True and the False 1/2 *Den Underbara Lognen* **1955** Two stories haunt the dreams of young bride-to-be Josephine (Hasso). When she falls asleep reading Balzac's "La Grande Breteche," Josephine dreams that she and fiance Louis (Langford) are living out the story of infidelity and revenge. In Guy de Maupassant's "The Old Maid" a disfigured young girl loves a soldier who doesn't love her—until she inherits a fortune. In Swedish with subtitles; also available in an English-language version. **95m/B VHS.** Signe Hasso, William Langford, Ragnor Arvedson, Ann Bibby; ***D:*** Schamyl Bauman, Mike Road; ***W:*** Bob Condon; ***C:*** Sven Nykvist; ***M:*** Jules Sylvain.

True Believer 1/2 **1989 (R)** Cynical lawyer, once a '60s radical, now defends rich drug dealers. Spurred on by a young protege, he takes on the hopeless case of imprisoned Asian-American accused of gang-slaying. Tense thriller with good cast. **103m/C VHS, DVD.** James Woods, Robert Downey Jr., Yuji Okumoto, Margaret Colin, Kurtwood Smith, Tom Bower, Miguel Fernandes, Charles Hallahan; ***D:*** Joseph Ruben; ***W:*** Wesley Strick; ***C:*** John Lindley; ***M:*** Brad Fiedel.

True Blood 🦴🦴 **1989 (R)** A man returns to his home turf to save his brother from the same ruthless gang who set him up for a cop's murder. **100m/C VHS, DVD.** Chad Lowe, Jeff Fahey, Sherilyn Fenn; ***D:*** Peter Maris.

True Blue 🦴🦴 **2001 (R)** Rem Macy (Berenger) is supposed to be a seasoned NYPD detective. So why does he behave like a hormonally challenged rookie? He's investigating a severed hand found floating in a Central Park pond that turns out to belong to the roommate of Nikki (Heuring). Nikki begs protection from Macy and he lets her stay in his apartment—which the Hound is sure is standard police procedure. Naturally, this is a really dumb move. **101m/C VHS, DVD.** Tom Berenger, Lori Heuring, Barry Newman, Pamela Gridley, Soon-Teck Oh, Richard Chevolleau, Leo Lee; ***D:*** J.S. Cardone; ***W:*** J.S. Cardone; ***C:*** Darko Suvak; ***M:*** Timothy S. (Tim) Jones. **VIDEO**

True Colors 🦴🦴 ½ **1987 (PG-13)** A woman fights for her homeland of France in order to save the country from being taken over by Hitler. **160m/C VHS.** Noni Hazlehurst, John Waters, Patrick Ryecart, Shane Briant, Alan Andrews; ***D:*** Pino Amenta.

True Colors 🦴🦴 **1991 (R)** Law school buddies take divergent paths in post grad real world. Straight and narrow Spader works for Justice Department while dropout Cusack manipulates friends and acquaintances to further his position as Senator's aid. Typecast, predictable and, moralizing. **111m/C VHS, DVD.** John Cusack, James Spader, Imogen Stubbs, Mandy Patinkin, Richard Widmark, Paul Guilfoyle, Dina Merrill, Philip Bosco, Brad Sullivan, Don McManus; ***D:*** Herbert Ross.

True Confessions 🦴🦴🦴 **1981 (R)** Tale of corruption pits two brothers, one a priest and the other a detective, against each other. Nice 1940s period look, with excellent performances from De Niro and Duvall. Based on a true case from the Gregory Dunne novel. **110m/C VHS, DVD.** Robert De Niro, Robert Duvall, Kenneth McMillan, Charles Durning, Cyril Cusack, Ed Flanders, Burgess Meredith, Louisa Moritz; ***D:*** Ulu Grosbard; ***W:*** John Gregory Dunne, Joan Didion; ***C:*** Owen Roizman; ***M:*** Georges Delerue.

True Confessions of a Hollywood Starlet 🦴🦴 ½ **2008** Amusing Lifetime showbiz dramedy. Bratty teen Morgan Carter (Levesque) is a singer/actress whose success has led to completely out-of-control behavior. One drink too many lands her in rehab and then her worried mom (Boyd) sends Morgan to her Aunt Trudy (Bertinelli), who lives in Fort Wayne, Indiana. Morgan is supposed to learn how to live like a normal teenager in the boring Midwest, but she's not going to make it easy on anyone, including herself. **87m/C DVD.** Joanna "JoJo" Levesque, Valerie Bertinelli, Lynda Boyd, Justin Louis, Ian Nelson, Shenae Grimes; ***D:*** Tim Matheson; ***W:*** Elisa Bell; ***C:*** David Herrington; ***M:*** David Schwartz. **CABLE**

True Crime 🦴🦴 ½ *Dangerous Kiss* **1995 (R)** High school student turns detective when a classmate is killed, hooks up with a police cadet, and finds herself on the trail of a serial killer. **94m/C VHS, DVD.** Alicia Silverstone, Kevin Dillon, Bill Nunn, Michael Bowen; ***D:*** Pat Verducci; ***W:*** Pat Verducci; ***C:*** Chris Squires; ***M:*** Blake Leyh.

True Crime 🦴🦴 ½ **1999 (R)** Eastwood, who directs and stars, does a good job developing his character Steve Everett, a flawed reporter who has boozed and womanized his way out of the top of his profession. He is given the assignment to interview death row inmate Frank Beachum (Washington), who is scheduled to die in 24 hours. Everett becomes convinced that Beachum is innocent, and the plot erodes into a trite race against time to save the innocent man. Clint shows his acting chops before the story deflates, however, and his fans will certainly enjoy this one. **127m/C VHS, DVD.** Jack Kehler, Clint Eastwood, James Woods, Isaiah Washington IV, Denis Leary, Frances Fisher, Diane Venora, Mary McCormack, Lisa Gay Hamilton, Bernard Hill, Michael McKean, Michael Jeter, Hattie Winston, Laila Robins, Christine Ebersole, Anthony Zerbe, John Finn, Marissa Ribisi, Erik King, Graham Beckel, Sydney Tamiia Poitier, Penny Rae Bridges; ***D:*** Clint Eastwood; ***W:*** Larry Gross, Paul Brickman, Stephen Schiff; ***C:*** Jack N. Green; ***M:*** Lennie Niehaus.

True Friends 🦴🦴 **1998 (R)** Amateurish but earnest effort by the three lead actors (who also wrote, directed, and produced in various combinations). In 1980, three 12-year-old Bronx buddies witness local mob boss, Big Tony, kill a man. They've stayed friends and kept the secret for 15 years but now the crime comes back to haunt them. **98m/C VHS, DVD.** James Quattrochi, Loreto Mauro, Rodrigo Botero, Dan Lauria, MacKenzie Phillips, John Capodice, Peter Onorati, Bertila Damas, Leo Rossi; ***D:*** James Quattrochi; ***W:*** James Quattrochi, Rodrigo Botero; ***C:*** Jeff Baustert; ***M:*** Charles Dayton.

True Grit 🦴🦴🦴 **1969 (G)** Hard-drinking U.S. Marshal Rooster Cogburn (Wayne) is hired by a young girl (Darby) to find her father's killer. Won Wayne his only Oscar. Based on the Charles Portis novel. Prompted sequel, "Rooster Cogburn." **128m/C VHS, DVD.** Jeremy Slate, Dennis Hopper, Alfred Ryder, Strother Martin, Jeff Corey, Ron Soble, John Fiedler, James Westerfield, John Doucette, Donald Woods, Edith Atwater, Carlos Rivas, Wilford Brimley, Jay Silverheels, Hank Worden, John Wayne, Glen Campbell, Kim Darby, Robert Duvall; ***D:*** Henry Hathaway; ***W:*** Marguerite Roberts; ***C:*** Lucien Ballard; ***M:*** Elmer Bernstein. Oscars '69: Actor (Wayne); Golden Globes '70: Actor—Drama (Wayne).

True Heart 🦴🦴 ½ **1997 (PG)** Bonnie (Dunst) and brother Sam (Bryan) are lost in the British Columbian wilderness after surviving a plane crash. They are befriended by a Native American elder (Schellenberg), who guides them through the dangers and back to civilization. Corny dialogue and beautiful scenery. **92m/C VHS, DVD.** Kirsten Dunst, Zachery Ty Bryan, August Schellenberg, Dey Young, Michael Gross; ***D:*** Catherine Cyran; ***W:*** Catherine Cyran; ***C:*** Christopher Baffa; ***M:*** Eric Allaman.

True Heart Susie 🦴🦴 ½ **1919** A simple, moving story about a girl who is in love with a man who marries another girl from the city. Silent. **87m/B VHS, DVD.** Lillian Gish, Robert "Bobbie" Harron; ***D:*** D.W. Griffith.

True Identity 🦴🦴 **1991 (R)** Henry, a comic superstar in England, stars as an innocent black man marked for death by the Mafia. He hides by disguising himself as white and gets a taste of life on the other side of the color line. The interesting premise was based on a classic Eddie Murphy sketch on "Saturday Night Live," but isn't treated with sufficient imagination or humor here. **94m/C VHS.** Lenny Henry, Frank Langella, Anne-Marie Johnson, Charles Lane; ***D:*** Charles Lane; ***W:*** Andy Breckman.

True Lies 🦴🦴 ½ **1994 (R)** Brain candy with a bang offers eye popping special effects and a large dose of unbelievability. Sort of like a big screen "Scarecrow and Mrs. King" as supposed computer salesman Harry Trasker (Ah-nuld) keeps his spy work secret from mousy, neglected and bored wife Helen (Curtis), who has a few secrets of her own and inadvertantly ends up right in the thick of things. Raunchy and extremely sexist, but not without charm; the stupidity is part of the fun. Perfectly cast sidekick Arnold holds his own as a pig, but Heston is wasted as the head honcho. Tons of special effects culiminate in a smashing finish. Very loosely adapted from the 1991 French comedy "La Total." **114m/C VHS, DVD.** Arnold Schwarzenegger, Jamie Lee Curtis, Tom Arnold, Bill Paxton, Tia Carrere, Art Malik, Eliza Dushku, Charlton Heston, Grant Heslov; ***D:*** James Cameron; ***W:*** James Cameron; ***C:*** Russell Carpenter; ***M:*** Brad Fiedel. Golden Globes '95: Actress—Mus./Comedy (Curtis); Blockbuster '96: Action Actress, V. (Curtis).

True Love 🦴🦴🦴 **1989 (R)** Low-budget, savagely observed comedy follows the family and community events leading up to a Bronx Italian wedding. Authentic slice-of-life about two young people with very different ideas about what marriage and commitment mean. Acclaimed script and performances. **104m/C VHS, DVD.** Annabella Sciorra, Ron Eldard, Aida Turturro, Roger Rignack, Michael J. Wolfe, Star Jasper, Kelly Cinnante, Rick Shapiro, Suzanne Costallos, Vincent Pastore; ***D:*** Nancy Savoca; ***W:*** Nancy Savoca, Richard Guay; ***C:*** Lisa Rinzler. Sundance '89: Grand Jury Prize.

True Romance 🦴🦴 ½ **1993 (R)** Geeky Clarence (Slater) and wide-eyed call girl Alabama (Arquette) meet and fall instantly in love (and marriage). The inept duo inadvertantly steals her pimp's coke and they head to L.A. with the mob in pursuit. Gem performances in small roles include Walken's icily debonair mafioso; Clarence's dad (Hopper), an ex-cop who runs afoul of Walken; Pitt's space-case druggie; Oldman's crazed pimp; and the ghost of Elvis (Kilmer), whom Clarence talks to in times of stress. Horrific violence mixed with very black humor clicks most of the time. Tarantino helped finance "Reservior Dogs" when he sold this script, his first. Unrated version also available. **116m/C VHS, DVD, UMD.** Christian Slater, Patricia Arquette, Gary Oldman, Brad Pitt, Val Kilmer, Dennis Hopper, Christopher Walken, Samuel L. Jackson, Christopher Penn, Bronson Pinchot, Michael Rapaport, Saul Rubinek, Conchata Ferrell, James Gandolfini, Tom Sizemore, Ed Lauter, Maria Pitillo, Gregory Sporleder, Kevin Corrigan, Michael Beach, Frank Adonis, Victor Argo, Paul Ben-Victor, Paul Bates; ***D:*** Tony Scott; ***W:*** Quentin Tarantino; ***C:*** Jeffrey L. Kimball; ***M:*** Hans Zimmer, Mark Mancina.

True Stories 🦴🦴🦴 ½ **1986 (PG)** Quirky, amusing look at the eccentric denizens of a fictional, off-center Texas town celebrating its 150th anniversary. Notable are Kurtz as the Laziest Woman in America and Goodman as a blushing suitor. Directorial debut of Byrne. Worth a look. **89m/C VHS, DVD.** David Byrne, John Goodman, Swoosie Kurtz, Spalding Gray, Annie McEnroe, Pops Staples, Tito Larriva, Alix Elias, Scott Valentine, Jo Harvey Allen; ***D:*** David Byrne; ***W:*** Beth Henley, Stephen Tobolowsky, David Byrne; ***C:*** Edward Lachman; ***M:*** David Byrne.

True Vengeance 🦴🦴 **1997 (R)** Navy operative finds himself on the run from a group of bounty hunters. **90m/C VHS.** Daniel Bernhardt, Miles O'Keeffe, Beverly Johnson; ***D:*** David Worth; ***W:*** Kurt Johnstad; ***C:*** David Worth. **VIDEO**

True West 🦴🦴🦴 **1986** Filmed performance of the acclaimed Sam Shepard play about two mismatched brothers. **110m/C VHS.** John Malkovich, Gary Sinise; ***D:*** Allan Goldstein. **TV**

True Women 🦴🦴 ½ **1997 (PG-13)** Sarah McClure (Delany) leaves Georgia with husband Bartlett (Boothe), settles in Texas, and raises her orphaned sister Euphemia (Majorino and Gish), as well as her own family, while Bartlett's off being a Texas Ranger. Euphemia's eventually reunited with her best friend, southern plantation beauty Georgia (Jolie), who's trying to hide the fact that she's part-Cherokee. The ladies suffer through Comanche attacks, the Alamo and the Mexican Army, the Civil War, Reconstruction, and various romantic trials and tribulations, all while being gosh-darn heroic. TV miniseries based on the historical novel by Janice Woods Windle. **170m/C VHS, DVD.** Dana Delany, Annabeth Gish, Angelina Jolie, Powers Boothe, Tina Majorino, Rachael Leigh Cook, Jeffrey Nordling, Michael Greyeyes, Tony Todd, Terrence Mann, Michael York, Salli Richardson, Irene Bedard, Charles S. Dutton, Julie Carmen, Matthew Glave, John Schneider; ***D:*** Karen Arthur; ***W:*** Christopher Lofton; ***C:*** Thomas Neuwirth; ***M:*** Bruce Broughton. **TV**

Truly, Madly, Deeply 🦴🦴🦴 **1991 (PG)** The recent death of her lover Jamie (Rickman) drives Nina (Stevenson) into despair and anger, until he turns up at her apartment one day. And decides to bring some of his ghostly buddies and hang out. Tender and well written tale of love and the supernatural, with believable characters and plot-line. Playwright Minghella's directorial debut. **107m/C VHS, DVD.** *GB* Juliet Stevenson, Alan Rickman, Bill Paterson, Michael Maloney, Christopher Rozycki, Keith Bartlett, David Ryall, Stella Maris; ***D:*** Anthony Minghella; ***W:*** Anthony Minghella; ***C:*** Remi Adefarasin; ***M:*** Barrington Pheloung. Australian Film Inst. '92: Foreign Film; British Acad. '91: Orig. Screenplay.

Truman 🦴🦴 ½ **1995 (PG)** Cable bio follows "Give 'em Hell" Harry (Sinise) from 1917 to 1968. The 33rd U.S. President, derided as a political hack, was determined to prove himself against the odds and by making the tough decisions, including authorizing use of the A-bomb on Japan. Sinise gives the appropriate no-nonsense performance, matched by Scarwid as ever-loyal wife Bess. Based on David McCullough's Pulitzer Prize-winning book. **135m/C VHS, DVD.** Gary Sinise, Diana Scarwid, Colm Feore, Richard Dysart, James Gammon, Tony Goldwyn, Pat Hingle, Harris Yulin, Leo Burmester, Zeljko Ivanek, David Lansbury, Marian Seldes, Lois Smith, Richard Venture, Daniel von Bargen; ***D:*** Frank Pierson; ***W:*** Thomas (Tom) Rickman; ***C:*** Paul Elliott; ***M:*** David Mansfield. **CABLE**

The Truman Show 🦴🦴🦴🦴 **1998 (PG)** Flawless execution of an eerie, yet fantastical premise, marked by outstanding performances, make this surreal fable a joy to watch from start to finish. Unbeknownst to insurance salesman Truman Burbank, (Carrey) his entire life has been broadcast live on TV in a 24-hour soap opera. When evidence of Truman's fabricated life begins to surface, he plans his escape, upsetting the grand scheme of producer, director and charismatic artist Christof (Harris in a stand-out performance). Carrey's sympathetic, low-key portrayal will make people forget the disappointment of "Cable Guy." Weir handles his satirical theme with craftmen-like precision, never letting his commentary on the power of the tube become too heavy-handed. Carrey reportedly took a pay cut from his $20 million fee in order to star. **102m/C VHS, DVD, Blu-ray Disc.** Jim Carrey, Ed Harris, Laura Linney, Noah Emmerich, Natascha (Natasha) McElhone, Holland Taylor, Paul Giamatti, Philip Baker Hall, Brian Delate, Una Damon; ***D:*** Peter Weir; ***W:*** Andrew Niccol; ***C:*** Peter Biziou; ***M:*** Philip Glass, Burkhard Dallwitz. British Acad. '98: Director (Weir), Orig. Screenplay; Golden Globes '99: Actor—Drama (Carrey), Support. Actor (Harris), Score; MTV Movie Awards '99: Male Perf. (Carrey); Natl. Bd. of Review '98: Support. Actor (Harris).

Trumbo 🦴🦴🦴 ½ **2007 (PG-13)** Dalton Trumbo was one of Hollywood's most fierce, original, and ultimately tarnished screenwriters of the 1950's. Blacklisted by the House Un-American Activities Committee, he was forced to pen scripts under a pseudonym and fake identity, winning an Oscar in the process. Based on his son Christopher's play of the same title, this first-hand account documents his days in the limelight and under the microscope, with Nathan Lane reprising his stage role, but oddly includes eight other actors, reading excerpts from a 1999 volume of Trumbo's collected letters, "Additional Dialogue." Nothing new to Hollywood historians and old-time fans, yet a fascinating examination of a dark period in America. **96m/C DVD.** *US* ***D:*** Peter Askin; ***W:*** Christopher Trumbo; ***C:*** Frank Prinzi, Jonathan Furmanski, Fred Murphy, Christopher Norr; ***M:*** Robert Miller.

The Trumpet of the Swan 🦴 ½ **2001 (G)** Disappointing animated adaptation of E.B. White's 1970 children's book has Louis, a mute trumpeter swan, trying to overcome his disability. Louis befriends a human boy who persuades him to learn to read and write, which doesn't help him much in the animal world, but brings him fame in the human one. His father, distraught over his son's "defect," steals a trumpet for him, and Louis learns to play, becoming famous enough to assuage his father's guilt over the theft by paying for the instrument. The animation, story, and (surprisingly) the score, all seem flat, while the script provides nothing in the way of magic. Only the youngest (under 5) of viewers will be distracted, but probably not for very long. **75m/C VHS, DVD.** *US* ***D:*** Richard Rich, Terry L. Noss; ***W:*** Judy Rothman Rofe; ***M:*** Marcus Miller; ***V:*** Dee Bradley Baker, Jason Alexander, Mary Steenburgen, Reese Witherspoon, Seth Green, Carol Burnett, Joe Mantegna, Sam Gifaldi.

Trumps 🦴🦴 *Enormous Changes at the Last Minute* **1983 (R)** Three dramas about women and contemporary relationships in New York City. Based on three stories—"Faith's Story," "Virginia's Story," and "Alexandra's Story"—by Grace Paley. **90m/C VHS.** Ellen Barkin, Kevin Bacon, Maria Tucci, Ron McLarty, Zvee Scooler, David Strathairn,

Jeffrey DeMunn, Sudie Bond; *D:* Mirra Bank, Ellen Hovde; *W:* John Sayles, Susan Rice.

Trust **1991 (R)** An obnoxious girl, tossed out by her family after becoming pregnant, forms a loving bond with a strange, possibly deranged guy from an abusive household. Similar in style and theme to Hartley's "The Unbelievable Truth"—a peculiar sardonic comedy/drama not for every taste. **107m/C VHS.** Adrienne Shelly, Martin Donovan, Merritt Nelson, Edie Falco, John MacKay, Marko Hunt; *D:* Hal Hartley; *W:* Hal Hartley; *C:* Michael Spiller; *M:* Phil Reed. Sundance '91: Screenplay.

Trust Me **1989 (R)** A cynical L.A. art dealer decides to promote a young artist's work and then kill him off to increase the value of his paintings. Satirical view of the Los Angeles art crowd. **94m/C VHS.** Adam Ant, Talia Balsam, David Packer, Barbara Bain, Joyce Van Patten, William De Acutis; *D:* Bobby Houston.

Trust the Man **2006 (R)** Relationship flick finds two Manhattan couples whining and dining in local eateries complaining about each other. Successful actress Rebecca (Moore, real-life wife of director Freundlich) is married to sex-addict stay-at-home dad Tom (Duchovny), and Elaine (Gyllenhaal) is an aspiring writer and live-in girlfriend of Rebecca's brother Tobey (Crudup), a commitment-phobic but cute schlub. Everyone ponders the state of their unions while dabbling in infidelity and self-pity, and despite a few too many moments that are cloying, cliched, or contrived, the leads are good and make things watchable. Tom and Rebecca's two kids are played by Moore and Freundlich's real offspring. **103m/C DVD.** *US* Julianne Moore, David Duchovny, Billy Crudup, Maggie Gyllenhaal, Garry Shandling, Eva Mendes, Ellen Barkin, James LeGros, Liam Broggy, Dagmara Dominczyk, Justin Bartha; *D:* Bart Freundlich; *W:* Bart Freundlich; *C:* Tim Orr; *M:* Clint Mansell.

Trusting Beatrice **1/2 1992 (PG)** Lame comedy finds feckless landscaper Claude (Jacobs) the bewildered caretaker of Beatrice (Jacob), a Frenchwoman stranded in America without a green card and with a young Cambodian refugee girl. So Claude decides to take Beatrice home to his determinedly eccentric family. Tries for quirky but fails miserably. **86m/C VHS.** Irene Jacob, Mark Evan Jacobs, Leonardo Cimino, Charlotte Moore, Steve Buscemi, Pat McNamara; *D:* Cindy Lou Johnson; *W:* Cindy Lou Johnson.

The Truth about Cats and Dogs **1996 (PG-13)** Funny, intelligent Abby (Garofalo) hosts a popular radio call-in show for pet lovers. When a handsome Brit photographer (Chaplin) phones in with a Great Dane problem, he becomes intrigued by her voice, and asks for a date. Insecure about her looks, Abby asks her beautiful-but-dim girlfriend Noelle (Thurman) to fill in. Naturally, both women fall for the shy Englishman. Charming, updated version of "Cyrano de Bergerac" theme works because of strong lead performances, especially Garofalo, who steals the show with her dry, self-effacing wit. Entertaining romantic comedy features some nice scenes of Santa Monica, too. **97m/C VHS, DVD.** Bob Odenkirk, Janeane Garofalo, Uma Thurman, Ben Chaplin, Jamie Foxx, Richard Coca, Stanley DeSantis; *D:* Michael Lehmann; *W:* Audrey Wells; *C:* Robert Brinkmann; *M:* Howard Shore.

The Truth About Charlie **1/2 2002 (PG-13)** Jonathan Demme's remake of the Cary Grant-Audrey Hepburn vehicle "Charade" has the same Paris setting and convoluted plot, but not much of the carefree attitude of the original. Regina (Newton) comes home from a vacation and finds that her husband Charlie has been murdered, and that he was more than he seemed, as the police produce several passports that show Charlie with a different name and disguise. She also discovers that she now has a trio of her husband's former colleagues following her, looking for his hidden six million dollars. As an homage to the French New Wave cinema that was blooming when the original was filmed, Demme includes cameos of several luminaries of the genre. **104m/C VHS, DVD.** *US* Mark Wahlberg, Thandie Newton, Tim Robbins, Joong-Hoon Park, Ted Levine, Lisa Gay Hamilton, Christine Boisson, Stephen (Dillon) Dillane; ***Cameos:*** Charles Aznavour, Anna Karina; *D:* Jonathan Demme; *W:* Jonathan Demme, Stephen Schmidt, Jessica Bendinger; *C:* Tak Fujimoto; *M:* Rachel Portman.

The Truth About Jane **1/2 2000** Fifteen-year-old Jane (muth) is experiencing her first love. Unfortunately for her family and friends, it's with another girl and they just can't cope. Her mom, Janice (Channing), is especially upset and may lose Jane if she can't find a way to accept her. **91m/C VHS, DVD.** Stockard Channing, Ellen Muth, James Naughton, RuPaul Charles, Noah Fleiss, Kelly Rowan, Jenny O'Hara, Alicia Lagano; *D:* Lee Rose; *W:* Lee Rose; *C:* Eric Van Haren Noman; *M:* Terence Blanchard. **CABLE**

The Truth About Love **2004** Prudish and plain nurse Alice (Hewitt) gets an anonymous Valentine's Day card and assumes it's meant for her philandering husband. Alice and sister Felicity (Miles) conspire, cooking up their own anonymous love letter to Alice's husband Sam (Mistry) in hopes of proving his infidelity. Twists and turns are plentiful in the Brit love caper along the lines of Bridget Jones or Love Actually. **90m/C VHS, DVD.** *GB* Jennifer Love Hewitt, Kate Miles, Jimi Mistry, Dougray Scott, Branka Katic; *D:* John Hay; *W:* John Hay, Peter Blore, William Johnston, Rik Carmichael; *C:* Graham Frake; *M:* Debbie Wiseman. **VIDEO**

Truth about Women **1958** An old aristocrat recounts his youthful adventures to his son-in-law. A pale British comedy of manners. **107m/C VHS.** *GB* Laurence Harvey, Julie Harris, Mai Zetterling, Eva Gabor, Wilfrid Hyde-White, Derek Farr; *D:* Muriel Box.

Truth or Consequences, N.M. **1997 (R)** Yes, the name of the town is real. No, Bob Barker is not the mayor. Dim parolee Raymond (Gallo) and his even dimmer girlfriend Addy (Dickens) are reunited and just want to settle down, to tell the truth. Instead, they fall immediately back into a life of crime. Along with their accomplices Marcus (Williamson) and Curtis (Sutherland), they plan to rip off a drug dealer for big bucks (no whammies!). The heist, of course, goes bad; they steal an RV and kidnap its owners Gordon (Pollack) and Donna (Phillips). An attempt to unload the drugs on a powerful Mafia boss (Steiger) also goes awry, and that starts a real family feud. As the mob hit man (Sheen), the cops, and the crooks all converge on the eponymous New Mexico town, everyone is in jeopardy. Not logical, not original and not good. Directorial debut for Sutherland, who should really quit playing coked-up psychopathic murderers. **106m/C VHS, DVD.** Vincent Gallo, Kim Dickens, Kiefer Sutherland, Mykelti Williamson, Grace Phillips, Kevin Pollak, Martin Sheen, Rod Steiger, Rick Rossovich, John C. McGinley, Max Perlich; *D:* Kiefer Sutherland; *W:* Brad Mirman; *C:* Ric Waite; *M:* Jude Cole.

Truth or Dare? **1986** The childhood game of truth or dare turns deadly in this violent thriller. **87m/C VHS.** John Brace, Mary Fanaro, Geoffrey Lewis Miller; *D:* Tim Ritter; *W:* Tim Ritter.

Truth or Dare **1/2** *In Bed with Madonna; Madonna Truth or Dare* **1991 (R)** A quasi-concert-documentary—here is music superstar Madonna tarted up in fact, fiction, and fantasy—exhibitionism to the nth power. Tacky, self-conscious,and ultimately, if you are a Madonna fan, moving. On camera Madonna stings ex-boyfriend Warren Beatty, disses admirer Kevin Costner, quarrels with her father, reminisces, and does sexy things with a bottle. Oh yes, she occasionally sings and dances. Both those who worship and dislike the Material Girl will find much to pick apart here. **118m/C VHS, DVD.** Madonna; *D:* Alek Keshishian.

Truth or Die *Doing Life* **1986 (PG-13)** This trite, cliched TV movie chronicles the life of convict Jerry Rosenberg, the first prisoner to earn a law degree from his cell. Still, an uncharacteristic role for sitcom guy Danza. Based on Rosenberg's book "Doing Life." **96m/C VHS, DVD.** Tony Danza, Jon (John) DeVries, Lisa Langlois, Rocco Sisto; *D:* Gene Reynolds.

Try and Get Me *Sound of Fury* **1950** A small town is incited into a manhunt for kidnappers who murdered their victim. Suspenseful melodrama analyzes mob rule and the criminal mind. **91m/B VHS.** Lloyd Bridges, Kathleen Ryan, Richard Carlson, Frank Lovejoy, Katherine Locke; *D:* Cy Endfield; *W:* Cy Endfield, Jo Pagano; *C:* Guy Roe.

The Trygon Factor **1/2 1966** There's an over-abundance of plot in this confusing crime comedy. Impoverished Livia Embarday (Nesbitt) and her family set up a phony convent in their ancestral home as a front for a stolen-goods operation. Their latest scheme is to melt down gold from a bank heist and smuggle it out of the country but Scotland Yard inspector Cooper-Smith (Granger) is on the case. **88m/C VHS.** *GB* Stewart Granger, Susan Hampshire, Cathleen Nesbitt, Robert Morley, Eddi Arent, Sophie Hardy, James Robertson-Justice, James Culliford; *D:* Cyril Frankel; *W:* Stanley Munro, Derry Quinn; *C:* Harry Waxman; *M:* Peter Thomas.

Tryst **1/2 1994 (R)** Julia plots to kill her husband with the help of a detective, but when her housekeeper's son arrives, Julia decides another pawn is just what her deceitful plan needs. **101m/C VHS.** Barbara Carrera, Louise Fletcher, David Warner, Steve Bond, Andy Romano, Johnny LaSpada; *D:* Peter Foldy; *W:* Peter Foldy; *M:* Tom Howard.

The Tsar's Bride *Tsarskaya Nevesta* **1966** A lovely young woman is chosen to be the bride of the horrible Tsar Glebov but when the Tsar's bodyguard falls for her, romantic difficulties ensue. A hybrid of the 1899 Rimsky-Korsakov opera and an 1849 play. **95m/B VHS.** *RU* Raisa Nedashkovskaya, Natalya Rudnaya, Otar Koberidze; *D:* Vladimir Gorikker.

Tsotsi **1/2 2005 (R)** Young Tsotsi and his gang of urban thugs pillage their shantytown-turf outside Johannesburg, South Africa. After stealing a BMW from a wealthy black woman, Tsotsi discovers he's also nabbed her infant son in the backseat. The child's affect on this criminal becomes the centerpiece and eventual redemption behind the story. Unpredictable, violent, and compassionate. Director Gavin Hood constructs a world foreign to most Western audiences, in every sense of the word. **94m/C DVD.** Kenneth Nkosi, Zenzo Ngqobe, Presley Chweneyagae, Terry Pheto, Mothusi Magano, Israel Makoe, Percy Matsemela, Benny Moshe, Benny Moshe, Nambitha Mpumlwana, Rapulana Seiphemo, Ian Roberts, Jerry Mofokeng; *D:* Gavin Hood; *W:* Gavin Hood; *C:* Lance Gewer; *M:* Mark Kilian, Paul Hepker. Oscars '05: Foreign Film.

Tsui Hark's Vampire Hunters *Vampire Hunters; The Era of the Vampires* **2002 (R)** Don't expect any sense just watch the kung fu sequences. There are four vampire hunters named Wind, Thunder, Lightning, and Rain who are assigned by their master to find and destroy the zombie-like vampires. They have several sword fights with some human opponents as well. Cantonese with subtitles. **90m/C VHS, DVD.** *HK JP* Lam Suet, Kwok-Kwan Chan, Ken Chang, Michael Chow Man-Kin; *D:* Wellson Chin; *W:* Tsui Hark; *C:* Herman Yau, Joe Chan, Sunny Tsang Tat Sze; *M:* J.M. Logan.

Tube *Tyubeu* **2003 (R)** After suffering a shocking personal loss, police detective Jay (Kim) finds himself relegated to the ranks of subway cop. He toils away until that fateful day when the good-guy-gone-bad (Park) takes control of the train and terrorizes the community, giving Jay the chance to be a hero again and save the day. While the action in director Woon-hak's Seoul-based debut zips along, the effort lacks that "certain something" (like a well-developed plot) that made its obvious inspirations—"Die Hard" and "Speed"—smash hits. Korean, with English subtitles. **112m/C VHS, DVD.** Seok-hun Kim, Du-na Bae, Samg-min Park, Byeong-ho Son, Oh-jung Gweon; *D:* Woon-hak Baek; *W:* Woon-hak Baek, Weon-mi Byeon, Jeong-min Kim, Min-ju Kim; *C:* Hong-shik Yun; *M:* Sang-jun Hwang. **VIDEO**

Tuck Everlasting **1/2 2002 (PG)** Director Jay Russell does an admirable job adapting the beloved 1975 children's novel by Natalie Babbitt into a feature film. Winnie (Bledel) is chafing under the strict discipline of her parents, particularly the rule that forbids her from playing in the nearby woods. One day while sneaking into the forbidden forest, she meets Jesse, a boy from the rough and tumble Tuck clan. He tells her not to drink from a certain spring, but immediately after the warning she is abducted by Jesse's brother Miles (Bairstow). At the Tuck residence, Jesse's parents inform her that the spring is a fountain of youth and that she is not allowed to return home with that knowledge. She begins to fall for young Jesse although she discovers that he is actually 104 years old. **90m/C VHS, DVD.** *US* Alexis Bledel, Jonathan Jackson, Sissy Spacek, William Hurt, Scott Bairstow, Ben Kingsley, Amy Irving, Victor Garber; *D:* Jay Russell; *W:* James V. Hart, Jeffrey Lieber; *C:* James L. Carter; *M:* William Ross; ***Nar:*** Elisabeth Shue.

Tucker: The Man and His Dream **1988 (PG)** Portrait of Preston Tucker, entrepreneur and industrial idealist, who in 1946 tried to build the car of the future and was effectively run out of business by the powers-that-were. Ravishing, ultra-nostalgic lullaby to the American Dream. Watch for Jeff's dad, Lloyd, in a bit role. **111m/C VHS, DVD.** Jeff Bridges, Martin Landau, Dean Stockwell, Frederic Forrest, Mako, Joan Allen, Christian Slater, Lloyd Bridges, Elias Koteas, Nina Siemaszko, Corin "Corky" Nemec, Marshall Bell, Don Novello, Peter Donat, Dean Goodman, Patti Austin; *D:* Francis Ford Coppola; *W:* Arnold Schulman, David Seidler; *M:* Joe Jackson, Carmine Coppola. Golden Globes '89: Support. Actor (Landau); N.Y. Film Critics '88: Support. Actor (Stockwell).

Tuesdays with Morrie **1/2 1999** Detroit sportswriter Mitch Albom (Azaria) spots his old college prof, 78-year-old Morrie Schwartz (Lemmon), on ABC's "Nightline" discussing his battle with ALS and his thoughts on death. The workaholic Albom, who has not seen Morrie in 16 years, decides to pay his one-time mentor a visit in Boston. The relationship rekindles and they begin to meet every Tuesday, with Albom coming to question the path his life is taking. Based on Albom's best-selling book. **89m/C VHS, DVD.** Jack Lemmon, Hank Azaria, John Carroll Lynch, Wendy Moniz, Bonnie Bartlett, Caroline Aaron, Aaron Lustig, Bruce Nozick; *D:* Mick Jackson; *W:* Thomas (Tom) Rickman; *C:* Theo van de Sande; *M:* Marco Beltrami. **TV**

Tuff Turf **1985 (R)** The new kid in town must adjust to a different social lifestyle and a new set of rules when his family is forced to move to a low-class section of Los Angeles. He makes enemies immediately when he courts the girlfriend of one of the local toughs. Fast-paced with a bright young cast. Music by Jim Carroll, Lene Lovich, and Southside Johnny. **113m/C VHS, DVD.** James Spader, Kim Richards, Paul Mones, Matt Clark, Olivia Barash, Robert Downey Jr., Catya (Cat) Sassoon, Claudette Nevins; *D:* Fritz Kiersch; *W:* Jette Rinck; *C:* Willy Kurant; *M:* Jonathan Elias.

Tugboat Annie **1933** A colossal MGM hit for the very popular Dressler, with Beery as her drunken husband Terry. Son Alec (Young) is the captain of an ocean liner who's in love with Patricia (O'Sullivan), the daughter of liner owner Red Severn (Robertson). Alec wants his mom to leave his dad and come work with him but the loyal Annie refuses, even after Terry crashes the tugboat. Sold at auction and turned into a garbage scow, Annie continues to run the vessel and one stormy night, the ocean liner sends out an SOS and it's the little-scow-that-could to the rescue! Based on a series of Norman Reilly Raine stories published in the "Saturday Evening Post." **88m/B DVD.** Marie Dressler, Wallace Beery, Robert Young, Maureen O'Sullivan, Willard Robertson, Tammany Young, Frankie Darro; *D:* Mervyn LeRoy; *W:* Zelda Sears, Eve Greene; *C:* Gregg Toland.

Tulips **1/2 1981 (PG)** Would-be suicide takes a contract out on himself, and then meets a woman who makes life worth living again. Together they attempt to evade the gangland hit man. Limp comedy. **91m/C VHS.** *CA* Gabe Kaplan, Bernadette Peters, Henry Gibson; *D:* Stan Ferris.

Tully *What Happened to Tully; The Truth About Tully* **2000 (R)** Quiet and convincing adaptation of Tom Neal's 1992 short story is set on a Nebraska dairy farm owned by taciturn Tully Coates Sr. (Burrus), who is hiding family secrets from his two sons. Handsome Tully Jr. (Mount) is the local womanizer while younger brother Earl (Fitzgerald) is shy and sensitive. Both have a soft spot for recently-returned neighbor Ella Smalley (Nicholson), who is too smart to fall for Tully's lines even as their friendship veers toward romance. **107m/C VHS, DVD.** *US* Anson Mount, Julianne Nicholson, Glenn Fitzgerald, Bob Burrus, Catherine Kellner, Natalie Canerday, John Diehl, V. Craig Heidenreich; ***D:*** Hilary Birmingham; ***W:*** Hilary Birmingham, Matt Drake; ***C:*** John Foster; ***M:*** Marcelo Zarvos.

Tulsa **1949** High-spirited rancher's daughter begins crusade to save her father's oil empire when he's killed. Having become ruthless and determined to succeed at any cost, she eventually sees the error of her ways. Classic Hayward. **96m/C VHS, DVD.** Susan Hayward, Robert Preston, Chill Wills, Ed Begley Sr., Pedro Armendariz Sr.; ***D:*** Stuart Heisler; ***C:*** Winton C. Hoch.

Tumbledown Ranch in Arizona **1941** After a rodeo accident, an unconscious college student dreams of adventure out west. Part of the "Range Busters" series. **60m/B VHS.** Ray Corrigan, John "Dusty" King, Max Terhune, Sheila Darcy, Marian Kerby; ***D:*** S. Roy Luby.

Tumbleweed Trail ½ **1942** Action-packed thundering western. **57m/B VHS.** William Boyd, Art Davis, Lee Powell, Jack Rockwell; ***D:*** Sam Newfield.

Tumbleweeds **1925** William S. Hart's last western. Portrays the last great land rush in America, the opening of the Cherokee Strip in the Oklahoma Territory to homesteaders. Preceded by a sound prologue, made in 1939, in which Hart speaks for the only time on screen, to introduce the story. Silent, with musical score. **114m/B VHS, DVD.** William S. Hart, Lucien Littlefield, Barbara Bedford; ***D:*** King Baggot.

Tumbleweeds ½ **1998 (PG-13)** Mary Jo Walker (McTeer) has been married numerous times and been in even more relationships. 12-year-old daughter Ava (Brown) knows that when things go wrong with mom's romantic prospects they pack up and hit the road, which is why they're on their way to San Diego. Of course, Mary Jo meets trucker Jack (O'Connor) along the way and decides to shack up with him when they reach their destination, while the remarkably resilient Ava settles into another new life. But since Mary Jo has such lousy judgment (except about her love for Ava) this mother-daughter duo is headed for rocky times ahead. **104m/C VHS, DVD.** Janet McTeer, Kimberly J. Brown, Gavin O'Connor, Jay O. Sanders, Lois Smith, Laurel Holloman, Michael J. Pollard, Noah Emmerich; ***D:*** Gavin O'Connor; ***W:*** Angela Shelton, Gavin O'Connor; ***C:*** Dan Stoloff; ***M:*** David Mansfield. Golden Globes '00: Actress—Mus./Comedy (McTeer); Ind. Spirit '00: Debut Perf. (Brown); Natl. Bd. of Review '99: Actress (McTeer); Sundance '99: Filmmakers Trophy.

Tundra ½ *The Mighty Thunder* **1936** Quasi adventure-drama/documentary set in the Alaskan tundra. A young man, known only as the "Flying Doctor," tends to the sick in small villages throughout the wilderness. But his own survival is at stake when his small plane crashes. Filmed on location. **72m/B VHS.** Del Cambre; ***D:*** Norman Dawn.

The Tune **1992** 30,000 ink and watercolor drawings make up this animated gem which tells the story of Del (Neiden), a failed songwriter who gets a fresh start when he makes a wrong turn on the freeway and winds up in Flooby Nooby. The strange inhabitants of this town teach Del to throw out his rhyming dictionary and write about his experiences. Plympton's first full-length animated feature. Also includes "The Making of The Tune" and the animated short "Draw." **80m/C VHS, DVD.** ***D:*** Bill Plympton; ***W:*** Maureen McElheron, Bill Plympton, P.C. Vey; ***C:*** John Donnelly; ***M:*** Maureen McElheron; ***V:*** Daniel Neiden, Maureen McElheron, Marty Nelson, Emily Bindiger, Chris Hoffman.

Tune in Tomorrow **1990 (PG-13)** Lovesick young Martin (Reeves) wants to woo divorced older babe aunt-by-marriage Julia (Hershey) and is romantically counseled by wacky soap opera writer Pedro (Falk). Seems even soap operas draw on real life, and Martin's story is immortalized on the airwaves, circa 1951 New Orleans. The story-within-a-story also features Pedro's radio characters coming to hammy life. Sometimes funny, sometimes not (the Albanian jokes are tiresome). Adapted from the novel "Aunt Julia and the Scriptwriter" by Mario Vargas Llosa. **90m/C VHS, DVD.** Barbara Hershey, Keanu Reeves, Peter Falk, Bill McCutcheon, Patricia Clarkson, Peter Gallagher, Dan Hedaya, Buck Henry, Hope Lange, John Larroquette, Elizabeth McGovern, Robert Sedgwick, Henry Gibson; ***D:*** Jon Amiel; ***W:*** William Boyd; ***C:*** Robert M. Stevens; ***M:*** Wynton Marsalis.

Tunes of Glory ½ **1960** Guinness and Mills are wonderful in this well made film about a brutal, sometimes lazy colonel and a disciplined and educated man moving up through the ranks of the British military. York's film debut. From the novel by James Kennaway, who adapted it for the screen. **107m/C VHS, DVD.** *GB* Alec Guinness, John Mills, Dennis Price, Kay Walsh, Susannah York; ***D:*** Ronald Neame; ***M:*** Malcolm Arnold.

The Tunnel ½ **1989 (R)** Obsessive romance film with a trace of suspense. Artist sees the woman of his dreams at a showing of his work. Her marriage, and her trepidation, don't keep his obsession from consuming him. **99m/C VHS.** Jane Seymour, Peter Weller, Fernando Rey; ***D:*** Antonio Drove.

The Tunnel ½ *Der Tunnel* **2001** Originally produced for German television broadcast. Based on the true story of Harry Melchior (Ferch), an East German swimming champ who fled to West Berlin in 1961 as the wall was going up. Melchior is so committed to getting his sister Lotte (Lara) and her family out of East Berlin that he hatches a plan to dig a tunnel under the wall. Naturally the tunnel becomes a massive undertaking requiring the clandestine enlistment of other West Berliners with loved ones behind the wall. This tense drama is packed with story lines and looming disaster—a rare gem with top notch production values. **157m/C DVD.** *GE* Heino Ferch, Nicolette Krebitz, Sebastian Koch, Mehmet Kurtulus, Alexandra Maria Lara, Felix Eitner; ***D:*** Roland Suso Richter; ***W:*** Johannes W. Betz; ***C:*** Martin Langer; ***M:*** Harald Kloser, Thomas Wanker. **TV**

The Tunnel of Love ½ **1958** Day and Widmark are a married couple who find themselves over their heads in red tape when they try to adopt a baby. A beautiful, disapproving adoption investigator also causes more problems for the couple when she believes Widmark is less than ideal father material. Widmark is not in his element at comedy but Day and Young (as their next-door neighbor) are fine in this lightweight adaptation of the Joseph Fields-Peter DeVries play. **98m/B VHS.** Doris Day, Richard Widmark, Gig Young, Gia Scala, Elisabeth Fraser, Elizabeth Wilson; ***D:*** Gene Kelly; ***W:*** Jerome Chodorov.

Tunnel Rats *1968 Tunnel Rats* **2008** A tense and competent actioner from Boll set during the Vietnam War. A special unit of American soldiers, led by Sgt. Hollowborn (Pare), is assigned to infiltrate the maze-like, booby-trapped tunnels used by the Viet Cong. Not for the claustrophobic. **92m/C DVD.** *GE* Michael Pare, Wilson Bethel, Mitch Eakins, Brandon Fobbs, Erik Eiden, Rocky Marquette, Jane Le; ***D:*** Uwe Boll; ***W:*** Uwe Boll; ***C:*** Mathias Neumann; ***M:*** Jessica de Rooij.

Tunnel Vision ½ **1995 (R)** Detective Kelly Wheatstone (Kensit) and her partner Frank Yanovitch (Reynolds) are after a serial killer whose victims are all beautiful women killed in a ritualistic fashion. But all the clues begin to point to Yanovitch as the one committing the crimes. This one is routine all the way. **100m/C VHS, DVD.** *AU* Patsy Kensit, Robert Reynolds, Rebecca Rigg, Shane Briant; ***D:*** Clive Fleury; ***W:*** Clive Fleury; ***C:*** Paul Murphy; ***M:*** David Hirschfelder.

Tunnelvision ½ **1976 (R)** A spoof of TV comprised of irreverent sketches. Fun to watch because of the appearances of several now-popular stars. **70m/C VHS, DVD.** Chevy Chase, John Candy, Laraine Newman, Joe Flaherty, Howard Hesseman, Gerrit Graham, Al Franken, Tom Davis, Ron Silver; ***D:*** Neal Israel.

Turbo: A Power Rangers Movie **1996 (PG)** The Power Rangers must battle the evil Divatox (Turner), who's kidnapped the wizard Lerigot so she can use his power to free her even more evil boyfriend Maligore. It's all around cheesy but if you're a five-year-old you may still enjoy the action. **99m/C VHS, DVD.** Jason David Frank, Stephen Antonio Cardenas, John Yong Bosch, Catherine Sutherland, Nakia Burrise, Blake Foster, Paul Schrier, Jason Narvy, Amy Jo Johnson, Austin St. John, Hilary Shepard Turner, Jon Simanton; ***D:*** David Winning, Shuki Levy; ***W:*** Shuki Levy, Shell Danielson; ***C:*** Ilan Rosenberg; ***M:*** Shuki Levy.

Turbulence ½ **1996 (R)** When you fly, it's usually the turbulence that makes you throw up. Well, this movie isn't that bad, but you may experience a touch of nausea. Flight attendant Teri (Holly) is pushing the drink cart on a strangely vacant New York to L.A. Christmas Eve run. Among the passengers are convicted felons Ryan (Liotta) and Stubbs (Gleeson), who are either on their way to a more secure prison or fulfilling the "consumption of airline food" portion of their sentence. The prisoners seize a gun from the marshals and accidentally rub out the cockpit crew. With all the passengers locked away, Teri must battle the serial rapist/killer Ryan as well as learn to fly the plane through a horrible storm. Passengers on the left of the screen may look out and see "Passenger 57," while those on the right can see the ancient monument of "Airport 75." **103m/C VHS, DVD.** Ray Liotta, Lauren Holly, Hector Elizondo, Brendan Gleeson, Ben Cross, Rachel Ticotin, Jeffrey DeMunn, John Finn, Catherine Hicks; ***D:*** Robert Butler; ***W:*** Jonathan Brett; ***C:*** Lloyd Ahern II; ***M:*** Shirley Walker.

Turbulence 2: Fear of Flying **1999** Group of scared to fly passengers try to overcome their fears aboard a jumbo 747. They will never set foot off the ground again after severe turbulance damages the plane and a nerve gas-carrying terrorist commandeers it. **100m/C VHS, DVD.** Tom Berenger, Craig Sheffer, Jennifer Beals, Jeffrey Nordling; ***D:*** David Mackay; ***W:*** Kevin Bernhardt, Brendan Broderick, Rob Kerchner. **VIDEO**

Turbulence 3: Heavy Metal WOOF! **2000 (R)** Wannable shock rocker Slade Craven (Mann) wants to make his last concert a spectacular affair, so he has a passenger jet modified so he can give his performance, which will be broadcast over the Internet, in mid-air to a select audience. But the plane is hijacked and FBI agent Kate Hayden (Anwar), who just happens to be on board, and hacker Nick Watts (Sheffer) try to prevent a disaster. Stupid plot, stupid characters—all around cheese. **96m/C VHS, DVD.** Craig Sheffer, Gabrielle Anwar, Monica Schnarre, Rutger Hauer, Joe Mantegna, John Mann; ***D:*** Jorge Montesi; ***W:*** Wade Ferley; ***C:*** Philip Linzey; ***M:*** John McCarthy. **VIDEO**

Turf Boy *Mr. Celebrity* **1942** Desperate for cash, a boy and his uncle try to get an old horse into prime condition for racing. A minor equine melodrama, just the right length for an old-time matinee double-feature. **68m/B VHS.** Robert "Buzzy" Henry, James Seay, Doris Day, William (Bill) Halligan, Gavin Gordon; ***D:*** William Beaudine.

Turistas **2006 (R)** Young, sexy, and often-naked travelers are stuck in Brazil after a bus accident. That doesn't stop them from partying, however, until they wake up the next morning to the not-so-shocking realization that they've been drugged and robbed. The overly-friendly locals aren't what they seem, and soon a crazed surgeon straight out of the book of urban legends is blathering about economic inequality and carving out the visitors' vital organs. Dopey, dull, and not very scary (unless xenophobia counts). **89m/C DVD.** *US* Josh Duhamel, Melissa George, Olivia Wilde, Desmond Askew, Beau Garrett, Max Brown, Agles Steib, Miguel Lunardi; ***D:*** John Stockwell; ***W:*** Michael Arlen Ross; ***C:*** Enrique Chediak; ***M:*** Paul Haslinger.

Turk 182! ½ **1985 (PG-13)** The angry brother of a disabled fireman takes on City Hall in order to win back the pension that he deserves. He attacks through his graffiti art. Hutton is too heavy for the over-all comic feel of this mostly silly film. **96m/C VHS, DVD.** Timothy Hutton, Robert Culp, Robert Urich, Kim Cattrall, Peter Boyle, Darren McGavin, Paul Sorvino; ***D:*** Bob (Benjamin) Clark.

Turkish Delight ½ **1973** Free spirit sculptor falls in love with free spirit gal from bourgeois family and artsy soft porn ensues. That is until a brain tumor puts an end to their fun, and he's left to wallow in flashbacks and more artsy soft porn. Dubbed. Verhoeven later became big boxoffice in the U.S. with "Total Recall." **100m/C VHS, DVD.** *NL* Monique Van De Ven, Rutger Hauer, Tonny Huurdeman, Wim Van Den Brink; ***D:*** Paul Verhoeven; ***W:*** Gerard Soeteman; ***C:*** Jan De Bont.

Turn It Up **2000 (R)** Diamond (Pras) is a talented musician who's involved in the drug trade with childhood friend Gage (Ja Rule). He wants to go legit so he can pursue his music dreams but Gage is a hothead who gets them into more trouble. Then Diamond's girlfriend announces she's pregnant, his mother unexpectedly dies, and his estranged father (Curtis-Hall) turns up. **87m/C VHS, DVD.** Pras, Vondie Curtis-Hall, Ja Rule, Tamala Jones, Jason Statham, Eugene Clark; ***D:*** Robert Adetuyi; ***W:*** Robert Adetuyi; ***C:*** Hubert Taczanowski; ***M:*** Gary Jones, Happy Walters.

Turn of the Blade **1997** Predictable thriller finds photographer Sam Peyton (Christensen) upset that his wife Kelly (Owens) is more interested in her acting career than in having a baby. It may be safer to have the kid, since Kelly's the lust object for a seedy film director and then a dangerous stalker. Meanwhile, Sam has his own problems with his associate Wendy, who wants their relationship to get personal and wants Kelly out of the way. **91m/C VHS, DVD.** David Christensen, Crystal Owens, David Keith Miller, Julie Horvath; ***D:*** Bryan Michael Stoller; ***W:*** Mark Bark; ***C:*** Richard A. Jones; ***M:*** Greg Edmonson. **VIDEO**

The Turn of the Screw **1974** Supernatural powers vie with a young governess for control of the souls of the two children in her charge. Redgrave does well in this chilling film adapted from the Henry James story. **120m/C VHS, DVD.** Lynn Redgrave, Jasper Jacobs, Eva Griffith; ***D:*** Dan Curtis.

The Turn of the Screw **1989 (R)** The young charges of an English nanny are sought for their souls by a dark, unimaginable evil in the mansion. Another version of the Henry James classic. **60m/C VHS, DVD.** Amy Irving, David Hemmings; ***D:*** Graeme Clifford.

The Turn of the Screw **1992 (R)** Yet another version of the Henry James classic as a young governess struggles with sexual obsession and the two children in her care who are possessed by evil. **95m/C VHS.** Julian Sands, Patsy Kensit, Stephane Audran, Marianne Faithfull; ***D:*** Rusty Lemorande; ***M:*** Simon Boswell.

The Turn of the Screw ½ **1999** Solid TV adaptation of the Henry James novel boasts some fine performances in a now familiar story. Miss (May) is the young, too-impressionable governess at Bly manor, whose charges are the overly well-behaved Miles (Sowerbutts) and his younger sister, Flora (Robinson). Soon Miss is seeing ghosts—those of the former governess and another servant, Peter Quint (Salkey), whom she believes are corrupting her innocent children. But maybe the emotional young woman is simply crazy. **80m/C VHS, DVD.** *GB* Jodhi May, Pam Ferris, Colin Firth, Joe Sowerbutts, Grace Robinson, Jason Salkey, Caroline Pegg, Jenny Howe; ***D:*** Ben Bolt; ***W:*** Nick Dear; ***C:*** David Odd; ***M:*** Adrian Johnston. **TV**

Turn the River **2007 (R)** Kailey (a de-glamorized Janssen) is a downtrodden pool hustler who is allowed no contact with her 11-year-old son Gulley (Doman), so they meet secretly. Kailey's trying to put together the cash so she can just take the kid from his toxic father (Ross) and head for Canada but she makes some majorly dumb mistakes (there's a gun involved). **92m/C DVD.** Famke Janssen, Jamie Dornan, Rip Torn, Matt Ross, Lois Smith, Terry Kinney, Marin Hinkle, John Juback; ***D:*** Christopher Eigeman; ***W:*** Christopher Eigeman; ***C:*** H. Michael Otano; ***M:*** Clogs.

Turnaround 1987 (R) Unusual action/suspense film set in a small town. Relentless gang rampages the citizens. Finally, a man decides he's had enough, and turns on the heathens with his knowledge of magic. **97m/C VHS.** Doug McKeon, Tim Maier, Eddie Albert, Gayle Hunnicutt; ***D:*** Ola Solum.

Turner and Hooch 1989 (PG) A dog witnesses a murder, and a fussy cop is partnered with the drooling mutt and a weak script in his search for the culprit. Drool as a joke will only go so far, but Hanks is his usual entertaining self. **99m/C VHS, DVD.** Tom Hanks, Mare Winningham, Craig T. Nelson, Scott Paulin, J.C. Quinn; ***D:*** Roger Spottiswoode; ***W:*** Michael Blodgett, Jim Cash, Jack Epps Jr.; ***C:*** Adam Greenberg; ***M:*** Charles Gross.

The Turning 1/2 *Home Fires Burning* **1992** Twenty-two-year-old Cliff Harnish (Dolan) returns home after a four-year absence to shock his family with his strident Neo-Nazi beliefs. May be of curiosity value to Anderson's "X-Files" fans, since she appears (relatively briefly and partially nude) as the guy's girlfriend in a kitchen sex scene. Based on the play by Ceraso. **92m/C VHS, DVD.** Michael Dolan, Raymond J. Barry, Karen Allen, Tess Harper, Gillian Anderson; ***D:*** L.A. Puopolo; ***W:*** L.A. Puopolo, Chris Ceraso; ***C:*** J. Michael McClary.

The Turning Point 1/2 1977 (PG) A woman who gave up ballet for motherhood must come to terms as her daughter launches a ballet career and falls for the lead male dancer. The mother finds herself threatened by her daughter's affection toward an old friend who sacrificed a family life for the life of a ballerina. Baryshnikov's film debut. Melodramatic ending and problems due to ballet sequences. **119m/C VHS, DVD.** Shirley MacLaine, Anne Bancroft, Tom Skerritt, Leslie Browne, Martha Scott, Marshall Thompson, Mikhail Baryshnikov; ***D:*** Herbert Ross; ***W:*** Arthur Laurents; ***C:*** Robert L. Surtees. Golden Globes '78: Director (Ross), Film—Drama; L.A. Film Critics '77: Director (Ross); Natl. Bd. of Review '77: Actress (Bancroft), Support. Actor (Skerritt); Writers Guild '77: Orig. Screenplay.

Turtle Diary 1986 (PG) Two lonely Londoners collaborate to free giant turtles from the city aquarium with the aid of a zoo-keeper, and the turtles' freedom somehow frees them as well. Jackson and Kingsley are stunning. Adapted by Harold Pinter from the Russell Hoban book. **90m/C VHS.** *GB* Ben Kingsley, Glenda Jackson, Richard Johnson, Michael Gambon, Rosemary Leach, Jeroen Krabbe, Eleanor Bron; ***D:*** John Irvin; ***W:*** Harold Pinter; ***M:*** Geoffrey Burgon.

Turtles Can Fly 1/2 *Lakposhtha ham parvaz mikonand* **2004** Director Ghobadi's stark and engrossing tale of the unending daily sufferings of refugee children living on the Iraq-Turkey border as they await the U.S.-led invasion in early 2003. Essentially absent of adults, Ghobadi centers on 13-year-old Satellite (Ebrahim)—who uses his technical savvy to bring TV to the camp so they can watch news channels—along with his rival Hengov, disfigured by landmines, and Hengov's withdrawn sister Agrin who rebuffs Satellite's romantic advances. In Kurdish, with English subtitles. **95m/C DVD.** *FR IA IQ* Soran Ebrahim, Avaz Latif, Hirsh Feyssal, Saddam Hossein Feysal, Hiresh Feysal Rahman, Abdol Rahman Karim, Ajil Zibari; ***D:*** Bahman Ghobadi; ***W:*** Bahman Ghobadi; ***C:*** Shahriar Assadi; ***M:*** Hossein Alizadeh.

Turumba 1984 A quiet satire about a family of papier-mache animal makers in a Philippine village who get a gargantuan order in time for the Turumba holiday, and desperately try to fill it. In Tagalog with English subtitles. **94m/C VHS.** *PH* Claudia Adires, Johnny Ching, Maria Pehipol; ***D:*** Kidlat Tahimik; ***W:*** Kidlat Tahimik.

The Tuskegee Airmen 1995 (PG-13) Cable drama based on the formation and WWII achievements of the U.S. Army Air Corps' first squadron of black combat fighter pilots, the "Fighting 99th" of the 332nd Fighter Group. They were nicknamed after the segregated military outpost where they trained in Tuskegee, Alabama and distinguished themselves in combat, never losing a single bomber, and receiving more than 800 medals. Cast all do a fine job in what turns out to essentially be a standard action/war movie. Based on a story by former Tuskegee airman, Robert W. Williams. **107m/C VHS, DVD.** Laurence Fishburne, Cuba Gooding Jr., Allen Payne, Malcolm Jamal Warner, Courtney B. Vance, Andre Braugher, John Lithgow, Rosemary Murphy, Christopher McDonald, Vivica A. Fox, Daniel Hugh-Kelly, David Harrod, Eddie Braun, Bennet Guillory; ***D:*** Robert Markowitz; ***W:*** Paris Qualles, Ron Hutchinson, Trey Ellis; ***C:*** Ronald Orieux; ***M:*** Lee Holdridge. **CABLE**

Tusks 1/2 *Fire in Eden* **1989 (R)** A ruthless hunter tries to kill elephants. **99m/C VHS, DVD.** Andrew Stevens, John Rhys-Davies, Lucy Gutteridge, Julian Glover; ***D:*** Tara Hawkins Moore.

Tut & Tuttle 1/2 *Through the Magic Pyramid* **1981** Young dabbler in magic is transported to ancient Egypt where he is able to demonstrate courage and wits against the evil Horemheb, who has kidnapped Prince Tut. **97m/C VHS.** James Hampton, Kario Salem, Jo Anne Worley, Sydney Penny, Olivia Barash, Elaine Giftos, Chris Barnes, Eric Greene, Hans Conried, Vic Tayback; ***D:*** Ron Howard; ***W:*** Rance Howard; ***C:*** Gary Graver; ***M:*** Joe Renzetti. **TV**

The Tuttles of Tahiti 1942 The Tuttles lead a life of leisure in the South Seas. Laughton's child becomes enamoured of his rival's offspring, causing problems between the two families. More interesting than it sounds. **91m/C VHS.** Charles Laughton, Jon Hall, Peggy Drake, Victor Francen, Gene Reynolds, Florence Bates, Mala, Alma Ross, Curt Bois; ***D:*** Charles Vidor.

The Tuxedo 1/2 2002 (PG-13) After an unusual opening non sequiter, movie pits kickmaster Chan against the evil Banning (Coster) out to dehydrate the world via a deadly ingredient in the water supply. Mild mannered taxi driver Jimmy (Chan) takes a job chauffeuring Clark Devlin (Isaacs), a wealthy spy with a secret weapon: the title's near-magical tuxedo that turns the wearer into a martial arts fighting machine. After Devlin's injured, Jimmy dons the supersuit and joins agent Del (Hewitt) in the fight against Banning. Chan is his usual amiable, entertaining self even against this extremely silly backdrop of a movie. Highlight is Chan's stint as a stand-in for soul man James Brown. **98m/C VHS, DVD.** *US* Jackie Chan, Jennifer Love Hewitt, Jason Isaacs, Debi Mazar, Ritchie Coster, Peter Stormare, Romany Malco, Mia Cottet; ***D:*** Kevin Donovan; ***W:*** Michael J. Wilson, Michael Leeson; ***C:*** Stephen Windon; ***M:*** John Debney, Christophe Beck.

Tuxedo Warrior 1/2 1982 Set in South Africa, this film involves the adventures of a well-dressed mercenary who is caught between the police, diamond thieves, and an old girlfriend's bank robbing. **93m/C VHS.** John Wyman, Carol Royle, Holly Palance; ***D:*** Andrew Sinclair.

The TV Set 1/2 2006 (R) Art vs. commerce in an amusing satire. Writer Mike (Duchovny) is trying to sell a personal project for TV development to a network headed by the predatory Lenny (Weaver). Lenny willfully prefers the mediocre and sleazy as long as it bring in ratings and advertising dollars. She ignores his original vision, but Mike is reassured by new programming head Richard McAllister (Gruffudd) that he'll have his say. Mike is doomed to disappointment. Kasdan worked on "Freaks and Geeks" and "Undeclared" so he knows the territory—maybe too well for those who aren't insiders. **87m/C DVD.** David Duchovny, Sigourney Weaver, Ioan Gruffudd, Judy Greer, Fran Kranz, Lindsay Sloane, Justine Bateman, Lucy Davis; ***D:*** Jake Kasdan; ***W:*** Jake Kasdan; ***C:*** Uta Briesewitz; ***M:*** Michael Andrews.

Tweek City 1/2 2005 Bumpy indie follows San Francisco drug dealer Bill, who has a crystal meth problem that fuels his insecurities about his half-Latino heritage, his sexuality, and his troubled childhood. Bill can't get past his ex-high school girlfriend getting married and goes on a bender before crashing the wedding. Writer/director Johnson ultimately doesn't know where to take his character or story. **86m/C DVD.** Giuseppe Andrews, Keith Brunsmann, Elizabeth Bogush, Eva Fisher; ***D:*** Eric Johnson; ***W:*** Eric Johnson; ***C:*** Barry Stone; ***M:*** Jim Latham.

Twelfth Night 1/2 1996 (PG) Director Nunn's take on Shakespeare's gender-bending, romantic-comedy, which is now set in the 1890s. Shipwrecked on an unfriendly Illyrian shore, Viola (Stubbs), believing twin brother Sebastian (Mackintosh) to be dead, disguises herself in male attire and joins the retinue of the lovesick Duke Orsino (Stephens). He's pining for the Countess Olivia (Bonham Carter) and decides to use Viola-turned-Cesario as a surrogate wooer. Too bad Olivia's becoming more interested in her effeminate pseudo-suitor and that Orsino's having a few sexual quandries of his own. **133m/C VHS, DVD.** *GB* Imogen Stubbs, Helena Bonham Carter, Toby Stephens, Steven Mackintosh, Richard E. Grant, Nigel Hawthorne, Ben Kingsley, Imelda Staunton, Mel Smith, Nicholas Farrell; ***D:*** Trevor Nunn; ***W:*** Trevor Nunn; ***C:*** Clive Tickner; ***M:*** Shaun Davey.

12 2007 (PG-13) Despite the PG-13 rating, it's unlikely any teens will be interested in a Russian courtroom drama inspired by the 1957 film "12 Angry Men." In Mikhalkov's operatic drama, 12 Muscovites (who are nameless) are sent to a decrepit high school gym so they can deliberate a case where an 18-year-old Chechan is accused of murdering his adoptive Russian father. Eleven of the jurors quickly vote guilty while a contrary engineer insists they need to consider the consequences of acquiescing to the government's case without debate. Russian with subtitles. **159m/C DVD.** *RU* Sergei Makovetsky, Alexei Petrenko, Nikita Mikhalkov, Sergei Garmash, Valentin Gaft, Yuri Stoyanov, Sergei Gazarov, Mikhail Efremov, Apti Magamaev; ***D:*** Nikita Mikhalkov; ***W:*** Nikita Mikhalkov, Alexander Novototsky, Vladimir Moiseenko; ***C:*** Vladislav Opeliants; ***M:*** Edward Artemiev.

Twelve 2010 White Mike (Crawford) drops out of school to deal drugs to his trust-fund acquaintances but there's trouble with supplier Lionel (Jackson) that brings in the cops. Title refers to a new street drug. Adaptation of then-17-year-old Nick McDonell's novel. **94m/C DVD.** *US* Chace Crawford, Curtis "50 Cent" Jackson, Emma Roberts, Rory Culkin, Jeremy White, Billy Magnussen, Emily Meade, Esti Ginzburg; ***D:*** Joel Schumacher; ***W:*** Jordan Melamed; ***C:*** Steven Fierberg; ***M:*** Harry Gregson-Williams; ***Nar:*** Kiefer Sutherland.

12 and Holding 2005 (R) Rudy (Donovan) and his fat buddy Leonard (Camacho) spend the night in their tree house, which is torched by bullies. Leonard is injured (he loses his sense of taste) but Rudy dies. His twin Jacob is barely able to cope (he already has self-esteem issues since a birthmark covers half his face), especially when confronted with his parents' grief and rage. Leonard's survival inspires him to lose weight and get in shape, much to the resentment of his obese parents. Meanwhile, their friend Malee (Weizenbaum) becomes precociously interested in one of her therapist mom's (Sciorra) patients, a hunky construction worker (Renner). First-rate work by all, with much uncomfortably honest depiction of adolescent bewilderment and fear. **95m/C DVD.** *US* Zoe Weizenbaum, Jeremy Renner, Conor Donovan, Jesse Camacho, Annabella Sciorra, Linus Roache, Jayne Atkinson, Marcia DeBonis, Michael Fuchs; ***D:*** Michael Cuesta; ***W:*** Anthony Cipriano; ***C:*** Romeo Tirone; ***M:*** Pierre Foldes.

Twelve Angry Men 1957 Fonda sounds the voice of reason as a jury inclines toward a quick-and-dirty verdict against a boy on trial. Excellent ensemble work. Lumet's feature film debut, based on a TV play by Reginald Rose. **95m/B VHS, DVD.** Henry Fonda, Martin Balsam, Lee J. Cobb, E.G. Marshall, Jack Klugman, Robert Webber, Ed Begley Sr., John Fiedler, Jack Warden, George Voskovec, Edward Binns, Joseph Sweeney; ***D:*** Sidney Lumet; ***W:*** Reginald Rose; ***C:*** Boris Kaufman; ***M:*** Kenyon Hopkins. Berlin Intl. Film Fest. '57: Golden Berlin Bear; British Acad. '57: Actor (Fonda), Natl. Film Reg. '07.

Twelve Angry Men 1/2 1997 (PG-13) Cable TV update of the 1954 "Studio One" teleplay/1957 movie (both written by Rose) that brings together an all-male jury (now with four black jurors) to decide the fate of a Latino murder suspect. Lemmon has the Henry Fonda role of the juror with reasonable doubts, determined to provide a fair hearing. **117m/C VHS.** George C. Scott, Jack Lemmon, Hume Cronyn, Tony Danza, Mykelti Williamson, Edward James Olmos, Courtney B. Vance, Ossie Davis, Armin Mueller-Stahl, Dorian Harewood, James Gandolfini, William L. Petersen, Mary McDonnell, Douglas Spain; ***D:*** William Friedkin; ***W:*** Reginald Rose. **CABLE**

The Twelve Chairs 1970 (PG) Take-off on Russian folktale first filmed in Yugoslavia in 1927. A rich matron admits on her deathbed that she has hidden her jewels in the upholstery of one of 12 chairs that are no longer in her home. A Brooksian treasure hunt ensues. **94m/C VHS, DVD.** Mel Brooks, Dom DeLuise, Frank Langella, Ron Moody, Bridget Brice; ***D:*** Mel Brooks; ***W:*** Mel Brooks; ***C:*** Djordje Nikolic; ***M:*** Mel Brooks, John Morris.

The Twelve Days of Christmas Eve 1/2 2004 (PG) Business exec Calvin Carter (Weber) neglects those closest to him in his pursuit of success. When he winds up in the hospital on Christmas Eve, nurse/guardian angel Angie (Shannon) informs Calvin he has 12 chances to make amends and find his true holiday spirit or suffer the consequences. Manages to be more mildly sarcastic than sugary despite its holiday theme. **120m/C DVD.** Steven Weber, Molly Shannon, Patricia Velasquez, Teryl Rothery, Chad Willett, Vincent Gale, Stefanie von Pfetten; ***D:*** Martha Coolidge; ***W:*** J.B. White; ***C:*** Derick Underschultz; ***M:*** Jennie Muskett. **CABLE**

The Twelve Dogs of Christmas 1/2 2005 Sappy Christmas story set in the Depression. 12-year-old Emma O'Connor (Green) is sent to live with her aunt in a small town and finds out that dogs are newly banned in the community (grrrrr). So it's up to Emma, a large number of pooches, and a school holiday pageant to make everything right. Cute dogs, cute kid—probably tolerable for the younger set. Based on the book by Emma Kragen. **107m/C DVD.** Jordan-Claire Green, John Billingsley, Richard Riehle, Eric Lutes, Bonita Friedericy, Mindy Sterling, John-Kevin Hilbert; ***D:*** Keith Merrill; ***W:*** Keith Merrill, Emma Kragen; ***C:*** Michael Fimognari. **VIDEO**

12 Monkeys 1995 (R) Forty years after a plague wipes out 99 percent of the human population and sends the survivors underground, scientists send prisoner James Cole (Willis) to the 1990s to investigate the connection between the virus and seriously deranged fanatic Jeffrey Goines (Pitt), whose father happens to be a renowned virologist. Director Gilliam's demented vision is a bit tougher and less capricious than usual, and the convoluted plot and accumulated detail require a keen attention span, but as each piece of the puzzle falls into place the story becomes a fascinating sci-fi spectacle. Pitt drops the pretty-boy image with a nutzoid performance that'll make revelers stop swooning in a heartbeat. Inspired by the 1962 French short "La Jetee." **131m/C VHS, DVD, HD DVD.** Bruce Willis, Madeleine Stowe, Brad Pitt, Christopher Plummer, David Morse, Frank Gorshin, Jon Seda; ***D:*** Terry Gilliam; ***W:*** David Peoples, Janet Peoples; ***C:*** Roger Pratt; ***M:*** Paul Buckmaster. Golden Globes '96: Support. Actor (Pitt).

Twelve o'Clock High 1/2 1949 Epic drama about the heroic 8th Air Force, with Peck as bomber-group commander sent to shape up a hard-luck group, forced to drive himself and his men to the breaking point. Compelling dramatization of the strain of military command. Includes impressive footage of actual WWII battles. Best-ever flying fortress movie. **132m/B VHS, DVD.** Gregory Peck, Hugh Marlowe, Gary Merrill, Millard Mitchell, Dean Jagger, Paul Stewart, Robert Arthur, John Kellogg, Sam Edwards, Russ Conway, Lawrence (Larry) Dobkin; ***D:*** Henry King; ***W:*** Sy Bartlett, Beirne Lay Jr.; ***C:*** Leon Shamroy; ***M:*** Alfred Newman. Oscars '49: Sound, Support. Actor (Jagger), Natl. Film Reg. '98.

12:01 1/2 1993 (PG-13) It's the "Groundhog Day" premise played for thrills. Barry Thompson (Silverman) is an employee at a scientific research firm who finds himself reliving the same 24-hour period over and over again. And what a day it is—he discovers a secret project is causing the mysterious time warp, falls in love with beauteous scientist Lisa (Slater) and watches as she gets murdered. Can Barry figure out how to stop what's going on and change things enough to save her? Adaptation of the short story "12:01" by Richard Lupoff, which was previously made into a short film. **92m/C VHS, DVD.** Jonathan Silverman, Helen Slater, Martin Landau, Nicolas Surovy, Jeremy Piven; ***D:*** Jack Sholder. **TV**

12 Plus 1 ♂♂♂ *The Thirteen Chairs* **1970 (R)** A man sells 13 chairs left to him by his aunt, only to find that one of them contained a hidden fortune. He chases across Europe in search of each of them. Some good cameos help move this re-make of a Russian folk-tale along, but it remains lightweight. Tate's last movie, before her death at the hands of Manson and his "family." **94m/C VHS.** *FR IT* Sharon Tate, Orson Welles, Vittorio Gassman, Mylene Demongeot, Terry-Thomas, Tim Brooke; ***Cameos:*** Vittorio De Sica; ***D:*** Nicolas Gessner.

12 Rounds ♂♂ **2009 (PG-13)** During an FBI sting to capture the notorious Irish terrorist, Miles Jackson (Gillen), things go wrong and detective Danny Fisher (Cena) accidentally kills the terrorist's girlfriend. One year later Jackson busts out of prison and kidnaps Fisher's wife in an act of revenge. The detective then must pass 12 violent challenges in order to save her and take down the deadly con on the streets of New Orleans during Mardi Gras. Veteran action director Harlin loads up on the standard barrage of car chases and fist-pumping action, but a shoddy script leaves much to be explained. WWE wrestler Cena proves capable of handling his new career but he's no Dwayne "The Rock" Johnson, as sad as that may sound. **108m/C DVD.** *US* John Cena, Aidan Gillen, Steve Harris, Ashley Scott, Brian White, Taylor Cole, Ray Santiago; ***D:*** Renny Harlin; ***W:*** Daniel Kunka; ***C:*** David Boyd; ***M:*** Trevor Rabin.

Twentieth Century ♂♂♂♂ **1934** Maniacal Broadway director Barrymore transforms shop girl Lombard into a smashing success adored by public and press. Tired of Barrymore's manic-excessive ways, she heads for the Hollywood hills, pursued by the Profile in fine form. **91m/B DVD.** Carole Lombard, John Barrymore, Walter Connolly, Roscoe Karns, Edgar Kennedy, Ralph Forbes, Charles Lane, Etienne Girardot, Snow Flake; ***D:*** Howard Hawks; ***W:*** Charles MacArthur, Ben Hecht.

Twenty Bucks ♂♂♂ **1993 (R)** Whimsical film follows a $20 bill from its "birth" at a cash machine to its "death" as it is returned to the bank, tattered and torn, for shredding. The bill is passed from owner to owner, sometimes simply and briefly, sometimes altering fate. The original screenplay is nearly 60 years old: Endre Bohem originally drafted it in 1935, and his son revised and updated it. Clever transitions allow the various stories and characters to blend almost seamlessly. The strongest character is Shue's, a young waitress and aspiring writer. Rosenfeld's directorial debut is worth a look. Filmed in Minneapolis. **91m/C VHS, DVD.** Linda Hunt, David Rasche, George Morfogen, Brendan Fraser, Gladys Knight, Elisabeth Shue, Steve Buscemi, Christopher Lloyd, Sam Jenkins, Kamal Holloway, Melora Walters, William H. Macy, Diane Baker, Spalding Gray, Matt Frewer, Concetta Tomei, Nina Siemaszko; ***D:*** Keva Rosenfeld; ***W:*** Leslie Bohem, Endre Bohem; ***C:*** Emmanuel Lubezki; ***M:*** David Robbins. Ind. Spirit '94: Support. Actor (Lloyd).

20 Dates ♂♂ ½ **1999 (R)** Writer/director Myles Berkowitz, recently divorced and having career problems, decided to combine these two problems into one. He filmed himself going on 20 dates, sometimes without the dates' knowledge (until he sprung the release form on 'em at the end of the night). Some of it's real, some staged, but all of it focuses on Berkowitz. He talks about himself, and the project, incessantly, which gets annoying after awhile, but the film has its moments. When one of the dates actually works out, and turns into a budding romance, he has to tell the girl that he's still obligated to play out the string. Some of the funnier moments are his conversations with his financial backer, who thought he was getting a sex romp flick. **88m/C VHS.** ***D:*** Myles Berkowitz; ***W:*** Myles Berkowitz; ***C:*** Adam Biggs; ***M:*** Bob Mann, Steve Tyrell.

Twenty Dollar Star ♂ ½ **1991 (R)** Steamy thriller about an prominent actress who leads a double life as a cheap hooker, and consequent occupational hazards. The title may as well refer to the budget. **92m/C VHS.** Rebecca Holden, Bernie (Bernard) White, Eddie Barth, Marilyn Hassett, Dick Sargent; ***D:*** Paul Leder.

25th Hour ♂♂ ½ **2002 (R)** Moody, atmospheric character study follows the last 24 hours of freedom for convicted drug dealer Monty Brogan (Norton) before he begins a seven-year sentence. Brogan says his good-byes to his father, a retired firefighter who now runs a bar paid for with Monty's drug money; his longtime buddies Frank (Pepper), a Wall Street shark, and Jacob (Hoffman), a high school teacher with low self-esteem and a crush on one of his students (Paquin); and girlfriend Naturelle (Dawson), whom he suspects of turning him in. All feel different levels of guilt over letting Monty become involved in "the life." If Lee had stuck to these stories, it would've worked much better, but instead he lays the spectre of 9/11 over the proceedings, creating jarring scenes that sometimes work, but mostly distract from some impressive performances. **132m/C VHS, DVD.** *US* Edward Norton, Philip Seymour Hoffman, Barry Pepper, Rosario Dawson, Anna Paquin, Brian Cox, Isiah Whitlock Jr., Michael Genet, Tony Siragusa, Levani Outchanechvili, Misha Kuznetsov; ***D:*** Spike Lee; ***W:*** David Benioff; ***C:*** Rodrigo Prieto; ***M:*** Terence Blanchard. Golden Globes '03: Score.

The 24th Day ♂ ½ **2004 (R)** Tom learned 24 days ago that he and his wife are infected with HIV and Tom blames Dan—a man whom he had a one-night-stand with five years before. Off he goes to not merely confront Dan—who doesn't even remember Tom—but to take him hostage while his blood is tested with plans for a slow, painful death if it comes back positive. Adapted from writer-director Piccirillo's own stage play—where it should have stayed. **92m/C VHS, DVD.** Sofia Vergara, James Marsden, Scott Speedman; ***D:*** Tony Piccirillo; ***W:*** Tony Piccirillo; ***C:*** Alan Hostetter; ***M:*** Kevin Manthei. **VIDEO**

20 Million Miles to Earth ♂♂ ½ **1957** A spaceship returning from an expedition to Venus crashes on Earth, releasing a fast-growing reptilian beast that rampages throughout Rome. Another entertaining example of stop-motion animation master Ray Harryhausen's work, offering a classic battle between the monster and an elephant. **82m/B DVD, Blu-ray Disc.** William Hopper, Joan Taylor, Frank Puglia, John Zaremba, Thomas B(rowne). Henry, Jan Arvan; ***D:*** Nathan "Jerry" Juran; ***W:*** Christopher Knopf, Bob Williams; ***C:*** Irving Lippman; ***M:*** Mischa Bakaleinikoff.

29th & Gay ♂♂ **2005** A year in the life of a 29-year-old gay man, James Sanchez, who longs for love and success. But the average-looking, unemployed actor is trapped by his own idea of what his life should be. Charming if clichéd. **87m/C DVD.** James Vasquez, Mike Doyle, Kail Rocha, Michael Emerson, Nicole Marcks, David McBean, Annie Hinton; ***D:*** Carrie Preston; ***C:*** Mark Holmes; ***M:*** John Avila.

20,000 Leagues under the Sea ♂♂♂ **1916** Outstanding silent adaptation of Jules Verne's "20,000 Leagues Under the Sea" and "The Mysterious Island" filmed with a then revolutionary underwater camera. Much octopus fighting. Look for newly mastered edition. **105m/B VHS, DVD.** Matt Moore, Allen Holubar, June Gail, William Welsh, Chris Benton, Dan Hamlon; ***D:*** Stuart Paton; ***W:*** Stuart Paton; ***C:*** Eugene Gaudio.

20,000 Leagues under the Sea ♂♂♂ ½ **1954** From a futuristic submarine, Captain Nemo wages war on the surface world. A shipwrecked scientist and sailor do their best to thwart Nemo's dastardly schemes. Buoyant Disney version of the Jules Verne fantasy. **127m/C VHS, DVD.** James Mason, Kirk Douglas, Peter Lorre, Paul Lukas, Robert J. Wilke, Carleton Young; ***D:*** Richard Fleischer; ***W:*** Earl Felton; ***C:*** Franz Planer; ***M:*** Paul J. Smith. Oscars '54: Art Dir./Set Dec., Color.

20,000 Leagues Under the Sea ♂ ½ **1997** Silly TV version of the oft-told Verne tale finds marine biologist Aronnax (Crenna) and his assistant/daughter Sophie (Cox) prisoners on Captain Nemo's (Cross) submarine. In the original Verne version, Sophie was a young man—the sex change now means there's lots of boring eye-batting between Sophie, harpoonist Ned Land (Gross), and the jealous Nemo. The underwater photography is nifty but the fish also provide more excitement than the cast. **91m/C VHS, DVD.** Ben Cross, Richard Crenna, Paul Gross, Julie Cox, Michael Jayston; ***D:*** Michael Anderson Sr.; ***W:*** Joe Wiesenfeld; ***C:*** Alan Hume; ***M:*** John Scott. **TV**

20,000 Years in Sing Sing ♂♂ ½ **1933** Based on the book by Sing Sing's reform-minded warden Lewis E. Lawes, who allowed the movie to be shot at the prison with actual prisoners in the crowd scenes. Tough guy Tom Connors (Tracy) soon finds out he's a nobody when he winds up in the joint, so he joins in an escape plan. When things go wrong, Tom decides to work with Warden Long (Byron) and earn a parole instead. Meanwhile, girlfriend Fay (Davis in an ill-fitting ingenue role) turns to sleazy lawyer Finn (Calhern) for help and gets in a serious car crash. And things get worse for Tom. Remade in 1940 as "Castle on the Hudson" with John Garfield in the Tracy role. **81m/B DVD.** Spencer Tracy, Bette Davis, Bruce Byron, Lyle Talbot, Louis Calhern, Grant Mitchell, Warren Hymer; ***D:*** Michael Curtiz; ***W:*** Brown Holmes, Courtney Terrett, Wilson Mizner, Robert Lord; ***M:*** Bernhard Kaun.

23 Paces to Baker Street ♂♂ ½ **1956** Blind writer Phillip Hannon (Johnson), who lives on London's Baker Street, overhears a kidnapping plot but can't get the police to believe him. So Phillip asks former fiancee Jean (Miles) and his secretary Matthews (Parker) to help him find the criminals. Some good twists in a tight B-movie crime/mystery. **103m/C DVD.** Maurice Denham, Estelle Winwood; ***D:*** Henry Hathaway, James B. Clark; ***W:*** Nigel Balchin; ***C:*** Milton Krasner; ***M:*** Leigh Harline.

2012 ♂ *Twenty Twelve* **2009 (PG-13)** The ending of the Mayan calendar on 12/12/2012 brings about a number of natural disasters and predicts the end of the world. The king of the CGI apocalypse, director Emmerich delivers just that once again and little else. What there is of an actual tale focuses on sci-fi writer Jackson Curtis (Cusack, much too good of an actor for this), his failed marriage to Kate (Peet), and their kids—who Jackson of course has taken on a trip to Yellowstone Park before the world comes unhinged. An hour-too-long, preposterous exercise in computer-generated graphics. **158m/C DVD.** *US* John Cusack, Amanda Peet, Danny Glover, Chiwetel Ejiofor, Oliver Platt, Thandie Newton, Woody Harrelson, Thomas (Tom) McCarthy; ***D:*** Roland Emmerich; ***W:*** Roland Emmerich, Harald Kloser; ***C:*** Dean Semler; ***M:*** Harald Kloser, Thomas Wanker.

20 Years After ♂ ½ **2008 (R)** A post-apocalyptic saga with bombs and plagues leaving only a few survivors. Sarah (Skye) is pregnant with the first child to be born in 15 years and her only solace is listening to pirate radio DJ Michael (Leonard), whom she turns to for help when her pregnancy is put in danger. Sounds like somebody was reading "Children of Men." **95m/C DVD.** Azura Skye, Joshua Leonard, Reg E. Cathey, Diane Salinger, Charlie Talbert, Nathan Baesel; ***D:*** Jim Torres; ***W:*** Ron Harris, Jim Torres; ***C:*** William Sweikart; ***M:*** John Heitzenrater, Chris Johnson. **VIDEO**

Twenty-One ♂♂ ½ **1991 (R)** Modern morality tale of a young English woman who moves to the U.S. to make a new start, but falls into the same old habits. Kensit is frank and charming, in spite of difficulties with her drug addict boyfriend and the illegal alien she marries. Director Boyd leaves it to the viewer to decide between right and wrong and where Kensit fits. **92m/C VHS.** *GB* Patsy Kensit, Jack Shepherd, Patrick Ryecart, Maynard Eziashi, Rufus Sewell, Sophie Thompson, Susan Wooldridge, Julia Goodman; ***D:*** Don Boyd; ***W:*** Don Boyd; ***C:*** Keith Goddard; ***M:*** Michael Berkeley.

21 ♂ ½ **2008 (PG-13)** Lacking the $300,000 needed to attend Harvard, wide-eyed med student Ben Campbell (Sturgess) joins a secret gang of MIT geeks who spend their weekends raking in millions from Vegas casinos. Led by sneaky math prof Mickey Rose (Spacey), who teaches the ways of card counting and hand signals, and under the spell of his new girlfriend Jill (Bosworth), Ben quickly turns to the dark side. Very loosely based on the true exploits in Ben Mezrich's book "Bringing Down the House." Director Luketic should've stayed closer to the original material, but instead focuses solely on Ben and his predictable rise-and-fall drama as high roller who leaves his buddies behind, and the story suffers for it. **122m/C DVD.** *US* Jim Sturgess, Kevin Spacey, Kate (Catherine) Bosworth, Aaron Yoo, Jacob Pitts, Laurence Fishburne, Liza Lapira, Sam Golzari, Jack Gilpin, Helen Carey, Josh Gad, Spencer Garrett, Jack McGee; ***D:*** Robert Luketic; ***W:*** Peter Steinfeld, Allan Loeb; ***C:*** Russell Carpenter; ***M:*** David Sardy.

21 Days ♂♂ ½ *Twenty-One Days Together; The First and the Last* **1937** Dull film somewhat redeemed by its stars. Leigh is a married woman carrying on with Olivier. When her husband confronts them, Olivier accidentally kills him in a fight. They keep quiet but then a mentally deranged man is taken into custody for the crime. Since he will be held 21 days before coming to trial, the lovers decide to spend the time together before Olivier confesses. Based on the play "The First and the Last" by John Galsworthy. **75m/C VHS, DVD.** *GB* Vivien Leigh, Laurence Olivier, Leslie Banks, Francis L. Sullivan, Hay Petrie, Esme Percy, Robert Newton; ***D:*** Basil Dean; ***W:*** Graham Greene, Basil Dean.

21 Grams ♂♂♂ ½ **2003 (R)** In his second film (his first in English), Inarritu takes what could have, in the wrong hands, become a trite Lifetime movie, and elevates it in an unusual and compelling fashion. Jack (DelToro), is imprisoned and born-again. Paul (Penn) has a terminal heart disease and needs a transplant. Christina (Watts), a recovering addict, mourns the loss of her family. Of course, the lives of these characters collide. Stellar performances by an excellent cast combine with beautiful cinematography to create a powerful film. Title refers to the amount of weight a body loses upon death. **125m/C VHS, DVD.** *US* Sean Penn, Benicio Del Toro, Naomi Watts, Charlotte Gainsbourg, Melissa Leo, Clea DuVall, Danny Huston, Paul Calderon; ***D:*** Alejandro Gonzalez Inarritu; ***W:*** Guillermo Arriaga; ***C:*** Rodrigo Prieto; ***M:*** Gustavo Santaolalla. L.A. Film Critics '03: Actress (Watts); Natl. Bd. of Review '03: Actor (Penn).

21 Hours at Munich ♂♂♂ **1976** Made-for-TV treatment of the massacre of Israeli athletes by Arab terrorists at the 1972 Olympics. Well-done. The film was produced using the actual Munich locations. **100m/C VHS, DVD.** William Holden, Shirley Knight, Franco Nero, Anthony Quayle, Noel Willman; ***D:*** William A. Graham.

2103: Deadly Wake ♂♂ **1997** A cargo ship is carrying deadly waste, unbeknowst to its crew, which is also unaware that the ship is intended to be sunk (with the crew). **100m/C VHS, DVD.** *CA GB* Malcolm McDowell, Michael Pare, Heidi von Palleske, Gwynyth Walsh, Hal Eisen; ***D:*** G. Philip Jackson; ***W:*** Timothy Lee, Andrew Dowler, Doug Bagot. **VIDEO**

23 1/2 Hours Leave ♂♂ **1937** Amusing WWI service comedy as a barracks wiseacre bets that by the following morning he'll be breakfasting with a general. It's a song-filled remake of a 1919 film, whose star Douglas MacLean later produced this. **73m/B VHS.** James Ellison, Terry Walker, Morgan Hill, Arthur Lake, Paul Harvey; ***D:*** John Blystone.

Twenty-Four Eyes ♂♂♂ *Nijushi No Hitomi* **1954** Miss Oishi (Takamine), a teacher on a remote Japanese island in the 1920s, attempts to transmit peaceful values to her 12 pupils amidst the clamor of a nation gearing up for war. As she watches them grow up, many of them doomed to an early death, she remains a pillar of quiet strength. In Japanese with English subtitles. **158m/B VHS.** *JP* Hideko Takamine, Chishu Ryu, Toshiko Kobayashi; ***D:*** Keisuke Kinoshita.

24 Hour Party People ♂♂ **2001 (R)** Winterbottom's tribute to the late '70s through early '90s punk rock/rave/acid culture of his native Manchester as seen through the bleary eyes of real-life figure Tony Wilson (Coogan). Wilson is a presenter for Granada TV when he's inspired by a Sex

Pistols performance to open a club, the Hacienda, to showcase local bands, including Joy Division (which morphs into New Order) and the Happy Mondays. He also starts Factory Records—both of which eventually fail, thanks to drugs and general craziness. Filmed in a semi-documentary style with Wilson's asides to camera commenting on the scenes. **115m/C VHS, DVD.** *GB* Steve Coogan, Lennie James, Shirley Henderson, Paddy Considine, Andy Serkis, John Simm, Danny Cunningham, Keith Allen, Sean Harris, Chris Coghill, Paul Popplewell; ***D:*** Michael Winterbottom; ***W:*** Frank Cottrell-Boyce; ***C:*** Robby Muller.

The 24 Hour Woman 🦴🦴 ½ **1999 (R)** Perez is Grace, a morning TV talk show producer who has her pregnancy announced on the air, to the surprise of the baby's father (and the show's co-host) Serrano. Heartless executive producer LuPone milks the pregnancy for every ratings point, then callously turns her back on her employee's problems once the baby is delivered. Pressured by the demands of her job and motherhood, Grace has a major mental meltdown in which she confronts her harpy boss on air. Perez shows a more mature side while still retaining her Latina buzzsaw comic gifts. **93m/C VHS.** Rosie Perez, Marianne Jean-Baptiste, Patti LuPone, Karen Duffy, Wendell Pierce, Melissa Leo, Aida Turturro, Diego Serrano, Rosanna Desoto, Alicia Renee Washington; ***D:*** Nancy Savoca; ***W:*** Nancy Savoca, Richard Guay; ***C:*** Teresa Medina; ***M:*** Louis Vega, Kenny Gonzalez.

24 Hours in a Woman's Life 🦴🦴 **1961** A girl in love with an irresponsible guy hears a cautionary tale from grandma Bergman, who once had a whirlwind romance with a young gambler and naively thought she could reform him. A static TV adaptation of an oft-filmed Stefan Zweig novel, unusually lavish for its time but on the dull side. **90m/C VHS.** Ingrid Bergman, Rip Torn, John Williams, Lili Darvas, Jerry Orbach; ***D:*** Silvio Narizzano; ***W:*** John Mortimer.

24 Hours in London 🦴🦴 **2000 (R)** In 2009's London, organized crime openly vies with the police for control of the streets. Mob boss Christian (Olsen) has just 24 hours to prevent witness Martha (Smith) from testifying against him for murder or watch his criminal empire vanish. Violent. **91m/C VHS, DVD.** *GB* Gary Olsen, Tony London, Anjela Lauren Smith, David Sonnethal, Wendy Cooper, Sara Stockbridge, Luke Garrett; ***D:*** Alexander Finbow; ***W:*** Alexander Finbow; ***C:*** Chris Plevin; ***M:*** Edmund Butt.

24 Hours to Midnight 🦴 ½ **1992** A widow uses her ninja skills to wipe out the crime bosses and henchmen who killed her husband. **91m/C VHS.** Cynthia Rothrock, Stack Pierce; ***D:*** Leo Fong.

24 Nights 🦴🦴 ½ **1999** Twenty-four-year-old Jonathan Parker has never stopped believing in Santa Claus after a magical encounter at the age of four. Now a pot-smoking loser at life and love, he writes a letter to Santa asking for true romance. When Jonathan meets new co-worker Toby, he decides his letter has been answered even though Toby has a longtime boyfriend. But Jonathan will do anything to get what he believes is his Christmas wish. **97m/C VHS, DVD.** Kevin Isola, Aida Turturro, Steven Mailer, David Burtka, Mary Louise Wilson; ***D:*** Kieran Turner; ***W:*** Kieran Turner; ***C:*** Scott Barnard.

24 : Redemption 🦴🦴 **2008** TV movie is set between the sixth and seventh seasons of the series. Jack Bauer has been contacted by his Special Forces buddy Carl Benton (Carlyle), who now runs an orphanage in the small (fictional) African nation of Sangala. A local warlord is planning a coup and forcing boys to become child soldiers. Jack comes to their rescue (over the mealy-mouthed objections of the bureaucrats at the U.S. embassy) while back home President-Elect Allison Taylor (Jones) should be watching out for unsavory elements in the Capitol. **88m/C DVD.** Kiefer Sutherland, Robert Carlyle, Cherry Jones, Tony Todd, Powers Boothe, Jon Voight, Gil Bellows, Peter MacNichol, Bob Gunton, Eric Lively, Colm Feore, Sebastien Roche; ***D:*** Jon Cassar; ***W:*** Howard Gordon; ***M:*** Sean Callery. **TV**

24-7 🦴🦴 **1997 (R)** Title is local Midlands English slang for 24 hours a day, seven days a week. And in this case it refers to the boredom suffered by the aimless, unemployed youth who live in the local housing estates in Thatcher's depressed '80s England. Middle-aged ex-boxer Alan Darcy (Hoskins in a sincere and sweet performance) decides to help the lads by reviving the amateur boxing club which saved him in his youth. Although it seems to work for a time, things slide downward as, eventually, does the distraught Darcy himself. Meadows' feature directorial debut. **96m/B VHS.** *GB* Bob Hoskins, Danny Nussbaum, James Hooton, Darren O. Campbell, Mat Hand, Jimmy Hynd, Justin Brady, Karl Collins, Johann Myers, Anthony Clarke, Bruce Jones, Frank Harper, Pamela Cundell; ***D:*** Shane Meadows; ***W:*** Shane Meadows, Paul Fraser; ***C:*** Ashley Rowe; ***M:*** Neil MacColl, Boo Hewerdine.

25 Fireman's Street 🦴🦴🦴 *Almok a hazrol; Tuzolto utca 25* **1973** An evocative drama about the residents of an old house in Hungary which is about to be torn down, and their evening of remembrances of life before, during and after WWII. In Hungarian with English subtitles. **97m/C VHS, DVD.** *HU* Rita Bekes, Peter Muller, Lucyna Winnicka, Andras Balint; ***D:*** Istvan Szabo; ***W:*** Istvan Szabo, Luca Karall; ***C:*** Sandor Sara.

27 Dresses 🦴 ½ **2008 (PG-13)** You know the drill: Hopeless romantic Jane (Heigl) simply adores weddings but is the perennial bridesmaid—literally—with 27 (oft hideous) bridesmaid dresses to prove it. Jane crushes on her boss George (Burns), but he has eyes for her sister Tess (Akerman). In the meantime perennial cynic Kevin (Marsden) has a thing for Jane, but she's too hooked on her boss to pay any attention. What she doesn't realize is that Kevin is actually the writer of a marriage column that Jane has been clipping for years. What ensues is pure romantic-comedy rehash. Heigl's adorable, but alas, this silly chick flick is much less so. **107m/C DVD, Blu-ray Disc.** *US* Katherine Heigl, James Marsden, Malin Akerman, Judy Greer, Edward Burns, Melora Hardin, Brian Kerwin, Maulik Pancholy; ***D:*** Anne Fletcher; ***W:*** Aline Brosh McKenna; ***C:*** Peter James; ***M:*** Randy Edelman.

The 27th Day 🦴🦴 ½ **1957** Temperate cold war allegory has aliens deliver five mysterious capsules to five Earthlings from different countries. Each capsule, if opened, is capable of decimating the population of the entire planet, but is rendered ineffective after 27 days or upon the death of the holder. Wild ending. Based on John Mantley novel. **75m/B VHS.** Gene Barry, Valerie French, George Voskovec, Arnold Moss, Stefan Schnabel, Ralph Clanton, Friedrich Ledebur, Mari Tsien; ***D:*** William Asher; ***W:*** John Mantley; ***C:*** Henry Freulich; ***M:*** Mischa Bakaleinikoff.

28 Days 🦴🦴 ½ **2000 (PG-13)** Hard-partying New York journalist Gwen (Bullock) manages to destroy her sister's wedding reception when she gets drunk and manages to get arrested for DUI. The film's title refers to the amount of time Gwen must spend at a rehab clinic. Naturally, Gwen doesn't really believe she has a problem and that's the first attitude adjustment she has to make. Cliches galore although Bullock is welcomingly spiky rather than sweet. **103m/C VHS, DVD.** Sandra Bullock, Viggo Mortensen, Dominic West, Diane Ladd, Elizabeth Perkins, Steve Buscemi, Alan Tudyk, Reni Santoni, Marianne Jean-Baptiste, Michael O'Malley, Azura Skye, Margo Martindale; ***D:*** Betty Thomas; ***W:*** Susannah Grant; ***C:*** Declan Quinn; ***M:*** Richard Gibbs.

28 Days Later 🦴🦴 ½ **2002 (R)** Jim (Murphy) wakes up in a London hospital after an accident and finds the building deserted. London seems deserted as well—until he nearly becomes a victim of blood-drinking zombies. Rescued by Selena (Harris) and Mark (Huntley), Jim learns that animal rights activists released lab chimps who carried a blood-transmitted plague that decimated the population within 28 days. The few uninfected survivors have banded together and decide to head to Manchester, where a military installation is said to be a safe haven. Ick and gore galore. **108m/C VHS, DVD.** *GB US* Cillian Murphy, Megan Burns, Brendan Gleeson, Naomie Harris, Christopher Eccleston, Noah Huntley; ***D:*** Danny Boyle; ***W:*** Alex Garland; ***C:*** Anthony Dod Mantle; ***M:*** John Murphy.

28 Weeks Later 🦴🦴 ½ **2007 (R)** Sequel to "28 Days Later" serves up new flawed protagonists and same old angry zombies ravaging Britain. Don (Carlyle), attacked by a horde infected by the rage virus, leaves his wife Alice (McCormack) behind. Reunited in an American-run safe zone in London, Alice infects Don and all hell breaks loose and American occupiers must fight for their lives, sometimes at the expense of morality. Brutally terrifying and relentlessly paced, director Fresnadillo also injects wit and allegory, although both get buried as the movie progresses into a full-blown bloodfest. **99m/C DVD.** *GB US* Robert Carlyle, Rose Byrne, Jeremy Renner, Harold Perrineau Jr., Catherine McCormack, Idris Elba; ***D:*** Juan Carlos Fresnadillo; ***W:*** Juan Carlos Fresnadillo, Rowan Joffe, Jesus Olmo, Enrique Lopez Lavigne; ***C:*** Enrique Chediak.

29th Street 🦴🦴 ½ **1991 (R)** Compelling comedy-drama based on the true story of Frank Pesce, a New York actor who won $6 million in that state's first lottery. Great performance from Aiello, as usual, but the direction falters in the dramatic sequences. Based on the book by Frank Pesce and James Franciscus. **101m/C VHS, DVD.** Danny Aiello, Anthony LaPaglia, Lainie Kazan, Frank Pesce, Donna Magnani, Rick Aiello, Vic Manni, Ron Karabatsos, Robert Forster, Joe Franklin, Pete Antico; ***D:*** George Gallo; ***W:*** George Gallo; ***C:*** Steven Fierberg; ***M:*** William Olvis.

2046 🦴🦴 ½ **2004 (R)** Wong's quasi-sequel to 2001's "In the Mood for Love" is a swoony, hopeless romance about lovers who meet each other at the wrong time to fall in love. Womanizing Chow (Leung Chui-wai) is a pulp fiction writer who moves into Room 2047 of Hong Kong's Hotel Oriental and gets involved with the beautiful women who briefly occupy Room 2046 ("2046" is also the name of the sci-fi novel Chow is writing). There are two ex-girlfriends named Su Li (Gong Li and Cheung), whom he left behind in Singapore; Lulu/Mimi (Lau), who is murdered; prostitute Bai Ling (Zhang), who becomes Chow's confidante; and Jing (Wong), the daughter of the hotel's owner who's in love with a man her father disapproves of. It certainly looks gorgeous; Japanese and Mandarin with subtitles. **129m/C DVD.** *CH HK FR GE* Tony Leung Chiu-Wai, Gong Li, Takuya Kimura, Faye Wong, Zhang Ziyi, Carina Lau, Chang Chen, Maggie Cheung, Wang Sum, Lam Siu-ping, Thongchai McIntyre, Dong Jie; ***D:*** Wong Kar-Wai; ***W:*** Wong Kar-Wai; ***C:*** Christopher Doyle, Lai Yiu-fai, Kwan Pun-leung; ***M:*** Peer Raben, Shigeru Umebayashi. N.Y. Film Critics '05: Cinematog.; Natl. Soc. Film Critics '05: Cinematog.

Twentynine Palms 🦴 ½ **2003** Director Dumont's first feature made in the U.S. is a grim, moody thriller than grinds on monotonously until a twist near the end triggers an intense situation. L.A. residents David (Wissak) and his French-speaking girlfriend Katia (Golubeva) embark on a trip to the California desert locale of the title. The action mostly consists of motel stops where the eerily laconic couple, who mostly just drive around and bicker, copulate graphically and frequently out of boredom. David accidentally hits a dog, to Katia's horror, but not much else happens until they get hit from behind by a strange vehicle which sets off horrific violence. Seemingly pointless exercise in gratuitous sex and violence. Mostly in English with some French dialogue. **119m/C VHS, DVD.** *GE FR* Yekaterina (Katia) Golubeva, David Wissak; ***D:*** Bruno Dumont; ***W:*** Bruno Dumont; ***C:*** Georges Lechaptois; ***M:*** Takashi Hirayasu, Bob Brozman.

Twice a Judas 🦴 *Dos Veces Judas; Due Volte Guida* **1969** An amnesiac is swindled and has his family killed by a ruthless renegade. He wants to get even, even though he can't remember who anyone is. **90m/C VHS.** *IT SP* Klaus Kinski, Antonio (Tony) Sabato, Emma Baron, Franco Beltramme, Jose Calvo; ***D:*** Nando Cicero; ***W:*** Jaime Jesus Balcazar; ***C:*** Francis Marin; ***M:*** Carol Pes.

Twice a Woman 🦴 *Twee Vrouwen* **1979 (R)** Man and woman divorce, and then both fall in love with the same provocative young woman. It's complicated. **90m/C VHS.** *NL* Bibi Andersson, Anthony Perkins, Sandra Dumas, Charles Gormley; ***D:*** George Sluizer; ***W:*** George Sluizer; ***C:*** Mat van Hensbergen; ***M:*** Willem Breuker.

Twice Dead WOOF! **1988** A family moves into a ramshackle mansion haunted by a stage actor's angry ghost. The ghost helps them battle some attacking delinquent boys. Uninteresting story, poorly done. Never released in theatres. **94m/C VHS.** Tom Breznahan, Jill Whitlow, Sam Melville, Brooke Bundy, Todd Bridges, Jonathan Chapin, Christopher Burgard; ***D:*** Bert L. Dragin; ***M:*** David Bergeaud.

Twice in a Lifetime 🦴🦴🦴 **1985 (R)** Middle-aged man takes stock of his life when he's attracted to Ann-Margret. Realizing he's married in name only, he moves in with his new love while his former wife and children struggle with shock, disbelief, and anger. Well-acted, realistic, and unsentimental. **117m/C VHS, DVD.** Gene Hackman, Ellen Burstyn, Amy Madigan, Ann-Margret, Brian Dennehy, Ally Sheedy; ***D:*** Bud Yorkin; ***W:*** Colin Welland.

Twice-Told Tales 🦴🦴🦴 *Nathaniel Hawthorne's "Twice Told Tales"* **1963** Horror trilogy based loosely on three Nathaniel Hawthorne tales, "Dr. Heidegger's Experiment," "Rappaccini's Daughter," and "The House of Seven Gables." Price is great in all three of these well-told tales. **120m/C VHS, DVD.** Beverly Garland, Richard Denning, Vincent Price, Sebastian Cabot, Brett Halsey; ***D:*** Sidney Salkow; ***W:*** Robert E. Kent; ***C:*** Ellis W. Carter; ***M:*** Richard LaSalle.

Twice upon a Yesterday 🦴🦴 *The Man With Rain in His Shoe; If Only* **1998 (R)** Struggling London actor Victor (Henshall) is a romantic swine. He two-timed girlfriend Sylvia (Headey) and she wisely dumped him and found another guy, Dave (Strong), and they're going to get married. Through some time-travelling magic, Victor is able to relive his fateful moment and prevent Sylvia's going. But she winds up meeting Dave anyway while a confused Victor finds a sympathetic bartender, Louise (Cruz), to listen to his romantic trials. Things are just a little too sappy and meandering but the cast (especially Cruz) are worth watching. **94m/C VHS, DVD.** *GB* Douglas Henshall, Lena Headey, Mark Strong, Penelope Cruz, Elizabeth McGovern, Eusebio Lazaro, Charlotte Coleman, Gustavo Salmeron, Neil Stuke; ***D:*** Maria Ripoli; ***W:*** Rafa Russo; ***C:*** Javier Salmones.

Twilight 🦴🦴🦴 *The Magic Hour* **1998 (R)** It's a pleasure to see pros at work, even if the story is a familiar one. In the noir world of L.A., ex-cop, ex-drunk, ex-P.I. Harry Ross (Newman) is living above the garage at the estate of movie star marrieds Jack (Hackman) and Catherine (Sarandon) Ames, for whom Harry has done several jobs. The cancer-stricken Jack asks Harry to handle a blackmail payoff, which seems to resurrect the circumstances of femme fatale Catherine's first husband's alleged suicide. Also involved is Harry's colleague Raymond Hope (Garner)and Harry's ex-flame, Verna (Channing), a cop investigating a murder with ties to the entire ugly situation. **94m/C VHS, DVD.** Paul Newman, Susan Sarandon, Gene Hackman, James Garner, Stockard Channing, Reese Witherspoon, Giancarlo Esposito, Liev Schreiber, Margo Martindale, John Spencer, M. Emmet Walsh; ***D:*** Robert Benton; ***W:*** Robert Benton, Richard Russo; ***C:*** Piotr Sobocinski; ***M:*** Elmer Bernstein.

Twilight 🦴🦴 ½ **2008 (PG-13)** Misfit Bella Swan (Stewart) moves in with her divorced sheriff father in small-town Forks, Washington, where she struggles to fit into her new high school. However, after being saved from certain death in the school parking lot by mysterious hunk Edward Cullen (Pattinson), she discovers romance and the dark secret behind his family tree: they're all vampires. A pop-culture phenomenon with teen girls, mostly due to Pattinson's instant heartthrob status, but like most book-to-screen translations, some fans of Stephanie Meyer's novel will likely be disappointed. **121m/C DVD.** *US* Kristen Stewart, Robert Pattinson, Taylor Lautner, Billy Burke, Peter Facinelli, Elizabeth Reaser, Nikki Reed, Jackson Rathbone, Ashley Greene, Kellan Lutz, Cam Gigandet, Rachelle Lefevre, Edi Gathegi, Anna Kendrick, Michael Welch, Gil Birmingham, Justin Chon, Christian Serratos; ***D:*** Catherine Hardwicke; ***W:*** Melissa Rosenberg; ***C:*** Elliot Davis; ***M:*** Carter Burwell.

The Twilight Girls 🦴🦴 *Les Collegiennes* **1957** Escaping a family scandal, Catherine Royner (Arnaud) enters an exclusive girls boarding school and is immediately introduced to a clique of wealthy girls—one of whom, Monica (Laurent) develops a amourous attraction to the newcomer. Film was originally banned in New York because of the frankness of its lesbian scenes. Deneuve's film debut (under the family name Dorleac) as Adelaide. Her scenes were cut in the version originally released in the U.S. but are restored on the DVD. **83m/B VHS, DVD.** *FR* Marie-Helene Arnaud, Agnes Laurent, Elga Andersen, Henri Guisol, Estella Blain, Catherine Deneuve; ***D:*** Andrew Hunebelle; ***W:*** Jean Lambertie, Jacques Lancien; ***C:*** Paul Cotteret.

Twilight in the Sierras 1/2 **1950** Lots of heroics and music in this action-packed western. An ex-outlaw gone straight is kidnapped for his notorious criminal finesse. Rogers must come to rescue. **67m/C VHS, DVD.** Roy Rogers, Dale Evans, Estelita Rodriguez, Pat Brady, Russ Vincent, George Meeker; ***D:*** William Witney.

Twilight Man 1/2 **1996 (R)** University professor and novelist Jordan Cooper (Matheson) finds his great life turned upside down when a brief altercation with a stranger turns into a nightmare. Turns out the stranger is very strange indeed—computer hacker Hollis Dietz (Stockwell) has made Cooper his own deadly obsession. Suddenly his medical records say he's schizophrenic and even a killer and Cooper must elude police to clear his name. **99m/C VHS.** Tim Matheson, Dean Stockwell, L. Scott Caldwell, Yvette Nipar, Georgann Johnson; ***D:*** Craig R. Baxley; ***W:*** Pablo F. Fenjves, Jim Korris; ***C:*** David Connell; ***M:*** Gary Chang.

Twilight of the Cockroaches 1/2 *Gokiburi* **1990** Mr. Saito is a slovenly bachelor who winds up leaving the remains of his meals for the anthropomorphic cockroaches that infest his apartment. The cockroaches have had it so good for so long that they don't know about insecticides and fearing humans. That is, until Mr. Saito's fastidious new girlfriend makes her appearance and declares war on the vermin. A lifelessly animated tale too dumb for both children and adults and with decidedly unpleasant subject matter, despite the singing, dancing insects. In Japanese with English subtitles. **105m/C VHS.** *JP* ***D:*** Hiroaki Yoshida; ***V:*** Kaoru Kobayashi, Setsuko Karamsumarau.

The Twilight of the Golds 1/2 **1997 (PG-13)** The upper-middle class Jewish Gold family seem conventional if fretful: there's doctor dad Walter (Marshall), concerned mom Phyllis (Dunaway), married daughter Suzanne (Beals), and aspiring theatrical producer son David (Fraser), who's gay. It seems everyone's dealt with David's homosexuality until Suzanne's geneticist husband, Rob Stein (Tenney), informs his pregnant wife that tests on their unborn son show genes statistically link to him being gay. (The theory is unproven.) Suzanne considers abortion and David is understandably upset when no one tries to talk her out of it, beginning a family estrangement. Based on the play by Tolins. **90m/C VHS, DVD.** Garry Marshall, Faye Dunaway, Jennifer Beals, Brendan Fraser, Jon Tenney, Jack Klugman, Sean O'Bryan, Rosie O'Donnell; ***D:*** Ross Kagen Marks; ***W:*** Jonathan Tolins, Seth Bass; ***C:*** Tom Richmond; ***M:*** Lee Holdridge. **CABLE**

The Twilight of the Ice Nymphs **1997** Welcome once again to filmmaker Maddin's weird world. Peter Glahn (Whitney) is released from prison and travels back to his mythical home in Mandragora, where the sun never sets. At the family ostrich farm, his sister Amelia (Duvall) is smitten with Dr. Solti (Thompson) who has unearthed a mysterious statue of Venus that apparently has strange powers. And Peter gets involved with two women, Zephyr (Krige) and Julianna (Bussieres), who also have ties to the doctor. Deliberately artificial and hallucinatory. **91m/C VHS, DVD.** *CA* Pascale Bussieres, R.H. Thomson, Alice Krige, Nigel Whitmey, Shelley Duvall, Frank Gorshin, Ross McMillan; ***D:*** Guy Maddin; ***W:*** George Toles; ***C:*** Michael Marshall; ***M:*** John McCulloch.

Twilight on the Rio Grande **1941** Autry runs into a female knife thrower and some jewel smugglers in this far-fetched western. **54m/B VHS.** Gene Autry, Sterling Holloway, Adele Mara, Bob Steele; ***D:*** Frank McDonald.

Twilight on the Trail **1941** Cattle rustlers disappear and Hopalong Cassidy and his sidekicks become "dude" detectives to solve the crime. **54m/B VHS, DVD.** William Boyd, Brad King, Andy Clyde, Jack Rockwell, Wanda McKay, Howard Bretherton; ***D:*** Howard Bretherton; ***W:*** J. Benton Cheney, Ellen Corby, Cecile Kramer; ***C:*** Russell Harlan; ***M:*** John Leipold.

Twilight People **WOOF!** *Beasts* **1972 (PG)** When a mad scientist's creations turn on him for revenge, he runs for his life. Boring, gory, with bad make-up and even poorer acting. This one should fade away into the night. **84m/C VHS, DVD.** *PH* John Ashley, Pat(ricia) Woodell, Jan Merlin, Pam Grier, Eddie Garcia; ***D:*** Eddie Romero.

The Twilight Saga: Eclipse **2010** The 3rd film from Stephenie Meyer's books. Bella Swan (Stewart) is reunited with vampire love Edward Cullen (Pattinson) but doesn't want to give up her friendship with werewolf Jacob Black (Lautner), who's still Edward's rival. Vamp Victoria (Howard) wants revenge against Bella and may be behind a series of Seattle kills that are moving closer to Bella's hometown. Also, as Bella nears high school graduation, she still wants Edward to change her so they can be immortal together, but he's reluctant. **m/C DVD.** *US* Kristen Stewart, Robert Pattinson, Taylor Lautner, Ashley Greene, Peter Facinelli, Elizabeth Reaser, Kellan Lutz, Nikki Reed, Jackson Rathbone, Bryce Dallas Howard, Billy Burke, Anna Kendrick, Dakota Fanning, Jodelle Ferland, Michael Welch, Gil Birmingham, Christian Serratos, Julia Jones, Cameron Bright, Kirsten Prout, Sarah Clarke, Catalina Sandino Moreno, Chaske Spencer, Leah Gibson, Alex Meraz; ***D:*** David Slade; ***W:*** Melissa Rosenberg; ***C:*** Javier Aguirresarobe; ***M:*** Howard Shore.

The Twilight Saga: New Moon *New Moon; Twilight: New Moon* **2009 (PG-13)** When Bella's (Stewart) 18th birthday party at the Cullens' nearly proves fatal for her, vampire beau Edward (Pattinson) abruptly leaves, fearing his attraction might be the death of her. Despondent, Bella and her now-superbuff childhood pal Jacob Black (Lautner) reconnect, leading to a romantic triangle—sort of. Thing is Jacob has his own secret and Bella is drawn into his Native American world of werewolves, the ancestral enemies of the vampires. But her devotion to Edward causes Bella to put herself in harm's way hoping he will return and "save" her. Meanwhile, Edward is in Italy trying to provoke the vampire counsel of the Volturri into killing him, as sister Alice (Greene) and Bella race to save him. Slow moving and overly mopey, but sure to suck in fanatics by staying true to the second book in the Stephenie Meyer's series. **130m/C DVD.** *US* Kristen Stewart, Robert Pattinson, Taylor Lautner, Ashley Greene, Peter Facinelli, Elizabeth Reaser, Kellan Lutz, Nikki Reed, Jackson Rathbone, Chaske Spencer, Rachelle Lefevre, Edi Gathegi, Billy Burke, Dakota Fanning, Cameron Bright, Michael Sheen, Chris Heyerdahl, Graham Greene, Anna Kendrick, Michael Welch, Justin Chon, Christian Serratos; ***D:*** Chris Weitz; ***W:*** Melissa Rosenberg; ***C:*** Javier Aguirresarobe; ***M:*** Alexandre Desplat.

The Twilight Samurai 1/2 *Tasogare Seibei* **2002** Director Yamada's long-awaited foray into samurai cinema that was definitely worth the wait. Story takes place in mid-19th century feudal Japan and centers on Seibei (Sanada), a very capable but low-level samurai who must single-handedly take care of his aged, senile mother and two young daughters after the recent death of his wife. The hard-working Seibei makes very little from his clan-appointed jobs and spends the rest of his time doing household chores. Still grieving his wife, the staunchly single Seibei slowly begins to soften to the idea of love until suddenly being dispatched by the clan to take on the rebel Yogo (Tanaka), a master swordsman. Yamada lets the human drama takes center stage over the spectacular swordfighting usually found in this genre. Based on a novel by Shuhei Fujiwara. **129m/C DVD.** *JP* Hiroyuki (Henry) Sanada, Ren Osugi, Miki Ito, Rie Miyazawa, Nenji Kobayashi, Mitsuru Fukikoshi, Hiroshi Kanbe, Min Tanaka, Erina Hashiguchi; ***D:*** Yoji Yamada; ***W:*** Yoji Yamada, Yoshitaka Asama; ***C:*** Mutsuo Naganuma; ***M:*** Isao Tomita.

Twilight Zone: The Movie 1/2 **1983 (PG)** Four short horrific tales are anthologized in this film as a tribute to Rod Sterling and his popular TV series. Three of the episodes, "Kick the Can," "It's a Good Life" and "Nightmare at 20,000 Feet," are based on original "Twilight Zone" scripts. Morrow was killed in a helicopter crash during filming. **101m/C VHS, Blu-ray Disc, HD DVD.** Steven Williams, Dan Aykroyd, Albert Brooks, Vic Morrow, Kathleen Quinlan, John Lithgow, Billy Mumy, Scatman Crothers, Kevin McCarthy, Bill Quinn, Selma Diamond, Abbe Lane, John Larroquette, Jeremy Licht, Patricia Barry, William Schallert, Burgess Meredith, Cherie Currie, Nancy Cartwright, Dick Miller, Stephen Bishop; ***D:*** John Landis, Steven Spielberg, George Miller, Joe Dante; ***W:*** John Landis, George Clayton Johnson, Richard Matheson; ***C:*** Allen Daviau, John Hora, Stevan Larner; ***M:*** Jerry Goldsmith.

Twilight's Last Gleaming 1/2 **1977 (R)** A maverick general takes a SAC missile base hostage, threatening to start WWIII if the U.S. government doesn't confess to its Vietnam policies and crimes. Gripping film, with good performances. Based on a novel by Walter Wager, "Viper Three." **144m/C VHS.** Burt Lancaster, Charles Durning, Richard Widmark, Melvyn Douglas, Joseph Cotten, Paul Winfield, Burt Young, Roscoe Lee Browne, Richard Jaeckel, William Marshall, Vera Miles, Leif Erickson, Charles McGraw, William (Bill) Smith, John Ratzenberger; ***D:*** Robert Aldrich; ***W:*** Ronald M. Cohen; ***C:*** Robert B. Hauser; ***M:*** Jerry Goldsmith.

Twin Beds 1/2 **1942** Screwball comedy has newlyweds Mike and Julie Abbott (Brent and Bennett) trying to get a little alone time away from their overly friendly neighbors. The interruptions include Julie's exboyfriend Larky (Truex) who's on the lookout for imaginary burglars, and an inebriated Russian (Auer) who can't find his own room. Both of their wives just add to the fun. Provides plenty of laughs, especially when Auer's on screen. Adapted from the Margaret Mayo/Salisbury Field play. **85m/B VHS.** Joan Bennett, George Brent, Mischa Auer, Glenda Farrell, Ernest Truex, Una Merkel, Margaret Hamilton, Charles Arnt, Charles Coleman, Cecil Cunningham, Thurston Hall; ***D:*** Tim Whelan; ***W:*** Eddie Moran, Kenneth Earl, Curtis Kenyon; ***C:*** Hal Mohr; ***M:*** Dimitri Tiomkin.

Twin Dragons *Shuang Long Hui* **1992 (PG-13)** Re-edited and redubbed English version of the Asian all-star film "Seung Lung Wui," a benefit for the Director's Guild of Hong Kong. Stealing the plot from Jean-Claude Van Damme of all people, Chan plays a dual role as twins separated at birth (as if there were any other kinds of twins in movie scripts) who grow up and cross paths. Chan's likable personality saves the trite, allegedly funny comedy jokelets from bouncing too hard, and the action is chop-sockety good. Cameos from Hong Kong big shots like Tsui Hark, Ringo Lam and John Woo. **89m/C VHS, DVD.** *HK* Jackie Chan, Maggie Cheung, Anthony Chan, Philip Chan, Nina Li Chi, Sylvia Chang, James Wong, Kirk Wong, Ringo Lam, John Woo, Tsui Hark, Teddy Robin; ***D:*** Ringo Lam, Tsui Hark; ***W:*** Barry Wong, Tsui Hark; ***C:*** Wing-Hung Wong, Wong Ngor Tai; ***M:*** Michael Wandmacher, Phe Loung.

Twin Falls Idaho **1999 (R)** Eerie romantic drama about a lonely pair of conjoined twins, Francis (Michael Polish) and Blake (Mark Polish) Falls. The handsome 25-year-olds are celebrating their birthday in a shabby hotel room on Idaho Street, which is where hooker Penny (Hicks) shows up. Blake (the strong twin) intends Penny as a present for his fragile brother Francis, whose weakened heart is seemingly kept beating by Blake's sheer will. Initially repulsed, Penny becomes fascinated by their situation and begins to fall for Blake. But just what will happen if Francis does indeed die? The talented Polish brothers are identical but not "Siamese" twins. **110m/C VHS, DVD.** Michael Polish, Mark Polish, Michele Hicks, Jon(athan) Gries, Patrick Bauchau, Garrett Morris, William Katt, Lesley Ann Warren, Teresa Hill, Holly Woodlawn; ***D:*** Michael Polish; ***W:*** Michael Polish, Mark Polish; ***C:*** M. David Mullen; ***M:*** Stuart Matthewman.

Twin Peaks: Fire Walk with Me **1992 (R)** Prequel to the cult TV series is weird and frustrating, chronicling the week before Laura Palmer's death. Suspense is lacking since we know the outcome, but Lynch manages to intrigue with dream-like sequences and interestingly offbeat characters. On the other hand, it's exploitative and violent enough to alienate series fans. Includes extremely brief and baffling cameos by Bowie as an FBI agent and Stanton as the manager of a trailer park. Several of the show's regulars are missing, and others appear and disappear very quickly. On the plus side are the strains of Badalamenti's famous theme music and Isaak as an FBI agent with amazingly acute powers of observation. **135m/C VHS, DVD.** *FR* Kyle MacLachlan, Sheryl Lee, Moira Kelly, David Bowie, Chris Isaak, Harry Dean Stanton, Ray Wise, Kiefer Sutherland, Peggy Lipton, Dana Ashbrook, James Marshall, David Lynch, Catherine Coulson, Julee Cruise, Eric (DaRe) Da Re, Miguel Ferrer, Heather Graham, Madchen Amick, Jurgen Prochnow, Grace Zabriskie; ***D:*** David Lynch; ***W:*** David Lynch; ***C:*** Ron Garcia; ***M:*** Angelo Badalamenti.

Twin Sisters 1/2 **1991** Woman discovers her missing twin sister was a high-priced prostitute and a detective tries to protect her from the lowlifes sis was involved with. **92m/C VHS, DVD.** Stephanie Kramer, Susan Almgren, Frederic Forrest, James Brolin; ***D:*** Tom Berry; ***M:*** Lou Forestieri.

Twin Town 1/2 **1997** Dark comedy about class warfare, escalating revenge, and drug abuse in a small seaside Welsh town features sharp, profane, and very funny dialogue, well-developed and played characters, and uneven direction. Brothers Julian (Evans) and Jeremy (Ifans) like to steal expensive cars and get high on any substance they can find and control. They live with their handyman dad Fatty (Ceredig) and massage parlor receptionist sister (Scorgie) on the wrong side of the tracks. Dad falls off a roof while working for the local contractor/drug kingpin (Thomas) and is not fairly compensated. This starts a cycle of revenge that begins with public urination and gets nasty from there. Sort of a Welsh "Trainspotting," which featured a cameo by "Twin" writer/director Allen. Some scenes may be too much for some viewers (especially animal lovers). **101m/C VHS.** *GB* Llyr Evans, Rhys Ifans, Huw Ceredig, William Thomas, Dorien Thomas, Dougray Scott; ***D:*** Kevin Allen; ***W:*** Kevin Allen, Paul Durden; ***C:*** John Mathieson; ***M:*** Mark Thomas.

Twin Warriors 1/2 *The Tai-Chi Master; Tai ji Zhang San Feng* **1993 (R)** Junbao (Li) and Tianbao (Siu-hou) grow up together in a Shaolin temple where they secretly learn kung fu by observing the monks in training. Eventually, they're kicked out and Junbao joins a group of rebels while Tianbao enlists in the imperial army. He betrays the rebels and Junbao works to become a Tai Chi master in order to defeat his old friend. Dubbed from Cantonese. **91m/C VHS, DVD.** *HK* Jet Li, Chin Siu-hou, Michelle Yeoh; ***D:*** Woo-ping Yuen; ***W:*** Kwong Kim Yip; ***C:*** Tom Lau; ***M:*** Wai Lap Wu.

Twinkletoes **1926** Twink Minasi (Moore) wants to use her dancing skills to escape her life of poverty in London's Limehouse district. Married prizefighter Chuck (Harland) falls for Twink but she resists him until he can free himself from his bitter, drunken wife Cissie (Brockwell). **78m/B DVD.** Colleen Moore, Kenneth Harlan, Gladys Brockwell, Tully Marshall, Warner Oland, Lucien Littlefield; ***D:*** Charles Brabin; ***W:*** Winifred Dunn; ***C:*** James Van Trees.

Twins 1/2 **1988 (PG)** A genetics experiment gone awry produces twins rather than a single child. One is a genetically engineered superman, the other a short, lecherous petty criminal. Schwarzenegger learns he has a brother, and becomes determined to find him, despite their having been raised separately. The two meet and are immediately involved in a contraband scandal. Amusing pairing of Schwarzenegger and DeVito. **107m/C VHS, DVD.** Arnold Schwarzenegger, Danny DeVito, Kelly Preston, Hugh O'Brian, Chloe Webb, Bonnie Bartlett, Marshall Bell, Trey Wilson, Nehemiah Persoff; ***D:*** Ivan Reitman; ***W:*** William Davies, William Osborne, Timothy Harris, Herschel Weingrod; ***C:*** Andrzej Bartkowiak; ***M:*** Georges Delerue, Randy Edelman.

Twins of Evil *The Gemini Twins; Twins of Dracula; The Virgin Vampires* **1971** Beautiful female twins fall victim to the local vampire, and their God-fearing uncle is out to save/destroy them. Hammer sex and blood-sucking epic starring the Collinsons, who were featured in the October 1970 issue of "Playboy" as the first twin Playmates. **86m/C VHS.** *GB* Madeleine Collinson, Mary Collinson, Peter Cushing, Kathleen Byron, Dennis Price, Damien Thomas, David Warbeck, Katya Wyeth, Maggie Wright, Luan Peters, Kristen Lindholm, Judy Matheson; ***D:*** John Hough; ***W:*** Tudor Gates; ***C:*** Dick Bush.

Twinsanity 🦴 *Goodbye Gemini* **1970 (R)** Evil twins are charged with the murder of a man who attempted to blackmail them. **91m/C VHS.** *GB* Judy Geeson, Martin Potter, Alexis Kanner, Michael Redgrave, Freddie Jones, Peter Jeffrey; ***D:*** Alan Gibson; ***W:*** Edmund Ward; ***M:*** Christopher Gunning.

Twinsitters 🦴🦴 1/2 **1995 (PG-13)** Twins Peter and David Falcone (Peter and David Paul) find themselves unexpectedly saving the life of corrupt businessman Frank Hillhurst (Martin). Hillhurst is turning state's evidence on his crooked operations and his disturbed partners have threatened both his life and the lives of his twin 10-year-old nephews. So Hillhurst hires the Falcones to protect his hellacious pint-sized relatives—who manage to get themselves kidnapped. **93m/C VHS, DVD.** Peter Paul, David Paul, Christian Cousins, Joseph Cousins, Jared Martin, George Lazenby, Rena Sofer, Mother Love; ***D:*** John Paragon; ***W:*** John Paragon.

Twirl 🦴🦴 **1981** Satirical look at the cut-throat world of baton twirling. Parents apply relentless pressure on their daughters to win a contest. Decent made-for-TV movie. **100m/C VHS.** Stella Stevens, Charles Haid, Lisa Whelchel, Erin Moran, Edd Byrnes, Sharon Spelman, Matthew Tobin, Donna McKechnie, Rosalind Chao, Heather Locklear, Deborah Richter, Jamie Rose, Tracy Scoggins; ***D:*** Gus Trikonis.

Twist 🦴 1/2 *Folies Bourgeoises; Pazzi borghesi; Die Verruckten Reichen* **1976** A tepid French drama chronicling the infidelities of various wealthy aristocrats. The aristocrats are boring, as is the film. In French with English subtitles or dubbed. **105m/C VHS.** *FR* Bruce Dern, Stephane Audran, Ann-Margret, Sydne Rome, Jean-Pierre Cassel, Curt Jurgens, Maria Schell, Charles Aznavour; ***D:*** Claude Chabrol; ***M:*** Manuel De Sica.

Twist 🦴🦴🦴 **2003** Dark adaption of the Charles Dicken's Oliver Twist novel set amongst the street hustlers and heroin junkies of Toronto's streets. Oliver (Close), a teenage runaway meets up with Dodge (Stahl), a young prostitute. Dodge introduces him to the life of street hustling and the protective wing of Fagin (Farmer), the local pimp. A mindful presence, but not seen on screen is Bill the drug dealer, who controls both Fagin and his lover Nancy (Pelletier), a waitress at the diner where Fagin's boys often hang out. Despite what the title would suggest, the focus of the movie is Dodge as he plies his trade to further his heroin addiction. Works mainly because the young actors are so genuine and compelling. **97m/C DVD.** *CA* Nick Stahl, Gary Farmer, Michelle-Barbara Pelletier, Joshua Close, Brigid Tierney, Stephen McHattie, Gary Farmer, Tygh Runyan; ***D:*** Jacob Tierney; ***W:*** Jacob Tierney; ***C:*** Gerald Packer; ***M:*** Ron Proulx.

Twist & Shout 🦴🦴🦴 *Hab Og Karlighed* **1984 (R)** Sequel to the popular Danish import "Zappa," in which two teenage lovers discover sex and rock and roll. Transcends the teens discovering sex genre. Danish with English subtitles. Profanity, nudity, and sex. **107m/C VHS, DVD.** *DK* Lars Simonsen, Adam Tonsberg, Ulrikke Juul Bondo, Camilla Soeberg; ***D:*** Bille August; ***W:*** Bille August; ***C:*** Jan Weincke, Aldo (G.R. Aldo) Graziatti.

Twisted 🦴🦴 **1986 (R)** This curio from Slater's early career came out on tape to take advantage of his rising stardom. He's properly creepy as a brilliant but evil teen using electronics, psychology, and swordplay to terrorize victims. The suspense isn't too bad when direction doesn't go overboard, which unfortunately is half the time. Based on the play "Children! Children!" by Jack Horrigan. **87m/C VHS.** Lois Smith, Christian Slater, Tandy Cronyn, Brooke Tracy, Dina Merrill, Dan Ziskie, Karl Taylor, Noelle Parker, John Cunningham, J.C. Quinn; ***D:*** Adam Holender.

Twisted 🦴🦴 **1996** Apt title for a contemporary gay version of "Oliver Twist" set in New York. Homeless 10-year-old orphan Lee (Graves) is brought into the seedy world of brothel owner Andre (Hickey). The youngster is befriended by Angel (Norona) a drug-addicted hustler who's under the sway of abusive pimp Eddie (Crivello). Along with big-hearted drag queen Shiniqua (Porter), Angel tries to rescue Lee from a sordid life. A stylized, operatic melodrama. **100m/C VHS, DVD.** Keivyn McNeil Graves, William Hickey, David Norona, Anthony Crivello, Billy Porter; ***D:*** Seth Michael Donsky; ***W:*** Seth Michael Donsky; ***C:*** Hernan Toto.

Twisted 🦴🦴 **1996 (PG-13)** Four people become trapped in a fantasy world where nothing is as it seems. An airline passenger loses his identity, a houswife finds romance, a con man find a new mark, and a hired killer decides to retire—or at least that's what they believe. From the Australian TV series "Twisted Tales." **86m/C VHS, DVD.** *AU* Geoffrey Rush, Rachel Ward, Bryan Brown, Kimberly Davies, Shane Briant; ***D:*** Samantha Lang, Christopher Robbin Collins, Gregor Jordan, Catherine Millar; ***C:*** James Bartle; ***M:*** Nerida Tyson-Chew; ***Nar:*** Bryan Brown. **TV**

Twisted 🦴 1/2 **2004 (R)** Judd stars as police detective Jessica Shepard in a sleazy, predictable thriller. Jessica likes to drink herself into blackout stupors and have one-night stands, until her hook-ups start turning up dead. Somehow, she ends up in charge of the murder investigation and must hunt down the killer while wondering what she has to do with the crimes. Partner Mike (Garcia) and Police Commissioner Mills (Jackson) are there to keep the pressure on. Oh yeah, and her father went crazy and killed a bunch of people, too. Convoluted backstory, lame plot, and yet another "Ashley Judd in trouble" role adds up to a mediocre turkey and a precipitous step down for director Kaufman. **96m/C DVD.** *US* Ashley Judd, Samuel L. Jackson, Andy Garcia, Russell Wong, David Strathairn, Camryn Manheim, Mark Pellegrino, Titus Welliver, D.W. Moffett, Richard T. Jones, Leland Orser; ***D:*** Philip Kaufman; ***W:*** Sarah Thorp; ***C:*** Peter Deming; ***M:*** Mark Isham.

Twisted Brain 🦴 *Horror High* **1974 (R)** An honor student develops a serum that makes him half man and half beast. Now he can exact revenge on all the jocks and cheerleaders who have humiliated him in the past. Cardi is okay, the rest of the cast is awful. Silly, horrific teen monster epic. **89m/C VHS, DVD.** Pat Cardi, Austin Stoker, Rosie Holotik, John Niland, Joyce Hash, Jeff Alexander, Joe "Mean Joe" Greene; ***D:*** Larry N. Stouffer.

Twisted Justice 🦴 1/2 **1989** Set in 2020, Heavener is a cop determined to stop a ruthless killer. Matters become complicated, however, when his gun is taken away. Now he's forced to rely on his cunning to outwit his sadistic opponent. **90m/C VHS, DVD.** David Heavener, Erik Estrada, Jim Brown, Shannon Tweed, James Van Patten, Don Stroud, Karen Black, Lori Warren; ***D:*** David Heavener; ***W:*** David Heavener; ***C:*** David Hue.

Twisted Love 🦴 1/2 **1995 (R)** Wallflower becomes obsessed with the most popular guy in school. He has a motorcycle accident-that-was-no-accident and winds up in her tender care. Sounds like "Misery" to me. **80m/C VHS.** Lisa Dean Ryan, Mark Paul Gosselaar, Soleil Moon Frye; ***D:*** Eb Lottimer.

Twisted Nightmare 🦴 **1987 (R)** The people responsible for a young retarded boy's death are hunted by a strange figure lurking in the shadows. **95m/C VHS.** Rhonda Gray, Cleve Hall, Angelia High, Robert Padilla; ***D:*** Paul Hunt.

Twisted Obsession 🦴🦴 **1990 (R)** A man becomes passionately obsessed with a woman, and it leads to murder. **109m/C VHS, DVD.** Jeff Goldblum, Miranda Richardson, Anemone, Dexter Fletcher, Daniel Ceccaldi, Liza Walker, Jerome Natali, Arielle Dombasle; ***D:*** Fernando Trueba; ***C:*** Jose Luis Alcaine; ***M:*** Antoine Duhamel.

Twister 🦴🦴 **1989 (PG-13)** An intriguing independent feature about a bizarre midwestern family, its feverish eccentricities and eventual collapse. Awaiting a cult following. **93m/C VHS, DVD.** Dylan McDermott, Crispin Glover, Harry Dean Stanton, Suzy Amis, Jenny Wright, Lindsay Christman, Lois Chiles, William S. Burroughs, Tim Robbins; ***D:*** Michael Almereyda; ***W:*** Michael Almereyda; ***C:*** Renato Berta; ***M:*** Hans Zimmer.

Twister 🦴🦴 1/2 **1996 (PG-13)** Director De Bont's sophomore directorial effort is another non-stop adrenaline drive, but instead of a mad bomber, nature is the bad guy. Hunt leads a team of storm chasing scientists through Oklahoma in hopes of placing robotic sensors inside a tornado. Hunt's soon-to-be ex-husband Paxton rejoins the chase, to spice things up when the skies clear. There's a lot of things flying around, including trucks, houses, cows and the plausibility of the plot. Some nice chemistry between Hunt and Paxton, apparently the only people who can still look attractive in high winds and blowing debris. **105m/C VHS, DVD, Blu-ray Disc.** Bill Paxton, Helen Hunt, Cary Elwes, Jami Gertz, Alan Ruck, Lois Smith, Sean M. Whalen, Gregory Sporleder, Abraham Benrubi, Jake Busey, Joey Slotnick, Philip Seymour Hoffman, Jeremy Davies, Zach Grenier, Richard Lineback, Rusty Schwimmer, Alexa Vega; ***D:*** Jan De Bont; ***W:*** Michael Crichton, Anne-Marie Martin; ***C:*** Jack N. Green; ***M:*** Mark Mancina. MTV Movie Awards '97: Action Seq.

Twists of Terror 🦴🦴 1/2 **1998** Three horror stories narrated by an agoraphobic Los Angelenos. In "The People You Meet," a couple are terrorized while in the country; "The Clinic" has Mancuso confined to a hospital after a vicious dog attack, but the patient learns he can't check out; while "Stolen Moments" finds one young woman and two playboys with murder on their minds. **90m/C VHS.** Jennifer Rubin, Nick Mancuso, Carl Marotte, Francoise Robertson, Andrew Jackson; ***D:*** Douglas Jackson.

Twitch of the Death Nerve 🦴🦴 *Bay of Blood; Last House on the Left, Part 2; Carnage* **1971 (R)** Four vacationers are relentlessly pursued by a homicidal maniac armed with a sickle, bent on decapitation. Supposedly the inspiration for the "Friday the 13th" series. **87m/C VHS, DVD.** *IT* Claudine Auger, Chris Avran, Isa Miranda, Laura Betti, Luigi Pistilli, Sergio Canvari, Anna M. Rosati; ***D:*** Mario Bava; ***W:*** Mario Bava, Filippo Ottoni, Joseph McLee, Gene Luotto; ***C:*** Mario Bava; ***M:*** Stelvio Cipriani.

Twitches 🦴🦴 1/2 **2005 (PG)** Tweener girls should enjoy the fantasy adventures of twins Camryn and Alex (Tamera & Tia Mowry) who were separated at birth and raised under very different circumstances. Meeting at 21, the twins learn that they were spirited away from their magical kingdom for their own safety and that they are powerful witches. Now they must learn to use their abilities and work together to defeat their evil uncle, Thantos (Fabian). **86m/C DVD.** Tamera Mowry, Tia Mowry, Kristen Wilson, Jenny Robertson, Patrick Fabian, Patrick Kelly, Arnold Pinnock, Jessica Grieco, Karen Holness; ***D:*** Stuart Gillard; ***W:*** Daniel Berendsen, Melissa Gould; ***C:*** Manfred Guthe; ***M:*** John Van Tongeren. **CABLE**

Twitches Too 🦴🦴 1/2 **2007** Our twin witches return—continuing to learn to control their magical abilities while dealing with living as a family and going to college and having boyfriends and other girl stuff. But the darkness follows Alex and Camryn into the mortal world, so they must return to Coventry to defeat it once and for all. **83m/C DVD.** Tamera Mowry, Tia Mowry, Kristen Wilson, Patrick Kelly, Kevin Jubinville, Arnold Pinnock, Leslie Seiler, Patrick Fabian, Karen Holness, Chris Gallinger, Nathan Stephenson; ***D:*** Stuart Gillard; ***W:*** Daniel Berendsen; ***C:*** Manfred Guthe; ***M:*** John Van Tongeren. **CABLE**

Two Alone 🦴 1/2 **1934** Romantic melodrama. Orphaned Mazie (Parker) is mistreated by farmer Slag (Byron) and his wife (Bondi). When reform school runaway Adam (Brown) shows up, he suffers similar abuse but does have Mazie's love. The lovebirds are rescued from despair by farmhand Marshall (Robertson) who has a secret of his own. Adapted from the play "Wild Birds" by Dan Totheroh. **75m/B VHS.** Jean Parker, Tom Brown, Arthur Byron, Beulah Bondi, Willard Robertson, Zasu Pitts, Charley Grapewin; ***D:*** Elliott Nugent; ***W:*** Joseph Moncure March, Joseph Lovett; ***C:*** Lucien N. Andriot.

Two Bits 🦴🦴 1/2 *A Day to Remember* **1996 (PG-13)** Depression-era drama tells the story of a 12-year-old boy and his emotional coming of age. Title refers to a quarter Gennaro (Barone, in his film debut) seeks in order to attend the grand opening of a glamorous, air-conditioned movie palace. A heavily made-up Pacino (looking suspiciously like Marlon Brando in the garden scene of "The Godfather"), co-stars as the boy's grandfather, who leaves him his last quarter. Gramps promises that he can collect later that day, when, he says, he will die. Fine performances all around and some powerful scenes go a long way toward masking the fact that the material is a bit too thin to stretch over an entire feature film. **85m/C VHS, DVD.** Al Pacino, Gerlando Barone, Mary Elizabeth Mastrantonio, Joe Grifasi, Joanna Merlin, Andy Romano, Ron McLarty, Donna Mitchell, Patrick Borriello, Mary Lou Rosato, Rosemary DeAngelis; ***D:*** James Foley; ***W:*** Joseph Stefano; ***C:*** Juan Ruiz-Anchia; ***M:*** Jane Musky; ***V:*** Alec Baldwin.

Two Bits & Pepper 🦴🦴 1/2 **1995 (PG)** Bumbling criminals (both played by Piscopo) still manage to kidnap a a young girl and her friend and it's up to the title characters, a pet horse and a pony, to attempt a daring rescue. **90m/C VHS, DVD.** Joe Piscopo, Lauren Eckstrom, Rachel Crane, Perry Stephens, Kathrin Lautner, Dennis Weaver; ***D:*** Corey Michael Eubanks; ***W:*** Corey Michael Eubanks; ***C:*** Jacques Haitkin; ***M:*** Louis Febre.

Two Brothers 🦴🦴 1/2 **2004 (PG)** Kiddy fare about tiger brothers whose happy cubhood is shattered by the intrusion of Man. Great White Hunter (Pearce) guns down their father, and the cubs are snatched away into captivity. One cub is bought by a cruel circus owner (Scarito); the other becomes a child's (Highmore) pet. Neither can be tamed though, and circumstances reunite them with predictably tender results. Set in Indochina in the 1920s, with gorgeous backdrops of crumbling temples and lush jungles. The tigers are great, but human characters are exaggerated and unbelievable. Director Annaud shows great talent working with animals, as in previous work, "The Bear." Perhaps next time he'll leave out the humans. **109m/C VHS, DVD.** *FR GB* Guy Pearce, Jean-Claude Dreyfus, Freddie Highmore, Philippine Leroy-Beaulieu, Moussa Maaskri, Vincent Scarito, Mai Anh Le, Oanh Nguyen, Stephanie Lagarde; ***D:*** Jean-Jacques Annaud; ***W:*** Jean-Jacques Annaud; ***C:*** Jean-Marie Dreujou; ***M:*** Stephen Warbeck.

2 Brothers & a Bride 🦴🦴 1/2 *A Foreign Affair* **2003 (PG-13)** Simple-minded siblings Jake (Arquette) and Josh (Nelson) need to find a good (yet equally simple-minded) woman to tend to the chores on the farm since dear old mom passed away. They figure they'll find that lucky girl waiting for them somewhere in Russia. **92m/C DVD.** David Arquette, Tim Blake Nelson, Emily Mortimer, Larry Pine, Lois Smith, Allyce Beasley, Megan Follows, Redmond M. Gleeson; ***D:*** Helmut Schleppi; ***W:*** Geert Heetebrij; ***C:*** M. David Mullen; ***M:*** Todd Holden Capps.

Two by Forsyth 🦴🦴 *No Comebacks* **1986** Two short films based on stories by Frederick Forsyth, one dealing with a dying millionaire's clever efforts to prevent his fortune from being inherited by greedy relatives, the other about a mild-mannered stamp dealer who avenges himself on a nasty gossip columnist. **60m/C VHS.** Dan O'Herlihy, Cyril Cusack, Milo O'Shea, Shirley Anne Field; ***D:*** Michael O'Herlihy; ***W:*** Michael Callan; ***C:*** Jack Conroy; ***M:*** Bill Whelan.

2 by 4 🦴🦴 **1998** Johnnie (Smallhorne) is an Irish construction worker employed by his hard-living Uncle Trump (O'Neill) in New York. Though he's got a steady job, good friends, and a loving girlfriend in Maria (Topper), Johnnie's plagued by nightmares of something that happened in his childhood. And his apparent childhood abuse leads him to drugs, drink, and a certain sexual ambiguity as his repressed memories try to force their way to the surface. **90m/C VHS, DVD.** Jimmy Smallhorne, Chris O'Neill, Bradley Fitts, Joe Holyoake, Terrence McGoff, Michael Liebman, Ronan Carr, Leo Hamill, Seamus McDonagh, Kimberly Topper; ***D:*** Jimmy Smallhorne; ***W:*** Fergus Tighe, Jimmy Smallhorne, Terrence McGoff; ***C:*** Declan Quinn. Sundance '98: Cinematog.

Two Can Play That Game 🦴 1/2 **2001 (R)** Upwardly mobile Shante (Fox) seems to be the fountain of knowledge for her romantically challenged girlfriends Diedre (Mo'Nique), Karen (Robinson) and Trayce (Jones) on the subject of how to keep a man in line. When she sees her boyfriend Keith (Chestnut) grinding on another woman at a nightclub, however, her credibility takes a blow. She decides on a 10-day plan of action to force Keith back under her thumb. Clued in by his worldly wise buddy Tony (Anderson), however, Keith is well versed in the battle tactics of the opposite sex. Familiar material (director Brown also wrote "How to Be a Player"), spotty performances and the incessant narration by Fox's character make this a game you may want to quit halfway through. **90m/C VHS, DVD.** *US* Vivica A. Fox, Morris Chestnut, Anthony Anderson, Gabrielle Union, Wendy Raquel Robinson, Tamala Jones, Mo'Nique, Ray Wise, Bobby Brown, Dondre T. Whitfield; ***D:*** Mark Brown; ***W:*** Mark Brown; ***C:*** Alexander Grusynski; ***M:*** Marcus Miller.

Two Daughters 🦴🦴🦴 *Teen Kanya* **1961** Director Ray wrote the scripts for two stories based on the writings of Nobel Prize winner Rabindranath Tagore. "The Postmaster" covers the relationship between an ambitious young man who befriends his servant without realizing the consequences of his actions. "The Conclusion" finds a solemn young scholar declining to marry the girl arranged to be his intended and instead marrying a high-spirited young woman who doesn't want to give up her freedoms. Bengali with English subtitles. **114m/B VHS.** *IN* Chandana Banerjee, Anil Chatterjee, Soumitra Chatterjee; ***D:*** Satyajit Ray; ***W:*** Satyajit Ray; ***C:*** Soumendu Roy; ***M:*** Satyajit Ray.

Two Days 🦴🦴 **2003** What could be more depressing than being a dejected wanna-be actor? Apparently, not much as Paul Miller (Rudd) decides life isn't much worth living if he can't make it there (or, anywhere). In typical Hollywood fashion, he clings to his last 15 minutes (er, 48 hours) of fame by having his final two days put down on film. Will the filmmakers, his family, or his friends try to stop him? While Rudd tries his best to breathe life into it, this unconventional journey and its requisite destination proves too haphazardly constructed for anyone to truly care. **87m/C VHS, DVD.** Paul Rudd, Donal Logue, MacKenzie Astin, Adam Scott, Joshua Leonard, Caroline Aaron, Graham Beckel, Marguerite Moreau, Stacey Travis; ***D:*** Sean McGinly; ***W:*** Sean McGinly; ***C:*** Jens Sturup; ***M:*** Alan Ari Lazar. **VIDEO**

2 Days in Paris 🦴🦴🦴 **2007 (R)** Vacationing couple Jack (Goldberg) and Marion (writer/director Julie Delpy) stop off in Paris to see Marion's parents before they go home to New York. Unfortunately for neurotic Jack, the visit isn't exactly how he wanted to wrap up their trip, as he's forced to confront his fear of terrorist attacks, lunch with Marion's French-speaking parents (Delpy's real-life parents Albert Delpy and Pillet), and encounter her ex-boyfriends. The ensuing stresses and culture clash begin to highlight the differences between the two. A funny, if occasionally mean, anti-romantic comedy. **96m/C DVD.** *FR GE* Julie Delpy, Adam Goldberg, Albert Delpy, Marie Pillet, Adan Jodorowsky, Daniel Bruehl, Alexia Landeau, Alex Nahon; ***D:*** Julie Delpy; ***W:*** Julie Delpy; ***C:*** Lubomir Bakchev.

Two Days in the Valley 🦴🦴🦴 **1996 (R)** Film adds two days with ten characters in one locale and one half dozen separate plots and tries to come up with a dark comedy/thriller and winning debut for Herzfeld. It succeeds, mostly. San Fernando Valley is the backdrop, with a diverse ensemble of disturbed characters thrown together by the murder of a philandering spouse. Disjointed, and some plot threads are left hanging, but there's some fine comic moments and interesting character development, especially Aiello's culinary hitman, Dosmo Pizzo. Theron's Helga adds eye candy. For those too young to remember "Dynasty," you may want to check out the intense cat-fight between Hatcher's Becky Foxx and Helga. **105m/C VHS, DVD.** Danny Aiello, Jeff Daniels, Marsha Mason, Teri Hatcher, Glenne Headly, James Spader, Eric Stoltz, Greg Cruttwell, Peter Horton, Charlize Theron, Keith Carradine, Louise Fletcher, Austin Pendleton, Paul Mazursky, Kathleen Luong; ***D:*** John Herzfeld; ***W:*** John Herzfeld; ***C:*** Oliver Wood; ***M:*** Anthony Marinelli.

Two Deaths 🦴🦴 **1994 (R)** Sex, brutality, power, madness, death, revolution—sounds like a Roeg concoction. In 1989 Romania, the Ceaucescu government is under siege and a civil war rages outside. But inside the opulent apartment of cynical Dr. Daniel Pavenic (Gambon) calmness prevails, as three longtime friends join him for their annual reunion dinner. Dinner is served by Pavenic's housekeeper Ana (Braga), who has a strange, disturbing relationship with the possessive doctor that he relates to his friends. His candor leads to similar revelations by his companions. Based on the novel "The Two Deaths of Senora Puccini" by Stephen Dobyns. **102m/C VHS, DVD.** *GB* Michael Gambon, Sonia Braga, Patrick Malahide, Nickolas Grace, John Shrapnel, Ion Caramitru; ***D:*** Nicolas Roeg; ***W:*** Allan Scott; ***C:*** Witold Stok; ***M:*** Hans Zimmer.

Two Drifters 🦴 *Odete* **2005** Overwrought tearjerker. Rui is devastated when his lover Pedro is killed in a car accident. This leaves him vulnerable when he meets Odete, whose obsession to have a baby has left her unhinged. She happens to know Pedro's mother Teresa and claims she's carrying Pedro's child and things just go downhill from there. Portuguese with subtitles. **98m/C DVD.** *PT* Ana Christine de Oliveira, Teresa Madruga, Nuno Gil, Joao Carreira; ***D:*** Joao Pedro Rodrigues; ***W:*** Joao Pedro Rodrigues, Paulo Rebelo; ***C:*** Rui Pocas; ***M:*** Frank Beauvais.

Two English Girls 🦴🦴🦴 1/2 *Les Deux Anglaises et le Continent; Anne and Muriel* **1972 (R)** A pre-WWI French lad, with a possessive mother, loves two English sisters, one an impassioned, reckless artist, the other a repressed spinster. Tenderly delineates the triangle's interrelating love and friendship over seven years. Based on the novel "Les Deux Anglaises et le Continent" by Henri-Pierre Roche. In French with English subtitles. **130m/C VHS, DVD.** *FR* Jean-Pierre Leaud, Kika Markham, Stacey Tendeter, Sylvia Marriott, Marie Mansert, Philippe Leotard; ***D:*** Francois Truffaut; ***W:*** Francois Truffaut; ***C:*** Nestor Almendros; ***M:*** Georges Delerue.

Two Evil Eyes 🦴🦴 *Due Occhi Diabolici* **1990 (R)** Horror kings Romero and Argento each direct an Edgar Allan Poe tale in this release, hence the title. Barbeau, the scheming younger wife of a millionaire, hypnotizes her husband with the help of her lover in "The Facts in the Case of M. Valdemar." When hubby dies too soon to validate changes made in his will, the lovers decide to freeze him for two weeks in order that death can be recorded at the correct time. In "Black Cat" a crime photographer used to photographing gore adopts a feline friend and starts getting sick on the job. **121m/C VHS, DVD.** *IT* Adrienne Barbeau, Ramy Zada, Harvey Keitel, Madeleine Potter, Bingo O'Malley, E.G. Marshall, John Amos, Sally Kirkland, Kim Hunter, Martin Balsam, Tom Atkins; ***D:*** George A. Romero, Dario Argento; ***W:*** George A. Romero, Dario Argento, Franco Ferrini; ***C:*** Giuseppe Maccari, Peter Reniers; ***M:*** Pino Donaggio.

Two-Faced Woman 🦴🦴🦴 **1941** Garbo, in her last film, attempts a ruse when she finds her husband may be interested in an old flame. Pretending to be her twin sister in an attempt to lure Douglas away from the other woman, she's fooled a little herself. Romantic comedy unfortunately miscasts Garbo as an Americanized ski bunny. **90m/B VHS.** Greta Garbo, Melvyn Douglas, Constance Bennett, Roland Young, Ruth Gordon, Robert Sterling, George Cleveland, Frances Carson; ***D:*** George Cukor; ***C:*** Joseph Ruttenberg.

The Two Faces of Dr. Jekyll 🦴🦴 1/2 *House of Fright; Jekyll's Inferno* **1960** Henry Jekyll's (Massie) experiments lead to the release of his suave alter ego Edward Hyde. When Hyde discovers that Jekyll's long-suffering wife has taken up with his best friend, Hyde pits everyone against each other, while Jekyll struggles to retain control over his insidious other half. **87m/C VHS.** *GB* Paul Massie, Dawn Addams, Christopher Lee, David Kossoff, Francis De Wolff, Oliver Reed, Norma Marla, Terry Quinn; ***D:*** Terence Fisher; ***W:*** Wolf Mankowitz; ***C:*** Jack Asher.

The Two Faces of Evil 🦴 **1982** A family's vacation turns into a night of unbearable terror when they pick up a sinister hitchhiker. **60m/C VHS, DVD.** Anna Calder-Marshall, Gary Raymond, Denholm Elliott, Pauline Delany, Philip Latham; ***D:*** Peter Sasdy, Alan Gibson.

Two Family House 🦴🦴 1/2 **1999 (R)** The '50s aren't exactly a time of happiness and prosperity for factory worker Buddy Rispoli. He's a frustrated singer, still haboring dreams of the big time, with a number of failed moneymaking schemes behind him. His latest venture is buying a two-family house where he and his family can live upstairs while he turns the downstairs into a bar. But the current tenants, a pregnant Irish teen and her abusive husband, have other ideas. **109m/C VHS, DVD.** Michael Rispoli, Kelly Macdonald, Kathrine Narducci, Matt Servitto, Kevin Conway, Michele Santopietro; ***D:*** Raymond De Felitta; ***W:*** Raymond De Felitta; ***C:*** Mike Mayers; ***M:*** Stephen Endelman. Sundance '00: Aud. Award.

2 Fast 2 Furious 🦴🦴 **2003 (PG-13)** 2 dumb 2 believe, but no one seems to care. Walker reprises his role as now-disgraced undercover cop Brian O'Connor, and he's once again upstaged by his co-star. This time it's Tyrese, as childhood pal and new partner-in-undercover-crime Roman. It doesn't really matter, though, because everyone is upstaged by the lovingly photographed cars and the chaos they cause. The continuous action is now in Miami, as the buddies infiltrate the street-racing circuit to bust a Colombian drug ring and some bad cops. **94m/C VHS, DVD, UMD, HD DVD.** *US* Paul Walker, Tyrese Gibson, Cole Hauser, Eva Mendes, Ludacris, Devon Aoki, James Remar, Thom Barry, Michael Ealy, Mark Boone Jr.; ***D:*** John Singleton; ***W:*** Derek Haas, Michael Brandt; ***C:*** Matthew F. Leonetti; ***M:*** David Arnold.

Two Fathers' Justice **1985** Two dads, one tough and one a wimp, seek revenge on the men who killed their kids. **100m/C VHS.** Robert Conrad, George Hamilton, Brooke Bundy, Catherine Corkill, Whitney Kershaw, Greg Terrell; ***D:*** Rod Holcomb. **TV**

Two Fisted Justice 🦴 **1931** A cowboy protects a town against a daring and deadly Indian attack. **45m/B VHS.** Tom Tyler, Barbara Weeks, Bobby Nelson, William Walling, Yakima Canutt, John Elliott; ***D:*** George Arthur Durlam; ***W:*** George Arthur Durlam; ***C:*** Archie Stout.

Two-Fisted Justice 🦴 **1943** The Range Busters do their part to maintain law and order in the old West. **55m/B VHS.** John "Dusty" King, David Sharpe, Max Terhune, Gwen Gaze, John Elliott, Charles "Blackie" King, George Chesebro, Frank Ellis; ***D:*** Robert Emmett Tansey; ***W:*** William Nolte; ***C:*** Robert E. Cline.

Two-Fisted Law 🦴 1/2 **1932** McCoy plays a rancher who borrows big bucks from the corrupt Oakman, who's actually a land grabber. McCoy then teams up with a posse to bring the evildoer to justice. Early (and small) screen roles for Wayne and Brennan. **58m/B VHS, DVD.** Tim McCoy, Tully Marshall, Wheeler Oakman, Alice Day, Wallace MacDonald, John Wayne, Walter Brennan; ***D:*** David Ross Lederman; ***W:*** Kurt Kempler; ***C:*** Benjamin (Ben H.) Kline.

Two for Texas 🦴🦴 1/2 **1997** Young buck Holland (Bairstow) and grizzled adventurer Allison (Kristofferson) manage to escape from a Louisiana chain gang and decide to head to Texas so they can join in the Texas Volunteer Army under Sam Houston (Skerritt). Soon, they're part of a group sent to San Jacinto in order to avenge the massacre at the Alamo. Kind of plodding western based on the novel by James Lee Burke. **96m/C VHS.** Kris Kristofferson, Scott Bairstow, Tom Skerritt, Peter Coyote, Irene Bedard, Victor Rivers, Rodney A. Grant, Marco Rodriguez, Richard Jones; ***D:*** Rod Hardy; ***W:*** Larry Brothers; ***C:*** David Connell; ***M:*** Lee Holdridge. **CABLE**

Two for the Money 🦴🦴 **2005 (R)** Another bigger-than-life role for Al Pacino who plays Walter, the owner of a sports betting advice empire. Walter takes on Brandon Lang (McConaughey) after his incredible football game-picking accuracy gains notice. Brandon, whose NFL hopes were shot down by a career-ending knee injury, moves to Manhattan where under the mentoring of Walter he becomes a game-picking superstar, rocketing into a world of wealth and glamour. Predictably Brandon's hot streak cools, plunging him back to earth. If you can't get enough of Pacino's "Hoo-WAH!" roles, you'll love this one, which borders on self-parody. **124m/C DVD.** *US* Al Pacino, Matthew McConaughey, Rene Russo, Armand Assante, Jeremy Piven, Jaime (James) King, Kevin Chapman, Gedde Watanabe, Carly Pope, Gerard Plunkett, James Kirk; ***D:*** D.J. Caruso; ***W:*** Dan Gilroy; ***C:*** Conrad W. Hall; ***M:*** Christophe Beck.

Two for the Road 🦴🦴🦴 1/2 **1967** On a road trip to the French Riviera, Mark (Finney) and Joanna (Hepburn) look back on more than a decade of marriage and find only fragments of their relationship. Flashbacks to their first meeting and subsequent vacations detail what when wrong and if their love is worth saving. Mancini score adds poignancy to the couple's reflections on their stormy life. Well-acted but the very sixties look has dated badly. **112m/C VHS, DVD.** *GB* Audrey Hepburn, Albert Finney, Eleanor Bron, William Daniels, Claude Dauphin, Nadia Gray, Jacqueline Bisset, Georges Descrieres, Gabrielle Middleton, Judy Cornwell, Irene Hilda, Roger Dann, Libby Morris, Yves Barsac; ***D:*** Stanley Donen; ***W:*** Frederic Raphael; ***C:*** Christopher Challis; ***M:*** Henry Mancini.

Two for the Seesaw 🦴🦴🦴 **1962** Mitchum stars as a Nebraska attorney who comes to New York and gets involved with MacLaine. Humorous and touching comedy-drama worked better on stage, because the large screen magnified the talkiness of Gibson's play. Unusual casting of Mitchum as a Midwest lawyer and MacLaine as a New York Jewish bohemian. **119m/B VHS, DVD.** Robert Mitchum, Shirley MacLaine, Edmon Ryan, Elisabeth Fraser, Eddie Firestone, Billy Gray, Vic Lundin; ***D:*** Robert Wise; ***W:*** Isobel Lennart; ***M:*** Andre Previn.

Two Friends 🦴🦴 **1986** Campion's first feature, made for Australian TV, depicts the severing of the friendship between 15-year-olds Kelly (Bidenko) and Louise (Coles). Separated physically and emotionally as they begin growing up and attending different schools, the film flashes back to moments in their once inseparable friendship. **76m/C VHS, DVD.** *AU* Kris Bidenko, Emma Coles, Peter Hehir, Kris McQuade; ***D:*** Jane Campion; ***W:*** Helen Garner; ***C:*** Julian Penney; ***M:*** Martin Armiger.

Two Girls and a Guy 🦴🦴🦴 **1998 (R)** Graham and Wagner find out that Downey's been two-timing them and they confront him at his apartment. Only don't expect the usual revenge scenario. Yeah, it's talky, but the dialogue (much of it improvised) is great. Downey is at his best, playing an irresistibly charismatic actor backed into a (real and figurative) corner by his lifestyle while Graham and Wagner avoid the wronged-woman cliches. In one of the all-time male fantasies ever, Downey's character still gets to have sex with one of the women even after his lie has been exposed. The MPAA had a little problem with that, since that scene, like most of the rest of the movie, was shot in real time. The uncut NC-17 version is also available. **92m/C VHS, DVD.** Robert Downey Jr., Heather Graham, Natasha Gregson Wagner, Angel David, Frederique van der Wal; ***D:*** James Toback; ***W:*** James Toback; ***C:*** Barry Markowitz.

Two Girls and a Sailor 🦴🦴🦴 **1944** Wartime musical revue loosely structured around a love triangle involving a sailor on leave. Vintage hokum with lots of songs. ♫ Paper Doll; The Young Man with a Horn; Concerto for Index Finger; Take it Easy; Ritual Fire Dance; Inka Dinka Doo; My Mother Told Me; A Love Like Ours; In A Moment of Madness. **124m/B VHS.** June Allyson, Gloria De Haven, Van Johnson, Xavier Cugat, Jimmy Durante, Tom Drake, Lena Horne, Harry James, Gracie Allen, Virginia O'Brien, Jose Iturbi, Carlos Ramirez, Donald Meek, Ben Blue; ***Cameos:*** Buster Keaton; ***D:*** Richard Thorpe; ***C:*** Robert L. Surtees.

Two Gladiators 🦴 1/2 *I Due Gladiatori* **1964** Loyal Roman senator Tarrunio (Solaro) needs to find the long-lost twin brother (Harrison) of cruel new emperor Commodus (Palmara) and convince him to take his rightful place as ruler. Dubbed. **90m/C DVD.** *IT* Richard Harrison, Moira Orfei, Mimmo Palmara, Pierro Lulli, Alberto (Albert Farley) Farnese, Gianni Solaro, Mirko Ellis; ***D:*** Mario Caiano; ***W:*** Mario Caiano, Alfonso Brescia; ***C:*** Pier Ludovico Pavoni; ***M:*** Carlo Franci.

The Two Great Cavaliers ✓ **1973** A Ming warrior has a hard time with the Manchurian army, fending it off as he must with only his bare instep, heel, and wrist. **95m/C VHS, DVD.** Chen Shing, Mao Ying; ***D:*** Yeung Ching Chen.

Two Gun Man ✓ 1/2 **1931** America's first singing cowboy, Ken Maynard, performs hair-raising stunts in this old oater. One of the first "talkies!" **60m/B VHS, DVD.** Ken Maynard, Lafe (Lafayette) McKee, Charles "Blackie" King, Tom London, Lucille Powers; ***D:*** Phil Rosen.

Two-Gun Man from Harlem **1938** Big city guy travels to the wild West in search of a little truth. **60m/B VHS.** Herbert Jeffries, Marguerite Whitten, Mantan Moreland, Matthew "Stymie" Beard; ***D:*** Richard C. Kahn.

Two-Gun Troubador ✓ *The Lone Troubador* **1937** A masked singing cowboy struggles to uncovers his father's murderer. **59m/B VHS.** Fred Scott, Claire Rochelle, John Merton; ***D:*** Bernard B. Ray; ***W:*** Phil Dunham, Richard Bare; ***C:*** Walter Bluemel.

Two Hands ✓✓✓ **1998** Black comedy/thriller stars Aussie heartthrob Ledger as teen Jimmy who's got a nothing job in Sydney and would like to improve his prospects. So he agrees to deliver a cash-filled envelope for local gang boss, Pando (Brown), and then promptly loses the money. This sends Jimmy on the run to avoid Pando's retribution. (But the kid still finds some time to romance naive Alex (Byrne).) **104m/C VHS, DVD.** *AU* Heath Ledger, Bryan Brown, David Field, Rose Byrne, Susie Porter, Tom Long, Steven Vidler; ***D:*** Gregor Jordan; ***W:*** Gregor Jordan; ***C:*** Malcolm McCulloch; ***M:*** Chris Gough. Australian Film Inst. '99: Director (Jordan), Film, Film Editing, Orig. Screenplay, Support. Actor (Brown).

200 Cigarettes ✓✓ **1998 (R)** Directorial debut from former casting director Garcia follows the adventures of various self-absorbed hipsters on New Year's Eve in early '80s New York. The excellent ensemble cast is given spotty material, however. The primary goal of all these rather unlikable characters is to find someone (or anyone) to sleep with before the night is over. They all hook up in this ode to the high life of pre-AIDS promiscuity, but you don't really care about them at all. Chapelle provides the most entertainment as a philosophy-spouting disco cabbie who schleps the shallow party-goers to and fro. **101m/C VHS, DVD.** Ben Affleck, Casey Affleck, Jay Mohr, Dave Chappelle, Gaby Hoffman, Courtney Love, Christina Ricci, Paul Rudd, Catherine Kellner, Martha Plimpton, Janeane Garofalo, Guillermo Diaz, Angela Featherstone, Brian McCardie, Nicole Ari Parker, Kate Hudson, Elvis Costello; ***D:*** Risa Bramon Garcia; ***W:*** Shana Larsen; ***C:*** Frank Prinzi; ***M:*** Mark Mothersbaugh, Bob Mothersbaugh.

200 Motels ✓ 1/2 **1971 (R)** Rambling, non-narrative self-indulgent video album by and about Frank Zappa and the Mothers of Invention, as they document a long and especially grueling road tour. For fans only. **99m/C VHS.** Ringo Starr, Theodore Bikel, Keith Moon, Janet Ferguson, Lucy Offerall; ***D:*** Frank Zappa; ***W:*** Frank Zappa; ***C:*** Gillian Lynne; ***M:*** Frank Zappa.

Two If by Sea ✓ 1/2 *Stolen Hearts* **1995 (R)** Small-time hood Frank (Leary) and his girlfriend Roz (Bullock) hole up in a New England mansion after Frank steals a valuable Matisse painting. Between verbal sparring matches, the two try to mingle with the upper crusty residents with predictable results. Pursuing the pair are the FBI, led by the deluded O'Malley (Kotto), and Frank's bonehead cousin Beano (Robson) and his trio of dim henchmen. Tries to be a caper/romantic comedy but fails to deliver on all fronts. The usually caustic Leary takes some of the edge off of his trademark bitter humor, and the alleged witty repartee is just plain annoying as a result. Nova Scotia turns in a fine performance as New England. **96m/C VHS, DVD.** Sandra Bullock, Denis Leary, Stephen (Dillon) Dillane, Yaphet Kotto, Wayne Robson, Jonathan Tucker, Mike Starr, Michael Badalucco, Lenny Clarke, John Friesen; ***D:*** Bill Bennett; ***W:*** Denis Leary, Mike Armstrong; ***C:*** Andrew Lesnie.

The Two Jakes ✓✓ **1990 (R)** Ten years have passed and Jake Gittes is still a private investigator in this sequel to 1974's "Chinatown." When a murder occurs while he's digging up dirt on an affair between the wife of a real estate executive and the executive's partner, Jake must return to Chinatown to uncover the killer and face the painful memories buried there. Despite solid dialogue and effective performances, it's unreasonably difficult to follow if you haven't seen "Chinatown." Outstanding photography by Vilmos Zsigmond. **137m/C VHS, DVD.** Jack Nicholson, Harvey Keitel, Meg Tilly, Madeleine Stowe, Eli Wallach, Ruben Blades, Frederic Forrest, David Keith, Richard Farnsworth, Tracey Walter; ***D:*** Jack Nicholson; ***W:*** Robert Towne; ***C:*** Vilmos Zsigmond; ***M:*** Van Dyke Parks.

Two Kinds of Love ✓✓ **1985** Adapted from Peggy Mann's novel "There Are Two Kinds of Terrible," this is the story of a young boy who learns to love his distant, workaholic father after his protective mother suddenly dies. **94m/C VHS.** Rick Schroder, Lindsay Wagner, Peter Weller, Rossie (Ross) Harris; ***D:*** Jack Bender. **TV**

Two Lane Blacktop ✓✓✓ **1971** Counterculture critics darling that failed at the box-office but has since developed a cult following. The Driver (Taylor) and the Mechanic (Wilson) are car freaks in a '55 Chevy, driving the southwestern backroads looking for a race. They meet up with Oates who's at the wheel of a brand-new G.T.O. He proposes they cross-country to D.C. and the winner gets the loser's car. Along the way, everyone's enthusiasm wanes and they part, with Wilson and Taylor driving down a two-lane blacktop as the film literally melts into a bright light. Music includes The Doors, Kris Kristofferson, and Ray Charles. **103m/C VHS, DVD.** James Taylor, Dennis Wilson, Warren Oates, Laurie Bird, Harry Dean Stanton; ***D:*** Monte Hellman; ***W:*** Rudy Wurlitzer, Will Corry; ***C:*** Jackson Deerson.

Two Lost Worlds **WOOF!** **1950** A young hero battles monstrous dinosaurs, pirates, and more in this cheapy when he and his shipmates are shipwrecked on an uncharted island. Don't miss the footage from "Captain Fury," "One Billion B.C.," and "Captain Caution" and Arness long before his Sheriff Dillon fame, and his "big" role in "The Thing." **63m/B VHS, DVD.** James Arness, Laura Elliott, Bill Kennedy; ***D:*** Norman Dawn; ***W:*** Tom Hubbard; ***C:*** Harry Neumann.

Two Lovers ✓✓✓ **2009 (R)** Brooklynite Leonard (Phoenix) is torn between family friend Sandra (Shaw), whom his parents want him to marry, and volatile new neighbor Michelle (Paltrow). Leonard falls in love with Michelle despite the fact that she is being kept by a married man. Gray, known for hard-edged, tough-guy themes, keeps things dark but deeply sensitive in this effectively moody character study of love, loss and the struggle between. Sadly this excellent second collaboration between writer/director Gray and Phoenix (*The Yards*) could be the last if Phoenix follows through on his claim of trading acting for, a-hem, rapping. **110m/C DVD.** *US FR* Joaquin Rafael (Leaf) Phoenix, Gwyneth Paltrow, Vinessa Shaw, Isabella Rossellini, Elias Koteas, Moni Moshonov; ***D:*** James Gray; ***W:*** James Gray, Richard Menello; ***C:*** Joaquin Baca-Asay.

Two Men & a Wardrobe ✓✓ 1/2 **1958** Polanski's project while a student at the Polish Film Institute. Consideration of modern man's lack of privacy and made without dialogue. Two men emerge from the sea carrying nothing but a large piece of furniture. Absurd and funny. **19m/B VHS.** ***D:*** Roman Polanski.

Two Men Went to War ✓ 1/2 **2002** Silly comedy that falls into the "truth is stranger than fiction" category. In 1942, Sgt. King (Cranham) and Pvt. Cuthbertson (Bill), both assigned to the Army Dental Corps, decide to go AWOL in order to see some action. They take a bag of grenades, steal a boat, sneak into France, and go after some Nazi targets. Adapted from Raymond Foxall's book "Amateur Commandos." **108m/C DVD.** *GB* Kenneth Cranham, Leo Bill, Derek Jacobi, Phyllida Law, James Fleet, Julian Glover, Anthony Valentine, David Ryall, Rosanna Lavelle; ***D:*** John Henderson; ***W:*** Christopher Villiers, Richard Everett; ***C:*** John Ignatius; ***M:*** Richard Harvey.

Two Minute Warning ✓ **1976 (R)** A sniper plans to take out the president of the United States at an NFL playoff game in this boring, pointless, disaster film that goes on forever. Features all the ready-made characters inherent in the genre, but, until its too late, precious little of the mayhem. To get caught watching the TV version, which features more characters and an additional subplot, would be truly disastrous. **116m/C VHS, DVD.** Charlton Heston, John Cassavetes, Martin Balsam, Beau Bridges, Marilyn Hassett, David Janssen, Jack Klugman, Walter Pidgeon, Gena Rowlands; ***D:*** Larry Peerce; ***W:*** Ed Hume; ***C:*** Gerald Hirschfeld; ***M:*** Charles Fox.

2 Minutes Later ✓✓ **2007** Graham is sassy and Molina is hunky in this noirish thriller. Mild-mannered insurance agent Michael Dalmar (Molina) goes looking for his missing twin brother Kyle, a Philadelphia photographer who specialized in kink and was notorious for being a jerk. Take-charge private eye Abigail Marks (Graham) teams up with Michael and they decide he should pose as Kyle to see what shakes lose. They get a digital-camera chip from Kyle's last shoot, which points them in a dangerous direction. **70m/C DVD.** J. Matthew Miller, Michael Molina, Jessica Graham, Peter Sickles; ***D:*** Robert Gaston; ***W:*** Robert Gaston; ***C:*** Jeff Schirmer. **VIDEO**

The Two Mrs. Carrolls ✓✓ 1/2 **1947** Bogart is a psycho-killer/artist who paints portraits of his wives as the Angel of Death—and then kills them. The married Bogart falls for Stanwyck, poisons his current wife, and the two marry. After a few years, Bogart falls for Smith and decides to rid himself of Stanwyck in the same manner as his first killing. Stanwyck, however, becomes increasingly suspicious and calls on an old beau for help. Melodrama cast Bogart against type (not always successfully). Filmed in 1945, but was unreleased until 1947. **99m/B VHS.** Humphrey Bogart, Barbara Stanwyck, Alexis Smith, Nigel Bruce, Pat O'Moore, Ann Carter; ***D:*** Peter Godfrey.

Two Moon Junction ✓ 1/2 **1988 (R)** A soon-to-be-wed Southern debutante enters into a wild love affair with a rough-edged carnival worker. Poorly acted, wildly directed, with many unintentional laughs. **104m/C VHS, DVD.** Sherilyn Fenn, Richard Tyson, Louise Fletcher, Burl Ives, Kristy McNichol, Millie Perkins, Don Galloway, Herve Villechaize, Dabbs Greer, Milla Jovovich, Screamin' Jay Hawkins; ***D:*** Zalman King; ***W:*** Zalman King; ***C:*** Mark Plummer; ***M:*** Jonathan Elias. Golden Raspberries '88: Worst Support. Actress (McNichol).

Two Much ✓ 1/2 **1996 (PG-13)** Banderas does double duty as a con man pretending to be twins in order to romance two sisters (Griffith and Hannah). Embarrassingly light comedy suffers from a complicated plot (which still manages to leave holes), weak or non-existent characterization, and a general lack of humor. About the only thing it has going for it is Cusack as a wisecracking secretary. It was on the set of this film that Banderas and Griffith started their real-life romance. While that may have helped the boxoffice and gossip columns in Banderas's homeland, the fireworks didn't find their way to the screen. **118m/C VHS, DVD.** Melanie Griffith, Antonio Banderas, Daryl Hannah, Joan Cusack, Danny Aiello, Eli Wallach, Vincent Schiavelli; ***D:*** Fernando Trueba; ***W:*** Fernando Trueba, David Trueba; ***C:*** Jose Luis Alcaine; ***M:*** Michel Camilo.

Two Mules for Sister Sara ✓✓✓ **1970 (PG)** American mercenary in 19th century Mexico gets mixed up with a cigar-smoking nun and the two make plans to capture a French garrison. MacLaine and Eastwood are great together. Based on a Boetticher story. **105m/C VHS, DVD.** Clint Eastwood, Shirley MacLaine; ***D:*** Donald Siegel; ***W:*** Albert (John B. Sherry) Maltz; ***M:*** Ennio Morricone.

Two Nights with Cleopatra ✓ 1/2 *Due Notti Con Cleopatra* **1954** A piece of Italian pizza involving Cleopatra's double (also played by Loren) falling in love with one of the guards. Notable only for the 19-year-old Sophia's brief nudity. **77m/C VHS, DVD.** *IT* Sophia Loren, Ettore Manni, Alberto Sordi, Paul Muller, Alberto Talegalli, Rolf Tasna, Gianni Cavalieri, Nando (Fernando) Bruno, Riccardo Garrone, Carlo Dale; ***D:*** Mario Mattoli; ***W:*** Nino Maccari, Ettore Scola.

Two Ninas ✓ 1/2 **2000 (R)** Dreary romantic comedy finds mopey aspiring writer Marty (Livingston) meeting sarcastic Nina Cohen (Buono) at a party. The two hit it off but then Marty literally runs into Nina 2, i.e. wealthy Nina Harris (Peet), while rollerblading in Central Park. He starts dating her as well. Now Marty has to keep his stories straight and hope the two Ninas never meet, which, of course, they do. **90m/C VHS, DVD.** *US* Ron Livingston, Cara Buono, Amanda Peet, Bray Poor, Jill(ian) Hennessey; ***D:*** Neil Turitz; ***W:*** Neil Turitz; ***C:*** Joaquin Baca-Asay; ***M:*** Joseph Saba.

Two of a Kind ✓✓ 1/2 **1982** In his TV movie debut, Burns plays an elderly man whose mentally handicapped grandson helps him put the starch back in his shirt. Sensitively produced and performed. **102m/C VHS.** George Burns, Robby Benson, Cliff Robertson, Barbara Barrie, Frances Lee McCain, Geri Jewell, Ronny Cox; ***D:*** Roger Young. **TV**

Two of a Kind ✓ **1983 (PG)** Angels make a bet with God—two selfish people will redeem themselves or God can blow up the Earth. Bad acting, awful direction, and the script needs divine intervention. **88m/C VHS, DVD.** John Travolta, Olivia Newton-John, Charles Durning, Beatrice Straight, Scatman Crothers, Oliver Reed; ***D:*** John Herzfeld; ***C:*** Fred W. Koenekamp.

The Two of Us ✓✓✓ 1/2 *Le Vieil Homme Et L'Enfant; Claude; The Old Man and the Boy* **1968** Young Jewish boy flees Nazi-occupied Paris to live in the country with an irritable, bigoted guardian. Sensitive, eloquent movie about racial prejudice and anti-Semitism. In French with English subtitles. **86m/B VHS, DVD.** *FR* Michel Simon, Alain Cohen, Luce Fabiole, Roger Carel, Paul Preboist, Charles Denner; ***D:*** Claude Berri; ***W:*** Claude Berri; ***C:*** Jean Penzer; ***M:*** Georges Delerue.

Two of Us ✓✓ **2000 (PG-13)** A "what-if" look at the friendship between ex-Beatles Paul McCartney and John Lennon. In 1976, Paul (Quinn) is in New York to publicize a concert with his band Wings and he decides to visit estranged mate John (Harris) at the Dakota in a bittersweet effort to make peace with their relationship. **90m/C VHS, DVD.** Aidan Quinn, Jared Harris; ***D:*** Michael Lindsay-Hogg; ***W:*** Mark Stanfield; ***C:*** Miroslaw Baszak; ***M:*** David Schwartz. **CABLE**

Two or Three Things I Know about Her ✓✓ *Deux ou Trois Choses Que Je Sais d'Elle* **1966** Inspired by a magazine article about housewife-prostitutes, Godard takes on the bourgeoise. Juliette (Vlady) is a wife and mother who lives in the suburbs of Paris and goes into the city once a week to work as a prostitute in order to buy consumer goods. French with subtitles. **95m/C VHS, DVD.** *FR* Marina Vlady, Anny (Annie Legras) Duperey, Roger Montsoret, Jean Narboni, Raoul Levy; ***D:*** Jean-Luc Godard; ***W:*** Jean-Luc Godard; ***C:*** Raoul Coutard.

Two Plus One ✓✓ **1995** Triangular drama about Yuppie relationships, set in Philadelphia. Romantic couple searches for happiness and decides to invite a third person to join their relationship. Newcomer Lewis is the sister of actress Juliette. **85m/C VHS.** William Sage, Deirdre Lewis, Tony Vinto; ***D:*** Eugene Martian.

Two Rode Together ✓✓ 1/2 **1961** A Texas marshal and an army lieutenant negotiate with the Comanches for the return of captives, but complications ensue. **109m/C VHS.** James Stewart, Richard Widmark, Shirley Jones, Linda Cristal, Andy Devine, John McIntire; ***D:*** John Ford.

Two Seconds ✓✓ **1932** Hammy crime melodrama. The press arrives at a prison to witness the electric chair execution of convicted murderer John Allen (Robinson). Flashbacks detail the trouble that derails the friendship of ironworker Allen and his pal Bud Clark (Foster) which eventually leads to Allen winding up on Death Row. Title refers to the time it takes the electrical current to reach the chair's occupant. **68m/B DVD.** Edward G. Robinson, Preston Foster, Vivienne Osborne, J. Carrol Naish, Guy Kibbee, Berton Churchill; ***D:*** Mervyn LeRoy; ***W:*** Harvey Thew; ***C:*** Sol Polito.

2 Seconds ✓✓ *Deux Secondes* **1998 (R)** Laurie (Laurier) has spent most of her life as a mountain bike racer but a two second hesitation costs her a race and forces her retirement. She returns to Montreal and meets Lorenzo (Tavarone), a cantankerous, elderly former racer who runs a bike shop. Laurie gets a job as a bike courier and begins to re-evaluate her life. French with subtitles. **101m/C VHS, DVD.** *CA* Charlotte Laurier, Suzanne Clement, Yves Pelletier, Dino Tavarone; ***D:*** Manon Briand; ***W:*** Manon Briand; ***C:*** Louise Archambault, Pierre Crepo; ***M:*** Dominic Grand, Sylvain-Charles Grand.

Two Shades of Blue ½ **1998 (R)** Surprisingly dull erotic thriller. Writer Hunter is framed for the murder of fiancee Busey, so she assumes the alter ego identity of her novel's sexy heroine in order to hunt for the killer herself. She takes a job as a relay telephone operator for the deaf so she can contact deaf D.A. Matlin. But Matlin has a sexually obsessive relationship with boyfriend Roberts (who's in whacko mode) and Hunter begins to take a voyeuristic delight in their conversations. **103m/C VHS, DVD.** Rachel Hunter, Marlee Matlin, Eric Roberts, Gary Busey; ***D:*** James D. Deck; ***W:*** Ted Williams. **VIDEO**

The Two Sisters 1937 Goldstein, in her only film role, plays an older sister who sacrifices everything for the younger. The younger thanks her by stealing her fiance. In Yiddish with English subtitles. **70m/B VHS.** Sylvia Dell, Muni Seroff, Harvey Kier, Jacob Wexler, Jenney Goldstein, Michael Rosenberg; ***D:*** Ben Blake; ***W:*** Samuel Cohen; ***C:*** George Hinners; ***M:*** Joseph Rumshinsky.

Two Small Bodies 1993 Police detective Brann investigates the disappearance of two young children, suspecting their mother Eileen may have murdered them. Two character study set in Eileen's home with both verbally recreating versions of the possible crime. Based on the play by Neal Bell. **85m/C VHS.** *GE* Fred Ward, Suzy Amis; ***D:*** Beth B; ***W:*** Beth B, Neal Bell; ***C:*** Phil Parmet.

2000 Maniacs ½ **1964** One of cult director Lewis' most enjoyably watchable films. A literal Civil War "ghost town" takes its revenge 100 years after being slaughtered by renegade Union soldiers by luring unwitting "yankee" tourists to their centennial festival. The hapless Northerners are then chopped, crushed, ripped apart etc. while the ghostly rebels party. Quite fun in a cartoonishly gruesome sort of way. Filmed in St. Cloud, FL. **75m/C VHS, DVD.** William Kerwin, Connie Mason, Jeffrey Allen, Ben Moore, Gary Bakeman, Jerome (Jerry Stallion) Eden, Shelby Livingston, Michael Korb, Yvonne Gilbert, Mark Douglas, Linda Cochran, Vincent Santo, Andy Wilson; ***D:*** Herschell Gordon Lewis; ***W:*** Herschell Gordon Lewis; ***C:*** Herschell Gordon Lewis; ***M:*** Herschell Gordon Lewis, Larry Wellington.

2001: A Space Odyssey
1968 Space voyage to Jupiter turns chaotic when a computer, HAL 9000, takes over. Seen by some as a mirror of man's historical use of machinery and by others as a grim vision of the future, the special effects and music are still stunning. Critically acclaimed and well accepted by some, simply confusing to others. Martin Balsam originally recorded the voice of HAL, but was replaced by Rain. From Arthur C. Clarke's short story "The Sentinel." Followed by a sequel "2010: The Year We Make Contact." **139m/C VHS, DVD, Blu-ray Disc, HD DVD.** *GB* Keir Dullea, Gary Lockwood, William Sylvester, Dan Richter, Leonard Rossiter, Margaret Tyzack, Robert Beatty, Vivian Kubrick; ***D:*** Stanley Kubrick; ***W:*** Stanley Kubrick, Arthur C. Clarke; ***C:*** Geoffrey Unsworth, John Alcott; ***V:*** Douglas Rain. Oscars '68: Visual FX; AFI '98: Top 100, Natl. Film Reg. '91.

2001: A Space Travesty ½ **2000 (R)** Nielsen continues his tradition of parodies starring as none-too-bright Marshal "Dick" Dix who must rescue the U.S. president who has been kidnapped by aliens and replaced by a clone. He joins forces with sexy Cassandra (Winter) and heads to planet Vegan on his mission. **99m/C VHS, DVD.** Leslie Nielsen, Ezio Greggio, Peter Egan, Ophelie Winter; ***D:*** Allan Goldstein; ***W:*** Alan Shearman; ***C:*** Sylvain Brault; ***M:*** Claude Foisy.

2010: The Year We Make Contact **1984 (PG)** Based on Arthur C. Clarke's novel, which is his sequel to "2001: A Space Odyssey." Americans and Russians unite to investigate the abandoned starship Discovery's decaying orbit around Jupiter and try to determine why the HAL 9000 computer sabotaged its mission years before, while signs of cosmic change are detected on and around the giant planet. **116m/C VHS, DVD.** Roy Scheider, John Lithgow, Helen Mirren, Bob Balaban, Keir Dullea, Madolyn Smith, Mary Jo Deschanel; ***D:*** Peter Hyams; ***W:*** Peter Hyams, Arthur C. Clarke; ***C:*** Peter Hyams; ***M:*** David Shire; ***V:*** Douglas Rain, Candice Bergen.

2020 Texas Gladiators WOOF! 1985 (R) In the post-nuclear holocaust world, two groups, one good, one evil, battle for supremacy. **91m/C VHS.** *IT* Harrison Muller, Al Cliver, Daniel Stephen, Peter Hooten, Hal Yamanouchi, Sabrina Santi; ***D:*** Kevin Mancuso.

2069: A Sex Odyssey ½ **1978 (R)** Team of beautiful, sensuous astronauts are sent to Earth to obtain male sperm which they must bring back to Venus. Tongue-in-cheek soft core sci-fi spoof. **73m/C VHS, DVD.** Alena Penz, Nina Fredric, Gerti Sneider, Raoul Retzer, Catherine Conti, Heidi Hammer, Michael Mein, Herb Heesel; ***D:*** George Keil; ***W:*** Willi Frisch; ***C:*** Michael Marszalek, Georg Mondi; ***M:*** Hans Hammerschmid.

Two Tickets to Broadway ½ **1951** A small-town singer and a crooner arrange a hoax to get themselves on Bob Crosby's TV show. Appealing but lightweight. ♫ Let the Worry Bird Worry For You; Pagliacci; There's No Tomorrow; Manhattan; Big Chief Hole in the Ground; The Closer You Are; Baby, You'll Never Be Sorry; Pelican Falls High; It Began In Yucatan. **106m/C VHS.** Tony Martin, Janet Leigh, Gloria De Haven, Joi Lansing; ***D:*** James V. Kern; ***M:*** Leo Robin, Jule Styne.

Two Tickets to Paradise *Dirt Nap* **2006** Three middle-aged buddies finally have to accept the fact that their glory days are behind them—but they're not going down without a fight. Mark's (McGinley) family life is hurt by his serious gambling problem, McGriff (Sweeney) can't give up his rock 'n' roll dreams despite his marital troubles, and nerdy Jason (Hipp) still lives with his parents who run his life. When Jason wins tickets to the College Football Championship Bowl, it makes for an eventful road trip to Florida. Sweeney's directorial debut. **91m/C DVD.** D.B. Sweeney, John C. McGinley, Paul Hipp, Moira Kelly, Janet Jones, Ed Harris, Ned Bellamy, Pat Hingle; ***D:*** D.B. Sweeney; ***W:*** D.B. Sweeney, Brian Currie; ***C:*** Claudio Rocha; ***M:*** John E. Nordstrom.

Two to Tango ½ **1988 (R)** A hired assassin goes to Buenos Aires to kill a crime boss, and falls in love with his tango-dancing mistress. Based on the novel by J.P. Feinman. **87m/C VHS.** *AR* Don Stroud, Adrienne Sachs; ***D:*** Hector Olivera.

Two Tough Guys ½ *Dos Tipos Duros* **2003** Spanish hitman Paco (Resines) owes money to his boss Don Rodrigo (Alexandre) so he's willing to help out by looking after the Don's dim nephew Alex (Vilches). This includes paying for good-time girl Tatiana (Anaya) although Paco doesn't think this should mean that she can tag along on their next job. Uneasy mix of comedy and violence. Spanish with subtitles. **100m/C DVD.** *SP* Antonio Resines, Jordi Vilches, Elena Anaya, Rosa Maria Sarda, Manuel Alexandre; ***D:*** Juan Martinez Moreno; ***W:*** Juan Martinez Moreno; ***C:*** Gonzalo F. Berridi; ***M:*** Alex Martinez.

Two-Way Stretch ½ **1960** Three prison inmates in a progressive jail plan to break out, pull a diamond heist, and break back in, all in the same night. Fast-paced slapstick farce. **84m/B VHS, DVD.** *GB* Peter Sellers, Wilfrid Hyde-White, Liz Fraser, David Lodge; ***D:*** Robert Day.

Two Weeks ½ **2006 (R)** Wan and predictable family drama with a lot of unlikable characters (but not our Sally!). Four squabbling siblings unexpectedly find themselves together for two weeks in order to deal with their mother's upcoming death. Filmmaker Keith (Chaplin) decides to record interviews with mom Anita (Field) while the others cope (or not) in their own ways. **102m/C DVD.** Sally Field, Ben Chaplin, Julianne Nicholson, Glenn Howerton, Thomas Cavanaugh, Clea DuVall, James Murtaugh; ***D:*** Steve Stockman; ***W:*** Steve Stockman; ***C:*** Stephen Kazmierski; ***M:*** Hector Pereira.

Two Weeks in Another Town
1962 Douglas and Robinson are a couple of Hollywood has-beens who set out to make a comeback picture but meet with adversity at every turn. Extremely sappy melodrama is based on Irwin Shaw's trashy novel and represents one of director Minnelli's poorer efforts. **107m/C VHS.** Kirk Douglas, Edward G. Robinson, Cyd Charisse, George Hamilton, Daliah Lavi, Claire Trevor, James Gregory, Rosanna Schiaffino, George Macready, Stefan Schnabel, Vito Scotti, Leslie Uggams; ***D:*** Vincente Minnelli; ***C:*** Milton Krasner.

Two Weeks Notice ½ **2002 (PG-13)** We know that Bullock and Grant are master charmers and they've both done romantic comedies, so perhaps our slight disappointment in this routine pairing can be understood. Irresponsible New York playboy and real estate developer George Wade (Grant) has a history of hiring female attorneys based on looks and not professional ability. Environmental activist Lucy Kelson (Bullock) is somehow roped in as George's latest lawyer/babysitter but she eventually has enough and hands in her, well, the title says it all. Of course, the ditzy duo need to figure out that they're made for each other. **100m/C VHS, DVD.** *US* Sandra Bullock, Hugh Grant, Alicia Witt, Dana Ivey, Robert Klein, Heather Burns, David Haig, Dorian Missick; ***D:*** Marc Lawrence; ***W:*** Marc Lawrence; ***C:*** Laszlo Kovacs; ***M:*** John Powell.

Two Weeks to Live ½ **1943** The comedy team inherits a railroad line, only to find it's a pile of junk. **60m/B VHS, DVD.** Franklin Pangborn, Kay Linaker, Irving Bacon, Chester Lauck, Norris Goff; ***D:*** Malcolm St. Clair; ***W:*** Roswell Rogers, Michael L. Simmons; ***C:*** Jack MacKenzie; ***M:*** Lucien Moraweck.

Two Weeks with Love 1950 Reynolds and family wear funny bathing suits in the Catskills in the early 1900s while the Debster sings songs and blushes into young adulthood. ♫ Aba Daba Honeymoon; The Oceana Roll; A Heart That's Free; By the Light of the Silvery Moon; My Hero; Row, Row, Row; That's How I Need You; Beautiful Lady. **92m/C VHS.** Debbie Reynolds, Jane Powell, Ricardo Montalban, Louis Calhern, Ann Harding, Phyllis Kirk, Carleton Carpenter, Clinton Sundberg, Gary Gray; ***D:*** Roy Rowland.

Two Women *La Ciociara* **1961** Widowed Cesira (Loren) and her 13-year-old daughter Rosetta (Brown) travel war-torn Italy during WWII and must survive lack of food, bombings, and brutal soldiers. Tragic, moving, well-directed. Loren received well-deserved Oscar. Based on the novel by Alberto Moravia. In Italian with English subtitles or dubbed. **99m/B VHS, DVD.** *IT* Sophia Loren, Raf Vallone, Eleonora Brown, Jean-Paul Belmondo; ***D:*** Vittorio De Sica; ***W:*** Cesare Zavattini, Vittorio De Sica; ***C:*** Gabor Pogany; ***M:*** Armando Trovajoli. Oscars '61: Actress (Loren); British Acad. '61: Actress (Loren); Cannes '61: Actress (Loren); Golden Globes '62: Foreign Film; N.Y. Film Critics '61: Actress (Loren).

The Two Worlds of Jenny Logan ½ **1979** A woman travels back and forth in time whenever she dons a 19th century dress she finds in her old house. She is also able to fall in love twice, in different centuries. Adapted from "Second Sight," a novel by David Williams. Stylish and well made. **97m/C VHS.** Lindsay Wagner, Marc Singer, Alan Feinstein, Linda Gray, Constance McCashin, Henry Wilcoxon, Irene Tedrow, Joan Darling, Allen Williams, Pat Corley, Gloria Stuart; ***D:*** Frank De Felitta. **TV**

Two Wrongs Make a Right **1989** A quiet nightclub owner beats and clubs his way through his tough neighborhood to protect himself and his woman. Low budget actioner with standard plot and cool, atmospheric tone. **85m/C VHS.** Ivan Rogers, Ron Blackstone, Rich Komenich; ***D:*** Robert Brown; ***W:*** Ivan Rogers.

Two Years before the Mast ½ **1946** Charles Stewart (Ladd) is the privileged son of a ship owner who discovers just how difficult a sailor's life in the 1840s can be. Drinking in a Boston waterfront dive, he's shanghaied and pressed into service aboard the S.S. Pilgrim, which is bound for California. Sadistic Captain Thompson (da Silva) brutalizes the men in an effort to set a record time for the voyage. Stewart and the crew eventually mutiny and face trial back in Boston. Based on the novel by Richard Henry Dana. **98m/B VHS.** Alan Ladd, Howard da Silva, Brian Donlevy, William Bendix, Barry Fitzgerald, Albert Dekker, Darryl Hickman, Esther Fernandez; ***D:*** John Farrow; ***W:*** George Bruce, Seton I. Miller; ***C:*** Ernest Laszlo; ***M:*** Victor Young.

2B Perfectly Honest ½ *2BPerfectlyHonest* **2004** Frank and Josh try to strike it rich on the Internet but their agency sinks, making Frank ditch his posh Manhattan digs and—gulp—move back in with ma and pa. Another shot at success appears doomed when they find out their new investors are up to no good. **88m/C VHS, DVD.** Adam Trese, Andrew McCarthy, John Turturro, Michael Badalucco, Aida Turturro, Robert Vaughn, Hayley Mills, Mark Margolis, Kathleen Chalfant, Bruce MacVittie; ***D:*** Randel Cole; ***W:*** Randel Cole; ***C:*** Christopher La Vasseur; ***M:*** Jason Frederick. **VIDEO**

Twogether ½ **1994 (R)** Struggling artist John (Cassavettes) and environmentalist Allison (Bakke) have this lust thing going on. It leads to a drunken Las Vegas wedding and a quickie divorce but they still don't keep their hands off of each other (or any other body parts) and Allison gets pregnant. They decide to become partners in raising the baby but first they'll have to do some growing up of their own. Also available unrated. **108m/C VHS.** Brenda Bakke, Nick Cassavetes, Jeremy Piven, Jim Beaver; ***D:*** Andrew Chiaramonte; ***W:*** Andrew Chiaramonte; ***C:*** Eugene Shlugleit; ***M:*** Nigel Holton.

Tycoon ½ **1947** Wayne goes to Latin America to build a road for an American industrialist. When the industrialist insists on a shorter but more dangerous route, Wayne must satisfy his own sense of honor. Meanwhile, he's found romance with the industrialist's half-Spanish daughter. Long, but well-acted. **129m/C VHS.** John Wayne, Laraine Day, Cedric Hardwicke, Judith Anderson, James Gleason, Anthony Quinn, Jan Sterling, Grant Withers, Paul Fix, Charles Trowbridge; ***D:*** Richard Wallace; ***W:*** Borden Chase, John Twist; ***C:*** William Howard Greene, Harry Wild; ***M:*** Leigh Harline.

Tycus **1998 (R)** Journalist Jake Lowe (Onorati) investigates a suspicious mining company and discovers that visionary Peter Crawford (Hopper) has been building his own vast underground city as a modern-day Noah's Ark. Seems the Tycus comet is on a destruco course with Earth and not much is expected to survive. And when the rest of the world finds out, it'll be a race against time. **94m/C VHS, DVD.** Dennis Hopper, Peter Onorati, Finola Hughes, Chick Vennera; ***D:*** John Putch; ***W:*** Kevin Goetz; ***C:*** Ross Berryman; ***M:*** Alexander Baker, Clair Marlo. **VIDEO**

Tyler Perry's Meet the Browns ½ *Meet the Browns* **2008 (PG-13)** Single mother Brenda (Bassett) learns that her father, a man she's never met, has died, so she packs up the family and heads to Georgia for the funeral. There, she and her three children are greeted with varying degrees of Southern hospitality by a batch of half-siblings she never knew existed. Brenda then meets Harry (Fox, in a role not far from home), a handsome retired basketball player who sweeps Brenda off her feet (surprise, surprise). Typical Perry fare, loaded with racial commentary, monologues on family values, and conversations about economic struggle. **101m/C DVD, Blu-ray Disc.** *US* Angela Bassett, Rick Fox, Margaret Avery, Frankie Faison, Jenifer Lewis, Sofia Vergara, Lamman Rucker, Irma P. Hall, Tyler Perry, Lance Gross, David Mann, Tamela Mann, Judy Rhee; ***D:*** Tyler Perry; ***W:*** Tyler Perry; ***C:*** Sandi Sissel; ***M:*** Aaron Zigman.

Tyler Perry's Why Did I Get Married? ½ *Why Did I Get Married?* **2007 (PG-13)** Four couples—all friends who met as undergrads at a historically black college—navigate the rollercoaster of marriage as they gather for their annual couples retreat. Each is successful (there's a psychologist, lawyer, and pediatrician), but each relationship hides secrets and they begin to unfold over the retreat. One couple argues over having a second child; someone's sleeping with his wife's best friend; another couple fights about everything. Perry, with God's help (a theme throughout most of his work), wraps things up a bit too neatly by the end of the retreat. Despite the drama, though, the characters are both smart and refreshing. **113m/C DVD.** *US* Tyler Perry, Janet Jackson, Jill Scott, Malik Yoba, Richard T. Jones, Michael Jai White, Lamman Rucker, Sharon Leal, Tasha Smith, Denise Boutte; ***D:*** Tyler Perry; ***W:*** Tyler Perry; ***C:*** Toyomichi Kurita; ***M:*** Aaron Zigman.

Tyler Perry's Why Did I Get Married Too? *Why Did I Get Married Too* **2010** Four couples take their annual vacation together in the Bahamas and spend their time examining their marriages. Sequel to Perry's 2007 film. **m/C DVD.** Tyler Perry, Janet Jackson, Malik Yoba, Sharon Leal, Michael Jai White, Tasha Smith, Amber Stevens, Richard T. Jones, Louis Gossett Jr., Cicely Tyson; ***D:*** Tyler Perry; ***W:*** Tyler Perry; ***C:*** Toyomichi Kurita.

Typhoon *Taepung* **2006 (R)** Melodramatic action flick, filmed in Korea, Russia, and Thailand, follows North Korean exile Myong-sin (Jang), who's plotting to unleash chemical weapons during a typhoon on both South and North Korea. His family was betrayed and murdered while trying to escape the oppressive regime and he wants payback. Kang (Lee) is the military officer who must stop him. Korean with subtitles. **103m/C DVD.** *KN* Dong-Kun Jang, Lee Miyeon, Lee Jung-jae; ***D:*** Kwak Kyung-taek; ***W:*** Kwak Kyung-taek; ***C:*** Hong Kyeng-pyo.

Typhoon Treasure **1939** Whilst recovering his sunken treasure, the hero battles bad guys, savage natives and a crocodile, all of whom could probably have made a more sophisticated film. **68m/B VHS.** *AU* Campbell Copelin, Gwen Munro, Joe Valli, Douglas Herald; ***D:*** Noel Monkman.

Tyson **1995** Based on the life of former World Heavyweight Champion, Mike Tyson (White) who rose from the streets of Brownsville to a million dollar lifestyle and a spectacular fall to a rape conviction and a prison term (which are handled in voiceover). Story begins with trainer Cus D'Amato (Scott) finding unpolished and troubled young Tyson and training him for the Junior Olympics. When promoter Don King (Winfield) enters the picture, Tyson's career really takes off. Pulls no punches about Tyson's short fuse and brutal abilities. Based on the book "Fire and Fear: The Inside Story of Mike Tyson" by Jose Torres. **90m/C VHS.** Michael Jai White, Paul Winfield, George C. Scott, Malcolm Jamal Warner, Tony LoBianco, James B. Sikking, Clark Gregg, Kristen Wilson, Sheila Wills, Holt McCallany, Lilyan Chauvin, Georg Stanford Brown, Joe Santos, Charles Napier; ***D:*** Uli Edel; ***W:*** Robert P. Johnson; ***M:*** Stewart Copeland.

Tyson **1/2 2008 (R)** Toback uses his longtime friendship with the boxer to draw out the volatile former heavyweight championship in this complex bio. Toback delves into Tyson's troubled childhood, his various boxing triumphs and defeats, his relationships and prison stint, drug addiction and rehabilitation, and what happened after he hung up the gloves for good. **90m/C DVD.** *US* Mike Tyson; ***D:*** James Toback; ***C:*** Lawrence McConkey; ***M:*** Salaam Remi.

U-Boat Prisoner **1944** Bennett is an American sailor who's captured by a Nazi U-boat. He promptly defeats the crew, leaving the U-boat to the mercy of a U.S. destroyer. Silly, silly, silly. **65m/B VHS.** Bruce Bennett, John Abbott, John Wengraf, Kenneth MacDonald, Erik Rolf; ***D:*** Lew Landers.

U-571 **1/2 2000 (PG-13)** U.S sub crew is sent to steal an Enigma encryption device from a disabled Nazi U-boat before the Germans can send help. When their own sub is sunk, the Americans, led by Lt. Tyler (McConaughey), take over the German sub and try to make their way back home through enemy destroyers. Long on loud and impressive action sequences, but short on characterization and good dialogue, this one will work best for adrenalin junkies and those with theatre-quality entertainment systems. **116m/C VHS, DVD, HD DVD.** Matthew McConaughey, Bill Paxton, Harvey Keitel, Jon Bon Jovi, Jake Weber, David Keith, Terrence "T.C." Carson, Jack Noseworthy, Tom Guiry, Thomas Kretschmann, Erik Palladino, Will Estes, Matthew Settle, Dave Power, Derk Cheetwood; ***D:*** Jonathan Mostow; ***W:*** Jonathan Mostow, David Ayer, Sam Montgomery; ***C:*** Oliver Wood; ***M:*** Richard (Rick) Marvin. Oscars '00: Sound FX Editing.

U-Turn **1/2** *Stray Dogs* **1997 (R)** Bobby (Penn) is a two-bit gambler on his way to pay off the balance of a debt in Las Vegas (the down payment was two of his fingers) when he is stranded in the town of Superior, Arizona. He becomes mixed up with a married couple (Nolte and Lopez), each of whom want Bobby to kill the other. Adding to the fun in this Mayberry on mescaline are the walking grease pit of a mechanic (Thornton) and a local tough guy named TNT (Phoenix), who thinks Bobby is making a play for his nymphet girlfriend (Danes). Also appearing is the stock issue Oliver Stone wise old Indian who dispenses wisdom, or something like it. The characters meet for the predestined showdown in the desert, with predictable results. Stone has a good time taking stereotypical noir characters and putting his unique twist on them, although you may not have as much fun watching them. **125m/C VHS, DVD.** Sean Penn, Jennifer Lopez, Claire Danes, Nick Nolte, Joaquin Rafael (Leaf) Phoenix, Powers Boothe, Billy Bob Thornton, Jon Voight, Abraham Benrubi, Julie Hagerty, Bo Hopkins, Valery (Valeri Nikolayev) Nikolaev, Aida Linares, Laurie Metcalf, Liv Tyler; ***D:*** Oliver Stone; ***W:*** John Ridley; ***C:*** Robert Richardson; ***M:*** Ennio Morricone.

UFO: Target Earth **1974 (G)** Scientist attempts to fish flying saucer out of lake and costs studio $70,000. **80m/C VHS.** Nick Plakias, Cynthia Cline, Phil Erickson; ***D:*** Michael de Gaetano.

Uforia **1981** Two rival evangelists meet up with a UFO-infatuated girl. Under her guidance, they wait for UFO encounters they intend to use to milk their revivalist audiences. Sometimes clumsy, but more often fun. **92m/C VHS.** Cindy Williams, Harry Dean Stanton, Fred Ward, Hank Worden, Beverly Hope Atkinson, Harry Carey Jr., Diane Adair, Robert Gray, Ted Harris; ***D:*** John Binder; ***W:*** John Binder; ***C:*** David Myers; ***M:*** Richard Baskin.

Ugetsu **1/2** *Ugetsu Monogatari* **1953** The classic film that established Mizoguchi's reputation outside of Japan. Two 16th century Japanese peasants venture from their homes in pursuit of dreams, and encounter little more than their own hopless folly and a bit of the supernatural. A wonderful mix of comedy and action with nifty camera movement. Based on the stories of Akinara Ueda. In Japanese with English subtitles. **96m/B VHS, DVD.** *JP* Machiko Kyo, Masayuki Mori, Kinuyo Tanaka, Eitaro (Sakae, Saka Ozawa) Ozawa; ***D:*** Kenji Mizoguchi; ***W:*** Yoshikata Yoda; ***C:*** Kazuo Miyagawa; ***M:*** Fumio Hayasaka. Venice Film Fest. '53: Silver Prize.

The Ugly **1/2 1996** Confessed serial killer Simon (Rotondo) has celebrity shrink Karen (Hobbs) evaluate him to determine whether he's cured or has to stand trial for his crimes. Through flashbacks, dream sequences, and fantasies (both Simon's and the doc's), Simon's screwed-up past is revealed: mentally and physically abused by an unstable mother (Ward-Leeland) and picked on by bullies, he commits his first murder at 13. First-time director Reynolds' use of red herrings, alternate points of view, and mixing of perspectives can be hard to follow, but they do ratchet up the suspense. He also doesn't scrimp on the gore, which is highly stylized and effective. **93m/C VHS, DVD.** *NZ* Paolo Rotondo, Rebecca Hobbs, Jennifer Ward-Lealand, Roy Ward, Vanessa Byrnes; ***D:*** Scott Reynolds; ***W:*** Scott Reynolds; ***C:*** Simon Raby; ***M:*** Victoria Kelly.

The Ugly American **1/2 1963** A naive American ambassador to a small, civil-war-torn Asian country fights a miniature Cold War against northern communist influence. Too preachy, and the "Red Menace" aspects are now very dated, but Brando's performance is worth watching. Based on the William J. Lederer novel. **120m/C VHS, DVD.** Marlon Brando, Sandra Church, Eiji Okada, Pat Hingle, Arthur Hill; ***D:*** George Englund; ***W:*** Stewart Stern.

The Ugly Dachshund **1/2 1965** Jones and Pleshette are married dog lovers who raise Dachshunds. When Ruggles convinces them to take a Great Dane puppy, the fun begins! The Great Dane thinks he is a Dachshund because he has been raised with them—just imagine what happens when such a large dog acts as if he is small! Kids will love this wacky Disney film. **93m/C VHS, DVD.** Dean Jones, Suzanne Pleshette, Charlie Ruggles, Kelly Thordsen, Parley Baer, Mako; ***D:*** Norman Tokar; ***W:*** Albert Aley; ***C:*** Edward Colman; ***M:*** George Bruns.

The Ugly Truth **WOOF! 2009 (R)** This is NOT what adult women want. Shrewish prude Abby (Heigl) is a morning TV show producer with a long list of requirements for the perfect man, so it's no wonder she's still single. Then loutish ape Mike (Butler), a cable shock jock, is hired to improve ratings with his outrageously chauvinistic rants. He presumes to give Abby advice about man's typical caveman behavior, encouraging her into such ridiculously superficial changes as hair extensions, push-up bras, and vibrating panties. Since apparently Abby has absolutely no pride or dignity, she's easy to dismiss and the flick is all too predictable. A humiliating throwback (or throw-up) in more ways than one and an ugly, desperate example of what is passing for romantic comedy. **95m/C DVD.** *US* Katherine Heigl, Gerard Butler, Eric Winter, Bonnie Sommerville, Bree Turner, Nick Searcy, Cheryl Hines, John Michael Higgins, Kevin Connolly, Yvette Nicole Brown, Nathan Corddry, Noah Matthews; ***D:*** Robert Luketic; ***W:*** Kirsten Smith, Nicole Eastman, Karen McCullah; ***C:*** Russell Carpenter; ***M:*** Aaron Zigman.

UHF **1989 (PG-13)** A loser is appointed manager of a bargain-basement UHF television station. He turns it around via bizarre programming ideas. Some fun parodies of TV enhance this minimal story. Developed solely as a vehicle for Yankovic. **97m/C VHS, DVD.** Weird Al Yankovic, Kevin McCarthy, Victoria Jackson, Michael Richards, David Bowe, Anthony Geary, Stan Brock, Trinidad Silva, Gedde Watanabe, Dr. Demento, Fran Drescher, John Paragon, Emo Philips, Billy Barty; ***D:*** Jay Levey; ***W:*** Jay Levey, Weird Al Yankovic; ***C:*** David Lewis; ***M:*** John Du Prez.

UKM: The Ultimate Killing Machine **2006** Action trash. After turning war hero Dodds (Northwood) into an uncontrollable killing machine, the army decides to experiment on a group of misfits instead, in an effort to turn them into supersoldiers. The side-effects are uncontrollable rage and uncontrollable lust and since this is a co-ed group, the latter wouldn't appear to be a problem. But the human guinea pigs escape, as does the raging Dodds, and the hunt is on! **90m/C DVD.** *CA* Michael Madsen, John Evans, Simon Northwood, Mak Fyfe, Steve Arbuckle, Victoria Nestorowicz, Erin Mackinnon, Deanna Dezmari; ***D:*** David Mitchell; ***W:*** Tyler Levine, Tim McGregor; ***C:*** Marcus Elliott; ***M:*** Craig McConnell. **VIDEO**

Ulee's Gold **1997 (R)** Slow-paced, deliberate character study, set in the Florida panhandle. Ulysses "Ulee" Jackson (Fonda) is a widowed, middle-aged Vietnam vet who puts most of his energies into his work as a beekeeper, much to the detriment of his family. Son Jimmy (Wood) is in prison and druggie daughter-in-law Helen (Dunford) has disappeared, leaving the taciturn Ulee to care for his troubled granddaughters, teenaged Casey (Biel) and nine-year-old Penny (Zima). But their ordinary lives change when Helen turns up in Orlando with two violent hoods from Jimmy's past and Ulee must not only rescue her but find the emotional release to make them all a home. Splendidly moving performance from Fonda. **111m/C VHS, DVD.** Peter Fonda, Tom Wood, Vanessa Zima, Jessica Biel, Christine Dunford, Patricia Richardson, Steve Flynn, Dewey Weber, J. Kenneth Campbell; ***D:*** Victor Nunez; ***W:*** Victor Nunez; ***C:*** Virgil Marcus Mirano; ***M:*** Charles Engstrom. Golden Globes '98: Actor—Drama (Fonda); N.Y. Film Critics '97: Actor (Fonda).

Ulterior Motives **1/2 1992 (R)** P.I. Jack Blaylock agrees to protect a pretty reporter from Japanese gangsters. He finds himself caught up in deception and betrayal and uses all his considerable, and violent, skills to make certain he does his job. **90m/C VHS.** Thomas Ian Griffith, Mary Page Keller, Joe Yamanaka, Ellen Crawford, Ken Howard, Tyra Ferrell; ***D:*** James Becket.

Ultimate Desires **1991 (R)** When a high class hooker is brutally killed, beautiful Scoggins puts on what there is of the victim's clothes in order to solve the mystery. But trouble lies in wait as she actually begins to enjoy her funky new double life. Can she solve the crime before becoming lost in her own hot fantasy world? **93m/C VHS.** Tracy Scoggins, Brion James, Marc Singer, Marc Baur, Marc Bennett, Suzy Joachim, Jason Scott, John Wood; ***D:*** Lloyd A. Simandl.

The Ultimate Gift **1/2 2007 (PG)** Sentimental, sometimes preachy drama based on Jim Stovall's novel. Trust-fund twentysomething playboy Jason Stevens (Fuller) expects nothing from his estranged grandfather Red's (Garner) will. But Red, via videotaped messages, leaves Jason a fortune—with stipulations that are intended to teach him to be a better person, including bonding with young cancer patient Emily (Breslin). Pic veers off track when Jason goes to Ecuador and gets kidnapped by bandits but manages to right itself. And it's a pleasure to see old pros like Garner, Dennehy, and Cobb at work. **114m/C DVD.** *US* Drew Fuller, James Garner, Ali Hillis, Abigail Breslin, Lee Meriwether, Brian Dennehy, Bill Cobbs; ***D:*** Michael O. Sajbel; ***W:*** Cheryl McKay; ***C:*** Brian Baugh; ***M:*** Mark McKenzie, Anthony Short.

The Ultimate Imposter **1979** A secret agent acquires voluminous knowledge through a computer brain linkup, but can only retain the knowledge for 72 hours. In that timespan he has to rescue a defecting Russian from hordes of assassins. **97m/C VHS.** Keith Andes, Erin Gray, Joseph Hacker, Macon McCalman; ***D:*** Paul Stanley. **TV**

The Ultimate Thrill **1/2** *The Ultimate Chase* **1974 (PG)** Businessman's paranoia about his wife's affairs leads him to follow her to Colorado on a ski holiday and stalk her lovers. Well-filmed skiing scenes and not much else. **84m/C VHS.** Britt Ekland, Barry Brown, Michael Blodgett, John Davis Chandler, Eric (Hans Gudegast) Braeden; ***D:*** Robert Butler.

The Ultimate Warrior **1/2 1975 (R)** Yul Brynner must defend the plants and seeds of a pioneer scientist to help replenish the world's food supply in this thriller set in 2012. **92m/C VHS.** Yul Brynner, Max von Sydow, Joanna Miles, Richard Kelton, Lane Bradbury, William (Bill) Smith; ***D:*** Robert Clouse; ***W:*** Robert Clouse.

The Ultimate Weapon **1997 (R)** Mercenary Hogan destroys an IRA base camp when he realizes he's been double-crossed. **110m/C VHS, DVD.** Hulk Hogan, Carl Marotte, Cynthia (Cyndy, Cindy) Preston, Lynne Adams, Daniel Pilon; ***D:*** Jon Cassar; ***C:*** Bert Tougas; ***M:*** Marty Simon. **VIDEO**

Ultra Warrior **1/2** *Welcome to Oblivion* **1992 (R)** A basic post-apocalyptic adventure tale of a radioactive earth, mutants, and various battles by the good guys to save the planet. **80m/C VHS.** Dack Rambo, Meshach Taylor, Clare Beresford; ***D:*** Kevin Tent, Augusto Tamayo San Roman; ***W:*** Len Jenkin, Dan Kleinman; ***C:*** Cusi Barrio; ***M:*** Kevin Klingler.

Ultrachrist! **2003** It's the 21st century and Jesus is back in town—New York City, to be exact—but soon realizes that the old ways of getting his word out aren't cutting. So he dons a skin-tight superhero suit and assumes the alias Ultrachrist. But Dad isn't thrilled with this newfangled approach and Christ must prove himself, while battling his archenemy the Antichrist. Further proof that one person's blasphemy is another's fun. **92m/C VHS, DVD.** Jonathan C. Green, Celia A. Montgomery, Dara Shindler, Jordan Hoffman, Danielle Langlois, Samantha Dark, Nathaniel Graves, Bob Cohen, Jurgen Fauth, Marty Grillo, Rob Haussman, Ryan V. McCallum, Steve Montague, Leila Nelson, Michael R. Thomas; ***D:*** Kerry Douglas Dye; ***W:*** Kerry Douglas Dye, Jordan Hoffman; ***C:*** Peter Olsen; ***M:*** Howard Leshaw. **VIDEO**

Ultraviolet **1/2 1991 (R)** Another warning against playing the good samaritan. Young couple on vacation in Death Valley try to help a stranded stranger only to have him turn on them. **80m/C VHS.** Esai Morales, Stephen Meadows, Patricia Healy; ***D:*** Mark Griffiths.

Ultraviolet ☠☠ ½ **1998** Vampires walk among us. Humans are their food source and now they are threatened by humanity's ability to destroy itself and the vamps want to take control. The CIB, a secret government operation, is determined to prevent that situation. Atmospheric British miniseries in which the term "vampire" is never used—the bloodsuckers are referred to as Code Fives and the title refers to the ultraviolet light that the CIB uses in its work. **360m/C VHS, DVD.** *GB* Jack Davenport, Susannah Harker, Philip Quast, Idris Elba, Corin Redgrave, Stephen Moyer, Thomas Lockyer, Collette Brown, Fiona Dolman; ***D:*** Joe Ahearne; ***W:*** Joe Ahearne; ***C:*** Peter Greenhalgh; ***M:*** Sue Hewitt. **TV**

Ultraviolet ☠ **2006 (PG-13)** After being given a virus by the military to create a group of superhumans, sexy vamp Violet (Jovovich) must kick some major butt to save their lives when the powers-that-be decide to terminate them. Their ultimate survival rests within a boy named Six (Bright), whom Violet must protect. Set in a "Matrix"-like future world—a world where no shirt exists that properly fits Violet—writer/director Wimmer seems proud to crudely rip off a mishmash of other such action flicks as "Tomb Raider" and "Kill Bill," not to mention "Resident Evil." **89m/C DVD, Blu-ray Disc, UMD.** *US* Milla Jovovich, Cameron Bright, Nicholas Chinlund, William Fichtner, Sebastien Andrieu; ***D:*** Kurt Wimmer; ***W:*** Kurt Wimmer; ***C:*** Arthur Wong Ngok Tai; ***M:*** Klaus Badelt.

Ulysses ☠☠ ½ *Ulisse* **1955** An Italian made version of the epic poem by Homer, as the warrior returns to his homeland and the ever-faithful Penelope after the Trojan war. Ambitious effort provides for the ultimate mixed review. Douglas is good in the role and his stops along the ten-year way are well visualized. Sometimes sluggish with poor dubbing. Seven writers helped bring Homer to the big screen. **104m/C VHS, DVD.** *IT* Kirk Douglas, Silvana Mangano, Anthony Quinn, Rossana Podesta; ***D:*** Mario Camerini.

Ulysses ☠☠ ½ **1967** James Joyce's probably unfilmable novel was given a noble effort in this flawed film covering a day in the life of Leopold Bloom as he wanders through Dublin. Shot in Ireland with a primarily Irish cast. **140m/B VHS, DVD.** Milo O'Shea, Maurice Roeves, T.P. McKenna, Martin Dempsey, Sheila O'Sullivan, Barbara Jefford; ***D:*** Joseph Strick; ***W:*** Joseph Strick, Fred Haines; ***C:*** Wolfgang Suschitzky; ***M:*** Stanley Myers.

Ulysses' Gaze ☠☠ *The Look of Ulysses; To Vlemma Tou Odyssea; The Gaze of Ulysses* **1995** Nameless Greek-American filmmaker (Keitel) journeys across the Balkans from Athens to Sarajevo while making a documentary on pioneer filmmakers, the Manakia brothers, who ignored national and ethnic strife in order to record the lives of ordinary people. Keitel has heard that some undeveloped film shot by the brothers has turned up in Sarajevo and he's determined to see it despite the turmoil in Bosnia. Moving and pessimistic depiction of the Balkan conflict seen through a filmmaker's eyes. English and Greek with subtitles. **173m/C VHS, DVD.** *GR FR IT* Harvey Keitel, Maia Morgenstern, Erland Josephson, Thanassis Vengos, Yorgos Michalokopoulos, Dora Volonaki; ***D:*** Theo Angelopoulos; ***W:*** Theo Angelopoulos, Tonino Guerra, Petros Markaris; ***C:*** Yorgos Arvanitis; ***M:*** Eleni Karaindrou. Cannes '95: Grand Jury Prize.

Ulzana's Raid ☠☠☠ **1972 (R)** An aging scout and an idealistic Cavalry lieutenant lock horns on their way to battling a vicious Apache chieftain. A violent, gritty western that enjoyed critical re-evaluation years after its first release. **103m/C VHS, DVD.** Burt Lancaster, Bruce Davison, Richard Jaeckel, Lloyd Bochner, Jorge Luke; ***D:*** Robert Aldrich; ***W:*** Alan Sharp; ***C:*** Joseph Biroc; ***M:*** Frank DeVol.

Umberto D ☠☠☠☠ **1955** A government pensioner, living alone with his beloved dog, struggles to keep up a semblance of dignity on his inadequate pension. De Sica considered this his masterpiece. A sincere, tender treatment of the struggles involved with the inevitability of aging. In Italian with English subtitles. Laser edition features letterboxed print. **89m/B VHS, DVD.** *IT* Carlo Battista, Maria Pia Casilio, Lina Gennari; ***D:*** Vittorio De Sica; ***W:*** Cesare Zavattini, Vittorio De Sica; ***M:*** Alessandro Cicognini. N.Y. Film Critics '55: Foreign Film.

Umbrellas of Cherbourg ☠☠☠ ½ *Les Parapluies de Cherbourg; Die Regenschirme von Cherbourg* **1964** A bittersweet film operetta with no spoken dialog. Genevieve (Deneuve) is the teenaged daughter of a widow (Vernon) who owns an umbrella shop. She and her equally young boyfriend Guy (Castelnuovo) are separated by his military duty in Algeria. Finding she is pregnant, Genevieve marries the wealthy Roland (Michel), and when her former lover returns, he too marries someone else. But when they meet once again will their love be rekindled? Lovely photography and an evocative score enhance the story. French with subtitles; also available dubbed in English (not with the same effectiveness). **90m/C VHS, DVD.** *FR* Catherine Deneuve, Nino Castelnuovo, Anne Vernon, Ellen Farner, Marc Michel, Mireille Perrey, Jean Champion, Alfred Wolff, Dorothee Blanck; ***D:*** Jacques Demy; ***W:*** Jacques Demy; ***C:*** Jean Rabier; ***M:*** Michel Legrand. Cannes '64: Film.

Un Air de Famille ☠☠ *Respectable Families; Family Resemblances* **1996** Comedy, adapted from a play, about a dysfunctional family. They're meeting at the family's rundown bar to celebrate the birthday of son Philippe's (Yordanoff) silly wife, Yolande (Frot). The bar is run by his brother Henri (Bacri), whose wife calls to say she's left him, while their tactless mother (Maurier) frets over their sister, Betty (Jaoui), who's 30 and still single. What no one knows is that Betty has been secretly seeing Denis (Darroussin), the bartender, whom everyone thinks is simple but is actually the only one with any clue to the family's hypocrisy. French with subtitles. **107m/C VHS, DVD.** *FR* Jean-Pierre Bacri, Agnes Jaoui, Jean-Pierre Darroussin, Catherine Frot, Claire Maurier, Wladimir Yordanoff; ***D:*** Cedric Klapisch; ***W:*** Jean-Pierre Bacri, Agnes Jaoui, Cedric Klapisch; ***C:*** Benoit Delhomme. Cesar '97: Support. Actor (Darroussin), Support. Actress (Frot), Writing.

Un Chien Andalou ☠☠☠☠ *An Andalusian Dog* **1928** Masterful surrealist short features a host of classic sequences, including a razor across an eye, a severed hand lying in the street, ants crawling from a hole in a man's hand, priests, dead horses, and a piano dragged across a room. A classic. Score features both Wagner and tango. **20m/B VHS, DVD.** *FR* Pierre Batcheff, Simone Mareuil, Jaime Miravilles, Luis Bunuel, Salvador Dali; ***D:*** Luis Bunuel, Salvador Dali; ***W:*** Luis Bunuel, Salvador Dali.

Un Coeur en Hiver ☠☠ ½ *A Heart in Winter* **1993** An anti-romance romantic drama where passion is frozen and real emotion is reserved for the inanimate. Serious Stephane (Auteuil) is a master craftsman at repairing violins; his partner Maxime (Dussollier) runs the business side and deals with the musicians, including beautiful violinist Camille (Beart) with whom he has fallen in love. Camille is single-mindedly fixated on her career and she recognizes a kindred spirit in Stephane but their calculated emotional seduction causes problems for all. Can be frustrating since the smooth surface of the characters is rarely cracked. In French with English titles. **100m/C VHS, DVD.** *FR* Emmanuelle Beart, Daniel Auteuil, Andre Dussollier, Elisabeth Bourgine, Brigitte Catillon, Maurice Garrel, Miriam Boyer; ***D:*** Claude Sautet; ***W:*** Jacques Fieschi, Jerome Tonnerre; ***C:*** Yves Angelo. Cesar '93: Director (Sautet), Support. Actor (Dussollier).

Un Singe en Hiver ☠☠ ½ *A Monkey in Winter; It's Hot in Hell* **1962** A young wanderer (Belmondo) befriends a crusty old alcoholic (Gabin) who has kept his vow to abstain since his village survived the German bombing of WWII. Moving tale of regret and the passage of time. In French with English subtitles. **105m/B VHS.** Jean-Paul Belmondo, Jean Gabin, Suzanne Flon, Paul Frankeur; ***D:*** Henri Verneuil.

Unaccompanied Minors ☠☠ ½ **2006 (PG)** Mildly goofy holiday comedy meant for the pre-adolescent crowd finds a disparate group of kids left by various adults at a midwestern airport to begin their solo travels on Christmas Eve. Only there's a blizzard and all flights are cancelled, leaving the little darlings to plot their escape from the control of airport stooge Mr. Porter (Black) and more sympathetic staffer Zach (Valderrama). Mayhem ensues. **87m/C DVD.** *US* Brett Kelly, Lewis Black, Wilmer Valderrama, Paget Brewster, Tyler James Williams, Dyllan Christopher, Gina Mantegna, Quinn Shephard, Dominique Saldana, Jessica Walter, David Koechner, Rob Corddry, Teri Garr, Michelle Sandler; ***D:*** Paul Feig; ***W:*** Jacob Meszaros, Mya Stark; ***C:*** Christopher Baffa; ***M:*** Michael Andrews.

The Unapproachable ☠☠ ½ **1982** A rendition of the Polish director's two one-act plays concerning a reclusive aging stage star being manipulated by her hangers-on. **92m/C VHS.** *PL* Leslie Caron, Danny (Daniel) Webb, Leslie Malton; ***D:*** Krzysztof Zanussi.

The Unbearable Lightness of Being ☠☠☠ ½ **1988 (R)** Tomas (Day Lewis), a young Czech doctor in the late 1960s, leads a sexually and emotionally carefree existence with a number of women, including provocative artist Olin. When he meets the fragile Binoche, he may be falling in love for the first time. On the eve of the 1968 Russian invasion of Czechoslovakia the two flee to Switzerland, but Binoche can't reconcile herself to exile and returns, followed by the reluctant Tomas who has lost his position because of his new-found political idealism. They lead an increasingly simple life, drawn ever closer together. The haunting ending caps off superb performances. Based on the novel by Milan Kundera. **172m/C VHS, DVD.** Daniel Day-Lewis, Juliette Binoche, Lena Olin, Derek de Lint, Erland Josephson, Pavel Landovsky, Donald Moffat, Daniel Olbrychski, Stellan Skarsgard, Tormek Bork, Bruce Myers, Pavel Slaby, Pascale Kalensky, Jacques Ciron, Anne Lonnberg, Laszlo Szabo, Vladimir Valenta, Clovis Cornillac, Leon Lissek, Consuelo de Haviland; ***D:*** Philip Kaufman; ***W:*** Jean-Claude Carriere, Philip Kaufman; ***C:*** Sven Nykvist; ***M:*** Mark Adler, Ernie Fosselius, Leos Janacek. British Acad. '88: Adapt. Screenplay; Ind. Spirit '89: Cinematog.; Natl. Soc. Film Critics '88: Director (Kaufman), Film.

The Unbelievable Truth ☠☠ ½ **1990 (R)** Ex-con Robocop-to-be Burke meets armageddon-obsessed model and sparks fly until bizarre murder occurs. Quirky black comedy shot in less than two weeks. **100m/C VHS, DVD.** Adrienne Shelly, Robert John Burke, Christopher Cooke, Julia Mueller, Julia McNeal, Mark Bailey, Gary Sauer, Kathrine Mayfield; ***D:*** Hal Hartley; ***W:*** Hal Hartley; ***C:*** Michael Spiller; ***M:*** Jim Coleman.

The Unborn ☠ ½ **1991 (R)** An infertile wife gets inseminated at unorthodox clinic. But once pregnant she suspects that her unborn baby is a monstrous being. Tasteless B-movie with an A-performance from Adams; if the rest had been up to her standard this could have been another "Stepford Wives." Instead it cops out with cheap gore. **85m/C VHS, DVD.** Brooke Adams, Jeff Hayenga, James Karen, K. Callan, Jane Cameron; ***D:*** Rodman Flender; ***W:*** John Brancato; ***C:*** Wally Pfister; ***M:*** Gary Numan, Michael R. Smith.

The Unborn ☠ **2009 (PG-13)** Fabulously-gorgeous co-ed Casey Beldon (Yustman) begins seeing disturbing images of a frightening young boy. Fearing she may be losing her sanity as her mother had years before, Casey turns to a Holocaust survivor (Alexander), who explains the events through a family connection to medical experiments performed by the Nazis on Casey's unborn twin brother nicknamed Jumby, who died in utero. Unnerving bugs, a freakish dog, scary mirrors, and the fact that Jumby wants to be born signals the need for Rabbi Sendak (Oldman) to perform an exorcism. The whole Nazi tie-in is a stretch and the final scene stalls, but heck, the Jewish exorcism theme is at least somewhat novel. **86m/C DVD.** *US* Odette Yustman, Gary Oldman, Cam Gigandet, Meagan Good, Jane Alexander, Idris Elba, Carla Gugino, James Remar; ***D:*** David S. Goyer; ***W:*** David S. Goyer; ***C:*** James Hawkinson; ***M:*** Ramin Djawadi, Spring Aspers.

The Unborn 2 ☠ **1994 (R)** Greene's blood-craving baby thinks nothing of feasting off the babysitter until a gun-wielding avenger comes to the rescue. Some notably gross scenes. **84m/C VHS, DVD.** Michele Greene, Scott Valentine, Robin Curtis; ***D:*** Rick Jacobson.

Unborn but Forgotten ☠☠ *Hayanbang; White Room* **2002 (R)** A female journalist investigates why pregnant women who visit an abortion web site called the White Room all die within 15 days after having given birth. Of course she visits it herself, and the clock starts ticking as she suddenly becomes pregnant. Coincidentally she also finds out from the families none of the other women were supposed to be pregnant either. Should only cause minor computer phobia seeing as it's not nearly as interesting as the description makes it sound. **90m/C DVD.** *KN* Jun-ho Jeong, Eun-ju Lee; ***D:*** Chang-jae Lim; ***W:*** Hyon-geun Han; ***C:*** Hui-ju Park; ***M:*** Jeong-a Kim.

Unbreakable ☠☠ ½ **2000 (PG-13)** Willis reteams with "The Sixth Sense" writer/director Shyamalan for another spooky saga. He's not only the sole survivor of a train crash but he emerged without a scratch, which intrigues Jackson, who suffers from brittle bone disease. Shyamalan still knows how to hold attention, and the look and feel of the movie are mesmerizing, but this time the story doesn't quite hold up. You'll either find this one a keeper or a head-scratcher. **107m/C VHS, DVD.** Bruce Willis, Samuel L. Jackson, Robin Wright Penn, Spencer (Treat) Clark, Charlaine Woodard, James Handy, Elizabeth Lawrence, Leslie Stefanson, Eamonn Walker; ***D:*** M. Night Shyamalan; ***W:*** M. Night Shyamalan; ***C:*** Eduardo Serra; ***M:*** James Newton Howard.

Uncaged ☠ *Angel in Red* **1991 (R)** Five beautiful young prostitutes hit Sunset Strip, each of them dreaming of a better life. When a crazy pimp brutally murders one of their friends, they set out to avenge that girl, and her broken dreams. **78m/C VHS.** Leslie Bega, Jeffrey Dean Morgan, Pamella D'Pella, Gregory Millar, Henry Brown, Jason Oliver, Elena Sahagun; ***D:*** William Duprey; ***W:*** Robert Alden, Joan Freeman, Catherine Cyran.

The Uncanny WOOF! **1978** Horror anthology of three tales concerned with feline attempts to control the world. Waste of good cast and cats on silly stories. Not released in the U.S. **85m/C VHS.** *GB* Peter Cushing, Ray Milland, Samantha Eggar, Donald Pleasence; ***D:*** Denis Heroux.

Uncertain Glory ☠☠ **1944** Errol plays a French thief who's willing to pretend to be a saboteur and die for his country. Based on a story by Joe May and Laszlo Vadnay. **102m/B VHS.** Errol Flynn, Paul Lukas, Jean Sullivan, Lucile Watson, Faye Emerson, James Flavin, Douglass Dumbrille, Dennis Hoey, Sheldon Leonard; ***D:*** Raoul Walsh; ***W:*** Laszlo Vadnay, Max Brand.

The Unchastened Woman ☠☠ **1925** A married couple is torn apart by infidelity despite their impending parenthood, and wife Bara heads overseas to run wild and have the baby. She returns with a foreign flame, whom she dumps when erstwhile husband finds fatherly feelings in his heart. One of Bara's last films. **52m/B VHS.** Theda Bara, Wyndham Standing, Dale Fuller, John Miljan; ***D:*** James L. Young.

Uncivilized ☠☠ *Endangered* **1994** Young couple, on a vacation in the mountains, run into a gang of drug runners who don't want their whereabouts revealed. So, the duo have to play a deadly game of hide-and-seek to survive. **90m/C VHS.** Sandra Hess, Dale Dye, Renee Estevez, Richard Hench, Martin Kove, Rick Aiello; ***D:*** Nick Kellis; ***W:*** Nick Kellis; ***C:*** Arnold Peterson; ***M:*** Peter Waldman.

Uncle Buck ☠☠☠ **1989 (PG)** When Mom and Dad have to go away suddenly, the only babysitter they can find is good ol' Uncle Buck, a lovable lout who spends much of his time smoking cigars, trying to make up with his girlfriend, and enforcing the teenage daughter's chastity. More intelligent than the average slob/teen comedy with a heart, due in large part to Candy's dandy performance. Memorable pancake scene. **100m/C VHS, DVD.** John Candy, Amy Madigan, Jean (Louisa) Kelly, Macaulay Culkin, Jay Underwood, Gaby Hoffman, Laurie Metcalf, Elaine Bromka, Garrett M. Brown; ***D:*** John Hughes; ***W:*** John Hughes; ***C:***

Ralf Bode; ***M:*** Ira Newborn.

Uncle Moses 1/2 **1932** The clash of old-world values and new-world culture in a story of East European Jewish immigrants transplanted to turn of the century New York's Lower East Side. Patriarch Uncle Moses struggles to keep traditional family values as romantic difficulties and labor union struggles intrude. Based on the novel by Sholem Asch. In Yiddish with English subtitles. **87m/B VHS.** Maurice Schwartz, Rubin Goldberg, Judith Abarbanel, Zvee Scooler; ***D:*** Sidney Goldin, Aubrey Scotto.

Uncle Nino 1/2 **2003 (PG)** Financially comfortable, but mildly dysfunctional, family headed by clueless dad (Mantegna) gets an unexpected visit from their colorful Italian uncle (Mascarino). He injects a little chaos into their lives, helping them to relax and smell the roses. Saccharin sweet family movie destined to please the masses. **104m/C** *US* Joe Mantegna, Anne Archer, Pierrino Mascarino, Trevor Morgan, Gina Mantegna; ***D:*** Robert Shallcross; ***W:*** Robert Shallcross; ***C:*** Hugo Cortina; ***M:*** Larry Pecorella.

Uncle Sam **1996 (R)** The box art is cool but this is basically a video horror. Desert Storm hero Sam Harper (Fralick) returns home—in a coffin. Only he doesn't stay dead and decides to liven up his small town's Fourth of July celebration by dressing up as Uncle Sam and going on a killing spree. **91m/C VHS, DVD.** David "Shark" Fralick, Timothy Bottoms, Robert Forster, Isaac Hayes, Bo Hopkins; ***D:*** William Lustig; ***W:*** Larry Cohen; ***C:*** James Lebovitz; ***M:*** Mark Governor. **VIDEO**

Uncle Tom's Cabin **1914** Satisfying version of Harriet Beecher Stowe's tale from the view of a founder of the underground railroad. Lucas was the first black actor to garner a lead role. **54m/C VHS.** Mary Eline, Irving Cummings, Sam Lucas; ***D:*** William Robert Daly.

Uncle Tom's Cabin 1/2 **1927** Universal Studios' $2 million production was one of the costliest of the silent era, with more than 2400 actors, and a shooting schedule of 19 months. It follows Harriet Beecher Stowe's abolitionist novel about a black family torn apart by slavery. This version contains heroine Eliza's (Fischer) flight across the ice floes, which was borrowed by D.W. Griffith for his film "Way Down East." **112m/B VHS, DVD.** James B. Lowe, Margarita Fischer, George Siegmann, Virginia Grey; ***D:*** Harry A. Pollard; ***W:*** Harry A. Pollard, Harvey Thew; ***C:*** Charles Stumar, Jacob Kull; ***M:*** Erno Rapee.

Uncle Tom's Cabin 1/2 *Onkel Toms Hutte; La Case de L'Oncle Tom; Cento Dollari D'Odio; Cica Tomina Koliba* **1969 (G)** Ambitious adaptation of Harriet Beecher Stowe's stirring book about the Southern slavery and the famous underground railroad devised to aid those most determined to reach freedom. The film has the habit of drifting away from the facts. Though set in Kentucky, the picture was filmed in Yugoslavia with an international cast. **120m/C VHS.** *FR IT YU GE* Herbert Lom, John Kitzmiller, Otto Wilhelm Fischer, Eleanora Rossi-Drago, Mylene Demongeot, Juliette Greco; ***D:*** Geza von Radvanyi; ***V:*** Ella Fitzgerald.

Uncle Tom's Cabin 1/2 **1987** The first American sound version of this film. Excellent cast and interestingly adapted script are perfect for a message that is still socially relevant today. Based on the novel by Harriet Beecher Stowe. **110m/C VHS.** Avery Brooks, Kate Burton, Bruce Dern, Paula Kelly, Phylicia Rashad, Kathryn Walker, Edward Woodward, Frank Converse, George Coe, Albert Hall; ***D:*** Stan Lathan. **TV**

Uncle Was a Vampire *Tempi Duri per i Vampiri; Hard Times for Vampires* **1959** An impoverished Italian count has turned his castle into a hotel. But staying there could be hazardous to a guest's health since the count was bitten by a vampire. **85m/C VHS.** *IT* Christopher Lee, Kai (Kay) Fischer, Renato Rascel, Sylva Koscina, Lia Zoppelli, Susanne Loret; ***D:*** Steno; ***W:*** Edoardo Anton; ***C:*** Marco Scarpelli.

Uncommon Valor 1/2 **1983 (R)** After useless appeals to the government for information on his son listed as "missing in action" in Vietnam, Colonel Rhodes takes matters into his own hands. Hackman is solid and believable as always, surrounded with good cast in generally well-paced film. **105m/C VHS, DVD.** Gene Hackman, Fred Ward, Reb Brown, Randall "Tex" Cobb, Robert Stack, Patrick Swayze, Harold Sylvester, Tim Thomerson; ***D:*** Ted Kotcheff; ***C:*** Stephen Burum; ***M:*** James Horner.

Unconditional Love **2003 (PG-13)** Watch it for Bates's performance because otherwise there's not much here (or maybe there's too much going on). Chicago housewife Grace Beasley (Bates) is abruptly dumped by hubby Max (Aykroyd) who needs his space. Meanwhile, a Chicago serial killer has just offed closeted lounge singer Victor Fox (Pryce), leaving his in-the-shadows lover Dirk (Everett) to battle with Victor's sister Nola (Redgrave) over his estate. Fan Grace meets Dirk at Victor's funeral, they bond, and decide to hunt for Victor's killer together. Hey, it's one way to deal with unresolved feelings. **122m/C VHS, DVD.** Kathy Bates, Rupert Everett, Lynn Redgrave, Meredith Eaton, Dan Aykroyd, Jonathan Pryce, Peter Sarsgaard, Stephanie Beacham, Richard Briers, Jack Noseworthy, Daniel Wyllie; ***D:*** P.J. Hogan; ***W:*** P.J. Hogan, Jocelyn Moorhouse; ***C:*** Remi Adefarasin; ***M:*** James Newton Howard.

Unconquered 1/2 **1947** Silly epic about America finds indentured servant Abby (Goddard), meeting Virignia militia man Christopher Holden (Cooper). He nobly buys her contract and frees her but scurvy trader Martin Garth (da Silva) manages to get Abby working in his saloon. Garth also illegally sells guns to the local Seneca Indian tribe and persuades their chief, Guyasuta (Karloff), to attack the colonists. Cooper has to keep rescuing Goodard throughout the movie, as well as battling da Silva and helping the settlers fight Indians. Based on the novel "The Judas Tree" by Neil H. Swanson. **147m/C VHS, DVD.** Gary Cooper, Paulette Goddard, Howard da Silva, Boris Karloff, Cecil Kellaway, Ward Bond, Katherine DeMille, Henry Wilcoxon, Sir C. Aubrey Smith, Victor Varconi, Virginia Grey, Mike Mazurki, Porter Hall; ***D:*** Cecil B. DeMille; ***W:*** Charles Bennett, Jesse Lasky Jr., Frederic M. Frank; ***C:*** Ray Rennahan; ***M:*** Victor Young.

Unconquered Bandit 1/2 **1935** Tom Morgan is seeking revenge for his father's death at the hands of cattle rustling outlaws controlled by crooked San Diego politician Frank Cleyburn. Cleyburn's new scheme is running off the local landowners, who have discovered gold on their properties. Tom bargains with local bandito the Night Hawk to assume his identity so Tom can raid Cleyburn's properties. Tom also begins to court Helen, Cleyburn's niece, in order to use her as a pawn in a marriage scheme but naturally falls in love with her and has to change his plans. **59m/B DVD.** Tom Tyler, Slim Whitaker, Lillian Gilmore, William (Bill) Gould, John Elliott, Earl Dwire, Joe de la Cruz; ***D:*** Harry S. Webb; ***W:*** Lewie Borden; ***C:*** J. Henry Kruse.

Uncorked 1/2 *At Sachem Farm; Higher Love* **1998 (PG)** British ex-pats gather together in Simi Valley, California to essentially drive each other crazy. Ross (Sewell) is visiting his family in order to close a deal on selling some rare wines so he can get the money to support another get-rich-quick scheme. But he's thwarted by his eccentric Uncle Cullen (Hawthorne) who wants Ross to do something he passionately believes in (which happens to be music). Ross also has a reclusive, nutty brother Paul (Rodgers), and then there's his snooty girlfriend Kendal (Driver) who really wants her ex-boyfriend, Tom (Sporleder) back. It's predictable but pleasant. **95m/C VHS, DVD.** Rufus Sewell, Nigel Hawthorne, Minnie Driver, Michael E. Rodgers, Gregory Sporleder, Amelia Heinle, Keone Young; ***D:*** John Huddles; ***W:*** John Huddles; ***C:*** Mark Vicente; ***M:*** Jeff Danna.

Uncovered *La Tabla de Flandes* **1994 (R)** Julia (Beckinsale at the beginning of her career) is restoring a 500-year-old painting of a chess game when she discovers an inscription hidden on the painting that says "Who killed the knight?". Some investigation indicates the painter was telling the story of a series of killings that followed the pattern of play in the painting, and that pattern is being duplicated in the present day. Complex and interesting story is undermined by poor acting (Beckinsale's inexperience shows) and inconsistent direction. **112m/C VHS, DVD.** *GB SP* Kate Beckinsale, John Wood, Sinead Cusack, Peter Wingfield, Helen McCrory, Michael Gough, Art Malik, James Villiers, Paudge Behan; ***D:*** Jim McBride; ***W:*** Jim McBride, Jack Baran, Michael Hirst; ***C:*** Alfonso Beato; ***M:*** Philippe Sarde. **VIDEO**

Uncovered: The War on Iraq 1/2 **2004** Documentary presents case against Bush administration's decision to go to war with Iraq through interviews with authorities ranging from weapons inspectors and C.I.A. analysts to ex-military and diplomatic figures. Another in a slew of anti-Bush documentaries released in election year of 2004. Drier and less theatrical than political heavyweight Michael Moore, but the straightforward style make it effective and convincing. **83m/C DVD.** ***D:*** Robert Greenwald; ***C:*** Richard Perez, Glen Pearcy, Bob Sullivan, Scott Williams, Hamish Campbell, Marc Levy, Bob Seeberger; ***M:*** Jim Ervin, Brad Chiet, Mars Lasar.

The Undead **1957** A prostitute is accidentally sent back to the Middle Ages as the result of a scientific experiment and finds herself condemned to die for witchcraft. Early Corman script filled with convoluted storylines, laughable characters, violence, and heaving bosoms. **75m/B VHS, DVD.** Paul Blaisdell, Pamela Duncan, Richard Garland, Allison Hayes, Mel Welles, Richard Devon, Billy Barty, Dick Miller, Val Dufour, Dorothy Neumann, Aaron Saxon, Bruno VeSota; ***D:*** Roger Corman; ***W:*** Charles B. Griffith, Mark Hanna; ***C:*** William Sickner; ***M:*** Ronald Stein.

Undead 1/2 **2005 (R)** A freakish meteor shower falls upon the residents of Berkeley, Queensland, tainting the water supply and causing the locals to morph into brain-munching zombies, except, of course, for a few lucky(?) unaffected folks who band together at an outback farmhouse with the area's resident kooky gun nut. As they try to fend off the mutants some aliens arrive. Not much of a point, but then it is a zombie flick. If you like your zombies with an Aussie accent, give this one a try, but don't say you weren't warned. **100m/C DVD.** Felicity Mason, Mungo McKay, Lisa Cunningham, Dirk Hunter, Dirk Hunter, Emma Randall, Steve Greig, Noel Sheridan, Gaynor Wensley, Eleanor Stillman, Peter Spierig; ***D:*** Peter Spierig, Michael Spierig; ***W:*** Peter Spierig, Michael Spierig; ***C:*** Andrew Strahorn; ***M:*** Cliff Bradley.

Undead or Alive **2007 (R)** Unlikely cowboy Luke (Kattan) and his new partner, army deserter Elmer (Denton), run a con on a corrupt sheriff and escape into the desert. Only they're pursued by angry Sheriff Claypool (Besser) and his posse. The duo meets up with Native American Sue (Rawat) and learn that because of Geronimo's curse all the local white settlers and soldiers are turning into zombies. About as dumb as you can imagine. **91m/C DVD.** Chris Kattan, James Denton, Navi Rawat, Matt Besser, Christopher Coppola; ***D:*** Glasgow Phillips; ***W:*** Glasgow Phillips; ***C:*** Thomas Callaway; ***M:*** Ivan Koutikov. **VIDEO**

Undeclared War **1991 (R)** Suspenseful espionage thriller that takes you behind the scenes of an international terrorist plot, which has been cleverly disguised as a bloody global revolution. Intense action heightened by conflicts between worldwide intelligence networks, the news media and terrorist organizations. **103m/C VHS, DVD.** Vernon Wells, David Hedison, Olivia Hussey, Peter Lapis; ***D:*** Ringo Lam.

Undefeatable 1/2 **1994 (R)** Rothrock is out to avenge the murder of her sister at the hands of a serial killer who, coincidentally, happens to be a martial arts expert. You watch for Cynthia to kick butt not for plot anyway. **88m/C VHS.** Cynthia Rothrock, Don Niam, John Miller, Donna Jason; ***D:*** Godfrey Ho.

The Undefeated **1969 (G)** A Confederate and Yankee find they must team up on the Rio Grande. They attempt to build new lives in the Spanish held Mexico territory, but are caught in the battle for Mexican independence. Standard fare made palatable only by Wayne and Hudson. **119m/C VHS, DVD.** John Agar, John Wayne, Rock Hudson, Lee Meriwether, Merlin Olsen, Bruce Cabot, Ben Johnson, Jan-Michael Vincent, Harry Carey Jr., Antonio Aguilar, Roman Gabriel; ***D:*** Andrew V. McLaglen; ***C:*** William Clothier.

Undefeated **2003** Leguizamo stars and makes his directorial debut in this too-familiar boxing tale. Lex Vargas (Leguizamo) is a tough amateur boxer from Queens who comes under the tutelage of Victor (Serrano). Victor believes in a slow and steady rise but manager Mack (Miller) and promoter Scott Green (Forster) offer up a more enticing proposal. And then Vargas falls for Mack's girlfriend Lizette (Ferlito), who's stringing both men along. As Vargas climbs the boxing ladder, it's suggested that maybe he should take a dive with next opponent, Beveaqua (De Los Reyes), in order to get a bigger payday down the road. Leguizamo broods effectively. **90m/C VHS, DVD.** John Leguizamo, Nestor Serrano, Omar Benson Miller, Robert Forster, Vanessa Ferlito, Kamar De Los Reyes, Clifton (Gonzalez) Collins Jr., Guillermo Diaz; ***D:*** John Leguizamo; ***W:*** Frank Pugliese; ***C:*** Enrique Chediak; ***M:*** Roy Nathanson, Bill Ware. **CABLE**

Under California Stars *Under California Skies* **1948** Shady gang making a living rounding up wild horses decides they can make more money by capturing Rogers' horse, Trigger. **71m/C VHS, DVD.** Roy Rogers, Andy Devine, Jane Frazee; ***D:*** William Witney.

Under Capricorn 1/2 **1949** Bergman is an Irish lass who follows her convict husband Cotten out to 1830s Australia where he makes a fortune. She turns to drink, perhaps because of his neglect, and has her position usurped by a housekeeper with designs on her husband. When Bergman's cousin (Wilding) arrives, Cotten may have cause for his violent jealousy. There's a plot twist involving old family skeletons, but this is definitely lesser Hitchcock. Adapted from the Helen Simpson novel. Remade in 1982. **117m/C VHS, DVD.** *GB* Ingrid Bergman, Joseph Cotten, Michael Wilding, Margaret Leighton, Jack Watling, Cecil Parker, Denis O'Dea; ***D:*** Alfred Hitchcock; ***C:*** Jack Cardiff.

Under Capricorn **1982** An Australian remake of the 1949 Hitchcock film about family secrets, an unhappy marriage, and violence set in 1830s' Australia. **120m/C VHS.** *AU* Lisa Harrow, John Hallam, Peter Cousens, Julia Blake, Catherine Lynch; ***D:*** Rod Hardy.

Under Colorado Skies 1/2 **1947** Medical student Hale is accused of robbery and escapes the law to clear his name. **65m/C VHS.** Monte Hale, Adrian Booth, Paul Hurst, Tom London; ***D:*** R.G. Springsteen; ***W:*** Louise Rousseau; ***C:*** Alfred S. Keller.

Under Fire 1/2 **1983 (R)** Three foreign correspondents, old friends from the past working together, find themselves in Managua, witnessing the 1979 Nicaraguan revolution. In a job requiring objectivity, but a situation requiring taking sides, they battle with their ethics to do the job right. Fine performances, including Harris as a mercenary. Interesting view of American media and its political necessities. **128m/C VHS, DVD.** Gene Hackman, Nick Nolte, Joanna Cassidy, Ed Harris, Richard Masur, Hamilton Camp, Jean-Louis Trintignant; ***D:*** Roger Spottiswoode; ***W:*** Clayton Frohman, Ron Shelton; ***C:*** John Alcott; ***M:*** Jerry Goldsmith.

Under Heavy Fire 1/2 *Going Back* **2001 (R)** Formulaic "war is hell" story that has lots of flashbacks filled with rather graphic violence. In 1968, the Marines of Echo company came under a friendly fire bombing during a raid on an enemy village in 'Nam. The men blamed their captain, Ramsey (Van Dien), for the incident. Some 30 years later, the survivors (including Ramsey) meet up in Saigon at the request of journalist Kathleen (Otis) to get to the truth. **118m/C VHS, DVD.** Casper Van Dien, Carre Otis, Jaimz Woolvett, Bobby Hosea, Daniel Kash, Martin Kove; ***D:*** Sidney J. Furie; ***W:*** Greg Mellott; ***C:*** Curtis Petersen; ***M:*** Amin Bhatia.

Under Hellgate Bridge **1999 (R)** Familiar New York crime drama is set in the Astoria neighborhood of Queens. Ryan (Rodrick) is just outa prison (it was a bum rap) and heads home to find slick wiseguy Vincent (LaPaglia) has taken over his territory and his old girlfriend, Carla (Bayne). The situation gets messy. **87m/C VHS, DVD.** *US* Brian Vincent, Careena Melia, Michael Rodrick,

Jonathan LaPaglia, Jordan Bayne, Frank Vincent, Vincent Pastore, Dominic Chianese; ***D:*** Michael Sergio; ***W:*** Michael Sergio; ***C:*** Leland Krane; ***M:*** Stephan Moccio.

Under Investigation 1/2 **1993 (R)** Burned out cop Hamlin is after a crazed killer. His cool lover Pacula turns out to be the prime suspect. Who's deceiving who? **94m/C VHS.** Harry Hamlin, Joanna Pacula, Ed Lauter, Richard Beymer, Lydie Denier; ***D:*** Kevin Meyer; ***W:*** Kevin Meyer.

Under Milk Wood 1/2 **1973 (PG)** An adaptation of the Dylan Thomas play about the lives of the residents of a village in Wales. Burton and O'Toole are wonderful in this uneven, but sometimes engrossing film. **90m/C VHS, DVD.** *GB* Richard Burton, Elizabeth Taylor, Peter O'Toole, Glynis Johns, Vivien Merchant; ***D:*** Andrew Sinclair.

Under Montana Skies 1/2 **1930** An early talkie western features music and comedy in abundance, relegating the action to second place. A singing cowboy protects a travelling burlesque show from evildoers. **55m/B VHS.** Kenneth Harlan, Dorothy Gulliver, Lafe (Lafayette) McKee, Ethel Wales, Slim Summerville; ***D:*** Richard Thorpe.

Under Nevada Skies 1/2 **1946** Fairly good matinee-era western centers on a missing map to a uranium deposit, climaxing with Rogers heading a posse of Indian allies to the rescue. The Sons of the Pioneers contribute songs. **69m/B VHS, DVD.** Roy Rogers, George "Gabby" Hayes, Dale Evans, Douglass Dumbrille, Tristram Coffin, Rudolph Anders, Iron Eyes Cody; ***D:*** Frank McDonald.

Under Oath *Urban Justice; Blood Money* **1997 (R)** Financially strapped cops Scalia and Velez accidentally kill a drug runner in a shakedown and then learn he was an undercover ATF agent. Then they're assigned to investigate their own crime. Cast does good work in slick genre fare. **89m/C VHS, DVD.** Jack Scalia, James Russo, Eddie Velez, Richard Lynch, Abraham Benrubi, Beth Grant, Clint Howard, Robert LaSardo; ***D:*** Dave Payne; ***W:*** Scott Sandin; ***C:*** Mike Michiewicz; ***M:*** Roger Neil. **VIDEO**

Under One Roof 1/2 **2002** Cute Daniel Chang (Wong) is a Chinese-American guy living with his tradition-bound mother (Lee) in San Francisco. She wants grandchildren and keeps introducing her son to suitable Chinese girls. Daniel is keeping secret the fact that he's gay—until mom rents out the basement flat to new-to-the-city Robert (Marks). Daniel's attracted and if Robert reciprocates, Mother Chang is in for a big surprise. Sweet story if unevenly told. **76m/C VHS, DVD.** Jay Wong, James Marks, Sandra Lee, Vivian Kobayashi; ***D:*** Todd Wilson; ***W:*** David Lewis; ***C:*** Dan Schmeltzer; ***M:*** Jack Curtis Dubowsky.

Under Pressure **1998 (R)** What do you do when your neighbor tries to run your life? It's hot, the kids are cranky, you're cranky, and the guy next door comes over to complain about everything you do. Only he doesn't just complain—he threatens you, but the cops won't do anything to help. **88m/C VHS.** Charlie Sheen, Mare Winningham, John Ratzenberger, David Andrews; ***D:*** Craig R. Baxley; ***W:*** Betsy Giffen Nowrasteh.

Under Satan's Sun *Under the Sun of Satan; Sous le Soleil de Satan* **1987** A rural priest is tortured by what he sees as his sins and failings to his parishioners. He is further tempted from the straight path by a beautiful murderess, a worldly priest, and, perhaps by Satan in disguise. Stylized film is not easily accessible, but Depardieu's performance is worth the effort. Based on the Georges Bernanos book "Diary of a Country Priest." In French with English subtitles. **97m/C VHS.** *FR* Gerard Depardieu, Sandrine Bonnaire, Yann Dedet, Alain Artur, Maurice Pialat; ***D:*** Maurice Pialat; ***W:*** Maurice Pialat. Cannes '87: Film.

Under Siege **1992 (R)** The USS Missouri becomes the battleground for good-guy-with-a-secret-past Seagal. He's up against the deranged Jones, as an ex-Special Forces leader, and Busey, a corrupt naval officer looking to steal the battleship's nuclear arsenal. May be predictable (especially the graphic violence) but the action is fast, the villains swaggering, and Seagal efficient at dispatching the enemy. Work for "Die Hard 3" was reportedly scrapped after Warner announced this film because DH's John McClane was supposed to save the passengers of a boat from terrorists. Sound familiar? **100m/C VHS, DVD, Blu-ray Disc.** Steven Seagal, Tommy Lee Jones, Gary Busey, Patrick O'Neal, Erika Eleniak, Dale Dye, Richard Jones; ***D:*** Andrew Davis; ***W:*** J.F. Lawton; ***C:*** Frank Tidy; ***M:*** Gary Chang.

Under Siege 2: Dark Territory **1995 (R)** Kicking terrorists' butts and slinging hash have worn out ex-Navy SEAL and gourmet chef Casey Ryback (Seagal), so he takes a little vacation to the Rocky Mountains. By coincidence, the train he boards is command central for psychotic computer expert Dane's (Bogosian) scheme to control the world's deadliest satellite. Pretty familiar territory for Seagal, who's acting technique consists of "look mad and hurt poeple." Bigger budget means bigger, and more frequent, explosions. Bogosian takes over the Jones/Busey role of evil villain-talented actor. **100m/C VHS, DVD.** Steven Seagal, Eric Bogosian, Katherine Heigl, Morris Chestnut, Everett McGill, Andy Romano, Nick Mancuso, Brenda Bakke, Dale Dye; ***D:*** Geoff Murphy; ***W:*** Richard Hatem; ***C:*** Robbie Greenberg; ***M:*** Basil Poledouris.

Under Suspicion 1/2 **1992 (R)** Christmas 1959 in Brighton finds seedy private eye Tony Aaron and his wife faking adultery cases for those desperate to get around England's strict divorce laws. Sordid tale takes a turn when Tony bursts in to snap incriminating photos and finds both his wife and their client, a famous artist, murdered. Dark who-dunnit has some interesting twists that could have made it exceptional rather than the conventional melodrama it turned out to be. Neeson is very good as the charmingly sleazy Tony but nobody else stands out, except the unfortunately miscast San Giacomo. Theatrical feature debut for director Moore. **99m/C VHS, DVD.** *GB* Liam Neeson, Laura San Giacomo, Alphonsia Emmanuel, Kenneth Cranham, Maggie O'Neill, Martin Grace, Stephen Moore; ***D:*** Simon Moore; ***W:*** Simon Moore; ***C:*** Vernon Layton; ***M:*** Christopher Gunning. **TV**

Under Suspicion 1/2 **2000 (R)** Not much tension in what aims to be a tension-filled thriller. Hackman is accused of raping and murdering several Puerto Rican women and spends the film being interrogated by detectives Freeman and Jane. Lots of talk but little to connect with in this remake of Claude Miller's very well respected "Garde a Vue." Both Hackman and Freeman co-executive produced. **111m/C VHS, DVD.** Morgan Freeman, Gene Hackman, Thomas Jane, Monica Bellucci; ***D:*** Stephen Hopkins; ***W:*** W. Peter Iliff, Tom Provost; ***C:*** Peter Levy.

Under the Biltmore Clock **1985** F. Scott Fitzgerald's story, "Myra Meets His Family," is the basis for this American Playhouse installment for PBS. It is outwit or be outwitted in this tale of a fortune-hunting '20s flapper who is outsmarted by the man she has set her sights on when he hires actors to play his eccentric "family." **80m/C VHS, DVD.** Sean Young, Lenny Von Dohlen, Barnard Hughes; ***D:*** Neal Miller. **TV**

Under the Boardwalk 1/2 **1989 (R)** A pair of star-crossed teenage lovers struggle through familial and societal differences in 1980s California. This is, like, bogus, ya know. **102m/C VHS.** Keith Coogan, Danielle von Zerneck, Richard Joseph Paul, Hunter von Leer, Tracey Walter, Roxana Zal, Dick Miller, Sonny Bono, Corky Carroll; ***D:*** Fritz Kiersch; ***C:*** Don Burgess. **VIDEO**

Under the Bombs *Sous les Bombes* **2007** During a ceasefire in the 2006 Lebanon-Israel conflict, Christian taxi driver Tony agrees to drive Shiite Zeina into the still dangerous southern countryside. She is searching for her young son, who was staying with her sister in a small village while she and her soon-to-be-ex husband were in Dubai. The two discover nothing but the rubble of bombed-out towns and a frantic Zeina comes to depend on Tony's sympathy and care. Filmed on location in Lebanon during the actual ceasefire with the two leads the only professionals in the cast. Arabic with subtitles. **98m/C DVD.** *FR* Nada Abou Farhat, Georges Khabbaz; ***D:*** Philipe Aractingi; ***W:*** Philipe Aractingi, Michel Leviant; ***C:*** Nidal Abedel Khalek; ***M:*** Rene Aubry, Lazare Boghossian.

Under the Cherry Moon 1/2 **1986 (PG-13)** Prince portrays a fictional musician of the 1940s who travels to the French Riviera, seeking love and money. Songs include "Under the Cherry Moon," "Kiss," "Another-loverholeinyohead," "Sometimes It Snows in April," and "Mountains." A vanity flick down to its being filmed in black and white. **100m/B VHS, DVD.** Prince, Jerome Benton, Francesca Annis, Kristin Scott Thomas; ***D:*** Prince; ***C:*** Michael Ballhaus. Golden Raspberries '86: Worst Picture, Worst Actor (Prince), Worst Support. Actor (Benton), Worst Director (Prince), Worst Song ("Love or Money").

Under the Domim Tree 1/2 *Etz Hadomim Tafus* **1995** Sequel to "The Summer of Aviya," set in 1953, finds 15-year-old Aviya (Cohen) living in an Israeli community with other teenagers who were scarred by the Holocaust. As they get to know one another, each must deal with their own tormented memories. Based on a memoir by Almagor, who plays Aviya's institutionalized mother. Hebrew with subtitles. **102m/C VHS, DVD.** *IS* Kaipo Cohen, Julino Mer, Ohad Knoller, Orli Perl, Riki Blich, Gila Almagor; ***D:*** Eli Cohen; ***W:*** Gila Almagor, Eyal Sher; ***C:*** David Gurfinkel; ***M:*** Benny Nagari.

Under the Earth *Debajo del Mundo* **1986 (R)** An Argentine-Czech coproduction, depicting the plight of a family of Polish Jews forced to live underground for two years to avoid the Nazis. Harrowing and critically well-received. In Spanish with subtitles. **100m/C VHS.** *SP* Victor Laplace; ***D:*** Beda Docampo Feijoo, Juan Bautista Stagnaro.

Under the Flag of the Rising Sun *Gunki hataweku motoni* **1972** A grieving widow (Hidari) is determined to find the truth behind her husband's court martial and execution on the New Guinea front during the final days of World War II. Interviewing surviving members of her husband's garrison, she encounters conflicting testimonies that form a heart-breaking tapestry of wartime atrocity and desperate measures taken for survival. Subtitled. **96m/C DVD.** *JP* Sachiko Hidari, Tetsuro Tamba, Kanemon Nakamura, Noboru Mitani, Sanae Nakahara; ***D:*** Kinji Fukasaku; ***W:*** Kinji Fukasaku, Kaneto Shindo, Norio Osada; ***C:*** Hiroshi Segawa; ***M:*** Hikaru Hayashi.

Under the Greenwood Tree 1/2 **2005** Fancy Day, a local beauty from a wealthy family, is the new schoolteacher in the village of Mellstock. She attracts the romantic interests of wealthy landowner Farmer Shiner, young vicar Reverend Maybold, and laborer Dick Dewey. A loose adaptation of the 1872 novel by Thomas Hardy, much sweeter than his similar quadrangle in "Far from the Madding Crowd." **100m/C DVD.** *GB* Keeley Hawes, Ben Miles, Tony Haygarth, James Murray, Steve Pemberton; ***D:*** Nicholas Laughland; ***W:*** Ashley Pharoah; ***C:*** John Aspinall; ***M:*** John Lunn, Jim Williams. **TV**

Under the Gun **1988 (R)** A cop recruits a lawyer to help him find the man who murdered his brother. Action drives this formulaic plot along. **89m/C VHS.** Sam Jones, Vanessa L(ynne) Williams, John Russell, Michael Halsey; ***D:*** James Sbardellati; ***W:*** James Sbardellati, Almer John Davis.

Under the Gun 1/2 **1995 (R)** Debt-ridden club owner Frank Torrance (Norton) is in trouble with everyone he knows. But he can't clear his debts just by quitting the business, so he decides to fight back. **90m/C VHS, DVD.** Jane Badler, Peter Lindsey, Richard Norton, Kathy Long; ***D:*** Matthew George; ***W:*** Matthew George; ***C:*** Dan Burstall; ***M:*** Frank Strangio.

Under the Hula Moon 1/2 **1995 (R)** Buzzard (Baldwin) and Betty (Lloyd) Wall are living unhappily in the charmless desert town of Cactus Gulch. Their trailer home is festooned in faux-Hawaiian finery and the duo dream of the day they can actually move to their island paradise. Buzz's invented an ultraprotective sunscreen that may be their ticket out, if his prison-escapee, trigger-happy half-brother Turk (Penn), who's also kidnapped Betty, doesn't get them all killed first. Charming lead performances—very lightweight story. **94m/C VHS.** Stephen Baldwin, Emily Lloyd, Christopher Penn, Musetta Vander, Edie McClurg, Pruitt Taylor Vince, Billy Campbell, Carel Struycken, R. Lee Ermey; ***D:*** Jeff Celentano; ***W:*** Jeff Celentano; ***C:*** Phil Parmet.

Under the Lighthouse Dancing 1/2 **1997** What began as a vacation for six friends on a picturesque Australian island turns into a mad scramble to fulfill Emma's dying wish to marry Harry. Flat, despite being drawn from actual events. **94m/C VHS, DVD.** *AU* Jack Thompson, Jacqueline McKenzie, Naomi Watts, Aden (John) Gillett, Philip Holder, Zoe Bertram; ***D:*** Graeme Rattigan; ***W:*** David Giles, Graeme Rattigan; ***C:*** Paul Murphy; ***M:*** Nerida Tyson-Chew. **VIDEO**

Under the Moonlight **2001** A young seminary students gets the education he truly needs to serve the people when, after his vestments are stolen by a hustling street kid, he must enter the homeless subculture to retrieve them. In Farsi with English subtitles. **96m/C DVD.** Hossein Parastar, Hamad Rajabali; ***D:*** Seyyed Reza Mir-Karimi; ***W:*** Seyyed Reza Mir-Karimi; ***C:*** Hamid Khozui-Abyaneh; ***M:*** Mohammad Reza Alighori. **VIDEO**

Under the Pampas Moon 1/2 **1935** Rakish gaucho Cesar (Baxter) heads to Buenos Aires in search of his stolen horse and discovers beautiful singing senorita Yvonhe (Gallian) instead. He figures out that her manager may also be a horse thief. Features Rita Hayworth (credited under Rita Cansino) as a dancehall girl. **78m/B VHS.** Warner Baxter, Ketti Gallian, J. Carrol Naish, John Miljan, Jack LaRue, Ann Codee; ***D:*** James Tinling; ***W:*** Bradley King, Ernest Pascal; ***C:*** Chester Lyons.

Under the Pavement Lies the Strand *Unter dem Pflaster Ist der Strand* **1975** Grischa and Heinrich were fervent radicals during Germany's 1968 student demonstrations. Now stage actors in Berlin, they are feeling older and insignificant until they decide to put their passion into fighting a new abortion bill. But their zeal is tempered by an unexpected pregnancy. First film from Sanders-Brahms; German with subtitles. **106m/B DVD.** *GE* Grischa Huber, Heinrich Giskes; ***D:*** Helma Sanders-Brahms; ***W:*** Grischa Huber, Heinrich Giskes, Helma Sanders-Brahms; ***C:*** Thomas Mauch.

Under the Pear Tree *Unterm Birnbaum* **1973** Classic crime based on a novella by Theodor Fontane. Bankrupt restaurant owner Hradschek and his wife come up with a plan to foil the debt collector at their door. But when the man's carriage is found—empty—by the river, the neighbors remember Hradschek digging under the pear tree the night before. German with subtitles. **86m/C VHS.** *GE* Angelica Domrose, Manfred Karge, Erik S. Klein, Agnes Kraus, Norbert Christian; ***D:*** Ralf Kirsten; ***W:*** Ralf Kirsten.

Under the Piano 1/2 **1995** Regina Bailio (Stratas) is a failed opera singer-turned-voice teacher whose bitterness leads to her over-protecting her autistic daughter Rosetta (Follows). Meanwhile, Regina's handicapped older daughter Franny (Plummer) tries to help her sister lead the fullest life possible. Set in the 1940s. **92m/C DVD.** *CA* Teresa Stratas, Amanda Plummer, Megan Follows, James Carroll, Richard Blackburn, Dan Lett, John Juliani, Jackie Richardson; ***D:*** Stefan Scaini; ***W:*** Blair Ferguson; ***C:*** Robert Saad; ***M:*** Christopher Dedrick. **TV**

Under the Rainbow **WOOF!** **1981 (PG)** Comic situations encountered by a talent scout and a secret service agent in a hotel filled with Munchkins during filming of "The Wizard of Oz." Features midgets, spies, and a prevailing lack of taste. International intrigue adds to the strange attempt at humor. **97m/C VHS.** Chevy Chase, Carrie Fisher, Eve Arden, Joseph Maher, Robert Donner, Mako, Pat McCormick, Billy Barty, Zelda Rubinstein; ***D:*** Steve Rash; ***W:*** Pat McCormick, Martin Smith, Harry Hurwitz, Fred Bauer, Pat Bradley.

Under the Red Robe 1/2 **1936** A French soldier of fortune is trapped into aiding Cardinal Richelieu in his persecution of the Huguenots and winds up falling in love with the sister of his intended victim. Good costume adventure-drama. Sjostrom's last film as a director. **82m/B VHS, DVD.** *GB* Raymond Massey, Conrad Veidt, Annabella, Romney Brent; ***D:*** Victor Sjostrom; ***C:*** James Wong Howe.

Under the Roofs of Paris ½ *Sous les Toits de Paris* **1929** An early French sound film about the lives of young Parisian lovers. A gentle, highly acclaimed melodrama. In French with English subtitles. **95m/B VHS, DVD.** *FR* Albert Prejean, Pola Illery, Gaston Modot, Edmond T. Greville; ***D:*** Rene Clair; ***W:*** Rene Clair; ***C:*** Georges Perinal; ***M:*** Armand Bernard.

Under the Same Moon ½ *La Misma Luna* **2007 (PG-13)** A heart-tugger that usually stays just this side of sentimentality. Young Carlitos (Alonso) lives in Mexico with his grandma while his mother Rosario (del Castillo) works illegally as a maid in L.A. Every Sunday she calls him from the same pay phone. When grandma dies, Carlitos decides to cross the border to reunite with his mom. He makes it to Texas but it's a problematic journey from there to California that may be for naught since the fed-up Rosario is deciding whether to return home. English and Spanish with subtitles. **109m/C DVD.** *US* Adrian Alonso, Maya Zapata, Kate del Castillo, Eugenio Derbez, Gabriel Porras; ***D:*** Patricia Riggen; ***W:*** Ligiah Villalobos; ***C:*** Checco Varese; ***M:*** Carlo Siliotto.

Under the Sand *Sous le Sable* **2000** Middleaged Marie (Rampling) has been married for many years to Jean (Cremer). They are vacationing at their summer house and Jean goes for a swim while Marie takes a nap. When she awakens, he has disappeared. A search reveals nothing and Marie must eventually return to Paris and try to go on with her life. But Marie is deep in denial—she speaks as if Jean were still alive and, in fact, she continues to see and interact with—well, whatever spirit of Jean that she has conjured up. Bravura performance from Rampling. French with subtitles. **95m/C VHS, DVD.** *FR* Charlotte Rampling, Bruno Cremer, Jacques Nolot, Alexandra Stewart, Pierre Vernier, Andree Tainsey; ***D:*** Francois Ozon; ***W:*** Francois Ozon, Marina de Van, Emmanuele Bernheim, Marcia Romano; ***C:*** Jeanne Lapoirie, Antoine Heberle; ***M:*** Philippe Rombi.

Under the Skin **1997** After their mother's unexpected death, 19-year-old Iris (Morton) and her married, pregnant older sister Rose (Rushbrook) deal with their grief in very different ways. The dreamy Iris decides to explore all her sexual fantasies after she has a spontaneous sexual encounter with a stranger, Tom (Townsend), and drifts into promiscuity. The fragile Iris pushes her limits to find some kind of comfort while her remaining family ties steadily disintegrate. Astonishing no-holds-barred performance by Morton. **81m/C VHS.** *GB* Samantha Morton, Claire Rushbrook, Rita Tushingham, Stuart Townsend, Christine Tremarco, Mark Womack, Odette Springer; ***D:*** Carine Adler; ***W:*** Carine Adler; ***C:*** Barry Ackroyd; ***M:*** Ilona Sekacz.

Under the Sun *Under Solen* **1998** In 1956, 40-year-old virgin, Olof (Lassgard), lives on his rather rundown farm in western Sweden—his only friend being the younger Erik (Widerberg), who takes advantage of Olof's generosity. Then Ellen (Bergstrom) turns up in answer to Olof's ad for a housekeeper and the unlikely duo become a romantic couple much to Erik's dismay. So he decides to find out what a beautiful city girl is doing on a remote farm. Based on a short story by H.E. Bates. Swedish with subtitles. **118m/C VHS, DVD.** *SW* Rolf Lassgard, Helena Bergstrom, Johan Widerberg, Jonas Falk, Linda Ulvaeus; ***D:*** Colin Nutley; ***W:*** Colin Nutley; ***C:*** Jens Fischer; ***M:*** Paddy Moloney.

Under the Tuscan Sun ½ **2003 (PG-13)** Very loose adaptation of the Frances Mayes bestseller has beautiful scenery—both from its leads and Italy. Still in shock from her recent divorce, writer Frances (Lane) is given a change-of-scenery trip by her lesbian best friend Patti (Oh). While traveling in Tuscany, Frances comes across a rundown villa, which she impulsively buys and proceeds to renovate with the aid of some displaced Polish workmen. She begins to make friends with the locals, including handsome Marcello (Bova), with whom she is soon getting romantic. Lane is exuberant as the newly risk-taking Frances but Oh supplies much humor when Patti shows up, pregnant and deserted by her lover, to join Frances's new household. **113m/C VHS, DVD.** *US* Diane Lane, Sandra Oh, Lindsay Duncan, Raoul Bova, Vincent Riotta, Guilia Steigerwalt, Pawel Szajda, Valentine Pelka, Sasa Vulicevic, David Sutcliffe, Kate Walsh; ***D:*** Audrey Wells; ***W:*** Audrey Wells; ***C:*** Geoffrey Simpson; ***M:*** Christophe Beck.

Under the Volcano **1984** An alcoholic British ex-consul finds his life further deteriorating during the Mexican Day of the Dead in 1939. His half-brother and ex-wife try to save him from himself, but their affair sends him ever-deeper into his personal hell. Finney's performance is pathetic and haunting. Adapted from the novel by Malcolm Lowry. **112m/C VHS.** Albert Finney, Jacqueline Bisset, Anthony Andrews, Katy Jurado; ***D:*** John Huston; ***M:*** John Beal, Alex North. L.A. Film Critics '84: Actor (Finney).

Under the Yum-Yum Tree ½ **1963** When womanizing landlord Hogan's (Lemmon) ex-fiance Irene (Adams) moves out, he doesn't pine. Instead he plots to romance her niece Robin (Lynley) who's just moved into his building. But his romantic shenanigans are thwarted by the presence of fiance David (Jones), who's living platonically with Robin to test their compatibility. Silly sex comedy based on the play by Roman. **110m/C VHS.** Jack Lemmon, Carol Lynley, Dean Jones, Edie Adams, Imogene Coca, Paul Lynde, Robert Lansing, Bill Bixby; ***D:*** David Swift; ***W:*** David Swift, Lawrence Roman; ***C:*** Joseph Biroc; ***M:*** Frank DeVol.

Under Western Stars **1938** Roy's first starring vehicle. A newly elected congressman goes to Washington and fights battles for his constituents, caught in the middle of the Dust Bowl and drought. **83m/B VHS, DVD.** Roy Rogers, Smiley Burnette; ***D:*** Jean Yarbrough. Natl. Film Reg. '09.

The Underachievers **1988 (R)** A night school is the scene for typical libido-oriented gags, but this time instead of teenagers it's adult education providing the plot. Only a few real laughs in this one. **90m/C VHS.** Barbara Carrera, Edward Albert, Michael Pataki, Vic Tayback, Garrett Morris, Susan Tyrrell; ***D:*** Jackie Kong.

Underclassman WOOF! **2005 (PG-13)** Venice beach bike cop, Tre (Cannon), gets assigned to prep school to investigate a murder. Sounds like it might have promise, but nope. Even the juxtaposition of Tre—the only African American on the starkly white prep school campus—falls flat amidst cheap jokes and predictably cliched circumstances. Poor Cheech Marin, who plays Tre's boss, adds another thankless role to his resume. Why Tre, a trouble-finding high school dropout, is a cop in the first place, is beyond logic. **95m/C DVD.** *US* Nick Cannon, Shawn Ashmore, Roselyn Sanchez, Kelly Hu, Ian Gomez, Hugh Bonneville, Richard "Cheech" Marin, Mary Pat Gleason, Angelo Spizzirri, Kaylee DeFer; ***D:*** Marcos Siega; ***W:*** David T. Wagner, Brent Goldberg; ***C:*** David Hennings; ***M:*** BT (Brian Transeau).

Undercover ½ **1987 (R)** Routine cop action film in which an eastern detective finds himself undercover in a southern high school in search of a cop-murdering drug ring. Plagued with cliches. Director Stockwell is appropriately better known for his role as "Cougar" in "Top Gun." **92m/C VHS.** David Neidorf, Jennifer Jason Leigh, Barry Corbin, David Harris, Kathleen Wilhoite; ***D:*** John Stockwell; ***M:*** Bruce Smeaton.

Undercover ½ **1994 (R)** Police detective (and hot babe) Cindy Hanen (Massey) gets an undercover assignment to capture a murderer who's targeted an upscale brothel. It's an excuse for interesting undies (or less). **93m/C VHS, DVD.** Athena Massey, Tom Tayback, Anthony Guidera, Rena Riffel, Jeffrey Dean Morgan, Meg Foster; ***D:*** Alexander Gregory (Gregory Dark) Hippolyte; ***W:*** Oola Bloome, Lalo Wolf; ***C:*** Philip Hurn; ***M:*** Ashley Irwin.

Undercover Angel ½ **1999 (PG-13)** Predictably cheesy but still entertaining movie that features the chubby-cheeked blonde girl from the Welch's Juice TV commercials. Six-year-old Young is left in the care of struggling writer Winters, her mom's old boyfriend. He's attracted to Bleeth and the little moppet charges into the woman's life in order to get the duo together. Oh yeah, and then Young and Winters discover that he's actually her biological father. **93m/C VHS, DVD.** Yasmine Bleeth, Dean Winters, Emily Mae Young, Lorraine Ansell, Casey Kasem, Richard Eden, James Earl Jones; ***D:*** Bryan Michael Stoller; ***W:*** Bryan Michael Stoller; ***C:*** Bruce Alan Greene; ***M:*** Greg Edmonson. **VIDEO**

Undercover Blues ½ **1993 (PG-13)** Comedy-thriller starring Turner and Quaid as married spies Jane and Jeff Blue, on parental leave from the espionage biz, who are on vacation with their 11-month-old daughter in New Orleans. But the holiday is interrupted when they're recruited by their boss to stop an old adversary from selling stolen weapons. The leads play cute together and the baby is adorable but this is strictly routine escapism. Stick with "The Thin Man" instead. **90m/C VHS, DVD.** Kathleen Turner, Dennis Quaid, Fiona Shaw, Stanley Tucci, Larry Miller, Obba Babatunde, Park Overall, Tom Arnold, Saul Rubinek, Michelle Schuelke; ***D:*** Herbert Ross; ***W:*** Ian Abrams; ***M:*** David Newman.

Undercover Brother ½ **2002 (PG-13)** Funny but padded spoof of secret agents and blaxploitation movies. Brother (Griffin) is a secret agent from the B.R.O.T.H-.E.R.H.O.O.D. sent to rescue a black war hero turned presidential candidate (the always-cool Williams) who has been brainwashed in a plot by The Man to destroy African-American culture. More-hit-than-miss comedy finds many targets of all stripes to lampoon, and does so with just the right amount of funk. **85m/C VHS, DVD.** *US* Eddie Griffin, Chris Kattan, Denise Richards, Dave Chappelle, Chi McBride, Aunjanue Ellis, Neil Patrick Harris, Billy Dee Williams, Jack Noseworthy, Gary Anthony Williams, James Brown, Robert Trumbull; ***D:*** Malcolm Lee; ***W:*** John Ridley, Michael McCullers; ***C:*** Tom Priestley; ***M:*** Stanley Clarke; ***Nar:*** J.D. Hall.

Undercover Cop **1994** True story of Sergeant George Aguilar and the high-speed chase that left one dead and the police dealing their revenge on all the offenders. **90m/C VHS.** Danny Trejo, Kevin Anthony Cole; ***D:*** Martin Greene; ***W:*** Glenn A. Bruce; ***M:*** Randall Kent Heddon.

The Undercover Kid **1995 (PG)** Ten-year-old Max Anderson's (Pierce) dog has told him that the President is going to be assassinated. Can he get anyone to believe him? Harmless actiony adventure for the kiddies. **81m/C VHS.** Bradley Michael Pierce, Melora Hardin, Nicolas Surovy, Erik Avari, Trishalee Hardy, Sven-Ole Thorsen, Erik Avari, Susan Dolan; ***D:*** Linda Shayne; ***W:*** Dennis Carr; ***C:*** Jacek Laskus; ***M:*** Steve Dorff; ***V:*** Robert Knepper, Victoria Jackson.

Undercover Man ½ **1936** A Wells Fargo agent goes undercover to expose a crooked sheriff. **57m/B VHS.** Johnny Mack Brown, Suzanne Kaaren, Ted Adams, Lloyd Ingraham, Horace Murphy; ***D:*** Albert Ray.

The Undercover Woman ½ *Passkey to Danger* **1946** Private eye Marcia Conroy (Bachelor) is on the case at a dude ranch gathering evidence for a divorce when guest and philanderer Gregory Vixon (Fraser) winds up dead. Comedy-mystery-romance pits small-town (guy) sheriff against big-city (gal) detective, as they hunt for the least likely suspect. **56m/B DVD.** Stephanie Bachelor, Robert "Bob" Livingston, Richard Fraser, Isabel Withers, Helene Heigh; ***D:*** Thomas Carr; ***W:*** Sylvia G.L. Dannet, Sherman Lowe.

Undercurrent ½ **1946** Minnelli's only foray into film noir is high-gloss melodrama based on the novel "You Were There" by Thelma Strabel. Innocent Ann (Hepburn) marries Alan (Taylor) after a whirlwind romance and then discovers he's not the man she thinks. He may be a murderer and there's some chicanery involving his brother Michael (Mitchum) and the family business. Taylor's in a rare bad guy role while Hepburn seems too sophisticated for her naive wife and Mitchum just seems tired. **116m/B VHS, DVD.** Katharine Hepburn, Robert Taylor, Robert Mitchum, Edmund Gwenn, Marjorie Main, Clinton Sundberg, Dan Tobin, Jayne Cotter; ***D:*** Vincente Minnelli; ***W:*** Marguerite Roberts, Edward Chodorov, George Oppenheimer; ***C:*** Karl Freund; ***M:*** Herbert Stothart.

Undercurrent **1999 (R)** Ex-cop Lamas arrives in Puerto Rico to run a nightclub and is blackmailed into an affair with a mobster's wife. **99m/C VHS, DVD.** Lorenzo Lamas, Frank Vincent, Brenda Strong; ***D:*** Frank Kerr; ***C:*** Carlos Gaviria; ***M:*** Christopher Lennertz. **VIDEO**

The Underdog ½ **1943** After the bank forecloses, a farm family must move to the city. The family's young son has only his loyal dog to turn to for friendship, but the gallant animal proves his mettle by rounding up a gang of spies plotting some WWII sabotage. Believe it if you dare. **65m/B VHS.** Barton MacLane, Bobby Larson, Jan Wiley; ***D:*** William Nigh.

Underdog **2007 (PG)** Live-action/CGI combo finds the TV cartoon character making his feature film debut. Beagle Underdog (Lee) goes from ordinary to extraordinary, thanks to an accident in the lab of Dr. Simon Barsinister (Dinklage). He can even talk, which is a big surprise to young owner Jack (Neuberger). Now Underdog's new mission is to protect the citizens of Capitol City, especially lovely spaniel "Sweet" Polly Purebred (Adams), from Barsinister's...well...sinister plans to take over. With a dog as a superhero, there's no way this should have missed. Unfortunately, a handful of inspired moments aren't enough to overcome the generally disjointed and rushed feel of the whole thing. **84m/C DVD, Blu-ray Disc.** *US* Peter Dinklage, Patrick Warburton, Alex Neuberger, Taylor Momsen, John Slattery, Brad Garrett, James Belushi; ***D:*** Frederick Du Chau; ***W:*** Adam Rifkin, Joe Piscatella, Craig A. Williams; ***C:*** David Eggby; ***M:*** Randy Edelman; ***V:*** Jason Lee, Amy Adams.

Undergrads **1985** A bright generational Disney comedy with Carney, estranged from his stick-in-the-mud son, deciding to attend college with his free-thinking grandson. **102m/C VHS.** Art Carney, Chris Makepeace, Jackie Burroughs, Len Birman; ***D:*** Steven Hilliard Stern. **TV**

Underground ½ **1941** Eric (Dorn) is a member of the German underground working against the Nazis. But he must conceal his activities from his loyal solider brother Kurt (Lynn). Topical wartime drama still hits home with its story of divided loyalties. **95m/B VHS, DVD.** Philip Dorn, Jeffrey Lynn, Martin Kosleck, Karen Verne, Mona Maris, Peter Whitney, Ilka Gruning; ***D:*** Vincent Sherman; ***W:*** Charles Grayson; ***C:*** Sid Hickox; ***M:*** Adolph Deutsch.

Underground *Once Upon a Time There Was a Country; Il Etait une Fois un Pays* **1995** Exhausting black comedy, set in Yugoslavia from 1941 to 1992, follows the adventures of Marko (Manojlovic) and his best friend Blacky (Ristovski). They run a black-market operation and lead Communist Party meetings while trying to avoid the Gestapo in WWII Belgrade. Hiding out in a cellar, where refugees have put together a munitions factory, the treacherous Marko manages to convince everyone that the war is still going on—20 years later in fact—until the truth unexpectedly comes out (thanks to a pet monkey). The final section sees Marko unscrupulously dealing arms and drugs amidst the breakup of Yugoslavia in a civil war and the violence on all sides. **192m/C VHS, DVD.** *FR GE HU* Miki (Predrag) Manojlovic, Lazar Ristovski, Mirjana Jokovic, Slavko Stimac, Ernst Stotzner, Srdan Todorovic, Mirjana Karanovic, Milena Pavlovic, Danilo Stojkovic, Bora Todorovic, Davor Dujmovic, Branislav Lecic, Dragan Nikolic, Hark Bohm; ***Cameos:*** Emir Kusturica; ***D:*** Emir Kusturica; ***W:*** Emir Kusturica, Dusan Kovacevic; ***C:*** Vilko Filac; ***M:*** Goran Bregovic. Cannes '95: Film.

The Underground **1997 (R)** A rap artist is gunned down by a gang and Sgt. Brian Donnegan (Fahey) and his partner Scully (Tigar) are on the investigation. But when Scully is killed by the same scum, Donnegan is partnered with a rookie (McFall) and the duo must infiltrate L.A.'s music scene to get their suspects. **92m/C VHS, DVD.** Jeff Fahey, Ken Tigar, Michael McFall; ***D:*** Cole McKay; ***W:*** William Lawlor; ***C:*** Ken Blakey; ***M:*** John Gonzalez.

Underground Aces WOOF! **1980 (PG)** A group of parking lot attendants transforms a sheik into an attendant in order to help him meet the girl of his dreams. A bad "Car Wash" spinoff. **93m/C VHS.** Dirk Benedict, Melanie Griffith, Frank Gorshin, Jerry Orbach, Robert Hegyes, Audrey Landers; ***D:*** Robert Butler; ***W:*** James (Jim) Carabatsos.

Underground Agent 1/2 **1942** Probably proved more exciting during its WWII release timeframe than it will for modern sensibilities. Government agent Lee Graham (Bennett) is hired to stop enemy eavesdropping at a defense plant. He invents a scrambler that confuses the Axis and then rounds up the saboteurs. Pretty standard B fare. **70m/B VHS.** Bruce Bennett, Leslie Brooks, Frank Albertson, Julian Rivero, Rhys Williams, Henry Victor, Addison Richards, Hans Conried; ***D:*** Michael Gordon; ***W:*** J. Robert Bren, Gladys Atwater; ***C:*** L.W. O'Connell.

Underground Rustlers **1941** The Range Busters are commissioned by the government to stop unscrupulous gold-marketeers. **58m/B VHS.** Ray Corrigan, Max Terhune, John "Dusty" King; ***D:*** S. Roy Luby.

Underground Terror **1988** A gang of murderers, organized by a psychopath, rampages through the New York City subway system. One cop enthusiastically tries to snuff out each one. **91m/C VHS.** Doc Dougherty, Lenny Y. Loftin; ***D:*** James McCalmont.

Underground U.S.A. **1984** Street hustler picks up a has-been underground movie star at the chic New York new wave disco, The Mudd Club. **85m/C VHS.** Patti Astor, Eric Mitchell; ***D:*** Eric Mitchell.

Undermind 1/2 **2003** Dissolute corporate lawyer Derrick (Trammell) wakes up in an altered reality as a low-life criminal named Zane. While Zane's enjoying the perks of Derrick's life, Derrick's finding it hard to manage Zane's bottom-feeder existence. Everything gets tied up neatly. Dwek's debut effort. **113m/C DVD.** Sam Trammell, Erik Jensen, Susan May Pratt, Tara Subkoff, Celia Weston, Ellen Pompeo, Aasif Mandai, Michael Ryan Segal; ***D:*** Nevil Dwek; ***W:*** Nevil Dwek; ***C:*** Wolfgang Held; ***M:*** Joel Goodman.

The Underneath **1995 (R)** Recovering gambling addict Michael Chambers (Gallagher) returns home after skipping out on his debts and his wife Rachel (sultry newcomer Elliott) several years before. Old passions ignite in more ways than one, and Michael's lust for his ex, now married to a hot-tempered hoodlum, leads him to risk it all for a final big score. Moody and tense study of the complexities of emotion is capped by smart lead performances but style wins out over substance and the finale definitely leaves more questions than answers. Remake of the 1949 film noir classic "Criss Cross," based on Don Tracy's novel of the same name. **99m/C VHS, DVD.** Shelley Duvall, Richard Linklater, Dennis Hill, Peter Gallagher, Alison Elliott, William Fichtner, Elisabeth Shue, Adam Trese, Paul Dooley, Joe Don Baker, Anjanette Comer, Harry Goz, Vincent Gaskins, Tony Perenski, Helen Cates, John Martin, David Jensen, Joseph Chrest; ***D:*** Steven Soderbergh; ***W:*** Steven Soderbergh, Daniel Fuchs; ***C:*** Elliot Davis; ***M:*** Cliff Martinez.

Undersea Kingdom **1936** Adventure beneath the ocean floor. In 12 chapters of 13 minutes each; the first chapter runs 20 minutes. Later re-edited into one film, "Sharad of Atlantis." **226m/B VHS, DVD.** Ray Corrigan, Lon Chaney Jr., Lois Wilde, Monte Blue, William Farnum, Smiley Burnette; ***D:*** B. Reeves Eason.

Understudy: The Graveyard Shift 2 1/2 **1988 (R)** Vampire survives poorly directed cliche-riddled original to be cast as a vampire cast as a vampire in a horror movie within a horrible sequel. **88m/C VHS.** *CA* Wendy Gazelle, Mark Soper, Silvio Oliviero, Ilse von Glatz, Tim Kelleher; ***D:*** Gerard Ciccoritti; ***C:*** Barry Stone.

The Undertaker and His Pals **1967** Undertaker teams up with diner owners in murder scheme to improve mortician's business and expand restaurateurs' menu. Pretty violent stuff, with some good laughs and a campy flare, but not for every one's palate. **70m/C VHS, DVD.** Ray Dannis, James Westmoreland, Larrene Ott, Robert Lowery, Sally Frei; ***D:*** David C. Graham; ***C:*** Andrew Janczak.

The Undertaker's Wedding **1997 (R)** Undertaker Mario Bellini (Brophy) fakes the death and burial of mob boss Rocco (Wincott) to stem a local mob war but then makes the big mistake of falling in love with the new "widow," Maria (Wuhrer). **90m/C VHS, DVD.** *CA* Adrien Brody, Jeff Wincott, Kari Wuhrer, Burt Young, Holly Gagnier, Nicholas Pasco; ***D:*** John Bradshaw; ***W:*** John Bradshaw; ***C:*** Edgar Egger.

Undertow 1/2 **1930** Lighthouse keeper Paul (Brown) marries Sally (Nolan) but when he goes blind she's ripe for Coast Guardsman Jim's (Ellis) attentions. **65m/B VHS.** Mary Nolan, Johnny Mack Brown, Robert Ellis, Churchill Ross, Audrey Ferris; ***D:*** Harry A. Pollard; ***W:*** Edward T. Lowe, Kristen Overdurf; ***C:*** Jerome Ash.

Undertow **1995 (R)** Drifter Jack Ketchum (Phillips) loses control of his car in a storm and wakes up in the secluded cabin of paranoid Lyle Yates (Dance) and his terrified wife, Willie (Sara). Since the storm's worse, Jack can't leave—too bad for him that Willie's so darn attractive and Lyle's so crazy. **90m/C VHS.** Lou Diamond Phillips, Mia Sara, Charles Dance; ***D:*** Eric Red; ***W:*** Kathryn Bigelow, Eric Red; ***C:*** Geza Sinkovics; ***M:*** John (Gianni) Frizzell. **CABLE**

Undertow **2004 (R)** Over-heated southern gothic. Rebellious teen Chris (Bell) lives on a hardscrabble hog farm with widowed dad John (Mulroney) and sickly 10-year-old bro Tim (Alan). Then wicked Uncle Deel (Lucas) shows up, fresh outta prison and with a lot of pent-up resentment and anger toward John (seems John's late wife was Deel's gal first). He demands his share of some rare gold coins bequeathed to him and John, which John believes are cursed. Deel goes all Cain and Abel, which forces the younger duo to grab the gold and take off running. Brit boy Bell manages his Southern twang with aplomb. Filmed on location around Savannah, Georgia. **107m/C DVD.** *US* Jamie Bell, Josh(ua) Lucas, Dermot Mulroney, Shiri Appleby, Patricia Healy, Bill McKinney, Alan Devon; ***D:*** David Gordon Green; ***W:*** David Gordon Green; ***C:*** Tim Orr; ***M:*** Philip Glass.

Undertow *Contracorriente* **2010** Despite his seemingly happy marriage and his wife's pregnancy, Peruvian fisherman Miguel (Mercado) is secretly having an affair with gay artist Santiago (Cardona). Spanish with subtitles. **100m/C DVD.** *PV* Manolo Cardona, Christian Mercado, Tatiano; ***D:*** Javier Fuentes-Leon; ***W:*** Javier Fuentes-Leon; ***C:*** Mauricio Vidal; ***M:*** Selma Mutal.

Underwater! **1955** A team of skin divers faces danger when they try to retrieve treasure from a Spanish galleon. The second film after "The Outlaw" masterminded by Howard Hughes, primarily to show off Russell's figure. **99m/C VHS.** Jane Russell, Richard Egan, Gilbert Roland, Jayne Mansfield; ***D:*** John Sturges.

Underworld **1927** Inspired gangster saga finds bank robber Bull Weed (Bancroft) befriending a genteel bum, known as Rolls Royce (Brook), and taking him into his gang. The bum has brains and soon makes Weed king of the underworld but there's jealousy when Weed's moll Feathers (Brent) falls for Royce. Climactic shootout set a standard for the genre. **85m/B VHS.** George Bancroft, Clive Brook, Evelyn Brent, Larry Semon, Fred Kohler Sr.; ***D:*** Josef von Sternberg. Oscars '28: Story.

Underworld **1996 (R)** Considering the on-screen talent, this crime comedy/thriller is a disappointment. Ex-wiseguy Johnny Crown (Leary) studied psychotherapy in the joint and, when he's released, decides to put his new knowledge to work on bossman Frank Gavilan (Mantegna), who may be behind the hit on Johnny's old man. Contrived dialogue and story but a sleek-looking production. **95m/C VHS, DVD.** Denis Leary, Joe Mantegna, Annabella Sciorra, Larry Bishop, Abe Vigoda, James Tolkan, Robert Costanzo; ***D:*** Roger Christian; ***W:*** Larry Bishop; ***C:*** Steven Bernstein; ***M:*** Anthony Marinelli.

Underworld **2003 (R)** Vampires and Lycans (werewolves) wage a centuries old battle of survival. The aristocratic vampires have been in control, but the lycans have a plan to turn the tide. It involves human med student Michael (Speedman), who has the blood of both in his family. Head vampire warrior Selene (Beckinsale) inexplicably falls in love with him, precipitating a final showdown. Despite the almost constant gunplay and fight scenes, style vs. substance is the overriding battle here, even though it's no contest. Substance gets its butt handed to it, suffering from the absence of allies plot and characterization. On the bright side, Beckinsale can handle the action stuff, and looks great doing it. **121m/C VHS, DVD, Blu-ray Disc, UMD.** *US GB GE HU* Kate Beckinsale, Scott Speedman, Michael Sheen, Shane Brolly, Bill Nighy, Erwin Leder, Sophia Myles, Robbie Gee, Wentworth Miller; ***D:*** Len Wiseman; ***W:*** Danny McBride; ***C:*** Tony Pierce-Roberts; ***M:*** Paul Haslinger.

Underworld: Evolution 1/2 **2005 (R)** Selene and Michael are still on the run and still trying to figure out the depths of the various betrayals and who, if anyone, they can trust. This time out they have to deal with the O.G. vampire and werewolf, and there are a few family issues to work out.There's also plenty of backstory, and more of what made the first installment a hit: Beckinsale in black leather, frenetic vampire-on-werewolf battle action, blood, and gunplay. As a bonus, there's a much better villain and script that brings everything home (but don't rule out another sequel). **106m/C DVD, Blu-ray Disc, UMD.** Kate Beckinsale, Scott Speedman, Tony Curran, Shane Brolly, Derek Jacobi, Bill Nighy, Steven Mackintosh, Brian Steele, John Mann, Michael Sheen, Sophia Myles, Richard Cetrone; ***D:*** Len Wiseman; ***W:*** Len Wiseman, Danny McBride; ***C:*** Simon Duggan; ***M:*** Marco Beltrami.

Underworld: Rise of the Lycans 1/2 **2009 (R)** Third installment in the "Underworld" franchise serves as a prequel for the earlier offeringsand is set a thousand years prior to the original. Explains the origin of the epic conflict between the werewolves and vampires born in the dark ages. Favored Lycan member Lucian (Sheen) falls in love with Sonja (Mitra), the daughter of chief vampire and villain Viktor (Nighy). The affair provokes Viktor's wrath while in turn Lucian instigates an uprising among the Lycans. The two clans do magical battle in mostly inky dark settings with the exception of the blood, which shoots across the screen like fireworks. Nothing surprising or interesting, but hard-core fans will appreciate the history behind the discord. **93m/C DVD.** *US* Michael Sheen, Rhona Mitra, Bill Nighy, Shane Brolly, Steven Mackintosh, Kevin Grevioux, Elizabeth Hawthorne, Kate Beckinsale, David Aston, Larry Rew; ***D:*** Patrick Tatopoulos; ***W:*** Danny McBride, Howard McCain, Dirk Blackman; ***C:*** Ross Emery; ***M:*** Paul Haslinger.

Underworld Scandal *Big Town Scandal* **1947** An editor attempts to break up a ring of basketball game fixers. Based on the radio program "Big Town." **60m/C VHS.** Philip Reed, Hillary Brooke, Stanley Clements, Darryl Hickman, Carl "Alfalfa" Switzer; ***D:*** William C. Thomas; ***W:*** Milton Raison; ***C:*** Ellis W. Carter; ***M:*** Darrell Calker.

The Underworld Story 1/2 **1950** Big city journalist at large moves to small-town New England after losing job for unethical reporting and uncovers scheme to frame innocent man for murder. Solid performances. **90m/B VHS.** Dan Duryea, Herbert Marshall, Gale Storm, Howard da Silva, Michael O'Shea, Mary Anderson, Gar Moore, Melville Cooper, Frieda Inescort, Art Baker, Harry Shannon, Alan Hale Jr., Steve (Stephen) Dunne, Roland Winters; ***D:*** Cy Endfield.

Underworld, U.S.A. **1960** A man infiltrates a tough crime syndicate to avenge his father's murder, which winds up with him caught between the mob and the feds. A well-acted and directed look at the criminal underworld. **99m/B VHS.** Cliff Robertson, Dolores Dorn, Beatrice Kay, Robert Emhardt, Larry Gates, Paul Dubov; ***D:*** Samuel Fuller; ***W:*** Samuel Fuller; ***C:*** Hal Mohr.

Underworld USA 1/2 **1961** Tolly's (Robertson) petty criminal father was murdered by four men who work for a crime syndicate headed by Earl Conners (Emhardt). When Tolly lands in the joint, he befriends one of the killers (who's dying) and gets the names of his cohorts. Tolly then wangles his way into Conners organization to get his revenge, although he's sidetracked when he falls for moll Cuddles (Dorn). Federal agent Driscoll (Gates) persuades Tolly to work undercover to bring down the criminals, which doesn't work out as intended. **98m/B DVD.** Cliff Robertson, Dolores Dorn, Robert Emhardt, Larry Gates, Beatrice Kay, Paul Dubov, Gerald Milton, Richard Rust, Allan Gruener; ***D:*** Samuel Fuller; ***W:*** Samuel Fuller; ***C:*** Hal Mohr; ***M:*** Harry Sukman.

Undesirable *With a Vengeance* **1992** Dull thriller-wannabe. Amnesiac Jenna King (Gilbert) has no memory of her childhood and only knows that she alone survived the murder of her family. Now working as a nanny, Jenna's life is in danger when that same killer finally decides to finish the job. **93m/C VHS.** Melissa Gilbert, Jack Scalia, Matthew Lawrence, Michael Gross, Roger Aaron Brown, John Cullum, Russell Johnson, Robert Donner; ***D:*** Michael Switzer; ***W:*** Renee Longstreet; ***C:*** Rob Draper; ***M:*** J. Peter Robinson. **TV**

Undiscovered **2005 (PG-13)** Model Brier (James) and songwriter Luke (Strait) meet in New York's subway but Luke is soon off to L.A. to ply his trade. Some time later, Brier heads to the coast to try her luck as an actress and just happens to find Luke again. Brier decides to create some media buzz to help Luke's career, but her plans backfire. Price of fame cliches abound and the music is egregiously bad (although the leads are attractive). **97m/C DVD.** Pell James, Steven Strait, Kip Pardue, Fisher Stevens, Ashlee Simpson, Shannyn Sossamon, Peter Weller, Carrie Fisher, Stephen Moyer; ***D:*** Meiert Avis; ***W:*** John Galt; ***C:*** Danny Hiele; ***M:*** David Baerwald.

Undisputed 1/2 **2002 (R)** Champion boxer James "Ice Man" Chambers is locked up in Sweetwater maximum-security prison for rape, which he claims he didn't commit. Snipes is Monroe Hutchens, a lifer at Sweetwater and fellow boxer, sentenced for beating a man to death. Hutchens is also the prison's undefeated champ of the illegal boxing matches set up by a rough prison guard (Rooker). Smacking of real-life boxer Tyson, Chambers desperately tries to find honor in his unhappy situation and wants to be the first to break Hutchen's winning streak, but Monroe has his reasons for avoiding a smack-down with Chambers. Short on dialogue, pic is a well-cast, lean, mean movie machine. **96m/C VHS, DVD.** *US* Wesley Snipes, Ving Rhames, Peter Falk, Michael Rooker, Jon Seda, Wes Studi, Fisher Stevens, Dayton Callie, Amy Aquino, Nils Allen Stewart, Denis Arndt, Rose Rollins; ***D:*** Walter Hill; ***W:*** Walter Hill, David Giler; ***C:*** Lloyd Ahern II; ***M:*** Stanley Clarke.

Undisputed II: Last Man Standing **2006 (R)** An unnecessary sequel that has few ties to the first pic. Ex-boxing champ George Chambers (White) is making vodka commercials in Russia when he lands in prison on trumped-up charges. Seems the Russian mob wants to pit Chambers against the prison's best fighter, Uri Boyka (Adkins), in a televised match they expect will bring in big gambling bucks. The fights between the leads are impressive but scant as is the rest of the action. **98m/C DVD.** Michael Jai White, Eli Danker, Ben Cross, Scott Adkins; ***D:*** Isaac Florentine; ***W:*** David White, James Townsend; ***C:*** Ross Clarkson; ***M:*** Stephen (Steve) Edwards. **VIDEO**

The Undying Monster 1/2 *The Hammond Mystery* **1942** Upper crusty Brit is werewolf with insatiable appetite. Familiar story with lots of atmosphere and style. **63m/B VHS.** James Ellison, Heather Angel, John Howard, Bramwell Fletcher, Heather Thatcher, Aubrey Mather, Halliwell Hobbes, Heather Wilde; ***D:*** John Brahm; ***W:*** Lillie Hayward, Michael Jacoby; ***C:*** Lucien Ballard; ***M:*** Cyril Mockridge, David Raksin, Arthur Lange.

Une Femme Mariee *A Married Woman* **1964** A series of moments in the life of married Charlotte, a vain, trivial woman who cheats on her pilot husband with an actor. When Charlotte gets pregnant and isn't sure who the father is, she has to decide between the two men. For Godard completists. French with subtitles. **95m/B DVD.** *FR* Macha Meril, Phillippe LeRoy, Bernard Noel; ***D:*** Jean-Luc Godard; ***W:*** Jean-Luc Godard; ***C:*** Raoul Coutard.

Une Parisienne 1/2 **1958** Gallic fluff starring sex kitten Bardot finds her an unhappy newlywed whose husband (Vidal) is enjoying being a bon vivant a little too much. So she decides to make him jealous by heading off to the Riviera with an aging Prince (Boyer). French with subtitles. **85m/C VHS.** *FR* Brigitte Bardot, Charles Boyer, Henri Vidal, Andre Luguet, Nadia Gray, Madeleine Le-Beau, Noel Roquevert; ***D:*** Michel Boisrond; ***W:*** Michel Boisrond, Annette Wademant, Jean Aurel; ***C:*** Marcel Grignon; ***M:*** Hubert Rostaing.

Unearthed **2007 (R)** It should be re-buried as soon as possible. In this cliched creature feature an alien being, buried by the Anasazi tribe centuries ago, is unearthed during an archeological dig near a small New Mexico town. And now that it's awake it's angry and hungry. The beautiful Vaugier plays the town's troubled, alcoholic sheriff. **93m/C DVD.** Emmanuelle Vaugier, Luke Goss, Charlie (Charles Q.) Murphy, Beau Garrett, M.C. Gainey, Russell Means; ***D:*** Matthewer Leutwyler; ***W:*** Matthewer Leutwyler; ***C:*** Ross Richardson, Ross Richardson.

The Unearthing **1993 (R)** An unwanted pregnancy seems to find a happy solution when a woman decides to marry the heir to a wealthy estate and pass off her child as his. Only the family has some very strange tastes, including a taste for the blood of the unborn. Based on a Filipino vampire legend (!). **83m/C VHS, DVD.** Norman Moses, Tina Ona Paukstelis; ***D:*** Wyre Martin, Barry Poltermann; ***W:*** Wyre Martin, Barry Poltermann.

The Unearthly 1/2 **1957** A mad scientist is trying to achieve immortality through his strange experiments, but all he winds up with is a basement full of mutants. When his two latest about-to-be victims fall in love, the doctor's mutant assistant decides enough is enough and things come to an unpleasant end. Carradine is typecast. Absurd, but fun. **76m/B VHS, DVD.** John Carradine, Tor Johnson, Allison Hayes, Myron Healey, Karl Johnson; ***D:*** Boris L. Petroff.

The Unearthly Stranger 1/2 **1964** Earth scientist marries woman and decides she's from another planet. Not a nineties style gender drama; seems she's part of an invading alien force, but really does love her earth man. Surprisingly good low-budget sci-fi. **75m/B VHS.** *GB* John Neville, Gabriella Licudi, Philip Stone, Patrick Newell, Jean Marsh, Warren Mitchell; ***D:*** John Krish.

Uneasy Terms **1948** Rennie is a detective investigating the murder of one of his own clients. Evidence points to stepchildren and inheritance money but things may not be as they seem. Written for the screen by Peter Cheyney, adapted from his own novel. **91m/B VHS.** *GB* Michael Rennie, Moira Lister, Faith Brook, Joy Shelton, Patricia Goddard, Barry Jones, Nigel Patrick, Paul Carpenter, Marie Ney, Sydney Tafler, J.H. Roberts, John Robinson; ***D:*** Vernon Sewell; ***W:*** Peter Cheyney; ***C:*** Ernest Palmer.

An Unexpected Family 1/2 **1996 (PG)** Barbara Whitney (Channing) is a Manhattan career woman who is unwillingly thrust into the role of surrogate mom when her irresponsible sister, Ruth (Ebersole), dumps her two children at Barbara's door. Along with her friend Sam (Collins), Barbara and the children slowly make a new family but, after a year, Ruth returns, demanding her children back. Predictable plot is redeemed by good performances from Channing and Ebersole. **93m/C VHS.** Stockard Channing, Stephen Collins, Christine Ebersole, Noah Fleiss, Chelsea Russo; ***D:*** Larry Elikann; ***W:*** Lee Rose; ***C:*** Eric Van Haren Noman; ***M:*** Tom Scott. **CABLE**

An Unexpected Life 1/2 **1997 (PG)** Sequel to 1996's "An Unexpected Family." Barbara Whitney (Channing) has moved to the country and is raising her niece Megan (Russo) and nephew Matt (Fleiss) with the help of boyfriend Sam (Collins). Then Babs discovers she's pregnant—not altogether welcome news. Neither is Barbara's sister Ruth (Ebersole) deciding her life is back on track and she wants to regain custody of her kids or Sam's estrangement from his own visiting mother (Stritch). This blended family needs a good therapist. **92m/C VHS.** Stockard Channing, Stephen Collins, Christine Ebersole, Elaine Stritch, Noah Fleiss, Chelsea Russo, RuPaul Charles; ***D:*** David Hugh Jones; ***W:*** Lee Rose. **CABLE**

Unexplained Laughter **1989** A cynical journalist vacations in Wales with her timid vegetarian friend and stumbles across a mystery in this darkly comic British TV-movie. **85m/C VHS.** *GB* Diana Rigg, Elaine Page, Jon Finch; ***D:*** Gareth Davies; ***W:*** Alun Owen; ***C:*** Ashley Rowe.

Unfaithful **2002 (R)** Director Lyne may be known for such hot-blooded features as "9 1/2 Weeks," "Fatal Attraction," and "Lolita" but he takes a cooler approach to adultery in this melodrama, which was inspired by Claude Chabrol's 1969 film "La Femme Infidele." Connie (a luscious Lane) is a suburban mom, complacently married to regular guy Edward (Gere), who cannot resist having a hot, hot, hot affair with French bookseller Paul (Martinez), whom Connie meets cute while shopping in New York. Edward gets suspicious, Connie tries to break things off, and it turns out there's nothing like a MAN who gets scorned to bring trouble. **123m/C VHS, DVD, Blu-ray Disc.** *US* Richard Gere, Diane Lane, Olivier Martinez, Erik Per Sullivan, Dominic Chianese, Zeljko Ivanek, Kate Burton, Chad Lowe, Gary Basaraba, Margaret Colin; ***D:*** Adrian Lyne; ***W:*** Alvin Sargent, William Broyles Jr.; ***C:*** Peter Biziou; ***M:*** Jan A.P. Kaczmarek. N.Y. Film Critics '02: Actress (Lane), Actress (Lane).

Unfaithfully Yours 1/2 **1948** A conductor suspects his wife is cheating on him and considers his course of action. He imagines punishment scenarios while directing three classical works. Well-acted by all, but particularly by Harrison as the egotistical and jealous husband. Another of Sturges' comedic gems. Remade in 1984. **105m/B VHS, DVD.** Rex Harrison, Linda Darnell, Kurt Kreuger, Rudy Vallee, Lionel Stander, Edgar Kennedy; ***D:*** Preston Sturges; ***C:*** Victor Milner.

Unfaithfully Yours **1984 (PG)** A symphony conductor suspects his wife of fooling around with a musician; in retaliation, he plots an elaborate scheme to murder her with comic results. No match for the 1948 Preston Sturges film it's based on. **96m/C VHS, DVD.** Dudley Moore, Nastassja Kinski, Armand Assante, Albert Brooks, Cassie Yates, Richard Libertini, Richard B. Shull; ***D:*** Howard Zieff; ***W:*** Valerie Curtin, Barry Levinson, Robert Klane; ***M:*** Bill Conti.

The Unfaithfuls *Le Infedeli* **1960** Infidelity among upper-class Italian society couples leads to divorce, blackmail, suicide, and (amazingly enough) some laughs. One philandering husband tries to catch his wife fooling around so he can get a divorce and hook up with his girlfriend. **89m/B VHS.** *IT* Gina Lollobrigida, May Britt, Irene Papas, Pierre Cressoy, Marina Vlady, Franco Rossi; ***D:*** Mario Monicelli, Steno; ***W:*** Mario Monicelli, Steno, Franco Brusati, Ivo Perilli; ***C:*** Aldo Tonti; ***M:*** Armando Trovajoli.

Unfinished Business 1/2 **1989** A 17 year-old girl leads a troubled adolescent life with her divorced parents. She decides running away will ease her problems—not a smart move. Sequel to "Nobody Waved Goodbye." **88m/C VHS.** *CA* Isabelle Mejias, Peter Kastner, Leslie Toth, Peter Spence, Chuck Shamata, Julie Biggs; ***D:*** Don Owen.

An Unfinished Life 1/2 **2005 (PG-13)** Crusty Wyoming rancher Einar Gilkyson (Redford) has a rundown property he works a little with his best friend, Mitch Bradley (Freeman), who has been severely mauled by a bear. This furry nemesis was captured and unhappily resides in a local animal park. (That's the symbolism you're smelling, not the bear.) Jean Gilkyson (Lopez), Einar's widowed daughter-in-law has been abused by her lowlife boyfriend Gary (Lewis) for the last time and unwillingly seeks shelter at the ranch with her tough-talking, 11-year-old daughter Griff (Gardner). Einar, who blames Jean for his son's death, grudging allows them to stay temporarily and gradually thaws towards his spunky granddaughter. Much gruff bonding and a family reconciliation finally ensue (with the bear playing its part). Tomboyish Gardner is a delight, though Lopez has little to do and makes an equally slight impression. Best are the interactions between pros Redford and Freeman, whose characters squabble and fuss like a longtime married couple. Co-writer Spragg adapted from his novel. **107m/C DVD.** *US* Robert Redford, Morgan Freeman, Jennifer Lopez, Josh(ua) Lucas, Damian Lewis, Camryn Manheim, Becca Gardner; ***D:*** Lasse Hallstrom, Andrew Mondshein; ***W:*** Mark Spragg; ***C:*** Oliver Stapleton; ***M:*** Christopher Young.

An Unfinished Piece for a Player Piano 1/2 **1977** A general's widow invites family and friends to a weekend house party in 1910 Russia. Romantic and familial entanglements begin to intrude in a lyrical adaptation of Chekov's play "Platonov." In Russian with English subtitles. **100m/C VHS, DVD.** *RU* Alexander Kalyagin, Elena Solovei, Antonina Shuranova, Oleg Tabakov, Yuri Bogatyrev, Nikita Mikhalkov; ***D:*** Nikita Mikhalkov.

Unforgettable **1996 (R)** Unfortunately, the film doesn't live up to its title. On-the-edge medical examiner David Krane (Liotta) has barely escaped conviction for his wife's brutal murder. Living under a cloud of suspicion, he turns to university researcher Martha Briggs (Fiorentino, wasted as a nerdy scientist), whose experiments in memory transference lead David to believe he can uncover the killer. But, like a Chinese puzzle box, one discovery only leads to a further complication. Too many, in fact, for the story to stay focused (and the ending is less than satisfying). **116m/C VHS, DVD.** Ray Liotta, Linda Fiorentino, Peter Coyote, Christopher McDonald, Kim Cattrall, David Paymer, Kim Coates, Duncan Fraser, Garwin Sanford; ***D:*** John Dahl; ***W:*** Bill Geddie; ***C:*** Jeffrey Jur; ***M:*** Christopher Young.

An Unforgettable Summer 1/2 **1994** The elegant Marie-Therese Dumitriu (Scott Thomas) has married Army officer Petre (Bleont) and tried to focus on maintaining a serene life, following the Communist takeover of Romania. When Petre is transferred to an isolated border town, he and his family are caught between what the Army demands and what is just. The local Bulgarian peasants are accused of attrocities against the soldiers and Petre is ordered to execute a group of them as an example—guilty or not. Set in 1925 and based on the short story "La Salade" by Petru Dumitriu. English, French, and Romanian with subtitles. **82m/C VHS.** *RO* Kristin Scott Thomas, Claudiu Bleont, Olga Tudorache, George Constantin; ***D:*** Lucian Pintilie; ***W:*** Lucian Pintilie; ***C:*** Calin Ghibu; ***M:*** Anton Suteu.

The Unforgiven **1960** A western family is torn asunder when it is suspected that the eldest daughter is of Indian birth. Film takes place in 1850s' Texas. One of Huston's weakest ventures, but viewed in terms of 1950s' prejudices it has more resonance. Fine acting from all the cast, especially Gish. Watch for the stunning Indian attack scene. **123m/C VHS, DVD.** Burt Lancaster, Audrey Hepburn, Lillian Gish, Audie Murphy, John Saxon, Charles Bickford, Doug McClure, Joseph Wiseman, Albert Salmi; ***D:*** John Huston.

Unforgiven 1/2 **1992 (R)** Will Munny (Eastwood) lives a quiet life with his stepchildren on his failing pig farm, but his desperado past catches up with him when the Schofield Kid invites him to a bounty hunt. Munny reluctantly agrees, mistakenly believing that once the killing is through he can take up his peaceful ways again. Enter sadistic sheriff Little Bill Daggett (Hackman), who doesn't want any gunmen messing up his town. Eastwood uses his own status as a screen legend to full advantage as the aging gunman who realizes too late that his past can never be forgotten. Director Eastwood is also in top form with his well-seasoned cast and myth-defying Old West realism. Surprising critical and boxoffice hit. **131m/C VHS, DVD, Blu-ray Disc.** Clint Eastwood, Gene Hackman, Morgan Freeman, Richard Harris, Jaimz Woolvett, Saul Rubinek, Frances Fisher, Anna Thomson, David Mucci, Rob Campbell, Anthony James; ***D:*** Clint Eastwood; ***W:*** David Peoples; ***C:*** Jack N. Green; ***M:*** Lennie Niehaus. Oscars '92: Director (Eastwood), Film Editing, Picture, Support. Actor (Hackman); AFI '98: Top 100; British Acad. '92: Director (Eastwood), Film, Support. Actor (Hackman); Directors Guild '92: Director (Eastwood); Golden Globes '93: Director (Eastwood), Support. Actor (Hackman); L.A. Film Critics '92: Actor (Eastwood), Director (Eastwood), Film, Screenplay, Support. Actor (Hackman); N.Y. Film Critics '92: Support. Actor (Hackman); Natl. Soc. Film Critics '92: Director (Eastwood), Film, Screenplay, Support. Actor (Hackman).

The Unholy 1/2 **1988 (R)** A New Orleans priest battles a demon that's killing innocent parishioners. Confusing and heavy-handed. **100m/C VHS.** Ben Cross, Hal Holbrook, Trevor Howard, Ned Beatty, William Russ, James Dennis (Jim) Carroll; ***D:*** Camilo Vila; ***W:*** Philip Yordan; ***M:*** Roger Bellon.

Unholy **2007** After widowed Martha's daughter commits suicide, she and son Lucas decide to investigate, which leads them to brainwashing techniques and government conspiracies. Dull, drab, and confusing. **86m/C DVD.** Adrienne Barbeau, Nicholas Brendon, Siri Baruc; ***D:*** Daryl Goldberg; ***W:*** Sam Freeman; ***C:*** Jeff Maher. **VIDEO**

Unholy Four 1/2 *A Stranger Came Home* **1954** An amnesiac returns home after three years to attempt to find out which of his three fishing buddies left him for dead. Confusing at times, but has some suspenseful moments. **80m/B VHS.** *GB* Paulette Goddard, Paul Carpenter, William Sylvester, Patrick Holt, Russell Napier; ***D:*** Terence Fisher; ***W:*** Michael Carreras; ***C:*** Walter J. (Jimmy W.) Harvey; ***M:*** Ivor Slaney, Leonard Salzedo.

Unholy Rollers *Leader of the Pack* **1972 (R)** Jennings stars as a factory worker who makes it big as a tough, violent roller derby star. Typical "Babes-on-Wheels" film that promises nothing and delivers even less. **88m/C VHS.** Claudia Jennings, Louis Quinn, Betty Anne Rees, Roberta Collins, Alan Vint, Candice Roman; ***D:*** Vernon Zimmerman.

The Unholy Three 1/2 **1925** Ventriloquist Chaney, working with other carnival cohorts, uses his talent to gain entrance to homes which he later robs. Things go awry when two of the gang strike out on their own and the victim is killed. When the wrong man is accused, his girl, one of Chaney's gang, begs Chaney to get him free, which he does by using his vocal talents. Chaney decides being a criminal is just too hard and goes back to his ventriloquism. **70m/B VHS.** Lon Chaney Sr., Harry Earles, Victor McLaglen, Mae Busch, Matt Moore, Matthew Betz, William Humphreys; ***D:*** Tod Browning.

The Unholy Three **1930** Chaney remade his silent hit of 1925 for his first and only talking picture (he died before the film was released). The story is essentially the same. Chaney is a ventriloquist who, with his circus friends, work as scam artists and thieves. When an innocent man is accused of their crimes Chaney tries his ventriloquist tricks to come to his aid, only in this version Chaney is exposed as a fraud and is sent to prison. Rumors that Chaney was a mute had him agreeing to appear in a "talkie" and he actually used five different voices for his various roles. **75m/B VHS.** Lon Chaney Sr., Lila Lee, Elliott Nugent, Harry Earles, John Miljan; ***D:*** Jack Conway.

Unholy Wife 1/2 **1957** A young woman plans to murder her wealthy husband, but her plan goes awry when she accidentally kills someone else. Muddled and heavy-handed, with Steiger chewing scenery. **94m/C VHS.** Rod Steiger, Diana Dors, Tom Tryon, Marie Windsor, Beulah Bondi; ***D:*** John Farrow. .

Unhook the Stars 1/2 **1996 (R)** Director Cassavetes does mom Rowlands proud (and she him) with the lead role of widowed Mildred, who discovers there's life after the kids leave the nest. At loose ends, Mildred befriends her wild young neighbor Monica (Tomei), who conveniently needs a babysitter for her solemn six-year-old son, J.J. (Lloyd). Monica also tries to get Mildred to loosen up by taking her to a local joint, where French-Canadian trucker Tommy (Depardieu) knows a good woman when he sees one. Mildred makes some tentative steps towards independence and we get to enjoy the stellar Rowlands once again. **105m/C VHS, DVD.** Gena Rowlands, Marisa Tomei, Gerard Depardieu, Moira Kelly, Jake Lloyd, David Sherrill, David Thornton; ***D:*** Nick Cassavetes; ***W:*** Nick Cassavetes, Helen Caldwell; ***C:*** Phedon Papamichael; ***M:*** Steven Hufsteter.

Unidentified Flying Oddball 1/2 **1979 (G)** An astronaut and his robotic buddy find their spaceship turning into a time machine that throws them back into Arthurian times and at the mercy of Merlin the magician. Futuristic version of Twain's "A Connecticut Yankee at King Arthur's Court." **92m/C VHS, DVD.** Dennis Dugan, Jim Dale, Ron Moody, Kenneth More, Rodney Bewes; ***D:*** Russ Mayberry; ***W:*** Don Tait; ***C:*** Paul Beeson; ***M:*** Ronald Goodwin.

Uniform *Zhifu* **2003** A young man goes to work in the family shop in order to help pay his father's medical bills. When a policeman leaves his uniform to be tailored, the young man puts it on and gains instant respect, especially from Zheng, who is also leading another life—as a prostitute. Mandarin with subtitles. **92m/C DVD.** *CH* Kai Han, Hongli Liang, Hua Qin; ***D:*** Diao Yinan; ***W:*** Diao Yinan; ***C:*** Jingsong Dong; ***M:*** Zi Wan.

The Uninvited **1944** Roderick Fitzgerald (Milland) and his sister Pamela (Hussey) buy a house in Cornwall, only to find it is haunted. Doors open and close by themselves, strange scents fill the air, and they hear sobbing during the night. Soon they are visited by a woman (Russell) with an odd link to the house—her mother is the spirit who haunts the house. Chilling and unforgettable, this is one of the first films to deal seriously with ghosts. Based on the novel by Dorothy Macardle. **99m/B VHS.** Ray Milland, Ruth Hussey, Donald Crisp, Cornelia Otis Skinner, Gail Russell, Alan Napier, Dorothy Stickney; ***D:*** Lewis Allen; ***W:*** Dodie Smith, Frank Partos; ***C:*** Charles B(ryant) Lang Jr.; ***M:*** Victor Young.

The Uninvited WOOF! **1988** A mutant cat goes berserk onboard a luxury yacht, killing the passengers one by one with big, nasty, pointy teeth. **89m/C VHS.** George Kennedy, Alex Cord, Clu Gulager, Toni Hudson, Eric Larson, Shari Shattuck, Austin Stoker; ***D:*** Greydon Clark.

Uninvited 1/2 **1993 (R)** Grady is a mysterious old man who leads eight misfits to the top of a sacred mountain with the promise of finding gold. But the fortune hunters have trespassed in a sacred Indian burial ground and find their nightmares becoming a violent reality. **90m/C VHS, DVD.** Jack Elam, Christopher Boyer, Erin Noble, Bari Buckner, Jerry Rector, Zane Paolo, Dennis Gibbs, Ted Haler, Eno Brutto; ***D:*** Michael Derek Bohusz; ***W:*** Michael Derek Bohusz.

The Uninvited 1/2 **2009 (PG-13)** Institutionalized for months after a suicide attempt, Anna (Browning) returns home for the first time since the tragic death of her ill mother (Masser) to find that her father (Strathairn) is engaged to Rachel (Banks), mom's nurse during her illness. Suspicious of Rachel's overly saccharin behavior, Anna and sister Alex (Kebbel) soon see Rachel's dark side. By then Anna begins seeing disturbing visions—among them the ghost of her mother delivering a message of doom about the soon-to-be stepmom. Remake of the 2003 Korean horror hit "Changhwa Hongryeon" (A Tale of Two Sisters), its great cinematography and even better locations fall short of delivering the original's uneasy suspense, though the final plot twist is definitely creepy. **87m/C DVD.** *US* Emily Browning, Elizabeth Banks, Arielle Kebbel, David Strathairn, Maya Massar, Thomas Guard, Jesse Moss, Dean Paul Gibson; ***D:*** Charles Guard; ***W:*** Doug Miro, Carlo Bernard, Craig Rossenberg; ***C:*** Dan Landin; ***M:*** Christopher Young.

Uninvited Guest 1/2 *An Invited Guest* **1999 (R)** Smooth-talking Silk (Phifer) comes to the suburban home of Howard (Jackson) and Debbie (Morrow) and asks to use their phone. The couple agree and let the stranger in and he promptly takes them and their friends captive. A twist comes unexpected early and takes a little away from the real ending. **103m/C VHS, DVD.** Mekhi Phifer, Mari Morrow, Mel Jackson, Kim Fields, Malinda Williams; ***D:*** Timothy Wayne Folsome; ***W:*** Timothy Wayne Folsome; ***C:*** Wayne Sells; ***M:*** Gregory Darryl Smith. **VIDEO**

Union City **1981 (R)** Deborah "Blondie" Harry's husband gets a little edgy when someone steals the milk. Murder ensues, and they're on the run from the law. Intended as a film noir spoof, and not without some good moments. **82m/C VHS, DVD.** Deborah Harry, Everett McGill, Dennis Lipscomb, Pat Benatar, Irina Maleeva, Terina Lewis, Sam McMurray, Paul Andor, Tony Azito, CCH Pounder; ***D:*** Mark Reichert; ***W:*** Mark Reichert; ***C:*** Edward Lachman; ***M:*** Chris Stein.

Union Depot 1/2 **1932** Chic (Fairbanks Jr.) and Scrap Iron (Kibbee) are tramps who find their luck changing when they hang around a train station. First Chic finds some dough and a nice suit in the washroom and gives himself a makeover. Then Scrap Iron finds a checkroom claim ticket—lost by con man The Baron (Hale Sr.)—and redeems it for a violin case full of dough. Meanwhile, stranded chorus girl Ruth (Blondell) is doing a little vamping of Chic so he'll give her the fare to get to her gig in Salt Lake City. But there's trouble when G-men start looking for counterfeit money being passed around the station. **68m/B DVD.** Douglas Fairbanks Jr., Joan Blondell, Guy Kibbee, Alan Hale, George Rosener, David Landau, Earle Foxe; ***D:*** Alfred E. Green; ***W:*** Kubec Glasmon, John Bright, Walter DeLeon, Kenyon Nicholson; ***C:*** Sol Polito.

Union Pacific **1939** Full DeMille treatment highlights this saga about the building of America's first transcontinental railroad. Jeff Butler (McCrea) is the construction overseer who must battle saboteurs and Indians (although the U.S. Cavalry does arrive to save the day). He also gets to fall for self-sufficient postmistress Mollie Monahan (Stanwyck). DeMille borrowed the actual golden spike used to drive in the last rail in 1869 for his reenactment of the completion celebration. Based on the book "Trouble Shooters" by Ernest Haycox. **136m/B VHS, DVD.** Joel McCrea, Barbara Stanwyck, Robert Preston, Brian Donlevy, Akim Tamiroff, Lynne Overman, Robert Barrat, Anthony Quinn, Stanley Ridges, Henry Kolker, Evelyn Keyes, Regis Toomey; ***D:*** Cecil B. DeMille; ***W:*** Walter DeLeon, Jesse Lasky Jr., C. Gardner Sullivan; ***C:*** Victor Milner.

Union Station **1950** Holden plays the chief of the railway police for Chicago's Union Station. He learns the station is to be used as a ransom drop in a kidnapping; but for all his security, the main thug gets away with the money, and the hunt is on. Good acting raises this film above the ordinary. **80m/B VHS.** William Holden, Barry Fitzgerald, Nancy Olson, Jan Sterling, Lee Marvin, Allene Roberts, Lyle Bettger; ***D:*** Rudolph Mate; ***C:*** Daniel F. Fapp.

United 93 **2006 (R)** Greengrass' intense, emotional drama covers the hijacking of United Airlines Flight 93 on September 11, 2001. Events alternate between what is happening onboard as the passengers and crew try to disarm the hijackers and what is happening at the FAA, air defense headquarters, and airport control towers as realization dawns about the scope of the disaster and what, if anything, can be done. The Boeing 757 eventually crashed near Shanksville, Pennsylvania, with a total loss of life. Greengrass filmed in the U.K., and a number of the cast are nonprofessionals playing themselves. **111m/C DVD.** *US* David Alan Basche, Richard Bekins, Susan Blommaert, Christian Clemenson, Ray Charleson, Gregg Henry, Polly Adams, Denny Dillon, Khalid Abdalla, Lewis Alsamari, Ben Sliney, Maj. James Fox, Trish Gates, Cheyenne Jackson; ***D:*** Paul Greengrass; ***W:*** Paul Greengrass; ***C:*** Barry Ackroyd; ***M:*** John Powell. British Acad. '06: Director (Greengrass), Film Editing.

U.S. Marshals **1998 (PG-13)** Jones reprises his Oscar-winning role from "The Fugitive" as the hound dog U.S. Marshal Sam Gerard in this lackluster sequel. Gerard tracks down Sheridan (Snipes) who is framed for a double homicide of two federal agents. Gerard's probing reveals that Sheridan really isn't the average Joe he seems, and the presence of shifty agent Downey Jr. further confirms Gerard's suspicions of a government cover-up. Jones remains solid in a popular role, supported well by his sidekick Cosmo (Pantolino). The stunts equal if not better its predecessor, yet a poorly developed Sheridan, compounded by Snipes's lack of intensity drag this chase movie down to a slow crawl. **133m/C VHS, DVD.** Tommy Lee Jones, Robert Downey Jr., Wesley Snipes, Joe Pantoliano, Kate Nelligan, Irene Jacob, Daniel Roebuck, Tom Wood, LaTanya Richardson Jackson, Michael Paul Chan; ***D:*** Stuart Baird; ***W:*** John Pogue; ***C:*** Andrzej Bartkowiak; ***M:*** Jerry Goldsmith.

U.S. Navy SEALS: Dead or Alive 1/2 **2002 (R)** Lots of action, not much plot, which doesn't really matter with these sorts of movies. Terrorist Casper has promised to sell a cluster bomb to some renegades, although he doesn't have it yet. A team of Navy SEALS is assigned to locate and take possession of the bomb before Casper gets to it. **93m/C VHS, DVD.** Tyler Christopher, Bentley Mitchum, John Simon Jones, Gary Murphy; ***D:*** Franklin A. Vallette; ***W:*** Steve Latshaw; ***C:*** Don E. Fauntleroy. **VIDEO**

United States of Leland **2003 (R)** Low-key high school student Leland (Gosling) senselessly stabs his ex-girlfriend's autistic brother to death at the beginning of this bleak flick. Director Hoge then spends the rest of his debut film juggling the pieces attempting to define Leland's motivation. Was it his heroin-addicted girlfriend (Malone) who left him for her dealer? Or his emotionally absent novelist father, Albert (Spacey)? Or something else? Meanwhile, Pearl (Cheadle), an aspiring but struggling writer, is Leland's juvenile detention counselor who sees in him an opportunity for his first novel and the hidden agenda has its own consequences. While those encounters provide some lively scenes, and Spacey, Cheadle, and Malone give capable performances, there's no sustaining this disjointed piece. **108m/C DVD.** *US* Ryan Gosling, Don Cheadle, Chris Klein, Jena Malone, Lena Olin, Kevin Spacey, Michelle Williams, Martin Donovan, Ann Magnuson, Kerry Washington, Sherilyn Fenn, Matt Malloy, Michael Pena, Ron Canada, Troy Winbush, Yolonda Ross, Jim Haynie, Kimberly Scott, Ryan Malgarini, Clyde Kusatsu, Sheeri Rappaport, Angela Paton, Michael Welch; ***D:*** Matthew Ryan Hoge; ***W:*** Matthew Ryan Hoge; ***C:*** James Glennon; ***M:*** Jeremy Enigk.

U.S. Seals **1998 (R)** Absolutely undistinguished action flick pits a team of Navy SEALs against pirates from Kazakhstan. The heroes are jut-jawed guys with crewcuts and cute kids. Lots of stuff blows up. Production values are strictly of the made-for-cable quality. **90m/C DVD.** Jim (James) Fitzpatrick, Greg Collins, J. Kenneth Campbell; ***D:*** Yossi Wein.

U.S. Seals 2 1/2 **2001 (R)** An ex-SEAL is planning to launch a nuclear strike on the U.S. from a secret Russian missile base unless the good guys can stop him. **95m/C VHS, DVD.** Damian Chapa, Mike Worth, Marshall Teague, Sophia Crawford; ***D:*** Isaac Florentine; ***W:*** Michael D. Weiss; ***C:*** Peter Belcher; ***M:*** Stephen (Steve) Edwards. **VIDEO**

U.S. SEALs: Dead or Alive *Frogmen Operation Stormbringer; U.S. SEALs 3: Frogmen* **2002 (R)** A team of Navy SEALs must locate a cluster bomb before terrorists sell it to the Albania government. The producers no doubt hope the action with be enough cover for the dumb plot and subpar acting, but they're wrong. **93m/C DVD.** Tyler Christopher, John Simon Jones, Bentley Mitchum, Gary Murphy, George Stanchev; ***D:*** Franklin A. Vallette; ***W:*** Steve Latshaw; ***C:*** Don E. Fauntleroy; ***M:*** Serge Colbert. **VIDEO**

The U.S. Vs. John Lennon **2006 (PG-13)** A look at peace advocate John Lennon's post-Beatles contributions to music and popular culture that leaves out the man's dark edges (the documentary was made with the cooperation of Yoko Ono, so no surprise there). The focus is on the Nixon's administration paranoid view of Lennon as an enemy to national security and his subjection to wiretapping, surveillance, and a deportation order. Music from Lennon's solo career highlights the visuals and it features an odd group of talking heads, from Geraldo Rivera to Gore Vidal. **99m/C DVD.** *US* ***D:*** David Leaf, John Scheinfeld; ***W:*** David Leaf, John Scheinfeld; ***C:*** James Mathers.

Universal Soldier **1992 (R)** A reporter discovers a secret government project to design perfect robo-soldiers by using the bodies of dead GIs, including tough guys Lundgren and Van Damme who were killed in Vietnam. But the knowledge is going to get her killed until Van Damme has flashbacks of his past (the soldier's memories have supposedly been erased) and agrees to help her. Lundgren doesn't have the same compassion and goes after them both. Big-budget thriller with some good action sequences and a lot of violence. **98m/C VHS, DVD, UMD.** Jean-Claude Van Damme, Dolph Lundgren, Ally Walker, Ed O'Ross, Jerry Orbach; ***D:*** Roland Emmerich; ***W:*** Dean Devlin, Christopher Leitch, Richard Rothstein; ***C:*** Karl Walter Lindenlaub; ***M:*** Christopher Franke.

Universal Soldier 2: Brothers in Arms **1998 (R)** Cable actioner not to be confused with the 1999 big-screen sequel "Universal Soldier: The Return" starring Jean-Claude Van Damme. Here, Luc Devereaux (Battaglia), who works for the top-secret UniSol military operation, teams up with journalist Veronica Roberts (West) to expose UniSol's plan to re-animate dead soldiers into unstoppable killing machines. **93m/C VHS.** Matt Battaglia, Chandra West, Gary Busey, Jeff Wincott; ***D:*** Jeff Woolnough; ***W:*** Peter M. Lenkov; ***C:*** Russ Goozee; ***M:*** Ivan Dorochuk, John Kastner, Steve Pecile. **CABLE**

Universal Soldier 3: Unfinished Business 1/2 **1998 (R)** An ex-soldier and a journalist try to stop a billion-dollar robbery and discover the deadly (and dead) military men are active once again. **95m/C VHS.** Matt Battaglia, Chandra West, Burt Reynolds, Jeff Wincott; ***D:*** Jeff Woolnough; ***W:*** Peter M. Lenkov; ***C:*** Russ Goozee; ***M:*** Ivan Dorochuk, John Kastner, Steve Pecile. **CABLE**

Universal Soldier: Regeneration **2009 (R)** Hardcore action in this fifth flick, which reunites Van Damme and Lundgren, as a futuristic terrorist (Arlovski) and his crew take over the Chernobyl nuclear reactor and threaten a meltdown. Dormant universal soldier Luc Deveraux (Van Damme) is reactivated to stop them but the bad guys have UniSol's version (Lundgren) to help them. **98m/C DVD.** Dolph Lundgren, Jean-Claude Van Damme, Andrei Arlovski, Mike Pyle, Garry Cooper; ***D:*** John Hyam; ***W:*** Victor Ostrovsky; ***C:*** Peter Hyams. **VIDEO**

Universal Soldier: The Return **1999 (R)** The creators of superwarrior Van Damme have double-crossed him and he's out to get even in this sequel (although technically it's the fourth installment after two straight-to-cable releases). After Defense Department cutbacks short circuit the Universal Soldier program, the cyborgs start a rebellion led by an evil computer. Van Damme must battle the renegade warriors while attempting to not muss his hair. The Muscles from Brussels goes back to a proven winner after a series of boxoffice stinkers in hopes that he can kick-start his flagging career. **82m/C VHS, DVD.** Jean-Claude Van Damme, Michael Jai White, Daniel von Bargen, Heidi Schanz, Xander Berkeley, Justin Lazard; ***D:*** Mic Rodgers; ***W:*** John Fasano, William Malone; ***C:*** Michael A. Benson; ***M:*** Don Davis.

The Unkissed Bride *Mother Goose A Go-Go* **1966 (PG)** A young newlywed couple are driven to distraction by the husband's inexplicable fainting spells and his strange obsession with Mother Goose. **82m/C VHS, DVD.** Tommy Kirk, Anne Helm, Danica D'Hondt, Henny Youngman; ***D:*** Jack H. Harris.

The Unknown 1/2 **1927** Typically morbid Chaney fare has him working as a circus freak while trying to win the heart of his assistant. After drastic romancing he's still rejected by her, so he plots to kill the object of her intentions. Ghoulish as it is, the picture is really top-notch. **60m/B VHS, DVD.** Lon Chaney Sr., Norman Kerry, Joan Crawford, Nick De Ruiz, Frank Lanning, John St. Polis; ***D:*** Tod Browning.

Unknown Island 1/2 **1948** Scientists travel to a legendary island where dinosaurs supposedly still exist. Bogus dinosaurs and cliche script. **76m/C VHS, DVD.** Virginia Grey, Philip Reed, Richard Denning, Barton MacLane; ***D:*** Jack Bernhard; ***W:*** Jack Harvey, Robert T. Shannon; ***C:*** Fred W. Jackman; ***M:*** Ralph Stanley.

Unknown Origin *The Alien Within; Roger Corman Presents: The Alien Within* **1995 (R)** Scientific crew is stuck in an underwater installation with a deadly parasite. It's "Aliens" under the sea but a few twists will tweak your interest. **75m/C VHS, DVD.** Roddy McDowall, Melanie Shatner, Alex Hyde-

White, Don Stroud; *D:* Scott Levy; *W:* Alex Simon; *M:* Christopher Lennertz. **CABLE**

Unknown Powers WOOF! 1980 (PG) Science and drama are combined to examine ESP and magic. Are they gifts or curses, and how are peoples' lives affected by them? Members of the cast introduce various sections of this totally inept film. **97m/C VHS, DVD.** Samantha Eggar, Jack Palance, Will Geer, Roscoe Lee Browne; *D:* Don Como.

The Unknown Ranger 1/2 **1936** Allen's first cowboy role has him foiling a gang of rustlers. The real highlight turns out to be the battle between his horse and a wild stallion. Eat your heart out, Trigger! **57m/B VHS.** Robert "Tex" Allen, Harry Woods, Martha Tibbetts, Hal Taliaferro, Robert "Buzzy" Henry; *D:* Spencer Gordon Bennet.

The Unknown Soldier 1/2 **1998** Fine performances in an ultimately depressing drama, with some unexpected twists, focusing on the tragedy of war. When aristocratic Sophia Carey's (Aubrey) ancestral home is turned into a private hospital for WWI soldiers, she seriously takes up her nursing duties. One of her latest patients is an amnesiac, initially mute soldier nicknamed Angel (Mavers) by the men who rescued him in France. Sophia falls hopelessly in love with the traumatized Angel but the working-class Jenny (McGuckin) claims Angel is actually her fiance John and the military police believe he's a deserter wanted for murder. **180m/C VHS, DVD.** *GB* Juliet Aubrey, Gary Mavers, Aislin McGuckin; *D:* David Drury; *W:* Peter Barwood. **TV**

Unknown White Male 1/2 **2005 (PG-13)** Spellbinding documentary following the lost life of Doug Bruce, a man with retrograde amnesia. Two years prior Doug took a subway trip to Coney Island; once he arrived he didn't know where he was or why he was there. Since that time, for reasons no one knows, his entire memory has been wiped out. His family, his girlfriend, his home have become pieces in a puzzle he's unable to fit back together. Completely absorbing and provocative. Would make for a wicked psycho-drama. **88m/C DVD.** *US* *D:* Rupert Murray; *C:* Orlando Stuart; *M:* Mukul.

The Unknown Woman 1/2 *La Sconoscuita* **2006 (R)** Ukrainian Irina was forced into the life of a sex slave but escaped with money stolen from her brutal pimp Muffa. Having made her way to Trieste, Irina gets a job as the nanny to Thea, the fragile adopted daughter of the Adachers, who are gold dealers. Irina has a secret (about a black market baby scam) and Muffa is still determined to find her. Highly disturbing situations and brutal violence involving women and children. Italian with subtitles. **120m/C DVD.** *IT* Kseniya Rappoport, Michele Placido, Claudia Gerini, Pierfrancesco Favino, Clara Dossena, Piera Degli Esposti; *D:* Giuseppe Tornatore; *W:* Giuseppe Tornatore; *C:* Fabio Zamarion; *M:* Ennio Morricone.

Unknown World **1951** A group of scientists tunnel to the center of the Earth to find a refuge from the dangers of the atomic world. Big start winds down fast. Director Terry Morse sometimes credited as Terrell O. Morse. **73m/B VHS, DVD.** Bruce Kellogg, Marilyn Nash, Victor Kilian, Jim Bannon; *D:* Terry Morse; *M:* Ernest Gold.

Unlawful Entry **1992 (R)** After a break-in, Karen and Michael Carr naturally call the cops. Handsome, polite policeman Pete Davis responds to the call and agrees to help burglar-proof their home. But Pete has some definite quirks—he falls for the beauteous Karen and begins stalking the couple, deciding to get rid of Michael in order to have his wife. A lurid combination of the worst moments of "Internal Affairs" and "Fatal Attraction" undermines this usually talented cast. **107m/C VHS, DVD.** Kurt Russell, Ray Liotta, Madeleine Stowe, Roger E. Mosley, Ken Lerner, Deborah Offner, Carmen Argenziano, Andy Romano, Barry W. Blaustein, Dick Miller; *D:* Jonathan Kaplan; *W:* Lewis Colick; *C:* Jamie Anderson; *M:* James Horner.

Unlawful Passage **1994 (R)** Vacation turns into a nightmare when a man's wife is kidnapped. **?m/C VHS.** Lee Horsley, William Zabka, Felicity Waterman; *D:* Camilo Vila; *W:* Peter Dixon; *C:* Henry Vargas.

Unleashed *Danny the Dog* **2005 (R)** Fight scenes are taken to seat-jolting heights by renowned martial-arts choreographer Yuen Wo Ping in this live-action cyberpunk cartoon starring Jet Li as Danny the human pit bull. Enslaved from childhood and conditioned to kill without conscience by his ruthless London mobster "owner" Bart (Hoskins), Danny maims and mutilates delinquent debtors when his collar is removed. With the collar he's passive and docile. His accidental liberation sends him to the only person who was ever kind to him, a blind piano tuner (Freeman), who through piano music helps connect him with his humanity. The gangster, alas, returns for Danny resulting in one last showdown of canine love and loyalty. **102m/C DVD, UMD, HD DVD.** *US FR GB HK* Jet Li, Morgan Freeman, Bob Hoskins, Michael Jenn, Kerry Gordon, Christian Gazio, Carole Ann Wilson; *D:* Louis Leterrier; *W:* Luc Besson; *C:* Pierre Morel; *M:* Massive Attack.

Unlikely Angel 1/2 **1997** Brassy singer Ruby Diamond (Parton) dies suddenly in an accident but is having some trouble entering heaven. St. Peter (McDowall) thinks she's a likely prospect but Ruby needs a few more good deeds before she can get her wings. So she's sent to help a frazzled widower (Kerwin) who's the father of two lonely preteens. **90m/C VHS, DVD.** Dolly Parton, Roddy McDowall, Brian Kerwin; *D:* Michael Switzer.

An Unmarried Woman **1978 (R)** Suddenly divorced by her husband of 17 years, a woman deals with change. She enters the singles scene, copes with her daughter's growing sexuality, and encounters a new self-awareness. Mazursky puts real people on screen from start to finish. **124m/C VHS, DVD.** Jill Clayburgh, Alan Bates, Cliff Gorman, Michael Murphy; *D:* Paul Mazursky; *W:* Paul Mazursky; *M:* Bill Conti. Cannes '78: Actress (Clayburgh); L.A. Film Critics '78: Screenplay; N.Y. Film Critics '78: Screenplay; Natl. Soc. Film Critics '78: Screenplay.

Unmasked Part 25 1/2 **1988** A second-generation serial killer takes up where dad left off. This one is intended to be a parody of slasher films, but it's still very bloody. **85m/C VHS.** *GB* Gregory Cox, Fiona Evans, Edward Brayshaw, Debbie Lee London; *D:* Anders Palm.

Unmasking the Idol **1986** A suave hero with tongue firmly in check battles Ninja warlords. Sequel to "Order of the Black Eagle." **90m/C VHS.** *GB* Ian Hunter, William T. Hicks, Charles K. Bibby; *D:* Worth Keeter.

The Unmistaken Child *Ha-Gilgul* **2008** Israeli documentary chronicles Nepalese monk Tenzin Zopa's years-long search for the reincarnation of a deceased Buddhist master. Senior lamas in India consult Taiwanese astrologers for clues that have disciple Zopa examining a number of young children on his travels to find the new embodiment of Geshe Lama Konchog. Tibetan, Nepali, Hindi, and Taiwanese with subtitles. **104m/C DVD.** *IS* *D:* Nati Baratz; *W:* Nati Baratz, Ilil Alexander; *C:* Yaron Orbach; *M:* Cyril Morin.

The Unnamable **1988** The adaptation of the H.P. Lovecraft story about a particular New England ancestral home haunted by a typically Lovecraftian bloodthirsty demon borne of a woman hundreds of years before. College students, between trysts, investigate the myths about it. Uncut version, unseen in theatres, available only on video good for a few giggles and thrills. **87m/C VHS.** Charles King, Mark Kinsey Stephenson, Alexandra Durrell, Laura Albert, Eben Ham, Blane Wheatley, Mark Parra, Katrin Alexandre; *D:* Jean-Paul Ouellette; *W:* Jean-Paul Ouellette; *C:* Tom Fraser.

The Unnamable 2: The Statement of Randolph Carter 1/2 *H.P. Lovecraft's The Unnamable Returns; The Unnamable Returns* **1992 (R)** Randolph Carter is investigating a series of murders at Miskatonic University. Evidence leads Carter back to a 17th-century warlock who had the misfortune to summon an evil creature known as Alyda. The half-demon, half-woman now wants to permanently return to the mortal plane and every new victim just helps her evil purpose along. Based on a story by H.P. Lovecraft. **104m/C VHS, DVD.** Mark Kinsey Stephenson, John Rhys-Davies, David Warner, Julie Strain, Maria Ford, Charles Klausmeyer; *D:* Jean-Paul Ouellette; *W:* Jean-Paul Ouellette; *C:* Greg Gardiner.

Unnatural 1/2 **1952** A mad scientist creates a souless child from the genes of a murderer and a prostitute. The child grows up to be the beautiful Neff, who makes a habit of seducing and destroying men. Dark, arresting film from a very popular German story. **90m/B VHS, DVD.** Hildegarde Knef, Erich von Stroheim, Karl-Heinz Boehm, Harry Meyen, Harry Helm, Denise Vernac, Julia Koschka; *D:* Arthur Maria Rabenalt.

Unnatural Causes **1986** A dying Vietnam vet believes that his illness is the result of exposure to Agent Orange. With the help of a VA counselor, they lobby for national programs to assist other veterans who have been exposed to the chemical and together bring publicity to the issue. A TV drama that is exceptionally well-acted. **96m/C VHS, DVD.** John Ritter, Patti LaBelle, Alfre Woodard, John Sayles, Sean McCann, John Vargas, Gwen E. Davis; *D:* Lamont Johnson; *W:* John Sayles; *M:* Charles Fox. **TV**

Unnatural Pursuits **1991** Playwright Simon Gray's black comic look at a British playwright's sojourn from London to L.A., Dallas, and New York and the Broadway debut of his new work. Alcoholic Hamish Partt (Bates), in the throes of a midlife crisis, is plagued by ego, indignities, and hostile actors, audiences, and critics as he tries desperately to work. Made for British TV. **60m/C VHS.** *GB* Alan Bates, Keith Szarabajka, Deborah Rush, John Mahoney, Tom Hickey, Richard Wilson, David Healy, Jack Gilpin, Paul Zimet, Bob Balaban; *W:* Simon Gray. **TV**

Uno 1/2 **2004** Living in Oslo with his dying father, withdrawn mother, and mentally-challenged brother proves too much for 25-year-old David (Hennie) who seeks refuge with the wrong crowd at the local gym and ends up under arrest. The distasteful change of scenery makes him grasp the meaning of life so he rats out the bad guys to get out of jail and rushes to his dad's deathbed to make amends. Unfortunately the crooks aren't so forgiving and unleash an overwhelming wave of violence that's not for the meek. Lead actor Hennie also wrote and directed. In Norwegian with English subtitles. **99m/C DVD.** Bjorn Floberg, Aksel Hennie, Nicolai Cleve Broch, Espen Juul Kristiansen, Ahmed Zeyan, Martin Skaug; *D:* Aksel Hennie; *W:* Aksel Hennie; *C:* John Andreas Andersen; *M:* Tom McRae. **VIDEO**

An Unreasonable Man **2006** Straightforward look at the career of crusading consumer advocate Ralph Nader and his presidential aspirations. The self-righteous workaholic frequently exasperated his colleagues and was heavily criticized for siphoning votes away from Al Gore during the contested 2000 election. Documentary is a mix of contemporary interviews and archival footage. **122m/C DVD.** *US* Ralph Nader; *D:* Henriette Mantel, Stephen Skrovan; *C:* Mark Raker; *M:* Joe Kraemer.

An Unremarkable Life **1989 (PG)** Two aging sisters live symbiotically together, until one views the other's romantic attachment to a charming widower as destructive to her own life. **97m/C VHS, DVD.** Shelley Winters, Patricia Neal, Mako, Rochelle Oliver, Charles S. Dutton, Lily Knight; *D:* Amin Qamar Chaudhri.

The Unsaid 1/2 *The Ties That Bind* **2001 (R)** After psychologist Michael Hunter's (Garcia) teenaged son commits suicide, he becomes estranged from his wife and daughter and gives up hands-on therapy. But he's persuaded by his former student, Barbara (Polo), to look into one of her social work cases. Now nearly-18, Tommy (Kartheiser) discovered the body of his murdered mother when he was a boy and his father (Bottoms) is in prison for the crime. But Tommy has been keeping a lot of secrets. **110m/C DVD.** *US CA* Andy Garcia, Vincent Kartheiser, Teri Polo, Linda Cardellini, Sam Bottoms, August Schellenberg, Chelsea Field, Trevor Blumas, Brendan Fletcher; *D:* Tom McLoughlin; *W:* Miguel Tejada-Flores, Scott Williams; *C:* Lloyd Ahern II; *M:* Don Davis.

Unsane 1/2 *Shadow; Sotto gli Occhi dell'Assassino; Tenebrae; Tenebre* **1982** A mystery novelist realizes that a series of bizarre murders strangely resembles the plot of his latest book. Bloody fun from Argento. **91m/C VHS, DVD.** *IT* Anthony (Tony) Franciosa, John Saxon, Daria Nicolodi, Giuliano Gemma, Christian Borromeo, Mirella D'Angelo, Veronica Lario, Ania Pieroni, Carola Stagnaro, John Steiner, Lara Wendel; *D:* Dario Argento; *W:* Dario Argento; *C:* Luciano Tovoli; *M:* The Goblins, Claudio Simonetti.

The Unseen 1/2 **1980** Three young women from a TV station are covering a story in a remote area of California. Before nightfall, two are horribly killed, leaving the third to come face to face with the terror. **91m/C VHS.** Barbara Bach, Sydney Lassick, Stephen Furst; *D:* Peter Foleg.

The Unseen **2005** College professor Roy Clemens (Harris) returns to his rural Georgia hometown to deal with the death of his father. This also means confronting his estranged childhood friend, volatile redneck Harold Dickerson (Harold). Whatever dark secret they share has also impacted the life of Sammy (Bloch), Harold's blind, simple-minded younger brother who's kept a near-prisoner at home. Southern gothic anchored by some good performances. **99m/C DVD.** Steve Harris, Catherine Dent, Michelle Clunie, Judah Friedlander, Gale Harrold, Phillip Bloch; *D:* Jim Hunter; *W:* Jim Hunter; *C:* Jim Hunter; *M:* Dean Parker.

Unseen Evil **1999 (R)** A group of archeological students accompany their professor to an ancient burial ground for a dig. Unfortunately, the prof wants to uncover a powerful alien force and is prepared to sacrifice anyone necessary. **90m/C VHS, DVD.** Richard Hatch, Tim Thomerson, Robbie (Reist) Rist, Cindi Braun, Frank Ruotolo, Jere Jon, Cindy Pena; *D:* Jay Woelfel; *W:* Scott Spears; *C:* Scott Spears. **VIDEO**

Unsettled Land **1988 (PG)** Young Israeli settlers try to survive the elements and Bedouin attackers in Palestine during the 1920s. **109m/C VHS.** *IS* Kelly McGillis, John Shea, Arnon Zadok, Christine Boisson; *D:* Uri Barbash.

Unshackled 1/2 **2000 (PG-13)** Slightly overdone melodrama tells the true story of Harold Morris, who was sentenced to life at 20 for armed robbery and murder and later helped organize the first interracial basketball team at Georgia State Prison. The team led the way to fully integrating the prison. Eventually paroled, Morris goes on to steer kids away from drugs and crime. Often heavy-handed, but the message is supposed to be inspirational (hence the PG13 rating), and it will be, to some. **106m/C VHS, DVD.** Burgess Jenkins, James Black, Stacy Keach, Morgan Fairchild; *D:* Bart Patton; *W:* Harold Morris; *C:* Paul Varrieur; *M:* Jeffrey Scott Pearson.

The Unsinkable Molly Brown **1964** A spunky backwoods girl is determined to break into the upper crust of Denver's high society and along the way survives the sinking of the Titanic. This energetic version of the Broadway musical contains many Meredith Willson ("Music Man") songs and lots of hokey, good-natured fun. ♫ Colorado Is My Home; Leadville Johnny Brown (Soliloquy); I Ain't Down Yet; Belly Up to the Bar, Boys; He's My Friend; I've Already Started; The Beautiful People of Denver; I May Never Fall in Love with You; Up Where the People Are. **128m/C VHS, DVD.** Debbie Reynolds, Harve Presnell, Ed Begley Sr., Martita Hunt, Hermione Baddeley; *D:* Charles Walters; *C:* Daniel F. Fapp; *M:* Meredith Willson.

Unspeakable 1/2 **2000** James (Cline) and Alice Fhelleps have a nasty, unsatisfying marriage until a car accident turns their life together into a true horror. From that premise, Chad Ferrin spins out a relatively realistic tale of madness and murder. For hard-core horror fans only. **81m/C DVD.** Robert Cline, Timothy Muskatell, Tina Birchfield, Wolf Dangler; *D:* Chad Ferrin; *W:* Chad Ferrin; *C:* Nicholas Loizides.

Unspeakable 1/2 **2002 (R)** A shrink is sickened when her fancy-pants mind machine shows lots of icky and—could it be?—

inhuman stuff going on inside the serial killer's head. Things get funky when he flies the coop after outlasting the electric chair, making the hotheaded warden (Hopper) lose face (really). **109m/C VHS, DVD.** Michele J. Wolff, Marco Rodriguez, Dina Meyer, Lance Henriksen, Dennis Hopper, Luke McCoubrey, Jim Helton, Jonah Moran, Ron Pantane, Adam Zuckerman; ***D:*** Thomas J. Wright; ***W:*** Luke McCoubrey; ***C:*** Antonio Calvache; ***M:*** Jeff Marsh. **VIDEO**

The Unstoppable Man 🦴 1/2 **1959** The son of an American businessman is kidnapped while they are in London. No pushover he, dad develops his own plan to destroy the criminals, eventually pursuing them with a flame thrower. **68m/B VHS.** *GB* Cameron Mitchell, Marius Goring, Harry H. Corbett, Lois Maxwell, Denis Gilmore; ***D:*** Terry Bishop.

Unstrung Heroes 🦴🦴 1/2 **1995 (PG)** Semi-autobiographical tale of Steven Lidz (Watt), growing up in 1960s California with a mother who is dying of cancer (MacDowell) and a nutty professor-type father (Turturro) who refuses to accept her illness. A desperate Steven goes to live with his two oddball uncles (Richards and Chaykin) who provide understanding and insight for the youngster, as well as a new name, Franz. Moving and quirky without being sappy, Keaton's feature debut avoids what would've been easy stereotypes. Based on the autobiography by Franz Lidz. **93m/C VHS, DVD.** Andie MacDowell, John Turturro, Michael Richards, Maury Chaykin, Nathan Watt, Kendra Krull; ***D:*** Diane Keaton; ***W:*** Richard LaGravenese; ***C:*** Phedon Papamichael; ***M:*** Thomas Newman.

Unsuitable Job for a Woman 🦴🦴 1/2 **1982** Independent Cordelia Gray, following the death of her boss, takes over his detective agency and gets involved with murder. Based on the novel by P.D. James. **94m/C VHS.** *GB* Pippa Guard, Paul Freeman, Billie Whitelaw; ***D:*** Christopher Petit.

The Unsuspected 🦴🦴 1/2 **1947** Complicated noir-thriller involving murder, blackmail, amnesia, and an inheritance. Rains is appropriately suave and creepy as Victor Grandison, the host of a successful crime-mystery radio program. Of course it's because Victor is a murderous crazy who is planning to take over the inheritance of allegedly dead niece Matilda (Caulfield). Matilda makes a surprising return to her home, temporarily thwarting Victor, who must also alter his plans when suspicious Steven Howard (North) becomes involved after Steven's friend (and Grandison's secretary) is found dead. **103m/B DVD.** Claude Rains, Joan Caulfield, Ted North, Audrey Trotter, Hurd Hatfield, Constance Bennett, Fred Clark, Jack Lambert; ***D:*** Michael Curtiz; ***W:*** Ranald MacDougall; ***C:*** Elwood "Woody" Bredell; ***M:*** Franz Waxman.

The Untamable 🦴🦴 **1923** Unusual silent about volatile woman suffering from schizophrenia. **65m/B VHS.** Gladys Walton, Malcolm McGregor, John St. Polis, Etta Lee; ***D:*** Herbert Blache.

Untamable Angelique 🦴🦴 1/2 *Indomptable Angelique* **1967** The fourth in the series, following "Angelique and the King." Angelique learns that Joffrey is alive and leaves the court to find him, but her ship is attacked by pirates. Angelique jumps overboard without knowing that the pirate chief is Joffrey in disguise. She's rescued by d'Escrainville (Pigaut) but when she refuses his advances he threatens to sell her at the Candia slave market. Followed by "Angelique and the Sultan." French with subtitles. **95m/C DVD.** *FR* Michele Mercier, Robert Hossein, Roger Pigaut, Ettore Manni, Bruno Dietrich; ***D:*** Bernard Borderie; ***W:*** Francis Cosne; ***C:*** Henri Persin; ***M:*** Michel Magne.

Untamed Heart 🦴🦴 1/2 **1993 (PG-13)** Adam (Slater), the painfully shy busboy with a heart condition, loves Caroline (Tomei), the bubbly waitress, from afar. She doesn't notice him until he saves her from some would-be rapists and their love blooms in the coffee shop where they both work. Tomei and Slater are both strong in the leads and Perez, as Caroline's best buddy Cindy, hurls comic barbs with ease. Charmingly familiar surroundings help set this formulaic romance apart. Filmed on location in Minneapolis. **102m/C VHS, DVD.** Christian Slater, Marisa Tomei, Rosie Perez, Kyle Secor, Willie Garson; ***D:*** Tony Bill; ***W:*** Tom Sierchio; ***C:*** Jost Vacano; ***M:*** Cliff Eidelman. MTV Movie Awards '93: Most Desirable Male (Slater), Kiss (Christian Slater/Marisa Tomei).

Untamed Youth 🦴 1/2 **1957** Campy '50s rock 'n' roll youth exploitation flick finds sisters Penny (Van Doren) and Janey (Nelson) arrested in the rural south for hitchhiking and vagrancy. It's all a scam to get them sentenced to a prison farm, which means free labor for head man Tropp's (Russell) cotton-picking operation. Apparently the teens do find the time to bop around to the juke box, with Van Doren's jiggling physical assets on notable display. **80m/B DVD.** Mamie Van Doren, Lori Nelson, John Russell, Lurene Tuttle, Eddie Cochran, Don Burnett; ***D:*** Howard W. Koch; ***W:*** John C. Higgins; ***C:*** Carl Guthrie; ***M:*** Les Baxter.

Until September 🦴🦴 **1984 (R)** An American tourist becomes stranded in Paris. She meets and falls in love with a married banker while she is stuck in her hotel. Routine romance. **96m/C VHS, DVD.** Karen Allen, Thierry Lhermitte, Christopher Cazenove, Johanna Pavlis; ***D:*** Richard Marquand; ***M:*** John Barry.

Until the End of the World 🦴🦴🦴 1/2 *Bis ans Ende der Welt; Jusqu'au Bout du Monde* **1991 (R)** Convoluted road movie set in 1999 follows the travails of Sam Farber (Hurt) through 15 cities in eight countries on four continents as he is chased by Dommartin, her lover (Neill), a bounty hunter, a private detective, and bank robbers, until all wind up in the Australian outback. And this is only the first half of the movie. For true cinematic satisfaction, don't expect logic—just go with the flow. Visually stunning, unexpectedly humorous, with excellent performances from an international cast. Footage created with high definition (HDTV) video technology is a technological first. The soundtrack features Lou Reed, David Byrne, U2, and others. **158m/C VHS.** *AU GE FR* William Hurt, Solveig Dommartin, Sam Neill, Max von Sydow, Ruediger Vogler, Ernie Dingo, Jeanne Moreau, David Gulpilil; ***D:*** Wim Wenders; ***W:*** Wim Wenders, Peter Carey; ***C:*** Robby Muller; ***M:*** Graeme Revell.

Until They Get Me 🦴 1/2 **1918** Northern Mountie rides horse in silence as he tracks criminal to the edge of the earth. **58m/B VHS.** Pauline Starke, Joe King, Jack Curtis, Wilbur Higby, Anna Dodge, Walter Perry; ***D:*** Frank Borzage; ***W:*** Kenneth B. Clarke; ***C:*** C.H. Wales.

Until They Sail 🦴🦴 1/2 **1957** Soap opera set in New Zealand during WWII. Plot centers around the lives of four sisters involved in love and murder. Dee's film debut. Based on a story by James Michener. **95m/B VHS.** Jean Simmons, Joan Fontaine, Paul Newman, Piper Laurie, Charles Drake, Sandra Dee, Wally Cassell, Alan Napier; ***D:*** Robert Wise; ***W:*** Robert Anderson.

(Untitled) 🦴🦴 **2009 (R)** Parker offers an absurdist look at the contemporary New York art and music scenes and the differences between commerce and personal expression. Humorless Adrian (Goldberg) is a self-important avant-garde composer and his brother Josh (Bailey) is a superficial commercially-successful artist. Adrian begrudges his brother's success, especially since Adrian himself is neither successful nor a particularly good composer. However, ambitious Chelsea art gallery owner Madeleine (Shelton) commissions Adrian for a performance piece to be played during an exhibition by pretentious bad boy Brit Ray (Jones) and his luck may finally change. **96m/C DVD.** *US* Adam Goldberg, Marley Shelton, Eion Bailey, Vinnie Jones, Lucy Punch, Zak Orth, Michael Panes, Janet Carroll, Ben Hammer, Ptolemy Slocum; ***D:*** Jonathan Parker; ***W:*** Jonathan Parker, Catherine Di Napoli; ***C:*** Svetlana Cvetko; ***M:*** David Lang.

Untold Scandal 🦴🦴 *Joseon Namnyeo Sangyeol Ji Sa* **2003** The scandalous 18th-century French novel "Les Liaisons Dangereuses" is transported to Korea during the publicly conservative (and privately wicked) Chosun dynasty. Jo Weon (Bae) is a pleasure-seeking artist whose manipulative cousin, Lady Jo (Mi-suk Lee), wants him to seduce virginal teen Soh-ok (So-yeon Lee), who's about to become her husband's concubine. Jo Weon is more interested in the virtuous Catholic widow, Lady Jeong (Jeon), as a challenge. If you've seen any of the other film versions of the novel, you know what's coming. Korean with subtitles. **124m/C DVD.** *KN* Bae Yong-jun, Lee Mi-suk, Jeon Do-yeon; ***D:*** Je-yong Lee; ***C:*** Kim Byeong-il.

The Untold Story 🦴🦴 *The Untold Story: Human Meat Roast Pork Buns; Ba Xian Fan Dian Zhi Ren Rou Cha Shao Bao; Bunman; Human Meat Pies* **1993** New restaurant owner Wong discovers that the previous owner and his family mysteriously disappeared. Then the police detective (Lee) on the case makes a very shocking discovery. Modern cult classic includes footage cut from the original Hong Kong release and its violence is not for the squeamish. Cantonese with subtitles. **95m/C VHS, DVD.** *HK* Anthony Wong, Danny Lee, Emily Kwan, Fui-On Shing; ***D:*** Herman Yau, Danny Lee.

The Untold Story of Emmett Louis Till 🦴🦴🦴 **2005 (PG-13)** Documentary was released to coincide with the 50th anniversary of the 1955 murder of Till, a 14-year-old African American from Chicago who went to visit his grandfather in Money, Mississippi, where he was tortured and killed for allegedly whistling at a white woman. Till's murder became a pivotal moment in the civil rights movement. The Justice Department reopened the case when new evidence came to light, thanks to the years-long investigation of director Beauchamp. Includes TV and newsreel footage and numerous interviews. **70m/C DVD.** *US* ***D:*** Keith Beauchamp; ***C:*** Rondrick Cowins, Sikay Tang; ***M:*** Jim Papoulis.

The Untouchables 🦴🦴🦴 1/2 **1987 (R)** Big-budget, fast-paced, and exciting re-evaluation of the popular TV series about the real-life battle between Treasury officer Eliot Ness (Costner) and crime boss Al Capone (De Niro) in 1920s Chicago. History sometimes takes a back seat to Hollywood's imagination in the screenplay, but it doesn't really matter since there are splendid performances by De Niro and Connery as Ness' mentor Jimmy Malone to help it look realistic. Costner does a fine job showing the change in Ness from naive idealism to steely conviction. Beautifully filmed with excellent special effects. Note DePalma's long train station/baby carriage scene that's an homage to the 1925 silent Russian classic, "Battleship Potemkin." **119m/C VHS, DVD, Blu-ray Disc, HD DVD.** Kevin Costner, Sean Connery, Robert De Niro, Andy Garcia, Charles Martin Smith, Billy Drago, Richard Bradford, Jack Kehoe; ***D:*** Brian De Palma; ***W:*** David Mamet; ***C:*** Stephen Burum; ***M:*** Ennio Morricone. Oscars '87: Support. Actor (Connery); Golden Globes '88: Support. Actor (Connery); Natl. Bd. of Review '87: Support. Actor (Connery).

Untraceable 🦴 1/2 **2008 (R)** Agent Jennifer Marsh (Lane) is an FBI "cybercrime" expert who must find a killer whose elaborate, torturous murders are broadcast live on the Internet. The twist? The more hits the killer's website gets, the faster he kills his victims. Eventually, Marsh must work to stop the killer and protect her own family as well. Cynical movie that aspires to condemn people's love of exploitative violence while serving up lots of violent exploitation without a shred of irony to redeem it. **100m/C DVD, Blu-ray Disc.** *US* Diane Lane, Billy Burke, Colin Hanks, Joseph Cross, Mary Beth Hurt, Ty(rone) Giordano, Perla Haney-Jardine, Peter Lewis, Tim De Zarn; ***D:*** Gregory Hoblit; ***W:*** Allison Burnett, Robert Fyvolent, Mark R. Brinker; ***C:*** Anastas Michos; ***M:*** Christopher Young.

Unveiled 🦴🦴 1/2 **1994 (R)** Stephanie Montgomery's (Zane) friend falls victim to a killer in Marrakesh. So Steph sets out to trap the killer, with the help of government offficial Peter (Hubley). **103m/C VHS.** Lisa Zane, Whip Hubley, Nicholas Chinlund, Martha Gehman; ***D:*** William Cole; ***W:*** Michael Diamond, Roger Kumble; ***M:*** Christopher Tyng.

Unveiled 🦴🦴 *Fremde Haut; Foreign Skin* **2005** Translator Fariba (Tabatabai) is persecuted in Iran because she's a lesbian. She flees the country and takes the identity of male refugee Siamak (Akhavan), who commits suicide before learning that he has been granted temporary asylum in Germany. Passing herself off as a young man, Fariba gets a job in a factory where she meets Anne (Sarnau,) who seemingly never realizes that the male she is infatuated with is actually a woman. But then Fariba's ruse begins to unravel. Farsi and German with subtitles. **97m/C DVD.** *GE* Jasmin Tabatabai, Anneke Kim Sarnau, Navid Akhavan, Hinnerk Schoenemann, Jens Munchow; ***D:*** Angelina Maccarone; ***W:*** Judith Kaufmann, Angelina Maccarone; ***C:*** Judith Kaufmann; ***M:*** Hartmut Ewert, Jacob Hansons.

Unzipped 🦴🦴🦴 **1994 (R)** Witty, behind-the-scenes look at whiz-kid fashion designer Isaac Mizrahi as he prepares for the showing of his 1994 collection. Alternately filmed in black-and-white and color in a variety of film stocks, Keeve (Mizrahi's former lover) captures Mizrahi's varying moods, from his creative struggles to his unique sense of humor and gift for mimicry. Highlights include scenes with Mizrahi's doting mother. Fashionphiles will love every minute, and strictly off-the-rack viewers can enjoy the supermodels on parade. **76m/C VHS, DVD.** ***D:*** Douglas Keeve; ***C:*** Ellen Kuras. Sundance '95: Aud. Award.

Up 🦴🦴🦴 1/2 **2009 (PG)** Going the lawn chair one better. In Pixar's stunning 10th animated adventure (the first in 3-D), grumpy 78-year-old widower Carl Fredricksen (Asner), a retired balloon salesman, ties thousands of helium balloons to his house so it will be able to float. Carl wants to fulfill the lifelong dream of his late wife by traveling to Paradise Falls in South America in the footsteps of his discredited explorer hero Charles F. Muntz (Plummer). However, he doesn't expect to have a stowaway—enthusiastic eight-year-old Russell (Nagai), who thinks his experience as a Junior Wilderness Explorer will come in handy. Carl and Russell not only find Muntz but a gawky bird and some talking dogs, an odd-couple friendship, and a lot of action. **96m/C DVD.** *US* ***D:*** Pete Docter, Bob Peterson; ***W:*** Bob Peterson; ***C:*** Patick Lin; ***M:*** Michael Giacchino; ***V:*** Ed Asner, Jordan Nagai, Christopher Plummer, John Ratzenberger, Delroy Lindo, Bob Peterson, Jerome Ranft. Oscars '09: Animated Film, Orig. Score; British Acad. '09: Animated Film, Orig. Score; Golden Globes '10: Animated Film, Orig. Score.

Up Against the Eight Ball 🦴 1/2 **2004 (R)** Best friends Monique (Dahl) and Krista (La'Shawn) need money for their last year of college tuition. So they take their pool-hustling skills to a tournament in Vegas with various troubles (romantic and otherwise) accompanying them. Way too predictable in a you-go-girl way. **90m/C VHS, DVD.** Kym E. Whitley, Iva La'Shawn, Tawny Dahl, Jay Cooper, T. Ashanti Mozelle; ***D:*** Miguel A. Nunez Jr., Troy Curvey Jr.; ***W:*** Keith Sagoes. **VIDEO**

Up Against the Wall 🦴🦴 **1991 (PG-13)** A black kid from the Chicago projects attends school in the affluent suburbs, but there too he must resist temptation, crime and violence. A well-intentioned but didactic cautionary drama, adapted from the book by African-American author/commentator Dr. Jawanza Kunjufu. **103m/C VHS.** Marla Gibbs, Stoney Jackson, Catero Colbert, Ron O'Neal, Salli Richardson; ***D:*** Ron O'Neal.

Up and Down 🦴🦴 *Horem Padem* **2004 (R)** Overstuffed character drama begins with a couple of Czech lowlifes who are transporting a group of illegal immigrants from India. They discover a baby has been left behind in their truck, which they sell to a pawnshop owner who in turn sells the infant to a desperate childless couple who change their lives (breaking off from their hooligan friends) to try starting over as a family. Then there's a second scenario involving a man who's visiting his divorced parents for the first time in 20 years (he'd immigrated to Australia). Martin discovers that his dad lives with Martin's ex-girlfriend and they have an 18-year-old daughter. This makes for a very awkward family lunch, which includes Martin's resentful (and racist) mother. Czech with subtitles. **108m/C DVD.** Jan Triska, Jaroslav Dusek, Petr Forman, Emilia Vasaryova, Jiri Machacek, Natasa Burger, Ingrid Timkova, Kristyna Liska-Bokova, Pavel Liska, Marek Daniel, Jan Budar, Zdenek Suchy; ***Cameos:*** Vaclav Havel; ***D:*** Jan Hrebejk; ***W:*** Jan Hrebejk; ***C:*** Jan Malir; ***M:*** Ales Brezina.

Up at the Villa 🦴🦴 1/2 **2000 (PG-13)** The British and American expatriate community in 1938 Florence is the setting for the unlikely romantic travails of respectable British widow Mary Panton (Scott Thomas). She is courted by longtime (and older) friend/diplomat Sir Edgar (Fox) who will offer her a comfortable if dull life in India. But at a party, Mary is paired off with confident American Rowley Flint (Penn), who must unexpectedly help Mary out of a jam involving a dead body. However, politics also plays its part with the rise of fascism. Scott Thomas and Penn may not have any romantic sparks but they do well individually and Bancroft is an amusing scene stealer as a wealthy socialite. Based on a novella by W. Somerset Maugham. **115m/C VHS, DVD.** *GB* Kristin Scott Thomas, Sean Penn, Anne Bancroft, Derek Jacobi, Jeremy Davies, James Fox, Massimo Ghini; ***D:*** Philip Haas; ***W:*** Belinda Haas; ***C:*** Maurizio Calvesi; ***M:*** Pino Donaggio.

Up Close and Personal **1996 (PG-13)** Ambitious Reno card dealer Tally Atwater (Pfeiffer) wants to get into broadcasting and finds her chance at a Miami TV station where she's mentored by successful veteran-reporter-turned-producer Warren Justice (Redford). They fall in love but find their careers clashing as Tally climbs the media success ladder. Originally inspired by the tragic life of NBC reporter Jessica Savitch, whose problems with drugs and abusive relationships led to a sad ending, film turned into a star-powered romance with media trappings and another variation of "A Star is Born." It's now "suggested" by Alanna Nash's book "Golden Girl." **124m/C VHS, DVD.** Michelle Pfeiffer, Robert Redford, Kate Nelligan, Stockard Channing, Joe Mantegna, Glenn Plummer, James Rebhorn, Noble Willingham, Scott Bryce, Raymond Cruz, Dedee Pfeiffer, Miguel (Michael) Sandoval, James Karen; ***D:*** Jon Avnet; ***W:*** Joan Didion, John Gregory Dunne; ***C:*** Karl Walter Lindenlaub; ***M:*** Thomas Newman.

Up/Down/Fragile *Haut Bas Fragile* **1995** New Wavish musical following the fortunes of three young women in Paris. Louise (Denicourt) has just emerged from a coma after several years and is living in a tiny apartment though she has inherited the antiques-filled home of an aunt; Ninon (Richard) has fled from her gangster boyfriend and gotten a job as a delivery girl; and the adopted Ida (Cote) has become obsessed with learning the identities of her biological parents. Their link is Roland (Marcon) who knows all three. The mood's more important than the plot anyway. French with subtitles. **169m/C VHS.** *FR* Marianne (Cuau) Denicourt, Laurence Cote, Nathalie Richard, Andre Marcon, Anna Karina; ***D:*** Jacques Rivette; ***C:*** Christophe Pollock; ***M:*** Francois Breant.

Up for Grabs ½ **2005** The story of the controversy over ownership of Barry Bonds's record-setting homer is actually more interesting than all the hype leading up to the history-making hit. Following the frenzied scramble for the ball, two men stepped forward into the spotlight—one with the ball and the other claiming he had caught the ball only to have it ripped from his hand in the ensuing struggle. Using news footage of the event as well as eyewitness accounts, documentarian Michael Wranovics shines a light on the absurd clash, which ends up with the two parties in court. **88m/C DVD.** *US* ***D:*** Michael Wranovics; ***W:*** Michael Wranovics; ***C:*** Zack Richard, Josh Keppel.

Up from the Depths ½ **1979 (R)** Something from beneath the ocean is turning the paradise of Hawaii into a nightmare. Prehistoric fish are returning to the surface with one thing on their minds—lunch. "Jaws" rip-off played for humor. **85m/C VHS.** Sam Bottoms, Suzanne Reed, Virgil Frye; ***D:*** Charles B. Griffith; ***W:*** Alfred Sweeney; ***M:*** James Horner.

Up in Arms **1944** Danny Kaye's first film presents a typical Kaye scenario: he plays a twitching hypochondriac who is drafted into the Army and sneaks his girlfriend aboard the troopship bound for the Pacific. Features an appearance by the Goldwyn Girls. Remake of the film "The Nervous Wreck." ♫ Theatre Lobby Number; Now I Know; All Out for Freedom; Tess's Torch Song; Melody in 4-F. **105m/C VHS.** Danny Kaye, Dinah Shore, Constance Dowling, Dana Andrews, Margaret Dumont, Lyle Talbot, Louis Calhern, Charles Halton; ***D:*** Elliott Nugent; ***C:*** Ray Rennahan.

Up in Central Park ½ **1948** Poor adaptation of the hit Broadway musical (the studio removed much of Romberg's score) about Irish immigrant lass Rosie Moore (Durbin), who teams up with New York reporter John Matthews (Haymes) to expose corrupt politician Boss Tweed (Price). Without the songs, the plot is shown to be wafer-thin. ♫ When She Walks in the Room; Carousel in the Park; Oh Say Do You See What I See?; Pace, Pace Mio Dio. **88m/B VHS.** Deanna Durbin, Dick Haymes, Vincent Price, Albert Sharpe, Tom Powers, Hobart Cavanaugh, Thurston Hall; ***D:*** William A. Seiter; ***W:*** Dorothy Fields, Herbert Fields, Karl Tunberg; ***C:*** Milton Krasner; ***M:*** Sigmund Romberg.

Up in the Air **1940** Darro and Moreland have ambitions as radio comedians, and their friend Reynolds wants to be a singer. Their break comes when other performers are murdered on the air. First, though, they must solve the killings. **62m/B VHS, DVD.** Frankie Darro, Marjorie Reynolds, Mantan Moreland, Gordon Jones, Tristram Coffin, John Holland, Carleton Young; ***D:*** Howard Bretherton; ***W:*** Edmond Kelso; ***C:*** Fred H. Jackman Jr.; ***M:*** Edward Kay, Johnny Lange, Lew Porter.

Up in the Air **2009 (R)** Corporate downsizer Ryan Bingham (Clooney) attributes his commitment phobia to his work, though he seems naturally inclined to distancing himself from too many messy human emotions. Bingham loves his airport life and is deeply offended when his boss (Bateman) pairs him with young go-getter Natalie (Kendrick) whose big idea is to fire people via the Internet. Then Ryan gets distracted by the more mature beauty and wit of fellow traveler Alex (Farmiga), who's equally amenable to no-strings sex. Clooney is made for this role—a debonair, intelligent if somewhat ruthless, man who's become complacent until he finds his own working life threatened, which leads to some midlife questioning. Thankfully, writer/director Reitman refrains from mawkishness and expected changes. Adapted from Walter Kirn's 2002 novel. **109m/C DVD.** *US* George Clooney, Vera Farmiga, Jason Bateman, Melanie Lynskey, Anna Kendrick, Danny McBride, Chris Lowell, Amy Morton, Sam Elliott, Zach Galifianakis, J.K. Simmons; ***D:*** Jason Reitman; ***W:*** Jason Reitman, Sheldon Turner; ***C:*** Eric Steelberg; ***M:*** Rolfe Kent. British Acad. '09: Adapt. Screenplay; Golden Globes '10: Screenplay; Writers Guild '09: Adapt. Screenplay.

Up Periscope ½ **1959** Garner is a demolitions expert unwillingly assigned to a submarine commanded by O'Brien. His mission: to sneak onto a Japanese-held island and steal a top-secret code book. Trouble is, O'Brien may not wait for Garner to complete his mission before taking the sub back underwater. A routine submarine film. **111m/C VHS, DVD.** James Garner, Edmond O'Brien, Andra Martin, Alan Hale Jr., Carleton Carpenter, Frank Gifford, Richard Bakalyan; ***D:*** Gordon Douglas.

Up River **1979** Wealthy land baron rapes and murders the wife of a simple pioneer, who is beaten and whose homestead is burned by the baron as well. The pioneer lives to seek terrible vengeance. **90m/C VHS.** Jeff Corey, Morgan Stevens, Debbie AuLuce; ***D:*** Carl Kitt.

Up the Academy *Mad Magazine's Up the Academy; The Brave Young Men of Weinberg* **1980 (R)** Four teenaged delinquents are sent to an academy for wayward boys where they encounter a sadistic headmaster and a gay dance instructor. Sometimes inventive, often tasteless fare from "Mad" magazine. **88m/C VHS, DVD.** Ron Leibman, Ralph Macchio, Barbara Bach, Tom Poston, Stacey Nelkin, Wendell Brown, Tom Citera; ***D:*** Robert Downey.

Up the Creek **1958** Crazy antics abound in this tale of an old British destroyer, a black-market scheme run by the crew, and the new skipper whose hobby is rocket building. Followed by "Further Up the River." **83m/B VHS.** *GB* David Tomlinson, Wilfrid Hyde-White, Peter Sellers, Vera Day, Michael Goodliffe, Lionel Jeffries; ***D:*** Val Guest.

Up the Creek ½ **1984 (R)** Four college losers enter a whitewater raft race to gain some respect for their school. The soundtrack features songs by Heart, Cheap Trick and The Beach Boys. Routine. **95m/C VHS.** Tim Matheson, Jennifer Runyon, Stephen Furst, John Hillerman, James B. Sikking, Julia Montgomery, Jeana Tomasina; ***D:*** Robert Butler; ***M:*** William Goldstein.

Up the Down Staircase **1967** A naive, newly trained New York public school teacher is determined to teach the finer points of English literature to a group of poor students. She almost gives up until one student actually begins to learn. Good production and acting. Based on Bel Kaufman's novel. **124m/C VHS.** Sandy Dennis, Patrick Bedford, Eileen Heckart, Ruth White, Jean Stapleton, Sorrell Booke; ***D:*** Robert Mulligan.

Up the Ladder **1925** Presumably that's the ladder of success. Heiress Jane Cornwall (Valli) secretly finances her boyfriend James Van Clinton's (Stanley) latest invention: a telephone that allows both parties to see each other while talking. When it's a success, Jane and James get married. After a few years James gets bored and messes things up. **70m/B DVD.** Virginia Valli, Forrest Stanley, Margaret Livingston, Holmes Herbert, Priscilla Moran, George Fawcett; ***D:*** Edward Sloman; ***W:*** Grant Carpenter, Tom McNamara; ***C:*** Jackson Rose.

Up the River ½ **1930** Tracy's film debut as convict St. Louis. He breaks out of jail with sidekick Dan (Hymer) and the two go their separate ways but can't keep out of trouble. They wind up back in the joint, this time sharing a cell with rich boy Steve (Bogart). Steve gets blackmailed after his release and his two prison buddies break out again to come to his aid. Ford reworked the original dramatic script into a comedy and shot the film in two weeks. **90m/B DVD.** Spencer Tracy, Warren Hymer, Humphrey Bogart, Morgan Wallace, Robert Emmett O'Connor, Clare Luce, Joan Lawes; ***D:*** John Ford; ***W:*** Maurine Watkins, William "Buster" Collier Jr.; ***C:*** Joseph August.

Up the Sandbox **1972 (R)** A bored housewife fantasizes about her life in order to avoid facing her mundane existence. Fine acting from Streisand, with real problems of young mothers accurately shown. **98m/C VHS, DVD.** Barbra Streisand, David Selby, Jane Hoffman, Barbara Rhoades; ***D:*** Irvin Kershner; ***W:*** Paul Zindel; ***C:*** Gordon Willis; ***M:*** Billy Goldenberg.

Up to a Certain Point *Up to a Point; Hasta Clerto Punto* **1983** Writer Oscar believes he has a liberal attitude (to go along with Cuban political ideology) but his belief is shaken when he interviews workers on the Havana docks about their notions of machismo. Seems when Oscar falls for a sexy dockworker his ideas of maleness and a woman's place are more traditional than he imagines. Spanish with subtitles. **70m/C VHS.** *CU* Oscar Alvarez, Mirta Ibarra, Omar Valdes, Coralia Veloz, Rogelio Blain, Ana Vina; ***D:*** Tomas Gutierrez Alea; ***W:*** Tomas Gutierrez Alea; ***M:*** Leo Brouwer.

Up to His Neck ½ **1954** A sailor abandoned by his ship on a south sea island becomes a native islander and all is well until a decade later they remember him and send a ship to his rescue. Overly silly and under developed. **90m/B VHS.** Ronald Shiner, Brian Rix, Laya Raki; ***D:*** Jack Paddy Carstairs; ***W:*** Jack Paddy Carstairs. **VIDEO**

Up Your Alley **1989 (R)** A female reporter, pursuing a story on homelessness, and a skidrow bum find romance. Langston, who produced and co-wrote the film, is better known as "The Unknown Comic." **90m/C VHS.** Linda Blair, Murray Langston, Ruth Buzzi, Johnny Dark, Bob Zany, Yakov Smirnoff; ***D:*** Bob Logan.

Uphill All the Way **1985** A couple of card-cheatin' good old boys are pursued by posses and cavalry alike, and end up killing real outlaws. **91m/C VHS.** Roy Clark, Mel Tillis, Glen Campbell, Trish Van Devere, Burl Ives, Burt Reynolds; ***D:*** Frank Q. Dobbs. **TV**

The Uppercrust ½ *Den Tuchtigen Gehart die Welt* **1981** Boring tale of corruption and greed that takes place at the highest levels of American business and government. **95m/C VHS.** *AT* Frank Gorshin, Broderick Crawford, Pavel Landovsky, Franz Buchrieser; ***D:*** Peter Patzak; ***W:*** Peter Patzak, Helmut Zenker; ***C:*** Walter Kinder.

The Uprising **1981** A Nicaraguan drama filmed just months after the 1979 Sandinista revolution, wherein a young guard of Somoza retains his job for the money, while his father is active in the revolutionary forces. In Spanish with English subtitles. **96m/C VHS.** *SP* Oscar Catillo, Carlos Catania, Augustin Pereira, Guido Sanz; ***D:*** Peter Lilienthal; ***W:*** Peter Lilienthal; ***C:*** Michael Balhaus; ***M:*** Claus Bantzer.

Uprising **2001** Well-done, realistic miniseries depicts the Warsaw Ghetto uprising of 1943, when Polish Jews, facing deportation to death camps, held off the Nazis for a month using guerilla tactics. Solid script, which avoids melodrama and over-sentimentality, leaves room to show the politics and motivations involved between the people who wanted to negotiate with the Nazis, those who collaborated for self-preservation, and the fighters. Though the whole cast is up to the task, Sobieski's performance stands out, and Schwimmer makes a better showing here than he did in "Band of Brothers." **177m/C VHS, DVD.** Leelee Sobieski, Hank Azaria, David Schwimmer, Jon Voight, Donald Sutherland, Cary Elwes, Stephen Moyer, Sadie Frost, Radha Mitchell, Mili Avital, Alexandra Holden, John Ales, Eric Lively, Jesper Christensen; ***D:*** Jon Avnet; ***W:*** Jon Avnet, Paul Brickman; ***C:*** Denis Lenoir; ***M:*** Maurice Jarre. **TV**

The Upside of Anger **2005 (R)** Allen gives new meaning to the term ferocious as betrayed suburban Detroit wife Terry Wolfmeyer. Her husband has apparently left Terry and their four beautiful daughters (Witt, Christensen, Russell, Wood) for his secretary. Terry takes to alcohol, anger, and rebellion while the girls run the household. When neighbor Denny (Costner) finds out about her plight, he's eager to make Terry a drinking buddy and possible romantic partner. Genial Denny, who's bored and lonely, is a retired Detroit Tigers pitcher turned radio talk show host. (He's also entranced by the sheer femaleness of the Wolfmeyer home.) There's a certain comfortable, angsty camaraderie to the whole situation that's appealing. Writer/director Binder also takes a small role as Denny's lecherous producer. **118m/C DVD.** *US* Joan Allen, Kevin Costner, Erika Christensen, Evan Rachel Wood, Keri Russell, Alicia Witt, Mike Binder, Dane Christensen, Holt McCallany; ***D:*** Mike Binder; ***W:*** Mike Binder; ***C:*** Richard Greatrex; ***M:*** Alexandre Desplat, Stephen (Steve) Edwards.

Uptown Angel **1990 (R)** A young woman is determined to work her way out of her home on the wrong side of town. Black cast brings new life to old premise. **90m/C VHS.** Caron Tate, Cliff McMullen, Gloria Davis Hill, Tracy Hill; ***D:*** Joy Shannon; ***W:*** Joy Shannon.

Uptown Girls ½ **2003 (PG-13)** Cloying female buddy comedy pits a ditsy, down-on-her-luck socialite against an extremely precocious and well-off 8-year-old with annoying results. After her financial manager embezzles her inheritance, spoiled New York trust-fund kid Molly (Murphy) is forced to get a (shudder!) job. She becomes a nanny to young Ray (Fanning), who is largely abandoned by her record exec mum (Locklear in an especially unappealing performance). The two butt heads immediately, but through a series of uninspired events predictably do the role reversal bit—learning from each other how to act more their own ages. Murphy's performance is forced and just plain weird at times. Fanning holds her own against her flaky co-star and dismal script. **93m/C VHS, DVD.** *US* Brittany Murphy, Dakota Fanning, Heather Locklear, Donald Adeosun Faison, Marley Shelton, Austin Pendleton, Jesse Spencer, Polly Adams; ***D:*** Boaz Yakin; ***W:*** Mo Ogrodnik, Julia Dahl, Lisa Davidowitz; ***C:*** Michael Ballhaus; ***M:*** Joel McNeely.

Uptown New York **1932** A young man pressured by his family marries a rich girl instead of the woman he loves, who in turn marries a man she does not love. Routine melodrama. **81m/B VHS.** Jack Oakie, Shirley Green, Leon Ames, Shirley Grey, George Cooper, Raymond Hatton; ***D:*** Victor Schertzinger.

Uptown Saturday Night ½ **1974 (PG)** Two working men attempt to recover a stolen lottery ticket from the black underworld after being ripped off at an illegal gambling place. Good fun, with nice performances from both leads and from Belafonte doing a black "Godfather" parody of Brando. Followed by "Let's Do It Again." **104m/C VHS, DVD.** Sidney Poitier, Bill Cosby, Harry Belafonte,

Flip Wilson, Richard Pryor, Calvin Lockhart; *D:* Sidney Poitier; *W:* Richard Wesley; *C:* Fred W. Koenekamp.

The Upturned Glass ♂ 1/2 **1947** Brooding crime melodrama told in flashbacks, with an unsatisfying ending and a nonsensical title. London brain surgeon Michael Joyce falls in love with married Emma Wright after saving the life of her young daughter. Unwilling to get caught in a scandal, they break their romance off. When Emma dies in a suspicious fall, Michael is certain she was murdered by jealous sister-in-law Kate and takes his revenge. **90m/B DVD.** *GB* James Mason, Rosamund John, Pamela Kellino, Brefni O'Rorke, Ann Stephens, Jane Hylton, Morland Graham; *D:* Lawrence Huntington; *W:* Pamela Kellino; *C:* Reg Wyer; *M:* Bernard Stevens.

The Uranium Conspiracy ♂ 1/2 *Agenten Kennen Keine Tranen* **1978** A secret agent and a mercenary soldier try to stop a shipment of uranium out of Zaire from falling into enemy hands. It won't be easy. German with subtitles. **100m/C VHS, DVD.** *GE IS IT* Fabio Testi, Janet Agren, Assaf Dayan, Siegfried Rauch, Herbert (Fuchs) Fux; *D:* Gianfranco Baldanello, Menahem Golan; *W:* David Paulsen, August Rieger; *C:* Adam Greenberg; *M:* Coriolano Gori, Dov Seltzer.

Uranus ♂♂♂ **1991 (R)** After WWII a French provincial town has been liberated from Nazi invaders—but not its own suspicions, as citizens try to rebuild knowing some of them collaborated with the enemy. An important subject is heavily talked over in static fashion, with a robust Depardieu either a standout or a ham as the earthy saloonkeeper. Based on a novel by Marcel Ayme, himself accused of pro-Vichy leanings during the era. In French with English subtitles. **100m/C VHS.** *FR* Gerard Depardieu, Michel Blanc, Jean-Pierre Marielle, Philippe Noiret, Gerard Desarthe, Michel Galabru, Fabrice Luchini, Daniel Prevost; *D:* Claude Berri; *W:* Claude Berri; *M:* Jean-Claude Petit.

Urban Cowboy ♂♂ 1/2 **1980 (PG)** A young Texas farmer comes to Houston to work in a refinery. After work he hangs out at Gilley's, a roadhouse bar, where he and his friends drink, fight, and prove their manhood by riding a mechanical bull. Film made Winger a star, was an up in Travolta's roller coaster career, and began the craze for country western apparel and dance and them there mechanical bulls. Ride 'em, cowboy! **135m/C VHS, DVD.** John Travolta, Debra Winger, Scott Glenn, Madolyn Smith, Barry Corbin; *D:* James Bridges; *W:* James Bridges, Aaron Latham; *C:* Reynaldo Villalobos; *M:* Ralph Burns.

Urban Crossfire ♂♂ 1/2 **1994 (PG-13)** Two veteran white Brooklyn detectives investigating gang violence are aided by a young black patrolman whose partner was killed by a gang leader. Solid cast, fast paced action. **95m/C VHS, DVD.** Mario Van Peebles, Ray Sharkey, Peter Boyle, Michael Boatman; *D:* Dick Lowry.

Urban Ghost Story ♂♂ **1998 (R)** Saddled with guilt after surviving a car wreck that killed her friend, 12-year-old Lizzie suspects that her near-death experience released a nasty ghost that's purposely tormenting her. When no one believes her, her mom enlists the aid of a journalist to prove Lizzie's claims—which only makes life worse as a gaggle of scientists and voyeurs swarm their grungy Glasgow home. **82m/C VHS, DVD.** Jason Connery, Stephanie Buttle, Heather Ann Foster, Nicola Stapleton, James Cosmo, Elizabeth Berrington, Siri Neal, Andreas Wisniewski, Kenneth Bryans, Carolyn Bonnyman, Alan Owen, Stephen MacDonald, Julie Austin, Nicola Greene, Nick Von Schlippe, David Haddow, Richard Syms, Andy McEwan, Aaron White, Joss Castell-Gydesen; *D:* Genevieve Jolliffe; *W:* Genevieve Jolliffe, Chris Jones; *C:* Jon Walker; *M:* Rupert Gregson-Williams. **VIDEO**

Urban Justice ♂ **2007 (R)** If you're looking for a brainless, violent flick, then here it is because nothing else is offered. When the police department doesn't pursue the criminals who killed a cop in a drive-by shooting, his dad (Seagal) decides to take on the 'hood and blow the bad guys away himself. **92m/C DVD.** Steven Seagal, Eddie Griffin, Danny Trejo, Kirk B.R. Woller, Carmen Serano, Cory Hart; *D:* Don E. Fauntleroy; *W:* Gilmar Fortis II; *C:* Don E. Fauntleroy; *M:* Peter Meisner. **VIDEO**

Urban Legend ♂ **1998 (R)** Another in the nudge-and-wink genre of horror movies. Screen scream alumni litter the screen in this ode to modern tall tales that may have actually happened to the friend of a cousin of a friend of yours. Natalie (Watt) is the standard good girl who doesn't know why her friends are getting knocked off, even though her folklore prof (Englund) is the guy who played Freddy Krueger, and the voice of Chucky the evil doll is now coming out of her gas station attendant (Dourif). The killer uses urban legends as the theme of his crimes, but he never makes anyone eat Pop Rocks then drink Pepsi. Characters are so irritating you'll cheer when they die. **100m/C VHS, DVD.** Alicia Witt, Jared Leto, Rebecca Gayheart, Loretta Devine, Joshua Jackson, Tara Reid, John Neville, Robert Englund, Brad Dourif, Natasha Gregson Wagner, Danielle Harris, Michael Rosenbaum; *D:* Jamie Blanks; *W:* Silvio Horta; *C:* James Chressanthis; *M:* Christopher Young.

Urban Legends 2: Final Cut ♂ 1/2 **2000 (R)** This entry in the current trend of tongue-in-cheek slasher flicks proves that the genre is like its crazed killer characters. It refuses to die and is getting really ugly. Nearly abandoning the urban legend aspect of the original, the "movie within a movie" schtick is stolen from the "Scream" series as film students compete for the career-starting Hitchcock award at a prestigious film school. Amy (Morrison) decides to base her movie on urban legends after a chat with Reese (Devine), the only returning cast member of the original. Soon, fellow students and their projects get killed in development. Composer and film editor Ottman, making his directorial debut, seems more intent on giving movie cliches a slight twist and making film industry inside jokes than actually delivering a coherent plot. **94m/C VHS, DVD.** Jenny (Jennifer) Morrison, Anthony Anderson, Joseph Lawrence, Matthew Davis, Hart Bochner, Loretta Devine, Marco Hofschneider, Eva Mendes, Michael Bacall, Anson Mount, Jessica Cauffiel, Chas Lawther; *D:* John Ottman; *W:* Paul Harris Boardman, Scott Derrickson; *C:* Brian Pearson; *M:* John Ottman.

Urban Legends: Bloody Mary ♂ 1/2 **2005 (R)** Mary (Fields) dies during prom night because of a jock prank gone wrong. Years later, some slumber party babes giggle and do the "Bloody Mary" chant, only to rouse the restless Mary's spirit, causing her to start playing her own bloody tricks on another group of equally thoughtless jocks. **93m/C DVD.** Kate Mara, Tina Lifford, Ed Marinaro, Lilith Fields, Robert Vito, Haley McCormick, Olesya Rulin; *D:* Mary Lambert; *W:* Michael Dougherty, Dan Harris; *C:* Ian Fox; *M:* Jeff Rona. **VIDEO**

Urban Menace ♂♂ **1999 (R)** Another "the future sucks" urban nightmare. A quarantined wasteland known as "The Downs" is the killing ground for a serial maniac. Two men, Harper and Crow, try to stop the mayhem and discover their murderer isn't even human. Features a hard-core rap and hip-hop soundtrack. **73m/C VHS, DVD.** Snoop Dogg, Big Pun, Ice-T, Fat Joe, T.J. Storm, Vincent Klyn, Romany Malco, Tahitia, Karen Dyer, Ernie Hudson; *D:* Albert Pyun; *W:* Tim Story; *C:* Philip Alan Waters. **VIDEO**

Urban Warriors ♂ **1987** Savage barbarians roam and pillage a post-nuclear war Earth, but one invincible warrior ushers them out. **90m/C VHS.** *IT* Maurice Poli, Malisa Longo, Brigitte Porsche, Bruno Bilotta, Alex Vitale, Deborah Keith; *D:* Joseph Warren; *W:* Piero Regnoli.

Urbania ♂♂ **2000 (R)** Urban legends and painful flashbacks are plentifully featured in this disturbing film that finds Charlie (Futterman) restlessly wandering the streets of New York in search of the handsome homophobic stranger (Ball) who turns out to be responsible for the death of Charlie's boyfriend Chris (Keeslar). Directorial debut of Shear; based on Daniel Reitz's play "Urban Folk Tales." **104m/C VHS, DVD.** Dan Futterman, Matt Keeslar, Josh Hamilton, Samuel Ball, William Sage, Megan Dodds, Alan Cumming, Lothaire Bluteau, Barbara Sukowa, Paige Turco, Gabriel Olds; *D:* Jon Shear; *W:* Daniel Reitz; *C:* Shane Kelly; *M:* Marc Anthony Thompson.

Urge to Kill ♂ **1984 (PG)** A man returning from a mental hospital after pleading temporary insanity to the murder of his girlfriend returns to her town and tries to uncover the truth, with the help of her younger sister. **96m/C VHS.** Karl Malden, Holly Hunter, William Devane, Alex McArthur; *D:* Mike Robe. **TV**

Ursus in the Valley of the Lions ♂ 1/2 *The Mighty Ursus; Ursus* **1962** Ursus attempts to rescue his love from druids but is dismayed to find that she has taken up homicide in her free time. **92m/C VHS.** *IT SP* Ed Fury, Luis Prendes, Moira Orfei, Cristina Gajoni, Maria Luisa Merlo; *D:* Carlo Campogalliani.

Used Cars ♂♂♂ **1980 (R)** A car dealer is desperate to put his jalopy shop competitors out of business. The owners go to great lengths to stay afloat. Sometimes too obnoxious, but often funny. **113m/C VHS, DVD.** Kurt Russell, Jack Warden, Deborah Harmon, Gerrit Graham, Joe Flaherty, Michael McKean, David Lander, Al Lewis, Wendie Jo Sperber, Dick Miller, Rita Taggart; *D:* Robert Zemeckis; *W:* Robert Zemeckis, Bob Gale; *C:* Donald M. Morgan; *M:* Patrick Williams.

Used People ♂♂ 1/2 **1992 (PG-13)** A study in ethnicity and characterization, three Oscar-winning actresses lead a talented cast playing a Jewish family living in Queens in 1969. When the father dies, Joe (Mastroianni), an old friend with an old torch for the widow, Pearl (MacLaine), shows up at the funeral and manages to charm her into a date for coffee. Pearl's new relationship with her Italian suitor affects each of the somewhat off-balance family members and washes the whole clan with a sense of hope and renewal. Adpated from screenwriter Graff's play "The Grandma Plays" that was based on memories of his grandmother. Director Kidron's American debut. **116m/C VHS.** Shirley MacLaine, Marcello Mastroianni, Kathy Bates, Marcia Gay Harden, Jessica Tandy, Sylvia Sidney, Bob (Robert) Dishy, Joe Pantoliano, Matthew Branton, Louis Guff, Charles Cioffi, Doris Roberts, Helen Hanft; *D:* Beeban Kidron; *W:* Todd Graff; *M:* Rachel Portman.

Users ♂♂ **1978** Small-town girl who worked as a prostitute meets a faded film star and becomes involved in the movie business. Ode to decadent Hollywood. Based on the Joyce Haber novel. **125m/C VHS.** Jaclyn Smith, Tony Curtis, John Forsythe, Red Buttons, George Hamilton; *D:* Joseph Hardy; *M:* Maurice Jarre. **TV**

Ushpizin ♂♂ *Ha'Ushpizin* **2004 (PG-13)** Depiction of the ultra-Orthodox Jewish community of Jerusalem is a gentle fable about a childless couple, Moshe and Malli (Rand and his wife Michal), whose prayers are answered in unexpected ways. It's considered a blessing to share the Sukkot festival with others (the title means "holy guests") but the couple are too poor to do so until an expected windfall comes their way—both monetary and in the form of Eliahu (Mizrahi) and Yosef (Gannai), once friends of the younger Moshe who turn out to be prison escapees. Hebrew with subtitles. **90m/C DVD.** Shuli Rand, Shaul Mizrahi, Michal Bat-Sheva Rand, Ilan Ganani, Avraham Abutboul, Yonathan Danino, Rabbi Daniel Dayan, Michael Vaigel, Daniel Rand, Yizhak Levkovits, Shmuel Ovadia; *D:* Gidi Dar; *W:* Shuli Rand; *C:* Amit Yasur; *M:* Nathaniel Mechaly.

The Usual Suspects ♂♂♂ 1/2 **1995 (R)** Twisted noir-thriller about some crooks, a $91 million heist, and mysterious crime lord Keyser Soze. Customs agent Kujan (Palminteri) tries to get a straight story out of small-time con man "Verbal" Kint (Spacey) about a burning tanker in the San Pedro harbor, 27 dead bodies, and the other four tempermental criminals involved: ex-cop-turned thief Keaton (Byrne), explosives expert Hockney (Pollak), and hot-headed partners McManus (Baldwin) and Fenster (Del Toro). Nothing is as it seems, and the ending keeps everyone guessing, right up to the final credits. Terrific performances from all complement the intelligent, humorous script. And yes, the title does come from the famous line in "Casablanca." **105m/C VHS, DVD, Blu-ray Disc.** Louis Lombardi, Kevin Spacey, Gabriel Byrne, Chazz Palminteri, Kevin Pollak, Stephen Baldwin, Benicio Del Toro, Giancarlo Esposito, Pete Postlethwaite, Dan Hedaya, Suzy Amis, Paul Bartel, Peter Greene; *D:* Bryan Singer; *W:* Christopher McQuarrie; *C:* Newton Thomas (Tom) Sigel; *M:* John Ottman. Oscars '95: Orig. Screenplay, Support. Actor (Spacey); British Acad. '95: Orig. Screenplay; Ind. Spirit '96: Screenplay, Support. Actor (Del Toro); Natl. Bd. of Review '95: Support. Actor (Spacey); N.Y. Film Critics '95: Support. Actor (Spacey); Broadcast Film Critics '95: Support. Actor (Spacey).

Utah ♂♂ **1945** A musical comedy star who inherits a ranch wishes to sell it to finance one of her shows. She is persuaded not to by Rogers, the ranch foreman. **54m/B VHS, DVD.** Roy Rogers, Dale Evans, George "Gabby" Hayes; *D:* John English.

Utah Trail ♂ **1938** Lawman Ritter is hired to stop a gang of cattle rustlers. Cheapie oater made for Grand National, which went bankrupt soon after. **57m/B VHS, DVD.** Tex Ritter; *D:* Al(bert) Herman.

Utamaro and His Five Women ♂♂ 1/2 *Five Women Around Utamaro; Utamaro O Meguru Gonin No Onna* **1946** Utamaro is a legendary 19th-century Edo artist who gained inspiration from Tokyo's "floating world," of courtesans, brothels, drinking parties, and violent passions. His gorgeous portraits worship women but he dislikes the complications that flesh-and-blood females bring. Heavily stylized look at the artistic impulse. In Japanese with English subtitles. **89m/B VHS.** *JP* Minnosuke Bando, Kinuyo Tanaka, Kotaro Bando, Hisato Osawa, Tamezo Mochizuki, Hiroko Kawasaki; *D:* Kenji Mizoguchi; *W:* Yoshikata Yoda; *C:* Shigeto Miki; *M:* Hisato Osawa, Tamezo Mochizuki.

Utilities ♂ 1/2 *Getting Even* **1983 (PG)** A frustrated social worker enlists the help of his friends in his efforts to impress an attractive policewoman by taking on a large corporate utility. **94m/C VHS.** *CA* Robert Hays, Brooke Adams, John Marley, Ben Gordon, Helen Burns, Helene Winston; *D:* Harvey Hart.

Utopia ♂♂ *Atoll K; Robinson Crusoeland; Escapade* **1951** Laurel and Hardy inherit a paradisaical island, but their peace is disturbed when uranium is discovered. Final screen appearance of the team is diminished by poor direction and script. **82m/B VHS, DVD.** *FR* Stan Laurel, Oliver Hardy, Suzy Delair, Max Elloy; *D:* Leo Joannon; *W:* Rene Wheeler, Piero Tellini, Monte (Monty) Collins Jr.; *C:* Louis Nee, Armand Thirard; *M:* Paul Misraki.

The Utopian Society ♂ 1/2 **2003** Low-budget and predictable story about six college students realizing they're not so different after all. The students are supposed to have been working on a group sociology project to describe what they would consider a utopian society. But they blew it off until the night before the paper is due and now seem more interested in bickering and other foolishness than getting down to work, even if it means failing the class. **93m/C DVD.** Kelvin Yu, Malin Akerman, Austin Nichols, Kristen Ariza, Sam Doumit, Mat Hostetler; *D:* John P. Aguirre; *W:* Jason Preston; *C:* Eric Petersen; *M:* Eric Hester.

Utu ♂♂♂ **1983 (R)** A Maori tribesman serving with the colonizing British army in 1870 explodes into ritual revenge when his home village is slaughtered. Filmed in New Zealand. **122m/C VHS, DVD.** *NZ* Anzac Wallace, Kelly Johnson, Tim Elliot, Bruno Lawrence; *D:* Geoff Murphy; *W:* Geoff Murphy, Keith Aberdein; *C:* Graeme Cowley; *M:* John Charles.

U2: Rattle and Hum ♂♂ 1/2 **1988 (PG-13)** Very-well-done concert/documentary, focusing on the Irish band U2 and their 1988 U.S. tour. Filmed in black-and-white and color. **90m/C VHS, DVD.** *D:* Phil Joanou; *C:* Robert Brinkmann, Jordan Cronenweth.

Utz ♂♂ 1/2 **1993** The Baron von Utz (Mueller-Stahl) collects both women and priceless porcelain figures. When his friend, art dealer Marius Fischer (Riegert), travels to Prague for a visit he finds that both Utz's housekeeper (Fricker), who has suffered from unrequited love, and the porcelain have disappeared. So Marius teams up with the Baron's old friend Dr. Orlick (Scofield) to find out what's going on. Based on the novel by Bruce Chatwin. **95m/C VHS.** *GB GE IT* Armin Mueller-Stahl, Peter Riegert, Brenda Fricker, Paul Scofield; *D:* George Sluizer.

Uzumaki 🦴 1/2 *Spiral* **2000** In what was originally a manga by famed horror writer Junji Ito, the inhabitants of the small town of Kurozu-cho are obsessed with spirals, which is the symbol of some entity that transforms or destroys anything it encounters. The comic is written in 20 episodes, seven of which make it into the film, which ultimately fails to live up to the spirit of the comic due to its lower budget effects and a lack of closure. **90m/C DVD.** *JP* Hinako Saeki, Eun-Kyung Shin, Ren Osugi, Denden, Taro Suwa, Eriko Hatsune, Fhi Fan, Keiko Takahashi, Masami Horiuchi, Tooru Teduka, Sadao Abe, Asumi Miwa, Saori Nakane, Yasuki Tanaka, Yuki Murakama, Maki Hamada, Tomoo Fukatsu, Akira Matsuda, Takuto Oyama, Hasseí Takano; ***D:*** Higuchinsky; ***W:*** Junji Ito, Kengo Kaji, Takao Nitta, Chika Yasuo; ***C:*** Gen Kobayashi; ***M:*** Keiichi Suzuki, Tetsuro Kashibuchi.

V 🦴🦴🦴 **1983** Very creepy sci-fi miniseries that spawned a short-lived TV show. Advanced aliens, known as the Visitors, come to Earth on a seemingly friendly quest. But their human-like appearance is a facade—as is their mission. Fake skin masks a repitilian hide and what they want is complete planetary control. Naturally, some earthlings don't fall for their smooth talk and a resistance movement is born. Followed by miniseries conclusion "V: The Final Battle." **190m/C VHS, DVD.** Marc Singer, Jane Badler, Faye Grant, Robert Englund, Michael Durrell, Peter Nelson, Neva Patterson, Andrew Prine, Richard Herd, Rafael Campos; ***D:*** Kenneth Johnson; ***W:*** Kenneth Johnson. **TV**

V for Vendetta 🦴🦴 1/2 **2006 (R)** The Wachowskis and director McTeigue bring Alan Moore's 1980s graphic novel to the big screen (though Moore disowned the film). In the year 2020, disease and chaos have swept America off the top of the global food chain, and dictator Sutler (Hurt) has used the resultant fear to turn Britain into a totalitarian regime. V (Weaving), a masked avenger who uses the legend of Guy Fawkes as both disguise and inspiration, strikes at the government by blowing up Big Ben, promising to return in a year to bring about revolution. On the same night, he also happens to save Evey (Portman) from being raped by the police. She becomes an important ally in his fight. Covers a lot of philosophical ground, but at times glosses over the ideas it presents, costing it much real depth. But it does so with a goodly amount of flash, and not a little artistry. **132m/C DVD, HD DVD.** *US* Hugo Weaving, Natalie Portman, Stephen Rea, Stephen Fry, John Hurt, Tim Pigott-Smith, Rupert Graves, Roger Allam, Ben Miles, Sinead Cusack, Eddie Marsan, Natasha Wightman; ***D:*** James McTeigue; ***W:*** Andy Wachowski, Larry Wachowski; ***C:*** Adrian Biddle; ***M:*** Dario Marianelli.

V: The Final Battle 🦴🦴 1/2 **1984** It's four-months since the Visitors appeared on earth, proclaiming their false friendship. But a resistance movement knows these reptiles, who hide behind a human appearance, are only interested in harvesting earth's inhabitants as a new food source. Continuation of the TV miniseries "V." **285m/C VHS, DVD.** Marc Singer, Robert Englund, Michael Ironside; ***D:*** Richard T. Heffron.

Va Savoir 🦴🦴 1/2 *Who Knows?* **2001 (PG-13)** Romantic farce involving theatre folk. French actress Camille (Balibar) returns to Paris as the star of an Italian theatrical company. She's involved with company director Ugo (Castellitto) but sees her ex, Pierre (Bonaffre), who has a new girlfriend, Sonia (Basler). Meanwhile, Ugo is searching for a lost play by 18th-century writer Goldoni, aided by grad student Do (de Fougerolles) who gets a crush on him, despite her half-brother Arthur's (Todeschini) dislike of the situation. That everyone will interact in each other's lives is a given. French with subtitles. **154m/C VHS, DVD.** *FR IT GE* Jeanne Balibar, Sergio Castellitto, Jacques Bonnaffe, Marianne Basler, Helene de Fougerolles, Bruno Todeschini, Catherine Rouvel, Claude Berri; ***D:*** Jacques Rivette; ***W:*** Jacques Rivette, Christine Laurent, Pascal Bonitzer; ***C:*** William Lubtchansky.

Vacancy 🦴 1/2 **2007 (R)** Standard slasher flick finds bickering estranged couple David (Wilson) and Amy (Beckinsale) stuck in a fleabag motel after having car trouble along a deserted backroad. Their in-room entertainment consists of dusty videotapes of torture snuff flicks they soon realize happened in the very room they're in. Then they figure out they're being watched. Wilson and Beckinsale give their characters a little more depth than the pic probably deserves. **80m/C DVD, Blu-ray Disc.** *US* Luke Wilson, Kate Beckinsale, Frank Whaley, Ethan (Randall) Embry; ***D:*** Nimrod Antal; ***W:*** Mark Smith; ***C:*** Andrzej Sekula; ***M:*** Paul Haslinger.

Vacancy 2: The First Cut 🦴 **2008 (R)** A generally cheap, dreary, and dumb prequel story to the 2007 studio release. Two sleazoids tape the sexual encounters of their no-tell motel guests for fun and profit. A serial killer rents a room and they catch him killing a hooker on video and the killer proposes they team up and turn from sex tapes to snuff films. Then three friends check-in and are about to become the first "stars." **86m/C DVD.** Agnes Bruckner, David Moscow, Arjay Smith, Trevor Wright, Beau Billingslea, Brian Klugman, JAMES MCARTHUR; ***D:*** Eric Bross; ***W:*** Mark L. Smith; ***C:*** Horacio Marquinez; ***M:*** Jerome Dillon. **VIDEO**

Vacas 🦴🦴 *Cows* **1991** The political and social climate of the Basque region of Spain is frequently dangerous but the region's cows (the "vacas" of the title) placidly continue as always despite what happens to the humans around them. Covering more than 50 years, from 1875 through the Spanish Civil War, the lives of two families are interwined in emotional conflict through three generations. Spanish with subtitles. **96m/C VHS, DVD.** *SP* Carmelo Gomez, Ana Torrent, Emma Suarez, Pilar Bardem, Kandito Uranga; ***D:*** Julio Medem; ***W:*** Julio Medem, Michel Gaztambide; ***C:*** Carlos Gusi; ***M:*** Alberto Iglesias.

The Vacillations of Poppy Carew 🦴🦴 1/2 **1994** Free-spirited Poppy is just trying to make funeral arrangements for her father when she becomes involved in a series of unexpected and complicated romances. Based on a novel by Mary Wesley. **109m/C VHS.** *GB* Tara Fitzgerald, Sian Phillips, Charlotte Coleman, Samuel West, Edward Atterton, Joseph Fiennes, Daniel Massey; ***D:*** James Cellan Jones; ***W:*** William Humble; ***C:*** David Feig; ***M:*** Richard Holmes. **TV**

Vacuuming Completely Nude in Paradise 🦴🦴 1/2 **2001** Not only is Pete's (Begley) girlfriend tired of stripping to support them but she won't put out until he gets a real job. Off he goes to the local door-to-door vacuum sales office and is placed under the dubious tutelage of polar opposite Tommy (Spall)—a frantic, morally bankrupt, yet very experienced and successful salesman. The jocularity is plentiful in this BBC-TV production as the contest for the "Golden Hoover" pits all the sales folks against Tommy. Spall excels in punching out his frenzied lines while director Boyle's use of the digital video format captures the essence of office life in this grim send-up. **75m/C VHS, DVD.** Timothy Spall, Michael Begley, Katy Cavanagh, Caroline Ashley; ***D:*** Danny Boyle; ***W:*** Jim Cartwright; ***C:*** Anthony Dod Mantle; ***M:*** John Murphy. **TV**

The Vagabond 🦴🦴 **1916** The Little Tramp is a pathetic fiddler making a scanty living who rescues a damsel in distress. Silent with musical soundtrack added. **20m/B VHS, DVD.** Charlie Chaplin, Edna Purviance, Eric Campbell, Albert Austin; ***D:*** Charlie Chaplin.

Vagabond 🦴🦴🦴 1/2 *Sans Toit Ni Loi* **1985** Bleak, emotionally shattering, powerful and compelling, this film traces the peripatetic life of an amoral and selfish young French woman who has no regard for social rules and tremendous fear of responsibility in her drifting yet inexorable journey into death. Told via flashbacks from the moment when she is found dead, alone, and unaccounted for by the roadside, this film will not leave you unscathed. Written by New Wave director Varda. In French with English subtitles. **105m/C VHS, DVD.** *FR* Sandrine Bonnaire, Macha Meril, Stephane Freiss, Elaine Cortadellas, Marthe Jarnias, Yolande Moreau; ***D:*** Agnes Varda; ***W:*** Agnes Varda; ***C:*** Patrick Blossier; ***M:*** Joanne Bruzdowicz. Cesar '86: Actress (Bonnaire); L.A. Film Critics '86: Actress (Bonnaire), Foreign Film.

Vagabond Lover 🦴🦴 1/2 **1929** The amusing tale of the loves, hopes, and dreams of an aspiring saxophone player. Rudy croons through his megaphone in his movie debut. Appealing, with Dressler sparkling in the role of the wealthy aunt. ♫If You Were the Only Girl in the World; A Little Kiss Each Morning; Heigh Ho Everybody; Piccolo Pete; I Love You; I'll Be Reminded of You; I'm Just a Vagabond Lover. **66m/B VHS, DVD.** Rudy Vallee, Sally Blane, Marie Dressler, Charles Sellon, Eddie Nugent; ***D:*** Marshall Neilan; ***W:*** James A. Creelman; ***C:*** Leo Tover.

The Vagrant 🦴 **1992 (R)** Run-of-the-mill creeper with a mind-game playing derelict inhabiting the home of a young exec. A series of murders has this wimp yuppie wondering how to get rid of his unwelcome intruder. **91m/C VHS.** Bill Paxton, Michael Ironside, Marshall Bell, Stuart Pankin; ***D:*** Chris Walas.

The Valachi Papers 🦴🦴 1/2 **1972 (R)** Joe Valachi (Bronson), serving a life sentence, recouns his life and times as a small-time soldier in the mob. The Feds want him to tell them how the outfit works, and the the mob wants him dead. Sometimes violent but overall flatly told story of low-life mob life can be seen as a precursor to the Scorsese mob epics that came later. Bronson turns in a good performance. **125m/C DVD.** Charles Bronson, Lino Ventura, Jill Ireland, Walter Chiari, Joseph Wiseman, Gerald S. O'Loughlin, Amedeo Nazzari, Fausto Tozzi, Angelo Infanti, Pupella Maggio; ***D:*** Terence Young; ***W:*** Stephen Geller; ***C:*** Aldo Tonti; ***M:*** Riz Ortolani, Armando Trovajoli.

Valdez Is Coming 🦴🦴 1/2 **1971 (PG-13)** Though not a world-class western, this filmed-in-Spain saga does feature a probing script (based on an Elmore Leonard novel) on the nature of race relations. Fine performance by Lancaster as a Mexican-American who ignites the passions of a town, and ultimately confronts the local land baron. **90m/C VHS, DVD.** Burt Lancaster, Susan Clark, Jon Cypher, Barton Heyman, Richard Jordan, Frank Silvera, Hector Elizondo; ***D:*** Edwin Sherin; ***W:*** David Rayfiel; ***M:*** Charles Gross.

Valentin 🦴🦴 1/2 **2002 (PG-13)** Valentin is the overly adorable, 9-year-old, horn-rimmed glasses wearing hero of Agresti's semi-autobiographical drama set in 1960s Buenos Aires. Valentin (Noya) lives with his kooky grandmother (Maura) after being abandoned by his mother and playboy father, (director Agresti) who have long separated. Valentin attempts to rebuild his family by playing Cupid with his dad's current girlfriend, the beautiful and attentive Leticia (Cardinali) while simultaneously charming and inspiring various local, hardened grown-ups. The precocious boy is also an aspiring astronaut, a fact which allows him to dress up in a far-less-than-homemade looking get-up and look cute, which he does for far too much of this sometimes saccharine heart-tugger. Does boast some genuinely touching moments. **86m/C DVD.** *AR NL* Carmen Maura, Rodrigo Noya, Alejandro Agresti, Jean Pierre Noher, Mex Urtizberea, Julieta Cardinali; ***D:*** Alejandro Agresti; ***W:*** Alejandro Agresti; ***C:*** Jose Luis Cajaraville; ***M:*** Luis Salinas, Paul M. van Brugge.

Valentin 🦴 1/2 **2003** Spanish sex comedy. A theater company is putting on traditional performances of Shakespeare with male actors in the female roles. Director Ricardo (Homar) suddenly becomes obsessed with their new male ingenue Valentin (Font), provoking a jealous rage in Jaime (Del Rio), the actor whose parts he's taken. Valentin is supposed to be irresistibly charming but you'll be hard-pressed to understand why since he seems only shallow and petulant. Spanish with subtitles. **110m/C DVD.** *SP* Lluis Homar, Armando Del Rio, Elisa Matilla, Inaki Font, Jorge Bosch; ***D:*** Juan Luis Iborra; ***W:*** Juan Luis Iborra, Marc Cases; ***C:*** Porfirio Enriquez; ***M:*** Juan Carlos Cuello.

Valentina's Tango 🦴🦴 **2007** Valentina (Quiroga) is an obsessive tango dancer who owns a Hollywood nightclub with her husband Eduardo (Caballero), where their dancing together has also kept their passion alive. Good son Eddie (Perez) is about to enter the seminary while bad boy Victor (Rubio) hangs around gangster Sonny (Larraza). Sonny is pressuring Victor to get his parents to sell the club, but things turn dramatic and tragic. **98m/C DVD.** Jordi Caballero, Jack Rubio, George Perez, Yelba Osorio, Guillermina Quiroga, Mario Larraza, Dianna Miranda, Allen Walls; ***D:*** Rogelio Lobato; ***W:*** Rogelio Lobato; ***C:*** Irv Goodnoff; ***M:*** Albert Guinovart.

Valentine 🦴 **2001 (R)** Slasher film with a former nerd of a killer in a Cupid mask wreaking revenge upon the snooty girls who dissed him in junior high. After one victim's funeral, the remaining four get some threatening Valentines, which they, of course, promptly ignore. Boreanaz is among the doomed babes' boyfriends and a prime suspect. After yet another of the girls falls victim to the demented deity-wannabe, the remaining three grieve by throwing a bash at a swanky mansion with rambling vacant rooms that just scream, well, you get it. Eye-candy cast with mild suspense mix with dubious scripting. The only real victim here is your precious time. **96m/C VHS, DVD.** *US* David Boreanaz, Denise Richards, Marley Shelton, Jessica Capshaw, Katherine Heigl, Johnny Whitworth, Hedy Burress, Jessica Cauffiel, Fulvio Cecere, Daniel Cosgrove; ***D:*** Jamie Blanks; ***W:*** Donna Powers, Wayne Powers, Gretchen J. Berg, Aaron Harberts; ***C:*** Rick Bota; ***M:*** Don Davis.

Valentine's Day 🦴 **2010 (PG-13)** There are only two things missing from this star-studded romantic comedy from schmaltz-meister Marshall. Unfortunately, those things are romance and comedy. Linking the stories of lust, love, and revenge together is the flower store owned by Reed (Kutcher), who is proposing to his conflicted girlfriend Morley (Alba). Stars such as Julia Roberts, Shirley MacLaine, and Anne Hathaway are wasted in this movie that has so many plot lines and characters that nothing is able to emerge as anything other than two-dimensional. The celebrity cameos might have seemed like a good idea, but it's more like "The Love Boat" hit an iceberg and sank. **125m/C DVD.** Julia Roberts, Anne Hathaway, Jessica Alba, Jessica Biel, Jennifer Garner, Shirley MacLaine, Queen Latifah, Bradley Cooper, Ashton Kutcher, Jamie Foxx, Topher Grace, Emma Roberts, Taylor Swift, Hector Elizondo, George Lopez, Patrick Dempsey, Eric Dane; ***D:*** Garry Marshall; ***W:*** Abby Kohn, Marc Silverstein; ***C:*** Charles Minsky; ***M:*** John Debney.

Valentino 🦴🦴 **1977 (R)** Another one of director Russell's flamboyantly excessive screen biographies, this time of silent screen idol Rudolph Valentino (Nureyev). The details hardly matter but the movie is told in flashback from Valentino's funeral to his beginnings as a dance instructor and his eventual success as a screen lover. Nureyev is noticeably stiff in his screen debut but at least he possesses some charisma. **127m/C VHS.** *GB* Rudolf Nureyev, Leslie Caron, Michelle Phillips, Carol Kane, Felicity Kendal, Seymour Cassel, Peter Vaughan, William Hootkins, Huntz Hall, David de Keyser, Alfred Marks, Anton Diffring; ***D:*** Ken Russell; ***W:*** Mardik Martin, Ken Russell, John Byrum; ***C:*** Peter Suschitzky; ***M:*** Ferde Grofe Jr.

Valentino Returns 🦴🦴 **1988 (R)** A kid in 1955 California buys a pink Cadillac he nicknames "Valentino Returns," thinking it will help him meet girls, as his parents undergo a stormy divorce. Weak script fades fast from fine premise, good start. Nice period feel. **97m/C VHS.** Frederic Forrest, Veronica Cartwright, Jenny Wright, Barry Tubb; ***D:*** Peter Hoffman.

Valentino: The Last Emperor 🦴🦴 1/2 **2008 (PG-13)** Debuting director Tynauer's documentary examines haute couture and the career of Italian fashion designer Valentino (who retired in 2007 shortly after the two-year shoot was completed). Included are a celebration of the designer's 45-year career and his longtime personal and professional relationship with partner Giancarlo Giammaetti. **96m/C DVD.** *US*

The Valet 🦴🦴 1/2 *La Doublure* **2006 (PG-13)** Venal tycoon Pierre Levasseur (Auteuil) is in big trouble when a paparazzo takes a photo of him and supermodel mistress Elena (Taglioni). Seems Pierre's wife Christine (Scott Thomas) owns the majority share of company stock and he can't afford a divorce. Ah, but valet Francois (Elmaleh) was also in the picture, so Pierre pays him (and Elena) to pretend that they are a couple. Francois wants the money to help out true (if oblivious) love Emilie (Ledoyen) but the complications increase in Veber's amusing bedroom farce. French with subtitles. **85m/C DVD.** *FR* Daniel Auteuil, Kristin Scott Thomas, Virginie Ledoyen, Richard Berry, Gad Elmaleh,

Alice Taglioni, Dany Boon; *D:* Francis Veber; *W:* Francis Veber; *C:* Robert Fraisse; *M:* Alexandre Desplat.

Valhalla Rising **2009** Mute Viking warrior One-Eye (Mikkelsen), imprisoned in England, slays his captors and sets out for home before falling in with a band of Christian Vikings who plan to sail for Jerusalem (and conquer it). **90m/C DVD.** *DK* Mads Mikkelsen, Maarten Stevenson, Gordon Brown, Andrew Flanagan, Gary Lewis, Gary McCormack, Alexander Morgan, Jamie Sieves; *D:* Nicolas Winding Refn; *W:* Nicolas Winding Refn, Roy Jacobsen; *C:* Morten Soborg; *M:* Peter Kyed.

Valiant 🦴 1/2 **2005 (G)** Feature-length film based on the WWII homing pigeons used by the British Armed Forces is cute and short, which should please the kids but the plot development never really gets off the ground. Classic "misfit gets his chance and saves the day" story focuses on Valiant (McGregor), who has not been allowed to join the Royal Homing Pigeon Service until they discover how to turn his short-falling into an asset. Plenty of jokes spoofing war movies of days-gone-by. **80m/C DVD.** *GB US* *D:* Gary Chapman; *W:* Jordan Katz, George Webster, George Melrod; *C:* John Fenner; *M:* George Fenton; *V:* Ewan McGregor, Tim Curry, Jim Broadbent, Hugh Laurie, Daniel Roberts, John Cleese, John Hurt, Pip Torrens, Ricky Gervais, Brian Lonsdale, Olivia Williams, Rik Mayall, Sharon Horgan.

Valkyrie 🦴🦴 1/2 **2008 (PG-13)** Following the loss of an eye, a hand, and a couple of fingers during an air raid, Claus von Stauffenberg (Cruise), a Colonel in Hitler's Third Reich, realizes he can no longer participate in the destruction and mass murders being carried out by the Fuhrer's SS troops. With several like-minded officers (Branagh, Nighy and Stamp), von Stauffenberg hatches a covert plan to assassinate Hitler (Bamber) and bring back honor to Germany. The historically known failure of the June 1944 plot hangs the story's interest on the thoughts and motivations of those involved and on the plan's details. Much of the action is restrained due to the nature of the career military officers being portrayed, but the suspense of the many near misses and close calls makes for an interesting second half. **120m/C DVD.** *US GE* Tom Cruise, David Bamber, Matthias Freihof, Carice van Houten, Kenneth Branagh, Eddie Izzard, Thomas Kretschmann, Bill Nighy, Terence Stamp, Kevin McNally, Christian Berkel, Tom Hollander, Kenneth Cranham; *D:* Bryan Singer; *W:* Christopher McQuarrie, Nathan Alexander; *C:* Newton Thomas (Tom) Sigel; *M:* John Ottman.

Valley Girl 🦴🦴 1/2 *Bad Boyz* **1983 (R)** Slight but surprisingly likeable teen romantic-comedy inspired by Frank Zappa novelty tune. Title stereotype falls for a leather-jacketed rebel. Really. It may look like a music video, but the story is straight from "Romeo and Juliet" via Southern California. Helped launch Cage's career. Music by Men at Work, Culture Club, and others. **95m/C VHS, DVD.** Nicolas Cage, Deborah Foreman, Colleen Camp, Frederic Forrest, Lee Purcell, Elizabeth (E.G. Dailey) Daily, Michael Bowen, Cameron Dye, Heidi Holicker, Michelle Meyrink; *D:* Martha Coolidge; *W:* Wayne Crawford, Andrew Lane; *C:* Frederick Elmes; *M:* Marc Levinthal, Scott Wilk.

The Valley Obscured by the Clouds 🦴🦴 *La Vallee* **1970** A group of dropouts and seekers search for the valley of the gods in the wilds of New Guinea, and experience a sexual and spiritual metamorphosis. In French with English subtitles. **106m/C VHS, DVD.** *FR* Bulle Ogier, Michael Gothard, Jean-Pierre Kalfon, Jerome Beauvarlet, Monique Giraudy; *D:* Barbet Schroeder; *W:* Barbet Schroeder; *C:* Nestor Almendros; *M:* Pink Floyd.

The Valley of Decision 🦴🦴🦴 **1945** Entertaining poor-girl-meets-rich-boy story with Peck as a wealthy mill owner who falls in love with beautiful housemaid Garson (the Queen of MGM at the time). Set in 1870 Pittsburgh; based on Marcia Davenport's novel. **111m/B VHS.** Gregory Peck, Greer Garson, Donald Crisp, Lionel Barrymore, Preston Foster, Gladys Cooper, Marsha Hunt, Reginald Owen, Dan Duryea, Jessica Tandy, Barbara Everest; *D:* Tay Garnett; *W:* John Meehan, Sonya Levien; *C:* Joseph Ruttenberg.

Valley of Fire 🦴🦴 **1951** Autry is the mayor of a boom town that suffers from a lack of women. He decides to import a caravan of brides for the men in town but villains attempt to kidnap the women. **63m/B VHS, DVD.** Gene Autry, Gail Davis, Pat Buttram; *D:* John English.

The Valley of Gwangi 🦴🦴🦴 **1969 (G)** One of the best prehistoric-monster-westerns out there. Cowboys discover a lost valley of dinosaurs and try to capture a vicious, carnivorous allosaurus. Bad move, kemosabe! The creatures move via the stop-motion model animation by f/x maestro Ray Harryhausen, here at his finest. **95m/C VHS, DVD.** James Franciscus, Gila Golan, Richard Carlson, Laurence Naismith, Freda Jackson, Gustavo Rojo, Dennis Kilbane, Mario De Barros, Curtis Arden, Jose Burgos; *D:* James O'Connolly; *W:* William Bast, Julian More; *C:* Erwin Hillier; *M:* Jerome Moross.

Valley of Terror 🦴 1/2 **1938** Maynard is framed for cattle rustling. Can he prove his innocence? **59m/B VHS.** Kermit Maynard, Harley Wood, John Merton, Jack Ingram, Dick Curtis, Roger Williams; *D:* Al(bert) Herman.

Valley of the Dolls 🦴🦴 **1967 (PG)** Camp/trash classic was rated as a bomb by many critics but is really of the so-bad-it's-good variety. Three beauties, Jennifer (Tate), Neely (Duke), and Anne (Parkins), dream of Hollywood stardom but fall victim to Hollywood excess, including drug dependency (the "dolls" of the title). There's unhappy love affairs, porno parts, health risks, and hysterics of various kinds—all designed to have you dropping your jaw in disbelief. The bathroom scene between Duke and Hayward involving a wig is not to be missed. Based on the novel by Jacqueline Susann who has a bit part as a reporter. Remade for TV as "Jacqueline Susann's Valley of the Dolls" in 1981. **123m/C VHS, DVD.** Barbara Parkins, Patty Duke, Sharon Tate, Paul Burke, Tony Scotti, Martin Milner, Susan Hayward, Charles Drake, Lee Grant, Alex Davion, Robert H. Harris, Robert Viharo, Joey Bishop, George Jessel, Richard Dreyfuss; ***Cameos:*** Jacqueline Susann; *D:* Mark Robson; *W:* Dorothy Kingsley, Helen Deutsch, Jacqueline Susann; *C:* William H. Daniels; *M:* John Williams.

Valley of the Eagles 🦴 1/2 **1951** When his wife and partner take off into the Lapland wilderness with his new invention, a scientist leads the police across the tundra in pursuit. Setting is at least a plus. **83m/B VHS.** *GB* Jack Warner, Nadia Gray, John McCallum, Martin Boddey, Christopher Lee; *D:* Terence Young; *M:* Nino Rota.

Valley of the Heart's Delight 🦴 1/2 **2007** Old-fashioned and somewhat flat retelling of a true crime story from 1933. The title refers to Silicon Valley's previous incarnation as an agricultural area. Ambitious rookie reporter Jack Daumier is assigned to a society story when Blake Walsh, son of local bigwig Horace, gets a job promotion. However, Jack is more interested in dating Blake's sister Helen (Harrison). When Blake is kidnapped, Jack thinks there's a cover-up. **100m/C DVD.** Gabriel Mann, Pete Postlethwaite, Emily Harrison, Diana Scarwid, Bruce McGill, Tom Bower, Ron Rogge, Joe Mandragona, Michael Sommers, Cully Fredricksen; *D:* Tim Boxell; *W:* Miles Murphy; *C:* Hiro Narita; *M:* Richard Gibbs, Nicholas O'Toole. **VIDEO**

Valley of the Kings 🦴🦴 1/2 **1954** Corny big dig movie that does have some nice Egyptian scenery. Archeologist Mark Brandon (Taylor) is searching for the treasure of pharoah Ra-Hotep in 1900s Egypt. Ann (Parker) would like to prove that several Bible stories are, in fact, true while her husband Philip (Thompson) is supposed to be helping Mark but is only out for himself. Although he does seem a little upset when Mark and Ann begin making goo-goo eyes at each other. **86m/C VHS.** Robert Taylor, Eleanor Parker, Kurt Kasznar, Carlos Thompson, Victor Jory, Leon Askin, Aldo Silvani; *D:* Robert Pirosh; *W:* Robert Pirosh, Karl Tunberg; *C:* Robert L. Surtees; *M:* Miklos Rozsa.

Valley of the Lawless 🦴 **1936** A cowboy rides into trouble aplenty while out searching for treasure. A routine western for Brown fans only. **59m/B VHS.** Johnny Mack Brown; *D:* Robert North Bradbury; *W:* Robert North Bradbury.

Valley of the Sun 🦴🦴🦴 **1942** A government agent tracks a crooked Indian liaison to prevent an Indian uprising in Arizona. Ball, well before her "Lucy" days, plays the restaurant owner both men romance. Better than average, with good cast, some laughs, and lots of excitement. **84m/B VHS.** Lucille Ball, James Craig, Cedric Hardwicke, Dean Jagger, Peter Whitney, Billy Gilbert, Tom Tyler, Antonio Moreno, George Cleveland, Hank Bell; *D:* George Marshall.

Valley of Wanted Men 🦴 1/2 **1935** Three cons escape during a jailbreak and one uses his wits and nerve to prove another was framed. **56m/B VHS, DVD.** Leroy Mason, Russell Hopton, Grant Withers, Paul Fix, Drue Layton, Frankie Darro; *D:* Alan James; *W:* Barry Barrington, Forrest Barnes; *C:* Arthur Reed.

Valmont 🦴🦴🦴 **1989 (R)** Another adaptation of the Choderlos de Laclos novel "Les Liaisons Dangereuses." Various members of the French aristocracy in 1782 mercilessly play each other for fools in a complex game of lust and deception. Firth and Bening are at first playfully sensual, then the stakes get too high. They share an interesting bathtub scene. Well-acted, the 1988 Frears version, "Dangerous Liaisons," is edgier. Seeing the two films together makes for interesting comparisons of characters and styles. **137m/C VHS, DVD.** Colin Firth, Meg Tilly, Annette Bening, Fairuza Balk, Sian Phillips, Jeffrey Jones, Fabia Drake, Henry Thomas, Vincent Schiavelli, T.P. McKenna, Ian McNeice; *D:* Milos Forman; *W:* Jean-Claude Carriere; *M:* Christopher Palmer. Cesar '90: Art Dir./Set Dec., Costume Des.

The Vals 🦴 1/2 **1985 (R)** The glibly hip lethargy which is characteristic of four southern California teenaged girls turns to socially conscious resolve when a local orphanage is threatened. Like, for sure. **100m/C VHS.** Jill Carroll, Elana Stratheros, Gina Calabrese, Michelle Laurita, Chuck Connors, Sonny Bono, John Carradine, Michael Leon; *D:* James Polakof.

Vamp 🦴 1/2 **1986 (R)** Two college freshmen encounter a slew of weird, semi-vampiric people in a seamy red-light district nightclub. Starts cute but goes kinky. Jones is great as the stripping vampire. **93m/C VHS, DVD.** Grace Jones, Chris Makepeace, Robert Rusler, Gedde Watanabe, Sandy Baron, Dedee Pfeiffer, Billy Drago, Lisa Lyons; *D:* Richard Wenk; *W:* Richard Wenk; *C:* Elliot Davis; *M:* Jonathan Elias.

Vamping 🦴 1/2 **1984 (PG)** Struggling musician plans to burglarize a wealthy widow's home. Once inside, he finds himself attracted to his proposed victim. Tedious going. **110m/C VHS.** Patrick Duffy, Catherine Hyland, Rod Arrants, Fred A. Keller; *D:* Frederick King Keller.

The Vampire 🦴🦴 *Mark of the Vampire* **1957** Pale man with big teeth attempts to swindle a beautiful babe out of fortune. Followed by "The Vampire's Coffin." **95m/B VHS, DVD.** *MX* Abel Salazar, Ariadne Welter, German Robles, Carmen Montejo, Jose Luis Jimenez; *D:* Fernando Mendez.

Vampire Assassin 🦴 **2005 (PG-13)** Martial artist Hall is a would-be triple threat in this dull vampire story in which he stars as Derek Washington, an ambitious cop who has a phobia about blood. Which is bad news when Derek realizes bad guy Slovak (Novak) is a blood-sucker. Derek teams up with vampire hunter Master Kao (Okamura) but soon figures out he may have to become what he hates in order to fight this evil. **87m/C VHS, DVD.** Ron Hall, Mel Novak, Rudy Ray Moore, Gerald Okamura, Anthony Chow, Merry Everest; *D:* Ron Hall; *W:* Ron Hall; *C:* Ed Tillman. **VIDEO**

Vampire at Midnight 🦴 1/2 **1988** Fairly stupid homicide detective stalks a rampaging vampire in Los Angeles. Occasional moments of gratuitous sex thrown in for good measure. **93m/C VHS.** Jason Williams, Gustav Vintas, Jeanie Moore, Christina Whitaker, Leslie Milne; *D:* Gregory McClatchy.

The Vampire Bat 🦴🦴 1/2 **1932** A mad scientist and a vampire bat and its supernatural demands set the stage for murders in a small town. Sets and actors borrowed from Universal Studios in this low-budget flick that looks and plays better than it should. Weird and very exploitative for 1932, now seems dated. **69m/B VHS, DVD.** Lionel Atwill, Fay Wray, Melvyn Douglas, Dwight Frye, Maude Eburne, George E. Stone; *D:* Frank Strayer; *W:* Edward T. Lowe; *C:* Ira Morgan.

Vampire Centerfolds 🦴🦴 *Vampire Conspiracy* **1998** Innocent college cheerleader (Williamson) seeks to try out her thespian skills when she's cast in a cult film about vampiric bloodlust. Then she discovers that the models and actresses involved are a secret coven of sex obsessed vamps! **125m/C VHS.** Elaine Juliette Williamson, Jasmine Jean, Tonya Qualls, Joan A. Teeter; *D:* Geoffrey De Vallois. **VIDEO**

Vampire Circus 🦴🦴 1/2 **1971 (R)** A circus appears in an isolated Serbian village in the 19th century but instead of bringing joy and happiness, this circus brings only death, mutilation and misery. It seems all the members are vampires who have the unique ability to transform themselves into animals. They intend to take revenge on the small town, whose inhabitants killed their evil ancestor 100 years previously. Excellent Hammer production. **84m/C** *GB* Adrienne Corri, Laurence Payne, Thorley Walters, John Moulder-Brown, Lynne Frederick, Elizabeth Seal, Anthony (Corlan) Higgins, Richard Owens, Domini Blythe, David Prowse; *D:* Robert W. Young; *W:* Judson Kinberg; *C:* Moray Grant.

Vampire Cop 🦴 1/2 **1990 (R)** A vampire cop (not to be confused with zombie, maniac, midnight, psycho, future or Robo) teams up with a beautiful reporter to 'collar' a drug kingpin. **89m/C VHS.** Melissa Moore, Ed Cannon, Terence Jenkins; *D:* Donald Farmer.

Vampire Effect 🦴🦴 1/2 *The Twins Effect; Chin gei bin* **2003 (R)** The evil Duke Dekotes (Hardt) wants to take over the world (and who wouldn't?) but he needs to snuff out Prince Kazaf (Chen)—the last offshoot of European vampire royalty—and round up his blood to do so. When Kazaf attempts to elude the Duke by going to Hong Kong, he unexpectedly falls for Helen (Chen)—who, of course, just happens to the sister of butt-kicking vampire-killer, Reeve (Cheng). There's more! Helen's friend, Gypsy (Chung) wants to get in on the action and so all three band together in an effort to foil the Duke's dastardly plot. Jackie Chan cameos in this supernatural romp. Cantonese, with English subtitles. **88m/C VHS, DVD.** *HK* Ekin Cheng, Anthony Wong, Jackie Chan, Josie Ho, Charlene (Cheuk-Yin) Choi, Gillian (Yan-Tung) Chung, Edison Chen, Mickey Hardt, Karen Mok; *D:* Dante Lam; *W:* Jack Ng; *C:* Man Po Cheung; *M:* Kwong Wing Chan, Robert Duncan. **VIDEO**

The Vampire Happening 🦴 1/2 **1971 (R)** An actress travels to Translyvania to sell the family castle and discovers to her chagrin that her ancestors were vampires after she unknowingly releases them to party hearty on the local villagers. **101m/C VHS, DVD.** *GE* Ferdinand "Ferdy" Mayne, Pia Degermark, Thomas Hunter, Yvor Murillo, Ingrid van Bergen, Raoul Retzer; *D:* Freddie Francis; *W:* Karl Heinz Hummel, August Rieger; *C:* Gerard Vandenburg; *M:* Jerry Van Rooyen.

The Vampire Hookers 🦴 *Cemetery Girls; Sensuous Vampires; Night of the Bloodsuckers; Twice Bitten* **1978 (R)** Man in makeup recruits bevy of beautiful bloodsuckers to lure warm blooded victims to his castle. High ham performance by Carradine. **82m/C VHS.** *PH* John Carradine, Bruce Fairbairn, Trey Wilson, Karen Stride, Lenka Novak, Katie Dolan, Lex Winter; *D:* Cirio H. Santiago.

Vampire in Brooklyn 🦴 **1995 (R)** Murphy switches gears to play a Carribean vampire traveling to New York in search of his vampiric lady love—who turns out to be half-vamp-half-cop Bassett. As in "Coming to America," Murphy plays multiple characters, but that's three times the disappointment. Stale humor and cheap horror effects do little to break the zombie curse plaguing Murphy's career. Three days into filming, a stunt double for Bassett was killed after doing a routine jump on the set, providing a bad omen Murphy should have heeded. **103m/C VHS, DVD.** Eddie Murphy, Angela Bassett, Kadeem Hardison, Allen Payne, Zakes Mokae, John Witherspoon, Jsu Garcia; *D:* Wes Craven; *W:* Charles Murphy, Christopher Parker, Michael Lucker; *C:* Mark Irwin; *M:* J. Peter Robinson.

Vampire Journals 🦴🦴 1/2 **1996 (R)** Revenge-minded Zachary (Gunn) vows to destroy Ash (Morris), the ancient vampire who created him centuries before, especially when they both become interested in the same mortal woman, Sofia (Cerre). Shot on location in Transylvania. **82m/C VHS, DVD.** David Gunn, Jonathan Morris, Kirsten Cerre, Starr Andreeff; ***D:*** Ted Nicolaou; ***W:*** Ted Nicolaou; ***C:*** Adolfo Bartoli; ***M:*** Richard Kosinski.

Vampire Killers 1/2 *Lesbian Vampire Killers* **2009 (R)** Slapdash, deadpan horror comedy. Lesbian vampire Carmilla (Colloca) has plagued the secluded village of Craigswich for centuries. She turns all the young women at 18 and the men only remain alive if they agree to trick visitors into becoming blood donors. During a hiking trip, milquetoast Jimmy (Horne) and his oversized, lager-swilling best bud Fletch (Corden) meet fellow hiker Lotte (Burning), whose friends have already been converted, and a vampire-killing vicar (McGann) with a plan to stop Carmilla once and for all. Special effects are good (lots of gushing geysers of gore) but it's still surprisingly bland. **86m/C DVD.** *GB* Mathew Horne, James Corden, MyAnna Buring, Silvia Colloca, Vera Filatova, Ashley Mulheron, Paul McGann, Louise Dylan, Lucy Gaskell; ***D:*** Phil Claydon; ***W:*** Paul Hupfield, Stewart Williams; ***C:*** David Higgs; ***M:*** Debbie Wiseman.

The Vampire Lovers 1/2 **1970 (R)** An angry father goes after a lesbian vampire who has ravished his daughter and other young girls in a peaceful European village. Innovative story was soon used in countless other vampire vehicles. Hammer Studio's first horror film with nudity, another addition to the genre which spread rapidly. Based on the story "Carmilla" by Sheridan Le Fanu. Followed by "Lust for a Vampire." **91m/C VHS, DVD.** *GB* Ingrid Pitt, Pippa Steele, Madeleine Smith, Peter Cushing, George Cole, Dawn Addams, Kate O'Mara, Ferdinand "Ferdy" Mayne, Douglas Wilmer, Harvey Hall, Charles Farrell; ***D:*** Roy Ward Baker; ***W:*** Tudor Gates; ***C:*** Moray Grant.

Vampire Night WOOF! **2000** Pretty Peggy (Metcalfe) runs off to Hollywood with stars in her eyes and winds up with an agent, Vezrech (Ryan), whose main talent is supplying fresh blood to his stable of vampire babes. Peggy's brother, Carl (Jerman), gets worried and comes to the big, bad city to find his sis. How can a movie with vampire babes be so dull? **76m/C VHS, DVD.** Jimmy Jerman, Heather Metcalfe, Robert Michael Ryan, Pat Downey, Eden Rae; ***D:*** John Robert Stephens; ***W:*** John Robert Stephens; ***C:*** Dennis Devine; ***M:*** Jonathan Price.

The Vampire People 1/2 *The Blood Drinkers* **1966 (PG)** A dwarf-assisted vampire attempts to save the life of his true love by transplanting her sister's heart. Typical Filipino vampire movie. In color and sepiatone. **79m/C VHS, DVD.** *PH* Ronald Remy, Amalia Fuentes, Eddie Fernandez, Eva Montez; ***D:*** Gerardo (Gerry) De Leon.

Vampire Raiders—Ninja Queen WOOF! **1989** The white ninjas versus the black ninjas. The evil black ninjas are plotting to infiltrate the hotel industry. The white ninjas come to the rescue. **90m/C VHS.** Agnes Chan, Chris Petersen; ***D:*** Godfrey Ho.

Vampire Time Travelers WOOF! **1998** Four college gals try to pledge a strange sorority and wind up battling vampires and other supernatural creepies. It's hard to tell if the comedy is accidental or deliberate. Low-budget amateur night. **80m/C VHS.** Micky Levy, J.J. Rodgers, Jimmy Jerman, Robert Ginty, Kat Facchino, Lori Morrissey, Jillien Weisz; ***D:*** Les Sekely; ***W:*** Les Sekely; ***C:*** Dennis Devine; ***M:*** Les Sekely.

Vampire Vixens from Venus **1994** Three hideous drug smuggling aliens transform themselves into bodacious babes on earth so they can get what they came for. Seems their drug fix is derived from the life essence of men and they plan to drain every last drop they can. **90m/C VHS, DVD.** J.J. North, Leslie Glass, Michelle (McClellan) Bauer, Leon Head, Charlie Callas, Theresa Lynn; ***D:*** Tewd A. Bohus; ***W:*** Tewd A. Bohus; ***C:*** Curtis Mattikow; ***M:*** Ariel Shallit.

Vampirella 1/2 *Roger Corman Presents: Vampirella* **1996 (R)** Inhabitants of the planet Drakulon use a synthetic concoction to quench their thirst for blood. When Vampirella's (Soto) stepfather is murdered by rebels, led by Vlad Tepes (Daltrey), she must pursue them to earth to get justice. There she finds two opposing forces—the vampires led by Tepes and a paramilitary group led by Adam Van Helsing (Paul), who's out to cleanse the planet of the interlopers. But it's Vampirella who wants a final confrontation with Tepes (in Las Vegas, no less). **90m/C VHS, DVD.** Talisa Soto, Roger Daltrey, Richard Joseph Paul, Angus Scrimm, Tom Deters, Cirnna Harney, Brian Bloom; ***D:*** Jim Wynorski; ***W:*** Gary Gerani; ***C:*** Andrea V. Rossotto; ***M:*** Joel Goldsmith. **CABLE**

The Vampire's Coffin 1/2 *El Ataud Del Vampiro; El Ataud Del Coffin* **1958** Count Lavud is relieved when faithful servant removes stake implanted in his heart. **86m/B VHS.** *MX* Abel Salazar, Ariadne Welter, German Robles; ***D:*** Fernando Mendez.

The Vampire's Ghost **1945** A 400-hundred-year-old vampire/zombie, doomed to walk the earth forever, heads the African underworld. He can't be killed and can even go out during the day if he wears sunglasses. His future's so bright he's just gotta wear shades. **59m/B VHS.** John Abbott, Peggy Stewart; ***D:*** Lesley Selander.

Vampire's Kiss **1988 (R)** Cage makes this one worthwhile; his twisted transformation from pretentious post-val dude to psychotic yuppie from hell is inspired. If his demented torment of his secretary (Alonso) doesn't give you the creeps, his scene with the cockroach will. Cage fans will enjoy his facial aerobics; Beals fans will appreciate her extensive sucking scenes (she's the vamp of his dreams). More for psych majors than horror buffs. **103m/C VHS, DVD.** Nicolas Cage, Elizabeth Ashley, Jennifer Beals, Maria Conchita Alonso, Kasi Lemmons, Bob Lujan, David Hyde Pierce, Jessica Lundy, John Michael Higgins, Amy Stiller, Marc Coppola, Debbie Rochon; ***D:*** Robert Bierman; ***W:*** Joe Minion; ***C:*** Stefan Czapsky; ***M:*** Colin Towns.

Vampires of Sorority Row: Kickboxers From Hell **1999** Trailer-trash princess Cindy (Glass) goes to college and pledges a sorority, only to find domineering pledge mistress Denise (Lydon) and a gaggle of vampires causing a commotion. T&A competes with kickboxing action and self-mocking humor (that really works!) for viewers' attention spans. You could do worse on a Saturday night when "Gandhi" is rented and you need a laugh. **80m/C VHS, DVD.** Christine Lydon, Rich Ward, Kathryn Glass, Rita Fiora, Erika Gardener, Christian Caitlin, Angelica Hayden; ***D:*** Dennis Devine, Kathryn Glass; ***W:*** Dennis Devine; ***M:*** Jonathan Price.

Vampyr *Vampyr, Ou l'Etrange Aventure de David Gray; Vampyr, Der Traum des David Gray; Not against the Flesh; Castle of Doom; The Strange Adventure of David Gray; The Vampire* **1931** Dreyer's classic portrays a hazy, dreamlike world full of chilling visions from the point of view of a young man who believes himself surrounded by vampires and who dreams of his own burial in a most disturbing way. Evil lurks around every corner as camera angles, light and shadow sometimes overwhelm plot. A high point in horror films based on a collection of horror stories by Sheridan Le Fanu. In German with English subtitles. **75m/B VHS, DVD.** *GE FR* Julian West, Sybille Schmitz, Henriette Gerard, Maurice Schutz, Rena Mandel, Jan Hieronimko, Albert Bras; ***D:*** Carl Theodor Dreyer; ***W:*** Carl Theodor Dreyer, Christen Jul; ***C:*** Rudolph Mate, Louis Nee; ***M:*** Wolfgang Zeller.

The Vampyr **1992** Uncut version of the BBC musical production about a lustful vampire. Text sets present-day lyrics to the 1827 opera by Heinrich Marschner. Vampire Ripley (Ebrahim) has just been set free in London after having been trapped in an underground tomb for 200 years. Unless he puts the bite on three lovely ladies within three days he will be condemned to eternal damnation. Everyone gets to sing in the nude. Surreally amusing. **115m/C VHS.** *GB* Omar Ebrahim, Willemijn Van Gent, Fiona O'Neill, Sally-Ann Shepherdson; ***D:*** Nigel Finch; ***C:*** Chris Seager.

Vampyres 1/2 *Vampyres, Daughters of Dracula; Blood Hunger; Satan's Daughters; Daughters of Dracula; Vampire Orgy* **1974 (R)** Alluring female vampires coerce unsuspecting motorists to their castle for a good time, which ends in death. Anulka was the centerfold girl in "Playboy"'s May 1973 issue. **90m/C VHS, DVD.** *GB* Marianne Morris, Anulka, Murray Brown, Brian Deacon, Sally Faulkner, Michael Byrne, Karl Lanchbury, Bessie Love, Elliott Sullivan; ***D:*** Joseph (Jose Ramon) Larraz; ***W:*** Diane Daubeney; ***C:*** Harry Waxman; ***M:*** James Clark.

The Van *Chevy Van* **1977 (R)** A recent high school graduate passes on the college scene so he can spend more time picking up girls in his van. A lame sex (and sexist) comedy. **92m/C VHS, DVD.** Stuart Getz, Deborah White, Danny DeVito, Harry Moses, Maurice Barkin; ***D:*** Sam Grossman; ***W:*** Robert J. Rosenthal, Celia Susan Cotelo; ***C:*** Irv Goodnoff; ***M:*** Steve Eaton.

The Van **1995 (R)** The last of writer Roddy Doyle's Barrytown trilogy (following "The Commitments" and "The Snapper") is set in 1989-90, in Dublin, where baker Bimbo (O'Kelly) has just lost his job. Tired of sitting around the pub, he takes his redundancy money and buys a filthy, dilapidated fish 'n' chips van, which he decides to run with best friend Larry (Meany), with their families helping out. The months pass quickly and their venture turns out to be a big success but the close quarters puts a strain on the mens' friendship until Bimbo has another idea. **105m/C VHS, DVD.** *GB* Donal O'Kelly, Colm Meaney, Ger Ryan, Caroline Rotwell, Neili Conroy, Ruaidhri Conroy; ***D:*** Stephen Frears; ***W:*** Roddy Doyle; ***C:*** Oliver Stapleton; ***M:*** Eric Clapton, Richard Hartley.

Van Gogh **1992 (R)** "One doesn't produce 100 masterpieces in a state of depression—Van Gogh died from having had a glimpse of happiness." This is the way director Pialat sums up his approach to the last 67 days in the life of Vincent Van Gogh. Dutronc is skillful in portraying Van Gogh as a man with no excuses, and even a sense of humor. Not a psychological portrait and offers no answers—it's simply one artist's view of another. In French with English subtitles. **155m/C VHS, DVD.** *FR* Jacques Dutronc, Alexandra London, Gerard Sety, Bernard Le Coq, Corinne Bourdon; ***D:*** Maurice Pialat; ***W:*** Maurice Pialat; ***C:*** Gilles Henry, Emmanuel Machuel; ***M:*** Edith Vesperini. Cesar '92: Actor (Dutronc).

Van Helsing **2004 (PG-13)** Bram Stoker's title character takes on Frankenstein's monster, the Wolf Man and Count Dracula. Hollywood's macho "Indiana Jones meets James Bond" Van Helsing (Jackman) is a high-tech bow and arrow-slinging, creature-slaying hero who travels with sidekick Carl (Wenham), to Transylvania to kill the head vampire himself (Roxburgh). Sexy gypsy Anna (Beckinsale) turns up seeking to vanquish Dracula and lift a curse her family has suffered for centuries. With chase scenes, a masked ball, nonstop adventure, monsters galore, and a script that doesn't take itself too seriously, this f/x extravaganza will find something to appeal to everyone. **132m/C DVD, UMD, HD DVD.** *US CZ* Hugh Jackman, Kate Beckinsale, Richard Roxburgh, David Wenham, Shuler Hensley, Elena Anaya, Will(iam) Kemp, Kevin J. O'Connor, Alun Armstrong, Thomas (Tom) Fisher, Samuel West, Robbie Coltrane, Silvia Colloca, Josie Maran, Stephen H. Fisher; ***D:*** Stephen Sommers; ***W:*** Stephen Sommers; ***C:*** Allen Daviau; ***M:*** Alan Silvestri.

Van Nuys Blvd. 1/2 **1979 (R)** The popular boulevard is the scene where the cool southern California guys converge for cruising and girl watching, so naturally it's where a country hick comes to test his drag racing skills and check out the action. **93m/C VHS, DVD.** Bill Adler, Cynthia Wood, Dennis Bowen, Melissa Prophet; ***D:*** William Sachs.

Van Wilder: Freshman Year 1/2 **2008 (R)** The third flick in the franchise is a prequel detailing how Van Wilder (Bennett) became the ultimate college party animal. As he starts his freshman year at Coolidge College, Van Wilder must deal with an uptight Dean and a campus full of girls who have taken a vow of chastity even as he pursues ultimate babe Kaitlin (Cavallari). **100m/C DVD.** Jonathan Bennett, Steven Talley, Kurt Fuller, Kristin Cavallari, Jerry Shea; ***D:*** Harvey Glazer; ***C:*** Shawn Maurer; ***M:*** Nathan Wang. **VIDEO**

Vanessa 1/2 **2007** Vanessa runs away from home to escape her abusive stepfather and only survives on the streets by turning to prostitution. Just when she decides that suicide is the only way out, she meets a stranger who offers her hope. **88m/C DVD.** Nick Mancuso, Candice Prentice; ***D:*** Bozidar D. Benedikt; ***W:*** Bozidar D. Benedikt. **VIDEO**

Vanilla Gorilla **2009** Young Nikki (Carroll) befriends Gogo, the world's only albino gorilla in captivity. They communicate through sign language and Nikki decides Gogo would be much happy back in her African wilderness. So she decides to break the gorilla out and get her back home. **m/C DVD.** *US* Madeline Carroll, Pierce Brosnan, Dennis Haysbert, Peter Anthony Elliott; ***D:*** Tim Loane; ***W:*** Craig Gardner; ***C:*** Roman Osin; ***M:*** Stephen Warbeck.

Vanilla Sky 1/2 **2001 (R)** Director Crowe goes existential in this puzzling, surreal thriller, a remake of Alejandro Amenabar's 1997 Spanish film, "Abre los Ojos." Cruise plays David Aames, a publishing magnate and playboy who's got it all except for real love. Just when he thinks he's found it in the form of aspiring dancer Sofia (Cruz, reprising her role from the original), a bitter ex-lover (Diaz) changes the game by inadvertently changing David's pretty face. Fairly straightforward allegory becomes science fiction, where David (and the audience) can't tell dream from reality. Thought-provoking, even deliberately confusing plot may frustrate some. But for those who like to sink their brains into a film, it'll will be rewarding, whether you like the explain-it-all ending or not. Decent acting, dreamy cinematography, and an engaging soundtrack will provide entertainment at the very least. **135m/C VHS, DVD.** *US* Tom Cruise, Penelope Cruz, Cameron Diaz, Jason Lee, Kurt Russell, Noah Taylor, Timothy Spall, Tilda Swinton, Alicia Witt, Johnny Galecki, Michael Shannon; ***D:*** Cameron Crowe; ***W:*** Cameron Crowe; ***C:*** John Toll; ***M:*** Nancy Wilson.

Vanina Vanini 1/2 **1961** An acclaimed Rossellini historical drama about the daughter of an Italian aristocrat in 1824 who nurses and falls in love with a wounded patriot hiding in her house. Based on a Stendhal short story. In Italian with English subtitles. **113m/B VHS.** *IT* Sandra Milo, Laurent Terzieff; ***D:*** Roberto Rossellini.

Vanished *Danielle Steel's Vanished* **1995 (PG)** Marielle and Charles are happily married in 1920 Paris until the tragic death of their son breaks them up. Marielle remarries and has another child who gets kidnapped and her estranged husband is arrested for the crime. **120m/C DVD.** George Hamilton, Lisa Rinna, Robert Hays, Maurice Godin, Alex D. Linz; ***D:*** George Kaczender; ***W:*** Kathleen Rowell; ***C:*** Pierre Mignot; ***M:*** Francois Dompierre. **CABLE**

The Vanishing *Spoorloos* **1988** When his wife suddenly disappears, a young husband finds himself becoming increasingly obsessed with finding her. Three years down the road, his world has become one big, mad nightmare. Then, just as suddenly, the answer confronts him, but the reality of it may be too horrible to face. Well-made dark thriller based on "The Golden Egg" by Tim Krabbe. In French and Dutch with English subtitles. Remade by Sluizer in 1992. **107m/C VHS, DVD.** *NL FR* Barnard Pierre Donnadieu, Johanna Ter Steege, Gene Bervoets, Gwen Eckhaus, Bernadette Le Sache, Tania Latarjet, Lucille Glenn, Roger Souza; ***D:*** George Sluizer; ***W:*** George Sluizer, Tim Krabbe; ***C:*** Toni Kuhn; ***M:*** Henny Vrienten.

The Vanishing 1/2 **1993 (R)** Director Sluizer remakes his own 1988 Dutch film "Spoorloos" to lesser effect. Tense thriller about the disappearance of a woman (Bullock) at a highway rest stop. Her boyfriend (Sutherland) becomes obsessed with locating her, searching for some three years as he is haunted by her memory. Unlike the Dutch original, the remake resorts to a clumsy ending designed for feel-good appeal. Based on the novel "The Golden Egg" by Tim Krabbe. **110m/C VHS, DVD.** Jeff Bridges, Kiefer Sutherland, Nancy Travis, Sandra Bullock, Park Overall, Lisa Eichhorn, George Hearn, Maggie Linderman, Lynn Hamilton; ***D:*** George Sluizer; ***W:*** Todd Graff; ***M:*** Jerry Goldsmith.

Vanishing Act 🦴🦴 1/2 **1988 (PG)** While on his honeymoon, Harry Kenyon reports his wife missing to the local police. Within a short period of time his wife is found, but Harry says the woman is an impostor. This thriller follows Harry's desperate attempt to get to the truth. **94m/C VHS.** Mike Farrell, Margot Kidder, Elliott Gould, Fred Gwynne, Graham Jarvis; ***D:*** David Greene; ***W:*** Richard Levinson, William Link; ***C:*** Laszlo George; ***M:*** Kenneth Wannberg. **TV**

The Vanishing American 🦴🦴 **1925** The mistreatment of the American Indian is depicted in this sweeping Western epic that stars Dix as Navajo chieftain Nophaie. Nophaie must reconcile the heritage of his people with the 20th century and deal with a crooked government agent. Filmed in Monument Valley and the Betatkin Cliff Dwellings of Arizona. Based on the novel by Zane Grey. **109m/B VHS, DVD.** Richard Dix, Noah Beery Sr., Lois Wilson; ***D:*** George B. Seitz; ***W:*** Lucien Hubbard, Ethel Doherty; ***C:*** Harry Perry, Charles E. Schoenbaum.

Vanishing Legion 🦴🦴 **1931** Western serial with outdoor action and gunplay. Twelve chapters, 13 minutes each. **156m/B VHS.** Frankie Darro, Harry Carey Sr.; ***D:*** B. Reeves Eason.

Vanishing Point 🦴🦴 **1971 (R)** An ex-racer makes a bet to deliver a souped-up car from Denver to San Francisco in 15 hours. Taking pep pills along the way, he eludes police, meets up with a number of characters, and finally crashes into a roadblock. Rock score helps attract this film's cult following. **98m/C VHS, DVD, Blu-ray Disc.** Barry Newman, Cleavon Little, Gilda Texter, Dean Jagger, Paul Koslo, Robert Donner, Severn Darden, Victoria Medlin; ***D:*** Richard Sarafian; ***W:*** Guillermo Cain; ***C:*** John A. Alonzo; ***M:*** Jim Bowen, Peter Carpenter.

The Vanishing Westerner 🦴🦴 **1950** A cowboy, falsely accused of murder, works to vindicate himself and uncovers a series of robberies. This one has enough plot twists to take it out of the routine. **60m/B VHS.** Monte Hale, Arthur Space, Aline Towne, Paul Hurst, Roy Barcroft, Richard Anderson, William Phipps, Rand Brooks; ***D:*** Philip Ford.

Vanity Fair 🦴🦴 **1932** Loy stars in this tale of a wily and manipulative woman looking for the perfect marriage. This was the 58th film for the 27-year-old Loy, but even she couldn't save it. Of course, none of the three films based on the story by Thackeray have done it justice. **67m/B VHS, DVD.** Myrna Loy, Conway Tearle, Barbara Kent, Walter Byron, Anthony Bushell, Billy Bevan, Montagu Love, Mary Forbes; ***D:*** Chester M. Franklin.

Vanity Fair 🦴🦴 1/2 **1967** BBC TV adaptation of William Makepeace Thackeray's satire on human folly in 19th-century England. Amoral governess (and anti-heroine) Becky Sharp (Hampshire) will stop at nothing to climb the social ladder, aided by a wealthy marriage and her own audacity, which ultimately leads to scandal. **250m/C VHS.** *GB* Susan Hampshire, Robert Flemyng, Richard Caldicot, Barbara Couper, Roy Marsden, Bryan Marshall; ***D:*** David Giles. **TV**

Vanity Fair 🦴🦴 1/2 **1999** Orphaned Becky Sharp (Little) is beautiful, clever and, despite her poverty, determined to get ahead in society so she can enjoy the same privileges as her posh childhood friend, Amelia Sedley (Grey). And she's not too particular about how she stakes her claim. Based on the novel by William Makepeace Thackeray, this Brit miniseries loses the author's acerbic voice which makes for a bland, though typically lavish, production. **300m/C VHS, DVD.** Natasha Little, Frances Grey, Nathaniel Parker, Philip Glenister, Jeremy Swift, Roger Ashton-Griffiths, Eleanor Bron, Anton Lesser, Miriam Margolyes, Michele Dotrice, David Bradley, David Ross; ***D:*** Marc Munden; ***W:*** Andrew Davies; ***C:*** Oliver Curtis. **TV**

Vanity Fair 🦴🦴 1/2 **2004 (PG-13)** In William Makepeace Thackeray's novel "Vanity Fair," Becky Sharp is an unrepentant social climber. But with Witherspoon tackling Becky in director Nair's version, such calculation just wouldn't do. Becky still aspires to climb the slippery social ladder in early 19th century Britain, but here she has a heart. Becky first flirts with the wealthy, foppish brother (Maudsley) of her sweet-but-dim friend Amelia (Garai) but cannot bring him to marriage. She then rolls the dice with dashing gambler/soldier Rawdon Crawley (Purefoy). However, things never quite turn out for greedy Becky. Nair's hard-pressed to cover the novel's 30 years and multiple subplots so the film has a rushed feeling. Witherspoon is plucky but the supporting cast of British stalwarts (Hoskins, Atkins, Broadbent, etc.) gives the endeavor its panache. **137m/C VHS, DVD.** *US GB* Reese Witherspoon, Eileen Atkins, Jim Broadbent, Gabriel Byrne, Romola Garai, Bob Hoskins, Rhys Ifans, Geraldine McEwan, James Purefoy, Jonathan Rhys Meyers, Douglas Hodge, Natasha Little, Tony Maudsley; ***D:*** Mira Nair; ***W:*** Matthew Faulk, Mark Skeet, Julian Fellowes; ***C:*** Declan Quinn; ***M:*** Mychael Danna.

Vantage Point 🦴 1/2 **2008 (PG-13)** Do they celebrate Groundhog day in Spain? U.S. President Ashton (Hurt) has just arrived in Spain to give the opening speech at a global "War on Terror" conference when he's shot. Sheer chaos ensues as eight different versions of the event unfold from eigh points of view. American tourist Howard Lewis (Whitaker) with his videocam; Secret Service agents Thomas Barnes (Quaid) and Kent Taylor (Fox); news producer Rex Brooks (Weaver) and others all saw the event, but in different ways. Is it terrorists or a conspiracy? Sure, each version adds another piece of the puzzle, but by the time it all actually comes together, the audience may be too confused or bored to care. **90m/C DVD, Blu-ray Disc.** *US* Dennis Quaid, Matthew Fox, Forest Whitaker, William Hurt, Sigourney Weaver, Bruce McGill, Edgar Ramirez, Said Taghmaoui, Ayelet Zurer, Zoe Saldana, Eduardo Noriega, Richard T. Jones, Holt McCallany, Leonardo Nam, James LeGros; ***D:*** Stuart Baird, Pete Travis; ***W:*** Barry L. Levy; ***C:*** Amir M. Mokri; ***M:*** Atli Orvarsson.

Vanya on 42nd Street 🦴🦴🦴 1/2 **1994 (PG)** Group of actors in street clothes rehearse a workshop production of Chekhov's play, "Uncle Vanya," in New York's dilapidated New Amsterdam Theater. Theatrical director Gregory first gets his group together in 1989, with Mamet's contemporary adaptation, and they continue to work in private until Malle films their production some four years later before a small, select audience. Shawn, best known for "My Dinner with Andre" portrays Vanya with depth and complexity. The other actors shine as well, often against type, in this complex Russian drama of desperation. **119m/C VHS, DVD.** Wallace Shawn, Julianne Moore, Brooke Smith, Larry Pine, George Gaynes, Lynn Cohen, Madhur Jaffrey, Phoebe Brand, Jerry Mayer, Andre Gregory; ***D:*** Louis Malle; ***W:*** Andre Gregory, David Mamet; ***C:*** Declan Quinn; ***M:*** Joshua Redman.

Varan the Unbelievable 🦴 *Daikaiju Baran; The Monster Baran* **1961** A chemical experiment near a small island in the Japanese archipelago disturbs a prehistoric monster beneath the water. The awakened monster spreads terror on the island. Most difficult part of this movie is deciding what the rubber monster model is supposed to represent. **70m/B VHS, DVD.** *JP* Myron Healey, Tsuruko Kobayashi; ***D:*** Inoshiro Honda.

Varian's War 🦴🦴 1/2 **2001** Based on the true story of American Varian Fry (Hurt), who is the editor of a foreign affairs publication when he witnesses the Nazi rise in Berlin and decides he must help Europe's Jews despite American neutrality. He heads off to Marseilles where a number of artists and intellectuals wait to escape Vichy France and establishes an underground rescue organization. **120m/C VHS, DVD.** William Hurt, Julia Ormond, Matt Craven, Maury Chaykin, Alan Arkin, Lynn Redgrave, Remy Girard, Chris Heyerdahl, Vlasta Vrana, Gloria Carlin, John Dunn-Hill; ***D:*** Lionel Chetwynd; ***W:*** Lionel Chetwynd; ***C:*** Daniel Jobin; ***M:*** Neil Smolar. **CABLE**

Variety 🦴🦴🦴🦴 *Vaudeville; Variete* **1925** Simple and tragic tale of a scheming young girl and the two men of whom she takes advantage. The European circus in all its beautiful sadness is the setting. Extraordinary cast and superb cinematography. Silent. **104m/B VHS, DVD.** *GE* Emil Jannings, Lya de Putti, Warwick Ward, Werner Krauss; ***D:*** E.A. Dupont; ***W:*** E.A. Dupont; ***C:*** Karl Freund.

Variety 🦴 1/2 **1983** Christine (McLeod) gets a job selling tickets at a porno theatre near Times Square and starts getting curious about the milieu. Her relationships begin to change as her interest in pornography becomes all-consuming. **97m/C VHS.** Sandy McLeod, Will Patton, Richard Davidson; ***D:*** Bette Gordon; ***W:*** Kathy Acker; ***C:*** Tom DiCillo; ***M:*** John Lurie.

Variety Girl 🦴🦴 1/2 **1947** More than 55 Paramount stars appear in this salute to the Variety Club charitable organization, so the plot is the least important element. Catherine (Hatcher) and Amber (San Juan) have both made their way to Hollywood with stars in their eyes and eventually find themselves on the studio lot. Your basic extravaganza-type show, benefitting the charity, concludes the picture. **93m/B VHS.** Mary Hatcher, Olga San Juan, DeForest Kelley; ***D:*** George Marshall; ***W:*** Edmund Hartmann, Frank Tashlin, Monte Brice, Robert L. Welch; ***C:*** Lionel Lindon, Stuart Thompson.

Variety Lights 🦴🦴🦴 1/2 *Luci del Varieta; Lights of Variety* **1951** Fellini's first (albeit joint) directorial effort, wherein a young girl runs away with a travelling vaudeville troupe and soon becomes its main attraction as a dancer. Filled with Fellini's now-familiar delight in the bizarre and sawdust/tinsel entertainment. In Italian with English subtitles. **93m/B VHS, DVD.** *IT* Giulietta Masina, Peppino de Filippo, Carla Del Poggio, Folco Lulli; ***D:*** Federico Fellini, Alberto Lattuada; ***W:*** Federico Fellini, Alberto Lattuada, Tullio Pinelli, Ennio Flaiano; ***C:*** Otello Martelli; ***M:*** Felice Lattuada.

Varsity Blues 🦴🦴 1/2 **1998 (R)** After star quarterback Lance (Walker) goes down with an injury, backup Mox (Van Der Beek) learns the perks of stardom in a small Texas town obsessed with high school football. It's not all free six-packs and groupies in whipped cream bikinis, however. He butts heads with blood-and-guts Coach Kilmer (Voight), whose win-at-all-costs philosophy is injuring his players. Mox leads the players in a rebellion against the coach, leaving the usual doubts about the inevitable "big game." The young cast does an admirable job lifting the material above the average jock flick, but it lurches into the gutter a little too often for some tastes. **103m/C VHS, DVD.** James Van Der Beek, Jon Voight, Paul Walker, Ron Lester, Scott Caan, Richard Lineback, Amy Smart, Thomas F. Duffy, Tony Perenski, Tiffany C. Love, Eliel Swinton, Jill Parker Jones, Joe Pichler, Ali Larter; ***D:*** Brian Robbins; ***W:*** W. Peter Iliff; ***C:*** Charles Cohen; ***M:*** Mark Isham. MTV Movie Awards '99: Breakthrough Perf. (Van Der Beek).

Varsity Show 🦴🦴 **1937** Broadway producer Chuck Daly (Powell) is an alumnus of Winfield College and offers to produce the annual varsity show to the delight of Betty (Lane) and her fellow students. Only their conservative faculty advisor, Prof. Biddle (Catlett), opposes their choice and Daly bows out to prevent trouble. The students travel to New York on spring break to convince Daly to change his mind and wind up putting on the show there. The big Busby Berkeley dance finale is a tribute to the nation's colleges and got the choreographer an Oscar nomination. Beware the edited version released at 80 minutes. **120m/B DVD.** Dick Powell, Priscilla Lane, Fred Waring, Walter Catlett, Rosemary Lane, Sterling Holloway, Ted Healy, Mabel Todd, Lee Dixon, Lee Dixon; ***D:*** William Keighley; ***W:*** Warren Duff, Sid Herzig, Richard Macaulay, Jerry Wald; ***C:*** Sol Polito, George Barnes.

Vasectomy: A Delicate Matter
WOOF! *Vasectomy* **1986 (PG-13)** A mother of eight issues a final decree to her husband about their sex life. He must get a vasectomy or there won't be any. As good as it sounds. **92m/C VHS.** Paul Sorvino, Abe Vigoda, Cassandra Edwards, Lorne Greene, Ina Balin, June Wilkinson, William Marshall; ***D:*** Robert Burge; ***W:*** Robert Burge.

Vatel 🦴🦴 **2000 (PG-13)** Lavish period drama suffers from a dull screenplay and a lack of gusto. In 1671, Sun King Louis XIV (Sands) is ruling with the usual decadence when he and his court are invited to the country chateau of the Prince de Conde (Glover), who's hoping to curry favor. Conde leaves the plans for the royal visit to his steward, Francois Vatel (Depardieu). He must supply food and entertainment to keep the court amused but Vatel provokes envy as well. Depardieu is efficient but the English language cast seems to be primping more than acting. **117m/C VHS, DVD.** *GB FR* Gerard Depardieu, Uma Thurman, Tim Roth, Julian Glover, Julian Sands, Timothy Spall, Arielle Dombasle, Hywel Bennett, Richard Griffiths, Feodor Atkine, Phillippe LeRoy, Murray Lachlan Young; ***D:*** Roland Joffe; ***W:*** Jeanne Labrune, Tom Stoppard; ***C:*** Robert Fraisse; ***M:*** Ennio Morricone.

Vatican Conspiracy 🦴 1/2 **1981** The members of the Vatican's College of Cardinals do everything in their power to discredit a newly appointed radical pontiff. **90m/C VHS.** *IT* Fabrizio Bentivoglio, Gabriele Ferzetti, Paula Molina, Antonio Marsina, Terence Stamp; ***D:*** Marcello Aliprandi; ***W:*** Marcello Aliprandi; ***C:*** Alejandro Ulloa; ***M:*** Pino Donaggio.

The Vault 🦴🦴 **2000 (R)** Teacher Mr. Burnett (Lyde) takes four students—Dezaray (Pride), Willy (Priester), Zipper (Walker), and Kyle (Davis) to visit an old high school, which is scheduled to be demolished. (The four kids fit the stereotypes of cheerleader, jock, nerd, and tough guy.) The school was originally a way-station for slaves and the group hopes to rescue some historical items (or something like that). Once they arrive at the school, they meet the eerie security guard Spangler (Papi), who warns them to not venture into the basement. You see, there's a very old locked door in the basement, and behind that door is...ultimate evil. Unfortunately, the film ends just as it's beginning to get interesting. **85m/C DVD.** Ted Lyde, Shani Pride, Austin Priester, Kyle Walker, Michael Cory Davis, Leopold Papi; ***D:*** James Black.

Vault of Horror 🦴🦴 1/2 *Tales from the Crypt II* **1973 (R)** A collection of five terrifying tales based on original stories from the E.C. comic books of the 1950s. Stories include, "Midnight Mess," "Bargain in Death," "This Trick'll Kill You," "The Neat Job," and "Drawn and Quartered." **86m/C VHS, DVD.** *GB* Terry-Thomas, Curt Jurgens, Glynis Johns, Dawn Addams, Daniel Massey, Tom Baker, Michael Craig, Anna Massey, Denholm Elliott; ***D:*** Roy Ward Baker; ***W:*** Milton Subotsky.

The Vector File 🦴 1/2 **2003 (R)** Little Mattie got her hands on a wicked DNA code that threatens the world if not kept under wraps forcing dear old dad to fend off the terrorists in pursuit of it. Stars real-life family—Van Dien is Oxenberg's husband and India is her daughter. **92m/C VHS, DVD.** Casper Van Dien, Catherine Oxenberg, Timothy Balme, William Wallace, Katherine Kennard, India Oxenberg, Roz Turnbull, George Henare, Laurie Foel, Stephen Hall, David Stott, Chic Littlewood, Craig Hall, Paddy Wilson, Paul Norell, Roz Worthington, Chris Easley; ***D:*** Eliot Christopher; ***W:*** Iain McFadyen; ***C:*** Kevin Riley; ***M:*** Bruce Lynch. **VIDEO**

Vegas 🦴 **1978** A private detective, with Las Vegas beauties as assistants and pursuers, solves the murder of a teenage runaway girl. Pilot for a TV series. Scriptwriter Mann went on to do "Miami Vice." **74m/C VHS.** Robert Urich, June Allyson, Tony Curtis, Will Sampson, Greg Morris; ***D:*** Richard Lang; ***W:*** Michael Mann. **TV**

Vegas in Space WOOF! **1994** Four male astronauts take a secret mission to the planet Clitoris, the all-female pleasure plant where men are forbidden to trod. To capture a heinous villainous, they swallow gender-reversal pills in order to infiltrate the resort as show-girls. Typical Troma trash. Boasts an all-transvestite cast. **85m/C VHS, DVD.** Doris Fish, Miss X, Ginger Quest, Ramona Fischer, Lori Naslund, Timmy Spence, Silvana Nova, Sandelle Kincaid, Tommy Pace, Arturo Galster, Jennifer Blowdryer, Freida Lay, Tippi; ***D:*** Phillip R. Ford; ***W:*** Phillip R. Ford, Doris Fish, Miss X; ***C:*** Robin Clark; ***M:*** Ramona Fischer, Timmy Spence.

The Vegas Strip Wars 🦴🦴 *Las Vegas Strip War* **1984** Rival casino owners battle it out in the land of lady luck. Unmemorable except for Jones's Don King impersonation and the fact that it was Hudson's last TV movie. **100m/C VHS, DVD.** Rock Hudson, James Earl Jones, Noriyuki "Pat" Morita, Sharon Stone, Robert Costanzo; ***D:*** George Englund.

Vegas Vacation 🦴 **1996 (PG)** It may not have come out under the "National Lampoon" banner but you'll recognize both the characters and the situations. The innocent Griswold clan head from their Chicago home to the bright lights and gambling temptations of Las Vegas. Clark (Chase) blows all their money, Ellen (D'Angelo) reveals a hidden passion for Wayne Newton, daughter Audrey (Nichols) decides to become a go-go dancer, and son Rusty (Embry) turns into a high roller who draws the attention of the mob. Oh yeah, dimwit cousin Eddie (Quaid) also tries to supply a few yucks. **98m/C VHS, DVD.** Chevy Chase, Beverly D'Angelo, Randy Quaid, Ethan (Randall) Embry, Miriam Flynn, Marisol Nichols, Shae D'Lyn, Wallace Shawn, Wayne Newton; ***Cameos:*** Sid Caesar, Julia Sweeney, Christie Brinkley; ***D:*** Stephen Kessler; ***W:*** Elisa Bell; ***C:*** William A. Fraker; ***M:*** Joel McNeely.

Vegas Vice 🦴 1/2 *Hard Vice* **1994** Tweed and Jones are Vegas cops after a serial killer, who might be a hooker. Routine. **83m/C VHS, DVD.** Sam Jones, Shannon Tweed, James Gammon, Tom Fridley, Rebecca Ferratti, Branscombe Richmond; ***D:*** Joey Travolta; ***W:*** Joey Travolta; ***M:*** Jeff Lass.

The Velocity of Gary 🦴 1/2 *The Velocity of Gary* (*Not His Real Name)* **1998 (R)** Melodrama about love, death, and what makes a family is undone by a weak script, strained humor, and a screechy performance by Hayek. Gary's (Jane) a hustler in New York City who's attracted to bisexual porn star Valentino (D'Onofrio). Valentino has a possessive waitress girlfriend, Mary Carmen (Hayek), and she and Gary immediately hate each other and constantly compete for Valentino's affections. But when Valentino falls ill with AIDS, the three move into together and try to put aside their differences. **98m/C VHS, DVD.** Vincent D'Onofrio, Salma Hayek, Thomas Jane, Olivia D'Abo; ***D:*** Dan Ireland; ***W:*** James Still; ***C:*** Claudio Rocha.

Velocity Trap 🦴🦴 **1999 (R)** In 2150, electronic crime and piracy run rampant throughout the galaxy. Cop Raymond Stokes (Gruner) is assigned to escort a federal banking ship through a section of space, known as the Velocity Run, that's equivalent to the Bermuda Triangle. Along with ship's navigator, Beth Sheffield (Coppola), Stokes must prevent thieves from grabbing the ship's loot and an asteroid from destroying the ship itself. **90m/C VHS, DVD.** Olivier Gruner, Alicia Coppola, Ken Olandt, Bruce Weitz, Craig Wasson; ***D:*** Phillip J. Roth; ***W:*** Phillip J. Roth. **VIDEO**

Velvet Goldmine 🦴🦴 **1998 (R)** Director Haynes takes on the excesses of the '70s British glam-rock era. In 1984, journalist Arthur Stuart (Bale) is assigned to write a "Whatever Happened to" article on the 10-year disappearance of vanished superstar Brian Slade (Rhys Meyers as a cross between T-Rex's Marc Bolan and a Ziggy Stardust-era David Bowie). This leads fan Arthur to Slade's viperish ex-wife Mandy (Collette) and his ex-manager Jerry Divine (Izzard). But Arthur discovers the most important relationship in Brian's life was to self-destructive cult idol Curt Wild (MacGregor, channelling Iggy Pop). The flamboyant duo had an equally flamboyant affair that eventual lead to a downward spiral for them both. The story might be average but the visuals are spectacular and MacGregor, especially, is mesmerizing. **120m/C VHS, DVD.** *GB* Ewan McGregor, Jonathan Rhys Meyers, Christian Bale, Toni Collette, Eddie Izzard, Emily Woof, Michael Feast; ***D:*** Todd Haynes; ***W:*** Todd Haynes; ***C:*** Maryse Alberti; ***M:*** Carter Burwell. British Acad. '98: Costume Des.; Ind. Spirit '99: Cinematog.

Velvet Smooth 🦴 **1976 (R)** A protection agency's sultry boss, Velvet Smooth, gets involved solving the problems of a numbers racket. **89m/C VHS, DVD.** Johnnie Hill; ***D:*** Janace Fink.

Velvet Touch 🦴🦴🦴 **1948** Well-engineered thriller about an actress who craftily murders her producer. A theatre-loving police detective winds up accusing the wrong woman—sending the overwrought murderess into a moral tailspin. Things don't work out as you may expect. Fine acting. **97m/B VHS.** Rosalind Russell, Leo Genn, Claire Trevor, Sydney Greenstreet, Leon Ames, Frank McHugh, Walter Kingsford, Dan Tobin, Lex Barker, Nydia Westman; ***D:*** John Gage; ***W:*** Leo Rosten.

The Velvet Vampire 🦴🦴 *Cemetery Girls; Through the Looking Glass; The Waking Hour* **1971 (R)** Yarnall is a sexy, sun-loving, dune buggy-riding vampiress who seduces a young, sexy, swinging, Southern California couple in her desert home. Lots of atmosphere to go along with the blood and nudity. **82m/C VHS, DVD.** Michael Blodgett, Sherry Miles, Celeste Yarnall, Gene Shane, Jerry Daniels, Sandy Ward, Paul Prokop, Chris Woodley, Robert Tessier; ***D:*** Stephanie Rothman; ***W:*** Stephanie Rothman, Maurice Jules, Charles S. Swartz; ***C:*** Daniel Lacambre.

Vendetta 🦴 1/2 **1985** A woman gets herself arrested and sent to the penitentiary in order to exact revenge there for her sister's death. Acting and pacing make this better than the average sexploitation flick. **89m/C VHS.** Karen Chase, Sandy Martin, Durga McBroom, Kin Shriner, Eugene Robert Glazer; ***D:*** Bruce Logan; ***M:*** David Newman.

Vendetta 🦴🦴 **1999 (R)** Based on a true story. New Orleans politicians and businessman seek to wrest away control of the docks from the Italian family that controls it. An unleashed angry mob leads to the largest lynching in American history. Adapted from the book by Richard Gambino. **117m/C VHS, DVD.** Christopher Walken, Clancy Brown, Bruce Davison, Joaquim de Almeida, Edward Herrmann, Kenneth Welsh; ***D:*** Nicholas Meyer; ***W:*** Tim Prager; ***C:*** David Franco; ***M:*** John Altman. **CABLE**

Vendetta for the Saint 🦴 **1968** A feature-length episode of the TV series "The Saint," in which Simon Templar pursues a Sicilian mobster on a personal vendetta. **98m/C VHS, DVD.** *GB* Ian Hendry, Aimi MacDonald, Rosemary Dexter, George Pastell, Roger Moore; ***D:*** James O'Connolly; ***W:*** Harry Junkin, John Kruse; ***C:*** Brendan Stafford; ***M:*** Edwin Astley. **TV**

Vengeance 🦴🦴 **1937** A police officer resigns in shame after failing to thwart a holdup. He attempts to redeem himself by working on his own to infiltrate the same gang. **61m/B VHS.** Lyle Talbot, Wendy Barrie, Wally Albright, Marc Lawrence; ***D:*** Del Lord.

Vengeance 🦴 **1980** Four burglars take hostages after their robbery is bungled, but they won't get away—especially after the hostages die. **92m/C VHS.** Sally Lockett, Nicholas Jacquez, Bob Elliott; ***D:*** Bob Blizz.

Vengeance 🦴 **1986** A low-budget film about rebels fighting off an authoritarian government. **114m/C VHS.** Jason Miller, Lea Massari; ***D:*** Antonio (Isasi-Isasmendi) Isasi.

Vengeance 🦴🦴 *Vengeance: The Story of Tony Cimo* **1989 (R)** A bereaved young man strikes out against the injustice of his parents' murder. His revenge against the killers takes him several steps beyond the law, and he's not so sure it was the right idea. **90m/C VHS.** Brad Davis, Roxanne Hart, Brad Dourif, William Conrad; ***D:*** Marc Daniels. **TV**

Vengeance is a Golden Blade 🦴 1/2 *Fei yan jin dao; Fei yin gam do* **1969** Li Chih Shan (Ching Tang) returns from adventures abroad to find his wife has been sleeping around with his rivals. She conspires with them to steal the Golden Dragon Blade, which is said to make its wielder invincible. Li escapes with his daughter and servant to hide in the mountains but a foolish mistake puts them in harm's way. **99m/C DVD.** *HK* Hsiung Chao, Ping Chin, Pao-Shu Kao, Wen Chung Ku, Peng-fei Li, Han Lo, Peng Peng, Ching Tang, Ping-Ao Wei, Hua Yueh; ***D:*** Meng Hua Ho; ***W:*** Yun Chih Tu, Meng Hua Ho; ***C:*** Kuo-Hsiang Lin; ***M:*** Fu-ling Wang.

Vengeance Is Mine WOOF! **1974 (R)** A demented farmer captures three criminals and tortures them in horrifyingly sadistic ways. Gratuitously grisly. **90m/C VHS, DVD.** Ernest Borgnine, Michael J. Pollard, Hollis McLaren, Louis Zorich, Cec Linder, Vladimir Valenta, Al Waxman, Tim Henry, Susan Petrie; ***D:*** John Trent; ***W:*** John Trent, David Main; ***C:*** Marc Champion; ***M:*** Paul Hoffert.

Vengeance Is Mine 🦴🦴🦴 *Fukusho Suruwa Ware Ni Ari* **1979** Told in flashbacks, the film focuses on the life of a habitual criminal whose life of deprivation leads to murder. Contains violence and nudity. Based on a true story. In Japanese with English subtitles. **129m/C VHS.** *JP* Ken Ogata, Rentaro Mikuni, Mitsuko Baisho, Chocho Miyako, Mayumi Ogawa, Nijiko Kiyokawa; ***D:*** Shohei Imamura; ***W:*** Masuru Baba; ***C:*** Sinsaku Himeda; ***M:*** Shinichiro Ikebe.

The Vengeance of Fu Manchu 🦴 **1967** The third in the Lee series finds Fu Manchu and daughter Lin Tang (Chin) plotting revenge on Scotland Yard commissioner Nayland Smith (Wilmer). He's kidnapped and replaced with a murderous double in order to further the crime syndicate plans of the villains. Based on the characters created by Sax Rohmer. **91m/C VHS.** *GE* Christopher Lee, Tsai Chin, Douglas Wilmer, Tony Ferrer, Noel Trevarthen, Horst Frank, Wolfgang Kieling, Suzanne Roquette; ***D:*** Jeremy Summers; ***W:*** Harry Alan Towers; ***C:*** John von Kotze; ***M:*** Malcolm Lockyer.

The Vengeance of She 🦴 *The Return of She* **1968** Carol (Berova) is taken for the reincarnation of 2,000-year-old queen, Ayesha, by her immortal lover, King Killikrates (Richardson). The king promises high priest Man Hari (Godfrey) immortality if he can restore Ayesha's soul. But Carol's shrink boyfriend (Judd) isn't crazy about the idea and tries to convince the king otherwise. **101m/C VHS, DVD.** *GB* Olinka (Schoberova) Berova, John Richardson, Derek Godfrey, Edward Judd, Colin Blakely; ***D:*** Cliff Owen; ***W:*** Peter O'Donnell; ***C:*** Peter Suschitzky; ***M:*** Mario Nascimbene.

Vengeance of the Dead 🦴 1/2 **2001** Homegrown horror flick never manages to live up to the big ideas it introduces. Eric (Galvin) journeys to the town of Harvest, to visit his Grandpa (Vollmers). (Although we're never told where he's been or given an idea of how long he's going to stay.) Once he's settled in, Eric has strange nightmares concerning a little girl, an act of violence, and a burning house. These dreams lead him to sleepwalk through the town and commit strange acts of vengeance. The dreams and Eric's behaviors are linked to a crime from many years ago, and a ghostly presence is seeking revenge on those responsible. Despite an interesting premise, the film is slow, boring, and hard to follow at times. Kudos to filmmakers Adams and Picardi for squeezing as much as possible out of their limited budget, but this movie can't overcome its amateur roots. **85m/C DVD.** Michael Galvin, Mark Vollmers; ***D:*** Don Adams, Harry James Picardi.

Vengeance of the Zombies 🦴 1/2 **1972** A madman seeks revenge by setting an army of walking corpses to stalk the streets of London. **90m/C VHS, DVD.** *SP* Paul Naschy; ***D:*** Leon Klimovsky.

Vengeance Valley 🦴🦴 **1951** Lancaster and Walker are foster brothers with Walker being an envious weasel who always expects Lancaster to get him out of scrapes. Lancaster is even accused of a crime committed by Walker and must work to clear himself. Good cast is let down by uneven direction. **83m/C VHS, DVD.** Burt Lancaster, Joanne Dru, Robert Walker, Sally Forrest, John Ireland, Hugh O'Brian; ***D:*** Richard Thorpe; ***W:*** Irving Ravetch; ***C:*** George J. Folsey; ***M:*** Rudolph Kopp.

Venice, Venice 🦴🦴 1/2 **1992 (R)** Alternately earnest and satirical, Jaglom pokes fun at himself and movie-making in a movie about, well, himself and movie-making. Consciously straddling the genre fence, he uses real people and events, but adopts a pseudonym, Dean. In Venice, Italy, young filmmaker Alard decides to make a film about Dean/Jaglom, a plot which creates the effect of two mirrors reflecting each other into infinity. Dean/Jaglom and Alard return to Venice, California, where he conducts auditions for a movie in which he will star and direct. Art imitating life or life imitating art? More importantly, does it really matter? **108m/C VHS, DVD.** Nelly Alard, Henry Jaglom, Suzanne Bertish, Melissa Leo, Daphna Kastner, David Duchovny, Diane Salinger, Zack Norman, Marshall Barer, John Landis, Pierre Cottrell, Edna Fainaru, Klaus Hellwig; ***D:*** Henry Jaglom; ***W:*** Henry Jaglom; ***C:*** Hanania Baer.

Venom WOOF! **1982 (R)** Deadly black mamba is loose in an elegant townhouse, terrorizing big-name cast. The snake continually terrorizes an evil kidnapper, his accomplices and his kidnapped victim. Participants walk through tired cliches with that far-away look in their eyes—like they wish they were anywhere else. Original director Tobe Hooper was replaced. **92m/C VHS, DVD.** *GB* Sterling Hayden, Klaus Kinski, Sarah Miles, Nicol Williamson, Cornelia Sharpe, Susan George, Michael Gough, Oliver Reed; ***D:*** Piers Haggard; ***W:*** Robert B. Carrington; ***M:*** Michael Kamen.

Venom 🦴🦴 **2005 (R)** Swamp-set slasher flick offers redneck Ray (Cramer) getting bitten by a suitcase full of snakes that happened to belong to a voodoo priestess. Ray gets resurrected and goes after all the pretty teens (male and female) who annoyed Ray when he was alive. Hits all the genre highlights, so if voodoo and zombies and gore, oh my, are what you're searching for, look no further. **87m/C DVD.** *US* Agnes Bruckner, Joshua Jackson, Rick Cramer, Meagan Good, Bijou Phillips, Method Man, Laura Ramsey, Pawel Szajda, Stacey Travis, James Pickens Jr., Davetta Sherwood, D.J. Cotrona, Marcus Lyle Brown, Deborah Duke; ***D:*** Jim Gillespie; ***W:*** Flint Dille, Brandon Boyce; ***C:*** Steve Mason; ***M:*** James L. Venable.

Venomous 🦴🦴 **2001 (PG-13)** Genetically altered poisonous snakes make their presence felt in a small town by spreading a deadly virus among the human population. To cover up the source of the disease, the military (the snakes are one of their experiments gone wrong) plans to blow up the town. **97m/C VHS, DVD.** Treat Williams, Mary Page Keller, Brian Poth, J.B. Gaynor, Hannes Jaenicke, Geoffrey Pierson, Catherine Dent; ***D:*** Fred Olen Ray; ***W:*** Dan Golden, Sean McGinley; ***C:*** Andrea V. Rossotto; ***M:*** Neal Acree. **VIDEO**

Venus 🦴🦴🦴 **2006 (R)** The ever-charismatic, though now frail, O'Toole plays a mildly famous charmer of an actor who still takes an interest in a pretty girl, even if the flesh is weak. Maurice's best friend is his grumpy (and equally aged) fellow thespian Ian (Phillips). Ian's grand-niece Jessie (Whittaker) has ostensibly arrived to help him out but the sullen, lower-class teen is more concerned with her own interests. This doesn't prevent Maurice from becoming interested in her, though it might be more a nod to his rogue past than to Jessie herself. Funny and poignant without mawkishness; also notable is the appearance of Redgrave as Maurice's understanding ex-wife. **94m/C DVD.** *GB* Peter O'Toole, Leslie Phillips, Richard Griffiths, Jodie Whittaker, Vanessa Redgrave; ***D:*** Roger Michell; ***W:*** Hanif Kureishi; ***C:*** Haris Zambarloukos; ***M:*** David Arnold, Corinne Bailey Rae.

Venus Against the Son of Hercules 🦴 *Marte, Dio Della Guerra* **1962** Our hero must use all his genetically procured musculature in his battle against the lovely but deadly Venus. **?m/C VHS.** *IT* Jackie Lane, Roger Browne, Massimo Serato, Linda Sini, Dante DiPaolo; ***D:*** Marcello Baldi; ***W:*** Ernesto Gastaldi.

Venus Beauty Institute 🦴🦴 1/2 **1998 (R)** Fortyish Angele (Baye) works at a Paris beauty salon along with proprietor Nadine (Ogier) and younger colleagues Samantha (Seigner) and Marie (Tantou). Angele refuses to fall in love and picks up men strictly for sex—until she's pursued by Antoine (Le Bihan), a young sculptor who insists he fell in love with her at first sight. (He basically stalks her but Angele is intrigued rather than repulsed by his devotion.) The Institute also has a parade of frequently neurotic customers in romantic dilemmas. French with subtitles. **105m/C VHS, DVD.** *FR* Nathalie Baye, Bulle Ogier, Samuel Le Bihan, Jacques Bonnaffe, Mathilde Seigner, Robert Hossein, Claire Nebout, Audrey Tautou; ***D:*** Tonie Marshall; ***W:*** Tonie Marshall; ***C:*** Gerard de Battista; ***M:*** Khalil Chahine. Cesar '00: Director (Marshall), Film, Screenplay.

Venus in Furs 🦴 1/2 *Paroxismus; Puo Una Morta Rivivere Per Amore?; Venus in Peltz* **1970 (R)** Jazz musician working in Rio de Janeiro becomes obsessed with a mysterious woman; she resembles a murder victim whose body he discovered months earlier. Weird mix of horror, sadism, black magic, and soft porn. **70m/C VHS, DVD.** *GB IT GE* James Darren, Klaus Kinski, Barbara McNair, Dennis Price, Maria Rohm, Margaret Lee, Jess (Jesus) Franco; ***D:*** Jess (Jesus) Franco; ***W:*** Milo G. Cuccia, Malvin Wald, Jess (Jesus) Franco; ***C:*** Angelo Lotti.

Venus Rising 🦴🦴 **1995 (R)** In the year 2000, Eve and August manage to escape from the island prison on which they were raised. They discover that the mainland world features emotions that are controlled by drugs and love is only a game on the virtual reality network. Hunted, the fugitives try to fit in and figure out what's real and what's fantasy. Be forewarned—Fairchild's role is very small. **91m/C VHS, DVD.** Audie England, Costas Mandylor, Billy Wirth, Morgan Fairchild; ***D:*** Leora Barish; ***W:*** Leora Barish.

Vera Cruz 1/2 **1953** Two soldiers of fortune become involved in the Mexican Revolution of 1866, a stolen shipment of gold, divided loyalties, and gun battles. Less than innovative plot is made into an exciting action flick. **94m/C VHS, DVD.** Gary Cooper, Burt Lancaster, Denise Darcel, Cesar Romero, George Macready, Ernest Borgnine, Charles Bronson, Jack Elam; ***D:*** Robert Aldrich; ***W:*** Roland Kibbee, James R. Webb; ***C:*** Ernest Laszlo; ***M:*** Hugo Friedhofer.

Vera Drake **2004 (R)** Compassionate, complex drama with a stellar performance by Staunton in the title role. Set in the drab postwar London of 1950, Vera is a cozy, middle-aged married house cleaner who is relentlessly cheery and helpful to all those around her. This includes the poor young women who find themselves "in trouble." Vera, as it happens, is the local abortionist—something her family discovers only when the police descend on them after one of Vera's procedures goes wrong. Her subsequent trial highlights the hypocrisy of the proceedings (matched against Vera's bewildered decency) without becoming overbearing. **125m/C DVD.** Imelda Staunton, Philip Davis, Peter Wright, Adrian Scarborough, Heather Craney, Alex Kelly, Daniel Mays, Eddie Marsan, Sally Hawkins, Ruth Sheen, Helen Coker; ***D:*** Mike Leigh; ***W:*** Mike Leigh; ***C:*** Dick Pope; ***M:*** Andrew Dickson. British Acad. '04: Actress (Staunton), Costume Des., Director (Leigh).

Verboten! 1/2 **1959** In post-war occupied Berlin, an American G.I. falls in love with a German girl. Good direction maintains a steady pace. **93m/B VHS.** James Best, Susan Cummings, Tom Pittman, Paul Dubov; ***D:*** Samuel Fuller; ***W:*** Samuel Fuller; ***C:*** Joseph Biroc.

Verdi *The Life and Music of Giuseppe Verdi* **1953** The story of the Italian operatic composer and the loves of his life. Italian with subtitles. **80m/C VHS.** *IT* Pierre Cressoy, Gaby Andre; ***D:*** Raffaello Matarazzo; ***W:*** Leonardo Benvenuti; ***C:*** Tino Santoni.

The Verdict 1/2 **1946** Siegel made his directorial feature film debut in the last film Greenstreet and Lorre would appear in together. In 1890 London, aging Scotland Yard superintendent Grodman (Greenstreet) is forced into retirement after a convicted murderer is found to be innocent—after his execution. He's replaced by pompous Buckley (Coulouris) who soon has a locked room murder on his hands. Naturally he arrests the wrong man (a friend of Grodman's) and then the case turns even more complicated. **86m/B DVD.** Sydney Greenstreet, Peter Lorre, George Coulouris, Joan Lorring; ***D:*** Terry Morse; ***C:*** Arthur L. Todd; ***M:*** Max Steiner.

The Verdict **1982 (R)** Frank Galvin (Newman) is an alcoholic failed attorney reduced to ambulance chasing. A friend gives him a supposedly easy malpractice case that pits Frank against a powerful establishment Catholic hospital in Boston in what turns out to be a last chance at redeeming himself and his career. Adapted from the novel by Barry Reed. One of Newman's finest performances. **122m/C VHS, DVD.** Paul Newman, James Mason, Charlotte Rampling, Jack Warden, Milo O'Shea, Lindsay Crouse, Edward Binns, Roxanne Hart, James Handy, Wesley Addy, Joe Seneca, Julie Bovasso; ***D:*** Sidney Lumet; ***W:*** David Mamet; ***C:*** Andrzej Bartkowiak; ***M:*** Johnny Mandel. Natl. Bd. of Review '82: Director (Lumet).

Verdict in Blood 1/2 **2002 (R)** When the judge she covered is murdered, reporter Joanne Kilbourne's hunt for the culprit exposes scandalous family secrets. Based on Gail Bowen's serial novel. **90m/C VHS, DVD.** Wendy Crewson, Shawn Doyle, Zachary Bennett, Neil Crone, Robert Davi, Richard Fitzpatrick, Ken James, Sally Kellerman, Kristen Lehman, Reagan Pasternak, Elizabeth Shepherd, Walter Alza, Alex Campbell, Diego Chambers, Pablo Coffey, Callahan Connor, Angela Gei, Kristen Gutoskie, Natasha La Force, Shawn Laurence, Tony Munch, Paul Robbins, Pamela Wallin, Lila Yee, Jean Yoon, Gail Bowen, Janet Maclean, Andrew Wreggitt; ***D:*** Stephen Williams; ***W:*** Jeremy Hole; ***C:*** David Herrington; ***M:*** Robert Carli. **TV**

Verdict on Auschwitz: The Frankfurt Auschwitz Trial 1963—1965 *Strafsache 4 Ks 2/63: Auschwitz Vor Dem Frankfurter Schwurgericht* **1993** Originally made for German TV, where it was shown as a 3-part documentary. (It was also released in 2005 in a 60-minute version.) This re-release is a loosely structured examination of the 1963-65 trial of 22 Auschwitz SS officers, based on 430 hours of audiotapes. Directors Bickel and Wagner divide this chilling recounting into the investigation, the trial (which included testimony by more than 200 survivors), and the verdict. Testimony is illustrated with footage and photographs as well as archival material. English, German, Polish, and Russian with subtitles. **180m/C DVD.** *GE* ***D:*** Rolf Bickel, Dietrick Wagner; ***W:*** Rolf Bickel, Dietrick Wagner; ***C:*** Armin Alker, Dominik Schunk; ***Nar:*** Edgar M. Boehke.

Vermont Is for Lovers 1/2 **1992** Prewedding jitters consume stressed-out Manhattanites Marya (Cohn) and George (Thrush) when they travel to bucolic Tunbridge, Vermont to get married on Marya's Aunt Ann's farm. After continuously arguing, they decide to spend the day before the wedding apart and George wanders around the community asking marriage advice from various old-timers. The Yuppie leads aren't terribly compelling and neither is the improvised dialogue. **86m/C VHS.** George Thrush, Marya Cohn, Ann O'Brien; ***D:*** John O'Brien; ***C:*** John O'Brien; ***M:*** Tony Silbert.

Verne Miller **1988 (R)** A film of the true story of Verne Miller, Al Capone's hit man. After rescuing a friend from the Feds, Miller is hunted down by both the cops and the mob. **95m/C VHS.** Scott Glenn, Barbara Stock, Thomas G. Waites, Lucinda Jenney, Sonny Carl Davis; ***D:*** Rod Hewitt.

Vernie **2004** Sean and Kristi were once best friends and they reunite when Sean is diagnosed with an inoperable brain tumor. When Sean asks Kristi to have his child, she surprises herself by agreeing. But the ensuing months prove to be more difficult than either of them imagined. A tearjerker with humor, which makes for a generally winning combo. **86m/C DVD.** Amy Colon, John Riedlinger, Patrick Coyle, Allyson Kearns, Adam Whisner, Heidi Jo Langseth; ***D:*** David Tufford; ***W:*** Kevin Ross; ***C:*** David Doyle; ***M:*** Todd Syring.

The Vernonia Incident 1/2 **1989** Urban guerillas invade a small town, killing the police chief. The townspeople gather up their shotguns and fight back. That's entertainment. **95m/C VHS.** David Jackson, Shawn Stevens, Floyd Ragner, Ed Justice, Robert Louis Jakson; ***D:*** Ray Etheridge; ***W:*** Ray Etheridge.

Veronica Guerin 1/2 **2003 (R)** A less than inspired script is nonetheless brought to life by the brilliant acting of Blanchett in the title role of the real-life Irish reporter, who took on a Dublin drug lord in the 1990s. Despite threats and extreme violence, the plucky wife and mother was relentless in her pursuit of the truth. While Guerin pays for her anti-drug crusade with her life, gunned down at a red light in 1996 by a suspected drug-world henchman, pic tones down the martyr factor by presenting a well-rounded character. Hinds effectively plays a sympathetic Guerin informant who tries to warn her of her impending doom. **98m/C VHS, DVD.** *US* Cate Blanchett, Gerard McSorley, Ciaran Hinds, Brenda Fricker, Barry Barnes, David Murray, Joe Hanley, David Herlihy, Gerry O'Brien, Don Wycherley, Colin Farrell, Alan Devine; ***D:*** Joel Schumacher; ***W:*** Carol Doyle, Mary Agnes Donoghue; ***C:*** Brendan Galvin; ***M:*** Harry Gregson-Williams.

Veronico Cruz 1/2 *La Dueda Interna; The Debt* **1987** Despite its sincerity, Pereira's feature debut offers muddled response to the human waste incurred by the Falklands War. Set in a tiny remote village in the Argentinean mountains, the film's narrative is derived from the growing friendship between a shepherd boy and a teacher from the city. Well-meaning anti-war movie. In Spanish with English subtitles. **96m/C VHS, DVD.** *AR GB* Juan Jose Camero, Gonzalo Morales, Rene Olaguivel, Guillermo Delgado; ***D:*** Miguel Pereira; ***W:*** Miguel Pereira, Eduardo Leiva Muller; ***C:*** Gerry Feeny; ***M:*** David Eppel, Jaime Torres.

Veronika Voss *Die Sehns Ucht Der Veronika Voss* **1982 (R)** Highlights the real life of fallen film star Sybille Schmitz who finally took her own life out of despair. Played by Zech, Voss is exploited by her physician to turn over all of her personal belongings for morphine. A lover discovers the corruption and reveals it to the authorities. This causes great upheaval resulting in Voss' suicide. Highly metaphoric and experimental in its treatment of its subject. In German with English subtitles. **105m/C VHS, DVD.** *GE* Rosel Zech, Hilmar Thate, Conny Froboess, Anna Marie Duringer, Volker Spengler; ***D:*** Rainer Werner Fassbinder; ***W:*** Pea Frolich, Peter Marthesheimer; ***C:*** Xaver Schwarzenberger; ***M:*** Peer Raben.

Versus 1/2 **2000 (R)** There are 666 portals to the other side, and the 444th (the Forest of Resurrection) is set in Japan, where the local Yakuza have been using it to get rid of dead bodies. Two prisoners have recently taken a girl hostage to escape from a maximum security prison, and the yakuza are supposed to pick them up in the forest and take them to a safe house. Instead a gunfight erupts, after which the dead reanimate and attack the living. One of the prisoners escapes into the forest with the girl, and they desperately search for a way out from their undead pursuers. Over-the-top gore and martial arts fights commence. **119m/C DVD.** *JP* Tak Sakaguchi, Hideo Sakaki, Chieko Masaki; ***D:*** Ryuhei Kitamura; ***W:*** Ryuhei Kitamura, Yudai Yamaguchi; ***C:*** Takumi Furuya; ***M:*** Nobuhiko Morino.

Vertical Limit **2000 (PG-13)** Photographer O'Donnell joins a team of mountain climbers in order to rescue his sister Tunney, who is part of a group trapped on K2. Plot serves mainly as connective tissue for the numerous heart-stopping (and well-done) action sequences. Mountain-fodder cast has few standouts, except maybe Glenn in the crazy-but-wise-old-coot role. **126m/C VHS, DVD, Blu-ray Disc.** Chris O'Donnell, Robin Tunney, Bill Paxton, Scott Glenn, Izabela Scorupco, Temuera Morrison, Stuart Wilson, Nicholas Lea, Alexander Siddig, Robert Taylor, Roshan Seth, David Hayman, Ben Mendelsohn, Steve Le Marquand; ***D:*** Martin Campbell; ***W:*** Robert King, Terry Hayes; ***C:*** David Tattersall; ***M:*** James Newton Howard.

The Vertical Ray of the Sun 1/2 **2000 (PG-13)** Slow-moving visual treat set in Hanoi. Three sisters plan a commemorative meal in honor of the anniversary of their mother's death. The two eldest sisters have marital problems and the youngest is so close to their brother that many believe the twosome are sexually involved. Over the course of a month (which ends with the anniversary of their father's death), the women deal with their emotional entanglements. Vietnamese with subtites. **112m/C VHS, DVD.** *VT FR* Tran Nu Yen-Khe, Nguyen Nhu Quynh, Le Khanh, Tran Manh Cuong, Chu Ngoc Hung, Ngo Quang Hai; ***D:*** Tran Anh Hung; ***W:*** Tran Anh Hung; ***C:*** Mark Lee Ping-Bin; ***M:*** Ton That Tiet.

Vertigo **1958 (PG)** Hitchcock's romantic story of obsession, manipulation and fear. Stewart plays a detective forced to retire after his fear of heights causes the death of a fellow policeman and, perhaps, the death of a woman he'd been hired to follow. The appearance of her double (Novak), whom he compulsively transforms into the dead girl's image, leads to a mesmerizing cycle of madness and lies. Features Herrmann's haunting music. **126m/C VHS, DVD.** James Stewart, Kim Novak, Barbara Bel Geddes, Tom Helmore, Ellen Corby, Henry Jones, Raymond Bailey, Lee Patrick; ***D:*** Alfred Hitchcock; ***W:*** Samuel A. Taylor; ***C:*** Robert Burks; ***M:*** Bernard Herrmann. AFI '98: Top 100, Natl. Film Reg. '89.

Very Annie Mary 1/2 **2000** Sentimental comedy set in a small Welsh village filled with eccentrics. That would include singing baker Jack (Pryce), a tyrannical widower who dominates his gauche, 30-ish daughter Annie-Mary (Griffiths). She's saving up to buy a house of her own when her father is felled by a severe stoke and she must take over running the family bakery (for which she has no talent). What Annie-Mary can do is sing and she decides to enter a talent contest in Cardiff in order to fund a trip to Disneyland for her dying friend Bethan (Page). Very twee. **105m/C VHS, DVD.** *GB FR* Rachel Griffiths, Jonathan Pryce, Ioan Gruffudd, Matthew Rhys, Kenneth Griffiths, Ruth Madoc, Joanna Page, Radcliffe Grafton; ***D:*** Sara Sugarman; ***W:*** Sara Sugarman; ***C:*** Barry Ackroyd; ***M:*** Stephen Warbeck.

Very Bad Things **1998 (R)** What begins as a not-so-innocent prenuptial bachelor party in Vegas quickly disintegrates into a murderous blood bath. Kyle (Favreau), the groom-to-be, escapes the clutches of his control-freak fiance Laura (Diaz) with some pals, including unscrupulous yuppie Boyd (Slater). When the hired "entertainment" is killed in a freak accident involving a towel hook, Boyd comes up with the idea of burying her body in the desert and going on with the wedding. A pitch-dark comedy of errors ensues. Peter Berg's first stab at writing and directing has some funny moments, mostly the kind you realize afterwards you shouldn't find funny, but relies too heavily on gratuitous gore and shock value. **100m/C VHS, DVD.** Jon Favreau, Christian Slater, Cameron Diaz, Jeremy Piven, Daniel Stern, Leland Orser, Jeanne Tripplehorn, Joey Zimmerman; ***D:*** Peter Berg; ***W:*** Peter Berg; ***C:*** David Hennings; ***M:*** Stewart Copeland.

A Very Brady Christmas **1988** Many of the original Bradys returned for this yuletide special. After Mike and Carol's vacation plans go awry, they decide to invite the whole bunch home for a family reunion. This was the highest rated TV movie in 1989. Spawned yet another unsuccessful "Brady" series sequel. **94m/C VHS.** Florence Henderson, Robert Reed, Ann B. Davis, Maureen McCormick, Eve Plumb, Jennifer Runyon, Barry Williams, Christopher Knight, Michael (Mike) Lookinland, Jerry Houser, Caryn Richman; ***D:*** Peter Baldwin. **TV**

A Very Brady Sequel 1/2 **1996 (PG-13)** They're back! The cast from the surprise hit "The Brady Bunch Movie" returns and Brady mom Carol (Long) is shocked when her presumed dead first husband Roy Martin (Matheson) suddenly appears on their doorstep. The Bradys must travel to Hawaii to attempt to save the family (based on a three-part episode from the original TV series). The stuck-in-the-'70s gang is still too far-out for the '90s, but in Hawaii it's always a sunshine day. Not as good as the first, but still worth a few laughs. **90m/C VHS, DVD.** Shelley Long, Gary Cole, Tim Matheson, Christopher Daniel Barnes, Christine Taylor, Paul Sutera, Jennifer Elise Cox, Henriette Mantel, Olivia Hack, Jesse Lee, RuPaul Charles, Whip Hubley, John Hillerman, Richard Belzer, David Spade, Barbara Eden; ***Cameos:*** Zsa Zsa Gabor, Rosie O'Donnell; ***D:*** Arlene Sanford; ***W:*** Harry Elfont, Deborah Kaplan, Stan Zimmerman, James Berg; ***C:*** Mac Ahlberg; ***M:*** Guy Moon.

A Very British Coup **1988** McAnally plays Harry Perkins, a former steelworker who gets involved in British politics. Although a left-wing radical, the charismatic Perkins is actually elected Prime Minister. However, his radical policies cause the entrenched government officials to conspire to bring him down. And you thought American politics were dirty! **180m/C VHS, DVD.** *GB* Ray McAnally, Alan MacNaughton, Keith Allen, Geoffrey Beevers, Jim Carter, Philip Madoc, Tim (McInnerny) McInnery; ***D:*** Mick Jackson; ***W:*** Alan Plater; ***C:*** Ernest Vincze; ***M:*** John Keane. **TV**

Very Close Quarters **1984** Thirty people face many trials and tribulations as they share an apartment in Moscow. Interesting cast is wasted in this mostly un-funny flick. **97m/C VHS.** Shelley Winters, Paul Sorvino, Theodore Bikel, Farley Granger; ***D:*** Vladmir Rif.

A Very Curious Girl 1/2 *La Fiancee du Pirate; Dirty Mary; Pirate's Fiancee* **1969 (R)** A peasant girl realizes she is being used by the male population of her village, and decides to charge them for sex, creating havoc. In French with English subtitles.

105m/C VHS. *FR* Bernadette LaFont, Georges Geret, Michel Constantin, Julien Guiomar, Claire Maurier; ***D:*** Nelly Kaplan; ***W:*** Nelly Kaplan, Claude Makovski; ***C:*** Jean Badal; ***M:*** Georges Moustaki.

The Very Edge ½ **1963** A pregnant woman suffers a miscarriage after being brutally attacked. The repercussions nearly destroy her marriage until her attacker is caught. A disturbing psycho-drama. **90m/B VHS.** *GB* Anne Heywood, Richard Todd, Jeremy Brett, Jack Hedley, Barbara Mullen, Maurice Denham, William Lucas, Gwen Watford, Patrick Magee; ***D:*** Cyril Frankel; ***W:*** Elizabeth Jane Howard; ***C:*** Robert Huke.

Very Important Person **1961** British satire of wartime POW flicks. Irascible Sir Ernest Pease (Justice) is an eminent scientist on a WWII reconnaissance flight that's testing his new radar invention. When the plane is shot down, Pease winds up in a German POW camp under an alias so the Nazis won't realize his importance. But his fellow Brits think the unpleasant chappie is a snitch or spy. When they realize Pease's value to the war effort, they plan an escape without much cooperation from their VIP. **90m/B DVD.** *GB* James Robertson Justice, Leslie Phillips, Stanley Baker, Eric Sykes, Richard Wattis, Colin Gordon, Norman Bird, John Forrest, John Le Mesurier; ***W:*** Jeremy Lloyd, Ken Annakin, Jack Davies, Henry Blyth; ***C:*** Ernest Steward; ***M:*** Reg Owen.

A Very Long Engagement *Un long dimanche de fiancailles* **2004 (R)** Jeunet reteams with his "Amelie" star Tautou in a bittersweet WWI-era weepie about a young woman who refuses to believe her fiance has died on the battlefield. In 1917, Manech (Ulliel) is the youngest of five soldiers court-martialed and condemned to certain death in a frontline trench. Two years later, Mathilde (Tautou) is equally certain that Manech is still alive, especially when she receives a letter from one of Menach's fellow soldiers. She hires detective Pire (Holgado) to help her investigate; in a parallel story, Tina (Cotillard), the girlfriend of another soldier, is also looking for answers, although for a much-deadlier purpose. French with subtitles; based on the 1991 novel by Sebastien Japrisot. **133m/C DVD.** *FR* Audrey Tautou, Gaspard Ulliel, Jean Becker, Clovis Cornillac, Marion Cotillard, Jodie Foster, Jean-Claude Dreyfus, Albert Dupontel, Andre Dussollier, Ticky Holgado, Tcheky Karyo, Denis Lavant, Francois Levantal, Chantal Neuwirth, Dominique Pinon, Dominique Bettenfeld, Jean-Pierre Daroussin, Jerome Kircher, Jean-Paul Rouve, Rodolphe Pauly; ***D:*** Jean-Pierre Jeunet; ***C:*** Bruno Delbonnel; ***M:*** Angelo Badalamenti.

A Very Natural Thing **1973** Twenty-six-year-old Jason leaves the priesthood to pursue a gay lifestyle in New York. He becomes a teacher, meets ad exec David, and finds love. Considered to be the first film to explore homosexuality in a realistic manner, made by a gay director, and given national, commercial distribution. **85m/C VHS, DVD.** Robert Joel, Curt Gareth, Bo White; ***D:*** Christopher Larkin; ***W:*** Christopher Larkin, Joseph Coencas; ***C:*** C.H. Douglass; ***M:*** Gordon Gottlieb, Bert Lucarelli.

A Very Old Man with Enormous Wings *Un Senor Muy Viejo Con Unas Alas Enormes* **1988** An angel, battered during a hurricane, seeks refuge on a tiny Caribbean island. There, two men keep him and charge an increasingly curious world admission to view the creature. A colorful, musical expose of human failings based on a story by Gabriel Garcia Marquez. In Spanish with English subtitles. **90m/C VHS.** *SP IT* Daisy Granados, Asdrubal Melendez, Luis Alberto Ramirez, Fernando Birri; ***D:*** Fernando Birri.

A Very Private Affair ½ *La Vie Privee; Vita Privata* **1962** A movie star finds that she has no privacy from the hordes of fans and paparazzi who flock to her side. The glare of publicity helps to destroy her relationship with a married director, and to fuel her desire for privacy, a desire that ends tragically. An appealing, better-than-average Bardot vehicle, it is nonetheless below-average (early) Malle. In French with English subtitles. **95m/C VHS.** *FR* Marcello Mastroianni, Brigitte Bardot; ***D:*** Louis Malle.

A Very Serious Person **2006** Precocious, orphaned 13-year-old Gil (Verhoest) lives with his grandma, Mrs. A (Bergen), and loves their beachside summers. She accepts his budding sexuality (a queen in the making) although he can't accept the fact that she is dying. Mrs. A needs professional nursing that companion Betty (Ivey) can't handle, so she hires prim Danish male nurse Jan (Busch—mostly out of drag). Jan and Gil become friends, but Jan is also overprotective. Knowing that the boy will soon be living with distant relatives, he urges Gil to an unwilling (and unlikely) conformity. **96m/C DVD.** Charles Busch, Polly Bergen, Dana Ivey, Julie Halston, P.J. Verhoest, Carl Andress; ***D:*** Charles Busch; ***W:*** Charles Busch, Carl Andress; ***C:*** Joseph Parlagreco; ***M:*** Andrew Sherman.

The Very Thought of You ½ *Martha, Meet Frank, Daniel and Laurence* **1998 (PG-13)** Limp romantic comedy finds a trio of longtime London friends clashing over their interest in the same woman. Actor Frank (Sewell), music exec Daniel (Hollander), and painter Laurence (Fiennes) all separately encounter Martha (Potter) and pick her up—without anyone realizing (until late in the movie) how they're all connected. However, Martha's character comes across as a imperious nag, while the men are either petulant, arrogant, or wimpy. You won't care who Martha finally ends up with. **88m/C VHS, DVD.** *GB* Monica Potter, Rufus Sewell, Joseph Fiennes, Tom Hollander, Ray Winstone; ***D:*** Nick Hamm; ***W:*** Peter Morgan; ***C:*** David C(lark) Johnson; ***M:*** Ed Shearmur.

The Veteran ½ **2006** Crazed from his time as a Vietnam War POW, Doc (Ironside) is bent on avenging his abandonment by his comrades and targets Ray (Hosea), who is now a preacher with high political aspirations. Doc lures Ray back to Vietnam and holds him hostage in a hotel while rehashing painful memories (done via vivid flashbacks), not knowing that a government agent (Sheedy) investigating MIAs is trailing the pair. **89m/C DVD.** Michael Ironside, Bobby Hosea, Ally Sheedy, Kenneth Johnson, Colin Glazer; ***D:*** Sidney J. Furie; ***W:*** J. Stephen Maunder. **VIDEO**

V.I. Warshawski **1991 (R)** The filmmakers seem to think they can slum with the oldest cliches in detective shows just as long as the tough gumshoe is a woman. They're wrong. Turner is terrific as the leggy shamus of the title (from a popular series of books by Sara Paretsky), but the plot is nothing special, featuring stock characters in the killing of a pro athlete and a real-estate deal. **89m/C VHS, DVD.** Stephen (Steve) Root, Kathleen Turner, Jay O. Sanders, Angela Goethals, Charles Durning; ***D:*** Jeff Kanew; ***W:*** Nick Thiel, David Aaron Cohen; ***M:*** Randy Edelman.

Via Appia **1992** Fictional documentary about Frank, a German airline steward who brings a film crew with him when travels back to Rio de Janeiro in search of the street hustler who gave him AIDS. Grim guided tour of the city's gay subculture along the "Via Appia," the Rio district where the male prostitutes hang out. Film is firmly unapologetic for its sexual explicitness and lack of moralizing. In German and Portuguese with English subtitles. **90m/C VHS.** *GE BR* Peter Senner, Guilherme de Padua, Yves Jansen, Margarita Schmidt, Luiz Kleber; ***D:*** Jochen Hick; ***W:*** Jochen Hick.

Vibes **1988 (PG)** Two screwball psychics are sent on a wild goose chase through the Ecuadorean Andes in search of cosmic power and, of course, fall in love. Flat offering from the usually successful team of writers, Lowell Ganz and Babaloo Mandel ("Splash" and "Night Shift"). Lauper's first starring role (and so far, her last). **99m/C VHS.** Jeff Goldblum, Cyndi Lauper, Julian Sands, Googy Gress, Peter Falk, Elizabeth Pena; ***D:*** Ken Kwapis; ***W:*** Babaloo Mandel, Lowell Ganz; ***C:*** John Bailey; ***M:*** James Horner.

Vibration *Lejonsommar* **1968** Writer Mauritz (Taube) travels to an island off the Swedish coast to enjoy some fun in the sun and immediately becomes involved with the tempting Barbro (Sjodin). But she can't compete with sex kitten Eliza (Persson), a film star who says she wants to be alone—although her actions say something quite different. Sixties Swedish erotica. **84m/B VHS, DVD.** *SW* Sven-Bertil Taube, Essy Persson, Margareta Sjodin; ***D:*** Torbjorn Axelman; ***W:*** Torbjorn Axelman; ***C:*** Hans Dittmer; ***M:*** Ulf Bjorlin.

Vibrations ½ **1994 (R)** Anamika (Applegate), a dance club manager, befriends TJ (Marshall), a homeless, alcoholic, once-promising musician who lost his hands in a brutal attack. The duo find romance as Anamika encourages TJ to try again. **104m/C VHS, DVD.** James Marshall, Christina Applegate, Faye Grant, Paige Turco, Bruce Altman, David Burke, Scott Cohen, Shane Butterworth; ***D:*** Michael Paseornek; ***W:*** Michael Paseornek; ***M:*** Bob Christianson.

Vice ½ **2008 (R)** Familiar crime thriller but Madsen makes an effort. Cop Max Walker (Madsen) is on a downhill slide that gains momentum after an undercover drug bust goes bad and the heroin goes missing. As members of his team get offed, Walker turns to fellow cops Sampson (Williamson) and Salt (Hannah) to help him out, especially since the killer may be one of their own. **98m/C DVD.** Michael Madsen, Daryl Hannah, Mykelti Williamson, Mark Boone Jr., Kurupt, Nicholas Lea, John Cassini; ***D:*** Raul Inglis; ***W:*** Raul Inglis; ***C:*** Andrzej Sekula; ***M:*** Cliff Martinez. **VIDEO**

Vice Academy ½ **1988 (R)** Two females join the Hollywood vice squad. Allen was a former porn queen. **90m/C VHS, DVD.** Linnea Quigley, Ginger Lynn Allen, Karen Russell, Jayne Hamil, Ken Abraham, Stephen Steward, Jeannie Carol; ***D:*** Rick Sloane.

Vice Academy 2 **1990 (R)** Two vice cop babes try to stop a female crime boss from dumping aphrodesiacs in the city's water supply. **90m/C VHS, DVD.** Linnea Quigley, Ginger Lynn Allen, Jayne Hamil, Scott Layne, Jay Richardson, Joe Brewer, Marina Benvenga, Teagan Clive; ***D:*** Rick Sloane.

Vice Academy 3 **WOOF!** **1991 (R)** The worst of the series, and not just because cult actress Linnea Quigley is absent. Wit, pacing and even sets are nonexistent as the girls battle a toxic villainess called Malathion. **88m/C VHS, DVD.** Ginger Lynn Allen, Elizabeth Kaitan, Julia Parton, Jay Richardson, Johanna Grika, Steve Mateo; ***D:*** Rick Sloane; ***W:*** Rick Sloane.

Vice Girls ½ **1996 (R)** Three undercover female cops (all babes naturally) use their brains and bodies to capture a serial killer who gets his jollies by filming his victims before he kills them. Sexy fun. **85m/C VHS, DVD.** Lana Clarkson, Liat Goodson, Kimberly Roberts, A. Michael Baldwin, Richard Gabai, Caroline Keenan, Hoke Howell; ***D:*** Richard Gabai; ***W:*** A. Michael Baldwin; ***C:*** Gary Graver.

Vice Squad **1931** Lukas is forced to turn police informer to save his own neck, which almost ruins him. Just when he thinks he's free of the cops they come back threatening the woman he loves unless he plays stoolie again. Rather flat, but the different cop/criminal angle makes for some unusual twists. **80m/B VHS.** Paul Lukas, Kay Francis, Helen Johnson, William B. Davidson, Esther Howard; ***D:*** John Cromwell; ***C:*** Charles B(ryant) Lang Jr.

Vice Squad **WOOF!** **1982 (R)** Violent and twisted killer-pimp goes on a murderous rampage, and a hooker helps a vice squad plainclothesman trap him. Sleazy and disturbing, with little to recommend it. **97m/C VHS, DVD.** Wings Hauser, Season Hubley, Gary Swanson, Cheryl "Rainbeaux" Smith; ***D:*** Gary Sherman; ***W:*** Robert Vincent O'Neil.

Vice Versa **1988 (PG)** Another 80s comedy about a workaholic father and his 11-year-old son who switch bodies, with predictable slapstick results. Reinhold and Savage carry this, appearing to have a great time in spite of over-done story. **97m/C VHS, DVD.** Judge Reinhold, Fred Savage, Swoosie Kurtz, David Proval, Corinne Bohrer, Jane Kaczmarek, William Prince, Gloria Gifford; ***D:*** Brian Gilbert; ***W:*** Dick Clement, Ian La Frenais; ***M:*** David Shire.

Vicious **1988** A bored young woman falls in with people your mother warned you about and soon their high school hi-jinks turn into murder. Graphic violence. **88m/C VHS.** Tamblyn Lord, Craig Pearce, Tiffany Dowe; ***D:*** Karl Zwicky.

The Vicious Circle ½ *The Circle* **1957** A prominent London physician becomes involved in murder and an international crime ring when he agrees to perform an errand for a friend. Good performances and tight pacing. **84m/B VHS.** *GB* John Mills, Wilfrid Hyde-White, Rene Ray, Lionel Jeffries, Noelle Middleton; ***D:*** Gerald Thomas.

Vicious Circles **1997 (R)** Decidedly kinky erotic thriller finds Dylan (Hipp) getting arrested for drug possession in Paris. So his half-sister and lover Andi (Lowery) decides to help raise the money for his release by working as a hooker for mystery man March (Gazzara). As Andi gets more involved in her new lifestyle, she also discovers that March was somehow connected to the death of a tycoon's daughter. **90m/C VHS.** Carolyn Lowery, Ben Gazzara, Paul Hipp; ***D:*** Alexander Whitelaw; ***W:*** Alexander Whitelaw; ***M:*** Robert Lockhart.

The Vicious Kind **2009 (R)** Misogynistic Caleb (Scott) rants to his innocent younger brother Peter (Frost) that his new girlfriend Emma (Snow), who's coming to Thanksgiving dinner, is basically a slut. Caleb is protesting too much since he's got a sexual thing for Emma he won't willingly admit to as well as a corrosive relationship with their brutal father (Simmons). Writer/director Krieger is good at dialogue and characters although the dysfunctional family plot is familiar. **93m/C DVD.** Adam Scott, Brittany Snow, Alex Frost, J.K. Simmons; ***D:*** Lee Toland Krieger; ***W:*** Lee Toland Krieger; ***C:*** Bradley Stonesifer; ***M:*** Jeff Cardoni.

Vicky Cristina Barcelona ½ **2008 (PG-13)** Two best friends, Vicky (Hall), the stable engaged one, and Cristina (Johansson), the risk-taking impulsive one, decide to spend the summer in Barcelona at the home of Vicky's relatives, Judy and Mark (Clarkson and Dunn). Both are drawn to an eccentric local artist, Juan Antonio (Bardem), and eventually they are charmed into considering a shared romance with the smooth-talker. They're unaware, however, that he is still passionately (and violently) involved with his tempestuous ex-wife (Cruz). Similar in theme and style with most of Woody Allen's later work; as always, Allen's characters speak intelligently and never follow the Hollywood formulas. Cruz infuses the otherwise languid film with needed spark. **96m/C DVD, Blu-ray Disc.** *US SP* Javier Bardem, Rebecca Hall, Scarlett Johansson, Penelope Cruz, Patricia Clarkson, Kevin Dunn, Chris Messina; ***D:*** Woody Allen; ***W:*** Woody Allen; ***C:*** Javier Aguirresarobe; ***V:*** Christopher Evan Welch. Oscars '08: Support. Actress (Cruz); British Acad. '08: Support. Actress (Cruz); Golden Globes '09: Film—Mus./Comedy; Ind. Spirit '09: Screenplay, Support. Actress (Cruz).

Victim ½ **1961** A successful married English barrister (Bogarde) with a hidden history of homosexuality is threatened by blackmail after the death of his ex-lover. When the blackmailers, who are responsible for his lover's suicide, are caught, Bogarde decides to prosecute them himself, even though it means revealing his hidden past. One of the first films to deal straightforwardly with homosexuality. Fine performances. **100m/B VHS, DVD.** *GB* Dirk Bogarde, Sylvia Syms, Dennis Price, Peter McEnery, Nigel Stock, Donald Churchill, Anthony Nicholls, Hilton Edwards, Norman Bird, Derren Nesbitt, Alan MacNaughton, Noel Howlett, Charles Lloyd-Pack, John Barrie, John Bennett; ***D:*** Basil Dearden; ***W:*** John McCormick, Janet Green; ***C:*** Otto Heller; ***M:*** Philip Green.

Victim of Beauty **1991** A small-town girl comes to the big city and becomes a successful model. However, she then becomes the victim of a fatal attraction killer as all her would-be suitors get killed off one by one. **90m/C VHS, DVD.** Jennifer Rubin, Sally Kellerman, Stephen Shellen, Peter Outerbridge; ***Cameos:*** Michael Ironside; ***D:*** Paul Lynch. **CABLE**

Victim of Desire ½ **1994 (R)** Mysterious death of an embezzler is investigated, only the investigator falls for the sexy widow and begins to doubt her innocence. Also available in an unrated version. **85m/C VHS.** Marc Singer, Wings Hauser, Johnny Williams, Jay Richardson, Shannon Tweed, Julie Strain; ***D:*** Jim Wynorski; ***W:*** William Martell; ***C:*** Carlos Gonzalez; ***M:*** Ross Wright.

Victim of Love 1991 **(PG-13)** A therapist doesn't know whom to believe when she finds out she and one of her more neurotic patients are sharing the same boyfriend. Only the patient claims the man murdered his wife to be with his lover. Who will be the next victim? **92m/C VHS, DVD.** Pierce Brosnan, JoBeth Williams, Virginia Madsen, Georgia Brown; ***D:*** Jerry London, James Desmarais; ***C:*** Billy Dickson; ***M:*** Richard Stone. **TV**

Victimless Crimes 1990 **(R)** The seemingly victimless crime of robbing art galleries turns deadly when betrayal and murder enter the picture. **85m/C VHS.** Debra Sandlund, Craig Bierko, Larry Brandenburg, Peggy Dunne, Richard Redlin, Cheryl Lynn Bruce; ***D:*** Peter Hawley.

Victor/Victoria 1982 **(PG)** Victoria (Andrews), an unsuccessful actress in Depression-era Paris, impersonates a man impersonating a woman and becomes a star. Luscious music and sets. Warren as confused showgirl Norma, and Preston as Andrews' gay mentor Toddy are right on target; Garner is charming as gangster King Marchan, who falls for the woman he thinks she is, with Karras amusing as his bodyguard with a secret, Squash. ♫You and Me; The Shady Dame from Seville; Le Jazz Hot; Crazy World; Chicago Illinois; Gay Peree. **133m/C VHS, DVD.** Julie Andrews, James Garner, Robert Preston, Lesley Ann Warren, Alex Karras, John Rhys-Davies, Norman Chancer, Peter Arne; ***D:*** Blake Edwards; ***W:*** Blake Edwards; ***C:*** Dick Bush; ***M:*** Henry Mancini. Oscars '82: Orig. Song Score and/or Adapt.; Cesar '83: Foreign Film; Golden Globes '83: Actress—Mus./Comedy (Andrews); Natl. Bd. of Review '82: Support. Actor (Preston); Writers Guild '82: Adapt. Screenplay.

Victoria & Albert 1/2 2001 In this BBC production, fabulous sets and costumes frame the story of Victoria, the girl who would be Queen, and Albert, the husband she weds by arrangement. This is a romantic tale of two people who are put together through politics but come to depend on and love each other through trust and mutual respect. The story is historically accurate, but little things pertaining to the personal relationship and family life are painted a little too rosy. Literary license aside, this is a great, romantic, period drama that makes historical figures from a distant land accessible and friendly while teaching you a little about potentially dry English history. **200m/C VHS, DVD.** Victoria Hamilton, Jonathan Firth, David Suchet, Diana Rigg, Patrick Malahide, Penelope Wilton, Peter Ustinov, Nigel Hawthorne; ***D:*** John Erman; ***W:*** John Goldsmith; ***C:*** Tony Imi; ***M:*** Alan Parker. **TV**

Victoria Regina 1961 In a succession of vignettes, the life of Queen Victoria is viewed, from her ascension to the throne of England in 1837 through the celebration of her Diamond Jubilee. A presentation from "George Schaefer's Showcase Theatre." **76m/C VHS.** Julie Harris, James Donald, Felix Aylmer, Pamela Brown, Basil Rathbone; ***D:*** George Schaefer. **TV**

The Victors 1/2 1963 Anti-war drama follows Allied soldiers in Europe in the waning days of the war. The men's romantic endeavors with European women are intercut with images of the common brutality and chaos of war. The young ensemble cast, most of whom went on to stardom, do an excellent job, but the material gets a little heavy-handed at times. From the Alexander Baron novel "The Human Kind." **156m/B** George Peppard, George Hamilton, Eli Wallach, Vince Edwards, Jim Mitchum, Peter Fonda, Romy Schneider, Rosanna Schiaffino, Jeanne Moreau, Albert Finney, Elke Sommer, Michael Callan, Mervyn Johns, Melina Mercouri, Vanda Godsell, Patrick Jordan, Alf Kjellin, Albert Lieven, Peter Vaughan, Senta Berger, James Chase, Maurice Ronet; ***D:*** Carl Foreman; ***W:*** Carl Foreman; ***C:*** Christopher Challis; ***M:*** Sol Kaplan.

Victory 1/2 1981 **(PG)** Soccer match between WWII American prisoners of war and a German team is set up so that the players can escape through the sewer tunnels of Paris. Of course they want to finish the game first. Not particularly believable as either a soccer flick (even with Pele and other soccer stars) or a great escape, but watchable. **116m/C VHS, DVD.** Sylvester Stallone, Michael Caine, Max von Sydow, Pele, Carole Laure, Bobby Moore, Daniel Massey; ***D:*** John Huston; ***W:*** Jeff Maguire, Djordje Milicevic; ***C:*** Gerry Fisher; ***M:*** Bill Conti.

The Victory *This Time Forever; Yesterday* 1981 **(PG)** In 1967 Montreal, an American college exchange student falls in love with a French-Canadian co-ed. Can love survive their different cultures? **95m/C VHS.** Vincent Van Patten, Cloris Leachman, Eddie Albert, Claire Pimpare, Nicholas (Nick) Campbell, Jack Wetherall, Jacques Godin, Marthe Mercure; ***D:*** Larry Kent; ***W:*** John Dunning, Bill LaMond; ***C:*** Richard Ciupka; ***M:*** Paule Baillargeon.

Victory 1/2 1995 **(R)** In 1913, Axel Heyst (Dafoe) is living on a remote island in the Dutch East Indies. He makes a trip to the port town of Surabaya and becomes enamored of Alma (Jacob), a violinist who plays in the hotel's orchestra. Alma is being coerced by hotel owner Schomberg (Yanne) into becoming his mistress and Axel decides to take her with him back to his island. Schomberg then sends a couple of thieves (Neill, Sewell) after them by falsely saying that Axel has amassed a fortune. No happy endings; based on the novel by Joseph Conrad. **99m/C VHS, DVD.** Willem Dafoe, Irene Jacob, Sam Neill, Rufus Sewell, Jean Yanne, Simon Callow; ***D:*** Mark Peploe; ***W:*** Mark Peploe; ***C:*** Bruno de Keyzer; ***M:*** Richard Hartley.

Victory at Entebbe 1/2 1976 An all-star cast in a made-for-TV movie that aired within five months of the actual July 4, 1976, incident in which the PLO hijacked an Air France flight with a number of Israeli and Jewish passengers aboard. Israeli leaders Yitzhak Rabin and Shimon Perez go into action to put a military rescue team together while the plane sits on the tarmac at the Entebbe airport in Uganda, which is under the control of bombastic dictator Idi Amin. **119m/C VHS.** Helmut Berger, Theodore Bikel, Linda Blair, Kirk Douglas, Richard Dreyfuss, Stefan Gierasch, David Groh, Julius W. Harris, Helen Hayes, Anthony Hopkins, Burt Lancaster, Christian Marquand, Elizabeth Taylor, Jessica Walter, Harris Yulin; ***D:*** Marvin J. Chomsky; ***W:*** Ernest Kinoy; ***C:*** Jim Kilgore; ***M:*** Charles Fox. **TV**

The Video Dead WOOF! 1987 **(R)** Gore-farce in which murderous zombies emerge from a possessed TV and wreak havoc. **90m/C VHS.** Roxanna Augesen, Rocky Duvall, Michael St. Michaels; ***D:*** Robert Scott.

Video Murders 1987 A police detective tracks down a rapist/murderer who tapes all his own crimes. **90m/C VHS.** Eric Brown, Virginia Loridans, John Ferita; ***D:*** Jim McCullough Sr.; ***W:*** Jim McCullough Jr.; ***C:*** Joseph M. Wilcots; ***M:*** Robert Sprayberry.

Video Violence 1987 A gory spoof about a video store owner who discovers that his customers have grown bored with the usual Hollywood horror movies and decide to shoot some flicks of their own. **90m/C VHS, DVD.** Art Neill, Jackie Neill, William Toddie, Bart Sumner; ***D:*** Gary P. Cohen.

Video Violence Part 2... The Exploitation! 1987 Two sickos named Howard and Eli run a cable TV network where talk show guests are spindled and mutilated. **90m/C VHS, DVD.** Uke, Bart Sumner, Lee Miller; ***D:*** Gary P. Cohen.

Video Voyeur: The Susan Wilson Story 1/2 2002 Based on the true story of Lousiana wife and mother Susan Wilson. Susan (Harmon), husband Gary (Midkiff), and their kids move into her dream house. Next-door neighbor Steve Glover (Sheridan) is an old friend but Susan becomes concerned about his overly helpful nature. Then she discovers that Steve installed video surveillance equipment prior to the Wilson's moving in and has been spying on them every since. This prompts Wilson to lobby for a state law (which passed in 1999) making video voyeurism a felony. **91m/C VHS, DVD.** Angie Harmon, Jamey Sheridan, Dale Midkiff, Tegan Moss, Garry Chalk, Teryl Rothery; ***D:*** Tim Hunter; ***W:*** Kathleen Rowell; ***C:*** Peter Woeste; ***M:*** Daniel Licht. **VIDEO**

Video Wars WOOF! 1984 Video games explode randomly. A wicked computer whiz is behind it all in a blackmail scheme. **90m/C VHS.** George Diamond.

Videodrome 1983 Woods is a cable TV programmer with a secret yen for sex and violence, which he satisfies by watching a pirated TV show. "Videodrome" appears to show actual torture and murder, and also seems to control the thoughts of its viewers—turning them into human VCRs. Cronenberg's usual sick fantasies are definitely love 'em or leave 'em. Special effects by Rick Baker. **87m/C VHS, DVD.** *CA* James Woods, Deborah Harry, Sonja Smits, Peter Dvorsky; ***D:*** David Cronenberg; ***W:*** David Cronenberg; ***C:*** Mark Irwin; ***M:*** Howard Shore. Genie '84: Director (Cronenberg).

Vietnam, Texas 1990 **(R)** Vietnam vet leaves his past to become a priest. But he returns to violence when he discovers his Vietnamese daughter is in the hands of Houston's most relentless gangster. **101m/C VHS.** Robert Ginty, Haing S. Ngor, Tamlyn Tomita, Tim Thomerson; ***D:*** Robert Ginty; ***W:*** C. Courtney Joyner, Tom Badal.

View from the Top 2003 **(PG-13)** Does for "stewardess-in-training" films what "Feds" did for the buddy-cop genre. Don't remember that one? Exactly. The problem isn't that it's a bad film, it's that it doesn't know what kind of a bad film to be (romance, comedy, or fish-out-of water success story). Paltrow is small-town girl Donna, who aspires to a more worldly life (as a stewardess). After leaving for the big blue, Donna falls in love with Ted (Ruffalo) then loses him. She finds him again only to lose him for a shot at the big time. Other tedious stew school hijinks are involved. "Showgirls" showed more depth and logic. Only Mike Myers's lampooning saves it from being completely dreadful. **87m/C VHS, DVD.** *US* Gwyneth Paltrow, Christina Applegate, Mark Ruffalo, Candice Bergen, Kelly Preston, Rob Lowe, Joshua Malina, Mike Myers; ***D:*** Bruno Barreto; ***W:*** Eric Wald; ***C:*** Alfonso Beato; ***M:*** Theodore Shapiro.

A View to a Kill 1985 **(PG)** This James Bond mission takes him to the United States, where he must stop the evil Max Zorin from destroying California's Silicon Valley. Feeble and unexciting plot with unscary villain. Duran Duran performs the catchy title tune. Moore's last appearance as 007. **131m/C VHS, DVD.** *GB* Roger Moore, Christopher Walken, Tanya Roberts, Grace Jones, Patrick Macnee, Lois Maxwell, Dolph Lundgren, Desmond Llewelyn, Robert Brown; ***D:*** John Glen; ***W:*** Michael G. Wilson; ***C:*** Alan Hume; ***M:*** John Barry.

Vigil 1984 A stark, dreamy parable about a young girl, living on a primitive farm in a remote New Zealand valley, who watches her family collapse after a stranger enters their territory. Visually ravishing and grim; Ward's first American import. Predecessor to "The Navigator." **90m/C VHS.** *NZ* Penelope Stewart, Bill Kerr, Fiona Kay, Gordon Shields, Frank Whitten; ***D:*** Vincent Ward; ***W:*** Vincent Ward.

Vigilante WOOF! *Street Gang* 1983 **(R)** Frustrated ex-cop, tired of seeing criminals returned to the street, joins a vigilante squad dedicated to law and order. Often ridiculous and heavy handed. **91m/C VHS, DVD.** Robert Forster, Fred Williamson, Carol Lynley, Rutanya Alda, Richard Bright, Woody Strode, Donald Blakely, Joseph Carberry, Joe Spinell, Frank Pesce; ***D:*** William Lustig; ***W:*** Richard Vetere; ***C:*** James (Momel) Lemmo; ***M:*** Jay Chattaway.

The Vigilantes Are Coming 1936 "The Eagle" sets out to avenge his family and upsets a would-be dictator's plot to establish an empire in California. In 12 chapters; the first is 32 minutes, and additional chapters are 18 minutes each. **230m/B VHS, DVD.** Robert "Bob" Livingston, Kay Hughes, Guinn "Big Boy" Williams, Raymond Hatton, William Farnum; ***D:*** Mack V. Wright, Ray Taylor.

Vigilantes of Boom Town 1/2 1946 A championship prize fight is the cover for a bank robbery which must be foiled by Red Ryder. **54m/B VHS, DVD.** Allan "Rocky" Lane, Robert (Bobby) Blake, Peggy Stewart, Martha Wentworth, Roscoe Karns, Roy Barcroft, George Turner, John Dehner; ***D:*** R.G. Springsteen; ***Nar:*** Leroy Mason.

The Viking 1928 Viking Leif Ericsson (Crisp) sails off in search of new lands after disagreeing with his father Eric the Red (Randolf). Leif must also compete with his friend Egil (Woods) and English slave Alwin (Mason) for the affections of Nordic beauty Helga (Starke). Filmed in two-strip Technicolor. **90m/C DVD.** Donald Crisp, Anders Randolf, Pauline Starke, Harry Woods, Leroy Mason; ***D:*** Roy William Neill; ***W:*** Jack Cunningham; ***C:*** George Cave.

The Viking Queen 1967 Babe and swordplay saga. After her father dies, Salina (Carita) becomes queen and must protect her British tribe from the Roman occupation. But after tribal rebels attack the Centurions, Roman commander Justinian (Murray) refuses her father a proper burial, even though he and Salina are getting romantic. Then Salina falls into the hands of the evil Octavian (Keir) and he begins a war against the tribes while Justinian is away. When Salina escapes, she joins the fighting. **91m/C VHS, DVD.** *GB* Carita, Don Murray, Andrew Keir, Donald Houston, Adrienne Corri, Niall MacGinnis, Nicola Pagett, Patrick Troughton; ***D:*** Don Chaffey; ***W:*** Clarke Reynolds; ***C:*** Stephen Dade; ***M:*** Gary Hughes.

The Viking Sagas 1995 **(R)** Kjartan (Moeller) is the warrior who must avenge his father's execution, defend his people, and fight for his country's survival against evil oppressors. At least there's a beautiful babe around to offer him some comfort. The Icelandic scenery is the best thing about the movie. **83m/C VHS, DVD.** Ralph (Ralf) Moeller, Ingibjorg Stefansdottir, Sven-Ole Thorsen; ***D:*** Michael Chapman; ***W:*** Dale Herd, Paul R. Gurian; ***M:*** George S. Clinton.

The Vikings 1/2 1958 A Viking king and his son kidnap a Welsh princess and hold her for ransom. Depicts the Vikings' invasion of England. Great location footage of both Norway and Brittany. Basic costume epic with good action scenes. Narrated by Welles. **116m/C VHS, DVD.** Kirk Douglas, Ernest Borgnine, Janet Leigh, Tony Curtis, James Donald, Alexander Knox; ***D:*** Richard Fleischer; ***W:*** Calder Willingham; ***C:*** Jack Cardiff; ***M:*** Mario Nascimbene, Gerard Schumann; ***Nar:*** Orson Welles.

Vile 21 1/2 1999 Let's see, a drug developed by Dr. Walter Hall on government orders turns an unsuspecting derelict into a part man/part reptile/part alien monster (the title character) that goes on a rampage. And now Hall must come up with a way to destroy the creature. **80m/C VHS.** Daniel Skinner, Ronnie Sortor, Steve Kelly, Byron Blakey, Brian Southwick, Tammi Strain; ***D:*** Mike Strain Jr.; ***W:*** Mike Strain Jr. **VIDEO**

Villa Rides 1968 A flying gun-runner aids Francisco "Pancho" Villa's revolutionary Mexican campaign. Considering the talent involved, this one is a disappointment. Check out Brynner's hair. **125m/C VHS, DVD.** Yul Brynner, Robert Mitchum, Charles Bronson, Herbert Lom, Jill Ireland, Robert Towne, Robert Viharo, Frank Wolff, Fernando Rey, Alexander Knox, Diana Lorys; ***D:*** Buzz Kulik; ***W:*** Robert Towne, Sam Peckinpah; ***C:*** Jack Hildyard; ***M:*** Maurice Jarre.

The Village 2004 **(PG-13)** So is Shyamalan a one-trick director or are we just anticipating a trick in every film he directs? This solemn supernatural thriller is set in a 19th Century village whose insular, fearful inhabitants have formed an uneasy, unspoken truce with the monsters that live in the woods that surround it. The village elders forbid anyone to go beyond the perimeter but Lucius (Phoenix) becomes determined to defy them. Lucius is in love with blind Ivy (Howard), who is also loved by the village idiot Noah (Brody in an unfortunate role). Except that it's Ivy who finally enters the woods and is soon hearing scary noises coming in her direction. The payoff doesn't measure up to the portentousness. Maybe it's time Shyamalan does a comedy. **120m/C DVD.** *US* Joaquin Rafael (Leaf) Phoenix, William Hurt, Sigourney Weaver, Adrien Brody, Bryce Dallas Howard, Judy Greer, Jayne Atkinson, Frank Collison, Brendan Gleeson, Cherry Jones, Liz Stauber, Celia Weston, Michael Pitt, John Christopher Jones, Fran Kranz; ***D:*** M. Night Shyamalan; ***W:*** M. Night Shyamalan; ***C:*** Roger Deakins; ***M:*** James Newton Howard.

A Village Affair 1/2 1995 Ward is a young wife and mother, living what appears to be a perfect life in a quiet English village, when she meets a neighbor's daughter (Fox) who's just returned from America. Fox makes her interests clear and soon the two women are having an affair that shatters the peacefulness around them. Based on a novel by Joanna Trollope. **108m/C VHS.** *GB* Sophie Ward, Kerry Fox, Nathaniel Parker, Claire Bloom, Michael Gough, Barbara Jefford, Jeremy Northam, Rosalie Crutchley; ***D:*** Moira Armstrong; ***W:*** Alma Cullen; ***C:*** John Else. **TV**

The Village Barbershop 2008 **(R)** Gruff Reno widower Arthur Leroldi has just buried his longtime barbershop partner. His greedy landlord wants to break the lease and Arthur is having money trouble. He reluctantly hires cosmetologist Gloria, who can also keep the books straight. Gloria seems tough but she's just found out she's pregnant by the guy who just dumped her and the two lost souls find someone they can lean on. **99m/C DVD.** John Ratzenberger, Shelly Cole, Cindy Pickett, Amos Glick, Josh Hutchinson; ***D:*** Chris Ford; ***W:*** Chris Ford; ***C:*** Cliff Traiman; ***M:*** Michael Tremante.

Village of Dreams 1997 Middle-aged identical twin brothers recall the sweetness of their childhood in a rural Japanese village in 1948. As mischievous eight-year-olds, the duo spend their time playing pranks, spying on their neighbors, and entertaining themselves in the woods and streams. Based on the memoir "The Village of My Paintings" by Seizo Tashima. Japanese with subtitles. **112m/C VHS, DVD.** *JP* Keigo Matsuyama, Shogo Matsuyama; ***D:*** Yoichi Higashi; ***W:*** Takehiro Nakajima, Yoichi Higashi; ***C:*** Yoshio Shimizu.

Village of the Damned 1960 A group of unusual children are born in a small English village. They avoid their fathers and other men, except for the one who is their teacher. He discovers they are the vanguard of an alien invasion and leads the counter-attack. Exciting and bone-chilling low-budget thriller. From the novel, "The Midwich Cuckoos," by John Wyndham. **78m/B VHS, DVD.** *GB* George Sanders, Barbara Shelley, Martin Stephens, Laurence Naismith, Michael Gwynn, John Phillips, Richard Vernon, Jenny Laird, Richard Warner, Thomas Heathcote, Charlotte Mitchell, John Stuart, Bernard Archard; ***D:*** Wolf Rilla; ***W:*** Wolf Rilla, Stirling Silliphant, George Harley; ***C:*** Geoffrey Faithfull; ***M:*** Ronald Goodwin.

Village of the Damned 1/2 1995 **(R)** The quiet town of Midwich, California, has been enveloped by a strange force that seems to have impregnated the local women. The albino children born of this incident have disturbing telepathic powers that they display through their bright orange and red eyes—supposedly precipitating a plot to take control. A pale remake of the 1960 British horror classic, which was based on John Wyndham's novel "The Midwich Cuckoos." Fails to capture the eeriness of it's predecessor and is bogged down with awkward casting, absurd dialogue, and a brood of children with glowing eyes that make them less like a threat and more like Nintendo addicts. **98m/C VHS, DVD.** Christopher Reeve, Kirstie Alley, Linda Kozlowski, Mark Hamill, Meredith Salenger, Michael Pare, Peter Jason, Constance Forslund, Karen Kahn; ***D:*** John Carpenter; ***W:*** John Carpenter, David Himmelstein; ***C:*** Gary B. Kibbe; ***M:*** John Carpenter, Dave Davies.

Village of the Giants 1965 A group of beer-guzzling teenagers become giants after eating a mysterious substance invented by a 12-year-old genius. Fun to pick out all the soon-to-be stars. Totally silly premise with bad special effects and minimal plot follow-through. Based on an H.G. Wells story. **82m/C VHS, DVD.** Ron Howard, Johnny Crawford, Tommy Kirk, Beau Bridges, Freddy Cannon, Toni Basil, Tisha Sterling, Tim Rooney, Charla Doherty, Joe Turkel; ***D:*** Bert I. Gordon; ***W:*** Alan Caillou; ***C:*** Paul Vogel; ***M:*** Jack Nitzsche.

Village Tale 1935 Relentlessly nasty drama about the harm gossip can do. Small town know-nothings gather at the general store to spread lies about their neighbors, leading to suicide and attempted murder. Adapted from the Philip Strong novel. **80m/B VHS.** Randolph Scott, Kay Johnson, Dorothy Burgess, Donald Meek, Andy Clyde, Guinn "Big Boy" Williams, Arthur Hohl, Robert Barrat, Janet Beecher, Edward Ellis; ***D:*** John Cromwell; ***C:*** Nicholas Musuraca.

The Villain 1/2 *Cactus Jack* 1979 **(PG)** An unfunny spoof of "B" westerns that is almost like a live-action "Roadrunner" cartoon. Douglas plays Cactus Jack, a highwayman who keeps trying to kidnap fair damsel Ann-Margret. Hero Schwarzenegger keeps rescuing her. Lynde is amusing as the uptight Indian chief Nervous Elk. **93m/C VHS, DVD.** Kirk Douglas, Ann-Margret, Arnold Schwarzenegger, Paul Lynde, Foster Brooks, Ruth Buzzi, Jack Elam, Strother Martin, Robert Tessier, Mel Tillis; ***D:*** Hal Needham; ***W:*** Robert G. Kane; ***C:*** Bobby Byrne; ***M:*** Bill Justis.

The Villain Still Pursued Her 1941 A poor hero and rich villain vie for the sweet heroine in this satire of old-fashioned temperance melodrama. Keaton manages to shine as the hero's sidekick. **67m/B VHS, DVD.** Anita Louise, Alan Mowbray, Buster Keaton, Hugh Herbert; ***D:*** Edward F. (Eddie) Cline.

Vince Vaughn's Wild West Comedy Show *Wild West Comedy Show* 2006 **(R)** Part comedy concert film, part backstage documentary follows comedy tour mastermind Vaughn and four up-and-coming comics on a tour across the southern U.S. in 2005. Outside of a visit to a camp of people who had just been displaced by Hurricane Katrina, the film doesn't break out of its basic concept, focusing on the backgrounds of comedians Caparule, Ernst, Maniscalco, and Ahmed and their time on the road, which seems to involve very little partying or getting into trouble. The result is a tour movie that's not particularly wild. For stand-up fans. **100m/C DVD.** *US Cameos:* Vince Vaughn, Ahmed Ahmed, John Caparulo, Bret Ernst, Sebastian Mansicalco; ***D:*** Ari Sandel; ***M:*** John O'Brien.

Vincent & Theo 1/2 1990 **(PG-13)** The story of Impressionist painter Vincent van Gogh (Roth), and his brother Theo (Rhys), a gallery owner who loved his brother's work, yet could not get the public to buy it. Increasing despair and mental illness traps both men, as each struggles to create beauty in a world where it has no value. Altman has created a stunning portrait of "the artist" and his needs. The exquisite cinematography will make you feel as if you stepped into van Gogh's work. **138m/C VHS, DVD.** Tim Roth, Paul Rhys, Johanna Ter Steege, Wladimir Yordanoff; ***D:*** Robert Altman; ***W:*** Julian Mitchell; ***C:*** Jean Lepine.

Vincent, Francois, Paul and the Others *Vincent, Francois, Paul et les Autres* 1976 Three middle-aged Frenchmen rely on their friendships to endure a host of mid-life crises. In French with English subtitles. **113m/C VHS.** *FR* Yves Montand, Gerard Depardieu, Michel Piccoli, Stephane Audran, Serge Reggiani, Marie DuBois; ***D:*** Claude Sautet; ***W:*** Claude Sautet, Jean-Loup Dabadie, Claude Neron; ***C:*** Jean Boffety; ***M:*** Philippe Sarde.

Vincent: The Life and Death of Vincent van Gogh 1987 Van Gogh's work and creativity is examined in a documentary manner through his life and his letters. Thoughtful and intriguing production. Narrated by John Hurt as van Gogh. **99m/C VHS, DVD.** *AU* ***D:*** Paul Cox; ***W:*** Paul Cox; ***M:*** Norman Kaye; ***V:*** John Hurt.

The Vindicator *Frankenstein '88* 1985 **(R)** A scientist killed in a lab accident is transformed into a cyborg who runs amok and murders indiscriminately. A modernized Frankenstein, with interesting special effects and well drawn characters. **92m/C VHS.** *CA* Terri Austin, Richard Cox, David McIlwraith, Pam Grier; ***D:*** Jean-Claude Lord.

The Vineyard 1989 **(R)** Hapless victims are lured to a Japanese madman's island, where he drinks their blood and maintains a questionable immortality. **95m/C VHS, DVD.** James Hong, Karen Witter, Michael Wong; ***D:*** James Hong, Bill Rice.

Vintage Model *Modelo Antiguo* 1992 Carmen hosts a radio program giving romantic advice, though she's lonely and lives on her memories of the past. When she learns she only has a short time to live, Carmen hires a chauffeur to drive her around Mexico City so she can remember. Spanish with subtitles. **97m/C VHS, DVD.** *MX* Silvia Pinal, Alonso Echanove; ***D:*** Raul Araiza; ***W:*** Consuelo Garrido, Alejandro Pelayo; ***C:*** Rosalio Solano; ***M:*** Osni Cassab.

Violated 1953 Pathetic production about New York police attempting to track down a sex-maniac murderer who slays his victims and then gives them a haircut. Unbelievably bad. **78m/B VHS.** Ian Roberts, Lili Dawn, Mitchell Kowal, Vicki Carlson, William Martell; ***D:*** Walter Strate.

Violated **WOOF!** 1984 A detective endeavors to implicate a local businessman in the rapes of two beautiful women. Exploitative and dreary. **88m/C VHS.** John Heard, J.C. Quinn, April Daisy White, Samantha Fox; ***D:*** Richard Cannistraro.

Violence 1/2 1947 Magazine writer Ann (Coleman) goes undercover to shed light on a scam outfit, the United Defenders—a public service organization that's actually a racket. While hunting down the bad guys, she suffers a bout of amnesia which threatens to blow her cover. **72m/B DVD.** Nancy Coleman, Michael O'Shea, Sheldon Leonard; ***D:*** Jack Bernhard; ***W:*** Lewis Lantz, Stanley Rubin.

Violence at Noon 1966 Highly disturbing film in which two women protect a brutal sex murderer from the law. Living among a quiet community of intellectuals, this conspiracy ends in a shocking finale in Oshima's stylized masterpiece. In Japanese with English subtitles. **99m/B VHS.** *JP* Saeda Kawaguchi, Akiko Koyama; ***D:*** Nagisa Oshima.

Violent Breed 1983 A CIA operative is sent on a mission to put a black marketeer out of business. **91m/C VHS.** *IT* Henry Silva, Harrison Muller, Woody Strode; ***D:*** Fernando Di Leo.

Violent Cop *Sono Otoko, Kyobo ni Tsuki* 1989 Think "Dirty Harry" to the nth power and you'll have some idea of the kind of cop Detective Azuma (Kitano) is. However, he also gets results, so the boss is willing to overlook the violent way Azuma does his job. His latest case involves a drug-related murder, a sadistic killer, a corrupt friend, and the kidnapping of Azuma's own mentally unstable sister. Not for the squeamish. Japanese with subtitles. **103m/C VHS, DVD.** *JP* Takeshi "Beat" Kitano, Shiro Sano, Maiko Kawakami, Makoto Ashikawa, Shigeru Hiraizumi, Mikiko Otonashi; ***D:*** Takeshi "Beat" Kitano; ***W:*** Hisahi Nozawa; ***C:*** Yasushi Sasakibara; ***M:*** Daisaku Kume.

The Violent Men 1/2 *Rough Company* 1955 Big-time land baron Robinson is trying to push out all other landowners in the valley, including Ford. At first Ford refuses to fight back, but after one of Robinson's henchmen kills one of his hired hands, he starts an all-out war against Robinson to save his land. Stanwyck as Robinson's wife and Keith as his brother are wicked as the two urging him on and having an affair behind his back. Based on the novel "Rough Company" by Donald Hamilton. **95m/C VHS, DVD.** Glenn Ford, Barbara Stanwyck, Edward G. Robinson, Dianne Foster, Brian Keith, May Wynn; ***D:*** Rudolph Mate; ***C:*** Burnett Guffey.

Violent Ones **WOOF!** 1968 Three men who are suspected of raping a young girl are threatened with lynching by an angry mob of townspeople. Badly acted, poorly directed, uneven and feeble. **96m/C VHS.** Fernando Lamas, David Carradine; ***D:*** Fernando Lamas.

Violent Professionals 1/2 *La Polizia vuole Giustizia* 1973 Suspended cop runs into resistance inside and outside the force when he infiltrates the mob to get the goods on a crime boss. **100m/C VHS, DVD.** *IT* Richard Conte, Luc Merenda; ***D:*** Sergio Martino.

Violent Women 1959 Five female convicts escape and embark on a bloody journey through the countryside, pursued by the authorities. Shows women can be just as brutal as any man. **61m/C VHS.** Jennifer Slater, Jo Ann Kelly, Sandy Lyn, Eleanor Blair, Pati Magee; ***D:*** Barry Mahon.

The Violent Years **WOOF!** *Female* 1956 Spoiled high-school debutantes form a vicious all-girl gang and embark on a spree that includes murder, robbery, and male rape. Justice wins out in the end. Exploitive trash written by Wood, who directed the infamous "Plan 9 from Outer Space." **60m/B VHS, DVD.** Jean Moorehead, Barbara Weeks, Glenn Corbett, Theresa Hancock, I. Stanford Jolley, Arthur Millan; ***D:*** Edward D. Wood Jr., Franz Eichhorn, William M. Morgan; ***W:*** Edward D. Wood Jr.; ***C:*** William C. Thompson.

Violent Zone 1989 Mercenaries go on a supposed rescue mission in the wilderness. **92m/C VHS, DVD.** John Douglas, Chard Hayward, Christopher Weeks; ***D:*** John Garwood; ***W:*** David Pritchard, John Bushelman.

Violets Are Blue 1/2 1986 **(PG-13)** Two high-school sweethearts are reunited in their hometown years later and try to rekindle their romance—even though the man is married. **86m/C VHS.** Kevin Kline, Sissy Spacek, Bonnie Bedelia, John Kellogg, Augusta Dabney, Jim Standford; ***D:*** Jack Fisk; ***W:*** Naomi Foner; ***C:*** Ralf Bode; ***M:*** Patrick Williams.

Violette *Violette Noziere* 1978 **(R)** Fascinating true-life account of a 19-year-old French girl in the 1930s who, bored with her life and wanting to be with her lover, decides to poison her parents so she can receive her inheritance. Her mother survives but her father dies, and the girl is sent to prison for murder. Extraordinary performance by Huppert and the film is visually stunning. **122m/C VHS, DVD.** *FR* Isabelle Huppert, Stephane Audran, Jean Carmet, Jean-Francoise Garreaud, Bernadette LaFont; ***D:*** Claude Chabrol; ***W:*** Odile Barski, Frederic Grendel; ***C:*** Jean Rabier; ***M:*** Pierre Jansen. Cannes '78: Actress (Huppert); Cesar '79: Support. Actress (Audran).

VIP, My Brother Superman 1990 The Vips are modern-day descendants of super-beings about to become legends in their own times. SuperVip is broad of chest and pure in spirit while his brother MiniVip possesses only limited powers. From the creator of "Allegro Non Troppo" comes this enticing, amusing piece of animation. **90m/C VHS.** *IT* ***D:*** Bruno Bozzetto; ***W:*** Bruno Bozzetto; ***C:*** Luciano Marzetti; ***M:*** Franco Godi.

Viper 1988 A woman battles a cryptic anti-terrorist band to avenge the murder of her husband. **96m/C VHS.** Linda Purl, Chris Robinson, James Tolkan; ***D:*** Peter Maris.

Vipers 2008 **(R)** Genetically-enhanced snakes escape during a break-in at a research lab. Since they reproduce at an alarming rate, they're soon devouring all the locals, who happen to be stuck on an isolated island. Lots of bad acting and shoddy CGI effects. **89m/C DVD.** Tara Reid, Jonathan Scarfe, Corbin Bernsen, Don S. Davis, Jessica Steen, Mark Humphrey, Genevieve Buechner; ***D:*** Bill Cocoran; ***W:*** Brian Katkin; ***C:*** Thomas Burstyn; ***M:*** Lawrence Shragge. **VIDEO**

The V.I.P.'s 1963 Slick, sophisticated drama set in the V.I.P. lounge of a British airport. Trapped by fog, several of the passengers get acquainted and are forced to face their problems as they spend the night in the airport lounge. Taylor stars as Frances Andros, a wealthy young woman leaving her husband (Burton) for life in the U.S. with her lover, Jourdan. A movie tycoon, an Australian entrepreneur, his secretary, and a duchess are among the other passengers grounded by the fog. Both Rutherford and Smith give excellent performances and it was a tossup as to which actress would be nominated for the Oscar. **119m/C VHS, DVD.** *GB* Elizabeth Taylor, Richard Burton, Louis Jourdan, Elsa Martinelli, Margaret Rutherford, Maggie Smith, Rod Taylor, Orson Welles, Linda Christian, Dennis Price; ***D:*** Anthony Asquith; ***W:*** Terence Rattigan; ***C:*** Jack Hildyard; ***M:*** Miklos Rozsa. Oscars '63: Support. Actress (Rutherford); Golden Globes '64: Support. Actress (Rutherford); Natl. Bd. of Review '63: Support. Actress (Rutherford).

Virgil Bliss 2001 Virgil (Jordan) is a mild-mannered career thief from Mississippi who's been paroled to a Brooklyn halfway house after 12 years in the joint. So what's the first thing he does? Well, he listens to his new roomie Manny (Gorman) who maybe wants Virgil to do another job and who introduces him to tough hooker/junkie Ruby (Russell). Naturally, Virgil falls for her and there's more trouble a-coming. **94m/C VHS, DVD.** Clint Jordan, Kirsten Russell, Anthony Gorman; ***D:*** Joe Maggio; ***W:*** Joe Maggio; ***C:*** Harlan Bosmajian.

Virgin 2003 **(R)** Fundamentalist's rebellious daughter becomes pregnant after being drugged and date-raped. Not remembering the assault, she declares herself Virgin Mother to the Second Coming, and is not surprisingly attacked by her family and community. Odd feminist parable seems unsure whether to take itself seriously or not. Intense and unforgettable central performance by Moss does little to rid film of its contrived weirdness. **114m/C DVD.** Robin Wright Penn, Elisabeth (Elissabeth, Elizabeth, Liz) Moss, Daphne Rubin-Vega, Dr. Charles Socarides, Socorro Santiago, Peter Gerety, Stephanie Gatchet; ***D:*** Deborah Kampmeier; ***W:*** Deborah Kampmeier; ***C:*** Ben Wolf.

Virgin among the Living Dead 𝒻 **1971 (R)** Young woman travels to remote castle when she hears of relative's death. Once there, she finds the residents a tad weird and has bad dreams in which zombies chase her. Bizarre even for Franco, who seems to have been going through a "Pasolini" phase while making this one. **90m/C VHS, DVD.** *SP* Christina von Blanc, Britt Nichols, Howard Vernon, Anne Libert, Rose Kiekens, Paul Muller; ***D:*** Jess (Jesus) Franco.

The Virgin and the Gypsy 𝒻𝒻 ½ **1970 (R)** An English girl brought up in a repressive household in 1920s England falls in love with a gypsy. Based on the novel by D.H. Lawrence. Directorial debut of Miles. **92m/C VHS, DVD.** *GB* Joanna Shimkus, Franco Nero, Honor Blackman, Mark Burns; ***D:*** Christopher Miles; ***W:*** Alan Plater.

Virgin High 𝒻 **1990 (R)** Three young men sneak into an all-girls Catholic boarding school with hilarious consequences. Ward (TV's Robin, from "Batman") makes a special appearance in bondage in this sex farce. **90m/C VHS.** Burt Ward, Linnea Quigley, Tracy Dali, Richard Gabai, Catherine McGuiness, Chris Dempsey; ***D:*** Richard Gabai; ***W:*** Richard Gabai, Jeff Neal.

Virgin Machine 𝒻𝒻 *Jungfrauenmaschine* **1988** Lesbian journalist Dorothy Muller (Blum) is unhappy in her native Hamburg and decides to move to California to pursue her idea of romantic love. English and German with English subtitles. **91m/B VHS, DVD.** *GE* Ina Blum, Susie Bright, Shelley Mars, Dominique Gaspar; ***D:*** Monika Treut; ***W:*** Monika Treut; ***C:*** Elfi Mikesch.

The Virgin of Nuremberg 𝒻 ½ *Horror Castle; Terror Castle; Castle of Terror; La Vergine de Norimberga* **1965** A young woman enters her new husband's ancestral castle and is stalked by the specter of a legendary sadist. **82m/C VHS, DVD.** *IT* Rossana Podesta, George Riviere, Christopher Lee, Jim Dolen; ***D:*** Anthony M. Dawson.

The Virgin Queen 𝒻𝒻𝒻 **1955** Davis stars in this historical drama, which focuses on the stormy relationship between the aging Queen and Sir Walter Raleigh. Collins is the lady-in-waiting who is the secret object of Raleigh's true affections. Previously, Davis played Queen Elizabeth I in "Elizabeth and Essex." Davis holds things together. **92m/C VHS.** Bette Davis, Richard Todd, Joan Collins, Herbert Marshall, Dan O'Herlihy, Jay Robinson, Romney Brent; ***D:*** Henry Koster.

Virgin Queen of St. Francis High 𝒻 **1988 (PG)** Two high school foes make a bet that one of them can take the "virgin" title away from gorgeous Christensen by summer's end. She has to fight off their advances, but grows to like Straface. **89m/C VHS.** *CA* Joseph R. Straface, Stacy Christensen, J.T. Wotton; ***D:*** Francesco Lucente.

Virgin Sacrifice 𝒻 **1959** A great white hunter looking for zoo-bound jaguars confronts the virgin-sacrificing, Tiger God-revering natives of Guatemala. **67m/C VHS, DVD.** David DaLie, Antonio Gutierrez, Angelica Morales, Fernando Wagner; ***D:*** Fernando Wagner.

The Virgin Soldiers 𝒻𝒻 ½ **1969 (R)** A British comedy about greenhorn military recruits stationed in Singapore, interested in women as well as battle, and their struggles to overcome both situations. A good cast raises this above the usual low-brow sex farce. Based on the novel by Leslie Thomas. Followed by "Stand Up Virgin Soldiers." **96m/C VHS.** *GB* Hywel Bennett, Nigel Davenport, Lynn Redgrave, Nigel Patrick, Rachel Kempson, Jack Shepherd, Tsai Chin; ***D:*** John Dexter; ***W:*** John Hopkins.

The Virgin Spring 𝒻𝒻𝒻 ½ *Jungfrukallan* **1959** Based on a medieval ballad and set in 14th-century Sweden. The rape and murder of young innocent Karin (Pattersson) spurs her father Tore (Van Sydow) to vengeance and he kills her attackers. Over the girl's dead body, the father questions how God could have let any of it happen, but he comes to find solace and forgiveness when a spring bursts forth from the spot. Stunning Bergman compositions. In Swedish with English subtitles; also available in dubbed version. **88m/B VHS, DVD.** *SW* Max von Sydow, Birgitta Valberg, Gunnel Lindblom, Brigitta Pattersson, Axel Duborg; ***D:*** Ingmar Bergman; ***W:*** Ulla Isaakson; ***C:*** Sven Nykvist; ***M:*** Erik Nordgren. Oscars '60: Foreign Film; Golden Globes '61: Foreign Film.

The Virgin Suicides 𝒻𝒻 **1999 (R)** The five teenaged Lisbon sisters are all blonde, lovely, and isolated in their 70s suburban life. Mom (Turner) is a rigid, religious harridan while Dad (Woods) is a wimpy math teacher. After 13-year-old Cecilia (Hall) tries to off herself, her parents are encouraged to let the girls socialize and the story becomes the recollections of the narrator (Ribisi), one of the boys fascinated by the quintet. Much of the movie focuses on sexually provocative Lux (Dunst) and her hunky would-be beau, Trip (Hartnett). There's a floaty, listlessly romantic air to the whole production (Coppola's directorial debut), which is based on the novel by Jeffrey Eugenides. **97m/C VHS, DVD.** Kirsten Dunst, Kathleen Turner, James Woods, Josh Hartnett, Hanna Hall, Chelse Swain, A.J. Cook, Leslie Hayman, Danny DeVito, Scott Glenn, Jonathan Tucker, Anthony DeSimone; ***D:*** Sofia Coppola; ***W:*** Sofia Coppola; ***C:*** Edward Lachman; ***Nar:*** Giovanni Ribisi.

Virgin Territory 𝒻 ½ **2007 (R)** If you're expecting a version of "Casanova," this isn't it. Instead, it's a dull rather than swaggering would-be romp with a couple of weak leads. In 14th-century Florence, penniless rogue Lorenzo (Christensen) is known for deflowering the local lovelies. His next likely conquest is Pampinea (Barton), who's also being pursued by a Russian count (Rhys) and an obsessed Italian nobleman (Roth), but of course the two youngsters actually love each other. **97m/C DVD.** Hayden Christensen, Mischa Barton, Matthew Rhys, Tim Roth, Christopher Ega; ***D:*** David Leland; ***W:*** David Leland; ***C:*** Benjamin Davis; ***M:*** Ilan Eshkeri.

The Virgin Witch 𝒻 ½ *Lesbian Twins* **1970 (R)** Two beautiful sisters are sent to the British countryside, ostensibly for a modeling job. They soon find themselves in the midst of a witches' coven however, and discover one of them is to be sacrificed. The Michelles were "Playboy" magazine's first sister centerfolds. **89m/C VHS, DVD.** *GB* Anne Michelle, Vicki Michelle, Patricia Haines, Keith Buckley, James Chase, Neil Hallett; ***D:*** Ray Austin.

Virginia City 𝒻𝒻𝒻 **1940** Action-packed western drama set during the Civil War. Flynn is a Union soldier who escapes from a Confederate prison run by Scott, after learning of a gold shipment being sent by Southern sympathizers to aid the Confederacy. He ends up in Virginia City (where the gold-laden wagon train is to leave from) and falls for a dance-hall girl (Hopkins) who turns out to be a Southern spy working for Scott but who falls for Flynn anyway. Bogart is miscast as a half-breed outlaw who aids Scott but wants the gold for himself. Considered a follow-up to "Dodge City." **121m/C VHS.** Errol Flynn, Miriam Hopkins, Randolph Scott, Humphrey Bogart, Frank McHugh, Alan Hale, Guinn "Big Boy" Williams, Douglass Dumbrille, Charles Halton; ***D:*** Michael Curtiz; ***M:*** Max Steiner.

The Virginia Hill Story 𝒻𝒻 **1976** Fictionalized biography of mobster Bugsy Siegel's girlfriend who, in the mid-'50s, was subpoenaed to appear before the Kefauver investigation on crime in the U.S. As the examining lawyer presents questions regarding her background and connections with the underworld, we see the story of her life. **90m/C VHS, DVD.** Dyan Cannon, Harvey Keitel, Robby Benson, Allen (Goorwitz) Garfield, John Vernon; ***D:*** Joel Schumacher. **TV**

The Virginian 𝒻𝒻 ½ **1923** The second silent version of Owen Wister's classic western novel, inferior to both the 1914 Cecil B. DeMille silent and the 1929 Victor Fleming talkie. Harlan plays the title role as the cowpoke who leads a posse against cattle rustlers and falls in love with a schoolteacher. **79m/B VHS.** Kenneth Harlan, Florence Vidor, Russell Simpson, Pat O'Malley, Raymond Hatton; ***D:*** Tom Forman.

The Virginian 𝒻𝒻𝒻 **1929** A classic early-talkie western about a ranch-hand defeating the local bad guys. One line of dialogue has become, with modification, a standard western cliche: "If you want to call me that, smile." Based on the novel by Owen Wister. With this starring role, Cooper broke away from the juvenile lovers he had been playing to the laconic, rugged male leads he would be known for. Huston is perfectly cast as the outlaw leader. **95m/B VHS.** Gary Cooper, Walter Huston, Richard Arlen, Chester Conklin, Eugene Pallette; ***D:*** Victor Fleming.

The Virginian 𝒻𝒻 ½ **1946** Cowboy good guy, known as the Virginian (McCrea), and his best pal Steve (Tufts) both fall for Molly (Britton), the Eastern-bred schoolmarm who's come to their Wyoming town. Steve wants to make some quick money and joins up with leader Trampas' (Donlevy) cattle rustling gang. So the Virginian is forced to chose between friendship and the code of the west and Molly wonders if she can accepts the country's harsh ways. Based on Owen Wister's 1902 novel. **87m/C VHS.** Joel McCrea, Sonny Tufts, Barbara Britton, Brian Donlevy, Fay Bainter, Tom Tully, Henry O'Neill, William Frawley; ***D:*** Stuart Gilmore; ***W:*** Frances Goodrich, Albert Hackett; ***C:*** Harry Hallenberger; ***M:*** Daniele Amfitheatrof.

The Virginian 𝒻𝒻 ½ **1999** Yet another remake (this one unremarkable but watchable) of Owen Wister's 1902 novel. Pullman (who also directed) is the cowboy of the title, who is out for a brutal brand of justice against an unscupulous rancher. But his methods upset his schoolmarm sweetie (Lane). **95m/C VHS.** Bill Pullman, Diane Lane, John Savage, Dennis Weaver; ***D:*** Bill Pullman; ***W:*** Larry Gross. **CABLE**

Viridiana 𝒻𝒻𝒻𝒻 **1961** Innocent Viridiana (Pinal), with strong ideas about goodness, visits her worldly uncle, Don Jaime's (Rey), home before she takes her vows as a nun. He has developed a sick obsession for her, but after drugging Viridiana, Don Jaimefinds he cannot violate her purity. He tells her, however, she is no longer chaste so she will not join the church. After her uncle's suicide, Viridiana learns she and his illegitimate son Jorge (Rabal) have inherited her uncle's rundown estate. Viridiana opens the house to all sorts of beggars, who take shameless advantage, while Jorge works slowly to restore the estate and improve the lives of those around him. Considered to be one of Bunuel's masterpieces and a bitter allegory of Spanish idealism versus pragmatism and the state of the world. Spanish with subtitles. **90m/B VHS, DVD.** *SP MX* Silvia Pinal, Francisco Rabal, Fernando Rey, Margarita Lozano, Victoria Zinny; ***D:*** Luis Bunuel; ***W:*** Luis Bunuel, Julio Alajandro; ***C:*** Jose F. Aguayo. Cannes '61: Film.

Virtual Assassin 𝒻𝒻 *Cyberjack* **1995 (R)** 21st century sci-fi actioner finds the crooked Zef (James) leading his band of thugs into a research lab to steal a powerful computer virus. Naturally, the janitor (Dudikoff) just happens to be an ex-cop with a score to settle with Zef. Predictable but with decent special effects. **99m/C VHS, DVD.** *CA JP* Michael Dudikoff, Brion James, Jon Cuthbert, Suki Kaiser, James Thom; ***D:*** Robert Lee; ***W:*** Eric Poppen.

Virtual Combat 𝒻𝒻 **1995 (R)** Ex-cop Quarry (Wilson) teams up with some cybergirls to stop a madman who's able to manipulate virtual reality programs into living beings and releases a killer who wants to lead a destructive virtual army. **97m/C VHS, DVD.** Don "The Dragon" Wilson, Athena Massey, Loren Avedon, Kenneth McLeod, Turhan Bey, Stella Stevens, Michael Bernardo; ***D:*** Andrew Stevens; ***W:*** William Martell; ***C:*** David J. Miller; ***M:*** Claude Gaudette.

Virtual Desire 𝒻 ½ **1995 (R)** Brad Collins is bored with his marriage and finds some excitement via sexual games on the Internet. But someone is taking a very close interest in Brad's virtual amours and when his wife is murdered, Brad becomes the prime suspect. **92m/C VHS, DVD.** Michael Meyer, Julie Strain, Gail Harris; ***D:*** Noble Henri; ***W:*** Pete Slate; ***C:*** Gary Graver; ***M:*** Leo Nichols.

Virtual Encounters 𝒻𝒻 ½ **1996 (R)** Top-drawer soft-core fluff follows busy executive Amy (Elizabeth Kaitan), whose birthday present is a session of virtual wish fulfillment at a high-tech fantasyland. The fantasies involve masks, leather, desks, broccoli...well, O.K., the broccoli is an exaggeration. This is sexy and kinky, not sick. The action is slickly staged and well photographed by director Richards. Also available in an unrated version at 84 minutes. **80m/C VHS, DVD.** Elizabeth Kaitan, Taylore St. Claire, Rob Lee; ***D:*** Cybil (Sybil) Richards; ***C:*** Cybil (Sybil) Richards.

Virtual Girl 𝒻𝒻 **2000 (R)** Computer programmer John Lewis (Dixon) is working on an erotic virutal reality program that features a cyber-slut (Curtis). When said vixen gets rejected by her creator, she gets very, very angry. Erotica that makes the best use of its low-budget and Curtis' assets. **84m/C VHS, DVD.** Richard Gabai, Charlie Curtis, Max Dixon; ***D:*** Richard Gabai. **VIDEO**

Virtual Seduction 𝒻𝒻 **1996 (R)** Liam's (Fahey) taken a job testing a virtual reality pod that can interpret what the user wants—and Liam wants to see his dead girlfriend Paris (Genzel). Only he spends so much time with the virtual Paris, that his real-life gal Laura (Dolenz) is worried about his health and sanity—too bad project developer Grant (Novak) isn't so concerned. **84m/C VHS.** Jeff Fahey, Ami Dolenz, Carrie Genzel, Frank Novak, Meshach Taylor; ***D:*** Paul Ziller.

Virtual Sexuality 𝒻𝒻 **1999 (R)** Teen comedy, set in London, that has an amusing virtual reality plot. Cute 17-year-old Justine (Fraser) decides school stud Alex (O'Brien) is the perfect guy to lose her virginity to. But he's only interested in school vamp, "Hoover" (Bell). So Justine enters a virtual reality makeover machine at a technology fair in order to create an electronic facsimile of her perfect man. But a malfunction causes Justine to split in two—herself (with amnesia) and her perfect man, the bewildered male creation Jake (Penry-Jones). Based on the novel by Chloe Rayban. **92m/C VHS, DVD.** *GB* Laura Fraser, Rupert Penry-Jones, Kieran O'Brien, Luke De Lacey, Natasha Bell, Steve John Shepherd, Laura Macaulay, Marcelle Duprey; ***D:*** Nick Hurran; ***W:*** Nick Fisher; ***C:*** Brian Tufano; ***M:*** Rupert Gregson-Williams.

Virtue's Revolt 𝒻 ½ **1924** A small-town girl is corrupted by the sleazy world of showbiz. Silent. **51m/B VHS.** Florence Lee, Eddie (Edward) Phillips, Betty Morrissey, Charles Cruz, Edith Thornton, Crauford Kent; ***D:*** James Chapin; ***W:*** Frederick Chapin; ***C:*** Ernest Miller.

Virtuosity 𝒻 ½ **1995 (R)** Ex-cop-with-a-tragic-past Parker Barnes (Washington) is sprung from prison to help capture computer-generated killer Sid 6.7 (Crowe), who escapes from cyberspace and goes on a rampage in 1997 Los Angeles. Seems this virtual reality bad guy has a personality composed of some 200 serial killers and criminal minds so Parker's got his work cut out for him. But criminal-behavior psychologist Madison Carter (Lynch) is around to lend her expert advice. Both the charismatically evil Crowe and the sufferingly noble Washington are wasted in this effects-laden thriller that sacrifices character for flash. **105m/C VHS, DVD.** Denzel Washington, Russell Crowe, Kelly Lynch, Stephen Spinella, William Forsythe, Louise Fletcher, William Fichtner, Costas Mandylor, Kevin J. O'Connor; ***D:*** Brett Leonard; ***W:*** Eric Bernt; ***C:*** Gale Tattersall; ***M:*** Christopher Young.

Virus 𝒻𝒻 *Fukkatsu no Hi* **1982 (PG)** After nuclear war and plague destroy civilization, a small group of people gather in Antarctica and struggle with determination to carry on life. A look at man's genius for self-destruction and his endless hope. **102m/C VHS, DVD.** *JP* George Kennedy, Sonny Chiba, Glenn Ford, Robert Vaughn, Stuart Gillard, Stephanie Faulkner, Ken Ogata, Bo Svenson, Olivia Hussey, Chuck Connors, Edward James Olmos; ***D:*** Kinji Fukasaku.

Virus 𝒻 ½ **1996 (PG-13)** Secret Service agent Ken Fairchild (Bosworth) finds out that biological-warfare chemicals have been spilt in a national park that's the site for an ecological summit between the president and world leaders. It's up to Fairchild and a park ranger (Pinsent) to battle the minions of the chemical's manufacturer who wants to keep the whole thing quiet. **90m/C VHS, DVD.** Brian Bosworth, Leah K. Pinsent; ***D:*** Allan Goldstein.

Virus 🦴 1/2 **1998 (R)** Curtis, Sutherland, and Baldwin are members of a tugboat crew whose boat has been wrecked by a typhoon. They take refuge aboard a Russian research ship only to discover the Russian crew has been eliminated by a strange life form. The electricity-based alien considers humanity a virus and begins making bizarre killing machines out of body parts and machinery. The plot also seems pieced together from other sci-fi horror movies that did it better. **100m/C VHS, DVD.** Jamie Lee Curtis, William Baldwin, Donald Sutherland, Joanna Pacula, Sherman Augustus, Clifford Curtis, Marshall Bell, Julio Oscar Mechoso, Yuri Chervotkin, Keith Flippen; ***D:*** John Bruno; ***W:*** Chuck Pfarrer, Dennis Feldman; ***C:*** David Eggby; ***M:*** Joel McNeely.

The Vision 🦴🦴 **1987** Suspenseful British production about televangelists who attempt to control their viewers' minds through worldwide satellite broadcasting. **103m/C VHS.** *GB* Lee Remick, Dirk Bogarde, Helena Bonham Carter, Eileen Atkins; ***D:*** Norman Stone.

Vision Quest 🦴🦴 1/2 *Crazy for You* **1985 (R)** A high school student wants to win the Washington State wrestling championship and the affections of a beautiful older artist. He gives it his all as he trains for the meet and goes after his "visionquest." A winning performance by Modine raises this above the usual teen coming-of-age movie. Madonna sings "Crazy for You" in a nightclub. Based on novel by Terry Davis. **107m/C VHS, DVD.** Matthew Modine, Linda Fiorentino, Ronny Cox, Roberts Blossom, Daphne Zuniga, Charles Hallahan, Michael Schoeffling, Forest Whitaker, Gary Kasper, James Gammon, Harold Sylvester, Raphael Sbarge; ***D:*** Harold Becker; ***W:*** Darryl Ponicsan; ***C:*** Owen Roizman; ***M:*** Tangerine Dream.

Visions 🦴 1/2 **1990** A man's ability to "see" murders before they happen leads police to suspect him of committing them, and he must clear himself. **90m/C VHS.** Joe Balogh, Alice Villarreal, Tom Taylor, A.R. Newman, J.R. Pella; ***D:*** Stephen E. Miller.

Visions of Evil 🦴 *So Sad About Gloria* **1975** A young woman, recently released from a mental institution, is plagued by a series of terrifying visions when she moves into a house where a brutal axe murder took place. **85m/C VHS, DVD.** Robert Ginnaven, Lou Hoffman, Seymour Trietman, Linda Wyse, Lori Sanders, Dean Jagger; ***D:*** Harry Z. Thomason; ***W:*** Marshall Riggan; ***C:*** James Roberson; ***M:*** Jerald Reed.

Visions of Light: The Art of Cinematography 🦴🦴🦴 **1993** Excellent documentary on the way films look and how the art of photographing movies can contribute as much, if not more, than cast, director, and script. Scenes from 125 films, from "Birth of a Nation" to "GoodFellas" are shown, with commentary from a number of cinematographers, including Gordon Willis, William A. Fraker, Conrad Hall, Ernest Dickerson, Vilmos Zsigmond, and Michael Chapman, on how they achieved certain effects and their collaborations with the director of the film. **95m/C VHS, DVD.** ***D:*** Arnold Glassman, Stuart Samuels, Todd McCarthy; ***W:*** Todd McCarthy; ***C:*** Nancy Schreiber. N.Y. Film Critics '93: Feature Doc.; Natl. Soc. Film Critics '93: Feature Doc.

Visions of Sugarplums 🦴 **1999** Amateurish and filled with stereotypes that makes for more bah-humbug than a jolly holiday. Happy gay New Yorkers Joey and Bruce are thrown into a panic by the sudden visit of Joey's conservative parents, who don't know about their son's alternative lifestyle. Bruce is temporarily kicked out of the apartment but the truth comes out anyway. **78m/C DVD.** Edward Fasulo, Mark Hardin, Mary Jean Feton, Vincent Wares; ***D:*** Edward Fasulo; ***W:*** Anthony Bruce; ***C:*** Chun Lee; ***M:*** Marty Dunayer. **VIDEO**

The Visit 🦴🦴🦴 **2000 (R)** Harper leads an excellent cast in this story of Alex, a man imprisoned for a rape he may not have committed who only seeks the acceptance and love of his family. Through visits with his estranged, successful brother (Obatunde), his loving mother (Gibbs), and his disapproving father (Williams), as well as a prison psychiatrist (Rashad) and a childhood friend (Chong), Alex finds the peace he seeks. Yes, it sounds hokey, but the excellent performances and steady, subtle direction make it all work. The parole board scene is a highlight. **107m/C VHS, DVD.** *US* Hill Harper, Obba Babatunde, Billy Dee Williams, Marla Gibbs, Rae Dawn Chong, Phylicia Rashad, Talia Shire, David Clennon, Glynn Turman, Efrain Figueroa, Amy Stiller; ***D:*** Jordan Walker-Pearlman; ***W:*** Jordan Walker-Pearlman; ***C:*** John L. (Ndiaga) Demps Jr.; ***M:*** Michael Bearden.

Visitants 🦴 **1987** Aliens descend irreverently on a small town in the 1950s, with unexpected comedic results. **93m/C VHS.** Marcus Vaughter, Johanna Grika, Joel Hile, Nicole Rio; ***D:*** Rick Sloane.

Visiting Hours 🦴 *The Fright; Get Well Soon* **1982 (R)** Psycho-killer slashes his female victims and photographs his handiwork. Grant is one of his victims who doesn't die, so the killer decides to visit the hospital and finish the job. Fairly graphic and generally unpleasant. **101m/C VHS, DVD.** *CA* Lee Grant, William Shatner, Linda Purl, Michael Ironside; ***D:*** Jean-Claude Lord; ***W:*** Brian Taggert; ***M:*** Jonathan Goldsmith.

The Visitor 🦴 1/2 **1980 (R)** Affluent handsome doctor and mate conspire with grisly devil worshippers to conceive devil child. **90m/C VHS.** Mel Ferrer, Glenn Ford, Lance Henriksen, John Huston, Shelley Winters, Joanne Nail, Sam Peckinpah; ***D:*** Giullo Paradisi.

The Visitor 🦴🦴🦴 1/2 **2007 (PG-13)** Ubiquitous character actor Jenkins runs away with his lead role in McCarthy's humanistic drama. Widowed professor Walter Vale reeks of being stuck in his lonely, boring rut of a life. On a rare visit to New York, Walter finds immigrants Tarek (Sleiman) and his girlfriend Zainab (Gurira) living in his infrequently-used city apartment, the victims of a renter's scam. Walter allows them to stay until something can be figured out and is befriended by the gregarious Tarek, a musician. Unfortunately, Tarek runs into a bureaucratic nightmare (he's outstayed his visa) when he's arrested and incarcerated in a detention center. This brings Tarek's mother Mouna (Abbass) into the picture, which furthers Walter's re-emergence as a participant rather than a mere observer of life. **108m/C DVD, Blu-ray Disc.** *US* Richard Jenkins, Hiam Abbass, Haaz Sleiman, Danai Gurira; ***D:*** Thomas (Tom) McCarthy; ***W:*** Thomas (Tom) McCarthy; ***C:*** Oliver Bokelberg; ***M:*** Jan A.P. Kaczmarek. Ind. Spirit '09: Director (McCarthy).

Visitor from the Grave 🦴 **1981** When an American heiress and her boyfriend dispose of a dead man's body, his spirit comes back to haunt them. This annoys them. Part of the BBC's "Hammer House of Horror" TV series. **60m/C VHS, DVD.** *GB* Simon MacCorkindale, Kathryn Leigh Scott, Garner "Skip" Thomas, Mia Nadasi; ***D:*** Peter Sasdy. **TV**

Visitor Q 🦴🦴 *Bijita Q* **2001 (R)** Director Takashi Miike is known for surreal, disturbing films, and this is him at his most over the top. In a very unusual family, the father is a reality television host/reporter shunned by his fellow workers (in a documentary on young women becoming prostitutes he tries to convince his own daughter to sleep with him). The mother is a heroin addict so far gone she can barely communicate. Her son, bullied brutally at school, has taken to torturing her for relief. To say they have 'mental issues' is seriously downplaying it. Then one day a young man hits the father over the head with a rock, moves in, and begins terrorizing the family in one of the most hallucinatory films ever made. **90m/C DVD.** *JP* Kenichi Endo, Shaun Hood, Joel Hookey, Virginia Carraway, Charlie Fitzgerald, Iain Kelso, Mia Blake; ***D:*** Takashi Miike; ***W:*** David Fane; ***C:*** Hideo Yamamoto; ***M:*** Koji Endo.

The Visitors 🦴 1/2 **1989 (R)** Ghosts come to stay at a young family's dream house in Sweden. Not exactly a novel treatment or a novel premise. **102m/C VHS.** *SW* Keith Berkeley, Lena Endre, John Force, John Olsen, Joanna Berg, Brent Landiss, Patrick Ersgard; ***D:*** Joakim (Jack) Ersgard.

The Visitors 🦴🦴 *Les Visiteurs* **1995 (R)** Time travel comedy features 12th-century knight Godefroy (Reno) and his vassal Jacquasse (Clavier) crossing paths with a powerful witch (and evidently pissing her off) since she casts a spell causing Godefroy to accidentally kill his father-in-law. So Godefroy contacts a wizard to give him a time travel potion so he can go back and stop the shooting. Too bad the potion hurls knight and vassal forward into present-day France. French with subtitles. **106m/C VHS, DVD.** *FR* Jean Reno, Christian Clavier, Mariann (Marie-Anne) Chazel, Valerie Lemercier, Christian Bujeau; ***D:*** Jean-Marie Poire; ***W:*** Christian Clavier, Jean-Marie Poire; ***C:*** Jean-Yves Le Mener; ***M:*** Eric Levi.

Visitors 🦴 1/2 **2003 (R)** Supernatural thriller that turns a bit silly. After six months on a solo sailing trip aournd the world, Georgia's (Mitchell) sloop is becalmed for several days. Not very stable to begin with (she has the requisite dark past), Georgia begins to hallucinate, only these ghostly encounters leave behind physical reminders of their presence. **88m/C VHS, DVD.** *AU* Radha Mitchell, Susannah York, Ray Barrett, Tottie Goldsmith; ***D:*** Richard Franklin; ***W:*** Everett De Roche; ***C:*** Ellery Ryan; ***M:*** Nerida Tyson-Chew.

Vital Signs 🦴 **1990 (R)** Hackneyed drama about six medical students enduring the tribulations of their profession. **102m/C VHS, DVD.** Adrian Pasdar, Diane Lane, Jack Gwaltney, Laura San Giacomo, Jane Adams, Tim Ransom, Bradley Whitford, Lisa Jane Persky, William Devane, Norma Aleandro, Jimmy Smits, James Karen, Telma Hopkins; ***D:*** Marisa Silver; ***W:*** Jeb Stuart; ***M:*** Miles Goodman.

Viva Knievel **WOOF!** *Seconds to Live* **1977 (PG)** Crooks plan to sabotage Knievel's daredevil jump in Mexico and then smuggle cocaine back into the States in his coffin. Unintentionally campy. **106m/C VHS, DVD.** Evel Knievel, Gene Kelly, Lauren Hutton, Red Buttons, Leslie Nielsen, Cameron Mitchell, Marjoe Gortner, Albert Salmi, Dabney Coleman; ***Cameos:*** Frank Gifford; ***D:*** Gordon Douglas; ***C:*** Fred H. Jackman Jr.; ***M:*** Charles Bernstein.

Viva Las Vegas 🦴🦴 1/2 *Love in Las Vegas* **1963** Race car driver Elvis needs money to compete against rival Danova in the upcoming Las Vegas Grand Prix. He takes a job in a casino and romances fellow employee Ann-Margret, who turns out to be his rival for the grand prize in the local talent competition. Good pairing between the two leads, and the King does particularly well with the title song. ♫ The Lady Loves Me; Viva Las Vegas; What'd I Say; I Need Somebody to Lean On; Come On, Everybody; Today, Tomorrow and Forever; If You Think I Don't Need You; Appreciation; My Rival. **85m/C VHS, DVD, Blu-ray Disc, HD DVD.** Elvis Presley, Ann-Margret, William Demarest, Jack Carter, Cesare Danova, Nicky Blair, Larry Kent; ***D:*** George Sidney; ***C:*** Joseph Biroc.

Viva Maria! 🦴🦴 1/2 **1965 (R)** Tongue-in-cheek comedy with Bardot and Moreau as two dancers (both named Maria) in a show traveling through Mexico. The two become incensed by the poverty of the peasants and decide to turn revolutionary (especially after Moreau has an affair with revolutionary leader Hamilton, who promptly gets killed). The two French sex symbols are a fine match. **119m/C VHS, DVD.** *FR IT* Jeanne Moreau, Brigitte Bardot, George Hamilton, Paulette Dubost, Claudio Brook; ***D:*** Louis Malle; ***W:*** Louis Malle, Jean-Claude Carriere; ***C:*** Henri Decae; ***M:*** Georges Delerue.

Viva Max 🦴🦴 1/2 **1969** A blundering modern-day Mexican general and his men recapture the Alamo, and an equally inept American force, headed by Winters, is sent to rout them out. Mostly works, with some very funny scenes. Ustinov is great. **93m/C VHS.** Peter Ustinov, Jonathan Winters, John Astin, Pamela Tiffin, Keenan Wynn; ***D:*** Jerry Paris.

Viva Villa! 🦴🦴🦴 **1934** Exciting action biography of Mexican revolutionary Pancho Villa, well-portrayed by the exuberant Beery. The film follows the early Robin Hood-like exploits of Villa and his men who soon join Walthall and his peasant army in overthrowing the government. But Villa's bandito instincts and ego cause problems and a power struggle ensues. Director Howard Hawks went uncredited for his work on the film, being fired by the studio after an incident while on location in Mexico. **115m/B VHS.** Wallace Beery, Fay Wray, Stuart Erwin, Leo Carrillo, Donald Cook, George E. Stone, Joseph Schildkraut, Henry B. Walthall, Katherine DeMille, David Durand, Frank Puglia; ***D:*** Jack Conway; ***W:*** Ben Hecht.

Viva Zapata! 🦴🦴🦴🦴 **1952** Chronicles the life of Mexican revolutionary Emiliano Zapata. Brando is powerful as he leads the peasant revolt in the early 1900s, only to be corrupted by power and greed. Quinn well deserved his Best Supporting Actor Oscar for his performance as Zapata's brother. Based on the novel "Zapata the Unconquered" by Edgcumb Pinchon. **112m/B VHS, DVD.** Marlon Brando, Anthony Quinn, Jean Peters, Margo, Arnold Moss, Joseph Wiseman, Mildred Dunnock; ***D:*** Elia Kazan; ***W:*** John Steinbeck; ***M:*** Alex North. Oscars '52: Support. Actor (Quinn); British Acad. '52: Actor (Brando); Cannes '52: Actor (Brando).

Vivacious Lady 🦴🦴🦴 **1938** Romantic comedy about a mild-mannered college professor who marries a chorus girl. Problems arise when he must let his conservative family and his former fiancee in on the marriage news. Good performances. Appealing. **90m/B VHS.** Ginger Rogers, James Stewart, James Ellison, Beulah Bondi, Charles Coburn, Jack Carson, Franklin Pangborn, Dorothy Moore; ***D:*** George Stevens.

Vive l'Amour 🦴🦴 *Aiqing Wansui* **1994** A furnished Taipei luxury apartment is the setting for three characters who make use of the space but have little connection to each other. Guimei is the real estate agent who's trying to sell the apartment and uses it for casual sex, including an encounter with street vendor Zhaorong. The third part of the triangle is young salesman Kangsheng, who's broken into the place to commit suicide but is forestalled by Zhaorong, with whom Kangsheng then becomes sexually intrigued. The trio come and go, mostly alone, so dialogue is at a minimum. Taiwanese with subtitles. **118m/C VHS, DVD.** *TW* Yang Guimei, Chen Zhaorong, Li Kangsheng; ***D:*** Tsai Ming-Liang; ***W:*** Tsai Ming-Liang; ***C:*** Pen-jung Liao, Ming-kuo Lin.

Vlad 🦴 1/2 **2003** Four grad students travel to Romania to study the vile legend of Vlad Drakul (aka Dracula) per a Bucharest professor's request. While inside his tomb (what could possibly go wrong?) they end up taking a harrowing trip back in time thanks to a mysterious necklace. **98m/C VHS, DVD.** Billy Zane, Brad Dourif, Francesco Quinn, John Rhys-Davies, Claudiu Bleont, Paul Popowich, Kam Heskin, Nicholas Irons, Monica Davidescu, Iva Hasperger, Emil Hostina, Guy Siner, Mircea Stoian, Andreea Macelaru, Alin Panc, Alexandera Velniciuc, Zoltan Butuc, Anca-Ioana Androne, Adrian Pintea, Ian Ionescu, Catalin Rotaru, Cristian Popa; ***D:*** Michael D. Sellers; ***W:*** Michael D. Sellers, Tony Shawkat; ***C:*** Viorel Sergovici Jr.; ***M:*** Christopher Field. **VIDEO**

Vogues of 1938 🦴🦴 *All This and Glamour Too; Vogues* **1937** As a lark, a rich girl takes a job as a fashion model and incurs the displeasure of Baxter, the owner of the chic fashion house where she works. An early Technicolor fashion extravaganza. ♫ That Old Feeling; Lovely One; Turn On the Red Hot Heat (Burn the Blues Away); King of Jam. **110m/C VHS.** Joan Bennett, Warner Baxter, Helen Vinson, Mischa Auer, Hedda Hopper, Penny Singleton, Alan Mowbray; ***D:*** Irving Cummings.

The Voice of Merrill 🦴🦴 1/2 *Murder Will Out* **1952** Has a blackmailing secretary been killed by unhappy publisher Ronald Parker (Kendall)? Or ailing, unpleasant, but successful writer Jonathan Roach (Justice)? Or Roach's unhappy wife Alycia (Hobson) who is having an affair with struggling author Hugh Allen (Underdown)? Scotland Yard investigates. Title refers to the radio serial, penned but disowned by Roach, which leads to a final twist. **83m/B DVD.** *GB* Valerie Hobson, Edward Underdown, James Robertson Justice, Henry Kendall, Garry Marsh; ***D:*** John Gilling; ***W:*** John Gilling; ***C:*** Monty Berman; ***M:*** Frank Cordell.

Voices 🦴 1/2 *Du Saram-yida; Someone Behind You* **2008 (R)** Ga-in Kim (Jin-seo Yun) sees her Aunt murdered at her wedding by her own sister, who tells Kim that she felt she was required to murder her due to intense feelings of jealousy. Poor Kim seems to suddenly elicit this same response afterwards, as suddenly all her friends and family feel an overwhelming desire to kill her. **84m/C DVD.** *KN* Jin-seo Yun, Gi-woong Park, Ki-woo Lee, Yu-seon Ham, So-eun Kim, Yu-mi Jeong, Kan-hie Lee, Yu-Jeong Seo; ***D:*** Ki-Hwan Oh; ***W:*** Ki-Hwan Oh, Lee Hyo-Chul, Kang Kyung-ok, Lee Shin-ae; ***C:*** Yong-heung Kim; ***M:*** Jun-Seok Kim.

Voices from a Locked Room ✓✓ *Voices* **1995 (R)** Very loosely based on the life of British composer Peter Warlock (1894-1930) and music critic Philip Heseltine. Heseltine detests Warlock's music, Warlock threatens Heseltine, and Heseltine's fiancee (Bergen) is the girl in the middle. Of course, what's really bizarre is that Warlock is Heseltine's pseudonym. Film does have a nice period look. **93m/C VHS.** *GB* Jeremy Northam, Tushka Bergen, Allan Corduner, Hilton McRae; ***D:*** Malcolm Clarke; ***W:*** Peter Barnes; ***C:*** Ann T. Rossetti; ***M:*** Elliot Goldenthal.

Voices from Beyond ✓ 1/2 *Voci dal Profondo* **1990** After wealthy Giorgio Mainardi hemorrhages to death, his daughter Rosy (Huff) returns home from college to attend the funeral. She soon begins to have strange dreams in which her father claims that he was murdered, and begs Rosy to discover the identity of the killer. In flashbacks, we learn that Giorgio did something to enrage everyone in the household before he died, so there are many suspects. While the revelation of the murderer is actually surprising, the rest of the film is a boring mess. While director Fulci is well-known for his liberal use of gore and his occasionally creepy visuals, this film has neither. The acting isn't very good, and the atrocious dubbing only makes matters worse. **91m/C DVD.** *IT* Dulio Del Prete, Karina Huff, Pascal Persiano, Lorenzo Flaherty, Bettina Giovannini, Damiano Azzos; ***D:*** Lucio Fulci; ***W:*** Piero Regnoli; ***M:*** Stelvio Cipriani.

Voices of Iraq ✓✓✓ **2004** In April of 2004 a crew of American filmmakers distributed 150 video cameras to citizens of Iraq. Given full artistic and legal license to speak at will, the citizens participate in an unbiased experiment showing the true sentiment of the war-torn country. Surprisingly, there is little complaint of the U.S. and coalition's occupying troops and rampant hatred against their former dictator, Saddam Hussein; which leads us to believe that perhaps the cameras were given to select sects, rather that random citizens, or likely a dictatorship in the editing room. Still, it makes for an empowering tool in the struggle of a wounded country. **79m/C DVD.** *US* ***M:*** Narcicyst, Euphrates.

The Void ✓ 1/2 **2001 (R)** Physicist Eva Soderstrom (Tapping) discovers that industrialist Thomas Abernathy (McDowell) is experimenting with creating an artificial black hole on Earth. This isn't a good thing so Eva hooks up with Dr. Steven Price (Paul) to stop Abernathy. So-so thriller. **90m/C VHS, DVD.** Amanda Tapping, Adrian Paul, Malcolm McDowell, Andrew McIlroy; ***D:*** Gilbert M. Shilton; ***W:*** Gilbert M. Shilton, Geri Cudia Barger; ***C:*** Attila Szalay; ***M:*** Ross Vannelli.

Volcano ✓✓ **1997 (PG-13)** L.A. has already had to deal with earthquakes, mudslides, raging fires, riots and the acting career of Anna Nicole Smith. Now it's completely roasted by millions of gallons of molten lava. This overblown Rescue 911 has Mike Roark (Jones), the standard take-charge guy, trying to avert total destruction while being assisted by the brainy-but-beautiful seismologist Dr. Amy Barnes (Heche). Many tongue-in-cheek jokes about the general state of chaos in L.A. even on the best of days; but aside from these, the dialogue is cheesy beyond belief. The special effects are very impressive, however. Wilshire Blvd. was actually recreated on a 17-acre set (believed to be the biggest ever) in order to meet its fiery doom. **120m/C VHS, DVD.** Tommy Lee Jones, Anne Heche, Gaby Hoffman, Don Cheadle, Keith David, John Corbett, Michael Rispoli, John Carroll Lynch, Jacqueline Kim; ***D:*** Mick Jackson; ***W:*** Billy Ray, Jerome Armstrong; ***C:*** Theo van de Sande; ***M:*** Alan Silvestri.

Volcano: Fire on the Mountain ✓ 1/2 *Fire on the Mountain* **1997 (PG)** Cheesy TV disaster flick finds geologist Peter Slater (Cortese) trying to convince both his boss and the residents of Angel Falls, California that a nearby volcano is about to blow. **99m/C VHS.** Dan Cortese, Cynthia Gibb, Brian Kerwin; ***D:*** Graeme Campbell; ***C:*** Tobias Schliessler; ***M:*** David Michael Frank.

Volere Volare ✓✓ 1/2 **1992 (R)** Shy sound engineer Nichetti shares a studio with his brother. The brother employs a bevy of beauties to dub sound effects onto soft-core porn films while Nichetti works on dubbing classic cartoons. He becomes so involved in his work he actually turns into a cartoon figure, which does nothing for his love life. Then he meets Martina, who's strangely attracted to this cartoon figure. Quirky comedy mixes animation and live action with too many gimmicks and not enough heart. In Italian with English subtitles. **92m/C VHS.** *IT* Maurizio Nichetti, Angela Finocchiaro, Mariella Valentini, Patrizio Roversi, Remo Remotti, Renato Scarpa; ***D:*** Maurizio Nichetti, Guido Manuli; ***W:*** Maurizio Nichetti, Guido Manuli. Montreal World Film Fest. '92: Director (Nichetti).

Volpone ✓✓✓ **1939** A classic adaptation of Ben Jonson's famous tale. A greedy merchant pretends he is dying, leaving a fortune behind, in order see what his family will do to become his heir. In French with English subtitles. **95m/B VHS.** *FR* Harry Baur, Louis Jouvet, Fernand Ledoux; ***D:*** Maurice Tourneur.

Volunteers ✓✓ **1985 (R)** Ivy League playboy joins the newly formed Peace Corps to escape gambling debts and finds himself on a bridge-building mission in Thailand. Has its comedic moments, especially with Candy. **107m/C VHS, DVD.** Tom Hanks, John Candy, Rita Wilson, Tim Thomerson, Gedde Watanabe, George Plimpton, Ernest Harada; ***D:*** Nicholas Meyer; ***W:*** David Isaacs, Ken Levine; ***C:*** Ric Waite; ***M:*** James Horner.

Volver ✓✓✓ *To Return* **2006 (R)** Almodovar and the women. The writer/director tackles domestic melodrama when frustrated cleaner Raimunda (Cruz) is forced into drastic action to protect her daughter Paula (Cobo). In addition, Raimunda's hairdresser sister Sole (Duenas) is suddenly confronted by their mother Irene's (Maura) ghost, who takes up residence with Sole and helps out in her salon in order to rectify some mistakes she made with her daughters. Much sly humor and female bonding and yes, Cruz is wearing a prosthetic backside to give her that sexy sway. Spanish with subtitles. **111m/C DVD, Blu-ray Disc.** *SP* Penelope Cruz, Lola Duenas, Carmen Maura, Chus (Maria Jesus) Lampreave, Blanca Portillo, Yohana Cobo, Maria Isabel Diaz, Antonio de la Torre, Carlos Blanco, Leonardo Rivera; ***D:*** Pedro Almodovar; ***W:*** Pedro Almodovar; ***C:*** Jose Luis Alcaine; ***M:*** Alberto Iglesias.

Von Ryan's Express ✓✓✓ **1965** An American Air Force colonel leads a group of prisoners-of-war in taking control of a freight train in order to make their exciting escape from a WWII P.O.W. camp in Italy. Strong cast. **117m/C VHS, DVD.** Frank Sinatra, Trevor Howard, Brad Dexter, Raffaella Carra, Sergio Fantoni, John Leyton, Vito Scotti, Edward Mulhare, Adolfo Celi, James Brolin, James B. Sikking, Wolfgang Preiss, John van Dreelen, Richard Bakalyan, Michael Goodliffe, Michael St. Clair, Ivan Triesault; ***D:*** Mark Robson; ***W:*** Wendell Mayes, Joseph Landon; ***C:*** William H. Daniels; ***M:*** Jerry Goldsmith.

Voodoo ✓✓ **1995 (R)** College student Andy (Feldman) must battle a fraternity, lead by an evil voodoo priest, when they decide to make his girlfriend their next human sacrifice. **91m/C VHS, DVD.** Corey Feldman, Sarah Douglas, Jack Nance, Joel J. Edwards; ***D:*** Rene Eram; ***W:*** Brian DiMuccio, Dino Vindeni; ***C:*** Dan Gillham; ***M:*** Keith Bilderbeck.

Voodoo Academy ✓✓ **2000** Imagine an episode of "Scooby Doo" crossed with a Calvin Klein ad and you'll get the idea of what video veteran Dave DeCoteau is doing in what he calls "the first horror film made for girls." A Bible college is a front for voodoo activity. The all-male students run around in their underwear trying to figure out what's going on. **100m/C DVD.** Riley Smith, Chad Burns, Debra Meyer; ***D:*** David DeCoteau.

Voodoo Black Exorcist ✓ *Vudu Sangriento* **1973** Some 3000 years ago, a black prince was buried alive for messin' with another man's woman. Now he's back...and he's mad—real mad. He's prepared to kill just about everyone. Can he be stopped before all in the modern world are dead?? **88m/C VHS, DVD.** *SP* Aldo Sambrel, Tenyeka Stadle, Fernando (Fernand) Sancho; ***D:*** Manuel Cano; ***W:*** Santiago Moncada; ***C:*** Roberto Ochoa; ***M:*** Fernando Garcia Morcillo.

Voodoo Dawn ✓✓ **1989 (R)** Two New Yorkers travel to the Deep South to visit a friend who, it turns out, is the latest victim in a series of really gross voodoo murders. A beautiful girl is written into the plot, and the New York guys have an excuse to stay in voodooville, even though bimbolina's southern accent comes and goes for no discernable reason. Filmed near Charleston, South Carolina, and co-written by Russo of "Night of the Living Dead" fame. **83m/C VHS.** Raymond St. Jacques, Theresa Merritt, Gina Gershon, Kirk Baily, Billy "Sly" Williams, J. Grant Albrecht, Tony Todd; ***D:*** Steven Fierberg; ***W:*** John A. Russo, Jeffrey Delman.

Voodoo Dawn ✓✓ 1/2 **1999** Crazy con Frank Barlow (Madsen) has learned voodoo rites in prison and is using his power to get revenge on his brother's killer. Predictable crime drama despite the occult trappings. **93m/C VHS, DVD.** Michael Madsen, Rosanna Arquette, Balthazar Getty, Phillip Glasser, James Russo; ***D:*** Andrzej Sekula. **VIDEO**

Voodoo Moon ✓ 1/2 **2005** More silly than scary. Cole (Mabius) and Heather (Carpenter) were the only survivors when a demonic presence destroyed their town. For many years, Cole has been learning how to destroy the demon and now returns with his psychic sis to put his knowledge to the test. **89m/C DVD.** Eric Mabius, Charisma Carpenter, Alison Grace, Jeffrey Combs, Jayne Heitmeyer, John Amos, Dee Wallace; ***D:*** Kevin VanHook; ***W:*** Kevin VanHook; ***C:*** Matt Steinauer; ***M:*** Ludek Drizhal. **CABLE**

Voodoo Woman ✓ **1957** An innocent girl is lured into the jungle by an evil scientist who is trying to create the perfect woman to commit murders. He turns the girl into an ugly monster in an attempt to get her to obey his telepathic commands. A campy classic that's as bad as it sounds. **77m/B VHS.** Marla English, Tom Conway, Mike Connors, Lance Fuller, Paul Blaisdell; ***D:*** Edward L. Cahn.

Vortex ✓ 1/2 **1981** Punk/film noir style in which a female private eye becomes immersed in corporate paranoia and political corruption. **87m/C VHS.** Lydia Lunch, James Russo, Bill Rice, Richard France, Ann Magnuson, Haoui Montaug, Adele Bertei, Bill Landis; ***D:*** Scott B, Beth B; ***W:*** Scott B, Beth B; ***C:*** Steven Fierberg; ***M:*** Lydia Lunch, Adele Bertei.

Voulez-Vous Danser avec Moi? ✓✓ 1/2 *Come Dance with Me; Do You Want to Dance with Me?* **1959** Lighthearted comedy-mystery with a sexy Bardot starring as the newly married Virginie. After a quarrel with her husband Herve (Vidal), she follows him to a dance studio and finds him incriminated in the murder of the studio's owner. So Virginie decides to go undercover as an instructor to clear her husband's name. Based on the novel "The Blonde Died Dancing" by Kelley Roos. French with subtitles. **91m/C VHS, DVD.** *FR IT* Brigitte Bardot, Henri Vidal, Dawn Addams, Philippe Nicaud, Serge Gainsbourg, Dario Moreno; ***D:*** Michel Boisrond; ***W:*** Annette Wademant; ***C:*** Robert Lefebvre; ***M:*** Henri Crolla.

A Vow to Kill ✓✓ 1/2 **1994 (PG-13)** Predictable cable thriller finds the wealthy Phillips marrying the charming Grieco after a whirlwind courtship. Then, on their honeymoon, she accidentally learns that her new husband has contacted her family and is masquerading as a kidnapper—demanding a large ransom for her safe release. But maybe it's not such a masquerade after all. **91m/C VHS.** Julianne Phillips, Richard Grieco, Gordon Pinsent, Peter MacNeill, Tom Cavanagh, Nicole Oliver; ***D:*** Harry S. Longstreet; ***W:*** Harry S. Longstreet, Sean Silas, Renee Longstreet; ***C:*** Francois Protat; ***M:*** John Keane. **CABLE**

Voyage ✓ 1/2 **1993 (R)** Boring rip-off of "Dead Calm" and other couple-in-peril-from-psycho-on-boat films. Hauer and Allen are having marital problems and decide to sail away from their troubles with new-found friends Roberts and Nielson. Only their guests are sociopaths. Hauer takes a breather from his psycho roles for a turn as the good guy while Roberts could do his patented crazy act in his sleep. **88m/C VHS.** Rutger Hauer, Karen Allen, Eric Roberts, Connie Nielsen; ***D:*** John MacKenzie. **CABLE**

Voyage en Balloon ✓✓ 1/2 **1959** This is the delightful story of a young boy (played by the star of "The Red Balloon") who stows away on his grandfather's hot air balloon for an adventurous trip across France. **82m/C VHS.** *FR* Pascal Lamorisse, Andre Gille, Maurice Baquet; ***D:*** Albert Lamorisse; ***W:*** Albert Lamorisse; ***Nar:*** Jack Lemmon.

Voyage en Douce ✓✓ **1981** Helene and Lucie have been friends since childhood. Helene wants to rent a summer house, and Lucie, fed up with her marriage, agrees to join her on a leisurely journey through the south of France. Thoughtful look at friendship among women. French with subtitles. **95m/C VHS.** *FR* Dominique Sanda, Geraldine Chaplin; ***D:*** Michel DeVille.

Voyage in Italy ✓✓ 1/2 *Viaggio in Italia; Voyage to Italy; The Lonely Woman; Strangers* **1953** Narrative of a marriage finds unhappy English couple Bergman and Sanders travelling by car to Naples. However, various crises manage to reunite them. Critically mauled upon its release, this third collaboration between Bergman and Rossellini, following "Stromboli" and "Europa '51," later became a big hit with New Wave directors. **83m/B VHS.** *IT* Ingrid Bergman, George Sanders; ***D:*** Roberto Rossellini; ***W:*** Roberto Rossellini, Vitaliano Brancatti; ***C:*** Enzo Serafin; ***M:*** Renzo Rossellini.

Voyage of Terror: The Achille Lauro Affair ✓✓ 1/2 **1990** Recounting of the 1985 Italian cruise-ship hijacking by four Palestinians. Lancaster is the wheelchair-bound Leon Klinghoffer and Saint is wife Marilyn. Miniseries was shot on the actual ship and route where the tragedy occurred. **120m/C VHS.** Burt Lancaster, Eva Marie Saint, Robert Culp, Brian Bloom, Dominique Sanda, Rebecca Schaeffer, Joseph Nasser, Gabriele Ferzetti, Renzo Montagnani; ***D:*** Alberto Negrin. **TV**

Voyage of the Damned ✓✓✓ **1976 (G)** The story of one of the most tragic incidents of WWII. In 1939, 1,937 German-Jewish refugees fleeing Nazi Germany are bound for Cuba aboard the Hamburg-America liner S.S. St. Louis. They are refused permission to land in Cuba (and everywhere else) and must sail back to Germany and certain death. Based on the novel by Gordon Thomas and Max Morgan-Witts. **155m/C VHS, DVD.** *GB* Faye Dunaway, Max von Sydow, Oskar Werner, Malcolm McDowell, Orson Welles, James Mason, Lee Grant, Katharine Ross, Ben Gazzara, Lynne Frederick, Wendy Hiller, Jose Ferrer, Luther Adler, Sam Wanamaker, Denholm Elliott, Nehemiah Persoff, Julie Harris, Maria Schell, Jonathan Pryce, Janet Suzman, Helmut Griem, Michael Constantine, Victor Spinetti; ***D:*** Stuart Rosenberg; ***W:*** Steve Shagan, David Butler; ***C:*** Billy Williams; ***M:*** Lalo Schifrin. Golden Globes '77: Support. Actress (Ross).

Voyage of the Heart ✓✓ **1990** An aging fisherman meets up with a sexy college girl and the passion begins. **88m/C VHS.** Dunja Djordjenic, Bill Ackridge, Jeremy Slate, Geoffrey Dunn, Liz Rolfe; ***D:*** Mark Schwartz; ***W:*** Geoffrey Dunn; ***C:*** Gene Evans; ***M:*** Randy Masters.

Voyage of the Rock Aliens ✓ **1987** A quasi-satiric space farce about competing alien rock stars. **97m/C VHS, DVD.** Pia Zadora, Tom Nolan, Craig Sheffer, Rhema, Ruth Gordon, Michael Berryman, Jermaine Jackson, Alison La Placa; ***D:*** James Fargo; ***W:*** Edward Gold, S. James Guidotti; ***C:*** Gilbert Taylor; ***M:*** Jack White.

The Voyage of the Yes ✓✓ **1972 (PG)** Two teenagers, one white and one black, in a small sailboat hit rough weather and battle the elements while learning about themselves. Average TV movie. **100m/C VHS, DVD.** Desi Arnaz Jr., Mike Evans, Beverly Garland, Skip Homeier, Della Reese, Scoey Mitchell; ***D:*** Lee H. Katzin. **TV**

A Voyage 'Round My Father 𝒜𝒜𝒜 **1989** John Mortimer's adaptation of his semi-autobiographical stage play. Olivier is the eccentric, opinionated blind barrister-father and Bates the exasperated son as both try to come to terms with their stormy family relationship. Well-acted and directed. **85m/C VHS.** *GB* Laurence Olivier, Alan Bates, Jane Asher, Elizabeth Sellars; ***D:*** Alvin Rakoff. **TV**

Voyage Suprise 𝒜𝒜𝒜 **1946** A slapstick comedy about a crazy old man who runs a mystery tour from a dilapidated bus as he takes an unknowing mob of tourists on a cross-country escapade through a brothel, a wedding, criminals, police, terrorists and the Haute-Provence. In French with English subtitles. **108m/B VHS.** *FR* Martine Carol, Sioel; ***D:*** Pierre Prevert; ***C:*** Jean (Yves, Georges) Bourgoin.

Voyage to the Beginning of the World 𝒜𝒜𝒜 *Journey to the Beginning of the World; Viagem ao Principio do Mundo* **1996** Autobiographical piece by 88-year-old director de Oliveira, who has been making movies since the silent film era. Mastroianni, in his last role, plays the somewhat fictionalized director named Manoel who travels to Portugal to shoot a film. Along the way he points out crumbling landmarks that he remembers from his childhood, an apt metaphor for the memories where the majority of his life now resides. Along with him is French actor Afonso (Gautier), who makes a visit to an elderly aunt (de Castro) who poignantly tells Afonso about his father and the way things used to be. Slow moving but lyrical ode to aging and the changing perspective it gives. French and Portuguese with subtitles. **93m/C VHS, DVD.** *PT* Marcello Mastroianni, Jean-Yves Gautier, Leonor Silveira, Diogo Doria, Isabel de Castro; ***D:*** Manoel de Oliveira; ***W:*** Manoel de Oliveira; ***C:*** Renato Berta; ***M:*** Emmanuel Nunes.

Voyage to the Bottom of the Sea 𝒜𝒜𝒜 **1961** The crew of an atomic submarine must destroy a deadly radiation belt which has set the polar ice cap ablaze. Fun stuff, with good special effects and photography. Later became a TV series. **106m/C VHS, DVD.** Walter Pidgeon, Joan Fontaine, Barbara Eden, Peter Lorre, Robert Sterling, Michael Ansara, Frankie Avalon; ***D:*** Irwin Allen; ***W:*** Charles Bennett, Irwin Allen; ***C:*** Winton C. Hoch; ***M:*** Paul Sawtell, Bert Shefter.

Voyage to the Planet of Prehistoric Women **WOOF!** *Gill Woman; Gill Women of Venus* **1968** Astronauts journey to Venus, where they discover a race of gorgeous, sea-shell clad women led by Van Doren, as well as a few monsters. Incomprehensible but fun. The third film incorporating the Russian "Planeta Burg" footage. Directed (and narrated) by Bogdanovich under the pseudonym Derek Thomas. **78m/C VHS, DVD.** Mamie Van Doren, Mary Mark, Paige Lee, Aldo Roman, Margot Hartman; ***D:*** Peter Bogdanovich; ***W:*** Henry Ney; ***Nar:*** Peter Bogdanovich.

Voyage to the Prehistoric Planet 𝒜 ½ *Voyage to a Prehistoric Planet* **1965** In the year 2020, an expedition to Venus is forced to deal with dinosaurs and other perils. In the making of this movie, Roger Corman edited in special effects and additional footage from a recently acquired Russian film, "Planeta Burg," and his own "Queen of Blood." **80m/C VHS, DVD.** Basil Rathbone, Faith Domergue, Marc Shannon, Christopher Brand; ***D:*** Curtis Harrington.

Voyager 𝒜𝒜𝒜 **1991 (PG-13)** Restless, middle-aged engineer Walter Faber (Shepherd) tells his life story in a series of flashbacks. Twenty years before (the film starts in 1957) he abandons his pregnant girlfriend who promises to get an abortion. He laters hears she married, had a child, and divorced. While sailing to New York from France Walter falls in love with a young student and accompanies her to Greece to visit her mother. Only then does he realize her true identity, leading to a tragic conclusion. Shepherd's is a glum, repressed performance (in keeping with the character) while Delpy personifies youthful sweetness. Based on the novel "Homo Faber" by Max Frisch. **110m/C VHS.** *FR GE* Sam Shepard, Julie Delpy, Barbara Sukowa, Dieter Kirchlechner, Traci Lind, Deborra-Lee Furness, August Zirner, Thomas Heinze; ***D:*** Volker Schlondorff; ***W:*** Volker Schlondorff, Rudy Wurlitzer.

The Voyeur 𝒜 **1994** After ten years of marriage, a couple tries to ignite those sexual fires by spending a weekend in Napa Valley and indulging in erotic sexual games. Based on Lonnie Barbach's book "Erotic Edge." **80m/C VHS.** Al Sapienza, Kim (Kimberly Dawn) Dawson; ***D:*** Deborah Shames; ***W:*** Udana Power.

Vukovar 𝒜𝒜𝒜 **1994** Vukovar is a Croat town just across the Danube river from Serbia, in the former Yugoslavia, where different ethnic groups had managed to coexist peacefully. When Croatian Anna (Jokovic) marries her childhood sweetheart, the Serbian Toma (Isakovic), however, their celebration is marred by nationalist demonstrations. Soon Anna's pregnant, Toma has been drafted, and the town comes under siege, with Tomas' parents fleeing, Anna's family killed in a bombing, and Ann herself struggling to survive. Film was condemned by the Croatian government as pro-Serbian propaganda though director Draskovic, a Serbian whose parents are Croatian and Bosnian, strove to be nonpartisan. Serbo-Croatian with subtitles. **94m/C VHS.** *YU* Mirjana Jokovic, Boris Isakovic, Monica Romic; ***D:*** Boro Draskovic; ***W:*** Boro Draskovic, Maja Draskovic; ***C:*** Aleksandar Petkovic.

Vulcan God of Fire **WOOF!** *Vulcan, Son of Jupiter* **1962** Flash is a muscle-bound Vulcan fighting off cheesy monsters in an effort to win the hand of Venus. **76m/C VHS.** *IT* Rob Flash, Gordon Mitchell, Bella Cortez; ***D:*** Emmimo Salvi.

Vulture 𝒜 **1967** In an attempt to carry out a curse on the descendants of the man who killed his forefather, a scientist tries an atomic transmutation experiment and winds up combining himself with a bird. **91m/C VHS.** Robert Hutton, Akim Tamiroff, Broderick Crawford, Diane Clare, Philip Friend, Patrick Holt, Annette Carell; ***D:*** Lawrence Huntington.

Vultures 𝒜 **1984** A dying patriarch summons his predatory family to his home in order to straighten out the distribution of inheritance. One by one, they fall victim to a mysterious murderer. **101m/C VHS.** Yvonne De Carlo, Stuart Whitman, Jim Bailey, Meredith MacRae, Aldo Ray; ***D:*** Paul Leder.

Vulture's Eye 𝒜 **2004** Why is it that a bunch of sexy ladies can't roam the pleasant Virginia countryside without having some creepy evil-doer Count lurking about? Thank goodness there's a stereotypical coot of a Southern doctor around to try to save the poor women's souls. That and the special strength they get from just being friends. Who knew that just having pals keeps ya from joining the undead! **100m/C DVD.** Brooke Paller, Anne Flosnik, Jason King, Fred Iacovo, James Nalitz, Eve Young; ***D:*** Frank Sciurba; ***W:*** Frank Sciurba. **VIDEO**

W 𝒜 ½ *I Want Her Dead* **1974 (PG)** A woman and her husband are terrorized and must find out why. A single letter "W" is found at the scene of the crimes. Notable only as model Twiggy's first film. **95m/C VHS, DVD.** Twiggy, Dirk Benedict, John Vernon, Eugene Roche; ***D:*** Richard Quine.

W. 𝒜𝒜𝒜 **2008 (PG-13)** Stone's take on the life and times of President George W. Bush is surprisingly conventional and restrained. Bush (played convincingly by Brolin) spends his early years as a troubled alcoholic, rebelling against his privileged upbringing, fighting his father (Cromwell), and watching as his brother Jeb became the chosen one. Still, somehow, he climbs the political ladder high enough to become the leader of the free world. All the key players are here—vice-presidential strategist Dick Cheney (Dreyfuss), master political consultant Karl Rove (Jones), Defense Secretary Donald Rumsfeld (Glenn), and first lady Laura Bush (Banks). Told in non-linear fashion, flashing back to key moments in W.'s upbringing and to the major decisions he was forced to make as president, it's a solid drama, but nothing out of the ordinary from most celebrity biopics. Ultimately, it highlights both his incompetence, and his humanity. **131m/C DVD, Blu-ray Disc.** *US* Josh Brolin, Elizabeth Banks, Thandie Newton, Richard Dreyfuss, Scott Glenn, Ioan Gruffudd, James Cromwell, Ellen Burstyn, Noah Wyle, Jason Ritter, Jeffrey Wright, Jesse Bradford, Rob Corddry, Toby Jones, Sayed Badreya, Michael Gaston; ***D:*** Oliver Stone; ***W:*** Stanley Weiser; ***C:*** Phedon Papamichael; ***M:*** Paul Cantelon.

Wackiest Ship in the Army 𝒜𝒜 ½ **1961** A completely undisciplined warship crew must smuggle an Australian spy through Japanese waters during WWII. Odd, enjoyable mixture of action and laughs. Became a TV series. In the middle of the war effort, Nelson straps on a guitar and sings "Do You Know What It Means to Miss New Orleans." **99m/C VHS, DVD.** Jack Lemmon, Ricky Nelson, Chips Rafferty, John Lund, Mike Kellin, Patricia Driscoll; ***D:*** Richard Murphy.

Wackiest Wagon Train in the West 𝒜 **1977 (G)** Hapless wagon master is saddled with a dummy assistant as they guide a party of five characters across the West. Based on the minor TV sitcom "Dusty's Trail." Produced by the same folks who delivered the similarly premised TV series "Gilligan's Island" and "The Brady Bunch." **86m/C VHS, DVD.** Ivor Francis, Lori Saunders, Bob Denver, Forrest Tucker, Jeannine Riley, William Cort; ***D:*** Elroy Schwartz; ***W:*** Sherwood Schwartz, Elroy Schwartz. **TV**

The Wackness 𝒜𝒜 ½ **2008 (R)** Loner Luke Shapiro (Peck) peddles pot and navel-gazes as he contemplates graduation, the long summer prior to college, parental issues, and a serious lack of confidence with girls. He strikes up an unlikely yet drug-based friendship with his therapist, Dr. Squires (Kingsley, who although a jack-of-all-trades actor is kinda creepy as a pot-head), who has issues of his own, namely a failing marriage and a general lack of maturity. The good doctor seems to have an undue interest in getting Luke laid, although he's not hip to Luke's interest in his own stepdaughter Stephanie (Thirlby). The coming-of-age storyline meanders in a stoner haze around 1994 New York, which doesn't seem long ago enough to be treated in a period movie. **95m/C DVD, Blu-ray Disc.** *US* Josh Peck, Ben Kingsley, Famke Janssen, Olivia Thirlby, Mary-Kate Olsen, Jane Adams, Method Man, Talia Balsam, David Wohl, Bob (Robert) Dishy; ***D:*** Jonathan Levine; ***W:*** Jonathan Levine; ***C:*** Petra Korner; ***M:*** David Torn.

Wacko **WOOF!** **1983 (PG)** Group of nymphettes and tough guys get caught up in a wild Halloween-pumpkin-lawnmower murder. This spoof of the "Halloween" series works too hard for as few laughs as it gets. **84m/C VHS.** Stella Stevens, George Kennedy, Joe Don Baker, Andrew (Dice Clay) Silverstein; ***D:*** Greydon Clark.

The Wacky World of Wills & Burke 𝒜𝒜 **1985** Comedy based on the adventures of Wills and Burke, the two 19th-century explorers who led the first unsuccessful expedition across the outback—the Lewis and Clark of Australia, if you will. In real life they died during the adventure, a less than wacky finale. "Burke and Wills," out the same year, was a serious treatment of the same story. **102m/C VHS.** *AU* Garry McDonald, Kim Gyngell, Peter Collingwood, Jonathan Hardy, Mark Little; ***D:*** Bob Weis.

Wag the Dog 𝒜𝒜 ½ **1997 (R)** Based on the book "American Hero" by Larry Beinhart and adapted by Hilary Henkin and David Mamet. Over-the-top Hollywood producer (Hoffman) is hired by White House officials to stage a military attack against the U.S. to divert media attention from accusations that the President fondled a Girl Scout. Show biz insiders say Hoffman's Motss resembles one-time studio head Robert Evans; Washington insiders wonder if it's a documentary. In fact, the entire film is one big insider's joke. Luckily, it's smart enough, and short enough, to avoid becoming tiresome. Look for cameos by Woody Harrelson and Willie Nelson. Filmed in a speedy 29 days on a $15 million budget. **96m/C VHS, DVD.** Dustin Hoffman, Robert De Niro, Anne Heche, Woody Harrelson, Denis Leary, Willie Nelson, Andrea Martin, Suzanne Cryer, John Michael Higgins, Suzy Plakson, Kirsten Dunst, William H. Macy, Michael Belson; ***D:*** Barry Levinson; ***W:*** Hilary Henkin, David Mamet; ***C:*** Robert Richardson; ***M:*** Mark Knopfler. Natl. Bd. of Review '97: Support. Actress (Heche).

Wager of Love 𝒜𝒜 **1990** While vacationing on their annual pleasure cruise, four women bet on their individual power of seduction. They find themselves competing for passion as each woman's erotic adventure unravels in this exciting and sensual tale. **75m/C VHS.** Steve Landers, Shelly Johnson, Elliot Silverman, Lisa Cook; ***D:*** Jason Holt.

Wages of Fear 𝒜𝒜𝒜𝒜 *Le Salaire de la Peur* **1955** American oil company controls a desolate Central American town whose citizens desperately want out—so desperately that four are willing to try a suicide mission to deliver nitroglycerine to put out a well-fire raging 300 miles away. The company's cynical head has offered $2000 to each man, enough to finance escape from the hell-hole they live in. Complex, multi-dimensional drama concentrates on character development for the first half—crucial to the film's greatness. This is the restored version. Remade by William Friedkin as "Sorcerer" in 1977. Based on a novel by Georges Arnaud. In French with English subtitles. **138m/B VHS, DVD.** *FR* Yves Montand, Charles Vanel, Peter Van Eyck, Vera Clouzot, Folco Lulli, William Tubbs; ***D:*** Henri-Georges Clouzot; ***W:*** Henri-Georges Clouzot; ***C:*** Armand Thirard; ***M:*** Georges Auric. British Acad. '54: Film; Cannes '53: Actor (Vanel), Film.

Wagner: The Complete Epic 𝒜𝒜 **1985** The unedited version of the epic miniseries dramatizing the life of German composer Richard Wagner. The excellent photography does justice to the elaborate production, shot on some 200 different locations. The actors cringe in the presence of the subject's grandeur; Burton, a shell of his former cinematic self, is painful to watch in his last released film. Frankly, this is way too long. Also available in a edited 300-minute version, which is still too long. **540m/C VHS, DVD.** *GB HU* Richard Burton, Vanessa Redgrave, Ralph Richardson, John Gielgud, Laurence Olivier, Franco Nero; ***D:*** Tony Palmer. **TV**

Wagner: The Movie 𝒜 ½ **1985** Slightly half it's original length, the world's biggest biopic is still huge, sweeping, and long. Incoherent and over-acted. Wagner's music is conducted by Sir Georg Solti. Made for television. **300m/C VHS.** *GB HU* Richard Burton, Vanessa Redgrave, John Gielgud, Franco Nero, Laurence Olivier; ***D:*** Tony Palmer.

Wagon Master 𝒜𝒜𝒜 **1950** Two cowboys are persuaded to guide a group of Mormons, led by Bond, in their trek across the western frontier. They run into a variety of troubles, including a band of killers who joins the wagon train to escape a posse. Sensitively directed, realistic and worthwhile. Inspired the TV series "Wagon Train." Also available colorized. **85m/B VHS.** Ben Johnson, Joanne Dru, Harry Carey Jr., Ward Bond, Jane Darwell, James Arness; ***D:*** John Ford.

Wagon Tracks 𝒜𝒜 ½ **1919** Hart searches for the man responsible for his brother's death. **64m/B VHS, DVD.** William S. Hart, Jane Novak, Robert McKim, Lloyd Bacon; ***D:*** Lambert Hillyer.

Wagon Trail 𝒜𝒜 ½ **1935** The sheriff's son is blackmailed into helping a gang of robbers, with terrible consequences for himself and his father (Carey), who is fired from his job after the son breaks jail. The new sheriff is secretly chief of the outlaw band. Carey rides back into town and eventually virtue triumphs. Good, tense—but not too tense—western. **59m/B VHS, DVD.** Gertrude Messinger, Edward Norris, Roger Williams, Earl Dwire, Harry Carey Sr.; ***D:*** Harry Fraser; ***W:*** Harry Fraser; ***C:*** Robert E. Cline.

Wagon Wheels 𝒜𝒜 *Caravans West* **1934** Recycling was in vogue in '34, when unused footage from "Fighting Caravans" (1931) with Gary Cooper was used to remake the very same plot. The result is biodegradable. Settlers heading to Oregon are ambushed by bad guy Blue, employed by fur traders. Blue sics Injuns on them too, but don't worry, they make it. Adapted from Zane Grey's novel "Fighting Caravans." **54m/B VHS, DVD.** Randolph Scott, Monte Blue, Gail Patrick, Billy Lee; ***D:*** Charles T. Barton.

Wagons East 𝒜 **1994 (PG-13)** Fed up with prairie hardships, pioneers decide to hitch up to a wagon train and head east. Candy (who died during filming) plays the drunken former wagonmaster hired to get them back home, with Lewis (out of his depth) as a neurotic ex-doctor, and McGinley stuck in the role of a gay bookseller that reeks of stereotypical mannerisms. Script is desperate for humor, which it never finds, and it's hard to watch Candy's performance knowing this mess was his last role. **100m/C VHS, DVD.** Melinda Culea, John Candy, Richard Lewis, Ellen Greene, John C. McGinley, Robert Picardo, William Sanderson, Thomas F. Duffy, Russell Means, Rodney A. Grant, Michael Horse, Gailard Sartain, Lochlyn Munro, Stuart Proud Eagle Grant; ***D:*** Peter Markle; ***W:*** Matthew Carlson, Jerry Abrahamson.

The Wagons Roll at Night 1/2 **1941** The circus wagons that is. Remake of 1937's "Kid Galahad" transfers the action from the boxing arena to the circus arena. Nick Coster (Bogart) is the owner of the failing enterprise, romancing fortune teller Flo (Sidney) while trying to protect his innocent sister, Mary (Leslie) from the seedy side of life. This would have been easier if sis hadn't fallen for the new lion tamer, Matt Varney (Albert). Nick tries to break up the lovebirds with predictable results. Based on the novel by Francis Wallace. **84m/B VHS.** Humphrey Bogart, Sylvia Sidney, Eddie Albert, Joan Leslie, Sig Rumann, Cliff Clark, Charles Foy, Frank Wilcox; ***D:*** Ray Enright; ***W:*** Barry Trivers, Fred Niblo Jr.; ***C:*** Sid Hickox; ***M:*** Heinz Roemheld.

Wagons Westward 1/2 **1940** Twin brothers David (Warren Hull) and Tom (Wayne Hull) Cook can't be more different, and when their father dies they take very different paths. Tom moves in with Uncle Hardtack (Hayes) in New Mexico and David stays home to care for their mother (Brissac). As adults, Tom (Morris) becomes an outlaw gunman and David (Morris) becomes a Marshall, eventually charged with apprehending his brother. While classically western, the story adds the twists of mistaken identity and double-crossing as it creeps to a final confrontation. **70m/B DVD.** Wayne Hull, Warren Hull, Chester Morris, Anita Louise, Buck Jones, Ona Munson, George "Gabby" Hayes; ***D:*** Lew Landers; ***W:*** Harrison Jacobs, Joseph Moncure March; ***C:*** Ernest Miller.

Wah-Wah **2005 (R)** Grant debuts as a writer/director in an autobiographical family story set in Swaziland in the late 1960s on the eve of the African nation's independence from Britain. Young Ralph (Fox) catches his mother Lauren (Richardson) committing adultery. Lauren walks out on the family, and husband/father Harry (Byrne) takes to drink, sending Ralph to boarding school. When the boy returns (now played by Hoult), he discovers his father has suddenly married a brash American, Ruby (Watson). Ruby becomes the teenager's ally, which is a good thing since the ex-pat colony is breaking apart, Harry's drinking makes him violent, and Ralph's mother suddenly decides to return. **97m/C DVD.** *GB FR* Gabriel Byrne, Miranda Richardson, Emily Watson, Julie Walters, Nicholas Hoult, Celia Imrie, Julian Wadham, Fenella Woolgar, Sid Mitchell, Zachary Fox, Ian Roberts; ***D:*** Richard E. Grant; ***W:*** Richard E. Grant; ***C:*** Pierre Aim; ***M:*** Patrick Doyle.

Waikiki 1/2 **1980** Two private eyes set out to prove that their friend is not the "cane field murderer" who is terrorizing the Hawaiian island of Oahu. Harmless but pointless TV pilot. **96m/C VHS.** Dack Rambo, Steve Marachuk, Donna Mills, Cal Bellini, Darren McGavin; ***D:*** Ron Satlof. **TV**

Waikiki Wedding **1937** Enjoyable musical about a scheming pineapple promoter (Crosby) who meets the woman of his dreams in a contest he concocted. Contest winner Ross dislikes Hawaii and wants to go home and Crosby must keep her from going...first for business reasons and later, for love. Supporting cast includes Hawaiian Prince Leilani and a pig. Lots of song and dance and Hawaiian sunsets, along with Burns and Raye, the other couple destined for love on the islands, keep the story moving. ♫ Sweet Leilani; Sweet Is the Word for You; In a Little Hula Heaven; Blue Hawaii; Okolehao; Nani Ona Pua. **89m/B VHS, DVD.** Bing Crosby, Bob Burns, Martha Raye, Shirley Ross, George Barbier, Leif Erickson, Grady Sutton, Granville Bates, Anthony Quinn; ***D:*** Frank Tuttle; ***W:*** Frank Butler, Don Hartman, Walter DeLeon, Francis Martin; ***C:*** Karl Struss; ***M:*** Leo Robin, Ralph Rainger. Oscars '37: Song ("Sweet Leilani").

The Wailer 1/2 *La Llorona* **2006** Low-budget and cliched horror story based on a Mexican legend. Six vacationing Americans are offered a mountain cabin by a local. Only the place is haunted by the ghost of a crying woman who murdered her children to be with her lover. For some reason, the ghost decides to dispense with her visitors. **85m/C DVD.** Vanessa Rice q, John Patrick Jordan, Hugo Medina, Brenda Lynn Mejia, Monique Barajas, Nicole Daniels, Rocael Leiva; ***D:*** Andres Navia; ***W:*** Rafy Rivera; ***C:*** Curtis Petersen; ***M:*** Richard John Baker. **VIDEO**

Waist Deep **2006 (R)** Violent urban gangsta pic more or less delivers as expected. Parolee O2 (Gibson) is trying to live the straight and narrow when he gets carjacked with his son sleeping in the back seat. Was it a deliberate snatch and did his snarling mad dog rival Meat (The Game) have something to do with it? No matter—O2 is gonna get his little boy back at any cost—with some help from street-smart honey Coco (Good). **97m/C DVD, HD DVD.** *US* Tyrese Gibson, Meagan Good, Larenz Tate, Kimora Lee Simmons, H. Hunter Hall, The Game; ***D:*** Vondie Curtis-Hall; ***W:*** Vondie Curtis-Hall, Darin Scott; ***C:*** Shane Hurlbut; ***M:*** Terence Blanchard.

Wait Till Your Mother Gets Home **1983** "Mr. Mom"-like zaniness abounds as a football coach cares for the kids and does chores while his wife takes her first job in 15 years. Almost too darn cute, but well written. **97m/C VHS.** Paul Michael Glaser, Dee Wallace, Peggy McCay, David Doyle, Raymond Buktenica, James Gregory, Joey Lawrence, Lynne Moody; ***D:*** Bill Persky. **TV**

Wait until Dark **1967** A photographer unwittingly smuggles a drug-filled doll into New York, and his blind wife, alone in their apartment, is terrorized by murderous crooks in search of it. A compelling thriller based on the Broadway hit by Frederick Knott, who also wrote "Dial M for Murder." The individual actors' performances were universally acclaimed in this spinetingler. **105m/C VHS, DVD.** Audrey Hepburn, Alan Arkin, Richard Crenna, Efrem Zimbalist Jr., Jack Weston; ***D:*** Terence Young; ***W:*** Robert B. Carrington; ***C:*** Charles B(ryant) Lang Jr.; ***M:*** Henry Mancini.

Wait until Spring, Bandini 1/2 **1990 (PG-13)** A flavorful immigrant tale about a transplanted Italian family weathering the winter in 1925 Colorado, as seen through the eyes of a young son. Alternately funny and moving, with one of Dunaway's scenery-chewing performances as a local temptation for the father. Based on the autobiographical novel by John Fante, co-produced by Francis Ford Coppola. **104m/C VHS.** Joe Mantegna, Faye Dunaway, Burt Young, Ornella Muti, Alex Vincent, Renata Vanni, Michael Bacall, Daniel Wilson; ***D:*** Dominique Deruddere; ***W:*** Dominique Deruddere; ***M:*** Angelo Badalamenti.

Waiting **2000** Actor wannabe/slacker/waiter Sean (Keenan) is told by his dad that he has 30 days to find a job, an apartment, and something to do with his life. And dad doesn't mean that Sean should continue to wait tables at a South Philly mob-run Italian eatery—and maybe he could find a nice girl as well. **80m/C VHS, DVD, UMD.** Will Keenan, Hannah Dalton, Kerri Kenney, Harry Philabosian, Lloyd Kaufman, Ron Jeremy; ***D:*** Patrick Hasson; ***W:*** Patrick Hasson; ***C:*** Michael Pearlman.

Waiting WOOF! **2005 (R)** Any laughs that might have been squeezed from this comedy set at ShenaniganZ—an eatery more mall-generic than a blend of Bennigan's and Applebee's—have been derailed by the genuinely pathetic lives of the staff and their patrons. Solid cast, led by Reynolds, is given table scraps in the form of predictable food pranks and self-loathing gags. **93m/C DVD, Blu-ray Disc.** *US* Ryan Reynolds, Anna Faris, Justin Long, David Koechner, Luis Guzman, Chi McBride, Alanna Ubach, Vanessa Lengies, Max Kasch, Dane Cook, Jordan Ladd, Emmanuelle Chriqui, Wendie Malick, John Francis Daley, Kaitlin Doubleday, Robert Patrick Benedict, Andy Milonakis; ***D:*** Rob McKittrick; ***W:*** Rob McKittrick; ***C:*** Matthew Irving; ***M:*** Adam Gorgoni.

Waiting for Guffman **1996 (R)** The eccentric citizens of Blaine, Missouri, plan an original musical ("Red, White, and Blaine") to celebrate the town's 150th anniversary with the aid of former New Yorker and semi-hysteric Corky St. Claire (Guest) as their director. Everyone's very game—and almost completely talentless. The Guffman of the title is the Broadway producer Corky knows and whom he's invited to see their disaster-in-the-making. A little too deliberately quirky for its own good. **84m/C VHS, DVD.** Bob Odenkirk, Christopher Guest, Eugene Levy, Catherine O'Hara, Parker Posey, Fred Willard, Lewis Arquette, Matt Keeslar, Paul Dooley, Paul Benedict, Bob Balaban, Larry Miller, Brian Doyle-Murray; ***D:*** Christopher Guest; ***W:*** Christopher Guest, Eugene Levy; ***C:*** Roberto Schaefer; ***M:*** Michael McKean, Harry Shearer, Christopher Guest.

Waiting for Superman **2010** Guggenheim's expose of the failing U.S. educational system with its monetary waste, unfulfilled potential, and social and generational failure. Title comes from a comment made by educational reformer Geoffrey Canada. **102m/C DVD.** *US* ***D:*** Davis Guggenheim; ***W:*** Davis Guggenheim, Billy Kimball; ***C:*** Erich Roland; ***M:*** Christophe Beck.

Waiting for the Light 1/2 **1990 (PG)** When a woman takes over a small-town diner, she gets the surprise of her life. Seems an angel has made his home there and now the townsfolk are flocking to see him. MacLaine is wonderful and Garr is fetching and likeable. Set during the Cuban missile crisis. Enjoyable, tame comedy. **94m/C VHS, DVD.** Shirley MacLaine, Teri Garr, Vincent Schiavelli, John Bedford Lloyd; ***D:*** Christopher Monger; ***W:*** Christopher Monger.

Waiting for the Moon 1/2 **1987 (PG)** Hunt as Alice B. Toklas is a relative treat in this ponderous, frustrating biopic about Toklas and Gertrude Stein, her lover. Made for "American Playhouse" on PBS. **88m/C VHS, DVD.** Linda Hunt, Linda Bassett, Andrew McCarthy, Bruce McGill, Jacques Boudet, Bernadette LaFont; ***D:*** Jill Godmilow; ***W:*** Mark Magill; ***C:*** Andre Neau. Sundance '87: Grand Jury Prize. **TV**

The Waiting Game 1/2 **1998** College friends Sarah (West) and Amy (Abdul) work at the same art gallery but things start to get dicey when Sarah gets dragged into a mystery involving her Uncle Lowell (Hinkle), undercover CIA agent Adrian (Potter), and some smuggled artifacts. From the Harlequin Romance Series; adapted from the Jayne Ann Krentz novel. **95m/C DVD.** *CA* Chandra West, Chris Potter, Paula Abdul, Jonathan Crombie, John Pyper-Ferguson, Art Hinkle; ***D:*** Vic Sarin; ***W:*** Barbara O'Kelly, Peter Lauterman, Jennifer Black; ***C:*** Vic Sarin; ***M:*** John McCarthy. **TV**

The Waiting Game **1999** Group of actor wannabes are working in a New York restaurant while waiting for the proverbial big break. They fall in and out of lust and love and suffer audition humiliation and other trials. **81m/C VHS, DVD.** Michael Raynor, Will Arnett, Terumi Matthews, Dan Riordan, Debbon Ayer; ***D:*** Ken Liotti; ***W:*** Ken Liotti; ***C:*** Rich Eliano; ***M:*** Jim Farmer.

The Waiting Time 1/2 **1999** Post-Cold War thriller based on the novel by Gerald Seymour. Tracy Barnes (Turner) is a corporal in the British Intelligence Corps who makes a seemingly unprovoked attack on German politician Dieter Krause (Becker). Befriended by solicitor's clerk Joshua Mantle (Thaw), the duo travel to Berlin to make sense of things but Joshua finds himself involved in the decade-old murder of Tracy's German lover and with the dreaded East German secret police. **150m/C VHS, DVD.** *GB* John Thaw, Zara Turner, Hartmut Becker, Mark Pegg, Struan Rodger, Colin Baker, Christien Anholt; ***D:*** Stuart Orme; ***W:*** Patrick Harbinson; ***C:*** Peter Middleton; ***M:*** Colin Towns. **TV**

Waiting to Exhale **1995 (R)** Adaptation of Terry McMillan's novel about four African-American women hoping to reach the point in their love lives when they can relax and stop waiting for the right man. After the string of dogs and users they choose, you want to tell them not to hold their breath. The women are supposed to be close friends, but all of their stories are broken up into vignettes. This erodes the ensemble feeling of the movie, but performances are strong all around. Retaining the book's feel of just-between-friends girl talk, it may be a little harsh for those who are, shall we say, estrogen-challenged. A lush R&B soundtrack is the perfect backdrop for the ladies' soulful yearning for real love. **120m/C VHS, DVD.** Whitney Houston, Angela Bassett, Loretta Devine, Lela Rochon, Gregory Hines, Dennis Haysbert, Mykelti Williamson, Michael Beach, Leon, Wendell Pierce, Donald Adeosun Faison, Jeffrey D. Sams, Lamont Johnson; ***Cameos:*** Wesley Snipes; ***D:*** Forest Whitaker; ***W:*** Ronald Bass; ***C:*** Toyomichi Kurita; ***M:*** Kenneth "Babyface" Edmonds. MTV Movie Awards '96: Song ("Sittin' Up in My Room").

Waitress WOOF! *Soup to Nuts* **1981 (R)** Three beautiful girls are waitresses in a crazy restaurant where the chef gets drunk, the kitchen explodes, and the customers riot. Awful premise, worse production. **85m/C VHS, DVD.** Jim Harris, Carol Drake, Carol Bever; ***D:*** Lloyd Kaufman; ***W:*** Charles Kaufman, Michael Stone; ***C:*** Lloyd Kaufman.

Waitress **2007 (PG-13)** Sweet as, well, pie. Waitress Jenna (the radiantly appealing Russell) is a pie-baking phenom in her southern community. She's also fixing to leave her abusive jerk husband Earl (Sisto) when she discovers she's pregnant. Jenna looks for support from her diner co-workers while baking up outrageous concoctions ("I Hate My Husband Pie") that reflect her changing moods. She also decides to have a fling with her sweetly flustered OB-GYN (Fillion), and from there, the tale is uneven but cute nonetheless. Writer/director/actress Shelly (who plays Dawn) was murdered in November 2006 just after completing the film. **107m/C DVD.** *US* Keri Russell, Nathan Fillion, Cheryl Hines, Lew Temple, Jeremy Sisto, Edward Jemison, Andy Griffith, Darby Stanchfield, Adrienne Shelly; ***D:*** Adrienne Shelly; ***W:*** Adrienne Shelly; ***C:*** Matthew Irving; ***M:*** Andrew Hollander.

Wake Island **1942** After Pearl Harbor, a small group of Marines face the onslaught of the Japanese fleet on a small Pacific Island. Although doomed, they hold their ground for 16 days. Exciting, realistic, and moving. The first film to capitalize on early "last stands" of WWII; also among the most popular war movies. Shown to soldiers in training camps with great morale-raising success. **88m/B VHS, DVD.** Robert Preston, Brian Donlevy, William Bendix, MacDonald Carey, Albert Dekker, Walter Abel, Rod Cameron, Barbara Britton, Mikhail Rasumny, Bill Goodwin, Damian O'Flynn, Frank Albertson, Hugh Beaumont, Hillary Brooke, James Brown, Don Castle, Frank Faylen, Mary Field, William Forrest, Alan Hale Jr., Charles Trowbridge, Philip Van Zandt, Phillip Terry; ***D:*** John Farrow; ***W:*** W.R. Burnett, Frank Butler; ***C:*** William Mellor, Theodor Sparkuhl; ***M:*** David Buttolph. N.Y. Film Critics '42: Director (Farrow).

Wake of the Red Witch 1/2 **1949** Wayne captains the ship of the title and battles shipping tycoon Adler for a fortune in pearls and the love of a beautiful woman (Russell). Wayne shows impressive range in a non-gun-totin' role. **106m/B VHS, DVD.** John Wayne, Gail Russell, Gig Young, Luther Adler, Henry Daniell; ***D:*** Edward Ludwig.

Waking Life 1/2 **2001 (R)** Linklater's innovative and visually groundbreaking look at dreams, life, and philosophy doesn't really seem to have a plot. What it does have is several vignettes of people mostly just talking about the above subjects. What makes it stunning is the look of the project. Linklater "filmed" the scenes on digital video, then had a group of artists digitally "paint" over the footage, assigning different artists different scenes or actors so as to have a variety of styles. The result is a trippy experiment that might not appeal to many people except philosophy majors, computer geeks, or chemically altered college students. Film buffs looking for something new would do well to check it out. **99m/C VHS, DVD.** *US* Richard Linklater, Glover Gill, Julie Delpy, Wiley Wiggins, Ethan Hawke, Adam Goldberg, Nicky Katt, Steven Soderbergh; ***D:*** Richard Linklater; ***W:*** Richard Linklater; ***C:*** Richard Linklater, Tommy Pallotta; ***M:*** Glover Gill. N.Y. Film Critics '01: Animated Film.

Waking Ned Devine 1/2 **1998 (PG)** Old Ned Devine has the winning ticket for the Irish National Lottery—unfortunately, the shock has killed him. Jackie O'Shea

(Bannen) and the other 50 still-living residents of Tulaigh Morh conspire to fool a bored lottery official (Dempsey) into thinking that Michael O'Sullivan (Kelly) is Devine, so that they can share the wealth. As each obstacle to the payoff is overcome, a larger hurdle appears, and the comedy becomes more and more screwball until it reaches its darkly comic conclusion. Warm and full of blarney, but never becomes too sappy, or contrived. Filmed on the beautiful Isle of Man and accented with a fine score full of Celtic melodies. Veteran cast carries off even the most improbable gags (including Kelly's buck-naked motorcycle ride). **91m/C VHS, DVD.** Ian Bannen, David Kelly, Fionnula Flanagan, Susan Lynch, James Nesbitt, Maura O'Malley, Robert Hickey, Paddy Ward, James Ryland, Fintan McKeown, Matthew Devitt, Eileen Dromey, Dermot Kerrigan, Brendan F. Dempsey; ***D:*** Kirk Jones; ***W:*** Kirk Jones; ***C:*** Henry Braham; ***M:*** Shaun Davey.

Waking the Dead 🦴🦴 1/2 **2000 (R)** Director Gordon's uneven but earnest adaptation of the Scott Spencer novel features Crudup as Fielding Pierce, an aspiring politician haunted by the death ten years earlier of his activist girlfriend Sarah (Connelly) in a car bombing. As Fielding begins a run at the Senate, he starts to see Sarah in crowds, wondering if the reports of her death were exaggerated, and doubting his sanity. The love story angle gets a lot of play, yet manages to be unconvincing, and the frequent jumps back and forth in time are jarring. Crudup and Connelly seem in over their heads at times. **105m/C VHS, DVD.** Billy Crudup, Jennifer Connelly, Molly Parker, Janet McTeer, Paul Hipp, Sandra Oh, Hal Holbrook, Lawrence Dane; ***D:*** Keith Gordon; ***W:*** Robert Dillon; ***C:*** Tom Richmond; ***M:*** Tomandandy.

Waking Up in Reno 🦴 1/2 **2002 (R)** Redneck road pic where romance goes awry for two couples on the way to a monster truck show in Nevada. Ringleader is Little Rock car dealer Lonnie Earl (Thornton), who fools around on his wife Darlene (Richardson) with the aptly named Candy (Theron) under the nose of his best friend and Candy's husband Roy (Swayze). Candy, who desperately wants to get pregnant, is always fooling around in the back seat with Roy while Lonnie enters a steak eating contest. Cruz appears as a hooker Roy meets in a sleazy hotel bar. Flimsy setup gives way to the disappointing payoff, and you soon realize its all over but the shouting. **100m/C VHS, DVD.** *US* Billy Bob Thornton, Charlize Theron, Patrick Swayze, Natasha Richardson, Holmes Osborne, Chelcie Ross, Brent Briscoe, Wayne Federman, Penelope Cruz, Mark Fauser; ***Cameos:*** Tony Orlando; ***D:*** Jordan Brady; ***W:*** Brent Briscoe, Mark Fauser; ***C:*** William A. Fraker; ***M:*** Marty Stuart.

Waking Up Wally 🦴🦴 1/2 **2005** Innocuously-told true story based on hockey dad Walter Gretzky (McCamus), whose debilitating brain aneurysm made him forget, among other things, his famous son Wayne's (Holden-Reid) sports achievements. The family struggles through rehabilitation as Walter's lack of short-term memory leads to frustration before he (and they) can accept his limitations. Based on the memoir "Walter Gretzky: On Family, Hockey and Healing." **?m/C DVD.** *CA* Tom McCamus, Kris Holden-Ried, Victoria Snow, Tara Spencer-Nairn, Carey Feeham; ***D:*** Dean Bennett; ***W:*** Carol Hay; ***C:*** Roger Vernon; ***M:*** Christopher Dedrick. **TV**

Wal-Mart: The High Cost of Low Price 🦴🦴🦴 1/2 **2005** Greenwald's latest documentary investigates the economic impact of the retail giant on everyday people, from its own workers to competing business owners in rural areas to the consumer in general. Gives voice to the views of those opposed to the practices of the company. **98m/C DVD.** *US* ***D:*** Robert Greenwald; ***C:*** Kristy Tully; ***M:*** John (Gianni) Frizzell.

Walk, Don't Run 🦴🦴 1/2 **1966** Romantic comedy involving a British businessman (Grant) unable to find a hotel room in Tokyo due to the crowds staying for the 1964 summer Olympic Games. He winds up renting a room from an Embassy secretary (Eggar) and then meets and invites Hutton, a member of the U.S. Olympic walking team, also without a place to stay, to share it with him. Grant then proceeds to play matchmaker, despite the fact that Eggar has a fiance. Grant's last film. Innocuous, unnecessary remake of "The More the Merrier." **114m/C VHS, DVD.** Cary Grant, Samantha Eggar, Jim Hutton, John Standing, Miiko Taka; ***D:*** Charles Walters; ***M:*** Quincy Jones.

Walk Hard: The Dewey Cox Story 🦴 1/2 **2007 (R)** Yet another double entendre smut-fest from screenwriter Apatow (and director/writer Kasdan), who mock every music bio cliche they can twang a guitar at. Reilly goes silly for his title role as a white boy singer (with a family tragedy that haunts him) who gets that devil rock 'n' roll in his soul and finds it leads to drugs and debauchery, if not the love of a woman (Fisher) too good for him. Much like a novelty record it's clever for a moment but repeated exposure may cause brain damage. **96m/C DVD.** *US* John C. Reilly, Jenna Fischer, Raymond J. Barry, Kristen Wiig, Tim Meadows, Harold Ramis, Margo Martindale, Chris Parnell, Matt Besser, David Krumholtz, Frankie Muniz, Jack White, Justin Long, Paul Rudd, Jason Schwartzman, Rance Howard, Martin Starr, Jack McBrayer, Jane Lynch, Simon Helberg, Jack Black, John Michael Higgins, Jonah Hill, Craig Robinson; ***D:*** Jake Kasdan; ***W:*** Jake Kasdan, Judd Apatow; ***C:*** Uta Briesewitz; ***M:*** Michael Andrews.

A Walk in the Clouds 🦴🦴 1/2 **1995 (PG-13)** Gorgeously photographed, if sappy, romantic fantasy finds WWII vet Paul Sutton (Reeves), returning to his unhappy marriage and salesman job. So when the good-hearted Paul meets beautiful Victoria (Sanchez-Gijon), the pregnant and unmarried daughter of a possessive Napa vineyard owner (Giannini), he's more than happy to help by posing as her husband. Naturally, dad is livid at their "marriage" and Paul falls in love with his sham bride. Quinn gets to do his part as wise family patriarch and yes, there's even a grape harvest (and some grape stomping) to put everyone in the proper romantic mood. Based on the 1942 Italian film "Four Steps in the Clouds." **103m/C VHS, DVD.** Keanu Reeves, Aitana Sanchez-Gijon, Giancarlo Giannini, Anthony Quinn, Angelica Aragon, Evangelina Elizondo, Freddy Rodriguez, Debra Messing; ***D:*** Alfonso Arau; ***W:*** Robert Mark Kamen; ***C:*** Emmanuel Lubezki; ***M:*** Leo Brouwer. Golden Globes '96: Score.

Walk in the Spring Rain 🦴🦴 1/2 **1970 (PG)** The bored wife of a college professor follows him to rural Tennessee when he goes on sabbatical, where she meets the married Quinn and the two begin an affair. When Quinn's disturbed son learns of the affair, he attacks the woman, with tragic results. Fine cast should have had better effect on low-key script. **98m/C VHS.** Ingrid Bergman, Anthony Quinn, Fritz Weaver, Katherine Crawford, Tom Fielding, Virginia Gregg; ***D:*** Guy Green; ***W:*** Stirling Silliphant; ***C:*** Charles B(ryant) Lang Jr.; ***M:*** Elmer Bernstein.

A Walk in the Sun 🦴🦴🦴 1/2 *Salerno Beachhead* **1946** The trials of a group of infantrymen in WWII from the time they land in Italy to the time they capture their objective, a farmhouse occupied by the Germans. Excellent ensemble acting shows well the variety of civilians who make up any fighting force and explores their fears, motivations, and weaknesses. Producer and director Milestone also made "All Quiet on the Western Front" and the Korean War masterpiece "Pork Chop Hill." Released in the final days of the war, almost concurrently with two other WWII films of the first echelon, "The Story of G.I. Joe" and "They Were Expendable." **117m/B VHS, DVD.** Dana Andrews, Richard Conte, John Ireland, Lloyd Bridges, Sterling Holloway, George Tyne, Norman Lloyd, Herbert Rudley, Richard Benedict, Huntz Hall, James B. Cardwell, George Offerman Jr., Steve Brodie, Matt Willis, Alvin Hammer, Chris Drake, Victor Cutler, Jay Norris; ***D:*** Lewis Milestone; ***W:*** Robert Rossen, Harry Brown; ***C:*** Russell Harlan; ***M:*** Freddie Rich, Earl Robinson.

Walk into Hell 🦴🦴 **1957** A mining engineer and his assistant searching for oil meet the primitive natives of New Guinea. Tedious at times and dated, but pleasant enough. **91m/C VHS.** *AU* Chips Rafferty, Francoise Christophe, Reg Lye; ***D:*** Lee Robinson.

Walk Like a Man 🦴 1/2 **1987 (PG)** In a take-off of Tarzan movies, Mandel plays a man raised by wolves. Comic problems arise when he is found by his mother and the family attempts to civilize him. Juvenile script wastes fine cast. **86m/C VHS, DVD.** Howie Mandel, Christopher Lloyd, Cloris Leachman, Colleen Camp, Amy Steel, George DiCenzo; ***D:*** Melvin Frank.

A Walk on the Moon 🦴🦴 1/2 **1999 (R)** Goldwyn's promising directorial debut has 30-ish, vaguely restless Jewish housewife Pearl (Lane) vacationing in the Catskills in the summer of 1969 with her family: teenage daughter Alison (Paquin), son Daniel (Boriello), and intrusive mother-in-law Lillian (Feldshuh). Hubby Marty (Schreiber) is working in the city and visits on the weekends. When sensitive hippie blouse peddler Walker (Mortensen) catches her eye, she decides it's time to catch up on the '60s and her lost teenage years. When she takes off for Woodstock and happens upon her daughter, the family drama is intensified. Pearl's turmoil and motivations are handled well by Lane and the screenwriter Gray, and neither of the men vying for her are cardboard stereotypes, but the abruptly feel-good ending may not work for some. **107m/C VHS, DVD.** Diane Lane, Liev Schreiber, Viggo Mortensen, Anna Paquin, Tovah Feldshuh, Bobby Boriello, Lisa Bronwyn Moore; ***D:*** Tony Goldwyn; ***W:*** Pamela Gray; ***C:*** Anthony B. Richmond; ***M:*** Mason Daring.

Walk on the Wild Side 🦴🦴 **1962** In 1930s New Orleans, a man searches for his long-lost love, finds her working in a whorehouse and fights to save her from the lesbian madame Stanwyck. Melodrama, based only loosely on the Nelson Algren novel and adapted by cult novelist John Fante, with Edmund Morris. Much-troubled on the set, and it shows. **114m/B VHS, DVD.** Jane Fonda, Laurence Harvey, Barbara Stanwyck, Capucine, Anne Baxter; ***D:*** Edward Dmytryk; ***W:*** Edmund Morris, John Fante, Ben Hecht; ***C:*** Joe MacDonald; ***M:*** Elmer Bernstein.

Walk Softly, Stranger 🦴🦴 **1950** Two-bit crook is reformed by the love of an innocent peasant girl. If you can stand the cliche masquerading as a plot, the performances are good. **81m/B VHS.** Alida Valli, Joseph Cotten, Spring Byington, Paul Stewart, Jack Paar, Jeff Donnell, John McIntire; ***D:*** Robert Stevenson.

Walk the Line 🦴🦴🦴 1/2 **2005 (PG-13)** Phoenix embodies The Man in Black, warts and all in this excellent biopic showing Johnny Cash's family strife, rise as an early 50s rock star, through his battle with drugs, and his long courtship of June Carter (an equally brilliant Witherspoon). Script and actors never shy away from the more disturbing aspects of Cash's personality and life, which makes for a powerful, if not always comfortable, film. Phoenix and Witherspoon did all their own singing, and they do it well enough to make you wonder if it's the real thing. **135m/C DVD.** *US* Joaquin Rafael (Leaf) Phoenix, Reese Witherspoon, Ginnifer Goodwin, Robert Patrick, Dallas Roberts, Larry Bagby, Dan John Miller, Shelby Lynne, Tyler Hilton, Waylon Malloy Payne, Shooter Jennings; ***D:*** James Mangold; ***W:*** James Mangold, Gill Dennis; ***C:*** Phedon Papamichael; ***M:*** T-Bone Burnett. Oscars '05: Actress (Witherspoon); British Acad. '05: Actress (Witherspoon), Sound; Golden Globes '06: Actor—Mus./Comedy (Phoenix), Actress—Mus./Comedy (Witherspoon), Film—Mus./Comedy; N.Y. Film Critics '05: Actress (Witherspoon); Natl. Soc. Film Critics '05: Actress (Witherspoon); Screen Actors Guild '05: Actress (Witherspoon).

Walk the Proud Land 🦴🦴 1/2 **1956** Story of Indian agent John Clum (Murphy), who fights for the rights of the Apache in 1870s Arizona and who convinces their leader Geronimo (Silverheels) to surrender to the authorities. Adapted from the biography "Apache Agent" by Woodworth Clum. **88m/C VHS.** Audie Murphy, Jay Silverheels, Anne Bancroft, Pat(ricia) Crowley, Charles Drake; ***D:*** Jesse Hibbs; ***W:*** Jack Sher, Gil Doud; ***C:*** Harold Lipstein.

A Walk to Remember 🦴🦴 **2002 (PG)** **101m/C VHS, DVD.** *US* Mandy Moore, Shane West, Peter Coyote, Daryl Hannah, Lauren German, Clayne Crawford; ***D:*** Adam Shankman; ***W:*** Karen Janszen; ***C:*** Julio Macat; ***M:*** Mervyn Warren.

Walkabout 🦴🦴🦴 1/2 **1971 (PG)** Beautifully told and filmed story (by Roeg in his debut) about a nameless young brother (John, Roeg's six-year-old son) and sister (Agutter), who are abandoned in the Australian outback when their father kills himself. The children wander, with little chance of survival, until a young aborigine (Gumpilil) finds them. He interrupts his own "walkabout," a rite of passage, to teach them to survive, leading to betrayal and tragedy. Based on a novel by James Vance Marshall. **100m/C VHS, DVD.** *AU* Jenny Agutter, Lucien John, David Gulpilil, John Meillon; ***D:*** Nicolas Roeg; ***W:*** Edward Bond; ***C:*** Nicolas Roeg; ***M:*** John Barry.

Walker 🦴🦴 **1987 (R)** Slapdash, tongue-in-cheek historical pastiche about the real-life American William Walker (played previously in "Burn!" by Marlon Brando), and how he led a revolution in Nicaragua in 1855 and became its self-declared president. A bitter, revisionist farce never for a moment attempting to be accurate. Matlin's unfortunate, though fortunately brief, follow-up to her Oscar-winning performance. **95m/C VHS.** Ed Harris, Richard Masur, Peter Boyle, Rene Auberjonois, Marlee Matlin, Miguel (Michael) Sandoval; ***D:*** Alex Cox; ***W:*** Rudy Wurlitzer; ***M:*** Joe Strummer.

The Walker 🦴 1/2 **2007 (R)** Carter (Harrelson), an extravagantly gay DC insider who spends most of his time escorting rich married women to public events, ends up in the middle of the investigation of the murder of a powerful Beltway lobbyist who was having an affair with Carter's married friend Lynn (Scott Thomas). In order to protect her and clear his own name, Carter must try and find the real killer himself while his carefully cultivated status in DC society collapses. Harrelson's performance stands out, but otherwise this is a run-of-the mill crime drama that flirts awkwardly with political commentary. **107m/C DVD.** *GB US* Woody Harrelson, Kristin Scott Thomas, Lauren Bacall, Lily Tomlin, Moritz Bleibtreu, Ned Beatty, Willem Dafoe, Geff Francis, Steven Hartley, Mary Beth Hurt; ***D:*** Paul Schrader; ***W:*** Paul Schrader; ***C:*** Chris Seager; ***M:*** Anne Dudley.

Walker Payne 🦴 1/2 **2006 (R)** Self-conscious drama with some strongly suggestive scenes of cruelty to animals. Walker Payne (Patric) is a divorced ex-con who's laid off from his mining job in rural Illinois in the late 1950s. Walker's hateful ex-wife Luanne (de Matteo) won't let him near his daughters until he hands over $5K so she can go to nursing school. His one potential asset is entering his faithful pit bull Brute in a backwoods dogfighting match. **117m/C DVD.** Jason Patric, Drea De Matteo, KaDee Strickland, Sam Shepard, Bruce Dern; ***D:*** Matt Williams; ***W:*** Alex Paraskevas; ***C:*** James L. Carter; ***M:*** Mason Daring.

Walker: Texas Ranger: One Riot, One Ranger 🦴🦴 1/2 **1993 (PG-13)** Norris sticks with the action-adventure mode with this tv pilot movie about Cordell Walker, a good guy with a code and some martial arts skills, who teams up with an ex-gridiron star and a female district attorney to go after lawbreakers. This time its bank robbers and three hoods after a teenaged girl. **96m/C VHS.** Chuck Norris, Sheree J. Wilson, Clarence Gilyard Jr., Gailard Sartain, Floyd "Red Crow" Westerman, James Drury; ***D:*** Virgil W. Vogel; ***W:*** Louise McCann. **TV**

Walking and Talking 🦴🦴 1/2 **1996 (R)** Low-budget, lighthearted estrogen romp through the lives of two best friends in New York, Amelia (Keener) and Laura (Heche), going through commitment crises. Freshman writer/director Holofcener scores by making a lackluster story imminently watchable. Likable cast of mostly unknowns (Heche was deemed a rising star at a recent Cannes Festival) deliver Holofcener's clever and humorous exchanges. Corrigan's video store clerk and all-around "ugly guy" is a highlight. Brit Bragg brings in a worthy score. **86m/C VHS, DVD.** Anne Heche, Catherine Keener, Liev Schreiber, Todd Field, Kevin Corrigan, Randall Batinkoff, Joseph Siravo, Vincent Pastore, Lynn Cohen, Andrew Holofcener; ***D:*** Nicole Holofcener; ***W:*** Nicole Holofcener; ***C:*** Michael Spiller; ***M:*** Billy Bragg.

Walking Back 🦴🦴 **1926** Troubled teens go for joyride and bash mirthmobile to smithereens. The body shop agrees to give them a different car, but they find themselves in the middle of a heist at a plant belonging to the father of one of the boys. **53m/B VHS.** Sue Carol, Richard Walling, Ivan Lebedeff, Robert Edeson, Florence Turner, Arthur (L.) Rankin; ***D:*** Rupert Julian.

The Walking Dead **1994 (R)** Depicts the Vietnam War from the perspectives of four black and one white Marine assigned to rescue POWs from a North Vietnam camp in 1972. Fairly routine story with stock characters (by-the-book sergeant, family man, naive youngster, cynical hustler) and flashbacks to depict their back home struggles. Cast tries but is defeated by a one-dimensional script. **89m/C VHS.** Joe Morton, Eddie Griffin, Allen Payne, Vonte Sweet, Roger Floyd; ***D:*** Preston A. Whitmore II; ***W:*** Preston A. Whitmore II; ***C:*** John L. (Ndiaga) Demps Jr.; ***M:*** Gary Chang.

Walking on Air **1987** Ray Bradbury's story comes to life as a handicapped boy dreams of completing a real space walk. Originally aired on PBS as part of the "Wonderworks" series. **60m/C VHS.** Lynn Redgrave, Jordan Marder, James Treuer, Katheryn Trainor; ***D:*** Ed Kaplan.

Walking on Water **2002** Gavin (Bonney) has been suffering from leukemia for a long time and has asked his friends and housemates—Charlie (Colosimo), Anna (Theodorakis), and Frank (Bishop)—to help him die with dignity at home. In the end, this means Charlie must quietly assist Gavin's suicide, which leaves him haunted by grief and guilt. He's not the only one unable to cope as Gavin's friends and family all struggle in their separate ways. **90m/C VHS, DVD.** *AU* Vince Colosimo, Maria Theodorakis, Nicholas Bishop, Nathaniel Dean, Judi Farr, David Bonney, Anne Lise Phillips, Daniel Roberts; ***D:*** Tony Ayres; ***W:*** Roger Monk; ***C:*** Robert Humphreys; ***M:*** Antony Partos. Australian Film Inst. '02: Actor (Dean), Actress (Theodorakis), Screenplay, Support. Actress (Farr).

Walking Tall **½ 1973 (R)** A Tennessee sheriff takes a stand against syndicate-run gambling and his wife is murdered in response. Ultra-violent crime saga wowed the movie going public and spawned several sequels and a TV series. Based on the true story of folk-hero Buford Pusser, admirably rendered by Baker. **126m/C VHS, DVD.** Joe Don Baker, Elizabeth Hartman, Noah Beery Jr., Gene Evans, Rosemary Murphy, Felton Perry; ***D:*** Phil Karlson; ***W:*** Mort Briskin; ***C:*** Jack Marta; ***M:*** Walter Scharf.

Walking Tall **½ 2004 (PG-13)** Changes abound in this ho hum retelling of the 1973 version as the good guy now goes by Chris Vaughn (The Rock) who's single and lives in Washington. Luckily, he's still carrying the big stick and taking care of business (although, oddly enough, director Bray contemplated swapping it out for an aluminum bat—c'mon, is nothing sacred?) And he does just that with the authority one would expect from The Rock, whose presence is commanding yet surprisingly subtle (something he could not have learned from his wrestling days) allowing him to rise above the mediocre script and sub-par character development. Johnny Knoxville effectively serves as the comic-relief/sidekick guy while Neal McDonough sleepwalks through what could have been a fun villain role. **86m/C VHS, DVD.** *US* Dwayne "The Rock" Johnson, Johnny Knoxville, Neal McDonough, Kristen Wilson, Khleo Thomas, John Beasley, Barbara Tarbuck, Michael Bowen, Ashley Scott; ***D:*** Kevin Bray; ***W:*** David Klass, Channing Gibson, David Levien, Brian Koppelman; ***C:*** Glen MacPherson; ***M:*** Graeme Revell.

Walking Tall: Lone Justice **2007 (R)** Low-grade actioner that has nothing to do with the original franchise. Sheriff Nick Prescott (Sorbo) has retired but it doesn't last long when he's caught up in a federal case against a drug lord and his gang who are determined to wipe out all witnesses. **94m/C DVD.** Kevin Sorbo, Haley Ramm, Laurent Martin, Rodrigo De La Rosa, Jennifer Sipes; ***D:*** Tripp Reed; ***W:*** Joe Halpin, Ben Strassmann; ***C:*** Jas Shelton; ***M:*** Eric Wurst, David Wurst. **VIDEO**

Walking Tall: Part 2 **1975 (PG)** Club-wielding Tennessee sheriff Buford Pusser, this time played less memorably by Svenson, attempts to find the man who killed his wife. Even more violent than the original. **109m/C VHS, DVD.** Bo Svenson, Noah Beery Jr., Angel Tompkins, Richard Jaeckel; ***D:*** Earl Bellamy.

Walking Tall: The Final Chapter **½ 1977 (PG)** The final months in the life of Tennessee sheriff Buford Pusser and the mystery surrounding his death. It wasn't the final chapter. Still to come: a TV flick and series. **112m/C VHS, DVD.** Bo Svenson, Forrest Tucker, Leif Garrett, Morgan Woodward; ***D:*** Jack Starrett; ***C:*** Robert B. Hauser.

Walking the Edge **½ 1983 (R)** A widow hires a taxi driver to help her seek vengeance against the men who killed her husband and her son. Forster does what he can with the lousy story and script. **94m/C VHS, DVD.** Robert Forster, Nancy Kwan, Joe Spinell, Aarika Wells; ***D:*** Norbert Meisel; ***W:*** Curt Allen; ***C:*** Ernie Poulos; ***M:*** Jay Chattaway.

Walking Through the Fire **½ 1980** A young woman's real-life struggle with Hodgkin's disease. Her fight for her own and her unborn baby's survival is a stirring testament to the power of faith. Absorbing drama. **143m/C VHS.** Bess Armstrong, Tom Mason, Bonnie Bedelia, Richard Masur, Swoosie Kurtz, J.D. Cannon, June Lockhart; ***D:*** Robert Day. **TV**

Walking Thunder **½ 1994 (PG)** The McKay family are stranded in the Rocky Mountains in 1850 when their wagon is destroyed by a grizzly bear. But they're rescued by a mountain man (Read) and a Sioux medicine man (Thin Elk), who introduce young Jacob to a number of adventures. It's wholesome, old-fashioned kid entertainment. **95m/C VHS, DVD.** John Denver, James Read, David Tom, Chief Ted Thin Elk; ***D:*** Craig Clyde; ***W:*** Craig Clyde; ***M:*** John Scott; ***Nar:*** Brian Keith.

The Wall **½** *Guney's The Wall; Le Mur; Duvar* **1983** The last film by Guney, author of "Yol," about orphaned boys in prison in the Turkish capitol of Ankara trying to escape and/or rebel after ceaseless rapings, beatings and injustice. An acclaimed, disturbing film made from Guney's own experience. He died in 1984, three years after escaping from prison. Brutal and horrifying. In Turkish with English subtitles. **117m/C VHS, DVD.** *TU* Ayse Emel Mesci, Saban, Sisko; ***D:*** Yilmaz Guney; ***W:*** Yilmaz Guney.

The Wall **1999** Three stories that focus on the Vietnam Veterans Memorial and some of the objects left there. "The Pencil Holder" finds young Ben Holst (Blumas) living with his stiff-necked Army colonel father (Olmos) in Saigon in 1969 where he's mistaken by a dying soldier (Chevolleau) for his own son. "The Badge" is the good-luck toy sheriff's badge that black soldier Bracey Mitchell (Glover) clings to as he hides from the Vietcong and dreams of home. "The Player" is conniving wheeler-dealer Bishop (Whaley), who runs a base nightclub and gets his comeuppance from self-sacrificing soldier Luis (DeLorenzo), who's a guitar-playing whiz. **94m/C VHS, DVD.** Edward James Olmos, Richard Chevolleau, Trevor Blumas, Dean McDermott, Savion Glover, Ruby Dee, Martin Roach, Linette Robinson, Frank Whaley, Michael Delorenzo, Ron White, Matthew Ferguson; ***D:*** Joseph Sargent; ***W:*** Scott Abbott, Charles Fuller, Patrick Sheane Duncan; ***C:*** Donald M. Morgan; ***M:*** Larry Brown. **CABLE**

Wall **½** *Mur* **2004** Documentary from veteran filmmaker Simone Bitton. This time she takes on the security fence being erected to divide Israel from the West Bank. Use of the term "wall" gives a hint of the filmmaker's opinion of the security fence. Israeli officials resist the use of any term apart from "fence." The strength of this documentary is in its balanced view. While showing the wall from many locations it is never clear what side of the wall is being viewed. Ultimately the wall reveals itself as a divider of people and land that neither Israelis nor Palestinians embrace. **98m/C DVD.** ***D:*** Simone Bitton; ***W:*** Simone Bitton; ***C:*** Jacques Bouquin.

WALL-E **½ 2008 (G)** Another winner from Pixar that's both sweet and edgy (that whole global disaster thing is a bummer). Lonely robot WALL-E (Waste Allocation Load Lifter Earth-Class) has been cleaning up Earth for 700 years after it was abandoned by those destructive, messy humans. Sleek droid EVE (Extra-terrestrial Vegetation Evaluator) comes calling to see if it's okay for humans to return and WALL-E is instantly smitten. So when EVE completes her assignment, WALL-E latches on and returns with her to Axiom, the giant spaceship housing the couch potato consumers that barely pass for human to let them know the big news. Oscar-winning sound designer Ben Burtt provides WALL-E's beeps, boops, and other noises. **97m/C DVD.** *US* ***D:*** Andrew Stanton; ***W:*** Andrew Stanton, Jim Reardon; ***C:*** Jeremy Lasky; ***M:*** Thomas Newman; ***V:*** Fred Willard, Jeff Garlin, Ben Burtt, Sigourney Weaver, Kathy Najimy, John Ratzenberger, Elissa Knight. Oscars '08: Animated Film; British Acad. '08: Animated Film; Golden Globes '09: Animated Film.

Wall Street **1987 (R)** Stone's energetic, high-minded big business treatise in which naive, neophyte stockbroker Bud Fox (Charlie Sheen) is seduced into insider trading by sleek entrepreneur Gordon Gekko (Douglas), much to his blue-collar father's (Martin Sheen) chagrin. A fast-moving drama of '80s-style materialism with a mesmerizing, award-winning performance by Douglas as greed personified. Expert direction by Stone, who co-wrote the not-very-subtle script. His father, to whom this film is dedicated, was a broker. Look for Stone in a cameo. **126m/C VHS, DVD, Blu-ray Disc.** Paul Guilfoyle, Michael Douglas, Charlie Sheen, Martin Sheen, Daryl Hannah, Sean Young, James Spader, Hal Holbrook, Terence Stamp, Richard Dysart, John C. McGinley, Saul Rubinek, James Karen, Josh Mostel, Millie Perkins, Cecilia Peck, Grant Shaud, Franklin Cover, Oliver Stone; ***D:*** Oliver Stone; ***W:*** Stanley Weiser, Oliver Stone; ***C:*** Robert Richardson; ***M:*** Stewart Copeland. Oscars '87: Actor (Douglas); Golden Globes '88: Actor—Drama (Douglas); Natl. Bd. of Review '87: Actor (Douglas); Golden Raspberries '87: Worst Support. Actress (Hannah).

Wall Street 2: Money Never Sleeps **2010** Gordon Gekko's "greed is good" credo from Stone's 1987 pic is updated when he tries for a second chance after being released from prison. Gordon's daughter Winnie is engaged to young Wall Street broker Jake Moore so things may not be so different after all. **m/C DVD.** Michael Douglas, Shia LaBeouf, Carey Mulligan, Frank Langella, Josh Brolin, Susan Sarandon, Vanessa Ferlito; ***D:*** Oliver Stone; ***W:*** Allan Loeb; ***C:*** Rodrigo Prieto.

Wall Street Cowboy **1939** When his land is threatened, a cowboy fights big business in the big city. **54m/B VHS.** George "Gabby" Hayes, Raymond Hatton, Pierre Watkin, Ann Baldwin, Roy Rogers; ***D:*** Joseph Kane; ***W:*** Gerald Geraghty, Norman S. Hall; ***C:*** Jack Marta.

Wallaby Jim of the Islands **1937** The singing captain of a pearl fishing boat must protect his treasure from marauding pirates. Pleasant enough musical adventure. **61m/B VHS, DVD.** George Houston, Douglas Walton; ***D:*** Charles Lamont.

Wallace & Gromit in The Curse of the Were-Rabbit **½ 2005 (G)** Will appeal to adult audiences more than a stop-action animation film would at first seem to warrant. But don't worry, there's still plenty for the kiddies. The dynamic duo is faced with the responsibility of guarding the gardens for miles around in preparation for the annual Giant Vegetable Fete. But rabbits are eating all of the vegetables! Inventor Wallace comes up with a humane way to solve the pesky bunny issue, but it's more complicated than that. The painstakingly millimeter by millimeter claymation is impressive enough. That the characters manage to be expressive, and hilarious, is sheer brilliance. **85m/C DVD.** *GB* ***D:*** Nick Park, Steve Box; ***W:*** Nick Park, Steve Box, Bob Baker, Mark Burton; ***C:*** Tristan Oliver, Dave Alex-Riddett; ***M:*** Julian Nott, Hans Zimmer; ***V:*** Peter Sallis, Ralph Fiennes, Helena Bonham Carter, Nicholas C. Smith, Liz Smith, Peter Kay. Oscars '05: Animated Film; L.A. Film Critics '05: Animated Film; Broadcast Film Critics '05: Animated Film.

Wallander: Firewall **2008** Two teenaged girls are accused of murdering a cab driver; a body is found near a cash machine and the victim was an IT expert; a new computer system disrupts the work at the police station and power outages occur. Wallander ties the various crimes together and finds they relate to global monetary systems and revenge. **90m/C DVD.** *GB* Kenneth Branagh, Jeany Sparks, Sarah Smart, Sadie Shimmin, Tom Beard, Tom Hiddleston, Richard McCabe, Orla Brady, Luke Allen-Gale; ***D:*** Niall MacCormic; ***W:*** Richard Cottan, Richard McBrien; ***C:*** Jan Jonaeus; ***M:*** Martin Phipps, Vincent Pope. **TV**

Wallander: One Step Behind **2008** Three teenagers are murdered in the woods as they celebrate Midsummer's Eve. Then detective Wallander discovers the dead body of his colleague Svedberg, which ties in with the triple murder. A fourth teenager, Isa, is in danger and more murders occur before Wallander makes all the connections. **90m/C DVD.** *GB* Kenneth Branagh, Jeany Sparks, Sarah Smart, Sadie Shimmin, Tom Beard, Tom Hiddleston, Flora Spencer-Longhurst, Richard McCabe; ***W:*** Richard Cottan; ***C:*** Anthony Dod Mantle; ***M:*** Martin Phipps. **TV**

Wallander: Sidetracked **2008** World-weary Swedish detective Kurt Wallander (Branagh) works in the seaside town of Ystad and carries a lot of personal baggage. In his latest case, a teenaged girl burns herself to death before Wallander's horrified gaze but does her death have anything to do with a series of hatchet murders of the town's prominent male citizens? Adaptation of the Henning Mankell mystery series. **90m/C DVD.** *GB* Kenneth Branagh, David Warner, Sarah Smart, Tom Hiddleston, Richard McCabe, Jeany Sparks, Sadie Shimmin, Tom Beard; ***D:*** Philip Martin; ***W:*** Richard Cottan; ***C:*** Anthony Dod Mantle; ***M:*** Martin Phipps. **TV**

The Walloping Kid **½ 1926** A B-western with photography done in Monument Valley. Silent with original organ music. **67m/B VHS.** Kit Carson, Pauline Curley; ***D:*** Robert J. Horner.

Walls of Glass **½** *Flanagan* **1985 (R)** An aging New York cabby tries to make it as an actor. Effective performances by all override the thin plot. Slow and uneven, but involving. **85m/C VHS, DVD.** Geraldine Page, Philip Bosco, William Hickey, Olympia Dukakis, Brian Bloom, Linda Thorson; ***D:*** Scott Goldstein.

The Walls of Hell *Intramuros* **1964** Lt. Jim Sorenson (Mahoney) leads guerilla fighters into the city of Manila, aided by freedom fighter Nardo (Poe), to defeat desperate Japanese troops hold up in the city. **88m/B VHS, DVD.** *PH* Jock Mahoney, Fernando Poe Jr., Mike Parsons; ***D:*** Gerardo (Gerry) De Leon, Eddie Romero; ***W:*** Eddie Romero, Cesar Amigo, Ferde Grofe Jr.; ***C:*** Felipe Sacdalan; ***M:*** Tito Arevalo.

The Walls of Malapaga *Au-Dela des Grilles; Le Mura di Malapaga* **1949** Frenchman Gabin, who's killed his mistress, stows away aboard a ship to Italy. He arrives in Genoa only to have all his money and papers stolen. Gabin then meets Miranda, a lonely waitress with a young daughter, and the two fall in love. But it's only temporary as the authorities come closing in. French with subtitles. **91m/C VHS.** *FR IT* Jean Gabin, Isa Miranda, Vera Talchi, Andrea Checchi, Robert Dalban; ***D:*** Rene Clement; ***W:*** Jean Aurenche, Pierre Bost; ***M:*** Roman Vlad. Oscars '50: Foreign Film.

Walpurgis Night *Valborgmassoafton* **1941** Soapy Swedish drama about abortion was racy for its time. Office gal Bergman secretly loves her boss (Hanson). His wife refuses to have children and goes through an abortion. An unscrupulous fellow blackmails her with this knowledge. Bergman bides her time. Stay tuned... Interesting document on the mores of another time. In Swedish with English subtitles. **82m/B VHS.** *SW* Lars Hanson, Karin Carlsson, Victor Sjostrom, Ingrid Bergman, Erik "Bullen" Berglund, Sture Lagerwall, Georg Rydeberg, Georg Blickingberg; ***D:*** Gustaf Edgren.

Walter and Henry **2001** Walter (Larroquette) and his 12-year-old son Henry (Braun) live in a trailer in Brooklyn and (barely) make ends meet as street musicians in the city. However, after Walter has a psychotic breakdown and is institutionalized, Henry is forced to live with his rigid grandfather (Coburn) from whom Walter has been estranged for years. And slowly, Henry begins to adapt, and even enjoy, his new life. **90m/C VHS, DVD.** John Larroquette, James Coburn, Kate Nelligan, Nicholas Braun; ***D:*** Daniel Petrie; ***W:*** Geoffrey Sharp; ***C:*** Michael Storey; ***M:*** Christopher Dedrick. **CABLE**

The Waltons: The Christmas Carol 🦴🦴 **1980** The winter solstice brings no special joy to Walton's mountain; WWII has taken many men, with short wave reports indicating the Nazi terror spreading across Europe. But huddled in the glow of Walton's barn, the children rediscover the true meaning of Christmas. **94m/C VHS.** Judy Norton-Taylor, Jon Walmsley, Mary (Elizabeth) McDonough, Eric Scott, Kami Cotler, Joe Conley, Ronnie Clare, Leslie Winston, Peggy Rea; ***D:*** Lawrence (Larry) Dobkin. **TV**

Waltz across Texas 🦴🦴 1/2 **1983** Young oil man Jastrow and good-lookin' rock scientist Archer at first don't take to each other, but there's something in the air, and romance blossoms. Jastrow and Archer cowrote and coproduced, and cohabitated as spouses in real-life. **100m/C VHS, DVD.** Terry Jastrow, Anne Archer, Mary Kay Place, Richard Farnsworth; ***D:*** Ernest Day; ***C:*** Robert Elswit.

Waltz King 🦴🦴 **1963** Typically hokey Disney biography of the young composer Johann Strauss during his Old Viennese heyday. Fine music, pretty German locations. Well-made family fare. **94m/C VHS.** Kerwin Mathews, Senta Berger, Brian Aherne; ***D:*** Steve Previn.

Waltz of the Toreadors 🦴🦴🦴 *The Amorous General* **1962** Retired general Sellers doesn't care for his wealthy, shrewish wife and tries to re-kindle a 17-year-old romance with a French woman. It doesn't work out (seems his illegitimate son also has a soft spot for the lady), but the general decides to keep his eyes open for other possibilities. Interestingly cast adaptation of Jean Anouilh's play. Sellers is hilarious, as usual. **105m/C VHS, DVD.** *GB* Peter Sellers, Dany Robin, Margaret Leighton, Cyril Cusack; ***D:*** John Guillermin; ***W:*** Wolf Mankowitz; ***C:*** John Wilcox; ***M:*** Richard Addinsell.

A Waltz Through the Hills 1988 Two orphans head into the Australian outback and experience many adventures en route to the coast where they can set sail for England and their grandparents. Aired on PBS as part of the "Wonderworks" series. **116m/C VHS, DVD.** Tina Kemp, Andre Jansen, Ernie Dingo, Dan O'Herlihy; ***D:*** Frank Arnold.

Waltz with Bashir 🦴🦴🦴 1/2 *Vals in Bashir* **2008 (R)** Animated autobiographical account of director Folman's experiences as a former member of the Israeli army and participant in the 1982 Israeli-Lebanese war—the brutal massacre of civilians in response to the assassination of Lebanese president Bashir Gemayel—and the role his military unit played. Folman's repressed memories first play out as frightening images in the recurring dream of a friend who is also a combat survivor, then proceed to scenes of war, conversations in a cafe, and a final realistic glimpse of war's aftermath. The visions are psychedelic while the realism is stark and uncomfortable. In Hebrew with subtitles. **87m/C DVD.** *FR IS GE* ***D:*** Ari Folman; ***W:*** Ari Folman; ***M:*** Max Richter. Directors Guild '08: Feature Doc.; Golden Globes '09: Foreign Film.

Waltzing Anna 🦴 1/2 **2006 (PG-13)** Greedy Dr. Charlie Keegan gets nailed for insurance fraud and must work six months in an upstate New York nursing home to keep his license. The place is run by an equally shady operator and Keegan just passes the time until his conscience is pricked by beautiful nurse Jill. Well-meaning but predictable and maudlin. **108m/C DVD.** Emmanuelle Chriqui, Pat Hingle, Betsy Palmer, Artie Lange, Robert Capelli Jr., Mackenzie Milone, Paige Turco, Grant Shaud, Marilyn Chris, Casey Siemaszko; ***D:*** Doug Bollinger; ***W:*** Robert Capelli Jr., Doug Bollinger; ***C:*** Yaron Orbach; ***M:*** Tony McAnany. **VIDEO**

Wanda Nevada 🦴 1/2 **1979 (PG)** Gambler Fonda wins nubile young Shields in a poker game, so he drags her with him to the Grand Canyon to look for gold. Director/star Fonda sure picked a lemon for his only screen appearance with dad Henry (a grizzled old varmint appearing briefly). Shields is in her usual form—stellar for a shampoo commercial. **105m/C VHS.** Peter Fonda, Brooke Shields, Henry Fonda, Fiona Lewis, Luke Askew, Ted Markland, Severn Darden, Paul Fix; ***D:*** Peter Fonda.

Wanda, the Sadistic Hypnotist 🦴 **1967** A comely vixen hypnotizes an innocent pedestrian, ties him up and whips him to indulge her whims. Despite the "victim's" protests, she unleashes a gang of sexually playful women on him, and he is subjected to a multitude of "tortures." **70m/C VHS, DVD.** Katharine Shubeck, Janice Sweet, Dick Dangerfield, Daryl Cobinot; ***D:*** Gregory Corarito.

The Wanderer 🦴🦴 *Le Grand Meaulnes* **1967** Two friends fall in love—Frantz with Valentine and his friend Augustin with Frantz's sister, Yvonne. When the two women disappear on Frantz's wedding day, the two men begin a search to find both the women and the reasons for their disappearance. In French with English subtitles. **108m/C VHS.** *FR* Brigitte Fossey, Jean Blaise, Alain Noury, Juliette Villard; ***D:*** Jean-Gabriel Albicocco.

Wanderers 🦴🦴🦴 1/2 **1979 (R)** Richard Price's acclaimed novel about youth gangs coming of age in the Bronx in 1963. The "Wanderers," named after the Dion song, are a gang of Italian-American teenagers about to graduate high school, who prowl the Bronx with the feeling that something is slipping away from them. Fascinating, funny and touching. Manz is unforgettable as a scrappy gal. A wonderful 60s soundtrack (Dion, the Four Seasons) colors this "coming of age the hard way" film. **113m/C VHS, DVD.** Erland van Lidth, Ken Wahl, John Friedrich, Karen Allen, Linda Manz, Richard Price, Toni Kalem, Tony Ganios, Alan Rosenberg, Jim Youngs, Val Avery, Dolph Sweet, Olympia Dukakis; ***D:*** Philip Kaufman; ***W:*** Philip Kaufman, Rose Kaufman; ***C:*** Michael Chapman.

Wandering Jew 🦴🦴 1/2 **1920** An excellent print of the rare Austrian film version of the classic legend, one of at least three silent versions. A Jew is condemned to wander the earth for eternity. **65m/B VHS.** *AT* Ernst Bath, Else Osterheim, Josef Schreiter, Rudolf Schildkraut, Joseph Schildkraut; ***D:*** Otto Kreisler; ***W:*** Heinrich Glucksmann.

The Wandering Swordsman 🦴🦴 *You xia er; Yau hap yi* **1970** Often aptly referred to as director Chang Cheh's retelling of the Robin Hood legend. Yu Hsieh Erh (David Tiang) steals from thieves, but instead of returning the money to its owners he gives it away to whoever he encounters that might need it. Surprisingly this works out pretty good for him until he's tricked into stealing from an escort service and has to clear his name before they kill him. Apparently even in medieval China you don't mess with pimps. **103m/C DVD.** *HK* David Chiang, Lily Li, Pei-Shan Chang, Lei Cheng, Liu Hung, Kang Liu, Ma Wu, Bolo Yeung, Sing Chen, Wei Lieh Lan, Kuang Yu Wang; ***D:*** Cheh Chang; ***W:*** Kuang Ni; ***C:*** Shan Hua; ***M:*** Fu-ling Wang.

Wannabes 🦴🦴 **2001** Angelo (DeMeo) and his younger brother Paulie (Dubin) are waiters in a New York neighborhood joint where the local mob boss is Santo (Vitrelli). Tired of being abused, particularly by Santo's spoiled son Vinny (D'Onofrio), Angelo, Paulie and a couple of their buds become successful bookies and go into loansharking and other criminal activities. Santo likes Angelo's gumption and makes him his protege, much to Vinny's anger. Familiar stereotypes abound. **110m/C VHS, DVD.** Joe (Johnny) Viterelli, Joseph (Joe) D'Onofrio, William DeMeo, Conor Dubin, Raymond Serra; ***D:*** William DeMeo, Charles A. Addessi; ***W:*** William DeMeo.

The Wannsee Conference 🦴🦴🦴 1/2 *Wannseekonferenz* **1984** A startling, important film depicting, in real time, the conference held at the Wannsee on January 20, 1942, during which 14 members of the Nazi hierarchy decided in 85 minutes the means and logistics of effecting the Final Solution. Recreated from the original secretary's notes. Horrifying and chilling. Along with "Shoah," a must-see for understanding the Holocaust and the psychology of genocide. In German with English subtitles. **87m/C VHS, DVD.** *GE* Dietrich Mattausch, Gerd Brockmann, Friedrich Beckhaus, Robert Atzorn, Jochen Busse, Hans-Werner Bussinger, Harald Dietl, Peter Fitz, Reinhard Glemnitz, Dieter Groest, Martin Luttge, Anita Mally, Gerd Riegauer; ***D:*** Heinz Schirk; ***W:*** Paul Mommertz; ***C:*** Horst Schier.

Wanted 🦴 1/2 **1998 (R)** Jimmy Scrico (Sutton) has accidentally shot a mob boss. Naturally, this means he's on the run from the vengeful wiseguys and he finds sanctuary in a Catholic school where Jimmy's befriended by Father Donnelly (Busfield). Then the bad guys catch up with him. **90m/C VHS, DVD.** Michael Sutton, Timothy Busfield, Robert Culp, Tracey Gold, James Quattrochi; ***D:*** Terence M. O'Keefe; ***W:*** Terence M. O'Keefe, Mark Evan Schwartz; ***C:*** Richard A. Jones.

Wanted 🦴🦴🦴 **2008 (R)** Russian-born director Bekmambetov keeps the pace smoking and makes Michael Bay (and others of his ilk) look like hacks and wimps. Or like Wesley Gibson (McAvoy) when we first meet him—a humiliated office drone. Picked up by Fox (Jolie), Wesley's informed that the dad he never knew was just killed and also happened to be an assassin who belonged to a secret society called the Fraternity. Wesley is taken to meet boss Sloan (Freeman) and told to man up so he can get revenge on rogue Cross (Kretschmann), who offed his pops. After some brutal training, Wes heads for his confrontation. The violence is as excessive as it is ridiculous. So what? It's also well-done. Adapted from Mark Millar and J.G. Jones's cult comic. **110m/C DVD, Blu-ray Disc.** *US* James McAvoy, Angelina Jolie, Morgan Freeman, Terence Stamp, Thomas Kretschmann, Common, Marc Warren, David O'Hara, Kristi Hager, Konstantin Khabensky, Dato Bakhtadze; ***D:*** Timur Bekmambetov; ***W:*** Michael Brandt, Derek Haas, Chris Morgan; ***C:*** Mitchell Amundsen; ***M:*** Danny Elfman.

Wanted: Babysitter WOOF! 1975 A young student accidentally becomes involved by her roommate in a plot to kidnap the child she is babysitting. Schneider is truly awful; Italian comic Pazzetto is at sea in a bad role as her boyfriend. Also released as "The Babysitter." **90m/C VHS.** Robert Vaughn, Vic Morrow, Maria Schneider, Renato Pozzetto, Nadja Tiller, Carl Mohner, Sydne Rome; ***D:*** Rene Clement.

Wanted Dead or Alive 🦴 1/2 **1986 (R)** Ex-CIA agent Hauer is now a high-tech bounty hunter assigned to bring in an international terrorist. When the terrorist kills Hauer's friend and girlfriend, he forgets the $50,000 bonus for bringing him in alive. Official "sequel" to the Steve McQueen TV series with Hauer as the McQueen character's great-grandson. The link is meaningless, and the plot is a thin excuse for much violence and anti-terrorist flag-waving. **104m/C VHS, DVD.** Rutger Hauer, Gene Simmons, Robert Guillaume, William Russ, Jerry Hardin, Mel Harris; ***D:*** Gary Sherman; ***W:*** Brian Taggert; ***C:*** Alex Nepomniaschy; ***M:*** Joe Renzetti.

Wanted: The Perfect Guy 🦴🦴 1/2 **1986** Danny and Melanie try to find Mister Right for their divorced Mom (Kahn). An Emmy Award winner about single parents and their children. **45m/C VHS.** Ben Affleck, Pam Potillo, Keith Szarabajka, Madeline Kahn, Melanie Mayron; ***D:*** Caitlin Adams; ***W:*** Mary P. Willis; ***C:*** Tom Hurwitz; ***M:*** Jonathan Sheffer.

The War 🦴🦴 1/2 **1994 (PG-13)** Post-Vietnam war drama, set in 1970 Mississippi, centers on a children's battle over a treehouse but becomes a sermon on love, death, family values, pacifism, and the physical and spiritual wounds of war. After helping son Stu (Wood) and daughter Lidia (Randall) build their treehouse, troubled Vietnam vet Stephen Simmons (Costner) tries to coax Stu to make peace with the bullies trying to take it over. However cliched, director Avnet allows a talented cast of kids to thoughtfully express a child's view of the world but gosh-darn-it the preachy tone can get down-right annoying. **126m/C VHS, DVD, HD DVD.** Elijah Wood, Kevin Costner, Lexi (Faith) Randall, Mare Winningham, Christine Baranski, Bruce A. Young, Gary Basaraba, Raynor Scheine, Nick Searcy, Lucas Black; ***D:*** Jon Avnet; ***W:*** Kathy McWorter; ***C:*** Geoffrey Simpson; ***M:*** Thomas Newman.

War 🦴 **2007 (R)** Yet another of Jet Li's urban action/martial arts flicks, this time featuring British action import Statham. Rogue (Li) is an assassin manipulating two crime families into a bloody gang war. Crawford (Statham) is the FBI agent chasing him. Did Rogue kill Crawford's partner? Why is Rogue starting a gang war? Does it matter? The movie is mostly about explosions and gunfire, at the expense of the charisma and action skills of Statham and Li. What plot exists owes much to "Yojimbo" and "A Fistful of Dollars," minus the depth and the appeal of the Asian martial-arts movies that gave Li his start, leaving a noisy, forgettable mess. **103m/C DVD, Blu-ray Disc.** *US* Jet Li, Jason Statham, John Lone, Devon Aoki, Luis Guzman, Saul Rubinek, Ryo Ishibashi, Sung Kang, Mathew St. Patrick, Nadine Velazquez; ***D:*** Philip G. Atwell; ***W:*** Lee Anthony Smith, Gregory J. Bradley; ***C:*** Pierre Morel; ***M:*** Brian Tyler.

War & Love 🦴🦴 **1984 (PG-13)** Two Jewish teenagers in Warsaw are torn apart by WWII and Nazi persecution. After the war they search for each other. Sincere, but not adequately developed, drama based on the book "The Survivors" by film's producer Jack Eisner. **112m/C VHS.** Sebastian Keneas, Kyra Sedgwick; ***D:*** Moshe Mizrahi.

War and Peace 🦴🦴 1/2 **1956** Lengthy adaptation of Tolstoy's great (and likewise lengthy) novel about three families caught up in Russia's Napoleonic Wars from 1805 to 1812; filmed in Rome. Bad casting and confused script (by six writers) are somewhat overcome by awesome battle scenes and Hepburn. Remade in 1968. **208m/C VHS, DVD.** Audrey Hepburn, Mel Ferrer, Henry Fonda, Anita Ekberg, Vittorio Gassman, John Mills, Oscar Homolka, Herbert Lom, Helmut Dantine, Tullio Carminati, Barry Jones, Milly Vitale, Maria Ferrero, Wilfred Lawson, May Britt, Jeremy Brett, Lea Seidl, Patrick Crean, Sean Barrett, Richard Dawson; ***D:*** King Vidor; ***W:*** King Vidor, Bridget Boland, Mario Camerini, Ennio de Concini, Ivo Perilli, Irwin Shaw, Robert Westerby; ***C:*** Jack Cardiff, Aldo Tonti; ***M:*** Nino Rota. Golden Globes '57: Foreign Film.

War and Peace 🦴🦴🦴 **1968** The massive Russian production of Leo Tolstoy's masterpiece, adapting the classic tome practically scene by scene. All of the production took place in the Soviet Union. So painstaking that it took more than five years to finish, no other adaptation can touch it. Hugely expensive ($100 million, claimed the Russians), wildly uneven production. Great scenes of battle and aristocratic life. Though this version is far from perfect, one asks: Is it humanly possible to do screen justice to such a novel? In Russian with English subtitles. On four tapes. (Beware the two-part, poorly dubbed version that was also released.) **373m/C VHS, DVD.** *RU* Lyudmila Savelyeva, Sergei Bondarchuk, Vyacheslav Tihonor, Hira Ivanov-Golarko, Irina Gubanova, Antonina Shuranova; ***D:*** Sergei Bondarchuk; ***C:*** Jack Cardiff. Oscars '68: Foreign Film; Golden Globes '69: Foreign Film; N.Y. Film Critics '68: Foreign Film.

War and Peace 🦴🦴 1/2 **1973** Lengthy BBC production of the lengthy Tolstoy masterpiece that follows the trials and triumphs of two Russian families whose lives intersect against a backdrop of the Napoleonic Wars. On 6 cassettes. **750m/C VHS, DVD.** *GB* Anthony Hopkins, Alan Dobie, Faith Brook, Morag Hood, Colin Baker, Neil Stacey; ***D:*** John (Howard) Davies; ***W:*** Jack Pulman.

War & Remembrance 🦴 1/2 **1988** Tedious sequel to the epic TV miniseries "The Winds of War," based on the novel by Herman Wouk. Historical fiction is created around the events of WWII, including Nazi persecution and naval battles in the Pacific. Followed by "War and Remembrance: The Final Chapter." On seven cassettes. **840m/C VHS, DVD.** Charles Lane, Robert Mitchum, Jane Seymour, Hart Bochner, Victoria Tennant, Barry Bostwick, Polly Bergen, David Dukes, Michael Woods, Sharon Stone, Robert Morley, Sami Frey, Chaim Topol, John Rhys-Davies, Ian McShane, William Schallert, Jeremy Kemp, Steven Berkoff, Robert Hardy, Ralph Bellamy, John Gielgud; ***D:*** Dan Curtis. **TV**

War & Remembrance: The Final Chapter 🦴 1/2 **1989** The final episodes of Herman Wouk's sweeping saga, following "The Winds of War" and "War and Remembrance," deal with the struggle of a Jewish family in war-torn Europe. Natalie and her son, Louis, are trapped in a ghetto under the reign of a vicious Nazi, who considers a bribe for the sake of the mother and son. On five cassettes. **600m/C VHS.** Robert Mitchum, Jane Seymour, Hart Bochner, Victoria Tennant, Polly Bergen, David Dukes, Michael Woods, Sharon Stone, Robert Morley, Sami Frey, Chaim Topol, John Rhys-Davies, Ian McShane, William Schallert, Jeremy Kemp, Steven Berkoff, Robert Hardy, Ralph Bellamy, John Gielgud; ***D:*** Dan Curtis. **TV**

War Arrow 🦴🦴 **1953** Army Major Howell Brady (Chandler) is sent by Washington to end the Kiowa uprisings in Texas in this cavalry vs. Indians western. Along the way, he tries to win the heart of O'Hara. **79m/C VHS, DVD.** Maureen O'Hara, Jeff Chandler, Suzan Ball, John McIntire, Noah Beery Jr., Henry (Kleinbach) Brandon, Dennis Weaver, Jay Silverheels; ***D:*** George Sherman; ***W:*** John Michael Hayes.

The War at Home 🦴 ½ **1996 (R)** In 1972 Vietnam vet Jeremy Collier (Estevez) has been home in the Dallas suburbs for a year but the war and its effects still linger. Mom Maureen (Bates) is a conservative control freak and dad Bob (Sheen) just can't connect, while teenaged sis Karen (Williams) is going through her own rebellion. The tense situation comes to a bitter head over a Thanksgiving weekend. Based on the 1984 play "Home Front" by James Duff. **124m/C VHS, DVD.** Kathy Bates, Martin Sheen, Emilio Estevez, Kimberly Williams, Carla Gugino, Geoffrey Blake, Corin "Corky" Nemec, Ann Hearn; ***D:*** Emilio Estevez; ***W:*** James Duff; ***C:*** Peter Levy; ***M:*** Basil Poledouris.

War Between the Tates 🦴🦴 **1976** A college professor's affair with a female student is the basis for a tension filled stand-off with his wife. Mediocre adaptation of the Allison Lurie novel, somewhat redeemed by Ashley's performance. **90m/C VHS.** Mina (Badiyi) Badie, Ann Wedgeworth, Annette O'Toole, Colin Fox, Harvey Atkin, Michael J. Reynolds, Richard Crenna, Elizabeth Ashley, Granville Van Dusen; ***D:*** Lee Philips; ***W:*** Barbara Turner; ***M:*** John Barry. **TV**

The War Boy 🦴🦴 ½ **1985 (R)** Difficulties encountered by a young Canadian boy as he grows up in Central Europe during WWII. Not to be compared with "Empire of the Sun" or "Hope and Glory," both of which were released later; successful in its modest ambitions. Beautiful performance from 12-year-old star Hopely. **86m/C VHS.** *CA* Helen Shaver, Kenneth Welsh, Jason Hopely; ***D:*** Allan Eastman.

The War Bride 🦴🦴 **2001** Slow and sometimes tedious homefront drama but Friel's a firecracker. Cockney Lily (Friel) makes a whirlwind wartime marriage to Canadian soldier Charlie (Young) and is eventually granted citizenship and shipped off to her husband's home country. Lily's in for a rude shock when she sees that she'll be living on a small hardscrabble ranch in rural Alberta with her unwelcoming in-laws—Charlie's mother Betty (Fricker) and polio-stricken sister Sylvia (Parker). But this city sparrow is determined to make the best of things, although it's not going to be easy. **96m/C DVD.** *GB CA* Anna Friel, Brenda Fricker, Molly Parker, Aden Young, Loren Dean, Julie Cox; ***D:*** Lyndon Chubbuck; ***C:*** Ronald Orieux; ***M:*** John Sereda.

War Brides 🦴 **1980** Civil War brides confront life after the war. Low-budget drama. **100m/C VHS.** *CA* Elizabeth Richardson, Sharry Fleet, Sonja Smits; ***D:*** Martin Lavut. **TV**

War Bus Commando 🦴 **1989** A fully loaded bus is the only way out when soldiers are caught behind enemy lines in Afghanistan. A case of the spoof coming first: The plot is almost exactly the same as "Stripes"—only this one isn't funny. In Hi-Fi. **90m/C VHS.** *IT* Savina Gersak, Mark Gregory, John Vernon; ***D:*** Frank (Pierluigi Ciriaci) Valenti.

War in Space 🦴 *Battle of the Stars; Anno Zero - Guerra Nello Spazio; Year Zero - War in Sace* **1977** Powerful U.N. Space Bureau Starships and UFOs band together to battle alien invaders among the volcanoes and deserts of Venus. **91m/C VHS, DVD.** *IT* John Richardson, Gaetano Balestrieri, Yanti Sommer; ***D:*** Alfonso Brescia; ***W:*** Alfonso Brescia; ***C:*** Silvio Fraschetti; ***M:*** Marcello Giombini.

War, Inc. 🦴 ½ **2008 (R)** Over-the-top black comedy lampoons American wartime operations in Iraq. Hauser (Cusack) is a hitman sent to Turaquistan, a fictional country occupied by U.S. troops and run by an American corporation called Tamerlane, to assassinate a Middle Eastern oil barren named Omar Sharif (not actually played by Omar Sharif, of course). While there he falls for a reporter (Tomei), who mistakes him for another money-hungry executive. Several prominent political figures are roasted, including Dan Akroyd's obvious take on Dick Cheney as an ex-veep and current head of Tamerlane, running the corporation while sitting on the toilet (literally). Still, it's a little too angry and smug to work, as it awkwardly pushes its self-important sermon amid the silly jokes. **107m/C DVD, Blu-ray Disc.** *US* John Cusack, Hilary Duff, Marisa Tomei, Joan Cusack, Ben Kingsley, Dan Aykroyd, Lyubomir Neikov, Ben Cross, Ned Bellamy, Shirly Brener; ***D:*** Joshua Seftel; ***W:*** John Cusack, Jeremy Pikser, Mark Leyner; ***C:*** Zoran Popovic; ***M:*** David Robbins.

The War Lord 🦴🦴🦴 **1965** Set in the 11th century, Heston stars as Chrysagon, a Norman knight and war lord who commands a peasant village. While battling his enemies, he becomes enamored of a peasant girl named Bronwyn (Forsyth), who is unfortunately engaged to someone else. Pulling rank, Chrysagon uses an ancient law that allows noblemen the first night with a bride and the two fall in love. The two vow to never part, but that sets the stage for even more bloody battles. Fine acting and great production values make this a well-adapted version of the play "The Lovers" by Leslie Stevens. **121m/C VHS, DVD.** Charlton Heston, Richard Boone, Rosemary Forsyth, Guy Stockwell, Niall MacGinnis, Henry Wilcoxon, James Farentino, Maurice Evans, Michael Conrad; ***D:*** Franklin J. Schaffner; ***W:*** John Collier, Millard Kaufman; ***C:*** Russell Metty.

War Lover 🦴🦴 ½ **1962** An American daredevil flying captain and his co-pilot find themselves vying for the affections of a woman during WWII in England. Seeks human frailty beneath surface heroism. McQueen is impressive, no thanks to mediocre script. Excellent aerial photography, and featuring one of only a very few serviceable WWII B-17s then remaining. Based on John Hersey's novel. **105m/B VHS, DVD.** *GB* Steve McQueen, Robert Wagner, Shirley Anne Field, Bill Edwards, Gary Cockrell; ***D:*** Philip Leacock; ***W:*** Howard Koch.

War of the Buttons 🦴🦴 ½ **1995 (PG)** Two sleepy Irish fishing villages provide childish battle grounds for two groups of local lads. The Ballys (Ballydowse village), lead by Fergus (Fitzgerald), and the Carricks (Carrickdowse), with leader Geronimo (Coffey), have an intense rivalry and capture by the other gang leads to the removal of every clothing button for the unfortunate captive. When Fergus becomes a Carrick victim, he organizes a retaliatory strike, and emotions threaten to overwhelm all concerned. Based on the French novel "La Guerre des Boutons" by Louis Pergaud. Filmed on location in West Cork, Ireland. **94m/C VHS.** Gregg Fitzgerald, John Coffey, Liam Cunningham, Paul Batt, Eveanna Ryan, Colm Meaney, Johnny Murphy; ***D:*** John Roberts; ***W:*** Colin Welland; ***C:*** Bruno de Keyzer; ***M:*** Rachel Portman.

The War of the Colossal Beast 🦴 ½ *The Terror Strikes* **1958** This sequel to "The Amazing Colossal Man" finds the 70-foot Colonel Manning even angrier at the attempts to kill him than he was in the first film. So he wreaks more havoc until scolded by his sister into committing suicide for being such a troublemaker. Cheesy special effects but good for a laugh. **68m/B VHS, DVD.** Dean Parkin, Sally Fraser, Russ Bender, Roger Pace, Charles Stewart; ***D:*** Bert I. Gordon.

War of the Gargantuas 🦴 *Duel of the Gargantuas; Frankenstein Monsters: Sanda vs. Gairath; Furankenshutain No Kaiju: Sanda tai Gailah; Sanda tai Gailah* **1970 (G)** Tokyo is once again the boxing ring for giant monsters. This time it's a good gargantua (half human, half monster) against a bad gargantua. This is a strange one. **92m/C VHS.** *JP* Russ Tamblyn, Kumi Mizuno, Kenji Sahara, Jun Tazaki, Kipp Hamilton, Haruo Nakajima, Nobuo Nakamura, Ikio Sawamura, Yoshifumi Tajima; ***D:*** Inoshiro Honda; ***W:*** Inoshiro Honda, Takeshi Kimura, Kaoru Mabuchi; ***C:*** Hajime Koizumi; ***M:*** Akira Ifukube.

The War of the Roses 🦴🦴🦴 **1989 (R)** Acidic black comedy about a well-to-do suburban couple who can't agree on a property settlement in their divorce so they wage unreserved and ever-escalating combat on each other, using their palatial home as a battleground. Expertly and lovingly (if that's the word) directed by DeVito, who plays the lawyer. Turner and Douglas are splendid. Adapted from the novel by Warren Adler. **116m/C VHS, DVD.** Michael Douglas, Kathleen Turner, Danny DeVito, Marianne Saegebrecht, Sean Astin, G.D. Spradlin, Peter Donat, Heather Fairfield, Dan Castellaneta, Danitra Vance, Tony Crane; ***D:*** Danny DeVito; ***W:*** Michael Leeson; ***C:*** Stephen Burum; ***M:*** David Newman.

War of the Wildcats 🦴🦴 ½ *In Old Oklahoma* **1943** Fast-moving western with Wayne as a tough cowboy battling a powerful land baron. They fight over land, oil and a woman. Unusual because Wayne's character acts on behalf of the Indians to drill and transport oil. **102m/B VHS, DVD.** John Wayne, Martha Scott, Albert Dekker, George "Gabby" Hayes, Sidney Blackmer; ***D:*** Albert Rogell.

War of the Wizards 🦴 ½ *Phoenix* **1983 (PG)** Low-budget sci-fi thriller about an alien woman with supernatural powers who comes to take over the Earth. But, lucky for all earthlings, she's challenged by a herotype just in the nick of time. **90m/C VHS.** Charles Lang, Betty Noonan, Richard Kiel; ***D:*** Richard Caan; ***W:*** F. Kenneth Lin; ***C:*** Sokei Tomioka; ***M:*** Lawrence Borden.

The War of the Worlds 🦴🦴🦴 ½ **1953** H.G. Wells's classic novel of the invasion of Earth by Martians, updated to 1950s California, with spectacular special effects of destruction caused by the Martian war machines. Pretty scary and tense; based more on Orson Welles's radio broadcast than on the book. Still very popular; hit the top 20 in sales when released on video. Classic thriller later made into a TV series. Produced by George Pal, who brought the world much sci-fi, including "The Time Machine," "Destination Moon," and "When Worlds Collide," and who appears here as a street person. **85m/C VHS, DVD.** Gene Barry, Ann (Robin) Robinson, Les Tremayne, Lewis Martin, Robert Cornthwaite, Sandro Giglio, George Pal, Jack Kruschen, Carolyn Jones, Alvy Moore, William Phipps, Paul Frees; ***D:*** Byron Haskin; ***W:*** Barre Lyndon; ***C:*** George Barnes; ***M:*** Leith Stevens; ***V:*** Cedric Hardwicke.

War of the Worlds 🦴🦴🦴 **2005 (PG-13)** Spielberg and Cruise re-team in this modern sci-fi remake of the H.G. Wells classic 1898 novel (George Pal produced the 1953 film version) though the M-word (Martians, that is) is never actually uttered here. Dockworker Ray Ferrier (Cruise) is a distant dad forced together with his teenage son Robbie (Chatwin) and 10-year-old daughter Rachel (Fanning) for the weekend. That dysfunctional scene is cut short by powerful lightning strikes that activate massive underground three-legged alien machines bent on destroying every human in sight, which puts Ray and his brood on the run. Typical breathtaking Spielberg special effects abound; Cruise shows why he's an A-lister. **118m/C DVD.** *US* Tom Cruise, Dakota Fanning, Miranda Otto, Tim Robbins, Justin Chatwin, Rick Gonzalez, David Alan Basche, Yul Vazquez, Lenny Venito, Lisa Ann Walter, Ann (Robin) Robinson, Gene Barry; ***D:*** Steven Spielberg; ***W:*** David Koepp, Josh Friedman; ***C:*** Janusz Kaminski; ***M:*** John Williams; ***Nar:*** Morgan Freeman.

War Party 🦴🦴 **1989 (R)** During a 100-year commemoration of an Indian massacre in the Midwest, a murder occurs and a lynch mob chases a pack of young Blackfeet into the mountains before the inevitable showdown. A feeble attempt at portraying the unfair treatment of Native Americans. Unsubtle, Hollywood style, this time in favor of the Indians, and therefore un-serious. Too bad; the premise had potential. **99m/C VHS.** Kevin Dillon, Billy Wirth, Tim Sampson, M. Emmet Walsh; ***D:*** Franc Roddam; ***C:*** Brian Tufano.

The War Room 🦴🦴🦴 **1993 (PG)** Eye opening, sometimes disturbing documentary presents a behind the scenes peek at what really goes on during a Presidential campaign. When filming began in June '92 Bill Clinton was an unknown political quantity and advisors George Stephanopoulos and James Carville were masterminding his campaign. The "War Room" refers to the building in Little Rock where they struggled to organize a small army of volunteers into a winning team. Highlights include the Democratic National Convention, the North Carolina leg of Clinton's campaign bus tour, three Presidential debates, and the week leading up to election night. **93m/C VHS, DVD.** ***D:*** Chris Hegedus, D.A. Pennebaker; ***C:*** D.A. Pennebaker, Kevin Rafferty. Natl. Bd. of Review '93: Feature Doc.

War Tapes 🦴🦴🦴 **2006** Director Scranton gave digital video cameras to members of a New Hampshire National Guard unit deployed to Iraq. They filmed what they saw, did, and experienced, and sent the footage back. She gave them tips on improving technique and edited it down to a 97-minute movie. The experiment works best when showing the day-to-day dangers of the war. **97m/C DVD.** ***D:*** Dan Wallin; ***C:*** P.H. O'Brien, Peter Ciardelli; ***M:*** Norman Arnold.

The War Wagon 🦴🦴🦴 **1967** The Duke plans revenge on Cabot, the greedy mine owner who stole his gold claim and framed him for murder for which he spent years in prison. He assembles a gang to aid him, including a wise-cracking Indian (Keel) and the man sent by Cabot to kill him (Douglas). Wayne's plan is to steal the gold being shipped in Cabot's armor-plated stagecoach, the "war wagon." Well-written, good performances, lots of action. Based on the book "Badman" by Clair Huffaker. **101m/C VHS, DVD.** John Wayne, Kirk Douglas, Howard Keel, Robert Walker Jr., Keenan Wynn, Bruce Dern, Bruce Cabot, Joanna Barnes; ***D:*** Burt Kennedy; ***W:*** Clair Huffaker; ***C:*** William Clothier; ***M:*** Dimitri Tiomkin.

The War Within 🦴🦴 **2005 (R)** Pakistani student Hassan (Akhtar) is kidnapped from his Paris home and tortured for three years in a detention center during which time he becomes a radicalized Jihadist. After being released he is smuggled into New York where he is to play a key role in a plot to bomb targets in the city. Hassan's friend Sayeed (Bamji) allows him to stay in his home in New Jersey while Hassan is working within a sleeper cell. This sets up a sharp contrast between the western lifestyle of Sayeed's family and the extremist activities of Hassan and his cell. The chilling plausibility of the storyline makes up for any weakness in execution. **90m/C DVD.** *US* Ayad Akhtar, Nandana Sen, Firdous Bamji, Sarita Choudhury, John Ventimiglia, Mike McGlone, Firdous Bamji, Charles Daniel Sandoval, Varun Sriram, Anjeli Chapman, Ajay Naidu, Aasif Mandvi; ***D:*** Joseph Castelo; ***W:*** Joseph Castelo, Ayad Akhtar, Tom Glynn; ***C:*** Lisa Rinzler; ***M:*** David Holmes.

The War Zone 🦴🦴 **1998 (R)** Harrowing and uncompromising look at a working class British family torn apart by incest and abuse. Dad (Winstone) has just moved the family to a small Devon town—a move resented by his children, 18-year-old Jessie (Belmont) and 15-year-old Tom (Cunliffe). Mum (Swinton) is too busy with a new baby to see what's going on but lonely Tom gradually (and later graphically) becomes aware that something not right is happening between Jessie and their father. Roth's disquieting directing debut; based on Stuart's novel. **98m/C VHS, DVD.** *GB* Ray Winstone, Tilda Swinton, Lara Belmont, Freddie Cunliffe, Aisling O'Sullivan, Colin Farrell, Annabelle Apsion, Kate Ashfield; ***D:*** Tim Roth; ***W:*** Alexander Stuart; ***C:*** Seamus McGarvey; ***M:*** Simon Boswell.

Warbirds 🦴🦴 **1988 (R)** American pilots are off to quell a revolution in a Middle East country. Too little action fails to support mediocre plot and characters. **88m/C VHS.** Jim Eldert, Cully Holland, Bill Brinsfield; ***D:*** Ulli Lommel; ***W:*** Ulli Lommel.

Warbirds **WOOF!** **2008** This WWII-set creature feature woofer has slightly better CGI than your typical Sci Fi Channel original but it doesn't make up for the bad acting and beyond dumb plot. Officer Jack Toller (Krause) is involved in a secret mission that has a crew of female pilots transporting a weapon to a Pacific island. A storm forces the plane down on the wrong island, which is the land that time forgot since it's populated by flying dinosaurs (and Japanese soldiers). **86m/C DVD.** David Jensen, Brian Kruase, Jamie Elle Mann, Tohoru Masamune, Lucy Faust; ***D:*** Kevin Gendreau; ***W:*** Kevin Gendreau; ***C:*** Adolfo Bartoli; ***M:*** Margaret Guinee. **CABLE**

Warbus 🦴🦴 **1985 (R)** Marines lead a school bus load of Americans through war-torn Vietnam to safety. Decent action and surprisingly enjoyable characters. Otherwise mediocre. **90m/C VHS.** Daniel Stephen, Romano Kristoff, Urs Althaus; ***D:*** Ted Kaplan.

WarCat 🦴 *Angel of Vengeance* **1988** The daughter of a green beret fights for her life against a blood-thirsty gang. **78m/C VHS.** Macka Foley, Jannina Poynter, David O'Hara, Carl Erwin; ***D:*** Ted V. Mikels.

Ward Six 🦴🦴 *Pavilion 6* **1978** An insane asylum is the setting for various analogies regarding the perception of reality as defined by societal values. When it is felt that the residing physician is no more sane than his patients, he is placed among them, in Ward Six. Adapted from a story by Anton Chekhov. In Serbian with English subtitles. **93m/C VHS.** *YU* Ljuba Tadic, Slobodan Perovic, Zoran Radmilovic, Slavko Simic; ***D:*** Lucian Pintilie; ***W:*** Lucian Pintilie; ***C:*** Milorad Jaksic-Fandjo.

Warden of Red Rock 🦴🦴 ½ **2001 (PG-13)** Ex-criminal John Flinders (Caan) has been an upstanding citizen a long time. In fact, he's now the warden of the Red Rock prison in Arizona, which is where his old partner, Mike Sullivan (Carradine), has just been sent to serve a life sentence. Instead, Sullivan engineers a bloody jail break and Flinders must set out with a posse to hunt them down. (And as expected, there's a final showdown between the two.) **89m/C VHS.** James Caan, David Carradine, Rachel Ticotin, Brian Dennehy; ***D:*** Stephen Gyllenhaal; ***W:*** James Lee Barrett; ***C:*** Henner Hofmann; ***M:*** Michel Colombier. **CABLE**

Wardogs 🦴 ½ *The Assassination Team* **1987** A man tries to rescue his brother from becoming one of an elite, brainwashed group of ex-Vietnam vets trained by the government as professional assassins. Might not have been quite so bad; promising inversion of many 'Nam cliches wrecked by unnecessary violence and bad acting. **95m/C** *SW* Tim Earle, Bill Redvers; ***D:*** Daniel Hubenbecker.

WarGames 🦴🦴 ½ **1983 (PG)** A young computer whiz, thinking that he's sneaking an advance look at a new line of video games, breaks into the country's NORAD missile-defense system and challenges it to a game of Global Thermonuclear Warfare. The game might just turn out to be the real thing. Slick look at the possibilities of an accidental start to WWIII. Entertaining and engrossing, but with a B-grade ending. **110m/C VHS, DVD.** Matthew Broderick, Dabney Coleman, John Wood, Ally Sheedy; ***D:*** John Badham; ***W:*** Walter F. Parkes, Lawrence Lasker; ***C:*** William A. Fraker; ***M:*** Arthur B. Rubinstein.

WarGames 2: The Dead Code 🦴 **2008 (PG-13)** Computer whiz Will Farmer (Lanter) hacks into a restricted online gaming network called Ripley. Only it's actually a secret government defense project designed to catch would-be terrorists, since the object of the game is to launch a successful attack on a U.S. city. Will gets targeted, goes on the run with gal pal Annie (Walsh), winds up in custody, and figures out Ripley has decided to play for keeps unless the hacker can stop the game. The 1983 original still has an anachronistic charm but this is just silly. **100m/C DVD.** Matt Lanter, Amanda Walsh, Maxim Roy, Colm Feore, Susan Glover, Chuck Shamata; ***D:*** Stuart Gillard; ***W:*** Randall Badat; ***C:*** Bruce Chun; ***M:*** John Van Tongeren. **VIDEO**

Warhead 🦴 ½ **1996 (R)** Special Forces Ranger Tannen (Zagarino) has to stop a renegade military group, led by his former compatriot Craft (Lara), that have stolen a nuclear warhead and are threatening Washington. **97m/C VHS, DVD.** Frank Zagarino, Joe Lara, Elizabeth Giordano; ***D:*** Mark Roper; ***W:*** Jeff Albert; ***C:*** Rod Stewart; ***M:*** Robert O. Ragland.

Warkill 🦴🦴 ½ **1965** WWII action set in the jungles of the Philippines. Journalist who idolizes violent, hard-edged colonel, loses his illusions, but gains a more genuine respect for his men. Not-bad war flick. **99m/C VHS.** George Montgomery, Tom Drake, Eddie Infante; ***D:*** Ferde Grofe Jr.; ***W:*** Ferde Grofe Jr.

Warlock 🦴🦴🦴 **1959** Claustrophic, resonant town-bound tale of a marshal (Fonda) and his adoring sidekick (Quinn) who clean up a town which then turns against him. Unusual story, fine performances carry this well beyond the run-of-the-mill cow flick. Fonda re-established himself at the box office as a western star, after "Stage Struck" and "Twelve Angry Men." From the novel by Oakley Hall. Look for "Bones" McCoy from "Star Trek" in a bit part. **122m/C VHS, DVD.** Henry Fonda, Anthony Quinn, Richard Widmark, Dorothy Malone, Wallace Ford, Richard Arlen, Regis Toomey, DeForest Kelley; ***D:*** Edward Dmytryk; ***W:*** Robert Alan Aurthur.

Warlock 🦴🦴 ½ **1991 (R)** It's 1691 and the most powerful warlock (Sands) in the New World is only hours away from execution. Luckily, his pal, Satan, whisks him (and witchhunter Grant, by mistake) three hundred years in the future to present-day Los Angeles, where he crash-lands in Singer's house. Surprisingly witty dialogue and neat plot twists outshine occasionally cheesy special effects. **103m/C VHS, DVD.** Richard E. Grant, Julian Sands, Lori Singer, Mary Woronov, Richard Kuss, Kevin O'Brien, Anna Levine, Allan Miller, David Carpenter; ***D:*** Steve Miner; ***W:*** David N. Twohy; ***C:*** David Eggby; ***M:*** Jerry Goldsmith.

Warlock 3: The End of Innocence 🦴🦴 **1998 (R)** Kris (Laurence) decides to spend a weekend in the abandoned 16th-century family manor that she has inherited. Disturbed by visions, she comes to realize that her family has a legacy of witchcraft and now she is the sacrifical target of a warlock (Payne). Predictable, although Payne is sufficiently chilling. **94m/C VHS, DVD.** Bruce Payne, Ashley Laurence, Angel Boris, Boti Ann Bliss, Paul Francis, Rick Hearst, Jan Schweiterman; ***D:*** Eric Freiser; ***W:*** Eric Freiser, Bruce David Eisen. **VIDEO**

Warlock Moon 🦴 ½ **1973** Young woman is lured to a secluded spa and falls prey to a coven of witches. **75m/C VHS, DVD.** *MX* Laurie Walters, Joe Spano, Edna Macafee, Ray Goman, Steve Solinsky, Charles Raino; ***D:*** Bill Herbert.

Warlock: The Armageddon 🦴🦴 ½ **1993 (R)** Sequel finds Sands back again as the sinister Warlock. This time he's out to gather six Druidic rune stones which have the power to summon Satan's emissary (in the wrong hands) or to stop his nefarious activities (in the right ones). A sect in a small California town serves as the keeper of the stones, only their designated champions are two unprepared teenagers. Sands has all the fun, gleefully dispatching his would-be opponents with some good special effects. **93m/C VHS, DVD.** Julian Sands, Chris Young, Paula Marshall, Steve Kahan, Charles Hallahan, R.G. Armstrong, Bruce Glover, Zach Galligan, Dawn Ann Billings, Joanna Pacula; ***D:*** Anthony Hickox; ***W:*** Kevin Rock, Sam Bernard; ***C:*** Gerry Lively; ***M:*** Mark McKenzie.

Warlords 🦴 ½ **1988 (R)** Lone soldier Carradine battles mutant hordes in a post-apocalyptic desert. Amateurish futuristic drivel. **87m/C VHS.** David Carradine, Sid Haig, Ross Hagen, Fox Harris, Robert Quarry, Victoria Sellers, Brinke Stevens, Dawn Wildsmith; ***D:*** Fred Olen Ray.

Warlords *Tou Ming Zhuang* **2008 (R)** Set during the Taiping Rebellion of the 1860s. General Pang, surviving a massacre of his soldiers, joins with bandits Er-Hu and Wen-Xiang and the three pledge their loyalty as blood brothers. But their loyalty is tested by circumstance, including the romantic triangle that develops between Pang, Er-Hu, and courtesan Lian. Mandarin with subtitles. **110m/C DVD.** *CH HK* Jet Li, Andy Lau, Takeshi Kaneshiro, Jinglei Xu; ***D:*** Peter Chan; ***W:*** Tin Chun, Jojo Hui, Oi Wah Lam, Huang Jianxin, Lan Xu; ***C:*** Arthur Wong; ***M:*** Kwong Wing Chan, Peter Kam, Leon Ko.

Warlords from Hell **WOOF!** **1987 (R)** Two young men motorcycling through Mexico are captured by a bloodthirsty gang and forced to do hard labor in the marijuana fields. We can only hope that they just learn to say no. **76m/C VHS.** Brad Henson, Jeffrey Rice; ***D:*** Clark Henderson.

Warlords of the 21st Century 🦴 ½ *Battletruck* **1982** Bandit gang speed around the galaxy in an indestructible battle cruiser. Then the boys are challenged by a space lawman. Gratuitously violent action pic lacking real action. Filmed on planet New Zealand. **91m/C VHS.** Michael Beck, Annie McEnroe, James Wainwright; ***D:*** Harley Cokliss; ***W:*** Harley Cokliss, Irving Austin, John Beech; ***C:*** Chris Menges.

Warlords 3000 🦴 ½ **1993 (R)** In the future, Earth is a barren wasteland ravaged by raging electrical storms. Deadly cancers are rampant and the few people who have survived take their comfort in a hallucinogenic drug that provides a temporary pleasure and a permanent madness. Drug lords control the planet but one man is out to eliminate the scum and save the future. **92m/C VHS.** Jay Roberts Jr., Denise Marie Duff, Steve Blanchard, Wayne Duvall; ***D:*** Faruque Ahmed; ***W:*** Ron Herbst, Faruque Ahmed.

Warm Blooded Killers 🦴🦴 **2001 (R)** Quirky, likeable comedy has brother/sister hitmen (hitpersons?) John and Vicky doing well for themselves until Vicky's boyfriend angers John. Being what he is, John ices the guy, then finds out he was the boss's godson. Disorganized crime hi-jinks ensue. **84m/C DVD.** Mick Murray, Constance Zimmer, F. William Parker, Carmen Argenziano; ***D:*** Nicholas Siapkaris, Stephen Langford; ***W:*** Stephen Langford; ***C:*** Charles L. Barbee; ***M:*** Matthew Olivo. **VIDEO**

Warm Nights on a Slow-Moving Train 🦴🦴 **1987 (R)** A hot-blooded schoolteacher turns tricks for cash to support her brother on the Sunday-night train to Melbourne, until she meets a stranger who has a deadly masquerade of his own. Interestingly different; much sex, as you can imagine. Australian-made. **90m/C VHS.** *AU* Wendy Hughes, Colin Friels, Norman Kaye, John Clayton, Peter Whitford; ***D:*** Bob Ellis; ***W:*** Bob Ellis, Denny Lawrence; ***C:*** Yuri Sokol.

Warm Summer Rain 🦴 ½ **1989 (R)** A young couple meet under unusual circumstances and develop a relationship in a desert cabin as they reflect on their unfulfilled pasts. Lust, self-doubt and longing for something to hold onto draw them together as the days pass. Thoroughly self-indulgent romantic comedy that's oddly self-pitying and poorly directed. **85m/C VHS, DVD.** Kelly Lynch, Barry Tubb; ***D:*** Joe Gayton.

The Warning 🦴 **1980** A pair of proverbial honest cops investigate ties between the mob and the police department. Hard to follow. **101m/C VHS.** *IT* Martin Balsam, Giuliano Gemma, Giancarlo Zanetti; ***D:*** Damiano Damiani.

Warning from Space 🦴 ½ *The Mysterious Satellite; The Cosmic Man Appears in Tokyo; Space Men Appear in Tokyo; Unknown Satellite Over Tokyo; Uchujin Tokyo Ni Arawaru* **1956** Aliens visit Earth to warn of impending cosmic doom. When it becomes apparent that the one-eyed starfish look is off-putting, they assume human form. Japanese sci fi. **87m/B VHS, DVD.** *JP* Toyomi Karita, Keizo Kawasaki, Isao Yamagata, Shozo Nanbu, Buntaro Miake, Mieko Nagai, Kiyoko Hirai; ***D:*** Koji Shima.

Warning Shadows 🦴🦴🦴 **1923** Classic example of interior German Expressionism. Brilliantly portrays a jealous husband's emotions and obsessions through shadows. Innocent events seem to reek of sin. A seldom-seen study of the oft-precarious distinction between love and obsession; directly influenced by the classic "The Cabinet of Dr. Caligari." Silent with German and English titles. **93m/B VHS, DVD.** *GE* Ruth Weyher, Alexander Granach, Rudolf Klein-Rogge, Max Gulstorff, Fritz Kortner; ***D:*** Arthur Robison; ***W:*** Arthur Robison; ***C:*** Fritz Arno Wagner.

Warning Sign 🦴 ½ **1985 (R)** A high-tech thriller in which a small town is terrorized by the accidental release of an experimental virus at a research facility. Shades of "The Andromeda Strain" and "The China Syndrome," though less originality and quality. **99m/C VHS, DVD.** Sam Waterston, Kathleen Quinlan, Yaphet Kotto, Richard Dysart, Rick Rossovich; ***D:*** Hal Barwood; ***W:*** Hal Barwood, Matthew Robbins; ***C:*** Dean Cundey.

The Warrior 🦴🦴 **1981 (R)** If you've ever watched a samurai movie, this effort will seem familiar (although less violent). Warrior Lafcadia (Khan) is an indentured enforcer in the northwest Indian state of Rajasthan. During his latest pillage with his men, Lafcadia has a mystical vision and decides to lay down his sword, which enrages his master who sends other warriors after him. Seeking redemption, Lafcadia follows his vision into the Himalayas accompanied by a young thief (Mani) and a blind woman (Marfatia) on a pilgrimage. Hindi with subtitles; there is also an English-language version. **86m/C DVD.** Irfan Khan, Puru Chhibber, Mandakini Goswami, Sunita Sharma, Noor Mani, Damayanti Marfatia, Firoz Khan, Anupam Shyam; ***D:*** Asif Kapadia; ***W:*** Tim Miller, Asif Kapadia; ***C:*** Roman Osin; ***M:*** Dario Marianelli.

The Warrior 🦴🦴🦴 *Musa: The Warrior; Musa; The Warrior Princess; Wu Shi* **2001 (R)** Set in 1375, the Ming Dynasty is beginning to settle into power, and Korea sends an envoy to make start diplomatic relations with China's new rulers. Upon arrival, the lead diplomat is jailed and the rest are exiled for spying. The survivors attempt to get back to Korea, and incidentally rescue a Ming Princess who has been kidnapped by a deposed Chinese faction. Deciding that protecting her may be their best option for survival, they make for a lonely military outpost in the hopes they can get help. **157m/C DVD.** *CH KN* Ziyi Zhang, Woo-sung Jung, Sung-kee Ahn, Jin-mo Ju, Yong-woo Park, Jeong-hak Park, Hye-jin Yu, Seok-yong Jeong, Du-il Lee, Yeong-mak Han; ***D:*** Sung-su Kim; ***W:*** Sung-su Kim; ***C:*** Hyung-ku Kim; ***M:*** Shiroh Sagisu.

The Warrior & the Sorceress 🦴 ½ **1984 (R)** Mercenary Carradine offers his services to rival factions fighting for control of a water well in an impoverished desert village located on a planet with two suns. He attempts to aggravate the conflicts between the factions, playing the shifty go-between. The sorceress is topless throughout. "A Fistful of Dollars" goes to outer space. Inoffensive, except that better judgment is expected of Carradine. **81m/C VHS, DVD.** David Carradine, Luke Askew, Maria Socas, Harry Townes; ***D:*** John Broderick; ***W:*** John Broderick.

Warrior of Justice 🦴 **1996** Karate instructor has one of his students disappear after competing in a secret tournament. He then uncovers a black market ring specializing in selling human organs that's run by a former opponent. **90m/C VHS, DVD.** Richard Lynch, Jorge (George) Rivero, Nick (Nicholas, Niko) Hill, Ian Jacklin, Jorgo Ognenovski; ***D:*** Jorgo Ognenovski, Mike Tristano.

Warrior of the Lost World **WOOF!** **1984** A warrior must destroy the evil Omega Force who tyrannically rules the world in the distant future, etcetera, etcetera. One-size-fits-all premise; horrible special effects; miserably directed. Only for really hard-core Pleasence fans. **90m/C VHS, DVD.** Robert Ginty, Persis Khambatta, Donald Pleasence; ***D:*** David Worth.

Warrior Queen 🦴 **1987 (R)** Long ago in ancient Rome, overly histrionic mayor Pleasence married porn queen with a wandering eye Fox, and much gratuitous sex and erupting volcanoes resulted. Even the score blows. Also available in an "Unrated" version. Brit pop star Fox is billed as Stasia Micula. **69m/C VHS.** Sybil Danning, Donald Pleasence, Richard (Rick) Hill, Josephine Jacqueline Jones, Tally Chanel, Samantha Fox; ***D:*** Chuck Vincent; ***W:*** Rick Marx; ***C:*** Gianlorenzo Battaglia; ***M:*** Ian Shaw.

Warrior Queen 🦴🦴 ½ **2003** Boudica (Kingston) is the leader of her tribe in first-century Briton, which is under Roman rule. Sickened by the increasing demands of the Emperor Nero and his occupying troops, Boudica unites the fractious Celt tribes to lead an onslaught on the Roman camps. But the Romans did not conquer the world by giving in. **90m/C VHS, DVD.** *GB* Alex Kingston, Steven Waddington, Hugo Speer, Gary Lewis, Emily Blunt, Leanne Rowe, Ben Faulks; ***D:*** Bill Anderson; ***W:*** Andrew Davies; ***C:*** Tudor Lucaciu; ***M:*** Nina Humphreys. **TV**

Warrior Spirit 1/2 **1994 (PG-13)** After getting kicked out of their prep school, two boys decide to head for the Yukon and search for gold. **94m/C VHS.** Lukas Haas, Jimmy Herman, Allan Musy; ***D:*** Rene Manzor.

The Warriors 1/2 *The Dark Avenger* **1955** Swashbuckling adventure about Prince Edward's valiant rescue of Lady Joan and her children from the clutches of the evil Count De Ville. Flynn looks old and pudgy, but buckles his way gallantly through intrepid adventure. Also the last Flynn to see: fun, but more or less completely derivative and familiar. Filmed in England. **85m/C VHS.** *GB* Errol Flynn, Peter Finch, Joanne Dru, Yvonne Furneaux, Noel Willman, Michael Hordern; ***D:*** Henry Levin.

The Warriors 1/2 **1979 (R)** Action story about a turf battle between NYC street gangs that rages from Coney Island to the Bronx. Silly plot works because of fine performances and direction, excellent use of action and color, and nonstop pace. Fight scenes are very carefully, even obviously, choreographed. **94m/C VHS, DVD, Blu-ray Disc, HD DVD.** Michael Beck, James Remar, Deborah Van Valkenburgh, Thomas G. Waites, David Patrick Kelly, Mercedes Ruehl, Dorsey Wright, David Harris, Brian Tyler, Tom McKitterick, Steve James, Robert Kevin Townsend, Lynne Thigpen, Terry Michos; ***D:*** Walter Hill; ***W:*** Walter Hill, David Shaber; ***C:*** Andrew Laszlo; ***M:*** Barry DeVorzon.

Warriors **1994 (R)** Col. Frank Vail (Busey) is the leader of a top secret government anti-terrorist hit squad, considered so deadly that its members are confined behind the walls of a military prison. But when Vail escapes, it's up to his lethal protege Colin Newl (Pare) to hunt him down. **100m/C VHS.** Gary Busey, Michael Pare; ***D:*** Shimon Dotan.

Warriors 1/2 *Guerreros* **2002** Spanish troops are sent by NATO to Kosovo as non-combatants in the midst of the Serbian-Albanian war in 1999. Their job is to restore electricity to a local village. Not getting involved in the bloodshed proves futile and they face a life-and-death struggle to bail out and return to their base. In Spanish, with subtitles. **96m/C VHS, DVD, UMD.** Eloy Azorin, Eduardo Noreiga, Ruben Ochandiano; ***D:*** Daniel Calparsoro; ***W:*** Daniel Calparsoro; ***C:*** Josep Civit; ***M:*** Najwa Nimri, Carlos Jean. **VIDEO**

Warriors from Hell 1/2 **1990 (R)** Western forces in a small African country battle rebel fighters who threaten the hapless native villagers. **90m/C VHS.** Deon Stewardson, Shayne Leith, Adrienne Pierce, Glen Gabela, Hector Manthanda, Ivan Dean, Connie Chume; ***D:*** Ronnie Isaacs; ***W:*** Ronnie Isaacs.

Warriors of Heaven and Earth 1/2 *Tian di ying xiong* **2003 (R)** Grand epic Chinese western has two men of honor face off against one another in frontier Asia circa 700 A.D., but soon join forces to protect an ancient relic and its bearer from marauding bandits. Beautifully filmed and rousing adventure that is frequently confusing and corny, but always a terrific ride. Particularly fun is Wang Xueqi as a flamboyant villain who looks strangely like Harvey Keitel's Sport in "Taxi Driver." **114m/C DVD, Blu-ray Disc.** *CH* Jiang Wen, Kiichi Nakai, Wang Xueqi, Harrison Liu, Zhao Wei, Hasi Bagen, He Tao, Zhou Yun; ***D:*** He Ping; ***W:*** He Ping, Zhang Rui; ***C:*** Fei Zhao; ***M:*** A.R. Rahman.

Warriors of the Apocalypse WOOF! *Searchers of the Voodoo Mountain; Time Raiders* **1985 (R)** After a nuclear holocaust, heavily sworded and loin-clothed men search for the secret of eternal life and instead find an Amazon realm in the jungle. A terrible waste of post-apocalyptic scenery. **96m/C VHS.** Michael James, Debrah Moore, Ken Metcalfe, Franco Guerrero; ***D:*** Bobby Suarez.

Warriors of the Wasteland WOOF! *The New Barbarians; I Nuovi Barbari* **1983 (R)** It's the year 2019, and the world has been devastated by a nuclear war. The few survivors try to reach a distant land which emits radio signals indicating the presence of human life. They are hindered by attacks from the fierce homosexual Templars, led by a self-proclaimed priest called One. Mindless rip-off of "Road Warrior" and obviously made on the proverbial shoestring budget. Dubbed. **92m/C VHS, DVD.** *IT* Fred Williamson, Giancarlo Prete, Anna Kanakis; ***D:*** Enzo G. Castellari.

Warriors of Virtue 1/2 **1997 (PG)** Teenaged Ryan Jefers (Yedidia) is transported to the land of Tao where he learns the five virtues (righteousness, benevolence, integrity, wisdom, and loyalty) from the kangaroo-like Warmblood warriors, who live in harmony with humans. Then he must use his knowledge to fight the evil Komodo (MacFadyen), who wishes to steal the energy from Tao to make himself immortal. Nice message for the kids, with enough action to keep them interested, but the Warmbloods are dorky-looking. **101m/C VHS, DVD.** Mario Yedidia, Angus MacFadyen, Marley Shelton, Chao-Li Chi; ***D:*** Ronny Yu; ***W:*** Michael Vickerman, Hugh Kelley; ***C:*** Peter Pau; ***M:*** Don Davis.

Wasabi 1/2 **2001 (R)** This is one Japanese dip you probably won't care to sample. Hubert (Reno) is a hard-assed, violence-prone French cop, who is forced to take a vacation. He winds up in Tokyo at the funeral of a woman he loved years before. He also discovers he's been left a screechy punk daughter, Yumi (Hirosue), he didn't know about, a mysterious key, and 200 million (in dollars) in the bank. And then the yakuza get involved. High-concept and fast-paced but not particularly entertaining. French and Japanese with subtitles. **94m/C VHS, DVD.** *FR JP* Jean Reno, Michel Muller, Carole Bouquet, Ryoko Hirosue; ***D:*** Gerard Krawczyk; ***W:*** Luc Besson; ***C:*** Gerard Sterin; ***M:*** Eric Serra.

The Wash **1988** Quiet domestic drama about a couple who drift apart after 40 years of marriage. Set interestingly among Japanese-Americans in California; treats social and cultural factors with intelligence. Superb cast takes it a notch higher. **94m/C VHS.** Mako, Nobu McCarthy, Sab Shimono; ***D:*** Michael Toshiyuki Uno; ***W:*** Philip Kan Kotanda; ***C:*** Walt Lloyd.

The Wash **2001 (R)** Sean (Dre) loses his job and has his car booted, so pal Dee Loc (Snoop Dogg) helps him out with some news about an opening at the car wash where he works. Soon Sean is assistant manager under crusty owner Mr. Washington (Wallace). Between dealing with the resentment of Loc, and the kidnapping of the boss, along with the usual supply of quirky characters and subplots, Sean has his hands full in this very laid-back, low-key tribute to 1977's "Car Wash." Appealling performances, moments of inspired comedy, and plenty of cameos to watch for make this a pleasant way to kill some time. **96m/C VHS, DVD.** Snoop Dogg, Dr. Dre, DJ Pooh, George Wallace, Tommy (Tiny) Lister, Alex Thomas, Arif S. Kinchen, Demetrius Navarro, Thomas Chong, Pauly Shore, Lamont Bentley, Bruce Bruce, Shari Watson, Shawn Fonteno, Angell Conwell; ***D:*** DJ Pooh; ***W:*** DJ Pooh; ***C:*** Keith L. Smith.

Washington Affair **1977 (PG)** A tale of intrigue in the nation's capital. Sullivan is a businessman who uses women and blackmail to capture government contracts. Selleck is the hapless bureaucrat he preys on. Remake of Stoloff's own "Intimacy" was not released until "Magnum P.I." became a hit. **90m/C VHS.** Tom Selleck, Carol Lynley, Barry Sullivan; ***D:*** Victor Stoloff.

Washington Heights **2002 (R)** Washington Heights is an upper west side Manhattan neighborhood largely populated by immigrants from the Dominican Republic. Widower Eddie Ramirez (Milian) provides for his family by running a bodega and would like his twenty-something son Carlos (Perez) to take over the business. But Carlos is a cartoonist with dreams of his own, who wants to move out of the 'hood, although his girlfriend Maggie (Navedo) is reluctant. Then Eddie is shot and Carlos is forced to mind the store, which makes the son feel even more trapped by circumstance. An effective portrayal (warts-and-all) that has something of a pat ending. **85m/C VHS, DVD.** *US* Manny Perez, Tomas Milian, Danny Hoch, Andrea Navedo, Jude Ciccolella, Bobby Cannavale, Judy Reyes, Callie (Calliope) Thorne, David Zayas; ***D:*** Alfredo de Villa; ***W:*** Alfredo de Villa, Nat Moss; ***C:*** Claudio Chea; ***M:*** Leigh Roberts.

Washington Mistress 1/2 **1981** Emminently ordinary made-for-TV grist about Capitol Hill aide Arnaz, politician Jordan, and their affair. Listless performances. **96m/C VHS.** Lucie Arnaz, Richard Jordan, Tony Bill; ***D:*** Peter Levin.

Washington Square **1997 (PG)** Adaptation of Henry James' novel, which was previously filmed as "The Heiress." Set in 19th-century New York City (filmed in Baltimore), wealthy spinster Catherine Sloper (Leigh), against the will of her overbearing father (Finney), is pursued by a handsome fortune hunter (Chaplin). Director Holland tends to bluntly simplify James' complex undertones, and Leigh's facial ticks can't equal "The Heiress'" Olivia de Havilland's painful plainness; nonetheless, definitely worth seeing. **115m/C VHS, DVD.** Jennifer Jason Leigh, Ben Chaplin, Albert Finney, Maggie Smith, Judith Ivey, Betsy Brantley, Jennifer Garner, Peter Maloney, Robert Stanton, Scott Jaeck; ***D:*** Agnieszka Holland; ***W:*** Carol Doyle; ***C:*** Jerzy Zielinski; ***M:*** Jan A.P. Kaczmarek.

The Wasp Woman 1/2 **1959** In her quest for eternal beauty, a woman uses a potion made from wasp enzymes. Naturally, she turns into a wasp monster at night. Good fun, courtesy of Corman. **84m/B VHS, DVD.** Susan Cabot, Anthony Eisley, Barboura Morris, Michael Marks, William Roerick, Frank Gerstle, Bruno VeSota, Frank Wolff, Lynn Cartwright, Roy Gordon; ***D:*** Roger Corman; ***W:*** Leo Gordon; ***C:*** Harry Neumann; ***M:*** Fred Katz.

The Wasp Woman **1996 (R)** Equally campy cable remake of the 1959 flick finds ex-supermodel-turned-cosmetics company exec Janice Starlin (Rubin) discovering that her fading beauty is causing problems both with her company and her love life. So she turns to a mysterious doctor for help and injects herself with his untested serum, an experimental wasp hormone. She's hoping to discover a fountain of youth and is instead transformed into a nasty-tempered giant insect. Cool, disgusting makeup/costuming. **81m/C VHS.** Jennifer Rubin, Daniel J. Travanti, Maria Ford, Doug Wert; ***D:*** Jim Wynorski; ***W:*** Daniella Purcell; ***M:*** Terry Plumeri. **CABLE**

Wassup Rockers **2006 (R)** A group of South Central Salvadoran teens hang out, skateboarding, working their punk-rock band, chasing girls—two of whom happen to be rich, so the boys travel to Beverly Hills and get into trouble and then scamper back to their 'hood. The teens are first-time actors basically playing themselves and, for Clark, the film is almost surprisingly sweet. **99m/C DVD.** *US* Carlos Ramirez, Jonathan Velasquez, Francisco Pedrasa, Milton Valesquez, Usvaldo Panameno, Eddie Velasquez, Luis Rojas Salgado, Iris Zelaya, Rosalia, Laura Cellner, Jessica Steinbaum; ***D:*** Larry Clark; ***W:*** Larry Clark; ***C:*** Steve Gainer; ***M:*** Harry Cody.

Wasted *Farewell Bender* **2006 (R)** Impressive debut for Oates despite the seemingly familiar plot. In 1996, three high school buddies reunite several years after graduation for the funeral of their friend Bender. Mitch (Pardue) is a golden college boy, nice guy Stan (Thomas) is a municipal worker, and Dixon (Cooke) is perpetually wasted and blaming himself for being unable to rescue Bender from drowning. The trio takes to reliving their hell-raising teen exploits before realizing it's time to face reality, grow up, and move on. **92m/C DVD.** Kip Pardue, Eddie Kaye Thomas, Josh Cooke, Kaley Cuoco, Marisa Coughlan, Alexandra Holden; ***D:*** Mat Oates; ***W:*** Mat Oates, Jeremiah Lowder; ***C:*** Paul Marshall; ***M:*** Tree Adams.

Watch It **1993 (R)** Four self-absorbed 20-something guys share a house in Chicago for the summer. They pursue a post-adolescent game, consisting of increasingly complicated practical jokes, where the unsuspecting victim is set up for a "watch it" gag. The rivalry escalates, and turns increasingly unpleasant, when cousins John and Michael vie for the affections of Anne, who's wary of involvement because of male selfishness. A first-rate cast with recognizable situations and emotions. **102m/C VHS.** Jon Tenney, Peter Gallagher, Suzy Amis, John C. McGinley, Tom Sizemore, Lili Taylor, Cynthia Stevenson, Terri Hawkes, Jordanna Capra; ***D:*** Tom Flynn; ***W:*** Tom Flynn; ***M:*** Stanley Clarke.

Watch Me **1996 (R)** Photog Paul (Medford) is inspired by new neighbor babe Elise (Burns) and secretly snaps her through the window. Meanwhile, Elise is peeking in on Paul's would-be gal Samantha (Burton) who's having sex with his best bud Alex (Sherwin). Paul of course wants to get more personally involved with Elise (especially after he finds out about Samantha). Lots of nudity—no heat. **90m/C VHS, DVD.** Robert Medford, Kelly Burns, Jennifer Burton, Steven Sherwin; ***D:*** Lipo Ching; ***W:*** Beth Salmon; ***C:*** Andreas Kossak; ***M:*** Yoav Goren.

Watch Me When I Kill *Il Gatto Dagli Occhi di Giada; The Cat With the Jade Eyes* **1977 (R)** We'd rather not. A young nightclub dancer stops by a drugstore seconds after the owner was killed. She doesn't see the killer's face, but his rasping voice remains to torment her and the viewer. Dubbed. **95m/C VHS, DVD.** *IT* Corrado Pani, Paola Tedesco, Franco Citti, Fernando Ceruli, Paolo Malco; ***D:*** Antonio Bido; ***W:*** Antonio Bido; ***C:*** Mario Vulpiani.

Watch on the Rhine 1/2 **1943** Couple involved with the anti-Nazi underground has escaped the country, but is pursued and harassed by Nazi agents. Adapted by Hammett and Hellman from her play. Performed on stage before the U.S. entered the war, it was the first American play and movie to portray the ugliness of fascism as an ideology, as opposed to the more devious evil of its practical side. The Production Code at the time required that a killer always be punished; the murderer (whose screen motives had been noble) refused to film the offending scene, which explains the tacked-on ending. Superb drama from a pair of highly gifted writers and a great cast. Shumlin also directed the play. **114m/B VHS.** Bette Davis, Paul Lukas, Donald Woods, Beulah Bondi, Geraldine Fitzgerald, George Coulouris, Henry Daniell, Helmut Dantine, Donald Buka, Anthony Caruso, Clyde Fillmore, Howard Hickman, Creighton Hale, Kurt Katch, Clarence Muse, Alan Hale Jr., Frank Reicher, Mary (Marsden) Young; ***D:*** Herman Shumlin; ***W:*** Lillian Hellman, Dashiell Hammett; ***C:*** Hal Mohr, Merritt B. Gerstad; ***M:*** Max Steiner. Oscars '43: Actor (Lukas); Golden Globes '44: Actor—Drama (Lukas); N.Y. Film Critics '43: Actor (Lukas), Film.

Watch the Birdie 1/2 **1950** It's Skelton three times over as cameraman, father, and grandfather! First, he accidentally films a scam that would send the lovely Miss Dahl filing for bankruptcy. Later a crazy chase scene unfolds, that will have viewers rolling, as Skelton the cameraman nabs the bad guys and turns them over to the cops. Light fun that will charm Skelton fans. **70m/B VHS.** Red Skelton, Arlene Dahl, Ann Miller, Leon Ames; ***D:*** Jack Donohue.

Watched **1973** A former U.S. attorney, gone underground, has a nervous breakdown and kills the narcotics agent who has him under surveillance. Self-important, too serious social/political conspiracy drama of the Watergate era. Keach and Yulin are good, but not good enough to save it. **95m/C VHS.** Stacy Keach, Harris Yulin, Bridgit Polk; ***D:*** John Parsons.

The Watcher **2000 (R)** Serial killer Reeves leaves clues for burned-out FBI agent Spader as to who his next victim will be so Spader will get back in the game. Start with a direct-to-video feel, add a plot cribbed from better serial killer thrillers, throw in a bunch of showy visual effects and Reeves' hysterical line readings, and you've got a night of talking back to the TV, MST3K-style. It's ridiculous, but that's half the fun. **97m/C VHS, DVD.** Keanu Reeves, James Spader, Marisa Tomei, Ernie Hudson, Chris Ellis, Robert Cicchini, Jenny (Jennifer) McShane, Yvonne Niami, Gina Alexander, Joe Sikora, Rebekah Louise Smith; ***D:*** Joe Charbanic; ***W:*** Joe Charbanic, David Elliott, Clay Ayers; ***C:*** Michael Chapman; ***M:*** Marco Beltrami.

The Watcher in the Attic 1/2 *Edogawa Rampo ryoki-kan: Yaneura no sanpo sa* **1976** Based on loose adaptations of Edogawa Rampo's short stories "The Human Chair" and "The Attic Stroller," this is one of Studio Nikkatsu's more bizarre entries in the Roman Porno subgenre of exploitation films. Set in a boarding house in the 1920s, a landlord spies on his eccentric boarders from the attic. One of them is a bored aristocrat turned prostitute who murders men for fun, and he decides she is his obvious soulmate upon discovering this. **77m/C DVD.** *JP* Junko Miyashita, Renji Ishibashi; ***D:*** Noboru Tanaka; ***W:*** Akio Ido, Rampo Edogawa; ***C:*** Masaru Mori; ***M:*** Jiro Sarashina.

The Watcher in the Woods **1981 (PG)** When an American family rents an English country house, the children are haunted by the spirit of a long-missing young girl. A very bland attempt at a ghost story. **83m/C VHS, DVD.** Bette Davis, Carroll Baker, David McCallum, Ian Bannen, Lynn-Holly Johnson, Kyle Richards, Frances Cuka, Richard Pasco; ***D:*** John Hough; ***W:*** Brian Clemens; ***C:*** Alan Hume; ***M:*** Stanley Myers.

Watchers **1988 (R)** From the suspense novel by Dean R. Koontz, a secret experiment goes wrong, creating half-human monsters. A boy and his extremely intelligent dog are soon pursued. Low-budget, Corman-influenced production is tacky but effective. **99m/C VHS, DVD.** Barbara Williams, Michael Ironside, Corey Haim, Duncan Fraser, Blu Mankuma, Dale Wilson, Colleen Winton; ***D:*** Jon Hess; ***W:*** Bill Freed; ***C:*** Richard Leiterman; ***M:*** Joel Goldsmith.

Watchers 2 **1990 (R)** Sequel to "Watchers" follows the further adventures of a super-intelligent golden retriever who leads a Marine to an animal psychologist and then attempts to warn them both of a mutant killer. The dog says woof, but this movie doesn't quite. Fun for lovers of hounds or horror flicks. **101m/C VHS, DVD.** Marc Singer, Tracy Scoggins; ***D:*** Thierry Notz; ***M:*** Rick Conrad.

Watchers 3 1/2 **1994 (R)** A secret military outpost in the South American jungles is attacked by a carnivorous predator. Ex-military convicts are sent to rescue the remaining survivors and to make certain the government experiment that started the terror never comes to light. **95m/C VHS, DVD.** Wings Hauser, Gregory Scott Cummins, Daryl Roach, John K. Linton, Lolita Ronalds, Frank Novak; ***D:*** Jeremy Stanford.

Watchers Reborn **1998 (R)** Genetically engineered mutants stalk the innocent with only a hyper-intelligent golden retriever (of course!) able to stop them. Based on the novel "Watchers" by Dean R. Koontz. **83m/C VHS, DVD.** Mark Hamill, Lisa Wilcox, Stephen Macht, Lou Rawls, Floyd Levine, Gary Collins, Kane Hodder; ***D:*** John Carl Buechler; ***W:*** Sean Dash; ***M:*** Terry Plumeri.

Watching the Detectives 1/2 **2007** Oddball romantic comedy that fails to deliver on the appeal of its leads. Movie geek/video store owner Neil (Murphy) is obsessed with film noir and he can spot a femme fatale when she walks into his joint. Violet (Liu) is big on spontaneity, but when they start dating, her penchant for increasingly dangerous practical jokes has Neil questioning her sanity. Bogie never had this kind of trouble with Bacall. **91m/C DVD.** Cillian Murphy, Lucy Liu, Michael Panes, Jason Sudeikis, Callie (Calliope) Thorne; ***D:*** Paul Soter; ***W:*** Paul Soter; ***C:*** Christopher Lanzenberg; ***M:*** Nathan Barr. **VIDEO**

Watchmen **2009 (R)** In an alternate reality of 1985, superheroes have been outlawed or taken under government control. Vigilante Rorschach (Haley) investigates the murder of a former superhero, which reunites him with some old, albeit flawed, colleagues: Dr. Manhattan (Crudup), a giant glowing blue nudist; Silk Spectre II (Akerman), the sexy daughter of a former superhero; and Nite Owl (Wilson), a Batman-knock off. After investigation, the Watchmen uncover a conspiracy to discredit and kill the retired crimefighters. The unconventional structure and focus on backstories often make it difficult to follow. Director Snyder's highly-anticipated and ambitious attempt to bring Alan Moore's post-modern cult graphic novel to the big screen will inevitably upset some fanboys, and send others to orgasmic heights, but overall, it's an uneven disappointment. **161m/C DVD.** *US* Jackie Earle Haley, Billy Crudup, Jeffrey Dean Morgan, Matthew Goode, Carla Gugino, Malin Akerman, Stephen McHattie, Patrick Wilson, Matt Frewer; ***D:*** Zack Snyder; ***W:*** David Hayter, Alex Tse; ***C:*** Larry Fong; ***M:*** Tyler Bates.

Water **1985 (PG-13)** The resident governor of a Caribbean British colony juggles various predatory interests when a valuable mineral water resource is found. The good cast is wasted in this all-too-silly effort. **89m/C VHS, DVD.** *GB* Michael Caine, Brenda Vaccaro, Leonard Rossiter, Valerie Perrine, Jimmie Walker; ***Cameos:*** Eric Clapton, George Harrison, Fred Gwynne, Ringo Starr; ***D:*** Dick Clement; ***W:*** Dick Clement, Ian La Frenais, Bill Persky.

Water **2005 (PG-13)** Following Hindu custom in 1938 India, when child bride Chuyia's (Sarala) aged husband dies, her family sends her to live in exile in an ashram for widows. Chuyia can't understand and rebels against the restrictions until she is befriended by religious, middle-aged Shankuntala (Biswas) and beautiful, young Kalyani (Ray). Kalyani is forced to work as a prostitute to help support the ashram but falls in love with Narayan (Abraham), whose progressive views are inspired by Gandhi. However, their involvement leads to both tragedy and freedom. The last of Mehta's trilogy following "Fire" and "Earth." Hindi with subtitles. **117m/C DVD.** *CA* Seema Biswas, Lisa Ray, Raghuvir Yadav, Kulbashan Kharbanda, John Abraham, Sarala, Manorama, Vidula Javalgekar, Vinay Pathak, Seema Biswas, Gerson Da Cunha, Mohan Jhanjiani; ***D:*** Deepa Mehta; ***C:*** Giles Nuttgens; ***M:*** Mychael Danna, A.R. Rahman.

Water Babies *Slip Slide Adventures* **1979 (G)** When a chimney sweep's 12-year-old apprentice is wrongly accused of stealing silver, the boy and his dog fall into a pond and eventually rescue some of the characters they find there. Combination of live-action and animated fairy-tale story set in 19th-century London. Boring, unless you're a young child with equivalent standards. Based on the book by Charles Kingsley. **93m/C VHS, DVD.** *GB* James Mason, Billie Whitelaw, David Tomlinson, Paul Luty, Sammantha Coates; ***D:*** Lionel Jeffries.

Water Drops on Burning Rocks *Gouttes d'Eau sur Pierres Brulantes* **1999** Director Ozon pays tribute to late German director Rainer Werner Fassbinder by resurrecting his unproduced play. In the '70s, 50-year-old businessman Leopold (Giraudeau) picks up 19-year-old Franz (Zidi), who winds up moving in, though the mismatched duo fight constantly. When Franz's former girlfriend, Anna (Sagnier), shows up, Leopold even begins seducing her. Then transexual Vera (Thomson), Leopold's ex-girlfriend, also comes back. And it's a very messy foursome, indeed. French with subtitles. **82m/C VHS, DVD.** *FR* Bernard Giraudeau, Anna Thomson, Malik Zidi, Ludivine Sagnier; ***D:*** Francois Ozon; ***W:*** Francois Ozon; ***C:*** Jeanne Lapoirie.

The Water Engine 1/2 **1992** Charles Lang (Macy) is a luckless machinist struggling to survive in Depression-era Chicago. Lang invents a remarkable engine, that runs on water, and holds the promise of limitless, cheap power. To protect his invention he finds a seedy patent attorney (Mahoney), which leads to the sinister Oberman (Mantegna), a mysterious and powerful figure who wants Lang's invention—at any cost. Based on the play by David Mamet. **110m/C VHS.** Charles Durning, Patti LuPone, William H. Macy, John Mahoney, Joe Mantegna, Joanna Miles, Mike Nussbaum, Treat Williams, Andrea Marcovicci, Peter Michael Goetz, David Mamet; ***D:*** Steven Schachter; ***W:*** David Mamet; ***C:*** Bryan England. **CABLE**

The Water Horse: Legend of the Deep 1/2 **2007 (PG)** The water horse turns out to be the Loch Ness Monster and this charming family film explains how it got into that Scottish loch. Lonely young Angus (Etel) is living with his stern housekeeper mum (Watson) and sister Kirstie (Xi) on a Scottish estate while dad is off fighting in WWII. Angus finds an egg on the beach that hatches into a cute, mischievous critter Angus names Crusoe that soon grows to mammoth size. So he must secretly be transported to the loch under the noses of snooty British soldiers stationed on the property. Visual effects are good. Based on the novel by Dick King-Smith. **111m/C DVD.** *GB US* Alex(ander Nathan) Etel, Emily Watson, Ben Chaplin, David Morrissey, Priyanka Xi, Brian Cox; ***D:*** Jay Russell; ***W:*** Robert Nelson Jacobs; ***C:*** Oliver Stapleton; ***M:*** James Newton Howard.

Water Lilies *Naissance des Pieuvres; Birth of Octopuses* **2007** Gawky 15-year-old Marie (Acquart) and her chubby friend Anne (Blachere) are interested in the local synchronized swim team. Marie approaches star swimmer, the beautiful Floriane (Haenel), so they'll be allowed into the practices. Marie is infatuated with Floriane, who has a reputation, and she uses Marie to meet her boyfriend Francois (Jacquin), whom Anne also likes. But Floriane's reputation proves to be misleading as her friendship with Marie deepens. French with subtitles. **85m/C DVD.** *FR* Pauline Acquart, Adele Haenel, Louise Blanchere, Warren Jacquin; ***D:*** Celine Sciama; ***W:*** Celine Sciama; ***C:*** Crystal Fournier; ***M:*** Jean-Baptiste de Laubier.

The Water Margin *Outlaws of the Marsh; Seven Blows of the Dragon; Sui Woo Juen; Shui Hu Zhuan* **1972** War epic based loosely on the book "All Men Are Brothers" which was inspired by the true story of the Mountain Brothers, a group of 108 rebels who repeatedly held off invasions by the armies of the Sung Dynasty. Fans of the Shaw Brothers' Kung-Fu films will enjoy the all-star cast of many of the actors working for them at the time. A bit short as the book has so many characters and subplots the only way to do it justice would be a series. **81m/C DVD.** *HK* David Chiang, Lung Ti, Kuan Tai Chen, Chung Wang, Tetsuro Tanba, Feng Ku, Lily Ho, Toshio Kurosawa, Feng Chin, Miao Ching; ***D:*** Cheh Chang, Hsueh Li Pao, Ma Wu; ***W:*** Guanzhong Luo, Kuang Ni; ***C:*** Mu-To Kung; ***M:*** Yung-Yu Chen.

Water Rustlers 1/2 **1939** Unscrupulous land baron builds a dam on his side of the creek with the intention of drying out the cattle pastures. Heroine Page, whose pop has been rubbed out by varmints, and good guy/lover O'Brien save her property and avenge her father. Second of three Page westerns. **55m/B VHS.** Dorothy Page, Dave O'Brien; ***D:*** Samuel Diege.

The Waterboy **1998 (PG-13)** Another in a continuing line of deliberately stupid comedies finds Sandler a not-too-bright, constantly picked-on waterboy for a lousy Louisiana college football team. After a player taunts him once too often, he tackles the big guy, and is suddenly promoted to player—much to the title the dismay of his over-protective mother, Bates. Loser player turns loser team into winners after some contrived obstacles: you've seen it before, but Sandler cultists (and less discerning football fans) will love it anyway. **90m/C VHS, DVD.** Adam Sandler, Kathy Bates, Henry Winkler, Fairuza Balk, Jerry Reed, Larry (Lawrence) Gilliard Jr., Blake Clark, Rob Schneider, Clint Howard, Allen Whiting, Robert Kokol; ***D:*** Frank Coraci; ***W:*** Tim Herlihy, Adam Sandler; ***C:*** Steven Bernstein; ***M:*** Alan Pasqua.

The Waterdance **1991 (R)** Autobiographical film based on the experiences of writer/co-director Jimenez. When writer Joel Garcia (Stoltz) is paralyzed in a hiking accident he finds himself dealing with not only the rehab process itself but his feelings, the feelings of his married lover, and those of his fellow patients. Deals unsentimentally with all the physical adjustments, including the sexual ones. Resolutions may be predictable but the performances rise above any script weaknesses. The title refers to Hill's dream of dancing on water—and the fear of drowning if he stops. **106m/C VHS, DVD.** Eric Stoltz, Wesley Snipes, William Forsythe, Helen Hunt, Elizabeth Pena, Grace Zabriskie; ***D:*** Neal Jimenez, Michael Steinberg; ***W:*** Neal Jimenez; ***C:*** Mark Plummer; ***M:*** Michael Convertino. Ind. Spirit '93: First Feature, Screenplay; Sundance '92: Screenplay, Aud. Award.

Waterfront 1/2 **1939** Dreary dockside melodrama, with drinking and brawling longshoreman Jim (Morgan) avenging his brother's death. Based on the play "Blindspot" by Kenyon Nicholson. **59m/B VHS.** Dennis Morgan, Gloria Dickson, Marie Wilson, Larry Williams, Sheila (Manors) Mannors, Ward Bond, Frank Faylen; ***D:*** Terry Morse; ***W:*** Arthur Ripley, Lee Katz.

Waterfront **1944** Nazis coerce German-Americans into helping them in WWII-era San Francisco. Credulity defying spy doings, but that's okay. Fairly entertaining wartime drama about paranoia on the home front. **68m/B VHS, DVD.** John Carradine, J. Carrol Naish, Terry Frost, Maris Wrixon, Edwin Maxwell; ***D:*** Steve Sekely.

Waterfront 1/2 **1983** Effective romantic drama set in Melbourne, Australia. Australian workers strike after taking forced pay cuts. As a result, Italian immigrants are hired as scabs to keep the docks going. Despite the tension, an Italian woman and an Australian man fall deeply in love, only to find that they must struggle to keep that love alive. **294m/C VHS.** *AU* Jack Thompson, Greta Scacchi, Frank Gallacher, Tony Rickards, Mark Little, Jay Mannering, Ray Barrett, Chris Haywood, Warren Mitchell, Noni Hazlehurst, John Karlsen, Elin Jenkins; ***D:*** Chris Thomson.

Waterhole Number 3 1/2 **1967 (PG)** Three Confederate army buddies steal a fortune in gold bullion from the Union Army and hide it in a waterhole in the desert. One of the funnier entries in the Western comedy genre. **95m/C VHS, DVD.** James Coburn, Carroll O'Connor, Margaret Blye, Claude Akins, Bruce Dern, Joan Blondell, James Whitmore; ***D:*** William A. Graham; ***C:*** Robert Burks; ***M:*** Dave Grusin.

Waterland **1992 (R)** Meandering drama about a history teacher who tries to solve a personal crisis by using his class as a sounding board to describe his troubled past in England. Dark secrets abound, including incest, madness, murder, and the terrifying love between the teacher and his childhood bride. Melancholy, overwrought but partially redeemed by the lead performances of Irons and his (real-life and cinematic) wife, Cusack. The film's setting has been unfortunately moved from London to Pittsburgh, destroying story links. Based on the novel by Graham Swift. **95m/C VHS, DVD.** Jeremy Irons, Ethan Hawke, Sinead Cusack, John Heard, Grant Warnock, Lena Headey, Pete Postlethwaite, Cara Buono; ***D:*** Stephen Gyllenhaal; ***W:*** Peter Prince; ***C:*** Robert Elswit; ***M:*** Carter Burwell.

Waterloo **1971 (G)** Massive chronicle of Napoleon's European conquests and eventual defeat at the hands of Wellington. Filmed on location in Italy and the Ukraine, it bombed due largely to Steiger's bizarre rendition of Napoleon. **122m/C VHS.** *IT RU* Rod Steiger, Orson Welles, Virginia McKenna, Michael Wilding, Donal Donnelly, Christopher Plummer, Jack Hawkins, Dan O'Herlihy, Terence Alexander, Rupert Davies, Ivo Garrani, Gianni "John" Garko, Ian Ogilvy, Andrea Checchi, Jean Louis, Willoughby Gray, John Savident, Adrian Brine, Jeffrey Wickham, Sergei Zakariadze, Richard Heffer, Aldo Cecconi, Peter Davies, Eugene Samoilov; ***D:*** Sergei Bondarchuk; ***W:*** Sergei Bondarchuk, H.A.L. Craig, Vittorio Bonicelli; ***C:*** Armando Nannuzzi; ***M:*** Nino Rota.

Waterloo Bridge **1940** In London during WWI, Capt. Roy Cronin (Taylor), a soldier from an aristocratic family, begins a tragic romance with ballet dancer Myra Lester (Leigh) when they meet by chance on the foggy Waterloo Bridge. She loses her job and when Roy is listed as dead, Myra's despair turns her to prostitution. But when Roy returns from POW camp, they once again meet by accident on Waterloo Bridge, and their romance resumes, with Myra struggling to conceal her shameful secret. Four-hanky drama with fine performances by Leigh (her first after "Gone with the Wind") and Taylor. Based on the play by Robert E. Sherwood. **109m/B VHS, DVD.** Vivien Leigh, Robert Taylor, Lucile Watson, Sir C. Aubrey Smith, Maria Ouspenskaya, Virginia Field; ***D:*** Mervyn LeRoy; ***W:*** S.N. Behrman, George Froeschel, Hans Rameau; ***C:*** Joseph Ruttenberg; ***M:*** Herbert Stothart.

Waterloo Road **1944** Jim (Mills) is off fighting in France when he receives a letter from his sister Ruby (Leggatt) intimating that Jim's lonely wife Tillie (Shelton) is succumbing to the sleazy charms of shirker Ted (Granger). Jim goes AWOL from the army and returns to London to sort out his marriage while trying to avoid getting caught by the military police. **77m/B DVD.** *GB* John Mills, Joy Shelton, Stewart Granger, Alastair Sims, Alison Leggatt, Beatrice Varley, George Carney; ***D:*** Sidney Gilliat; ***W:*** Sidney Gilliat; ***C:*** Arthur Crabtree.

Watermelon Man **1970 (R)** The tables are turned for a bigoted white guy when he wakes up one morning to discover he has become a black man. Broad comedy with not much place to go is still engaging. Cambridge takes on both roles, appearing in unconvincing white makeup. **97m/C VHS, DVD.** Godfrey Cambridge, Erin Moran, Estelle Parsons, Howard Caine, D'Urville Martin, Kay

Kimberly, Paul Williams; *D:* Melvin Van Peebles; *W:* Herman Raucher; *C:* Herman Raucher; *M:* Melvin Van Peebles.

The Watermelon Woman **1997** Cheryl (Dunye) is a young, black, lesbian video store clerk who wants to be a documentary filmmaker. She becomes obsessed with a black actress seen in some 1930s black films, who was known only as the "Watermelon Woman." Doing research, Cheryl discovers the woman's name was Fae Richards (Bronson) and that she was a lesbian who had an affair with her white director. While deciding to film a documentary about Fae, Cheryl's personal life begins to parallel Fae's when she briefly falls for white customer, Diana (Turner). **85m/C VHS, DVD.** Cheryl Dunye, Valerie Walker, Guinevere Turner, Lisa Marie Bronson; *D:* Cheryl Dunye; *W:* Cheryl Dunye; *C:* Michelle Crenshaw; *M:* Paul Shapiro.

Waterproof **1999 (PG-13)** Reynolds is oddly cast but very effective as Eli, a Jewish shopkeeper who is shot by a young would-be robber, Thaniel (Dye). To protect him from prosecution, Thaniel's mother, Tyree (Grace), whisks her son and Eli to her childhood home in Waterproof, Louisiana. She's been away for 15 years and finds a great deal of tension with her family, but they are willing to take Tyree and Thaniel in to assist them. The film examines the struggles that exist between family members and individuals from differing ethnic backgrounds. Without becoming overwrought, the film delivers positive message while being entertaining. Special kudos to Jones, who overcomes his comic reputation by portraying a man with severe brain damage. **94m/C DVD.** Burt Reynolds, April Grace, Cordereau Dye, Whitman Mayo, Anthony Lee, Orlando Jones, Ja'net DuBois; *D:* Barry Berman.

Water's Edge **½ 2003 (R)** Tense little thriller finds New Yorkers Robert (Fillion) and Molly (West) relocating to a small town and the rustic lakeside cabin that Robert inherited from his father. But this friendly town hides some dirty secrets, including blackmail and murder. **?m/C VHS, DVD.** Nathan Fillion, Chandra West, Emmanuelle Vaugier, Daniel Baldwin, Andrew Moxham; *D:* Harvey Kahn; *W:* Craig Brewer. **VIDEO**

Watership Down **½ 1978 (PG)** Wonderfully animated story based on Richard Adams's allegorical novel about how a group of rabbits escape fear and overcome oppression while searching for a new and better home. It's really an adult theme with sufficient violence to the poor wittle wabbits to scare the kiddies. **92m/C VHS, DVD.** *GB* *D:* Martin Rosen; *W:* Martin Rosen; *V:* Richard Briers, Ralph Richardson, Zero Mostel, John Hurt, Denholm Elliott, Harry Andrews, Michael Hordern, Joss Ackland.

Waterworld **½ 1995 (PG-13)** "The Man From Atlantis" meets "Mad Max." Industry knives sharpened with glee before release, with some insiders calling this luck-impaired project "Fishtar" and "Kevin's Gate." Most of the estimated $150 million budget seems to have ended up on screen, which makes for a visually striking, and at times daunting, film. Costner, who did just about everything but cater the meals, stars as Mariner, a mutant man-fish who reluctantly helps human survivors search for the mythical Dryland since the polar ice caps melted, flooding the earth. The bad guys are the Smokers, led by the evil Hopper, who can play these roles in his sleep. Entertaining, but not riveting, as the budget and PR hype leads one to expect. The floating set was anchored (not very well, apparently) off the Hawaiian coast and was lost once during a tropical storm. Costner bet the boat on this one and lost more than just money. **135m/C VHS, DVD, HD DVD.** Jack Kehler, Zakes Mokae, Sab Shimono, Jack Black, Kim Coates, John Toles-Bey, Ari Barak, Sean M. Whalen, Robert LaSardo, Lee Arenberg, Kevin Costner, Dennis Hopper, Jeanne Tripplehorn, Tina Majorino, Michael Jeter, R.D. Call, Robert Joy; *D:* Kevin Reynolds; *W:* Peter Rader, Marc Norman, David N. Twohy; *C:* Dean Semler; *M:* James Newton Howard. Golden Raspberries '95: Worst Support. Actor (Hopper).

Wavelength **½ 1983 (PG)** A rock star living in the Hollywood Hills with his girlfriend stumbles on an ultra-secret government project involving friendly aliens from outer space recovered from a recent UFO crash site. Fun, enthusiastically unoriginal cheap sci-fi. Soundtrack by Tangerine Dream. **87m/C VHS.** Bobby DiCicco, Robert Carradine, Cherie Currie, Keenan Wynn; *D:* Mike Gray; *W:* Mike Gray; *M:* Tangerine Dream.

Wavelength **½ 1996 (R)** Physicist and Oxford professor Paul Higgins (Piven) has a few problems—a wife, Claire (Williams), a girlfriend, Lucy (Walker), Lucy's father who just happens to be the head of the physics department, and a mysterious presence (Attenborough) who's trying to help Paul with his research on nuclear fission. Piven's character is so selfish you'll wonder why either woman wants him and the happy ending feels contrived. **94m/C VHS.** *GB* Jeremy Piven, Kelli Williams, Liza Walker, James Villiers, James Faulkner, Richard Attenborough, Byrne Piven, Nicholas Marco, Dominic West; *D:* Benjamin Fry; *W:* Benjamin Fry; *C:* Chris Middleton; *M:* Michael Storey.

Wax Mask **½** *M.D.C. Maschera di Cera* **1997** Liner notes state that this loose remake of "House of Wax" was to have been directed by Lucio Fulci ("Zombie," "The Black Cat") who died before he could begin work. It was produced in part by Dario Argento, but the important thing for horror fans to know is that this one owes just as much to Stuart Gordon's "Re-Animator." It takes the same gleeful approach to outrageous medical horror and sex, though overall, it is a much more polished looking film with expensive production values, an attractive (if unknown in America) young cast, and a sharply focused image. The setting is Paris and Rome in the early 20th century. Sonia (Mondello) witnessed the brutal murder of her parents as a child. Years later, she goes to work for Boris Volkoff (Hossein), whose macabre wax museum hides terrible secrets. Director Sergio Stivaletti came to the job through special effects expertise and his work here (in both capacities) is very good. This is a man to watch. The plot goes much too far for the film ever to find a large mainstream audience, and that's the point of Grand Guignol horror. **98m/C DVD.** *IT FR* Robert Hossein, Romina Mondello, Ricardo Serventi Longhi; *D:* Sergio Stivaletti; *W:* Lucio Fulci; *C:* Sergio Salvati. **VIDEO**

Wax, or the Discovery of Television among the Bees **1993** Intricate and eccentric fable dealing with alternate realities and perceptions. Jacob Maker (Blair) keeps a hive of very unusual bees, a family legacy passed down from his grandfather. Jacob begins experiencing a eerie communication with his bees and suffering mysterious blackouts, which cause him to perceive the world through blurred bee vision. New Mexico desert setting provides a surreal and desolate landscape. **85m/C VHS.** David Blair, Meg Savlov, Florence Ormezzano, William S. Burroughs; *D:* David Blair; *W:* David Blair; *M:* Beo Morales, Brooks Williams.

Waxwork **½ 1988 (R)** A wax museum opens up, and it is soon evident that the dummies are not what they seem. Garbled nonthriller. Available in a 100-minute unrated version. **97m/C VHS, DVD.** Zach Galligan, Deborah Foreman, Michelle Johnson, Dana Ashbrook, Miles O'Keeffe, Patrick Macnee, David Warner, John Rhys-Davies; *D:* Anthony Hickox; *W:* Anthony Hickox; *C:* Gerry Lively; *M:* Roger Bellon.

Waxwork 2: Lost in Time **½** *Lost in Time* **1991 (R)** A young couple (Galligan and Schnarre) barely escape with their lives when the infamous waxworks museum burns down. A severed hand also gets loose and follows Schnarre home and murders her stepfather, leaving her to take the blame. In order to prove her innocence, the couple must travel through a bizarre time machine. Extraordinary special effects, strange plot twists, and recreations of scenes from past horror movies make this a highly entertaining sequel. **104m/C VHS, DVD.** Zach Galligan, Alexander Godunov, Bruce Campbell, Michael Des Barres, Monica Schnarre, Martin Kemp, Sophie Ward, Marina Sirtis, Juliet Mills, John Ireland, Patrick Macnee, David Carradine, Drew Barrymore; *D:* Anthony Hickox; *W:* Anthony Hickox; *C:* Gerry Lively.

Waxworks **1924** A major achievement in German Expressionism, in which a poet imagines scenarios in a wax museum fairground that involve Jack the Ripper, Ivan the Terrible, and Haroun al-Rashid. Influential and considered ahead of its time. Silent. **63m/B VHS, DVD.** *GE* William Dieterle, Emil Jannings, Conrad Veidt, Werner Krauss, John Gottowt, Olga Belajeff; *D:* Paul Leni; *W:* Henrik Galeen.

Way Back Home *Old Greatheart; Other People's Business* **1932** Man wants to adopt a boy to release him from the clutches of his cruel guardian. Minor role for the then unknown Davis. **81m/B VHS.** Phillips Lord, Frank Albertson, Bette Davis; *D:* William A. Seiter; *M:* Max Steiner.

Way Down East **1920** Melodramatic silent drama of a country girl who is tricked into a fake marriage by a scheming playboy. The famous final scene of Gish adrift on the ice floes is in color. One of Griffith's last critical and popular successes. This tape includes the original Griffith-approved musical score. Remade in 1935 with Henry Fonda. **107m/B VHS, DVD.** Lillian Gish, Richard Barthelmess, Lowell Sherman, Creighton Hale, Burr McIntosh, Kate Bruce, Florence Short; *D:* D.W. Griffith; *W:* D.W. Griffith, Joseph R. Grismer; *C:* Billy (G.W.) Bitzer, Hendrik Sartov.

Way Down South **½ 1939** The orphan son of a plantation owner tries to take over his father's estate, only to find out that the place has been run into the ground by a corrupt lawyer and a cruel slave driver. Black poet Hughes and actor Muse collaborated on the screenplay. German-born director Vorhaus was in his second year in Hollywood, after making his mark in Britain directing talkies. ♫Good Ground; Louisiana; Nobody Know De Trouble I See; Sometimes I Feel Like a Motherless Child; Lord I You Can't Come Send One Angel Down. **62m/B VHS, DVD.** Bobby Breen, Alan Mowbray, Ralph Morgan, Clarence Muse, Steffi Duna, Sally Blane, Edwin Maxwell, Matthew "Stymie" Beard, Lillian Yarbo, Charles Middleton; *D:* Bernard Vorhaus; *W:* Clarence Muse, Langston Hughes.

Way He Was **1976 (R)** A satirical re-enactment of the events that led up to the Watergate burglary and the coverup that followed. **87m/C VHS.** Steve Friedman, Al Lewis, Merrie Lynn Ross, Doodles Weaver; *D:* Mark L. Lester.

The Way Home **½ 2001 (PG)** Because his mother has lost her job, a seven-year-old boy (Yoo) is forced to leave the city of Seoul to stay with his wizened mute grandmother (Kim) in her ranshackle rural hut. The spoiled kid can't believe he has to do without fast food, let alone indoor plumbing and other modern conveniences. But what the boy eventually comes to realize is that his grandmother loves him unconditionally. Korean with subtitles. **85m/C VHS, DVD.** *KN* Seung-Ho Yoo, Eul-Boon Kim, Hyo-Hee Dong; *D:* Jeong-Hyang Lee; *W:* Jeong-Hyang Lee; *C:* Hong-Shik Yoon; *M:* Dae-Hong Kim, Yan-Hee Kim.

A Way of Life **½ 2004** One of those unrelentingly bleak British kitchen-sink dramas with a completely unsympathetic lead. Leigh-Anne is a young, trouble-prone, unemployed single mum who hangs out with a bunch of racist losers to the concern of her granny, who wants custody of Leigh-Ann's baby daughter. When she takes the baby to the hospital after a minor accident, suspicious doctors insist on keeping the child and paranoid Leigh-Anne blames her immigrant neighbor for her problems, resulting in more tragedy. **91m/C DVD.** Brenda Blethyn, Nathan Jones, Stephanie James, Gary Sheppeard, Dean Wong, Sara Gregory, Oliver Haden; *D:* Amma Asante; *W:* Amma Asante; *C:* Ian Wilson; *M:* David Gray.

Way of the Black Dragon **1981** When slave-trading drug traffickers threaten the moral fiber of our nation, two commandoes join forces to halt their operation. **88m/C VHS, DVD.** Ron Van Clief, Carter Wang, Charles Bonet; *D:* Chan Wui Ngai.

Way of the Gun **½ 2000 (R)** Two unsuccessful career criminals (Phillippe and Del Toro) take up kidnapping and hold a surrogate mother (Lewis) for ransom. Only the parents-to-be are mobbed up and send two thugs (Diggs and Katt) and a philosophical enforcer (Caan) to get her back unharmed. McQuarrie shows that he still has the knack for twisty plots, surprise revelations, and cool dialogue, but he lets the proceedings drag on a little longer than they need to. He's also not shy about heaping on the violence and crude language (which isn't necessarily bad, just consider yourself forewarned). **118m/C VHS, DVD.** Ryan Phillippe, Benicio Del Toro, Juliette Lewis, James Caan, Taye Diggs, Nicky Katt, Scott Wilson, Kristen Lehman, Geoffrey Lewis, Dylan Kussman; *D:* Christopher McQuarrie; *W:* Christopher McQuarrie; *C:* Dick Pope; *M:* Joe Kraemer.

Way of the West **½ 1935** Them durn pesky sheepherders are up to it again! Okay, so the cow/sheep thing is a classic western plot, but here it's offered perfunctorily. **52m/B VHS.** Wally Wales, William Desmond, Art Mix, Jim Sheridan, Bobby Nelson; *D:* Robert Emmett Tansey.

The Way of War **½ 2008 (R)** Paramilitary operative David Wolfe (Gooding Jr.) is assigned to kill a Middle Eastern terrorist. While on the job (which goes bad), David learns about a U.S. government conspiracy and tries to expose the truth before getting silenced himself. Plot feels like a tired retread of other military and conspiracy flicks. **87m/C DVD.** Cuba Gooding Jr., J.K. Simmons, John Terry, Lance Reddick; *D:* John Carter; *W:* John Carter, Scott Schafer; *M:* James Melvin. **VIDEO**

The Way Out *Dial 999* **1956** Average crime drama starring Nelson as a fugitive accused of killing a bookie. **90m/C VHS.** *GB* Gene Nelson, Mona Freeman, John Bentley, Michael Goodliffe, Sydney Tafler; *D:* Montgomery Tully.

Way Out West **1937** The classic twosome journey way out west to deliver the deed to a gold mine to the daughter of their late prospector pal. The obligatory romance is missing, but you'll be laughing so hard you won't notice. One of Stan and Ollie's best. Score includes the song "Trail of the Lonesome Pine." Also included on this tape is a 1932 Todd and Pitts short, "Red Noses." Available colorized. **86m/B VHS, DVD.** Stan Laurel, Oliver Hardy, Rosina Lawrence, James Finlayson, Sharon Lynne, Zasu Pitts, William Haines; *D:* James W. Horne.

Way Past Cool **2000 (R)** Two gangs, both made up of pre-teens, are pitted against each other by a 16-year-old drug dealer, with all the gang staples, including turf battles, shootouts, drinking (and we're not talking juice boxes), and swearing. Sorry, can't think of a single redeeming thing about it. **96m/C VHS, DVD.** Wayne Collins, Adam Davidson, Terence Williams, Kareem Woods, Wes Charles Jr., Jonathan Roger Neal, Luchisha Evans, D'andre Jenkins, D'esmond Jenkins, Partap Khalsa; *D:* Adam Davidson; *W:* Yule Caise, Jess Mowry; *C:* Amy Vincent; *M:* Zen Amen. **VIDEO**

The Way To Fight *Kenka no hanamichi: Oosaka saikyo densetsu* **1996** Kazuyoshi Tamai is a serious street brawler and the toughest guy in his school. Similarly Takeshi Hamada is the toughest boy of his school, and they have challenged one another to see who is the best. Due to a series of missteps they miss one another, and years later Kazuyoshi is a Bantamweight boxing champion while Takeshi has become a famous pro wrestler. Meeting once again, they decide to continue their rivalry. Unusually normal fare for director Takashi Miike. **114m/C DVD.** *JP* Takeshi Caesar, Ryoko Imamura, Kazuki Kitamura; *D:* Takashi Miike; *W:* Masa Nakamura, Seijun Ninomiya; *C:* Hideo Yamamoto.

The Way We Live Now **½ 2002** Based on the 1875 novel by Anthony Trollope, this adaptation centers around shady financier Augustus Melmotte (Suchet). An economic boom is sweeping through Europe in the 1870s and Melmotte arrives in London with a scheme to buy himself a place in Victorian society. Melmotte is even willing to sacrifice his daughter Marie (Henderson) who has developed an infatuation for debt-ridden but aristocratic Sir Felix Carbury (Macfadyen). The question for all this greedy bunch is who will get the better of whom? **300m/C VHS, DVD.** *GB* David Suchet, Shirley Henderson, Matthew MacFadyen, Cheryl Campbell, Paloma Baeza, Douglas Hodge, Miranda Otto, Cillian Murphy, Michael Riley, Allan Corduner, David Bradley, Jim Carter, Oliver Ford Davies, Joanna David; *D:* David Yates; *W:* Andrew Davies; *C:* Chris Seager; *M:* Nicholas Hooper. **TV**

The Way We Were ♂♂♂ **1973 (PG)** Big boxoffice hit follows a love story between opposites from the 1930s to the 1950s. Streisand is a Jewish political radical who meets the handsome WASP Redford at college. They're immediately attracted to one another, but it takes years before they act on it and eventually marry. They move to Hollywood where Redford is a screenwriter and left-wing Streisand becomes involved in the Red scare and the blacklist, much to Redford's dismay. Though always in love, their differences are too great to keep them together. An old-fashioned and sweet romance, with much gloss. Hit title song sung by Streisand. Adapted by Arthur Laurents from his novel. ♫The Way We Were. **118m/C VHS, DVD.** Barbra Streisand, Robert Redford, Bradford Dillman, Viveca Lindfors, Herb Edelman, Murray Hamilton, Patrick O'Neal, James Woods, Sally Kirkland, Lois Chiles, Susan Blakely, Allyn Ann McLerie, Marcia Mae Jones, Diana Ewing, George Gaynes; *D:* Sydney Pollack; *W:* Arthur Laurents; *C:* Harry Stradling Jr.; *M:* Marvin Hamlisch. Oscars '73: Song ("The Way We Were"), Orig. Dramatic Score; Golden Globes '74: Song ("The Way We Were").

The Way West ♂ 1/2 **1967** A wagon train heads to Oregon. A poor and muddled attempt at recreating the style of a John Ford western. What really galls is that it's based on the Pulitzer-winning novel by A.B. Guthrie Jr. Boy, is the book better than the movie. Field's first film. **122m/C VHS.** Kirk Douglas, Robert Mitchum, Richard Widmark, Lola Albright, Michael Witney, Stubby Kaye, Sally Field, Jack Elam; *D:* Andrew V. McLaglen; *C:* William Clothier.

Wayne Murder Case ♂♂♂ *A Strange Adventure* **1932** A fast-moving, cleverly constructed murder mystery. A rich old man dies just as he is about to sign a new will. Though no one was standing near him, a knife is found stuck in his back. **61m/B VHS, DVD.** June Clyde, Regis Toomey, Jason Robards Sr., Lucille LaVerne; *D:* Hampton Del Ruth, Philip H. (Phil, P.H.) Whitman; *W:* Arthur Hoerl; *C:* Leon Shamroy.

Wayne's World ♂♂♂ **1992 (PG-13)** Destined to become one of the top movies of all time—Not! This "Saturday Night Live" skit proved to be so popular that it got its own movie, not unlike the plot, which has slimy producer Benjamin Oliver (Lowe) take the public access "Wayne's World" into the world of commercial television. The zany duo of Wayne (Myers) and Garth (Carvey) are as much fun on the big screen as they were on SNL and there are many funny moments, several of which are destined to become comedy classics. A huge boxoffice hit that spawned a sequel. It also spawned Lorne Michaels's desperate attempts to match its success with other non-bigscreen worthy skits from the show. **93m/C VHS, DVD.** Mike Myers, Dana Carvey, Rob Lowe, Tia Carrere, Brian Doyle-Murray, Lara Flynn Boyle, Kurt Fuller, Colleen Camp, Donna Dixon, Ed O'Neill, Alice Cooper, Meat Loaf Aday; *D:* Penelope Spheeris; *W:* Mike Myers, Bonnie Turner, Terry Turner; *C:* Theo van de Sande; *M:* J. Peter Robinson. MTV Movie Awards '92: On-Screen Duo (Mike Myers/Dana Carvey).

Wayne's World 2 ♂♂ **1993 (PG-13)** Good-natured rerun of the original has plenty of sophomoric gags, but feels tired. Wayne and Garth are on their own, planning a major concert, Waynestock. "If you book them they will come," Jim Morrison says in a dream. Meanwhile, Wayne's girlfriend (Carrere) is falling for slimeball record promoter Walken. Offers a few brilliantly funny segments. If you liked the "Bohemian Rhapsody" spot in the original, get ready for the Village People here. Heston has a funny cameo, and Walken and Basinger push the limits without going over the top. Feature film debut for director Surjik. **94m/C VHS, DVD.** Mike Myers, Dana Carvey, Tia Carrere, Christopher Walken, Ralph Brown, Kim Basinger, James Hong, Chris Farley, Ed O'Neill, Olivia D'Abo, Kevin Pollak, Drew Barrymore, Charlton Heston, Rip Taylor, Bob Odenkirk, Michael A. (M.A.) Nickles; *D:* Stephen Surjik; *W:* Bonnie Turner, Terry Turner, Mike Myers; *C:* Francis Kenny; *M:* Carter Burwell.

The Wayward Wife ♂♂ *La Provinciale* **1952** Young woman, married to a university professor, is blackmailed over her less-than-respectable past. Based on the novel by Alberto Moravia. Italian with subtitles. **92m/B VHS.** *IT* Gina Lollobrigida, Gabriele Ferzetti, Franco Interlenghi, Renato Baldini; *D:* Mario Soldati.

We All Fall Down ♂♂ **2000** Disturbing urban drama about addiction and friendship. The death of his mother propels struggling Vancouver actor Michael (Belsher) deeper into his drug habit, which suits his best friend, junkie/artist Kris (Cummins), just fine. Following a friend's drug-related death, Michael struggles to get clean, pushing away from Kris and his temptations. Ryan (Robertson), Kris' girlfriend, is also fed up and looks to Michael for solace, adding an extra complication. **92m/C DVD.** *CA* Martin Cummins, Francoise Robertson, Helen Shaver, Nicholas (Nick) Campbell, Darcy Belsher, Rene Auberjonois, Barry Pepper, Ryan Reynolds; *D:* Martin Cummins; *W:* Martin Cummins, Richard C. Burton; *C:* Andreas Poulsson; *M:* Jim Byrnes.

We All Loved Each Other So Much ♂♂♂ 1/2 **1977** Sensitive comedy follows three friends over 30 years, beginning at the end of WWII. All three have loved the same woman, an actress. Homage to friendship and to postwar Italian cinema. Includes a full-scale re-creation of the fountain scene in "La Dolce Vita." In Italian with English subtitles. **124m/C VHS, DVD.** *IT* Vittorio Gassman, Nino Manfredi, Stefano Satta Flores, Stefania Sandrelli, Marcello Mastroianni, Federico Fellini, Anita Ekberg, Vittorio De Sica; *D:* Ettore Scola.

We Are Marshall ♂♂ 1/2 **2006 (PG)** The tight-knit community of Huntington, West Virginia, grieves after the real-life tragedy of a plane crash that killed 75 Marshall University football players, coaches, staff, and boosters in 1970. The school's president decides to end the program until the student body gathers together with its "We are Marshall!" pep-rally chant (repeated often throughout). Enter coach Jack Lengyel (a spirited McConaughey) to lead the piecing together of the team and win over the doubters. Occasional goosebumpy moments give way to a dull script and, oddly enough, entirely too much on-field action. **131m/C DVD, Blu-ray Disc, HD DVD.** *US* Matthew McConaughey, Matthew Fox, Anthony Mackie, David Strathairn, Ian McShane, Kate Mara, January Jones, Kimberly Williams; *D:* McG; *W:* Jamie Linden; *C:* Shane Hurlbut; *M:* Christophe Beck.

We Are the Children ♂♂ **1987** Cynical reporter covering the famine in Ethiopia meets an idealistic nurse who's been living there for years. Romance blossoms among the starving in made-for-TV drama co-produced by Danson. **92m/C VHS.** Ally Sheedy, Ted Danson, Judith Ivey, Zia Mohyeddin; *D:* Robert M. Young.

We Dive at Dawn ♂♂♂ **1943** Interesting, tense British submarine drama. The "Sea Tiger" attempts to sink the German battleship "Brandenburg" off Denmark. Good cast. Mills prepared for the role by riding an actual submarine, turning "a pale shade of pea-green" when it crash-dived. **98m/B VHS, DVD.** *GB* Eric Portman, John Mills; *D:* Anthony Asquith; *W:* Val Valentine; *C:* Jack Cox.

We Don't Live Here Anymore ♂♂ **2004 (R)** A quartet of 30-somethings discover adultery and betrayal have repercussions in this adaptation of two novellas by Andre Dubus. Best friends Jack (Ruffalo) and Hank (Krause) teach at a small college; Jack's married to Terry (Dern), Hank to Edith (Watts). Both couples have children; neither marriage is happy. Jack and Edith are in lust and enjoy woodland trysts while waiting to get caught. Serial womanizer Hank is seemingly unconcerned when he finds out but Terry is driven by fury to punish Jack by screwing Hank and then telling her husband—who doesn't react as expected. They're whiny, indecisive, self-involved, angry, weak, occasionally passionate, but not a group you'd want to spend a lot of time with (despite the capable performances from all four actors). **101m/C DVD.** *US* Mark Ruffalo, Laura Dern, Peter Krause, Naomi Watts, Jennifer Bishop, Sam Charles, Haili Page; *D:* John Curran; *W:* Larry Gross; *C:* Maryse Alberti; *M:* Lesley Barber, Laurie Parker.

We of the Never Never ♂♂♂ **1982 (G)** In turn-of-the-century Australia a city-bred woman marries a cattle rancher and moves from civilized Melbourne to the barren outback of the Northern Territory. Based on the autobiographical story written by Jeannie Gunn, the first white woman to travel in the aboriginal wilderness. She finds herself fighting for her own rights as well as for those of the aborigines in this sincere, well-done film. **136m/C VHS, DVD.** *AU* Angela Punch McGregor, Arthur Dignam, Tony Barry; *D:* Igor Auzins.

We Own the Night ♂♂ **2007 (R)** Nightclub manager Bobby (Phoenix) has distanced himself from his cop father Bert (Duvall) and brother Joseph (Wahlberg) to work for Russian mobster Marat (Moshonov) and his drug-dealing nephew Vadim (Veadov). After a raid, Vadim attacks Joseph, and Bobby nervously agrees to become an informant. The performances are okay (everyone's done better work) but Mendes is inarguably hot as Bobby's personal party girl. Set in late 1980s Brooklyn, this stark crime story superficially harkens back to the police dramas of the 70s. **117m/C DVD, Blu-ray Disc.** *US* Joaquin Rafael (Leaf) Phoenix, Mark Wahlberg, Robert Duvall, Eva Mendes, Moni Moshonov, Alex Veadov, Danny Hoch, Tony Musante, Antoni Corone; *D:* James Gray; *W:* James Gray; *C:* Joaquin Baca-Asay; *M:* Wojciech Kilar.

We the Living ♂♂ 1/2 **1942** The torpid long-lost and restored Italian version of Ayn Rand's unique political tome. Deals with a young Soviet woman in revolutionary Petrograd who is slowly ruined by the system and her affair with a romantic counter-revolutionary. Made under the Fascists' nose during WWII. A fascinating dialectic between utopian melodrama and Rand dogma. In Italian with subtitles. **174m/B VHS.** *IT* Alida Valli, Rossano Brazzi, Fosco Giachetti; *D:* Goffredo Alessandrini.

We Think the World of You ♂♂♂ **1988 (PG)** When bisexual Oldman goes to prison, his lover Bates, whose feelings are unresolved and complex, finds friendship with Oldman's dog. Odd, off-bitter comedy-drama of love and loyalty characterized by excellent acting and respectful, gentle direction. From the novel by Joseph R. Ackerly. **94m/C VHS.** *GB* Alan Bates, Gary Oldman, Frances Barber, Liz Smith, Max Wall, Kerry Wise; *D:* Colin Gregg.

We Were Dancing ♂♂ 1/2 **1942** Shearer made only one more film after this frothy effort before retiring from acting and it's a loose adaptation of Noel Coward's play "Tonight at 8:30." Penniless Vicki (Shearer) is engaged to wealthy Hubert Tyler (Bowman) but abandons him for dashing Nicki (Douglas) under the impression he has dough. He thinks the same about her and they get married before realizing they're a couple of cons. Trying another scam, the duo are exposed by Nicki's ex-lover Linda (Patrick) but it doesn't stop them for long. **94m/B DVD.** Norma Shearer, Melvyn Douglas, Gail Patrick, Lee Bowman, Marjorie Main, Reginald Owen, Alan Mowbray, Florence Bates; *D:* Robert Z. Leonard; *W:* George Froeschel, Claudine West, Hans Rameau; *C:* Robert Planck; *M:* Bronislau Kaper.

We Were One Man ♂♂ *Nous Etions Un Seul Homme* **1980** In 1943, simple French peasant Guy finds wounded German soldier Rolf hiding in the woods and brings him to his cottage to recover. Eventually, Guy and Rolf's growing friendship turns sexual but when Rolf realizes he needs to leave for fear of capture, Guy makes a shocking decision. French with subtitles. **105m/C DVD.** *FR* Serge Avedikian, Piotr Stanislas, Catherine Albin; *D:* Philippe Vallois; *W:* Philippe Vallois; *C:* Francois About; *M:* Jean-Jacques Ruhlmann.

We Were Soldiers ♂♂♂ 1/2 **2002 (R)** Writer-director Wallace once again tackles the fact-based miltary epic, with outstanding results. Recounting the battle of the Ia Drang Valley in 1965, the first major land battle for U.S. troops in Vietnam, the story focuses on Lt. Col. Hal Moore (Gibson) and his leadership of the 7th Air Cavalry at LZ X-Ray. Moore's combination of experience, leadership, instinct, knowledge, and genuine concern for his men make him seem too good to be true, but Gibson's portrayal, and the fact that Moore is real, help to erase disbelief. Inevitable comparisons with "Black Hawk Down" are justified, as both pics deal with chaotic battlefields and the heroism of the soldiers who must fight their way out of situations they were trained, but not quite prepared, for. But this movie goes beyond the battle to show the impact to families back home, as well as giving a nod of respect to the enemy. Elliot stands out as Moore's right-hand man, as does Pepper as reporter Galloway, while Stein, Russell, and Kinnear do well playing against type. Based on the book "We Were Soldiers Once...and Young" by Lt. Gen. Harold G. Moore (Ret.) and Joseph L. Galloway. **137m/C VHS, DVD, Blu-ray Disc, HD DVD.** *US* Mel Gibson, Madeleine Stowe, Greg Kinnear, Sam Elliott, Chris Klein, Keri Russell, Barry Pepper, Don Duong, Ryan Hurst, Marc Blucas, Jsu Garcia, Clark Gregg, Desmond Harrington, Blake Heron, Dylan Walsh, Robert Bagnell, Josh Daugherty, Jon Hamm, Erik MacArthur, Simbi Khali, Mark McCracken, Taylor Momsen, Daniel Roebuck, Keith Szarabajka, Sloane Momsen, Matthew Lang, Edwin Morrow, Billinger C. Tran; *D:* Randall Wallace; *W:* Randall Wallace; *C:* Dean Semler; *M:* Nick Glennie-Smith.

We Will Not Enter the Forest ♂♂♂ **1979** Moral dilemmas afflict a group of French Resistance fighters during WWII when they must decide what to do with four German deserters they've captured. In French with subtitles. **88m/C VHS.** *FR* Richard Leduc, Siegfried Rauch, Jacques Higelin, Georges Claisse, Sylvain Joubert, Marie-France Pisier; *D:* Georges Dumoulin; *W:* Catherine Varlin; *C:* Alain Derobe; *M:* Michel Sendrez.

The Weaker Sex ♂♂ 1/2 **1949** Typical patriotic British weepie finds a British widow and her daughters trying to hold on to hope as D-Day approaches. **89m/B VHS.** *GB* Ursula Jeans, Cecil Parker, Joan Hopkins, Derek Bond, Lana Morris; *D:* Roy Ward Baker.

Weapons of Mass Distraction ♂♂ **1997 (R)** Two megalomanical multimedia tycoons set out to destroy each other in this black comedy. Lionel Powers (Byrne) wants to buy pro football's Tucson Titans and so does his arch-rival Julian Messenger (Kingsley). So there's bribery and blackmail and airing of dirty family laundry all over the place. No heroes here but occassionally some sharp satire. **105m/C VHS, DVD.** Gabriel Byrne, Ben Kingsley, Mimi Rogers, Jeffrey Tambor, Illeana Douglas, Paul Mazursky, Kathy Baker, Chris Mulkey, R. Lee Ermey, Caroline Aaron, Jason Lee, Christina Pickles; *D:* Stephen Surjik; *W:* Larry Gelbart; *C:* Alar Kivilo; *M:* Don Davis. **CABLE**

Weather Girl ♂♂ **2009 (R)** Seattle TV weather girl Sylvia Miller (O'Kelley) trashes her career in a spectacular on-air rant when she publicly reviles her boyfriend, clueless host Dale Waters (Harmon), after discovering that he is cheating on her. Unable to land another broadcast job, Sylvia moves in with her slacker younger brother Walt (Devlin), finds a job as a waitress, and takes up the offer of Walt's friend Byron (Adams) to be her rebound guy. It's all about the sex since neither are looking for any commitments or romance and you can see where this is going, can't you. **92m/C DVD.** *US* Tricia O'Kelley, Patrick Adams, Ryan Devlin, Mark Harmon, Kaitlin Olson, Jane Lynch, Marin Hinkle, Jon Cryer, Blayne Weaver, Alex Kapp Horner; *D:* Blayne Weaver; *W:* Blayne Weaver; *C:* Brandon Trost; *M:* Andrew Hollander.

Weather in the Streets ♂ 1/2 **1984 (PG)** A young woman enters into an ill-fated love affair after spending a few moments with an aristocratic married man. Cliched drama set in England between the two world wars. **108m/C VHS, DVD.** Michael York, Joanna Lumley, Lisa Eichhorn, Isabel Dean, Norman Pitt; *M:* Carl Davis.

The Weather Man ♂♂ 1/2 **2005 (R)** David Spitz (Cage) is a weatherman in Chicago. Not really much of a movie in that fact alone. What makes this story move is that, as his Pulitzer Prize-winning father Robert (Caine) points out, he isn't a particularly good one. David's life seems to consistently point out to him the fact that he's not actually good at much at all. To illustrate the point, strangers on the street thank him for his rotten forecast with fast food showers. Just as Dave's life sinks to a new low, he is offered a prestigious position on a morning show in New York. Cage and Caine are excellent. **102m/C DVD.** *US* Nicolas Cage, Michael Caine, Hope Davis, Gemmenne de la Pena, Nicholas Hoult, Michael Rispoli, Gil Bellows, Judith McConnell, Anne Marie Howard; ***D:*** Gore Verbinski; ***W:*** Steve Conrad; ***C:*** Phedon Papamichael; ***M:*** Hans Zimmer.

The Weather Underground **2002** Documentary insightfully studies the Weather Underground, the radical group that called for and practiced violence and unrest as an alternative to the peaceful, and in their view, ineffectual protests that were going on at the time. Also explores the issues and atmosphere of the times that bhrough about the division in society that made the Weather Underground a semi-viable movement for a time, before disillusionment set in. **92m/C DVD.** *US* ***D:*** Sam Green, Bill Siegel; ***C:*** Andrew Black, Federico Salsano; ***M:*** Dave Cerf, Amy Domingues.

Web of Deceit ½ **1990 (PG-13)** Defense lawyer Purl returns to her Southern hometown to defend an unjustly accused teenager. She falls in love with the prosecutor, but could he be the killer? Shades of "Jagged Edge." Good, suspenseful made-for-TV movie. **93m/C VHS.** Linda Purl, James Read, Paul DeSouza, Larry Black, Len Birman, Barbara Rush; ***D:*** Sandor Stern; ***W:*** Sandor Stern.

Web of Deception **1971 (R)** A jewel thief disappears with $5 million worth of jewels. When the case turns to murder, a private detective becomes the prime suspect. **90m/C VHS.** *SP* Thomas Hunter, Aelina Nathaniel, Gabriele Tinti, Marilia Branco; ***D:*** Massimo Castellani; ***W:*** Italo Gasperini, Armando Merandi; ***C:*** Giorgio Tonti; ***M:*** Daniele Patucchi.

Web of the Spider *Nella Stretta M Orsa Del Ragno; In the Grip of the Spider; Dracula in the Castle of Blood; And Comes the Dawn...But Colored Red* **1970** Kinski as Poe is really the only good thing about this run-of-the-mill horror outing. A man stays the night in a spooky house to prove it's not haunted. Remake of "Castle of Blood." **94m/C VHS, DVD.** *GE FR IT* Anthony (Tony) Franciosa, Klaus Kinski, Michele Mercier, Peter Carsten, Karin (Karen) Field; ***D:*** Anthony M. Dawson.

Webmaster *Skyggen; The Shadow* **1998 (R)** The futureworld Technotropolis is run by tyrant industrialist Stoiss. Hacker JB is forced to work surveillance for Stoiss and when a thief breaks into Stoiss' cyber empire, JB is given a mechanical heart that will stop in 35 hours unless he finds the intruder first. Dubbed from Danish. **102m/C VHS, DVD.** *DK* Jorgen Kiil, Lars Bom, Puk Scharbau; ***D:*** Thomas Borch Nielsen; ***C:*** Lars Beyer.

Webs **2003** Electrical workers investigating a power source coming from an abandoned building discover a deserted lab. They accidentally activate a device that transports them to a savage parallel universe occupied by cannibalistic spider-people with a very hungry queen. But does she mate first before biting your head off? A Sci-Fi Channel original. **87m/C DVD.** Richard Grieco, Kate Greenhouse, Colin Fox, Richard Yearwood, Jeff Douglas, Dylan Bierk; ***D:*** David Wu; ***W:*** Greenville Case, Robinson Young; ***C:*** Richard Wincenty; ***M:*** Lawrence Shragge. **CABLE**

A Wedding ½ **1978 (PG)** The occasion of a wedding leads to complications galore for the relatives and guests on the happy day. Silent film legend Gish's 100th screen role. Miserable, self-indulgent outing for Altman, who went through quite a dry spell after "Nashville." **125m/C VHS, DVD.** Tim Thomerson, Allan Nicholls, Pam Dawber, Dennis Franz, Bert Remsen, Gavan O'Herlihy, Mia Farrow, Carol Burnett, Lillian Gish, Lauren Hutton, Viveca Lindfors, Geraldine Chaplin, Paul Dooley, Howard Duff, Dennis Christopher, Peggy Ann Garner, John Considine, Nina Van Pallandt, Dina Merrill, Pat McCormick, Vittorio Gassman, Desi Arnaz Jr.; ***D:*** Robert Altman; ***W:*** Robert Altman, Allan Nicholls, Patricia Resnick, John Considine.

Wedding Band **1989** Episodic comedy about a rock 'n' roll band that plays all sorts of weddings. Thin and lame but inoffensive. **95m/C VHS.** William Katt, Joyce Hyser, Tino Insana, Fran Drescher, David Rasche, Joe Flaherty, Tim Kazurinsky, James Belushi; ***D:*** Daniel Raskov.

The Wedding Banquet *Xiyan; Hsi Yen* **1993 (R)** Charming story about a clash of customs and secrets. Naturalized American Wai Tung (Chao, in his film debut) lives comfortably with his lover Simon (Lichtenstein) while hiding the fact that he's gay from his Chinese parents. To appease his parents and get his "wife" (Chin) a green card, he marries for convenience and watches as the deception snowballs. Comedy of errors was shot on a small budget ($750,000) and examines small details with as much care as the larger ones. A fine effort from director Lee that's solidly humorous, but also poignant. In English and Chinese with subtitles. **111m/C VHS, DVD.** *TW* Winston Chao, May Chin, Mitchell Lichtenstein, Sihung Lung, Ah-Leh Gua, Michael Gaston, Jeffrey Howard; ***D:*** Ang Lee; ***W:*** Ang Lee, Neil Peng, James Schamus; ***C:*** Jong Lin.

Wedding Bell Blues **1996 (R)** Three 30ish single friends/roommates cope with a variety of crises. Pregnant Tanya (Porikova) learns that her boyfriend Tom (Edson) has no intention of marrying her, Micki's (Warner) fiance has just called off their wedding, and Jasmine's (Douglas) conservative parents are upset by their promiscuous daughter's approach to life. Stressed, the women decide to seek their fortunes in Vegas—preferably through some quickie marriages and even quickier divorces. Looks like it was shot on a shoestring budget and the lighting could be better, but the dialogue rings true and the actors do a decent job. Look for Seinfeld's TV mom as Micki's overbearing mother and Jackson as a disgruntled shopper. Reynolds plays herself. **100m/C VHS, DVD.** Illeana Douglas, Paulina Porizkova, Julie Warner, John Corbett, Jonathan Penner, Richard Edson, Charles Martin Smith, Stephanie Beacham, Carla Gugino, Leo Rossi, John Capodice, Victoria Jackson, Jeff Seymour; ***Cameos:*** Debbie Reynolds; ***D:*** Dana Lustig; ***W:*** Annette Goliti Gutierrez; ***C:*** Kent Wakeford; ***M:*** Paul Christian Gordon, Tal Bergman.

The Wedding Bros. *The Marconi Bros* **2008 (R)** Anthony and Carmine Marconi dutifully work in the family carpet business while Anthony takes classes at the community college and Carmine gambles in Atlantic City in an effort to change their lives. An unexpected meeting with Long Island wedding video producer Mo Brown has the brothers impulsively deciding to become crazy Mo's new assistants, which doesn't go so well. **83m/C DVD.** Dan Fogler, Brendan Sexton III, Jon Polito, Patti D'Arbanville, Zoe Lister-Jones, Steven Randazzo, Yul Vasquez; ***D:*** Michael Canzoniero, Marco Ricci; ***W:*** Michael Canzoniero, Marco Ricci; ***C:*** Brian Hubbard; ***M:*** Carlo Giacco.

Wedding Crashers **2005 (R)** Womanizing buds John (Wilson) and Jeremy (Vaughn) are divorce mediators who crash weddings in order to pick up Ms. Right Now. Only John really falls for engaged Claire (McAdams), who's the daughter of eccentric politician William Cleary (Walken), and the duo find themselves spending the weekend at the family's waterfront estate. Harkens back to the "Animal House/Blues Brothers/Caddyshack" glory days of R-rated comedy, earning the rating and plenty of laughs. Vaughn and Wilson do what they do best, and have great chemistry. Walken, though underused, is effective. Stumbles a little toward the end, but not enough to spoil the festivities. **119m/C DVD, Blu-ray Disc, UMD.** *US* Owen Wilson, Vince Vaughn, Rachel McAdams, Christopher Walken, Jane Seymour, Will Ferrell, Ellen A. Dow, Isla Fisher, Bradley Cooper, Ron Canada, Henry Gibson, Keir O'Donnell, Dwight Yoakam, Rebecca De Mornay, David Conrad, Larry Joe Campbell, Jennifer (Jenny) Alden, Geoff Stults, Diora Baird; ***D:*** David Dobkin; ***W:*** Bob Fisher, Steve Faber; ***C:*** Julio Macat; ***M:*** Rolfe Kent.

The Wedding Date ½ **2005 (PG-13)** Complete waste of two attractive, amusing leads. High-strung New Yorker Kat (Messing) must fly to London for her self-absorbed half-sister Amy's (Adams) wedding. To her horror, the best man is her ex-fiance Jeff (Sheffield), who dumped her. Refusing to appear alone and needy, especially to her critical mother Bunny (Taylor), Kat decides to hire handsome escort Nick (Mulroney) to accompany her as her new beau. Nick is intelligent and somewhat mysterious; Kat is confused. There are various pre-wedding complications as sub-plots. Predictability rules. **90m/C DVD, HD DVD.** *US* Debra Messing, Dermot Mulroney, Amy Adams, Jack Davenport, Jeremy Sheffield, Peter Egan, Holland Taylor, Sarah Parish, Jolyon James, C. Gerod Harris, Martin Barrett, Jay Simon, Stephen Lobo; ***D:*** Clare Kilner; ***W:*** Dana Fox; ***C:*** Oliver Curtis.

Wedding Daze ½ *The Pleasure of Your Company* **2006 (R)** Muddled and somewhat vulgar rom com that tries too hard for yuks. Anderson's (Biggs) been in a funk since his fiancee died after an embarrassing incident. Best pal Ted (Weston) thinks Anderson should get back in the dating game but, instead, he proposes to the next woman he meets, who happens to be quirky coffee shop waitress Katie (Fisher). And she accepts. **90m/C DVD.** Jason Biggs, Isla Fisher, Joe Pantoliano, Joanna Gleason, Edward Herrmann, Mark Consuelos, Rob Corddry, Margo Martindale, Chris Diamantopoulos, Matt Malloy, Jay O. Sanders, Heather Goldenhersch; ***D:*** Michael Ian Black; ***W:*** Michael Ian Black; ***C:*** Dan Stoloff; ***M:*** Peter Nashel.

The Wedding Director ½ *Il Regina di Matrimoni* **2006** Troubled film director Franco Elica unexpectedly winds up in a small Sicilian town where he becomes the guest of fan Enzo Baiocco, the local wedding videographer. Franco is asked if he will shoot some footage of an upcoming wedding but he falls in love with bride-to-be Bona the instant he meets her. Italian with subtitles. **100m/C DVD.** *FR IT* Sergio Castellitto, Sami Frey, Maurizio Donadoni, Donatella Finocchiaro, Bruno Cariello, Simona Nobili, Gianni Carina; ***D:*** Marco Bellocchio; ***W:*** Marco Bellocchio; ***C:*** Pasquale Mari; ***M:*** Riccardo Giagni.

The Wedding Gift *Wide-Eyed and Legless* **1993 (PG-13)** Offbeat charm and humor go a long way to overcome the inherent tragedy in this true story made for British TV. Longtime happily marrieds Diana (Walters) and Deric (Broadbent) Longden are struggling to cope with Diana's mysterious and increasingly debilitating illness, which causes blackouts, pain, and the inability to use her limbs. Diana comes to accept the fact that she's going to die and decides to find her hubby a new wife, aided by Deric's friendship with a blind novelist (Thomas). Terrific performances keep the mawkishness at bay. Based on Deric Longden's books "Diana's Story" and "Lost for Words." **87m/C VHS, DVD.** *GB* Julie Walters, Jim Broadbent, Sian Thomas, Thora Hird, Andrew Lancel, Anastasia Mulrooney; ***D:*** Richard Loncraine; ***W:*** Jack Rosenthal; ***C:*** Remi Adefarasin. **TV**

Wedding in Blood *Les Noces Rouges* **1974 (PG)** Two French lovers plot to kill their respective spouses, and proceed to do so amid calamity and much table-turning. Sharp social satire and suspenseful mystery. Based on a true story. In French with English subtitles. **98m/C VHS, DVD.** *FR IT* Claude Pieplu, Stephane Audran, Michel Piccoli; ***D:*** Claude Chabrol; ***W:*** Claude Chabrol; ***C:*** Jean Rabier.

A Wedding in Galilee *Noce In Galilee* **1987** The elder of a Palestinian village is given permission to have a traditional wedding ceremony for his son if Israeli military officers can attend as the guests of honor. As the event approaches, conflicts arise among the villagers, the family, and the Israelis. Long but fascinating treatment of traditional culture in the modern world amidst political tension. In Arabic and Hebrew, with English subtitles. **113m/C VHS, DVD.** *BE FR* Ali M. El Aleili, Nazih Akleh, Anna Achdian; ***D:*** Michel Khleifi.

Wedding in White **1972 (R)** A rape and out-of-wedlock pregnancy trouble a poor British clan living in Canada during WWII. Sad, glum way to spend an evening. Kane is good in a non-comic role. Her screen father cares more for her honor than he does for her. **103m/C VHS, DVD.** *CA* Donald Pleasence, Carol Kane, Leo Phillips; ***D:*** William Fruet.

The Wedding March **1928** Von Stroheim's famous silent film about romantic couplings in pre-WWI Vienna. The director also stars as a prince preparing to marry for money, who falls in love with a beautiful, but poor woman. Romance and irony, with a memorable finale. Like many of his other great films, it was taken from him and re-edited. Initially the first of two halves; the second, "The Honeymoon," has been lost. Next to "Greed," his most successful film. **113m/B VHS.** Erich von Stroheim, Fay Wray, Zasu Pitts, George Fawcett, Maud(e) (Ford) George, Matthew Betz, George Nicholls, Cesare Gravina; ***D:*** Erich von Stroheim; ***C:*** Hal Mohr; ***M:*** Gaylord Carter. Natl. Film Reg. '03.

The Wedding Party ½ **1969** Apprehensive groom is overwhelmed by his too-eager bride and her inquisitive relatives at a prenuptial celebration. Hokey, dull, would-be comedy. First screen appearances of both Clayburgh and De Niro (spelled DeNero in the credits). **90m/C VHS, DVD.** Jill Clayburgh, Robert De Niro, William Finley; ***D:*** Brian De Palma, Cynthia Munroe, Wilford Leach; ***W:*** Brian De Palma.

The Wedding Party ½ *Thank God He Met Lizzie* **1997 (R)** Predictable wedding comedy has thirtysomething Guy (Roxburgh) searching for the perfect woman. Finally he meets Lizzie (Blanchett) and the twosome are soon involved in lavish wedding preparations before they really have a chance to get to know each other. In fact, Guy begins dreaming of former love, Jenny (O'Connor), in the middle of the ceremony! **91m/C VHS, DVD.** *AU* Richard Roxburgh, Cate Blanchett, Frances O'Connor, Linden Wilkinson, Michael Ross, John Gaden, Genevieve Mooy, Rhett Walton, Deborah Kennedy; ***D:*** Cherie Nowlan; ***W:*** Alexandra Long; ***C:*** Kathryn Milliss; ***M:*** Martin Armiger. Australian Film Inst. '97: Support. Actress (Blanchett).

The Wedding Planner ½ **2001 (PG-13)** A film that's a bridesmaid instead of a bride. Mary Fiore (Lopez) is a workaholic wedding planner in San Francisco who has no love life of her own. The driven Mary meets cute with aw-shucks doctor Steve Edison (McConaughey) who, naturally, turns out to be the fiance of Mary latest client, heiress Fran (Wilson). Not that the attractive duo can stay away from each other despite their good intentions. The leads nearly carry the film on charm alone before the script finally lets them down. **105m/C VHS, DVD.** *US* Jennifer Lopez, Matthew McConaughey, Bridgette Wilson-Sampras, Justin Chambers, Alex Rocco, Judy Greer, Kevin Pollak, Joanna Gleason, Charles Kimbrough, Fred Willard, Kathy Najimy; ***D:*** Adam Shankman; ***W:*** Michael Ellis, Pamela Falk; ***C:*** Julio Macat; ***M:*** Mervyn Warren.

Wedding Present **1936** After "Big Brown Eyes," Grant and Bennett were reteamed for this screwy—but not very funny—screwball comedy. Rusty (Bennett) and Charlie (Grant) are newspaper reporters. When Charlie gets a promotion to editor, he becomes insufferable and Rusty quits. She decides to marry boring writer Dodacker (Nagel) and Charlie goes out of his way to find her the perfect wedding present, which turns out to be himself. Grant's last contract film for Paramount. **81m/B DVD.** Cary Grant, Joan Bennett, Conrad Nagel, Gene Lockhart, William Demarest, Inez Courtney; ***D:*** Richard Wallace; ***W:*** Joseph Anthony; ***C:*** Leon Shamroy.

Wedding Rehearsal ½ **1932** A young nobleman thwarts his grandmother's plans to marry him off by finding suitors for all the young ladies offered to him until he finally succumbs to the charms of his mother's secretary. Enjoyable, fun comedy. First featured roles for actresses Oberon, Barrie, and Gardner. **84m/B VHS.** Merle Oberon, Roland Young, John Loder, Wendy Barrie, Maurice Evans, Joan Gardner; ***D:*** Alexander Korda.

The Wedding Singer ½ **1997 (PG-13)** Despite almost nonexistent pacing and a script full of holes, "Singer" is an enjoyably goofy look at the mid '80s. Surprisingly toned-down and appealing Sandler is Robbie Hart, wedding singer, ultimate nice guy, and rock-star wanna-be, who's jilted at the altar. Waitress Barrymore is engaged to a skirt-chasing stock broker. It's immediately clear that they belong together, and the rest of the movie is spent on them chasing each other through various contrived obstacles, to the obvious ending. Features great cameos by punk-rocker Billy Idol, Jon Lovitz (as a rival wedding singer), and Steve Buscemi (excellent as the groom's jealous "dad always liked you best" brother). Musical highlight is Sandler's heartfelt rendition of the J. Geils Band's "Love Stinks." Isn't it a little scary that we're already spoofing the '80s? **96m/C VHS, DVD.** Adam Sandler, Drew Barrymore, Christine Taylor, Allen Covert, Matthew Glave, Ellen A. Dow, Angela Featherstone, Alexis Arquette, Christina Pickles, Jon Lovitz, Steve Buscemi, Kevin Nealon; ***Cameos:*** Billy Idol; ***D:*** Frank Coraci; ***W:*** Tim Herlihy; ***C:*** Tim Suhrstedt; ***M:*** Teddy Castellucci. MTV Movie Awards '98: Kiss (Adam Sandler/Drew Barrymore).

Wedding Wars ✓✓ 1/2 **2006** Fluff comedy with a serious message. Shel (Stamos) is a gay wedding planner who's in charge of brother Ben's (Dane) nuptials to Maggie (Somerville), the daughter of the governor of Maine. When Shel learns that Ben's boss, Governor Welling (Brolin), opposes gay marriage, he picks up a picket sign and goes on strike. Soon, gays across the country are leaving their jobs to join in Shel's protest, and the wedding, which has been turned over to the tacky Mrs. Fairfield (Kash), is a disaster waiting to happen. **87m/C DVD.** John Stamos, Eric Dane, Bonnie Somerville, James Brolin, Sean Maher, Linda Kash, Rosemary Dunsmore, Jayne (Jane) Eastwood, Sean McCann; ***D:*** Jim Fall; ***W:*** Stephen Mazur; ***C:*** Ron Stannett. **CABLE**

Wee Willie Winkie ✓✓✓ **1937 (PG)** A precocious little girl is taken in by a British regiment in India. Sugar-coated. If you're a cinematic diabetic, be warned. If you're a Temple fan, you've probably already seen it. If not, you're in for a treat. Inspired by the Rudyard Kipling story. **99m/B VHS.** Shirley Temple, Victor McLaglen, Sir C. Aubrey Smith, June Lang, Michael Whalen, Cesar Romero, Constance Collier; ***D:*** John Ford; ***C:*** Arthur C. Miller.

Weeds ✓✓✓ **1987 (R)** A highly fictionalized account of the career of Rick Cluchey, who, as a lifer in San Quentin federal prison, wrote a play. He was eventually paroled and went on to form a theatre group made up of ex-cons. Original and often enjoyable with a tight ensemble performance. Filmed on location at Stateville Correctional Center in Illinois, with inmates serving as extras. **115m/C VHS.** Nick Nolte, Rita Taggart, William Forsythe, Lane Smith, Joe Mantegna, Ernie Hudson, John Toles-Bey, Mark Rolston, Anne Ramsey, Charlie Rich; ***D:*** John Hancock; ***W:*** John Hancock, Dorothy Tristan; ***M:*** Angelo Badalamenti.

Week-End in Havana ✓✓ 1/2 **1941** Set in pre-revolution Cuba, this frothy musical finds salesgirl Faye on a long-awaited cruise when her ship gets stranded in Havana. She's escorted around town by shipping-official Payne and catches the eye of gambler-lothario Romero, who has a jealous girlfriend in Miranda. Fun fluff. ♫ Romance and Rhumba; Tropical Magic; The Nango; A Weekend in Havana; When I Love, I Love; Maria Inez; Rebola a Bola. **80m/C VHS, DVD.** Alice Faye, John Payne, Cesar Romero, Carmen Miranda, Cobina Wright Jr., George Barbier, Sheldon Leonard, Billy Gilbert; ***D:*** Walter Lang; ***W:*** Karl Tunberg; ***M:*** Alfred Newman.

Weekend ✓✓✓ **1967** A Parisian couple embark on a drive to the country. On the way they witness and are involved in horrifying highway wrecks. Leaving the road they find a different, equally grotesque kind of carnage. Godard's brilliant, surreal, hyper-paranoiac view of modern life was greatly influenced by the fact that his mother was killed in an auto accident in 1954 (he himself suffered a serious motorcycle mishap in 1975). In French with English subtitles. **105m/C VHS, DVD.** *FR IT* Mireille Darc, Jean Yanne, Jean-Pierre Kalfon, Valerie Lagrange, Jean-Pierre Leaud, Yves Beneyton; ***D:*** Jean-Luc Godard; ***W:*** Jean-Luc Godard; ***M:*** Antoine Duhamel.

The Weekend ✓✓ 1/2 **2000** Marian (Unger) and John (Harris) Kerr are hosting a weekend for family and friends at their upstate New York home to remember John's half-brother Tony (Sweeney) who died of AIDS a year before. Gathered are Tony's lover Lyle (Conrad) and his new boyfriend Robert (Duval) as well as neighbors Laura (Rowlands) and her daughter Nina (Shields). Turns out that mostly everybody was enamored of Tony and some unpleasant truths come out after too much wine. Good cast in a very gabby drama. Based on the novel by Peter Cameron. **97m/C VHS, DVD.** *GB US* Deborah Kara Unger, Jared Harris, Gena Rowlands, D.B. Sweeney, Brooke Shields, David Conrad, James Duval, Gary Jourdan; ***D:*** Brian Skeet; ***W:*** Brian Skeet; ***C:*** Ron Fortunato; ***M:*** Dan (Daniel) Jones, Sarah Class.

Weekend at Bernie's ✓✓ 1/2 *Hot and Cold* **1989 (PG-13)** Two computer nerds discover embezzlement at their workplace after being invited to their boss's beach house for a weekend party. They find their host murdered. They endeavor to keep up appearances by (you guessed it) dressing and strategically posing the corpse during the party. Kiser as the dead man is memorable, and the two losers gamely keep the silliness flowing. Lots of fun. **101m/C VHS, DVD.** Andrew McCarthy, Jonathan Silverman, Catherine Mary Stewart, Terry Kiser, Don Calfa, Louis Giambalvo; ***D:*** Ted Kotcheff; ***W:*** Robert Klane; ***C:*** Francois Protat; ***M:*** Andy Summers.

Weekend at Bernie's 2 ✓ 1/2 **1993 (PG)** Unlikely but routine sequel to the original's cavorting cadaver slapstick, except now McCarthy and Silverman are frantically hunting for Bernie's (Kiser) cash stash, a quest that takes them and poor dead Bernie to the Caribbean. See Bernie get stuffed in a suitcase, see Bernie hang glide, see Bernie tango, see Bernie attract the opposite sex. Thin script with one-joke premise done to death but fun for those in the mood for the postmortem antics of a comedic stiff. Plenty of well-executed gags involving the well-preserved corpse (particularly one that's been dead for two films now) should lure back fans of the 1989 original. **89m/C VHS, DVD.** Andrew McCarthy, Jonathan Silverman, Terry Kiser, Steve James, Troy Beyer, Barry Bostwick; ***D:*** Robert Klane; ***W:*** Robert Klane; ***M:*** Peter Wolf.

Weekend at the Waldorf ✓✓✓ **1945** Glossy, americanized remake of "Grand Hotel" set at the famous Park Avenue hotel, the Waldorf-Astoria, in New York City. Turner and Rogers star in the roles originated by Joan Crawford and Greta Garbo. Johnson and Pidgeon play their love interests. Combining drawing room comedy with slapstick and a touch of romance proved to be a hit, as this film was one of the top grossers of 1945 and was just what war-weary moviegoers wanted to see. Based on the play "Grand Hotel" by Vicki Baum. **130m/B VHS.** Ginger Rogers, Walter Pidgeon, Van Johnson, Lana Turner, Robert Benchley, Edward Arnold, Leon Ames, Warner Anderson, Phyllis Thaxter, Keenan Wynn, Porter Hall, Samuel S. Hinds; ***D:*** Robert Z. Leonard; ***W:*** Samuel Spewack, Bella Spewack, Guy Bolton.

A Weekend in the Country ✓✓ 1/2 **1996 (R)** Ensemble comedy finds a varied group of couples and would-be couples traveling to California's wine country for a weekend of relaxation at a bed and breakfast inn. Nothing quite works out as planned but Cupid's arrow does strike. Filmed on location in Temecula, CA. **94m/C VHS.** Rita Rudner, Faith Ford, Christine Lahti, Jack Lemmon, Richard Lewis, Dudley Moore, Betty White, Dan Cortese, Jennifer Elise Cox; ***D:*** Martin Bregman; ***W:*** Rita Rudner, Martin Bregman; ***M:*** Patrick Williams. **CABLE**

Weekend of Shadows ✓✓✓ **1977** Confident, moralistic murder drama about a posse after an innocent immigrant they believe has killed a woman. Police sergeant Roberts is interested only in his reputation, not in justice. Posse member Waters begins to sympathize with the hunted man and defends his innocence. Intelligent, well-conceived, and professionally directed. **94m/C VHS.** John Waters, Melissa Jaffer, Graeme Blundell, Wyn Roberts, Barbara West, Graham Rouse; ***D:*** Tom Jeffrey.

Weekend Pass ✓ **1984 (R)** Moronic rookie sailors who have just completed basic training are out on a weekend pass, determined to forget everything they have learned. They find this surprisingly easy to do. **92m/C VHS, DVD.** D.W. Brown, Peter Ellenstein, Phil Hartman, Patrick Hauser, Chip McAllister; ***D:*** Lawrence Bassoff; ***W:*** Lawrence Bassoff; ***C:*** Bryan England.

Weekend War ✓✓ 1/2 **1988 (PG-13)** A group of National Guardsmen are sent to the Honduras for their annual tour of duty. But when a guerilla war between Honduras and Nicaragua breaks out, the Guardsmen are forced to fight for their lives. The "Bridge on the River Kwai" finale features the dilemma over a bridge linking the two countries. **96m/C VHS.** Daniel Stern, Stephen Collins, Charles Haid, Evan Mirand, Michael Beach, Scott Paulin, James Tolkan; ***D:*** Steven Hilliard Stern; ***M:*** Brad Fiedel. **TV**

Weekend Warriors ✓ 1/2 **1986 (R)** Young film-studio employees evade the draft in 1961 by enlisting for National Guard weekend duty. Grade "C" dumb comedy from professional celebrity and first-time director Convy. **88m/C VHS.** Chris Lemmon, Lloyd Bridges, Daniel Greene, Tom Villard, Vic Tayback; ***D:*** Bert Convy; ***W:*** Bruce Belland; ***M:*** Perry Botkin.

Weekend with the Babysitter **WOOF!** *Weekend Babysitter* **1970 (R)** Sordid teen drama about a weekend babysitter who goes to a film director's house and babysits everyone but the kids, running into a heroin-smuggling ring along the way. Casting-couch story with a twist. **93m/C VHS, DVD.** Susan (Suzan) Roman, George E. Carey, James Almanzar, Luanne Roberts; ***D:*** Don Henderson.

Weep No More My Lady ✓✓ **1993 (PG-13)** Suspense-filled whodunit about a wealthy businessman who comes between two sisters and a sibling rivalry that turns into a deadly game of murder. Based on the best-selling book by Mary Higgins Clark. **92m/C VHS.** Daniel J. Travanti, Shelley Winters, Kristin Scott Thomas; ***D:*** Michel Andrieu; ***W:*** Michel Andrieu; ***C:*** Renan Polles; ***M:*** Rene Marc Bini.

Weeping Meadow ✓✓ *Trilogia: To Livadi pou dakryzei; Trilogy: The Weeping Meadow; Eleni; La Sorgente del fiume; La Terre qui pleure* **2004** Greek tragedy? Part one of Theo Angelopoulos' historical trilogy starts with a family fleeing Russia's Bolshevik Revolution in Russia and landing in Greece. Eleni (Aidini) and Alexis (Poursadinis) are stepsiblings who fall in love and struggle to forge and remain their romantic relationship, though the fates are continually against them. Eleni bears twins she is forced to give up for adoption. Story weaves through time as the sons grow and tragedy after tragedy besets all involved. **168m/C DVD.** Alexandra Aidini, Nikos Poursanidis, Yorgos Armenis, Vasilis Kolovos, Eva Kotamanidou, Toula Stothopoulou, Mihalis Yannatos, Thalia Argyriou, Grigoris Evangelatos; ***W:*** Tonino Guerra, Petros Markaris, Giorgio Silvagni; ***C:*** Andreas Sinanos; ***M:*** Eleni Karaindrou.

The Weight of Water ✓✓ **2000 (R)** Photographer Jean (McCormack) arrives at Smuttynose Island, off the coast of New Hampshire, to research an infamous 1873 ax-murder case involving two Norwegian immigrant women (Cartlidge, Shaw) a local man (Hinds), and an unreliable witness (Polley). You see their story in flashback as Jean struggles with her own domestic dilemmas—her drunken poet husband Thomas (Penn), his brother Rich (Lucas), and Rich's sexy girlfriend Adaline (Hurley). Jealousy, lies, and betrayal abound in both stories. Based on the novel by Anita Shreve. **105m/C VHS, DVD.** *US* Catherine McCormack, Sarah Polley, Sean Penn, Josh(ua) Lucas, Elizabeth Hurley, Ciaran Hinds, Ulrich Thomsen, Anders W. Berthelsen, Katrin Cartlidge, Vinessa Shaw; ***D:*** Kathryn Bigelow; ***W:*** Alice Arlen, Christopher Kyle; ***C:*** Adrian Biddle; ***M:*** David Hirschfelder.

Weird Science ✓✓ **1985 (PG-13)** Hall is appealing, and Hughes can write dialogue for teens with the best of them. However, many of the jokes are in poor taste, and the movie seems to go on forever. Hall and his nerdy cohort Mitchell-Smith use a very special kind of software to create the ideal woman who wreaks zany havoc in their lives from the outset. **94m/C VHS, DVD.** Kelly Le Brock, Anthony Michael Hall, Ilan Mitchell-Smith, Robert Downey Jr., Bill Paxton; ***D:*** John Hughes; ***W:*** John Hughes; ***C:*** Matthew F. Leonetti; ***M:*** Ira Newborn.

Weird Woman ✓✓ 1/2 **1944** Professor Chaney and his South Seas bride suffer the wrath of a jealous woman. Based on radio's "The Inner Sanctum Mysteries." **63m/B VHS.** Lon Chaney Jr., Evelyn Ankers, Ralph Morgan, Lois Collier, Douglass Dumbrille, Elena Verdugo, Anne Gwynne, Milburn Stone, Martin Kosleck; ***D:*** Harold Young, Reginald LeBorg; ***W:*** Brenda Weisberg, Bernard Schubert, Lucille Ward.

Weird World of LSD ✓ 1/2 **1967** Cheap exploitation film featuring the evil effects of LSD. **75m/B VHS.** Terry Tessem, Ann Lindsay, Yolanda Morino; ***D:*** Robert Ground.

The Weirdo ✓ **1989** "The Jerk" meets Freddie Krueger. This film is absolutely wretched, even by horror movie standards. **91m/C VHS.** Steve Burlington, Jessica Straus; ***D:*** Andy Milligan.

Weirdsville ✓ 1/2 **2007 (R)** Heroin addict pals Dexter (Speedman) and Royce (Bentley) live in tiny Weedsville in Northern Ontario. They owe their dealer Omar (Bhaneja) and agree to deal drugs for him to settle their account. Royce's girlfriend and sometimes-hooker Matilda (Manning) seemingly overdoses on Omar's goods, and the brilliant pair decide to get rid of her by burying her in the boiler room of a drive-in theatre where Dexter briefly worked. But they run into complications. 1) She's still alive, and 2) they figure this out only after they've accidentally stumbled upon some Satanists in the middle of a human sacrifice. Pursued by the Satanists, they've still got to figure out how to pay Omar. Some would doubt the humor in heroin addiction, and this pic will definitely reinforce that doubt. **90m/C DVD.** *CA* Scott Speedman, Wes Bentley, Taryn Manning, Matt Frewer, Greg Bryk, Maggie Castle, Raoul Bhaneja, Joe Dinicol, Jordan Prentice, Dax Ravina; ***D:*** Allan Moyle; ***W:*** Willem Wennekers; ***C:*** Adam Swica; ***M:*** Michael Doherty, John Rowley.

Welcome Back Mr. Fox **1983** An award-winning science fiction short wherein an obnoxious movie producer cheats death by being cryogenically frozen, and then wakes up years later no wiser for the experience. Suitably, he receives his comeuppance. **21m/C VHS.** E.D. Phillips, Gustav Vintas; ***D:*** Walter W. Pitt III.

Welcome Home ✓✓ **1989 (R)** A missing-in-action Vietnam vet (Kristofferson) leaves his wife and children in Cambodia to return to America more than 15 years after he was reported dead. He finds his first wife remarried and discovers a teenaged son he unknowingly fathered. This plotless, sporadically moving film was Schaffner's last. **92m/C VHS.** Kris Kristofferson, JoBeth Williams, Sam Waterston, Brian Keith, Trey Wilson, Thomas Wilson Brown; ***D:*** Franklin J. Schaffner; ***C:*** Fred W. Koenekamp; ***M:*** Henry Mancini. **CABLE**

Welcome Home Roscoe Jenkins ✓ 1/2 **2008 (PG-13)** Cultures clash and cliches abound when hotshot Hollywood talk-show host Roscoe Jenkins (Lawrence) returns home to small-town Georgia with his dim fiancee (Bryant) and young son for his parents' 50th wedding anniversary. His unimpressed family-including horndog sister Betty (Mo'Nique), studly brother Otis (Duncan), slick cousin Reggie (Epps), and nemesis Clyde (Cedric the Entertainer)—doesn't exactly roll out the red carpet. In no time, old rivalries make for put-downs, pot-shots, and sight gags that alternate between amusing and embarrassing, until a not-unexpected but somewhat ironic dose of schmaltz finally ends the tedium. **113m/C DVD.** *US* Martin Lawrence, Margaret Avery, James Earl Jones, Joy Bryant, Michael Clarke Duncan, Cedric the Entertainer, Mike Epps, Mo'Nique, Louis C.K., Nicole Ari Parker, Damani Roberts; ***D:*** Malcolm Lee; ***W:*** Malcolm Lee; ***C:*** Greg Gardiner; ***M:*** David Newman.

Welcome Home, Roxy Carmichael ✓✓ **1990 (PG-13)** Ryder, as a young misfit, is the bright spot in this deadpan, would-be satire. Hollywood star Roxy Charmichael returns to her small Ohio hometown and begins fantasizing that she is really her mother. It is obvious why this deadpan, hard-to-follow movie was a boxoffice flop. **98m/C VHS, DVD.** Winona Ryder, Jeff Daniels, Laila Robins, Dinah Manoff, Ava Fabian, Robbie Kiger, Sachi (MacLaine) Parker; ***D:*** Jim Abrahams; ***C:*** Paul Elliott.

Welcome Says the Angel ✓✓ **2001** Drifter Joshua (Jacobs) winds up at a seedy bar in Hollywood where he's picked up by Ana (Hauer) and the two go off to her loft. In the morning, Josh finds himself handcuffed, his wallet and Ana gone. She returns after getting her heroin fix but refuses to let Josh go. They begin to bond (must be Stockholm Syndrome) and Josh vows to get her off drugs when he finally gets free. Maybe he wants to handcuff her instead. No-budgeter but the leads work well together. **90m/C VHS, DVD.** Jon Jacobs, Aysha Hauer; ***D:*** Philippe Dib; ***W:*** Jon Jacobs, Philippe Dib; ***C:*** Gabor Satanyl; ***M:*** Nels Cline, George Lockwood.

Welcome Stranger 1/2 **1947** New doctor's ideas clash with the old doctor's ways in a small town until the younger saves the live of the elder. Crosby and Fitzgerald star as the two clashing medics in this reunion of the cast of "Going My Way." He wins the heart of the town and the heart of local teacher Caulfield in the meantime. Sheekman's script calls for Marx Brothers'-like comedy and director Nugent appears in a cameo as another doctor. **107m/B VHS.** Bing Crosby, Barry Fitzgerald, Joan Caulfield, Wanda Hendrix, Frank Faylen, Elizabeth Patterson, Robert Shayne, Don Beddoe, Percy Kilbride, Larry Young; ***Cameos:*** Elliott Nugent; ***D:*** Elliott Nugent; ***W:*** Arthur Sheekman; ***C:*** Lionel Lindon; ***M:*** Johnny Burke, James Van Heusen.

Welcome to Blood City 1/2 **1977** An anonymous totalitarian organization kidnaps a man and transports him electronically to a fantasy western town where the person who murders the most people becomes the town's "kill master." Amateurish and low-budget. **96m/C VHS.** Jack Palance, Keir Dullea, Samantha Eggar, Barry Morse; ***D:*** Peter Sasdy; ***W:*** Stephen Schneck, Michael Winder; ***C:*** Reginald Morris; ***M:*** Roy Budd.

Welcome to Collinwood **2002 (R)** Ensemble comedy by the brothers Russo is a remake of the 1958 Italian classic, "Big Deal on Madonna Street." Collinwood is home to a group of hopelessly inept, dim wanna-be criminals. The dubious crew consists of single father Riley (Macy), Leon (Washington), Toto (Jeter), Pero (Rockwell) and Basil (Davoli). Broad character bits are highlighted by the always brilliant Macy and an amusing Rockwell. Producer Clooney provides a highlight as a wheelchair-bound safe cracker. A little too over-the-top, but accurately cops original's hilarious comic climax as the boys break down a wall to get at the safe. **86m/C VHS, DVD.** *US* Luis Guzman, Michael Jeter, Patricia Clarkson, Andrew Davoli, Isaiah Washington IV, William H. Macy, Sam Rockwell, Gabrielle Union, Jennifer Esposito, George Clooney; ***D:*** Anthony Russo, Joe Russo; ***W:*** Anthony Russo, Joe Russo; ***C:*** Lisa Rinzler, Charles Minsky; ***M:*** Mark Mothersbaugh.

Welcome to 18 **1987 (PG-13)** Three girls, just out of high school, take summer jobs at a dude ranch, work a local casino, flirt, tease and get in trouble. The movie isn't funny in the least, and is filled with utter nonsense. Hargitay is the daughter of actress Jayne Mansfield. **91m/C VHS.** Courtney Thorne-Smith, Mariska Hargitay, Jo Ann Willette, Christine Kaufmann; ***D:*** Terry Carr.

Welcome to Hollywood **2000** Filmmaker Rifkin plays himself in this mockumentary that follows the career of actor Nick Decker (Markes) from wannabe to superstar, which includes his romance with married actress Everhart (playing herself). **89m/C VHS, DVD.** Adam Rifkin, Tony Markes, Angie Everhart; ***D:*** Adam Rifkin, Tony Markes.

Welcome to L.A. **1977 (R)** Rudolph's ambitious directorial debut focuses on the sexual escapades of a group of Southern Californians. Based on the music suite "City of the One Night Stands" by Baskin, which also (unfortunately) serves as the soundtrack. Rudolph improved greatly after this initial effort. **106m/C VHS.** Allan Nicholls, Sissy Spacek, Sally Kellerman, Keith Carradine, Geraldine Chaplin, Lauren Hutton, Viveca Lindfors, Harvey Keitel, John Considine; ***D:*** Alan Rudolph; ***W:*** Alan Rudolph; ***M:*** Richard Baskin.

Welcome to Mooseport 1/2 **2004 (PG-13)** Romano's big-screen debut is a weak-scripted mess that has him running for mayor of his stock-character quirky small town against former president Hackman. Romano plays average schlub (Everybody Loves) Handy Harrison, who gets into politics when ex-President Monroe "Eagle" Cole (Hackman) hits on his long-time, waiting-for-commitment girlfriend (Tierney). A golf match for the town and her heart ensues. Hackman turns in a dependable performance but Romano shuffles through, depending too much on the audience's familiarity with his TV character while Tierney taps her foot impatiently. Riddled with stereotypical characters, the movie never moves past utterly predictable, and the laughs are few and far between. Director Petrie obviously wants to conjure the charm of old Frank Capra movies, but only manages to reach the level of a bad sitcom pilot that drags on for far too long. **110m/C DVD.** *US* Ray Romano, Gene Hackman, Marcia Gay Harden, Maura Tierney, Christine Baranski, Fred Savage, Rip Torn, June Squibb, Wayne Robson, John Rothman, Karl Pruner; ***D:*** Donald Petrie; ***W:*** Tom Schulman, Doug Richardson; ***C:*** Victor Hammer; ***M:*** John Debney.

Welcome to Paradise 1/2 **2007 (PG)** Uplifting family drama has single mom and controversial preacher Debbie Laramie (Bernard) transferred from her large urban ministry to the small, depressed town of Paradise, Texas. She meets a lot of resistance from her parishioners and the church's charter is in danger of being revoked. But when the church burns down, everyone finds a reason to work together. **105m/C DVD.** Crystal Bernard, Brian Dennehy, Bobby Edner, Nick Searcy, Brad Stine, Beth Grant, Ken Jenkins, William Shockley; ***D:*** Brent Huff; ***W:*** William Shockley, Brent Huff; ***C:*** Robert Hayes; ***M:*** Steve Pierson.

Welcome to Sarajevo 1/2 **1997 (R)** Fresh, unusual take on the siege of Sarajevo in 1992. A group of news correspondents, including British reporter Michael Henderson (Dillane), find themselves in the middle of the siege, and become disillusioned when the conflict is largely ignored by the rest of the world. Film sheds perspective when a particularly bloody massacre takes a backseat to the marital troubles of the royal family. Henderson becomes personally involved when his daily coverage of an orphanage sparks him to become a hero to the orphaned Emily (Sarajevan actress Nusevic). Intermingling actual news footage, Winterbottom shows the violence on a personal level. Solid supporting characters include Harrelson as the wonderfully egotistic American celeb journalist. Strong emotional content is tempered by the smart and savvy gallows humor, which keeps melodrama miles away. Loosely based on a true story by ITN reporter, Michael Nicholson. **102m/C VHS, DVD.** Stephen (Dillon) Dillane, Woody Harrelson, Marisa Tomei, Kerry Fox, Emily Lloyd, Goran Visnjic, Juliet Aubrey, Emira Nusevic, James Nesbitt, Igor Dzambazov, Gordana Gadzic, Drazen Sivak, Vesna Orel; ***D:*** Michael Winterbottom; ***W:*** Frank Cottrell-Boyce; ***C:*** Daf Hobson; ***M:*** Adrian Johnston.

Welcome to Spring Break 1/2 *Nightmare Beach* **1988 (R)** College co-eds are stalked by a killer on the beaches of Florida. **92m/C VHS, DVD.** Nicolas De Toth, Sarah Buxton, Lance LeGault, Rawley Valverde, John Saxon, Michael Parks; ***D:*** Umberto Lenzi; ***W:*** Umberto Lenzi; ***M:*** Claudio Simonetti.

Welcome to the Dollhouse 1/2 **1995 (R)** Eleven-year-old, glasses-wearing Dawn Wiener (Matarazzo) is the middle child of a middle-class family in an average New Jersey town. It's her first year in junior high and Dawn's bewildered—by school, by family, by life in general, and where she fits in. Puberty sucks. **87m/C VHS, DVD.** Heather Matarazzo, Brendan Sexton III, Daria Kalinina, Matthew Faber, Angela Pietropinto, Eric Mabius; ***D:*** Todd Solondz; ***W:*** Todd Solondz; ***C:*** Randy Drummond; ***M:*** Jill Wisoff. Ind. Spirit '97: Debut Perf. (Matarazzo); Sundance '96: Grand Jury Prize.

Welcome II the Terrordome 1/2 **1995 (R)** Yet another future apocalypse. Terrordome is a city collapsing under pollution, filled with corrupt police, where blacks are confined to ghettos with rampant gang violence and drugs. Spike's young nephew is killed in a police raid and his sister goes on a shooting spree, which draws more rage and has Spike being forced to choose between his homies and his preggers white girlfriend. **98m/C VHS, DVD.** *GB* Saffron Burrows, Valentine Nonyela, Suzette Llewellyn, Felix Joseph; ***D:*** Ngozi Onwurah; ***W:*** Ngozi Onwurah.

Welcome to Woop Woop 1/2 **1997 (R)** Hit-or-miss (mostly miss) comedy about a con man meeting his match in a small Australian town of redneck eccentrics. On the lam, Teddy (Schaech) nevertheless offers a ride to buxom blonde Angie (Porter), whom he meets at a gas station. The next thing he knows (having been drugged), Teddy wakes up in the nightmarish community of Woop Woop, where Angie announces they've gotten married. And Angie's violent father, Daddy-O (Taylor), makes it clear his new son-in-law has no chance of making it out alive. Based on the book "The Dead Heart" by Douglas Kennedy. **97m/C VHS.** *AU* Johnathon Schaech, Rod Taylor, Susie Porter, Dee Smart, Richard Moir, Rachel Griffiths, Barry Humphries; ***D:*** Stephan Elliott; ***W:*** Michael Thomas; ***C:*** Mike Molloy; ***M:*** Stewart Copeland.

The Well **1951** A young black girl disappears and a white man (Morgan) is accused of kidnapping her. When it is discovered that the girl is trapped in a deep well, Morgan's expertise is needed to help free her. **85m/B VHS, DVD.** Richard Rober, Harry (Henry) Morgan, Barry Kelley, Christine Larson; ***D:*** Leo Popkin, Russell Rouse; ***C:*** Ernest Laszlo.

The Well **1997** Repression, isolation, and tragedy set in barren rural Australia. Drab, middleaged Hester (Rabe) hires spirited teenager Katherine (Otto) to help out on her bleak farm. Hester soon becomes emotional dependent on Katherine, who eventually convinces her to sell the property so they can travel to Europe. (Yes, "The Servant" will come to mind.) But a car accident (caused by Katherine) claims the life of a mystery man and Hester decides to hide the body in an unused well. Then they discover all their money has been stolen, probably by their dead friend, and just who's going down the well to retrieve it? Based on a novel by Elizabeth Jolley. **101m/C VHS, DVD.** *AU* Pamela Rabe, Miranda Otto, Paul Chubb; ***D:*** Samantha Lang; ***W:*** Laura Jones; ***C:*** Mandy Walker; ***M:*** Stephen Rae. Australian Film Inst. '97: Actress (Rabe), Adapt. Screenplay, Art Dir./Set Dec.

Well-Digger's Daughter *La Fille Du Puisatier* **1946** As her lover goes off to war, a well-digger's daughter discovers that she is pregnant causing both sets of parents to feud over who's to blame. This is the first film made in France after the end of WWII and marks the return of the French film industry. In French with English subtitles. **142m/B VHS.** *FR* Raimu, Josette Day, Fernandel, Charpin; ***D:*** Marcel Pagnol.

We'll Meet Again 1/2 **1982** Cliched but touching miniseries set in a quiet English town in 1943. At least the town was quiet until the arrival of a bomber group from the U.S. Army Eighth Air Force. Soon the Yanks are chasing the local girls and getting into trouble while their commander (Shannon) finds himself falling for a married doctor (York). **690m/C VHS, DVD.** *GB* Michael J. Shannon, Susannah York, Ronald Hines, Ed Devereaux, Christopher Malcolm, Patrick O'Connell, Joris Stuyck; ***D:*** Christopher Hodson. **TV**

We'll Meet Again 1/2 **2002 (PG-13)** Having been unjustly thrown in the slammer for six years for her husband's slaying makes the strong-willed Molly intent on hunting down the real killer with the aide of reporter pal Fran. But, as often is the case in these Mary Higgins Clark adaptations, the truth could have deadly results for the women. **100m/C VHS, DVD.** Laura Leighton, Brandy Ledford, Andrew Jackson, Anne Openshaw, Bryan Genesse, Beverley Elliott, Paul Campbell, Gedeon Burkhard, Paula Shaw, Steve Archer, Karin Konoval, Michael Eklund, Eva DeViveiros, Patti Allan, Sam MacMillan, Taayla Markell; ***D:*** Michael Storey; ***W:*** Michael Thoma, John Benjamin Martin; ***C:*** Henry Lebo; ***M:*** Claude Foisy. **TV**

Wend Kuuni *God's Gift* **1982** A fable for modern times set in Burkina Faso before the coming of Islam or Christianity. A mute, memoryless child is found by a peddler and adopted by the peddler's village. One day the boy finds a body hanging from a tree. Shocked, he recovers his speech and tells the story of his tragic past, when he and his mother were cast out of their own village. When his mother dies, the boy is bereft of family and tradition. Without these ties to his history he loses both speech and memory. In More with English subtitles. **70m/C VHS.** Serge Yanogo, Rosine Yanogo, Joseph Nikiema, Colette Kabore; ***D:*** Gaston Kabore.

The Wendell Baker Story 1/2 **2005 (PG-13)** Con man Wendell (Luke Wilson) bumbles from a fake-ID con to prison to working at a seedy retirement hotel where the nurses (Griffin and Owen Wilson) are scamming Medicare, stealing medicine, and forcing the residents to work for food. Wendell takes the side of the residents (Cassel, Stanton, and Kristofferson) and lazy hijinks ensue. Or something. All three Wilsons (including director Andrew) try hard to make a lazy 70s stoner comedy but mostly coast on their proven talent while rehashing themes done better elsewhere. **95m/C DVD.** *US* Luke Wilson, Owen Wilson, Seymour Cassel, Eddie Griffin, Kris Kristofferson, Eva Mendes, Harry Dean Stanton, Jacob Vargas, Spencer Scott, Buck Taylor, Jo Harvey Allen, Azura Skye, Paul M. Wright, Mathew Greer, Will Ferrell; ***D:*** Luke Wilson, Andrew Wilson; ***W:*** Luke Wilson; ***C:*** Steve Mason; ***M:*** Aaron Zigman.

Wendigo 1/2 **2001 (R)** Manhattanites George (Weber), Kim (Clarkson), and their eight-year-old son Miles (Sullivan) are heading out of the city for a weekend at a friend's farmhouse in upstate New York. Distracted George hits a deer, which enrages backwoods hunter Otis (Speredakos) who was trailing the buck. Quiet Miles notices the tension between his parents but weird things really begin to happen when a mysterious man gives Miles a Wendigo figure, a creature in Native American mythology that has destructive powers, which Miles now seems to command. **91m/C VHS, DVD.** *US* Patricia Clarkson, Jake Weber, Erik Per Sullivan, John Speredakos, Christopher Winkoop; ***D:*** Larry Fessenden; ***W:*** Larry Fessenden; ***C:*** Terry Stacey; ***M:*** Michelle DiBucci.

Wendy and Lucy **2008 (R)** Director Reichhardt crafts a stripped-down and poignant gem of Wendy's (Williams) never-quite-finished and financially challenged journey from Indiana to Alaska, where she attempts to free herself from an unemployed, dead-end existence. With her lovable mutt, Lucy, as her sole traveling companion, Wendy just can't seem to catch a break along the way. In Oregon her beat-up Honda breaks down and she finds herself locked up, hit with a fine, and dogless after trying to lift some jerky and dog food from the local market. An honest but not sentimental portrait of the realities of life in America normally hidden away. **80m/C DVD.** *US* Michelle Williams, William Oldham, John Robinson, Will Patton, Larry Fessenden, Wally Dalton; ***D:*** Kelly Reichardt; ***W:*** Kelly Reichardt, Jonathan Raymond; ***C:*** Sam Levy.

Went to Coney Island on a Mission from God... Be Back by Five **1998 (R)** Daniel (Cryer), Stan (Stear), and Richie (Baez) were all best neighborhood friends while growing up in Brooklyn. Now it's years later and Stan and Daniel have lost touch with Richie, whom they hear is a mentally ill vagrant living under the boardwalk at Coney Island. So they decide to ditch their boring lives and track him down. Flashbacks to earlier incidents get confusing if not tedious. **94m/C VHS, DVD, Blu-ray Disc.** Jon Cryer, Rick Stear, Rafael Baez, Ione Skye, Frank Whaley, Peter Gerety, Akili Prince, Aesha Waks, Dominic Chianese; ***D:*** Richard Schenkman; ***W:*** Richard Schenkman, Jon Cryer; ***C:*** Adam Beekman; ***M:*** Midge Ure.

We're Back! A Dinosaur's Story 1/2 **1993 (G)** Animated adventures of a pack of revived dinosaurs who return to their old stomping grounds—which are now modern-day New York City. Smart-mouth human boy Louie and his girlfriend Cecilia take the dinos under their wing (so to speak), wise them up to modern life, and try to prevent their capture by the evil Professor Screweyes. Slow-moving with some violence. Adapted from the book by Hudson Talbott. **78m/C VHS.** ***D:*** Dick Zondag, Ralph Zondag, Phil Nibbelink, Simon Wells; ***W:*** John Patrick Shanley; ***V:*** John Goodman, Felicity Kendal, Walter Cronkite, Joey Shea, Jay Leno, Julia Child, Kenneth Mars, Martin Short, Rhea Perlman, Rene LeVant, Blaze Berdahl, Charles Fleischer, Yeardley Smith.

We're in the Legion Now 1/2 **1937** Denny and Barnett star as a couple of American gangsters who join the French Foreign

Legion to escape rival hoods from back home. **56m/B VHS.** Eleanor Hunt, Claudia Dell, Robert Frazer, Rudolph Anders, Reginald Denny, Vince Barnett, Esther Ralston; ***D:*** Crane Wilbur; ***W:*** Roger Whately.

We're in the Navy Now **1927** The famed comedy duo is back again with another armed forces farce. A mild successor to "Behind the Front." **60m/B VHS.** Chester Conklin, Tom Kennedy, Donald Keith, Lorraine Eason, Wallace Beery, Raymond Hatton; ***D:*** A. Edward Sutherland; ***W:*** Monte Brice; ***C:*** Charles P. Boyle.

We're No Angels 🦴🦴🦴 **1955** Three escapees from Devil's Island hide out with the family of a kindly French storekeeper on Christmas Eve. Planning to rob the family, they end up helping them with various financial, romantic, and familial problems. Somewhat stagey, but great dialogue and excellent cast make for enjoyable holiday fare. One of Bogart's few comedies. From the French stage play of the same name, later remade with De Niro and Penn. **103m/C VHS, DVD.** Humphrey Bogart, Aldo Ray, Joan Bennett, Peter Ustinov, Basil Rathbone, Leo G. Carroll, Lea Penman, John Smith, Gloria Talbott, John Baer; ***D:*** Michael Curtiz; ***W:*** Ranald MacDougall; ***C:*** Loyal Griggs; ***M:*** Frederick "Friedrich" Hollander.

We're No Angels 🦴🦴 ½ **1989 (R)** Two escaped cons disguise themselves as priests and get in the appropriate series of jams. De Niro and Penn play off each other well, turning in fine comic performances. Distantly related to the 1955 film of the same name and the David Mamet play. **110m/C VHS, DVD.** Robert De Niro, Sean Penn, Demi Moore, Hoyt Axton, Bruno Kirby, James Russo, John C. Reilly, Ray McAnally, Wallace Shawn; ***D:*** Neil Jordan; ***W:*** David Mamet; ***C:*** Philippe Rousselot; ***M:*** George Fenton.

We're Not Dressing 🦴🦴🦴 **1934** Loose musical adaptation of J.M. Barrie's "The Admirable Crichton" with the butler transformed into singing sailor Crosby. Fabulously wealthy heiress Lombard invites her pals for a South Seas yachting adventure. Only the ship gets wrecked and everyone winds up on a small island where the practical Crosby whips everyone into shape (and romances Lombard). Burns and Allen supply additional comedy as a pair of botanists who just happen to be studying the local fauna. ♫Good Night Lovely Little Lady; I'll Sing About the Birds and the Bees; It's Just a New Spanish Custom; Let's Play House; Love Thy Neighbor; May I?; Once in a Blue Moon; She Reminds Me of You. **74m/B VHS, DVD.** Bing Crosby, Carole Lombard, George Burns, Gracie Allen, Ethel Merman, Leon Errol, Ray Milland; ***D:*** Norman Taurog; ***W:*** Horace Jackson, Francis Martin; ***M:*** Harry Revel, Mack Gordon.

We're Not Married 🦴🦴🦴 **1952** Five couples learn that they are not legally married when a judge realizes his license expired before he performed the ceremonies. The story revolves around this quintet of couples who now must cope with whether or not they really do want to be married. Although the episodes vary in quality, the Allen-Rogers sequence is excellent. Overall, the cast performs well in this lightweight comedy. **85m/B VHS, DVD.** Ginger Rogers, Fred Allen, Victor Moore, Marilyn Monroe, Paul Douglas, David Wayne, Eve Arden, Louis Calhern, Zsa Zsa Gabor, James Gleason, Jane Darwell, Eddie Bracken, Mitzi Gaynor, Selmer Jackson, Lee Marvin; ***D:*** Edmund Goulding; ***W:*** Nunnally Johnson, Dwight Taylor; ***C:*** Leo Tover; ***M:*** Cyril Mockridge.

We're Talkin' Serious Money 🦴🦴 ½ **1992 (PG-13)** Sal and Charlie are a couple of loser scam-artists always after the elusive big score. They borrow $10,000 from the mob for another get-rich-quick scheme and wind up over their heads with both the mob and the FBI out to get them. **92m/C VHS.** Dennis Farina, Leo Rossi, Fran Drescher, John Lamotta; ***D:*** James (Momel) Lemmo; ***W:*** Leo Rossi, James (Momel) Lemmo; ***M:*** Scott Grusin.

Were the World Mine 🦴🦴 ½ **2008** Timothy is out and proud, which makes him a target at his private boys' high school. He also has a crush on jock Jonathan and gets a chance when he's cast as Puck in the school production of 'A Midsummer Night's Dream.' Tim discovers a magic love potion that makes the target of the potion fall hopelessly in love with the first person they see, which Tim makes sure are of the same sex, thus turning a bunch of homophobes into lovesick fools. A musical teen fantasy with risk-taking pizzazz. **95m/C DVD.** Wendy Robie, Zelda Williams, David Darlow, Tanner Cohen, Nathaniel David Becker, Judy McLane, Ricky Goldman, Jill Larson; ***D:*** Tom Gustafson; ***W:*** Tom Gustafson, Cory James Krueckeberg; ***C:*** Kira Kelly; ***M:*** Jessica Fogle.

Werewolf 🦴 **1995 (R)** A remote desert town is stricken by an ancient curse that turns its occupants into werewolves at the full moon. This doesn't help the tourism industry. **99m/C VHS, DVD.** Jorge (George) Rivero, Fred Cavalli, Adrianna Miles, Richard Lynch, Joe Estevez, R(ichard) C(arlos) Bates, Heidi Bjorn, Randall Oliver, Nena Belini, Tony Zarindast; ***D:*** Tony Zarindast; ***W:*** Tony Zarindast; ***C:*** Robert Hayes, Dan Gilman.

Werewolf in a Girl's Dormitory 🦴 *Lycanthropus; The Ghoul in School* **1961** Girls' school headmaster undergoes dental transformation at night. Atrocious dubbing, with equally atrocious theme song "The Ghoul in School." **82m/B VHS, DVD.** *IT* Barbara Lass, Carl Schell, Curt Lowens, Maurice Marsac; ***D:*** Richard Benson.

Werewolf of London 🦴🦴 ½ **1935** A scientist searching for a rare Tibetan flower is attacked by a werewolf. He scoffs at the legend, but once he's back in London, he goes on a murderous rampage every time the moon is full. Dated but worth watching as the first werewolf movie made. **75m/B VHS, DVD.** Henry Hull, Warner Oland, Valerie Hobson, Lester Matthews, Spring Byington, Lawrence Grant, Zeffie Tilbury; ***D:*** Stuart Walker; ***W:*** Robert H. Harris, John Colton; ***C:*** Charles Stumar.

Werewolf of Washington 🦴🦴 **1973 (PG)** Stockwell is a White House press secretary with a problem—he turns into a werewolf. And bites the President, among others. Sub-plot involves a short mad scientist who operates a secret monster-making lab in a White House bathroom. Occasionally engaging horror spoof and political satire made during Watergate era. **90m/C VHS, DVD.** Dean Stockwell, Biff McGuire, Clifton James, Jane House, Beeson Carroll, Michael Dunn, Nancy Andrews, Stephen Cheng, Barbara Siegel; ***D:*** Milton Moses Ginsberg; ***W:*** Milton Moses Ginsberg; ***C:*** Robert M. "Bob" Baldwin Jr.; ***M:*** Arnold Freed.

The Werewolf vs. the Vampire Woman 🦴 ½ *Shadow of the Werewolf; Blood Moon; Night of Walpurgis; La Noche de Walpurgis* **1970 (R)** Hirsute Spanish wolfman teams with two female students in search of witch's tomb. One is possessed by the witch, and eponymous title results. **82m/C VHS, DVD.** *SP GE* Paul Naschy, Gaby Fuchs, Barbara Capell, Patty (Patti) Shepard, Valerie Samarine, Julio Pena, Andres Resino; ***D:*** Leon Klimovsky; ***W:*** Paul Naschy; ***C:*** Leopoldo Villasenor; ***M:*** Anton Abril.

Werewolves on Wheels WOOF! **1971 (R)** A group of bikers are turned into werewolves due to a Satanic spell. A serious attempt at a biker/werewolf movie, however, too violent and grim, not at all funny, and painful to sit through. McGuire had a hit with "Eve of Destruction." **85m/C VHS, DVD.** Stephen Oliver, Severn Darden, D.J. Anderson, Duece Barry, Billy Gray, Barry McGuire; ***D:*** Michel Levesque.

Wes Craven Presents Mind Ripper 🦴🦴 *Mind Ripper* **1995 (R)** A top secret government experiment, intended to produce a superhuman, goes wrong and traps the scientists in a remote desert outpost with their deadly, pissed-off creation. **90m/C VHS.** Lance Henriksen, John Diehl, Natasha Gregson Wagner, Dan Blom, Claire Stansfield; ***D:*** Joe Gayton; ***W:*** Jonathan Craven, Phil Mittleman; ***C:*** Fernando Arguelles; ***M:*** J. Peter Robinson.

Wes Craven Presents: They 🦴 ½ *They* **2002 (PG-13)** Maybe Wes should stop presenting this stuff and start writing and directing it again. It might turn out better. Derivative horror flick has psych grad student Julia (Regan) visited by childhood friend and fellow nightmare sufferer Billy, who tells her that something's after them. She doesn't believe him until her old nightmares return and spooky things start happening. Starts off genuinely creepy and appropriately scary, but loses itself in cliches and other plot devices you've seen done better elsewhere. Regan gives a good debut performance, though. **100m/C VHS, DVD.** *US* Laura Regan, Marc Blucas, Ethan (Randall) Embry, Dagmara Dominczyk, Jon Abrahams, Jay Brazeau, Alexander Gould; ***D:*** Robert Harmon; ***W:*** Brendan William Hood; ***C:*** Rene Ohashi; ***M:*** Elia Cmiral.

Wes Craven's New Nightmare 🦴🦴🦴 *Nightmare on Elm Street 7* **1994 (R)** Seems the six previous conjurings of Freddy's tortured but fictional soul have inadvertently created a real supernatural force bent on tormenting the lives of retired scream queen Langenkamp, her son (Hughes), writer-director Craven, and surprisingly mild alter-ego Englund. Craven's solution is to write a script that reunites series principals for a final showdown with the slashmaster in Hell. Clever and original in a genre known for neither trait, this movie-in-a-movie-about-a-movie is equal parts playful gimmick and inspired terror that will give even the most seasoned Kruegerphile the heebie-jeebies. **112m/C VHS, DVD.** Robert Englund, Heather Langenkamp, Miko Hughes, David Newsom, Tracy Middendorf, Fran Bennett, John Saxon, Wes Craven, Robert Shaye, Sara Risher, Marianne Maddalena; ***D:*** Wes Craven; ***W:*** Wes Craven; ***C:*** Mark Irwin; ***M:*** J. Peter Robinson.

West Beirut 🦴🦴 *West Beyrouth* **1998** Muslim teenagers Tarek (Doueiri, the director's younger brother) and Omar (Chamas) and their new friend, the Christian May (Al Amin), live in an apartment complex in Muslim-controlled West Beirut in 1975. The date is significant since Muslim and Christian militias are battling for control of the Lebanese city and, since their school is closed, the teens have little better to do than to explore the forbidden. Arabic with subtitles. **105m/C VHS, DVD.** *FR* Rami Doueiri, Mohamad Chamas, Rola Al Amin, Leila Karam; ***D:*** Ziad Doueiri; ***W:*** Ziad Doueiri; ***C:*** Ricardo Jacques Gale; ***M:*** Stewart Copeland.

West-Bound Limited 🦴🦴 ½ **1923** A Romantic adventurer rescues a girl from certain death as a train is about to hit her, and the two fall in love. Lucky for him, she happens to be the boss' daughter. This film is a good example of classic silent melodrama with music score. **70m/B VHS.** John Harron, Ella Hall, Claire McDowell; ***D:*** Emory Johnson.

West Is West 🦴🦴 **1987** Vikram arrives in San Francisco from Bombay to attend university and discovers that his sponser has returned to India. With little money, he gets a room in a seedy hotel run by an Indian immigrant, who also gives Vikram a menial job. As he begins to explore the city Vikram meets arty punk Sue, but with his visa running out and the INS ready to deport him, Vikram needs to convince Sue to a green card marriage. **80m/C VHS.** Ashutosh Gowariker, Heidi Carpenter, Pearl Padamsee; ***D:*** David Rathod; ***W:*** David Rathod; ***C:*** Christopher Tufty.

West New York 🦴🦴 **1996 (R)** Ex-cop Tom Coletti (Vincent) has a job in Jersey, disposing of old bank bonds. He comes up with a scheme to skim some of the bonds but the news leaks to the local mob boss, Carmine (Pastore). He's unhappy he's not being cut in and decides to put out a hit to show his displeasure, so Coletti has to get to him first. **90m/C VHS, DVD.** Frank Vincent, Vincent Pastore, Victor Colicchio, Brian Burke, Gian DiDonna, Gloria Darpino, Brian McCormick; ***D:*** Phil Gallo.

West of Cimarron 🦴 ½ **1941** The Mesquiteers return to Texas after the Civil War only to find themselves caught between warring carpetbaggers and local bushwackers. They discover some rotten eggs within the army post are swindling the citizens and work to expose them and calm the volatile situation down. The 41st film in the series. **56m/B DVD.** Bob Steele, Tom Tyler, Rufe Davis, Lois Collier, James Bush, Guy Usher, Budd Buster, Roy Barcroft, Hugh Prosser; ***D:*** Les(ter) Orlebeck; ***W:*** Albert DeMond, Don Ryan; ***C:*** Ernest Miller; ***M:*** Cy Feuer.

West of Here 🦴 ½ **2002 (R)** Predictable and dull road story that's the directorial debut of Masterson, whose sister does him the favor of co-starring. When Josiah (Butz) is killed in a car crash, his cousin and songwriting partner Gil (Hamilton) decides to leave his boring life in Boston and hit the road to San Francisco to settle Josiah's affairs. Along the way, Gil just happens to reconnect with his old college flame (Masterson), and she comes along for the ride. **80m/C DVD.** Josh Hamilton, Norbert Lee Butz, Mary Stuart Masterson, Guillermo Diaz, Tate Donovan; ***D:*** Peter Masterson; ***W:*** Jay Sweet; ***C:*** Peter Masterson; ***M:*** Timothy Cutler, Todd Park Mohr.

West of Nevada 🦴🦴 **1936** A rare film, featuring the former Lieutenant Governor of Nevada (and Clara Bow's husband) in a fast-moving adventure about a band of Indians who must protect their gold from thieves. Bell is the good guy who aids the Indians. **59m/B VHS, DVD.** Georgia O'Dell, Forrest Taylor, Rex Bell, Joan Barclay, Al "Fuzzy" St. John, Steve Clark; ***D:*** Robert F. "Bob" Hill; ***W:*** Robert F. "Bob" Hill; ***C:*** Robert E. Cline.

West of Pinto Basin 🦴🦴 **1940** The Range Busters are riding around checking the territory for badmen in this tale of the old west. The music score includes "That Little Prairie Gal of Mine," "Rhythm of the Saddle," and "Ridin' the Trail Tonight." **60m/B VHS.** Ray Corrigan, Max Terhune, John "Dusty" King, Gwen Gaze, Tristram Coffin, George Chesebro, Bud Osborne, Jack Perrin; ***D:*** S. Roy Luby; ***W:*** Earle Snell; ***C:*** Edward Linden.

West of the Divide 🦴🦴 ½ **1933** A young cowboy (Wayne) impersonates an outlaw in order to hunt down his father's killer and find his missing younger brother. He saves a proud rancher and his feisty daughter along the way. A remake of "Partners of the Trail," and a solid early Wayne oater. **53m/B VHS, DVD.** John Wayne, George "Gabby" Hayes, Lloyd Whitlock, Yakima Canutt; ***D:*** Robert North Bradbury; ***W:*** Robert North Bradbury; ***C:*** Archie Stout.

West of the Law 🦴🦴 **1942** A group of ranchers turn to lawmen for protection from a band of outlaws. Part of the Rough Riders series. **60m/B VHS.** Buck Jones, Tim McCoy, Raymond Hatton; ***D:*** Howard Bretherton.

West of the Pecos 🦴🦴 ½ **1945** Rill (Hale) is a society gal on her way to the family ranch in Texas. She's disguised as a boy for safety, which turns out to be a smart idea when outlaws attack the stagecoach. Fortunately, Pecos Smith (Mitchum) is also around to lend a hand. Based on the novel by Zane Grey; first filmed in 1935. **66m/B VHS, DVD.** Robert Mitchum, Barbara Hale, Richard Martin, Thurston Hall, Rita (Paula) Corday, Russell Hopton, Harry Woods; ***D:*** Edward Killy; ***C:*** Russell Metty.

West of Zanzibar 🦴🦴 ½ **1928** Chaney plays an ivory trader, ruling a jungle kingdom, who lives for revenge on the man who left him a cripple. He decides to ruin the man's daughter and turn her into a prostitute but his plan backfires. Chaney and director Browning offer a steamy atmosphere amidst a number of script flaws. **63m/B VHS.** Lon Chaney Sr., Lionel Barrymore, Warner Baxter, Mary Nolan; ***D:*** Tod Browning.

West Point 🦴🦴 **1927** Typical role for Haines as he plays wealthy practical joker Brice Wayne who angers his fellow West Point cadets with his arrogance despite his stardom on the gridiron. Brice falls for local girl Betty (Crawford), who's more than his match although even she tires of his juvenile ways. Brice sulkily resigns after clashing with his coach until he finally realizes he has to man up when the big Army-Navy game is at stake. **95m/B DVD.** William Haines, Joan Crawford, William "Billy" Bakewell, Neil Neely, Ralph Emerson, Leon Kellar; ***D:*** Edward Sedwick; ***W:*** Joe Farnham; ***C:*** Ira Morgan.

The West Point Story 🦴🦴 ½ *Fine and Dandy* **1950** Cagney stars as an on-the-skids Broadway director offered a job staging a show at West Point. Seems cadet MacRae has written a musical and his uncle happens to be a producer. Cagney, with girlfriend Mayo, finds all the rules and regulations getting the better of his temper, so much so that he's told unless he can conform to academy standards the show won't go on! Day is the showgirl MacRae falls for. Cagney's energy and charm carry the too-long film but it's not one of his better musical efforts. ♫Ten Thousand Sheep; You Love Me; By the Kissing Rock; Long Before I Knew You; Brooklyn; It Could Only Happen in Brooklyn; Military Polka. **107m/B VHS, DVD.** James Cagney, Virginia Mayo, Gordon MacRae, Doris Day, Roland Winters, Gene Nelson, Alan Hale Jr., Wilton Graff, Jerome Cowan; ***D:*** Roy Del Ruth; ***W:*** John Monks Jr., Charles Hoffman, Irving Wallace; ***M:*** Sammy Cahn, Jule Styne.

West Side Story 1/2 **1961** Gang rivalry and ethnic tension on New York's West Side erupts in a ground-breaking musical. Loosely based on Shakespeare's "Romeo and Juliet," the story follows the Jets and the Sharks as they fight for their turf while Tony and Maria fight for love. Features frenetic and brilliant choreography by co-director Robbins, who also directed the original Broadway show, and a high-caliber score by Bernstein and Sondheim. Wood's voice was dubbed by Marni Nixon and Jimmy Bryant dubbed Beymer's. ♫Prologue; Jet Song; Something's Coming; Dance at the Gym; Maria; America; Tonight; One Hand, One Heart; Gee, Officer Krupke. **151m/C VHS, DVD.** Yvonne Wilder, Natalie Wood, Richard Beymer, Russ Tamblyn, Rita Moreno, George Chakiris, Simon Oakland, Ned Glass; ***D:*** Robert Wise, Jerome Robbins; ***W:*** Ernest Lehman; ***C:*** Daniel F. Fapp; ***M:*** Leonard Bernstein, Stephen Sondheim. Oscars '61: Art Dir./Set Dec., Color, Color Cinematog., Costume Des. (C), Director (Wise), Film Editing, Picture, Sound, Support. Actor (Chakiris), Support. Actress (Moreno), Scoring/Musical; AFI '98: Top 100; Directors Guild '61: Director (Wise), Director (Robbins); Golden Globes '62: Film—Mus./Comedy, Support. Actor (Chakiris), Support. Actress (Moreno), Natl. Film Reg. '97;; N.Y. Film Critics '61: Film.

West to Glory 1/2 **1947** Glory isn't necessarily exciting, as the hero helps a Mexican rancher save his gold and jewels from evildoers in this slow-paced oater. **61m/B VHS.** Eddie Dean, Roscoe Ates, Dolores Castle, Gregg Barton, Alex Montoya, Harry Vejar; ***D:*** Ray Taylor.

The West Wittering Affair **2005** Kathy (Sutcliffe) borrows a weekend retreat and invites her friends Jaime (Scheinmann) and Natasha (Cardinale), whose boyfriend Greg (Anneh) is also supposed to come. But Natasha suspects him of cheating and shows up alone, leading to an evening of too much booze and confessions and Jaime having sex with both women (separately). And this misbegotten experience still resounds with problems three years later. Ensemble comedy/drama that was frequently improvised. **90m/C DVD.** *GB* Danny Scheinmann, Sarah Sutcliffe, Rebecca Cardinale, David Annen; ***D:*** David Scheinmann; ***W:*** Danny Scheinmann, Sarah Sutcliffe; ***C:*** David Scheinmann; ***M:*** Marc Tschantz.

Westbound **1958** One of the lesser western collaborations between Boetticher and Scott. Union officer John Hayes (Scott) is charged with starting up a stagecoach line that will deliver gold shipments from California. Setting up in the small Colorado town of Julesberg, Hayes runs into serious opposition from Confederate supporter (and town leader) Clay Putnam (Duggan) and his henchmen. **72m/C DVD.** Randolph Scott, Virginia Mayo, Andrew Duggan, Karen Steele, Michael Dante, Michael Pate, Wally Brown; ***D:*** Budd Boetticher; ***W:*** Berne Giler; ***C:*** J. Peverell Marley; ***M:*** David Buttolph.

Western **1996** Spaniard Paco (Lopez), a traveling rep for a shoe manufacturer in France, picks up hitchhiking Russian emigre Nino (Bourdo) and soon finds himself minus car, shoe samples, and luggage. He's rescued by local beauty Marinette (Vitali) and, since he's been fired, decides to hang around the town where she lives. But when Paco spots Nino again, he promptly beats him up, sending the Russian to the hospital. Oddly, this serves as a bond for the two men and they decide to do a little traveling through Brittany together, with Paco trying to teach the naive Nino how to pick up pretty girls. Funny, if extended, French road trip. French with subtitles. **136m/C VHS.** *FR* Sergi Lopez, Sacha Bourdo, Elisabeth Vitali, Marie Matheron, Basile Siekoua; ***D:*** Manuel Poirier; ***W:*** Jean-Francois Goyet, Manuel Poirier; ***C:*** Nara Keo Kosal; ***M:*** Bernardo Sandoval. Cannes '97: Special Jury Prize.

Western Courage 1/2 **1935** Spoiled city girl Gloria (Mitchell) causes all sorts of trouble for dude ranch foreman Ken Baxter (Maynard), including getting him fired. But he stays on as a guest because he suspects that Gloria's beau Eric (Keefe) is just a fortune hunter. Ken foils Gloria's elopement but then the stupid girl gets herself kidnapped and held for ransom by bad guy LaCrosse (Bond) and his henchmen. **61m/B DVD.** Ken Maynard, Geneva Mitchell, Charles French, Ward Bond, Betty Blythe, Cornelius Keefe, Renee Whitney; ***D:*** Spencer Gordon; ***W:*** Nate Gatzert; ***C:*** Herbert Kirkpatrick.

Western Frontier **1935** Ordinary cowpoke Maynard is called on to lead the fight against a band of outlaws led by the Indian-raised sister he never knew he had. Action-packed, fast, and fun. Maynard's first outing for Columbia. **56m/B VHS.** Ken Maynard, Lucille Browne, Nora Lane, Robert "Buzzy" Henry, Frank Yaconelli; ***D:*** Al(bert) Herman.

Western Gold **1937** Western set during the Civil War in which Smith Ballew is sent west to stop thieves who are stealing gold from the Union. **57m/C VHS.** Smith Ballew, Heather Angel, Leroy Mason, Howard Hickman, Ben Alexander, Frank McGlynn, Otis Harlan, Tom London, Bud Osborne; ***D:*** Howard Bretherton.

Western Justice **1935** Good Guy Steele brings western-style justice to a lawless town. Ordinary oater with horses, etc., and a few chuckles on the side. **56m/B VHS.** Rene Borden, Julian Rivero, Arthur Loft, Lafe (Lafayette) McKee, Bob Steele; ***D:*** Robert North Bradbury; ***W:*** Robert North Bradbury; ***C:*** William (Bill) Hyer.

Western Mail **1942** Yet another western in which the hero goes undercover so he can bring the bad guys to justice. Yaconelli plays a guitar tune, accompanied by his monkey. **54m/B VHS.** Tom Keene, Frank Yaconelli, Leroy Mason, Jean Trent, Fred Kohler Jr.; ***D:*** Robert Emmett Tansey.

Western Pacific Agent **1951** A Western Pacific agent chases an outlaw who has committed robbery and murder. The agent falls in love with the victim's sister and, of course, prevails. Rather violent. **62m/B VHS.** Kent Taylor, Sheila Ryan, Mickey Knox, Robert Lowery; ***D:*** Sam Newfield; ***Nar:*** Jason Robards Sr.

Western Trails **1938** Forgettable western about the clean-up of a Wild West town terrorized by outlaws. Thin script, bad acting, and a little singin' and funnin' around. **59m/B VHS.** Bob Baker, Marjorie Reynolds, Robert Burns; ***D:*** George Waggner.

Western Union 1/2 **1941** A lavish, vintage epic romantically detailing the political machinations, Indian warfare, and frontier adventure that accompanied the construction of the Western Union telegraph line from Omaha, Nebraska, to Salt Lake City, Utah, during the Civil War. A thoroughly entertaining film in rich Technicolor. This was Lang's second western, following his personal favorite, "The Return of Frank James." Writer Carson utilized the title, but not the storyline, of a Zane Grey book. The German Lang showed himself a master of the most American of genres, yet made only one more western, "Rancho Notorious" (1952), another masterpiece. **94m/C VHS.** Randolph Scott, Robert Young, Dean Jagger, Slim Summerville, Virginia Gilmore, John Carradine, Chill Wills, Barton MacLane, Minor Watson, Charles Middleton, Irving Bacon; ***D:*** Fritz Lang.

The Westerner 1/2 **1940** Cooper stars as Cole Hardin, a sly, soft-spoken drifter who champions Texas border homesteaders in a land war with the legendary Judge Roy Bean (Brennan). Known as "The Law West of the Pecos," Bean sentences Hardin hang as a horse thief, but he breaks out of jail. Hardin then falls for damsel Jane-Ellen (Davenport) and stays in the area, advocating the rights of homesteaders, and has to have a final confrontation with the judge. Brennan's Bean is unforgettable and steals the show from Cooper. Film debuts of actors Tucker and Andrews. Amazing cinematography; Brennan's Oscar was his third, making him the first performer to pull a hat trick. **100m/B VHS, DVD.** Gary Cooper, Walter Brennan, Doris Davenport, Fred Stone, Chill Wills, Dana Andrews, Forrest Tucker, Charles Halton, Lupita Tovar, Tom Tyler, Lillian Bond; ***D:*** William Wyler; ***W:*** Jo Swerling, Niven Busch, W.R. Burnett; ***C:*** Gregg Toland; ***M:*** Dimitri Tiomkin. Oscars '40: Support. Actor (Brennan).

Westfront 1918 **1930** A dogmatic anti-war film by the German master (his first talkie), about German and French soldiers on the fields of WWI, dying together without victory. Stunning in its portrayal of war's futility, with excellent photography that achieves a palpable realism. In German with English subtitles. **90m/B VHS.** *GE* Gustav Diesl, Fritz Kampers, Claus Clausen, Hans Joachim Moebis; ***D:*** G.W. Pabst.

Westler: East of the Wall **1985** West Berliner Felix takes a day trip to East Berlin and falls in love with Thomas. Their time together is frustrating since Felix must return before the midnight curfew and the border guards become suspicious of his frequent trips. Eventually, Felix and Thomas decide that Thomas must escape to the west. German with subtitles. **94m/C VHS.** *GE* Sigurd Rachman, Rainer Strecker, Sasha Kogo, Andy Lucas; ***D:*** Wieland Speck; ***W:*** Wieland Speck; ***C:*** Klemens Becker; ***M:*** Engelbert Rehm.

Westward Bound 1/2 **1930** Rich boy Bob Lansing (Wilsey) gets mixed up in a publicity incident at a nightclub where he meets Montana rancher Marge Holt (Ray). Having embarrassed his senator father, Bob and his chauffeur Ben (Corbett) are sent out west where they are mistaken for a couple of rustlers. Bob also meets Marge again but she's reluctant to clear up their identity problems. **65m/B DVD.** Jay Wilsey, Allene Ray, Ben (Benny) Corbett, Buddy Roosevelt, Yakima Canutt, Tom London, Fern Emmett; ***D:*** Harry S. Webb; ***W:*** Carl Krusada; ***C:*** William Nobles.

Westward Bound 1/2 **1944** Maynard's last series western features the Trail Blazers coming to the aid of Montana ranchers who are being forced off their land by greedy developers. **54m/B DVD.** Ken Maynard, Hoot Gibson, Bob Steele, Harry Woods, Betty Miles, Karl Hackett, Weldon Heyburn, John Bridges; ***D:*** Robert Emmett Tansey; ***W:*** Elizabeth Beecher, Frances Kavanaugh; ***C:*** Marcel Le Picard.

Westward Ho 1/2 **1935** Wayne is determined to bring to justice his parents' slayer. Haven't we seen this one before? Seems the bad guys have corrupted his brother. Wayne's group of vigilantes is called "The Singing Riders," so naturally he sings—or is made to appear to. He looks and sounds ridiculous. **55m/B VHS, DVD.** John Wayne, Sheila (Manors) Mannors; ***D:*** Robert North Bradbury.

Westward Ho, the Wagons! 1/2 **1956** The promised land lies in the west, but to get there these pioneers must pass unfriendly savages, thieves, villains, and scoundrels galore. Suitable for family viewing, but why bother? Well, the cast does include four Mouseketeers. **94m/B VHS.** Fess Parker, Kathleen Crowley, Jeff York, Sebastian Cabot, George Reeves; ***D:*** William Beaudine; ***M:*** George Bruns.

Westward the Women **1951** Buck Wyatt (Taylor) is a scout hired to wagon-train 150 mail-order brides from Chicago to California. When his lustful hired hands turn out to be all hands, Buck and the ladies must fight off attacking Indians on their own. Notable film allowing women to be as tough as men is not your typical western. Based on the Frank Capra story. **116m/C VHS.** Robert Taylor, Denise Darcel, Hope Emerson, John McIntire, Beverly Dennis, Lenore Lonergan, Marilyn Erskine, Julie Bishop, Renata Vanni, Frankie Darro, George Chandler; ***D:*** William A. Wellman; ***W:*** Charles Schnee; ***C:*** William Mellor; ***M:*** Jeff Alexander.

Westworld **1973 (PG)** Crichton wrote and directed this story of an adult vacation resort of the future which offers the opportunity to live in various fantasy worlds serviced by lifelike robots. Brolin and Benjamin are businessmen who choose a western fantasy world. When an electrical malfunction occurs, the robots begin to go berserk. Brynner is perfect as a western gunslinging robot whose skills are all too real. **90m/C VHS, DVD.** Yul Brynner, Richard Benjamin, James Brolin, Dick Van Patten, Majel Barrett; ***D:*** Michael Crichton; ***W:*** Michael Crichton; ***C:*** Gene Polito; ***M:*** Fred Karlin.

Wet and Wild Summer WOOF! **1992 (R)** Topless beach resort is the playground for stud lifeguards and sexy resort owners. **95m/C VHS.** Christopher Atkins, Elliott Gould, Julian McMahon, Rebecca Cross; ***D:*** Maurice Murphy.

Wet Gold **1984** A beautiful young woman and three men journey to retrieve a sunken treasure. Nice scenery. Proves that it is possible to make "The Treasure of the Sierra Madre" without making a classic. John Huston, where are you? **90m/C VHS.** Brooke Shields, Brian Kerwin, Burgess Meredith, Tom Byrd; ***D:*** Dick Lowry. **TV**

Wet Hot American Summer **2001 (R)** Send-up of late 70s/early 80s camp flicks like "Meatballs" and "Little Darlings" focuses on the counselors trying to get laid and/or stoned on the last weekend of a Maine summer camp in 1981 while the youngsters in their charge are thrown around like chew toys. Beth (Garofalo) is the camp director with the hots for an astrophysicist (Pierce) who finds that the camp is in danger of being crushed by Skylab. The plot also involves many other cast members trying to sleep with many other cast members, but to detail more of the story would take crucial print space away from the genius that is the Vietnam vet camp cook (Meloni), whose spiritual advisor is a can of mixed vegetables. Take that whatever way you want, but trust us, you really have to see it to believe it. **97m/C VHS, DVD.** *US* Janeane Garofalo, David Hyde Pierce, Michael Showalter, Marguerite Moreau, Paul Rudd, Zak Orth, Christopher Meloni, A.D. Miles, Molly Shannon, Bradley Cooper, Michael Ian Black, Amy Poehler, Marisa Ryan, Elizabeth Banks, Kevin Sussman, Gideon Jacobs; ***D:*** David Wain; ***W:*** Michael Showalter, David Wain; ***C:*** Ben Weinstein; ***M:*** Theodore Shapiro, Craig (Shudder to Think) Wedren.

Wetbacks **1956** Fishing boat skipper Jim Benson (Bridges) agrees to help the U.S. Immigration Department nab smugglers who want to use Benson's vessel to carry illegal immigrants from Mexico into the U.S. **89m/C VHS.** Lloyd Bridges, Nancy Gates, Barton MacLane, John Hoyt, Harold (Hal) Peary, Nacho Galindo; ***D:*** Hank McCune; ***W:*** Pete LaRoche; ***C:*** Brydon Baker; ***M:*** Les Baxter.

Wetherby **1985 (R)** Playwright David Hare's first directorial effort, which he also wrote, about a Yorkshire schoolteacher whose life is shattered when a young, brooding stranger comes uninvited to a dinner party, and then shoots himself in her living room. Compelling but oh, so dark. Richardson, who plays a young Redgrave, is actually Redgrave's daughter. **97m/C VHS, DVD.** *GB* Vanessa Redgrave, Ian Holm, Judi Dench, Joely Richardson, Tim (McInnerny) McInnery, Suzanna Hamilton; ***D:*** David Hare; ***W:*** David Hare; ***M:*** Nick Bicat. Berlin Intl. Film Fest. '85: Golden Berlin Bear; Natl. Soc. Film Critics '85: Actress (Redgrave).

Whacked! **2002 (R)** Adopted brothers Mark and Tony go from the rough streets of Brooklyn to jobs as professional killers: one for the Mob, the other for the CIA. The discovery of a plot to steal millions from the government reunites them to protect a witness and bring down the scheme. Standard actioner has some good stunt work going for it. **91m/C DVD.** Paul Sampson, Patrick Muldoon, Carmen Electra, Judge Reinhold, Michael (Mike) Papajohn; ***D:*** James Bruce; ***W:*** Paul Sampson, Matthew Goodman; ***C:*** Dan Heigh.

Whale for the Killing 1/2 **1981** An ecologist stranded in a remote Alaskan fishing village battles to save a beached humpbacked whale from a malicious Russian fisherman. Platitudinous and self-congratulatory, if well-meaning. From a book by Farley Mowat. **145m/C VHS.** Richard Widmark, Peter Strauss, Dee Wallace, Bruce McGill, Kathryn Walker; ***D:*** Richard T. Heffron; ***M:*** Basil Poledouris. **TV**

Whale Music **1994** Off-beat saga of a burned-out rock star and the runaway who invades his life. Desmond Howl (Chaykin) has retreated to a tumbledown estate in the Pacific Northwest, tired of the music grind, and wanting to devote himself to his masterwork—a symphony for whales. Runaway Claire (Preston) provides a surprisingly welcome presence in contrast to Howl's other visitors—ex-wife Fay (Dale), who wants him to sell the estate, rapacious recording exec Kenneth (Welsh), and Howl's brother, singer Daniel (Gross), who happens to be dead and haunting his sibling. Haphazard direction helps dissipate powerful lead performances. Adapted from the novel by Paul Quarrington. **100m/C VHS.** *CA* Maury Chaykin, Cynthia (Cyndy, Cindy) Preston, Jennifer Dale, Kenneth Welsh, Paul Gross; ***D:*** Richard J. Lewis; ***W:*** Paul Quarrington, Richard J. Lewis; ***C:*** Vic Sarin; ***M:*** George Blondheim. Genie '94: Actor (Chaykin), Song ("Claire"), Sound.

Whale of a Tale 🦴 **1976 (G)** A young boy trains a killer whale to appear in the big show in the main tank at "Marineland." **90m/C VHS.** William Shatner, Marty Allen, Abby Dalton, Andy Devine, Nancy O'Conner; ***D:*** Ewing Miles Brown.

Whale Rider 🦴🦴🦴 ½ **2002 (PG-13)** Pai (Castle-Hughes, wonderful in her film debut) is a very determined 12-year-old Maori girl whose very traditional grandfather Koro (Paratene) is the tribal chief. Pai's father (Curtis) should be the next in line but after the death of his wife and Pai's infant twin brother, he's left the family. Although the stubborn Koro loves Pai, he refuses to see his granddaughter as a possible successor and won't train her in the customs that he teaches to the Maori boys. So Pai observes and learns on her own—ready to show everyone that she has what it takes. Title refers to the legend that their ancestor arrived in their land on the back of a whale. Adapted from the 1986 novel by Witi Ihimaera. **105m/C VHS, DVD.** *NZ GE* Keisha Castle-Hughes, Rawiri Paratene, Vicky Haughton, Clifford Curtis; ***D:*** Niki Caro; ***W:*** Niki Caro; ***C:*** Leon Narbey; ***M:*** Lisa Gerrard. Ind. Spirit '04: Foreign Film.

The Whales of August 🦴🦴🦴 ½ **1987** Based on the David Berry play, the story of two elderly sisters—one caring, the other cantankerous, blind, and possibly senile—who decide during a summer in Maine whether or not they should give up their ancestral house and enter a nursing home. Gish and Davis are exquisite to watch, and the all-star supporting cast is superb—especially Price as a suave Russian. Lovingly directed by Anderson in his first US outing. **91m/C VHS, DVD.** Lillian Gish, Bette Davis, Vincent Price, Ann Sothern, Mary Steenburgen, Harry Carey Jr., Tisha Sterling, Margaret Ladd; ***D:*** Lindsay Anderson; ***W:*** David Berry; ***C:*** Mike Fash. Natl. Bd. of Review '87: Actress (Gish).

Wham-Bam, Thank You Spaceman 🦴 ½ **1975 (R)** Very silly stuff about aliens with fiberglass heads and balloon ears that inflate when they become excited. They transport themselves to Earth in a tiny set decorated with tinfoil where most of the action takes place. Their mission: to impregnate Earth women to save their race. Though the female nudity is abundant, the sexual action is pretty tame by today's standards. **79m/C DVD.** Jay Rasumny, Samuel Mann, Dyanne Thorne, Maria Arnold, Valda Hansen, Sandy Carey, John Ireland Jr.; ***D:*** William A. Levey; ***W:*** Shlomo D. Weinstein; ***C:*** David Platnik; ***M:*** Miles Goodman, David White.

The Wharf Rat 🦴🦴 **1995 (R)** Waterfront con man Petey Martin (Phillips) teams up with journalist Dexter Ireland (Ticotin) to avenge the murder of his policeman brother by a group of corrupt cops lead by the crazy Doc (Reinhold). **88m/C VHS.** Lou Diamond Phillips, Rachel Ticotin, Judge Reinhold, Rita Moreno, Scott Cohen; ***D:*** Jimmy Huston; ***W:*** Jimmy Huston; ***C:*** Levie Isaacks; ***M:*** Mervyn Warren. **CABLE**

What a Carve-Up! 🦴🦴 *No Place Like Homicide* **1962** A group of relatives gather in an old, spooky mansion to hear the reading of a will. Tries too hard. Remake of "The Ghoul." **87m/B VHS, DVD.** *GB* Kenneth Connor, Sidney James, Shirley Eaton, Donald Pleasence, Dennis Price, Michael Gough; ***D:*** Pat Jackson.

What a Girl Wants 🦴🦴 ½ **2003 (PG)** Another movie intended for the tweenie girl set ala "The Princess Diaries." Spunky Daphne Reynolds (Bynes) lives in Manhattan with her single bohemian mom Libby (Preston). Daphne has never met her Dad, a once-adventurous English lord, Sir Henry Dashwood (Firth), who has gone all staid and stuffy. So Daph takes off for London to introduce herself. Henry's got a political career to think about so the arrival of this brash American teen is a less than happy occasion, especially to Henry's fiancee, manipulative Glynnis (Chacellor) and her snobby daughter Clarissa (Cole). But you just know that Daphne will get everything she wants (including this really cute English boy). Adapted from a play and previously filmed as 1958's "The Reluctant Debutante" with Sandra Dee. **104m/C VHS, DVD.** *US* Amanda Bynes, Colin Firth, Kelly Preston, Eileen Atkins, Anna Chancellor, Jonathan Pryce, Oliver James, Christina Cole, Sylvia Syms, Ben Scholfield; ***D:*** Dennie Gordon; ***W:*** Elizabeth Chandler, Jenny Bicks; ***C:*** Andrew Dunn; ***M:*** Rupert Gregson-Williams.

What a Life 🦴 ½ **1939** High school student Henry Aldrich (Cooper) needs to quit the pranks and clean up his image of being the worst kid in school, made harder by his dad's former status as big man on campus at Princeton. Fortunately Henry pulls it all together. This character was so popular that subsequent films were spawned. **75m/B DVD.** Jackie Cooper, Betty Field, John Howard, Janice Logan, Vaughan Glaser; ***D:*** Theodore Reed; ***W:*** Charles Brackett, Clifford Goldsmith; ***C:*** Victor Milner.

What a Way to Die 🦴 ½ **1970 (R)** An evil assassin plots dispatching with a difference. **87m/C VHS.** William Berger, Anthony Baker, Helga Anders, Georgia Moll; ***D:*** Helmut Foernbacher.

What a Woman! 🦴🦴 ½ *La Fortuna di Essere Donna; Lucky to Be a Woman* **1956** Shop girl Antonietta (Loren) becomes a star thanks to a sensational photo of her taken by a paparazzo (Mastroianni) that appears on the cover of a popular magazine. With the aid of a talent agent (Boyer), Antonietta becomes a famous fashion model. Only our photographer gets jealous when she ignores him for the debonair agent. **95m/B VHS.** *IT* Sophia Loren, Marcello Mastroianni, Charles Boyer, Elisa Cegani, Nino Besozzi; ***D:*** Alessandro Blasetti; ***W:*** Ennio Flaiano, Suso Cecchi D'Amico, Alessandro Continenza; ***C:*** Otello Martelli.

What about Bob? 🦴🦴🦴 **1991 (PG)** Bob, a ridiculously neurotic patient, follows his psychiatrist on vacation, turning his life upside down. The psychiatrist's family find Bob entertaining and endearing. Murray is at his comedic best; Dreyfuss's overly excitable characterization occasionally wears thin. **99m/C VHS, DVD.** Richard Dreyfuss, Bill Murray, Julie Hagerty, Charlie Korsmo, Tom Aldredge, Roger Bowen, Fran Brill, Kathryn Erbe, Doris Belack, Susan Willis; ***D:*** Frank Oz; ***W:*** Tom Schulman, Alvin Sargent; ***C:*** Michael Ballhaus; ***M:*** Miles Goodman.

What About Your Friends: Weekend Getaway 🦴🦴 ½ **2002** Heartfelt adventures of three bright African-American high school friends as they seek out college scholarships at a weekend retreat and begin to realize the powerful life changes that await them—including the possibility that they'll be heading in different directions. **89m/C VHS, DVD.** Keisha Knight Pulliam, Angell Conwell, Monica McSwain, Kym E. Whitley, Edwin Morrow, Salim Grant, Alexis Fields, Louis Gossett Jr., Denise Dowse, Ella Joyce, Troy Winbush; ***D:*** Niva Dorell; ***W:*** Kim Watson; ***C:*** Jurgen Baum; ***M:*** Andre Mayon. **TV**

What Comes Around 🦴🦴 **1985 (PG)** A good-ole-boy drama about a doped-up country singer who is kidnapped by his brother for his own good. The singer's evil manager sends his stooges out to find him. Might have been funny, but isn't. But is it meant to be? Good Reed songs; mildly interesting plot. **92m/C VHS, DVD.** Jerry Reed, Bo Hopkins, Arte Johnson, Barry Corbin; ***D:*** Jerry Reed.

What Did You Do in the War, Daddy? 🦴 ½ **1966** Unfunny comedy set in WWII about a group of weary American soldiers trying to get a small town in Sicily to surrender. Things don't go smoothly thanks to a combination soccer game/wine festival, not to mention the Germans deciding to attack. Director Edwards comedic verve deserted him. **119m/C VHS.** Dick Shawn, James Coburn, Sergio Fantoni, Giovanna Ralli, Aldo Ray, Harry (Henry) Morgan, Carroll O'Connor, Jay Novello, Vito Scotti; ***D:*** Blake Edwards; ***W:*** William Peter Blatty, Blake Edwards; ***M:*** Henry Mancini.

What Doesn't Kill You 🦴🦴 **2008 (R)** Brian (Ruffalo) and his childhood pal Paulie (Hawke) have been doing low-end work for local South Boston hood Pat (Goodman) for years. Paulie is impatient to break away for more lucrative work, but the married Brian has become a drug addict and Pat knows how to keep him in line. A prison stint has Brian trying to go straight but he's terrified at the changes surrounding him. Especially good performances from leads Ruffalo and Hawke though the story may seem familiar. **100m/C DVD.** *US* Mark Ruffalo, Ethan Hawke, Amanda Peet, Will Lyman, Lenny Clarke, Angela Featherstone, Donnie Wahlberg, Brian Goodman; ***D:*** Brian Goodman; ***W:*** Donnie Wahlberg, Brian Goodman, Paul T. Murray; ***C:*** Christopher Norr; ***M:*** Alex Wurman.

What Dreams May Come 🦴🦴 **1998 (PG-13)** Romantic idea and lushly colorful computer imagery combine with sappy dialogue to turn surreal fantasy into very average digital hocus-pocus. Dr. Chris Neilsen (Williams) and his artist-wife Annie (Sciorra) lose their two children to a traffic accident. Four years later the doctor himself is killed in a freak accident. He finds that his heaven is much like a painting done by his wife (or Monet or Van Gogh) of their dream cottage. Chris is just getting used to the "rules" when he learns that his wife has committed suicide, damning her to hell. Unable to accept eternal separation, he begins an odyssey to find her. For the first half hour, Williams alternates between a "Patch Adams" rehearsal and over-emoting into the tear-filled eyes of Sciorra. Very loosely adapted from a 20-year-old Richard Matheson novel. **113m/C VHS, DVD, HD DVD.** Rosalind Chao, Robin Williams, Annabella Sciorra, Cuba Gooding Jr., Max von Sydow, Jessica Brooks Grant, Josh Paddock; ***D:*** Vincent Ward; ***W:*** Ronald Bass; ***C:*** Eduardo Serra; ***M:*** Michael Kamen. Oscars '98: Visual FX.

What Ever Happened To... 🦴🦴 ½ *What Ever Happened to Baby Jane* **1993** Sisters play sisters as the Redgraves (in their first film together) tackle this remake of "What Ever Happened to Baby Jane?" in all its demented glory. Former actress Blanche (Vanessa) and former child star "Baby Jane" (Lynn) are living in a decaying mansion, which Blanche, confined to a wheelchair, is talking about selling. "Baby" snaps (not that she was ever very stable) and proceeds to torment her sis (more than usual). **94m/C VHS, DVD.** Vanessa Redgrave, Lynn Redgrave, Bruce A. Young, Amy Steel, John Scott Clough, John Glover; ***D:*** David Greene; ***W:*** Brian Taggert.

What Ever Happened to Baby Jane? 🦴🦴🦴 ½ **1962** Davis and Crawford portray aging sisters and former child stars living together in a decaying mansion. When the demented Jane (Davis) learns of her now-crippled sister's (Crawford) plan to institutionalize her, she tortures the wheelchair-bound sis. Davis plays her part to the hilt, unafraid of Aldrich's unsympathetic camera, and the viciousness of her character. She received her 10th Oscar nomination for the role. **132m/B VHS, DVD.** Bette Davis, Joan Crawford, Victor Buono, Anna Lee, B.D. Merrill, Maidie Norman; ***D:*** Robert Aldrich; ***W:*** Lukas Heller; ***C:*** Ernest Haller; ***M:*** Frank DeVol.

What Goes Up 🦴 **2009 (R)** Depressed New York reporter Babbitt comes to the Concord, New Hampshire hometown of teacher Christa McAuliffe to interview high school students about her space shuttle mission. But everyone's lives are affected when the Challenger mission proves fatal. Too much teen angst (and bad acting) and odd plot threats (suicide, pregnancy, bogus stories) to make this pic watchable. **115m/C DVD.** Steve Coogan, Hilary Duff, Olivia Thirlby, Josh Peck, Molly Shannon, Molly Price, Max Hoffman, Andrea Brooks; ***D:*** Jonathan Glatzer; ***W:*** Jonathan Glatzer, Robert Lawson; ***C:*** Antonio Calvache; ***M:*** Roddy Bottum. **VIDEO**

What Happened to Rosa? 🦴🦴🦴 **1921** This early Goldwyn release, a whimsical Cinderella story, casts Normand as an endearing shop girl duped by a gypsy's bogus predictions. Believing herself to be the reincarnation of a Castillian noblewoman she dons a fancy gown, attends a fancy shipboard ball and captures the heart of the fancy doctor of her dreams. But fearing his rejection of her true identity she slips away during the chaos of a brawl, leading the good doctor to believe that she is dead. A comedy of errors unfolds before they meet again and live happily ever after. No doubt it jerked a few tears in its day. **42m/B VHS.** Mabel Normand, Hugh Thompson, Doris Pawn, Tully Marshall, Eugenie Besserer, Buster Trow; ***D:*** Victor Schertzinger.

What Happened Was... 🦴🦴 **1994 (R)** Two-character study about a weirdly nightmarish first date. Law secretary Jackie (Sillas) has been eyeing bookish paralegal Michael (Noonan) and finally invites him for dinner at her loft. The two struggle to relax and make small talk that turns into some unexpected soul baring. Emotionally distant Michael is unexpectedly hostile about his job and claims to be writing an expose of their law firm while overly friendly Jackie is writing a children's book, which turns out to be jarringly violent and apparently autobiographical. Provides an idiosyncratic, if limited, appeal thanks to a compelling performance by Sillas. **92m/C VHS.** Tom Noonan, Karen Sillas; ***D:*** Tom Noonan; ***W:*** Tom Noonan; ***C:*** Joe DeSalvo; ***M:*** Tom Noonan. Sundance '94: Screenplay, Grand Jury Prize.

What Happens in Vegas 🦴 ½ **2008 (PG-13)** Wanna bet how this one's gonna go? Strangers Jack (Kutcher) and Joy (Diaz) are in Vegas escaping their respective personal bad luck when when a hotel snafu sticks them in the same room. Several cocktails and one wild night later, they wake up married. Too bad they hate each other, because thanks to a twist in the already ridiculous and deteriorating plot, a quarter gets tossed in a slot and the newlyweds are rich. So who makes off with the $3 million? And might these impossibly good-looking losers be made for each other after all? Queen Latifah's appearance as a marriage counselor is lackluster, while pretty much everyone else overacts and over gesiculates in an attempt to make the gags funny, with little success. Note to Hollywood: Don't base movies on catchy marketing slogans if you can't make them at least half as clever as a 30-second commercial. **99m/C DVD.** *US* Cameron Diaz, Ashton Kutcher, Lake Bell, Rob Corddry, Queen Latifah, Treat Williams, Dennis Miller, Dennis Farina, Zach Galifianakis, Jason Sudeikis, Michelle Krusiec, Krysten Ritter, Deirdre O'Connell; ***D:*** Tom Vaughan; ***W:*** Dana Fox; ***C:*** Matthew F. Leonetti; ***M:*** Christophe Beck.

What Have I Done to Deserve This? 🦴🦴🦴 *Que He Hecho Yo Para Merecer Estol?* **1985** A savage parody on Spanish mores, about a speed-addicted housewife who ends up selling her son and killing her husband with a ham bone. Black, black comedy, perverse and funny as only Almodovar can be. In Spanish with subtitles. Nudity and profanity. **100m/C VHS, DVD.** Carmen Maura, Chus (Maria Jesus) Lampreave; ***D:*** Pedro Almodovar; ***W:*** Pedro Almodovar.

What It's All About 🦴 ½ *El Perque de Tot Plegat* **1995** Fifteen brief comic stories, set in Barcelona, that explore faith, desire, love, doubt, and other emotions. Based on the book by Quim Monzo. Spanish with subtitles. **96m/C DVD.** *SP* Lluis Homar, Alex Casanovas, Camilo Rodriguez, Rosa Gamiz, Pepa Lopez, Rosa Novell; ***D:*** Ventura Pons; ***W:*** Ventura Pons; ***C:*** Carles Gusi; ***M:*** Carles Cases.

What Just Happened 🦴🦴 ½ **2008 (R)** Fictionalized version of producer Art Linson's memoirs follows two weeks in the course of A-list Hollywood producer Ben (DeNiro), who is suddenly caught up in a massive career snag. His Sean Penn movie is tanking at test screening, and now, Bruce Willis refuses to lose a few pounds or shave his beard for a new part. It's funny at times, but unlike the exaggerated, flashy television series "Entourage" or Altman's satire "The Player," this realistic behind-the-scenes look at Hollywood unconsciously appeals mostly to those involved in the industry. However, DeNiro's sharp, subtle performance is a welcome return to more grounded material, after a long stretch of goofy or over-hyped roles. *CNT Language, some violent images, sexual content and some drug material. **113m/C DVD.** *US* Robert De Niro, Bruce Willis, Sean

Penn, Stanley Tucci, John Turturro, Robin Wright Penn, Michael Wincott, Catherine Keener, Kristen Stewart, Lily Rabe; *D:* Barry Levinson; *W:* Art Linson; *C:* Stephane Fontaine; *M:* Marcelo Zarvos.

What Lies Beneath 🦴🦴 **2000 (PG-13)** Empty-nester Pfeiffer wanders around a seemingly haunted house suspecting neighbors of murder and finding out more about her scientist husband's past than she'd like. Zemeckis shoots for Hitchcockian suspense but manages mostly intermittent jolts and occasional wit. The "surprise" ending, telegraphed by the film's marketing campaign, has nothing to do with the film's first hour, which has everything to do with atmosphere and setting up distractions. **130m/C VHS, DVD.** Harrison Ford, Michelle Pfeiffer, Diana Scarwid, Joe Morton, James Remar, Miranda Otto, Amber Valletta, Katharine Towne, Victoria Birdwell; *D:* Robert Zemeckis; *W:* Clark Gregg; *C:* Don Burgess; *M:* Alan Silvestri.

What Love Is 🦴 ½ **2007 (R)** Trouble, that's what it is, especially in this talky production. Nice guy Tom (Gooding) has his live-in girlfriend (Pratt) leave him on Valentine's Day just as he was about to propose. His buds come over (followed by their gals) to offer relationship advice despite being equally clueless. **93m/C DVD.** Cuba Gooding Jr., Matthew Lillard, Anne Heche, Gina Gershon, Sean Astin, Tamala Jones, Judy Tylor, Shiri Appleby, Mars Callahan, Victoria Pratt, Andrew Daily; *D:* Mars Callahan; *W:* Mars Callahan; *C:* David G. Stump; *M:* Erik Godal.

What Matters Most 🦴🦴 ½ **2001** High school basketball star Lucas Warner (Allen) is the son of a prominent family in their small Texas community. His father (Teague) doesn't approve of Lucas falling in love with wrong-side-of-the-tracks Heather (Cole). When Heather becomes pregnant, the teens plan to run away and get married but an accident leaves Lucas in a coma. **105m/C DVD.** Chad Allen, Marshall Teague, Polly Cole, Shonda Farr, Tamara Clatterbuck, Gary Driver; *D:* Jane Cusumano; *W:* Jane Cusumano; *C:* Michael Goi; *M:* Sean Morris.

What! No Beer? 🦴🦴 **1933** Two dimbulb friends decide to put their money into a defunct brewery hoping for the end of Prohibition. They start up operations too soon and wind up attracting the unwelcome attentions of gangster bootleggers and the cops. Mediocre comedy and Keaton's last starring role as his own problems with alcohol affected his work. **66m/B VHS.** Buster Keaton, Jimmy Durante, Phyllis Barry, Roscoe Ates, John Miljan, Henry Armetta, Edward Brophy; *D:* Edward Sedgwick.

What Planet Are You From? 🦴🦴 **2000 (R)** Two jokes, no waiting! Shandling's feature film debut tries to be a comment on how differently men and women view sex and relationships, but it spends most of its time with a humming penis. Shandling is an alien sent from a planet of test tube people to impregnate an earth woman, once he's given the proper equipment (which has the previously mentioned unfortunate feature). He disguises himself as Harold, a bank executive, and gets dating tips from a philandering co-worker (Kinnear) who recommends AA meetings as a great pickup place. His direct approach ("You smell nice") somehow attracts a recovering alcoholic (Bening) who's on the biological clock. The other joke (and better of the two) involves a hen-pecked FAA inspector who's suspicious of Harold's origins. Shandling's limited range is exposed, and the juvenile script doesn't do him any favors. **107m/C VHS, DVD.** Garry Shandling, Annette Bening, Greg Kinnear, Ben Kingsley, Linda Fiorentino, John Goodman, Richard Jenkins, Caroline Aaron, Judy Greer, Nora Dunn, Ann Cusack, Camryn Manheim, Janeane Garofalo, Stacey Travis, Willie Garson, Sarah Silverman; *D:* Mike Nichols; *W:* Garry Shandling, Michael Leeson, Edward Solomon, Peter Tolan; *C:* Michael Ballhaus; *M:* Carter Burwell.

What Price Glory? 🦴🦴🦴 **1952** Remake of the 1926 silent classic about a pair of comradely rivals for the affections of women in WWI France. Strange to have Ford directing an offbeat comedy, but it works: masterful direction, good acting. Demarest broke both legs in a motorcycle accident during shooting. **111m/C VHS, DVD.** James Cagney, Dan Dailey, Corinne Calvet, William Demarest, James Gleason, Robert Wagner, Max (Casey Adams) Showalter, Craig Hill, Marisa Pavan; *D:* John Ford.

What Price Hollywood? 🦴🦴🦴 **1932** Aspiring young starlet decides to crash film world by using an alcoholic director as her stepping stone. Bennett is lovely; Sherman is superb as an aging, dissolute man who watches his potential slip away. From a story by Adela Rogers St. Johns. Remade three times as "A Star is Born." **88m/B VHS.** Constance Bennett, Lowell Sherman, Neil Hamilton; *D:* George Cukor; *W:* Robert Presnell Sr., Gene Fowler Sr., Jane Murfin, Ben Markson, Allen Rivkin, Rowland Brown; *C:* Charles Rosher; *M:* Max Steiner.

What the #$*! Do We Know? 🦴 ½ **2004** Excruciatingly upbeat New Agers' guide to the perplexed. Follows a confused woman (Maitlin) through the troubles of daily life with annoying animation and talking heads helping her search for meaning. Supposed exploration of quantum theory and its impact is a queasy mishmash of pop- and pseudo-science, with some mysticism made to please the starry-eyed and vacant. **108m/C VHS, DVD.** *US* Marlee Matlin, Elaine Hendrix, John Ross Bowie, Robert Bailey Jr., Barry Newman, Larry Brandenburg; *D:* Mark Vicente, William Arntz, Betsy Chasse; *W:* William Arntz, Betsy Chasse, Matthew Hoffman; *C:* David Bridges; *M:* Christopher Franke.

What the Deaf Man Heard 🦴🦴🦴 **1998** Sly comedy starts off in the '40s with 10-year-old Sammy (Muniz) winding up alone in the small town of Barrington, Georgia after his single mother (Peters) vanishes. Since she told him to keep silent, Sammy continues to obey her—even when he's taken in by kindly bus station manager Norm (Skerritt). Soon everyone believes Sammy is deaf and mute and this doesn't change as Sammy grows to adulthood (Modine) as the local handyman. In fact, everyone is happy to confide in Sammy so he knows everyone's secrets—not always a happy situation. Based on the novel "What the Deaf-Mute Heard" by G.D. Gearino. **107m/C VHS, DVD.** Matthew Modine, Tom Skerritt, Judith Ivey, Claire Bloom, James Earl Jones, Jerry O'Connell, Anne Bobby, Stephen Spinella, Jake Weber, Bernadette Peters, Frankie Muniz; *D:* John Kent Harrison; *W:* Robert W. Lenski; *C:* Eric Van Haren Noman; *M:* J.A.C. Redford. **TV**

What the Moon Saw 🦴🦴 ½ **1990** When a young boy is confronted by a less than friendly theatre owner, he uses favorite scenes from "Sinbad" to deal with the aggressor. **86m/C VHS.** *AU* Max Phipps, Danielle Spencer, Andrew Shepherd, Kim Gyngell, Gary Sweet, Robyn Gibbes, Pat Evison; *D:* Pino Amenta; *W:* Frank Howson; *C:* David Connell; *M:* John Capek.

What the Peeper Saw 🦴🦴 *Night Hair Child; Child of the Night; Diabolica Malicia* **1972** The wife of a wealthy author finds her comfortable life turning into a terrifying nightmare when her young stepson starts acting funny. Juicy and terrifying. **97m/C VHS, DVD.** Britt Ekland, Mark Lester, Hardy Kruger, Lilli Palmer, Harry Andrews; *D:* Andrea Bianchi; *W:* Andrea Bianchi; *C:* Luis Cuadrado, Harry Waxman; *M:* Stelvio Cipriani.

What Time Is It There? 🦴🦴 **2001** Hsiao Kang (Lee) earns a living on the streets of Taipei by selling cheap wristwatches. Shiang-Chyi (Chen) wants to buy the watch Hsiao is wearing because it displays two time zones and she is flying to Paris. After she leaves, Hsiao suddenly decides to change all the watches on display to Paris time—and then all the watches and clocks he can find all around the city, even a gigantic clock on a building—in order to keep a connection with her. French and Chinese with subtitles. **116m/C VHS, DVD.** *TW* Kangsheng Lee, Shiang-chyi Chen, Tien Miao, Yiching Lu; ***Cameos:*** Cecilia Yip, Jean-Pierre Leaud; *D:* Ming-liang Tsai; *W:* Ming-liang Tsai, Pi-ying Yang; *C:* Benoit Delhomme.

What to Do in Case of Fire 🦴🦴 ½ *Was Tun, Wenn's Brennt?* **2002 (R)** In 1987, six friends, part of an anarchist group in Berlin, make a bomb and place it in an empty building. It sits there until it's inadvertently detonated 15 years later. Although no one is injured, there is no statute of limitations on their crime. Veteran police detective Manowsky (Lowitsch) knows just who to look for and goes after the group's two remaining holdouts Tim (Schweiger) and Hotte (Feifel). The cops find incriminating materials and the buddies must now seek out their four former members in order to get them all off the hook. German with subtitles. **101m/C VHS, DVD.** *GE* Til Schweiger, Sebastian Blomberg, Nadja Uhl, Martin Feifel, Matthias Matschke, Doris Schretzmayer; *D:* Gregor Schnitzler; *W:* Stefan Dahnert, Anne Wild; *C:* Andreas Berger; *M:* Stephan Zacharias, Stephan Gade.

What Up? 🦴 *The Sweep* **2008 (R)** Nothing much, that's for sure in this dumb comedy with an overly-familiar plot. Janitors Tyrone (Hardison) and Jerome (Godfrey) find a briefcase full of cash and blow it all. Then they discover it was mob money and they have a week to pay it back—or else. **82m/C DVD.** Kadeem Hardison, Godfrey, Sonny Bermudez; *D:* Dale Stelly; *W:* Dale Stelly, Marvin Hayes; *C:* Keith L. Smith; *M:* Jason Solowsky.

What Waits Below 🦴 ½ **1983 (PG)** A scientific expedition encounters a lost race living in caves in South America. Good cast, bad acting, and lousy script. Might have been much better. **88m/C VHS.** Dick Curtis, Timothy Bottoms, Robert Powell, Lisa Blount; *D:* Don Sharp.

What We Do Is Secret 🦴🦴 ½ **2007 (R)** Clear, engagingly personal take on the California punk scene and a self-destructive icon. Jan Paul Beahm recreates himself as Darby Crash (West), songwriter and leader of 1970s SoCal punk band the Germs—and a junkie. A man with a five-year plan, Crash is a rule-breaker determined to find success his way and then kill himself (which he did in 1980). The look seems remarkably accurate, and surviving bandmate Pat Smear also taught the actors to recreate the Germs' performances. **92m/C DVD.** Shane West, Bijou Phillips, Rick Gonzalez, Noah Segan, Ashton Holmes, Tina Majorino, Azura Skye, Ray Park, Sebastien Roche; *D:* Rodger Grossman; *W:* Rodger Grossman; *C:* Andrew Huesbscher; *M:* Anna Waronker.

What Women Want 🦴🦴 ½ **2000 (PG-13)** Male-chauvinist Gibson gets electrocuted in his bathroom and suddenly has the power to hear women's thoughts, which aren't very complimentary towards him. Gibson, obviously enjoying himself, shines in this intermittently funny, lightweight but enjoyable romantic comedy. Sublety and restraint are in short supply, but Gibson's performance, especially when he's doing his neo-Rat Pack act, makes up for the overindulgences. **123m/C VHS, DVD.** Mel Gibson, Helen Hunt, Marisa Tomei, Lauren Holly, Bette Midler, Mark Feuerstein, Ashley Johnson, Judy Greer, Alan Alda, Delta Burke, Valerie Perrine, Lisa Edelstein, Sarah Paulson, Ana Gasteyer, Loretta Devine, Eric Balfour, Logan Lerman; *D:* Nancy Meyers; *W:* Josh Goldsmith, Cathy Yuspa; *C:* Dean Cundey; *M:* Alan Silvestri.

What Your Eyes Don't See 🦴🦴 *Ojos Que No Ven* **1999** Abelardo Sachs is the owner/editor of a political magazine. He's murdered in his home by a masked gunman. As the police start investigating, everyone in Sachs's life has their own theory on whether the killing was political or personal. Spanish with subtitles. **90m/C VHS, DVD.** *AR* Mauricio Dayub, Luis Luque, Malena Solda, Gaston Pauls, Alejandra Flechner; *D:* Beda Docampo Feijoo; *W:* Beda Docampo Feijoo, Enrique Cortes; *C:* Ricardo Rodriguez; *M:* Ivan Wyszogrod.

Whatever 🦴🦴 **1998 (R)** Straightforward teenage coming of age story set in a small New Jersey town in the early 80s. Focuses on the friendship of two high school seniors, aspiring artist Anna (Weil) and party animal Brenda (Morgan). Anna copes with her bitter single mom (Rossetter) and bratty little brother and hopes to escape to a prestigious art school in New York, but is in danger of being dragged down by Brenda. The two girls numb their mostly grim home lives with drugs, alcohol and casual sex at joyless parties. The revelation that Brenda is being sexually abused at home moves the plot into the TV movie realm. **112m/C VHS.** Liza Weil, Chad Morgan, Kathryn Rossetter, Frederic Forrest; *D:* Susan Skoog; *W:* Susan Skoog; *C:* Michael Barrow, Mike Mayers.

Whatever Happened to Aunt Alice? 🦴🦴🦴 **1969 (PG)** After murdering her husband to inherit his estate, a poor, eccentric widow develops an awful habit: she hires maids, only to murder them and steal their savings. The only evidence is a growing number of trees by the drive. Sleuth Ruth Gordon (of "Harold and Maude" fame, acting here just as odd) takes the job in hopes of solving the mystery. Thoroughly amusing. **101m/C VHS, DVD.** Geraldine Page, Ruth Gordon, Rosemary Forsyth, Robert Fuller, Mildred Dunnock; *D:* Lee H. Katzin; *W:* Theodore Apstein; *C:* Joseph Biroc; *M:* Gerald Fried.

Whatever It Takes 🦴 ½ **2000 (PG-13)** Dopey teen romancer, with the usual attractive cast, that tries to be a modern version of "Cyrano de Bergerac." Ya got cutie boy-next-door-type Ryan (West) and his sensitive best pal Maggie (Sokoloff), who is, of course, his unknown soulmate. But Ryan pines for snobby hottie Ashley (O'Keefe). Meanwhile, Maggie has won the eye of jock Chris (Franco). So Chris and Ryan team up so that each can get their dream girl before the prom. You know how everything turns out. **94m/C VHS, DVD.** Marla Sokoloff, Jodi Lyn O'Keefe, Shane West, James Franco, Julia Sweeney, Richard Schiff, Aaron Paul, Colin Hanks; *D:* David Raynr; *W:* Mark Schwahn; *C:* Tim Suhrstedt; *M:* Ed Shearmur.

Whatever Works 🦴 ½ **2009 (PG-13)** You'd think Allen (in his 42nd film) would get tired of trotting out the same old obsessions and characters, although the script is allegedly recycled from the 1970s. Allen's protagonist is even more mopey, misanthropic, and ridiculous than usual: aging New Yorker Boris (David), a self-proclaimed scientific genius, who upends his uptown life and moves into a dingy apartment near Chinatown. A chance meeting with beautiful young southern runaway Melody (Wood) leads to an odd relationship (and then marriage) until her repressed, conservative parents (Clarkson, Begley Jr.) show up and there are further extreme character transformations. **92m/C DVD.** *US FR* Larry David, Evan Rachel Wood, Patricia Clarkson, Ed Begley Jr., Henry Cavill, Michael McKean; *D:* Woody Allen; *W:* Woody Allen; *C:* Harris Savides.

Whatever You Say 🦴🦴 *Mon Idole; My Idol* **2002** Bastien (Canet) works as the abused assistant to Philippe (Lefebvre), the egotistical host of a popular TV reality show. He puts up with the humiliations for a chance to pitch his own ideas to producer Broustal (Berleand), who suddenly invites Bastien to his country home for the weekend. Bastien soon figures out that his TV opportunity is tied to pleasing Broustal's younger wife Clara (Kruger) but there's something so unsettling about the situation that all Bastien wants is a way out. Directorial debut for Canet; French with subtitles. **110m/C DVD.** *FR* Guillaume Canet, Francois Berleand, Diane Kruger, Philippe Lefebvre, Daniel Prevost, Clotilde Courau; *D:* Guillaume Canet; *W:* Guillaume Canet, Philippe Lefebvre; *C:* Christophe Offenstein; *M:* Alexandra Sinclair.

What's Cooking? 🦴🦴🦴 **2000 (PG-13)** Follows the Thanksgiving tradition of feasting amid household tension through the stories of four American families: one Jewish, one Latino, one Vietnamese, and one African American. Culture clashes, generation gaps, sexual identities, divorce, and other family flash points get addressed with sincere writing and delicate acting by all involved. Written by India-born English director Chadha and her Japanese-American husband Berges—you can't more all-American than that. **109m/C VHS, DVD.** Alfre Woodard, Joan Chen, Julianna Margulies, Mercedes Ruehl, Kyra Sedgwick, Lainie Kazan, Dennis Haysbert, Victor Rivers, Douglas Spain, A. Martinez, Maury Chaykin, Estelle Harris, Will Yun Lee, Kristy Wu; *D:* Gurinder Chadha; *W:* Gurinder Chadha, Paul Mayeda Berges; *C:* Jong Lin; *M:* Craig Pruess.

What's Eating Gilbert Grape 🦴🦴🦴 *Gilbert Grape* **1993 (PG-13)** Offbeat is mildly descriptive. Depp stars as Gilbert Grape, the titular head of a very dysfunctional family living in a big house in a small Iowa town. His Momma (Cates) weighs more than 500 pounds and hasn't left the house in seven years, he has two squabbling teenage sisters, and 17-year-old brother Arnie (DiCaprio) is mentally retarded and requires constant supervision. What's a good-hearted grocery clerk to do? Well, when free-spirited Becky (Lewis) is momentarily marooned in town, Gilbert may have found a true soulmate. Performances, especially DiCaprio's, save this from the oddball/cute factor although flick would have benefitted from streamlining, particularly the scenes involving Depp and bad-haircut Lewis. Based on the novel by Hedges. **118m/C VHS, DVD.** Johnny Depp, Leonardo DiCaprio, Juliette Lewis, Mary Steenburgen, Darlene Cates, Laura Harrington, Mary Kate Schellhardt, Kevin Tighe, John C. Reilly, Crispin Glover, Penelope Branning; ***D:*** Lasse Hallstrom; ***W:*** Peter Hedges; ***C:*** Sven Nykvist; ***M:*** Alan Parker, Bjorn Isfalt. Natl. Bd. of Review '93: Support. Actor (DiCaprio).

What's Good for the Goose 1/2 **1969** Stuffy, married financial institution executive's lifestyle receives a major overhaul when he attends a banking conference and meets a beautiful and free-spirited young woman whom he takes as a lover. Unfortunately, he perpetually finds her in bed with other men, and then his wife gets in on the act, too. Classic British humor. **104m/C VHS, DVD.** *GB* Norman Wisdom, Sarah Atkinson, Sally Bazely, Sally Geeson, Derek Francis, Terence Alexander, David Lodge; ***D:*** Menahem Golan; ***W:*** Norman Wisdom, Menahem Golan; ***C:*** William Brayne; ***M:*** Reg Tilsley.

What's Love Got to Do with It? 1/2 **1993 (R)** Energetic biopic of powerhouse songstress Tina Turner. Short sequences cover her early life before moving into her abusive relationship with Ike and solo comeback success. Bassett may not look like Tina, but her exceptionally strong performance leaves no question as to who she's supposed to be, even during on-stage Tina sequences. Some credibility is lost when Turner is shown in the final concert sequence—Gibson would have been wise to let Bassett finish what she started. Fishburne is a sympathetic but still chilling Ike, rising to the challenge of showing both Ike's initial charm and longtime cruelty. Based on "I, Tina" by Turner and Kurt Loder. **118m/C VHS, DVD.** Angela Bassett, Laurence Fishburne, Vanessa Bell Calloway, Jenifer Lewis, Phyllis Stickney, Khandi Alexander, Pamela Tyson, Penny Johnson, Rae'ven (Alyia Larrymore) Kelly, Robert Miranda, Chi McBride, Damon Hines; ***D:*** Brian Gibson; ***W:*** Kate Lanier; ***C:*** Jamie Anderson; ***M:*** Stanley Clarke. Golden Globes '94: Actress—Mus./Comedy (Bassett); Blockbuster '95: Female Newcomer, V. (Bassett).

What's New Pussycat? *Quoi De Neuf, Pussycat?* **1965** A young engaged man, reluctant to give up the girls who love him, seeks the aid of a married psychiatrist who turns out to have problems of his own. Allen's first feature as both actor and screenwriter. Oscar-nominated title song sung by Tom Jones. **108m/C VHS, DVD.** Peter Sellers, Peter O'Toole, Romy Schneider, Paula Prentiss, Woody Allen, Ursula Andress, Capucine; ***D:*** Clive Donner; ***W:*** Woody Allen; ***M:*** Burt Bacharach, Hal David.

What's the Matter with Helen? 1/2 **1971 (PG)** Two women, the mothers of murderous sons, move to Hollywood to escape their past and start a new life. They open a school for talented children, and seem to be adjusting to their new lives until strange things start happening. It is soon revealed that one of the mothers is a psychotic killer, and the other mother becomes part of an eerie finale. A fine starring vehicle for two aging actresses. Great score. **101m/C VHS, DVD.** Debbie Reynolds, Shelley Winters, Dennis Weaver, Agnes Moorehead, Michael MacLiammoir; ***D:*** Curtis Harrington.

What's the Worst That Could Happen? **2001 (PG-13)** Billionaire DeVito catches thief Lawrence robbing his mansion and, in retaliation, takes the man's lucky charm ring. Since Lawrence just received the ring from new girlfriend Ejogo, he'll do anything to get it back. It becomes an escalating, and ultimately tiresome, war of revenge and humiliation. The large and talented cast are given neither the script or the room to really shine, but some of the supporters fare well. Leguizamo, Fichtner, and Headly stand out, but Lawrence and DeVito should've been reined in a bit. **95m/C VHS, DVD.** *US* Martin Lawrence, Danny DeVito, Nora Dunn, William Fichtner, Glenne Headly, John Leguizamo, Bernie Mac, Carmen Ejogo, Larry Miller, Richard Schiff, Ana Gasteyer, Sascha Knopf, Siobhan Fallon Hogan, GQ, Lenny Clarke; ***D:*** Sam Weisman; ***W:*** Matthew Chapman; ***C:*** Anastas Michos; ***M:*** Tyler Bates.

What's Up, Doc? **1972 (G)** A shy musicologist from Iowa (Ryan) travels to San Francisco with his fiance (Kahn) for a convention. He meets the eccentric Streisand at his hotel and becomes involved in a chase to recover four identical flight bags containing top secret documents, a wealthy woman's jewels, the professor's musical rocks, and Streisand's clothing. Bogdanovich's homage to the screwball comedies of the '30s. Kahn's feature film debut. **94m/C VHS, DVD.** Barbra Streisand, Ryan O'Neal, Kenneth Mars, Austin Pendleton, Randy Quaid, Madeline Kahn; ***D:*** Peter Bogdanovich; ***W:*** David Newman, Buck Henry, Robert Benton; ***M:*** Artie Butler. Writers Guild '72: Orig. Screenplay.

What's Up Front 1/2 *The Fall Guy; A Fourth for Marriage* **1963** Occasionally funny '60s gag-fest about an ogle-eyed bra salesman who decides to sell door-to-door in order to save a failing brassiere company. Filmed in "Girl-O-Rama" by the young Vilmos Zsigmond. Dated and weird, with camp value. No nudity. Costumes were done by Frederick's of Hollywood. **90m/C VHS.** Tommy Holden, Marilyn Manning, Carolyn Walker, William Watters; ***D:*** Bob Wehling.

What's Up, Scarlet? **2005** Successful L.A. matchmaker Scarlet Zabrinski is constantly at odds with her overbearing mother Ruth and her pothead brother Benjamin. Scarlet has no interest in a relationship of her own until a fender-bender introduces her to scatter-brained but sultry actress Sabrina. Learning Sabrina's homeless, Scarlet impulsively invites her to stay at her home, but is clueless about her burgeoning feelings for Sabrina until Ben makes a play for her. **84m/C DVD.** Musetta Vander, Sally Kirkland, Jere Burns, Susan Priver; ***D:*** Anthony Caldarella; ***W:*** Anthony Caldarella; ***C:*** Geza Sinkovics; ***M:*** Stephen Graziano.

What's Up, Tiger Lily? **1966** This legitimate Japanese spy movie—"Kagi No Kag" (Key of Keys), a 1964 Bond imitation—was re-edited by Woody Allen, who added a new dialogue track, with hysterical results. Characters Terri and Suki Yaki are involved in an international plot to secure egg salad recipe; Allen's brand of Hollywood parody and clever wit sustain the joke. Music by the Lovin' Spoonful, who make a brief appearance. **90m/C VHS, DVD.** *JP* Tatsuya Mihashi, Mie Hama, Akiko Wakabayashi, China Lee, Eisei Amamoto, Kumi Mizuno, Tadao Nakamura, The Lovin' Spoonful; ***D:*** Senkichi Taniguchi, Woody Allen; ***W:*** Julie Bennett, Frank Buxton, Louise Lasser, Mickey Rose, Bryan Wilson, Kazuo Yamada, Woody Allen; ***C:*** Kazuo Yamada; ***M:*** Jack Lewis, The Lovin' Spoonful; ***Nar:*** Woody Allen.

Wheel of Fortune *A Man Betrayed; Citadel of Crime* **1941** A shrewd small-town lawyer, working on a case in the big city, is forced to expose his girlfriend's father as a crooked politician. Strange to see the Duke here in the lead, but what the hey. Not great, but interesting. **83m/B VHS.** John Wayne, Frances Dee, Edward Ellis, Ward Bond, Wallace Ford; ***D:*** John H. Auer.

The Wheeler Dealers *Separate Beds* **1963** Garner plays a supposedly penniless investor (actually a Texas millionaire) who comes to New York stock analyst Remick for investment advice. Her shyster boss (Backus) tells her to sell the aw-shucks cowboy worthless stock which turns out to be worth a fortune. Zany spoof of Wall Street ethics. **100m/C VHS.** James Garner, Lee Remick, Jim Backus, Phil Harris, Shelley Berman, Chill Wills, John Astin, Louis Nye; ***D:*** Arthur Hiller.

Wheels of Fire *Vindicator* **1984 (R)** The earth is a wasteland controlled by sadistic highway hoodlums. When they kidnap the hero's sister, he fights back in a flame-throwing car. Horrible "Road Warrior" rip-off. **81m/C VHS.** Gary Watkins, Lynda Wiesmeier; ***D:*** Cirio H. Santiago.

Wheels of Terror **1990 (R)** Possessed black car stalks children in isolated village. Bus driver Cassidy gets behind the wheel of V-8 super-charged school bus to initiate most interminable chase scene in screen history. **86m/C VHS.** Joanna Cassidy, Marcie Leeds, Carlos Cervantes, Arlen Dean Snyder; ***D:*** Christopher Cain; ***C:*** Rick Bota; ***M:*** Jay Gruska.

When a Man Falls in the Forest *Desires of a Housewife* **2007 (R)** Three former high school classmates meet middle age. Architect Gary (Hutton) is disillusioned by his job and estranged from his equally depressed wife (Stone); Travis (Vince) still suffers the effects from a long-ago accident; and Bill (Baker), a janitor at Gary's office, listens to an instructional tape on lucid dreaming, imaging a life he will never have the nerve to live. It's all low-key and bleak. **86m/C DVD.** Timothy Hutton, Dylan Baker, Pruitt Taylor Vince, Sharon Stone, Nicholas Elia; ***D:*** Ryan Eslinger; ***W:*** Ryan Eslinger; ***C:*** Lawrence Sher; ***M:*** Billy Corgan, John Sereda.

When a Man Loves **1927** Adaptation of the novel "Manon Lescault" by Abbe Prevost. Chevalier Fabien des Grieux (Barrymore) rescues Manon (Costello) after her brother offers her to the Comte de Morfontaine (de Grasse) but she eventually returns to him because Manon likes what Morfontaine's wealth brings. When des Grieux reenters her life, he tries cheating at cards as a way to support them but that only gets Manon imprisoned on a convict ship. **112m/B DVD.** John Barrymore, Dolores Costello, Sam De Grasse, Warner Oland, Holmes Herbert, Stuart Holmes, Bertram Grassby; ***D:*** Alan Crosland; ***W:*** Bess Meredyth; ***C:*** Byron Haskin.

When a Man Loves a Woman 1/2 *To Have and to Hold; Significant Other* **1994 (R)** Time to get suspicious when song titles become film titles. Alice Green (Ryan) is the mother in a perfect little family, with a loving husband (Garcia), two little girls, and a satisfying career. She's also a closet alcoholic. Less about her alcoholism than the effect on her family and her hubby in particular, shown as a '90s sort of guy who allows Alice to keep her secret. Ryan's detox treatments and struggle back to sobriety are fertile ground for psycho-babble and 12-step cliches, but solid performances save this picture from drying out. **126m/C VHS, DVD.** Meg Ryan, Andy Garcia, Lauren Tom, Philip Seymour Hoffman, Tina Majorino, Mae Whitman, Ellen Burstyn, Eugene Roche, LaTanya Richardson Jackson; ***D:*** Luis Mandoki; ***W:*** Ronald Bass, Al Franken; ***C:*** Lajos Koltai; ***M:*** Zbigniew Preisner. Blockbuster '95: Drama Actress, V. (Ryan).

When a Man Rides Alone **1933** Tyler relieves trains of their gold shipments in order to reimburse swindled investors. Lovely Lacey frowns on his initiative, so he kidnaps her to keep her quiet. The two fall in love, and the man who rides alone works beside his beloved. **60m/B VHS.** Tom Tyler, Adele Lacey, Alan Bridge, Robert Burns, Frank Ball, Alma Chester, Bud Osborne; ***D:*** J(ohn) P(aterson) McGowan.

When a Man Sees Red 1/2 **1934** Jones is a ranch foreman whose new boss is Campbell (she inherited the property). The two argue constantly but then come to realize all the fighting is just hiding true love. **60m/B VHS.** Buck Jones, Peggy Campbell, Dorothy Revier, Syd Saylor, Leroy Mason, Charles French, Robert F. (Bob) Kortman; ***D:*** Alan James.

When a Man's a Man 1/2 *Saga of the West* **1935** Nick Gambert refuses to help out neighboring rancher Dean Baldwin when a landslide diverts the water from Baldwin's property onto his own. Larry Knight takes a job with Gambert so he can divert the water back but his plan is put in jeopardy. **60m/B DVD.** George O'Brien, Dorothy Wilson, Paul Kelly, Harry Woods, Jimmy Butler, Richard Carlyle; ***D:*** Edward Kline; ***W:*** Frank Mitchell, Agnes Christine Johnston; ***C:*** Frank B. Good.

When a Stranger Calls 1/2 **1979 (R)** Babysitter is terrorized by threatening phone calls and soon realizes that the calls are coming from within the house. Story was expanded from director Walton's short film "The Sitter." Distasteful and unlikely, though the first half or so is tight and terrifying. **97m/C VHS, DVD.** Carol Kane, Charles Durning, Colleen Dewhurst, Rachel Roberts, Rutanya Alda, Carmen Argenziano, Kirsten Larkin, Ron O'Neal, Tony Beckley; ***D:*** Fred Walton; ***W:*** Fred Walton, Steve Feke; ***C:*** Don Peterman.

When a Stranger Calls **2006 (PG-13)** The call is still coming from (gasp!) inside the house in this remake of the 1979 nail-biter, except the house is now a modern high-tech glass palace (strangely without caller ID though)—in the middle of nowhere, of course (because that's where most palaces are). The violence that marked the original is toned down to make it more teen-friendly. Unfortunately, so is the suspense. **100m/C DVD, UMD.** *US* Camilla Belle, Tommy Flanagan, Tessa Thompson, Brian Geraghty, Clark Gregg, Derek de Lint, David Denman, Madeleine Carroll, Kate Jennings Grant, Arthur Young, Steve Eastin, Katie Cassidy; ***D:*** Simon West; ***W:*** Jake Wade Wall; ***C:*** Peter Menzies Jr.; ***M:*** James Dooley; ***V:*** Lance Henriksen.

When a Stranger Calls Back 1/2 **1993 (R)** Sequel to "When a Stranger Calls" finds college student Julia Jenz (Schoelen) still trying to put her life together five years after a terrifying ordeal with a stalker. She turns to her advisor Jill (Kane), who went through a similar fate, but once Jill becomes involved she again becomes the pawn of a psychopath. It's up to retired detective John Clifford (Durning), who saved Jill before, to do his heroics once again. Scary opening sequence but suspense peters out toward the end. **94m/C VHS, DVD.** Carol Kane, Charles Durning, Jill Schoelen, Gene Lythgow, Karen Austin; ***D:*** Fred Walton; ***W:*** Fred Walton; ***C:*** David Geddes; ***M:*** Dana Kaproff. **CABLE**

When a Woman Ascends the Stairs *Onna Ga Kaidan O Agaru Toki* **1960** A young widow with an elderly mother and a useless brother supports them all by working as a Ginza bar hostess. As she approaches the perilous professional age of 30, Keiko must decide whether to open her own bar or marry once again. In Japanese with English subtitles. **110m/B VHS, DVD.** *JP* Hideko Takamine, Tatsuya Nakadai, Masayuki Mori; ***D:*** Mikio Naruse.

When Angels Fly **1982** In this emotional tale of love and murder, a young woman sets out to find the exact circumstances surrounding the mysterious death of her sister. **96m/C VHS.** *CA* Patricia Collins, David Gardner, Robert Hawkins, Joan Fowler, Jennifer Dale, Robin Ward; ***D:*** Jack Nixon-Browne; ***W:*** Mary Stuart; ***M:*** Brian Koonin. **TV**

When Brendan Met Trudy **2000** Irish romantic comedy by the writer of such standout novels as "The Commitments" and "The Snapper." Brendan (McDonald) is somewhat of a pansy-boy who attracts his polar opposite Trudy (Montgomery), a street-smart sort of girl and falls in love. Brendan, a straitlaced schoolteacher, soon learns that Trudy moonlights as a thief, and after the initial shock wears off, joins his outlaw honey in some good old-fashioned felonious fun. The true fun of the film, though, is its constant classic film references, such as when a misadventure lands Brendan in the gutter, he is reminded of William Holden in "Sunset Boulevard." Even if you're not a film buff, thought, you'll still enjoy this offbeat comic romp. **95m/C VHS, DVD.** *IR GB* Peter McDonald, Flora Montgomery, Marie Mullen, Pauline McLynn, Don Wycherley; ***D:*** Kieron J. Walsh; ***W:*** Roddy Doyle; ***C:*** Ashley Rowe; ***M:*** Richard Hartley.

When Danger Follows You Home 1/2 **1997 (PG-13)** Ann Werden (Williams), a psychologist at a county mental health facility, becomes interested in the case of a disturbed patient who calls himself Gogel, a computer genius with an FBI file. When Gogel mysteriously dies in Anne's home, she finds herself accused of manslaughter—and then her son is kidnapped. Anne's got a lot to figure out if she wants her life to go back to normal. **92m/C VHS.** JoBeth Williams, William Russ, Michael Manasseri, Vanessa King, Susan Hogan, Duncan Fraser, Nicolas Surovy; ***D:*** David Peckinpah; ***W:*** Sharon Elizabeth Doyle; ***C:*** Robert Hudececk; ***M:*** Charles Bernstein. **CABLE**

When Did You Last See Your Father? 1/2 **2007 (PG-13)** Blake (Firth) returns to the town where he was born to reconnect with his dying father (Broadbent), realizing it's too late to say the things he's wanted to say for so long. Told in episodes, with flashbacks to a past when the two would go camping together and dad was teaching son to drive. Director Tucker tells this sad story with lush landscape photography and a melodramatic score, often framing the characters in mirrors, as if they're only reflecting, and not truly there. It all works; it's just not very pleasant. **92m/C DVD.** Jim Broadbent, Colin Firth, Juliet Stevenson, Gina McKee, Matthew "Stymie" Beard, Sarah Lancashire, Elaine Cassidy, Claire Skinner; ***D:*** Anand Tucker; ***W:*** David Nicholls; ***C:*** Howard Atherton; ***M:*** Barrington Pheloung.

When Dinosaurs Ruled the Earth 1970 (G) When "One Million Years B.C." ruled the boxoffice the Brits cranked out a few more lively prehistoric fantasies. A sexy cavegirl, exiled because of her blond hair, acquires a cave-beau and a dinosaur guardian. Stop-motion animation from Jim Danforth, story by J.G. Ballard. Under the name Angela Dorian, Vetri was Playmate of the Year in 1968 (A.D.). **96m/C VHS.** *GB* Victoria Vetri, Robin Hawdon, Patrick Allen, Drewe Henley, Sean Caffrey, Magda Konopka, Imogen Hassall, Patrick Holt, Jan Rossini; ***D:*** Val Guest; ***W:*** Val Guest; ***C:*** Dick Bush.

When Do We Eat? 1/2 2005 (R) Stereotypical dysfunctional family comedy. The Stuckman family's Passover Seder doesn't go smoothly since no one seems to get along. Although patriarch Ira (Lerner) is feeling no pain after stoner son Zeke (Feldman) doses him with ecstasy. **86m/C DVD.** *US* Michael Lerner, Lesley Ann Warren, Ben Feldman, Jack Klugman, Shiri Appleby, Mili Avital, Meredith Scott Lynn, Adam Lamberg, Max Greenfield, Cynda Williams; ***D:*** Salvador Litvak; ***W:*** Salvador Litvak, Nina Davidovich; ***C:*** M. David Mullen; ***M:*** Mark Adler.

When Eight Bells Toll 1971 MacLean adapted his own adventure novel in which naval secret service agent Philip Calvert (Hopkins) discovers that millions in gold bullion is being stolen. He and agent Hunslett (Redgrave) travel to Scotland, posing as marine biologists; there they encounter hostile Scottish locals and a suspicious Greek tycoon, Skouras (Hawkins), who has a very attractive companion (Delon). Hawkins had lost his voice to throat cancer so his lines were dubbed by actor Charles Gray. **94m/C VHS, DVD.** *GB* Anthony Hopkins, Corin Redgrave, Jack Hawkins, Nathalie Delon, Robert Morley, Derek Bond, Ferdinand "Ferdy" Mayne, Maurice Roeves; ***D:*** Etienne Perier; ***W:*** Alistair MacLean; ***C:*** Arthur Ibbetson; ***M:*** Angela Morley.

When Every Day Was the Fourth of July 1/2 1978 A nine-year-old girl asks her father, a lawyer, to defend a mute handyman accused of murder, knowing this will bring on him the contempt of the community. Well handled, but see "To Kill a Mockingbird" first. Based on producer/director Curtis's childhood. Sequel: "The Long Days of Summer." **100m/C VHS.** Katy Kurtzman, Dean Jones, Louise Sorel, Harris Yulin, Chris Petersen, Geoffrey Lewis, Scott Brady, Henry Wilcoxon, Michael Pataki; ***D:*** Dan Curtis. **TV**

When Evil Calls 1/2 2006 (R) Well, don't answer! In this horror parody, a sleazy narrator (Pertwee) informs the audience of the consequences of a deadly text message circulating among high school students. The message grants the recipient's wish—to be popular, thin, beautiful, etc.—as long as the text gets passed on to two more students. Of course the wish is "granted" in the most gory (and often naked) way possible. Originally a 20-episode series made to be downloaded to a cell phone and then re-edited. **76m/C DVD.** *GB* Jennifer Lim, Dominique Pinon, Sean Pertwee, Sean Brosnan, Chris (Christopher) Barrie, Rick Warden, Chris Barrie; ***D:*** Johannes Roberts; ***W:*** Johannes Roberts; ***C:*** John Raggett; ***M:*** Alex Taylor. **VIDEO**

When Father Was Away on Business 1/2 *Otac na Sluzbenom Putu* 1985 (R) Set in 1950s Yugoslavia. A family must take care of itself when the father is sent to jail for philandering with a woman desired by a Communist Party offical. The moving story of the family's day-to-day survival is seen largely through the eyes of the father's six-year-old son, who believes dad is "away on business." In Yugoslavian with English subtitles. **144m/C VHS, DVD.** *YU* Moreno D'E Bartolli, Miki (Predrag) Manojlovic, Mirjana Karanovic; ***D:*** Emir Kusturica; ***W:*** Abdullah Sidran; ***C:*** Vilko Filac; ***M:*** Zoran Simjanovic. Cannes '85: Film.

When Gangland Strikes 1956 A country lawyer, blackmailed by the mob, tries to protect his family without caving in. Unexceptional remake of "Main Street Lawyer." **70m/B VHS.** Raymond Greenleaf, Marjie Millar, Anthony Caruso, Jack Perrin, John Hudson; ***D:*** R.G. Springsteen; ***M:*** Van Alexander.

When Good Ghouls Go Bad 1/2 2001 (PG) Twelve-year-old Danny has just moved to a new town where he discovers that because of a town curse no one is allowed to celebrate Halloween. So Danny teams up with his recently departed Uncle Fred (Lloyd) to drive away the prankster ghouls who have been causing all the mischief. Based on a story by R.L. Stine. **93m/C VHS, DVD.** Christopher Lloyd, Tom Amandes, Joe Pichler; ***D:*** Patrick Read Johnson; ***W:*** Patrick Read Johnson; ***C:*** Brian J. Breheny; ***M:*** Christopher Gordon. **TV**

When Harry Met Sally... 1989 (R) Romantic comedy follows the long relationship between two adults who try throughout the changes in their lives (and their mates) to remain platonic friends—and what happens when they don't. Wry and enjoyable script is enhanced by wonderful performances. Another directorial direct hit for "Meathead" Reiner, and a tour de force of comic screenwriting for Ephron, with improvisational help from Crystal. Great songs by Sinatra sound-alike Connick. **96m/C VHS, DVD.** Billy Crystal, Meg Ryan, Carrie Fisher, Bruno Kirby, Steven Ford, Lisa Jane Persky, Michelle Nicastro, Harley Jane Kozak, Tracy Reiner; ***D:*** Rob Reiner; ***W:*** Nora Ephron; ***C:*** Barry Sonnenfeld; ***M:*** Harry Connick Jr., Marc Shaiman. British Acad. '89: Orig. Screenplay.

When Hell Broke Loose 1/2 1958 Routine WWII actioner about a small-time crook (Bronson) who joins the Army, changes his ways because of the love of a good woman, and gets a chance to be a hero when he stumbles upon a Nazi assassination plot against General Eisenhower. **78m/B VHS.** Charles Bronson, Violet Rensing, Richard Jaeckel, Arvid Nelson, Robert Easton; ***D:*** Kenneth Crane; ***W:*** Oscar Brodney.

When Hell Was in Session 1982 In more than seven years as a prisoner of the Viet Cong, Holbrook is subjected to torture, starvation, and psychological warfare to break his will. Based on the true story of Navy Commander Jeremiah Denton. Painful and violent. **98m/C VHS.** Mako, Sab Shimono, Paul Mantee, Rod Browning, Richard Evans, James Hong, Tom Bower, Stephen Keep, Nicole Eggert, Pat Hingle, Hal Holbrook, Eva Marie Saint, Ronny Cox; ***D:*** Paul Krasny. **TV**

When He's Not a Stranger 1989 Lyn is a college freshman who goes to a campus party hosted by the football team. When Ron, the star quarterback, invites Lyn to his dorm room, the situation gets out of hand. Only Lyn calls it rape and Ron calls her a liar. Intense performances are a highlight of this well-done story. **100m/C VHS, DVD.** Annabeth Gish, John Terlesky, Kevin Dillon, Paul Dooley, Kim Meyers; ***D:*** John Gray. **TV**

When I Close My Eyes *Ko Zaprem Oci* 1993 First independent film from Slovenia is a thriller in which rural postal employee Ana uses one crime to cover another. When a motorcyclist robs the post office while Ana is working, she uses his crime to steal some money for herself. But then Ana becomes obsessed with the thief and decides to track him down. Slovenian with subtitles. **94m/C VHS, DVD.** Petra Govc, Mario Selih, Mira Sardo; ***D:*** Franci Slak; ***W:*** Franci Slak, Silvan Furlan; ***C:*** Sven Pepeonik.

When I Close My Eyes *Love Letter* 1995 (PG-13) After attending a memorial service for her fiance, Hiroko (Nakayama) discovers his high school yearbook and an old address. She impulsively writes a letter to the address and is shocked to receive a reply from a young woman, Itsuki (also played by Nakayama), who bears the same name as her dead lover and even went to high school with him. The two women begin to correspond, as Hiroko asks what Itsuki remembers about the young man (Kashiwabara), and the mock resentment/friendship the two maintained in school. Eventually, Hiroko decides to meet Itsuki in person, hoping that she can get over the past that haunts her. Japanese with subtitles. **116m/C VHS.** *JP* Miho Nakayama, Takashi Kashiwabara, Etsushi Toyokawa; ***D:*** Shunji Iwai; ***W:*** Shunji Iwai; ***C:*** Noboru Shinoda.

When I Find the Ocean 2006 (PG) It's 1965. Lily (Holly) is 12 and lives in Alabama with her mother Jenny (Redford) and her grandparents (Ladd, Majors). She's still heartbroken over her sailor father's disappearance at sea and is keeping secret the fact that her mother's new boyfriend Dean (Tyson) has been abusing her. Lily finally decides to escape to the ocean—in a rowboat—to feel closer to her father's memory. **104m/C DVD.** Amy Redford, Diane Ladd, Lee Majors, Richard Tyson, Graham Greene, Bernie Casey, David "Shark" Fralick, Lily Matland Holly; ***D:*** Tonya S. Holly; ***W:*** Tonya S. Holly; ***C:*** Mario DiLeo; ***M:*** Flavio Motalla.

When in Rome 2009 (PG-13) Unlucky in love, Beth Harper (Bell) travels to Rome to see her newlywed sister. She impulsively steals some coins from the city's magical fountain of love and must deal with the men who suddenly fall hopelessly in love with her in this chemistry-free romantic comedy. What little potential the flimsy premise contains is trampled by the terrible script, one-note characters, and utterly inept direction. The cast is left trying too hard for laughs that were never there to begin with. **91m/C DVD.** *US* Kristen Bell, Josh Duhamel, Will Arnett, Jon Heder, Anjelica Huston, Alexis Dziena, Kate Micucci, Bobby Moynihan; ***D:*** Mark Steven Johnson; ***W:*** David Diamond, David Weissman; ***C:*** John Bailey; ***M:*** Christopher Young.

When Justice Fails 1998 (R) Vigilante goes after rapists. **90m/C VHS, DVD.** Jeff Fahey, Marlee Matlin, Monique Mercure, Carl Marotte; ***D:*** Allan Goldstein; ***W:*** Tony Kayden; ***C:*** Barry Gravelle.

When Knights Were Bold 1/2 1936 An English nobleman living in India inherits a castle in his native land. Returning home, he is knocked unconscious by a falling suit of armor while trying to impress a young lady and dreams himself back to medieval days. Enjoyable comedy about that ubiquitous British class hierarchy. **55m/B VHS.** Fay Wray, Jack Buchanan, Martita Hunt; ***C:*** Frederick A. (Freddie) Young.

When Ladies Meet 1/2 *Strange Skirts* 1941 Entertaining story of a love quadrangle that features several of MGM's top stars of the '40s. In this remake of the 1933 film, Crawford plays a novelist and an early proponent of the women's liberation movement. She falls in love with her publisher (Marshall), who just happens to be married to Garson. Meanwhile, Taylor, who is in love with Crawford, attempts to show her that he isa more suitable match for her than Marshall, but Crawford has yet to catch on.The lengthy dialogue on women's rights is badly dated, but the real-life rivalry between Crawford and Garson adds a certain bite to their witty exchanges. **105m/B VHS.** Joan Crawford, Robert Taylor, Greer Garson, Herbert Marshall, Spring Byington; ***D:*** Robert Z. Leonard; ***W:*** Anita Loos, S.K. Lauren.

When Lightning Strikes WOOF! 1934 Lightning the Wonder Dog prevents the owner of a rival lumber company from stealing his master's land. He gets to use his talents of running, swimming, barking, and smoking cigars. Proves that real woofers were made way back when, even though in 1934 they didn't feature scantily clad babes. Part of Video Yesteryear's Golden Turkey series. **51m/B VHS.** Francis X. Bushman, Alice Dahl, William Desmond, J(ohn) P(aterson) McGowan; ***D:*** Burton King, Harry Revier.

When Love Comes 1998 Katie Keen (Owen) is a 40ish one-hit pop singer who decides to return home to New Zealand to rethink her fading career and life with her manager/lover Eddie (Westaway). Her best pal is still Stephen (Prast) who is involved with the younger Mark (O'Gorman), a songwriter. Mark's friends Fig (Brunning) and Sally (Hawthorne) have a band and ask Katie to sing on a recording. Everyone eventually winds up at Katie's seaside home trying to make potentially life-altering decisions. **94m/C DVD.** *NZ* Rena Owen, Dean O'Gorman, Simon Prast, Nancy Brunning, Simon Westaway, Sally Hawthorne; ***D:*** Garth Maxwell; ***W:*** Garth Maxwell, Peter Wells, Rex Pilgrim; ***C:*** Darryl Ward; ***M:*** Chris Anderton.

When Nature Calls WOOF! 1985 (R) A city family "gets back to nature" in this collection of mostly ineffective gags and poor satirical ideas. Probably your first and last chance to see Liddy and Mays on screen together. **76m/C VHS, DVD.** David Orange, Barbara Marineau, Nicky Beim, Tina Marie Staiano, Willie Mays, G. Gordon Liddy; ***D:*** Charles Kaufman.

When Night Is Falling 1995 (R) Camille (Bussieres) is a professor of mythology at a Calvinist college in Toronto and engaged to theologian Martin (Czerny). Vaguely unsatisfied, Camille meets Petra (Crawford), a trapeze artist in a traveling circus, gets drawn into her world, falls in love, and must decide what she wants from her life. Lots of yearning, romance, and fantasy. Lesbian lovemaking scenes caused a ratings problem (the MPAA originally deemed them worthy of NC-17). **96m/C VHS.** *CA* Pascale Bussieres, Rachael Crawford, Henry Czerny, David Fox, Don McKellar, Tracy Wright; ***D:*** Patricia Rozema; ***W:*** Patricia Rozema; ***C:*** Douglas Koch; ***M:*** Lesley Barber.

When Pigs Fly 1993 A story with two ghosts, a rocking chair, and a lonely, struggling musician. Lilly (Faithful) and young Ruthie (Bella) are the ghosts, who both happen to have died in the same rocking chair a century apart. The chair is now in the possession of down-and-out jazz musician Marty (Molina), who doesn't know how to react to his unworldly visitors. Whimsical but not cloying. **94m/C VHS.** Marianne Faithfull, Alfred Molina, Seymour Cassel, Rachael Bella; ***D:*** Sara Driver; ***W:*** Ray Dobbins; ***C:*** Robby Muller; ***M:*** Joe Strummer.

When Saturday Comes 1/2 1995 Feel-good working-class drama follows Sheffield-born Jimmy Muir (Bean), whose life revolves around a job in a brewery, the local pub, chasing girls, and playing football (soccer) on the weekends. He gets involved with co-worker Annie (Lloyd), whose Uncle Ken (Postlethwaite) coaches the local semi-pro team and who offers Jimmy a chance to play. His success leads to a trial with the pros, Sheffield United, which Jimmy blows by getting drunk. After losing his job, his girl, and having his brother die in an accident, Jimmy struggles to pull himself together, and maybe get a second chance. **97m/C VHS.** *GB* Sean Bean, Emily Lloyd, Pete Postlethwaite, John McEnery, Ann Bell, Craig Kelly; ***D:*** Maria Giese; ***W:*** Maria Giese; ***C:*** Gerry Fisher; ***M:*** Anne Dudley.

When Taekwondo Strikes 1983 (R) One brave Taekwondo master leads the Korean freedom fighters against the occupying army of WWII Japan. **95m/C VHS, DVD.** Jhoon Rhee, Ann Winton, Angela (Mao Ying) Mao, Huang Ing Sik; ***D:*** Raymond Chow.

When the Bough Breaks 1986 A psychologist helps the police with the case of a murder-suicide witnessed by a child. He finds one sick secret society at work in this unkinder, ungentler TV thriller, based on the novel by Jonathan Kellerman. Danson co-produced. **100m/C VHS, DVD.** Ted Danson, Richard Masur, Rachel Ticotin, David Huddleston, James Noble, Kim Miyori, Merritt Butrick; ***D:*** Waris Hussein.

When the Bough Breaks 1993 (R) A Texas police chief (Sheen) discovers seven severed hands and turns to a forensic expert (Walker) for help. But then the specialist discovers a psychic link between a mentally disturbed child and the serial killer. **103m/C VHS, DVD.** Ally Walker, Martin Sheen, Ron Perlman; ***D:*** Michael Cohn; ***W:*** Michael Cohn; ***C:*** Michael Bonvillain.

When the Bullet Hits the Bone 1996 (R) Particularly nasty vigilante flick as EMS doc Jack Davies (Wincott) decides to get even with a drug cartel, after being seriously wounded while trying to help drug-addicted hooker Lisa (Johnson) get away from her vicious pimp. **82m/C VHS.** Jeff Wincott, Michelle Johnson, Doug O'Keefe, Richard Fitzpatrick; *D:* Damian Lee; *W:* Damian Lee.

When the Cat's Away *Chacun Cherche Son Chat* **1996 (R)** Touching Gallic frolic finds introverted Parisian make-up artist face-to-face with adventure while searching for her lost cat. Chloe (Clavel) eventually comes out of her shell, as the search for little Gris-Gris brings her into contact with a wide variety of characters, some lonely, like herself, played by real people and real cats. Best non-actor kudos to Renee Le Calm as Madame Renee, the kooky neighborhood cat lady, with her network of cat fanciers acting as the reconnaissance party for the runaway feline. Director Klapisch's comedy also tackles weightier topics along the way, including lonliness, homelessness, racism, and the moderization of a city steeped with history. Stylishly spare with adept photography, seems almost semi-documentary. **91m/C VHS.** *FR* Garance Clavel, Zinedine Soualem, Olivier Py, Renee Le Calm, Romain Duris; *D:* Cedric Klapisch; *W:* Cedric Klapisch; *C:* Benoit Delhomme.

When the Clouds Roll By ½ **1919** Psycho-satire pits demented doctor against Fairbanks in experiment to make him suicidal basket case. Fairbanks seems to contract ferocious nightmares, passionate superstitions, a spurning lover, and a warrant for his arrest, none of which suppresses his penchant for acrobatics. **77m/B VHS.** Douglas Fairbanks Sr., Herbert Grimwood, Kathleen Clifford, Frank Campeau, Ralph Lewis, Daisy Robinson, Albert MacQuarrie; *D:* Victor Fleming.

When the Dark Man Calls ½ **1995 (R)** Shock ending and a strong lead performance by Van Ark enhance this cable mystery. Call-in radio shrink Julianne Kaiser (Van Ark) is stalked by ex-con Parmenter (Lewis). Twenty-five years ago she testified that he murdered her parents although the bitter man's always proclaimed his innocence. Now Kaiser is having grisly flashbacks to her childhood but can she figure out the truth before Parmenter kills her? Based on a novel by Stuart M. Kaminsky. **89m/C VHS.** Joan Van Ark, Geoffrey Lewis, Chris Sarandon, James Read, Frances Hyland, Janet-Laine Green; *D:* Nathaniel Gutman; *W:* Pablo F. Fenjves. **CABLE**

When the Greeks *Ton Kero Ton Hellinon* **1981** At the turn of the century, a rich young landowner is kidnapped by a group of nationalist bandits who demand a hefty ransom. But soon the young man realizes he's seeing his true Greek heritage for the first time and begins to identify with his captors. Greek with subtitles. **100m/C VHS.** *GR* Alexis Damianos, Kostas Arzoglou, George Sampanis, Stavros Mermighis; *D:* Lakis Papastathis; *W:* Lakis Papastathis; *M:* George Papadakis.

When the Last Sword is Drawn *Mibu gishi den* **2002** In the last days of the Tokugawa Shogunate a group of samurai known as the Shinsegumi remain loyal to the Shogun after the Emperor decides to modernize Japan by eliminating the Shogun and his samurai because he feels they are unnecessary, touching off a civil war. Told mostly in flashback it is the story of one misunderstood samurai and his friend caught in the middle between the countries current and former governments, and his tragic story. **143m/C DVD.** *JP* Kiichi Nakai, Koichi Sato, Yui Natsukawa, Takehiro Murata, Miki Nakatani, Yuji Miyake; *D:* Yojiro Takita; *W:* Takehiro Nakajima, Jiro Asada; *C:* Takashi Hamada; *M:* Joe Hisaishi.

When the Legends Die **1972 (PG)** A Ute Indian strives to preserve his heritage in an often harsh modern world. Recorded in hi-fi. **105m/C VHS.** Richard Widmark, Frederic Forrest; *D:* Stuart Millar.

When the Line Goes Through **1973** A drifter arrives in a small West Virginia town and changes the lives of two pretty sisters. **90m/C VHS.** Martin Sheen, Davey Davison, Beverly Washburn; *D:* Clyde Ware; *W:* Clyde Ware; *C:* Jackson Deerson; *M:* Lyle Ritz.

When the North Wind Blows **1974 (G)** An old, lone trapper hunts for and later befriends the majestic snow tiger of Siberia in the Alaskan wilderness. A good family film. **113m/C VHS.** Henry (Kleinbach) Brandon, Herbert Nelson, Dan Haggerty; *D:* Stewart Raffill.

When the Party's Over ½ **1991 (R)** Twenty-somethings share a southern California house and a hip—but ultimately empty—lifestyle. **114m/C VHS, DVD.** Rae Dawn Chong, Fisher Stevens, Elizabeth Berridge, Sandra Bullock, Brian McNamara, Kris Kamm; *D:* Matthew Irmas.

When the Screaming Stops **1973 (R)** A hunter is hired to find out who has been cutting the hearts out of young women who reside in a small village near the Rhine River. Turns out it's a she-monster who rules a kingdom beneath the river. Bad effects; gory gore; outlandish plot. All the ingredients, in other words, of a classic dog. **86m/C VHS.** *SP* Tony Kendall, Helga Line, Silvia Tortosa; *D:* Armando de Ossorio.

When the Sky Falls **1999** Gritty bio loosely focuses on the last years of crusading Dublin journalist Veronica Gerin, who was murdered in 1996. Sinead Hamilton (Allen) has angered Dublin politicians, the IRA, police, and crime bosses with her investigation into the city's drug scene. She ticks off bad guy Dave Hackett (Flynn) and even tough detective Mackey (Bergin) tries to warn her but threats only make Hamilton more determined to do her expose. **107m/C VHS, DVD.** *IR* Joan Allen, Patrick Bergin, Liam Cunningham, Gerard Flynn, Kevin McNally, Jimmy Smallhorne, Jason Barry, Pete Postlethwaite, Des McAleer, Ruaidhri Conroy; *D:* John MacKenzie; *W:* Michael J. Sheridan, Ronan Gallagher, Colum McCann; *C:* Seamus Deasy; *M:* Pol Brennan.

When the Time Comes **1991 (PG-13)** A woman dying of cancer wants to take her own life, but when her husband refuses, she seeks the help of a male friend. Excellent acting doesn't provide the needed depth. Less a disease-of-the-week TV movie, more of an ethical-dilemma-of-the-week, and just as trivial. **94m/C VHS.** Bonnie Bedelia, Brad Davis, Terry O'Quinn, Karen Austin, Donald Moffat, Wendy Schaal; *D:* John Erman; *M:* Marvin Hamlisch.

When the West Was Young ½ *Wild Horse Mesa* **1932** An outdoor adventure about rounding up horses in the Old West. Based on a novel by Zane Grey. **58m/B VHS, DVD.** Randolph Scott, Sally Blane, Guinn "Big Boy" Williams; *D:* Henry Hathaway.

When the Whales Came ½ **1989 (PG)** A conservationist fable about two children and a grizzled old codger living on a remote British isle during WWI. They try to avert disaster as mysterious narwhal whales descend on the island. Moralistic and uninvolving; poorly acted; slumber-inducing. Adapted from the novel by Morpugo. **100m/C VHS.** *GB* Paul Scofield, Helen Mirren, David Threlfall, David Suchet, Jeremy Kemp, Max Rennie, Helen Pearce, Barbara Jefford; *D:* Clive Rees; *W:* Michael Morpugo; *M:* Christopher Gunning, Ruth Rennie.

When the Wind Blows **1986** An animated feature about a retired British couple when their peaceful—and naive—life in the country is destroyed by nuclear war. Poignant, sad, and thought-provoking, and just a little scary. Features the voices of Ashcroft and Mills; Roger Waters, David Bowie, Squeeze, Genesis, Hugh Cornell, and Paul Hardcastle all contribute to the soundtrack. Based on the novel by Raymond Briggs. **80m/C VHS.** *GB D:* Jimmy T. Murakami; *V:* Peggy Ashcroft, John Mills.

When Thief Meets Thief ½ **1937** A cat burglar finds his world turned upside down when he begins to fall in love with one of his victims. Not much happening except a few nice stunts by Fairbanks. **85m/B VHS.** *GB* Douglas Fairbanks Jr., Valerie Hobson, Alan Hale, Jack Melford, Leo Genn, Ian Fleming; *D:* Raoul Walsh.

When Time Expires **1997 (PG-13)** Extraterrestrial scientist Travis Beck (Grieco) time travels from the future to present-day earth to stop the planet's destruction by evil forces. **93m/C VHS.** Richard Grieco, Cynthia Geary, Mark Hamill, Tim Thomerson, Chad Everett; *D:* David Bourla; *W:* David Bourla; *C:* Dean Lent; *M:* Todd Hayen. **CABLE**

When Time Ran Out **1980 (PG)** A volcano erupts on a remote Polynesian island covered with expensive hotels and tourists with no way to escape. Contains scenes not seen in the theatrically released print of the film. A very good cast is wasted in this compilation of disaster film cliches. **144m/C VHS.** Paul Newman, Jacqueline Bisset, William Holden, Ernest Borgnine, Edward Albert, Barbara Carrera, Valentina Cortese, Burgess Meredith, Noriyuki "Pat" Morita, Red Buttons; *D:* James Goldstone; *W:* Stirling Silliphant; *C:* Fred W. Koenekamp; *M:* Lalo Schifrin.

When Trumpets Fade ½ **1998 (R)** Private Manning (Eldard) is the only survivor of his platoon, which is caught in the Battle of the Hurtgen Forest along the Belgian-German border in 1944. Manning is interested in nothing more than his own survival but his skills attract the attention of an officer (Donovan) who promptly promotes him to sgt. (and soon, lieutenant) and gives him his own platoon of raw recruits to whip into shape. **93m/C VHS, DVD.** Ron Eldard, Zak Orth, Frank Whaley, Dylan Bruno, Martin Donovan, Timothy Olyphant, Dan Futterman, Dwight Yoakam, Devon Gummersall, Jeffrey Donovan; *D:* John Irvin; *W:* William W. Vought; *C:* Thomas Burstyn; *M:* Geoffrey Burgon. **CABLE**

When We Were Kings ½ **1996 (PG)** Chronicles the 1974 heavyweight championship fight, held in Zaire, between underdog Muhammad Ali and George Foreman. Gast uses original footage of the prefight hype as well as current interviews from George Plimpton and Norman Mailer (who covered the fight at the time) and Spike Lee. **94m/C VHS, DVD.** *D:* Leon Gast. Oscars '96: Feature Doc.; Broadcast Film Critics '96: Feature Doc.

When Will I Be Loved ½ **2004 (R)** Cynical, chilly wannabe thriller stars Campbell as wealthy dilettante Vera Barrie who's involved with a shady, sometimes violent street hustler named Ford (Weller). Needing money, Ford sells Vera's favors to a visiting Italian media mogul (Chianese), but manipulative Vera turns the tables by working out her own devious deal. Despite its brief length, film's rambling and semi-improvised dialogue and structure does the story no favors, although the city of New York is richly displayed. **81m/C DVD.** *US* Neve Campbell, Dominic Chianese, Frederick Weller, Karen Allen, Barry Primus, Abdullah Ibrahim, James Toback, Joelle Carter; *D:* James Toback; *W:* James Toback; *C:* Lawrence McConkey; *M:* Oli "Power" Grant.

When Willie Comes Marching Home **1950** An insightful (and funny) satire from Ford with equally well-done dramatic moments. William Kluggs (Dailey) wants to become a hero when he enlists, but instead he's assigned to be the gunnery instructor in his own hometown. A town joke, Bill finally gets his chance as a B-17 gunner but winds up being rescued by members of the French Resistance. After aiding them, he does become a hero but is sworn to secrecy by his superiors. Bill then has to endure more abuse from the folks at home until everything is revealed. **90m/C DVD.** Dan Dailey, William Demerest, Bill Calvert, Lloyd Corrigan, Colleen Townsend, James Lydon, Evelyn Varden; *D:* John Ford; *W:* Mary Loos, Richard Sale; *C:* Leo Tover; *M:* Alfred Newman.

When Wolves Cry ½ *The Christmas Tree* **1969 (G)** Tearjerker about an estranged father and young son reunited on a Corsican vacation. Their newfound joy sours when the lad is diagnosed with a fatal illness. Hardly one of Holden's best films. **108m/C VHS.** William Holden, Virna Lisi, Brook Fuller, Andre Bourvil; *D:* Terence Young.

When Women Had Tails ½ *Quando De Donne Avevando La Coda* **1970 (R)** A primitive comedy about prehistoric man's discovery of sex. And boy, did they ever discover it. Harmless (more or less), though not exactly cerebral. Followed by "When Women Lost Their Tails." **99m/C VHS.** *IT* Senta Berger, Frank Wolff; *D:* Pasquale Festa Campanile; *M:* Ennio Morricone.

When Women Lost Their Tails **1975 (R)** Ostensible sequel to "When Women Had Tails" about prehistoric cavemen and their sexual habits. **94m/C VHS, DVD.** *IT* Senta Berger; *D:* Pasquale Festa Campanile; *M:* Ennio Morricone.

When Worlds Collide ½ **1951 (G)** Another planet is found to be rushing inevitably towards earth, but a select group of people attempt to escape in a spaceship; others try to maneuver their way on board. Oscar-quality special effects and plot make up for cheesy acting and bad writing. **81m/C VHS, DVD.** Richard Derr, Barbara Rush, Larry Keating, Peter Hansen; *D:* Rudolph Mate; *W:* Sydney (Sidney) Boehm; *C:* William Howard Greene; *M:* Leith Stevens.

When Your Lover Leaves **1983** Alleged comedy about a woman, dumped by her married boyfriend, who gets involved in a short-lived relationship with a neighbor. When that also doesn't work out, she decides she must first do something to please herself. Here endeth the lesson. Produced by Fonzie and Richie of "Happy Days." **100m/C VHS.** Valerie Perrine, Betty Thomas, David Ackroyd, Ed O'Neill, Dwight Schultz, Shannon Wilcox; *D:* Jeff Bleckner; *M:* Randy Edelman. **TV**

When's Your Birthday? ½ **1937** Brown stars in this comedy about a prize-fighter who is working his way through astrology school with his fighting skills. The stars, in turn, tell him when to fight. Lame zaniness (what other kind is there?) meant as a vehicle for Brown, though Kennedy is funnier. The opening sequence, an animated cartoon showing the influence of the moon over the planets, was filmed in Technicolor. **77m/B VHS.** Joe E. Brown, Marian Marsh, Edgar Kennedy; *D:* Harry Beaumont.

Where **1990** Young man living in Budapest begins a psycho-sexual relationship with a young woman that explores the nature of domination and submission. After moving to Los Angeles, he subjects himself to the whims of a student. In English and Hungarian with subtitles. **?m/C VHS.** *HU* Miklos Acs, Dennis Cornell; *D:* Gabor Szabo; *C:* Nyika Jancso.

Where Angels Fear to Tread **1991 (PG)** Another turn-of-the-century tale of the English in Italy from the pen of E.M. Forster. Widowed, 40ish Lilia (Mirren) is urged by her stuffy in-laws to spend some time in Italy. Much to everyone's dismay she impulsively marries a 21-year-old Italian—with disastrous consequences. Based on Forster's first novel, the characters are more stereotypical and the story less defined than his later works and the movies made from them. Impressive performances and beautiful settings make up for a somewhat lackluster direction that isn't up to the standards set by the team of Merchant Ivory, responsible for the Forster films "A Room with a View" and "Howard's End." **112m/C VHS, DVD.** *GB* Rupert Graves, Helena Bonham Carter, Judy Davis, Helen Mirren, Giovanni Guidelli, Barbara Jefford, Thomas Wheatley, Sophie Kullman; *D:* Charles Sturridge; *W:* Charles Sturridge, Tim Sullivan, Derek Granger; *C:* Michael Coulter; *M:* Rachel Portman.

Where Angels Go, Trouble Follows ½ **1968** Follow-up to "The Trouble with Angels," with Russell reprising her role as the wise Mother Superior challenged by her mischief loving students. Younger, modern nun Stevens tries to convince Russell to update her old-fashioned ways and persuades her to take the convent students on a bus trip to a California peace rally. A very young Saint James is one of the convent's irrepressible troublemakers. Very dated but still mildly amusing. **94m/C VHS, DVD.** Rosalind Russell, Stella Stevens, Binnie Barnes, Mary Wickes, Susan St. James, Dolores Sutton, Alice Rawlings; *Cameos:* Milton Berle, Arthur Godfrey, Van Johnson, Robert Taylor; *D:* James Neilson; *W:* Blanche Hanalis.

Where Are the Children? ½ **1985 (R)** Based on Mary Higgins Clark's best-seller. A woman who was cleared of murdering the children from her first marriage remarries. Then the children from her second marriage are kidnapped. Sustains suspense completely, until it falls apart. **92m/C VHS.** Jill Clayburgh, Max Gail, Barnard Hughes, Clifton James, Harley Cross, Elisabeth Harnois, Elizabeth Wilson, Frederic Forrest; *D:* Bruce Malmuth.

Where Danger Lives 1950 Tough guy Mitchum plays a patsy. Young Dr. Jeff Cameron is intrigued when he treats beautiful Margo (Domergue), who attempted suicide. After Jeff gets all hot and bothered, he learns that the older man (a sneering Rains) he thought was her father, is actually her husband. During a boozy confrontation, the cuckold husband winds up dead, the doc gets a concussion, and Margo insists they have to make a run for the border. The French Domergue was a sultry, but not particularly talented, protege of Howard Hughes. **82m/B DVD.** Robert Mitchum, Faith Domergue, Claude Rains, Maureen O'Sullivan, Charles Kemper, Billy House, Philip Van Zandt, Ralph Duke; ***D:*** John Farrow; ***W:*** Charles Bennett; ***C:*** Nicholas Musuraca; ***M:*** Roy Webb.

Where Eagles Dare 1968 (PG) During WWII, a small group of Allied commandos must rescue an American general held by the Nazis in a castle in the Bavarian Alps. Relentless plot twists and action keep you breathless. Well-made suspense/adventure. Alistair MacLean adapted his original screenplay into a successful novel. **158m/C VHS, DVD.** *GB* Clint Eastwood, Richard Burton, Mary Ure, Michael Hordern, Anton Diffring, Ingrid Pitt, Patrick Wymark, Robert Beatty, Donald Houston, Derren Nesbitt, Ferdinand "Ferdy" Mayne, Peter Barkworth, William Squire, Neil McCarthy, Brook Williams, Vincent Ball; ***D:*** Brian G. Hutton; ***W:*** Alistair MacLean; ***C:*** Arthur Ibbetson; ***M:*** Ronald Goodwin.

Where East Is East 1/2 1929 In Indochina a badly scarred trapper (Chaney) lives with his daughter (Velez) and sells wild animals to circuses. Velez falls in love with a circus owner's son but finds out her own mother, seeking revenge on her ex-husband, trying to seduce the young man. A gorilla figures in the plot as well. Chaney's makeup, which contributed to his "Man of a Thousand Faces" nickname, highlights a contrived movie. **140m/B VHS.** Lon Chaney Sr., Lupe Velez, Estelle Taylor, Lloyd Hughes; ***D:*** Tod Browning.

Where God Left His Shoes 2007 Stabile's drama stacks the deck against his homeless boxer but, thanks to a strictly unsentimental performance by lead Leguizamo, refrains from schmaltz. Frank is a washed-up fighter who is forced into a New York homeless shelter with his family right before Christmas. He has a chance at low-income housing if Frank can quickly find a job but he's illiterate and has a criminal record that's further limiting his prospects. It's so real and awkward it can be hard to watch but worth the effort. **110m/C DVD.** Leonor Varela, David Castro, Samantha Rose, John Leguizamo; ***D:*** Salvatore Stabile; ***W:*** Salvatore Stabile; ***C:*** Vanja Cernjul; ***M:*** Jeff Beal.

Where Have All the People Gone? 1974 Solar explosion turns most of Earth's inhabitants to dust while the Anders family vacations in a cave. The family tries to return home amid the devastation. Bad timing, bad acting, bad script. **74m/C VHS.** Peter Graves, Kathleen Quinlan, Michael-James Wixted, George O'Hanlon Jr., Verna Bloom; ***D:*** John Llewellyn Moxey. **TV**

Where in the World Is Osama Bin Laden? 2006 (PG-13) Daddy-to-be Spurlock decides he needs to make the world safer for his first child by hunting down Osama bin Laden. Not quite serious documentary, not quite comedy, although it would benefit from picking a side and sticking with it. Surprisingly he's only assaulted once, in an Orthodox Jewish neighborhood in Israel. Apparently they didn't find him amusing. **90m/C DVD.** Morgan Spurlock, Alexandra Jamieson; ***D:*** Morgan Spurlock; ***W:*** Morgan Spurlock, Jeremy Chilnick; ***C:*** Daniel Marracino. **VIDEO**

Where Is My Child? 1/2 1937 Immigration to the New World brings only misfortune and betrayal in this tale of Jews in Eastern Europe between 1911 and 1937, as many experience the loss of family ties and religion. In Yiddish with English subtitles. **92m/B VHS.** Celia Adler, Anna Lillian, Morris Strassberg; ***D:*** Abraham Leff, Harry Lynn.

Where Is My Friend's House? *Where is the Friend's Home?; Khaneh-Je Doost Kojast?* 1987 At the village school, Mohamed is told by his teacher that he'll be expelled if he doesn't do his homework in the required exercise book. But that evening schoolmate Ahmed realizes he's taken Mohamed's book by mistake so he sets off to find his friend's house in a neighboring village. However, Ahmed gets lost and none of the adults he meets will help him. Farsi with subtitles. Followed by "Life and Nothing More..." and "Through the Olive Trees." **90m/C VHS, DVD.** *IA* Babek Ahmed Poor, Ahmed Ahmed Poor, Kheda Barech Defai; ***D:*** Abbas Kiarostami; ***W:*** Abbas Kiarostami; ***C:*** Farhad Saba.

Where Love Has Gone 1/2 1964 A soaper about a teenage daughter who kills her nympho mother's current boyfriend. Her divorced parents end up dragging the ordeal out in a murder trial/custody battle and a lot of family skeletons come out of their closets. Davis is the manipulative grand dame grandmother. Based on the novel by Harold Robbins. **114m/C VHS.** Bette Davis, Susan Hayward, Joey Heatherton, Jane Greer, George Macready; ***D:*** Edward Dmytryk; ***W:*** John Michael Hayes.

Where Sleeping Dogs Lie 1991 (R) A struggling writer moves into an abandoned California home five years after a wealthy family was murdered there. While doing research for his novel on their brutal killings, he revives their ghosts as well as the very real presence of their killer. **92m/C VHS, DVD.** Dylan McDermott, Tom Sizemore, Sharon Stone; ***D:*** Charles Finch.

Where the Boys Are 1/2 1960 Four college girls go to Fort Lauderdale to have fun and meet boys during their Easter vacation. Features the film debuts of Francis, who had a hit single with the film's title song, and Prentiss. Head and shoulders above the ludicrous '84 remake. **99m/C VHS, DVD.** George Hamilton, Jim Hutton, Yvette Mimieux, Connie Francis, Paula Prentiss, Dolores Hart, Frank Gorshin, Barbara Nichols, Rory Harrity, Chill Wills, Jack Kruschen; ***D:*** Henry Levin; ***W:*** George Wells; ***C:*** Robert J. Bronner; ***M:*** Pete Rugolo, Georgie Stoll.

Where the Boys Are '84 WOOF! 1984 (R) Horrible remake of the 1960 comedy still features girls searching for boys during spring break in Fort Lauderdale. Telling about its era: charm gives way to prurience. **95m/C VHS.** Lisa Hartman Black, Wendy Schaal, Lorna Luft, Lynn-Holly Johnson, Christopher McDonald; ***D:*** Hy Averback; ***W:*** Jeff Burkhart; ***C:*** James A. Contner; ***M:*** Sylvester Levay. Golden Raspberries '84: Worst Support. Actress (Johnson).

Where the Buffalo Roam 1/2 1980 (R) Early starring role for Murray as the legendary "gonzo" journalist Hunter S. Thompson. Meandering satire based on Thompson's books "Fear and Loathing in Las Vegas" and "Fear and Loathing on the Campaign Trail '72." Either confusing or offensively sloppy, depending on whether you've read Thompson. Music by Neil Young, thank goodness, or this might be a woof. **98m/C VHS, DVD.** Danny Goldman, Leonard Frey, Bill Murray, Peter Boyle, Susan Kellerman, Bruno Kirby, Rene Auberjonois, R.G. Armstrong, Rafael Campos, Craig T. Nelson; ***D:*** Art Linson; ***W:*** John Kaye; ***C:*** Tak Fujimoto; ***M:*** Neil Young.

Where the Bullets Fly 1966 Fast-paced Bond spoof. A British spy takes on the intelligence forces of several governments in his search for a new fuel elixir. Fun, if not scintillating. **88m/C VHS.** *GB* Tom Adams, Dawn Addams, Michael Ripper, Tim Barrett; ***D:*** John Gilling.

Where the Day Takes You 1/2 1992 (R) Runaways on Hollywood Boulevard are depicted in an unfortunately heavy-handed drama. King (Mulroney) is the slightly older leader of a group of street kids who tries to discourage his friends from getting involved in the violence and drugs they see all around them. He falls in love with new runaway Heather (Boyle) but their love is blighted by the relentless bleakness of their lives. Among the other members of King's "family" are Astin, as a young druggie in thrall to his older dealer (MacLachlan) and Getty, as a young hustler drawn to violence. The story's predictability undercuts some convincing acting. **105m/C VHS, DVD.** Dermot Mulroney, Lara Flynn Boyle, Balthazar Getty, Sean Astin, James LeGros, Ricki Lake, Kyle MacLachlan, Robert Knepper, Peter Dobson, Stephen Tobolowsky, Will Smith, Adam Baldwin, Christian Slater, Nancy McKeon, Alyssa Milano, David Arquette, Leo Rossi, Rachel Ticotin; ***D:*** Marc Rocco; ***W:*** Michael Hitchcock, Kurt Voss, Marc Rocco; ***M:*** Mark Morgan; ***V:*** Laura San Giacomo.

Where the Eagle Flies *Pickup on 101* 1972 (PG) Ersatz '60s rock 'n' roll road movie shuffles together free spirited college coed, hobo with heart of gold, and rock and roller who's making a lane change out of the fast track. **93m/C VHS.** Jack Albertson, Lesley Ann Warren, Martin Sheen, Michael Ontkean; ***D:*** John Florea.

Where the Green Ants Dream 1/2 *Wo Die Grunen Ameisen Traumen* 1984 A mining excavation in the Outback is halted by Aborigines who declare ownership of the sacred place where the mythical green ants are buried. A minor entry in the Herzog vision of modern-versus-primal civilization. Too obvious and somehow unsure of itself artistically. **99m/C VHS, DVD.** *GE* Bruce Spence, Wandjuk Marika, Roy Marika, Ray Barrett, Norman Kaye, Colleen Clifford; ***D:*** Werner Herzog.

Where the Heart Is 1990 (R) Wealthy dad Coleman kicks his spoiled kids out on the streets to teach them the value of money. Meant as farce with a message. Flops in a big way; one senses it should have been much better. **111m/C VHS, DVD.** Dabney Coleman, Uma Thurman, Joanna Cassidy, Suzy Amis, Crispin Glover, Christopher Plummer, David Hewlett, Maury Chaykin, Dylan Walsh, Ken Pogue, Sheila Kelley, Robbie Coltrane; ***D:*** John Boorman; ***W:*** John Boorman, Telsche Boorman; ***C:*** Peter Suschitzky; ***M:*** Peter Martin. Natl. Soc. Film Critics '90: Cinematog.

Where the Heart Is *Home Is Where the Heart Is* 2000 (PG-13) Pregnant 17-year-old Novalee Nation (Portman) is on her way to California with her no-good boyfriend Willy Jack (Bruno), who abandons her at an Oklahoma WalMart. Without friends or funds, Novalee hides out in the store until she gives birth there. Suddenly a local celeb, Novalee finds shelter with eccentric Sister Husband (Channing) and becomes best pals with fecund single mom, Lexi (Judd). Novalee also gets a potential romance with shy librarian Forney (Frain). Superficially one-note sap and Portman seems miscast. Based on the novel by Billie Letts. **115m/C VHS, DVD.** Natalie Portman, Ashley Judd, Stockard Channing, James Frain, Dylan Bruno, Joan Cusack, Keith David, Richard Jones, Sally Field; ***D:*** Matt Williams; ***W:*** Lowell Ganz, Babaloo Mandel; ***C:*** Richard Greatrex; ***M:*** Mason Daring.

Where the Hot Wind Blows *La Legge; La Loi; The Law* 1959 Marietta (Lollobrigida) is a poor girl in a Sicilian fishing village who's in love with Enrico (Mastroianni), an equally impoverished engineer. But she comes up with a unique way to get money for her dowry even as she's pursued by every male in town. Meanwhile, local mobster Brigante (Montand) wants to make sure than his son Francisco (Mattioli) doesn't get too involved with the unsuitable Lucrezia (Mercouri). Italian with subtitles. **120m/B VHS, DVD.** *FR IT* Gina Lollobrigida, Marcello Mastroianni, Yves Montand, Melina Mercouri, Raf Mattioli, Pierre Brasseur, Paolo Stoppa; ***D:*** Jules Dassin; ***W:*** Jules Dassin, Francoise Giroud; ***C:*** Otello Martelli; ***M:*** Roman Vlad.

Where the Lilies Bloom 1974 (G) The touching story of four backwoods children who are left orphans when their father dies. They don't report his death to authorities, because they are afraid the family will be separated and sent to an orphanage. Stanton is great as the crusty landlord the children gradually accept as a friend. Based on the book by Vera and Bill Cleaver. **96m/C VHS.** Julie Gholson, Jan Smithers, Matthew Burrill, Helen Harmon, Harry Dean Stanton, Rance Howard, Sudie Bond, Tom Spratley, Helen Bragdon, Alice Beardsley; ***D:*** William A. Graham.

Where the Money Is 1/2 2000 (PG-13) Famed bank robber Henry (Newman) fakes a stroke so he can get transferred from prison to a nursing home. Carol (Fiorentino) is the bored former prom queen nurse who knows he's faking and enlists his help in pulling one more job. She also brings along dull but devoted hubby Wayne (Mulroney). The characters, and the superb actors playing them, are the main reasons to see this one. Newman is still more charismatic than 90% of the leading men around, while Fiorentino and Mulroney seem inspired just by being on the same set with him. The lightweight script depends heavily on the audience's knowledge of Newman's filmography and the standard caper comedy conventions, but still manages to entertain. **90m/C VHS, DVD.** Paul Newman, Linda Fiorentino, Dermot Mulroney, Susan Barnes, Bruce MacVittie, Dorothy Gordon, Anne Pitoniak, Irma St. Paule; ***D:*** Marek Kanievska; ***W:*** E. Max Frye, Topper Lilien, Carroll Cartwright; ***C:*** Thomas Burstyn; ***M:*** Mark Isham.

Where the North Begins 1947 A Mountie ransacks the Canadian countryside in search of crime. **41m/B VHS.** Russell Hayden, Jennifer Holt, Tristram Coffin, Denver Pyle, Steve Barclay; ***D:*** Howard Bretherton; ***W:*** Betty Burbridge.

Where the Red Fern Grows 1/2 1974 (G) A young boy in Dust Bowl-era Oklahoma learns maturity from his love and responsibility for two Redbone hounds. Well produced, but tends to be hokey; good family fare. Followed by a sequel nearly 20 years later. **97m/C VHS, DVD.** James Whitmore, Beverly Garland, Jack Ging, Lonny (Lonnie) Chapman, Stewart Petersen; ***D:*** Norman Tokar; ***W:*** Douglas Day Stewart, Eleanor Lamb; ***C:*** Dean Cundey; ***M:*** Lex de Azevedo.

Where the Red Fern Grows: Part 2 1/2 1992 (G) Sequel to one of the most popular family movies of all time starring Brimley as Grandpa Coleman. Set deep in the Louisiana woods, this magical coming of age tale will touch the hearts of young and old viewers alike. **105m/C VHS, DVD.** Wilford Brimley, Doug McKeon, Lisa Whelchel, Chad McQueen; ***D:*** Jim McCullough Sr.; ***W:*** Samuel Bradford; ***C:*** Joseph M. Wilcots; ***M:*** Robert Sprayberry.

Where the River Runs Black 1986 (PG) An orphaned Indian child is raised in the Brazilian jungles by river dolphins. He is eventually befriended by a kindly priest who brings him into the modern world of violence and corruption. Slow pace is okay until the boy arrives at the orphanage, at which point the dolphin premise sadly falls by the wayside. **96m/C VHS.** Charles Durning, Peter Horton, Ajay Naidu, Conchata Ferrell, Alessandro Rabelo, Castulo Guerra; ***D:*** Christopher Cain; ***C:*** Juan Ruiz-Anchia; ***M:*** James Horner.

Where the Rivers Flow North 1/2 1994 (PG-13) Vermont logger Noel Lord (Torn) has lived on the land all his life and doesn't want to sell out to the power company. His blunt-talking Indian housekeeper/lover Bangor (Cardinal) knows it's best to take the money and move on. Set in 1927 and adapted from the novella by Howard Frank Mosher. Flat storytelling with a good performance by Cardinal. **104m/C VHS, DVD.** Rip Torn, Tantoo Cardinal, Bill Raymond, Mark Margolis, John Griesemer, Amy Wright, Dennis Mientka, Jusef Bulos, Michael J. Fox, Treat Williams; ***D:*** Jay Craven; ***W:*** Jay Craven, Don Bredes; ***C:*** Paul Ryan.

Where the Sidewalk Ends 1/2 1950 Preminger and Hecht are credited with developing the character of the rogue cop/detective who uses violence to get justice. The son of a career criminal, detective Mark Dixon (Andrews) is over-zealous in his pursuit of bad guys. He accidentally beats to death gambler/murder suspect Ken Paine (Stevens) while trying to put away mob boss Tommy Scalise (Merrill). Dixon attempts to make the death look like a mob hit but innocent cabbie Taylor (Tully) becomes the prime suspect because his daughter Morgan (Tierney) was married to the louse. Dixon falls for the widow and tries to clear her pop while still wanting to nail Scalise. **94m/B DVD.** Dana Andrews, Gene Tierney, Gary Merrill, Bert Freed, Tom Tully, Karl Malden, Craig Stevens, Ruth Donnelly, Robert F. Simon; ***D:*** Otto Preminger; ***W:*** Ben Hecht; ***C:*** Joseph LaShelle; ***M:*** Cyril Mockridge.

Where the Spirit Lives 1/2 1989 (PG) Native children kidnapped by Canadian government agents are forced to live in dreadful boarding schools where they are abused emotionally and physically. St. John is a new arrival who refuses to put up with it and tries to escape. Engrossing and moving. **97m/C VHS.** *CA* Kim Fox, Marianne Jones, Gus Chief Moon, Clayton Julian, Michelle St. John; *D:* Bruce Pittman; *W:* Keith Ross Leckie; *C:* Rene Ohashi; *M:* Buffy Sainte-Marie.

Where the Truth Lies 🦴🦴 ½ **1999** Dana Sue Lacey (Matlin) is the deaf campaign manager for a candidate who has just been murdered. When she becomes the prime suspect and goes to trial, attorney Lillian Rose Martin (King) has her work cut out for her since Dana refuses to cooperate. But the past and its secrets cannot stay hidden any longer. **92m/C VHS, DVD.** Marlee Matlin, Regina King, Philip Lester, Robert Blanche, Linden Ashby, Brian McNamara, Susan Walters; *D:* Nelson McCormick; *W:* Marshall Goldberg; *C:* Bill Roe; *M:* Peter Manning Robinson. **CABLE**

Where the Truth Lies 🦴🦴 **2005** Lanny (Bacon) and Vince (Firth) were a successful '50s showbiz duo (think Martin & Lewis) whose act broke up in 1957 over a sensational scandal involving a dead blonde (Blanchard) in a bathtub. Fifteen years later, ambitious and nubile blonde journalist Karen (a miscast Lohman) is trying to write Vince's bio and wants to know what really happened. Except truth is a subjective idea at best and the men still prefer their secrets to remain that way. A menage a trois scene upset the MPAA so director Egoyan released his voyeuristic noir drama unrated. Adapted from the novel by Rupert Holmes. **107m/C DVD.** *US CA GB* Kevin Bacon, Colin Firth, Alison Lohman, Rachel Blanchard, David Hayman, Maury Chaykin, Kristin Adams, Sonja Bennett, Deborah Grover, Beau Starr; *D:* Atom Egoyan; *W:* Atom Egoyan; *C:* Paul Sarossy; *M:* Mychael Danna.

Where the Wild Things Are 🦴🦴 **2009 (PG)** You have to wonder who writer/director Jonze's audience is truly meant to be since the pic's anarchic sophistication seems geared to adults who grew up with Maurice Sendak's 1963 picture book, although children will see the appeal of Max's own wild behavior and facing their fears. Having tested his frazzled single mom's (Keener) patience once too often, tantrum-throwing Max (newcomer Records) is sent to his room. Instead, wearing his white wolf costume, Max runs outside, boards a boat, and makes his way to the island where the Wild Things (who now have names and distinctive personalities) live. They crown Max their ruler but there are lots of parallels to the world—and troubles—Max left behind. The Wild Things, as created by Jim Henson's Creature Shop, are particularly amazing. **101m/C DVD.** *US* Catherine Keener, James Gandolfini, Paul Franklin Dano, Max Records; *D:* Spike Jonze; *W:* Spike Jonze, Dave Eggers; *C:* Lance Acord; *M:* Carter Burwell; *V:* Forest Whitaker, Catherine O'Hara, Tom Noonan, Lauren Ambrose.

Where There's a Will 🦴 ½ **1955** Mild comedy about a Cockney family that inherits a rundown Devon farm. Alfie (Dwyer), aided by housekeeper Annie (Harrison), is determined to rebuild and make a go of the property despite the reluctance of the rest of his family who want to return to London. **79m/B DVD.** *GB* Leslie Dwyer, Kathleen Harrison, George Cole, Thelma Ruby, Ann Hanslip, Dandy Nichols; *D:* Vernon Sewell; *W:* Vernon Sewell, R.F. Delderfield; *C:* Basil Emmott; *M:* Robert Sharples.

Where There's Life 🦴🦴 ½ **1947** Wisecracking Hope is a New York DJ about to be married to Marshe when he discovers he's the heir to the kingdom of Borovia (whose last king was assassinated). Hasso works her feminine wiles as the general who's guarding Hope when the assassins come after him. Oh, and Marshe and her cop brother Bendix are tracking him down to go through with the wedding ceremony. Frantic antics. **75m/B VHS, DVD.** Bob Hope, Signe Hasso, William Bendix, Vera Marshe, George Coulouris, George Zucco, Dennis Hoey, John Alexander; *D:* Sidney Lanfield; *W:* Melville Shavelson, Allen Boretz.

Where Time Began 🦴🦴 **1977 (G)** The discovery of a strange manuscript of a scientist's journey to the center of the earth leads to the decision to re-create the dangerous mission. Based on Jules Verne's classic novel "Journey to the Center of the Earth," but not anywhere near as fun or stirring. **87m/C VHS, DVD.** Kenneth More, Pep Munne, Jack Taylor; *D:* J(uan) Piquer Simon.

Where Trails Divide 🦴 ½ **1937** Keene is a U.S. Marshal who poses as a lawyer to bring a gang of thieves to justice. Lacks action. **54m/B VHS, DVD.** Tom Keene, Eleanor Stewart, Warner Richmond, David Sharpe, Charles French, Hal Price, Bud Osborne; *D:* Robert North Bradbury.

Where Trails End 🦴🦴 **1942** Novel sci-fi western set during WWII with just about everything, including phosphorescent-clothed good guys, Nazis, scoundrels, literate horses, and Gallic sidekicks. Interestingly different. **54m/B VHS.** Tom Keene, Joan Curtis, Charles "Blackie" King; *D:* Robert Emmett Tansey.

Where Truth Lies 🦴🦴 **1996 (R)** After a severe breakdown, troubled psychiatrist Ian Lazarre (Savage) is sent to a clinic run by the sinister Dr. Renquist (McDowell). Lazarre's given an experimental drug that causes him to have visions of executed serial killer Jonas Keller (Forrest) and also to develop ESP. The plot doesn't make much sense in any case. **92m/C VHS, DVD.** John Savage, Kim Cattrall, Malcolm McDowell, Sam Jones, Eric Pierpoint, Candice Daly, Dennis Forrest; *D:* William H. Molina; *W:* Ted Perkins; *C:* William H. Molina; *M:* David Wurst, Eric Wurst.

Where Were You When the Lights Went Out? 🦴 ½ **1968 (PG)** A complicated, unsuccessful farce about a retiring Broadway actress, her jealous, possibly philandering husband, her greedy agent, an embezzler, and a citywide blackout. Film was actually not based on the 1965 New York City blackout but on a French play, "Monsieur Masure" by Claude Magnier, which was written nine years before. **94m/C VHS.** Doris Day, Patrick O'Neal, Robert Morse, Terry-Thomas, Lola Albright, Steve Allen, Jim Backus, Ben Blue, Pat Paulsen; *D:* Hy Averback.

Where's Marlowe? 🦴🦴 **1998 (R)** Sendup of both indie filming and the private eye genre in a b&w and color combo. NYU film school grads Crawley (Def) and Edison (Livingston) decide to make a documentary about private investigators and choose nearly bankrupt L.A. detectives Boone (Ferrer) and Murphy (Slattery) as their subjects. The dicks latest case seems to involve a wife, a mistress, and, soon, Murphy's demise and the two film students decide to lend a more active hand in solving the case. **99m/C VHS, DVD.** Miguel Ferrer, John Slattery, John Livingston, Mos Def, Allison Dean, Clayton Rohner, Barbara Howard, Elizabeth Schofield; *D:* Daniel Pyne; *W:* Daniel Pyne, John Mankiewicz; *C:* Greg Gardiner; *M:* Michael Convertino.

Where's Piccone 🦴🦴🦴 **1984** A woman attempts, with the assistance of a two-bit hustler, to locate her missing husband, only to discover that he has led a double life in the Neapolitan underworld. Giannini as the sleazy hubby is perfectly cast. On-target social and political satire. In Italian with English subtitles. **110m/C VHS.** *IT* Giancarlo Giannini, Lina Sastri, Aldo Guiffre, Clelia Rondinelli; *D:* Nanni Loy.

Where's Poppa? 🦴🦴🦴 *Going Ape* **1970** A Jewish lawyer's senile mother constantly ruins his love life, and he considers various means of getting rid of her, including dressing up as an ape to scare her to death. Filled with outlandish and often tasteless humor, befitting its reign as a black comedy cult classic. Adapted by Robert Klane from his novel. **84m/C VHS, DVD.** George Segal, Ruth Gordon, Trish Van Devere, Ron Leibman, Rae Allen, Vincent Gardenia, Barnard Hughes, Paul Sorvino, Rob Reiner, Garrett Morris; *D:* Carl Reiner; *W:* Robert Klane; *C:* Jack Priestley; *M:* Jack Elliott.

Where's the Money, Noreen? 🦴🦴 ½ **1995 (PG-13)** Noreen's (Phillips) out on parole and trailed by the police who believe she knows the whereabouts of the $3 million she helped to steal 12 years before. **93m/C VHS.** Julianne Phillips, A. Martinez, Nigel Bennett, Colm Feore; *D:* Artie Mandelberg; *W:* Carla Jean Wagner; *C:* Brenton Spencer; *M:* Richard Bellis. **CABLE**

Where's Willie? 1977 (G) Willie is a very bright boy; perhaps a little too bright. When he reveals his latest invention to the folks in his small town, everyone is out to get him. **91m/C VHS.** Guy Madison, Henry Darrow, Kate Woodville, Marc Gilpin; *D:* John Florea.

Which Way Home 🦴🦴 **1990** A Red Cross nurse attempts to flee Cambodia with four young orphans. An Australian smuggler befriends and helps her. Way too long and wandering, though like many a TV movie, it means well. **141m/C VHS.** Cybill Shepherd, John Waters, Peta Toppano, John Ewart, Ruben Santiago-Hudson, Marc Gray; *D:* Carl Schultz; *W:* Michael Lawrence.

Which Way Home 2009 Cammisa's documentary looks primarily at the freight train journey of four migrant children—two from Honduras and two from Mexico—who are trying to illegally enter the United States. English and Spanish with subtitles. **90m/C DVD.** *D:* Rebecca Cammisa; *C:* Rebecca Cammisa, Lorenzo Hagerman, Eric Goethals; *M:* James Lavino.

Which Way Is Up? 🦴🦴 ½ **1977 (R)** Pryor plays three roles in this story of an orange picker who accidentally becomes a union hero. He leaves his wife and family at home while he seeks work in Los Angeles. There he finds himself a new woman, starts a new family, and sells out to the capitalists. American version of the Italian comedy "The Seduction of Mimi" tries with mixed success for laughs. Pryor as a dirty old man is the high point. **94m/C VHS, DVD.** Richard Pryor, Lonette McKee, Margaret Avery, Morgan Woodward, Marilyn Coleman; *D:* Michael A. Schultz; *W:* Carl Gottlieb; *C:* John A. Alonzo.

Which Way to the Front? 🦴 ½ **1970 (G)** Assorted Army rejects form a guerilla band and wage their own small-scale war during WWII. **96m/C VHS.** Jerry Lewis, Jan Murray, George L. Baxt, Steve Franken; *D:* Jerry Lewis; *W:* Dee Caruso.

Whiffs 🦴 **1975 (PG)** A gullible man plays guinea pig in an Army experiment on germ warfare which leaves him with the intellect of a chimpanzee. Naturally, he then devises a plan to use the volatile gas in a chain of bank robberies. The title is appropriate—this movie is a stinker. **91m/C VHS.** Elliott Gould, Eddie Albert, Harry Guardino, Godfrey Cambridge, Jennifer O'Neill, Alan Manson; *D:* Ted Post; *W:* Malcolm Marmorstein.

While I Live 🦴 ½ **1947** Woman meets female pianist with uncanny resemblance to sister who's been dead 25 years and rethinks her position on reincarnation. **85m/B VHS.** *GB* Tom Walls, Clifford Evans, Carole Raye, Patricia Burke, Sonia Dresdel, John Warwick; *D:* John Harlow; *C:* Frederick A. (Freddie) Young.

While She Was Out 🦴 **2008 (R)** Dopey woman-in-jeopardy flick. Abused wife Della (Basinger) heads to the mall on Christmas Eve and attracts the unwanted attention of four teen sociopaths. She finds herself running to a deserted construction site with a toolbox and a desire to kick some male tail. **88m/C DVD.** Kim Basinger, Lukas Haas, Craig Sheffer, Jamie Starr, Leonard Wu, Luis Chavez; *D:* Susan Montford; *W:* Susan Montford; *C:* Steve Gainer; *M:* Paul Haslinger.

While the City Sleeps 🦴🦴🦴 **1956** Three newspaper reporters vie to crack the case of a sex murderer known as "The Lipstick Killer" with the editorship of their paper the prize. Good thriller-plus with the emphasis on the reporters' ruthless methods of gaining information rather than on the killer's motivations. Lang's last big success. Based on "The Bloody Spur" by Charles Einstein. **100m/B VHS.** Dana Andrews, Rhonda Fleming, George Sanders, Howard Duff, Thomas Mitchell, Ida Lupino, Vincent Price, Mae Marsh; *D:* Fritz Lang; *C:* Ernest Laszlo.

While You Were Sleeping 🦴🦴🦴 **1995 (PG)** Feel-good romantic comedy finds lonely Lucy Moderatz (Bullock) collecting tokens for the Chicago train system and admiring Yuppie lawyer Peter Callaghan (Gallagher) as he commutes to and fro. Fate conspires to throw them together when Lucy rescues Peter after a mugging. Trouble is, he's not conscious so Lucy goes to the hospital with him, where she's mistaken for his fiancee. She continues the charade and is warmly welcomed by the Callaghan family, with the exception of Peter's brother, Jack (Pullman), who smells a rat even as he falls under the token collector's spell. Meanwhile, Peter remains in a coma, allowing Jack and Lucy to supply romantic comedy. Gallagher brings a serenity to his role as the unconscious Peter, while Bullock and Pullman take the predictable plot and deliver performances that earn them another notch on the climb to stardom. **103m/C VHS, DVD.** Sandra Bullock, Bill Pullman, Peter Gallagher, Jack Warden, Peter Boyle, Glynis Johns, Micole Mercurio, Jason Bernard, Michael Rispoli, Ally Walker, Monica Keena; *D:* Jon Turteltaub; *W:* Fred Lebow, Daniel G. Sullivan; *C:* Phedon Papamichael; *M:* Randy Edelman. Blockbuster '96: Comedy Actress, V. (Bullock), Comedy Actress, T. (Bullock).

The Whip and the Body 🦴🦴 ½ *Night Is the Phantom; What* **1963** Mario Bava's 19th-century ghost/love/revenge story makes a belated arrival on home video. Nevena (Lavi) is about to be married when her ex-lover Kurt (Lee), soon to be her brother-in-law, shows up. The rest of the action is almost pure Gothic with a moody castle for setting, secret passages, ladies wandering the hallways late at night in their diaphanous gowns. Though the story doesn't quite live up to the title, it is very sexually charged for its time and Lee turns in an aggressive performance. **88m/C DVD.** *IT* Christopher Lee, Daliah Lavi, Tony Kendall, Harriet Medin, Isli Oberon; *D:* Mario Bava; *W:* Ernesto Gastaldi, Ugo Guerra, Luciano Martino; *C:* Ubaldo Terzano; *M:* Carlo Rustichelli.

Whip It 🦴🦴🦴 **2009 (PG-13)** Desperate to break from the clutches of her controlling mom (Harden) and her small-town Texas beauty pageant life, misfit teen Bliss (Page) is drawn to all-girls roller derby. After secretly joining the Hurl Scouts team in nearby Austin, she quickly becomes a crowd favorite as Babe Ruthless. Adapted by Cross from her 2007 novel "Derby Girl," this coming-of-age story might not be unique but is dipped in the delicious roller derby culture where girls rule. And not only did Barrymore craft an engaging female-power action comedy for her directorial debut, but she also dons some skates as tough chick Smashley Simpson—a particular treat is seeing her and Page do much of their own skating. **111m/C DVD.** *US* Ellen Page, Kristen Wiig, Juliette Lewis, Eve, Zoe Bell, Alia Shawkat, Ari Graynor, Sydney Bennett, Marcia Gay Harden, Daniel Stern, Jimmy Fallon, Drew Barrymore; *D:* Drew Barrymore; *W:* Shauna Cross; *C:* Robert Yeoman; *M:* The Section Quartet.

Whipped 🦴 **2000 (R)** It's probably aiming for sophisticated, adult romantic comedy but all it achieves is smut. Sexpot Mia (Peet) is forced to deal with the arrested development of three Manhattan yuppies (Van Holt, Domke, Abrahams) who have prehistoric attitudes towards women. They all discover they are dating her but none wants to give Mia up and they become rivals for her questionable affections. Very unlikeable characters; very unpleasant. **82m/C VHS, DVD.** Amanda Peet, Brian Van Holt, Judah Domke, Zorie Barber, Jonathan Abrahams, Callie (Calliope) Thorne; *D:* Peter M. Cohen; *W:* Peter M. Cohen; *C:* Peter B. Kowalsk; *M:* Michael Montes.

Whipsaw 🦴🦴 ½ **1935** Vivian (Loy), Ed (Stephens), and Harry (Clement) are jewel thieves who make their way from Paris to New York with stolen pearls. Vivian meets Ross (Tracy), who's trying to pass himself off as a crook but Vivian soon figures out he's a G-man. Still, he comes in handy when Vivian skips out on her partners—only to be followed cross-country by a rival gang after the goods. Loy is lovely and Tracy does right by her as the hero who falls for the shady dame. **88m/B DVD.** Myrna Loy, Spencer Tracy, Harvey Stephens, Clay Clement, William Harrigan, Robert Gleckler, Robert Warwick; *D:* Sam Wood; *W:* Howard Emmett Rogers; *C:* James Wong Howe; *M:* William Axt.

Whirlpool 🦴🦴 **1949** Ann Sutton (Tierney) has managed to keep her kleptomania from her L.A. shrink husband William (Conte). When she gets caught shoplifting, sinister hypnotist David Korvo (Ferrer) comes to her rescue and takes her on as a patient. However, he's setting Ann up to take the fall for the murder of his mistress (O'Neill), whom William happened to be treating. With Ann a suspect, William teams up with detective Colton (Bickford) and uses hypnosis to turn the tables on Korvo. Screenwriter Hecht was on the blacklist so he used the pseudonym Lester Barstow for Preminger's paint-by-numbers noir. **97m/B DVD.** Gene Tierney, Richard Conte, Jose Ferrer, Charles Bickford, Barbara O'Neil, Eduard Franz, Constance Collier; ***D:*** Otto Preminger; ***W:*** Ben Hecht, Andrew Solt; ***C:*** Arthur C. Miller; ***M:*** David Raskin.

Whirlwind Horseman **1938** Substandard horse opera. Maynard's search for a gold prospector friend leads him to a rancher and his pretty daughter. He beats up some bad guys, etcetera. **60m/B VHS.** Ken Maynard, Joan Barclay, Bill Griffith; ***D:*** Robert F. "Bob" Hill.

Whirlygirl **2004 (R)** Naive prep school student James (Morris) follows an exotic dancer known as Whirlygirl (Mazur) to New York, ditching school to learn about life. Based on a true story. **95m/C DVD.** Monet Mazur, Julian Morris, Fran Kranz, Daniel Franzee; ***D:*** Jim Wilson; ***W:*** Pete McCormack; ***C:*** Christo Bakalov; ***M:*** Deborah Lurie. **VIDEO**

Whiskers **½ 1996 (G)** Mischievous Jed and his cat Whiskers can't seem to stay out of trouble and Jed thinks his parents may force him to get rid of his furry friend. So he makes a plea to an Egyptian goddess (they worshiped cats, you know) and Whiskers is suddenly turned into a human being. **94m/C VHS.** *CA* Michael Caloz, Brent Carver, Steve Adams, Mark Bromilow; ***D:*** Jim Kaufman; ***W:*** Wendy Biller, Christopher Hawthorne; ***C:*** Francois Protat; ***M:*** Daniel Lavoie.

Whiskey Galore **½** *Tight Little Island* **1948** During WWII, a whiskey-less Scottish island gets a lift when a ship, carrying 50,000 cases of spirits, wrecks off the coast. A full-scale rescue operation and the evasion of both local and British government authorities ensue. The classic Ealing studio comedy is based on the actual wreck of a cargo ship off the Isle of Eriskay in 1941. **81m/B VHS, DVD.** *GB* Basil Radford, Joan Greenwood, Gordon Jackson, James Robertson Justice; ***D:*** Alexander MacKendrick.

Whiskey Mountain **1977 (PG)** Two couples go on a treasure hunt to Whiskey Mountain but instead find terror. **95m/C VHS.** Christopher George, Preston Pierce, Linda Borgeson, Roberta Collins, Robert Leslie; ***D:*** William Grefe.

Whisper **½ 2007 (R)** Kidnappers (Holloway, Callies, Edgerton, Rooker) abduct the 10-year-old adoptive son (Woodruff) of a wealthy socialite only to find out that the boy is one of those demon spawn kiddies with his own agenda. Woodruff is a lot scarier than the kid they got for "The Omen" remake so this routine horror show has something going for it. **95m/C DVD.** Josh Holloway, Sarah Wayne Callies, Blake Woodruff, Joel Edgerton, Michael Rooker, Dule Hill, Teryl Rothery; ***D:*** Stewart Hendler; ***W:*** Christopher Borrelli; ***C:*** Dean Cundey; ***M:*** Jeff Rona. **VIDEO**

A Whisper to a Scream **1988 (R)** An actress, in researching a film part, takes a job at a telephone sex service, creating different personas as she talks to keep herself interested. Soon, women resembling the personas are being murdered. Great premise fails to deliver fully, though there is some suspense. **96m/C VHS.** *CA* Nadia Capone, Yaphet Kotto, Lawrence Bayne, Silvio Oliviero; ***D:*** Robert Bergman; ***W:*** Robert Bergman, Gerard Ciccoritti.

The Whispering **1994 (R)** Scary little low-budget tale about an insurance investigator who's checking out several suicides and meets up with the Grim Reaper (who just happens to be female). **88m/C VHS.** Leif Garrett, Leslie Danon, Tom Patton, Maxwell Rutherford, Mette Holt; ***D:*** Gregory Gieras; ***W:*** Leslie Danon.

Whispering City **1947** A female reporter receives an inside tip incriminating a prominent attorney in a murder committed several years earlier. She tries to get the evidence she needs before she becomes his latest victim. Highly suspenseful, thanks to competent scripting and directing. **89m/B VHS, DVD.** *CA* Helmut Dantine, Mary Anderson, Paul Lukas; ***D:*** Fedor Ozep.

Whispering Corridors **½** *Yeogo Goedam* **1998 (R)** If this film is correct, girl's schools in South Korea are filled with cruel, sadistic teachers who spend their time harming students with vain, bloated egos. In this first film of the Ghost School Trilogy, students, teachers, and even a molester preying on the girls are savagely murdered one by one. One even appears to commit suicide, but unknown to the students she didn't put the rope around her own neck. Has the ghost of a prior student returned to haunt the school? And if so what does she want? And why are all these people dying? Not a typical horror film, it plays out more as a slow drama that also happens to be a ghost story. **105m/C DVD.** *KN* Kang-hie Choi, Gyu-ri Kim, Mi-yeon Lee, Jin-hie Park, Yong-soo Park, Ji-hye Yun, Min-jung Kim, Roe-ha Kim, Yu-seok Kim, Yong-nyeo Lee, Yi Shin; ***D:*** Ki-hyeong Park; ***W:*** Ki-hyeong Park, Jung-Ok In; ***M:*** Sung-heon Moon.

Whispering Shadow **1933** Serial starring the master criminal known as the "faceless whisperer." Twelve chapters, 13 minutes each. **156m/B VHS, DVD.** Bela Lugosi, Robert Warwick; ***D:*** Al(bert) Herman, Colbert Clark.

Whispers **1989 (R)** Psycho Le Clerc repeatedly bothers writer Tennant even though she seems to have killed him. This dismays police guy Sarandon. Based on the novel by Dean R. Koontz. **96m/C VHS.** Victoria Tennant, Chris Sarandon, Jean LeClerc; ***D:*** Douglas Jackson; ***W:*** Anita Doohan, Don Carmody.

Whispers: An Elephant's Tale **½ 2000 (G)** Odd anthropomorphic film made up entirely of nature footage is similar in some respects to "The Adventures of Milo & Otis." As with that film, here we have animals photographed in the wilds of Africa, with various actors supplying voices for the animals. The film opens with the birth of Whispers (Derryberry), an elephant. While his herd is roaming, he gets lost and can't find his mother Gentle Heart (Archer). Wandering through the bush, he meets another elephant named Groove (Bassett). Groove isn't very fond of Whispers at first, but she ultimately decides to help him find his mom. Along the way, they meet a variety of interesting animals and encounter some evil poachers. An entertaining film, but it also feels very artificial. The end result is a film with some amazing photography, but a story which comes across as hollow. **72m/C DVD.** ***D:*** Dereck Joubert; ***W:*** Dereck Joubert, Jordan Moffet, Holly Goldberg Sloan; ***C:*** Dereck Joubert; ***M:*** Trevor Rabin; ***V:*** Debi Derryberry, Anne Archer, Angela Bassett, Joanna Lumley, Kevin M. Richardson, Alice Ghostley, Betty White, Kathryn Cressida, Joan Rivers.

Whispers in the Dark **1992 (R)** A psychiatrist counsels two odd patients—one is an ex-con turned painter with a violent streak, the other is a woman who reveals her kinky sexual experiences with a mystery man. Things get interesting when the doctor finds out her new lover is her patient's mystery man, and the patient turns up murdered. Confusing thriller seems forced but the experienced cast is worth watching. **103m/C VHS, DVD.** Annabella Sciorra, Jamey Sheridan, Anthony LaPaglia, Jill Clayburgh, John Leguizamo, Deborah Kara Unger, Alan Alda, Anthony Heald; ***D:*** Christopher Crowe; ***W:*** Christopher Crowe; ***C:*** Michael Chapman; ***M:*** Thomas Newman.

Whispers of White **½ 1993 (R)** Bridgetown's mayor has been trying for years to put a stop to the drug dealing going on in his fair community. Finally, his new Chief of Police decides to deploy a special task force to clean-up the streets—using whatever methods are necessary (and they're all violent). **98m/C VHS.** Nicholette Goulet, Anthony De Sando, Tony Craig, April Bransome, Ron Gorton Sr.; ***D:*** Ron Gorton Sr.; ***W:*** Ron Gorton Sr.

The Whistle Blower **1987** A young government worker in England with a high-security position mysteriously dies. His father, a former intelligence agent, begins investigating his son's death and discovers sinister Soviet-related conspiracies. A lucid, complex British espionage thriller. Adapted from the John Hale novel by Julian Bond. **98m/C VHS, DVD.** *GB* Michael Caine, Nigel Havers, John Gielgud, James Fox, Felicity Dean, Gordon Jackson, Barry Foster, David Langton; ***D:*** Simon Langton; ***W:*** Julian Bond; ***C:*** Fred Tammes; ***M:*** John Scott.

Whistle down the Wind **½ 1961** Three children of strict religious upbringing find a murderer hiding in their family's barn and believe him to be Jesus Christ. A well done and hardly grim or dull allegory of childhood innocence based on a novel by Mills's mother, Mary Hayley Bell. For a film relying heavily on child characters, it's important to portray childhood well and realistically. That is done here, as in "To Kill a Mockingbird." Mills is perfect. The film is Forbes's directorial debut and Richard Attenborough's second production. **99m/B VHS.** *GB* Hayley Mills, Bernard Lee, Alan Bates, Norman Bird, Elsie Wagstaff, Diane Holgate, Alan Barnes, Roy Holder, Barry Dean, Diane Clare, Patricia Heneghan; ***D:*** Bryan Forbes; ***W:*** Keith Waterhouse, Willis Hall; ***C:*** Arthur Ibbetson; ***M:*** Malcolm Arnold.

Whistle Stop **1946** A small-town girl divides her attentions between low-life gambler Raft, and villainous nightclub owner McLaglen, who plans a robbery-murder to get rid of any rivals. A forgettable gangster drama. **85m/B VHS, DVD.** George Raft, Ava Gardner, Victor McLaglen; ***D:*** Leonide Moguy; ***W:*** Philip Yordan.

Whistlin' Dan **1932** Yet another lead cowpoke sets out to avenge the murder of a close relative. Maynard whistles while he walks (and rides) woodenly through this one. **60m/B VHS, DVD.** Ken Maynard, Joyzelle Joyner, Lew Meehan, Georges Renavent, Dan Terry, Harlan E. Knight, Bud McClure, Hank Bell, Iron Eyes Cody, Frank Ellis; ***D:*** Phil Rosen.

Whistling Bullets **½ 1936** Action galore in the story of an undercover Texas Ranger infiltrating a gang of thieves. The low budget doesn't detract from an exciting script and tight direction. **58m/B VHS, DVD.** Kermit Maynard, Jack Ingram; ***D:*** John English.

Whistling in Brooklyn **½ 1943** Skelton again plays radio crime-solver Wally Benton in this third and last entry following "Whistling in the Dark" and "Whistling in Dixie." A cop-killer and the Brooklyn Dodgers baseball team figure in the mystery, which finds Skelton a suspect in the crimes. **87m/B VHS.** Red Skelton, Ann Rutherford, Jean Rogers, Rags Ragland, Ray Collins, Henry O'Neill, William Frawley, Sam Levene; ***D:*** S. Sylvan Simon; ***W:*** Wilkie Mahoney, Nat Perrin; ***C:*** Lester White; ***M:*** George Bassman.

Whistling in Dixie **½ 1942** The second appearance of Skelton as radio sleuth Wally "The Fox" Benton (following "Whistling in the Dark") finds him traveling to Georgia with girlfriend Carol (Rutherford). She's worried about an ex-sorority sister who knows the secret of a hidden Civil War treasure. When Wally gets involved, humorous trouble follows. Followed by "Whistling in Brooklyn." **73m/B VHS.** Red Skelton, Ann Rutherford, George Bancroft, Guy Kibbee, Diana Lewis, Peter Whitney, Rags Ragland; ***D:*** S. Sylvan Simon; ***W:*** Nat Perrin, Wilkie Mahoney; ***C:*** Clyde De Vinna.

Whistling in the Dark **1941** Skelton plays Wally Benton, a radio sleuth nicknamed "The Fox," in the first of a three-film series. Veidt (an always excellent villain) is the leader of a phony religious cult, after the money of one of his followers. He decides to kidnap Skelton and have him come up with a plan for the perfect murder but of course there are all sorts of comic complications. Skelton's first starring role is a clever comic mystery and a remake of the 1933 film. Followed by "Whistling in Dixie" and "Whistling in Brooklyn." **78m/B VHS.** Red Skelton, Ann Rutherford, Conrad Veidt, Virginia Grey, Rags Ragland, Eve Arden, Donald "Don" Douglas, Don Costello, Paul Stanton, William Tannen, Reed Hadley; ***D:*** S. Sylvan Simon; ***W:*** Harry Clork, Albert Mannheimer, Robert MacGunigle; ***C:*** Sidney Wagner.

Whitcomb's War **½ 1987** Small town becomes a battleground among a host of comic characters who are unaware who really is in charge. **67m/C VHS.** Patrick Pankhurst, Leon Charles, Bill Morey, Robert Denison, Garnett Smith; ***D:*** Russell S. Doughten Jr.

White Badge **1992** Opening with the 1979 assassination of South Korean President Park Chung Hee, film depicts the trauma and struggle of the more than 300,000 Korean soldiers sent to Vietnam to fight alongside the Americans. Reporter, and war vet, Han (Ahn) is assigned to write about the conflict, which takes on unexpected personal conflicts as he encounters traumatized war buddy Pyon (Lee) and tries to deal with his own repressed memories of the war. Adapted from the novel by Jung Hyo Ahn. **125m/C VHS, DVD.** Sung-Ki Ahn, Kyung-Young Lee, Hye-Jin Shim; ***D:*** Ji-Yong Chung.

White Badge **1997** Kiju Han (Ahn) was a youthful infantry soldier in the South Korean Army's decorated White Horse Division, which fought alongside American troops in Vietnam. Now a writer, and having long suffered from post-tramatic stress, Han decides to use his experiences for his latest work. Flashbacks showcase a reconnaissance mission behind enemy lines that caused one of Han's men to go insane and in the present, Han has a reunion with this soldier in order to confront his own painful past. Korean with subtitles. **122m/C VHS, DVD.** *KN* Sung-Ki Ahn, Kyung-Young Lee, Hye-Jin Shim, Junho Huh, Sejun Kim, Yongjae Tokko; ***D:*** Ji-Yong Chung; ***W:*** Ji-Yong Chung.

The White Balloon **½** *Badkonake Sefid* **1995** Beautifully told story from the viewpoint of determined seven-year-old Tehranian Razieh (Mohammadkhani), who wants to properly celebrate the Islamic New Year by buying a particularly plump goldfish (a symbol of harmony) from the pet shop. She manages to beg the money from her mother and sets off but, distracted by the street sights, Reziah loses the banknote, which falls into a street grate. Various characters seek to help her out but it's Reziah's resourceful brother Ali (Kafili) who gets a balloon seller to finally retrieve the money. Farsi with subtitles. **85m/C VHS, DVD.** *IA* Aida Mohammadkhani, Mohsen Kalifi, Fereshteh Sadr Orfani, Anna Bourkowska, Mohammad Shahani, Mohammad Bahktiari; ***D:*** Jafar Panahi; ***W:*** Abbas Kiarostami; ***C:*** Farzad Jowdat. N.Y. Film Critics '96: Foreign Film.

White Boyz *Whiteboys* **1999 (R)** Flip (Hoch) and his friends long to be gangsta rappers, despite being white and from Iowa. He fantasizes about duets with his idol Snoop Doggy Dogg while dealing baking soda passed off as cocaine to dimwit yuppie disco patrons. He befriends recent Chicago transplant Khalid (Bird) and persuades him to take Flip and his poseur posse to the Cabrini Green projects, where Flip discovers his gangsta fantasy pales in comparison to the real thing. Uneven performances and a rather phat-free script water down an undeniably good premise. **92m/C VHS, DVD.** Danny Hoch, Dash Mihok, Eugene Bird, Mark Webber, Piper Perabo, Bonz Malone; ***D:*** Marc Levin; ***W:*** Danny Hoch, Marc Levin, Richard Stratton, Garth Belcon; ***C:*** Mark Benjamin.

The White Buffalo *Hunt to Kill* **1977 (PG)** A strange, semi-surreal western parable about the last days of Wild Bill Hickok (Bronson) and his obsession with a mythical white buffalo that represents his fear of mortality. Something of a "Moby Dick" theme set in the Wild West. Clumsy but intriguing. **97m/C VHS.** Charles Bronson, Jack Warden, Will Sampson, Kim Novak, Clint Walker, Stuart Whitman, John Carradine, Slim Pickens, Cara Williams, Douglas Fowley; ***D:*** J. Lee Thompson; ***M:*** John Barry.

White Cargo **½ 1942** Lamarr holds the corny story together with one of her best-known roles as sultry native girl Tondelayo. Pidgeon is a cynical African rubber planter who advises new assistant Carlson against Lamarr's sarong-clad charms. But hormones speak louder than warnings and Pidgeon has to take some strong action to save Carlson from this femme fatale. Based on the novel "Hell's Playground" by Ida Vera Simonton and adapted for both stage and screen by Gordon. **90m/B VHS.** Hedy Lamarr, Walter Pidgeon, Richard Carlson, Frank Morgan, Reginald Owen, Bramwell Fletcher, Henry O'Neill, Clyde Cook, Richard Ainley; ***D:*** Richard Thorpe; ***W:*** Leon Gordon; ***M:*** Bronislau Kaper.

White Cargo **½ 1996** Detective Joe Hargatay is investigating a series of fashion model murders that lead him to Chinatown gangsters, corrupt cops, and the crazy world of model agencies. **92m/C VHS.** David Bradley, Shannon Tweed, Lydie Denier, Tommy (Tiny) Lister, David Groh; ***D:*** Daniel Reardon.

White Chicks 🦴½ **2004 (PG-13)** Two African-American FBI agents (Shawn and Marlon Wayans) are assigned to protect two wealthy white heiresses from a kidnapping plot. When the sisters are bruised and refuse to be seen in public, the guys disguise themselves as the heiresses to uncover the kidnappers. Hilarity allegedly ensues. Crazy premise could've been mined for class, culture and gender clash material, but instead lunges down the easy path of junior high humor. Too bad, since the Wayans brothers can be very funny when they play it smart. Disconcerting layers of latex and makeup make them look more like bizarre androgynous aliens than debutantes. **108m/C DVD, UMD.** *US* Marlon Wayans, Shawn Wayans, Brittany Daniel, Jaime (James) King, Jessica Cauffiel, Busy Philipps, Frankie Faison, John Heard, Lochlyn Munro, Maitland Ward, Anne Dudek, Terry Crews, Eddie Velez, Faune A. Chambers, Rochelle Aytes, Jennifer Carpenter, Drew Sidora, Casey Lee, Suzy Joachim; ***D:*** Keenen Ivory Wayans; ***W:*** Marlon Wayans, Shawn Wayans, Keenen Ivory Wayans, Michael Anthony Snowden, Andrew McElfresh, Xavier Cook; ***C:*** Steven Bernstein; ***M:*** Teddy Castellucci.

White Christmas 🦴🦴🦴 **1954** Two ex-army buddies become a popular comedy team and play at a financially unstable Vermont inn at Christmas for charity's sake. Many swell Irving Berlin songs rendered with zest. Paramount's first Vista Vision film. ♫The Best Things Happen While You're Dancing; Love, You Didn't Do Right By Me; Choreography; Count Your Blessings Instead of Sheep; What Can You Do With a General; Mandy; The Minstrel Show; Sisters; Heat Wave. **120m/C VHS, DVD.** Bing Crosby, Danny Kaye, Rosemary Clooney, Vera-Ellen, Dean Jagger; ***D:*** Michael Curtiz; ***W:*** Norman Panama; ***C:*** Loyal Griggs.

The White Cliffs of Dover 🦴🦴🦴 **1944** Prime example of a successful 40s "women's weepie." American Dunne goes to England in 1914, falls in love, and marries the British Marshal. He joins the WWI troops and is killed, without knowing he had a son. Dunne raises the boy in England as a new threat looms with the rise of Hitler. Now grown, he goes off to do his duty and she joins the Red Cross, where she sees him again among the wounded, another victim of the ravages of war. Dunne is fine in her noble, sacrificing role. McDowall is the young son with Taylor (with whom he'd already worked in "Lassie Come Home") as a childhood friend. Based on the poem by Alice Duer Miller. Bring the hankies. **126m/B VHS.** Irene Dunne, Alan Marshal, Frank Morgan, Peter Lawford, Gladys Cooper, May Whitty, Sir C. Aubrey Smith, Roddy McDowall, Van Johnson, Elizabeth Taylor, June Lockhart, John Warburton, Jill Esmond, Norma Varden, Tom Drake, Arthur Shields, Brenda Forbes, Edmund Breon, Clyde Cook, Isobel Elsom, Lumsden Hare, Miles Mander, Ian Wolfe; ***D:*** Clarence Brown; ***W:*** George Froeschel, Jan Lustig, Claudine West; ***C:*** George J. Folsey; ***M:*** Herbert Stothart.

White Coats 🦴½ *Intern Academy* **2004** Low-brow comedy about the misadventures (medical and personal) of the interns at chaotic St. Albert's Hospital. Many gross-out jokes and familiar comedy names, but not much else to recommend it. **98m/C DVD.** *CA* Dave Thomas, Patrick Kelly, Viv Leacock, Dave Foley, Peter Oldring, Ingrid Kavelaars, Dan Aykroyd, Maury Chaykin, Carly Pope, Matt Frewer, Saul Rubinek; ***C:*** John Spooner.

White Comanche 🦴½ **1967** Half-breed twins battle themselves and each other to a rugged climax. **90m/C VHS, DVD.** William Shatner, Joseph Cotten, Perla Cristal, Rossana Yanni; ***D:*** Gilbert Kay.

The White Countess 🦴🦴🦴½ **2005 (PG-13)** As you might expect from a Merchant Ivory production, the period styling is gorgeous even if the story is a little finicky. Set on the eve of Japan's WWII invasion of China in 1936, the film follows Sofia (Richardson) who lives in Shanghai, where she supports her family of exiled Russian aristocrats by scratching out a living as an exotic dancer and prostitute. She meets expatriate American Todd Jackson (Fiennes), who recognizes Sofia as the ideal hostess for his new nightclub, The White Countess. Richardson and Fiennes truly make the viewer care about their wounded characters, even as their business and personal relationships spirals downwards thanks to the chaos of war. **138m/C DVD.** *US CH GB GE* Ralph Fiennes, Natasha Richardson, Vanessa Redgrave, Hiroyuki (Henry) Sanada, Lynn Redgrave, Allan Corduner, Da(nniel) Ying, Jean-Pierre Lorit, Lee Pace, Madeleine Potter, John Wood, Madeleine Daly, Dan Herzberg, Pierre Seznec, Luoyong Wang; ***D:*** James Ivory; ***W:*** Kazuo Ishiguro; ***C:*** Christopher Doyle; ***M:*** Richard Robbins.

The White Dawn 🦴🦴½ **1975 (PG)** Three whalers are stranded in the Arctic in the 1890s and are taken in by an Eskimo vilage. They teach the villagers about booze, gambling, and other modern amenities. Resentment grows until a clash ensues. All three leads are excellent, especally Oates. Much of the dialogue is in an Eskimo language, subtitled in English, as in "Dances with Wolves." **110m/C VHS, DVD.** Warren Oates, Timothy Bottoms, Louis Gossett Jr., Simonie Kopapik, Joanasie Salomonie; ***D:*** Philip Kaufman; ***C:*** Michael Chapman; ***M:*** Henry Mancini.

The White Diamond 🦴🦴🦴 **2004** Herzog's documentary (which he also narrates) begins with a brief history of flight and then moves on to the eccentricities of British aeronautical engineer Graham Dorrington, who designs a two-person airship meant to be used for scientific research in the Amazon rain forest. Herzog records their expedition to Guyana as they try to get Dorrington's aircraft to fly. Dorrington's crew is supported by local Guyanese diamond miners, including Mark Anthony Yhap, whose christening of the airship gives the film its title. **90m/C DVD.** *GE GB JP* ***D:*** Werner Herzog; ***C:*** Henning Brummer, Klaus Scheurich; ***M:*** Ernst Reijseger, Eric Spitzer-Marlyn.

White Dog 🦴🦴 **1982** Young actress Julie Sawyer (McNichol) finds a white stray dog that she adopts, but she soon learns that the dog has been conditioned to kill blacks. She takes the dog to black animal trainer Keys (Winfield), who believes that the dog can be re-trained. Fuller's controversial drama about racism scared off the studio (Paramount) who dumped the picture without more than a token release. **90m/C DVD.** Kristy McNichol, Paul Winfield, Burl Ives, Jameson Parker, Lynne Moody, Samuel Fuller; ***D:*** Samuel Fuller; ***W:*** Samuel Fuller, Curtis Hanson; ***C:*** Bruce Surtees; ***M:*** Ennio Morricone.

White Dwarf 🦴½ **1995** Confusing sci-fi adventure finds edgy Manhattan internist Driscoll Rampart (McDonough) serving his residency on Rusta, a war-torn planet located in a white-dwarf star system. The planet is divided into two hemispheres, one in perpetual darkness and the other in constant light. Rampart learns the ropes from mystical doc Akada (Winfield), who's also involved in a peace accord between Rusta's warring leaders. Visually striking but overly ambiguous—probably because it was intended as the pilot for a weekly series. **91m/C VHS.** Paul Winfield, Neal McDonough, CCH Pounder, Ele Keats, Michael McGrady, Katy Boyer; ***D:*** Peter Markle; ***W:*** Bruce Wagner; ***M:*** Stewart Copeland. **TV**

White Eagle 🦴🦴 **1932** A white man who believes himself to be an Indian gets a job as a Pony Express rider and gets mixed up with horse rustlers. When he finds out who he really is, he is free to marry the white woman he's had his eye on. Interesting plot twist caused by the narrow-mindedness of the Hays Office. **64m/B VHS.** Buck Jones, Barbara Weeks, Robert Ellis, Jason Robards Sr., Robert Elliott, Jim Thorpe, Ward Bond; ***D:*** Lambert Hillyer.

White Fang 🦴🦴🦴 **1991 (PG)** Boy befriends canine with big teeth and both struggle to survive in third celluloid rendition of Alaska during the Gold Rush. Beautiful cinematography. Fun for the entire family based on Jack London's book. Followed by "White Fang 2: The Myth of the White Wolf." **109m/C VHS, DVD.** Klaus Maria Brandauer, Ethan Hawke, Seymour Cassel, James Remar, Susan Hogan; ***D:*** Randal Kleiser; ***W:*** Jeanne Rosenberg, Nick Thiel, David Fallon; ***C:*** Tony Pierce-Roberts; ***M:*** Basil Poledouris.

White Fang 2: The Myth of the White Wolf 🦴🦴 **1994 (PG)** White boy and his wolf-dog lead starving Native American tribe to caribou during the Alaskan Gold Rush. Simplistic story with obvious heroes and villains, yes, but this is also wholesome (and politically correct) family fare compliments of Disney. Focuses less on the wolf, a flaw, and more on Bairstow and his love interest Craig, a Haida Indian princess, while exploring Native American mythology and dreams in sequences that tend to stop the action cold. Still, kids will love it, and there are plenty of puppies to achieve required awwww factor. Beautiful scenery filmed on location in Colorado and British Columbia. **106m/C VHS, DVD.** Scott Bairstow, Alfred Molina, Geoffrey Lewis, Charmaine Craig, Victoria Racimo, Paul Coeur, Anthony Michael Ruivivar, Al Harrington; ***Cameos:*** Ethan Hawke; ***D:*** Ken Olin; ***W:*** David Fallon; ***M:*** John Debney.

White Fang and the Hunter 🦴🦴 **1985 (G)** The adventures of a boy and his dog who survive an attack from wild wolves and then help to solve a murder mystery. Loosely based on the novel by Jack London. **87m/C VHS, DVD.** Pedro Sanchez, Robert Woods; ***D:*** Al (Alfonso Brescia) Bradley.

White Fire 🦴🦴 *Three Steps to the Gallows* **1953** Brady, in search of his lost brother, gets involved in a smuggling ring. Seems the brother is falsely accused of murder and about to hang. Brady and bar singer Castle solve the case. Good photography; bad script. **82m/C VHS.** *GB* Scott Brady, Mary Castle, Ferdinand "Ferdy" Mayne; ***D:*** John Gilling.

White Fire 🦴 **1984** Two jewel thieves will stop at nothing to own White Fire, a two hundred-carat diamond. **90m/C VHS, DVD.** Robert Ginty, Fred Williamson, Belinda Mayne, Jess Hahn; ***D:*** Jean Marie Pallardy; ***W:*** Edward John Francis; ***C:*** Roger Fellous; ***M:*** Vicky Brown.

White Fury 1990 Couples on a campout are victimized by sleazy hoodlums during a snowstorm. **89m/C VHS.** Deke Anderson, Sean Holton, Douglas Harter, Christine Shinn, Chastity Hammons; ***D:*** David A. Prior.

White Ghost 🦴 **1988 (R)** An Intelligence Officer who disappeared in the jungles of Asia 18 years ago is ready to come back to the United States, but not everyone wants to see him again. **90m/C VHS.** William Katt, Rosalind Chao, Martin Hewitt, Wayne Crawford, Reb Brown; ***D:*** B.J. Davis.

White Gold 🦴🦴🦴 **1928** Shepherd's son weds Mexican woman and his disgruntled father contrives apparent rendezvous between the wife and a ranch-hand, who's found dead in her bedroom. Seems no one believes the wife's story. Unprecedented, dark, silent drama. **73m/B VHS.** Jetta Goudal, Kenneth Thomson, George Bancroft, George Nicholls Jr., Clyde Cook; ***D:*** William K. Howard.

White Heat 🦴🦴🦴½ **1949** A classic gangster film with one of Cagney's best roles as a psychopathic robber/killer with a mother complex. The famous finale—perhaps Cagney's best-known scene—has Cagney trapped on top of a burning oil tank shouting "Made it, Ma! Top of the world!" before the tank explodes. Cagney's character is allegedly based on Arthur "Doc" Barker and his "Ma," and his portrayal is breathtaking. Also available colorized. **114m/B VHS, DVD.** James Cagney, Virginia Mayo, Edmond O'Brien, Margaret Wycherly, Steve Cochran, John Archer, Wally Cassell; ***D:*** Raoul Walsh; ***W:*** Ivan Goff, Ben Roberts; ***C:*** Sid Hickox; ***M:*** Max Steiner. Natl. Film Reg. '03.

White Hot 🦴½ **1988 (R)** A young businessman loses his prestigious Wall Street job, and in order to live the good life, he resorts to selling drugs. Benson stars and directs. **95m/C VHS.** Robby Benson, Tawny Kitaen, Danny Aiello, Sally Kirkland, Judy Tenuta; ***D:*** Robby Benson.

White Hot: The Mysterious Murder of Thelma Todd 🦴🦴 **1991** Thelma Todd was a Hollywood starlet found dead under strange circumstances in 1935. Buffs have sought a solution to the maybe-murder ever since; this treatment (based on the book "Hot Toddy" by Andy Edmunds) leaves too many loose ends for purists and isn't sufficiently gripping for the uninitiated. **95m/C VHS, DVD.** Loni Anderson, Robert Davi, Paul Dooley, Lawrence Pressman; ***D:*** Paul Wendkos.

White Hunter, Black Heart 🦴🦴🦴 **1990 (PG)** Eastwood casts himself against type as Hustonesque director who is more interested in hunting large tusked creatures than shooting the film he came to Africa to produce. Based on Peter Viertel's 1953 account of his experiences working on James Agee's script for Huston's "African Queen." Eastwood's Huston impression is a highlight, though the story occasionally wanders off with the elephants. **112m/C VHS, DVD.** Clint Eastwood, Marisa Berenson, George Dzundza, Jeff Fahey, Timothy Spall, Charlotte Cornwell, Mel Martin, Alun Armstrong, Richard Vanstone; ***D:*** Clint Eastwood; ***W:*** Peter Viertel, James Bridges, Burt Kennedy; ***C:*** Jack N. Green; ***M:*** Lennie Niehaus.

White Huntress 🦴½ *Golden Ivory* **1957** Two brothers venturing into the jungle encounter a beautiful young woman, the daughter of a settlement leader. Meanwhile, a killer is on the loose. **86m/C VHS, DVD.** *GB* Robert Urquhart, John Bentley, Susan Stephen; ***D:*** George Breakston.

The White Legion 🦴½ **1936** Workers and engineers push their way through steaming jungles and reeking swamps while building the Panama Canal. Many fall victim to yellow fever. Physician Keith does some medical sleuthing and saves the day. Plodding, predictable drama. **81m/B VHS.** Ian Keith, Tala Birell, Snub Pollard; ***D:*** Karl Brown.

White Lie 🦴🦴½ **1991 (PG-13)** Len Madison Jr. (Hines), a press secretary for the mayor of New York, receives an old photo of a lynched black man who he learns is his father, hung for raping a white woman. Madison returns to his Southern hometown to find out the truth behind his father's death, assisted by a white doctor (O'Toole) whose mother was a rape victim. They fall in love, adding to an already complicated situation, and incur the wrath of locals who are trying to keep the truth hidden. Based on the novel "Louisiana Black" by Samuel Charters. **93m/C VHS.** Gregory Hines, Annette O'Toole, Bill Nunn; ***D:*** Bill Condon.

White Lies 🦴🦴 **1998 (R)** Catherine (Polley), a freshman college student at a liberal university, feels alienated from her peers and finds solace in an online chat room. She becomes increasingly involved with the shadowy National Identity Movement and becomes their spokesperson before understanding what they really represent and that they're a group of neo-Nazis. **92m/C VHS, DVD.** *CA* Sarah Polley, Tanya Allen, Jonathan Scarfe, Lynn Redgrave, Joseph Kell, Albert Schultz; ***D:*** Keri Skogland; ***W:*** Dennis Foon. **TV**

White Light 🦴🦴 **1990 (R)** "Flatliners" with a flatfoot; after a near-death experience a cop returns with memories of a beautiful woman. He tries to find out who she is/was in plodding fashion. The voyage to the afterlife is represented by a jog through a storm sewer. **96m/C VHS.** Martin Kove, Allison Hossack, Martha Henry, Heidi von Palleske, James Purcell, Bruce Boa; ***D:*** Al Waxman.

White Lightning 🦴🦴½ *McKlusky* **1973 (PG)** Good ol' boy Reynolds plays a moonshiner going after the crooked sheriff who murdered his brother. Good stunt-driving chases enliven the formula. The inferior sequel is "Gator." **101m/C VHS, DVD.** Burt Reynolds, Ned Beatty, Bo Hopkins, Jennifer Billingsley, Louise Latham; ***D:*** Joseph Sargent; ***W:*** William W. Norton Sr.; ***M:*** Charles Bernstein.

White Line Fever 🦴🦴½ **1975 (PG)** A young trucker's search for a happy life with his childhood sweetheart is complicated by a corrupt group in control of the long-haul trucking business. Well-done action film of good triumphing over evil. **89m/C VHS.** Jan-Michael Vincent, Kay Lenz, Slim Pickens, L.Q. Jones, John David Garfield; ***D:*** Jonathan Kaplan; ***W:*** Jonathan Kaplan, Ken Friedman; ***C:*** Fred W. Koenekamp.

The White Lioness 🦴🦴 *Den Vita Lejoninnan* **1996** A young woman is found murdered in the Swedish countryside and the small town cop investigating realizes it's a more complicated case than he can handle. Especially when the crime leads him to Russia and South Africa and an international terrorist organization. Based on the novel by Henning Mankell. Swedish with subtitles. **104m/C VHS, DVD.** *SW* Rolf Lassgard, Basil Appollis, Jesper Christensen, Nelson Mandela; ***D:*** Per (Pelle) Berglund; ***W:*** Lars Bjorkman; ***C:***

Tony Forsberg; **M:** Thomas Lindahl.

White Mama **1980** A poor widow (Davis, in a splendid role) takes in a streetwise black kid (Harden) in return for protection from the neighborhood's dangers, and they discover friendship. Poignant drama, capably directed by Cooper, featuring sterling performances all around Made-for-TV drama at its best. **96m/C VHS.** Bette Davis, Ernest Harden Jr., Eileen Heckart, Virginia Capers, Lurene Tuttle, Anne Ramsey; **D:** Jackie Cooper.

White Mane **1952** The poignant, poetic story of a proud and fierce white stallion that continually eludes attempts by ranchers to capture it. In French with English subtitles. **38m/B VHS.** Alain Emery, Frank Silvera; **D:** Albert Lamorisse. Cannes '52: Film.

White Man's Burden **1995 (R)** In a world where blacks have all the wealth and power, and whites comprise the struggling underclasses, Caucasian factory worker Louis Pinnock (John Travolta) is fired by his bigoted black CEO (Belafonte) due to a misunderstanding. Driven by poverty-level financial strain, Louis kidnaps his wealthy boss to show him how the other half lives. Gimmicky premise is full of reversed stereotypes, such as black cops beating a white guy, and skinheads taking over as inner-city gangsters. Treads too lightly, and rehashes too many familiar stories, to make any real impact. Travolta had to be talked into this role by "Pulp Fiction" producer Lawrence Bender. **89m/C VHS, DVD.** John Travolta, Harry Belafonte, Kelly Lynch, Margaret Avery, Tom Bower, Carrie Snodgress, Sheryl Lee Ralph; **D:** Desmond Nakano; **W:** Desmond Nakano; **C:** Willy Kurant; **M:** Howard Shore.

White Men Can't Jump **1992 (R)** Sometimes they can't act either. Small-time con man Harrelson stands around looking like a big nerd until someone dares him to play basketball and he proves to be more adept than he looks. After he beats Snipes, they become friends and start hustling together. Harrelson lays to rest the rumor that he can't act; here, he proves it. Fast-paced, obscenity-laced dialogue does not cover up for the fact that the story hovers between dull and dismal, redeemed only by the surreal "Jeopardy" game show sequence and the convincing b-ball action. Snipes manages to rise above the material as well as the rim, while Perez, as wooden Woody's spitfire Hispanic girlfriend, is appropriately energetic. **115m/C VHS, DVD.** Wesley Snipes, Woody Harrelson, Rosie Perez, Tyra Ferrell, Cylk Cozart, Kadeem Hardison, Ernest Harden Jr., John Jones; **D:** Ron Shelton; **W:** Ron Shelton; **C:** Russell Boyd; **M:** Bennie Wallace.

White Mile ½ **1994 (R)** Abusive L.A. advertising exec Dan Cutler (Alda) invites his top execs and important clients on a white-water rafting expedition along the Chilko River in the Canadian Rockies (filmed at Northern California's Russian River). But competition and arrogance causes the deaths of several participants and the widow of one sues the agency for damages. Alda excels in arrogant, self-serving nastiness. Fact-based TV movie based on court transcripts. **97m/C VHS, DVD.** Alan Alda, Peter Gallagher, Robert Loggia, Fionnula Flanagan, Dakin Matthews, Bruce Altman, Robert Picardo, Max Wright, Jack Gilpin, Ken Jenkins; **D:** Robert Butler; **W:** Michael Butler.

White Mischief **1988 (R)** An alternately ghastly and hilarious indictment of the English upper class between the World Wars, and the decadence the British colonists perpetrated in Kenya, which came to world attention with the murder of the philandering Earl of Errol in 1941. Exquisitely directed and photographed. Acclaimed and grandly acted, especially by Scacchi; Howard's last appearance. **108m/C VHS.** Greta Scacchi, Charles Dance, Joss Ackland, Sarah Miles, John Hurt, Hugh Grant, Geraldine Chaplin, Trevor Howard, Murray Head, Susan Fleetwood, Alan Dobie, Jacqueline Pearce; **D:** Michael Radford; **W:** Michael Radford; **C:** Roger Deakins; **M:** George Fenton.

White Nights *Le Notti Bianche* **1957** Based on a love story by Dostoyevski. A young woman pines for the return of her sailor while a mild-mannered clerk is smitten by her. Both of their romantic fantasies are explored the dance-hall cadence is mixed with dreamy, fantastic flashbacks. In Italian with English subtitles. Equally good Soviet version made in 1959. **107m/C VHS, DVD.** *IT FR* Maria Schell, Jean Marais, Marcello Mastroianni, Clara Calamai, Giorgio Listuzzi; **D:** Luchino Visconti; **W:** Luchino Visconti, Suso Cecchi D'Amico; **C:** Giuseppe Rotunno; **M:** Nino Rota.

White Nights ½ **1985 (PG-13)** A Russian ballet dancer who defected to the U.S. (Baryshnikov) is a passenger on a jet that crashes in the Soviet Union. With the aid of a disillusioned expatriate tap dancer (Hines), he plots to escape again. The excellent dance sequences elevate the rather lame story. ♫Say You, Say Me. **135m/C VHS, DVD.** Mikhail Baryshnikov, Gregory Hines, Isabella Rossellini, Helen Mirren, Jerzy Skolimowski, Geraldine Page; **D:** Taylor Hackford; **C:** David Watkin; **M:** Michel Colombier. Oscars '85: Song ("Say You, Say Me"); Golden Globes '86: Song ("Say You, Say Me").

White Noise **2005 (PG-13)** Despite an eerily effective marketing campaign—touting the science behind Electronic Voice Phenomenon (EVP), in which ghosts use electric static to contact the living—this cheap Michael Keaton vehicle should have gone straight to video. After architect Jonathan Rivers (Keaton) loses his wife Anna (West) in a suspicious accident, he retreats into despair. That is, until a stranger (McNeice) convinces Rivers that Anna is sending him messages from beyond the grave via EVP. Rivers becomes obsessed with the transmissions, which awakens a malevolent force unamused with his meddling. The last hour plays like a low budget "Final Destination" retread. **101m/C VHS, DVD, HD DVD.** *US* Michael Keaton, Chandra West, Deborah Kara Unger, Ian McNeice, Sarah Strange, Nicholas Elia, Mike Dopud; **D:** Geoffrey Sax; **W:** Niall Johnson; **C:** Chris Seager; **M:** Claude Foisy.

White Noise 2: The Light ½ **2007 (PG-13)** After Abe Dale's (Fillion, playing it straight and dull) family is killed and he is saved from an attempted suicide, Abe comes back from his near-death experience seeing white auras around people who are about to die. But in preventing their deaths, Abe learns there's an unexpected price to pay, since those he saves turn into demons after 72 hours—unless they die again. **99m/C DVD, HD DVD.** Nathan Fillion, Katee Sackhoff, Craig Fairbrass, Teryl Rothery, Adrian Homes, William Macdonald; **D:** Patrick Lussier; **W:** Matt Venne; **C:** Brian Pearson; **M:** Normand Corbeil. **VIDEO**

White of the Eye **1988 (R)** A murdering lunatic is on the loose in Arizona, and an innocent man must find him to acquit himself of the murders. A tense, effective thriller; dazzling technique recalls the experimental films of the 1960s. **111m/C VHS.** David Keith, Cathy Moriarty, Art Evans, Alan Rosenberg, Michael Greene, Alberta Watson, Marc Hayashi; **D:** Donald Cammell; **W:** China Cammell, Donald Cammell; **M:** Nick Mason, Rick Fenn, George Fenton.

White Oleander ½ **2002 (PG-13)** Pfieffer plays against type as an ice cold mother who controls her daughter Astrid's (Lohman) life from the prison where she's serving a life sentence for murder. Astrid is forced into an odyssey through the foster care system, where she is taken in by a string of damaged foster moms, including a born-again ex-stripper (Wright Penn), a needy ex-actress (Zellweger) and a greedy Russian ragpicker (Efremova). Astrid changes her looks as well as her psyche for each of these faux-mothers, but finally learns to break away and become her own person with some help from fellow foster child Paul (Fugit). The performances are good across the board, but director Kosminsky seems more interested in making the all-star cast of actresses look good then giving them an interesting story to tell. **110m/C VHS, DVD.** *US* Alison Lohman, Michelle Pfeiffer, Robin Wright Penn, Renee Zellweger, Patrick Fugit, Billy Connolly, Cole Hauser, Noah Wyle, Amy Aquino, Svetlana Efremova; **D:** Peter Kosminsky; **W:** Mary Agnes Donoghue; **C:** Elliot Davis; **M:** Thomas Newman.

The White Orchid **1954** Romantic triangle ventures into the wilds of Mexico in search of Toltec ruins. Exceptional sets. **81m/C VHS, DVD.** William Lundigan, Peggy Castle, Armando Silvestre, Rosenda Monteros; **D:** Reginald LeBorg.

White Palace ½ **1990 (R)** Successful widowed Jewish lawyer Spader is attracted to older, less educated hamburger waitress Sarandon, and ethnic/cultural strife ensues, as does hot sex. Adapted from the Glenn Savan novel, it starts out with promise but fizzles toward the end. **103m/C VHS, DVD.** Susan Sarandon, James Spader, Jason Alexander, Eileen Brennan, Griffin Dunne, Kathy Bates, Steven Hill, Rachel Levin, Corey Parker, Spiros Focas, Renee Taylor, Kim Myers; **D:** Luis Mandoki; **W:** Alvin Sargent, Ted Tally; **C:** Lajos Koltai; **M:** George Fenton.

White Phantom: Enemy of Darkness **1987** Ninja warriors in modern day society battling against other evil ninjas. **89m/C VHS.** Page Leong, Jay Roberts Jr., Bo Svenson; **D:** Dusty Nelson; **W:** David Hamilton, Chris Gallagher.

White Pongo **WOOF!** **1945** A policeman goes undercover with a group of British biologists to capture a mythic white gorilla believed to be the missing link. A camp jungle classic with silly, cheap special effects. **73m/B VHS, DVD.** Richard Fraser, Maris Wrixon, Lionel Royce, Al Eben, Gordon Richards, Michael Dyne, George Lloyd; **D:** Sam Newfield; **W:** Raymond L. Schrock; **C:** Jack Greenhalgh.

The White Raven **1998 (R)** Nazi war criminal Markus Straud (Rubes) agrees to be interviewed only by Chicago journalist Tully Windsor (Silvers). During the war, Straud hid a priceless diamond and various factions think he's finally going to reveal where the stone is. But Straud only offers a series of cryptic clues that lead Windsor back home, with the bad guys in pursuit. **92m/C VHS, DVD.** Ron Silver, Jan Rubes, Joanna Pacula, Roy Scheider; **D:** Andrew Stevens; **W:** Michael Blodgett; **C:** Michael Slovis; **M:** David Wurst, Eric Wurst.

The White Ribbon *Das Weisse Band* **2009 (R)** Gorgeously filmed in black-and-white, Haneke's disturbing drama is best-suited to film aficionados. Misfortunes befall the small German Protestant agricultural town of Eichwald shortly before World War I, changing from minor disturbances to outright atrocities as longtime neighbors turn suspicious and vengeful. Narrated by the town's schoolteacher (Friedel)—years after the events have taken place—the town has a strict and brutal moral code and hierarchy with the children (and women) being punished for the slightest suspected infraction while the adult males carry on as they please. It comes as neither a surprise that the abused children are behind the havoc nor that the horrors depicted are only a prelude to the horrors of the upcoming war. German with subtitles. **150m/B DVD.** *GE AT FR IT* Ulrich Tukur, Burghart Klaussner, Josef Bierbichler, Christian Friedel, Leonie Benesch, Ursina Lardi, Steffi Kuhnert, Rainer Bock, Gariela Maria Shcmeide; **D:** Michael Haneke; **W:** Michael Haneke; **C:** Christian Berger; **Nar:** Ernst Jacobi. Golden Globes '10: Foreign Film.

White River *The White River Kid* **1999 (R)** Embarassingly bad would-be comedy based on the book "The Little Brothers of St. Mortimer" by John Fergus Ryan. Broth Edgar (Hoskins) is a fake monk, teamed up with illegal immigrant Morales Pittman (Banderas), in a scam involving selling cheap "socks for God." Traveling through Arkansas they meet up with serial killer "The White River Kid" (Bentley), his girlfriend Apple Lisa Weed (Dickens) and her eccentric family, a blind prostitute (Barkin), and a singing, corrupt sheriff (Travis). Not that you'll be interested in any of them. **99m/C VHS, DVD.** Bob Hoskins, Antonio Banderas, Wes Bentley, Kim Dickens, Ellen Barkin, Randy Travis, Beau Bridges, Swoosie Kurtz; **D:** Arne Glimcher; **W:** David Leland; **C:** Michael Chapman; **M:** John (Gianni) Frizzell.

The White Rose **1923** An aspiring minister travels to see the world he intends to save, and winds up falling from grace. Complicated menage a trois is finally sorted out at the end. Silent. **120m/B VHS.** Mae Marsh, Carol Dempster, Ivor Novello, Neil Hamilton, Lucille LaVerne; **D:** D.W. Griffith.

The White Rose *Die Weisse Rose* **1983** The true story of a group of dissident students in Munich in 1942, who put their lives in danger by distributing leaflets telling the truth of what was going on in the concentration camps. Hans Scholl was an Army officer who discovered the truth and told the others. In the end, most of the students were captured by the Gestapo and executed. "The White Rose" was the name of the group, but none survived to tell where the name came from. Verhoeven's film telling is engrossing and compelling, with excellent acting from the young cast. In German with English subtitles. **108m/C VHS.** *GE* Lena Stolze, Wulf Kessler, Oliver Siebert, Ulrich Tucker, Werner Stocker, Martin Benrath, Anja Kruse, Ulf-Jurgen Wagner, Mechthild Reinders, Peter Kortenbach, Gerhard Friedrich, Sabine Kretzschmar, Heinz Keller, Suzanne Seuffert, Christina Schwartz; **D:** Michael Verhoeven; **W:** Michael Verhoeven, Mario Krebs; **C:** Axel de Roche; **M:** Konstantin Wecker.

White Sands ½ **1992 (R)** When a dead man's body is found at a remote Indian reservation clutching a gun and a briefcase filled with $500,000, the local sheriff (Dafoe) takes his identity to see where the money leads. Using a phone number found on a piece of paper in the dead man's stomach, the sheriff follows clues until he finds himself mixed up with a rich woman (Mastrantonio) who sells black market weapons and uses the money to support "worthy" causes, and an FBI man (Jackson) who uses him as bait to lure a CIA turncoat/arms dealer (Rourke). Sound confusing? It is, and despite the strong cast and vivid scenery of the southwest United States, this film just doesn't cut it. **101m/C VHS, DVD.** Jack Kehler, Willem Dafoe, Mary Elizabeth Mastrantonio, Mickey Rourke, Mimi Rogers, Samuel L. Jackson, M. Emmet Walsh, James Rebhorn, Maura Tierney, Beth Grant, Miguel (Michael) Sandoval, John Lafayette; ***Cameos:*** Fred Dalton Thompson, John P. Ryan; **D:** Roger Donaldson; **W:** Daniel Pyne; **C:** Peter Menzies Jr.; **M:** Patrick O'Hearn.

White Shadows in the South Seas ½ **1929** Alcohol, drugs, and prostitution take their toll on the native population of Tahiti in this early talkie. Blue plays a western doctor who marries the daughter of a native chief. However, he finds greed for the island's pearl treasures drawing other unscrupulous westerners to destroy the unspoiled paradise. **88m/B VHS.** Monte Blue, Robert Anderson, Raquel Torres; **D:** Woodbridge S. Van Dyke; **C:** Clyde De Vinna. Oscars '29: Cinematog.

The White Sheik *Lo Sceicco Bianco* **1952** Fellini's first solo effort. A newly wed bride meets her idol from the comic pages (made with photos, not cartoons; called fumetti) and runs off with him. She soon finds he's as ordinary as her husband. Brilliant satire in charming garb. Remade as "The World's Greatest Lover." Woody Allen's "The Purple Rose of Cairo" is in a similar spirit. In Italian with subtitles. **86m/B VHS, DVD.** *IT* Alberto Sordi, Giulietta Masina, Brunella Bovo, Leopoldo Trieste; **D:** Federico Fellini; **W:** Federico Fellini, Tullio Pinelli, Ennio Flaiano; **C:** Arturo Galea; **M:** Nino Rota.

The White Sin **1924** An innocent country girl hires on as maid of a rich woman and is seduced and abandoned by the woman's profligate son, but everything turns out all right by the end of the third handkerchief. Silent with original organ music. **93m/B VHS.** Madge Bellamy, John Bowers, Billy Bevan; **D:** William A. Seiter.

The White Sister ½ **1923** Gish is an Italian aristocrat driven from her home by a conniving sister. When her true love (Colman) is reported killed she decides to become a nun and enters a convent. When her lover does return he tricks her into leaving the convent but before he can persuade her to renounce her vows Vesuvius erupts and he goes off to warn the villagers, dying for his efforts. Gish then re-dedicates herself to her faith. Colman's first leading role, which made him a romantic star. Filmed on location in Italy. **108m/B VHS.** Lillian Gish, Ronald Colman, Gail Kane, J. Barney Sherry, Charles Lane; **D:** Henry King.

White Slave *Amazonia: The Catherine Miles Story* **1986 (R)** An Englishwoman is captured by bloodthirsty cannibals and, rather than being eaten, is tormented and made a slave. **90m/C VHS, DVD.** Elvive Avoray, Will Gonzales, Andrew Louis Coppola; ***D:*** Mario Gariazzo.

White Squall 1/2 **1996 (PG-13)** Based on the 1960 true story of 13 young men who become students at Ocean Academy, a year-long adventure spent aboard the brigantine Albatross. Bridges plays the ship's captain and surrogate dad. The boys agonize over their various crises, making the first half of the movie into a veritable "Dead Poets Yachting Society." However, a sudden storm overtakes the ship in the Caribbean and several crew members are killed. There's a shift to a "Caine Mutiny" type trial in which Bridges must prove the tragedy was not his fault while the survivors rally to his defense. Director Scott excels at showing the fury of nature in the prolonged storm scene, but takes his time getting there. **128m/C VHS, DVD.** Jeff Bridges, Scott Wolf, Caroline Goodall, Balthazar Getty, John Savage, Jeremy Sisto, Jason Marsden, David Selby, Zeljko Ivanek, Ryan Phillippe, David Lascher, Eric Michael Cole, Julio Oscar Mechoso, Ethan (Randall) Embry; ***D:*** Ridley Scott; ***W:*** Todd Robinson; ***C:*** Hugh Johnson; ***M:*** Jeff Rona.

White Tiger 1/2 **1923** Three crooks pull off a major heist and hide out in a mountain cabin where their mistrust of each other grows. **81m/C VHS.** Priscilla Dean, Matt Moore, Raymond Griffith, Wallace Beery; ***D:*** Tod Browning.

White Tiger 1/2 **1995 (R)** DEA agent Mike Ryan (Daniels) decides to take the law into his own fists when his partner Grogan (Craven) is murdered by Chinese gang/drug leader Victor Chow (Tagawa). **93m/C VHS, DVD.** Gary Daniels, Matt Craven, Cary-Hiroyuki Tagawa, Julia Nickson-Soul; ***D:*** Richard Martin; ***W:*** Gordon Melbourne; ***C:*** Gregory Middleton; ***M:*** Graeme Coleman.

The White Tower **1950** Five men and a woman set out to scale the infamous White Tower in the Alps. Each person's true nature is revealed as he or she scales the peak, which has defied all previous attempts. Slightly overwrought, but exciting. Filmed in Technicolor on location in the Swiss Alps. **98m/C VHS.** Glenn Ford, Claude Rains, Cedric Hardwicke, Oscar Homolka, Lloyd Bridges; ***D:*** Ted Tetzlaff; ***W:*** Paul Jarrico.

White Water Summer 1/2 *Rites of Summer* **1987 (PG)** A group of young adventurers trek into the Sierras, and find themselves struggling against nature and each other to survive. Bacon is the rugged outdoorsman (yeah, sure) who shows them what's what. Chances are it was never at a theatre near you, and with good reason. **90m/C VHS, DVD.** Kevin Bacon, Sean Astin, Jonathan Ward, Matt Adler, K.C. Martel; ***D:*** Jeff Bleckner; ***M:*** Michael Boddicker.

White Wolves 2: Legend of the Wild 1/2 **1994 (PG)** Troubled teens are on a school assignment involving a conservation foundation's rescue of a pair of young wolves. They must overcome lots of obstacles, including the fact that they can't stand each other. Average teens-in-the-woods adventure. **95m/C VHS, DVD.** Corin "Corky" Nemec, Justin Whalin, Jeremy London, Elizabeth Berkley, Ernie Reyes Jr., Ele Keats; ***D:*** Terence H. Winkless; ***C:*** John Aronson.

White Wolves 3: Cry of the White Wolf 1/2 **1998 (PG)** A plane crash strands three teens in the wilderness where they must depend on themselves, and the mystical white wolf, for survival. **82m/C VHS, DVD.** Rodney A. Grant, Mercedes McNab, Robin Clarke, Tracy Brooks Swope, Mick Cain, Margaret Howell; ***D:*** Victoria Muspratt.

The White Zombie **1932** Lugosi followed his success in "Dracula" with the title role in this low-budget horror classic about the leader of a band of zombies who wants to steal a beautiful young woman from her new husband. Set in Haiti; the first zombie movie. Rich and dark, though ludicrous. Based on the novel "The Magic Island" by William Seabrook. **73m/B VHS, DVD.** Bela Lugosi, Madge Bellamy, John Harron, Joseph Cawthorn, Robert Frazer, Brandon Hurst, George Burr Macannan, John Peters, Dan Crimmins, Clarence Muse; ***D:*** Victor Halperin; ***W:*** Garnett Weston; ***C:*** Arthur Martinelli; ***M:*** Xavier Cugat.

WhiteForce **1988 (R)** A secret agent tracks an enemy. His government tracks him. He runs around with a big machine gun and a couple of hand grenades. He fires the gun and throws the grenades. **90m/C DVD.** Sam Jones, Kimberly Pistone; ***D:*** Eddie Romero.

Whiteout 1/2 **2009 (R)** Disturbingly violent thriller is set in Antarctica's Amundsen-Scott Station days before the winter closes down travel. Carrie Stetko (Beckinsale), the only U.S. Marshal assigned to the post, hopes to wrap up an uneventful two-year stint, but the station's first homicide victim shows up just as a brutal storm approaches. Stetko's not going anywhere, right? Yeah, and neither is this movie. As dead scientists pile up, Stetko gets assistance from mentoring father figure/pilot Doc (Skerritt) and special UN investigator, Robert (Macht). Flashbacks to a Russian plane crash in 1957 hint at the back-story but the storm, big parkas, and frenetically filmed action make it difficult to follow the unfolding mystery. On a good note, the gorgeous Beckinsale delivers her obligatory disrobing and shower scene very early in the film so, guys, if you doze off in the final third...you're good. **101m/C DVD.** *US* Kate Beckinsale, Gabriel Macht, Tom Skerritt, Columbus Short, Alex O'Loughlin, Shawn Doyle; ***D:*** Dominic Sena; ***W:*** Chad Hayes, Carey Hayes, Jon Hoeber, Erich Hoeber; ***C:*** Christopher Soos; ***M:*** John (Gianni) Frizzell.

Whitewash: The Clarence Brandley Story 1/2 **2002 (R)** Black farmer Dan Brandley is shot to death in broad daylight on the main street of Conroe, Texas, in 1940. No one is ever brought to trial, even though his white killer is known. Forty years later, grandson Clarence Brandley discovers the murdered body of a white teenaged girl and learns that racism and corruption still hold sway. Clarence is tried, convicted, and sentenced to death. Now, his lawyer must prevent an innocent man's execution. **108m/C VHS.** Courtney B. Vance, Gil Bellows, Eamonn Walker, Chuck Shamata, Richard Eden, Joseph Ziegler; ***D:*** Tony Bill; ***W:*** Abby Mann; ***C:*** Jean Lepine. **CABLE**

Whitewater Sam 1/2 **1978 (G)** Whitewater Sam and his Siberian Husky, Sybar, embark on an exciting trip through the uncharted wilds of the Great Northwest. The likeable, intelligent hound steals the show. Good family adventure. **87m/C VHS.** Keith Larsen; ***D:*** Keith Larsen; ***W:*** Keith Larsen.

Whity **1970** Whity (Kaufman) is the illegitimate mulatto son of the wealthy white man for whom he works. An equally exploited barmaid (Schygulla) convinces Whity his one chance for freedom is to murder his masters. Kaufman was one of Fassbinder's boyfriends and the personal tensions and obsessions of their relationship spilled onto the screen. German with subtitles. **102m/C DVD.** *GE* Rainer Werner Fassbinder, Gunther Kaufman, Hanna Schygulla, Ulli Lommel, Harry Baer; ***D:*** Rainer Werner Fassbinder; ***W:*** Rainer Werner Fassbinder; ***C:*** Michael Ballhaus; ***M:*** Peer Raben.

Who Am I This Time? **1982** Two shy people can express their love for each other only through their roles in a local theatre production of "A Streetcar Named Desire." Good cast responds well to competent direction from Demme; poignant, touching, and memorable. Based on a story by Kurt Vonnegut Jr. **60m/C VHS, DVD.** Susan Sarandon, Christopher Walken, Robert Ridgely, Mike Bacarella, Aaron Freeman, Caitlin Hart; ***D:*** Jonathan Demme; ***M:*** John Cale. **TV**

Who Done It? **1942** Average Abbott and Costello comedy about two would-be radio mystery writers, working as soda-jerks, who play detective after the radio station's president is murdered. **77m/B VHS, DVD.** Bud Abbott, Lou Costello, William Gargan, Patric Knowles, Louise Allbritton, Don Porter, Jerome Cowan, William Bendix, Mary Wickes; ***D:*** Erle C. Kenton.

Who Done It? 1/2 **1956** Film debut of the rakish Hill as ice-rink sweeper, Hugo Dill. When Dill comes into some money and a dog, he launches a private investigating firm. A woman enters the picture and Hugo discovers his sleuthing has gotten him in over his head. Lots of typical gags and car chases. **85m/B VHS, DVD.** *GB* Benny Hill, Belinda Lee, David Kossoff, Ernest Thesiger, Garry Marsh, George Margo, Denis Shaw, Fred Schiller, Jeremy Hawk, Thorley Walters, Philip Stainton, Stratford Johns; ***D:*** Basil Dearden; ***W:*** T.E.B. Clarke; ***C:*** Otto Heller; ***M:*** Philip Green.

Who Framed Roger Rabbit 1/2 **1988 (PG)** Technically marvelous, cinematically hilarious, eye-popping combination of cartoon and live action create a Hollywood of the 1940s where cartoon characters are real and a repressed minority working in films. A 'toon-hating detective is hired to uncover the unfaithful wife of 2-D star Roger, and instead uncovers a conspiracy to wipe out all 'toons. Special appearances by many cartoon characters from the past. Coproduced by Touchstone (Disney) and Amblin (Spielberg). Adapted from "Who Censored Roger Rabbit?" by Gary K. Wolf. **104m/C VHS, DVD.** Bob Hoskins, Christopher Lloyd, Joanna Cassidy, Alan Tilvern, Stubby Kaye; ***D:*** Robert Zemeckis; ***W:*** Jeffrey Price, Peter S. Seaman; ***C:*** Dean Cundey; ***M:*** Alan Silvestri; ***V:*** Charles Fleischer, Mae Questel, Kathleen Turner, Amy Irving, Mel Blanc, June Foray, Frank Sinatra. Oscars '88: Film Editing, Visual FX.

Who Gets to Call It Art? 1/2 **2005** Jumbled documentary about the unlikely career of Metropolitan Museum of Art curator Henry Geldzahler, who died in 1994, and his 1969 landmark 408-piece exhibition entitled "New York Painting and Sculpture: 1940-1970" that showcased works from 43 artists, including Jackson Pollock, Jasper Johns, Willem de Kooning, Andy Warhol, and David Hockney. **80m/C DVD.** *US*

Who Has Seen the Wind? **1977** Two boys grow up in Saskatchewan during the Depression. So-so family viewing drama. Ferrer as a bootlegger steals the otherwise small-paced show. **102m/C VHS.** *CA GB* Brian Painchaud, Patricia Hamilton, Gordon Pinsent, Chapelle Jaffe, Helen Shaver, Cedric Smith, Jose Ferrer; ***D:*** Allan King; ***W:*** Patricia Watson; ***C:*** Richard Leiterman; ***M:*** Eldon Rathburn.

Who is Cletis Tout? 1/2 **2002 (R)** This nostalgic spoof of/homage to classic movies revolves around the efforts of cornered man Trevor (Slater) to convince a film-loving hitman that he is not Cletis Tout, a reporter that the mob wants dead. Critical Jim (Allen) is a button man with time on his hands, so he has Trevor tell him the story like he was pitching a movie idea to a studio executive. The tale contains many obvious Hollywood plot machinations and references including a prison break, a pretty girl, elaborate con jobs and true love. Trevor is also not above taking cues from Jim, changing the story when his captor is displeased by part of it. Good premise tends to get too cute with the material, but all in all a fun ride. **92m/C VHS, DVD.** Tim Allen, Christian Slater, Portia de Rossi, Richard Dreyfuss, Billy Connolly, Peter MacNeill, Richard Chevolleau, RuPaul Charles; ***D:*** Christopher Ver Wiel; ***W:*** Christopher Ver Wiel; ***C:*** Jerzy Zielinski; ***M:*** Randy Edelman.

Who Is Harry Kellerman and Why Is He Saying Those Terrible Things About Me? 1/2 **1971 (R)** Hoffman stars as a successful composer/singer who finds money didn't bring him happiness. **108m/C VHS.** Dustin Hoffman, Barbara Harris, Jack Warden, Dom DeLuise; ***D:*** Ulu Grosbard.

Who Is Killing the Great Chefs of Europe? *Too Many Chefs; Someone is Killing the Great Chefs of Europe* **1978 (PG)** A fast-paced, lightly handled black comedy. When a gourmand, well-played by Morley, learns he must lose weight to live, a number of Europe's best chefs are murdered according to their cooking specialty. A witty, crisp, international mystery based on Ivan and Nan Lyon's novel. **112m/C VHS.** George Segal, Jacqueline Bisset, Robert Morley, Jean-Pierre Cassel, Philippe Noiret, Jean Rochefort, Joss Ackland, Nigel Havers; ***D:*** Ted Kotcheff; ***M:*** Henry Mancini. L.A. Film Critics '78: Support. Actor (Morley).

Who Is the Black Dahlia? **1975** In L.A. in 1947, a detective tries to find out who murdered a star-struck 22-year-old woman nicknamed "The Black Dahlia" (Arnaz). Based on a famous unsolved murder case which was later the basis for "True Confessions." Made for TV. **96m/C VHS.** Efrem Zimbalist Jr., Lucie Arnaz, Ronny Cox, MacDonald Carey, Linden Chiles; ***D:*** Joseph Pevney; ***W:*** Robert W. Lenski. **TV**

Who Killed Baby Azaria? **1983** Parents are arrested for infanticide after they claim their baby was stolen by a wild dog while vacationing on a supposedly haunted Australian mountain, or was it an aboriginal spirit that absconded with the tyke? Less compelling than the American remake, "A Cry in the Dark." Made for Australian TV. **96m/C VHS.** *AU* Elaine Hudson, John Hamblin, Peter Carroll; ***D:*** Judy Rymer. **TV**

Who Killed Bambi? 1/2 *Qui a tu Bambi?* **2003** Proving that hospitals are creepy in any language, this French thriller uses the hygienic facade of the medical profession as its backdrop for terror. Isabelle (Quinton) is a nursing student, beginning her first residency at a large, isolated hospital. After she faints on the job, her cousin Veronique (Jacob) nicknames her "Bambi," due to her inability to stay on her feet. When the stoic, handsome Dr. Philipp (Lucas) believes that Isabelle's fainting spells might be cured by an operation, she goes under his care, only to discover that Philipp has a penchant for molesting female patients while they're unconscious. Thus begins a protracted cat-and-mouse struggle between doctor and nurse, which reaches increasingly improbable heights. **121m/C DVD.** Laurent Lucas, Catherine Jacob, Sophie Quinton, Doc Mateo; ***D:*** Gilles Marchand; ***C:*** Pierre Milon; ***M:*** Alexandre Beaupain, Lily Margot, Francois Eudes.

Who Killed Doc Robbin? *Sinister House; Curley and His Gang in the Haunted Mansion* **1948** A group of youngsters try to clear their friend, Dan, the town handyman, when the sinister Dr. Robbin is murdered. The follow-up to "The Adventures of Curly and His Gang"; intended as part of a Roach kid-comedy series in the manner of "Our Gang." Fast pace and lots of slapstick give a first impression of spirited juvenile hijinks, but not much is genuinely funny. And the names of the two black kids—"Dis" and "Dat"—aren't funny either. **50m/C VHS, DVD.** Peter Miles, George Zucco, Paul Hurst, Larry Olsen, Don Castle, Eilene Janssen, Virginia Grey; ***D:*** Bernard Carr; ***W:*** Dorothy Davenport Reid, Maurice Geraghty; ***C:*** John Boyle; ***M:*** Marvin Hatley.

Who Killed Mary What's 'Er Name? *Death of a Hooker* **1971 (PG)** A diabetic ex-fighter tracks a prostitute's killer through Greenwich Village. Illogical, incredible and disjointed attempt at comedy/mystery. Odd, unsatisfying ending, with the boxer going into a coma. Good supporting cast. **90m/C VHS.** Red Buttons, Sylvia Miles, Conrad Bain, Ron Carey, David Doyle, Sam Waterston; ***D:*** Ernest Pintoff.

Who Killed the Electric Car? 1/2 **2006 (PG)** Advocate Paine looks at the history of the EV1, the first mass-produced electric automobile, introduced by General Motors in California in 1996 after the state passed legislation requiring automakers to make a portion of their vehicles with zero-emission engines. Despite protests, GM pulled the cars (which were only available by lease) in 2000, citing lack of consumer interest among other reasons. Paine uncovers the EV1's ultimate fate—crushed at GM's Nevada desert proving ground. **92m/C DVD.** *US* ***D:*** Charles Paine; ***W:*** Charles Paine; ***C:*** Thaddeus Wadleigh; ***M:*** Michael Brook.

Who Made the Potatoe Salad? **2005 (R)** Vulgar comedy that wastes a lot of potential. Bumbling San Diego cop Michael (White) proposes to his girlfriend Ashley (Frederique) and insists that they travel to L.A. for Thanksgiving to inform her family. Ashley has been keeping everyone in the dark—Michael knows nothing about them and they know nothing about him, so let the trouble begin. It seems Ashley's dad (Powell) is a former Black Panther who doesn't want a pig for a son-in-law, her brother June Bug (Davis) is a hip-hop slinging thug, and her ex (Griffin) is a con. **90m/C DVD.** Jaleel White, Clifton Powell, DeRay Davis, Eddie Griffin, Jenna Frederique, Ella Joyce, Tommy (Tiny) Lister; ***D:*** Damon "Coke" Daniels; ***W:*** Damon "Coke" Daniels; ***C:*** Geary McLeod; ***M:*** Geoff Levin. **VIDEO**

Who Saw Her Die? 𝒫𝒫 *Chi l'Ha Vista Morire* **1972** Sculptor Franco (Lazenby) is visited by his preteen daughter Roberta (Elmi) at his Venice home. Roberta goes missing and is found dead in a canal. When Franco and his estranged wife Elizabeth (Strindberg) investigate, they learn that there has been a cover-up concerning the murders of several other children. Italian with subtitles. **94m/C DVD.** *IT* George Lazenby, Anita Strindberg, Nicoletta Elmi, Adolfo Celi, Peter Chatel; ***D:*** Aldo Lado; ***W:*** Aldo Lado, Francesco Barilli; ***M:*** Ennio Morricone.

Who Shot Pat? 𝒫𝒫 ½ *Who Shot Patakango?; Brooklyn Love Story* **1992 (R)** Funny, nostalgic, coming of age story set in '50s Brooklyn. Knight stars as Bic Bickham, the leader of a clean-living "gang" of seniors at a Brooklyn vocational school. Memorable vintage soundtrack features hits by legendary artists Chuck Berry and Bo Diddly. **102m/C VHS, DVD.** David Edwin Knight, Sandra Bullock, Kevin Otto, Aaron Ingram, Brad Randall; ***D:*** Robert Brooks; ***W:*** Robert Brooks, Halle Brooks; ***C:*** Robert Brooks.

Who Slew Auntie Roo? 𝒫𝒫 ½ *Whoever Slew Auntie Roo?; Gingerbread House* **1971 (PG)** An updated twist on the Hansel and Gretel fairy tale. Features Winters as an odd, reclusive widow mistaken for the fairy tale's children-eating witch by one of the orphans at her annual Christmas party—with dire consequences. **90m/C VHS, DVD.** Shelley Winters, Ralph Richardson, Mark Lester, Lionel Jeffries, Hugh Griffith; ***D:*** Curtis Harrington; ***W:*** Robert Blees.

Who Wants to Kill Jessie? 𝒫𝒫 **1965** Lunatic Czech comedy about a jealous wife and a comic strip babe. A scientist has invented a device that makes dreams visible and she decides to see what goes on in her meek hubby's subconscious. He's dreaming about another inventor—Jessie, an imperiled va-va-voom comic strip character. When wifey interferes, the side effect is that the dreams show up in reality and Jessie brings along the villains who are chasing her. Lots of sight gags; Czech with subtitles. **79m/B DVD.** *CZ* Dana Medricka, Jiri Sovak, Olga Shoberova, Karel Effa, Juraj Visny; ***D:*** Vaclav Vorkicek; ***W:*** Vaclav Vorkicek, Milos Macourek; ***C:*** Jan Nemecek; ***M:*** Svatopluk Havelka.

Whodunit 𝒫 **1982 (R)** The bad horror flicks always seem to have (usually young) characters murdered one at a time, often on a remote island. This loser is no exception. **82m/C VHS.** Rick Bean, Gary Phillips; ***D:*** Bill Naud; ***W:*** Anthony Shaffer.

Whole New Thing 𝒫𝒫 **2005** Precocious 13-year-old Emerson (Webber in his feature debut) has been home-schooled by his hippie parents Kaya (Jenkins) and Rog (Joy). Worried about his social skills, Kaya decides androgynous Emerson should now attend public school, where he's promptly beaten up, which Emerson takes with remarkable poise. He's not so self-possessed about his gay middle-aged English teacher, Don (McIvor), on whom Emerson develops a major crush. Don fends off Emerson's inappropriate advances while suffering through a midlife crisis—one shared by Emerson's parents, who are having marital problems. **92m/C DVD.** *CA* Rebecca Jenkins, Robert Joy, Callum Keith Rennie, Daniel McIvor, Aaron Webber; ***D:*** Amnon Buchbinder; ***W:*** Daniel McIvor, Amnon Buchbinder; ***C:*** Christopher Ball; ***M:*** David Buchbinder.

The Whole Nine Yards 𝒫𝒫 ½ **2000 (PG-13)** Wimpy dentist Oz (Perry) has his life turned to chaos when former hit man Jimmy (Willis) moves in next door, inspiring his wife Sophie (Arquette), who's bored and wants Oz dead for the insurance money, and Jill, Oz's receptionist, who aspires to be a hit woman herself. Sophie nags Oz into a plot to alert Jimmy's former employers of his whereabouts, which brings in a whole bunch of new over-the-top characters, all of whom want somebody dead. While it's true that most of the plot elements are not only ridiculous, but cribbed from other hit man movies, this one works because the actors all do fine jobs (except maybe Arquette), and seem to be having a good time. One of those movies that plays much better on video than on the big screen. **101m/C VHS, DVD.** Bruce Willis, Matthew Perry, Michael Clarke Duncan, Natasha Henstridge, Amanda Peet, Rosanna Arquette, Kevin Pollak, Harland Williams; ***D:*** Jonathan Lynn; ***W:*** Mitchell Kapner; ***C:*** David Franco; ***M:*** Randy Edelman.

The Whole Shebang 𝒫𝒫 **2001** Low-key, sentimental romantic comedy. After the heir to the Barzini fireworks company blows himself up during a little extra-marital nookie, Pop (Giannini) sends for Neapolitan cousin Giovanni (Tucci, heavy on the shtick) to come to New Jersey as a replacement. Giovanni has been suicidally lovesick over a heartless beauty (Champa) but his luck may change when he meets his cousin's not-so-brokenhearted widow, Val (Fonda). Val is being wooed by Joey Zito (DeSando), whose family is eager to learn Pop's pyrotechnical secrets. A big fireworks competition (which was filmed in Naples) adds some pow. **97m/C DVD.** *US CA* Stanley Tucci, Bridget Fonda, Giancarlo Giannini, Talia Shire, Anthony DeSando, Anna Maria Alberghetti, Jo Champa, Alexander Milani; ***D:*** George Zaloom; ***W:*** Jeff Rothberg, George Zaloom; ***C:*** Jacek Laskus; ***M:*** Evan Lurie.

The Whole Shootin' Match 𝒫𝒫𝒫 **1979** Two 30-something Texas nobodies chase the American Dream via a sure-fire invention called the Kitchen Wizard, after failing in the small-animal biz and polyurethane. Offbeat, very low-budget independent feature shot interestingly in sepia tones. Sympathetic and human. **108m/C VHS.** Matthew Perry, Sonny Carl Davis, Doris Hargrave; ***D:*** Eagle Pennell.

The Whole Ten Yards 𝒫 ½ **2004 (PG-13)** Apparently, this is one yard too many. Stretching the premise of the original into a better-left-undone mess, sequel reunites dorky dentist Oz (Perry) with ex-hitman Jimmy the Tulip (Willis) and his still-aspiring hit woman wife Jill (Peet), who are trying to live on the down-low in Mexico. Jill is still trying (and failing) to become an assassin while Jimmy's attempts at blending in consist of pretending to be a house-husband to terrifically bad comic effect. Oz, meanwhile is living in L.A. with wife Cynthia (Henstridge). Shred of a plot centers around the revenge scheme of Lazlo Gogolak (Pollack), whose son Janni (also Pollack) was whacked by Oz and the Tulip in the not great but infinitely better original. Joyless performances by all underscored by a spectacularly bad Pollack. **99m/C DVD.** *US* Bruce Willis, Matthew Perry, Amanda Peet, Kevin Pollak, Natasha Henstridge, Frank Collison, Johnny Messner, Silas Weir Mitchell, Tasha Smith; ***D:*** Howard Deutch; ***W:*** Mitchell Kapner, George Gallo; ***C:*** Neil Roach; ***M:*** John Debney.

The Whole Town's Talking 𝒫𝒫𝒫 **1935** Meek clerk Arthur Jones (Robinson) usually leads an uneventful life, until the police arrest him, thinking he's escaped mobster Killer Mannion (Robinson again). Arthur manages to prove his identity and is issued an ID card to settle the confusion, but the mix-up has hit the papers and when Mannion finds out about his double, he steals the card and kidnaps Arthur's Aunt Agatha (Ellsler) and coworker Wilhelmina (Arhtur) to ensure his cooperation. Mannion goes on a crime spree and Arthur must figure a way out of his double trouble. Based on a novel by William R. Burnett. **95m/B VHS.** Edward G. Robinson, Jean Arthur, Arthur Hohl, Wallace Ford, Arthur Byron, Donald Meek, Paul Harvey, Effie Ellsler; ***D:*** John Ford; ***W:*** Jo Swerling, Robert Riskin; ***C:*** Joseph August.

The Whole Wide World 𝒫𝒫𝒫 **1996 (PG)** Adaptation of Novalyne Price Ellis' memoirs about her friendship with "Conan the Barbarian" pulp writer Robert E. Howard. In 1933, proper young Cross Plains, Texas schoolteacher (and aspiring writer) Price (Zellweger) arranges an introduction to local eccentric Howard (D'Onofrio), who lives with his overprotective, dying mother (Wedgeworth) and respected doctor father (Presnell) while churning out his bloody tales. Howard has few, if any, social skills but his unpredictability appeals to the sensible Price and the two have a turbulent emotional relationship that never blooms into a full romance. Howard committed suicide in 1936 at the age of 30. **111m/C VHS, DVD.** Renee Zellweger, Vincent D'Onofrio, Ann Wedgeworth, Harve Presnell, Helen Cates, Benjamin Mouton, Michael Corbett, Marion Eaten, Leslie Berger, Chris Shearer, Sandy Walper, Dell Aldrich, Libby Villari, Antonia Bogdanovich, Elizabeth D'Onofrio, Stephen Marshall; ***D:*** Dan Ireland; ***W:*** Michael Scott Myers, Novalyne Price Ellis; ***C:*** Claudio Rocha; ***M:*** Hans Zimmer, Harry Gregson-Williams.

Who'll Save Our Children? 𝒫𝒫𝒫 **1982** Two children are abandoned and left on the doorstep of a middle-aged, childless couple. Years later the natural parents, now reformed, attempt to reclaim their children. Well cast and topical. **96m/C VHS.** Shirley Jones, Len Cariou, Conchata Ferrell, Frances Sternhagen, Cassie Yates, David Hayward; ***D:*** George Schaefer. **TV**

Who'll Stop the Rain? 𝒫𝒫𝒫 ½ *Dog Soldiers* **1978 (R)** A temperamental Vietnam vet (Nolte) is enlisted in a smuggling scheme to transport a large amount of heroin into California. An excellent blend of drama, comedy, action, suspense, and tragedy. Based on Robert Stone's novel "Dog Soldiers." Outstanding period soundtrack by Creedence Clearwater Revival, including title song. Violent and compelling tale of late-'60s disillusionment. **126m/C VHS, DVD.** Nick Nolte, Tuesday Weld, Michael Moriarty, Anthony Zerbe, Richard Masur, Ray Sharkey, David Opatoshu, Charles Haid, Gail Strickland; ***D:*** Karel Reisz; ***W:*** Judith Rascoe; ***C:*** Richard H. Kline; ***M:*** Laurence Rosenthal.

Wholly Moses! **WOOF!** **1980 (PG)** Set in biblical times, this alleged comedy concerns a phony religious prophet who begins to believe that his mission is to lead the chosen. Horrible ripoff of "Life of Brian," released the previous year. What a cast—what a waste! **125m/C VHS, DVD.** Dudley Moore, Laraine Newman, James Coco, Paul Sand, Dom DeLuise, Jack Gilford, John Houseman, Madeline Kahn, Richard Pryor, John Ritter; ***D:*** Gary Weis.

Whoopee! 𝒫𝒫 **1930** Cantor stars in his first sound picture as a rich hypochondriac sent out west for his health, where he encounters rugged cowboys and Indians. Filmed in two-color Technicolor and based on Ziegfeld's 1928 Broadway production with the same cast. Dances supervised by Busby Berkeley. ♫The Song of the Setting Sun; Mission Number; Makin' Whoopee; A Girlfriend of a Boyfriend of Mine; My Baby Just Cares for Me; I'll Still Belong to You; Stetson. **93m/C VHS.** Eddie Cantor, Ethel Shutta, Paul Gregory, Eleanor Hunt, Betty Grable; ***D:*** Thornton Freeland.

The Whoopee Boys 𝒫 **1986 (R)** A New York lowlife in Palm Beach tries to reform himself by saving a school for needy children so his rich girlfriend will marry him. Full of unfunny jokes and very bad taste, with no redeeming qualities whatever. **89m/C VHS, DVD.** Michael O'Keefe, Paul Rodriguez, Denholm Elliott, Carol(e) Shelley, Eddie Deezen, Marsha Warfield, Elizabeth Arlen, Joe Spinell, Robert Gwaltney, Stephen Davies, Taylor Negron, Greg Germann, David Keith, Noelle Parker, Dan O'Herlihy, Lucinda Jenney; ***D:*** John Byrum; ***W:*** Jeff Buhai; ***C:*** Ralf Bode; ***M:*** Jack Nitzsche.

Whoops Apocalypse 𝒫𝒫 ½ **1983** T.V. series that offers a satiric account of events leading up to WWIII. Invasion in South America leads British prime minister to suggest nuclear retaliation. Uneven, lacking in the Strangelovian element, but funny in spots. **137m/C VHS.** *GB* John Cleese, John Barron, Richard Griffiths, Peter Jones, Bruce Montague, Barry Morse, Rik Mayall, Ian Richardson, Alexei Sayle, Herbert Lom, Joanne Pearce; ***D:*** John Reardon; ***W:*** Andrew Marshall, David Renwick.

Whore 𝒫𝒫 *If You Can't Say It, Just See It* **1991 (R)** Ken Russell's gritty night in the life of cynical prostitute Theresa Russell is strong medicine, a powerful antidote to sappy Hollywood films that glorify streetwalking. Also available in the 92-minute original uncut version, an 85-minute NC-17 version, and an alternate R-Rated version. **80m/C VHS.** Theresa Russell, Antonio Vargas; ***D:*** Ken Russell; ***W:*** Ken Russell, Deborah Dalton.

Whore 2 𝒫 ½ *Bad Girls* **1994 (R)** Jack is a middle-aged writer who moves into Hell's Kitchen in order to do research for a book about prostitutes. Then Jack gets involved with two of the girls—the tough, jealous Lori and childlike Mary Lou. **85m/C VHS.** Amos Kollek, Marla Sucharetza, Mari Nelson; ***D:*** Amos Kollek; ***W:*** Amos Kollek.

Who's Afraid of Virginia Woolf? 𝒫𝒫𝒫𝒫 **1966 (R)** Nichols debuts as a director in this biting Edward Albee play. A teacher and his wife (Segal and Dennis) are invited to the home of a burned-out professor and his foul-mouthed, bitter, yet seductive wife (Burton and Taylor). The guests get more than dinner, as the evening deteriorates into brutal verbal battles between the hosts. Taylor and Dennis won Oscars; Burton's Oscar-nominated portrait of the tortured husband is magnificent. Richard and Liz's best film together. **127m/B VHS, DVD.** Richard Burton, Elizabeth Taylor, George Segal, Sandy Dennis; ***D:*** Mike Nichols; ***W:*** Ernest Lehman; ***C:*** Haskell Wexler; ***M:*** Alex North. Oscars '66: Actress (Taylor), Art Dir./Set Dec., B&W, B&W Cinematog., Costume Des. (B&W), Support. Actress (Dennis); British Acad. '66: Actor (Burton), Actress (Taylor), Film; Natl. Bd. of Review '66: Actress (Taylor); N.Y. Film Critics '66: Actress (Taylor).

Who's Got the Action? 𝒫 ½ **1963** Martin and Turner are a husband and wife divided by his love of playing the ponies. In order to keep his gambling under control Turner schemes to become his new bookie. But when Martin suddenly goes on a winning streak, the new bookie is in trouble with her former competition, who just happen to be the Mob. Strained, flat comedy with Turner especially miscast. **93m/C VHS.** Lana Turner, Dean Martin, Walter Matthau, Eddie Albert, Nita Talbot, Margo, Paul Ford, John McGiver, Jack Albertson; ***D:*** Daniel Mann; ***W:*** Jack Rose.

Who's Harry Crumb? 𝒫 ½ **1989 (PG-13)** Bumbling detective Candy can't even investigate a routine kidnapping! His incompetence is catching: the viewer can't detect a single genuinely funny moment. Candy is the only likeable thing in this all-around bad, mindless farce. **95m/C VHS, DVD.** John Candy, Jeffrey Jones, Annie Potts, Tim Thomerson, Barry Corbin, Shawnee Smith, Valri Bromfield, Renee Coleman, Joe Flaherty, Lyle Alzado, James Belushi, Stephen Young; ***D:*** Paul Flaherty; ***W:*** Robert Conte; ***M:*** Michel Colombier.

Who's Minding the Mint? 𝒫𝒫𝒫 **1967** A money checker at the U.S. Mint must replace $50,000 he accidentally destroyed. He enlists a retired money printer and an inept gang to infiltrate the mint and replace the lost cash, with predictable chaos resulting. Non-stop zaniness in this wonderful comedy that never got its due when released. Thieves who befriend Hutton include Denver of "Gilligan's Island" and Farr, later of "M*A*S*H." **97m/C VHS.** Jim Hutton, Dorothy Provine, Milton Berle, Joey Bishop, Bob Denver, Walter Brennan, Jamie Farr; ***D:*** Howard Morris; ***C:*** Joseph Biroc.

Who's Minding the Store? 𝒫𝒫 ½ **1963** Well, it's certainly not Lewis, who plays poodle sitter Raymond Phiffier who's in love with rich girl Barbara (St. John). Barbara's imperious mother (Moorehead) is determined to break up the duo and hires Raymond to work at the family department store (hoping he'll be a disaster), instead he becomes a success in his own slapstick way. **90m/C VHS.** Jerry Lewis, Jill St. John, Agnes Moorehead, John McGiver, Ray Walston, Nancy Kulp; ***D:*** Frank Tashlin; ***W:*** Frank Tashlin, Harry Tugend; ***C:*** Wallace Kelley; ***M:*** Joseph J. Lilley.

Who's That Girl? 𝒫 **1987 (PG)** A flighty, wrongly convicted parolee kidnaps her uptight lawyer and they have wacky adventures as she goes in search of the crumb that landed her in the pokey. Plenty of Madonna tunes, if that's what you like; they briefly keep you from wondering why you're not laughing. Kind of a remake (a bad one) of "Bringing Up Baby" (1938). **94m/C VHS, DVD.** Madonna, Griffin Dunne, John Mills, Haviland (Haylie) Morris, Albert "Poppy" Popwell; ***D:*** James Foley; ***C:*** Jan De Bont. Golden Raspberries '87: Worst Actress (Madonna).

Who's That Knocking at My Door? 𝒫𝒫𝒫 *J.R.; I Call First* **1968** Interesting debut for Scorsese, in which he exercises many of the themes and techniques that he polished for later films. An autobiographical drama about an Italian-American youth growing up in NYC, focusing on street life, Catholicism and adolescent bonding. Begun as a student film called "I Call First"; later developed into a feature.

Keitel's film debut. **90m/B VHS, DVD.** Harvey Keitel, Zena Bethune; ***D:*** Martin Scorsese.

Who's the Man? **1993 (R)** Two clowning companions who work in a barbershop in Harlem get recruited onto the police force to investigate a murder. Doctor Dre and Ed Lover (themselves) make use of their hip-hop music connections and full-throttle slapstick humor to enliven the search. Salt of "Salt 'n' Pepa," is the female lead and Ice-T plays a gangster. First-time director Demme works his star duo for both foolish and vulgar humor. Filming done mostly on location in Harlem. Includes a lengthy list of cameo appearances by several hip-hop performers. For fans; based on a story by Dre, Lover, and Seth Greenland. **124m/C VHS, DVD.** Ed Lover, Cheryl "Salt" James, Ice-T, Jim Moody, Colin Quinn, Kim Chan, Rozwill Young, Badja (Medu) Djola, Richard Bright, Denis Leary, Andre B. Blake, Bill Bellamy, Louis Freese; ***D:*** Ted (Edward) Demme; ***W:*** Seth Greenland; ***M:*** Michael Wolff.

Who's Who **1978** In a satire on climbing the British social ladder, workers in a London brokerage firm struggle with class issues and find the higher you climb, the more you find greed, pettiness, and stupidity. **75m/C VHS, DVD.** *GB* Bridget Kane, Simon Chandler, Adam Norton, Philip Davis, Joolia Cappleman; ***D:*** Mike Leigh; ***W:*** Mike Leigh. **TV**

Who's Your Caddy? 1/2 **2007 (PG-13)** Rap mogul C-Note (Patton) tries to become a member at the conservative Carolina Pines country club, where he's opposed by snobby club president Cummings (Jones). But C-Note blackmails his way in, causing predictable havoc. Vulgarity and stereotypes abound. **93m/C DVD.** Antwan Andre Patton, Jeffrey Jones, Sherri Shepherd, Faizon Love, Jenifer Lewis, Tamala Jones, Andy Milonakis, Chase Tatum; ***D:*** Don Michael Paul; ***W:*** Don Michael Paul, Bradley Allenstein, Robert Henny; ***C:*** Thomas Callaway; ***M:*** Jon Lee.

Who's Your Monkey 1/2 *Throwing Stars* **2007 (R)** Four longtime buddies are in a crisis after doctor Mark (Grimes) kills a threatening local drug dealer and they need to get rid of the body. And, uh, animal porn is a main plot point, which would explain the monkey. **86m/C DVD.** Scott Grimes, Jason London, Scott Michael Campbell, David DeLuise, Kevin Durand, Wayne Knight, Ali Hillis, Susan May Pratt; ***D:*** Todd Breau; ***W:*** Ryan Steckloff; ***C:*** Michael Jacob Kerber; ***M:*** Ron Alan Cohen. **VIDEO**

Whose Child Am I? **1975 (R)** A woman so desperately wants a child of her own that she doesn't mind who the father is. Ludicrous and vulgar. **90m/C VHS.** Kate O'Mara, Paul Freeman, Edward Judd, Felicity Devonshire; ***D:*** Lawrence Britten.

Whose Life Is It Anyway? 1/2 **1981 (R)** Black humor abounds. Sculptor Dreyfuss is paralyzed from the neck down in an auto accident. What follows is his struggle to persuade the hospital authorities to let him die. Excellent cast headed impressively by Dreyfuss; Lahti as his doctor and hospital head Cassavetes also are superb. From Brian Clark's successful Broadway play. **118m/C VHS, DVD.** Richard Dreyfuss, John Cassavetes, Christine Lahti, Bob Balaban, Kenneth McMillan, Kaki Hunter, Thomas Carter; ***D:*** John Badham; ***W:*** Reginald Rose, Brian Clark.

Why Change Your Wife? 1/2 **1920** A rare, recently re-discovered silent comedy. Swanson and Meighan play married couple Beth and Robert who find themselves drifting apart after ten years of marriage. Robert becomes involved with someone else and Beth demands a divorce. After Robert remarries, Beth decides she wants him back and the real fun begins as she tries every trick in the book to regain her ex-husband. Piano scored. **100m/B VHS, DVD.** Gloria Swanson, Thomas Meighan, Bebe Daniels; ***D:*** Cecil B. DeMille.

Why Do Fools Fall in Love? **1998 (R)** Frankie Lymon was a teen do-wop singing sensation in the mid-'50s but a career slide led to heroin addiction and an OD death at the age of 25 in 1968. The other thing Frankie liked to do was marry—without bothering to get divorced. So there are three would-be widows battling for what's left of Lymon's estate: R&B singer Zola Taylor (Berry), goodtime girl and single mom Elizabeth Waters (Fox), and churchgoing schoolteacher Emira Eagle (Rochon). The ladies pull out of the stops but Lymon remains a mystery. **115m/C VHS, DVD.** Larenz Tate, Halle Berry, Lela Rochon, Vivica A. Fox, Paul Mazursky, Pamela Reed, Little Richard, Ben Vereen, Lane Smith, Alexis Cruz; ***D:*** Gregory Nava; ***W:*** Tina Andrews; ***C:*** Edward Lachman; ***M:*** Stephen James Taylor.

Why Do They Call It Love When They Mean Sex? *Por Que Lo Llaman Amor Cuando Quieren Decir Sexo?* **1992** Gloria (Forque) works in a live-sex act but is forced to change partners and work with inexperienced Manu (Sanz), who needs some quick cash because of gambling debts. But everything goes well until Manu's respectable parents meet Gloria and think the duo are just a nice conventional couple. **115m/C VHS, DVD.** *SP* Jorge Sanz, Veronica Forque, Fernando Colomo, Fernando Guillen, Rosa Maria Sarda, Alejandra Grepi, Elisa Matilla, Isabel Ordaz; ***D:*** Manuel Gomez Pereira; ***W:*** Manuel Gomez Pereira; ***C:*** Hans Burman; ***M:*** Manuel Tena.

Why Does Herr R. Run Amok? *Warum Lauft Herr R Amok?* **1969** Notorious Fassbinder black comedy about a middle-class man, unable to cope with the increasing problems of modern life, who suddenly murders his family. The characters are called by the actors' names to heighten the sense of reality. Film is based on a case history. In German with English subtitles. **88m/C VHS, DVD.** *GE* Kurt Raab, Lilith Ungerer, Amadeus Fengler, Hanna Schygulla, Franz Maron; ***D:*** Rainer Werner Fassbinder, Michael Fengler; ***W:*** Rainer Werner Fassbinder, Michael Fengler.

Why Has Bodhi-Darma Left for the East **1989** Set in a remote monastery in the Korean mountains, film follows an old master, close to death, who must lead his disciples in their search for spiritual freedom. The film's title is a Zen koan—an unanswerable riddle that serves as an aid on the path to enlightenment. Korean with subtitles. **135m/C VHS, DVD.** *KN* Hae-Jin Huang, Su-Myong Ko, Yi Pan-Yong, Sin Won-Sop; ***D:*** Bae Young-kyun; ***W:*** Bae Young-kyun; ***C:*** Bae Young-kyun.

Why Me? **1990 (R)** Two jewel thieves unknowingly steal an enormously valuable ruby ring and are in over their heads trying to evade the cops and everyone else. In the same vein as the much-funnier "Nuns on the Run," this caper is done in by bad acting and too much ill-conceived slapstick. Adapted by Donald E. Westlake from his own novel. **96m/C VHS.** Christopher Lambert, Christopher Lloyd, Kim Greist, J.T. Walsh, Michael J. Pollard, Tony Plana, John Hancock, Lawrence Tierney; ***D:*** Gene Quintano; ***W:*** Donald E. Westlake.

Why Must I Die? 1/2 *Thirteen Steps to Death* **1960** Low-budget sensationalism from AIP and director Del Ruth's last pic. Singer Lois King (Moore) walks out on her crook boyfriend Eddie (Ames) to make a new life. She falls for club owner Kenny Randall (Harvey) before Eddie and his hard-boiled new squeeze Dottie (Paget) show up, wanting Lois to help them rob the joint. Trigger-happy Dottie kills Kenny but it's Lois who's tried, convicted, and sentenced to death row. When unrepentant Dottie is imprisoned on another crime, can Lois convince her to tell the truth or will she soon be getting the shock of her life? **86m/B DVD.** Terry Moore, Debra Paget, Bert Freed, Juli Reding, Phil Harvey, Lionel Ames, Fred Sherman; ***D:*** Roy Del Ruth; ***W:*** Richard Bernstein, George Waters; ***C:*** Ernest Haller; ***M:*** Richard LaSalle.

Why Shoot the Teacher **1979** A young teacher sent to a one-room schoolhouse in a small prairie town in Saskatchewan during the Depression gets a cold reception on the cold prairie. One of the more popular films at the Canadian box office. Cort was Harold in "Harold and Maude." Based on the novel by Max Braithwaite. **101m/C VHS.** *CA* Bud Cort, Samantha Eggar, Chris Wiggins; ***D:*** Silvio Narizzano; ***W:*** James DeFelice.

The Wicked *Outback Vampires* **1989** Though packaged as serious horror, this is a cheap, tacky spoof with folks stranded at the country residence of a vampire family. Sole point of interest: these Transylvanian cliches take place in the Australian outback. Kids might actually like this (gore isn't severe), if they can surmount the thick Down Under accents. **87m/C VHS, DVD.** Brett Cumo, Richard Morgan, Angela Kennedy, Maggie Blinco, John (Roy Slaven) Doyle; ***D:*** Colin Eggleston.

Wicked **1998 (R)** Fourteen-year-old Ellie (Stiles) has a big Electra complex—she's desperate to get Daddy Ben's (Moses) attention (he's too busy boffing their au pair) and get rid of Mom Karen (Field). Then Karen is murdered and Detective Boland (Parks) first suspects their sleazy neighbor, Lawson (Muldoon), with whom Karen had been carrying on. But Inger, Ellie's younger sister, notices that things aren't, well, normal between her sibling and their pop. But the twists aren't done yet. **87m/C VHS, DVD.** Julia Stiles, William R. Moses, Chelsea Field, Patrick Muldoon, Michael Parks, Vanessa Zima; ***D:*** Michael Steinberg; ***W:*** Eric Weiss; ***C:*** Bernd Heinl; ***M:*** Eric Martinez.

Wicked City **1989** Wild and woolly anime is similar in tone to a James Bond movie. In fact, the whole production has a mid-'60s look. A young man named Taki is picked up by a sexy woman in a bar and regrets his decision when she does one of those really icky transformations. Seems she's a visitor from the parallel Black World of monsters. He's an agent of the Black Guard, a secret intelligence organization that protects the Earth from these supernatural bad guys. The story revolves around Guiseppi Mayart, a strange little character who looks (and acts!) like an oversexed E.T., and is the key to a treaty between the two worlds. Taki and his reluctant female partner Makea are assigned to guard the debauched diplomat. **82m/C DVD.** *JP* ***D:*** Yoshiaki Kawajiri; ***W:*** Kisei Choo; ***C:*** Kinichi Ishikawa; ***V:*** Greg Snegoff, Michael J. Reynolds, Alexandra Kenworthy.

Wicked City **1992** Humans are uneasily coexisting with Reptoids (creatures that can assume human shape) in this sci-fi tale based on a Japanese comic strip. Then Hong Kong police discover a plot by the Reptoids to destroy mankind and rule the world (what else is new). Nifty special effects. Available dubbed or in Cantonese with subtitles. **88m/C VHS, DVD.** *HK* Tatsuya Nakadai, Yuen Woo Ping, Roy Cheung, Jacky Cheung, Leon Lai, Michelle Li; ***D:*** Peter Mak; ***W:*** Tsui Hark, Roy Szeto; ***C:*** Wai Keung (Andrew) Lau, Joe Chan; ***M:*** Richard Yuen.

The Wicked Lady **1945** Posh but lame costume drama about a bored 17th century noblewoman who takes to highway robbery to spice up her life. Credulity-stretcher extraordinaire. Based on "The Life and Death of Wicked Lady Skelton" by Magdalen King-Hall. Mason is cheeky as a fellow highwayman. Remade in 1983 with Faye Dunaway. **103m/B VHS.** *GB* James Mason, Margaret Lockwood, Patricia Roc, Michael Rennie, Felix Aylmer, Enid Stamp-Taylor, Griffith Jones; ***D:*** Leslie Arliss.

The Wicked Lady 1/2 **1983 (R)** Remake of the 1945 costumer about a 17th-century noblewoman trying her hand at highway robbery. More noted for its low-cut costumes and racy humor than any talent involved. **99m/C VHS.** *GB* Faye Dunaway, John Gielgud, Denholm Elliott, Alan Bates, Glynis Barber, Oliver Tobias, Prunella Scales; ***D:*** Michael Winner; ***W:*** Michael Winner; ***C:*** Jack Cardiff; ***M:*** Tony Banks.

Wicked Lake 1/2 **2008** Four lesbian witches go to a remote mountain cabin to perform a ritual, get insulted and assaulted by the local rednecks, and take bloody revenge at midnight when their powers spontaneously pop into being. There's no one to root for in this film—not the doltish cowardly men, not the smart slutty psychopaths who like to get naked and make out when they're not getting even in the bloodiest of ways. Wait, maybe there is someone to root for. **95m/C DVD.** Will Keenan, Robin Sydney, Tim Thomerson, Carlee Baker, Frank Birney, Michael Esparza, Eryn Joslyn, Eve Mauro, Mark Senter; ***D:*** Zach Passero; ***W:*** Chris Sivertson, Adam Rockoff; ***C:*** Stephen Osborn; ***M:*** Al Jourgensen. **VIDEO**

Wicked Stepmother **1989 (PG-13)** A family discovers that an aged stepmother is actually a witch. Davis walked off the film shortly before she died, and was replaced by Carrera. Davis's move was wise; the result is dismal, and would have been had she stayed. As it is the viewer wonders: How come the stepmother isn't Davis anymore? Davis's unfortunate last role. **90m/C VHS.** Bette Davis, Barbara Carrera, Colleen Camp, Lionel Stander, David Rasche, Tom Bosley, Seymour Cassel, Evelyn Keyes, Richard Moll, Laurene Landon, James Dixon; ***D:*** Larry Cohen; ***W:*** Larry Cohen; ***C:*** Bryan England; ***M:*** Robert Folk.

Wicked Ways *A Table for One* **1999 (R)** Matt Draper (Rooker) is a bigamist. And when wife Ruth (De Mornay) discovers his other life, she becomes determined to make the vow "till death do us part" a reality. Watchable cast in a familiar storyline. **110m/C VHS, DVD.** Rebecca De Mornay, Michael Rooker, Lisa Zane, Mark Rolston, Peter Dobson; ***D:*** Ron Senkowski; ***W:*** Ron Senkowski; ***C:*** Chris Walling; ***M:*** Evan Evans. **VIDEO**

The Wicked, Wicked West *Painted Angels* **1997 (R)** Follows the desolate lives of several prostitutes and their pragmatic madam Annie Ryan (Fricker) in a prairie town bordello in the 1870s. **108m/C VHS, DVD.** Brenda Fricker, Kelly McGillis, Bronagh Gallagher, Meret Becker, Lisa Jakub; ***D:*** Jon Sanders; ***W:*** Jon Sanders; ***C:*** Gerald Packer.

The Wicker Man 1/2 **1975** The disappearance of a young girl leads a devoutly religious Scottish policeman to an island whose denizens practice bizarre pagan sexual rituals. An example of occult horror that achieves its mounting terror without gratuitous gore. The first original screenplay by playwright Shaffer. Beware shortened versions that may still lurk out there; the 103-minute restored director's cut is definitive. **103m/C VHS, DVD.** *GB* Edward Woodward, Christopher Lee, Britt Ekland, Diane Cilento, Ingrid Pitt, Lindsay Kemp, Irene Sunters, Walter Carr, Geraldine Cowper, Lesley Mackie; ***D:*** Robin Hardy; ***W:*** Anthony Shaffer; ***C:*** Harry Waxman; ***M:*** Paul Giovanni.

The Wicker Man WOOF! **2006 (PG-13)** What was originally creepily foreboding (with a shocker ending) has turned into a laughable muddle in this remake of the 1973 Brit horror pic. An overwrought Cage stars as troubled cop Edward Malus, who looks into the disappearance of ex-fiance Willow's (Beahan) young daughter. This involves traveling to an isolated island community off the Washington coast, where Malus discovers a matriarchal community of beekeepers led by Sister Summerisle (Burstyn) practicing pagan goddess rites. Why LaBute wanted to do this story in the first place is a bigger mystery than why it turned out so badly. **97m/C DVD.** *US* Nicolas Cage, Ellen Burstyn, Kate Beahan, Frances Conroy, Molly Parker, Leelee Sobieski, Diane Delano; ***D:*** Neil LaBute; ***W:*** Neil LaBute; ***C:*** Paul Sarossy; ***M:*** Angelo Badalamenti.

Wicker Park **2004 (PG-13)** A sluggish homage to the 1996 French thriller "L'Appartement." Chicago advertising exec Matthew (Hartnett) is engaged to Rebecca (Pare), his boss' sister, when he thinks he sees his one true love, Lisa (Kruger), who disappeared from his life two years before. Matt cancels a business trip and tells no one except best bud Luke (Lillard) as he hunts for the dame. This leads him to an apartment rented by the mysterious Alex (Byrne), who was Lisa's neighbor. Romantic obsession, stalking, and many confusing flashbacks ensue and everyone, except for the goofy Lillard, seems quite glum. **115m/C DVD.** *US* Josh Hartnett, Rose Byrne, Matthew Lillard, Diane Kruger, Christopher Cousins, Jessica Pare; ***D:*** Paul McGuigan; ***W:*** Brandon Boyce; ***C:*** Peter Sova; ***M:*** Cliff Martinez, Liza Richardson.

Wide Awake 1/2 **1997 (PG)** After the death of his beloved grandfather (Loggia), a young Catholic school boy (Cross) begins a mission to find God in order to find out if his grandpa is O.K. He asks difficult questions of his parents (Leary and Delaney) and teachers, including O'Donnell as a sports obsessed nun who compares Jesus and his disciples to a baseball team. He explores Judaism, Islam and Buddhism as well as Christianity. Finally he has an encounter with an angel that restores his faith. While Cross comes across well, the fellow youngsters in the movie have a stagy stiffness to their lines and expressions that lend the movie a hokey feel. **88m/C VHS, DVD.** Joseph Cross, Dana Delany, Rosie O'Donnell, Denis Leary, Robert Loggia, Dan Lauria, Timothy Reifsnyder, Camryn Manheim; ***D:*** M. Night Shyamalan; ***W:*** M. Night Shyamalan; ***C:*** Adam Holender; ***M:*** Edmund Choi.

The Wide Blue Road *La Grande Strada Azzurra* **1957** Neo-realist melodrama stars Montand as stubborn fisherman Squarcio, who lives with his family in a small village off the Adriatic Sea. Determined to support his family by any means, he scorns the nets used by his fellow fisherman and instead goes illegal dynamite fishing. Successful at first, this practice leads to tragedy for Squarcio and his family. Pontecorvo's debut film; Italian with subtitles. **99m/C VHS, DVD.** *IT* Yves Montand, Alida Valli, Francisco Rabal, Frederica Ranchi, Ronaldo Bonacchi; ***D:*** Gillo Pontecorvo; ***W:*** Gillo Pontecorvo, Franco Solinas; ***C:*** Mario Montuori; ***M:*** Carlo Franci.

Wide Open Faces **1938** Every crook in town is looking for some missing stolen loot. Soda jerk Brown outwits them all in his own inimitable way. The story may be predictable, but Brown's physical humor keeps things interesting. **67m/B VHS.** Joe E. Brown, Jane Wyman, Alison Skipworth, Alan Baxter, Lucien Littlefield, Sidney Toler, Berton Churchill, Barbara Pepper, Stanley Fields, Horace Murphy; ***D:*** Kurt Neumann; ***C:*** Paul Vogel.

Wide Sargasso Sea **1992 (NC-17)** Jamaica in the 1840s is a seething, mysterious paradise—a former British slave colony with a mix of powerful voodoo culture, beauty, and eroticism providing a very potent brew, a perfect setting for this soaper. Based on the novel by Jean Rhys, which is something of a prequel to Charlotte Bronte's "Jane Eyre." Properly English Edward Rochester meets and marries the tragic Antoinette—the same mad wife locked in the attic in the Bronte novel. Explicit nudity and sex earn the NC-17, but the film is tragic without being sensationalized. Also available in an edited R-rated and unrated versions. **98m/C VHS, DVD.** *AU* Karina Lombard, Nathaniel Parker, Rachel Ward, Michael York, Martine Beswick, Claudia Robinson, Rowena King, Huw Christie Williams; ***D:*** John Duigan; ***W:*** Jan Sharp, Carole Angier, John Duigan; ***C:*** Geoff Burton; ***M:*** Stewart Copeland.

Wide Sargasso Sea 1/2 **2006** TV adaptation made for the BBC that's based on the 1966 novel by Jean Rhys, which she wrote as a prequel to Charlotte Bronte's "Jane Eyre." Young Edward Rochester (Spall) goes to Jamaica to make his fortune and meets Creole beauty Antoinette Cosway-Mason (Hall). Her family offers a substantial dowry and they swiftly marry—before Edward learns about Antoinette's tragic past or the madness that runs in her family. Lust, betrayal, and revenge follow. Previously (and explicitly) filmed in 1993. **84m/C DVD.** *GB* Rafe Spall, Rebecca Hall, Nina Sosanya, Victoria Hamilton, Fraser Ayres, Karen Meagher, Lorraine Burroughs, Alex Robertson; ***D:*** Brendan Maher; ***W:*** Stephen Greenhorn; ***C:*** David Luther; ***M:*** Nina Humphreys. **TV**

The Widow **1976** A story about a woman slowly learning to deal with her own grief, her children's traumas, and monetary worries after the death of her husband. Straightforward, passable domestic drama based on Lynn Caine's best-selling novel. **99m/C VHS.** Michael Learned, Farley Granger, Bradford Dillman, Robert Lansing; ***D:*** J. Lee Thompson. **TV**

Widow Couderc **1974** A provincial widow unknowingly includes an escaped murderer among her liaisons. Based on a novel by Georges Simenon. In French with English subtitles. **92m/C VHS.** *FR* Simone Signoret, Alain Delon; ***D:*** Pierre Granier-Deferre.

The Widow of Saint-Pierre *La Veuve de Saint-Pierre* **2000 (R)** Saint-Pierre is a remote French-run island off the coast of Newfoundland. In 1849, drunken sailor Neel Auguste (Kusturica) is involved in a murder and condemned to death via guillotine—known as the "widow." But the island doesn't have one and it must be sent from another French colony. In the meantime, Auguste is in the custody of the local military officer, Le Capitaine (Auteuil), whose compassionate wife (Binoche) has a repentent Auguste released to do chores for the islanders. But the more Auguste becomes part of the community, the more the townspeople become uneasy about the rightness of his fate. French with subtitles. **112m/C VHS, DVD.** *FR* Juliette Binoche, Daniel Auteuil, Emir Kusturica, Michel Duchaussoy, Sylvie Moreau, Sarah McKenna, Reynald Bouchard, Philippe Magnan; ***D:*** Patrice Leconte; ***W:*** Claude Faraldo; ***C:*** Eduardo Serra; ***M:*** Pascal Esteve.

The Widowing of Mrs. Holroyd **1995** Adapted from an early play by D.H. Lawrence and based on memories of his parents' tempestuous marriage. Mrs. Holroyd (Wanamaker) wishes her blustering coal miner husband (Firth) dead after she falls in love with another man (Dillane). When he suddenly does die, she finds her life changing in unexpected ways. **90m/C DVD.** *GB* Zoe Wanamaker, Colin Firth, Stephen (Dillon) Dillane, Brenda Bruce; ***D:*** Katie Mitchell. **TV**

Widows 1/2 **2002 (PG-13)** A gang of professional thieves are double-crossed and killed during the attempted theft of a Vermeer from an art gallery. When the police bring in their widows for questioning, Dolly (Ruehl) gets suspicious about the circumstances. So she recruits the other women to avenge their men's deaths and to carry out the original heist. **168m/C VHS, DVD.** Mercedes Ruehl, Brooke Shields, Rosie Perez, N'Bushe Wright, Jay O. Sanders, Nigel Bennett, Colm Feore, Rod Wilson, Jacob Davis, Lark Voorhies; ***D:*** Geoffrey Sax; ***W:*** Lynda La Plante; ***C:*** Alan Caso; ***M:*** Simon Boswell. **TV**

Widow's Kiss **1994 (R)** Sean Sager (Astin) is suspicious when his wealthy dad Justin (Davison) dies in the arms of sexy, widowed Vivian (D'Angelo). So he hires detective Eddie Costello (Haysbert), who learns that the widow has left a number of dead husbands behind. But Sean's in desperate trouble when he discovers Vivian gets dad's fortune if Sean should die. Rather dull cable drama wastes its talented cast. **103m/C VHS.** MacKenzie Astin, Beverly D'Angelo, Bruce Davison, Dennis Haysbert, Michael Woolson, Barbara Rush, Anna Maria Horsford, Michael Des Barres, Claudette Nevins; ***D:*** Peter Foldy; ***W:*** Peter Foldy, Mark Donnelly; ***C:*** Doyle Smith; ***M:*** Robert Sprayberry. **CABLE**

Widow's Nest **1977** Three widowed sisters live in a bizarre fantasy world when they lock themselves in a dingy mansion in Cuba of the 1930s. Filmed in Spain. **90m/C VHS.** Patricia Neal, Susan Oliver, Lila Kedrova, Valentina Cortese; ***D:*** Tony Navarro.

Widow's Peak 1/2 **1994 (PG)** 1920s Irish community is run by a dictatorship of well-to-do widows with Mrs. Doyle-Counihan (Plowright) at the helm. Troubles begin for the town non-widow (Farrow) upon the arrival of recently widowed Broome (Richardson), who attracts Dunbar, the nitwit son of Plowright. Entertaining performances (Farrow shows that success is possible after the Wood-man) and beautiful scenery help boost a script that seems torn between whimsical comedy and dark drama. **102m/C VHS, DVD.** *GB* Mia Farrow, Joan Plowright, Natasha Richardson, Adrian Dunbar, Jim Broadbent, John Kavanagh, Gerard McSorley, Anne Kent, Rynagh O'Grady, Michael James Ford, Garrett Keogh; ***D:*** John Irvin; ***W:*** Hugh Leonard; ***C:*** Ashley Rowe; ***M:*** Carl Davis.

Wieners **2008 (R)** Typically infantile gross-out comedy. Buddies Joel (Kranz), Ben (Levi), and Wyatt (Thompson) travel cross-country in a custom weiner van in order to confront smarmy daytime talk show therapist Dr. Dwayne (Hammond). The doc encouraged Joel's girlfriend to break up with him, humiliating Joel live and nationwide. Along the route the boys pass out free hot dogs and encounter a number of disgusting situations and weird people. And beware—McCarthy (as the trio's hot-for-teacher fantasy) has only one scene despite her promo prominence. **93m/C DVD.** Fran Kranz, Zachary Levi, Darrell Hammond, Jenny McCarthy, Keenan Thompson, Andy Milonakis; ***D:*** Mark Steilen; ***W:*** Suzanne Francis, Gabe Grifoni; ***C:*** Walt Lloyd; ***M:*** David Kitay. **VIDEO**

The Wife **1995 (R)** The routine of married psychotherapists Jack (Noonan) and Rita (Hagerty), who live in an isolated Vermont farmhouse, is disrupted by the unexpected (and unwelcome) appearance of Jack's patient Cosmo (Shawn), who's in crisis, and his wife Arlie (Young). Everyone's got secrets and marital dilemmas that come spilling out over too much wine. A variation on "Who's Afraid of Virginia Woolf?" **101m/C VHS, DVD.** Tom Noonan, Julie Hagerty, Karen Young, Wallace Shawn; ***D:*** Tom Noonan; ***W:*** Tom Noonan; ***C:*** Joe DeSalvo; ***M:*** Tom Noonan.

Wife Versus Secretary 1/2 **1936** Excellent acting against type creates a near-perfect picture of romantic relationships. Harlow and Gable play a secretary and her boss who have a wonderful professional relationship, but Loy worries something else is afoot. Could have been a heavy-handed soap opera, but the witty dialogue and Brown's fine pacing make it much more. Stewart later claimed that he purposely messed up his romantic scenes with Harlow in order to spend more time in her arms. **89m/B VHS, DVD.** Clark Gable, Jean Harlow, Myrna Loy, May Robson, Hobart Cavanaugh, James Stewart, George Barbier, Gilbert Emery, Gloria Holden; ***D:*** Clarence Brown; ***W:*** John Lee Mahin, Norman Krasna, Alice Duer Miller; ***C:*** Ray June; ***M:*** Herbert Stothart, Edward Ward.

Wifemistress 1/2 *Mogliamante; Lover, Wife* **1979 (R)** In the early 1900s, an invalid wife resents her neglectful husband. When he goes into hiding because of a murder he didn't commit, she begins to drift into a world of sexual fantasies. Fine performances. Italian dialogue with English subtitles. **101m/C VHS.** *IT* Marcello Mastroianni, Laura Antonelli; ***D:*** Marco Vicario.

Wigstock: The Movie 1/2 **1995 (R)** Documentary of the eponymous annual Labor Day event in Manhattan, billed as the Super Bowl of drag. Shils intercuts stage numbers with interviews from a variety of the talented, witty festival performers, such as Lypsinka, Mistress Formika, and RuPaul. One of the best numbers is performed by the Dueling Bankheads (as in Tallulah) singing "Born to Be Wild." Like the event itself, documentary is more a celebration than a probing, psychological look at drag. Won't appeal to everyone, but a lot of fun for those who can appreciate high hair and high fashion. **92m/C VHS, DVD.** RuPaul Charles, John (Lypsinka) Epperson, Alexis Arquette; ***D:*** Barry Shils; ***C:*** Wolfgang Held, Michael Barrow; ***M:*** Peter Fish, Robert Reale.

Wilbur Wants to Kill Himself **2002 (R)** Indeed, Wilbur (Sives) does want to die as the opening sequence shows him eager to swallow some pills in one of his many, varied attempts to join his deceased parents. When he becomes homeless his responsible, easy-going brother, Harbour (Rawlins), who lives above their father's old dingy bookstore, provides refuge even after Harbour's new wife and her nine-year-old daughter move in. With this unconventional family unit, Danish director Scherfig's first English offering exquisitely spans the spectrum of human emotion as it shuffles between humor as dark and dreary as its backdrop (Glasgow) and the morbidity inherent in such a tale. **106m/C DVD.** *SW GB DK FR* Adrian Rawlins, Shirley Henderson, Jamie Sives, Lisa McKinlay, Mads Mikkelsen, Susan Vidler, Julia Davis; ***D:*** Lone Scherfig; ***W:*** Lone Scherfig, Anders Thomas Jensen; ***C:*** Jorgen Johansson; ***M:*** Joachim Holbek.

The Wilby Conspiracy **1975 (PG)** A political activist and an Englishman on the wrong side of the law team up to escape the clutches of a prejudiced cop in apartheid Africa. The focus of the film is on the chase, not the political uprising taking place around it. Well-done chase film with fine performances throughout. **101m/C VHS, DVD.** Sidney Poitier, Michael Caine, Nicol Williamson, Prunella Gee, Persis Khambatta, Saeed Jaffrey, Rutger Hauer, Helmut Dantine; ***D:*** Ralph Nelson; ***W:*** Rod Amateau.

The Wild 1/2 **2006 (G)** No, it's not "Madagascar 2" although you'd be forgiven for thinking so. Here young lion cub Ryan (Cipes) decides he needs to get out from under his dad Samson's (Sutherland) roar, so he escapes from a New York zoo and stows away on an Africa-bound ship. Dad follows along with opinionated giraffe Bridget (Garofalo) and her bossy squirrel admirer, Benny (Belushi); dopey anaconda Larry (Kind); and snooty, campy koala, Nigel (a very enjoyable Izzard). When they get to Africa, Nigel gets mistaken for a god by a herd of wildebeests, led by the sinister Kazar (Shatner), who challenges Samson for supremacy. **85m/C DVD, Blu-ray Disc.** *US* ***D:*** Steve "Spaz" Williams; ***W:*** Edward Decter, John J. Strauss, Mark Gibson, Philip Halprin; ***M:*** Alan Silvestri; ***V:*** Kiefer Sutherland, James Belushi, Eddie Izzard, Janeane Garofalo, Greg Cipes, Richard Kind, William Shatner, Colin Hay, Don Cherry, Lenny Venito, Patrick Warburton, Kevin M. Richardson.

Wild America **1997 (G)** Warner Bros. invades Disney's well-marked territory of family-friendly real-life adventure with this bio of famed nature documentarians Mark, Marty, and Marshall Stouffer. Pic focuses on the origins of the boys' fascination with animals, which started when their parents gave them a used 16mm camera to mess around with. After getting some footage of backyard wildlife, they're hooked, and hit the road to find more dangerous (and endangered) beasts to shoot (in the good way). As you would expect, the scenery and camera work are splendid, and any expected wild animal gore and violence has been toned way down. There's plenty to hold the interest of adults as well as children, with a big assist going to the clever script. Title is taken from Marty Stouffer's long-running PBS nature series. **105m/C VHS, DVD.** Sonny Shroyer, Jonathan Taylor Thomas, Devon Sawa, Scott Bairstow, Jamey Sheridan, Frances Fisher, Tracey Walter, Don Stroud; ***D:*** William Dear; ***W:*** David Michael Wieger; ***C:*** David Burr; ***M:*** Joel McNeely.

The Wild and the Free **1980** Light-hearted comedy about research chimps. The lab-raised bunch become the instruments for radioactive experimenting. Scheming scientists return the chimps to their home to save them from their demise. Made for TV. **100m/C VHS.** Granville Van Dusen, Linda Gray, Bill Gribble; ***D:*** James Hill. **TV**

Wild & Wooly 1/2 **1978** In 1903, a tough cowgirl and her friends must prevent the assassination of the President. **120m/C VHS.** Chris DeLisle, Susan Bigelow, Elyssa Davalos, Jessica Walter, Doug McClure, David Doyle, Ross Martin, Vic Morrow, Charles Seibert, Sherry Bain, Paul Burke; ***D:*** Philip Leacock; ***M:*** Charles Bernstein. **TV**

The Wild Angels 1/2 **1966 (PG)** Excessively violent film but B-movie classic about an outlaw biker gang and the local townspeople. Typical Corman fodder was one of AIP's most successful productions. **124m/C VHS, DVD.** Peter Fonda, Nancy Sinatra, Bruce Dern, Diane Ladd, Michael J. Pollard, Gayle Hunnicutt, Peter Bogdanovich, Dick Miller; ***D:*** Roger Corman; ***W:*** Charles B. Griffith, Peter Bogdanovich; ***C:*** Richard Moore; ***M:*** Michael Curb.

Wild at Heart 1/2 **1990 (R)** Dern and Cage are on the lam, going across country to escape her mother, his parole officer, and life. Humorous and frightening, sensual and evocative as only Lynch can be. Sweet love story of Sailor and Lula is juxtaposed with the violent and bizarre, obsessive brand of love of the people they encounter. Unmistakable Wizard of Oz imagery sprinkled throughout, as are some scenes of graphic violence. Ladd is unnerving as Dern's on-screen mother (she also has the role off-screen). **125m/C VHS, DVD.** Nicolas Cage, Laura Dern, Diane Ladd, Willem Dafoe, Isabella Rossellini, Harry Dean Stanton, Crispin Glover, Grace Zabriskie, J.E. Freeman, Freddie Jones, Sherilyn Fenn, Sheryl Lee, Albert "Poppy" Popwell, Jack Nance, Charlie Spradling, William Morgan Sheppard; ***D:*** David Lynch; ***W:*** David Lynch; ***C:*** Frederick Elmes; ***M:*** Angelo Badalamenti. Cannes '90: Film; Ind. Spirit '91: Cinematog.

The Wild Beasts WOOF! *Savage Beasts* **1985** Children and animals clash violently after drinking water tainted with PCP. Disgusting premise; unredeemably violent. **92m/C VHS.** John Aldrich, Lorraine (De Sette) De Selle; ***D:*** Franco Prosperi.

Wild Bill 1/2 **1995 (R)** Realistic, unheroic portrait of Wild Bill Hickok (Bridges), seen mostly in flashback. From trapper and lawman to his last days in Deadwood, South Dakota, focus is on the events haunting the glaucoma-stricken, opium-addicted legend in his later years, such as twice deserting his true love (Lane). Action packed first 20 minutes mellows along with the aging Hickok and the rest gets a bit talky for a Western, albeit an arty one. Bridges's Hickok is brilliant, but Barkin is given a somewhat tedious Calamity Jane. Based on the novel "Deadwood" by Pete Dexter and the play "Fathers and Sons" by Thomas Babe. **97m/C VHS, DVD.** Jeff Bridges, Ellen Barkin, John Hurt, Diane Lane, Keith Carradine, Christina Applegate, Bruce Dern, James Gammon, David Arquette, Marjoe Gortner; ***D:*** Walter Hill; ***W:*** Walter Hill; ***C:*** Lloyd Ahern II; ***M:*** Van Dyke Parks.

Wild Boys of the Road 1933 **77m/B DVD.** Frankie Darro, Rochelle Hudson, Sterling Holloway, Minna Gombell, Robert Barrat, Edwin Phillips, Dorothy Coonan; ***D:*** William A. Wellman; ***W:*** Earl Baldwin; ***C:*** Arthur L. Todd.

Wild Brian Kent 1/2 **1936** Polo-playing sponger Brian (Bellamy) stops in a Kansas town and manages to talk Sue Prentice (Lowell) into letting him stay on her farm. He tries romancing her niece Betty (Clarke) but it's not until Brian prevents a crooked real estate agent from claiming the property and stops a fire that Betty decides he's okay after all. **60m/B DVD.** Ralph Bellamy, Mae Clarke, Stanley Andrews, Lew Kelly, Helen Lowell; ***D:*** Howard Bretherton; ***W:*** Don Swift, Earle Snell, James Gruen; ***C:*** Harry Neumann.

The Wild Bunch **1969 (R)** Acclaimed western about a group of aging outlaws on their final rampage, realizing time is passing them by. Highly influential in dialogue, editing style, and lyrical slow-motion photography of violence; Peckinpah's main claim to posterity. Holden and Ryan create especially memorable characters. Arguably the greatest western and one of the greatest American films of all times. Beware of shortened versions; after a pre-release showing to the East Coast critics, producer Feldman cut key scenes without Peckinpah's knowledge or consent. **145m/C VHS, DVD, Blu-ray Disc, HD DVD.** William Holden, Ernest Borgnine, Robert Ryan, Warren Oates, Strother Martin, L.Q. Jones, Albert Dekker, Bo Hopkins, Edmond O'Brien, Ben Johnson, Jaime Sanchez, Emilio Fernandez, Dub Taylor; ***D:*** Sam Peckinpah; ***W:*** Walon Green, Sam Peckinpah; ***C:*** Lucien Ballard; ***M:*** Jerry Fielding. AFI '98: Top 100, Natl. Film Reg. '99;; Natl. Soc. Film Critics '69: Cinematog.

Wild Cactus **1992 (R)** Philip and Alexandria Marcus decide to take a romantic vacation at a desert resort where they meet up with a homicidal ex-con and his seductive girlfriend. The two couples find themselves entangled in some violent and kinky games. An unrated version is also available. **92m/C VHS.** David Naughton, India Allen, Gary Hudson, Michelle Moffett, Kathy Shower, Robert Z'Dar, Paul Gleason, Anna Karin, David Wells; ***D:*** Jag Mundhra; ***W:*** Carl Austin.

The Wild Card 1/2 **2003** Four crooks take on a new task by kidnapping a trophy wife—who's been fooling around with a gangster—but their Vegas luck runs out once the typical backstabbing seeps in. **90m/C VHS, DVD.** Ron Dean, Mik Scriba, Jim Petersmith, Timothy Patrick Klein, Marty Maguire, Hillary Tuck, Barbara Alyn Woods, John J. Dalesandro, Zelda Rubinstein; ***D:*** Tom Whitus; ***W:*** Tom Whitus; ***C:*** Richard Siegel; ***M:*** Trebor Murray, Terry Quiet, Sugar Free Allstars, Deon Vozov. **VIDEO**

The Wild Child 1/2 *L'Enfant Sauvage* **1970 (G)** The brilliant film based on the journal of a 19th century physician who attempts to educate and civilize a young boy who has been found living in the wilderness, without any comprehension of human life. Tenderly told coming of age tale, with surprising sensitivity for its subject. In French with English subtitles. **85m/B VHS, DVD.** *FR* Jean-Pierre Cargol, Francois Truffaut, Jean Daste, Francoise Seigner, Paul Ville; ***D:*** Francois Truffaut; ***W:*** Jean Gruault, Francois Truffaut; ***C:*** Nestor Almendros; ***M:*** Antoine Duhamel. Natl. Bd. of Review '70: Director (Truffaut); Natl. Soc. Film Critics '70: Cinematog.

Wild Child 1/2 **2008 (PG-13)** When pampered Malibu teen Poppy (Roberts) finally crosses the line, her fed-up dad (Quinn) packs her off to an all-girls British boarding school where the brash American is instantly disliked by the reigning clique, headed by Harriet (King). Poppy eventually learns from headmistress Mrs. Kingsley (Richardson) that her mysterious mother attended the school and she finds some teen romance with Mrs. Kingsley's son, Freddie (Pettyfer). A bit choppy but sweet for tweens as girl power rules. **98m/C DVD.** *GB* Emma Roberts, Natasha Richardson, Alex Pettyfer, Shirley Henderson, Aidan Quinn, Kimberly Nixon, Georgia King, Juno Temple, Sophie Wu, Daisy Donovan, Shelby Young, Nick Frost; ***D:*** Nick Moore; ***W:*** Lucy Dahl; ***C:*** Chris Seager; ***M:*** Michael Price. **VIDEO**

Wild Country 1/2 **1947** Tame western. A U.S. Marshal races to stop the bad guy from killing the late sheriff's daughter and snatching her ranch. **57m/B VHS.** Eddie Dean, Roscoe Ates, Peggy Wynn, Douglas Fowley, I. Stanford Jolley, William "Bill" Fawcett; ***D:*** Ray Taylor; ***C:*** Robert E. Cline.

The Wild Country 1/2 *The Newcomers* **1971 (G)** Children's fare detailing the trials and tribulations of a Pittsburgh family moving into an inhospitable Wyoming ranch in the 1880s. Based on the novel "Little Britches" by Ralph Moody. **92m/C VHS.** Steve Forrest, Ron Howard, Clint Howard, Rance Howard; ***D:*** Robert Totten; ***M:*** Robert F. Brunner.

Wild Country 1/2 **2005 (R)** The low budget is something of a problem since the beastie in this teen horror flick isn't very scary. Kelly Ann (Shields) is on a hike in the Scottish Highlands with some friends when they find an abandoned baby. As they try to get the tyke to safety, a wolf-life creature starts stalking and killing them. **72m/C DVD.** *GB* Martin Compston, Peter Capaldi, Kevin Quinn, Samantha Shields, Nicola Muldoon, Jamie Quinn; ***D:*** Craig Strachan; ***W:*** Craig Strachan; ***C:*** Jan Pester.

The Wild Duck 1/2 **1984 (PG)** A father discovers that his beloved daughter is illegitimate and turns against her. To regain his love, she plans to sacrifice her most prized possession. Irons overacts; Ullmann almost disappears into the woodwork. Child star Jones is insufferable, and the whole family squeaks with "literary" pomposity. A horrid adaptation of the classic Ibsen play. **96m/C VHS.** *AU* Jeremy Irons, Liv Ullmann, Lucinda Jones, Arthur Dignam; ***D:*** Henri Safran.

Wild Frontier 1/2 **1947** A rugged old lawman and his sons team up to rid a town of outlaws. Lane, playing a character with his own name for first time, takes over from his murdered father and roots out the evildoer (Holt). Decent, enjoyable, good-guys-win western. **59m/B VHS.** Allan "Rocky" Lane, Jack Holt, Eddy (Eddie, Ed) Waller, Pierre Watkin, Roy Barcroft; ***D:*** Philip Ford; ***W:*** Albert DeMond; ***C:*** Alfred S. Keller.

Wild Geese **1978 (R)** The adventure begins when a veteran band of mercenaries land deep inside Africa to rescue the imprisoned leader of an emerging African nation, in the interest of protecting British commercial interest. Their mission meets an unexpected turn when they are betrayed by their financial backers. Too much training in the early part; too long; too much dialogue. Where's the action? **132m/C VHS, DVD.** *GB* Richard Burton, Roger Moore, Richard Harris, Hardy Kruger, Stewart Granger, Frank Finlay, Jeff Corey; ***D:*** Andrew V. McLaglen; ***W:*** Reginald Rose.

Wild Geese 2 1/2 **1985 (R)** Lame sequel to the flamed and overlong "Wild Geese," which depended on its name stars. More of the same, this time sans Burton, Harris and Moore. Sure, it's got Olivier, but it still stinks. **124m/C VHS.** *GB* Laurence Olivier, Edward Fox, Scott Glenn, Barbara Carrera, Robert Webber; ***D:*** Peter Hunt; ***W:*** Reginald Rose.

Wild Grizzly 1/2 **1999 (PG)** A grizzly escapes from a mountain community and rampages through the small town of Pine Lake. Teenaged newcomer John Harding, Ranger Frank Bradford, wildlife tracker Jack Buck, and land developer Harlan Adams are all on a bear hunt for their own reasons. **100m/C VHS, DVD.** Daniel Baldwin, Fred (John F.) Dryer, Michele Greene, Steve Reevis, Brendan O'Brien, John Hurley, Courtney Peldon, Riley Smith; ***D:*** Sean McNamara. **VIDEO**

Wild Guitar **WOOF!** **1962** A swinging youth cycles into Hollywood and, improbably, becomes an instant teenidol. Considered a top contender for "Worst Picture of All Time" honors. **92m/B VHS, DVD.** Arch Hall Jr., Ray Dennis Steckler, Ray Dennis Steckler, Carolyn Brandt, Bob Crumb, Nancy Czar, Marie Denn, Arch (Archie) Hall Sr.; ***D:*** Ray Dennis Steckler; ***W:*** Joe Thomas, Bob Wehling, Arch (Archie) Hall Sr.; ***C:*** Joseph Mascelli; ***M:*** Alan O'Day.

Wild Gypsies **1969** A band of gypsies seek revenge against a renegade member who returned to rape and pillage. Without merit except for the good photography of Steven Burum, who has become respected doing cinematographically intriguing films like "Rumblefish." **85m/C VHS.** Todd Grange, Gayle Clark, Laurel Welcome, Wayne Lundy; ***D:*** Marc B. Ray; ***W:*** Marc B. Ray; ***C:*** Stephen Burum; ***M:*** Richard LaSalle.

Wild Hearts Can't Be Broken **1991 (G)** Depicts the true-life story of Sonora Webster, a small town Georgia girl who runs away from a foster home to join a carnival in the early 1930s, hoping to become a stunt rider. She becomes a horse-diver (a Depression-era sideshow phenomena) and is blinded in a diving accident, but returns to find romance and ride again. Storyline has little screen tension, but it doesn't detract from this fresh family film with a feisty heroine, a sweet romance, and horses. Nice U.S. screen debut for British actress Anwar. **89m/C VHS, DVD.** Gabrielle Anwar, Cliff Robertson, Dylan Kussman, Michael Schoeffling, Kathleen York, Frank Renzulli; ***D:*** Steve Miner; ***W:*** Oley Sassone; ***M:*** Mason Daring.

Wild Hogs **2007 (PG-13)** Four middle-aged buddies in Cincinnati get together on the weekends to indulge their mild sides by putting on their leather jackets and riding their hogs around town. Then Woody (Travolta) gets the bright idea to go on a road trip. Their first blunder is enraging a true outlaw biker gang, led by Jack (Liotta). Their second is to get stuck in a desert nowheres-ville, which at least allows shy Dudley (Macy) to go gaga over waitress Maggie (Tomei). And yes, there's a showdown between the biker boys. You'll laugh, but you'll probably wonder why in the morning. **99m/C DVD, Blu-ray Disc.** *US* John Travolta, Tim Allen, Martin Lawrence, William H. Macy, Ray Liotta, Marisa Tomei, Kevin Durand, M.C. Gainey, Jill(ian) Hennessey, Tichina Arnold, Stephen Tobolowsky, John C. McGinley; ***D:*** Walt Becker; ***W:*** Brad Copeland; ***C:*** Robbie Greenberg; ***M:*** Teddy Castellucci.

Wild Horse 1/2 *Silver Devil* **1931** Gibson is the lead (in his favorite talking role), but his magnificent mount Mut commands most of the attention. Interesting historically as an example of stars' (Gibson's in this case) difficulty adjusting to talking pictures. **68m/B VHS, DVD.** Hoot Gibson, Stepin Fetchit, Edmund Cobb, Alberta Vaughn; ***D:*** Richard Thorpe, Sidney Algier.

Wild Horse Canyon **1925** Yakima Canutt, the man credited with creating the profession of stunt man, stars in this tale about a lady rancher who requires saving from her evil foreman. The climactic stampede scene gives Yakima a chance to demonstrate a high dive off a cliff and a somersault onto his horse. Silent, with musical score. **68m/B VHS.** Yakima Canutt, Edward Cecil, Helene Rosson, Jay Talbet; ***D:*** Ben F. Wilson.

Wild Horse Canyon 1/2 **1939** One of those westerns designed to run as half of a double-feature, this one's shorter than most, but hardly notable. The hero goes after a rustler who shot his brother. **57m/B VHS.** Addison "Jack" Randall, Dorothy Short, Frank Yaconelli, Dennis Moore, Warner Richmond, Charles "Blackie" King, Sherry Tansey; ***D:*** Robert F. "Bob" Hill.

Wild Horse Hank **1979** A young woman risks everything to save a herd of wild mustangs from being slaughtered for use as dog food. Creena is good; otherwise, it's sentimental family fare. Based on the novel "The Wild Horse Killers" by Mel Ellis. **94m/C VHS.** *CA* Linda Blair, Richard Crenna, Michael Wincott, Al Waxman; ***D:*** Eric Till.

Wild Horse Phantom **1944** A Wild West banker plans to fake a robbery in a diabolical deception to part honest ranchers from their lands. Surely this man's not a member of the F.D.I.C. Okay sagebrush saga. **56m/B VHS, DVD.** Buster Crabbe, Al "Fuzzy" St. John, Charles "Blackie" King, John Merton, Lane Chandler, Edward Cassidy, Bud Osborne; ***D:*** Sam Newfield.

Wild Horse Rodeo 1/2 **1937** When a gunman appears at a rodeo, trouble starts. Part of "The Three Mesquiteers" series. Ordinary action-packed western, the good guys win. Actor Dick Weston, who sings, later gained fame as singing cowboy Roy Rogers. **53m/B VHS.** Robert "Bob" Livingston, Ray Corrigan, Max Terhune, June Martel, Walter Miller, Edmund Cobb, William (Bill) Gould, Jack Ingram, Roy Rogers; ***D:*** George Sherman; ***W:*** Betty Burbridge; ***C:*** William Nobles.

Wild Horse Valley 1/2 **1940** When Bob Evans' prized Arabian stallion is stolen he tracks the horse to the Kimball ranch, where crooked foreman Raymer is using the stallion as a decoy. He and his henchmen round up the horses who have followed the stallion in a hidden corral, intending to sell them cross the border unless Evans can stop them. **55m/B DVD.** Bob Steele, Phyllis Adair, Lafe (Lafayette) McKee, Jimmy Aubrey, Ted Adams, George Chesebro, Bud Osborne, Buzz Barton; ***D:*** Ira Webb; ***W:*** Carl Krusada; ***C:*** Edward Kull.

Wild Horses **1982** A man attempts to make a living by capturing and selling wild horses. Adventure fans will love this film which deals with the common theme of man against nature. **88m/C VHS, DVD.** *NZ* Keith Aberdein, John Bach, Robyn Gibbes; ***D:*** Derek Morton.

Wild Horses **1984** Ex-rodeo champ Rogers is hankering to escape his dull life. He joins a roundup of wild horses and with Dawber's help exposes a bureaucrat's scheme for them. Rogers is likable and sings, but the supporting cast carries this one. Made for TV. **90m/C VHS, DVD.** Kenny Rogers, Pam Dawber, Ben Johnson, Richard Masur, David Andrews, Karen Carlson; ***D:*** Dick Lowry. **TV**

Wild Horses *Caballos Salvajes* **1995** Elderly Jose (Alterio) resorts to bank robbery to recover his $15,000 nest egg. Young employee Pedro (Sbarablia) gives him $500,000 and offers to be the old man's hostage. The unlikely duo hit the road for Patagonia and send the press messages detailing the money's suspects origins and their own good intentions. Spanish with subtitles. **122m/C VHS, DVD.** *AR* Hector Alterio, Leonardo Sbaraglia, Cecilia Dopazo; ***D:*** Marcelo Pineyro; ***W:*** Marcelo Pineyro, Aida Bortnik; ***C:*** Alfredo Mayo; ***M:*** Andres Calamaro.

Wild in the Country 1/2 **1961** Backwoods delinquent Presley is aided in his literary aspirations by woman psychiatrist Lange. Okay, so that's fairly novel. Strange plot lines but in general Elvis is going to college and reading and writing and singing and playing his guitar. Meanwhile Weld wanders around seductively to provide that hint of Tennessee Williams ambience as interpreted by Odet but hey, who cares? Interesting if convoluted Elvis dramatic turn. ♫ Wild in the Country; In My Way; I Slipped, I Stumbled, I Fell; Lonely Man. **114m/C VHS, DVD.** Elvis Presley, Hope Lange, Tuesday Weld, Millie Perkins, John Ireland, Gary Lockwood, Alan Napier; ***D:*** Philip Dunne; ***W:*** Clifford Odets; ***C:*** William Mellor.

Wild in the Streets 1/2 **1968** Satire set in the future, where a malcontent rock star becomes president after the voting age is lowered to 14. Adults over 30 are imprisoned and fed a daily dose of LSD. The president gets his comeuppance when challenged by even younger youths. Very groovy, very political in its own way, very funny. **97m/C VHS, DVD.** Christopher Jones, Shelley Winters, Hal Holbrook, Richard Pryor, Diane Varsi, Millie Perkins, Ed Begley Sr., Barry Williams, Dick Clark; ***D:*** Barry Shear; ***W:*** Robert Thom; ***C:*** Richard Moore; ***M:*** Les Baxter.

Wild Iris 1/2 **2001 (R)** After Iris Bravard's (Linney) husband commits suicide, she and her young son are forced to move back in with her overbearing yet charming mother Min (Rowlands) and work in the family bridal shop. Eight years later, Iris is an alcoholic shrew who blames her mother for everything bad in her life. Meanwhile, Iris's now-teenaged son Lonnie (Hirsch) is tired of being a referee and walking through the family minefield. **93m/C VHS.** Laura Linney, Gena Rowlands, Emile Hirsch, Lee Tergesen, Miguel (Michael) Sandoval, Fred Ward; ***D:*** Daniel Petrie; ***W:*** Kent Broadhurst; ***C:*** Rene Ohashi; ***M:*** Laurence Rosenthal. **CABLE**

The Wild Life **1984 (R)** A recent high school graduate takes on a wild and crazy wrestler as his roommate in a swinging singles apartment complex. The same writer and producer as "Fast Times at Ridgemont High" but lacks that film's commercial success. Just as adolescent, though. **96m/C VHS.** Christopher Penn, Randy Quaid, Rick Moranis, Hart Bochner, Eric Stoltz, Jenny Wright, Lea Thompson, Sherilyn Fenn, Lee Ving, Ashley St. John, Francesca "Kitten" Natividad; ***D:*** Art Linson; ***W:*** Cameron Crowe.

Wild Man **1989** A Las Vegas gambling magnate with supernatural powers decides to avenge the murder of his friend and sets out on an adventure to find the killer. Crummy acting in yet another "ex-agent called back for one more mission" yarn. **106m/C VHS.** Ginger Lynn Allen, Michelle (McClellan) Bauer, Don Scribner, Kathleen Middleton; ***D:*** Fred J. Lincoln.

The Wild Man of the Navidad 1/2 **2008** A flick made to be seen at a drive-in, where its cheesy low-budget aesthetic can be properly appreciated. A legendary bloodthirsty creature has been terrorizing the town of Sublime, Texas along the Navidad River for over 200 years. Wimpy Dale S. Rogers (Meek) nightly leaves a dead rabbit to appease the beast but when Rogers finally allows hunting on his land and the Wild Man gets winged, he also gets mighty perturbed. **85m/C DVD.** Justin Meeks, Tony Wolford, Charlie Hurtin, Alex Garcia, Stacy Meeks, Edmond Geyer, Bob Wood; ***D:*** Justin Meeks, Duane Graves; ***W:*** Justin Meeks, Duane Graves; ***C:*** Duane Graves; ***M:*** Charlie Hurtin.

Wild Mustang 1/2 **1935** Sheriff's son (Gordon) joins some outlaws to help father (Carey) spring a trap. The plan is sidetracked, and Gordon is captured and nearly branded by the baddies. Don't worry, though; everything turns out all right. Good western. **62m/B VHS.** Harry Carey Sr., Robert F. (Bob) Kortman, George Chesebro, Del Gordon; ***D:*** Harry Fraser.

The Wild One 1/2 **1954** The original biker flick: two motorcycle gangs descend upon a quiet midwestern town and each other. Brando is the leader of one (Marvin leads the other), struggling against social prejudices and his own gang's lawlessness to find love and a normal life. The classic tribute to 1950s rebelliousness. Based vaguely on a real incident in California. Quaint after nearly 40 years, but still the touchstone for much that has come since, and still a central role in Brando's now-long career. Brando himself believes it failed to explore motivations for youth gangs and violence, only depicting them. Banned in Britain until 1967. **79m/B VHS, DVD.** Marlon Brando, Lee Marvin, Mary Murphy, Robert Keith, Jerry Paris, Alvy Moore, Jay C. Flippen, Peggy Maley, Bruno VeSota; ***D:*** Laszlo Benedek; ***W:*** John Paxton; ***C:*** Hal Mohr; ***M:*** Leith Stevens.

Wild Ones on Wheels **WOOF!** *Drivers to Hell* **1962** A gang of teenage hot-rod punks meet an ex-con in the Mojave desert who is searching for the half-a-million bucks he buried there years earlier. Before they find out where the money is, they kill him. In an attempt to find the stash, they kidnap the dead con's wife, hoping she'll sing like a bird. Plenty of unintended laughter. **92m/B VHS.** Francine York, Edmund Tontini, Robert Blair, Ray Dennis Steckler; ***D:*** Rudolph Cusumano; ***W:*** Eugene Pollack; ***C:*** Ray Dennis Steckler.

Wild Orchid **1990 (R)** One of the most controversial theatrical releases of 1990. Rourke is a mystery millionaire involved with two beautiful women in lovely Rio de Janeiro. Bisset is strange as an international real estate developer with unusual sexual mores. Very explicit sex scenes, but otherwise mostly boring and unbelievable. Rourke allegedly took his method-acting technique to the limit in the last love scene with Otis. Available in an unrated version as well. From the producers of "9 1/2 Weeks." Followed by an unrelated sequel. **107m/C VHS, DVD.** Mickey Rourke, Jacqueline Bisset, Carre Otis, Assumpta Serna, Bruce Greenwood; ***D:*** Zalman King; ***W:*** Zalman King; ***C:*** Gale Tattersall; ***M:*** Simon Goldenberg, Geoff MacCormack.

Wild Orchid 2: Two Shades of Blue **WOOF! 1992 (R)** Blue's jazz-musician, heroin-addict dad dies after a bad fix and she's sold into prostitution, until she runs away to find her true love and live a "normal" life. Effort from soft-core expert King has nothing to do with the first "Wild Orchid" and is almost laughably bad. Siemaszko is whiny, the plot is unbelievable, and the dialogue is unintentionally funny. Yes, you get sex, lots of it, but rather than passionate, it merely looks staged. Also available in an unrated version at 111 minutes. **105m/C VHS, DVD.** Nina Siemaszko, Wendy Hughes, Brent Fraser, Robert Davi, Tom Skerritt, Joe Dallesandro, Christopher McDonald, Liane (Alexandra) Curtis; ***D:*** Zalman King; ***W:*** Zalman King.

Wild Orchids 1/2 **1928** A husband suspects his wife of infidelity while they take a business cruise to Java. One of Garbo's earliest silent films. Garbo is lushly surrounded with great scenery, costumes and sets, making the best of her as she makes the best of a cheery tale. **119m/B VHS.** Greta Garbo, Lewis Stone, Nils Asther; ***D:*** Sidney Franklin; ***C:*** William H. Daniels.

The Wild Pair 1/2 *Hollow Point; Devil's Odds* **1987 (R)** Two cops track down a cocaine smuggling ring and uncover a private army planning to conquer the United States. Lloyd Bridges is memorable as a rabid right-winger, and the wild pairing of Bubba and Beau inspires head-scatching. Otherwise, what we have here is a typical action pic, complete with car chases. Beau Bridges' inauspicious feature directing debut. **89m/C VHS.** Beau Bridges, Bubba Smith, Lloyd Bridges, Gary Lockwood, Raymond St. Jacques; ***D:*** Beau Bridges; ***M:*** John Debney.

Wild Palms **1993** In 2007 Los Angeles, Harry (Belushi) takes a job at a TV station that offers virtual reality programming to viewers, only this isn't benign technology. Delany is stuck in a thankless role as his wife, Cattrall is his former lover, but Dickinson has the most fun as Harry's power-mad mother-in-law who's also a sadistic co-conspirator of a nasty senator (Loggia). Lesson in weird style over substance really doesn't make much sense, but unlike "Twin Peaks" (to which this TV miniseries was heavily compared) it at least has an ending. Executive producer Stone has a cameo which concerns the JFK conspiracy. Based on the comic strip by Wagner. In two parts. **300m/C VHS, DVD.** James Belushi, Robert Loggia, Dana Delany, Kim Cattrall, Angie Dickinson, Ernie Hudson, Bebe Neuwirth, Nick Mancuso, Charles Hallahan, Robert Morse, David Warner, Ben Savage, Bob Gunton, Brad Dourif, Charles Rocket; ***Cameos:*** Oliver Stone; ***D:*** Phil Joanou, Kathryn Bigelow, Keith Gordon, Peter Hewitt; ***W:*** Bruce Wagner; ***C:*** Phedon Papamichael; ***M:*** Ryuichi Sakamoto.

The Wild Parrots of Telegraph Hill **2003 (G)** This cute little documentary is for the birds. But the birds are cool, man. Free-spirit Mark Bittner moved to San Francisco during the dawn of the hippie age with dreams of becoming a professional musician. Instead of flocking fans, he acquired a flock of parrots. Over the next 25 years these escaped tropical pets often roosted on his front porch, finding the climate nice and the owner quite hospitable. Soon enough they began following him everywhere, even when he was forced to move. Bittner grows to be a local icon and tourist attraction, kind of like the Birdman of San Francisco. A tender little character study about the bohemian nature of life. **83m/C DVD.** *US* ***D:*** Judy Irving; ***C:*** Judy Irving.

Wild Party 1/2 **1974 (R)** It's 1929, a year of much frivolity in Hollywood. Drinking, dancing, maneuvering and almost every sort of romance are the rule of the night at silent film comic Jolly Grimm's sumptuous, star-studded party that climaxes with, among other things, a murder. Well performed but somehow hollow; ambitious Ivory effort unfortunately falls short. Based on Joseph Moncure March's poem, and loosely on the Fatty Arbuckle scandal. **90m/C VHS, DVD.** Raquel Welch, James Coco, Perry King, David Dukes, Royal Dano, Tiffany Bolling; ***D:*** James Ivory; ***C:*** Walter Lassally.

Wild Pony **1983** A young boy spurns his new stepfather, preferring to live with his pony instead. Reversal of the evil-stepmother-and-girl-loves-horse theme. **87m/C VHS, DVD.** Marilyn Lightstone, Art Hindle, Josh Byrne; ***D:*** Kevin Sullivan; ***M:*** Hagood Hardy.

Wild Rebels **1971 (R)** A two-faced member of a ruthless motorcycle gang informs the police of the gang's plans to rob a bank. Lots of bullet-flying action. Dumb, ordinary biker flick; star Pastrano was a former boxing champ in real life. **90m/C VHS.** Steve Alaimo, Willie Pastrano, John Vella, Bobbie Byers; ***D:*** William Grefe.

Wild Reeds *Les Roseaux Sauvages* **1994** Emotional coming of age tale set in 1962 (at the end of the French war in Algeria) and focusing on three classmates at a French boarding school. Sensitive Francois (Morel) is just coming to the realization that he likes boys, particularly working-class Serge (Rideau) who's attracted to Francois's confidante Maite (Bouchez). The provocateur is Algerian-born Henri (Gorny), a bitter political militant who enjoys his battles with classmates and teachers alike. Politics and youthful passions are forced into crises. French historical/political context may prove a barrier. French with subtitles. **110m/C VHS, DVD.** *FR* Gael Morel, Stephane Rideau, Elodie Bouchez, Frederic Gorny, Michele Moretti; ***D:*** Andre Techine; ***W:*** Gilles Taurand, Olivier Massart, Andre Techine; ***C:*** Jeanne Lapoirie; ***M:*** Chubby Checker. Cesar '95: Director (Techine), Film, Writing; L.A. Film Critics '95: Foreign Film; Natl. Soc. Film Critics '95: Foreign Film.

The Wild Ride *Velocity* **1960** Nicholson, in an early starring role, portrays a rebellious punk of the Beat generation who hotrods his way into trouble and tragedy. He kidnaps now-straight ex-buddy Bean's squeeze (Carter); kills a few cops; then is killed. Interesting only if you're interested in Nicholson. **59m/B VHS, DVD.** Jack Nicholson, Georgianna Carter, Robert Bean; ***D:*** Harvey Berman; ***W:*** Marion Rothman.

Wild Riders **WOOF!** *Angels for Kicks* **1971 (R)** Two ruthless, amoral bikers molest, kidnap, rape, and beat two beautiful, naive young society ladies. Despicable story, with deplorable acting, but the ending, in which a husband slays a biker with a cello, surely is unique. **91m/C VHS.** Alex Rocco, Elizabeth Knowles, Sherry Bain, Arell Blanton; ***D:*** Richard Kanter.

Wild Rovers **1971 (PG)** An aging cowboy and his younger colleague turn to bank robbing and are pursued by a posse in a wacky comedy-adventure from director Edwards. Uneven script and too much referential baggage (faint shades of "Butch Cassidy") doom this valiant effort, with the two stars hanging right in there all the way. **138m/C VHS.** William Holden, Ryan O'Neal, Karl Malden, Lynn Carlin, Tom Skerritt, Joe Don Baker, Rachel Roberts, Moses Gunn; ***D:*** Blake Edwards; ***W:*** Blake Edwards; ***M:*** Jerry Goldsmith.

Wild Side **1995 (R)** Bank employee Alex (Heche) moonlights as a hooker and gets caught in a federal sting operation. Forced to inform on one of her clients, Bruno (Walken), who's involved in a money-laundering scheme, Alex complicates matters by falling in love with Bruno's mistress, Victoria (Chen). The unrated version is 96 minutes. Original director Cammell (who retained his screenwriter's credit) removed his name from the film after disagreeing with cuts made by the production company. **90m/C VHS, DVD.** Anne Heche, Christopher Walken, Joan Chen, Steven Bauer; ***D:*** Franklyn Brauner; ***W:*** Donald Cammell, China Cammell.

Wild Strawberries *Smultron-Stallet* **1957** Bergman's landmark film of fantasy, dreams and nightmares. An aging professor, on the road to accept an award, must come to terms with his anxieties and guilt. Brilliant performance by Sjostrom, Sweden's first film director and star. Excellent use of flashbacks and film editing. An intellectual and emotional masterpiece. In Swedish with English subtitles. **90m/B VHS, DVD.** *SW* Victor Sjostrom, Bibi Andersson, Max von Sydow, Ingrid Thulin, Gunnar Bjornstrand, Folke Sundquist, Bjorn Bjelvenstam; ***D:*** Ingmar Bergman; ***W:*** Ingmar Bergman; ***C:*** Gunnar Fischer; ***M:*** Erik Nordgren. Golden Globes '60: Foreign Film.

Wild Style **1983** Zoro, a mild-mannered Bronx teenager, spends his evenings spray-painting subway cars. Intended as a depiction of urban street life, including graffiti, breakdancing and rap music. Mildly interesting social comment, but unconvincing as cinema. Too "realistic," with too little vision. **82m/C VHS, DVD.** Lee George Quinones, Fredrick Braithwaite, Dondi White; ***D:*** Charlie Ahearn; ***M:*** Fred Brathwaite.

Wild Thing 1/2 **1987 (PG-13)** A modern variation on the Wild Child/Tarzan myth, as a feral kid stalks a crime-ridden ghetto. Sayles, a usually imaginative writer and director, really takes a dive here. And of course, the Troggs' overplayed title hit is abused as the theme. **92m/C VHS.** Kathleen Quinlan, Robert Knepper, Robert Davi, Betty Buckley, Maury Chaykin; ***D:*** Max Reid, Ken Cameron; ***W:*** John Sayles; ***M:*** George S. Clinton, Guy Moon.

Wild Things **1998 (R)** Titillating pulp friction can't decide between modern noir and swampy spoof. Miami guidance counselor and high school heartthrob fodder Sam Lombardo (Dillon) lectures on sex crimes and gets accused of rape by two school girls: snotty rich Kelly (Richards) and trailer trash Suzie (Campbell). The seemingly upright investigator (Bacon) tries to figure out who's telling the truth. Murray pops up doing his best Bill Murray, but his hilarious presence doesn't play next to the oh-so-serious Dillon and gang. Even more out of place is Wagner's wooden cameo as Kelly's lawyer. Speaking of wooden, the normally fine Russell is reduced to similar stereotype as Kelly's vampy, conniving mother. Endless exercise in audience manipulation has plot twists and turns relentlessly continue through the credits for no apparent reason. **108m/C VHS, DVD, Blu-ray Disc.** Matt Dillon, Neve Campbell, Kevin Bacon, Denise Richards, Theresa Russell, Daphne Rubin-Vega, Bill Murray, Robert Wagner, Carrie Snodgress, Jeff(rey) Perry, Marc Macaulay; ***D:*** John McNaughton; ***W:*** Stephen Peters; ***C:*** Jeffrey L. Kimball; ***M:*** George S. Clinton. L.A. Film Critics '98: Support. Actor (Murray).

Wild Things 2 **2004 (R)** Bad-girl classmates Brittney (Ward) and Maya (Arcieri) try to get their hands on an inheritance and insurance money by using their looks and other talents to doublecross each other or anyone else who might be after the same thing. Basically the same scenario as the original, only not as well plotted or acted. Seems like the only reason it got made was to get a new pair of girls to make out in a pool. Not that there's anything wrong with that. **95m/C DVD.** Susan Ward, Leila Arcieri, Katie Stuart, Anthony John (Tony) Denison, Linden Ashby, Joe Michael Burke, Isaiah Washington IV, Dylan Kussman, Ron Dean, Kathy Neff; ***D:*** Jack Perez; ***W:*** Ross Helford, Andy Hurst; ***M:*** Andrew Feltenstein, John Nau. **VIDEO**

The Wild Thornberrys Movie 1/2 **2002 (PG)** Big-screen adaptation of the popular Nickelodeon toon provides all the action, sly wit, and fully-realized characters that fans would expect. Newcomers will be entertained as well, no matter what age. The Thornberrys are nature documentary filmmakers, led by dad Nigel (Curry) and mom Marianne (Carlisle). Their intrepid brood includes angsty teen Debbie and half-feral Donnie, but the real star is daughter Eliza (Chabert), who can communicate with the animals and has a sarcastic monkey pal, Darwin (Kane). When Eliza's new playmate, a cheetah cub, is taken by poachers (Everett and Tomei), she has to escape a stuffy boarding school, where she was sent by her proper English grandmum, to save him and her family. African setting and rollicking action translate well to the big screen, but shouldn't lose anything when it returns to your TV for the numerous video viewings. Some scenes involving the poachers may be a little scary for younger kids. **88m/C VHS, DVD.** *US* ***D:*** Jeff McGrath, Cathy Malkasian; ***W:*** Kate Boutilier; ***M:*** Drew Neumann; ***V:*** Lacey Chabert, Tom Kane, Tim Curry, Lynn Redgrave, Danielle Harris, Flea, Jodi Carlisle,

Rupert Everett, Marisa Tomei, Kevin M. Richardson, Obba Babatunde, Alfre Woodard, Melissa Greenspan, Brock Peters, Brenda Blethyn.

Wild Tigers I Have Known ½ **2006** Experimental and abstract debut feature by Archer. 13-year-old Logan (Stumpf) and his best friend, science nerd Joey (Paradise), seem to be physically developing slower than their classmates, much to Joey's dismay. Logan, however, is emotionally maturing and discovering that he likes boys, especially rugged ninth-grader Rodeo (White), whose own feelings towards his precocious worshipper are ambiguous. Originally released at 98 minutes. **88m/C DVD.** Malcolm Stumpf, Fairuza Balk, Kim Dickens, Tom Gilroy, Patrick White, Max Paradise; ***D:*** Cam Archer; ***W:*** Cam Archer; ***C:*** Aaron Platt; ***M:*** Nate Archer.

Wild Times **1979** Too long but pleasant rendition of the life of High Candill, early Wild West showman. Based on the novel by Brian Garfield. Made for TV, originally in two parts. **200m/C VHS.** Sam Elliott, Trish Stewart, Ben Johnson, Dennis Hopper, Pat Hingle; ***D:*** Richard Compton. **TV**

Wild West *Prairie Outlaws* **1946** The hero and loyal companions (with names like Skinny, Stormy, and Soapy) tackle desperadoes trying to stop telegraph line construction. More mild than wild, it was later trimmed and released under its alternate title, but here you're getting the original. **73m/C VHS.** Eddie Dean, Roscoe Ates, Lash LaRue, Robert "Buzzy" Henry, Sarah Padden, Louise Currie, Warner Richmond, Chief Yowlachie, Bud Osborne; ***D:*** Robert Emmett Tansey; ***W:*** Frances Kavanaugh; ***C:*** Fred H. Jackman Jr.

Wild West **1993** Three Pakistani brothers, living in London, decide to form an American-style country and western band they call the Honky Tonk Cowboys and dream of making it big in Nashville. A little romance, lots of energy, but too many gags leave the film unfocused. **83m/C VHS.** *GB* Naveen Andrews, Sarita Choudhury, Ronny Jhutti, Ravi Kapoor, Bhasker; ***D:*** David Attwood; ***W:*** Harwant Bains; ***C:*** Nicholas D. Knowland.

Wild Wheels WOOF! 1969 (PG) A group of dune-buggy enthusiasts seek revenge against a gang of motorcyclists who have ravaged a small California beach town. **81m/C VHS.** Casey Kasem, Dovie Beams, Terry Stafford, Robert Dix; ***D:*** Ken Osborne; ***W:*** Ken Osborne; ***C:*** Ralph Waldo; ***M:*** Harley Hatcher.

Wild, Wild Planet ½ **1965** Alien beings from a distant planet are miniaturizing Earth's leaders in a bid to destroy our planet, and a dubbed, wooden hero comes to the rescue. A rarely seen Italian SF entry, great fun for genre fans. A must for "robot girls in skin tight leather outfits" completists. **93m/C VHS.** *IT* Tony Russell, Lisa Gastoni, Massimo Serato, Franco Nero; ***D:*** Anthony M. Dawson.

Wild Wild West **1999 (PG-13)** A wild, wild waste of time, money, and star power that saw director Sonnenfeld and star Smith re-team (after "Men In Black") for this western spy spoof based on the 60s TV series. Government agents James T. West (Smith) and master-of-disguise Artemus Gordon (Kline) are sent to stop diabolical wheelchair-bound scientist, Dr. Arliss Loveless (Branagh), from assassinating President Ulysses S. Grant in 1867. The budget was $100 million but the elaborate sets and effects are more hokey than cool and some money should have been spent on the script. And a black James West just doesn't work, no matter Smith's charm. **105m/C VHS, DVD.** Will Smith, Kevin Kline, Kenneth Branagh, Salma Hayek, M. Emmet Walsh, Ted Levine, Musetta Vander, Bai Ling, Rodney A. Grant, Frederique van der Wal, Garcelle Beauvais, Sofia Eng; ***D:*** Barry Sonnenfeld; ***W:*** Brent Maddock, S.S. Wilson, Jeffrey Price, Peter S. Seaman; ***C:*** Michael Ballhaus; ***M:*** Elmer Bernstein. Golden Raspberries '99: Worst Picture, Worst Director (Sonnenfeld), Worst Screenplay, Worst Song ("Wild Wild West").

Wild, Wild West Revisited ½ **1979** A feature-length reprise of the tongue-in-cheek western TV series. Irreverent and fun, in the spirit of its admirable predecessor—though it's probably just as well the proposed new series didn't see fruition. **95m/C VHS.** Robert Conrad, Ross Martin, Harry (Henry) Morgan, Rene Auberjonois; ***D:*** Burt Kennedy. **TV**

Wild Women **1953** Extremely hilarious schlocker about a safari of white men captured by a savage tribe of jungle women. Total camp. **62m/B VHS.** Lewis Wilson, Frances Dubay, Dana Wilson; ***D:*** Norman Dawn.

Wild Women ½ **1970** Five female convicts are released during the Texas/Mexico dispute to help smuggle arms to American forces. Innocuous western, original in a made-for-TV kind of way. **90m/C VHS.** Hugh O'Brian, Anne Francis, Marilyn Maxwell, Marie Windsor; ***D:*** Don Taylor. **TV**

Wild Women of Wongo ½ **1959** The denizens of a primitive isle, essentially beautiful women and ugly men, meet the natives of a neighboring island, handsome men and ugly women. Not quite bad enough to be true camp fun, but stupidly silly in a low-budget way. **73m/C VHS, DVD.** Pat Crowley, Ed Fury, Adrienne Bourbeau, Jean Hawkshaw, Johnny Walsh; ***D:*** James L. Wolcott; ***W:*** Cedric Rutherford; ***C:*** Harry Walsh.

The Wild World of Batwoman *She Was a Hippy Vampire* **1966** A campy cult film in which Batwoman and a bevy of Bat Girls are pitted against an evil doctor in order to find the prototype of an atomic hearing aid/nuclear bomb. **70m/C VHS.** Katherine Victor, George Andre, Steve Brodie, Richard Banks, Lloyd Nelson, Steve Conte, Mel Oshins, Bruno VeSota, Bob Arbogast, Lucki Winn, Suzanne Lodge, Pam Garry, Sylvia Holiday, Francis Bryan, Leah London; ***D:*** Jerry Warren; ***W:*** Jerry Warren; ***C:*** William G. Troiano; ***M:*** Erich Bromberg.

Wild Zero **2000** KISS had "Phantom of the Park," and the Japanese punk band Guitar Wolf has this film. Young fan Ace goes to see his favorite band Guitar Wolf in concert, and they have a gunfight with their soon-to-be-former manager—then aliens invade and turn people into flesh-eating zombies. Ace finds a girlfriend who wasn't always a girl and summons the band to whoop some behind. Meant to be campy with cheesy effects, it has a trippy charm. **98m/C DVD.** *JP* Shiro Namiki, Yoshiyuki Morishita, Guitar Wolf, Bass Wolf, Drum Wolf, Masasahi Endo, Kwancharu Endo, Makoto Inamiya, Haruka Nakajo, Taneko, Masao, Tawaki Fusamori, Akihiko Murata, Kae Egawa, Hideaki Skiguchi; ***D:*** Tetsuro Takeuchi; ***W:*** Tetsuro Takeuchi, Satoshi Takagi; ***C:*** Motoki Kobayashi; ***M:*** Guitar Wolf.

Wild Zone **1989 (R)** An American ex-soldier combats mercenaries in Africa in order to rescue his kidnapped father. **100m/C VHS.** Edward Albert, Philip Brown, Carla Herd; ***D:*** Percival Rubens.

Wildcard ½ **1992 (PG-13)** When a veteran pilot is killed in a helicopter crash, a friend suspects foul play. He calls in Preacher, a special forces veteran, to investigate and what he discovers is murder, greed, and corruption. **86m/C VHS.** Powers Boothe, Cindy Pickett, Rene Auberjonois, Terry O'Quinn, M. Emmet Walsh, John Lacy; ***D:*** Mel Damski; ***W:*** Scobie Richardson.

The Wildcat **1926** Manager takes his fighter to an isolated ranch in order to recover from his boozing but the boxer winds up getting involved with a pretty girl and a robbery. **52m/B VHS.** Gordon Clifford, Charlotte Pierce, Frank Bond, Hooper Phillips, Ervin Renard, Arthur Millett; ***D:*** Harry Fraser.

Wildcat **1942** Crabbe, famous as the serials' Flash Gordon, is a villain in this petrochemical adventure. The hero overextends his credit when he buys an oil well and must produce a gusher or else. **73m/B VHS.** Richard Arlen, Arline Judge, Buster Crabbe, William Frawley, Arthur Hunnicutt, Elisha Cook Jr., William Benedict; ***D:*** Frank McDonald; ***W:*** Maxwell Shane; ***C:*** Fred H. Jackman Jr.

Wildcats **1986 (R)** A naive female phys-ed teacher (Hawn) is saddled with the job of coach for a completely undisciplined, inner city, high school football team. Formulaic, connect-the-dots comedy; moderately funny, and of course Hawn triumphs in adversity, but at nearly two hours a very long sitcom episode. **106m/C VHS, DVD.** Goldie Hawn, James Keach, Swoosie Kurtz, Bruce McGill, M. Emmet Walsh, Woody Harrelson, Wesley Snipes, Tab Thacker, Jsu Garcia; ***D:*** Michael Ritchie; ***M:*** James Newton Howard.

Wilde **1997 (R)** The witty Wilde is making something of a resurgence in film, plays, and books. The Irish author/playwright (portrayed by look-alike Fry) is enjoying the London limelight and his family life with wife Constance (Ehle) and their two sons, while privately acknowledging his attraction to men. Unfortunately, this leads Oscar into a mad passion for sulky, neurotic pretty boy Bosie Douglas (Law), whose aristocratic father, the Marquess of Queensbury (Wilkinson), wants moral revenge on Wilde. His affair with Bosie leads to a celebrated trial for Oscar and a tragic outcome. Adapted from the biography by Richard Ellman. **115m/C VHS, DVD.** *GB* Stephen Fry, Jude Law, Vanessa Redgrave, Jennifer Ehle, Michael Sheen, Zoe Wanamaker, Tom Wilkinson, Gemma Jones, Judy Parfitt; ***D:*** Brian Gilbert; ***W:*** Julian Mitchell; ***C:*** Martin Fuhrer; ***M:*** Debbie Wiseman.

Wilder **2000 (R)** Maverick cop Della Wilder (Grier) and her partner Harlan Lee (Orzari) are assigned to investigate the murder of the ex-lover of Dr. Sam Charney (Hauer). He seems the most likely suspect but the detectives find out that this is one in a series of deaths and it's not the usual sort of serial killer. In fact, the crimes are tied into a giant pharmaceutical company and Della decides to use Charney's medical expertise to prove it—if they can survive the investigation. **92m/C VHS, DVD.** *CA* Pam Grier, Rutger Hauer, Romano Orzari, John Dunn-Hill, Eugene Clark, Serge Houde; ***D:*** Rodney Gibbons; ***W:*** Terry Abrahamson; ***C:*** Bert Tougas; ***M:*** Michael Corriveau, Robert Marchaud. **VIDEO**

Wilder Napalm ½ **1993 (PG-13)** Lame comedy about two at-odds brothers, the woman they both love, and their dangerous pyrokinetic abilities. Wilder (Howard) and Wallace (Quaid) Foudroyant have been feuding for years—and not just over the fact that Wallace is in love with Wilder's wife Vida (Winger). Wallace wants to use their family "gift" to become rich and famous but Wilder doesn't want them to exploit their fiery powers. They finally decide on an incendiary showdown to settle the score once and for all. Good actors lost in witless characters and a incoherent plot. **109m/C VHS, DVD.** Dennis Quaid, Arliss Howard, Debra Winger, M. Emmet Walsh, Jim Varney, Mimi Lieber, Marvin J. McIntyre; ***D:*** Glenn Gordon Caron; ***W:*** Vince Gilligan; ***M:*** Michael Kamen.

Wilderness ½ **1996 (R)** Quiet British librarian Alice White (Ooms) is keeping quite a secret. It seems when there's a full moon, she gets a little furry. She tries to cope with her affliction by seeing a shrink (Kitchen) but the weasel just wants to exploit her. And just try explaining you're a werewolf to the new guy (Teale) in your life. Think gothic romance more than straight horror. Made for British TV. **90m/C VHS, DVD.** *GB* Amanda Ooms, Michael Kitchen, Owen Teale, Gemma Jones; ***D:*** Ben Bolt; ***W:*** Andrew Davies, Bernadette Davis. **TV**

Wilderness Love ½ *Personally Yours* **2002** Handsome Alaskan rancher Jesse (Nordling) is a divorced dad and since his kids worry he'll never find someone to love again, they decide to submit his photo to a lonely-hearts magazine. His profile draws attention from lots of eligible women but Jesse's perfect romance may still be his ex-wife Susannah (Bertinelli). **90m/C DVD.** Jeffrey Nordling, Valerie Bertinelli, Brittney Irvin, Michael Welch, Donnelly Rhodes, Andrea Roth, Emily Tennant; ***D:*** Jeff Reiner; ***W:*** Jill Blotevogel; ***C:*** Feliks Parnell; ***M:*** Don Davis. **TV**

The Wildest Dream: Conquest of Everest **2010** In 1999, American mountaineer Conrad Anker was part of a team that recovered the body of George Mallory—75 years after the British explorer vanished in 1924, along with climbing partner Andrew Irvine, while attempting to make the first ascent to the summit of Mount Everest. Includes recreations of the climb and recovery efforts along with readings from Mallory's letters and other narration. **m/C DVD.** ***D:*** Anthony Geffen; ***W:*** mark Halliley; ***C:*** Chris Openshaw; ***M:*** John Douek; ***V:*** Hugh Dancy, Ralph Fiennes, Natasha Richardson, Alan Rickman; ***Nar:*** Liam Neeson.

Wildest Dreams ½ *Bikini Genie* **1990 (R)** Released from its bottle by a lovely nebbish, a genie puts a love spell on one beautiful girl after another in order to find him the right one, resulting in a bevy of women clamoring for our hero's attention. **84m/C VHS.** James Davies, Heidi Paine, Deborah Blaisdell, Ruth (Coreen) Collins, Jane (Veronica Hart) Hamilton; ***D:*** Chuck Vincent.

Wildfire ½ **1945** Two horse traders come to the aid of ranchers beset by horse thieves. Early color outing for Steele. Harmless, ordinary oater. **60m/C VHS.** Bob Steele, Sterling Holloway, John Miljan, William Farnum, Eddie Dean, Sarah Padden, Frank Ellis; ***D:*** Robert Emmett Tansey.

Wildfire **1988 (PG)** As teenagers, Frank and Kay run away to get married but Frank is sent to prison for robbing a bank and Kay winds up making a new life for herself. Released from prison after eight years, Frank discovers Kay is married with two children and doesn't want anything further to do with him. But when Frank violates his parole, Kay discovers she can't leave him again and the two go on the run together. **98m/C VHS.** Steven Bauer, Linda Fiorentino, Will Patton, Marshall Bell; ***D:*** Zalman King; ***W:*** Zalman King, Matthew Bright; ***C:*** Bill Butler; ***M:*** Maurice Jarre.

Wildflower **1991** Set in the Depression-era South, Alice is a 17 year-old partially deaf girl who also suffers from epilepsy. Her stepfather believes she's possessed and confines her to a shed. Growing up ignorant and abused Alice is befriended by a neighboring brother and sister who decide to rescue her. A three-hankie family picture with moving performances and inspirational themes. Based on the novel "Alice" by Sara Flanigan. **94m/C VHS, DVD.** Patricia Arquette, Beau Bridges, Susan Blakely, William McNamara, Reese Witherspoon, Collin Wilcox-Paxton, Norman (Max) Maxwell, Heather Lynch, Allison Smith, Richard Olsen, Mary Page; ***D:*** Diane Keaton; ***W:*** Sara Flanigan; ***C:*** Janusz Kaminski; ***M:*** Jon Gilutin, Ken Edwards. **CABLE**

Wildflowers ½ *Wild Flowers* **1999 (R)** Cathy (DuVall) is a 17-year-old tomboy who lives on a houseboat with her single dad (Arana). Longing for a female role model, Cally stumbles across hippie artist Sabine (Hannah) and gets involved in her life and a past that has some secrets Cally may not want to uncover. Especially fine performance by DuVall. **98m/C VHS, DVD.** Clea DuVall, Daryl Hannah, Tomas Arana, Eric Roberts, Irene Bedard, James Gandolfini, John Doe; ***D:*** Melissa Painter; ***W:*** Melissa Painter; ***C:*** Paul Ryan.

Wilding ½ **1990** A pair of cops are on the trail of a gang of kids who go "wilding," which involves sprees of killing, raping and looting. Exploitive fare based on horrible, recent events in New York. The filmmakers skirt controversy by making the criminals rich suburban kids. **92m/C VHS.** Wings Hauser, Joey Travolta, Karen Russell, Steven Cooke; ***D:*** Eric Louzil.

Wildrose **1985** Eichhorn is memorable as a recent divorcee who must assert herself among her otherwise all-male coworkers at a Minnesota strip mine. She finds a new love, and tries to put her life back together. Filmed on location. **96m/C VHS.** Lisa Eichhorn, Tom Bower, James Cada; ***D:*** John Hanson; ***W:*** John Hanson, Eugene Corr.

Will: G. Gordon Liddy ½ **1982** The life of the Watergate conspirator, based on his autobiography. Made for TV. Producer/star Conrad reportedly objected strongly to cuts from the original three-hour length, apparently with cause: the first half is superficial pap. The portrayal of Liddy's time in prison, though, is fascinating, and Conrad is excellent. **100m/C VHS.** Robert Conrad, Katherine (Kathy) Cannon, Gary Bayer, Peter Ratray, James Rebhorn, Red West, Maurice Woods, Danny Lloyd; ***D:*** Robert Lieberman. **TV**

Will It Snow for Christmas? *Y'aura t'il de la Niege a Noel?* **1996** A single mother and her seven children live in a drafty farmhouse in rural southern France. Their father is married, has another family, and uses his mistress and the children as cheap farm labor. He treats them all badly and their mother begins to sink into despair as the seasons pass. Finally, on Christmas Eve, everything comes to an unexpected conclusion. French with subtitles. **90m/C VHS.** *FR* Dominique Reymond, Daniel Duval; ***D:*** Sandrine Veysset; ***W:*** Sandrine Veysset; ***C:*** Helene Louvart.

Will Penny 1/2 **1967** Just back from a cattle drive, a range-wandering loner looks for work in the wrong place and offends a family of outlaws who come after him. His escape from them leads to another kind of trap—one set by a love-hungry woman (Hackett, in a strong performance). Heston considers this film his personal best, and he's probably right. Superbly directed western, with excellent cinematography and professional, realistic portrayals, flopped in theatres, moviegoers preferring simultaneous Heston outing "Planet of the Apes." **109m/C VHS, DVD.** Charlton Heston, Joan Hackett, Donald Pleasence, Lee Majors, Bruce Dern, Anthony Zerbe, Ben Johnson, Clifton James, Jon(athan) Gries; ***D:*** Tom Gries; ***W:*** Tom Gries; ***C:*** Lucien Ballard; ***M:*** Elmer Bernstein.

Will Success Spoil Rock Hunter? 1/2 **1957** Dated advertising satire finds ad man Hunter (Randall) hoping to get the key to the executive washroom but he may instead find himself on the unemployment line unless he can convince the profitable Stay-Put lipstick account not to change agencies. One day Rock sees movie star Rita Marlowe (Mansfield), and her kissable lips, on TV and tries to convince her to endorse the product. But she'll only agree if he'll pose as her new boyfriend to make ex-beau Bobo (Mansfield's real-life hubby Hargitay) jealous. Naturally, the lipstick ads take off bigtime but success does indeed spoil Rock (at least temporarily). Very slightly based on the play by George Axelrod. **94m/C VHS, DVD.** Tony Randall, Jayne Mansfield, Betsy Drake, Mickey Hargitay, John Williams, Henry Jones, Joan Blondell; ***Cameos:*** Groucho Marx; ***D:*** Frank Tashlin; ***W:*** Frank Tashlin; ***C:*** Joe MacDonald; ***M:*** Cyril Mockridge. Natl. Film Reg. '00.

Willa **1979** Raffin, a hash-joint waitress with two kids and one in the pipeline, is deserted by her husband and determines to get ahead by becoming a trucker. Okay made-for-TV drama. **95m/C VHS.** Cloris Leachman, Deborah Raffin, Clu Gulager, John Amos, Diane Ladd; ***D:*** Claudio Guzman, Joan Darling; ***M:*** John Barry.

Willard **1971 (PG)** Willard is a lonely, psychotic youngster who trains a group of rats, his only friends, to attack his enemies. Not as disgusting as it might have been (rated PG), but pretty weird and not redeemed by any sense of style or humor. Popular at the boxoffice; followed by inferior "Ben." Based on Stephen Gilbert's novel "Ratman's Notebooks." **95m/C VHS.** Bruce Davison, Ernest Borgnine, Elsa Lanchester, Sondra Locke, Michael Dante, J. Pat O'Malley, Jody Gilbert, William Hansen; ***D:*** Daniel Mann; ***W:*** Gilbert Ralston; ***C:*** Robert B. Hauser; ***M:*** Alex North.

Willard **2003 (PG-13)** Willard is back (in the form of Glover) and he brought the rats with him. He's the beaten-down son to a hateful, domineering mom, and the punching bag for his brutish boss (Ermey). The twist in this one is that he communicates with fuzzy, white Socrates, instead of the apparently steroid-fueled giant rat Ben, which causes a vermin power struggle. Sometimes clever (the original Willard, Bruce Davison, is seen in a painting as this Willard's deceased father), but mostly soulless remake does have the advantage of Glover's presence in a role that seems made for him. He goes all-out and over-the-top to portray Willard's swirling psychosis and ever-escalating delusions of grandeur. **95m/C VHS, DVD.** *US* Crispin Glover, R. Lee Ermey, Laura Elena Harring, Jackie Burroughs, David Parker; ***D:*** Glen Morgan; ***W:*** Glen Morgan; ***C:*** Robert McLachlan; ***M:*** Shirley Walker.

William Faulkner's Old Man 1/2 *Old Man* **1997 (PG)** TV adaptation of a part of Faulkner's 1939 novel "The Wild Palms" that is set in the '20s. The "Old Man" in question is the mighty Mississippi, which has flooded leaving a pregnant Addie (Tripplehorn), abandoned by her husband, stranded and about to give birth. But prison-farm inmate J.J. Taylor (Howard) is sent by the warden to row to her rescue, becoming a surrogate father when the baby is born, and traveling the river to New Orleans to get mother and child to safety. **98m/C VHS.** Jeanne Tripplehorn, Arliss Howard, Leo Burmester; ***D:*** John Kent Harrison; ***W:*** Horton Foote; ***C:*** Kees Van Oostrum; ***M:*** Lawrence Shragge. **TV**

William Shakespeare's A Midsummer Night's Dream 1/2 *A Midsummer Night's Dream* **1999 (PG-13)** Shakespeare's fantasy/romance/comedy is transported to turn-of-the-century Tuscany where Oberon (Everett), King of the Fairies, is fighting with his queen, Titania (Pfeiffer). Their spats lead to trouble for a variety of humans, including the hapless Bottom (Kline), who winds up with a donkey's head replacing his own. Kline is the most at ease with his role (Everett and Pfeiffer, primarily, have to look beautiful, which they do), while the younger foursome of would-be lovers (Flockhart, Bale, Friel, and West) prove to be less than memorable, as does the entire production. **115m/C VHS, DVD.** Rupert Everett, Michelle Pfeiffer, Kevin Kline, Stanley Tucci, Calista Flockhart, Dominic West, Christian Bale, David Strathairn, Sophie Marceau, John Sessions, Anna Friel, Roger Rees, Max Wright, Gregory Jbara, Bill Irwin, Sam Rockwell, Bernard Hill; ***D:*** Michael Hoffman; ***W:*** Michael Hoffman; ***C:*** Oliver Stapleton; ***M:*** Simon Boswell.

William Shakespeare's Romeo and Juliet *Romeo and Juliet* **1996 (PG-13)** Bright, loud update of Shakespeare's tragedy of feuding families and first love. Contemporary fantasy setting, Verona Beach, and attitude (the Montagues and the Capulets are business rivals), with the 16th-century Elizabethan language intact, although Luhrmann's said to have cut half the text. Hot-blooded Romeo (DiCaprio) takes one look at angelic Juliet (Danes) and falls immediately in love/lust. This doesn't please Juliet's family, including quick-tempered cousin Tybalt (Leguizamo) who goes after Romeo with far-reaching consequences. DiCaprio's remarkable and the young duo look wonderful together. A big hit with the teens. Filmed in Mexico City. **120m/C VHS, DVD.** Leonardo DiCaprio, Claire Danes, John Leguizamo, Paul Sorvino, Brian Dennehy, Diane Venora, Pete Postlethwaite, Paul Rudd, Harold Perrineau Jr., Jesse Bradford, Miriam Margolyes, Vondie Curtis-Hall, Christina Pickles, M. Emmet Walsh; ***D:*** Baz Luhrmann; ***W:*** Baz Luhrmann, Craig Pearce; ***C:*** Donald McAlpine; ***M:*** Nellee Hooper. British Acad. '97: Adapt. Screenplay, Art Dir./Set Dec., Director (Luhrmann), Score; MTV Movie Awards '97: Female Perf. (Danes).

Willie & Phil 1/2 **1980 (R)** At the start of the '70s, two buddies (Ontkean and Sharkey) fall for the same girl (Kidder). They become a threesome and are entangled in each other's lives for the rest of the decade. Insightful comedy-drama. **111m/C VHS.** Michael Ontkean, Margot Kidder, Ray Sharkey, Jan Miner, Julie Bovasso, Natalie Wood, Laurence Fishburne, Louis Guss, Kaki Hunter, Kristine DeBell; ***D:*** Paul Mazursky; ***W:*** Paul Mazursky; ***C:*** Sven Nykvist; ***M:*** Claude Bolling.

The Willies **1990 (PG-13)** Three youngsters gross each other out with juvenile tales of horror and scariness while camping out in the backyard. Pointless but not without a few yuks (in both senses of the term). **120m/C VHS.** James Karen, Sean Astin, Kathleen Freeman, Jeremy Miller; ***D:*** Brian Peck.

Willow 1/2 **1988 (PG)** Blockbuster fantasy epic combines the story of Moses with "Snow White," dwarves and all. Willow is the little Nelwyn who finds the lost baby Daikini and is assigned the task of returning her safely to her people. Willow discovers that the girl is actually a sacred infant who is destined to overthrow the evil queen Bavmorda and rule the land. As you might expect from executive producer George Lucas, there is much action and plenty of clever, high-quality special effects. But the "Star Wars"-esque story (by Lucas) is strangely predictable, and a bit too action-packed. Not really for children. **118m/C VHS, DVD.** Warwick Davis, Val Kilmer, Jean Marsh, Joanne Whalley, Billy Barty, Pat Roach, Ruth Greenfield, Patricia Hayes, Gavan O'Herlihy, Kevin Pollak; ***D:*** Ron Howard; ***W:*** Bob Dolman; ***C:*** Adrian Biddle; ***M:*** James Horner.

Willy Wonka & the Chocolate Factory 1/2 **1971 (G)** When the last of five coveted "golden tickets" falls into the hands of sweet but very poor Charlie, he and his Grandpa Joe get a tour of the most wonderfully strange chocolate factory in the world. The owner is the most curious hermit ever to hit the big screen. He leads the five young "winners" on a thrilling and often dangerous tour of his fabulous factory. Adapted from Roald Dahl's "Charlie and the Chocolate Factory." Without a doubt one of the best "kid's" movies ever made; a family classic worth watching again and again. ♫The Candy Man; Cheer Up, Charlie; (I've Got a) Golden Ticket; Pure Imagination; Oompa Loompa; I Want It Now. **100m/C VHS, DVD, HD DVD.** Gene Wilder, Jack Albertson, Denise Nickerson, Peter Ostrum, Roy Kinnear, Aubrey Woods, Michael Bollner, Ursula Reit, Leonard Stone, Dodo Denney, Julie Dawn Cole, Gunter Meisner; ***D:*** Mel Stuart; ***W:*** Roald Dahl; ***C:*** Arthur Ibbetson; ***M:*** Leslie Bricusse, Anthony Newley, Walter Scharf.

Wilma **1977** Based on the true story of Wilma Rudolph, a young black woman who overcame childhood illness to win three gold medals at the 1960 Olympics. Plodding made-for-TV biography suffers from sub-par script and acting. **100m/C VHS, DVD.** Shirley Jo Finney, Joe Seneca, Cicely Tyson, Jason Bernard, Denzel Washington, Larry B. Scott, Norman Matlock; ***D:*** Bud Greenspan; ***C:*** Arthur Ornitz; ***M:*** Irwin Bazelon. **TV**

Wilson **1944** Biography of Woodrow Wilson from his days as the head of Princeton University, to the governorship of New Jersey, and as U.S. President during WWI. After the war, Wilson conceives of the League of Nations but is unable to sell it to a U.S. still bent on isolationism. This lavish film won critical plaudits but was a major moneyloser. **154m/C VHS.** Alexander Knox, Charles Coburn, Geraldine Fitzgerald, Thomas Mitchell, Ruth Nelson, Cedric Hardwicke, Vincent Price, William Eythe, Mary Anderson, Sidney Blackmer, Stanley Ridges, Eddie Foy Jr., Charles Halton; ***D:*** Henry King; ***W:*** Lamar Trotti; ***C:*** Leon Shamroy; ***M:*** Alfred Newman. Oscars '44: Color Cinematog., Film Editing, Orig. Screenplay, Sound; Golden Globes '45: Actor—Drama (Knox).

Wimbledon 1/2 **2004 (PG-13)** Harmlessly predictable romantic comedy set in the tennis world, where weary 30-something Brit Peter Colt (Bettany) is coming to the end of his career with his final Wimbledon tournament. He meets cute with aggressive American super-player Lizzie Bradbury (Dunst), who's managed by her control-freak dad, Dennis (Neill). Lizzie's up for a little serve-and-volley and Peter suddenly finds his game (not to mention his love life) reinvigorated. Suddenly, he's a contender! But Lizzie is having second thoughts when love interferes with her concentration. After all, love in tennis is a big zero. Bettany is all self-deprecating charm while Dunst manages to be both smug and vulnerable. **98m/C DVD.** *US* Kirsten Dunst, Paul Bettany, Sam Neill, Jon Favreau, Bernard Hill, Eleanor Bron, Nikolaj Coster-Waldau, Austin Nichols, Robert Lindsay, James McAvoy; ***D:*** Richard Loncraine; ***W:*** Adam Brooks, Jennifer Flackett, Marc Levin; ***C:*** Darius Khondji; ***M:*** Ed Shearmur.

Wimps **1987 (R)** A collegiate wimp is subjected to a brutal fraternity initiation, but eventually gets the girl. Cheap ripoff of Cyrano de Bergerac, turned into a teen sex flick. **94m/C VHS.** Louie Bonanno, Jim Abele, Deborah Blaisdell; ***D:*** Chuck Vincent.

Win a Date with Tad Hamilton! **2004 (PG-13)** Typical young-love romance has small-town girl Rosalee (Bosworth) fall for actor-outsider Tad (Duhamel) while boy-next-door Pete (Grace) pines away in silence for her. Tad's agent (Lane) and manager (Hayes)—both oh so cleverly sharing the same name, Richard Levy—concoct the "win a date" contest to fix the bad boy image that's made him tabloid fodder. Rosalee is chosen and, to no one's surprise, Tad becomes intrigued. He pursues her much to Pete's dismay, and the usual dance ensues. Bosworth's down-to-earth appeal saves the formulaic concept but one wonders what prompted Broadway success Lane to take the bit role. **96m/C VHS, DVD.** *US* Kate (Catherine) Bosworth, Topher Grace, Ginnifer Goodwin, Josh Duhamel, Nathan Lane, Sean P. Hayes, Gary Cole, Kathryn Hahn, Stephen Tobolowsky, Amy Smart, Octavia L. Spancer; ***D:*** Robert Luketic; ***W:*** Victor Levin; ***C:*** Peter Lyons Collister; ***M:*** Ed Shearmur.

Win, Place, or Steal 1/2 *The Big Payoff; Three For the Money; Just Another Day at the Races* **1972 (PG)** Lame comedy set at the racetrack about three grown men and their adolescent schemes to win big. Better you should scratch. **88m/C VHS.** McLean Stevenson, Alex Karras, Dean Stockwell; ***D:*** Richard Bailey.

Winchell 1/2 **1998 (R)** Flamboyant biopic of powerful journalist/radio personality Walter Winchell (Tucci), whose career stretched from the 1930s into the '50s. Winchell blurred the line between hard news and tabloid gossip and used his influence politically to re-elect President Roosevelt and get the U.S. involved in WWII. But he was also arrogant and mean-spirited and his grandiosity eventually proved to be his downfall. Based on the 1976 book "Walter Winchell: His Life and Times" by Winchell's longtime ghostwriter Herman Klurfeld. **105m/C VHS.** Stanley Tucci, Paul Giamatti, Glenne Headly, Christopher Plummer, Xander Berkeley, Kevin Tighe, Frank Medrano, Vic Polizos, Megan Mullally, Victoria Platt; ***D:*** Paul Mazursky; ***W:*** Scott Abbott; ***C:*** Robbie Greenberg; ***M:*** Bill Conti. **CABLE**

Winchester '73 1/2 **1950** Superb acting and photography characterize this classic, landmark western. Simple plot—cowboy Stewart pursues his stolen state-of-the-art rifle as it changes hands—speeds along and carries the viewer with it, ending with an engrossing and unforgettable shootout. Almost singlehandedly breathed new life into the whole genre. Laser videodisc version contains a special narration track provided by Stewart. Mann's and Stewart's first teaming. **82m/C VHS, DVD.** James Stewart, Shelley Winters, Stephen McNally, Dan Duryea, Millard Mitchell, John McIntire, Will Geer, Jay C. Flippen, Rock Hudson, Tony Curtis, Charles Drake; ***D:*** Anthony Mann; ***C:*** William H. Daniels.

The Wind **1928** One of the last great silents still stands as a magnificent entertainment. Gish, in possibly her best role, is an innocent Easterner who finds herself married to a rough cowpoke and raped by a married man in a bleak frontier town. Director Sjostrom has a splendid feel for landscape, and the drama—climaxing with a tumultuous desert storm—is intense yet fully believable. Based on the novel by Dorothy Scarborough. **74m/B VHS.** Lillian Gish, Lars Hanson, Montagu Love, Dorothy (Dorothy G. Cummings) Cumming, Edward Earle, William Orlamond; ***D:*** Victor Sjostrom; ***W:*** Frances Marion. Natl. Film Reg. '93.

The Wind **1987** Foster is terrorized by Hauser while attempting to write her next thriller in Greece. Let's hope her book is more exciting than this movie. Shot on location in Greece. **92m/C VHS, DVD.** Meg Foster, Wings Hauser, Steve Railsback, David McCallum, Robert Morley; ***D:*** Nico Mastorakis; ***W:*** Nico Mastorakis, Fred C. Perry; ***C:*** Andreas Bellis; ***M:*** Stanley Myers, Hans Zimmer.

Wind 1/2 **1992 (PG-13)** Sailor Will Parker (Modine) chooses the opportunity to be on the America's Cup team over girlfriend Grey and then has the dubious honor of making a technical error that causes their loss. Undaunted, he locates Grey and her new engineer boyfriend (Skarsgard) and convinces them to design the ultimate boat for the next set of races. ESPN carried extensive coverage of the America's Cup races for the first time in the summer of '92 and viewers discovered that a little goes a long way. The same holds true for "Wind" which has stunning race footage, but little else. The script lacks substance and was written as filming progressed, and it shows. **123m/C VHS, DVD.** Matthew Modine, Jennifer Grey, Cliff Robertson, Jack Thompson, Stellan Skarsgard, Rebecca Miller, Ned Vaughn; ***D:*** Carroll Ballard; ***W:*** Rudy Wurlitzer, Mac Gudgeon; ***C:*** John Toll; ***M:*** Basil Poledouris.

Wind and Cloud: The Storm Riders *Tian xia; Storm Riders* **2004** This disc by Tai Seng is marketed as a sequel to the original "Storm Riders" film, but it is instead a film cobbled together from a TV series that's a sequel to a similar film. Since the series is 30 hours long, and this film is less than three hours, the plot suffers. It has been 12 years since Wind and Cloud fought their duel, and a new Evil has arisen to plague the land. It's assumed Wind and Cloud will come together, but an evil pill has turned Wind to the dark side. **109m/C DVD.** *HK* Sonny Chiba, Aaron Kwok, Yiu-Cheung Lai, Kristy Yang, Ekin Chang; ***D:*** Raymond Lee, Shui Chung Yuet; ***W:*** Wing-Shing Ma; ***M:*** Akira Inoue.

The Wind and the Lion 🦴🦴🦴 **1975 (PG)** In turn-of-the-century Morocco, a sheik (Connery) kidnaps a feisty American woman (Bergen) and her children and holds her as a political hostage. President Teddy Roosevelt (Keith) sends in the Marines to free the captives, who are eventually released by their captor. Directed with venue and style by Milius. Highly entertaining, if heavily fictionalized. Based very loosely on a historical incident. **120m/C VHS, DVD.** Sean Connery, Candice Bergen, Brian Keith, John Huston, Geoffrey Lewis, Steve Kanaly, Vladek Sheybal, Nadim Sawalha, Roy Jenson, Larry Cross, Simon Harrison, Polly Gottesmann, Marc Zuber; ***D:*** John Milius; ***W:*** John Milius; ***C:*** Billy Williams; ***M:*** Jerry Goldsmith.

Wind Chill 🦴🦴 **2007 (R)** Two college students are heading home for Christmas break. Driving in whiteout conditions, they get stuck in a snowbank on a deserted road without heat or a phone signal. But staying alive through the night may not be just a matter of the weather as it seems the ghosts of those who died on that road would like some more company. **91m/C DVD.** *US* Emily Blunt, Ashton Holmes, Martin Donovan, Ned Bellamy; ***D:*** Gregory Jacobs; ***W:*** Steven Katz, Joesph Gangemi; ***C:*** Dan Laustsen; ***M:*** Clint Mansell.

A Wind from Wyoming 🦴 ½ **1994 (R)** Lea's boyfriend leaves her for her mother. Her father is determined to win back his wife by means of a hypnotist. Her chubby sister is obsessed with a celebrated author who somehow falls for Lea. When the hypnotist decides he wants Lea he turns the author into a woman-hater. Humorous look at dysfunctional families and the mysteries of love through a plot that is a bit hard to follow. Subtitled. **99m/C VHS, DVD.** *CA FR* Francois Cluzet, France Castel, Michel Cote, Marc Messier, Sarah-Jeanne Salvy, Celine Bonnier, Donald Pilon; ***D:*** Andre Forcier; ***W:*** Andre Forcier, Patrice Arbour, Jacques Marcotte; ***C:*** Georges Dufaux; ***M:*** Christian Gaubert.

A Wind Named Amnesia 🦴🦴 **1993** A strange amnesia wind sweeps away all of mankind's knowledge and human civilization vanishes. Then a mysterious young man is miraculously re-educated and searches for those who destroyed man's memories. In Japanese with English subtitles. **80m/C VHS, DVD.** *JP* ***D:*** Kazuo Yamazaki; ***W:*** Hideyuki Kikuchi; ***M:*** Hidenobu Takimoto, Kazuhiko Toyama; ***V:*** Susan Baker, Denica Fairman, Adam Henderson, Peter Marinker, Lee Tyler.

Wind River 🦴🦴 ½ **1998 (PG-13)** In 1855 Utah, there's trouble between the settlers and the Shoshone tribe. The wife of Chief Washakie (Means) dreams that a wolf threatens the tribe and a young blond warrior saves them. So the chief sends Moragoni (Martinez) to find the boy. Moragoni meets 15-year-old settler Nicolas Wilson (Heron) and believes him to be the dream warrior and Nicolas agrees to live with the Shoshone and learn their ways. But eventually, Nicolas must choose between his real and adopted families. Based on "The White Indian Boy" by Elijah Nicolas, which was inspired by actual events. **97m/C VHS, DVD.** Blake Heron, A. Martinez, Russell Means, Wes Studi, Karen Allen, Patricia Van Ingen, Joe Wandell; ***D:*** Tom Shell; ***W:*** Tom Shell, Elizabeth Hansen; ***C:*** Lawrence Schweich; ***M:*** Jeff Marsh. **VIDEO**

The Wind That Shakes the Barley 🦴🦴🦴 **2006** Loach's take on the Irish fight for independence from Great Britain, which resulted in the partitioning of the country. In 1920, Damien O'Donovan (Murphy) is expecting to study medicine in London, but repeated run-ins with British soldiers find him joining his activist brother, Teddy (Delaney), in the IRA. However, following the Anglo-Irish Peace Agreement, the brothers find themselves on opposite sides—Teddy is willing to support an Irish Free State while the zealous Damien continues pursuing the dream of a totally independent country. Loach is unafraid to show the ruthlessness on both sides and the bitterness and tragedy that still lingers. **127m/C DVD.** *SP IT GE IR GB* Cillian Murphy, Liam Cunningham, Mary Murphy, Padraic Delaney, Orla Fitzgerald, Mary Riordan, Laurence Barry; ***D:*** Ken Loach; ***W:*** Paul Laverty; ***C:*** Barry Ackroyd; ***M:*** George Fenton.

Windhorse 🦴🦴 **1998** In a Tibetan village in 1979, Dolkar and her brother Dorjee watch as two Chinese soldiers execute their grandfather for espousing Tibetan freedom. Eighteen years later, Dolkar has become a popular singing star by cooperating with the Chinese while her brother has become a sullen, cynical drunk. But as the Chinese initiate further crackdowns, the Tibetans decide to protest. Title refers to the prayers, written on bits of paper, that the Tibetans throw to the winds. Tibetan and Chinese with subtitles. **97m/C VHS, DVD.** Dadon, Jampa Kolsang, Richard Chang; ***D:*** Paul Wagner; ***W:*** Paul Wagner, Thupten Tsering, Julia Elliott; ***C:*** Steven Schecter; ***M:*** Tommy Hayes.

Windjammer 🦴🦴 **1937** Western star O'Brien took a break from the lone prairie to make this seafaring rescue drama. He is a deputy state's attorney who signs up for a yacht race in order to serve a subpoena. Bad guys arrive on the scene, and the initially moody yacht denizens rely on our trusty hero to save them. Decent adventure. **75m/B VHS, DVD.** George O'Brien, Constance Worth; ***D:*** Sam Newfield.

Windmills of the Gods 🦴🦴 ½ *Sidney Sheldon's Windmills of the Gods* **1988** Glamor, romance, intrigue, and politics all mixed together in eastern Europe. Smith is named ambassador to Romania, finds the suave Wagner in residence, and becomes the target of assassins. Based on the novel by Sidney Sheldon. **95m/C VHS.** Jaclyn Smith, Robert Wagner, Franco Nero, Christopher Cazenove, David Ackroyd, Jean-Pierre Aumont, Ruby Dee, Jeffrey DeMunn, Michael Moriarty, Ian McKellen, Susan Tyrrell; ***D:*** Lee Philips; ***W:*** John Gay; ***M:*** Perry Botkin. **TV**

Windom's Way 🦴🦴🦴 **1957** Finch, in a strong role in this intriguing political drama, is an idealistic doctor in a remote village in Malaysia. He juggles a failing marriage and a budding romance, then finds himself caught in a local labor dispute. He works for a peaceful solution, but is captured by an insurgent army. Disillusioned, he plans to leave the country, but his wife persuades him to stay and tend the wounded. Based on a novel by James Ramsey Ullman. **90m/B VHS.** *GB* Peter Finch, Mary Ure; ***D:*** Ronald Neame.

The Window 🦴🦴🦴 ½ **1949** A little boy (Disney star Driscoll, intriguingly cast by director, Tetzlaff) has a reputation for telling lies, so no one believes him when he says he witnessed a murder...except the killers. Almost unbearably tense, claustrophobic thriller about the helplessness of childhood. Tetzlaff clearly learned more than a thing or two from the master, Hitchcock, for whom he photographed "Notorious." Based on the novella "The Boy Who Cried Murder" by Cornell Woolrich. Driscoll was awarded a special miniature Oscar as Outstanding Juvenile for his performance. **73m/B VHS.** Bobby Driscoll, Barbara Hale, Arthur Kennedy, Ruth Roman; ***D:*** Ted Tetzlaff.

Window Shopping 🦴🦴 ½ **1986** Multiple, confusing romances occur at the "Toison d' Or" shopping mall in Paris. A modern, French homage to the classic Hollywood musical. In French with English subtitles. **96m/C VHS.** *FR* Delphine Seyrig, Charles Denner, Fanny Cottencon, Miriam Boyer, Lio, Pascale Salkin, Jean-Francois Balmer; ***D:*** Chantal Akerman; ***W:*** Chantal Akerman.

Window Theory 🦴 **2004 (R)** Aimless Ethan (Large) returns to his hometown to stop the wedding of his high school honey Stephanie (O'Dell) to his ex-best friend Jeff (Flynn). Ethan wants her back but he's such an immature jerk—especially to women—that Steph is well rid of him. Since the lead is so unpleasant you really want him to get pummeled but that's about all. **?m/C DVD.** *CA* Luke Kirby, Alexandra Holden, Carly Pope, James Duval, Corey Large, Jennifer O'Dell, Luke Flynn, Paul Johannson, Tom Lenk, John Cassini; ***D:*** Andrew Putschoegl; ***W:*** Kyle Kramer; ***C:*** Andrew Huebscher; ***M:*** Miles Ito.

Window to Paris 🦴🦴 **1995 (PG-13)** East and West meet unexpectedly when a young music teacher (Dontsov) rents a room in St. Petersburg with a secret window that opens onto a Paris rooftop. Loony adventures ensue as Dontsov and his friends escape their dreary existence to exploit the bounties of Western capitalism in this sharp satire of Russian social ills. Relentless humor based on cross-cultural stereotypes wears thin (the Russians are cantankerous drunks; the Parisians, self-important snobs), but it keeps a sunny cast upon what could have been a scathing commentary. Russian and French with subtitles. **92m/C VHS.** *RU FR* Serguej Dontsov, Agnes Soral, Viktor Michailov, Nina Oussatova; ***D:*** Yuri Mamin; ***W:*** Arkadi Tigai, Yuri Mamin; ***M:*** Aleksei Zalivalov, Yuri Mamin.

Windows 🦴 **1980 (R)** A lonely lesbian (Ashley) becomes obsessed with her quiet neighbor (Shire) and concocts a plot to get close to her. Director Willis is known for his unbeatable cinematography, most notably for Woody Allen in "Manhattan." His debut in the chair is a miserable, offensive flop. **93m/C VHS.** Talia Shire, Joe Cortese, Elizabeth Ashley, Kay Medford, Linda Gillin; ***D:*** Gordon Willis; ***C:*** Gordon Willis; ***M:*** Ennio Morricone.

Windrider 🦴 ½ **1986** Simple love story made in Australia. A wind surfer and a rock star become lovers. Self-indulgent overwrought garbage with rare moments of promise. **83m/C VHS.** *AU* Tom Burlinson, Nicole Kidman, Charles "Bud" Tingwell, Jill Perryman, Simon Chilvers; ***D:*** Vincent Monton.

Windrunner 🦴🦴 ½ **1994 (PG)** Angry at his football-star dad and rejected by the local high school team, Greg Cima (Wiles) finds an unlikely ally in the spirit of Native American Olympic hero Jim Thorpe (Means). Seems Thorpe needs some aid to return to the spirit world and, by coaching Cima, he'll also get the help he needs. Believable performances and an exploration of the power of Native American mysticism help the unlikely premise along. **110m/C VHS, DVD.** Russell Means, Jason Wiles, Amanda Peterson, Margot Kidder, Jake Busey, Max Casella, Bruce Weitz; ***D:*** William Clark; ***W:*** Mitch Davis; ***M:*** Arthur Kempel.

The Winds of Jarrah 🦴 ½ **1983** English woman runs from broken heart to Australia to become nanny for misogynist, and Harlequin code prevails. Based on a Harlequin romance novel. **78m/C VHS.** *AU* Terence Donovan, Susan Lyons; ***D:*** Mark Egerton; ***M:*** Bruce Smeaton.

The Winds of Kitty Hawk 🦴🦴 **1978** Visually interesting but talky account of the Wright brothers attempt to beat their rival Glenn Curtiss and his backer, phone man Alexander Graham Bell. Rule of thumb: Fast-forward through the parts when they are on the ground, or see Stacy Keach's public-TV version instead. **96m/C VHS.** Michael Moriarty, David Huffman, Kathryn Walker, Eugene Roche, John Randolph, Scott Hylands; ***D:*** E.W. Swackhamer; ***M:*** Charles Bernstein.

Winds of Terror 🦴 ½ *WW3* **2001** FBI special agent Larry Sullivan (Hutton) is called in to investigate the sudden and mysterious deaths of a number of passengers aboard a cruise ship. It turns out to be biological terrorism and Sullivan must find out who's behind the act before they strike again. **100m/C VHS, DVD.** Timothy Hutton, Terry O'Quinn, Lane Smith, Marin Hinkle, Michael Constantine, Vanessa L(ynne) Williams; ***D:*** Robert Mandel; ***W:*** Daniel Taplitz; ***C:*** Claudio Chea. **TV**

Winds of the Wasteland 🦴🦴 ½ **1936** Would-be Pony Express contractors, Wayne and Chandler, race rivals to land government work. Competent western that put Wayne on the Hollywood map. **54m/B VHS, DVD.** John Wayne, Phyllis Fraser, Lane Chandler, Yakima Canutt; ***D:*** Mack V. Wright; ***W:*** Joseph Poland; ***C:*** William Nobles.

The Winds of War 🦴🦴 **1983** Excruciatingly long and dull miniseries based on Herman Wouk's bestseller about WWII. The book was much better; Mitchum appears to be fighting sleep unsuccessfully for much of the show. Two follow-ups were produced: "War and Remembrance" and "War and Remembrance: The Final Chapter." **900m/C VHS, DVD.** Charles Lane, Robert Mitchum, Ali MacGraw, Ralph Bellamy, Polly Bergen, Jan-Michael Vincent, David Dukes, John Houseman, Victoria Tennant, Peter Graves, Chaim Topol, Ben Murphy, Jeremy Kemp, Anton Diffring, Lawrence Pressman, Andrew Duggan, Barbara Steele; ***D:*** Dan Curtis. **TV**

Windtalkers 🦴🦴 **2002 (R)** Woo's WW II drama squanders a promising premise and turns it into a by-the-book war flick. The plot is inspired by the true story of Navaho Native Americans recruited by the Marines in order to use their language as an unbreakable code. Sgt. Enders (Cage) is a Marine assigned to protect one of these men, Pvt. Yahzee (Beach), but he also has orders to kill him if capture is imminent to protect the secrets of the code. The stage is then set for some of Woo's favorite themes: betrayal, duty and explosive bloody violence. Unfortunately, the characters are trite and the violence a bit overwhelming. **134m/C VHS, DVD, Blu-ray Disc.** *US* Nicolas Cage, Adam Beach, Christian Slater, Noah Emmerich, Mark Ruffalo, Peter Stormare, Brian Van Holt, Frances O'Connor, Jason Isaacs, Martin Henderson, Roger Willie; ***D:*** John Woo; ***W:*** John Rice, Joe Batteer; ***C:*** Jeffrey L. Kimball; ***M:*** James Horner.

Windwalker 🦴🦴🦴 **1981** Howard, the only cast member who is not a Native American, is an aged chief who shares the memories of his life with his grandchildren. Filmed in the Crow and Cheyenne Indian languages and subtitled in English throughout. A beautifully photographed, intelligent independent project. **108m/C VHS, DVD.** Trevor Howard, James Remar, Dusty Iron Wing McCrea; ***D:*** Keith Merrill.

Windy City 🦴🦴 **1984 (R)** A group of seven childhood friends must come to terms with the harsh realities of their failed ambitions when they meet for a weekend in Chicago. Told from the point of view of one of the group, recounting the sorts of memories we all prefer to forget. Typical and overwrought '80s yuppie reunion/regret drama. Aren't these people too young to be unhappy? **103m/C VHS.** John Shea, Kate Capshaw, Josh Mostel, Jeffrey DeMunn, Lewis J. Stadlen, James Sutorius; ***D:*** Armyan Bernstein; ***W:*** Armyan Bernstein; ***M:*** Jack Nitzsche.

Wine, Women and Horses 🦴🦴 ½ **1937** Well cast and powerfully presented remake of "Dark Hazard" follows a gambling man (MacLane) as he tries to leave 'the life' behind and be obedient to his self-righteous wife's wishes by taking a respectable $20-week job. **64m/B VHS.** Barton MacLane, Ann Sheridan, Dick Purcell, Peggy Bates; ***D:*** Louis King; ***W:*** Roy Chanslor. **VIDEO**

A Wing and a Prayer 🦴🦴🦴 **1944** Better-than-average WWII Air Force action flick. Battles rage throughout the Pacific theater and the men aboard the aircraft carrier struggle to do their part to save the world for freedom. Fine cast receives Hathaway's excellent unsentimental direction. **97m/B VHS, DVD.** Don Ameche, Dana Andrews, William Eythe, Charles Bickford, Cedric Hardwicke, Kevin O'Shea, Richard Jaeckel, Harry (Henry) Morgan; ***D:*** Henry Hathaway; ***W:*** Jerome Cady; ***C:*** Glen MacWilliams; ***M:*** Hugo Friedhofer.

Wing Chun 🦴🦴 **1994** Wing Chun (Yeoh) battles horse stealing bandits and the male chauvinists around her that don't think a woman can be strong and independent (as well as a fighting expert). Chinese with subtitles or dubbed. **93m/C VHS, DVD.** *HK* Michelle Yeoh, Donnie Yen, Waise Lee; ***D:*** Yuen Woo Ping.

Wing Commander WOOF! **1999 (PG-13)** Unintentionally amusing sci-fi action flick combines elements from old WWII pilot movies, "Top Gun," and "Star Trek." Hot-shot space pilots (Prinz Jr. and Lillard) battle an evil race of aliens that resembles a heavily armed version of the cast of "Cats." Their real battle is with the heinous dialogue and techno-babble they are forced to regurgitate. Adapted from a video game. **105m/C VHS, DVD.** Freddie Prinze Jr., Matthew Lillard, Saffron Burrows, Tcheky Karyo, Jurgen Prochnow, David

Suchet, David Warner; *D:* Chris Roberts; *W:* Kevin Droney; *C:* Thierry Arbogast; *M:* Kevin Kiner.

Winged Migration 1/2 *Le Peuple Migrateur; Traveling Birds* **2001 (G)** Exhilarating documentary that follows the migratory patterns of birds. Shot from 1998 to 2001 by some 15 cinematographers throughout 40 countries, using a variety of gliders, balloons, and long-lensed cameras to get close enough to record the working muscles on a crane's back, among other sights. Terns float on arctic ice, rockhopper penguins waddle, gannets feed, sand grouse perform their mating dance, and flocks fly. The minimal narration identifies the birds and their journeys. English and French with subtitles. **89m/C VHS, DVD, Blu-ray Disc.** *FR GE SP IT SI D:* Jacques Perrin; *W:* Jacques Perrin, Stephane Durand; *C:* Bernard Lutic, Thierry Machado, Olli Barbe, Michel Benjamin, Sylvie Carcedo, Laurent Charbonnier, Luc Drion, Laurent Fleutot, Philippe Garguil, Dominique Gentil, Stephane Martin, Fabrice Moindrot, Ernst Sasse, Michel Terasse, Thierry Thomas; *M:* Bruno Coulais; *Nar:* Jacques Perrin.

Wings 1/2 **1927** The silent classic about friends, Rogers and Arlen, their adventures in the Air Corps during WWI, and their rivalry for the hand of a woman. Contains actual footage of combat flying from the Great War. Won the very first Best Picture Oscar. Too-thin plot hangs on (barely) to the stirring, intrepid dogfight scenes. **139m/B VHS, DVD.** Clara Bow, Charles "Buddy" Rogers, Richard Arlen, Gary Cooper, Jobyna Ralston, El Brendel, Richard Tucker, Henry B. Walthall, Roscoe Karns, Gunboat Smith, Julia Swayne Gordon, Arlette Marchal, Carl von Haartman, William A. Wellman; *D:* William A. Wellman; *W:* Hope Loring, John Monk Saunders, Louis D. Lighton; *C:* Harry Perry; *M:* J.S. Zamecnik. Oscars '28: Picture, Natl. Film Reg. '97.

Wings in the Dark 1/2 **1935** The first (of three) pairings for Grant and Loy. Pilot Ken Gordon (Grant) is working on expanding airplane safety equipment when he meets stunt aviatrix Sheila Mason (Loy). Ken is blinded in an explosion and, unbeknownst to him, Sheila begins helping him financially. When she gets into trouble while flying in heavy fog, Ken is able to come to her rescue using his new safety instruments. Good flying sequences. **75m/B DVD.** Cary Grant, Myrna Loy, Roscoe Karns, Hobart Cavanaugh, Dean Jagger, Bert Hanlon; *D:* James Flood; *W:* Dale Van Every, Jack Kirkland, Frank Partos, E. H. Robinson; *C:* Dewey Wrigley, William Mellor.

Wings of Danger *Dead on Course* **1952** A pilot tries to save his friend from blackmailing gold smugglers. **72m/B VHS, DVD.** *GB* Zachary Scott, Kay Kendall, Robert Beatty, Naomi Chance; *M:* Malcolm Arnold.

Wings of Desire 1/2 *Der Himmel Uber Berlin* **1988 (PG-13)** An ethereal, haunting modern fable about angels Damiel (Ganz) and Cassiel (Sander), who observe human life in and above the broken existence of Berlin. Their attention is particularly focused on Homer (Bois), an elderly poet, American actor Peter Falk (playing himself), and a lovely French trapeze performer named marion (Dommartin). But the more Damiel observes, the more he longs to experience desire—emotional and physical—as humans do. A moving, unequivocable masterpiece, with as many beautiful things to say about spiritual need as about the schizophrenic emptiness of contemporary Germany; Wenders' magnum opus. German with subtitles, and with black-and-white sequences. **130m/C VHS, DVD.** *GE* Bruno Ganz, Peter Falk, Solveig Dommartin, Otto Sander, Curt Bois; *D:* Wim Wenders; *W:* Wim Wenders, Peter Handke; *C:* Henri Alekan; *M:* Jurgen Knieper. Ind. Spirit '89: Foreign Film; L.A. Film Critics '88: Cinematog., Foreign Film; N.Y. Film Critics '88: Cinematog.; Natl. Soc. Film Critics '88: Cinematog.

Wings of Eagles 1/2 **1957** Hollywood biography of Frank 'Spig' Wead, a famous WWI aviation pioneer turned screenwriter. Veers wildly from comedy to stolid drama, though Bond's lampoon of Ford as "John Dodge" is justly famous. **110m/C VHS, DVD.** John Wayne, Ward Bond, Maureen O'Hara, Dan Dailey, Edmund Lowe, Ken Curtis, Kenneth Tobey, Sig Rumann, Veda Ann Borg; *D:* John Ford; *C:* Paul Vogel.

Wings of Fame 1/2 **1993 (R)** Comic afterlife fantasy skewering celebrity status. Recently departed celebs check into a posh hotel, but as their fame on earth declines so do their afterlife accomodations, until they reach the state of oblivion. The latest hotel arrivals are a renowned, arrogant actor (O'Toole) and the frustrated writer (Firth) whose claim to fame has come from murdering him. **109m/C VHS.** Peter O'Toole, Colin Firth; *D:* Otakar Votocek; *W:* Herman Koch, Otakar Votocek.

The Wings of the Dove 1/2 **1997 (R)** Beautifully acted and filmed romance "inspired by" Henry James's 1902 novel. Updated to 1910, this triangular tale focuses on well-bred- but-penniless Kate Croy (Bonham Carter), who's been taken in by her imperious Aunt Maude (Rampling) with the expectation that she marry well. And this doesn't mean Kate's present beau, poor journalist Milton Densher (Roache). But when Kate meets gentle American heiress Millie Theale (Elliott), learns she's dying, and that she's also intrigued by Merton, the wheels begin to turn. A trip to Vehice sets Kate's plan in motion but leads to unexpected developments for all concerned. **101m/C VHS, DVD.** *GB* Helena Bonham Carter, Linus Roache, Alison Elliott, Elizabeth McGovern, Charlotte Rampling, Alex Jennings, Michael Gambon; *D:* Iain Softley; *W:* Hossein Amini; *C:* Eduardo Serra; *M:* Gabriel Yared. British Acad. '97: Cinematog., Makeup; L.A. Film Critics '97: Actress (Bonham Carter); Natl. Bd. of Review '97: Actress (Bonham Carter); Broadcast Film Critics '97: Actress (Bonham Carter).

Wings of the Morning 1/2 **1937** Maria (Annabella), a descendant of Spanish gypsies, comes to Ireland with her grandmother (Vanbrugh) who's entering a horse in the Epsom Downs Derby. Maria disguises herself as a boy so she can ride in the race but is discovered by Canadian horse-trainer Kerry (Fonda), who promptly falls in love with her. Legendary tenor John McCormack sings several songs. The first British movie to be filmed in Technicolor. **89m/C VHS, DVD.** *GB* Annabella, Henry Fonda, Edward Underdown, Irene Vanbrugh, Leslie Banks, Stewart Rome; *D:* Harold Schuster; *W:* Tom Geraghty; *C:* Jack Cardiff, Henry Imus, Ray Rennahan; *M:* Arthur Benjamin.

Wings over the Pacific 1/2 **1943** Love and his daughter Cooper are living quietly on a Pacific island when a pair of pilots, American Norris and the Nazi Guttman, crash-land after a dogfight. The island is strategic because of its oil supply but Norris manages to prevent the Nazis from taking control and wins Cooper's love in the process. Veteran actor Love died shortly before the film's release. **60m/B VHS, DVD.** Montagu Love, Inez Cooper, Edward Norris, Henry Guttman, Robert Armstrong, Ernie Adams; *D:* Phil Rosen; *W:* George Wallace Sayre.

The Winner **1996 (R)** Philip (D'Onofrio) is on a winning streak at the Vegas Pair-A-Dice casino and the target of estranged brother Wolf (Madsen), tempermental lounge singer Louise (DeMornay), and various other con artists and thugs, all of whom want to separate him from his winnings. Lots of good actors but this Vegas story is nothing new. Based on the play "A Darker Purpose" by Riss. **90m/C VHS.** Vincent D'Onofrio, Michael Madsen, Rebecca De Mornay, Delroy Lindo, Frank Whaley, Billy Bob Thornton, Richard Edson; *D:* Alex Cox; *W:* Wendy Riss; *C:* Denis Maloney; *M:* Daniel Licht.

A Winner Never Quits 1/2 **1986 (PG)** A true story based on the life of 1940s baseball player Pete Gray. As a boy Gray lost his right arm above the elbow in an accident. He's determined to prove himself as a baseball player and during WWII is given a tryout, although his teammates consider him a sideshow freak. A Memphis sportswriter takes an interest in Pete's career and Gray's success on the field leads to a career with the St. Louis Browns. Along the way he becomes the inspiration to a young fan, who's also lost an arm. **96m/C VHS.** Keith Carradine, Mare Winningham, Huckleberry Fox, Dennis Weaver, Dana Delany, G.W. Bailey, Charles Hallahan, Fionnula Flanagan, Jack Kehoe; *D:* Mel Damski; *W:* Burt Prelutsky. **TV**

Winner Takes All *The Boy Who Had Everything* **1984 (R)** A young college student during the Vietnam War comes to grips with maturity and growing pains. **94m/C VHS, DVD.** *AU* Lewis Fitz-Gerald, Ian Gilmour, Laura Williams, Jason Connery, Diane Cilento; *D:* Stephen Wallace; *W:* Stephen Wallace; *C:* Geoff Burton; *M:* Ralph Schneider.

Winner Takes All 1/2 **1998 (R)** In 1978, two childhood buddies turn to crime to support their families, but a botched robbery finds one doing time and the other fleeing the scene, getting a new identity, and becoming a drug enforcement agent. Years later, the two are reunited over an assassination plot involving a mob boss. **103m/C VHS.** AMG, Louis Freese, Reegus Flenory, Flesh N Bone, Robert Hayes III, Marlon Parry, Daniel Zirilli; *D:* Daniel Zirilli; *W:* Robert Hayes III, Marlon Parry, Daniel Zirilli; *C:* David West.

Winners of the West **1940** A landowner schemes to prevent a railroad from running through his property. The railroad's chief engineer leads the good guys in an attempt to prevent sabotage. A fun serial in 13 chapters, full of shooting, blown-up bridges, locomotives afire, etc., and, of course, the requisite damsel in distress. **250m/B VHS, DVD.** Anne Nagel, Dick Foran, James Craig, Harry Woods; *D:* Ray Taylor, Ford Beebe.

Winners Take All **1987 (PG-13)** A handful of friends compete in Supercross races. Spirited but thoroughly cliche sports flick. **103m/C VHS, DVD.** Gerardo Mejia, Don Michael Paul, Kathleen York, Robert Krantz; *D:* Fritz Kiersch.

Winning **1969 (PG)** A race car driver (Newman) will let nothing, including his new wife (Woodward), keep him from winning the Indianapolis 500. Newman does his own driving. Thomas' film debut. **123m/C VHS, DVD.** Paul Newman, Joanne Woodward, Robert Wagner, Richard Thomas, Clu Gulager; *D:* James Goldstone; *W:* Howard Rodman; *C:* Richard Moore; *M:* Dave Grusin.

Winning Girls Through Psychic Mind Control **2002** Highly convoluted and slightly comedic story of a drummer in a lounge act who becomes possessed by four wise entities after listening to an audiotape on psychic mind control. This new 'power' works its way into the act wherein he mind-reads audience members revealing where items are lost, if they're pregnant, and where they have hidden tattoos. The two-guys-talking effect wears out easily and the comedy, although clever, is not enough to make up for the exceedingly thin plot line. **93m/C** *US* Bronson Pinchot, Ruben Santiago-Hudson, Amy Carlson, Christopher Murney; *D:* Barry Alexander Brown; *W:* Dan Harnden; *C:* Scott Maher; *M:* Griffin Richardson, Adam Asarnow, Bill Simms Jr.

The Winning of Barbara Worth 1/2 **1926** Orphaned Barbara (Banky) has been raised by rancher Jefferson Worth (Lane), whose dream is to irrigate the desert. She's in love with foreman Abe Lee (young and gorgeous Cooper) until Willard Holmes (Colman) comes to town. Holmes is an engineer who has been hired by a land speculator to dam the local river but the speculator cheats the ranchers and uses cheap materials on the dam, setting up a spectacular disaster that has Holmes and Lee joining forces. King filmed on location in Nevada. Based on the novel by Harold Bell Wright. **89m/B DVD.** Vilma Banky, Ronald Colman, Gary Cooper, Charles Lane, E.J. Ratcliffe; *D:* Henry King; *W:* Frances Marion; *C:* Gregg Toland, Georges Barens; *M:* Ted Henkel.

Winning of the West **1953** Yodelin' ranger Autry vows to protect a crusading publisher from unscrupulous crooks, including his own dog-gone brothers. The brothers see the light, and the two corral the varmints. Autry tunes include "Cowboy Blues," "Cowpoke Poking Along," and "Find Me My 45." **57m/B VHS.** Gene Autry, Smiley Burnette, Gail Davis, Richard Crane; *D:* George Archainbaud.

The Winning Team 1/2 **1952** Reagan stars in this biography of baseball legend Grover Cleveland Alexander and Day plays his dedicated wife. Some controversial issues were glossed over in the film, such as Alexander's real-life drinking problem and the fact that he had epilepsy. Although this was one of Reagan's favorite roles, he was upset by the studio's avoidance of all-too-human problems. Nonetheless, it's an entertaining enough movie about a very talented ballplayer. **98m/B VHS, DVD.** Doris Day, Ronald Reagan, Frank Lovejoy, Eve Miller, James Millican, Russ Tamblyn; *D:* Lewis Seiler.

The Winslow Boy 1/2 **1948** A cadet at the Royal Naval College is wrongly accused of theft and expelled. Donat as the boy's lawyer leads a splendid cast. Despite consequences for his family, the boy's father (Hardwicke) sues the government and fights his son's battle, as the case makes the papers and he approaches bankruptcy. Plot would seem far-fetched if it weren't based on fact. Absorbing. Based on a play by Rattigan, who co-wrote the script. **112m/B VHS.** *GB* Robert Donat, Cedric Hardwicke, Margaret Leighton, Frank Lawton, Kathleen Harrison, Basil Radford; *D:* Anthony Asquith; *W:* Terence Rattigan; *C:* Frederick A. (Freddie) Young.

The Winslow Boy **1998 (G)** Mamet successfully treads on unfamiliar ground with this English period piece in which young Ronnie Winslow (Edwards) is accused of stealing and expelled from military school. His father (Hawthorne) becomes determined to clear his name at whatever cost. And the cost is to be high, for his family, his health, and his moderate fortune. He hires renowned lawyer Sir Robert Morton (Northam), also with consequences for family and bank balance. Although based on a real case, the story largely ignores the main events of the scandal, focusing on its effects on the various family members. Strong performances are led by Northam and Hawthorne. Based on Terence Rattigan's play. **104m/C VHS, DVD.** Nigel Hawthorne, Jeremy Northam, Rebecca Pidgeon, Gemma Jones, Guy Edwards, Matthew Pidgeon, Colin Stinton, Aden (John) Gillett, Perry Fenwick, Sarah Flind, Sara Stewart, Alan Polanski, Neil North; *D:* David Mamet; *W:* David Mamet; *C:* Benoit Delhomme; *M:* Alaric Jans.

Winter Break 1/2 *Sheer Bliss* **2002 (R)** Cheesy-but-amusing comedy for those who liked "American Pie." College grad Matt (Ventimigila) is wondering what to do about getting a job when his best bud, Peter (Thomas), persuades him to join their friends in Aspen for the winter. They're basically out to enjoy themselves—until Matt finds romance with Michelle (Lawson). **98m/C VHS, DVD.** Milo Ventimiglia, Eddie Kaye Thomas, Maggie Lawson, Justin Urich, Eddie Mills, George Lazenby, Rachel Wilson; *D:* Marni Banack; *W:* Mark Botvinick; *C:* George Mooradian; *M:* Hope Botvinick. **VIDEO**

Winter Flight **1984** A small, gentle British drama about an RAF recruit and a barmaid who quickly become lovers, and then are confronted with her pregnancy. **105m/C VHS.** *GB* Reece Dinsdale, Nicola Cowper, Gary Olsen; *D:* Roy Battersby.

The Winter Guest **1997 (R)** Rickman's directorial debut looks at the lives of eight people living in a remote and icy Scottish village, focusing on the fictional relationship between real-life mother and daughter Law and Thompson. Introspective and somewhat stagey, but fine performances and excellent use of the desolate landscape make this a worthwhile debut effort. Based on the play by Sharman Macdonald, which he and Rickman adapted for the screen. **106m/C VHS, DVD.** *GB* Emma Thompson, Phyllida Law, Sheila Reid, Sandra Voe, Gary Hollywood, Arlene Cockburn, Douglas Murphy, Sean Biggerstaff, Tom Watson; *D:* Alan Rickman; *W:* Alan Rickman, Sharman MacDonald; *C:* Seamus McGarvey; *M:* Michael Kamen.

Winter in Wartime *Oorlogswinter* **2010** In January, 1945, the Nazis occupy Holland and bored 14-year-old Michiel is disgusted that his father, the town's mayor, placates their leaders. Instead, the teenager hopes to help out the Resistance and gets his chance when he witnesses an RAF plane get shot down and the pilot bail out. Dutch with subtitles. **103m/C DVD.** *NL* Yorick Van Wageningen, Jamie Campbell Bower, Martijn Lakemeier, Raymond Thir, Melody Klaver; *D:* Martin Koolhoven; *W:* Paul Jan Nelissen, Martin Koolhoven, Mieke de Jong; *C:* Guido van Gennep; *M:* Pino Donaggio.

Winter Kill **1974** A failed TV pilot finds Griffith starring as the sheriff of a ski resort town troubled by a serial killer who spray-paints messages near his victims. The town council wants the crimes solved before tourist season begins or sheriff Sam will be out of a job. **97m/C DVD.** Andy Griffith, John Calvin, Sheree North, Lawrence Pressman, Eugene Roche, John Larch, Nick Nolte, Joyce Van Patten, Tim O'Connor; ***D:*** Jud Taylor; ***W:*** John Michael Hayes, David Karp; ***C:*** Frank Stanley; ***M:*** Jerry Goldsmith. **TV**

Winter Kills **1979 (R)** Distinctive political black comedy suffers a hilariously paranoid version of American public life. Nick Kegan (Bridges) has been drifting through life ever since his older brother, a U.S. president, was assassinated 15 years earlier. His eccentric father (Huston) wants to draw Nick back into the family by claiming a conspiracy, but as Nick begins to dig into the past, he does uncover political machinations. Uneven, but well worth seeing; flopped at the boxoffice, but was re-edited (with the original ending restored) and re-released in 1983. Elizabeth Taylor (as Lola Comante) went unbilled. Basèd on the novel by Richard Condon. **97m/C VHS, DVD.** Jeff Bridges, John Huston, Anthony Perkins, Richard Boone, Sterling Hayden, Eli Wallach, Ralph Meeker, Belinda Bauer, Dorothy Malone, Toshiro Mifune, Elizabeth Taylor, Donald Moffat, Tisa Farrow, Brad Dexter, Joe Spinell; ***D:*** William Richert; ***W:*** William Richert; ***C:*** Vilmos Zsigmond; ***M:*** Maurice Jarre.

The Winter Light **1/2** *Nattvardsgaesterna* **1962** The second film in Bergman's famous trilogy on the silence of God, preceded by "Through a Glass Darkly" and followed by "The Silence." Bleak and disturbing view of a tortured priest who searches for the faith and guidance he is unable to give his congregation. Hard to swallow for neophyte Bergmanites, but challenging, deeply serious and rewarding for those accustomed to the Swede's angst. Polished and personal. In Swedish with English subtitles. **80m/B VHS, DVD.** *SW* Gunnar Bjornstrand, Ingrid Thulin, Max von Sydow; ***D:*** Ingmar Bergman; ***W:*** Ingmar Bergman; ***C:*** Sven Nykvist.

Winter Lily **1998** Disturbing shocker. Photographer Peter (Gilmore) checks into a remote B&B where the only inhabitants are owner Agatha (Berryman) and her 14-year-old daughter Lily (Laferriere) who is confined to her bedroom by illness. When Peter finds Lily's diary, he discovers that she is dying because her parents are refusing her medical aid. Is this as a punishment for her affair with a much-older man? And just where is Lily's violent absent father (Bergeron) anyway? **90m/C VHS, DVD.** *CA* Dorothee Berryman, Danny Gilmore, Jean-Pierre Bergeron, Kimberley Laferriere; ***D:*** Roshel Bissett; ***W:*** Roshel Bissett.

Winter Meeting **1948** Overwrought drama with Bette Davis starring as a spinster poetess who falls in love with a war hero who wants to be a priest. Very talky script, of interest only as the sole romantic lead for James Davis, whose claim to fame was westerns and the TV series "Dallas." **104m/B VHS.** Bette Davis, Janis Paige, James Davis, John Hoyt, Florence Bates, Walter Baldwin, Ransom Sherman; ***D:*** Bretaigne Windust; ***M:*** Max Steiner.

Winter of Frozen Dreams **2008** Based on the 1970s true crime murder case of Barbara Hoffman, a Madison, Wisconsin college student who worked as a massage parlor hooker. When her jittery fiance Jerry Davies reports finding a body frozen in the snow, it's not long until Detective Lulling makes them the prime suspects. Turns out Barb seduces her clients into leaving her money and then kills them. The first televised murder trial in the United States. **92m/C DVD.** Thora Birch, Brendan Sexton III, Leo Fitzpatrick, Dean Winters, Keith Carradine, Scott Cohen, Dan Moran; ***D:*** Eric Mandelbaum; ***W:*** Eric Mandelbaum; ***C:*** Brian O'Carroll; ***M:*** Kenneth Lampl.

The Winter of Our Dreams **1/2** **1982** Down Under slice of seamy life as a heroin-addicted prostitute becomes involved with an unhappy bookshop owner. Davis shines in otherwise slow and confusing drama. **89m/C VHS.** *AU* Judy Davis, Bryan Brown, Cathy Downes, Baz Luhrmann, Peter Mochrie, Mervyn Drake, Margie McCrae, Marcie Deane-Johns; ***D:*** John Duigan. Australian Film Inst. '81: Actress (Davis).

Winter Passing **1/2 2005 (R)** Reese (Deschanel) is a disillusioned actress living an empty life in New York, trying not to acknowledge the fact that her mother has recently died and she hasn't seen her father, a reclusive, alcoholic, once-famous novelist, in years. Motivated by an editor's (Madigan) offer of big money for potential love letters written by her parents long ago, Reese reluctantly returns to Michigan to reconnect with her mislaid father. Upon her arrival she's greeted by Corbit (Ferrell), her father's spaced-out caretaker, and Shelly (Warner), who handles her father's business matters. Dancing between humor and affection, the characters all carefully paint a portrait of loneliness and awakening. However, that dance is often a little too slow. Inspired performances, especially in Ferrell's wise restraint. **98m/C DVD.** *US* Zooey Deschanel, Ed Harris, Will Ferrell, Amelia Warner, Amy Madigan, Dallas Roberts, Deirdre O'Connell, Robert Beitzel; ***D:*** Adam Rapp; ***W:*** Adam Rapp; ***C:*** Terry Stacey; ***M:*** John Kimbrough, John Kimbrough.

Winter People **1/2 1989 (PG-13)** A clock-making widower and a woman living alone with her illegitimate son experience tough times together with feuding families in a Depression-era Appalachian community. Silly, rehashed premise doesn't deter McGillis, who gamely gives a fine performance. Based on the novel by John Ehle. **109m/C VHS, DVD.** Kurt Russell, Kelly McGillis, Lloyd Bridges, Mitchell Ryan, Jeffrey Meek, Eileen Ryan, Amelia Burnette; ***D:*** Ted Kotcheff; ***W:*** Carol Sobieski; ***M:*** John Scott.

Winter Sleepers **1/2** *Winterschlafer* **1997** Angsty and slow (completely unlike the director's breakthrough "Run Lola Run"). Rebecca (Daniel) is waiting at a mountain chalet for her boyfriend Marco (Ferch) to show up. When Marco leaves his keys in his car, Rene (Matthes) takes it for a joy ride and gets into an accident, eventually meeting Laura (Sellem) the nurse, who owns the chalet. The foursome wind-up together but nothing much matters. Based on the novel "Expense of the Spirit" by Pyszora, who co-wrote the screenplay. German with subtitles. **124m/C VHS, DVD.** *GE* Heino Ferch, Floriane Daniel, Ulrich Matthes, Marie-Lou Sellem, Josef Bierbichler; ***D:*** Tom Tykwer; ***W:*** Tom Tykwer, Anne-Francois Pyszora; ***C:*** Frank Griebe; ***M:*** Tom Tykwer, Johnny Klimek, Reinhold Heil.

Winter Solstice **2004 (R)** Such a sad, sad gut-wrencher. But it's so good at being sad. Jim Winters (LaPaglia) is the struggling father of a motherless family still trying to get by without her, five years after a tragic car accident. Jim's two sons, Gabe and Peter, don't want to grab hold when he reaches out to them. They're mad at the life they live. Thankfully, writer/director Josh Sternfeld doesn't bother with much plot, something that normally distracts from emotion and character examination in these types of films. These people live and suffer, and let us watch—we wonder what'll happen to them when the movie ends. Its effect lingers long after the credits. **90m/C DVD.** *US* Anthony LaPaglia, Aaron Stanford, Mark Webber, Allison Janney, Michelle Monaghan, Ron Livingston, Brandon Sexton III, Ebon Moss-Bachrach; ***D:*** Josh Sternfeld; ***W:*** Josh Sternfeld; ***C:*** Harlan Bosmajian; ***M:*** John Leventhal.

A Winter Tan **1/2 1988** True story of New Yorker Maryse Holder (Burroughs), who's an alcoholic, drug-addicted, promiscuous one-time teacher who has decided to lose herself in the degradations Acapulco has to offer. Holder's eventually murdered by a pimp and her letters to a friend are posthumously published as "Give Sorrow Words." Self-destruction as its worst. **90m/C VHS.** *CA* Jackie Burroughs; ***D:*** Jackie Burroughs, John Frizzell, John Walker, Louise Clark; ***W:*** Jackie Burroughs; ***C:*** John Walker, Louise Clark. Genie '89: Actress (Burroughs).

The Winter War *Talvisota* **1989** One of Finnish films ever tells the story of the Russian war on Finland and the Finnish defense in 1939-41. **195m/C VHS.** Esko Nikkari, Tomi Salmela, Vesa Vierikko, Samuli Edelmann, Teemu Koskinen, Esko Kovero, Eero Maenpaa, Konsta Makela, Taneli Makela, Heikki Paavilainen, Antti Raivio, Miitta Sorvali, Martti Suosalo, Timo Torikka; ***D:*** Pekka Parikka; ***W:*** Pekka Parikka; ***C:*** Kari Sohlberg; ***M:*** Jukka Haavisto, Juha Tikko.

Winterbeast **1992** Winter resort community dwellers begin mysteriously disappearing until somebody remembers that the resort was built over a sacred Indian burial ground. Sgt. Bill Whitman, the valiant park ranger and his Barney Fife-like assistant Stillman, question the town's wise old sage, Sheldon, who's sitting on a secret that could threaten the entire community. **77m/C VHS.** Bob Harlow, Charles Majka, Dori May Kelly, Tim R. Morgan, Mike Magri; ***D:*** Christopher Thies; ***W:*** Christopher Thies; ***M:*** Michael Perilstein.

Winterhawk **1976 (PG)** A Blackfoot Indian seeks smallpox serum from a nearby trapper camp for his stricken tribe. When he's attacked for his efforts, he takes revenge by kidnapping two of the settlement's children. Exceptional cinematography of the breathtaking scenery can't hide the cliched, melodramatic story and waste of a fine cast. This was Hunnicutt's last screen appearance. **98m/C VHS.** Leif Erickson, Woody Strode, Denver Pyle, L.Q. Jones, Elisha Cook Jr., Arthur Hunnicutt, Dennis Fimple, Dawn Wells, Jimmy Clem, Michael Dante, Charles B. Pierce, Seamon Glass; ***D:*** Charles B. Pierce; ***W:*** Charles B. Pierce, Earl E. Smith; ***C:*** Jim Roberson; ***M:*** Lee Holdridge.

Winter's Bone **2010** Teenager Ree (Lawrence) lives in an impoverished Missouri Ozarks community and must look after her siblings because her drug-dealer father has disappeared after being released from jail. Threatened with the loss of their home and land, Ree is determined to find her dad though she's warned off by his hostile associates. Adaptation of the Daniel Woodrell novel. **99m/C DVD.** *US* Jennifer Lawrence, John Hawkes, Kevin Breznahan, Dale Dickey, Garret Dillahunt, Sheryl Lee, Lauren Sweetser, Tate Taylor; ***D:*** Debra Granik; ***W:*** Debra Granik, Anne Rosellini; ***C:*** Michael McDonough; ***M:*** Dickon Hinchliffe.

Winterset **1/2 1936** A son seeks to clear his father's name of a falsely accused crime 15 years after his electrocution. Powerful at the time, though time has lessened its impact. Loosely based on the trial of Sacco and Vanzetti and adapted from Maxwell Anderson's Broadway play, with stars in the same roles. Meredith's film debut. **85m/B VHS, DVD.** Burgess Meredith, Margo, John Carradine; ***D:*** Alfred Santell.

Wintertime **1/2 1943** Forgettable and mindless Henie musical. Plot revolves around Henie travelling in Canada with her wealthy uncle, and saving an old, run-down hotel. An appearance by Woody Herman and his Orchestra give the film a much-needed boost. Based on a story by Arthur Kober. **82m/B VHS.** Sonja Henie, Jack Oakie, Cesar Romero, Carole Landis, S.Z. Sakall, Cornel Wilde, Woody Herman; ***D:*** John Brahm; ***W:*** E. Edwin Moran, Jack Jevne, Lynn Starling.

Wired **1989 (R)** A justly lambasted, unintentionally hilarious biography of comic genius and overdose victim John Belushi, very loosely based on Bob Woodward's best-selling muckraking book. The chronicle of addiction and tragedy is tried here as a weird sort of comedy; was it meant as a tribute to its off-kilter subject? If so, it misses by a mile. And, we're sorry, but Chiklis doesn't cut it as Belushi—who would?! **112m/C VHS.** Michael Chiklis, Ray Sharkey, Patti D'Arbanville, J.T. Walsh, Gary Groomes, Lucinda Jenney, Alex Rocco, Jere Burns, Billy Preston; ***D:*** Larry Peerce; ***W:*** Earl MacRauch; ***C:*** Tony Imi; ***M:*** Basil Poledouris.

Wired to Kill **WOOF! 1986 (R)** In a futuristic world, two teenagers seek justice for their parents' murder by building a remote-controlled erector set programmed for revenge. Laughably porous plot drops any pretence of credibility. Dizzyingly bad. **96m/C VHS.** Merritt Butrick, Emily Longstreth, Devin Hoelscher, Frank Collison; ***D:*** Francis Schaeffer.

Wirey Spindell **1999** Self-indulgent clap-trap about a self-satisfied creep. The title character (Schaeffer) is engaged to beautiful Tabatha (Thorne) but has become suddenly impotent due to extreme premarital jitters. This little dilemma leads Wirey to explore his childhood and druggie high school/college years (when the character is played by Mabius), his first love, and his falling for Tabatha. Problem is Wirey isn't a very interesting character. **101m/C VHS, DVD.** Eric Schaeffer, Callie (Calliope) Thorne, Eric Mabius, Samantha Buck; ***D:*** Eric Schaeffer; ***W:*** Eric Schaeffer; ***C:*** Kramer Morgenthau; ***M:*** Amanda Kravat.

Wisdom **1/2 1987 (R)** Unemployed young guy (Estevez) becomes a bank robber with Robin Hood aspirations, coming to the aid of American farmers by destroying mortgage records. Estevez became the youngest person to star in, write, and direct a major motion picture. And, my goodness, it shows. **109m/C VHS.** Emilio Estevez, Demi Moore, Tom Skerritt, Veronica Cartwright; ***D:*** Emilio Estevez; ***M:*** Danny Elfman.

Wise Blood **1/2 1979 (PG)** Gothic drama about a drifter who searches for sin and becomes a preacher for a new religion, The Church Without Christ. Excellent cast in achingly realistic portrayal of ersatz religion, southern style. Many laughs are more painful than funny. Superb, very dark comedy from Huston. Adapted from the Flannery O'Connor novel. **106m/C VHS.** Brad Dourif, John Huston, Ned Beatty, Amy Wright, Harry Dean Stanton; ***D:*** John Huston; ***M:*** Alex North.

Wise Guys **1/2 1986 (R)** Two small-time hoods decide to rip off the mob. When their boss figures out their plan he decides to set them up instead. Lame black comedy that has too few moments. **100m/C VHS, DVD.** Joe Piscopo, Danny DeVito, Ray Sharkey, Captain Lou Albano, Dan Hedaya, Julie Bovasso, Patti LuPone; ***D:*** Brian De Palma; ***M:*** Ira Newborn.

Wisecracks **1993** Women comics perform and talk about their work in this documentary directed by Gail Singer. The comics featured have, in some cases, little more in common than their work, but all share interesting perspectives on what they do. Interesting mix of performance clips and interviews sometimes includes banal comments about the nature of comedy, but is more often insightful, especially remarks by seasoned vet Phyllis Diller. Although there exists here the potential for an angry feminist diatribe on gender-based humor, the focus is more towards talented women who are just plain funny. **93m/C VHS, DVD.** ***D:*** Gail Singer.

Wisegal **1/2 2008** Tough Brooklyn widow Patty Montanari (Milano) has two young sons to support. While selling contraband smokes for some local wiseguys, Patty catches the eye of married crime boss Frank Russo (Gedrick), who gives Patty a nightclub to manage. Then mob honcho Salvatore Palmeri (Caan) insists Patty transport cash from New York across the border to his Canadian operations. Patty eventually wants out, especially when the feds start closing in. Inspired by a true story; an original Lifetime movie. **89m/C DVD.** Alyssa Milano, Jason Gedrick, James Caan, Janet Wright, Alessandro Costantini, Kyle Harrington; ***D:*** Jerry Ciccoritti; ***W:*** Shelley Evans; ***C:*** Gerald Packer; ***M:*** John (Gianni) Frizzell. **CABLE**

Wisegirls *Wise Girls* **2002** Estrogen-injected mob flick follows Meg (Sorvino), a med school grad who moves back to New York and takes a job waitressing in a mob-infested restaurant. Trying to divorce herself from a disastrous past, Meg gets wise to just which family owns this family-owned establishment. She's less than thrilled but the worst she has to deal with is reluctantly accepting money from their boss (Nascarelli), who admires her medical skills, and fending off advances from his odious son (Maelen), until she witnesses a murder and finds herself on the wrong side of the law. Plot contains interesting twists right down to the satisfying end. Sorvino performs ably while Walters is a standout and Carey proves she has stuff to make it on the big screen. Tired premise, however, takes some of the fun out this gangster chick flick. **96m/C VHS, DVD.** Mira Sorvino, Mariah Carey, Melora Walters, Arthur J. Nascarelli, Christian Maelen, Joseph Siravo; ***D:*** David Anspaugh; ***W:*** John Meadows; ***C:*** Johnny E. Jensen; ***M:*** Keith Forsey.

Wish Me Luck **1/2 1995** A babe genie (Avalon) has a dilemma—unless she can make a man of a geek college student (Gesner) in 48 hours, she'll become the property of an evil sorcerer for a thousand years. She gets three equally bodacious college cheerleaders to help her out. Also available in an edited version that cuts six minutes worth of fleshy fantasies. **91m/C VHS.** Avalon Anders, Zen Gesner; ***D:*** Philip Jones.

Wish upon a Star ✓✓ 1/2 **1996 (PG)** Battling teenage sisters Alexia (Heigl) and Haley (Harris) wind up switching identities when bookish Haley wishes on a falling star to be like popular Alexia. Naturally, this confuses everyone but the sisters get to see how their other sibling feels. **90m/C VHS, DVD.** Scott Wilkinson, Mary Parker Williams, Don Jeffcoat, Lois Chiles, Katherine Heigl, Danielle Harris; ***D:*** Blair Treu; ***W:*** Jessica Barondes; ***C:*** Brian Sullivan; ***M:*** Ray Colcord.

Wish You Were Dead ✓✓ 1/2 **2000 (R)** Schnook insurance adjuster MacBeth (Elwes) naively signs over his million dollar life insurance policy to slutty "girlfriend" Sally (Steenburgen), who promptly hires hit woman Jupiter (Hendrix) to get rid of the excess baggage. Only Jupiter can't get over what a nice guy MacBeth is and falls in love with him instead—which doesn't mean Sally is giving up. **89m/C VHS, DVD.** Cary Elwes, Mary Steenburgen, Elaine Hendrix, Christopher Lloyd, Billy Ray Cyrus, Robert Englund, Sally Kirkland, Gene Simmons, Shannon Tweed; ***D:*** Valerie McCaffrey; ***W:*** Scott Firestone; ***C:*** David Klein. **VIDEO**

Wish You Were Here ✓✓✓ *Too Much* **1987** Poignant yet funny slice of British postwar life roughly based on the childhood memoirs of famous madame, Cynthia Payne. A troubled and freedom-loving teenager expresses her rebellion in sexual experimentation. Mum is dead and Dad just doesn't understand, so what's a girl to do, but get the boys excited? Lloyd, in her first film, plays the main character with exceptional strength and feistiness. Payne's later life was dramatized in the Leland-scripted "Personal Services." **92m/C VHS, DVD.** *GB* Emily Lloyd, Tom Bell, Clare Clifford, Barbara Durkin, Geoffrey Hutchings, Charlotte Barker, Chloe Leland, Trudy Cavanagh, Jesse Birdsall, Geoffrey Durham, Pat Heywood; ***D:*** David Leland; ***W:*** David Leland; ***C:*** Ian Wilson; ***M:*** Stanley Myers. British Acad. '87: Orig. Screenplay; Natl. Soc. Film Critics '87: Actress (Lloyd).

Wishful Thinking ✓✓ **1992** A lovelorn screenwriter rescues a peculiar man from mysterious assassins and receives a magical writing pad for his efforts. It seems that whatever Michael writes on the paper will come true, so he decides to write himself into the life of the luscious Diane. **94m/C VHS, DVD.** Murray Langston, Michelle Johnson, Ruth Buzzi, Billy Barty, Johnny Dark, Ray "Boom Boom" Mancini, Vic Dunlop, Kip Addotta; ***D:*** Murray Langston.

Wishful Thinking ✓✓ 1/2 **1996 (R)** Elizabeth (Beals) and Max (Le Gros) have been living together for four years. When Max doesn't want to get married, Elizabeth becomes withdrawn but Max decides she's having an affair. As he becomes more and more jealous, a third party enters the picture. Lena (Barrymore) decides she wants Max herself and devises a plan to get him at any cost. **89m/C VHS, DVD.** Drew Barrymore, Jennifer Beals, James LeGros, Mel Gorham, Eric Thal, Jon Stewart; ***D:*** Adam Park; ***W:*** Adam Park.

The Wishing Ring ✓✓✓ **1914** Light and charming romance, beautifully filmed by Tourneur, based on Owen Davis' play. The son of an earl in Old England is expelled from college and told by his father he must earn half a crown on his own before the family will take him back. With the help of a minister's daughter, he sets things right. **50m/B VHS, DVD.** Vivian Martin, Alec B. Francis, Chester Barnett, Simeon Wiltsie, Walter Morton; ***D:*** Maurice Tourneur; ***W:*** Maurice Tourneur.

The Wishing Stairs ✓✓ 1/2 *Yeogo Goedam 3: Yeowoo Gyedan; Whispering Corridors 3* **2003 (R)** There is a legend at the Yongwha Art Institute, a specialized school for girls. If you climb the 28 steps to the dormitories, and count each one aloud, a 29th step will appear when you reach the top. If you climb that last step, and wish really hard, the Fox Spirit may grant it out of pity. Considering the bad reputation of Fox Spirits in Asia you'd think more of the school's students would think twice before doing it. But jealousy and emotion abound at the school, and it isn't long before the spirit has plenty of students willing to risk their lives and sanity to find that 29th step. The third film in the Ghost School Trilogy. **97m/C DVD.** *KN* Ji-yeon Park, Ji-hyo Song, Han-byeol Park, An Jo, Su-a Hong, Ji-min Kwak, Jung-Hee Moon; ***D:*** Jae-yeon Yun; ***W:*** Soyoung Lee; ***C:*** Jeong-min Seo.

Wishman ✓✓ 1/2 **1993** Hollywood hustler Basie Banks (Le Mat) meets Hitch (Lewis), a two million-year-old genie whose magic bottle has been stolen. In exchange for Banks' help in recovering his home, Hitch agrees to help Banks get the girl of his dreams. **89m/C VHS.** Paul LeMat, Geoffrey Lewis, Paul Gleason, Quin Kessler, Nancy Parsons, Gailard Sartain, Brion James; ***D:*** Mike Marvin; ***W:*** Mike Marvin.

Wishmaster ✓ *Wes Craven Presents Wishmaster* **1997 (R)** An evil genie grants wishes to those who stumble upon him, but he also gets his kicks by destroying the lives of those naive enough to play along. Anemic horror tale that's as thin on plot as it is on scares. Standard-issue exploding chest cavities and flying heads can't easily erase the boredom. Make-up artist turned director Kurtzman should have wished for some directorial skills, because he hasn't got a clue. Don't be misled by Wes Craven's name, his association with this dud is meant to lure the least discriminating of horror fans. **90m/C VHS, DVD.** Tammy Lauren, Andrew Divoff, Robert Englund, Chris Lemmon, Tony Crane, Wendy Benson, Jenny O'Hara, Tony Todd, Kane Hodder; ***D:*** Robert Kurtzman; ***W:*** Peter Atkins; ***C:*** Jacques Haitkin; ***M:*** Harry Manfredini.

Wishmaster 2: Evil Never Dies ✓✓ **1998 (R)** The Djinn is awakened by thief Morgana during a botched robbery and, in order to gain the souls he needs, the Djinn allows himself to be put in prison where he can offer wishes to the prisoners. But Morgana, aided by a priest, tries to stop him before the Djinn can destroy humanity. **96m/C VHS, DVD.** Andrew Divoff, Paul Johansson, Holly Fields, Bokeem Woodbine, Tommy (Tiny) Lister; ***D:*** Jack Sholder; ***W:*** Jack Sholder; ***C:*** Carlos Gonzalez; ***M:*** David Williams. **VIDEO**

Wishmaster 3: Beyond the Gates of Hell ✓ 1/2 **2001 (R)** Baxter College history prof Joel Barash (Connery) has a crush on student Diana (Cook) who has been helping him out. Unfortunately, her help includes releasing the demonic Djinn from its puzzle box. The Djinn then possesses Barash and goes after Diana to grant her three wishes. Diana knows there's a trick but her fellow students aren't so smart and their wishes have nasty results. Diana can wish to spare her friends but the only thing that will really destroy the evil is the magical Sword of Justice. **92m/C VHS, DVD.** A.J. Cook, Jason Connery, Tobias Mehler, Aaron Smolinksi, Louisette Geiss, John Novak; ***D:*** Chris Angel; ***W:*** Alexander Wright. **VIDEO**

Wishmaster 4: The Prophecy Fulfilled ✓ **2002 (R)** Same old, same old. The Djinn (Novak) gets released by Lisa (Spencer-Nairn) whose boyfriend Steven (Trucco) has been paralyzed in an accident. She gets the usual three wishes that don't come out the way she intended. This time if Lisa does her third wish, the Djinn brotherhood are released from hell—or something like that. Usual gore and Spencer-Nairn takes her clothes off and has a gratuitous sex scene. **92m/C VHS, DVD.** John Novak, Tara Spencer-Nairn, Michael Trucco, Victor Webster, John Benjamin Martin; ***D:*** Chris Angel; ***W:*** John Benjamin Martin; ***M:*** Daryl Bennett, Jim Guttridge. **VIDEO**

The Wistful Widow of Wagon Gap ✓✓ *The Wistful Widow* **1947** Lou, a traveling salesman, accidentally kills a man, and according to the law of the west he has to take care of the dead man's widow and children—all seven of them. Because the family is so unsavory, Lou knows that no other man will kill him, so he allows himself to be appointed sheriff and clears the town of lowlifes. Usual Abbott & Costello fare is highlighted with their zany antics. **78m/B VHS, DVD.** Bud Abbott, Lou Costello, Marjorie Main, George Cleveland, Gordon Jones, William Ching, Peter Thompson, Glenn Strange, Olin Howlin; ***D:*** Charles T. Barton.

Wit ✓✓✓ **2001** A tough topic buoyed by Thompson's fierce performance and Nichols expert direction. Middleaged scholar Vivian Bearing (Thompson) has dedicated her work to studying the holy sonnets of John Donne. The poet's life-and-death issues take on new meaning when Vivian learns she has stage-four ovarian cancer and she agrees to undergo the most aggressive treatment available. She puts herself in the care of veteran researcher Dr. Kelekian (Lloyd) and his internist Dr. Posner (Woodward), a former student of Vivian's. Their insensitivity sparks her bitter wit as Vivian realizes the inevitable truth. Based on the 1997 Pulitzer Prize-winning play by Margaret Edson. **98m/C VHS, DVD.** Emma Thompson, Christopher Lloyd, Audra McDonald, Jonathan M. Woodward, Eileen Atkins, Harold Pinter; ***D:*** Mike Nichols; ***W:*** Emma Thompson, Mike Nichols; ***C:*** Seamus McGarvey. **CABLE**

The Witch ✓ 1/2 *La Strega in Amore; Aura* **1966** Historian hired by family to assemble the late father's works falls in love with beautiful daughter. Seems she's no angel. **103m/B VHS, DVD.** *IT* Rosanna Schiaffino, Richard Johnson, Sarah Ferrati, Gian Marie Volonte, Margherita Guzzinati; ***D:*** Damiano Damiani.

Witch Hunt ✓✓ 1/2 **1994 (R)** Mock fantasy/mystery set in 1953 Hollywood. Private eye H. Phillip Lovecraft (Hopper) is hired by actress Kim Hudson (Miller) to shadow her philandering studio hubby Gottlieb (Rosenberg), who dies in an untimely fashion. The kicker is that witchcraft is commonplace, with the studio hiring witches and warlocks to cast spells. Also, a blowhard senator (Bogosian) is heading a McCarthy-like campaign to ban magic and Lovecraft fears his sorceress friend (Ralph) is going to be the scapegoat for Gottlieb's murder. Great special effects; fuzzy plot. **101m/C VHS.** Dennis Hopper, Penelope Ann Miller, Eric Bogosian, Sheryl Lee Ralph, Julian Sands, Alan Rosenberg, Valerie Mahaffey, Debi Mazar; ***D:*** Paul Schrader; ***W:*** Joseph Dougherty; ***M:*** Angelo Badalamenti.

Witch Who Came from the Sea ✓ 1/2 **1976 (R)** Witch terrorizes all the ships at sea, but doesn't exactly haunt the viewer. **98m/C VHS, DVD.** Millie Perkins, Lonny (Lonnie) Chapman, Vanessa Brown, Peggy (Margaret) Feury, Rick Jason; ***D:*** Matt Cimber.

A Witch Without a Broom ✓ 1/2 *Una Bruja Sin Escoba* **1968** Shoestring time travel fantasy. When an American professor catches the eye of a 15th century apprentice witch, the trip begins. Since the witch is only learning the ropes, they end up visiting a number of periods other than their own before the professor gets home. **78m/C VHS.** *SP* Jeffrey Hunter, Maria Perschy, Perla Cristal, Gustavo Rojo; ***D:*** Joe Lacy.

Witchboard ✓✓ 1/2 **1987 (R)** During a college party, a group of friends bring out the Ouija board and play with it for laughs. One of the girls discovers she can use the board to communicate with a small boy who died years before. In her effort to talk with him she unwittingly releases the evil spirit of an ax murderer who haunts and murders members of the group. An entertaining, relatively inoffensive member of its genre that displays some attention to characterization and plot. **98m/C VHS, DVD.** Todd Allen, Tawny Kitaen, Stephen Nichols, Kathleen Wilhoite, Burke Byrnes, Rose Marie, James W. Quinn, Judy Tatum, Gloria Hayes, J.P. Luebsen, Susan Nickerson; ***D:*** Kevin S. Tenney; ***W:*** Kevin S. Tenney; ***C:*** Roy Wagner; ***M:*** Dennis Michael Tenney.

Witchboard 2: The Devil's Doorway ✓✓ 1/2 **1993 (R)** There seem to be a lot of doorways to hell because someone is always finding a new one (and making a movie about it). This time it's the innocent Paige Benedict (Dolenz), who moves into an artist's loft and finds an old Ouija board in a closet. Through the board, Paige is contacted by a former tenant who claims to be a murder victim. Soon her fellow tenants are dying in violent and mysterious ways and Paige's dreams are haunted by evil. What hath she wrought—and can she get it back in the closet where it belongs. **98m/C VHS.** Ami Dolenz, Laraine Newman, Timothy Gibbs, John Gatins, Julie Michaels, Marvin Kaplan; ***D:*** Kevin S. Tenney; ***W:*** Kevin S. Tenney; ***C:*** David Lewis; ***M:*** Dennis Michael Tenney.

Witchboard 3: The Possession ✓✓ 1/2 **1995 (R)** A Ouija board opens the gates to hell (yet again or we wouldn't have a movie) and the board's spirit steals Brian's soul and takes control of his body—much to the bewilderment of his girlfriend Julie. **93m/C VHS, DVD.** David Nerman, Locky Lambert, Cedric Smith, Donna Sarrasin; ***D:*** Peter Svatek; ***W:*** Kevin S. Tenney, Jon Ezrine; ***C:*** Barry Gravelle.

Witchcraft WOOF! **1988 (R)** A young mother meets a couple killed three centuries ago for performing witchcraft. They want her baby, of course, to be the son of the devil. "Rosemary's Baby" rip-off, that is thoroughly predictable. **90m/C VHS, DVD.** Anat "Topol" Barzilai, Gary Sloan, Mary Shelley, Deborah Scott, Alexander Kirkwood, Lee Kisman, Edward Ross Newton; ***D:*** Robert Spera; ***W:*** Jody Savin; ***C:*** Jens Sturup; ***M:*** Randy Miller.

Witchcraft 2: The Temptress ✓ **1990 (R)** A sensuous woman seduces an innocent young man into the rituals of witchcraft and the occult. Sequel to "Witchcraft" does not succeed where original failed, but does have a fair share of sex and violence. **88m/C VHS, DVD.** Charles Solomon, Mia Ruiz, Delia Sheppard; ***D:*** Mark Woods; ***W:*** Jim Hanson, Sal Manna; ***C:*** Jens Sturup; ***M:*** Miriam Cutler.

Witchcraft 3: The Kiss of Death ✓✓ **1990 (R)** Once a master of the occult, William Spanner now seeks only to live a normal life. His plans are changed, however, when a sensual creature from Hell is sent to seduce him. More sex and violence, with an emphasis on sex. The best of the "Witchcraft" trio, for those trying to plan a festive evening. **85m/C VHS.** Charles Solomon, Lisa Toothman, William L. Baker, Lena Hall; ***D:*** R.L. Tillmanns.

Witchcraft 4: Virgin Heart ✓ **1992 (R)** Supernatural horror continues as attorney Will Spanner sinks even deeper into his enemy's satanic trap in this shocking sequel to the popular series. His only hope is to use his own black magic powers and to enlist the help of a seductive stripper (Penthouse Pet Strain). **92m/C VHS, DVD.** Charles Solomon, Julie Strain, Clive Pearson, Jason O'Gulihar, Lisa Jay Harrington, Barbara Dow; ***D:*** James Merendino.

Witchcraft 5: Dance with the Devil ✓ **1992 (R)** This undistinguished horror series continues with several successful people finding the unpleasant loopholes in their satanic contracts. A demon named Cain is behind all the trouble. The horror special effects are cheap but there are several softcore sex scenes (pointless to the plot) which provide a minimal interest. An unrated version is also available. **94m/C VHS.** Marklen Kennedy, Carolyn Taye-Loren, Nicole Sassaman, Aysha Hauer; ***D:*** Talun Hsu.

Witchcraft 6: The Devil's Mistress ✓ **1994 (R)** Police detectives Lutz and Garner's new case involves young women turning up naked and dead. Turns out satanic disciple Savanti is expected to impress the boss with a virgin sacrifice before an impending eclipse. But since virgins are scarce, he's having a real tough time. Practically no gore but lots of skin, along with hit-or-miss humor. **86m/C VHS, DVD.** Kurt Alan, John E. Holiday, Bryan Nutter, Jerry Spicer, Shannon Lead; ***D:*** Julie Davis; ***W:*** Julie Davis.

Witchcraft 7: Judgement Hour ✓ **1995 (R)** Modern-day warlock must sacrifice his earthly existence to kill an evil vampire. **91m/C VHS, DVD.** David Byrnes, April Breneman, Alisa Christensen, John Cragen, Loren Schmalle; ***D:*** Michael Paul Girard; ***W:*** Peter Fleming; ***C:*** Denis Maloney; ***M:*** Miriam Cutler.

Witchcraft 8: Salem's Ghost ✓✓ *Salem's Ghost* **1995 (R)** Warlock Simon Winfrough (Van Landingham) was burned at the stake in 1692 but if you could keep a bad satanist in his grave there'd be no movie. So when Simon's spirit is accidentally awakened by the Dunaways (Grober and Korf) in their Salem home, they seek the help of exorcist McArthur (Overmyer). **90m/C VHS.** Lee Grober, Kim Kopf, Tom Overmyer, Jack Van Landingham, David Weills,

Anthoni Stuart; ***D:*** Joseph John Barmettler Jr.; ***W:*** Joseph John Barmettler Jr.; ***C:*** Denis Maloney.

Witchcraft 9: Bitter Flesh **1996 (R)** Yet another sequel to the endless erotic horror series finds the LAPD investigating a series of murders. They get a tip from a strange call girl who claims to be chanelling the spirit of a warlock, who's about to open the gates to hell. **90m/C VHS, DVD.** Landon Hall, David Byrnes, Stephanie Beaton, Mikul Robins; ***D:*** Michael Paul Girard; ***W:*** Stephen J. Downing; ***C:*** Jeff Gateman; ***M:*** Michael Paul Girard.

Witchcraft 10: Mistress of the Craft **1998** Witch Celeste Sheridan has been hunting Raven and her band of vampires outside London. Meanwhile, LAPD detective Lucy Lutz arrives in London with an extradition order for Satanic serial killer, Hyde. But Raven and her vamps free Hyde in order to have him help in a ritual power-enhancing ceremony. After Celeste finds out, she teams up with Lucy and Interpol agent Chris Dixon to hunt down Raven and Hyde before they can finish their demonic work. **90m/C VHS, DVD.** Wendy Cooper, Eileen Daly, Stephanie Beaton, Kerry Knowlton, Sean Harry, Frank Scantori, Emily Bouffante, Lynn Michelle; ***D:*** Elisar Cabrera; ***W:*** Elisar Cabrera; ***C:*** Alvin Leong. **VIDEO**

Witchcraft 11: Sisters in Blood **1/2 2000** A college production of "Macbeth" resurrects three long-dead witches. Full of fuzzy occult logic and semi-undressed girls in peril. **m/C VHS, DVD.** Stephanie Beaton, Mikul Robins, James Servais, Miranda Odell, Laura Ian Richards, Kathleen St. Lawrence; ***D:*** Ron Ford; ***W:*** Ron Ford; ***C:*** Scott Spears. **VIDEO**

Witchery *La Casa 4; Ghosthouse 2; Witchcraft* **1988** A photographer and his girlfriend vacation at a New England hotel where they discover a horrifying, satanic secret. One by one (as always, in this kind of bad flick, in the interest of "suspense"), people are killed off. Seems it's a witch, bent on revenge. Forget room service and bar the door. Laurenti used the pseudonym Martin Newlin. **96m/C VHS, DVD.** David Hasselhoff, Linda Blair, Catherine Hickland, Hildegarde Knef, Leslie Cumming, Bob Champagne, Richard Farnsworth, Michael Manches; ***D:*** Fabrizio Laurenti.

The Witches **1/2** *The Devil's Own* **1966** Gwen Mayfield (Fontaine) accepts a teaching position at Haddaby School. She wants to put terrifying memories of work in Africa behind her, but finds that the bucolic English country town is just as dangerous. The sense of menace isn't as strong as it is in the similar "Wicker Man," and the film isn't one of the strongest entries from the Hammer Studio, but it is up to their high standards in terms of production values and acting. **90m/C DVD.** Joan Fontaine, Kay Walsh, Alec McCowen, Ann Bell, John Collin, Michele Dotrice, Gwen Ffrangcon Davies, Ingrid Brett; ***D:*** Cyril Frankel; ***W:*** Nigel Kneale; ***C:*** Arthur Grant; ***M:*** Richard Rodney Bennett.

The Witches **1/2 1990 (PG)** Nine-year-old boy on vacation finds himself in the midst of a witch convention, and grand high witch Huston plans to turn all children into furry little creatures. The boy, with the help of his good witch grandmother, attempts to prevent the mass transmutation of children into mice. Top-notch fantasy probably too spooky for the training wheel set. Wonderful special effects; the final project of executive producer Jim Henson. Based on Roald Dahl's story. **92m/C VHS, DVD.** Anjelica Huston, Mai Zetterling, Jasen Fisher, Rowan Atkinson, Charlie Potter, Bill Paterson, Brenda Blethyn, Jane Horrocks; ***D:*** Nicolas Roeg; ***W:*** Allan Scott; ***C:*** Harvey Harrison; ***M:*** Stanley Myers. L.A. Film Critics '90: Actress (Huston); Natl. Soc. Film Critics '90: Actress (Huston).

Witches' Brew **1979 (PG)** Three young women try to use their undeveloped skills in witchcraft and black magic to help Garr's husband get a prestigious position at a university, with calamitous results. Oft-funny spoof is silly and oft-predictable. Turner's role is small as an older, experienced witch. **98m/C VHS.** Teri Garr, Richard Benjamin, Lana Turner, Kathryn Leigh Scott; ***D:*** Richard Shorr, Herbert L. Strock.

The Witches Hammer **WOOF! 2006 (R)** An action-horror woofer with a stupid plot, bad acting, and lame action and CGI effects. Rebecca is turned into a vampire and then recruited by a secret organization to battle a power-hungry vamp who wants to rule over humans. Title refers to a book of magic that falls into the bad vamp's hands. **91m/C DVD.** Claudia Coulter, Stephanie Beacham, Tom Dover, Harold Gasnier, Sally Reeve, Jonathan Sidgwick, Jason Tompkins, Maga Rodriguez; ***D:*** James Eaves; ***W:*** James Eaves; ***C:*** John Raggett; ***M:*** Mark Conrad Chambers. **VIDEO**

Witches' Mountain **1971** A troubled couple is captured by a coven of witches in the Pyrenees. Dull and pointless. **98m/C VHS.** ***MX*** Patty (Patti) Shepard, John Caffari, Monica Randall; ***D:*** Raul Artigot.

The Witches of Eastwick **1/2 1987 (R)** "Mad Max" director Miller meets Hollywood in this unrestrained, vomit-filled treatment of John Updike's novel about three lonely small-town New England women and their sexual liberation. A strange, rich, overweight and balding, but nonetheless charming man knows their deepest desires and makes them come true with decadent excess. Raunchy fun, with Nicholson over-acting wildly as the Mephisto. Miller lends a bombastic violent edge to the effort, sometimes at the expense of the story. Filmed on location in Cohasset, Massachusetts. **118m/C VHS, DVD.** Jack Nicholson, Cher, Susan Sarandon, Michelle Pfeiffer, Veronica Cartwright, Richard Jenkins, Keith Joakum, Carel Struycken; ***D:*** George Miller; ***W:*** Michael Cristofer; ***C:*** Vilmos Zsigmond; ***M:*** John Williams. L.A. Film Critics '87: Actor (Nicholson); N.Y. Film Critics '87: Actor (Nicholson).

Witches of the Caribbean **2005 (R)** Troubled teen Angela (Cavazos) is plagued by nightmares of a witch being burned at the stake. She heads to a Caribbean retreat to participate in a program organized by psychotherapist Professor Avebury (Cassidy) but evil things happen when her fellow patients start to disappear. The scenery is pretty but there's little else to recommend in this standard witch tale. **82m/C DVD.** Joanna Cassidy, Nicole Cavazos, Nicole Marie Monica, Kelly Giddish, Michael King, Nina Tapanin, Kyle Jordan; ***D:*** David DeCoteau; ***W:*** Jana K. Arnold; ***C:*** Robert Hayes. **VIDEO**

Witchfire **1986 (R)** After their psychiatrist dies in an automobile accident, three maniacal women escape from an asylum and hide out in the woods. Winters then holds seances to contact the dead doctor, but instead captures a young, very much alive hunter. For dedicated fans of Winters. **92m/C VHS.** Shelley Winters, Gary Swanson, David Mendenhall, Corinne Chateau; ***D:*** Vincent J. Privitera; ***W:*** Vincent J. Privitera.

The Witching **WOOF!** *Necromancy* **1972** Poorly made story of man's continuing quest for supernatural power. Welles slums as the high priest out to get victim Franklin. **90m/C VHS.** Orson Welles, Pamela Franklin, Michael Ontkean, Lee Purcell, Lisa James, Harvey Jason, Terry Quinn; ***D:*** Bert I. Gordon; ***W:*** Bert I. Gordon, Gail March; ***C:*** Winton C. Hoch.

The Witching of Ben Wagner **1/2 1995 (G)** Strange occurrences have Ben believing his friend Regina and her grandmother may be witches. But, if so, they're friendly ones as they help Ben adjust to a new home and neighborhood. **96m/C VHS.** Justin Gocke, Harriet Hall, Sam Bottoms; ***D:*** Paul Annett.

Witching Time **1/2 1984** Elvira presents this film, in which a young composer is visited by a horny 17th-century witch while his wife is away from home. When the wife returns, both women fight to possess him. **60m/C VHS, DVD.** Jon Finch, Prunella Gee, Patricia Quinn, Ian McCulloch; ***D:*** Don Leaver.

The Witchmaker *Legend of Witch Hollow; Witchkill* **1969** Remote, crocodile-infested bayou in Louisiana is the scene of witchcraft and the occult as young girls are murdered in order for a group of witches to become youthful again. **101m/C VHS, DVD.** John Lodge, Alvy Moore, Thordis Brandt, Anthony Eisley, Shelby Grant, Robyn Millan, Helene Winston; ***D:*** William O. Brown; ***W:*** William O. Brown.

Witchouse **1999 (R)** Elizabeth (McKinney), a modern-day witch, invites some fellow college students to an off-campus party at her creepy mansion. But it turns out they are all descendants of witch-hunters who burned Elizabeth's ancestor at the stake. And now it's time for revenge. **90m/C VHS, DVD.** David Oren Ward, Ashley Mckinney, Matt Raftery, Monica Serene Garnich, Brooke Muller, Ariauna Albright, Marissa Tait, Dane Northcutt, Kimberly Pullis; ***D:*** Jack Reed; ***W:*** Matthew Jason Walsh; ***C:*** Viorel Sergovici Jr. **VIDEO**

Witchouse 2: Blood Coven **1/2 2000 (R)** Four unmarked graves are discovered by a strange house that is about to be torn down. The graves may be related to Lilith, a witch burned to death in the area. When a professor and her students come to investigate they find the locals aren't very friendly—especially after people start dying. Has Lilith return to take revenge? **82m/C VHS, DVD.** Ariauna Albright, Andrew Prine, Nicholas Lanier, Elizabeth Hopgood; ***D:*** J.R. Bookwalter. **VIDEO**

Witchouse 3: Demon Fire **2001 (R)** Stevie (Rochon) and Rose (Krause) are filming a documentary on witchcraft, when their old friend Annie (Dempsey) comes to visit. Annie is seeking refuge from her abusive boyfriend and her buddies are glad to oblige. As part of the documentary, the three women conduct a mock seance, and inadvertently raise the spirit of the evil witch Lilith (Stevens). Soon, strange things happen and the corpses start piling up. Is Lilith real, or has one of the girls gone insane? As with the other films in this series, director Bookwalter is able to put every nickel up on-screen and create an interesting movie. This one isn't great art, nor does it want to be. It's simply a horror film that offers cheap thrills, attractive ladies, and a brief escape from reality. **77m/C DVD.** Debbie Rochon, Tanya Dempsey, Tina Krause, Brinke Stevens; ***D:*** J.R. Bookwalter.

The Witch's Mirror **1960** A sorceress plots to destroy the murderer of her god-daughter. The murderer, a surgeon, begins a project to restore the disfigured face and hands of his burned second wife, and he doesn't care how he gets the materials. For true fans of good bad horror flicks. Badly dubbed (which adds to the charm); dark (of course); and offbeat (naturally). **75m/B VHS, DVD.** ***MX*** Rosita (Rosa) Arenas, Armando Calvo, Isabela Corona, Dina De Marco; ***D:*** Chano Urueto.

WitchTrap **1989 (R)** Lame sequel to "Witchboard." A mansion's new owner hires psychics to exorcise the disturbed ghost of his predecessor. **87m/C VHS.** James W. Quinn, Kathleen Bailey, Linnea Quigley; ***D:*** Kevin S. Tenney.

With a Friend Like Harry *Harry, He's Here to Help; Harry, un Ami Qui Vous Veut du Bien; Harry, A Friend Who Wishes You Well* **2000 (R)** Twisted, surprisingly funny black comedy about a sociopath. Michel (Lucas), wife Claire (Seigner), and their three young daughters have embarked on the vacation from hell as they head to their summer home. At a rest stop, Michel happens to meet Harry (Lopez), a high school acquaintance who remembers Michel very well. Before they know it, Claire and Michel are sharing their farmhouse with Harry and his sexy girlfriend, the aptly named Plum (Guillemin). Harry's a very, very generous (if off-kilter) guy—in fact, he'll do anything to make Michel's life better, even kill. French with subtitles. **117m/C VHS, DVD.** ***FR*** Sergi Lopez, Laurent Lucas, Mathilde Seigner, Sophie Guillemin; ***D:*** Dominik Moll; ***W:*** Dominik Moll, Gilles Marchand; ***C:*** Mathieu Poirot-Delpech; ***M:*** David Whitaker. Cesar '01: Actor (Lopez), Director (Moll), Film Editing, Sound.

With a Song in My Heart **1952** Showbiz drama based on the life of singer Jane Froman, with a stellar performance by Hayward. Told in flashback; Jane (Hayward) gets her first big break in radio and decides to marry mentor Don (Wayne), who becomes increasingly jealous of her success. During a WWII troop tour, Jane's plane crashes near Lisbon and she's rescued by pilot John Burn (Calhoun), who falls in love as Jane slowly recuperates. Aided by faithful nurse Clancy (Ritter), Jane is eventually strong enough to try for a comeback and Don finally realizes that their marriage is over. Froman herself dubbed the singing for Hayward. **117m/C DVD.** Susan Hayward, Thelma Ritter, Rory Calhoun, David Wayne, Robert Wagner, Helen Westcott, Una Merkel, Leif Erickson; ***D:*** Walter Lang; ***W:*** Lamar Trotti; ***C:*** Leon Shamroy; ***M:*** Alfred Newman. Oscars '53: Orig. Score.

With Friends Like These **1998 (R)** Johnny DeMartino (Constanzo) is a small time character actor in Hollywood. He, along with his three other actor buddies, makes a living playing small bit roles of Mafia henchmen, when one day he is approached with an opportunity to audition for Martin Scorsese to play the role of a lifetime, Al Capone (Scorsese wants an unknown actor). Although he was sworn to secrecy about the audition, Johnny can't help spread the good news to his friends. Faster than you can say "sleeps with the fishes," every character actor in town is trying to wrangle their own audition and practicing their best mobster impressions. Clever and funny look inside the non-glamorous side of the movie industry, with all its faults and insecurities attached. **105m/C VHS.** Adam Arkin, Robert Costanzo, Beverly D'Angelo, Elle Macpherson, Amy Madigan, David Strathairn, Jon Tenney, Lauren Tom, Carmine Costanzo, Garry Marshall, Michael McKean, Ashley Peldon, Jon Polito, Heather Stephens, Bill Murray, Martin Scorsese, Laura San Giacomo, Tom La Grua, Armando Pucci, Andrew Schaifer; ***D:*** Philip Messina; ***W:*** Philip Messina; ***C:*** Brian Reynolds.

With Honors **1/2 1994 (PG-13)** Pesci is a bum who finds desperate Harvard student Fraser's Honors thesis, and, like any quick-witted bum with a yen for literature, holds it for ransom. Desperate to salvage his future gold card, Fraser and his roommates agree to fix Joe's homeless state. Self-involved students learn something about love and life while Madonna drones in the background. Fraser is believable as the ambitious student about to endure Pesci's enlightenment. Pesci is Pesci, doing his best to overcome numerous script difficulties. **100m/C VHS, DVD.** Joe Pesci, Brendan Fraser, Moira Kelly, Patrick Dempsey, Josh Hamilton, Gore Vidal; ***D:*** Alek Keshishian; ***W:*** William Mastrosimone; ***C:*** Sven Nykvist; ***M:*** Patrick Leonard.

With Kit Carson over the Great Divide **1/2 1925** A large-scale silent western about a doctor's family gone asunder and then reunited during the Fremont expeditions out of St. Louis in the 1840s. Snow's final screen appearance. Recently refound. Fun cinematic history (in two senses of the phrase). Beautiful landscape. **72m/B VHS.** Roy Stewart, Henry B. Walthall, Marguerite Snow, Sheldon Lewis, Earl Metcalfe; ***D:*** Frank S. Mattison.

With Six You Get Eggroll *A Man in Mommy's Bed* **1968 (G)** A widow with three sons and a widower with a daughter elope and then must deal with the antagonism of their children and even their dogs. Brady Bunch-esque family comedy means well, but doesn't cut it. Hershey's debut. Jamie Farr, William Christopher, and Vic Tayback have small parts. To date, Day's last big-screen appearance. **95m/C VHS, DVD.** Doris Day, Brian Keith, Pat Carroll, Alice Ghostley, Vic Tayback, Jamie Farr, William (Bill) Christopher, Barbara Hershey; ***D:*** Howard Morris; ***C:*** Harry Stradling Jr.

Within the Rock **1996 (R)** Space crew must shift a wandering moon before it collides with earth but beyond that problem they've got an alien predator that's escaped. **91m/C VHS, DVD.** Xander Berkeley, Bradford Tatum, Brian Krause, Caroline Barclay, Calvin Levels, Earl Boen, Dale Dye; ***D:*** Gary J. Tunnicliffe; ***W:*** Gary J. Tunnicliffe; ***C:*** Adam Kane; ***M:*** Tony Fennell, Rod Gammons.

Withnail and I **1/2 1987 (R)** A biting and original black comedy about a pair of unemployed, nearly starving English actors during the late 1960s. They decide to retreat to a country house owned by Withnail's uncle, for a vacation and are beset by comic misadventures, particularly when the uncle, who is gay, starts to hit on his nephew's friend. Robinson, who scripted "The Killing Fields," makes his successful directorial debut, in addition to drafting the screenplay from his own novel. Co-produced by George Harrison and Richard Starkey (Ringo

Starr). **108m/C VHS, DVD.** *GB* Richard E. Grant, Paul McGann, Richard Griffiths, Ralph Brown, Michael Elphick; ***D:*** Bruce Robinson; ***W:*** Bruce Robinson; ***C:*** Peter Hannan; ***M:*** David Dundas.

Without a Clue 🦴🦴 ½ **1988 (PG)** Spoof of the Sherlock Holmes legend, in which Holmes is actually portrayed by a bumbling, skirt-chasing actor, and Watson is the sole crime-solving mastermind, hiring the actor to impersonate the character made famous by the doctor's published exploits. The leads have some fun and so do we; but laughs are widely spaced. **107m/C VHS, DVD.** *GB* Michael Caine, Ben Kingsley, Jeffrey Jones, Lysette Anthony, Paul Freeman, Nigel Davenport, Peter Cook, Pat Keen; ***D:*** Thom Eberhardt; ***W:*** Gary Murphy, Larry Strawther; ***M:*** Henry Mancini.

Without a Paddle 🦴🦴 ½ **2004 (PG-13)** A harmlessly stupid buddy flick finds three lifelong friends—phobic Dan (Green), surfer dude Jerry (Lillard), and loudmouth Tom (Shepard)—mourning the unexpected death of pal Billy. Uneasily pushing 30, these faux grown-ups decide to pursue a childhood fantasy by heading into the Oregon woods to search for the lost treasure of '70s crime legend, D.B. Cooper. Now the real fun begins as they deal with growling bears, canoeing the rapids, redneck pot farmers, tree-huggers, and, briefly, a charismatically grizzled Burt Reynolds. There's a lot of standard scatological and slapstick humor as well as many nostalgic '70s and '80s references that may be lost on a younger crowd. **99m/C VHS, DVD, UMD.** *US* Seth Green, Matthew Lillard, Dax Shepard, Ethan Suplee, Abraham Benrubi, Rachel Blanchard, Burt Reynolds, Christina Moore, Bonnie Somerville, Ray Baker; ***D:*** Steven Brill; ***W:*** Jay Leggett, Mitch Rouse, Fred Wolf, Harris Goldberg, Tom Nursall; ***C:*** Jonathan Brown; ***M:*** Christophe Beck.

Without a Paddle: Nature's Calling 🦴 ½ **2009 (PG-13)** Doofus buddy comedy. Workaholic Ben (James) and easy-going Zach (Turner) were childhood buds who drifted apart. Ben's one outside interest is his longtime crush on would-be sweetheart Heather (Riley), now a tree hugger living in the wilderness. Zach decides he and Ben can reconnect, accompanied by Brit nature enthusiast Nigel (Young), by heading into the woods and tracking Heather down so Ben can finally tell her how he feels. **90m/C DVD.** Kristopher Turner, Oliver James, Amber McDonald, Rik Young, Madison Riley, Jerry Rice; ***D:*** Ellory Elkayem; ***W:*** Stephen Mazur; ***C:*** Thomas Callaway. **VIDEO**

Without a Trace 🦴🦴 **1983 (PG)** One morning, a six-year-old boy is sent off to school by his loving mother, never to return. The story of the mother's relentless search for her son. Cardboard characters, wildly unrealistic ending that is different from the real-life incident on which it's based. Scripted by Gutcheon from her book "Still Missing." Jaffe's directorial debut. **119m/C VHS, DVD.** Kate Nelligan, Judd Hirsch, Stockard Channing, David Dukes; ***D:*** Stanley R. Jaffe; ***C:*** John Bailey; ***M:*** Jack Nitzsche.

Without Anesthesia 🦴🦴 *Rough Treatment; Bez Znieczulenia* **1978** Journalist Jerzy returns from a trip abroad to discover his wife has left him for an obnoxious young writer. Against advice, Jerzy fights the divorce and searches for an explanation. Meanwhile, he has mysteriously fallen out of political favor and finds his career falling apart as well. Polish with English subtitles. **111m/C VHS.** *PL* Zbigniew Zapasiewicz, Ewa Dalkowska, Krystyna Janda, Andrzej Seweryn; ***D:*** Andrzej Wajda; ***W:*** Agnieszka Holland, Andrzej Wajda.

Without Evidence 🦴🦴 **1996** When Oregon correctional director Michael Francke (Garrett) is visiting younger brother Kevin (Plank) in Florida, he mentions his suspicions about an operation within his department involving drugs in prison. Then the next phone call Kevin gets is that Michael's been murdered. When he heads to Oregon, Kevin seems to be getting the official runaround and becomes increasingly suspicious about a coverup. A tension-building true story that remains unsolved. **90m/C VHS, DVD.** Scott Plank, Anna Gunn, Andrew Prine, Angelina Jolie, Paul Perri, Allen Nause, Ernie Garrett; ***D:*** Gill Dennis; ***W:*** Gill Dennis, Phil Stanford; ***C:*** Victor Nunez; ***M:*** Franco Piersanti.

Without Honors 🦴🦴 **1932** A man seeks to restore the reputation of his dead brother, accused of murder and theft. He joins the Texas Rangers and brings the real criminals to justice. Excellent location shooting lifts ordinary early western. **62m/B VHS.** Harry Carey Sr., Mae Busch, Gibson Gowland, George "Gabby" Hayes; ***D:*** William Nigh.

Without Limits 🦴🦴🦴 *Pre* **1997 (PG-13)** Second biopic about '70s long-distance runner Steve Prefontaine (after 1996's "Prefontaine") focuses mainly on Prefontaine's (Crudup) relationship with his University of Oregon coach Bill Bowerman (Sutherland), who later was a co-founder of Nike. Also explores the heartbreak of the 1972 Olympics. Crudup does a fine job exploring the runner's playful arrogance, fearlessness, and iconoclasm (especially when dealing with the corrupt AAU). Sutherland, playing a three-dimensional character for the first time in a while, gives a fine performance. Kenny Moore, a close friend and fellow '72 Olympian, wrote the script with director Towne, with the full cooperation of Bowerman and Prefontaine's girlfriend. **117m/C VHS, DVD.** Billy Crudup, Donald Sutherland, Monica Potter, Jeremy Sisto, Matthew Lillard, Billy Burke, Dean Norris, Gabriel Olds, Judith Ivey; ***D:*** Robert Towne; ***W:*** Robert Towne, Kenny Moore; ***C:*** Conrad L. Hall; ***M:*** Randy Miller.

Without Love 🦴🦴 ½ **1945** Tracy is a scientist, Hepburn, a woman with an empty basement for his laboratory. Since the neighbors would be scandalized by the idea of unmarried people living together, however platonically, they decide to get married, although each has sworn off romance. Snappy dialogue, expertly rendered by the Tracy/Hepburn team. Terrific supporting cast keeps this minimally plotted outing afloat. Adapted from the play of the same name by Philip Barry. **113m/B VHS, DVD.** Spencer Tracy, Katharine Hepburn, Lucille Ball, Keenan Wynn, Carl Esmond, Patricia Morison, Felix Bressart; ***D:*** Harold Bucquet; ***W:*** Donald Ogden Stewart; ***C:*** Karl Freund.

Without Love 🦴🦴 **1980** Ambitious young journalist experiences resentment from her peers because of her aggressive methods, and they decide to teach her a lesson by drawing her into a situation destined for disaster. In Polish with English subtitles. **104m/C VHS.** *PL* Malgorzata Zajaczkowska, Dorota Stalinska, Wladyslaw Kowalski; ***D:*** Barbara Sass; ***W:*** Barbara Sass; ***C:*** Wieslaw Zdort; ***M:*** Seweryn Krajewski.

Without Mercy 🦴 ½ **1995 (R)** Marine platoon is shafted by the government when they're left to die while on a U.N. peacekeeping mission in Africa. POW survivor John Carter (Zagarino) then winds up in Asia and gets set up by ex-soldier and general bad guy Larsen (Kove), who he must constantly battle in order to survive. **88m/C VHS.** Frank Zagarino, Martin Kove, Ayu Azhari, Frans Tumbuan; ***D:*** Robert Anthony; ***W:*** Robert Anthony.

Without Orders 🦴 **1936** Playboy pilot Len (Haworth) vies with dull good guy pilot Wad (Armstrong) for the affections of stewardess Kay (Eilers). But when Len cowardly parachutes out of a crippled airplane, Kay must take over the controls, guided by Wad from the control tower. And no, this was not played for laughs. **64m/B VHS.** Sally Eilers, Robert Armstrong, Vinton (Hayworth) Haworth, Charley Grapewin, Ward Bond, Frances Sage; ***D:*** Lew Landers; ***W:*** J. Robert Bren, Edmund L. Hartman; ***C:*** J. Roy Hunt.

Without Reservations 🦴🦴 ½ **1946** Hollywood-bound novelist Colbert encounters Marine flyer Wayne and his pal (DeFore) aboard a train. She decides he would be perfect for her newest movie. They both dislike her famous book and don't realize they're traveling with the renowned author. Misadventures and misunderstandings abound as this trio make their way to Tinseltown. Of course, Colbert and Wayne fall in love. Boxoffice success with a tired script and too few real laughs. The Duke is interesting but miscast. Based on the novel "Thanks, God, I'll Take It From Here" by Jane Allen. **101m/B VHS.** Claudette Colbert, John Wayne, Don DeFore, Phil Brown, Frank Puglia; ***Cameos:*** Louella Parsons, Cary Grant, Jack Benny; ***D:*** Mervyn LeRoy; ***C:*** Milton Krasner.

Without Warning 🦴🦴 ½ *The Story Without A Name* **1952** Inexperienced director and actors pull out a minor success in this fairly ordinary murder mystery, about a serial killer of beautiful blondes. **75m/C VHS, DVD.** *FR* Maurice Ronet, Adam Williams, Gloria Franklin, Edward Binns; ***D:*** Arnold Laven.

Without Warning: The James Brady Story 🦴🦴🦴 **1991 (R)** White House Press Secretary Brady took a bullet in the brain during the 1981 shooting of President Reagan, and made a slow, grueling recovery. This fine cable film spares none of it, concentrating on the stricken man and his family, and opting out of disease-of-the-week cliches (though the pic's politics won't please the gun-adorers). Based on Mollie Dickinson's biography "Thumbs Up." **120m/C VHS.** Beau Bridges, Joan Allen, David Strathairn, Christopher Bell, Gary Grubbs, Bryan Clark, Steve Flynn, Christine Healy, Susan Brown; ***D:*** Michael Toshiyuki Uno; ***W:*** Robert Bolt. **CABLE**

Witless Protection **WOOF!** **2008 (PG-13)** Another unsuccessful, unnecessary, and unfunny vehicle for Larry the Cable Guy. This time around Larry plays a dimwitted cop who kidnaps a woman in witness protection because he thinks the FBI agents at her side are ruthless drug dealers. Genius screenplay! It take about 90 minutes for him to realize his mistake, allowing plenty of time to insert lame fart jokes and zingers about Arabs along the way. Larry needs to start making like a real cable guy and keep us waiting a long time before we see the likes of him on screen again. **97m/C DVD, Blu-ray Disc.** *US* Larry the Cable Guy, Ivana Milicevic, Yaphet Kotto, Peter Stormare, Jenny McCarthy, Eric Roberts, Joe Mantegna; ***D:*** Charles Robert Carner; ***W:*** Charles Robert Carner; ***C:*** Michael Goi; ***M:*** Eric Allaman.

Witness 🦴🦴🦴 ½ **1985 (R)** A young Amish boy, Samuel Lapp (Haas), traveling from his father's funeral witnesses a murder in a Philadelphia bus station. Investigating detective John Book (Ford, in one of his best roles) soon discovers the killing is part of a conspiracy involving corruption in his department. He follows the child and his young widowed mother, Rachel (McGillis) to their home in the country. A thriller with a difference, about the encounter of alien worlds, with a poignant love story. McGillis, in her first major role, is luminous as the Amish mother, while Ford is believable as both a cop and a sensitive man. An artfully crafted drama, richly focusing on the often misunderstood Amish lifestyle. **112m/C VHS, DVD.** Harrison Ford, Kelly McGillis, Alexander Godunov, Lukas Haas, Josef Sommer, Danny Glover, Patti LuPone, Viggo Mortensen, Robert Earl Jones; ***D:*** Peter Weir; ***W:*** William Kelley, Earl W. Wallace; ***C:*** John Seale; ***M:*** Maurice Jarre. Oscars '85: Film Editing, Orig. Screenplay; Writers Guild '85: Orig. Screenplay.

The Witness 🦴 ½ *Fish Out of Water* **1999 (PG)** Teen discovers an arsonist's plot to burn down a historic museum. Cheesy Canadian 'action' flick fails to deliver any thrillls, spills, or, well, action. **95m/C VHS, DVD.** John Heard, Susan Almgren, Patrick Thomas, Chris Heyerdahl; ***D:*** Geoffrey Edwards; ***W:*** Richard Gourdreau; ***C:*** Georges Archambault; ***M:*** Jerry Devilliers. **VIDEO**

The Witness Files 🦴 ½ **2000 (R)** Sandy (Butler) has been imprisoned for the murder of her abusive husband. Corrupt politician Frank Sutton (Flatman) arranges for her release so he can use her special talents (she does makeup special effects) for his own nefarious ends. But Sandy hooks up with a detective (Nerman) to doublecross Sutton. Watch "F/X" instead unless you're a particular fan of Butler. **97m/C VHS, DVD.** Yancy Butler, David Nerman, Barry Flatman, Matthew Harbour; ***D:*** Douglas Jackson. **VIDEO**

Witness for the Prosecution 🦴🦴🦴 ½ **1957** An unemployed man is accused of murdering a wealthy widow whom he befriended. Ailing defense attorney Laughton can't resist taking an intriguing murder case, and a straightforward court case becomes increasingly complicated in this energetic adaptation of an Agatha Christie story and stage play. Outstanding performances by Laughton, with excellent support by real life wife, Lanchester, as his patient nurse. Power, as the alleged killer, and Dietrich, as his enigmatic wife, are top-notch. **116m/B VHS, DVD.** Charles Laughton, Tyrone Power, Marlene Dietrich, Elsa Lanchester, John Williams, Henry Daniell, Una O'Connor, Ian Wolfe, Torin Thatcher, Norma Varden, Francis Compton, Philip Tonge, Ruta Lee, Ottola Nesmith, J. Pat O'Malley; ***D:*** Billy Wilder; ***W:*** Harry Kurnitz, Billy Wilder; ***C:*** Russell Harlan; ***M:*** Matty Malneck. Golden Globes '58: Support. Actress (Lanchester).

Witness Protection 🦴🦴🦴 **1999** Highly watchable performances raise this cable movie about mobsters above the average. Boston goodfella Bobby Batton (Sizemore) turns state's evidence after he's betrayed by his cronies. He and his family are placed in the witness protection program under the eye of a U.S. marshal (Whitaker) but living as a regular mook proves difficult. Bobby's wife (Mastrantonio) is bitter, his kids are angry and confused, and there are no easy endings. Based on a 1996 New York Times Magazine article by Robert Sabbag. **105m/C VHS, DVD.** Tom Sizemore, Forest Whitaker, Mary Elizabeth Mastrantonio, Shawn Hatosy, Richard Portnow; ***D:*** Richard Pearce; ***W:*** Daniel Therriault; ***C:*** Fred Murphy; ***M:*** Cliff Eidelman. **CABLE**

Witness to the Execution 🦴🦴 **1994 (PG-13)** It's 1999 and Tycom Entertainment, a pay-per-view network, is looking for some hot entertainment. Top exec Jessica (Young) decides to televise the electric chair execution of convicted criminal Dennis Casterline (Daly). But Casterline claims to be innocent and as the execution date nears Jessica is unsettled by new evidence that may supports his claim. The cutthroat TV execs provide amusement but this TV movie fare quickly becomes muddled. **92m/C VHS.** Sean Young, Timothy Daly, Len Cariou, George Newbern; ***D:*** Tommy Lee Wallace; ***W:*** Thomas Baum.

Witness to the Mob 🦴 ½ **1998 (R)** Originally an NBC miniseries, this mob saga tells the true story of Sammy "The Bull" Gravano (Turturro), who turned state's evidence against his boss, John Gotti. Manages to hit every cliche and stereotype along the way. **172m/C VHS.** Nicholas Turturro, Tom Sizemore, Debi Mazar, Frankie Valli, Abe Vigoda, Philip Baker Hall, Frank Vincent, Michael Imperioli, Lenny Venito, Vincent Pastore, Kirk Acevedo, Richard Bright; ***D:*** Thaddeus O'Sullivan; ***W:*** Stanley Weiser; ***C:*** Frank Prinzi; ***M:*** Stephen Endelman. **TV**

The Witnesses 🦴🦴 *Les Temoins* **2007** Set in 1984, friends are forced to consider their fears when confronted by the early days of the AIDS epidemic. Writer Sarah (Beart) and her cop husband Mehdi (Bouajila) have an arrangement allowing liaisons. Sarah's close friend Adrien (Blanc), a middle-aged gay doctor, is enamored of provincial young Manu (Libereau) who agrees to be his platonic companion. When Adrien and Manu visit Sarah and Mehdi during a summer holiday, Manu and Mehdi begin a secret affair. Then Manu gets sick, Adrien becomes an early fighter against the new disease, and Sarah learns what's been going on and reacts unexpectedly. French with subtitles. **115m/C DVD.** *FR* Emmanuelle Beart, Michel Blanc, Johan Libereau, Julie Depardieu, Sami Bouajila; ***D:*** Andre Techine; ***W:*** Andre Techine, Laurent Guyot, Viviane Zingg; ***C:*** Julien Hirsch; ***M:*** Philippe Sarde.

Wittgenstein 🦴🦴 **1993** Complicated, experimental portrait of Viennese-born philosopher Ludwig Wittgenstein (Johnson), executed as a series of blackout sketches (that feature a green Martian dwarf and such friends as Bertrand Russell and Ottoline Morrell). Assumes a familiarity with the eccentric Wittgenstein's ideas but does manage to convey some emotion and wit. **75m/C VHS.** *GB* Karl Johnson, Michael Gough, Tilda Swinton, John Quentin, Nabil Shaban; ***D:*** Derek Jarman; ***W:*** Derek Jarman, Terry Eagleton, Ken Butler.

Wives and Daughters 🦴🦴 ½ **2001** Charming adaptation of Elizabeth Gaskell's 1864 chronicle of family ties, romance, and scandal set in an 1820s English country town. Our heroine is modest Molly Gibson (Waddell), whose widower doctor father (Paterson) marries ambitious Hyacinth (Annis), who has a beautiful daughter, Cynthia (Hawes), who's Molly's age. Then there's the local gentry, Squire Hamley (Gambon), and his two sons, the poetic Osborne (Hollander) and the scientific Roger (Howell). Molly becomes everyone's confidante, but also has her own secrets. **300m/C VHS, DVD.** *GB* Justine Waddell, Keeley Hawes, Francesca Annis, Bill Paterson, Michael Gambon, Penelope Wilton, Tom Hollander, Anthony Howell, Ian Carmichael, Iain Glen, Barbara Leigh-Hunt, Tonia Chauvet, Shaughan Seymour, Barbara Flynn, Deborah Findlay; ***D:*** Nicholas Renton; ***W:*** Andrew Davies. **TV**

Wives under Suspicion 1/2 **1938** While prosecuting a man who murdered his wife out of jealousy, a district attorney finds his own home life filled with similar tension. Director Whale's unnecessary remake of his own earlier film, "The Kiss Before the Mirror." He is best known for "Frankenstein." **75m/B VHS, DVD.** Warren William, Gail Patrick, Constance Moore, William Lundigan; ***D:*** James Whale.

The Wiz **1978 (G)** Black version of the long-time favorite "The Wizard of Oz," based on the Broadway musical. Ross plays a Harlem schoolteacher who is whisked away to a fantasy version of NYC in a search for her identity. Some good character performances and musical numbers, but generally an overblown and garish effort with Ross too old for her role. Pryor is poorly cast, but Jackson is memorable as the Scarecrow. High-budget ($24 million) production with a ton of name stars, lost $11 million, and cooled studios on black films. Horne's number as the good witch is the best reason to sit through this one. ♫ The Feeling That We Have; Can I Go On Not Knowing; Glinda's Theme; He's the Wizard; Soon as I Get Home; You Can't Win; Ease on Down the Road; What Would I Do If I Could Feel?; Slide Some Oil to Me. **133m/C VHS, DVD.** Diana Ross, Michael Jackson, Nipsey Russell, Ted Ross, Mabel King, Thelma Carpenter, Richard Pryor, Lena Horne; ***D:*** Sidney Lumet; ***W:*** Joel Schumacher; ***C:*** Oswald Morris; ***M:*** Quincy Jones.

The Wizard 1/2 **1989 (PG)** Facing the dissolution of his dysfunctional family, a youngster decides to take his autistic, video game-playing little brother across the country to a national video competition. Way too much plot in pretentious, blatantly commercial feature-length Nintendo ad, featuring the kid from "The Wonder Years." For teen video addicts only. **99m/C VHS, DVD.** Fred Savage, Beau Bridges, Christian Slater, Luke Edwards, Jenny Lewis; ***D:*** Todd Holland; ***W:*** David Chisholm.

The Wizard of Gore **1970 (R)** The prototypical Lewis splatter party, about a magician whose on-stage mutilations turn out to be messily real. High camp and barrels of bright movie blood. **96m/C VHS, DVD.** Ray Sager, Judy Cler, Wayne Ratay, Phil Laurensen, Jim Rau, Don Alexander, Monika Blackwell, Corinne Kirkin, John Elliott; ***D:*** Herschell Gordon Lewis; ***W:*** Allen Kahn; ***C:*** Alex Ameri, Daniel Krogh; ***M:*** Larry Wellington.

The Wizard of Gore **2007 (R)** Remake of the 1970 flick lives up to its title. Underground magician Montag the Magnificent (a perfect fit for Glover) has an extremely graphic act where he dismembers chosen females from the audience, although they reappear healthy. Too bad they don't stay that way. Amateur detective Edmund Bigelow (Pardue) learns the women are later found in pieces in the exact same way as in the magic show. As Bigelow keeps digging, his sanity becomes suspect, especially since Montag is ever only seen onstage. Maybe he doesn't exist at all? **97m/C DVD.** Crispin Glover, Kip Pardue, Bijou Phillips, Jeffrey Combs, Brad Dourif, Joshua John Miller; ***D:*** Jeremy Kasten; ***W:*** Zach Chassler; ***C:*** Christopher Duddy; ***M:*** Steve Porcaro.

The Wizard of Loneliness 1/2 **1988 (PG-13)** A disturbed young boy goes to live with his grandparents during WWII, and slowly discovers family secrets centering on his aunt. Excellent performances barely save an aimless plot with an overdone denouement. Based on the novel by John Nichols. **110m/C VHS.** Lukas Haas, Lea Thompson, John Randolph, Lance Guest, Anne Pitoniak, Jeremiah Warner, Dylan Baker; ***D:*** Jenny (H. Anne Riley) Bowen; ***W:*** Nancy Larson; ***C:*** Richard Bowen; ***M:*** Michel Colombier.

The Wizard of Oz 1/2 **1925** An early silent version of the L. Frank Baum fantasy, with notable plot departures from the book and later 1939 adaptation, starring long-forgotten comedian Semon as the Scarecrow, supported by a pre-Laurel Hardy as the Tin Woodman. With music score. **96m/B VHS, DVD.** Larry Semon, Dorothy Dwan, Bryant Washburn, Charles Murray, Oliver Hardy, Josef Swickard, Virginia Pearson; ***D:*** Larry Semon; ***W:*** L. Frank Baum Jr., Larry Semon; ***C:*** Leonard Smith, Frank B. Good, Hans Koenekamp.

The Wizard of Oz **1939** From the book by L. Frank Baum. Fantasy about a Kansas farm girl (Garland, in her immortal role) who rides a tornado to a brightly colored world over the rainbow, full of talking scarecrows, munchkins and a wizard who bears a strange resemblance to a Kansas fortuneteller. She must outwit the Wicked Witch if she is ever to go home. Delightful performances from Lahr, Bolger, and Hamilton; King Vidor is uncredited as co-director. Director Fleming originally wanted Deanna Durbin or Shirley Temple for the role of Dorothy, but settled for Garland who made the song "Over the Rainbow" her own. She received a special Academy Award for her performance. For the 50th anniversary of its release, "The Wizard of Oz" was restored and includes rare film clips of Bolger's "Scarecrow Dance" and the cut "Jitterbug" number, and shots by Buddy Ebsen as the Tin Man before he became ill and left the production. Another special release of the film, "The Ultimate Oz," contains a documentary on the making of the film, a reproduction of the original script, still photos, and liner notes. ♫ Munchkinland; Ding Dong the Witch is Dead; Follow the Yellow Brick Road; If I Only Had a Brain/a Heart/the Nerve; If I Were the King of the Forest; The Merry Old Land of Oz; Threatening Witch; Into the Forest of the Wild Beast; The City Gates are Open. **101m/C VHS, DVD.** Judy Garland, Margaret Hamilton, Ray Bolger, Jack Haley, Bert Lahr, Frank Morgan, Charley Grapewin, Clara Blandick, Mitchell Lewis, Billie Burke; ***D:*** Victor Fleming; ***W:*** Noel Langley; ***C:*** Harold Rosson; ***M:*** Herbert Stothart. Oscars '39: Song ("Over the Rainbow"), Orig. Score; AFI '98: Top 100, Natl. Film Reg. '89.

The Wizard of Speed and Time 1/2 **1988 (PG)** A special-effects wizard gets the break of his life when he's hired by a movie studio, but there's more to this particular studio than he realizes. Jittlov, a real special-effects expert, plays himself in this personally financed production. Although brimming with inside jokes and references, this self-indulgence succeeds with its enthusiasm and ambition, despite being rather obviously self-produced. Unique special effects make it memorable. **95m/C VHS.** Mike Jittlov, Richard Kaye, Page Moore, David Conrad, Steve Brodie, John Massari, Frank Laloggia, Philip Michael Thomas, Angelique Pettyjohn, Arnetia Walker, Paulette Breen, Forrest J Ackerman; ***D:*** Mike Jittlov; ***W:*** Deven Chierighino, Mike Jittlov, Richard Kaye; ***C:*** Russell Carpenter; ***M:*** John Massari.

Wizards 1/2 **1977 (PG)** A good, bumbling sorcerer battles for the sake of a magic kingdom and its princess against his evil brother who uses Nazi propaganda films to inspire his army of mutants. Profane, crude, & typically Bakshian fantasy with great graphics. Animated. **81m/C VHS, DVD.** ***D:*** Ralph Bakshi; ***W:*** Ralph Bakshi; ***M:*** Andrew Belling; ***V:*** Bob Holt, Jesse Wells, Richard Romanus, David Proval.

Wizards of the Demon Sword **1994 (R)** Group of warriors battle over a sword with the power to control the world. **90m/C VHS, DVD.** Lawrence Tierney, Michael Berryman, Russ Tamblyn, Lyle Waggoner, Blake Bahner, Heidi Paine, Dan Speaker, Jay Richardson, Dawn Wildsmith; ***D:*** Fred Olen Ray; ***W:*** Dan Golden, Ernest Farino.

Wizards of the Lost Kingdom 1/2 **1985 (PG)** A boy magician, aided by various ogres and swordster Svenson battles an all-powerful wizard for control of his kingdom. Family fare a bit too clean and harmless. **76m/C VHS.** Bo Svenson, Vidal Peterson, Thom Christopher; ***D:*** Hector Olivera.

Wizards of the Lost Kingdom 2 **1989 (PG)** A boy wizard is charged with vanquishing the evil tyrants from three kingdoms. Barely a sequel; no plot continuation or cast from earlier kiddie sword epic. **80m/C VHS.** David Carradine, Bobby Jacoby, Lana Clarkson, Mel Welles, Susan Lee Hoffman, Sid Haig; ***D:*** Charles B. Griffith.

The Wizards of Waverly Place: The Movie 1/2 **2009 (G)** In this Disney Channel original (derived from the TV series), Alex (Gomez), Max (Austin), Justin (Henrie), and their parents go on a Caribbean vacation but 16-year-old Alex gets pouty over being told what to do. She inadvertently wishes her parents had never met and makes them forget all about their family. Max tries to prevent his parents from endangering their future while Alex and Justin try to find the Stone of Dreams to reverse the spell. **98m/C DVD.** Selena Gomez, David Henrie, Jake T. Austin, Maria Canals-Barrera, David DeLuise, Jennifer Stone, Steve Valentine; ***D:*** Lev L. Spiro; ***W:*** Daniel Berendsen; ***C:*** David Makin; ***M:*** Kenneth Burgomaster. **CABLE**

Wolf **1986** To everyone's lasting regret, an ex-Vietnam POW strives to rescue an American ambassador kidnapped by Central American rebels. **95m/C VHS.** J. Antonio Carreon, Ron Marchini; ***D:*** Charlie Ordonez.

Wolf 1/2 **1994 (R)** Harrison's original script is massaged by Nichols into an upscale new age men's movement horror spectacle lacking a suitable climax. Stressed out Manhattan book editor Will Randall's (Nicholson) car hits a wolf on a country road and he's bitten when he tries to help the animal. Normally a wishy-washy guy, he notices some distinctly hairy changes to both his body and personality, leading him to make some drastic changes at work by knocking off his firm's greedy honchos and taking over. Talk about being ruthless in business. Boss' daughter Pfeiffer takes a shine to Randall's new animal magnetism, but is just visual candy. Walks a fine line between black comedy, camp, romance, and horror, though Jack baying at the moon seems sort of campy. **125m/C VHS, DVD.** Oz (Osgood) Perkins II, Jennifer Nicholson, Jack Nicholson, Michelle Pfeiffer, James Spader, Kate Nelligan, Christopher Plummer, Richard Jenkins, Om Puri, Eileen Atkins, David Hyde Pierce, Ron Rifkin, Prunella Scales; ***D:*** Mike Nichols; ***W:*** Wesley Strick, Jim Harrison; ***C:*** Giuseppe Rotunno; ***M:*** Ennio Morricone.

The Wolf at the Door 1/2 **1987 (R)** A well-appointed, sincere biography of impressionist Paul Gauguin in the middle period of life, during his transition from the petty demands of his Parisian life to the freedom of Tahiti. Not definitive or compelling, but serves the purpose of a biography—arousing interest in the subject's life and art. **90m/C VHS.** *DK FR* Donald Sutherland, Jean Yanne, Sofie Grabol, Ghita Norby, Max von Sydow, Merete Voldstedlund, Fanny Bastien, Valerie Morea; ***D:*** Henning Carlsen; ***W:*** Christopher Hampton; ***M:*** Roger Bourland.

Wolf Blood 1/2 **1925** When Dick (Chesebro) is hurt in an accident, Dr. Horton uses wolf's blood for a transfusion. Soon there are unexplained deaths and Dick fears he's becoming a man-beast. Early precursor to the wolfman films. **68m/B VHS.** George Chesebro, Marguerite Clayton, Ray Hanford, Roy Watson, Milburn (Milt) Morante; ***D:*** George Chesebro, George Mitchell.

Wolf Call 1/2 **1939** Carroll plays the son of a miner who travels with his devoted hound to see his father's old mine and start it working again. Gangsters and a beautiful Indian maiden get in his way. Master and pooch both find romance, and both sing. From the Jack London novel. **62m/B VHS.** John Carroll, Movita, Wheeler Oakman, Peter George Lynn; ***D:*** George Waggner; ***W:*** George Waggner; ***C:*** Fred H. Jackman Jr.; ***M:*** Edward Kay.

Wolf Creek **2005 (R)** In the Australian Outback, three young adults, Ben (Phillips), Liz (Magrath) and Kristy (Morassi) are on a cross-country car trip. Having purchased a cheap junker for the trek, the threesome find they've been stranded in the bush when the car fails to start. In an unlikely stroke of luck, a tow truck-driving bushman named Mick (Jarratt) appears and assures them he can repair the car but must tow them back to his compound. So begins the unrelenting stream of torturous (to them and the audience) horrors. More than a wee bit over the top. **95m/C DVD, HD DVD.** John Jarratt, Kestie Morassi, Nathan Phillips, Cassandra Magrath; ***D:*** Greg Mclean; ***W:*** Greg Mclean; ***C:*** William Gibson; ***M:*** Francois Tetaz.

Wolf Dog **1933** A boy and his dog. Outdoor action and adventure. Twelve chapters, 13 minutes each. **156m/B VHS.** Frankie Darro, Patricia "Boots" Mallory; ***D:*** Harry Fraser, Colbert Clark.

Wolf Lake 1/2 **1979** WWII veteran, whose son was killed in Vietnam, and a Vietnam army deserter clash with tragic consequences during their stay at a Canadian hunting lodge. Steiger gives it a go, but overwrought revenge pic resists quality upgrade. **90m/C VHS.** Rod Steiger, David Hoffman, Robin Mattson, Jerry Hardin, Richard Herd, Paul Mantu; ***D:*** Burt Kennedy.

The Wolf Man 1/2 **1941** Fun, absorbing classic horror with Chaney as a man bitten by werewolf Lugosi. His dad thinks he's gone nuts, his screaming gal pal just doesn't understand, and plants on the Universal lot have no roots. Ouspenskaya's finest hour as the prophetic gypsy woman. Ow-ooo! Chilling and thrilling. **70m/B VHS, DVD.** Lon Chaney Jr., Claude Rains, Maria Ouspenskaya, Ralph Bellamy, Bela Lugosi, Warren William, Patric Knowles, Evelyn Ankers, Forrester Harvey, Fay Helm; ***D:*** George Waggner; ***W:*** Curt Siodmak; ***C:*** Joseph Valentine; ***M:*** Charles Previn, Hans J. Salter, Frank Skinner.

Wolf Trap *Vlci Jama* **1957** Trapped indeed—small town veterinarian is suffocating in a marriage to an older, domineering and needy wife. The two adopt an orphaned teenager, which turns out to be a big mistake as the unhappy husband gradually falls in love with the girl. Czech with subtitles. **95m/C VHS.** *CZ* Jirinaova Sejbalova, Jana Brecjchova, Miroslav Dolezal, Jaroslav Pucha; ***D:*** Jiri Weiss; ***W:*** Jiri Weiss; ***C:*** Vaclav Hanus.

Wolfen **1981 (R)** Surrealistic menace darkens this original and underrated tale of super-intelligent wolf creatures terrorizing NYC. Police detective Finney tries to track down the beasts before they kill again. Notable special effects in this thriller, which covers environmental and Native American concerns while maintaining the tension. Feature film debuts of Hines and Venora. Based on the novel by Whitley Strieber. **115m/C VHS, DVD.** Albert Finney, Gregory Hines, Tom Noonan, Diane Venora, Edward James Olmos, Dick O'Neill, Dehl Berti, Peter Michael Goetz, Sam Gray, Ralph Bell; ***D:*** Michael Wadleigh; ***W:*** Michael Wadleigh, David Eyre; ***C:*** Gerry Fisher; ***M:*** James Horner.

Wolfheart's Revenge **1925** An honest cowboy, helped by Wolfheart the Wonder Dog, steps in when a sheep rancher is murdered. Silent film with original organ score. **64m/B VHS.** S.J. Bingham, Kathleen Collins, Larry Fisher, Helen Walton, Guinn "Big Boy" Williams; ***D:*** Charles Seeling.

The Wolfman **1982** Colin Glasgow is summoned back to his family manor to attend the funeral of his father. Unbeknownst to Colin, his father was actually murdered by his children who are in thrall to a Satanist priest. The family stalls Colin, hoping their father's "curse" will be passed on to him at the next full moon. It does, and Colin turns into a werewolf and begins a small rural rampage. Extremely amateurish gothic horror attempt in the Universal/"Dark Shadows" vein. The sets and models look flimsy and the acting is like that of a bad stage-play. **102m/C VHS, DVD.** Earl Owensby, Kristina Reynolds, Sid Rancer, Julian Morton; ***D:*** Worth Keeter; ***W:*** Worth Keeter; ***C:*** Darrell Cathcart; ***M:*** David Floyd, Arthur Smith.

The Wolfman **2009 (R)** Inspired by the 1941 horror classic starring Lon Chaney, this foggy homage shows what happens when family dysfunction gets hairy. Lawrence Talbot (Del Toro) returns to his family's estate to help his brother's fiance Gwen (Blunt) after said brother ends up gnawed and gnarly. Reunited with his estranged father (Hopkins), Lawrence learns that a bloodthirsty creature is feasting on the villagers. While strolling on the moors, Lawrence is also attacked but survives. Now a werewolf, Lawrence must deal with his bestial nature, a family secret, and Scotland Yard detective Aberline (Weaving). Fairly true to the spirit of the original, you will be rooting for the reluctant Wolfman by the end. **102m/C DVD.** *US* Benicio Del Toro, Emily Blunt, Anthony Hopkins, Hugo Weaving, Geraldine Chaplin, Art Malik, Asa Butterfield, Simon Merrells; *D:* Joe Johnston; *W:* Andrew Kevin Walker; *C:* Shelly Johnson; *M:* Danny Elfman.

Wolverine ✗✗ *Code Name: Wolverine* **1996 (R)** Former Navy SEAL Harry Gordini (Sabato Jr.) and his family are vacationing in Italy where he becomes an unwitting drug smuggler. After the drug cartel kidnaps his wife and son, Harry uses his training to attempt a rescue before the authorities intervene. Based on the book by Frederick Forsyth. Supplies the required action quotient. **91m/C VHS, DVD.** Antonio Sabato Jr., Richard Brooks, Traci Lind, Daniel Quinn; *D:* David S. Jackson; *W:* Robert T. Megginson; *C:* Denis Maloney; *M:* Christopher Franke. **TV**

The Wolves ✗✗✗ *Shussho Iwai* **1982** Gosha shows the world of the yakuza (gangster) during the 1920s. Reminiscent of the samurai, the movie combines ancient Japanese culture with the rapidly changing world of 20th century Japan. In Japanese with English subtitles. **131m/C VHS.** *JP* Tatsuya Nakadai, Noboru Ando, Komake Kurihara, Kyoko Enami, Isao Natsuyagi, Noboru Ando; *D:* Hideo Gosha; *W:* Hideo Gosha; *C:* Kozo Okazaki; *M:* Masaru Sato.

The Wolves ✗✗ **1995 (PG-13)** Blackie (Dalton) and his sister Barbara (Hocking) have inherit some land in the Alaskan wilderness that evil businessman King (Harmstorf) wants to use as a toxic waste dump. But when Blackie befriends native guide Chilkoot (Cardinal) and rescues an injured wolf, he decides to fight King and his henchmen. **87m/C VHS.** Darren Dalton, Kristen Dalton, Raimund Harmstorf, Ben Cardinal, John Furey; *D:* Steve Carver; *W:* Stephen Peters, Art Bernd; *C:* Eugene Shlugleit.

Wolves in the Snow ✗✗ *Des Chiens dans la Neige* **2002** When Lucie finds out her husband Antoine has been cheating on her for years, she accidentally kills him in a rage. Unwilling to go to jail, she tries to figure out how to dispose of the body. But cheating wasn't all Antoine was hiding—he was also involved in money laundering for the mob. When a couple of hoods show up to question Lucie about Antoine's whereabouts, she lies. Now they think he's skipped out of town with a bag of missing cash and that Lucie knows more than she's telling. French with subtitles. **95m/C DVD.** *CA* Marie Josee Croze, Jean-Philippe Ecoffey, Romano Orzari, Anne Roussel, Frederic Gilles, Antoine Lacomblez; *D:* Michael Welterlin; *W:* Antoine Lacomblez, Michael Welterlin; *C:* Yves Belanger; *M:* Alain Mouysset.

The Wolves of Kromer ✗✗ **1998** A modern-day fairytale set in the rural English town of Kromer. The hypocritical townspeople are mean-spirited gossips who look down upon the local wolf population (in this case very attractive young human/beasts in fur coats and long tails). Seth (Williams) has just "come out" as a wolf and fallen for promiscuous Gabriel (Layton). Meanwhile, two servants are poisoning their cruel mistress and plan to point accusing fingers at the wolves, giving the human populace the excuse they need for violence. Based on the play by Lambert, who wrote the screenplay. **77m/C VHS, DVD.** *GB* Lee Williams, James Layton, Rita Davies, Margaret Towner, Rosemary Dunham, Angharad Rees, Kevin Moore, Leila Lloyd-Evelyn, Matthew Dean, David Prescott; *D:* Will Gould; *W:* Charles Lambert, Matthew Read; *C:* Laura Remacha; *M:* Basil Moore-Asfouri; *Nar:* Boy George.

A Woman and a Woman ✗✗ **1980** Covers a ten-year period in the friendship of Barbara and Irena and how it survives their professional and personal conflicts. In Polish with English subtitles. **99m/C VHS.** *PL* Halina Labonarska, Anna Romantowska; *D:* Richard Bugajski.

The Woman and the Stranger ✗✗ *Die Frau und der Fremde* **1984** Two German soldiers, Karl and Richard, are imprisoned by the Russians in WWI. Richard shares stories about his wife Anna and Karl falls vicariously in love with her. When Karl escapes, he goes to Anna for refuge and she begins to reciprocate his feelings. Then Richard returns. German with subtitles; based on the novel by Leonhard Frank. **97m/C DVD.** *GE* Kathrin Waligura, Joachim Latsch, Peter Zimmermann, Katrin Knappe, Christine Schorn, Ulrich Muhe; *D:* Rainer Simon; *W:* Rainer Simon; *C:* Roland Dressel; *M:* Reiner Bredemeyer.

A Woman at Her Window ✗✗ ½ *Une Femme a sa Fentre* **1977** Aristocratic, jaded Margot (Schneider), the wife of dissolute nobleman Rico (Orsini), is pursued by capitalistic businessman Raoul (Noiret). But Margot herself is taken by idealistic Michel (Lanoux), a communist evading the secret police in 1936 Greece, and has a daughter from their brief and ultimately tragic union. Years later, Margot's now-grown daughter returns to Greece to learn more about her parents. Adapted from the novel by Pierre Drieu La Rochelle. French with subtitles. **110m/C VHS.** *FR* Romy Schneider, Philippe Noiret, Victor Lanoux, Umberto Orsini, Delia Boccardo, Gastone Moschin, Carl Mohner; *D:* Pierre Granier-Deferre; *W:* Pierre Granier-Deferre, Jorge Semprun.

A Woman at War ✗✗ ½ **1994 (PG-13)** True-story of a young woman's heroic fight against the Nazis. Nineteen-year-old Helene Moskiewicz (Plimpton) has had her parents arrested by the Gestapo in occupied Brussels, Belgium. She joins the resistance and falls for Franz Boehler (Stoltz), a young businessman who is not above lining his pockets with Nazi profits. When persecution of the Jews intensifies, Helene risks infiltrating Gestapo headquarters in order to save lives. **115m/C VHS.** Martha Plimpton, Eric Stoltz; *D:* Edward Bennett; *W:* Edward Bennett.

A Woman Called Golda ✗✗✗ **1982** Political drama following the life and career of Golda Meir, the Israeli Prime Minister and one of the most powerful political figures of the 20th century. Davis portrays the young Golda, Bergman taking over as she ages. Superior TV bio-epic. **192m/C VHS.** Ingrid Bergman, Leonard Nimoy, Anne Jackson, Ned Beatty, Robert Loggia, Judy Davis; *D:* Alan Gibson; *W:* Steven Gethers, Harold Gast. **TV**

A Woman Called Moses ✗✗ ½ **1978** The story of Harriet Ross Tubman, who bought her freedom from slavery, founded the underground railroad, and helped lead hundreds of slaves to freedom before the Civil War. Wonderful performance by Tyson but the telefilm is bogged down by a so-so script. Based on the novel by Marcy Heldish. **200m/C VHS, DVD.** Cicely Tyson, Dick Anthony Williams, Will Geer, Robert Hooks, Hari Rhodes, James Wainwright; *D:* Paul Wendkos; *W:* Lonnie Elder III; *M:* Coleridge-Taylor Perkinson. **TV**

Woman Condemned ✗ ½ **1933** A reporter's attempt to clear a woman of murder leads to a mysterious mental hospital run by a mad scientist. Not much to recommend this low-level melodrama, unless you like to see shameless mugging and overacting. **58m/B VHS, DVD.** Mischa Auer, Lola Lane, Claudia Dell, Richard Hemingway, Jason Robards Sr., Louise Beavers, Paul Ellis; *D:* Dorothy Davenport Reid; *W:* Dorothy Davenport Reid, Willis Kent; *C:* James Diamond; *M:* Lee Zahler.

Woman Hater ✗✗ **1949** Delightful farce about the belief in the single life. Confirmed bachelor plays games with a single woman. They eventually disregard their solitary ways in favor of romance. **101m/B VHS.** Stewart Granger, Edwige Feuillere, Ronald Squire, Mary Jerrold; *D:* Terence Young.

The Woman He Loved ✗✗ ½ **1988** The infamous romance of Edward VIII, who gave up the throne of England for American divorcee, Wallis Warfield Simpson. Seymour and Andrews are fine in their roles but the drama is slow-going. **100m/C VHS.** Anthony Andrews, Jane Seymour, Olivia de Havilland, Lucy Gutteridge, Julie Harris, Robert Hardy, Phyllis Calvert; *D:* Charles Jarrott. **TV**

A Woman, Her Men and Her Futon ✗✗ **1992 (R)** A beautiful woman tries to find her identity by having a number of lovers but none can satisfy her every need. **90m/C VHS, DVD.** Jennifer Rubin, Lance Edwards, Grant Show, Michael Ceveris, Delaune Michel, Robert Lipton; *D:* Mussef Sibay; *W:* Mussef Sibay; *C:* Michael J. Davis; *M:* Joel Goldsmith.

Woman Hunt WOOF! *The Highest Bidder* **1972 (R)** Men kidnap women, then hunt them in the jungle for fun. So deeply offensive, we would give it negative bones if we could. "Hee Haw" bimbo Todd plays a sadistic lesbian. **81m/C VHS.** John Ashley, Lisa Todd, Eddie Garcia, Laurie Rose; *D:* Eddie Romero.

A Woman Hunted ✗ ½ **2003 (PG-13)** Lainie Wheeler's (Paul) car breaks down in the middle of nowhere and she's happy when good samaritan Harry (Higgins) stops and offers her a ride. She shouldn't be. **94m/C DVD.** *CA* Alexandra Paul, Linden Ashby, Michele Greene, Jonathan Higgins, Maxim Roy; *D:* Morrie Ruvinsky; *W:* Morrie Ruvinsky; *C:* Bruno Philip; *M:* Richard Bowers. **VIDEO**

The Woman Hunter ✗ ½ **1972** A wealthy woman recovering from a traffic accident in Mexico believes someone is after her for her jewels and possibly her life. Eden dressed well, if nothing else; suspense builds ploddingly to a "Yeah, sure" climax. **73m/C VHS, DVD.** Barbara Eden, Robert Vaughn, Stuart Whitman, Sydney Chaplin, Larry Storch, Enrique Lucero; *D:* Bernard L. Kowalski. **TV**

A Woman in Berlin ✗✗ *Anonyma: Eine Frau in Berlin* **2008** Too-long drama based on an anonymous diary. A German journalist (Hoss) is hiding in her damaged apartment building during the waning days of WWII as Russian soldiers rape and pillage the city. She finally finds a Russian officer (Sidikhin) who listens to her complaints and she then turns to him for protection. German and Russian with subtitles. **131m/C DVD.** *GE* Nina Hoss, Evgeny Sikikhin, Irm Hermann, August Diehl, Ruediger Vogler, Ulrike Krumbiegel, Rolf Kanies; *D:* Max Faerberboeck; *W:* Max Faerberboeck; *C:* Benedict Neuenfels; *M:* Zbigniew Preisner.

Woman in Black ✗✗ ½ **1989** Chilling ghost story set in 1925 and adapted from the novel by Susan Hill. Soliciter Arthur Kidd is sent to a remote house to settle the estate of a client. He's haunted by the mysterious figure of a woman in black, who according to the locals, has put a curse on the village. Arthur's driven close to the edge of sanity by the ghostly figure and the tragedy that haunts the past. **100m/C VHS, DVD.** *GB* Adrian Rawlins, Bernard Hepton, David Daker, Pauline Moran; *D:* Herbert Wise; *W:* Nigel Kneale. **TV**

Woman in Brown ✗✗ ½ *The Vicious Circle; The Circle* **1948** It's Hungary, 1882, and five Jewish men are on trial for the murder of a man who actually committed suicide. Despite the prejudice and hatred from the locals, their lawyer believes in and fights for their innocence. **77m/B VHS.** Conrad Nagel, Fritz Kortner, Reinhold Schunzel, Philip Van Zandt, Eddie LeRoy, Edwin Maxwell; *D:* W. Lee Wilder.

A Woman in Flames ✗✗✗ *Die Flambierte Frau* **1984 (R)** A bored middle-class housewife leaves her overbearing husband and becomes a high-priced prostitute. She has a passionless affair with an aging bisexual gigolo. Dark and dreary tale of human relationships and the role of sex in people's lives. Interesting but depressing. **106m/C VHS.** *GE* Gudrun Landgrebe, Robert Van Ackeren, Matthieu Carriere, Gabriele Lafari, Hanns Zischler; *D:* Robert Van Ackeren.

The Woman in Green ✗✗ *Sherlock Holmes and the Woman in Green* **1949** Murder victims are found with missing index fingers, and it's up to Holmes and Watson to try to solve this apparently motiveless crime. Available colorized. **68m/B VHS, DVD.** Basil Rathbone, Nigel Bruce, Hillary Brooke, Henry Daniell, Paul Cavanagh, Frederick Worlock, Mary Gordon, Billy Bevan; *D:* Roy William Neill; *W:* Bertram Millhauser; *C:* Virgil Miller.

A Woman in Grey ✗✗ **1920** A man and a woman battle wits when they attempt to locate and unravel the Army Code while staying one step ahead of J. Haviland Hunter, a suave villain after the same fortune. Silent. **205m/B VHS.** Arline Pretty, Henry Sell, Fred C. Jones, John Heenan, Margaret Fielding, Ann Brody; *D:* James Vincent; *W:* Walter R. Hall.

The Woman in Question ✗✗ ½ *Five Angles on Murder* **1950** When carnival fortune teller Astra (Kent) is murdered, Police Inspector Lodge (MacRae) finds that all her acquaintances have differing views about her character, making his investigation even more difficult. **82m/B VHS.** *GB* Jean Kent, Dirk Bogarde, Susan Shaw, Duncan MacRae, John McCallum, Hermione Baddeley, Charles Victor, Lana Morris, Vida Hope, Joe Linnane, Duncan Lamont, Bobbie Scroggins, Anthony Dawson, John Boxer, Julian D'Albie, Josephine Middleton, Everley Gregg, Albert Chevalier, Richard Pearson; *D:* Anthony Asquith; *W:* John Cresswell; *C:* Desmond Dickinson; *M:* John Wooldridge.

The Woman in Red ✗✗ ½ **1984 (PG-13)** Executive Wilder's life unravels when he falls hard for stunning Le Brock. Inferior Hollywood-ized remake of the ebulliant "Pardon Mon Affaire." Somehow the French seem to do the sexual force thing with more verve, but this one has its moments, and Wilder is likeable. Music by Stevie Wonder. ♫ I Just Called to Say I Love You; Don't Drive Drunk; It's More Than You; It's You; Love Light in Flight; Moments Aren't Moments; Weakness; Woman in Red. **87m/C VHS, DVD.** Gene Wilder, Charles Grodin, Kelly Le Brock, Gilda Radner, Judith Ivey, Joseph Bologna; *D:* Gene Wilder; *W:* Gene Wilder; *M:* John Morris. Oscars '84: Song ("I Just Called to Say I Love You"); Golden Globes '85: Song ("I Just Called to Say I Love You").

Woman in the Dunes ✗✗✗✗ *Suna No Onna; Woman of the Dunes* **1964** Splendid, resonant allegorical drama. A scientist studying insects in the Japanese sand dunes finds himself trapped with a woman in a hut at the bottom of a pit. Superbly directed and photographed (by Hiroshi Segawa). Scripted by Kobo Abe from his acclaimed novel. In Japanese with English subtitles. **123m/B VHS, DVD.** *JP* Eiji Okada, Kyoko Kishida, Koji Mitsui, Hiroko Ito, Sen Yano; *D:* Hiroshi Teshigahara; *W:* Kobe Abe; *C:* Hiroshi Segawa; *M:* Toru Takemitsu. Cannes '64: Grand Jury Prize.

Woman in the Moon ✗✗ ½ *By Rocket to the Moon; Girl in the Moon* **1929** Assorted people embark on a trip to the moon and discover water, and an atmosphere, as well as gold. Lang's last silent outing is nothing next to "Metropolis," with a rather lame plot (greedy trip bashers seek gold), but interesting as a vision of the future. Lang's predictions about space travel often hit the mark. Silent with music. **115m/B VHS, DVD.** *GE* Klaus Pohl, Willy Fritsch, Gustav von Wagenheim, Gerda Maurus; *D:* Fritz Lang.

Woman in the Shadows ✗✗ **1934** A ex-con retreats to the woods for serenity and peace, but is assaulted by mysterious women, jealous lovers, and gun-slinging drunks, until he explodes. A man can only take so much. From a Dashiell Hammett story. **70m/B VHS.** Fay Wray, Ralph Bellamy, Melvyn Douglas, Roscoe Ates, Joe King; *D:* Phil Rosen; *C:* Joseph Ruttenberg.

The Woman in the Window ✗✗✗ **1944** Psycho-melodrama finds staid college professor Richard Wanley straying off the straight and narrow into a world of trouble—thanks to beautiful model Alice (Bennett). She invites him over but when her jealous boyfriend Claude (Loft) arrives unexpectedly, he attacks them both and Richard kills Claude in self-defense. Thinking no one will believe them, and afraid of scandal, the inept duo bury the body in the woods. Too bad Richard's best friend Frank (Massey) is the D.A. and there's a blackmailer around. Or is there? Surprise ending. Based on the novel "Once Off Guard" by J.H. Wallis. **99m/B VHS.** Edward G. Robinson, Joan Bennett, Raymond Massey, Arthur Loft, Dan Duryea, Edmund Breon, Dorothy Peterson, Robert (Bobby) Blake; *D:* Fritz Lang; *W:* Nunnally Johnson; *C:* Milton Krasner; *M:* Arthur Lange.

The Woman in White ✗✗ ½ **1997** The happy hours half-sisters, outgoing Marian (Fitzgerald) and shy Laura (Waddell), spend with their eccentric Uncle Fairlie (Richardson) soon turn sinister when Laura is married off to the seemingly charming Sir Percival Glyde (Wilby). Sir Percival quickly appears to be conspiring with the suspicious Count Fosco (Callow) to take control of Laura's money. When Marian visits her sister, she's alarmed by Laura's decline and equally unnerved by the mysterious woman in white,

Anne (Vidler), who seems to know Glyde and tries to warn the sisters of impending danger. Based on the novel by Wilkie Collins, who also wrote "The Moonstone." **120m/C VHS, DVD.** *GB* Tara Fitzgerald, Justine Waddell, James Wilby, Simon Callow, Ian Richardson, Andrew Lincoln, Susan Vidler, John Standing, Corin Redgrave; *D:* Tim Fywell; *W:* David Pirie; *M:* David Ferguson. **TV**

The Woman Inside 1/2 **1983 (R)** Low-budget gender-bender depicts the troubled life of a Vietnam veteran who decides on a sex-change operation to satisfy his inner yearnings. Blondell's unfortunate last role as his/her aunt. Cheesy like Limburger; almost too weird and boring even for camp buffs. **94m/C VHS, DVD.** *CA* Gloria Manon, Dave Clark, Joan Blondell; *D:* Joseph Van Winkle; *W:* Steve(n) Fisher.

A Woman Is a Woman *Une Femme Est une Femme; La Donna E Donna* **1960** Godard's affectionate sendup of Hollywood musicals is a hilarious comedy about a nightclub dancer (Karina) who desperately wants a baby. When boyfriend Belmondo balks, she asks his best friend Brialy. Much ado is had, with the three leads all splendid. Godard's first film shot in color and cinemascope, with great music. In French with English subtitles. **88m/C VHS, DVD.** *FR* Jean-Claude Brialy, Jean-Paul Belmondo, Anna Karina, Marie DuBois; *D:* Jean-Luc Godard; *W:* Jean-Luc Godard; *C:* Raoul Coutard; *M:* Michel Legrand.

Woman Is the Future of Man *Yeojaneun namjaui miraeda* **2004** While meeting for lunch, two old Korean friends Mun-ho (Ji-tae) and Hyeon-gon (Tae-woo) reminisce over too much rice wine about a girl they both dated years before, Seon-hwa (Hyeon-a), and how each regrets mistreating her. Even though the men have moved on with their lives—Mun-ho is a married college art lecturer while Hyeon-gon is a hopeful filmmaker—they decide to visit Seon-hwa but find that life has not gone quite as well for her. In Korean, with English subtitles. **88m/C DVD.** Yoo Jitae, Kim Taewoo, Sung Hyunah; *D:* Hong Sang-soo; *W:* Hong Sang-soo; *C:* Kim Hyungkoo; *M:* Chong Yongjin.

A Woman Named Jackie 1/2 **1991 (PG)** Three-part TV miniseries covering the life of Jacqueline Bouvier Kennedy Onassis. Downey offers a pretty picture as the enigmatic and beleagured heroine but this version is simplistic at best. Based on the book by C. David Heymann. On three cassettes. **246m/C VHS.** Roma Downey, Stephen Collins, William Devane, Joss Ackland, Rosemary Murphy, Wendy Hughes, Josef Sommer; *D:* Larry Peerce; *W:* Roger O. Hirson. **TV**

The Woman Next Door *La Femme d'a Cote* **1981 (R)** One of Truffaut's last films before his sudden death in 1984. The domestic drama involves a suburban husband who resumes an affair with a tempestuous now-married woman after she moves next door, with domestic complications all around. An insightful, humanistic paean to passion and fidelity by the great artist, though one of his lesser works. Supported by strong outings from the two leads. In French with English subtitles. **106m/C VHS, DVD.** *FR* Gerard Depardieu, Fanny Ardant, Michele Baumgartner, Veronique Silver, Roger Van Hool; *D:* Francois Truffaut; *W:* Suzanne Schiffman; *C:* William Lubtchansky; *M:* Georges Delerue.

A Woman Obsessed *Bad Blood* **1993 (R)** Pathetic, over-cooked drama about a woman obsessed with her long-lost son. "Ruth Raymond" is really porn-flick vet Georgina Spelvin. Soon-to-be camp classic takes itself with utter seriousness. **105m/C VHS, VHS.** Ruth Raymond, Gregory Patrick, Troy Donahue, Linda Blair; *D:* Chuck Vincent; *W:* Craig Horrall; *C:* Larry Revene; *M:* Joey Mennona.

A Woman of Affairs **1928** Garbo, who can't have the guy she really loves (Gilbert), marries scoundrel. When she finds out husband's true profession, he kills himself and Gilbert comes back. In order to preclude happy ending, she decides the affair wasn't meant to be and expires. Tragically. Silent. **90m/B VHS.** Greta Garbo, John Gilbert, Lewis Stone, Johnny Mack Brown, Douglas Fairbanks Jr., Hobart Bosworth, Dorothy Sebastian; *D:* Clarence Brown.

Woman of Desire **1993 (R)** Christina Ford (Derek) is a femme fatale who is yachting with rich boyfriend Ted when there is a terrible storm. Christina, Ted, and yacht captain Jack are washed overboard and Jack is found washed ashore with no memory. When Christina turns up she claims Jack killed Ted. So Jack gets a lawyer, Walter J. Hill (played by the redoubtable Mitchum) but is he wily enough to discredit the deceitful Christina? Bo's body is once again on display. Also available in an unrated version. **97m/C VHS, DVD.** Bo Derek, Jeff Fahey, Steven Bauer, Robert Mitchum; *D:* Robert Ginty; *W:* Robert Ginty; *C:* Hanro Mohr; *M:* Rene Veldsman.

A Woman of Distinction **1950** Slapstick comedy with potential to be ordinary is taken over the top by a good, vivacious cast. Russell, the stuffy Dean of a women's college, is driven to distraction by a reporter linking her romantically to Milland, a visiting professor. **85m/C VHS.** Ray Milland, Rosalind Russell, Edmund Gwenn, Francis Lederer; *Cameos:* Lucille Ball; *D:* Edward Buzzell.

A Woman of Independent Means **1994 (PG)** Leisurely family miniseries, based on the 1979 novel by Elizabeth Forsythe Hailey. Fields stars as the title character, Bess Steed Garner (based on the author's maternal grandmother), a well-off Texas belle who marries childhood sweetheart Robert Steed (Goldwyn) in 1907 and settles down to family life. Of course, nothing is settled as Beth bears children, Robert tries to make a go of his insurance business, their families interfere, and tragedy strikes. **316m/C VHS.** Sally Field, Tony Goldwyn, Brenda Fricker, Charles Durning, Ron Silver, Sheila McCarthy, Ann Hearn; *D:* Robert Greenwald.

A Woman of Rome *La Romana* **1956** Standard Italian star vehicle, with Lollobrigida portraying a successful prostitute in Rome who decides to change her life. Dubbed. **93m/B VHS.** *IT* Gina Lollobrigida, Daniel Gelin, Franco Fabrizi, Raymond Pellegrin; *D:* Luigi Zampa.

Woman of Straw 1/2 **1964** Connery plays off his Bond role with a villainous twist. He's Anthony Richmond, the nephew of dying tycoon Charles Richmond (Richardson), who won't write him into the will. Uncle is very fond of his nurse (Lollobrigida), who in turn falls in love with Anthony. He convinces her to marry the old coot and get him into the will, but Charles dies, leaving her a murder suspect. Compelling thriller does well, despite plot holes, on the strength of performances by Richardson and Connery, portraying members of a family no one would want to see at a reunion. **115m/C VHS.** Sean Connery, Gina Lollobrigida, Ralph Richardson, Alexander Knox, Johnny Sekka, Peter Madden, George Curzon, Noel Howlett, Andre Morell, Douglas Wilmer; *D:* Basil Dearden; *W:* Stanley Mann, Michael Relph; *C:* Otto Heller.

A Woman of Substance 1/2 **1984** The woman of the title, Emma Harte, rises from poverty to wealth and power through self-discipline, enduring various romantic disappointments and tragedies along the way. Based on the novel by Barbara Taylor Bradford. Followed by "Hold the Dream." **300m/C VHS, DVD.** Jenny Seagrove, Barry Bostwick, Deborah Kerr, Liam Neeson, Diane Baker, George Baker, Peter Chelsom, Peter Egan, Christopher Gable, Christopher Guard, Gayle Hunnicutt, John Mills, Nicola Pagett, Saskia Reeves, Miranda Richardson; *D:* Don Sharp; *W:* Lee Langley; *C:* Ernest Vincze; *M:* Nigel Hess. **TV**

The Woman of the Town 1/2 **1944** Frontier marshal and newspaperman Bat Masterson is portrayed convincingly by Dekker as a very human hero who seeks justice when the woman he loves, a dance hall girl who works in the town for social causes, is killed by an unscrupulous rancher. Fictionalized but realistic western shows "heroes" as good, ordinary people. **90m/B VHS.** Claire Trevor, Albert Dekker, Barry Sullivan, Henry Hull, Porter Hall, Percy Kilbride; *D:* George Archainbaud; *M:* Miklos Rozsa.

A Woman of the World **1925** After being betrayed in love, sophisticated Italian Countess Elnora (Negri) decides to visit distant cousins in their conservative Iowa town. She causes a scandal with her liberated behavior that both disturbs and intrigues stuffy DA Granger (Herbert) and he tries to run her out of town. Outraged, Elnora uses a handy horsewhip to teach him some manners, which apparently—uh—excites the guy since he changes his mind. Definitely offers a melodramatic shock. **70m/B DVD.** Pola Negri, Holmes Herbert, Chester Conklin, Lucille Ward, Charles Emmet Mack, Blanche Mehaffey, Guy Oliver; *D:* Malcolm St.Clair; *W:* Lucille Ward, Pierre Collings; *C:* Bert Glennon.

Woman of the Year **1942** First classic Tracy/Hepburn pairing concerns the rocky marriage of a renowned political columnist and a lowly sportswriter. Baseball scene with Hepburn at her first game is delightful. Hilarious, rich entertainment that tries to answer the question "What really matters in life?" Tracy and Hepburn began a close friendship that paralleled their quarter-century celluloid partnership. Hepburn shepherded Kamin and Lardner's Oscar-winning script past studio chief Louis B. Mayer, wearing four-inch heels to press her demands. Mayer caved in, Tracy was freed from making "The Yearling," and the rest is history. **114m/B VHS, DVD.** Spencer Tracy, Katharine Hepburn, Fay Bainter, Dan Tobin, Reginald Owen, Roscoe Karns, William Bendix, Minor Watson; *D:* George Stevens; *W:* Ring Lardner Jr., Michael Kanin; *C:* Joseph Ruttenberg; *M:* Franz Waxman. Oscars '42: Orig. Screenplay, Natl. Film Reg. '99.

The Woman on Pier 13 1/2 **1950** Brad Collins (Ryan) is now the VP of a San Francisco shipping company but in his wayward youth (and under another name), he was a dockworker who joined the Communist Party. Now he's being blackmailed by Commie Vanning (Gomez), who wants Brad to call a strike or else. Wife Nan (Day) is confused by Brad's strange behavior, which leads to all sorts of complications in this Red Scare melodrama. The title makes no sense but audiences disliked the preview title "I Married a Communist." **73m/B DVD.** Robert Ryan, Laraine Day, John Agar, Thomas Gomez, Janis Carter, Richard Rober, William Talman; *D:* Robert Stevenson; *W:* Charles Grayson, Robert D. (Robert Hardy) Andrews; *C:* Nicholas Musuraca; *M:* Leigh Harline.

Woman on Top 1/2 **2000 (R)** Mildly amusing romantic comedy that's held together by the charm of its lead. Beautiful Brazilian Isabella (Cruz) suffers from extreme motion sickness, which means she must always be in control. She's a whiz in the kitchen and her talents make her husband's (Benicio) restaurant a big success. But Izzie takes off for San Francisco when she discovers Toninho with another gal. Thanks to her culinary skills (and some magical realism), Isabella soon has her own cable cooking show and men (literally) falling at her feet. First there's "Like Water for Chocolate," then there's "Simply Irresistible," and now "Woman" completes the trifecta of food overwhelming the emotions. **93m/C VHS, DVD.** Penelope Cruz, Harold Perrineau Jr., Mark Feuerstein, Murilo Benicio, John de Lancie; *D:* Fina Torres; *W:* Vera Blasi; *C:* Thierry Arbogast; *M:* Luis Bacalov.

A Woman Rebels 1/2 **1936** A young Victorian woman challenges Victorian society by fighting for women's rights. Excellent performance from Hepburn lifts what might have been a forgettable drama. Screen debut of Van Heflin. Based on Netta Syrett's "Portrait of a Rebel." **88m/B VHS.** Katharine Hepburn, Herbert Marshall, Elizabeth Allan, Donald Crisp, Van Heflin; *D:* Mark Sandrich.

Woman, Thou Art Loosed 1/2 **2004 (R)** Critics may have been divided on this pic's merits but female audiences gave it strong word-of-mouth support. Based on the self-help novel by charismatic Bishop T.D. Jakes (who plays himself), "Woman" follows the lifelong misfortunes of Michelle (a ferocious Elise), a young black victim of poverty, rape, drug addiction, and eventual imprisonment for murder. The flashback structure of the story (Jakes offers a compassionate ear as Michelle tells her story) is somewhat distracting, but Foster's script offers multi-dimensional characters even if it's a little self-conscious. **99m/C DVD.** Kimberly Elise, Loretta Devine, Debbi (Deborah) Morgan, Michael Boatman, Clifton Powell, Sean Blakemore, Ricky Harris; *D:* Michael A. Schultz; *C:* Reinhart Pesche.

Woman Times Seven 1/2 *Sept Fois Femme; Sette Volte Donna* **1967 (PG)** Italian sexual comedy: seven sketches, each starring MacLaine with a different leading man. Stellar cast and good director should have delivered more, but what they have provided has its comedic moments. **99m/C VHS.** *IT FR* Shirley MacLaine, Peter Sellers, Rossano Brazzi, Vittorio Gassman, Lex Barker, Elsa Martinelli, Robert Morley, Alan Arkin, Michael Caine, Patrick Wymark, Anita Ekberg, Philippe Noiret, Elspeth March; *D:* Vittorio De Sica.

A Woman under the Influence **1974 (R)** Strong performances highlight this overlong drama about a family's disintegration. Rowlands is the lonely, middle-aged housewife who's having a breakdown and Falk is her blue-collar husband who can't handle what's going on. **147m/C VHS, DVD.** Gena Rowlands, Peter Falk, Matthew Cassel, Matthew Laborteaux, Christina Grisanti; *D:* John Cassavetes; *W:* John Cassavetes; *C:* Caleb Deschanel, Mitch Breit. Golden Globes '75: Actress—Drama (Rowlands); Natl. Bd. of Review '74: Actress (Rowlands), Natl. Film Reg. '90.

Woman Undone 1/2 *Joshua Tree* **1995 (R)** Husband Allen Hansen (Quaid) and wife Terri (McDonnell) are involved in a car crash on a lonely stretch of desert highway. He dies, she's thrown clear, but an autopsy reveals he was actually shot in the head before the accident. Then attorney Ross Bishop (Elliott) gets involved and in a California courtroom Terri must prove that her unhappy marriage wasn't ended by murder. **91m/C VHS.** Mary McDonnell, Randy Quaid, Sam Elliott, Benjamin Bratt; *D:* Evelyn Purcell; *W:* William Mickelberry; *C:* Toyomichi Kurita; *M:* Daniel Licht.

Woman Wanted **1998 (R)** Vivacious Emma Riley (Hunter) is hired by as a live-in housekeeper by widowed professor Richard Goddard (Moriarty) and his troubled son Wendell (Sutherland). Both men fall in love with her and Emma, who loves Richard, nevertheless has a one-nighter with Wendell. Then she winds up pregnant. Rather yakky but these are actors who are worth watching. Based on the novel by Glass, who also wrote the screenplay. **110m/C VHS.** Holly Hunter, Michael Moriarty, Kiefer Sutherland; *D:* Kiefer Sutherland; *W:* Joanna McClelland Glass. **CABLE**

The Woman Who Came Back **1945** A young woman who believes she suffers from a witch's curse returns to her small hometown with unhappy results. Good cast; bad script. Indifference inducing. **69m/B VHS, DVD.** Nancy Kelly, Otto Kruger, John Loder, Ruth Ford, Jeanne Gail; *D:* Walter Colmes; *W:* Dennis J. Cooper, Lee Willis; *C:* Henry Sharp; *M:* Edward Plumb.

The Woman Who Loved Elvis 1/2 **1993 (PG-13)** TV movie about an obsessive fan who converts her home into an Elvis shrine. **?m/C VHS, DVD.** Roseanne, Tom Arnold, Cynthia Gibb, Sally Kirkland, Danielle Harris, Joe Guzaldo; *D:* Bill Bixby. **TV**

The Woman Who Willed a Miracle **1983** TV drama has a devoted mother encouraging her mentally retarded son to pursue his interest in the piano. **72m/C VHS.** Cloris Leachman, James Noble; *D:* Sharron Miller. **TV**

Woman with a Past 1/2 **1992 (PG-13)** Reed gets out of an abusive marriage only to have her ex kidnap their kids. Since the law's no help she hires a bounty hunter to find them—committing armed robbery to pay the fees. Caught and imprisoned, Reed escapes, changes her identity, remarries, and even is reunited with her sons. Then she's suddenly arrested when her fugitive status comes to light 10 years later. Based on a true story; made for TV melodrama. **95m/C VHS.** Pamela Reed, Dwight Schultz, Paul LeMat, Carrie Snodgress, Richard Lineback; *D:* Mimi Leder. **TV**

A Woman Without Love **1951** A rarely seen film from Bunuel's Mexican period based on a classic Guy de Maupassant tale about a forbidden romance. Family tragedy results later when the husband "misbequeaths" his fortune. Minor but fascinating bug-the-bourgeoisie Bunuel. In Spanish with English subtitles. **91m/C VHS.** *MX* Rosario Granados, Julio Villareal, Tito Junco; ***D:*** Luis Bunuel.

The Womaneater **1959** This '50s oddity makes a belated appearance on home video. Dr. James Moran (Coulouris) returns from the depths of the Amazon jungle (obviously a set filled with plastic plants) with a miraculous tree that's a close cousin of "Audrey" in the original "Little Shop of Horrors." To maintain its healing powers, the doctor must feed it a steady diet of young women. Not a good sign for his sexy housekeeper Sally (Day). It's every bit as silly as it sounds, swiftly paced and short. **71m/B VHS, DVD.** *GB* Vera Day, George Coulouris, Robert MacKenzie, Norman Claridge, Marpessa Dawn, Jimmy Vaughan; ***D:*** Charles Saunders; ***W:*** Brandon Fleming; ***C:*** Ernest Palmer; ***M:*** Edwin Astley.

A Woman's a Helluva Thing **2001 (R)** Lewd men's magazine publisher Houston loses his macho swagger when he heads home for his mother's funeral and learns that not only did she have a lesbian lover but that it's his ex-girlfriend, and that she stands to inherit the entire estate. **94m/C VHS, DVD.** Angus MacFadyen, Penelope Ann Miller, Ann-Margret, Kathryn Harrold, Mary Kay Place, Barry Del Sherman, Paul Dooley, Jonas Chernick, John Robinson; ***D:*** Karen Leigh Hopkins; ***W:*** Karen Leigh Hopkins; ***C:*** Barry Parrell; ***M:*** Louis Febre, Thomas Kilzer. **VIDEO**

A Woman's Face *En Kvinnas Ansikte* **1938** An unpleasant, bitter woman with a hideous scar on her face blackmails illicit lovers as a form of revenge for a happiness she doesn't know. She even plots to murder a child for his inheritance. But after plastic surgery, she becomes a nicer person and doubts her plan. Lean, tight suspense with a bang-up finale. In Swedish with English subtitles. Remade in Hollywood in 1941. **100m/B VHS.** *SW* Ingrid Bergman, Anders Henrikson, Karin Carlsson, Georg Rydeberg, Goran Bernhard, Tore Svennberg; ***D:*** Gustaf Molander.

A Woman's Face **1941** A physically and emotionally scarred woman becomes part of a blackmail ring. Plastic surgery restores her looks and her attitude. Begins with a murder trial and told in flashbacks; tight, suspenseful remake of the 1938 Swedish Ingrid Bergman vehicle. Climax will knock you out of your chair. **107m/B VHS.** Joan Crawford, Conrad Veidt, Melvyn Douglas, Osa Massen, Reginald Owen, Albert Bassermann, Marjorie Main, Donald Meek, Charles Quigley, Henry Daniell, George Zucco, Robert Warwick; ***D:*** George Cukor; ***W:*** Donald Ogden Stewart, Elliot Paul; ***C:*** Robert Planck; ***M:*** Bronislau Kaper.

A Woman's Guide to Adultery **1/2 1993** Four female friends, living and working in London, find their lives turned upside down by their passions for unavailable men. Political advisor Jo (Donohoe) is involved with married politician Martin (McElhinney) while art tutor Jennifer (Gillies) wants her student David (Morrissey), despite his having a live-in girlfriend. Ad execs Helen (Lacey) and Michael (Dunbar) find their marriage in tatters when Helen admits to an affair with their boss and photographer Rose (Russell) breaks her own rule about adultery by getting involved with married university instructor Paul (Bean). Based on the novel by Carol Clewlow. Made for TV. **145m/C VHS, DVD.** *GB* Theresa Russell, Amanda Donohoe, Sean Bean, Adrian Dunbar, Ingrid Lacey, Fiona Gillies, Neil Morrissey, Danny (Daniel) Webb, Ian McElhinney, Julie Peasgood, Caroline Lee-Johnson; ***D:*** David Hayman; ***W:*** Frank Cottrell-Boyce; ***C:*** Graham Frake; ***M:*** Daemion Barry. **TV**

A Woman's Secret **1949** O'Hara admits to murder she didn't commit. Why? It's as indiscernible as why the plot should be muddled by flashbacks. RKO lost big bucks on this one. **85m/B VHS.** Maureen O'Hara, Melvyn Douglas, Gloria Grahame, Bill Williams, Victor Jory, Jay C. Flippen; ***D:*** Nicholas Ray; ***W:*** Herman J. Mankiewicz.

A Woman's Tale **1992 (PG-13)** The superlative performance of Florence highlights this look at aging and death. Martha, 78, has been diagnosed with terminal lung cancer. She is looked after by a much-younger nurse and in turn looks after the older friends who share her apartment house. This gentle story quietly depicts the feisty, joyous Martha's last days and the simple pleasures she derives from her remaining time. Florence herself died from cancer not long after completing the film. **94m/C VHS.** *AU* Sheila Florance, Gosia Dobrowolska, Norman Kaye, Chris Haywood, Myrtle Woods, Ernest Gray, Monica Maughan, Bruce Myles, Alex Menglet; ***D:*** Paul Cox; ***W:*** Paul Cox. Australian Film Inst. '91: Actress (Florance).

A Woman's World **1954** Slick, sophisticated look at big business in the '50s, with Webb as the boss who chooses his next general manager based on the suitability of the executive's wives. Beautiful costumes, witty dialogue, and good acting make this worthwhile viewing. Plus, film offers a nostalgic look at New York in the '50s, with several shots of Fifth Avenue, Macy's, Park Avenue, and the long-gone Stork Club. Based on a story by Mona Williams. **94m/C VHS.** Clifton Webb, June Allyson, Van Heflin, Lauren Bacall, Fred MacMurray, Arlene Dahl, Cornel Wilde, Elliott Reid, Margalo Gillmore, Alan Reed, David Hoffman, George Melford; ***D:*** Jean Negulesco; ***W:*** Claude Binyon, Richard Sale, Mary Loos, Howard Lindsay, Russel Crouse; ***C:*** Joe MacDonald; ***M:*** Cyril Mockridge.

Wombling Free **1977** An English girl makes friends with a race of tiny, litter-hating furry creatures called Wombles. The creatures are visible only to the little girl because she is the only one who believes. Together they try to clean up a dirty world. British society is less cutting-edge about social roles, etc. than our enlightened one; be prepared for retrograde characterizations. Fun scene with Kelly/Astaire-style dance number. **86m/C VHS.** *GB* Bonnie Langford, David Tomlinson; ***D:*** Lionel Jeffries; ***M:*** George Bassman.

The Women **1/2 1939** A brilliant adaptation of the Clare Boothe Luce stage comedy about a group of women who destroy their best friends' reputations at various social gatherings. Crawford's portrayal of the nasty husband-stealer is classic, and the fashion-show scene in Technicolor is one not to miss. Hilarious bitchiness all around. Remade semi-musically as "The Opposite Sex." Another in that long list of stellar 1939 pics. **133m/B VHS, DVD.** Norma Shearer, Joan Crawford, Rosalind Russell, Joan Fontaine, Mary Boland, Lucile Watson, Margaret Dumont, Paulette Goddard, Ruth Hussey, Marjorie Main; ***D:*** George Cukor; ***W:*** Anita Loos; ***C:*** Joseph Ruttenberg. Natl. Film Reg. '07.

The Women **1/2** *Les Femmes; The Vixen* **1968** Plodding romantic comedy about a blocked writer and his muse. Dizzy Clara (Bardot) is secretary to middle-aged womanizer Jerome (Ronet), who is attempting to work on his memoirs. Inspired by her beauty, Jerome sets out to seduce Clara, which also reinvigorates his writing. But he's thinking fling and she's thinking something more permanent. French with subtitles. **86m/C VHS, DVD.** *FR IT* Brigitte Bardot, Maurice Ronet, Anny (Annie Legras) Duperey, Jean-Pierre Marielle, Christina Holme; ***D:*** Jean Aurel; ***W:*** Jean Aurel, Cecil Saint-Laurent; ***C:*** Claude Lecomte; ***M:*** Luis Fuentes Jr.

Women **1/2** *Elles* **1997** Linda (Maura) is a journalist who asks her equally middleaged female friends what they would do with three wishes. Wishes may not help as the ladies suffer through career and family crises, infidelity, affairs, and aging. French with subtitles. **94m/C VHS, DVD.** *FR* Carmen Maura, Miou-Miou, Marthe Keller, Marisa Berenson, Guesch Patti, Joaquim de Almeida, Didier Flamand, Morgan Perez; ***D:*** Luis Galvao Teles; ***W:*** Don Bohlinger, Luis Galvao Teles; ***C:*** Alfredo Mayo; ***M:*** Alejandro Masso.

The Women **1/2 2008 (PG-13)** Only borrowing the title and a few ideas from the 1939 film, and mostly just taking inspiration for the original play by Clare Booth Luce—this all-female comedy is very much its own. Wiser and funnier than the women in "Sex and the City," four close friends help each other get through the ups and downs of life—one married with four kids (Messing), one married to a Wall Street millionaire who's cheating on her (Ryan), one a successful fashion magazine editor (Bening), and one who's simply a lesbian (Smith), nothing more. However, even with sharp, honest dialogue and an amazing cast, the introduction of too many characters and too much melodrama ruins what could have been truly great. By the way, take the title literally: not a single man is ever on screen. **m/C DVD.** Meg Ryan, Annette Bening, Eva Mendes, Debra Messing, Jada Pinkett Smith, Bette Midler, Candice Bergen, Carrie Fisher, Cloris Leachman, Debi Mazar, Joanna Gleason, Ana Gasteyer, India Ennenga, Lynn Whitfield; ***D:*** Diane English; ***W:*** Diane English; ***C:*** Anastas Michos; ***M:*** Mark Isham.

Women & Men: In Love There Are No Rules **1/2 1991 (R)** Extravaganza chronicling the relationships of three couples, each adapted from the short story of a renowned author. Irwin Shaw's "Return to Kansas City" tells of a young boxer who is prematurely pushed into a match by his ambitious wife. In Carson McCullers' "A Domestic Dilemma," a marriage begins to crumble thanks to an alcoholic wife. Finally, Henry Miller's "Mara" has an aging man and a young Parisian prostitute spending a revealing evening together. **90m/C VHS.** Matt Dillon, Kyra Sedgwick, Ray Liotta, Andie MacDowell, Scott Glenn, Juliette Binoche, Jerry Stiller; ***D:*** Kristi Zea, Walter Bernstein, Mike Figgis. **CABLE**

Women & Men: Stories of Seduction **1/2 1990** Three famous short stories are brought to the screen in this made-for-TV collection. Mary McCarthy's "The Man in the Brooks Brothers Shirt," Dorothy Parker's "Dusk Before Fireworks," and Hemingway's "Hills Like White Elephants" between them cover every aspect of male-female relationships. Since there are three casts and three directors, there is little to join the stories in style, calling attention to some flaws in pacing and acting ability; still, worth watching. **90m/C VHS, DVD.** James Woods, Melanie Griffith, Peter Weller, Elizabeth McGovern, Beau Bridges, Molly Ringwald; ***D:*** Ken Russell, Tony Richardson, Frederic Raphael.

Women from the Lake of Scented Souls **1994** Mournful film, set in a rural Chinese village, focuses on matriarchal businesswoman Xiang (Gaowa), who runs the local sesame oil making factory that has just attracted the attention of Japanese investors. Seems the water of the nearby lotus-covered lake, scene of local tragedies, is Xiang's special ingredient. With her newfound wealth, Xiang is able to purchase a very reluctant bride, Huanhuan (Yujuan), for her mentally retarded son—a disaster in the making. Rich detail and nuanced performances; Chinese with subtitles. **105m/C VHS, DVD.** *CH* Siqin Gaowa, Wu Yujuan, Lei Luosheng, Chen Baoguo; ***D:*** Xie Fei; ***W:*** Xie Fei; ***C:*** Bao Xianran; ***M:*** Wang Liping.

Women in Cell Block 7 **WOOF!** *Diario Segreto Di Un Carcere Femminele* **1977 (R)** Exploitative skinfest about women in prison suffering abuse from their jailers and each other. Seems that one of the prisoners knows the location of massive heroin stash. Badly dubbed. **100m/C VHS, DVD.** *IT* Anita Strindberg, Eve Czemeys, Olga Bisera, Jane Avril, Valeria Fabrizi, Jenny Tamburi; ***D:*** Rino Di Silvestro.

Women in Fury **WOOF! 1984** A woman is sentenced to imprisonment in a mostly lesbian Brazilian jail, and subsequently leads a breakout. **94m/C VHS, DVD.** *IT BR* Suzanne Carvalno, Gloria Cristal, Zeni Pereira, Leonardo Jose; ***D:*** Michele Massimo Tarantini; ***W:*** Michele Massimo Tarantini; ***C:*** Edson Batista; ***M:*** Remo Usai.

Women in Love **1970 (R)** Atmospheric drama of two steamy affairs, based on D.H. Lawrence's classic novel. Forward-thinking artist Gudrun (Jackson) and her teacher sister Ursula (Linden) are introduced to Gerald (Reed) and Rupert (Bates). The more conventional Ursual and Rupert marry while Gudrun and Gerald have an affair that ends violently when Gudrun takes up with another man. Deservedly Oscar-winning performance by Jackson; controversial nude wrestling scene with Bates and Reed is hard to forget. Followed nearly two decades later (1989) by a "prequel": "The Rainbow," also from Lawrence, also directed by Russell and featuring Jackson. **129m/C VHS, DVD.** *GB* Glenda Jackson, Jennie Linden, Alan Bates, Oliver Reed, Michael Gough, Eleanor Bron, Vladek Sheybal; ***D:*** Ken Russell; ***W:*** Larry Kramer; ***C:*** Billy Williams; ***M:*** Georges Delerue. Oscars '70: Actress (Jackson); Golden Globes '71: Foreign Film; Natl. Bd. of Review '70: Actress (Jackson); N.Y. Film Critics '70: Actress (Jackson); Natl. Soc. Film Critics '70: Actress (Jackson).

Women in Prison *Women without Names* **1949** A pseudo-documentary style expose of the hardships endured by women in Italian detention camps following WWII. Controversial for its examination of such themes as human rights, abortion, lesbianism, and sexuality. English, French, Italian, with English subtitles. **94m/C VHS.** *IT* Simone Simon; ***D:*** Geza Radvanyi; ***W:*** Geza Radvanyi.

Women in Trouble **2009 (R)** Director Gutierrez unleashes an uninhibited soap opera about the intersecting lives of a number of women dealing with life-altering crises. Newly pregnant porn star Elektra (Gugino) gets stuck in an elevator with nervous neurotic Doris (Britton). Meanwhile her X-rated co-star Holly Rocket (Palicki) takes on a private client with her pal Bambi (Chriqui). As the plotlines intertwine, the characters are linked by a series of coincidences and their effects. Raunchy behavior and dialogue may offend those with delicate sensibilities. Shot in twelve days on a low budget, this is the first installment in a planned trilogy. The soundtrack is by esteemed alt-rocker Robyn Hitchcock. **95m/C DVD.** *US* Adrianne Palicki, Isabella Gutierrez, Carla Gugino, Connie Britton, Emmanuelle Chriqui, Sarah Clarke, Marley Shelton, Rya Kihlstedt, Caitlin Keats, Cameron Richardson, Josh Brolin, Simon Baker, Joseph Gordon-Levitt, Robyn Hitchcock; ***D:*** Sebastian Gutierrez; ***W:*** Sebastian Gutierrez; ***C:*** Cale Finot; ***M:*** Robyn Hitchcock.

Women of All Nations **1931** Buddies in the Marines, Quirt and Flagg (McLaglen and Lowe) fought together in WWI and Panama and are post-war buddies stateside in New York, but now they find themselves fighting for the love of the beautiful Else, whom they meet in Sweden. But first they go to Nicaragua to help earthquake victims. After that, strangely, they're off to Egypt where Else's somehow gotten herself a spot in Prince Hassan's (Lugosi) harem. Apparently Humphrey Bogart was in this film, but all his scenes were cut. **72m/B VHS.** Victor McLaglen, Edmund Lowe, Greta Nissen, El Brendel; ***D:*** Raoul Walsh; ***W:*** Maxwell Anderson.

The Women of Brewster Place **1989** Seven black women living in a tenement fight to gain control of their lives. (Men in general don't come out too well.) Excellent, complex script gives each actress in a fine ensemble headed by Winfrey (in her TV dramatic debut) time in the limelight. Pilot for the series "Brewster Place." Based on the novel by Gloria Naylor. Winfrey was executive producer. **180m/C VHS, DVD.** Oprah Winfrey, Mary Alice, Olivia Cole, Robin Givens, Moses Gunn, Jackee, Paula Kelly, Lonette McKee, Paul Winfield, Cicely Tyson; ***D:*** Donna Deitch; ***W:*** Karen Hall; ***C:*** Alexander Grusynski; ***M:*** David Shire. **TV**

Women of the Prehistoric Planet **WOOF! 1966** On a strange planet, the members of a space rescue mission face deadly perils. Typical bad sci-fi of its era, with horrid special effects, including "giant" lizards. Get this: there's one woman, and she's not of the planet in question. See if you can last long enough to catch the amazing plot twist at the end. **87m/C VHS.** John Agar, Wendell Corey, Irene Tsu, Robert Ito, Stuart Margolin, Lyle Waggoner, Adam Roarke, Merry Anders; ***D:*** Arthur C. Pierce.

Women of Valor **1/2 1986** During WWII, a band of American nurses stationed in the Philippines are captured by the Japanese and struggle to survive in a brutal POW camp. TV feature was made 40 years too late, adding up to a surreal experience. **95m/C VHS, DVD.** Susan Sarandon, Kristy McNichol, Alberta Watson, Valerie Mahaffey, Suzanne Lederer, Pat Bishop, Terry O'Quinn, Neva

Patterson; *D:* Buzz Kulik; *C:* Mike Fash; *M:* Georges Delerue. **TV**

The Women on the Roof *Kvinnorna pa Taket* **1989** Naive Linnea (Ooms) rents an attic apartment in Stockholm, just before the start of WWI. Her neighbor is Anna (Bergstrom), an artist working on a tableaux that soon involves Linnea, as the women become friends and then lovers. The reappearance of Anna's former boyfriend Willy (Skarskard) leads to a menage a trois until an accident compels Anna to reveal secrets that alter their lives. Swedish with subtitles. **86m/C VHS.** *SW* Helena Bergstrom, Amanda Ooms, Stellan Skarsgard; *D:* Carl-Gustaf Nykvist; *W:* Carl-Gustaf Nykvist, Lasse Summanen; *C:* Jorgen Persson, Ulf Brantas.

Women on the Verge of a Nervous Breakdown 1/2 *Mujeres al Borde de un Ataque de Nervios* **1988 (R)** Surreal and hilarious romp through the lives of film dubber Maura, her ex-lover, his crazed wife, his new lover, his son, and his son's girlfriend. There's also Maura's friend Barranco, who inadvertantly lent her apartment to Shiite terrorists and now believes the police are after her as an accomplice in an airline hijacking. They meet in a comedy of errors, missed phone calls, and rental notices, while discovering the truth and necessity of love. Fast-paced and full of black humor, with loaded gazpacho serving as a key element. Introduced Almodovar to American audiences. In Spanish with English subtitles. **88m/C VHS, DVD.** *SP* Carmen Maura, Fernando Guillen, Julieta Serrano, Maria Barranco, Rossy de Palma, Antonio Banderas; *D:* Pedro Almodovar; *W:* Pedro Almodovar; *C:* Jose Luis Alcaine; *M:* Bernardo Bonezzi. N.Y. Film Critics '88: Foreign Film.

Women Unchained WOOF! 1972 (R) Five women escape from a maximum security prison and make a run for the Mexican border, shunning civilized behavior along the way. Much less-than-honorable entry in desperate women genre. **82m/C VHS.** Carolyn Judd, Teri Guzman, Darlene Mattingly, Angel Colbert, Bonita Kalem; *D:* Kent Osborne; *W:* Kent Osborne.

Women vs. Men **2002 (R)** Michael (Mantegna) is a typical married guy bewildered when Dana (Lahti), his wife of 20 years, begins behaving out of character. (She's basically fed up with her hubby and their boring marriage.) His best bud Bruce (Reiser) decides they should go to a strip club and commiserate but doesn't know that Dana is following them. Furious, Dana reports the guys' sleazy night out to Bruce's wife, Brita (Headley). Equally peeved, they kick their husbands out, leading Michael and Bruce to get advice from their swinger divorced buddy Nick (Pastorelli). Basic battle-of-the-sexes flick. **88m/C VHS, DVD.** Joe Mantegna, Christine Lahti, Paul Reiser, Glenne Headly, Jennifer Coolidge, Robert Pastorelli, Marshall Herskovitz, Jon Polito; *D:* Chazz Palminteri; *W:* David J. Burke. **CABLE**

Women Without Men *Zanan Bedoone Mardan* **2009** In 1953 in Iran, a CIA-backed coup topples the government and installs the Shah. Munis kills herself after hearing the news while the unhappily married Fakhri leaves her army officer husband to occupy a rundown house where prostitute Zarin also takes refuge. Based on the novella by Shahrnush Parsipur; Farsi with subtitles. **100m/C DVD.** *AT FR GE* Pegah Ferydoni, Artia Shahrzad, Shabnam Toloui, Orsi Toth, Bijan Daneshmand; *D:* Shirin Neshat, Shoja Azari; *W:* Shirin Neshat, Shoja Azari, Steven Henry Madoff; *C:* Martin Gschlacht; *M:* Ryuichi Sakamoto, Abbas Bakhtiari.

Women's Club 1/2 **1987 (R)** Table-turning sex comedy about a wealthy matron who patronizes a talented (?) young movie writer, but really wants—you know what. She begins lending his services to friends—and does he ever get worn out! This excuse may be intended to be uproarious, but it's hard to tell. And all that sex gets very perfunctory after awhile. **89m/C VHS.** Michael Pare, Maud Adams, Eddie Velez; *D:* Sandra Weintraub; *M:* Paul Antonelli.

Women's Prison Escape 1/2 *Cell Block Girls; Thunder County* **1974** Four tough broads blow the pen and are forced to high-tail it through the Everglades. They can't decide which is worse, the snakes and 'gators, or the corrupt and sleazy life they left behind. Only cinematic pairing of Rooney and Lurch. **90m/C VHS, DVD.** Ted Cassidy, Chris Robinson, Mickey Rooney; *D:* Chris Robinson.

Women's Prison Massacre WOOF! 1985 Four male convicts temporarily detained at a woman's prison (why?) violently take hostages and generally make trouble for the authorities and the women. Horribly dubbed. **89m/C VHS, DVD.** *IT* Laura Gemser, Lorraine (De Sette) De Selle, Francois Perrot, Ursula Flores, Gabriele Tinti; *D:* Gilbert Roussel.

Wonder Bar **1934** This Pre-Hays Code Jolson pic pushes the limits for suggestiveness with Busby Berkeley doing his usual extravagant choreography. Al Wonder (Jolson) is the owner of a Paris nightspot who's in love with dancer Inez (Del Rio). So's band singer Tommy (Powell) but Inez only has eyes for her gigolo partner Harry (Cortez). Harry's cheating with married socialite Liane (Francis) and there's a bunch more subplots about the customers and such. Jolson (in blackface) does the now-very dated (not to mention strange) song 'I'm Going to Heaven on a Mule' accompanied by a number of black children with all the angels black as well. **84m/B DVD.** Al Jolson, Dick Powell, Dolores Del Rio, Ricardo Cortez, Kay Francis, Guy Kibbee, Ruth Donnelly, Louise Fazenda; *D:* Lloyd Bacon; *W:* Earl Baldwin; *C:* Sol Polito.

Wonder Boys **2000 (R)** Curis Hanson's excellent follow up to "L.A. Confidential" pits professor and former literary star Grady (Douglas in his finest performance in years) against a strange case of writer's block, his flamboyant New York editor (Downey), an approaching literary festival, and several converging mid-life crises. His wife's just left, he's having an affair with the school chancellor (McDormand), who's the wife of his boss and has just informed him that she's pregnant, and his prize pupil is a death-obsessed compulsive liar (Maguire) who shoots his boss's dog and steals a valuable piece of memorabilia. On paper it seems chaotic, but the screwball comedy manages to be subtle and understated. Based on Michael Chambon's novel. **112m/C VHS, DVD.** Michael Douglas, Tobey Maguire, Frances McDormand, Katie Holmes, Robert Downey Jr., Richard Thomas, Rip Torn, Philip Bosco, Jane Adams; *D:* Curtis Hanson; *W:* Steve Kloves; *C:* Dante Spinotti; *M:* Christopher Young. Oscars '00: Song ("Things Have Changed"); Golden Globes '01: Song ("Things Have Changed").

Wonder Man 1/2 **1945** When a brash nightclub entertainer (Kaye) is killed by gangsters, his mild-mannered twin brother (Kaye) takes his place to smoke out the killers. One of Kaye's better early films. The film debuts of Vera-Ellen and Cochran. Look for Mrs. Howell of "Gilligan's Island." ♫ So In Love; Bali Boogie; Ortchi Chornya; Opera Number. **98m/C VHS, DVD.** Danny Kaye, Virginia Mayo, Vera-Ellen, Steve Cochran, S.Z. Sakall, Otto Kruger, Natalie Schafer; *D:* H. Bruce Humberstone; *W:* Jack Jevne, Eddie Moran, Don Hartman, Melville Shavelson, Philip Rapp; *C:* Victor Milner; *M:* Ray Heindorf.

The Wonderful Ice Cream Suit 1/2 **1998 (PG)** Slapstick hokum based on Bradbury's 1957 story "The Magic White Suit." Cash-poor barrio sharpster Gomez (Mantegna) would like to buy a flashy white suit he sees in a shop window and manages to convince four more men of roughly the same size to pony up some money and have shares in the suit. Each take a turn wearing the garment and find their various dreams coming true. **77m/C VHS.** Joe Mantegna, Esai Morales, Edward James Olmos, Clifton (Gonzalez) Collins Jr., Gregory Sierra, Liz Torres, Sid Caesar, Howard Morris, Lisa Vidal, Mike Moroff; *D:* Stuart Gordon; *W:* Ray Bradbury; *C:* Mac Ahlberg.

Wonderful World 1/2 **2009 (R)** Once a semi-successful children's music performer, discontented, pot-smoking misanthrope Ben Singer (Broderick playing the ultimate mope) is now floundering in his proofreading job and as a weekend dad. He's such a hopeless downer that even his tween daughter Sandra (Ferland) is refusing his custodial visits. Ben's only friendship is with his Sengalese roommate Ibou (Williams), who falls into a diabetic coma and then becomes part of a managed medical care nightmare. Ben decides a lawsuit against the city is the way to go but that has unexpected consequences, including the arrival of Ibou's hopeful sister Khadi (Lathan) who moves in with Ben (and starts him rethinking his depressing ways) while her brother's fate is being decided. **95m/C DVD.** *US* Matthew Broderick, Michael K. Williams, Sanaa Lathan, Jodelle Ferland, Ally Walker, Philip Baker Hall, Jesse Tyler Ferguson; *D:* Joshua Goldin; *W:* Joshua Goldin; *C:* Daniel Shulman; *M:* Craig Richey.

The Wonderful World of the Brothers Grimm 1/2 **1962** Big-budget fantasy based very loosely on the Grimm Brothers' lives and three of their stories: "The Dancing Princesses," "The Cobbler and the Elves," and "The Singing Bone." Good, fun Puppetoon scenes, but leaves much else to be desired. A megawatt cast and the ubiquitous hand of producer-director Pal are not enough to cover the flaws. The biographical parts are hokey, and the tales used are the wrong ones. Disappointing but historically interesting. The second-ever story film done in Cinerama. ♫ The Theme From the Wonderful World of the Brothers Grimm; Gypsy Rhapsody; Christmas Land; Ah-Oom; Above the Stars; Dee-Are-A-Gee-O-En (Dragon). **134m/C VHS.** Laurence Harvey, Karl-Heinz Boehm, Claire Bloom, Buddy Hackett, Terry-Thomas, Russ Tamblyn, Yvette Mimieux, Oscar Homolka, Walter Slezak, Beulah Bondi, Martita Hunt, Otto Kruger, Barbara Eden, Jim Backus, Arnold Stang; *D:* Henry Levin, George Pal; *W:* William Roberts; *C:* Paul Vogel. Oscars '62: Costume Des. (C).

Wonderland *The Fruit Machine* **1988** Campy thriller follows two young gay boys in England, inadvertent witnesses to a murder, who find themselves on the run. Fast paced, dreamy atmosphere makes up for the sometimes confusing plot. Often overlooked British import. **103m/C VHS.** *GB* Emile Charles, Tony Forsyth, Robert Stephens, Clare Higgins, Bruce Payne, Robbie Coltrane; *D:* Philip Saville; *W:* Frank Clarke; *C:* Dick Pope; *M:* Hans Zimmer.

Wonderland **1999** Slice of London pic covers four November days in the lives of sisters Debbie (Henderson), Nadia (McKee), and Molly (Parker) and their daily struggles—single parenthood, bad dates, pregnancy, separation, unemployment, and their equally frustrated parents. Yet the film is about the ability to survive rather than about succumbing to despair. **108m/C VHS, DVD.** *GB* Shirley Henderson, Gina McKee, Molly Parker, Ian Hart, John Simm, Stuart Townsend, Kika Markham, Jack Shepherd; *D:* Michael Winterbottom; *W:* Laurence Coriat; *C:* Sean Bobbitt; *M:* Michael Nyman.

Wonderland **2003 (R)** Inferior true-crime drama about down-on-his-luck, druggie porn star John C. Holmes (Kilmer) who got mixed up in a 1981 quadruple homicide at 8763 Wonderland Avenue, where Holmes partied and bought his drugs. Kudrow, in a standout performance, plays his long-suffering wife Sharon and Bosworth his much-younger girlfriend Dawn. While emphasis is on the crime and what role Holmes played in it, pic may have benefited from further exploring the relationship between Sharon and Dawn, who became life-long friends. The anatomically gifted Holmes, is adequately portrayed by Kilmer. Told in confused, back and forward chronology, events and motivations muddle an interesting story much better articulated in director Anderson's fictitious but far superior ode to the porno industry, "Boogie Nights." **99m/C VHS, DVD.** *US* Val Kilmer, Kate (Catherine) Bosworth, Lisa Kudrow, Dylan McDermott, Eric Bogosian, Josh(ua) Lucas, Christina Applegate, Tim Blake Nelson, Ted Levine, Natasha Gregson Wagner, Janeane Garofalo, Franky G., M.C. Gainey, Carrie Fisher, Faizon Love; *D:* James Cox; *W:* James Cox, Captain Mauzner, Todd Samovitz, D. Loriston Scott; *C:* Michael Grady; *M:* Michael A. Levine.

Wonderland Cove **1975** Seafaring adventurer adopts five orphan children and embarks on journeys to exotic locales. **78m/C VHS.** Clu Gulager, Sean Marshall, Randi Kiger, Lori Walsh; *D:* Jerry Thorpe.

The Wonders of Aladdin 1/2 *Les Mille Et Une Nuits; Le Meraviglie Di Aladino* **1961** Slapstick comedy based on the ancient rubbed-lamp-and-genie chestnut. Kids'll love it; adults will yawn. **93m/C VHS.** *IT FR* Donald O'Connor, Vittorio De Sica; *D:* Henry Levin, Mario Bava.

Wonderwall: The Movie 1/2 **1969** Bizarre characters trip over themselves in love while groovy music plays in background. **82m/C VHS, DVD.** *GB* Jack MacGowran, Jane Birkin, Irene Handl; *D:* Joe Massot; *C:* Harry Waxman; *M:* George Harrison, Eric Clapton, Ravi Shankar.

Wondrous Oblivion **2006 (PG)** Though 11-year-old David (Smith) loves the sport of cricket, he lacks the skills, so when a cricket-loving Jamaican family moves in next door he's overjoyed. The family's patriarch, Dennis Samuels (Lindo) offers to teach him. While the young Jewish boy at first has no qualms about befriending the Samuels, the rest of their South London neighbors aren't so accepting, it being the racially-charged 1960s and all, and eventually David finds himself in an awkward situation. Avoids being sappy, and Lindo really rules as the father. **106m/C DVD.** Sam Smith, Jo Stone-Fewings, Emily Woof, Leagh Conwell, Dominic Barklem, Delroy Lindo, Carol MacReady, Yasmin Paige, Stanley Townsend; *D:* Paul Morrison; *W:* Paul Morrison; *C:* Nina Kellgren; *M:* Ilona Sekacz. **VIDEO**

Wonsan Operation **1978** U.N. soldiers plunge into the muddy depths of enemy territory in search of secret information that would end the Korean War. Dubbed. **100m/C VHS.** Lew Montania, Frederick Hill; *D:* Terrence Sul.

Woo **1997 (R)** Knock-out party girl Darlene "Woo" Bates (Pinkett Smith) agrees to a blind date with nice-guy law student Tim (Davidson) on the advice of her cross-dressing psychic. Tim wants to do the right thing and be honorable, but Woo seduces, endangers, and humiliates him at every turn. When Tim finally stands up for himself, she has a change of heart and appreciates his better qualities. Somewhat mean-spirited comedy trods familiar urban cliches and blind-date disaster territory, but Pinkett Smith's turn could be a star-maker. **80m/C VHS, DVD.** Jada Pinkett Smith, Tommy Davidson, Duane Martin, Dave Chappelle, LL Cool J, Paula Jai Parker, Darrell Heath, Pam Grier, Jsu Garcia, Isaac Hayes; *D:* Daisy von Scherler Mayer; *W:* David C(lark) Johnson; *C:* Jean Lepine; *M:* Michel Colombier.

The Wood 1/2 **1999 (R)** Follows the friendship of three young black men growing up together during the 80s in Inglewood, California. Through the use of flashbacks, their lives are traced from junior high to the imminent wedding day of one of the trio. Mike (Epps) and Slim (Jones) are also forced to track down reluctant groom Roland (Diggs), sober him up, and get him to the church on time. Newcomer Famuyiwa based the script on his own life. Good cast is left with little interesting to do in this likable, but bland, nostalgia-fest. **107m/C VHS, DVD.** Omar Epps, Sean Nelson, Richard T. Jones, Taye Diggs, Trent Cameron, Malinda Williams, Duane Finley, Sanaa Lathan, De'Aundre Bonds, LisaRaye, Cynthia Martells, Tamala Jones, Elayne J. Taylor; *D:* Rick Famuyiwa; *W:* Rick Famuyiwa; *C:* Steven Bernstein; *M:* Robert Hurst.

Woodchipper Massacre WOOF! 1989 Aunt Tess is frozen in the freezer, waiting to be turned into whatever the fleshy equivalent of woodchips is by her three unloving relations, and her totally evil son has just broken out of prison looking to retrieve his inheritance. You think you have problems? You'll have one less if you leave this one on the shelf. **90m/C VHS, DVD.** Jon McBride, Patricia McBride; *D:* Jon McBride.

The Wooden Gun 1/2 *Roveh Huliot* **1979** Conflicts arise between two teenage factions in 1950s Tel Aviv: native Israelis, and the children of Jews arrived from Europe since WWII. In Hebrew with English subtitles. **91m/C VHS, DVD.** *IS* Nadav Brenner, Nissim Eliaz, Michael Kafir, Arik Rosen, Louis Rosenberg; *D:* Ilan Moshenson; *W:* Ilan Moshenson; *C:* Gadi Danzig; *M:* Yossi Mar-Haim.

Wooden Horse **1950** Lean thriller of British POWs escaping a Nazi camp through a tunnel beneath their exercise horse. Based on a true incident in 1943 and on "The Tunnel Escape" by Eric Williams; set the tone for all British prison-camp movies to follow: stiff upper lip and all that, and adolescent-style trickery reminiscent of English boarding schools. **98m/C VHS.** Anthony Steel, Leo Genn, David Tomlinson, Bryan Forbes, Peter Finch; ***D:*** Jack Lee.

The Wooden Man's Bride
1994 The inhabitants of this austere 1920s, northwest Chinese community live in stone fortresses, fearful of being attacked by roving armed bandits. Which is what happens to the bridal party of Young Mistress (Lan), who's kidnapped by bandit leader Tang (Mingjun). She's released unharmed when her servant Kui (Shih) impresses Tang with his bravery but her bridegroom has been killed in a freak accident and formidable Madame Liu (Yumei), who runs the fortress, forces her to marry a wooden likeness of the deceased. Despairing Young Mistress begins an affair with Kui, which can only end badly. Mandarin with subtitles. **114m/C VHS, DVD.** *CH* Wang Lan, Chang Shih, Wang Yu-mei, Kao Mingjun; ***D:*** Huang Jianxin; ***W:*** Yang Zhengguang; ***C:*** Zhang Xiaoguang; ***M:*** Zhang Dalong.

The Woods **2003 (R)** In 1965, isolated Falburn Academy is an all-girls New England boarding school. Troublesome new student Heather (Bruckner) is determined to get thrown out so she can return home, but she's got other problems. It seems the surrounding woods are giving Heather nightmares, her classmates start disappearing, and sinister headmistress Mrs. Traverse (Clarkson) wants to recruit Heather as a witch. Campbell is briefly seen as Heather's clueless pop. **91m/C DVD.** Agnes Bruckner, Patricia Clarkson, Rachel Nichols, Bruce Campbell; ***D:*** Lucky McKee; ***W:*** David Ross; ***C:*** John R. Leonetti; ***M:*** John (Gianni) Frizzell. **VIDEO**

The Woodsman **2004 (R)** Kassell's feature debut is not for the fainthearted. How do you not depict a convicted pedophile of young girls as a monster? It's a measure of Bacon's talents as Walter that if you can't sympathize with his character (and you're not asked to), you do come to some understanding of his torment. Recently paroled after a 12-year prison term, Walter finds a job in a lumberyard and an apartment opposite a grade school. As Walter struggles to keep his sexual impulses in check, he starts his first adult relationship with equally scarred co-worker Vickie (Bacon's wife Sedgwick), even as receptionist Mary-Kay (Eve) and cop Lucas (Mos Def) become suspicious of withdrawn Walter's behavior. Disturbing without becoming explicit and with a sliver of hopefulness in its resolution. Co-writer Fechter adapted from his play. **87m/C DVD.** *US* Kevin Bacon, Kyra Sedgwick, Eve, Mos Def, David Alan Grier, Benjamin Bratt, Michael Shannon, Hannah Pilkes, Carlos Leon; ***D:*** Nicole Kassell; ***W:*** Nicole Kassell, Steven Fechter; ***C:*** Xavier Perez Grobet; ***M:*** Nathan Larson.

Woodstock **1970 (R)** Step into the way-back machine and return to the times of luv, peace, and understanding. Powerful chronicle of the great 1969 Woodstock rock concert celebrates the music and lifestyle of the late '60s. More than 400,000 spectators withstood lack of privacy, bathrooms, parking, and food while wallowing in the mud for four days to catch classic performances by a number of popular performers and groups. Martin Scorcese helped edit the documentary, trail-blazing in its use of split-screen montage. A director's cut is available at 225 minutes. **180m/C VHS, DVD.** ***D:*** Michael Wadleigh. Oscars '70: Feature Doc., Natl. Film Reg. '96.

Woodstock '94 **1/2 1994** The 25th anniversary of the original festival was celebrated with a three-day music explosion (complete with mud). Includes backstage footage and interviews with some of the 30 acts, including Aerosmith, Peter Gabriel, Blind Melon, Metallica, and the Red Hot Chili Peppers. **165m/C VHS.** ***D:*** Bruce Gowers.

The Word **1/2 1978** Intriguing premise has an archeologist finding a perviously unknown text purporting to be written by the younger brother of Jesus. If authentic and publicized, it would wreak theological havoc. Janssen is off to Italy to check up; he finds murder and skullduggery. Well-acted, interesting story. **300m/C VHS.** David Janssen, James Whitmore, Florinda Bolkan, Eddie Albert, Geraldine Chaplin, Hurd Hatfield, John Huston, Kate Mulgrew, Janice Rule, Nicol Williamson; ***D:*** Richard Lang; ***M:*** Alex North.

Word Wars: Tiles and Tribulations on the Scrabble Circuit
2004 Four unconventional competitors make their way to the 2002 National Scrabble Tournament in San Diego pursing the $25, 000 grand prize. The characters are authentic oddballs, their world becomes more arcane and peculiar the longer you're in it, and the suspense approaches desperation at the end, all of which makes the film watchable in this age of reality TV. **80m/C DVD.** ***D:*** Eric Chaikin, Julian Petrillo; ***C:*** Laela Kilbourn; ***M:*** Thor Madsen.

Wordplay **2006** Creadon looks at the passion of crossword puzzle fans and champions by following "New York Times" crossword puzzle editor Will Shortz as he prepares for the 28th annual American Crossword Puzzle Tournament in 2005. He interviews puzzle designers, competitors, and such crossword puzzlers as John Stewart, Bill Clinton, and Ken Burns. **90m/C DVD.** *US* ***D:*** Patrick Creadon; ***W:*** Patrick Creadon, Christine O'Malley; ***C:*** Patrick Creadon; ***M:*** Peter Golub.

Words and Music **1/2 1948** Plot based on the careers of Rodgers and Hart is little more than a peg on which to hang lots of classic songs, sung by a parade of MGM stars. Also includes Kelly's dance recreation of "Slaughter on Tenth Avenue." Good advice: if no one's singing or dancing, fast forward. **122m/C VHS.** Mickey Rooney, Tom Drake, Judy Garland, Gene Kelly, Lena Horne, Mel Torme, Cyd Charisse, Marshall Thompson, Janet Leigh, Betty Garrett, June Allyson, Perry Como, Vera-Ellen, Ann Sothern; ***D:*** Norman Taurog; ***M:*** Richard Rodgers.

Words by Heart **1984** An African American family in turn of the century Missouri faces issues of discrimination and prejudice. Twelve-year-old Lena wins a speech contest and begins to question their place in the community and their aspirations for a better life. Based on a book by Ouida Sebestyen. Aired by PBS as part of the "Wonderworks" family movie series. **116m/C VHS, DVD.** Charlotte Rae, Robert Hooks, Alfre Woodard; ***D:*** Robert Thompson.

The Worker and the Hairdresser *Metalmeccanico e Parrucchiera in un Turbine di Sesso e di Politica* **1996** Married Tunin is a leftist labor organizer who falls instantly into lust with right-wing business zealot Rossella when he spots her at a political rally. The opposites may attract but Rosella is determined to put the would-be Lothario in his place. Italian with subtitles. **104m/C VHS.** *IT* Tullio Solenghi, Gene Gnocchi, Veronica Pivetti, Cyrielle Claire; ***D:*** Lina Wertmuller; ***W:*** Lina Wertmuller, Leonardo Benvenuti, Piero De Bernardi; ***C:*** Blasco Giurato.

Working Girl **1988 (R)** Romantic comedy set in the Big Apple has secretary Tess McGill (Griffith) working her way to the top in spite of her manipulative boss Katherine Parker (Weaver in a powerful parody). Tess gets her chance to shine when Katherine breaks a leg and she strikes a business deal with Jack Trainer (Ford)that turns to romance. A 1980s Cinderella story that's sexy, funny, and sharply written and directed. Nice work by Ford, but this is definitely Griffith's movie. And keep an eye on Tess's gal pal Cynthia (Cusack). ♫Let the River Run. **115m/C VHS, DVD.** Melanie Griffith, Harrison Ford, Sigourney Weaver, Joan Cusack, Alec Baldwin, Philip Bosco, Ricki Lake, Nora Dunn, Olympia Dukakis, Oliver Platt, James Lally, Kevin Spacey, Robert Easton; ***D:*** Mike Nichols; ***W:*** Kevin Wade; ***C:*** Michael Ballhaus; ***M:*** Carly Simon, Rob Mounsey. Oscars '88: Song ("Let the River Run"); Golden Globes '89: Actress—Mus./Comedy (Griffith), Film—Mus./Comedy, Song ("Let the River Run"), Support. Actress (Weaver).

Working Girls **1975 (R)** Three girls who share an apartment in Los Angeles are willing to do anything for money. And they do. For lack of anything else to recommend, watch for the striptease by Peterson, better known as Elvira on TV. **80m/C VHS, DVD.** Sarah Kennedy, Laurie Rose, Mark Thomas, Cassandra Peterson; ***D:*** Stephanie Rothman.

Working Girls **1987** An acclaimed, controversial look by independent filmmaker Borden into lives of modern brothel prostitutes over the period of one day. The sex is realistically candid and perfunctory; the docudrama centers on a prostitute who is a Yale graduate and aspiring photographer living with a female lover. Compelling, touching, and lasting, with sexually candid language and scenery. **93m/C VHS, DVD.** Amanda Goodwin, Louise Smith, Ellen McElduff, Maurisia Zach, Janne Peters, Helen Nicholas; ***D:*** Lizzie Borden; ***W:*** Sandra Kay, Lizzie Borden; ***C:*** Judy Irola; ***M:*** David Van Tiegham.

The World *Shijie* **2004** Beijing's World Park is a theme park featuring small reproductions of international landmarks such as the Eiffel Tower and the Taj Mahal. We get a behind the scenes look at the lives of some of the park's young workers, many of whom have moved from small villages to the big city to make new lives. These include dancer Tao (Zhao) and her security guard boyfriend, Taisheng (Chen), who are caught up in the dead-end artifice surrounding them. Mandarin and Shanxi dialect with subtitles. **139m/C DVD.** Zhao Tao, Chen Taisheng, Jing Jue, Jiang Zhongwei, Wang Yiqun, Hongwei Wang, Liang Jingdong, Xiang Wan, Liu Juan; ***D:*** Jia Zhang-ke; ***W:*** Jia Zhang-ke; ***M:*** Lim Giong.

The World According to Garp **1982 (R)** Comedy turns to tragedy in this relatively faithful version of John Irving's popular (and highly symbolic) novel, adapted by Steve Tesich. Chronicles the life of T.S. Garp, a struggling everyman beset by the destructive forces of modern society. Nevertheless, Garp maintains his optimism even as his life unravels around him. At the core of the film is a subplot involving a group of extreme feminists inspired in part by Garp's mother, the author of "A Sexual Suspect." Close and Lithgow (as a giant transsexual) are spectacular, while Williams is low-key and tender as the beleagured Garp. Ultimately pointless, perhaps, but effectively and intelligently so. **136m/C VHS, DVD.** Robin Williams, Mary Beth Hurt, John Lithgow, Glenn Close, Hume Cronyn, Jessica Tandy, Swoosie Kurtz, Amanda Plummer, Warren Berlinger, Brandon Maggart, George Roy Hill; ***D:*** George Roy Hill; ***W:*** Steve Tesich; ***C:*** Miroslav Ondricek; ***M:*** David Shire. L.A. Film Critics '82: Support. Actor (Lithgow), Support. Actress (Close); Natl. Bd. of Review '82: Support. Actress (Close); N.Y. Film Critics '82: Support. Actor (Lithgow).

The World Accuses **1/2 1935** A woman takes a job in a nursery, unaware that one child is her own, put up for adoption after her wealthy husband died. Then, her ex-lover shows up in her attic after escaping from prison and takes her hostage. Whew! Everything works out, except that the viewer is left confused and incredulous. **62m/B VHS.** Vivian Tobin, Dickie Moore, Russell Hopton, Cora Sue Collins, Mary Carr; ***D:*** Charles Lamont.

World and Time Enough **1/2 1995** Sculptor Mark's (Guidry) father compulsively designed Gothic cathedrals and after his death Mark decides to build his own version in a field belonging to a sympathetic cleric. Meanwhile, his equally eccentric lover, garbage-collector Joey (Giles), goes on a search for his birth parents. Lots of symbols, not much sense. **90m/C VHS, DVD.** Matt Guidry, Gregory G. Giles, Kraig Swartz, Peter Macon; ***D:*** Eric Mueller; ***W:*** Eric Mueller; ***C:*** Kyle Bergersen; ***M:*** Eugene Huddleston.

A World Apart **1/2 1988 (PG)** Cinematographer Menges' first directoral effort is a blistering, insightful drama told from the point of view of a 13-year-old white girl living in South Africa, oblivious to apartheid until her crusading journalist mother is arrested under the 90-Day Detention Act, under which she might remain in prison permanently. Political morality tale is also a look at the family-vs-cause choices activists must make. Heavily lauded, with good reason; the autobiographical script is based on Slovo's parents, persecuted South African journalists Joe Slovo and Ruth First. **114m/C VHS, DVD.** *GB* Barbara Hershey, Jodhi May, Linda Mvusi, David Suchet, Jeroen Krabbe, Paul Freeman, Tim Roth, Jude Akuwidike, Albee Lesotho; ***D:*** Chris Menges; ***W:*** Shawn Slovo; ***C:*** Peter Biziou; ***M:*** Hans Zimmer. British Acad. '88: Orig. Screenplay; Cannes '88: Actress (Hershey), Actress (May, Mvusi), Grand Jury Prize; N.Y. Film Critics '88: Director (Menges).

The World Gone Mad **1/2** *The Public Be Hanged; Public Be Damned* **1933** During Prohibition, a tough reporter discovers the district attorney is the intended victim of a murder plot involving crooked Wall Street types. Full circle: this interesting drama of white-collar crime is again topical, though dialogue heavy and desultory. **70m/B VHS, DVD.** Pat O'Brien, Louis Calhern, J. Carrol Naish; ***D:*** Christy Cabanne.

World Gone Wild **1/2 1988 (R)** Action yarn about a post-apocalyptic world of the future where an evil cult leader brainwashes his disciples. Together they battle a small band of eccentrics for the world's last water source. Stale rehash (with ineffective satiric elements) of the Mad Max genre, served with Ant for campy appeal. **95m/C VHS.** Bruce Dern, Michael Pare, Adam Ant, Catherine Mary Stewart, Rick Podell; ***D:*** Lee H. Katzin; ***C:*** Don Burgess.

The World in His Arms **1/2**
1952 Action and romance, circa 1850. Seal hunter Jonathan Clark (Peck) and his crew are in San Francisco when he meets beautiful Countess Marina Selanova (Blyth), who's fleeing an arranged marriage and is anxious to join her Uncle (Rumann), who happens to be the Governor General of Alaska (which is under Russian control). The twosome fall quickly in love but Marina's kidnapped by her would-be fiance, Prince Semyon (Esmond), who takes off for Alaska and Clark must go to rescue his love. Based on the book by Rex Beach. **104m/C VHS.** Gregory Peck, Ann Blyth, Anthony Quinn, Carl Esmond, Sig Rumann, John McIntire, Hans Conried, Andrea King; ***D:*** Raoul Walsh; ***W:*** Borden Chase; ***C:*** Russell Metty; ***M:*** Frank Skinner.

The World Is Full of Married Men **WOOF! 1980 (R)** A philandering ad exec gets involved with a reckless model, inspiring his fed-up wife also to look for extramarital sex. Promiscuously raunchy melodrama was written by the queen of sleaze, Jackie Collins, based on her novel. **106m/C VHS.** *GB* Anthony (Tony) Franciosa, Carroll Baker, Sherrie Croon, Gareth Hunt, Paul Nicholas; ***D:*** Robert W. Young; ***W:*** Jackie Collins.

The World Is Not Enough **1/2**
1999 (PG-13) Brosnan returns in the 19th James Bond adventure in which 007 is sent to protect Elektra King (Marceau), the daughter of a murdered oil tycoon who was also an old friend of M's (Dench). The threat appears to come from terrorist Renard (Carlyle), who has a bullet in the brain courtesy of MI6 that has made him impervious to pain. Renard's playing the nuclear explosion card, which leads to this episode's Bond girl, nuclear weapons expert (!) Dr. Christmas Jones (Richards), who has minimal impact but looks fetching and (of course) falls for the dashing spy's charms. The numerous action sequences overwhelm the characters and Bond has little to pit himself against since the villains are so low-key. There is a welcome darker edge to both Bond's character and the plot that the franchise should build on, rather than trying to top its death-defying stunts each time. **125m/C VHS, DVD.** Pierce Brosnan, Sophie Marceau, Denise Richards, Robert Carlyle, Judi Dench, John Cleese, Desmond Llewelyn, Robbie Coltrane, Samantha Bond, Michael Kitchen, Colin Salmon, Maria Grazia Cucinotta, David Calder, Serena Scott Thomas, Ulrich Thomsen, Goldie; ***D:*** Michael Apted; ***W:*** Neal Purvis, Robert Wade, Bruce Feirstein; ***C:*** Adrian Biddle; ***M:*** David Arnold. Golden Raspberries '99: Worst Support. Actress (Richards).

The World Moves On **1934** In 1825, the Girards and the Warburtons are the most prominent families in the New Orleans cotton industry. A will unites them in business, which expands overseas to England, France, and Germany. But after some four generations, their business empire is destroyed by WWI and the stock market crash. Tone plays a Girard and Carroll a Warburton who find love over several incarnations. **104m/B DVD.** Madeleine Carroll, Franchot Tone, Lumsden Hare, Reginald Denny, Raul Roulien, Sig Rumann, Louise Dresser, Stepin

Fetchit, Dudley Digges; *D:* John Ford; *W:* Reginald Berkeley; *C:* George Schneiderman; *M:* Hugo Friedhofer.

The World of Apu *Apu Sansat; Apur Sansar* **1959** Finale of director Ray's acclaimed Apu trilogy (following "Pather Panchali" and "Aparajito"). Aspiring writer Apu drops out of the university for want of money and takes up with an old chum. An odd circumstance leads him to marry his friend's cousin, whom he comes to love. She dies in childbirth (though her baby boy lives); Apu is deeply distraught, destroys the novel he was working on, and becomes a wanderer. His friend finds him five years later and helps him begin again with his young son. Wonderfully human, hopeful story told by a world-class director. From the novel "Aparajito" by B. Bandopadhaya. In Bengali with English subtitles. **103m/B VHS, DVD.** *IN* Soumitra Chatterjee, Sharmila Tagore, Alok Charkravarty, Swapan Makerji; *D:* Satyajit Ray; *W:* Satyajit Ray; *M:* Ravi Shankar.

The World of Henry Orient 1/2 **1964** Charming, eccentric comedy about two 15-year-old girls who, madly in love with an egotistical concert pianist, pursue him all around New York City. Sellers is hilarious, Walker and Spaeth are adorable as his teen groupies; Bosley and Lansbury are great as Walker's indulgent parents. For anyone who has ever been uncontrollably infatuated. Screenplay by the father/daughter team, Nora and Nunnally Johnson, based on Nora Johnson's novel. **106m/C VHS, DVD.** Peter Sellers, Tippy Walker, Merrie Spaeth, Tom Bosley, Angela Lansbury, Paula Prentiss, Phyllis Thaxter, Bibi Osterwald; *D:* George Roy Hill; *W:* Nunnally Johnson, Nora Johnson; *C:* Boris Kaufman; *M:* Elmer Bernstein.

A World of Strangers **1962** A harsh look at apartheid through the eyes of an Englishman who has traveled to South Africa to manage a publishing house. Filmed in strict secrecy in Johannesburg due to the film's aggressive condemnation of the practice. Based on a novel by Nadine Gordimer. **89m/B VHS.** *DK* Ivan Jackson, Zakes Mokae; *D:* Henning Carlsen.

The World of Suzie Wong **1960** Asian prostitute Kwan plays cat-and-mouse with American painter Holden. She lies to him about her profession, her family, and herself. His association with her ruins relationships in his life. Why, then, does he not get a clue? Good question, not answered by this soap opera that would be a serious drama. Offensively sanitized picture of the world of prostitution in an Asian metropolis. On the other hand, it's all nicely shot, much of it on location in Hong Kong. Based on Paul Osborn's play which was taken from Richard Mason's novel. **129m/C VHS, DVD.** *GB* William Holden, Nancy Kwan, Sylvia Syms, Michael Wilding, Laurence Naismith, Jacqueline "Jackie" Chan; *D:* Richard Quine; *C:* Geoffrey Unsworth.

World of the Depraved *Mundo Depravados* **1967** Tango (Storm) runs an exercise club for young lovelies that are systematically being stalked by the mysterious full moon sex killer. Enter police detectives Riley and Hamilton (Decker, Reed), joking types who peep on their charges through keyholes, etc. When the plot finally gets around to the issue of the killer, the point of the movie has already been made clear. Silly, trivial, sophomoric humor lacking a trace of sincerity. Volume 6 of Frank Henenlotter's Sexy Shockers series. **73m/C VHS, DVD.** Tempest Storm, Johnnie Decker, Larry Reed; *D:* Herbert Jeffries; *W:* Herbert Jeffries.

The World Owes Me a Living **1947** Melodrama about pilot Farrar losing his memory in a plane crash and Campbell trying to spark his recollection of the past. **91m/B VHS.** *GB* David Farrar, Judy Campbell, Jack Livesey, John Laurie; *D:* Vernon Sewell; *W:* Vernon Sewell.

The World Sinks Except Japan WOOF! *Nihon igai zenbu chinbotsu* **2006** Based on a novel from the seventies, due to seismic activity the entire world has moved to Japan because their home countries are underwater. Needless to say the Japanese aren't exactly happy with the sudden huge immigrant population when the horde of survivors arrives. **98m/C DVD.** *JP* Kenji Kohashi, Masatoshi Matsuo, Shuuji Kashiwabara; *D:* Minoru Kawasaki; *W:* Minoru Kawasaki, Yasutaka Tsutsui, Masakazu Migita; *C:* Takashi Suga; *M:* Masako Ishii.

World Trade Center **2006 (PG-13)** Stone directs a 9/11 drama about John McLoughlin (Cage) and Will Jimeno (Pena), two Port Authority policemen trapped in the World Trade Center after they went in as part of the rescue team. Film follows their efforts at survival and escape with the efforts of others to save them, and the fears of their families. Stone shot in chronological order to heighten the reality and tension and had the survivors and their families on the set as well. He puts aside the cynicism and paranoia for an elegantly told tale of extraordinary heroism by ordinary people. **129m/C DVD, Blu-ray Disc, HD DVD.** *US* Nicolas Cage, Michael Pena, Maria Bello, Maggie Gyllenhaal, Jay Hernandez, Stephen Dorff, Michael Shannon; *D:* Oliver Stone; *W:* Andrea Berloff; *C:* Seamus McGarvey; *M:* Craig Armstrong.

World Traveler 1/2 **2001 (R)** One day, thirtysomething NYC architect Cal (Crudup) leaves his wife and son, gets into the family station wagon, and hits the road to drive cross country in this frustrating film. Although Crudup is a fine actor, the viewer never learns Cal's motives for leaving his life behind except that he's not the nicest guy around, considering the way he treats some of the people he meets on his trip, including construction worker Carl (Derricks) whose marriage Cal damages, and various female hitchhikers. Not a lot really happens as Cal searches for himself (apparently) and the film ultimately falls flat. **104m/C VHS, DVD.** *US CA* Billy Crudup, Julianne Moore, Cleavant Derricks, David Keith, Mary McCormack, James LeGros, Karen Allen, Liane Balaban; *D:* Bart Freundlich; *W:* Bart Freundlich; *C:* Terry Stacey; *M:* Clint Mansell.

World War II: When Lions Roared 1/2 **1994** The "Lions" are Franklin Delano Roosevelt, Winston Churchill, and Joseph Stalin. The three Allied leaders formed an uneasy alliance to crush Hitler and Mussolini, all against much internal treachery. Uses lots of WWII newsreel footage. **186m/C VHS.** John Lithgow, Bob Hoskins, Michael Caine, Ed Begley Jr., Jan Triska; *D:* Joseph Sargent; *W:* David W. Rintels; *C:* John A. Alonzo. **TV**

World War III 1/2 **1986** How's that for a title? A Russian plot is afoot to seize and destroy the Alaskan pipeline. When the plot is discovered, negotiation is needed to prevent world war. Executive branch showdown ensues between U.S. prez Hudson and Soviet chief Keith. Director Boris Sagal was killed on location, whereupon Greene took over, and shooting was moved indoors with dramatic tension lost in the transition. **186m/C VHS.** Brian Keith, David Soul, Rock Hudson, Cathy Lee Crosby, Katherine Helmond, Robert Prosky, James Hampton, Richard Yniguez, Herbert Jefferson Jr.; *D:* David Greene; *W:* Robert L. Joseph. **TV**

The Worldly Madonna 1/2 **1922** Young plays two roles as Janet, a convent novitiate, and her cabaret dancer sister, Lucy. Lucy thinks she's killed a man and Janet agrees to change places with her. **47m/B VHS.** Clara Kimball Young, Richard Tucker, George Hackathorne, William P. Carleton, Jean De Limur, William Marion, Milla Davenport; *D:* Harry Garson.

The World's Fastest Indian **2005 (PG-13)** Burt Munro (a refreshingly un-scary Hopkins) is the town "crazy old guy," a kooky New Zealander with a dream of setting a land-speed motorcycle record at Bonneville Flats, Utah. The Indian in the title is the bike, a 1920 Indian Scout, which, with Munro's constant tinkering, flies at a blistering 201 mph across the desert with Munro at its helm. A true story, told here by the same director of the 1971 documentary about Munro, "Offerings to the God of Speed." Mildly schmaltzy, but well-told and all heart. **127m/C DVD.** *US NZ* Anthony Hopkins, Diane Ladd, Aaron Murphy, Paul Rodriguez, Chris(topher) Williams, Christopher Lawford, Annie Whittle; *D:* Roger Donaldson; *W:* Roger Donaldson; *C:* David Gribble; *M:* J. Peter Robinson.

The World's Greatest Athlete **1973 (G)** Lame Disney comedy about a Tarzan-like jungle-man (Vincent) recruited by an unsuccessful American college coach (Amos) and his bumbling assistant (Conway). Fun special effects, weak script add up to mediocre family fare. Cameo by Howard Cosell as—who else?—himself. **89m/C VHS, DVD.** Jan-Michael Vincent, Tim Conway, John Amos, Roscoe Lee Browne, Dayle Haddon; ***Cameos:*** Howard Cosell; *D:* Robert Scheerer; *W:* Dee Caruso; *M:* Marvin Hamlisch.

World's Greatest Dad **2009** Sweet-yet-twisted story of failed writer/high school teacher/single dad Lance Clayton (Williams) whose life unexpectedly takes a turn for the better after his jackass, porn-obsessed, teenage son Kyle (Sabara), accidentally kills himself by auto-erotic asphyxiation. Lance rearranges the scene to appear as though Kyle hung himself, even composing a suicide letter. The note becomes public and Kyle is remembered with great affection by those who hours before hated him, or never even knew him, and Lance is suddenly a much sought-after instructor. This unintended attention leads Lance to compose an entire diary of Kyle's, which also gets out-of-control recognition. Williams remarkably laces this heavy-handed material with just the right dollop of comedy while writer/director Goldthwait continues to emerge as a dark comedy genius. **99m/C DVD.** *US* Robin Williams, Daryl Sabara, Alexie Gilmore, Henry Simmons, Evan Martin, Tom Kenny, Mitzi McCall, Jermaine Williams, Toby Huss, Michael Thomas Moore, Lorraine Nicholson; *D:* Bob(cat) Goldthwait; *W:* Bob(cat) Goldthwait; *C:* Horacio Marquinez; *M:* Gerald Brunskill.

World's Greatest Lover 1/2 **1977 (PG)** Milwaukee baker Rudi Valentine, played oft-hilariously by Wilder, tries to make it big in 1920s Hollywood. He has a screen test as a Hollywood movie sheik, but his wife (Kane) leaves him for the real McCoy. Episodic and uneven, it's alternately uproarious, touching and downright raunchy. **89m/C VHS, DVD.** Gene Wilder, Carol Kane, Dom DeLuise, Fritz Feld, Carl Ballantine, Michael Huddleston, Matt Collins, Ronny Graham; *D:* Gene Wilder; *W:* Gene Wilder.

The World's Oldest Living Bridesmaid 1/2 **1992** Hokey romantic comedy about a successful woman attorney who just can't find Mr. Right. Brenda feels even worse when she attends yet another friend's wedding. However, when she hires a younger, male secretary (former model Wimmer) the romantic sparks fly. An appealing and attractive cast helps this TV fare. **100m/C VHS.** Donna Mills, Brian Wimmer, Beverly Garland, Winston Rekert, Art Hindle, Laura Press; *D:* Joseph L. Scanlan. **TV**

The Worm Eaters WOOF! **1977 (PG)** Mean developers want to take over a reclusive worm farmer's land. He unleashes his livestock on them. The bad guys turn into—eeck!—"worm people." A truck runs over our hero nearly 75 minutes too late to save the viewer. **75m/C VHS, DVD.** Herb Robins, Barry Hostetler, Lindsay Armstrong Black, Joseph Sacket, Robert Garrison, Mike Garrison; *D:* Herb Robins; *W:* Herb Robins; *C:* Willis Hawkins; *M:* Theodore Stern.

The Worst Witch 1/2 **1986 (G)** Fantasy about a school for young witches where the educational lessons never go quite as planned. Adapted from the children's book "The Worst Witch" by Jill Murphy. **70m/C VHS, DVD.** Diana Rigg, Charlotte Rae, Tim Curry, Fairuza Balk; *D:* Robert M. Young.

Worth Winning 1/2 **1989 (PG-13)** A notoriously eligible Philadelphia bachelor takes a bet to become engaged to three women within three months, and finds himself in hot water. A critically dead-in-the-water chucklefest. **103m/C VHS, DVD.** Mark Harmon, Lesley Ann Warren, Madeleine Stowe, Maria Holvoe, Mark Blum, Andrea Martin, Alan Blumenfeld, Brad Hall, Tony Longo; *D:* Will MacKenzie; *W:* Sara Parriott, Josann McGibbon.

The Would-Be Gentleman 1/2 **1958** The Comedie Francaise troupe performs Moliere's famous farce-comedy. Valuable as a record of the famous troupe on stage. When they're long gone, our grandkids can enjoy this. We can too (if we can't afford the trip to France), though it's less a film than a filming of a play. In French with English subtitles. **93m/C VHS.** *FR* Louis Seigner, Jean Meyer, Jean Piat; *D:* Jean Meyer; *C:* Henri Alekan.

Wounded **1997 (R)** Game warden Julie Clayton (Amick) vows to get even with poacher Hanghan (Pasdar) after he murders her fiance and assaults her. The FBI tell her to stay clear but Julie is determined to track Hanaghan down. **91m/C VHS.** Madchen Amick, Adrian Pasdar, Graham Greene, Richard Joseph Paul, Daniel Kash; *D:* Richard Martin; *W:* Harry S. Longstreet, Lindsay Bourne; *C:* Gregory Middleton; *M:* Ross Vannelli. **CABLE**

The Wounds *Rane* **1998** In 1991, 16-year-old Pinki (Pekic) and Kraut (Maric) are two relatively innocent Serbians who, by 1996, have fallen under the pernicious influence of Dickie (Bjelogrlic), a flashy black marketeer. With brutality everywhere in their war-torn country, the young men have become amoral brutes who only understand an eye-for-an-eye—even with each other. Serbo-Croatian with subtitles. **103m/C VHS, DVD.** Dragan Bjelogric, Dusan Pekic, Milan Maric, Branka Katic; *D:* Srdjan Dragojevic; *W:* Srdjan Dragojevic; *C:* Dusan Joksimovic; *M:* Aleksandar Habic.

Woyzeck **1978** Chilling portrayal of a man plunging into insanity. Mired in the ranks of the German Army, Woyzeck is harassed by his superiors and tortured in scientific experiments, gradually devolving into homicidal maniac. Based on Georg Buchner play. In German with English subtitles. **82m/C VHS, DVD.** *GE* Klaus Kinski, Eva Mattes, Wolfgang Reichmann, Josef Bierbichler; *D:* Werner Herzog; *W:* Werner Herzog; *C:* Jorge Schmidt-Reitwein.

Woyzeck **1994** Woyzeck (Kovacs) is a flagman in a decaying trainyard—caught between his cruel employer, poverty, and his distant wife. In order to make a little extra money, he agrees to take part in a bizarre medical experiment. Increasingly pushed to the edge, Woyzeck snaps when he learns his wife is having an affair. Based on the play by Georg Buchner. Hungarian with subtitles. **93m/B VHS.** *HU* Lajos Kovacs, Diana Vacaru, Aleksandr Porokhovshchikov, Sandor Gaspar; *D:* Janos Szasz; *W:* Janos Szasz; *C:* Tibor Mathe.

Wozzeck **1947** The corpse of murderer Franz Wozzeck (Meisel) is being used in an anatomy lecture, while medical student Buchner (Eckard) tells Wozzeck's tragic story in flashbacks. A soldier, Wozzeck endures humiliation in order to barely support his wife Marie (Zulch) and their child. The beautiful Marie allows herself to be seduced by another soldier (Haussler), as Wozzeck's physical and mental health declines. And then Franz learns of her infidelity. Based on the drama by Georg Buchner. German with subtitles. **94m/B VHS.** Kurt Meisel, Helga Zulch, Richard Haussler, Max Eckard; *D:* Georg C. Klaren; *W:* Georg C. Klaren; *C:* Bruno Mondi; *M:* Herbert Trantow.

WR: Mysteries of the Organism **1971** Makavejev's breakthrough film, a surreal, essayist exploration of the conflict/union between sexuality and politics—namely, Wilheim Reich and Stalin. A raunchy, bitterly satiric non-narrative that established the rule-breaking Yugoslav internationally. In Serbian with English subtitles. **84m/C VHS, DVD.** Milena Dravic, Jagoda Kaloper, Tuli Kupferberg, Jackie Curtis; *D:* Dusan Makavejev; *W:* Dusan Makavejev.

The Wraith 1/2 **1987 (PG-13)** Drag-racing Arizona teens find themselves challenged by a mysterious, otherworldly stranger. Hot cars; cool music; little else to recommend it. Lousy script; ludicrous excuse for a premise. Most of the stars herein are related to somebody famous. **92m/C VHS, DVD.** Charlie Sheen, Nick Cassavetes, Sherilyn Fenn, Randy Quaid, Matthew Barry, Clint Howard, Griffin O'Neal; *D:* Mike Marvin; *W:* Mike Marvin.

Wrangler 1/2 **1988** When an Australian rancher dies his daughter tries to hang on to the family ranch from a ruthless creditor. She also has to deal with the attentions of two men—one a businessman and the other a cattleman, both equally dashing and handsome. Beautiful scenery of the Australian Outback as well as romance and adventure.

93m/C VHS, DVD. Jeff Fahey, Tushka Bergen, Steven Vidler, Richard Moir, Shane Briant, Drew Forsythe, Cornelia Frances, Sandy Gore, Frederick Parslow; ***D:*** Ian Barry; ***W:*** John Sexton; ***M:*** Mario Millo.

Wrath of Daimajin 🦴🦴 ½ *Daimajin ikaru; The Return of Giant Majin; Daimajin 2: Wrath of Daimajin* **1966** Daimajin's statue is now located on an island between two countries of happy citizens. There is of course a country of depressed citizens nearby, and their lord decides invading and assassinating the leaders of the other two is a good way to get to know his neighbors. To further cheese people off, he blows up the statue of their God, despite what happened in the first movie. Much drama ensues, along with spooky unexplained events, before the god Daimajin once again whoops the bad guys while inflicting massive damage on the surrounding countryside. All things considered, there seems to be a reason the peasants try to avoid summoning him in these films. **90m/C DVD.** *JP* Kojiro Hongo, Riki Hashimoto, Shiho Fujimura; ***D:*** Kenji Misumi; ***W:*** Tetsuro Yoshida; ***M:*** Akira Ifukube.

The Wrath of the Gods 🦴🦴 **1914** Boyish American sailor Tom Wilson (Borzage) is shipwrecked near a Japanese village. He soon falls in love with local beauty, Toya San (Aoki). But their forbidden romance leads to divine retribution (she's under a curse) in the form of a volcanic eruption. **?m/B DVD.** Frank Borzage, Sessue Hayakawa, Tsuru Aoki, Kisaburo Kurihara; ***D:*** Reginald Barker; ***W:*** Thomas Ince.

The Wreck of the Mary Deare 🦴🦴 ½ **1959** Slow-moving adventure drama focusing on the wreck of the freighter called the Mary Deare. Heston plays a ship salvager who comes upon a seemingly empty ship one night and Cooper is the only crew member on board. Special effects are the main attraction in this interesting sea drama. Film originally was to be directed by Hitchcock, but he turned down the offer to do "North by Northwest." **105m/C VHS, DVD.** *GB* Gary Cooper, Charlton Heston, Michael Redgrave, Emlyn Williams, Cecil Parker, Alexander Knox, Virginia McKenna, Richard Harris; ***D:*** Michael Anderson Sr.; ***W:*** Eric Ambler.

The Wrecking Crew 🦴🦴 **1968** The fourth and final of Martin's Matt Helm spy spoof series. Matt and bumbling babe Freya (Tate) must save the world from economic doom when evildoer Massimo (Green) steals $1 billion in gold. Tate was murdered several months after the film's release. **105m/C VHS, DVD.** Dean Martin, Sharon Tate, Nigel Green, Elke Sommer, Nancy Kwan, Tina Louise, John Larch, Wilhelm von Homburg, Tony Giorgio; ***D:*** Phil Karlson; ***W:*** William McGivern; ***C:*** Sam Leavitt; ***M:*** Hugo Montenegro.

The Wrecking Crew 🦴 ½ **1999 (R)** Ice-T heads the title "crew," a government-sponsored (secret) hit squad that's sent to the Motor City to clean up the mess made by gangmaster Snoop Dogg. **81m/C VHS, DVD.** Ice-T, Snoop Dogg, David Askew, Ernie Hudson Jr.; ***D:*** Albert Pyun; ***W:*** Hannah Blue. **VIDEO**

The Wrestler 🦴 **1973** All-star wrestling, which is fictional anyway, gets said treatment in the appropriate way. Honest promoter (yeah, sure) bumps heads with bad-guy crooks who want in on the action. Made-for-TV opportunity for Asner to slum. **103m/C VHS, DVD.** Ed Asner, Elaine Giftos, Verne Gagne, Harold Sakata; ***D:*** James Westman; ***W:*** Eugene Gump; ***C:*** Gil Hubbs; ***M:*** William Allen Castleman.

The Wrestler 🦴🦴🦴🦴 **2008 (R)** In the 1980's, Randy "The Ram" Robinson was a huge star in a small wrestling circuit. Over the years, his health has deteriorated, his daughter (Wood) has turned her back on him, and his trailer in New Jersey can't keep out winter. However, a proposed 20th anniversary rematch with his legendary nemesis lures him back into the ring for one more shot at glory. This prayer for redemption is financed by his part-time supermarket job, but, unfortunately, the affection from his stripper girlfriend (Tomei) runs cold once the money's tucked away. Heart-wrenching, funny, and never succumbs to cheap sports-movie melodrama. A triumphant comeback for Rourke with his infamously abused face and body, guided by cult director Darren Aronofsky. **109m/C DVD.** *US* Mickey Rourke, Marisa Tomei, Evan Rachel Wood; ***D:*** Darren Aronofsky; ***W:*** Robert Siegel; ***C:*** Maryse Alberti; ***M:*** Clint Mansell. British Acad. '08: Actor (Rourke); Golden Globes '09: Actor—Drama (Rourke), Song ("The Wrestler"); Ind. Spirit '09: Actor (Rourke), Cinematog., Film.

Wrestling Ernest Hemingway 🦴🦴 **1993 (PG-13)** A shy barber and a rollicking sea captain, both 75 and retired, form an unlikely companionship in a Florida retirement mecca. Duvall is the persnickety introvert who quietly follows routine and Harris is the would-be ladies' man whose endless tall tales include having tangled with Papa Hemingway in his youth. They share walks in the park, little league baseball from the bleachers, and coffee klatches that reveal the emptiness of their lives. Director Haines' focus on the principals' emotional baggage considerably dampens the proceedings. Depression in the elderly may be a topic that is not quite ready to come out of Hollywood's closet. **123m/C VHS.** Robert Duvall, Richard Harris, Piper Laurie, Shirley MacLaine, Sandra Bullock; ***D:*** Randa Haines; ***W:*** Steve Conrad; ***C:*** Lajos Koltai; ***M:*** Michael Convertino.

Wrestling with Alligators 🦴🦴 ½ **1998** Quiet, coming-of-ager stars Palladino as Maddy, a teenager escaping a tragic past in Florida and finding comfort in her new-found friends at an all-female boarding house on the New Jersey shore in 1959. Lulu's Look Out offers the tough teenager a place to find herself, with the help of proprietor Lulu (Bloom), an eccentric silent-screen star, and residents Mary (Shelly), an artist, and the beautiful Claire (Richardson), a French war widow. Tomboy Maddy finds herself attracted to a man for the first time when she meets carnival worker Will (Trammell). Then, when Claire becomes pregnant by the local garage owner (Sanders), Maddy finds herself growing up even more as she comes to the aid of her newfound family, which is beginning to show signs of serious strain. Unassuming portrait of four very different women is a worthy effort, with the leads displaying convincing chemistry. **95m/C VHS, DVD.** Aleksa Palladino, Joely Richardson, Claire Bloom, Adrienne Shelly, Sam Trammell, Jay O. Sanders, Tom Guiry, Sloane Shelton, Angelica Torn, Schuyler Grant; ***D:*** Laurie Weltz; ***W:*** Laurie Weltz; ***C:*** Richard Dallett; ***M:*** Andrew Hollander.

Wrestling Women vs. the Aztec Mummy **WOOF!** *Las Luchadoras Contra la Momia; Rock and Roll Wrestling Women vs. the Aztec Mummy* **1959** Women, broad of shoulder, wrestle an ancient Aztec wrestler who comes to life. Furnished with a new rock soundtrack. **88m/C VHS, DVD.** *MX* Lorena Lalazquez, Armando Silvestre, Elizabeth Campbell, Maria Eugenia San Martin, Ramon Bugarini, Victor Velaquez, Chabela Romero; ***D:*** Rene Cardona Sr.; ***W:*** Alfredo Salazar, Guillermo Calderon; ***C:*** Ezequiel Carrasco.

Wristcutters: A Love Story 🦴🦴 **2006 (R)** What could be worse than a miserable life? A miserable afterlife, that's what. Croatian director Goran Dukic takes a stark and quirky peek at the limbo that exists between the two. Zia (Fugit) is dumped by girlfriend Desiree (Bibb) and decides to end it all, hoping for relief from his misery. But he finds himself stuck in an afterlife that is marginally like the one he just left, only duller, and with worse jobs. A cast of kooky characters who have also offed themselves shares the limbo world, two of which are wild Russian rocker Eugene (Whigham) and derelict clown Kneller (an aptly-cast Waits). Zia cheers up just a bit when he finds out that Desiree followed his lead and he goes on a roadtrip to find her, but ends up falling for Mikal (Sossamon), who swears she's there by mistake and is trying to get home. **88m/C DVD.** *US* Patrick Fugit, Shannyn Sossamon, Shea Whigham, Leslie Bibb, Tom Waits, Mark Boone Jr., Mary Pat Gleason, Abraham Benrubi, Will Arnett, Clayne Crawford, John Hawkes, Jake Busey, Sarah Roemer, Azura Skye, Eddie Steeples, Nick Offerman; ***D:*** Goran Dukic; ***W:*** Goran Dukic; ***C:*** Vanja Cernjul; ***M:*** Bobby Johnston.

Write to Kill 🦴 ½ **1991 (R)** A young mystery writer seeks revenge when his brother is murdered by a ring of counterfeiters. **120m/C VHS.** Scott Valentine, Chris Mulkey, Joan Severance, G.W. Bailey, Ray Wise; ***D:*** Ruben Preuss.

Writer's Block 🦴🦴 **1991 (R)** Fairchild is a successful thriller writer whose latest books feature a serial killer. She decides to kill the character off and is soon stalked by a psycho who is using her plots for some copy-cat killings. Tepid cable movie with San Diego locations the only highlight. **90m/C VHS.** Morgan Fairchild, Joe Regalbuto, Michael Praed, Cheryl Anderson, Mary Ann Pascal, Douglas Rowe, Ned Bellamy; ***D:*** Charles Correll; ***W:*** Elisa Bell. **CABLE**

Written on the Wind 🦴🦴🦴 ½ **1956** Sirk's frenzied, melodrama-as-high-art dissection of both the American Dream and American movies follows a Texas oil family's self-destruction through wealth, greed and unbridled lust. Exaggerated depiction of and comment on American ambition and pretension, adapted from Robert Wilder's novel. **99m/C VHS, DVD.** Lauren Bacall, Rock Hudson, Dorothy Malone, Robert Stack, Robert Keith, Grant Williams, Edward Platt, Harry Shannon; ***D:*** Douglas Sirk; ***W:*** George Zuckerman; ***C:*** Russell Metty. Oscars '56: Support. Actress (Malone).

The Wrong Arm of the Law 🦴🦴🦴 **1963** Loopy gangster yarn about a trio of Aussie gangsters who arrive in London and upset the local crime balance when they dress up as cops and confiscate loot from apprehended robbers. General confusion erupts among the police, the local crooks, and the imposters. Riotous and hilarious, with Sellers leading a host of familiar faces. **94m/B VHS, DVD.** *GB* Peter Sellers, Lionel Jeffries, Nanette Newman, Bernard Cribbins, Dennis Price; ***D:*** Cliff Owen; ***M:*** Richard Rodney Bennett.

The Wrong Box 🦴🦴🦴 **1966** Two elderly Victorian brothers try to kill each other so that one of them may collect the large inheritance left to them. Based on a Robert Louis Stevenson novel. Well-cast black comedy replete with sight gags, many of which flop. **105m/C VHS.** *GB* Peter Sellers, Dudley Moore, Peter Cook, Michael Caine, Ralph Richardson, John Mills; ***D:*** Bryan Forbes; ***W:*** Larry Gelbart; ***M:*** John Barry.

The Wrong Guy 🦴🦴 **1996 (PG-13)** Hit-and-miss spoof of "man on the run" movies. Nerdy exec Nelson Hibbert (Foley) threatens his boss in front of a bunch of people and is later seen running from the man's office, screaming, covered in blood, and holding a knife. Although the police quickly figure out Nelson is not the killer, Nelson doesn't know this and he keeps ending up in the wrong place at the wrong time. **87m/C VHS, DVD.** *CA* Dave Foley, David Anthony Higgens, Jennifer Tilly, Joe Flaherty, Alan Scarfe, Kenneth Welsh, Enrico Colantoni, Colm Feore; ***D:*** David Steinberg; ***W:*** Dave Foley, David Anthony Higgens, Jay Kogen; ***C:*** David Makin; ***M:*** Lawrence Shragge.

The Wrong Guys 🦴 **1988 (PG)** Five giants of stand-up comedy star as a group of men who reunite their old boy scout pack and go camping. A crazed convict mistakes them for FBI agents. It's supposed to get zany after that, but succeeds only in being clumsy and embarassing. **86m/C VHS, DVD.** Richard Lewis, Richard Belzer, Louie Anderson, Tim Thomerson, Franklin Ajaye, John Goodman, Ernie Hudson, Timothy Van Patten; ***D:*** Danny Bilson; ***W:*** Danny Bilson, Paul DeMeo.

Wrong Is Right 🦴🦴 *The Man With The Deadly Lens* **1982 (R)** A black action comedy about international terrorism, news reporting and the CIA. Connery is terrific, as usual, as a TV reporter in a head-scratching attempt at satire of our TV-influenced society. **117m/C VHS, DVD.** Sean Connery, Katharine Ross, Robert Conrad, George Grizzard, Henry Silva, G.D. Spradlin, John Saxon, Leslie Nielsen, Robert Webber, Rosalind Cash, Hardy Kruger, Dean Stockwell, Ron Moody, Jennifer Jason Leigh; ***D:*** Richard Brooks; ***W:*** Richard Brooks; ***C:*** Fred W. Koenekamp.

The Wrong Man 🦴🦴🦴 ½ **1956** Nightclub musician Fonda is falsely accused of a robbery and his life is destroyed. Taken almost entirely from the real-life case of mild-mannered bass player "Manny" Balestrero; probes his anguish at being wrongly accused; and showcases Miles (later to appear in "Psycho") and her character's agony. Harrowing, especially following more light-hearted Hitchcock fare such as "The Trouble with Harry." Part of the "A Night at the Movies" series, this tape simulates a 1956 movie evening with a color Bugs Bunny cartoon, "A Star Is Bored," a newsreel and coming attractions for "Toward the Unknown." **126m/B VHS, DVD.** Henry Fonda, Vera Miles, Anthony Quayle, Nehemiah Persoff; ***D:*** Alfred Hitchcock; ***C:*** Robert Burks.

The Wrong Man 🦴🦴 ½ **1993 (R)** American sailor Alex Walker (Anderson) is framed for the murder of a Mexican smuggler. He eludes the police and winds up hitching a ride from wacko couple Phillip (Lithgow) and Missy Mills (Arquette). Missy does topless table dancing and is very interested in their fugitive passenger. Alex may be better off with the police. **98m/C VHS.** Kevin Anderson, John Lithgow, Rosanna Arquette, Robert Harper; ***D:*** Jim McBride; ***C:*** Alfonso Beato. **CABLE**

The Wrong Move 🦴🦴 ½ **1978** A loose adaptation of Goethe's "Sorrows of Young Werther" by screenwriter Peter Handke. Justly acclaimed and engrossing, though slow. Kinski's first film. A young poet, searching for life's meaning, wanders aimlessly through Germany. In German with English subtitles. **103m/C VHS, DVD.** *GE* Nastassja Kinski, Hanna Schygulla, Ruediger Vogler, Hans-Christian Blech; ***D:*** Wim Wenders.

The Wrong Road 🦴 ½ **1937** A young couple embark on a robbery spree, and subsequently end up in prison. On their release, they search for the loot they had previously hidden, but find the man who was holding it for them has died. Will they ever recover their ill-gotten stash? **62m/B VHS, DVD.** Richard Cromwell, Helen Mack, Lionel Atwill, Horace McMahon, Russ Powell, Billy Bevan, Marjorie Main, Rex Evans; ***D:*** James Cruze.

Wrong Turn 🦴 ½ **2003 (R)** Six friends are involved in a car crash that strands them in the West Virginia mountains where they are hunted by disfigured, inbred, cannibalistic mountain men. Typical victim-by-number horror flick offers no twists on the genre and only slight wit by its doomed cast. Don't expect to see this one on the West Virginia Tourist Board's recommended list. **85m/C VHS, DVD.** *US* Eliza Dushku, Jeremy Sisto, Emmanuelle Chriqui, Desmond Harrington, Lindy Booth, Kevin Zegers, Julian Richings, Garry Robbins, Ted Clark, Yvonne Gaudry, David Huband, Joel Harris, Wayne Robson, James Downing; ***D:*** Rob Schmidt; ***W:*** Alan B. McElroy; ***C:*** John Bartley; ***M:*** Elia Cmiral.

Wrong Turn 2: Dead End 🦴 **2007 (R)** Retired special forces officer Dale Murphy (Rollins) is the host of a reality TV show where contestants must survive in a remote West Virginia wilderness. But they don't expect to find themselves being hunted by an inbred family of cannibals. Just as sleazy and gross as it sounds. **93m/C DVD.** Henry Rollins, Erica Leerhsen, Daniella Alonso, Texas Battle, Crystal Lowe, Aleksa Palladino, Steve Braun, Kimberly Caldwell; ***D:*** Joe Lynch; ***W:*** Turi Meyer, Al Septien; ***C:*** Robin Loewen; ***M:*** Bear McCreary. **VIDEO**

Wrong Turn 3: Left for Dead 🦴 **2009** This franchise, featuring lots of gore and violence, should be left as well but continues to carry on with its typical plot. Three Finger and his inbred cannibal clan get a two-fer when a group of innocent campers take a wrong turn and then a bunch of escaped cons also become prey for the stabbings, decapitations, vivisections, and various other graphically-depicted deaths. **92m/C DVD.** Janet Montgomery, Tamer Hassan, Chucky Venice, Gil Kolirin, Borislav Iliev, Tom Frederic; ***D:*** Declan O'Brien; ***W:*** Connor James Delaney; ***C:*** Lorenzo Senatore; ***M:*** Claude Foisy. **VIDEO**

The Wrong Woman 🦴🦴 ½ **1995 (PG-13)** When Melanie Brooke's (McKeon) boss is murdered, she's framed to take by rap by the company's sleazy comptroller (Field). Melanie begins a desperate hunt for the real culprit with the killer and the cops both after her. **90m/C VHS.** Michelle Scarabelli, Gary Hudson, Stephen Shellen, Nancy McKeon, Chelsea Field; ***D:*** Douglas Jackson; ***W:*** Douglas Soesbe; ***C:*** Peter Benison; ***M:*** Marty Simon.

Wrongfully Accused 🦴 ½ **1998 (PG-13)** Yet another Nielsen spoof, with "The Fugitive" (along with several other movies) the target this time around. He's violinist Ryan Harrison who has a tryst with socialite Lauren Goodhue (Le Brock) and then gets convicted of her husband Hibbing's (York) murder. Harrison escapes, determined to find the actual killer—the one-armed, one-legged, and one-eyed man—while being hunted by Marshal Fergus Falls (Crenna). This is one genre that's definitely had its day, with more clunkers than chuckles. **85m/C VHS, DVD.** Leslie Nielsen, Richard Crenna, Kelly Le Brock, Melinda McGraw, Michael York, Sandra Bernhard; ***D:*** Pat Proft; ***W:*** Pat Proft; ***C:*** Glen MacPherson; ***M:*** Bill Conti.

Wuthering Heights **1939** The first screen adaptation of Emily Bronte's romantic novel about the doomed love between Heathcliff and Cathy on the Yorkshire moors. Dynamically captures the madness and ferocity of the classic novel, remaining possibly the greatest romance ever filmed. Excellent performances from Wyler's sure direction, particularly Olivier's, which made him a star, and Oberon in her finest hour as the exquisite but selfish Cathy. Remade twice, in 1953 (by Luis Bunuel) and in 1970. **104m/B VHS, DVD.** Laurence Olivier, Merle Oberon, David Niven, Geraldine Fitzgerald, Flora Robson, Donald Crisp, Cecil Kellaway, Leo G. Carroll, Miles Mander, Hugh Williams; ***D:*** William Wyler; ***W:*** Ben Hecht, Charles MacArthur; ***C:*** Gregg Toland; ***M:*** Alfred Newman. Oscars '39: B&W Cinematog.; AFI '98: Top 100, Natl. Film Reg. '07;; N.Y. Film Critics '39: Film.

Wuthering Heights ½ *Abismos de Pasion; Cumbres Borrascosas* **1953** Bunuel tackles the Bronte classic during his Mexican period, and comes up with a film containing little passion, but much of the customary Bunuel manic cynicism. The 1939 version is far superior, but fans of Bunuel will probably enjoy this one. Loosely adapted; in Spanish with English subtitles. Remade in another English-language version in 1970. **90m/B VHS.** *MX* Irasema Dilian, Jorge Mistral, Lilia Prado, Ernesto Alonso; ***D:*** Luis Bunuel.

Wuthering Heights ½ **1970 (G)** The third screening of the classic Emily Bronte romance about two doomed lovers. Fuest's version features excellent photography, and Calder-Marshall's and Dalton's performances are effective, but fail even to approach the intensity and pathos of the 1939 film original (or of the book). Filmed on location in Yorkshire, England. **105m/C VHS, DVD.** *GB* Anna Calder-Marshall, Timothy Dalton, Harry Andrews, Pamela Brown, Judy Cornwell, James Cossins, Rosalie Crutchley, Hilary Dwyer, Hugh Griffith, Ian Ogilvy; ***D:*** Robert Fuest; ***W:*** Patrick Tilley; ***C:*** John Coquillon; ***M:*** Michel Legrand.

Wuthering Heights ½ **1998** Yet another adaptation of Emily Bronte's 1847 gothic romance. Cavanah plays the embittered Heathcliff while Brady is the wilfull Cathy, whose desire for a life of ease places them both on a tragic path that haunts them even after death. **120m/C VHS.** *GB* Robert Cavanah, Orla Brady, Crispin Bonham Carter, Peter Davison; ***W:*** David Skynner; ***M:*** Warren Bennett, Neil McKay. **TV**

Wuthering Heights **2009** Umpteenth version of the Emily Bronte tragedy is well-staged but an intense Hardy isn't well-matched by petulant newcomer Riley. Heathcliff (Hardy) is a poor Gypsy boy adopted into the Earnshaw family where he and Cathy (Riley) find they are soulmates. Unfortunately, Cathy chooses to marry proper aristocrat Edgar Linton (Lincoln) and a furious Heathcliff, who has made his own fortune, decides on a spiteful revenge. **150m/C DVD.** *GB* Thomas (Tom) Hardy, Burn Gorman, Andrew Lincoln, Rebecca Night, Tom Payne, Sarah Lancashire, Charlotte Riley, Rosalind Halstead; ***D:*** Coky Giedroyc; ***W:*** Peter Bowken; ***C:*** Ulf Brantas; ***M:*** Ruth Barrett. **TV**

Wyatt Earp ½ **1994 (PG-13)** Revisionist epic suffers from bad timing as it follows "Tombstone" in telling the story of tarnished badge Earp (Costner), his brothers, and tubercular friend Doc Holliday (Quaid). Costner is barely believable as a 20-something lad, but fares better as he ages. Forty pounds lighter and likely delusional from lack of food, Quaid is unrecognizable but terrific, hacking his way to supporting Oscar territory. 'Course, Val Kilmer got there first. Huge cast finds screen time precious, even though film is some 40 minutes too long, due to prolonged intro to early Wyatt life. Originally envisioned as a TV miniseries till sheriff Costner took a hankering to bring tall tale to the big screen. Filmed on location in Sante Fe, New Mexico. For the full Earp effect, see it with "Tombstone" and relive the legend. **191m/C VHS, DVD, Blu-ray Disc, HD DVD.** James Gammon, Randle Mell, Lewis Smith, Ian Bohen, Alison Elliott, MacKenzie Astin, John Dennis Johnston, Jack Kehler, Kris Kamm, Michael Huddleston, John Doe, Kevin Costner, Dennis Quaid, Gene Hackman, Jeff Fahey, Mark Harmon, Michael Madsen, Catherine O'Hara, Bill Pullman, Isabella Rossellini, Tom Sizemore, JoBeth Williams, Mare Winningham, Betty Buckley, Adam Baldwin, Rex Linn, Todd Allen, David Andrews, Linden Ashby, Annabeth Gish, Joanna Going, Martin Kove, Tea Leoni, James (Jim) Caviezel, Karen Grassle, Owen Roizman; ***D:*** Lawrence Kasdan; ***W:*** Dan Gordon, Lawrence Kasdan; ***C:*** Owen Roizman; ***M:*** James Newton Howard. Golden Raspberries '94: Worst Remake/Sequel, Worst Actor (Costner).

Wyatt Earp: Return to Tombstone ½ **1994** O'Brian, who starred in TV's "The Life and Legend of Wyatt Earp" from 1955 to 1961, returns to Tombstone in 1914. Colorized clips from the series are used for flashbacks. Filmed on location in Tombstone, Arizona. **94m/C VHS.** Hugh O'Brian, Bruce Boxleitner, Paul Brinegar, Harry Carey Jr., Bo Hopkins, Martin Kove, Don Meredith, Alex Hyde-White, Jay Underwood; ***D:*** Frank McDonald; ***W:*** Daniel Ullman; ***C:*** James Roberson; ***M:*** Dana Walden. **TV**

Wyoming Outlaw **1939** Based on an actual incident, the story revolves around a small-town man who kills an outlaw. Barry, in the role that made him a western star, is forced into crime after a corrupt politician extorts money from him in exchange for a job. Lincoln, the screen's first Tarzan, appears in a supporting role. **62m/B VHS.** John Wayne, Ray Corrigan, Raymond Hatton, Donald (Don "Red") Barry, Pamela Blake, Leroy Mason, Charles Middleton, Elmo Lincoln, Jack Ingram, Yakima Canutt, Curley Dresden; ***D:*** George Sherman.

Wyvern **2009** Sci Fi Channel movie has global warming thawing out the non-fire breathing dragon that's been stuck in the ice in Alaska. Naturally hungry, the wyvern chows down on the residents of isolated Beaver Mills who are celebrating the summer solstice. This time the CGI of the flying beastie is actually acceptable. Last role for Don S. Davis who plays the town's retired military kook. **89m/C DVD.** Nicholas Chinlund, Erin Karpluk, Barry Corbin, Elaine Miles, Don S. Davis, John Shaw; ***D:*** Stephen R. Monroe; ***W:*** Jason Bourque; ***C:*** C. Kim Miles; ***M:*** Pinar Toprak. **CABLE**

The Wyvern Mystery **2000** Confusing and stodgy Gothic mystery based on an 1869 novel by Sheridan Le Fanu. As a child, Alice is taken in by Squire Fairfield (Jacobi) when her tenant father dies. Alice grows up into a beautiful young woman (Watts) and the Squire has lustful designs on her but is bested when Alice runs off and marries Fairfield's son Charles (Glen). The newlyweds wind up at an isolated Fairfield property that apparently has a curse on it and a now-pregnant Alice begins to have nightmares of tragedy. Watts is demure and Jacobi chews the scenery; everything else is a follow-the-numbers folly. **118m/C VHS, DVD.** *GB* Naomi Watts, Derek Jacobi, Iain Glen, Jack Davenport, Aisling O'Sullivan, Ellie Haddington; ***D:*** Alex Pillai; ***W:*** David Pirie; ***C:*** Simon Maggs; ***M:*** Philip Appleby. **TV**

The X-Files ½ *The X-Files: Fight the Future* **1998 (PG-13)** The TV series' fifth-season cliffhanger continues in the big screen adaptation, which supposedly has a plot clear enough so viewers unfamiliar with the series can still figure out what's going on. Creator Chris Carter uses the show's "mythology" episodes to have FBI agents Mulder (Duchovny) and Scully (Anderson) battling a global conspiracy involving the Cigarette-Smoking Man (Davis) and an international syndicate, colonizing aliens, and related paranormal perplexities. The big budget allows for some big action sequences and special effects and the two leads have a comfortable partnership. **120m/C VHS, DVD.** David Duchovny, Gillian Anderson, Martin Landau, William B. Davis, John Neville, Armin Mueller-Stahl, Blythe Danner, Mitch Pileggi, Terry O'Quinn, Jeffrey DeMunn, Lucas Black, Glenne Headly; ***D:*** Rob Bowman; ***W:*** Chris Carter, Frank Spotnitz; ***C:*** Ward Russell; ***M:*** Mark Snow.

The X Files: I Want to Believe **2008 (PG-13)** A decade after the first movie and six years since the TV series ended its run, the dynamic paranormal-investigating duo of Mulder (Duchovny) and Scully (Anderson) are drawn back to their FBI roots. While investigating a string of bizarre, though not particularly supernatural murders, they are prodded along by a disgraced priest (played by an unexpectedly low-key Connolly) and his seemingly psychic visions. The X-philes audience will enjoy them back in action, but will likely miss those wacky aliens. **104m/C DVD.** *US* David Duchovny, Gillian Anderson, Billy Connolly, Xzibit, Amanda Peet, Callum Keith Rennie, Adam Godley, Mitch Pileggi; ***D:*** Chris Carter; ***W:*** Chris Carter, Frank Spotnitz; ***C:*** Bill Roe; ***M:*** Mark Snow.

X from Outer Space **1967 (PG)** A space voyage to Mars brings back a giant rampaging creature. Badly dubbed. **85m/C VHS.** *JP* Eiji Okada, Peggy Neal, Toshiya Wazaki, Itoko Harada, Shinichi Yanagisawa, Franz Gruber, Keisuke Sonoi, Mike Daning, Torahiko Hamada; ***D:*** Nazui Nihonmatsu.

X Marks the Spot **1942** When a police sergeant is killed, his detective son investigates his murder. He's drawn into a crime ring which smuggles rubber (a scarce commodity during WWII). Quick pacing enlivens standard cliches. **55m/B VHS, DVD.** Damian O'Flynn, Helen Parrish, Dick Purcell, Jack La Rue, Neil Hamilton, Robert E. Homans, Anne Jeffreys, Dick Wessel, Vince Barnett; ***D:*** George Sherman.

X-Men ½ **2000 (PG-13)** The Marvel Comics characters, who were born with genetic mutations that give them superpowers, get their shot at the big screen. Wheelchair-bound telepath Charles Xavier (Stewart), AKA Professor X, runs a school to help others learn to use their mutant powers. The good guys, who seeks to work with humans, fight against the Magneto (McKellen)-led Brotherhood, who feel mankind is expendable. The story is simple enough for newbies to follow and takes itself seriously (no camp allowed) but doesn't have a lot of surprises and, except for Wolverine (Jackman), the characters aren't very involving. The setup calls for a sequel, which may flesh things out. **104m/C VHS, DVD, UMD.** Patrick Stewart, Ian McKellen, Famke Janssen, Hugh Jackman, James Marsden, Halle Berry, Rebecca Romijn, Ray Park, Tyler Mane, Anna Paquin, Bruce Davison, Shawn Ashmore; ***D:*** Bryan Singer; ***W:*** David Hayter; ***C:*** Newton Thomas (Tom) Sigel; ***M:*** Michael Kamen.

X-Men Origins: Wolverine **2009 (PG-13)** Jackman stars as the angry, adamantium-clawed mutant for the fourth time in this conventional, though briskly moving, popcorn flick from the Marvel Comics universe as we learn how James became Logan/Wolverine. James and his half-brother Victor (Schreiber) join in various wars throughout the decades. Eventually this draws the attention of nefarious General William Stryker (Huston) and his Team X mutant Army unit. Wolverine comes to regret his participation but will never be allowed to lead a peaceful life. Other mutants make appearances, with Reynolds (as Deadpool) and Kitsch (as Gambit) making the most of their screen time. **107m/C DVD.** *US* Hugh Jackman, Liev Schreiber, Ryan Reynolds, Dominic Monaghan, Taylor Kitsch, Kevin Durand, Danny Huston, will.i.am, Daniel Henney, Lynn Collins; ***D:*** Gavin Hood; ***W:*** David Benioff, Skip Woods; ***C:*** Donald McAlpine; ***M:*** Harry Gregson-Williams.

X-Men: The Last Stand ½ *X-Men 3* **2006 (PG-13)** Last stand? More like "can't stand." Hack-a-licious director Brett Ratner tarnishes the legacy of Bryan Singer's above-average superhero series with this lazy, unimaginative bore. Forget all the subtlety and coolness from the first two X-Men movies, because Ratner's replaced them with cheap-looking FX, incoherent storytelling, and barely disguised misogyny. Professor X's merry mutants have to contend with a resurrected Jean Grey (reborn as the all powerful Phoenix) and a new "cure" that threatens to wipe out mutantkind forever. Sounds intriguing, but you won't believe how often your eyes will involuntarily roll as major characters die stupidly, plot holes run rampant, and Wolverine cries like a wuss every ten minutes. **104m/C DVD, Blu-ray Disc.** *US* Patrick Stewart, Ian McKellen, Hugh Jackman, Famke Janssen, Halle Berry, Anna Paquin, Rebecca Romijn, Kelsey Grammer, Ben Foster, James Marsden, Shawn Ashmore, Daniel Cudmore, Ellen Page, Aaron Stanford, Vinnie Jones, Dania Ramirez, Olivia Williams, Shohreh Aghdashloo, Cameron Bright, Michael Murphy, Bill Duke, Eric Dane, Haley Ramm, Josef Sommer, Connor Widdows, Shauna Kain, Ken Leung, Kea Wong, Anthony Heald, Makenzie Vega; ***D:*** Brett Ratner; ***W:*** Zak Penn, Simon Kinberg; ***C:*** Dante Spinotti; ***M:*** John Powell.

X: The Man with X-Ray Eyes *The Man with the X-Ray Eyes; X* **1963** First-rate Corman has Milland gain power to see through solid materials. Predates Little Caesars campaign. **79m/C VHS, DVD.** Ray Milland, Diana Van Der Vlis, Harold J. Stone, John Hoyt, Don Rickles, Dick Miller, Jonathan Haze, Morris Ankrum, Barboura Morris; ***D:*** Roger Corman; ***W:*** Ray Russell, Robert Dillon; ***C:*** Floyd Crosby; ***M:*** Les Baxter.

X The Unknown ½ **1956** Geologist Adam Royston (Jagger) is sent to investigate a radioactive spot where a mysterious and deadly fissure has appeared. Seems a mud something that feeds on radiation bursts out of the Earth's surface every 50 years or so and kills. Now, it's expanding its territory. **78m/B VHS, DVD.** Dean Jagger, Leo McKern, Edward Chapman, John Harvey, William Lucas, Anthony Newley; ***D:*** Leslie Norman; ***W:*** Jimmy Sangster; ***C:*** Gerald Gibbs; ***M:*** James Bernard.

X2: X-Men United *X-Men 2* **2003 (PG-13)** The regulars are back as Prof. Xavier's X-Men must join forces with Magneto's mutants to battle a greater evil: a power-mad, mutant-hating general (Cox) out to find and eliminate all mutants. Cox is great as the general, full of self-righteousness and silky menace, properly denying his character the small moments of sympathy allowed to McKellan's Magneto. The story is better than in the original, even though it jams as much, if not more exposition into the plot and lingers too long on the teen romance between Rogue and Iceman. Script provides a well-executed and exciting central plot, while leaving plenty of threads and new characters that audiences will be anxious to follow in "X-Men 3." Special effects are fantastic, but they don't overshadow the story. **134m/C VHS, DVD, UMD.** *US* Patrick Stewart, Ian McKellen, Famke Janssen, Hugh Jackman, James Marsden, Halle Berry, Rebecca Romijn, Anna Paquin, Shawn Ashmore, Brian Cox, Alan Cumming, Kelly Hu, Bruce Davison, Aaron Stanford, Katie Stuart, Cotter Smith, Daniel Cudmore, Peter Wingfield, Michael Reid MacKay, Keely Purvis, Jill Teed, Alf Humphreys, James Kirk; ***D:*** Bryan Singer; ***W:*** Michael Dougherty, Daniel P. "Dan" Harris; ***C:*** Newton Thomas (Tom) Sigel; ***M:*** John Ottman.

X, Y & Zee ½ *Zee & Co* **1972 (R)** A brassy, harsh version of the menage a trois theme, wherein the vicious wife (Taylor) of a philanderer (Caine) decides to avenge herself by seducing his mistress. An embarrassment for everyone involved. **110m/C VHS.** Michael Caine, Elizabeth Taylor, Susannah York, Margaret Leighton; ***D:*** Brian G. Hutton; ***W:*** Edna O'Brien; ***C:*** Billy Williams.

Xala *The Curse; Impotence* **1975** Sembene is at the height of his powers in this bitter and brilliantly witty tale of a self-satisfied, "Europeanized" black businessman (he washes his Mercedes with Evian) who is suddenly struck down by the dreaded 'xala' curse, which causes impotence. As he searches desperately—and in all the wrong places—for a cure, his refusal to recognize the genesis of his condition explodes into both a tragic portrait of cultural enslavement and a sharp satire of man's endless capacity for self-delusion. Despite being heavily censored in Senegal, it is nevertheless one of Sembene's most widely seen and thoroughly entertaining films. Be prepared: the last sequence is sobering and unsparing. **123m/C DVD.** Douta Seck, Makhouredia Gueye, Thierno Leye, Dieynaba Niang, Miriam Niang, Illamane Sagna, Seune Samb, Abdoulaye Seck, Younouss Seye; ***D:*** Ousmane Sembene; ***W:*** Ousmane Sembene; ***C:***

Georges Caristan, Orlando L. Lopez, Seydina D. Saye, Farba Seck; *M:* Samba Diabara Samb.

Xanadu WOOF! 1980 (PG) Dorky star-vehicle remake (of 1947's "Down to Earth") eminently of its era, which is now better forgotten. Newton-John is a muse who descends to Earth to help two friends open a roller disco. In the process she proves that as an actor, she's a singer. Kelly attempts to soft shoe some grace into the proceedings, though he seems mystified as anyone as to why he's in the movie. Don Bluth adds an animated sequence. ♫ I'm Alive; The Fall; Don't Walk Away; All Over the World; Xanadu; Magic; Suddenly; Dancing; Suspended in Time. **96m/C VHS, DVD.** Olivia Newton-John, Michael Beck, Gene Kelly, Sandahl Bergman; *D:* Robert Greenwald; *W:* Richard Danus; *C:* Victor Kemper; *M:* Barry DeVorzon. Golden Raspberries '80: Worst Director (Greenwald).

Xchange *X Change* **2000 (R)** In the near future, bio-technology advances allow people to transfer their minds into the bodies of others. The process called "floating" lets anyone "travel" by having his or her consciousness transmitted anywhere in the world. When anti-corporate terrorists assassinate a powerful CEO, Baldwin is called in to investigate the murder. He is transported to San Francisco, where he ends up occupying the body of the lead terrorist (MacLachlan). Then he must fight to reclaim his body. The concept is more than compelling, and the action sequences generally overcome the relative low budget of the production. **110m/C VHS, DVD.** *CA* Stephen Baldwin, Kyle MacLachlan, Kim Coates, Pascale Bussieres; *D:* Allan Moyle. **VIDEO**

Xica 1976 A diamond rush in 18th century Brazil transformed that country's interior into a place of undreamed wealth and excess. Black slave Xica uses her sexual allure to rise out of poverty and capture the attentions of Joao, the governor of the diamond-mining town. She gleefully wields her increasing wealth and power, becoming the unofficial Empress of Brazil. Reportedly based on a real-life character. In Portuguese with English subtitles. **109m/C VHS.** *BR* Zeze Motta, Walmor Chagas, Altair Lima, Jose Wilker, Marcus Vinicius, Elke Maravilha; *D:* Carlos Diegues; *W:* Joao Felicio.

Xiu Xiu: The Sent Down Girl *Tian Yu* **1997 (R)** To foil Chinese censors, first-time director Chen was forced into guerilla filmmaking (accounting for the film's somewhat rough look) in this moving effort set during the Cultural Revolution. In 1975, teenaged city girl Xiu-Xiu (Lu Lu) is sent down to a remote corner of Tibet to learn horse training from peasant Lao Jin (Lopsang). She expects only to be gone six-months but is instead stuck, forgotten, on the plains. In desperation, Xiu-Xiu begins to trade sexual favors in exchange for the chance to return home. Based on the novel "Tian Yu" (Heavenly Bath) by co-writer Geling. Mandarin with subtitles. **99m/C VHS, DVD.** Lu Lu, Lopsang; *D:* Joan Chen; *W:* Joan Chen, Yan Geling; *C:* Lu Yue; *M:* Johnny Chen.

Xtro WOOF! 1983 (R) An Englishman, abducted by aliens three years before, returns to his family with a deadly, transforming disease. Slime-bucket splatter flick notable for the scene where a woman gives birth to a full-grown man, and various sex slashings. **80m/C VHS, DVD.** *GB* Philip Sayer, Bernice Stegers, Danny Brainin, Simon Nash, Maryam D'Abo, David Cardy, Anna Wing, Peter Mandell, Robert Fyfe; *D:* Harry Bromley-Davenport; *W:* Robert Smith, Iain Cassie; *C:* John Metcalfe; *M:* Harry Bromley-Davenport.

Xtro 2: The Second Encounter 1991 (R) Research facility conducts an experiment to transfer people to a parallel dimension. Out of the three researchers sent to the other side, only one returns, unconscious. Turns out that he is playing host to a biohazardous creature brought over from the other dimension who escapes into the air shafts and threatens to kill everyone in the building. One more problem: if the creature isn't killed, the computer system will fill the building with radiation. Sound familiar? It should, because this is a low-budget remake of "Alien." Good photography, adequate acting, but Vincent just isn't credible as a brilliant scientist. A sequel to "Xtro" in name only. **92m/C VHS, DVD.** *CA* Jan-Michael Vincent, Paul Koslo, Tara Buckman, Jano Frandsen, Nicholas Lea, W.F. Wadden, Rolf Reynolds, Nic Amoroso, Tracy Westerholm; *D:* Harry Bromley-Davenport.

Xtro 3: Watch the Skies 1995 (R) Military unit arrives at a remote island where the government has covered up a UFO landing. However, the island is now inhabited by a pissed-off alien whose mate has been killed. **90m/C VHS, DVD.** Sal Landi, Jim Hanks, Robert Culp, Andrew Divoff, Karen Moncrieff; *D:* Harry Bromley-Davenport; *W:* Daryl Haney.

XX/XY 1/2 2002 (R) In 1993, Coles Burroughs (Ruffalo) is studying film at Sarah Lawrence, meets fellow students Sam (Stange) and Thea (Robertson), and tries a menage a trois until pairing up with Sam for awhile. Ten years later, Coles is an ad exec living with longtime girlfriend Claire (Wright), Thea runs a restaurant with husband Miles (Thornton), and Sam has just returned from London after breaking her engagement. Sam and Coles meet accidentally and they're soon rekindling their long-ago flame. The sexual intrigue comes to a head during a weekend in the Hamptons. **91m/C VHS, DVD.** *US* Mark Ruffalo, Maya Stange, Kathleen Robertson, Petra Wright, David Thornton, Kel O'Neill, Joshua Spafford, Zach Shaffer; *D:* Austin Chick; *W:* Austin Chick; *C:* Uta Briesewitz.

XXX 1/2 2002 (PG-13) Director Rob Cohen attempts to update the secret agent flick for the X Games crowd with this stunt-riddled explosion fest. Xander "XXX" Cage (Diesel) is a former extreme athlete recruited by NSA agent Gibbons (Jackson) after he's busted stealing a senator's car. Xander is given a choice between jail time or becoming a special ops agent. He then spends the rest of the movie jumping off, sliding down and blowing up plot devices. If you're looking for an introspective drama about feelings, move along. If you're looking to watch things go "Boom!" while a thick-necked mumbling guy acts like a jackass, then put it in and get some popcorn. Cohen and Diesel previously teamed up on the unexpected hit "The Fast and the Furious," so the bets on the duo remaking "Steel Magnolias" as their next project have officially been taken off the board. **111m/C VHS, DVD, Blu-ray Disc, UMD.** *US* Vin Diesel, Samuel L. Jackson, Asia Argento, Marton Csokas, Danny Trejo, Michael Roof, Tom Everett, Richy Muller, Werner Daehn; *D:* Rob Cohen; *W:* Rich Wilkes; *C:* Dean Semler; *M:* Randy Edelman.

XXX: State of the Union 2005 (PG-13) Ice Cube replaces Vin Diesel (whose character, Xander Cage, is pointedly and dismissively pronounced dead about 20 minutes in) as Darius Stone, a former Navy SEAL in Gibbons' (Jackson) old unit jailed nine years ago for leading a mutiny against a general. When members of that old SEAL unit begin disappearing and Gibbons' XXX HQ is attacked, the two team up to find out why. What they find is an attempted military coup by the Secretary of Defense (Dafoe). To no one's surprise, there's plenty of explosions, gunplay, car chases, and mayhem, and none of it makes a damn bit of sense. But for those who enjoy that sort of thing, it is a wild ride. Don't expect anything resembling believability, though. **94m/C DVD, Blu-ray Disc, UMD.** *US* Ice Cube, Samuel L. Jackson, Willem Dafoe, Scott Speedman, Peter Strauss, Nona Gaye, Michael Roof, Sunny Mabrey, Xzibit, John G. Connolly; *D:* Lee Tamahori; *W:* Simon Kinberg; *C:* David Tattersall; *M:* Marco Beltrami.

Y Tu Mama Tambien 1/2 *And Your Mother Too* **2001** Mexican teenagers Julio (Bernal) and Tenoch (L'una) envision a guilt-free, sex-filled summer when their girlfriends go to Europe on vacation. At a wedding, they meet Luisa (Verdu), the wife of Tenoch's cousin, and begin a flirtation, telling her of their planned trip to a secluded (and non-existent) beach. When Luisa discovers her husband's infidelity, she decides to join the boys on their trip, and their adolescent sexual fantasies turn to emotional upheaval when she seduces them separately. Believe it or not, this is a comedy (and a funny one), with "American Pie" type jokes and shenanigans sprinkled throughout. But since this movie has a brain, and something of a soul, the consequences aren't always slapstick-funny. Spanish with subtitles. **105m/C VHS, DVD.** *MX* Gael Garcia Bernal, Diego Luna, Maribel Verdu; *D:* Alfonso Cuaron; *W:* Alfonso Cuaron, Carlos Cuaron; *C:* Emmanuel Lubezki. Ind. Spirit '03: Foreign Film; L.A. Film Critics '02: Foreign Film; N.Y. Film Critics '02: Foreign Film; Natl. Soc. Film Critics '02: Foreign Film.

Y2K 1/2 1999 (R) The gimmick of the Y2K bug is what this tame actioner hangs its plot on. A secret U.S. nuclear facility, established by the CIA in the Colombian jungle 30 years ago, is becoming destablized because its computer thinks it's 1969 and that the U.S. is under nuclear attack. A Y2K expert (Woolvett), a crazy general (McDowell), a CIA officer (O'Ross), and the facility's designer (Gossett), among others, all try to head off disaster. **103m/C VHS.** Jaimz Woolvett, Louis Gossett Jr., Ed O'Ross, Malcolm McDowell, Sarah Chalke, Ismael Carlo; *D:* Richard Pepin; *W:* Terry Cunningham, Mick Dalrymple; *C:* Ronald Orieux; *M:* John Sponsler.

Yaaba 1/2 *Grandmother* **1989** Young Nopoko and her cousin Bila chance to meet an old woman named Sana, who was outcast from their village as a witch years before. When Nopoko falls seriously ill, Bila wants Sana to help save her but the villagers refuse to let the old woman near. So Sana journeys to find a doctor in hopes that he can provide a cure the suspicious villagers will accept. Moore with subtitles. **90m/C VHS.** Assita Ouedraogo, Rasmane Ouedraogo, Fatimata Sanga, Noufou Ouedraogo, Roukietou Barry, Adama Ouedraogo, Amade Toure, Sibidou Ouedraogo, Adame Sidibe, Kinda Moumouni, Zenabou Ouedraogo, Ousmane Sawadogo; *D:* Idrissa Ouedraogo; *W:* Idrissa Ouedraogo; *C:* Matthias Kalin; *M:* Francis Bebey.

The Yakuza 1/2 *Brotherhood of the Yakuza* **1975 (R)** An ex G.I. (Mitchum) returns to Japan to help an old army buddy find his kidnapped daughter. He learns the daughter has been kidnapped by the Japanese version of the Mafia (the Yakuza) and he must call on old acquaintances to help free her. A westernized oriental gangster drama with a nice blend of buddy moments, action, ancient ritual, and modern Japanese locations. **112m/C VHS, DVD.** Robert Mitchum, Richard Jordan, Ken Takakura, Brian Keith, Herb Edelman; *D:* Sydney Pollack; *W:* Paul Schrader, Leonard Schrader, Robert Towne; *M:* Dave Grusin.

Yanco 1964 A young Mexican boy makes visits to an island where he plays his homemade violin. Unfortunately, no one can understand or tolerate his love for music, save for an elderly violinist, who gives him lessons on an instrument known as "Yanco." Not exactly riveting, but sensitively played. Spanish with subtitles. **95m/B VHS.** *MX* Ricardo Ancona, Jesus Medina, Maria Bustamante; *D:* Servando Gonzalez; *W:* Servando Gonzalez; *C:* Alex Phillips Jr.; *M:* Gustavo Cesar Carrion.

A Yank in Australia 1943 Australian farce/war mystery/romance/documentary tells the story of two WWII newspaper reporters whose ship gets torpedoed, stranding them in the Australian outback, where they manage to foil a Japanese invasion. **56m/B VHS.** *AU* Al Thomas, Hartney Arthur, Kitty Bluett, Jane Conolly, Graham Wicker; *D:* Alfred Goulding; *W:* Alfred Goulding; *C:* George Malcolm.

Yank in Libya 1/2 1942 No, not the American bombing raid of Khadafy, rather a low-budget WWII adventure pitting an American man and an English girl against Libyan Arabs and Nazis. **65m/B VHS, DVD.** Walter Woolf King, Joan Woodbury, H.B. Warner, Parkyakarkus (Harry Einstein); *D:* Al(bert) Herman; *W:* Arthur St. Claire, Sherman Lowe; *C:* Edward Linden.

A Yank in the R.A.F. 1/2 1941 Power's enthusiastic performance as a brash American pilot boosts this dated WWII adventure. He and his British allies seem more concerned over who gets showgirl Betty Grable than in the Nazis, but climactic air attacks retain excitement. Produced by Darryl F. Zanuck to drum up American support for embattled Britain and France. **98m/B VHS, DVD.** Tyrone Power, Betty Grable, John Sutton, Reginald Gardiner; *D:* Henry King.

Yankee Buccaneer 1/2 1952 With the arrival of impulsive Lt. David Farragut (Brady), Naval Captain David Porter's (Chandler) frigate is given a new assignment. The crew and ship are to sail to the Caribbean, disguised as pirates, and stop the criminals who have been preying on America's merchant fleet. Portuguese countess Donna (Ball) comes aboard since the pirates are threatening to overthrow her government, but when she and Farragut are captured, it's the noble Porter to their rescue. **86m/C DVD.** Jeff Chandler, Scott Brady, Suzan Ball, Joseph Calleia, George Mathews, Rodolfo Acosta, David Janssen; *D:* Fred de Cordova; *W:* Charles K. Peck Jr.; *C:* Russell Metty; *M:* Milton Rosen.

Yankee Clipper 1/2 1927 Deceit, treachery, and romance are combined in this depiction of a fierce race from China to New England between the American ship Yankee Clipper, and the English ship Lord of the Isles. Silent. **68m/B VHS.** William Boyd, Elinor Fair, Frank "Junior" Coghlan, John Miljan, Walter Long; *D:* Rupert Julian.

Yankee Doodle Dandy 1942 Nostalgic view of the Golden Era of show business and the man who made it glitter—George M. Cohan. His early days, triumphs, songs, musicals and romances are brought to life by the inexhaustible Cagney in a rare and wonderful song-and-dance performance. Told in flashback, covering the Irishman's struggling days as a young song writer and performer to his salad days as the toast of Broadway. Cagney, never more charismatic, dances up a storm, reportedly inventing most of the steps on the spot. ♫ Give My Regards to Broadway; Yankee Doodle Dandy; You're a Grand Old Flag; Over There; I Was Born in Virginia; Off the Record; You're a Wonderful Girl; Blue Skies, Grey Skies; Oh You Wonderful Girl. **126m/B VHS, DVD.** James Cagney, Joan Leslie, Walter Huston, Richard Whorf, Irene Manning, Rosemary DeCamp, Jeanne Cagney, S.Z. Sakall, Walter Catlett, Frances Langford, Eddie Foy Jr., George Tobias, Michael Curtiz; *D:* Michael Curtiz; *W:* Robert Buckner; *C:* James Wong Howe. Oscars '42: Actor (Cagney), Sound, Scoring/Musical; AFI '98: Top 100, Natl. Film Reg. '93;; N.Y. Film Critics '42: Actor (Cagney).

Yankee Doodle in Berlin 1/2 1919 A spoof of WWI dramas, with the hero dressing up as a woman and seducing the Kaiser into giving up his war plans. Typical Sennett slapstick with a music and effects score added to the silent film. **60m/B VHS.** Ford Sterling, Ben Turpin, Marie Prevost, Bothwell Browne; *D:* F. Richard Jones; *W:* Mack Sennett; *C:* Fred W. Jackman.

Yankee Zulu 1995 (PG) A young black boy, Zulu, and a young white boy, Rhino, begin a friendship in their South African homeland that is torn apart by apartheid. Twenty-five years later, they are reunited by chance and forced into race-reversal roles that lead to a number of comedic disasters and a renewal of their boyhood friendship. **89m/C VHS.** *SA* Leon Schuster, John Matshikiza, Wilson Dunster, Terri Treas; *D:* Gray Hofmeyr; *W:* Leon Schuster, Gray Hofmeyr.

Yanks 1979 An epic-scale but uneventful drama depicts the legions of American soldiers billeted in England during WWII, and their impact—mostly sexual—on the staid Britons. No big story, no big deal, despite a meticulous recreation of the era. **139m/C VHS, DVD.** Richard Gere, Vanessa Redgrave, William Devane, Lisa Eichhorn, Rachel Roberts, Chick Vennera, Arlen Dean Snyder, Annie Ross; *D:* John Schlesinger; *W:* Colin Welland, Walter Bernstein; *C:* Dick Bush; *M:* Richard Rodney Bennett. British Acad. '79: Support. Actress (Roberts); Natl. Bd. of Review '79: Director (Schlesinger).

The Yards 1/2 2000 (R) Director James Gray presents a gloomy, tragic New York story once again in his follow-up to "Little Odessa." Just out of the joint, Leo (Wahlberg) returns home to find that his mother Val (Burstyn) is suffering from a heart condition and his girl Erica (Theron) has taken up with his best friend Willie (Phoenix). Deciding to do right by mom, Leo decides to get a job with his Uncle Frank (Caan), whose company makes and repairs New York City trains. He discovers that his uncle isn't as squeaky clean as he thought when he joins Willie's crew, running highly illegal errands for Frank. On a sabotage mission to a competing company, Willie murders a security guard and tries to pin the crime on Leo. Leo is now chased by the cops and Uncle Frank's "family." Gray's writing is superb and the cast turns in good performances as well, although Theron's Noo Yawk accent tends to grate. **115m/C VHS, DVD.** Mark Wahlberg, James Caan, Charlize Theron, Joaquin Rafael (Leaf) Phoenix, Ellen Burstyn, Faye Dunaway, Tony Musante, Steve Lawrence, Victor Argo, Tomas Milian, Victor Arnold, Chad Aaron, Andrew Davoli, Robert Montano; ***D:*** James Gray; ***W:*** James Gray, Matt Reeves; ***C:*** Harris Savides; ***M:*** Howard Shore. Natl. Bd. of Review '00: Support. Actor (Phoenix).

The Yarn Princess 1/2 **1994** With her family threatened by separation, mentally retarded Marjorie Thomas (Smart) must prove to state authorities that she has the ability to take care of her six sons when husband Jake (Pastorelli) falls victim to severe schizophrenia. Boutsikaris plays Smart's defense lawyer. Average made for TV movie about a handicapped woman beating the odds. **92m/C VHS, DVD.** Jean Smart, Robert Pastorelli, Dennis Boutsikaris, Peter Crook; ***D:*** Tom McLoughlin; ***W:*** Dalene Young. **TV**

A Year in Provence **1989** Retired London executive Peter Mayle and his wife Annie decide to leave England to live in the south of France. They buy a 200-year-old farmhouse and experience all the trials and amusements of forging a new life in a different country, complete with different language and customs. They hoped for tranquility and what they got were eccentric neighbors, endless renovations, lots of company, and a taste for good food and drink. Based on Mayle's autobiographical novels "A Year in Provence" and "Tonjours Provence" and filmed on location. **360m/C VHS, DVD.** *GB* John Thaw, Lindsay Duncan, Bernard Spiegel, Jean-Pierre Delage, Maryse Kuster, Louis Lyonnet; ***D:*** David Tucker; ***W:*** Michael Sadler. **TV**

The Year My Parents Went on Vacation *O Ano em que Mus Pais Sairam de Ferais* **2007 (PG)** In 1970, Brazil is ruled by a military dictatorship, which forces the activist parents of 12-year-old Mauro (Joelsas) to go underground to escape arrest. So Mauro finds himself being cared for by his grandfather's grumpy neighbor Shlomo (Haiut), a member of the Orthodox Jewish community in San Paulo. Mauro's naturally confused and lonely as he tries to adjust to his new circumstances in this fairly familiar and sentimental tale. Portuguese, Hebrew, and Yiddish with subtitles. **103m/C DVD.** *BR* Caio Blat, Michel Joelsas, Germano Haiut, Daniela Piepszyk, Liliana Castro, Simone Spoladore, Eduardo Moreira, Paulo Autran; ***D:*** Cao Hamburger; ***W:*** Braulio Mantovani, Cao Hamburger, Claudio Galperin, Anna Muylaert; ***C:*** Adriano Goldman; ***M:*** Beto Villares.

The Year My Voice Broke **1987 (PG-13)** Above-average adolescent drama: a girl breaks a boy's heart by getting pregnant by a tougher, older boy, then leaves town. Blues-inducing, explicit, and not pleasant, but good acting from newcomers carries the day. Followed by "Flirting." **103m/C VHS, DVD.** *AU* Noah Taylor, Leone Carmen, Ben Mendelsohn, Graeme Blundell, Lynette Curran, Malcolm Robertson, Judi Farr, Bruce Spence; ***D:*** John Duigan; ***W:*** John Duigan; ***C:*** Geoff Burton; ***M:*** Christine Woodruff. Australian Film Inst. '87: Film.

The Year of Living Dangerously 1/2 **1982 (PG)** Political thriller features Gibson as immature, impulsive Australian journalist Guy Hamilton, who's covering a political story in Indonesia, circa 1965. During the coup against President Sukarno, he becomes involved with British attache Jill Bryant (Weaver) at the height of the bloody fighting and rioting in Jakarta. Hunt is excellent as male photographer Billy Swan, central to the action as the moral center. Rumored to be based on the activities of CNN's Peter Arnett, although the original source is a novel by C.J. Koch, who reportedly collaborated/battled with Weir on the screenplay. Fascinating, suspenseful film, set up brilliantly by Weir, with great romantic chemistry between Gibson and Weaver. Shot on location in the Philippines (then moved to Sydney after cast and crew were threatened). First Australian movie financed by a U.S. studio. **114m/C VHS, DVD.** *AU* Mel Gibson, Sigourney Weaver, Linda Hunt, Michael Murphy, Noel Ferrier, Bill Kerr; ***D:*** Peter Weir; ***W:*** Peter Weir, David Williamson; ***C:*** Russell Boyd; ***M:*** Maurice Jarre. Oscars '83: Support. Actress (Hunt); L.A. Film Critics '83: Support. Actress (Hunt); Natl. Bd. of Review '83: Support. Actress (Hunt); N.Y. Film Critics '83: Support. Actress (Hunt).

Year of the Comet **1992 (PG-13)** Amusing adventure/romantic comedy throws straightlaced Maggie (Miller) together with carefree Oliver (Daly) in a quest for a rare bottle of wine. Fine wine is Maggie's passion, and snagging this particular bottle will boost her status in the family business. Oliver is a pretzels and beer kind of guy, but his boss wants this bottle and will pay a lot to get it. Wants to be another "Romancing the Stone," but plot and characters are too thin. Nice chemistry between Miller and Daly sort of saves this one despite a disappointing script. Beautiful location shots of Scotland. **135m/C VHS.** Penelope Ann Miller, Timothy Daly, Louis Jourdan, Art Malik, Ian Richardson, Ian McNeice, Timothy Bentinck, Julia McCarthy, Jacques Mathou; ***D:*** Peter Yates; ***W:*** William Goldman; ***M:*** Hummie Mann.

Year of the Dog **2007 (PG-13)** Peggy (Shannon) is your basic single, middle-aged office drone whose one true love is her beagle, Pencil. When Pencil suddenly dies, Peggy goes off the deep end in her grief. Looking for a sense of purpose, Peggy takes up the cause of animal rights, with the encouragement of fellow activist Newt (Sarsgaard), and also adopts every stray she sees. Shannon plays her character absolutely straight: Peggy might be nuts, she might be unsympathetic sometimes, but she's completely sincere and those animals are lucky to have her. Screenwriter (and actor) White makes his directorial debut. **98m/C DVD.** *US* Molly Shannon, Peter Sarsgaard, Laura Dern, Thomas (Tom) McCarthy, Regina King, John C. Reilly, Josh Pais; ***D:*** Mike White; ***W:*** Mike White; ***C:*** Tim Orr; ***M:*** Christophe Beck.

Year of the Dragon 1/2 **1985 (R)** Polish police Captain Stanley White of the NYPD vows to neutralize the crime lords running New York's Chinatown. Brilliant cinematography, well-done action scenes with maximum violence, a racist hero you don't want to root for, murky script, and semi-effective direction are the highlights of this tour through the black market's underbelly and hierarchy. Based on Robert Daley's novel. **136m/C VHS, DVD.** Jack Kehler, Mickey Rourke, John Lone, Ariane, Leonard Termo, Raymond J. Barry; ***D:*** Michael Cimino; ***W:*** Oliver Stone, Michael Cimino.

Year of the Gun 1/2 **1991 (R)** McCarthy is an American journalist in Rome who begins a novel based on the political instability around him, using the names of real people in his first draft. Soon, ambitious photojournalist Stone wants to collaborate with him, and the Red Brigade terrorist group wants to "remove" anyone associated with the book. Although failing on occasion to balance the thin line it establishes between reality and perception, "Gun" aspires to powerful drama, offering a realistic look at the lives and priorities of political terrorists. Love scenes between Stone and McCarthy are torrid. **111m/C VHS, DVD.** Andrew McCarthy, Sharon Stone, Valeria Golino, John Pankow, Mattia Sbragia, George Murcell; ***D:*** John Frankenheimer; ***W:*** David Ambrose, Jay Presson Allen; ***M:*** Bill Conti.

Year of the Horse **1997 (R)** Jarmusch's documentary on the nearly 30-year rock phenomenon of Neil Young & Crazy Horse. Looking as gritty as some of Horse's riffs sound, pic intercuts footage of the band's performances in '76, '86, and the latest '96 European and U.S. tours shot on Super-8, High Fi-8 video, and 16 mm. Jarmusch wisely lets songs run full-length with complete performances intact, though lesser fans of the band may not be as thrilled about that. Falls short in capturing the spirit and essence of the band and their drive to stay together after all these years, but does show some cool behind-the-scenes moments that make it worthwhile to rock fans. **107m/C VHS, DVD.** ***D:*** Jim Jarmusch.

Year of the Quiet Sun 1/2 **1984 (PG)** A poignant, acclaimed love story about a Polish widow and an American soldier who find each other in the war-torn landscape of 1946 Europe. Beautifully rendered, with a confident sense of time and place, making this much more than a simple love story. In Polish with English subtitles. **106m/C VHS, DVD.** *PL GE* Scott Wilson, Maja Komorowska; ***D:*** Krzysztof Zanussi. Venice Film Fest. '84: Film.

Year One 1/2 **2009 (PG-13)** Comic shtick filled with jokes that were old when the Old Testament wasn't. Jack Black naturally looks like a caveman and Michael Cera naturally looks like a dweeb, which happen to fit their characters, who are dumb hunter-gatherers who get kicked out of their tribe for not pulling their weight. Somehow these Neanderthals stumble into various biblical situations, such as witnessing Cain kill Abel, and wind up in Sodom where Zed decides it would be fun to proclaim himself a religious deity (good for getting chicks). **97m/C DVD.** *US* Jack Black, Michael Cera, Olivia Wilde, June Raphael, David Cross, Oliver Platt, Hank Azaria, Christopher Mintz-Plasse, Paul Rudd, Harold Ramis, Vinnie Jones; ***D:*** Harold Ramis; ***W:*** Harold Ramis, Gene Stupnitsky, Lee Eisenberg; ***C:*** Alar Kivilo; ***M:*** David Kitay, Theodore Shapiro.

A Year Without Love 1/2 *Un Ano Sin Amor* **2005** Pablo (Minujin) is a young Argentinian writer living with AIDS who is boldly facing the physical effects of the disease while seeking a cure. As a clock sound ticks off the minutes of his fading life, Pablo still hopefully pursues a new love while partaking in the painful pleasure of S&M at various gay clubs in Buenos Aires. Taken from the real-life diaries of Pablo Perez. **95m/C DVD.** Juan Minujin, Mimi Ardu, Javier Van de Couter, Carlos Echevarria, Barbara Lombardo, Osmar Nunez; ***D:*** Anahi Berneri; ***W:*** Anahi Berneri, Pablo Perez; ***C:*** Lucio Bonelli; ***M:*** Leo Garcia, Martin Bauer.

Year Zero 1/2 *Shnat Effes* **2004** Similar in nature to the American-made "Crash." Several people, living in Israel at a pivotal point in their lives find their paths crossing as they work toward redemption from past wrongs. Laudable cast and intriguing soundtrack. Hebrew with subtitles. **131m/C DVD.** *IS* Dan Toren, Moni Moshonov, Sarah Adler, Uri Klauzner, Danny Geva, Ezra Kafri, Menashe Noy, Keren Mor; ***D:*** Joseph Pitchadze; ***W:*** Joseph Pitchadze, Dov Steuer; ***C:*** Itai Neeman; ***M:*** Ishai Adar.

The Yearling 1/2 **1946** This family classic is a tear-jerking adaptation of the Marjorie Kinnan Rawlings novel about a young boy's love for a yearling fawn during the post Civil-War era. His father's encouragement and his mother's bitterness play against the story of unqualified love amid poverty and the boy's coming of age. Wonderful footage of Florida. Jarman was awarded a special Oscar as outstanding child actor. **128m/C VHS, DVD.** Gregory Peck, Jane Wyman, Claude Jarman Jr., Chill Wills, Henry Travers, Jeff York, Forrest Tucker, June Lockhart, Margaret Wycherly; ***D:*** Clarence Brown; ***C:*** Charles Rosher. Oscars '46: Color Cinematog.; Golden Globes '47: Actor—Drama (Peck).

The Yearling 1/2 **1994** TV remake of the classic Marjorie Kinnan Rawlings novel about a boy and his orphaned fawn. The Baxters are struggling in '30s Florida: Pa Penny (Strauss) is a hardscrabble farmer and severe Ma Ora (Smart) has lost three of her four children. Surviving son, 12-year-old Jody (Horneff), gets more than his share of life's hard lessons—with even his adored pet causing problems. On the cloying side, the 1946 big-screen version is still the one to watch. Filmed in South Carolina. **98m/C VHS.** Peter Strauss, Jean Smart, Wil Horneff, Brad Greenquist, Jarred Blanchard, Philip Seymour Hoffman, Nancy Moore Atchison; ***D:*** Rod Hardy; ***W:*** Joe Wiesenfeld; ***M:*** Lee Holdridge.

Yella **2007** Yella, a woman from the former East Germany, lands a job in the western city of Hanover, where she plans to break free of her violent, estranged husband Ben. Despite the abuse, Yella continues to give in to her husband's demands and finds that her past will not stop haunting her. She bounces from one strange encounter to another as writer-director Petzold slices a tightly wound psychological thriller out of a timeline that weaves from present to past. **89m/C DVD.** *GE* Hinnerk Schoenemann, David Striesow, Christian Redl, Michael Wittenborn; ***D:*** Christian Petzold; ***W:*** Christian Petzold; ***C:*** Hans Fromm.

Yellow **1998** Eight Korean-American teens have big plans for their graduation night in L.A. but they didn't originally include trying to help Sin Lee (Chung) recover the large sum of his dad's dough that he lost. They get into more trouble trying to round up the cash and Sin reacts to their friendly efforts by running away and making things worse for himself. **90m/C VHS, DVD.** Soon-Teck Oh, Amy Hill, Michael Chung, Burt Bulos, Angie Suh, Mia Suh, Jason J. Tobin, Lela Lee, Mary Chen, John Cho; ***D:*** Chris Chan Lee; ***W:*** Chris Chan Lee; ***C:*** Ted Cohen; ***M:*** John Oh.

Yellow **2006 (R)** Cliched though energetic follow-your-dreams pic. Classically trained dancer Amaryllis (very sultry Sanchez) moves from San Juan to New York hoping to dance on Broadway. Needing a job while she auditions, Amaryllis works as a stripper (whose nom de pole is "Yellow") and soon has a favorite client, depressed doctor Christian (Sweeney), who wants to sweep Amaryllis away from all the sleaze. **90m/C DVD.** Roselyn Sanchez, D.B. Sweeney, Bill Duke, Manny Perez, Jamie Tirelli, Erika Michaels; ***D:*** Alfredo de Villa; ***W:*** Roselyn Sanchez, Nacoma Whobery; ***C:*** Claudio Chea; ***M:*** Andre Abujamra.

Yellow Asphalt *Asphalt Zahov* **2001** Writer-director Verete presents a collection of three fictional stories that highlight real-world cultural differences between Arabic Bedouin tribes and the Jewish community in Israel: the accidental death of a Bedouin boy at the hands of two callous Israelis, a German woman attempting to flee her stifling Bedouin marriage with her daughters, and a Bedouin maid caught having a forbidden affair. Grand view of the Middle East's desert. In Hebrew and Arabic, with English subtitles. **87m/C VHS, DVD.** Sami Samir, Tatjana Blacher, Raida Aden, Moshe Ivgy, Zavik Raz, Abed Zuabi, Motti Katz; ***D:*** Dan Verete; ***W:*** Dan Verete; ***C:*** Yoram Millo; ***M:*** Yves Touati. **VIDEO**

The Yellow Cab Man 1/2 **1950** Skelton plays a cab driver who is also an inventor of safety gadgets. When he invents unbreakable elastic glass he finds various crooks after him for the formula. Skelton's wacky inventions are amusing and the movie culminates in a breakneck chase through a home show exposition. **85m/B VHS.** Red Skelton, Gloria De Haven, Walter Slezak, Edward Arnold, James Gleason, Jay C. Flippen, Paul Harvey; ***D:*** Jack Donohue.

Yellow Cargo **1936** Ingenious "B" movie about a pair of undercover agents who blow the lid off a smuggling scam. It seems that the smugglers have been masquerading as a movie crew, and use disguised Chinese "extras" to transport their goods. The agents pose as actors to infiltrate the gang. **70m/B VHS.** Conrad Nagel, Eleanor Hunt, Vince Barnett, Jack La Rue, Claudia Dell; ***D:*** Crane Wilbur; ***W:*** Crane Wilbur.

Yellow Dust 1/2 **1936** Dull story of a gold miner (Dix) who hits a big strike but before he can make good on it he's accused of a series of stagecoach robberies. So he goes undercover to clear his name. Based on the play "Mother Lode" by Dan Totheroh and George O'Neil. **68m/B VHS.** Richard Dix, Leila Hyams, Andy Clyde, Onslow Stevens, Moroni Olsen, Jessie Ralph; ***D:*** Wallace Fox.

Yellow Earth 1/2 *Huang Tudi* **1989** In 1939 a soldier arrives in a small Chinese village to research folk songs. He becomes involved in the lives of a local peasant family, including a 14-year-old girl who wishes to escape from a pre-arranged marriage. Mixture of poetry, dance, music, and drama set against the barren landscape of the title. In Mandarin Chinese with English subtitles. **89m/C VHS.** *CH* Xue Bai, Wang Xueqi, Tan Tuo, Liu Qiang; ***D:*** Chen Kaige; ***W:*** Zhang Ziliang.

The Yellow Fountain *La Fuente Amarilla* **1999** Following the mysterious suicide of her boyfriend, Lola (Abascal) heads for Madrid to research the Chinese side of her family, and to get clues surrounding her beau's strange behavior. There, she meets Sergio (Noriega), a nerdy government employee whose hobby is collecting data on

Chinese immigrants. Together, they uncover an illegal immigrant smuggling ring, and Lola decides to take on the ruthless Triads. Director Santesmases allows the film to unfold at a deliberate pace, as another piece of the puzzle is revealed every few minutes. The problem is that most of the story seems very hackneyed. We've all seen the movie where the fearless girl influences the bookish guy, and the image of Chinese only being gangsters is getting very old. The bright spot in the film is Noriega, who sheds his playboy image and is quite good as the quiet Sergio. **94m/C DVD.** *SP* Silvia Abascal, Eduardo Noriega, Carlos Wu, Chuen Lam; *D:* Miguel Santesmases; *W:* Miguel Santesmases; *C:* Javier Aguirresarobe.

Yellow Hair & the Fortress of Gold ✓ 1/2 *Yellow Hair and the Pecos Kid* **1984 (R)** Princess who's part Indian and her sidekick fight bad guys and seek gold. Well-meaning, self-conscious parody. **102m/C VHS, DVD.** *SP* Laurene Landon, Ken Robertson; *D:* Matt Cimber; *W:* Matt Cimber.

The Yellow Handkerchief ✓✓✓ **2008 (PG-13)** Just out of prison, Brett (Hurt) is hoping his ex-wife May (Bello) will take him back, so he hitches a ride with teenage misfits Martine (Stewart) and Gordy (Redmayne) back to Louisiana. As they travel the three strangers come to trust, understand, and help one another. Hurt leads with an excellent performance in this movie that's unafraid to sit back and let the character dynamics unfold slowly and gracefully, avoiding excessive sentimentality. Title refers to Brett's request that May should hang a yellow handkerchief outside the house if she says yes. Adapted from a 1971 short story by Pete Hamill. **102m/C DVD.** *US* William Hurt, Maria Bello, Kristen Stewart, Eddie Redmayne, Veronica Russell; *D:* Udayan Prasad; *W:* Erin Dignam; *C:* Chris Menges; *M:* Eef Barzelay, Jack Livesey.

The Yellow Rose of Texas ✓✓ **1944** Rogers works as an undercover insurance agent (he's singing on a river boat) to clear the name of an old man falsely accused of a stagecoach robbery. The usual melodious Rogers lead. **55m/B VHS, DVD.** Roy Rogers, Dale Evans, Grant Withers, Harry Shannon; *D:* Joseph Kane.

Yellow Submarine ✓✓✓ 1/2 **1968 (G)** The acclaimed animated fantasy based on a plethora of mid-career Beatles songs, sees the Fab Four battle the Blue Meanies for the sake of Sgt. Pepper, the Nowhere Man, Strawberry Fields, and Pepperland. The first full-length British animated feature in 14 years features a host of talented cartoonists. Fascinating LSD-esque animation and imagery. Speaking voices provided by John Clive (John), Geoff Hughes (Paul), Peter Batten (George), and Paul Angelis (Ringo). The Beatles themselves do appear in a short scene at the end of the film. Martin fills in as music director, and Segal of "Love Story" fame co-scripts. ♫ Yellow Submarine; All You Need is Love; Hey, Bulldog; When I'm Sixty Four; Nowhere Man; Lucy in the Sky With Diamonds; Sgt. Pepper's Lonely Hearts Club Band; A Day in the Life; All Together Now. **87m/C VHS, DVD.** *GB D:* George Duning, Dick Emery; *W:* Erich Segal, Al Brodax, Jack Mendelsohn, Lee Minoff; *M:* George Martin, George Harrison, John Lennon, Paul McCartney, Ringo Starr; *V:* John Clive, Geoff Hughes, Peter Batten, Paul Angelis, Dick Emery, Lance Percival, George Harrison, John Lennon, Paul McCartney, Ringo Starr.

Yellowbeard ✓✓ **1983 (PG)** An alleged comedy with a great cast who wander about with little direction. Follows the efforts of an infamous pirate (Chapman) to locate a buried treasure using the map tattooed on the back of his son's head. Final role for Feldman, who died during production. **97m/C VHS, DVD.** Graham Chapman, Peter Boyle, Richard "Cheech" Marin, Thomas Chong, Peter Cook, Marty Feldman, Martin Hewitt, Michael Hordern, Eric Idle, Madeline Kahn, James Mason, John Cleese, Susannah York, David Bowie, Monte Landis, Kenneth Mars, Ferdinand "Ferdy" Mayne, Beryl Reid; *D:* Mel Damski; *W:* Bernard McKenna, Graham Chapman, Peter Cook; *C:* Gerry Fisher; *M:* John Morris.

Yellowneck ✓✓ **1955** A handful of Confederate Army soldiers desert, hoping to cross the Florida Everglades and eventually reach Cuba. The swamp takes its toll, however, and one by one the men fall by the wayside. A sole survivor reaches the coast. Will the escape boat be waiting for him? **83m/C VHS, DVD.** Lin McCarthy, Stephen Courtleigh, Berry Kroeger, Harold Gordon, Bill Mason; *D:* R. John Hugh.

Yellowstone ✓✓ **1936** An ex-con is murdered at Yellowstone National Park, at the site of a hidden cache of money, of which assorted folks are in search. Uncomplicated, well-meaning mystery. **65m/B VHS, DVD.** Andy Devine, Ralph Morgan, Judith Barrett; *D:* Arthur Lubin.

Yentl ✓✓ 1/2 **1983 (PG)** The famous Barbra adaptation of Isaac Bashevis Singer's story set in 1900s Eastern Europe about a Jewish girl who masquerades as a boy in order to study the Talmud, and who becomes enmeshed in romantic miscues. Lushly photographed, with a repetitive score that nevertheless won an Oscar. Singer was reportedly appalled by the results of Streisand's hyper-controlled project. ♫ A Piece of Sky; No Matter What Happens; This Is One of Those Moments; Tomorrow Night; Where Is It Written; No Wonder; The Way He Makes Me Feel; Papa, Can You Hear Me; Will Someone Ever Look at Me That Way?. **134m/C VHS.** Barbra Streisand, Mandy Patinkin, Amy Irving, Nehemiah Persoff, Steven Hill, Allan Corduner, Ruth Goring, David de Keyser, Bernard Spear; *D:* Barbra Streisand; *C:* David Watkin; *M:* Michel Legrand, Alan Bergman, Marilyn Bergman. Oscars '83: Orig. Song Score and/or Adapt.; Golden Globes '84: Director (Streisand), Film—Mus./Comedy.

Yerma ✓✓ **1999** Yerma (Sanchez-Gijon) desperately wants a child but is unable to conceive. The village wise woman (Papas) puts the blame on Yerma's husband Juan (Diego). As her obsession grows so does Yerma's hatred of her husband and she is tempted to seduce shepherd Victor (Cabrero) to fulfill her longings, which are now driving her to the edge of insanity. Based on a drama by Federico Garcia Lorca. Spanish with subtitles. **118m/C VHS, DVD.** *SP* Aitana Sanchez-Gijon, Irene Papas, Juan Diego, Jesus Cabrero; *D:* Pilar Tavora; *W:* Pilar Tavora; *C:* Acacio De Almeida; *M:* Vincente Sanchez.

Yes ✓✓ 1/2 **2004 (R)** When She (Allen) and He (Abkarian) cross paths in London some serious sexual fireworks go off and, at first, they ignore their cultural differences—She's an Irish-American scientist trapped in a dead-end marriage to a rich politician and He's a Lebanese refugee and surgeon-turned-chef. All good things must come to an end, though, as he despises Western culture while she questions Islamic values. Tries too hard to push its post-9/11 political message, as it awkwardly uses poetic meter for dialogue. **99m/C DVD.** *US* Joan Allen, Simon Abkarian, Sam Neill, Shirley Henderson, Sheila Hancock, Samantha Bond, Gary Lewis, Raymond Waring, Stephanie Leonidas, Wil Johnson; *D:* Sally Potter; *C:* Alexei Rodionov; *M:* Sally Potter.

Yes, Giorgio ✓✓ **1982 (PG)** Opera singer Pavarotti in his big-screen debut. He has an advantage over other non-actors trapped in similar situations (e.g., Hulk Hogan): He can sing (but of course, not wrestle). Lame plot (famous opera star falls for lady doctor) is the merest excuse for the maestro to belt out "If We Were in Love," "I Left My Heart in San Francisco," and arias by Verdi, Donizetti, and Puccini. **111m/C VHS.** Luciano Pavarotti, Kathryn Harrold, Eddie Albert, James Hong; *D:* Franklin J. Schaffner; *W:* Norman Steinberg; *M:* John Williams.

Yes Man ✓✓ **2008 (PG-13)** After a heartbreaking divorce, glum bank employee Carl (Carrey) attends a self-help seminar, where the eccentric speaker convinces him to stop saying "no" and start saying "yes"—to everything. Soon he finds himself bungee jumping off a bridge, learning Korean, and somehow becoming an overall better person through his new positive mantra, even meeting a girl (Deschanel—who's much too young for Carrey). A simple premise comes across as tame and shallow while goofball Carrey stretches it to the limit with very few glimpses of his true talents. Based on the memoir by Danny Wallace, an actual participator in the "yes" self-help program. **104m/C DVD.** *US* Jim Carrey, Zooey Deschanel, Terence Stamp, Sasha Alexander, Bradley Cooper, Danny Masterson, Molly Sims, Rhys Darby, Fionnula Flanagan, John Michael Higgins; *D:* Peyton Reed; *W:* Nicholas Stoller, Jarrad Paul, Andrew Mogel; *C:* Robert Yeoman; *M:* Lyle Workman, Mark Oliver Everett.

The Yes Men ✓✓ **2003 (R)** Documentary follows a couple of anti-government pranksters, Andy Bichlbaum and Mike Bonanno, who travel around impersonating representatives of the World Trade Organization. They disrupt various economic conferences, give fake interviews and speeches, and generally behave like nitwits. They also seem to be the only ones getting the supposed joke. Fighting the man has never been so bland. **80m/C DVD.** *D:* Chris Smith, Dan Ollman, Sarah Price; *C:* Chris Smith, Dan Ollman, Sarah Price.

Yes Nurse! No Nurse! ✓ 1/2 *Ja Zuster Nee Zuster* **2002** Residents at Nurse Klivia's Rest Home use a series of musical production numbers and a very slight storyline to fight the efforts of a nasty landlord who wants them evicted. **97m/C DVD.** *NL* Loes Luca, Paul Kooij, Tjitske Reidinga, Waldemar Torenstra, Paul de Leeuw, Edo Brunner, Lennart Vader, Frits Lambrechts; *D:* Pieter Kramer; *W:* Harry Bannink, Frank Houtappels; *C:* Piotr Kukla; *M:* Raymund van Santen, Ferdinand Boland.

Yes, Sir, Mr. Bones ✓ 1/2 **1951** Entertaining but dated musical about a boy who wanders into a rest home and inspires the old folks there to reminisce about their days as riverboat minstrels. ♫ I Want to Be a Minstrel Man; Stay Out of the Kitchen; Is Your Rent Paid Up in Heaven?; Flying Saucers; Memphis Bill; Southland. **60m/B VHS.** Pete Daily, Jimmy O'Brien, Sally Anglim, Cotton Watts, Chick Watts, Chet Davis, F.E. (Flourney) Miller, Scatman Crothers; *D:* Ron Ormond; *W:* Ron Ormond.

The Yesterday Machine WOOF! **1963** Camp sci-fi: A mad doctor tries to bring back Hitler. Don't worry, though: the good guys win. Predictable, dumb drivel. **85m/B VHS, DVD.** Tim Holt, James Britton, Jack Herman; *D:* Russ Marker.

Yesterday, Today and Tomorrow ✓✓✓ 1/2 *Ieri, Oggi E Domani; She Got What She Asked For* **1964** Trilogy of comic sexual vignettes featuring Loren and her many charms. She plays a black marketeer, a wealthy matron, and a prostitute. Funny, and still rather racy. Loren at her best, in all senses; includes her famous striptease for Mastroianni. **119m/C VHS, DVD.** *IT FR* Sophia Loren, Marcello Mastroianni, Tony Pica, Giovanni Ridolfi; *D:* Vittorio De Sica. Oscars '64: Foreign Film; British Acad. '64: Actor (Mastroianni).

Yesterday's Hero ✓ 1/2 **1979** A fading soccer star finds his career and love-life on the upswing. Poor production with equally lame pop music score. **95m/C VHS.** *GB* Ian McShane, Suzanne Somers, Adam Faith, Paul Nicholas, Glynis Barber, Sandy Ratcliff; *D:* Neil Leifer; *W:* Jackie Collins.

Yesterday's Target ✓✓ **1996 (R)** Paul (Baldwin), Jessica (Haiduk), and Carter (Carter) all possess special psychic powers in their future society, which is on the verge of destruction. They're sent back in time to rescue a young boy who may hold the key to saving their world but a glitch leaves them with collective amnesia and ruthless hunter Holden (McDowell) on their trail. **80m/C VHS.** Daniel Baldwin, Stacy Haiduk, T.K. Carter, LeVar Burton, Malcolm McDowell, Trevor Goddard; *D:* Barry Samson.

Yeti: A Love Story WOOF! **2008** Along with importing cheap products to Walmart, China apparently now also imports homosexual rapist Yetis from Tibet for the use of homicidal American cultists. Or so you'd believe after watching this film, which also implies that pillow fights are life-altering events that convince women to turn lesbian, and that by sharing chocolate and talking afterwards, victims of rape and their attackers can fall in love. Just beyond bad. **90m/C DVD.** Adam Balivet, Brie Bouslaugh, Laura Glascott, Eric Gosselin, Adam Malamut, Joe Mande, Jim Martin, Loren Mash, David Paige, Noah Wolfe; *D:* Eric Gosselin, Adam Deyoe; *W:* Eric Gosselin, Jim Martin, Adam Deyoe, Moses Roth; *C:* Eric Gosselin, Adam Deyoe. **VIDEO**

Yi Yi ✓✓ *A One and a Two* **2000** N.J. Jian is a middle-aged partner in a Taipei computer firm that needs to innovate if the business is to stay profitable. NJ thinks about teaming up with Japanese games designer, Ota, but a number of family difficulties begin to distract him and things unravel even more while NJ is on a business trip to Japan. Japanese and Mandarin with subtitles. **173m/C VHS, DVD.** *JP TW* Elaine Jin, Nianzhen Wu, Kelly Lee, Jonathan Chang, Issey Ogata, Suyun Ke; *D:* Edward Yang; *W:* Edward Yang; *C:* Weihan Yang; *M:* Kai-li Peng. Cannes '00: Director (Yang); L.A. Film Critics '00: Foreign Film; N.Y. Film Critics '00: Foreign Film; Natl. Soc. Film Critics '00: Film.

Yidl Mitn Fidl ✓✓ *Yiddle with a Fiddle; Castle in the Sky* **1936** Disguised as a man, a young woman travels about the countryside with a group of musicians, revealing her female identity only after falling for a man. One of Picon's finest roles and Green's biggest successes. Vaudevillian fare in Yiddish with English subtitles. ♫ Yiddle With His Fiddle; Arye With His Bass. **92m/B VHS.** *PL* Molly Picon, Simche Fostel, Max Bozyk, Leon Liebgold; *D:* Joseph Green.

Yin & Yang of Mr. Go ✓ **1971 (R)** A CIA operative must retrieve the stolen plans of an awesome weapons system. Set in Hong Kong, features a strong cast in a tangled tale of no particular merit. Unworthy spoof of Oriental intrigue flicks. **89m/C VHS.** Jeff Bridges, James Mason, Broderick Crawford, Burgess Meredith; *D:* Burgess Meredith; *W:* Burgess Meredith.

Yodelin' Kid from Pine Ridge ✓ 1/2 *The Hero of Pine Ridge* **1937** Autry tries to stop a war between cattlemen and woodsmen in Georgia. Standard horse opera notable for its location. **59m/B VHS, DVD.** Gene Autry, Smiley Burnette, Betty Bronson, Charles Middleton, Art Mix; *D:* Joseph Kane.

Yog, Monster from Space ✓ *Kessen Nankai No Daikaiju; Nankai No Daikaiju; The Space Amoeba* **1971 (G)** When a spaceship crashes somewhere near Japan, the aliens in it create monsters out of ordinary critters in order to destroy all the cities. A promoter gets a gleam in his eye and sees the potential for a vacation spot featuring the viscious creatures. Standard Japanese monster flick utilizing the usual out-of-synch dub machine. Dubbed. **105m/C VHS, DVD.** *JP* Akira Kubo, Yoshio Tsuchiya, Kenji Sahara, Atsuko Takahashi, Yukiko Kobayashi, Yu Fujiki, Noritake Saito; *D:* Inoshiro Honda; *W:* Ei Ogawa; *C:* Taiichi Kankura; *M:* Akira Ifukube.

Yojimbo ✓✓✓✓ **1961** Two clans vying for political power bid on the services of a laconic masterless samurai Sanjuro (Mifune), who comes to their small town in 1860. The samurai sells his services to both parties, with devastating results for all. Japanese with subtitles or dubbed. Re-made by Sergio Leone as the 1964 western "A Fist Full of Dollars." **110m/B VHS, DVD.** *JP* Toshiro Mifune, Eijiro Tono, Isuzu Yamada, Seizaburo Kawazu, Kamatari (Keita) Fujiwara, Takashi Shimura, Tatsuya Nakadai, Daisuke Kato, Yoshio Tsuchiya, Susumu Fujita, Hiroshi Tachikawa, Kyu Sazanka, Ko Nishimura, Ikio Sawamura, Yoko Tsukasa; *D:* Akira Kurosawa; *W:* Akira Kurosawa, Hideo Oguni, Ryuzo Kikushima; *C:* Kazuo Miyagawa; *M:* Masaru Sato.

Yol ✓✓✓ 1/2 *The Way* **1982 (PG)** Five Turkish prisoners are granted temporary leave to visit their families. An acclaimed, heartfelt film, written by Guney while he himself was in prison. A potent protest against totalitarianism. In Turkish with English subtitles. **126m/C VHS.** *TU* Tarik Akan, Serif Sezer; *D:* Yilmaz Guney, Serif Goren; *W:* Yilmaz Guney; *M:* Sebastian Argol. Cannes '82: Film.

Yolanda and the Thief ✓✓ 1/2 **1945** A charming, forgotten effort from the Arthur Freed unit about a con man who convinces a virginal South American heiress that he is her guardian angel. Songs include a lengthy Dali-esque ballet built around "Will You Marry Me?" ♫ This is the Day for Love; Angel; Yolanda; Coffee Time; Will You Marry Me. **109m/C VHS.** Fred Astaire, Lucille Bremer, Leon Ames, Mildred Natwick; *D:* Vincente Minnelli; ***C:*** Charles Rosher; ***M:*** Arthur Freed, Harry Warren.

Yongkari Monster of the Deep 🦴 *Dai Koesu Yongkari; Monster Yongkari; Great Monster Yongkari* **1967 (PG)** A giant burrowing creature is causing earthquakes and generally ruining scores of Japanese models. Dubbed. **79m/C VHS, DVD.** *KN* Oh Young Il, Nam Chung-Im; ***D:*** Kim Ki-dak.

Yonkers Joe 🦴 1/2 **2008 (R)** Palminteri is in familiar territory as a crooked gambler and bad dad. Joe heads up a group of con artists who scam unsuspecting marks at various gambling venues from Atlantic City to Vegas. One thing not going his way is the sudden reappearance of his mentally-handicapped 20-year-old son, Joe Jr. (Guiry), whose aggression has gotten him kicked out of his group home. The kid resents dad's parental neglect and dad resents the kid upsetting his plans. Think they can find some common ground and come to an understanding? **102m/C DVD.** *US* Chazz Palminteri, Christine Lahti, Tom Guiry, Michael Lerner, Linus Roache, Michael Rispoli, Roma Maffia; ***D:*** Robert Celestino; ***W:*** Robert Celestino; ***C:*** Michael Fimognari; ***M:*** Chris Hajian.

Yor, the Hunter from the Future 🦴 *Il Mondo Di Yor; The World of Yor* **1983 (PG)** Lost in a time warp where the past and the future mysteriously collide, Yor sets out on a search for his real identity, with his only clue a golden medallion around his neck. **88m/C VHS.** *IT* Reb Brown, Corinne Clery, John Steiner; ***D:*** Anthony M. Dawson; ***W:*** Anthony M. Dawson, Robert Bailey.

Yossi & Jagger 🦴🦴 **2002** Lior (Levi) and Yossi (Knoller) are soldiers stationed at a remote and snowy Army base on the Israeli-Lebanese border. They also happen to be lovers. They're discreet—Yossi is a career military officer—but Lior, who's nicknamed "Jagger" because of his charisma, is ready to leave the service and come out of the closet so they can live together. Tensions are heightened when two female soldiers, Goldie (Furstenberg) and Yaeli (Koren), arrive and Yaeli immediately makes a play for Jagger. Just as the truth about Yossi and Jagger seems certain to come out, the unit is sent on a dangerous night mission. Restraint is the word for director Fox, which only makes the situation more intense. Hebrew with subtitles. **71m/C DVD.** *IS* Ohad Knoller, Yehuda Levi, Hani Furstenberg, Aya Koren, Assi Cohen, Sharon Reginiano, Erez Kahana; ***D:*** Eytan Fox; ***W:*** Avner Bernheimer; ***C:*** Yaron Sharf; ***M:*** Ivri Lider.

You and Me 🦴🦴 1/2 **1938** Joe Dennis (Raft) is an ex-con now employed at the same department store as Helen (Sidney). They fall in love and marry without Helen admitting she's on parole herself and the rules forbid her to wed. When Joe realizes his marriage is illegal (and his wife's a liar), he picks up with his old gang and plans a robbery. Schizophrenic film is an uneasy mixture of comedy, pathos, romance, crime, and even some songs by Lang's associate Kurt Weill. **90m/B VHS.** George Raft, Sylvia Sidney, Harry Carey Sr., Robert Cummings, Barton MacLane, Warren Hymer, Roscoe Karns, George E. Stone; ***D:*** Fritz Lang; ***W:*** Virginia Van Upp; ***C:*** Charles B(ryant) Lang Jr.; ***M:*** Boris Morros.

You and Me 🦴🦴 *Toi et Moi* **2006** Ariane (Depardieu) writes for illustrated romance magazines but her own life is lovelorn since her boyfriend Farid (Sisley) isn't about to commit to her. Meanwhile, Ariane is oblivious to the interest of mason Pablo (Mencheta), who's working in her apartment building. Ariane's serious sister Lena (Cotillard), a classical cellist, has a dull boyfriend and is ready to succumb to the cocky charms of rakish violinist Mark (Zaccai) but it's a brief interlude that disrupts Lena's life more than she could have imagined. French with subtitles. **95m/C DVD.** *FR* Julie Depardieu, Marion Cotillard, Jonathan Zaccai, Tomer Sisley, Sergio Peris-Mencheta, Eric Berger, Chantal Lauby; ***D:*** Julie Curval; ***W:*** Julie Curval; ***C:*** Philippe Guilert; ***M:*** Sebastien Schuller.

You Are Here * 🦴🦴 **2000 (R)** You are a big loser. (Well, maybe not you personally but you get the idea.) Your job sucks, your love life sucks, life sucks in general. So you decide to quit your job and do what you've always wanted to do. And then your boss comes along and offers you a promotion. Now what? This indie feature gives you some possibilities. **86m/C VHS, DVD.** Todd Peters, Randall Jaynes, Ajay Naidu, Caroline Hall, Larry Fessenden, Heather Burns; ***D:*** Jeff Winner; ***W:*** Jeff Winner; ***C:*** Bryan Pryzpek; ***M:*** Byron Estep.

You Are Not Alone 🦴🦴 *Due Er Ikke Alene* **1978** Two boarding school boys find their friendship turning into first love. But the film doesn't completely dwell on this—when a fellow student is about to be expelled for a prank, the classmates organize a strike against the stern headmaster. Danish with subtitles. **90m/C DVD.** *CZ* Ove Sprogoe, Anders Agenso, Peter Bjerg; ***D:*** Ernst Johansen, Lasse Nielsen; ***W:*** Lasse Nielsen, Bent Petersen; ***C:*** Henrik Herbert.

You Belong to Me 🦴🦴 **2007** Whether you want to or not. Jeffrey (Sauli) thinks Rene (Lucas) is the man of his dreams and impulsively decides to move into the same New York apartment building. Overly-attentive landlady Gladys (D'Arbanville, properly horrific) doesn't have a good explanation as to why the previous tenant left all his stuff behind and it's too late to leave when Jeffrey discovers Rene has a live-in lover. Jeffrey starts getting creeped out by the strange goings-on and suspicious when he hears a faint voice calling for help. **82m/C DVD.** Daniel Serafini Sauli, Patti D'Arbanville, Heather Alicia Simms, Duane Boutte, Julien Lucas; ***D:*** Sam Zalutsky; ***W:*** Sam Zalutsky; ***C:*** Jonathan Furmanski; ***M:*** John Turner. **VIDEO**

You Can Count On Me 🦴🦴🦴 **1999 (R)** Sammy (Linney) is a single mom who works at the local bank in her small hometown. Orphaned at an early age, she has grown apart from her younger brother Terry (Ruffalo), who's become a self-destructive wanderer. When Terry comes for a visit, the love they still share as siblings conflicts with their unease over their adult selves and what they now expect from each other. Great performances and no pat resolutions. **109m/C VHS, DVD.** Laura Linney, Mark Ruffalo, Matthew Broderick, Jon Tenney, Rory Culkin; ***Cameos:*** Kenneth Lonergan; ***D:*** Kenneth Lonergan; ***W:*** Kenneth Lonergan; ***C:*** Stephen Kazmierski; ***M:*** Lesley Barber. Ind. Spirit '01: First Feature, Screenplay; L.A. Film Critics '00: Screenplay; N.Y. Film Critics '00: Actress (Linney), Screenplay; Natl. Soc. Film Critics '00: Actress (Linney), Screenplay; Sundance '00: Screenplay, Grand Jury Prize; Writers Guild '00: Orig. Screenplay.

You Can't Cheat an Honest Man 🦴🦴🦴 **1939** The owner of a misfit circus suffers a variety of headaches including the wisecracks of Charlie McCarthy. Contains Field's classic ping-pong battle and some of his other best work. **79m/B VHS, DVD.** W.C. Fields, Edgar Bergen, Constance Moore, Eddie Anderson, Mary Forbes, Thurston Hall; ***D:*** George Marshall; ***C:*** Milton Krasner.

You Can't Fool Your Wife 🦴🦴 **1940** Ball in two roles gives zip to this otherwise ordinary marital comedy. Previously blah hubby has a fling; previously blah better half wins him back with glamour. **69m/C VHS.** Lucille Ball, James Ellison, Robert Coote, Emma Dunn, Nita Naldi; ***D:*** Ray McCarey.

You Can't Hurry Love 🦴 **1988 (R)** A jilted-at-the-altar Ohio bachelor moves to Los Angeles and flounders in the city's fast-moving fast lane. A dull film with Fonda, daughter of "Easy Rider" Peter, playing a minor role. **92m/C VHS, DVD.** David Leisure, Scott McGinnis, Sally Kellerman, Kristy McNichol, Charles Grodin, Anthony Geary, Bridget Fonda, David Packer, Frank Bonner; ***D:*** Richard Martini; ***C:*** Peter Lyons Collister.

You Can't Take It with You 🦴🦴🦴 1/2 **1938** The Capra version of the Kaufman-Hart play about an eccentric New York family and their non-conformist houseguests. Alice Sycamore (Arthur), the stable family member of an offbeat clan of free spirits, falls for Tony Kirby (Stewart), the down-to-earth son of a snooty, wealthy and not always quite honest family. Amidst the confusion over this love affair, the two families rediscover the simple joys of life. **127m/B VHS, DVD.** James Stewart, Jean Arthur, Lionel Barrymore, Spring Byington, Edward Arnold, Mischa Auer, Donald Meek, Samuel S. Hinds, Ann Miller, H.B. Warner, Halliwell Hobbes, Dub Taylor, Mary Forbes, Eddie Anderson, Harry Davenport, Lillian Yarbo; ***D:*** Frank Capra; ***W:*** Robert Riskin. Oscars '38: Director (Capra), Picture.

You Can't Take It with You 🦴🦴🦴 **1984** Taped performance of the Kaufman and Hart comedy about the strange pastimes of the Sycamore family who must behave themselves to impress their daughter's boyfriend's stuffy family. **116m/C VHS.** Colleen Dewhurst, James Coco, Jason Robards Jr., Elizabeth Wilson, George Rose; ***D:*** Ellis Rabb.

You Don't Mess with the Zohan 🦴🦴 **2008 (PG-13)** Over-the-top comedy featuring Adam Sandler's latest incarnation, the Zohan—an Israeli commando who fakes his death in order to move to New York and fulfill his dream of becoming a hairdresser. Armed with a superhero-sized crotch and a desire to please the babes, the Zohan becomes a minor celebrity in the Big Apple, but runs into trouble once his homeland finds out. Vulgar and unapologetic, as Sandler will say or do just about anything to anyone (even a cat) for a laugh--but not very funny. Still, it's nice to see Sandler as something other than a dull dad or soft-hearted boyfriend. **113m/C DVD, Blu-ray Disc.** *US* Adam Sandler, John Turturro, Emmanuelle Chriqui, Nick Swardson, Rob Schneider, Barry Livingston, Shelley Berman, Omid Abtahi, Lainie Kazan, Dave Matthews, Ido Mosseri, Michael Buffer; ***Cameos:*** Mariah Carey; ***D:*** Dennis Dugan; ***W:*** Adam Sandler, Robert Smigel, Judd Apatow; ***C:*** Michael Barrett; ***M:*** Rupert Gregson-Williams.

You Got Served 🦴🦴 **2004 (PG-13)** Friends David (Grandberry) and Elgin (Houston)—both from real-life hip hop groups, B2K and IMx, respectively—have a falling out before the big street-dance contest that could earn them $50,000. David is a bit of a tomcat and wants to date Elgin's cute sister, Liyah (Freeman). There's also the issue of the busted drug run. This is about as complex as the story gets. Rookie writer-director Stokes—also of B2K with music-video directing credits—puts all the dancers' energy and talent out there but chops up the segments, thus diminishing the overall effect. Oh and, just to be clear, "you got served" means "I beat you...and BAD." So there. **94m/C DVD, UMD.** *US* Marques Houston, Michael "Bear" Taliferro, Omari (Omarion) Grandberry, Jarell (J-Boog) Houston, DeMario (Raz B) Thornton, Dreux (Lil' Fizz) Frederic, Jennifer Freeman, Christopher Jones, Meagan Good, Steve Harvey, Jackee, Malcolm David Kelly; ***Cameos:*** Kimberly (Lil' Kim) Jones; ***D:*** Christopher B. Stokes; ***W:*** Christopher B. Stokes; ***C:*** David Hennings; ***M:*** Tyler Bates.

You Gotta Stay Happy 🦴🦴 1/2 **1948** Heiress Dee Dee Dillwood (Fontaine) marries the man (Parker) her family approves of and realizes her mistake on their wedding night honeymoon in New York. Distraught, she manages to hide out in the room of failing airplane cargo company owner Marvin Payne (Stewart). He takes her with him on a California-bound cargo flight that winds up crashlanding in a field. By this time Dee Dee and Marvin are in love but then he finds out the truth about his would-be fiancee. **101m/B VHS, DVD.** James Stewart, Joan Fontaine, Eddie Albert, Willard Parker, Roland Young, Halliwell Hobbes, Stanley Prager, Mary Forbes, Percy Kilbride, William "Billy" Bakewell, Arthur Walsh; ***D:*** H.C. Potter; ***W:*** Karl Tunberg; ***C:*** Russell Metty; ***M:*** Daniele Amfitheatrof.

You Kill Me 🦴🦴🦴 **2007 (R)** Hit man in love. Frank (Kingsley) is a killer for his Polish mob family in Buffalo. Only his drinking problem wrecks havoc and he screws up eliminating rival Irish mob boss O'Leary (Farina). So Frank's Uncle Roman (Hall) sends him to San Francisco to sober up. Frank begins attending AA meetings (which are hilarious given Frank's profession) and gets a job at a funeral home. He also finds a grown-up romance with tough sales exec Laurel (a breezy Leoni), who doesn't faze easily. Still, Frank's family back home is being squeezed. Kingsley, who's done a lot of crap lately, proves again why the Brits bothered to knight him. **92m/C DVD.** *US* Ben Kingsley, Tea Leoni, Dennis Farina, Philip Baker Hall, Bill Pullman, Luke Wilson, Jayne (Jane) Eastwood, John Dahl, Marcus Thomas, Alison Sealy-Smith; ***W:*** Christopher Markus, Stephen McFeely; ***C:*** Jeffrey Jur; ***M:*** Marcelo Zarvos.

You Know My Name 🦴🦴🦴 **1999** Elliott is perfectly cast in this true story of legendary lawman-turned-moviemaker Bill Tilghman. Tilghman was connected to the Earp Brothers and then segued into early filmmaking, trying to produce authentic silent westerns in what turned out to be an ill-fated venture. In 1924, toward the end of his life, Tilghman is called upon by the law-abiding citizens of oil-rich boomtown Cromwell, Oklahoma to clean up its dens of iniquity. But Tilghman finds himself unexpectedly opposed by corrupt federal agent Wiley (Howard). **94m/C VHS, DVD.** Sam Elliott, Arliss Howard, Carolyn McCormick, James Gammon, R. Lee Ermey, Sheila McCarthy, Jonathan Young, Nataalia Rey, James Parks; ***D:*** John Kent Harrison; ***W:*** John Kent Harrison; ***C:*** Kees Van Oostrum; ***M:*** Lawrence Shragge. **CABLE**

You Light Up My Life **WOOF!** **1977 (PG)** Sappy sentimental story of a young singer trying to break into the music business. Debbie Boone's version of the title song was a radio smash, the constant playing of which drove many people over the edge. ♫ You Light Up My Life. **91m/C VHS, DVD.** Didi Conn, Michael Zaslow, Melanie Mayron, Joe Silver, Stephen Nathan; ***D:*** Joseph Brooks; ***W:*** Joseph Brooks; ***C:*** Eric Saarinen; ***M:*** Joseph Brooks. Oscars '77: Song ("You Light Up My Life"); Golden Globes '78: Song ("You Light Up My Life").

You, Me and Dupree 🦴🦴 **2006 (PG-13)** Call it "The Marriage Crasher." Having recently lost his job, home, and car, down-and-out Dupree (Wilson) becomes the houseguest from hell of his best friend Carl (Dillon) and Carl's reluctant new bride, Molly (Hudson). Dupree strings together rude and crude antics while his hosts react with predictable dismay and lack of confrontation skills; a mugging Douglas adds further strain as a menacing father-in-law who stirs the pot. But Dupree's sleazy charm contrasts with Carl's uptight angst, giving Molly plenty of opportunities to offer cute and soulful looks. Too bad they couldn't be funnier in the process. **108m/C DVD, HD DVD.** *US* Owen Wilson, Matt Dillon, Kate Hudson, Michael Douglas, Amanda Detmer, Seth Rogen, Todd Stashwick, Harry Dean Stanton; ***D:*** Anthony Russo, Joe Russo, Peter Ellis; ***W:*** Michael LeSieur; ***C:*** Charles Minsky; ***M:*** Rolfe Kent.

You Move You Die 🦴 1/2 **2007** Micro-budget Kiwi crime comedy, filmed in real time, that actually improves as it rolls along. Despite being a professional criminal, Mike (Sterling) gets mugged and robbed of the engagement ring he's just bought. He and psycho pal Rob (Harrison) have no problem resorting to violence as they careen through various Auckland neighborhoods in an effort to retrieve his property. **92m/C DVD.** *NZ* Bruce Hopkins, Ketzal Sterliing, Julian Harisson, Patrick Clarke; ***D:*** Ketzal Sterliing; ***W:*** Ketzal Sterliing; ***C:*** Ketzal Sterliing.

You Must Remember This **1992** When Uncle Buddy (Guillaume) receives a mysterious trunk, Ella's curiosity gets the best of her. She opens the trunk to discover a number of old movies made by W.B. Jackson—Uncle Buddy. Ella takes the films to a movie archive to find out about her uncle's past as an independent black filmmaker. After researching the history of black cinema, Ella convinces her uncle to be proud of his contribution to the film world. Includes a viewers' guide. Part of the "Wonderworks" series. **110m/C VHS, DVD.** Robert Guillaume, Tim Reid, Daphne Maxwell Reid, Vonetta McGee.

You Only Live Once 🦴🦴 1/2 **1937** Ex-con Fonda wants to mend his ways and tries to cross into Canada with his girlfriend in tow. Impressively scripted, but a glum and dated Depression-era tale. **86m/B VHS, DVD.** Henry Fonda, Sylvia Sidney, Ward Bond, William Gargan, Barton MacLane, Margaret Hamilton, Jean Dixon, Warren Hymer, Charles "Chic" Sale, Guinn "Big Boy" Williams, Jerome Cowan, John Wray, Jonathan Hale, Ben Hall, Jean Stoddard, Wade Boteler, Henry Taylor, Walter DePalma; ***D:*** Fritz Lang; ***W:*** C. Graham Baker, Gene Towne; ***C:*** Leon Shamroy.

You Only Live Twice 🦴🦴 1/2 **1967 (PG)** 007 travels to Japan to take on archnemesis Blofeld, who has been capturing Russian and American spacecraft in an attempt to start WWIII. Great location photography; theme sung by Nancy Sinatra. Implausible plot, however, is a handicap, even though this is Bond. **125m/C VHS, DVD.** *GB* Sean Connery, Mie Hama, Akiko Wakabayashi, Tetsuro Tamba, Karin Dor, Charles Gray, Donald Pleasence, Tsai Chin, Bernard Lee, Lois Maxwell, Desmond Llewelyn; ***D:*** Lewis Gilbert; ***W:*** Roald Dahl; ***C:*** Frederick A. (Freddie) Young; ***M:*** John Barry.

You So Crazy 🦴 1/2 *Martin Lawrence You So Crazy* **1994** Scandalous star of TV show "Martin" and host of HBO's "Def Comedy Jam" follows in the footsteps of raunchy humorists Richard Pryor and Eddie Murphy. Threatened with an NC-17 rating, Lawrence refused to edit and Miramax, the original distributor, dropped it. It was picked up by Samuel Goldwyn, who released the original version, uncut and unrated. Filmed live at the Brooklyn Academy of Music, Lawrence displays too little of his considerable talent, and too much vulgarity and poor taste. **85m/C VHS, DVD.** Martin Lawrence; ***D:*** Thomas Schlamme; ***W:*** Martin Lawrence; ***C:*** Arthur Albert.

You Stupid Man 🦴 1/2 **2002** Actually, "you stupid movie" would be more appropriate. First-timer Burns (brother of Ed) does his own NY romantic-comedy to mixed effect. Geeky writer Owen (Krumholtz) loses hot blonde girlfriend Chloe (Richards) to L.A.'s bright lights and TV fame. So he goes on a blind date and meets brunette babe Nadine (Jovovich) and they eventually get cozy. Then Chloe's TV show gets cancelled and she comes home to the Big Apple and wants Owen back. Is this a Woody Allen fantasy or what? **95m/C DVD.** David Krumholtz, Denise Richards, Milla Jovovich, William Baldwin, Dan Montgomery Jr., Jessica Cauffiel; ***D:*** Brian Burns; ***W:*** Brian Burns; ***C:*** David Herrington; ***M:*** David Schwartz.

You Talkin' to Me? 🦴 **1987 (R)** Fledgling actor who idolizes De Niro moves to the West Coast for his big break. He fails, so he dyes his hair blond and digs the California lifestyle. Embarrassingly bad. **97m/C VHS.** Chris Winkler, Jim Youngs, Faith Ford; ***D:*** Charles Winkler; ***W:*** Charles Winkler.

You Tell Me 🦴🦴 **2006** Three twenty-something slacker buddies on New York's Lower East Side continue to screw up their romantic lives by listening to each other's bad advice. Flint (Fenkart) has been dumped and is crashing at Jeff's (Ledoux) apartment; Jeff has just discovered that both his girlfriend and his mother (who's left his dad) have been cheating; and floundering Gray's (Cary) talented girlfriend is about to break big in the art world, leaving him even more insecure. **88m/C DVD.** Jack Davidson, Joshua Cary, David Ledoux, Bryan Fenkart, Amber McDonald, Maren Levin, Ciara Pressler; ***D:*** Joshua Cary; ***W:*** Joshua Cary, David Ledoux, Bryan Fenkart; ***C:*** Colin Bressler; ***M:*** Charles Newman. **VIDEO**

You Were Never Lovelier 🦴🦴🦴 1/2 **1942** Charming tale of a father who creates a phony Romeo to try to interest his daughter in marriage. Astaire appears and woos Hayworth in the flesh. The dancing, of course, is superb, and Hayworth is stunning. ♫ Dearly Beloved; I'm Old Fashioned; Shorty George; Wedding in the Spring; You Were Never Lovelier. **98m/B VHS, DVD.** Fred Astaire, Rita Hayworth, Leslie Brooks, Xavier Cugat, Adolphe Menjou, Larry Parks; ***D:*** William A. Seiter; ***M:*** Jerome Kern, Johnny Mercer.

You'll Find Out 🦴🦴 **1940** A comic mix of music and mystery as Kay Kyser and his Band, along with a debutante in distress, are terrorized by Lugosi, Karloff, and Lorre. ♫ The Bad Humor; I'd Know You Anywhere; You've Got Me This Way; Like the Fella Once Said; I've Got a One-Track Mind; Don't Think it Ain't Been Charming. **97m/B VHS.** Peter Lorre, Kay Kyser, Boris Karloff, Bela Lugosi, Dennis O'Keefe, Helen Parrish; ***D:*** David Butler.

You'll Get Over It 🦴🦴 *A Cause d'un Garcon* **2002** Seventeen-year-old high schooler Vincent (Baumgartner) is the star of the swim team; has a pretty girlfriend, Noemie (Maraval); and a best pal, Stephane (Comar). But Vincent is also seeing the older Bruno (Ohlund) and struggling with maintaining his secret. Then, new student Benjamin (Elkaim) obviously pursues Vincent and he's outted before the whole school—resulting in feelings of betrayal on all fronts. Soon, Vincent is discovering who his friends really are. French with subtitles. **90m/C DVD.** *FR* Julien Baumgartner, Francois Comar, Julie Marawal, Nils Ohlund, Jeremie Elkaim; ***D:*** Fabrice Cazeneuve; ***W:*** Vincent Molina; ***C:*** Stephan Massis; ***M:*** Michel Portal. **TV**

You'll Like My Mother 🦴🦴 1/2 **1972 (PG)** Surprisingly tense thriller finds preggers Francesca (Duke) traveling to Minnesota to meet the family of her recently deceased husband. Mrs. Kinsolving (Murphy) refuses to acknowledge her but Fran is forced to stay the night because of a snowstorm. She meets the rest of the clan, including mentally retarded Kathleen (Allen) and homicidal Kenny (Thomas). When she learns the truth about these various relations, all the strain pushes Fran into labor and no one's about to let her go to the hospital. Adapted from the novel by Naomi A. Hintze. **92m/C VHS.** Patty Duke, Rosemary Murphy, Richard Thomas, Sian Barbara Allen; ***D:*** Lamont Johnson; ***W:*** Jo Heims; ***C:*** Jack Marta; ***M:*** Gil Melle.

You'll Never Get Rich 🦴🦴🦴 **1941** A Broadway dance director is drafted into the Army, where his romantic troubles cause him to wind up in the guardhouse more than once. He of course gets the girl. Exquisitely funny. ♫ Since I Kissed My Baby Goodbye; The A-stairable Rag; Shootin' the Works for Uncle Sam; Wedding Cake Walk; Dream Dancing; Boogie Barcarolle; So Near and Yet So Far. **88m/B VHS, DVD.** Fred Astaire, Rita Hayworth, Robert Benchley; ***D:*** Sidney Lanfield.

Young Adam 🦴🦴🦴 1/2 **2003 (NC-17)** Writer/director Mackenzie uses the grim backdrop of 1950s Scotland for the richly dark character drama of his second feature. McGregor is Joe, a sexually charged but emotionally and morally devoid transient who finds work, room, and board on a barge owned by Les (Mullan) and his wife Ella (Swinton) who share a loveless marriage. When the body of a young woman washes up and is fished out by the barge-dwellers it sets off various reactions in all three. Joe seduces Ella under the nose of the emotionally repressed Les and a series of flashbacks reveal more about Joe's past and his relationship with Cathie (Mortimer), a young woman who reminds him of the deceased. Moody, noirish and visually engaging with stellar portrayals by all. Based on a novel by Alexander Trocchi. **98m/C DVD.** *FR GB* Ewan McGregor, Tilda Swinton, Peter Mullan, Emily Mortimer, Alan Cooke, Jack McElhone; ***D:*** David Mackenzie; ***W:*** David Mackenzie; ***C:*** Giles Nuttgens; ***M:*** David Byrne.

Young America 🦴🦴 **1932** Juvenile delinquent Arthur (Conlon) is paroled by Judge Blake (Bellamy) into the care of his strict aunt (Graham) but he runs away to stay with his best friend Nutty (Borzge) and Nutty's grandma (Mercer). When grandma gets sick, the boys steal medicine from druggist Jack Doray (Tracy) and get caught. Soft-hearted Mrs. Doray (Kenyon) takes Arthur in over hubby's objections but the kid becomes a hero after witnessing a robbery at the drugstore and outwitting the crooks. **70m/B DVD.** Spencer Tracy, Doris Kenyon, Ralph Bellamy, Beryl Mercer, Anne Shirley, Robert E. Homans, Tommy Conlon, Raymond Borzage, Betty Jane Graham; ***D:*** Frank Borzage; ***W:*** William Counselman; ***C:*** George Schneiderman; ***M:*** George Lipschultz.

The Young Americans 🦴🦴 **1993 (R)** Tough New York cop John Harris (Keitel) is sent to London to aid the police with their investigations into a series of killings related to a drug smuggling operation working out of the club scene. Harris wants to tie everything to the sleazeball gangster Carl Frazer (Mortensen) that he's been trailing. Slick formula with hard-working cast. Debut for 25-year-old director Cannon. **108m/C VHS, DVD.** *GB* Harvey Keitel, Viggo Mortensen, Iain Glen, John Wood, Keith Allen, Craig Kelly, Thandie Newton, Terence Rigby; ***D:*** Danny Cannon; ***W:*** Danny Cannon, David Hilton; ***M:*** David Arnold.

Young & Free 🦴 1/2 **1978** Following the death of his parents, a young man must learn to face the perils of an unchartered wilderness alone. Ultimately he must choose between returning to civilization, or remain with his beloved wife and life in the wild. **87m/C VHS.** Eric Larsen; ***D:*** Keith Larsen.

Young and Innocent 🦴🦴🦴 *The Girl Was Young* **1937** Somewhat uneven thriller about a police constable's daughter who helps a fugitive prove he didn't strangle a film star. **80m/B VHS, DVD.** *GB* Derrick DeMarney, Nova Pilbeam, Percy Marmont, Edward Rigby, Mary Clare, John Longden, George Curzon, Basil Radford, Pamela Carme, George Merritt, J.H. Roberts, Jerry Verno, H.F. Maltby, Beatrice Varley, Syd Crossley, Frank Atkinson, Torin Thatcher; ***D:*** Alfred Hitchcock; ***W:*** Charles Bennett, Alma Reville, Gerald Savory, Antony Armstrong, Edwin Greenwood; ***C:*** Bernard Knowles; ***M:*** Louis Levy.

The Young and the Guilty 🦴🦴 **1958** Two star-crossed teenagers are frustrated in their romance when their parents find one of their love letters and hit the ceiling. Told not to see each other again, the two take to sneaking around, which adds an edge to their relationship. Moving performances by the two young leads. **65m/B VHS.** Phyllis Calvert, Andrew Ray, Edward Chapman, Janet Munro, Campbell Singer; ***D:*** Peter Cotes.

Young and Willing 🦴🦴 1/2 *Out of the Frying Pan* **1942** A group of struggling actors gets hold of a terrific play and tries various schemes to get it produced. Based on the Broadway Play "Out of the Frying Pan" by Francis Swann. Unexceptional but enjoyable comedy. **83m/B VHS.** William Holden, Susan Hayward, Eddie Bracken, Robert Benchley, Martha O'Driscoll, Barbara Britton; ***D:*** Edward H. Griffith; ***W:*** Virginia Van Upp; ***C:*** Leo Tover; ***M:*** Victor Young.

Young Aphrodites 🦴🦴 1/2 *Mikres Aphrodites* **1963** Two young teenagers of a primitive Greek tribe discover sexuality. An acclaimed film retelling the myth of Daphnis and Chloe. Narrated in English. **87m/B VHS, DVD.** *GR* Takis Emmanuel, Kleopatra Rota, Vangelis Ioannidis, Eleni Prokopiou; ***D:*** Nikos Koundouros; ***W:*** Kostas Sfikas, Vassilis Vassilikos, Giovanni Varriano; ***M:*** Giannis Markopoulos. Berlin Intl. Film Fest. '63: Director (Koundouros).

Young at Heart 🦴🦴 1/2 **1954** Fanny Hurst's lighthearted tale of a cynical hard-luck musician who finds happiness when he falls for a small town girl. A remake of the 1938 "Four Daughters." ♫ Young at Heart; Someone to Watch Over Me; One for My Baby; Hold Me in Your Arms; Ready, Willing and Able; Till My Love Comes Back to Me; There's a Rising Moon For Every Falling Star; You, My Love. **117m/C VHS, DVD.** Frank Sinatra, Doris Day, Gig Young, Ethel Barrymore, Dorothy Malone, Robert Keith, Elisabeth Fraser, Alan Hale Jr.; ***D:*** Gordon Douglas; ***W:*** Julius J. Epstein, Liam O'Brien.

YoungHeart 🦴🦴🦴 **2007 (PG)** The other side of the spectrum from Don Argott's documentary "Rock School." This time around director Walker spotlights the Young at Heart Chorus, an eclectic nursing home choir that specializes in classic and indie rock. They run through staples by the Clash, the Bee Gees, and David Bowie, while struggling to learn Sonic Youth's "Schizophrenia" and James Brown's "I Feel Good." Lead by pseudo-radical teacher Bob Cilman, who probably spends too much time gushing over his pupils but never backs down from the challenge. Begins light and peppy, with corny jokes from the singers, but gradually darkens as their stories turn to age, depression, and death. Don't worry; it's wrapped up nice and pretty. **107m/C DVD.** *US* ***D:*** Stephen Walker; ***C:*** Edward Marritz; ***Nar:*** Stephen Walker.

Young Bess 🦴🦴🦴 1/2 **1953** Simmons and real-life husband Granger star in this splashy costume drama about 16th century England's young Queen. Features outstanding performances by Simmons as Elizabeth I and Laughton (repeating his most famous role) as Henry VIII. Based on the novel by Margaret Irwin. **112m/C VHS.** Jean Simmons, Stewart Granger, Deborah Kerr, Charles Laughton, Kay Walsh, Guy Rolfe, Kathleen Byron, Cecil Kellaway, Rex Thompson; ***D:*** George Sidney; ***W:*** Jan Lustig, Arthur Wimperis; ***C:*** Charles Rosher; ***M:*** Miklos Rozsa.

Young Bill Hickok 🦴🦴 **1940** A Rogers vehicle in the form of a very fictionalized biography of the famous gunfighter. **54m/B VHS, DVD.** Roy Rogers, George "Gabby" Hayes, Julie Bishop, John Miljan, Sally Payne, Monte Blue, Archie Twitchell; ***D:*** Joseph Kane; ***W:*** Olive Cooper, Norton S. Parker; ***C:*** William Nobles.

Young Blood 🦴🦴 **1933** A cowboy robs from the rich to help the poor. He's also interested in a foreign actress having trouble bonding with the townfolk. Lots of old fashioned western violence. **61m/B VHS, DVD.** Bob Steele, Charles "Blackie" King, Helen Foster; ***D:*** Phil Rosen.

The Young Bruce Lee 🦴🦴 **1980** A young boy named Bruce Lee and his friend both learn the martial arts in order to defend themselves from bullies. As they grow up Lee sets his sights on becoming a movie star while his friend performs in acrobatic stage shows. Though Lee achieves stardom, he finds himself hounded by martial artists that want to challenge him. This unauthorized biopic follows the major events in Bruce Lee's life but most of it is cliched fabrication. The film is cheap and poorly crafted, but Lung (AKA Bruce Li) does a fairly successful job of mimicking Lee and he's helped by an accurate hairdo and wardrobe. As far as Bruce Lee wannabe films, you could do a lot worse. Despite the packaging, there is no Lee footage in the film—only a newsphoto of his body. **80m/C VHS, DVD.** *HK* Bruce Li, Bolo Yeung, Bruce Le, Lily Hua; ***D:*** Bruce Le; ***C:*** Alardar Kline.

Young Buffalo Bill 🦴🦴 **1940** Buffalo Bill battles the Spanish land-grant patrons. **54m/B VHS, DVD.** Roy Rogers, George "Gabby" Hayes, Pauline Moore; ***D:*** Joseph Kane.

Young Caruso 🦴🦴 *Enrico Caruso: Leggenda di Una Voce* **1951** Dramatic biography of legendary tenor Enrico Caruso, following his life from childhood poverty in Naples to the beginning of his rise to fame. Dubbed in English. **78m/B VHS, DVD.** *IT* Gina Lollobrigida, Ermanno Randi, Gino Saltamerenda, Maria V. Tasnady; ***D:*** Giacomo Gentilomo; ***W:*** Giacomo Gentilomo; ***C:*** Tino Santoni; ***M:*** Carlo Franci.

Young Catherine 🦴🦴🦴 **1991** Made-for-TV account of Russia's strongest female ruler, the girl who would be Catherine the Great. Star-studded cast and excellent production values. Script and strong cast make Ormond look like a lightweight. Filmed in Leningrad. Also available in 186-minute version. **150m/C VHS.** Vanessa Redgrave, Christopher Plummer, Marthe Keller, Franco Nero, Julia Ormond, Maximilian Schell, Reece Dinsdale, Mark Frankel; ***D:*** Michael Anderson Sr.; ***W:*** Chris Bryant.

Young Charlie Chaplin 🦴🦴 **1988** A British-made TV biography of the legendary silent screen comic. **160m/C VHS.** Ian McShane, Twiggy; ***M:*** Rachel Portman.

A Young Connecticut Yankee in King Arthur's Court 🦴🦴 1/2 **1995** A modern-day teenager timetravels back to the court of King Arthur and Camelot. Based on the book by Mark Twain. **93m/C VHS.** Michael York, Theresa Russell, Nick Mancuso, Philippe Ross, Jack Langedijk, Polly Shannon, Paul Hopkins; ***D:*** Ralph L. (R.L.) Thomas; ***W:*** Ralph L. (R.L.) Thomas, Frank Encarnacao; ***C:*** John Berrie; ***M:*** Alan Reeves.

Young Doctors in Love 🦴🦴 **1982 (R)** Spoof of medical soap operas features a chaotic scenario at City Hospital, where the young men and women on the staff have better things to do than attend to their patients. Good cast keeps this one alive, though many laughs are forced. Includes cameos by real soap star, including then-General Hospital star Moore. **95m/C VHS, DVD.** Dabney Coleman, Sean Young, Michael McKean, Harry Dean Stanton, Hector Elizondo, Patrick Macnee, Pamela Reed, Saul Rubinek; ***Cameos:*** Demi Moore, Janine Turner; ***D:*** Garry Marshall; ***W:*** Michael Elias, Rich Eustis; ***M:*** Maurice Jarre.

Young Einstein 🦴🦴 **1989 (PG)** A goofy, irreverent Australian farce starring, directed, co-scripted and co-produced by Serious, depicting Einstein as a young Outback clod who splits beer atoms and invents rock and roll. Winner of several Aussie awards. Fun for the kids. **91m/C VHS, DVD.** *AU* Yahoo Serious, Odile Le Clezio, John Howard, Pee Wee Wilson, Su Cruickshank, Lulu Pinkus, Kaarin Fairfax, Jonathan Coleman; ***D:*** Yahoo

Serious; *W:* David Roach, Yahoo Serious; *C:* Jeff Darling; *M:* Martin Armiger, William Motzing, Tommy Tycho.

Young Frankenstein 1974 **(PG)** Young Dr. Frankenstein (Wilder), a brain surgeon, inherits the family castle back in Transylvania. He's skittish about the family business, but when he learns his grandfather's secrets, he becomes obsessed with making his own monster. Wilder and monster Boyle make a memorable song-and-dance team to Irving Berlin's "Puttin' on the Ritz," and Hackman's cameo as a blind man is inspired. Garr ("What knockers!" "Oh, sank you!") is adorable as a fraulein, and Leachman ("He's vass my—boyfriend!") is wonderfully scary. Wilder saves the creature with a switcheroo, in which the doctor ends up with a certain monster-sized body part. Hilarious parody. **108m/B VHS, DVD, Blu-ray Disc.** Peter Boyle, Gene Wilder, Marty Feldman, Madeline Kahn, Cloris Leachman, Teri Garr, Kenneth Mars, Richard Haydn, Gene Hackman, Liam Dunn, Monte Landis; *D:* Mel Brooks; *W:* Mel Brooks, Gene Wilder; *C:* Gerald Hirschfeld; *M:* John Morris. Natl. Film Reg. '03.

The Young Girl and the Monsoon 1/2 **1999** Successful photojournalist and divorced dad Hank (Kinney) agrees to take care of 13-year-old daughter Constance (Muth) while her mother, with whom she usually lives, is out of town. Constance is a mass of teenage contradictions—constantly testing her boundaries (and Hank's sanity and patience). Hank has kept his work and life, including the fact that his girlfriend is a twentysomething model named Erin (Avital), from Constance but there's an explosion in every conversation. **93m/C VHS, DVD.** Terry Kinney, Ellen Muth, Mili Avital, Diane Venora, Tim Guinee, Domenick Lombardozzi; *D:* James Ryan; *W:* James Ryan; *C:* Ben Wolf; *M:* David Carbonara.

The Young Girls of Rochefort 1/2 *Les Demoiselles de Rochefort* **1968** Twins sisters Delphine and Solange (played by sisters Deneuve and Dorleac) dream of romance, which first appears in the forms of salesmen Etienne (Chakiris) and Bill (Dale), who are minor distractions for the real thing—artistic sailor Maxence (Perrin) and concert pianist Andy (Kelly). Demy's followup to the more compelling "The Umbrellas of Cherbourg" is still an equally candy-colored musical fantasy. Rochefort (like Cherbourg) is an actual town that Demy took over for filming. **125m/C VHS, DVD.** *FR* Catherine Deneuve, Francoise Dorleac, George Chakiris, Grover Dale, Gene Kelly, Jacques Perrin, Danielle Darrieux, Michel Piccoli, Pamela Hart, Jacques Riberolles, Leslie North; *D:* Jacques Demy; *W:* Jacques Demy; *C:* Ghislan Cloquet; *M:* Michel Legrand.

The Young Graduates 1971 **(PG)** Hormonally imbalanced teens come of age in spite of meandering plot. Features "Breaking Away" star Christopher in big screen debut. **99m/C VHS.** Patricia Wymer, Steven Stewart, Gary Rist, Bruce Kirby, Jennifer Ritt, Dennis Christopher; *D:* Robert Anderson.

Young Guns 1/2 **1988 (R)** A sophomoric Wild Bunch look-alike that ends up resembling a western version of the Bowery Boys. Provides a portrait of Billy the Kid and his gang as they move from prairie trash to demi-legends. Features several fine performances by a popular group of today's young stars. **107m/C VHS, DVD, Blu-ray Disc, UMD.** Emilio Estevez, Kiefer Sutherland, Lou Diamond Phillips, Charlie Sheen, Casey Siemaszko, Dermot Mulroney, Terence Stamp, Terry O'Quinn, Jack Palance, Brian Keith, Patrick Wayne, Sharon Thomas; *D:* Christopher Cain; *W:* John Fusco; *C:* Dean Semler; *M:* Anthony Marinelli, Brian Backus, Brian Banks.

Young Guns 2 **1990 (PG-13)** Brat Pack vehicle neo-Western sequel about Billy the Kid (Estevez) and his gang. Told as an account by Brushy Bill Roberts who, in 1950, claims to be the real Billy the Kid and recounts his continuing adventures with Doc (Sutherland), Chavez (Phillips) and Pat Garrett (Petersen). Not bad for a sequel, thanks mostly to Petersen. **105m/C VHS, DVD.** Emilio Estevez, Kiefer Sutherland, Lou Diamond Phillips, Christian Slater, William L. Petersen, Alan Ruck, R.D. Call, James Coburn, Balthazar Getty, Jack Kehoe, Robert Knepper, Jenny Wright, Tracey Walter, Ginger Lynn Allen, Jon Bon Jovi, Viggo Mortensen, Leon Rippy, Bradley Whitford, Scott Wilson, John Hammil; *D:* Geoff Murphy; *W:* John Fusco; *C:* Dean Semler; *M:* Alan Silvestri. Golden Globes '91: Song ("Blaze of Glory").

Young Hercules 1/2 **1997 (PG-13)** Seventeen-year-old Herc (Bohen) is a confused teen, torn between his mortal and immortal sides. So concerned mom Alcmene sends the kid to Cherion's academy where Herc can learn to be a warrior and where he'll meet friends and rivals Iolus (O'Gorman), Prince Jason (Conrad), and the beautiful Yvenna (Stewart). Oh yes, war god Ares (Smith) also shows up, trying to prevent half-brother Herc and his friends from obtaining the golden fleece for Jason's dying father. **93m/C VHS, DVD.** Ian Bohen, Dean O'Gorman, Johna Stewart, Chris Conrad, Kevin Smith; *D:* T.J. Scott; *W:* Robert Tapert, Andrew Dettmann, Daniel Truly; *C:* John Mahaffie; *M:* Joseph LoDuca. **VIDEO**

The Young in Heart **1938** A lonely, old woman allows a family of con-artists into her life for companionship. Impressed by her sweet nature, the parasitic brood reforms. The cute comedy was a real crowd-pleaser in its day, especially after the bittersweet ending was replaced with a happier variety. Based on the novel "The Gay Banditti" by I.A.R. Wylie. **90m/C VHS, DVD.** Janet Gaynor, Douglas Fairbanks Jr., Paulette Goddard, Roland Young, Billie Burke, Minnie Dupree, Richard Carlson, Charles Halton; *D:* Richard Wallace; *W:* Charles Bennett, Paul Osborn.

Young Ivanhoe 1/2 **1995** Ivanhoe learns how to be a warrior, with some help from Robin Hood and the Black Knight, inspiring others to follow him into battle to save their land from seizure by the Norman invaders. **96m/C VHS, DVD.** Stacy Keach, Nick Mancuso, Margot Kidder, Kris Holden-Ried, Rachel Blanchard, Matthew Daniels; *D:* Ralph L. (R.L.) Thomas; *W:* Ralph L. (R.L.) Thomas, Frank Encarnacao; *C:* John Berrie; *M:* Alan Reeves.

Young Lady Chatterly 2 1/2 **1985** A poor sequel to the popular MacBride film, with only the name of the Lawrence classic. Chatterly inherits the family mansion and fools around with the servants and any one else who comes along. Unrated version with 13 minutes of deleted footage is also available. **87m/C VHS, DVD.** Sybil Danning, Adam West, Harlee MacBride; *D:* Alan Roberts.

The Young Land 1/2 **1959** Less-than-inspiring western does feature a good performance by Hopper as malcontent bully Hatfield Carnes. Carnes kills a respected Mexican in a barroom gunfight in 1848 California and sheriff Jim Ellison (Wayne) is quick to call territorial judge Isham (O'Herlihy) to ensure a fair trial—with the rest of the Spanish-speaking town looking on in skepticism. Based on the story "Frontier Frenzy" by John Reese. **88m/C VHS, DVD.** Dennis Hopper, Patrick Wayne, Dan O'Herlihy, Yvonne Craig, Ken Curtis, Pedro Gonzalez-Gonzalez; *D:* Ted Tetzlaff; *W:* Norman S. Hall; *C:* Winton C. Hoch, Henry Sharp; *M:* Dimitri Tiomkin.

The Young Lions **1958** A cynical WWII epic following the experiences of a young American officer and a disillusioned Nazi in the war's last days. Martin does fine in his first dramatic role. As the Nazi, Brando sensitively considers the belief that Hitler would save Germany. A realistic anti-war film. **167m/B VHS, DVD.** Marlon Brando, Montgomery Clift, Dean Martin, Hope Lange, Barbara Rush, Lee Van Cleef, Maximilian Schell, May Britt, Dora Doll, Liliane Montevecchi, Parley Baer, Arthur Franz, Hal Baylor, Richard Gardner, Herbert Rudley, L.Q. Jones; *D:* Edward Dmytryk; *W:* Edward Anhalt; *C:* Joe MacDonald; *M:* Hugo Friedhofer.

Young Love, First Love 1/2 **1979** TV movie about a young woman who must decide whether to have sex with her boyfriend. Sound familiar? Pretty blah, earnest story, though well cast. **100m/C VHS.** Valerie Bertinelli, Leslie Ackerman, Timothy Hutton, Arlen Dean Snyder, Fionnula Flanagan; *D:* Steven Hilliard Stern. **TV**

Young Love—Lemon Popsicle 7 **1987 (R)** Three hunks stalk the beaches in search of babes. **91m/C VHS.** Yftach Katzur, Zachi Noy, Jonathan Sagalle, Sonja Martin; *D:* Walter Bennett.

Young Man with a Horn **1950** Dorothy Baker's novel, which was loosely based on the life of jazz immortal Bix Beiderbecke, was even more loosely adapted for this film, featuring Kirk as an angst-ridden trumpeter who can't seem to hit that mystical "high note." ♫The Very Thought of You; I May be Wrong; The Man I Love; Too Marvelous for Words; With a Song in My Heart; Pretty Baby; I Only Have Eyes for You; Limehouse Blues; Melancholy Rhapsody. **112m/B VHS, DVD.** Kirk Douglas, Doris Day, Lauren Bacall, Hoagy Carmichael; *D:* Michael Curtiz.

Young Master **1980** Chan, searching for his missing brother, is mistaken for a fugitive and has to save himself from bounty hunters and police. Oh, and get the real bad guys so he can clear his name. Chinese with subtitles or dubbed. **90m/C VHS, DVD.** *HK* Jackie Chan, Pai Wei, Ing-Sik Whang, Kien Shih; *D:* Jackie Chan; *W:* Jackie Chan; *M:* Akira Inoue.

Young Mr. Lincoln 1/2 **1939** A classy Hollywood biography of Lincoln in his younger years from log-cabin country boy to idealistic Springfield lawyer. A splendid drama, and one endlessly explicated as an American masterpiece by the French auteur critics in "Cahiers du Cinema." **100m/B VHS, DVD.** Henry Fonda, Alice Brady, Marjorie Weaver, Arleen Whelan, Eddie Collins, Ward Bond, Donald Meek, Richard Cromwell, Eddie Quillan, Charles Halton; *D:* John Ford; *W:* Lamar Trotti. Natl. Film Reg. '03.

The Young Nurses *Nightingale; Young L.A. Nurses 3* **1973 (R)** The fourth entry in the Roger Corman produced "nurses" series. Three sexy nurses uncover a drug ring run from their hospital, headed by none other than director Fuller. Also present is Moreland, in his last role. Preceded by "The Student Nurses," "Private Duty Nurses," "Night Call Nurses," followed by "Candy Stripe Nurses." Also on video as "Young L.A. Nurses 3." **77m/C VHS, DVD.** Jean Manson, Ashley Porter, Angela Gibbs, Zack Taylor, Dick Miller, Jack La Rue, William Joyce, Sally Kirkland, Allan Arbus, Mary Doyle, Don Keefer, Nan Martin, Mantan Moreland, Samuel Fuller; *D:* Clinton Kimbrough; *W:* Howard R. Cohen; *M:* Greg Prestopino.

Young Nurses in Love **1989 (R)** Low-budget sex farce in which a foreign spy poses as a nurse to steal sperm from a sperm bank donated by world leaders, celebrities and geniuses. **82m/C VHS.** Jeanne Marie, Alan Fisher, Barbra Robb, James Davies; *D:* Chuck Vincent.

The Young One 1/2 *La Joven; Island of Shame* **1961** Traver (Hamilton) is a black jazz musician who escapes from his southern town when he's wrongly accused of raping a white woman. He hides out on a small island which is used as a private hunting ground for rich sportsmen, overseen by Miller (Scott), the game keeper. Hamilton gets work as the new handyman and becomes close to the young Evalyn (Meersman). When Miller rapes Evalyn, it's Traver who's once again accused until things can be put right. Racist elements are heavy-handed; one of Bunuel's lesser efforts. Based on the story "Travelin' Man" by Peter Matthiessen. **94m/B VHS.** *MX* Bernie Hamilton, Zachary Scott, Kay Meersman, Claudio Brook, Graham Denton; *D:* Luis Bunuel; *W:* Hugo Butler, Luis Bunuel.

Young People 1/2 **1940 (G)** Temple's 12 in this lesser vehicle and almost-adolescence doesn't serve her well with this tired plot. She's an orphan adopted by show-biz team Oakie and Greenwood who've decided to retire to rural life. They even get to put on a show to prove to the small-minded small-towners what a swell trio they are. Temple's last film for 20th-Century Fox does include nostalgic clips from earlier Shirley hits, including "Stand Up and Cheer" and "Curly Top," to explain her character's background. ♫Tra-La-La; Fifth Avenue; I Wouldn't Take a Million; The Mason-Dixon Line; Young People. **78m/C VHS.** Shirley Temple, Jack Oakie, Charlotte Greenwood, Arleen Whelan, George Montgomery, Kathleen Howard; *D:* Allan Dwan; *W:* Edwin Blum, Don Ettlinger.

The Young Philadelphians *The City Jungle* **1959** Ambitious young lawyer Newman works hard at making an impression on the snobbish Philadelphia upper crust. As he schemes and scrambles, he woos debutante Rush and defends buddy Vaughn on a murder charge. Long, but worth it. Part of the "A Night at the Movies" series, this package simulates a 1959 movie evening with a Bugs Bunny cartoon, "People Are Bunny," a newsreel and coming attractions for "The Nun's Story" and "The Hanging Tree." **136m/B VHS, DVD.** Paul Newman, Barbara Rush, Alexis Smith, Billie Burke, Brian Keith, John Williams, Otto Kruger, Robert Vaughn; *D:* Vincent Sherman; *C:* Harry Stradling Sr.; *M:* Ernest Gold.

The Young Pioneers 1/2 **1976** Teenaged newlyweds David and Molly Beaton head for the Dakota Territory in the 1870s to secure a homestead. They're faced with a blizzard, an army of grasshoppers that destroy their crop, and Molly's pregnancy and find their survival harder than expected. Pilot TV movie for the brief 1978 series. **96m/C VHS.** Linda Purl, Roger Kern, Robert Donner, Mare Winningham, Robert Hays; *D:* Michael O'Herlihy. **TV**

The Young Poisoner's Handbook **1994 (R)** Based on the true story of London teenager Graham (O'Conor), who's obsessed with chemistry and at odds with his stepmother. So, he poisons her chocolates and she dies. Sent to Broadmoor prison for the criminally insane, Graham comes under the care of Dr. Ziegler (Sher), who, eight years later, recommends Graham for parole. Now working in a photographic lab, Graham decides to experiment with doctoring his co-workers tea—which results in eight more deaths before Graham is caught. Locked up again, Graham spends his time writing a poisoner's handbook for Dr. Ziegler. Be warned that the sufferings of the poisoned victims are gruesome. **99m/C VHS, DVD.** *GB* Hugh O'Conor, Anthony Sher, Ruth Sheen, Charlotte Coleman, Roger Lloyd-Pack, Paul Stacey, Samantha Edmonds, Charlie Creed-Miles; *D:* Benjamin Ross; *W:* Benjamin Ross, Jeff Rawle; *C:* Hubert Taczanowski; *M:* Robert (Rob) Lane, Frank Strobel.

The Young Savages **1961** Gang warfare in New York's East Harlem. Three Italian teenagers are accused of murdering another teen—a blind Puerto Rican boy. Assistant DA Hank Bell (Lancaster), who grew up on the same mean streets, doesn't think the case is as cut-and-dry as presented and determines that the deceased was not the innocent victim he's portrayed to be. Routine juvenile delinquent drama based on the novel "A Matter of Conviction" by Evan Hunter. **103m/B VHS.** Burt Lancaster, Dina Merrill, Edward Andrews, Shelley Winters, Vivian Nathan, Larry Gates, Telly Savalas, John Davis Chandler, Neil Nephew, Stanley Kristien; *D:* John Frankenheimer; *W:* Edward Anhalt, J.P. Miller; *C:* Lionel Lindon; *M:* David Amram.

Young Sherlock Holmes **1985 (PG-13)** Holmes and Watson meet as schoolboys. They work together on their first case, solving a series of bizarre murders gripping London. Watch through the credits for an interesting plot twist. Promising "what if" sleuth tale crashes and burns, becoming a typical high-tech Spielberg film. Second half bears too strong a resemblance to "Indiana Jones and the Temple of Doom." **109m/C VHS, DVD.** Nicholas (Nick) Rowe, Alan Cox, Sophie Ward, Freddie Jones, Michael Hordern; *D:* Barry Levinson; *W:* Chris Columbus; *M:* Bruce Broughton.

Young Tiger **WOOF!** *Police Woman; Rumble in Hong Kong* **1974 (R)** A really cheesy Chan movie where he plays a bad guy, followed by a 12-minute documentary featuring Jackie Chan, kung-fu sensation, demonstrating his skills. **102m/C VHS, DVD.** *HK* Jackie Chan, Qui Yuen, Ken Jeong, Gam Woo; *D:* Hdeng Tsu.

Young Tom Edison 1/2 **1940** Two teenaged years in the life of Thomas Alva Edison, as he drives his family crazy with his endless experiments on his way to becoming the famed inventor. Rooney manages to be enthusiastic without being overwhelming. Followed by "Edison the Man," with Spencer Tracy in the adult role. **82m/B VHS.** Mickey Rooney, Fay Bainter, George Bancroft, Virginia Weidler, Eugene Pallette, Victor Kilian, Bobby Jordan, Lloyd Corrigan; ***D:*** Norman Taurog; ***W:*** Dore Schary, Bradbury Foote, Hugo Butler.

The Young Victoria **2009 (PG)** Depicting the early years of the reign of Queen Victoria (Blunt), period piece artfully blends the court intrigues and eventual emotion that led to her marriage to Prince Albert (Friend). Victoria must learn to rule as well as navigate the manipulations of her mother (Richardson) and uncle (Kretschmann), who both wish to be the power behind the throne. Victoria and Albert begin to warm to each other in their mutual dislike of their meddling elders, and love blossoms. Producers include Martin Scorsese and Sarah Ferguson, Duchess of York, whose daughter Beatrice appears as a lady-in-waiting. Sadly, inquiries concerning Prince Albert in a can remain unanswered as this edition went to print. **104m/C DVD.** *US* Emily Blunt, Rupert Friend, Paul Bettany, Miranda Richardson, Jim Broadbent, Thomas Kretschmann, Mark Strong, Jesper Christensen, Harriet Walter, Julian Glover, Michael Maloney, Julian Fellowes, Michaela Brooks; ***D:*** Jean-Marc Vallee; ***W:*** Julian Fellowes; ***C:*** Hagen Bogdanski; ***M:*** Ilan Eshkeri. Oscars '09: Costume Des.; British Acad. '09: Costume Des., Makeup.

Young Warlord **1975** Arthur roams western England in 500 AD, leading a band of guerrilla cavalrymen. When the Saxons invade, Arthur unites the tribe, holds off the attack and becomes king. **97m/C VHS.** Oliver Tobias, Michael Gothard, Jack Watson, Brian Blessed; ***D:*** Peter Sasdy.

Young Warriors **1/2 1983 (R)** Frat boys turn vigilante to avenge a street gang murder. Weird mix of teen sex comedy, insufferable self-righteous preachiness, and violence. **104m/C VHS.** Ernest Borgnine, James Van Patten, Richard Roundtree, Lynda Day George, Dick Shawn; ***D:*** Lawrence Foldes; ***W:*** Lawrence Foldes, Richard Matheson, Russell W. Colgin; ***C:*** Mac Ahlberg.

Young Winston **1972 (PG)** Based on Sir Winston Churchill's autobiography "My Early Life: A Roving Commission." Follows him through his school days, journalistic career in Africa, early military career, and his election to Parliament at the age of 26. Ward is tremendous as the prime minister-to-be. **145m/C VHS.** *GB* Simon Ward, Robert Shaw, Anne Bancroft, John Mills, Jack Hawkins, Ian Holm, Anthony Hopkins, Patrick Magee, Edward Woodward, Jane Seymour; ***D:*** Richard Attenborough. Golden Globes '73: Foreign Film.

Youngblood **1986 (R)** An underdog beats the seemingly insurmountable odds and becomes a hockey champion. Some enjoyable hockey scenes although the success storyline is predictable. **111m/C VHS, DVD.** Rob Lowe, Patrick Swayze, Cynthia Gibb, Ed Lauter, George Finn, Fionnula Flanagan, Keanu Reeves; ***D:*** Peter Markle.

Younger & Younger **1/2 1994 (R)** Jonathan Younger (Sutherland) is forced to run the family storage business after his long-suffering wife Penny (Davidovich) dies. The business starts to fail, even after Jonathan's son (Fraser) arrives to help out, and the widower begins having visions of the woman he mistreated. And each time he sees her she looks younger and more beautiful than ever. **97m/C VHS.** Donald Sutherland, Brendan Fraser, Lolita (David) Davidovich, Sally Kellerman, Julie Delpy, Linda Hunt; ***D:*** Percy Adlon; ***W:*** Percy Adlon, Felix Adlon; ***C:*** Bernd Heinl; ***M:*** Hans Zimmer.

Your Friends & Neighbors **1998 (R)** If these are your friends and neighbors, you should reconsider your decisions and address. Six yuppies lie, cheat and deceive their way around the block in La Bute's tale of modern suburban immorality. Weasel Jerry (Stiller) sleeps with Mary (Brenneman), the supposedly happy wife of his old friend Barry (Eckhart). Meanwhile, his live-in girlfriend (Keener) is having a lesbian affair with art gallery employee Cheri (Kinski), and chilly misogynist Cary (Patric) seduces and discards a string of women. Excellent performances by the entire cast bring this nasty group to life and La Bute provides riveting if unsettling material for them. **99m/C VHS, DVD.** Jason Patric, Nastassja Kinski, Ben Stiller, Catherine Keener, Aaron Eckhart, Amy Brenneman; ***D:*** Neil LaBute; ***W:*** Neil LaBute; ***C:*** Nancy Schreiber.

Your Place or Mine **1/2 1983** Self-indulgent yuppie pap about middle-aged singles trying to find the right mate. **100m/C VHS.** Bonnie Franklin, Robert Klein, Peter Bonerz, Tyne Daly, Penny Fuller; ***D:*** Robert Day; ***M:*** Gerald Alters. **TV**

Your Ticket Is No Longer Valid **1984 (R)** Prurient excuse for a serious drama. Impotent failed businessman has disturbing erotic dreams about his girlfriend. Adapted from a novel by Romain Gary. **96m/C VHS.** *CA* Richard Harris, George Peppard, Jeanne Moreau; ***D:*** George Kaczender.

Your Turn Darling *A Toi de Faire, Mignonne; L'Agente Federale Lemmy Caution; Ladies Man* **1963** French espionage thriller with Constantine once again playing Lemmy Caution, a U.S. secret agent involved with a gang of spies. **93m/B VHS.** *FR* Eddie Constantine, Gaia Germani, Elga Andersen; ***D:*** Bernard Borderie; ***W:*** Bernard Borderie; ***C:*** Henri Persin; ***M:*** Paul Misraki.

Your Vice is a Closed Room and Only I Have the Key **1/2** *Il tuo vizio e una stanza chiusa e solo io ne ho la chiave; Excite Me; Eye of the Black Cat; Gently Before She Dies* **1972** Italian writer Oliviero (Pistilli) enjoys tormenting and belittling women, especially his wife. When one of his mistresses is brutally murdered, followed by similar crimes, he becomes a suspect. His behavior toward his wife worsens and is witnessed by his scheming niece and the family's cat. Satisfying giallo heavily influenced by Poe. **96m/C DVD.** *IT* Luigi Pistilli, Anita Strindberg, Edwige Fenech, Ivan Rassimov; ***D:*** Sergio Martino; ***W:*** Adriano Bolzoni, Ernesto Gastaldi, Luciano Martino, Sauro Scavolini; ***C:*** Giancarlo Ferrando; ***M:*** Bruno Nicolai.

You're a Big Boy Now **1966** Kastner, a virginal young man working in the New York Public Library, is told by his father to move out of his house and grow up. On his own, he soon becomes involved with man-hating actress Hartman and a discotheque dancer. A wild and weird comedy. Coppola's commercial directorial debut. **96m/C VHS.** Elizabeth Hartman, Geraldine Page, Peter Kastner, Julie Harris, Rip Torn, Michael Dunn, Tony Bill, Karen Black; ***D:*** Francis Ford Coppola; ***W:*** Francis Ford Coppola.

You're Jinxed, Friend, You've Met Sacramento **1970** The tongue-in-cheek adventures of a cool-headed cowboy as he passes from town to colorful town. Great title, too. **99m/C VHS.** *IT* Ty Hardin, Christian Hay, Jenny Atkins; ***D:*** George Cristallini.

Yours, Mine & Ours **1/2 1968** Bigger, better, big screen version of "The Brady Bunch." It's the story of a lovely lady (Ball) with eight kids who marries a a widower (Fonda) who has ten. Imagine the zany shenanigans! Family comedy manages to be both wholesome and funny. Based on a true story. **114m/C VHS, DVD.** Lucille Ball, Henry Fonda, Van Johnson, Tim Matheson, Tom Bosley, Tracy Nelson, Morgan Brittany; ***D:*** Melville Shavelson; ***W:*** Melville Shavelson; ***C:*** Charles F. Wheeler; ***M:*** Fred Karlin.

Yours, Mine & Ours **2005 (PG)** Over-the-top slapstick, remake of the 1968 Lucille Ball/Henry Fonda farce about blending a large family. Helen (Russo) and Frank (Quaid) shared a brief high school romance. Now it's 30 years (and 18 kids) later, they're both single, and the romance rekindles at a reunion. Conflict between the kids, their jobs, and their differing child-raising philosophies ensues, as do sporadic fits of humor. Fun and safe enough family viewing. **90m/C VHS, DVD.** *US* Dennis Quaid, Rene Russo, Rip Torn, Linda Hunt, Jerry O'Connell, David Koechner, Sean Faris, Katija Pevec, Tyler Patrick Jones, Danielle Panabaker, Drake Bell, Miranda Cosgrove, Dean Collins, Haley Ramm, Brecken Palmer, Bridger Palmer, Ty Panitz, Miki Ishikawa, Slade Pearce, Little JJ, Andrew Vo, Jennifer Habib, Jessica Habib, Nicholas Roget-King; ***D:*** Raja Gosnell; ***W:*** Ron Burch, David Kidd; ***C:*** Theo van de Sande; ***M:*** Christophe Beck.

Youth Aflame **WOOF!** *Hoodlum Girls* **1944** Trash film that tells the tale of two sisters—one good, one bad. Poor dialogue and weak performances do, however, make for some great camp. Based on a story by Helen Kiedy. **61m/B VHS.** Joy Reese, Warren Burr, Kay Morley, Michael Owen, Rod Rogers; ***D:*** Elmer Clifton; ***W:*** Elmer Clifton.

Youth in Revolt **2010 (R)** In this dark comedy about love and surviving puberty, over-bright, under-sexed teenage intellectual Nick Twisp (Cera) meets dream girl Sheeni (Doubleday) in a trailer park and is determined to be with her at any cost, no matter how absurd. Along the path to her heart, he lies, cheats, steals, invents a French bad-boy persona, destroys a city block, and becomes a fugitive from the police, all while dealing with his divorced parents (Smart, Buscemi), sleazy authority figures, and oddball peers. Cera puts a funny twist on the "awkward teenager" cliche as Nick and his remorseless alter ego, Francois, whose bad judgment, faux-Frenchman accent, and raging hormones turn dysfunction into chaos wherever he goes. Based on the cult novel by C.D. Payne, the zany moments abound but the manic pace sometimes misses the biting satire and insight of the source. **90m/C DVD.** *US* Michael Cera, Steve Buscemi, Jean Smart, Justin Long, Portia Doubleday, Ray Liotta, Ari Graynor, Fred Willard, Zach Galifianakis, Erik Knudsen, M. Emmet Walsh, Mary Kay Place; ***D:*** Miguel Arteta; ***W:*** Gustin Nash; ***C:*** Chuy Chavez; ***M:*** John Swihart.

Youth of the Beast *Yaju No Seishun* **1963** A cop in disgrace plots to avenge the murder of a friend by infiltrating two rival yakuza gangs and having them destroy each other. Flamboyant visuals and filled with Suzuki's soon-to-be trademarked sex and violence. Japanese with subtitles. **91m/C VHS.** *JP* Joe Shishido, Shoji Kobayashi, Ichiro Kijima, Misako Suzuki; ***D:*** Seijun Suzuki.

Youth on Parole **1/2 1937** Same old story: Boy gets paroled. Girl gets paroled. Parolee meets parolette and romance blossoms as they beat a further rap. **60m/B VHS.** Miles Mander, Margaret Dumont, Milburn Stone, Marian Marsh, Gordon Oliver; ***D:*** Phil Rosen; ***W:*** Hershal Rebuas; ***C:*** Edward Snyder.

Youth Without Youth **2007 (R)** A disappointing return to directing for Francis Ford Coppola after a ten-year hiatus. Dominic (Roth) is a 70-year-old Romanian linguist who fears he'll die alone a failure and, on the eve of World War II, decides to kill himself. But his suicide plans are interrupted when he's struck by lightning and somehow begins to grow younger. Scientists of the Third Reich snatch him up for observation and soon he meets Veronica (Lara), a sexy German spy who is coincidentally also struck by lightning, but begins to age rapidly. A muddled and tiring story that would've been better suited as a "Twilight Zone" episode. **124m/C DVD, Blu-ray Disc.** *US* Tim Roth, Alexandra Maria Lara, Bruno Ganz, Andre Hennicke, Alexandra Pirici; ***D:*** Francis Ford Coppola; ***W:*** Francis Ford Coppola; ***C:*** Mihai Malaimare Jr.; ***M:*** Osvaldo Golijoy.

You've Got Mail **1/2 1998 (PG)** Third remake of "The Shop Around the Corner" ("In the Good Old Summertime" was number 2) finds independent bookstore owner Ryan battling Hank's bookstore conglomerate to stay in business. How does this qualify as a romantic comedy? Because they're flirting with each other anonymously by e-mail. Third teaming of Ryan and Hanks relies, almost too much, on their considerable chemistry. Soundtrack music was chosen for maximum on-screen and record store effect. Must-see for hopeless romantics and fans of Hanks and/or Ryan. Others must decide based on tolerance for meet-cute situations and lightweight romantic comedy. **119m/C VHS, DVD.** Meg Ryan, Tom Hanks, Parker Posey, Greg Kinnear, Jean Stapleton, Steve Zahn, Dave Chappelle, Dabney Coleman, John Randolph, Michael Badalucco, Heather Burns, Hallee Hirsh; ***D:*** Nora Ephron; ***W:*** Nora Ephron; ***C:*** John Lindley; ***M:*** George Fenton.

You've Got to Have Heart *La Moglie Vergine; The Virgin Wife* **1977 (R)** A young bridegroom's life gets complicated after he does not sexually satisfy his bride on their wedding night. **98m/C VHS.** *IT* Carroll Baker, Edwige Fenech, Ray Lovelock, Renzo Montagnani; ***D:*** Marino Girolami; ***W:*** Marino Girolami.

You've Ruined Me, Eddie *The Touch of Flesh* **1958** A spoiled rich girl gets knocked up and her boyfriend will never know peace again. Meanwhile, their once quiet town is outraged. **76m/B VHS, DVD.** Charles Martin, Robert Cannon, Ted Marshall, Jeanne Rainer, Sue Ellis, Josie Hascall; ***D:*** R. John Hugh; ***C:*** Charles T. O'Rork.

Yu-Gi-Oh! The Movie: Pyramid of Light **2004 (PG)** Yu-Gi-Oh hits the big screen with the television cartoon's storyline (picking up at the end of the series' third season) and gameplay in tow, meaning only fans (and their suffering parents) need to see it. Yu-GI-Oh, whose body hosts an Egyptian spirit, plays a combat monster game, apparently for the future of humanity and occasionally for the players' souls. The Pyramid of Light in question is the most powerful card, and controls the destiny of the players. If your kids aren't fans, count yourself lucky. If they are, keep in mind that game cards were given out as inticement to get people into the theater. **89m/C VHS, DVD.** *JP* ***D:*** Hatuki Tsuji; ***W:*** Norman Grossfeld, Matthew Drdek, Lloyd Goldfine; ***C:*** Hiroaki Edamitsu; ***M:*** Elik Alvarez; ***V:*** Eric Stuart, Dan Green, Maddie (Maddeleine) Blaustein, Wayne Grayson, Scottie Ray, Tara Jayne, Frank Frankson.

Yukon Flight **1940** A Renfrew of the Mounties adventure. The hero finds illegal gold mining operations and murder in the Yukon. **57m/B VHS, DVD.** James Newill, Dave O'Brien, Louise Stanley, Warren Hull, Karl Hackett, Roy Barcroft; ***D:*** Ralph Staub; ***W:*** Edward Halperin; ***C:*** Mack Stengler.

The Yum-Yum Girls **1/2 1978 (R)** Pair of innocent girls arrive in NYC to pursue their dreams. Gives an inside looks at the fashion industry. Not as funny or as cute as it wants to be. **89m/C VHS, DVD.** Judy Landers, Tanya Roberts, Barbara Tully, Michelle Daw; ***D:*** Barry Rosen.

Yuma **1970** An old-style Western about a sheriff (Walker) who rides into town, cleans it up, and saves his own reputation from a plot to discredit him. Dull in places, but action-packed ending saves the day. **73m/C VHS, DVD.** Clint Walker, Barry Sullivan, Edgar Buchanan; ***D:*** Ted Post; ***M:*** George Duning. **TV**

Yuri Nosenko, KGB **1/2 1986** Fact-based account of a KGB defector and the CIA agent who must determine if he's on the up-and-up. **85m/C VHS, DVD.** *GB* Tommy Lee Jones, Oleg Rudnik, Josef Sommer, Ed Lauter, George Morfogen, Stephen D. Newman; ***D:*** Mick Jackson. **TV**

Z **1969** The assassination of a Greek nationalist in the 1960s and its aftermath are portrayed by the notorious political director as a gripping detective thriller. Excellent performances, adequate cinematic techniques, and important politics in this highly acclaimed film. **128m/C VHS, DVD.** *FR* Yves Montand, Jean-Louis Trintignant, Irene Papas, Charles Denner, Georges Geret, Jacques Perrin, Francois Perier, Marcel Bozzuffi; ***D:*** Constantin Costa-Gavras; ***W:*** Constantin Costa-Gavras; ***M:*** Mikis Theodorakis. Oscars '69: Film Editing, Foreign Film; Cannes '69: Special Jury Prize, Actor (Trintignant); Golden Globes '70: Foreign Film; N.Y. Film Critics '69: Director (Costa-Gavras), Film; Natl. Soc. Film Critics '69: Film.

Zabriskie Point **1970 (R)** Antonioni's first U.S. feature. A desultory, surreal examination of the American way of life. Worthy but difficult. Climaxes with a stylized orgy in Death Valley. **112m/C VHS.** Mark Frechette, Daria Halprin, Paul Fix, Rod Taylor, Harrison Ford, G.D. Spradlin; ***D:*** Michelangelo Antonioni; ***W:*** Michelangelo Antonioni, Sam Shepard, Fred Gardner, Tonino Guerra, Clare Peploe.

Zachariah **1/2 1970 (PG)** A semi-spoof '60s rock western, wherein two gunfighters given to pursuing wealth-laden bands of outlaws separate and experience quixotic journeys through the cliched landscape. Scripted by members of The Firesign Theater and featuring appearances by Country Joe and The Fish, The New York Rock Ensemble, and The James Gang. **93m/C**

VHS, DVD. Don Johnson, John Rubinstein, Pat Quinn, Dick Van Patten, William Challee, Country Joe McDonald, Elvin Jones, Doug Kershaw, Lawrence Kubik, Hank Worden; *D:* George Englund; *W:* Peter Bergman, Joe Massot, Phil(ip) Proctor, Philip Austin, David Ossman; *C:* Jorge Stahl Jr.; *M:* Jimmie Haskell.

Zack and Miri Make a Porno ☙☙☙ **2008 (R)** Longtime platonic friends Zack (Rogan) and Miri (Banks), in desperate need of quick cash, decide to, as the title warns, make their own skin flick. Rather than sexy or smutty, they aim for goofy and ridiculous, particularly when converting "Star Wars" to "Star Whores." And, since this is actually a well-disguised romantic comedy, Zack and Miri eventually find they may be more than friends. Luckily, their on-screen chemistry keeps the perfect balance of nasty and nice. Rogan's signature crude charm is still fresh despite often-inconsistent Kevin Smith writing and directing in place of usual suspect Judd Apatow. **101m/C DVD.** *US* Seth Rogen, Elizabeth Banks, Craig Robinson, Jason Mewes, Jeff Anderson, Traci Lords, Ricky Mabe, Brandon Routh, Katie Morgan, Justin Long, Gerry Bednob; *D:* Kevin Smith; *W:* Kevin Smith; *C:* David Klein; *M:* James L. Venable.

Zack & Reba ☙☙ **1998 (R)** When Reba (Murphy) calls off her wedding a week before the ceremony, her fiance commits suicide. Guilt-ridden, Reba returns to her hometown of Spooner and its eccentric residents, which include shotgun-toting grandma, Beulah (Reynolds), and her grief-stricken grandson Zack (Flanery), who can't seem to get over the death of his wife. Naturally, Beulah thinks Zack and Reba are just made for each other. **91m/C VHS, DVD.** Sean Patrick Flanery, Brittany Murphy, Debbie Reynolds, Kathy Najimy, Martin Mull, Michael Jeter; *D:* Nicole Bettauer; *W:* Jay Stapleton; *C:* Mark Irwin; *M:* Joel McNeely.

Zafarinas ☙☙ *Moriras en Chafarinas* **1994 (R)** Zafarinas is an ancient walled city on the island of Melilla that houses a military barracks. Two suspicious deaths force Commander Contreras (Ladoire) to release zealous corporal Jaime (Sanz) and Corporal Cidraque (Albala) from the stockades to investigate. Then there's a third death and things just aren't what they seem. Spanish with subtitles. **85m/C VHS.** *SP* Jorge Sanz, Javier Albala, Oscar Ladoire, Maria Barranco; *D:* Pedro Olea; *W:* Pedro Olea, Fernando Lalana; *C:* Paco Femenia.

Zalmen or the Madness of God ☙☙ ½ **1975** Elie Wiesel's mystical story about a rabbi's struggle against religious persecution in post-Stalin Russia. **120m/C VHS, DVD.** Joseph Wiseman, Dianne Wiest; *D:* Peter Levin; *W:* Elie Wiesel. **TV**

Zandalee WOOF! **1991 (R)** The sexual adventures of a bored sexy young woman who has a fling with her husband's friend. Bad script, graphic sex. Also available in an unrated version. **100m/C VHS, DVD.** Nicolas Cage, Judge Reinhold, Erika Anderson, Viveca Lindfors, Aaron Neville, Joe Pantoliano, Ian Abercrombie, Marisa Tomei, Zach Galligan; *D:* Sam Pillsbury; *W:* Mari Kornhauser.

Zandy's Bride ☙ ½ **1974 (PG)** Basic story about a rancher who sents for a mail-order bride. She's shocked by his ill-treatment of her and stands up to his bullying, thus winning his respect and love. Beautiful scenery, courtesy of Big Sur, California, but predictable all-around and essentially a waste of an experienced cast. Based on the novel "The Stranger" by Lillian Bos Ross. **97m/C VHS.** Gene Hackman, Liv Ullmann, Eileen Heckart, Harry Dean Stanton, Joe Santos, Sam Bottoms, Susan Tyrrell, Frank Cady; *D:* Jan Troell; *W:* Marc Norman; *C:* Jordan Cronenweth; *M:* Michael Franks.

The Zany Adventures of Robin Hood ☙ **1984** Hackneyed spoof of the Robin Hood legend. Medieval man robs from the rich to help the poor. Not nearly as funny as Mel Brooks' TV series that spoofed "Robin Hood." **95m/C VHS.** George Segal, Morgan Fairchild, Roddy McDowall, Roy Kinnear, Janet Suzman, Tom Baker; *D:* Ray Austin.

Zapped! ☙ **1982 (R)** Teen genius discovers he possesses telekinetic powers. He does the natural thing, using his talent to remove clothing from nearby females. A teen boy's dream come true. **98m/C VHS, DVD.** Scott Baio, Willie Aames, Robert Mandan, Felice Schachter, Scatman Crothers, Roger Bowen, Marya Small, Greg Bradford, Hilary Beane, Sue Ane Langdon, Heather Thomas, Merritt Butrick, LaWanda Page, Rosanne Katon; *D:* Robert J. Rosenthal; *M:* Charles Fox.

Zapped Again ☙ **1989 (R)** The lame-brained sequel to 1982's "Zapped" about a high schooler who has telekinetic powers and lust on his mind. **93m/C VHS, DVD.** Todd Eric Andrews, Kelli Williams, Reed Rudy, Linda Blair, Karen Black, Lyle Alzado, Rossie (Ross) Harris; *D:* Doug Campbell.

Zardoz ☙☙ **1973** A surreal parable of the far future (2293), when Earth society is broken into strict classes: a society of intellectuals known as the Eternals, a society of savages called the Brutals, and an elite unit of killers, naturally named the Exterminators, who keep the order. The Exterminators worship a stone god named Zardoz, but killer Zed (Connery) discovers that it's merely a futuristic version of "The Wizard of Oz" and that the Eternals have been manipulating the social order. His presence causes chaos and destruction (but he does get all the babes). Visually interesting but pretentious. **105m/C VHS, DVD.** *GB* Sean Connery, Charlotte Rampling, John Alderton, Sara Kestelman, Sally Anne Newton, Niall Buggy, Christopher Casson, Bosco Hogan, Jessica Swift; *D:* John Boorman; *W:* John Boorman; *C:* Geoffrey Unsworth; *M:* David Munrow.

Zarkorr! The Invader ☙ **1996 (PG)** Aliens studying earth decide humans need a challenge (like we don't have enough problems of our own) so they send a 185-foot tall, laser-eyed monster to crush (American) cities and cause general terror in the population. And who's our hero? A postal worker—aided by a five-inch tall alien girl. Low-budget spoof has its moments, but eventually wears thin. **80m/C VHS, DVD.** Rhys Pugh, Deprise Grossman, Mark Hamilton, Charles Schneider, Eileen Wesson; *D:* Aaron Osborne; *W:* Benjamin Carr; *C:* Joe C. Maxwell; *M:* Richard Band.

Zathura ☙☙☙ **2005 (PG)** Ten year old Walter (Hutcherson) and six year old Danny (Bobo) both fight for overstressed dad's (Robbins) attention, but he's too busy. Older sister Lisa (Stewart) is charged with babysitting the two, but she could care less. Until they all find themselves trapped in the bizarre space-world of Zathura, a game which comes to life as they play. Sort-of sequel to "Jumanji," also done by Chris Van Allsburg. Fabulous special effects and a fantastical plot is exciting stuff for both children and adults. **113m/C DVD, UMD.** *US* Jonah Bobo, Josh Hutcherson, Dax Shepard, Kristen Stewart, Tim Robbins; *D:* Jon Favreau; *W:* David Koepp, John Kamps; *C:* Guillermo Navarro; *M:* John Debney; *V:* Frank Oz.

Zatoichi ☙☙☙ ½ *The Blind Swordsman: Zatoichi* **2003 (R)** Versatile and popular filmmaker Kitano (who also takes on the lead role under his actor's pseudonym) kicks butt as a legendary 19th-century samurai (an iconic figure in Japanese film and TV). The blind masseur/gambler hides his sword in his walking stick and the plot, such as it is, involves loner Zatoichi helping out geisha Okino (Daike) and her cross-dressing brother Osei (Tachibana) in their quest for revenge on the Ginzo gang, who slaughtered their family and who are now threatening the local peasants. Which makes a good excuse for Zatoichi to challenge the gang and their own formidable samurai Hattori (Asano). Lots of stylized violence and some slapstick gags; Japanese with subtitles. **115m/C DVD.** *JP* Tadanobu Asano, Takeshi "Beat" Kitano, Michiyo Ogusu, Guadalcanal Taka, Daigoro Tachibana, Yuko Daike, Ittoku Kishibe, Saburo Ishikura; *D:* Takeshi "Beat" Kitano; *W:* Takeshi "Beat" Kitano; *C:* Katsumi Yanagijima; *M:* Keiichi Suzuki.

Zatoichi: Master Ichi and a Chest of Gold ☙☙ **1964** A violent thriller about a blind gambler and former samurai who tries to clear his name after being framed for a gold robbery. Adapted from a novel by Kazuo Miyagawa. In Japanese with English subtitles. **83m/C VHS, DVD.** *JP* Shintaro Katsu, Tomisaburo Wakayama; *D:* Kazuo Ikehiro; *W:* Shozaburo Asai; *C:* Kazuo Miyagawa; *M:* Ichiro Saito.

Zatoichi: The Blind Swordsman and the Chess Expert ☙☙ **1965** Zatoichi, the blind gambler and former samurai, befriends a master chess player and gets involved with Japanese gangsters. In Japanese with English subtitles. **87m/C VHS, DVD.** *JP* Shintaro Katsu, Mikio Narita, Chizu Hayashi, Kaneko Iwasaki, Gaku Yamamoto; *D:* Kenji Misumi; *W:* Daisuke Ito; *C:* Chishi Makiura; *M:* Akira Ifukube.

Zatoichi: The Blind Swordsman and the Fugitives ☙☙ *Zatoichi and the Fugitives* **1968** This time Zatoichi, the blind masseur and master swordsman, is pitted against a band of outlaws. When the local bandits brutalize the countryside Zatoichi steps in to defend the weak and faces a showdown with outlaw leader Genpachiro. In Japanese with English subtitles. **82m/C VHS, DVD.** *JP* Shintaro Katsu, Yumiko Nogawa, Kayo Mikimoto, Kyosuke Machida; *D:* Kimiyoshi Yasuda.

Zatoichi: The Blind Swordsman's Vengeance *Zatoichi's Vengeance* **1966** Zatoichi defends a dying man against a group of gangsters who have taken over an isolated village. In Japanese with English subtitles. **83m/C VHS, DVD.** *JP* Shintaro Katsu, Shigeru Amachi, Kei Sato, Mayumi Ogawa; *D:* Tokuzo Tanaka.

Zatoichi: The Life and Opinion of Masseur Ichi ☙☙ *The Tale of Zatoichi* **1962** The first film in the action series about the Zen-like blind masseur, gambler, and swordsman. Zatoichi is drawn into a revenge match between two ruthless gangs. When one gang tries to hire him the other hires a savage killer. This sets in motion a war between the yakuza gangs and mercenary samurai. In Japanese with English subtitles. **96m/C VHS, DVD.** *JP* Shintaro Katsu, Masayo Mari, Ryuzo Shimada, Gen Mitamura, Shigeru Amachi; *D:* Kenji Misumi.

Zatoichi vs. Yojimbo ☙☙☙ ½ *Zatoichi Meets Yojimbo; Zato Ichi To Yojimbo* **1970** The legendary blind warrior-samurai, Zatoichi, wants to retire, but his village is being held captive by outlaws. He is forced to fight Yojimbo, the crude wandering samurai without a master, and the sparks really fly! This was a comic send-up of Akiro Kurosawa's "Yojimbo" with Mifune recreating his role here and playing it for laughs. Subtitled. **90m/C VHS, DVD.** *JP* Toshiro Mifune, Shintaro Katsu, Osamu Takizawa; *D:* Kihachi Okamoto; *W:* Tetsuro Yoshida.

Zatoichi: Zatoichi's Flashing Sword ☙☙ **1964** Blind swordsman Zatoichi gets caught up in a feud between two competing yakuza bosses. When Zatoichi declares his alliegence to Tsumugi, the unhappy Yasu tries to get his revenge. In Japanese with English subtitles. **82m/C VHS, DVD.** *JP* Shintaro Katsu, Mayumi Nagisa, Naoko Kubo, Ryutaro Gami, Yutaka Nakamura; *D:* Kazuo Ikehiro.

Zazie dans le Metro ☙☙☙ ½ *Zazie in the Underground; Zazie in the Subway* **1961** One of Malle's early movies, this is one of the best of the French New Wave comedies. A young girl, wise beyond her years, visits her drag queen uncle in Paris. She wants to ride the subway, but the ensuing hilarious adventures keep her from her goal. In French with English subtitles. **92m/C VHS.** *FR* Catherine Demonget, Philippe Noiret, Carla Marlier; *W:* Louis Malle.

Zebra Force ☙ **1976 (R)** Group of army veterans embark on a personal battle against organized crime, using their military training with deadly precision. Non-distinguished substandard action-adventure. **81m/C VHS.** Mike Lane, Richard X. Slattery, Rockne Tarkington, Glenn Wilder, Anthony Caruso; *D:* Joe Tornatore.

Zebra in the Kitchen ☙☙ ½ **1965** A 12-year-old boy living in a small town is upset when he sees the run-down condition of the local zoo. So he decides to set all the animals free, which causes pandemonium in the town. Pleasant family fare. **92m/C VHS, DVD.** Jay North, Martin Milner, Andy Devine, Joyce Meadows, Jim Davis; *D:* Ivan Tors.

Zebra Lounge ☙☙ **2001** Wendy (Swanson) and Alan (Baldwin) Barnet feel their marriage has gotten dull, so they place an ad in a swingers' magazine that leads them to the Zebra Lounge. There they meet the more experienced Jack (Daddo) and Louise (Ledford) Bauer who take them on a new sexual trip. But the Barnets soon discover that their new partners are not the emotionally stable people to get involved with. **92m/C VHS, DVD.** *CA* Stephen Baldwin, Kristy Swanson, Cameron Daddo, Brandy Ledford; *D:* Keri Skogland; *W:* Claire Montgomery, Monte Montgomery; *C:* Barry Parrell. **VIDEO**

Zebrahead ☙☙☙ **1992 (R)** Zack and Nikki are two high schoolers in love—which would be okay except Zack's white and Nikki's black. Writer/director Drazan's expressive debut features one of last appearances by Sharkey as Zack's dad. Outstanding performances by the young and largely unknown cast, particularly Rapaport and Wright, and a great musical score enrich the action. Filmed on location in Detroit, with plenty of authentic Motown scenery to chew on, including Cody High School and a shootout at the eastside Skateland. Developed with assistance by the Sundance Institute. **102m/C VHS, DVD.** Michael Rapaport, N'Bushe Wright, Ray Sharkey, DeShonn Castle, Ron Johnson, Marsha Florence, Paul Butler, Abdul Hassan Sharif, Dan Ziskie, Candy Ann Brown, Helen Shaver, Luke Reilly, Martin Priest, Kevin Corrigan; *D:* Tony Drazan; *W:* Tony Drazan; *C:* Maryse Alberti; *M:* Taj Mahal. Sundance '92: Filmmakers Trophy.

Zebraman ☙☙ ½ *Zeburaman* **2004** Junior high teacher Shinichi is a failure at life. His wife hates him, his daughter is slutty, and his son spends his days being bullied. Shinichi spends most of his time daydreaming about his favorite TV show from his childhood, "Zebraman" (think "Power Rangers" on drugs). Eventually he begins dressing up as Zebraman and going out into the city streets at night. At some point he meets a villain named Crabhead and kicks him unconscious. Then the aliens invade and begin possessing people and killing young girls, turning Shinichi into a superhero, whether he wants the job or not. Oddly lighthearted for a Takashi Miike flick. **115m/C DVD.** *JP* Sho Aikawa, Atsuro Watabe, Akira (Tsukamoto) Emoto, Ren Osugi, Kyoka Suzuki, Yui Ichikawa, Koen Kondo, Ryo Iwamatsu, Teruyoshi Uchimura; *D:* Takashi Miike; *W:* Kankuro Kudo; *C:* Kazunari Tanaka; *M:* Koji Endo.

A Zed & Two Noughts ☙☙☙ **1988** A serio-comic essay by the acclaimed British filmmaker. Twin zoologists, after their wives are killed in an accident, explore their notions of death by, among other things, filming the decay of animal bodies absconded from the zoo. Heavily textured and experimental; Greenaway's second feature film. **115m/C VHS, DVD.** *GB* Eric Deacon, Brian Deacon, Joss Ackland, Andrea Ferreol, Frances Barber; *D:* Peter Greenaway; *W:* Peter Greenaway; *C:* Sacha Vierny; *M:* Michael Nyman.

Zeder ☙☙ ½ *Revenge of the Dead; Zeder: Voices from Beyond* **1983** A young novelist (Lavia) discovers fragments of curious documents on the ribbon of a used typewriter bought by his wife (Canovas). He comes to think that they suggest research into immortality. The rest of the film combines elements of suspense with horror in a fairly slow-moving, serious plot with references to Val Lewton's "Cat People." **98m/C VHS, DVD.** *IT* Gabriele Lavia, Anne Canovos; *D:* Pupi Avati; *W:* Pupi Avati, Antonio Avati, Maurizio Costanzo.

Zelary ☙☙☙ ½ **2003 (R)** Eliska (Geislerova) is a confident young medical student in 1943 Prague whose life is interrupted by the Nazi invasion. She joins the resistance, but her cell is soon discovered, forcing her to flee with a sympathetic patient (Cserhalmi) to a rural village. In order to avert suspicion, she must marry the man and try to fit in. Slowly and gracefully follows Eliska's initial hesitation with her new benefactor and environment until she is won over by their kindness and strength of character. Lovingly shot and acted, if a bit overlong. **150m/C DVD.** *CZ AT* Anna Geislerova, Ivan Trojan, Jan Hrusinsky, Iva Bittova, Tomas Zatecka, Jaroslava Adamova; *D:* Ondrej Trojan; *W:* Petr Jarchovsky; *C:* Asen Sopov; *M:* Petr Ostouchov.

Zelig ☙☙☙ ½ **1983 (PG)** Documentary spoof stars Allen as Leonard Zelig, the famous "Chameleon Man" of the 1920s, whose personality was so vague he would assume the characteristics of those with whom he came into contact, and who had a habit of showing up among celebrities and at historic events. Filmed in black-and-white; intersperses bits of newsreel and photographs with live action. Allen-style clever filmmaking at its best. **79m/B VHS, DVD.** Woody Allen, Mia Farrow, Susan Sontag, Saul Bellow, Irving Howe; ***D:*** Woody Allen; ***W:*** Woody Allen; ***C:*** Gordon Willis. N.Y. Film Critics '83: Cinematog.

Zelly & Me *Phoebe* **1988 (PG)** A strange little drama about a young orphan living with her maniacally possessive grandmother, who forces the child into her own interior life through humiliation and isolation from anyone she cares for. Well-acted and interesting film that suffers from an overly introspective plot and confusing gaps in the narrative. Look for director Lynch on the other side of the camera. **87m/C VHS.** Isabella Rossellini, Alexandra Johnes, David Lynch, Glynis Johns, Kaiulani Lee, Joe Morton; ***D:*** Tina Rathborne; ***W:*** Tina Rathborne; ***C:*** Mikael Salomon; ***M:*** Pino Donaggio.

Zemsta *The Revenge* **2002** In the 17th century, two feuding noblemen occupy different parts of the same crumbling castle because of their declining fortunes. They live to make each other miserable and marry money. Papkin (Polanski), a boastful popinjay, is enlisted by Czesnik to help him woo a supposedly wealthy widow in return for the chance at romancing Czesnik's pretty niece, who has her own romantic plans. Adapted from the play by Aleksander Fredro. Polish with subtitles. **100m/C VHS, DVD.** *PL* Roman Polanski, Janusz Gajos, Andrzej Seweryn, Kasia (Katarzyna) Figura, Agata Buzek, Rafal Krolikowski; ***D:*** Andrzej Wajda; ***W:*** Andrzej Wajda; ***C:*** Pawel Edelman; ***M:*** Wojciech Kilar.

Zentropa *Europa* **1992 (R)** Clever cinematic allusions and visuals aside, this is essentially a conventional thriller. German-American pacifist Leopold travels to Germany in 1945 to help in the postwar rebuilding. He finds work as a sleeping-car conductor for a giant railway system called Zentropa and finds himself romancing the mysterious Katharina, who draws the hapless Leopold into an intrigue involving Nazi sympathizers. Director von Trier uses the voice of Von Sydow as an omniscient narrator to address the audience and move the story along. Filmed primarily in black-and-white with bursts of color denoting dramatic moments. In English and German with English subtitles. **112m/C VHS, DVD.** *GE* Jean-Marc Barr, Barbara Sukowa, Udo Kier, Eddie Constantine; ***D:*** Lars von Trier; ***W:*** Niels Vorsel, Lars von Trier; ***Nar:*** Max von Sydow.

Zeppelin 1/2 **1971 (G)** During WWI, the British enlist the aid of York as a double agent. His mission is to steal Germany's plans for a super-dirigible. Accompanying the Germans on the craft's maiden voyage, York discovers they are actually on a mission to steal British treasures. Although the script is poor, the battle scenes and the airship itself are very impressive. **102m/C VHS.** *GB* Michael York, Elke Sommer, Peter Carsten, Marius Goring, Anton Diffring, Andrew Keir, Rupert Davies, Alexandra Stewart; ***D:*** Etienne Perier.

Zeram *Zeiram; Zeiramu* **1991** Zeram is a giant renegade space alien lured to earth by a female bounty hunter. How does she expect to capture it? Why with a warp machine, space bazooka, electric shield, and a computer named Bob, of course. Dubbed. **92m/C VHS, DVD.** *JP* Yuko Moriyama, Yukihiro Hotaru, Kunihiko Ida; ***D:*** Keita Amemiya; ***W:*** Hajime Matsumoto; ***C:*** Hiroshi Kidokoro; ***M:*** Hirokazu Ohta.

Zeram 2 *Zeiram 2; Zeiramu* **1994** Moriyama returns to play Investigator Iria, an intergalactic bounty hunter, who is assisted by her computer, Bob. Iria has been given a new android as a trainee, but it malfunctions during a battle and turns on her. The android is infected with a Zeram, an evil alien force. To make matters worse, Iria's partner Fujikuro (Sabu) has betrayed her and is trying to steal an ancient artifact which Iria possesses. Trapped and in need of assistance, Iria calls on her old friends Teppei (Iida) and Kamiya (Hotaru), two bumbling electricians to help her. The film is non-stop fun, as it mixes amazing action scenes, gross monsters, and slapstick comedy seamlessly to create an entertaining sci-fi treat. **100m/C DVD.** *JP* Yukihiro Hotaru, Kunihiko Iida, Yuko Moriyama; ***D:*** Keito Amamiya.

Zero 1984 WWII story about the building of the zero fighter that was used to devastating effect in the invasion of Pearl Harbor. **128m/C VHS.** Yuzo Kayama, Tetsuro Tamba; ***D:*** Toshio Masuda.

Zero Boys WOOF! 1986 (R) Teenage survivalists in the Californian wilderness are stalked by a murderous lunatic. Exploitative and mean-spirited. **89m/C VHS, DVD.** Daniel Hirsch, Kelli Maroney, Nicole Rio, Joe Estevez; ***D:*** Nico Mastorakis; ***W:*** Nico Mastorakis, Fred C. Perry; ***C:*** Steve (Steven) Shaw; ***M:*** Stanley Myers, Hans Zimmer.

Zero Degrees Kelvin 1/2 *Zero Kelvin; Kjaerlighetens Kjotere* **1995** Brrrr! Get the ice scraper ready, because you may have to clear off your TV screen in this chilly tale of trappers in 1920s Greenland. Henrik Larsen (Eidsvold), a poet living in Oslo, decides to join the band of trappers after his girlfriend Gertrude (Martens) spurns his marriage proposal. On his arrival in the stark and frozen landscape, he is forced to share a cabin with the stoic, silent Holm (Sundquist) and the lewd, violent Randbaek (Skarsgard). Randbaek holds the newcomer and his city-boy ways in disdain, creating an air of tension and menace that inevitably results in a clash between the two. Instead of dwelling on the action aspect, director Moland uses the minimalist landscape to echo the psychological battles the men must face with the frigid terrain and between themselves. Norwegian with subtitles. **113m/C VHS, DVD.** *NO* Gard B. Eidsvold, Stellan Skarsgard, Bjorn Sundquist, Camilla Martens; ***D:*** Hans Petter Moland; ***W:*** Hans Petter Moland, Lars Bill Lundheim; ***C:*** Philip Ogaard; ***M:*** Terje Rypdal.

Zero Effect 1/2 **1997 (R)** A cross between Howard Hughes and Sherlock Holmes, brilliant, eccentric detective Daryl Zero (Pullman), who, along with his harried helper Steve Arlo (Stiller), takes on the case of a blackmailed timber tycoon (O'Neal) in this comedic whodunit. The normally reclusive sleuth bites the bullet and agrees to trek to Oregon to personally investigate the particularly intriguing case, which also involves an attractive paramedic (Dickens). Pullman pulls off another quirky leading man performance with flair. Stiller is stellar as the exasperated assistant. Fresh idea and hip humor mark this debut for 22-year-old writer/director Kasdan, son of director Lawrence Kasdan. **150m/C VHS, DVD.** Bill Pullman, Ben Stiller, Ryan O'Neal, Kim Dickens, Angela Featherstone; ***D:*** Jake Kasdan; ***W:*** Jake Kasdan; ***C:*** Bill Pope.

Zero for Conduct *Zero de Conduit* **1933** Vigo's classic French fantasy about an outrageous rebellion of schoolboys against bureaucratic adults. More of a visual poem than a drama, it inspired Lindsay Anderson's "If...." One of only four films created by Vigo before his early death. Banned across Europe at release. In French with English subtitles. **49m/B VHS.** *FR* Jean Daste, Robert Le Flon, Louis Lef'evre, Constantin Kelber, Gerard de Bedarieux; ***D:*** Jean Vigo; ***W:*** Jean Vigo; ***C:*** Boris Kaufman.

Zero Hour! 1/2 **1957** Passengers and crew aboard an airliner become sick from food poisoning and the only way to avoid disaster is to find someone on board who can fly the plane—and hasn't had fish for dinner! Yep, it's the film that inspired the classic spoof "Airplane!" And for that, it deserves an extra half bone. **81m/B DVD.** Dana Andrews, Linda Darnell, Sterling Hayden, Geoffrey Toone, Jerry Paris, Peggy King, Charles Quinlivan, Patricia Tiernan, Elroy "Crazylegs" Hirsch, Willis Bouchey, Robert Stevenson, Mary Newton; ***D:*** Hall Bartlett; ***W:*** Hall Bartlett, John C. Champion, Arthur Hailey; ***C:*** John F. Warren; ***Nar:*** William Conrad.

Zero Patience **1994** Yes, it's an audacious film musical about AIDS myths and ghosts and Victorian explorers—among other things. Infamous Patient Zero (Fauteux) is the Canadian flight attendant reputed to have carried the virus to North America. Ghostly Zero pleads for someone to tell his story and his cause is taken up by Victorian explorer Sir Richard Francis Burton (Robinson), who happens to have achieved eternal life after an encounter with the Fountain of Youth, and who is also preparing an exhibit on contagious diseases. Sharp mix of politics, humor, and fantasy. **100m/C VHS, DVD.** *CA* John Robinson, Normand Fauteux, Dianne Heatherington, Ricardo Keens-Douglas; ***D:*** John Greyson; ***W:*** John Greyson; ***M:*** Glenn Schellenberg.

Zero Population Growth 1/2 *Z.P.G* **1972** In the 21st century the government has decreed that no babies may be born for a 30-year span in order to control the population. But Chaplin and Reed secretly have a child and when they are discovered are sent to be executed. Maudlin and simplistic. **95m/C VHS.** Bill Nagy, Sheila Reid, David Markham, Oliver Reed, Geraldine Chaplin, Diane Cilento, Don Gordon; ***D:*** Michael Campus; ***W:*** Frank De Felitta, Max Ehrlich; ***C:*** Mikael Salomon, Michael Reed; ***M:*** Jonathan Hodge.

Zero to Sixty **1978 (PG)** Newly divorced man finds his car has been repossessed for nonpayment. Seeking out the manager of the finance company, he gets a job as a repo man with a sassy 16-year-old girl as his assistant. Repartee develops, stuff happens, and the movie ends. **96m/C VHS.** Darren McGavin, Sylvia Miles, Denise Nickerson, Joan Collins; ***D:*** Don Weis; ***M:*** John Beal.

Zero Tolerance 1/2 **1993 (R)** FBI agent Jeff Douglas (Patrick) is assigned to travel to Mexico and pick up a drug-runner who works for the White Hand cartel, whose latest product is liquid heroin. When they are ambushed Douglas is forced to carry a shipment of drugs across the border—the lives of his wife and child hang in the balance. But after the dirty deed is done, Douglas finds his family has been murdered anyway. So he sets out to execute the cartel druglords. **92m/C VHS, DVD.** Robert Patrick, Miles O'Keeffe, Mick Fleetwood, Titus Welliver, Jeffrey Anderson-Gunter, Gustav Vintas, Michael Gregory, Maurice Lamont; ***D:*** Joseph Merhi; ***W:*** Jacobsen Hart.

Zertigo Diamond Caper **1982** Utilizing his heightened senses, a blind boy solves a diamond caper and proves his mother's innocence. **50m/C VHS.** Adam Rich, David Groh, Jane Elliot; ***D:*** Paul Asselin; ***W:*** David Hoffman, Leslie Zerg; ***C:*** Erik Daarstad.

Zeta One *Alien Women; The Love Factor* **1969** A soft-core British science fiction yarn about scantily clad alien babes and the special agent who's trying to uncover their secret. It's all very sketchy, silly and campy, though pleasantly cast with plenty of lovely British actresses. **86m/C VHS, DVD.** *GB* James Robertson Justice, Charles Hawtrey, Robin Hawdon, Anna Gael, Brigitte Skay, Dawn Addams, Valerie Leon, Yutte Stensgaard, Wendy Lingham, Rita Webb, Caroline Hawkins; ***D:*** Michael Cort; ***W:*** Michael Cort, Christopher Neame, Alistain McKenzie; ***C:*** Jack Atcheler; ***M:*** John Hawksworth.

Zeus and Roxanne **1996 (PG)** Hey, I know! Let's combine "Flipper" and "Benji" with "The Parent Trap!" You know, for the kids! Marine biologist and single mom Mary Beth (Quinlan) meets her unconventional (and conveniently widowed) new neighbor Terry (Guttenberg) and his dog Zeus. Cuteness ensues. Mary Beth's daughters and Terry's young son go about getting the two adults together. Meanwhile, Zeus and Roxanne, Mary Beth's dolphin, strike up a unique friendship of their own. Showing up to provide drama is evil guy Claude (Vosloo), who is vying for the same grant as Mary Beth. Unlikely animal couple steals the show, and the story would have benefitted from focusing on the entertaining bond between those two and less on the human romance. Not much appeal for anyone over the age of nine. **98m/C VHS, DVD.** Kathleen Quinlan, Steve Guttenberg, Arnold Vosloo, Miko Hughes, Dawn McMillan, Majandra Delfino; ***D:*** George Miller; ***W:*** Tom Benedek; ***C:*** David Connell; ***M:*** Bruce Rowland.

Zhou Yu's Train 1/2 *Zhou Yu de Huoche* **2002 (PG-13)** Gong Li stars in this slick romantic drama as porcelain painter, Zhou Yu, who's in love with teacher/poet Chen Ching (Leung Kar-fai). Because he lives in a distant village, Zhou takes the train twice a week so they can be together. Chen begins to feel overwhelmed and transfers to an even farther away town; meanwhile, Zhou becomes friendly with another train passenger, Zhang (Honglei). Gong also plays another character, Xiu, who's involved with Chen and wants to know about his time with Zhou. Except maybe nothing is what it first seems since director's Sun's theme is that love is how you want it to appear (or something like that). Based on the novella "Zhou Yu's Cry" by Bei Cun. Mandarian with subtitles. **97m/C DVD.** Honglei Sun, Gong Li, Tony Leung Kar-fai, Li Zhixiong, Shi Chunling, Liu Wei, Gao Jingwen, Dai Ke, Pan Weiyan, Huang Mo; ***D:*** Sun Zhou; ***W:*** Sun Zhou, Bei Cun, Zhang Mei; ***C:*** Wang Yu; ***M:*** Shingeru Umebayashi.

Ziegfeld Follies 1/2 **1946** A lavish revue of musical numbers and comedy sketches featuring many MGM stars of the WWII era. Highlights include Astaire and Kelly's only duet and a Astaire-Bremer ballet number. ♫ Bring on Those Wonderful Men; Bring on Those Beautiful Girls; The Drinking Song; La Traviata; This Heart is Mine; Love; When Television Comes; There's Beauty Everywhere; The Babbitt and the Bromide. **115m/C VHS, DVD.** Fred Astaire, Judy Garland, Gene Kelly, Red Skelton, Fanny Brice, William Powell, Jimmy Durante, Edward Arnold, Lucille Bremer, Hume Cronyn, Victor Moore, Lena Horne, Lucille Ball, Esther Williams; ***D:*** Vincente Minnelli; ***C:*** Charles Rosher.

Ziegfeld Girl **1941** Three star-struck girls are chosen for the Ziegfeld follies and move on to success and heartbreak. Lavish costumes and production numbers in the MGM style. ♫ You Stepped Out of a Dream; I'm Always Chasing Rainbows; Minnie from Trinidad; Mr. Gallagher & Mr. Shean; You Never Looked So Beautiful. **131m/B VHS, DVD.** James Stewart, Judy Garland, Hedy Lamarr, Lana Turner, Tony Martin, Jackie Cooper, Ian Hunter, Charles Winninger, Al Shean, Edward Everett Horton, Philip Dorn, Paul Kelly, Eve Arden, Dan Dailey, Fay Holden, Felix Bressart, Mae Busch, Reed Hadley; ***D:*** Robert Z. Leonard.

ZigZag **2002 (R)** Louis "ZigZag" Fletcher (Jones) is an autistic 15-year-old who lives in fear of his dad Fletcher (Sniper), an abusive drug addict. ZigZag works after school as a dishwasher for the foul-mouthed Toad (Platt) and his one caring friend is his volunteer Big Brother, Dean (Leguizamo), who has cancer. As if things are bad enough, after a confrontation with Fletcher, ZigZag steals $9,000 from Toad to give to his dad and Dean goes to a loan shark (Goss) to get the money to return to Toad's safe before he realizes it's missing. Based on the novel by Landon J. Napoleon; Goyer's directorial debut. The sort of story that can easily descend into sap but doesn't thanks to some fearless performances and Goyer's tight control. **101m/C VHS, DVD.** Sam Jones III, John Leguizamo, Wesley Snipes, Oliver Platt, Natasha Lyonne, Sherman Augustus, Luke Goss, Michael Greyeyes, Elizabeth Pena; ***D:*** David S. Goyer; ***W:*** David S. Goyer; ***C:*** James L. Carter; ***M:*** Grant Lee Phillips.

Zipperface **1992** A Palm Beach serial killer is making mincemeat of the local prostitutes. In order to capture the scum, the prerequisite beautiful police detective goes undercover only to find herself the killer's biggest thrill. **90m/C VHS.** Dona Adams, Jonathan Mandell, David Clover, Trisha Melynkov, Richard Vidan, Harold Cannon, Bruce Brown, Rikki Brando, Timothy D. Lechner, John Dagnen; ***D:*** Mansour Pourmand; ***W:*** Barbara Bishop; ***C:*** F. Smith Martin; ***M:*** Jim Halfpenny.

Zis Boom Bah 1/2 **1941** Musical-comedy star buys a cafe for her college son. He and his friends transform the place into a restaurant-theatre with predictable results. ♫ Annabella; It Makes No Difference When You're In the Army; Put Your Trust in the Moon; Zis Boom Bah; Good News Tomorrow; I've Learned to Smile Again. **61m/B VHS, DVD.** Richard "Skeets" Gallagher, Jan Wiley, Peter Lind Hayes, Mary Healy, Grace Hayes, Huntz Hall, Benny Rubin; ***D:*** William Nigh; ***W:*** Harvey Gates, Jack Henley; ***C:*** Marcel Le Picard.

Zita 1/2 **1968** Young, shy Ann (Shimkus) learns that her adored Aunt Zita (Paxinqu) is dying, but she's unable to accept the idea of parting from her great friend and confidant. She also finds it too heartbreaking to remain in the house with the deathly ill Zita, so she runs off into the Parisian night, looking to lose herself in the clubs and cafes, and meeting a young man in the process.

When Ann returns home, she's able to face the situation through newly opened eyes. Shimkus turns in a sweet, sympathetic performance, and the cinematography is both otherworldly and intoxicating. Rarely seen, quietly contemplative film is a knockout. **92m/C DVD.** Suzanne Flon, Katina Paxinou, Joanna Shimkus; ***D:*** Robert Enrico; ***C:*** Jean Boffety; ***M:*** Francois de Roubaix.

The Zodiac **2005 (R)** Under-realized account of the notorious Zodiac Killer, who infamously terrorized the San Francisco area in the late '60s and has eluded the police to this day. Depressingly bland and straightforward, unintentionally looking like an episode of "Columbo." The killer is seen in shadow and cops are bogged down in exposition and melodrama. Do not confuse this clunker with the masterful David Fincher-helmed "Zodiac" (although they probably hope you will). **92m/C DVD.** *US* Justin Chambers, Robin Tunney, Rory Culkin, William Mapother, Brad William Henke, Rex Linn, Philip Baker Hall, Ian Scott Mcgregor, Marty Lindsey, Shelby Alexis Irey, Natassia Costa, Kris Palm, Nate Dushku, Katelin Chesna, Jodi Feder, Kathryn Howell, George Maguire, Carolyne Smith, Munda Razooki; ***D:*** Alexander Bulkley; ***W:*** Kelly Bulkley; ***C:*** Denis Maloney; ***M:*** Michael Suby.

Zodiac 1/2 **2007 (R)** Drawn-out and detailed examination (with strong performances) of the still-unsolved Bay Area serial killings from the 1970s. The self-named Zodiac sends cryptic messages to the San Francisco Chronicle, where dissolute reporter Paul Avery (Downey Jr.) is on the crime beat. The paper's editorial cartoonist, Robert Graysmith (Gyllenhaal), figures out the killer's cipher and becomes obsessed with helping out. Then, SFPD detectives Dave Toschi (Ruffalo) and William Armstrong (Edwards) are assigned to the case, which eventually goes cold. Graysmith later wrote about the killings and drew his own conclusions as to the Zodiac's identity. **156m/C DVD, Blu-ray Disc, HD DVD.** *US* Mark Ruffalo, Jake Gyllenhaal, Robert Downey Jr., Brian Cox, Chloe Sevigny, John Carroll Lynch, Charles Fleischer, Zach Grenier, Philip Baker Hall, Elias Koteas, Donal Logue, Dermot Mulroney, John Terry, John Getz, Adam Goldberg, Candy Clark, John Lacy, James Le Gros; ***D:*** David Fincher; ***W:*** James Vanderbilt; ***C:*** Harris Savides; ***M:*** David Shire.

The Zodiac Killer 1/2 **1971 (R)** Based on a true story, this tells the violent tale of the San Francisco murders that occurred in the late 1960s. Doesn't have the suspense it should. **87m/C VHS, DVD.** Tom Pittman, Hal Reed, Bob Jones, Ray Lynch; ***D:*** Tom Hanson.

Zoe 1/2 **2001** Teenager Zoe (Zima) longs to escape her abusive homelife and explore her Native American heritage through a Cherokee spirit guide. So she and two girlfriends (who want to go to Hollywood) run away from home and start their journey, eventually crossing paths with middle-aged Englishwoman Cecilia (Seagrove) whose mother's last request was to have her ashes scattered in the mountains of New Mexico. Recognizing a kindred spirit, Zoe leaves her friends to follow Cecilia and find her spirit guide. **92m/C VHS, DVD.** Vanessa Zima, Jenny Seagrove, Stephi Lineburg, Victoria Davis, Gordon Tootoosis, Kim Greist; ***D:*** Deborah Attoinese; ***W:*** Deborah Attoinese, Amy Dawes; ***C:*** Samuel Ameen; ***M:*** Dan Pinnella.

Zoltan... Hound of Dracula 1/2 *Dracula's Dog* **1978** The vampire and his bloodthirsty dog go to Los Angeles to find the last of Count Dracula's living descendants. Campy and just original enough to make it almost worth watching. **85m/C VHS, DVD.** Michael Pataki, Reggie Nalder, Jose Ferrer, Jan Shutan, Libbie Chase, John Levin, Cleo Harrington, Simmy Bow, JoJo D'Amore; ***D:*** Albert Band; ***W:*** Frank Ray Perilli; ***C:*** Bruce Logan; ***M:*** Andrew Belling.

Zombie *Zombie Flesh-Eaters; Island of the Living Dead; Zombi 2* **1980** Italian-made white-men-in-the-Caribbean-with-flesh-eating-zombies cheapie. **91m/C VHS, DVD.** *IT* Tisa Farrow, Ian McCulloch, Richard Johnson, Al Cliver, Auretta Gay, Olga Karlatos, Stefania D'Amario, Lucio Fulci, Ugo Bologna, Monica Zanchi; ***D:*** Lucio Fulci; ***W:*** Elisa Briganti, Dardano Sacchetti; ***C:*** Sergio Salvati; ***M:*** Fabio Frizzi, Giorgio Tucci.

Zombie and the Ghost Train *Zombie ja Kummitusjuna* **1991** Absurdist punk comedy about the vicissitudes of a down-and-out bass player. Finnish with subtitles. **88m/C VHS.** *FI* Silu Seppala, Matti Pellonpaa, Marjo Leinonen, Vieno Saaristo; ***D:*** Mika Kaurismaki; ***W:*** Mika Kaurismaki; ***C:*** Olli Varja; ***M:*** Mauri Sumen.

The Zombie Army **1993** Tough drill sergeant tries to whip a bunch of raw female recruits up to muster for a special mission. Toward that end, the government has conveniently bought a defunct lunatic asylum as a training ground. Only problem is that a few of the former inmates have been left behind and are able to menace the troops with their penchant for psychotic weirdness. **80m/C VHS.** Steve Roberts, John Kalinowski, Jody Amato, Eileen Saddow; ***D:*** Betty Stapleford; ***W:*** Roger Scearce.

Zombie High *The School That Ate My Brain* **1987 (R)** Students at a secluded academy are being lobotomized by the school president. Mindless, in two senses of the word. **91m/C VHS.** Virginia Madsen, Richard Cox, Kay E. Kuter, James Wilder, Sherilyn Fenn, Paul Williams, Scott Coffey, Clare Carey, Walter Addison; ***D:*** Ron Link; ***W:*** Aziz Ghazal, Tim Doyle, Elizabeth Passerelli; ***C:*** Brian Coyne, David Lux; ***M:*** Daniel May.

Zombie Honeymoon **2004** Generally successful mix of pathos, comedy, and horror. Denise (Coogan) and Danny (Sibley) are on their honeymoon when Danny is attacked by a zombie. Denise is inconsolable until Danny returns—a changed man. Neither his increasing bloodlust or physical disintegration can drive Denise away. Is that true love or what? **83m/C DVD.** *US* Neal Jones, Tracy Coogan, Graham Sibley, Tonya Cornelisse, David M. Wallace, Phil Catalano; ***D:*** Dave Gebroe; ***W:*** Dave Gebroe; ***C:*** Ken Seng; ***M:*** Michael Tremante.

Zombie Island Massacre **1984 (R)** In this trying film, tourists travel to see a voodoo ritual, and then are systematically butchered by the rite-inspired zombies. Featuring former congressional wife and "Playboy" magazine model Jenrette. **89m/C VHS, DVD.** Rita Jenrette, David Broadnax; ***D:*** John N. Carter.

Zombie Lake *El Lago de los Muertos Vivientes; The Lake of the Living Dead* **1980** Killed in an ambush by villagers during WWII, a group of Nazi soldiers turned zombies reside in the town's lake, preying on unsuspecting swimmers, especially dog paddling nude young women. Laughable FX, almost bad enough to be good. From the team that produced "Oasis of the Zombies." **90m/C VHS, DVD.** *FR SP* Howard Vernon, Pierre Escourrou, Anouchka, Anthony (Jose, J. Antonio, J.A.) Mayans, Nadine Pascale, Jean Rollin; ***D:*** J.A. Laser, Jean Rollin; ***W:*** Jess (Jesus) Franco, Julian Esteban.

Zombie Nightmare **WOOF!** **1986 (R)** A murdered teenager is revived by a voodoo queen and slaughters his punk-teen assailants. Cheap and stupid just about sums this one up. Music by Motorhead, Death Mask, Girlschool, and Thor. **89m/C VHS.** Adam West, Jon Mikl Thor, Tia Carrere, Frank Dietz, Linda Singer, Mandn E. Turbride, Hamibh McEwen; ***D:*** John Bravman.

Zombie Strippers **2008** The Bush administration, elected to a fourth term, creates a virus to reanimate dead tissue in order to ensure a supply of eternal soldiers to fight the never-ending Iraq war. Unfortunately the virus is only stable in women, and it eventually spreads from the lab to a nearby illegal strip club run by Ian (Englund). His best stripper Kat (Jameson) becomes infected, and suddenly the local rednecks can't spend enough money to watch her take her clothes off, causing jealousy in the other dancers, who promptly infect themselves to make more money. A subtle little film with perhaps some political commentary. **94m/C DVD, Blu-ray Disc.** Robert Englund, Joey Medina, John Hawkes, Whitney Anderson, Jenna Jameson, Roxy Saint, Shamron Moore, Penny Drake, Jeniffer Holland, Jeanette Sousa, Calvin Green, Catero Colbert, Carmit Levite, Zak Kilberg, Billy Beck, Adam Smith, Jen Alex Gonzalez, Laura Bach, Jessica Custodio, Travis Wood, Brad Milne, Shannon Malone, Gary Kraus, Jim Roof, Asante Jones, David O'Kelley; ***D:*** Jay Lee; ***W:*** Jay Lee; ***C:*** Jay Lee; ***M:*** Billy White Acre. **VIDEO**

Zombieland 1/2 **2009 (R)** The world is overrun by the undead and a rag-tag group of survivors must cling together to outwit and outgun the relentless zombie scourge. Teaming up are two unlikely survivors—a pathetically frightened kid from Ohio, Columbus (Eisenberg), and the fearsome Twinkie-loving zombie slayer, Tallahassee (Harrelson)—who face down the rotting menace with dark wit and shotgun blasts to the head. They connect with Wichita (Stone) and Little Rock (Breslin) and the four unleash a ghoulish road movie that somehow remains light-hearted and charming. Eventually the foursome makes it to California and a hoped-for respite at a supposedly zombie-free amusement park. **88m/C DVD.** *US* Woody Harrelson, Jesse Eisenberg, Emma Stone, Abigail Breslin, Amber Heard, Bill Murray, Derek Graf; ***D:*** Ruben Fleischer; ***W:*** Rhett Reese, Paul Wernick; ***C:*** Michael Bonvillain; ***M:*** David Sardy.

Zombies of Moratau **WOOF!** **1957** A diver and his girlfriend seek to retrieve an undersea treasure of diamonds protected by zombies. So boring you'll want to die. **70m/B VHS.** Gregg (Hunter) Palmer, Allison Hayes, Autumn Russel, Joel Ashley; ***D:*** Edward L. Cahn.

Zombies of the Stratosphere *Satan's Satellites* **1952** A serial in 12 chapters in which a cosmic policeman fights Zombies attempting to blow the Earth out of orbit. Also available in a 93-minute, colorized version. **152m/B VHS.** Judd Holdren, Aline Towne, Leonard Nimoy, John Crawford, Ray Boyle, Craig G. Kelly; ***D:*** Fred Brannon.

Zombies on Broadway 1/2 *Loonies on Broadway* **1944** Two press agents travel to the Caribbean in search of new talent, but find Lugosi performing experiments on people and turning them into sequel material. RKO hoped this would be equally successful follow-up to "I Walked with a Zombie." **68m/B VHS.** Wally Brown, Alan Carney, Bela Lugosi, Anne Jeffreys, Sheldon Leonard, Frank Jenks, Russell Hopton, Joseph (Joe) Vitale, Ian Wolfe, Louis Jean Heydt, Darby Jones, Sir Lancelot; ***D:*** Gordon Douglas; ***W:*** Robert E. Kent, Lawrence Kimble; ***C:*** Jack MacKenzie; ***M:*** Roy Webb.

Zone of the Dead **1978** A mortician is using his morgue for other than embalming—and it isn't pretty! **81m/C VHS, DVD.** John Ericson, Ivor Francis, Charles Aidman, Bernard Fox.

Zone 39 **1996** Sci-fi thriller vibrates with impending doom. A 40-year war results in an uneasy peace between two rival factions. Guard Leo (Phelps) has gone a little loopy after the death of his wife and is assigned to patrol the remote outpost of Zone 39, where a severe contamination is spreading. Thanks to the illegal drug Novan that Leo keeps taking, he's also experiencing flashbacks of his wife and other ghostly figures. The spectacularly desolate setting is a dry salt lake located in Woomera, Australia. **93m/C VHS, DVD.** *AU* Peter Phelps, William Zappa, Caroline Beck, Brad Byquar, Alex Menglet, Jeff Kovski; ***D:*** John Tatoulis; ***W:*** Deborah Parsons; ***C:*** Peter Zakhavor; ***M:*** Burkhard Dallwitz.

Zone Troopers 1/2 **1984 (PG)** Five American G.I.'s in WWII-ravaged Europe stumble upon a wrecked alien spacecraft and enlist the extraterrestrial's help in fending off the Nazis. **86m/C VHS.** Timothy Van Patten, Tim Thomerson, Art LaFleur, Biff Manard; ***D:*** Danny Bilson; ***W:*** Danny Bilson, Paul DeMeo; ***C:*** Mac Ahlberg; ***M:*** Richard Band.

Zontar, the Thing from Venus **1966** Scientist is taken over by alien batlike thing from Venus, and attempts to take over the Earth. A parody of itself. **68m/C VHS, DVD.** John Agar, Anthony Huston, Susan Bjorman, Pat Delaney, Warren Hammack, Neil Fletcher; ***D:*** Larry Buchanan; ***W:*** Larry Buchanan, Hillman Taylor; ***C:*** Robert Alcott. **TV**

The Zoo Gang 1/2 **1985 (PG-13)** A group of teens want to open a nightclub. Will they bring their dream to fruition, or will the mean rival gang foil their plans? **96m/C VHS.** Jackie Earle Haley, Tiffany Helm, Ben Vereen, Jason Gedrick, Eric Gurry; ***D:*** John Watson, Pen Densham; ***W:*** John Watson, Pen Densham; ***M:*** Patrick Gleeson.

Zoolander 1/2 **2001 (PG-13)** Stiller plays Derek Zoolander, an absurdly vacuous and successful male model who's brainwashed into becoming an assassin by over-the-top designer Mugatu (Ferrell). It seems that a foreign prime minister is committed to cutting off the supply of cheap third world labor for the fashion industry, and Zoolander is the only model stupid enough to have his noggin scrubbed clean. He develops a friendship with arch-rival model Hansel (Wilson), and the dim duo try to stop the nefarious plot. Packed to the gills with celebrity cameos, including Heidi Klum, Donald Trump and, yes, Fabio. Ran into unexpected controversy because the intended target is the prime minister of Malaysia (and the Malaysians naturally objected). **89m/C VHS, DVD.** *US* Ben Stiller, Owen Wilson, Christine Taylor, Will Ferrell, Milla Jovovich, Jerry Stiller, Jon Voight, David Duchovny; ***D:*** Ben Stiller; ***W:*** Ben Stiller, John Hamburg, Drake Sather; ***C:*** Barry Peterson; ***M:*** David Arnold.

Zoom **2006 (PG)** Superhero Captain Zoom (Allen) has retired and gotten soft. But he's called back into action when he's needed to turn a group of misfit kids into the next generation of superheroes so that the world can be saved once again. Based on the graphic novel by Jason Lethcote. Definitely the weak link in the "kids dealing with superpowers" genre. **88m/C DVD.** *US* Tim Allen, Courteney Cox, Spencer Breslin, Chevy Chase, Kate Mara, Rip Torn, Kevin Zegers, Ryan Newman, Michael Cassidy, Thomas F. Wilson, Willie Garson; ***D:*** Peter Hewitt; ***W:*** Adam Rifkin, David Berenbaum; ***C:*** David Tattersall; ***M:*** Christophe Beck.

Zooman **1995 (R)** Hard-hitting message on violence and responsibility. Gang member Zooman (Kain) spots members of a rival gang in a Brooklyn neighborhood, whips out his gun, and begins firing. When the shooting stops, a little girl sitting on her stoop is dead—what's even worse for her estranged parents is the fact that obvious witnesses refuse to identify the gunman for fear of their own safety. So father Reuben (Gossett Jr.) puts up a sign about their plight, attracting lots of media attention, and neighborhood hostility. Based on Fuller's 1978 play "Zooman and the Sign." **95m/C VHS.** Louis Gossett Jr., Charles S. Dutton, Khalil Kain, Cynthia Martells, CCH Pounder, Vondie Curtis-Hall, Hill Harper; ***D:*** Leon Ichaso; ***W:*** Charles Fuller. **CABLE**

Zoot Suit **1981 (R)** Based on Luis Valdez' play, this murder mystery/musical is rooted in the historical Sleepy Lagoon murder in the 1940s. Valdez plays a Mexican-American accused of the crime. His friends (and defense lawyers) rally around him to fight this travesty of justice. Lots o'music and dancing. **104m/C VHS, DVD.** Edward James Olmos, Daniel Valdez, Tyne Daly, Charles Aidman, John Anderson; ***D:*** Luis Valdez; ***W:*** Luis Valdez.

Zora Is My Name! 1/2 *My Name Is Zora* **1990** The funny, moving story of Zora Neal Hurston, a Black writer known for her stories and folklore of the rural South of the '30s and '40s. From PBS's American Playhouse. **90m/C VHS, DVD.** Roger E. Mosley, Flip Wilson, Ruby Dee, Louis Gossett Jr.; ***D:*** Neema Barnette; ***W:*** Ann Wallace; ***M:*** Olu Dara.

Zorba the Greek 1/2 *Zormba* **1964** A young British writer (Bates) comes to Crete to find himself by working his father's mine. He meets Zorba, an itinerant Greek laborer (Quinn), and they take lodgings together with an aging courtesan, who Zorba soon romances. The writer, on the other hand, is attracted to a lovely young widow. When she responds to him, the townsmen jealously attack her. Zorba teaches the young man the necessary response to life and its tragedies. Based on a novel by Nikos Kazantzakis. Masterpiece performance from Quinn. Beautifully photographed, somewhat overlong. Film later written for stage production. **142m/B VHS, DVD.** Anthony Quinn, Alan Bates, Irene Papas, Lila Kedrova; ***D:*** Michael Cacoyannis; ***C:*** Walter Lassally. Oscars '64: Art Dir./Set Dec., B&W, B&W Cinematog., Support. Actress (Kedrova); Natl. Bd. of Review '64: Actor (Quinn).

Zorro ♂♂ 1/2 *El Zorro la belva del Colorado; El Zorro* **1974 (G)** Italian take on the Zorro legend is a light romp, with Delon as the masked one careful not to take the proceedings too seriously. Recently arrived California governor Diego runs afoul of corrupt officials and dons the famous cape and mask to help the peasants. Mostly aims to please the kids but should keep adults interested, too. **120m/C VHS.** *IT FR* Alain Delon, Stanley Baker, Adriana Asti, Marino (Martin) Mase, Giacomo "Jack" Rossi-Stuart, Moustache, Ottavia Piccolo, Giampiero Albertini, Enzo Cerusico; ***D:*** Duccio Tessari; ***W:*** Giorgio Arlorio; ***C:*** Giulio Albonico; ***M:*** Guido de Angelis, Maurizio de Angelis.

Zorro Rides Again ♂♂ **1937** Zorro risks his life to outwit gangsters endeavoring to secure ancestor's property. In 12 chapters; the first runs 30 minutes, the rest 17. **217m/B VHS, DVD.** John Carroll, Helen Christian, Noah Beery Sr., Duncan Renaldo; ***D:*** William Witney, John English.

Zorro, the Gay Blade ♂♂ 1/2 **1981 (PG)** Tongue-in-cheek sword play with Hamilton portraying the swashbuckling crusader and his long-lost brother, Bunny Wigglesworth, in this spoof of the Zorro legend. The fashion-conscious hero looks his best in plum. Leibman is fun to watch. **96m/C VHS, DVD.** George Hamilton, Lauren Hutton, Brenda Vaccaro, Ron Leibman, Donovan Scott, James Booth, Helen Burns, Clive Revill; ***D:*** Peter Medak; ***W:*** Greg Alt; ***C:*** John A. Alonzo; ***M:*** Ian Fraser.

Zorro's Black Whip ♂♂ **1944** A young girl dons the mask of her murdered brother (Zorro) to fight outlaws in the old West. Serial in 12 episodes. **182m/B VHS, DVD.** George Lewis, Linda Stirling, Lucien Littlefield, Francis McDonald, Tom London; ***D:*** Spencer Gordon Bennet; ***W:*** Wallace Grissell.

Zorro's Fighting Legion ♂♂ **1939** Zorro forms a legion to help the president of Mexico fight a band of outlaws endeavoring to steal gold shipments. A serial in 12 chapters. **215m/B VHS, DVD.** Edmund Cobb, John Merton, C. Montague Shaw, Budd Buster, Carleton Young, Reed Hadley, Sheila Darcy; ***D:*** William Witney, John English; ***W:*** Barney A. Sarecky, Frank (Franklyn) Adreon, Morgan Cox; ***C:*** Reggie Lanning; ***M:*** William Lava.

Zotz! ♂♂ **1962** The holder of a magic coin can will people dead by uttering "zotz"; spies pursue the mild-mannered professor who possesses the talisman. Adapted from a Walter Karig novel. Typical William Castle fare; his gimic in the theatrical release of the movie was to distribute plastic "zotz" coins to the theatre patrons. **87m/B VHS.** Tom Poston, Julia Meade, Jim Backus, Fred Clark, Cecil Kellaway, Margaret Dumont, Jimmy Hawkins; ***D:*** Ray Russell, William Castle; ***W:*** Ray Russell; ***C:*** Gordon Avil; ***M:*** Bernard Green.

Zou Zou ♂♂ 1/2 **1934** Lavish backstage musical/drama of a laundress who fills in for the leading lady on opening night and becomes a hit. Baker's talking picture debut. In French with English subtitles. **92m/B VHS, DVD.** *FR* Josephine Baker, Jean Gabin; ***D:*** Marc Allegret.

Zu Warriors ♂ *Shu shan zheng zhuan; The Legend of Zu* **2001 (PG-13)** Back in the 1980s, director Tsui Hark made a neat little fantasy film called "Zu: Warriors of the Magic Mountain." In the 1990s he decided to update it, and did a cgi remake called "Legend of Zu." Eventually Miramax got the U.S. release rights to it and decided to rename it as "Zu Warriors" (which the original film is also called, causing some confusion), cutting 20 minutes of time from the length and dubbing and re-editing the chopped-up remainder. The result is an incomprehensible mess that was universally panned, which is why it didn't get a theatrical release like the other properties Miramax acquired. **80m/C DVD.** *HK* Zhang Ziyi, Cecilia Cheung, Louis Koo, Sammo Hung, Patrick Tam, Kelly Lin, Jacky Wu, Ekin Cheng; ***D:*** Tsui Hark; ***W:*** Tsui Hark; ***C:*** Hang-Seng Poon, Herman Yau, William Yim; ***M:*** Ricky Ho.

Zu: Warriors from the Magic Mountain ♂♂ *Shu Shan* **1983** The forces of evil are plotting to take over the world and a warrior endures the perils of the Zu Mountains in order to find the Twin Swords, the only weapons capable of defeating the demons. Cantonese with subtitles or dubbed. **98m/C VHS, DVD.** *HK* Adam Cheng, Yuen Biao, Brigitte Lin, Sammo Hung, Moon Lee; ***D:*** Tsui Hark; ***C:*** Bill Wong.

Zulu ♂♂ 1/2 **1964** In 1879, a small group of British soldiers try to defend their African outpost from attack by thousands of Zulu warriors. Amazingly, the British win. Dated colonial epic based on an actual incident; battle scenes are magnificent. Prequel "Zulu Dawn" (1979) depicts British mishandling of the situation that led to the battle. **139m/C VHS, DVD.** Michael Caine, Jack Hawkins, Stanley Baker, Nigel Green, Ulla Jacobsson, James Booth, Paul Daneman, Neil McCarthy, Gary Bond, Patrick Magee, Dickie Owen, Larry Taylor, Dennis Folbigge, Ivor Emmanuel, Glynn Edwards, David Kernan; ***D:*** Cy Endfield; ***W:*** Cy Endfield, John Prebble; ***C:*** Stephen Dade; ***M:*** John Barry; ***Nar:*** Richard Burton.

Zulu Dawn ♂♂♂ **1979 (PG)** An historical epic about British troops fighting the Zulus at Ulandi in 1878. Shows the increasing tensions between the British colonial government and the Zulus. Stunning landscapes unfortunately don't translate to the small screen. Good but unoriginal colonial-style battle drama. **117m/C VHS, DVD.** Burt Lancaster, Peter O'Toole, Denholm Elliott, Nigel Davenport, John Mills, Simon Ward, Bob Hoskins, Freddie Jones; ***D:*** Douglas Hickox; ***M:*** Elmer Bernstein.

Zus & Zo ♂♂ *This and That; Hotel Paraiso* **2001** Sisters Michelle (Poorta), Wanda (Blok), and Sonja (Hendrickx) are dismayed to learn that their gay younger brother Nino (Derwig) is going to marry Bo (Reijn) in order to collect on an inheritance. Thanks to a clause in their parents' will, he will become the sole owner of the family's waterfront hotel in Portugal, which each sister thinks should come to her, and which each believes that Nino will soon sell. So they scheme to break up the couple while avoiding their own domestic crises. Dutch with subtitles. **100m/C VHS, DVD.** *NL* Sylvia Poorta, Anneke Blok, Monic Hendrickx, Jacob Derwig, Halina Reijn, Theu Boermans, Jaap Spijkers, Pieter Embrechts, Annet Nieuwenhuyzen; ***D:*** Paula van der Oest; ***W:*** Paula van der Oest; ***C:*** Bert Pot; ***M:*** Fons Merkies.

Zvenigora ♂♂♂♂ **1928** Dovzhenko's first major film, and a lyrical revelation in the face of Soviet formality: a passionate, funny fantasy tableaux of 1,000 years of Ukrainian history, encompassing wild folk myths, poetic drama, propaganda and social satire. Silent. **73m/B VHS.** *RU* Nikolai Nademsky, Alexander Podorozhny, Semyon Svashenko; ***D:*** Alexander Dovzhenko.

Category List

The Category Index contains genre, sub-genre, thematic, or significant scene classifications, ranging from the very general terms (Western, Sports Comedies) to the fairly particular (Heists: Casinos, Ninjas, Grandparents). The terms are defined (more or less) below. We've done our best to provide serious subject references while also including fun categories and lists to make your video viewing experience a little more enjoyable. No one list is all-inclusive. We are continuously reclassifying, adding, and subtracting movies. Many of the categories in this list are new, and therefore represent only a beginning. We're also trying to pare down some of the bigger categories, like **Cops**, by creating more focused subject categories, such as **Alien Cops** or **FBI**. *VideoHound* invites readers to participate in this pastime by sending in suggestions for new categories and adding movies to existing ones. **An asterisk (*) denotes a new category for this edition.**

Action-Drama: Things go Boom!, but in a dramatic way

Action-Thriller: Things go Boom!, but in a suspenseful way

Adoption & Orphans: Cute kids lacking permanent authority figures, ranging from *Annie* to *Wild Hearts Can't Be Broken*

Adultery: Gettin' a little on the side; usually ends badly

Adventure Drama: Action with more attention to dramatic content—*Apocalypse Now* to *Robin Hood, Prince of Thieves*

Advertising: Corporate shenanigans at the agency—*How to Get Ahead in Advertising* to *The Horse in the Gray Flannel Suit*

Africa: *Out of Africa* to *Zulu Dawn*

African America: Dominant African American themes

AIDS: Someone usually dies; *An Early Frost* to *Longtime Companion*

Air Disasters: Contraptions up in the sky, but not for long

Airborne: Contraptions up in the sky

Alaska: The 49th state, home of the Iditarod and site of many manly Jack London adventures

Alcatraz: Prison island off San Francisco, aka *The Rock*

Alien Babes: Women who possess otherworldly beauty (and appetites)

Alien Beings—Benign: Friendly space visitors, including *Howard the Duck* and little buddy *E.T.*

Alien Beings—Vicious: Not-so-friendly space visitors, notably the multi-jawed *Alien* continually harassing Sigourney Weaver

Alien Cops: The long arm (tentacle?) of the outer space law

Aliens Are People, Too: Space visitors pretend to be human, or just take over the bodies—*Invasion of the Body Snatchers* kinda stuff

Amateur Sleuths: ...and I woulda gotten away with it, too, if it weren't for those meddling kids!

American South: Theatrics amid much brow mopping and drawling; *A Streetcar Named Desire* rattling down *Flamingo Road*

Amnesia: Phone call for *Anastasia*

Amsterdam: City in the Netherlands where many vices are legal—just ask Vincent Vega

Amusement Parks: Cotton candy, ferris wheels, Coney Island, *Godzilla on Monster Island, Rollercoaster*

Angels: Benevolent winged visitors from above: *Wings of Desire*

Animated Musicals: Boys, girls, dogs, ducks, birds, mice, and monkeys croon; many of Disney vintage, including *Aladdin* and *Sleeping Beauty*

Animated Sci-Fi: To boldly go where no cartoon has gone before!

Animation & Cartoons: Antics of Daffy, Donald, Bugs, Mickey, Chip, Dale, Tom, Jerry, Fred, Wilma, Charlie, and the rest of the gang

Anime: Animated cartoons from Japan with cult following

Anthology: More than one story to a package

Anti-Heroes: From *Billy Jack* to *Dirty Harry* to *Thelma & Louise*

Anti-War War Movies: Recognizes that war really is hell—from *All Quiet on the Western Front* to *Paths of Glory*

Apartheid: Afrikaans term for racial segregation in South Africa

Apartments & Apartment Buildings: Why do they call 'em apartments when they're all together? The building or an apartment becomes important to the plot.

Arab Culture: Dominant Arab-American themes.

Architects & Architecture: People designing buildings for other people to build

Army Training, Sir Tales of basic training, or boot camp, if you prefer. Are those *Stripes* on your *Full Metal Jacket*?

Art & Artists: They paint, pause, and propagate with equal passion

Asia: *China White, Red Dust, Sand Pebbles*

Asian America: Asian experience in the US—*The Joy Luck Club, Come See the Paradise*

Assassinations: Lincoln, *JFK, La Femme Nikita, Times of Harvey Milk*, and more

Astronauts: Houston, we have a problem.

At the Drive-In: Scenes in which people watch movies...at the drive-in.

At the Movies: The movie within a movie or movies about watching the movies, from *The Purple Rose of Cairo* to *Last Action Hero* to *Matinee*

At the Video Store: Scenes from a video store, *Clerks, Remote Control*

Atlanta: Home of the Braves, Ted Turner, CNN, and that annoying Tomahawk Chop. Sherman dropped in a while back with some rowdy friends.

Atlantic City: Gambling mecca of the East Coast, aka Trumptown

Auditions: Trying to get that part that'll be the Big Break

Aunts & Uncles, Nieces & Nephews: Extended family members you usually spend Thanksgiving with. In the movies, they're usually causing trouble

Autism: Tales of families dealing with the mysterious condition

Babysitting: Supervision of small-fry pranksters not your own; *Uncle Buck* to *The Hand that Rocks the Cradle*

Bachelor Party: The groom's last foray into debauchery before the big day; all hell generally breaks loose

Bad Bosses: When he says he wants that report by 5:00 or heads will roll...it may not be a figure of speech

Bad Dads: Daddy-Os with unpredictable mean streak: *The Shining, Kiss Daddy Goodbye*

Ballet: On your toes—*The Turning Point*

Ballooning: Up, up and away, or *Around the World in 80 Days*

Baltimore: Take a look at the Maryland city, hometown of director Barry Levinson and favorite digs of John Waters

Bar & Grill: Most, if not all, of the action takes place in a drinking establishment.

Barcelona: Second largest city in Spain is the capital of Catalonia; setting for recent Olympics, and some cool movies.

Baseball: Action on the diamond, ranging from *Bull Durham* to *A League of Their Own* to *Rookie of the Year*

Basketball: Roundball thrillers, including the memorable *The Fish that Saved Pittsburgh* and *White Men Can't Jump*

Bats: Flying rodents that fly into your hair and sometimes turn into centuries-old Eastern European aristocrats with strange eating habits

Beach Blanket Bingo: Annette, Frankie, sand, surf, bikinis

Bears: Most of "em are looking for more than just pic-i-nic baskets

Beatniks: Jazz beards, bongos, poetry that doesn't rhyme, berets

Beauty Pageants: From the heartless to the hilarious, beauty is a big business—*Smile* girls!

Beer: Mmmmm, beer. The cause and solution to all of Homer's problems. The cities of St. Louis and Milwaukee are fueled by it...so is your brother-in-law

Behind the Scenes: Peek behind show business curtain, from *A Chorus Line* to *Truth or Dare*

Bees: Flying insects that whore around with every flower they can get their hairy little legs on, and then make delicious honey.

* = new to this edition

Sometimes they get mad and go on mass stinging sprees

Belfast: Northern Ireland city, Van Morrison's hometown (but that's not what it's famous for)

Berlin: City in Germany divided after WWII, now it's one big happy city again

***Bermuda Triangle:** That place in the Pacific where ships, planes, and plot continuity tend to disappear

Betrayal: Somebody done somebody wrong. Could be a spouse, could be a partner, could be the intelligence agency that used to employ you that now wants you dead

Beverly Hills: Fancy-pants area of L.A., home of Cops, Troops, Vamps, and 30-year-old teenagers

Bicycling: Two wheels, no motor, much leg action and sweating

Big Battles: Big-budget (or at least illusion of such) clash of large, opposing military forces, from *Cromwell* to *Ran*

Big Budget Bombs: Millions spent for no apparent reason

Big Cats: Lions and Tigers and Panthers and Jaguars and other large felines that sports teams get named after.

Big Digs: Anthropology and archaeology, from Indiana Jones to various mummy on-the-loose stories

Big Ideas: Philosophy, ideology and other semi-mental pursuits somehow translated to film

Big Rigs: *Smokey and the Bandit* speed down *Thieves' Highway* in a *Convoy*

Bigfoot/Yeti: Large, hairy, seldom-seen beast with really big feet

Bikers: Usually with a mean streak and traveling in leather-clad packs

Biopics—Artists: True stories of artists' lives. Find out if they were really starving or not

Biopics—Cops & Robbers: True stories of real life criminals and the real life cops who arrested 'em

Biopics—Military: True stories of the men and women who fought this (and other) country's wars

Biopics—Musicians: From European composers to punk rock icons, they usually end up being tales of over-indulgence and others ripping them off

Biopics—Politics: True stories of the politicians who lead countries, states, and municipalities

Biopics—Religious: Life stories of church leaders, reformers, saints, and the occasional deity

Biopics—Royalty: Life stories of kings, queens, czars. They ran things before politicians were invented

Biopics—Science/Medical: Life stories of the people who invented the medicine and products that make modern life…modern

Biopics—Showbiz: Life stories of those who entertain us. It ain't always all glamour and happy endings

Biopics—Sports: Life stories of those we admire for their athletic prowess

Biopics—Writers: Life stories of those who put thoughts, stories, or manifestos to paper and became famous for it

Birds: Beaks, feathers, talons, bird #%!; *The Birds, Beaks: The Movie, Howard the Duck*

Birthdays: Congratulations on making it through another year!

Bisexuality: Going both ways—*Basic Instinct, Three of Hearts*

Black Comedy: Funny in a biting or despairing sort of way, from *The Addams Family* to *The Hospital*

Black Gold: Oil, that is; aka *Oklahoma Crude*

Blackmail: I'm gonna tell, unless… *The Last Seduction, Letter to My Killer*

Blackout: Boom Boom, Out go the lights! In the whole city, usually

Blaxploitation: '70s remakes of horror classics, as well as B-movies made with the black audience in mind

Blind Date: Usually set up by friends or family members with the best of intentions, they rarely result in the best of relationships

Blindness: Can't see or sight impaired; *Afraid of the Dark*

Blizzards: Big snow storms, usually overblown by over-excited local weather people.

Bloody Messages: Cryptic warnings to the living written in the blood of the poor slob who was just killed—Redrum

Bodyguards: Costner looks after Whitney's personal business

Bookies: Place your bets!…illegally with these guys

Books and Bookstores: Literary works (such as this) and the places where they can be found, as a major plot device: *La Lectrice* to *Crossing Delancey*

Boom!: Really big explosions, bombs, and other noisy or fiery messes popular in big budget action flicks

Boomer Reunions: thirty-somethings gather and reminisce: *The Big Chill*

Bootleggers: Fine purveyors of illegal booze, usually back in the 1920s…or in the backwoods of the South

Bosnia: Has played host to Olympics and ethnic strife

Boston: Beantown, where everybody knows your name.

Bounty Hunters: Bring 'em back dead or alive—for a price

Bowling: Heavy round ball is thrown down waxed alley toward club-like pins; all fall down

Boxing: Yo, Adrian!

Brains!: Disturbing scenes of brains being extracted, forcibly, from the brainpan

Brainwashed: Minds get scrubbed clean of what they used to know so someone can put in whatever they want; generally orders to do bad things

Break-Ups: They usually happen in the second act of romantic comedies, before the happy ending. Although sometimes they are the plot

Bridges: For crossing, or if you're in a war movie, defending and/or blowing up

Bringing Up Baby: *Look Who's Talking* to *Raising Arizona*, plus infants with that little something different—*Alien 3, Enemy Mine, Basket Case 3: The Progeny*

Brothers & Sisters: Siblings getting along and sometimes not

Buddhism: Eastern religion with bald guys

Buddies: Butch and Sundance, Bill and Ted, Rubin and Ed, *Thelma and Louise*

Buddy Cops: Couple of police hanging together, usually practicing limited repartee at a donut shop; *Lethal Weapon, Tango and Cash*

***Buffalo, NY:** Upstate New York city that's home to lots of snow and a famously perennial runner-up football team

Bullfighters & Bullfighting: "Sport" pitting Spaniards with red capes and swords vs. future Big Macs with horns

Burglars: Thievery by stealth, usually at night, and using cool equipment, like in *Entrapment*

Buried Alive: I'm not quite dead, yet! Hello, Mr. grave digger person, hello!

Buses: Large truck-like passenger vehicles—*Speed, The Big Bus, The Trip to Bountiful*

Cabbies: Where to, Mac?

Calcutta: Big, overpopulated city in India

Camelot (New): The exploits of JFK, Jackie, and various relatives and hangers-on

Camelot (Old): The exploits of King Arthur and his *Knights of the Round Table*

Cambodia: Small country in Southeast Asia bordering Vietnam. Haven't had much luck with politics in the last few decades

Campus Capers: What really goes on at college—*Assault of the Party Nerds*

Canada: Renfrew of the Mounties plus lots of wilderness and the occasional hockey puck

Canadian Mounties: The Great White North version of cops. They always get their man

Cannibalism: People who eat people are the luckiest people; *Alive, Rabid Grannies, Cannibal Women in the Avocado Jungle of Death, The Cook, the Thief, His Wife & Her Lover*

Capitol Capers: Hollywood versions of hijinks in Washington, D.C.—*Dave, Mr. Smith Goes to Washington, All the President's Men*

Carnivals & Circuses: Big top, little top, domes: *Shakes the Clown* to *Rollercoaster*, plus *Big Top Pee Wee, State Fair*, and metaphoric circuses: *Brewster McCloud, La Strada*

***Casbah:** Come with me…we will make beautiful musics togezher

Catholic School: Educational arm of the church of Rome, usually run by ruler-wielding nuns

Cats: Lesser vertebrate nonetheless much beloved by Hollywood

Cattle Drive: Git along little doggies!

Cave People: From the most primitive (*The Clan of the Cave Bear*) to the fairly modernized (*The Flintstones*)

Caves: Holes in the ground where monsters, bats, and Flintstones live

Checkered Flag: *Eat My Dust;* racing in the street or on the track; *The Last American Hero*

Cheerleaders: Give me an A! *The Positively True Adventures of the Alleged Texas Cheerleader-Murdering Mom* meets *Revenge of the Cheerleaders*

Chefs: The fancy-schmancy preparers of fancy-schmancy foods at fancy-schmancy eateries. They have cool hats that make them seem a lot taller

Chess: Game that involves much strategy and forward thinking…as well as a lot of staring, sitting, and generally looking unconscious. Not a really good spectator sport

Chicago: City in Illinois, right at the bottom of Lake Michigan

Child Abuse: Not very funny at all—*Mommie Dearest, Fallen Angel*

Childhood Buddies: The pals we hang around with before puberty hits

Childhood Visions: Stories dominated by the kid point of view, or by an adult flashbacking to childhood; *Au Revoir Les Enfants, Home Alone*

China: *The Last Emperor* to *Red Sorghum* to *The World of Suzie Wong*

Christmas: Reindeer, Santa, children make appearance amid much sentimentality

Church Choirs: Big groups of singers in robes who sing in…church (Duh!). Can I get an Amen?

CIA/NSA: Men and women of the Agency. You know, the good spies…uh, usually

Cincinnati: Southern Ohio city, home to German immigrants, Jerry Springer, and the Big Red Machine (and we're not talking about Ivan Drago)

Cinderella Stories: Gal down on her luck meets fairy godmother (or father) and finds true love—*Pretty Woman, Flashdance, Cinderella*

City-Squishing Behemoths: "Don't you hate it when you keep stepping on those little cars?" "Yeah! The little critters inside are always so noisy!"

Civil Rights: Fighting for equality—*The Autobiography of Miss Jane Pittman, Mississippi Burning*

Civil War: The Yankees against the Confederates; aka *The Blue and the Gray*

Civil War (non-U.S.): People in the same (foreign) country fighting and killing over religion, politics, tribal affiliation, or anything else that makes people kill their own countrymen

Classic Horror: Boris Karloff, Vincent Price, piercing screams

Clergymen: Non-Catholic (they're covered elsewhere) men and women of the cloth

Cleveland: "The Mistake by the Lake," home to the Rock 'n' Roll Hall of Fame, a very cinematic baseball team, and some of the most 'rabid' football fans in the country

Cloning Around: Makin' copies—of people or animals. *Multiplicity* to *Jurassic Park*

Clowns: Big red noses, huge feet, painted smiles frighten many

***Coaches/Managers:** They design the plays, pick the players, and make the speeches for the teams that win all those improbably 'underdog defies the odds' movies

Coast Guard: They, well, guard the coast, and help boaters, and bust smugglers, as well as other cool maritime duties

Cockroaches: Creepy crawlies signifying the work of the supernatural, or a lack of housekeeping skills

Cold Spots: Set in a frost-bitten locale with lots of shivering; *Ice Station Zebra, Never Cry Wolf, Quest for Fire*

Cold War Spies: Spy vs. Spy pitting various U.S. and British alphabet soup agencies against the Commies

Coma: Some sort of head trauma usually leads to extended nap time

Comedy Anthologies: More than one yuk fest on a cassette

Comedy Drama: Drama with a comedic touch or comedy underwired with drama—*Avalon, The Big Chill, Fried Green Tomatoes, One Flew Over the Cuckoo's Nest, Tootsie*

Comedy Mystery: Wacky whodunits like *Murder by Death, Clue*

Comedy Sci-Fi: Laughs in space! *Spaceballs*

Comic Adventure: Adventurous romps liberally laced with humor: *Romancing the Stone* to *Bird on a Wire* to *Crocodile Dundee*

Comic Books: Colorful tales of superheroes and adventure play a big part in the plot, unless your mom threw 'em out

Comic Cops: Police officers that catch laughs as they catch the bad guys. Think Axel Foley or those cut-ups from the *Police Academy* series

Coming of Age: Hard-fought adolescent battle for adulthood, led by *American Graffiti, The Apprenticeship of Duddy Kravitz, The Karate Kid*

Communists & Communism: Way left-wingers politically. They used to run Eastern Europe, but now they just rant in coffee-houses. The ones in Asia are still around, though

Computers: Bits and bytes play major role

Concentration/Internment Camps: Nazis used them for their "final solution" while the U.S. used them to imprison Japanese-Americans

Concert Films: Rock or comedy concerts—from *Woodstock* to *Divine Madness* to *Eddie Murphy: Raw*

Contemporary Musicals: Thematically modern and made during last 20 years; *All That Jazz*

Contemporary Noir: Dark and moody or tributes to dark and moody that pay homage to the original Film Noir genre—*Blue Velvet, 9½ Weeks, sex, lies, and videotape, Wild Orchid*

Cops: Police and pseudo-police work, including *Action Jackson, Blue Steel, The Choirboys, RoboCop, Lethal Weapon, National Lampoon's Loaded Weapon 1*

Corporate Shenanigans: Big Business runs amuck—*Barbarians at the Gate, Wall Street*

Cousins: Progeny of your parents' sibs.

* = new to this edition

Creepy Houses: Scary dwellings—*Amityville Horror* 1 through 33

Crime Doesn't Pay: When the perfect crime...isn't.

Crime Drama: Gangster family dysfunction, heists gone awry, packin' pathos with your piece. *The Godfather, Goodfellas, Reservoir Dogs.*

Crime Sprees: Bad guy, gal or couple goes on a crime binge and other tales of obsessive criminal activity, including *Bonnie & Clyde, The Boys Next Door*

Crimedy: formerly *So I Amuse You?* Wisenheimer Guys—funny felons, amusing miscreants, if you will

Crimes of Passion: Love, sex, and death

Criminally Insane: They don't really care if crime pays, they're just following orders from the voices.

The Crusades: "Holy" wars between Christians and Muslims in the middle ages.

Cuba: Fidel's Island, where the survivors vote themselves off and the winners make it 90 miles north to become high-priced baseball players.

Cubicle Hell: Toiling thanklessly in the land of Dilbert

Cults: Something like a gang but more intense and usually governed by a state of mind similar to irrationality—*Helter Skelter*

Culture Clash: Hilarity ensues (or sometimes not) as people from vastly different backgrounds try to interact. *Deliverance, Witness, George of the Jungle*

Custody Battles: People, mostly divorced couples, fight over who keeps the kids. *Kramer vs. Kramer, Losing Isaiah*

Cuttin' Heads: Barber shops and Beauty salons are the scenes of all or most of the "action"

Cyberpunk: Dark, moody, futuristic flicks—*Blade Runner, Freejack, Tank Girl*

Dads: Fathers play a major role

Dallas: Big city in Texas. Home of the Cowboys, J.R., and scandal among the rich

Dance Fever: Whole lotta foot-tapping going on, including *An American in Paris, Daddy Long Legs,* and *Dirty Dancing*

Dates from Hell: Fun evening for two singles turns into a nightmare for one of them—*Bye Bye Love, Singles, Something Wild*

Day Care/Nursery School: Babysitting warehouse where parents drop off their kids while they make money to pay for daycare

A Day In The Life: All the action takes place within a 24-hour period

DEA: G-men on the front lines of America's War on Drugs

Deadly Implants: Where is that ticking coming from?

Deafness: Can't hear or hearing impaired; *Bridge to Silence, The Miracle Worker*

Death & The Afterlife: Could be ghosts, could be voices from the beyond, could be any number of post-dead things—*Beetlejuice, Carnival of Souls, Flatliners, Poltergeist, Weekend at Bernie's*

Death Row: Waitin' for a call from the Governor; *Dead Man Walking, Angels with Dirty Faces*

Dedicated Teachers: From *The Dead Poet's Society* to *The Blackboard Jungle* to *The Miracle Worker*

Deep Blue: The sea around us, including *ffolkes* and *Splash*

***Deep Woods Offed:** People go into the woods, but they don't come out. Gonna make 'em squeal like a...well, you know...

Demons & Wizards: Swords, sorcery and wrinkled old men with wands—*The Alchemist, The Hobbit, The Sword & the Sorcerer*

Dental Mayhem: Toothpickin' uproars; *Marathon Man, The Dentist*

Desert War/Foreign Legion: Big battles among the dunes

Deserts: Endless beach minus the water—*Ishtar, Lawrence of Arabia*

Detective Spoofs: Putting together clues in humorous fashion—*The Adventures of Sherlock Holmes' Smarter Brother, The Naked Gun*

Detroit: The Motor City, home of Motown, lots of cars, and...VideoHound

Devils: Some may meet on *Judgment Day*

Devil's Island: French Island prison in the South Atlantic

Diner: Most of the story, or at least important parts of it, occur in the smallish, very informal eating establishment

Dinosaurs: *Jurassic Park* and other less animated thundering lizards

Disaster Flicks: Natural and man-made, including 47 *Airport* sequels

Disco Musicals: '70s tackiness reigns supreme, from *Saturday Night Fever* to *Xanadu*

Disease of the Week: Bulimia, anorexia, polio, cancer, and so on

Disorganized Crime: Stupid crime, including *Amos and Andrew, Dog Day Afternoon, Home Alone, Quick Change*

Divorce: Breaking up is hard to do; *Accidental Tourist, Heartburn, Kramer vs. Kramer*

Doctors & Nurses: Men and women in scrubs concerned about health of complete strangers for profit, often to the dismay of the patient—*Autopsy, Candy Stripe Nurses, Dead Ringers*

Docudrama: *The Thin Blue Line* between documentaries and drama

Documentary: Real life manipulated on film—*A Brief History of Time, The Last Waltz, Paris Is Burning, Roger and Me*

Dogs In Peril: Manipulative plot device, usually in disaster flicks, where things blow up just as Fido high-tails it out of there.

Domestic Abuse: *This Boy's Life, The Burning Bed, What's Love Got to Do With It?*

Doublecross!: Usually happens when there's no more honor among thieves, like in *Payback*

Down Under: Australian, New Zealand settings—*The Rescuers Down Under, Gallipoli, The Man from Snowy River, The Thorn Birds*

***Downsized:** Getting the pink slip, precipitating new opportunities, or maybe some unlawful activity

Dragons: Legendary medieval lizards, usually with fiery dispositions; *Dragonheart, Pete's Dragon*

Dream Girls: Product of male mid-life crisis; *Battling Amazons, Cycle Vixens, The Doll Squad, The Woman in Red*

Dropouts People who just couldn't finish what they started...it all seemed so promising back in kindergarten

Drug Abuse: Life with a drugstore cowboy; consumption of drugs, mostly illegal or in extra-large dosages

Dublin: Irish capitol city, home to *The Commitments*

Dying for a Promotion: ...or killing for one. Guess those business ethics seminars were a waste of money

Ears!: Bloody detachment and general maiming of...

Earthquakes: The Earth moved! Common occurrence in California

Easter: Holiday in the early spring celebrated with giant rabbits, eggs, chocolate, bonnets...and gruesome movies depicting the crucifixion

Eastern Europe: Basically everything east of Germany and west of Asia

Eat Me: Characters end up as food. *Jurassic Park, Soylent Green, Alive*

Eco-Vengeance!: Nature wreaks havoc on man—watch out for *Alligators, Frogs* and *Piranhas*

Edibles: Something's cooking—*Babette's Feast, Like Water for Chocolate*

Edinburgh: Scottish capital city. They pronounce it "Goff" instead of "Golf" according to Judge Smails.

Egypt-Ancient: Mummies, Pharaohs, Pyramids, when they were brand new

Elephants: Pachyderms play a BIG part in the plot—*Dumbo, Larger Than Life*

Elevators: Sometimes the oddest things happen in them...

Emerging Viruses: Deadly virus spreads like wildfire as frantic medical personnel search for a cure; think ebola

The Empire State Building: *King Kong* liked to hang there.

Erotic Thrillers: Hot sex and murder, including *Basic Instinct, Body of Evidence*

Errant Educators: Teachers, coaches, or principals who may not have the kids' best interests in mind, maybe because they're aliens (*The Faculty*), or they're just mean (*Teaching Mrs. Tingle*)

Escaped Cons: They busted outta the joint, now they're makin' a run for it. *Con Air, We're No Angels, Papillon, Fled*

Eskimos: Native North Americans who reside in particularly frosty climates

Ethics & Morals: Examination of values (or lack thereof)—*Crimes & Misdemeanors, Judgment at Nuremberg*

Etiquette: Usually comedy of manners: *Educating Rita, My Fair Lady*

Evil Doctors: Don't go to these guys for a checkup—*Malice, Dead Ringers,* and *Doctor X*

Ex-Cons: Former guests of state or federal penal institutions

Ex-Cops: Former members of the law enforcement community

Exchange Students: Kids come over here to sample our educational wares, and maybe some host family's nubile offspring...or we go over there and do the Ugly American thing

Executing Revenge: Bad guys come back from being executed to cause more trouble. *Fallen, Shocker*

Exorcism & Exorcists: Priests try to evict evil spirits from pea-soup-spewing, head-twirling victims of possession.

Exploitation: Rigged to take advantage of viewer, including historic treats like *Reefer Madness* and more recent ventures such as *Sleazemania*

Explorers: Going boldly where no man or woman has regularly gone before

Extraordinary Pairings: Jesse James meets Frankenstein's Daughter

Eyeballs!: Unnerving scenes involving pupils, irises, lids, and occasionally, lashes

Fairs & Expositions: Short term amusement parks: *State Fair*

Family Adventure: Families find themselves in perilous or thrilling predicaments; ingenuity and derring-do usually ensues

Family Comedy: Families find themselves in amusing situations; hilarity may or may not ensue

Family Drama: Families struggling through tragedy, daily life, difficult circumstances, or too few bathrooms; teardrops and recriminations are usually involved

Family Reunions: Vacations or picnics where extended family members get together to reintroduce themselves to each other, eat a lot of food, and pretend they have something in common besides surnames.

Family Ties: Blood runs deep—*Back to the Future, Five Easy Pieces, The Godfather, Homeward Bound, Lorenzo's Oil, The Mosquito Coast, Rocket Gibraltar*

Fantasy: Tales of the imagination, including *Alice* and her looking glass, *E.T., Ladyhawke, My Stepmother Is an Alien*

Farm Livin': Down on the farm; *Bitter Harvest, Pelle the Conqueror, Jean de Florette, The River*

Fatsuit Acting: Actors get big parts, and lots of padding to go with 'em

FBI: The Bureau. Federal cops with an internal focus and a dress code

Female Bonding: Women get together, usually to the men's dismay; *Waiting to Exhale*

Female Spies: The fairer sex uses its feminine assets and wiles to get the other side's secrets

Femme Fatale: She done him and him and him wrong

Fencing: En garde, dude

Film History: *America at the Movies;* includes movies important to film history

Film Noir: Dark and moody or tributes to dark and moody—*Farewell, My Lovely, The Postman Always Ring Twice, The Third Man, Who Framed Roger Rabbit?*

Filmmaking: The making of a film within a film: *The Player*

Firemen: *Backdraft, Frequency,* and other tales of brave people with hoses

Fires: *Frankenstein, Quest for Fire, Pyrates*

The First Time: Y'know, the first time you had...when you broke your...when you made...when you first...uh, did it...with another person

Flashback: Why, I remember like it was yesterday. It all started when... *The Usual Suspects, Casablanca*

Flatulence: Embarrassing gaseous emissions

Floods: Water, water everywhere

Florida: Beaches, retirement communities, swamps, Spring Training, Disney World.

Florence: Not Alice's grits-kissing pal, but the city in Italy.

Folklore & Legend: Age-old adult tales covering Atlantis, little people, faeries, Paul Bunyan, and the like

Football: Everything from terrorist attacks on the Superbowl (*Black Sunday*) to prison competition (*The Longest Yard*) plus *Diner*

Foreign Cops: The long arm of the law I n other countries, or visiting law enforcement representatives helping catch international baddies here in the good ole U.S. of A.

Foreign Intrigue: Overseas mystery, with emphasis on accent and location

Frame-ups: Someone's set up to take the rap: *My Cousin Vinny* to *Consenting Adults*

France: From *Dirty Rotten Scoundrels* to *The Moderns* to *Gigi* to *The Last Metro* to *Killer Tomatoes Eat France*

Fraternities & Sororities: Those fun-lovin' campus cutups who're always pulling pranks or getting offed in bad slasher flicks

Front Page: *Citizen Kane, All the President's Men, The Philadelphia Story,* and other journalistic stories

Fugitives: Running from the law; *Breathless, Nowhere to Hide, Posse*

Funerals: The final goodbye—*Four Weddings and a Funeral, Gardens of Stone, The Big Chill*

Funny Money: Counterfeiting, and all the action movie stuff that goes with it

Future Cop: The future of law enforcement

Future Shock: Someone from our past comes to our present, or someone from our present goes to our future; *Sleeper, Just Visiting*

Gambling: Aces and Eights, *The Color of Money, Eight Men Out, Honeymoon in Vegas*

Game Shows: *The Running Man* and *Queen for a Day*

Gangs: Criminally enterprising teens and adults running in packs: *State of Grace, Miller's Crossing, Public Enemy, The Wanderers*

Gays: Gay themes—*Kiss of the Spider Woman, The Hunger*

Gender Bending: *The Crying Game, La Cage aux Folles, Her Life as a Man* and other instances of boys becoming girls and vice versa

Generation X: Slacking in the '90s—*Reality Bites, Singles*

* = *new to this edition*

Genetics: Fooling with the double helix—*The Fly*

Genies: *Aladdin* finds magic lamp filled with compressed Robin Williams

Genocide/Ethnic Cleansing: One ethnic group thinks it is so superior to another that the other group must be completely destroyed. Words cannot describe the stupidity of this view

Genre Spoofs: Wacky takes on serious films, starting with the granddaddy of them all: *Airplane!*

Germany: *The Blue Angel, Wings of Desire*

Ghosts, Ghouls, & Goblins: *Ghostbusters, Topper, Poltergeist*

Giants: *The Amazing Colossal Man* visits *Village of the Giants*

Gifted Children: Kids show amazing talents that astound adults, from *Rookie of the Year* to *Little Man Tate*

Glasgow: Scottish city, not the capital of Scotland.

Go Fish: Casting a line in the river that runs through it; *Man of Aran, A Fish Called Wanda, Captains Courageous*

Going Native: Outsiders try to blend in; *Dances with Wolves, The Swiss Family Robinson*

Going Postal: Neither rain, snow, sleet, nor dead of night....Hello, Newman

Going Straight: Trying to stay on the right side of the law so you can stay on the right side of prison bars, after you've already sampled the wrong side of both

Golf: Slow boring game best experienced on screen ("Be the ball, Danny")

Gospel Music: Inspirational music usually sung by people in church or who really like church

Grand Hotel: Checkout time is noon; *Blame It on the Bellboy*

Grand Theft Auto: Boosting cars for fun and/or profit. Just like on *Cops*, chases usually ensue

Grandparents: Your parents' parents, the ones who spoil you and drive your folks crazy

Great Britain: Thwarted royals (*Charles & Diana: A Palace Divided, Edward and Mrs. Simpson*), kings (*King Ralph*), queens (*The Naked Civil Servant*), class distinctions (*The Ruling Class*), vanished empires (*Cromwell, A Man for All Seasons*), criminals (*The Krays, The Long Good Friday*) plus multiple stiff upper lips, the Brontes, and Dickens

Great Death Scenes: Signing off with style or elaboration; *Buffy the Vampire Killer, Bonnie and Clyde, Breaker Morant*

Great Depression: The era, not the state of mind—*Bound for Glory, Of Mice and Men, The Grapes of Wrath, Rambling Rose*

Great Escapes: Seizing the day for freedom—*The Big Doll House, Escape from Alcatraz, Papillon*

Greece—Ancient: In the immortal words of Socrates, "I drank what?"

Greece—Modern: They don't walk around in sheets and philosophize anymore, at least not in public

Grim Reaper: Time's up when the pale bald guy wearing a hood and carrying garden implements comes looking for you.

Growing Older: *On Golden Pond, *batteries not included, Cocoon, Driving Miss Daisy, The Shootist, The Wild Bunch*

Gunslingers: Old West killers for hire. Sometimes they killed the bad guys, sometimes they were the bad guys

***Gym Class:** The bane of un-athletic schoolkids throughout the country

Gymnastics: Human pretzels like *Nadia*

Gypsies: Fortune tellers with scarves around their heads and vaguely—European accents, or modern day con men are the two basic movie types

Hackers: Computer whiz kids cause havoc—or just change their grades

Halloween: *Trick or Treat!*

Hallucinations/Illusions: Stuff looks real, but it's all in yer head, man!

Handyman Specials: Houses that need a little work to be livable...unless you're a ghost, serial killer, or otherwise disinclined to hire an inspector

Hard Knock Life: Poverty and bad luck; *City of Joy, The Match Factory Girl*

Harlem: Part of New York City you don't see in the tourism brochures

Hawaii: The 50th state, fun in the sun, if the volcanoes are behaving.

Heads! Disturbing (or fun) scenes of heads being forcibly removed from the bodies they formerly controlled

Hearts!: Unnerving scenes involving human hearts, generally seen by the audience and almost always still pumping

Heaven Sent: Visits or returns from the place where good souls and all dogs go—*Field of Dreams* to *Made in Heaven* to *Oh God!*

Heists: The big lift

Heists—Armored Car: Crooks plan and carry out jobs on armored cars

Heists—Art: Crooks plan and carry out jobs to steal works of art, *The Thomas Crown Affair*

Heists—Bank: Crooks plan and carry out early withdrawals, sometimes incurring substantial penalties

Heists—Casinos: Crooks plan to steal from the one-armed bandits; *Ocean's Eleven* are *3000 Miles From Graceland*

Heists—Gold/Precious Metals: Elaborate plans to go for the gold, or silver, or platinum. Bronze isn't that valuable in this game

Heists—Jewels: Ya gotta be cool to get the ice, just ask the *Reservoir Dogs*

Heists—Trains: Not the whole train, just the good stuff inside it. *Butch Cassidy and the Sundance Kid* liked the choo-choos

Hell: Not a place you wanna end up. The forecast calls for continued hot, with a 0% chance of freezing over.

Hell High School: Place where adolescents gather against their will; also known as *Rock 'n' Roll High School*

The Help—Female: Maids, nannies, governesses, cooks, housekeepers

The Help—Male: Butlers, chauffeurs, manservants, valets

Hide the Dead Guy: What to do with those pesky bodies after the killing's done?

High School: This is for those few movies where high school isn't treated like the hellish experience we all seem to remember it being

High School Reunions: Adults gather to impress other adults they didn't like as adolescents

Hijacked!: Terrorists take over various modes of transportation, causing much action-movie heriocs

Hispanic America: Dominant Hispanic American themes (*Salsa, Mi Vida Loca*)

***Historical Comedy:** Famous and not-so-famous events of the past, played for laughs

Historical Detectives: It's elementary! Sherlock, meet Elliot Ness.

Historical Drama: Usually at least loosely based on a real incident or personality

Historical Romance: Smooches, longing looks, and other activities exchanged between historical personages

Hit Men/Women: Boys and girls armed with silencers; *Prizzi's Honor, Romeo is Bleeding*

Hockey: *Slap Shot* and other icy tales of passing the puck

Holidays: Easter, Thanksgiving, New Year's, Halloween, but generally not Christmas

Holocaust: *Playing for Time, Schindler's List*

Home Alone: Kids find themselves without adult supervision—*Adventures in Babysitting* to *Young Sherlock Holmes*

Home Invasion: Uninvited guests drop by...usually intent on larceny, mayhem, or a place to hide out

The Homefront—England: Air raids, stiff upper lips, they were a lot closer to the action, and were just as worried about their sons and husbands.

The Homefront—U.S./Canada: The war at home during WWII—looking for spies, rationing, waiting for word about "the boys."

Homeless: Street people with no homes

Homicide: Murder most foul! It's what usually gets those wacky buddy-cop movies started

Honeymoon: Where the bride and groom go after the wedding's over to...get acquainted

Hong Kong: Land of the really cool action flick; Chow Yun-Fat and Jackie Chan became stars there. Great Britain gave it back to the Chinese

Horrible Holidays: Holidays with a ghoulish twist—*Bloody New Year, Halloween, My Bloody Valentine, Silent Night, Bloody Night*

Horror: Modern cut 'em up scare theater

Horror Anthologies: More than one scarefest per package

Horror Comedy: Tongue-in-bloody cheek—*The Fearless Vampire Killers, Piranha, Sorority Babes in the Slimeball Bowl-A-Rama*

Horses: Can you say *Black Beauty?*

Hospitals & Medicine: Dysfunctional institutional health care—*Article 99, The Hospital, One Flew Over the Cuckoo's Nest, Young Doctors in Love*

Hostage!: People held against their will for bargaining purposes

Housesitting: Watching a friend's house while he's gone. You know, in case it gets the idea to run away or something

Houston: That big city in Texas where J.R. didn't live, but Roger Clemens does.

Hunted!: Humans tracking humans for trophy purposes

Hunting: Where's dat wascally wabbit? *Caddyshack, The Bear, White Hunter, Black Heart*

Hurling: What goes down sometimes comes back up—*The Exorcist, Parenthood*

I Was a Teenage Criminal: When teenagers steal, kill, or generally have a total lack of respect for the law . It's that damn rock 'n' roll music, I tell ya!

***Illegal Immigration:** Give us your tired, your poor, your huddled masses...unless they try to sneak in

I'm Not Dead, Yet! Reports of their demise have been greatly exaggerated

Immigration: Melting pot stories—*Avalon, Far and Away, Living on Tokyo Time*

Immortality: I wanna live forever

Impending Retirement: Gold watch, a party, some tearful goodbyes...but there's always those darn loose ends to tie up first

In-Laws: The family you marry into; usually a source of conflict and punchlines

Incest: Implied or actual relationships among family members—*The Grifters, Spanking the Monkey*

India: On the road to *Bombay*

The Inquisition, What a Show!: The Spanish Inquisition, that is. No one expects it. Spanish Catholic Church officials got a little, um, enthusiastic, in their recruiting efforts in the late 1400s

Insomnia: Can't sleep at night

Insurance: Usually the cure for the above category, unless someone's killing, scamming, or frauding for the money it pays

Internet Borne: It's not just for naughty pics or fantasy sports anymore. You can find either love or death on the World Wide Web.

Interpol: International police force that fights crime and terrorism when it crosses many borders

Interracial Affairs: Couple from different racial backgrounds cause trauma for family and friends—*Mississippi Masala, Jungle Fever*

Interviews: When asked questions, people talk

Inventors & Inventions: Those wacky folks and their newfangled machines; *Chitty Chitty Bang Bang*

Invisibility: Now you see 'em, now you don't

Iraq: Maybe you've heard of it...oil-rich country in the Middle East? We've been poking around there for a while now?

Ireland: Aye, make that a pint for take away; *The Field, Cal, The Playboys*

Islam: Religious themes, concentrating on Muslims

Island Fare: Thin, isolated stretch of land surrounded by water; notorious for encouraging natural appetites in men and women

Israel: *Cast a Giant Shadow, Exodus*

Istanbul, not Constantinople: Former seat of the Eastern Roman Empire, now the Turks run things.

Italy: Passion, vino, lust, vino, Sophia Loren

It's a Conspiracy, Man!: Just because you're paranoid doesn't mean they're not out to get you

Jamaica: Caribbean Island country to head to when you need to hear some reggae, inhale, or get your groove back

Japan: *Land of the Rising Sun, Godzilla, Hiroshima, Mon Amour*

Jazz & Blues: Uniquely American music form performed mostly by tragic figures...in the movies, anyway.

Jerusalem: Much-fought-over Holy City, it's ground zero for much of the world's religious population.

Jockeying for Position: Horse racing flicks like *Seabiscuit*

Joke and Dagger: *Spies Like Us* can be funny, even when the mission is *Top Secret!*

Judaism: *Fiddler on the Roof* meets *Funny Girl*

Jungle Stories: Tarzan, tribes, trees, treasure, temperature, temptresses, tigers

Junior Jocks: Kids got out onto the field, court, pitch, or rink to emulate their sports heroes, or just for fun, or to please their vicariously-thrilled parents.

Justice Prevails?: The verdict's in, but is it fair? *And Justice for All, In the Name of the Father, Presumed Innocent*

Karaoke: This Japanese import usually runs best on alcohol

KGB: Not the crazy Russian poker player from *Rounders* but the former Soviet Union's spy organization

Kiddie Viddy: Stuff aimed at kids that's actually suitable for the little nippers to watch

Kidnapped!: Held for ransom or just for the heck of it—*A Perfect World, Raising Arizona*

Killer Apes and Monkeys: *King Kong* lives on *The Planet of the Apes*

Killer Appliances: Defrosted refrigerator goes on killing binge

Killer Beasts: Cloned dinosaurs run amuck in backyard, destroying patio

Killer Brains: Literally has a mind of its own, i.e., *The Brain That Wouldn't Die*

Killer Bugs: Giant and/or miserably mean spiders, ants, bees, worms, flies, slugs, tarantulas, wasps, and other creepy things

Killer Cars: You should have changed *Christine*'s oil

Killer Clowns: Confirming what everybody knows: clowns are evil

Killer Dogs: Fido takes a walk on the wild side—*Cujo*, baby

* = new to this edition

Killer Dreams: More like nightmares on elm street

Killer Kats: Kitties with a killer instinct

Killer Pigs: Evil swine

Killer Plants: Too much fertilizer produces killer tomatoes (stewed)

Killer Reptiles: *Godzilla* and pals, not rampaging lawyers

Killer Rodents: Nasty mice, rats, bats, and shrews

Killer Sea Critters: Just when you thought it was safe to go back in the water; formerly *Sea Critter Attack*

Killer Spouses: Watch their eyes very closely when you get to the "...until death do you part" portion of the vows

Killer Toys: Demented play things develop homicidal urges; why hello, Chucky

Killing Sprees: A person, or sometimes a couple, decides that a bunch of people need killin' in a short amount of time

Kindness of Strangers: Baffling altruistic behavior

King of Beasts (Dogs): Need we say more?

Korean War: *M*A*S*H* and friends

L.A.: Smoggy city in California also known as Los Angeles or the City of Angels; includes Hollywood & Beverly Hills

Labor & Unions: *Hoffa* and other working stiffs

***Lacrosse:** It's like hockey, on grass

Late Bloomin' Love: Better late than not blooming at all

Law & Lawyers: Tom Cruise joins *The Firm* and other realistic legal adventures

Leprechauns: The wee mischievous people of Irish lore who carry around pots o' gold

Lesbians: Lesbian themes—*Lianna, Bar Girls*

Libraries & Librarians: Important things happen where you can't talk—sometimes people even read!

Lifeguards: Rescuers of the swimming-challenged

Little People: Dwarves, munchkins, leprechauns, oompa-loompas and the like

London: City in merry old England, home to many generations of the most famous royals

Loner Cops: *Dirty Harry* Syndrome

Look Ma! I'm on TV!: TV becomes real life—*The Truman Show*, live from *Pleasantville*

Lost Worlds: From *Brigadoon* to *The People That Time Forgot*

Lottery Winners: Ordinary schmoes get rich quick. Be careful what you wish for...

Louisiana: Southern state on the bayou; where the Mississippi ends and the party begins (at Mardi Gras time)

Lovable Loonies: Crazy, but not Norman Bates crazy; *Crazy People, Benny & Joon*

Lovers on the Lam: Couples commit crimes and find themselves on the run—*Badlands, Natural Born Killers, True Romance*

Mad Scientists: *The Brain That Wouldn't Die* spends an evening with *Frankenhooker*

Madrid: Capital of Spain, it has museums, great nightlife, and a pretty famous soccer team

Magic: Hocus pocus, often with evil intent

Magic Carpet Rides: *Aladdin* joins *Sinbad the Sailor* for *The Golden Voyage of Sinbad*

Mail-Order Brides: Shipping is okay, but I've got a problem with this handling charge!

***Makeovers:** When 'ugly' people become pretty by taking off glasses and putting on makeup, or letting their hair out of a bun

Making Friends: Using spare parts to create semi-articulate, reasonable facsimiles of people. *Young Frankenstein* meets *Frankenhooker*

Marriage: Wedding bells, honeymoons, affairs, divorce, and growing old together, as well as the occasional unfortunate marital union with a blood-sucking vampire or knife-wielding Satanist

Marriage Hell: Divorce is the preferred exit strategy, but an uncooperative spouse usually has other ideas

Marriages of Convenience: Will you marry me so I can inherit boatloads of cash or not get deported? Oh, how romantic!

Mars: The Red Planet, which gave us (supposedly) little green men and the Illudium-Q Explosive Space Modulator.

Martial Arts: Fists of Aluminum Foil; much head-kicking, rib-crunching, chop-socky action

Martyred Pop Icons: For us, they gave their all; Buddy Holly, Elvis, Marilyn, James Dean, *Stardust Memories*

Mass Media: From *Network* to *Broadcast News* to *My Favorite Year*

Masseurs: People who knead people...

Mathemagicians: Smarties with a good head for figures, but sometimes balancing the fine edge of sanity

May-December Romance: Older people meet younger people and the romantic sparks fly; *Harold and Maude* visit *Atlantic City.*

The Meaning of Life: The search for the elusive answer—*My Life, The Remains of the Day, Shadowlands*

Medieval Romps: Dirty peasants, deodorized and glorified kings and queens, splendid knights in shining armor, and one for all and all for one

Meltdown: Or how I learned to stop worrying and love the bomb; also bad wiring at local nuclear plants

Memphis: The other city in Tennessee; Elvis' home

Men: What is man? Is he neither fish nor fowl? Or perhaps linoleum?

Men in Prison: Working on a chain gang; what we have here is a failure to communicate

Mental Hospitals: Storage area for those not on speaking terms with Mr. Reality

Mental Retardation: *Bill, Charly*, Dominick, Lenny, Raymond (definitely)

Mercenaries: *Dogs of War* who like the killin' if they get paid enough

Mermaids: Half woman, half fish, alright! *The Little Mermaid* makes a big *Splash*

Metamorphosis: Ch-ch-ch-changes—From *The Fly* to *Wolf*

Meteors, Asteroids & Comets: Chunks of stuff wizzing through space, sometimes they land and cause problems

Mexico: *South of Santa Fe* and *Against All Odds*

Miami: Extremely warm coastal city in southern Florida

Middle East: Desert fare and camel close-ups ranging from *Ishtar* to *Lawrence of Arabia* to *The Jewel of the Nile*

Midlife Crisis: The point in a man's life when he trades in his car and wife for a newer, faster model. Neither decision ends well, usually

Military: Air Force: Flyboys fight America's aerial battles

Military: Army: GIs, Grunts, Dogfaces

Military Comedy: Marching to a different drummer, including *Stripes, M*A*S*H* and *No Time for Sergeants*

Military Crimes & Trials: Courtroom drama in the Armed Forces; *A Few Good Men* didn't follow the *Rules of Engagement* on their *Paths to Glory*

Military: Foreign: Armed forces of other nations are the focus

Military: Marines: Jarheads. The first ones in and the last ones out.

Military: Navy: Fighting on the high seas and in the air

Military School: Kids get sent there to learn discipline, the art of war, and how to march in a straight line.

Sometimes they learn too well and take over (*Taps*)

Military Westerns: Here comes the cavalry! Occasionally, *They Died with Their Boots On*

Milwaukee: Wisconsin home of beer, brats, the Brewers, Bucks, and lots and lots of snow

Miners & Mining: Helmets with the little flashlights are nifty; *Matewan* and *McCabe & Mrs. Miller*

Minnesota: Northern state that makes Michigan seem like the tropics. Home of the Twin cities and Prince, eh?

Missing Persons: People who disappear for a variety of reasons, sometimes because other people have taken them away

Missionaries: On a mission from God to save native populations

Mistaken Identity: You mean to say you're not the King of France?

Mockumentary: Movies in which actors pretend to be real people being followed around by fake documentary crews that are actually real filmmaking crews; *This is Spinal Tap*'s genre, and they're still *Best in Show* at it.

Model Behavior: Fashion and models are the center of attention—but isn't that the point? *Looker, Gia, Unzipped, Ready to Wear*

Modern Cowboys: Fun-lovin' rascals adept at riding horses through busy city streets or with a yen to experience mid-life crisis by doing a rodeo

Moms: Maternal figures have a prominent role

Monkeyshines: Critters from the jungle, sometimes cute and fluffy, often wreaking havoc—*Congo, Monkey Trouble, Outbreak*

Monks: Of the Catholic-Friar-Tuck, Tibetan-Buddhist and *Bulletproof* varieties

Monster Moms: Loving on the outside, evil on the inside—*Mommie Dearest, Serial Mom*

Monster Yuks: Monster movies where the creatures are more funny, or cuddly, than scary

Montana: Northern plains state, home to wide-open spaces and the occasional wide-eyed loon living on a "compound"

Monte Carlo/Monaco: European playgrounds of the rich, famous, and occasional suave secret agent

Montreal: Cosmopolitan city of francophones currently in Canada

Mormons: Religious sect headquartered in Utah; they're big on knocking on strangers' doors, polygamy, and *Reservoir Dogs* wardrobes

Moscow: City in Russia (the country formerly known as USSR) that has the Kremlin and Lenin's corpse

Moscow Mafia: The Russian Mob

Motor Vehicle Dept.: *Chitty Chitty Bang Bang* at the *Car Wash*, plus *Tucker, Herbie*, and the *Repo Man*

Mountaineering: *Cliffhangers*

Mummies: Dead guys with leather-like skin, often wrapped in sheets

Murderous Children: *Children of the Corn* hang out on the outskirts of the *Village of the Damned*...isn't that near the 7-Eleven of Doom?

Museums: Big buildings that contain old paintings, sculptures, treasures...and the occasional ancient man-eating beastie

Musical Comedy: Laughter, singing, and dancing

Musical Drama: Singing and dancing, less laughter, more tension

Musical Fantasy: Singing and dancing in a figment of someone's imagination

Musicals: High-energy singing and dancing, often for no particular reason

Mutiny: Gang of disgruntled sailors takes over the ship

Mystery & Suspense: Edge-of-the-couch thrillers and whodunits

Nannies & Governesses: Musically-inclined women raise kids for rich people too busy to do it themselves

Nashville: Tennessee city that country music and Robert Altman made famous

Nashville Narratives: *Honkytonk Man* elopes with the *Coal Miner's Daughter*

National Guard: Branch of the military that goes where they're needed most. Sometimes it's natural disasters in their own back yard, sometimes it's a tense social situation where order is needed, sometimes it's a patch of desert thousands of miles away

Native America: Dancing with the wolves on *Pow Wow Highway*

Nazis & Other Paramilitary Slugs: *The Boys from Brazil* and *The Dirty Dozen* plus SS she-wolf *Ilsa* and modern David Duke adaptations

Near-Death Experiences: Brushes with the Reaper, usually resulting in some extra powers upon the victim's return

Negative Utopia: Things seemed so perfect until...

Netherlands: Not to be confused with the nether regions, which are often prominently displayed in some areas of Amsterdam.

New Black Cinema: Spike is Godfather

New Jersey Butt of too many New Yorkers' jokes; home of The Chairman, The Boss, The Trump, and Jay & Silent Bob

New Orleans: City in Louisiana that boasts the Mardi Gras and cajun cookin'

New Year's Eve: Stay up late, count down with Dick Clark, drink too much, greet the New Year feeling like...

New York, New York: It's a hell of a town...

Newlyweds: Ah, the first year of marriage; the honeymoon, settling into your new life together, hanging out with Bob Eubanks...

News at 11: Broadcast "journalism" in which some local hairdo spends most of a half-hour telling you what he's gonna tell you, and the rest of the time scaring the bejeezus outta ya

Niagara Falls: Little upstate New York border town where honeymooners and barrel riders gather. Oh yeah, they have some water thing there, too...

Nice Mice: Cute anthropomorphic or cartoon rodents, rather than the disease-carrying vermin variety

Nightclubs: *Casablanca*, of course

9/11: Films dealing with the events and aftermath of that day

Ninjas: Stealthy martial arts assassins in pajamas

No-Exit Motel: Sleazy motels with extremely lenient late-checkout policies

Not-So-True Identity: People pass themselves off as something else; *Soul Man, Gentleman's Agreement*

Nuns & Priests: Collars and habits; *Agnes of God, The Cardinal, Going My Way, Nuns on the Run, Sister Act*

Nuns With Guns: Sister Mary Margaret has traded up from the ol' yardstick. Better practice that penmanship.

Nursploitation!: *Night Call Nurses* offer *Tender Loving Care* in *The Hospital of Terror*

Obsessive Love: You like me. You really, really, *really* like me.

Occult: Witches, warlocks, devil worshippers, spell makers, spell breakers, haunted houses, and so on

Office Surprise: Office supplies used as weapons

Ohio: Midwestern Rust Belt state most famous for being really flat.

Oldest Profession: It's not accounting

The Olympics: *Chariots of Fire* and other tales of athletic discipline

On the Rocks: Alcoholism, alcohol, barflies, moonshining, Prohibition—*Arthur, Days of Wine and Roses, Papa's Delicate Condition, My Favorite Year*

** = new to this edition*

One Last Job: Crooks just wanna retire to a warm climate and enjoy their ill-gotten booty, but someone is always pullin' 'em back in!

Only the Lonely: 50 ways to play solitaire—*The Cemetery Club, The Heart Is a Lonely Hunter, Sleepless in Seattle*

Opera: Shouting in a melodic way while in costume

Order in the Court: Courtroom tales, including *The Accused, And Justice for All, A Few Good Men, Witness for the Prosecution*

Organ Transplants: Taking parts from one body that doesn't need 'em anymore and putting 'em into a body that does.

Organized Crime: Gangsters with Franklin Planners

Otherwise Engaged: Couple buys ring, sets date, and gets ready to march down the aisle, sometimes with a new fiancee—*Moonstruck, Only You, Sleepless in Seattle*

Out of Order: Movies in which the director's vision was not chronologically 20/20. Think *Memento* or any Quentin Tarantino movie

Out of This World Sex: Doin' the intergalactic nasty, usually with unfortunate results for earthlings

Pacific Islands: Hawaii, Tahiti, Philippines, etc.

Paperboys: Kids who toss papers everywhere but your front porch

Parades & Festivals: *Animal House* and *Ferris Bueller's Day Off*

Paradise Gone Awry: You'd think it'd be perfect, but you'd be mistaken

Parallel Universes: There's a whole other world out there—*Cool World, Who Framed Roger Rabbit?*

Pardners: Buddies in the Old West; Butch & Sundance, Wyatt Earp & Doc Holliday, the guys from *Silverado*

Paramedics: Part doctor, part fireman, part delivery driver. Cool!

Parenthood: Moms, dads, substitutes—*Dutch, Ma Barker's Killer Brood, Father of the Bride, Three Men and a Baby, Yours, Mine, and Ours, Raising Arizona*

Paris: Ze city in France with rude occupants and ze Eiffel Tower

Party Hell: *Psycho Girls* have fun at a sleepover until *Monsters Crash the Pajama Party* and it becomes *The Slumber Party Massacre*

Patriotism & Paranoia: Run the flag up the pole and salute it—Rambo, Patton, Norris, etc.

Peace: *Friendly Persuasion, Gandhi*

Pen Pals: Strangers correspond through the mail (or cyberspace) and become friends...or sometimes more

Penguins: Cute waddling flightless birds from Antarctica in tuxedos

Period Piece: Costume epics or evocative of a certain time and place; now divided into eras for your time traveling pleasure

15th Century—*Braveheart* and other tales of the end of the Middle Ages

16th Century—The Renaissance; rebirth of culture, art, science

17th Century—The Enlightenment, or Age of Reason

18th Century—Revolutions all over the place

19th Century—more war, plus the Industrial Revolution

20th Century—Epics that span more than one decade

1900s—the decade that began the now-completed 20th century

1910s—stories not involving World War I

1920s—Roaring '20s, Age of Jazz, Prohibition, Babe Ruth

1930s—stories not involving the Depression

1940s—stories not involving World War II

1950s—Rock 'n' Roll, Elvis, Eisenhower, McCarthyism, Civil Rights movement begins

1960s—assassinations, hippies, Vietnam, along with more mundane concerns

1970s—bad clothes, Watergate, disco, Elvis dies...let's just forget this decade happened

1980s—Reagan, Iran-Contra, John Hughes angstfests, big hair, and greed

Persian Gulf War: Smart bombs away

Philadelphia: Famous Pennsylvania city that's home to *Rocky*, the Liberty Bell, cheesesteaks, and M. Night Shyamalan films

Phobias!: Ee-eeeeeeeeeeeeeek!

Phone Sex: Is it really the next best thing to being there?

Phone Terror: *Don't Answer the Phone*

Physical Problems: *My Left Foot, Coming Home, The Elephant Man, The Other Side of the Mountain, Untamed Heart, The Waterdance*

Pigs: Loveable swine—*Gordy, Babe the Gallant Pig*

Pirates: Avast, ye scurvy dogs! *Captain Blood* drops in on *Treasure Island*

Pittsburgh: City in western Pennsylvania, home of sports teams fond of the colors black and yellow.

Plastic Surgery: Using surgery to give you what nature didn't, or to take away some of the unwanted stuff with which nature was overly generous

Poetry: Not exactly a booming category, but think of *Poetic Justice*

Poisons: *Arsenic and Old Lace* and *D.O.A.*

Poker: Card game where fortunes, property, wives, etc can be won or lost in a myriad of ways: Texas Hold 'em; Stud, Draw (particularly in the Old West)

Police Detectives: They get paid to bust open the big cases amid wild car chases and gunplay.

Politics: *Bob Roberts, Mandela, Whoops Apocalypse*

***Polygamy:** I now pronounce you man and wife, and wife...and wife. You may kiss the brides

Pool: *The Hustler*

Pornography: *Hardcore, Body Double*

Portland (Oregon, not Maine): Northwestern city, home to lots of trees and rain, beautiful scenery, and the Trailblazers

Post Apocalypse: No more convenience stores

Postwar: After effects of war, generally WWI or WWII but sometimes the Civil War, the War of 1812, the Revolutionary War, and the Ohio Automobile Dealers War

POW/MIA: Captured by the enemy

Pregnant Men: Ahh-nuld fails the *Rabbit Test*

Pregnant Pauses: Humorous takes on pregnancy and birth—*Nine Months, She's Having a Baby*

Prep School: Where the children of the elite meet to learn how to be upper-crusty

Presidency: Mr. Lincoln, *JFK*, LBJ, FDR, and, of course, *Dave*

Price of Fame: What goes up...

Private Eyes: There's no such thing as a simple little case...

Prom: A night you'll always remember...which isn't necessarily a good thing. Right, *Carrie*?

Propaganda: Deliberately stretching the truth in order to persuade

Protests: Hell no, we won't go (to bad movies)! Make popcorn, not war!

Psychic Abilities: I see dead people! Or the future, or read minds, or have telekenesis...

Psycho-Thriller: It's all in your mind—*Bad Influence, House of Games, The Silence of the Lambs*

Psychotics/Sociopaths: *Killer Inside Me, Reservoir Dogs, The Stepfather*

Publicists: People who suck up to the press so celebrities don't have to

Punk Rock: Anarchic semi-musical revolution of the late 70s, where the message (if you could decipher it) was more important that the melody. Way, way more important.

Puppets: Usually with strings, but also muppets

Pure Ego Vehicles: Big stars doing their big star thing—*Hudson Hawk, Harlem Nights, Yes, Giorgio*

Rabbis: Jewish clergy

Rabbits: *Harvey* has a *Fatal Attraction* for the *Nasty Rabbit*

Race Against Time: Tick, tock, tick, tock—*China Syndrome, Lorenzo's Oil*

Radio: Over the airwaves—*Choose Me, The Fisher King, Radio Days, Sleepless in Seattle*

Rags to Riches: Grit, determination, and hustling (or just pure dumb luck) lead to fortune—*Trading Places, Working Girls*

Rape: Victims and often their revenge

Rats!: Rodent critters who obviously went with a different PR firm than their mouse cousins

Real Estate: Everyone's gotta live somewhere, and most want to live on land they own. That's where agents, scams, and deals come in

REALLY Bad TV: When TV sucks...you into another dimension. How can there be anything good on when your TV is possessed?

Rebel With a Cause: Bucking the establishment for a reason

Rebel Without a Cause: Bucking the establishment just because it's the establishment

The Red Cross: Organization that helps those in need of blood, disaster relief, and war relief; also monitors treatment of POWs

Red Scare: Cold War and Communism—*The Commies Are Coming, The Commies Are Coming, Reds*

Reefer Madness: Tales of the demon weed.

Reggae: Jamaican musical style that fits well with the island's laid-back vibe and is also strangely apropos for the preceding category

Rehab: Drying out, sobering up...walking around in bathrobes.

Reincarnation: Why is everyone somebody famous in a past life?

Religion: *Witness, The Last Temptation of Christ*

Religious Epics: Charlton Heston parts the Red Sea—religion on a really big scale

Renegade Body Parts: Hands, fingers, eyes, brains with a life of their own

Repressed Men: Often British (*see* Anthony Hopkins or Hugh Grant), always with plenty of stiffness in upper lip and little elsewhere

Rescue Missions: I'll save you—*The Searcher, Free Willy*

Rescue Missions Involving Time Travel: I'll save you in another dimension—*Back to the Future*

The Resistance: WWII rebels with an anti-Nazi cause

Reunited: Usually after a long absence caused by extreme circumstances

Revenge: A key motivation—*Death and the Maiden, Death Wish*

Revolutionary War: Fought over tea

Rio: As in de Janeiro—that swingin' South American party town.

A River Runs Through the Plot: Long, sometimes winding and narrow body of water the main characters may have to get over, around, through or travel down, or fish in to get to the end of the story

Road Trip: Escapism courtesy of two- and four-wheel vehicles—*Easy Rider, Coupe de Ville, Pee Wee's Big Adventure, Wild at Heart*

Robots/Androids: Mechanical but fascinating, like the one Tom replaced Katie with; *Blade Runner* and *The Terminator*

Rock Flicks: Movies about real or made up rockers, starring rock stars, or featuring bands in concert; *Eddie & the Cruisers, The Last Waltz, Almost Famous*

Rock Stars on Film: But can they act? Prince (Symbol), Sting, Elvis, Lennon, The Monkees, Whitney, and so on

Rodeos: Rope tricks with steers

Rogue Cops: Corruption in the PD, cops on the take, etc. Usually, *Internal Affairs* gets involved

Role Reversal: Vice versa; empathy test—*Freaky Friday, My Fair Lady, Switch, Soul Man*

Romantic Adventures: Love among the chases and explosions—*The African Queen, Romancing the Stone*

Romantic Comedy: Falling in love has its hilarious moments—*French Kiss, Crossing Delancey, Modern Romance, Much Ado About Nothing*

Romantic Drama: Love thing leads to tension and anxiety—*Cyrano de Bergerac, Far and Away, Sommersby, Tender Mercies*

Romantic Mystery: Like there's a bigger mystery than the opposite sex??

Romantic Triangles: Three where there's only room for two—*The Age of Innocence, Casablanca, Three of Hearts*

Rome—Ancient Emperors ran the show, feeding Christians to the lions, using V for U, having orgies, and throwing up on purpose...those were the days!

Rome—Modern: Capital city of Italy. The Pope has a little place there

Roommates from Hell: Sometimes they won't do the dishes, sometimes they're homicidal—*Single White Female*

Royalty: Emperors, kings, queens, princes, princesses, crowns, scepters

Royalty, British: Emperors, kings, queens, etc in Merry Olde England

Royalty, French: Kings and queens who ran France when they didn't surrender to any foreigner who happened by

Royalty, Russian: Emperors, czars, and czarinas who ran things in Moscow till those mean old Bolsheviks showed up

***Runaways:** Kids leave home without permission, bad things usually ensue

Running: Jogging, panting, collapsing

Russia/USSR: Back in what used to be the USSR

Russian Revolution: 1917, when the Bolsheviks kicked out the Czar, set up the Soviet Union, and got Russia out of WWI

Rwanda: Troubled country in Africa being torn apart by war, poverty, and disease

Sail Away: Vessels on the water—*Mutiny on the Bounty, Erik the Viking, Mister Roberts*

St. Petersburg: The one in Russia, seat of the old monarchy. You wouldn't wanna have spring break here

Saints: *Bernadette, Saint Joan, A Time for Miracles*

Salespeople: Have I got a deal for you...

Samurai: Bodyguards to royalty and nobility in ancient Japan, sometimes they had to freelance

San Diego: Sunny (is there any other kind?) Southern California city close to Mexico

San Francisco: Set in the Northern California city known for hills and sourdough bread

Sanity Check: Inmates running the asylum; also deviant mental states

Satanism: *Speak of the Devil*

Satire & Parody: Biting social commentary or genre spoofs, including *Being There, Airplane!, Down and Out in Beverly Hills, I'm Gonna Git You Sucka, Monty Python's The Meaning of Life, The Player*

Savannah: the city in Georgia, with the southern belles and the big social events

Savants: Half-minded geniuses; *Rain Man, Forrest Gump*

** = new to this edition*

Scams, Stings & Cons: The hustle—*The Billionaire Boys Club, The Color of Money, A Fish Called Wanda, The Grifters, The Sting*

Scared 'Chuteless: Jumping out of airplanes without the proper equipment. Good candidates for a bad case of cement poisoning

***Sci-Fi Romance:** Lookin' for love in space. And we're not just talkin' about Capt. Kirk makin' it with green chicks

School Daze: Education, school, and teachers, generally grammar school days—*Lean on Me, Dead Poet's Society, To Sir, with Love, Teachers*

Sci Fi: Imagination fueled by science and a vision of the future

Sci-Fi Westerns: You ain't from around heah, is ya?

Science & Scientists: *Altered States, Darkman, Them, They, Son of Flubber, The Story of Louis Pasteur*

Scotland: Lush hills, thick brogues, kilts, bagpipes, and *Whiskey Galore*

Scotland Yard: British coppers oddly not located anywhere near Scotland.

Screwball Comedy: Snappy repartee between a man and a woman dealing with an impossibly silly situation

Scuba: Wet suits, including *The Abyss, Navy SEALS*

Sculptors: Artists who like to work with clay, rock, hammers, and chisels

Sea Disasters: We've sprung a leak—*The Poseidon Adventure*

Seattle: Showcases the city in Washington state where it rains a lot; the home of grunge rock

Second Chance: Another opportunity to set things right, fix mistakes, redeem yourself, or all of the above

Secret Service: Bodyguards to the First Family, they also investigate counterfeiting

Serial Killers: They just won't stop—*Henry: Portrait of a Serial Killer, The Rosary Murders*

Serials: Segmented adventures; Heyday was in the 1930s—*The Adventures of Red Ryder, The Little Rascals, Flash Gordon*

Sex & Sexuality: Focus is on lust, for better or worse—*Alfie, Barbarella, Emmanuelle, Looking for Mr. Goodbar, Rambling Rose, She's Gotta Have It*

Sex on the Beach: Flashing the fish and getting sand in the darnedest places; the most famous couple was in *From Here to Eternity* and *Airplane!* lost no time making fun of them

Sexcapades: The wilder edge of the whole sex thing

Sexploitation: Softcore epics usually lacking in plot but not skin—*The Erotic Adventures of Pinocchio*

Sexual Abuse: Victims and their stories—*Twin Peaks, Fire Walk with Me*

Sexual Harassment: When I say no, I mean it

Shipwrecked: Stranded on an island when your boat sinks

Shops & Shopping: When commerce at the mall is a major plot point.

Showbiz Comedies: Laughter behind the scenes in Hollywood or on Broadway

Showbiz Dramas: Tension behind the scenes in Hollywood or on Broadway

***Showbiz Horror:** Bloody mayhem or creepy goings-on behind the scenes in Hollywood or on Broadway

Showbiz Musicals: Singing and dancing behind the scenes in Hollywood or on Broadway

Showbiz Thrillers: Screaming behind the scenes in Hollywood or on Broadway

Shrinkage: People become very, very small. Honey, I Shrunk Rick Moranis's Career

Shrinks: Psychiatry or equivalent, with *The Prince of Tides, One Flew Over the Cuckoo's Nest*

Shutterbugs: Photographers and their pictures—*The Public Eye, The Eyes of Laura Mars, Peeping Tom*

Sibling Rivalry: Brothers and sisters fighting over...well, anything, but usually romance or parental affection or wealth.

Silent Films: No small talk/no big talk/no talk talk

Silent Horror/Fantasy Classics: Silent screams, expressions of terror

Single Parents: Divorced or widowed, they're doing the work of two—and they're back in the dating scene, usually assisted by matchmaking kids

Singles: Not always swinging but still solidly unmarried—*About Last Night, Singles, When Harry Met Sally*

Skateboarding: Teens on wheels—*Gleaming the Cube*

Skating: Roller and ice, including *The Cutting Edge, Xanadu*

Skiing: Slap on a couple of waxed boards and off you go—*Downhill Racer, Swinging Ski Girls*

Skinheads: Nazi wannabes wreak havoc and cause trouble

Skydiving: Jumping from a plane with a polyester slip

Slapstick Comedy: Humor of the physical sort, including Abbott and Costello, the Marx Brothers, sports comedies, Ernest, Pink Panther, Home Alone, the Three Stooges

Slasher Flicks: Horror movies in which unsuspecting and promiscuous teens get sliced, diced, and julienned by knife, machete, drill, chainsaw, and/or farm implement-wielding maniacs

Slavery: *Roots, Spartacus*

Slob Comedy: Happily dumb comedies that provide plenty of laughs and quotes for adolescent boys of all ages. *Animal House, Stripes, Caddyshack* are the Holy Trinity

Small-Town Sheriffs: Think Sly in *Cop Land*, or Buford Pusser of *Walking Tall* fame

Smuggler's Blues: Making, transporting, and selling the drugs. Don't *Blow* your cool in the *Traffic*.

Snakes: Slithering creatures who frighten many—*Raiders of the Lost Ark*

Sniper: Military (and sometimes not) sharpshooters who can kill from a distance

Snowboarding: Kinda like skiing, except it's one big board attached to your feet, instead of two skinny ones. Oh, and no poles

Soccer: Known as football outside of the USA—*Victory, Ladybugs*

South America: Right below North America—*Aguirre, the Wrath of God, The Mission*

Southern Belles: Southern gals ooze charm—*Blaze, Driving Miss Daisy, Steel Magnolias*

Space Operas: Going where no spam has gone before—*Alien, Star Trek, 2001: A Space Odyssey, Apollo 13*

Spaghetti Western: Clint with a squint, *A Fistful of Dollars, My Name is Nobody, Once Upon a Time in the West*

Spain: Southern European country that's been home to conquerors, explorers, Moors, and Antonio Banderas

Spanish Civil War: Franco and the Fascists vs. the defenders of the newly-elected Socialist government. A preview of how WWII would be fought

Spiders: Eight-legged creepy crawlies spinning their webs, sometimes in the service of cartoon pigs

Spies & Espionage: Trench coats, dark glasses, Bond, *North by Northwest*

Sports Comedies: Humorous athletic tales, generally not based on a true story

Sports Documentaries: Non-fiction examinations of athletes and the games they play

Sports Dramas: Intense athletic tales, often based on a true story

Spring Break: Colleges and high schools empty their kids into the streets of Florida, Mexico and other exotic locales, where they search for beer and sex...if we remember correctly

Spy Kids: Agents with a safe house on Sesame Street

Stagestruck: Stories of the theatre; *Broadway Melody* sung at the *Stage Door* by *The Dolly Sisters*

Stalked: No, I do not want to switch to MCI

Star Gazing: Not Hollywood stars, astrology/astronomy type stars

Stay-at-Home Dads: *Mr. Mom* takes care of the kids while Mom goes to the office...or just goes

Stepparents: New spouse hiding either alien origins or sociopathic tendencies greets existing clan

Stewardesses: *Three Guys Named Mike* go to *Stewardess School* and meet *Blazing Stewardesses*

Stolen from Asia: American remakes of Asian classics—usually Kurosawa's; *Seven Samurai* becomes *The Magnificent Seven*

Stolen from Europe: American remakes of European fare; *A Walk in the Clouds, The Vanishing, Scent of a Woman*

Stolen From France: Hollywood goes to its favorite remake well; *Diabolique, Cousins, Nine Months, Three Men and a Baby*

Storytelling: *Amazing Stories, Grim Prairie Tales*

Strained Suburbia: Neighborhood is not what it seems—*Dennis the Menace, Neighbors, Edward Scissorhands*

Strippers: Take it off, take it all off

Struggling Artists: It's hard not to struggle when your work only becomes valuable after you're dead

Struggling Musicians: Talented, but still reaching for the top

Stuntmen: Guys (and gals) paid to take the fall (and punch, and crash) for the stars

Stupid Is...: Stupidity on purpose—*Billy Madison, Dumb and Dumber,* or dumbness as a plot device—*Being There, Forrest Gump*

Submarines: Deep sea diving; *Das Boot, Up Periscope, Run Silent, Run Deep, Hunt for Red October*

Subways: A train for shorter trips—*Speed, The Taking of Pelham One Two Three*

Suicide: Self-inflicted premature ends—*The Big Chill, Scent of a Woman, Romeo and Juliet*

Summer Camp: Where children go to misbehave, including *Meatballs* and *Sleepaway Camp*

Super Heroes: Men and women of extraordinary strength and abilities wearing silly- looking costumes

Supernatural Comedies: *Beetlejuice* marries *She-Devil* and they take *The Ghost Train* to their *Haunted Honeymoon*

Supernatural Horror: Forces from beyond terrorize those who are here

Supernatural Martial Arts: Kung fu *From Beyond the Grave*

Supernatural Westerns: Forces from beyond terrorize cowboys in the Old West

Surfing: Awesome wave, dude! *Mad Wax, The Surf Movie, Surf Nazis Must Die, Endless Summer*

Survival: *Alive, The Bridge over the River Kwai, Testament*

Suspended Animation: Frozen in time—*Coma, Late for Dinner*

Swashbucklers: Crossed swords and rope swinging, including *Robin Hood*, Zorro, various Musketeers, *Captain Blood, The Three Amigos*

Swimming: Ranging from *Gremlins* to *Jaws* to *The Swimmer* to *Cocoon*

Swingers: *Bob & Carol & Ted & Alice* try *Group Marriage* and Carol and Alice become *Swinging Wives*

Sword & Sandal: *See* Arnold Schwarzenegger's early career

Sydney: Big Aussie city; recent site of Olympic glory

Tale of the Tape: Videocassettes or audiocassettes are important plot devices...so remember to rewind

Talking Animals: *Dr. Doolittle* treats *Babe*

Tattoos: *The Illustrated Man* visits *Cape Fear* to do battle with *Cyber Bandits*

Taxing Situations: The IRS comes looking for the gummint's cut of the action. Gol' dang revenooers!

Team Efforts: Working together pays off—*Hoosiers, Memphis Belle, Renaissance Man*

Tearjerkers: Crying fests—*Love Story, Steel Magnolias, Old Yeller*

Technology—Rampant: Machines that wreak havoc—*Metropolis, Death Ray 2000, Blade Runner*

Teen Angst: Adolescent anxieties, including *Baby It's You* and almost everything produced or directed by John Hughes

Teen Comedy: Teenagers yuk it up in school or out. Usually has a lot to do with sex, bodily functions, and defying authority (preferably all three at once)

Teen Drama: Kinda redundant. Teenagers deal with VERY IMPORTANT issues, or stuff that seems that way at the time, anyway.

Teen Horror: Horror flicks where the body count is skewered toward the 15-19 demographic (isn't that pretty much all of 'em?)

Teen Musicals: Teens sing and dance, probably while texting their BFF. OMG!

Teen Romance: Teenagers falling in love, or lust

Televangelists: Salesmen on late-night or Sunday morning TV with plastic hair and shiny suits who want to help you get to heaven...if you have the cash

Tennis: Anyone?

Terminal Confusion: Luggage gets mixed up at the airport, bus station, etc. Trouble usually follows

Terminal Illness: Someone's gonna die a tragic death from a horrible disease, but probably not before falling in love or doing something inspirational. Usually not considered comedy premise

Terror in Tall Buildings: From *Die Hard* to *Speed* to *The Towering Inferno*

Terrorism: Love affairs with hidden bombs

Texas: Southern state that once was a country...and they never let anyone forget it. Apparently everything is bigger there.

Thanksgiving: Huge dinner, football, familial angst, turkey coma, Christmas shopping may now commence

There Goes the Neighborhood: Those nice new neighbors turn out out to be psychos, terrorists, aliens, or worse...tool borrowers!

The Third Degree: Where were you on the night of...

This Is My Life: Autobiographies starring the subject—Muhammed Ali in *The Greatest*, Audie Murphy goes *To Hell and Back*

This Is Your Life: Biography and autobiography, including *The Babe Ruth Story, Amazing Howard Hughes, Amadeus, Catherine the Great, Great Balls of Fire, Raging Bull, What's Love Got to Do With It?*

3-D Flicks: Bring your special glasses

Thumbs Up: Hitchin' a ride—*Even Cowgirls Get the Blues, The Hitcher*

Tibet: So I says "Hey, Lama, how's about a little somethin' for the effort..."

Tijuana: City in Mexico that holds a special allure for Americans looking for various flavors of debauchery

Time Travel: Fast forward or reverse with Bill and Ted, *Dr. Who, Back to the Future,* and *Peggy Sue Got Married*

Time Warped: You wake up in an era not your own; *Austin Powers*, the Bradys and the Cleavers coping with the '90s

Titanic: The unsinkable ship that hit an iceberg its first time out...and sunk. It was

* = new to this edition

in all the papers

To the Moon!: *Apollo 13, From the Earth to the Moon*

Tokyo: Crowded city in Japan terrorized by Godzilla

Torn in Two (or More): *Sybil* and *Dr. Jekyll and Mr. Hyde* are *Raising Cain* leading *Separate Lives* on the *Edge of Sanity*

Toronto: Big city in Canada where they don't make you speak French. Home of Skydome and the Hockey Hall of Fame

Torrid Love Scenes: Steamy and/or sticky—*Angel Heart, Bull Durham, From Here to Eternity, Risky Business, The Unbearable Lightness of Being*

Toys: *Babes in Toyland, The Toy, Toys*

Tragedy: The fate of humankind, magnified—*King Lear, Madame Bovary, Tess, The World According to Garp*

Trains: Rhythm of the clackity clack—*Romance on the Orient Express, Throw Momma from the Train, Running Scared, The Silver Streak*

Trapped with a Killer!: And there's no escape—*Dead Calm, Misery, The Shining*

Treasure Hunt: Looking for hidden riches—*Klondike Fever, Treasure of Sierra Madre, Romancing the Stone*

Trees & Forests: Can't see one for the other, that wilderness paradox—includes *Mr. Sycamore* and *The Wizard of Oz*

Triads: Chinese organized crime outfit. Chow-Yun Fat is always shooting it out with 'em in John Woo flicks

True Crime: Based on fact, including *The Boston Strangler, The Executioner's Song, Helter Skelter*

True Stories: Approximations of real-life events often significantly fictionalized for the screen, including *All The President's Men, Chariots of Fire, Cry Freedom, Heart Like a Wheel, The Killing Fields, Silkwood*

TV Pilot Movies: Some became series; some did not

TV Series: Collections, anthologies, and individual episodes of memorable shows—*I Love Lucy, Star Trek, The Fugitive*

Twins: *Double Trouble, Double Vision, Mirror Images*

Twister!: The big wind not caused by Mexican food that picks up heavy things (houses, cows, trucks) and deposits them elsewhere

Under My Skin: People (or cartoon characters) get inside a guy's pelt, and crawl around for a little while

Undercover Cops: Cops pretend they're bad guys to catch more bad guys, but sometimes they get *In Too Deep*

Unexplained Phenomena: No apparent reason for an event

Unhappy Meals Dining experience is marred by familial angst, unfortunate incidents, or people keeling over dead

U.S. Marshals: Law enforcement branch that transports prisoners, hunts down fugitives, and in the Old West, handled the showdown duties

Up All Night: Movie takes place mostly after the sun goes down and *Before Sunrise*

Urban Comedy: Taking the *Soul Plane* to the *Car Wash*, and then to the *Barbershop*. Then maybe head to *The Cookout. Are We There Yet?*

Urban Drama: *American Me* to *Boyz N the Hood* to *Grand Canyon* to *Zebrahead*

Urban Gangstas: Gangs fight it out for their piece of the mean streets of the inner city; *Colors, New Jack City*

The USO: Entertained the troops through two world wars and a variety of police actions—with Bob Hope usually leading the way

Vacation Hell: When the annual two-week respite from work goes horribly wrong. Usually starts with someone asking the skeevy gas station attendant for directions

Vacations: Getting away from it all, yet bringing the family.

Vampire Babes: Blood sucking dames—*The Brides of Dracula*

Vampire Spoof: Comedic blood suckers, including *Buffy, Andy Warhol's Dracula, Dracula Sucks*

Vampires: More serious vein of blood sucking varmint, including *Dracula* in his many manifestations

Venice: Italian city of gondolas

Veterans: Retired fighting men (and women)—*Alamo Bay* to *Who'll Stop the Rain*

Veterinarians: Animal doctors. Plasma! Dog Plasma!

Videogames Interactive digital games that long ago replaced human interacton and eye contact as the preferred method of home entertainment for kids and geeks all over the world

Vietnam War: *Platoon, Hamburger Hill, Apocalypse Now, Good Morning, Vietnam*

Vigilantes: Individuals take the law into their own hands—*Death Wish, The Outlaw Josey Wales*

Vikings: Rowdy guys with horns on their hats who like boat trips...Not those guys, the ones from Scandinavia!

Virtual Reality: High-tech video game that seems real...to computer geeks

Viva Las Vegas!: Celebrating America's tackiest city—*Honeymoon in Vegas, Sister Act*

Volcanoes: Mountain blowing off steam, including *Joe Versus the Volcano*

Volleyball: *Side Out* used to be the only one till we remembered the bare-chested boys from *Top Gun*

Voodoo: From *Angel Heart* to *How to Stuff a Wild Bikini* to *Weekend at Bernie's 2*

Vote for Me!: Political campaigns for various offices, from student council (*Election*) to U.S. President (*The Candidate*)

Wagon Train: Westward, Ho! Prairie Schooners play a big part in Westerns...such as getting people to the West

Waitresses: *Alice Doesn't Live Here Anymore*, she went to *Atlantic City* to get some *Mystic Pizza*

***Wall Street:** The financial capital of the U.S., makers of vast sums of money and occasional global financial crises

War Between the Sexes: Men and women battle for supremacy—*It Happened One Night, The King and I, He Said, She Said, Romancing the Stone, When Harry Met Sally, The War of the Roses, Thelma & Louise*

***War Brides:** Soldier meets girl and they get hitched, then he bring her home to his mother country

War, General: Generally any conflict that defies other classification—*The Alamo, Gunga Din, The Last of the Mohicans*

Weathermen: Guys on the news who stand in front of a map and "predict" whether or not it will rain. Isn't there always a 50% chance of rain? Either it'll rain or it won't

Wedding Bells: Memorable weddings; *Father of the Bride, Four Weddings and a Funeral, Sixteen Candles, The Wedding*

Wedding Hell: Horror-filled or anxiety-ridden weddings; *The Blood Spattered Bride, The Brides Wore Blood, The Graduate, Wedding Banquet*

Werewolves: Full moon wonders, like *Wolf*

Western Comedy: Gags and horses—*Ballad of Cable Hogue, Blazing Saddles, Rancho Deluxe, Support Your Local Sheriff*

Westerns: Cowboys, cowgirls, horses and jingle jangling spurs on the frontier

Westrogens: The Old West through women's eyes

Whales: Really big seafaring mammals. It's best to just stay out of their way...Just ask *Pinocchio*

Whitewater Rafting: Wild ride down a raging river, often in the company of a psycho

Widows & Widowers: The one who's left when a spouse dies; *Dragonfly, Sleepless in Seattle*

Wild Kingdom: Animals on their own and interacting with confused humans, including *The Bear, Dumbo, Born Free, Free Willy, Never Cry Wolf*

Wilderness: More trees than a forest, plus wild critters—*The Life and Times of Grizzly Adams*

Wine & Vinyards: Spirits from the grape, and the places the grapes came from

Wisconsin: Chilly northern state, makers of beer and dairy products, land of Cheeseheads.

Witchcraft: From *Hocus Pocus* to *Three Sovereigns for Sarah* to *The Wizard of Oz*

Witness Protection Program: Rat out your "associates," get a new identity

Women: Impressive women, less than impressive women, and issues concerning women—*Crimes of the Heart, My Brilliant Career, Passion Fish, Working Girls*

Women Cops: Female officers of the law

Women in Prison: The things that go on in the big doll house

Women in War: Nurses, WACs, WAVES, USO performers, sometimes prisoners—they also served...

Wonder Women: *Attack of the 50-Foot Woman, Ripley, La Femme Nikita, Supergirl*

Words Come to Life: Characters literally jump off the page

Workin' for a Livin': Focuses on working stiffs and their jobs

World War I: The First Big One, including *African Queen, Gallipoli, Grand Illusion*

World War I Spies: Espionage in the Great War. Think *Mata Hari*

World War II: The Last Big One, including *A Bridge Too Far, Guadalcanal Diary, The Guns of Navarone, Hope and Glory, Memphis Belle, Tora! Tora! Tora!*

World War II Spies: British and American agents who used stealth and deception to fight the Nazis

Wrestling: Choreographed sport involving men and women—*No Holds Barred, All the Marbles, Wrestling Women vs. the Aztec Ape*

Writers: Tortured souls who put pen to paper when they're not putting bottle to lips. Does not include the ink-stained wretches of the journalistic trade

The Wrong Man: ...has been accused or convicted. *The Fugitive* is in a *Frenzy* because *Jack's Back*.

Wrong Side of the Tracks: Often involves relationship with someone on the right side—*Cannery Row, The Flamingo Kid, Pretty in Pink, White Palace*

Yakuza: Japanese version of the Mafia, very organized crime

Yoga: Exercise you do sitting in one place that makes you all bendy

You Are Getting Sleepy!: Hypnosis, its practitioners, and effects, including glazed looks and strange behavior...Right, Katie, er, Kate?

You Big Dummy!: Ventriloquists have wooden dolls do their talking (or killing) for them

You Lose, You Die: Sports goes nuts—only the winner survives; *Arena, Rollerball, Tron*

Yuppie Nightmares: Young adults find best-laid plans for attaining wealth and privilege going astray—*Baby Boom, Desperately Seeking Susan, The Mighty Ducks, Pacific Heights, Something Wild, Wall Street*

Zombie Soldiers: Recently undead in the army—*They Saved Hitler's Brain*

Zombies: Recently undead everywhere—*I Walked with a Zombie, Night of the Living Dead*

** = new to this edition*

Category Index

The Category Index includes subject terms ranging from straight genre descriptions (Crime Drama, Romantic Comedy, etc.) to more off-the-wall themes (Nuns with Guns, Eyeballs!). These terms can help you identify unifying themes (Baseball, Heists), settings (Miami, Period Piece: 1950s), events (The Great Depression, World War II), occupations (Clowns, Police Detectives, Doctors & Nurses), or suddenly animate objects (Killer Appliances, Killer Cars). Category definitions and cross-references precede the index; category terms are listed alphabetically. Release year is now included in this index. **A tipped triangle indicates a video rated three bones or higher.**

Abortion

Balzac and the Little Chinese Seamstress *'02*
The Choice *'81*
Choices *'86*
The Cider House Rules *'99* ▸
Citizen Ruth *'96*
The Crime of Father Amaro *'02* ▸
Critical Choices *'97*
Daddy's Gone A-Hunting *'69* ▸
Dogma *'99*
Eye of God *'97* ▸
Family Life *'71*
Fast Times at Ridgemont High *'82* ▸
Flanders *'06*
4 Months, 3 Weeks and 2 Days *'07* ▸
Goldstein *'64*
Happy Endings *'05*
If These Walls Could Talk *'96*
Listen to Me *'89*
Maria's Child *'93*
Men in White *'34*
Palindromes *'04* ▸
Panic in Needle Park *'71* ▸
A Private Matter *'92* ▸
Rain Without Thunder *'93*
Roe vs. Wade *'89* ▸
Rude *'96*
Signs & Wonders *'00*
Silent Victim *'92*
The Story of Women *'88* ▸
Things You Can Tell Just by Looking at Her *'00*
Unborn but Forgotten *'02*
Vera Drake *'04* ▸
Walpurgis Night *'41* ▸

Action-Adventure

see *Action-Comedy; Action-Drama; Action-Thriller; Adventure Drama; Boom!; Comic Adventure; Disaster Flicks; Martial Arts; Romantic Adventures; Swashbucklers*

Battlefield Baseball *'03*
Bionic Ninja *'85*
Bionicle 3: Web of Shadows *'05*
Black Dawn *'05*
Blonde Comet *'41*
Blood Stained Tradewind *'90*
Caesar the Conqueror *'63*
Call of the Wild *'04*
Call of the Yukon *'38*
Captain Calamity *'36*
The Challenge *'05*
Dororo *'07*
Five Element Ninjas *'82*
Forbidden Valley *'38*
Goyokin *'69* ▸
Have Sword, Will Travel *'69*
Heaven & Hell *'78*
The Houdini Serial *'20*
House of Traps *'81*
Human Lanterns *'82*
Life Gamble *'04*
Lightning Hutch *'26*
The Losers *'10*
Master of the Flying Guillotine *'75*
Ong Bak 2 *'08*
Prince of Persia: The Sands of Time *'10*
The Prisoner of Zenda *'22*
The Restless *'06*
Sars Wars: Bangkok Zombie Crisis *'04*
Seal Team *'08*
The Shadow Whip *'71*
She *'65*
Shogun's Samurai—The Yagyu Clan Conspiracy *'78*
The Sky Crawlers *'08*
The Spider Returns *'41*
The Spider's Web *'38*
Sword Masters: Brothers Five *'70*
Sword Masters: The Battle Wizard *'77*
10,000 A.D.: The Legend of the Black Pearl *'08*
The Wandering Swordsman *'70*
Wind and Cloud: The Storm Riders *'04*

Action-Comedy

see also *Action-Adventure; Comedy*

The Accidental Spy *'01*
After the Sunset *'04*
Agent Cody Banks 2: Destination London *'04*
Around the World in 80 Days *'04*
Bait *'00*
Beverly Hills Chihuahua *'08*
Bon Cop Bad Cop *'06*
Bounty Hunters 2: Hardball *'97*
Camouflage *'00*
Chandni Chowk to China *'09*
Charlie's Angels *'00*
Charlie's Angels: Full Throttle *'03*
Chill Factor *'99*
D.E.B.S. *'04*
Double Agent 73 *'80*
Double Take *'01*
G-Force *'09*
Get Smart *'08*
Gorgeous *'99*
Hancock *'08*
Hot Fuzz *'07* ▸
Hot Rod *'07*
Hot Tamale *'06*
House of Fury *'05*
I Spy *'02*
The Incredibles *'04* ▸
Kelly's Heroes *'70*
Killers *'10*
Kiss Kiss Bang Bang *'05* ▸
Knight and Day *'10*
Kung Fu Hustle *'04*
Legend of the Liquid Sword *'93*
The Librarian: Curse of the Judas Chalice *'08*
The Librarian: Quest for the Spear *'04*
The Librarian: Return to King Solomon's Mines *'06*
The Machine Girl *'07*
The Man *'05*
Man of the House *'05*
The Medallion *'03*
Meltdown *'95*
Miracles *'89*
Miss Congeniality 2: Armed and Fabulous *'05*
My Super Ex-Girlfriend *'06*
New York Minute *'04*
Next Day Air *'09*
Night at the Museum: Battle of the Smithsonian *'09*
Nim's Island *'08*
Ocean's Twelve *'04*
Oh! My Zombie Mermaid *'04*
The Other Guys *'10*
The Pacifier *'05*
Partners *'99*
Pineapple Express *'08* ▸
Pirates of the Caribbean: At World's End *'07*
Project A *'83*
Project A: Part 2 *'87*
The Rundown *'03*
Running on Karma *'03*
Rush Hour *'98*
Rush Hour 3 *'07*
Sahara *'05*
Scooby-Doo 2: Monsters Unleashed *'04*
Scott Pilgrim vs. the World *'10*
Seoul Raiders *'05*
Shaolin Soccer *'01*
South Sea Woman *'53*
Spider-Man 2 *'04* ▸
The Spy Next Door *'10*
Starsky & Hutch *'04*
Taxi *'04*
Thunderbirds *'04*
Tropix *'02*
The Tuxedo *'02*
Underclassman *'05*
Underdog *'07*
Warm Blooded Killers *'01*
White Chicks *'04*
The Whole Ten Yards *'04*
You Don't Mess with the Zohan *'08*
Zebraman *'04*

Action-Drama

The A-Team *'10*
Assault on Precinct 13 *'05*
Blast *'04*
Bound by Lies *'05*
Breaking News *'04*
The Celestine Prophecy *'06*
Constantine *'05*
Domino *'05*
Doom *'05*
Elektra *'05*
Fighting *'09*
Flight of the Phoenix *'04*
Flyboys *'06*
The Great Raid *'05*
Green Street Hooligans *'05* ▸
Hostage *'05*
Illegal Tender *'07*
Inglourious Basterds *'09* ▸
Into the Blue *'05*
It's All About Love *'03*
Jarhead *'05*
Journey to the Center of the Earth *'08*
King Kong *'05* ▸
The Last Legion *'07*
The Legend of Suriyothai *'02*
Lethal *'04*
Letters from Iwo Jima *'06* ▸
Lord of War *'05* ▸
The Master *'80*
The Memory of a Killer *'03*
Miami Vice *'06*
Mountain Patrol: Kekexili *'04*
National Treasure *'04*
Never Back Down *'08*
New Police Story *'04*
North Face *'08* ▸
Oldboy *'03* ▸
Ong-Bak *'03* ▸
Pathfinder *'07*
The Promise *'05*
The Proposition *'05*
Purple Butterfly *'03* ▸
Rebel Run *'94*
Redbelt *'08* ▸
Robin Hood *'10*
Rocky Balboa *'06*
The Sentinel *'06*
Serenity *'05* ▸
Sin City *'05*
16 Blocks *'06* ▸
Soldiers of Change *'06*
A Sound of Thunder *'05*
State Property 2 *'05*
Steamboy *'05*
Stryker *'04*
Submerged *'05*
Supercross: The Movie *'05*
Superman Returns *'06*
Sword Masters: Two Champions of Shaolin *'80*
The Three Burials of Melquiades Estrada *'05* ▸
Transporter 2 *'05*
24 : Redemption *'08*
Typhoon *'06*
Vengeance is a Golden Blade *'69*
The Veteran *'06*
Waist Deep *'06*
Warlords *'08*
The Warrior *'01* ▸
The Water Margin *'72*
The Way To Fight *'96*
World Trade Center *'06* ▸

Action-Thriller

Aeon Flux *'05*
Alone in the Dark *'05*
Anti-Terrorist Cell: Manhunt *'01*
Archangel *'05*

▸ = *rated three bones or higher*

Art of War 2: The Betrayal '08
The Art of War 3: Retribution '08
Bangkok Dangerous '08
Black Heat '76
Blade: Trinity '04
Blood Diamond '06
Body of Lies '08
Bohachi Bushido: Code of the Forgotten Eight '73
Breakaway '02
The California Kid '74
The Chairman '69
China Heat '90
Chrysalis '07
The City of Violence '06
Cleaner '07
Cloverfield '08
Command Performance '09
Conspiracy of Fear '96
Crimson Rivers 2: Angels of the Apocalypse '05
Dead or Alive '02
The Deal '05
Death Row Girls '08
Death Sentence '07
Death Trance '05
Deja Vu '06
Delinquent Girl Boss: Blossoming Night Dreams '70
Depth Charge '08
The Detonator '06
District B13 '04
District 13: Ultimatum '09
Domino '05
Eagle Eye '08
88 Minutes '08
Fast & Furious '09
The Fast and the Furious: Tokyo Drift '06
Feast 2: Sloppy Seconds '08
Female Prisoner Sigma '06
Firewall '06
Flash Point '07
Flightplan '05
The Flock '07
From Paris With Love '10
Fudoh: The New Generation '96
Full Time Killer '01
Ghost Rider '07
The Ghost Writer '10
Hard As Nails '01
Higher Ground '88
Hitman '07
Honor '06
The Hunt for Eagle One: Crash Point '06
The Incredible Hulk '08
Indiana Jones and the Kingdom of the Crystal Skull '08
The International '09
Iron Man 2 '10
Jumper '08
The Keeper '09
King Kong '05 ▸
The Kingdom '07
Kiss Kiss Bang Bang '05 ▸
Knowing '09
Layer Cake '05 ▸
Legends of the Poisonous Seductress 1: Female Demon Ohyaku '68
Legends of the Poisonous Seductress 2: Quick Draw Okatsu '69
Legends of the Poisonous Seductress 3: Okatsu the Fugitive '69
Live Free or Die Hard '07
Lost '05
Masked Rider—The First '05
The Memory of a Killer '03
Mexican Blow '02
Mirror Wars: Reflection One '05
Munich '05 ▸
Naked Weapon '03
National Treasure '04
National Treasure: Book of Secrets '07
The Net 2.0 '06
Next '07
No Blood No Tears '02 ▸
Oldboy '03 ▸
Opium and Kung-Fu Master '84 ▸
Pandemic '09
A Perfect Getaway '09
Public Enemy '02
Push '09
Quantum of Solace '08
Red Eye '05 ▸
The Red Spectacles '87
Rica '72
Rica 2: Lonely Wanderer '73
Rica 3: Juvenile's Lullaby '73
Running on Karma '03
Running Out of Time 2 '06
Running Scared '06
Salt '10
The Secret Invasion '64
Serenity '05 ▸
Sex and Fury '73
Shoot 'Em Up '07
Shooter '07
Sin City '05
6ixtynin9 '99
Sky Captain and the World of Tomorrow '04
The Soul Guardians '98
Stray Dog '91
Sympathy for Mr. Vengeance '02 ▸
Syriana '05 ▸
Taken '08
The Taking of Pelham 123 '09
Total Force '98
Trade '07
Transporter 3 '08
Typhoon '06
Ultraviolet '06
Underworld: Evolution '05
Vantage Point '08
Versus '00
The Veteran '06
Waist Deep '06
Wanted '08 ▸
War '07
The Way of War '08
When Eight Bells Toll '71
Whiteout '09
The Witness '99
XXX: State of the Union '05

Adolescence

see *Coming of Age; Hell High School; Summer Camp; Teen Angst; Teen Comedy; Teen Drama; Teen Horror; Teen Musicals; Teen Romance*

The Black Balloon '09

Adoption & Orphans

see also *Custody Battles; Hard Knock Life; Only the Lonely*

A la Mode '94
Across the Great Divide '76
Adoption '75 ▸
Adoration '08
The Affair of the Necklace '01
After the Wedding '06 ▸
Agata and the Storm '04
Aladdin '92 ▸
Alex Rider: Operation Stormbreaker '06
Aliens '86 ▸
All Mine to Give '56
Alone in the Dark '05
The Amazing Mrs. Holiday '43
Anastasia '97
Andre '94
Angel in a Taxi '59
Anne of Green Gables '34 ▸
Anne of Green Gables '85 ▸
Annie '82
Annie '99 ▸
August Rush '07
Azumi '03 ▸
Babes on Broadway '41
Bachelor Mother '39 ▸
Back to the Secret Garden '01
Ballet Shoes '07
Bambi '42 ▸
Batman Begins '05 ▸
Batman Forever '95 ▸
Battle Hymn '57
The Beniker Gang '83
Beshkempir the Adopted Son '98
Big Daddy '99
Big Red '62
Black Dynamite '09
The Blind Side '09
Blossoms in the Dust '41
Blues Brothers 2000 '98
Bobbie's Girl '02
Bogus '96
Born Free '66 ▸
Born in America '90
The Boy with the Green Hair '48 ▸
Brand Upon the Brain! '06 ▸
The Breaks '99
Bright Eyes '34
Brute '97
Casa de los Babys '03 ▸
Catfish in Black Bean Sauce '00
The Chateau '01
The Children of An Lac '80
The Children of Huang Shi '08
Children of the Corn 3: Urban Harvest '95
Christmas Eve '47
Christmas Lilies of the Field '84
Chronicle of a Boy Alone '64
The Cider House Rules '99 ▸
City Boy '93 ▸
Close to My Heart '51
The Country Bears '02
A Cry from the Streets '57
Crystalstone '88
Daddy Long Legs '19
Daddy Long Legs '55 ▸
Dangerous Orphans '86
D.A.R.Y.L. '85
David Copperfield '35 ▸
David Copperfield '70
David Copperfield '99
Days of Being Wild '91 ▸
Deadly Sanctuary '68
Dear Wendy '05
December Boys '07
Defiant '70
Despicable Me '10
The Devil's Backbone '01
Dick Tracy '90 ▸
Dondi '61
Don't Cry, It's Only Thunder '82
Eagle's Shadow '84
Earthling '80
The Education of Little Tree '97 ▸
Emile '03
Escape to Witch Mountain '75 ▸
The Family Holiday '07
Family Jewels '65
Family of Strangers '93
The Father Clements Story '87
Fighting Father Dunne '48
First Love '39
The Flamingo Rising '01
Flirting with Disaster '95 ▸
Four Brothers '05
Free Willy '93
The Geisha Boy '58
Gigantic '08
Glass House: The Good Mother '06
Gloria '98
Great Expectations '34
Great Expectations '46 ▸
Great Expectations '81
Great Expectations '89 ▸
Great Expectations '99
Great Expectations: The Untold Story '87
The Great Water '04
Happy Endings '05
Heaven on Earth '89
Heroes of the Saddle '40
Home at Last '88
A Home at the End of the World '04
A Home of Our Own '75
Hoodoo Ann '16
Hotel for Dogs '09
Hurt '09
I Am David '04
Immediate Family '89
Intimate Relations '95
Invisible Mom 2 '99
The Italian '05
The Jack Knife Man '20 ▸
James and the Giant Peach '96 ▸
Jane Eyre '34
Jane Eyre '44 ▸
Jane Eyre '83 ▸
Jane Eyre '96 ▸
Jane Eyre '97
Juno '07 ▸
The Kid '21 ▸
The Kid Who Loved Christmas '90
Kidnapped '05 ▸
King, Queen, Knave '72 ▸
Kings and Queen '04 ▸
Korczak '90 ▸
La Passante '83 ▸
Lady from Yesterday '85
The Lady Is Willing '42
The Land Before Time '88 ▸
Lemony Snicket's A Series of Unfortunate Events '04
Like Mike '02
Lilo & Stitch '02 ▸
The Little Kidnappers '90
Little Men '98
Little Orphan Annie '18
Little Orphan Annie '32
The Little Princess '87
Little Secrets '02
Loggerheads '05 ▸
A Long Way Home '81
Losing Isaiah '94 ▸
The Lost Child '00
Love Come Down '00
Love Finds a Home '09
Love Takes Wing '09
Lovely & Amazing '02 ▸
The Loves of Edgar Allen Poe '42
Love's Unending Legacy '07
Mad Max: Beyond Thunderdome '85
Madeline '98
The Magic Christian '69 ▸
Major Payne '95
Man, Woman & Child '83
Manny's Orphans '78
Marion Bridge '02
Martian Child '07
Meet the Robinsons '07
The Memory Keeper's Daughter '08
Mercury Rising '98
Mighty Aphrodite '95
Mighty Joe Young '49
Mighty Joe Young '98
Milwaukee, Minnesota '03
Min & Bill '30
The Mistress of Spices '05
Moll Flanders '96
Mon Amie Max '94
Mondo '96
Monsieur Ibrahim '03 ▸
Mostly Martha '01 ▸
Mother and Child '09
My Blue Heaven '50
My Dog Shep '46
My Little Girl '87
My Name is Modesty: A Modesty Blaise Adventure '04
Mystery of the Million Dollar Hockey Puck '75
Nacho Libre '06
Napoleon and Samantha '72 ▸
Nice Girl Like Me '69
No Reservations '07
Norbit '07
Nothing But the Night '72
The Odyssey of the Pacific '82
Off Season '01
The Official Story '85 ▸
Oliver! '68 ▸
Oliver & Company '88
Oliver Twist '22 ▸
Oliver Twist '33
Oliver Twist '48 ▸
Oliver Twist '82 ▸
Oliver Twist '85
Oliver Twist '97
Oliver Twist '00 ▸
Oliver Twist '05 ▸
Oliver Twist '07
On the Right Track '81
One Good Cop '91
The Orphan '79
Orphan '09
Orphan Train '79 ▸
The Orphanage '07 ▸
Orphans '87 ▸
Orphans of the Storm '21 ▸
Our Very Own '50
The Outsiders '83
Paper Moon '73 ▸
Peck's Bad Boy '34
Pennies from Heaven '36
Penny Serenade '41 ▸
Perfume: The Story of a Murderer '06
Phantasm '79
Pictures of Hollis Woods '07
Pixote '81 ▸
A Place for Annie '94
Pollyanna '20
Pollyanna '60 ▸
The Poor Little Rich Girl '36
The Prince of Central Park '77 ▸
Prison for Children '93
Problem Child '90
Queen Kelly '29 ▸
The Quest '96
The Quiet '05
Rags to Riches '87
Raising Heroes '97
Rebecca of Sunnybrook Farm '17
Record of a Tenement Gentleman '47
Red Cherry '95
Redwood Curtain '95
Relative Strangers '06
Rent-A-Kid '95
The Rescuers '77 ▸
The Revolt of Job '84 ▸
Rikisha-Man '58 ▸
The Road Home '95
The Road to Life '31
Rodeo Rhythm '42
Room for One More '51
Rose Hill '97
The Royal Tenenbaums '01 ▸
Sally '29
Sally of the Sawdust '25
Samantha '92
Santa with Muscles '96
Scaramouche '23
Scout's Honor '80
The Sea Serpent '85
Second Best '94 ▸
The Secret Garden '49 ▸
The Secret Garden '84
The Secret Garden '87 ▸
The Secret Garden '93
Secrets and Lies '95
Shep Comes Home '49
Shooting Fish '98
Sidewalks of London '38 ▸
A Simple Twist of Fate '94
Sioux City '94
The Sleepy Time Gal '01
Snow Dogs '02
Snow White and the Seven Dwarfs '37 ▸
Sois Belle et Tais-Toi '58
A Soldier's Daughter Never Cries '98
Spin '04
Station Jim '01
The Story of an African Farm '04
Strange Relations '02
The Stranger Who Looks Like Me '74
A Stranger's Heart '07
Streetwise '84 ▸
Stuart Little '99
Sugar Cane Alley '83 ▸
The Sugarland Express '74 ▸
Sundays & Cybele '62 ▸
Superman: The Movie '78 ▸
Susannah of the Mounties '39
Tarzan Finds a Son '39 ▸
Then She Found Me '07
They Still Call Me Bruce '86
The Thief Lord '06
Three Secrets '50
The Tie That Binds '95
To Each His Own '46 ▸
Tom Jones '98 ▸
Torch Singer '33
The Tunnel of Love '58
24 : Redemption '08
Twisted '96
Two Alone '34
The Unknown Woman '06
Up/Down/Fragile '95
Vanity Fair '04
A Very Serious Person '06
Way Back Home '32
Weeping Meadow '04
Welcome to Sarajevo '97 ▸
Whacked! '02
Where the River Runs Black '86
Which Way Home '90
Who'll Save Our Children? '82 ▸
Wild Hearts Can't Be Broken '91 ▸
The World Accuses '35
Wuthering Heights '09
Young & Free '78
Young People '40
Yours, Mine & Ours '05

Adultery

A Coeur Joie '67
All the Good Ones Are Married '07
An American Affair '09
Angela '02
Another Life '01
Asylum '05
The Babysitters '07
Back Street '41
Battle in Heaven '05
Bed and Board '70 ▸
Before the Devil Knows You're Dead '07 ▸
Before the Rains '07
Bloom '03
Blue Blood '07
Bread and Tulips '01 ▸
The Bridges of Madison County '95 ▸
Brothers '04 ▸
Burn After Reading '08
The Burning Plain '08
Calling Dr. Death '43
Car Trouble '85
Chicago '02 ▸
Closer '04 ▸
Coastlines '02
Coco Chanel & Igor Stravinksy '09
Cool and the Crazy '94
Counsellor-at-Law '33 ▸
Cover '08
Curse of the Golden Flower '06
Daisy Kenyon '47
Dangerous Liaisons '03
Darkness Falls '98
Day-Time Wife '39
Dead Gorgeous '02
The Decalogue '88 ▸
Derailed '05
The Devil and the Deep '32
The Devil Wears Prada '06
Dial Red O '55
Diary of a Mad Black Woman '05
Die Mommie Die! '03
The Divine Lady '29
Doctor Zhivago '65 ▸
Doctor Zhivago '03
The Door in the Floor '04 ▸
Dot the I '03
The Duchess '08 ▸
The Dying Gaul '05 ▸
Extract '09
Faithless '00 ▸
Familia '05
The Family That Preys '08
Fatal Attraction '87 ▸
Flashbacks of a Fool '08
The Foot Fist Way '08
Fracture '07
From the Terrace '60
The Golden Bowl '00
The Good Girl '02 ▸
Happily Ever After '04
Haunted Highway '05
Head On '04
The Healer '02
Heart '99
The Heart of Me '02
Heart of Stone '01
Heights '04

▸ = rated three bones or higher

Hitched '01
Hollywoodland '06
I Take This Woman '40
I Think I Love My Wife '07
The Ice Storm '97 ▸
In My Country '04
In the Mood for Love '00
Incendiary '08
The Innocent '76
Jarhead '05
Just Another Love Story '08
Just Before Nightfall '71
The Kids Are All Right '10
The Killer Must Kill Again '75
La Femme Infidele '69 ▸
La Mujer de Mi Hermano '06
Lady Chatterley '06 ▸
Lansdown '01
Lantana '01 ▸
Le Divorce '03
Leo '02
Lies & Alibis '06
Little Chenier: A Cajun Story '06
Little Children '06 ▸
Lord of War '05 ▸
Lovely & Amazing '02 ▸
Loving '70
Lymelife '08
The Man Who Wasn't There '01 ▸
Match Point '05 ▸
Meet Bill '07
Melinda and Melinda '05
Melo '86
The Monkey's Mask '00
Motives '03
My Life Without Me '03
Nathalie '03
Never Forever '07
Night Life in Reno '31
Nina Takes a Lover '94
No Money Down '97
No Other Woman '33
Nora Prentiss '47
Obsession '49
One Hour Photo '02 ▸
100 Mile Rule '02
The Other Man '08
The Other Side of the Bed '03
Out of Time '03
The Painted Veil '06
Petulia '68 ▸
Pleasure '31
Possession '02
Rain '01
The Reckoning '03 ▸
Reconstruction '03
Resistance '03
Revolutionary Road '08
Romance & Cigarettes '05
Romulus, My Father '07 ▸
Say Nothing '01
The Scarlet Letter '34
The Scarlet Letter '73 ▸
The Scarlet Letter '79 ▸
The Scarlet Letter '95
Second Skin '99
The Sentinel '06
A Serious Man '09 ▸
The Shooting Party '85 ▸
Sidewalks of New York '01
Signs & Wonders '00
Six Days, Six Nights '94
Sleep Easy, Hutch Rimes '00
Sleuth '07
Smart Woman '31
Snow Angels '07 ▸
Someone Behind the Door '71
Sordid Lives '00
Steam: A Turkish Bath '96 ▸
Suckerfish '99
Summer of '04 '06
A Summer Place '59
Summer Storm '44
Sylvia '03
The Taste of Others '00 ▸
Tempted '01
Therese Raquin '80
Thirst '09 ▸
Three Blondes in His Life '61
Three Monkeys '08
3-Way '04
Tick Tock '00 ▸
Time Regained '99
Town and Country '01
Tristan & Isolde '06
The Two Jakes '90
Undertow '30
Undertow '10
Une Femme Mariee '64
Unfaithful '02 ▸
Unfaithfully Yours '48 ▸
Unfaithfully Yours '84
The Unfaithfuls '60
Up the Ladder '25
The Valet '06
The Voice of Merrill '52
Wah-Wah '05
Waitress '07 ▸
Waking Up in Reno '02
The Walker '07
We Don't Live Here Anymore '04
The Witnesses '07
The Women '08
Y Tu Mama Tambien '01
Yes '04
Young Adam '03 ▸

Adventure Drama

see also ***Action-Adventure; Boom!; Drama***

Abandon Ship '57
Ace of Aces '33
Act of Piracy '89
Action in the North Atlantic '43
The Admirable Crichton '57
The Adventures of Frontier Fremont '75
The Adventures of Huck Finn '93 ▸
The Adventures of Huckleberry Finn '39 ▸
The Adventures of Huckleberry Finn '78
The Adventures of Milo & Otis '89 ▸
The Adventures of the Wilderness Family '76
The Adventures of Tom Sawyer '38 ▸
Air Force '43 ▸
Air Force One '97 ▸
Alaska '96
Alexander Nevsky '38 ▸
Ali Baba and the Forty Thieves '43
All the Rivers Run '84
Allan Quatermain and the Lost City of Gold '86
Alligator Alley '72
Aloha, Bobby and Rose '74
The Amazing Panda Adventure '95
Amazon '90
The Amazons '84
America '24
American Empire '42
American Roulette '88
The American Scream '88
American Tiger '89
And I Alone Survived '78
Angels of the City '89
Anzacs: The War Down Under '85 ▸
Apocalypse Now '79 ▸
Apocalypto '06 ▸
Apollo 13 '95 ▸
Appointment with Crime '45
The Arab Conspiracy '76
Archer's Adventure '85
Arctic Blue '93
Arizona Heat '87
Around the World in 80 Days '56 ▸
Around the World in 80 Days '89
The Ascent '94
Assassination '87
The Aviator '85
Azumi '03 ▸
Back in the USSR '92
Backdraft '91
Backlash '86
Bang Rajan '00 ▸
Barbary Coast '35 ▸
The Baron '88
Bataan '43
Battle Hell '56
The Battle of El Alamein '68
Battle of the Eagles '79
The Battle of the Japan Sea '70
Battleforce '78
Bear Island '80
Beau Geste '39 ▸
The Beautiful Country '04
Beneath the 12-Mile Reef '53
Benji: Off the Leash! '04
Benji the Hunted '87
Beowulf '07 ▸
Beowulf & Grendel '06
The Berlin Conspiracy '91
Between Heaven and Hell '56 ▸
Beyond Rangoon '95
Big Bad Mama '74
The Big Push '75
The Big Scam '79
The Big Turnaround '88
Bigfoot: The Unforgettable Encounter '94
Billy Budd '62 ▸
Black Arrow '48 ▸
The Black Arrow '84
Black Bikers from Hell '70
Black Moon Rising '86
Blackout '78
Blood and Sand '41 ▸
Blood Debts '83
Blood Diamond '06
Bloom '03
Blowing Wild '54
Blown Away '94
The Blue and the Gray '82
Blue Fin '78
The Blue Lamp '49 ▸
Blue Thunder '83
The Bodyguard from Beijing '94
Bomb at 10:10 '67
Bombardier '43
Border Blues '03
Born Wild '95
Botany Bay '53
The Bounty '84
The Bourne Supremacy '04 ▸
Breakdown '96 ▸
The Breed '01
Brighty of the Grand Canyon '67
Brotherhood of Death '76
A Bullet Is Waiting '54
Burke & Wills '85
The Butterfly '02 ▸
By Way of the Stars '92
Cadence '89
California Gold Rush '81
Call of the Wild '72
Camel Boy '84
Casablanca Express '89
The Castilian '63
Casualties of War '89 ▸
The Cat '66
Catwoman '04
Cellular '04
Chain Reaction '80
Chain Reaction '96
Chains of Gold '92
The Challenge '38 ▸
Challenge of a Lifetime '85
The Charge of the Light Brigade '36 ▸
The Children of Huang Shi '08
Children of the Wild '37
China Gate '57 ▸
Chrome Soldiers '92
Clarence, the Cross-eyed Lion '65 ▸
Claws '77
Clear and Present Danger '94
The Climb '87
The Coast Patrol '25
Code Name: Emerald '85
Cold Heat '90
Cold Justice '89
Command Decision '48
Commando Attack '67
Con Air '97 ▸
Conspiracy Theory '97 ▸
Contagious '96
Coogan's Bluff '68 ▸
The Cop & the Girl '86
Cop-Out '91
The Corruptor '99 ▸
Corsair '31
The Count of Monte Cristo '12
The Count of Monte Cristo '34 ▸
The Count of Monte Cristo '74
The Count of Monte Cristo '99
The Count of Monte Cristo '02
Courage Mountain '89
Courage of Black Beauty '57
Courage of Rin Tin Tin '57
Crimebusters '79
Crimson Romance '34
Crimson Tide '95 ▸
Dam Busters '55 ▸
Danger Beneath the Sea '02
Dangerous Ground '96
Dangerous Moonlight '41 ▸
Dangerous Passage '44
Daring Game '68
Dark Before Dawn '89
Dark Mountain '44
Dark Tide '93
The Darkside '87
The Dawson Patrol '78
The Day Will Dawn '42 ▸
Days of Thunder '90
Deadlock '91
Deadlock 2 '94
Deadly Sanctuary '68
Death in the Garden '56
The Death Merchant '91
Death Stalk '74
The Deceivers '88
Deliverance '72 ▸
Desert Warrior '88
Destination Tokyo '43
Dick Tracy '90 ▸
Dick Turpin '25
Die Hard '88 ▸
Die Hard 2: Die Harder '90 ▸
Die Hard: With a Vengeance '95
A Different Loyalty '04 ▸
Dinosaur Island '93
Diplomatic Immunity '91
Dive Bomber '41 ▸
Doomsdayer '99
Down to the Sea in Ships '22
Dragon Storm '04
Dragonfly Squadron '54
Duma '05 ▸
Dust '85 ▸
Each Dawn I Die '39
The Eagle Has Landed '77 ▸
East of Borneo '31
Edge of Honor '91
Eight Below '06
84 Charlie MoPic '89 ▸
The Elusive Pimpernel '50
The Emerald Forest '85 ▸
Enchanted Island '58
Enemy Below '57 ▸
Enemy of the State '98
The Enforcer '51
Eraser '96
Escape to Witch Mountain '75 ▸
Evel Knievel '72
Executive Decision '96
The Expendables '89
The Expendables '10
Eye of the Wolf '95
Fangs of the Wild '54
Fantastic Seven '79
Far from Home: The Adventures of Yellow Dog '94
A Far Off Place '93
Farewell to the King '89
The Fencing Master '92
Ferry to Hong Kong '59
55 Days at Peking '63 ▸
The Fighting Prince of Donegal '66
Fire Alarm '32
Fire in the Night '85
Fireball 500 '66
Firepower '79
Flame of Araby '51
Flame Over India '60 ▸
The Flash '90
Flight of the Grey Wolf '76
Flipper '63 ▸
Flying Leathernecks '51 ▸
Flying Tigers '42
Follow Me '69
For Whom the Bell Tolls '43 ▸
Fort Saganne '84
Fortunes of War '94
Forty Thousand Horsemen '41
The Four Feathers '39 ▸
The Four Feathers '78
F.P. 1 '33
F.P. 1 Doesn't Answer '33
Free Grass '69
Free Willy '93
Free Willy 2: The Adventure Home '95
Free Willy 3: The Rescue '97
Freelance '71
The Fugitive '93 ▸
Fugitive Champion '99
Full Eclipse '93
Fury to Freedom: The Life Story of Raul Ries '85
Future Zone '90
Game for Vultures '86
The Gaucho '27 ▸
The Ghost and the Darkness '96
Glory & Honor '98
God's Country '46
The Golden Compass '07
Goldrush: A Real Life Alaskan Adventure '98
Goliath Awaits '81
Gone in 60 Seconds '74
Great Adventure '75
The Great Elephant Escape '95
The Great Escape '63 ▸
The Great Escape 2: The Untold Story '88
The Great Locomotive Chase '56
The Great Train Robbery '79 ▸
The Green Glove '52
Greystoke: The Legend of Tarzan, Lord of the Apes '84
Grizzly Mountain '97
Guadalcanal Diary '43
The Guardian '00
Gun Cargo '49
Gunblast '74
Gunga Din '39 ▸
The Gunrunner '84
Hackers '95
The Halls of Montezuma '50
Hamlet '90 ▸
Hangfire '91
Hard Knocks '80
Harley '90
Harry Potter and the Goblet of Fire '05 ▸
Harry Potter and the Prisoner of Azkaban '04
Hawk and Castile '67
The Heartbreak Kid '07
Hell Commandos '69
Hell in the Pacific '69 ▸
Hell River '75
Hell Squad '58
Hell Squad '85
Hell to Eternity '60
Hellcats of the Navy '57
Hellfighters '68
Hell's Angels '30 ▸
Hell's Brigade: The Final Assault '80
Here Come the Littles: The Movie '85
The Heroes of Desert Storm '91
Heroes Three '84
Hidalgo '04
Himalaya '99 ▸
Himatsuri '85 ▸
Hired to Kill '73
Hiroshima: Out of the Ashes '90 ▸
Hit! '73
Homeward Bound: The Incredible Journey '93 ▸
Horatio Hornblower '99 ▸
Horatio Hornblower: The Adventure Continues '01 ▸
Hostile Waters '97
Huck and the King of Hearts '93
The Hunt for Red October '90 ▸
Hurricane Smith '92
Hustler Squad '76
Immortal Sergeant '43
In Enemy Hands '04
In Harm's Way '65
In Love and War '91
In Search of a Golden Sky '84
In the Name of the King: A Dungeon Siege Tale '08
In Which We Serve '43 ▸
The Indian Tomb '59 ▸
Indiana Jones and the Kingdom of the Crystal Skull '08
Indiana Jones and the Last Crusade '89 ▸
Indiana Jones and the Temple of Doom '84 ▸
Inferno in Paradise '88
Into Thin Air: Death on Everest '97
The Intruder '04 ▸
The Iron Mask '29
Iron Will '93
Island in the Sky '53 ▸
Island of the Blue Dolphins '64
Island Trader '71
Islands '87
Isle of Forgotten Sins '43
Istanbul '90
It Rained All Night the Day I Left '78
Jack London's The Call of the Wild '97
JAG '95
Jaguar '56
Jamaica Inn '39
Jamaica Inn '82
Jason and the Argonauts '00
Jaws of Justice '33
Jenny's War '85
Jet Pilot '57
Joey '98
Johnny Mnemonic '95
The Journey of Natty Gann '85 ▸
Journey to the Center of the Earth '88
Joy Ride to Nowhere '78
Juggernaut '74 ▸
Jungle '52
Jungle Goddess '49
Jurassic Park '93 ▸
Jurassic Park 3 '01
Kamikaze '89 '83 ▸
The Karate Kid '84 ▸
The Karate Kid: Part 2 '86
The Karate Kid: Part 3 '89
Kashmiri Run '69
Kavik the Wolf Dog '80
Keeper of the City '92
The Keeper: The Legend of Omar Khayyam '05
Keeping Track '86
Kid Colter '85
Kidnapped '48
Kidnapped '60
Kidnapped '05 ▸
The Killer '90 ▸
The Killer Elite '75
Killer Instinct '92
King Arthur '04
King of New York '90 ▸
King Solomon's Mines '50 ▸
King Solomon's Mines '85
King Solomon's Treasure '76
Kingfisher Caper '76
Kings of the Sun '63
Kiss and Kill '68
Klondike Fever '79
Knives of the Avenger '65
Kojiro '67 ▸
K2: The Ultimate High '92
La Guerre Est Finie '66 ▸
Lady Avenger '89
Lady Cocoa '75
Landslide '92
Lassie: Adventures of Neeka '68
Lassie, Come Home '43

▸ = rated three bones or higher

Lassie: Well of Love '70
Lassiter '84
The Last Hunter '80
Last Man Standing '87
The Last of the Finest '90
The Last of the Mohicans '32
The Last of the Mohicans '36
The Last of the Mohicans '92 ▸
The Last Place on Earth '85
The Last Riders '90
The Last Season '87
Legend of Billie Jean '85
The Legend of Cryin' Ryan '98
The Legend of Johnny Lingo '03
Legend of Lobo '62
The Legend of Sea Wolf '75
The Legend of the Sea Wolf '58
The Legend of Wolf Mountain '92
Lethal Pursuit '88
Lethal Weapon 2 '89 ▸
Liane, Jungle Goddess '56
Life & Times of Grizzly Adams '74
The Lion Man '36
Lion of the Desert '81 ▸
The Live Wire '34
Loaded Guns '75
Lockdown '90
Lost '83
Lost '86
The Lost World: Jurassic Park 2 '97
Lost Zeppelin '29
Macao '52 ▸
The Mad Bomber '72
Made for Love '26
Magnificent Adventurer '63
The Man from Beyond '22
The Man in the Iron Mask '39 ▸
The Man in the Iron Mask '97
The Man in the Iron Mask '98 ▸
Man of Legend '71
Manhunt for Claude Dallas '86
The Mask of Zorro '98 ▸
Massacre in Dinosaur Valley '85
The Master of Ballantrae '53
The McConnell Story '55
Memphis Belle '90 ▸
Men in War '57
Men of Steel '77
Merlin and the Sword '85
Miami Vice '84
Midnight Crossing '87
Midway '76
Milo & Otis '89
MirrorMask '05
Ms. 45 '81 ▸
Mission Phantom '79
Mr. Kingstreet's War '71
Moby Dick '56 ▸
Moby Dick '98
Money Movers '78
Money Train '95
The Moon-Spinners '64
Moran of the Lady Letty '22
Mountain Family Robinson '79
Mountain of the Cannibal God '79
Moving Target '89
Murder Without Motive '92
The Mutiny of the Elsinore '39
Mutiny on the Blackhawk '39
My Dog Shep '46
Naked Jungle '54 ▸
The Navy Comes Through '42
Ned Kelly '03
The Negotiator '98
Night Crossing '81
The Night Train to Kathmandu '88
Nightstick '87
No Greater Love '43
No More Women '34
No Time to Die '84
Noon Sunday '75
Norseman '78
The North Star '43 ▸
Northern Pursuit '43
Northwest Passage '40 ▸
Number One with a Bullet '87
Objective, Burma! '45 ▸
Obsessed '88
Oceans of Fire '86
The Odyssey '97
Omega Syndrome '87
On Wings of Eagles '86
One Armed Executioner '80
One Man Force '89
One Minute to Zero '52
One of Our Aircraft Is Missing '41 ▸
One That Got Away '57 ▸
Operation Cross Eagles '69
Operation Haylift '50
Operation Julie '85
Operation 'Nam '85
Operation Thunderbolt '77
Operation Warzone '89
Opposing Force '87
Oubliette '14
Outbreak '94 ▸
Outlaw Blues '77
Outlaw Force '87
The Package '89
Paco '75
Palais Royale '88
Palindromes '04 ▸
Papillon '73 ▸
Party Line '88
Passenger 57 '92
Passion '92
Pathfinder '87 ▸
The Patriot '86
Patriot Games '92 ▸
Payoff '91
The Peacemaker '97
Penitentiary '79
Penitentiary 2 '82
Penitentiary 3 '87
The Perils of Gwendoline '84
Permission To Kill '75
The Phantom '96
Pharaoh '66
Pirates of the High Seas '50
Place in Hell '69
Platoon '86 ▸
Platoon Leader '87
Plunder Road '57
Plunge Into Darkness '77
Policewomen '73
Pork Chop Hill '59 ▸
Portrait of a Hitman '77
Pray for the Wildcats '74
The Presidio '88
Prime Target '91
Prince Brat and the Whipping Boy '95 ▸
Prisoner in the Middle '74
Private Investigations '87
PT 109 '63
Pursuit of the Graf Spee '57
Queen's Messenger II '01
Radio Patrol '37
Raid on Entebbe '77 ▸
Raid on Rommel '71
Raiders of the Lost Ark '81 ▸
Rainbow Warrior '94
Rambo '08
Ran '85 ▸
Raw Courage '84
The Real Glory '39 ▸
Reap the Wild Wind '42
Red Barry '38
Red Flag: The Ultimate Game '81
Remedy '05
Renegades '89
The Replacement Killers '98
Report to the Commissioner '74 ▸
The Rescue '88
Retreat, Hell! '52
Revelation '00
Revenge '90
Riot in Cell Block 11 '54 ▸
The River Pirates '88
The River Wild '94
Robbery '67
Robbery '85
Robin Hood: Prince of Thieves '91
RoboCop '87 ▸
Ronin '98
Rudyard Kipling's The Jungle Book '94
Runaway Train '85 ▸
Running Free '00
Running out of Time '99 ▸
The Saint '97
The St. Valentine's Day Massacre '67
San Demetrio, London '47
The Sand Pebbles '66 ▸
Sands of Iwo Jima '49 ▸
Sardinia Kidnapped '75
Savage Hunger '84
Savage Justice '88
Savage Sam '63
Savage Streets '83
Scaramouche '52 ▸
The Scarlet Car '17
Scarlet Spear '54
Scorchy '76
Scott of the Antarctic '48
Sea Chase '55
Sea Devils '31
Sea Devils '53
Sea Gypsies '78
The Sea Hawk '40 ▸
The Sea Shall Not Have Them '55
Sea Wolves '81
Search and Destroy '81
Secret of Stamboul '36
Secret Weapon '90
Self-Defense '83
Sell Out '76
Sergeant York '41 ▸
Seven Alone '75
Sex Crimes '92
The Shadow '94
Shadow Force '92
Shame '87
Shame '92
Shark! '68
She '35
She Came to the Valley '77
Shell Shock '63
Shogun Assassin '80
Shooting Stars '85
Shout at the Devil '76
The Siege '98
The Siege of Firebase Gloria '89
The Silent Enemy '58
Silent Raiders '54
Silk '86
The Silver Stallion: King of the Wild Brumbies '93
Sinai Commandos '68
The Sinister Urge '60
Sink the Bismarck '60 ▸
Sins of Rome '54
Six Pack '82
Sky Riders '76
Slow Moves '84
Smugglers '75
The Sniper '78
Sniper '92
Sniper 2 '02
Sniper 3 '04
Sno-Line '85
The Snow Walker '03
Sodom and Gomorrah '62
Soldier of Fortune '55
Sonny Boy '87
Sorcerer '77
Soul Vengeance '75
Souls at Sea '37
South of Hell Mountain '70
Spawn of the North '38
Special Forces '68
The Specialist '94
Speed '94 ▸
Spider-Man 2 '04 ▸
Spin '04
Spirit of the Eagle '90
The Spring '89
Squanto: A Warrior's Tale '94 ▸
Stanley and Livingstone '39 ▸
Star Trek: Insurrection '98
The Starfighters '63
Steamboy '05
The Steel Claw '61
The Steel Helmet '51 ▸
Steele Justice '87
Steele's Law '91
The Sting '73 ▸
The Stone Killer '73
Strange Days '95 ▸
Street Crimes '92
Street War '76
Streets of Fire '84
Strike Force '75
Striker '88
Striker's Mountain '87
Sub Down '97
Submarine Seahawk '59
Sudden Death '95
Sundown '41
Sunset Grill '92
Sunset Heat '92
Surabaya Conspiracy '75
Surfacing '84
Survival Run '80
The Swiss Family Robinson '60 ▸
Switchback '97
The Taking of Pelham One Two Three '74 ▸
Tank '83
Taps '81
Target of Opportunity '04
The Ten Million Dollar Getaway '91
10,000 B.C. '08
Terminal Error '02
Thelma & Louise '91 ▸
They Were Expendable '45 ▸
Thirty-Six Hours of Hell '77
Those Calloways '65
The 317th Platoon '65 ▸
The Three Musketeers '16
The Three Musketeers '21 ▸
Three the Hard Way '74
Throw Down '00
Thunder Alley '67
Thunderbirds '04
Thunderground '89
Tides of War '90
Tiger Fangs '43
A Tiger Walks '64
Tim Tyler's Luck '37
Tom Sawyer '73
Top Gun '86
Tour of Duty '87
Toy Soldiers '91
The Transporter '02
Tribulation '00
Triple Cross '67 ▸
Trouble in Paradise '88
True Blood '89
True Heart '97
Truth or Die '86
Turnaround '87
2012 '09
Twisted Justice '89
Two Brothers '04
Two Years before the Mast '46
Unconquered '47
Underworld '27 ▸
U.S. Marshals '98
U.S. Seals '98
Up Periscope '59
Valley of Wanted Men '35
The Vector File '03
Violent Breed '83
Von Ryan's Express '65 ▸
Wake Island '42 ▸
A Walk in the Sun '46 ▸
Walking Back '26
A Waltz Through the Hills '88
The War Boy '85
Warkill '65
The Warrior '81
Warriors '02
Warriors of Heaven and Earth '03
We Dive at Dawn '43 ▸
Weekend War '88
What a Way to Die '70
Wheel of Fortune '41
When the Last Sword is Drawn '02 ▸
Where the Spirit Lives '89
White Fire '53
White Fury '90
White Hot '88
White Squall '96
The White Tower '50 ▸
White Wolves 2: Legend of the Wild '94
The Wicked Lady '83
The Wild Pair '87
Wild Riders '71
Wild Thing '87
A Wing and a Prayer '44 ▸
Winning '69 ▸
Wooden Horse '50 ▸
The World in His Arms '52
World War III '86
The Year of Living Dangerously '82 ▸
Yellowneck '55
Young & Free '78
A Young Connecticut Yankee in King Arthur's Court '95
Young Warlord '75
Young Warriors '83
Zafarinas '94
Zeppelin '71
Zulu '64
Zulu Dawn '79 ▸

Advertising

see also Front Page; Mass Media

Advertising Rules! '01
The Agency '81
Beauty School '93
Beer '85
Bliss '85 ▸
Bounce '00
Carpool Guy '05
C.O.D. '83
Crazy People '90
Dear Me: A Blogger's Tale '08
Derailed '05
DROP Squad '94
Eros '04
A Fool and His Money '88
The Girl Can't Help It '56
Giving It Up '99
Her Husband's Affairs '47
The Horse in the Gray Flannel Suit '68
How to Get Ahead in Advertising '89 ▸
How to Lose a Guy in 10 Days '03
The Hucksters '47 ▸
I Married a Woman '56
Image of Passion '86
In Good Company '04 ▸
The Joneses '10
Kids in the Hall: Brain Candy '96
Kramer vs. Kramer '79 ▸
Lost in America '85 ▸
Lover Come Back '61
Loving '70
The Man in the Gray Flannel Suit '56
Mr. Blandings Builds His Dream House '48 ▸
Mr. Mom '83 ▸
Mr. Write '92
No Marriage Ties '33
Nothing in Common '86
Nothing to Lose '96
One Night Stand '97 ▸
Perfect Stranger '07
Picture Perfect '96
Pray for the Wildcats '74
Pretty Baby '50
Pursuit of Happiness '01
Putney Swope '69 ▸
Renaissance Man '94
Revolution 9 '01
Santa Claus: The Movie '85
Son of the Mask '05
Surviving Christmas '04
Sweet November '01
Ten Speed '76
Thanks for Everything '38
Think Dirty '70
The Thrill of It All! '63
Thunder in the City '37 ▸
Transformers: The Movie '86
Waikiki Wedding '37 ▸
What Women Want '00
White Mile '94
Will Success Spoil Rock Hunter? '57

Africa

see also Apartheid

Abdulla the Great '56
Ace Ventura: When Nature Calls '95
The Adventurers '51
Africa Screams '49
An African Dream '90
African Journey '89
The African Queen '51 ▸
African Rage '78
The Air Up There '94
Albino '76
Algiers '38 ▸
Allan Quatermain and the Lost City of Gold '86
Amin: The Rise and Fall '82
Amistad '97 ▸
And Now Ladies and Gentlemen '02
The Ascent '94
Babel '06 ▸
Bamako '06
Beyond Borders '03
Black Force '75
Black Hawk Down '01 ▸
Black Jesus '68
Black Terrorist '85
Blood Diamond '06
Blood Monkey '07
Boesman & Lena '00
Bopha! '93 ▸
Born Wild '95
Borom Sarret '66 ▸
The Boys of Baraka '05
The Bride & the Beast '58
The Bushbaby '70
Call Me Bwana '63
Cape of Good Hope '04
Changing Times '04
Cheetah '89
Chocolat '88 ▸
City of Blood '88
The Claw '27
Cobra Verde '88
The Color of Freedom '07
Coming to America '88 ▸
Congo '95
The Constant Gardener '05 ▸
Curious George '06
Curse 3: Blood Sacrifice '90
Dangerous Ground '96
Darfur Now '07
Dark of the Sun '68
Darkest Africa '36
Darwin's Nightmare '04 ▸
The Desert Fox '51 ▸
Desert Nights '29
The Devil Came on Horseback '07
Dingaka '65
Disgrace '08
District 9 '09 ▸
The Dogs of War '81
Dominion: Prequel to the Exorcist '05
Drums of Africa '63
A Dry White Season '89 ▸
Duma '05 ▸
East of Kilimanjaro '57
The Egyptian '54
An Elephant Called Slowly '69
Endgame '09
Ernest Goes to Africa '97
Eyes of a Witness '94
Faces of Women '85
A Far Off Place '93
The Fighting Rats of Tobruk '44
Firefall '94
Five Weeks in a Balloon '62
The Flame Trees of Thika '81 ▸
Fort Saganne '84
The Four Feathers '02
Friends '95
Ganja and Hess '73
The Garden of Allah '36 ▸
George of the Jungle '97 ▸
The Ghost and the Darkness '96
God Grew Tired of Us '06 ▸
The Gods Must Be Crazy '84 ▸
The Gods Must Be Crazy 2 '89
Golden Dawn '30
The Golden Salamander '51
A Good Man in Africa '94
Gorillas in the Mist '88 ▸
The Great Elephant Escape '95
Greystoke: The Legend of Tarzan, Lord of the Apes '84
Guns at Batasi '64
Half-Caste '04

▸ *= rated three bones or higher*

African America

see also ***New Black Cinema***

Our Family Wedding '10
Our Song '01 ▶
Out of Sync '95
Paid in Full '02
Panther '95
Parallel Sons '95
Paris Is Burning '91 ▶
Passing Glory '99 ▶
Pastime '91 ▶
A Patch of Blue '65
Paul Robeson '77
Penitentiary '79
The Perfect Holiday '07
Perfume '91
Personals '00
Phat Beach '96
Phat Girlz '06
The Piano Lesson '94 ▶
Pinky '49 ▶
Poetic Justice '93
Pootie Tang '01
The Preacher's Wife '96
Preaching to the Choir '05
Precious: Based on the Novel by Sapphire '09 ▶
Pride '07
The Princess and the Frog '09 ▶
The Proud Family Movie '05
Purlie Victorious '63
Purple Rain '84
The Pursuit of Happyness '06
Putney Swope '69 ▶
Quartier Mozart '92
Quiet Fire '91
Race '99
Race to Freedom: The Story of the Underground Railroad '94
Radio '03
A Rage in Harlem '91 ▶
A Raisin in the Sun '61 ▶
A Raisin in the Sun '08
Raising the Heights '97
Rappin' '85
The Reading Room '05
Rebound: The Legend of Earl "The Goat" Manigault '96
The Red Sneakers '01
Return of Superfly '90
Rhapsody '01
Ricochet '91 ▶
Ride '98
The River Niger '76
Rock the Paint '05
Rockwell: A Legend of the Wild West '93
Roll Bounce '05 ▶
Roll of Thunder, Hear My Cry '78
Romeo Must Die '00
Roots '77 ▶
Roots: The Gift '88
Roots: The Next Generation '79 ▶
The Rosa Parks Story '02
Rosewood '96 ▶
Ruby Bridges '98
Rude '96
The Salon '05
Santa and Pete '99
Saving God '08
Scar of Shame '27
School Daze '88 ▶
The Secret Life of Bees '08 ▶
Selma, Lord, Selma '99
Separate but Equal '91 ▶
Sepia Cinderella '47
Sergeant Rutledge '60 ▶
Set It Off '96
Seventeen Again '00
The '70s '00
Shadows '60 ▶
Shaft '71 ▶
Shaft '00 ▶
Shaft's Big Score '72
Shanty Tramp '67
She Hate Me '04
Sheba, Baby '75
She's Gotta Have It '86 ▶
The Show '95
The Simple Life of Noah Dearborn '99
A Simple Promise '07
Six Degrees of Separation '93
The '60s '99
Slam '98
Small Time '91
Snow Dogs '02
A Soldier's Story '84 ▶
Something New '06
Song of Freedom '36
Sophisticated Gents '81 ▶
Soul Food '97
Soul Men '08
Soul of the Game '96 ▶
Soul Plane '04
Soul Survivor '95
Soul Vengeance '75
Sounder '72 ▶
South Central '92
Spark '98
Sparkle '76
Sprung '96
Stomp the Yard '07
Straight out of Brooklyn '91
Strange Fruit '04
Strange Justice: The Clarence Thomas and Anita Hill Story '99
A Stranger in the Kingdom '98
Strapped '93
Sudie & Simpson '90 ▶
Sugar Hill '94
Summer's End '99
Sun Ra & His Intergalactic Solar Arkestra: Space Is the Place '74
Superfly '72
Superfly T.N.T. '73
Sweet Love, Bitter '67
Sweet Sweetback's Baadasssss Song '71 ▶
Tales from the Hood '95
Talk to Me '07
Tap '89
Tar '97
The Temptations '98
The Tenants '06
They Call Me Sirr '00
Thicker than Water '99
A Thin Line Between Love and Hate '96
30 Years to Life '01
This Christmas '07
Three Can Play That Game '07
Three Strikes '00
Three the Hard Way '74
The Tiger Woods Story '98
A Time to Kill '96 ▶
To Sir, with Love '67
To Sleep with Anger '90 ▶
Tougher Than Leather '88
Trippin' '99
Truck Turner '74
Turn It Up '00
The Tuskegee Airmen '95 ▶
Two Can Play That Game '01
Tyler Perry's Meet the Browns '08
Tyler Perry's Why Did I Get Married? '07
Tyler Perry's Why Did I Get Married Too '10
Tyson '95
Uncle Tom's Cabin '14
Uncle Tom's Cabin '69
Uncle Tom's Cabin '87
Undercover Brother '02
Undisputed '02
The Untold Story of Emmett Louis Till '05 ▶
Up Against the Eight Ball '04
Uptown Angel '90
Vicky Cristina Barcelona '08
Waist Deep '06
Waiting to Exhale '95 ▶
The Walking Dead '94
The Wash '01
Watermelon Man '70
The Watermelon Woman '97
Way Down South '39
Welcome Home Roscoe Jenkins '08
What About Your Friends: Weekend Getaway '02
What Up? '08
What's Love Got to Do with It? '93
When We Were Kings '96 ▶
White Chicks '04
White Dog '82
White Man's Burden '95
White Men Can't Jump '92
Whitewash: The Clarence Brandley Story '02
Who Made the Potatoe Salad? '05
Who's Your Caddy? '07
The Wiz '78
Woman, Thou Art Loosed '04
The Women of Brewster Place '89 ▶
The Wood '99
Words by Heart '84
You Got Served '04
You Must Remember This '92
You So Crazy '94
Zebrahead '92 ▶
Zooman '95 ▶
Zora Is My Name! '90

AIDS

***see also** Disease of the Week*

Alive and Kicking '96
All About My Mother '99 ▶
Amazing Grace '92
And the Band Played On '93 ▶
Angels in America '03 ▶
As Is '85
Because of You '95
Before Night Falls '00 ▶
Behind the Red Door '02
Blue '93
Boys on the Side '94
Close My Eyes '91
Close to Leo '02
Common Threads: Stories from the Quilt '89
Conspiracy of Silence '03
The Constant Gardener '05 ▶
The Cure '95
Darwin's Nightmare '04 ▶
An Early Frost '85 ▶
The Event '03
Forrest Gump '94 ▶
Gia '98
Green Plaid Shirt '96
Heaven's a Drag '94
A Home at the End of the World '04
The Hours '02 ▶
In the Gloaming '97 ▶
Intimate Contact '87 ▶
It's My Party '95
Jeanne and the Perfect Guy '98
Jeffrey '95
Joey Breaker '93 ▶
Kids '95
Les Nuits Fauves '92 ▶
Life '95
Life Support '07 ▶
Loggerheads '05 ▶
Longtime Companion '90 ▶
Love Thy Neighbor '02
Love! Valour! Compassion! '96
The Man I Love '97
Men in Love '90
A Mother's Prayer '95
My Own Country '98
No One Sleeps '01
One Night Stand '97 ▶
Our Sons '91
Parting Glances '86 ▶
The Perfect Son '00
Peter's Friends '92
Philadelphia '93 ▶
A Place for Annie '94
Playing by Heart '98
Postcards from America '95
Remembering the Cosmos Flower '99
Rent '05
A River Made to Drown In '97
Sex Positive '09
Sweet Jane '98
This Girl's Life '03
The Trip '02
The 24th Day '04
The Velocity of Gary '98
Via Appia '92
The Visit '00 ▶
The Witnesses '07
A Year Without Love '05
Zero Patience '94

Air Disasters

***see also** Airborne; Disaster Flicks; Sea Disasters*

Air Force One '97 ▶
Airport '70 ▶
Airport '75 '75
Airport '77 '77
Alaska '96
Alive '93
Apollo 13 '95 ▶
The Assassination of Richard Nixon '05
Bounce '00
Broken Arrow '95
The Buddy Holly Story '78 ▶
Cast Away '00 ▶
Con Air '97 ▶
The Concorde: Airport '79 '79
The Crash of Flight 401 '78
Crocodile 2: Death Swamp '01
Die Hard 2: Die Harder '90 ▶
Escape from Wildcat Canyon '99
Executive Decision '96
Extreme Limits '01
Fearless '93 ▶
Fire and Rain '89
Flight of the Living Dead: Outbreak on a Plane '07
Flight of the Phoenix '04
Flight to Fury '66
The Forgotten '04
Get Shorty '95 ▶
The Great Plane Robbery '40
Ground Control '98
Heaven's Prisoners '95
Hero '92 ▶
The High and the Mighty '54 ▶
The Hindenburg '75
Into the Fire '05
Island in the Sky '53 ▶
Jet Over the Atlantic '59
Jurassic Park 3 '01
Killing Moon '00
Madam Satan '30
Mayday at 40,000 Feet '76
Mercy Mission '93
The Note '07
Nowhere to Land '00
Operation Intercept '95
Ordeal in the Arctic '93
Pandora's Clock '96
Panic in the Skies '96
Passengers '08
The Pilot's Wife '01
Restless Spirits '99
Seven Were Saved '47
Snakes on a Plane '06
Sole Survivor '84
Soul Plane '04
Submerged '00
Subterfuge '98
Survivor '80
Tailspin: Behind the Korean Airline Tragedy '89
A Thousand Heroes '92
The Ticket '97
Tragedy of Flight 103: The Inside Story '91 ▶
Turbulence '96
Turbulence 2: Fear of Flying '99
Turbulence 3: Heavy Metal '00
United 93 '06 ▶
U.S. Marshals '98
We Are Marshall '06
With a Song in My Heart '52 ▶
Zero Hour! '57

Airborne

***see also** Air Disasters*

Above and Beyond '53 ▶
Ace Drummond '36
Ace of Aces '33
Aces: Iron Eagle 3 '92
Active Stealth '99
Adventures of Smilin' Jack '43
Afterburn '92 ▶
Air America '90
Air Force '43 ▶
Air Force One '97 ▶
Air Hawk '84
Air Rage '01
Airborne '98
Airboss '97
Airplane! '80 ▶
Airplane 2: The Sequel '82
Airport '70 ▶
Airport '75 '75
Airport '77 '77
Always '89
Amelia '09
Amelia Earhart: The Final Flight '94
And I Alone Survived '78
Angels One Five '54
Attack Squadron '63
The Aviator '85
Bail Out at 43,000 '57
The Bamboo Blonde '46
Battle of Britain '69
Battle of the Eagles '79
Beyond the Time Barrier '60
Biggles '85
Birds of Prey '72
Black Box Affair '66
Black Thunder '98
The Blue Max '66
Blue Thunder '83
Blue Tornado '90
Boeing Boeing '65
Bombardier '43
Bombers B-52 '57
Brewster McCloud '70 ▶
Bulldog Drummond at Bay '37
Bulletproof '96
Bush Pilot '47
By Dawn's Early Light '89
Captains of the Clouds '42
Ceiling Zero '35 ▶
Chain Lightning '50
Christopher Strong '33
Con Air '97 ▶
The Concorde: Airport '79 '79
The Crash of Flight 401 '78
Crimson Romance '34
The Crowded Sky '60
Danger in the Skies '79
Dangerous Moonlight '41 ▶
Dark Blue World '01
Dawn Patrol '38 ▶
Deadly Encounter '72 ▶
Delta Force '86
Desert Thunder '99
Devil Dogs of the Air '35
Die Hard 2: Die Harder '90 ▶
Disney's The Kid '00
Dive Bomber '41 ▶
Dr. Strangelove, or: How I Learned to Stop Worrying and Love the Bomb '64 ▶
The Dogfighters '95
The Doomsday Flight '66
Dragonfly Squadron '54
Drop Zone '94
Dumbo '41 ▶
The Eagle and the Hawk '33 ▶
Enola Gay: The Men, the Mission, the Atomic Bomb '80
Executive Decision '96
Family Jewels '65
Fighter Attack '53
Fighting Pilot '35
Final Approach '91
Final Approach '08
Final Destination '00
Final Mission '93
Fire Birds '90
Firefox '82
Five Came Back '39
Five Weeks in a Balloon '62
Flaming Signal '33
Flat Top '52
Flight from Glory '37
Flight from Singapore '62
Flight of Black Angel '91
Flight of the Intruder '90
The Flight of the Phoenix '65 ▶
Flight to Fury '66
Flightplan '05
Fly Away Home '96 ▶
Fly Boy '99
Flyboys '06
Flying Blind '41
The Flying Deuces '39 ▶
Flying Down to Rio '33
Flying High '31
The Flying Irishman '39
Flying Leathernecks '51 ▶
Flying Tigers '42
For the Moment '94
Forget Paris '95
Freedom Strike '98
French Kiss '95
The Geisha Boy '58
God is My Co-Pilot '45
The Great Skycopter Rescue '82
The Great Waldo Pepper '75 ▶
A Guy Named Joe '44
Gypsy Angels '94
Hell's Angels '30 ▶
High Road to China '83
Higher Ground '88
Hostage '87
Hot Shots! '91 ▶
The Hunters '58
Independence Day '96 ▶
Interceptor '92
Into the Sun '92
Iron Eagle '86
Iron Eagle 2 '88
Iron Eagle 4 '95
The Island at the Top of the World '74
It Happened at the World's Fair '63
Jack Brown, Genius '94
Jet Over the Atlantic '59
Jet Pilot '57
Keep 'Em Flying '41
La Bamba '87 ▶
La Grande Vadrouille '66 ▶
Lafayette Escadrille '58
L'Annee Sainte '76
The Left Hand of God '55 ▶
The Lion Has Wings '40
Look Who's Talking Now '93
Lost Squadron '32
Love Affair '94
Mach 2 '00
Malta Story '53
The Man with the Golden Gun '74
The McConnell Story '55
Memphis Belle '90 ▶
Men of Steel '77
Men of the Fighting Lady '54 ▶
Mercy Mission '93
Millennium '89
Mirror Wars: Reflection One '05
Moon Pilot '62
Murder on Flight 502 '75
Mystery Squadron '33
Night Flight '33
1941 '79
No Highway in the Sky '51 ▶
October Sky '99 ▶
One of Our Aircraft Is Missing '41 ▶
Only Angels Have Wings '39 ▶
Operation Dumbo Drop '95
Out of Control '85
Pancho Barnes '88
Pandora's Clock '96
Paradise, Hawaiian Style '66
Party Plane '90
Passenger 57 '92
Pearl Harbor '01
The Phantom '96
Phantom of the Air '33
Phone Call from a Stranger '52
Piece of Cake '88
Power Dive '41
The Pursuit of D.B. Cooper '81
Pushing Tin '99 ▶
Reach for the Sky '56
Red Eye '05 ▶
Red Flag: The Ultimate Game '81
Return to Earth '76
Revenge of the Red Baron '93
The Right Stuff '83 ▶
Robot Pilot '41
Sabre Jet '53
Saint-Ex: The Story of the Storyteller '95

▶ = rated three bones or higher

Savage Hunger '84
Shadow of the Eagle '32
Shadow on the Sun '88
Six Days, Seven Nights '98
633 Squadron '64
Sky Hei$t '75
Sky Liner '49
Sky Parade '36
Sky Riders '76
Snakes on a Plane '06
The Sound Barrier '52
Spirit of St. Louis '57 ►
Spitfire '42 ►
The Starfighters '63
Starflight One '83
Steal the Sky '88
Stealth '05
Stealth Fighter '99
Stephen King's The Langoliers '95
Stephen King's The Night Flier '96
Strategic Air Command '55
Stuart Little 2 '02 ►
Stunt Pilot '39
Survivor '80
Tactical Assault '99
Tailspin: Behind the Korean Airline Tragedy '89
The Taking of Flight 847: The Uli Derickson Story '88 ►
Tarnished Angels '57 ►
Task Force '49
Terminal Velocity '94
Test Pilot '38 ►
Texas Buddies '32
Those Endearing Young Charms '45
Those Magnificent Men in Their Flying Machines '65 ►
Thunder Birds '42
Today We Live '33
Top Gun '86
Tragedy of Flight 103: The Inside Story '91 ►
Turbulence '96
The Tuskegee Airmen '95 ►
Twelve o'Clock High '49 ►
Up in the Air '09 ►
View from the Top '03
War Lover '62
Warbirds '88
The Wedding Singer '97
We'll Meet Again '82
The White Diamond '04 ►
Who Is Harry Kellerman and Why Is He Saying Those Terrible Things About Me? '71
The Winds of Kitty Hawk '78
A Wing and a Prayer '44 ►
Wings '27
Wings in the Dark '35
Wings of Danger '52
Wings of Eagles '57
Without Orders '36
The World Owes Me a Living '47
You Gotta Stay Happy '48
Zeppelin '71
Zero '84

Airplanes

see *Air Disasters; Airborne*

Alaska

see also *Cold Spots*
Alaska '96
Avalanche '99
Balto '95
The Big White '05
Call of the Wild '72
Call of the Wild '93
Cry Vengeance '54
Dead Ahead: The Exxon Valdez Disaster '92 ►
Deep Winter '08
The Edge '97
Extreme Limits '01
Eye of the Beholder '99
First Descent '05
The Fourth Kind '09
The Gold Rush '25 ►
Goldrush: A Real Life Alaskan Adventure '98
Grizzly Man '05 ►
Higher Ground '88
Insomnia '02 ►
Into the Wild '07 ►
Jack London's The Call of the Wild '97
Klondike Annie '36
Klondike Fever '79
The Last Winter '06
Limbo '99
Mystery, Alaska '99
Never Cry Wolf '83 ►
North to Alaska '60 ►
On Deadly Ground '94
The Proposal '09
The Road to Utopia '46 ►
Runaway Train '85 ►
The Simpsons Movie '07 ►
Snow Buddies '08
Spawn of the North '38
The Spoilers '14
The Spoilers '42 ►
Spoilers of the North '47
30 Days of Night '07
The Trail of '98 '28
Wilderness Love '02
Wyvern '09

Alcatraz

see also *Great Escapes; Men in Prison*
Birdman of Alcatraz '62 ►
Dark Passage '47
The Enforcer '76
Escape from Alcatraz '79 ►
Half Past Dead '02
King of Alcatraz '38
The Last Gangster '37
Murder in the First '95
Point Blank '67
The Rock '96 ►
X-Men: The Last Stand '06

Alcoholism

see *On the Rocks*

Alien Babes

see also *Alien Beings—Benign; Alien Beings—Vicious; Aliens Are People, Too*
Alien Visitor '95
Beach Babes 2: Cave Girl Island '95
Beach Babes from Beyond '93
Cat Women of the Moon '53
Cocoon '85 ►
Decoys '04
Decoys: The Second Seduction '07
Dude, Where's My Car? '00
Interceptor Force 2 '02
Invasion of the Star Creatures '63
Last Exit to Earth '96
Leprechaun 4: In Space '96
Mars Attacks! '96
Men in Black 2 '02
My Stepmother Is an Alien '88
Planet of Blood '66
Queen of Outer Space '58
The Sender '98
Species '95
Species 2 '98
Species 3 '04
Species 4: The Awakening '07
Star Portal '97
Star Trek: First Contact '96 ►
Starlight '97
Vampire Vixens from Venus '94
Vampirella '96

Alien Beings—Benign

see also *Alien Babes; Alien Beings—Vicious; Alien Cops; Aliens Are People, Too; Out of This World Sex; Space Operas*
The Abyss '89 ►
Aftershock '88
Alien from L.A. '87
Alien Nation '88
Alien Nation: Body and Soul '95
Alien Nation: Dark Horizon '94
Alien Nation: Millennium '96
Alien Nation: The Enemy Within '96
Alien Private Eye '87
Amanda and the Alien '95
Aqua Teen Hunger Force Colon Movie Film for Theaters '07
The Aurora Encounter '85
Avatar '09 ►
*batteries not included '87
Battle for Terra '09 ►
The Big Empty '04
Big Meat Eater '85
The Brother from Another Planet '84 ►
Can of Worms '00
The Cat from Outer Space '78
Chicken Little '05
Close Encounters of the Third Kind '77 ►
Cocoon '85 ►
Cocoon: The Return '88
Communion '89
Coneheads '93
The Cosmic Eye '71 ►
The Cosmic Man '59
Dark City '97
The Day the Earth Stood Still '51 ►
The Day the Earth Stood Still '08
District 9 '09 ►
Doctor Who '96
Doin' Time on Planet Earth '88
Earth Girls Are Easy '89
Earth vs. the Flying Saucers '56
The Empire Strikes Back '80 ►
Enemy Mine '85
Escape to Witch Mountain '75 ►
E.T.: The Extra-Terrestrial '82 ►
The Ewok Adventure '84
The Ewoks: Battle for Endor '85
Explorers '85
Femalien '96
Femalien 2 '98
Fire in the Sky '93
Flight of the Navigator '86
Galaxy Quest '99
Gremlins '84 ►
Gremlins 2: The New Batch '90 ►
Groom Lake '02
The Hidden '87 ►
The Hitchhiker's Guide to the Galaxy '05 ►
Howard the Duck '86
Hyper-Sapien: People from Another Star '86
I'll Believe You '07
Intruders '92
It Came from Outer Space '53 ►
Josh Kirby... Time Warrior: Chapter 5, Journey to the Magic Cavern '96
Labyrinth '86 ►
The Last Mimzy '07
The Last Starfighter '84
Lilo & Stitch '02 ►
Lilo & Stitch 2: Stitch Has a Glitch '05
Mac and Me '88
Man Facing Southeast '86 ►
The Man from Atlantis '77
The Man Who Fell to Earth '76 ►
Martians Go Home! '90
Masters of Venus '62
The Mating Habits of the Earthbound Human '99
Men in Black '97 ►
Missile to the Moon '59
Moon Pilot '62
Morons from Outer Space '85
Munchie '92
Muppets from Space '99
My Favorite Martian '98
My Stepmother Is an Alien '88
My Uncle: The Alien '96
Mysterious Two '82
Nukie '93
Official Denial '93
Pajama Party '64
Pet Shop '94
The Phantom Planet '61
Planet 51 '09
Project: Genesis '93
Purple People Eater '88
Real Men '87
Repo Man '83 ►
Return of the Jedi '83 ►
Search for the Gods '75
Simon '80
Spaced Invaders '90
Star Knight '85
Star Trek '09 ►
Star Trek 3: The Search for Spock '84
Star Trek 4: The Voyage Home '86 ►
Star Trek: First Contact '96 ►
Star Wars '77 ►
Star Wars: Episode 1—The Phantom Menace '99 ►
Stardust Memories '80
Starlight '97
Starman '84 ►
Starship Invasions '77
Stranded '87
Suburban Commando '91
Super Mario Bros. '93
Supergirl '84
Superman: The Movie '78 ►
Superman 2 '80 ►
Superman 3 '83
Superman 4: The Quest for Peace '87
Teenage Mutant Ninja Turtles 2: The Secret of the Ooze '91
The Terrornauts '67
The 27th Day '57
UFO: Target Earth '74
Vegas in Space '94
Voyage of the Rock Aliens '87
Warning from Space '56
Wavelength '83
What Planet Are You From? '00
When Time Expires '97
Zarkorr! The Invader '96
Zeta One '69

Alien Beings—Vicious

see also *Alien Babes; Alien Beings—Benign; Alien Cops; Aliens Are People, Too; Out of This World Sex; Space Operas*
The Adventures of Buckaroo Banzai Across the Eighth Dimension '84 ►
Alien '79 ►
Alien 3 '92
The Alien Agenda: Endangered Species '97
The Alien Agenda: Out of the Darkness '96
The Alien Agenda: Under the Skin '97
Alien Agent '07
Alien Cargo '99
Alien Contamination '81
Alien Dead '79
The Alien Factor '78
Alien Fury: Countdown to Invasion '00
Alien Massacre '67
Alien Nation: Dark Horizon '94
Alien Predators '80
Alien Prey '78
Alien Raiders '08
Alien: Resurrection '97 ►
Alien Seed '89
Alien Siege '05
Alien Space Avenger '91
Alien Terminator '95
Alien 3000 '04
Alien Trespass '09
Alien vs. Predator '04
Alienator '89
Aliens '86 ►
Aliens Are Coming '80
Aliens in the Attic '09
Aliens vs. Predator: Requiem '07
The Alpha Incident '76
The Ambushers '67
The Angry Red Planet '59
The Arrival '96
The Arrival 2 '98
The Astounding She-Monster '58
The Astro-Zombies '67
Atomic Submarine '59
Attack from Mars '88
Backlash: Oblivion 2 '95
Bad Channels '92
Bad Taste '88 ►
Battle Beyond the Stars '80
Battle of the Worlds '61
Battlefield Earth '00
Battlestar Galactica '78
Beware! The Blob '72
Bio Hazard '85
The Blob '58
The Blob '88 ►
Bloodsuckers from Outer Space '83
Blue Flame '93
Blue Monkey '87
Body Snatchers '93
The Borrower '89
The Brain '88
The Brain Eaters '58
The Brain from Planet Arous '57
Breeders '86
Breeders '97
Cat Women of the Moon '53
Class of Nuke 'Em High 3: The Good, the Bad and the Subhumanoid '94
Cold and Dark '05
The Colony '98
The Cosmic Monsters '58
Creature '85
Creeping Terror '64
The Cremators '72
Crimson Force '05
Critters '86
Critters 2: The Main Course '88
Critters 3 '91
Critters 4 '91
Crossworlds '96
The Curse '87
D-Day on Mars '45
The Dark '79
Dark Breed '96
Dark Star '74 ►
Dark Universe '93
Day the World Ended '55
The Day the World Ended '01
Day Time Ended '80
Dead Space '90
Dead Weekend '95
Deceit '89
Deep Red '94
Deep Space '87
Destroy All Planets '68
Devil Girl from Mars '54
Dr. Alien '88
Doctor Who '96
Dollman '90
Dracula vs. Frankenstein '69
Dragon Storm '04
Dreamcatcher '03
Earth vs. the Flying Saucers '56
Eat and Run '86
The Empire Strikes Back '80 ►
Encounter at Raven's Gate '88
End of the World '76
Endangered Species '02
Epoch: Evolution '03
Escape from Galaxy Three '81
Escapes '86
Evil Alien Conquerors '02
Evils of the Night '85
Evolution '01
The Eye Creatures '65
Eyes Behind the Stars '72
The Faculty '98
Fantastic Four: Rise of the Silver Surfer '07
The Fear Chamber '68
Feeders '96
The Fifth Element '97
Final Fantasy: The Spirits Within '01
First Man into Space '59
Flight to Mars '52
Forbidden World '82
Forbidden Zone: Alien Abduction '96
Frankenstein Meets the Space Monster '65
Freezer Burn: The Invasion of Laxdale '08
From Beyond '86 ►
From Other Worlds '04
Funky Forest: The First Contact '06
Galaxy Invader '85
Galaxy of Terror '81
Galaxy Quest '99
Gamera vs. Guiron '69
Gamera vs. Zigra '71
Genesis II '73
Ghidrah the Three Headed Monster '65
The Giant Claw '57
The Giant Spider Invasion '75
God Told Me To '76
Godzilla vs. King Ghidora '91
Godzilla vs. the Cosmic Monster '74
Grand Tour: Disaster in Time '92
The Green Slime '68
Gremlins '84 ►
Gremlins 2: The New Batch '90 ►
The Guyver '91
Guyver 2: Dark Hero '94
Hands of Steel '86
The Hidden '87 ►
The Hidden 2 '94
The High Crusade '92
High Desert Kill '90
The Hitchhiker's Guide to the Galaxy '05 ►
Horror of the Blood Monsters '70
The Human Duplicators '64
Hybrid '97
I Come in Peace '90
I Married a Monster from Outer Space '58
Impostor '02
Independence Day '96 ►
Inseminoid '80
Interceptor Force '99
Invader '91
The Invaders '95
Invaders from Mars '53
Invaders from Mars '86
Invasion '65
Invasion! '99
The Invasion '07
Invasion: Earth '98
Invasion Earth: The Aliens Are Here! '87
Invasion of the Animal People '62
Invasion of the Bee Girls '73 ►
Invasion of the Body Snatchers '56 ►
Invasion of the Body Snatchers '78 ►
Invasion of the Body Stealers '69
Invasion of the Girl Snatchers '73
Invasion of the Saucer Men '57
Invasion of the Space Preachers '90
Invisible Adversaries '77
Invisible Invaders '59
Island of the Burning Doomed '67
It Came from Outer Space '53 ►
It Came from Outer Space 2 '95
It Conquered the World '56
It! The Terror from Beyond Space '58
J-Men Forever! '79 ►
Jimmy Neutron: Boy Genius '01

► = rated three bones or higher

John Carpenter's Ghosts of Mars '01
Killer Klowns from Outer Space '88
Killer Tongue '96
Killers from Space '54
Killings at Outpost Zeta '80
Kronos '57
Laboratory '80
Laserhawk '99
Leviathan '89
Lifeform '96
Liquid Sky '83 ▸
Lords of the Deep '89
Lost in Space '98
Mars Attacks! '96
Mars Needs Women '66
The Martian Chronicles: Part 3 '79
Masters of Venus '62
Men in Black '97 ▸
Men in Black 2 '02
Metallica '85
Mindwarp '91
Mission Mars '67
Mom and Dad Save the World '92
Monolith '93
The Monolith Monsters '57
Monster '78
Monster a Go-Go! '65
Monster High '89
Monsters vs. Aliens '09
Moontrap '89
Munchies '87
The Mysterians '58
Negadon: The Monster from Mars '05
Night Beast '83
Night Caller from Outer Space '66
Night of the Blood Beast '58
Night of the Creeps '86
Night Skies '07
No Survivors, Please '63
Not of This Earth '88
Not of This Earth '96
Oblivion '94
The Outer Limits: Sandkings '95 ▸
Outlander '08
The P.A.C.K. '96
Peacemaker '90
Pet Shop '94
Phantom from Space '53
The Phantom Planet '61
The Pink Chiquitas '86
Pitch Black '00 ▸
Plan 9 from Outer Space '56
Plan 10 from Outer Space '95
Planet of Blood '66
Planets Against Us '61
Predator '87
Predator 2 '90
Predators '10
Progeny '98
The Puppet Masters '94
Quatermass 2 '57 ▸
Quatermass and the Pit '58
The Quatermass Experiment '56 ▸
Radar Men from the Moon '52
Reactor '78
Remote Control '88
Reptilian '99
The Return '80
Return of the Aliens: The Deadly Spawn '83
Return of the Jedi '83 ▸
Returner '02
Revenge of the Teenage Vixens from Outer Space '86
Robin Cook's Invasion '97
Robot Monster '53
Rock 'n' Roll Nightmare '85
Scared to Death '80
Sci-Fighters '96
Showdown at Area 51 '07
Signs '02 ▸
The Silencers '95
The Sinister Invasion '68
Slapstick of Another Kind '84
Slaughterhouse Five '72
Space Chimps '08
Space Jam '96
Space Master X-7 '58
Species '95
Species 2 '98
Specimen '97
Spider-Man 3 '07
Split '90
Split Second '92
Star Crystal '85
Star Hunter '95
Star Trek '09 ▸
Star Trek: The Motion Picture '79
Star Trek 3: The Search for Spock '84
Star Trek: First Contact '96 ▸
Star Wars '77 ▸
Star Wars: Episode 1—The Phantom Menace '99 ▸
Stargate '94
Stargate: Continuum '08
Starship Invasions '77
Stephen King's The Langoliers '95
Stephen King's The Tommyknockers '93
Strange Invaders '83 ▸
The Stranger from Venus '54
Super Mario Bros. '93
Superman 2 '80 ▸
Supernova '99
Taken '02
A Taste for Flesh and Blood '90
Teen Alien '78
Teenagers from Outer Space '59
Terminal Invasion '02
Terror of Mechagodzilla '78
They '77
They Came from Beyond Space '67
They Live '88
The Thing '51 ▸
The Thing '82
This Island Earth '55
Threshold '03
Thrill Seekers '99
Time Runner '92
Time Walker '82
Transformers '07
Transformers: Revenge of the Fallen '09
Tripods: The White Mountains '84
20 Million Miles to Earth '57
2001: A Space Travesty '00
Undead '05
Unearthed '07
The Unearthly Stranger '64
Unknown Origin '95
Unseen Evil '99
V '83 ▸
V: The Final Battle '84
Vampire Vixens from Venus '94
Village of the Damned '60 ▸
Village of the Damned '95
Virus '98
War in Space '77
War of the Wizards '83
The War of the Worlds '53 ▸
War of the Worlds '05 ▸
When Time Expires '97
Wicked City '92
Wild, Wild Planet '65
Wild Zero '00
Within the Rock '96
Women of the Prehistoric Planet '66
The X-Files '98
X from Outer Space '67
Xtro '83
Xtro 2: The Second Encounter '91
Xtro 3: Watch the Skies '95
Zarkorr! The Invader '96
Zathura '05 ▸
Zebraman '04
Zeram '91
Zeram 2 '94 ▸
Zombies of the Stratosphere '52
Zontar, the Thing from Venus '66

Alien Cops

***see also** Alien Babes; Alien Beings—Benign; Alien Beings—Vicious; Aliens Are People, Too; Extraordinary Pairings; Sci Fi; Space Operas*

Alien Trespass '09
The Hidden '87 ▸
The Hidden 2 '94
Peacemaker '90
The Silencers '95

Aliens Are People, Too

***see also** Alien Babes; Alien Beings—Benign; Alien Beings—Vicious*

The Adventures of Buckaroo Banzai Across the Eighth Dimension '84 ▸
Alien '79 ▸
Alien 3 '92
The Alien Agenda: Under the Skin '97
Alien Avengers '96
Alien: Resurrection '97 ▸
Alien Trespass '09
Aliens '86 ▸
The Arrival '96
Artifacts '08
The Astronaut's Wife '99
Body Snatchers '93
The Chronicles of Riddick '04
Earth Girls Are Easy '89
The Faculty '98
The Hidden '87 ▸
The Hidden 2 '94
The Hitchhiker's Guide to the Galaxy '05 ▸
I Married a Monster '98
I Married a Monster from Outer Space '58
Impostor '02
InAlienable '08
Infected '08
The Invader '96
The Invaders '95
Invaders from Mars '53
Invaders from Mars '86
Invasion of the Body Snatchers '56 ▸
Invasion of the Body Snatchers '78 ▸
K-PAX '01
Mars Attacks! '96
Meet Dave '08
Men in Black '97 ▸
Men in Black 2 '02
My Favorite Martian '98
My Stepmother Is an Alien '88
Not Like Us '96
Outlander '08
Planet of the Vampires '65
Predator Island '05
The Puppet Masters '94
Species 2 '98
Species 3 '04
Specimen '97
Star Portal '97
Starlight '97
Starman '84 ▸
Starship Troopers 2: Hero of the Federation '04
Superman Returns '06
Taken '02
Terminal Invasion '02
The Thing '51 ▸
The Thing '82
Thrill Seekers '99
V '83 ▸
V: The Final Battle '84

Amateur Sleuths

Ace Ventura Jr.: Pet Detective '08
After the Thin Man '36 ▸
Agatha Christie's A Caribbean Mystery '83
Agatha Christie's Murder is Easy '82
Agatha Christie's Murder with Mirrors '85
Alibi for Murder '36
The Body in the Library '84
Clubhouse Detectives '96
Deathmask '69
The Detective '54 ▸
Dirkham Detective Agency '83
Emil and the Detectives '64
Ex-Mrs. Bradford '36 ▸
Fletch '85
Fletch Lives '89
Footsteps in the Dark '41
Frog and Wombat '98
Get a Clue '02
The Glass Key '42 ▸
Gumshoe '72
Hard-Boiled Mahoney '47
Having Wonderful Crime '45
In Your Dreams '07
Irish Luck '39
Killing 'Em Softly '85
Kit Kittredge: An American Girl '08 ▸
The Lady in Question '99
Lying Lips '39
Man from Cairo '54
The Mandarin Mystery '37
Manhattan Murder Mystery '93 ▸
Matinee Idol '33
Messenger of Death '88
Mr. Arkadin '55 ▸
Murder Ahoy '64
Murder at the Gallop '63 ▸
Murder by the Book '87
Murder in a Small Town '99
A Murder Is Announced '87
Murder Most Foul '65 ▸
Murder She Purred: A Mrs. Murphy Mystery '98
Murder She Said '62
Mystery Kids '99
Mystery Liner '34
Nancy Drew '07
Nancy Drew, Reporter '39
A Plumm Summer '08
Ruby in the Smoke '06
The Shadow in the North '07
Shadow of the Thin Man '41 ▸
Shooting Stars '85
A Shot in the Dark '33
A Shot in the Dark '35
The Silent Passenger '35
Song of the Thin Man '47
Speedy Death '99 ▸
Star of Midnight '35
They Might Be Giants '71 ▸
The Thin Man '34 ▸
The Thin Man Goes Home '44
13th Guest '32
Tomorrow at Seven '33
Unconditional Love '03
Voulez-Vous Danser avec Moi? '59
Whistling in Brooklyn '43
Whistling in Dixie '42
Whistling in the Dark '41 ▸
The Wizard of Gore '07

American Indians

***see** Native America*

American South

***see also** Atlanta; Memphis; Miami; Nashville; Nashville Narratives; New Orleans; Savannah; Southern Belles*

Ain't No Way Back '89
All the King's Men '06
All the Real Girls '03 ▸
Alligator Alley '72
An American Haunting '05
Among Brothers '05
Andersonville '95 ▸
Angel Baby '61
Angel City '80
Angel Heart '87
The Apostle '97 ▸
As Summers Die '86
The Autobiography of Miss Jane Pittman '74 ▸
The Baby Dance '98 ▸
Baby Doll '56 ▸
Bad Georgia Road '77
The Ballad of the Sad Cafe '91
Ballast '08
Bandwagon '95
Bastard out of Carolina '96
Beer for My Horses '08
The Beguiled '70 ▸
Belizaire the Cajun '86
Between Heaven and Hell '56 ▸
Beulah Land '80
Big Bad Love '02
Big Boy '30
The Big Easy '87 ▸
Big Fish '03 ▸
Big Momma's House '00
Black Like Me '64
Black Snake Moan '07
Blind Vengeance '90
Blue Ridge Fall '99
Boxcar Bertha '72
Boycott '02 ▸
Bright Leaf '50
Broken Bridges '06
Bucktown '75
Camilla '94
Cape Fear '61 ▸
Cat on a Hot Tin Roof '58 ▸
Cat on a Hot Tin Roof '84
The Chamber '96
Charms for the Easy Life '02
Chiefs '83
Children On Their Birthdays '02
Christy '94
Cold Mountain '03 ▸
Cold Sassy Tree '89 ▸
Colonel Effingham's Raid '45
The Color Purple '85 ▸
Come Early Morning '06
The Con '98
Cookie's Fortune '99 ▸
Cool Hand Luke '67 ▸
Crazy in Alabama '99
Crazy Like a Fox '04
Cries of Silence '97
Crossroads '86
CSA: The Confederate States of America '04
Cypress Edge '99
Daddy & Them '99
Daltry Calhoun '05
Dancer, Texas—Pop. 81 '98 ▸
Dead Birds '04
Dead Right '68
The Delta '97
Delta Heat '92
Dirty Laundry '07
Divine Secrets of the Ya-Ya Sisterhood '02
Dixiana '30
Down in the Delta '98 ▸
Driving Miss Daisy '89 ▸
The Drowning Pool '75
Drum '76
Due East '02
The Dukes of Hazzard '05
Elizabethtown '05
Eve's Bayou '97 ▸
A Family Thing '96 ▸
The Fighting Temptations '03
Final Cut '88
Fire in the Night '85
Fireball 500 '66
First Love, Last Rites '98
The First Saturday in May '08
Flamingo Road '49 ▸
Fled '96
Fletch Lives '89
Follow That Car '80
For Real '02
For Sale by Owner '09
Forrest Gump '94 ▸
Foxfire '87 ▸
Frailty '02 ▸
Freedom Song '00 ▸
Fried Green Tomatoes '91 ▸
The Fugitive Kind '60
The General's Daughter '99
George Wallace '97
Get Low '09
Gettysburg '93 ▸
Ghosts of Mississippi '96
The Gift '00
The Gingerbread Man '97
The Girl from Tobacco Row '66
The Glass Menagerie '87 ▸
Gods and Generals '03
God's Little Acre '58 ▸
Gone with the Wind '39 ▸
A Good Baby '99
Goodbye Solo '08
The Grass Harp '95
The Grave '95
Great Balls of Fire '89
The Great Santini '80 ▸
Great World of Sound '07
The Green Mile '99
Hannah Montana: The Movie '09
Hard Drivin' '60
Harlan County War '00
The Heart Is Deceitful Above All Things '04
The Heart of Dixie '89
Heavens Fall '06
Heroes of the Heart '94
Home from the Hill '60 ▸
The Home Front '02
Hometown Legend '02
Honeydripper '07
Hooch '76
Hootch Country Boys '75
Hope '97
Hot Spell '58
Hounddog '08
A House Divided '00
The Hunley '99
Hunter's Blood '87
Hunter's Moon '97
Hurricane Season '08
Hush, Hush, Sweet Charlotte '65 ▸
I Know Why the Caged Bird Sings '79 ▸
I Walk the Line '70
I'd Climb the Highest Mountain '51 ▸
In a Shallow Grave '88
In Old Kentucky '35
In the Electric Mist '08
In the Flesh '97
In the Heat of the Night '67 ▸
Inherit the Wind '99
Intruder in the Dust '49 ▸
Invitation to a Gunfighter '64
Jezebel '38 ▸
John Grisham's The Rainmaker '97
The Journey of August King '95
Judge Horton and the Scottsboro Boys '76
Judge Priest '34 ▸
Kentucky Kernels '34
Kiss of Fire '98
The Klansman '74
Lady for a Night '42
Lady from Louisiana '42
The Ladykillers '04
Lake City '08
The Last Confederate: The Story of Robert Adams '05
Last Dance '96
The Last Song '10
The Legend of Gator Face '96
A Lesson Before Dying '99 ▸
Life '99
The Life and Assassination of the Kingfish '76
Lily in Winter '94
A Lion in the Streets '53
A Lion Is in the Streets '53 ▸
The List '07
Little Chenier: A Cajun Story '06
The Little Colonel '35 ▸
Little Richard '00
Lone Star State of Mind '02
The Lords of Discipline '83
The Loss of a Teardrop Diamond '08
Louisiana '87
Louisiana Story '48 ▸
Macon County Line '74
Madea's Family Reunion '06
Manderlay '05
Mandingo '75
Many Rivers to Cross '55
Meeting Daddy '98
The Member of the Wedding '97
Midnight in the Garden of Good and Evil '97
Miss Evers' Boys '97
Miss Firecracker '89 ▸
Mississippi '35
Mississippi Burning '88 ▸
Mississippi Masala '92 ▸
Mr. & Mrs. Loving '96 ▸
Misty '61
Monster's Ball '01 ▸

Moonshine Highway '96
Moonshine Mountain '64
Morgan's Ferry '99
Morning Glory '93
The Mothman Prophecies '02
Murder in Coweta County '83
The Murder of Mary Phagan '87 ►
Murder on the Bayou '91 ►
Murder She Purred: A Mrs. Murphy Mystery '98
My Cousin Vinny '92 ►
My Dog Skip '99 ►
My Louisiana Sky '02
My Mom's New Boyfriend '08
My Own Country '98
My Sweet Charlie '70
Mystery of the Riverboat '44
The Neon Bible '95
Netherworld '90
No Mercy '86
Norma Rae '79 ►
North and South Book 1 '85 ►
North and South Book 2 '86 ►
The Notebook '04
Nothing but a Man '64
O Brother Where Art Thou? '00
An Occasional Hell '96
Ode to Billy Joe '76
On the Run '73
On Valentine's Day '86
Once Upon a Time ... When We Were Colored '95 ►
One False Move '91 ►
100 Proof '96
The Only Thrill '97
Orpheus Descending '91
Other Voices, Other Rooms '95
Outside Chance '78
Paradise '91 ►
Paris Trout '91
Passion Fish '92 ►
The Patriot '00
Perfect Harmony '91
Plain Dirty '04
The Ponder Heart '01
Poor Pretty Eddie '73
Poor White Trash '57
Poor White Trash 2 '75
Primary Colors '98
The Prince of Tides '91 ►
Princess Protection Program '09
Psycho from Texas '75
Purlie Victorious '63
Queen Bee '55
Radio '03
Rambling Rose '91 ►
A Real American Hero '78
The Reaping '07
Red Dirt '99
Reflections in a Golden Eye '67
The Relic '96
Return to Mayberry '85
Return to Two Moon Junction '93
Rich in Love '93
Ride the Wild Fields '00
Ride with the Devil '99
Ripe '97
The Rising Place '02
Riverbend '89
Road to Nashville '67
Roll of Thunder, Hear My Cry '78
Rooster: Spurs of Death! '83
Roots '77 ►
Roots: The Next Generation '79 ►
The Rosa Parks Story '02
The Rose Tattoo '55 ►
Rosewood '96 ►
Ruby Gentry '52
Ruby's Bucket of Blood '01
The Runaway '00
Running Mates '86 ►
Rustin '01
The St. Francisville Experiment '00
Saratoga Trunk '45
Scarlett '94
Scorchers '92
The Secret Life of Bees '08 ►
Selma, Lord, Selma '99
Shadrach '98
Shag: The Movie '89 ►
Shanty Tramp '67
Sherman's March '86 ►
Shy People '87 ►
The Simple Life of Noah Dearborn '99
Sins of the Father '01 ►
Sister, Sister '87
Sixteen '72
Sling Blade '96 ►
A Slipping Down Life '99
Smokey Bites the Dust '81
Snuffy Smith, Yard Bird '42
Soldier's Girl '03 ►
Something for the Boys '44
Something to Talk About '95
Sonny '02
Sounder '72 ►
Southern Comfort '81 ►
The Southerner '45 ►
Sparrows '26 ►
Storm Warning '51
Stormswept '95
Storyville '92
Strange Fruit '04
The Strangers '08
A Streetcar Named Desire '51 ►
A Streetcar Named Desire '84 ►
A Streetcar Named Desire '95
Summer and Smoke '61
The Summer of Ben Tyler '96
Summer's End '99
The Supernaturals '86
Swamp Fire '46
Sweet Bird of Youth '62 ►
Sweet Bird of Youth '89
Sweet Country Road '83
Sweet Home Alabama '02
Swimming '00
Tammy and the Bachelor '57
Tammy and the Doctor '63
Tank '83
The Tempest '99
Texasville '90
That Evening Sun '09 ►
They Won't Forget '37 ►
This Stuff'll Kill Ya! '71
Tigerland '00 ►
A Tiger's Tale '87
A Time to Kill '96 ►
To Kill a Mockingbird '62 ►
The Trail of the Lonesome Pine '36 ►
Tribute '09
The Trip to Bountiful '85 ►
Tune in Tomorrow '90
Two Moon Junction '88
2000 Maniacs '64
Tyler Perry's Meet the Browns '08
Uncle Tom's Cabin '14
Uncle Tom's Cabin '69
Undertow '04
The Unseen '05
Untamed Youth '57
The Untold Story of Emmett Louis Till '05 ►
Uphill All the Way '85
Video Voyeur: The Susan Wilson Story '02
Voodoo Dawn '89
Vulture's Eye '04
Waitress '07 ►
Walk in the Spring Rain '70
A Walk to Remember '02
Walking Tall '73
Walking Tall: Part 2 '75
Walking Tall: The Final Chapter '77
The War '94
The Waterboy '98
We Are Marshall '06
Welcome Home Roscoe Jenkins '08
What Comes Around '85
When I Find the Ocean '06
Where the Lilies Bloom '74 ►
White Lie '91
The White Rose '23 ►
Wild Things '98
Wildflower '91 ►
William Faulkner's Old Man '97
Wise Blood '79 ►
A Woman Called Moses '78
Wrong Turn '03
The Yellow Handkerchief '08 ►

Amnesia

The Addams Family '91
Amateur '94 ►
Amnesia '96
Anastasia '56 ►
Anastasia: The Mystery of Anna '86
Another Woman '94
Armistead Maupin's More Tales of the City '97
As You Desire Me '32 ►
Battle Shock '56
Black Out '96
Blackout '85
Blind Horizon '04
The Blonde '92
The Blue Gardenia '53 ►
The Bourne Identity '88 ►
The Bourne Identity '02 ►
The Bourne Supremacy '04 ►
The Bourne Ultimatum '07 ►
The Bumblebee Flies Anyway '98
Clean Slate '94
Code Name: The Cleaner '07
Crack-Up '46
Crossroads '42
Cure '97 ►
Dead Again '91 ►
Desperately Seeking Susan '85
Diabolically Yours '67
Empire of the Wolves '05
Eternal Sunshine of the Spotless Mind '04 ►
Experiment '05
Facing Windows '03
Fall Guy '47
50 First Dates '04
Final Approach '91
Forger of London '61
The Forgotten '04
The Ghost '04
The Great Dictator '40 ►
Gypsy Angels '94
Hana & Alice '04 ►
Hancock '08
Hardwired '09
Hellhole '85
High Stakes '93
Horrors of Malformed Men '69
Hysteria '64
I Love a Bandleader '45
I Love You Again '40 ►
Identity Unknown '45
The Immoral One '80
Inferno '99
Into the Arms of Strangers '07
Istanbul '57
The Jacket '05
Jackie Chan's Who Am I '98
Jane Doe '83
Jericho '01
The Killing Jar '96
Kiss Me Deadly '08
Landslide '92
Last Rites '98
The Lazarus Man '96
The Long Kiss Goodnight '96
Lost Honeymoon '47
Love Letters '45
The Majestic '01
The Man Without a Past '02 ►
Memories of Murder '90
The Memory of a Killer '03
Men in Black '97 ►
Men in Black 2 '02
Mirage '66 ►
Mission of Death '97
Moment to Moment '66
Mulholland Drive '01 ►
The Muppets Take Manhattan '84 ►
Murder by Night '89
Never Forget '08
Overboard '87
Palombella Rossa '89
Paycheck '03
The Perfect Daughter '96
A Pure Formality '94
Random Harvest '42 ►
The Red Squirrel '93
Regarding Henry '91 ►
Return of the Soldier '82 ►
The Road to Hong Kong '62
The Saddest Music in the World '03
San Saba '08
Santa with Muscles '96
The Second Woman '51
The Sender '82
Shattered '91
Shock '79
Siesta '87
Singapore '47
Snow 2: Brain Freeze '08
Someone Behind the Door '71
Somewhere in the Night '46
Southland Tales '06
Speed Dating '07
Spellbound '45 ►
Strange Awakening '58
The Stranger '87 ►
Summer's Children '79
Sundays & Cybele '62 ►
XIII '08
36 Hours '64 ►
The Three Lives of Karen '97
Till Human Voices Wake Us '02
Time Lapse '01
Total Recall '90 ►
Twice a Judas '69
Undesirable '92
Unholy Four '54
The Unknown Soldier '98
Unknown White Male '05 ►
The Unsuspected '47
Virtual Sexuality '99
While I Live '47
A Wind Named Amnesia '93

Amsterdam

The Amsterdam Connection '78
The Amsterdam Kill '78
Amsterdamned '88
Anne Frank: The Whole Story '01 ►
The Attic: The Hiding of Anne Frank '88
The Bourne Supremacy '04 ►
Broken Mirrors '85
Business is Business '71
Deuce Bigalow: European Gigolo '05
The Diary of Anne Frank '59 ►
The Diary of Anne Frank '08
Gay in Amsterdam '04
Hostel '06
Katie Tippel '75
Ocean's Twelve '04
Operation Amsterdam '60
Paid '06
Puppet on a Chain '72
Snapshots '02

Amusement Parks

***see also** Carnivals & Circuses; Fairs & Expositions*

Adventureland '09 ►
The Beast from 20,000 Fathoms '53
Bebe's Kids '92
Beverly Hills Cop 3 '94
Big '88 ►
Carnival of Blood '71
Carnival of Souls '62 ►
The Crying Game '92 ►
Curse of the Headless Horseman '72
Dr. Giggles '92
Dragonworld '94
Fatal Attraction '87 ►
Final Destination 3 '06
Funland '89
Gangster World '98
Getting Even with Dad '94
Godzilla on Monster Island '72
Jimmy Neutron: Boy Genius '01
KISS Meets the Phantom of the Park '78
The Lady from Shanghai '48 ►
Little Fugitive '06
Luv '67
Mighty Joe Young '98
My Life '93
National Lampoon's Vacation '83 ►
1941 '79
Omega Doom '96
Postal '07
Rollercoaster '77
Rugrats in Paris: The Movie '00 ►
Scooby-Doo '02
A Slipping Down Life '99
Strangers on a Train '51 ►
Strike Me Pink '36
The Third Man '49 ►
3 Ninjas: High Noon at Mega Mountain '97
Tremors 3: Back to Perfection '01
The World '04
Zombieland '09 ►

Angels

***see also** Heaven Sent*

Almost an Angel '90
Always '89
Angel-A '05
The Angel Levine '70
Angels in America '03 ►
Angels in the Endzone '98
Angels in the Infield '00
Angels in the Outfield '51 ►
Angels in the Outfield '94
The Bishop's Wife '47 ►
Cabin in the Sky '43 ►
Christmas at Water's Edge '04
The Christmas Box '95
Circus Angel '65 ►
City of Angels '98
Clarence '91
Click '06
The Contractor '07
Cowboys and Angels '00
Creation of Adam '93
Date with an Angel '87
Defending Your Life '91 ►
Dogma '99
Down to Earth '01
Fallen '97
Faraway, So Close! '93
Fear No Evil '80
Field of Dreams '89 ►
For Heaven's Sake '79
Forever Darling '56
Gabriel & Me '01
Gabriel Over the White House '33 ►
Get Smart '08
Green Pastures '36 ►
A Guy Named Joe '44
Heart and Souls '93
Heaven Can Wait '78 ►
The Heavenly Kid '85
Here Comes Mr. Jordan '41 ►
The Horn Blows at Midnight '45 ►
I Married an Angel '42
It Came Upon a Midnight Clear '84
It's a Wonderful Life '46 ►
The Kid with the Broken Halo '82
Kindergarten Ninja '94
La Merveilleuse Visite '74
Legion '10
Levitation '97
A Life Less Ordinary '97
The Littlest Angel '69
Lover's Knot '96
Made in Heaven '87
Michael '96
Miracle in Milan '51 ►
Neil Gaiman's NeverWhere '96
$9.99 '08
No News from God '01
Northfork '03
One Magic Christmas '85
A Perfect Day '06
The Perfect Holiday '07
The Preacher's Wife '96
The Prophecy '95
The Prophecy 2: Ashtown '97
The Prophecy 3: The Ascent '99
Raging Angels '95
A Season for Miracles '99
Slam Dunk Ernest '95
Soultaker '90
Stairway to Heaven '46 ►
The Twelve Days of Christmas Eve '04
Two of a Kind '83
Unlikely Angel '97
Waiting for the Light '90
Wide Awake '97
Wings of Desire '88 ►

Animals

***see** Bears; Birds; Cats; Horses; King of Beasts (Dogs); Penguins; Wild Kingdom*

Animated Musicals

***see also** Animation & Cartoons; Musicals*

Adam Sandler's 8 Crazy Nights '02
Aladdin '92 ►
All Dogs Go to Heaven '89
All Dogs Go to Heaven 2 '95
American Pop '81
An American Tail '86
An American Tail: Fievel Goes West '91
Anastasia '97
Beauty and the Beast '91 ►
Cats Don't Dance '97
Charlotte's Web '73
Cinderella '50 ►
Fantasia/2000 '00
Gay Purr-ee '62
Happy Feet '06 ►
Hercules '97 ►
Home on the Range '04
Hoodwinked '05 ►
The Hunchback of Notre Dame '96 ►
The Jungle Book '67 ►
The King and I '99
Lady and the Tramp '55 ►
The Lion King '94 ►
The Little Mermaid '89 ►
The Magic Voyage '93
Melody Time '48 ►
Mulan '98
The Nightmare Before Christmas '93 ►
The Pebble and the Penguin '94
Pink Floyd: The Wall '82
Pinocchio '40 ►
Pocahontas '95 ►
Prince of Egypt '98 ►
The Princess and the Frog '09 ►
Quest for Camelot '98
The Return of Jafar '94
The Road to El Dorado '00
Robin Hood '73 ►
Rock-a-Doodle '92
Shinbone Alley '70
Sleeping Beauty '59 ►
Snow White and the Seven Dwarfs '37 ►
South Park: Bigger, Longer and Uncut '99
The Swan Princess '94
The Swan Princess 2: Escape from Castle Mountain '97
The Thief and the Cobbler '96 ►
Thumbelina '94
Tim Burton's Corpse Bride '05 ►
The Trumpet of the Swan '01
The Tune '92
Water Babies '79
Yellow Submarine '68 ►

Animated Sci-Fi

Battle for Terra '09 ►
Bionicle 3: Web of Shadows '05
Despicable Me '10
Final Fantasy: The Spirits Within '01
Fly Me to the Moon '08
Heavy Metal '81 ►

► = rated three bones or higher

Howl's Moving Castle *'04*
The Incredibles *'04* ▸
Inspector Gadget's Biggest Caper Ever *'05*
The Iron Giant *'99* ▸
Jimmy Neutron: Boy Genius *'01*
Meet the Robinsons *'07*
Monsters vs. Aliens *'09*
9 *'09* ▸
Planet 51 *'09*
Pokemon 3: The Movie *'01*
Renaissance *'06*
Space Chimps *'08*
Star Wars: The Clone Wars *'08*
Steamboy *'05*
Titan A.E. *'00*
Transformers: The Movie *'86*
WALL-E *'08* ▸
Yu-Gi-Oh! The Movie: Pyramid of Light *'04*

Animation & Cartoons

see also ***Animated Musicals***
The Adventures of Ichabod and Mr. Toad *'49* ▸
The Adventures of Mark Twain *'85* ▸
Aladdin and the King of Thieves *'96*
Alice in Wonderland *'50*
Alice in Wonderland *'51* ▸
Allegro Non Troppo *'76* ▸
Animal Farm *'55* ▸
The Ant Bully *'06*
Antz *'98* ▸
Aqua Teen Hunger Force Colon Movie Film for Theaters *'07*
The Aristocats *'70* ▸
Astro Boy *'09*
Atlantis: The Lost Empire *'01*
Babar: The Movie *'88*
Balto *'95*
Bambi *'42* ▸
Barnyard *'06*
Batman: Mask of the Phantasm *'93*
Beavis and Butt-Head Do America *'96*
Bebe's Kids *'92*
Bee Movie *'07*
Beowulf *'07* ▸
The Black Cauldron *'85*
Bolt *'08* ▸
Bon Voyage, Charlie Brown *'80*
A Bug's Life *'98* ▸
Butterfly Ball *'76*
Cars *'06* ▸
Chicago 10 *'07* ▸
Chicken Little *'05*
Chicken Run *'00* ▸
A Christmas Carol *'09*
Clifford's Really Big Movie *'04*
Cloudy with a Chance of Meatballs *'09*
Cool World *'92*
Coraline *'09* ▸
The Cosmic Eye *'71* ▸
Curious George *'06*
The Dagger of Kamui *'85* ▸
Delgo *'08*
Dinosaur *'00*
Disney's Teacher's Pet *'04* ▸
Dr. Seuss' Horton Hears a Who! *'08* ▸
Doogal *'05*
Doug's 1st Movie *'99* ▸
DuckTales the Movie: Treasure of the Lost Lamp *'90*
Dumbo *'41* ▸
Everyone's Hero *'06*
Evil Toons *'90*
Fantasia *'40* ▸
Fantastic Mr. Fox *'09* ▸
Fantastic Planet *'73* ▸
Felix the Cat: The Movie *'91*
Ferngully: The Last Rain Forest *'92*
Finding Nemo *'03* ▸
Fire and Ice *'83*
Flight of Dragons *'82*
Flushed Away *'06* ▸
The Fox and the Hound *'81* ▸
Freddie the Frog *'92*
Fritz the Cat *'72* ▸
Garfield: A Tail of Two Kitties *'06*
Garfield: The Movie *'04*
Gargoyles, The Movie: The Heroes Awaken *'94*
Ghost in the Shell *'95* ▸
The Good, the Bad, and Huckleberry Hound *'88*
A Goofy Movie *'94*
The Great Mouse Detective *'86* ▸
Grendel, Grendel, Grendel *'82*
Gulliver's Travels *'39*
Gulliver's Travels *'77*
Gumby: The Movie *'95*
Happily Ever After *'93*
Happily N'Ever After *'07*
Heavy Metal 2000 *'00*
Heavy Traffic *'73* ▸
Here Come the Littles: The Movie *'85*
Hey Arnold! The Movie *'02*
Hey Good Lookin' *'82*
Hey There, It's Yogi Bear *'64*
The Hobbit *'78* ▸
Home on the Range *'04*
Hoodwinked *'05* ▸
Hoodwinked Too! Hood vs. Evil *'10*
Hoppity Goes to Town *'41*
How to Train Your Dragon *'10*
Huckleberry Finn *'81*
Hugo the Hippo *'76*
Ice Age *'02* ▸
Ice Age: Dawn of the Dinosaurs *'09*
Ice Age: The Meltdown *'06*
Igor *'08*
The Incredibles *'04* ▸
Jetsons: The Movie *'90*
Journey Back to Oz *'71*
Kaena: The Prophecy *'03*
The Land Before Time *'88* ▸
The Land Before Time 2: The Great Valley Adventure *'94*
The Land Before Time 3: The Time of the Great Giving *'95*
The Land Before Time 4: Journey Through the Mists *'96*
The Land Before Time 5: The Mysterious Island *'97*
The Land Before Time 6: The Secret of Saurus Rock *'98*
Land Before Time 7: The Stone of Cold Fire *'00*
The Last Unicorn *'82*
The Legend of Sleepy Hollow *'49*
Lensman *'84*
Light Years *'88*
Lilo & Stitch 2: Stitch Has a Glitch *'05*
The Lion King 1 1/2 *'04* ▸
The Little Mermaid *'75*
Little Nemo: Adventures in Slumberland *'92*
Looney Looney Looney Bugs Bunny Movie *'81* ▸
The Lord of the Rings *'78*
Mad Monster Party *'68*
Madagascar *'05*
Madagascar: Escape 2 Africa *'08*
Man from Button Willow *'65*
The Many Adventures of Winnie the Pooh *'77*
Marco Polo, Jr. *'72*
Marquis *'90*
Mary and Max *'09*
The Miracle Maker: The Story of Jesus *'00*
Monster House *'06* ▸
Monsters, Inc. *'01* ▸
Mouse and His Child *'77*
Nine Lives of Fritz the Cat *'74*
$9.99 *'08*
The Nutcracker Prince *'91*
Oliver & Company *'88*
Once Upon a Forest *'93*
101 Dalmatians *'61* ▸
1001 Arabian Nights *'59*
Open Season *'06*
Over the Hedge *'06* ▸
Persepolis *'07* ▸
Peter Pan *'53* ▸
Phantom Tollbooth *'69* ▸
Phantom 2040 Movie: The Ghost Who Walks *'95*
Piglet's Big Movie *'03*
The Pirates Who Don't Do Anything: A VeggieTales Movie *'08*
The Plague Dogs *'82*
The Point *'71*
The Polar Express *'04*
Ponyo *'08* ▸
Pooh's Heffalump Movie *'05*
Popeye's Voyage: The Quest for Pappy *'04*
Pound Puppies and the Legend of Big Paw *'88*
The Powerpuff Girls Movie *'02* ▸
The Princess and the Goblin *'94*
The Proud Family Movie *'05*
The Puppetoon Movie *'87*
Queer Duck: The Movie *'06*
Race for Your Life, Charlie Brown *'77*
Ratatouille *'07* ▸
The Rescuers *'77* ▸
The Rescuers Down Under *'90*
The Return of the King *'80*
Return to Never Land *'02*
Robots *'05*
Rock & Rule *'83*
Rover Dangerfield *'91*
Rugrats Go Wild! *'03*
Rugrats in Paris: The Movie *'00* ▸
The Rugrats Movie *'98* ▸
The Secret of Kells *'09*
The Secret of NIMH *'82* ▸
The Secret of NIMH 2 *'98*
Shame of the Jungle *'75*
Shark Tale *'04*
Shrek *'01* ▸
Shrek 2 *'04* ▸
Shrek Forever After *'10*
Shrek the Third *'07*
The Simpsons Movie *'07* ▸
Sinbad and the Eye of the Tiger *'77*
Sinbad: Legend of the Seven Seas *'03*
The Singing Princess *'49*
Sky Blue *'03*
Spirit: Stallion of the Cimarron *'02*
Spirited Away *'01*
The SpongeBob SquarePants Movie *'04*
Starchaser: The Legend of Orin *'85*
Steamboy *'05*
Streetfight *'75*
Surf's Up *'07*
The Sword in the Stone *'63* ▸
The Tale of Despereaux *'08*
Tarzan *'99* ▸
The Three Caballeros *'45*
Tiny Toon Adventures: How I Spent My Vacation *'91* ▸
TMNT (Teenage Mutant Ninja Turtles) *'07*
Todd McFarlane's Spawn *'97* ▸
Tom and Jerry: The Movie *'93*
Tom Thumb *'58* ▸
Toy Story *'95* ▸
Toy Story 2 *'99* ▸
Toy Story 3 *'10*
The Triplets of Belleville *'02* ▸
A Troll in Central Park *'94*
Up *'09* ▸
Valiant *'05*
VIP, My Brother Superman *'90*
Waking Life *'01*
Wallace & Gromit in The Curse of the Were-Rabbit *'05* ▸
Watership Down *'78*
We're Back! A Dinosaur's Story *'93*
When the Wind Blows *'86* ▸
The Wild Thornberrys Movie *'02* ▸
Wizards *'77*
Yu-Gi-Oh! The Movie: Pyramid of Light *'04*

Anime

see also ***Animation & Cartoons***
Akira *'89*
The Castle of Cagliostro *'80*
The Dagger of Kamui *'85* ▸
Dragonball: Evolution *'09*
Funky Forest: The First Contact *'06*
Grave of the Fireflies *'88* ▸
Howl's Moving Castle *'04*
Lensman *'84*
My Neighbor Totoro *'88*
Otaku No Video *'91* ▸
Paprika *'06*
Party 7 *'00*
Pokemon: The First Movie *'99*
Pokemon the Movie 2000: The Power of One *'00*
Pom Poko *'94*
Princess Mononoke *'98* ▸
Sky Blue *'03*
The Sky Crawlers *'08*
Spriggan *'98*
Steamboy *'05*
Talking Head *'92*
Toward the Terra *'80*
Twilight of the Cockroaches *'90*
Wicked City *'89* ▸
A Wind Named Amnesia *'93*

Anthology

see also ***Comedy Anthologies; Horror Anthologies; Serials***
The Acid House *'98*
Actors and Sin *'52*
The Air I Breathe *'07*
America at the Movies *'76*
American Tickler *'76*
America's Dream *'95* ▸
Amore *'48* ▸
Beyond the Clouds *'95*
Black Sabbath *'64* ▸
Boys in Love *'95*
Boys Life *'94*
Cat's Eye *'85*
The Chaplin Revue *'58*
Charade *'53*
Coffee and Cigarettes *'03* ▸
Common Ground *'00*
Cosmic Slop *'94*
Crash *'05* ▸
Dark Eyes *'87* ▸
Deadtime Stories *'86*
The Decameron *'70* ▸
Decameron Nights *'53*
The Discovery Program *'89*
Dogville Shorts *'30*
Dolls *'02* ▸
Eros *'04*
Erotique *'94*
Escapes *'86*
Fallen Angels 1 *'93* ▸
Fallen Angels 2 *'93* ▸
Fantasia/2000 *'00*
Four Rooms *'95*
From Beyond the Grave *'73*
A Girl Thing *'01*
The Great New Wonderful *'06*
Halfmoon *'95*
Hotel Room *'93*
If These Walls Could Talk *'96*
If These Walls Could Talk 2 *'00*
It's a Big Country *'51*
Kaos *'85* ▸
Kisses in the Dark *'97*
Kurt Vonnegut's Monkey House *'91*
Kwaidan *'64* ▸
Le Plaisir *'52*
Letters from My Windmill *'54* ▸
The Little Theatre of Jean Renoir *'78* ▸
Loggerheads *'05* ▸
Love in the City *'53* ▸
Love Songs *'99*
Mama Africa *'02*
Melody Time *'48* ▸
Mickey the Great *'39*
More American Graffiti *'79*
Mystery Train *'89* ▸
New York, I Love You *'09*
Night Gallery *'69* ▸
Night on Earth *'91* ▸
Nightmares *'83*
Nine Lives *'05* ▸
Noel *'04*
Once Upon a Midnight Scary *'90*
Paisan *'46* ▸
Paris, je t'aime *'06*
Personal Velocity: Three Portraits *'02* ▸
Picture Windows *'95*
Prison Stories: Women on the Inside *'91* ▸
Pulp Fiction *'94* ▸
Red Shoe Diaries *'92*
Red Shoe Diaries 2: Double Dare *'92*
Red Shoe Diaries 3: Another Woman's Lipstick *'93*
Red Shoe Diaries 4: Auto Erotica *'93*
Red Shoe Diaries 5: Weekend Pass *'95*
Red Shoe Diaries 6: How I Met My Husband *'95*
Red Shoe Diaries 7: Burning Up *'96*
Red Shoe Diaries 8: Night of Abandon *'97*
Red Shoe Diaries: Four on the Floor *'96*
Red Shoe Diaries: Luscious Lola *'00*
Red Shoe Diaries: Strip Poker *'96*
Red Shoe Diaries: Swimming Naked *'00*
Rendezvous in Paris *'95*
Renoir Shorts *'27* ▸
The Robert Benchley Miniatures Collection *'35*
Robot Stories *'03*
RoGoPaG *'62*
Route 30 *'08*
Seven Deadly Sins *'53* ▸
Short Cuts *'93* ▸
The Silent Mr. Sherlock Holmes *'12*
Sin City *'05*
Six in Paris *'68*
Slacker *'91* ▸
Strictly G.I. *'44*
Subway Stories *'97*
Tales from the Crypt *'89*
Tales of Erotica *'93*
Tales of Manhattan *'42* ▸
Tales of the Unexpected *'91*
Tales That Witness Madness *'73*
The Ten *'07*
Terrorgram *'90*
That's Dancing! *'85* ▸
That's Entertainment *'74* ▸
That's Entertainment, Part 2 *'76*
That's Entertainment, Part 3 *'93*
Things 2 *'97*
Three Cases of Murder *'55* ▸
Three Days of Rain *'02*
Three Times *'05*
To Die (Or Not) *'99*
Tokyo! *'09*
Trick 'r Treat *'08* ▸
Twice-Told Tales *'63* ▸
Twilight Zone: The Movie *'83*
Twisted *'96*
Two Days in the Valley *'96* ▸
The Unapproachable *'82*
The Uncanny *'78*
Vanishing Legion *'31*
The Wall *'99* ▸
What It's All About *'95*
Women & Men: In Love There Are No Rules *'91*
Women & Men: Stories of Seduction *'90*

Anti-Heroes

see also ***Rebel With a Cause***
Aeon Flux *'05*
Belly *'98*
Big Bad Love *'02*
Billy Jack *'71*
Blade *'98*
Bonnie & Clyde *'67* ▸
Born Losers *'67*
Butch Cassidy and the Sundance Kid *'69* ▸
Casino *'95* ▸
A Civil Action *'98*
The Dead Pool *'88*
Dirty Harry *'71* ▸
Easy Rider *'69* ▸
The Enforcer *'76*
Gang Related *'96*
H *'90*
Hero *'92* ▸
Hulk *'03*
Hustle *'04*
In a Lonely Place *'50* ▸
Last Man Standing *'96*
Lock, Stock and 2 Smoking Barrels *'98* ▸
Magnum Force *'73*
Niagara, Niagara *'97*
The Night Watchman *'02*
Palookaville *'95* ▸
Playing God *'96*
The Punisher *'04*
Rebel without a Cause *'55* ▸
Robin Hood: Prince of Thieves *'91*
The Secret Agent *'96*
Set It Off *'96*
Shaun of the Dead *'04* ▸
16 Blocks *'06* ▸
Steal This Movie! *'00*
Street Kings *'08*
Sudden Impact *'83*
Surviving Picasso *'96*
Ten Benny *'98*
Thelma & Louise *'91* ▸
Things to Do in Denver When You're Dead *'95* ▸
To Wong Foo, Thanks for Everything, Julie Newmar *'95*
Traveller *'96* ▸
The Trial of Billy Jack *'74*
Trojan Eddie *'96* ▸
True Crime *'99*
12 Monkeys *'95* ▸
Twin Town *'97*
U-Turn *'97*
Ultraviolet *'06*
V for Vendetta *'06*
The Weather Man *'05*
Wisdom *'87*
Yojimbo *'61* ▸

Anti-War War Movies

see also ***Satire & Parody***
The Adventures of Werner Holt *'65*
All Quiet on the Western Front *'30* ▸
All Quiet on the Western Front *'79*
Amazing Grace & Chuck *'87*
Apocalypse Now *'79* ▸
Beaufort *'07* ▸
The Big Parade *'25* ▸
Born on the Fourth of July *'89* ▸
The Bridge *'59*
The Bridges at Toko-Ri *'55* ▸
The Burmese Harp *'56* ▸
Castle Keep *'69* ▸
Catch-22 *'70* ▸
The Charge of the Light Brigade *'68*
Civilization *'16* ▸
Come and See *'85* ▸
Coming Home *'78* ▸
The Cuckoo *'02*
Cup Final *'92*
Dr. Strangelove, or: How I Learned to Stop Worrying and Love the Bomb *'64* ▸
The Eagle and the Hawk *'33* ▸
Fahrenheit 9/11 *'04* ▸
Field of Honor *'87*
Fiesta *'95*
Fires on the Plain *'59* ▸
Forbidden Games *'52* ▸
The Four Horsemen of the Apocalypse *'21* ▸
The Four Horsemen of the Apocalypse *'62*
Gallipoli *'81* ▸
Glory *'89* ▸

▸ = rated three bones or higher

Apartheid

Apartments & Apartment Buildings

Arab Culture

Archaeology

Architects & Architecture

Army Training, Sir!

Art & Artists

Asia

▶ = rated three bones or higher

Oldboy '03 ▸
Ong-Bak '03 ▸
Purple Butterfly '03 ▸
The Quest '96
The Quiet American '02 ▸
Rambo '08
Red Dust '32 ▸
Rogue Trader '98
S21: The Khmer Rouge Killing Machine '03 ▸
The Sand Pebbles '66 ▸
The Scent of Green Papaya '93 ▸
Shanghai Surprise '86
Singapore '47
The Story of the Weeping Camel '03 ▸
A Tale of Two Sisters '03 ▸
That's the Way I Like It '99
The 13th Mission '91
Three ... Extremes '04
Three Seasons '98
Three Times '05
Tigershark '87
Two Brothers '04
The Two Great Cavaliers '73
Typhoon '06
The Ugly American '63
Untold Scandal '03
The Vertical Ray of the Sun '00
Wake Island '42 ▸
White Ghost '88
Woman Is the Future of Man '04 ▸

Asian America

American Fusion '05
The Beautiful Country '04
Better Luck Tomorrow '02 ▸
Chan Is Missing '82 ▸
Charlotte Sometimes '02
Color of a Brisk and Leaping Day '95
Combination Platter '93
Come See the Paradise '90 ▸
Dim Sum: A Little Bit of Heart '85 ▸
Dim Sum Funeral '08
Double Happiness '94 ▸
Eat a Bowl of Tea '89 ▸
Golden Gate '93
Green Dragon '01
The Joy Luck Club '93 ▸
Living on Tokyo Time '87
Old San Francisco '27
Only the Brave '06
Red Doors '05
Romeo Must Die '00
Shanghai Kiss '07
Strawberry Fields '97
A Thousand Years of Good Prayers '07
The Wedding Banquet '93 ▸
Yellow '98

Assassination

see also *Camelot (New); Foreign Intrigue; Hit Men/Women; Spies & Espionage*
Abraham Lincoln '30
Ace of Hearts '85
Act of Vengeance '86
An Affair in Mind '89
African Rage '78
All the King's Men '49 ▸
The American Friend '77 ▸
The American Soldier '70
Antonio Das Mortes '68
The Arab Conspiracy '76
Ashes and Diamonds '58 ▸
Assassination '87
The Assassination Bureau '69 ▸
The Assassination File '96
The Assassination Game '92
The Assassination of Jesse James by the Coward Robert Ford '07 ▸
The Assassination of Richard Nixon '05
The Assignment '78
Azumi '03 ▸
Azumi 2 '05
Beautiful Beast '95
Beautiful Hunter '94
Belfast Assassin '84
Black Sunday '77
Blind Horizon '04
Blood for Blood '95
Blow Out '81 ▸
Bobby '06
The Bourne Identity '02 ▸
The Bourne Ultimatum '07 ▸
Brass Target '78
The Break '97
Brother Orchid '40 ▸
The Brotherhood of the Rose '89
The Burning Season '94 ▸
Cal '84 ▸
Caracara '00
Center of the Web '92
Cleopatra '99
The Clockmaker '73 ▸
Cold Front '89
Coming Out Alive '84
Counterstrike '03
The Criminal Mind '93
Dagger Eyes '83
The Dallas Connection '94
Dangerous Pursuit '89
The Day of the Dolphin '73
The Day of the Jackal '73 ▸
The Day That Shook the World '78
Dead Zone '83 ▸
Deadly Exposure '93
Death Force '78
Death to Smoochy '02
The Destructors '74
Diamond Run '90
The Dirty Dozen: The Next Mission '85
Disappearance '81
The Domino Principle '77
Eagle Eye '08
The Eagle Has Landed '77 ▸
The Eagle Has Two Heads '48 ▸
Elizabeth '98 ▸
Emmanuelle, the Queen '79
The Emperor and the Assassin '99
End Game '06
Enigma '82
Equalizer 2000 '86
The Evil That Men Do '84
Excellent Cadavers '99
Excessive Force 2: Force on Force '95
Executive Action '73
Expert Weapon '93
F/X '86 ▸
Fatal Justice '93
Flashpoint '84
Flirting with Fate '16 ▸
Foul Play '78 ▸
Friday Foster '75
From Russia with Love '63 ▸
Funeral for an Assassin '77
Gandhi '82 ▸
Ghosts of Mississippi '96
Hangmen Also Die '42
Hard Way '80
Harum Scarum '65
Hero '03 ▸
Hidden Assassin '94
Hit Lady '74
The Hunted '94
The Hunted '03
I Spit on Your Corpse '74
In the Line of Fire '93 ▸
The Informant '97 ▸
The Interpreter '05 ▸
Interview with the Assassin '02
Invitation to a Gunfighter '64
Jack Higgins' Midnight Man '96
Jack Higgins' On Dangerous Ground '95
The Jackal '97
JFK '91 ▸
Judgment Night '93
Kill Castro '80
The Killer Elite '75
Killer Likes Candy '78
The Killing Device '92
King Richard and the Crusaders '54
Kingfish: A Story of Huey P. Long '95
La Femme Nikita '91 ▸
La Passante '83 ▸
La Scorta '94 ▸
The Last Boy Scout '91
The Long Kiss Goodnight '96
Love and Anarchy '73 ▸
Love Kills '91
Loves & Times of Scaramouche '76
Lumumba '01 ▸
Malcolm X '92 ▸
The Man Who Knew Too Much '34 ▸
The Man Who Knew Too Much '56
The Man with the Golden Gun '74
The Manchurian Candidate '62 ▸
Maniac '77
Mark of the Beast '87
The Mercenaries '80
Mercury Rising '98
Michael Collins '96 ▸
Most Wanted '97
Munich '05 ▸
My Little Assassin '99
Nashville '75 ▸
Nick of Time '95
A Night of Love '87
Night of the Assassin '77
Ninja Assassin '09
Ninja Death Squad '87
November Conspiracy '96
The November Men '93
Nowhere to Hide '83
The Odd Job '78
Omar Khayyam '57
On the Run '83
One Man Out '89
Operation C.I.A. '65
The Ordeal of Dr. Mudd '80 ▸
The Parallax View '74 ▸
Paris Belongs to Us '60
Point of No Return '93
Programmed to Kill '86
PT 109 '63
Puerto Vallarta Squeeze '04
Queen's Messenger II '01
Quicker Than the Eye '88
Quiet Thunder '87
Red Eye '05 ▸
Red King, White Knight '89
Red Scorpion '89
Revenge of the Pink Panther '78
RFK '02
Rogue Male '76
Ruby '92
Running Against Time '90
Russian Roulette '75
Sabotage '96
Scorpio '73
Seven Days in May '64 ▸
Shinobi no Mono '62 ▸
Shinobi no Mono 2: Vengeance '63 ▸
Shiri '99
Shooter '07
Silent Trigger '97
Snake Eyes '98
Soul Assassin '01
Spenser: The Judas Goat '94
Stalking Danger '86
State of Siege '73 ▸
Steele's Law '91
Stopover Tokyo '57
Suddenly '54 ▸
Supreme Sanction '99
Target: Favorite Son '87
Taxi Driver '76 ▸
The Terminator '84 ▸
The Terrorist '98
XIII '08
This Gun for Hire '90
Times of Harvey Milk '83 ▸
Two Minute Warning '76
Vantage Point '08
Veronica Guerin '03
Wardogs '87
What a Way to Die '70
When Hell Broke Loose '58
Where There's Life '47
Windmills of the Gods '88
Winter Kills '79 ▸
Without Warning: The James Brady Story '91 ▸
Xchange '00 ▸
XXX: State of the Union '05
Yojimbo '61 ▸
Z '69 ▸
Zoolander '01

Astronauts

see also *Space Operas*
Apollo 13 '95 ▸
Armageddon '98
The Astronaut Farmer '07
The Astronaut's Wife '99
Beneath the Planet of the Apes '70
Capricorn One '78 ▸
Countdown '68
Crimson Force '05
Deep Impact '98
Earth II '71
Escape from Mars '99
Fantastic Four '05
Fly Me to the Moon '08
From the Earth to the Moon '98 ▸
Gattaca '97 ▸
In the Shadow of the Moon '07 ▸
Marooned '69
Mission to Mars '00
Moon '09
Pandorum '09
Planet 51 '09
Planet of the Apes '68 ▸
Planet of the Apes '01 ▸
Red Planet '00
The Reluctant Astronaut '67
The Right Stuff '83 ▸
RocketMan '97
Solaris '02
Space Buddies '08
Space Chimps '08
Space Cowboys '00 ▸
Species 2 '98
2001: A Space Odyssey '68 ▸
2010: The Year We Make Contact '84 ▸

Astronomy & Astrology

see *Star Gazing*

At the Drive-In

see also *At the Movies*
Dead End Drive-In '86
Drive-In '76
Drive-In Massacre '74
The Flamingo Rising '01
Grease '78 ▸
Lone Star '95 ▸
The Outsiders '83
Pee-wee's Big Adventure '85 ▸
Targets '68 ▸
Twister '96

At the Movies

see also *Behind the Scenes*
Alien Trespass '09
Anguish '88
Apartment Zero '88 ▸
Attack from Mars '88
The Aviator '04 ▸
Bonnie & Clyde '67 ▸
Boogie Nights '97 ▸
Brutal Massacre: A Comedy '07
The Cheetah Girls: One World '08
Cinema Paradiso '88 ▸
Come See the Paradise '90 ▸
Coming Up Roses '87
CQ '01
The Creeps '97
Cyxork 7 '06
Day for Night '73 ▸
The Deal '08
Demons '86
Desperately Seeking Susan '85
The Dying Gaul '05 ▸
Entropy '99
For Ever Mozart '96
Foul Play '78 ▸
Full Frontal '02
Get Shorty '95 ▸
Goodbye, Dragon Inn '03
Gremlins '84 ▸
Gremlins 2: The New Batch '90 ▸
The Hard Way '91 ▸
Hollywood Hotel '37
I Love Your Work '03
In and Out '97 ▸
In the Electric Mist '08
Inglourious Basterds '09 ▸
The Inner Circle '91 ▸
Into the West '92 ▸
Invasion Earth: The Aliens Are Here! '87
Johnny Dangerously '84
The Kid and I '05
L.A. Twister '04
Last Action Hero '93
The Last Picture Show '71 ▸
The Last Shot '04
The Long Day Closes '92 ▸
Love and Death on Long Island '97
Marigold '07
Matinee '92
Merton of the Movies '47
Military Intelligence and You! '06
Mr. Bean's Holiday '07
The Movie House Massacre '78
My Faraway Bride '06
A Nightmare on Elm Street 4: Dream Master '88
One Summer Love '76
Otto: Or, Up with Dead People '08
Passion '82
Polyester '81
Popcorn '89
The Projectionist '71 ▸
The Proprietor '96
The Purple Rose of Cairo '85 ▸
The Real Blonde '97
Reel Paradise '05 ▸
The Replacement Killers '98
Rorret '87 ▸
Sabotage '36 ▸
Scenes from a Mall '91
Scream '96 ▸
Scream 2 '97 ▸
Scream 3 '00
Shadow of the Vampire '00 ▸
Sherlock, Jr. '24 ▸
Simone '02
Slippery Slope '06
Slipstream '07
Something Short of Paradise '79
South Park: Bigger, Longer and Uncut '99
Tampopo '86 ▸
Tartuffe '25
Things to Do in Denver When You're Dead '95 ▸
Trailer, the Movie '99
Tristram Shandy: A Cock and Bull Story '05
Trojan Eddie '96 ▸
Tropic Thunder '08 ▸
Two Bits '96
Variety '83
Venice, Venice '92
Wes Craven's New Nightmare '94 ▸
What Just Happened '08
What the Moon Saw '90
White Heat '49 ▸
Who Framed Roger Rabbit '88 ▸
With Friends Like These '98 ▸
Zack and Miri Make a Porno '08 ▸

At the Video Store

see also *At the Drive-In; At the Movies*
Be Kind Rewind '08
Cafe Ole '00
Clerks '94 ▸
EDtv '99
Film Geek '06
The Fisher King '91 ▸
Heart of the Beholder '05 ▸
How to be a Serial Killer '08
Jersey Girl '04
Little Fish '05 ▸
Love and Death on Long Island '97
Remote Control '88
Scream '96 ▸
The Sisterhood of the Traveling Pants 2 '08
Tainted '98
Video Violence '87
Watching the Detectives '07
The Watermelon Woman '97

Atlanta

see also *American South*
Beauty Shop '05 ▸
Blast '96
Cyborg '89
Daddy's Little Girls '07
Diary of a Mad Black Woman '05
Driving Miss Daisy '89 ▸
The Dukes of Hazzard '05
Echo of Murder '00
Gone with the Wind '39 ▸
The Gospel '05 ▸
In the Flesh '97
Let's Do It Again '75
Midnight Blue '96
The Murder of Mary Phagan '87 ▸
Run for the Dream: The Gail Devers Story '96
Scarlett '94
Sharky's Machine '81
Sherman's March '86 ▸
Stomp the Yard '07
Three Can Play That Game '07

Atlantic City

Atlantic City '81 ▸
Beaches '88 ▸
Convention Girl '35
Duane Hopwood '05 ▸
$5 a Day '08
Gunshy '98 ▸
The King of Marvin Gardens '72
The Lemon Sisters '90
Owning Mahowny '03
Snake Eyes '98
Sour Grapes '98
Where the Truth Lies '05
Yonkers Joe '08

Auditions

Audition '99
Billy Elliot '00 ▸
Center Stage: Turn It Up '08
Chain of Souls '00
Dickie Roberts: Former Child Star '03
The Dolly Sisters '46
Every Little Step '08
Fame '80 ▸
Flashdance '83
Girls Just Want to Have Fun '85
Great World of Sound '07
The Guru '02
Hairspray '88 ▸
Hollywood Homicide '03
Hollywood, Je T'Aime '09
Honkytonk Man '82
I Want Someone to Eat Cheese With '06
Inside Daisy Clover '65
Kiss Kiss Bang Bang '05 ▸
Love Songs '84
Make It Happen '08
National Lampoon Presents Cattle Call '06
Never Say Macbeth '07
Pipe Dream '02
Shakespeare in Love '98 ▸
Showgirls '95
Smiley Face '07
The Thing Called Love '93
Three Sailors and a Girl '53
True Romance '93
Undiscovered '05
Weeds '87 ▸
Yellow '06
You Light Up My Life '77

Aunts & Uncles, Nieces & Nephews

see also *Brothers & Sisters; Family Ties*
The Addams Family '91
Addams Family Values '93
Airborne '93
Alex Rider: Operation Stormbreaker '06
All in a Night's Work '61
American Movie '99 ▸
Arsenic and Old Lace '44 ▸

▸ = *rated three bones or higher*

Australia

Autism

Automobiles

Babysitting

Bachelor Party

Bad Bosses

Bad Dads

▸ = rated three bones or higher

Stakeout '62
Star Maps '97
Steel City '06
The Stepfather '87 ▶
Stepfather 2: Make Room for Daddy '89
Stepfather 3: Father's Day '92
Swimming Upstream '03
Talladega Nights: The Ballad of Ricky Bobby '06
Tetro '09
That Evening Sun '09 ▶
This Boy's Life '93 ▶
A Thousand Acres '97
Thumbsucker '05 ▶
Toll of the Desert '35
Transfixed '01
Turn It Up '00
U-Turn '97
Underworld: Evolution '05
Virgin '03
Wannabes '01
The War Zone '98
Washington Square '97 ▶
When Did You Last See Your Father? '07
Where the Hot Wind Blows '59
Yonkers Joe '08
ZigZag '02 ▶

Ballet

***see also** Dance Fever*

Alive and Kicking '96
An American in Paris '51 ▶
Angel in a Taxi '59
The Bacchantes '63
Ballet Russes '05 ▶
Black Tights '60
Body Beat '88
Brain Donors '92
Center Stage '00
Center Stage: Turn It Up '08
The Children of Theatre Street '77 ▶
The Company '03 ▶
The Cowboy & the Ballerina '84
Dance '90
Dance, Girl, Dance '40
The Dancer Upstairs '02
Dancers '87
George Balanchine's The Nutcracker '93
Gold Diggers in Paris '38
Grand Hotel '32 ▶
Invitation to the Dance '56
Limelight '52 ▶
Little Ballerina '47
Meet Me in Las Vegas '56
Mirrors '85
Never Let Me Go '53
Nijinsky '80
Nine Months '95
Nutcracker Sweet '84
Nutcracker: The Motion Picture '86
The Red Shoes '48 ▶
Shadow Dancing '88 ▶
Shall We Dance '37 ▶
Spectre of the Rose '46
The Story of Three Loves '53
Summer Interlude '50 ▶
Suspiria '77 ▶
Tales of Beatrix Potter '71 ▶
The Tales of Hoffmann '51
Talk to Her '02 ▶
The Turning Point '77
Waterloo Bridge '40 ▶

Ballooning

The Adventures of Baron Munchausen '89 ▶
Around the World in 80 Days '56 ▶
Around the World in 80 Days '89
Around the World in 80 Days '04
Charlie and the Great Balloon Chase '82
Cloud Waltzing '87
Danny Deckchair '03
Enduring Love '04
Fantastic Balloon Voyage '76
Five Weeks in a Balloon '62
Flight of the Eagle '82
Frankenstein Island '81
The Great Race '65
Lost Zeppelin '29
Men Don't Leave '89
Mysterious Island '61 ▶
Night Crossing '81
Octopussy '83
Olly Olly Oxen Free '78
Police Academy 4: Citizens on Patrol '87
Queen of the Jungle '35
The Red Balloon '56 ▶
Those Magnificent Men in Their Flying Machines '65 ▶
Voyage en Balloon '59
The Wizard of Oz '39 ▶

Baltimore

The Alien Factor '78
And Justice for All '79
Avalon '90 ▶
The Boys of Baraka '05
Breathing Lessons '94 ▶
Cause of Death '00
The Climb '97
Crash and Burn '07
Diner '82 ▶
A Dirty Shame '04
Duck '05
First Sunday '08
Hairspray '88 ▶
Hairspray '07 ▶
He Said, She Said '91
He's Just Not That Into You '09
The Hit '01
Homicide: The Movie '00
Ladder 49 '04
Liberty Heights '99
Management '09
Pecker '98
Polyester '81
The Salon '05
Seven Days of Grace '06
Sleepless in Seattle '93 ▶
Step Up 2 the Streets '08
The Sum of All Fears '02
Tin Men '87

Bar & Grill

***see also** Nightclubs*

Albino Alligator '96
Americano '05
Ash Wednesday '02
Bar Girls '95
Bar Hopping '00
Barb Wire '96
Barfly '87 ▶
Bedazzled '68 ▶
Before Sunrise '94
Bottoms Up '06
The Bowery '33 ▶
The Broken Hearts Club '00 ▶
Bucktown '75
Burnzy's Last Call '95
Cocktail '88
Coyote Ugly '00
Crocodile Dundee '86 ▶
Death in Brunswick '90
Death Proof '07
Dinner Rush '00 ▶
The Exiles '61
Feast '06
Feast 2: Sloppy Seconds '08
Flickering Lights '01
The Florentine '98
From Dusk Till Dawn '95
From Dusk Till Dawn 2: Texas Blood Money '98
From Dusk Till Dawn 3: The Hangman's Daughter '99
Headless Body in Topless Bar '96
Hedwig and the Angry Inch '00 ▶
Hi-Life '98
Hysterical Blindness '02
The Iceman Cometh '60 ▶
The Iceman Cometh '73
Intimacy '00
John Carpenter's Vampires '97
Kings '07
The Last Time I Committed Suicide '96
Lemonade Joe '64
Little Boy Blue '97
Luminarias '99
Margarita Happy Hour '01
Mondays in the Sun '02
Money Kings '98
Nobody '99
One Night at McCool's '01
Overnight '03 ▶
Pee-wee's Big Adventure '85 ▶
Phenomenon '96
Portland Expose '57
Rare Birds '01
Restaurant '98
Road House '89
Road House 2: Last Call '06
Roxanne '87 ▶
Ruby's Bucket of Blood '01
Stand-Ins '97
Stickmen '01
Still Waiting '08
Table One '00
The Taste of Others '00 ▶
The Tavern '00
Time Served '99
Tree's Lounge '96
Twice upon a Yesterday '98
Two Family House '99
Un Air de Famille '96
Urban Cowboy '80
Urbania '00
The White Countess '05 ▶

Barcelona

***see also** Madrid; Spain*

The Bobo '67
Body Armour '07
The Cheetah Girls 2 '06
Dark Habits '84
Food of Love '02
Gaudi Afternoon '01
Land and Freedom '95 ▶
L'Auberge Espagnole '02 ▶
Nico and Dani '00
The Sea Change '98
Vicky Cristina Barcelona '08
What It's All About '95

Baseball

Air Bud 4: Seventh Inning Fetch '02
Alibi Ike '35
Amazing Grace & Chuck '87
Angels in the Infield '00
Angels in the Outfield '51 ▶
Angels in the Outfield '94
The Babe '92
Babe Ruth Story '48
The Bad News Bears '76 ▶
The Bad News Bears '05
The Bad News Bears Go to Japan '78
The Bad News Bears in Breaking Training '77
Ball of Wax '03
Bang the Drum Slowly '56
Bang the Drum Slowly '73 ▶
Battlefield Baseball '03
Battling Orioles '24
The Benchwarmers '06
Bingo Long Traveling All-Stars & Motor Kings '76 ▶
Blood Games '90
Blue Skies Again '83
The Break-Up '06
Brewster's Millions '85
The Bronx Is Burning '07
Bull Durham '88 ▶
The Busher '19
The Catcher '98
Chasing Dreams '81
Chicken Little '05
Chu Chu & the Philly Flash '81
Cobb '94 ▶
Comeback Kid '80
The Comrades of Summer '92
Cooperstown '93
Damn Yankees '58 ▶
Diminished Capacity '08
Don't Look Back: The Story of Leroy "Satchel" Paige '81
Ed '96
Eight Men Out '88 ▶
Everyone's Hero '06
The Fan '96
Fear Strikes Out '57 ▶
Fever Pitch '05
Field of Dreams '89 ▶
The Final Season '07
Finding Buck McHenry '00
For Love of the Game '99
Frequency '00
Game 6 '05
The Geisha Boy '58
Hank Aaron: Chasing the Dream '95 ▶
Hardball '01
Headin' Home '20
Hustle '04
Ironweed '87 ▶
It Happens Every Spring '49 ▶
It's Good to Be Alive '74
It's My Turn '80
The Jackie Robinson Story '50 ▶
Jim Thorpe: All American '51
Joe Torre: Curveballs Along the Way '97
The Kid From Cleveland '49
The Kid from Left Field '79
Kill the Umpire '50
The King '05
A League of Their Own '92 ▶
Life '99
The Life and Times of Hank Greenberg '99 ▶
Little Big League '94
A Little Inside '01
Long Gone '87
Love Affair: The Eleanor & Lou Gehrig Story '77 ▶
Major League '89
Major League 2 '94
Major League 3: Back to the Minors '98
The Man from Left Field '93
Mean Streak '99
Mr. Baseball '92
Mr. Destiny '90
Mr. 3000 '04
The Natural '84 ▶
Night Game '89
One in a Million: The Ron LeFlore Story '78
The Open Road '09
Past the Bleachers '95
Pastime '91 ▶
Perfect Game '00
Pride of St. Louis '52
The Pride of the Yankees '42 ▶
Rhubarb '51
The Rookie '02 ▶
Rookie of the Year '93
The Sandlot '93 ▶
The Sandlot 2 '05
The Sandlot 3: Heading Home '07
The Scout '94
61* '01 ▶
The Slugger's Wife '85
Soul of the Game '96 ▶
Squeeze Play '79
Stealing Home '88
The Stratton Story '49 ▶
Sugar '09 ▶
Summer Catch '01
Take Me Out to the Ball Game '49
Taking Care of Business '90
Talent for the Game '91
Three Wishes '95
Tiger Town '83
Trading Hearts '87
Up for Grabs '05
The Upside of Anger '05 ▶
Wait until Spring, Bandini '90
Whistling in Brooklyn '43
Wide Awake '97
A Winner Never Quits '86
The Winning Team '52
Woman of the Year '42 ▶

Basketball

Above the Rim '94
The Absent-Minded Professor '61 ▶
Adam Sandler's 8 Crazy Nights '02
Air Bud '97
The Air Up There '94
Alien: Resurrection '97 ▶
Annie O '95
The Basket '99
The Basketball Diaries '95
Believe in Me '06
Big and Hairy '98
Big Mo '73
Big Shot: Confessions of a Campus Bookie '02
Black and White '99 ▶
Blue Chips '94
The Cable Guy '96
Campus Confessions '38
Celtic Pride '96
Coach '78
Coach Carter '05 ▶
The Cookout '04
Cornbread, Earl & Me '75
Crossover '06
Eddie '96
Fast Break '79
Final Exam '98
Final Shot: The Hank Gathers Story '92
Finding Forrester '00
The Fish that Saved Pittsburgh '79
Flubber '97
For Heaven's Sake '79
Forget Paris '95
Glory Road '06
Grown Ups '10
Guarding Eddy '04
Harvard Man '01
He Got Game '98
The Heart of the Game '05
Heaven Is a Playground '91
High School Musical 3: Senior Year '08
Hoop Dreams '94 ▶
Hoosiers '86 ▶
Hurricane Season '08
Inside Moves '80
John Tucker Must Die '06
Juwanna Mann '02
King of the Jungle '01
Like Mike '02
Love and Basketball '00 ▶
More Than a Game '08
O '01 ▶
One on One '77
Passing Glory '99 ▶
Pistol: The Birth of a Legend '90
Pleasantville '98 ▶
Porky's Revenge '85
Rebound '05
Rebound: The Legend of Earl "The Goat" Manigault '96
The Red Sneakers '01
Rock the Paint '05
The St. Tammany Miracle '94
A Season on the Brink '02
Semi-Pro '08
The Sixth Man '97
Slam Dunk Ernest '95
Space Jam '96
Sunset Park '96
Tall Story '60
Teen Wolf '85
That Championship Season '82
That Championship Season '99
Through the Fire '05 ▶
Tyler Perry's Meet the Browns '08
Underworld Scandal '47
Unshackled '00
White Men Can't Jump '92

Bats

***see also** Eco-Vengeance!; Up All Night; Wild Kingdom*

The Bat People '74
Batman Begins '05 ▶
Batman Forever '95 ▶
Batman Returns '92
Bats '99
Bats: Human Harvest '07
The Devil Bat '41
Nightwing '79
The Vampire Bat '32

Beach Blanket Bingo

***see also** Lifeguards; Sex on the Beach; Surfing; Swimming*

Back to the Beach '87
Baywatch the Movie: Forbidden Paradise '95
Beach Babes from Beyond '93
Beach Blanket Bingo '65 ▶
Beach Girls '82
The Beach Girls and the Monster '65
Beach House '82
Beach Party '63
Bikini Beach '64
Bikini Summer '91
Bikini Summer 3: South Beach Heat '97
Blue Crush '02 ▶
Body Waves '92
California Dreaming '79
Computer Beach Party '88
The Fat Spy '66
Horror of Party Beach '64
How to Stuff a Wild Bikini '65
Love! Valour! Compassion! '96
Malibu Beach '78
Maslin Beach '97
Muscle Beach Party '64
Nico and Dani '00
Pajama Party '64
Phat Beach '96
Psycho Beach Party '00
Ride the Wild Surf '64
Seaside Swingers '65
Shag: The Movie '89 ▶
South Beach Academy '96
A Summer's Tale '96
Surf Party '64
A Swingin' Summer '65
Too Good to Be True '98
Wet and Wild Summer '92
Where the Boys Are '60

Bears

***see also** Wild Kingdom*

Almost Heroes '97
The Bear '89 ▶
The Bears & I '74
Berserker '87
Brother Bear '03
Brother Bear 2 '06
The Capture of Grizzly Adams '82
Claws '77
The Country Bears '02
Deadtime Stories '86
Dr. Dolittle 2 '01
Earth '07
The Edge '97
Gentle Giant '67
The Golden Compass '07
The Great Outdoors '88
Grizzly '76
Grizzly Adams: The Legend Continues '90
Grizzly Falls '99
Grizzly Man '05 ▶
Grizzly Rage '07
The Hotel New Hampshire '84
The Jungle Book '67 ▶
The Jungle Book 2 '03
King of the Grizzlies '69
Kung Fu Panda '08 ▶
Legends of the Fall '94
Life & Times of Grizzly Adams '74
The Many Adventures of Winnie the Pooh '77
Ms. Bear '97
The Parent Trap '61
The Polar Bear King '94
Pooh's Heffalump Movie '05
Rudyard Kipling's The Jungle Book '94
Rudyard Kipling's the Second Jungle Book: Mowgli and Baloo '97
Starbird and Sweet William '73
True Heart '97
An Unfinished Life '05
Wild Grizzly '99
Without a Paddle '04

Beatniks

Beat Girl '60
A Bucket of Blood '59 ▶
Expresso Bongo '59
Funny Face '57 ▶
Hairspray '88 ▶

▶ = *rated three bones or higher*

The Last Time I Committed Suicide '96
The Prime Time '60
The Sleazy Uncle '89
So I Married an Axe Murderer '93

Beauty Pageants

see also *Dream Girls*
Beautiful '00
The Case of the Lucky Legs '35
Drop Dead Gorgeous '99
The Duchess of Idaho '50
Happy, Texas '99 ▸
I Know What You Did Last Summer '97 ▸
I Wanna Be a Beauty Queen '85
Little Miss Sunshine '06 ▸
Miss All-American Beauty '82
Miss Cast Away '04
Miss Congeniality '00
Miss Congeniality 2: Armed and Fabulous '05
Miss Firecracker '89 ▸
No Contest '94
Shag: The Movie '89 ▸
Slap Her, She's French '02
Smile '75 ▸
Sweet Beat '59
Waikiki Wedding '37 ▸

Beer

see also *On the Rocks*
Beer '85
Beer League '06
Beerfest '06
Happy Hour '87
The Jolly Boys' Last Stand '00
Kicked in the Head '97
The Lady Eve '41 ▸
The Nugget '02
The Saddest Music in the World '03
Smokey and the Bandit '77
Strange Brew '83
Swing Vote '08
Take This Job & Shove It '81
Young Einstein '89

Bees

see also *Killer Bugs and Slugs*
Bee Movie '07
The Bees '78
Candyman '92
Candyman 2: Farewell to the Flesh '94
Candyman 3: Day of the Dead '98
Microcosmos '96 ▸
The Secret Life of Bees '08 ▸
The Swarm '78

Behind Bars

see *Great Escapes; Men in Prison; Women in Prison*

Behind the Scenes

see also *At the Movies; Film History*
Abuse '82
Actors and Sin '52
Adaptation '02 ▸
The Affairs of Annabel '38
An Alan Smithee Film: Burn, Hollywood, Burn '97
Alexandria Again and Forever '90
American Virgin '98
America's Sweethearts '01
Anaconda '96
...And God Spoke '94
The Audrey Hepburn Story '00
Augustin '95
Auto Focus '02 ▸
The Bad and the Beautiful '52 ▸
Beaumarchais the Scoundrel '96
Best Friends '82
Beware of a Holy Whore '70
Bewitched '05
Big Fat Liar '02
The Big Knife '55 ▸
The Big Picture '89
Big Shot's Funeral '01
Big Show '37
Bloodbath '98
Body Chemistry 3: Point of Seduction '93
The Bodyguard '92
Bollywood Hero '09
Bombay Talkie '70
Borat: Cultural Learnings of America for Make Benefit Glorious Nation of Kazakhstan '06 ▸
Boy Meets Girl '38 ▸
Break a Leg '03
Broadway Rhythm '44
Bruno '09
Brutal Massacre: A Comedy '07
Bullets over Broadway '94 ▸
Cannes Man '96
Cats Don't Dance '97
Cecil B. Demented '00
Celebrity '98 ▸
Chaplin '92 ▸
The Chaplin Revue '58
A Chorus Line '85
A Chorus of Disapproval '89
Chuck Berry: Hail! Hail! Rock 'n' Roll '87 ▸
Come as You Are '05
The Confessional '95 ▸
Contempt '64 ▸
Cosi '95 ▸
CQ '01
Crimetime '96
Crocodile Dundee in Los Angeles '01
Crossover Dreams '85
Cut '00
Dames '34 ▸
Dance of Life '29
Dancing in September '00
Dancing Lady '33
Dangerous Game '93
Danny Roane: First Time Director '06
Darlings of the Gods '90
Day at the Beach '98
Day for Night '73 ▸
The Death Kiss '33
Delirious '91
The Disappearance of Kevin Johnson '95
Don't Let Your Meat Loaf '95
Double Threat '92
The Dresser '83 ▸
Ed Wood '94 ▸
The End of Violence '97
Entropy '99
Everything for Sale '68
Evil Ed '96
Expresso Bongo '59
Face the Music '92
Factory Girl '06
Fall Guy '82
Festival at Cannes '02
5 Dark Souls '96
Flickers '80
The Fluffer '01
Footlight Parade '33 ▸
For Ever Mozart '96
For Your Consideration '06
Free and Easy '30
Free Enterprise '98
The Freeway Maniac '88
French Exit '97
The French Lieutenant's Woman '81 ▸
Full Frontal '02
Full Tilt Boogie '97
Funny People '09
Get Shorty '95 ▸
The Ghost Walks '34
Give a Girl a Break '53
Glam '97
Gods and Monsters '98 ▸
Going Hollywood '33 ▸
The Goldwyn Follies '38
Good Times '67
Goodbye, Norma Jean '75
Goodnight, Sweet Marilyn '89
The Grace Kelly Story '83
The Great Buck Howard '09
Grief '94
Grunt! The Wrestling Movie '85
The Hard Way '91 ▸
He Said, She Said '91
The Hearst and Davies Affair '85
Hearts of Darkness: A Filmmaker's Apocalypse '91 ▸
Heckler '08
Help! '65 ▸
Hijacking Hollywood '97
Hindsight '97
Hollywood Boulevard '76
Hollywood Cavalcade '39
Hollywood Confidential '97
Hollywood Ending '02
Hollywood Kills '06
Hollywood Man '76
Hollywood Mystery '34
Hollywood North '03
Hollywood Shuffle '87
Hollywoodland '06
Hooper '78
Hughes & Harlow: Angels in Hell '77
I Could Never Be Your Woman '06
I Want Candy '07
The Ice Rink '99
Identification of a Woman '82
I'll Do Anything '93
I'm Going Home '00 ▸
In a Moment of Passion '93
In the Shadows '01
In the Soup '92
The Independent '00
Inland Empire '06
Inside Daisy Clover '65
Into the Sun '92
Introducing Dorothy Dandridge '99 ▸
Irma Vep '96
It Happened in Hollywood '37
James Dean '01
The Jayne Mansfield Story '80
Joey Breaker '93 ▸
The Killing of Sister George '69
L.A. Confidential '97 ▸
La Dolce Vita '60 ▸
L.A. Goddess '92
The Last Don 2 '98
The Last Shot '04
The Last Word '95
Le Polygraphe '96
Le Schpountz '38
The Leading Man '96
Legs '83
Lies '83
Lisbon Story '94
Living in Oblivion '94 ▸
Lobster Man from Mars '89
The Lonely Lady '83
Lucky Devils '33
Make a Wish '37
A Man in Love '87 ▸
Man of a Thousand Faces '57 ▸
Matinee '92
Me and Orson Welles '09
Meet the Feebles '89
A Midwinter's Tale '95
Miss All-American Beauty '82
Mistress '91
Modern Romance '81 ▸
The Moguls '05
The Moon & the Stars '07
Movie Maker '86
Movies Money Murder '96
The Mozart Brothers '86 ▸
Mulholland Drive '01 ▸
The Muppets Take Manhattan '84 ▸
The Muse '99
My Life's in Turnaround '94
My Wife is an Actress '01
Naked in New York '93
New Faces of 1952 '54
A Night for Crime '42
Night of the Living Dead, 25th Anniversary Documentary '93
Nine '09
The Nines '07 ▸
Nixon '95 ▸
Noises Off '92
Notting Hill '99 ▸
The November Men '93
On an Island with You '48
On with the Show '29
Open Season '95
Opening Night '77
The Oscar '66
Paradise, Texas '05
Paris When It Sizzles '64
Passion '82
Pastime '91 ▸
People I Know '02
The Perils of Pauline '47
The Phantom Lover '95
Pick a Star '37
The Pickle '93
The Player '92 ▸
Portraits Chinois '96
Postcards from the Edge '90 ▸
Quicksand '01
Rave Review '95
Ready to Wear '94
Rented Lips '88
Return to Cabin by the Lake '01
Rhythm on the River '40
Ringmaster '98
RKO 281 '99 ▸
Roadie '80
Rorret '87 ▸
Sally '29
Scream 3 '00
Search and Destroy '94
Searching for Bobby D '05
Secret Honor '85 ▸
Sex Is Crazy '79
Shadow of the Vampire '00 ▸
Shoot or Be Shot '02
The Shot '96
The Show '95
Show Girl in Hollywood '30
Silent Motive '91
Simone '02
Sioux City Sue '46
Skeleton Crew '09
Slaves of Hollywood '99
Slings & Arrows: Season 2 '05 ▸
Slipstream '07
S.O.B. '81
Somewhere in Time '80
Son of Gascogne '95
Souls for Sale '23
Spice World: The Movie '97
Stage Door '37 ▸
Stand-In '85
Stand-Ins '97
The Star Maker '95
Star Spangled Rhythm '42 ▸
State and Main '00 ▸
State of Things '82 ▸
The Stranger: Kabloonak '95
The Stunt Man '80 ▸
Stunts '77
The Suburbans '99
Sugar Sweet '02
Sugar Town '99
Sullivan's Travels '41 ▸
Summer Stock '50 ▸
Sunset '88
Sunset Boulevard '50 ▸
Sweet Liberty '86
Sweet Perfection '90
Swimming with Sharks '94 ▸
Tango '98
Teenager '74
10 Items or Less '06
That Thing You Do! '96 ▸
These Old Broads '01
They Bite '95
Through the Olive Trees '94 ▸
Tie Me Up! Tie Me Down! '90
Time Code '00
Tootsie '82 ▸
The Travelling Players '75
Tropic Thunder '08 ▸
Truth or Dare '91
The TV Set '06
Ulysses' Gaze '95
Under the Rainbow '81
Users '78
Valley of the Dolls '67
Velvet Touch '48 ▸
Venice, Venice '92
A Very Private Affair '62
Wag the Dog '97
Waiting for Guffman '96
The Waiting Game '99
The Watermelon Woman '97
Welcome to Hollywood '00
Wes Craven's New Nightmare '94 ▸
The West Point Story '50
What Just Happened '08
What Price Hollywood? '32 ▸
Where's Marlowe? '98
White Hunter, Black Heart '90 ▸
Whodunit '82
Wild Party '74
Witch Hunt '94
Zou Zou '34

Belfast

see also *Dublin; Ireland*
Belfast Assassin '84
Cal '84 ▸
Circle of Deceit '94
The Devil's Own '96 ▸
An Everlasting Piece '00
Fifty Dead Men Walking '08
Four Days in July '85
Hennessy '75
In the Name of the Father '93 ▸
The Informant '97 ▸
Mad About Mambo '00
The Merry Gentleman '08
The Mighty Celt '05
Nothing Personal '95 ▸
Quiet Day in Belfast '74 ▸
Resurrection Man '97
This Is the Sea '96

Berlin

see also *Germany*
Adam Resurrected '08
Aimee & Jaguar '98
The Alley Cats '65
Anita, Dances of Vice '87
The Apple '80
The Assignment '97
Before the Fall '04
Bent '97
Berlin Alexanderplatz '80 ▸
The Berlin Conspiracy '91
Berlin Tunnel 21 '81
The Blue Hour '91
Born in '45 '65
The Bourne Supremacy '04 ▸
Cabaret '72 ▸
The Captain from Koepenick '56
Charlie Chan at the Olympics '37
Cherry Blossoms '08
Chinese Boxes '84
Club Extinction '89
Cold Room '84
The Company '07
David '79 ▸
Dead Pigeon on Beethoven Street '72
Demons '86
Dr. Ehrlich's Magic Bullet '40
Downfall '04 ▸
The Edukators '04
80 Minutes '08
Eurotrip '04
Faraway, So Close! '93
Fatherland '94
Flightplan '05
Forbidden '85
A Foreign Affair '48 ▸
Funeral in Berlin '66 ▸
Go for Zucker '05
Good Bye, Lenin! '03 ▸
The Good German '06
Gotcha! '85
Hidden Agenda '99
I Am a Camera '55 ▸
Indiana Jones and the Last Crusade '89 ▸
The Innocent '93
Invincible '01
Judgment in Berlin '88
Kamikaze '89 '83 ▸
King of Thieves '04
Kuhle Wampe, Or Who Owns the World? '32
The Legend of Rita '99
The Lives of Others '06 ▸
Lola and Billy the Kid '98
The Looking Glass War '69
The Mistake '91
Mother Night '96 ▸
The Murderers Are Among Us '46
My Fuhrer '07
Obsession '97
The Oppermann Family '82
Otto: Or, Up with Dead People '08
The Promise '94
Run Lola Run '98 ▸
Salmonberries '91
The Search '48 ▸
The Serpent's Egg '78
Shining Through '92
Solo Sunny '80
The Song of Songs '33
Summer Palace '06 ▸
Taking Sides '01 ▸
The Third Sex '57
The Tigress '93
Timecop 2: The Berlin Decision '03
The Truce '96 ▸
The Tunnel '01 ▸
Under the Pavement Lies the Strand '75
Verboten! '59
The Waiting Time '99
What to Do in Case of Fire '02
Wings of Desire '88 ▸
A Woman in Berlin '08

Bermuda Triangle

Airport '77 '77
The Bermuda Depths '78
The Land That Time Forgot '09
Lost Voyage '01
Starship Invasions '77
The Triangle '01

Betrayal

Amores Perros '00 ▸
Assault on Precinct 13 '05
Benedict Arnold: A Question of Honor '03
The Betrayed '08
Black Belt '07
Blade 2 '02
Blue Car '03 ▸
Blue Hill Avenue '01
Body of Lies '08
Book of Love '04
Breach '07
The Business '05
The Business of Fancydancing '02
The Business of Strangers '01
The Butcher '07
The Casino Job '08
Chill Factor '99
The Count of Monte Cristo '02
Cruel Intentions 3 '04
Cypher '02 ▸
Dangerous Liaisons '03
The Departed '06 ▸
The Devil's Backbone '01
The Devil's Dominoes '07
Die Another Day '02
Enigma '01
Esther Kahn '00
The Expendables '10
Extremely Dangerous '99
Familia '05
Far from Heaven '02 ▸
The Fast Runner '01 ▸
Good '08
The Good Shepherd '06
The Great Water '04
Hangover Square '45
The Hard Word '02
Heart '99
Heist '01 ▸
Hitman '07
In the Mood for Love '00
The Kite Runner '07 ▸
Lady Jayne Killer '03
The League of Extraordinary Gentlemen '03
The Legend of Suriyothai '02
A Lion in the Streets '53
Lord of War '05 ▸
The Losers '10
Lost in Beijing '07
Love in the Time of Cholera '07
Mad Love '01
Medea '88

The Messenger: The Story of Joan of Arc *'99*
Mindstorm *'01*
Mongol *'07* ▸
Munich *'05* ▸
Once Upon a Time in America *'84* ▸
One Day You'll Understand *'08*
Pack of Lies *'87*
Philby, Burgess and MacLean: Spy Scandal of the Century *'84*
Relative Strangers *'99*
Resistance *'03*
Ripley's Game *'02* ▸
Road House *'48*
The Room *'03*
Signs & Wonders *'00*
Smiley's People *'82*
Star Wars: Episode 2—Attack of the Clones *'02* ▸
Star Wars: Episode 3—Revenge of the Sith *'05* ▸
This Gun for Hire *'42* ▸
Tick Tock *'00* ▸
Tinker, Tailor, Soldier, Spy *'80* ▸
Tropix *'02*
25th Hour *'02*
The Weight of Water *'00*
Wicker Park *'04*
The Women *'08*

Beverly Hills

Allie & Me *'97*
Anywhere But Here *'99*
B.A.P.'s *'97*
Beverly Hills Chihuahua *'08*
Beverly Hills Cop *'84*
Beverly Hills Cop 2 *'87*
Beverly Hills Cop 3 *'94*
Beverly Hills Madam *'86*
Clueless *'95* ▸
Down and Out in Beverly Hills *'86*
The Hollywood Knights *'80*
Housewife *'72*
Just Married *'03*
The Kreutzer Sonata *'08*
Legally Blonde *'01*
Pretty Woman *'90* ▸
The Return of the Beverly Hillbillies *'81*
Scenes from the Class Struggle in Beverly Hills *'89*
Slums of Beverly Hills *'98* ▸
Troop Beverly Hills *'89*
Wassup Rockers *'06*

Bicycling

American Flyers *'85*
And Soon the Darkness *'70*
Beijing Bicycle *'01*
The Bicycle Thief *'48* ▸
Blood Trails *'06*
BMX Bandits *'83*
Breaking Away *'79* ▸
Butch Cassidy and the Sundance Kid *'69* ▸
E.T.: The Extra-Terrestrial *'82* ▸
The Flying Scotsman *'06*
Go Further *'03*
Isn't Life Wonderful *'24* ▸
Off the Mark *'87*
Pee-wee's Big Adventure *'85* ▸
Quicksilver *'86*
Rad *'86*
Rush It *'77*
Ten Speed *'76*
The Triplets of Belleville *'02* ▸
2 Seconds *'98*

Big Battles

see also *Civil War; Korean War; Korean War; Persian Gulf/Iraq War; Revolutionary War; Vietnam War; World War I; World War II*

The Alamo *'60* ▸
The Alamo *'04*
Alexander Nevsky *'38* ▸
Alexander the Great *'55*
Aliens *'86* ▸
Anzio *'68*
Apocalypse Now *'79* ▸
The Arena *'73*
Arena *'89*
Attila *'01*
Avatar *'09* ▸
Back to Bataan *'45*
Barry Lyndon *'75* ▸
Battle Beyond the Sun *'63*
Battle of Britain *'69*
The Battle of El Alamein *'68*
Battle of the Bulge *'65*
The Battle of the Japan Sea *'70*
Battle of the Worlds *'61*
Battleground *'49* ▸
The Battleship Potemkin *'25* ▸
Ben-Hur *'26* ▸
Beowulf *'07* ▸
Beowulf & Grendel *'06*
The Big Parade *'25* ▸
The Big Red One *'80* ▸
The Birth of a Nation *'15* ▸
Braveheart *'95* ▸
A Bridge Too Far *'77*
The Bruce *'96*
Cage 2: The Arena of Death *'94*
Captain Caution *'40*
The Castilian *'63*
Chasing the Deer *'94*
The Chronicles of Narnia: Prince Caspian *'08*
Cold Mountain *'03* ▸
Crazy Horse *'96* ▸
Cromwell *'70*
Cross of Iron *'76*
The Crossing *'00*
The Crusades *'35*
Das Boot *'81* ▸
Days of Glory *'06*
Diamonds Are Forever *'71* ▸
Dragonheart *'96*
Dragonslayer *'81* ▸
Druids *'01*
El Cid *'61* ▸
Elizabeth: The Golden Age *'07*
The Emperor and the Assassin *'99*
The Empire Strikes Back *'80* ▸
Enemy Below *'57* ▸
Eragon *'06*
Excalibur *'81* ▸
The Fall of the Roman Empire *'64* ▸
The Fighting Sullivans *'42* ▸
First Knight *'95*
Flags of Our Fathers *'06* ▸
The Four Feathers *'02*
Gallipoli *'81* ▸
Gettysburg *'93* ▸
The Giant of Marathon *'60*
Giants of Rome *'63*
Gladiator *'00* ▸
Gladiators 7 *'62*
Glory *'89* ▸
Godzilla vs. the Smog Monster *'72*
Goldfinger *'64* ▸
The Guns of Navarone *'61* ▸
Heaven & Earth *'90* ▸
Helen of Troy *'03*
Henry V *'44* ▸
Henry V *'89* ▸
Hercules vs. the Sons of the Sun *'64*
Highlander *'86* ▸
I Bombed Pearl Harbor *'60*
In the Name of the King: A Dungeon Siege Tale *'08*
Independence Day *'96* ▸
Jeanne la Pucelle *'94*
Joan of Arc *'99*
John Paul Jones *'59*
Joyeux Noel *'05* ▸
The King of the Kickboxers *'91*
Kings of the Sun *'63*
The Last Command *'55*
The Last Samurai *'03* ▸
Letters from Iwo Jima *'06* ▸
The Lighthorsemen *'87* ▸
The Long Riders *'80* ▸
The Longest Day *'62* ▸
Lord of the Rings: The Fellowship of the Ring *'01* ▸
Lord of the Rings: The Two Towers *'02* ▸
Lord of the Rings: The Return of the King *'03* ▸
The Magical Legend of the Leprechauns *'99*
The Man Who Would Be King *'75* ▸
Mars Attacks! *'96*
Master and Commander: The Far Side of the World *'03* ▸
Memphis Belle *'90* ▸
The Messenger: The Story of Joan of Arc *'99*
Midway *'76*
Mists of Avalon *'01* ▸
Mongol *'07* ▸
The Mongols *'60*
Monty Python and the Holy Grail *'75* ▸
Moonraker *'79*
Motel Hell *'80*
Mulan *'98*
The Mummy Returns *'01*
Napoleon *'03*
Night Watch *'04*
A Nightmare on Elm Street *'84*
The Odyssey *'97*
The Patriot *'00*
Patton *'70* ▸
Pearl *'78*
Pirates of the Caribbean: At World's End *'07*
Raiders of the Lost Ark *'81* ▸
Ran *'85* ▸
Rawhide *'50* ▸
Red Cliff *'08* ▸
Red Dawn *'84*
Return of the Jedi *'83* ▸
Revolution *'85*
Ring of Fire *'91*
Rob Roy *'95* ▸
Robo Warriors *'96*
Robot Jox *'90*
Samson and His Mighty Challenge *'64*
The Sand Pebbles *'66* ▸
Sands of Iwo Jima *'49* ▸
Saving Private Ryan *'98* ▸
The Siege of Firebase Gloria *'89*
The Silk Road *'92*
Soldier *'98*
Son of the Morning Star *'91* ▸
Stalingrad *'94*
Star Crash *'78*
Star Trek: Nemesis *'02*
Star Wars *'77* ▸
Star Wars: Episode 1—The Phantom Menace *'99* ▸
Star Wars: Episode 2—Attack of the Clones *'02* ▸
Star Wars: Episode 3—Revenge of the Sith *'05* ▸
Star Wars: The Clone Wars *'08*
Street Hunter *'90*
Tales from a Parallel Universe: I Worship His Shadow *'97*
Ten Days That Shook the World *'27* ▸
Terminator Salvation *'09*
They Died with Their Boots On *'41* ▸
The 13th Warrior *'99*
300 *'07*
The 300 Spartans *'62*
Thunderball *'65*
To Hell and Back *'55*
Tora! Tora! Tora! *'70*
Transformers *'07*
The Trench *'99*
The Trojan Horse *'62*
Troy *'04*
Twelve o'Clock High *'49* ▸
Two for Texas *'97*
The Viking Queen *'67*
War and Peace *'56*
War and Peace *'68* ▸
War and Peace *'73*
The War Lord *'65* ▸
Warrior Queen *'03*
The Wild Bunch *'69* ▸
Zulu *'64*
Zulu Dawn *'79* ▸

Big-Budget Bombs

see also *Pure Ego Vehicles*

The Adventurers *'70*
Alexander *'04*
Alexander the Great *'55*
American Anthem *'86*
Annie *'82*
The Bonfire of the Vanities *'90*
Boom! *'68*
Christopher Columbus: The Discovery *'92*
Cleopatra *'63*
The Conqueror *'56*
The Cotton Club *'84* ▸
Dune *'84*
Harlem Nights *'89*
Heaven's Gate *'81*
Howard the Duck *'86*
Hudson Hawk *'91*
I'll Do Anything *'93*
Ishtar *'87*
Last Action Hero *'93*
The Long Ships *'64*
The Lovers on the Bridge *'91*
Midway *'76*
Money Train *'95*
Moon in the Gutter *'83*
1941 *'79*
One from the Heart *'82*
Pirates *'86*
Rambo 3 *'88*
Santa Claus: The Movie *'85*
The Scarlet Letter *'95*
The Shoes of the Fisherman *'68*
The Silver Chalice *'54*
Sphere *'97*
Summer Holiday *'48*
Supergirl *'84*
Tora! Tora! Tora! *'70*
Toys *'92*
Two Minute Warning *'76*
Two of a Kind *'83*
Waterloo *'71*

Big Cats

see also *Jungle Stories; Wild Kingdom*

Across the Moon *'94*
The Adventures of Tarzan *'21*
Androcles and the Lion *'52*
The Big Cat *'49*
Bringing Up Baby *'38* ▸
Cat People *'42* ▸
Charlie the Lonesome Cougar *'67*
Cheetah *'89*
Doctor Dolittle *'67*
The Ghost and the Darkness *'96*
The Gladiator *'38* ▸
I Dreamed of Africa *'00*
Ice Age *'02* ▸
Island of Lost Souls *'32* ▸
Jungle Hell *'55*
The Leopard Man *'43*
The Lion King *'94* ▸
The Lost Jungle *'34*
Passion in the Desert *'97*
Rugrats Go Wild! *'03*
So This Is Africa *'33*
Talladega Nights: The Ballad of Ricky Bobby *'06*
Terror Is a Man *'59*
A Tiger Walks *'64*
The Wild *'06*

Big Digs

Ancient Evil: Scream of the Mummy *'00*
Ancient Relic *'02*
Around the Bend *'04*
Belphegar: Phantom of the Louvre *'01*
Blood from the Mummy's Tomb *'71*
The Body *'01*
Charlie Chan in Egypt *'35*
The Curse of King Tut's Tomb *'80*
Dead Are Alive *'72*
Deadly Intent *'88*
Exorcist: The Beginning *'04*
The Golden Salamander *'51*
Indiana Jones and the Last Crusade *'89* ▸
Indiana Jones and the Temple of Doom *'84* ▸
King of the Forest Rangers *'46*
The Last Templar *'09*
Legend of the Lost Tomb *'97*
The Librarian: Return to King Solomon's Mines *'06*
The Lost Treasure of the Grand Canyon *'08*
March or Die *'77*
The Mask *'61*
The Mole People *'56*
The Mummy *'32* ▸
The Mummy *'99*
The Mummy's Hand *'40*
The Mummy's Shroud *'67*
National Treasure: Book of Secrets *'07*
Pimpernel Smith *'42*
Raiders of the Lost Ark *'81* ▸
The Ruins *'08*
Russell Mulcahy's Tale of the Mummy *'99*
Search for the Gods *'75*
Secre of the Andes *'98*
Sound of Horror *'64*
Specters *'87*
Stargate *'94*
Tomb *'86*
Tower of the Firstborn *'98*
Unseen Evil *'99*
Valley of the Kings *'54*
The Word *'78*

Big Ideas

see also *Ethics & Morals*

The Addiction *'95*
The Air I Breathe *'07*
Amazing Grace *'06* ▸
Barefoot in Athens *'66*
Being Human *'94*
Bickford Shmeckler's Cool Ideas *'06*
The Big Kahuna *'00*
Blaise Pascal *'71* ▸
Blue *'93*
A Brief History of Time *'92* ▸
The Buddha of Suburbia *'92* ▸
Cold Souls *'09*
Contact *'97*
Dead Man *'95*
The Designated Mourner *'97*
Destiny *'97*
Diary of a Seducer *'95*
Eat, Pray, Love *'10*
Faraway, So Close! *'93*
Final Destination *'00*
First Snow *'07*
The Fountain *'06*
Four Days in September *'97*
Harvard Man *'01*
Holy Man *'98*
The Incredible Shrinking Man *'57* ▸
I.Q. *'94*
Jonathan Livingston Seagull *'73*
Judgment at Nuremberg *'61* ▸
Kicking and Screaming *'95* ▸
The Life Before Her Eyes *'07*
Life Is a Bed of Roses *'83*
Meetings with Remarkable Men *'79*
Melvin Goes to Dinner *'03*
The Messiah *'75* ▸
Metropolitan *'90* ▸
Mindwalk: A Film for Passionate Thinkers *'91* ▸
Mission to Mars *'00*
Mr. North *'88*
My Brother Is an Only Child *'07*
My Dinner with Andre *'81* ▸
$9.99 *'08*
1900 *'76* ▸
Nostradamus *'93*
The Passion of Ayn Rand *'99*
The Quarrel *'93*
The Razor's Edge *'46* ▸
The Razor's Edge *'84*
Return to Eden *'89*
Samurai 3: Duel at Ganryu Island *'56* ▸
Sans Soleil *'82* ▸
The Seventh Seal *'56* ▸
Sliding Doors *'97*
Sorceress *'88* ▸
Sunshine *'07*
That Championship Season *'82*
Time of the Wolf *'03* ▸
The Triumph of Love *'01*
Up to a Certain Point *'83*
Waking Life *'01*
What Dreams May Come *'98*
What It's All About *'95*
What the $*! Do We Know? *'04*
What to Do in Case of Fire *'02*
Wittgenstein *'93*
The Wrong Move *'78*
Zabriskie Point *'70* ▸

Big Rigs

see also *Motor Vehicle Dept.; Road Trip*

The Art of War 3: Retribution *'08*
Big Trouble in Little China *'86*
Black Dog *'98*
Breakdown *'96* ▸
Breaker! Breaker! *'77*
California Straight Ahead *'25*
California Straight Ahead! *'37*
Citizens Band *'77* ▸
Coast to Coast *'80*
Convoy *'78*
Desperate *'47*
Driving Force *'88*
Duel *'71* ▸
Every Which Way But Loose *'78*
F.I.S.T. *'78*
Flatbed Annie and Sweetiepie: Lady Truckers *'79*
Great Smokey Roadblock *'76*
Hi-Jacked *'50*
High Ballin' *'78*
Joy Ride *'01* ▸
Joy Ride 2: Dead Ahead *'08*
Larger Than Life *'96*
The Long Haul *'57*
Maximum Overdrive *'86*
The National Tree *'09*
The Other Side of the Mountain, Part 2 *'78*
Pee-wee's Big Adventure *'85* ▸
Road Games *'81*
Road Rage *'01*
Rolling Vengeance *'87*
Smokey and the Bandit *'77*
Smokey and the Bandit 2 *'80*
Smokey and the Bandit, Part 3 *'83*
Smokey & the Hotwire Gang *'79*
Sorcerer *'77*
Steel Cowboy *'78*
The Sure Thing *'85* ▸
They Drive by Night *'40* ▸
Think Big *'90*
Trucker *'08*
Trucks *'97*
Wages of Fear *'55* ▸
White Line Fever *'75*
Willa *'79*

Bigfoot/Yeti

The Abominable Snowman *'57*
Big and Hairy *'98*
Big Foot *'72*
Bigfoot: The Unforgettable Encounter *'94*
The Capture of Bigfoot *'79*
Clawed: The Legend of Sasquatch *'05*
Frostbiter: Wrath of the Wendigo *'94*
Half Human *'58*
Harry and the Hendersons *'87*
Legend of Boggy Creek *'75*
Little Bigfoot *'96*

▸ *= rated three bones or higher*

Bikers

Biography

Biopics: Artists

Biopics: Cops & Robbers

Biopics: Military

Biopics: Musicians

Biopics: Politics

► = *rated three bones or higher*

Magnificent Doll *'46*
The Magnificent Yankee *'50* ▶
Mandela *'87* ▶
Michael Collins *'96* ▶
Monsieur N. *'03* ▶
Mosley *'98*
The Motorcycle Diaries *'04* ▶
Mussolini & I *'85*
Napoleon *'03*
Nixon *'95* ▶
Path to War *'02*
Pinochet's Last Stand *'06*
Prince Jack *'83*
The Reagans *'04*
RFK *'02*
Robert Kennedy and His Times *'90*
Rudy: The Rudy Giulani Story *'03*
Sadat *'83*
Sakharov *'84* ▶
Secret Honor *'85* ▶
The Sicilian *'87*
Simon Bolivar *'69*
Stalin *'92*
Sunrise at Campobello *'60* ▶
Truman *'95*
Viva Zapata! *'52* ▶
W. *'08* ▶
Will: G. Gordon Liddy *'82*
Wilson *'44* ▶
Without Warning: The James Brady Story *'91* ▶
A Woman Called Golda *'82* ▶
Young Mr. Lincoln *'39* ▶

Biopics: Religious

***see also** Islam; Judaism; Religion*

Augustine of Hippo *'72* ▶
Bernadette *'90*
Brother Sun, Sister Moon *'73*
The Courageous Mr. Penn *'41*
The Eyes of Tammy Faye *'00*
The Flowers of St. Francis *'50* ▶
From a Far Country: Pope John Paul II *'81*
Have No Fear: The Life of Pope John Paul II *'05*
The Hoodlum Priest *'61* ▶
Jesus of Nazareth *'77* ▶
Joan of Arc *'48*
Joan of Arc *'99*
Kundun *'97* ▶
Loyola, the Soldier Saint *'52*
Luther *'03*
The Messenger: The Story of Joan of Arc *'99*
Passion of Joan of Arc *'28* ▶
The Passion of the Christ *'04* ▶
Saint Joan *'57*
St. Patrick: The Irish Legend *'00*
The Scarlet & the Black *'83*
Sebastiane *'79* ▶
Sister Aimee: The Aimee Semple McPherson Story *'06*
The Song of Bernadette *'43* ▶
Therese *'86* ▶
Therese: The Story of Saint Therese of Lisieux *'04*
A Time for Miracles *'80*

Biopics: Royalty

***see also** Politics; Royalty; Royalty, British; Royalty, Russian; True Stories*

The Abdication *'74*
Bonnie Prince Charlie *'48*
Caesar the Conqueror *'63*
Catherine the Great *'34*
Catherine the Great *'95*
Charlemagne *'95*
Diana: Her True Story *'93*
The Duchess *'08* ▶
Edward and Mrs. Simpson *'80*
Elizabeth *'98* ▶
Elizabeth R *'72* ▶
Elizabeth I *'05* ▶
Elizabeth: The Golden Age *'07*
Elizabeth, the Queen *'68*
Lady Jane *'85* ▶
Ludwig *'72*
Mad Love *'01*
Marie Antoinette *'38*
Mary of Scotland *'36* ▶
Nicholas and Alexandra *'71*
Peter the Great *'86* ▶
The Queen's Sister *'05*
The Rise of Louis XIV *'66* ▶
Six Wives of Henry VIII *'71* ▶
Victoria Regina *'61*
The Virgin Queen *'55* ▶
Warrior Queen *'03*
The Woman He Loved *'88*

Biopics: Science/ Medical

***see also** This Is My Life; This Is Your Life*

A Beautiful Mind *'01* ▶
Bethune *'77*
Breaking the Code *'95*
Darwin's Darkest Hour *'09*
The Doctor *'91*
Dr. Bethune *'90* ▶
Dr. Ehrlich's Magic Bullet *'40*
The Elephant Man *'80* ▶
The Five of Me *'81*
Flash of Genius *'08*
Florence Nightingale *'85*
Florence Nightingale *'08*
The Great Moment *'44*
Holy Terror *'65*
Infinity *'96*
Kinsey *'04* ▶
Korczak *'90* ▶
Lamp at Midnight *'66*
Long Journey Back *'78*
Madame Curie *'43* ▶
A Matter of Life and Death *'81*
The Miracle Worker *'62* ▶
The Miracle Worker *'79* ▶
The Miracle Worker *'00*
Nurse Edith Cavell *'39* ▶
The Prisoner of Shark Island *'36*
Sakharov *'84* ▶
The Secret Diary of Sigmund Freud *'84*
The Sound and the Silence *'93*
The Story of Alexander Graham Bell *'39* ▶
The Story of Dr. Wassell *'44*
The Story of Louis Pasteur *'36* ▶
Theremin: An Electronic Odyssey *'95* ▶
Young Tom Edison *'40*

Biopics: Showbiz

***see also** Price of Fame*

Actor: The Paul Muni Story *'78*
Alex in Wonderland *'70*
All That Jazz *'79* ▶
The Amazing Howard Hughes *'77*
The Ann Jillian Story *'88*
The Audrey Hepburn Story *'00*
Auto Focus *'02* ▶
The Aviator *'04* ▶
Baadasssss! *'03* ▶
Beyond the Sea *'04*
Blonde *'01*
The Bodyguard *'92*
Bogie: The Last Hero *'80*
Bojangles *'01*
Bruce Lee: Curse of the Dragon *'93* ▶
Bud and Lou *'78*
Can You Hear the Laughter? The Story of Freddie Prinze *'79*
The Cat's Meow *'01*
Cecil B. Demented *'00*
Celine *'08*
Chaplin *'92* ▶
Coco Before Chanel *'09*
Confessions of a Dangerous Mind *'02*
Darlings of the Gods *'90*
Dear Brigitte *'65*
The Dolly Sisters *'46*
Dragon: The Bruce Lee Story *'93* ▶
Ed Wood *'94* ▶
Eight Miles High *'07*
Eight Miles High *'08*
Enter Laughing *'67*
Ernie Kovacs: Between the Laughter *'84*
F. Scott Fitzgerald in Hollywood *'76*
Factory Girl *'06*
Flynn *'96*
Frances *'82* ▶
From the Journals of Jean Seberg *'95*
Funny Girl *'68* ▶
Funny Lady *'75*
The George Raft Story *'61*
Go West, Young Man *'36*
The Goddess *'58* ▶
Gods and Monsters *'98* ▶
Goodbye, Norma Jean *'75*
Goodnight, Sweet Marilyn *'89*
The Grace Kelly Story *'83*
The Great Ziegfeld *'36* ▶
Gypsy *'62* ▶
Gypsy *'93*
Harlow *'65*
Haywire *'80*
The Helen Morgan Story *'57*
Henri Langlois: The Phantom of the Cinematheque *'04* ▶
Houdini *'53*
How to Eat Your Watermelon in White Company (and Enjoy It) *'05* ▶
Hughes & Harlow: Angels in Hell *'77*
In Person *'35*
The Incredible Sarah *'76*
Introducing Dorothy Dandridge *'99* ▶
Isadora *'68* ▶
James Dean *'76*
James Dean *'01*
James Dean: Live Fast, Die Young *'97*
The Jayne Mansfield Story *'80*
Jolson Sings Again *'49*
The Jolson Story *'46* ▶
The Josephine Baker Story *'90* ▶
La Vie en Rose *'07*
Legend of Valentino *'75*
Lenny *'74* ▶
Life with Judy Garland—Me and My Shadows *'01* ▶
Lillian Russell *'40*
Lillie *'79* ▶
Livin' for Love: The Natalie Cole Story *'00*
Look for the Silver Lining *'49*
The Love Goddesses *'65* ▶
Lucy and Desi: Before the Laughter *'91*
Madame Sata *'02*
Mae West *'84*
Man in the Mirror: The Michael Jackson Story *'04*
Man of a Thousand Faces *'57* ▶
Man on the Moon *'99*
Marilyn & Bobby: Her Final Affair *'94*
Marilyn: The Untold Story *'80* ▶
Mayor of the Sunset Strip *'03* ▶
Merton of the Movies *'47*
Mommie Dearest *'81*
My Favorite Year *'82* ▶
My Wicked, Wicked Ways *'84*
Nijinsky *'80*
Norma Jean and Marilyn *'95*
The Notorious Bettie Page *'06*
Paul Robeson *'77*
The Perils of Pauline *'47*
Permanent Midnight *'98*
Prisoner of Paradise *'02* ▶
Queenie *'87*
Quiet Days in Hollywood *'97*
Rainbow *'78*
The Reagans *'04*
Rita Hayworth: The Love Goddess *'83*
RKO 281 *'99* ▶
Rock Hudson's Home Movies *'92*
Roman Polanski: Wanted and Desired *'08*
Roseanne: An Unauthorized Biography *'94*
Rosie: The Rosemary Clooney Story *'82*
The Seven Little Foys *'55* ▶
Sinatra *'92*
So This Is Love *'53*
Sophia Loren: Her Own Story *'80*
Star! *'68*
The Story of Vernon and Irene Castle *'39* ▶
Superstar: The Life and Times of Andy Warhol *'90* ▶
Talk to Me *'07*
Taxi zum Klo *'81* ▶
Tell Them Who You Are *'05*
That's Entertainment *'74* ▶
That's Entertainment, Part 2 *'76*
That's Entertainment, Part 3 *'93*
This Is Elvis *'81*
Thursday's Child *'43*
Topsy Turvy *'99* ▶
Up Close and Personal *'96* ▶
Valentino *'77*
Veronika Voss *'82* ▶
What Ever Happened to Baby Jane? *'62* ▶
White Hot: The Mysterious Murder of Thelma Todd *'91*
White Hunter, Black Heart *'90* ▶
Wired *'89*
Yankee Doodle Dandy *'42* ▶
Young Charlie Chaplin *'88*

Biopics: Sports

***see also** Baseball; Basketball; Football; Hockey; The Olympics; Running; Soccer; Sports Dramas; Team Efforts*

Ali *'01*
Babe! *'75* ▶
The Babe *'92*
Babe Ruth Story *'48*
Big Mo *'73*
The Blind Side *'09*
Bobby Jones: Stroke of Genius *'04*
Boy in Blue *'86*
Breaking the Surface: The Greg Louganis Story *'96*
Brian's Song *'71* ▶
Brian's Song *'01*
Carnera: The Walking Mountain *'08*
Champions *'84*
Chariots of Fire *'81* ▶
Cinderella Man *'05* ▶
Coach Carter *'05* ▶
Cobb *'94* ▶
Dempsey *'83*
Don King: Only in America *'97*
Don't Look Back: The Story of Leroy "Satchel" Paige *'81*
The Express *'08*
Fallen Champ: The Untold Story of Mike Tyson *'93* ▶
Fast Company *'78*
Final Shot: The Hank Gathers Story *'92*
The Flying Scotsman *'06*
Follow the Sun *'51*
Gentleman Jim *'42* ▶
Going for the Gold: The Bill Johnson Story *'85*
Grambling's White Tiger *'81*
Greased Lightning *'77*
The Great White Hope *'70*
The Greatest *'77*
Harmon of Michigan *'41*
Headin' Home *'20*
Heart Like a Wheel *'83*
Heart of a Champion: The Ray Mancini Story *'85*
Hustle *'04*
It's Good to Be Alive *'74*
The Jackie Robinson Story *'50* ▶
The Jesse Owens Story *'84*
Jim Thorpe: All American *'51*
Joe and Max *'02* ▶
The Joe Louis Story *'53*
Joe Torre: Curveballs Along the Way *'97*
The Junction Boys *'02*
Knute Rockne: All American *'40* ▶
The Last American Hero *'73* ▶
The Loneliest Runner *'76*
Marciano *'79*
Miracle *'04* ▶
One in a Million: The Ron LeFlore Story *'78*
Pistol: The Birth of a Legend *'90*
Prefontaine *'96*
Pride *'07*
Pride of St. Louis *'52*
The Pride of the Yankees *'42* ▶
Raging Bull *'80* ▶
Rebound: The Legend of Earl "The Goat" Manigault *'96*
Richard Petty Story *'72*
The Rocket *'05* ▶
Rocky Marciano *'99*
The Rookie *'02* ▶
Run for the Dream: The Gail Devers Story *'96*
Running Brave *'83*
Seabiscuit *'03* ▶
A Season on the Brink *'02*
61* *'01* ▶
Somebody Up There Likes Me *'56* ▶
Through the Fire *'05* ▶
The Tiger Woods Story *'98*
Tyson *'95*
Tyson *'08*
Wilma *'77*
A Winner Never Quits *'86*
The Winning Team *'52*
Without Limits *'97* ▶

Biopics: Writers

The Adventures of Mark Twain *'44* ▶
Agatha *'79*
Agatha Christie: A Life in Pictures *'04*
Almost Famous *'00* ▶
An Angel at My Table *'89* ▶
Balzac: A Life of Passion *'99* ▶
The Barretts of Wimpole Street *'34* ▶
Becoming Colette *'92*
Before Night Falls *'00* ▶
Borstal Boy *'00*
Bright Star *'09*
Byron *'03*
Capote *'05* ▶
Celeste *'81* ▶
Children of the Century *'99*
Coming Through *'85*
Cross Creek *'83*
Daphne *'07*
Dash and Lilly *'99*
The Disappearance of Garcia Lorca *'96*
Dreams with Sharp Teeth *'07* ▶
The Edge of Love *'08*
Finding Neverland *'04* ▶
Forbidden Passion: The Oscar Wilde Movie *'85*
Goldeneye: The Secret Life of Ian Fleming *'89*
Gonzo: The Life and Work of Dr. Hunter S. Thompson *'08* ▶
Gothic *'87* ▶
Hammett *'82*
Hans Christian Andersen *'52*
Haunted Summer *'88*
Heart Beat *'80*
Henry & June *'90* ▶
How to Lose Friends & Alienate People *'08*
I Shot Andy Warhol *'96* ▶
In the Realms of the Unreal *'04* ▶
Infamous *'06*
Iris *'89*
Iris *'01* ▶
Isn't She Great *'00*
Jack London *'44*
James Joyce: A Portrait of the Artist as a Young Man *'77* ▶
James Joyce's Women *'85* ▶
The Keeper: The Legend of Omar Khayyam *'05*
Last Call: The Final Chapter of F. Scott Fitzgerald *'02*
The Last Station *'09*
The Lost Boys *'78* ▶
The Loves of Edgar Allen Poe *'42*
Meteor & Shadow *'85*
Mishima: A Life in Four Chapters *'85* ▶
Miss Austen Regrets *'07*
Miss Potter *'06*
Mrs. Parker and the Vicious Circle *'94*
My Apprenticeship *'39* ▶
My Childhood *'38* ▶
My Left Foot *'89* ▶
My Universities *'40* ▶
Nerolio *'96*
Nora *'00*
The Passion of Ayn Rand *'99*
Pinero *'01*
Postcards from America *'95*
Quiet Days in Clichy *'90*
The Road from Coorain *'02*
Roughly Speaking *'45*
Saint-Ex: The Story of the Storyteller *'95*
The Secret Life of Mrs. Beeton *'06*
Shadowlands *'85* ▶
Shadowlands *'93* ▶
The Spectre of Edgar Allen Poe *'73*
Spymaker: The Secret Life of Ian Fleming *'90*
Stevie *'78*
Swann *'96*
Sylvia *'03*
Tom & Viv *'94* ▶
Total Eclipse *'95*
The Trials of Oscar Wilde *'60* ▶
Trumbo *'07* ▶
Veronica Guerin *'03*
Wilde *'97*
The Wonderful World of the Brothers Grimm *'62*
Zora Is My Name! *'90*

Birds

Babe *'95* ▶
Batman Returns *'92*
Beaks: The Movie *'87*
Birdman of Alcatraz *'62* ▶
The Birds *'63* ▶
The Birds 2: Land's End *'94*
Blade Master *'84*
Blood Freak *'72*
The Blue Bird *'40* ▶
A Breed Apart *'84*
Brewster McCloud *'70* ▶
Chicken Run *'00* ▶
Chronicle of the Raven *'04*
Clash of the Titans *'81*
Cockfighter *'74* ▶
Continental Divide *'81*
The Crow *'93*
The Crow 2: City of Angels *'96*
Cry of the Penguins *'71*
Duck *'05*
Flu Birds *'08*
Fly Away Home *'96* ▶
The Giant Claw *'57*
The Golden Child *'86*
The Goodbye Bird *'93*
The Hawk Is Dying *'06*
High Anxiety *'77*
Hoot *'06*
Howard the Duck *'86*
Ladyhawke *'85*
Love Happens *'09*
Magic in the Mirror: Fowl Play *'96*
Mating Season *'81*
Million Dollar Duck *'71*
No Fear, No Die *'90*
Paulie *'98*
The Pebble and the Penguin *'94*
Queer Duck: The Movie *'06*

▶ *= rated three bones or higher*

Fuel '08 ▸
Gas Pump Girls '79
Giant '56 ▸
The Guns and the Fury '83
Hellfighters '68
Intruder Within '81
The Last Winter '06
Legend of Frenchie King '71
Lie Down with Lions '94
Local Hero '83 ▸
Louisiana Story '48 ▸
The Madwoman of Chaillot '69
Mission in Morocco '59
Naked Gun 2 1/2: The Smell of Fear '91
'Neath the Arizona Skies '34
Oceans of Fire '86
Oklahoma Crude '73
On Deadly Ground '94
Red Rock West '93 ▸
Roughnecks '80
The Stars Fell on Henrietta '94
There Will Be Blood '07 ▸
Thunder Bay '53 ▸
Tulsa '49 ▸
Waltz across Texas '83
War of the Wildcats '43
Wildcat '42
The World Is Not Enough '99
Written on the Wind '56 ▸

Blackmail

see also *Corporate Shenanigans; Crime & Criminals; Disorganized Crime; Organized Crime*

The Art of Murder '99
Barocco '76
The Big Brass Ring '99
Big Nothing '06
Billion Dollar Brain '67
Black Angel '46 ▸
Blackmale '99
Blonde for a Day '46
Bon Voyage '03 ▸
Burn After Reading '08
Cafe Metropole '37
Captives '94
Charlie Chan at Treasure Island '39
Choke '00
Christie's Revenge '07
Clue '85
Crossroads '42
The Crusader '32
Dead Pigeon on Beethoven Street '72
Death at a Funeral '07
Death at a Funeral '10
The Deep End '01 ▸
Derailed '05
Devil in the Flesh '98
Dogville '03
El Crimen Perfecto '04
Feeling Minnesota '96
First Degree '98
The First Wives Club '96
A Gentleman After Dark '42
The Golden Spiders: A Nero Wolfe Mystery '00
Good People, Bad Things '08
Goodbye, Lover '99
The Guilty '99
Happy Endings '05
Hard Evidence '94
Heart of the Beholder '05 ▸
Here's Flash Casey '38
High Heels and Low Lifes '01
Hoffman '70
An Ideal Husband '47
An Ideal Husband '99 ▸
The Immoral One '80
The Informant '97 ▸
Interstate '07
It Seemed Like a Good Idea at the Time '75
Johnny Skidmarks '97
Keys to Tulsa '96
The Killer Must Kill Again '75
Kiss Tomorrow Goodbye '00
Ladies' Man '62
A Lady of Chance '28
Legal Deceit '95
Letter to My Killer '95
Little Sweetheart '90
Lost in Beijing '07
Love Walked In '97
Lucky Numbers '00
Madame O '67
Man of the World '31
Mrs. Winterbourne '96
Mulholland Falls '95
Murder Is My Business '46
Mysterious Mr. Moto '38
Mystery Street '50
The Notorious Landlady '62
100 Mile Rule '02
The Opposite of Sex '98
Paparazzi '04
Parallel Corpse '83
Perfect Lies '97
A Perfect Murder '98
The Player '92 ▸
Portrait in Black '60
Pretty Persuasion '05
Punch-Drunk Love '02 ▸
Resilience '06
The Sentinel '06
Shockproof '49
The Silent Partner '78 ▸
Slackers '02
A Slight Case of Murder '99
The Strange Mrs. Crane '48
Tick Tock '00 ▸
Time to Kill '42
Twilight '98 ▸
Undercurrent '99
The Unsuspected '47
Up the River '30
Victim '61 ▸
The Voice of Merrill '52
Water's Edge '03
The Woman on Pier 13 '50
Zero Effect '97

Blackout

City of Ember '08
City Unplugged '95
Dark Town '04
Fear of the Dark '02
Love at First Bite '79
Mirage '66 ▸
100 Girls '00
Where Were You When the Lights Went Out? '68

Blaxploitation

see also *African America; New Black Cinema*

Across 110th Street '72
Avenging Disco Godfather '76
Baadasssss! '03 ▸
Big Score '83
Black Belt Jones '74
Black Caesar '73
Black Dynamite '09
Black Gestapo '75
Black Godfather '74
Black Gunn '72
Black Heat '76
Blackenstein '73
Blacula '72
Bones '01
Bucktown '75
Cleopatra Jones '73
Cleopatra Jones & the Casino of Gold '75
Coffy '73
Cotton Comes to Harlem '70 ▸
Detroit 9000 '73
Dr. Black, Mr. Hyde '76
Dolemite '75
Dolemite 2: Human Tornado '76
Foxy Brown '74
Friday Foster '75
Ganja and Hess '73
The Guy from Harlem '77
Hell Up in Harlem '73
Hot Potato '76
J.D.'s Revenge '76
Let's Do It Again '75
The Mack '73
Mean Johnny Barrows '75
Miracle in Harlem '48
Monkey Hustle '77
Moon over Harlem '39
No Way Back '74
One Down, Two to Go! '82
Return of Superfly '90
Savage! '73
Scream Blacula Scream '73
Shaft '71 ▸
Shaft in Africa '73
Shaft's Big Score '72
Sheba, Baby '75
Slaughter '72
Slaughter's Big Ripoff '73
Soul Vengeance '75
Superfly '72
Superfly T.N.T. '73
Sweet Sweetback's Baadasssss Song '71 ▸
That Man Bolt '73
Three the Hard Way '74
Top of the Heap '72
Truck Turner '74
Undercover Brother '02

Blind Date

All About Steve '09
Betrayal of the Dove '92
Blind Date '87
Blind Date '08
Blind Dating '06
Caffeine '06
Carry On Loving '70
Coffee Date '06
Dirty Love '05
Friends with Money '06
I'll Take You There '99
I'm with Lucy '02
Internet Dating '08
Knight and Day '10
Last Chance Harvey '08
Mating Dance '08
Must Love Dogs '05
The Perfect Man '05
Pride of the Marines '45 ▸
Return to Me '00
Something New '06
This Above All '42
Weather Girl '09
You Stupid Man '02

Blindness

see also *Physical Problems*

Afraid of the Dark '92
Alligator Eyes '90
Amazing Grace '06 ▸
Amy '81
Ashes of Time '94 ▸
At First Sight '98
Aurora '84
Ballad in Blue '66
Balls of Fury '07
Blacklight '98
Blackout '50
Blind Date '84
Blind Dating '06
Blind Fear '89
Blind Fury '90
Blind Justice '94
Blind Man's Bluff '91
Blind Witness '89
Blindness '08
Blink '93
Breaking Free '95
Broken Embraces '09 ▸
Butterflies Are Free '72 ▸
Cactus '86
Can You Feel Me Dancing? '85
City for Conquest '40 ▸
City Lights '31 ▸
The Color of Paradise '99
Connor's War '06
Crazy Love '07 ▸
Crimes & Misdemeanors '89 ▸
Dancer in the Dark '99
Daredevil '03
The Dark Angel '35
Dead Man's Eyes '44
Don't Look Now '73 ▸
Eight Witnesses '54
Elmer '76
The Eye '02
The Eye '08
Eye on the Sparrow '91
A Family Thing '96 ▸
Good Luck '96
Happy Times '00
The Haunting of Marsten Manor '07
Hollywood Ending '02
The Human Monster '39
Ice Castles '79
If You Could See What I Hear '82
Incantato '03
Jennifer 8 '92
The Killer '90 ▸
La Roue '23 ▸
La Symphonie Pastorale '46 ▸
Last Game '80
Life on a String '90
The Lookout '07 ▸
Lost for Words '99 ▸
Love at First Sight '76
Love Leads the Way '84
Magnificent Obsession '35
Mask '85 ▸
Minnesota Clay '65
The Miracle Worker '62 ▸
The Miracle Worker '79 ▸
The Miracle Worker '00
Mr. Magoo '97
Night Gallery '69 ▸
Night Is My Future '47
Nowhere in Sight '01
Octavia '82
On Dangerous Ground '51 ▸
Once Upon a Time in Mexico '03 ▸
Ordinary Heroes '85
Other Men's Women '31
A Patch of Blue '65
People Who Own the Dark '75
Places in the Heart '84 ▸
Possessed '05
Pride of the Marines '45 ▸
Proof '91 ▸
Ray '04 ▸
Red Dragon '02
Return of the Evil Dead '75
The Scent of a Woman '75
Scent of a Woman '92 ▸
Schlock '73
Second Sight '99 ▸
See No Evil '71 ▸
See No Evil, Hear No Evil '89
Seven Pounds '08
7th Heaven '27
Sketch Artist 2: Hands That See '94
Sneakers '92
Someone Else's America '96 ▸
They Watch '93
Things You Can Tell Just by Looking at Her '00
This Woman Is Dangerous '52
To Race the Wind '80
Touch the Top of the World '06
The Toxic Avenger '86
23 Paces to Baker Street '56
Undertow '30
Unleashed '05
The Unseen '05
Until the End of the World '91 ▸
The Village '04
A Voyage 'Round My Father '89 ▸
Wait until Dark '67 ▸
The Whales of August '87 ▸
The White Countess '05 ▸
Wild Hearts Can't Be Broken '91 ▸
Wings in the Dark '35
Year Zero '04
Young Frankenstein '74 ▸
Zatoichi '03 ▸
Zatoichi: The Blind Swordsman and the Chess Expert '65
Zatoichi: The Blind Swordsman's Vengeance '66
Zertigo Diamond Caper '82

Blizzards

see also *Cold Spots*

Babes in Toyland '86
Cold Comfort '90
The Day of the Outlaw '59
Donner Pass: The Road to Survival '84
8 Women '02 ▸
The Last Stop '99
One Special Night '99
Operation Haylift '50
Ravenous '99
The Shining '80
Snow Day '00
Snowbound: The Jim and Jennifer Stolpa Story '94
Stephen King's The Storm of the Century '99
Terminal Invasion '02
Trapped in Paradise '94
You'll Like My Mother '72

Bloody Messages

Die Hard '88 ▸
Fatal Vision '84
The Hades Factor '06
Harold and Maude '71 ▸
Helter Skelter '76
In the Blood '06
The Jagged Edge '85
Seven '95 ▸
The Shining '80
Stephen King's The Night Flier '96
The Untouchables '87 ▸

Boating

see *Sail Away*

Bodyguards

Absolute Power '97
Assassination '87
Avenging Angelo '02
Be Cool '05
Black Belt '92
Blackjack '97
Body Armour '07
The Bodyguard '92
The Bodyguard from Beijing '94
The Chase '46
Drillbit Taylor '08
Eastern Promises '07 ▸
Fatal Beauty '87
Fatal Past '94
Final Voyage '99
Finish Line '08
First Kid '96
Genuine Risk '89
Get Shorty '95 ▸
The Girl From Monaco '08
Guarding Tess '94
Half a Loaf of Kung Fu '78
Heat '87
His Bodyguard '98
In the Line of Fire '93 ▸
In the Mix '05
Incognito '99
The Keeper '09
La Scorta '94 ▸
The Librarian: Quest for the Spear '04
Man on Fire '87
Man on Fire '04
Mr. Nanny '93
My Bodyguard '80 ▸
Night Eyes 4: Fatal Passion '95
On Guard! '03 ▸
The Princess Diaries 2: Royal Engagement '04
Protecting the King '07
Pushed to the Limit '92
Sabotage '96
Second Chance '53
Secret Window '04
Social Error '35
The Taste of Others '00 ▸
Time and Tide '00
Transporter 2 '05
The Tsar's Bride '66 ▸

Bookies

see also *Gambling; Organized Crime*

Bad Lieutenant '92 ▸
Big Shot: Confessions of a Campus Bookie '02
Bloodhounds of Broadway '52
Bookies '03
Buffalo 66 '97 ▸
Dinner Rush '00 ▸
Even Money '06
40 Pounds of Trouble '62
Guys and Dolls '55 ▸
Hollywood or Bust '56
Little Miss Marker '34 ▸
Little Miss Marker '80
Lucky Number Slevin '06
Player 5150 '08
The Runner '99
Saratoga '37
Shadow of the Thin Man '41 ▸
Snatch '00 ▸
Sorrowful Jones '49
Starsky & Hutch '04
Three Men on a Horse '36 ▸
U-Turn '97

Books & Bookstores

see also *Storytelling*

Agata and the Storm '04
Ambition '91
The Answer Man '09
Army of Darkness '92 ▸
Better Than Chocolate '99
Bickford Shmeckler's Cool Ideas '06
The Book of Eli '10
Breakin' All The Rules '04
Burglar '87
Capote '05 ▸
Careless '07
Cross Creek '83
Crossing Delancey '88 ▸
The Edge of Heaven '07 ▸
84 Charing Cross Road '86 ▸
Everything You Want '05
Evil Dead '83
Fahrenheit 451 '66 ▸
Falling in Love '84
Funny Face '57 ▸
A Girl Cut in Two '07
Halloween II '09
The Hitchhiker's Guide to the Galaxy '05 ▸
The Hoax '06
Hocus Pocus '93
I, Madman '89
In the Mouth of Madness '95
Inkheart '09
The Jane Austen Book Club '07 ▸
La Lectrice '88
The Love Letter '99
The Mysteries of Pittsburgh '08
The NeverEnding Story '84 ▸
A Night to Remember '42 ▸
The Ninth Gate '99
Not So Dusty '56
Notting Hill '99 ▸
The Pagemaster '94
The Paper Chase '73 ▸
Phenomenon '96
Priest of Love '81
Providence '77 ▸
QB VII '74 ▸
The Reader '08
The Russia House '90
The Seven Year Itch '55 ▸
Snapshots '02
The Spiderwick Chronicles '08 ▸
Stone Reader '02 ▸
Suburban Girl '07
Tristram Shandy: A Cock and Bull Story '05
Warlock '91
Wilbur Wants to Kill Himself '02 ▸
You've Got Mail '98

Boom!

see also *Action-Adventure; Fires*

The Adventures of Ford Fairlane '90
Airport '70 ▸
Arlington Road '99
Armageddon '98
Atomic Train '99
Australia '08
Bad Company '02
Ballistic: Ecks vs. Sever '02
Black Dog '98
Blown Away '94
Bridge of Dragons '99
Broken Arrow '95
Casino '95 ▸
Catch a Fire '06
Chain Reaction '96
Chill Factor '99
Clear and Present Danger '94
Collateral Damage '02
Con Air '97 ▸
The Core '03

Crackerjack 2 *'97*
Cutthroat Island *'95*
Dante's Peak *'97*
The Dark Knight *'08* ▸
The Day After *'83* ▸
Daylight *'96*
Dead in a Heartbeat *'02*
Deep Rising *'98*
Deja Vu *'06*
Detention *'03*
Die Another Day *'02*
Die Hard *'88* ▸
Die Hard 2: Die Harder *'90* ▸
Die Hard: With a Vengeance *'95*
District B13 *'04*
Dr. Strangelove, or: How I Learned to Stop Worrying and Love the Bomb *'64* ▸
Earthquake *'74*
Enemy of the State *'98*
The English Patient *'96* ▸
Eraser *'96*
Extreme Limits *'01*
Face/Off *'97* ▸
The Fifth Element *'97*
Fight Club: ' *'99* ▸
The Final Cut *'96*
Fire Down Below *'97*
Firestorm *'97*
Friends *'95*
From Dusk Till Dawn *'95*
The Fugitive *'93* ▸
Get Smart *'08*
Goldeneye *'95* ▸
Gone Fishin' *'97*
Greenmail *'01*
Grosse Pointe Blank *'97* ▸
Heaven *'01*
Hiroshima: Out of the Ashes *'90* ▸
Hoodlum *'96*
Human Bomb *'97*
The Hurt Locker *'08* ▸
I Am Omega *'07*
Independence Day *'96* ▸
The Inglorious Bastards *'78*
The Inspectors *'98*
Jackass: The Movie *'02*
John Carpenter's Vampires *'97*
The Kingdom *'07*
Lethal Weapon 3 *'92*
Lethal Weapon 4 *'98*
Live Free or Die Hard *'07*
Live Wire: Human Timebomb *'95*
Magnum Force *'73*
The Marine *'06*
Mission: Impossible *'96* ▸
My House in Umbria *'03* ▸
Nowhere to Land *'00*
Path to Paradise *'97*
The Peacemaker *'97*
Pearl Harbor *'01*
Riot *'96*
The Rock *'96* ▸
Sabotage *'36* ▸
Sea of Sand *'58*
The Secret Agent *'96*
Serial Bomber *'96*
Shakedown *'02*
Shattered City: The Halifax Explosion *'03*
The Siege *'98*
Simon Sez *'99*
The Specialist *'94*
Speed *'94* ▸
Spider-Man *'02* ▸
Spy Train *'43*
The State Within *'06*
Stealth Fighter *'99*
Steel *'97*
Sudden Death *'95*
The Sum of All Fears *'02*
Sweepers *'99*
Swordfish *'01*
The Terminator *'84* ▸
The Terrorist Next Door *'08*
Testament *'83* ▸
Thirty Seconds Over Tokyo *'44* ▸
Thr3e *'07*
Ticker *'01*
Total Recall *'90* ▸
Traitor *'08*
Transformers *'07*
The Transporter *'02*
True Lies *'94*
U.S. Navy SEALS: Dead or Alive *'02*
U.S. SEALs: Dead or Alive *'02*
The Usual Suspects *'95* ▸
V for Vendetta *'06*
Vantage Point *'08*
What to Do in Case of Fire *'02*
The Whole Shebang *'01*
The X-Files *'98*
XXX *'02*
XXX: State of the Union *'05*

Boomer Reunions

***see also** Period Piece: 1960s*

The Big Chill *'83* ▸
The Brutal Truth *'99*
Come as You Are *'05*
Everything Relative *'96*
Far Harbor *'96*
The Foursome *'06*
I Think I Do *'97*
Indian Summer *'93*
Infested: Invasion of the Killer Bugs *'02*
Lifeguard *'76*
A Mighty Wind *'03* ▸
Old Joy *'06* ▸
Parallel Lives *'94*
Peter's Friends *'92*
Return of the Secaucus 7 *'80* ▸
Spin the Bottle *'97*
Standing Still *'05*
That Championship Season *'99*

Bootleggers

***see also** Beer; On the Rocks; Organized Crime; Prohibition Gangs*

The Boob *'26*
Bugsy Malone *'76*
The Crusader *'32*
Dixie Jamboree *'44*
The Helen Morgan Story *'57*
Hell's House *'32*
Izzy & Moe *'85*
Lady for a Day *'33* ▸
Last Man Standing *'96*
The Little Giant *'33*
Moonshine County Express *'77*
Moonshine Highway *'96*
Once Upon a Time in America *'84* ▸
Pocketful of Miracles *'61* ▸
Public Enemy *'31* ▸
The Roaring Twenties *'39* ▸
Scarface *'31* ▸
A Slight Case of Murder *'38*
Smokey and the Bandit *'77*
The Untouchables *'87* ▸
What! No Beer? *'33*

Bosnia

Beautiful People *'99*
Behind Enemy Lines *'01*
For Ever Mozart *'96*
Go West *'05*
Grbavica: The Land of My Dreams *'06*
Harrison's Flowers *'02*
The Hunting Party *'07*
No Man's Land *'01*
Pretty Village, Pretty Flame *'96* ▸
Savior *'98* ▸
Shot Through the Heart *'98* ▸
Sniper 2 *'02*
Ulysses' Gaze *'95*
Underground *'95* ▸
Vukovar *'94* ▸
Welcome to Sarajevo *'97* ▸
The Wounds *'98*

Boston

The Actress *'53*
Adrenalin: Fear the Rush *'96*
Alex & Emma *'03*
Athena *'54*
Bad Manners *'98*
A Beautiful Mind *'01* ▸
Before and After *'95*
Behind the Red Door *'02*
Black Irish *'07*
Blown Away *'94*
Body Count *'97*
Boondock Saints *'99*
The Boondock Saints II: All Saints Day *'09*
The Boston Strangler *'68*
The Boston Strangler: The Untold Story *'08*
Breeders *'97*
A Case of Deadly Force *'86* ▸
Celtic Pride *'96*
Coma *'78* ▸
Criminal Law *'89*
Dealing: Or the Berkeley-to-Boston Forty-Brick Lost-Bag Blues *'72*
The Departed *'06* ▸
Dr. Jekyll and Mr. Hyde *'08*
Edge of Darkness *'10*
Everybody Wants to Be Italian *'08*
Fear Strikes Out *'57* ▸
Fever Pitch *'05*
The Forbidden Kingdom *'08*
Fuzz *'72*
Game 6 *'05*
Gentleman Bandit *'81*
Gone Baby Gone *'07* ▸
Good Will Hunting *'97*
The Great Moment *'44*
H.M. Pulham Esquire *'41*
Infected *'08*
Jill the Ripper *'00*
Johnny We Hardly Knew Ye *'77*
Legally Blonde *'01*
Lemony Snicket's A Series of Unfortunate Events *'04*
Little Men *'98*
Little Shots of Happiness *'97*
Love Story *'70* ▸
The Matchmaker *'97*
Money Kings *'98*
Monument Ave. *'98*
My Best Friend's Girl *'08*
Mystic River *'03* ▸
Never Met Picasso *'96*
Next Stop, Wonderland *'98*
The Parent Trap *'61*
The Parent Trap *'98*
The Proposition *'97*
The Rendering *'02*
The Scarlet Letter *'34*
The Scarlet Letter *'73* ▸
The Scarlet Letter *'95*
Sci-Fighters *'96*
See How She Runs *'78* ▸
The Seekers *'79*
Shuttle *'09*
Small Vices: A Spenser Mystery *'99*
Southie *'98*
Spenser: Ceremony *'93*
Spenser: Pale Kings & Princes *'94*
Spenser: The Judas Goat *'94*
Spraggue *'84*
Squeeze *'97*
Thin Air *'00*
Tuesdays with Morrie *'99*
21 *'08*
Two Years before the Mast *'46*
The Verdict *'82* ▸
What Doesn't Kill You *'08*
What's the Worst That Could Happen? *'01*
Witness Protection *'99* ▸

Bounty Hunters

All About the Benjamins *'02*
American Streetfighter 2: The Full Impact *'97*
Avenging Angel *'07*
The Awakening *'95*
Banjo Hackett *'76*
The Bounty Hunter *'10*
Bounty Hunter 2002 *'94*
Bounty Hunters *'89*
Bounty Hunters *'96*
Bounty Hunters 2: Hardball *'97*
The Bounty Man *'72*
Bounty Tracker *'93*
Cold Harvest *'98*
Constantine *'05*
Critters *'86*
Critters 2: The Main Course *'88*
Dead or Alive *'02*
Domino *'05*
The Empire Strikes Back *'80* ▸
A Fistful of Dollars *'64* ▸
For a Few Dollars More *'65*
Ghost Rider *'07*
The Glove *'78*
The Good, the Bad and the Ugly *'67* ▸
Home for Christmas *'93*
The Hunter *'80*
Jonah Hex *'10*
Kidnapped *'05* ▸
Kill Zone *'08*
The Last of the Dogmen *'95*
Lethal *'04*
Midnight Run *'88* ▸
Most Wanted *'97*
Moving Target *'96*
No Country for Old Men *'07* ▸
Past Perfect *'98*
Return of the Jedi *'83* ▸
The Rundown *'03*
Showdown at Boot Hill *'58*
Slipstream *'89*
Smokin' Aces 2: Assassins' Ball *'10*
Star Wars *'77* ▸
Star Wars: Episode 2—Attack of the Clones *'02* ▸
Subhuman *'04*
Terminal Impact *'95*
The Tracker *'88*
True Vengeance *'97*
Wanted Dead or Alive *'86*

Bowling

Alley Cats Strike *'00*
The Big Lebowski *'97* ▸
Dream with the Fishes *'97*
Dreamer *'79*
The Family Man *'79*
Family Man *'00*
The Flintstones *'94*
Fright Night 2 *'88*
Grease 2 *'82*
Greedy *'94*
Kingpin *'96*
League of Ordinary Gentlemen *'04* ▸
Mr. Wonderful *'93*
Pleasantville *'98* ▸
Spare Me *'92*
Strike *'07*
Uncle Buck *'89* ▸

Boxing

Abbott and Costello Meet the Invisible Man *'51* ▸
Against the Ropes *'04*
Ali *'01*
Animal 2 *'07*
Annapolis *'06*
Any Which Way You Can *'80*
Arena *'89*
Back Roads *'81*
Battling Bunyon *'24*
Battling Butler *'26*
Be Yourself *'30*
Before the Fall *'04*
Belle of the Nineties *'34*
Best of the Best *'89*
The Big Man: Crossing the Line *'91* ▸
Black Cloud *'04*
Blade Boxer *'97*
Body and Soul *'47* ▸
Body & Soul *'81*
Body and Soul *'98*
Bowery Blitzkrieg *'41*
Boxcar Blues *'90*
The Boxer *'97*
The Boxer and Death *'63* ▸
Breakdown *'53*
Brutal Glory *'89*
The Cage *'89*
Cain and Mabel *'36*
Carnera: The Walking Mountain *'08*
The Champ *'32* ▸
The Champ *'79*
Champion *'49* ▸
Cinderella Man *'05* ▸
Circle Man *'87*
City for Conquest *'40* ▸
Cock & Bull Story *'03*
Confessions of a Pit Fighter *'05*
Confessions of Tom Harris *'72*
Counter Punch *'71*
Dempsey *'83*
Diggstown *'92*
Don King: Only in America *'97*
Dynamite Dan *'24*
Fallen Champ: The Untold Story of Mike Tyson *'93* ▸
Far and Away *'92*
Fat City *'72* ▸
Fight Club: ' *'99* ▸
Fight for the Title *'57*
The Fighter *'52* ▸
Fighting *'09*
Fighting Champ *'33*
Firepower *'93*
Fist Fighter *'88*
Gentleman Jim *'42* ▸
Girlfight *'99* ▸
Gladiator *'92*
Golden Boy *'39* ▸
Golden Gloves *'40*
Great Guy *'36*
The Great White Hope *'70*
The Great White Hype *'96*
The Greatest *'77*
The Hammer *'07*
Hard Times *'75* ▸
The Harder They Fall *'56* ▸
Heart *'87*
Heart of a Champion: The Ray Mancini Story *'85*
Hell's Kitchen NYC *'97*
Here Comes Mr. Jordan *'41* ▸
The Hitter *'79*
Hollywood Stadium Mystery *'38*
Homeboy *'75*
Homeboy *'88*
Honeyboy *'82*
The Hurricane *'99* ▸
I Spy *'02*
Joe and Max *'02* ▸
The Joe Louis Story *'53*
Jump In! *'07*
Keep Punching *'39*
Kelly the Second *'36*
The Kid *'97*
Kid Dynamite *'43*
Kid from Brooklyn *'46*
Kid Galahad *'37* ▸
Kid Galahad *'62*
Kid Monk Baroni *'52*
Killer McCoy *'47*
Killer's Kiss *'55*
The Last Fight *'82*
Last Man Standing *'87*
Les Miserables *'95*
Like It Is *'98* ▸
Little Old New York *'23*
Love Come Down *'00*
Love Songs *'99*
Made *'01*
The Main Event *'79*
Mandingo *'75*
Marciano *'79*
Matilda *'78*
Meatballs 2 *'84*
Milky Way *'36*
Million Dollar Baby *'04* ▸
Miracle Kid *'42*
Mr. Moto's Gamble *'38*
Movie, Movie *'78*
Navy Way *'44*
Night and the City *'92* ▸
No News from God *'01*
Ocean's Eleven *'01* ▸
Off Limits *'53*
On the Waterfront *'54* ▸
One-Punch O'Day *'26*
The Opponent *'89*
The Opponent *'01*
Opposite Corners *'96*
Palooka *'34*
Penitentiary *'79*
Penitentiary 2 *'82*
Penitentiary 3 *'87*
Percy & Thunder *'93*
Play It to the Bone *'99*
Poor Man's Game *'06* ▸
The Power of One *'92*
Price of Glory *'00*
Pride of the Bowery *'41*
Prison Shadows *'36*
Prize Fighter *'79*
The Prizefighter and the Lady *'33* ▸
Pulp Fiction *'94* ▸
The Quest *'96*
The Quiet Man *'52* ▸
Raging Bull *'80* ▸
Requiem for a Heavyweight *'56* ▸
Requiem for a Heavyweight *'62* ▸
Resurrecting the Champ *'07*
Ricky 1 *'88*
The Ring *'27*
The Ring *'52*
Ring of Death *'08*
Ringside *'49*
Rip Roarin' Buckaroo *'36*
Roaring City *'51*
Rocky *'76* ▸
Rocky 2 *'79*
Rocky 3 *'82*
Rocky 4 *'85*
Rocky 5 *'90*
Rocky Balboa *'06*
Rocky Marciano *'99*
Rude *'96*
Schizo *'04*
The Set-Up *'49* ▸
Shiner *'00*
Snake Eyes *'98*
Snatch *'00* ▸
Somebody Up There Likes Me *'56* ▸
Spike of Bensonhurst *'88*
The Spirit of Youth *'37*
Split Decisions *'88*
The Sting 2 *'83*
Street Crimes *'92*
Streets of Gold *'86*
Teen Wolf Too *'87*
They Made Me a Criminal *'39*
They Never Come Back *'32*
Thunderground *'89*
Title Shot *'81*
Tough Enough *'83*
Tough Kid *'39*
Triumph of the Spirit *'89* ▸
Trouble Chasers *'45*
24-7 *'97*
Tyson *'95*
Tyson *'08*
Undefeated *'03*
Undisputed *'02*
Undisputed II: Last Man Standing *'06*
Vigilantes of Boom Town *'46*
When We Were Kings *'96* ▸
When's Your Birthday? *'37*
The Wildcat *'26*
A Wind from Wyoming *'94*

Brains!

***see also** Eyeballs!; Heads!; Renegade Body Parts*

The Black Sleep *'56*
Bride of Re-Animator *'89*
Dawn of the Dead *'78* ▸
Gamebox 1.0 *'04*
George A. Romero's Land of the Dead *'05* ▸
Hannibal *'01*
Hardwired *'09*
Igor *'08*
Indiana Jones and the Temple of Doom *'84* ▸
The Man with Two Brains *'83* ▸
Messiah of Evil *'74*
Night of the Living Dead *'68* ▸
Return of the Living Dead: Rave to the Grave *'05*

Brainwashed

Angel Dust *'96*
Awakening of Candra *'81*
Becky Sharp *'35*
Brainwashed *'60*
Circle of Power *'83*
A Clockwork Orange *'71* ▸
Cypher *'02* ▸
Disturbing Behavior *'98*
DROP Squad *'94*
In Like Flint *'67*
The Ipcress File *'65* ▸
Killzone *'85*
The Manchurian Candidate *'62* ▸
The Manchurian Candidate *'04* ▸
The Mind Benders *'63*

▸ *= rated three bones or higher*

Mind Snatchers '72
1984 '56 ▶
No Dead Heroes '87
On Her Majesty's Secret Service '69 ▶
Patty Hearst '88
Simon '80
Split Image '82 ▶
Timebomb '91
Unholy '07
Zoolander '01

Break-Ups

see also *Divorce; Romantic Comedy; Romantic Drama*

Annie Hall '77 ▶
The Break-Up '06
The Breakup Artist '04
The Broken Hearts Club '00 ▶
Casablanca '42 ▶
Cashback '06
The Devil Wears Prada '06
(500) Days of Summer '09
Flannel Pajamas '06
Forgetting Sarah Marshall '08
Gone with the Wind '39 ▶
Homecoming '09
The Hottest State '06
Inside Paris '06
The Jane Austen Book Club '07 ▶
Jour de Fete '48 ▶
Le Divorce '03
My Blueberry Nights '07
Nick & Norah's Infinite Playlist '08 ▶
Nights and Weekends '08
Postcards from the Edge '90 ▶
Prime '05
Puccini for Beginners '06
Room at the Top '59 ▶
St. Elmo's Fire '85
Sweet November '68
2 Days in Paris '07 ▶
Under the Tuscan Sun '03
Valentine's Day '10
The Way We Were '73 ▶
What Love Is '07

Bridges

Bataan '43
The Bridge '59
The Bridge at Remagen '69
The Bridge of San Luis Rey '44 ▶
The Bridge of San Luis Rey '05
The Bridge on the River Kwai '57 ▶
Bridge to Hell '87
A Bridge Too Far '77
The Bridges at Toko-Ri '55 ▶
The Bridges of Madison County '95 ▶
Carnival of Souls '62 ▶
Crossing the Bridge '92
Dream with the Fishes '97
For Whom the Bell Tolls '43 ▶
George of the Jungle '97 ▶
The Ghost and the Darkness '96
The Girl on the Bridge '98 ▶
Graffiti Bridge '90
It's a Wonderful Life '46 ▶
The Longest Day '62 ▶
The Lovers on the Bridge '91
Ode to Billy Joe '76
Saturday Night Fever '77
Saving Private Ryan '98 ▶
Tarzan's New York Adventure '42
The Truman Show '98 ▶
Volunteers '85
Waterloo Bridge '40 ▶

Bringing Up Baby

see also *Parenthood; Pregnant Men; Pregnant Pauses*

Addams Family Values '93
And Baby Makes Six '79
Angie '94
Baby '00
The Baby and the Battleship '56
Baby Boom '87
Baby Boy '01
Baby Broker '81
Baby Geniuses '98
Babyfever '94
Baby's Day Out '94
Bachelor Mother '39 ▶
Basket Case 3: The Progeny '92
Being Two Isn't Easy '62
Blondie Brings Up Baby '39
Brink of Life '57
The Brood '79
Bundle of Joy '56
By Design '82
The Child '05
Close to My Heart '51
Cotton Mary '99
Court Jester '56 ▶
The Cradle '06
Dad On the Run '00
East Side of Heaven '39
Eastern Promises '07 ▶
The Ex '07
Eye on the Sparrow '91
The Family Man '79
Family Man '00
Fanny '61 ▶
Fear of Fear '75
For Keeps '88
Four and a Half Women '05
Four Days in July '85
Fran '85
From Here to Maternity '85
Ghost Son '06
The Girls of Huntington House '73
A Good Baby '99
Grave of the Vampire '72
The Great Lie '41 ▶
A Hole in the Head '59
I Don't Want to Be Born '75
In Search of a Golden Sky '84
It's Alive '74 ▶
It's Alive 2: It Lives Again '78
It's Alive 3: Island of the Alive '87
Jack and Sarah '95
Lazybones '25
The Lightning Incident '91
Lion's Den '08
Little Man '06
Little Man Tate '91 ▶
Look Who's Talking '89 ▶
Look Who's Talking, Too '90
Mamele '38
Meet the Fockers '04
Monika '52
Nanny Insanity '06
Night Cries '78
Nobody's Baby '01
Not of This World '99
Novel Romance '06
The Omen '06
Paternity '81
Penny Serenade '41 ▶
Problem Child 2 '91
Psycho 4: The Beginning '90
Raising Arizona '87 ▶
Robin-B-Hood '06
Robot Stories '03
Rock-A-Bye Baby '57
Rosemary's Baby '68 ▶
The Rugrats Movie '98 ▶
Rumpelstiltskin '86
Sacred Ground '83
The Saga of the Draculas '72
Sarah's Child '96
Scarred '84
Secrets '94
Sex and Lucia '01
She's So Lovely '97
Shoot 'Em Up '07
The Snapper '93 ▶
Son of Godzilla '66
Song o' My Heart '30
A Song of Innocence '05
A Stranger in Town '95
The Sugarland Express '74 ▶
Superbabies: Baby Geniuses 2 '04
Susan Slade '61
The Switch '10
Table for Five '83
The Tender Years '47
The Terminator '84 ▶
Test Tube Babies '48
That's My Baby! '88
The 13th Floor '88
Thomas Graal's First Child '18 ▶
Three Men and a Baby '87 ▶
Three Men and a Cradle '85 ▶
Three Men and a Little Lady '90
Tomorrow's Child '82
Tomorrow's Children '34
Tsotsi '05 ▶
The 24 Hour Woman '99
The Unborn 2 '94
Unnatural '52
Up and Down '04
The War Zone '98
A Way of Life '04
Willa '79
Willow '88
A Woman Is a Woman '60 ▶

Brothers & Sisters

see also *Family Adventure; Family Comedy; Family Drama; Sibling Rivalry; Twins*

ABCD '99
About Adam '00
Above Suspicion '95
The Accidental Tourist '88 ▶
Across the Plains '39
Across to Singapore '28
Adam Had Four Sons '41
The Addams Family '91
Agata and the Storm '04
Agnes and His Brothers '04
Alaska '96
Alice Upside Down '07
All About You '01
All Fall Down '62
All My Sons '86 ▶
All the Brothers Were Valiant '53
Almost an Angel '90
Alpine Fire '89
American Flyers '85
American History X '98
American Outlaws '01
American Samurai '92
American Streetfighter '96
American Wedding '03
America's Sweethearts '01
Amores Perros '00 ▶
Amreeka '09 ▶
And You Thought Your Parents Were Weird! '91
Angela '94
Angels in the Endzone '98
Angus, Thongs and Perfect Snogging '08
Anne Frank: The Whole Story '01 ▶
Anne Rice's The Feast of All Saints '01
The Anniversary '68
Arabian Nights '42
Arabian Nights '00
The Aristocrats '99
Armored '09
Ash Wednesday '02
Ask Any Girl '59
At Any Cost '00
At Close Range '86 ▶
ATL '06
Atonement '07 ▶
Au Pair '99
Au Pair 2: The Fairy Tale Continues '01
Au Pair 3: Adventure in Paradise '09
Audrey's Rain '03
August '08
Autumn Sonata '78 ▶
The Avenging '92
Backdraft '91
Bad Blood '94
Bad Boys 2 '03
Bare Knees '28
Barjo '93
Based on an Untrue Story '93
The Basket '99
Basket Case '82 ▶
Basket Case 2 '90
Beau Geste '39 ▶
Beautiful Ohio '06
Because I Said So '07
Bee Season '05 ▶
Beerfest '06
Before the Devil Knows You're Dead '07 ▶
Behind the Red Door '02
Behind the Sun '01
Belle Epoque '92 ▶
Benny & Joon '93
Best of Youth '03 ▶
Betsy's Wedding '90
Better Dayz '02
Better Than Chocolate '99
Between Love & Goodbye '08
Big Brother Trouble '00
Big Business '88
Big Night '95
The Big White '05
Birds of America '08
Black Cadillac '03
Black Gunn '72
Black Irish '07
The Black Room '35 ▶
Black Sheep '96
Black Sheep '06
Blind Dating '06
Blinded by the Light '82
Blood Angels '05
Blood Creek '09
Blood Rage '87
Blood Relatives '77
Bloodlink '86
The Bloodstained Shadow '78
Bloodstream '00
Bloody Mama '70
Blue Car '03 ▶
Blue Crush '02 ▶
Blue River '95
Bobbie's Girl '02
The Bodyguard '92
Bollywood Hero '09
The Book of Stars '99
Boondock Saints '99
Born Killers '05
Born to Run '93
The Boys and Girl From County Clare '03
Bra Boys '07
Brand Upon the Brain! '06 ▶
Bread and Roses '00
The Bread, My Sweet '01
Breathing Fire '91
Brideshead Revisited '08
The Bridesmaid '04
Brilliant Lies '96
Bring It On '00
Broadway Melody '29
Broken Trust '93
The Brontes of Haworth '73
Brother '97
Brother Bear '03
Brotherhood of the Wolf '01
Brothers '04 ▶
Brothers '09
The Brothers Bloom '09
The Brothers Grimm '05
The Brothers Karamazov '58 ▶
Brother's Keeper '92 ▶
Brother's Keeper '02
A Brother's Kiss '97
The Brothers McMullen '94 ▶
Brothers of the Head '06
The Brothers Rico '57
The Brothers Solomon '07
Brothers Three '07
Buchanan Rides Alone '58
Bush Pilot '47
The Butterfly Effect 3: Revelation '09
Bye-Bye '96
Cadillac Ranch '96
Cafe Ole '00
The Cake Eaters '07
The Captive: The Longest Drive 2 '76
Carolina '03
Carolina Skeletons '92
Carriers '09
Carrie's War '04
Carry Me Back '82
Cassandra's Dream '07
Cat People '42 ▶
Cat People '82
Catacombs '07
Catherine Cookson's The Dwelling Place '94
Catherine Cookson's The Fifteen Streets '90
Catherine Cookson's The Wingless Bird '97
Cavalcade of the West '36
Cavalry Charge '51
Cellblock Sisters: Banished Behind Bars '95
The Cement Garden '93
Chain of Souls '00
Chameleon 3: Dark Angel '00
Chasing the Green '09
The Chateau '01
Cheaper by the Dozen '03
Cheetah '89
Chicken Tikka Masala '05
Children of Heaven '98
Children of the Corn 3: Urban Harvest '95
Christmas Comes to Willow Creek '87
Christmas in Wonderland '07
The Chronicles of Narnia: Prince Caspian '08
The Chronicles of Narnia: The Lion, the Witch and the Wardrobe '05
Chutney Popcorn '99
City of Industry '96
Close My Eyes '91
Code Unknown '00
Come Undone '00
The Confession '20
The Confessional '95 ▶
The Conrad Boys '06
Cookie's Fortune '99 ▶
Corky Romano '01
Counterstrike '03
Coupe de Ville '90
Cow Belles '06
Cowboy Up '00
Cracker: Brotherly Love '95 ▶
Crazy on the Outside '10
The Crew '08
Cria Cuervos '76 ▶
Cries and Whispers '72 ▶
Crimes of the Heart '86
Criminal '04
The Criminal Mind '93
Cruel and Unusual '01
Curly Top '35
Cursed '04
Cyclo '95
Daddy's Little Girls '07
Dancing at Lughnasa '98
Dangerous Ground '96
A Dangerous Place '94
Daniel '83
Danielle Steel's Kaleidoscope '90
Daring Daughters '33
The Darjeeling Limited '07 ▶
Dark Mirror '46 ▶
Dark Odyssey '57
Dead in the Water '06
Dead Man's Shoes '04
Death at a Funeral '07
Death of a Salesman '51 ▶
Deathfight '93
Deathlands: Homeward Bound '03
December Bride '91
Deep Winter '08
Defiance '08
Delightfully Dangerous '45
Deliver Us from Eva '03
Demons in the Garden '82 ▶
Desperate Remedies '93
Deuces Wild '02
The Devil's Daughter '39
Devil's Knight '03
The Devil's Web '74
Diamond Girl '98
Diamonds '72
Dick Tracy '37
Die Sister, Die! '74
Dim Sum Funeral '08
Dinotopia '02
Dirty Dancing: Havana Nights '04
Dixie Dynamite '76
Dr. Seuss' The Cat in the Hat '03
A Dog's Breakfast '07
The Dolly Sisters '46
Dominick & Eugene '88 ▶
Don't Tell '05
Double Dragon '94
Doughboys '08
Down in the Valley '05
Dream Street '21
The Dreamers '03
Driven '01
Drop Zone '94
Duel in the Sun '46 ▶
Dust '01
East of Eden '54 ▶
East of Eden '80
East Side Kids '40
EDtv '99
El Norte '83 ▶
The Elephant King '06
Elizabethtown '05
Emile '03
Empire Falls '05
Endplay '75
Enid Is Sleeping '90
Entertaining Mr. Sloane '70
Erskinville Kings '99
Eurotrip '04
Evening '07
Everybody's Fine '09
Experiment in Terror '62 ▶
Eye of the Storm '91
Eyes of a Stranger '81
The Fabulous Baker Boys '89 ▶
The Fabulous Dorseys '47
Face/Off '97 ▶
Faceless '88
The Fall of the House of Usher '49
The Fall of the House of Usher '60 ▶
The Fall of the House of Usher '80
Falling Angels '03
The Family Stone '05
Fanny and Alexander '83 ▶
Fantastic Four '05
Far Side of the Moon '03
Farinelli '94
The Fast Runner '01 ▶
Fatal Passion '94
The Favorite Son '94 ▶
Fear of the Dark '02
Feeling Minnesota '96
Female Perversions '96
Ferris Bueller's Day Off '86 ▶
A Few Days in September '06
Fiddler on the Roof '71 ▶
50 First Dates '04
The Fighting Sullivans '42 ▶
Final Analysis '92
Final Appeal '93
The Finger Man '55
Flexing with Monty '10
The Florentine '98
Flowers in the Attic '87
The Flying Fool '29
Fool for Love '86
For Better or Worse '95
Force of Evil '49 ▶
40 Days and 40 Nights '02
Forty Guns '57
Four Brothers '05
Four Christmases '08
Four Daughters '38 ▶
Four Men and a Prayer '38
Four Sheets to the Wind '07
Four Sons '28
Frailty '02 ▶
Frank and Jesse '94
Frayed '07
Fred Claus '07
Freddy Got Fingered '01
Freud Leaving Home '91
From Dusk Till Dawn '95
The Game '97 ▶
Gas Food Lodging '92 ▶
The Gene Generation '07
George White's Scandals '45
Georgia '95 ▶
Get Over It! '01
Ghosts of Girlfriends Past '09
Gigantic '08
Ginger Snaps '01
Ginger Snaps: Unleashed '04
The Girl with a Suitcase '60
Give Me a Sailor '38
Give Me Your Hand '09
Gladiator '00 ▶
The Glass House '01
Glass House: The Good Mother '06

▶ = rated three bones or higher

▶ = rated three bones or higher

Whacked! '02
Whale Music '94
The Whales of August '87 ▶
What Ever Happened To... '93
What Ever Happened to Baby Jane? '62 ▶
What's Eating Gilbert Grape '93 ▶
What's Up, Scarlet? '05
When Angels Fly '82
When Brendan Met Trudy '00 ▶
Where the Lilies Bloom '74 ▶
Where the Wild Things Are '09
Wild America '97 ▶
Wild West '93
Wilder Napalm '93
The Wind That Shakes the Barley '06 ▶
Windhorse '98
Wish upon a Star '96
Without Evidence '96
The Wizard '89
The Wolves '95
The Woman in White '97
Wonderful World '09
Wonderland '99
Wyatt Earp '94
X-Men Origins: Wolverine '09
You and Me '06
You Can Count On Me '99 ▶
You Got Served '04
The Young Girls of Rochefort '68
Zathura '05 ▶
Zatoichi '03 ▶
Zus & Zo '01

Buddhism

The Calamari Wrestler '04
The Covenant '06
The Cup '99
Green Snake '93
The Judgement '04
Kundun '97 ▶
Little Buddha '93
Omaha (the movie) '95
Raw Force '81
Seven Years in Tibet '97
Siddhartha '72
Spring, Summer, Fall, Winter... and Spring '03 ▶
Temptation of a Monk '94
The Unmistaken Child '08
Why Has Bodhi-Darma Left for the East '89
Windhorse '98

Buddies

***see also** Buddy Cops*
Abbott and Costello Meet Frankenstein '48 ▶
Adios Amigo '75
The Adventures of Huck Finn '93 ▶
The Adventures of Huckleberry Finn '78
The Adventures of Milo & Otis '89 ▶
The Adventures of Rusty '45
Against the Wall '04
Ain't No Way Back '89
The Alamo '60 ▶
All Saint's Day '98
All the Real Girls '03 ▶
American Pie '99 ▶
An American Story '92
Amongst Friends '93
Andre '94
Another 48 Hrs. '90
Another You '91
Anzacs: The War Down Under '85 ▶
As Tears Go By '88 ▶
Asian Stories '06
At First Sight '95
ATL '06
The Baby-Sitters' Club '95
Babyfever '94
Bachelor Party '84
Bachelor Party Vegas '05
Backbeat '94 ▶
Bad Company '72 ▶
Bad Girls '94
Band of Brothers '01 ▶
BASEketball '98
The Basketball Diaries '95
The Battle of Blood Island '60
The Bear '89 ▶
Beautiful Girls '96 ▶
Beavis and Butt-Head Do America '96
Beer League '06
Belly '98
Benji: Off the Leash! '04
A Better Tomorrow, Part 1 '86
A Better Tomorrow, Part 2 '88
Between Heaven and Hell '56 ▶
The Big Chill '83 ▶
Big Deadly Game '54
Big Eden '00
Big Fan '09
Big Mo '73
Big Shots '87
The Big Slice '90
Bigfoot: The Unforgettable Encounter '94
Bill & Ted's Bogus Journey '91
Birdy '84 ▶
Black Beauty '46
Black Cadillac '03
Black Fox: The Price of Peace '94
Blackrock '97
Blonde in Black Leather '77
Blood Brothers '07
Blowin' Smoke '99
Blue De Ville '86
Blue Juice '95
The Blue Lamp '49 ▶
Blue Ridge Fall '99
Blue Skies '46 ▶
The Blue Tooth Virgin '09
Body Shots '99
Bogus '96
Bookies '03
Boot Hill '69
Boots Malone '52
Born to Be Wild '38
Born to Be Wild '95
Boston Kickout '95
The Bowery '33 ▶
A Boy and His Dog '75
The Boy Who Could Fly '86 ▶
The Boys in the Band '70
The Boys Next Door '96
Branded Men '31
Breaking the Rules '92
Breakout '98
Brian's Song '01
Bride of Killer Nerd '91
Broadway Melody of 1940 '40
Brooklyn Rules '07
The Brothers '01 ▶
The Bucket List '07
The Buddy System '83
A Bullet in the Head '90 ▶
Bulletproof '96
The Bumblebee Flies Anyway '98
Bundle of Joy '56
The Business of Fancydancing '02
The Butterfly '02 ▶
Bye Bye Braverman '67
The Cable Guy '96
The Caddy '53
Calendar Girl '93
Cambridge Spies '03
The Campus Corpse '77
Campus Man '87
Capitaine Conan '96 ▶
Captive Hearts '87
The Cat '66
Catch and Release '07
Celtic Pride '96
Charlie's Ghost: The Secret of Coronado '94
Chasing Amy '97
Cheap Shots '91
Chill Factor '99
Circle of Two '80
The Cisco Kid '94
City of Men '07 ▶
City Slickers '91 ▶
City Slickers 2: The Legend of Curly's Gold '94
Class Act '91
Class of '61 '92
Clay Pigeons '98
Clayton County Line '78
Clerks '94 ▶
Clerks 2 '06 ▶
Clown Murders '83
Cock & Bull Story '03
Colombian Love '04
The Color Purple '85 ▶
Colorado Serenade '46
Company Business '91
The Concrete Cowboys '79
Convict Cowboy '95
Cops and Robbers '73
Corleone '79
Country Gentlemen '36
Courage of Black Beauty '57
Crack Up '97
Crime Busters '78
Crime Lords '91
Crime Spree '03
Crossfire '89
Crossing the Bridge '92
Crossover '06
Cry Freedom '87
The Cure '95
Curtis's Charm '96
Cycle Vixens '79
Dancer, Texas—Pop. 81 '98 ▶
Dark Blue World '01
Day Zero '07
Dead Presidents '95
Dead Reckoning '47 ▶
Deadlock '91
Deadly Surveillance '91
December '91
The Deer Hunter '78 ▶
Defenseless '91
The Defiant Ones '58 ▶
Delta Farce '07
Detroit Rock City '99
The Devil's Dominoes '07
Die Hard: With a Vengeance '95
Digger '94
Diggers '06
Diner '82 ▶
Dirty Work '97
Dish Dogs '98
Dogfight '91 ▶
Donnie Brasco '96 ▶
Donovan's Reef '63 ▶
Don't Look Back '96 ▶
Dopamine '03
Double Down '01
Double Team '97
Down Under '86
Downtown '89
Dragonheart '96
Dragonworld '94
Dream a Little Dream 2 '94
The Dream Catcher '99
Dream with the Fishes '97
Dreamcatcher '03
The Dresser '83 ▶
Driving Miss Daisy '89 ▶
Drop Dead Fred '91
Drums in the Deep South '51
Dude, Where's My Car? '00
Dumb & Dumber '94
Dumb and Dumberer: When Harry Met Lloyd '03
The Eagle and the Hawk '33 ▶
Easy Rider '69 ▶
Eat the Peach '86
Ed's Next Move '96
The Eighth Day '95
El Dorado '67 ▶
Elling '01
Elmer '76
The Emperor's New Groove '00 ▶
Enemy Mine '85
Enemy of the State '98
Entre-Nous '83 ▶
Eurotrip '04
Every Which Way But Loose '78
Extreme Prejudice '87
Extremedays '01
F/X 2: The Deadly Art of Illusion '91
The Falcon and the Snowman '85 ▶
Fanboys '09
Far from Home: The Adventures of Yellow Dog '94
Father's Day '96
Federal Hill '94
Ferris Bueller's Day Off '86 ▶
Fight Club: ' '99 ▶
Finder's Fee '01
First Kid '96
5 Against the House '55
The Five Heartbeats '91 ▶
(500) Days of Summer '09
Fled '96
Flickering Lights '01
The Flintstones '94
The Flintstones in Viva Rock Vegas '00
Floating '97
Flyboys '06
For the Moment '94
Forgive and Forget '99
Forsaking All Others '35
Fortunes '05
The 40 Year Old Virgin '05 ▶
The Four Feathers '02
Francis in the Navy '55
Free Enterprise '98
Free Willy '93
Free Willy 2: The Adventure Home '95
Free Willy 3: The Rescue '97
Freeze-Die-Come to Life '90 ▶
The Frisco Kid '79
Frontier Fugitives '45
Full Count '06
The Full Monty '96 ▶
Funny People '09
Funny Valentine '05
Galaxies Are Colliding '92
Gallipoli '81 ▶
Garden State '04 ▶
Geek Mythology '08
Gerry '02
Get Over It! '01
Getting Even '92
A Girl, 3 Guys and a Gun '01
A Girl in Every Port '28
Glory Daze '96
Going All the Way '97
Going Back '83
Going Greek '01
Gold Diggers: The Secret of Bear Mountain '95
Gold of the Seven Saints '61
The Golden Boys '08
Gone Fishin' '97
The Good Humor Man '05
Good Luck '96
Good Will Hunting '97
Goodfellas '90 ▶
Gordy '95
Gossip '99
Grand Illusion '37 ▶
Gridlock'd '96 ▶
Grilled '06
Grind '03
The Groomsmen '06
Grown Ups '10
Grumpier Old Men '95
Grumpy Old Men '93 ▶
Guarding Tess '94
A Guide to Recognizing Your Saints '06
Gunga Din '39 ▶
Gunmen '93
Hangin' with the Homeboys '91 ▶
The Hangover '09
Hank and Mike '08
Hard Core Logo '96
Hard Eight '96 ▶
Hard Luck '01
Harley Davidson and the Marlboro Man '91
Harold and Kumar Go to White Castle '04
Harriet the Spy '96
Harsh Times '05
The Hasty Heart '86
Hate '95 ▶
Hats Off '37
Hawaii Calls '38
He Died With a Felafel in His Hand '01
Heartaches '82 ▶
Heartbreakers '84 ▶
Heavenly Creatures '94 ▶
Henry & Verlin '94
Hercules '97 ▶
The Hi-Lo Country '98
The Highest Honor '84
Highway '01
Hired Hand '71
Hollywood or Bust '56
Home Free All '84
Homeward Bound 2: Lost in San Francisco '96
Hong Kong Nights '35
Hong Kong 1941 '84
Honor '06
Hoot '06
Hot Tub Time Machine '10
Huck and the King of Hearts '93
Humpday '09
The Hunters '58
Hurlyburly '98
Hurricane Streets '96
Husbands '70
I Got Five on It '05
I Hope They Serve Beer in Hell '09
I Love You, Man '09 ▶
I Now Pronounce You Chuck and Larry '07
I Shot a Man in Vegas '96
I Spy '02
I Went Down '97 ▶
Ice Age: Dawn of the Dinosaurs '09
Ice Age: The Meltdown '06
Ice Men '04
If I Had My Way '40
If Lucy Fell '95
I'll Remember April '99
I'm Not Rappaport '96
The In-Laws '79 ▶
In the Navy '41
Indian Summer '93
Inn of Temptation '73
Intimate Lighting '65
The Iron Giant '99 ▶
Ishtar '87
Ivan and Abraham '94
Jackass Number Two '06
Jay and Silent Bob Strike Back '01
Jimmy Hollywood '94
Jindabyne '06
Johnny Come Lately '43
Johnny Holiday '49
The Jolly Boys' Last Stand '00
Joy Ride to Nowhere '78
Joyride '97
Judgment Night '93
Juice '92
Juke Girl '42
Jules and Jim '62 ▶
Junior Army '42
Just a Little Harmless Sex '99
Just Between Friends '86
Just Like the Son '06
K-9000 '89
The Kansas Terrors '39
The Karate Kid '84 ▶
The Karate Kid: Part 2 '86
The Karate Kid: Part 3 '89
Kazaam '96
Keeping the Faith '00
Killer Bud '00
Killer Pad '06
The Killing Fields '84 ▶
King of the Mountain '81
Kingpin '96
Kings of the Road—In the Course of Time '76 ▶
Knock Off '98
Knockaround Guys '01
Knocked Up '07
K2: The Ultimate High '92
L.A. Twister '04
Ladies on the Rocks '83
The Land Before Time 5: The Mysterious Island '97
Lansky '99
Larry McMurtry's Dead Man's Walk '96
Last American Virgin '82
The Last Boy Scout '91
The Last Kiss '06
Last Orders '01 ▶
Last Stop for Paul '08
Last Summer '69
The Last Time I Committed Suicide '96
Late Last Night '99
Lawn Dogs '96
Le Beau Serge '58 ▶
Le Doulos '61 ▶
Leaving Normal '92
Les Apprentis '95 ▶
Les Comperes '83 ▶
The Lesser Evil '97
Let 'er Go Gallegher '28
Let's Do It Again '75
Liar's Poker '99
L.I.E. '01
Life '99
The Life of Jesus '96
Linda Linda Linda '05 ▶
The Lion King 1 1/2 '04 ▶
Little City '97
The Littlest Outlaw '54
The Lives of a Bengal Lancer '35 ▶
The Long Voyage Home '40 ▶
Looking for Miracles '90
Lords of Dogtown '05
The Lords of Flatbush '74
Lost in the Barrens '91
Love Goggles '99
Love Letters '45
Love Thy Neighbor '02
Love! Valour! Compassion! '96
Lovelife '97
Love's Labour's Lost '00
The Low Down '00
Macaroni '85
Mad Dog and Glory '93 ▶
Made '01
Made of Honor '08
Mallrats '95
The Man on the Train '02 ▶
The Man Who Would Be King '75 ▶
Managua '97
Manhattan Melodrama '34 ▶
Manpower '41
March or Die '77
Master and Commander: The Far Side of the World '03 ▶
McHale's Navy '97
Me and Him '89
Mean Frank and Crazy Tony '75
Meet Danny Wilson '52
Men Men Men '95
The Men's Club '86
Metroland '97
Midnight Cowboy '69 ▶
Midnight Run '88 ▶
The Mighty '98 ▶
The Mighty Quinn '89
Mikey & Nicky '76
Mina Tannenbaum '93
Miss March '09
Misunderstood '87
Molly and Gina '94
Mondays in the Sun '02
Money Talks '97
Money to Burn '94
Monster Man '03
Monsters, Inc. '01 ▶
Monument Ave. '98
Moola '07
Moon over Miami '41 ▶
Moonlight and Valentino '95
Mortal Thoughts '91
The Mosaic Project '95
The Motorcycle Diaries '04 ▶
Mulligan '00
MXP: Most Xtreme Primate '03
My Beautiful Laundrette '85 ▶
My Best Friend's Girl '84
My Best Friend's Girl '08
My Best Friend's Wedding '97
My Dinner with Andre '81 ▶
My Effortless Brilliance '08
My First Mister '01
My Giant '98
My Girl '91
My Name Is Joe '98
Mystic Pizza '88 ▶
Mystic River '03 ▶
Naked Youth '59
The Naughty Nineties '45
Neil Simon's The Odd Couple 2 '98
The New Twenty '08
Night Beat '48
Nightforce '86
The Nightingale '83 ▶

▶ = rated three bones or higher

1915 '82
No Blood No Tears '02 ▸
No Money Down '97
No Sleep 'Til Madison '02
Nothing to Lose '96
Now and Then '95
The Nugget '02
Ocean's 11 '60
Ocean's Eleven '01 ▸
Ocean's Thirteen '07 ▸
The Odd Couple '68 ▸
Old Dogs '09
Old Explorers '90
Old Joy '06 ▸
Oliver & Company '88
On the Fiddle '61
On the Line '01
One Crazy Summer '86
100 Days Before the Command '90
One Last Thing '05
One Sings, the Other Doesn't '77
The Opposite Sex and How to Live With Them '93
Ordinary Sinner '02
Out to Sea '97
The Pacific and Eddy '07
Palo Alto '07
Palookaville '95 ▸
Pals '87
Papillon '73 ▸
Parallel Lives '94
Past the Bleachers '95
Peck's Bad Boy with the Circus '38
The Penitent '88
The Perfect Clown '25
Perfectly Normal '91
Peter's Friends '92
Petits Freres '00
The Phantom of 42nd Street '45
Phat Beach '96
Piece of Cake '88
Pigs '07
Pineapple Express '08 ▸
P.K. and the Kid '85
Plan B '97
Platoon '86 ▸
Play It to the Bone '99
Playmates '72
A Pleasure Doing Business '79
Plunder Road '57
The Poker Club '08
The Pompatus of Love '95
Portrait of a Showgirl '82
Psycho Cop 2 '94
P.U.N.K.S. '98
Push '06
Racing with the Moon '84 ▸
Rafferty & the Gold Dust Twins '75
Rape '76
The Rat Pack '98
Ready to Rumble '00
The Red Balloon '56 ▸
Red Meat '98
Reign Over Me '07
The Reivers '69 ▸
Relax... It's Just Sex! '98
Reno and the Doc '84
Reprise '06
Requiem for Dominic '91 ▸
The Return of Grey Wolf '22
The Return of the Musketeers '89
Return of the Secaucus 7 '80 ▸
Return to Paradise '98 ▸
Revenge of the Nerds '84
Revenge of the Nerds 2: Nerds in Paradise '87
Rich and Famous '81
Ride the High Country '62 ▸
Ride with the Devil '99
Rio Conchos '64 ▸
The Road to El Dorado '00
The Road to Hong Kong '62
The Road to Morocco '42 ▸
Road Trip '00
Road Trip: Beer Pong '09
Roadside Prophets '92
Robby '68
Robert et Robert '78 ▸
Romy and Michele's High School Reunion '97
Roommates '95
Rory O'Shea Was Here '04
Rubin & Ed '92
Rules of Engagement '00
The Run of the Country '95 ▸
The Rundown '03
Running Scared '86
Russkies '87
Rusty's Birthday '49
St. Elmo's Fire '85
The Saint of Fort Washington '93
Saints and Sinners '95
Salut l'Artiste '74 ▸
Same River Twice '97
The Sandlot '93 ▸
Saving Silverman '01
The Search for One-Eye Jimmy '96
Searching for Bobby D '05
Searching For Wooden Watermelons '01
A Separate Peace '04
Seven Days Ashore '44
7 Virgins '05
The Seventh Veil '46 ▸
Sex Drive '08
Shag: The Movie '89 ▸
Shaking the Tree '92
Shanghai Knights '03
Shaolin & Wu Tang '81 ▸
Shaun of the Dead '04 ▸
She Gods of Shark Reef '56
Sherman's Way '08
Shipmates Forever '35
Shiri '99
The Shot '96
Shot Through the Heart '98 ▸
Showdown in Little Tokyo '91
Shrek the Third '07
Shut Up and Kiss Me '05
Sideways '04 ▸
Silence Like Glass '90
Slackers '02
Slappy and the Stinkers '97
The Slaughter Rule '01
Sleepers '96
Sling Blade '96 ▸
Snow White and the Seven Dwarfs '83 ▸
So This Is Washington '43
Some Like It Hot '59 ▸
Someone Else's America '96 ▸
Something of Value '57 ▸
Son of Rusty '47
Songwriter '84
Sophisticated Gents '81 ▸
The Souler Opposite '97
Souls at Sea '37
Sparkler '99
Spawn of the North '38
Spies Like Us '85
Spittin' Image '83
Spotlight Scandals '43
Spring Forward '99
Sprung '96
Stag '97
Stand by Me '86 ▸
Star Trek 4: The Voyage Home '86 ▸
Starbird and Sweet William '73
State of Grace '90 ▸
The Station Agent '03 ▸
Stealing Home '88
Steaming '86
The Steel Helmet '51 ▸
Stickmen '01
Sticks and Stones '96
Stir Crazy '80
Stolen Summer '02
The Stoned Age '94
Stop-Loss '08 ▸
Strange Bedfellows '04
Stranger than Fiction '99
Strawberry and Chocolate '93 ▸
Stricken '98
Stuckey's Last Stand '80
The Substitute 3: Winner Takes All '99
subUrbia '96
Sudden Death '50
Summer City '77
Sunny Skies '30
The Sunshine Boys '75 ▸
Superbad '07 ▸
Superheroes '07
The Sweetest Thing '02
Swingers '96 ▸
T Bone N Weasel '92
Take Care of My Cat '01
Talladega Nights: The Ballad of Ricky Bobby '06
Tape '01 ▸
Target of Opportunity '04
The Tavern '00
Ten Benny '98
Ten Who Dared '60
Tenacious D in the Pick of Destiny '06
Tequila Sunrise '88
Terminal Bliss '91
That Championship Season '99
That Sinking Feeling '79 ▸
Thelma & Louise '91 ▸
Things to Do '06
Think Tank '06
Three Amigos '86
Three Days to Vegas '07
Three Legionnaires '37
Three Men and a Baby '87 ▸
Three Men and a Cradle '85 ▸
Three Men in a Boat '56
The Three Musketeers '33
The Three Musketeers '35
The Three Musketeers '48
The Three Musketeers '74 ▸
The Three Musketeers '93
Thunder in the Pines '49
Thursday's Game '74 ▸
Tiger Shark '32
Tin Cup '96 ▸
To Forget Venice '79
To Wong Foo, Thanks for Everything, Julie Newmar '95
Tombstone '93 ▸
Tomcats '01
Top Dog '95
Top Gun '86
Tough Guys '86
Tour of Duty '87
Toy Story '95 ▸
Toy Story 2 '99 ▸
Trainspotting '95 ▸
Tree's Lounge '96
The Triangle '01
Trippin' '99
True Colors '91
True Friends '98
The Turning Point '77
12 and Holding '05 ▸
25th Hour '02
Twin Warriors '93
2 Fast 2 Furious '03
Two Tickets to Paradise '06
Two Weeks to Live '43
2B Perfectly Honest '04
Ugetsu '53 ▸
Under the Lighthouse Dancing '97
Under the Sun '98
Underworld '27 ▸
Unholy Four '54
Vampire Killers '09
The Van '95 ▸
Veronico Cruz '87
Very Bad Things '98
The Very Thought of You '98
Vincent, Francois, Paul and the Others '76 ▸
The Virginian '46
The Virginian '99
Walking and Talking '96
Walking on Water '02
Warrior Spirit '94
Wasted '06
Wayne's World '92 ▸
Wayne's World 2 '93
We All Fall Down '00
Wedding Crashers '05 ▸
Weirdsville '07
Went to Coney Island on a Mission from God... Be Back by Five '98
We're in the Legion Now '37
Western '96
What Price Glory? '52 ▸
When Harry Met Sally... '89 ▸
Where Is My Friend's House? '87
Where the River Runs Black '86
Whipped '00
White Badge '92
White Christmas '54 ▸
White Mama '80 ▸
White Men Can't Jump '92
White Nights '85
Who's the Man? '93
Who's Your Monkey '07
Why Me? '90
Wieners '08
Wild Hogs '07
Wild Horses '95
The Wild Life '84
Wild Rovers '71
Windy City '84
Winners Take All '87
Winter Break '02
With a Friend Like Harry '00 ▸
With Friends Like These '98 ▸
Withnail and I '87 ▸
Without a Paddle: Nature's Calling '09
The Wood '99
Wrestling Ernest Hemingway '93
The Wrong Guys '88
The Wrong Road '37
Y Tu Mama Tambien '01
The Yakuza '75
Yankee Zulu '95
Year One '09
Yes Man '08
You Are Here * '00
You, Me and Dupree '06
You Move You Die '07
You Tell Me '06
Young Hercules '97
Zorba the Greek '64 ▸

Buddy Cops

***see also** Cops; Women Cops*

Another 48 Hrs. '90
Another Stakeout '93
Arizona Heat '87
Bad Boys '95
Bad Boys 2 '03
The Black Dahlia '06
Blue Streak '99
Bon Cop Bad Cop '06
Car 54, Where Are You? '94
City Heat '84
Collision Course '89
Cop Land '97 ▸
Cop Out '10
The Corruptor '99 ▸
Dirty '05
Exit to Eden '94
48 Hrs. '82 ▸
The Glimmer Man '96
The Hard Way '91 ▸
Hollywood Homicide '03
Hot Fuzz '07 ▸
Internal Affairs '90
La Chevre '81 ▸
Lethal Weapon '87 ▸
Lethal Weapon 2 '89 ▸
Lethal Weapon 3 '92
Lethal Weapon 4 '98
Liberty & Bash '90
The Man '05
A Man Apart '03
Men in Black '97 ▸
Metro '96
Miami Vice '06
Money Train '95
Mulholland Falls '95
National Lampoon's Loaded Weapon 1 '93
Night Children '89
Nighthawks '81
The Other Guys '10
The Presidio '88
Red Heat '88
Renegades '89
The Rookie '90
Rush Hour 2 '01
Rush Hour 3 '07
Shakedown '88
Shoot to Kill '88 ▸
Simon Sez '99
Speed '94 ▸
Stakeout '87
Starsky & Hutch '04
Tango and Cash '89
Taxi '04
White Chicks '04

Buffalo, NY

Best Friends '82
Bruce Almighty '03
Buffalo 66 '97 ▸
Dames '34 ▸
Evan Almighty '07
Frozen River '08 ▸
Gypsy '62 ▸
The Last Seduction '94 ▸
Manna from Heaven '02
The Savages '07 ▸
You Kill Me '07 ▸

Bullfighters & Bullfighting

***see also** Spain*

Around the World in 80 Days '56 ▸
Around the World in 80 Days '89
Blood and Sand '22
Blood and Sand '41 ▸
Blood and Sand '89
The Bobo '67
Bolero '84
Bullfighter & the Lady '50
Bullfighters '45
Carnage '02
El Matador '03
Jamon, Jamon '93
The Magnificent Matador '55
Matador '86
The Matador '06 ▸
Pandora and the Flying Dutchman '51
Sand and Blood '87
Talk to Her '02 ▸
Torero '56

Burglars

***see also** Crime Doesn't Pay; Crime Drama; Disorganized Crime; Heists*

Absolute Power '97
After Hours '85 ▸
Allie & Me '97
Breaking and Entering '06
Bullet '94
Burglar '87
Canvas: The Fine Art of Crime '92
Circus Angel '65 ▸
Criss Cross '48 ▸
The Doll '62
The Edukators '04
Entrapment '99
Family Business '89
Federal Hill '94
Floating '97
Following '99
Gambit '66
The General '98 ▸
Home Alone '90 ▸
The Hot Rock '70 ▸
Hudson Hawk '91
I Hate Blondes '83
Kid Sister '45
Laurel & Hardy: Night Owls '30
Let Him Have It '91 ▸
Little Sweetheart '90
Millions '05 ▸
Murph the Surf '75
The Night They Robbed Big Bertha's '75
Picture Windows '95
Ping! '99
The Pink Panther '64 ▸
Poor White Trash '00
P.S. Your Cat is Dead! '02
Raffles '30 ▸
Row Your Boat '98
The Set Up '95
The Spree '96
Sworn to Justice '97
The Thief of Paris '67 ▸
Thrillkill '84
Vamping '84
Vengeance '80
When Thief Meets Thief '37

Buried Alive

Buried '10
Buried Alive '90
Buried Alive 2 '97
The Fall of the House of Usher '49
The Fall of the House of Usher '60 ▸
The Fall of the House of Usher '80
The House of Usher '88
Kill Bill Vol. 2 '04 ▸
La Chute de la Maison Usher '28 ▸
The Oblong Box '69
Oxygen '99
Premature Burial '62
Seed '08
Simon the Magician '99
Three ... Extremes '04

Buses

The Adventures of Priscilla, Queen of the Desert '94 ▸
All God's Children '80
Almost Famous '00 ▸
Beavis and Butt-Head Do America '96
The Big Bus '76
Boycott '02 ▸
Bull Durham '88 ▸
Bus Stop '56 ▸
Bustin' Loose '81 ▸
Dirty Harry '71 ▸
Exit Speed '08
Ferris Bueller's Day Off '86 ▸
Forrest Gump '94 ▸
The Fugitive '93 ▸
The Gauntlet '77
Get On the Bus '96 ▸
Heart and Souls '93
Incident at Deception Ridge '94
The Interpreter '05 ▸
Jeepers Creepers 2 '03
Keane '04 ▸
The King Is Alive '00
Lady on the Bus '78
The Laughing Policeman '74
A League of Their Own '92 ▸
Long Journey Back '78
Love Field '91
Magical Mystery Tour '67
A Man of No Importance '94 ▸
Mexican Bus Ride '51
My Life in Ruins '09
National Lampoon's Senior Trip '95
Pardon My Sarong '42
Planes, Trains & Automobiles '87
Ride '98
The Runaway Bus '54
Selena '96
Shuttle '09
Siam Sunset '99
The Siege '98
Sixteen Candles '84 ▸
Speed '94 ▸
Spice World: The Movie '97
Still Crazy '98 ▸
Sunday in New York '63
The Sweet Hereafter '96 ▸
Swordfish '01
Three Days to Vegas '07
The Trip to Bountiful '85 ▸
Vince Vaughn's Wild West Comedy Show '06
Wassup Rockers '06
Wheels of Terror '90
Where Angels Go, Trouble Follows '68

Cabbies

All or Nothing '02
Better Than Sex '00
The Bishop's Wife '47 ▸
Blood & Donuts '95
Born Romantic '00
Carry On Cabby '63
Chicago Cab '98
Claire Dolan '97
Collateral '04 ▸
Conspiracy Theory '97 ▸
Crocodile Dundee '86 ▸
Crossing Delancey '88 ▸
Daylight '96
D.C. Cab '84
Doc Hollywood '91
Drowning on Dry Land '00
Escape from New York '81
Extremely Dangerous '99
Fall '97
Family Jewels '65
The Fifth Element '97
For Hire '98

▸ = rated three bones or higher

The Glass Jungle '88
Goodbye Solo '08
Look Who's Talking '89 ►
The Love Trap '29
Mexico City '00
My Best Friend '06
My Son the Fanatic '97 ►
Nick and Jane '96
Night on Earth '91 ►
Pulp Fiction '94 ►
Race to Witch Mountain '09
Radio Cab Murder '54
Scrooged '88
She's the One '96
Sorry, Haters '05
Sorum '01
Stir Crazy '80
Taxi '04
Taxi Blues '90 ►
Taxi Driver '76 ►
The Taxi Mystery '26
They Met in a Taxi '36
3 A.M. '01 ►
Three Days of Rain '02
Too Bad She's Bad '54
Total Recall '90 ►
The Town Is Quiet '00
200 Cigarettes '98
Under the Bombs '07
Vintage Model '92
The Yellow Cab Man '50

Calcutta

***see also** India*
The Adversary '71
Baraka '93 ►
Born Into Brothels: Calcutta's Red Light Kids '04
Calcutta '47
City of Joy '92
Days and Nights in the Forest '70
The Quest '96

Cambodia

***see also** Asia; Vietnam War*
Apocalypse Now '79 ►
City of Ghosts '03
The Expendables '89
Fortunes of War '94
The Girl Who Spelled Freedom '86 ►
The Killing Fields '84 ►
No Retreat, No Surrender 2 '89
S21: The Khmer Rouge Killing Machine '03 ►
Swimming to Cambodia '87 ►

Camelot (New)

***see also** Assassination; Presidency*
Jackie, Ethel, Joan: The Kennedy Women '01
Jacqueline Bouvier Kennedy '81
JFK '91 ►
The JFK Conspiracy '91
JFK: Reckless Youth '93
Kennedy '83
Prince Jack '83
PT 109 '63
Robert Kennedy and His Times '90
Ruby '92
Thirteen Days '00 ►

Camelot (Old)

***see also** Medieval Romps; Swashbucklers*
Arthur's Quest '99
Camelot '67
A Connecticut Yankee '31 ►
A Connecticut Yankee in King Arthur's Court '49
Excalibur '81 ►
First Knight '95
A Kid in King Arthur's Court '95
Kids of the Round Table '96
King Arthur '04
King Arthur, the Young Warlord '75
A Knight in Camelot '98
Knights of the Round Table '53
Merlin '98 ►
Merlin and the Book of Beasts '09
Merlin and the Sword '85
Merlin's Apprentice '06
Mists of Avalon '01 ►
Monty Python and the Holy Grail '75 ►
Prince Valiant '54
Prince Valiant '97
Quest for Camelot '98
The Sword in the Stone '63 ►
Sword of Lancelot '63
Sword of the Valiant '83
A Young Connecticut Yankee in King Arthur's Court '95

Campus Capers

***see also** Fraternities & Sororities; Hell High School; School Daze*
Abandon '02
The Absent-Minded Professor '61 ►
Accepted '06
Accident '67
The Affairs of Dobie Gillis '53
All-American Murder '91
American Pie Presents: Beta House '07
American Pie Presents: The Naked Mile '06
American Psycho 2: All American Girl '02
American Tiger '89
American Virgin '09
Animal Behavior '89
Assault of the Party Nerds '89
Baby Love '83
Bachelor of Hearts '58
Back to School '86
A Beautiful Mind '01 ►
Berkeley '05
Beware '46
Beyond Dream's Door '88
Bickford Shmeckler's Cool Ideas '06
Big Man on Campus '89
Big Shot: Confessions of a Campus Bookie '02
Black Christmas '75
Black Tower '50
Blondie Goes to College '42
Blood Cult '85
Blood Sisters '86
Blue Chips '94
Boogeyman 3 '08
Boys and Girls '00
Breeders '97
Bride of Killer Nerd '91
Bring It On Again '03
Campus Confessions '38
The Campus Corpse '77
Campus Knights '29
Campus Man '87
Carnal Knowledge '71 ►
Charley's Aunt '41 ►
The Cheerleaders '72
Cheers for Miss Bishop '41
A Chump at Oxford '40
Circle of Friends '94
College '27 ►
College '08
College Humor '33
College Swing '38
Computer Beach Party '88
The Computer Wore Tennis Shoes '69
Confessions of Sorority Girls '94
The Cousins '59 ►
The Crimson Rivers '01
Cruel Intentions 3 '04
Cult '07
The Curve '97
Dark Matter '07
Dead Man on Campus '97
Deadly Lessons '94
Deadly Obsession '88
Deadly Possession '88
Dealing: Or the Berkeley-to-Boston Forty-Brick Lost-Bag Blues '72
Death Screams '83
Decoys '04
Decoys: The Second Seduction '07
Defying Gravity '99
Devil in the Flesh 2 '00
Didn't You Hear? '83
Divided We Stand '00
Doctor in the House '53 ►
Dorm That Dripped Blood '82
Down to You '00
Drumline '02 ►
The Duke of West Point '38
Elegy '08
Ernest Rides Again '93
Escapade in Florence '62
The Express '08
Father Was a Fullback '49
Final Exam '81
First Affair '83
First Daughter '04
First Love '77
First Time '82
Flubber '97
Foreign Student '94
Francis Goes to West Point '52
Fraternity Vacation '85
The Freshman '25 ►
The Freshman '90
Freshman Orientation '04
Fright Night 2 '88
Getting Away With Murder '96
Getting In '94
Ghoulies 3: Ghoulies Go to College '91
Girl Crazy '43 ►
Girls Night Out '83
The Gladiator '38 ►
Glory Daze '96
Going Greek '01
Good '08
Good News '47
Good Will Hunting '97
Goodbye My Fancy '51
Gossip '99
Gotcha! '85
The Great Debaters '07 ►
Gross Anatomy '89
Gross Misconduct '93
Hamburger... The Motion Picture '86
Happy Hell Night '92
Harmon of Michigan '41
Harold and Kumar Go to White Castle '04
Harrad Experiment '73
Harrad Summer '74
Harvard Man '01
HauntedWeen '91
The Heart of Dixie '89
Heart of Stone '01
Hell Night '81
Higher Education '88
Higher Learning '94
Horse Feathers '32 ►
H.O.T.S. '79
The House Bunny '08
House of the Dead 2: Dead Aim '05
The House on Sorority Row '83
House Party 2: The Pajama Jam '91
How High '01
How I Got into College '89
How I Spent My Summer Vacation '97
The Human Stain '03
I Don't Buy Kisses Anymore '92
I'll Be Home for Christmas '98
In the Blood '06
The Initiation '84
Initiation of Sarah '78
The Initiation of Sarah '06
I.Q. '94
Iris '01 ►
Is There Life Out There? '94
Jock Petersen '74
The Junction Boys '02
Kicking and Screaming '95 ►
The Kid with the 200 I.Q. '83
A Killer in Every Corner '74
Killer Me '01
Killer Party '86
A Killing Spring '02
Knock Outs '92
Lady Killer '97
Legally Blonde '01
Let's Go Collegiate '41
Life 101 '95
Little Sister '92
A Little Stiff '91
Loser '00
Love and Basketball '00 ►
Love and Debate '06
Love and Other Catastrophes '95
Lover's Knot '96
Lucky Jim '58
Maker of Men '31
The Male Animal '42
Malice '93
Man of the House '05
A Matter of Degrees '90
Mazes and Monsters '82
Me Without You '01
Midnight Madness '80
The Mirror Has Two Faces '96
The Misadventures of Merlin Jones '63
Mona Lisa Smile '03
The Monkey's Mask '00
Monkey's Uncle '65
Monster on the Campus '59
Mortuary Academy '91
Mugsy's Girls '85
Murder on the Campus '52
My Lucky Star '38
My Sex Life... Or How I Got into an Argument '96
National Lampoon's Adam & Eve '05
National Lampoon's Animal House '78 ►
National Lampoon's Van Wilder '02
National Lampoon's Van Wilder 2: The Rise of Taj '06
Navy Blue and Gold '37
Necessary Roughness '91
New Best Friend '02
A Night in the Life of Jimmy Reardon '88
Night of the Creeps '86
Nightwish '89
Nobel Son '08
Now You See Him, Now You Don't '72
The Nutty Professor '63 ►
The Nutty Professor '96 ►
Nutty Professor 2: The Klumps '00
An Occasional Hell '96
Odd Jobs '85
Old School '03
Oleanna '94
100 Girls '00
Ordinary Sinner '02
The Paper Chase '73 ►
Parallel Lives '94
Party Animal '83
P.C.U. '94
Pieces '83
Pigskin Parade '36
The Plastic Age '25
Pledge Night '90
Poison Ivy 4: The Secret Society '08
Poster Boy '04
Preppies '82
The Prince & Me '04
The Prodigy '98
The Program '93
Prozac Nation '01
Pumpkin '02
Real Genius '85 ►
A Reason to Believe '95
Red Letters '00
Return Engagement '78
Return to Halloweentown '06
Revenge of the Nerds '84
Revenge of the Nerds 2: Nerds in Paradise '87
Revenge of the Nerds 3: The Next Generation '92
Ring of Terror '62
Ripper: Letter from Hell '01
Road Trip '00
Road Trip: Beer Pong '09
Roommate '84
Roommates '95
Rosalie '38
R.P.M.* (*Revolutions Per Minute) '70
Rudy '93
The Rules of Attraction '02
Rush Week '88
Scent of a Woman '92 ►
School Daze '88 ►
School Spirit '85
Scream 2 '97 ►
The Secret Life of Girls '99
The Seniors '78
Sensation '94
Senseless '98
A Serious Man '09 ►
Shallow Grave '87
Silent Madness '84
Silent Scream '80
The Sixth Man '97
The Skulls '00
The Skulls 2 '02
Sky High '84
Slackers '02
Slipping into Darkness '88
A Small Circle of Friends '80
Smart People '08
Sniper '75 ►
Social Error '35
Sorority Babes in the Slimeball Bowl-A-Rama '87
Sorority Boys '02
Sorority Girl '57
Sorority House Massacre '86
Sorority House Massacre 2: Nighty Nightmare '92
Sorority House Party '92
Sorority House Vampires '95
Sorority Row '09
Soul Man '86
Soul Survivors '01
South Beach Academy '96
Spellbound '41
The Spirit of West Point '47
Splatter University '84
Splitz '84
Spring Break '83
Starter for Ten '06
The Sterile Cuckoo '69 ►
Stitches '85
Stomp the Yard '07
Stonebrook '98
Storytelling '01 ►
Stricken '98
The Strongest Man in the World '75
The Student Affair '97
The Substitute 3: Winner Takes All '99
Summer Palace '06 ►
The Sure Thing '85 ►
Surviving Desire '91 ►
Sweet Young Thing '79
Sydney White '07
Sylvia '03
Tag: The Assassination Game '82
Talking Walls '85
Tall Lie '53
Tall Story '60
Teen Wolf Too '87
Thesis '96
Three in the Attic '68
Three in the Cellar '70
Threesome '94
Toga Party '77
Transylmania '09
21 '08
Underclassman '05
Undergrads '85 ►
Unforgettable '96
The Unnamable '88
The Unnamable 2: The Statement of Randolph Carter '92
Up the Creek '84
Urban Legend '98
Urban Legends 2: Final Cut '00
The Utopian Society '03
Vampires of Sorority Row: Kickboxers From Hell '99
Van Wilder: Freshman Year '08
Varsity Show '37
The Victory '81
Voodoo '95
Voodoo Academy '00
Waking the Dead '00
War Between the Tates '76
The Waterboy '98
Wavelength '96
We Are Marshall '06
What Lies Beneath '00
When He's Not a Stranger '89 ►
The Wild Life '84
Wish Me Luck '95
Wishmaster 3: Beyond the Gates of Hell '01
Witchboard '87
Witches' Brew '79
With Honors '94
Wonder Boys '00 ►
Zis Boom Bah '41

Canada

***see also** Cold Spots; Hockey*
Abducted '86
The Adjuster '91
The Agency '81
All Hat '07
American Boyfriends '89
The Amityville Curse '90
And Then You Die '88 ►
Angel Square '92
Angela '77
Anne of Avonlea '87 ►
Anne of Green Gables '34 ►
Anne of Green Gables '85 ►
The Apprenticeship of Duddy Kravitz '74 ►
Ararat '02 ►
Atlantic City '81 ►
Autumn Hearts: A New Beginning '07
The Bay Boy '85
Beautiful Dreamers '92
Big Bear '98
The Big Crimewave '86
Big Meat Eater '85
Big Red '62
Black Christmas '75
Black Robe '91 ►
Blades of Courage '88
Blood Clan '91
Blood of the Hunter '94
Blood Relations '87
The Bloody Brood '59
Blue State '07
Boy in Blue '86
The Boys '97
The Boys Club '96
The Boys of St. Vincent '93 ►
Brand Upon the Brain! '06 ►
Breaking All the Rules '85
The Brood '79
Buffalo Jump '90 ►
Bullies '86
Bush Pilot '47
Busted Up '86
By Design '82
By Way of the Stars '92
Bye Bye Blues '89
Cafe Romeo '91
Camilla '94
Canada's Sweetheart: The Saga of Hal C. Banks '85
Canadian Bacon '94
Candy Mountain '87
The Cariboo Trail '50
Cathy's Curse '77
The Changeling '80
Christina '74
Circle of Two '80
City on Fire '78
Class of 1984 '82
Clean '04
Clean, Shaven '93
Clearcut '92
Close to Home '86
Cold Comfort '90
Concrete Angels '87
The Confessional '95 ►
Confidential '86
Conquest '98
Covergirl '83
Cross Country '83
A Cry in the Wild '90 ►
Curtains '83
Dan Candy's Law '73
Dance Me Outside '95
Dancing in the Dark '86
Danger Ahead '40
Daughter of Death '82
The Dawson Patrol '78
Dead Ringers '88 ►
Death Ship '80
Death Weekend '76
Deathdream '72
The Decline of the American Empire '86 ►
Decoy '95
Deranged '74 ►
The Deserters '83

► = rated three bones or higher

Canadian Mounties

Cannibalism

Capitol Capers

Carnivals & Circuses

Casbah

Kismet '55
Pepe Le Moko '37 ►

Catholic School

Absolution '81
Boys Town '38 ►
The Craft '96
The Dangerous Lives of Altar Boys '02 ►
Doubt '08 ►
Going My Way '44 ►
The Gospel According to Vic '87
Heaven Help Us '85
House of D '04
Kentucky Fried Movie '77 ►
Loving Annabelle '06
Perfect Parents '06
Prom Queen '04
Ready? OK! '08
Sister Act 2: Back in the Habit '93
Stolen Summer '02
True Crime '95

Cats

see also *Killer Kats*
The Adventures of Milo & Otis '89 ►
After the Revolution '90
Alice in Wonderland '50
Alice in Wonderland '51 ►
Alice in Wonderland '85
Alice in Wonderland '99
Alien '79 ►
An American Tail '86
Angus, Thongs and Perfect Snogging '08
The Aristocats '70 ►
Austin Powers: International Man of Mystery '97 ►
Babe '95 ►
Babe: Pig in the City '98
Batman Returns '92
The Big Cat '49
The Black Cat '34 ►
The Black Cat '41
The Black Cat '81
Black Cat '90
Bolt '08 ►
The Cat '66
The Cat from Outer Space '78
Cat Girl '57
Cat People '82
Cats & Dogs '01
Cats & Dogs: The Revenge of Kitty Galore '10
Cats Don't Dance '97
Cat's Eye '85
Catwoman '04
The Corpse Grinders '71
Disney's Teacher's Pet '04 ►
Dr. Seuss' The Cat in the Hat '03
Felix the Cat: The Movie '91
Fritz the Cat '72 ►
Garfield: A Tail of Two Kitties '06
Garfield: The Movie '04
Gay Purr-ee '62
Harry and Tonto '74 ►
Hocus Pocus '93
Homeward Bound 2: Lost in San Francisco '96
Homeward Bound: The Incredible Journey '93 ►
The Incredible Journey '63
Ju-On: The Grudge '03
Kiki's Delivery Service '98
The Late Show '77 ►
Le Chat '75 ►
Meet the Fockers '04
Men in Black '97 ►
Milo & Otis '89
Mouse Hunt '97 ►
Murder She Purred: A Mrs. Murphy Mystery '98
Night of a Thousand Cats '72
Oliver & Company '88
Pet Sematary '89
Puss 'n Boots '84 ►
Return of Chandu '34
Rhubarb '51
Rubin & Ed '92
Sabrina the Teenage Witch '96
Seven Deaths in the Cat's Eye '72
Shrek 2 '04 ►
The Stars Fell on Henrietta '94
Stuart Little '99
Stuart Little 2 '02 ►
That Darn Cat '65
That Darn Cat '96
The Three Lives of Thomasina '63 ►
Tom and Jerry: The Movie '93
Two Evil Eyes '90
The Uncanny '78
The Uninvited '88
When the Cat's Away '96 ►
Whiskers '96
Your Vice is a Closed Room and Only I Have the Key '72

Cattle Drive

see also *Pardners; Westerns; Westrogens*
Alvarez Kelly '66
Australia '08
Born Free '66 ►
Canyon River '56
The Cowboys '72 ►
Far Country '55 ►
Hills of Oklahoma '50
Lonesome Dove '89 ►
Overlanders '46 ►
The Proposition '97
Saddle Tramp '47
The Showdown '50
The Tall Men '55
Trail Drive '33

Cave People

Beach Babes 2: Cave Girl Island '95
Being Human '94
The Cave '05
Cave Girl '85
Caveman '81
The Clan of the Cave Bear '86
Creatures the World Forgot '70
Encino Man '92
The Flintstones '94
The Flintstones in Viva Rock Vegas '00
History of the World: Part 1 '81
Iceman '84 ►
Ironmaster '82
National Lampoon's The Stoned Aged '07
One Million B.C. '40
Prehistoric Women '50
Quest for Fire '82 ►
Teenage Caveman '58
10,000 B.C. '08
When Dinosaurs Ruled the Earth '70
When Women Had Tails '70
When Women Lost Their Tails '75
Year One '09

Caves

Ace in the Hole '51 ►
Afghan Knights '07
The Bat People '74
The Cavern '05
The Descent '05
Fixed Bayonets! '51 ►
George and the Dragon '04
The Hills Have Eyes 2 '07
Invasion of the Star Creatures '63
Turistas '06

Central America

see also *Mexico; South America*
Apocalypto '06 ►
Appointment in Honduras '53
The Art of Travel '08
Carla's Song '97
Che '08
Cyclone Cavalier '25
Delta Force Commando '87
Devil Wears White '86
El Norte '83 ►
The Evil That Men Do '84
Exiled in America '90
The Firing Line '91
Hombres Armados '97 ►
Last Plane Out '83
Latino '85
Marie Galante '34 ►
The Mosquito Coast '86
No Turning Back '01
Noriega: God's Favorite '00
Panama Menace '41
Panama Patrol '39
Romero '89
Salvador '86 ►
The Silence of Neto '94
Solo '96
Sugar '09 ►
The Tailor of Panama '00 ►
Torrid Zone '40
Toy Soldiers '84
Under Fire '83 ►
Virgin Sacrifice '59
Wages of Fear '55 ►

Checkered Flag

see also *Motor Vehicle Dept.*
American Graffiti '73 ►
Baffled '72
Banzai Runner '86
The Big Wheel '49
Bobby Deerfield '77
Born to Race '88
Born to Run '93
Brewster McCloud '70 ►
Bullitt '68 ►
Cannonball '76
Cannonball Run '81
Cannonball Run 2 '84
Cannonball Run Europe: The Great Escape '05
Car Crash '80
Cars '06 ►
Catch Me... If You Can '89
The Checkered Flag '63
The Circuit '08
Daddy-O '59
Days of Thunder '90
Death Driver '78
Death Race '08
Death Race 2000 '75
Desert Steel '94
The Devil on Wheels '47
Diamonds Are Forever '71 ►
Dirty Mary Crazy Larry '74 ►
Dragstrip Girl '57
Dragstrip Girl '94
Driven '01
The Dukes of Hazzard '05
Dust to Glory '05 ►
Eat My Dust '76
The Fast and the Furious '54
The Fast and the Furious: Tokyo Drift '06
Fast Company '78
Fast Girl '07
Faster, Pussycat! Kill! Kill! '65
Finish Line '08
Fireball 500 '66
The First Auto '27
Fury on Wheels '71
Genevieve '53 ►
Goldfinger '64 ►
Grand Prix '66
Grandview U.S.A. '84
Grease '78 ►
Greased Lightning '77
The Great Race '65
Gumball Rally '76
Hard Drivin' '60
Heart Like a Wheel '83
The Heavenly Kid '85
Hell on Wheels '67
Herbie: Fully Loaded '05
Herbie Goes Bananas '80
Herbie Goes to Monte Carlo '77
High Gear '33
Hot Rod '79
Hot Rod Girl '56
King of the Mountain '81
The Last American Hero '73 ►
Last Chase '81
Le Mans '71 ►
The Love Bug '97
A Man and a Woman: 20 Years Later '86
Pit Stop '67 ►
Private Road: No Trespassing '87
Race for Life '55
Race the Sun '96
The Racers '55
Rebel without a Cause '55 ►
Red Line '96
Red Line 7000 '65
Redline '07
Return to Macon County '75
Richard Petty Story '72
Road Racers '59
Roaring Roads '35
Safari 3000 '82
Sahara '83
Shaker Run '85
Six Pack '82
Smash Palace '82
Smokey and the Bandit '77
Speed Racer '08
Speed Zone '88
Speedway '29
Speedway '68
Spinout '66
Stroker Ace '83
Talladega Nights: The Ballad of Ricky Bobby '06
Those Daring Young Men in Their Jaunty Jalopies '69
Thunder Alley '67
To Please a Lady '50
2 Fast 2 Furious '03
Van Nuys Blvd. '79
Vanishing Point '71
Viva Las Vegas '63
Winning '69 ►
The Wraith '87

Cheerleaders

see also *Campus Capers; Hell High School*
American Beauty '99 ►
BASEketball '98
Bring It On '00
Bring It On Again '03
Bring It On: All or Nothing '06
Bring It On: Fight to the Finish '09
Bring It On: In It to Win It '07
Buffy the Vampire Slayer '92 ►
But I'm a Cheerleader '99
Cheering Section '73
Cheerleader Camp '88
The Cheerleaders '72
Cheerleaders' Wild Weekend '85
Death Proof '07
Fired Up! '09
Flesh Gordon 2: Flesh Gordon Meets the Cosmic Cheerleaders '90
Gimme an F '85
Grease '78 ►
I Love You, Beth Cooper '09
Jeepers Creepers 2 '03
John Tucker Must Die '06
Kids in America '05
Lucas '86 ►
The Majorettes '87
Man of the House '05
National Lampoon's Animal House '78 ►
The New Guy '02
Pandemonium '82
Pep Squad '98
Pom Pom Girls '76
The Positively True Adventures of the Alleged Texas Cheerleader-Murdering Mom '93 ►
Raising Genius '04
Ready? OK! '08
The Replacements '00
Revenge of the Cheerleaders '76
Satan's Cheerleaders '77
Slap Her, She's French '02
Starsky & Hutch '04
Sugar & Spice '01 ►
The Swinging Cheerleaders '74
Varsity Blues '98

Chefs

see also *Edibles*
Angels Fall '07
April's Shower '03
Autumn in New York '00
Big Night '95
Chef's Special '08
Felicia's Journey '99 ►
A Fine Mess '86
Funny About Love '90
Julie & Julia '09 ►
Kitchen Privileges '00
Last Holiday '50 ►
Love and Mary '07
Mostly Martha '01 ►
No Reservations '07
Oldboy '03 ►
The Ramen Girl '08
Ratatouille '07 ►
Soul Kitchen '09
South Park: Bigger, Longer and Uncut '99
Tampopo '86 ►
301, 302 '94
Tortilla Soup '01
Who Is Killing the Great Chefs of Europe? '78 ►

Chess

Alice Through the Looking Glass '66
Black and White As Day and Night '78
Brainwashed '60
The Chess Player '27
The Chinese Cat '44
Dangerous Moves '84 ►
Fresh '94
The Invisible Boy '57
Knight Moves '93
Knights of the South Bronx '05
The Luzhin Defence '00
The Mighty Pawns '87
The Other Man '08
Searching for Bobby Fischer '93 ►
The Seventh Seal '56 ►
Stalag 17 '53 ►
Swept from the Sea '97
The Thomas Crown Affair '68 ►
Treasure of Fear '45
Zatoichi: The Blind Swordsman and the Chess Expert '65

Chicago

Above the Law '88
Adventures in Babysitting '87
The Alien Agenda: Under the Skin '97
Amreeka '09 ►
Angel Eyes '01
The Architect '06
Baby Face Nelson '97
Baby on Board '08
Bad City '06
Barbershop '02 ►
The Beast of the City '32
Beauty Shop '05 ►
Beginning of the End '57
Big Town '87
The Blues Brothers '80 ►
Blues Brothers 2000 '98
Bomb Squad '97
Bordertown '06
The Break-Up '06
Cadillac Records '08 ►
Call Northside 777 '48 ►
Candyman '92
Category 6 : Day of Destruction '04
Chain Reaction '96
Chasing Papi '03
Chicago '02 ►
Chicago Cab '98
Chicago 10 '07 ►
Christmas With the Kranks '04
City That Never Sleeps '53
Code of Silence '85
The Company '03 ►
Crime Spree '03
Deadline '00
Derailed '05
Diminished Capacity '08
Down in the Delta '98 ►
Dragonfly '02
Everyone's Hero '06
A Family Thing '96 ►
Ferris Bueller's Day Off '86 ►
First Time Felon '97
The Fixer '97
For Hire '98
The Front Page '74
The Fugitive '93 ►
Go Into Your Dance '35
Goldstein '64
The Grudge 3 '09
Hardball '01
Heaven Is a Playground '91
Hey! Hey! USA! '38
High Fidelity '00 ►
Holiday Heart '00
Home Alone '90 ►
Home Alone 3 '97
Hoopla '33
I, Robot '04
I Want Someone to Eat Cheese With '06
Jerry and Tom '98
John Q '02
Just Visiting '01
Keeper of the City '92
Kissing a Fool '98
The Lake House '06
Let No Man Write My Epitaph '60
Lethal Tender '96
Love and Action in Chicago '99
Love Jones '96 ►
Mad Dog and Glory '93 ►
Make It Happen '08
Mercury Rising '98
The Merry Gentleman '08
Mickey One '65
Miss March '09
My Best Friend's Wedding '97
My Big Fat Greek Wedding '02
My Reputation '46
The Negotiator '98
Never Been Kissed '99
The Newton Boys '97
Next of Kin '89
Nights and Weekends '08
Nothing Like the Holidays '08
On the Line '01
Our America '02
Outing Riley '04
Primal Fear '96
The Promotion '08
Proof '05 ►
Public Enemies '09
A Raisin in the Sun '08
The Relic '96
Resurrection '99
Return to Me '00
Risky Business '83 ►
Robin and the 7 Hoods '64
Roll Bounce '05 ►
Running Scared '86
Save the Last Dance '01
Shall We Dance? '04
Shattered '07
The Song of the Lark '01
Stir of Echoes '99
Stir of Echoes 2: The Homecoming '07
Stolen Summer '02
Straight Talk '92
Stranger Than Fiction '06
Studs Lonigan '60
Surviving Christmas '04
Taking Care of Business '90
The Third Miracle '99
Three to Tango '99
The Time Traveler's Wife '09
Uncle Buck '89 ►
Uncle Nino '03
Unconditional Love '03
U.S. Marshals '98
The Untouchables '87 ►
Wanted '08 ►
The Watcher '00
The Water Engine '92
The Weather Man '05
While You Were Sleeping '95 ►
The White Raven '98
The Whole Nine Yards '00
Wicker Park '04
Witless Protection '08

► = *rated three bones or higher*

Child Abuse

Abuse '82
Alias Betty '01
America '09
An American Crime '07
Antwone Fisher '02 ▸
Any Place But Home '97
Bad Education '04 ▸
Bastard out of Carolina '96
Blind Fools '40
Born Into Brothels: Calcutta's Red Light Kids '04
The Boys of St. Vincent '93 ▸
A Brother's Kiss '97
Brute '97
The Butterfly Effect '04
Capturing the Friedmans '03 ▸
Close to Home '86
Cries of Silence '97
Cronicas '04
Darkness '02
Dear Frankie '04
Dolores Claiborne '94 ▸
Dominick & Eugene '88 ▸
Don't Tell '05
El Bola '00
Ellen Foster '97
Evil '03 ▸
Evil Has a Face '96
Fallen Angel '81
Fatal Confinement '64
Father Hood '93
The Final Cut '04
Gardens of the Night '08
The Great Water '04
The Hanging Garden '97
The Heart Is Deceitful Above All Things '04
Hollow Reed '95 ▸
Holly '07
Impulse '74
Indictment: The McMartin Trial '95 ▸
Joe the King '99
Johnny Belinda '82
Judgment '90 ▸
Killer Me '01
Lamb '85
Lime Salted Love '06
The Lost Son '98
Love's Unending Legacy '07
Mockingbird Don't Sing '01
Mommie Dearest '81
Monsoon Wedding '01 ▸
Monster's Ball '01 ▸
The Mudge Boy '03
Mysterious Skin '04 ▸
The Offence '73 ▸
Oliver Twist '05 ▸
Osama '03 ▸
The Poker House '09
Postcards from America '95
Precious: Based on the Novel by Sapphire '09 ▸
Psychopath '73
A Question of Guilt '78
Radio Flyer '92
Raising Cain '92
Ripe '97
The River is Red '48
Runaway '05
Running Scared '06
The Scamp '57
Seeing Red '99
Short Eyes '79 ▸
Shot in the Heart '01 ▸
Sleepers '96
Sleepwalking '08
South Bronx Heroes '85
The Stepdaughter '00
Stolen Childhoods '05
The Stolen Children '92 ▸
This Boy's Life '93 ▸
Threat of Exposure '02
Towelhead '07
Transamerica '05 ▸
Turn the River '07
2 by 4 '98
When I Find the Ocean '06
Where the Spirit Lives '89
The White Ribbon '09
Who Killed Baby Azaria? '83
Wildflower '91 ▸
The Woodsman '04
ZigZag '02 ▸

Childhood Buddies

***see also** Childhood Visions*

Ace Ventura Jr.: Pet Detective '08
Aliens in the Attic '09
Because of Winn-Dixie '05
Bloodhounds of Broadway '52
Bridge to Terabithia '07
Children On Their Birthdays '02
Cross My Heart '91
Dreamcatcher '03
El Bola '00
I'm Not Scared '03
Julia '77 ▸
The Jungle Book 2 '03
Keeping the Faith '00
Kit Kittredge: An American Girl '08 ▸
The Kite Runner '07 ▸
Let the Right One In '08
Lilo & Stitch '02 ▸
Mysterious Skin '04 ▸
Now and Then '95
Once Upon a Time in America '84 ▸
Paradise Now '05 ▸
The Robin Hood Gang '98
Shorts: The Adventures of the Wishing Rock '09
Stand by Me '86 ▸
A Time for Dancing '00
What About Your Friends: Weekend Getaway '02
Without a Paddle '04

Childhood Visions

***see also** Home Alone*

A. I.: Artificial Intelligence '01
About a Boy '02 ▸
The Adventures of Sharkboy and Lavagirl in 3-D '05
Afraid of the Dark '92
Akeelah and the Bee '06
Alice in Wonderland '99
All I Want for Christmas '91
All I Want for Christmas '07
All My Loved Ones '00
All Roads Lead Home '08
Alone in the Woods '95
Along with Ghosts '69
Alsino and the Condor '82 ▸
The Amazing Mrs. Holiday '43
American Girl: Chrissa Stands Strong '09
American Heart '92 ▸
Amy '98
And Now Miguel '66
Andre '94
Angela '94
Angela's Ashes '99
Angels in the Outfield '94
The Ant Bully '06
Army Brats '84
Arthur and the Invisibles '06
Au Revoir les Enfants '87 ▸
August Rush '07
The Baby-Sitters' Club '95
Back to the Secret Garden '01
The Bad News Bears '05
Balloon Farm '97
Bastard out of Carolina '96
Beethoven Lives Upstairs '92
The Beniker Gang '83
Beyond Silence '96
Big '88 ▸
Big Bully '95
Big Daddy '99
Big Fella '37
Billy Elliot '00 ▸
Black Beauty '94 ▸
The Black Stallion '79 ▸
Blame It on Fidel '06
Blank Check '93
Bless the Child '00
The Blue Bird '40 ▸
The Blue Butterfly '04
Bogus '96
The Borrowers '97
The Boy in the Striped Pajamas '08 ▸
Boys Will Be Boys '97
Brand Upon the Brain! '06 ▸
Breakout '98
Bridge to Terabithia '07
Brighton Beach Memoirs '86
Broken Harvest '94
But Where Is Daniel Wax? '74
The Butcher Boy '97 ▸
Butterfly '98 ▸
Cameron's Closet '89
Camp Nowhere '94
Canvas '06
Captain January '36
Careful, He Might Hear You '84 ▸
Carrie's War '04
Casey's Shadow '78
Casper '95 ▸
The Cat '66
Catherine Cookson's The Rag Nymph '96
Cathy's Curse '77
Celia: Child of Terror '89
The Cellar '90
Central Station '98 ▸
Charlie and the Chocolate Factory '05 ▸
Charlotte's Web '06 ▸
Child in the Night '90
Child Star: The Shirley Temple Story '01
The Children Are Watching Us '44 ▸
Children of Divorce '80
Children of Heaven '98
Child's Play '88
China, My Sorrow '89
Chocolat '88 ▸
The Christmas Box '95
The Christmas Miracle of Jonathan Toomey '07
A Christmas Reunion '93
A Christmas Story '83 ▸
Chronicle of a Boy Alone '64
The Chronicles of Narnia: Prince Caspian '08
Cider with Rosie '99
Cinema Paradiso '88 ▸
The Clay Bird '02
The Client '94
Clifford '92
Close to Leo '02
Clubhouse Detectives '96
The Color of Paradise '99
Comedy of Innocence '00
Coraline '09 ▸
Cria '76 ▸
Cria Cuervos '76 ▸
Crooklyn '94 ▸
Cross My Heart and Hope to Die '94
Crows '94
Cuban Blood '03
Curly Sue '91
Curly Top '35
Dam Street '05
D.A.R.Y.L. '85
David Copperfield '35 ▸
David Copperfield '70
David Copperfield '99
The Day the World Ended '01
Days of Heaven '78 ▸
Dead Silent '99
Deadly Game '98
A Death in the Family '02
Demons in the Garden '82 ▸
Dennis the Menace '93
A Dennis the Menace Christmas '07
Dennis the Menace Strikes Again '98
Desert Bloom '86 ▸
Deutschland im Jahre Null '47 ▸
The Devil's Backbone '01
The Diary of Anne Frank '59 ▸
Digger '94
Digging to China '98
Disney's The Kid '00
Diva '82 ▸
Dodson's Journey '01
Domestic Disturbance '01
Don't Tell Mom the Babysitter's Dead '91
The Dress Code '99
D3: The Mighty Ducks '96
Earth '98
The Education of Little Tree '97 ▸
The Elementary School '91
Ellen Foster '97
Eloise at the Plaza '03
Emma's Shadow '88 ▸
Empire of the Sun '87 ▸
Escapade '55 ▸
E.T.: The Extra-Terrestrial '82 ▸
Eternity and a Day '97
Eve's Bayou '97 ▸
Eye Witness '70
FairyTale: A True Story '97
The Fall '06
The Fallen Idol '49 ▸
Family Jewels '65
Family Tree '00
Fanny and Alexander '83 ▸
Far Away and Long Ago '74
Father '67 ▸
Fido '06
Finding Buck McHenry '00
Firehouse Dog '07
The Flame Trees of Thika '81 ▸
Flight of the Grey Wolf '76
Flight of the Innocent '93
Flight of the Red Balloon '08
Flowers in the Attic '87
Fly Away Home '96 ▸
For a Lost Soldier '93
Forbidden Games '52 ▸
Forever Together '00
48 Angels '06
Freedom Song '00 ▸
Fresh '94
Gabriel & Me '01
Girl from Hunan '86 ▸
A Girl of the Limberlost '90
The Golden Compass '07
The Golden Seal '83
Good Boy! '03
Goodnight, Mr. Tom '99
The Goonies '85
The Green House '96
Grizzly Falls '99
Grizzly Mountain '97
Gypsy Colt '54
Happiness '98 ▸
Hardball '01
Harriet the Spy '96
Heart of America '03
Hearts in Atlantis '01
Heavyweights '94
Heidi '37
Heidi '52
Heidi '65 ▸
Heidi '67
Heidi '93 ▸
Hidden '05 ▸
Holes '03 ▸
Home Alone '90 ▸
Home Alone 2: Lost in New York '92
Home Alone 3 '97
Home for Christmas '90
Home of Angels '94
A Home of Our Own '93
Homecoming '96
Honey, I Shrunk the Kids '89
Hook '91
Hope '97
Hope and Glory '87 ▸
Hounddog '08
House Arrest '96
House of Cards '92
How Green Was My Valley '41 ▸
How to Kill Your Neighbor's Dog '01
Huck and the King of Hearts '93
Hue and Cry '47 ▸
I Was Born But... '32 ▸
I'll Remember April '99
Imagine That '09
In America '02 ▸
In Desert and Wilderness '01
The Indian in the Cupboard '95
Inkheart '09
Into the West '92 ▸
Invaders from Mars '53
Invaders from Mars '86
The Iron Giant '99 ▸
The Island on Bird Street '97
The Italian '05
Jack '96
Jack Be Nimble '94
Jacob Two Two Meets the Hooded Fang '99
Jacquot '91
James and the Giant Peach '96 ▸
Jimmy the Kid '82
Joey '98
John and Julie '55
John John in the Sky '00
Josh and S.A.M. '93
Journey for Margaret '42 ▸
Jurassic Park '93 ▸
Just Like the Son '06
The Karate Kid '10
Kazaam '96
A Kid for Two Farthings '55
The Kid from Left Field '79
The Kid with the Broken Halo '82
The Kid with the X-Ray Eyes '99
Kids of the Round Table '96
Kikujiro '99
The King of Masks '99 ▸
King of the Hill '93 ▸
Kit Kittredge: An American Girl '08 ▸
The Kitchen Toto '87 ▸
Kolya '96 ▸
The Lady in White '88 ▸
Lamb '85
Landscape in the Mist '88 ▸
Lassie's Great Adventure '62
Last Action Hero '93
The Last Airbender '10
The Last Days of Summer '07
The Last Mimzy '07
The Last Winter '89
Lawn Dogs '96
Lawnmower Man 2: Beyond Cyberspace '95
Lazarillo '59
Le Grand Chemin '87 ▸
Leave It to Beaver '97
Leolo '92 ▸
Les Violons du Bal '74
Let the Right One In '08
Lies My Father Told Me '75 ▸
Life According to Muriel '97
Life Is a Bed of Roses '83
Life-Size '00
Little Big League '94
Little Buddha '93
Little Devil '07
Little Fugitive '53 ▸
Little Fugitive '06
Little Lord Fauntleroy '95
Little Man Tate '91 ▸
Little Manhattan '05
Little Monsters '89
The Little Princess '39 ▸
A Little Princess '95 ▸
The Little Rascals '94
The Littlest Horse Thieves '76
Lloyd '00
Locked in Silence '99
Long Life, Happiness and Prosperity '02
The Longshots '08
Look Who's Talking '89 ▸
Look Who's Talking, Too '90
Lord of the Flies '63 ▸
Lord of the Flies '90
Lost in Yonkers '93
Louisiana Story '48 ▸
Love Film '70
Luminous Motion '00
Ma Vie en Rose '97 ▸
Madeline '98
Magic in the Mirror: Fowl Play '96
Magic in the Water '95
Magic of Lassie '78
The Magnet '50
Man of the House '95
Margot at the Wedding '07
Martian Child '07
Matilda '96 ▸
The Member of the Wedding '97
Mendel '98 ▸
Mermaid '00
The Messengers '07
The Mighty '98 ▸
Miracle in Lane Two '00
The Miracle Maker: The Story of Jesus '00
The Miracle of Marcelino '55
The Mirror '75 ▸
Ms. Bear '97
Mrs. Doubtfire '93
Mr. Magorium's Wonder Emporium '07
Mr. Rice's Secret '00
Mom, Can I Keep Her? '98
Mommie Dearest '81
Mondo '96
Monster House '06 ▸
Mosby's Marauders '66
Mother of Mine '05 ▸
My Childhood '38 ▸
My Dog Skip '99 ▸
My Friend Flicka '43 ▸
My Life As a Dog '85 ▸
My Life So Far '98
My Louisiana Sky '02
My Mother's Castle '91 ▸
My Name Is Ivan '62 ▸
My Teacher Ate My Homework '98
Mystery Kids '99
National Velvet '44 ▸
The Neon Bible '95
New York Stories '89 ▸
The Night of the Shooting Stars '82 ▸
Nim's Island '08
North '94
Northfork '03
Not One Less '99
Nothing Personal '95 ▸
Now and Then '95
Off Season '01
Old Swimmin' Hole '40
Oliver! '68 ▸
Oliver Twist '97
Oliver Twist '00 ▸
Oliver Twist '07
One Christmas '95
100 Monsters '68
One Little Indian '73
One Small Hero '99
The Optimists '73
An Orphan Boy of Vienna '37
The Orphanage '07 ▸
The Orphans '77 ▸
Osama '03 ▸
The Other '72 ▸
Other Voices, Other Rooms '95
The Others '01 ▸
The Pagemaster '94
Pan's Labyrinth '06 ▸
Paradise '91 ▸
Paranormal Activity '09 ▸
The Parent Trap '98
Parents '89 ▸
Paulie '98
Pay It Forward '00
Peck's Bad Boy '21
Pelle the Conqueror '88 ▸
Perfect Game '00
Peter Pan '24
Peter Pan '03
Pete's Meteor '98
Phoebe in Wonderland '08
Pictures of Hollis Woods '07
The Pillow Book '95
Pixote '81 ▸
Pokemon 3: The Movie '01
Pollyanna '60 ▸
Poltergeist '82 ▸
Poltergeist 2: The Other Side '86
Poltergeist: The Legacy '96
Ponette '95
Ponyo '08 ▸
A Poor Little Rich Girl '17 ▸
The Poor Little Rich Girl '36
Possessed '00
Powder '95
Prancer Returns '01
Prince of Central Park '00
Psycho 4: The Beginning '90
Pure '02 ▸
The Quest '96
The Quiet Room '96
Rabbit-Proof Fence '02 ▸
Radio Flyer '92
Rails & Ties '07
The Railway Children '70 ▸
The Railway Children '00 ▸
Ratcatcher '99
Ready? OK! '08
Real Genius '85 ▸

▸ = rated three bones or higher

The Real Howard Spitz '98
The Red Balloon '56 ►
The Red Pony '49 ►
The Red Pony '76 ►
The Reflecting Skin '91
Return from Witch Mountain '78
Return to Never Land '02
Richie Rich '94
Ride the Wild Fields '00
The Road '09
Rock-a-Doodle '92
Roll of Thunder, Hear My Cry '78
Romulus, My Father '07 ►
Ruby Blue '07
Ruby Bridges '98
Running Free '94
A Safe Place '71
Safety Patrol '98
Salaam Bombay! '88 ►
Savage Sam '63
Saving Sarah Cain '07
Searching for Bobby Fischer '93 ►
Second Chances '98
A Secret '07 ►
The Secret Garden '49 ►
The Secret Garden '84
The Secret Garden '87 ►
The Secret Garden '93
The Secret Life of Bees '08 ►
The Secret of Kells '09
Selma, Lord, Selma '99
The Seven Little Foys '55 ►
Shiloh 2: Shiloh Season '99
Shorts: The Adventures of the Wishing Rock '09
Sidekicks '93
The Silence of Neto '94
The Silences of the Palace '94 ►
Simon Birch '98
The Sixth Sense '99 ►
The Skateboard Kid 2 '94
Slappy and the Stinkers '97
Sling Blade '96 ►
The Slingshot '93 ►
Small Change '76 ►
Snap Decision '01
Snow Day '00
Snow in August '01
Son of Rambow '07
Sounds of Silence '91
South Park: Bigger, Longer and Uncut '99
Sparrows '26 ►
Spirit of the Beehive '73 ►
Spirited Away '01
Spook Warfare '68
Spy Kids '01 ►
Square Shoulders '29
Star Kid '97 ►
Star Wars: Episode 1—The Phantom Menace '99 ►
Stealing Home '88
Stephen King's It '90
Stir '98
Stir of Echoes '99
Stolen Summer '02
Sudie & Simpson '90 ►
The Summer of Aviya '88
A Summer to Remember '61 ►
Sunday Daughters '80 ►
Sunday's Children '94 ►
Taps '81
Tea with Mussolini '99
Three Wishes '95
Tideland '05
The Tin Drum '79 ►
Tito and Me '92 ►
To Kill a Mockingbird '62 ►
The Tooth Fairy '06
Tooth Fairy '10
Toothless '97
Toto le Heros '91 ►
Toy Story '95 ►
Trading Mom '94
Train to Hollywood '86 ►
Treasure Island '34 ►
Treasure Island '50 ►
Treasure Island '99
Treehouse Hostage '99
Treeless Mountain '08
The Trial of Old Drum '00
Trucker '08
Turf Boy '42
The Turn of the Screw '74
The Turn of the Screw '92
The Turn of the Screw '99
The Twelve Dogs of Christmas '05
12 Monkeys '95 ►
Twisted '96
Under the Same Moon '07
Undercover Angel '99
An Unexpected Family '96
Up '09 ►
Village of Dreams '97
Wait until Spring, Bandini '90
Walkabout '71 ►
Walking Thunder '94
The War '94
The War Boy '85
Water '05
The Water Horse: Legend of the Deep '07
The Way Home '01
Welcome to Sarajevo '97 ►
Welcome to the Dollhouse '95
Wendigo '01
What the Moon Saw '90
When Father Was Away on Business '85 ►
Where the Wild Things Are '09
Where's Willie? '77
Whistle down the Wind '61 ►
White Fang '91 ►
Wide Awake '97
The Wild Country '71
Will It Snow for Christmas? '96
Willy Wonka & the Chocolate Factory '71 ►
The Witching of Ben Wagner '95
The Wizard of Loneliness '88
Wombling Free '77
A World Apart '88 ►
Yaaba '89 ►
The Year My Parents Went on Vacation '07
The Yearling '46 ►
Yes, Sir, Mr. Bones '51
Zazie dans le Metro '61 ►
Zero for Conduct '33 ►
Zeus and Roxanne '96

Children

***see** Animated Musicals; Animation & Cartoons; Childhood Visions; Kiddie Viddy; Storytelling*

China

***see also** Asia*

Adventures of Smilin' Jack '43
The Amazing Panda Adventure '95
Ashes of Time Redux '08
Balzac and the Little Chinese Seamstress '02
Beijing Bicycle '01
Bethune '77
Beyond the Next Mountain '87
The Bitter Tea of General Yen '33 ►
Black Mask '96
Blood Brothers '07
The Blue Kite '93 ►
Blush '95
Charlie Chan in Shanghai '35
The Children of Huang Shi '08
China '43
China Cry '91
China, My Sorrow '89
Chinese Box '97
Crows and Sparrows '49 ►
Curse of the Golden Flower '06
Dam Street '05
The Day the Sun Turned Cold '94 ►
Deadly Target '94
Dragon Seed '44
East Palace, West Palace '96
The Emperor and the Assassin '99
The Emperor's Shadow '96
Empire of the Sun '87 ►
Ermo '94
Farewell My Concubine '93
Fleeing by Night '00
Flowers of Shanghai '98
The Forbidden Kingdom '08
Formula 17 '04
The General Died at Dawn '36 ►
Girl from Hunan '86 ►
The Good Earth '37 ►
Goodbye, Dragon Inn '03
A Great Wall '86 ►
Happy Times '00
Hero '03 ►
The Horse Thief '87 ►
House of Flying Daggers '04 ►
The Inn of the Sixth Happiness '58 ►
Iron & Silk '91
Jet Li's Fearless '06
The Joy Luck Club '93 ►
Ju Dou '90 ►
The Karate Kid '10
Kashmiri Run '69
The Keys of the Kingdom '44 ►
Kill Bill Vol. 2 '04 ►
The Killer '90 ►
The King of Masks '99 ►
Kung Fu Hustle '04
Kung Fu Panda '08 ►
Lan Yu '01
The Last Emperor '87 ►
The Leatherneck '28
The Lost Empire '01
Lust, Caution '07
M. Butterfly '93
Marco Polo '07
Mission: Impossible 3 '06 ►
The Mountain Road '60
Mulan '98
The Mummy: Tomb of the Dragon Emperor '08
Not One Less '99
Once Upon a Time in China '91 ►
Once Upon a Time in China III '93 ►
The Painted Veil '06
Pavilion of Women '01
Princess Yang Kwei Fei '55 ►
The Promise '05
Purple Butterfly '03 ►
Raise the Red Lantern '91 ►
Red Cliff '08 ►
Red Corner '97
Red Firecracker, Green Firecracker '93
Red Sorghum '87 ►
The Red Violin '98
The Reincarnation of Golden Lotus '89 ►
Rhapsody of Spring '98
Riding Alone for Thousands of Miles '05
The Road Home '01 ►
The Sand Pebbles '66 ►
Seventh Moon '08
Shadow Magic '00
Shadows of the Orient '37
Shadows over Shanghai '38
Shanghai '09
Shanghai Express '32 ►
Shanghai Triad '95 ►
The Silk Road '92
Smile '05
Soldier of Fortune '55
Song of the Exile '90
Spy Game '01
The Story of Qiu Ju '91 ►
The Story of Xinghua '93
Summer Palace '06 ►
Tai-Pan '86
Temptation of a Monk '94
Temptress Moon '96
Thank you, Mr. Moto '37
Think Fast, Mr. Moto '37
To Live '94 ►
Together '02
2046 '04
Typhoon '06
Warlords '08
Warriors of Heaven and Earth '03
The White Countess '05 ►
Windhorse '98
Women from the Lake of Scented Souls '94
The Wooden Man's Bride '94
The World '04
The World of Suzie Wong '60
Xiu Xiu: The Sent Down Girl '97 ►
Zhou Yu's Train '02

Christmas

***see also** Holidays; Horrible Holidays*

ABC Stage 67: Truman Capote's A Christmas Memory '66
All I Want for Christmas '91
All I Want for Christmas '07
Alvin and the Chipmunks '07
An American Christmas Carol '79
American Gun '02 ►
Babes in Toyland '61
Babes in Toyland '86
Bad Santa '03
Batman Returns '92
Bernard and the Genie '91
The Bishop's Wife '47 ►
Black Christmas '75
Black Christmas '06
Blast of Silence '61
Bloodbeat '85
A Boyfriend for Christmas '04
Breakaway '02
Breathing Room '96
Call Me Claus '01
Cast Away '00 ►
Chasing Christmas '05
Christmas at Water's Edge '04
The Christmas Blessing '05
The Christmas Box '95
Christmas Caper '07
The Christmas Card '06
A Christmas Carol '38 ►
A Christmas Carol '51 ►
A Christmas Carol '54
A Christmas Carol '84 ►
A Christmas Carol '99
A Christmas Carol '09
Christmas Child '03
The Christmas Choir '08
The Christmas Coal Mine Miracle '77
Christmas Comes to Willow Creek '87
The Christmas Cottage '08
Christmas Do-Over '06
Christmas Eve '47
Christmas Evil '80
Christmas in Connecticut '45 ►
Christmas in Connecticut '92
Christmas in July '40 ►
Christmas in the Clouds '01
Christmas in Wonderland '07
The Christmas Kid '68
Christmas Lilies of the Field '84
The Christmas Miracle of Jonathan Toomey '07
A Christmas Proposal '08
A Christmas Reunion '93
The Christmas Shoes '02
A Christmas Story '83 ►
A Christmas Tale '08 ►
The Christmas That Almost Wasn't '66
A Christmas to Remember '78
Christmas Town '08
The Christmas Wife '88
Christmas With the Kranks '04
A Christmas Without Snow '80
The Crossing '00
The Day of the Beast '95
The Dead '87 ►
Deck the Halls '06
A Dennis the Menace Christmas '07
Die Hard '88 ►
Diner '82 ►
Dr. Seuss' How the Grinch Stole Christmas '00
A Dog Named Christmas '09
The Dog Who Saved Christmas '09
Dondi '61
Don't Open Till Christmas '84
Dorm That Dripped Blood '82
A Dream for Christmas '73 ►
Ebenezer '97
Elf '03 ►
Elves '89
Ernest Saves Christmas '88
Exit Speed '08
The Family Holiday '07
Family Man '00
The Family Stone '05
Felicidades '00
Four Christmases '08
Fred Claus '07
Friday After Next '02
Friends & Lovers '99
Frozen River '08 ►
Funny Farm '88
The Gathering '77
The Gathering: Part 2 '79
George Balanchine's The Nutcracker '93
The Gift of Love '90
Go '99 ►
A Grandpa for Christmas '07
Gremlins '84 ►
Heidi '37
Heidi '52
Heidi '65 ►
Heidi '67
Heidi '93 ►
Here Comes Santa Claus '84
Hi-Life '98
Hobo's Christmas '87
Hogfather '06
The Holiday '06
Holiday Affair '49
Holiday Affair '96
Holiday in Handcuffs '07
Holiday Inn '42 ►
Home Alone '90 ►
Home Alone 2: Lost in New York '92
Home Alone 3 '97
Home for Christmas '90
Home of Angels '94
Homecoming '09
Homecoming: A Christmas Story '71
A House Without a Christmas Tree '72
The Ice Harvest '05
I'll Be Home for Christmas '98
I'll Be Seeing You '44
It Came Upon a Midnight Clear '84
It Happened on 5th Avenue '47
It's a Wonderful Life '46 ►
Jack Frost '98
Jingle All the Way '96
Joyeux Noel '05 ►
Just Friends '05
The Kid Who Loved Christmas '90
Kramer vs. Kramer '79 ►
La Buche '00
Lady on a Train '45 ►
The Lemon Drop Kid '51
Lethal Weapon '87 ►
Lily in Winter '94
The Lion in Winter '68 ►
The Lion in Winter '03 ►
The Little Drummer Girl '84 ►
The Little Match Girl '84
The Little Match Girl '87
Little Women '94 ►
The Long Kiss Goodnight '96
Look Who's Talking Now '93
Love Actually '03
Ma Saison Preferee '93 ►
Make the Yuletide Gay '09
The Man in the Santa Claus Suit '79
The Man Upstairs '93
March of the Wooden Soldiers '34 ►
A Matter of Principle '83
Merry Christmas, Mr. Lawrence '83 ►
The Merry Gentleman '08
A Midnight Clear '92 ►
Midnight Clear '06
A Midwinter's Tale '95
Miracle at Sage Creek '05
Miracle Down Under '87
Miracle in the Wilderness '91
Miracle on 34th Street '47 ►
Miracle on 34th Street '94
Mrs. Santa Claus '96
Ms. Scrooge '97
Mr. Corbett's Ghost '90
Mr. St. Nick '02
Mixed Nuts '94
Moonlight & Mistletoe '08
The Most Wonderful Time of the Year '08
The Muppet Christmas Carol '92
Must Be Santa '99
My Uncle: The Alien '96
The Mystery of Edwin Drood '93
Naked City: A Killer Christmas '98
National Lampoon's Christmas Vacation '89
National Lampoon's Christmas Vacation 2: Cousin Eddie's Big Island Adventure '03
The National Tree '09
Nativity '78
The Night of the Hunter '55 ►
The Night They Saved Christmas '87
Night Train '09
The Nightmare Before Christmas '93 ►
Noel '04
Nothing Like the Holidays '08
The Nutcracker Prince '91
Nutcracker: The Motion Picture '86
Off Season '01
One Christmas '95
One Magic Christmas '85
P2 '07
Papa's Angels '00
Parental Guidance '98
A Perfect Day '06
The Perfect Holiday '07
The Polar Express '04
Powder Blue '09
Prancer '89
Prancer Returns '01
The Preacher's Wife '96
Pride and Glory '08
'R Xmas '01
The Railway Children '70 ►
Reckless '95
The Ref '93 ►
Reindeer Games '00
Remember the Night '40 ►
Riot '96
The Robe '53
Roots: The Gift '88
Santa and Pete '99
Santa Baby '06
Santa Buddies '09
Santa Claus '59
Santa Claus Conquers the Martians '64
Santa Claus: The Movie '85
The Santa Clause '94
The Santa Clause 2 '02
The Santa Clause 3: The Escape Clause '06
The Santa Trap '02
Santa with Muscles '96
Scrooge '35 ►
Scrooge '70
Scrooged '88
A Season for Miracles '99
Sheitan '06
Silent Night, Deadly Night '84
Silent Night, Deadly Night 2 '87
Silent Night, Deadly Night 3: Better Watch Out! '89
Silent Night, Deadly Night 5: The Toymaker '91
Silent Night, Lonely Night '69
Sleepless in Seattle '93 ►
A Smoky Mountain Christmas '86

► = rated three bones or higher

Snow '04
Snow 2: Brain Freeze '08
Snowglobe '07
Stalag 17 '53 ▸
The Sum of Us '94 ▸
Surviving Christmas '04
Susan Slept Here '54
A Tale of Winter '92
Thirteenth Day of Christmas '85
This Christmas '07
Three Godfathers '48 ▸
A Time to Remember '87
To All a Goodnight '80
To Grandmother's House We Go '94
Together Again for the First Time '08
Too Cool for Christmas '04
The Town That Banned Christmas '06
Trading Places '83
Trail of Robin Hood '50
Trapped in Paradise '94
Turbulence '96
The Twelve Days of Christmas Eve '04
The Twelve Dogs of Christmas '05
24 Nights '99
Unaccompanied Minors '06
Untamed Heart '93
A Very Brady Christmas '88
The Victors '63
Visions of Sugarplums '99
The Waltons: The Christmas Carol '80
Where God Left His Shoes '07
While She Was Out '08
While You Were Sleeping '95 ▸
White Christmas '54 ▸
Who Slew Auntie Roo? '71
Will It Snow for Christmas? '96

Church Choirs

see also *Gospel Music; Nuns & Priests*
The Chorus '04
The Christmas Choir '08
A Christmas Without Snow '80
The Fighting Temptations '03
First Sunday '08
The Gospel '05 ▸
The Preacher's Wife '96
Preaching to the Choir '05
Sister Act '92
Sister Act 2: Back in the Habit '93

CIA/NSA

see also *Foreign Intrigue; Spies & Espionage*
Acts of Betrayal '98
Agent Cody Banks '03
Agent on Ice '86
Aldrich Ames: Traitor Within '98
The Amateur '82
Assassin '89
The Assassination Game '92
The Assignment '97
Avalanche Express '79
Avenging Force '86
Bad Company '02
Ballistic: Ecks vs. Sever '02
A Beautiful Mind '01 ▸
The Berlin Conspiracy '91
Bionic Ninja '85
Black Dawn '05
Blink of an Eye '92
Bloodfist 8: Hard Way Out '96
Body of Lies '08
Bomb Squad '97
The Bourne Supremacy '04 ▸
The Bourne Ultimatum '07 ▸
Burn After Reading '08
Call Me Bwana '63
The Capitol Conspiracy '99
Chain Reaction '96
Charlie Wilson's War '07
Chu Chu & the Philly Flash '81
C.I.A.: Code Name Alexa '92
C.I.A. 2: Target Alexa '94
Class of 1999 2: The Substitute '93
Clear and Present Danger '94
Code Name Alpha '67
The Company '07
Company Business '91
Confessions of a Dangerous Mind '02
Connor's War '06
Conspiracy of Fear '96
Conspiracy Theory '97 ▸
Contract Killers '08
Crackerjack 3 '00
Crash & Byrnes '99
The Crocodile Hunter: Collision Course '02
Crossfire '99
Deadly Spygames '89
The Defector '66
The Detonator '06
Diplomatic Siege '99
Divided by Hate '96
Double Tap '98
Double Team '97
D.R.E.A.M. Team '99
The Eiger Sanction '75
Erik '90
Escape from the KGB '87
Exiled in America '90
Exterminator '80
Extreme Limits '01
Eye See You '01
Fay Grim '06
Felony '95
Femme Fontaine: Killer Babe for the C.I.A. '95
A Few Days in September '06
The Fourth Angel '01
Francis Gary Powers: The True Story of the U-2 Spy '76
The Glimmer Man '96
The Good Shepherd '06
Harold & Kumar Escape from Guantanamo Bay '08
Hudson Hawk '91
The Hunt for Red October '90 ▸
The In-Laws '03
Kill Castro '80
Killer Likes Candy '78
Knock Off '98
The Listening '06
The Long Kiss Goodnight '96
Lumumba '01 ▸
Man on Fire '04
Mankillers '87
Memoirs of an Invisible Man '92
Militia '99
Mission: Impossible '96 ▸
Mission: Impossible 2 '00 ▸
Most Wanted '97
My Brother's War '97
My Little Assassin '99
Nixon '95 ▸
No Safe Haven '87
Nothing But the Truth '08 ▸
The Objective '08
Once Upon a Time in Mexico '03 ▸
Operation C.I.A. '65
The P.A.C.K. '96
Pandora's Clock '96
Patriot Games '92 ▸
The Peacemaker '97
President's Target '93
Puerto Vallarta Squeeze '04
The Quiet American '02 ▸
The Recruit '03
Rendition '07
Rosebud '75
Royce '93
Sahara '05
Salt '10
S.A.S. San Salvador '84
The Shadow Conspiracy '96
Shadow Man '06
The Siege '98
Silent Partner '05
The Situation '06
Sky High '84
Sniper 3 '04
The Spanish Prisoner '97 ▸
Spartan '04 ▸
Spies Like Us '85
The Spook Who Sat by the Door '73
Spy Games '99
Sticks '98
Street Justice '89
Subterfuge '98
The Sum of All Fears '02
Sunstorm '01
Swordfish '01
Syriana '05 ▸
Taken Alive '95
Target '85
Target of Opportunity '04
357 Magnum '79
Time Lapse '01
To the Limit '95
Traitor '08
Violent Breed '83
The Waiting Game '98
White Ghost '88
White Sands '92
XXX '02
XXX: State of the Union '05
Yuri Nosenko, KGB '86

Cincinnati

Airborne '93
Beloved '98
Dirty Pictures '00
Eight Men Out '88 ▸
Fresh Horses '88
The Great Buck Howard '09
Hustle '04
Jimmy & Judy '06
Kit Kittredge: An American Girl '08 ▸
Pride of Jesse Hallum '81
Scream 2 '97 ▸
Wild Hogs '07
With a Song in My Heart '52 ▸

Cinderella Stories

Angus '95
Another Cinderella Story '08
Arthur '81 ▸
Au Pair '99
Au Pair 2: The Fairy Tale Continues '01
B.A.P.'s '97
Boogie Nights '97 ▸
Born Yesterday '50 ▸
Born Yesterday '93
Camp Rock '08
Celestial Clockwork '94
The Church Mouse '34
Cinderella '50 ▸
Cinderella Man '05 ▸
A Cinderella Story '04
Cinderfella '60
Dreamer: Inspired by a True Story '05
Ella Enchanted '04 ▸
Ever After: A Cinderella Story '98 ▸
Evita '96
First Love '39
Flashdance '83
For Real '02
Heaven or Vegas '98
Hero '92 ▸
Just Friends '05
The Little Mermaid '89 ▸
The Love Trap '29
Maid in Manhattan '02
Maid to Order '87
Milk Money '94
The Mirror Has Two Faces '96
Mrs. Winterbourne '96
My Fair Lady '64 ▸
Once Around '91
Picture This! '08
Pretty Woman '90 ▸
The Prince & Me '04
The Princess Diaries '01
The Princess Diaries 2: Royal Engagement '04
Pygmalion '38 ▸
The Red Mill '27
Saint Ralph '04
Sally '29
She's All That '99
The Slipper and the Rose '76
Splash '84
A Star Is Born '37 ▸
Stroke of Midnight '90
Up Close and Personal '96 ▸
Working Girl '88 ▸
The World of Suzie Wong '60

Circuses

see *Carnivals & Circuses; Clowns*

City-Squishing Behemoths

see also *Alien Beings—Vicious; Monster Yuks*
Cloverfield '08
Dragon Wars '07
Frankenstein Conquers the World '64
Gamera the Brave '06
Godzilla '98
Godzilla, King of the Monsters '56
Godzilla 1985 '85
Hellboy II: The Golden Army '08 ▸
King Kong Escapes '67
Legend of the Dinosaurs and Monster Birds '77
Negadon: The Monster from Mars '05
Tetsujin 28 '04

Civil Rights

see also *Apartheid; Slavery*
An African Dream '90
Ali '01
As Summers Die '86
The Autobiography of Miss Jane Pittman '74 ▸
Bloody Sunday '01 ▸
Boycott '02 ▸
Bucktown '75
The Color of Courage '98
The Color Purple '85 ▸
The Conversation '74 ▸
Crazy in Alabama '99
Crisis at Central High '80 ▸
Dangerous Evidence: The Lori Jackson Story '99
Driving Miss Daisy '89 ▸
A Dry White Season '89 ▸
Dutchman '67 ▸
The Ernest Green Story '93
The Express '08
Final Comedown '72
For Us, the Living '88 ▸
Free, White, and 21 '62
Freedom Road '79
Freedom Song '00 ▸
The Fringe Dwellers '86
Game for Vultures '86
Gang in Blue '96
George Wallace '97
Get On the Bus '96 ▸
Ghosts of Mississippi '96
Gospel Hill '08
The Great Debaters '07 ▸
Hairspray '07 ▸
Half Slave, Half Free '85
Hank Aaron: Chasing the Dream '95 ▸
Hawmps! '76
The Heart of Dixie '89
Hidden Agenda '90
Home of the Brave '49 ▸
The Killing Yard '01
King '78 ▸
The Kitchen Toto '87 ▸
Long Shadows '86
The Long Walk Home '89 ▸
Malcolm X: Make It Plain '95 ▸
The McMasters '70
Mean Streak '99
Mississippi Burning '88 ▸
Mr. & Mrs. Loving '96 ▸
A Nation Aflame '37
Panther '95
The Red Fury '84
The Ring '52
The Rising Place '02
The Rosa Parks Story '02
Rosewood '96 ▸
Ruby Bridges '98
The Secret Life of Bees '08 ▸
Selma, Lord, Selma '99
A Soldier's Story '84 ▸
The Two of Us '68 ▸
The Untold Story of Emmett Louis Till '05 ▸
We of the Never Never '82 ▸

Civil War

see also *American South; Southern Belles*
Abraham Lincoln '30
Alvarez Kelly '66
Andersonville '95 ▸
The Andersonville Trial '70 ▸
Bad Company '72 ▸
Band of Angels '57
The Beguiled '70 ▸
The Birth of a Nation '15 ▸
Blood at Sundown '88
Bloody Trail '72
The Blue and the Gray '82
The Bushwackers '52
Cavalry '36
Cavalry Charge '51
Charlotte Forten's Mission: Experiment in Freedom '85 ▸
Civil War Diary '90 ▸
Class of '61 '92
Cold Mountain '03 ▸
Colorado '40
Copper Canyon '50
CSA: The Confederate States of America '04
Dark Command '40 ▸
Dead Birds '04
Drums in the Deep South '51
Escape from Fort Bravo '53
Finger on the Trigger '65
The Fool Killer '65
Fort Yuma Gold '66
Friendly Persuasion '56 ▸
Frontier Pony Express '39
Frontier Scout '38
The General '26 ▸
General Spanky '36
Gettysburg '93 ▸
The Ghost Brigade '93
Glory '89 ▸
Gods and Generals '03
Gone with the Wind '39 ▸
The Good, the Bad and the Ugly '67 ▸
Gore Vidal's Lincoln '88
Great Day in the Morning '56
The Great Locomotive Chase '56
Hangman's Knot '52
Hellbenders '67
Hellgate '52
The Horse Soldiers '59
How the West Was Won '63 ▸
The Hunley '99
Innocent Voices '04
Ironclads '90
It Happened in New Orleans '36
Johnny Shiloh '63
Kansas Pacific '53
The Last Confederate: The Story of Robert Adams '05
Last Stand at Saber River '96
Little Women '33 ▸
Little Women '49 ▸
Little Women '78
Little Women '94 ▸
The Littlest Rebel '35
Louisiana '87
The Love Letter '98
Love Me Tender '56
Love's Savage Fury '79
Macho Callahan '70
The McMasters '70
Menace on the Mountain '70
Mosby's Marauders '66
Mysterious Island '61 ▸
No Drums, No Bugles '71
North and South Book 1 '85 ▸
North and South Book 2 '86 ▸
Of Human Hearts '38
The Old Maid '39 ▸
Oldest Confederate Widow Tells All '95 ▸
Operator 13 '34
The Ordeal of Dr. Mudd '80 ▸
The Outlaw Josey Wales '76 ▸
Pharoah's Army '95
The Private History of a Campaign That Failed '81
Queen '93 ▸
Raiders of Ghost City '44
Raintree County '57
Rebel Love '85
Rebel Vixens '69
The Red Badge of Courage '51 ▸
Ride with the Devil '99
Rocky Mountain '50
The Rose and the Jackal '90
Run of the Arrow '56
The Sacketts '79
Sahara '05
Shadow of Chikara '77
The Shadow Riders '82
Shenandoah '65 ▸
Sommersby '93
South of St. Louis '48
A Southern Yankee '48
The Supernaturals '86
The Tempest '99
Tramplers '66
Treason '33
True Women '97
The Undefeated '69
Virginia City '40 ▸
War Brides '80
Way Down South '39
Westbound '58
Western Gold '37
Yellowneck '55

Civil War (non U.S.)

see also *Genocide/Ethnic Cleansing; Spanish Civil War; War, General*
Darfur Now '07
Enough! '06
Rambo '08
To Kill a King '03
24 : Redemption '08

Classic Horror

see also *Horror Anthologies*
The Abominable Dr. Phibes '71 ▸
An American Haunting '05
And Now the Screaming Starts '73
The Ape '40
The Ape Man '43
The Appointment '82
Asylum '72
Asylum of Satan '72
Atom Age Vampire '61
Attack of the Beast Creatures '85
Attack of the Mayan Mummy '63
Attack of the Swamp Creature '75
Avenging Conscience '14
The Awakening '80
Barn of the Naked Dead '73
The Bat '26 ▸
The Bat '59
The Bat People '74
The Beast from Haunted Cave '60
The Beast Must Die '75
Bedlam '45 ▸
Before I Hang '40 ▸
The Birds '63 ▸
The Black Cat '34 ▸
The Black Room '35 ▸
Black Sabbath '64 ▸
The Black Scorpion '57
Black Sunday '60 ▸
Blood and Roses '61
Blood Beast Terror '67
Blood Island '68
Blood of Dracula '57
Blood of Dracula's Castle '69
Blood of the Vampire '58
The Bloodsuckers '70
Bluebeard '44
The Body Snatcher '45 ▸
The Bride '85
The Bride of Frankenstein '35 ▸
Bride of the Gorilla '51

Bride of the Monster '55
The Brute Man '46
Burn, Witch, Burn! '62 ▸
The Cabinet of Dr. Caligari '19 ▸
Calling Dr. Death '43
Carnival of Souls '62 ▸
Castle of Blood '64
Castle of Evil '66
Castle of the Living Dead '64
Cat Girl '57
Cat in the Cage '68
Cat People '42 ▸
Cat People '82
Cauldron of Blood '67
Cave of the Living Dead '65
Chamber of Horrors '40
The Changeling '80
Circus of Fear '67
Condemned to Live '35
The Conqueror Worm '68 ▸
Corridors of Blood '58
Count Dracula '71
Count Yorga, Vampire '70
The Crawling Eye '58
Creature from the Black Lagoon '54 ▸
Creature of Destruction '67
Creature of the Walking Dead '60
The Creature Walks among Us '56
Creature with the Blue Hand '70
The Creeper '48
The Creeping Flesh '72
Creeping Terror '64
Creepshow '82
Creepshow 2 '87
The Crime of Dr. Crespi '35
Crimes at the Dark House '39 ▸
Crimes of Dr. Mabuse '32 ▸
The Crimes of Stephen Hawke '36
The Crimson Cult '68
Crucible of Horror '69
Cry of the Banshee '70
Cry of the Werewolf '44
Crypt of the Living Dead '73
The Curse of Frankenstein '57
Curse of Nostradamus '60
Curse of the Devil '73
Curse of the Swamp Creature '66
Cyclops '56
Dance of the Damned '88
Darkness '02
Daughters of Darkness '71 ▸
Dead Man's Eyes '44
Dementia 13 '63
Demon Barber of Fleet Street '36
Demons of the Mind '72
The Devil Bat '41
The Devil Bat's Daughter '46
Devil Doll '36 ▸
Devil's Kiss '75
Dr. Death, Seeker of Souls '73
Dr. Jekyll and Mr. Hyde '20 ▸
Dr. Jekyll and Mr. Hyde '32 ▸
Dr. Jekyll and Mr. Hyde '41 ▸
Dr. Jekyll and Mr. Hyde '68
Dr. Jekyll and Mr. Hyde '73
Doctor X '32
Dolly Dearest '92
Dorian Gray '70
Dracula (Spanish Version) '31
Dracula '31 ▸
Dracula '73
Dracula '79
Dracula A.D. 1972 '72
Dracula 2000 '00
Dracula vs. Frankenstein '69
Dracula vs. Frankenstein '71
Dracula's Daughter '36 ▸
Dracula's Great Love '72
Dracula's Last Rites '79
Dracula's Widow '88
The Evil of Frankenstein '64
The Exorcist '73 ▸
Exorcist: The Beginning '04
Eye of the Demon '87
Eyes of Fire '84
Eyes of the Panther '90
The Fall of the House of Usher '49
The Fall of the House of Usher '60 ▸
The Fall of the House of Usher '80
Fangs of the Living Dead '68
The Fear Chamber '68
Fear No Evil '80
The Fog '78
Frankenstein '31 ▸
Frankenstein '73
Frankenstein '82
Frankenstein and the Monster from Hell '74
Frankenstein Created Woman '66 ▸
Frankenstein '80 '79
Frankenstein Island '81
Frankenstein Meets the Wolfman '42 ▸
Frankenstein Must Be Destroyed '69
Frankenstein Unbound '90 ▸
Frankenstein's Daughter '58
Fright Night '85
Fright Night 2 '88
The Fury '78
The Fury of the Wolfman '70
Genie of Darkness '62
George A. Romero's Land of the Dead '05 ▸
The Ghost of Frankenstein '42
The Ghoul '34
The Gorgon '64
Gothic '87 ▸
Grave of the Vampire '72
Graveyard Shift '90
The Greed of William Hart '48
Guardian of the Abyss '82
Halloween Night '90
The Hanging Woman '72
The Haunted '79
The Haunted Strangler '58
Haunted Summer '88
The Haunting '63 ▸
Haunting Fear '91
The Haunting of Morella '91
Haxan: Witchcraft through the Ages '22 ▸
The Head '59
The Horror of Dracula '58 ▸
House of Dark Shadows '70 ▸
House of Dracula '45
House of Frankenstein '44
House of the Black Death '65
The House of Usher '88
House of Wax '53 ▸
House on Haunted Hill '58
The House that Dripped Blood '71
How to Make a Monster '58
The Hunchback of Notre Dame '23 ▸
The Hunger '83
I Walked with a Zombie '43 ▸
I Was a Teenage Werewolf '57
Invasion of the Vampires '61
The Invisible Dr. Mabuse '62 ▸
The Invisible Man '33 ▸
The Invisible Ray '36
The Island of Dr. Moreau '77
Island of Lost Souls '32 ▸
Isle of the Dead '45
Jaws '75 ▸
Jaws 2 '78
Jaws 3 '83
Jaws: The Revenge '87
King of the Zombies '41
La Chute de la Maison Usher '28 ▸
Lady Frankenstein '72
The Lair of the White Worm '88 ▸
The Legend of Blood Castle '72
Legend of the Werewolf '75
The Legend of the Wolf Woman '77
Lemora, Lady Dracula '73
The Living Coffin '58
The Mad Monster '42
Malevolence '04
The Man They Could Not Hang '39
The Manson Family '04
Mark of the Vampire '35 ▸
Martin '77 ▸
Mary Shelley's Frankenstein '94
Masque of the Red Death '65 ▸
Masque of the Red Death '89
Matango '63
Miami Horror '87
Mirrors '78
The Mummy '32 ▸
The Mummy '59 ▸
Mummy & Curse of the Jackal '67
The Mummy's Curse '44
The Mummy's Ghost '44
The Mummy's Hand '40
The Mummy's Tomb '42
Murders in the Rue Morgue '32
Mystery of the Wax Museum '33 ▸
The Neighbor No. Thirteen '05
Night of Dark Shadows '71 ▸
Nosferatu '22 ▸
Once Upon a Midnight Scary '90
Pandora's Box '28 ▸
The Phantom of the Opera '25 ▸
The Phantom of the Opera '43 ▸
The Phantom of the Opera '89
Picture of Dorian Gray '45 ▸
Picture of Dorian Gray '74 ▸
Pillow of Death '45
The Pit and the Pendulum '61 ▸
The Pit & the Pendulum '91
Psycho '60 ▸
The Raven '35 ▸
Return of the Vampire '43
Revenge of the Creature '55
Revenge of the Zombies '43
Scared to Death '46
The Snow Creature '54
Son of Dracula '43 ▸
Son of Frankenstein '39 ▸
Teenage Frankenstein '58
Three ... Extremes '04
Undead '05
The Undying Monster '42
The Vampire '57
The Vampire Bat '32
The Vampire People '66
The Vampire's Coffin '58
The Vampire's Ghost '45
Vampyr '31 ▸
Van Helsing '04 ▸
Werewolf of London '35
The Werewolf vs. the Vampire Woman '70
When a Stranger Calls '06
The White Zombie '32 ▸
The Wolf Man '41 ▸

Clergymen

see also *Nuns & Priests; Religion; Religious Epics*

Angel Baby '61
Angels and Insects '95 ▸
The Apostle '97 ▸
Avenging Angel '07
Bear Ye One Another's Burden... '88
Because of Winn-Dixie '05
The Bishop's Wife '47 ▸
The Bridge of San Luis Rey '05
Changeling '08 ▸
Cold Turkey '71 ▸
Creation '09
Darklight '04
The Disappearance of Aimee '76 ▸
Dragnet '87
Elmer Gantry '60 ▸
The Europeans '79 ▸
First Sunday '08
Footloose '84
Get Low '09
The Gospel '05 ▸
Hallelujah! '29 ▸
Home Movie '08
The King '05
Little Church Around the Corner '23
Little Minister '34 ▸
A Man Called Peter '55 ▸
Mercy Streets '00
Middletown '06
Miss Sadie Thompson '53 ▸
The Night of the Hunter '55 ▸
The Preacher's Wife '96
Purlie Victorious '63
The Quick and the Dead '95
Rain '32
The Rector's Wife '94
Saving God '08
The Scarlet Letter '34
The Scarlet Letter '73 ▸
The Scarlet Letter '79 ▸
The Scarlet Letter '95
The Second Chance '06
Serious Charge '59
Signs '02 ▸
Sirens '94
Something Beneath '07
A Walk to Remember '02
Wise Blood '79 ▸
Woman, Thou Art Loosed '04

Cleveland

see also *Cincinnati; Ohio*

Against the Ropes '04
American Splendor '03 ▸
Antwone Fisher '02 ▸
The Fortune Cookie '66 ▸
Howard the Duck '86
The Kid From Cleveland '49
Light of Day '87
Major League '89
Major League 2 '94
The Oh in Ohio '06
The Rocker '08
The Soloist '09
Stranger than Paradise '84 ▸
Welcome to Collinwood '02

Cloning Around

Alien: Resurrection '97 ▸
Attack of the Sabretooth '05
The Boys from Brazil '78
The Clones '73
The Clonus Horror '79
Godsend '04
The Island '05
Jurassic Park '93 ▸
The Last Sentinel '07
The Lost World: Jurassic Park 2 '97
Moon '09
Multiplicity '96
Repli-Kate '01
Replicant '01
Resident Evil: Extinction '07
Resurrection of Zachary Wheeler '71
The 6th Day '00
Species '95
Species 2 '98
Species 4: The Awakening '07
Spy Kids '01 ▸
Star Trek: Nemesis '02
Star Wars: Episode 2—Attack of the Clones '02 ▸
2001: A Space Travesty '00

Clowns

see also *Carnivals & Circuses; Killer Clowns*

Carnival of Souls '98
Clown Murders '83
Clownhouse '88
Clowning Around '92
Clowning Around 2 '93
The Clowns '71 ▸
Court Jester '56 ▸
Family Jewels '65
The Funhouse '81
Funland '89
He Who Gets Slapped '24 ▸
House of 1000 Corpses '03
Killer Klowns from Outer Space '88
Make-Up '37
The Man Who Laughs '27 ▸
Mr. Jingles '06
Painted Hero '95
Pee-wee's Big Adventure '85 ▸
Poltergeist '82 ▸
Quick Change '90
Rize '05 ▸
Shakes the Clown '92
S.I.C.K. Serial Insane Clown Killer '03
Spawn '97 ▸
Stephen King's It '90
13 Moons '02
To Catch a Killer '92 ▸

Coast Guard

see also *Military: Navy; Sail Away*

Don Winslow of the Coast Guard '43
The Guardian '06
Sea Devils '37
Waking the Dead '00
Wetbacks '56
Yours, Mine & Ours '05

Cockroaches

see also *Killer Bugs and Slugs*

Addicted to Love '96
The Applegates '89
Bird on a Wire '90
The Craft '96
Creepshow '82
Honey, We Shrunk Ourselves '97
Joe's Apartment '96
Just Married '03
Men in Black '97 ▸
Mimic '97
The Nest '88
Pacific Heights '90 ▸
Shinbone Alley '70
Team America: World Police '04 ▸
Twilight of the Cockroaches '90
Vampire's Kiss '88 ▸
WALL-E '08 ▸

Cold Spots

The Abominable Snowman '57
Adam Sandler's 8 Crazy Nights '02
Alaska '96
Alien vs. Predator '04
Antarctica '84
Arctic Blue '93
Arctic Tale '07
Atomic Submarine '59
Avalanche '99
Balto '95
The Big Push '75
Black Cadillac '03
Boa '02
Bog '84
Call of the Wild '93
Challenge To Be Free '76
Chilly Dogs '01
Christmas Comes to Willow Creek '87
Cold Fever '95
Cool Runnings '93
Courage Mountain '89
Crackerjack '94
The Crimson Rivers '01
Cry of the Penguins '71
The Day the Earth Froze '59
Dead Ahead: The Exxon Valdez Disaster '92 ▸
Dead of Winter '87 ▸
Dead Snow '09
Devil's Island '96
Die Another Day '02
Doctor Zhivago '65 ▸
Downhill Willie '96
The Eiger Sanction '75
The Empire Strikes Back '80 ▸
Encounters at the End of the World '07 ▸
Extreme Ops '02
Fallen Angel '03
Far North '07
The Fast Runner '01 ▸
Firefox '82
Fixed Bayonets! '51 ▸
The Forbidden Quest '93
Fred Claus '07
Friends & Lovers '99
Frozen '10
Frozen River '08 ▸
Glory & Honor '98
The Golden Compass '07
Happy Feet '06 ▸
Heart of Light '97
The Heroes of Telemark '65
Ice Age '02 ▸
Ice Age: Dawn of the Dinosaurs '09
Ice Men '04
Ice Palace '60
The Ice Runner '93
Ice Spiders '07
Ice Station Zebra '68
L'Iceberg '05
Into Thin Air: Death on Everest '97
Intruder Within '81
Iron Will '93
Island in the Sky '53 ▸
Jack Frost '98
Jack Frost 2: Revenge of the Mutant Killer Snowman '00
Jack London's The Call of the Wild '97
The Juniper Tree '87
Kavik the Wolf Dog '80
Klondike Annie '36
The Last Place on Earth '85
The Last Stop '99
Lost in Alaska '52
Lost Zeppelin '29
Lovers of the Arctic Circle '98
Map of the Human Heart '93
Meltdown '06
MXP: Most Xtreme Primate '03
Mystery, Alaska '99
Never Cry Wolf '83 ▸
North Face '08 ▸
North Star '96
North to Alaska '60 ▸
Operation Haylift '50
Ordeal in the Arctic '93
Out Cold '01
Pathfinder '87 ▸
The Pebble and the Penguin '94
Pipe Dreams '76
Quest for Fire '82 ▸
Reindeer Games '00
Salmonberries '91
The Santa Clause 2 '02
The Santa Clause 3: The Escape Clause '06
Shackleton '02 ▸
Shadow of the Wolf '92
She '35
The Shining '80
Silent Hunter '94
A Simple Plan '98 ▸
Smilla's Sense of Snow '96
Snow Angels '07 ▸
Snow Day '00
Snow Dogs '02
The Snow Queen '02
The Snow Walker '03
Snowboard Academy '96
Snowbound: The Jim and Jennifer Stolpa Story '94
Sometimes They Come Back... For More '99
Spawn of the North '38
The Spoilers '42 ▸
Spy Games '99
Stargate: Continuum '08
The Stranger: Kabloonak '95
Sub Down '97
Suspended Animation '02
Tentacles of the North '26
The Thaw '09
The Thing '51 ▸
The Thing '82
30 Days of Night '07
Transsiberian '08 ▸
Unaccompanied Minors '06
Vertical Limit '00
The Viking Sagas '95
Virus '82
The White Dawn '75
White Fang 2: The Myth of the White Wolf '94
White Wolves 3: Cry of the White Wolf '98
Whiteout '09
Wind Chill '07

Cold War

Cold War Spies

Coma

Comedy

Comedy Anthologies

Comedy Drama

The Family Stone '05
Fandango '85
Far North '88
Fast Talking '86
Fatso '80
Feeling Minnesota '96
The Fifth Monkey '90
First Name: Carmen '83 ▸
The Fisher King '91 ▸
Five Corners '88 ▸
The Five Heartbeats '91 ▸
The Flamingo Kid '84 ▸
Flesh '68 ▸
Flickers '80
Flirting '89 ▸
Floundering '94
Flourish '06
FM '78
Follow the Leader '44
Foolish '99
For Keeps '88
For the Love of Benji '77
A Foreign Field '93
Forrest Gump '94 ▸
Four Adventures of Reinette and Mirabelle '89 ▸
Four and a Half Women '05
Four Days in July '85
Four Deuces '75
Four Friends '81 ▸
The Four Musketeers '75 ▸
The Four Seasons '81
Freud Leaving Home '91
Fried Green Tomatoes '91 ▸
From the Hip '86
From the Mixed-Up Files of Mrs. Basil E. Frankweiler '95
Full Moon in Blue Water '88
Fuzz '72
Game 6 '05
Garbo Talks '84
Generation '69
George! '70
Georgy Girl '66 ▸
Get Shorty '95 ▸
Getting Over '81
Getting Straight '70
Ghost Chasers '51
The Gig '85
Gin Game '84 ▸
Ginger & Fred '86 ▸
The Girl in the Cafe '05
Girl Play '04
The Girl with the Hat Box '27
Girlfriends '78 ▸
A Girl's Folly '17
Go '99 ▸
Go Now '96 ▸
The Gold of Naples '54 ▸
Gone Are the Days '63
Good Bye, Lenin! '03 ▸
Good Luck '96
A Good Man in Africa '94
Good Morning, Vietnam '87 ▸
Good Sam '48
A Good Woman '04
The Goodbye Bird '93
Goodbye Columbus '69 ▸
The Goodbye People '83
Goodnight, Michelangelo '89
The Gospel According to Vic '87
The Graduate '67 ▸
The Grand Role '04
Grandview U.S.A. '84
The Great Man Votes '38 ▸
The Great McGinty '40 ▸
The Great Moment '44
The Great New Wonderful '06
A Great Wall '86 ▸
The Great War '59
Gregory's Girl '80 ▸
Grief '94
The Groomsmen '06
Gross Anatomy '89
Grown Ups '80
Grumpy Old Men '93 ▸
Guess What We Learned in School Today? '70
Guess Who's Coming to Dinner '67 ▸
Half a Sixpence '67
Hana & Alice '04 ▸
Hangin' with the Homeboys '91 ▸
Hannah and Her Sisters '86 ▸
Happily Ever After '86
Happily Ever After '04
Happy Endings '05
Happy Hour '03
Happy Since I Met You '89 ▸
Hard Promises '92
The Hard Way '91 ▸
Harlem Nights '89
Harry and Max '04
The Hawks & the Sparrows '67
Head Winds '25
The Heartbreak Kid '72 ▸
Heartburn '86 ▸
Henry Poole Is Here '08 ▸
Here Come the Marines '52
Hero '92 ▸
Hero of the Year '85
Hey, Babu Riba '88
The Hideaways '73
Hideous Kinky '99
Highball '97 ▸
His Double Life '33
His First Command '29
Hold Your Man '33 ▸
The Hole '98
A Hole in the Head '59
Hollywood Heartbreak '89
Hollywood Vice Sqaud '86
Holy Man '98
Home for the Holidays '95
Home Free All '84
Homegrown '97
Homer and Eddie '89
Horsemasters '61
The Hot Line '69
The Hotel New Hampshire '84
House of Angels '92
Household Saints '93 ▸
The Householder '63
Housekeeping '87 ▸
I Live My Life '35
I Live with Me Dad '86
I Love You Phillip Morris '10
I Vitelloni '53 ▸
The Ice Flood '26
If You Could See What I Hear '82
Il Sorpasso '63
I'll Never Forget What's 'Isname '67 ▸
Illuminata '98
I'm Not Rappaport '96
Imaginary Heroes '05
Immediate Family '89
Impure Thoughts '86
In Her Shoes '05 ▸
In Praise of Older Women '78
In the Mood '87
In the Soup '92
Indian Summer '93
Inside Monkey Zetterland '93
Insignificance '85 ▸
International Lady '41
The Invention of Lying '09
Irish Jam '05
It Couldn't Happen Here '88
It Started in Naples '60 ▸
It's a Wonderful Life '46 ▸
It's All Gone, Pete Tong '04
Jack and Sarah '95
Jailbird's Vacation '65
Jamon, Jamon '93
The January Man '89
Jazzman '84 ▸
Jimmy Hollywood '94
Jo Jo Dancer, Your Life Is Calling '86
Joe '70
Joe's Bed-Stuy Barbershop: We Cut Heads '83
Johnny Suede '92
The Jolly Paupers '38
Joshua Then and Now '85 ▸
Judge Priest '34 ▸
Judy Berlin '99
Juno '07 ▸
Just Another Pretty Face '58
Kicking and Screaming '95 ▸
The Kid '21 ▸
Kid Dynamite '43
The Kid from Left Field '79
Kids in America '05
The Killing Game '67
A King in New York '57
King of California '07
King of the Corner '04 ▸
Kingdom Come '01
Kisses in the Dark '97
Kitchen Stories '03
Knights & Emeralds '87
Knots '05
Kolya '96 ▸
Kostas '79
Kotch '71 ▸
La Discrete '90 ▸
La Dolce Vita '60 ▸
La Ronde '51 ▸
Lady by Choice '34
Lady for a Day '33 ▸
The Lady Says No '51
Larks on a String '68 ▸
Lars and the Real Girl '07
The Last Days of Chez Nous '92
The Last Detail '73 ▸
Last Holiday '50 ▸
Last Night '98 ▸
The Last of Mrs. Cheyney '37 ▸
Last Summer In the Hamptons '96 ▸
Law and Disorder '74 ▸
Le Beau Serge '58 ▸
Le Petit Amour '87 ▸
A League of Their Own '92 ▸
Leap of Faith '92
Leave 'Em Laughing '81
The Lemon Sisters '90
Let's Talk About Sex '98
Letter to Brezhnev '86 ▸
Letters from My Windmill '54 ▸
Letting Go '85
Life '99
Life 101 '95
Like Water for Chocolate '93 ▸
Lily in Love '85
Little Annie Rooney '25
Little Miss Sunshine '06 ▸
Little Red Schoolhouse '36
A Little Sex '82
The Little Theatre of Jean Renoir '71 ▸
The Little Thief '89 ▸
Little Vegas '90
Little Voice '98 ▸
Live Nude Girls '95
Living Out Loud '98
Local Hero '83 ▸
Loch Ness '95
Lonesome Jim '06 ▸
Long Shot Kids '81
Look at Me '04 ▸
Loose Connections '87
The Lovable Cheat '49
Love and Human Remains '93 ▸
Love Finds Andy Hardy '38 ▸
Love in the City '53 ▸
Love Me if You Dare '03
Love! Valour! Compassion! '96
Lover Girl '97
Lovers and Other Strangers '70 ▸
Loves of a Blonde '65 ▸
Loving '70
The Low Life '95
Lucas '86 ▸
Ma Vie en Rose '97 ▸
Mac and Me '88
Madame Sousatzka '88 ▸
Made for Each Other '39 ▸
Made in USA '88
Madea Goes to Jail '09
Madea's Family Reunion '06
Magic Town '47
Make Room for Tomorrow '81
Mama Turns a Hundred '79 ▸
The Man Upstairs '93
Manny's Orphans '78
Mantrap '26
Marathon '80
Maria's Child '93
Marilyn Hotchkiss' Ballroom Dancing & Charm School '06
Marius '31 ▸
The Marriage of Maria Braun '79 ▸
Marry Me, Marry Me '69 ▸
The Marrying Kind '52
Masala '91
M*A*S*H '70 ▸
M*A*S*H: Goodbye, Farewell & Amen '83 ▸
The Matador '06 ▸
Mauvaise Graine '33
Max Dugan Returns '83
May Fools '90 ▸
Maybe Baby '99
Me and You and Everyone We Know '05 ▸
Me Myself I '99
Meantime '81
Mediterraneo '91 ▸
Melinda and Melinda '05
Melvin Goes to Dinner '03
Memories of Me '88
Men at Work '90
Men Don't Leave '89
Mermaids '90 ▸
Metropolitan '90 ▸
Mexican Bus Ride '51
Middle Age Crazy '80
Midnight Auto Supply '78
Mifune '99
The Mighty Ducks '92
The Mighty Quinn '89
The Milagro Beanfield War '88 ▸
Million Dollar Kid '44
Millions '05 ▸
Min & Bill '30
Miracle on 34th Street '94
Mischief '85
The Misfit Brigade '87
Miss Annie Rooney '42
Miss Pettigrew Lives for a Day '08 ▸
Mrs. 'Arris Goes to Paris '92
Mrs. Henderson Presents '05
Mrs. Palfrey at the Claremont '05
Mrs. Wiggs of the Cabbage Patch '34
Mr. Deeds Goes to Town '36 ▸
Mr. Mom '83 ▸
Mr. North '88
Mr. Saturday Night '92
Mr. Winkle Goes to War '44
M'Lady's Court '73
Mom, the Wolfman and Me '80
Money for Nothing '93
The Moneytree '93
Moon over Parador '88
Moonlighting '85
More American Graffiti '79
Morgan Stewart's Coming Home '87
Moscow, Belgium '08
Moscow on the Hudson '84 ▸
Mother '96
The Mozart Brothers '86 ▸
Murmur of the Heart '71 ▸
My Beautiful Laundrette '85 ▸
My Blue Heaven '50
My Bodyguard '80 ▸
My Dinner with Andre '81 ▸
My Girl '91
My Life As a Dog '85 ▸
My Other Husband '85
My Therapist '84
My Twentieth Century '90 ▸
My Wonderful Life '90
Mystic Pizza '88 ▸
Nadine '87
The Nanny Diaries '07
The Nasty Girl '90 ▸
Nea '78
'Neath Brooklyn Bridge '42
Never Let Go '60
The New Age '94
A New Life '88
New Year's Day '89 ▸
Next Stop, Greenwich Village '76 ▸
Next Summer '84 ▸
Night on Earth '91 ▸
9 Souls '03
1969 '89 ▸
1999 '98
90 Days '86 ▸
The Ninth Configuration '79 ▸
No Man of Her Own '32
No Money Down '97
No Small Affair '84
Nobody's Fool '94 ▸
Noi '03
Norman, Is That You? '76
North '94
North Dallas Forty '79 ▸
Nothing in Common '86
Nueba Yol '95
No. 3 '97
Nurse on Call '88
The Object of Beauty '91 ▸
The Object of My Affection '98
Oblomov '81 ▸
Off Your Rocker '80
Oh, Alfie '75
Oh, What a Night '92
O'Horten '09
Olly Olly Oxen Free '78
Omaha (the movie) '95
Once Around '91
One Arabian Night '21 ▸
One Flew Over the Cuckoo's Nest '75 ▸
One Last Thing '05
Only One Night '42
Only When I Laugh '81 ▸
Orphans '87 ▸
Other People's Money '91
Our Little Girl '35
Out '82
Outrageous! '77 ▸
Outside Chance of Maximillian Glick '88
Over the Brooklyn Bridge '83
Paddy '70
Padre Nuestro '85
Palm Springs Weekend '63
Palooka '34
The Paper '94 ▸
The Paper Chase '73 ▸
Parental Guidance '98
Parenthood '89 ▸
Paris, je t'aime '06
Parting Shots '98
Party 7 '00
Patch Adams '98
Patti Rocks '88 ▸
The Pentagon Wars '98
People Will Talk '51 ▸
Peppermint Soda '77 ▸
Perfect Timing '84
Perfumed Nightmare '89 ▸
Period of Adjustment '62 ▸
Pete 'n' Tillie '72
Peter's Friends '92
The Philadelphia Story '40 ▸
The Pickle '93
Pictures '81
Ping Pong '87
Ping Pong '02 ▸
Pink Cadillac '89
Pink Nights '87
P.K. and the Kid '85
Playboy of the Western World '62
The Players Club '98 ▸
Pocketful of Miracles '61 ▸
The Pointsman '86
Pollyanna '20
Pollyanna '60 ▸
Pontiac Moon '94
Popi '69 ▸
Portnoy's Complaint '72
Post Concussion '99 ▸
Power '28
Powwow Highway '89 ▸
A Prairie Home Companion '06
The Preacher's Wife '96
Pretty in Pink '86
Pretty Persuasion '05
Pride of the Bowery '41
Primrose Path '40
Prisoner of Second Avenue '74
Prisoners of Inertia '89
The Private History of a Campaign That Failed '81
Prizzi's Honor '85 ▸
Problem Child '90
Promised Land '88 ▸
Pronto '97
Provincial Actors '79
Punchline '88
Purple People Eater '88
Pushing Hands '92
Pushing Tin '99 ▸
Queen of Hearts '89 ▸
The Quiet Family '98 ▸
The Rachel Papers '89 ▸
Racquet '79
Rafferty & the Gold Dust Twins '75
Rags to Riches '87
Raining Stones '93
Raising Helen '04
The Rascals '81
Ratboy '86
The Reception '05
Reckless '97 ▸
Reckless: The Sequel '98 ▸
The Red Light Sting '84
Remedy for Riches '40
Reno and the Doc '84
Return of the Secaucus 7 '80 ▸
Rich and Famous '81
Ride the Wild Surf '64
Robert et Robert '78 ▸
Rocket Gibraltar '88 ▸
Rocket Science '07 ▸
Roll Bounce '05 ▸
Romance of a Horsethief '71
Roommate '84
Roommates '95
The Rules of the Game '39 ▸
The Runnin' Kind '89
Rupert's Land '98
Russian Dolls '05
The Saddest Music in the World '03
Sadie McKee '34 ▸
Samurai Fiction '99 ▸
Saved! '04
Saving Grace '86
Saving Grace '00
Say Anything '89 ▸
Scenes from a Mall '91
School of Life '06
Schultze Gets the Blues '03
Searching For Wooden Watermelons '01
Second Best '05
Second Thoughts '83
Secrets of Women '52 ▸
Seduced and Abandoned '64 ▸
The Seducer '69
A Self-Made Hero '95 ▸
The Seven-Per-Cent Solution '76 ▸
Seven Thieves '60 ▸
Sex and the City 2 '10
Shadows and Fog '92
Shag: The Movie '89 ▸
She Hate Me '04
She Must Be Seeing Things '87
Shirley Valentine '89 ▸
A Shock to the System '90 ▸
Shooters '89
Shopgirl '05 ▸
Short Cuts '93 ▸
Side Out '90
Sideways '04 ▸
Signs of Life '89
Simon Birch '98
Simon, King of the Witches '71
A Simple Twist of Fate '94
Single Bars, Single Women '84
Sisterhood of the Traveling Pants '05
The Sisterhood of the Traveling Pants 2 '08
Six in Paris '68
Six Weeks '82
Sizzle Beach U.S.A. '74
Skin Game '71 ▸
Slap Shot '77 ▸
Slaves of New York '89
SLC Punk! '99
Sliding Doors '97
Slightly Honorable '40
The Slingshot '93 ▸
The Slugger's Wife '85
Smart Alecks '42
Smart People '08
Smoke Signals '98

▸ = rated three bones or higher

Smugglers' Cove '48 ►
The Snapper '93 ►
Soldier in the Rain '63
Some Kind of Hero '82
Some Kind of Wonderful '87
Someone Else's America '96 ►
Something in Common '86
Something Special '86
Something to Talk About '95
Son of Rambow '07
Song of the Thin Man '47
Soul Food '97
Soul Man '86
Southern Belles '05
Spencer's Mountain '63
Spike of Bensonhurst '88
Spitfire '34 ►
Spoiled Children '77
Spook Busters '48
Spy Games '99
The Squid and the Whale '05 ►
Stage Door '37 ►
Star Maps '97
Star of Midnight '35
Star Spangled Girl '71
Stardust Memories '80
Starlight Hotel '90
The Stars Fell on Henrietta '94
Starting Over '79 ►
Staying Together '89
Stealing Beauty '96
Steamboat Bill, Jr. '28 ►
The Stepford Wives '04
Stoogemania '85
Storm in a Teacup '37
The Story of Seabiscuit '49
Strange Fits of Passion '99
Stranger than Paradise '84 ►
Strawberry Blonde '41 ►
Stray Dog '91
Street Music '81
Striptease '96
Strong Man '26 ►
Stroszek '77 ►
Stuck on You '84
Student Confidential '87
Sueno '05
Sugarbaby '85 ►
The Sugarland Express '74 ►
Summer Fantasy '84
Summer Snow '94
The Sunshine Boys '75 ►
Suppose They Gave a War and Nobody Came? '70
Swedenhielms '35
Sweet Adeline '26
Sweet Hearts Dance '88
Sweet Lorraine '87 ►
Sweet William '79 ►
Sweetie '89 ►
Swept Away... '75 ►
Swing Shift '84
Sylvia Scarlett '35
T Bone N Weasel '92
Table Settings '84
Take Down '79
Take This Job & Shove It '81
Take Your Best Shot '82
A Tale of Springtime '89
The Talent Given Us '04 ►
Tales of Manhattan '42 ►
Talk '94
Talking Walls '85
The Taste of Others '00 ►
The Taste of Tea '04 ►
Taxi Blues '90 ►
A Taxing Woman '87 ►
Teachers '84
Teacher's Pet '58 ►
Teddy at the Throttle '16
10 '79
Ten Things I Hate about You '99 ►
Teresa Venerdi '41 ►
Texasville '90
That Thing You Do! '96 ►
That's Life! '86
That's My Baby! '88
Then She Found Me '07
There Goes My Baby '92
They Might Be Giants '71 ►
The Thief of Paris '67 ►
The Thin Man Goes Home '44
Things Change '88 ►
Things I Never Told You '96
13 Moons '02
This Is My Life '92
Those Lips, Those Eyes '80
A Thousand Clowns '65 ►
Three for the Road '87
Three in the Attic '68
Three Men and a Baby '87 ►
Three Men and a Cradle '85 ►
Three Men and a Little Lady '90
Thunder in the City '37 ►
Thursday's Child '43
Thursday's Game '74 ►
A Tiger's Tale '87
The Time of Your Life '48 ►
Tin Men '87
The Tip-Off '31
Tito and Me '92 ►
To Please a Lady '50
To Sleep with Anger '90 ►
Toby Tyler '59 ►
Tom Brown's School Days '40
Tom Brown's School Days '51 ►
Tom Sawyer '30 ►
Tony Draws a Horse '51
Too Bad She's Bad '54
Too Pretty to Be Honest '72
Tootsie '82 ►
Topaze '33 ►
Topaze '51 ►
Torch Song Trilogy '88
Toys '92
Trading Hearts '87
The Tragedy of a Ridiculous Man '81
Train to Hollywood '86 ►
Traveller '96 ►
Travels with My Aunt '72
Trouble along the Way '53
Trouble in the Glen '54
True Love '89 ►
Truly, Madly, Deeply '91 ►
The Truman Show '98 ►
Trust '91
Truth about Women '58
Turk 182! '85
Turkish Delight '73
Twenty Bucks '93 ►
Twenty-One '91
The 24 Hour Woman '99
29th Street '91
Twister '89
Two for the Road '67 ►
Two for the Seesaw '62 ►
2B Perfectly Honest '04
Twogether '94
Ugetsu '53 ►
Under the Biltmore Clock '85
Under the Boardwalk '89
Underworld '96
The Unfaithfuls '60
An Unfinished Piece for a Player Piano '77 ►
Up and Down '04
Up the Down Staircase '67 ►
Up the Sandbox '72
Used People '92
Vacuuming Completely Nude in Paradise '01
The Vals '85
The Van '95 ►
Varsity Blues '98
Venice, Venice '92
Very Close Quarters '84
Vicky Cristina Barcelona '08
The Virgin Soldiers '69
Visitor Q '01
Volpone '39 ►
The Wackness '08
Wait until Spring, Bandini '90
Waitress '07 ►
Walls of Glass '85
Wassup Rockers '06
The Way To Fight '96
We Think the World of You '88 ►
The Weather Man '05
Weekend at the Waldorf '45 ►
Welcome Home, Roxy Carmichael '90
Went to Coney Island on a Mission from God... Be Back by Five '98
We're No Angels '55 ►
West Is West '87
The West Wittering Affair '05
What a Life '39
What the $*! Do We Know? '04
What's Cooking? '00 ►
When Your Lover Leaves '83
Where the Heart Is '90
Whitcomb's War '87
The Whole Shootin' Match '79 ►
The Whole Town's Talking '35 ►
Who's Who '78
Whose Life Is It Anyway? '81 ►
Widow's Peak '94
The Wife '95
Wild in the Streets '68
Willie & Phil '80
A Wind from Wyoming '94
Wings of Eagles '57
Winter Kills '79 ►
Wired '89
Wise Blood '79 ►
Wish upon a Star '96
Wish You Were Here '87 ►
With Honors '94
The Wizard '89
The Women '39 ►
Women of All Nations '31
The World According to Garp '82 ►
The World of Henry Orient '64 ►
WR: Mysteries of the Organism '71 ►
The Wrong Arm of the Law '63 ►
A Yank in Australia '43
A Year in Provence '89 ►
The Year My Voice Broke '87 ►
Year of the Dog '07
Yesterday, Today and Tomorrow '64 ►
You and Me '38
You Are Here * '00
The Young in Heart '38 ►
You're a Big Boy Now '66 ►
A Zed & Two Noughts '88 ►
Zombie Honeymoon '04

Comedy Mystery

see also Black Comedy; Comedy; Comedy Drama; Genre Spoofs; Horror Comedy; Satire & Parody

Charade '63 ►
Clubhouse Detectives '96
Clue '85
Curse of the Pink Panther '83
Deathtrap '82
Get a Clue! '98
Goodbye, Lover '99
The Gracie Allen Murder Case '39
Hard-Boiled Mahoney '47
High Anxiety '77
Hoodwinked '05 ►
Kiss Kiss Bang Bang '05 ►
Lady on a Train '45 ►
The Man with Two Faces '34
Mortal Transfer '01
Murder by Death '76
Mystery Kids '99
The Notorious Landlady '62
Off and Running '90
The Pink Panther '64 ►
The Pink Panther '06
The Pink Panther Strikes Again '76 ►
The Princess Comes Across '36 ►
Return of the Pink Panther '74
Revenge of the Pink Panther '78
Safe House '99
Scoop '06
A Shot in the Dark '64 ►
Trail of the Pink Panther '82
Trixie '00
Voulez-Vous Danser avec Moi? '59
Whistling in Brooklyn '43
Whistling in Dixie '42
Whistling in the Dark '41 ►
Zero Effect '97

Comedy Performance

see Concert Films

Comedy Sci-Fi

see also Comedy; Comic Adventure; Genre Spoofs; Satire & Parody; Sci Fi

The Absent-Minded Professor '61 ►
Alien Avengers '96
Aliens in the Attic '09
Beach Babes 2: Cave Girl Island '95
Beach Babes from Beyond '93
Bug Buster '99
Can of Worms '00
Class of Nuke 'Em High '86
Class of Nuke 'Em High 2: Subhumanoid Meltdown '91
Class of Nuke 'Em High 3: The Good, the Bad and the Subhumanoid '94
Clockstoppers '02
Coneheads '93
The Creature Wasn't Nice '81
Dinosaur Valley Girls '96
Doin' Time on Planet Earth '88
Earth Girls Are Easy '89
Evolution '01
Freezer Burn: The Invasion of Laxdale '08
From Other Worlds '04
Funky Forest: The First Contact '06
Galaxy Quest '99
Hell Comes to Frogtown '88
Hellboy '04
The Hitchhiker's Guide to the Galaxy '05 ►
Honey, I Blew Up the Kid '92
Honey, I Shrunk the Kids '89
Honey, We Shrunk Ourselves '97
Howard the Duck '86
Ice Pirates '84
The Incredibles '04 ►
Invasion! '99
Invasion of the Saucer Men '57
Invasion of the Star Creatures '63
Men in Black '97 ►
Men in Black 2 '02
My Favorite Martian '98
My Uncle: The Alien '96
Out There '95
Robots '05
The Sex Machine '75
Sleeper '73 ►
Son of Flubber '63
Spaceballs '87
Star Kid '97 ►
Theodore Rex '95
Wham-Bam, Thank You Spaceman '75
Zoom '06

Comic Adventure

see also Action-Adventure; Comedy

Adventures Beyond Belief '87
Adventures in Babysitting '87
Adventures in Spying '92
Adventures of a Private Eye '77
Adventures of a Taxi Driver '76
The Adventures of Bullwhip Griffin '66
Agent Cody Banks '03
Air America '90
Alien from L.A. '87
All the Lovin' Kinfolk '70
All the Way, Boys '73
The Amazing Dobermans '76
The Ambushers '67
The Americano '17
Andy and the Airwave Rangers '89
Angel of H.E.A.T. '82
Angels Hard As They Come '71
Another 48 Hrs. '90
Another Stakeout '93
The Ant Bully '06
Avenging Disco Godfather '76
Baby on Board '92
Back Roads '81
Back to the Future '85 ►
Back to the Future, Part 2 '89
Back to the Future, Part 3 '90 ►
Bad Guys '86
Bagdad Cafe '88 ►
The Baltimore Bullet '80
Bananas Boat '78
Behind the Front '26
Beverly Hills Cop '84
Beverly Hills Cop 2 '87
Beverly Hills Cop 3 '94
The Big Lebowski '97 ►
The Big Slice '90
The Big White '05
Big Zapper '73
Bingo '91
Bird on a Wire '90
Black Tight Killers '66 ►
Bloodstone '88
Blue Iguana '88
Body Trouble '92
Bon Voyage '03 ►
Boris and Natasha: The Movie '92
Bridget Jones: The Edge of Reason '04
Brink's Job '78 ►
Brothers O'Toole '73
Burglar '87
Butler's Dilemma '43
California Straight Ahead '25
Campus Knights '29
Cannibal Women in the Avocado Jungle of Death '89
Cannonball Run '81
Cannonball Run 2 '84
The Captain from Koepenick '56
Captain Swagger '25
Cartouche '62 ►
Chan Is Missing '82 ►
Chasers '94
Cheaper by the Dozen 2 '05
Chu Chu & the Philly Flash '81
City Heat '84
Club Med '83
Collision Course '89
The Concrete Cowboys '79
Crocodile Dundee '86 ►
Crocodile Dundee 2 '88
Danny Deckchair '03
Dirt Bike Kid '86
Doctor Detroit '83
Dog Pound Shuffle '75 ►
Dolemite 2: Human Tornado '76
Doogal '05
Double Crossbones '51
The Double O Kid '92
Down to Earth '17 ►
Drop Dead Sexy '05
Every Girl Should Have One '78
Explosion '69
Fast Getaway '91
Feds '88
The Fifth Musketeer '79
The Fighting American '24
Flatfoot '78
Flipper '96 ►
Flirting with Fate '16 ►
Forever Young '92
48 Hrs. '82 ►
Foul Play '78 ►
Free Ride '86
The Further Adventures of Tennessee Buck '88
Garfield: The Movie '04
Ghostbusters '84 ►
Ghostbusters 2 '89
Go for It '83
The Golden Child '86
Gozu '03
The Gumshoe Kid '89
Gunmen '93
Hambone & Hillie '84
Harriet the Spy '96
Hawthorne of the USA '19
Hellboy '04
Here We Go Again! '42
High Road to China '83
High Voltage '29
Highpoint '80
How to Eat Fried Worms '06
Hudson Hawk '91
In Like Flint '67
In 'n Out '86
It's in the Bag '45
Jackie Chan's Who Am I '98
Jake Speed '86
Jane & the Lost City '87
The Jewel of the Nile '85
Just Tell Me You Love Me '80
Kamikaze Girls '04
Kazaam '96
Kindergarten Cop '90
King Kung Fu '87
Kiss My Grits '82
Kuffs '92
Landlord Blues '87
Last Action Hero '93
Last Holiday '06
Lemony Snicket's A Series of Unfortunate Events '04
Leonard Part 6 '87
The Life Aquatic with Steve Zissou '04
Looking for Trouble '96
A Low Down Dirty Shame '94
Lucky Devil '25
Lunch Wagon '81
Lust in the Dust '85 ►
Mad About Money '37
Madigan's Millions '67
Magic Island '95
Magic Kid '92
A Man Called Sarge '90
The Man in the Raincoat '57
The Man Who Wasn't There '83
The Man with One Red Shoe '85
Master Mind '73
The Masters of Menace '90
Memoirs of an Invisible Man '92
Miami Supercops '85
Midnight Madness '80
Midnight Run '88 ►
Miracles '86
Mr. Billion '77
Mr. Nanny '93
Mr. Nice Guy '98
Mr. Robinson Crusoe '32
Mr. Superinvisible '73
Mitchell '75
Mo' Money '92
Mob Story '90
Mom and Dad Save the World '92
The Money '75
Money Talks '97
Monkey Hustle '77
Monkey's Uncle '65
Muppet Treasure Island '96
Mutants In Paradise '84
My African Adventure '87
My Dog, the Thief '69
My Science Project '85
No Deposit, No Return '76
O Brother Where Art Thou? '00
Oddball Hall '91
Odds and Evens '78
Off the Lip '04
Operation Condor 2: The Armour of the Gods '86
Operation Dumbo Drop '95
Our Man Flint '66
Over the Hill '93
Palookaville '95 ►
Pippi Goes on Board '69
Pippi in the South Seas '70
Pippi Longstocking '69
Pippi on the Run '70
Pirates '86
Pirates of the Caribbean: Dead Man's Chest '06
Pizza '05
Pootie Tang '01
Prehysteria '93
The Prince of Thieves '48
Red Lion '69
Reggie Mixes In '16 ►
The Reivers '69 ►
Rescue Me '93

► = rated three bones or higher

The Return of the Musketeers '89
Return of the Rebels '81
Riff-Raff '47
Romancing the Stone '84 ▸
Round Trip to Heaven '92
Royal Flash '75 ▸
Rumble in the Bronx '96
Running Scared '86
Rush Hour '98
Russkies '87
The Savage '75
Seven '79
Sherlock: Undercover Dog '94
She's Back '88
Shoot '92
Short Time '90 ▸
Shredder Orpheus '89
Shrek 2 '04 ▸
Silver Streak '76 ▸
Ski Patrol '89
Sky High '84
Slither '73 ▸
Smokey and the Bandit '77
Smokey and the Bandit 2 '80
Smokey and the Bandit, Part 3 '83
Smokey & the Judge '80
Smokey Bites the Dust '81
Spaghetti House '82
Special Delivery '76
Speed Zone '88
Speedy '28 ▸
Spies, Lies and Naked Thighs '91
Spy Trap '88
Spy with a Cold Nose '66
S*P*Y*S '74
The Squeeze '87
Stakeout '87
Stand-In '85
Steelyard Blues '73
Stepmonster '92
The Stick-Up '77
The Sting 2 '83
Stingray '78
Stop! or My Mom Will Shoot '92
Stop That Cab '51
Stuntwoman '81
Suburban Commando '91
Suffering Bastards '90
The Suitors '88
Summer Night with Greek Profile, Almond Eyes & Scent of Basil '87
Sunburn '79
Super Fuzz '81
Surf Nazis Must Die '87
Surf Ninjas '93
Survivors '83
Swashbuckler '76
The Tall Blond Man with One Black Shoe '72 ▸
Tall, Tan and Terrific '46
A Taxing Woman's Return '88 ▸
Teenage Mutant Ninja Turtles: The Movie '90
Teenage Mutant Ninja Turtles 2: The Secret of the Ooze '91
Teenage Mutant Ninja Turtles 3 '93
Terminal Exposure '89
That Man from Rio '64
That Sinking Feeling '79 ▸
They Met in Bombay '41
The Thief Who Came to Dinner '73
Think Big '90
This Time I'll Make You Rich '75
Those Daring Young Men in Their Jaunty Jalopies '69
Those Fantastic Flying Fools '67
Those Magnificent Men in Their Flying Machines '65 ▸
Three Amigos '86
Three Fugitives '89
Three Kinds of Heat '87
The Three Musketeers '74 ▸
3 Ninjas '92
3 Ninjas Kick Back '94
3 Ninjas Knuckle Up '95
Thunder and Lightning '77
Thunder in the Pines '49
Thursday '98
Title Shot '81
Toga Party '77
Tom and Huck '95 ▸
Too Hot to Handle '38 ▸
Top Dog '95
Topkapi '64 ▸
Tough Guys '86
Treasure of the Moon Goddess '88
Trenchcoat '83
TripleCross '85
Trouble in Store '53
The Trouble with Spies '87
True Lies '94
12 Plus 1 '70 ▸
Twin Dragons '92
Twins '88
Ultrachrist! '03
Under the Hula Moon '95
Under the Rainbow '81
Up the Creek '84
Uphill All the Way '85
Uptown Saturday Night '74
Vampire Effect '03
Van Nuys Blvd. '79
Vice Academy '88
Vice Academy 2 '90
Vice Academy 3 '91
Viva Maria! '65
Wackiest Ship in the Army '61
Wallace & Gromit in The Curse of the Were-Rabbit '05 ▸
We're No Angels '89
When the Clouds Roll By '19 ▸
Who Killed Mary What's 'Er Name? '71
The Wild and the Free '80
Wishman '93
Without a Paddle '04
Women of All Nations '31
World Gone Wild '88
Wrong Is Right '82
Year of the Comet '92
The Yum-Yum Girls '78

Comic Books

American Splendor '03 ▸
Artists and Models '55
Chasing Amy '97
Comic Book: The Movie '04 ▸
The Dangerous Lives of Altar Boys '02 ▸
Dark Justice '00
I Want to Go Home '89
Jay and Silent Bob Strike Back '01
Mallrats '95
Son of the Mask '05

Comic Cops

see also *Disorganized Crime*
The Animal '01
Big Trouble '02
Cop Out '10
Dragnet '87
Feds '88
Find the Lady '76
Freebie & the Bean '74
Inspector Clouseau '68
It Seemed Like a Good Idea at the Time '75
K-9 '89
Mambo Italiano '03
Me, Myself, and Irene '00 ▸
The Naked Gun: From the Files of Police Squad '88 ▸
Naked Gun 33 1/3: The Final Insult '94
Naked Gun 2 1/2: The Smell of Fear '91
National Lampoon's Loaded Weapon 1 '93
Police Academy '84
Police Academy 2: Their First Assignment '85
Police Academy 3: Back in Training '86
Police Academy 4: Citizens on Patrol '87
Police Academy 5: Assignment Miami Beach '88
Police Academy 6: City under Siege '89
Police Academy 7: Mission to Moscow '94
Reno 911! Miami '07
The Rug Cop '06
Rush Hour '98
Rush Hour 2 '01
Super Troopers '01
Superbad '07 ▸
Taxi '04
Turner and Hooch '89

Coming of Age

see also *Teen Angst*
A la Mode '94
A Nos Amours '84 ▸
The Abe Lincoln of Ninth Avenue '39
Across the Great Divide '76
The Affairs of Annabel '38
Ah, Wilderness! '35 ▸
Alan & Naomi '92
Alexandria... Why? '78
All Fall Down '62
All I Wanna Do '98
All I Want '02
All Over Me '96 ▸
All the Right Moves '83
All Things Fair '95
Aloha Summer '88
Alpine Fire '89
Amarcord '74 ▸
American Boyfriends '89
American Graffiti '73 ▸
An American Rhapsody '01 ▸
An American Summer '90
Americano '05
Among the Cinders '83
... And the Earth Did Not Swallow Him '94
Angele '34 ▸
Angelo My Love '83 ▸
Anne Frank: The Whole Story '01 ▸
Anne of Green Gables '85 ▸
Anthony Adverse '36
Anywhere But Here '99
Aparajito '58 ▸
The Apprenticeship of Duddy Kravitz '74 ▸
Au Revoir les Enfants '87 ▸
An Awfully Big Adventure '94
Babe '95 ▸
Baby It's You '82 ▸
Back Door to Heaven '39 ▸
Barnyard '06
Batman Begins '05 ▸
The Battle of Shaker Heights '03
Battling Bunyon '24
Beautiful Ohio '06
Beautiful Thing '95 ▸
Beshkempir the Adopted Son '98
Big '88 ▸
The Big Bet '85
The Big Red One '80 ▸
Billy Bathgate '91
The Birch Interval '78
Black Cloud '04
Black Peter '63
Blue Car '03 ▸
Blue Fin '78
Blue Jeans '78
The Blue Kite '93 ▸
The Blue Lagoon '80
Blue River '95
Blue Velvet '86 ▸
Bonjour Monsieur Shlomi '03 ▸
Borstal Boy '00
Boss' Son '78 ▸
The Boys in Company C '77
Boys Life '94
The Boys of 2nd Street Park '03 ▸
Brave New Girl '04
Breaking Away '79 ▸
Breaking Home Ties '87
Bridge to Terabithia '07
Brighton Beach Memoirs '86
A Bronx Tale '93 ▸
Brother to Brother '04
The Buddha of Suburbia '92 ▸
Buddy's Song '91
Buffalo Boy '04
Butterfly '98 ▸
By Way of the Stars '92
Calendar Girl '93
Can You Feel Me Dancing? '85
Can't Buy Me Love '87
Carnal Knowledge '71 ▸
Carry Me Home '04
Catherine Cookson's The Cinder Path '94
Catherine Cookson's The Dwelling Place '94
Catherine Cookson's The Glass Virgin '95
The Chicken Chronicles '77
China, My Sorrow '89
The Chorus '04
Christy '94
The Cider House Rules '99 ▸
Circle of Friends '94
City Boy '93 ▸
Civil War Diary '90 ▸
Class '83
Class of '44 '73
The Claw '27
Closely Watched Trains '66 ▸
Clowning Around 2 '93
Cocktail '88
Cold Sassy Tree '89 ▸
The Color of Money '86 ▸
Come and See '85 ▸
Come Undone '00
Coming Home '98
Coming Soon '99
Courage Mountain '89
Courtship '87 ▸
Cowboys & Angels '04 ▸
Crazy Moon '87
Cria '76 ▸
The Crossing '92
Crossing the Bridge '92
Crutch '04
A Cry in the Wild '90 ▸
Cry of Battle '63
Culpepper Cattle Co. '72
Dakota '88
Dallas 362 '03
Damien: Omen 2 '78
Dancer, Texas—Pop. 81 '98 ▸
The Dangerous Lives of Altar Boys '02 ▸
The Dark Side of the Sun '88
David Copperfield '70
David Copperfield '99
David Holzman's Diary '67 ▸
Dead Beat '94
Dead Poets Society '89 ▸
December '91
December Boys '07
The Deer Hunter '78 ▸
Desert Bloom '86 ▸
The Devil's Playground '76 ▸
Diner '82 ▸
Dirty Dancing '87 ▸
The Doe Boy '01
Dogfight '91 ▸
Dragstrip Girl '57
Dreamland '06 ▸
Driving Lessons '06
D3: The Mighty Ducks '96
Dutch Girls '87
Eat Drink Man Woman '94 ▸
Edge of Seventeen '99
The Education of Little Tree '97 ▸
Edward Scissorhands '90 ▸
Ellen Foster '97
Emanon '86
Eragon '06
Ernesto '79
Experience Preferred... But Not Essential '83
The Eyes of Youth '19
Eyes Right! '26
Family Prayers '91
Fandango '85
Fast Times at Ridgemont High '82 ▸
Father '67 ▸
Feelin' Screwy '90
Fellini Satyricon '69 ▸
Fierce People '05
Fiesta '95
The Fire in the Stone '85
First Affair '83
First Love '70
First Love '77
The First Time '69
The Flamingo Kid '84 ▸
For a Lost Soldier '93
For Love Alone '86
Forever '78
Forever Young '85
Four and a Half Women '05
The 400 Blows '59 ▸
Foxes '80
Freedom Is Paradise '89 ▸
Freud Leaving Home '91
Friends Forever '86 ▸
A Friendship in Vienna '88
Gas Food Lodging '92 ▸
A Generation '54 ▸
A Gentleman's Game '01
Get Real '99
The Getting of Wisdom '77
Gidget '59
Ginger Snaps '01
Girl '98
A Girl of the Limberlost '90
Girlfight '99 ▸
Girls Can't Swim '99
Go Tell It on the Mountain '84
Going All the Way '97
The Gold & Glory '88
The Good Humor Man '05
Goodbye Columbus '69 ▸
Goodbye, Miss 4th of July '88
Goodbye, My Lady '56
The Graduate '67 ▸
The Grass Harp '95
The Great Outdoors '88
The Great Santini '80 ▸
The Great Water '04
Gregory's Girl '80 ▸
Grown Ups '80
A Guide to Recognizing Your Saints '06
Hairspray '88 ▸
Hammers over the Anvil '91
Hangin' with the Homeboys '91 ▸
Happy Birthday, Gemini '80
Hard Choices '84 ▸
Harry Potter and the Order of the Phoenix '07
Hearts in Atlantis '01
Heathers '89 ▸
Heaven Help Us '85
A Hero Ain't Nothin' but a Sandwich '78
Higher Education '88
Hole in the Sky '95
Holy Girl '04 ▸
Holy Matrimony '94
Homeboy '88
Homework '82
The Horse '82 ▸
The Horsemen '70
Hot Moves '84
Hounddog '08
The Hour of the Star '85 ▸
House of D '04
How I Learned to Love Women '66
Huck and the King of Hearts '93
The Human Comedy '43 ▸
Hurricane Streets '96
I Capture the Castle '02
I Don't Want to Talk About It '94
I Know Why the Caged Bird Sings '79 ▸
I Love You, I Love You Not '97
I Vitelloni '53 ▸
If Looks Could Kill '91
Il Sorpasso '63
I'm Not Scared '03
In Her Shoes '05 ▸
In Praise of Older Women '78
In the Custody of Strangers '82 ▸
The Incredible Mrs. Ritchie '03
Indian Paint '64
The Inheritors '82
Introducing the Dwights '07
Inventing the Abbotts '97
Invisible Circus '00
The Islander '88
Jacob Have I Loved '88
Jerry Maguire '96 ▸
JFK: Reckless Youth '93
Joe the King '99
Joey '85
Johnny Be Good '88
Jory '72
The Journey of Jared Price '00
The Journey of Natty Gann '85 ▸
Just Looking '99
Kamikaze Girls '04
The Karate Kid '84 ▸
The Karate Kid: Part 2 '86
The Karate Kid: Part 3 '89
Keeping Up with the Steins '06
Kicking and Screaming '95 ▸
King of the Gypsies '78
King of the Hill '93 ▸
Kings Row '41 ▸
Kipperbang '82
The Kitchen Toto '87 ▸
La Boum '81
La Symphonie Pastorale '46 ▸
Labyrinth '86 ▸
The Last Prostitute '91
Late Summer Blues '87
The Lawrenceville Stories '88
Le Grand Chemin '87 ▸
Le Sexe des Etoiles '93
The Learning Tree '69
The Legend of Johnny Lingo '03
Les Mistons '57 ▸
L'Homme Blesse '83 ▸
Liam '00
L.I.E. '01
Life 101 '95
Like A Bride '94 ▸
The Lion King '94 ▸
Little Ballerina '47
A Little Romance '79 ▸
Little Women '49 ▸
Little Women '78
The Littlest Viking '94
The Long Day Closes '92 ▸
The Lords of Flatbush '74
Lost Legacy: A Girl Called Hatter Fox '77
A Lost Year '93
Love Film '70
Lover Girl '97
Lucas '86 ▸
Maid to Order '87
Malena '00
The Man from Snowy River '82
The Man in the Moon '91 ▸
A Man of Passion '88
The Man Without a Face '93
The Mango Tree '77
Marking Time '03
Martha and I '91 ▸
Matinee '92
Me and Orson Welles '09
Mean Creek '04 ▸
Mean Streets '73 ▸
The Member of the Wedding '52 ▸
The Member of the Wedding '97
Memoirs of a Geisha '05
Men of Ireland '38
Metropolitan '90 ▸
Mickey '48
A Midnight Clear '92 ▸
Milk Money '94
Mirrors '85
Mischief '85
Monika '52
Monsieur Ibrahim '03 ▸
More American Graffiti '79
Mosby's Marauders '66
The Mudge Boy '03
Murmur of the Heart '71 ▸
My American Cousin '85 ▸
My Apprenticeship '39 ▸
My Bodyguard '80 ▸
My Brilliant Career '79 ▸
My Girl '91
My Girl 2 '94
My Life As a Dog '85 ▸
My Life on Ice '02
My One and Only '09
My Summer of Love '05
My Tutor '82
My Universities '40 ▸
Mystic Pizza '88 ▸
New Waterford Girl '99
Next Stop, Greenwich Village '76 ▸

▸ = rated three bones or higher

Communists & Communism

Computers

Concentration/ Internment Camps

Concert Films

Contemporary Musicals

Contemporary Noir

▸ = rated three bones or higher

Flypaper '97
Following '99
Forever Mine '99
The Girl in a Swing '89
Goodbye, Lover '99
The Grifters '90 ▶
Guncrazy '92
Hammett '82
Hard Eight '96 ▶
The Hi-Lo Country '98
Hit Me '96
Hollywoodland '06
The Horseplayer '91
The Hot Spot '90
Husbands and Lovers '91
The Hustle '75
I Want You '98
Inevitable Grace '94
Jigsaw '99
Kill Me Again '89
The Kill-Off '90
Killing Zoe '94
Kiss of Death '94
Kiss Tomorrow Goodbye '00
L.A. Confidential '97 ▶
The Last Seduction '94 ▶
Le Cercle Rouge '70 ▶
Le Samourai '67 ▶
Let the Devil Wear Black '99
Lights in the Dusk '06
The Limey '99 ▶
A Little Trip to Heaven '05
Live Flesh '97 ▶
The Locusts '97
The Long Goodbye '73 ▶
The Lookout '07 ▶
Love Walked In '97
The Manchurian Candidate '62 ▶
Manhunter '86 ▶
Marlowe '69
Mercy Streets '00
The Million Dollar Hotel '99
Mirage '94
Mulholland Falls '95
The Music of Chance '93
Narrow Margin '90
Night Moves '75 ▶
9 1/2 Weeks '86
No Good Deed '02
No Way Out '87 ▶
Nobody '07
Novocaine '01
One False Move '91 ▶
Palmetto '98
Payback '98 ▶
The Perfect Sleep '08
Performance '70 ▶
Place Vendome '98 ▶
Promised Land '88 ▶
The Public Eye '92 ▶
Pulp Fiction '94 ▶
Purple Noon '60 ▶
Red Rock West '93 ▶
Redbelt '08 ▶
Reservoir Dogs '92 ▶
The Rich Man's Wife '96
River of Grass '94
Romeo Is Bleeding '93
The Salton Sea '02
sex, lies and videotape '89 ▶
Shattered '91
The Silence of the Lambs '91 ▶
Simpatico '99
Sin City '05
A Slight Case of Murder '99
So Close to Paradise '98
Something Wild '86
The Spanish Prisoner '97 ▶
Spare Me '92
Sticks '98
Stormy Monday '88
Taxi Driver '76 ▶
Tequila Sunrise '88
Things to Do in Denver When You're Dead '95 ▶
This World, Then the Fireworks '97
Three Monkeys '08
To Live & Die in L.A. '85
Track 29 '88
Trouble in Mind '86 ▶
True Believer '89
True Confessions '81 ▶
Twilight '98 ▶
Two Days in the Valley '96 ▶
The Two Jakes '90
2 Minutes Later '07
U-Turn '97
The Underneath '95 ▶
Union City '81
The Usual Suspects '95 ▶
The Walker '07
Watching the Detectives '07
When Will I Be Loved '04
Where the Truth Lies '05
Who'll Stop the Rain? '78 ▶
Wild at Heart '90 ▶
Wild Orchid '90
Wild Orchid 2: Two Shades of Blue '92
Wild Things '98
You Kill Me '07 ▶

Cooking

***see** Chefs; Edibles*

Cops

***see also** Alien Cops; Biopics: Cops & Robbers; Buddy Cops; Comic Cops; DEA; FBI; Future Cop; Historical Detectives; Loner Cops; Police Detectives; Private Eyes; Rogue Cops; Small-Town Sheriffs; Undercover Cops; Women Cops*

Above Suspicion '95
Abraxas: Guardian of the Universe '90
Absence of the Good '99
Ace of Hearts '08
Across 110th Street '72
Across the Line '00
Adrenalin: Fear the Rush '96
The Adventures of a Gnome Named Gnorm '93
Affliction '97 ▶
Against the Law '98
Alien Nation '88
Alone in the Neon Jungle '87
American Cop '94
American Gangster '07 ▶
American Justice '86
The Amsterdam Kill '78
Angel Eyes '01
Animal Instincts '92
Antibodies '05
Apartment Complex '98
Assault on Precinct 13 '76 ▶
At Gunpoint '90
Back in Action '94
Backlash '99
Backstreet Justice '93
Badge 373 '73
Ballbuster '89
Band of the Hand '86
Bandits '99
Bang '95
The Beast of the City '32
Before Morning '33
Belfast Assassin '84
Bellamy '81
Beretta's Island '92
Best Kept Secrets '88
Best Seller '87 ▶
Beverly Hills Cop '84
Beverly Hills Cop 2 '87
Beverly Hills Cop 3 '94
Beyond Forgiveness '94
Big Chase '54
Big Combo '55 ▶
The Big Easy '87 ▶
The Big Heat '53 ▶
Big Score '83
The Big Slice '90
Bitter Sweet '98
Black and White '99 ▶
Black & White '99
Black Day Blue Night '95
Black Eliminator '78
The Black Marble '79 ▶
Black Mask '96
Black Rain '89
Blacklight '98
Blackout '85
Blade '72
Blade Boxer '97
Blind Eye '06
Blind Faith '98
Blood for Blood '95
Blood on the Badge '92
Bloodfist 7: Manhunt '95
Bloodhounds '96
Bloodlines '05
Blowback '99
Blown Away '94
Blue Desert '91 ▶
Blue Flame '93
The Blue Lamp '49 ▶
Blue Thunder '83
The Blues Brothers '80 ▶
Blues Brothers 2000 '98
Bodily Harm '95
The Bone Collector '99
Bopha! '93 ▶
Border Blues '03
Border Patrol '01
The Boston Strangler '68
Brainscan '94
Brannigan '75
Brass '85
Breach of Trust '95
Bread, Love and Dreams '53
Breaking News '04
Breaking Point '94
Broken Badge '85 ▶
Brooklyn's Finest '09
Bullet Down Under '94
Bulletproof '96
Bunco '77
Busting '74
The Butterfly Effect 3: Revelation '09
Cafe Society '97
Captive '97
Carmen, Baby '66
Caroline at Midnight '93
The Carpathian Eagle '81
Carpool '96
A Case of Deadly Force '86 ▶
The Caveman's Valentine '01
Cement '99
The Chase '66
The Chase '91
Chiefs '83
Children of Hannibal '98
China Heat '90
China Moon '91
Chinatown Connection '90
The Chinatown Murders: Man against the Mob '89
Choice of Weapons '76
The Choirboys '77
Chungking Express '95 ▶
City Hall '95 ▶
City That Never Sleeps '53
Clayton County Line '78
Clockers '95 ▶
Cobra '86
Cold Blooded '00
Cold Front '89
Cold Light of Day '95
Cold Steel '87
Coldfire '90
Colors '88 ▶
Confessions of a Police Captain '72
Conflict of Interest '92
Coogan's Bluff '68 ▶
Cop '88
Cop and a Half '93
Cop-Out '91
Cops and Robbersons '94
Cornbread, Earl & Me '75
Cotton Comes to Harlem '70 ▶
Cover Me '95
Cracker: Best Boys '95 ▶
Cracker: Brotherly Love '95 ▶
Cracker: Men Should Weep '94
Cracker: To Be a Somebody '94
Cracker: True Romance '95 ▶
Crime Busters '78
Crime Story '93
The Crimson Rivers '01
The Crow '93
The Custodian '94
Danger Ahead '40
The Dark '94
Dark Before Dawn '89
Dark City '97
Dead Badge '94
Dead End '98
Dead Heart '96 ▶
Dead Heat '88
Dead to Rights '93
Deadly Breed '89
Deadly Conspiracy '91
Deadly Diamonds '91
Deadly Game '98
Deadly Hero '75 ▶
Deadly Sins '95
Deadly Surveillance '91
Death Shot '73
The Death Squad '73
Deceiver '97
Deceptions '90
Deep Cover '92
Deep Space '87
The Delicate Delinquent '56
Delta Heat '92
Demolition Man '93
The Designated Mourner '97
Detroit 9000 '73
Devil in a Blue Dress '95 ▶
Devil's Angels '67
The Devil's Own '96 ▶
The Devil's Undead '75
Devlin '92
Dirty Mind of Young Sally '72
Distant Justice '92
Diva '82 ▶
Dog Bite Dog '06
Dollman '90
Dollman vs Demonic Toys '93
Double Edge '97
Double Take '97
Double Trouble '91
Drowning Mona '00
Drying Up the Streets '76
Dying Game '94
East Palace, West Palace '96
Edison Force '05
Electra Glide in Blue '73 ▶
Evil Has a Face '96
Ex-Cop '93
Exorcist 3: Legion '90
Extreme Justice '93
Extreme Prejudice '87
Extreme Vengeance '90
An Eye for an Eye '81
Eyes of Laura Mars '78
Eyewitness '81
Eyewitness to Murder '93
Fair Game '95
Fallen '97
Family of Cops '95
Family of Cops 2: Breach of Faith '97
Family of Cops 3 '98
The Fast and the Furious '01
Fatal Chase '77
Fatal Chase '92
Fatal Error '83
Fatal Instinct '92
Felony '95
The Female Jungle '56
Fever '88
Fever '99
Final Combination '93
Final Embrace '92
Final Equinox '95
Firepower '93
Fireworks '97
First Degree '95
Flashpoint '84
Flatfoot '78
Flipping '96
The Formula '80
Fort Apache, the Bronx '81 ▶
Fortune Dane '86
44 Minutes: The North Hollywood Shootout '03
Foul Play '76
Frame by Frame '95
Frame Up '91
The French Connection '71 ▶
French Connection 2 '75 ▶
French Quarter Undercover '85
French Silk '94
Frequency '00
From Dusk Till Dawn 2: Texas Blood Money '98
Full Count '06
Full Eclipse '93
Full Exposure: The Sex Tape Scandals '89
Future Cop '76
Future Force '89
Fuzz '72
Gang in Blue '96
Gen-X Cops '99
Get On the Bus '96 ▶
The Glass Shield '95
The Glitter Dome '84
Glitz '88
Go '99 ▶
Go for It '83
Gone Are the Days '84
The Good Thief '03 ▶
Goodbye, Lover '99
Gorky Park '83 ▶
Guilty by Association '03
Hands of a Stranger '87
The Happy Face Murders '99
Hard Justice '95
The Hard Truth '94
Hard Vice '94
Hardcase and Fist '89
Hate '95 ▶
Hawkeye '88
He Walked by Night '48 ▶
Hear No Evil '93
Heart of Dragon '85
Hellbound '94
Heroes in Blue '39
High & Low '62 ▶
High Crime '73
High Noon '09
Highway Patrolman '91
Hollywood Vice Sqaud '86
Hologram Man '95
Homicide '91 ▶
Homicide: The Movie '00
The Hot Rock '70 ▶
Humanity '99
The Hunted Lady '77
I Take This Oath '40
The Ice House '97 ▶
Illegal in Blue '95
Illtown '96
In the Kingdom of the Blind the Man with One Eye Is King '94
Indecent Behavior '93
The Indian Runner '91
Indiscreet '98
The Informant '97 ▶
Innocent Blood '92
The Innocent Sleep '95
Inside Information '34
Interpol Connection '92
It Could Happen to You '94
It's the Rage '99
Jackie Brown '97 ▶
Jailbait '93
The January Man '89
Jennifer 8 '92
Jigsaw '71
John Carpenter's Ghosts of Mars '01
Johnny Skidmarks '97
Jumanji '95
Jungleground '95
Just Cause '94
K-911 '99
K-9000 '89
Kamikaze '89 '83 ▶
Karate Cop '91
Keaton's Cop '90
Keeper of the City '92
Kidnapped '87
The Kill Reflex '89
Killer Condom '95
The Killer's Edge '90
The Killing Gene '07
The Killing Mind '90
The Killing Time '87
Killing Time '97
Kinatay '09
Kiss and Tell '96
Kiss & Tell '99
Kiss of Death '47 ▶
Kiss or Kill '97
The Klansman '74
Knife in the Head '78
Kuffs '92
L.627 '92 ▶
L.A. Bounty '89
L.A. Heat '88
L.A. Vice '89
L.A. Wars '94
Ladykiller '92
Laguna Heat '87
Laser Moon '92
Last Man Standing '95
The Last Marshal '99
The Last of the Finest '90
The Last Stop '99
The Laughing Policeman '74
Law and Disorder '74 ▶
Legacy of Lies '92
Les Miserables '95
Les Miserables '97 ▶
Les Voleurs '96 ▶
Lethal Obsession '87
Lethal Seduction '97
Lightblast '85
Like a Puppet Out of Strings '05
The Limbic Region '96
The Lives of Others '06 ▶
Lockdown '90
Lone Star Law Men '42
Lords of the Street '08
Love '05
Love on the Run '85
Love the Hard Way '01
Mad Dog and Glory '93 ▶
Mad Max '80 ▶
Madigan '68 ▶
Magic Hunter '96
Magnolia '99 ▶
Malarek '89
Man from Mallorca '84
A Man in Uniform '93
The Man Inside '76
Man on a String '71
The Man on the Roof '76
Mardi Gras for the Devil '93
Martial Law '90
Martial Law 2: Undercover '91
Mask of Death '97
Matter of Trust '98
Maximum Force '92
The Memory of a Killer '03
Miami Beach Cops '93
Miami Blues '90
Miami Cops '89
Miami Vice '84
Midnight Ride '92
Midnight Witness '93
Mimic 2 '01
Mind, Body & Soul '92
A Mind to Kill '95
Mind Twister '93
The Missing Gun '02
Mission of Justice '92
Mr. Inside, Mr. Outside '74
Mr. Reliable: A True Story '95
Mistrial '96
Mitchell '75
Model by Day '94
Money to Burn '94
Monolith '93
Moonshine Highway '96
Mortal Challenge '97
Mosquitoman '05
Moving Violations '85
The Murder of Stephen Lawrence '99 ▶
Murder Without Motive '92
Murdered Innocence '94
My Husband's Secret Life '98
Mystery Date '91
Nails '92
The Naked City '48 ▶
The Narrow Margin '52 ▶
The New Centurions '72
New Jack City '91
New Police Story '04
New York Cop '94
New York Ripper '82
Next of Kin '89
Night Game '89
Night of the Cyclone '90
Night Partners '83
The Night Patrol '26
Night Patrol '85
Night Vision '97
Nightmare '91
Nightstalker '02
Ninja Vengeance '93
No Code of Conduct '98
No Escape, No Return '93
No Good Deed '02
No Place to Hide '93
Octopus 2: River of Fear '02
Off the Wall '82
The Offence '73 ▶
100 Feet '08
One Man Force '89
One Man Jury '78
One Tough Cop '98
Organized Crime & Triad Bureau '93
Othello '01 ▶
Out in Fifty '99

▶ = rated three bones or higher

Outside the Law '95
The Painted Lady '97 ▸
Pair of Aces '90
Paper Bullets '99
Past Perfect '98
Past Tense '94
Pendulum '69
Phoenix '98
P.I. Private Investigations '87
Picture Snatcher '33
Point of Impact '93
Police '85
Portraits of a Killer '95
Post Mortem '99
Prime Target '91
Prince of the City '81 ▸
Private Investigations '87
Probable Cause '95
Profile for Murder '96
Pronto '97
The Prophecy '95
The Proposal '00
Provoked '89
Prowler '51
Public Enemy '02
Puppet on a Chain '72
A Pure Formality '94
Q & A '90
The Quarry '98
Question of Honor '80
Rage and Honor 2: Hostile Takeover '93
Rainbow Drive '90
Random Hearts '99
Rapid Fire '92
Raw Nerve '99
Raw Target '95
The Razor: Sword of Justice '72
Reach the Rock '98
Recruits '86
Red Sun Rising '94
Redbelt '08 ▸
Regular Guys '96
Renaissance '06
Renfrew of the Royal Mounted '37
The Replacement Killers '98
Replicant '01
Return to Macon County '75
Return to Mayberry '85
The Right to Remain Silent '95
Riot in the Streets '96
Rising Sun '93 ▸
The Road '00
Rock House '88
Rogue Force '99
Roots of Evil '91
Route 9 '98
Rumble in the Streets '96
Runaway '84
The Runaway '00
Running on Karma '03
Running Scared '86
The Rutherford County Line '87
Sands of Sacrifice '21
Santa Fe '97
The Satan Killer '93
Saw 4 '07
Sawbones '95
Scanner Cop '94
Scanner Cop 2: Volkin's Revenge '94
Scanners: The Showdown '94
Scarred City '98
Sci-Fighters '96
Scream 3 '00
Season for Assassins '71
Self-Defense '83
Sgt. Kabukiman N.Y.P.D. '94
Serial Killer '95
Seven Seconds '05
Shadow Force '92
Shadow of a Scream '97
Shadowhunter '93
Shameless '94
Sharon's Secret '95
Shoot It Black, Shoot It Blue '74
Shoot to Kill '90
Shootfighter 2: Kill or Be Killed! '96
Short Time '90 ▸
The Shot '96
Sirens '99
Sirens '02
Siringo '94
S.I.S. '08
Sketch Artist '92
Sketch Artist 2: Hands That See '94
Skins '02
Skull: A Night of Terror '88
Slipstream '89
Slow Burn '90
A Small Killing '81
Smokey & the Judge '80
Snake Eyes '98
Snapdragon '93
Soggy Bottom U.S.A. '84
Solar Force '94
Son of the Pink Panther '93
Soul Patrol '80
Speed 2: Cruise Control '97
Speedtrap '78
The Spirit '08
Stamp of a Killer '87
Steele's Law '91
The Stendahl Syndrome '95
Stephano Quantestorie '93
The Stone Killer '73
Stonewall '95 ▸
Stop! or My Mom Will Shoot '92
Strange Days '95 ▸
Stranger by Night '94
Street Asylum '90
Street Crimes '92
Street Kings '08
Street War '76
Strike Force '75
Strip Search '97
Super Force '90
Super Fuzz '81
Supercop '92
Supercop 2 '93
Supervixens '75
Surveillance '08
Suspicious Agenda '94
S.W.A.T. '03
Sweet Trash '70
Sword of Honor '94
T-Force '94
The Take '90
Taking the Heat '93
Tar '97
The Taxman '98
Terminal Justice: Cybertech P.D. '95
Terror Stalks the Class Reunion '93
Theodore Rex '95
They Crawl '01
They Only Kill Their Masters '72
Three Blind Mice '02
Three Strikes '00
Tightrope '84 ▸
Till Death Do Us Part '92
A Time to Die '91
Timecop '94
Timecop 2: The Berlin Decision '03
To Protect and Serve '92
Too Fast, Too Young '96
Top of the Heap '72
Total Recall 2070: Machine Dreams '99
Traces of Red '92
Trancers '84
Trancers 2: The Return of Jack Deth '90
Trancers 3: Deth Lives '92
Trancers 4: Jack of Swords '93
Trancers 5: Sudden Deth '94
Truth or Consequences, N.M. '97
Tunnel Vision '95
Twelve '10
Twin Sisters '91
Twisted Justice '89
Two Days in the Valley '96 ▸
Two Small Bodies '93
Ultraviolet '98
Under Investigation '93
Under Oath '97
Undercover '87
Undercover '94
Undercover Cop '94
The Underground '97
Underground Terror '88
Unforgettable '96
Union Station '50
The Untold Story '93
Urban Crossfire '94
Vampire Cop '90
Vampire in Brooklyn '95
Vegas Vice '94
Vengeance '37
Vice '08
Vice Academy '88
Vice Academy 2 '90
Vice Academy 3 '91
Virtuosity '95
Walker: Texas Ranger: One Riot, One Ranger '93
The Warning '80
We Own the Night '07
The Wharf Rat '95
When Danger Follows You Home '97
Where's the Money, Noreen? '95
Whispers of White '93
White Cargo '96
The White Lioness '96
The Wicker Man '06
The Wild Pair '87
Witchcraft 6: The Devil's Mistress '94
The Young Americans '93
Youth of the Beast '63
Zipperface '92

Corporate Shenanigans

***see also** Advertising; Dying for a Promotion; Salespeople; Workin' for a Livin'*

The Abduction of Allison Tate '92
Ablaze '00
Acceptable Risks '86
The Alarmist '98
The Alchemists '99
All in a Night's Work '61
All My Sons '48 ▸
All My Sons '86 ▸
Anacondas: Trail of Blood '09
And Nothing But the Truth '82
Antitrust '00
Any Wednesday '66
The Apartment '60 ▸
April Fools '69
As Young As You Feel '51 ▸
Ask Any Girl '59
The Associate '79
The Associate '96
Au Pair 2: The Fairy Tale Continues '01
August '08
Avalanche '99
Avatar '09 ▸
Baby Geniuses '98
Bad Company '94
The Bad Sleep Well '60 ▸
The Bank '01
Barbarians at the Gate '93 ▸
Barbershop 2: Back in Business '04 ▸
BASEketball '98
The Battle of the Sexes '60 ▸
Beggars in Ermine '34
Behind Office Doors '31
The Best of Everything '59 ▸
The Bible and Gun Club '96
Big Business '88
Big Business Girl '31
The Big One '98
Big Trees '52 ▸
The Bikini Car Wash Company '90
The Bikini Car Wash Company 2 '92
Blonde Ambition '07
Blood Red '88
Body & Soul '93 ▸
Body Language '92
Boiler Room '00 ▸
Bombshell '97
Bone Eater '07
Boom Town '40
Boomerang '92
The Boss of It All '06
Boys Will Be Boys '97
Bright Leaf '50
Burning Daylight '28
The Business of Strangers '01
Buy & Cell '89
The Caller '08
Capitalism: A Love Story '09
The Capture of Bigfoot '79
The Carpetbaggers '64
Cash McCall '60
Catherine & Co. '76
Catwoman '04
Chairman of the Board '97
Changing Lanes '02 ▸
Chasing the Green '09
The China Syndrome '79 ▸
China White '91
C.H.O.M.P.S. '79
Circle of Power '83
A Civil Action '98
Class of Nuke 'Em High 2: Subhumanoid Meltdown '91
Clockwatchers '97
The Closet '00
The Coca-Cola Kid '84 ▸
Cold Turkey '71 ▸
The Colombian Connection '91
The Colony '95
Comedy of Power '06
Comic Book: The Movie '04 ▸
Consuming Passions '88
Corporate Affairs '90
Corporate Affairs '07
The Corporate Ladder '97
The Corporation '96
Cow Belles '06
Crime of Honor '85
The Crime of Monsieur Lange '36 ▸
Cyborg 2 '93
Cypher '02 ▸
Dark River: A Father's Revenge '90
Dark Streets '08
Daybreakers '09
The Daydreamer '75
Deadlier Than the Male '67
Deadly Business '86 ▸
Deadly Conspiracy '91
Dealers '89
Death Chase '87
Death Collector '89
Death Machine '95
Demonlover '02
The Devil & Miss Jones '41 ▸
The Devil's Advocate '97
Devil's Crude '71
Dinner for Schmucks '10
Disclosure '94
Do or Die '03
Dr. Dolittle '98
Dodsworth '36 ▸
Double Play '96
Dragonfight '90
Duplicity '09
Dutch Treat '86
Ebbtide '94
Edge of Darkness '10
The Efficiency Expert '92
Empire '02
Empire Records '95
The Empty Beach '85
End of the Line '88
Enron: The Smartest Guys in the Room '05 ▸
Erin Brockovich '00 ▸
Escape: Human Cargo '98 ▸
Eternity '90
Executive Koala '06 ▸
Executive Suite '54 ▸
The Family That Preys '08
Fast Food Nation '06 ▸
Fatal Confinement '64
Fatal Skies '90
Feel the Motion '86
Fierce Creatures '96
Fire Down Below '97
Firetrap '01
First Degree '98
The First $20 Million is Always the Hardest '02
Flash of Genius '08
The Flintstones '94
FM '78
Food, Inc. '08
For Love or Money '93
Ford: The Man & the Machine '87
Forest Warrior '95
Freaked '93
Frozen Assets '92
Gas '81
Gas Pump Girls '79
Get to Know Your Rabbit '72
Glengarry Glen Ross '92 ▸
Good Burger '97
Good Neighbor Sam '64 ▸
Goodfellas '90 ▸
Gorgeous '99
Gremlins 2: The New Batch '90 ▸
Gung Ho '85
Hackers '95
Haiku Tunnel '00
Halloween 3: Season of the Witch '82
Hamlet '00 ▸
Happy Hour '87
The Harder They Come '72
Hardwired '09
Head Office '86
Heartbeat Detector '07
Her Husband's Affairs '47
Herbie Rides Again '74
Hey Arnold! The Movie '02
His Girl Friday '40 ▸
Hold the Dream '86
Home Town Story '51
Hoot '06
Hot Chocolate '92
How the West Was Fun '95
How to Get Ahead in Advertising '89 ▸
How to Succeed in Business without Really Trying '67 ▸
The Hucksters '47 ▸
The Hudsucker Proxy '93 ▸
I Heart Huckabees '04
I Love Trouble '94
I Witness '03
If I Were Rich '33
In Good Company '04 ▸
In the Company of Men '96
Indio 2: The Revolt '92
Infected '08
The Informant! '09
The Inheritance '76
The Insider '99 ▸
The International '09
Iron Man '08 ▸
Iron Man 2 '10
Ivory Tower '97
Jack and the Beanstalk: The Real Story '01
Janice Beard '99
Joe Somebody '01
John Grisham's The Rainmaker '97
Johnny Mnemonic '95
Journey to Spirit Island '92
The Kansan '43
Kids in the Hall: Brain Candy '96
Killer Wave '07
A Kiss Before Dying '91
La Truite '83 ▸
Ladies Who Do '63
Land of Promise '74
The Last Hour '91
The Last Time '06
The Late Shift '96
The Lavender Hill Mob '51 ▸
Lawnmower Man 2: Beyond Cyberspace '95
Le Bonheur Est Dans le Pre '95
Legal Deceit '95
Les Destinees '00
Let the Devil Wear Black '99
Letter to My Killer '95
Life Stinks '91
Limit Up '89
The List '07
The Listening '06
Little Bigfoot '96
Little Giant '46
Lloyds of London '36 ▸
Local Hero '83 ▸
Looney Tunes: Back in Action '03
The Loved One '65
Ma and Pa Kettle at Waikiki '55
Major League '89
Mama, There's a Man in Your Bed '89 ▸
The Man in the Gray Flannel Suit '56
The Man in the White Suit '51 ▸
The Man Inside '90
The Manchurian Candidate '04 ▸
Married to It '93
Material Girls '06
A Matter of WHO '62
Maxed Out: Hard Times, Easy Credit and the Era of Predatory Lenders '06
Meet Joe Black '98
Megaville '91
Memron '04
Michael Clayton '07 ▸
Micmacs '09
Millions '90
Miss Grant Takes Richmond '49
Missionary Man '07
Mr. Accident '99
Mr. Average '06
Mr. Destiny '90
Mo' Money '92
A Model Employee '02
Monkey Hustle '77
Monsters, Inc. '01 ▸
Moola '07
Moon 44 '90
Morals for Women '31
Mutants '08
Naked Gun 2 1/2: The Smell of Fear '91
Network '76 ▸
Never 2 Big '98
New Rose Hotel '98
Night of January 16th '41
The Night They Saved Christmas '87
9 to 5 '80
No Marriage Ties '33
No Room to Run '78
No Smoking '55
No Time to Die '84
Noble House '88
Nowhere to Run '93
Office Killer '97
Office Space '98
Oktober '98
One, Two, Three '61 ▸
Open Season '95
Other People's Money '91
The Other Side of Midnight '77
Out Cold '01
Outfoxed: Rupert Murdoch's War on Journalism '04 ▸
Outland '81
Overdrawn at the Memory Bank '83
The Pajama Game '57 ▸
The Paper '94 ▸
Parrish '61
Patterns '56 ▸
Paycheck '03
Perfume '01
The Pirates of Silicon Valley '99
Playback '95
The Player '92 ▸
Pootie Tang '01
Power '86
Primal Scream '87
The Prime Gig '00
The Prince '95
Private Parts '96
Private Wars '93
The Promotion '08
A Public Affair '62
P.U.N.K.S. '98
Purpose '02
Putney Swope '69 ▸
The Queen of Mean '90
Quicksand '01
Quicksand: No Escape '91
Race the Sun '96
Rancid Aluminium '00
Ravenhawk '95
Red Ensign '34
The Reluctant Agent '89
Return Fire '88
Richie Rich '94
Rick '03
Rising Sun '93 ▸
RoboCop '87 ▸
RoboCop 2 '90
RoboCop 3 '91
Robots '05
Roger & Me '89 ▸
Rogue Trader '98
Rollover '81
Sabrina '95

▸ = *rated three bones or higher*

Sahara '05
Santa with Muscles '96
Scrooged '88
The Search for John Gissing '01
The Secret of My Success '87
The Secretary '94
Secretary '02 ►
Sensations of 1945 '44
Shadow of China '91 ►
Shark Swarm '08
The Shawshank Redemption '94 ►
She Hate Me '04
Shining Star '75
A Shock to the System '90 ►
Side Effects '05
Silicon Towers '99
The Silver Horde '30
The Simple Life of Noah Dearborn '99
Sing Me a Love Song '37
Sins '85
The 6th Day '00
Ski Bum '75
Skyscraper Souls '32 ►
Smilla's Sense of Snow '96
Solid Gold Cadillac '56 ►
Solitary Man '10
Soul Assassin '01
The Spanish Prisoner '97 ►
Stand-In '37 ►
The State Within '06
Stormy Monday '88
The Story of O, Part 2 '87
Strange Bedfellows '65
Strange Brew '83
Strange Confession '45 ►
The Strongest Man in the World '75
The Summit '08
Sunshine State '02 ►
Swimming with Sharks '94 ►
Switching Channels '88
Synapse '95
Taffin '88
Take This Job & Shove It '81
The Taste of Others '00 ►
A Taxing Woman '87 ►
The Temp '93
There Will Be Blood '07 ►
They All Kissed the Bride '42
They Drive by Night '40 ►
3 Ninjas Knuckle Up '95
Tiger Heart '96
Tin Men '87
Tommy Boy '95
Topaze '33 ►
Topaze '51 ►
The Toxic Avenger, Part 3: The Last Temptation of Toxie '89
Toys '92
Trading Places '83
Tucker: The Man and His Dream '88 ►
The TV Set '06
Two Weeks Notice '02
Undercurrent '46
The Uppercrust '81
Utilities '83
Vendetta '99
Virus '96
The Void '01
Vortex '81
Wal-Mart: The High Cost of Low Price '05 ►
Wall Street '87 ►
Wall Street Cowboy '39
War, Inc. '08
Washington Affair '77
The Way We Live Now '02
Weapons of Mass Distraction '97
Weekend at Bernie's '89
Weekend at Bernie's 2 '93
The Wheeler Dealers '63 ►
Which Way Is Up? '77
White Mile '94
Who Killed the Electric Car? '06
Who's Who '78
Wilder '00
Wolf '94
A Woman's World '54 ►
Working Girl '88 ►
The World Gone Mad '33
The World Moves On '34
The Wrong Woman '95
Yella '07 ►
You've Got Mail '98

Courtroom Drama

see *Law & Lawyers; Order in the Court*

Cousins

see also *Aunts & Uncles, Nieces & Nephews; Brothers & Sisters; Family Ties*

ABC Stage 67: Truman Capote's A Christmas Memory '66
The Addams Family '91
The Age of Innocence '93 ►
Airborne '93
Almost Strangers '01 ►
American Cousins '02
American Pie Presents: Beta House '07
Arsenic and Old Lace '44 ►
Barbershop 2: Back in Business '04 ►
Barcelona '94 ►
Black Magic '92
Blanche Fury '48
Blood & Chocolate '07
Blood Relatives '77
Body Count '97
Born to Be Bad '50
Brighton Beach Memoirs '86
The Buttercup Chain '70
Bye-Bye '96
Cafe Romeo '91
The Camomile Lawn '92
Catherine Cookson's The Black Candle '92
Cheech and Chong's Next Movie '80
Coffee and Cigarettes '03 ►
Corky of Gasoline Alley '51
Cousin, Cousine '76 ►
The Cousins '59 ►
Cousins '89 ►
Desperate Motives '92
Doctor Zhivago '03
Dragonwyck '46
Dreaming About You '92
The Dukes of Hazzard '05
First Love '39
The Four Horsemen of the Apocalypse '21 ►
The Four Horsemen of the Apocalypse '62
Friday After Next '02
Go for Zucker '05
The Godfather, Part 3 '90 ►
Going Greek '01
The Good Son '93
Gothic '87 ►
The Great Outdoors '88
The Groomsmen '06
The Guru '02
A Guy Thing '03
The Heartbreak Kid '07
The Hellfire Club '61
The Hillside Strangler '89
The Hillside Strangler '04
I'll Be Seeing You '44
The Importance of Being Earnest '52 ►
The Importance of Being Earnest '02
The Intended '02
Invisible Mom 2 '99
Jude '96 ►
Jude the Obscure '71
Kiss of Death '94
Kissin' Cousins '64
Little Old New York '23
Madhouse '90
Mansfield Park '99
Mansfield Park '07
Maryam '00
Men Cry Bullets '00
Miss Firecracker '89 ►
Money from Home '53
My American Cousin '85 ►
My Baby's Daddy '04
My Cousin Vinny '92 ►
Nanny McPhee 2 '10
National Lampoon's Christmas Vacation '89
National Lampoon's Vacation '83 ►
Next Friday '00
Nora's Hair Salon 2: A Cut Above '08
On Guard! '03 ►
One Night at McCool's '01
Phat Girlz '06
The Players Club '98 ►
The Pope of Greenwich Village '84
Portrait of a Lady '67
Portrait of a Lady '96 ►
Prisoner of Zenda '37 ►
Rabbit-Proof Fence '02 ►
Ratas, Ratones, Rateros '99
Reducing '31
The Rugrats Movie '98 ►
The Secret Garden '49 ►
The Secret Garden '84
The Secret Garden '87 ►
The Secret Garden '93
Slums of Beverly Hills '98 ►
Smother '08
Sour Grapes '98
Stranger than Paradise '84 ►
Striking Distance '93
Summer of Fear '78
Traveller '96 ►
Twelfth Night '96
Under Capricorn '82
Vegas Vacation '96
We're No Angels '55 ►
West of Here '02
The Yards '00

Creepy Houses

The Abandoned '06
An American Werewolf in Paris '97
The Amityville Horror '79
Amityville 2: The Possession '82
Amityville 3: The Demon '83
Amityville 4: The Evil Escapes '89
The Amityville Curse '90
The Amityville Horror '05
Amityville 1992: It's About Time '92
Angel of the Night '98
The Attic '06
The Bat Whispers '30
Believe '99
Beneath '07
Beyond Darkness '92
Beyond Evil '80
The Black Castle '52
The Black Cat '41
Black Cat '90
The Black Widow '05
Blondie Has Trouble '40
Blood Island '68
Blood Legacy '73
Blue Blood '73
Bones '01
Burnt Offerings '76
Candles at Nine '44
Carnage '84
Casper '95 ►
Castle Freak '95
Castle in the Desert '42
Castle of Blood '64
Castle of the Living Dead '64
The Cat and the Canary '79
Celine and Julie Go Boating '74
Cellar Dweller '87
The Changeling '80
Chasing Sleep '00
Chronicle of the Raven '04
Clive Barker's Book of Blood '08
Cold Creek Manor '03
The Collector '09
The Colony '95
Contagion '87
The Cradle '06
The Craft '96
Crazed '82
Crescendo '69
Cthulhu Mansion '91
Dark Mirror '07
Dark Water '02
Darkness '02
Dead Birds '04
A Dead Calling '06
Deadline '09
Demon Seed '77 ►
Demon Wind '90
The Devil's Mercy '07
The Diary of Ellen Rimbauer '03
Die Sister, Die! '74
Dolls '87
Don't Be Afraid of the Dark '73
The Doorway '00
Dragonwyck '46
Dream Demon '88
Dream House '98
Endless Night '71
The Evictors '79
The Evil '78
Evil Laugh '86
Evil Toons '90
The Fall of the House of Usher '49
The Fall of the House of Usher '60 ►
Fatally Yours '95
Fear in the Night '47 ►
Flowers in the Attic '87
For Sale by Owner '09
Forever: A Ghost of a Love Story '92
Francis in the Haunted House '56
Fright House '89
Fright Night '85
Funnyman '94
The Ghastly Ones '68
The Ghost and Mr. Chicken '66
The Ghost Breakers '40 ►
Ghost in the Invisible Bikini '66
The Ghost of Dragstrip Hollow '59
Girls School Screamers '86
The Glass House '01
Goblin '93
The Good Witch '08
Great Expectations '97
Grindstone Road '07
The Grudge '04
The Grudge 2 '06
Halloween: Resurrection '02
Haunted '95
The Haunted Mansion '03
The Haunting '63 ►
The Haunting '99
The Haunting in Connecticut '09
The Haunting of Hell House '99
The Haunting of Marsten Manor '07
The Heirloom '05
Home Movie '08
House '86 ►
House 2: The Second Story '87
House 4: Home Deadly Home '91
House of Darkness '48
House of Mystery '34
House of 9 '05
The House of Secrets '37
House of the Dead '78
The House of the Devil '09 ►
House of the Living Dead '73
House of the Long Shadows '82
House of the Rising Sun '87
The House of the Seven Gables '40
The House of Usher '88
The House of Usher '06
House on Haunted Hill '58
House on Haunted Hill '99
The House on Tombstone Hill '92
The House that Bled to Death '81
The House that Dripped Blood '71
The House that Vanished '73
House Where Evil Dwells '82
The Innocents '61 ►
Ju-On 2 '00
Killer Pad '06
Knocking on Death's Door '99
La Chute de la Maison Usher '28 ►
Last Hour '08
The Legend of Hell House '73 ►
Malice '93
The Mephisto Waltz '71 ►
The Messengers '07
Midnight Bayou '09
Monster House '06 ►
Monsters Crash the Pajama Party '65
Mother's Day '80
Mouse Hunt '97 ►
Munster, Go Home! '66
Murder by Death '76
Murder Mansion '70
The Nesting '80
Nevermore '07
Next of Kin '82
Night Nurse '77
Night of the Demons '09
Night of the Demons 2 '94
Office Killer '97
The Old Dark House '32 ►
The Orphanage '07 ►
The Others '01 ►
Panic Room '02
Paperhouse '89 ►
Paranoiac '62
The People under the Stairs '91
The Perverse Countess '73
The Phantom '31
Psycho '60 ►
Psycho '98
Psycho 2 '83
Psycho 3 '86
Psycho 4: The Beginning '90
The Raven '07
Rest in Pieces '87
Restraint '08
Return to House on Haunted Hill '07
Revenge in the House of Usher '82
The Rocky Horror Picture Show '75 ►
Rooms for Tourists '04
The St. Francisville Experiment '00
Salem's Lot '79
Scary Movie 2 '01
The Screaming Skull '58
Secret Window '04
Seven Days to Live '01
The Shining '80
Shock '79
Silent Scream '80
Sister, Sister '87
The Skeleton Key '05
The Skeptic '09
Smart House '00
Spectre '96
Spirit Lost '96
Spookies '85
Stephen King's Rose Red '02
Stormswept '95
A Strange and Deadly Occurrence '74
Superstition '82
Tangled Destinies '32
Teenage Exorcist '93
Terror House '97
Terror in the Haunted House '58
Terror Tract '00
Things 2 '97
13 Ghosts '60
13 Ghosts '01
Three Cases of Murder '55 ►
Treasure of Fear '45
The Uninvited '44 ►
Visions of Evil '75
Warlock 3: The End of Innocence '98
Web of the Spider '70
What a Carve-Up! '62
Who Killed Doc Robbin? '48
Witchouse '99
Witchouse 2: Blood Coven '00
The Wyvern Mystery '00

Crime & Criminals

see *Biopics: Cops & Robbers; Crime Drama; Crime Sprees; Crimes of Passion; Disorganized Crime; Frame-Ups; Fugitives; Gangs; Grand Theft Auto; Heists; Hit Men/Women; Juvenile Delinquents; Killer Spouses; Organized Crime; Scams, Stings & Cons; Serial Killers; Smuggler's Blues; True Crime; Urban Drama; Vigilantes*

Crime Doesn't Pay

see also *Crime Drama; Crimedy; Disorganized Crime; Heists*

Alpha Dog '06
Armored '09
The Bank Job '08 ►
Blue Blood '07
Bookies '03
Burnt Money '00
Carnival of Wolves '96
City on Fire '87
Crime Wave '54
The Devil Is a Sissy '36
Double Indemnity '44 ►
The Elder Son '06
Federal Hill '94
Fool's Gold: The Story of the Brink's-Mat Robbery '92
44 Minutes: The North Hollywood Shootout '03
The Front Line '06
Graduation '07
Hero Wanted '08
How to Rob a Bank '07
Invisible Stripes '39
Julia '08
The Killing '56 ►
Klepto '03
The Ladykillers '04
Lansdown '01
Le Deuxieme Souffle '66
Lift '01
Living & Dying '07
The Lookout '07 ►
Love Is Colder Than Death '69
Macbeth '06
Nobel Son '08
Ocean's 11 '60
The Poker Club '08
The Postman Always Rings Twice '46 ►
The Postman Always Rings Twice '81
Pray '05
Pushover '54
The Red Lily '24
RocknRolla '08
Seance '00
A Slight Case of Murder '38
Sympathy for Mr. Vengeance '02 ►
T Bone N Weasel '92
Tread Softly Stranger '58
Two Tough Guys '03
Underworld USA '61
Vengeance '80
Young America '32

Crime Drama

see also *Drama*

Abandoned '47

► = *rated three bones or higher*

▶ = rated three bones or higher

What Doesn't Kill You '08
When the Sky Falls '99
Where the Sidewalk Ends '50
Whipsaw '35
Whirlpool '49
Whiteout '09
Without Evidence '96
Witness to the Mob '98
The Wounds '98
Wozzeck '47
The Yards '00
Young Adam '03 ▸
The Young Americans '93
Zodiac '07

Crime Sprees

see also Fugitives; Lovers on the Lam
America's Deadliest Home Video '91
Attack the Gas Station '99
Baise Moi '00
The Big Bounce '69
Bonnie & Clyde '67 ▸
Border Radio '88
Born Killers '05
The Boys Next Door '85
Burning Life '94
Butterfly Kiss '94
Cannonball Run Europe: The Great Escape '05
The Chant of Jimmie Blacksmith '78 ▸
Cop Killers '73
Cracker: Best Boys '95 ▸
Crackers '84
The Day of the Wolves '71
Enemy Gold '93
Explosion '69
Fatal Bond '91
15 Minutes '01
Flash & Firecat '75
Fudoh: The New Generation '96
Fun With Dick and Jane '05
Heat '95 ▸
High Rolling in a Hot Corvette '77
Idiot Box '97
In Cold Blood '96
Jessi's Girls '75
Lewis and Clark and George '97
Love and a .45 '94
Love Is Colder Than Death '69
Mad Dog Killer '77
Marshal Law '96
Messidor '77
Murder One '88
Naked Youth '59
Natural Born Killers '94
Normal Life '96
On the Run '73
The One '01
One Way Out '95
Piano Man '96
Public Enemies '96
Public Enemies '09
Rampage '87
Retribution '06
Road Kill USA '93
Saw '04
Saw 2 '05
Set It Off '96
She Came on the Bus '69
Shopping '93
Stander '03
Steelyard Blues '73
Sworn Enemies '96
Takers '10
That Sinking Feeling '79 ▸
Thieves Like Us '74 ▸
The Tie That Binds '95
Too Fast, Too Young '96
Twin Town '97
Virtuosity '95
Waist Deep '06
When Brendan Met Trudy '00 ▸
The Whole Town's Talking '35 ▸
Why Does Herr R. Run Amok? '69
The Wrong Road '37

Crimedy

see also Comic Cops; Disorganized Crime
Analyze That '02
Analyze This '98 ▸
Avenging Angelo '02
Beethoven's Big Break '08
Betsy's Wedding '90
Big Nothing '06
Big Trouble '02
Blonde and Blonder '07
Break '09
The Brooklyn Heist '08
The Brothers Bloom '09
Burn After Reading '08
The Busy Body '67
Carry On Matron '72
Chaos & Cadavers '03
Christmas in Wonderland '07
Cop Out '10
Corky Romano '01
Crazy on the Outside '10
The Crew '00
Criminal Ways '03
Dead Fish '04
Dead Lenny '06
Dog Gone '08
8 Heads in a Duffel Bag '96
Fakers '04
First Sunday '08
Forget About It '06
Friends and Family '01
Get Shorty '95 ▸
Gigli '03
Hoodlum & Son '03
Horror Island '41
The Inveterate Bachelor '58
The Jerky Boys '95
Kaleidoscope '66
Kangaroo Jack '02
Knockaround Guys '01
Larceny, Inc. '42
Lies & Alibis '06
Mad Dog and Glory '93 ▸
Mad Money '08
Mafia! '98
The Maiden Heist '08
The Man Who Wouldn't Die '42
Married to the Mob '88 ▸
The Mexican '01
Micmacs '09
My Mom's New Boyfriend '08
A New Wave '07
Next Day Air '09
Ocean's Thirteen '07 ▸
One More Time '70
Oscar '91
Paul Blart: Mall Cop '09
Pineapple Express '08 ▸
Postman's Knock '62
Prizzi's Honor '85 ▸
Robin-B-Hood '06
RocknRolla '08
Strictly Sinatra '01
Table One '00
They Met in a Taxi '36
The Tiger Woman '45
The Trygon Factor '66
The Undercover Woman '46
The Wendell Baker Story '05
The Whole Nine Yards '00
You Move You Die '07

Crimes of Passion

The Amy Fisher Story '93
Backfire '88
Bad Boy Bubby '93
Being at Home with Claude '92
The Big Clock '48 ▸
Bizarre '87
Blood Vows: The Story of a Mafia Wife '87
The Blue Dahlia '46 ▸
Born to Kill '47 ▸
Casque d'Or '52 ▸
Casualties of Love: The "Long Island Lolita" Story '93
China Moon '91
Concealed Weapon '94
Cracker: True Romance '95 ▸
Crime of Passion '57
The Crucible '96 ▸
A Dark Adapted Eye '93 ▸
Deadbolt '92
Deception '46 ▸
Diary '06
Dupont Lajoie '74
Fatal Attraction '87 ▸
For Your Love Only '79
The Gingerbread Man '97
The Girl '86
Homicidal Impulse '92
I Love You to Death '90
Intimate Relations '95
Jade '95
Knots '05
The Last Dance '93
Lethal Lolita—Amy Fisher: My Story '92
Love and Hate: A Marriage Made in Hell '90
The Love Flower '20
Make Haste to Live '54
The Man in the Attic '94
The Mask of Diijon '46
Men Are Not Gods '37
Murder in New Hampshire: The Pamela Smart Story '91
Murder Rap '87
Niagara '52
Passion '92
The People vs. Jean Harris '81 ▸
The Preppie Murder '89
Rancid '04
Roadhouse Girl '53
Secret Beyond the Door '48
Sex Crimes '92
Sharon's Secret '95
The Shooting Party '77
Single White Female '92
This World, Then the Fireworks '97
To Die For '95 ▸
Tomorrow Never Comes '77
Victim of Beauty '91
The Walls of Malapaga '49
The Watcher in the Attic '76
Woman in the Window '44 ▸
The Worldly Madonna '22
Wozzeck '47

Criminally Insane

see also Crime Sprees; Sanity Check; Torn in Two (or More)
Criminally Insane '75
The Dark Knight '08 ▸
Diary '06
High Tension '03
Last Resort '09
Ricochet '91 ▸
Shutter Island '09 ▸
Son of Sam '08
Unbreakable '00

The Crusades

The Adventures of Robin Hood '38 ▸
King Richard and the Crusaders '54
Kingdom of Heaven '05 ▸
Lionheart '90
Robin and Marian '76
Robin Hood: Prince of Thieves '91

Cuba

see also Red Scare
Assault of the Rebel Girls '59
Before Night Falls '00 ▸
Che '08
The Company '07
Company Man '00
Cuba '79 ▸
Cuban Blood '03
Dance with Me '98
Death of a Bureaucrat '66 ▸
Dirty Dancing: Havana Nights '04
A Few Good Men '92 ▸
Fidel '02 ▸
For Love or Country: The Arturo Sandoval Story '00
The Godfather, Part 2 '74 ▸
Guantanamera '95 ▸
Guantanamero '07
Havana '90
Hello, Hemingway '90
Key Largo '48 ▸
Lansky '99
The Last Supper '76 ▸
Letters from the Park '88 ▸
The Lost City '05
Memories of Underdevelopment '68
The Motorcycle Diaries '04 ▸
The Old Man and the Sea '58 ▸
The Old Man and the Sea '90
Original Sin '01
Our Man in Havana '59 ▸
A Paradise Under the Stars '99
The Perez Family '94
Plato's Run '96
Rough Riders '97
Ruby '92
Scarface '83 ▸
Sicko '07
Strawberry and Chocolate '93 ▸
Tamango '59
Thirteen Days '00 ▸
Up to a Certain Point '83

Cubicle Hell

see also Bad Bosses; Workin' for a Livin'
Clockwatchers '97
He Was a Quiet Man '07
Office Space '98
Tokyo Sonata '09 ▸

Cults

see also Occult; Satanism
Alien Nation: Millennium '96
Bad Dreams '88
Bandh Darwaza '90
Batman Begins '05 ▸
Because of the Cats '74
The Believers '87
Believers '07
Beware! Children at Play '95
Blinded by the Light '82
Blood Clan '91
Bloodbath '76
Borderland '07
Burial of the Rats '95
Chain of Souls '00
Children of the Corn 2: The Final Sacrifice '92
Cobra Woman '44
Cthulhu '08
Cult of the Cobra '55
The Dark Secret of Harvest Home '78
Deadly Blessing '81
Death of an Angel '86
The Deceivers '88
The Devil's Prey '01
Divided by Hate '96
Fatal Passion '94
Force: Five '81
Forever Evil '87
The Guyana Tragedy: The Story of Jim Jones '80
Hellraiser: Deader '05
Helter Skelter '76
Helter Skelter Murders '71
Holy Smoke '99
The House on Todville Road '95
In the Line of Duty: Ambush in Waco '93
Isaac Asimov's Nightfall '00
The Lightning Incident '91
Lord of Illusions '95
The Loved One '65
The Manson Family '04
The Mephisto Waltz '71 ▸
Mind, Body & Soul '92
Mindstorm '01
Next One '84
The Night God Screamed '71
Night of the Death Cult '75
Postal '07
Purana Mandir '84 ▸
Putney Swope '69 ▸
The Pyx '73 ▸
Raging Angels '95
The Reincarnate '71
Rest in Pieces '87
Revenge '86
Sabaka '55
Safe '95 ▸
Savage Messiah '02
Servants of Twilight '91
Shock 'Em Dead '90
The Snake Hunter Strangler '66
The Snake People '68
Soul's Midnight '06
The Spellbinder '88
Split Image '82 ▸
Steps from Hell '92
The Stranglers of Bombay '60
They Crawl '01
Thou Shalt Not Kill...Except '87
Ticket to Heaven '81 ▸
Treasure of the Four Crowns '82
Ultrachrist! '03
Withnail and I '87 ▸
Yeti: A Love Story '08

Culture Clash

ABCD '99
American Adobo '02
American Fusion '05
An American Rhapsody '01 ▸
American Venus '07
Amreeka '09 ▸
At Play in the Fields of the Lord '91 ▸
Babe: Pig in the City '98
Babel '06 ▸
The Baby Dance '98 ▸
The Beautiful Country '04
Before the Rains '07
The Bengali Night '88
The Beverly Hillbillies '93
Beverly Hills Chihuahua '08
Beyond Honor '05
Black Robe '91 ▸
Borat: Cultural Learnings of America for Make Benefit Glorious Nation of Kazakhstan '06 ▸
Breaking and Entering '06
Bride & Prejudice '04
Bringing Down the House '03
The Brother from Another Planet '84 ▸
Brothers in Trouble '95
Cabaret '72 ▸
Carla's Song '97
Caterina in the Big City '03
Catfish in Black Bean Sauce '00
The Chateau '01
Chicken Tikka Masala '05
Chutney Popcorn '99
City of Ghosts '03
City of Joy '92
The Class '08
The Comfort of Strangers '91 ▸
Coneheads '93
Conrack '74 ▸
The Cookout '04
Crash '05 ▸
crazy/beautiful '01
Crocodile Dundee '86 ▸
Crocodile Dundee in Los Angeles '01
Dark Matter '07
Dead Heart '96 ▸
Deliverance '72 ▸
Devdas '55 ▸
Devdas '02 ▸
Did You Hear About the Morgans? '09
Down in the Delta '98 ▸
The Dreamers '03
East Is East '99 ▸
The Emerald Forest '85 ▸
Encino Man '92
The Europeans '79 ▸
Everything is Illuminated '05 ▸
The Family Stone '05
The Fast and the Furious: Tokyo Drift '06
For Richer or Poorer '97
The Foul King '00
G '02
George of the Jungle '97 ▸
Georgia Rule '07
Gonzo: The Life and Work of Dr. Hunter S. Thompson '08 ▸
Gorillas in the Mist '88 ▸
The Great New Wonderful '06
Green Dragon '01
Greystoke: The Legend of Tarzan, Lord of the Apes '84
The Guru '02
Heart of Light '97
Heat and Dust '82 ▸
Hello Goodbye '08
Holy Man '98
Hotel Colonial '88
House of Angels '92
I Want to Go Home '89
Just Visiting '01
The Last Samurai '03 ▸
Late Marriage '01
L'Auberge Espagnole '02 ▸
Lawrence of Arabia '62 ▸
Le Divorce '03
Leningrad Cowboys Go America '89
Like A Bride '94 ▸
Lila Says '04
The Lost Child '00
Malibu's Most Wanted '03
Marigold '07
Marking Time '03
Maryam '00
Meet the Fockers '04
Meet the Parents '00 ▸
The Mission '86 ▸
Mississippi Masala '92 ▸
Mister Johnson '91 ▸
Mixing Nia '98
Moonlighting '82 ▸
Moscow on the Hudson '84 ▸
The Namesake '06 ▸
The Nephew '97
One Long Night '07
The Other End of the Line '08
Our Family Wedding '10
Outsourced '06
A Passage to India '84 ▸
Pathfinder '07
Pizzicata '96
Quigley Down Under '90
Red Doors '05
Rescue from Gilligan's Island '78
River Queen '05
Rock My World '02
Rodgers & Hammerstein's South Pacific '01
Rush Hour '98
Saving Face '04
The Science of Sleep '06
Shadow Magic '00
Shanghai Knights '03
Shanghai Noon '00
The Sheltering Sky '90 ▸
Shogun '80 ▸
Snow Dogs '02
The Snow Walker '03
Someone Else's America '96 ▸
Songcatcher '99 ▸
South Pacific '58 ▸
Spanglish '04
Splash '84
Starman '84 ▸
Strangers with Candy '06
Swept from the Sea '97
Thunderheart '92 ▸
Tokyo Cowboy '94
2 Brothers & a Bride '03
Uncle Nino '03
Wasabi '01
Wassup Rockers '06
West Is West '87
Witness '85 ▸
A Woman of the World '25
Wondrous Oblivion '06 ▸
Yes '04
Zorba the Greek '64 ▸

Custody Battles

see also Divorce; Order in the Court; Single Parents
Big Daddy '99
Careful, He Might Hear You '84 ▸
Changing Lanes '02 ▸
Daddy's Little Girls '07
Dark Water '02
Evelyn '02 ▸
Faithless '00 ▸
A Father's Choice '00
Gaudi Afternoon '01
The Good Mother '88
I Am Sam '01

▸ = rated three bones or higher

Irreconcilable Differences '84
Kramer vs. Kramer '79 ▶
Losing Isaiah '94 ▶
Mrs. Doubtfire '93
Rain Man '88 ▶

Cuttin' Heads

Abbott and Costello in Hollywood '45
Allie & Me '97
The Barber Shop '33 ▶
Barbershop '02 ▶
Barbershop 2: Back in Business '04 ▶
The Beautician and the Beast '97
The Big Tease '99
Black Shampoo '76
Blow Dry '00
Born to Win '71
Caramel '07 ▶
Chain of Fools '00
Claire Dolan '97
Coming to America '88 ▶
The Crying Game '92 ▶
Demon Barber of Fleet Street '36
Earth Girls Are Easy '89
Educating Rita '83 ▶
An Everlasting Piece '00
The French Touch '54
Frolics on Ice '39
Good Hair '09
The Hairdresser's Husband '92
Hairspray '88 ▶
Hellbent '04
Honey '03
House of Traps '81
Joe's Bed-Stuy Barbershop: We Cut Heads '83
The Man Who Wasn't There '01 ▶
Mississippi Burning '88 ▶
Nora's Hair Salon 2: A Cut Above '08
Nutty Professor 2: The Klumps '00
Poetic Justice '93
Reducing '31
Runaway Bride '99 ▶
The Salon '05
Shampoo '75
Slander House '38
Spotlight Scandals '43
Steel Magnolias '89 ▶
Stigmata '99
Sweeney Todd: The Demon Barber of Fleet Street '84
Sweeney Todd: The Demon Barber of Fleet Street '07
Venus Beauty Institute '98
The Village Barbershop '08
You Don't Mess with the Zohan '08

Cyberpunk

Arcade '93
Blade Runner '82 ▶
The Crow 2: City of Angels '96
Cyborg '89
Cyborg 2 '93
Cyborg Cop '93
Cyborg Soldier '94
Demolition Man '93
Electric Dragon 80,000V '01
Escape from L.A. '96
Escape from New York '81
The Fifth Element '97
Freejack '92
The Gene Generation '07
Hackers '95
Johnny Mnemonic '95
Killing Machine '02
The Lawnmower Man '92
Lawnmower Man 2: Beyond Cyberspace '95
Mad Max '80 ▶
Mad Max: Beyond Thunderdome '85
Megaville '91
Natural City '03
Nemesis '93
Overdrawn at the Memory Bank '83
Pinocchio 964 '92
The Road Warrior '82 ▶
RoboCop '87 ▶
RoboCop 2 '90
RoboCop 3 '91
Rubber's Lover '97
Stealing Candy '04
Tank Girl '94
TekWar '94
The Terminator '84 ▶
Terminator 2: Judgment Day '91 ▶
Tetsuo: The Iron Man '92
Tetsuo 2: Body Hammer '97
Total Recall '90 ▶
Tron '82
Universal Soldier '92
Universal Soldier 2: Brothers in Arms '98
Universal Soldier 3: Unfinished Business '98
Universal Soldier: The Return '99
Virtual Combat '95
Virtuosity '95
Webmaster '98

Dads

see also Bad Dads; Moms; Monster Moms; Parenthood

About Schmidt '02 ▶
Address Unknown '96
The Adventures of Pinocchio '96
After the Deluge '03 ▶
Alice et Martin '98
All My Sons '48 ▶
American Gun '02 ▶
American Heart '92 ▶
Animal '05
April Fool '26
Armageddon '98
Artemisia '97
Austin Powers In Goldmember '02
Author! Author! '82
Autumn Marathon '79
Back to School '86
The Ballad of Jack and Rose '05 ▶
Ballistic '94
Bandits '86
Barnyard '06
The Baron and the Kid '84
Beat Girl '60
The Bed You Sleep In '93
Behind Prison Walls '43
Betsy's Wedding '90
Between Men '35
Beyond Obsession '82
Big Daddy '99
Big Fish '03 ▶
A Bill of Divorcement '32
Billy Elliot '00 ▶
Billy Galvin '86
Billy Madison '94
The Birdcage '95 ▶
Black Eyes '39
Blood Diamond '06
Bloodfist 4: Die Trying '92
Bloodfist 8: Hard Way Out '96
Bloodlines '05
Blue Fin '78
Boiler Room '00 ▶
Bonjour Tristesse '57 ▶
Boomerang '76
Bopha! '93 ▶
Boss' Son '78 ▶
Bottle Shock '08
The Boys Are Back '09
The Brady Bunch Movie '95 ▶
Breaking Away '79 ▶
Bringing Down the House '03
Broken Angel '88
A Bronx Tale '93 ▶
The Buddha of Suburbia '92 ▶
Butterfly '82
Bye Bye, Love '94
Cal '84 ▶
Call of the Forest '49
The Capture of Grizzly Adams '82
Carbon Copy '81
Carousel '56 ▶
Carpool '96
Casanova Brown '44
Casper '95 ▶
Caterina in the Big City '03
Catherine Cookson's The Glass Virgin '95
Celine and Julie Go Boating '74
The Champ '32 ▶
The Champ '79
Chasing Destiny '00
Chasing the Deer '94
Chicken Little '05
The Circuit '08
City of Men '07 ▶
Class Action '91 ▶
Click '06
The Climb '97
Clown '53
Cody '77
Cold Comfort '90
College Road Trip '08
The Color of Paradise '99
Come and Get It '36 ▶
Common Ground '00
Complex World '92
Cookie '89
A Cool, Dry Place '98
The Cooler '03 ▶
Cop-Out '67
Corky Romano '01
The Courtship of Eddie's Father '62 ▶
crazy/beautiful '01
Crush '93
A Cry from the Mountain '85
Cry, the Beloved Country '51 ▶
Cry, the Beloved Country '95 ▶
Da '88
Dad '89
Dad On the Run '00
Daddy Day Camp '07
Daddy Nostalgia '90 ▶
Daltry Calhoun '05
Dan in Real Life '07
The Dance Goes On '92
The Dancer Upstairs '02
Dancing in Twilight '05
Daredevil '03
The Dark Side of the Sun '88
Daughter of Don Q '46
David '97
Dead to Rights '93
Deadlocked '00
Death of a Salesman '51 ▶
The Death of Richie '76
Definitely, Maybe '08 ▶
Demonstrator '71
Desert Blue '98
Desperate Measures '98
Diamonds '99
Dinner Rush '00 ▶
Disgrace '08
Distant Thunder '88
Django Strikes Again '87
Dr. T & the Women '00 ▶
Dodson's Journey '01
Domestic Disturbance '01
Donkey Skin '70 ▶
Donovan's Reef '63 ▶
The Dream Catcher '99
A Dream of Kings '69 ▶
Dreamer: Inspired by a True Story '05
Dreaming of Rita '94
Drifting Weeds '59 ▶
Duets '00
East and West '24 ▶
Eat Drink Man Woman '94 ▶
Eden Valley '94
Edge of Darkness '10
11:14 '03
Elisa, Vida Mia '77
The Emerald Forest '85 ▶
Empire Falls '05
The Enemy '01
Escape from Atlantis '97
Evelyn '02 ▶
Everybody's Famous! '00
Everybody's Fine '90
Everybody's Fine '09
Eyes of a Witness '94
Eyes of an Angel '91
Faceless '88
Family Business '89
Family Tree '00
The Fantasticks '95
Fast Getaway 2 '94
Fatal Justice '93
Father '90
Father and Scout '94
Father and Son '03
Father Figure '80
Father of the Bride '50 ▶
Father Was a Fullback '49
Fathers and Sons '92
A Father's Choice '00
Father's Day '96
A Father's Revenge '88
The Favorite Son '94 ▶
Fear '96
Finding Nemo '03 ▶
Fingers '78 ▶
Firehouse Dog '07
The First Auto '27
Five Easy Pieces '70 ▶
Floating '97
For Richer, for Poorer '92
Force on Thunder Mountain '77
Forty Shades of Blue '05
Fourth Wish '75
Free Willy 3: The Rescue '97
Freedom Is Paradise '89 ▶
Freedom Song '00 ▶
Frequency '00
Friday After Next '02
Friends & Lovers '99
The Game Plan '07
Gepetto '00
Ghost Dad '90
Gigantic '08
The Golden Bowl '72 ▶
The Golden Bowl '00
A Goofy Movie '94
The Gospel '05 ▶
Grace Is Gone '07 ▶
The Great Buck Howard '09
Green Eyes '76 ▶
The Green Promise '49
Grizzly Falls '99
Gunman's Walk '58
Gunslinger's Revenge '98
Happy Tears '09
Harry & Son '84
Heaven Tonight '93
Hidden Guns '56 ▶
Hidden in America '96
High & Low '62 ▶
High Command '37
His Greatest Gamble '34
Hobson's Choice '53 ▶
Hobson's Choice '83
A Hole in the Head '59
Holiday in Mexico '46
Home from the Hill '60 ▶
Home Is Where the Hart Is '88
Honey, We Shrunk Ourselves '97
The Horse '82 ▶
The Horse in the Gray Flannel Suit '68
The Horsemen '70
House Arrest '96
A House Divided '00
A House Without a Christmas Tree '72
Hud '63 ▶
I Am Sam '01
I Live with Me Dad '86
I Ought to Be in Pictures '82
I Was Born But... '32 ▶
Il Grido '57
I'll Be There '03
I'll Do Anything '93
I'm Not Rappaport '96
Imaginary Crimes '94 ▶
Imagine That '09
In Good Company '04 ▶
In His Father's Shoes '97
In the Gloaming '97 ▶
In the Name of the Father '93 ▶
In the Valley of Elah '07 ▶
The Incredibles '04 ▶
The Independent '00
Indiana Jones and the Last Crusade '89 ▶
Invisible Dad '97
It's a Date '40
Jack Frost '98
Jack the Bear '93
Jersey Girl '04
Jet Li's The Enforcer '95
Jingle All the Way '96
Joe Somebody '01
Joey '85
John Q '02
Johnny's Girl '95
Journey to the End of the Night '06
The Judgement '04
Jumanji '95
Jungle 2 Jungle '96
Just Like Dad '96
Just Write '97
Keeping Up with the Steins '06
Kicking & Screaming '05
The Kid and I '05
King of California '07
King of Texas '02 ▶
King of the Corner '04 ▶
Kings and Queen '04 ▶
Knockaround Guys '01
Kolya '96 ▶
Kramer vs. Kramer '79 ▶
La Deroute '98
The Lady Eve '41 ▶
The Lady Refuses '31
Lamb '85
Lara Croft: Tomb Raider '01
The Last Hard Men '76
The Last Hit '93
The Last Song '10
Late Spring '49 ▶
Laughing at Life '33
Le Sexe des Etoiles '93
The Legend of Zorro '05
Leon the Pig Farmer '93
Les Comperes '83 ▶
Les Destinees '00
Letter of Introduction '38
Liar Liar '97
Life Is Beautiful '98 ▶
Life with Father '47 ▶
Like Father, Like Son '87
The Limey '99 ▶
The Lion King '94 ▶
Little Dorrit, Film 1: Nobody's Fault '88 ▶
Little Dorrit, Film 2: Little Dorrit's Story '88 ▶
Little Indian, Big City '95
Little John '02
A Little Princess '95 ▶
The Lives of a Bengal Lancer '35 ▶
Lone Star '95 ▶
Looking for an Echo '99
Luna Park '91
Lust and Revenge '95
Magic in the Water '95
Maker of Men '31
Malibu's Most Wanted '03
Marci X '03
The Marshal's Daughter '53
The Mask of Zorro '98 ▶
Matchstick Men '03 ▶
Meet the Fockers '04
Meet the Parents '00 ▶
Meeting Daddy '98
Memories of Me '88
Men with Brooms '02
Missing Pieces '00
Mr. Mom '83 ▶
Mr. St. Nick '02
Mr. Troop Mom '09
Misunderstood '84
Misunderstood '87
Mom and Dad Save the World '92
Moonlight & Mistletoe '08
Mulan '98
Must Be Santa '99
Must Love Dogs '05
Mutual Respect '77
My Date with the President's Daughter '98
My Father Is Coming '91
My Father the Hero '93
My Old Man '79
My Son the Fanatic '97 ▶
My Stepmother Is an Alien '88
National Lampoon's Dad's Week Off '97
Never Down '06
Nick of Time '95
Night at the Museum '06
Night Falls on Manhattan '96 ▶
Night Zoo '87
No Turning Back '01
No Way Back '96
Noah '98
Nobody's Fool '94 ▶
Nothing in Common '86
Old Dogs '09
Oldest Living Graduate '80 ▶
On a Clear Day '05
On the Edge '86
On the Third Day '83
One Christmas '95
Our Vines Have Tender Grapes '45 ▶
Out of the Fog '41
Over the Top '86
The Patriot '00
Picture This! '08
The Pillow Book '95
Platinum High School '60
Pokemon 3: The Movie '01
Ponette '95
Pontiac Moon '94
Pop Always Pays '40
Pope Dreams '06
Popi '69 ▶
Princess of Thieves '01
Proof '05 ▶
Proud Men '87
The Pursuit of Happyness '06
Race to Space '01
Raining Stones '93
Raising Flagg '06
Reservation Road '07
Return to Lonesome Dove '93
Revenge of the Musketeers '94
Revolution '85
Riding Alone for Thousands of Miles '05
Rio Grande '50 ▶
The River Rat '84
A River Runs Through It '92 ▶
The Road '09
Road to Perdition '02 ▶
Rocky Balboa '06
Romulus, My Father '07 ▶
Rugrats in Paris: The Movie '00 ▶
The Run of the Country '95 ▶
Ruslan '09
The Santa Clause '94
The Santa Clause 2 '02
Sci-Fighter '04
Sea Devils '37
Second Best '94 ▶
Secre of the Andes '98
The Secret Agent Club '96
The Secret Passion of Robert Clayton '92
The Sender '98
Severance '88
Shadow Man '06
Shattered '21 ▶
The Shepherd of the Hills '41 ▶
She's the One '96
Shiner '00
Shower '00
Signs '02 ▶
A Simple Curve '05
A Simple Wish '97
Sin Nombre '09 ▶
Skeletons in the Closet '00
Slaughter of the Innocents '93
Sleepless in Seattle '93 ▶
Slums of Beverly Hills '98 ▶
Snow Dogs '02
So I Married an Axe Murderer '93
A Soldier's Daughter Never Cries '98
Spanglish '04
Special Olympics '78
Speed of Life '99
The Spring '00
Spring Forward '99
Star Spangled Rhythm '42 ▶
Stolen Summer '02
The Stupids '95
The Sum of Us '94 ▶
Superdad '73
Swing Vote '08
Taken '08
Tank '83
The Tempest '63
The Tempest '82 ▶
The Tempest '99
The 10th Kingdom '00
Texas Lightning '81

That's My Baby! '44
The Thing About My Folks '05
13 Moons '02
35 Shots of Rum '08
A Thousand Years of Good Prayers '07
The Three Lives of Thomasina '63 ▸
Three Men and a Cradle '85 ▸
Three Men and a Little Lady '90
The Tiger Woods Story '98
The Time of His Life '55
A Time to Kill '96 ▸
Time Without Pity '57
To Gillian on Her 37th Birthday '96
Together '02
The Tomorrow Man '01
Tortilla Soup '01
The Tracker '88
Tully '00 ▸
25th Hour '02
Two Kinds of Love '85
Undercover Angel '99
A Very Brady Sequel '96
A Voyage 'Round My Father '89 ▸
Wait Till Your Mother Gets Home '83
Walter and Henry '01 ▸
The War '94
The War at Home '96
War of the Worlds '05 ▸
Wasabi '01
Washington Heights '02
The Weather Man '05
What a Girl Wants '03
When Wolves Cry '69
Winter Solstice '04 ▸
Woman Wanted '98
Wonderful World '09
The Young Girl and the Monsoon '99

Dallas

***see also** Black Gold; Houston; Texas*

Asteroid '97
Big Show '37
A Cool, Dry Place '98
Dr. T & the Women '00 ▸
Free, White, and 21 '62
JFK '91 ▸
Love Field '91
The Night of the White Pants '06
North Dallas Forty '79 ▸
Pioneer Marshal '49
Ruby '92
Steele's Law '91
Suspect Zero '04
Talk Radio '88 ▸
The Thin Blue Line '88 ▸
A Woman of Independent Means '94 ▸
The X-Files '98

Dance Fever

***see also** Ballet; Disco Musicals*

Alive and Kicking '96
All That Jazz '79 ▸
An American in Paris '51 ▸
Anchors Aweigh '45 ▸
April in Paris '52
Assassination Tango '03 ▸
Babes in Arms '39
The Bacchantes '63
The Band Wagon '53 ▸
The Barefoot Contessa '54 ▸
The Barkleys of Broadway '49 ▸
Beat Street '84
Because of You '95
The Belle of New York '52
Bert Rigby, You're a Fool '89
Billy Elliot '00 ▸
Billy Rose's Jumbo '62 ▸
Black Orpheus '58 ▸
Blood Wedding '81 ▸
Body Moves '90
Body Rock '84
Bojangles '01
Boogie Nights '97 ▸
Bootmen '00
Born to Dance '36
Breakin' '84
Breakin' 2: Electric Boogaloo '84
Breakin' Through '84
Broadway '42
Broadway Melody of 1940 '40
Cabin in the Sky '43 ▸
Can-Can '60
Captain January '36
Carefree '38 ▸
Carmen '83 ▸
Center Stage '00
Center Stage: Turn It Up '08
Charleston '26 ▸
A Chorus Line '85
Chu Chu & the Philly Flash '81
Cover Girl '44 ▸
Curdled '95
Daddy Long Legs '55 ▸
Dames '34 ▸
Dance Flick '09
Dance or Die '87
Dance with Me '98
Dancehall Queen '97
Dancing Lady '33
Danzon '91 ▸
Deadly Dancer '90
Delightfully Dangerous '45
Delivery Boys '84
Dirty Dancing '87 ▸
Dirty Dancing: Havana Nights '04
The Discovery Program '89
Doll Face '46
The Eighties '83
El Amor Brujo '86 ▸
Everybody's Dancin' '50
Everyone Says I Love You '96 ▸
Everything I Have is Yours '52
Faith '90
Fame '80 ▸
Fame '09
Fass Black '77
Fast Forward '84
Faster, Pussycat! Kill! Kill! '65
Femmes de Paris '53
Flashdance '83
Flower Drum Song '61
Flying Down to Rio '33
Follies Girl '43
Follow the Fleet '36 ▸
Footlight Parade '33 ▸
Footloose '84
The Forbidden Dance '90
42nd Street '33 ▸
French Can-Can '55 ▸
From Dusk Till Dawn '95
The Full Monty '96 ▸
Funky Forest: The First Contact '06
The Gay Divorcee '34 ▸
Ginger & Fred '86 ▸
Girl in Gold Boots '69
Girls Just Want to Have Fun '85
Give a Girl a Break '53
The Glass Slipper '55
Gold Diggers of 1933 '33 ▸
Gold Diggers of 1935 '35 ▸
Grease '78 ▸
Grease 2 '82
Groove '00 ▸
Hair '79 ▸
Hairspray '88 ▸
Hairspray '07 ▸
Happy Feet '06 ▸
The Harvey Girls '46 ▸
Heavenly Bodies '84
Hit the Deck '55
Hocus Pocus '93
Holiday in Havana '49
Honey '03
How She Move '08
Human Traffic '99
Idiot's Delight '39 ▸
The In Crowd '88
Isadora '68 ▸
It Started in Naples '60 ▸
Kickin' It Old Skool '07
Kiss Me Kate '53 ▸
Lambada '89
Last Dance '91
The Last Dance '93
The Last Days of Disco '98 ▸
Le Bal '82 ▸
Legs '83
Les Girls '57
Let's Dance '50
Lilo & Stitch 2: Stitch Has a Glitch '05
Liquid Dreams '92
Little Ballerina '47
Look Who's Talking '89 ▸
Mad About Mambo '00
Mad Hot Ballroom '05 ▸
Mad Youth '40
Make It Happen '08
Mamma Mia! '08
Manhattan Merenque! '95
Mantis in Lace '68
Marigold '07
Marilyn Hotchkiss' Ballroom Dancing & Charm School '06
Meet Me in Las Vegas '56
Michael '96
Michael Jackson's This Is It '09
Midnight Dancer '87
Music in My Heart '40
Neurotic Cabaret '90
The Next Step '95
No Time for Romance '48
Nutcracker: The Motion Picture '86
Orgy of the Dead '65
Out to Sea '97
Paris Is Burning '91 ▸
Party Girl '58 ▸
Pennies from Heaven '81 ▸
The Pirate '48 ▸
Pizzicata '96
Portrait of a Showgirl '82
Portrait of a Stripper '79
Pulp Fiction '94 ▸
Queen of the Stardust Ballroom '75 ▸
Rhythm Romance '39
Risky Business '83 ▸
Rize '05 ▸
Roberta '35 ▸
Romance in Manhattan '34
Romy and Michele's High School Reunion '97
Rooftops '89
Roseland '77 ▸
Salome, Where She Danced '45
Salsa '88
Satin Rouge '02
Saturday Night Fever '77
Save the Last Dance '01
Scent of a Woman '92 ▸
Seamless '00
Second Chorus '40
Seven Brides for Seven Brothers '54 ▸
Shag: The Movie '89 ▸
Shall We Dance '37 ▸
Shall We Dance? '96 ▸
Shall We Dance? '04
Showgirls '95
Silk Stockings '57 ▸
Singin' in the Rain '52 ▸
Siren of the Tropics '27
Slashdance '89
So This Is Paris '26 ▸
Spirit of '76 '91
Staying Alive '83
Step Up '06
Step Up 3D '10
Step Up 2 the Streets '08
Stepping Out '91 ▸
Stomp the Yard '07
The Story of Vernon and Irene Castle '39 ▸
Strictly Ballroom '92 ▸
Stripped to Kill II: Live Girls '89
Summer Stock '50 ▸
Sunset Strip '91
Sweet Charity '69 ▸
Swing Kids '93
Swing Time '36 ▸
Take Me Out to the Ball Game '49
Take the Lead '06
Tango '36
Tango '98
Tango Bar '88
The Tango Lesson '97
Tap '89
Taxi Dancers '93
Teen Wolf '85
Thank God It's Friday '78
That's Dancing! '85 ▸
That's Entertainment, Part 2 '76
That's Entertainment, Part 3 '93
That's the Way I Like It '99
They Shoot Horses, Don't They? '69 ▸
Those Lips, Those Eyes '80
A Time for Dancing '00
Top Hat '35 ▸
The Turning Point '77
Twinkletoes '26
Urban Cowboy '80
Valentina's Tango '07
Voulez-Vous Danser avec Moi? '59
West Side Story '61 ▸
What's the Matter with Helen? '71
Words and Music '48
Yankee Doodle Dandy '42 ▸
Yellow '06
You Got Served '04
You Were Never Lovelier '42 ▸
You'll Never Get Rich '41 ▸
Zatoichi '03 ▸
Ziegfeld Follies '46
Ziegfeld Girl '41 ▸
Zou Zou '34

Dates from Hell

***see also** Singles*

After Hours '85 ▸
Blind Date '87
Body Shots '99
Bride of Chucky '98
The Brothers Solomon '07
Bye Bye, Love '94
Ed's Next Move '96
The 40 Year Old Virgin '05 ▸
Harold and Maude '71 ▸
Mr. Woodcock '07
My Best Friend's Girl '08
Night of the Creeps '86
Perfect Strangers '03
The Personals '98
Reality Bites '94
Singles '92 ▸
Something Wild '86
The Third Wheel '02
20 Dates '99
Walking and Talking '96
What Happened Was... '94
Woo '97

Day Care/Nursery School

***see also** Babysitting*

Daddy Day Camp '07
Daddy Day Care '03
Indictment: The McMartin Trial '95 ▸
Superbabies: Baby Geniuses 2 '04
Toy Story 3 '10

A Day in the Life...

***see also** Up All Night*

American Graffiti '73 ▸
Barbershop '02 ▸
Before Sunrise '94
Before Sunset '04 ▸
Bella '06
The Best Man '97
Bobby '06
Bomb Squad '97
Borom Sarret '66 ▸
The Boys '98 ▸
The Breakfast Club '85 ▸
Caffeine '06
Call It a Day '37
Conversations with Other Women '05
Crank '06
A Day in the Life '09
The Daytrippers '96
Deadlocked '00
Falling '06
Ferris Bueller's Day Off '86 ▸
Flypaper '97
For One More Day '07
Four Christmases '08
Full Frontal '02
Groundhog Day '93 ▸
Head On '98 ▸
Heights '04
In a Day '06
Interceptor Force '99
Judy Berlin '99
Killing Time '97
Last Night '98 ▸
The Life Before This '99
Little Athens '05
Love and Other Catastrophes '95
Magnolia '99 ▸
Mandabi '68 ▸
Marie and Bruce '04
Midaq Alley '95 ▸
Miss Pettigrew Lives for a Day '08 ▸
Mrs. Dalloway '97
Motherhood '09
My Mother's Courage '95
North Shore Fish '97
Nothing Personal '95 ▸
Nowhere '96
One Fine Day '96
100 Proof '96
Orphans '97
People I Know '02
Radiance '98
Say Hello to Yesterday '71
A Single Man '09 ▸
Spy Game '01
Sunday '96
Sunset Strip '99
Time Code '00
Training Day '01
Trapped '02
Trojan War '97
True Crime '99
12:01 '93
25th Hour '02
24 Hours in London '00
Ulysses '67
Working Girls '87 ▸

DEA

***see also** Buddy Cops; FBI; Smuggler's Blues; Undercover Cops*

Basic '03
Cash Crop '01
Codename: Wildgeese '84
Crash & Byrnes '99
Drug Wars: The Camarena Story '90 ▸
Drug Wars 2: The Cocaine Cartel '92
Gang Related '96
Hollow Point '95
Love Lies Bleeding '07
A Low Down Dirty Shame '94
A Man Apart '03
Marked for Death '90
Martial Outlaw '93
Ninja: American Warrior '90
Road House 2: Last Call '06
Traffic '00 ▸
White Tiger '95
Winner Takes All '98

Deadly Implants

Alien: Resurrection '97 ▸
Blind Date '84
Bombshell '97
Drive '96
Escape from L.A. '96
Escape from New York '81
Fortress '93
King of Kong Island '78
Live Wire: Human Timebomb '95
The Mosaic Project '95
Star Trek: First Contact '96 ▸
Street Asylum '90
Synapse '95
Terminal Impact '95
The Terminal Man '74
Total Recall '90 ▸

Deafness

***see also** Physical Problems*

Amy '81
Babel '06 ▸
Bangkok Dangerous '00
Beyond Silence '96
Bridge to Silence '89
Children of a Lesser God '86 ▸
Cop Land '97 ▸
Crazy Moon '87
Crossfire '98
Dead Silence '96
Dear Frankie '04
The Family Stone '05
For the First Time '59
Four Weddings and a Funeral '94 ▸
Goya in Bordeaux '99
Hear No Evil '93
The Heart Is a Lonely Hunter '68 ▸
His Bodyguard '98
Immortal Beloved '94
In the Company of Men '96
It's All Gone, Pete Tong '04
Johnny Belinda '48 ▸
Johnny Belinda '82
Mandy '53 ▸
The Miracle Worker '62 ▸
The Miracle Worker '79 ▸
The Miracle Worker '00
Mr. Holland's Opus '95 ▸
Murderer's Keep '70
Music Within '07
Orphan '09
Personal Effects '09
Psych-Out '68
The Quiet '05
Read My Lips '01
Secret of Yolanda '82
See No Evil, Hear No Evil '89
Silent Victory: The Kitty O'Neil Story '79 ▸
Sincerely Yours '56
The Sound and the Silence '93
Sound of Love '78
The Sphinx '33
The Story of Alexander Graham Bell '39 ▸
A Summer to Remember '84
Suspect '87
Sweet Nothing in My Ear '08
Tin Man '83
Two Shades of Blue '98
Where the Truth Lies '99

Death & the Afterlife

***see also** Angels; Funerals; Ghosts, Ghouls, & Goblins; Great Death Scenes; Heaven Sent; Hell; Immortality; Occult; Reincarnation; Suicide; Terminal Illness*

After Life '98
Afterwards '08
The Alchemist '81
Alive and Kicking '96
All About My Mother '99 ▸
All of Me '84
All That Jazz '79 ▸
Always '89
The Amityville Horror '79
Amityville 2: The Possession '82
Amityville 3: The Demon '83
Amityville 4: The Evil Escapes '89
The Amityville Curse '90
Amityville 1992: It's About Time '92
Angel Eyes '01
Angel Heart '87
Angel on My Shoulder '46 ▸
Angel on My Shoulder '80
Another Chance '88
The Asphyx '72 ▸
Audrey Rose '77
Avanti! '72
Baby Girl Scott '87
Backwoods '87
Beetlejuice '88 ▸
Beyond Tomorrow '40
Bill & Ted's Bogus Journey '91
Black Force 2 '78
Black Magic '92
Bliss '85 ▸
Blithe Spirit '45 ▸
Blood of the Vampire '58
Bloody New Year '87
The Bone Yard '90
Bowery at Midnight '42
Boys on the Side '94
The Bramble Bush '60
Breaking the Rules '92

Bulletproof Heart '95 ▶
Burnt Offerings '76
The Canterville Ghost '44
Carnival of Souls '62 ▶
Carousel '56 ▶
Carry Me Back '82
Castle of the Creeping Flesh '68
The Cat and the Canary '27 ▶
Cathy's Curse '77
Cemetery Man '95
The Chair '87
Chances Are '89 ▶
The Changeling '80
The Child '76
A Christmas Carol '38 ▶
A Christmas Carol '51 ▶
A Christmas Carol '54
A Christmas Carol '84 ▶
A Christmas Carol '99
City of Angels '98
Cold Heaven '92
Courage Under Fire '96 ▶
The Crow '93
The Crow 2: City of Angels '96
The Crow: Wicked Prayer '05
Curse of the Cat People '44 ▶
Curse of the Living Corpse '64
Da '88
Daddy's Dyin'... Who's Got the Will? '90
Dark of the Night '85
Dark Tower '87
Dark Victory '39 ▶
Daughter of Horror '55
The Day It Came to Earth '77
Dead Heat '88
Dead Leaves '98
Dead Mate '88
Death Be Not Proud '75 ▶
Death Becomes Her '92 ▶
The Death Curse of Tartu '66
Death Row Diner '88
Death Takes a Holiday '34 ▶
The Deaths of Ian Stone '07
Defending Your Life '91 ▶
Deja Vu '84
Departures '08
The Devil & Max Devlin '81
Devil's Kiss '75
The Diabolical Dr. Z '65
Diary of the Dead '76
Digging Up Business '91
D.O.A. '49 ▶
D.O.A. '88
Dr. Death, Seeker of Souls '73
Dr. Hackenstein '88
Doctor Phibes Rises Again '72
Dominique Is Dead '79
Dona Flor and Her Two Husbands '78 ▶
Donkey Skin '70 ▶
Donovan's Brain '53 ▶
Don't Go in the House '80
Don't Let Me Die on a Sunday '98
Doomed Love '83
Down to Earth '01
Dragonfly '02
The Duellists '77 ▶
Early Days '81
Earthling '80
Eleni '85
Emerald of Artama '67
Encounter with the Unknown '75
The End '78 ▶
The English Patient '96 ▶
Enrapture '90
The Entertainer '60 ▶
Estate of Insanity '64
Eternity and a Day '97
Evil Spirits '91
Executive Suite '54 ▶
The Eye '08
The Eyes, the Mouth '83
Fearless '93 ▶
The Fig Tree '87
The Final Destination '09
Flatliners '90
Fluke '95
For Roseanna '96
The Forgotten One '89
Frida '02
Friendly Fire '79 ▶
The Frighteners '96
Frightmare '81
Frisk '95
From the Dead of Night '89 ▶
The Funeral '84 ▶
Funeral Home '82
Garbo Talks '84
Gates of Hell '80
The Ghost '63
Ghost '90 ▶
The Ghost and Mrs. Muir '47 ▶
Ghost Writer '89
Ghosts Can Do It '87
Ghosts Can't Do It '90
Ghosts of Berkeley Square '47
Go Down Death '41
Gotham '88 ▶
The Granny '94
Grave Secrets '89
The Green Room '78
Griffin and Phoenix: A Love Story '76
Hachiko: A Dog's Tale '09
Hawks '89
Heart and Souls '93
Heart Condition '90
Heaven '87
Heaven Can Wait '43 ▶
Heaven Can Wait '78 ▶
The Heavenly Kid '85
Heaven's a Drag '94
Hello Again '87
Hercules the Legendary Journeys, Vol. 4: In the Underworld '94
Here Comes Mr. Jordan '41 ▶
Hideaway '94
High Plains Drifter '73
High Spirits '88
Highlander: Endgame '00
Highway 61 '91
Hocus Pocus '93
Hold That Ghost '41 ▶
Hollow Gate '88
Homeward Bound '80
The Hours '02 ▶
Human Nature '02
I Bury the Living '58 ▶
I Married a Witch '42 ▶
I Walked with a Zombie '43 ▶
I'm Losing You '98
Impure Thoughts '86
In an Old Manor House '84
In Between '92
In the Gloaming '97 ▶
The Indestructible Man '56
Infinity '96
Into the West '92 ▶
Intruso '93
The Invisible '07
It Came Upon a Midnight Clear '84
It Could Happen to You '39
It's a Wonderful Life '46 ▶
It's My Party '95
Jacob's Ladder '90
Judge & Jury '96
Just like Heaven '05
The Kid with the Broken Halo '82
Killing Grandpa '91
Kiss Me Goodbye '82
Kiss of Death '77
Kissed '96
La Vie Continue '82
The Lady in White '88 ▶
The Last Best Year '90
Last Light '93
Left in Darkness '06
The Legend of Hell House '73 ▶
Liliom '35 ▶
Living Doll '90
Look Both Ways '05
Loot... Give Me Money, Honey! '70
Love Letters '99 ▶
Love Unto Death '84
The Loved One '65
Macbeth '48 ▶
Macbeth '71 ▶
Macbeth '88
Made in Heaven '87
Magnolia '99 ▶
The Man from Elysian Fields '01 ▶
The Man with Two Lives '42
Mannequin '87
Marvin's Room '96
Mausoleum '83
Maxie '85
Meet Joe Black '98
Mermaid '00
The Midnight Hour '86
The Miracle of the Bells '48
Mr. Corbett's Ghost '90
Monkeybone '01
Monty Python's The Meaning of Life '83 ▶
Moonlight and Valentino '95
Moonlight Mile '02 ▶
Mortuary Academy '91
Mother and Son '97
A Mother's Prayer '95
Must Read After My Death '09
My Life '93
Necropolis '87
The Newlydeads '87
Night of the Death Cult '75
Night of the Demons '88
Night of the Demons 2 '94
Night of the Living Dead '68 ▶
Night of the Living Dead '90
The Nightcomers '72
Nightmare Castle '65
Oh Dad, Poor Dad (Momma's Hung You in the Closet & I'm Feeling So Sad) '67
Oh, Heavenly Dog! '80
On Borrowed Time '39 ▶
The Oracle '85
Our Sons '91
Out of the Rain '90
Over Her Dead Body '08
Papa's Angels '00
Passed Away '92
The Peanut Butter Solution '85
Pet Sematary '89
Phantasm '79
Phantasm 2 '88
Phantasm 3: Lord of the Dead '94
The Phantom Chariot '20
Phantom of the Ritz '88
The Plague '92
Playroom '90
Poltergeist '82 ▶
Poltergeist 2: The Other Side '86
Poltergeist 3 '88
Ponette '95
Portrait of Jennie '48 ▶
The Possessed '77
Premonition '71
The Premonition '75
Prison '88
Promises in the Dark '79
The Prophecy '95
P.S. I Love You '07
The Psychic '78
Psychomania '73
Purgatory House '04
The Reincarnation of Peter Proud '75
Resurrection of Zachary Wheeler '71
Retribution '88
Return '88
Revenge of the Dead '84
Riders to the Sea '88
Riding the Bullet '04
Rimfire '49
A River Made to Drown In '97
Robot Stories '03
The Rue Morgue Massacres '73
Saturn in Opposition '07
Savage Hearts '95
Saved by the Light '95
Scared Stiff '53 ▶
School Spirit '85
Scrooge '35 ▶
Scrooge '70
Scrooged '88
Seven Days to Live '01
The Seventh Seal '56 ▶
Shadow Play '86
She Waits '71
Shock Waves '77
Sibling Rivalry '90
Silence Like Glass '90
The Sixth Man '97
The Sixth Sense '99 ▶
Sole Survivor '84
Sometimes They Come Back '91
Somewhere Tomorrow '85
Soultaker '90
South Park: Bigger, Longer and Uncut '99
Spawn '97 ▶
Stand by Me '86 ▶
Star Trek 3: The Search for Spock '84
Stones of Death '88
Strangers of the Evening '32
The Substitute Wife '94
Supernatural '33
Tell Me a Riddle '80
Tequila Body Shots '99
Terror Eyes '87
They Came Back '04
They Watch '93
Things to Do in Denver When You're Dead '95 ▶
13 Ghosts '60
13 Moons '02
Tim Burton's Corpse Bride '05 ▶
To Dance with the White Dog '93 ▶
To Die (Or Not) '99
To Forget Venice '79
To Gillian on Her 37th Birthday '96
Tomb of Torture '65
Topper '37 ▶
Topper Returns '41 ▶
Topper Takes a Trip '39 ▶
Trick or Treat '86
Truly, Madly, Deeply '91 ▶
Truth or Dare? '86
12 and Holding '05 ▶
Twice Dead '88
Two Days '03
Two of a Kind '83
Under the Lighthouse Dancing '97
Under the Sand '00 ▶
Under the Skin '97
The Undertaker's Wedding '97
Undertow '10
The Unnamable '88
Unnatural '52
Unstrung Heroes '95
The Vacillations of Poppy Carew '94
The Vampire's Ghost '45
Vengeance '89
Visitor from the Grave '81
The Visitors '89
Vulture's Eye '04
Weekend at Bernie's '89
Weekend at Bernie's 2 '93
Welcome Back Mr. Fox '83
What Dreams May Come '98
Where the Lilies Bloom '74 ▶
Whispers '89
White Light '90
White Noise 2: The Light '07
The Widow '76
Wings of Fame '93
A Woman's Tale '92 ▶
Wristcutters: A Love Story '06
Young@Heart '07 ▶
A Zed & Two Noughts '88 ▶
Zone of the Dead '78

Death Row

see also ***Executing Revenge; Men in Prison; Women in Prison***

An American Tragedy '31
Angels with Dirty Faces '38 ▶
Beyond the Call '96
Black Angel '46 ▶
Bundy: A Legacy of Evil '08
Castle on the Hudson '40 ▶
The Chamber '96
The Condemned '07
Convicted '04
Crime of the Century '96
Daniel '83
A Dark Adapted Eye '93 ▶
Dead Man Out '89 ▶
Dead Man Walking '95 ▶
Decoy '46
Desperate Measures '98
The Detective '68 ▶
88 Minutes '08
The Executioner's Song '82
Gamer '09
The Green Mile '99
Hellblock 13 '97
I Want to Live! '58 ▶
Identity '03
In Cold Blood '67 ▶
In Cold Blood '96
Killer: A Journal of Murder '95
Last Dance '96
Last Rites '98
A Lesson Before Dying '99 ▶
Let Him Have It '91 ▶
Letters from a Killer '98
The Life of David Gale '03
Live! From Death Row '92
Lost Highway '96
Mommy 2: Mommy's Day '96
Monster's Ball '01 ▶
Nora Prentiss '47
Pennies from Heaven '36
A Place in the Sun '51 ▶
Prisoner '07
The Riverman '04
The Seventh Sign '88
Shot in the Heart '01 ▶
The State Within '06
The Sun Sets at Dawn '50
The Thin Blue Line '88 ▶
True Crime '99
20,000 Years in Sing Sing '33
Two Seconds '32
Under Suspicion '92
Whitewash: The Clarence Brandley Story '02
Why Must I Die? '60
The Widow of Saint-Pierre '00 ▶

Dedicated Teachers

see also ***Hell High School; School Daze***

Akeelah and the Bee '06
Amy '81
Anna and the King '99
Balance of Power '96
Blackboard Jungle '55 ▶
Born Yesterday '50 ▶
Born Yesterday '93
Bossa Nova '99
The Browning Version '94
Burn Witch, Burn! '62 ▶
Butterfly '98 ▶
Carried Away '95
Chalk '06
Cheaters '00
Cheers for Miss Bishop '41
A Child Is Waiting '63 ▶
Children of a Lesser God '86 ▶
The Chorus '04
Christy '94
Ciao, Professore! '94
The Class '08
Coach Carter '05 ▶
Comic Book: The Movie '04 ▶
Coming Out '89
Conrack '74 ▶
The Corn Is Green '45 ▶
The Corn Is Green '79 ▶
The Country Teacher '08
Dangerous Minds '95
Dead Poets Society '89 ▶
Detention '03
Disney's Teacher's Pet '04 ▶
Eden '98
Educating Rita '83 ▶
Election '99 ▶
The Elementary School '91
The Emperor's Club '02
Fever Pitch '05
Forever Mary '89 ▶
Freedom Writers '07
Friday Night Lights '04 ▶
Front of the Class '08
Girl's Dormitory '36
Goodbye, Mr. Chips '39 ▶
Goodbye, Mr. Chips '69
Goodbye, Mr. Chips '02
The Great Debaters '07 ▶
Half Nelson '06 ▶
Hamlet 2 '08 ▶
Happy-Go-Lucky '08 ▶
Heart of America '03
High School High '96
The History Boys '06
Homework '82
Hoosier Schoolboy '37
How You Look to Me '05
If Lucy Fell '95
The Incredible Mrs. Ritchie '03
Inherit the Wind '60 ▶
Inherit the Wind '99
Institue Benjamenta or This Dream People Call Human Life '95
Johnny Tiger '66
Kindergarten Cop '90
Knights of the South Bronx '05
Lean on Me '89 ▶
L'Eleve '95
A Lesson Before Dying '99 ▶
Life Is a Bed of Roses '83
Like Father Like Son '05
Lovey: A Circle of Children 2 '82
Luna e L'Altra '96
Mad Hot Ballroom '05 ▶
Madame Sousatzka '88 ▶
The Male Animal '42
Matilda '96 ▶
Miracle '04 ▶
The Miracle Worker '62 ▶
The Miracle Worker '79 ▶
The Miracle Worker '00
Mr. Holland's Opus '95 ▶
Mona Lisa Smile '03
Music of the Heart '99
My Fuhrer '07
Necessary Roughness '91
The Next Karate Kid '94
Night Visitor '89
Not One Less '99
October Sky '99 ▶
Oktober '98
187 '97
The Paper Chase '73 ▶
Paper Clips '04 ▶
Passion for Life '48
The Piano Teacher '01
Powder '95
Precious: Based on the Novel by Sapphire '09 ▶
The Prime of Miss Jean Brodie '69 ▶
The Principal '87
Race the Sun '96
Rachel, Rachel '68 ▶
Rachida '05 ▶
Rebound '05
Renaissance Man '94
The Road Home '01 ▶
The Rookie '02 ▶
School of Life '06
School of Rock '03 ▶
Shooting Dogs '05
Stand and Deliver '88 ▶
The Substitute '96
Summer School '87
Sunset Park '96
Take the Lead '06
Teachers '84
Term of Trial '63
To Sir, with Love '67
Twenty-Four Eyes '54 ▶
Up the Down Staircase '67 ▶
Wildcats '86

Deep Blue

see also ***Go Fish; Sail Away; Shipwrecked; Submarines***

The Abyss '89 ▶
Andre '94
Assault on a Queen '66
Baywatch the Movie: Forbidden Paradise '95
The Beast '96
The Big Blue '88
Crimson Tide '95 ▶
Danger Beneath the Sea '02
Deep Blue '03 ▶
Deep Blue Sea '99
ffolkes '80
Finding Nemo '03 ▶
Flipper '96 ▶
1492: Conquest of Paradise '92
Free Willy '93

Free Willy 2: The Adventure Home '95
Free Willy 3: The Rescue '97
Happy Feet '06 ▸
Hello Down There '69
Lords of the Deep '89
Men of Honor '00
Mission of the Shark '91 ▸
Moby Dick '98
Namu, the Killer Whale '66
Oceans '09
Pirates '86
Shipwrecked '90
The Silent Enemy '58
Splash '84
The Spy Who Loved Me '77
Waterworld '95
Whale of a Tale '76
Wind '92

Deep Woods Offed

Backwoods '08
Blackwoods '02
Dead Snow '09
Deliverance '72 ▸
Don't Go in the Woods '81
The Hills Have Eyes '06
The Hills Have Eyes '77
The Hills Have Eyes 2 '07
The Hills Have Eyes, Part 2 '84
Pumpkinhead '88
Undertow '04
Wolf Creek '05
Wrong Turn '03
Wrong Turn 2: Dead End '07
Wrong Turn 3: Left for Dead '09

Demons & Wizards

***see also** Occult*
The Alchemist '81
Archer: The Fugitive from the Empire '81
Army of Darkness '92 ▸
Arthur's Quest '99
Bandh Darwaza '90
Belphegar: Phantom of the Louvre '01
Beyond Darkness '92
Blood Creek '09
Blood: The Last Vampire '09
Bloodlust: Subspecies 3 '93
Bloodstone: Subspecies 2 '92
Blue Blood '73
Born of Fire '87
Bram Stoker's Shadowbuilder '98
Brotherhood of Blood '08
The Church '98 ▸
The Color of Magic '08
Conan the Barbarian '82 ▸
Conan the Destroyer '84
Constantine '05
The Convent '00
Cthulhu '08
Cthulhu Mansion '91
Curse 4: The Ultimate Sacrifice '90
Darklight '04
Dead Waters '94
Death Note '06 ▸
Death Note 2: The Last Name '07
Death Note 3: L, Change the World '08
The Deaths of Ian Stone '07
Deathstalker '83
Deathstalker 3 '89
Deathstalker 4: Match of Titans '92
Demon Rage '82
Demon Wind '90
Demonoid, Messenger of Death '81
The Demons '74
Demons '86
Demons of Ludlow '75
Demonstone '89
Demonwarp '87
Devil Woman '76
The Devil's Web '74
Dororo '07
El Barbaro '84
Eragon '06
Ernest Scared Stupid '91
Evil Dead '83
Evil Dead 2: Dead by Dawn '87
Evil Toons '90
Excalibur '81 ▸
Fantasia '40 ▸
Fire and Ice '83
Funnyman '94
The Gate '87
Gate 2 '92
Ghost Son '06
Ghosts That Still Walk '77
The Giants of Thessaly '60
Gor '88
The Guardian '00
Guardian '01
Harry Potter and the Goblet of Fire '05 ▸
Harry Potter and the Order of the Phoenix '07
Harry Potter and the Prisoner of Azkaban '04
The Hazing '04
Hellboy '04
Hellraiser '87
Hellraiser 4: Bloodline '95
Hellraiser: Deader '05
The Heroic Trio '93
The Hobbit '78 ▸
Howl's Moving Castle '04
The Immortal '01
In the Name of the King: A Dungeon Siege Tale '08
Jack-O '95
Jennifer's Body '09
Just Visiting '01
The King and I '99
Krull '83
Ladyhawke '85
The Legacy '79
Lord of the Rings: The Fellowship of the Ring '01 ▸
Lord of the Rings: The Two Towers '02 ▸
Lord of the Rings: The Return of the King '03 ▸
Max Payne '08
The Mephisto Waltz '71 ▸
Merlin and the Book of Beasts '09
Merlin's Apprentice '06
The Minion '98
Mirror, Mirror '90
Mother of Tears '08
My Name Is Bruce '08
Natas... The Reflection '83
Night of the Demons '09
Night of the Demons 3 '97
Nightmare Man '06
Outlaw of Gor '87
P '04
Possessed '00
Pumpkinhead '88
Pumpkinhead 2: Blood Wings '94
Pumpkinhead 3: Ashes to Ashes '06
Pumpkinhead 4: Blood Feud '07
Purana Mandir '84 ▸
Quest for the Mighty Sword '90
The Raven '63 ▸
Rawhead Rex '87
Red Sonja '85
The Return of the King '80
Rock & Rule '83
Savage Harvest 2: October Blood '06
Seizure '74
Silent Night, Deadly Night 4: Initiation '90
Sinthia: The Devil's Doll '70
Sorceress '82
The Soul Guardians '98
Spellcaster '91
Stay Awake '87
Supergirl '84
Survival Island '02
Sword & the Sorcerer '82
The Sword in the Stone '63 ▸
Tales from the Crypt Presents Demon Knight '94
Talisman '98
Terror Eyes '87
Trancers 4: Jack of Swords '93
Troll '86
Troll 2 '92
The Unholy '88
The Unnamable 2: The Statement of Randolph Carter '92
Voodoo Moon '05
Warlock '91
Warlock: The Armageddon '93
Willow '88
Witchcraft 5: Dance with the Devil '92
The Witchmaker '69
Wizards of the Lost Kingdom '85
Wizards of the Lost Kingdom 2 '89
The Wizards of Waverly Place: The Movie '09
Zu Warriors '01
Zu: Warriors from the Magic Mountain '83

Dental Mayhem

***see also** Doctors & Nurses; Evil Doctors*
Almost Heroes '97
Brazil '85 ▸
Captives '94
Charlie and the Chocolate Factory '05 ▸
Compromising Positions '85
The Dentist '32 ▸
The Dentist '96
The Dentist 2: Brace Yourself '98
Dentist In the Chair '60
Diabolique '55 ▸
Don't Raise the Bridge, Lower the River '68
Eversmile New Jersey '89
Finding Nemo '03 ▸
Ghost Town '08 ▸
Horsemen '09
Houseguest '94
The In-Laws '79 ▸
Little Shop of Horrors '60 ▸
Little Shop of Horrors '86 ▸
Marathon Man '76 ▸
Novocaine '01
One Sunday Afternoon '33
The Paleface '48 ▸
Poltergeist 2: The Other Side '86
Reign Over Me '07
Reuben, Reuben '83 ▸
The Secret Lives of Dentists '02 ▸
Serial Mom '94 ▸
The Shakiest Gun in the West '68
Snow Dogs '02
Strawberry Blonde '41 ▸
Toothless '97
12 Monkeys '95 ▸
The Whole Nine Yards '00
The Whole Ten Yards '04

Desert War/Foreign Legion

***see also** Deserts; Persian Gulf/Iraq War*
Abbott and Costello in the Foreign Legion '50
Beau Geste '39 ▸
Beau Travail '98
Delta Force 3: The Killing Game '91
The Flying Deuces '39 ▸
Follow That Camel '67
Gunga Din '39 ▸
Jarhead '05
The Last Remake of Beau Geste '77
Lionheart '90
Man of Legend '71
March or Die '77
Morocco '30 ▸
Nine Men '43
Occupation: Dreamland '05 ▸
Outpost in Morocco '49
Sahara '43 ▸
Secondhand Lions '03

Deserts

***see also** Desert War/Foreign Legion*
Adventure in Sahara '38
The Adventures of Priscilla, Queen of the Desert '94 ▸
Alien Trespass '09
American Strays '96
Ashes of Time Redux '08
Back of Beyond '95
Baja '95
The Barbarian '33
Beavis and Butt-Head Do America '96
The Big Empty '04
Bone Dry '07
Broken Arrow '95
Children of Dune '03
Dark Country '09
Death Valley '04
Desert Blue '98
The Desert Fox '51 ▸
Desert Gold '36
Desert Hearts '86 ▸
Desert Heat '99
Desert Nights '29
The Desert Rats '53 ▸
The Desert Song '53
Desert Winds '95
The Devil's Tomb '09
Drowning on Dry Land '00
Duma '05 ▸
Dune '84
Dune '00
Dune Warriors '91
Dust to Glory '05 ▸
The English Patient '96 ▸
Evolution '01
A Far Off Place '93
Faster, Pussycat! Kill! Kill! '65
Feast '06
Five Graves to Cairo '43 ▸
Flame of Araby '51
Flight of the Phoenix '04
The Forsaken '01
The Four Feathers '02
Frankenstein and Me '96
Grand Theft Parsons '03
Hidalgo '04
The Hill '65
The Hills Have Eyes '06
Holes '03 ▸
House of Sand '05 ▸
In the Army Now '94
Indiana Jones and the Last Crusade '89 ▸
Ishtar '87
It Came from Outer Space 2 '95
Japanese Story '03 ▸
The Jewel of the Nile '85
Kill Your Darlings '06
Larry McMurtry's Dead Man's Walk '96
The Last Templar '09
Lawrence of Arabia '62 ▸
Legend of the Lost Tomb '97
Legionnaire '98
Lost '05
Mad Max '80 ▸
Mad Max: Beyond Thunderdome '85
The Men Who Stare at Goats '09
Miss Cast Away '04
Mojave Moon '96
Morocco '30 ▸
The Mummy '99
Natural Born Killers '94
New Eden '94
Off the Map '03 ▸
Operation Condor '91
The Passenger '75 ▸
Passion in the Desert '97
Patriot Games '92 ▸
Picking Up the Pieces '99
The Prisoner '09
The Road to Morocco '42 ▸
The Road Warrior '82 ▸
Sahara '43 ▸
Sahara '83
Sahara '05
Samson and Delilah '96
Scorpion Spring '96
Sea of Sand '58
The Sheik '21 ▸
The Sheltering Sky '90 ▸
Shoot or Be Shot '02
Slow Burn '00
Son of the Sheik '26 ▸
Star Wars '77 ▸
Stargate '94
The Story of the Weeping Camel '03 ▸
Strawberry Fields '97
The Three Burials of Melquiades Estrada '05 ▸
Tower of the Firstborn '98
Tremors '89
Tremors 2: Aftershocks '96
Twentynine Palms '03
White Sands '92
The Wind and the Lion '75 ▸
Yellow Asphalt '01

Detective Spoofs

Ace Ventura Jr.: Pet Detective '08
Ace Ventura: Pet Detective '93
Ace Ventura: When Nature Calls '95
The Adventures of Sherlock Holmes' Smarter Brother '78 ▸
Assault of the Party Nerds 2: Heavy Petting Detective '95
Blondes Have More Guns '95
Camouflage '00
Carry On Dick '75
Carry On Screaming '66
The Cheap Detective '78 ▸
Clean Slate '94
Clue '85
The Crooked Circle '32
Cry Uncle '71
The Curse of the Jade Scorpion '01
Curse of the Pink Panther '83
Dead Men Don't Wear Plaid '82
Detective School Dropouts '85
Dragnet '87
Fatal Instinct '93
Gumshoe '72
The Hollywood Detective '89
Hollywood Harry '86
Hoodwinked '05 ▸
The Hound of the Baskervilles '77
How to Kill 400 Duponts '68
Inspector Gadget '99
Inspector Gadget 2 '02
Inspector Hornleigh '39
Love Happy '50
The Man with Bogart's Face '80
Master Mind '73
Murder by Death '76
My Favorite Brunette '47
The Naked Gun: From the Files of Police Squad '88 ▸
Naked Gun 33 1/3: The Final Insult '94
Naked Gun 2 1/2: The Smell of Fear '91
Night Patrol '85
Oh, Heavenly Dog! '80
One Body Too Many '44
The Pink Chiquitas '86
The Pink Panther '64 ▸
The Pink Panther Strikes Again '76 ▸
The Private Eyes '80
Pure Luck '91
Rentadick '72
Return of the Pink Panther '74
Revenge of the Pink Panther '78
Ryder P.I. '86
Second Sight '89
Secret Agent 00-Soul '89
Sherlock, Jr. '24 ▸
A Shot in the Dark '64 ▸
The Strange Case of the End of Civilization As We Know It '93
Terror 2000 '92
Trail of the Pink Panther '82
Who Done It? '42
Who Done It? '56
Who's Harry Crumb? '89
Without a Clue '88
Zero Effect '97

Detectives

***see** Amateur Sleuths; CIA/NSA; Cops; Detective Spoofs; FBI; Historical Detectives; Police Detectives; Private Eyes*

Detroit

***see also** Checkered Flag; Motor Vehicle Dept.*
Aspen Extreme '93
Assault on Precinct 13 '05
Beverly Hills Cop '84
Beverly Hills Cop 2 '87
Beverly Hills Cop 3 '94
Bird on a Wire '90
The Butterfly Effect 3: Revelation '09
Chameleon Street '89 ▸
Collision Course '89
The Color of Courage '98
Coupe de Ville '90
Crimewave '85
Crossing the Bridge '92
Crossover '06
Detroit 9000 '73
Detroit Rock City '99
The Dollmaker '84
Dreamgirls '06 ▸
8 Mile '02 ▸
Exit Wounds '01
Flash of Genius '08
Four Brothers '05
Gifted Hands: The Ben Carson Story '09
Gridlock'd '96 ▸
Grosse Pointe Blank '97 ▸
Hoffa '92 ▸
Indian Summer '93
The Last Word '95
Let's Kill All the Lawyers '93
The Life and Times of Hank Greenberg '99 ▸
The Man '05
Mirrors '85
Mr. Mom '83 ▸
Narc '02 ▸
One in a Million: The Ron LeFlore Story '78
Out of Sight '98 ▸
Paper Lion '68
Presumed Innocent '90 ▸
Private Parts '96
Renaissance Man '94
R.I.C.C.O. '02
Ringmaster '98
RoboCop '87 ▸
RoboCop 2 '90
RoboCop 3 '91
Roger & Me '89 ▸
The Rosary Murders '87
Scarecrow '73
Standing in the Shadows of Motown '02 ▸
Tainted '98
Tiger Town '83
True Romance '93
Tucker: The Man and His Dream '88 ▸
The Upside of Anger '05 ▸
The Wrecking Crew '99
Zebrahead '92 ▸

Devils

Beauty and the Devil '50
Bedazzled '68 ▸
Bedazzled '00
Constantine '05
The Craft '96
Crazy as Hell '02
Crocodile Tears '98
Damn Yankees '58 ▸
Dark Angel: The Ascent '94
Deal of a Lifetime '99
The Devil & Max Devlin '81
The Devils '71 ▸
The Devil's Advocate '97
Doktor Faustus '82
End of Days '99
The Exorcism of Emily Rose '05 ▸
Exorcist: The Beginning '04
Faust '26 ▸
Gates of Hell 2: Dead Awakening '96
Ghost Rider '07
God, Man and Devil '49
Guardian of the Abyss '82
Haunted Symphony '94
Hell's Belles '95
High Strung '91
Highway to Hell '92

Hocus Pocus '93
The Imaginarium of Doctor Parnassus '09
Judgment Day '88
Legend '86
Les Visiteurs du Soir '42 ▸
Little Nicky '00
Lost Souls '00
Magic Hunter '96
The Mangler '94
Mr. Frost '89
Mother Joan of the Angels '60 ▸
Needful Things '93
The Ninth Gate '99
No News from God '01
The Omen '06
The Prophecy '95
Second Time Lucky '84
The Sorrows of Satan '26 ▸
South Park: Bigger, Longer and Uncut '99
Stephen King's The Stand '94
Tales from the Hood '95
The Witches of Eastwick '87

Devil's Island

see also *Great Escapes; Men in Prison*
Condemned '29
Crescendo '69
The Life of Emile Zola '37 ▸
Mysterious Mr. Moto '38
Papillon '73 ▸
Passage to Marseilles '44 ▸
Strange Cargo '40
We're No Angels '55 ▸

Diner

see also *Bar & Grill; Edibles; Waiters & Waitresses*
Alice Doesn't Live Here Anymore '74
Alien Trespass '09
American East '07
American Strays '96
Blood Diner '87
The Box '03
Coffee and Cigarettes '03 ▸
Deterrence '00
Diner '82 ▸
Empire Falls '05
Exiled in America '90
Eye of the Storm '91
Five Easy Pieces '70 ▸
Flakes '07
Frankie and Johnny '91 ▸
Gasoline Alley '51
Gloomy Sunday '02 ▸
Heavy '94 ▸
Here on Earth '00
Into the Fire '88
It Could Happen to You '94
Kisses in the Dark '97
Legion '10
Leo '02
Loveless '83
The Maldonado Miracle '03
Monster's Ball '01 ▸
My Blueberry Nights '07
Nickel Mountain '85
Parallel Sons '95
Payback '94
Pennies from Heaven '36
Petrified Forest '36 ▸
Pulp Fiction '94 ▸
Queen of Hearts '89 ▸
Recipe for Disaster '03
A Season for Miracles '99
Sliding Doors '97
Swimming '00
Trouble in Mind '86 ▸
The Undertaker and His Pals '67
Waiting for the Light '90
Waitress '07 ▸
When Harry Met Sally... '89 ▸

Dinosaurs

see also *Killer Beasts*
Adventures in Dinosaur City '92
Anonymous Rex '04
At the Earth's Core '76
Baby... Secret of the Lost Legend '85
Barney's Great Adventure '98
Carnosaur '93
Carnosaur 2 '94
Carnosaur 3: Primal Species '96
Caveman '81
Clifford '92
The Crater Lake Monster '77
Dennis the Menace: Dinosaur Hunter '93
Dinosaur '00
Dinosaur Island '93
Dinosaur Valley Girls '96
Dinosaurus! '60
Dinotopia '02
Ganjasaurus Rex '87
Ice Age: Dawn of the Dinosaurs '09
Inspector Gadget's Biggest Caper Ever '05
Josh Kirby. . .Time Warrior: Chapter 1, Planet of the Dino-Knights '95
Journey to the Center of the Earth '08
Jurassic Park '93 ▸
Jurassic Park 3 '01
King Dinosaur '55
King Kong '05 ▸
The Land Before Time '88 ▸
The Land Before Time 2: The Great Valley Adventure '94
The Land Before Time 3: The Time of the Great Giving '95
The Land Before Time 4: Journey Through the Mists '96
The Land Before Time 5: The Mysterious Island '97
The Land Before Time 6: The Secret of Saurus Rock '98
Land Before Time 7: The Stone of Cold Fire '00
Land of the Lost '09
The Land That Time Forgot '75
The Land That Time Forgot '09
The Land Unknown '57
The Lost Continent '51
The Lost World '25
The Lost World '92
The Lost World '02
The Lost World: Jurassic Park 2 '97
Massacre in Dinosaur Valley '85
Meet the Robinsons '07
My Science Project '85
A Nymphoid Barbarian in Dinosaur Hell '94
One Million B.C. '40
One Million Years B.C. '66
One of Our Dinosaurs Is Missing '75
Pee-wee's Big Adventure '85 ▸
The People That Time Forgot '77
Planet of the Dinosaurs '80
Prehysteria '93
Prehysteria 2 '94
Prehysteria 3 '95
Pterodactyl Woman from Beverly Hills '97
Return to the Lost World '93
Sir Arthur Conan Doyle's The Lost World '98
Sound of Horror '64
Super Mario Bros. '93
Tammy and the T-Rex '94
Teenage Caveman '58
Theodore Rex '95
Toy Story '95 ▸
Toy Story 2 '99 ▸
Two Lost Worlds '50
Unknown Island '48
The Valley of Gwangi '69 ▸
Warbirds '08
We're Back! A Dinosaur's Story '93
When Dinosaurs Ruled the Earth '70

Disaster Flicks

see also *Action-Adventure; Air Disasters; Meltdown; Sea Disasters*
Accident '83
After the Shock '90
Aftershock: Earthquake in New York '99
Airport '70 ▸
Airport '75 '75
Airport '77 '77
Alive '93
The Andromeda Strain '08
Armageddon '98
Assignment Outer Space '61
Asteroid '97
Atomic Train '99
Avalanche '78
Avalanche '99
Avalanche Express '79
Beyond the Poseidon Adventure '79
The Big Bus '76
Britannic '99
Brittanic '00
The Cassandra Crossing '76
Category 7 : The End of the World '05
Category 6 : Day of Destruction '04
The China Syndrome '79 ▸
The Christmas Coal Mine Miracle '77
City Beneath the Sea '71
City on Fire '78
The Concorde: Airport '79 '79
The Crash of Flight 401 '78
The Crowded Sky '60
Dante's Peak '97
The Day After Tomorrow '04
The Day the Sky Exploded '57
Daybreak '01
Daylight '96
Dead Ahead: The Exxon Valdez Disaster '92 ▸
Deep Core '00
Deep Impact '98
Disaster Movie '08
The Doomsday Flight '66
Earthquake '74
Earthstorm '06
Falling Fire '97
Fallout '01
Fatal Contact: Bird Flu in America '06
Final Warning '90
Fire '77
Fire and Rain '89
Firestorm '97
Firestorm: 72 Hours in Oakland '93
Firetrap '01
Flood! '76
Flood '07
Flood: A River's Rampage '97
Gale Force '01
Gray Lady Down '77
Hard Rain '97
The High and the Mighty '54 ▸
The Hindenburg '75
The Hole '98
The Hurricane '37 ▸
Hurricane '74
Hurricane '79
In Old Chicago '37 ▸
Independence Day '96 ▸
Inferno '98
Judgment Day '99
Krakatoa East of Java '69
Last Days of Pompeii '35
The Last Voyage '60
The Last Warrior '99
The Last Woman on Earth '61
The Lost Missile '58
Magma: Volcanic Disaster '06
Mayday at 40,000 Feet '76
Meltdown '06
Meteor '79
Morning Departure '50
A Night to Remember '58 ▸
Pandemic '07
Pandora's Clock '96
Panic in the Skies '96
The Perfect Storm '00
Planet on the Prowl '65
Poseidon '06
The Poseidon Adventure '72
Power Play '02
The Rains Came '39
Raise the Titanic '80
Red Alert '77
Red Planet '00
Right at Your Door '06
St. Helen's, Killer Volcano '82
Scorcher '02
Snowblind '78
Snowbound: The Jim and Jennifer Stolpa Story '94
S.O.S. Titanic '79
Space: 1999—Alien Attack '79 ▸
Storm Cell '08
The Survivalist '87
Survivor '87
Tailspin: Behind the Korean Airline Tragedy '89
Terror on the 40th Floor '74
Tidal Wave '75
Titanic '97 ▸
The Towering Inferno '74
Tragedy of Flight 103: The Inside Story '91 ▸
2012 '09
Twister '96
Two Minute Warning '76
Tycus '98
Velocity Trap '99
Volcano '97
Volcano: Fire on the Mountain '97
When Time Ran Out '80
White Squall '96
Y2K '99
Zero Hour! '57

Disco Musicals

see also *Musicals*
Can't Stop the Music '80
Car Wash '76
KISS Meets the Phantom of the Park '78
Pirate Movie '82
The Rocky Horror Picture Show '75 ▸
Roll Bounce '05 ▸
Saturday Night Fever '77
Thank God It's Friday '78
The Wiz '78
Xanadu '80

Disease of the Week

see also *AIDS; Emerging Viruses*
The Affair '73 ▸
And Now Ladies and Gentlemen '02
The Ann Jillian Story '88
As Good As It Gets '97 ▸
Away From Her '06 ▸
Bang the Drum Slowly '56
Batman and Robin '97
Beaches '88 ▸
Bear Ye One Another's Burden... '88
The Best Little Girl in the World '81 ▸
Between Two Women '86
The Blue Butterfly '04
Bobby Deerfield '77
The Book of Stars '99
The Boy in the Plastic Bubble '76
Brian's Song '71 ▸
Brian's Song '01
Bubble Boy '01
Camille '36 ▸
The Carrier '87
The Cassandra Crossing '76
Champions '84
Checking Out '89
Children of the Corn 4: The Gathering '96
Chinese Box '97
A Christmas Tale '08 ▸
C.H.U.D. '84
Cleo from 5 to 7 '61 ▸
Cold Harvest '98
Contagious '96
The Contaminated Man '01
Crash Course '00
Cries and Whispers '72 ▸
Crystal Heart '87
The Curse '87
Damien: The Leper Priest '80
Daybreak '93
Dead Man Walking '88
Dead Space '90
Dick Barton, Special Agent '48
The Doctor '91
Dr. Akagi '98
Doctor Bull '33
Down in the Delta '98 ▸
A Dream of Kings '69 ▸
Duet for One '86
Dying Young '91
An Early Frost '85 ▸
East of Kilimanjaro '57
The End '78 ▸
Eric '75 ▸
Erin Brockovich '00 ▸
Extraordinary Measures '10
The First Deadly Sin '80
First Do No Harm '97
Fourth Wish '75
Gaby: A True Story '87 ▸
Germicide '74
Girls' Night '97
Glory Enough for All: The Discovery of Insulin '92
Go Now '96 ▸
Griffin and Phoenix: A Love Story '76
Hangman's Curse '03
Here on Earth '00
Hilary and Jackie '98 ▸
Incredible Melting Man '77
Interrupted Melody '55 ▸
Intimate Contact '87 ▸
Iris '01 ▸
Isle of the Dead '45
Isn't She Great '00
Jack '96
Jericho Fever '93
John Grisham's The Rainmaker '97
Killer on Board '77
L.A. Bad '85
The Last Best Year '90
Last Breath '96
The Last Man on Earth '64
Look Both Ways '05
Lorenzo's Oil '92 ▸
Love Affair: The Eleanor & Lou Gehrig Story '77 ▸
Love Story '70 ▸
Love Under Pressure '78
Mad Death '83
Marvin's Room '96
A Matter of WHO '62
Miles to Go '86
Miss Evers' Boys '97
Molokai: The Story of Father Damien '99
A Mother's Prayer '95
My Father's House '75
My Life '93
Nasty Rabbit '64
Niagara, Niagara '97
On Her Majesty's Secret Service '69 ▸
One True Thing '98 ▸
Osmosis Jones '01
The Painted Veil '06
Panic in Echo Park '77
Parting Glances '86 ▸
Philadelphia '93 ▸
Pictures of Hollis Woods '07
Pilgrim, Farewell '82
The Plague '92
The Plague Dogs '82
The Pride of the Yankees '42 ▸
Princes in Exile '90
Project: Alien '89
Promises in the Dark '79
The Proud Ones '53
Quarantine '89
Question of Faith '93
A Quiet Duel '49
Rabid '77
Rasputin: Dark Servant of Destiny '96 ▸
Reborn '81
Right of Way '84
The Road to Galveston '96 ▸
The Road to Wellville '94
Safe House '99
The Shadow Box '80 ▸
Shadowlands '93 ▸
A Shining Season '79 ▸
Silence Like Glass '90
The Silver Streak '34
Simon Birch '98
Six Weeks '82
A Snake of June '02
A Song for Martin '01
Steel Magnolias '89 ▸
Stepmom '98 ▸
Stigma '73
Strange Relations '02
Sunchaser '96
Terms of Endearment '83 ▸
Terror Creatures from the Grave '66
That Russell Girl '08
The Theory of Flight '98
The Tic Code '99
A Time to Live '85
A Time to Remember '03
Venomous '01
Waking Up Wally '05
Walking Through the Fire '80
The Wedding Gift '93 ▸
When the Time Comes '91
When Wolves Cry '69
The White Legion '36
Xtro '83
ZigZag '02 ▸

Disorganized Crime

see also *Comic Cops; Crime Doesn't Pay; Crimedy; Organized Crime*
The Adventures of Pluto Nash '02
The Adventures of Rocky & Bullwinkle '00
Airheads '94
Albino Alligator '96
All About the Benjamins '02
All Saint's Day '98
Allie & Me '97
Amos and Andrew '93
The Apple Dumpling Gang '75
The Apple Dumpling Gang Rides Again '79
Armed and Dangerous '86
Baby on Board '92
Baby's Day Out '94
Bait '00
Bandits '01
Beautiful Creatures '00
Before the Devil Knows You're Dead '07 ▸
Big Nothing '06
Big Trouble '02
Born Bad '97
Bottle Rocket '95
Buffalo 66 '97 ▸
Children of Hannibal '98
Cop and a Half '93
Crackers '84
Crime Spree '03
Disorganized Crime '89
Dr. Otto & the Riddle of the Gloom Beam '86
Drowning Mona '00
Dying to Get Rich '98
8 Heads in a Duffel Bag '96
Ernest Goes to Jail '90
Everybody's Famous! '00
Face '97
Fargo '96 ▸
Find Me Guilty '06 ▸
Finders Keepers '84
A Fine Mess '86
Fish in a Barrel '01
Get Shorty '95 ▸
Glitch! '88
Goodbye South, Goodbye '96
Gravesend '97
Gridlock'd '96 ▸
The Gun in Betty Lou's Handbag '92
Gun Shy '00
Happy New Year '87
Headless Body in Topless Bar '96
Held Up '00
Her Alibi '88
Herbie Goes Bananas '80
High Heels and Low Lifes '01

▸ = rated three bones or higher

Hit Me '96
Home Alone '90 ►
Home Alone 2: Lost in New York '92
Hoods '98
I Wonder Who's Killing Her Now? '76
Idiot Box '97
In Bruges '08
In the Country Where Nothing Happens '99
Inside the Law '42
The Italian Job '69
The Jerky Boys '95
Keys to Tulsa '96
Kicked in the Head '97
Kill Me Later '01
Killing Zoe '94
Knockaround Guys '01
The League of Gentlemen '60 ►
Leather Jackets '90
L.I.E. '01
Lock, Stock and 2 Smoking Barrels '98 ►
Love, Honour & Obey '00
Lucky Numbers '00
Lunch Wagon '81
A Man, a Woman, and a Bank '79
Man of the House '95
Menage '86 ►
Mexican Hayride '48
Milo Milo '79
Miss Grant Takes Richmond '49
Mixed Nuts '94
More Dogs Than Bones '00
Mutant on the Bounty '89
A New Wave '07
The Night They Robbed Big Bertha's '75
Ocean's 11 '60
Once in the Life '00
Once Upon a Crime '92
101 Dalmatians '96
102 Dalmatians '00
Out on a Limb '92
Palookaville '95 ►
Partners '99
The Perfect Score '04
Perpetrators of the Crime '98
Picking Up the Pieces '99
Ping! '99
Poor White Trash '00
Pouvoir Intime '87
Quick Change '90
Ransom Money '70
Reservoir Dogs '92 ►
The River is Red '48
Round Trip to Heaven '92
Ruthless People '86 ►
Safe Men '98
St. Benny the Dip '51
Scorched '02
See No Evil, Hear No Evil '89
See Spot Run '01
Shake Hands with Murder '44
Shark Tale '04
The Shot '96
Silver Bears '78
Sister Act '92
Sitting Ducks '80 ►
6ixtynin9 '99
A Slight Case of Murder '99
Small Time Crooks '00
Snatch '00 ►
Stealing Harvard '02
Stop! or My Mom Will Shoot '92
Stop That Cab '51
Suicide Kings '97
The Super '91
Survivors '83
Tall, Tan and Terrific '46
The Thief Who Came to Dinner '73
Things to Do in Denver When You're Dead '95 ►
Three Kinds of Heat '87
Thrilled to Death '88
Too Many Crooks '59
Trapped in Paradise '94
Triggermen '02
Trouble Chasers '45
Truth or Consequences, N.M. '97
Two If by Sea '95
Two Tough Guys '03
Warm Blooded Killers '01
Welcome to Collinwood '02
We're Talkin' Serious Money '92
What's the Worst That Could Happen? '01
With Friends Like These '98 ►
The Wrong Arm of the Law '63 ►
The Young in Heart '38 ►
Zoolander '01

Divorce

***see also** Marriage; Single Parents; Singles; Stepparents*

The Accidental Tourist '88 ►
All I Want for Christmas '91
All the Good Ones Are Married '07
Alpha Beta '73
Angels in America '03 ►
The Assassination of Richard Nixon '05
The Awful Truth '37 ►
Bart Got a Room '08
Between Friends '83
A Bill of Divorcement '32
Blue Car '03 ►
Breaking Up '78
Breaking Up Is Hard to Do '79
Bringing Down the House '03
Bye Bye, Love '94
California Suite '78 ►
Can She Bake a Cherry Pie? '83
Catch Me If You Can '02
Celebrity '98 ►
Cheaper to Keep Her '80
Children of Divorce '80
City by the Sea '02
Clara's Heart '88
Cold Heat '90
A Conspiracy of Love '87
A Cooler Climate '99
Cross My Heart '88
Cyrus '10
Daisy Kenyon '47
Dead Cool '04
Definitely, Maybe '08 ►
Desert Hearts '86 ►
Diary of a Mad Black Woman '05
Divorce American Style '67
Divorce His, Divorce Hers '72
Divorce—Italian Style '62 ►
The Divorcee '30
Dr. T & the Women '00 ►
Dodson's Journey '01
Duane Hopwood '05 ►
Duck Season '04 ►
Dying to Get Rich '98
Early Frost '84
Eat, Pray, Love '10
Edie & Pen '95
Empire Falls '05
Escapade '55 ►
E.T.: The Extra-Terrestrial '82 ►
Every Other Weekend '91 ►
The Ex '96
Expectations '97
Face the Music '92
Faces '68 ►
Faithless '00 ►
Falling Down '93
Family Pictures '93 ►
Father Figure '80
Fergie & Andrew: Behind Palace Doors '93
A Fight for Jenny '90
The First Wives Club '96
5x2 '04
Flirting with Forty '09
Fool's Gold '08
For Richer or Poorer '97
Found Alive '34
The Full Monty '96 ►
The Fury Within '98
The Good Father '87 ►
The Good Mother '88
Goodbye Love '34
Hard Promises '92
Haywire '80
The Healer '02
Heartbreakers '01
Heartburn '86 ►
High Society '56 ►
History Is Made at Night '37 ►
Hollow Reed '95 ►
Hope Floats '98
House Arrest '96
How to Break Up a Happy Divorce '76
How to Commit Marriage '69
How to Deal '03
Husbands and Wives '92 ►
In Love We Trust '07
Interiors '78 ►
Intolerable Cruelty '03
Irreconcilable Differences '84
It's Complicated '09
The Kiss You Gave Me '00
Kramer vs. Kramer '79 ►
The Last Gangster '37
The Last Song '10
Late Marriage '01
Laws of Attraction '04
Le Divorce '03
Les Destinees '00
Let Us Be Gay '30
Let's Make It Legal '51
Liar Liar '97
The Liberation of L.B. Jones '70
Living Out Loud '98
Love '05
Love and Hate: A Marriage Made in Hell '90
Love Matters '93
Marie '85 ►
Marriage on the Rocks '65
The Marrying Kind '52
Me & Mrs. Jones '02
Me and You and Everyone We Know '05 ►
Melanie '82
Misbehaving Husbands '41
The Misfits '61 ►
Mrs. Doubtfire '93
Mr. Skeffington '44 ►
Mr. Wonderful '93
Mother '96
Must Love Dogs '05
My Foolish Heart '49
My One and Only '09
Nadine '87
Naked Paradise '78
Necessary Parties '88
Never Say Goodbye '46
A New Life '88
Night Life in Reno '31
The Night of the White Pants '06
Nothing in Common '86
Now and Then '95
Ocean's Eleven '01 ►
The Odd Couple '68 ►
The Odd Job '78
Old School '03
One Cooks, the Other Doesn't '83
The Parent Trap '61
The Parent Trap '98
Patti Rocks '88 ►
Payment on Demand '51
Peggy Sue Got Married '86
The Personals '83
Petulia '68 ►
Pilgrim, Farewell '82
Play It Again, Sam '72 ►
The Prize Pulitzer '89
Reckless '97 ►
Rich in Love '93
Rich Kids '79
Riptide '34 ►
The Santa Clause '94
Saraband '03 ►
Scenes from a Marriage '73 ►
Second Best '05
Second Chance '80
Second Honeymoon '37
See You in the Morning '89
Serving Sara '02
Sex and the Single Parent '82
Shattered Silence '71
Signs & Wonders '00
The Solitary Man '82
Something's Gotta Give '03 ►
The Squid and the Whale '05 ►
The Starter Wife '07
Starting Over '79 ►
Stepmom '98 ►
Strange Bedfellows '65
Sweet Revenge '90
Table for Five '83
Tattle Tale '92
Tell It to the Judge '49
Tell Me That You Love Me '84
Tenth Month '79
Thank You for Smoking '06
That Old Feeling '96
Then She Found Me '07
Till Murder Do Us Part '92
Town and Country '01
Twister '96
Under the Tuscan Sun '03
An Unmarried Woman '78 ►
The Upside of Anger '05 ►
Valentino Returns '88
Wah-Wah '05
Wanted: The Perfect Guy '86
The War of the Roses '89 ►
The Weather Man '05
Welcome to Mooseport '04
Wilderness Love '02
Without Anesthesia '78
Yella '07 ►

Doctors & Nurses

***see also** AIDS; Dental Mayhem; Disease of the Week; Emerging Viruses; Evil Doctors; Hospitals & Medicine; Nursploitation!; Sanity Check; Shrinks*

Adam Resurrected '08
Afterwards '08
All Creatures Great and Small '74 ►
Alone in the Dark '82
And the Band Played On '93 ►
The Android Affair '95
Anne of Green Gables: The Continuing Story '99
Any Given Sunday '99 ►
Arachnophobia '90
Armistead Maupin's More Tales of the City '97
Arrowsmith '32
Article 99 '92
Ashanti, Land of No Mercy '79
The Asphyx '72 ►
At First Sight '98
Atonement '07 ►
Awake '07
Awakenings '90 ►
Baby Girl Scott '87
Bad Medicine '85
Battle Circus '53
Beautiful People '99
Behind the Mask '99
Bethune '77
Between Wars '74
Beyond Borders '03
Beyond Re-Animator '03
Bikini House Calls '96
Bikini Med School '98
The Black Dragons '42
Black Friday '40
Blade '98
Bless the Child '00
Blind Justice '94
Bliss '96
Blood Mania '70
Blood Work '02
Bloodlink '86
Body Parts '91
Bone Daddy '97
Botany Bay '53
Brain Dead '89 ►
The Bramble Bush '60
Breast Men '97
Broken Glass '96
The Broken Mask '28
Brute Force '47 ►
The Bumblebee Flies Anyway '98
Calling Dr. Death '43
Calling Paul Temple '48
Candy Stripe Nurses '74
Carry On Again Doctor '69
Carry On Doctor '68 ►
Carry On Matron '72
Castle of the Creeping Flesh '68
Caught '49 ►
Century '94
Charlie Bravo '80
Children of Rage '75
Children of the Century '99
Children of the Corn 4: The Gathering '96
China Beach '88 ►
Christie's Revenge '07
The Cider House Rules '99 ►
Circus of Horrors '60
The Citadel '38 ►
City of Angels '98
City of Joy '92
The Clonus Horror '79
Club Havana '46
Coastlines '02
Coma '78 ►
Contagious '96
Corregidor '43
Corridors of Blood '58
Courageous Dr. Christian '40
Cries of Silence '97
Crimes & Misdemeanors '89 ►
Crisis '50
Critical Care '97
Critical Choices '97
Crossover '82
Dante 01 '08
Dark City '97
Dead in a Heartbeat '02
Dead Ringers '88 ►
Dead Sleep '91
Death Becomes Her '92 ►
Death by Prescription '86
Death Nurse '87
The Death of Mr. Lazarescu '05
Decoy '46
Deep Crimson '96
Depth Charge '08
The Devil's Web '74
Dirty Pretty Things '03 ►
Doc Hollywood '91
The Doctor '91
Dr. Akagi '98
Dr. Alien '88
The Doctor and the Devils '85
Doctor at Large '57
Doctor at Sea '56
Dr. Bell and Mr. Doyle: The Dark Beginnings of Sherlock Holmes '00
Dr. Bethune '90 ►
Dr. Black, Mr. Hyde '76
Doctor Blood's Coffin '62
Doctor Bull '33
Doctor Butcher M.D. '80
Dr. Caligari '89
Dr. Christian Meets the Women '40
Dr. Cyclops '40
Dr. Death, Seeker of Souls '73
Doctor Detroit '83
Doctor Dolittle '67
Dr. Dolittle '98
Dr. Dolittle 2 '01
Dr. Ehrlich's Magic Bullet '40
Doctor Faustus '68
Dr. Frankenstein's Castle of Freaks '74
Dr. Heckyl and Mr. Hype '80
Doctor in Clover '66
Doctor in Distress '63
Doctor in Love '60
Doctor in the House '53 ►
Dr. Jekyll and Mr. Hyde '73
Dr. Jekyll & Mr. Hyde '99
Dr. Jekyll and Mr. Hyde '08
Dr. Kildare's Strange Case '40
Dr. Mabuse, The Gambler '22 ►
Dr. Mabuse vs. Scotland Yard '64
Dr. Petiot '90
Doctor Satan's Robot '40
Dr. T & the Women '00 ►
Doctor Takes a Wife '40 ►
Dr. Tarr's Torture Dungeon '75
Dr. Terror's House of Horrors '65
Doctor Who '96
Doctor X '32
Doctor Zhivago '65 ►
Doctor Zhivago '03
Doctors and Nurses '82
Doctors' Wives '70
Dominick & Eugene '88 ►
Donor Unknown '95
Don't Cry, It's Only Thunder '82
Don't Look in the Basement '73
Dragonfly '02
Drunken Angel '48 ►
East of Borneo '31
The Egyptian '54
The Elephant Man '80 ►
Emmanuelle in the Country '78
An Enemy of the People '77
The English Patient '96 ►
Extraordinary Measures '10
Extreme Measures '96
Eyes Wide Shut '99
False Faces '32
Fantastic Voyage '66 ►
A Farewell to Arms '57
Fatal Error '99
The Fifth Horseman Is Fear '64
First Do No Harm '97
Flatliners '90
The Flesh and the Fiends '60
Flesh Feast '69
Florence Nightingale '85
Florence Nightingale '08
Flowers for Algernon '00
Foreign Body '86
The Fortune Cookie '66 ►
Fragments '08
The Fugitive '93 ►
Gifted Hands: The Ben Carson Story '09
Girl, Interrupted '99
Glory Enough for All: The Discovery of Insulin '92
The Great Moment '44
Gross Anatomy '89
Guest in the House '44
Gun Shy '00
Halloween 2: The Nightmare Isn't Over! '81
Hands Up '81 ►
Hard to Kill '89
Harold and Kumar Go to White Castle '04
He Loves Me ... He Loves Me Not '02
Healer '36
Hellgate '52
High Heels '72
A Hole in One '04
Holy Girl '04 ►
Holy Terror '65
Hombres Armados '97 ►
The Home Front '02
Honor Among Thieves '68
The Horrible Dr. Hichcock '62
The Horror Chamber of Dr. Faustus '59 ►
Horror Hospital '73
The Hospital '71 ►
Hospital of Terror '78
House Calls '78 ►
How I Killed My Father '03 ►
Hybrid '07
I Love My... Wife '70
I Never Promised You a Rose Garden '77 ►
I Take This Woman '40
In Dreams '98
The In-Laws '79 ►
In Love and War '96
The Incredible Journey of Dr. Meg Laurel '79 ►
An Indecent Obsession '85
Internes Can't Take Money '37
The Interns '62
Invasion '65
Jekyll & Hyde... Together Again '82
Jesse '88
Johnny Belinda '48 ►
Johnny Belinda '82

Junior '94
Just like Heaven '05
Kidnapping of Baby John Doe '88
Killing Moon '00
Kiss and Make Up '34
Korczak '90 ▸
La Sentinelle '92
Larceny On the Air '37
The Last Angry Man '59 ▸
The Last Bridge '54
The Last Enemy '08
The Last King of Scotland '06 ▸
Laurel Canyon '02
The Lazarus Syndrome '79
Le Cas du Dr. Laurent '57 ▸
Les Patterson Saves the World '90
Let's Get Married '60
Lie Down with Lions '94
Life Is a Long Quiet River '88 ▸
The Light in the Jungle '91
Like Father, Like Son '87
Living Proof '08
Looking for an Echo '99
Love '05
Love Finds a Home '09
Love for Rent '05
Love in the Time of Cholera '07
Love Is a Many-Splendored Thing '55
Love Takes Wing '09
Lover's Knot '96
Love's Unfolding Dream '07
Mad Love '35 ▸
The Mad Monster '42
The Madness of King George '94 ▸
Magnificent Obsession '35
Make-Up '37
Making Love '82
Malice '93
A Man to Remember '39
Maniac Nurses Find Ecstasy '94
Marvin's Room '96
M*A*S*H '70 ▸
M*A*S*H: Goodbye, Farewell & Amen '83 ▸
The Mask of Fu Manchu '32
Master and Commander: The Far Side of the World '03 ▸
A Matter of Life and Death '81
Matter of Trust '98
Maze '01
The Medicine Show '01
Meet Dr. Christian '39
Memories of Me '88
The Memory Keeper's Daughter '08
Men in White '34
Men of Ireland '38
Mesmer '94
Metamorphosis: The Alien Factor '93
The Millerson Case '47
The Millionairess '60
Miss Evers' Boys '97
Mr. North '88
Mockingbird Don't Sing '01
Molly '99
The Money Trap '65
Monty Python's The Meaning of Life '83 ▸
Murder in Texas '81 ▸
Murder Once Removed '71
Murder or Mercy '74
My Own Country '98
National Lampoon Presents RoboDoc '08
Nell '94
Night Call Nurses '72
Night Monster '42
Night Nurse '31 ▸
Night Nurse '77
Nightbreaker '89 ▸
Nine Months '95
No One Man '32
No Way Out '50
Noel '04
Nomads '86
Nora Prentiss '47
Not as a Stranger '55
Not of This Earth '96
Nurse '80
The Nurse '97
Nurse Betty '00 ▸
Nurse Edith Cavell '39 ▸
Nurse Marjorie '20
Nurse on Call '88
Old Swimmin' Hole '40
One Flew Over the Cuckoo's Nest '75 ▸
One Man's Journey '33
Only Love '98
Operation Mad Ball '57
Opium: Diary of a Madwoman '07
The Ordeal of Dr. Mudd '80 ▸
Out of the Ashes '03
Outbreak '94 ▸
The Painted Veil '06
Pandemic '07
Panic in Echo Park '77
Panic in the Streets '50 ▸
Paper Mask '91
Patch Adams '98
Pathology '08
The Patriot '99
Pearl Harbor '01
People Will Talk '51 ▸
Perfect Assassins '98
Persona '66 ▸
Petulia '68 ▸
Phenomenon '96
A Place for Annie '94
The Plague '92
Planet Terror '07
Playing God '96
Praying Mantis '83
The Princess and the Warrior '00 ▸
The Prisoner of Shark Island '36
Private Duty Nurses '71
Promises in the Dark '79
Purple Hearts '84
A Quiet Duel '49
Race Against Time '00
Rage '72
Rasen '98
The Raven '35 ▸
Re-Generation '04
The Real Glory '39 ▸
Reckless '97 ▸
Reckless Disregard '84
Reckless: The Sequel '98 ▸
Red Beard '65 ▸
Restoration '94 ▸
Riot Squad '41
The Road to Wellville '94
Robin Cook's Terminal '96
Rodgers & Hammerstein's South Pacific '01
Roommates '95
Salem's Lot '04
Saw '04
Saw 3 '06
Sawbones '95
Say Goodbye, Maggie Cole '72
Say It With Songs '29
Scalpel '76
The Secret of Dr. Kildare '39
Seducing Doctor Lewis '03
Series 7: The Contenders '01
Serving in Silence: The Margarethe Cammermeyer Story '95 ▸
Shadows '07
The Singing Detective '03
The Sins of Rachel Cade '61
Sister Dora '77
Sister Kenny '46 ▸
Skeezer '82
The Skeleton Key '05
Slaughter Hotel '71
Smart People '08
So Proudly We Hail '43 ▸
Someone Behind the Door '71
Something's Gotta Give '03 ▸
Sour Grapes '98
South Pacific '58 ▸
Speed Dating '07
Spraggue '84
The Spring '00
State of Emergency '94
Stigma '73
Stitches '85
A Stolen Face '52
The Story of Dr. Wassell '44
Strange Confession '45 ▸
The Student Nurses '70
Sublime '07
Sunchaser '96
The Surgeon '94
Talk to Her '02 ▸
Tarzan's Fight for Life '58
Tarzan's Hidden Jungle '55
Tears of the Sun '03
Teenage Frankenstein '58
Tell No One '06 ▸
Tender Loving Care '73
Testament of Youth '79
Things You Can Tell Just by Looking at Her '00
30 Years to Life '01
This Woman Is Dangerous '52
Torture Ship '39
Touched '05
Trial by Media '00
Tundra '36
The Twelve Days of Christmas Eve '04
The Twilight of the Ice Nymphs '97
The Unbearable Lightness of Being '88 ▸
The Uninvited '09
The Unknown Soldier '98
The Upturned Glass '47
A Very Serious Person '06
The Vicious Circle '57
Vital Signs '90
Vulture's Eye '04
Waitress '07 ▸
Waltzing Anna '06
We Are the Children '87
Welcome Stranger '47
What Dreams May Come '98
When Did You Last See Your Father? '07
When the Bullet Hits the Bone '96
Where Danger Lives '50
Where the Money Is '00
White Coats '04
White Dwarf '95
Who Killed Bambi? '03
Wit '01 ▸
Witness for the Prosecution '57 ▸
The Witnesses '07
Woman of Straw '64
Women of Valor '86
The X Files: I Want to Believe '08
Yes '04
Yes Nurse! No Nurse! '02
Young Doctors in Love '82
The Young Nurses '73
Zelary '03 ▸
Zero Hour! '57

Docudrama

see also Documentary

Above Us the Waves '56 ▸
Adam '83 ▸
After the Shock '90
Al Capone '59 ▸
Alexandria Again and Forever '90
The Amy Fisher Story '93
And Starring Pancho Villa as Himself '03 ▸
And the Band Played On '93 ▸
Anvil! The Story of Anvil '09
Baadasssss! '03 ▸
Babyfever '94
The Battle of Algiers '66 ▸
Battle of the Rails '46 ▸
Beefcake '99
Blind Ambition '79
The Boston Strangler '68
Bound for Glory '76 ▸
Boycott '02 ▸
Call Me: The Rise and Fall of Heidi Fleiss '04
Call Northside 777 '48 ▸
Casualties of Love: The "Long Island Lolita" Story '93
Chasing Freedom '04
Christian the Lion '76
The Class '08
Close to Home '86
Cocaine: One Man's Seduction '83
Conspiracy: The Trial of the Chicago Eight '87 ▸
The Cool World '63
Countdown '68
The Courtesans of Bombay '85 ▸
Crown Heights '02
The Cruel Sea '53 ▸
A Cry in the Dark '88 ▸
DC 9/11: Time of Crisis '04
Edge of the World '37 ▸
8-A '92
Endgame '09
The Flaming Teen-Age '56
Free, White, and 21 '62
The General Line '29 ▸
H '90
Helter Skelter Murders '71
Henry: Portrait of a Serial Killer '90 ▸
Hiroshima '95 ▸
Hostages '93 ▸
Immortal Battalion '44 ▸
In Cold Blood '67 ▸
Inside the Third Reich '82
Iron & Silk '91
James Dean '76
The Jayne Mansfield Story '80
Journey Through Rosebud '72
Kamikaze Hearts '91
Kids '95
King '78 ▸
Lethal Lolita—Amy Fisher: My Story '92
The Lion Has Wings '40
Looking for Richard '96 ▸
Mandela and de Klerk '97
The Manson Family '04
Miss Evers' Boys '97
Moolaade '04
Murder in Texas '81 ▸
The Naked City '48 ▸
No Turning Back '01
Our Music '04
Panther '95
Pickpocket '59 ▸
The Poppy Is Also a Flower '66
Prince of the City '81 ▸
Qui Etes Vous, Mr. Sorge? '61
Real Life '79 ▸
The Red Menace '49
The Road to Guantanamo '06
Shaka Zulu '83 ▸
S.O.S. Titanic '79
Special Bulletin '83 ▸
The Spy Who Came in from the Cold '65 ▸
Stealing Sinatra '04
Tailspin: Behind the Korean Airline Tragedy '89
Take the Money and Run '69 ▸
Tarnation '03
Teenage Devil Dolls '53
Ten Days That Shook the World '27 ▸
That's Adequate '90
The Thin Blue Line '88 ▸
32 Short Films about Glenn Gould '93 ▸
This Revolution '05
Times of Harvey Milk '83 ▸
Touching the Void '03
Uprising '01 ▸
What the $*! Do We Know? '04
Women in Prison '49
Working Girls '87 ▸

Documentary

see also Docudrama

After Innocence '05 ▸
Aileen: Life and Death of a Serial Killer '03 ▸
Air Guitar Nation '06 ▸
American Fabulous '92
American Movie '99 ▸
American Teen '08
America's Heart and Soul '04
Anna '93 ▸
Arctic Tale '07
The Aristocrats '05 ▸
Assassination of Trotsky '72
The Atomic Cafe '82 ▸
Awesome! I F***in' Shot That! '06 ▸
Ballet Russes '05 ▸
The Big One '98
Bigger Stronger Faster '08
Born Into Brothels: Calcutta's Red Light Kids '04
Born to Boogie '72
Bowling for Columbine '02 ▸
The Boys of Baraka '05
The Boys of 2nd Street Park '03 ▸
Bra Boys '07
A Brief History of Time '92 ▸
Brother's Keeper '92 ▸
Bruce Lee: Curse of the Dragon '93 ▸
Buena Vista Social Club '99 ▸
Burden of Dreams '82 ▸
Bush's Brain '04
Cannonball Run Europe: The Great Escape '05
Capitalism: A Love Story '09
Capturing the Friedmans '03 ▸
Catfish '10
The Celluloid Closet '95 ▸
Chicago 10 '07 ▸
The Children of Theatre Street '77 ▸
Children Underground '03 ▸
Chuck Berry: Hail! Hail! Rock 'n' Roll '87 ▸
Ciao Federico! Fellini Directs Satyricon '69
The Clowns '71 ▸
Collapse '09
Common Threads: Stories from the Quilt '89
Control Room '04 ▸
The Cove '09
Crazy Love '07 ▸
Crumb '94 ▸
Dance Hall Racket '58
Darfur Now '07
Darwin's Nightmare '04 ▸
Dave Chappelle's Block Party '06 ▸
A Decade Under the Influence '02 ▸
December 7th: The Movie '91
Decline of Western Civilization 1 '81 ▸
Decline of Western Civilization 2: The Metal Years '88 ▸
Deep Blue '03 ▸
Derby '71 ▸
The Devil and Daniel Johnston '05 ▸
The Devil Came on Horseback '07
DIG! '04 ▸
Dreams with Sharp Teeth '07 ▸
Dust to Glory '05 ▸
Earth '07
The 11th Hour '07
Elvis in Hollywood '93 ▸
Encounter with the Unknown '75
Encounters at the End of the World '07 ▸
End of the Century: The Story of the Ramones '03 ▸
The Endless Summer '66 ▸
The Endless Summer 2 '94 ▸
Enron: The Smartest Guys in the Room '05 ▸
Every Little Step '08
The Eyes of Tammy Faye '00
Fade to Black '04 ▸
Fahrenheit 9/11 '04 ▸
Fallen Champ: The Untold Story of Mike Tyson '93 ▸
Fast, Cheap & Out of Control '97 ▸
Fellini: I'm a Born Liar '03
Festival Express '03 ▸
The Filth and the Fury '99
First Descent '05
The First Saturday in May '08
The Fog of War: Eleven Lessons from the Life of Robert S. McNamara '03 ▸
Food, Inc. '08
Fuel '08 ▸
Full Tilt Boogie '97
Germany in Autumn '78
Giuliani Time '05
Go Further '03
God Grew Tired of Us '06 ▸
The Goebbels Experiment '05
Going Upriver: The Long War of John Kerry '04
Gonzo: The Life and Work of Dr. Hunter S. Thompson '08 ▸
Good Hair '09
Gray's Anatomy '96
Grizzly Man '05 ▸
The Ground Truth '06
Guilty of Treason '50
Gunner Palace '04 ▸
Hank Aaron: Chasing the Dream '95 ▸
Harlan County, U.S.A. '76 ▸
Haxan: Witchcraft through the Ages '22 ▸
The Heart of the Game '05
Hearts of Darkness: A Filmmaker's Apocalypse '91 ▸
Heavy Petting '89
Heckler '08
Hell's Angels Forever '83 ▸
The Hellstrom Chronicle '71 ▸
Henri Langlois: The Phantom of the Cinematheque '04 ▸
Hide and Seek '80
Hijacking Catastrophe: 9/11, Fear and the Selling of America '04
Hoop Dreams '94 ▸
How to Eat Your Watermelon in White Company (and Enjoy It) '05 ▸
Hugh Hefner: Once Upon a Time '92 ▸
The Hunting of the President '04
I Wanna Be a Beauty Queen '85
In the Pit '06
In the Realms of the Unreal '04 ▸
In the Shadow of the Moon '07 ▸
Incident at Oglala: The Leonard Peltier Story '92 ▸
An Inconvenient Truth '06 ▸
Inside Deep Throat '05 ▸
The Ister '04 ▸
It Happened in the Park '56
It Might Get Loud '09
It's All True '93
Jesus Camp '06
The JFK Conspiracy '91
Joan Rivers: A Piece of Work '10
Journeys with George '02
Kicking It '08
The Kid Stays in the Picture '02 ▸
Kidco '83
The King of Kong: A Fistful of Quarters '07 ▸
The Last Waltz '78 ▸
LBJ: A Biography '91
Le Joli Mai '62 ▸
League of Ordinary Gentlemen '04 ▸
The Leopard Son '96 ▸
Let It Be '70
Let's Get Lost '88
The Life and Times of Hank Greenberg '99 ▸
Lighting in a Bottle '04 ▸
Long Shadows '86
Lost in La Mancha '03 ▸
Louisiana Story '48 ▸
The Love Goddesses '65 ▸
Love Meetings '64
Mad Hot Ballroom '05 ▸
Malcolm X: Make It Plain '95 ▸
Man in the Silk Hat '83 ▸
Man of Aran '34 ▸
Man on Wire '08

▸ = rated three bones or higher

The Man with the Movie Camera '29 ▶
Many Faces of Sherlock Holmes '86
March of the Penguins '05 ▶
Marjoe '72
Maxed Out: Hard Times, Easy Credit and the Era of Predatory Lenders '06
Mayor of the Sunset Strip '03 ▶
Metallica: Some Kind of Monster '04 ▶
Microcosmos '96 ▶
Moana, a Romance of the Golden Age '26 ▶
Mondo Cane '63
Mondo Cane 2 '64
Mondovino '04
Moon over Broadway '98 ▶
Murderball '05 ▶
Must Read After My Death '09
My Architect: A Son's Journey '03 ▶
My Date With Drew '05 ▶
Neil Young: Heart of Gold '06 ▶
New York Doll '05 ▶
Nico Icon '95 ▶
Night of the Living Dead, 25th Anniversary Documentary '93
No End in Sight '07 ▶
Occupation: Dreamland '05 ▶
Oceans '09
Of Time and the City '08
Only the Strong Survive '03 ▶
Orwell Rolls in His Grave '03
Our Brand Is Crisis '05 ▶
Outfoxed: Rupert Murdoch's War on Journalism '04 ▶
Outrage '09
Overnight '03 ▶
Paper Clips '04 ▶
Paris Is Burning '91 ▶
Peace, Propaganda & the Promised Land '04
Prelude to War '42
Prisoner of Paradise '02 ▶
Protocols of Zion '05 ▶
The Real Dirt on Farmer John '06 ▶
Reel Paradise '05 ▶
Religulous '08 ▶
Restrepo '10
Riding Giants '04
Rize '05 ▶
Rock Hudson's Home Movies '92
Rock School '05 ▶
Roger & Me '89 ▶
Roman Polanski: Wanted and Desired '08
S21: The Khmer Rouge Killing Machine '03 ▶
Sasquatch '76
The Seafarers '53
The September Issue '09
Sex and Buttered Popcorn '91
Sex Positive '09
Shake Hands With the Devil: The Journey of Romeo Dallaire '04 ▶
Sherman's March '86 ▶
Shine a Light '08
The Show '95
Sicko '07
Soft and Hard '85
The Sorrow and the Pity '71 ▶
Spellbound '02 ▶
Standard Operating Procedure '08 ▶
Standing in the Shadows of Motown '02 ▶
Step Into Liquid '03 ▶
Stolen Childhoods '05
Stone Reader '02 ▶
The Story of the Weeping Camel '03 ▶
Streetwise '84 ▶
Stripper '86
Super Size Me '04 ▶
Superstar: The Life and Times of Andy Warhol '90 ▶
Surfwise '07 ▶
Swimming to Cambodia '87 ▶
Tarnation '03
Taxi to the Dark Side '07 ▶
Tell Them Who You Are '05
Thank You & Good Night '91
Theremin: An Electronic Odyssey '95 ▶
The Thin Blue Line '88 ▶
39 Pounds of Love '05
This Film Is Not Yet Rated '06
Through the Fire '05 ▶
The Tillman Story '10
Tokyo-Ga '85 ▶
Tokyo Olympiad '66 ▶
Touching the Void '03
Triumph of the Will '34 ▶
The Troubles We've Seen '94
Trumbo '07 ▶
Truth or Dare '91
20 Dates '99
Tyson '08
Uncovered: The War on Iraq '04
The U.S. Vs. John Lennon '06
Unknown White Male '05 ▶
The Unmistaken Child '08
An Unreasonable Man '06 ▶
The Untold Story of Emmett Louis Till '05 ▶
Unzipped '94 ▶
Up for Grabs '05
Verdict on Auschwitz: The Frankfurt Auschwitz Trial 1963—1965 '93 ▶
Vince Vaughn's Wild West Comedy Show '06
Visions of Light: The Art of Cinematography '93 ▶
Voices of Iraq '04 ▶
Waiting for Superman '10
Wal-Mart: The High Cost of Low Price '05 ▶
Wall '04 ▶
Waltz with Bashir '08 ▶
The War Room '93 ▶
War Tapes '06 ▶
The Weather Underground '02 ▶
When We Were Kings '96 ▶
Where in the World Is Osama Bin Laden? '06
Which Way Home '09
The White Diamond '04 ▶
Who Gets to Call It Art? '05
Who Killed the Electric Car? '06
Wigstock: The Movie '95
The Wild Parrots of Telegraph Hill '03 ▶
The Wildest Dream: Conquest of Everest '10
Winged Migration '01 ▶
Wisecracks '93 ▶
Word Wars: Tiles and Tribulations on the Scrabble Circuit '04 ▶
Wordplay '06 ▶
Year of the Horse '97
The Yes Men '03
Young@Heart '07 ▶

Dolls That Kill

***see** Killer Toys*

Domestic Abuse

***see also** Sexual Abuse*

The Abduction '96
Angel Eyes '01
The Break Up '98
The Burning Bed '85 ▶
Cafe Ole '00
Casualties '97
Dangerous Child '01
Dangerous Game '93
Dear Frankie '04
Edge of Madness '02
Enough '02
Evil '03 ▶
Fallen Angel '99
Falling Down '93
Far Cry from Home '81
.45 '06
The Gift '00
Harm's Way '07
Honey & Ashes '96
The House Next Door '01
The Human Stain '03
The Ice House '97 ▶
In the Bedroom '01 ▶
Independence Day '83
Instinct to Kill '01
Intimate Strangers '77
John John in the Sky '00
Lea '96
Lift '01
Love Come Down '00
Love Letters '45
The Merry Gentleman '08
Mesmerized '84
Mortal Thoughts '91
Nil by Mouth '96
Olivia '83
100 Feet '08
The Opponent '01
Our Mother's Murder '97
Perfect Crime '97
Personal Velocity: Three Portraits '02 ▶
Plain Dirty '04
Prairie Fever '08
Remember Me '85
Ryna '05
Shattered Dreams '90
Sleep Easy, Hutch Rimes '00
Sleeping with the Enemy '91
Solas '99
Take My Eyes '03
The Tenant of Wildfell Hall '96
This Boy's Life '93 ▶
An Unfinished Life '05
Vanessa '07
Visitor Q '01
Waitress '07 ▶
What's Love Got to Do with It? '93
While She Was Out '08
Woman Undone '95
Woman with a Past '92
Your Vice is a Closed Room and Only I Have the Key '72

Doofus Dads

***see also** Bad Dads; Dads; Single Parents; Slapstick Comedy; Stepparents*

Caddyshack 2 '88
Cheaper by the Dozen '03
Cheaper by the Dozen 2 '05
Coraline '09 ▶
Daddy Day Camp '07
Father of the Bride '91
Father of the Bride Part 2 '95
Honey, I Shrunk the Kids '89
Kicking & Screaming '05
Little Miss Sunshine '06 ▶
National Lampoon's Christmas Vacation '89
National Lampoon's European Vacation '85
National Lampoon's Vacation '83 ▶
Parenthood '89 ▶
RV '06
Three Men and a Baby '87 ▶
Vegas Vacation '96
What about Bob? '91 ▶

Doublecross!

***see also** Crime Drama; Heists; Revenge; Scams, Stings & Cons*

Casino Royale '06 ▶
Circus '00
The Code '09
Colorado Territory '49
The Contractor '07
Criss Cross '48 ▶
Cypher '02 ▶
Decoy '46
Diamond Run '00
Direct Contact '09
Dot the I '03
The Family '70
Four Days '99
The Hades Factor '06
Heist '01 ▶
The Italian Job '03 ▶
Journey to the End of the Night '06
Killer '73
A Lady of Chance '28
Lucky Number Slevin '06
National Lampoon's Gold Diggers '04
Niagara '52
No Good Deed '02
Our America '02
Out of the Past '47 ▶
Partners '99
Payback '98 ▶
Pulse 2: Afterlife '08
Score '95
The Sentinel '06
Seoul Raiders '05
The Set Up '95
Shutter '05
Six Gun Trail '38
Sniper 3 '04
Swindled '04
Thicker than Water '99
Tick Tock '00 ▶
The Ultimate Weapon '97
Wild Things '98
Wild Things 2 '04

Down Under

The Adventures of Priscilla, Queen of the Desert '94 ▶
Age of Consent '69
The Alice '04
Alien Visitor '95
Alvin Purple '73
Anzacs: The War Down Under '85 ▶
Around the World in 80 Ways '86
Australia '08
Back of Beyond '95
Barry McKenzie Holds His Own '74
Battle Cry '55 ▶
Between Wars '74
Black Water '07
Blackrock '97
Blackwater Trail '95
Blood Surf '00
The Blue Lightning '86
Bootmen '00
Botany Bay '53
Boulevard of Broken Dreams '88
The Boys '98 ▶
Brides of Christ '91
Broken English '96
Burke & Wills '85
Caddie '76
Candy '06
The Cars That Ate Paris '74 ▶
Cass '78
The Castle '97
The Chant of Jimmie Blacksmith '78 ▶
Children of the Revolution '95
Chopper '00
Country Life '95
Crocodile Dundee '86 ▶
Crocodile Dundee 2 '88
Crocodile Dundee in Los Angeles '01
The Crocodile Hunter: Collision Course '02
A Cry in the Dark '88 ▶
The Custodian '94
Danny Deckchair '03
Dark Age '88
Dead Alive '93
Dead Easy '82
Dead Heart '96 ▶
Death of a Soldier '85
December Boys '07
The Desert Rats '53 ▶
Dingo '90
Disgrace '08
The Dish '00 ▶
Do or Die '01
Down Under '86
The Dunera Boys '85 ▶
Dusty '85
The Echo of Thunder '98
Erskinville Kings '99
Eureka Stockade '49
Fair Game '85
Fast Talking '86
Fierce Creatures '96
15 Amore '98
Finding Nemo '03 ▶
Forty Thousand Horsemen '41
Freedom '82
The Fringe Dwellers '86
Gallagher's Travels '87
Gallipoli '81 ▶
Garage Days '03
Geordie '55
The Getting of Wisdom '77
The Good Wife '86
Great Gold Swindle '84
Ground Zero '88 ▶
Hammers over the Anvil '91
The Hard Word '02
Head On '98 ▶
Heavenly Creatures '94 ▶
Heaven's Burning '97
Holy Smoke '99
Howling 3: The Marsupials '87
Hurricane Smith '92
The Incredible Journey of Mary Bryant '05
The Irishman '78
Jackie Chan's First Strike '96 ▶
Japanese Story '03 ▶
Jindabyne '06
Kangaroo Jack '02
Kings in Grass Castles '97
Kitty and the Bagman '82
Lantana '01 ▶
The Lighthorsemen '87 ▶
A Little Bit of Soul '97
Little Boy Lost '78
Love Serenade '96
Mad Dog Morgan '76
The Man from Snowy River '82
Marking Time '03
Maslin Beach '97
Miracle Down Under '87
Mission: Impossible 2 '00 ▶
Mr. Nice Guy '98
Mr. Reliable: A True Story '95
Money Movers '78
Monkey Grip '82 ▶
Moving Out '83
Muriel's Wedding '94 ▶
My Brilliant Career '79 ▶
The Naked Country '85
Nature's Grave '08
Ned Kelly '70
Ned Kelly '03
Nevil Shute's The Far Country '85
Newcastle '08
The Night We Called It a Day '03
The Nugget '02
On the Beach '59 ▶
On the Beach '00
Once Were Warriors '94 ▶
One Crazy Night '93
Only the Brave '94
Oscar and Lucinda '97
Overlanders '46 ▶
Palm Beach '79
Passion '99
Perfect Strangers '03
Phar Lap '84
Plum Role '07
Praise '98 ▶
Prince and the Great Race '83
Prisoners of the Sun '91 ▶
The Quest '86
Quigley Down Under '90
Rabbit-Proof Fence '02 ▶
Race the Sun '96
Rebel '85
Reckless Kelly '93
The Rescuers Down Under '90
Return to Snowy River '88 ▶
Ride a Wild Pony '75 ▶
The Right Hand Man '87
River Queen '05
The Road from Coorain '02
Robbery under Arms '57
Rogue '07
Romulus, My Father '07 ▶
Run, Rebecca, Run '81
Sara Dane '81
Savage Attraction '83
Shine '95 ▶
The Shrimp on the Barbie '90
Siam Sunset '99
Silver City '84
The Silver Stallion: King of the Wild Brumbies '93
Sirens '94
Sister Kenny '46 ▶
Soft Fruit '99
Sorrento Beach '95
Squizzy Taylor '84
Stingaree '34
Stones of Death '88
Strange Bedfellows '04
Strange Fits of Passion '99
Strictly Ballroom '92 ▶
Summer City '77
The Sundowners '60 ▶
Sweet Talker '91
Talk '94
The Tattooist '07
The Thorn Birds '83 ▶
Tim '79
Two Hands '98 ▶
Undead '05
Under Capricorn '49
Under Capricorn '82
Under the Lighthouse Dancing '97
The Wacky World of Wills & Burke '85
Walkabout '71 ▶
A Waltz Through the Hills '88
Waterfront '83
We of the Never Never '82 ▶
Welcome to Woop Woop '97
Where the Green Ants Dream '84
The Winds of Jarrah '83
The Winter of Our Dreams '82
Wolf Creek '05
Wrangler '88

Downsized

Capitalism: A Love Story '09
Days and Clouds '07
Falling Down '93
The Full Monty '96 ▶
Fun with Dick and Jane '77
Fun With Dick and Jane '05
Hank and Mike '08
Hardly Working '81
Love on the Dole '41 ▶
Mondays in the Sun '02
New in Town '09
Office Space '98
Roger & Me '89 ▶
Up in the Air '09 ▶

Dragons

***see also** Medieval Romps*

Beowulf '07 ▶
Beyond Sherwood Forest '09
Captain Sinbad '63
Dragon Storm '04
Dragon Wars '07
Dragonheart '96
Dragonheart: A New Beginning '00
Dragonslayer '81 ▶
Dragonworld '94
Dungeons and Dragons '00
Eragon '06
Erik the Viking '89
George and the Dragon '04
Ghidrah the Three Headed Monster '65
Goliath and the Dragon '61
Harry Potter and the Goblet of Fire '05 ▶
How to Train Your Dragon '10
Jabberwocky '77
Jack the Giant Killer '62 ▶
Jason and the Argonauts '63 ▶
Knights of Bloodsteel '09
The Magic Sword '62
Mulan '98
The Mummy: Tomb of the Dragon Emperor '08
The NeverEnding Story '84 ▶
Orochi, the Eight Headed Dragon '94
Pete's Dragon '77
Pufnstuf '70
Quest for Camelot '98
Reign of Fire '02
The Seventh Voyage of Sinbad '58 ▶
Shrek '01 ▶
Sleeping Beauty '59 ▶

Sword & the Dragon *'56*
The Wonderful World of the Brothers Grimm *'62*
Wyvern *'09*

Drama

see *Adventure Drama; Comedy Drama; Coming of Age; Crime Drama; Docudrama; Historical Drama; Musical Drama; Romantic Drama; Showbiz Dramas; Sports Dramas; Tearjerkers; Tragedy; Urban Drama*

Black Belt *'07*
Bone Dry *'07*
Breakaway *'02*
Father of the Kamikaze *'74*
Flower & Snake 2 *'05*
Flower & Snake '74 *'74*
Goyokin *'69* ►
Have Sword, Will Travel *'69*
My Bloody Roommates *'06*
Pom Poko *'94*
Raw Summer *'06* ►
Ronin Gai *'90*
Salty O'Rourke *'45*
Shogun's Samurai—The Yagyu Clan Conspiracy *'78*
301/302 *'95*
The Wandering Swordsman *'70*

Dream Girls

see also *Beauty Pageants*

A la Mode *'94*
Age of Consent *'69*
American Graffiti *'73* ►
Angelique *'64*
Angelique and the King *'66*
Angelique and the Sultan *'68*
Angelique: The Road to Versailles *'65*
Angus *'95*
The Arena *'73*
Barb Wire *'96*
The Barbarians *'87*
Baywatch the Movie: Forbidden Paradise *'95*
Beauties of the Night *'52*
Beautiful Girls *'96* ►
Beauty School *'93*
Bikini Bistro *'94*
The Bikini Car Wash Company *'90*
The Bikini Car Wash Company 2 *'92*
Bikini Drive-In *'94*
Bikini Island *'91*
Bikini Summer *'91*
Bikini Summer 3: South Beach Heat *'97*
Blondes Have More Guns *'95*
Bluebeard *'72*
Bolero *'84*
Burial of the Rats *'95*
Calendar Girl Murders *'84*
California Girls *'84*
Cannonball Run *'81*
Cannonball Run 2 *'84*
Can't Buy Me Love *'87*
Cheerleader Camp *'88*
The Chosen One: Legend of the Raven *'98*
City of Women *'81*
Cover Me *'95*
Creatures the World Forgot *'70*
Cupid *'96*
Cycle Vixens *'79*
Daddy-O *'59*
Day of the Warrior *'96*
Deadly Weapons *'70*
Def Jam's How to Be a Player *'97*
Desperate Cargo *'41*
Desperate Moves *'86*
Devil Girl from Mars *'54*
The Devil's Hand *'61*
Diamonds Are Forever *'71* ►
Dinosaur Valley Girls *'96*
Divine Nymph *'71*
Do or Die *'91*
Dr. Alien *'88*
Dr. Goldfoot and the Bikini Machine *'66*
Dr. No *'62* ►
The Doll *'62*
The Doll Squad *'73*
The Dolls *'83*
Domino *'88*
Downhill Willie *'96*
Dracula: Dead and Loving It *'95*
Dream Trap *'90*
Dreaming of Rita *'94*
Dumb & Dumber *'94*
Emmanuelle *'74*
Emmanuelle 4 *'84*
Emmanuelle & Joanna *'78*
Emmanuelle in the Country *'78*
Emmanuelle on Taboo Island *'76*
Emmanuelle, the Joys of a Woman *'76*
Emmanuelle, the Queen *'79*
Emmanuelle's Daughter *'79*
Enchanted *'07*
Enchanted Island *'58*
Evil Toons *'90*
Exotica *'94* ►
Fair Game *'82*
Fate *'90*
Femme Fontaine: Killer Babe for the C.I.A. *'95*
Fire Maidens from Outer Space *'56*
Fireballs *'90*
Forbidden Games *'95*
Forbidden Planet *'56* ►
Forbidden Zone: Alien Abduction *'96*
Foreign Exchange *'08*
Gamera vs. Guiron *'69*
Gator Bait *'73*
Ghosts Can't Do It *'90*
Girl Shy *'24* ►
Gold of the Amazon Women *'79*
Goldeneye *'95* ►
Good Luck Chuck *'07*
The Good Night *'07*
The Grace Kelly Story *'83*
Great Bikini Off-Road Adventure *'94*
Guns *'90*
Hard Hunted *'92*
Helen of Troy *'56*
Hell's Belles *'95*
Hercules and the Princess of Troy *'65*
Hired to Kill *'91*
Hollywood Boulevard 2 *'89*
Hollywood or Bust *'56*
The Hottie and the Nottie *'08*
The House Bunny *'08*
How I Learned to Love Women *'66*
How to Succeed with Girls *'64*
I, a Woman *'66*
I Love You, Beth Cooper *'09*
I Married a Centerfold *'84*
I Posed for Playboy *'91*
Interstate 60 *'02*
It Takes a Thief *'59*
Junk Mail *'97*
Just Looking *'99*
Kiss and Kill *'68*
Kiss and Make Up *'34*
La Collectionneuse *'67*
Last Dance *'91*
Les Girls *'57*
Les Mistons *'57* ►
The Lion of Thebes *'64* ►
Lost and Found *'99*
The Loves of Hercules *'60*
Malena *'00*
A Man with a Maid *'73*
Masseuse *'95*
The Mermaids of Tiburon *'62*
Mirror Images *'91*
Mirror Images 2 *'93*
Mirror, Mirror 3: The Voyeur *'96*
Miss March *'09*
Missile to the Moon *'59*
Mysterious Island of Beautiful Women *'79*
Mystery Date *'91*
Naked Souls *'95*
National Lampoon's Vacation *'83* ►
Never Say Never Again *'83*
Nine Ages of Nakedness *'69*
The Notorious Bettie Page *'06*
A Nymphoid Barbarian in Dinosaur Hell *'94*
Oxford Blues *'84*
Panther Squad *'84*
Party Incorporated *'89*
Phat Beach *'96*
Pin-Up Girl *'44*
Posed for Murder *'89*
Priceless Beauty *'90*
Princess Daisy *'83*
Private Affairs *'89*
Queen of Outer Space *'58*
Queen of the Jungle *'35*
The Reckless Way *'36*
Return to Savage Beach *'97*
Revenge of the Cheerleaders *'76*
Round Trip to Heaven *'92*
Savage Beach *'89*
Seduce Me: Pamela Principle 2 *'94*
The Seven Year Itch *'55* ►
She Gods of Shark Reef *'56*
She's Dressed to Kill *'79*
She's Out of My League *'10*
Sidekicks *'93*
Silk 'n' Sabotage *'94*
Sizzle Beach U.S.A. *'74*
Ski School 2 *'94*
Slumber Party Massacre *'82*
Some Like It Hot *'59* ►
Sorceress *'82*
Soup for One *'82*
South Beach Academy *'96*
Spinout *'66*
The Spring *'89*
Star Crash *'78*
The Story of a Love Story *'73*
Strawberry Blonde *'41* ►
The Sure Thing *'85* ►
Swimsuit *'89*
The Swinging Cheerleaders *'74*
Tammy and the Doctor *'63*
Tanya's Island *'81*
Tarzan, the Ape Man *'81*
Telling Lies in America *'96*
10 *'79*
Ten Things I Hate about You *'99* ►
There's Something about Mary *'98* ►
Thieves of Fortune *'89*
Thunder & Mud *'89*
To the Limit *'95*
Tomorrow Never Dies *'97*
Too Shy to Try *'78*
Total Exposure *'91*
Trojan War *'97*
Undercover *'94*
Underground Aces *'80*
Untamable Angelique *'67*
Vampire Vixens from Venus *'94*
Vampire's Kiss *'88* ►
Vice Academy 3 *'91*
Voyage to the Planet of Prehistoric Women *'68*
Wayne's World *'92* ►
Wayne's World 2 *'93*
Weird Science *'85*
Wet and Wild Summer *'92*
When Dinosaurs Ruled the Earth *'70*
Who Wants to Kill Jessie? *'65*
Will Success Spoil Rock Hunter? *'57*
Wish Me Luck *'95*
Wishful Thinking *'92*
The Woman in Red *'84*
Woo *'97*
You Only Live Twice *'67*
Young Nurses in Love *'89*
Youth in Revolt *'10*
Zeta One *'69*

Dropouts

Boiler Room *'00* ►
Choke *'08*
Frankenhooker *'90*
The Great Buck Howard *'09*
The Scar *'48*
Street Girls *'75*
Trust *'91*
Young Man with a Horn *'50* ►
Zabriskie Point *'70* ►

Drug Use & Abuse

see also *On the Rocks; Reefer Madness; Rehab*

Above the Law *'88*
Aces: Iron Eagle 3 *'92*
The Acid Eaters *'67*
Across the Tracks *'89*
Acts of Worship *'01*
Adventures in Spying *'92*
Afterschool *'08*
Air America *'90*
Alien Nation *'88*
All That Jazz *'79* ►
Alphabet City *'84*
Altered States *'80* ►
American Fabulous *'92*
Amongst Friends *'93*
The Amsterdam Connection *'78*
The Amsterdam Kill *'78*
And Then You Die *'88* ►
Angel's Brigade *'79*
The Anniversary Party *'01* ►
Another Day in Paradise *'98*
Another Lonely Hitman *'95*
Arc *'06*
Armistead Maupin's Tales of the City *'93*
Around the Fire *'98*
Assassin of Youth *'35*
At Any Cost *'00*
Autopsy: A Love Story *'02*
Avenging Disco Godfather *'76*
Awakenings of the Beast *'68*
B. Monkey *'97*
Back in Action *'94*
Bad Boys *'95*
Bad Lieutenant *'92* ►
Bad Lieutenant: Port of Call New Orleans *'09*
Bad Medicine *'85*
Baja *'95*
The Barbarian Invasions *'03* ►
The Basketball Diaries *'95*
Basquiat *'96* ►
The Beach *'00*
Beat *'00*
Belly *'98*
Beretta's Island *'92*
Best Revenge *'83*
The Betty Ford Story *'87* ►
The Big Lebowski *'97* ►
Bigger Stronger Faster *'08*
Bird *'88* ►
Black Circle Boys *'97*
Black Snow *'89*
Black Starlet *'74*
The Blackout *'97*
Blast-Off Girls *'67*
Blind Spot *'93*
Blindside *'88*
Blood & Concrete: A Love Story *'90*
Blood Freak *'72*
Blood In ... Blood Out: Bound by Honor *'93*
Bloodbath *'76*
The Bloody Brood *'59*
Blow *'01*
Blowin' Smoke *'99*
Blue Sunshine *'78*
Bongwater *'98*
Boogie Boy *'98*
Boogie Nights *'97* ►
The Boost *'88*
Borderline *'50*
Born to Lose *'99*
Born to Win *'71*
The Boys of 2nd Street Park *'03* ►
Breaking Point *'09*
Bright Lights, Big City *'88*
Bringing Out the Dead *'99*
Broken Vessels *'98* ►
Brotherhood of Justice *'86*
A Brother's Kiss *'97*
Bully *'01*
Burnt Money *'00*
Busting *'74*
Bye-Bye *'96*
Candy *'06*
Capital Punishment *'96*
Captain Blackjack *'51*
Captive Rage *'88*
Carlito's Way *'93* ►
Carlito's Way: Rise to Power *'05*
Caroline at Midnight *'93*
Cartel *'90*
Casino *'95* ►
Catch the Heat *'87*
Caught *'96*
Cause of Death *'90*
Cement *'99*
Chained Heat 2 *'92*
Chains of Gold *'92*
Cheech and Chong: Still Smokin' *'83*
Cheech and Chong: Things Are Tough All Over *'82*
Chelsea Walls *'01*
The Children of Times Square *'86*
China White *'91*
Chinatown Connection *'90*
Christiane F. *'82* ►
Chrome Soldiers *'92*
The Chumscrubber *'05*
Chungking Express *'95* ►
The Cider House Rules *'99* ►
Circuit *'02*
City by the Sea *'02*
City of Ghosts *'03*
Class of 1984 *'82*
Clean *'04*
Clean and Sober *'88* ►
Clockers *'95* ►
Club Life *'86*
Cocaine Cowboys *'79*
Cocaine Fiends *'36*
Cocaine: One Man's Seduction *'83*
Cocaine Wars *'86*
Coffy *'73*
Coldfire *'90*
The Colombian Connection *'91*
Commando Squad *'87*
Comrades in Arms *'91*
Confessions of a Vice Baron *'42*
The Connection *'61* ►
Contraband *'80*
The Cool World *'63*
The Corner *'00*
Corridors of Blood *'58*
Countryman *'83*
Courage *'86* ►
Covert Action *'88*
Crack House *'89*
crazy/beautiful *'01*
Crescendo *'69*
Crossing the Bridge *'92*
The Crow 2: City of Angels *'96*
Cruel Intentions *'98*
Crutch *'04*
A Cry for Love *'80*
The Curfew Breakers *'57*
Curtis's Charm *'96*
Cut and Run *'85*
Dance or Die *'87*
Dangerous Game *'93*
Dangerous Heart *'93*
Darkman 3: Die Darkman Die *'95*
Day of Atonement *'93*
Day of the Cobra *'84*
Day of the Maniac *'77*
Dazed and Confused *'93* ►
Dead Aim *'87*
Dead Presidents *'95*
Dead Ringers *'88* ►
Deadly Surveillance *'91*
Death Drug *'83*
The Death of Richie *'76*
Death Shot *'73*
Death Wish 4: The Crackdown *'87*
Deep Cover *'92*
Delta Heat *'92*
Desert Snow *'89*
Desperado *'95* ►
Desperate Lives *'82*
The Destructors *'74*
The Devil's Sleep *'51*
Dick *'99* ►
Dirty Laundry *'87*
Distant Justice *'92*
Dr. Jekyll and Mr. Hyde *'20* ►
Dr. Jekyll and Mr. Hyde *'32* ►
Dr. Jekyll and Mr. Hyde *'41* ►
Dr. Jekyll and Mr. Hyde *'68*
Dr. Jekyll and Mr. Hyde *'73*
Dogs in Space *'87*
Don't Look Back *'96* ►
The Doom Generation *'95* ►
Dot.Kill *'05*
Double-Crossed *'91*
Down & Dirty *'76* ►
Down in the Delta *'98* ►
Down to the Bone *'04*
Dream with the Fishes *'97*
Drug Wars 2: The Cocaine Cartel *'92*
Drugstore Cowboy *'89* ►
Drunks *'96*
Drying Up the Streets *'76*
Dusty and Sweets Mcgee *'71*
Easy Kill *'89*
Easy Rider *'69* ►
Ed Wood *'94* ►
Edge of Sanity *'89*
Edie in Ciao! Manhattan *'72*
8 Million Ways to Die *'85*
El Cantante *'06*
The End of Innocence *'90*
Enter the Dragon *'73* ►
Equilibrium *'02*
Exit Speed *'08*
Exposure *'91*
Extreme Prejudice *'87*
Factory Girl *'06*
Fall from Innocence *'88*
Fall Guy *'47*
Fast Money *'83*
Fatal Beauty *'87*
Fatal Fix *'80*
Fear and Loathing in Las Vegas *'98*
Federal Hill *'94*
Feelin' Screwy *'90*
Fever *'88*
Fierce People *'05*
The Fifth Floor *'80*
54 *'98*
The Finger Man *'55*
Fiona *'98*
Fire Birds *'90*
First Born *'84*
The Five Heartbeats *'91* ►
The Fix *'84*
The Flaming Teen-Age *'56*
Flashback *'89* ►
Flatfoot *'78*
Flesh *'68* ►
Fletch *'85*
Four Friends *'81* ►
Foxes *'80*
Frances *'82* ►
The French Connection *'71* ►
French Connection 2 *'75* ►
French Intrigue *'70*
Fresh *'94*
Fresh Kill *'87*
The Fury of the Wolfman *'70*
Ganjasaurus Rex *'87*
Garage Days *'03*
The Gene Krupa Story *'59*
Georgia *'95* ►
Gia *'98*
Ginger Snaps: Unleashed *'04*
Go *'99* ►
Godmoney *'97*
Gone Dark *'03*
The Good Thief *'03* ►
Goodfellas *'90* ►
Gordon's War *'73*
Gothic *'87* ►
Gracie's Choice *'04*
Gridlock'd *'96* ►
Gunmen *'93*
H *'90*
Hair *'79* ►
Half-Baked *'97*
Half Nelson *'06* ►
Hallucination *'67*
Hangman's Curse *'03*
Happy Tears *'09*
Hard Evidence *'94*
Hardcore *'04*
Harsh Times *'05*
Harvard Man *'01*
Haunted Summer *'88*
The Heart Is Deceitful Above All Things *'04*
Heart of America *'03*

Heat '72 ►
Heaven's Prisoners '95
Hell's Kitchen NYC '97
Help Wanted Female '68
Hendrix '00
A Hero Ain't Nothin' but a Sandwich '78
Heroes for Sale '33 ►
High Art '98
High Crime '73
High Risk '81
Hit! '73
Holding Trevor '07
Holiday Heart '00
A Home at the End of the World '04
Homegrown '97
The Hooked Generation '69
Horsey '99
How Come Nobody's On Our Side? '73
Hugo Pool '97
Human Traffic '99
Hussy '80
I Come in Peace '90
I Dreamt Under the Water '07
I Drink Your Blood '71
I Got Five on It '05
Idle Hands '99
Igby Goes Down '02 ►
Illtown '96
I'm Dancing as Fast as I Can '82
The Impostor '84
In Hot Pursuit '77
In the Flesh '97
In the Line of Duty: A Cop for the Killing '90
Inside Edge '92
The Invisibles '99
Iowa '05
Iron Horsemen '71
Island Monster '53
Jaguar Lives '79
Jane Doe '96
Jekyll and Hyde '90
Jekyll & Hyde... Together Again '82
Jesus' Son '99
Jo Jo Dancer, Your Life Is Calling '86
Jumpin' at the Boneyard '92
Kamikaze Hearts '91
Kandyland '87
Kemek '70
Keys to Tulsa '96
Kickboxer the Champion '91
Kicked in the Head '97
Kids '95
Kids in the Hall: Brain Candy '96
Kill or Be Killed '93
Killing Zoe '94
The Killing Zone '90
L.627 '92 ►
La Bamba '87 ►
La Vie en Rose '07
L.A. Wars '94
Lady Sings the Blues '72
Last Flight to Hell '91
The Last of the Finest '90
Lenny '74 ►
Less Than Zero '87
Let No Man Write My Epitaph '60
Lethal Obsession '87
Lethal Weapon '87 ►
Let's Get Harry '87
Let's Get Lost '88
License to Kill '89 ►
Life is Hot in Cracktown '08
Life Support '07 ►
Light Sleeper '92
Little Fish '05 ►
Live and Let Die '73
Livin' for Love: The Natalie Cole Story '00
Loaded '94
Loaded '08
Loaded Guns '75
London '05
London Kills Me '91
Long Day's Journey into Night '62 ►
Long Day's Journey into Night '88
Long Day's Journey Into Night '96 ►
Loser '97
Lost Angels '89
Love Come Down '00
Love Liza '02
Lovely... But Deadly '82
Lullaby '08
MacArthur Park '01
Madea Goes to Jail '09
Magnolia '99 ►
Mainline Run '98
The Man Inside '76
The Man with the Golden Arm '55 ►
Marihuana '36
Marked for Death '90
Max Payne '08
Maybe I'll Be Home in the Spring '70
Maybe I'll Come Home in the Spring '71
McBain '91 ►
McQ '74
The Messenger '87
Miami Vendetta '87
Midnight Cop '88
Midnight Express '78 ►
Mike's Murder '84
Mindfield '89
Mission Manila '87
Mrs. Parker and the Vicious Circle '94
Mixed Blood '84
Mob War '88
The Mod Squad '99
The Moneytree '93
Monkey Grip '82 ►
More '69
My Life and Times with Antonin Artaud '93 ►
The Mystery of Edwin Drood '35
Naked Lunch '91 ►
Narc '02 ►
The Narcotics Story '58
National Lampoon's Senior Trip '95
Never Die Alone '04
New Best Friend '02
New Jack City '91
New York Doll '05 ►
Newman's Law '74
Nico Icon '95 ►
Night Friend '87
The Night of the Iguana '64 ►
The Night of the White Pants '06
Night Zoo '87
Nil by Mouth '96
Ninja in the U.S.A. '88
No Escape, No Return '93
No Vacancy '99
Not My Kid '85
Nowhere '96
Olga's Girls '64
On the Edge: The Survival of Dana '79
On the Outs '05
One False Move '91 ►
100 Proof '96
One Man's Justice '95
Opium and Kung-Fu Master '84 ►
Opium: Diary of a Madwoman '07
The Organization '71 ►
Out of Sync '95
Out of the Rain '90
Over the Edge '79 ►
Pace That Kills '28
The Palermo Connection '91
Pandaemonium '00
Panic in Needle Park '71 ►
Party Monster '03
Passion for Power '85
People I Know '02
The People Next Door '70
The People vs. Larry Flynt '96 ►
Perception '06
The Perfect Daughter '96
Performance '70 ►
Permanent Midnight '98
Pete's Meteor '98
Pharmacist '32
Pigalle '95
Pinero '01
Platoon the Warriors '88
Point of No Return '93
The Poker House '09
Police '85
The Poppy Is Also a Flower '66
Postcards from the Edge '90 ►
Pot, Parents, and Police '71
Praise '98 ►
Premonition '71
Pretty Smart '87
Prey for Rock and Roll '03 ►
Prime Cut '72
Private Investigations '87
The Private Lives of Pippa Lee '09
Protector '85
Prozac Nation '01
Psych-Out '68
Pulp Fiction '94 ►
Punk Love '06
Puppet on a Chain '72
Pure '02 ►
Purgatory House '04
Pusher '96
Question of Honor '80
Quiet Cool '86
Rage and Honor '92
Rapid Fire '92
Rated X '00
Raw Target '95
Ray '04 ►
Rebound: The Legend of Earl "The Goat" Manigault '96
Reckless Disregard '84
Red Blooded American Girl '90
Red Heat '88
Red Surf '90
Remedy '05
Rent '05
Requiem for a Dream '00 ►
Resurrection Man '97
Retribution '98
Return of the Tiger '78
Return to Paradise '98 ►
Revenge of the Ninja '83
Revenge of the Stepford Wives '80
Ricochet '91 ►
Riding in Cars with Boys '01
Rip-Off '77
River's Edge '87 ►
Rock House '88
Rodrigo D.: No Future '91
The Rose '79 ►
The Royal Tenenbaums '01 ►
Rude '96
Running Out of Time '94
Running Scared '86
Running with Scissors '06
Rush '91 ►
Saigon Commandos '88
Saints and Sinners '95
The Salton Sea '02
Satan's Harvest '65
Savage Instinct '89
A Scanner Darkly '06
Scarface '83 ►
Schnelles Geld '84
Scorchy '76
Scorpion Spring '96
Secret Agent Super Dragon '66
The Seducers '70
The Seven-Per-Cent Solution '76 ►
The '70s '00
Severance '88
Shameless '94
She Shoulda Said No '49
Sherlock Holmes '09
The Show '95
Showdown in Little Tokyo '91
Shrooms '07
Sicilian Connection '72
Sid & Nancy '86 ►
Silk '86
The '60s '99
SLC Punk! '99
The Slender Thread '65 ►
The Snake People '68
SnakeEater 2: The Drug Buster '89
Sno-Line '85
Sorry, Wrong Number '89
Sorted '04
Special '06
Speed of Life '99
Spenser: Pale Kings & Princes '94
Spun '02
Stand Alone '85
Stella Does Tricks '96
Still Crazy '98 ►
Stoned '05
The Stoned Age '94
Straight Up '90
Strange Days '95 ►
Street Girls '75
Street Wars '91
Streetwalkin' '85
Strike Force '75
The Substitute '96
The Substitute 3: Winner Takes All '99
Sugarhouse '07
Suicide Kings '97
Sunset Heat '92
Sunset Strip '85
Super Bitch '73
Superfly '72
Surrender Dorothy '98
The Sweet Hereafter '96 ►
Sweet Jane '98
Sweet Nothing '96 ►
The Take '90
Talons of the Eagle '92
Target Eagle '84
Tchao Pantin '84 ►
Teenage Devil Dolls '53
TekWar '94
The Temptations '98
Temptress Moon '96
The Tesseract '03
Things We Lost in the Fire '07
The Third Man '49 ►
This Time I'll Make You Rich '75
Thunder Alley '85
Tideland '05
The Tingler '59 ►
To Die Standing '91
Tombstone '93 ►
The Tong Man '19
Tongs: An American Nightmare '88
Too Young to Die '90
Torchlight '85
Tough and Deadly '94
Toughlove '85
The Town Is Quiet '00
Traffic '00 ►
Traffik '90 ►
Trainspotting '95 ►
Transmutations '85
Trash '70
Trespass '92
The Trip '67
Tropic Thunder '08 ►
Tropical Snow '88
Trouble in Paradise '88
Tweek City '05
Twenty-One '91
21 Grams '03 ►
24 Hour Party People '01
24-7 '97
Twin Peaks: Fire Walk with Me '92
Twin Town '97
Twisted '96
Ulee's Gold '97 ►
Under Hellgate Bridge '99
Undercover '87
Valley of the Dolls '67
Vanishing Point '71
Velvet Goldmine '98
Vicious Circles '97
Virgil Bliss '01
Wait until Dark '67 ►
Walk Hard: The Dewey Cox Story '07
Walk the Line '05 ►
Wanda, the Sadistic Hypnotist '67
Warlords from Hell '87
Warlords 3000 '93
Watched '73
We All Fall Down '00
Weekend with the Babysitter '70
Weird World of LSD '67
Weirdsville '07
Welcome Says the Angel '01
What Doesn't Kill You '08
What Have I Done to Deserve This? '85 ►
What We Do Is Secret '07
Whispers of White '93
Who'll Stop the Rain? '78 ►
Why Do Fools Fall in Love? '98
Wild Bill '95
Wild in the Streets '68
The Wild Pair '87
The Winter of Our Dreams '82
A Winter Tan '88
Wired '89
Withnail and I '87 ►
Woman, Thou Art Loosed '04
Women on the Verge of a Nervous Breakdown '88 ►
Wonder Boys '00 ►
Wonderland '03
Woodstock '70 ►
The Young Americans '93
Zero Tolerance '93
ZigZag '02 ►
Zone 39 '96

Drugs

***see** Drug Use & Abuse*

Dublin

***see also** Ireland*

About Adam '00
Agnes Browne '99
Circle of Friends '94
The Commitments '91 ►
The Dead '87 ►
Disco Pigs '01
Echoes '88
Evelyn '02 ►
Frankie Starlight '95
The Front Line '06
The General '98 ►
Girl with Green Eyes '64
In Bruges '08
The Informer '35 ►
Into the West '92 ►
Leap Year '10
The Lonely Passion of Judith Hearne '87 ►
A Man of No Importance '94 ►
Michael Collins '96 ►
My Left Foot '89 ►
Nora '00
Once '06
Ordinary Decent Criminal '99
Pete's Meteor '98
The Quare Fellow '62
Red Roses and Petrol '03
Rory O'Shea Was Here '04
Shake Hands with the Devil '59 ►
The Snapper '93 ►
The Tiger's Tale '06
Ulysses '67
The Van '95 ►
Veronica Guerin '03
When Brendan Met Trudy '00 ►
When the Sky Falls '99

Dying for a Promotion

***see also** Bad Bosses; Corporate Shenanigans; Office Surprise*

El Crimen Perfecto '04
He Was a Quiet Man '07
Office Killer '97
The Promotion '08
Severance '06
A Shock to the System '90 ►
The Temp '93

Ears!

***see also** Eyeballs!; Renegade Body Parts*

Blue Velvet '86 ►
Django '68
Feeling Minnesota '96
High Plains Drifter '73
I, Madman '89
Lust for Life '56 ►
Reservoir Dogs '92 ►
Say It Isn't So '01
Van Gogh '92 ►
Vincent & Theo '90 ►
White Mischief '88 ►

Earthquakes

***see also** Disaster Flicks; L.A.; San Francisco*

After the Shock '90
Aftershock: Earthquake in New York '99
Black Scorpion 2: Ground Zero '96
Cyxork 7 '06
Daybreak '01
Disaster Movie '08
Earthquake '74
Earthquake in Chile '74
Escape from L.A. '96
The Great Los Angeles Earthquake '91
The Last Warrior '99
Life and Nothing More ... '92
Marshal Law '96
Old San Francisco '27
Phenomenon '96
Power Play '02
Quake '92
The Rains Came '39
San Francisco '36 ►
The Seventh Sign '88
Shakedown '02
The World Sinks Except Japan '06

Easter

***see also** Holidays; Religion; Religious Epics*

Angel of Death '02
Dead Snow '09
Easter Parade '48 ►
Fourth Wise Man '85
Hank and Mike '08
Jesus '00
Jesus Christ, Superstar '73 ►
Jesus of Montreal '89 ►
Jesus of Nazareth '28
Jesus of Nazareth '77 ►
The Long Good Friday '80 ►
Mary, Mother of Jesus '99
The Passion of the Christ '04 ►
Resurrection '99
The Robe '53
The Sacred Family '04

Eastern Europe

All My Loved Ones '00
Black Peter '63
Blood & Chocolate '07
Brute '97
The Courageous Heart of Irena Sendler '09 ►
Dark Blue World '01
The Death of Mr. Lazarescu '05
Divided We Fall '00
Dracula: The Dark Prince '01
Dust '01
Everything is Illuminated '05 ►
4 Months, 3 Weeks and 2 Days '07 ►
Ghouls '07
Gloomy Sunday '02 ►
The Good Fairy '35 ►
The Great Water '04
Hostel '06
I Am David '04
I Served the King of England '07 ►
Invincible '01
The Ister '04 ►
Katyn '07
Kontroll '03 ►
Last Holiday '06
Love '05
The Pianist '02 ►
Police, Adjective '09
Second in Command '05
The Secret Invasion '64
Severance '06
Special Forces '03
Transylmania '09
The Troubles We've Seen '94

Listen '96
The Little Death '95
Lonely Hearts '91
Love Is a Gun '94
The Man in the Attic '94
Maniac Nurses Find Ecstasy '94
Match Point '05 ▸
Mercy '00
Midnight Blue '96
Midnight Confessions '95
Midnight Tease '94
Midnight Tease 2 '95
Mind Twister '93
Mirror Images '91
Mirror Images 2 '93
Motel Blue '98
Night Eyes '90
Night Eyes 2 '91
Night Eyes 3 '93
Night Eyes 4: Fatal Passion '95
Night Fire '94
The Nightman '93
Object of Obsession '95
Outside the Law '95
Over the Wire '95
Payback '94
A Place Called Truth '98
Playback '95
Playmaker '94
Poison '01
Poison Ivy 2: Lily '95
Poison Ivy 3: The New Seduction '97
Possessed by the Night '93
Private Obsession '94
Rubdown '93
Running Wild '94
Saturday Night Special '92
Save Me '93
Scorned '93
Scorned 2 '96
Secret Games '92
Secret Games 2: The Escort '93
Secret Games 3 '94
The Seductress '00
Sexual Malice '93
Sexual Roulette '96
Shadow Dancer '96
Shame, Shame, Shame '98
The Showgirl Murders '95
Sinful Intrigue '95
Sins of Desire '92
Sins of the Night '93
Sliver '93
A Snake of June '02
Snapdragon '93
Spirit Lost '96
Stolen Hearts '95
Stormswept '95
Stormy Nights '97
Strike a Pose '93
Suite 16 '94
Sunset Grill '92
Sweet Evil '98
Sweet Killing '93
Temptation '94
Temptress '95
Terrified '94
3-Way '04
Trade Off '95
Tryst '94
Turn of the Blade '97
Two Shades of Blue '98
Under Investigation '93
Undercover '94
Vicious Circles '97
Victim of Desire '94
Virtual Desire '95
Virtual Girl '00
Vulture's Eye '04
When Will I Be Loved '04
Wild Cactus '92
Young Adam '03 ▸

Errant Educators

see also Dedicated Teachers; Hell High School

Blue Car '03 ▸
Disturbing Behavior '98
Dumb and Dumberer: When Harry Met Lloyd '03
The Faculty '98
Killing Machine '02
Loving Annabelle '06
Lower Learning '08
Notes on a Scandal '06 ▸
Teaching Mrs. Tingle '99
When Brendan Met Trudy '00 ▸
Wild Things '98

Escaped Cons

see also Fugitives; Great Escapes; Men in Prison

Another Man's Poison '52
Axe '06
Bandits '01
Big Momma's House '00
The Big Sweat '90
Black Cat Run '98
Bond of Fear '56
Chasers '94
Choice of Arms '83
Colorado Territory '49
Con Air '97 ▸
Cool Hand Luke '67 ▸
Crime Wave '54
Dark Passage '47
Dead of Night '99
Deadlock '91
Deadlock 2 '94
The Defiant Ones '58 ▸
Destiny Turns on the Radio '95
Do or Die '01
Double Jeopardy '99
Duets '00
The Escape '95
Escape from Alcatraz '79 ▸
Face/Off '97 ▸
The Falcon Takes Over '42
Firestorm '97
Fled '96
48 Hrs. '82 ▸
From Dusk Till Dawn '95
The Fugitive '93 ▸
Gang Busters '55
A Gentleman After Dark '42
The Goonies '85
Great Expectations '34
Great Expectations '46 ▸
Great Expectations '89 ▸
Great Expectations '97
Great Expectations '99
Great Expectations: The Untold Story '87
Gunfight at Comanche Creek '64
Happy, Texas '99 ▸
Harold & Kumar Escape from Guantanamo Bay '08
His Greatest Gamble '34
I Am a Fugitive from a Chain Gang '32 ▸
Identity '03
The Incredible Journey of Mary Bryant '05
Instinct to Kill '01
Jailbreakers '94
Jailbreakin' '72
Jeopardy '53
Johnny Was '05
King of Alcatraz '38
Larceny, Inc. '42
The Last Hard Men '76
The Last House on the Left '09
The Last Marshal '99
Le Cercle Rouge '70 ▸
Le Deuxieme Souffle '66
Lewis and Clark and George '97
Lonely Are the Brave '62 ▸
A Long Ride From Hell '68
Mad Dog Killer '77
The Man Who Broke 1,000 Chains '87
The Mighty '98 ▸
Moonbase '97
Morgan's Ferry '99
Next Friday '00
Night Screams '87
9 Souls '03
Nobody's Baby '01
Nothing to Lose '08
O Brother Where Art Thou? '00
One Way Passage '32
Out of Sight '98 ▸
Papillon '73 ▸
Parallel Sons '95
Passage to Marseilles '44 ▸
Passenger 57 '92
A Perfect World '93
The Pledge '08
Point Blank '98
Prison on Fire 2 '91
Proximity '00
Raising Arizona '87 ▸
Red Letters '00
Rites of Passage '99
Runaway Train '85 ▸
San Quentin '37
A Scandal in Paris '46
School's Out '99
Shutter Island '09 ▸
Slow Burn '00
Soft Deceit '94
Spider-Man 3 '07
Spoiler '98
Stakeout '87
The Stunt Man '80 ▸
T Bone N Weasel '92
Thunder County '74
Two for Texas '97
Up the River '30
Ushpizin '04
Warden of Red Rock '01
We're No Angels '55 ▸
We're No Angels '89
Where the Money Is '00
The Wrong Guys '88
Wrong Turn 3: Left for Dead '09
Wrongfully Accused '98

Eskimos/Inuit

Map of the Human Heart '93
On Deadly Ground '94
Shadow of the Wolf '92
Smilla's Sense of Snow '96
The White Dawn '75

Ethics & Morals

see also Big Ideas

All the King's Men '49 ▸
And Justice for All '79
Any Man's Death '90
The Assault '86 ▸
Barbarians at the Gate '93 ▸
The Best Man '64 ▸
Blame It on Rio '84
Blue Chips '94
Boiler Room '00 ▸
The Border '82 ▸
The Boy with the Green Hair '48 ▸
The Bridge on the River Kwai '57 ▸
Casualties of War '89 ▸
Changing Lanes '02 ▸
Chinese Roulette '86
Chloe in the Afternoon '72 ▸
Choose Connor '07
Circle of Power '83
The Citadel '38 ▸
City Hall '95 ▸
City of Ghosts '03
A Civil Action '98
Commandments '96
The Contender '00
The Conversation '74 ▸
The Corruptor '99 ▸
Crime and Punishment in Suburbia '00
Crimes & Misdemeanors '89 ▸
Cruel Intentions '98
Cutter's Way '81
A Dangerous Woman '93
The Deep End '01 ▸
Deep Six '58
The Defiant Ones '58 ▸
The Doctor '91
Double Identity '89
The Dreamlife of Angels '98 ▸
Election '99 ▸
The Elephant Man '80 ▸
Elmer Gantry '60 ▸
Extreme Measures '96
Fifth Day of Peace '72
The Fifth Seal '76
Filth '08
Force of Evil '49 ▸
Fortunes of War '94
The Funeral '84 ▸
Fury '36 ▸
Getting Away With Murder '96
Gossip '99
Harriet the Spy '96
The Ice Storm '97 ▸
The Image '89
InAlienable '08
It Could Happen to You '94
Jerry Maguire '96 ▸
Jezebel '38 ▸
The Judge and the Assassin '75 ▸
Judgment at Nuremberg '61 ▸
Keys to Tulsa '96
Kings Row '41 ▸
Knocks at My Door '93
La Ronde '51 ▸
La Truite '83 ▸
The Last of England '87 ▸
L'Avventura '60 ▸
The Lazarus Syndrome '79
License to Kill '84
Love with the Proper Stranger '63 ▸
The Magdalene Sisters '02 ▸
Malicious '74
The Man Inside '76
The Man Who Shot Liberty Valance '62 ▸
Manhattan Melodrama '34 ▸
Marihuana '36
A Matter of Dignity '57
Midnight '34
The Millionairess '60
Mindwalk: A Film for Passionate Thinkers '91 ▸
Mr. Smith Goes to Washington '39 ▸
Mom & Dad '47
Muriel '63 ▸
Network '76 ▸
News at Eleven '86
The Next Voice You Hear '50
Nixon '95 ▸
No Man's Land '87
Oedipus Rex '67 ▸
One Flew Over the Cuckoo's Nest '75 ▸
Other People's Money '91
Overture to Glory '40
The Ox-Bow Incident '43 ▸
Paris Trout '91
Penalty Phase '86
A Place in the Sun '51 ▸
Platoon '86 ▸
Playing God '96
The Ploughman's Lunch '83 ▸
Prime Suspect '82
The Prisoner '09
Private Hell 36 '54
The Proposition '97
Quiz Show '94 ▸
Rabbit-Proof Fence '02 ▸
Ran '85 ▸
Reckless Disregard '84
Resilience '06
Return to Paradise '98 ▸
Riel '79
The Sacrifice '86 ▸
Scandal Man '67
The Scarlet Letter '34
The Scarlet Letter '73 ▸
Shampoo '75
The Shootist '76 ▸
Silent Witness '85
Soul Man '86
S*P*Y*S '74
SS Girls '77
The Star Chamber '83
The Story of Women '88 ▸
Strangers When We Meet '60
Sweet Smell of Success '57 ▸
Test Tube Babies '48
The Things of Life '70 ▸
To Live & Die in L.A. '85
To Save a Life '10
A Touch of Class '73 ▸
The Toy '82
Tulsa '49 ▸
Twelve Angry Men '57 ▸
Twelve Angry Men '97
Twenty-One '91
Tycoon '47
Under Fire '83 ▸
Viridiana '61 ▸
Wall Street '87 ▸
Wall Street 2: Money Never Sleeps '10
The Wheeler Dealers '63 ▸
With Honors '94
Zabriskie Point '70 ▸
Zero Degrees Kelvin '95

Etiquette

Born Yesterday '50 ▸
Educating Rita '83 ▸
My Fair Lady '64 ▸
Papa's Delicate Condition '63 ▸
Phantom of Liberty '74 ▸
Pleasure '31
Pygmalion '38 ▸
The Ruling Class '72 ▸
True Love '89 ▸

Evil Doctors

see also Doctors & Nurses; Mad Scientists

The Abominable Dr. Phibes '71 ▸
Anatomy '00 ▸
The Awful Dr. Orloff '62
Baby Geniuses '98
Batman Begins '05 ▸
Bats: Human Harvest '07
Blackmale '99
Body Melt '93
The Curious Dr. Humpp '70
Curse of the Puppet Master: The Human Experiment '98
Dead Ringers '88 ▸
Death and the Maiden '94 ▸
The Dentist '96
Dr. Alien '88
The Doctor and the Devils '85
Dr. Black, Mr. Hyde '76
Doctor Blood's Coffin '62
Doctor Butcher M.D. '80
Dr. Caligari '89
Dr. Cyclops '40
Dr. Death, Seeker of Souls '73
Dr. Frankenstein's Castle of Freaks '74
Dr. Giggles '92
Dr. Goldfoot and the Bikini Machine '66
Dr. Hackenstein '88
Dr. Jekyll and Mr. Hyde '20 ▸
Dr. Jekyll and Mr. Hyde '41 ▸
Dr. Jekyll and Mr. Hyde '68
Dr. Jekyll and Mr. Hyde '73
Dr. Jekyll and Sister Hyde '71
Dr. Jekyll and the Wolfman '71
Dr. Jekyll's Dungeon of Death '82
Dr. Mabuse, The Gambler '22 ▸
Dr. Mabuse vs. Scotland Yard '64
Dr. No '62 ▸
Dr. Orloff and the Invisible Man '72
Dr. Otto & the Riddle of the Gloom Beam '86
Doctor Phibes Rises Again '72
Doctor Satan's Robot '40
Dr. Tarr's Torture Dungeon '75
Dr. Terror's House of Horrors '65
Doctor X '32
Extreme Measures '96
Feast for the Devil '71
Gallery of Horrors '67
The Haunted Airman '06
Insanitarium '08
Jekyll and Hyde '90
Mad Doctor of Blood Island '68
Malice '93
Night of the Bloody Apes '68
Night of the Bloody Transplant '86
Obsession '49
Prince of Poisoners: The Life and Crimes of William Palmer '98
Slaughter Hotel '71
Strange World of Coffin Joe '68
Subject Two '06
Turistas '06
The Two Faces of Dr. Jekyll '60
Who Killed Bambi? '03

Ex-Cons

see also Crime Drama; Escaped Cons; Men in Prison; Revenge; Women in Prison

A Nous la Liberte '31 ▸
All Hat '07
Always Outnumbered Always Outgunned '98 ▸
American Heart '92 ▸
American Madness '32
And Now My Love '74
The Anderson Tapes '71 ▸
Animal '05
Any Number Can Win '63
Appointment with Crime '45
Baby Boy '01
The Badlanders '58
Ballistic '94
Barbershop '02 ▸
Barbershop 2: Back in Business '04 ▸
Benefit of the Doubt '93
Beyond Desire '94
Beyond Suspicion '00
The Big Scam '79
Black Dog '98
Blastfighter '85
Bloody Mama '70
Bound '96
The Box '03
Boy A '07
Bug '06
Bustin' Loose '81 ▸
Carlito's Way '93 ▸
Caught Up '98
Chain Link '08
The Chase '91
Coastlines '02
Cold Creek Manor '03
The Collector '09
Confessions of a Pit Fighter '05
Crazy on the Outside '10
Crime Wave '54
Dead Heat '01
Dead Heat on a Merry-Go-Round '66 ▸
Deadly Past '95
Department Store '35
Disorganized Crime '89
Dolemite '75
The Dream Catcher '99
Drop Zone '94
Emma's Shadow '88 ▸
Enforcer from Death Row '78
Eye of God '97 ▸
Eye of the Tiger '86
Fallen Angels '95
Family Business '89
Farewell, My Lovely '75 ▸
Feeling Minnesota '96
Fever '91
The Finger Man '55
Force Five '75
Framed for Murder '07
Frankie and Johnny '91 ▸
Getting Out '94
The Glove '78
Going Places '74 ▸
Graveyard of Honor '02
Guncrazy '92
Hard Frame '70
Hard Knocks '80
The Hard Word '02
Headless Body in Topless Bar '96
The Heist '89
Hell's Kitchen NYC '97
Henry: Portrait of a Serial Killer '90 ▸
Hi-Jacked '50
High Country '81
Hitler: Dead or Alive '43
Home Team '98
The Hoodlum Priest '61 ▸
Hot Money '79
A House in the Hills '93
I Love You Phillip Morris '10
The Impostor '84
In Cold Blood '67 ▸
In Cold Blood '96
Invisible Stripes '39
Islander '06
I've Loved You So Long '08 ▸
Jada '08
Jail Party '04

▸ = rated three bones or higher

Jailbird's Vacation '65
Jon Jost's Frameup '93
Judge Dredd '95
Kansas City Confidential '52 ►
Keeping Mum '05
Killer '73
The Killing '56 ►
Kiss of Death '47 ►
Kiss of Death '94
Klepto '03
Larceny, Inc. '42
The Last Gangster '37
The Lazarus Project '08
Le Cercle Rouge '70 ►
Le Doulos '61 ►
Leo '02
Levity '03
Life During Wartime '09
The Limey '99 ►
Little Children '06 ►
Loan Shark '52
Luck of the Draw '00
Mad Bad '07
Manito '03 ►
Masked and Anonymous '03
Max Dugan Returns '83
Mercy Streets '00
The Mighty '98 ►
Morning Glory '93
Motive for Revenge '35
Murder at Devil's Glen '99
Murder, My Sweet '44 ►
My Baby's Daddy '04
My Summer of Love '05
Mystic River '03 ►
Nasty Hero '89
Never Down '06
New Pastures '62
Ocean's Eleven '01 ►
Oceans of Fire '86
Odds Against Tomorrow '59 ►
On the Run '73
One More Chance '90
The Onion Field '79 ►
Outlaw Blues '77
Palmetto '98
The Passion of Anna '70 ►
Payback '94
Pennies from Heaven '36
Pier 23 '51
Pinero '01
Played '06
Poor Man's Game '06 ►
Powder Blue '09
Q (The Winged Serpent) '82 ►
Raising Arizona '87 ►
Rappin' '85
Ratas, Ratones, Rateros '99
The Ravagers '65
Read My Lips '01
The Real Thing '97
Red Road '06
Red Water '01
Renegade Trail '39
Revolver '05
Riff Raff '92 ►
The River Rat '84
Row Your Boat '98
Rude '96
Saving God '08
Say It With Songs '29
Scarecrow '73
The Set Up '95
Sex, Love and Cold Hard Cash '93
Sherrybaby '06
Shooters '00
Sins of the Night '93
Slaughterday '77
Small Time Crooks '00
A Small Town in Texas '76
Spring Forward '99
Stakeout '62
Stand Off '93
Stealing Candy '04
Stick '85
Straight Time '78 ►
Strangers with Candy '06
Street Angel '28
Street Law '95
The Swap '71
Switchblade Sisters '75
Swordfish '01
Sympathy for the Underdog '71
Temptation '94
This Is Not a Love Song '02
Three Fugitives '89
3000 Miles to Graceland '01
Till the End of the Night '94
The Time of His Life '55
Tough Guys '86
2 Fast 2 Furious '03
The Unbelievable Truth '90
Under Capricorn '49
Underworld USA '61
Waist Deep '06
Wall Street 2: Money Never Sleeps '10
Weeds '87 ►
The Wendell Baker Story '05
When the Dark Man Calls '95
Whispers in the Dark '92
Wild Cactus '92
Wild Ones on Wheels '62
Woman in the Shadows '34
Wonderland '03
The Yellow Handkerchief '08 ►
Yellowstone '36
You and Me '38
You Only Live Once '37

Ex-Cops

see also *Private Eyes; Rent-a-Cop*

Albino '76
American Streetfighter 2: The Full Impact '97
Back to Back '96
A Better Way to Die '00
Black Scorpion '95
Bodily Harm '95
Body Chemistry 2: Voice of a Stranger '91
Breaking Point '94
Brown's Requiem '98
Choice of Weapons '76
Dark World '08
Day of the Cobra '84
Dead Evidence '00
Dead Heat '01
Deadly Force '83
The Death Squad '73
8 Million Ways to Die '85
End of Days '99
Face Down '97
Final Payback '99
Gang Boys '97
Girls Night Out '83
The Glove '78
The Heist '96
Hope Ranch '02
Hostage Hotel '00
Identity '03
Into the Homeland '87
The Invader '96
The Isle '01
It Had to Be You '00
Jill the Ripper '00
Kansas City Confidential '52 ►
Le Cercle Rouge '70 ►
Little Children '06 ►
Mad Max '80 ►
The Man on the Roof '76
Midnight Run '88 ►
Mirrors '08
The Morning After '86
Night of the Juggler '80
An Occasional Hell '96
Odds Against Tomorrow '59 ►
Once a Thief '96 ►
One Shoe Makes It Murder '82
The Onion Field '79 ►
Payoff '91
Persons Unknown '96
Physical Evidence '89
Piece of the Action '77
Prime Time Murder '92
Q & A '90
Question of Honor '80
Raising Arizona '87 ►
Raw Justice '93
Raw Nerve '99
Ripper Man '96
Romeo Must Die '00
Saw '04
Separate Lives '94
Sin '02
Street Corner Justice '96
Street Knight '93
Tchao Pantin '84 ►
36 Hours to Die '99
Till Death Do Us Part '92
Traxx '87
Trouble in Mind '86 ►
True Romance '93
Twilight '98 ►
Undercurrent '99
Underdog '07
The Usual Suspects '95 ►
Vigilante '83
Virtual Assassin '95
Virtual Combat '95
Virtuosity '95
West New York '96

Exchange Students

see also *Elementary School/ Junior High; High School; Teen Comedy; Teen Drama*

American Pie '99 ►
Better Off Dead '85
Bon Voyage, Charlie Brown '80
Cashback '06
The Comebacks '07
Grease '78 ►
Grease 2 '82
Hamburger... The Motion Picture '86
L'Auberge Espagnole '02 ►
Monster High '89
National Lampoon's Van Wilder '02
Porky's Revenge '85
Sixteen Candles '84 ►
Slap Her, She's French '02
Son of Rambow '07
Sydney White '07

Executing Revenge

see also *Death & the Afterlife; Death Row; Men in Prison; Revenge*

Before I Hang '40 ►
Blowback '99
Destroyer '88
Exorcist 3: Legion '90
Fallen '97
The First Power '89
Gallery of Horrors '67
The Horror Show '89
I Know What You Did Last Summer '97 ►
The Indestructible Man '56
Judge & Jury '96
The Lazarus Project '08
Lethal Dose '03
The Man They Could Not Hang '39
Munich '05 ►
Prison '88
Sherlock Holmes '09
Shocker '89
Soldier '98
The 3 Marias '03

Existentialism

see *The Meaning of Life*

Exorcism & Exorcists

see also *Nuns & Priests; Supernatural Horror*

The Amityville Horror '05
Dominion: Prequel to the Exorcist '05
Drag Me to Hell '09
The Exorcism of Emily Rose '05 ►
The Exorcist '73 ►
London Voodoo '04
Lost Souls '00
Naked Evil '66
The Possessed '77
Possessed '00
Possession '09
Repossessed '90
Scary Movie 2 '01
Teenage Exorcist '93
The Unborn '09
Whispering Corridors '98

Exploitation

see also *Sexploitation*

Abduction '75
Agony of Love '66
American Nightmare '81
Angel of H.E.A.T. '82
Angels of the City '89
Armed Response '86
Assassin of Youth '35
Bad Girls from Mars '90
Barn of the Naked Dead '73
Basic Training '86
Beatrice '88 ►
Betrayal '78
Beyond the Valley of the Dolls '70
Black Shampoo '76
Blackenstein '73
Blood Games '90
The Bloody Brood '59
Blue Movies '88
Bohachi Bushido: Code of the Forgotten Eight '73
Boss '74
The Cage '89
Caged Terror '72
Cannibal Holocaust '80
Certain Sacrifice '80
Chain Gang Girls '08
Chained for Life '51
Common Law Wife '63
Confessions of a Vice Baron '42
Cover Girl Models '75
The Curfew Breakers '57
The Cut Throats '69
Cycle Psycho '72
Cycle Vixens '79
Dance Hall Racket '58
Dangerous Obsession '88
The Dark Side of Love '79
Deadly Sanctuary '68
Death of a Centerfold '81
Def Jam's How to Be a Player '97
Devil Hunter '08
Devil's Wedding Night '73
Escape from Safehaven '88
Exterminator 2 '84
Five Minutes to Love '63
The Flaming Teen-Age '56
For Ladies Only '81
Fox and His Friends '75 ►
Foxy Brown '74
Ghoulies 3: Ghoulies Go to College '91
Girl on a Chain Gang '65
Gun Girls '56
Heat of the Flame '76
Hell Ride '08
High School Caesar '60
Hitler's Children '43 ►
Hollywood after Dark '65
Hollywood Dreams '94
The Hollywood Strangler Meets the Skid Row Slasher '79
House of Whipcord '75
In Trouble '67
Island of Lost Girls '68
Jock Petersen '74
Kidnapped '87
Kinjite: Forbidden Subjects '89
L.A. Heat '88
L.A. Vice '89
Last Call '90
Legends of the Poisonous Seductress 1: Female Demon Ohyaku '68
Legends of the Poisonous Seductress 2: Quick Draw Okatsu '69
Legends of the Poisonous Seductress 3: Okatsu the Fugitive '69
Little Girl... Big Tease '75
Little Miss Innocence '73
The Lonely Sex '59
Love Camp '81
The Mack '73
Malibu Express '85
Mandinga '77
M'Lady's Court '73
My Wonderful Life '90
The Naked Flame '68
Naked in the Night '58
Naked Vengeance '85
The Narcotics Story '58
Night Friend '87
Night of Evil '62
Nomugi Pass '79
One Down, Two to Go! '82
One Night Only '84
One Plus One '61
One Too Many '51
Overexposed '90
Paradise Motel '84
Party Incorporated '89
Pin Down Girls '51
Policewoman Centerfold '83
Poor Pretty Eddie '73
Raw Summer '06 ►
Reefer Madness '38
Rica '72
Rica 2: Lonely Wanderer '73
Rica 3: Juvenile's Lullaby '73
Ringmaster '98
The Road to Ruin '28
Satan's Cheerleaders '77
Savages from Hell '68
Screaming Dead '03
Secrets of Sweet Sixteen '74
Sensual Partners '87
Sex Adventures of the Three Musketeers '71
She Shoulda Said No '49
Sin You Sinners '63
Single Room Furnished '68
Slaughter '72
Slaughter's Big Ripoff '73
Slaves in Bondage '37
S.O.B. '81
Something Weird '68
SS Girls '77
Star 80 '83
Street of Forgotten Women '25
Student Confidential '87
Suite 16 '94
Summer School Teachers '75
Sunset Strip '91
Sunstorm '01
Swamp Women '55
Sweet Spirits '71
Taxi Dancers '93
The Teacher '74
Teenage Doll '57
Test Tube Babies '48
They're Playing with Fire '84
Three in the Attic '68
Thunder & Mud '89
Tokyo Gore Police '08
Tomorrow's Children '34
Violated '53
Warrior Queen '87
Weekend with the Babysitter '70
Weird World of LSD '67
Woman Hunt '72
Women's Club '87
Yesterday's Hero '79
Young Lady Chatterly 2 '85
Youth Aflame '44

Explorers

The Adventures of Marco Polo '38
Almost Heroes '97
Apollo 13 '95 ►
Atlantis: The Lost Empire '01
Cabeza de Vaca '90 ►
Call Me Bwana '63
Carry On Columbus '92
The Cavern '05
Christopher Columbus '49
Christopher Columbus '85
Christopher Columbus: The Discovery '92
Congo '95
The Conqueror & the Empress '64
The Far Horizons '55
The Forbidden Quest '93
Forgotten City '98
1492: Conquest of Paradise '92
Glory & Honor '98
How Tasty Was My Little Frenchman '71
King Solomon's Mines '50 ►
King Solomon's Mines '85
The Last Place on Earth '85
The Live Wire '34
The Lost World '92
The Lost World '02
The Magic Voyage '93
Marco Polo '07
Mountains of the Moon '90 ►
The New World '05 ►
Shackleton '02 ►
She '35
Sir Arthur Conan Doyle's The Lost World '98
The Sky Above, the Mud Below '61 ►
Up '09 ►
The Valley Obscured by the Clouds '70
The Wacky World of Wills & Burke '85
Wagon Wheels '34
Wake of the Red Witch '49

Extraordinary Pairings

Abbott and Costello Meet Frankenstein '48 ►
Alien vs. Predator '04
All About the Benjamins '02
Almost Heroes '97
Bela Lugosi Meets a Brooklyn Gorilla '52
Billy the Kid Versus Dracula '66
The Breed '01
Bulletproof Monk '03
Dr. Jekyll and the Wolfman '71
Doctor of Doom '62
Dracula vs. Frankenstein '71
Frankenstein Meets the Space Monster '65
Frankenstein Meets the Wolfman '42 ►
Freddy vs. Jason '03
The Hollywood Strangler Meets the Skid Row Slasher '79
Jesse James Meets Frankenstein's Daughter '65
King Kong vs. Godzilla '63
Living Out Loud '98
My Giant '98
Rush Hour '98
Santa Claus Conquers the Martians '64
Wrestling Women vs. the Aztec Mummy '59

Eyeballs!

see also *Hearts!*

Anguish '88
Austin Powers: International Man of Mystery '97 ►
The Birds '63 ►
A Clockwork Orange '71 ►
The Crawling Eye '58
Damien: Omen 2 '78
Demolition Man '93
Die Hard 2: Die Harder '90 ►
Evil Dead 2: Dead by Dawn '87
The Eye '08
The Eye Creatures '65
Eyeball '78
Eyes of Laura Mars '78
Friday the 13th, Part 3 '82
The Fury '78
The Godfather '72 ►
Halloween 2: The Nightmare Isn't Over! '81
Headless Eyes '83
Idle Hands '99
Minority Report '02 ►
Nightwatch '96
Peeping Tom '60 ►
The Phantom '96
Pitch Black '00 ►
Rocky '76 ►
Scanners '81
See No Evil '06
Silver Bullet '85
Sleepy Hollow '99 ►
Strange Behavior '81
Summer School '87
The Terminator '84 ►
True Lies '94
Un Chien Andalou '28 ►
Wild Palms '93
X: The Man with X-Ray Eyes '63 ►
Zombie '80

Fairs & Expositions

see also *Amusement Parks; Carnivals & Circuses*

Babe '95 ►
Charlotte's Web '73
Howling 6: The Freaks '90
It Happened at the World's Fair '63
Ma and Pa Kettle at the Fair '52

► = rated three bones or higher

Megasnake '07
My Girl '91
Shag: The Movie '89 ►
State Fair '45 ►
Swap Meet '79

Family Adventure

The Adventures of the Wilderness Family '76
Alaska '96
All Mine to Give '56
Call of the Forest '49
Chang: A Drama of the Wilderness '27 ►
The Chisholms '79
Crusade: A March through Time '06
Disappearances '06
Escape from Wildcat Canyon '99
Far from Home: The Adventures of Yellow Dog '94
Force on Thunder Mountain '77
Further Adventures of the Wilderness Family, Part 2 '77
The Happening '08
Inkheart '09
Little Bigfoot 2: The Journey Home '97
Little House on the Prairie '74 ►
The Mummy: Tomb of the Dragon Emperor '08
Nancy Drew '07
Nim's Island '08
Outlaw Trail '06
The River Wild '94
Rolling Family '04
Secret of the Cave '06
Speed Racer '08
The Spiderwick Chronicles '08 ►
The Swiss Family Robinson '60 ►
Those Calloways '65
Vanilla Gorilla '09
Wild America '97 ►
The Wild Thornberrys Movie '02 ►
The Wizards of Waverly Place: The Movie '09
Zeus and Roxanne '96

Family Comedy

***see also** Aunts & Uncles, Nieces & Nephews; Bad Dads; Brothers & Sisters; Cousins; Dads; Family Drama; Family Reunions; Moms; Monster Moms*

About Adam '00
Ace Ventura Jr.: Pet Detective '08
The Addams Family '91
Addams Family Values '93
Air Bud 5: Buddy Spikes Back '03
Alberto Express '92
Alvin and the Chipmunks '07
American Fusion '05
And Baby Makes Six '79
And You Thought Your Parents Were Weird! '91
Are Parents People? '25
Are We Done Yet? '07
Are We There Yet? '05
At Home with the Webbers '94
Au Pair '99
Au Pair 2: The Fairy Tale Continues '01
Au Pair 3: Adventure in Paradise '09
Aussie and Ted's Great Adventure '09
Baby of the Bride '91
Bedtime Stories '08
Beethoven's 4th '01
Belles on Their Toes '52
Bend It Like Beckham '02 ►
Betsy's Wedding '90
The Beverly Hillbillies '93
Beverly Hills Family Robinson '97
Big and Hairy '98
Big Bully '95
The Big Day '99
Bon Voyage! '62
The Brady Bunch Movie '95 ►
California Dreaming '07
Call It a Day '37
Car Babes '06
Cars '06 ►
Cheaper by the Dozen '50 ►
Cheaper by the Dozen '03
Cheaper by the Dozen 2 '05
Christmas Caper '07
Christmas Do-Over '06
Christmas in Wonderland '07
A Christmas Story '83 ►
Christmas Town '08
Christmas With the Kranks '04
Chutney Popcorn '99
Click '06
Coffee Date '06
Cold Comfort Farm '71
Cold Comfort Farm '94 ►
College Road Trip '08
Collier & Co.: Hot Pursuit '06
Coneheads '93
Cote d'Azur '05
Crazy on the Outside '10
Daddy & Them '99
Daddy Day Camp '07
Daddy's Dyin'... Who's Got the Will? '90
Dan in Real Life '07
The Daytrippers '96
Death at a Funeral '07
Dennis the Menace '93
A Dennis the Menace Christmas '07
Diary of a Wimpy Kid '10
Dirty Laundry '07
Dr. Dolittle '98
Dr. Dolittle 2 '01
Dog Gone '08
The Dog Who Saved Christmas '09
Doogal '05
East Is East '99 ►
East Side of Heaven '39
Eat a Bowl of Tea '89 ►
El Carro '04
Everybody's Fine '09
The Family Holiday '07
The Family Plan '05
The Family Stone '05
Fashion Victims '07
Father of the Bride '50 ►
Father of the Bride '91
Father of the Bride Part 2 '95
Father Was a Fullback '49
Father's Little Dividend '51 ►
Firehouse Dog '07
First Kid '96
Fishtales '07
Folks! '92
Four Christmases '08
Frank '07
Freaky Friday '76
Freaky Friday '03 ►
Fred Claus '07
The Game Plan '07
Garfield: A Tail of Two Kitties '06
Getting Even with Dad '94
The Girl Next Door '53
Go for Zucker '05
Good Morning '59 ►
The Great Outdoors '88
Grown Ups '10
Guess Who '05
Hannah Montana: The Movie '09
Happy Tears '09
The Happy Years '50
Harry and the Hendersons '87
Hello Down There '69
Holiday in Handcuffs '07
Honey, I Blew Up the Kid '92
Honey, I Shrunk the Kids '89
Honey, We Shrunk Ourselves '97
Hoot '06
Hotel for Dogs '09
House of Fury '05
Houseboat '58
How Sweet It Is! '68
Humble Pie '07
I Do '06
I Downloaded a Ghost '04
I-See-You.Com '06
Ice Age: The Meltdown '06
Imagine That '09
The Incredibles '04 ►
Introducing the Dwights '07
Invisible Mom 2 '99
Johnson Family Vacation '04
Jungle 2 Jungle '96
Juno '07 ►
Keeping Up with the Steins '06
The Kids Are All Right '10
Krippendorf's Tribe '98
The Last Request '06
Leave It to Beaver '97
Little Indian, Big City '95
A Little Romance '79 ►
The Little Vampire '00
The Longshots '08
Look Who's Talking '89 ►
Look Who's Talking Now '93
Look Who's Talking, Too '90
Madea's Family Reunion '06
Make the Yuletide Gay '09
Manna from Heaven '02
Marley & Me '08
Marmaduke '10
Meet the Fockers '04
Meet the Robinsons '07
Mr. Blandings Builds His Dream House '48 ►
Mr. Mom '83 ►
Mr. Troop Mom '09
Monster-in-Law '05
My Mother Likes Women '02
My One and Only '09
My Summer Story '94
Nanny McPhee '06
Nanny McPhee 2 '10
National Lampoon's Christmas Vacation '89
National Lampoon's European Vacation '85
National Lampoon's Vacation '83 ►
Never Too Late '65
The Night of the White Pants '06
No Dessert Dad, 'Til You Mow the Lawn '94
Nothing Like the Holidays '08
Our Family Wedding '10
Our Italian Husband '04
The Pacifier '05
The Parent Trap '61
The Parent Trap '98
Parenthood '89 ►
Please Don't Eat the Daisies '60
Post Grad '09
The Prince and the Pauper '07
The Proud Family Movie '05
Racing Stripes '05
Raising Flagg '06
Ramona and Beezus '10
Ratatouille '07 ►
Recipe for Disaster '03
Red Doors '05
Robots '05
The Rocker '08
Rudo y Cursi '09
Rumor Has It... '05
RV '06
Santa Baby '06
The Santa Trap '02
Saving Face '04
Secondhand Lions '03
Serial Mom '94 ►
The Shaggy Dog '06
Shorts: The Adventures of the Wishing Rock '09
The Simpsons Movie '07 ►
Smother '08
Snowglobe '07
Soccer Mom '08
Sordid Lives '00
Spanglish '04
Step Brothers '08
Stuart Saves His Family '94
The Stupids '95
Surviving Christmas '04
Swing Vote '08
A Tale of Two Pizzas '03
They Had to See Paris '29
The Thing About My Folks '05
This Christmas '07
Together Again for the First Time '08
The Tollbooth '04
Too Busy to Work '32
Trading Mom '94
Tyler Perry's Meet the Browns '08
Tyler Perry's Why Did I Get Married? '07
Uncle Buck '89 ►
Uncle Nino '03
Up and Down '04
Valiant '05
Vegas Vacation '96
A Very Brady Sequel '96
Wait Till Your Mother Gets Home '83
Wallace & Gromit in The Curse of the Were-Rabbit '05 ►
Welcome Home Roscoe Jenkins '08
What about Bob? '91 ►
When Do We Eat? '05
Where There's a Will '55
Who Made the Potatoe Salad? '05
Wilderness Love '02
Yours, Mine & Ours '68
Yours, Mine & Ours '05

Family Drama

***see also** Aunts & Uncles, Nieces & Nephews; Bad Dads; Brothers & Sisters; Cousins; Dads; Family Comedy; Family Reunions; Moms; Monster Moms*

The Accidental Tourist '88 ►
Across to Singapore '28
The Actress '53
Adam Had Four Sons '41
The Adventures of Sebastian Cole '99
Affliction '97 ►
After the Promise '87
Agnes Browne '99
Alice et Martin '98
Alice Upside Down '07
All Fall Down '62
All I Desire '53
All Mine to Give '56
All My Sons '48 ►
All My Sons '86 ►
All or Nothing '02
Alpha Male '06
American Beauty '99 ►
American East '07
An American Haunting '05
American Heart '92 ►
American History X '98
Amongst Women '98
Amreeka '09 ►
... And the Earth Did Not Swallow Him '94
Angela '77
Angela '94
Angela's Ashes '99
Angelo My Love '83 ►
Animal '05
Anne Frank: The Whole Story '01 ►
The Anniversary '68
Antonia's Line '95
Anywhere But Here '99
Apres Lui '07
Around the Bend '04
Astoria '00
The Astronaut Farmer '07
At Close Range '86 ►
Atonement '07 ►
August '95
August Rush '07
Aurora Borealis '06
Avalon '90 ►
Baaria '09
Badland '07
The Ballad of Jack and Rose '05 ►
Ballast '08
The Barbarian Invasions '03 ►
The Battle of Shaker Heights '03
Beautiful Ohio '06
Because of Winn-Dixie '05
Becoming Jane '07
Bee Season '05 ►
Behind the Sun '01
Beshkempir the Adopted Son '98
Best of Youth '03 ►
The Betsy '78
The Betty Ford Story '87 ►
Beyond Honor '05
Billy Elliot '00 ►
Birds of America '08
Black Irish '07
Blame It on Fidel '06
Blessing '94
Blind Spot '93
Bombers B-52 '57
The Boys Are Back '09
Brideshead Revisited '08
Bridge to Terabithia '07
Broken Bridges '06
Broken Wings '02 ►
The Brontes of Haworth '73
Brooklyn Lobster '05
Brothers '04 ►
Brothers '09
The Brothers Karamazov '58 ►
Buffalo Boy '04
The Burning Plain '08
The Butcher Boy '97 ►
The Cake Eaters '07
Canvas '06
Caterina in the Big City '03
Catherine Cookson's Colour Blind '98
Catherine Cookson's The Black Velvet Gown '92
Catherine Cookson's The Cinder Path '94
Catherine Cookson's The Fifteen Streets '90
Catherine Cookson's The Man Who Cried '93
Catherine Cookson's The Wingless Bird '97
The Celebration '98
Chain Link '08
Charlie & Me '08
Charms for the Easy Life '02
The Children Are Watching Us '44 ►
Chloe '09
The Christmas Blessing '05
The Christmas Box '95
The Christmas Cottage '08
The Christmas Shoes '02
A Christmas Tale '08 ►
The Chronicles of Narnia: The Lion, the Witch and the Wardrobe '05
Cider with Rosie '99
Cinderella Man '05 ►
The Circuit '08
Close to Leo '02
Cookie's Fortune '99 ►
The Crow Road '96
Daddy's Little Girls '07
Damage '92 ►
Dancing at Lughnasa '98
Daniel's Daughter '08
Dark Blue Almost Black '06
Daughters of the Dust '91 ►
Days of Being Wild '91 ►
Dear Frankie '04
The Derby Stallion '05
Desire Under the Elms '58
Distant Voices, Still Lives '88 ►
A Dog Named Christmas '09
Doing Time on Maple Drive '92
Don't Come Knocking '05
Don't Tell '05
Down in the Delta '98 ►
Down to the Bone '04
Dreamer: Inspired by a True Story '05
Duma '05 ►
Eat Drink Man Woman '94 ►
The Edge of Heaven '07 ►
Eighteen '04
Elizabethtown '05
Emile '03
Emma's Wish '98
Empire Falls '05
Evelyn '02 ►
The Evening Star '96
Every Second Counts '08
Eve's Bayou '97 ►
Extraordinary Measures '10
Eye of the Dolphin '06
Falling Angels '03
The Family '87 ►
Family Pictures '93 ►
Family Prayers '91
The Family That Preys '08
Fanny and Alexander '83 ►
A Father's Choice '00
The Favorite Son '94 ►
Feast of July '95
Fierce People '05
Finding Home '03
Fiorile '93 ►
Fireproof '08
Fish Tank '09 ►
Flambards '78
The Flame Trees of Thika '81 ►
Flash of Genius '08
Flicka '06
Flight of the Red Balloon '08
Floating Life '95
Follow the Stars Home '01
A Fond Kiss '04
For One More Day '07
Forbidden Choices '94
Four Men and a Prayer '38
Four Sheets to the Wind '07
Frailty '02 ►
Free Style '09
Fudoh: The New Generation '96
Gabriel & Me '01
Gas Food Lodging '92 ►
Georgia Rule '07
Giant '56 ►
Gideon's Daughter '05
God's Sandbox '02
Grace Is Gone '07 ►
Gracie '07
Gracie's Choice '04
Grey Gardens '09 ►
Grocer's Son '07
Hamlet '96 ►
Happiness '98 ►
The Haunting in Connecticut '09
Henry & Verlin '94
Hesher '10
Hidden Places '06
A History of Violence '05 ►
Home '08
Home for the Holidays '72
Home for the Holidays '95
A Home of Our Own '93
Homecoming '96
Hounddog '08
House of D '04
The House of the Spirits '93
The House of Yes '97
Household Saints '93 ►
How the Garcia Girls Spent Their Summer '05
Humboldt County '08
Hush Little Baby '93
I Remember Mama '48 ►
The Ice Storm '97 ►
Illegal Tender '07
Imaginary Heroes '05
In America '02 ►
In Her Shoes '05 ►
In the Gloaming '97 ►
In the Land of Women '06
The Inheritance '76
Inside Paris '06
The Intended '02
Into the West '92 ►
Inventing the Abbotts '97
I've Loved You So Long '08 ►
Jada '08
JFK: Reckless Youth '93
Joshua '07 ►
Julien Donkey-boy '99
Junebug '05 ►
Just Business '08
Kabei: Our Mother '08
Kill the Poor '06
Killer of Sheep '77 ►
King of the Corner '04 ►
King of the Gypsies '78
Kingdom Come '01
Kings and Queen '04 ►
Kit Kittredge: An American Girl '08 ►
Lake City '08
The Last Hard Men '76
The Last Mimzy '07
The Last Song '10
Last Summer In the Hamptons '96 ►
Leaving Barstow '08

Family Reunions

Family Ties

Discontent '16
Distortions '87
Divided by Hate '96
Dixie Lanes '88
Dr. Dolittle '98
Donnie Darko '01 ▶
Don't Drink the Water '69
Don't Go to Sleep '82
Double Happiness '94 ▶
Double Play '96
Down & Dirty '76 ▶
Down in the Valley '05
The Dress Code '99
Dummy '02
Dune '84
Dune '00
An Early Frost '85 ▶
Early Summer '51 ▶
The Echo of Thunder '98
Eight on the Lam '67
8 Women '02 ▶
18 Again! '88
The Eighteenth Angel '97
El Bola '00
El Matador '03
Electra '95
Eli Eli '40
Elizabeth of Ladymead '48 ▶
Ellen Foster '97
Embassy '85
The Emigrants '72 ▶
Emma '97 ▶
Encore '52 ▶
Endless Love '81
The Entertainer '60 ▶
Equinox Flower '58
Erendira '83
Ermo '94
Escape from Wildcat Canyon '99
Escape Velocity '99
The Eternal '99
Eternal Return '43
Eulogy '04
The Europeans '79 ▶
The Everlasting Secret Family '88
Every Mother's Worst Fear '98
Everyone Says I Love You '96 ▶
Everything That Rises '98
Excess Baggage '96
The Executioner '78
Exotica '94 ▶
Expectations '97
Eye of the Storm '98
The Eyes of the Amaryllis '82
The Eyes, the Mouth '83
Face to Face '76 ▶
Faces of Women '85
Fallen Angel '03
Falling from Grace '92
The Family '87 ▶
Family '94 ▶
Family Jewels '65
Family of Cops '95
Family of Cops 2: Breach of Faith '97
Family of Cops 3 '98
Family Reunion '79
Family Secrets '84
Family Sins '87
Family Viewing '87 ▶
Fangs of the Living Dead '68
Far North '88
Fast Talking '86
The Feud '90
Fiddler on the Roof '71 ▶
Field of Dreams '89 ▶
Fight for Your Life '77
Final Approach '04
Final Verdict '91
The Fire Next Time '93
First Do No Harm '97
The Fishing Trip '98
Five Days One Summer '82
The Fixer '97
Flash '98
The Flintstones '94
Flirting with Disaster '95 ▶
Fly Boy '99
Follow That Dream '61
Footlight Glamour '43
For Love or Money '63
For Which He Stands '98
Forbidden Planet '56 ▶
Forever and a Day '43 ▶
Forever Love '98
Forever Together '00
The Four Horsemen of the Apocalypse '21 ▶
The Four Horsemen of the Apocalypse '62
Freaky Friday '76
Freaky Friday '03 ▶
Friend of the Family '95
Friendly Fire '79 ▶
Friendly Persuasion '56 ▶
Friends and Family '01
The Fringe Dwellers '86
From the Terrace '60
Fulfillment '89
The Funeral '84 ▶
The Funeral '96 ▶
Funny Bones '94 ▶
Funnyman '94
Further Adventures of the Wilderness Family, Part 2 '77
The Fury '78
Fuzz '72
Gabbeh '96 ▶
The Game Is Over '66
Gang Boys '97
The Garden of Delights '70 ▶
The Garden of the Finzi-Continis '71 ▶
Garden State '04 ▶
The Gathering: Part 2 '79
Gaudi Afternoon '01
Generation '69
Gervaise '56 ▶
A Girl on Her Own '76
The Girl on the Train '09
Girly '70
The Go-Masters '82 ▶
The Godfather '72 ▶
The Godfather 1902-1959: The Complete Epic '81 ▶
The Godfather, Part 2 '74 ▶
The Godson '98
Golden Gate '93
Good Bye, Lenin! '03 ▶
The Good Earth '37 ▶
Good Fences '03
Goodbye, Miss 4th of July '88
Goodnight, Michelangelo '89
Gosford Park '01 ▶
Grand Avenue '96
The Grandfather '98
The Granny '94
The Grapes of Wrath '40 ▶
The Grass Is Always Greener Over the Septic Tank '78
Grave Indiscretions '96
Great Day '46
The Great Madcap '49
The Great Man Votes '38 ▶
A Great Wall '86 ▶
The Great Wallendas '78
Greedy '94
Green Horizon '80
The Green House '96
The Green Wall '70 ▶
Grown Ups '80
Grown Ups '86
Guess Who's Coming to Dinner '67 ▶
Gulliver's Travels '95
Habitat '97
The Habitation of Dragons '91
Halloween with the Addams Family '79
Hamlet '90 ▶
Hamlet '00 ▶
Hamlet '01
The Hand that Rocks the Cradle '92
The Hanging Garden '97
Happiness '98 ▶
Hard Target '93
Harriet the Spy '96
Harvest '98
The Hatfields & the McCoys '75
The Haunted Mansion '03
Head of the Family '71
Head On '98 ▶
Heart of a Nation '43 ▶
Heat '95 ▶
Height of the Sky '99
Heimat 1 '84
Heimat 2 '92
Henry Fool '98 ▶
Here Come the Nelsons '52
Here Comes Cookie '35
Hi Diddle Diddle '43
Hide in Plain Sight '80 ▶
Hideaway '94
High Heels '91 ▶
The Hit List '88
Hobo's Christmas '87
Hold the Dream '86
Hollow Reed '95 ▶
Hollywood Safari '96
The Holy Innocents '84 ▶
Holy Matrimony '94
Holy Smoke '99
Home Alone '90 ▶
Home at Last '88
A Home at the End of the World '04
Home of Angels '94
Home to Stay '79
Homecoming: A Christmas Story '71
Homeward Bound '80
Homeward Bound: The Incredible Journey '93 ▶
Honey, We Shrunk Ourselves '97
Honor Thy Father '73
Honor Thy Father and Mother: The True Story of the Menendez Brothers '94
Hook '91
Hope '97
Hope and Glory '87 ▶
A Horse for Danny '95
The Horse Whisperer '97
Horton Foote's Alone '97
Hot Spell '58
House Arrest '96
House of Dreams '64
House of Saddam '08
House of Sand and Fog '03 ▶
The House on Chelouche Street '73
The House that Bled to Death '81
Houseguest '94
How Green Was My Valley '41 ▶
How the West Was Won '63 ▶
How to Commit Marriage '69
How to Deal '03
The Howards of Virginia '40
Hugo Pool '97
Hurricane Streets '96
I Could Go on Singing '63
I Live in Fear '55 ▶
I Love You, I Love You Not '97
I Love You to Death '90
I Never Sang for My Father '70 ▶
I Want You '51
The Ice Flood '26
I'd Give My Life '36
If Things Were Different '79
I'm Losing You '98
Immediate Family '89
The Imported Bridegroom '89
In Cold Blood '96
In His Father's Shoes '97
In Search of a Golden Sky '84
In the Custody of Strangers '82 ▶
In the Heat of Passion 2: Unfaithful '94
In the Presence of Mine Enemies '97
In This Our Life '42
The Incredibles '04 ▶
Independence Day '83
The Inkwell '94
Innocence Unprotected '68
Innocent Lies '95
Inside Monkey Zetterland '93
Inspector Lynley Mysteries: A Great Deliverance '01
Internes Can't Take Money '37
Intimate Relations '95
The Invention of Lying '09
Invisible Child '99
Iphigenia '77 ▶
The Irishman '78
Is There Life Out There? '94
The Island '61 ▶
Islands in the Stream '77
It Came from the Sky '98
It Runs in the Family '03
It's a Great Life '43
It's a Wonderful Life '46 ▶
It's My Party '95
Ivan and Abraham '94
Jack '96
The Jacksons: An American Dream '92
Jacob '94
Jalsaghar '58
Jamon, Jamon '93
Jason Goes to Hell: The Final Friday '93
The Jazz Singer '27
The Jazz Singer '80
Jeremy's Family Reunion '04
John and the Missus '87
Joseph '95
Journey '95
Journey of Hope '90 ▶
Junebug '05 ▶
Juno and the Paycock '30
Just for You '52
K-PAX '01
Karmina '96
Kazaam '96
Keep the Change '92
The Kennedys of Massachusetts '95
The Kettles in the Ozarks '56
The Kettles on Old MacDonald's Farm '57
Keys to Tulsa '96
The Kid Who Loved Christmas '90
Kidnapping of Baby John Doe '88
Killing Grandpa '91
Killing of Randy Webster '81
Kind Hearts and Coronets '49 ▶
The King '05
The King and Four Queens '56
King Lear '71 ▶
King Lear '98 ▶
King of the Hill '93 ▶
Kingfisher Caper '76
Kings in Grass Castles '97
The Kiss '88
The Kissing Place '90
Kotch '71 ▶
Kristin Lavransdatter '95
Kuffs '92
Kuni Lemel in Tel Aviv '77
La Boum '81
La Ceremonie '95 ▶
La Chartreuse de Parme '48
La Silence de la Mer '47 ▶
La Symphonie Pastorale '46 ▶
La Terra Trema '48 ▶
Lady Audley's Secret '00
Lady Mobster '88
Lantern Hill '90
The Last Assassins '96
The Last Don '97
The Last Don 2 '98
The Last of the High Kings '96
Last Resort '86
The Last September '99
Last Stand at Saber River '96
The Last Winter '89
Late Marriage '01
Laurel Avenue '93
The Lawless Breed '52 ▶
Lawn Dogs '96
Leapin' Leprechauns '95
Left Luggage '98
Legacy of Lies '92
The Legend of Black Thunder Mountain '79
L'Eleve '95
Les Violons du Bal '74
Let the Devil Wear Black '99
Lethal Weapon '87 ▶
Lethal Weapon 4 '98
Let's Dance '50
The Letter '40 ▶
Letting the Birds Go Free '86
Liar Liar '97
Liar's Edge '92
Liar's Moon '82
Liberty Heights '99
License to Kill '84
The Lickerish Quartet '70
Lies My Father Told Me '75 ▶
Life and Nothing More ... '92
Life Is a Long Quiet River '88 ▶
Lift '01
Like Father, Like Son '87
Like Water for Chocolate '93 ▶
Lily Dale '96
Lily in Winter '94
The Lion in Winter '68 ▶
The Lion in Winter '03 ▶
The Lion King '94 ▶
The Lion King: Simba's Pride '98
The List of Adrian Messenger '63 ▶
Little Bigfoot '96
Little Buddha '93
The Little Death '95
Little House on the Prairie '74 ▶
The Little Kidnappers '90
Little Lord Fauntleroy '95
Little Nellie Kelly '40
Little Nicky '00
Little Odessa '94
Little Richard '00
Little Women '33 ▶
Little Women '49 ▶
Little Women '78
Little Women '94 ▶
The Littlest Viking '94
Locked in Silence '99
Lone Star '95 ▶
Long Day's Journey into Night '62 ▶
Long Day's Journey into Night '88
Long Day's Journey Into Night '96 ▶
The Long, Hot Summer '58 ▶
The Long, Hot Summer '86 ▶
The Long Kiss Goodnight '96
Lorna Doone '34
Lorna Doone '90
Lorna Doone '01 ▶
Lost Boundaries '49
The Lost Boys '87
Lost Honeymoon '47
Lost in Space '98
Lost in Yonkers '93
Lots of Luck '85
Lotto Land '95
The Lotus Eaters '93
Louder than Bombs '01
Love Finds Andy Hardy '38 ▶
Love, Honour & Obey '00
Love Kills '98
Love Laughs at Andy Hardy '46
Love Me Tender '56
Love on the Dole '41 ▶
Lover Girl '97
Lovers and Other Strangers '70 ▶
The Low Life '95
Lucky Stiff '88
Ma and Pa Kettle '49
Ma and Pa Kettle at Home '54
Ma and Pa Kettle at the Fair '52
Ma and Pa Kettle at Waikiki '55
Ma and Pa Kettle Back On the Farm '51
Ma and Pa Kettle Go to Town '50
Ma and Pa Kettle on Vacation '53
Ma Barker's Killer Brood '60
Ma Vie en Rose '97 ▶
Mad Max '80 ▶
M.A.D.D.: Mothers Against Drunk Driving '83
Made in America '93
The Madness of King George '94 ▶
Mafia! '98
Mafia Princess '86
Magenta '96
Magic Kid '92
The Magnificent Ambersons '42 ▶
Make Room for Tomorrow '81
The Maker '98
Mama Turns a Hundred '79 ▶
Mambo Italiano '03
Mame '74
Man & Boy '71
The Man from Laramie '55 ▶
The Man in the Gray Flannel Suit '56
The Man in the Santa Claus Suit '79
A Man of Passion '88
Man of the House '95
Man, Woman & Child '83
Mandy '53 ▶
Maniac '63
Mansfield Park '85
Mansfield Park '99
Margaret's Museum '95 ▶
Maria's Day '84 ▶
Marooned in Iraq '02
Martha and I '91 ▶
Martin Chuzzlewit '94
Marvin's Room '96
Masala '91
Masterminds '96
The Mating Game '59 ▶
A Matter of Principle '83
Maverick '94
May Fools '90 ▶
Maybe I'll Be Home in the Spring '70
Me and the Mob '94
Meet Me in St. Louis '44 ▶
Meet the Hollowheads '89
Meet the Parents '91
Meet the Parents '00 ▶
The Member of the Wedding '52 ▶
The Member of the Wedding '83
Memory of Us '74
Menace on the Mountain '70
Merlin '92
Miami Rhapsody '95
Midnight '34
The Migrants '74 ▶
Milk Money '94
The Million Dollar Kid '99
Min & Bill '30
Mind Games '89
The Miniver Story '50
Miracle at Midnight '98
Miracle Down Under '87
Miracle on 34th Street '47 ▶
Miracle on 34th Street '94
The Mirror Has Two Faces '96
Missing Brendan '03
Mississippi Masala '92 ▶
Missouri Traveler '58 ▶
Mrs. Doubtfire '93
Mrs. Miniver '42 ▶
Mrs. Parkington '44
Mr. & Mrs. Bridge '90 ▶
Mr. Hobbs Takes a Vacation '62 ▶
Mr. Skitch '33
Mob Boss '90
Model Behavior '00
Mom & Dad '47
Mom, Can I Keep Her? '98
Mon Oncle '58 ▶
A Mongolian Tale '94
Monkey Trouble '94
Monsieur Verdoux '47 ▶
Monsoon Wedding '01 ▶
Moonlight Mile '02 ▶
Moonstruck '87 ▶
The Mortal Storm '40 ▶
The Mosquito Coast '86
Mother '26 ▶
Mother '52 ▶
Mother '94
Mother '96
Mother & Daughter: A Loving War '80
Mother and Son '31
Mother Wore Tights '47 ▶
Mother's Boys '94
Mouchette '67 ▶
Moving '88
Multiplicity '96

▶ = rated three bones or higher

The Mummy Returns '01
Murder, He Says '45
Murders in the Doll House '79
Music from Another Room '97
Must Read After My Death '09
My Architect: A Son's Journey '03 ▶
My Best Girl '27 ▶
My Big Fat Greek Wedding '02
My Daughter's Keeper '93
My Father, My Mother, My Brothers and My Sisters '99
My Father's Glory '91 ▶
My Friend Walter '93
My Grandpa Is a Vampire '92
My Life '93
My Mother's Castle '91 ▶
My Other Husband '85
My Son, My Son '40
My Uncle Silas '01 ▶
Mystic River '03 ▶
Nadja '95 ▶
Naked Paradise '78
National Lampoon's The Don's Analyst '97
National Treasure '04
Natural Enemies '79
The Natural History of Parking Lots '90
The New Land '73 ▶
New Waterford Girl '99
New York Stories '89 ▶
Next of Kin '89
Next Stop, Greenwich Village '76 ▶
Next Summer '84 ▶
Nice Girl? '41
Nicholas Nickleby '46 ▶
Nicholas Nickleby '02 ▶
Night Crossing '81
Night Must Fall '37 ▶
Night of Terror '87
The Night of the Hunter '55 ▶
Night of the Twisters '95
Nights and Days '76
Nine Months '95
1900 '76 ▶
No End '84
No Laughing Matter '97
No Place to Hide '81
No Place to Run '72
Noah's Ark '99
Noon Wine '84 ▶
The Norman Conquests, Part 1: Table Manners '78 ▶
The Norman Conquests, Part 2: Living Together '78 ▶
The Norman Conquests, Part 3: Round and Round the Garden '78 ▶
North '94
Not in This Town '97
Not My Kid '85
Not Quite Human '87
Not Quite Human 2 '89
Now and Forever '34
Nowhere in Africa '02
Numero Deux '75
The Nutty Professor '96 ▶
Nutty Professor 2: The Klumps '00
The Object of My Affection '98
Off Season '01
Oh Dad, Poor Dad (Momma's Hung You in the Closet & I'm Feeling So Sad) '67
O'Hara's Wife '82
The Old Curiosity Shop '94
The Old Dark House '32 ▶
Old Yeller '57 ▶
Ollie Hopnoodle's Haven of Bliss '88
Olly Olly Oxen Free '78
On Moonlight Bay '51
On Valentine's Day '86
Once Around '91
Once Upon a Time in the Midlands '02
Once Upon a Time ... When We Were Colored '95 ▶
The One and Only, Genuine, Original Family Band '68 ▶
One Cooks, the Other Doesn't '83
One Good Cop '91
One More Chance '90
The Only Thrill '97
Only You '94
Orange County '02
Ordet '55 ▶
The Other Sister '98
Our Little Girl '35
Our Mother's Murder '97
Our Mutual Friend '98
Our Town '40 ▶
Our Town '77 ▶
Our Very Own '50
Out of the Blue '80 ▶
Out of Time '00
Out on a Limb '92
Outcasts of the Trail '49
Outside Chance of Maximillian Glick '88
Overboard '87
Overture to Glory '40
The Ox '91
Paco '75
Padre Nuestro '85
Padre Padrone '77 ▶
The Painted Lady '97 ▶
Panic in the Year Zero! '62
Papa's Angels '00
Paradise '91 ▶
A Paradise Under the Stars '99
Parental Guidance '98
Parrish '61
Passion '92
Pecker '98
Peg o' My Heart '22
Peggy Sue Got Married '86
The Perez Family '94
The Perfect Daughter '96
Perfect Family '92
A Perfect Little Murder '90
Personal Exemptions '88
Persuasion '71
Persuasion '95 ▶
Pet Sematary '89
Phaedra '61
Phedre '68
Philadelphia '93 ▶
Ping Pong '87
Pinocchio's Revenge '96
Pitfall '48 ▶
A Place in the World '92 ▶
Poil de Carotte '31
Poison Ivy '92
Poldark '75 ▶
Poldark '96
Poldark 2 '75 ▶
Polish Wedding '97
Pollyanna '60 ▶
Poltergeist '82 ▶
Poltergeist 2: The Other Side '86
Poltergeist: The Legacy '96
Popeye's Voyage: The Quest for Pappy '04
The Portrait '93 ▶
Prehysteria '93
Prehysteria 3 '95
Pretty in Pink '86
Pride and Prejudice '40 ▶
Pride and Prejudice '85
Pride and Prejudice '95 ▶
Prince of Pennsylvania '88
The Prince of Tides '91 ▶
Prizzi's Honor '85 ▶
The Prodigal '55
The Prodigal '83
Promised a Miracle '88
The Proposition '96
Psycho Sisters '98
Queen Margot '94 ▶
Queen of Hearts '89 ▶
The Quickie '01
Quiz Show '94 ▶
Radiance '98
Radio Flyer '92
Rage of Angels: The Story Continues '86
Raging Bull '80 ▶
Rainbow's End '35
A Raisin in the Sun '61 ▶
A Raisin in the Sun '89 ▶
Ran '85 ▶
Ransom '96 ▶
The Real Charlotte '91
Red Dirt '99
Red Firecracker, Green Firecracker '93
The Red Pony '49 ▶
The Red Pony '76 ▶
The Ref '93 ▶
Regarding Henry '91 ▶
Regina '83
Relative Fear '95
Remember the Night '40 ▶
Respiro '02
Return '88
The Return of the Borrowers '96 ▶
Return to Africa '89
Return to Me '00
Rhapsody in August '91
Rich in Love '93
Rich, Young and Pretty '51
Richie Rich '94
Riders of the Purple Sage '25
Riot in the Streets '96
Rivals '72
The River Niger '76
The River Wild '94
Road Racers '59
Road to Salina '68 ▶
Robert Kennedy and His Times '90
The Rocking Horse Winner '49
Roger Dodger '02 ▶
RoGoPaG '62
Roll of Thunder, Hear My Cry '78
Rolling Home '48
Romeo and Juliet '54
Romeo and Juliet '68 ▶
Romola '25
Ronnie and Julie '97
Roommates '95
Roosters '95
The Royal Bed '31
Royal Deceit '94
Ruby Bridges '98
A Rumor of Angels '00
Runaway Father '91
Running Mates '86 ▶
Running Wild '94
Saint Maybe '98 ▶
St. Patrick's Day '99
A Saintly Switch '99
Sallah '63 ▶
Samantha '92
Same Old Song '97 ▶
Sand '00
Sandra of a Thousand Delights '65
The Saphead '21
Sardinia Kidnapped '75
Satan in High Heels '61
Savage Is Loose '74
Savage Island '03
Saving Shiloh '06
Scarlett '94
Scent of a Woman '92 ▶
Scott Turow's The Burden of Proof '92
Scream for Help '86
The Sculptress '97
The Sea '02
The Search '48 ▶
Searching for Bobby Fischer '93 ▶
Searching For Wooden Watermelons '01
A Season for Miracles '99
Season of Change '94
Season of Fear '89
The Secret '93
Secrets '94
Seduced and Abandoned '64 ▶
The Seducers '70
See You in the Morning '89
The Seekers '79
Selena '96
Separate Vacations '86
7 Faces of Dr. Lao '63 ▶
Shadow of a Doubt '43 ▶
Shameless '94
The Shanghai Gesture '42
The Shell Seekers '89
Shenandoah '65 ▶
The Shepherd of the Hills '41 ▶
She's So Lovely '97
Shiloh '97
Shock '79
Shoot the Moon '82
Shot Through the Heart '98 ▶
Showdown '94
Shy People '87 ▶
Siberiade '79 ▶
Siblings '04
Silence '73
The Silence of Neto '94
The Silences of the Palace '94 ▶
Silent Rebellion '82
Silent Tongue '92
The Silver Stallion: King of the Wild Brumbies '93
Simple Justice '89
A Simple Plan '98 ▶
Since You Went Away '44 ▶
Sinners '89
Sins of the Mind '97
Sioux City '94
Sitcom '97
Six in Paris '68
Sixteen Candles '84 ▶
The '60s '99
'68 '87
Skag '79 ▶
Skeletons '96
Skin Game '31
The Sleazy Uncle '89
Sleeping Dogs Lie '06
The Slingshot '93 ▶
Smart House '00
Smilin' Through '33 ▶
Smoke '70
Smoke Signals '98
The Snapper '93 ▶
Snow Day '00
Snowbound: The Jim and Jennifer Stolpa Story '94
Sofie '92
The Solitary Man '82
Something in the Wind '47
Something to Talk About '95
Sometimes a Great Notion '71 ▶
Sometimes They Come Back... Again '96
Son-in-Law '93
Son of Flubber '63
Son of Frankenstein '39 ▶
Son of Fury '42 ▶
The Son of the Bride '01
The Song of Songs '33
Song of the Exile '90
Song of the Islands '42
Sons '89
Sorceress '94
Sorrows of Gin '79
The Sound of Music '65 ▶
Sous Sol '96
South Central '92
South Riding '37
The Southerner '45 ▶
Southie '98
Souvenir '88
Spectre '96
Spider '02 ▶
Spider Baby '64
Spirit Rider '93 ▶
Spitfire '94
Splendor '35
Split Decisions '88
Split Image '82 ▶
Splitting Heirs '93
Spraggue '84
Spy Kids '01 ▶
Spy Kids 3-D: Game Over '03
Star Maps '97
State Fair '45 ▶
State Fair '62
Steal This Movie! '00
Stealing Beauty '96
Steamboy '05
Stella Dallas '37 ▶
Stepmonster '92
Stepsisters '74
Still Not Quite Human '92
Stir of Echoes '99
The Stone Boy '84 ▶
The Storm Within '48 ▶
Storytelling '01 ▶
Storyville '92
The Strange Door '51
Strange Interlude '32 ▶
Strange Interlude '90
Strange Relations '02
The Stranger '92
Strangers in the City '62
Strangers: The Story of a Mother and Daughter '79 ▶
The Strauss Family '73
Street Girls '75
Street Hero '84
Street Justice '89
Struggle '31
Stuart Little '99
Stuck on You '84
The Subject Was Roses '68 ▶
The Substance of Fire '96
The Substitute Wife '94
Such a Long Journey '98 ▶
Suddenly, Last Summer '59 ▶
Sugar Cane Alley '83 ▶
Summer Holiday '48
Summer Magic '63
The Summer of Aviya '88
Summer of Fear '78
Summer of the Monkeys '98
A Sunday in the Country '84 ▶
Sunday's Children '94 ▶
Sunshine '99
Sure Fire '90
Surfwise '07 ▶
Susan and God '40 ▶
Susana '51 ▶
Suzanne '80
Swedenhielms '35
The Sweeper '95
The Sweet Hereafter '96 ▶
Sweet Home Alabama '02
Sweet Nothing '96 ▶
Sweet Thing '00 ▶
The Swiss Family Robinson '60 ▶
Switched at Birth '91
Table Settings '84
The Tale of Ruby Rose '87 ▶
A Tale of Winter '92
The Talent Given Us '04 ▶
Tarantella '95
The Taste of Tea '04 ▶
Tears in the Rain '88
Teenage Exorcist '93
Temptress Moon '96
Ten Days Wonder '72
The Tenant of Wildfell Hall '96
Teorema '68
Terminator 2: Judgment Day '91 ▶
Termini Station '89
Terranova '91
Testament '83 ▶
Tevye '39
Tex '82
A Texas Funeral '99
Thank You & Good Night '91
That Eye, the Sky '94
That's My Baby! '44
There's No Business Like Show Business '54 ▶
They Call Me Sirr '00
They Watch '93
The Thief '97
Things in Their Season '74
The Third Sex '57
This Boy's Life '93 ▶
This Happy Breed '47 ▶
This Is My Father '99
This Is My Life '92
This Is the Sea '96
This Property Is Condemned '66
A Thousand Clowns '65 ▶
Threads '85 ▶
Three Daring Daughters '48
The Three Lives of Karen '97
Three Wishes '95
Three's Trouble '85
Thunderbirds '04
Thursday's Child '43
The Ticket '97
Ticket to Heaven '81 ▶
The Tie That Binds '95
Tieta of Agreste '96
Tiger Warsaw '87
Time Indefinite '93
Time Out '01
A Time to Live '85
A Time to Live and a Time to Die '85
Timemaster '95
Tito and Me '92 ▶
T.N.T. '98
To Dance with the White Dog '93 ▶
To Die For 2: Son of Darkness '91
To Gillian on Her 37th Birthday '96
To Paris with Love '55
To Sleep with Anger '90 ▶
Toby McTeague '87
Tokyo Cowboy '94
Tokyo Story '53 ▶
Tollbooth '94
Tommy Boy '95
Toughlove '85
Tourist Trap '98
The Town Is Quiet '00
Toys '92
Toys in the Attic '63
Track 29 '88
Trade Secrets '86
Traffic Jam '91
The Trail of the Lonesome Pine '36 ▶
Tramp at the Door '87
Traps '93
Traveller '96 ▶
Treasure of the Sierra Madre '48 ▶
The Tree of Wooden Clogs '78 ▶
Trois Couleurs: Blanc '94 ▶
Trois Couleurs: Bleu '93 ▶
Tromeo & Juliet '95
True Love '89 ▶
True Women '97
Trusting Beatrice '92
Tuck Everlasting '02
The Turning '92
The Tuttles of Tahiti '42 ▶
29th Street '91
Twice in a Lifetime '85 ▶
Twister '89
2 by 4 '98
Two Small Bodies '93
Ulee's Gold '97 ▶
Uncle Moses '32
Uncle Nino '03
Uncommon Valor '83
Uncorked '98
Under the Boardwalk '89
Undergrads '85 ▶
Uneasy Terms '48
An Unexpected Life '97
The Unforgiven '60 ▶
Uno '04
The Unsaid '01
Up/Down/Fragile '95
Up the Sandbox '72
The Uprising '81 ▶
Used People '92
Vacas '91
The Vector File '03
Vera Drake '04 ▶
A Very Brady Christmas '88
A Very Brady Sequel '96
Vigil '84 ▶
Village of Dreams '97
Violette '78 ▶
Viridiana '61 ▶
The Visit '00 ▶
Voyage en Balloon '59
Voyager '91 ▶
Vultures '84
A Walk in the Clouds '95
Walk in the Spring Rain '70
Walking on Water '02
Walking Thunder '94
The Wall '99 ▶
The Waltons: The Christmas Carol '80
War & Remembrance '88
War & Remembrance: The Final Chapter '89
The War at Home '96
Waterproof '99 ▶
The Way We Live Now '02
The Wedding Banquet '93 ▶
Wedding Bell Blues '96
Wedding Crashers '05 ▶
Wedding in White '72
The Weekend '00
Welcome Home '89
Wendigo '01
What the Peeper Saw '72
When Nature Calls '85
When Saturday Comes '95
Where East Is East '29
Where Have All the People Gone? '74

▶ = rated three bones or higher

Where Love Has Gone '64
Where the Heart Is '90
While You Were Sleeping '95 ▸
The White Balloon '95 ▸
The White Cliffs of Dover '44 ▸
Whity '70
Why Do They Call It Love When They Mean Sex? '92
Why Does Herr R. Run Amok? '69
Wicked '98
Wicked Stepmother '89
Wide Awake '97
The Wide Blue Road '57 ▸
Widow's Kiss '94
The Wild Country '71
The Wild Duck '84
Wild Pony '83
The Wild Thornberrys Movie '02 ▸
Wild Zone '89
Wildflower '91 ▸
William Shakespeare's Romeo and Juliet '96 ▸
The Winds of War '83
The Winner '96
The Winslow Boy '98 ▸
The Winter Guest '97 ▸
Winter in Wartime '10
Winter Kills '79 ▸
Winter People '89
The Wistful Widow of Wagon Gap '47
With Six You Get Eggroll '68
Witness Protection '99 ▸
Wives and Daughters '01
The Wizard of Oz '39 ▸
A Woman under the Influence '74 ▸
Women on the Verge of a Nervous Breakdown '88 ▸
Woodchipper Massacre '89
The World Accuses '35
World and Time Enough '95
A World Apart '88 ▸
The World of Apu '59 ▸
The Yarn Princess '94
The Yearling '94
Yellow Earth '89
Yi Yi '00
You Can't Take It with You '38 ▸
You Can't Take It with You '84 ▸
You'll Like My Mother '72
Younger & Younger '94
Zack & Reba '98
Zertigo Diamond Caper '82
Zooman '95 ▸

Fantasy

see also *Animation & Cartoons; Musical Fantasy*

A Nous la Liberte '31 ▸
The Acid Eaters '67
Adventures in Dinosaur City '92
The Adventures of a Gnome Named Gnorm '93
The Adventures of Baron Munchausen '89 ▸
The Adventures of Mark Twain '85 ▸
The Adventures of Pinocchio '96
The Adventures of Sharkboy and Lavagirl in 3-D '05
Aladdin '86
Aladdin and His Wonderful Lamp '84
Alice '88 ▸
Alice in Wonderland '85
Alice in Wonderland '99
Alice in Wonderland '10
Alice Through the Looking Glass '66
Alien from L.A. '87
...Almost '90
Alone Against Rome '62
Amazing Mr. Blunden '72
The Amazing Spider-Man '77
Amazing Stories '85
Amazons '86
America 3000 '86
The Amphibian Man '61
Angel-A '05
Angel on My Shoulder '46 ▸
Angel on My Shoulder '80
Aquamarine '06
Arthur and the Invisibles '06
Ashik Kerib '88 ▸
Atlantis, the Lost Continent '61
Atlantis: The Lost Empire '01
Atlas '60
Atlas in the Land of the Cyclops '61
Ator the Fighting Eagle '83
Babe '95 ▸
Babe: Pig in the City '98
Baby... Secret of the Lost Legend '85
Barbarella '68
Barbarian Queen '85
Baron Munchausen '43 ▸
Batman '89 ▸
Batman and Robin '97
Batman Forever '95 ▸
Batman Returns '92
*batteries not included '87
Beanstalk '94
Beastly '10
Beastmaster '82
Beastmaster 2: Through the Portal of Time '91
Beastmaster 3: The Eye of Braxus '95
Beauties of the Night '52
Beauty and the Devil '50
Beowulf & Grendel '06
Bernard and the Genie '91
Between Heaven and Earth '93
Beyond Atlantis '73
Beyond Tomorrow '40
Big '88 ▸
Big Top Pee-wee '88
Biggles '85
Bill & Ted's Excellent Adventure '89
The Bishop's Wife '47 ▸
The Black Cauldron '85
Blade: Trinity '04
Blithe Spirit '45 ▸
The Blood of a Poet '30
BloodRayne '06
The Blue Bird '40 ▸
Blue Monkey '87
Boogiepop and Others '00
The Borrowers '93 ▸
The Boy Who Could Fly '86 ▸
The Boy Who Loved Trolls '84
Bridge to Terabithia '07
The Brothers Grimm '05
Brothers Lionheart '77
Cabin Boy '94
The Canterville Ghost '44
The Canterville Ghost '96
Cars '06 ▸
The Cat from Outer Space '78
The Cave of the Silken Web '67
Celine and Julie Go Boating '74
Cerberus '05
The Challenge '82
Charleston '26 ▸
Charley and the Angel '73
Charlie and the Chocolate Factory '05 ▸
The Children of Noisy Village '86
The Christmas That Almost Wasn't '66
The Chronicles of Narnia '89
The Chronicles of Narnia: Prince Caspian '08
The Chronicles of Narnia: The Lion, the Witch and the Wardrobe '05
Cinderella 2000 '78
Circus Angel '65 ▸
City of Ember '08
The City of Lost Children '95 ▸
The Clan of the Cave Bear '86
Clarence '91
Clash of the Titans '81
Clash of the Titans '10
Click '06
Cocoon '85 ▸
Cocoon: The Return '88
The Color of Magic '08
Come Drink with Me '65 ▸
The Company of Wolves '85 ▸
Conan the Barbarian '82 ▸
Conan the Destroyer '84
A Connecticut Yankee '31 ▸
A Connecticut Yankee in King Arthur's Court '89
Conquest '83
Conquest of Mycene '63
Constantine '05
Coraline '09 ▸
Coriolanus, Man without a Country '64
The Crazy Ray '22 ▸
Crossworlds '96
The Crow '93
The Crow 2: City of Angels '96
The Curious Case of Benjamin Button '08 ▸
Curse of the Cat People '44 ▸
Daimajin '66
Darby O'Gill & the Little People '59 ▸
The Dark Crystal '82 ▸
The Day the Earth Froze '59
Death Takes a Holiday '34 ▸
Death Trance '05
Deathstalker '83
Deathstalker 2: Duel of the Titans '87
Deathstalker 3 '89
Deathstalker 4: Match of Titans '92
Delgo '08
Desperate Living '77
The Devil & Max Devlin '81
Devil of the Desert Against the Son of Hercules '62
Diary of Forbidden Dreams '73 ▸
Digby, the Biggest Dog in the World '73
Dinotopia '02
Donkey Skin '70 ▸
Dororo '07
Dragon Wars '07
Dragonball: Evolution '09
Dragonheart '96
Dragonheart: A New Beginning '00
Dragonslayer '81 ▸
Dragonworld '94
Dream a Little Dream '89
Dream a Little Dream 2 '94
Dreamchild '85 ▸
Dreamscape '84
Drop Dead Fred '91
Dungeonmaster '83
Dungeons and Dragons '00
Edward Scissorhands '90 ▸
Elektra '05
Ella Enchanted '04 ▸
Emmanuelle 4 '84
Enchanted '07
The Enchanted Cottage '45
The Enchantress '85
Endgame '85
Epoch: Evolution '03
Eragon '06
Eraserhead '78 ▸
Erotic Escape '72
Erotic Touch of Hot Skin '65
Escape from Atlantis '97
Escapes '86
E.T.: The Extra-Terrestrial '82 ▸
Eternal Return '43
Everybody Says I'm Fine! '06
The Ewok Adventure '84
The Ewoks: Battle for Endor '85
Excalibur '81 ▸
Explorers '85
The Fantastic Night '42 ▸
Fantasy Island '76
Faraway, So Close! '93
Field of Dreams '89 ▸
The Final Programme '73
Fire and Ice '83
Five Element Ninjas '82
Flight of Dragons '82
Flight of the Navigator '86
Fluke '95
The Forbidden Kingdom '08
Francis Goes to the Races '51
Francis the Talking Mule '49 ▸
Frankenstein and Me '96
Freddie the Frog '92
French Quarter '78
From the Earth to the Moon '58
Galgameth '96
Gamera the Brave '06
Garuda '04
George and the Dragon '04
George's Island '91 ▸
The Ghost and Mrs. Muir '47 ▸
Ghost Chase '88
Ghost Writer '89
Ghosts Can't Do It '90
Ghostwarrior '86
The Giants of Thessaly '60
Gladiators 7 '62
The Glass Slipper '55
The Gnome-Mobile '67
The Golden Compass '07
Golden Voyage of Sinbad '73
The Golem '20 ▸
Goliath Against the Giants '63
Goliath and the Barbarians '60
Goliath and the Dragon '61
Goliath and the Sins of Babylon '64
The Good Night '07
Gor '88
The Great Land of Small '86
The Great Yokai War '05
Grendel, Grendel, Grendel '82
Gryphon '88
Gulliver's Travels '39
Gulliver's Travels '77
Gulliver's Travels '95
A Gun, a Car, a Blonde '97
A Guy Named Joe '44
Harry Potter and the Chamber of Secrets '02 ▸
Harry Potter and the Goblet of Fire '05 ▸
Harry Potter and the Order of the Phoenix '07
Harry Potter and the Prisoner of Azkaban '04
Harry Potter and the Sorcerer's Stone '01 ▸
Harvey '50 ▸
Hawk the Slayer '81
Heartbreak Hotel '88
Hearts & Armour '83
Heaven & Hell '78
Heaven Can Wait '43 ▸
Heaven Can Wait '78 ▸
Heavy Metal '81 ▸
Helen of Troy '56
Hellboy II: The Golden Army '08 ▸
Herbie Rides Again '74
Hercules '58
Hercules and the Captive Women '63
Hercules and the Princess of Troy '65
Hercules in the Haunted World '64
Hercules, Prisoner of Evil '64
Hercules Unchained '59
Here Come the Littles: The Movie '85
Here Comes Mr. Jordan '41 ▸
Hey There, It's Yogi Bear '64
Highlander 2: The Quickening '91
Highlander: Endgame '00
Highlander: The Final Dimension '94
The Hobbit '78 ▸
Hobgoblins '87
Hogfather '06
The Holes '72
Hook '91
Hoppity Goes to Town '41
Horrors of the Red Planet '64
Howl's Moving Castle '04
A Hungarian Fairy Tale '87 ▸
Hyper-Sapien: People from Another Star '86
I Married a Witch '42 ▸
The Immortal '01
In the Name of the King: A Dungeon Siege Tale '08
The Incredible Hulk '08
The Incredible Mr. Limpet '64
Incubus '65
The Indian in the Cupboard '95
Indiana Jones and the Last Crusade '89 ▸
Inhibition '76
Inkheart '09
The Invasion of Carol Enders '74
The Invincible Gladiator '63
Invisible Agent '42
The Invisible Kid '88
Invisible: The Chronicles of Benjamin Knight '93
Irish Cinderella '22
The Iron Crown '41
Iron Warrior '87
It Happened Tomorrow '44
It's a Wonderful Life '46 ▸
Jack Frost '98
Jack the Giant Killer '62 ▸
Jacob Two Two Meets the Hooded Fang '99
James and the Giant Peach '96 ▸
Jason and the Argonauts '63 ▸
Jason and the Argonauts '00
Jimmy, the Boy Wonder '66
Jonathan Livingston Seagull '73
Josh Kirby. . .Time Warrior: Chapter 1, Planet of the Dino-Knights '95
Josh Kirby... Time Warrior: Chapter 2, The Human Pets '95
Josh Kirby... Time Warrior: Chapter 3, Trapped on Toyworld '95
Josh Kirby... Time Warrior: Chapter 4, Eggs from 70 Million B.C. '95
Josh Kirby... Time Warrior: Chapter 5, Journey to the Magic Cavern '96
Journey Beneath the Desert '61
Journey to the Center of the Earth '59 ▸
Journey to the Center of the Earth '99
Journey to the Lost City '58
Julia and Julia '87
Julia Has Two Lovers '91
Jumanji '95
The Jungle Book '42
Jungle Boy '96
Jungle Hell '55
Just like Heaven '05
Just My Luck '06
Kaena: The Prophecy '03
Kazaam '96
A Kid in Aladdin's Palace '97
Kids of the Round Table '96
King Kong '33 ▸
King Kong '76
King Kong '05 ▸
Kiss Me Goodbye '82
Knights of Bloodsteel '09
Kriemhilde's Revenge '24 ▸
Krull '83
Kull the Conqueror '97
La Merveilleuse Visite '74
L.A. Story '91 ▸
Labyrinth '86 ▸
Lady in the Water '06
Ladyhawke '85
The Lake House '06
Land of Doom '84
The Land of Faraway '87
The Last Airbender '10
The Last Days of Pompeii '60
The Last Mimzy '07
The Last Unicorn '82
Le Magnifique '76
Leapin' Leprechauns '95
Legend '86
The Legend of Cryin' Ryan '98
The Legend of Suram Fortress '85
Legend of the Liquid Sword '93
Legion of Iron '90
Lemony Snicket's A Series of Unfortunate Events '04
Leprechaun 2 '94
Les Visiteurs du Soir '42 ▸
The Lickerish Quartet '70
Like Father, Like Son '87
The Lion of Thebes '64 ▸
The Little Mermaid '75
Little Monsters '89
Little Nemo: Adventures in Slumberland '92
Little Red Riding Hood '83 ▸
Logan's Run '76
Looking for Eric '09
The Lord of the Rings '78
Lord of the Rings: The Fellowship of the Ring '01 ▸
Lord of the Rings: The Two Towers '02 ▸
Lord of the Rings: The Return of the King '03 ▸
Lords of Magick '88
The Lost Continent '51
The Lost Empire '01
Love Notes '88
The Loves of Hercules '60
The Luck of the Irish '48
Maciste in Hell '60
Made in Heaven '87
The Magic Fountain '61
Magic Hunter '96
Magic in the Mirror: Fowl Play '96
Magic in the Water '95
Magic Island '95
Magic Serpent '66 ▸
The Magic Voyage of Sinbad '52
The Magical Legend of the Leprechauns '99
The Magician '58 ▸
Making Contact '86
The Man in the Santa Claus Suit '79
The Man Who Could Work Miracles '37 ▸
The Man Who Wagged His Tail '57
Mannequin 2: On the Move '91
Marco Polo, Jr. '72
The Martian Chronicles: Part 1 '79
The Martian Chronicles: Part 2 '79
The Martian Chronicles: Part 3 '79
Master of the World '61
Masters of the Universe '87
Maxie '85
Mazes and Monsters '82
Medusa Against the Son of Hercules '62
Meet Joe Black '98
Merlin '92
Merlin '98 ▸
Merlin and the Book of Beasts '09
Merlin and the Sword '85
Merlin's Apprentice '06
Messalina vs. the Son of Hercules '64
Michael '96
A Midsummer Night's Dream '35 ▸
Mighty Joe Young '49
Mighty Joe Young '98
Mighty Morphin Power Rangers: The Movie '95
Million Dollar Duck '71
Miracle Beach '92
Miracle in Milan '51 ▸
MirrorMask '05
Mr. Destiny '90
Mr. Magorium's Wonder Emporium '07
Mr. Rice's Secret '00
Mr. Sycamore '74
The Mistress of Spices '05
Mists of Avalon '01 ▸
Mole Men Against the Son of Hercules '61
Momentum '03
Monkeybone '01

▸ = rated three bones or higher

Moon over Tao '97 ▸
The Moon Stallion '85
More about the Children of Noisy Village '87
Mortal Kombat 1: The Movie '95
Mortal Kombat 2: Annihilation '97
Mouse and His Child '77
Munchie '92
The Muppets' Wizard of Oz '05
My Friend Walter '93
My Neighbor Totoro '88
My Science Project '85
My Stepmother Is an Alien '88
The Mysterious Stranger '82
Mystery Island '81
Nanny McPhee '06
Natas... The Reflection '83
The Navigator '88 ▸
Neil Gaiman's NeverWhere '96
Neutron vs. the Amazing Dr. Caronte '61
Neutron vs. the Death Robots '62
Neutron vs. the Maniac '62
The NeverEnding Story '84 ▸
NeverEnding Story 2: The Next Chapter '91
The NeverEnding Story 3: Escape from Fantasia '94
Night Tide '63
Night Watch '04
The Nightmare Before Christmas '93 ▸
Nine Lives of Fritz the Cat '74
November '05 ▸
Nutcracker: The Motion Picture '86
The Ogre '96
Once a Hero '88
100 Monsters '68
One Magic Christmas '85
1001 Arabian Nights '59
One Wish Too Many '55
Onmyoji '01
Onmyoji 2 '03
The Original Fabulous Adventures of Baron Munchausen '61
Orochi, the Eight Headed Dragon '94
Orpheus '49
Outlander '08
Outlaw of Gor '87
The Pagemaster '94
Painted Skin '93
Pandora and the Flying Dutchman '51
Pan's Labyrinth '06 ▸
Paperhouse '89 ▸
Parasite '03
Patchwork Girl of Oz '14
The Peanut Butter Solution '85
Peau D'Ane '71 ▸
Penelope '06
Percy Jackson & The Olympians: The Lightning Thief '10
Peter Pan '24
Peter Pan '53 ▸
Peter Pan '03
Pete's Dragon '77
The Phantom Chariot '20
Phantom Tollbooth '69 ▸
The Phoenix and the Magic Carpet '95
Piano Tuner of Earthquakes '05
The Plague Dogs '82
Pleasantville '98 ▸
The Point '71
The Polar Bear King '94
Pom Poko '94
Powder '95
Prancer '89
Prehistoric Bimbos in Armageddon City '93
Prehistoric Women '50
Prehysteria '93
Prehysteria 2 '94
Prehysteria 3 '95
Prelude to a Kiss '92
The Price of Milk '00
Prince of Persia: The Sands of Time '10
Princess: A Modern Fairytale '08
Private Passions '85
The Promise '05
Pufnstuf '70
The Puppetoon Movie '87
Quest for the Mighty Sword '90
Quest of the Delta Knights '93
Radio Flyer '92
Ratboy '86
Re-Cycle '06
Real Men '87
Reckless '95
The Red Balloon '56 ▸
Red Sonja '85
Renoir Shorts '27 ▸
The Rescuers Down Under '90
The Restless '06
Restless Spirits '99
Return from Witch Mountain '78
Return of Daimajin '66
The Return of Jafar '94
The Return of Peter Grimm '35
The Return of the Borrowers '96 ▸
Return of the Fly '59
The Return of the King '80
Return to Fantasy Island '77
Return to Never Land '02
Return to Oz '85
Return to the Lost World '93
Revolt of the Barbarians '64
The Rise & Rise of Daniel Rocket '86
Robots '05
Rock & Rule '83
Roland the Mighty '56
The Rook '99
Rookie of the Year '93
Salome's Last Dance '88
Samson '61
Samson Against the Sheik '62
Samson and His Mighty Challenge '64
Samson and the 7 Miracles of the World '62
Santa Claus '59
Santa Claus Conquers the Martians '64
Santa Claus: The Movie '85
The Saragossa Manuscript '65
The Scalawag Bunch '75
The Science of Sleep '06
Sea of Dreams '90
Sea People '00
The Sea Serpent '85
Search for the Gods '75
The Secret of NIMH '82 ▸
The Secret of Roan Inish '94 ▸
The Seeker: The Dark Is Rising '07
Serpent Island '54
7 Faces of Dr. Lao '63 ▸
Seven Magnificent Gladiators '84
The Seventh Voyage of Sinbad '58 ▸
The Shaggy Dog '59
The Shaggy Dog '06
She '25
She '83
She Gods of Shark Reef '56
Shredder Orpheus '89
Shrek '01 ▸
Shrek 2 '04 ▸
Shrek Forever After '10
Siegfried '24 ▸
A Simple Wish '97
Simply Irresistible '99
Sinbad and the Eye of the Tiger '77
Sinbad of the Seven Seas '89
Sky Blue '03
Slave Girls from Beyond Infinity '87
Sleepwalk '88
Snow White: A Tale of Terror '97
Snow White: The Fairest of Them All '02
Solarbabies '86
Some Call It Loving '73
Something Wicked This Way Comes '83
Son of Hercules in the Land of Darkness '63
Son of Kong '33
Son of Samson '62
Son of Sinbad '55
Song Spinner '95
Sorceress '82
A Sound of Thunder '05
Southland Tales '06
Space Raiders '83
Space Soldiers Conquer the Universe '40
Spellbreaker: Secret of the Leprechauns '96
The Spiderwick Chronicles '08 ▸
Splash '84
The Spring '89
Stairway to Heaven '46 ▸
Stalker '79 ▸
Stand Up and Cheer '34
Stardust '07 ▸
Starry Night '99
The Steagle '71
Steel Dawn '87
Story of a Cowboy Angel '81
Storybook '95
Student of Prague '13 ▸
Super Mario Bros. '93
Supergirl '84
Superman: The Movie '78 ▸
Superman 2 '80 ▸
Superman 3 '83
Superman 4: The Quest for Peace '87
Superman & the Mole Men '51
Superman Returns '06
Sword & the Dragon '56
Sword & the Sorcerer '82
The Sword in the Stone '63 ▸
Sword Masters: The Battle Wizard '77
Sword of the Valiant '83
Sylvia and the Phantom '45 ▸
Tales of Beatrix Potter '71 ▸
Tall Tale: The Unbelievable Adventures of Pecos Bill '95
Tammy and the T-Rex '94
Tank Girl '94
Tanya's Island '81
Teenage Mutant Ninja Turtles: The Movie '90
The Tempest '63
The 10th Kingdom '00
Terror of Rome Against the Son of Hercules '64
Terror of the Steppes '64
Test Tube Teens from the Year 2000 '93
The Testament of Dr. Cordelier '59 ▸
The Testament of Orpheus '59 ▸
They Came Back '04
The Thief and the Cobbler '96 ▸
The Thief Lord '06
The Thief of Bagdad '40 ▸
The Thief of Baghdad '24 ▸
Thief of Baghdad '61
The Thief of Baghdad '78
Thor and the Amazon Women '60
A Thousand and One Nights '45
Three Wishes '95
The Three Worlds of Gulliver '59
Throne of Fire '82
Thumbelina '82 ▸
Thunderbirds '04
Tideland '05
Tim Burton's Corpse Bride '05 ▸
Time Bandits '81
The Time of Their Lives '46
The Time Traveler's Wife '09
Timestalkers '87
Tin Man '07
Tobor the Great '54
Tom Thumb '58 ▸
Toy Story '95 ▸
Toy Story 2 '99 ▸
Trading Mom '94
Train to Hollywood '86 ▸
Transformers: The Movie '86
The Trip '67
A Troll in Central Park '94
Tropical Malady '04
Trouble in Mind '86 ▸
The Tune '92
Turbo: A Power Rangers Movie '96
20,000 Leagues under the Sea '54 ▸
20,000 Leagues Under the Sea '97
The Twilight of the Ice Nymphs '97
Twisted '96
Twitches '05
Twitches Too '07
The Two Worlds of Jenny Logan '79
Undersea Kingdom '36
Unidentified Flying Oddball '79
Ursus in the Valley of the Lions '62
Uzumaki '00
The Valley of Gwangi '69 ▸
Venus Against the Son of Hercules '62
A Very Old Man with Enormous Wings '88
Vibes '88
Vice Versa '88 ▸
Vulcan God of Fire '62
Walking on Air '87
The Warrior & the Sorceress '84
Warrior Queen '87
Warriors of Virtue '97
The Water Horse: Legend of the Deep '07
Watership Down '78
Wax, or the Discovery of Television among the Bees '93
Waxworks '24 ▸
What Dreams May Come '98
Where the Wild Things Are '09
The White Sheik '52 ▸
Wild Women of Wongo '59
Wildest Dreams '90
William Shakespeare's A Midsummer Night's Dream '99
Willow '88
Wind and Cloud: The Storm Riders '04
Window to Paris '95
Wings of Desire '88 ▸
Wings of Fame '93
Witch Hunt '94
A Witch Without a Broom '68
The Witching of Ben Wagner '95
The Wizard of Oz '25
The Wizard of Speed and Time '88
Wizards '77
Wizards of the Demon Sword '94
Wizards of the Lost Kingdom '85
Wizards of the Lost Kingdom 2 '89
The Wolves of Kromer '98
Wombling Free '77
The Wonderful World of the Brothers Grimm '62
The Worst Witch '86
Wrath of Daimajin '66
Yor, the Hunter from the Future '83
Youth Without Youth '07
Yu-Gi-Oh! The Movie: Pyramid of Light '04
Zapped! '82
Zardoz '73
Zathura '05 ▸
Zero for Conduct '33 ▸
Zone Troopers '84
Zu Warriors '01
Zu: Warriors from the Magic Mountain '83

Farm Livin'

All Roads Lead Home '08
... And the Earth Did Not Swallow Him '94
Animal Farm '99
Balloon Farm '97
Barnyard '06
Bitter Harvest '81 ▸
Blessing '94
Bloodsuckers from Outer Space '83
Born in 68 '08
Boy Takes Girl '83
The Bridges of Madison County '95 ▸
Broken Harvest '94
Buffalo Jump '90 ▸
The Cabin in the Cotton '32
Captain Boycott '47
Cash Crop '01
The Castaway Cowboy '74
Charlotte's Web '73
Charlotte's Web '06 ▸
Chicken Run '00 ▸
The Cider House Rules '99 ▸
City Girl '30
Clodhopper '17
Cold Comfort Farm '71
Cold Comfort Farm '94 ▸
Cold Mountain '03 ▸
Country '84 ▸
Country Life '95
The Curse '87
Curse of the Starving Class '94
Dark Before Dawn '89
Days of Heaven '78 ▸
Deadly Stranger '88
December Bride '91
Demon Wind '90
Desire Under the Elms '58
The Devil & Daniel Webster '41 ▸
Disgrace '08
Doc Hollywood '91
Dog Day '83
A Dog Named Christmas '09
The Dukes of Hazzard '05
Earth '30 ▸
Earthworm Tractors '36
The Echo of Thunder '98
Egg and I '47 ▸
Eli Eli '40
Fantastic Mr. Fox '09 ▸
Far from the Madding Crowd '97 ▸
The Farmer Takes a Wife '35
The Farmer's Other Daughter '65
The Field '90 ▸
15 Amore '98
Freezer Burn: The Invasion of Laxdale '08
The General Line '29 ▸
Giant '56 ▸
The Girl from Paris '02 ▸
God's Little Acre '58 ▸
The Good Old Boys '95
The Grapes of Wrath '40 ▸
The Green Promise '49
Harvest '37 ▸
Harvest '98
Harvest of Fire '95
Home on the Range '04
Horton Foote's Alone '97
In the Winter Dark '98
The Inheritors '98
Jean de Florette '87 ▸
The Kettles in the Ozarks '56
Kings in Grass Castles '97
The Land Girls '98
Little John '02
Ma and Pa Kettle at Home '54
The Mating Game '59 ▸
Messengers 2: The Scarecrow '09
Mifune '99
The Milagro Beanfield War '88 ▸
Missouri Traveler '58 ▸
Morning Glory '93
My Antonia '94
Nanny McPhee 2 '10
Northern Lights '79 ▸
Nowhere in Africa '02
Nowhere to Run '93
Oklahoma Bound '81
Our Daily Bread '34 ▸
The Outsider '02
A Painted House '03
Pearl Diver '04
Pelle the Conqueror '88 ▸
Places in the Heart '84 ▸
The Price of Milk '00
The Proposition '96
The Purchase Price '32
Rachel and the Stranger '48 ▸
Ride the Wild Fields '00
The River '84
The Road from Coorain '02
Rock-a-Doodle '92
Romulus, My Father '07 ▸
Ruggles of Red Gap '35 ▸
Sarah, Plain and Tall: Skylark '93
Sarah, Plain and Tall: Winter's End '99 ▸
Secondhand Lions '03
Signs '02 ▸
Sommersby '93
Son-in-Law '93
Sounder '72 ▸
The Southerner '45 ▸
Stacking '87
The Stars Fell on Henrietta '94
Steal Big, Steal Little '95
The Stone Boy '84 ▸
The Story of Xinghua '93
Summer of the Monkeys '98
Sunday Too Far Away '74 ▸
The Sundowners '60 ▸
Sunrise '27 ▸
That Evening Sun '09 ▸
This Is My Father '99
A Thousand Acres '97
Tomboy & the Champ '58
Total Western '00
The Tree of Wooden Clogs '78 ▸
Tully '00 ▸
2 Brothers & a Bride '03
Under the Sun '98
Vacas '91
The Well '97
Where There's a Will '55
Wild Brian Kent '36
Will It Snow for Christmas? '96
Wisdom '87
The Yearling '94
The Young Pioneers '76

Farming

see Farm Livin'

Fashion

A la Mode '94
Beau Brummell: This Charming Man '06
The Bitter Tears of Petra von Kant '72
Bratz '07
Chanel Solitaire '81
Coco Before Chanel '09
Coco Chanel '08
Coco Chanel & Igor Stravinksy '09
The Devil Wears Prada '06
Don't Tell Mom the Babysitter's Dead '91
The Dress '96
Fashion Victims '07
Fashions of 1934 '34
Fernandel the Dressmaker '57
The Garment Jungle '57
Hourglass '95
The House of Eliott '92
I'm Dangerous Tonight '90
Intern '00
Kill by Inches '99
Kinky Boots '06
A Life of Her Own '50
Lovely to Look At '52 ▸
Made in Paris '65
Maytime in Mayfair '49
Mrs. 'Arris Goes to Paris '92
My Lucky Star '38
102 Dalmatians '00
Perfume '01
Phat Girlz '06
Portraits Chinois '96

▸ = rated three bones or higher

- Princess Daisy '83
- Ready to Wear '94
- Ripple Effect '07
- Romy and Michele's High School Reunion '97
- Scruples '80
- Selena '96
- The September Issue '09
- Sins '85
- Stroke of Midnight '90
- Tales of Manhattan '42 ►
- 27 Dresses '08
- Unzipped '94 ►
- Valentino: The Last Emperor '08
- Vogues of 1938 '37
- Yours, Mine & Ours '05

Fatsuit Acting

- America's Sweethearts '01
- Austin Powers 2: The Spy Who Shagged Me '99 ►
- Austin Powers In Goldmember '02
- Big Momma's House '00
- Big Momma's House 2 '06
- Dance Flick '09
- Death Becomes Her '92 ►
- Hairspray '07 ►
- Just Friends '05
- Monty Python's The Meaning of Life '83 ►
- My Mom's New Boyfriend '08
- Norbit '07
- The Nutty Professor '96 ►
- Nutty Professor 2: The Klumps '00
- The Santa Clause '94
- The Santa Clause 2 '02
- The Santa Clause 3: The Escape Clause '06
- Shallow Hal '01
- Stephen King's Thinner '96
- Tropic Thunder '08 ►

FBI

see also CIA/NSA; Crime Drama

- Acts of Betrayal '98
- After the Sunset '04
- Airboss '97
- Along Came a Spider '01
- American East '07
- American Meltdown '04
- American Yakuza '94
- Analyze That '02
- Analyze This '98 ►
- The Art of War '00
- The Assassination File '96
- The Astronaut Farmer '07
- Back in Business '96
- Bait '00
- Ballistic: Ecks vs. Sever '02
- Balls of Fury '07
- Beavis and Butt-Head Do America '96
- Best Men '98
- Betrayed '88
- A Better Way to Die '00
- Big Momma's House '00
- Big Momma's House 2 '06
- Big Trouble '02
- Bird on a Wire '90
- Black Dog '98
- Black Moon Rising '86
- Black Sunday '77
- Black Widow '87 ►
- Blade: Trinity '04
- Blast '04
- Bless the Child '00
- Blood, Guts, Bullets and Octane '99
- Blood Work '02
- Bloodfist 5: Human Target '93
- Boondock Saints '99
- Boss of Bosses '99
- Breach '07
- The Breed '01
- Broken Trust '95
- Bugs '03
- Capone '89
- Captain Nuke and the Bomber Boys '95
- Caracara '00
- Catch Me If You Can '02
- The Cell '00
- The Cell 2 '09
- Chain Reaction '96
- Chasing Papi '03
- Children of Fury '94
- City of Ghosts '03
- Civic Duty '06
- Clay Pigeons '98
- The Clearing '04 ►
- The Client '94
- Cloak & Dagger '84
- Club Fed '90
- Code Name Alpha '67
- Confessions of a Nazi Spy '39
- Corky Romano '01
- Crash and Burn '07
- Crime Killer '85
- Crime Spree '03
- The Crimson Code '99
- Daughter of the Tong '39
- Dead Aim '87
- Dead Bang '89
- Dead Silence '96
- Death Rides the Range '40
- Deja Vu '06
- Desperate Hours '90
- Die Hard '88 ►
- Dillinger '73
- Dillinger and Capone '95
- Domino '05
- Donnie Brasco '96 ►
- Double Take '01
- Double Tap '98
- Double Vision '02
- Eagle Eye '08
- Echelon Conspiracy '09
- 88 Minutes '08
- F/X '86 ►
- Face/Off '97 ►
- Fast Getaway 2 '94
- FBI Girl '52
- The FBI Story '59 ►
- Federal Agents vs. Underworld, Inc. '49
- Feds '88
- Felony '95
- Final Approach '08
- Final Destination '00
- Finish Line '08
- The Firm '93 ►
- The Fix '84
- Flashback '89 ►
- Flight to Nowhere '46
- The Flock '07
- Follow That Car '80
- Frailty '02 ►
- Full Disclosure '00
- G-Force '09
- "G" Men '35 ►
- G-Men Never Forget '48
- Ginostra '02
- The Glass Jungle '88
- Golden Gate '93
- Government Agents vs. Phantom Legion '51
- Grosse Pointe Blank '97 ►
- Gun Grit '36
- Half Past Dead '02
- Hannibal '01
- Hard Cash '01
- Harvard Man '01
- Held for Ransom '38
- Hellboy '04
- Hell's Bloody Devils '70
- Higher Ground '88
- Hit Woman: The Double Edge '93
- Hollow Point '95
- Honor and Glory '92
- The House on Carroll Street '88
- House on 92nd Street '45 ►
- The Hunted '03
- I Was a Communist for the FBI '51
- I Was a Zombie for the FBI '82
- I'll Get You '53
- iMurders '08
- In the Line of Duty: The FBI Murders '88 ►
- The Informant! '09
- The Interpreter '05 ►
- J. Edgar Hoover '87
- The Jackal '97
- Johnnie Gibson F.B.I. '87
- Judas Kiss '98
- Kill Me Later '01
- Kill Switch '08
- The Kingdom '07
- The Last Shot '04
- The Last Templar '09
- Let 'Em Have It '35
- Lethal '04
- Little Nikita '88
- Live Wire '92
- Live Wire: Human Timebomb '95
- Lure of the Islands '42
- Man of the House '05
- Manhunter '86 ►
- Married to the Mob '88 ►
- Master Spy: The Robert Hanssen Story '02
- Maximum Risk '96
- Me and the Mob '94
- Mean Streak '99
- Medium Cool '69 ►
- Melvin Purvis: G-Man '74
- Mercury Rising '98
- Mickey Blue Eyes '99
- Midnight Murders '91
- Midnight Run '88 ►
- Mindhunters '05
- Mindstorm '01
- Minutemen '08
- Miss Congeniality '00
- Miss Congeniality 2: Armed and Fabulous '05
- Mississippi Burning '88 ►
- Momentum '03
- Most Wanted '97
- My Blue Heaven '90
- My Mom's New Boyfriend '08
- Naked Lies '98
- Next '07
- No Way Back '96
- Nowhere Land '98
- The Outfit '93
- Pandemic '07
- Panther '95
- Paradise Canyon '35
- Partners in Crime '99
- Path to Paradise '97
- Perfect Assassins '98
- Perfect Lies '97
- Plughead Rewired: Circuitry Man 2 '94
- The Private Files of J. Edgar Hoover '77
- Public Enemies '09
- The Punisher '04
- Pups '99
- The Rage '96
- Ransom '96 ►
- Raw Deal '86
- Red Dragon '02
- The Reluctant Agent '89
- The Return of Eliot Ness '91
- Revolver '92
- Road Ends '98
- Robin of Locksley '95
- The Rock '96 ►
- Rollercoaster '77
- Rush Hour '98
- Sabotage '96
- Saw 4 '07
- Saw 5 '08
- Saw 6 '09
- Scam '93
- See Spot Run '01
- Serial Bomber '96
- Shattered Image '93
- Shoot to Kill '88 ►
- Shooter '07
- The Siege '98
- Silence of the Hams '93
- The Silence of the Lambs '91 ►
- The Silencer '99
- Silk Degrees '94
- Sky Liner '49
- Slaughter of the Innocents '93
- Sleeper Cell '05
- Smashing the Rackets '38
- Smokin' Aces '07
- Smokin' Aces 2: Assassins' Ball '10
- Snakes on a Plane '06
- Spartan '04 ►
- Special Investigator '36
- Standoff '97
- The Stickup '01
- Stone Cold '91
- Sugartime '95
- Sunstorm '01
- Surveillance '08
- Suspect Zero '04
- Switchback '97
- Taking Lives '04
- 10th & Wolf '06
- That Darn Cat '65
- That Darn Cat '96
- This Woman Is Dangerous '52
- 3 Ninjas '92
- Thunderheart '92 ►
- Timber! '42
- Tom Clancy's Netforce '98
- Torque '04
- Tortured '08
- Trail of a Serial Killer '98
- Traitor '08
- Triplecross '95
- Turbulence 3: Heavy Metal '00
- Twin Peaks: Fire Walk with Me '92
- Undercover Blues '93
- Underworld USA '61
- Union Depot '32
- U.S. Marshals '98
- The Untouchables '87 ►
- The Usual Suspects '95 ►
- Valley of the Heart's Delight '07
- War '07
- The Watcher '00
- The Weather Underground '02 ►
- Whipsaw '35
- White Chicks '04
- White Sands '92
- Wild Side '95
- Winds of Terror '01
- Wisegal '08
- Witless Protection '08
- Wounded '97
- The X-Files '98
- The X Files: I Want to Believe '08
- Zero Tolerance '93

Female Bonding

see also Women; Wonder Women

- Across the Moon '94
- All I Wanna Do '98
- Allie & Me '97
- Amusement '08
- Antonia's Line '95
- Aquamarine '06
- Autumn Tale '98
- Baby Mama '08
- Bandits '99
- The Banger Sisters '02
- B.A.P.'s '97
- Beaches '88 ►
- Beautiful Creatures '00
- Bend It Like Beckham '02 ►
- Berkeley Square '98
- Between Strangers '02
- The Big Bad Swim '06
- Blonde and Blonder '07
- Blue Crush '02 ►
- Blush '95
- Bonneville '06
- Boys on the Side '94
- Bride Wars '09
- The Buccaneers '95 ►
- Burning Life '94
- The Business of Strangers '01
- Cadillac Ranch '96
- Calendar Girls '03
- Camilla '94
- Caramel '07 ►
- Casa de los Babys '03 ►
- The Cemetery Club '93
- Chaos '01
- Charms for the Easy Life '02
- Chasing Papi '03
- The Cheetah Girls '03
- The Cheetah Girls 2 '06
- Clockwatchers '97
- Cold Mountain '03 ►
- Collected Stories '02 ►
- The Color of Courage '98
- Coming Soon '99
- Confessions of a Teenage Drama Queen '04
- Connie and Carla '04
- A Cooler Climate '99
- The Craft '96
- Crossroads '02
- Crush '02
- Dancing at the Blue Iguana '00
- Daughters of the Dust '91 ►
- Dead Gorgeous '02
- Desert Hearts '86 ►
- Divine Secrets of the Ya-Ya Sisterhood '02
- Don't Tell '05
- Dreamgirls '06 ►
- Dreamland '06 ►
- The Dreamlife of Angels '98 ►
- 8 Women '02 ►
- Emma '96 ►
- Emma '97 ►
- Enough! '06
- Evening '07
- Everything Relative '96
- Falling '06
- The First Wives Club '96
- 4 Months, 3 Weeks and 2 Days '07 ►
- Foxfire '96
- Freeway 2: Confessions of a Trickbaby '99
- Fried Green Tomatoes '91 ►
- Friends with Money '06
- Georgia Rule '07
- Getting Played '05
- Girl, Interrupted '99
- A Girl Thing '01
- Girls Can't Swim '99
- Girls' Night '97
- Girls Town '95
- Grace & Glorie '98
- The Heidi Chronicles '95
- High Heels and Low Lifes '01
- Hilary and Jackie '98 ►
- Home Room '02 ►
- The House Bunny '08
- How to Make an American Quilt '95
- Hysterical Blindness '02
- The Ice House '97 ►
- It's My Turn, Laura Cadieux '98
- Jackie, Ethel, Joan: The Kennedy Women '01
- The Jane Austen Book Club '07 ►
- John Tucker Must Die '06
- The Joy Luck Club '93 ►
- Just a Little Harmless Sex '99
- The Killing Club '01
- The Land Girls '98
- The Last of the Blonde Bombshells '00
- The Lemon Sisters '90
- Let's Talk About Sex '98
- The Life Before Her Eyes '07
- Little Witches '96
- Live-In Maid '04
- Live Nude Girls '95
- Living Out Loud '98
- Losing Chase '96
- A Lost Year '93
- Love and Other Catastrophes '95
- Lover Girl '97
- Luminarias '99
- Mad Money '08
- The Magdalene Sisters '02 ►
- Mamma Mia! '08
- Manny & Lo '96 ►
- Margarita Happy Hour '01
- Me & Will '99
- Me Without You '01
- Miss Congeniality 2: Armed and Fabulous '05
- Miss Pettigrew Lives for a Day '08 ►
- Mists of Avalon '01 ►
- Mona Lisa Smile '03
- Moonlight and Valentino '95
- Morvern Callar '02
- My Very Best Friend '96
- Nevada '97
- 9 to 5 '80
- Nora's Hair Salon '04
- Notes on a Scandal '06 ►
- Now and Then '95
- One True Thing '98 ►
- Our Song '01 ►
- Passion Fish '92 ►
- Phat Girlz '06
- The Pink Conspiracy '07
- Prey for Rock and Roll '03 ►
- Private Benjamin '80
- P.S. I Love You '07
- Radiance '98
- Return to Cranford '09
- Rip It Off '02
- The Road to Galveston '96 ►
- Romy and Michele's High School Reunion '97
- The Runaways '10
- Secret Society '00
- Set It Off '96
- Seven Days of Grace '06
- Sex and the City 2 '10
- Sex and the City: The Movie '08
- Sisterhood of the Traveling Pants '05
- The Sisterhood of the Traveling Pants 2 '08
- The Smokers '00
- Some Mother's Son '96 ►
- Some Prefer Cake '97
- Spring Breakdown '08
- Stand-Ins '97
- The Starter Wife '07
- Steel Magnolias '89 ►
- Stepmom '98 ►
- Sugar & Spice '01 ►
- The Sweetest Thing '02
- Talk '94
- Tea with Mussolini '99
- Terranova '91
- Thelma & Louise '91 ►
- These Girls '05
- These Old Broads '01
- Things You Can Tell Just by Looking at Her '00
- Thirteen '03 ►
- This Matter of Marriage '98
- Two Can Play That Game '01
- Two Friends '86
- Under the Tuscan Sun '03
- Unhook the Stars '96
- Up Against the Eight Ball '04
- Uptown Girls '03
- Vulture's Eye '04
- Waiting to Exhale '95 ►
- Waitress '07 ►
- Walking and Talking '96
- Water '05
- Wedding Bell Blues '96
- The Well '97
- Where the Heart Is '00
- Whip It '09 ►
- Widows '02
- Wild Child '08
- Wildflowers '99
- Wisegirls '02
- A Woman's Guide to Adultery '93
- Women '97
- The Women '08
- Women in Trouble '09
- Zoe '01

Female Spies

see also Spy Kids; World War I Spies; World War II Spies

- The Abductors '72
- Call Me Bwana '63
- Call Out the Marines '42
- Caprice '67
- C.I.A.: Code Name Alexa '92
- Court Jester '56 ►
- D.E.B.S. '04
- Harriet the Spy '96
- Head in the Clouds '04
- Inglourious Basterds '09 ►
- Mata Hari '32 ►
- Mr. & Mrs. Smith '05 ►
- Monte Carlo '86
- My Favorite Blonde '42 ►
- Notorious '46 ►
- Operator 13 '34
- Salt '10
- Secret of Stamboul '36
- Shining Through '92
- Shiri '99
- Spy Kids '01 ►
- Spy Kids 2: The Island of Lost Dreams '02 ►
- Spy Kids 3-D: Game Over '03
- The World Is Not Enough '99

► = rated three bones or higher

Feminism

see *Women; Wonder Women*

Femme Fatale

see also *Wonder Women*

The Accused '48
Addams Family Values '93
Algiers '38 ▸
All About Eve '50 ▸
The Amy Fisher Story '93
Armored Command '61
Auntie Lee's Meat Pies '92
Austin Powers: International Man of Mystery '97 ▸
Austin Powers 2: The Spy Who Shagged Me '99 ▸
Azumi '03 ▸
Azumi 2 '05
Backstab '90
Basic Instinct '92
Basic Instinct 2 '06
Batman and Robin '97
Beautiful Beast '95
Beautiful Hunter '94
Bedelia '46 ▸
The Beneficiary '97
Beverly Hills Ninja '96
Beverly Hills Vamp '88
The Big Bounce '69
Big Town '87
Bitter Harvest '93
The Black Dahlia '06
Black Magic Woman '91
Black Widow '87 ▸
Blind Woman's Curse '70
Blood of Dracula '57
The Blood Spattered Bride '72
Blown Away '93
The Blue Angel '30 ▸
Blues in the Night '41
Body Heat '81 ▸
Body of Evidence '92
Body Trouble '92
Bound '96
The Bridesmaid '04
Broken Embraces '09 ▸
The Brothers Grimm '05
Brute Force '47 ▸
Buddy Boy '99
Bulletproof Heart '95 ▸
The Cabin in the Cotton '32
Caesar and Cleopatra '46
Carmen: A Hip Hopera '01
Carried Away '95
Casque d'Or '52 ▸
Casualties of Love: The "Long Island Lolita" Story '93
Champagne for Caesar '50 ▸
Clash by Night '52 ▸
Clean Slate '94
Cleopatra '34
Cleopatra '63
Cleopatra '99
Crime of Passion '57
Criss Cross '48 ▸
Cruel Intentions '98
Crush '93
The Crush '93
The Dallas Connection '94
The Damned Don't Cry '50
Dance Hall '41
Dangerous Ground '96
Dangerous Liaisons '88 ▸
Dangerous Liaisons '03
Daughter of the Tong '39
Dead Reckoning '47 ▸
Deadly Past '95
Death in Deep Water '74
Deception '08
Deceptions '90
Decoy '46
Detour '46 ▸
Detour '92
The Devil's Daughter '91
Diamond Run '00
Disclosure '94
Dishonored Lady '47
Dr. Caligari '89
Dr. Jekyll and Sister Hyde '71
Double Indemnity '44 ▸
Double Jeopardy '92
Dream Lover '93
Drowning by Numbers '87 ▸
Emmanuelle, the Queen '79
Eve of Destruction '90
Eye of the Beholder '99
The Fall '98
Fallen Angel '99
Fangs of the Living Dead '68
Far from the Madding Crowd '67 ▸
Faster, Pussycat! Kill! Kill! '65
Federal Agents vs. Underworld, Inc. '49
Femme Fatale '02
Final Analysis '92
First Name: Carmen '83 ▸
Flame of the Islands '55
The Flesh and the Devil '27 ▸
A Fool There Was '14
A Foreign Affair '48 ▸
Frankenhooker '90
The Gingerbread Man '97
The Girl from Tobacco Row '66
Girl Hunters '63
Girl in His Pocket '57
A Girl to Kill For '90
Girlfriend from Hell '89
Great Flamarion '45
Grievous Bodily Harm '89
The Grifters '90 ▸
The Hard Word '02
Heat Wave '54
Hedda '75
Hellgate '89
Hit Me '96
Hoopla '33
Hostel '06
Human Desire '54
I Spit on Your Corpse '74
I Want You '98
Illusions '91
Impact '49 ▸
Impulse '55
Inner Sanctum '91
International Lady '41
Intersection '93
Into the Fire '88
Invasion of the Bee Girls '73 ▸
The Iron Mistress '52
Irresistible Impulse '95
Jay and Silent Bob Strike Back '01
The Jayne Mansfield Story '80
Jezebel '38 ▸
Kill Bill Vol. 1 '03 ▸
Kill Bill Vol. 2 '04 ▸
Kill Cruise '90
The Killers '46 ▸
L'Addition '85
Lady and the Tramp '55 ▸
Lady for a Night '42
Lady Frankenstein '72
The Lady from Shanghai '48 ▸
Lady Snowblood '73 ▸
The Lair of the White Worm '88 ▸
The Last Seduction '94 ▸
The Last Seduction 2 '98
Le Samourai '67 ▸
Leave Her to Heaven '45 ▸
The Legend of the Wolf Woman '77
Lemora, Lady Dracula '73
The Leopard Woman '20
Les Vampires '15 ▸
Lethal Lolita—Amy Fisher: My Story '92
Lethal Seduction '97
The Lifetaker '89
Lights in the Dusk '06
Like a Fish Out of Water '99
Linda '93
The Little Death '95
The Little Foxes '41 ▸
Lonely Hearts '06
Love Is a Gun '94
Love Walked In '97
Mado '76 ▸
The Malibu Beach Vampires '91
Malice '93
Malicious '95
The Maltese Falcon '41 ▸
Mantis in Lace '68
Married to the Mob '88 ▸
Massacre '56
Mata Hari '32 ▸
Mata Hari '85
Medusa Against the Son of Hercules '62
Mesa of Lost Women '52
Mirage '94
Ms. 45 '81 ▸
A Model Employee '02
Mountaintop Motel Massacre '86
Mutual Needs '97
Nana '55 ▸
Nana '82
The Natural '84 ▸
Net Games '03
Night Angel '90
The Night Evelyn Came Out of the Grave '71
Night of the Cobra Woman '72
Night Tide '63
The Ninth Gate '99
No Good Deed '02
No Way Out '87 ▸
Novocaine '01
An Occasional Hell '96
Of Human Bondage '34 ▸
Of Human Bondage '64
On Her Majesty's Secret Service '69 ▸
One Night at McCool's '01
The Opposite of Sex '98
Out Cold '89
Out of the Past '47 ▸
Palmetto '98
The Pamela Principle '91
Party Girls '29
Pepe Le Moko '37 ▸
Perfect Alibi '94
Planet of Blood '66
Play Murder for Me '91
Playing God '96
Point of No Return '93
Poison Ivy '92
Poison Ivy 2: Lily '95
Poison Ivy 4: The Secret Society '08
Possession: Until Death Do You Part '90
The Postman Always Rings Twice '46 ▸
Praying Mantis '93
Pretty Poison '68 ▸
Prey of the Chameleon '91
Pushover '54
Queen Bee '55
The Quick and the Dead '95
The Rage: Carrie 2 '99
A Rage in Harlem '91 ▸
Ran '85 ▸
Range Renegades '48
Reckless '35
Ring of Steel '94
Roadhouse Girl '53
Salome '53
Salome '85
Samson and Delilah '50 ▸
Samson and Delilah '84
Samson and Delilah '96
Sand Trap '97
Satanik '69
Scandal '89 ▸
Scarlet Street '45 ▸
Schemes '95
Scorned '93
Sea of Love '89 ▸
Second Skin '00
Secret Weapons '85
The Secretary '94
Serpent's Lair '95
Seven Sinners '40 ▸
Sex and Death 101 '07
Sexpot '88
Shadows in the Storm '88
The Showgirl Murders '95
Sins of Jezebel '54
Sleep of Death '79
Sleepy Eyes of Death: The Chinese Jade '63
Snow White and the Seven Dwarfs '37 ▸
Some Came Running '58 ▸
Something Wild '86
The Specialist '75
Species '95
The Spirit '08
Stormy Nights '97
The Strange Woman '46
Sunrise '27 ▸
Sunset Boulevard '50 ▸
Suspicious Minds '96
The Temp '93
The Temptress '26
The Temptress '49
A Thin Line Between Love and Hate '96
Third Degree Burn '89
The Tiger Woman '45
Tomb '86
Tomie '99
Too Late for Tears '49 ▸
Torso '01
Trading Favors '97
Truth or Dare '91
U-Turn '97
Under Suspicion '92
The Untamable '23
Valmont '89 ▸
Vanity Fair '32
The Velvet Vampire '71
Venus Against the Son of Hercules '62
Venus in Furs '70
Victim of Desire '94
The Wasp Woman '59
Weird Woman '44
When Will I Be Loved '04
White Cargo '42
Who Framed Roger Rabbit '88 ▸
Wicked Ways '99
Widow's Kiss '94
Winter of Frozen Dreams '08
Witchcraft 3: The Kiss of Death '90
Woman of Desire '93
Wrongfully Accused '98
XXX: State of the Union '05

Fencing

see also *Swashbucklers*

By the Sword '93
Court Jester '56 ▸
Dangerous Beauty '98 ▸
The Fencing Master '92
The Last Musketeer '00
Ring of Steel '94
Rob Roy '95 ▸
Sunshine '99

Fifties

see *Period Piece: 1950s*

Film History

America at the Movies '76
Burden of Dreams '82 ▸
The Cat's Meow '01
The Celluloid Closet '95 ▸
A Decade Under the Influence '02 ▸
Forgotten Silver '96 ▸
Heavy Petting '89
Intervista '87 ▸
The Kid Stays in the Picture '02 ▸
A Kiss for Mary Pickford '27
The Little Theatre of Jean Renoir '71 ▸
Lost Squadron '32
The Love Goddesses '65 ▸
Many Faces of Sherlock Holmes '86
Roman Polanski: Wanted and Desired '08
Scenario du Film Passion '82 ▸
Sex and Buttered Popcorn '91
Shadow Magic '00
A Star Is Born '54 ▸
That's Dancing! '85 ▸
That's Entertainment '74 ▸
That's Entertainment, Part 2 '76
That's Entertainment, Part 3 '93
This Film Is Not Yet Rated '06
Trumbo '07 ▸
Visions of Light: The Art of Cinematography '93 ▸

Film Noir

see also *Contemporary Noir*

The Accused '48
Act of Violence '48
Al Capone '59 ▸
Amateur '94 ▸
Angel Face '52 ▸
The Asphalt Jungle '50 ▸
Beware, My Lovely '52
Beyond a Reasonable Doubt '56
The Big Clock '48 ▸
Big Combo '55 ▸
The Big Heat '53 ▸
The Big Sleep '46 ▸
Black Angel '46 ▸
Black Lizard '68
Black Widow '54
Blast of Silence '61
The Blue Dahlia '46 ▸
The Blue Gardenia '53 ▸
A Blueprint for Murder '53
Bob le Flambeur '55 ▸
Boomerang '47 ▸
Born to Kill '47 ▸
The Bribe '48
Brute Force '47 ▸
Caged '50 ▸
Calcutta '47
Cornered '45 ▸
Crack-Up '46
Crime Wave '54
Criss Cross '48 ▸
Crossfire '47 ▸
Dangerous Crossing '53
Dark Corner '46 ▸
Dark Mirror '46 ▸
Dark Passage '47
Dark Streets '08
David Harding, Counterspy '50
Dead Again '91 ▸
Dead Silence '90
Deadline at Dawn '46
Decoy '46
Delusion '91
Desperate '47
Detour '46 ▸
The Devil Thumbs a Ride '47 ▸
D.O.A. '49 ▸
Don't Bother to Knock '52
Double Indemnity '44 ▸
The Element of Crime '84
End of the Road '44
The Enforcer '51
Fallen Angels 1 '93 ▸
Fallen Angels 2 '93 ▸
Farewell, My Lovely '75 ▸
Fear in the Night '47 ▸
Force of Evil '49 ▸
Frantic '58 ▸
Gilda '46 ▸
The Glass Key '42 ▸
Gotham '88 ▸
Grand Central Murder '42
Gun Crazy '49 ▸
He Walked by Night '48 ▸
High & Low '62 ▸
High Sierra '41 ▸
The Hitch-Hiker '53 ▸
House of Bamboo '55
Human Desire '54
I Wouldn't Be in Your Shoes '48
In a Lonely Place '50 ▸
Jigsaw '49 ▸
Johnny Angel '45 ▸
Key Largo '48 ▸
The Killer That Stalked New York '47
The Killers '46 ▸
Killer's Kiss '55
The Killing '56 ▸
King Creole '58
Kiss Me Deadly '55 ▸
Kiss of Death '47 ▸
The Lady from Shanghai '48 ▸
Lady in the Death House '44
Lady in the Lake '46
The Las Vegas Story '52
Laura '44 ▸
Le Doulos '61 ▸
Leave Her to Heaven '45 ▸
The Long Night '47
Loophole '54
Macao '52 ▸
The Maltese Falcon '41 ▸
Man in the Vault '56
The Mask of Dimitrios '44 ▸
Mikey & Nicky '76
Mildred Pierce '45 ▸
Ministry of Fear '44 ▸
Mr. District Attorney '41
Murder, My Sweet '44 ▸
Mystery Street '50
The Naked City '48 ▸
Naked Kiss '64
The Narrow Margin '52 ▸
Niagara '52
Night and the City '50 ▸
Nightfall '56 ▸
Nightmare Alley '47
Nocturne '46
Nora Prentiss '47
Obsession '49
Odds Against Tomorrow '59 ▸
On Dangerous Ground '51 ▸
Our Man in Havana '59 ▸
Out of the Past '47 ▸
Panic in the Streets '50 ▸
Phantom Lady '44 ▸
Pickup on South Street '53 ▸
Pitfall '48 ▸
Plunder Road '57
Portland Expose '57
Portrait of an Assassin '49
The Postman Always Rings Twice '46 ▸
The Postman Always Rings Twice '81
Prowler '51
Railroaded '47
Raw Deal '48 ▸
The Red House '47 ▸
Rendez-vous '85 ▸
Road House '48
Rope '48 ▸
Scandal Sheet '52
The Scar '48
Scarlet Street '45 ▸
The Set-Up '49 ▸
Shockproof '49
Shoot to Kill '47
Side Street '50
Signal 7 '83
Slow Moves '84
Somewhere in the Night '46
Sorry, Wrong Number '48 ▸
Station '81
Story of a Love Affair '50
Strange Illusion '45
Strange Impersonation '46
The Strange Love of Martha Ivers '46 ▸
The Strange Mrs. Crane '48
Sudden Fear '52 ▸
Sunset Boulevard '50 ▸
Sweet Smell of Success '57 ▸
T-Men '47 ▸
Tchao Pantin '84 ▸
Tension '50
They Live by Night '49 ▸
The Third Man '49 ▸
This Gun for Hire '42 ▸
3-Way '04
Too Late for Tears '49 ▸
Touch of Evil '58 ▸
Undercurrent '46
The Unsuspected '47
Violence '47
Vortex '81
Where Danger Lives '50
Where the Sidewalk Ends '50
While the City Sleeps '56 ▸
Whirlpool '49
White Heat '49 ▸
The Window '49 ▸
A Woman's Secret '49
The Wrong Man '56 ▸

Filmmaking

see also *At the Movies; Behind the Scenes*

Abbott and Costello Meet the Keystone Kops '54
The Adjuster '91
An Alan Smithee Film: Burn, Hollywood, Burn '97
Alexandria Again and Forever '90
All the Wrong Places '00
An Almost Perfect Affair '79
An American Carol '08
American Movie '99 ▸
...And God Spoke '94
And Starring Pancho Villa as Himself '03 ▸
Ararat '02 ▸
Art House '98
Baadasssss! '03 ▸
Barton Fink '91 ▸

Be Kind Rewind *'08*
Beyond the Clouds *'95*
Big Show *'37*
Black Cat *'90*
The Blair Witch Project *'99*
Bloodbath in Psycho Town *'89*
Body Chemistry 3: Point of Seduction *'93*
Bombay Talkie *'70*
Bowfinger *'99* ▶
Cannes Man *'96*
Cass *'78*
Children Shouldn't Play with Dead Things *'72*
Ciao Federico! Fellini Directs Satyricon *'69*
Comment Ca Va? *'76*
Contempt *'64* ▶
The Cool Surface *'92*
CQ *'01*
Dangerous Game *'93*
Danny Roane: First Time Director *'06*
David Holzman's Diary *'67* ▶
The Dead Hate the Living *'99*
Dead Silence *'90*
A Decade Under the Influence *'02* ▶
Deep in the Heart (of Texas) *'98*
Don Quixote *'92*
Drifting *'82*
Dubeat-E-O *'84*
Ed Wood *'94* ▶
84 Charlie MoPic *'89* ▶
Elsa, Elsa *'85*
Elvis in Hollywood *'93* ▶
F/X 2: The Deadly Art of Illusion *'91*
Fellini: I'm a Born Liar *'03*
Festival at Cannes *'02*
Film Geek *'06*
Final Cut *'88*
Flickers *'80*
Full Tilt Boogie *'97*
Get Shorty *'95* ▶
Good Morning, Babylon *'87* ▶
Gosford Park *'01* ▶
Hearts of Darkness: A Filmmaker's Apocalypse *'91* ▶
Hi, Mom! *'70* ▶
Hit and Runway *'01*
Hollywood Chaos *'89*
Hollywood Mystery *'34*
Hotel *'01*
The House of Seven Corpses *'73*
How to Eat Your Watermelon in White Company (and Enjoy It) *'05* ▶
How to Make a Monster *'58*
I Want Candy *'07*
Identification of a Woman *'82*
I'll Do Anything *'93*
In a Moment of Passion *'93*
Intervista *'87* ▶
Invasion Force *'90*
Iron Cowboy *'68*
Island of Blood *'82*
It's All True *'93*
Jacquot *'91*
Kamikaze Hearts *'91*
The Kid Stays in the Picture *'02* ▶
The King of the Kickboxers *'91*
Kisses in the Dark *'97*
La Petite Lili *'03*
The Last Broadcast *'98* ▶
The Last Porno Flick *'74*
Les Violons du Bal *'74*
The Life of Lucky Cucumber *'08*
Living in Oblivion *'94* ▶
Loaded *'94*
Lost in La Mancha *'03* ▶
A Man Like Eva *'83* ▶
The Mirror Crack'd *'80*
Mistress *'91*
The Moon & the Stars *'07*
Movies Money Murder *'96*
Mute Witness *'95*
My Dream Is Yours *'49*
My Life's in Turnaround *'94*
Nightmare in Blood *'75*
Nightmare in Wax *'69*
Nudity Required *'90*
Of Time and the City *'08*
On an Island with You *'48*
Once in Paris... *'79*
One Hundred and One Nights *'95*
Overnight *'03* ▶
Passion *'82*
The Pickle *'93*
Pictures *'81*
Pipe Dream *'02*
The Player *'92* ▶
The Pornographer *'00*
The Red Raven Kiss-Off *'90*
RKO 281 *'99* ▶
Secret File of Hollywood *'62*
Seed of Chucky *'04*
Sex is Comedy *'02*
She Must Be Seeing Things *'87*
Shoot or Be Shot *'02*
Silent Motive *'91*
Skin Deep *'94*
A Slave of Love *'78* ▶
Slaves of Hollywood *'99*
Souls for Sale *'23*
Special Effects *'85*
Spenser: A Savage Place *'94*
Stand-In *'85*
Storytelling *'01* ▶
The Stunt Man *'80* ▶
Sullivan's Travels *'41* ▶
The Swap *'71*
Sweet Liberty *'86*
Swimming with Sharks *'94* ▶
Talking Head *'92*
The Tango Lesson *'97*
Tristram Shandy: A Cock and Bull Story *'05*
Two Weeks in Another Town *'62*
Ulysses' Gaze *'95*
Understudy: The Graveyard Shift 2 *'88*
Venice, Venice *'92*
Visions of Light: The Art of Cinematography *'93* ▶
Voyage to the Beginning of the World *'96* ▶
Wes Craven's New Nightmare *'94* ▶
Where's Marlowe? *'98*
White Hunter, Black Heart *'90* ▶
The Wizard of Speed and Time *'88*
You Know My Name *'99* ▶
You Must Remember This *'92*

Firemen

***see also** Fires*

Ablaze *'00*
The Accidental Husband *'08*
Always *'89*
Backdraft *'91*
Backfire! *'94*
Blast *'04*
Club Paradise *'86*
Collateral Damage *'02*
Evolution *'01*
Fahrenheit 451 *'66* ▶
15 Minutes *'01*
Fire Alarm *'32*
Fire Serpent *'07*
Fireballs *'90*
Firefight *'03*
Firehouse *'72*
Firehouse *'87*
Firehouse Dog *'07*
The Fireman *'16*
The Firemen's Ball *'68* ▶
Fireproof *'08*
Firestorm *'97*
Frequency *'00*
The Guys *'02* ▶
Hellfighters *'68*
I Heart Huckabees *'04*
I Now Pronounce You Chuck and Larry *'07*
Inferno in Paradise *'88*
Just One Time *'00*
Ladder 49 *'04*
Miss March *'09*
Point of Origin *'02*
Reign of Fire *'02*
Roxanne *'87* ▶
Smoke Jumpers *'08*
Suicide Squad *'35*
Trespass *'92*
Turk 182! *'85*
World Trade Center *'06* ▶

Fires

***see also** Boom!; Disaster Flicks; Firemen*

Ablaze *'00*
Always *'89*
Backdraft *'91*
Blue Smoke *'07*
The Burning Bed *'85* ▶
The Burning Plain *'08*
Burning Rage *'84*
Carrie *'76* ▶
City on Fire *'78*
The Claim *'00*
The Cremators *'72*
Dinosaurus! *'60*
Don't Go in the House *'80*
Endless Love *'81*
Erendira *'83*
Fire *'77*
Fire Alarm *'32*
Fire Serpent *'07*
Firefight *'03*
Firehead *'90*
The Fireman *'16*
Firestarter *'84*
Firestarter 2: Rekindled *'02*
Firestorm *'97*
Firestorm: 72 Hours in Oakland *'93*
Firetrap *'01*
The Flaming Urge *'53*
Flashfire *'94*
Frankenstein *'31* ▶
Ghost Rider *'07*
Hellboy II: The Golden Army *'08* ▶
In Old Chicago *'37* ▶
Inferno *'01*
Interview with the Vampire *'94*
Island of the Burning Doomed *'67*
Ladder 49 *'04*
The Lion King *'94* ▶
Little Men *'98*
Look Who's Talking, Too *'90*
Meet the Parents *'00* ▶
The Michigan Kid *'28*
Mighty Joe Young *'49*
Nice Girls Don't Explode *'87*
Night Alarm *'34*
Oil *'78*
The Outsiders *'83*
Point of Origin *'02*
Pretty Poison *'68* ▶
Pyrates *'91*
A Pyromaniac's Love Story *'95*
Quest for Fire *'82* ▶
Rosewood *'96* ▶
Save the Tiger *'73* ▶
Smoke Jumpers *'08*
Sounds of Silence *'91*
Specimen *'97*
Speeding Up Time *'71*
Spontaneous Combustion *'89*
Suicide Squad *'35*
SuperFire *'02*
Terror on the 40th Floor *'74*
Ticks *'93*
The Towering Inferno *'74*
The Triangle Factory Fire Scandal *'79*
12 and Holding *'05* ▶
Twin Town *'97*
Volcano *'97*
Wilder Napalm *'93*
The Witness *'99*

The First Time

***see also** Sex & Sexuality; Teen Angst*

American Pie *'99* ▶
Bart Got a Room *'08*
Biloxi Blues *'88*
The Crime of Father Amaro *'02* ▶
December Boys *'07*
Dreaming About You *'92*
Driving Lessons *'06*
Earth & Water *'99*
An Education *'09* ▶
Fast Times at Ridgemont High *'82* ▶
Food of Love *'02*
Getting It *'06*
Ginger and Cinnamon *'03*
Juno *'07* ▶
The Last Request *'06*
Little Darlings *'80*
Losin' It *'82*
Lymelife *'08*
Marie Antoinette *'06*
Miss March *'09*
My Tutor *'82*
National Lampoon's Adam & Eve *'05*
Nico and Dani *'00*
Porky's *'82*
Pretty Baby *'78* ▶
The Reader *'08*
Risky Business *'83* ▶
The Rules of Attraction *'02*
Running with Scissors *'06*
Sade *'00*
Sex Drive *'08*
Skipped Parts *'00*
Tadpole *'02*
Teeth *'07*
The Ten *'07*
The Wackness *'08*

Flashback

Adam Resurrected *'08*
Adoration *'08*
All In *'06*
All Over the Guy *'01*
All the King's Men *'06*
Alpha Male *'06*
Amazing Grace *'06* ▶
America *'09*
American Beauty *'99* ▶
Amores Perros *'00* ▶
Anne Rice's The Feast of All Saints *'01*
Antonia's Line *'95*
Antwone Fisher *'02* ▶
Ararat *'02* ▶
Autumn Hearts: A New Beginning *'07*
Back of Beyond *'95*
The Bamboo Blonde *'46*
Bandits *'01*
Batman Forever *'95* ▶
Beau Geste *'39* ▶
Beau Travail *'98*
Behind Enemy Lines 2: Axis of Evil *'06*
Behind the Red Door *'02*
Being at Home with Claude *'92*
Bella *'06*
Belles on Their Toes *'52*
Beloved *'98*
Best Laid Plans *'99*
Betrayal *'83*
Beyond Borders *'03*
Big Fish *'03* ▶
Black Book *'06* ▶
Black Christmas *'06*
Blackout *'07*
Blind Faith *'98*
Blood Brothers *'07*
Blood Creek *'09*
Blue Valentine *'10*
Bonanno: A Godfather's Story *'99*
Boondock Saints *'99*
Born Killers *'05*
Boss of Bosses *'99*
Boy A *'07*
Boys *'95*
Brand Upon the Brain! *'06* ▶
Breaking Up *'97*
The Broken *'08*
Broken Embraces *'09* ▶
Broken Harvest *'94*
Brothers Three *'07*
Brush with Fate *'03*
The Brutal Truth *'99*
The Business of Fancydancing *'02*
The Caller *'08*
The Camomile Lawn *'92*
Can't Hardly Wait *'98*
Carmen *'03*
Carrie *'02*
Carried Away *'95*
Casablanca *'42* ▶
Casanova *'05* ▶
Catch Me If You Can *'02*
Catfish in Black Bean Sauce *'00*
Cello *'05*
Cement *'99*
Chaos Theory *'08*
Character *'97*
Charming Billy *'98*
The Chorus *'04*
Citizen Kane *'41* ▶
Closing the Ring *'07*
Coco Chanel *'08*
Come Undone *'00*
Company Man *'00*
The Confessional *'95* ▶
The Constant Gardener *'05* ▶
Courage Under Fire *'96* ▶
Cover *'08*
Creation *'09*
Criminal Lovers *'99*
The Crowded Sky *'60*
Dad Savage *'97*
Danny Roane: First Time Director *'06*
Dark Blue World *'01*
Deceit *'06*
December Boys *'07*
Decoy *'46*
Deeply *'99*
Definitely, Maybe *'08* ▶
The Devil Is a Woman *'35* ▶
Diary of a Suicide *'73*
The Disappearance of Garcia Lorca *'96*
Divine Secrets of the Ya-Ya Sisterhood *'02*
The Diving Bell and the Butterfly *'07* ▶
A Dog Named Christmas *'09*
Dogfight *'91* ▶
Dolores Claiborne *'94* ▶
Don Juan (Or If Don Juan Were a Woman) *'73*
Don't Tell *'05*
Drowning Mona *'00*
Dust *'01*
Eddie and the Cruisers *'83*
Edward Scissorhands *'90* ▶
Eighteen *'04*
El Cantante *'06*
Emile *'03*
The Emperor's Club *'02*
The Escape *'95*
Eternity and a Day *'97*
Evening *'07*
Event Horizon *'97*
Eve's Bayou *'97* ▶
Exotica *'94* ▶
Extraordinary Rendition *'07*
Eye of God *'97* ▶
Facing Windows *'03*
Faithless *'00* ▶
Fallen Angel *'03*
A Family Thing *'96* ▶
Far North *'07*
Far Side of the Moon *'03*
Fear and Loathing in Las Vegas *'98*
Fever Pitch *'96*
Fight Club *'99* ▶
Final *'01*
Finding Home *'03*
Flags of Our Fathers *'06* ▶
Flashbacks of a Fool *'08*
The Forbidden Quest *'93*
The Forgotten *'04*
The 4th Dimension *'06*
Frailty *'02* ▶
Frankie Starlight *'95*
Front of the Class *'08*
Frozen *'98*
Fur: An Imaginary Portrait of Diane Arbus *'06*
Gangster No. 1 *'00*
Genealogies of a Crime *'97*
The General *'98* ▶
The General's Daughter *'99*
Ghosted *'09*
G.I. Joe: The Rise of Cobra *'09*
Gifted Hands: The Ben Carson Story *'09*
Gloomy Sunday *'02* ▶
God is My Co-Pilot *'45*
The Godfather, Part 2 *'74* ▶
Godmoney *'97*
Gods and Monsters *'98* ▶
God's Sandbox *'02*
Good *'08*
The Good Guy *'10*
The Good Shepherd *'06*
A Good Year *'06*
Graduation *'07*
The Great Water *'04*
Grey Owl *'99*
Grizzly Falls *'99*
Guantanamero *'07*
A Guide to Recognizing Your Saints *'06*
Halloween II *'09*
The Hanging Garden *'97*
Haywire *'80*
Headspace *'02*
Heart *'99*
The Heart of Me *'02*
Hearts in Atlantis *'01*
Hedwig and the Angry Inch *'00* ▶
Helas pour Moi *'94*
Hellraiser 4: Bloodline *'95*
Henry Poole Is Here *'08* ▶
Hero *'03* ▶
Hero Wanted *'08*
The Hi-Lo Country *'98*
Hidden *'05* ▶
High Fidelity *'00* ▶
Highlander: Endgame *'00*
Hiroshima, Mon Amour *'59* ▶
Hitman *'07*
H.M. Pulham Esquire *'41*
The Hole *'01*
Holes *'03* ▶
Hollywoodland *'06*
A Home at the End of the World *'04*
Horatio Hornblower: The Adventure Continues *'01* ▶
Houdini *'99*
A House Divided *'00*
How I Killed My Father *'03* ▶
The Human Stain *'03*
The Hunted *'03*
I Served the King of England *'07* ▶
I Shot a Man in Vegas *'96*
In His Life: The John Lennon Story *'00*
In Praise of Love *'01*
Inferno *'99*
Instinct *'99*
Into the Wild *'07* ▶
Invitation *'51*
Jackie's Back *'99*
Jacob's Ladder *'90*
Jadup and Boel *'81*
Jerry and Tom *'98*
Jet Li's Fearless *'06*
John John in the Sky *'00*
Johnny Dangerously *'84*
Julie & Julia *'09* ▶
Jungle Woman *'44*
Just Another Love Story *'08*
Just Married *'03*
Karla *'06*
Keillers Park *'05*
Kicking and Screaming *'95* ▶
Ladder 49 *'04*
Lansky *'99*
The Last Letter *'04*
Last Orders *'01* ▶
The Last Templar *'09*
The Lawless Breed *'52* ▶
Leave Her to Heaven *'45* ▶
The Legend of Bagger Vance *'00*
The Legend of 1900 *'98*
Les Voleurs *'96* ▶
The Lesser Evil *'97*
Liebestraum *'91*
Life *'99*
The Life Before Her Eyes *'07*
The Life Before This *'99*
The Life of David Gale *'03*
Life Tastes Good *'99*
Lime Salted Love *'06*
Lone Star *'95* ▶
The Long Night *'47*
Looking for Eric *'09*
The Loss of Sexual Innocence *'98*
Love Come Down *'00*
Love Letters *'99* ▶
Lumumba *'01* ▶
Mad Love *'01*
A Man to Remember *'39*
Marilyn Hotchkiss' Ballroom Dancing & Charm School *'06*

▶ = *rated three bones or higher*

Flatulence

Flight

see *Airborne*

Flood

see also *Disaster Flicks*

Florence

see also *Italy*

Florida

see also *American South; Miami*

Flying Saucers

see *Alien Babes; Alien Beings—Benign; Alien Beings—Vicious; Alien Cops; Aliens Are People, Too; Out of This World Sex; Space Operas*

Folklore & Legends

see also *Storytelling*

Food

see *Edibles*

Football

▸ = rated three bones or higher

Monday Night Mayhem '02
Navy Blue and Gold '37
Necessary Roughness '91
North Dallas Forty '79 ▶
The O.J. Simpson Story '94
One Night Only '84
Paper Lion '68
Pigskin Parade '36
Players '03
Possums '99
The Program '93
Quarterback Princess '85
Radio '03
Remember the Titans '00 ▶
The Replacements '00
Roberta '35 ▶
Romeo Must Die '00
Rudy '93
Rustin '01
A Saintly Switch '99
School Ties '92 ▶
Semi-Tough '77
The Slaughter Rule '01
The Spirit of West Point '47
They Call Me Sirr '00
Trouble along the Way '53
Two Minute Warning '76
Varsity Blues '98
The Waterboy '98
We Are Marshall '06
West Point '27
Wildcats '86
Windrunner '94

Foreign Cops

***see also** Foreign Intrigue; Interpol; Police Detectives*

The Bourne Supremacy '04 ▶
Carry On Constable '60
Collision Course '89
Cop Au Vin '85
Coup de Torchon '81 ▶
Cradle 2 the Grave '03
Dudley Do-Right '99
Framed '93 ▶
Hard-Boiled '92
Hot Fuzz '07 ▶
Infernal Affairs '02 ▶
Inspector Clouseau '68
Jet Li's The Enforcer '95
The Killer '90 ▶
The King of the Kickboxers '91
La Balance '82 ▶
La Scorta '94 ▶
Le Deuxieme Souffle '66
Mad Dog Killer '77
The Medallion '03
The Pink Panther '64 ▶
The Pink Panther '06
Police Story '85
Prime Suspect '92 ▶
Red Heat '88
The Return of Dr. Mabuse '61
Return of the Pink Panther '74
Revenge of the Pink Panther '78
Rush Hour '98
Rush Hour 2 '01
Rush Hour 3 '07
A Shot in the Dark '64 ▶
The Siege of Sidney Street '60
Slumdog Millionaire '08 ▶
Touch of Evil '58 ▶
Traffic '00 ▶
Transporter 3 '08
Transsiberian '08 ▶

Foreign Intrigue

***see also** Spies & Espionage*

Above Suspicion '43 ▶
Ambassador Bill '31
American Roulette '88
Anne of Green Gables: The Continuing Story '99
Austin Powers: International Man of Mystery '97 ▶
Battle Beneath the Earth '68
Bulldog Drummond at Bay '37
Call Him Mr. Shatter '74
Catch Me a Spy '71
Chinese Boxes '84
Chinese Web '78
Cover-Up '91
Crimson Tide '95 ▶
The Day of the Jackal '73 ▶
Deadly Alliance '78
The Destructors '74
Devil Wears White '86
Diamonds Are Forever '71 ▶
Diplomatic Courier '52 ▶
Dr. No '62 ▶
The Dogs of War '81
Don't Drink the Water '69
The Eiger Sanction '75
An Englishman Abroad '83 ▶
Enigma '82
Erik '90
Escapade in Florence '62
Escape from the KGB '87
Escape to Love '82
Escape to the Sun '72
The Executioner '70
The Experts '89
Exposed '83
Exposure '91
Federal Agent '36
Foreign Correspondent '40 ▶
The Fourth Protocol '87 ▶
Frederick Forsyth's Icon '05
The Glimmer Man '96
A Global Affair '63
Gunpowder '87
Half Moon Street '86
Hamlet '96 ▶
The Human Factor '75
The Hunt for Red October '90 ▶
In the Company of Spies '99
The Interpreter '05 ▶
Jaguar Lives '79
Jumpin' Jack Flash '86
The Key to Rebecca '85
La Passante '83 ▶
Lady L '65
License to Kill '89 ▶
The Little Drummer Girl '84 ▶
The Magnificent Two '67
Man from Headquarters '28
The Man Who Knew Too Little '97
The Man Who Knew Too Much '34 ▶
The Man Who Knew Too Much '56
Marathon Man '76 ▶
The Mask of Dimitrios '44 ▶
Natural Causes '94
The Odessa File '74
Overthrow '82
Panama Hattie '42
Postmark for Danger '56
Puzzle '78
Reilly: Ace of Spies '87 ▶
Return of the Man from U.N.C.L.E. '83
Return of the Tall Blond Man with One Black Shoe '74
Return to Paradise '98 ▶
Rollover '81
The Russia House '90
Saigon: Year of the Cat '87
Sebastian '68
The Secret Agent '96
The Spy Who Came in from the Cold '65 ▶
Strangers '91
Sweet Country '87
They Met in Bombay '41
The Third Man '49 ▶
Tokyo Joe '49
Too Bad She's Bad '54
Topaz '69 ▶
Torn Curtain '66
Undeclared War '91
The White Countess '05 ▶
The Wind and the Lion '75 ▶
Windmills of the Gods '88

Foreign Legion

***see** Desert War/Foreign Legion*

Frame-Ups

Abbott and Costello Meet the Invisible Man '51 ▶
Agatha Christie's The Pale Horse '96
Animal 2 '07
Another Pair of Aces: Three of a Kind '91 ▶
The Art of War '00
The Art of War 3: Retribution '08
Backfire '22
The Badlanders '58
Bedroom Eyes '86
Below the Deadline '29
Best Revenge '83
Beyond a Reasonable Doubt '09
The Big Clock '48 ▶
Big Score '83
The Big Sweat '90
The Big Switch '70
Bitter Vengeance '94
The Black Sleep '56
Blackout '54
Blade: Trinity '04
Blind Man's Bluff '91
The Blum Affair '48
Bombay Mail '34
The Bourne Supremacy '04 ▶
Breakdown '53
Buried Alive '39
Caged Fear '92
Candyman 3: Day of the Dead '98
Capital Punishment '96
Caught in the Act '93
Chain Reaction '96
A Challenge for Robin Hood '68
City Hall '95 ▶
Class of Fear '91
The Clay Pigeon '49
Consenting Adults '92
Cop-Out '91
Covered Wagon Days '40
Crime and Punishment in Suburbia '00
Cry Vengeance '54
Dancing Man '33
Dark Corner '46 ▶
Deadline at Dawn '46
Death Race '08
Death Sentence '74
Demons from Her Past '07
The Desperadoes '43
Deuce Bigalow: European Gigolo '05
Devil Doll '36 ▶
The Disappearance of Christina '93
Double Take '01
Each Dawn I Die '39
Eagle Eye '08
Escape from DS-3 '81
Executive Koala '06 ▶
Exit in Red '97
Extremely Dangerous '99
F/X '86 ▶
A Face to Kill For '99
Family of Cops '95
Fast Getaway 2 '94
The Fighting Rookie '34
Final Payback '99
Fingerprints Don't Lie '51
Fleshtone '94
Forfeit '07
Frame by Frame '95
Framed '75
Framed '93 ▶
Framed for Murder '07
Free to Love '25
The Fugitive '93 ▶
Gang Related '96
The Gay Buckaroo '32
Get Rita '75
The Ghost Camera '33
The Gilded Cage '54
The Girl in the News '41
Girls in Prison '56
The Glimmer Man '96
Hi-Jacked '50
How to Frame a Figg '71
The Inner Circle '46
An Innocent Man '89
Judge Dredd '95
Judicial Consent '94
Kentucky Blue Streak '35
Kill Switch '08
Killing 'Em Softly '85
The Killing Yard '01
Kiss of the Dragon '01
The Lady Confesses '45
Lady in the Death House '44
Left for Dead '78
Legacy of Rage '86
Les Miserables '95
Let's Go to Prison '06
Letters from a Killer '98
The Life & Times of the Chocolate Killer '88
Life Begins at Forty '35
The Life of Emile Zola '37 ▶
Linda '93
A Lizard in a Woman's Skin '71
Louisiana Purchase '41
Lucky Cisco Kid '40
Macon County Line '74
Malevolence '95
Man Outside '88
The Man Who Came Back '08
The Manhunt '86
The Mighty Quinn '89
Mr. Wise Guy '42
Most Wanted '97
Motel Blue '98
Moving Target '96
Moving Target '00
Murder '30 ▶
Murphy's Law '86
My Cousin Vinny '92 ▶
My Fellow Americans '96
Nasty Hero '89
The Net 2.0 '06
Never 2 Big '98
Nightmare in Badham County '76
Nightwatch '96
No Escape, No Return '93
North by Northwest '59 ▶
Now and Forever '82
The Obsessed '51
Off the Wall '82
Oklahoma Frontier '39
Old Mother Riley's New Venture '49
Out of the Past '47 ▶
Out of Time '03
Palmetto '98
Phantom Lady '44 ▶
Plato's Run '96
Powder Burn '96
Presumed Innocent '90 ▶
Prime Suspect '88
Prison Break '38
Prison on Fire '87
Red Corner '97
Return of the Frontiersman '50
The Rich Man's Wife '96
Ricochet '91 ▶
Road House '48
Rubdown '93
Sabotage '96
Saboteur '42 ▶
The Sentinel '06
The Shadow Conspiracy '96
Shakes the Clown '92
Shelter '98
Shooter '07
The Sphinx '33
Stir Crazy '80
Storm Catcher '99
Street Kings '08
Sunset Heat '92
Suspended Alibi '56
The Take '07
Tank '83
TekWar '94
Thick as Thieves '99
Today I Hang '42
Torque '04
Undisputed II: Last Man Standing '06
U.S. Marshals '98
White Fire '53
Wild Things '98
Woman Condemned '33
The Wrong Man '93
The Wrong Woman '95
The Yards '00

France

***see also** Paris*

A la Mode '94
The Accompanist '93
The Adventures of Felix '99
The Advocate '93 ▶
The Affair of the Necklace '01
Alice et Martin '98
The Ambassador's Daughter '56
An American in Paris '51 ▶
An American Werewolf in Paris '97
Anatomy of Hell '04
And Soon the Darkness '70
Angelique '64
Angelique and the King '66
Angelique and the Sultan '68
Angelique: The Road to Versailles '65
Apres-Vous '03
Arch of Triumph '48 ▶
Arch of Triumph '85
Army of Shadows '69 ▶
Ballet Russes '05 ▶
Battle of the Rails '46 ▶
Becoming Colette '92
Bedtime Story '63
Before Sunset '04 ▶
The Better 'Ole '26
Big Fella '37
Black Girl '66 ▶
Bluebeard's Eighth Wife '38
Bon Voyage '03 ▶
Borsalino '70 ▶
Breathless '59 ▶
Brotherhood of the Wolf '01
Buffet Froid '79 ▶
The Butterfly '02 ▶
Can-Can '60
Cannes Man '96
Captain Scarlett '53
Carnage '02
Carnival in Flanders '35 ▶
Carve Her Name with Pride '58
Catch Me If You Can '02
Catherine & Co. '76
Cesar '36 ▶
Charade '63 ▶
Charlotte Gray '01
Chasing Butterflies '94
The Chateau '01
Chocolat '00 ▶
The Chorus '04
Classe Tous Risque '60 ▶
Cloud Waltzing '87
Coco Chanel '08
Coco Chanel & Igor Stravinksy '09
Come Undone '00
The Count of Monte Cristo '02
Criminal Lovers '99
Danton '82 ▶
Days of Glory '06
Desiree '54
Diane '55
Dirty Rotten Scoundrels '88 ▶
Dr. Petiot '90
The Dreamlife of Angels '98 ▶
Dubarry '30
The Duellists '77 ▶
Dupont Lajoie '74
8 Women '02 ▶
The Elusive Corporal '62 ▶
Ever After: A Cinderella Story '98 ▶
Fanfan la Tulipe '51 ▶
The Fatal Image '90
Festival at Cannes '02
The Fighting Eagle '27
5x2 '04
Flyboys '06
The Foreman Went to France '42
Forget Paris '95
The 4 Musketeers '05
Frantic '88 ▶
French Connection 2 '75 ▶
French Intrigue '70
French Kiss '95
The French Lesson '86
French Postcards '79
The French Woman '79
Full Speed '96
Games of Love and Chance '03
The Gendarme of Saint-Tropez '64
Gentlemen Prefer Blondes '53 ▶
Gigi '58 ▶
Girls Can't Swim '99
The Good Thief '03 ▶
A Good Year '06
Goya in Bordeaux '99
Hail Mafia '65
Happily Ever After '04
Harvest '37 ▶
Hate '95 ▶
He Loves Me ... He Loves Me Not '02
Heart of a Nation '43 ▶
Hellraiser 4: Bloodline '95
Henri Langlois: The Phantom of the Cinematheque '04 ▶
Hidden '05 ▶
The Horseman on the Roof '95
How to Steal a Million '66 ▶
I Stand Alone '98
If Looks Could Kill '86
Impromptu '90 ▶
The Intruder '04 ▶
Is Paris Burning? '66 ▶
I've Loved You So Long '08 ▶
Jeanne la Pucelle '94
Jefferson in Paris '94
Joan of Arc '48
Joan of Arc '99
Joan of Paris '42 ▶
The Josephine Baker Story '90 ▶
Just Visiting '01
Killer Tomatoes Eat France '91
Killing Zoe '94
Kings and Queen '04 ▶
Kings Go Forth '58
A Knight's Tale '01
La Ceremonie '95 ▶
La Collectionneuse '67
La Marseillaise '37 ▶
La Passante '83 ▶
La Petite Jerusalem '05
La Petite Lili '03
La Silence de la Mer '47 ▶
La Vie de Boheme '93 ▶
La Vie Promise '02
The Lacemaker '77 ▶
Ladies' Man '62
Lafayette Escadrille '58
The Last Metro '80 ▶
Last Tango in Paris '73 ▶
The Last Time I Saw Paris '54
The Last Train '74
Le Bal '82 ▶
Le Complot '73 ▶
Le Corbeau '43 ▶
Le Joli Mai '62 ▶
Le Million '31 ▶
Lemming '05
Les Destinees '00
Les Grandes Manoeuvres '55 ▶
Les Miserables '35 ▶
Les Miserables '57 ▶
Les Miserables '78 ▶
Les Miserables '97 ▶
The Life of Emile Zola '37 ▶
Lila Says '04
The Longest Day '62 ▶
Love Me if You Dare '03
Lovely to Look At '52 ▶
Loves & Times of Scaramouche '76
Lucie Aubrac '98
Ma and Pa Kettle on Vacation '53
Madame Bovary '91 ▶
Madame Bovary '00
Mademoiselle Fifi '44
The Man in the Iron Mask '39 ▶
The Man in the Iron Mask '77 ▶
The Man in the Iron Mask '97
The Man in the Iron Mask '98 ▶
The Man of My Life '06
Man on the Eiffel Tower '48 ▶
Maniac '63
Manon '50
Marie Antoinette '38
Marie Antoinette '06
Marie Baie des Anges '97
Marius '31 ▶
Maximum Risk '96
May Fools '90 ▶
Me and the Colonel '58
Mr. Bean's Holiday '07

▶ = rated three bones or higher

Mr. Klein '76 ►
The Moderns '88 ►
Modigliani '04
Moliere '07
Moment to Moment '66
Mondo '96
Mondovino '04
Monkeys, Go Home! '66
Monsieur Beaucaire '24
Monsieur Beaucaire '46 ►
Monsieur N. '03 ►
Monsieur Verdoux '47 ►
The Moon and Sixpence '43 ►
The Moonraker '58
Moulin Rouge '52 ►
The Mountain '56
My Father's Glory '91 ►
My Life on Ice '02
Napoleon '27 ►
Napoleon '55
A New Kind of Love '63
New World '95
The Night and the Moment '94
The Old Lady Who Walked in the Sea '91
Operation Mad Ball '57
O.S.S. '46 ►
Passion '19
Passion '82
Passion of Joan of Arc '28 ►
Passion of Mind '00
Paths of Glory '57 ►
Piaf '81
Prisoner of Honor '91 ►
The Proprietor '96
Quality Street '37
Quatorze Juliet '32
Queen Margot '94 ►
Quiet Days in Clichy '90
Read My Lips '01
Ready to Wear '94
The Red Inn '51
Reign of Terror '49
Reunion in France '42
Revenge of the Musketeers '63
Revenge of the Musketeers '94
Ridicule '96 ►
Roman de Gare '07
Round Midnight '86 ►
The Rover '67
The Rules of the Game '39 ►
Sade '00
Saint Joan '57
The Scarlet Pimpernel '34 ►
The Scarlet Pimpernel '82 ►
The Scarlet Pimpernel '99
The Scarlet Pimpernel 2: Mademoiselle Guillotine '99
The Scarlet Pimpernel 3: The Kidnapped King '99
The Sergeant '68
Sex is Comedy '02
Shall We Kiss '09
Silk Stockings '57 ►
Sister My Sister '94
A Soldier's Daughter Never Cries '98
Spy of Napoleon '36
The Square Peg '58
The Statement '03
Straight into Darkness '04
Strayed '03 ►
Suite 16 '94
A Summer's Tale '96
Surviving Picasso '96
Sweet Ecstasy '62
Swimming Pool '03 ►
A Tale of Two Cities '36 ►
A Tale of Two Cities '58 ►
A Tale of Two Cities '80
A Tale of Winter '92
The Taste of Others '00 ►
Theatre of Death '67
Therese Raquin '80
Therese: The Story of Saint Therese of Lisieux '04
This Land Is Mine '43 ►
Those Magnificent Men in Their Flying Machines '65 ►
Timeline '03
To Catch a Thief '55 ►
Tous les Matins du Monde '92 ►
The Town Is Quiet '00
The Transporter '02
The Trench '99
Tropic of Cancer '70 ►
True Colors '87
Uncertain Glory '44
Untamable Angelique '67
Until September '84
Uranus '91 ►
Valmont '89 ►
Varian's War '01
Vatel '00
A Very Long Engagement '04 ►
The Victors '63
Waterloo '71
We Were One Man '80
Western '96
What Price Glory? '52 ►
When a Man Loves '27
Who Killed Bambi? '03
Will It Snow for Christmas? '96
Window to Paris '95
With a Friend Like Harry '00 ►
A Year in Provence '89 ►

Fraternities & Sororities

***see also** Campus Capers*
American Pie Presents: Beta House '07
Among Brothers '05
Black Christmas '75
Black Christmas '06
The Campus Corpse '77
College '08
Confessions of Sorority Girls '94
Dead Man on Campus '97
Defying Gravity '99
Freshman Orientation '04
Funny About Love '90
Going Greek '01
Happy Hell Night '92
Hell Night '81
H.O.T.S. '79
The House Bunny '08
The Initiation '84
Initiation of Sarah '78
The Initiation of Sarah '06
Insecticidal '05
Little Sister '92
Midnight Madness '80
Monsters Crash the Pajama Party '65
National Lampoon's Adam & Eve '05
National Lampoon's Animal House '78 ►
National Lampoon's Van Wilder '02
National Lampoon's Van Wilder 2: The Rise of Taj '06
Old School '03
Pumpkin '02
Revenge of the Nerds '84
Ring of Terror '62
Scream 2 '97 ►
Senseless '98
The Skulls 2 '02
Sorority Babes in the Slime-ball Bowl-A-Rama '87
Sorority Boys '02
Sorority Girl '57
Sorority House Massacre '86
Sorority House Massacre 2: Nighty Nightmare '92
Sorority House Party '92
Sorority House Vampires '95
Sorority Row '09
Stomp the Yard '07
Sydney White '07
Urban Legend '98
Vampire Time Travelers '98
Wimps '87

Friendship

***see** Buddies; Buddy Cops; Childhood Buddies; Female Bonding; Pardners*

Front Page

***see also** Mass Media; Paperboys; Shutterbugs*
Absence of Malice '81
Ace in the Hole '51 ►
Act of Passion: The Lost Honor of Kathryn Beck '83
Action in Arabia '44
The Adventures of Nellie Bly '81
Against the Ropes '04
Alice in the Cities '74 ►
All the President's Men '76 ►
American Autobahn '84
America's Sweethearts '01
AngKor: Cambodia Express '81
Anima '98
Another Time, Another Place '58
Anzio '68
The Average Woman '24
The Barcelona Kill '77
The Beniker Gang '83
Between the Lines '77 ►
Beyond a Reasonable Doubt '09
Beyond Re-Animator '03
Big Brown Eyes '36
The Big Hurt '87
Big News '29
Big Town '47
Big Town After Dark '47
Blessed Event '32 ►
Blonde for a Day '46
Bloody Proof '99 ►
The Blue Gardenia '53 ►
Boca '94
Boeing Boeing '65
Bordertown '06
The Bounty Hunter '10
The Boys Are Back '09
Brenda Starr '86
Bright Lights, Big City '88
Broadway Melody of 1936 '35 ►
Brown Sugar '02
Bruce Almighty '03
Brutal Massacre: A Comedy '07
Bulldog Edition '36
A Bunny's Tale '85
The Business of Fancydancing '02
Call Northside 777 '48 ►
Caroline at Midnight '93
The Case of the Scorpion's Tail '71
The Children of Huang Shi '08
Chinese Box '97
Circumstantial Evidence '35
Citizen Kane '41 ►
City in Fear '80 ►
Close to Home '86
Close to My Heart '51
Cobb '94 ►
Cold Blooded '00
Concrete Beat '84
Continental Divide '81
Control Room '04 ►
Cover Story '93
Crazy Heart '09
Criminal Act '88
Crocodile Dundee '86 ►
Crocodile Dundee in Los Angeles '01
Cry Freedom '87
Cut and Run '85
Dark Secrets '95
Dark Side of Genius '94
Dead Air '94
Dead Connection '94
Deadline '81
Deadline '87
Deadline '00
Deadly Exposure '93
Deep Impact '98
Defense of the Realm '85 ►
Diamond Trail '33
Diary of a Serial Killer '97
The Disappearance of Garcia Lorca '96
Don't Look Down '98
Don't Torture a Duckling '72
Double Cross '92
Double Edge '92
Double Exposure '82
Down Came a Blackbird '94
Each Dawn I Die '39
Easy to Wed '46
Echo of Murder '00
Eight Men Out '88 ►
End of the Road '44
Everything Happens at Night '39 ►
Extramarital '98
Eyes Behind the Stars '72
Eyes of a Stranger '81
A Face in the Fog '36
Far East '85
Fast Money '96
Father Hood '93
Fatherland '94
The Feminine Touch '95
Fever Pitch '85
Final Assignment '80
Finnegan Begin Again '84
Fit for a King '37
A Flash of Green '85
Fletch '85
Fletch Lives '89
Footsteps '98
The Forbidden Quest '93
Foreign Correspondent '40 ►
Four's a Crowd '38
Francis Covers the Big Town '53
Freeze Frame '92
The Front Page '31 ►
The Front Page '74
Full Disclosure '00
Full Frontal '02
Fun '94
Generation Kill '08 ►
Gentleman's Agreement '47 ►
Get a Clue '02
The Ghost and Mr. Chicken '66
Ghosted '09
G.I. War Brides '46
The Girl With the Dragon Tattoo '09 ►
Golden Gloves '40
Good Advice '01
The Great Muppet Caper '81 ►
Grown Ups '86
Gunshy '98 ►
The Guys '02 ►
Harrison's Flowers '02
Headline Woman '35
Heads '93
Heartaches '47
Heat Wave '90 ►
Hellraiser: Deader '05
Her Life as a Man '83
Here's Flash Casey '38
Hero '92 ►
His Girl Friday '40 ►
Hit the Ice '43
Hour of Decision '57
How to Lose a Guy in 10 Days '03
How to Lose Friends & Alienate People '08
The Hudsucker Proxy '93 ►
Hue and Cry '47 ►
Hustling '75 ►
I Cover the Waterfront '33
I Love Trouble '94
I Was Framed '42
The Image '89
Imagining Argentina '04
Impact Point '08
Impolite '92
In and Out '97 ►
In My Country '04
An Inconvenient Woman '91
Infected '08
The Infiltrator '95
The Innocent Sleep '95
The Insider '99 ►
Invasion of Privacy '92
Istanbul '90
It Happened Tomorrow '44
Joe Gould's Secret '00
Johnny Come Lately '43
Journey for Margaret '42 ►
The Jury's Secret '38
Just Off Broadway '42
Just One of the Guys '85
Keeper of the City '92
Keeper of the Flame '42
Kid from Not-So-Big '78
Kill Slade '89
The Killing Beach '92
The Killing Device '92
The Killing Fields '84 ►
A Killing Spring '02
Killing Stone '78
Kit Kittredge: An American Girl '08 ►
L.A. Confidential '97 ►
La Dolce Vita '60 ►
Lana in Love '92
The Last Debate '00
The Last Gangster '37
The Last Word '95
Late Extra '35
Leatherheads '08
Legalese '98
Let 'er Go Gallegher '28
Lethal Charm '90
Libeled Lady '36 ►
Life Begins at Forty '35
The Life of David Gale '03
Lip Service '88 ►
L'Odeur des Fauves '66
Lonelyhearts '58
Love Is a Many-Splendored Thing '55
Love Is News '37 ►
The Love Machine '71
The Luck of the Irish '48
Malarek '89
The Man Inside '90
Man of Iron '81 ►
Marley & Me '08
The Mask '94 ►
Me & Mrs. Jones '02
Mean Season '85
Meet John Doe '41 ►
The Men Who Stare at Goats '09
Message in a Bottle '98
Michael '96
Midnight Edition '93
Midnight in the Garden of Good and Evil '97
Midnight Warrior '89
Mrs. Parker and the Vicious Circle '94
Mr. Deeds '02
Mr. Deeds Goes to Town '36 ►
Mr. District Attorney '41
Mr. Nice Guy '98
Money Talks '97
The Mothman Prophecies '02
Murder on the Campus '52
Murder With Pictures '36
Murrow '86
My Wife is an Actress '01
Mystic Circle Murder '39
Natas... The Reflection '83
The Natural '84 ►
Never Been Kissed '99
News at Eleven '86
Newsbreak '00
Newsfront '78 ►
Newsies '92
Night Alarm '34
Night Hunter '95
The Night Stalker '71
The Night Strangler '72
The Nightmare Years '89
Nina Takes a Lover '94
No Man's Land '01
No Time to Die '84
Not for Publication '84
The Note '07
The Note 2: Taking a Chance on Love '09
Nothing But the Truth '08 ►
Nothing Sacred '37 ►
Notting Hill '99 ►
Novel Desires '92
November Conspiracy '96
The Odessa File '74
Off the Lip '04
On Our Merry Way '48
One Fine Day '96
One Man Out '89
One True Thing '98 ►
Optic Fiber '97
Orwell Rolls in His Grave '03
The Other Woman '92
Our Music '04
Outfoxed: Rupert Murdoch's War on Journalism '04 ►
The Outlaws Is Coming! '65
The Paper '94 ►
Paper Lion '68
The Payoff '43
The Pelican Brief '93
Perfect '85
The Philadelphia Story '40 ►
Platinum Blonde '31 ►
The Ploughman's Lunch '83 ►
Power of the Press '43
Power Play '02
Premonition '98
Primary Motive '92
Private Investigations '87
Profile '54
Qui Etes Vous, Mr. Sorge? '61
The Quiet American '02 ►
Reckless Disregard '84
Reed: Insurgent Mexico '73
Resurrecting the Champ '07
Resurrection Man '97
Resurrection of Zachary Wheeler '71
Retribution '98
Revenge of the Radioactive Reporter '91
The Riddle '07
Riding on Air '37
The Ring '02
Roman Holiday '53 ►
Roxie Hart '42
The Rumor Mill '86
Runaway Bride '99 ►
Safari 3000 '82
Salome, Where She Danced '45
Salvador '86 ►
Savage Capitalism '93
Saving Sarah Cain '07
Scandal '50
Scandal Sheet '52
Scandal Sheet '85
Scream 2 '97 ►
The Secrets of Wu Sin '32
Seeds of Doubt '96
Sex & Mrs. X '00
Sex and the Single Girl '64
Sex Through a Window '72
The Shadow Conspiracy '96
The Shaft '01
Shattered Glass '03 ►
The Shipping News '01
Shock Corridor '63 ►
Short Fuse '88
Shriek in the Night '33
Shy People '87 ►
Silver City '04
The Sixth Man '97
61* '01 ►
Skeletons '96
Sky Captain and the World of Tomorrow '04
Snake Eyes '98
Snow Falling on Cedars '99
The Soloist '09
Somewhere I'll Find You '42 ►
Soul Patrol '80
Special Bulletin '83 ►
Speed Reporter '36
Spice World: The Movie '97
Star Reporter '39
State of Play '03 ►
State of Play '09 ►
Stavisky '74 ►
Stay Tuned for Murder '88
Stephen King's The Night Flier '96
The Story of G.I. Joe '45 ►
Straight Talk '92
The Strange Love of Molly Louvain '32
Stranger on the Third Floor '40 ►
Street Smart '87
Sucker Money '34
The Sun Sets at Dawn '50
Superman: The Movie '78 ►
Sweet Rosie O'Grady '43
Sweet Smell of Success '57 ►
Sweetwater: A True Rock Story '99
Switching Channels '88
Tainted Blood '93
Tarnished Angels '57 ►
Teacher's Pet '58 ►
Texas Lady '56
That Certain Age '38
That Lucky Touch '75
That Wonderful Urge '48
The Theory of the Leisure Class '01
They All Kissed the Bride '42
They Got Me Covered '43
The Thin Blue Lie '00
Things Behind the Sun '01
The Thirteenth Man '37

► = rated three bones or higher

Thirteenth Reunion '81
Those Glory, Glory Days '83
Three Kings '99 ►
Three o'Clock High '87
Tomorrow at Seven '33
Too Hot to Handle '38 ►
Top Secret Affair '57
Tough Assignment '49
Tower of Terror '97
Trahir '93 ►
Transylvania 6-5000 '85
Traps '93
The Trojan Horse '08
True Crime '99
27 Dresses '08
Under Fire '83 ►
Under Heavy Fire '01
Underworld Scandal '47
The Underworld Story '50
Unexplained Laughter '89
Universal Soldier 2: Brothers in Arms '98
Universal Soldier 3: Unfinished Business '98
Up in Central Park '48
Up to a Certain Point '83
Up Your Alley '89
Valley of the Heart's Delight '07
Velvet Goldmine '98
Veronica Guerin '03
Violence '47
Virgin Machine '88
War, Inc. '08
Wedding Present '36
Welcome to Sarajevo '97 ►
The Wharf Rat '95
What Goes Up '09
When the Sky Falls '99
Where the Buffalo Roam '80
While the City Sleeps '56 ►
Whispering City '47 ►
White Badge '92
The White Raven '98
Winchell '98
Without Love '80
Woman Condemned '33
Woman of the Year '42 ►
A World Apart '88 ►
The World Gone Mad '33
The Year of Living Dangerously '82 ►

Fugitives

see also *Escaped Cons; Lovers on the Lam*

Agent on Ice '86
Bad Girls '94
Bail Jumper '89
Ball of Fire '41 ►
Ballad of Gregorio Cortez '83 ►
Bandits of Orgosolo '61
Barricade '49
Bed & Breakfast '92
The Big Fix '78 ►
Bloodfist 7: Manhunt '95
Bloodhounds of Broadway '52
Bobbie Jo and the Outlaw '76
The Boldest Job in the West '71
A Boy Called Hate '95
Boys on the Side '94
Brannigan '75
Breathless '83
Bushwhacked '95
Butch and Sundance: The Early Days '79
Butch Cassidy and the Sundance Kid '69 ►
Cadillac Ranch '96
Captured in Chinatown '35
Chain Reaction '96
The Chase '91
The Chronicles of Riddick '04
Connie and Carla '04
Cyber-Tracker 2 '95
Danger: Diabolik '68
Dead Easy '82
The Deserters '83
Desperate '47
Desperate Measures '98
The Desperate Trail '94
Dogville '03
Eddie Macon's Run '83
Eight on the Lam '67
The Escape '95
Escape 2000 '81
Exit Smiling '26
Father Hood '93
Fled '96
Frank and Jesse '94
Free Grass '69
The Fugitive '93 ►
Fugitive Among Us '92
Good Girls Don't '95
The Great Texas Dynamite Chase '76
Gridlock'd '96 ►
Hard Knocks '80
Hiding Out '87
Hold Me, Thrill Me, Kiss Me '93
Hollow Point '95
I Died a Thousand Times '55
I Met a Murderer '39
In the Middle of Nowhere '93
It Always Rains on Sunday '47
The Jesus Trip '71
Jungle Inferno '72
Keeping Track '86
Kill Zone '08
Kiss of Death '47 ►
Klondike Annie '36
La Vie Promise '02
Le Doulos '61 ►
Leather Jackets '90
Liberators '69
Loners '72
Long Pants '27 ►
The Love Flower '20
The Man Upstairs '93
Marked Man '96
Miami Cops '89
Miles from Home '88
Minority Report '02 ►
Moving Target '89
Moving Violation '76
North by Northwest '59 ►
Northwest Trail '46
Nowhere to Hide '83
On the Run '73
One Away '76
The Outlaw and His Wife '17
Outlaw Riders '72
Paris Express '53
A Perfect World '93
Posse '93 ►
The Pursuit of D.B. Cooper '81
The Quarry '98
The Red Half-Breed '70
Rider on the Rain '70 ►
River's End '05
Rough Cut '80
The Savage Woman '91
Scorpion Spring '96
Sea Devils '31
The Second Awakening of Christa Klages '78
The Secret Agent '96
Shallow Grave '87
Shoot to Kill '88 ►
Simple Men '92 ►
The Simpsons Movie '07 ►
Slate, Wyn & Me '87
Sonny and Jed '73
The Spy Within '94
The Statement '03
Storm Catcher '99
Stray Dog '49 ►
Stray Dog '91
Strike Back '80
Suspect Device '95
Teenage Bonnie & Klepto Clyde '93
Three Days of the Condor '75 ►
Three Fugitives '89
Three Strikes '00
Thunder County '74
Truth or Consequences, N.M. '97
Twilight Man '96
U.S. Marshals '98
The Walls of Malapaga '49
The Way Out '56
Woman with a Past '92
The Wrong Guy '96
The Wrong Man '93
Wrongfully Accused '98

Funerals

see also *Death & the Afterlife*

About Schmidt '02 ►
Adam '09
The Addams Family '91
The Adventures of Ford Fairlane '90
Apres Lui '07
The Big Chill '83 ►
Big Eden '00
Big Shot's Funeral '01
Blackwater Trail '95
Bonneville '06
The Burning Plain '08
The Business of Fancydancing '02
Bye Bye Braverman '67
The Camomile Lawn '92
Catch and Release '07
City Hall '95 ►
Closing the Ring '07
Crazy Eights '06
The Crow Road '96
Cruel Intentions '98
Dangerous Ground '96
Daniel's Daughter '08
Death at a Funeral '07
Death at a Funeral '10
A Death in the Family '02
Demons from Her Past '07
Dim Sum Funeral '08
El Camino '08
Elizabethtown '05
Erskinville Kings '99
Eulogy '04
The Evening Star '96
Falling '06
The Fighting Temptations '03
Final Cut '98
First Knight '95
The Flamingo Rising '01
Four Brothers '05
Four Sheets to the Wind '07
Four Weddings and a Funeral '94 ►
Full Count '06
The Funeral '84 ►
Funeral Home '82
Gardens of Stone '87
Get Low '09
Go for Zucker '05
Grand Theft Parsons '03
Guantanamera '95 ►
The Guys '02 ►
Harold and Maude '71 ►
Hearts in Atlantis '01
Heathers '89 ►
High Fidelity '00 ►
Himalaya '99 ►
Hope Floats '98
The House of Usher '06
I Love You, Alice B. Toklas! '68
I'll Bury You Tomorrow '02
Infested: Invasion of the Killer Bugs '02
Jack and Sarah '95
Just Buried '07
Kingdom Come '01
Kissed '96
La Buche '00
The Last Enemy '08
Last Orders '01 ►
Lawless Heart '01
Louder than Bombs '01
The Loved One '65
Malicious Intent '99
A Man to Remember '39
Men with Brooms '02
Mr. Saturday Night '92
Moonlight Mile '02 ►
My Girl '91
My Girl 2 '94
Nowhere Boy '09
Ocean's 11 '60
One Night Stand '97 ►
Only the Lonely '91
Orphans '97
The Pallbearer '95
Premonition '07
The Queen '06 ►
Red Roses and Petrol '03
Red, White & Busted '75
Reservation Road '07
The Road Home '01 ►
Roommates '95
Rupert's Land '98
Saving Sarah Cain '07
Senior Skip Day '08
Shotgun Stories '07
Simon Birch '98
Sleepless in Seattle '93 ►
Snow Cake '06
Sordid Lives '00
Steel Magnolias '89 ►
Terms of Endearment '83 ►
A Texas Funeral '99
Things We Lost in the Fire '07
Those Who Love Me Can Take the Train '98
The Three Burials of Melquiades Estrada '05 ►
Till Human Voices Wake Us '02
Tom and Huck '95 ►
24-7 '97
Tyler Perry's Meet the Browns '08
Under Hellgate Bridge '99
Walking on Water '02
Wasted '06
Wes Craven Presents: They '02
What's Eating Gilbert Grape '93 ►
The Wings of the Dove '97 ►
The Winter Guest '97 ►

Funny Money

see also *Crime Drama; Disorganized Crime; Organized Crime*

Bad Men of the Border '45
Beverly Hills Cop 3 '94
Beverly Hills Ninja '96
The Castle of Cagliostro '80
Christmas in Wonderland '07
The Clay Pigeon '49
The Counterfeiters '07 ►
Fighting Caballero '35
Hell's Bloody Devils '70
Honeymoon Academy '90
The In-Laws '79 ►
Kounterfeit '96
Lethal Weapon 4 '98
Luck of the Draw '00
The Magician '93
Mercy Streets '00
Murder on the Yukon '40
Naked Lies '98
Paradise Canyon '35
Phantom Ranger '38
Playing God '96
Renfrew of the Royal Mounted '37
Rush Hour 2 '01
Seoul Raiders '05
Spy Smasher '42
T-Men '47 ►
To Live & Die in L.A. '85
Treehouse Hostage '99
Twilight in the Sierras '50
Union Depot '32

Future Cop

see also *Cops*

Apprentice to Murder '88
The Believers '87
Demolition Man '93
The Dying Truth '86
The Fifth Element '97
The First Power '89
God Told Me To '76
I, Robot '04
The Last Sentinel '07
Maniac Cop '88
Maniac Cop 2 '90
Maniac Cop 3: Badge of Silence '93
Minority Report '02 ►
RoboCop '87 ►
RoboCop 2 '90
Rush Hour 2 '01
Split Second '92
Timecop '94
Wolfen '81 ►

Future Shock

see also *Post-Apocalypse; Time Travel; Time Warped*

A. I.: Artificial Intelligence '01
Aeon Flux '05
Austin Powers: International Man of Mystery '97 ►
Back to the Future, Part 2 '89
Bicentennial Man '99
Bill & Ted's Excellent Adventure '89
The Challenge '05
Children of Men '06 ►
Chrysalis '07
City of Ember '08
The Deal '05
Doomsday '08
Forever Young '92
The Fountain '06
Ghostwarrior '86
Idiocracy '06
Immortal '04
Just Visiting '01
Late for Dinner '91
Minority Report '02 ►
Natural City '03
The Philadelphia Experiment '84
Planet of the Apes '68 ►
The Postman '97
Privilege '67
Renaissance '06
Repo Men '10
Six: The Mark Unleashed '04
Sky Blue '03
Sleeper '73 ►
A Sound of Thunder '05
10,000 A.D.: The Legend of the Black Pearl '08
Ultraviolet '06
Universal Soldier: Regeneration '09
The Visitors '95
WALL-E '08 ►

Gambling

see also *Viva Las Vegas!*

Action for Slander '38
Alex & Emma '03
Alibi Ike '35
All In '06
All or Nothing at All '93
Any Number Can Play '49
Any Number Can Win '63
Atlantic City '81 ►
Back to the Future, Part 2 '89
Bad Lieutenant: Port of Call New Orleans '09
Barry Lyndon '75 ►
Big Shot: Confessions of a Campus Bookie '02
Big Town '87
A Billion for Boris '90
Birds & the Bees '56
Bitter Sweet '33
Bitter Sweet '40
Bob le Flambeur '55 ►
Bookies '03
The Boys '97
Buffalo 66 '97 ►
Bugsy '91 ►
Caddyshack '80 ►
Canyon Passage '46 ►
Casino '80
Casino '95 ►
Casino Royale '06 ►
Cassandra's Dream '07
Catch Me... If You Can '89
Catherine Cookson's The Gambling Man '98
Charlie Chan at Monte Carlo '37
Charlie Chan at the Race Track '36
The Cheat '31
The Cheaters '76
Circus '00
Cockfighter '74 ►
The Color of Money '86 ►
The Cooler '03 ►
Croupier '97 ►
The Dark Dealer '95
Dead Heat '01
Dead Lucky '60
Deadly Impact '84
The Debt '98
The Deli '97
Diamonds Are Forever '71 ►
Diggstown '92
Dinner Rush '00 ►
Dona Flor and Her Two Husbands '78 ►
Double Down '01
Double Dynamite '51
Doughboys '08
Draw! '81
The Duchess and the Dirtwater Fox '76
Duke of the Derby '62
Easy Money '83
Eight Men Out '88 ►
Even Money '06
Eyes of an Angel '91
Familia '05
Family Prayers '91
Fever Pitch '85
Finding Amanda '08
A Fine Mess '86
Firepower '93
Five Card Stud '68
Flame of the Barbary Coast '45
Flame of the Islands '55
The Flamingo Kid '84 ►
Force of Evil '49 ►
Four Rooms '95
Frankie and Johnny '65
The Gamble '88
Gamble on Love '86
The Gambler '74 ►
The Gambler '97
The Gambler & the Lady '52
The Gambler, the Girl and the Gunslinger '09
Gambling Ship '33
Get Shorty '95 ►
Gilda '46 ►
Glory Years '87
Golden Rendezvous '77
The Good Thief '03 ►
The Great Mike '44
Gun Crazy '69
Guys and Dolls '55 ►
Half a Lifetime '86
Hard Eight '96 ►
Hardball '01
The Harder They Fall '56 ►
Heat '95 ►
Heaven '99
Hell's Angels '69 '69
Here Come the Marines '52
Hi-Life '98
The Honeymoon Machine '61
Hoodlum '96
Household Saints '93 ►
Huck and the King of Hearts '93
Hustle '04
The Hustler '61 ►
In Like Flint '67
Indecent Proposal '93
Inn of Temptation '73
Inside Out '91
Intacto '01
Jinxed '82
Kaleidoscope '66
Killer McCoy '47
Lady for a Night '42
Lady from Louisiana '42
Las Vegas Hillbillys '66
Las Vegas Lady '76
The Las Vegas Story '52
Las Vegas Weekend '85
Le Million '31 ►
The Lemon Drop Kid '51
Let It Ride '89
Let's Do It Again '75
Let's Make It Legal '51
Liberty Heights '99
Little Miss Marker '34 ►
Little Miss Marker '80
Little Vegas '90
Living to Die '91
Lock, Stock and 2 Smoking Barrels '98 ►
Lookin' to Get Out '82
Lost in America '85 ►
Lucky You '07
Luckytown '00
Manhattan Melodrama '34 ►
The Marrying Man '91
Maverick '94
McCabe & Mrs. Miller '71 ►
McHale's Navy '64
Mean Machine '01
Meet Me in Las Vegas '56
Michael Clayton '07 ►
Michael Shayne: Private Detective '40
Mickey One '65
Mr. Lucky '43 ►

► = rated three bones or higher

Mr. Muggs Rides Again *'45*
Money from Home *'53*
Money Kings *'98*
Money Train *'95*
Monte Carlo *'30*
Mother and Son *'31*
Murderers' Row *'66*
My Blueberry Nights *'07*
My Darling Clementine *'46* ►
My Little Chickadee *'40* ►
Ninja, the Violent Sorcerer *'86*
No Man of Her Own *'32*
Ocean's Eleven *'01* ►
Ocean's Thirteen *'07* ►
Oklahoma Kid *'39* ►
The Old Curiosity Shop *'07*
One Last Ride *'03*
One Tough Cop *'98*
Order to Kill *'73*
Oscar and Lucinda *'97*
Our Man Flint *'66*
Out to Sea *'97*
Owning Mahowny *'03*
Paradise Island *'30*
Phoenix *'98*
Pink Cadillac *'89*
Player 5150 *'08*
Players *'03*
Pleasure Palace *'80*
Poker Alice *'87*
Poolhall Junkies *'02*
The Queen of Spades *'49* ►
Quintet *'79*
Rain Man *'88* ►
Rat Race *'01*
Riders of the Range *'50*
Rimfire *'49*
The Ringer *'05*
Roaring City *'51*
The Roaring Twenties *'39* ►
Robbery *'85*
Robin-B-Hood *'06*
The Rocking Horse Winner *'49*
Ruggles of Red Gap *'35* ►
The Runner *'99*
Saint John of Las Vegas *'09*
Salty O'Rourke *'45*
Say Yes! *'86*
Sgt. Bilko *'95*
Shade *'03*
The Shadow Man *'53*
The Shanghai Gesture *'42*
Shoot *'92*
Showgirls *'95*
Silver Queen *'42*
Sno-Line *'85*
Song of the Thin Man *'47*
Sorrowful Jones *'49*
Sour Grapes *'98*
Spent *'00*
The Squeeze *'87*
Stacy's Knights *'83*
Stickmen *'01*
The Sting *'73* ►
Strike It Rich *'90*
Support Your Local Sheriff *'69* ►
Swing Time *'36* ►
The Tailor of Panama *'00* ►
Taking Chances *'09*
Tall Story *'60*
Talons of the Eagle *'92*
Tax Season *'90*
Taxi Dancers *'93*
Ten Benny *'98*
Tennessee's Partner *'55*
Thief *'71*
Things Change *'88* ►
This Is a Hijack *'73*
Thoroughbreds Don't Cry *'37*
Three Men on a Horse *'36* ►
3000 Miles to Graceland *'01*
Tomcats *'01*
Too Many Winners *'47*
Trading Places *'83*
21 *'08*
29th Street *'91*
Two for the Money *'05*
Uncle Buck *'89* ►
The Underneath *'95* ►
Uphill All the Way *'85*
Uptown Saturday Night *'74*
The Vegas Strip Wars *'84*
Vegas Vacation *'96*
Violence *'47*
Walking Tall *'73*
Welcome to 18 *'87*
The Westerner *'40* ►
Wheel of Fortune *'41*
Who's Got the Action? *'63*
The Winner *'96*
Wise Guys *'86*
Yonkers Joe *'08*

Game Shows

Champagne for Caesar *'50* ►
The Computer Wore Tennis Shoes *'69*
Confessions of a Dangerous Mind *'02*
Deathrow Gameshow *'88*
Everything You Always Wanted to Know about Sex (But Were Afraid to Ask) *'72* ►
For Love or Money *'84*
Groundhog Day *'93* ►
The Low Down *'00*
Mallrats *'95*
Mr. Average *'06*
National Lampoon's European Vacation *'85*
Prize of Peril *'84*
Queen for a Day *'51*
Quiz Show *'94* ►
Reckless *'95*
The Running Man *'87*
Shock Treatment *'81*
Starter for Ten *'06*
10th Victim *'65* ►
White Men Can't Jump *'92*

Gangs

***see also** Juvenile Delinquents; Moscow Mafia; Organized Crime; Urban Gangstas*

Abduction of St. Anne *'75*
Alien Private Eye *'87*
All Dogs Go to Heaven *'89*
Alley Cat *'84*
Alvin Rides Again *'74*
American Me *'92* ►
Angel Town *'89*
Angels Die Hard *'70*
Apache Woman *'55*
Assault on Precinct 13 *'76* ►
Baby Face Morgan *'42*
Bad Bunch *'76*
Bad Guys *'79*
Ballbuster *'89*
Behave Yourself! *'52*
Bells of Death *'68*
Belly *'98*
A Better Tomorrow, Part 1 *'86*
A Better Tomorrow, Part 2 *'88*
Beyond the Law *'92*
Big Bad Mama *'74*
Big Bad Mama 2 *'87*
The Big Brawl *'80*
Black Bikers from Hell *'70*
Black Caesar *'73*
The Black Cobra *'87*
Black Gestapo *'75*
Blood Brothers *'97*
Blood In ... Blood Out: Bound by Honor *'93*
The Bloody Brood *'59*
Bloody Mama *'70*
Blue *'68*
Blues Busters *'50*
Bonnie & Clyde *'67* ►
Borderline *'50*
Boricua's Bond *'00*
Borsalino *'70* ►
Boss of Big Town *'43*
Boulevard Nights *'79*
Bowery Blitzkrieg *'41*
Boyz N the Hood *'91* ►
Bra Boys *'07*
Breaking Loose *'90*
Bring Me the Head of Alfredo Garcia *'74*
Broadway Danny Rose *'84* ►
The Bronx War *'90*
Brother Orchid *'40* ►
Buckeye and Blue *'87*
Buddy Buddy *'81*
Bulldog Drummond's Bride *'39*
Bulldog Edition *'36*
Bulldog Jack *'35* ►
Bullet *'94*
Bullets or Ballots *'38* ►
Cartouche *'62* ►
C.C. & Company *'70*
Chains *'89*
Chains of Gold *'92*
The Chase *'46*
China Girl *'87*
China O'Brien *'88*
Chrome and Hot Leather *'71*
City of God *'02*
City of Men *'07* ►
Class of 1984 *'82*
Class of 1999 *'90*
Class of 1999 2: The Substitute *'93*
Clipped Wings *'53*
Coach Carter *'05* ►
Code of Silence *'85*
Commando Squad *'87*
The Concentratin' Kid *'30*
Confidential *'35*
Contraband *'80*
Cookie *'89*
The Cool World *'63*
Cop in Blue Jeans *'78*
Corruption *'70*
Cosh Boy *'52*
The Cross & the Switchblade *'72*
The Crow: Wicked Prayer *'05*
Cruisin' High *'75*
Cry-Baby *'90* ►
Cry of a Prostitute: Love Kills *'72*
Cry Terror *'76*
Danger Zone *'87*
Danger Zone 2 *'89*
Dangerous Ground *'96*
Dangerous Mission *'54*
Dark Rider *'91*
Darktown Strutters *'74*
The Day It Came to Earth *'77*
Dead End City *'88*
Deadly Encounter *'72* ►
Deadly Revenge *'83*
Dear Wendy *'05*
Death Sentence *'07*
Defiance *'79*
Defiant *'70*
Delinquent Girl Boss: Blossoming Night Dreams *'70*
Delta Fox *'77*
Designing Woman *'57* ►
Deuces Wild *'02*
Devil's Angels *'67*
Dick Tracy vs. Cueball *'46*
Dillinger *'45* ►
Dillinger *'73*
Dirt Gang *'71*
Dirty *'05*
Dirty Laundry *'87*
Disorganized Crime *'89*
Diva *'82* ►
The Divine Enforcer *'91*
Dixie Jamboree *'44*
The Doberman Gang *'72*
The Dog Who Stopped the War *'84*
The Don Is Dead *'73*
Drive By *'01*
Each Dawn I Die *'39*
East L.A. Warriors *'89*
East Side Kids *'40*
The Education of Sonny Carson *'74*
Emil and the Detectives *'64*
Enemy Territory *'87*
The Enforcer *'51*
The Enforcer *'76*
Escape from L.A. *'96*
Escape from the Bronx *'85*
Every Which Way But Loose *'78*
Exterminator *'80*
Eye of the Tiger *'86*
Fear in the City *'81*
Fight Club: ' *'99* ►
The Final Alliance *'89*
Foolish *'99*
Forced Vengeance *'82*
Forever, Lulu *'87*
Four Deuces *'75*
Four Jacks and a Jill *'41*
Foxy Brown *'74*
Full Eclipse *'93*
"G" Men *'35* ►
The Gambler & the Lady *'52*
Gambler's Choice *'44*
Game of Death *'79*
Gang Boys *'97*
Gang Bullets *'38*
Gang Busters *'42*
Gang Justice *'94*
Gang Wars *'75*
Gangland *'00*
Gangs of New York *'02* ►
The Gangster *'47*
Gangster Wars *'81*
Gangway *'37*
Ghetto Blaster *'89*
The Ghost and the Guest *'43*
Ghost Chasers *'51*
Gimme Shelter *'70*
The Glory Stompers *'67*
Golden Lady *'79*
Gone Are the Days *'84*
Goodfellas *'90* ►
Gran Torino *'08* ►
The Great Mike *'44*
The Great Skycopter Rescue *'82*
Green Street Hooligans *'05* ►
The Grissom Gang *'71* ►
The Gumshoe Kid *'89*
Gun Girls *'56*
The Gunrunner *'84*
Guns Don't Argue *'57*
Hard As Nails *'01*
Hard-Boiled Mahoney *'47*
Hard Lessons *'86*
Harley *'90*
Hawk's Vengeance *'96*
Heartbreaker *'83*
Heat Street *'87*
Hell on Frisco Bay *'55*
Hellcats *'68*
High Ballin' *'78*
High Sierra *'41* ►
Hitz *'89*
Homeboy *'75*
Homeboys *'92*
Hoodlum Empire *'52*
I Died a Thousand Times *'55*
I, Mobster *'58*
I'd Give My Life *'36*
Illtown *'96*
Impulse *'55*
Inside the Law *'42*
Jinxed *'82*
Johnny Apollo *'40*
Johnny Dangerously *'84*
Jungleground *'95*
Just William's Luck *'47*
Key Largo *'48* ►
Killer Dill *'47*
Knights of the City *'85*
Kung Fu Hustle *'04*
L.A. Bad *'85*
La Balance *'82* ►
L.A. Gangs Rising *'89*
Lady from Nowhere *'36*
Lady in a Cage *'64* ►
Lady in Red *'79*
Last Flight to Hell *'91*
Last Man Standing *'96*
The Last Ride of the Dalton Gang *'79*
The Last Riders *'90*
Latin Dragon *'03*
Law of the Underworld *'38*
Leather Jackets *'90*
Lepke *'75*
Lethal Games *'90*
Lethal Obsession *'87*
Like a Puppet Out of Strings *'05*
Linewatch *'08*
Little Dragons *'80*
Little Laura & Big John *'73*
The Longshot *'86*
The Lost Capone *'90* ►
Love Me or Leave Me *'55* ►
Lucky Luciano *'74*
Ma Barker's Killer Brood *'60*
Machine Gun Kelly *'58*
Manhattan Merry-Go-Round *'37*
Marie Baie des Anges *'97*
Marked Woman *'37* ►
Marshal Law *'96*
The Masters of Menace *'90*
Master's Revenge *'71*
The Maverick Queen *'55*
Meet the Mob *'42*
Men of Respect *'91*
Menace II Society *'93* ►
The Meteor Man *'93*
Mexican Gangster *'08*
Mi Vida Loca *'94*
Midnight *'34*
Million Dollar Kid *'44*
Miracle in Harlem *'48*
Mr. Majestyk *'74*
Mob Boss *'90*
Mob Story *'90*
Mob War *'88*
Motorcycle Squad *'41*
Murda Muzik *'03*
My Samurai *'92*
Mystery Date *'91*
The Naked Angels *'69*
Nashville Beat *'89*
'Neath Brooklyn Bridge *'42*
Ned Kelly *'03*
The Neon Empire *'89*
Never a Dull Moment *'68*
Never Let Go *'60*
Never Love a Stranger *'58*
The New Kids *'85*
99 & 44/100 Dead *'74*
Ninja Brothers of Blood *'89*
No Trace *'50*
The Noose Hangs High *'48* ►
Omega Doom *'96*
One Man's Justice *'95*
Original Gangstas *'96*
The Outsiders *'83*
Paco *'75*
Paradise in Harlem *'40*
Parole, Inc. *'49*
The Payoff *'43*
Peacekillers *'71*
Performance *'70* ►
Petrified Forest *'36* ►
Pickup on South Street *'53* ►
Pierrot le Fou *'65* ►
Play Murder for Me *'91*
The Power of the Ninjitsu *'88*
Prayer of the Rollerboys *'91*
Prime Cut *'72*
The Prime Time *'60*
The Principal *'87*
Prize Fighter *'79*
Pulp *'72*
Punk Vacation *'90*
The Purifiers *'04*
Quatorze Juliet *'32*
The Racket *'51* ►
The Racketeer *'29*
Rapid Fire *'92*
The Reading Room *'05*
Renegades *'89*
Return of the Dragon *'73*
Return of the Rebels *'81*
Return of the Tiger *'78*
Revenge *'90*
Revenge of the Ninja *'83*
Ricochet *'91* ►
Riot Squad *'41*
The Rise and Fall of Legs Diamond *'60*
The Ritz *'76* ►
Rooftops *'89*
Rumble Fish *'83* ►
Rumble in the Bronx *'96*
Running Woman *'98*
Satan's Sadists *'69*
The Savage Seven *'68*
Scared Stiff *'53* ►
Scarface *'83* ►
The Sea Serpent *'85*
Second Chance *'53*
The Second Chance *'06*
The Set-Up *'49* ►
Sexton Blake and the Hooded Terror *'38*
Shaft *'71* ►
Shank *'09*
She's Back *'88*
Shining Star *'75*
Shoot the Piano Player *'62* ►
Showdown *'93*
Sidewalks of New York *'31*
16 Years of Alcohol *'03*
Slam *'98*
Small Faces *'95* ►
Smart Alecks *'42*
SnakeEater 3: His Law *'92*
Sno-Line *'85*
Some Like It Hot *'59* ►
South Central *'92*
Speedy *'28* ►
Spike of Bensonhurst *'88*
Splinter *'06*
Spook Busters *'48*
Star Reporter *'39*
Stavisky *'74* ►
Steel *'97*
Sticky Fingers *'88*
Stingray *'78*
Stone Cold *'91*
Straight Line *'88*
Street Corner Justice *'96*
Street Crimes *'92*
Street Hitz *'92*
The Street King *'02*
Street Knight *'93*
Street Soldiers *'91*
Street Warriors *'77*
Street Warriors, Part 2 *'79*
The Street with No Name *'48* ►
The Streets of L.A. *'79*
Stryker *'04*
The Substitute *'96*
'Sucker Free City *'05* ►
Sunnyside *'79*
The Sun's Burial *'60* ►
Switchblade Sisters *'75*
T-Bird Gang *'59*
Teenage Doll *'57*
Teenage Gang Debs *'66*
Teenage Wolfpack *'57*
Thicker than Water *'99*
This Time I'll Make You Rich *'75*
Three Strikes *'00*
Timber Queen *'44*
The Tin Soldier *'95*
The Tip-Off *'31*
Tongs: An American Nightmare *'88*
Too Late for Tears *'49* ►
Topaze *'51* ►
Torque *'04*
Tough Assignment *'49*
Tough Kid *'39*
Tough to Handle *'37*
Tropical Snow *'88*
Trouble in Store *'53*
Truck Stop Women *'74*
True Believer *'89*
True Blood *'89*
Tuff Turf *'85*
Two to Tango *'88*
The Underground *'97*
Underground Terror *'88*
The Underworld Story *'50*
Urban Crossfire *'94*
Vengeance *'37*
Verne Miller *'88*
Vietnam, Texas *'90*
Violent Professionals *'73*
The Violent Years *'56*
The Virginia Hill Story *'76*
Waist Deep *'06*
Wanderers *'79* ►
The Warriors *'79*
West Side Story *'61* ►
When Gangland Strikes *'56*
The Wild One *'54* ►
Wilding *'90*
Wonder Man *'45*
Wonderland *'88* ►
The Wrecking Crew *'99*
The Wrong Arm of the Law *'63* ►
Year of the Dragon *'85*
The Young Savages *'61*
Young Warriors *'83*
Zooman *'95* ►

Gays

***see also** Bisexuality; Gender Bending; Lesbians*

Abuse *'82*
Adam & Steve *'05*
The Adventures of Felix *'99*
AKA *'02*
Alive and Kicking *'96*
All Over the Guy *'01*
Amazing Grace *'92*
American Beauty *'99* ►
American Fabulous *'92*
Amor de Hombre *'97*
Anatomy of Hell *'04*
And the Band Played On *'93* ►
Angel *'82*
Angels in America *'03* ►
Another Country *'84*
Apart from Hugh *'94*

Gender

Arabian Nights '74 ►
Arizona Sky '08
Armistead Maupin's More Tales of the City '97
Armistead Maupin's Tales of the City '93
As Good As It Gets '97 ►
As Is '85
B. Monkey '97
Bad Education '04 ►
Bam Bam & Celeste '05 ►
Be Cool '05
Beat '00
Beautiful Thing '95 ►
Bedrooms and Hallways '98
Before I Forget '07
Before Night Falls '00 ►
Behind the Red Door '02
Beloved/Friend '99
Bent '97
The Best Way '76
Between Love & Goodbye '08
Between Something & Nothing '08
The Big Brass Ring '99
Big Eden '00
The Big Tease '99
Billy's Hollywood Screen Kiss '98
The Birdcage '95 ►
Blast from the Past '98
Blue '93
Boat Trip '03
Boondock Saints '99
Born in 68 '08
Borstal Boy '00
Boy Culture '06
Boyfriends '96
Boys in Love '95
The Boys in the Band '70
Boys Life '94
Boys Love '06
Boystown '07
Breaking the Code '95
Breaking the Surface: The Greg Louganis Story '96
Brideshead Revisited '08
Broadway Damage '98
Brokeback Mountain '05 ►
The Broken Hearts Club '00 ►
Brother to Brother '04
Bruno '09
The Bubble '06
Burnt Money '00
The Business of Fancydancing '02
B.U.S.T.E.D. '99
Cabaret '72 ►
Cambridge Spies '03
Camp '03
Carandiru '03
Caresses '97
Carrington '95
The Celluloid Closet '95 ►
Chef's Special '08
Chicken Tikka Masala '05
Children of Hannibal '98
Chuck & Buck '00
Circuit '02
City in Panic '86
Close to Leo '02
The Closet '00
Coffee Date '06
Colonel Redl '84 ►
Color Me Kubrick '05
Come Undone '00
Coming Out '89
Common Ground '00
The Conformist '71 ►
Connie and Carla '04
The Conrad Boys '06
Consenting Adult '85
Cote d'Azur '05
The Country Teacher '08
Cowboys and Angels '00
Cowboys & Angels '04 ►
Cracker: Best Boys '95 ►
Creatures from the Pink Lagoon '07
Crocodile Tears '98
Cruel Intentions '98
Cruising '80
The Crying Game '92 ►
Cthulhu '08
The Curiosity of Chance '06
Curse of the Queerwolf '87
David Searching '97
Days '02
De-Lovely '04
Dear Boys '80
Death in Venice '71 ►
D.E.B.S. '04
The Deep End '01 ►
Defying Gravity '99
The Delta '97
The Detective '68 ►
Die Mommie Die! '03
Different Story '78
Dirty Laundry '07
A Dirty Shame '04
Dog Gone Love '03
Doing Time on Maple Drive '92
Dress Gray '86 ►
Drift '00
Drifting '82
The Dying Gaul '05 ►
An Early Frost '85 ►
East Palace, West Palace '96
East Side Story '07
Eating Out 2: Sloppy Seconds '06
Eating Out 3: All You Can Eat '09
Eban and Charley '01
Eclipse '94
Edge of Seventeen '99
Edward II '92
El Diputado '78 ►
Eleven Men Out '05
The Embalmer '03 ►
An Empty Bed '90 ►
Enduring Love '04
An Englishman in New York '09
Entertaining Mr. Sloane '70
Ernesto '79
The Event '03
The Everlasting Secret Family '88
Execution of Justice '99
Facing Windows '03
Far from Heaven '02 ►
Fashion Victims '07
Finding North '97
First Love and Other Pains / One of Them '99
Fleeing by Night '00
Flipping '96
Flirt '95
Floating '97
The Fluffer '01
Food of Love '02
For a Lost Soldier '93
Forbidden Passion: The Oscar Wilde Movie '85
Forgive and Forget '99
Formula 17 '04
Fortune and Men's Eyes '71
Four Weddings and a Funeral '94 ►
Fox and His Friends '75 ►
Frank McKlusky, C.I. '02
Freshman Orientation '04
Friends and Family '01
Friends & Lovers '99
Frisk '95
Full Speed '96
Fun Down There '88
The Garden '90
The Gay Bed and Breakfast of Terror '07
The Gay Deceivers '69
Gay in Amsterdam '04
Get Real '99
Go Fish '94 ►
Go West '05
Gods and Monsters '98 ►
Goodbye, Dragon Inn '03
Gorgeous '99
The Graffiti Artist '04
Green Plaid Shirt '96
Grief '94
Guys and Balls '04
The Hanging Garden '97
Happy Endings '05
Happy, Texas '99 ►
Happy Together '96
Hard Pill '05
Harry and Max '04
Hate Crime '05
Head On '98 ►
Hearing Voices '90
Heaven's a Drag '94
Heights '04
Hellbent '04
Her and She and Him '69
Hey, Happy! '01
His Secret Life '01 ►
The History Boys '06
Hit and Runway '01
Holding Trevor '07
Hollow Reed '95 ►
Hollywood, Je T'Aime '09
A Home at the End of the World '04
Home for the Holidays '95
The Hours '02 ►
The Hours and Times '92 ►
Hustler White '96
I Can't Sleep '93
I Love You Baby '01
I Love You Phillip Morris '10
I Now Pronounce You Chuck and Larry '07
I Think I Do '97
Ice Men '04
If You Only Knew '00
Illuminata '98
In and Out '97 ►
In the Blood '06
In the Flesh '97
Infamous '06
The Iron Ladies '00
The Iron Ladies 2 '03
It's In the Water '96
It's My Party '95
It's the Rage '99
Jeffrey '95
Joey Breaker '93 ►
The Journey of Jared Price '00
Just One Time '00
Keillers Park '05
Killer Condom '95
Kiss Kiss Bang Bang '05 ►
Kiss Me Deadly '08
Kiss Me, Guido '97
Kiss of the Spider Woman '85 ►
Kiss the Bride '07
Km. 0 '00
La Cage aux Folles '78 ►
La Cage aux Folles 2 '81
La Cage aux Folles 3: The Wedding '86
La Leon '07
Lan Yu '01
The Laramie Project '02 ►
Last Days '05
Latter Days '04
Lawless Heart '01
The Leather Boys '63
Leather Jacket Love Story '98
Leaving Metropolis '02
Les Nuits Fauves '92 ►
L'Escorte '96
L'Homme Blesse '83 ►
L.I.E. '01
Lie Down with Dogs '95
Like a Brother '05
Like It Is '98 ►
Like It Never Was Before '95
Lilies '96
The Line of Beauty '06
Lisa Picard Is Famous '01
Little Miss Sunshine '06 ►
The Living End '92
Loggerheads '05 ►
Lola and Billy the Kid '98
Long-Term Relationship '06
Longtime Companion '90 ►
The Lost Language of Cranes '92 ►
Love and Death on Long Island '97
Love and Human Remains '93 ►
Love and Other Disasters '06
Love Is the Devil '98 ►
Love Kills '98
Love! Valour! Compassion! '96
Ludwig '72
Luminarias '99
Luster '02
Ma Saison Super 8 '05
Madagascar Skin '95
Madame Sata '02
Make the Yuletide Gay '09
Making Love '82
Mambo Italiano '03
The Man I Love '97
The Man of My Life '06
A Man of No Importance '94 ►
Maurice '87 ►
Maybe... Maybe Not '94
Men in Love '90
Men Men Men '95
Menage '86 ►
Merci Docteur Rey '04 ►
Meteor & Shadow '85
The Mexican '01
Midnight Cowboy '69 ►
Midnight Dancers '94
Midnight in the Garden of Good and Evil '97
Milk '08 ►
Mr. Right '06
The Moon & the Stars '07
Mouth to Mouth '95
The Mudge Boy '03
Mulligans '08
The Music Lovers '71
My Beautiful Laundrette '85 ►
My Best Friend's Wedding '97
My Father Is Coming '91
My Own Private Idaho '91 ►
Mysterious Skin '04 ►
The Naked Civil Servant '75 ►
Naked Lunch '91 ►
Nerolio '96
Never Met Picasso '96
Newcastle '08
The Next Best Thing '00
Next Year in Jerusalem '98
Nico and Dani '00
The Night Listener '06
Nighthawks '78
Nijinsky '80
No One Sleeps '01
Noah's Arc: Jumping the Broom '08
Norman, Is That You? '76
Nowhere '96
O Fantasma '00
The Object of My Affection '98
Okoge '93
On the Other Hand, Death '08
Open Cam '05
The Opposite of Sex '98
Ordinary Sinner '02
Other Voices, Other Rooms '95
Otto: Or, Up with Dead People '08
Our Lady of the Assassins '01
Our Sons '91
Out at the Wedding '07
Outing Riley '04
Outrage '09
The Painted Lady '97 ►
Parallel Sons '95
Paris Is Burning '91 ►
Parting Glances '86 ►
Partners '82
Pedale Douce '96
The Perfect Son '00
Perfume '01
The Perfume of Yvonne '94
Philadelphia '93 ►
The Pillow Book '95
Possible Loves '00 ►
Postcards from America '95
Poster Boy '04
Prick Up Your Ears '87 ►
Priest '94
Prom Queen '04
P.S. Your Cat is Dead! '02
Queer Duck: The Movie '06
Querelle '83
Quiet Days in Hollywood '97
Quinceanera '06 ►
Raising Heroes '97
The Raven '07
Ready to Wear '94
The Reception '05
Red Dirt '99
Redwoods '09
Reflections in a Golden Eye '67
Regular Guys '96
Relax... It's Just Sex! '98
Rent '05
Rites of Passage '99
The Ritz '76 ►
A River Made to Drown In '97
Rock Haven '07
Rock Hudson's Home Movies '92
The Rocky Horror Picture Show '75 ►
Rope '48 ►
Rude '96
Sand and Blood '87
Satan's Brew '76
Saturday Night at the Baths '75
Savage Grace '07
Save Me '07
Saved! '04
Say Uncle '05
The Sculptress '97
Second Best '05
Second Skin '99
Seducing Maarya '99
The Sergeant '68
Sergeant Matlovich vs. the U.S. Air Force '78
Sex Positive '09
The Shadows '07
Shank '09
Shelter '07
Shock to the System '06
A Single Man '09 ►
Sitcom '97
Smoke '93
Sordid Lives '00
Speedway Junky '99
Spent '00
Spring Fever '09
Spring Forward '99
The Sprinter '84
The State Within '06
Stealth '06
Steam: A Turkish Bath '96 ►
Stonewall '95 ►
Straight for the Heart '88
Strange Bedfellows '04
Strange Fits of Passion '99
Strange Fruit '04
Strawberry and Chocolate '93 ►
The Sum of Us '94 ►
Sunday, Bloody Sunday '71 ►
Surveillance 24/7 '07
Sweet November '01
Swoon '91 ►
Taboo '99
The Talented Mr. Ripley '99
Tamation '03
Taxi zum Klo '81 ►
Testosterone '03
These Foolish Things '06
Third Man Out: A Donald Strachey Mystery '05
The Third Sex '57
This Special Friendship '67
Those Who Love Me Can Take the Train '98
Three to Tango '99
Threesome '94
Tidy Endings '88
Time to Leave '05 ►
Times Have Been Better '06
Times of Harvey Milk '83 ►
To Forget Venice '79
To Play or to Die '91
The Toilers and the Wayfarers '97
Tomcats '01
Too Cool for Christmas '04
Too Much Sun '90
Torch Song Trilogy '88
Total Eclipse '95
Totally F***ed Up '94
Touch of Pink '04
Transamerica '05 ►
Trick '99 ►
The Trio '97
The Trip '02
Tropical Malady '04
The 24th Day '04
29th & Gay '05
24 Nights '99
The Twilight of the Golds '97
Twist '03 ►
Twisted '96
Unconditional Love '03
Under One Roof '02
Undertow '10
Urbania '00
Valentino: The Last Emperor '08
Very Annie Mary '00
A Very Natural Thing '73
A Very Serious Person '06
Via Appia '92
Victim '61 ►
Victor/Victoria '82 ►
Visions of Sugarplums '99
Vive l'Amour '94
The Walker '07
Walking on Water '02
Water Drops on Burning Rocks '99
We Think the World of You '88 ►
We Were One Man '80
The Wedding Banquet '93 ►
Wedding Wars '06
The Weekend '00
Were the World Mine '08
Westler: East of the Wall '85
When Love Comes '98
Whole New Thing '05
Wild Reeds '94 ►
Wild Tigers I Have Known '06
Wilde '97
Withnail and I '87 ►
The Witnesses '07
Wittgenstein '93
The Wolves of Kromer '98
Wonderland '88 ►
World and Time Enough '95
A Year Without Love '05
Yeti: A Love Story '08
Yossi & Jagger '02
You Belong to Me '07
You'll Get Over It '02
Zero Patience '94
Zus & Zo '01

Gender Bending

see also *Gays; Lesbians; Role Reversal*

Abroad with Two Yanks '44
The Adventures of Priscilla, Queen of the Desert '94 ►
The Adventures of Sebastian Cole '99
All About My Mother '99 ►
All the Queen's Men '02
Angel '82
Anything for Love '93
At War with the Army '50
Auntie '73
The Badge '02
The Ballad of Little Jo '93
Better Than Chocolate '99
Blue Murder at St. Trinian's '56 ►
Boy! What a Girl '45
Come Drink with Me '65 ►
Connie and Carla '04
The Crying Game '92 ►
The Damned '69
Desperate Living '77
Different for Girls '96 ►
Divine '90
Dr. Jekyll and Ms. Hyde '95
Dressed to Kill '80
Ed Wood '94 ►
First a Girl '35
Flawless '99
Forever Mary '89 ►
Gaudi Afternoon '01
Glen or Glenda? '53
Go West '05
Hairspray '88 ►
Happily Ever After '86
Hedwig and the Angry Inch '00 ►
Her Life as a Man '83
He's My Girl '87
Holiday Heart '00
I Like It Like That '94 ►
I Shot Andy Warhol '96 ►
I Wanna Be a Beauty Queen '85
I Want What I Want '72
I Was a Male War Bride '49 ►
In a Year of 13 Moons '78
The Iron Ladies '00
The Iron Ladies 2 '03
It's Pat: The Movie '94
Just Like a Woman '95
Just One of the Girls '93
Just One of the Guys '85
Kill Your Darlings '06
Kinky Boots '06
La Cage aux Folles '78 ►

► = rated three bones or higher

La Cage aux Folles 2 '81
La Cage aux Folles 3: The Wedding '86
Law of Desire '86 ▸
Le Sexe des Etoiles '93
Lilies '96
Little Old New York '23
Lola and Billy the Kid '98
Lust in the Dust '85 ▸
M. Butterfly '93
Ma Vie en Rose '97 ▸
Madame Sata '02
Mascara '87
The Merchant of Venice '04 ▸
Mrs. Doubtfire '93
Mr. Headmistress '98
Mixed Nuts '94
Mob Queen '98
Mutant on the Bounty '89
My Son, the Vampire '52
Myra Breckinridge '70
The Mystery of Alexina '86
The Newlydeads '87
Nobody's Perfect '90
Normal '03
Nowhere '96
Nuns on the Run '90
Old Mother Riley's Ghosts '41
On Each Side '07
Outrageous! '77 ▸
Paris Is Burning '91 ▸
Pink Flamingos '72
Polyester '81
Psycho '60 ▸
The Rocky Horror Picture Show '75 ▸
The Romance of Astrea and Celadon '07
Shadey '87
She's the Man '06
The Silence of the Lambs '91 ▸
Skin Deep '94
So This Is Africa '33
Soldier's Girl '03 ▸
Some Like It Hot '59 ▸
Sonny Boy '87
Sorority Boys '02
Stonewall '95 ▸
Surrender Dorothy '98
Switch '91 ▸
Those Who Love Me Can Take the Train '98
Tipping the Velvet '02
To Wong Foo, Thanks for Everything, Julie Newmar '95
Tootsie '82 ▸
Torch Song Trilogy '88
Transamerica '05 ▸
Transfixed '01
Trash '70
Twelfth Night '96
Twisted '96
Unveiled '05
Vegas in Space '94
Velvet Goldmine '98
Victor/Victoria '82 ▸
Water Drops on Burning Rocks '99
The Wedding Singer '97
White Chicks '04
Wigstock: The Movie '95
Wild Zero '00
The Woman Inside '83
Woman on Top '00
The World According to Garp '82 ▸
The Year of Living Dangerously '82 ▸
Yentl '83
Zatoichi '03 ▸
Zazie dans le Metro '61 ▸

Generation X

All the Wrong Places '00
Bandwagon '95
The Beach '00
Beautiful Girls '96 ▸
Before Sunrise '94
Blade '98
Bodies, Rest & Motion '93
Bottle Rocket '95
Charlie White '04
Chasing Amy '97
Clerks '94 ▸
Don't Do It '94
Dream for an Insomniac '96
Ed's Next Move '96
Empire Records '95
Flakes '07
Floundering '94
Gen-X Cops '99
Glory Daze '96
Half-Baked '97
Home '05
Into the Wild '07 ▸
Keys to Tulsa '96
Kicked in the Head '97
Kicking and Screaming '95 ▸
Knocked Up '07
Little Athens '05
A Little Stiff '91
Live Bait '95
Loaded '94
Love and Other Catastrophes '95
The Low Life '95
Mallrats '95
Mama's Boy '07
Meet the Deedles '98
Nowhere '96
Omaha (the movie) '95
101 Ways (The Things a Girl Will Do to Keep Her Volvo) '00
Party Girl '94
Reality Bites '94
S.F.W. '94
Singles '92 ▸
Slacker '91 ▸
Sleep with Me '94
Something More '99
Strange Fits of Passion '99
subUrbia '96
When the Party's Over '91

Genetics

***see also** Mad Scientists; Metamorphosis*

Alien Nation: Body and Soul '95
Biohazard: The Alien Force '95
The Boys from Brazil '78
Corn '02
District 9 '09 ▸
Ed's Next Move '96
Extraordinary Measures '10
The Fly '58 ▸
The Fly '86 ▸
The Fly 2 '89
Forbidden World '82
Gattaca '97 ▸
The Gene Generation '07
Godsend '04
The Island of Dr. Moreau '96
Metamorphosis: The Alien Factor '93
Mimic '97
Rats '83
Re-Generation '04
Sabretooth '01
The Sender '98
Species 2 '98
Splice '09
Tomcat: Dangerous Desires '93
The Twilight of the Golds '97
Wes Craven Presents Mind Ripper '95
X-Men: The Last Stand '06

Genies

***see also** Magic Carpet Rides*

Aladdin '92 ▸
Aladdin and His Wonderful Lamp '84
Aladdin and the King of Thieves '96
Arabian Nights '00
Bernard and the Genie '91
The Brass Bottle '63
Kazaam '96
A Kid in Aladdin's Palace '97
Miracle Beach '92
Naked Wishes '00
The Outing '87
Priceless Beauty '90
The Return of Jafar '94
The Thief of Bagdad '40 ▸
The Thief of Baghdad '24 ▸
The Thief of Baghdad '78
A Thousand and One Nights '45
Three Wishes '95
Wildest Dreams '90
Wish Me Luck '95
Wishman '93
Wishmaster '97
Wishmaster 4: The Prophecy Fulfilled '02
The Wonders of Aladdin '61

Genocide/Ethnic Cleansing

***see also** Civil War (non U.S.); The Holocaust*

Ararat '02 ▸
Beyond Borders '03
Blood Diamond '06
Darfur Now '07
The Devil Came on Horseback '07
Hotel Rwanda '04
The Killing Fields '84 ▸
The Last King of Scotland '06 ▸
S21: The Khmer Rouge Killing Machine '03 ▸
Shooting Dogs '05
Sometimes in April '05 ▸
Swimming to Cambodia '87 ▸
Tears of the Sun '03

Genre Spoofs

***see also** Comedy Sci-Fi; Detective Spoofs; Satire & Parody; Vampire Spoof; Western Comedy*

Airplane! '80 ▸
Airplane 2: The Sequel '82
All Through the Night '42 ▸
April Fool's Day '86
Austin Powers: International Man of Mystery '97 ▸
Austin Powers 2: The Spy Who Shagged Me '99 ▸
Based on an Untrue Story '93
Beverly Hills Ninja '96
The Big Bus '76
The Big Crimewave '86
Black Dynamite '09
Blazing Saddles '74 ▸
Blondes Have More Guns '95
Bloodbath at the House of Death '85
Bollywood Hero '09
Bordello '79
Bugsy Malone '76
Cairo '42
Cannibal! The Musical '96
Casino Royale '67
Code Name: Chaos '90
Code Name: The Cleaner '07
The Comebacks '07
Corky Romano '01
Creature from the Haunted Sea '60
The Creature Wasn't Nice '81
Creatures from the Pink Lagoon '07
Dance Flick '09
Date Movie '06
Disaster Movie '08
Dogville Shorts '30
Don't Be a Menace to South Central While Drinking Your Juice in the Hood '95
Drive-In '76
18 Fingers of Death '05
Epic Movie '07
Fatal Instinct '93
Fathom '67
Fay Grim '06
Ferocious Female Freedom Fighters '88
Flesh Gordon '72
Frankenstein General Hospital '88
Frankenstein's Great Aunt Tillie '83
Galactic Gigolo '87
Galaxina '80
Ganjasaurus Rex '87
Get Crazy '83
Get Smart '08
Ghoul School '90
The Godson '98
Happily N'Ever After '07
Hell Comes to Frogtown '88
Hercules '97 ▸
High Anxiety '77
The Hollywood Detective '89
Hollywood Harry '86
Hot Fuzz '07 ▸
Hot Shots! '91 ▸
Hot Shots! Part Deux '93
The Hound of the Baskervilles '77
Hysterical '83
I'm Gonna Git You Sucka '88 ▸
Invasion! '99
J-Men Forever! '79 ▸
Jake Speed '86
Jet Benny Show '86
Johnny English '03
Kentucky Fried Movie '77 ▸
Kung Fu Hustle '04
Kung Pow! Enter the Fist '02
Last Action Hero '93
Lemonade Joe '64
The Little Giant '33
Lust in the Dust '85 ▸
Mafia! '98
The Man Who Knew Too Little '97
The Man with Two Brains '83 ▸
Mars Attacks! '96
Meet the Spartans '08
Military Intelligence and You! '06
Mob Boss '90
Modesty Blaise '66
Monster in the Closet '86
Monty Python and the Holy Grail '75 ▸
Mosquitoman '05
Murder by Death '76
Mutant on the Bounty '89
My Name Is Bruce '08
The Naked Gun: From the Files of Police Squad '88 ▸
National Lampoon's Loaded Weapon 1 '93
99 & 44/100 Dead '74
Not Another Teen Movie '01
Once Bitten '85
Orgazmo '98
Pandemonium '82
A Perfect Little Murder '90
Phantom of the Paradise '74
The Pink Chiquitas '86
Plan 10 from Outer Space '95
Plump Fiction '97
Pros & Cons '99
Psycho Beach Party '00
Repossessed '90
Return of Captain Invincible '83
Ricky 1 '88
Robin Hood: Men in Tights '93
Robin of Locksley '95
The Rocker '08
Rustler's Rhapsody '85
Saturday the 14th '81
Saturday the 14th Strikes Back '88
Scary Movie 2 '01
Scary Movie 3 '03
Scary Movie 4 '06
Scream '96 ▸
Silence of the Hams '93
The Silencers '66
A Slight Case of Murder '38
A Slight Case of Murder '99
So This Is Africa '33
Soapdish '91 ▸
Space Truckers '97
Spaceballs '87
Spaceship '81
The Specials '00 ▸
Spy Hard '96
Strange Invaders '83 ▸
The Stuff '85
Super Capers '09
SuperGuy: Behind the Cape '02
Superhero Movie '08
Supersonic Man '78
Support Your Local Gunfighter '71 ▸
Support Your Local Sheriff '69 ▸
Surf Ninjas '93
Team America: World Police '04 ▸
Teenage Exorcist '93
Terror Eyes '87
That Man from Rio '64
They Call Me Bruce? '82
They Call Me Trinity '72
They Live '88
They Still Call Me Bruce '86
Three Amigos '86
Too Many Crooks '59
Top Secret! '84 ▸
Transylmania '09
Transylvania 6-5000 '85
Trinity Is Still My Name '75
Tromeo & Juliet '95
The Trouble with Spies '87
2069: A Sex Odyssey '78
UHF '89
Undercover Brother '02
Union City '81
Unmasked Part 25 '88
Vegas in Space '94
The Video Dead '87
Video Violence '87
Video Violence Part 2... The Exploitation! '87
The Villain '79
Voyage of the Rock Aliens '87
Wacko '83
Werewolf of Washington '73
Wet Hot American Summer '01 ▸
Who Framed Roger Rabbit '88 ▸
The Wrecking Crew '68
The Wrong Guy '96
Wrongfully Accused '98
Young Frankenstein '74 ▸
The Zany Adventures of Robin Hood '84
Zarkorr! The Invader '96

Germany

***see also** Berlin*

Ali: Fear Eats the Soul '74 ▸
Alice in the Cities '74 ▸
All the Queen's Men '02
The Baader Meinhof Complex '08
Backbeat '94 ▸
Beerfest '06
Berlin Alexanderplatz '80 ▸
The Blue Angel '30 ▸
The Boy in the Striped Pajamas '08 ▸
The Bridge '59
The Brothers Grimm '05
Buffalo Soldiers '01
Carnival Story '54
The Damned '69
The Desert Fox '51 ▸
Die Grosse Freiheit Nr. 7 '45
The Dirty Girls '64
Dr. Mabuse, The Gambler '22 ▸
Downfall '04 ▸
Dresden '06
The Edge of Heaven '07 ▸
The Edukators '04
The Empty Mirror '99
Faraway, So Close! '93
Flightplan '05
Flirt '95
Geheimakte WB1 '42
Germany, Pale Mother '80
G.I. Blues '60
The Girl of Your Dreams '99
Go for Zucker '05
The Goebbels Experiment '05
Good '08
Good Bye, Lenin! '03 ▸
The Hamburg Cell '04
The Harmonists '99
Hart's War '02
Head On '04
Hitler: The Last Ten Days '73
Hitler: The Rise of Evil '03
Human Bomb '97
I Was Nineteen '68
The Infiltrator '95
Isn't Life Wonderful '24 ▸
The Ister '04 ▸
Jew-Boy Levi '99
Jud Suess '40 ▸
Kapo '59 ▸
Kaspar Hauser '93
Knife in the Head '78
Landscape After Battle '70
The Legend of Paul and Paula '73
Luther '03
Marianne and Juliane '82 ▸
The Marriage of Maria Braun '79 ▸
Max '02
Mephisto '81 ▸
The Merchant of Four Seasons '71 ▸
Mr. Emmanuel '44
Mostly Martha '01 ▸
Mother Night '96 ▸
Munich '05 ▸
Nico Icon '95 ▸
The Ninth Day '04 ▸
Nuremberg '00
The Odessa File '74
The Ogre '96
Once Upon a Honeymoon '42
Operation Valkyrie '04
Porcile '69
Prelude to War '42
Prince Brat and the Whipping Boy '95 ▸
Prisoner of Paradise '02 ▸
The Promise '94
The Reader '08
Regular Guys '96
Schtonk '92
Schultze Gets the Blues '03
Something for Everyone '70
Sophie Scholl: The Final Days '05 ▸
The Sound of Music '65 ▸
SS Girls '77
The Stationmaster's Wife '77
Swing Kids '93
Tenderness of the Wolves '73
Terror 2000 '92
They Were So Young '55
Three Comrades '38 ▸
Tiefland '44
Town without Pity '61
Triumph of the Will '34 ▸
The Truce '96 ▸
The Tunnel '01 ▸
Underground '41
Unveiled '05
Valkyrie '08
Verdict on Auschwitz: The Frankfurt Auschwitz Trial 1963—1965 '93 ▸
Water Drops on Burning Rocks '99
When Trumpets Fade '98
The White Ribbon '09
Wings of Desire '88 ▸
Woyzeck '78 ▸

Ghosts, Ghouls, & Goblins

***see also** Death & the Afterlife; Demons & Wizards; Occult*

Addicted '02
Afghan Knights '07
All Souls Day '05
Along with Ghosts '69
Amazing Mr. Blunden '72
An American Affair '99
An American Carol '08
An American Haunting '05
An American Werewolf in Paris '97
Apartment 1303 '07
Beetlejuice '88 ▸
Believe '99
Beloved '98
Below '02
Beyond Tomorrow '40
The Black Gate '95
Black Ops '07
Blithe Spirit '45 ▸
Blondie Has Trouble '40
Blood Gnome '02
Blood Pledge '09
Bones '01
Boo! '05
Boogeyman '05
The Brothers Grimm '05
The Canterville Ghost '91
The Canterville Ghost '96
Carved '07
Casper '95 ▸
Cello '05

The Changeling '80
Charlie's Ghost: The Secret of Coronado '94
Children Shouldn't Play with Dead Things '72
A Christmas Carol '84 ►
A Christmas Carol '99
The Club '94
Cold Sweat '93
Conjurer '08
The Cradle '06
Crazy Eights '06
The Crying Child '96
Curse of the Blue Lights '88
Cursed '04
Curtain Call '97
Dark Remains '05
Dark Water '02
Darkness Falls '03
A Dead Calling '06
Dead Cool '04
Deadly Advice '93
Death Dreams '92
Death Magic '92
Death Tunnel '05
Dedication '07
The Devil's Backbone '01
Devil's Den '06
The Diary of Ellen Rimbauer '03
Diecovery '03
Dona Flor and Her Two Husbands '78 ►
Dragonfly '02
Ebenezer '97
El Crimen Perfecto '04
The Empire of Passion '76 ►
Encounter with the Unknown '75
Evil Dead Trap 2: Hideki '91
The Eye '02
The Eye '08
The Eye 2 '04
The Eye 3 '05
Fatally Yours '95
The Fog '78
The Fog '05
For One More Day '07
Forest Warrior '95
Forever: A Ghost of a Love Story '92
The Forgotten One '89
1408 '07
The Frighteners '96
The Fury Within '98
The Gate '87
Genghis Cohn '93
Ghost '90 ►
The Ghost '04
The Ghost and Mrs. Muir '47 ►
The Ghost and Mr. Chicken '66
The Ghost Breakers '40 ►
The Ghost Brigade '93
Ghost Dad '90
The Ghost Goes West '36 ►
Ghost in the Invisible Bikini '66
The Ghost of Dragstrip Hollow '59
The Ghost of Rashmon Hall '47
Ghost on the Loose '43
Ghost Rider '35
Ghost Rider '43
Ghost Ship '53
Ghost Ship '02
Ghost Story '81
Ghost Town '08 ►
Ghostbusters '84 ►
Ghostbusters 2 '89
Ghosts of Berkeley Square '47
Ghosts of Girlfriends Past '09
GhostWatcher '02
The Ghoul '34
Ghouls '07
The Great Yokai War '05
The Green Man '91 ►
The Grudge '04
The Grudge 2 '06
The Grudge 3 '09
Halloween II '09
Halloweentown '98
Halloweentown 2: Kalabar's Revenge '01
Halloweentown High '04
Hangman's Curse '03
The Happiness of the Katakuris '01
Haunted '95
Haunted '98
Haunted Highway '05
Haunted Honeymoon '86
The Haunted Mansion '03
The Haunting '99
The Haunting of Marsten Manor '07
Heart and Souls '93
Heart Condition '90
Heaven's a Drag '94
Hidden Floor '06
High Spirits '88
Hollywood's New Blood '88
House of Darkness '48
The House of Dies Drear '88
House Where Evil Dwells '82
I Downloaded a Ghost '04
The Innocents '61 ►
Inugami '01 ►
The Invisible '07
Ju-On 2 '00
Ju-On: The Grudge '03
Ju-Rei: The Uncanny '04
Just like Heaven '05
Kibakichi '04
Kibakichi 2 '04
The Kingdom '95 ►
The Kingdom 2 '97 ►
Kiss Me Goodbye '82
Knights of Bloodsteel '09
Knocking on Death's Door '99
Kwaidan '64 ►
The Legend of Bloody Mary '08
The Legend of Cryin' Ryan '98
The Legend of Lucy Keyes '06
Life During Wartime '09
Life in the Fast Lane '00
Little Orphan Annie '18
Lost Colony: The Legend of Roanoke '07
Love and Other Four Letter Words '07
Lurking Fear '94
Madhouse '04
The Maid '05
The Man Who Wouldn't Die '42
Memento Mori '00
The Messengers '07
Midnight Bayou '09
The Midnight Phantom '35
Mr. Barrington '03
Mr. Vampire '86
The Morgue '07
The Mummy's Ghost '44
My Friend Walter '93
Mystic Circle Murder '39
Neither the Sea Nor the Sand '73
Never Say Macbeth '07
Night of the Scarecrow '95
Nightmare '00
No End '84
O'Hara's Wife '82
Old Mother Riley's Jungle Treasure '51
100 Feet '08
100 Monsters '68
One Missed Call '03 ►
One Missed Call '08
One Missed Call 2 '05
One Missed Call 3: Final '06
Onmyoji '01
Onmyoji 2 '03
The Orphanage '07 ►
The Others '01 ►
Our Town '03
Over Her Dead Body '08
Paranormal Activity '09 ►
Phantasm 3: Lord of the Dead '94
The Phantom '31
Phantoms '97
Phone '02
Pirates of the Caribbean: Dead Man's Chest '06
Poltergeist '82 ►
Poltergeist 2: The Other Side '86
Poltergeist 3 '88
Poltergeist: The Legacy '96
Pray '05
The Princess and the Goblin '94
Pulse 2: Afterlife '08
Purgatory '99
R-Point '04
Racing Daylight '07
Rasen '98
Red Riding Hood '03
The Red Shoes '05
Reincarnation '05
Rest Stop: Don't Look Back '08
Restless Spirits '99
Retribution '06
Revenge of the Red Baron '93
Riding the Bullet '04
The Ring 2 '05
The Ring Virus '99
Ringu '98 ►
Ringu 0 '01
Ringu 2 '99
The St. Francisville Experiment '00
Sauna '08
Scary Movie 2 '01
Scoop '06
Screaming Dead '03
Seance '00
Seance '06
Seven Keys to Baldpate '17
Seven Keys to Baldpate '29
Seventh Moon '08
Shadow Dancing '88 ►
Shadows '07
Shutter '05
Shutter '08
Silent Hill '06
Silent Tongue '92
The Simian Line '99
The Sixth Man '97
The Sixth Sense '99 ►
Sleepy Hollow '99 ►
Slings & Arrows: Season 2 '05 ►
Snake Woman's Curse '68
Soft for Digging '01
Sometimes They Come Back... Again '96
Somewhere Tomorrow '85
Sorum '01
Soultaker '90
Special Unit 2002 '01
Spectre '96
The Speed Spook '24
The Spiderwick Chronicles '08 ►
Spirit Lost '96
Spirited Away '01
Spook Warfare '68
Stir of Echoes '99
Stir of Echoes 2: The Homecoming '07
Stormswept '95
The Supernaturals '86
Sylvia and the Phantom '45 ►
A Tale of Two Sisters '03 ►
Terror Taxi '04
Things '93
13 Ghosts '60
13 Ghosts '01
3 Extremes 2 '02
The Time of Their Lives '46
To Gillian on Her 37th Birthday '96
Tomie '99
Topper '37 ►
Topper Returns '41 ►
Topper Takes a Trip '39 ►
The Turn of the Screw '74
The Turn of the Screw '92
The Turn of the Screw '99
Twice Dead '88
Ugetsu '53 ►
The Unborn '09
Unborn but Forgotten '02
Under the Sand '00 ►
Undertow '10
The Uninvited '44 ►
The Uninvited '09
Urban Ghost Story '98
Uzumaki '00
Versus '00
Visitor from the Grave '81
The Visitors '89
Visitors '03
Volver '06 ►
The Wailer '06
The Watcher in the Woods '81
Whale Music '94
What Lies Beneath '00
When Good Ghouls Go Bad '01
When I Find the Ocean '06
When Pigs Fly '93
Whispering Corridors '98
White Noise '05
Wind Chill '07
Windrunner '94
The Wishing Stairs '03
Woman in Black '89
Wuthering Heights '98
Younger & Younger '94
Zero Patience '94

Giants

***see also** Monsters, General*
The Amazing Colossal Man '57
Attack of the 50 Foot Woman '58
Attack of the 50 Ft. Woman '93
Attack of the 60-Foot Centerfold '95
Beanstalk '94
Beavis and Butt-Head Do America '96
Big Fish '03 ►
Boggy Creek II '83
Bride of the Monster '55
Cyclops '56
Daimajin '66
The Deadly Mantis '57
Digby, the Biggest Dog in the World '73
Dr. Cyclops '40
Ella Enchanted '04 ►
Evil Alien Conquerors '02
Giant from the Unknown '58
Godzilla vs. Megalon '76
Honey, I Blew Up the Kid '92
Humongous '82
Igor '08
The Iron Giant '99 ►
Josh Kirby... Time Warrior: Chapter 2, The Human Pets '95
Kronos '57
Mighty Joe Young '49
Mighty Joe Young '98
My Giant '98
The Mysterians '58
The Nutty Professor '96 ►
The Phantom Planet '61
The Princess Bride '87 ►
Return of Daimajin '66
The Spy Who Loved Me '77
Starship Troopers '97 ►
Tarantula '55 ►
Teenage Mutant Ninja Turtles: The Movie '90
Teenage Mutant Ninja Turtles 2: The Secret of the Ooze '91
Them! '54 ►
Tremors '89
Tremors 2: Aftershocks '96
Village of the Giants '65
The War of the Colossal Beast '58
Wrath of Daimajin '66
Zarkorr! The Invader '96

Gifted Children

***see also** Childhood Visions*
And You Thought Your Parents Were Weird! '91
Bee Season '05 ►
Dangerous Holiday '37
Dear Brigitte '65
Escape to Witch Mountain '75 ►
Joshua '07 ►
Lemony Snicket's A Series of Unfortunate Events '04
Little Man Tate '91 ►
Loverboy '05
Matilda '96 ►
On the Right Track '81
Powder '95
Push '09
Real Genius '85 ►
Rookie of the Year '93
Searching for Bobby Fischer '93 ►
Valentin '02

Glasgow

***see also** Scotland*
American Cousins '02
Beautiful Creatures '00
The Big Tease '99
Carla's Song '97
Comfort and Joy '84 ►
Dear Frankie '04
Doomsday '08
A Fond Kiss '04
My Name Is Joe '98
Nina's Heavenly Delights '06
On a Clear Day '05
Orphans '97
The Purifiers '04
Red Road '06
Small Faces '95 ►
Wilbur Wants to Kill Himself '02 ►

Go Fish

***see also** Deep Blue; Killer Sea Critters*
Alamo Bay '85
Almost Heaven '06
Around the World Under the Sea '65
Bait Shop '08
Big Fish '03 ►
Black Water '94
Bright Future '03 ►
Calm at Sunset '96
Captains Courageous '37 ►
Captains Courageous '95
Darwin's Nightmare '04 ►
The Day of the Dolphin '73
Detour to Danger '45
Dodson's Journey '01
Doomwatch '72
Finding Nemo '03 ►
A Fish Called Wanda '88 ►
Flipper '96 ►
Forrest Gump '94 ►
Frankenfish '04
Free Willy '93
Gone Fishin' '97
Grumpier Old Men '95
Grumpy Old Men '93 ►
The Incredible Mr. Limpet '64
The Islander '88
Islander '06
The Isle '01
It Came from Beneath the Sea '55 ►
Jaws '75 ►
Jaws 2 '78
Jaws 3 '83
Jaws: The Revenge '87
Johnny Frenchman '46
Killer Fish '79
La Terra Trema '48 ►
The Life Aquatic with Steve Zissou '04
Like a Fish Out of Water '99
Limbo '99
Love Serenade '96
Maelstrom '00
Man of Aran '34 ►
Man's Favorite Sport? '63
Megalodon '03
Milwaukee, Minnesota '03
Mr. Peabody & the Mermaid '48
Moby Dick '56 ►
Moby Dick '98
My Summer Story '94
92 in the Shade '76 ►
Northern Extremes '93
The Old Man and the Sea '58 ►
The Old Man and the Sea '90
On Golden Pond '81 ►
Orca '77
Out of the Fog '41
Ponyo '08 ►
Red Water '01
Respiro '02
Riff Raff '35
A River Runs Through It '92 ►
Scorpion with Two Tails '82
The Sea '02
Seducing Doctor Lewis '03
The Seventh Stream '01
Shark Hunter '79
Shark Tale '04
Sixteen Fathoms Deep '34
Spawn of the North '38
Spoilers of the North '47
The SpongeBob SquarePants Movie '04
Tabu: A Story of the South Seas '31 ►
Thunder Bay '53 ►
Tiger Shark '32
The Treasure of Jamaica Reef '74
Undertow '10
Up from the Depths '79
Wallaby Jim of the Islands '37
Whale for the Killing '81
Where the Hot Wind Blows '59
The Wide Blue Road '57 ►
Zeus and Roxanne '96

Going Native

Apocalypse Now '79 ►
The Blue Lagoon '80
The Bounty '84
Congo '95
Dances with Wolves '90 ►
The Emerald Forest '85 ►
Farewell to the King '89
George of the Jungle '97 ►
Grizzly Adams: The Legend Continues '90
Jeremiah Johnson '72 ►
Jungle 2 Jungle '96
Krippendorf's Tribe '98
Little Indian, Big City '95
Lord of the Flies '63 ►
Lord of the Flies '90
A Man Called Horse '70 ►
The Mosquito Coast '86
Mutiny on the Bounty '35 ►
Mutiny on the Bounty '62
Pagan Island '60
Paradise '82
The Return of a Man Called Horse '76
Robinson Crusoe '36
A Stranger Among Us '92
The Swiss Family Robinson '60 ►
Up to His Neck '54

Going Postal

Cop Au Vin '85
Dead Letter Office '98
Dear God '96
84 Charing Cross Road '86 ►
Going Postal '98
He Was a Quiet Man '07
The Inspectors '98
The Inspectors 2: A Shred of Evidence '00
Junk Mail '97
Letter from an Unknown Woman '48 ►
A Letter to Three Wives '49 ►
Letters from a Killer '98
The Minus Man '99
Overnight Delivery '96
Postal Inspector '36
The Postman '94 ►
The Postman '97
Postman's Knock '62
See Spot Run '01
The Shop Around the Corner '40 ►
Side Street '50
You've Got Mail '98

Going Straight

***see also** Ex-Cons*
Action Man '67
Almost an Angel '90
Angels with Dirty Faces '38 ►
Baby, Take a Bow '34
The Badlanders '58
Barbershop '02 ►
Bloodhounds of Broadway '52
Bloodhounds of Broadway '89
Boogie Boy '98
Boy A '07
Carlito's Way '93 ►
Chain Link '08
Colorado Territory '49
Confessions of a Pit Fighter '05

► = rated three bones or higher

Golf

Gospel Music

Governesses

see The Help: Female; Nannies & Governesses

Grand Hotel

see also No-Exit Motel

Grand Theft Auto

Grandparents

Great Britain

see also Ireland; London; Scotland

► = rated three bones or higher

Goodbye, Mr. Chips '69
Goodbye, Mr. Chips '02
Goodnight, Mr. Tom '99
Gosford Park '01 ▸
Grave Indiscretions '96
Great Expectations: The Untold Story '87
The Great Muppet Caper '81 ▸
The Green Man '91 ▸
Greenfingers '00
Gulliver's Travels '95
Harnessing Peacocks '92
Harry Potter and the Goblet of Fire '05 ▸
Haunted '95
The Hellfire Club '61
High Hopes '88 ▸
The History Boys '06
The History of Mr. Polly '07
The Holiday '06
Hot Fuzz '07 ▸
The Hours '02 ▸
House of Cards '90 ▸
The House of Eliott '92
The House of Secrets '37
How Green Was My Valley '41 ▸
I Capture the Castle '02
I'll Be There '03
Imagine Me & You '06
The Importance of Being Earnest '02
In His Life: The John Lennon Story '00
The Innocents '61 ▸
Inspector Clouseau '68
Intimate Relations '95
Invincible Mr. Disraeli '63
Iris '01 ▸
The Iron Duke '34
Jack Higgins' On Dangerous Ground '95
Jamaica Inn '82
Jane Eyre '96 ▸
Jane Eyre '97
Johnny English '03
Jude '96 ▸
Killing Time '97
King Ralph '91
The King's Thief '55
Ladies in Lavender '04
Lady Chatterley '06 ▸
Lady Jane '85 ▸
The Lady's Not for Burning '87
The Land Girls '98
Lara Croft: Tomb Raider '01
The Last of England '87 ▸
Lawless Heart '01
The Libertine '05
Lillie '79 ▸
The Lion in Winter '68 ▸
Lipstick on Your Collar '94
Lloyds of London '36 ▸
Lock, Stock and 2 Smoking Barrels '98 ▸
The Long Day Closes '92 ▸
The Long Good Friday '80 ▸
Looking for Richard '96 ▸
Lorna Doone '34
Lorna Doone '90
Lorna Doone '01 ▸
Love for Lydia '79 ▸
Lucky Break '01
Madagascar Skin '95
Made in Heaven '52
The Madness of King George '94 ▸
A Man for All Seasons '66 ▸
A Man for All Seasons '88 ▸
The Man from the Pru '89
The Man in Grey '45 ▸
The Man Who Knew Too Little '97
Mapp & Lucia '85
Mary of Scotland '36 ▸
Merlin '98 ▸
A Midwinter's Tale '95
The Mill on the Floss '37
The Mill on the Floss '97
Millions '05 ▸
A Mind to Murder '96
Miss Potter '06
Mrs. Brown '97 ▸
Mrs. Miniver '42 ▸
Mrs. Palfrey at the Claremont '05
Mister Drake's Duck '50
Mr. Toad's Wild Ride '96
The Moonraker '58
Mosley '98
The Mother '03 ▸
Munster, Go Home! '66
Murder Elite '86
My Brother Tom '86
My Summer of Love '05
My Uncle Silas '01 ▸
Naked '93 ▸
The Naked Civil Servant '75 ▸
Nanny McPhee '06
National Lampoon's Van Wilder 2: The Rise of Taj '06
The New World '05 ▸
Night Must Fall '37 ▸
Nine Days a Queen '36 ▸
No Kidding '60
No Surrender '86 ▸
None But the Lonely Heart '44 ▸
Of Time and the City '08
Oh! What a Lovely War '69
Oliver Twist '05 ▸
The Omen '06
Once Upon a Time in the Midlands '02
Pack of Lies '87
Pandaemonium '00
Passport to Pimlico '49
Persuasion '95 ▸
Pictures '81
Pink String and Sealing Wax '45
Pirate Radio '09
Plenty '85
Poldark '75 ▸
Portrait of a Lady '96 ▸
Pride and Prejudice '95 ▸
Pride and Prejudice '05 ▸
Prince of Poisoners: The Life and Crimes of William Palmer '98
Princess Caraboo '94
The Proposition '96
Pure '02 ▸
The Queen's Sister '05
A Question of Attribution '91
Raffles '30 ▸
The Railway Children '70 ▸
The Railway Children '00 ▸
Reckless '97 ▸
Reckless: The Sequel '98 ▸
The Reckoning '03 ▸
The Red Violin '98
A Respectable Trade '98
The Return of the Native '94
Return to Cranford '09
Rhodes '97
Richard III '12
Richard III '95 ▸
The Riddle of the Sands '79
Riders '88
Riff Raff '92 ▸
Robbery '67
Room to Let '49
A Royal Scandal '96
Royal Wedding '51 ▸
The Ruling Class '72 ▸
The Saint '97
Say Hello to Yesterday '71
Scandal '89 ▸
The Scarlet Tunic '97
Scoop '06
The Secret Garden '49 ▸
Secret of the Black Trunk '62
The Seeker: The Dark Is Rising '07
Sense and Sensibility '95 ▸
The Serpent's Kiss '97
The Servant '63 ▸
Shadowlands '93 ▸
Shanghai Knights '03
Shaun of the Dead '04 ▸
Shopping '93
Silver Dream Racer '83
Six Wives of Henry VIII '71 ▸
Soldier in Love '67
Son of Rambow '07
South Riding '37
Speedy Death '99 ▸
Split Second '92
Starter for Ten '06
Station Jim '01
The Stick-Up '77
Stiff Upper Lips '96
Still Crazy '98 ▸
Strange Relations '02
Sweet Revenge '98
Swept from the Sea '97
Sylvia '03
Tess of the D'Urbervilles '08
Testament of Youth '79
That Sinking Feeling '79 ▸
This England '42
Those Magnificent Men in Their Flying Machines '65 ▸
To Play the King '93 ▸
Tom Jones '98 ▸
A Touch of Class '73 ▸
Tristan & Isolde '06
Tristram Shandy: A Cock and Bull Story '05
Tunes of Glory '60 ▸
24 Hour Party People '01
Under the Skin '97
Vacuuming Completely Nude in Paradise '01
Valiant '05
Vanity Fair '04
Velvet Goldmine '98
A Very British Coup '88 ▸
Victoria Regina '61
A Village Affair '95
The Virgin Queen '55 ▸
Wallace & Gromit in The Curse of the Were-Rabbit '05 ▸
Warrior Queen '03
We Think the World of You '88 ▸
We'll Meet Again '82
When Saturday Comes '95
Whiskey Galore '48 ▸
The Whistle Blower '87 ▸
The White Cliffs of Dover '44 ▸
Wives and Daughters '01
The Wolves of Kromer '98
The Woman He Loved '88
Woman in Black '89
A Woman of Substance '84
Wondrous Oblivion '06 ▸
Wuthering Heights '39 ▸
Yanks '79
Year of the Comet '92
The Young Americans '93
Young Bess '53 ▸
The Young Victoria '09 ▸
Young Winston '72 ▸

Great Death Scenes

see also *Death & the Afterlife; Funerals*
Bonnie & Clyde '67 ▸
Breaker Morant '80 ▸
Bring Me the Head of Alfredo Garcia '74
Buffy the Vampire Slayer '92 ▸
Butch Cassidy and the Sundance Kid '69 ▸
Camille '36 ▸
The Champ '79
Coquette '29
Dangerous Liaisons '88 ▸
Dark Victory '39 ▸
Demolition Man '93
Die Hard: With a Vengeance '95
Evita '96
Face/Off '97 ▸
From Dusk Till Dawn '95
Gallipoli '81 ▸
Gettysburg '93 ▸
Glory '89 ▸
The Godfather '72 ▸
The Green Mile '99
Highlander '86 ▸
Highlander: The Gathering '92
Jeanne la Pucelle '94
Joan of Arc '99
John Carpenter's Vampires '97
Johnny Mnemonic '95
Jude '96 ▸
Julius Caesar '53 ▸
Jurassic Park '93 ▸
The Last Temptation of Christ '88 ▸
The Lost World: Jurassic Park 2 '97
Mimi '35
Monty Python and the Holy Grail '75 ▸
The Omen '76
The Omen '06
The Passion of the Christ '04 ▸
Pat Garrett & Billy the Kid '73 ▸
Psycho '60 ▸
Public Enemy '31 ▸
Scream '96 ▸
Shadowlands '93 ▸
A Song to Remember '45 ▸
Starship Troopers '97 ▸
Strangers on a Train '51 ▸
Things to Do in Denver When You're Dead '95 ▸
Valmont '89 ▸
The Wizard of Oz '39 ▸

Great Depression

see also *Hard Knock Life; Homeless*
After the Promise '87
All the King's Men '49 ▸
American Madness '32
Angela's Ashes '99
Annie '99 ▸
Ask the Dust '06
The Assistant '97
Baby Face Nelson '97
The Ballad of the Sad Cafe '91
Big Bad Mama '74
Big Bad Mama 2 '87
Billy Bathgate '91
Bloody Mama '70
Bonnie & Clyde '67 ▸
Bound for Glory '76 ▸
Boxcar Bertha '72
Catherine Cookson's The Man Who Cried '93
Charley and the Angel '73
Chinatown '74 ▸
A Christmas to Remember '78
Cinderella Man '05 ▸
The Cradle Will Rock '99
Dance Fools Dance '31 ▸
Dillinger '45 ▸
Dillinger '73
Dillinger '91
Dillinger and Capone '95
Dogville '03
Dream Chasers '82
Eleanor & Franklin '76 ▸
Emperor of the North Pole '73 ▸
Falling for a Dancer '98
Fatty Finn '84
Four Deuces '75
Fresh Horses '88
The Funeral '96 ▸
The Grapes of Wrath '40 ▸
The Green Mile '99
The Group '66
Hallelujah, I'm a Bum '33
Hard Times '75 ▸
Hard Traveling '85
Henry & Verlin '94
Hidden Places '06
Hit the Dutchman '92
Homecoming: A Christmas Story '71
Honkytonk Man '82
Hoodlum '96
Hunter's Moon '97
In a Savage Land '99
The Inheritors '98
Inside Daisy Clover '65
Ironweed '87 ▸
It Happened One Night '34 ▸
The Journey of Natty Gann '85 ▸
Just Around the Corner '38
Kansas City '95 ▸
King Kong '05 ▸
The King of Masks '99 ▸
King of the Hill '93 ▸
Kingfish: A Story of Huey P. Long '95
Kit Kittredge: An American Girl '08 ▸
The Lady in Question '99
Last Man Standing '96
Laurel & Hardy: Below Zero '30
Life '99
The Life and Times of Hank Greenberg '99 ▸
Long Road Home '91
Love on the Dole '41 ▸
Make Way for Tomorrow '37
Melvin Purvis: G-Man '74
Mrs. Henderson Presents '05
Modern Times '36 ▸
Morning Glory '93
O Brother Where Art Thou? '00
Of Mice and Men '39 ▸
Of Mice and Men '81 ▸
Of Mice and Men '92 ▸
Oscar '91
Our Daily Bread '34 ▸
The Outfit '93
Paper Moon '73 ▸
Pennies from Heaven '81 ▸
The Piano Lesson '94 ▸
Places in the Heart '84 ▸
Possessed '31
The Postman Always Rings Twice '46 ▸
The Postman Always Rings Twice '81
Public Enemies '96
Public Enemies '09
Rambling Rose '91 ▸
The Road Home '95
The Saddest Music in the World '03
Seabiscuit '03 ▸
Shadrach '98
Sir Arthur Conan Doyle's The Lost World '98
Sounder '72 ▸
The Stars Fell on Henrietta '94
Street Scene '31 ▸
Sullivan's Travels '41 ▸
Sweet and Lowdown '99
The Tale of Ruby Rose '87 ▸
They Shoot Horses, Don't They? '69 ▸
Thieves Like Us '74 ▸
The Twelve Dogs of Christmas '05
Two Bits '96
Victor/Victoria '82 ▸
Voices from a Locked Room '95
The Water Engine '92
White Hot: The Mysterious Murder of Thelma Todd '91
Who Has Seen the Wind? '77
Why Shoot the Teacher '79 ▸
Wild Boys of the Road '33
Wild Hearts Can't Be Broken '91 ▸
Wildflower '91 ▸
William Faulkner's Old Man '97
Winter People '89
The Yearling '94
You Only Live Once '37

Great Escapes

see also *Men in Prison; POW/MIA; War, General; Women in Prison*
Alias, La Gringa '91
The Ascent '94
Assassination '87
Austin Powers: International Man of Mystery '97 ▸
Bandits '99
Before Night Falls '00 ▸
Berlin Tunnel 21 '81
The Big Doll House '71
Blindness '08
Blood on the Mountain '88
Born to Be Wild '95
Brady's Escape '84
The Break '97
Breakout '75
Brute Force '47 ▸
Butch Cassidy and the Sundance Kid '69 ▸
Caged Fear '92
Captain Nemo and the Underwater City '69
The Chase '66
Chasers '94
Chicken Run '00 ▸
Chronicle of an Escape '06
City of Fear '59
The Colditz Story '55
Con Air '97 ▸
Condition Red '95
Crashout '55
A Day in October '92
Deadlock 2 '94
Deadly Mission '78
Deadly Target '94
The Deer Hunter '78 ▸
Desperate '47
Desperate Measures '98
Diamonds of the Night '64 ▸
Die Hard '88 ▸
Die Hard: With a Vengeance '95
Dirty Heroes '71
Double Team '97
Down by Law '86 ▸
Era Notte a Roma '60 ▸
Escape '90
The Escape Artist '82 ▸
Escape from Alcatraz '79 ▸
Escape from Atlantis '97
Escape from Cell Block 3 '74
Escape from Death Row '73
Escape from El Diablo '83
Escape from Fort Bravo '53
Escape from Galaxy Three '81
Escape from Hell '79
Escape from L.A. '96
Escape from Mars '99
Escape from New York '81
Escape from Safehaven '88
Escape from Sobibor '87 ▸
Escape from the KGB '87
Escape: Human Cargo '98 ▸
Escape to Love '82
Escape to Witch Mountain '75 ▸
Escapist '83
Extremely Dangerous '99
Face/Off '97 ▸
Fantastic Voyage '66 ▸
The Fast Runner '01 ▸
Fast Walking '82
Feeling Minnesota '96
Flame Over India '60 ▸
Fled '96
Flight from Vienna '56
Follow the River '95
Fortress '93
Fortress 2: Re-Entry '99
The Four Feathers '02
Frenchman's Creek '44
Frenchman's Creek '98
Gang Busters '55
Girls in Prison '56
The Grave '95
The Great Escape '63 ▸
The Great Escape 2: The Untold Story '88
The Great Train Robbery '79 ▸
Hangfire '91
Harold & Kumar Escape from Guantanamo Bay '08
Hart's War '02
Heaven '01
Hellraiser 5: Inferno '00
Hide '08
The Horseman on the Roof '95
Hostile Intentions '94
Houdini '53
Houdini '99
I Am David '04
The Ice Runner '93
In Hot Pursuit '77
The Inglorious Bastards '78
Inside Out '75
Iron Eagle '86
The Island '05
Jailbreakin' '72
Kidnapped '95
La Nuit de Varennes '82 ▸
Ladyhawke '85
The Last Confederate: The Story of Robert Adams '05
The Last Samurai '90
Le Trou '59 ▸
Leaving Normal '92
Les Miserables '35 ▸
Les Miserables '57 ▸
Les Miserables '78 ▸
Les Violons du Bal '74
Lonely Are the Brave '62 ▸
The Long Riders '80 ▸
Lords of the Street '08
Lucky Break '01

▸ = *rated three bones or higher*

Macho Callahan '70
Madagascar '05
A Man Escaped '57 ▸
The Man Who Broke 1,000 Chains '87
The Manhunt '86
McKenzie Break '70 ▸
McVicar '80
Midnight Edition '93
Midnight Express '78 ▸
Missing in Action '84
Mrs. Soffel '84
The Mole People '56
Monte Cristo '22
Murder in the First '95
Murder One '88
The Muthers '76
Mysterious Island '61 ▸
Naked Youth '59
Night Crossing '81
No Escape '94
North by Northwest '59 ▸
Not Without My Daughter '90
On Wings of Eagles '86
One That Got Away '57 ▸
Operation Thunderbolt '77
Pacific Inferno '85
Papillon '73 ▸
Passage to Marseilles '44 ▸
A Perfect World '93
Poseidon '06
Prison Break '38
Prison Break: The Final Break '09
The Prize '63 ▸
The Promise '94
Public Enemies '09
Raiders of the Lost Ark '81 ▸
Raising Arizona '87 ▸
Raw Deal '48 ▸
Rescue Dawn '06 ▸
Ricochet '91 ▸
Rob Roy '95 ▸
The Rock '96 ▸
Romancing the Stone '84 ▸
Romeo Must Die '00
Run '91
Runaway Train '85 ▸
The Saint '97
St. Ives '98
Samar '62
The Secret War of Harry Frigg '68
The Seventh Cross '44 ▸
The Seventh Floor '93
The Shawshank Redemption '94 ▸
The Shining '80
Six: The Mark Unleashed '04
Skin Game '71 ▸
The Sound of Music '65 ▸
The Spy Who Came in from the Cold '65 ▸
Stalag 17 '53 ▸
Stalag Luft '93
Strange Cargo '40
Strike Back '80
The Sugarland Express '74 ▸
Sweet Poison '91
Tequila Sunrise '88
Teresa's Tattoo '94
Texas Payback '95
Three Days of the Condor '75 ▸
Thunder County '74
To Catch a Thief '55 ▸
Torn Curtain '66
Toy Story '95 ▸
Toy Story 2 '99 ▸
Train of Life '98
The Truman Show '98 ▸
UKM: The Ultimate Killing Machine '06
Venus Rising '95
Very Important Person '61
Victory '81
Violent Women '59
Von Ryan's Express '65 ▸
Warbus '85
Welcome to Woop Woop '97
We're No Angels '55 ▸
White Nights '85
The Wild '06
Women Unchained '72
Wooden Horse '50 ▸
XXX: State of the Union '05
Zebra in the Kitchen '65

Greece—Ancient

Alexander '04
Alexander the Great '55
Atlantis, the Lost Continent '61
Barefoot in Athens '66
Clash of the Titans '81
Clash of the Titans '10
Conquest of Mycene '63
Helen of Troy '56
Helen of Troy '03
Iphigenia '77 ▸
Jason and the Argonauts '63 ▸
Jason and the Argonauts '00
The Lion of Thebes '64 ▸
The Loves of Hercules '60
Medea '70
Medusa Against the Son of Hercules '62
Meet the Spartans '08
The Odyssey '97
300 '07
The 300 Spartans '62
The Triumph of Hercules '66
The Trojan Horse '62
Trojan Women '71
Troy '04

Greece—Modern

Captain Corelli's Mandolin '01
The Case of the Scorpion's Tail '71
Eleni '85
Fishtales '07
Forty Carats '73
I Live My Life '35
Jupiter's Thigh '81
Mamma Mia! '08
The Mediterranean in Flames '72
Murderball '05 ▸
My Life in Ruins '09
Shirley Valentine '89 ▸
Signs & Wonders '00
Sisterhood of the Traveling Pants '05
The Sisterhood of the Traveling Pants 2 '08
Weeping Meadow '04
Z '69 ▸

Grim Reaper

***see also** Death & the Afterlife*

The Adventures of Baron Munchausen '89 ▸
Bill & Ted's Bogus Journey '91
Death Takes a Holiday '34 ▸
El Crimen Perfecto '04
The Exorcist 2: The Heretic '77
Exorcist 3: Legion '90
Exorcist: The Beginning '04
Final Destination '00
Final Destination 2 '03
Final Destination 3 '06
The Frighteners '96
Last Action Hero '93
Meet Joe Black '98
Monty Python's The Meaning of Life '83 ▸
The Order '03
Riding the Bullet '04
The Seventh Seal '56 ▸
Soul Survivors '01

Growing Older

***see also** Death & the Afterlife; Grandparents; Impending Retirement; Late Bloomin' Love*

About Schmidt '02 ▸
After the Rehearsal '84 ▸
Age Isn't Everything '91
Age Old Friends '89 ▸
Amos '85
The Angel Levine '70
Anima '98
Anna '87 ▸
Another Lonely Hitman '95
Any Number Can Win '63
Around the Bend '04
Around the World in 80 Ways '86
As Young As You Feel '51 ▸
Atlantic City '81 ▸
Aurora Borealis '06
Autumn Leaves '56
Autumn Tale '98
Away From Her '06 ▸
The Ballad of Narayama '83 ▸
The Banger Sisters '02
*batteries not included '87
Before I Forget '07
Belle Toujours '06 ▸
The Best of Times '86
Better Late Than Never '79
Blue Moon '00
The Boynton Beach Club '05
Breathing Lessons '94 ▸
Bubba Ho-Tep '03 ▸
The Bucket List '07
Buena Vista Social Club '99 ▸
Bullet to Beijing '95
Camilla '94
Captain Kronos: Vampire Hunter '74 ▸
Casanova '05 ▸
The Cemetery Club '93
Central Station '98 ▸
Changing Times '04
Charles: Dead or Alive '69
Chasing Butterflies '94
The Cheyenne Social Club '70
Children of Nature '91
Chimes at Midnight '67 ▸
Choices '86
The Christmas Box '95
Citizen Kane '41 ▸
City Slickers '91 ▸
Cobb '94 ▸
Cocoon '85 ▸
Cocoon: The Return '88
Collected Stories '02 ▸
The Color of Evening '95
Come Along with Me '84
The Conductor '80
Cooperstown '93
Crazy Heart '09
The Curious Case of Benjamin Button '08 ▸
Dad '89
Daddy Nostalgia '90 ▸
Death Becomes Her '92 ▸
Death of a Salesman '86 ▸
The Death of Mr. Lazarescu '05
Diamonds '99
Don't Come Knocking '05
Dorian Gray '70
Draw! '81
Dream a Little Dream '89
Dream Chasers '82
Dreaming of Rita '94
Driving Miss Daisy '89 ▸
Duck '05
Duplex '03
Early Days '81
Easy Living '49
Eating '90
Ebony Tower '86
Elegy '08
Emma's Wish '98
An Empty Bed '90 ▸
The Enchanted Forest '45
Enemies of Laughter '00
An Englishman in New York '09
The Evening Star '96
Facing Windows '03
Family Upside Down '78 ▸
Fantasy Man '84
Father of the Bride Part 2 '95
The Field '90 ▸
The Final Hit '02
The Firemen's Ball '68 ▸
Fly Boy '99
Folks! '92
For Love of the Game '99
A Foreign Field '93
Forever Young '92
Forget About It '06
Forty Carats '73
Forty Shades of Blue '05
Foxfire '87 ▸
The Gathering Storm '02 ▸
Getting Up and Going Home '92
Gideon '99
Gin Game '84 ▸
Ginger & Fred '86 ▸
The Girl from Paris '02 ▸
The Godfather, Part 3 '90 ▸
Gods and Monsters '98 ▸
Going in Style '79 ▸
The Golden Boys '08
The Good Guys and the Bad Guys '69
The Good Old Boys '95
The Good Thief '03 ▸
The Goodbye People '83
Goodbye Solo '08
Goodnight, Mr. Tom '99
Grace & Glorie '98
Grace Quigley '84
Gran Torino '08 ▸
The Grandfather '98
Great Smokey Roadblock '76
Greedy '94
Grumpier Old Men '95
Grumpy Old Men '93 ▸
Hamsun '96
Hanging Up '99
Happy Tears '09
Harakiri '62 ▸
Hard Labour '73
Hardbodies '84
Harry and Tonto '74 ▸
Heading South '05 ▸
Home Free All '84
Home Is Where the Hart Is '88
Home to Stay '79
Homebodies '74
Horton Foote's Alone '97
How About You '07
The Hunger '83
Hurry Up or I'll Be Thirty '73
Husbands '70
Hush, Hush, Sweet Charlotte '65 ▸
I Can't Sleep '93
I'm Going Home '00 ▸
I'm Not Rappaport '96
In Custody '94
The Incredible Mrs. Ritchie '03
Iris '01 ▸
Iris Blond '98
Iron Horsemen '71
Is Anybody There? '08
Judy Berlin '99
Killing Grandpa '91
King Lear '98 ▸
The King of Masks '99 ▸
Kotch '71 ▸
Lamerica '95 ▸
Larry McMurtry's Streets of Laredo '95 ▸
The Last Days of Frankie the Fly '96
The Last Good Time '94
The Last Laugh '24 ▸
The Last Lieutenant '94
The Last Station '09
Late Chrysanthemums '54
The Leech Woman '59
Lifeguard '76
Light Sleeper '92
Lightning Jack '94
Lilian's Story '95
The Limey '99 ▸
Lip Service '88 ▸
Local Color '06
The Locket '02
Lost for Words '99 ▸
Love Among the Ruins '75 ▸
Love Comes Lately '07
Ma Saison Preferee '93 ▸
Mafia! '98
The Magic Bubble '93
Make Way for Tomorrow '37
Mama Turns a Hundred '79 ▸
The Man on the Train '02 ▸
The Man Upstairs '93
Marathon '80
Martin Chuzzlewit '94
Meet Joe Black '98
The Memory of a Killer '03
Middle Age Crazy '80
Mind the Gap '04
Miss Firecracker '89 ▸
Mrs. Dalloway '97
Mrs. Palfrey at the Claremont '05
Mr. Saturday Night '92
Money to Burn '83
Monte Walsh '70 ▸
Monte Walsh '03
Moving Malcolm '03
My Heroes Have Always Been Cowboys '91
Neil Simon's The Odd Couple 2 '98
Never Again '01
Next of Kin '82
The Next Step '95
No Sleep 'Til Madison '02
Nobody's Fool '94 ▸
The Notebook '04
Off Your Rocker '80
O'Horten '09
Old Explorers '90
The Old Lady Who Walked in the Sea '91
The Old Man and the Sea '58 ▸
The Old Man and the Sea '90
Oldest Living Graduate '80 ▸
On Golden Pond '81 ▸
One Hundred and One Nights '95
Our Lady of the Assassins '01
Out of the Fog '41
The Out-of-Towners '99
Over the Hill '93
Pals '87
Pastime '91 ▸
Pauline and Paulette '01
Pelle the Conqueror '88 ▸
A Piano for Mrs. Cimino '82 ▸
The Pickle '93
Picture of Dorian Gray '45 ▸
Picture of Dorian Gray '74 ▸
The Portrait '93 ▸
The Private Life of Henry VIII '33 ▸
Pushing Hands '92
Queens Logic '91
The Quiet American '02 ▸
Rabid Grannies '89
Ran '85 ▸
A Rather English Marriage '98
The Rejuvenator '88
Return of the Rebels '81
Rhapsody in August '91
The Road to Galveston '96 ▸
Rocket Gibraltar '88 ▸
Rocky Balboa '06
Roommates '95
Rooster Cogburn '75
Roses Bloom Twice '77
The Rounders '65
Ruby Jean and Joe '96
Safe House '99
Satanik '69
The Savages '07 ▸
Sea People '00
The Set-Up '49 ▸
Seven Thieves '60 ▸
The Shell Seekers '89
Shirley Valentine '89 ▸
A Shock to the System '90 ▸
The Shootist '76 ▸
Side by Side '88
The Silent Touch '94
The Simple Life of Noah Dearborn '99
Soft for Digging '01
The Son of the Bride '01
A Song for Martin '01
Space Cowboys '00 ▸
Standing in the Shadows of Motown '02 ▸
Star Trek: Insurrection '98
Starting Out in the Evening '07
Stephen King's Golden Years '91
The Stone Angel '07
The Straight Story '99 ▸
Strangers in Good Company '91 ▸
Street Music '81
Summer Snow '94
Summer Solstice '81
Summer Wishes, Winter Dreams '73
The Sunshine Boys '75 ▸
The Sunshine Boys '95
Tatie Danielle '91 ▸
Tell Me a Riddle '80
Texas Guns '90
That Evening Sun '09 ▸
That's Life! '86
These Old Broads '01
Things Change '88 ▸
30 Is a Dangerous Age, Cynthia '68
Three Days to Vegas '07
Three Strange Loves '49 ▸
To Dance with the White Dog '93 ▸
To Forget Venice '79
Tokyo Story '53 ▸
Toto le Heros '91 ▸
Tough Guys '86
Traveling Companion '96
Tuesdays with Morrie '99
Twilight '98 ▸
Two for the Road '67 ▸
Two of a Kind '82
2 Seconds '98
Two Weeks in Another Town '62
Umberto D '55 ▸
Unforgiven '92 ▸
Unhook the Stars '96
Up '09 ▸
Venus '06 ▸
Voyage of the Heart '90
Voyage to the Beginning of the World '96 ▸
Waltzing Anna '06
The Wasp Woman '59
The Wendell Baker Story '05
The Whales of August '87 ▸
When a Woman Ascends the Stairs '60
Where the Money Is '00
The Wild Bunch '69 ▸
Wild Horses '95
Wild Strawberries '57 ▸
A Woman's Tale '92 ▸
The World's Fastest Indian '05 ▸
Wrestling Ernest Hemingway '93
Yes Nurse! No Nurse! '02
Young@Heart '07 ▸

Gunslingers

***see also** Pardners; Second Chance; Western Comedy; Westerns; Westrogens*

Aces 'n Eights '08
Adios, Sabata '71
The Alamo '04
Angel and the Badman '09
Appaloosa '08 ▸
The Assassination of Jesse James by the Coward Robert Ford '07 ▸
Black Patch '57
Blind Justice '94
Cat Ballou '65 ▸
Cjamango '67
Dear Wendy '05
Death of a Gunfighter '69
Decision at Sundown '57
The Desperadoes '43
Dust '01
El Dorado '67 ▸
A Fistful of Dollars '64 ▸
For a Few Dollars More '65
Forty Guns '57
Four Fast Guns '59
From Noon Till Three '76
The Gambler, the Girl and the Gunslinger '09
A Gunfight '71
Gunfight at the O.K. Corral '57 ▸
The Gunfighter '50 ▸
Gunfighter '98
Gunfighter's Moon '96
Gunslinger '70
The Hanged Man '74
High Noon '52 ▸
High Noon '00
Jonah Hex '10
The Legend of Butch & Sundance '04
The Long Ride Home '01
The Magnificent Seven '60 ▸
Man From God's Country '58
The Man Who Shot Liberty Valance '62 ▸
More Dead Than Alive '68
My Darling Clementine '46 ▸
Once Upon a Time in the West '68 ▸
The Outsider '02
Panhandle '48

The Quick and the Dead '87
The Quick and the Dead '95
Return of Sabata '71
Rio Bravo '59 ▶
Sabata '69
Shane '53 ▶
Shanghai Noon '00
The Sheepman '58
The Shootist '76 ▶
Sukiyaki Western Django '08
Support Your Local Gunfighter '71 ▶
3:10 to Yuma '07 ▶
Ticket to Tomahawk '50
Tombstone '93 ▶
Unforgiven '92 ▶
Westworld '73 ▶
Wyatt Earp '94

Gymnastics

American Anthem '86
Breaking Free '95
Dream to Believe '85
The Gymnast '06
I Was a Teenage Werewolf '57
Nadia '84
Peaceful Warrior '06
Stick It '06

Gypsies

The Advocate '93 ▶
Angelo My Love '83 ▶
Babes in Toyland '61
Black Cat, White Cat '98 ▶
Carmen '83 ▶
Carmen '03
Chocolat '00 ▶
Drag Me to Hell '09
The Hunchback '97
The Hunchback of Notre Dame '23 ▶
The Hunchback of Notre Dame '39 ▶
The Hunchback of Notre Dame '57
The Hunchback of Notre Dame '82 ▶
The Hunchback of Notre Dame '96 ▶
In the Arms of My Enemy '07
Incredibly Strange Creatures Who Stopped Living and Became Mixed-Up Zombies '63
Into the West '92 ▶
King of the Gypsies '78
Le Gitan '75
Little Minister '34 ▶
Love Potion #9 '92
The Man Who Cried '00
The Raggedy Rawney '90
Snatch '00 ▶
Spring Parade '40
Stephen King's Thinner '96
Time of the Gypsies '90 ▶
Triumph of the Spirit '89 ▶
The Wolf Man '41 ▶

Hackers

see also Computers
Category 6 : Day of Destruction '04
Confess '05
The Core '03
Demolition Man '93
Die Hard '88 ▶
Double Play '96
Ferris Bueller's Day Off '86 ▶
Hackers '95
Hellraiser: Hellworld '05
Jumpin' Jack Flash '86
The Lather Effect '06
Live Free or Die Hard '07
Mission: Impossible '96 ▶
The Net '95
Nicotina '03
Real Genius '85 ▶
Sneakers '92
So Close '02
Superman 3 '83
Swordfish '01
Twilight Man '96
Wallander: Firewall '08
WarGames '83
WarGames 2: The Dead Code '08
Weird Science '85

Halloween

American Nightmare '00
Boo! '05
Casper '95 ▶
Clown Murders '83
Double Double Toil and Trouble '94
E.T.: The Extra-Terrestrial '82 ▶
The Fear: Halloween Night '99
Frankenstein and Me '96
Frankenstein Sings... The Movie '95
The Ghost of Dragstrip Hollow '59
Halloween '78 ▶
Halloween '07
Halloween 2: The Nightmare Isn't Over! '81
Halloween 3: Season of the Witch '82
Halloween 4: The Return of Michael Myers '88
Halloween 5: The Revenge of Michael Myers '89
Halloween 6: The Curse of Michael Myers '95
Halloween: H20 '98 ▶
Halloween II '09
Halloweentown '98
Halloweentown 2: Kalabar's Revenge '01
Halloweentown High '04
Hellbent '04
Hocus Pocus '93
The Hollywood Knights '80
House of 1000 Corpses '03
I Downloaded a Ghost '04
Idle Hands '99
I've Been Waiting for You '98
Jack-O '95
KISS Meets the Phantom of the Park '78
The Legend of Sleepy Hollow '86 ▶
The Midnight Hour '86
Mozart and the Whale '05
Night of the Demons '88
Night of the Demons '09
Night of the Demons 2 '94
Night of the Demons 3 '97
The Nightmare Before Christmas '93 ▶
Return of the Living Dead: Rave to the Grave '05
Return to Halloweentown '06
Revenge of the Living Zombies '88
Satan's Little Helper '04
Spaced Invaders '90
Stan Helsing '09
Teen Alien '78
Trick or Treat '86
Trick or Treats '82
Trick 'r Treat '08 ▶
Twin Falls Idaho '99 ▶
Wacko '83
When Good Ghouls Go Bad '01

Hallucinations/ Illusions

The Alphabet Killer '08
Angel of Death '09
Bad Lieutenant: Port of Call New Orleans '09
A Beautiful Mind '01 ▶
Between '05
Blind Date '08
Bug '06
Buried Alive '90
The Caveman's Valentine '01
The Cradle '06
The Craft '96
Cria Cuervos '76 ▶
Dark Water '02
The Devil's Tomb '09
Dillinger Is Dead '69
Double Vision '02
Evil Eyes '04
The Eye '08
The Fever '04
Final '01
Frontier of Dawn '08
Ghost of the Needle '03
Ghost Ship '02
The Good Night '07
Gothika '03
Gradiva '06
The Haunted Airman '06
The Haunting of Molly Hartley '08
Hellraiser: Hellseeker '02
Images '72
Impostor '02
Invisible Child '99
Killer Me '01
Klimt '06
Last Call: The Final Chapter of F. Scott Fitzgerald '02
A Light in the Darkness '02
Max Payne '08
Memory '06
Mirrors '78
Monkeybone '01
Moon '09
The Mothman Prophecies '02
Naked Lunch '91 ▶
Nightwish '89
The Nines '07 ▶
Operation Sandman: Warriors in Hell '00
Paranoia 1.0 '04
Pi '98
Rapturious '07
Repulsion '65 ▶
The Return '06
S. Darko: A Donnie Darko Tale '09
Shadows '07
The Singing Detective '03
A Snake of June '02
Soho Square '00
Solaris '02
Something Beneath '07
Stir of Echoes 2: The Homecoming '07
Trauma '04
The Unborn '09
The Uninvited '09
Visitors '03
Waking Life '01
Who Wants to Kill Jessie? '65

Handyman Specials

see also Real Estate
Are We Done Yet? '07
Behind the Wall '08
Cold Creek Manor '03
The Evictors '79
House of Sand and Fog '03 ▶
Life as a House '01
Mr. Blandings Builds His Dream House '48 ▶
The Money Pit '86
Pacific Heights '90 ▶
Please Don't Eat the Daisies '60
The Tooth Fairy '06
Tribute '09
Under the Tuscan Sun '03

Hard Knock Life

see also Great Depression; Homeless
After Tomorrow '32
Agnes Browne '99
All or Nothing '02
Always Outnumbered Always Outgunned '98 ▶
American Buffalo '95
An American Crime '07
Angel '82
Angela's Ashes '99
The Assistant '97
The Baby Dance '98 ▶
Ballast '08
Beggars in Ermine '34
Beijing Bicycle '01
Black Tower '50
Blessing '94
Boesman & Lena '00
A Brivele der Mamen '38 ▶
Broken Blossoms '19 ▶
Cafe Express '83
Captain Scarlett '53
Carrie '52 ▶
Catherine Cookson's The Rag Nymph '96
Charlie and the Chocolate Factory '05 ▶
The Child '05
Children of Heaven '98
City of Joy '92
Clockers '95 ▶
Code Unknown '00
The Cow '93
Crisscross '92
Crows and Sparrows '49 ▶
The Damned Don't Cry '50
Dancing at Lughnasa '98
Daughters of the Sun '00
David Copperfield '70
David Copperfield '99
Devil's Island '96
A Dog of Flanders '99
Dolores Claiborne '94 ▶
The Dreamlife of Angels '98 ▶
The Easiest Way '31
8 Mile '02 ▶
Elena and Her Men '56 ▶
Entertaining Angels: The Dorothy Day Story '96
Erin Brockovich '00 ▶
Explicit Ills '08
Extreme Measures '96
Eye of God '97 ▶
Foolish '99
Forbidden Choices '94
Frozen River '08 ▶
The Full Monty '96 ▶
Gifted Hands: The Ben Carson Story '09
The Good Earth '37 ▶
Grbavica: The Land of My Dreams '06
Gridlock'd '96 ▶
The Grim Reaper '62 ▶
Here Comes Cookie '35
Heroes of the Heart '94
Hidden in America '96
Hideous Kinky '99
Hollow City '04
A Home of Our Own '93
Hoosier Schoolboy '37
I Capture the Castle '02
In America '02 ▶
The Inheritors '98
The Italian '15
Joe Dirt '01
Jude '96 ▶
Jude the Obscure '71
Juke Girl '42
Juno and the Paycock '30
Killer of Sheep '77 ▶
The King of Masks '99 ▶
Kuhle Wampe, Or Who Owns the World? '32
La Vie en Rose '07
Lamerica '95 ▶
Laughing Sinners '31
Le Gitan '75
Les Miserables '35 ▶
Les Miserables '57 ▶
Les Miserables '78 ▶
Les Miserables '97 ▶
Liam '00
Lies My Father Told Me '75 ▶
Little Dorrit '08
Little Dorrit, Film 1: Nobody's Fault '88 ▶
Little Dorrit, Film 2: Little Dorrit's Story '88 ▶
Little Heroes '91
Little Women '94 ▶
Live-In Maid '04
Lolo '92
Lucky Star '29
Madame Sata '02
Mama Africa '02
Mama Flora's Family '98
Marius and Jeannette '97
The Match Factory Girl '90 ▶
Me You Them '00
Meantime '81
Mrs. Wiggs of the Cabbage Patch '34
Moll Flanders '96
Monster's Ball '01 ▶
Monument Ave. '98
Mother Teresa: In the Name of God's Poor '97
My Name Is Joe '98
Nicholas Nickleby '02 ▶
None But the Lonely Heart '44 ▶
Not One Less '99
The Old Curiosity Shop '94
The Old Curiosity Shop '07
An Old-Fashioned Thanksgiving '08
Oliver Twist '97
Oliver Twist '00 ▶
Oliver Twist '07
100 Proof '96
One Third of a Nation '39
The Optimists '73
Paid in Full '02
Pay It Forward '00
Petits Freres '00
Pocketful of Miracles '61 ▶
The Pope of Greenwich Village '84
The Pursuit of Happyness '06
Ratas, Ratones, Rateros '99
Ratcatcher '99
Restoration '94 ▶
The Road Home '01 ▶
Rosetta '99
Salaam Bombay! '88 ▶
Scrooged '88
Set It Off '96
Shadrach '98
Shotgun Stories '07
Slumdog Millionaire '08 ▶
Small Faces '95 ▶
Sparrows '26 ▶
Spider '02 ▶
Stakeout '62
The Stars Fell on Henrietta '94
Steel City '06
The Story of Fausta '88
Street Scene '31 ▶
Sugar '09 ▶
The Super '91
The Sweetest Gift '98
Tess '79 ▶
Tess of the D'Urbervilles '98
Tess of the D'Urbervilles '08
Tess of the Storm Country '22
They Call Me Sirr '00
This Is My Father '99
Tokyo Sonata '09 ▶
Twinkletoes '26
Under the Moonlight '01 ▶
Union Depot '32
The Unseen '05
Vagabond '85 ▶
Vanessa '07
A Way of Life '04
Wendy and Lucy '08 ▶
Where the Hot Wind Blows '59
White Man's Burden '95
The White Ribbon '09
The Wide Blue Road '57 ▶
Wild Boys of the Road '33
Will It Snow for Christmas? '96
Willy Wonka & the Chocolate Factory '71 ▶
Winter's Bone '10
Woyzeck '94
Year Zero '04
Yellow Earth '89

Harlem

see also New York, New York
American Gangster '07 ▶
Brother to Brother '04
A Brother's Kiss '97
The Cotton Club '84 ▶
Hoodlum '96
Machine Gun Blues '95
Never Die Alone '04
The Old Settler '01
Paid in Full '02
Preaching to the Choir '05
A Rage in Harlem '91 ▶
Ride '98

Hawaii

see also Island Fare
Acapulco Gold '78
The Big Bounce '04
The Black Camel '31
Blue Crush '02 ▶
Blue Hawaii '62
Charlie Chan in Honolulu '38
50 First Dates '04
Flirting with Forty '09
Forgetting Sarah Marshall '08
Hawaii '66 ▶
Hercules '83
In God's Hands '98
Into the Blue 2: The Reef '09
Lilo & Stitch '02 ▶
Lilo & Stitch 2: Stitch Has a Glitch '05
Magnum P.I.: Don't Eat the Snow in Hawaii '80
Miss Tatlock's Millions '48
Morning Light '08
Paradise, Hawaiian Style '66
Pearl '78
Pearl Harbor '01
A Perfect Getaway '09
Picture Bride '94
Punch-Drunk Love '02 ▶
Race the Sun '96
Riding Giants '04
Sailor Beware '52
Silk 2 '89
A Very Brady Sequel '96
Waikiki '80
Waikiki Wedding '37 ▶

Heads!

see also Brains!; Ears!; Eyeballs!; Renegade Body Parts
Azumi '03 ▶
Botched '07
The Brain that Wouldn't Die '63
Braveheart '95 ▶
8 Heads in a Duffel Bag '96
Highlander '86 ▶
Highlander 2: The Quickening '91
Highlander: The Final Dimension '94
The Hitchhiker's Guide to the Galaxy '81 ▶
The Incredible Two-Headed Transplant '71
Lost Boys: The Tribe '08
The Man with Two Brains '83 ▶
Master of the Flying Guillotine '75
Mystery Men '99
Seven '79
The Skull '65
Tropic Thunder '08 ▶

Hearts!

see also Eyeballs!
An American Werewolf in Paris '97
Angel Heart '87
Apocalypto '06 ▶
Article 99 '92
Awake '07
Blood Work '02
Brainstorm '83
City of Angels '98
Crank: High Voltage '09
Dead in a Heartbeat '02
Dumb & Dumber '94
From Dusk Till Dawn '95
Heart '99
Indiana Jones and the Temple of Doom '84 ▶
The Intruder '04 ▶
John Q '02
The Last of the Mohicans '92 ▶
Legends of the Fall '94
The Mad Ghoul '43
Mary Shelley's Frankenstein '94
My Bloody Valentine '81
My Bloody Valentine 3D '09
The Prophecy '95
The Prophecy 2: Ashtown '97
Pulp Fiction '94 ▶
Return to Me '00
Split Second '92
Tales from the Crypt '72 ▶
Tales from the Crypt Presents Bordello of Blood '96
The Terminator '84 ▶

Heaven Sent

see also Angels
All Dogs Go to Heaven '89
All Dogs Go to Heaven 2 '95
All of Me '84
Almost an Angel '90
Always '89

▶ = rated three bones or higher

Angel on My Shoulder '46 ▶
Angel on My Shoulder '80
The Bishop's Wife '47 ▶
Brewster McCloud '70 ▶
Brother John '70 ▶
Bruce Almighty '03
Carousel '56 ▶
Chances Are '89 ▶
Charley and the Angel '73
Clarence '91
Constantine '05
Date with an Angel '87
Defending Your Life '91 ▶
Dogma '99
Down to Earth '01
The Family Man '79
Family Man '00
Field of Dreams '89 ▶
Forever Darling '56
Ghost '90 ▶
Ghost Dad '90
A Guy Named Joe '44
He Sees You When You're Sleeping '02
Heading for Heaven '47
Heart Condition '90
Heaven '87
Heaven Can Wait '43 ▶
Heaven Can Wait '78 ▶
The Heavenly Kid '85
Hello Again '87
Here Comes Mr. Jordan '41 ▶
The Horn Blows at Midnight '45 ▶
I Married an Angel '42
It Came Upon a Midnight Clear '84
It's a Wonderful Life '46 ▶
Kiss Me Goodbye '82
Liliom '35 ▶
The Littlest Angel '69
The Lovely Bones '09
Made in Heaven '87
Miracle in Milan '51 ▶
Mr. Destiny '90
The Next Voice You Hear '50
No News from God '01
Noah '98
Oh, God! '77
Oh, God! Book 2 '80
Oh, God! You Devil '84
One Magic Christmas '85
The Preacher's Wife '96
The Return of Peter Grimm '35
Stairway to Heaven '46 ▶
Static '87
The Three Lives of Thomasina '63 ▶
To Gillian on Her 37th Birthday '96
Toothless '97
Truly, Madly, Deeply '91 ▶
Two of a Kind '83
What Dreams May Come '98
White Light '90
Wide Awake '97
Xanadu '80

Heists

see also *Scams, Stings & Cons*

Aladdin and the King of Thieves '96
Almost Partners '87
The Amazing Transparent Man '60
The Anderson Tapes '71 ▶
The Apple Dumpling Gang '75
Army of One '94
The Asphalt Jungle '50 ▶
Assault of the Rebel Girls '59
At Gunpoint '55
Back in the USSR '92
Bad Boys '95
Bad Santa '03
Bandits '86
Bank Robber '93
Bellman and True '88
Bells of Coronado '50
Belly '98
Best Men '98
Beyond Fear '75
The Bicycle Thief '48 ▶
Big Chase '54
Big Deal on Madonna Street '58 ▶
Bitter Vengeance '94
The Black Lash '52
Blind Justice '94
Blood & Wine '96
The Boatniks '70
Body Count '97
Bonnie & Clyde '67 ▶
Born Bad '97
Bottle Rocket '95
Bound '96
The Brain '69
Breathing Fire '91
The Brooklyn Heist '08
Butch and Sundance: The Early Days '79
Captain Blackjack '51
Casino '95 ▶
The Catamount Killing '74
C.I.A. 2: Target Alexa '94
City Unplugged '95
The Cobra Strikes '48
Cold Around the Heart '97
Crack Up '97
Crackerjack '94
Crime Broker '94
Crime Spree '03
Crooks & Coronets '69
Croupier '97 ▶
The Curse of Inferno '96
The Curse of the Jade Scorpion '01
Danger: Diabolik '68
Daring Dobermans '73
Dead Heat on a Merry-Go-Round '66 ▶
Dead Presidents '95
Deadly Diamonds '91
Death Tide '58
The Deputy Drummer '35
Desperate Cargo '41
The Desperate Trail '94
Destiny Turns on the Radio '95
Diamond Fleece '92
Diamond Trail '33
The Diamond Trap '91
Die Hard '88 ▶
Die Hard: With a Vengeance '95
Dog Eat Dog '64
The Dog Who Saved Christmas '09
Dollars '71 ▶
Double Deal '84
Double Trouble '91
Dunston Checks In '95
11 Harrowhouse '74 ▶
Extreme Honor '01
Face '97
Fast Money '96
Firetrap '01
Five Golden Dragons '67
The Florida Connection '74
Four Ways Out '57
Free Ride '86
French Kiss '95
The Getaway '72
The Getaway '93
Getting Even with Dad '94
Going in Style '79 ▶
Grand Larceny '92
Great Bank Hoax '78
Great Gold Swindle '84
The Green Glove '52
Grisbi '53
Gun Crazy '49 ▶
Gun Girls '56
Guns Don't Argue '57
Gypsy '75
Hand Gun '93
Happy New Year '87
Happy, Texas '99 ▶
Hard Cash '01
Hard Hunted '92
The Hard Truth '94
The Hard Word '02
Harley Davidson and the Marlboro Man '91
The Heist '89
High Risk '81
Hit Me '96
Holy Matrimony '94
The Hoodlum '51
The Horse Without a Head '63
Hot Target '85
Hot Touch '82
How to Steal a Million '66 ▶
I Died a Thousand Times '55
Ice '93
The Immortals '95
Incident at Deception Ridge '94
Inside Information '34
Interceptor '92
Joy Ride to Nowhere '78
Kelly's Heroes '70
Killer Force '75
The Killing '56 ▶
Killing in the Sun '73
Killing Zoe '94
King's Ransom '91
Lassiter '84
The Last of Mrs. Cheyney '37 ▶
Late Extra '35
The Lavender Hill Mob '51 ▶
The League of Gentlemen '60 ▶
Letting the Birds Go Free '86
A Life Less Ordinary '97
Lightning Jack '94
Like a Fish Out of Water '99
The Lion's Share '79
Lock, Stock and 2 Smoking Barrels '98 ▶
Loophole '83
Mad Money '08
A Man, a Woman, and a Bank '79
Man Trouble '92
Marbella '85
Marked Money '28
Master Touch '74
Midnight Limited '40
Mission Batangas '69
Money Movers '78
Money to Burn '83
Motorama '91
My Dog, the Thief '69
Normal Life '96
The Old Lady Who Walked in the Sea '91
Old Mother Riley's New Venture '49
On the Border '98
Once a Thief '96 ▶
Operation Condor 2: The Armour of the Gods '86
Out of Sight '98 ▶
Palookaville '95 ▶
Pardon My Sarong '42
Passionate Thief '60
The Perfect Score '04
Persons Unknown '96
The Pink Panther 2 '09
Point Break '91
Queen of Diamonds '70
The Real McCoy '93
The Real Thing '97
The Rebel Set '59
Reindeer Games '00
The Return of Boston Blackie '27
Rififi '54 ▶
The Rip Off '78
Robbery '67
Robbery '85
Rough Cut '80
R.P.M. '97
Scarlet Street '45 ▶
The Score '01
Set It Off '96
Sexy Beast '00 ▶
Shadow Man '75
Slaughterday '77
Sneakers '92
Spider's Web '01
The Spree '96
The Squeaker '65
The Squeeze '87
Stranger in the House '97
Styx '00
They Met in Bombay '41
Thick as Thieves '99
Thief '81 ▶
The Thief Who Came to Dinner '73
Three Kings '99 ▶
Time to Kill '42
To Catch a Thief '55 ▶
Too Many Crooks '59
Topkapi '64 ▶
Trapped in Paradise '94
Truth or Consequences, N.M. '97
Two If by Sea '95
Two-Way Stretch '60
The Underneath '95 ▶
The Usual Suspects '95 ▶
Velocity Trap '99
When I Close My Eyes '93
Where the Money Is '00
White Fire '84
White Tiger '23
Who'll Stop the Rain? '78 ▶
The Wrong Arm of the Law '63 ▶
The Wrong Road '37
X Marks the Spot '42

Heists: Armored Car

Armored '09
Armored Car Robbery '50
Burnt Money '00
Classe Tous Risque '60 ▶
Criss Cross '48 ▶
Firefight '03
Forfeit '07
Hard Rain '97
Heat '95 ▶
Kansas City Confidential '52 ▶
Le Deuxieme Souffle '66
Raven's Ridge '97
Seven Seconds '05
The Take '07

Heists: Art

Art Heist '05
Body Count '97
Canvas: The Fine Art of Crime '92
Entrapment '99
Four Dogs Playing Poker '00
Gambit '66
The Good Thief '03 ▶
Just Business '08
Love Among Thieves '86
The Maiden Heist '08
Milo Milo '79
My Mom's New Boyfriend '08
Once a Thief '90
Ordinary Decent Criminal '99
Our America '02
Running Out of Time 2 '06
St. Trinian's '07
The Thomas Crown Affair '68 ▶
The Thomas Crown Affair '99 ▶
Widows '02

Heists: Banks

Action Man '67
American Madness '32
Bandits '01
The Bank Dick '40 ▶
The Bank Job '08 ▶
Bank Shot '74 ▶
The Big Scam '79
Breaking News '04
Burning Life '94
Catch That Kid '04
Children of Hannibal '98
Crime Wave '54
The Dark Knight '08 ▶
Dead Birds '04
Dead Heist '07
The Desperadoes '43
Dillinger and Capone '95
Firewall '06
44 Minutes: The North Hollywood Shootout '03
Four Days '99
The Front Line '06
Fun With Dick and Jane '05
Graduation '07
The Great St. Louis Bank Robbery '59
Heat '95 ▶
Heaven's Burning '97
Hero Wanted '08
Hot Money '79
How to Rob a Bank '07
Inside Man '06 ▶
Inspector Gadget 2 '02
Kill Me Later '01
Killer '73
Larceny, Inc. '42
Living & Dying '07
The Lookout '07 ▶
Loophole '54
Lost '05
Love Is Colder Than Death '69
Malevolence '04
The Moonlighter '53
A New Wave '07
No Good Deed '02
Odds Against Tomorrow '59 ▶
Public Enemies '09
Pups '99
Radio Cab Murder '54
The Robin Hood Gang '98
Robin's Hood '03
Scorched '02
The Set Up '95
Shakedown '02
Small Time Crooks '00
Stander '03
Stark Raving Mad '02
The Stickup '01
Sugar & Spice '01 ▶
Swindle '02
Takers '10
Taxi '04
Three on a Ticket '47
Thunderbirds '04

Heists: Casinos

Any Number Can Win '63
The Aura '05 ▶
Bob le Flambeur '55 ▶
Carnival of Wolves '96
The Casino Job '08
5 Against the House '55
Ghost of a Chance '01
The Good Thief '03 ▶
The Hollywood Sign '01
The Ladykillers '04
My Name is Modesty: A Modesty Blaise Adventure '04
Ocean's 11 '60
Ocean's Eleven '01 ▶
Ocean's Thirteen '07 ▶
Rip It Off '02
Seven Thieves '60 ▶
3000 Miles to Graceland '01

Heists: Gold/Precious Metals

Adios, Sabata '71
Arizona Cyclone '41
B.A.D. Cats '80
The Badlanders '58
Border River '47
Carson City '52
City Beneath the Sea '71
Exiled '06
Fool's Gold: The Story of the Brink's-Mat Robbery '92
Heist '01 ▶
The Italian Job '69
The Italian Job '03 ▶
Plunder Road '57
Raiders of Ghost City '44
Red Desert '50
Sam Whiskey '69
The Trygon Factor '66
Western Gold '37
When Eight Bells Toll '71
The Wrecking Crew '68

Heists: Jewels

After the Sunset '04
All About the Benjamins '02
And Now Ladies and Gentlemen '02
Before the Devil Knows You're Dead '07 ▶
Big Brown Eyes '36
Bloodstone '88
Botched '07
City of Industry '96
City on Fire '87
The Code '09
The Collector '09
Columbus Day '08
Cradle 2 the Grave '03
Crimson Gold '03
Desert Nights '29
Diamond Run '00
Dog Gone '08
Every Girl Should Have One '78
Fathom '67
Femme Fatale '02
Fish in a Barrel '01
Flawless '07
The Frightened Man '52
The Hot Rock '70 ▶
Hot Tamale '06
I Hate Blondes '83
Le Cercle Rouge '70 ▶
Lift '01
Lights in the Dusk '06
Little Man '06
Mad Mission 3 '84
Mr. Moto Takes a Vacation '39
Modesty Blaise '66
The Moonstone '34
The Moonstone '72
Mr. Takes a Vacation '39
Murph the Surf '75
The Notorious Landlady '62
Ocean's Twelve '04
Once Upon a Time in America '84 ▶
One More Time '70
Operation Amsterdam '60
Picture Claire '01
The Pink Panther '64 ▶
The Pink Panther '06
Place Vendome '98 ▶
Recoil '53
Reservoir Dogs '92 ▶
Score '95
Six Gun Trail '38
Snatch '00 ▶
The Squeeze '80
They Met in a Taxi '36
Three Blondes in His Life '61
Triplecross '95
Welcome to Collinwood '02
Whipsaw '35

Heists: Trains

Alberto Express '92
Butch Cassidy and the Sundance Kid '69 ▶
Colorado Territory '49
The Great Train Robbery '79 ▶
The Grey Fox '83 ▶
House of Bamboo '55
Money Train '95
Night Passage '57
Tough Guys '86

Hell

see also *Death & the Afterlife; Devils; Religion; Satanism*

All Dogs Go to Heaven '89
Bill & Ted's Bogus Journey '91
Bliss '85 ▶
Constantine '05
Dark Angel: The Ascent '94
The Doorway '00
Faust: Love of the Damned '00
Freddy vs. Jason '03
Heaven Can Wait '43 ▶
Hellbound: Hellraiser 2 '88
Hellboy II: The Golden Army '08 ▶
Hellraiser '87
Hellraiser '09
Hellraiser 3: Hell on Earth '92
Hellraiser 4: Bloodline '95
Hellraiser 5: Inferno '00
Highway to Hell '92
Little Nicky '00
Rapturious '07
South Park: Bigger, Longer and Uncut '99
Spawn '97 ▶
What Dreams May Come '98
Witchery '88

Hell High School

see also *Cheerleaders; Dedicated Teachers; Errant Educators; High School; High School Reunions; Prom; School Daze; Teen Angst*

Afterschool '08
Angus '95
Animal Room '95
Anything for Love '93
Bad Reputation '05 ▶

▶ = rated three bones or higher

The Beat '88
Big Bully '95
Bill & Ted's Excellent Adventure '89
Billy Madison '94
Black Circle Boys '97
Blackboard Jungle '55 ▸
Blood of Dracula '57
Bloodmoon '90
Boltneck '98
Born Innocent '74
Boy's Reformatory '39
The Brady Bunch Movie '95 ▸
Brutal Fury '92
Buffy the Vampire Slayer '92 ▸
Carrie '76 ▸
Carrie '02
Catch Me... If You Can '89
Cemetery High '89
Cheaters '00
Cheering Section '73
Cherry Hill High '76
The Chicken Chronicles '77
A Cinderella Story '04
Class '83
Class Act '91
Class of Fear '91
Class of '44 '73
The Class of Miss MacMichael '78
Class of 1984 '82
Class of 1999 '90
Class of 1999 2: The Substitute '93
Class of Nuke 'Em High '86
Class of Nuke 'Em High 2: Subhumanoid Meltdown '91
Class of Nuke 'Em High 3: The Good, the Bad and the Subhumanoid '94
Class Reunion Massacre '77
The Club '94
Clueless '95 ▸
Coach '78
Coneheads '93
Cooley High '75 ▸
The Craft '96
Creepers '85
Crisis at Central High '80 ▸
Cruel Intentions 2 '99
Cry-Baby '90 ▸
Cutting Class '89
Dangerously Close '86
Dazed and Confused '93 ▸
Deadly Fieldtrip '74
Deal of a Lifetime '99
Death Goes to School '53
Demolition High '95
Detention '03
Disturbing Behavior '98
Echoes in the Darkness '87
Elephant '03 ▸
Ernest Goes to School '94
The Ernest Green Story '93
Evil '03 ▸
The Faculty '98
Fast Times at Ridgemont High '82 ▸
Fear '96
Ferris Bueller's Day Off '86 ▸
Finishing School '33
5 Dark Souls '96
Ginger Snaps '01
The Girl, the Body and the Pill '67
Girls in Chains '43
Girls Town '95
Grad Night '81
Graduation Day '81
Grease 2 '82
The Great St. Trinian's Train Robbery '66
Hadley's Rebellion '84
Halloween: H20 '98 ▸
Hangman's Curse '03
Hard Knox '83
Hard Lessons '86
Heart of America '03
Heathers '89 ▸
Hell High '86
Hide and Go Shriek '87
Hiding Out '87
High School Caesar '60
High School Confidential '58
High School High '96
High School USA '84
Hollywood High '77
Home Room '02 ▸
Homework '82
Hoosiers '86 ▸
Hostage High '97
I Was a Teenage Werewolf '57
I Was a Teenage Zombie '87
If... '69 ▸
The Impostor '84
The Invisible Kid '88
The Invisible Maniac '90
Joy of Sex '84
Just One of the Girls '93
Kids in America '05
Killing Mr. Griffin '97
The Lawrenceville Stories '88
Light It Up '99
Little Witches '96
Lone Wolf '88
Loose Screws '85
Lust for a Vampire '71
Major Payne '95
The Majorettes '87
Making the Grade '84
Massacre at Central High '76
Maya '82
Mean Girls '04 ▸
Mirror, Mirror '90
Mr. Woodcock '07
Monster High '89
My Bodyguard '80 ▸
Napoleon Dynamite '04
National Lampoon's Senior Trip '95
Night Visitor '89
Nowhere to Run '88
On the Edge: The Survival of Dana '79
187 '97
One Night Only '84
Only the Strong '93
Pandemonium '82
Peggy Sue Got Married '86
Pep Squad '98
Plain Clothes '88
Platinum High School '60
Porky's '82
Porky's 2: The Next Day '83
The Positively True Adventures of the Alleged Texas Cheerleader-Murdering Mom '93 ▸
Pretty Persuasion '05
Princess Academy '87
Prison for Children '93
Prom Night '80
Prom Night 3: The Last Kiss '89
Prom Night 4: Deliver Us from Evil '91
Pump Up the Volume '90
The Quiet '05
The Rage: Carrie 2 '99
Rebel High '88
Return to Horror High '87
Rock 'n' Roll High School '79 ▸
Rock 'n' Roll High School Forever '91
Rock, Pretty Baby '56
Satan's Cheerleaders '77
Satan's School for Girls '73
School Ties '92 ▸
School's Out '99
Screwballs '83
Senior Trip '81
Serial Killing 101 '04
Show Me Love '99
Showdown '93
Shriek If You Know What I Did Last Friday the 13th '00
Sidekicks '93
Sister Act 2: Back in the Habit '93
Sixteen Candles '84 ▸
Slaughter High '86
Some Kind of Wonderful '87
Speak '04 ▸
Spliced '03
Stay Awake '87
Strangers with Candy '06
Student Affairs '88
Student Bodies '81
The Substitute '93
The Substitute '96
Summer School '87
Sunset Park '96
Superstar '99
Teaching Mrs. Tingle '99
Teenage Strangler '64
Terror Squad '87
3:15—The Moment of Truth '86
Three o'Clock High '87
Tom Brown's School Days '51 ▸
Trick or Treat '86
Twisted Brain '74
Undercover '87
Valentine '01
Wanderers '79 ▸
Werewolf in a Girl's Dormitory '61
When Evil Calls '06
White Squall '96
Zero for Conduct '33 ▸
Zombie High '87

The Help: Female

Adelheid '69
Alex Rider: Operation Stormbreaker '06
Au Pair Girls '72
Backstairs at the White House '79 ▸
The Beautician and the Beast '97
Black Girl '66 ▸
Blue Crush '02 ▸
Boeing Boeing '65
The Brady Bunch Movie '95 ▸
The Chateau '01
Cora Unashamed '00
Cotton Mary '99
Cries and Whispers '72 ▸
Diary of a Chambermaid '46 ▸
Diary of a Chambermaid '64 ▸
Die Mommie Die! '03
Dillinger Is Dead '69
The Double Hour '09
Dreaming About You '92
8 Women '02 ▸
Elvira's Haunted Hills '02
End of Desire '62
Eternal '04
The Farmer's Daughter '47 ▸
For Love of Ivy '68
For Real '02
Friends with Money '06
Gaslight '44 ▸
Girl with a Pearl Earring '03 ▸
Gone with the Wind '39 ▸
Gosford Park '01 ▸
Grave Indiscretions '96
Hard to Get '38
His Butler's Sister '44
Houseboat '58
The Housekeeper '86
I Can't Sleep '93
If You Could Only Cook '36
Imitation of Life '34
Imitation of Life '59 ▸
In the White City '83 ▸
Jane Eyre '06
Kama Sutra: A Tale of Love '96
Keeping Mum '05
The King and I '99
La Ceremonie '95 ▸
The Long Walk Home '89 ▸
Love Actually '03
Loyalties '86
Made in Heaven '52
The Maid '90
The Maid '09 ▸
Maid in Manhattan '02
Maid to Order '87
Maid's Night Out '38
Mammoth '09
A Matter of Time '76
The Member of the Wedding '97
The Milk of Sorrow '09
Miss Pettigrew Lives for a Day '08 ▸
Mrs. Parkington '44
Murder by Death '76
My Chauffeur '86
The Omen '06
One Man's Journey '33
The Others '01 ▸
Personal Maid '31
Plain Jane '01
Poison '01
Private Lessons '75
Rebecca '40 ▸
Rebecca '97 ▸
The Remains of the Day '93 ▸
The Rules of the Game '39 ▸
Seraphine '08 ▸
The Silences of the Palace '94 ▸
Sister My Sister '94
The Skeleton Key '05
A Song of Innocence '05
Spanglish '04
Tartuffe '25
That Funny Feeling '65
That Obscure Object of Desire '77 ▸
Traveling Companion '96
Under the Same Moon '07
Under the Sun '98
Uptown Girls '03
A Very Brady Sequel '96
The Water Horse: Legend of the Deep '07
The Well '97
A Woman of Substance '84
Woman Wanted '98

The Help: Male

The Admirable Crichton '57
Arthur '81 ▸
Arthur 2: On the Rocks '88
Backstairs at the White House '79 ▸
B.A.P.'s '97
Batman '89 ▸
Batman and Robin '97
Batman Begins '05 ▸
Batman Forever '95 ▸
Batman Returns '92
Bernard and Doris '08 ▸
The Black Widow '05
Blue Blood '73
Bob the Butler '05
Breakfast for Two '37
Candleshoe '78
Casanova '05 ▸
Catherine Cookson's The Moth '96
The Chase '46
The Chateau '01
Clue '85
The Collector '09
The Cowboys '72 ▸
Crescendo '69
The Dark Knight '08 ▸
Double Harness '33
Driving Miss Daisy '89 ▸
The Duke '99
The Empty Acre '07
The Fallen Idol '49 ▸
Family Jewels '65
Fancy Pants '50
Far from Heaven '02 ▸
Fido '06
The Girl in the News '41
Gosford Park '01 ▸
Grave Indiscretions '96
Heaven Can Wait '78 ▸
If You Could Only Cook '36
Institue Benjamenta or This Dream People Call Human Life '95
The Kite Runner '07 ▸
The Ladies' Man '61
Lady Chatterley's Lover '55
Lady Chatterley's Lover '81
Lara Croft: Tomb Raider '01
The Luck of the Irish '48
Maurice '87 ▸
Miss Julie '99
Mrs. Brown '97 ▸
Murder by Death '76
My Man Godfrey '36 ▸
My Man Godfrey '57
Nothing But Trouble '44
On the Run '83
The Princess Diaries 2: Royal Engagement '04
Private Lessons '75
Racing Daylight '07
The Remains of the Day '93 ▸
Richie Rich '94
Ruggles of Red Gap '35 ▸
Screwed '00
The Servant '63 ▸
Sheitan '06
Sitting Pretty '48 ▸
Stiff Upper Lips '96
Trading Places '83
The Water Horse: Legend of the Deep '07

Hide the Dead Guy

Arsenic and Old Lace '44 ▸
Black Cat, White Cat '98 ▸
Blue Ridge Fall '99
Dark Country '09
Dead Bodies '03
Death at a Funeral '10
Drop Dead Sexy '05
El Crimen Perfecto '04
Enid Is Sleeping '90
Grand Theft Parsons '03
Head Above Water '96
I'll Bury You Tomorrow '02
Jawbreaker '98
Jindabyne '06
Just Buried '07
The Last Supper '96
Little Miss Sunshine '06 ▸
Living Doll '90
Lost Junction '03
Mortal Transfer '01
Pulp Fiction '94 ▸
Shallow Grave '94
Siblings '04
Silver City '04
A Slight Case of Murder '38
Sorority Row '09
The Three Burials of Melquiades Estrada '05 ▸
The Trouble with Harry '55 ▸
Up at the Villa '00
Very Bad Things '98
Volver '06 ▸
Waking Ned Devine '98 ▸
Who's Your Monkey '07
Wolves in the Snow '02

High School

see also ***Hell High School; Teen Angst***

American Gun '05
American Pie '99 ▸
American Teen '08
Angel Rodriguez '05
Apt Pupil '97
Bandslam '09
Believe in Me '06
Better Luck Tomorrow '02 ▸
Blackboard Jungle '55 ▸
Blue Car '03 ▸
The Boys of Baraka '05
Bratz '07
The Breakfast Club '85 ▸
Brick '06 ▸
Can't Buy Me Love '87
Can't Hardly Wait '98
Chalk '06
Charlie Bartlett '07 ▸
A Cinderella Story '04
The Class '08
Coach Carter '05 ▸
Confessions of a Teenage Drama Queen '04
The Craft '96
The Curiosity of Chance '06
Cynthia '47
Dance Flick '09
Dangerous Minds '95
Dare '09
Drillbit Taylor '08
Dumb and Dumberer: When Harry Met Lloyd '03
Election '99 ▸
Encino Man '92
Evergreen '04
Fame '09
The Fast and the Furious: Tokyo Drift '06
Ferris Bueller's Day Off '86 ▸
The Final Season '07
Fired Up! '09
Foreign Exchange '08
Freedom Writers '07
Friday Night Lights '04 ▸
Full of It '07
Full Ride '02
Games of Love and Chance '03
Get a Clue '02
Get Over It! '01
The Girl Next Door '04
The Good Student '08
Gracie '07
Grease '78 ▸
Hairspray '07 ▸
Halloweentown High '04
Hamlet 2 '08 ▸
The Heart of the Game '05
Her Best Move '07
High School High '96
High School Musical '06
High School Musical 3: Senior Year '08
High School USA '84
Hometown Legend '02
Hoosier Schoolboy '37
Hoosiers '86 ▸
The Hot Chick '02
How to Deal '03
Hurricane Season '08
Ice Princess '05
It's a Boy Girl Thing '06
Jawbreaker '98
John Tucker Must Die '06
Juno '07 ▸
Just Friends '05
Keith '08
Kids in America '05
Lean on Me '89 ▸
The Life Before Her Eyes '07
Linda Linda Linda '05 ▸
Lord Love a Duck '66
Love Don't Cost a Thing '03
Maryam '00
Mean Girls '04 ▸
Minutemen '08
Mr. Holland's Opus '95 ▸
More Than a Game '08
Murder in New Hampshire: The Pamela Smart Story '91
Napoleon Dynamite '04
Never Back Down '08
Never Been Kissed '99
The New Guy '02
Noi '03
Not Another Teen Movie '01
O '01 ▸
187 '97
Orange County '02
The Perfect Score '04
Picture This! '08
Platinum High School '60
Players '03
Porky's '82
Porky's 2: The Next Day '83
Porky's Revenge '85
Possums '99
Pretty in Pink '86
Princess Protection Program '09
The Principal '87
Queen Sized '08
Radio '03
The Red Sneakers '01
Rock 'n' Roll High School '79 ▸
Rock 'n' Roll High School Forever '91
Rock the Paint '05
Rocket Science '07 ▸
The Rookie '02 ▸
Rushmore '98 ▸
Rustin '01
Save the Last Dance '01
Saved! '04
Senior Skip Day '08
Seventeen Again '00
17 Again '09
She's All That '99
Sixteen Candles '84 ▸
Sky High '05 ▸
Slap Her, She's French '02
Some Kind of Wonderful '87
Stand and Deliver '88 ▸
Step Up '06
The Substitute '96
Sugar & Spice '01 ▸
Summer School '87
Swimfan '02
Take the Lead '06
Teachers '84
Ten Things I Hate about You '99 ▸
There Goes My Baby '92
They Call Me Sirr '00
Through the Fire '05 ▸
A Time for Dancing '00
To Save a Life '10
Twilight '08

▸ = rated three bones or higher

The Twilight Saga: Eclipse '10
Underclassman '05
Varsity Blues '98
Virgin '03
What a Life '39

High School Reunions

see also *School Daze*
Archie: Return to Riverdale '90
Beautiful Girls '96 ▸
Class Reunion '72
Class Reunion Massacre '77
Flying By '09
Grosse Pointe Blank '97 ▸
Grown Ups '10
Just Friends '05
Mutual Needs '97
National Lampoon's Class Reunion '82
Peggy Sue Got Married '86
Romy and Michele's High School Reunion '97
Since You've Been Gone '97
Something Wild '86
Terror Stalks the Class Reunion '93
Zack and Miri Make a Porno '08 ▸

Hijacked!

Agent Red '00
Air Force One '97 ▸
Airport '77 '77
The Annihilators '85
Appointment in Honduras '53
Cotton Comes to Harlem '70 ▸
Delta Force '86
Die Hard 2: Die Harder '90 ▸
Drop Zone '94
Final Approach '04
Final Approach '08
The Fourth Angel '01
The Hamburg Cell '04
Hi-Jacked '50
Hostage '87
Maiden Voyage: Ocean Hijack '04
Maniac '77
Overland Stage Raiders '38 ▸
Passenger 57 '92
The Pursuit of D.B. Cooper '81
Star Trek 5: The Final Frontier '89
The Taking of Pelham One Two Three '74 ▸
The Taking of Pelham 123 '09
Under Siege 2: Dark Territory '95
United 93 '06 ▸
Victory at Entebbe '76

Hinduism

Earth '98
Fire '96
Gandhi '82 ▸
The Guru '02
The Mystic Masseur '01
Water '05

Hip-Hop/Rap

Be Cool '05
Brown Sugar '02
Bulworth '98 ▸
Bunny Whipped '06
Carmen: A Hip Hopera '01
CB4: The Movie '93
Cool As Ice '91
Da Hip Hop Witch '00
Dave Chappelle's Block Party '06 ▸
A Day in the Life '09
8 Mile '02 ▸
Fade to Black '04 ▸
Fear of a Black Hat '94
Feel the Noise '07
Fly by Night '93
Friday '95
G '02
Get Rich or Die Tryin' '05
The Gospel '05 ▸
Hip Hop 4 Life '02
The Hit '06
Hollywood Homicide '03
Honey '03
House Party '90 ▸
House Party 2: The Pajama Jam '91
House Party 3 '94
Hustle & Flow '05 ▸
In the Mix '05
Irish Jam '05
Janky Promoters '09
Kickin' It Old Skool '07
Krush Groove '85
Leprechaun 5: In the Hood '99
Makin' Baby '02
Malibu's Most Wanted '03
Marci X '03
Murda Muzik '03
New Jersey Drive '95
Notorious '09
The Perfect Holiday '07
Rapturious '07
Rude Boy: The Jamaican Don '03
The Show '95
Snipes '01
State Property 2 '05
Step Up 2 the Streets '08
Tougher Than Leather '88
The Underground '97
Who's the Man? '93
You Got Served '04

Hispanic America

American Fusion '05
Barrio Wars '02
The Burning Plain '08
Chasing Papi '03
crazy/beautiful '01
The Dead One '07
Dragstrip Girl '94
East Side Story '07
Fools Rush In '97
Gabriela '01
Hitz '89
How the Garcia Girls Spent Their Summer '05
I Like It Like That '94 ▸
Illegal Tender '07
Lone Star '95 ▸
Lotto Land '95
Love and Debate '06
Luminarias '99
Maid in Manhattan '02
The Maldonado Miracle '03
Mambo Cafe '00
Manito '03 ▸
Maricela '88
Mexican Gangster '08
Mi Vida Loca '94
Miami Rhapsody '95
My Family '94 ▸
Our Song '01 ▸
Pinero '01
Quinceanera '06 ▸
Race '99
Raising Victor Vargas '03
Real Women Have Curves '02 ▸
The Ring '52
Roosters '95
Salsa '88
Selena '96
Spin '04
Stand and Deliver '88 ▸
Steal Big, Steal Little '95
The Street King '02
Sueno '05
Sugar '09 ▸
Sweet 15 '90
Tortilla Heaven '07
Tortilla Soup '01
Wassup Rockers '06
The Wind That Shakes the Barley '06 ▸
Zoot Suit '81 ▸

Historical Comedy

Almost Heroes '97
Amreeka '09 ▸
Caveman '81
History of the World: Part 1 '81
Love and Death '75 ▸
Monty Python and the Holy Grail '75 ▸
Monty Python's Life of Brian '79 ▸
1941 '79

Historical Detectives

The Adventures of Sherlock Holmes '39
The Alphabet Murders '65
Appointment with Death '88
The Barbary Coast '74
The Crucifer of Blood '91
Death on the Nile '78
Dressed to Kill '46
Evil under the Sun '82
Great K & A Train Robbery '26
The Great Mouse Detective '86 ▸
Hands of a Murderer '90
Heat of the Sun '99 ▸
The Hound of the Baskervilles '39 ▸
The Hound of the Baskervilles '59
The Hound of the Baskervilles '77
The Hound of the Baskervilles '83
The Hound of the Baskervilles '00
The Hound of the Baskervilles '02 ▸
House of Fear '45
Masks of Death '86
Murder at the Baskervilles '37
Murder by Decree '79 ▸
Murder on Approval '56
Murder on the Orient Express '74 ▸
The Name of the Rose '86
The Pearl of Death '44
The Private Life of Sherlock Holmes '70 ▸
Pursuit to Algiers '45
The Ripper '97
The Rose and the Jackal '90
Scarlet Claw '44 ▸
The Seven-Per-Cent Solution '76 ▸
Sherlock Holmes and the Deadly Necklace '62
Sherlock Holmes and the Incident at Victoria Falls '91
Sherlock Holmes and the Secret Weapon '42 ▸
Sherlock Holmes Faces Death '43 ▸
Sherlock Holmes in Washington '43
Sherlock Holmes: The Voice of Terror '42
The Sign of Four '83
The Sign of Four '01
The Silent Mr. Sherlock Holmes '12
The Speckled Band '31 ▸
Spider Woman '44 ▸
A Study in Scarlet '33
A Study in Terror '66 ▸
Terror by Night '46
The Triumph of Sherlock Holmes '35
The Woman in Green '49
Young Sherlock Holmes '85

Historical Drama

see also *Medieval Romps; Period Piece*
The Abdication '74
Abe Lincoln in Illinois '40 ▸
Across the Wide Missouri '51
A.D. '85
The Adventures of Tom Sawyer '73
The Affair of the Necklace '01
The Agony and the Ecstasy '65
The Alamo '60 ▸
The Alamo '04
The Alamo: Thirteen Days to Glory '87
Alexander '04
Alexander the Great '55
Almost Peaceful '02 ▸
Alone Against Rome '62
Amadeus '84 ▸
Amazing Grace '06 ▸
Anastasia '56 ▸
Anastasia: The Mystery of Anna '86
Andrei Rublev '66 ▸
Anne of the Thousand Days '69 ▸
Antony and Cleopatra '73
Apocalypto '06 ▸
Army of Shadows '69 ▸
Artemisia '97
Assassination of Trotsky '72
The Attic: The Hiding of Anne Frank '88
Attila '54
Attila '01
Augustine of Hippo '72 ▸
The Autobiography of Miss Jane Pittman '74 ▸
Backstairs at the White House '79 ▸
The Ballad of Narayama '83 ▸
Bang Rajan '00 ▸
Barabbas '62
Barefoot in Athens '66
The Bastard '78
The Battle of Algiers '66 ▸
Battle of Britain '69
Battle of the Bulge '65
Battle of Valiant '63
The Battleship Potemkin '25 ▸
Beau Brummel '54 ▸
Becket '64 ▸
Beethoven's Nephew '88
The Beloved Rogue '27 ▸
Ben-Hur '26 ▸
Ben-Hur '59 ▸
Beowulf '07 ▸
Beowulf & Grendel '06
Bhowani Junction '56
The Big Red One '80 ▸
The Birth of a Nation '15 ▸
Black Robe '91 ▸
Blaise Pascal '71 ▸
The Blue Yonder '86
Bonnie Prince Charlie '48
The Bounty '84
Braveheart '95 ▸
A Bridge Too Far '77
Brigham Young: Frontiersman '40
Brother Sun, Sister Moon '73
The Bruce '96
The Bushido Blade '80
Cabeza de Vaca '90 ▸
Cabiria '14
Caesar and Cleopatra '46
Caesar the Conqueror '63
Captain Caution '40
Captain from Castile '47 ▸
Carthage in Flames '60
Catherine Cookson's The Rag Nymph '96
Catherine the Great '34
Catherine the Great '95
Centennial '78 ▸
The Charge of the Light Brigade '36 ▸
The Charge of the Light Brigade '68
Chasing the Deer '94
Children of Paradise '44 ▸
Christopher Columbus '49
Christopher Columbus '85
Christopher Columbus: The Discovery '92
Cleopatra '34
Cleopatra '63
Condemned to Live '35
A Connecticut Yankee '31 ▸
Conquest '37 ▸
The Court Martial of Billy Mitchell '55 ▸
Crazy Horse '96 ▸
Creation '09
Crisis at Central High '80 ▸
Cromwell '70
The Crossing '00
The Crucible '96 ▸
The Crusades '35
Curse of the Golden Flower '06
Dances with Wolves '90 ▸
A Dangerous Man: Lawrence after Arabia '91 ▸
Danton '82 ▸
David and Bathsheba '51 ▸
David Copperfield '35 ▸
David Copperfield '70
David Copperfield '99
The Day That Shook the World '78
DC 9/11: Time of Crisis '04
De Mayerling a Sarajevo '40
Demetrius and the Gladiators '54
Desiree '54
The Devils '71 ▸
The Devil's Disciple '59 ▸
Diane '55
The Divine Lady '29
Doctor Zhivago '65 ▸
Doctor Zhivago '03
Downfall '04 ▸
Druids '01
Drums in the Deep South '51
Dynasty '76
Edward II '92
Eight Men Out '88 ▸
El Cid '61 ▸
Eleanor & Franklin '76 ▸
Eleanor: First Lady of the World '82
Elizabeth '98 ▸
Elizabeth R '72 ▸
Elizabeth: The Golden Age '07
Elizabeth, the Queen '68
The Emperor and the Assassin '99
The Emperor's Shadow '96
Erik, the Viking '65
The Eternal Waltz '54
Eureka Stockade '49
Extramuros '85
Fabiola '48 ▸
FairyTale: A True Story '97
The Fall of the Roman Empire '64 ▸
The Far Horizons '55
Fellini Satyricon '69 ▸
Fiesta '95
Fire Over England '37 ▸
The First Olympics: Athens 1896 '84
The First Texan '56
Flyboys '06
Forever and a Day '43 ▸
Forty Days of Musa Dagh '85
47 Ronin, Part 1 '42 ▸
47 Ronin, Part 2 '42 ▸
1492: Conquest of Paradise '92
Freedom Road '79
Gallipoli '81 ▸
Gangs of New York '02 ▸
Gate of Hell '54 ▸
The Gathering Storm '74
Geheimakte WB1 '42
Geronimo: An American Legend '93
Gettysburg '93 ▸
Giants of Rome '63
The Girl of Your Dreams '99
Gladiator of Rome '63
Glory '89 ▸
Gods and Generals '03
Gonza the Spearman '86
Good Night, and Good Luck '05 ▸
The Gospel of John '03
Goya's Ghosts '06
The Great Commandment '41
The Greatest Game Ever Played '05
The Greatest Story Ever Told '65
Guilty by Suspicion '91
Harem '99
Hawaii '66 ▸
The Hellfire Club '61
Henry V '44 ▸
Henry V '89 ▸
Hero '03 ▸
Hill Number One '51
Hiroshima '95 ▸
Hitler '62
The Horseman on the Roof '95
Hotel Rwanda '04
The Howards of Virginia '40
The Hunchback '97
The Hunchback of Notre Dame '57
The Hunchback of Notre Dame '82 ▸
Hunter in the Dark '80
I Beheld His Glory '53
I Shot Andy Warhol '96 ▸
If They Tell You I Fell '89
Ike: Countdown to D-Day '04
Imperial Venus '63
In Old Chicago '37 ▸
Innocent Voices '04
The Invaders '63
The Iron Crown '41
The Iron Duke '34
Ironclads '90
Ivan the Terrible, Part 1 '44 ▸
Ivan the Terrible, Part 2 '46 ▸
Ivanhoe '52 ▸
Ivanhoe '82
Ivanhoe '97 ▸
Jakob the Liar '99 ▸
Jeanne la Pucelle '94
Jefferson in Paris '94
Jesus of Nazareth '77 ▸
The Jew '96
The Jewel in the Crown '84 ▸
JFK '91 ▸
Joan of Arc '48
Joan of Arc '99
John Adams '08
Johnny Tremain & the Sons of Liberty '58
Joyeux Noel '05 ▸
Judith of Bethulia '14 ▸
Julius Caesar '53 ▸
Justin Morgan Had a Horse '81
Kama Sutra: A Tale of Love '96
Kaspar Hauser '93
Khartoum '66
King David '85
King Richard and the Crusaders '54
Kingdom of Heaven '05 ▸
Kolberg '45
Korea Patrol '47
Kundun '97 ▸
La Marseillaise '37 ▸
La Nuit de Varennes '82 ▸
The Lady and the Highwayman '89
Lady Godiva '55
Lady Jane '85 ▸
Last Days of Pompeii '35
The Last Emperor '87 ▸
Last Four Days '77
The Last Legion '07
The Last of the Mohicans '85
The Last Station '09
The Last Valley '71
Lawrence of Arabia '62 ▸
Le Complot '73 ▸
The Legend of Suriyothai '02
The Libertine '05
The Lighthorsemen '87 ▸
The Lindbergh Kidnapping Case '76 ▸
The Lion in Winter '68 ▸
The Lion in Winter '03 ▸
The Lion of Thebes '64 ▸
Lionheart '87
Little House on the Prairie '74 ▸
Lloyds of London '36 ▸
Long Shadows '86
The Lost City '05
Ludwig '72
Luther '74
The Magician of Lublin '79
The Mahabharata '89
Mahler '74 ▸
A Man for All Seasons '66 ▸
A Man for All Seasons '88 ▸
Mandela '87 ▸
Marie Antoinette '38
Marie Antoinette '06
The Marquise of O '76
Martin Luther '53
Mary of Scotland '36 ▸
Mary, Queen of Scots '71
Masada '81 ▸
Mata Hari '85
Mayerling '68
Mayflower: The Pilgrims' Adventure '79
The Messenger: The Story of Joan of Arc '99
Michael Collins '96 ▸

Historical

Missiles of October '74 ▶
The Mission '86 ▶
Mrs. Brown '97 ▶
Mockery '27
Moll Flanders '96
Mongol '07 ▶
Monsieur N. '03 ▶
The Moonraker '58
Moses '96
The Motorcycle Diaries '04 ▶
Mountain Man '77
Mountbatten: The Last Viceroy '86
Munich '05 ▶
Mutiny on the Bounty '35 ▶
Mutiny on the Bounty '62
Napoleon '27 ▶
Napoleon '03
The Nativity Story '06
Nefertiti, Queen of the Nile '64
The New World '05 ▶
Nicholas and Alexandra '71
Nightjohn '96
Nine Days a Queen '36 ▶
The Ninth Day '04 ▶
Nixon '95 ▶
Norseman '78
O Jerusalem '07
Omar Khayyam '57
The Ordeal of Dr. Mudd '80 ▶
Orphan Train '79 ▶
Orphans of the Storm '21 ▶
Overlanders '46 ▶
Passion in the Desert '97
Passion of Joan of Arc '28 ▶
The Passover Plot '75
The Pathfinder '94
Pathfinder '07
The Patriot '00
Peter and Paul '81
Peter the First: Part 1 '37
Peter the First: Part 2 '38
Peter the Great '86 ▶
Pharoah's Army '95
Portrait of a Lady '96 ▶
Portrait of a Rebel: Margaret Sanger '82
The Power of One '92
Pride and Prejudice '40 ▶
The Private Life of Henry VIII '33 ▶
The Private Lives of Elizabeth & Essex '39 ▶
Queen Christina '33 ▶
Queen Margot '94 ▶
Quo Vadis '12
Quo Vadis '51 ▶
Quo Vadis '85
Ragtime '81 ▶
Raintree County '57
Rasputin '85 ▶
Rasputin and the Empress '33 ▶
Rasputin: Dark Servant of Destiny '96 ▶
The Rebels '79
The Red and the Black '57 ▶
Red Cliff '08 ▶
Reign of Terror '49
A Respectable Trade '98
Restoration '94 ▶
Revolution '85
Richard III '55 ▶
The Right Stuff '83 ▶
Rikyu '90 ▶
The Rise of Louis XIV '66 ▶
Roanoak '86
Rob Roy—The Highland Rogue '53
The Robe '53
Robin and Marian '76
Robin Hood '10
Roots '77 ▶
Roots: The Gift '88
Roots: The Next Generation '79 ▶
Rosewood '96 ▶
Royal Deceit '94
A Royal Scandal '96
Saint Joan '57
St. Michael Had a Rooster '72
St. Patrick: The Irish Legend '00
Salome '53
Samson and Delilah '96
Samurai Banners '69
Samurai Reincarnation '81
Scarlet Empress '34 ▶
The Scarlet Letter '95
The Scarlet Pimpernel '34 ▶
The Scarlet Pimpernel '82 ▶
The Scarlet Pimpernel '99
The Scarlet Pimpernel 2: Mademoiselle Guillotine '99
The Scarlet Pimpernel 3: The Kidnapped King '99
The Scarlet Tunic '97
Sebastiane '79 ▶
The Seekers '79
Senso '54 ▶
Separate but Equal '91 ▶
September Dawn '07
Shaka Zulu '83 ▶
Shenandoah '65 ▶
Shin Heike Monogatari '55 ▶
The Sicilian '87
The Sign of the Cross '33
The Silk Road '92
Sins of Rome '54
Six Wives of Henry VIII '71 ▶
Soldier in Love '67
Soldier of Orange '78 ▶
Song of Love '47 ▶
Sophie Scholl: The Final Days '05 ▶
Soul of the Game '96 ▶
Spartacus '60 ▶
Spy of Napoleon '36
Sunrise at Campobello '60 ▶
Surviving Picasso '96
The Sword of El Cid '62
Tai-Pan '86
A Tale of Two Cities '89 ▶
Tamango '59
The Ten Commandments '23
The Ten Commandments '56 ▶
Ten Days That Shook the World '27 ▶
Ten Who Dared '60
Tharus Son of Attila '62
That Hamilton Woman '41 ▶
There Will Be Blood '07 ▶
Therese '86 ▶
They Died with Their Boots On '41 ▶
Thirteen Days '00 ▶
'38: Vienna before the Fall '88
This England '42
The Thorn Birds '83 ▶
300 '07
Three Sovereigns for Sarah '85
To End All Wars '01
To Kill a King '03
The Tower of London '39
Tower of London '62
Tower of Screaming Virgins '68
The Triangle Factory Fire Scandal '79
The Truce '96 ▶
True Women '97
The Tunnel '01 ▶
Uncle Tom's Cabin '14
Uncle Tom's Cabin '69
Untold Scandal '03
Uranus '91 ▶
Vanina Vanini '61 ▶
Victoria Regina '61
The Virgin Queen '55 ▶
Viva Zapata! '52 ▶
The Wannsee Conference '84 ▶
The War Lord '65 ▶
Warlords '08
Warrior Queen '03
The Warriors '55
Waterloo '71
Weeping Meadow '04
The White Rose '83 ▶
Who Has Seen the Wind? '77
The Winds of Kitty Hawk '78
The Winter War '89 ▶
A Woman Called Golda '82 ▶
A Woman Called Moses '78
Young Bess '53 ▶
Young Catherine '91 ▶
Young Mr. Lincoln '39 ▶

Historical Romance

see also *Historical Drama*
The Affair of the Necklace '01
The Agony and the Ecstasy '65
Alexander '04
Angelique '64
Angelique and the King '66
Angelique and the Sultan '68
Angelique: The Road to Versailles '65
Anne of the Thousand Days '69 ▶
Becoming Jane '07
Braveheart '95 ▶
Caesar and Cleopatra '46
Casanova '05
Catherine the Great '34
Catherine the Great '95
Clarissa '91 ▶
Cleopatra '34
Cleopatra '63
Cleopatra '99
David and Bathsheba '51 ▶
Doctor Zhivago '65 ▶
Doctor Zhivago '03
Eleanor & Franklin '76 ▶
The Hunchback of Notre Dame '57
The Hunchback of Notre Dame '82 ▶
The Hunchback of Notre Dame '96 ▶
Ivanhoe '52 ▶
Ivanhoe '82
Ivanhoe '97 ▶
Jefferson in Paris '94
Kama Sutra: A Tale of Love '96
The Last of the Mohicans '85
Love Happens '09
Mrs. Brown '97 ▶
The New World '05 ▶
Nicholas and Alexandra '71
The Other Boleyn Girl '08
Portrait of a Lady '67
Portrait of a Lady '96 ▶
Pride and Prejudice '40 ▶
The Private Life of Henry VIII '33 ▶
The Private Lives of Elizabeth & Essex '39 ▶
Ragtime '81 ▶
Silk '07
Untamable Angelique '67

Hit Men/Women

see also *Assassination; Organized Crime*
African Rage '78
Amateur '94 ▶
Amores Perros '00 ▶
Angel of Death '09
Angel's Dance '99
Asian Stories '06
Assassination Tango '03 ▶
Assassins '95
Back to Back '96
Baja '95
Ballistic: Ecks vs. Sever '02
Bangkok Dangerous '00
Bangkok Dangerous '08
Big City Blues '99
The Big Hit '98
Big Trouble '02
Blackjack '97
Blast of Silence '61
Blonde and Blonder '07
Body Armour '07
Body Count '95
The Bodyguard '92
The Bourne Identity '02 ▶
Break '09
Breakaway '95
Brother '97
Bulletproof Heart '95 ▶
Bulworth '98 ▶
The Casino Job '08
Chain of Fools '00
Chameleon '98
Codename: Jaguar '00
Cold Sweat '93
Collateral '04 ▶
The Collectors '99
Confessions of a Dangerous Mind '02
Confessions of a Hit Man '94
The Contract '98
The Contract '07
Contract Killers '08
The Contractor '07
Crank: High Voltage '09
Crossfire '98
Cybercity '99
Daredevil '03
DaVinci's War '92
Dead Fish '04
Deadlier Than the Male '67
Decay '98
Deja Vu '89
Deliberate Intent '01
Desert Saints '01
Desperado '95 ▶
Destination Vegas '95
Devils on the Doorstep '00
Diary of a Hitman '91
Dinner Rush '00 ▶
Direct Hit '93
Dog Bite Dog '06
Dumb & Dumber '94
8 Heads in a Duffel Bag '96
El Mariachi '93 ▶
Elmore Leonard's Gold Coast '97
Escape Clause '96
Exiled '06
Faithful '95
Fallen Angels '95
The Family '70
Fatal Chase '77
Fatal Justice '93
The Feminine Touch '95
A Few Days in September '06
Fighting with Anger '07
Final Mission '84
Firepower '79
Fish in a Barrel '01
Formula 51 '01
Full Disclosure '00
Full Time Killer '01
The Funeral '96 ▶
The Gene Generation '07
Ghost Dog: The Way of the Samurai '99
Gigli '03
Goodbye, Lover '99
Grosse Pointe Blank '97 ▶
Hail Mafia '65
Hard-Boiled '92
Her Name Is Cat '99
Hidden Agenda '01
The Hit '01
The Hit List '93
Hit Men '73
Hit Woman: The Double Edge '93
Hitman '07
Hitman's Journal '99
Hitman's Run '99
Hogfather '06
Hollow Point '95
Honor and Glory '92
Hotel '01
I Accidentally Domed Your Son '04
In Bruges '08
In the Shadows '01
Intolerable Cruelty '03
The Jackal '97
Jerry and Tom '98
The Job '03
Joyride '97
Kill Bill Vol. 1 '03 ▶
Kill Bill Vol. 2 '04 ▶
The Killer '90 ▶
The Killers '46 ▶
Killers '10
Killing Emmett Young '02
Killing Machine '02
Killing Time '97
Killshot '09
King of the Ants '03
Kiss Me Deadly '08
La Femme Nikita '91 ▶
Lady Jayne Killer '03
Lansdown '01
Last Chance '07
The Last Hit '93
The Last Hit Man '08
Le Choc '82
Le Samourai '67 ▶
Lethal Panther '90
Life Tastes Good '99
Life Without Dick '01
The Line '08
The Lineup '58
Little Odessa '94
The Lost Samaritan '08
Love '05
Love and Action in Chicago '99
Lucky Number Slevin '06
Made Men '99
The Man Who Knew Too Little '97
Man with a Gun '95
The Manchurian Candidate '62 ▶
The Matador '06 ▶
Max Payne '08
Mean Johnny Barrows '75
The Mechanic '72
The Memory of a Killer '03
The Merry Gentleman '08
The Mexican '01
Mr. & Mrs. Smith '05 ▶
Mr. Nice Guy '86
Montana '97
Murda Muzik '03
Murder by Contract '58
Mysterious Mr. Moto '38
The Naked City '48 ▶
Naked Weapon '03
Nemesis 4: Cry of Angels '97
Night of the Running Man '94
No Witness '04
Nobody '07
Nurse Betty '00 ▶
On the Edge '02
On the Run '83
Once Upon a Time in Mexico '03 ▶
One Night at McCool's '01
Our Lady of the Assassins '01
The Outside Man '73
Over the Wire '95
The Pact '99
Paid '06
Paid to Kill '54
Panic '00
Party 7 '00
Perfect Assassins '98
Perfect Killer '77
The Perfect Sleep '08
Pistol Opera '02
Pistol Whipped '08
The Pleasure Drivers '05
Point of No Return '93
Portrait of a Hitman '77
The Positively True Adventures of the Alleged Texas Cheerleader-Murdering Mom '93 ▶
Prisoner of Love '99
Prizzi's Honor '85 ▶
The Professional '94
Project: Kill! '77
Puerto Vallarta Squeeze '04
Pulp Fiction '94 ▶
Quick '93
Raising Heroes '97
Razor Blade Smile '98
Real Time '08
Red King, White Knight '89
Red Rock West '93 ▶
The Replacement Killers '98
R.I.C.C.O. '02
Rick '03
Ripley's Game '02 ▶
Road to Perdition '02 ▶
Sabotage '96
Sanctuary '98
Savage Hearts '95
Season for Assassins '71
The Shadow Conspiracy '96
Shadowboxer '06
Shark Skin Man and Peach Hip Girl '98
Shattered Image '98
Shoot 'Em Up '07
The Silencer '99
Sin City '05
Six Ways to Sunday '99
Sleepers '96
Smokin' Aces '07
Smokin' Aces 2: Assassins' Ball '10
Solo '06
The Specialist '75
The Specialist '94
Stiletto '69
Stiletto '08
Strangers on a Train '51 ▶
Suddenly '54 ▶
Suicide Ride '97
Ten 'Til Noon '06
The Tesseract '03
Things to Do in Denver When You're Dead '95 ▶
This Gun for Hire '42 ▶
The 3 Marias '03
Thrill Seekers '99
Too Hot to Handle '76
Triggermen '02
Two Days in the Valley '96 ▶
Two Tough Guys '03
U-Turn '97
Wanted '08 ▶
War '07
War, Inc. '08
Warm Blooded Killers '01
Whacked! '02
Who is Cletis Tout? '02
The Whole Nine Yards '00
The Whole Ten Yards '04
Wish You Were Dead '00
The Wrecking Crew '99
You Kill Me '07 ▶

Hitchhikers

see *Thumbs Up*

Hockey

see also *Skating*
Accident '83
Bon Cop Bad Cop '06
The Boys '97
The Cutting Edge '92
D3: The Mighty Ducks '96
D2: The Mighty Ducks '94
The Duke of West Point '38
Dutch Girls '87
Happy Gilmore '96
Hockey Night '84
The Ice Rink '99
It's a Pleasure '45
Jack Frost '98
Lethal Weapon 3 '92
The Love Guru '08
Love Story '70 ▶
The Mighty Ducks '92
Miracle '04 ▶
Miracle on Ice '81
MVP (Most Valuable Primate) '00
Mystery, Alaska '99
Mystery of the Million Dollar Hockey Puck '75
No Sleep 'Til Madison '02
Paperback Hero '73
The Rocket '05 ▶
Slap Shot '77 ▶
Slap Shot 2: Breaking the Ice '02
Sticks and Stones '08
Strange Brew '83
Sudden Death '95
Tooth Fairy '10
Touch and Go '86
Waking Up Wally '05
Youngblood '86

Holidays

see also *Christmas; Halloween; Horrible Holidays; New Year's Eve; Thanksgiving*
Adam Sandler's 8 Crazy Nights '02
An American Carol '08
Carry On Behind '75
Easter Parade '48 ▶
Groundhog Day '93 ▶
Grown Ups '10
I Hate Valentine's Day '09
Jack Frost '97
Plan B '97
Strange Days '95 ▶
Turumba '84 ▶
Two Weeks with Love '50
Valentine's Day '10
The White Balloon '95 ▶

The Holocaust

see also *Germany; Judaism; Nazis & Other Paramilitary Slugs; World War II*
Adam Resurrected '08
Alan & Naomi '92

▶ = rated three bones or higher

Almost Peaceful '02 ▶
Amen '02 ▶
Anne Frank: The Whole Story '01 ▶
The Assault '86 ▶
The Assisi Underground '84
The Attic: The Hiding of Anne Frank '88
Au Revoir les Enfants '87 ▶
The Boxer and Death '63 ▶
The Boy in the Striped Pajamas '08 ▶
A Call to Remember '97
Charlie Grant's War '80
Christabel '89
Cold Days '66
Conspiracy '01
The Counterfeiters '07 ▶
The Courageous Heart of Irena Sendler '09 ▶
David '79 ▶
A Day in October '92
The Devil's Arithmetic '99
Diamonds of the Night '64 ▶
The Diary of Anne Frank '59 ▶
Dominion: Prequel to the Exorcist '05
Enemies, a Love Story '89 ▶
Era Notte a Roma '60 ▶
Europa, Europa '91 ▶
Everything is Illuminated '05 ▶
The Execution '85
Facing Windows '03
Fateless '05 ▶
Forced March '90
The Garden of the Finzi-Continis '71 ▶
Genghis Cohn '93
Getting Away With Murder '96
The Girl of Your Dreams '99
God on Trial '08
The Goebbels Experiment '05
Good '08
Good Evening, Mr. Wallenberg '93
The Grey Zone '01
Hanna's War '88
The Hiding Place '75
Hitler '62
The Holcroft Covenant '85
Holocaust '78 ▶
Holocaust Survivors... Remembrance of Love '83
I Love You, I Love You Not '97
In a Glass Cage '86
In the Presence of Mine Enemies '97
Jacob the Liar '74
Jakob the Liar '99 ▶
Kanal '56 ▶
Kapo '59 ▶
Korczak '90 ▶
The Last Butterfly '92
The Last Metro '80 ▶
Les Miserables '95
Les Violons du Bal '74
Max and Helen '90
Mendel '98 ▶
Murderers Among Us: The Simon Wiesenthal Story '89 ▶
The Murderers Are Among Us '46
Never Forget '91
The Ninth Day '04 ▶
Out of the Ashes '03
Paper Clips '04 ▶
Passenger '61 ▶
The Pawnbroker '65 ▶
The Pianist '02 ▶
Playing for Time '80 ▶
Prisoner of Paradise '02 ▶
Rescuers: Stories of Courage—Two Couples '98 ▶
Reunion '88 ▶
The Revolt of Job '84 ▶
The Rose Garden '89
Rosenstrasse '03 ▶
Schindler's List '93 ▶
A Secret '07 ▶
The Serpent's Egg '78
The Shop on Main Street '65 ▶
Sophie's Choice '82 ▶
Speak Up! It's So Dark '93
The Substance of Fire '96
Sunshine '99
Transport from Paradise '65
Triumph of the Spirit '89 ▶
The Truce '96 ▶
Uprising '01 ▶
Verdict on Auschwitz: The Frankfurt Auschwitz Trial 1963—1965 '93 ▶
The Wannsee Conference '84 ▶
War & Love '84
The White Rose '83 ▶

Home Alone

***see also** Childhood Visions*
Adventures in Babysitting '87
And You Thought Your Parents Were Weird! '91
Anything for a Thrill '37
The Apple Dumpling Gang '75
Baby's Day Out '94
Blank Check '93
Bless the Beasts and Children '71
The Blue Lagoon '80
Boys Will Be Boys '97
Camp Nowhere '94
Christina's House '99
Cloak & Dagger '84
Cohen and Tate '88
Courage Mountain '89
Cross My Heart '91
Dirkham Detective Agency '83
Dirt Bike Kid '86
Don't Tell Mom the Babysitter's Dead '91
Duck Season '04 ▶
Explorers '85
Famous Five Get into Trouble '70
Fatal Skies '90
Fear of the Dark '02
Footsteps '03
Four Rooms '95
Gleaming the Cube '89
The Goonies '85
He Is My Brother '75
Home Alone '90 ▶
Home Alone 2: Lost in New York '92
Home Alone 3 '97
Honey, I Shrunk the Kids '89
Honey, We Shrunk Ourselves '97
Hook '91
The Horse Without a Head '63
House Arrest '96
Invaders from Mars '53
Invaders from Mars '86
Island Trader '71
Just William's Luck '47
Legend of Billie Jean '85
The Littlest Horse Thieves '76
Lord of the Flies '63 ▶
Lord of the Flies '90
Mr. Wise Guy '42
Monkey Trouble '94
The Monster Squad '87
Nightwaves '03
Nobody Knows '04
Paradise '82
Playing Dangerous '95
The Rescue '88
Return to the Blue Lagoon '91
Scream '96 ▶
Shipwrecked '90
Snow Treasure '67
3 Ninjas '92
3 Ninjas Kick Back '94
Tideland '05
2 Brothers & a Bride '03
A Waltz Through the Hills '88
The Window '49 ▶
Young Sherlock Holmes '85

Home Invasion

***see also** Yuppie Nightmares*
Crime Wave '54
Cul de Sac '66 ▶
Desperate Hours '55 ▶
Desperate Hours '90
Door to Door Maniac '61
Funny Games '97
Funny Games '07 ▶
If I Die Before I Wake '98
I'll Sleep When I'm Dead '03 ▶
The Killing Floor '06
Lady in a Cage '64 ▶
The Last House on the Left '09
Panic Room '02
Perfect Hideout '08
Romper Stomper '92
The Strangers '08
Straw Dogs '72 ▶
Wait until Dark '67 ▶

The Homefront: England

***see also** World War II*
The Affair '95
And a Nightingale Sang '91
Carrie's War '04
The Edge of Love '08
The Haunted Airman '06
Hope and Glory '87 ▶
The Land Girls '98
The Last of the Blonde Bombshells '00
Mrs. Henderson Presents '05
Mrs. Miniver '42 ▶
Nanny McPhee 2 '10
Salute John Citizen '42 ▶
This Above All '42
The Water Horse: Legend of the Deep '07
Waterloo Road '44
The Weaker Sex '49
The White Cliffs of Dover '44 ▶

The Homefront: U.S./ Canada

***see also** World War II*
Air Raid Wardens '43
Blondie for Victory '42
Bye Bye Blues '89
Come See the Paradise '90 ▶
Flags of Our Fathers '06 ▶
For the Moment '94
The Home Front '02
The Human Comedy '43 ▶
I'll Remember April '99
In Love and War '91
In the Mood '87
A League of Their Own '92 ▶
The Messenger '09 ▶
The More the Merrier '43 ▶
1941 '79
Racing with the Moon '84 ▶
Raggedy Man '81 ▶
Ride the Wild Fields '00
Saboteur '42 ▶
Since You Went Away '44 ▶
Stop-Loss '08 ▶
The Summer of My German Soldier '78 ▶
Swing Shift '84
The War Bride '01
Wedding in White '72

Homeless

***see also** Great Depression; Hard Knock Life; Yuppie Nightmares*
Accatone! '61 ▶
All Mine to Give '56
Amores Perros '00 ▶
August Rush '07
The Billion Dollar Hobo '78
Billy: Portrait of a Street Kid '77
Brother to Brother '04
Bums '93
Carpool Guy '05
Caught '96
The Caveman's Valentine '01
The Child '05
Children of Sanchez '79
Children Underground '03 ▶
The Christmas Choir '08
City Lights '31 ▶
Curly Sue '91
Distant Thunder '73 ▶
Dodes 'ka-den '70 ▶
Down, Out and Dangerous '95
Drillbit Taylor '08
Duck '05
Eddie Presley '92
Emanon '86
Emperor of the North Pole '73 ▶
Entry Level '07
First, Last and Deposit '00
The Fisher King '91 ▶
Gardens of the Night '08
Gigantic '08
God Bless the Child '88 ▶
The Grapes of Wrath '40 ▶
Guarding Eddy '04
Hank and Mike '08
Heater '99
Home for Christmas '90
Home of Angels '94
Homecoming '96
The Innocent Sleep '95
Into the West '92 ▶
It Happened on 5th Avenue '47
Joe Gould's Secret '00
Kanal '56 ▶
Kicking It '08
The Kid '21 ▶
Land of Plenty '04
Le Petit Lieutenant '05
Life Stinks '91
Los Olvidados '50 ▶
The Lovers on the Bridge '91
The Lower Depths '36 ▶
The Lower Depths '57 ▶
The Man from Left Field '93
The Man Without a Past '02 ▶
Michael Shayne: Private Detective '40
Midnight Cowboy '69 ▶
Mon Homme '96
Mondo '96
Noel '04
None But the Lonely Heart '44 ▶
Oliver! '68 ▶
Oliver Twist '22 ▶
Oliver Twist '33
Oliver Twist '48 ▶
Oliver Twist '82 ▶
Oliver Twist '85
Oliver Twist '97
Oliver Twist '00 ▶
Oliver Twist '05 ▶
Original Intent '91
An Orphan Boy of Vienna '37
Pardon My Trunk '52
Pinero '01
The Prince of Central Park '77 ▶
The Pursuit of Happyness '06
Resurrecting the Champ '07
The Saint of Fort Washington '93
Salaam Bombay! '88 ▶
Samaritan: The Mitch Snyder Story '86 ▶
Scarecrow '73
Show Me '04
Silas Marner '85 ▶
The Soloist '09
Sounder '72 ▶
The Stray '00
Streetwise '84 ▶
Sullivan's Travels '41 ▶
Summer Magic '63
They Shall Have Music '39
The Third Wheel '02
The Tiger's Tale '06
Times Square '80
Up Your Alley '89
The Vagrant '92
Where God Left His Shoes '07
Where the Day Takes You '92
The Wild Parrots of Telegraph Hill '03 ▶
With Honors '94

Homicide

Abandon '02
Absolute Power '97
Agatha Christie's Murder is Easy '82
Ajami '09 ▶
Alpha Dog '06
American Gun '05
The Amityville Horror '05
Among Brothers '05
Another Life '01
Bad Lieutenant: Port of Call New Orleans '09
The Badge '02
Basic '03
Beat '00
Behind the Sun '01
Behind the Wall '08
Between Your Legs '99
Big Brown Eyes '36
The Black Camel '31
The Black Dahlia '06
The Black Doll '38
The Blackheath Poisonings '92
The Bloodstained Shadow '78
The Blue Gardenia '53 ▶
A Blueprint for Murder '53
Bon Voyage '03 ▶
Borderline '02 ▶
Bordertown '06
Breaking Point '09
The Bridesmaid '04
Bright Future '03 ▶
Bubble '06
Bunny Whipped '06
The Butterfly Effect 3: Revelation '09
Calling Dr. Death '43
The Case of the Bloody Iris '72
The Case of the Scorpion's Tail '71
Cassandra's Dream '07
The Cat's Meow '01
Cause of Death '00
The Caveman's Valentine '01
Changeling '08 ▶
The Charlatan '29
Charlie Chan at Monte Carlo '37
Charlie Chan at the Circus '36
Charlie Chan in City of Darkness '39
Charlie Chan in Honolulu '38
Charlie Chan in Shanghai '35
Charlie Chan on Broadway '37
Charlie Chan's Murder Cruise '40
Chicago '02 ▶
City by the Sea '02
Close Your Eyes '02
Cop Au Vin '85
Crash '05 ▶
Crime and Punishment, USA '59
Criminal Lovers '99
The Cry: La Llorona '07
Day of Wrath '06
Dead Broke '99
A Dead Calling '06
The Dead Girl '06
Dead Gorgeous '02
Dead Man's Eyes '44
Dead Ringer '64
Dead Silence '07
Death on the Set '35
Die Mommie Die! '03
Dillinger Is Dead '69
Dr. Bell and Mr. Doyle: The Dark Beginnings of Sherlock Holmes '00
A Dog's Breakfast '07
Donkey Punch '08
Edge of Darkness '10
The Edge of Heaven '07 ▶
Edmond '05
8 Women '02 ▶
Elephant '03 ▶
11:14 '03
Eye of the Storm '98
Fascination '04
The Fast Runner '01 ▶
Fear X '03 ▶
Gangs of New York '02 ▶
The Garment Jungle '57
A Girl Cut in Two '07
The Good German '06
Gosford Park '01 ▶
Gothika '03
Hangover Square '45
Hate Crime '05
Heart of Stone '01
The Hole '01
Hollywood Homicide '03
Hollywoodland '06
Identity '03
I'm Not Scared '03
In the Bedroom '01 ▶
In the Cut '03
In the Valley of Elah '07 ▶
Insomnia '02 ▶
Inspector Lynley Mysteries: A Great Deliverance '01
Irreversible '02
The Jacket '05
Jesse Stone: Death in Paradise '06
Jesse Stone: Night Passage '06
Jesse Stone: Stone Cold '05
Jiminy Glick in LaLa Wood '05
Jindabyne '06
Ju-On: The Grudge '03
Juke Girl '42
Keeping Mum '05
Keillers Park '05
The Killer Inside Me '10
The Killer Must Kill Again '75
The Killing Club '01
The Killing of John Lennon '07
A Killing Spring '02
The King '05
La Femme Infidele '69 ▶
La Vie Promise '02
Le Petit Lieutenant '05
The Life Before Her Eyes '07
Like Father Like Son '05
The Lineup '58
Loaded '08
Lola and Billy the Kid '98
Lonely Hearts '06
Love '05
The Lovely Bones '09
Macbeth '06
Madeo '09
Malicious Intent '99
Man of the House '05
The Man Who Wasn't There '01 ▶
The Man with Two Faces '34
The Manson Family '04
Melissa '97
Memento '00 ▶
Merci pour le Chocolat '00 ▶
Miami Vice '06
A Mighty Heart '07 ▶
Moontide '42
Motives '03
Murder at Devil's Glen '99
Murder by Numbers '02
Murder in Greenwich '02
Murder in Greenwich Village '37
The Murder of Stephen Lawrence '99 ▶
Murderous Intent '06 ▶
Mystery Street '50
Mystic River '03 ▶
Never Forget '08
Night Train Murders '75
Nightwaves '03
Notorious '09
November '05 ▶
The Number 23 '07
Nutcracker: Money, Madness & Murder '87 ▶
The Omen '06
100 Mile Rule '02
One Kill '00 ▶
One to Another '06
One Way '06
One Way Out '02
Our Lady of the Assassins '01
Out of Time '03
The Outrage '64
Pathology '08
P.D. James: Death in Holy Orders '03
P.D. James: The Murder Room '04
Perfect Murder, Perfect Town '00
Perfect Stranger '07

▶ = rated three bones or higher

Perfume: The Story of a Murderer *'06*
Personal Effects *'09*
Pillow of Death *'45*
The Pink Panther *'06*
Posers *'02*
Protector *'97*
Quicksand *'01*
Recipe for Revenge *'98*
The Reckoning *'03* ▸
The Riddle *'07*
R.S.V.P. *'02*
Running Scared *'06*
Savage Grace *'07*
Saw 2 *'05*
Scandal Sheet *'52*
The Secret in Their Eyes *'09*
Series 7: The Contenders *'01*
Shadow *'56*
Shanghai *'09*
Signs & Wonders *'00*
The Silence *'06*
Sleep Easy, Hutch Rimes *'00*
Slow Burn *'05*
Soldier's Girl *'03* ▸
Spider *'02* ▸
Sudden Manhattan *'96*
Summer Storm *'44*
Surrogates *'09*
Taboo *'02*
Tell No One *'06* ▸
Three Blind Mice *'02*
Torso *'01*
Transsiberian *'08* ▸
The Truth About Charlie *'02*
Tsotsi *'05* ▸
Unfaithful *'02* ▸
United States of Leland *'03*
The Unsuspected *'47*
The Upturned Glass *'47*
Valentine *'01*
Veronica Guerin *'03*
The Village *'04*
The Voice of Merrill *'52*
Volver *'06* ▸
The Walker *'07*
Wallander: Firewall *'08*
Wallander: One Step Behind *'08*
Wallander: Sidetracked *'08*
Water's Edge *'03*
The Weight of Water *'00*
What Your Eyes Don't See *'99*
White Oleander *'02*
Whiteout *'09*
Winter of Frozen Dreams *'08*
With a Friend Like Harry *'00* ▸
The Wizard of Gore *'07*
Wonderland *'03*
The Wrong Guy *'96*

Homosexuality

***see** Bisexuality; Gays; Lesbians*

Honeymoon

***see also** Marriage; Newlyweds; Wedding Bells*

Above Suspicion *'43* ▸
Awakening of Candra *'81*
The Bat People *'74*
Battle Shock *'56*
Bees in Paradise *'44*
Beyond the Rocks *'22*
The Blood Spattered Bride *'72*
Bloodstone *'88*
The Bride & the Beast *'58*
Bulldog Drummond's Bride *'39*
Caged Fear *'92*
Cat Girl *'57*
Chaos & Cadavers *'03*
Dangerous Crossing *'53*
Dark Country *'09*
Dark Honeymoon *'08*
Devil's Pond *'03*
Diecovery *'03*
Dr. Jekyll & Mr. Hyde *'99*
The Ghost and the Guest *'43*
A Good Woman *'04*
Halfmoon *'95*
Haunted Honeymoon *'86*
Having Wonderful Crime *'45*
The Heartbreak Kid *'07*
Heaven's Burning *'97*
Honeymoon Academy *'90*
Honeymoon Horror *'82*
Honeymoon in Vegas *'92*
Jupiter's Thigh *'81*
Just Married *'03*
The Long, Long Trailer *'54*
Lucky Partners *'40*
Made in Heaven *'52*
The Moon's Our Home *'36*
Move Over, Darling *'63*
Murder on the Midnight Express *'74*
Never Say Die *'39*
The Newlydeads *'87*
Niagara *'52*
The Other Half *'06*
Out to Sea *'97*
The Palermo Connection *'91*
A Perfect Getaway *'09*
Photographing Fairies *'97*
Prelude to a Kiss *'92*
The Prince & Me 3: A Royal Honeymoon *'08*
Private Lives *'31* ▸
The Red Rope *'37*
Seventh Moon *'08*
Sextette *'78*
Shattered Image *'98*
The She-Beast *'65*
Shutter *'08*
Strike It Rich *'90*
Treacherous Crossing *'92*
True Romance *'93*
Vanishing Act *'88*
A Vow to Kill *'94*
You Gotta Stay Happy *'48*
Zombie Honeymoon *'04*

Hong Kong

***see also** Asia; China*

The Amsterdam Kill *'78*
The Art of War *'00*
Autumn Moon *'92*
A Better Tomorrow, Part 1 *'86*
Black Mask *'96*
Blade in Hong Kong *'85*
Bloodsport *'88*
Boarding Gate *'07*
Breaking News *'04*
Chinese Box *'97*
Chungking Express *'95* ▸
Cleopatra Jones & the Casino of Gold *'75*
Crime Lords *'91*
Detonator 2: Night Watch *'95*
Dr. Jekyll & Mr. Hyde *'99*
Double Impact *'91*
Dream Lovers *'86*
Enter the Dragon *'73* ▸
Eros *'04*
Fallen Angels *'95*
First Love and Other Pains / One of Them *'99*
Five Golden Dragons *'67*
Forced Vengeance *'82*
Gen-X Cops *'99*
Hong Kong 1941 *'84*
Hong Kong '97 *'94*
In the Mood for Love *'00*
Infernal Affairs *'02* ▸
Just Like Weather *'86* ▸
Knock Off *'98*
Koroshi *'67*
Kung Fu Hustle *'04*
La Moustache *'05*
Love Is a Many-Splendored Thing *'55*
The Medallion *'03*
New Police Story *'04*
Noble House *'88*
Once a Thief *'96* ▸
Push *'09*
Romeo Must Die *'00*
Rush Hour 2 *'01*
Shadow of China *'91* ▸
Silver Hawk *'04*
Tai-Pan *'86*
The Terror of the Tongs *'61*
That Man Bolt *'73*
TNT Jackson *'75*
To Live and Die in Hong Kong *'89*
2046 *'04*
Twin Dragons *'92*
Vampire Effect *'03*
Yin & Yang of Mr. Go *'71*

Hopping Vampires

Exorcist Master *'93*
Gods of Wu Tang *'83*

Horrible Holidays

***see also** Christmas; Halloween; Holidays; New Year's Eve; Thanksgiving; Vacation Hell*

American Gun *'02* ▸
April Fool's Day *'86*
April Fool's Day *'08*
Asian Stories *'06*
Bad Santa *'03*
Black Christmas *'75*
Black Christmas *'06*
Bloodbeat *'85*
Bloody New Year *'87*
Chasing Christmas *'05*
Christmas Evil *'80*
Columbus Day *'08*
Don't Open Till Christmas *'84*
Dorm That Dripped Blood *'82*
Frankenstein Sings... The Movie *'95*
Gremlins *'84* ▸
Halloween *'78* ▸
Halloween 2: The Nightmare Isn't Over! *'81*
Halloween 3: Season of the Witch *'82*
Halloween 4: The Return of Michael Myers *'88*
Halloween 5: The Revenge of Michael Myers *'89*
Halloween 6: The Curse of Michael Myers *'95*
Halloween: H20 *'98* ▸
Halloween Night *'90*
Happy Birthday to Me *'81*
Home for the Holidays *'72*
Home Sweet Home *'80*
I Still Know What You Did Last Summer *'98*
Jack-O *'95*
Jam *'06*
The Lottery Ticket *'10*
Mixed Nuts *'94*
Mother's Day *'80*
My Bloody Valentine *'81*
My Bloody Valentine 3D *'09*
The Myth of Fingerprints *'97*
New Year's Evil *'78*
The Night After Halloween *'79*
Night of the Demons *'88*
Night of the Demons 2 *'94*
Night of the Demons 3 *'97*
Piranha 3D *'10*
Pontypool *'09*
'R Xmas *'01*
Reckless *'95*
The Ref *'93* ▸
Resurrection *'99*
Sheitan *'06*
Silent Night, Bloody Night *'73*
Silent Night, Deadly Night *'84*
Silent Night, Deadly Night 2 *'87*
Silent Night, Deadly Night 3: Better Watch Out! *'89*
Silent Night, Deadly Night 4: Initiation *'90*
Silent Night, Deadly Night 5: The Toymaker *'91*
Teen Alien *'78*
Trick or Treats *'82*
Uncle Sam *'96*
Valentine *'01*
Wacko *'83*
What Love Is *'07*
When Do We Eat? *'05*

Horror Anthologies

Alien Massacre *'67*
Asylum *'72*
Body Bags *'93*
Campfire Tales *'98*
Creepshow *'82*
Creepshow 2 *'87*
Cremains *'00* ▸
The Dark Dealer *'95*
Dead of Night *'45* ▸
Dead of Night *'77*
Deadtime Stories *'86*
Dr. Terror's House of Horrors *'65*
Escapes *'86*
Freakshow *'95*
Fright House *'89*
Future Shock *'93*
Gallery of Horrors *'67*
Grim Prairie Tales *'89*
Hellblock 13 *'97*
The House that Dripped Blood *'71*
H.P. Lovecraft's Necronomicon: Book of the Dead *'93*
Into the Badlands *'92*
The Monster Club *'85*
Night Gallery *'69* ▸
Nightmares *'83*
The Offspring *'87*
Once Upon a Midnight Scary *'90*
Quicksilver Highway *'98*
Screamtime *'83*
Spirits of the Dead *'68* ▸
Strange Frequency 2 *'01*
Tales from the Crypt *'72* ▸
Tales from the Darkside: The Movie *'90*
Tales from the Hood *'95*
Tales of Terror *'62*
Tales That Witness Madness *'73*
Terror Tract *'00*
Things *'93*
Three ... Extremes *'04*
Torture Garden *'67*
Trilogy of Terror *'75*
Trilogy of Terror 2 *'96*
Twice-Told Tales *'63* ▸
Twilight Zone: The Movie *'83*
Twists of Terror *'98*
Two Evil Eyes *'90*
The Uncanny *'78*
Vault of Horror *'73*
The Willies *'90*

Horror Comedy

Adventures of Eliza Fraser *'76*
American Vampire *'97*
An American Werewolf in Paris *'97*
Andy Warhol's Dracula *'74* ▸
Andy Warhol's Frankenstein *'74*
April Fool's Day *'86*
Arachnophobia *'90*
Army of Darkness *'92* ▸
Atomic Dog *'98*
Attack Girls' Swim Team vs. the Undead *'07*
Attack of the Killer Tomatoes *'77*
Attack of the Robots *'66*
Auntie Lee's Meat Pies *'92*
Autopsy: A Love Story *'02*
Autopsy of a Ghost *'67*
Bachelor Party in the Bungalow of the Damned *'08*
Bad Channels *'92*
Bad Taste *'88* ▸
Battle Heater *'89*
Battlefield Baseball *'03*
Beauty on the Beach *'61*
Beetlejuice *'88* ▸
Bela Lugosi Meets a Brooklyn Gorilla *'52*
Beverly Hills Bodysnatchers *'89*
Beyond Re-Animator *'03*
Big Meat Eater *'85*
Billy the Kid Versus Dracula *'66*
Biozombie *'98*
Black Magic *'92*
Black Sheep *'06*
Blood & Donuts *'95*
Blood Angels *'05*
Blood Beach *'81*
Blood Hook *'86*
Bloodbath at the House of Death *'85*
Body Bags *'93*
The Bogus Witch Project *'00*
The Bone Yard *'90*
The Boogie Man Will Get You *'42*
Botched *'07*
Bowery Boys Meet the Monsters *'54*
Brain Damage *'88*
Bride of Chucky *'98*
Bride of Re-Animator *'89*
Bubba Ho-Tep *'03* ▸
A Bucket of Blood *'59* ▸
Bugged! *'96*
Carry On Screaming *'66*
Christmas Evil *'80*
C.H.U.D. *'84*
C.H.U.D. 2: Bud the Chud *'89*
The Comedy of Terrors *'64* ▸
Creature from the Haunted Sea *'60*
The Creeps *'97*
Critters *'86*
Critters 2: The Main Course *'88*
Critters 3 *'91*
Critters 4 *'91*
Cruel Restaurant *'08*
Curse of the Queerwolf *'87*
Cutting Class *'89*
Dance of the Dead *'08*
Dead Alive *'93*
Dead Heat *'88*
Dead Snow *'09*
Dr. Jekyll and Sister Hyde *'71*
Dog Soldiers *'01*
Dolls *'87*
Doom Asylum *'88*
Dracula Blows His Cool *'82*
Dracula: Dead and Loving It *'95*
Eat and Run *'86*
Ed and His Dead Mother *'93*
Elvira, Mistress of the Dark *'88*
Elvira's Haunted Hills *'02*
Evil Spawn *'87*
Exorcist Master *'93*
The Eye 3 *'05*
Face of the Screaming Werewolf *'59*
The Fearless Vampire Killers *'67* ▸
Feast 2: Sloppy Seconds *'08*
Fido *'06*
Frankenhooker *'90*
Frankenstein 1970 *'58*
Frankenstein Sings... The Movie *'95*
Frankenstein's Great Aunt Tillie *'83*
The Frighteners *'96*
From Beyond *'86* ▸
Funnyman *'94*
The Gay Bed and Breakfast of Terror *'07*
The Ghost Breakers *'40* ▸
Ghoulies *'84*
Ghoulies 2 *'87*
Ghoulies 3: Ghoulies Go to College *'91*
Ghoulies 4 *'93*
Goblin *'93*
Gore-Met Zombie Chef from Hell *'87*
The Granny *'94*
Gremlins *'84* ▸
Gremlins 2: The New Batch *'90* ▸
The Happiness of the Katakuris *'01*
Hard to Die *'90*
The Haunted Mansion *'03*
Head of the Family *'96*
Hellboy *'04*
Highway to Hell *'92*
Hillbillies in a Haunted House *'67*
Horror Island *'41*
The Horror of Frankenstein *'70*
House *'86* ▸
House 2: The Second Story *'87*
House of the Long Shadows *'82*
Human Beasts *'80*
Hysterical *'83*
I Married a Vampire *'87*
I Was a Teenage Zombie *'87*
Idle Hands *'99*
Incredibly Strange Creatures Who Stopped Living and Became Mixed-Up Zombies *'63*
Infestation *'09*
Insanitarium *'08*
The Invisible Maniac *'90*
Jack Frost 2: Revenge of the Mutant Killer Snowman *'00*
Jennifer's Body *'09*
Killer Condom *'95*
Killer Klowns from Outer Space *'88*
Killer Movie *'08*
Killer Pad *'06*
Killer Tomatoes Eat France *'91*
Killer Tomatoes Strike Back *'90*
Killer Tongue *'96*
The Kingdom *'95* ▸
The Kingdom 2 *'97* ▸
Little Shop of Horrors *'60* ▸
Little Shop of Horrors *'86* ▸
Mama Dracula *'80*
A Man with a Maid *'73*
The Mask *'94* ▸
Matinee *'92*
Microwave Massacre *'83*
Mindkiller *'87*
Mr. Vampire *'86*
Mom *'89*
Monster in the Closet *'86*
Monster Man *'03*
Motel Hell *'80*
Munchies *'87*
My Boyfriend's Back *'93*
My Demon Lover *'87*
My Grandpa Is a Vampire *'92*
My Mom's a Werewolf *'89*
My Name Is Bruce *'08*
My Son, the Vampire *'52*
Nature of the Beast *'07*
Near Dark *'87* ▸
Netherbeast Incorporated *'07*
Night of a Thousand Cats *'72*
Night of the Creeps *'86*
Night of the Laughing Dead *'75*
Nightlife *'90*
Nocturna *'79*
Nothing But Trouble *'91*
The Old Dark House *'32* ▸
Old Mother Riley's Ghosts *'41*
Once Bitten *'85*
Out of the Dark *'88*
Pep Squad *'98*
Phantom Brother *'88*
Phantom Empire *'87*
Piranha *'78*
Piranha 2: The Spawning *'82*
Pontypool *'09*
Psycho Girls *'86*
Psychos in Love *'87*
Q (The Winged Serpent) *'82* ▸
Rabid Grannies *'89*
Re-Animator *'84* ▸
Redneck Zombies *'88*
The Refrigerator *'91*
Repo! The Genetic Opera *'08*
Return of the Killer Tomatoes! *'88*
Return of the Living Dead *'85*
Return of the Living Dead 2 *'88*
Return of the Living Dead 3 *'93*
Revenge of the Red Baron *'93*
Roman *'06*
Sars Wars: Bangkok Zombie Crisis *'04*
Saturday the 14th *'81*
Saturday the 14th Strikes Back *'88*
Scary Movie 2 *'01*
Scary Movie 3 *'03*
Scary Movie 4 *'06*
Schlock *'73*
Seed of Chucky *'04*

▸ = rated three bones or higher

Severance '06
Shaun of the Dead '04 ▶
Sheitan '06
Shrunken Heads '94
Skeleton Key 2: 667, the Neighbor of the Beast '08
Son of Ingagi '40
Sorority Babes in the Slimeball Bowl-A-Rama '87
Speak of the Devil '90
Special Unit 2002 '01
Spider Baby '64
Spooks Run Wild '41
Stan Helsing '09
Strangers of the Evening '32
Street Trash '87
Student Bodies '81
The Stuff '85
Suck '09
Tainted '98
Tales from the Crypt Presents Bordello of Blood '96
Tales from the Crypt Presents Demon Knight '94
Teenage Exorcist '93
Teeth '07
Tequila Body Shots '99
Terror Taxi '04
Terror Tract '00
Terrorvision '86
Theatre of Blood '73 ▶
There's Nothing out There '90
The Thing with Two Heads '72
Three ... Extremes '04
The Thrill Killers '65
Tokyo Gore Police '08
The Toxic Avenger '86
The Toxic Avenger, Part 2 '89
The Toxic Avenger, Part 3: The Last Temptation of Toxie '89
Transylmania '09
Treasure of Fear '45
The Treat '98
Tremors '89
Tremors 2: Aftershocks '96
Tremors 3: Back to Perfection '01
The Tripper '06
Undead '05
The Undertaker and His Pals '67
Vamp '86
The Vampire Happening '71
Vampire in Brooklyn '95
Vampire Killers '09
Vampire Time Travelers '98
Vampires of Sorority Row: Kickboxers From Hell '99
When Evil Calls '06
When Good Ghouls Go Bad '01
Wild Zero '00
Yeti: A Love Story '08
Zombie Strippers '08
Zombies on Broadway '44

Horse Racing

see *Gambling; Horses; Jockeying for Position*

Horse Racing

see *Gambling; Horses; Jockeying for Position*

Salty O'Rourke '45

Horses

The Adventures of Gallant Bess '48
All Hat '07
All the Pretty Horses '00
The Appaloosa '66
Banjo Hackett '76
Bells of San Angelo '47
The Better 'Ole '26
Big Boy '30
Black Beauty '46
Black Beauty '71
Black Beauty '94 ▶
The Black Stallion '79 ▶
The Black Stallion Returns '83
Blazing Saddles '74 ▶
Blue Fire Lady '78
Broken Trail '06 ▶
By Dawn's Early Light '00
Call of the Forest '49
Casey's Shadow '78
Chino '75
City Slickers 2: The Legend of Curly's Gold '94
Come on Tarzan '32
Courage of Black Beauty '57
Courage of the North '35
Coyote Summer '96
Danielle Steel's Palomino '91
Danny '79
Dark Horse '92
David Harum '34
Day the Bookies Wept '39
Devil Horse '32
Dreamer: Inspired by a True Story '05
Eagle's Wing '79
Eden Valley '94 ▶
The Electric Horseman '79
Envy '04
Equus '77
Far North '88
The Fighting Stallion '26 ▶
The First Auto '27
Flash '98
Flicka '06
The Flying Deuces '39 ▶
Forbidden Trails '41
Francis Goes to the Races '51
A Girl in Every Port '52
The Golden Stallion '49
The Great Mike '44
Gypsy Colt '54
Hair '79 ▶
Half-Baked '97
Heart of the Rockies '51
Hell's Hinges '16
Hit the Saddle '37
The Horse in the Gray Flannel Suit '68
The Horse Whisperer '97
Horsemasters '61
The Horsemen '70
Hot to Trot! '88
In Old Kentucky '35
In Pursuit of Honor '95
In the Arms of My Enemy '07
Indian Paint '64
International Velvet '78
Into the West '92 ▶
It Ain't Hay '43
Italian Straw Hat '27 ▶
It's a Great Life '43
Justin Morgan Had a Horse '81
King of the Sierras '38
King of the Stallions '42
King of the Wild Horses '24 ▶
King of the Wild Stallions '59
King of the Wind '93
The Lighthorsemen '87 ▶
The Littlest Horse Thieves '76
The Littlest Outlaw '54
Lotna '64
Lucky Luke '94
The Man from Snowy River '82
Marshal of Cedar Rock '53
Meet Wally Sparks '97
Michael Shayne: Private Detective '40
The Miracle of the White Stallions '63
The Misfits '61 ▶
Misty '61
Moondance Alexander '07
My Friend Flicka '43 ▶
My Pal Trigger '46
National Lampoon's Animal House '78 ▶
The Phantom Pinto '41
Racing Stripes '05
A Rare Breed '81
The Red Fury '84
The Red Pony '49 ▶
The Red Pony '76 ▶
Return of Wildfire '48
Return to Snowy River '88 ▶
Ride a Wild Pony '75 ▶
Ride Him, Cowboy '32 ▶
Riders '88
Riding High '50
Rolling Home '48
The Rounders '65
Running Free '00
Running Wild '73
The Saddle Buster '32
Second Chances '98
Shooting Fish '98
Silver Stallion '41
The Silver Stallion: King of the Wild Brumbies '93
Simpatico '99
Something to Talk About '95
Speedy '28 ▶
Spirit: Stallion of the Cimarron '02
Sundown Saunders '36
Texas to Bataan '42
Toy Story 2 '99 ▶
Treacherous Beauties '94
Two Bits & Pepper '95
The Undefeated '69
Under the Pampas Moon '35
When the West Was Young '32
White Mane '52 ▶
Wild Hearts Can't Be Broken '91 ▶
Wild Horse Hank '79
Wild Horse Valley '40
Wild Horses '82
Wild Horses '84
Wild Pony '83

Hospitals & Medicine

see also *Disease of the Week; Doctors & Nurses; Emerging Viruses; Sanity Check; Shrinks*

Against the Dark '08
Article 99 '92
Asylum of the Damned '03
Awake '07
Awakenings '90 ▶
The Barbarian Invasions '03 ▶
BASEketball '98
Boo! '05
B.O.R.N. '88
Bringing Out the Dead '99
Britannia Hospital '82
Calendar Girls '03
Carry On Matron '72
Carry On Nurse '59
A Child Is Waiting '63 ▶
China Beach '88 ▶
City of Angels '98
City of Joy '92
The Clonus Horror '79
Coma '78 ▶
Come to the Stable '49 ▶
Crazy Eights '06
Critical Care '97
Critical Condition '86
Dead Ringers '88 ▶
The Death of Mr. Lazarescu '05
Desperate Measures '98
Disorderlies '87
Disorderly Orderly '64
Doctor at Large '57
Doctor in Clover '66
Dr. Kildare's Strange Case '40
Doctors' Wives '70
East of Kilimanjaro '57
The Egyptian '54
Extreme Measures '96
The Fall '06
For Roseanna '96
Frankenstein General Hospital '88
The Fugitive '93 ▶
Gifted Hands: The Ben Carson Story '09
Green for Danger '47
Gross Anatomy '89
Halloween 2: The Nightmare Isn't Over! '81
Hard-Boiled '92
Hard to Kill '89
The Hasty Heart '86
The Healer '02
Horror Hospital '73
The Hospital '71 ▶
Hospital Massacre '81
Hospital of Terror '78
In for Treatment '82 ▶
In Love and War '96
The Interns '62
Invasion '65
John Q '02
Junior '94
Just Another Love Story '08
The Kingdom '95 ▶
The Kingdom 2 '97 ▶
Lifespan '75
Like Father, Like Son '87
Merrily We Go to Hell '32
Miracle Dogs '03
Miss Evers' Boys '97
Naked Is Better '73
National Lampoon Presents RoboDoc '08
Nine Months '95
Nurse '80
One Flew Over the Cuckoo's Nest '75 ▶
Open Your Eyes '97 ▶
Patch Adams '98
Pathology '08
Planet Terror '07
Pride of the Marines '45 ▶
Range of Motion '00
The Red Squirrel '93
Saturn in Opposition '07
The Singing Detective '03
State of Emergency '94
A Stolen Face '52
A Stranger's Heart '07
Sublime '07
The Surgeon '94
Take Down '92
Tales from the Gimli Hospital '88
Talk to Her '02 ▶
Tender Loving Care '73
Terminator 2: Judgment Day '91 ▶
13 Moons '02
This Woman Is Dangerous '52
Threshold '83
12 Monkeys '95 ▶
28 Days '00
The Ugly '96
Vital Signs '90
Welcome Stranger '47
Where Truth Lies '96
While You Were Sleeping '95 ▶
White Coats '04
Whose Life Is It Anyway? '81 ▶
Young Doctors in Love '82

Hostage!

see also *Kidnapped!; Missing Persons*

The Abduction '96
Against the Wall '94 ▶
Air Force One '97 ▶
Air Rage '01
Airheads '94
Albino Alligator '96
Alien Raiders '08
Allie & Me '97
Amos and Andrew '93
Attack the Gas Station '99
Autumn Born '79
Bait '02
Bandits '01
The Betrayed '08
Black Cobra 2 '89
Black Fox: Good Men and Bad '94
Blackout '78
Blast '96
Blood of the Hunter '94
Body Count '97
Born Bad '97
Botched '07
The Boys Club '96
Breakaway '02
Breaking News '04
Cadillac Man '90
Captivity '07
Carpool '96
Chameleon 2: Death Match '99
The Chaos Experiment '09
Civic Duty '06
The Clearing '04 ▶
Codename: Vengeance '87
Cold Sweat '71
Command Performance '09
Crackerjack 2 '97
Cradle 2 the Grave '03
Cravings '06
Crime Wave '54
Crisis '50
Cube '98
Cube 2: Hypercube '02
Cul de Sac '66 ▶
Cyborg Soldier '08
Dark Heart '06
Days of Hell '84
Dead Ahead '96
Dead Silence '96
Deadlocked '00
Deadly Outbreak '96
Death and the Maiden '94 ▶
Death Stalk '74
Demolition High '95
Desert Nights '29
Desperate Hours '90
Die Hard '88 ▶
Die Hard 2: Die Harder '90 ▶
Diplomatic Siege '99
Distortions '87
Dog Day Afternoon '75 ▶
Door to Door Maniac '61
Escape from New York '81
Face the Evil '97
Fall Time '94
Fatal Mission '89
Field of Fire '92
Firestorm '97
Firewall '06
First Sunday '08
For Which He Stands '98
48 Hours to Live '60
Friends and Family '01
Funny Games '97
Funny Games '07 ▶
Gigli '03
Gone Dark '03
Half Past Dead '02
Headless Body in Topless Bar '96
The Heist '96
Held Up '00
Homecoming '09
Hostage '05
Hostage High '97
Hostage Hotel '00
Hostages '93 ▶
Housewife '72
Human Bomb '97
In Her Line of Fire '06
In the Middle of Nowhere '93
Inside '06
Inside Man '06 ▶
Iron Eagle '86
Jeopardy '53
The Jesus Trip '71
John Q '02
Johnny 100 Pesos '93
Kill Me Later '01
King of Comedy '82 ▶
The Last Samurai '90
The Legend of Wolf Mountain '92
Lethal Tender '96
Light It Up '99
Live! From Death Row '92
Living & Dying '07
Mad City '97
The Marine '06
The Marine 2 '09
Masterminds '96
Meltdown '95
Midnight Fear '90
Miss Congeniality 2: Armed and Fabulous '05
Mr. Reliable: A True Story '95
Mistrial '96
Morgan's Ferry '99
Munich '05 ▶
My Name is Modesty: A Modesty Blaise Adventure '04
The Negotiator '98
Nick of Time '95
No Contest '94
No Good Deed '02
Nothing to Lose '96
Nothing to Lose '08
One Way Out '95
Open Fire '94
Operation Thunderbolt '77
P2 '07
Perfect Hideout '08
Perfect Strangers '03
A Perfect World '93
Peril '00
Petrified Forest '36 ▶
A Prayer in the Dark '97
Provoked '89
P.S. Your Cat is Dead! '02
Pups '99
Quake '92
Quick Change '90
Raising the Heights '97
Rambo '08
Red Mercury '05
The Ref '93 ▶
Restraint '08
Rock All Night '57
Saw 2 '05
Saw 4 '07
Saw 5 '08
The Seventh Floor '93
Sex and the Other Man '95
S.F.W. '94
The Shot '96
16 Blocks '06 ▶
Skyscraper '95
Snatched '72
Space Marines '96
Spaghetti House '82
Special Forces '03
Speed 2: Cruise Control '97
Split Second '53
Stand Off '93
A Stranger Is Watching '82
The Strangers '08
Stranglehold '94
Stripteaser '95
Sudden Death '95
Suddenly '54 ▶
Suspended Animation '02
Sweet Hostage '75
Take Down '92
The Taking of Pelham One Two Three '74 ▶
The Taking of Pelham 123 '09
Terror Stalks the Class Reunion '93
This Gun for Hire '42 ▶
3 Ninjas: High Noon at Mega Mountain '97
The Trap '59
Truth or Consequences, N.M. '97
Tube '03
12 Monkeys '95 ▶
Uninvited Guest '99
Vengeance '80
Victory at Entebbe '76

Housekeepers

see *The Help: Female*

Housekeepers

see *The Help: Female*

Dim Sum Funeral '08
Emma '32
Where There's a Will '55

Housesitting

Deuce Bigalow: Male Gigolo '99
Hard to Kill '89
A House in the Hills '93
My Boss's Daughter '03
Opportunity Knocks '90

Houston

see also *Black Gold; Texas*

Apollo 13 '95 ▶
The Bad News Bears in Breaking Training '77
Brewster McCloud '70 ▶
Charlie Wilson's War '07
Dance with Me '98
Dancing in Twilight '05
Enron: The Smartest Guys in the Room '05 ▶
The Evening Star '96
Full Fathom Five '90
Jason's Lyric '94
Last Night at the Alamo '83 ▶
Lethal Force '00
Love and Mary '07
Night Game '89
Reality Bites '94
The Swarm '78
Terms of Endearment '83 ▶
Threshold '03
Thursday '98
Towelhead '07
Urban Cowboy '80
Vietnam, Texas '90

▶ = rated three bones or higher

Hunted!

see also *Survival*
Apocalypto '06 ▸
Arctic Blue '93
Beyond Fear '93
Beyond Rangoon '95
Bigfoot: The Unforgettable Encounter '94
Bounty Hunter 2002 '94
The Cursed Mountain Mystery '93
Cyborg 2 '93
Damned River '89
Deadly Game '91
Death Hunt '81
Decoy '95
Deliverance '72 ▸
Desperate Prey '94
Diary of a Hitman '91
Dominion '94
Ex-Cop '93
Eyes of the Beholder '92
Fair Game '82
Final Round '93
5 Dark Souls '96
Fortress '85
Freejack '92
Fugitive X '96
The Good Guys and the Bad Guys '69
Hard Target '93
The Hunted '94
The Hunted '98
The Hunted '03
Hunter's Blood '87
Hydra '09
Illegal Entry: Formula for Fear '93
Incident at Deception Ridge '94
Jumper '08
Jungleground '95
Killing at Hell's Gate '81
Ladykillers '88
The Last of the Dogmen '95
Last Witness '88
Little Bigfoot '96
Maximum Risk '96
Midnight Murders '91
Montana '97
The Most Dangerous Game '32 ▸
The Naked Prey '66 ▸
Nemesis 2: Nebula '94
Nightmare at Bittercreek '91
No Way Back '90
Open Season '06
Overkill '96
The Pest '96
Predators '10
Prey for the Hunter '92
Primeval '07
Project Shadowchaser 3000 '95
Rumble in the Streets '96
Seraphim Falls '06
Severance '06
Shadowhunter '93
Shoot to Kill '88 ▸
Skinwalkers '07
Solo '96
Southern Comfort '81 ▸
Star Hunter '95
Survival Quest '89
Surviving the Game '94
Tracked '98
Trial and Error '92
Uncivilized '94
Warriors '94
Wild Grizzly '99
Wounded '97
Wrong Turn '03
Yesterday's Target '96

Hunting

see also *Go Fish*
The Amazing Panda Adventure '95
The Bear '89 ▸
The Belstone Fox '73
The Bridge to Nowhere '86
Caddyshack '80 ▸
Dan Candy's Law '73
Deadly Prey '87
The Doe Boy '01
Escanaba in da Moonlight '01
First Blood '82
Forest of Little Bear '87
Frostbiter: Wrath of the Wendigo '94
The Ghost and the Darkness '96
Git! '65
Harry Black and the Tiger '58
The Hunt '65 ▸
Ice Men '04
The Last Hunt '56
The Last Safari '67
The Lion Hunters '47
Mogambo '53 ▸
Night of the Grizzly '66
No Country for Old Men '07 ▸
Primeval '07
Shoot '76
Shooting '82
Those Calloways '65
To Catch a Yeti '95
White Hunter, Black Heart '90 ▸

I Was a Teenage Criminal

see also *Teen Angst; Teen Comedy; Teen Drama; Teen Horror; Teen Musicals; Teen Romance*
Bad Boys '83 ▸
Badlands '74 ▸
The Basketball Diaries '95
Brick '06 ▸
A Clockwork Orange '71 ▸
Crime and Punishment in Suburbia '00
Criminal Lovers '99
Drive By '01
Freeway 2: Confessions of a Trickbaby '99
Graduation '07
Guncrazy '92
Juice '92
L.I.E. '01
Murder by Numbers '02
Naked Youth '59
The Outsiders '83
Punk Love '06
Shank '09
Small Faces '95 ▸
Tenderness '08
United States of Leland '03
While She Was Out '08

Illegal Immigration

The Border '82 ▸
Border Incident '49
Born in East L.A. '87
Bowfinger '99 ▸
Bread and Roses '00
Crossing Over '09
Dirty Pretty Things '03 ▸
El Norte '83 ▸
Frozen River '08 ▸
In America '02 ▸
La Promesse '96
The Last Enemy '08
No Turning Back '01
On the Line '83
Sin Nombre '09 ▸
Sweet 15 '90
The Visitor '07 ▸

I'm Not Dead, Yet!

Blackout '50
Dawn of the Dead '04 ▸
Elektra '05
Hello Again '87
Incubus '05
The Jacket '05
The Lazarus Man '96
The Morgue '07
Move Over, Darling '63
My Favorite Wife '40 ▸
The Mysterious Dr. Fu Manchu '29
The Return of Dr. Fu Manchu '30
The Return of Martin Guerre '83 ▸
The Roundup '41
Seed '08
Sommersby '93
Stuck '07
Three for the Show '55
A Very Brady Sequel '96

Immigration

The Adventures of Felix '99
An American Rhapsody '01 ▸
An American Tail '86
Arizona '86
Ask the Dust '06
Avalon '90 ▸
Baran '01
The Beautiful Country '04
Blood Red '88
Border Blues '03
Border Incident '49
Borderline '80
Bread and Chocolate '73 ▸
Bread and Roses '00
Break of Dawn '88
Breaking and Entering '06
Brothers in Trouble '95
Buck Privates Come Home '47 ▸
Bye-Bye '96
Chasing Freedom '04
Children of Men '06 ▸
Code 46 '03
Code Unknown '00
Combination Platter '93
Coming to America '88 ▸
The Cowboy Way '94
Crossing Over '09
Dancer in the Dark '99
Dirty Pretty Things '03 ▸
Does This Mean We're Married? '90
Drachenfutter '87 ▸
Driving Me Crazy '91
East Is East '99 ▸
The Edge of Heaven '07 ▸
El Super '79 ▸
The Emigrants '72 ▸
Enemies, a Love Story '89 ▸
ESL: English as a Second Language '05
Far and Away '92
Fast Food Nation '06 ▸
Floating Life '95
Four Sons '28
Frozen River '08 ▸
Gangs of New York '02 ▸
Gran Torino '08 ▸
The Great New Wonderful '06
Green Card '90
Heaven Before I Die '96
Hello Goodbye '08
Hester Street '75 ▸
House of Sand and Fog '03 ▸
I Can't Sleep '93
I Cover the Waterfront '33
The Immigrant '17 ▸
In America '02 ▸
The Italian '15
It's a Big Country '51
Journey of Hope '90 ▸
Kill the Poor '06
A King in New York '57
Kings in Grass Castles '97
La Promesse '96
Late Marriage '01
Letters from Alou '90
Liam '00
Living on Tokyo Time '87
The Maldonado Miracle '03
Manhattan Merenque! '95
The Manions of America '81
Maricela '88
Maryam '00
Miami Rhapsody '95
Midnight Auto Supply '78
The Mistress of Spices '05
Monkey Business '31 ▸
Moscow on the Hudson '84 ▸
My Girl Tisa '48
My Sweet Victim '85
The Namesake '06 ▸
Nanny Insanity '06
The New Land '73 ▸
No Turning Back '01
Nueba Yol '95
O Quatrilho '95
Out of the Ashes '03
Pelle the Conqueror '88 ▸
Petty Crimes '02
Saving Face '04
Sky High '22
Skyline '84 ▸
Sold for Marriage '16
Someone Else's America '96 ▸
Spanglish '04
Sueno '05
Tarantella '95
The Terminal '04
The Three Burials of Melquiades Estrada '05 ▸
Under the Same Moon '07
The Visitor '07 ▸
Wait until Spring, Bandini '90
West Is West '87
Wetbacks '56
Where Is My Child? '37
Which Way Home '09

Immortality

Bram Stoker's Way of the Vampire '05
Escape from the KGB '87
Highlander '86 ▸
Highlander 2: The Quickening '91
Highlander: Endgame '00
Highlander: The Final Dimension '94
Highlander: The Source '07
The Imaginarium of Doctor Parnassus '09
Immortal '04
The Man from Earth '07
The Medallion '03
The Mummy: Tomb of the Dragon Emperor '08
The Seeker: The Dark Is Rising '07
She '35
She '65
The Spring '00
Tomie '99
Tuck Everlasting '02
Youth Without Youth '07

Impending Retirement

see also *Growing Older; One Last Job*
Assault on Precinct 13 '05
The Blue Knight '75
Bombers B-52 '57
Brooklyn's Finest '09
Carry On Sergeant '58
Cellular '04
Chasing Ghosts '05
Crackerjack 3 '00
Diamond Men '01 ▸
Fallen Angels '95
Falling Down '93
Firetrap '01
The First Deadly Sin '80
The Flock '07
Half Broken Things '07
Hitman's Journal '99
In the Secret State '85
K-9 3: P.I. '01
K-911 '99
Law and Order '53
Lethal Weapon '87 ▸
Love to Kill '97
Loving Annabelle '06
Major League 3: Back to the Minors '98
The Mask of Zorro '98 ▸
Mission: Impossible 3 '06 ▸
Must Be Santa '99
O'Horten '09
The Pledge '00 ▸
The Princess Diaries 2: Royal Engagement '04
The Quickie '01
Schultze Gets the Blues '03
Seven '95 ▸
Sharpshooter '07
She Wore a Yellow Ribbon '49 ▸
Silent Venom '08
Solo '06
Sonatine '96 ▸
Spring Forward '99
Spy Game '01
Suicide Ride '97
To Live & Die in L.A. '85
The Wrestler '08 ▸

In-Laws

Affair in Trinidad '52
Ash Wednesday '02
August '95
Between Two Women '86
Bittersweet Love '76
Blacksnake! '73
Blood Relations '87
Brothers '09
Cal '84 ▸
Commandments '96
Deadly Blessing '81
Deliver Us from Eva '03
Diary of a Mad Old Man '88
Diary of the Dead '76
Die! Die! My Darling! '65
Easy Virtue '08
The Ex '07
For Better or Worse '95
Free Money '99
Girl with a Pearl Earring '03 ▸
Grace '09
The Grandfather '98
Hurt '09
Hush '98
I Met a Murderer '39
The In-Laws '79 ▸
The In-Laws '03
The Inheritance '76
The Inveterate Bachelor '58
Junebug '05 ▸
Kill the Umpire '50
Killers '10
La Rupture '70
The Last Days of Chez Nous '92
Lawless Heart '01
Le Divorce '03
Leila '97
Love '71 ▸
Love Crazy '41 ▸
Love Finds a Home '09
Love Liza '02
Love Songs '99
Madame X '37
The Man with Two Faces '34
Meet the Fockers '04
Meet the Parents '00 ▸
Mirele Efros '38
Monster-in-Law '05
Motive for Revenge '35
Move Over, Darling '63
Murder-in-Law '92
Mussolini & I '85
My Brother's Wife '89
Norman Loves Rose '82
Not Easily Broken '09
Onibaba '64 ▸
Passion in Paradise '89
Portrait of a Stripper '79
Possession '09
Pride and Glory '08
Reign Over Me '07
Rocky Balboa '06
The Santa Clause 3: The Escape Clause '06
Secrets of Women '52 ▸
Shrek the Third '07
Silent Witness '85
The Sister-in-Law '95
Son-in-Law '93
Stir of Echoes '99
Storm Warning '51
Summer Snow '94
A Time of Destiny '88
Together Again '43
The War Bride '01
The Weight of Water '00
You, Me and Dupree '06

Incest

see also *Family Ties*
Against the Wind '90
Alpine Fire '89
An American Haunting '05
Andy Warhol's Frankenstein '74
Angels and Insects '95 ▸
The Ballad of Jack and Rose '05 ▸
Black Christmas '06
Blood Relatives '77
Born Killers '05
Brotherhood of the Wolf '01
The Cement Garden '93
The Cider House Rules '99 ▸
Close My Eyes '91
Downloading Nancy '08
The Fishing Trip '98
Flowers in the Attic '87
The Grifters '90 ▸
Harry and Max '04
Horrors of Malformed Men '69
The House of Yes '97
I Stand Alone '98
Innocent Lies '95
The King '05
Little Boy Blue '97
Mad Cowgirl '06
My Sister, My Love '78
Natural Born Killers '94
Novocaine '01
Pola X '99
Precious: Based on the Novel by Sapphire '09 ▸
Ringmaster '98
Savage Grace '07
Say It Isn't So '01
Seducing Maarya '99
Sitcom '97
Spanking the Monkey '94 ▸
The Sweet Hereafter '96 ▸
Tarnation '03
This World, Then the Fireworks '97
A Thousand Acres '97
'Tis a Pity She's a Whore '73
U-Turn '97
Vicious Circles '97
Visitor Q '01
The War Zone '98
Waterland '92
The Weight of Water '00
Wicked '98
Woman, Thou Art Loosed '04

India

see also *Calcutta*
The Adversary '71
Aparajito '58 ▸
Autobiography of a Princess '75
Bandit Queen '94
Before the Rains '07
The Bengali Night '88
Bhowani Junction '56
The Big City '63
The Black Devils of Kali '55
Black Narcissus '47 ▸
Bollywood Hero '09
Bombay Mail '34
Born Into Brothels: Calcutta's Red Light Kids '04
The Bourne Supremacy '04 ▸
Bride & Prejudice '04
Carry On Up the Khyber '68
Chandni Chowk to China '09
Charulata '64
The Cheetah Girls: One World '08
City of Joy '92
Conduct Unbecoming '75
Cotton Mary '99
The Courtesans of Bombay '85 ▸
The Darjeeling Limited '07 ▸
The Deceivers '88
Distant Thunder '73 ▸
Drums '38
Earth '98
Eat, Pray, Love '10
Ele, My Friend '93
The Far Pavilions '84
Fire '96
Flame Over India '60 ▸
Gandhi '82 ▸
Gunga Din '39 ▸
Heat and Dust '82 ▸
The Home and the World '84 ▸
Hullabaloo over Georgie & Bonnie's Pictures '78
In Custody '94
In the Spider's Web '07
The Indian Tomb '21
Jalsaghar '58
The Jewel in the Crown '84 ▸
Journey to the Lost City '58
Jungle Boy '96
Jungle Hell '55
Kama Sutra: A Tale of Love '96
Kim '50 ▸
Kim '84
Lagaan: Once upon a Time in India '01
The Lives of a Bengal Lancer '35 ▸
Looking for Comedy in the Muslim World '06
The Mahabharata '89
The Man Who Would Be King '75 ▸

▸ = rated three bones or higher

Marigold '07
Masala '91
Maya '66
The Middleman '76
Mission Kashmir '00
The Mistress of Spices '05
Monsoon '97
Monsoon Wedding '01 ▶
Mother Teresa: In the Name of God's Poor '97
Mountbatten: The Last Viceroy '86
My Faraway Bride '06
The Namesake '06 ▶
Octopussy '83
Outsourced '06
A Passage to India '84 ▶
Pather Panchali '54 ▶
The Rains Came '39
The Razor's Edge '46 ▶
The River '51 ▶
Rudyard Kipling's The Jungle Book '94
Sabaka '55
Shakespeare Wallah '65 ▶
Sharpe's Challenge '06
Siddhartha '72
Slumdog Millionaire '08 ▶
Spices '86 ▶
Staying On '80
Stiff Upper Lips '96
The Stranglers of Bombay '60
Such a Long Journey '98 ▶
Tales of the Kama Sutra: The Perfumed Garden '98
Tiger of Eschnapur '59
Two Daughters '61 ▶
The Warrior '81
Water '05
Wee Willie Winkie '37 ▶
The World of Apu '59 ▶

Inheritance

All in a Night's Work '61
The Aristocats '70 ▶
The Bachelor '99
Bailey's Billion$ '05
Billy Madison '94
Black Widow '87 ▶
The Black Widow '05
Bleak House '05
A Blueprint for Murder '53
Brewster's Millions '45
Brewster's Millions '85
Broken Trust '93
Carry Me Back '82
Casper '95 ▶
Catherine Cookson's The Black Candle '92
The Chateau '01
The Cheyenne Social Club '70
Chilly Dogs '01
Christmas Eve '47
Chronicle of the Raven '04
The Cruise of the Jasper B '26
Cutthroat Island '95
Daddy's Dyin'... Who's Got the Will? '90
Dangerous Passage '44
Dawg '02
Die Mommie Die! '03
Double or Nothing '37
Easy Money '83
Elvira, Mistress of the Dark '88
Emma '32
The Fighting Temptations '03
Finding Home '03
Fletch Lives '89
Freaks '32 ▶
Gaslight '44 ▶
Ghost in the Invisible Bikini '66
The Glass House '01
Go for Zucker '05
Gold Diggers: The Secret of Bear Mountain '95
A Good Year '06
Greedy '94
The Hearse '80
Heart of Midnight '89
The Hellfire Club '61
Home to Danger '51
Hot to Trot! '88
I Capture the Castle '02
In the Heat of Passion 2: Unfaithful '94
The Inheritance '76
Invisible Mom 2 '99
Just Buried '07
Kidnapped '48
Kidnapped '05 ▶
King of Texas '02 ▶
La Cage aux Folles 3: The Wedding '86
Lake Dead '07
Larger Than Life '96
The Last Station '09
Lemony Snicket's A Series of Unfortunate Events '04
The List '07
Little Big League '94
Little Old New York '23
Lord of the Rings: The Fellowship of the Ring '01 ▶
Love Kills '98
Love's Unfolding Dream '07
Mail Order Bride '63
Meet Mr. Callaghan '54
Milwaukee, Minnesota '03
Miss Tatlock's Millions '48
Mr. Deeds '02
Mr. Deeds Goes to Town '36 ▶
Montana Sky '07
Moon over Miami '41 ▶
Mouse Hunt '97 ▶
No More Women '34
On Guard! '03 ▶
Oriana '85
Purlie Victorious '63
The Reception '05
Rhubarb '51
Scavenger Hunt '79
The Sea '02
Seven Chances '25 ▶
Shanghai Kiss '07
Siblings '04
The Skeptic '09
Snow Dogs '02
Splitting Heirs '93
Square Shooter '35
Strangers in Love '32
Summer Hours '08
Sundance and the Kid '69
Tartuffe '25
13 Ghosts '01
UHF '89
The Ultimate Gift '07
The Unsuspected '47
Violette '78 ▶
Where There's a Will '55
Wild Things 2 '04
Woman of Straw '64
A Woman's a Helluva Thing '01
Zus & Zo '01

The Inquisition, What a Show!

***see also** Period Piece: 15th Century*
Captain from Castile '47 ▶
Christopher Columbus: The Discovery '92
Fire Over England '37 ▶
Goya's Ghosts '06
History of the World: Part 1 '81
Man of La Mancha '72
Nostradamus '93
The Pit and the Pendulum '61 ▶
The Tempter '74

Insomnia

***see also** Up All Night*
Bringing Out the Dead '99
Dream for an Insomniac '96
Fight Club: ' '99 ▶
The Haunting '99
I Can't Sleep '93
The Machinist '04
Taxi Driver '76 ▶

Insurance

About Schmidt '02 ▶
The Adjuster '91
Alias Jesse James '59
Along Came Polly '04
Amnesia '96
The Apartment '60 ▶
Baby Face Morgan '42
Bedelia '46 ▶
Beyond Suspicion '00
The Big Squeeze '96
Big Trouble '86
The Big White '05
The Black House '00
Black House '07
Burning Down the House '01
The Case of the Scorpion's Tail '71
Cause of Death '00
Changing Lanes '02 ▶
City of Ghosts '03
Coast of Skeletons '63
Code 46 '03
The Connection '73
Counter Attack '84
Critical Care '97
The Crocodile Hunter: Collision Course '02
The Curse of the Jade Scorpion '01
Dangerous Summer '82
The Darwin Awards '06
Dead Cold '96
Dead Eyes of London '61
Deadlier Than the Male '67
Deadly Desire '91
Death Benefit '96
Death Collector '89
Dillinger and Capone '95
Double Indemnity '44 ▶
Dying to Get Rich '98
The Electronic Monster '57
Enchanted Island '58
Entrapment '99
Escape Clause '96
The Favorite Son '94 ▶
Firestarter 2: Rekindled '02
First Do No Harm '97
Flawless '07
Folks! '92
Four Dogs Playing Poker '00
Frank McKlusky, C.I. '02
Frauds '93
Gold Diggers of 1937 '36
Gold Raiders '51
Gone in 60 Seconds '74
Goodbye, Lover '99
The Great Plane Robbery '40
High Strung '91
Hook, Line and Sinker '30
The Hunted '98
I Now Pronounce You Chuck and Larry '07
I Wonder Who's Killing Her Now? '76
In the Mouth of Madness '95
John Grisham's The Rainmaker '97
Kafka '91
The Killers '46 ▶
Lady Ice '73
The Last Adventure '67
Linda '93
A Little Trip to Heaven '05
Lloyds of London '36 ▶
Love, Lies and Murder '91
Lush '01
The Man from the Pru '89
Master Touch '74
Murder, He Says '45
National Lampoon's Gold Diggers '04
The Odd Job '78
One Body Too Many '44
One Night in the Tropics '40
Paid to Kill '54
Pas Tres Catholique '93
Pitfall '48 ▶
Prince of Poisoners: The Life and Crimes of William Palmer '98
Quick '93
Risk '00
Saint John of Las Vegas '09
Save the Tiger '73 ▶
Schemes '95
The Settlement '99
Sicko '07
Sins of the Night '93
Sleep Easy, Hutch Rimes '00
Sleuth '72 ▶
Stranger in the House '97
Sunburn '79
Sweet Lies '88
They Call It Murder '71
Things Happen at Night '48
The Thomas Crown Affair '68 ▶
The Thomas Crown Affair '99 ▶
Three Blondes in His Life '61
Till Death Do Us Part '92
A Touch of Class '73 ▶
Towards Darkness '07
Tropical Heat '93
The Truman Show '98 ▶
The Whispering '94
The Whole Nine Yards '00
Wild Things 2 '04
Wish You Were Dead '00
A Woman of Independent Means '94 ▶
The Yellow Rose of Texas '44

Internet Borne

***see also** Computers; Hackers*
The Blair Witch Project '99
Catfish '10
Confess '05
Dee Snider's Strangeland '98
Devour '05
Dot.Kill '05
Every Mother's Worst Fear '98
Feardotcom '02
Feed '05
GhostWatcher '02
Halloween: Resurrection '02
Hard Candy '06
Hellraiser: Hellworld '05
I Downloaded a Ghost '04
Jay and Silent Bob Strike Back '01
Mail to the Chief '00
Must Love Dogs '05
The Net '95
Open Cam '05
Pulse '01
Pulse '06
Southland Tales '06
Suspicion '03
Tom Clancy's Netforce '98
Train Man: Densha Otoko '05
Turbulence 3: Heavy Metal '00
Untraceable '08
You've Got Mail '98

Interpol

Assassins '95
Black Cobra 2 '89
The Case of the Scorpion's Tail '71
The Castle of Fu Manchu '68
Cave of the Living Dead '65
Feed '05
Framed '90
Hitman '07
The International '09
The King of the Kickboxers '91
Lord of War '05 ▶
The Medallion '03
Nighthawks '81
Ninja Assassin '09
One More Time '70
The Return of Dr. Mabuse '61
Soul Assassin '01
Terror of Mechagodzilla '78

Interracial Affairs

According to Greta '08
After the Rain '99
Ali: Fear Eats the Soul '74 ▶
Barbershop 2: Back in Business '04 ▶
Beauty Shop '05 ▶
Bleeding Hearts '94
The Bodyguard '92
Broken Blossoms '19 ▶
Bulworth '98 ▶
Cafe au Lait '94 ▶
Cake '05
Cape of Good Hope '04
Chaos '05
Chinese Box '97
Colorz of Rage '97
Come See the Paradise '90 ▶
Corrina, Corrina '94
Crash '05 ▶
The Crimson Kimono '59
Dark Blue '03 ▶
Dear Wendy '05
The Delta '97
Driving Miss Daisy '89 ▶
The Family Stone '05
The Family That Preys '08
A Fight for Jenny '90
A Fond Kiss '04
Freedomland '06
Glory Road '06
The Grasshopper '69
Guess Who '05
Guess Who's Coming to Dinner '67 ▶
Hairspray '07 ▶
Heaven and Earth '93
The Human Stain '03
Hustle & Flow '05 ▶
In My Country '04
In the Mix '05
Japanese Story '03 ▶
Jungle Fever '91 ▶
Lakeview Terrace '08 ▶
The Liberation of L.B. Jones '70
Love Field '91
Love Is a Many-Splendored Thing '55
Love Song '00
Machine Gun Blues '95
Made in America '93
Manderlay '05
Marci X '03
Melinda and Melinda '05
Miami Rhapsody '95
Mississippi Masala '92 ▶
Mr. & Mrs. Loving '96 ▶
Monster's Ball '01 ▶
My Baby's Daddy '04
My Beautiful Laundrette '85 ▶
The Nephew '97
Never Die Alone '04
The New World '05 ▶
Norman, Is That You? '76
Not Easily Broken '09
November '05 ▶
Now & Forever '02
One Night Stand '97 ▶
Othello '22
Othello '52 ▶
Othello '65 ▶
Othello '95 ▶
Parallel Sons '95
A Patch of Blue '65
The Pianist '91
Pieces of April '03
Pinky '49 ▶
Pocahontas '95 ▶
Rachel Getting Married '08 ▶
Relax... It's Just Sex! '98
A Respectable Trade '98
Restaurant '98
Romeo Must Die '00
The Royal Tenenbaums '01 ▶
Ruby's Bucket of Blood '01
Save the Last Dance '01
The Second Chance '06
Shadowboxer '06
Shadows '60 ▶
Snow Falling on Cedars '99
Soldiers of Change '06
Something New '06
The Story of a Three Day Pass '68
Storytelling '01 ▶
Taxi Blues '90 ▶
The Tenants '06
The Tic Code '99
Walking Tall '04
Wassup Rockers '06
The Watermelon Woman '97
The Wedding Banquet '93 ▶
Welcome II the Terrordome '95
The Wrath of the Gods '14
Yes '04
Zebrahead '92 ▶

Interviews

***see also** This Is Your Life*
An American Haunting '05
America's Heart and Soul '04
Anvil! The Story of Anvil '09
Brief Interviews With Hideous Men '09
Catch a Fire '06
Chuck Berry: Hail! Hail! Rock 'n' Roll '87 ▶
Collapse '09
Crazy Love '07 ▶
A Decade Under the Influence '02 ▶
Dirty Pictures '00
Dreams with Sharp Teeth '07 ▶
Fellini: I'm a Born Liar '03
The Filth and the Fury '99
The First Saturday in May '08
The Fog of War: Eleven Lessons from the Life of Robert S. McNamara '03 ▶
Frost/Nixon '08 ▶
Good Hair '09
Having Our Say: The Delany Sisters' First 100 Years '99
Hearts of Darkness: A Filmmaker's Apocalypse '91 ▶
In the Shadow of the Moon '07 ▶
Interview '07 ▶
Interview with the Assassin '02
It Might Get Loud '09
The JFK Conspiracy '91
Joan Rivers: A Piece of Work '10
La Salamandre '71
The Laramie Project '02 ▶
The Life of David Gale '03
No End in Sight '07 ▶
Only the Strong Survive '03 ▶
Outrage '09
Paper Heart '09
Religulous '08 ▶
Restrepo '10
Roger & Me '89 ▶
Roman Polanski: Wanted and Desired '08
The September Issue '09
Sex Positive '09
Sicko '07
Standard Operating Procedure '08 ▶
Standing in the Shadows of Motown '02 ▶
Stone Reader '02 ▶
Stripper '86
Surf's Up '07
Surfwise '07 ▶
Taxi to the Dark Side '07 ▶
The Thin Blue Line '88 ▶
Waltz with Bashir '08 ▶
The Weather Underground '02 ▶
When We Were Kings '96 ▶
Wisecracks '93 ▶

Inventors & Inventions

***see also** Mad Scientists; Science & Scientists*
The Absent-Minded Professor '61 ▶
Back to the Future '85 ▶
Blonde Comet '41
A Bug's Life '98 ▶
Chairman of the Board '97
Chitty Chitty Bang Bang '68
C.H.O.M.P.S. '79
Cloudy with a Chance of Meatballs '09
The Demi-Paradise '43 ▶
Edison the Man '40
Envy '04
Flash of Genius '08
Flubber '97
Flying High '31
The Great Moment '44
Gremlins '84 ▶
Hello Down There '69
Hidden Enemy '40
Homewrecker '92
Honey, I Blew Up the Kid '92
Honey, I Shrunk the Kids '89
Honey, We Shrunk Ourselves '97
Invisible Mom '96
Iron Man '08 ▶
Iron Man 2 '10
Jack Brown, Genius '94
The Jerk '79
The Last Word '80
Longitude '00 ▶
The Machine '96

▶ = rated three bones or higher

The Man in the White Suit '51 ▸
The Man Who Fell to Earth '76 ▸
Mom's Outta Sight '01
The Mosquito Coast '86
Mystery Plane '39
Not Quite Human '87
Not Quite Human 2 '89
The Nut '21
Orgazmo '98
Primer '04 ▸
P.U.N.K.S. '98
Roaring Speedboats '37
Rogue's Gallery '44
Service De Luxe '38
So This Is Washington '43
Son of Flubber '63
The Sound and the Silence '93
The Spanish Prisoner '97 ▸
Spitfire '42 ▸
Steamboy '05
Still Not Quite Human '92
The Story of Alexander Graham Bell '39 ▸
Strange Impersonation '46
Theremin: An Electronic Odyssey '95 ▸
Time After Time '79 ▸
Time Chasers '95
Under the Hula Moon '95
Up the Ladder '25
Village of the Giants '65
The Water Engine '92 ▸
Where's Willie? '77
The Whole Shootin' Match '79 ▸
Witness for the Prosecution '57 ▸
The Yellow Cab Man '50
Young Tom Edison '40

Invisibility

Abbott and Costello Meet the Invisible Man '51 ▸
The Amazing Transparent Man '60
Clash of the Titans '81
The Dancing Princesses '84 ▸
Dick Tracy vs. Crime Inc. '41
Doctor Faustus '68
Dr. Orloff and the Invisible Man '72
Forbidden Planet '56 ▸
Golden Voyage of Sinbad '73
Hollow Man '00
Hollow Man 2 '06
Invisible Agent '42
The Invisible Avenger '58
Invisible Dad '97
The Invisible Dr. Mabuse '62 ▸
Invisible Invaders '59
The Invisible Kid '88
The Invisible Man '33 ▸
The Invisible Man Returns '40 ▸
The Invisible Maniac '90
The Invisible Man's Revenge '44
Invisible Mom '96
Invisible Mom 2 '99
The Invisible Monster '50
The Invisible Strangler '76
The Invisible Terror '63
Invisible: The Chronicles of Benjamin Knight '93
The Invisible Woman '40 ▸
The League of Extraordinary Gentlemen '03
Leapin' Leprechauns '95
Mad Monster Party '68
The Man Who Wasn't There '83
Memoirs of an Invisible Man '92
Mr. Superinvisible '73
Mom's Outta Sight '01
My Magic Dog '97
Mystery Men '99
The New Invisible Man '58
Now You See Him, Now You Don't '72
Orloff and the Invisible Man '70
Panama Menace '41
The Phantom Creeps '39
Phantom from Space '53
Phantom 2040 Movie: The Ghost Who Walks '95
Predator '87
Return of Chandu '34
Riding with Death '76
Sound of Horror '64

Iraq

***see also** Civil War (non U.S.); Genocide/Ethnic Cleansing; Middle East; Persian Gulf/Iraq War*

Buried '10
Generation Kill '08 ▸
Green Zone '10 ▸
The Ground Truth '06
House of Saddam '08
The Hurt Locker '08 ▸
Manticore '05
The Men Who Stare at Goats '09
No End in Sight '07 ▸
Redacted '07
Seal Team '08
Stop-Loss '08 ▸
War Tapes '06 ▸

Ireland

***see also** Belfast; Dublin*

American Women '00
Amongst Women '98
Angela's Ashes '99
Beloved Enemy '36 ▸
Bloody Sunday '01 ▸
Blown Away '94
Bobbie's Girl '02
The Boxer '97
The Boys and Girl From County Clare '03
The Break '97
Broken Harvest '94
The Brylcreem Boys '96
The Butcher Boy '97 ▸
Captain Boycott '47
Children in the Crossfire '84
Conspiracy of Silence '03
Cowboys & Angels '04 ▸
The Crying Game '92 ▸
Dancing at Lughnasa '98
Danny Boy '82 ▸
Darby O'Gill & the Little People '59 ▸
The Dawning '88
December Bride '91
Durango '99
Echoes '88
The Eternal '99
The External '99
Falling for a Dancer '98
Far and Away '92
The Field '90 ▸
The Fighting Prince of Donegal '66
Five Minutes of Heaven '09
Fools of Fortune '90
48 Angels '06
Hangman's House '28
Hear My Song '91 ▸
Hellboy II: The Golden Army '08 ▸
The Honeymooners '03
How About You '07
How Harry Became a Tree '01
I See a Dark Stranger '46 ▸
I Went Down '97 ▸
Images '72
The Informer '29
Irish Cinderella '22
Irish Jam '05
James Joyce: A Portrait of the Artist as a Young Man '77 ▸
Johnny Nobody '61
Lamb '85
The Last of the High Kings '96
The Last September '99
Laws of Attraction '04
Leap Year '10
Legend of the Bog '08
Leprechaun '93
Love and Rage '99
A Love Divided '01
The Luck of the Irish '48
The Magdalene Sisters '02 ▸
The Magical Legend of the Leprechauns '99
Man of Aran '34 ▸
The Manions of America '81
The Mapmaker '01
The Matchmaker '97
Men of Ireland '38
Middletown '06
Moondance '95
My Brother's War '97
The Nephew '97
Odd Man Out '47 ▸
Oh, Mr. Porter '37
Ordinary Decent Criminal '99
The Playboys '92 ▸
Poltergeist: The Legacy '96
Prayer for the Dying '87
P.S. I Love You '07
The Purple Taxi '77
The Quiet Man '52 ▸
Rawhead Rex '87
The Real Charlotte '91
River of Unrest '36
Rory O'Shea Was Here '04
The Run of the Country '95 ▸
Ryan's Daughter '70
St. Patrick: The Irish Legend '00
Scarlett '94
The Secret of Kells '09
The Secret of Roan Inish '94 ▸
Secret of the Cave '06
The Seventh Stream '01
She Creature '01
Shrooms '07
Snatch '00 ▸
Some Mother's Son '96 ▸
Song o' My Heart '29 ▸
Song o' My Heart '30
Spectre '96
Spellbreaker: Secret of the Leprechauns '96
Taffin '88
This Is My Father '99
Trojan Eddie '96 ▸
Troubles '88
Waking Ned Devine '98 ▸
War of the Buttons '95
Widow's Peak '94
The Wind That Shakes the Barley '06 ▸
Wings of the Morning '37

Islam

***see also** Middle East*

Beyond Honor '05
The Clay Bird '02
God's Sandbox '02
Hamsin '83 ▸
Honey & Ashes '96
The Keeper: The Legend of Omar Khayyam '05
Leila '97
Looking for Comedy in the Muslim World '06
Malcolm X: Make It Plain '95 ▸
The Message '77
Monsieur Ibrahim '03 ▸
My Son the Fanatic '97 ▸
Osama '03 ▸
Paradise Now '05 ▸
Persepolis '07 ▸
Red Mercury '05
Religulous '08 ▸
The Road to Guantanamo '06
Silent Waters '03
Sorry, Haters '05
The Stoning of Soraya M. '08
The Suitors '88
Traitor '08

Island Fare

***see also** Pacific Islands; Sex on the Beach*

The Admirable Crichton '57
The Adventures of Sadie '55
Affair in Trinidad '52
All the Brothers Were Valiant '53
Arachnid '01
Atlantis, the Lost Continent '61
Attack of the Sabretooth '05
Au Pair 3: Adventure in Paradise '09
The Ballad of Jack and Rose '05 ▸
Bare Essentials '91
Baywatch the Movie: Forbidden Paradise '95
The Beach '00
Bees in Paradise '44
The Bermuda Depths '78
Beverly Hills Family Robinson '97
Bikini Island '91
Bird of Paradise '32
Blacksnake! '73
Bleeders '97
The Blue Lagoon '80
Body Trouble '92
Boom! '68
The Bounty '84
Brand Upon the Brain! '06 ▸
The Breed '06
The Bribe '48
Cabin Boy '94
Captain Corelli's Mandolin '01
Captain Ron '92
Cast Away '00 ▸
The Castaway Cowboy '74
Chandu on the Magic Island '34
Cloudy with a Chance of Meatballs '09
Club Dread '04
Club Paradise '86
The Condemned '07
The Conqueror & the Empress '64
Couples Retreat '09
The Cover Girl Murders '93
Crusoe '89
Cthulhu '08
Cutthroat Island '95
Cyber Bandits '94
Dark Harbor '98
Dead of Night '99
Dead Waters '94
Deadly Currents '93
Deeply '99
Dinosaur Island '93
Dinotopia '02
DOA: Dead or Alive '06
Doomsdayer '99
Dungeon of Harrow '64
The Ebb-Tide '97
Echoes of Paradise '86
Emmanuelle on Taboo Island '76
Escape from Atlantis '97
Exit to Eden '94
Eye of the Dolphin '06
The Fat Spy '66
Father Goose '64
Finding Home '03
Flipper '96 ▸
Four Last Songs '06
F.P. 1 '33
From Hell It Came '57
Gale Force '01
Gargantua '98
Ginger and Cinnamon '03
Girl in Black '56
The Girl With the Dragon Tattoo '09 ▸
Hack! '07
Haven '04
Hawk of the Wilderness '38
Head Above Water '96
Heading South '05 ▸
Heaven Knows, Mr. Allison '57 ▸
Horrors of Spider Island '59
House of the Dead '03
How to Train Your Dragon '10
Hurricane '79
Hydra '09
Ibiza Dream '02
The Idol Dancer '20
In a Savage Land '99
In Her Line of Fire '06
The Invitation '03
The Island '80
Island in the Sun '57
The Island of Dr. Moreau '96
Island of Lost Souls '32 ▸
Island of the Blue Dolphins '64
Island of the Dead '00
Island of the Lost '68
Islander '06
Jack Frost 2: Revenge of the Mutant Killer Snowman '00
Jacob Two Two Meets the Hooded Fang '99
Joe Versus the Volcano '90
Jurassic Park '93 ▸
Jurassic Park 3 '01
Kidnapped in Paradise '98
Kilma, Queen of the Amazons '75
King Kong '05 ▸
King of the Damned '36
Kiss the Sky '98
The Kovak Box '06
The Land That Time Forgot '09
The Last Templar '09
L'Enfant d'Eau '95
The Lost World: Jurassic Park 2 '97
The Lunatic '92
Ma and Pa Kettle at Waikiki '55
Madagascar '05
Magic on Love Island '80
Mamma Mia! '08
A Man of Passion '88
Mararia '98
McHale's Navy '97
Mediterraneo '91 ▸
Melody in Love '78
Men of War '94
Mindhunters '05
Mr. Art Critic '07
Mr. Moto in Danger Island '39
Molokai: The Story of Father Damien '99
Mutiny on the Bounty '35 ▸
Mutiny on the Bounty '62
My Father the Hero '93
My Little Assassin '99
Mysterious Island '61 ▸
Mysterious Island of Beautiful Women '79
The Mystic Masseur '01
The Natalee Holloway Story '09
National Lampoon's Last Resort '94
Nim's Island '08
No Escape '94
No Man Is an Island '62
The Noah '75
Northern Extremes '93
Old Mother Riley's Jungle Treasure '51
On an Island with You '48
Once Upon a Wedding '05
One Night in the Tropics '40
The Other Side of Heaven '02
The Others '01 ▸
Pagan Island '60
Paradise '82
Passion in Paradise '89
The Passion of Anna '70 ▸
Pearl of the South Pacific '55
People '04
Perfect Strangers '03
Pippi in the South Seas '70
Pirates of Blood River '62
Pirates of the Caribbean: Dead Man's Chest '06
The Postman '94 ▸
The Prisoner of Shark Island '36
PT 109 '63
Pufnstuf '70
The Quest '96
Rapa Nui '93
The Ravagers '65
The Real Macaw '98
Reel Paradise '05 ▸
Rescue from Gilligan's Island '78
Respiro '02
Return to Paradise '53
Return to the Blue Lagoon '91
Robinson Crusoe '96
Rugrats Go Wild! '03
Savage Is Loose '74
The Sea God '30
The Seducers '70
The Seventh Dawn '64
Sex and Lucia '01
Shadow Warriors '97
Shelter Island '03
Signs of Life '68
Six Days, Seven Nights '98
The Sleeping Dictionary '02
The Snake People '68
Somewhere in Time '80
Son of Fury '42 ▸
Speed 2: Cruise Control '97
Spy Kids 2: The Island of Lost Dreams '02 ▸
Stephen King's The Storm of the Century '99
The Story of Dr. Wassell '44
Summer Affair '71
Surf's Up '07
Survival Island '02
Survival of the Dead '09
Swept Away... '75 ▸
Swept Away '02
A Swingin' Summer '65
Tales of the Kama Sutra 2: Monsoon '98
The Tempest '82 ▸
Terror in Paradise '90
Third World Cop '99
Trouble in Paradise '88
The Tuttles of Tahiti '42 ▸
Tyler Perry's Why Did I Get Married Too '10
Undercurrent '99
Up Periscope '59
Up to His Neck '54
Utopia '51
Vibration '68
Victory '95
Vipers '08
Waikiki Wedding '37 ▸
Warbirds '08
Week-End in Havana '41
The Weight of Water '00
We're Not Dressing '34 ▸
When Time Ran Out '80
Where the Wild Things Are '09
The Wicker Man '06
Wide Sargasso Sea '92
Wide Sargasso Sea '06
The Widow of Saint-Pierre '00 ▸
Wings over the Pacific '43
Witches of the Caribbean '05
The Wizards of Waverly Place: The Movie '09
Xtro 3: Watch the Skies '95

Israel

***see also** The Holocaust; Judaism*

Adam Resurrected '08
Ajami '09 ▸
Amazing Grace '92
Ancient Relic '02
The Band's Visit '07 ▸
Bonjour Monsieur Shlomi '03 ▸
Broken Wings '02 ▸
The Bubble '06
Cast a Giant Shadow '66
Children of Rage '75
Colombian Love '04
Cup Final '92
Diamonds '72
Double Edge '92
Eagles Attack at Dawn '70
Exodus '60 ▸
Free Zone '05
Hello Goodbye '08
Hide and Seek '80
Hill 24 Doesn't Answer '55 ▸
Intimate Story '81
James' Journey to Jerusalem '03
Japan Japan '07
Kippur '00 ▸
Land of Plenty '04
Late Marriage '01
Late Summer Blues '87
The Little Drummer Girl '84 ▸
The Man Who Captured Eichmann '96
Mother Night '96 ▸
Munich '05 ▸
O Jerusalem '07
Operation Thunderbolt '77
Or (My Treasure) '04
Paradise Now '05 ▸
The Secrets '07

The Seventh Coin '92
Sinai Commandos '68
Soldier of the Night '84
The Syrian Bride '04
39 Pounds of Love '05
Time of Favor '00
Under the Domim Tree '95
Ushpizin '04
Victory at Entebbe '76
Wall '04 ▸
Year Zero '04
Yellow Asphalt '01
You Don't Mess with the Zohan '08

Istanbul, not Constantinople

Climates '06 ▸
The Edge of Heaven '07 ▸
Fay Grim '06
From Russia with Love '63 ▸
Istanbul '57
Istanbul '85
Istanbul '90
Journey into Fear '42 ▸
The Mask of Dimitrios '44 ▸
The Net 2.0 '06
Steam: A Turkish Bath '96 ▸
Topkapi '64 ▸
The World Is Not Enough '99

Italy

***see also** Florence; Rome—Ancient; Rome—Modern; Venice*
Accatone! '61 ▸
Acla's Descent into Floristella '87
Acqua e Sapone '83
After Midnight '04
All Screwed Up '74 ▸
Amarcord '74 ▸
Angela '02
The Assisi Underground '84
Avanti! '72
Baaria '09
Best of Youth '03 ▸
Beyond the Clouds '95
The Bicycle Thief '48 ▸
A Blade in the Dark '83
Blame It on the Bellboy '92
Blood Feud '79
Bright Star '09
Catch-22 '70 ▸
Caterina in the Big City '03
Cemetery Man '95
The Children '90
Christ Stopped at Eboli '79 ▸
Ciao, Professore! '94
Cinema Paradiso '88 ▸
Cobra '25
Come September '61
The Conformist '71 ▸
Cry of a Prostitute: Love Kills '72
Death Takes a Holiday '34 ▸
The Divine Lady '29
Divorce—Italian Style '62 ▸
Dondi '61
Don't Torture a Duckling '72
Double Team '97
Eat, Pray, Love '10
1860 '33
The Eighteenth Angel '97
Elective Affinities '96
Enchanted April '92
Eros '04
Escapade in Florence '62
Europa '51 '52
Excellent Cadavers '99
Executioner of Venice '63
A Face in the Rain '63
The Fallen '05 ▸
Fellini's Roma '72
Fiances '63
Final Justice '84
For Roseanna '96
The Forbidden Christ '50
The 4th Tenor '02
Francesco '93
Gallowglass '95 ▸
The Garden of Redemption '97
The Garden of the Finzi-Continis '71 ▸
Ginostra '02
The Godfather, Part 3 '90 ▸
Gomorrah '08 ▸
A Good Woman '04
Heaven '01
His Secret Life '01 ▸
Hornet's Nest '70
Hotel '01
Il Divo '08
I'm Not Scared '03
In Love and War '96
In Love and War '01
It Started in Naples '60 ▸
Italian for Beginners '01
The Italian Job '03 ▸
Kaos '85 ▸
La Chartreuse de Parme '48
La Dolce Vita '60 ▸
La Scorta '94 ▸
La Terra Trema '48 ▸
The Leopard '63 ▸
Letters to Juliet '10
The Lickerish Quartet '70
Life Is Beautiful '98 ▸
The Lizzie McGuire Movie '03
Lost Moment '47
Love and Anarchy '73 ▸
Love in the City '53 ▸
The Love Light '21
The Luzhin Defence '00
Macaroni '85
Mafioso '62
Malena '00
Mamma Roma '62 ▸
A Man About the House '47
Massacre in Rome '73
Miracle at St. Anna '08
A Month by the Lake '95
Mussolini & I '85
My Brother Is an Only Child '07
My House in Umbria '03 ▸
My Mother's Smile '02
Night Sun '90
1900 '76 ▸
Nora '00
Nostalghia '83
Only You '94
Open City '45 ▸
Orchestra Rehearsal '78
The Organizer '64
Ossessione '42 ▸
The Other Man '08
Paisan '46 ▸
The Palermo Connection '91
Passion of Love '82 ▸
Pizzicata '96
The Postman '94 ▸
Prince of Foxes '49
Pronto '97
A Rare Breed '81
The Red Violin '98
Ripley's Game '02 ▸
The Roman Spring of Mrs. Stone '03
Rome Adventure '62
St. Michael Had a Rooster '72
The Scent of a Woman '75
Screw Loose '99
Season for Assassins '71
The Secret of Santa Vittoria '69
The Seven Hills of Rome '58
Shoeshine '47 ▸
The Sicilian '87
The Sky Is Falling '00
The Son's Room '00 ▸
Spice World: The Movie '97
Stealing Beauty '96
Stiff Upper Lips '96
The Stone Merchant '06
The Story of G.I. Joe '45 ▸
Street Angel '28
Taken Alive '95
The Talented Mr. Ripley '99
That Long Night in '43 '60
Three Coins in the Fountain '54
Too Bad She's Bad '54
The Tree of Wooden Clogs '78 ▸
The Truce '96 ▸
The Twilight Saga: New Moon '09
Two Women '61 ▸
Uncle Nino '03
Under the Tuscan Sun '03
The Unknown Woman '06
The Victors '63
Von Ryan's Express '65 ▸
Voyage in Italy '53
The Walls of Malapaga '49
What Did You Do in the War, Daddy? '66
Where Angels Fear to Tread '91 ▸
The Wide Blue Road '57 ▸
William Shakespeare's A Midsummer Night's Dream '99
Wolverine '96
Women in Prison '49
Year of the Gun '91

It's a Conspiracy, Man!

***see also** Capitol Capers; Mystery & Suspense*
Absolute Power '97
The Alchemists '99
All the President's Men '76 ▸
Anatomy '00 ▸
The Andromeda Strain '08
The Arrival '96
The Arrival 2 '98
The Assassination File '96
Attack Force '06
Backlash '99
The Bank Job '08 ▸
Before I Say Goodbye '03
Blind Horizon '04
The Capitol Conspiracy '99
Chain Reaction '96
Circadian Rhythm '05
City Hall '95 ▸
Company Business '91
Conspiracy Theory '97 ▸
The Constant Gardener '05 ▸
Cop Land '97 ▸
Crimson Rivers 2: Angels of the Apocalypse '05
Cyborg Soldier '08
The Da Vinci Code '06 ▸
Dead Bang '89
Deadly Game '77
Echelon Conspiracy '09
Echo of Murder '00
Edge of Darkness '10
End Game '06
The End of Violence '97
Enemy of the State '98
Eraser '96
Executive Action '73
The Feminine Touch '95
Final Payback '99
Fire Serpent '07
Flashpoint '84
The Forgotten '04
The Fourth Protocol '87 ▸
The Game '97 ▸
Hijacking Catastrophe: 9/11, Fear and the Selling of America '04
Interview with the Assassin '02
The Jackal '97
JFK '91 ▸
The Kovak Box '06
The Last Templar '09
The Legend of Zorro '05
Looking for Richard '96 ▸
The Machinist '04
Malevolence '95
Man from Mallorca '84
The Manchurian Candidate '62 ▸
The Manchurian Candidate '04 ▸
The Matrix '99 ▸
The Matrix Reloaded '03
The Matrix Revolutions '03 ▸
Mulholland Falls '95
Muppets from Space '99
Murder at 1600 '97
Nixon '95 ▸
No Way Out '87 ▸
November Conspiracy '96
Oktober '98
The Package '89
Pandemic '09
The Parallax View '74 ▸
Perfect Target '98
Pistol Whipped '08
Poodle Springs '98
Power Play '02
The Prisoner '09
Rage '72
Rangers '00
Red Corner '97
Renaissance '06
Robin Cook's Terminal '96
Rush Hour 2 '01
Seven Days in May '64 ▸
The Shadow Conspiracy '96
Shooter '07
16 Blocks '06 ▸
Sneakers '92
Southland Tales '06
The Star Chamber '83
The State Within '06
Storm Catcher '99
Storm Tracker '99
Submerged '05
The Summit '08
They Crawl '01
They Live '88
Three Days of the Condor '75 ▸
Time Bomb '08
Tom Clancy's Netforce '98
Traitor '08
Unholy '07
Venomous '01
Watchmen '09
The Way of War '08
Winter Kills '79 ▸
The X-Files '98

Jail

***see** Alcatraz; Death Row; Great Escapes; Men in Prison; Women in Prison*

Jamaica

***see also** Island Fare; Vacations*
Belly '98
Captain Blood '35 ▸
Clara's Heart '88
Cocktail '88
Cool Runnings '93
The Devil's Daughter '39
Dr. No '62 ▸
The Harder They Come '72
How Stella Got Her Groove Back '98
Joey Breaker '93 ▸
Marked for Death '90
The Mighty Quinn '89
Pirates of the Caribbean: Dead Man's Chest '06
Pirates of the Caribbean: The Curse of the Black Pearl '03 ▸
Rude Boy: The Jamaican Don '03
Swashbuckler '76
Third World Cop '99
The Treasure Seekers '79
Voodoo Black Exorcist '73
White Squall '96
Wide Sargasso Sea '92

Japan

***see also** Asia; Tokyo*
Akira '89
As You Like It '06
Azumi '03 ▸
The Ballad of Narayama '83 ▸
Barbarian and the Geisha '58
The Battle of the Japan Sea '70
Behind the Rising Sun '43
Black Rain '88 ▸
Black Rain '89
Blood on the Sun '45
Blood: The Last Vampire '09
Bright Future '03 ▸
Cafe Lumiere '05
Captive Hearts '87
Cold Fever '95
The Cove '09 ▸
The Cruel Story of Youth '60 ▸
Demonlover '02
Destination Tokyo '43
Dr. Akagi '98
Dodes 'ka-den '70 ▸
Dolls '02 ▸
The Eel '96 ▸
Eijanaika '81 ▸
Enjo '58
Escapade in Japan '57
Father of the Kamikaze '74
Flirt '95
Force of the Ninja '88
47 Ronin, Part 1 '42 ▸
47 Ronin, Part 2 '42 ▸
The Geisha Boy '58
Geisha Girl '52
Girls of the White Orchid '85
Gozu '03
The Grudge '04
Gung Ho '85
Harakiri '62 ▸
Heaven & Earth '90 ▸
The Hidden Blade '04
Hiroshima '95 ▸
Hiroshima Maiden '88
Hiroshima, Mon Amour '59 ▸
House Where Evil Dwells '82
The Hunted '94
The Idiot '51 ▸
The Imperial Japanese Empire '85
Journey of Honor '91
Kikujiro '99
King's Ransom '91
The Last Samurai '03 ▸
Letters from Iwo Jima '06 ▸
Life of Oharu '52 ▸
Lost in Translation '03 ▸
Love and Faith '78 ▸
MacArthur's Children '85 ▸
Madame Butterfly '95
A Majority of One '56
The Makioka Sisters '83 ▸
Memoirs of a Geisha '05
The Men Who Tread on the Tiger's Tail '45
Midway '76
Minbo—Or the Gentle Art of Japanese Extortion '92
Mishima: A Life in Four Chapters '85 ▸
Mr. Baseball '92
Mother '52 ▸
The Neighbor No. Thirteen '05
No '98
No Regrets for Our Youth '46 ▸
Nomugi Pass '79
Objective, Burma! '45 ▸
Okoge '93
Osaka Elegy '36
Otaku No Video '91 ▸
The Pillow Book '95
Ponyo '08 ▸
Prisoners of the Sun '91 ▸
Ran '85 ▸
Rashomon '51 ▸
Red Beard '65 ▸
Rikyu '90 ▸
Rising Sun '93 ▸
Saga of the Vagabond '59
Samurai Banners '69
Samurai Cowboy '93
Samurai Rebellion '67 ▸
Samurai Reincarnation '81
Sansho the Bailiff '54 ▸
Sayonara '57 ▸
Seven Samurai '54 ▸
Shall We Dance? '96 ▸
She and He '63
Shin Heike Monogatari '55 ▸
Shogun '80 ▸
Showdown in Little Tokyo '91
Silk '07
Sisters of the Gion '36
Snow Country '57
Sonatine '96 ▸
The Sun's Burial '60 ▸
Taboo '99
Teenage Mutant Ninja Turtles 3 '93
Thirty Seconds Over Tokyo '44 ▸
3 Ninjas Kick Back '94
Tokyo Decadence '91
Tokyo-Ga '85 ▸
Tokyo Pop '88
Tora! Tora! Tora! '70
Traffic Jam '91
Twenty-Four Eyes '54 ▸
The Twilight Samurai '02 ▸
Ugetsu '53 ▸
Under the Flag of the Rising Sun '72 ▸
Utamaro and His Five Women '46
Village of Dreams '97
Walk, Don't Run '66
What's Up, Tiger Lily? '66 ▸
When I Close My Eyes '95
The Wolves '82 ▸
The Wrath of the Gods '14
The Yakuza '75
You Only Live Twice '67
Zatoichi '03 ▸
Zatoichi vs. Yojimbo '70 ▸

Jazz & Blues

***see also** Price of Fame; Struggling Musicians*
Almost Blue '93
American Blue Note '89
The Benny Goodman Story '55
Big Business Girl '31
Billy's Holiday '95
Bird '88 ▸
Birth of the Blues '41
Bix '90
Blueberry Hill '88
The Blues Brothers '80 ▸
Blues Brothers 2000 '98
Blues in the Night '41
Cool Mikado '63
The Cotton Club '84 ▸
Crossroads '86
Dingo '90
The Duke Is Tops '38
Eubie! '82 ▸
The Five Pennies '59
Forty Shades of Blue '05
The Gene Krupa Story '59
G.I. Blues '60
Giant Steps '92
The Gig '85
The Glenn Miller Story '54 ▸
Hi-De-Ho '35
The Jazz Singer '27
The Jazz Singer '80
Jazzman '84 ▸
Kansas City '95 ▸
Killer Diller '04
King of Jazz '30
Lady Sings the Blues '72
Let's Get Lost '88
Lighting in a Bottle '04 ▸
Lost Highway '96
Lush Life '94 ▸
Machine Gun Blues '95
Mo' Better Blues '90
Moonlight Serenade '09
Mystery in Swing '40
New Orleans '47
New York, New York '77 ▸
Paris Blues '61
Pete Kelly's Blues '55
Ragtime '81 ▸
Ray '04 ▸
Rendez-vous de Juillet '49
Round Midnight '86 ▸
Schultze Gets the Blues '03
Sepia Cinderella '47
Shadows '60 ▸
Silver Hawk '04
Some Like It Hot '59 ▸
A Song Is Born '48 ▸
Stormy Monday '88
Sweet and Lowdown '99
Sweet Love, Bitter '67
Swing '98
Swing High, Swing Low '37
Swing It, Professor '37
The Talented Mr. Ripley '99
Wild Orchid 2: Two Shades of Blue '92
Young Man with a Horn '50 ▸

Jealousy

Amor de Hombre '97
Amores Perros '00 ▸
Between Love & Goodbye '08
Boys Love '06
The Break-Up '06
Cold Showers '05
The Crimson Kimono '59
Crush '02
Curse of the Golden Flower '06
Daddy & Them '99
The Devil and the Deep '32
The Devil's Backbone '01
Dirty Love '05
Do Not Disturb '65
The Edge of Love '08
Elegy '08
Enigma '01
Envy '04
The Fast Runner '01 ▸

▸ = rated three bones or higher

Fast Sofa '01
For Your Consideration '06
Getting Gertie's Garter '27
A Girl Cut in Two '07
The Girl in the Red Velvet Swing '55
Gosford Park '01 ▶
Heart '99
The Heavenly Body '44
Honeymoon Lodge '43
The King '05
The Kreutzer Sonata '08
The Last Man '00
Leaving Metropolis '02
Les Biches '68 ▶
Little Black Book '04
Little Chenier: A Cajun Story '06
Lonely Hearts '06
The Loss of a Teardrop Diamond '08
The Male Animal '42
Manpower '41
Me Without You '01
Merci pour le Chocolat '00 ▶
My Wife is an Actress '01
Nora '00
Othello '01 ▶
The Other Man '08
Out of Time '03
Pandaemonium '00
The Piano Teacher '01
The Prestige '06 ▶
The Price of Milk '00
Pumpkin '02
Revolutionary Road '08
Second Best '05
Sex and Breakfast '07
Signs & Wonders '00
Sleuth '07
Sylvia '03
Taboo '99
This Woman Is Dangerous '52
Tiger Shark '32
Time '06
Valentin '03
The Valet '06
The Weather Man '05
The Weight of Water '00
Weird Woman '44
Who Wants to Kill Jessie? '65
Wife Versus Secretary '36 ▶

Jerusalem

Appointment with Death '88
Ben-Hur '59 ▶
The Body '01
The Crusades '35
Every Time We Say Goodbye '86
Kadosh '99
Kingdom of Heaven '05 ▶
The Silver Chalice '54
Ushpizin '04

Jockeying for Position

Archer's Adventure '85
The Bashful Bachelor '42
Big Boy '30
Bite the Bullet '75 ▶
The Black Stallion '79 ▶
Boots Malone '52
Broadway Bill '34 ▶
Casey's Shadow '78
Champions '84
Cold Feet '89
A Day at the Races '37 ▶
Dead Heat '01
Devil on Horseback '54
The Devil's Cargo '48
Down Argentine Way '40 ▶
Dreamer: Inspired by a True Story '05
Duke of the Derby '62
Ex-Mrs. Bradford '36 ▶
Far and Away '92
A Fine Mess '86
The First Saturday in May '08
Flame of Araby '51
Francis Goes to the Races '51
Glory '56
Grand National Night '53
Great Dan Patch '49
Hidalgo '04
A Horse for Danny '95
Kentucky Blue Streak '35
Law of the Wild '34
Le Gentleman D'Epsom '62
The Lemon Drop Kid '51
Let It Ride '89
Lightning: The White Stallion '86
The Longshot '86
Ma and Pa Kettle at the Fair '52
Money from Home '53
Moon over Miami '41 ▶
My Old Man '79
National Velvet '44 ▶
Off and Running '90
On the Right Track '81
Phar Lap '84
Prince and the Great Race '83
The Quiet Man '52 ▶
Racing Blood '36
Racing Luck '35
The Red Stallion '47
Riding High '50
Run for the Roses '78
Saratoga '37
Seabiscuit '03 ▶
Shooting Fish '98
Simpatico '99
The Story of Seabiscuit '49
Sylvester '85
Tennessee Stallion '78
Thoroughbreds Don't Cry '37
Three Men on a Horse '36 ▶
Trail to San Antone '47
Turf Boy '42
Win, Place, or Steal '72
Winds of the Wasteland '36
Wings of the Morning '37

Joke and Dagger

see also Cold War Spies; Female Spies; Genre Spoofs; Satire & Parody; Spies & Espionage; Spy Kids; World War I Spies; World War II Spies

The Accidental Spy '01
The Adventures of Rocky & Bullwinkle '00
Agent Cody Banks '03
Agent Cody Banks 2: Destination London '04
Austin Powers: International Man of Mystery '97 ▶
Austin Powers 2: The Spy Who Shagged Me '99 ▶
Austin Powers In Goldmember '02
Boris and Natasha: The Movie '92
Call Me Bwana '63
Casino Royale '67
Chu Chu & the Philly Flash '81
Code Name: The Cleaner '07
Condorman '81
Dead Men Don't Wear Plaid '82
D.E.B.S. '04
Don't Raise the Bridge, Lower the River '68
The Double O Kid '92
Duck Soup '33 ▶
G-Force '09
Get Smart '08
Get Smart, Again! '89
Hopscotch '80 ▶
Hudson Hawk '91
I Dood It '43
I Spy '02
If Looks Could Kill '86
The In-Laws '79 ▶
The In-Laws '03
In Like Flint '67
Ishtar '87
Looney Tunes: Back in Action '03
The Man Who Knew Too Little '97
The Man with One Red Shoe '85
Max Rules '05
Memoirs of an Invisible Man '92
My Favorite Brunette '47
A Night in Casablanca '46 ▶
The Nude Bomb '80
OSS 117: Cairo, Nest of Spies '06
Our Man Flint '66
The President's Analyst '67 ▶
Real Men '87
Salt & Pepper '68
Secret Agent 00-Soul '89
The Shakiest Gun in the West '68
Spies Like Us '85
Spy Hard '96
S*P*Y*S '74
Top Secret! '84 ▶
True Lies '94
Undercover Brother '02
What's Up, Tiger Lily? '66 ▶
Zoolander '01

Journalism

see Front Page; News at 11

Judaism

see also The Holocaust; Israel; Rabbi

Adam Sandler's 8 Crazy Nights '02
Aimee & Jaguar '98
All My Loved Ones '00
Almost Peaceful '02 ▶
American Matchmaker '40
The Angel Levine '70
Angry Harvest '85 ▶
Anne Frank: The Whole Story '01 ▶
The Apprenticeship of Duddy Kravitz '74 ▶
The Assisi Underground '84
The Assistant '97
Atalia '85
The Attic: The Hiding of Anne Frank '88
Au Revoir les Enfants '87 ▶
Autumn Sun '98 ▶
Bee Season '05 ▶
The Believer '01
Black Book '06 ▶
The Blum Affair '48
A Brivele der Mamen '38 ▶
Broken Glass '96
Bye Bye Braverman '67
The Cantor's Son '37
Charlie Grant's War '80
The Chosen '81 ▶
Commissar '68 ▶
Conspiracy of Hearts '60 ▶
Counsellor-at-Law '33 ▶
The Courageous Heart of Irena Sendler '09 ▶
Crossfire '47 ▶
Crossing Delancey '88 ▶
Dad On the Run '00
Daniel Deronda '02
David '79 ▶
David '97
A Day in October '92
Deconstructing Harry '97
Defiance '08
The Devil's Arithmetic '99
The Diary of Anne Frank '59 ▶
The Diary of Anne Frank '08
Disraeli '79 ▶
Divided We Fall '00
Drifting '82
The Dunera Boys '85 ▶
The Dybbuk '37 ▶
East and West '24 ▶
Eli Eli '40
Enemies, a Love Story '89 ▶
Esther '98
Esther Kahn '00
Evan Almighty '07
Every Time We Say Goodbye '86
Everything is Illuminated '05 ▶
Exodus '60 ▶
Fateless '05 ▶
Fiddler on the Roof '71 ▶
The Fixer '68 ▶
Freud Leaving Home '91
A Friendship in Vienna '88
The Frisco Kid '79
Funny Girl '68 ▶
The Garden of the Finzi-Continis '71 ▶
Gentleman's Agreement '47 ▶
The Girl on the Train '09
Go for Zucker '05
God, Man and Devil '49
God on Trial '08
The Golem '20 ▶
Good Evening, Mr. Wallenberg '93
Goodbye, New York '85
The Grand Role '04
Green Fields '37
The Grey Zone '01
Hamsin '83 ▶
Hanna's War '88
The Harmonists '99
Hello Goodbye '08
Hester Street '75 ▶
Hill 24 Doesn't Answer '55 ▶
Holocaust '78 ▶
Homicide '91 ▶
The House on Chelouche Street '73
I Love You, Alice B. Toklas! '68
I Love You, I Love You Not '97
I Love You Rosa '72
In the Presence of Mine Enemies '97
The Infiltrator '95
Inglourious Basterds '09 ▶
Invincible '01
The Island on Bird Street '97
It Runs in the Family '03
Ivan and Abraham '94
Jacob the Liar '74
James' Journey to Jerusalem '03
The Jazz Singer '27
The Jazz Singer '80
Jeremiah '98
The Jew '96
Jew-Boy Levi '99
Jud Suess '40 ▶
Kadosh '99
Keeping the Faith '00
Keeping Up with the Steins '06
King David '85
King of the Corner '04 ▶
Kissing Jessica Stein '02
Kuni Lemel in Tel Aviv '77
La Petite Jerusalem '05
Lansky '99
The Last Metro '80 ▶
The Last Winter '84
Late Marriage '01
Left Luggage '98
Leon the Pig Farmer '93
Les Violons du Bal '74
Liberty Heights '99
Lies My Father Told Me '75 ▶
The Life and Times of Hank Greenberg '99 ▶
Life During Wartime '09
The Light Ahead '39
Loving Leah '09
The Mad Adventures of Rabbi Jacob '73 ▶
Madman '79
The Man Who Captured Eichmann '96
The Man Who Cried '00
Martha and I '91 ▶
Masada '81 ▶
Max '02
Me and the Colonel '58
Mendel '98 ▶
The Merchant of Venice '04 ▶
Miracle at Midnight '98
Miracle at Moreaux '86
Miss Rose White '92 ▶
Mr. Emmanuel '44
Moses '96
Munich '05 ▶
The Murder of Mary Phagan '87 ▶
My Fuhrer '07
My Michael '75 ▶
My Mother's Courage '95
The Nativity Story '06
Next Year in Jerusalem '98
No Way to Treat a Lady '68 ▶
Noa at Seventeen '82 ▶
November Moon '85
Nowhere in Africa '02
Once Upon a Time in America '84 ▶
One Day You'll Understand '08
The Only Way '70
Outside Chance of Maximillian Glick '88
Over the Brooklyn Bridge '83
The Pawnbroker '65 ▶
The Pianist '02 ▶
Playing Mona Lisa '00
Power '34
A Price above Rubies '97
Prime '05
The Proprietor '96
Protocols of Zion '05 ▶
The Quarrel '93
Radio Days '87 ▶
Religulous '08 ▶
Rescuers: Stories of Courage—Two Couples '98 ▶
Rescuers: Stories of Courage "Two Women" '97 ▶
The Revolt of Job '84 ▶
Safe Men '98
Sallah '63 ▶
Schindler's List '93 ▶
School Ties '92 ▶
A Secret '07 ▶
A Secret Space '88
The Secrets '07
A Serious Man '09 ▶
The Serpent's Egg '78
The Shop on Main Street '65 ▶
The Sky Is Falling '00
Snow in August '01
Sofie '92
Solomon '98
Solomon and Gaenor '98
The Sorrow and the Pity '71 ▶
Steel Toes '06
Stolen Summer '02
A Stranger Among Us '92
The Substance of Fire '96
The Summer of Aviya '88
The Summer of My German Soldier '78 ▶
Sunshine '99
Table Settings '84
The Taxman '98
Tevye '39
Then She Found Me '07
They Were Ten '61
'38: Vienna before the Fall '88
Time of Favor '00
The Tollbooth '04
Train of Life '98
Transport from Paradise '65
The Twilight of the Golds '97
The Two of Us '68 ▶
Uncle Moses '32
Under the Domim Tree '95
Under the Earth '86 ▶
Unsettled Land '88
Unstrung Heroes '95
Uprising '01 ▶
Used People '92
Ushpizin '04
Voyage of the Damned '76 ▶
Wall '04 ▶
Wandering Jew '20
War & Love '84
When Do We Eat? '05
Where Is My Child? '37
Where's Poppa? '70 ▶
The Wooden Gun '79
The Year My Parents Went on Vacation '07
Year One '09
Yellow Asphalt '01
Yentl '83
You Don't Mess with the Zohan '08
Zalmen or the Madness of God '75

Jungle Stories

see also Monkeyshines; Treasure Hunt

Ace Ventura: When Nature Calls '95
Active Stealth '99
Africa Screams '49
Aguirre, the Wrath of God '72 ▶
All the Way, Boys '73
Amazon '90
Amazon Jail '85
Anaconda '96
Anacondas: The Hunt for the Blood Orchid '04
The Art of Travel '08
At Play in the Fields of the Lord '91 ▶
Baby... Secret of the Lost Legend '85
Back from Eternity '56
Bat 21 '88
Bela Lugosi Meets a Brooklyn Gorilla '52
Beyond Rangoon '95
Black Cobra 3: The Manila Connection '90
The Black Devils of Kali '55
Blonde Savage '47
Brenda Starr '86
The Bride & the Beast '58
Bride of the Gorilla '51
Cannibal Holocaust '80
Cannibal Women in the Avocado Jungle of Death '89
Carry On Up the Jungle '70
Cobra Woman '44
Codename: Terminate '90
The Colombian Connection '91
Commando Invasion '87
Congo '95
Curious George '06
Death in the Garden '56
Delta Force Commando '87
Devil Hunter '08
The Diamond of Jeru '01
Diplomatic Immunity '91
DNA '97
Dr. Cyclops '40
Dr. Seuss' Horton Hears a Who! '08 ▶
East of Borneo '31
Elephant Boy '37 ▶
Elephant Walk '54
The Emerald Forest '85 ▶
Emerald Jungle '80
Emmanuelle 6 '88
End of the Spear '06
Enemy Unseen '91
Escape from Hell '79
Escape to Burma '55
Escape 2000 '81
Farewell to the King '89
Fatal Mission '89
Field of Fire '92
Field of Honor '86
Final Mission '84
Fire on the Amazon '93
Firehawk '92
Firewalker '86
Fitzcarraldo '82 ▶
Five Came Back '39
Flight from Singapore '62
Found Alive '34
The Further Adventures of Tennessee Buck '88
Fury '78
George of the Jungle '97 ▶
Gold of the Amazon Women '79
Gold Raiders '83
Gorillas in the Mist '88 ▶
Green Fire '55
Green Inferno '72
Green Mansions '59
Greystoke: The Legend of Tarzan, Lord of the Apes '84
Harry Black and the Tiger '58
Heart of Darkness '93
Hell's Headquarters '32
The Hive '08
How Tasty Was My Little Frenchman '71
Indio '90
Indio 2: The Revolt '92
Instinct '99
The Intended '02
Invincible Barbarian '83
Jane & the Lost City '87
Jumanji '95
Jungle '52
The Jungle Book '42
The Jungle Book '67 ▶
The Jungle Book 2 '03
Jungle Boy '96
Jungle Bride '33
Jungle Drums of Africa '53
Jungle Goddess '49
Jungle Heat '84

Jungle Hell '55
Jungle Inferno '72
Jungle Master '72
Jungle Patrol '48
Jungle Raiders '85
Jungle Siren '42
Jungle Warriors '84
Killers '88
Killing Heat '84
King of the Jungle '33
King of the Kongo '29
King Solomon's Treasure '76
Krippendorf's Tribe '98
The Land Unknown '57
Law of the Jungle '42
Liane, Jungle Goddess '56
The Lion Hunters '47
The Lion King '94 ▶
The Lion Man '36
Lion Man '75
The Lost City '34
Lost City of the Jungle '45
The Lost Continent '51
The Lost Jungle '34
The Lost Tribe '89
Lure of the Islands '42
Managua '97
Medicine Man '92
Mercenary 2: Thick and Thin '97
Merrill's Marauders '62
Mighty Jungle '64
The Mighty Peking Man '77
Miracles '86
Missing in Action '84
The Mission '86 ▶
Mister Lonely '07
Mistress of the Apes '79
Mogambo '53 ▶
The Mosquito Coast '86
The Muthers '76
Mysterious Island of Beautiful Women '79
Nabonga '44
Naked Jungle '54 ▶
The Naked Prey '66 ▶
The New Adventures of Tarzan '35
Night Creature '79
Nightforce '86
No Man Is an Island '62
Objective, Burma! '45 ▶
Omoo Omoo, the Shark God '49
Operation Dumbo Drop '95
Options '88
Overkill '96
Perils of the Darkest Jungle '44
The Phantom '96
The Pink Jungle '68
Predator '87
Prehistoric Women '67
Proof of Life '00
Queen of the Amazons '47
Queen of the Jungle '35
The Real Glory '39 ▶
Red Dust '32 ▶
River of Death '90
River of Evil '64
The Road to Zanzibar '41 ▶
Robbers of the Sacred Mountain '83
Romancing the Stone '84 ▶
Rudyard Kipling's The Jungle Book '94
Rudyard Kipling's the Second Jungle Book: Mowgli and Baloo '97
The Ruins '08
The Rundown '03
Samar '62
The Savage Girl '32
Shame of the Jungle '75
Sheena '84
Snakeman '05
Sniper '92
Solo '96
Son of Kong '33
Stormquest '87
Sweet Revenge '87
Tarzan '99 ▶
Tarzan and His Mate '34 ▶
Tarzan and the Green Goddess '38
Tarzan and the Lost City '98
Tarzan and the Lost Safari '57
Tarzan and the She-Devil '53
Tarzan and the Slave Girl '50
Tarzan and the Trappers '58
Tarzan Escapes '36 ▶
Tarzan Finds a Son '39 ▶
Tarzan of the Apes '17
Tarzan, the Ape Man '32 ▶
Tarzan, the Ape Man '81
Tarzan the Fearless '33
Tarzan the Magnificent '60
Tarzan the Tiger '29
Tarzana, the Wild Girl '69
Tarzan's Fight for Life '58
Tarzan's Greatest Adventure '59
Tarzan's Hidden Jungle '55
Tarzan's Magic Fountain '48
Tarzan's Peril '51
Tarzan's Revenge '38
Tarzan's Savage Fury '52
Tarzan's Secret Treasure '41
Tears of the Sun '03
Terror in the Jungle '68
Terror of the Bloodhunters '62
The Thin Red Line '98 ▶
The Thirsty Dead '74
Tiger Fangs '43
Trader Horn '31
Trap Them & Kill Them '77
The Treasure of the Amazon '84
Troma's War '88
Tropic Thunder '08 ▶
Tropical Heat '93
Tropical Malady '04
Turistas '06
Two Brothers '04
Typhoon Treasure '39
Virgin Sacrifice '59
Volunteers '85
Voodoo Woman '57
Wages of Fear '55 ▶
Warkill '65
Warriors of the Apocalypse '85
Watchers 3 '94
West of Zanzibar '28
Where the River Runs Black '86
White Cargo '42
White Ghost '88
White Huntress '57
The White Legion '36
The White Orchid '54
White Pongo '45
Wild Women '53
Woman Hunt '72
The World's Greatest Athlete '73
Y2K '99
Zombie Island Massacre '84

Junior Jocks

***see also** Baseball; Basketball; Childhood Buddies; Football; Hockey; Sports Comedies; Sports Dramas; Team Efforts*

Adam Sandler's 8 Crazy Nights '02
Amazing Grace & Chuck '87
The Bad News Bears '76 ▶
The Bad News Bears '05
Bend It Like Beckham '02 ▶
The Big Green '95
D2: The Mighty Ducks '94
Gym Teacher: The Movie '08
Kicking and Screaming '95 ▶
Ladybugs '92
Like Mike '02
Little Big League '94
Little Giants '94
The Longshots '08
Max Dugan Returns '83
The Mighty Ducks '92
Past the Bleachers '95
Rebound '05
The Sandlot '93 ▶
The Sandlot 2 '05
The Sandlot 3: Heading Home '07
Stick It '06
Sticks and Stones '08

Justice Prevails...?

***see also** Order in the Court*

Above Suspicion '95
Absence of Malice '81
The Accused '88 ▶
The Advocate '93 ▶
After Innocence '05 ▶
All-American Murder '91
American Violet '09
And Justice for All '79
Assault at West Point: The Court-Martial of Johnson Whittaker '94
The Avenging Angel '95
Bamako '06
Beau Geste '39 ▶
Better Off Dead '94
Beyond Reasonable Doubt '80
The Burning Season '94 ▶
A Case for Murder '93
Cause Celebre '87 ▶
Cause of Death '00
A Certain Justice '99
The Chamber '96
Changeling '08 ▶
Circumstantial Evidence '35
A Civil Action '98
Color of Justice '97
Comedy of Power '06
The Confession '98
Crash Course '00
Creature with the Blue Hand '70
Crime of the Century '96
Cross Examination '32
The Crucible '96 ▶
A Cry in the Dark '88 ▶
Cyber-Tracker '93
Dangerous Evidence: The Lori Jackson Story '99
Dark Justice '91
The Day the Sun Turned Cold '94 ▶
Dead Right '68
Deadlocked '00
Death Sentence '07
Dingaka '65
A Dry White Season '89 ▶
Eddie Macon's Run '83
Edwin '84
8-A '92
Emma '32
Erin Brockovich '00 ▶
Excellent Cadavers '99
Execution of Justice '99
The Execution of Private Slovik '74 ▶
An Eye for an Eye '95
False Arrest '92
Fatal Vision '84
Final Justice '98
Find Me Guilty '06 ▶
Forgotten Prisoners '90
Fracture '07
Frisco Jenny '32
Ghosts of Mississippi '96
The Good Fight '92
Guilty as Charged '92
Guilty as Sin '93
A Gun in the House '81
The Hanging Tree '59 ▶
Heart of the Beholder '05 ▶
Heavens Fall '06
Hollow Reed '95 ▶
Honor Thy Father and Mother: The True Story of the Menendez Brothers '94
I Am Sam '01
In Self Defense '93
In the Name of the Father '93 ▶
Indictment: The McMartin Trial '95 ▶
Invasion of Privacy '96
The Jack Bull '99
The Jagged Edge '85
Jasper, Texas '03
JFK '91 ▶
Judex '16
Judge Dredd '95
Judicial Consent '94
Jury Duty '95
Just Cause '94
The Killing Yard '01
Last Dance '96
Law Abiding Citizen '09
Lawman '71 ▶
Laws of Deception '97
Let Him Have It '91 ▶
Life & Times of Judge Roy Bean '72
Losing Isaiah '94 ▶
The Magnificent Yankee '50 ▶
Man in the Shadow '57
Melanie Darrow '97
Mr. & Mrs. Loving '96 ▶
Mother Night '96 ▶
Murder in the First '95
The Murder of Mary Phagan '87 ▶
The Murder of Stephen Lawrence '99 ▶
Music Box '89
Mutiny '99
Night Falls on Manhattan '96 ▶
Nothing But the Truth '08 ▶
Nuremberg '00
Nuts '87 ▶
One Kill '00 ▶
The Paper '94 ▶
Pinochet's Last Stand '06
Place of Execution '09
Presumed Innocent '90 ▶
The Prisoner of Shark Island '36
Prisoners of the Sun '91 ▶
The Quarry '98
Reservation Road '07
Restraining Order '99
Reversal of Fortune '90 ▶
Roe vs. Wade '89 ▶
Rules of Engagement '00
The Runaway '00
Runaway Jury '03 ▶
The Secret in Their Eyes '09
Separate but Equal '91 ▶
Shoot to Kill '90
The Shooting Party '77
Showdown '73
Sins of the Father '01 ▶
Sirens '99
Skin '89
Sleepers '96
Slow Burn '05
Snap Decision '01
Storm Warning '51
The Story of Qiu Ju '91 ▶
The Summer of Ben Tyler '96
A Time to Kill '96 ▶
A Town Has Turned to Dust '98
Trial & Error '62
Trial and Error '92
The Trials of Oscar Wilde '60 ▶
12 '07
An Unforgettable Summer '94
The Verdict '82 ▶
Weekend of Shadows '77 ▶
White Lie '91
Whitewash: The Clarence Brandley Story '02
Wilde '97
The Winslow Boy '98 ▶
Woman Undone '95
The Wrong Man '56 ▶
The Young Land '59
The Young One '61
The Young Savages '61

Juvenile Delinquents

***see also** Gangs; Hell High School; Teen Angst*

Angels with Dirty Faces '38 ▶
Bad Boys '83 ▶
Blackboard Jungle '55 ▶
Boys Town '38 ▶
The Chorus '04
Coach Carter '05 ▶
Crime School '38
The Day of the Outlaw '59
Detention '03
The Devil Is a Sissy '36
Flu Birds '08
Gridiron Gang '06
Holes '03 ▶
The Hoodlum Priest '61 ▶
Hope Ranch '02
Hothead '63
The Kid From Cleveland '49
The Mayor of Hell '33
See No Evil '06
Serious Charge '59
Step Up '06
Susan Slept Here '54
Total Western '00
12 and Holding '05 ▶
Young America '32
The Young Savages '61

Karaoke

The Astronaut's Wife '99
The Cable Guy '96
College Road Trip '08
Crossroads '02
Duets '00
High School Musical '06
I Still Know What You Did Last Summer '98
Jackpot '01
Junk Mail '97
A Life Less Ordinary '97
Lost in Translation '03 ▶
Love, Honour & Obey '00
My Best Friend's Wedding '97
Pushing Tin '99 ▶
Rush Hour 2 '01
A Smile Like Yours '96
The Watermelon Woman '97
When Harry Met Sally... '89 ▶

KGB

***see also** CIA/NSA; Cold War Spies; Russia/USSR*

American Roulette '88
Bionic Ninja '85
Black Eagle '88
Cambridge Spies '03
Codename Kyril '91
The Company '07
Company Business '91
East-West '99
Enigma '82
The Experts '89
Fair Game '95
The Fourth Protocol '87 ▶
From Russia with Love '63 ▶
Gorky Park '83 ▶
Indiana Jones and the Kingdom of the Crystal Skull '08
The Inner Circle '46
The Jigsaw Man '84
Lie Down with Lions '94
The Living Daylights '87 ▶
Munich '05 ▶
No Way Out '87 ▶
Red Dawn '84
Red Scorpion '89
The Second Front '05
Sleepers '96
Smiley's People '82
Spy Hard '96
The Spy Who Loved Me '77
Subterfuge '98
Telefon '77
Tinker, Tailor, Soldier, Spy '80 ▶
Topaz '69 ▶
White Nights '85
The World Is Not Enough '99

Kiddie Viddy

***see also** Animation & Cartoons*

Cars '06 ▶
Diary of a Wimpy Kid '10
Family Tree '00
Finding Nemo '03 ▶
Inspector Gadget's Biggest Caper Ever '05
The Land Before Time 6: The Secret of Saurus Rock '98
Monsters, Inc. '01 ▶
My Dog Skip '99 ▶
The Pirates Who Don't Do Anything: A VeggieTales Movie '08
Pooh's Heffalump Movie '05
Saving Shiloh '06
The SpongeBob SquarePants Movie '04
The Trial of Old Drum '00

Kidnapped!

***see also** Hostage!; Missing Persons*

Abducted '86
Abducted 2: The Reunion '94
Abduction '75
The Abduction of Allison Tate '92
The Abduction of Kari Swenson '87
Ace Ventura: Pet Detective '93
Act of Piracy '89
Action Man '67
Adam '83 ▶
African Rage '78
Against a Crooked Sky '75
Agent of Death '99
Air Bud 6: Air Buddies '06
An Alan Smithee Film: Burn, Hollywood, Burn '97
Alias Betty '01
All Over Town '37
Alone in the Woods '95
Along Came a Spider '01
Alpha Dog '06
American Kickboxer 2: To the Death '93
And Hope to Die '72
Any Place But Home '97
The Art of War '00
Ashanti, Land of No Mercy '79
The Atomic City '52
Autumn Born '79
Baby's Day Out '94
Ballistic: Ecks vs. Sever '02
Battle in Heaven '05
Beach Blanket Bingo '65 ▶
Beer for My Horses '08
Beethoven's 2nd '93
Beethoven's Big Break '08
Believers '07
Benji '74 ▶
Best Revenge '83
Beverly Hills Brats '89
Beverly Hills Chihuahua '08
Beyond Fear '75
Beyond Justice '92
Big Brother Trouble '00
The Big Hit '98
The Big Lebowski '97 ▶
Black Cat Run '98
Black Samurai '77
Blacklight '98
Bless the Child '00
Blind Heat '00
Blink of an Eye '92
Blood at Sundown '88
Blown Away '90
Borderland '07
Bound and Gagged: A Love Story '93
Buffalo 66 '97 ▶
Burial of the Rats '95
Buried '10
B.U.S.T.E.D. '99
The Butterfly '02 ▶
Captivity '07
Cecil B. Demented '00
Cellular '04
Celtic Pride '96
Charlie Chan at the Olympics '37
Charlie's Angels '00
The Chase '93
The Chumscrubber '05
The City of Lost Children '95 ▶
The Clearing '04 ▶
Clifford's Really Big Movie '04
Close Your Eyes '02
Cohen and Tate '88
Cold Blood '75
Collateral '04 ▶
The Collector '65 ▶
Commando '85 ▶
The Concentratin' Kid '30
Contraband '40
The Coroner '98
Crime of the Century '96
Crime Story '93
Crimebusters '79
Crows '94
The Crying Game '92 ▶
Dance with the Devil '97
Dead Air '94
The Deal '08
The Deep End of the Ocean '98
Dirty Little Secret '98

▶ = rated three bones or higher

Distant Justice '92
Django Strikes Again '87
Don't Say a Word '01
Door to Door Maniac '61
Double Play '96
Dumb & Dumber '94
Earthly Possessions '99
The Edukators '04
Emma's Shadow '88 ►
The End of Violence '97
Ernest Goes to Africa '97
Ernie Kovacs: Between the Laughter '84
Everybody's Famous! '00
Excess Baggage '96
Executive Target '97
Extraordinary Rendition '07
Extreme Dating '04
Eye '96
Faceless '88
Fargo '96 ►
Fatal Combat '96
Final Justice '98
Find the Lady '76
Fire in the Sky '93
Fireback '78
First Daughter '99
Five Fingers '06
Flightplan '05
Flower & Snake '04
Follow the River '95
Force of the Ninja '88
Four Days in September '97
Fugitive Champion '99
Gallowglass '95 ►
The Gay Desperado '36
The Gingerbread Man '97
A Girl, 3 Guys and a Gun '01
The Golden Compass '07
The Grissom Gang '71 ►
Guarding Tess '94
Gun Fury '53
Hangfire '91
Harem '86
Hearts & Armour '83
Held for Ransom '38
Hey! Hey! USA! '38
Hidalgo '04
Hide and Seek '00
Holiday in Handcuffs '07
Hollywood Cop '87
Honeybaby '74
Hostage for a Day '94
House of Fury '05
I'm Not Scared '03
Implicated '98
In a Stranger's Hand '92
In Desert and Wilderness '01
In Old New Mexico '45
In the Country Where Nothing Happens '99
In the Doghouse '98
In the Name of the King: A Dungeon Siege Tale '08
Incident at Deception Ridge '94
Inkheart '09
Invasion of Privacy '96
Island Monster '53
Jack and His Friends '92
Jailbait '93
Judas Kiss '98
Judgment Day '99
Julia '08
Kansas City '95 ►
Kentucky Jubilee '51
Kickboxer 3: The Art of War '92
Kid Colter '85
Kidnap Syndicate '76
Kidnapped '48
Kidnapped '87
Kidnapped '95
Kidnapped '05 ►
Kidnapped in Paradise '98
King's Ransom '05
Lake Consequence '92
The Last Assassins '96
The Last Hard Men '76
Last Lives '98
A Life Less Ordinary '97
The Light in the Forest '58
The Lightning Incident '91
The Lindbergh Kidnapping Case '76 ►
Live Free or Die Hard '07
The Lone Rider Crosses the Rio '41
Lorna Doone '22
Lullaby '08
Ma and Pa Kettle at Waikiki '55
Mad Dog Killer '77
Make Your Bets Ladies '65
Malibu's Most Wanted '03
Man on Fire '04
The Man Who Captured Eichmann '96
Manipulator '71
Manny & Lo '96 ►
Marrionnier '05
Martin's Day '85
Master of Disguise '02
Memphis '91
Mercy '96
Midnight in Saint Petersburg '97
The Mighty '98 ►
A Mighty Heart '07 ►
Miss Congeniality 2: Armed and Fabulous '05
The Missing '03 ►
Mission: Impossible 3 '06 ►
Mr. Nanny '93
The Money '75
Moran of the Lady Letty '22
The Mummy Returns '01
Munich '05 ►
MXP: Most Xtreme Primate '03
Mystery Men '99
Mystic River '03 ►
Naked Weapon '03
National Lampoon's The Don's Analyst '97
Never Say Die '94
New Blood '99
Nick of Time '95
The Night of the Following Day '69
The Nightmare Before Christmas '93 ►
Nightstick '87
No '98
No Deposit, No Return '76
No Way Back '96
Nobel Son '08
Obsession '49
Oldboy '03 ►
Oliver Twist '05 ►
Omega Syndrome '87
101 Dalmatians '96
One Small Hero '99
The Only Way Home '72
Operation Condor 2: The Armour of the Gods '86
Operation Delta Force 2: Mayday '97
Orphans '87 ►
Out of Sight '98 ►
Outlaw Force '87
Paper Bullets '99
Parker '84
Pay or Die '83
Perfect Strangers '03
A Perfect World '93
Perpetrators of the Crime '98
Pirates of the Caribbean: The Curse of the Black Pearl '03 ►
The Pirates Who Don't Do Anything: A VeggieTales Movie '08
The Pleasure Drivers '05
Pray '05
Prince of Pennsylvania '88
Private Obsession '94
Proof of Life '00
Public Enemies '96
Pulse '03
Queen's Messenger II '01
Quentin Durward '55
The Quest '96
'R Xmas '01
Racing Blood '36
Raising Arizona '87 ►
Ransom '96 ►
Ransom Money '70
A Rare Breed '81
The Real McCoy '93
Red Eye '05 ►
Remote Control '94
Renaissance '06
Rendition '07
Rescue Me '93
Return to Never Land '02
The Revenger '90
Riders of the Purple Sage '25
Ring of Fire 2: Blood and Steel '92
Ring of the Musketeers '93
Rio Diablo '93
Riot '96
The Road Killers '95
Robin-B-Hood '06
Rockabye '86
Rosebud '75
Rumpelstiltskin '96
Runaway Nightmare '84
Running Scared '06
Rush Hour '98
Ruthless People '86 ►
Sahara '83
Savage Abduction '73
Save the Green Planet '03
Saw '04
Screwed '00
Seance '00
Second Sight '89
Seven Hours to Judgment '88
Sexus '64
Shadow Man '06
Shanghai Noon '00
Sharpe's Challenge '06
Sharpe's Enemy '94
Shattered '07
Shattered Image '93
Show Me '04
Silver Hawk '04
Singapore '47
Sky Captain and the World of Tomorrow '04
Slate, Wyn & Me '87
Sloane '84
A Snake of June '02
SnakeEater '89
Snipes '01
So Close to Paradise '98
Social Error '35
Soldier Boyz '95
Soldier's Fortune '91
Son of the Pink Panther '93
Son of the Sheik '26 ►
Spartan '04 ►
Spy School '08
The Squeeze '77
Stakeout '62
Starved '97
Stealing Candy '04
Stealing Sinatra '04
Still Not Quite Human '92
Stingaree '34
Street Fighter '94
Suicide Kings '97
Sunchaser '96
Sunstroke '92
Sweet Poison '91
Switchback '97
Sympathy for Mr. Vengeance '02 ►
Taken '99
Taken '08
Taken Alive '95
The Tale of Despereaux '08
Tar '97
Tarzan and the Slave Girl '50
Tarzan's New York Adventure '42
Teaching Mrs. Tingle '99
Teresa's Tattoo '94
Terror Stalks the Class Reunion '93
Terror 2000 '92
That Darn Cat '96
That Man from Rio '64
Thin Air '00
Thou Shalt Not Kill...Except '87
The Three Burials of Melquiades Estrada '05 ►
Three Days to a Kill '91
3 Ninjas '92
3 Ninjas Knuckle Up '95
3-Way '04
Tie Me Up! Tie Me Down! '90
Till the End of the Night '94
To Grandmother's House We Go '94
Towards Darkness '07
Toy Story 2 '99 ►
Trade '07
The Transporter '02
Transporter 2 '05
The Trap '22
Trapped '02
Trapped '06
Trapped Alive '93
TripFall '00
The Triplets of Belleville '02 ►
Tropix '02
Try and Get Me '50
Tsotsi '05 ►
Tuck Everlasting '02
12 Rounds '09
The 24th Day '04
23 Paces to Baker Street '56
Twinsitters '95
Two Bits & Pepper '95
Under the Hula Moon '95
Unlawful Passage '94
Valley of the Heart's Delight '07
The Vanishing '93
A Vow to Kill '94
Waikiki Wedding '37 ►
Waist Deep '06
The Warrior '81
The Wash '01
Way of the Gun '00
Western Courage '35
When Danger Follows You Home '97
When the Greeks '81
Whistling in the Dark '41 ►
The Whole Ten Yards '04
The Wild Card '03
Wild Ones on Wheels '62
The Wind and the Lion '75 ►
Winterhawk '76
Wolverine '96
The World in His Arms '52

Killer Apes and Monkeys

***see also** Monkeyshines*

The Ape '40
A*P*E* '76
The Ape Man '43
Battle for the Planet of the Apes '73
The Beast That Killed Women '65
Beneath the Planet of the Apes '70
The Bride & the Beast '58
Congo '95
Conquest of the Planet of the Apes '72
Doctor of Doom '62
Dr. Orloff and the Invisible Man '72
Gorilla '56
In the Shadow of Kilimanjaro '86
Jungle Captive '45
Jungle Woman '44
King Kong '33 ►
King Kong '76
King Kong '05 ►
King Kong Lives '86
King Kong vs. Godzilla '63
King of Kong Island '78
Link '86
Mighty Joe Young '49
Mighty Joe Young '98
The Mighty Peking Man '77
Monkey Boy '90
Monkey Shines '88
Planet of the Apes '68 ►
Primal Rage '90
Rat Pfink a Boo-Boo '66
Return of the Ape Man '44
Son of Ingagi '40
Son of Kong '33

Killer Appliances

***see also** Technology—Rampant*

Battle Heater '89
Final Destination 2 '03
Ghost in the Machine '93
The Mangler '94
Maximum Overdrive '86
Microwave Massacre '83
The Refrigerator '91

Killer Beasts

***see also** Killer Apes and Monkeys; Killer Dogs; Killer Kats; Killer Pigs; Killer Rodents*

The Abomination '88
Attack of the Beast Creatures '85
Beaks: The Movie '87
Berserker '87
Bog '84
The Brain Eaters '58
The Cave '05
Chupacabra Terror '05
Clash of the Titans '81
Creepshow '82
Day of the Animals '77
Food of the Gods '76
Grizzly '76
Half-Caste '04
Hybrid '07
In the Shadow of Kilimanjaro '86
Island of Terror '66 ►
Jabberwocky '77
Jason and the Argonauts '63 ►
Jason and the Argonauts '00
Jaws of Satan '81
Jurassic Park '93 ►
The Lost World: Jurassic Park 2 '97
Mad Death '83
The Monster Walks '32
Monty Python and the Holy Grail '75 ►
Night of the Grizzly '66
The Rats Are Coming! The Werewolves Are Here! '72
Return to Boggy Creek '77
Rodan '56
Shakma '89
Shriek of the Mutilated '74
Sleepwalkers '92
The Slime People '63
Snowbeast '77
Subspecies '90
Swamp of the Lost Monster '65
Vulture '67
The Wild Beasts '85
Winterbeast '92

Killer Brains

***see also** Renegade Body Parts*

Black Friday '40
Blood of Ghastly Horror '72
Boltneck '98
The Brain '62
The Brain '88
Brain Damage '88
The Brain from Planet Arous '57
Brain of Blood '71
The Brain that Wouldn't Die '63
Donovan's Brain '53 ►
Fiend without a Face '58
The Machine '96
Mindkiller '87

Killer Bugs and Slugs

Ants '77
The Applegates '89
Arachnid '01
Arachnophobia '90
Attack of the Giant Leeches '59
The Bees '78
Beginning of the End '57
Bionicle 3: Web of Shadows '05
The Black Scorpion '57
Blood Beast Terror '67
Blue Monkey '87
Bug '75
Bug Buster '99
Bugged! '96
Bugs '03
Centipede '05
The Cosmic Monsters '58
Creepers '85
Creepshow '82
Curse of the Black Widow '77
The Deadly Mantis '57
DNA '97
Earth vs. the Spider '58
Earth vs. the Spider '01
Eight Legged Freaks '02
Empire of the Ants '77
Evil Spawn '87
Food of the Gods '76
The Giant Spider Invasion '75
The Glass Trap '04
Godzilla vs. Megalon '76
Godzilla vs. Mothra '64
The Hive '08
Horrors of Spider Island '59
Infestation '09
Infested: Invasion of the Killer Bugs '02
Insecticidal '05
Island of the Dead '00
Kingdom of the Spiders '77
Kiss of the Tarantula '75
The Lair of the White Worm '88 ►
Last Days of Planet Earth '74
Locusts: The 8th Plague '05
Lord of the Rings: The Return of the King '03 ►
Man of the House '95
Mimic 2 '01
Mimic 3: Sentinel '03
The Mist '07 ►
Monster from Green Hell '58
The Monster That Challenged the World '57
Mosquito '95
Mosquitoman '05
Mothra '62 ►
Mysterious Island '61 ►
Naked Jungle '54 ►
The Nest '88
Parasite '82
Phase 4 '74
Rebirth of Mothra '96
Rebirth of Mothra 2 '97
Return of the Fly '59
Sand Serpents '09
The Savage Bees '76
The Scorpion's Tail '71
Skeeter '93
Slither '06 ►
Slugs '87
Son of Godzilla '66
Spider Woman '44 ►
Spiders '00
Spiders 2: Breeding Ground '01
Squirm '76
Starship Troopers '97 ►
Starship Troopers 2: Hero of the Federation '04
Starship Troopers 3: Marauder '08
Subhuman '04
The Swarm '78
Tarantula '55 ►
Tarantulas: The Deadly Cargo '77
Terror Out of the Sky '78
The Thaw '09
Them! '54 ►
They Came from Within '75
They Crawl '01
Ticks '93
Tremors '89
Tremors 2: Aftershocks '96
Tremors 3: Back to Perfection '01
The Wasp Woman '59
The Wasp Woman '96
The Worm Eaters '77

Killer Cars

***see also** Motor Vehicle Dept.*

Black Cadillac '03
The Cars That Ate Paris '74 ►
Christine '84
Dark of the Night '85
Death Race 2000 '75
Death Sport '78
Duel '71 ►
The Hearse '80
Mad Max '80 ►
Mad Max: Beyond Thunderdome '85
Maximum Overdrive '86
One Deadly Owner '74
The Road Warrior '82 ►
Wheels of Terror '90

► = rated three bones or higher

Killer Clowns

***see also** Carnivals & Circuses; Clowns*

Carnival of Souls '98
Clownhouse '88
The Devil's Rejects '05
Final Draft '07
Frayed '07
House of 1000 Corpses '03
Killer Klowns from Outer Space '88
Killjoy '81
S.I.C.K. Serial Insane Clown Killer '03
Spawn '97 ▶
Stephen King's It '90
When Evil Calls '06

Killer Dogs

***see also** King of Beasts (Dogs)*

Atomic Dog '98
The Breed '06
Cerberus '05
Cujo '83
Devil Dog: The Hound of Hell '78
Dogs of Hell '83
The Hound of the Baskervilles '39 ▶
The Hound of the Baskervilles '59
The Hound of the Baskervilles '00
The Hound of the Baskervilles '02 ▶
Man's Best Friend '93
Mongrel '83
Monster Dog '82
The Omen '76
The Pack '77
Pet Sematary 2 '92
Play Dead '81
Resident Evil '02
Revenge '86
Zoltan... Hound of Dracula '78

Killer Dreams

Alias John Preston '56
Bad Dreams '88
Beneath '07
Blood Rage '87
Chronicle of the Raven '04
Dario Argento's Trauma '93
Dark Corners '06
Dead of Night '45 ▶
Deadly Dreams '88
Dream No Evil '70
Evil Eyes '04
Freddy's Dead: The Final Nightmare '91
In Dreams '98
In Your Dreams '07
Inception '10
Jack O'Lantern '04
The Lathe of Heaven '80
The Lathe of Heaven '02
A Lizard in a Woman's Skin '71
Mirrors '78
A Nightmare on Elm Street '84
A Nightmare on Elm Street '10
A Nightmare on Elm Street 2: Freddy's Revenge '85
A Nightmare on Elm Street 3: Dream Warriors '87
A Nightmare on Elm Street 4: Dream Master '88
A Nightmare on Elm Street 5: Dream Child '89
NightScreams '97
Paperhouse '89 ▶
Paprika '06
Phantasm '79
Premonition '07
Strange Impersonation '46
Twisted Nightmare '87
Waking Life '01
Wes Craven's New Nightmare '94 ▶
Witches of the Caribbean '05

Killer Kats

***see also** Cats*

Batman Returns '92
The Black Cat '81
Cat People '42 ▶
Cat People '82
Cat Women of the Moon '53
Claws '85
The Corpse Grinders '71
The Creeper '48
Curse of the Cat People '44 ▶
The Leopard Man '43
Maneater '07
Mutator '90
Night Creature '79
Night of a Thousand Cats '72
Pet Sematary '89
Seven Deaths in the Cat's Eye '72
Strays '91
Tromba, the Tiger Man '52
The Uncanny '78
The Uninvited '88

Killer Kiddies

***see also** Childhood Visions*

Alice Sweet Alice '76
The Bad Seed '56
The Bad Seed '85
Before and After '95
Case 39 '10
The Child '76
The Children '80
Children of the Corn '84
Children of the Corn 2: The Final Sacrifice '92
Children of the Corn 3: Urban Harvest '95
Children of the Corn 5: Fields of Terror '98
Children of the Corn: Revelation '01
Children of the Damned '63
Daddy's Girl '96
Damien: Omen 2 '78
Don't Go to Sleep '82
The Good Son '93
Grace '09
Gummo '97
Home Movie '08
Hurt '09
Joshua '07 ▶
The Little Girl Who Lives down the Lane '76
Milo '98
The Omen '76
The Omen '06
Orphan '09
The Other '72 ▶
Red Riding Hood '03
Relative Fear '95
Soft for Digging '01
Tropic Thunder '08 ▶
Village of the Damned '60 ▶
Village of the Damned '95
Way Past Cool '00
Whisper '07

Killer Pigs

***see also** Pigs*

The Amityville Horror '79
Evilspeak '82
Pigs '73
Razorback '84

Killer Plants

Attack of the Killer Tomatoes '77
Attack of the Mushroom People '63
Body Snatchers '93
Day of the Triffids '63 ▶
Dr. Terror's House of Horrors '65
The Freakmaker '73
Godzilla vs. Biollante '89
Invasion of the Body Snatchers '56 ▶
Invasion of the Body Snatchers '78 ▶
It Conquered the World '56
Killer Tomatoes Eat France '91
Killer Tomatoes Strike Back '90
Little Shop of Horrors '60 ▶
Little Shop of Horrors '86 ▶
Navy vs. the Night Monsters '66
Please Don't Eat My Mother '72
Return of the Killer Tomatoes! '88
The Ruins '08
Seedpeople '92
Seeds of Evil '76
Swamp Devil '08
The Womaneater '59
Yog, Monster from Space '71

Killer Reptiles

Alligator '80 ▶
Alligator 2: The Mutation '90
Anaconda 3: The Offspring '08
Black Water '07
Copperhead '84
Croc '07
Crocodile '81
Crocodile '00
Crocodile 2: Death Swamp '01
Dark Age '88
Destroy All Monsters '68
Dinosaurus! '60
Dragonslayer '81 ▶
Fangs '75
Frogs '72
Gamera, the Invincible '66
Gamera vs. Barugon '66
Gamera vs. Gaos '67
Gamera vs. Guiron '69
Gamera vs. Zigra '71
Gargantua '98
Gator King '70
The Giant Gila Monster '59
Godzilla '98
Godzilla, King of the Monsters '56
Godzilla 1985 '85
Godzilla on Monster Island '72
Godzilla Raids Again '55
Godzilla 2000 '99 ▶
Godzilla vs. Biollante '89
Godzilla vs. King Ghidora '91
Godzilla vs. Mechagodzilla II '93
Godzilla vs. Megalon '76
Godzilla vs. Monster Zero '68
Godzilla vs. Mothra '64
Godzilla vs. the Cosmic Monster '74
Godzilla vs. the Sea Monster '66
Godzilla vs. the Smog Monster '72
Godzilla's Revenge '69
Hell Comes to Frogtown '88
King Kong vs. Godzilla '63
Komodo '99
Lake Placid '99
Lake Placid 2 '07
The Mole People '56
Mothra '62 ▶
Primeval '07
Q (The Winged Serpent) '82 ▶
Rana: The Legend of Shadow Lake '75
Rattlers '76
The Relic '96
Reptilian '99
Reptilicus '62
Return to Frogtown '92
Rogue '07
Slithis '78
Spasms '82
Stanley '72
Venom '82
Yongkari Monster of the Deep '67

Killer Rodents

***see also** Bats; Nice Mice*

The Bat '59
The Bat People '74
Bats '99
Ben '72
Burial of the Rats '95
Deadly Eyes '82
The Devil Bat '41
Flushed Away '06 ▶
Food of the Gods '76
Food of the Gods: Part 2 '88
The Killer Shrews '59
Mulberry Street '06
Nezulla the Rat Monster '02
Night of the Lepus '72
Nightwing '79
Of Unknown Origin '83
Rats '83
The Rats '01
The Rats Are Coming! The Werewolves Are Here! '72
Trilogy of Terror 2 '96
Willard '71
Willard '03

Killer Sea Critters

***see also** Deep Blue; Go Fish; Killer Beasts*

Alligator '80 ▶
Around the World Under the Sea '65
Attack of the Giant Leeches '59
Attack of the Swamp Creature '75
Barracuda '78
The Beach Girls and the Monster '65
The Beast '96
The Beast from 20,000 Fathoms '53
Beneath Loch Ness '01
The Bermuda Depths '78
Beyond Atlantis '73
Blood Beach '81
Blood Surf '00
Bloodstalkers '76
The Cave '05
Creature from Black Lake '76
Creature from the Black Lagoon '54 ▶
Creature from the Haunted Sea '60
Creature of Destruction '67
The Creature Walks among Us '56
Creatures from the Abyss '94
Curse of the Swamp Creature '66
Deep Blue '03 ▶
Deep Blue Sea '99
Deep Rising '98
Deepstar Six '89
Demon of Paradise '87
Devil Monster '46
Devilfish '84
Eye of the Beast '07
Fer-De-Lance '74
Finding Nemo '03 ▶
The Flesh Eaters '64
Frankenfish '04
Godzilla vs. Mothra '64
Godzilla vs. the Sea Monster '66
Gorgo '61
The Great Alligator '81
Hello Down There '69
Horror of Party Beach '64
The Host '06 ▶
Humanoids from the Deep '80
Humanoids from the Deep '96
Into the Blue '05
Island Claw '80
It Came from Beneath the Sea '55 ▶
Jason and the Argonauts '63 ▶
Jaws '75 ▶
Jaws 2 '78
Jaws 3 '83
Jaws of Death '76
Jaws: The Revenge '87
Killer Fish '79
Kraken: Tentacles of the Deep '06
Legend of the Dinosaurs and Monster Birds '77
The Loch Ness Horror '82
Loch Ness Terror '07
The Man from Atlantis '77
The McConnell Story '55
Mean Streets '73 ▶
Mega Shark Vs. Giant Octopus '09
Megalodon '03
Memphis Belle '90 ▶
Monster from the Ocean Floor '54
The Monster of Piedras Blancas '57
The Monster That Challenged the World '57
Mysterious Island '61 ▶
New York, New York '77 ▶
None But the Brave '65
Obsession '76
Octaman '71
Octopus '00
Octopus 2: River of Fear '02
Orca '77
Parasite '03
The Phantom from 10,000 Leagues '56
Piranha '95
Piranha '78
Piranha 2: The Spawning '82
Piranha 3D '10
Reap the Wild Wind '42
Red Water '01
Revenge of the Creature '55
Scorpion with Two Tails '82
Screams of a Winter Night '79
Sea Beast '08
The Sea Serpent '85
Serpent Island '54
Shark! '68
Shark Attack '99
Shark Attack 2 '00
Shark Attack 3: Megalodon '02
Shark Swarm '08
She Creature '01
Snakehead Terror '04
Sphere '97
Swamp Thing '82
Tentacles '77
Terror in the Swamp '85
They Bite '95
Tiger Shark '32
Tintorera... Tiger Shark '78
20,000 Leagues under the Sea '54 ▶
20,000 Leagues Under the Sea '97
Up from the Depths '79
War of the Gargantuas '70
What Waits Below '83

Killer Spouses

***see also** Wedding Hell*

Black Widow '87 ▶
Body Heat '81 ▶
Deliberate Intent '01
Diabolique '55 ▶
Diabolique '96
Double Jeopardy '99
Dragonwyck '46
Four Flies on Grey Velvet '72
Fracture '07
High Stakes '93
The Kreutzer Sonata '08
Sleeping with the Enemy '91
Souls for Sale '23
What Lies Beneath '00
White Oleander '02

Killer Teens

Devon's Ghost: Legend of the Bloody Boy '05
Disturbing Behavior '98
Heathers '89 ▶
Little Sweetheart '90
River's Edge '87 ▶
Scream '96 ▶
Under One Roof '02
United States of Leland '03

Killer Toys

Amityville Dollhouse '96
Black Devil Doll from Hell '84
Bride of Chucky '98
Child's Play '88
Child's Play 2 '90
Child's Play 3 '91
Dance of Death '68
The Dead Pool '88
Dead Silence '07
Demonic Toys '90
Devil Doll '36 ▶
Devil Doll '64
Devil's Gift '84
Dollman vs Demonic Toys '93
Dolls '87
Dolly Dearest '92
Halloween 3: Season of the Witch '82
Magic '78
Marrionnier '05
Pinocchio's Revenge '96
Poltergeist '82 ▶
The Preacher's Wife '96
Puppet Master '89
Puppet Master 2 '90
Puppet Master 3: Toulon's Revenge '90
Puppet Master 4 '93
Puppet Master 5: The Final Chapter '94
Retro Puppet Master '99
Seed of Chucky '04
Silent Night, Deadly Night 5: The Toymaker '91
Small Soldiers '98
Tales from the Hood '95
Trilogy of Terror '75
Trilogy of Terror 2 '96
Wired to Kill '86

Killing Sprees

September Dawn '07

Kindness of Strangers

Amelie '01 ▶
Angels Over Broadway '40 ▶
The Big Push '75
Dear God '96
Forrest Gump '94 ▶
Good Sam '48
Goodbye Solo '08
Lilies of the Field '63 ▶
Major Barbara '41 ▶
The Matchmaker '97
Mr. Deeds '02
Mr. Deeds Goes to Town '36 ▶
Mr. Lucky '43 ▶
Mr. North '88
Powder '95
The Rich Man's Wife '96
She Couldn't Say No '52
Sincerely Yours '56
The Toll Gate '20
Touch & Go '80
Train Man: Densha Otoko '05
The Vals '85

King of Beasts (Dogs)

***see also** Killer Dogs*

The Accidental Tourist '88 ▶
Ace of Hearts '08
Across the Bridge '57
The Adventures of Milo & Otis '89 ▶
The Adventures of Rusty '45
After the Thin Man '36 ▶
Air Bud '97
Air Bud 2: Golden Receiver '98
Air Bud 3: World Pup '00
Air Bud 4: Seventh Inning Fetch '02
Air Bud 5: Buddy Spikes Back '03
All Dogs Go to Heaven '89
All Dogs Go to Heaven 2 '95
The Amazing Dobermans '76
Amores Perros '00 ▶
Antarctica '84
As Good As It Gets '97 ▶
Atomic Dog '98
Aussie and Ted's Great Adventure '09
The Awful Truth '37 ▶
Babe '95 ▶
Babe: Pig in the City '98
Bad Moon '96
Balto '95
Bark! '02
Baxter '89
Beautiful Creatures '00
Because of Winn-Dixie '05
Beethoven '92
Beethoven's 2nd '93
Beethoven's 3rd '00
Beethoven's 4th '01

▶ = rated three bones or higher

Beethoven's 5th '03
Behave Yourself! '52
Benji '74 ▶
Benji: Off the Leash! '04
Benji the Hunted '87
Best in Show '00 ▶
Big Red '62
Bingo '91
Blondie Brings Up Baby '39
Blondie in Society '41
Bolt '08 ▶
A Boy and His Dog '75
Buck and the Magic Bracelet '97
Call of the Wild '72
Call of the Wild '93
Captured in Chinatown '35
Cats & Dogs '01
Cats & Dogs: The Revenge of Kitty Galore '10
Challenge To Be Free '76
Challenge to Lassie '49
Challenge to White Fang '86
Children of the Wild '37
Chilly Dogs '01
Chips, the War Dog '90
C.H.O.M.P.S. '79
Clean Slate '94
Clifford's Really Big Movie '04
Cool Hand Luke '67 ▶
Courage of Lassie '46
Courage of Rin Tin Tin '57
Courage of the North '35
A Cry in the Dark '88 ▶
Cujo '83
Cybermutt '02
Danny Boy '46
Daring Dobermans '73
The Dawson Patrol '78
Dead Dog '00
Devil Dog: The Hound of Hell '78
Digby, the Biggest Dog in the World '73
Dirkham Detective Agency '83
Disgrace '08
Disney's Teacher's Pet '04 ▶
The Doberman Gang '72
Dr. Dolittle '98
Dr. Dolittle 4: Tail to the Chief '08
Dr. Dolittle: Million Dollar Mutts '09
Dr. Seuss' How the Grinch Stole Christmas '00
A Dog Named Christmas '09
A Dog of Flanders '59
A Dog of Flanders '99
Dog Park '98
Dog Pound Shuffle '75 ▶
The Dog Who Saved Christmas '09
The Dog Who Stopped the War '84
Dogs of Hell '83
Dogville Shorts '30
Doogal '05
Down and Out in Beverly Hills '86
The Duke '99
Dumb & Dumber '94
Dusty '85
The Echo of Thunder '98
Eight Below '06
Elmer '76
Eyes of an Angel '91
Eyes of Texas '48
Fabulous Joe '47
Familiar Strangers '08
Famous Five Get into Trouble '70
Fangs of the Wild '54
Far from Home: The Adventures of Yellow Dog '94
Finding Rin Tin Tin '07
Flaming Signal '33
Fluke '95
For the Love of Benji '77
The Fox and the Hound '81 ▶
Frank '07
Frankenweenie '84
The Gay Dog '54
George! '70
Ghetto Dawg '02
Ghetto Dawg 2: Out of the Pits '05
Git! '65
God's Country '46
Good Boy! '03
The Good, the Bad, and Huckleberry Hound '88
Goodbye, My Lady '56
A Goofy Movie '94
Great Adventure '75
Greyfriars Bobby '61
Hachiko: A Dog's Tale '09
Hambone & Hillie '84
Heart of the Rockies '51
Heavy Petting '07
Heck's Way Home '95
The Hills Have Eyes '77
Hollow Gate '88
Homeward Bound 2: Lost in San Francisco '96
Homeward Bound: The Incredible Journey '93 ▶
Hotel for Dogs '09
The Hound of the Baskervilles '59
I Am Legend '07 ▶
In the Doghouse '98
The Incredible Journey '63
Inside Information '34
Iron Will '93
It's a Dog's Life '55
Jack London's The Call of the Wild '97
The Jerk '79
Jury Duty '95
K-9 '89
K-911 '99
K-9000 '89
Kavik the Wolf Dog '80
Lady and the Tramp '55 ▶
Lassie '94
Lassie: Adventures of Neeka '68
Lassie, Come Home '43
Lassie: Well of Love '70
Lassie's Great Adventure '62
Laurel & Hardy: Laughing Gravy '31
Legally Blonde '01
Legally Blonde 2: Red White & Blonde '03
Lightning Warrior '31
Little Heroes '91
Little Nicky '00
The Little Rascals '94
The Lone Defender '32
Look Who's Talking Now '93
Lost and Found '99
Love Leads the Way '84
Magic of Lassie '78
The Man From Oklahoma '26
Man Trouble '92
The Man Who Wagged His Tail '57
Man's Best Friend '93
Marley & Me '08
Marmaduke '10
The Mask '94 ▶
Meet the Fockers '04
Men in Black 2 '02
The Mexican '01
Michael '96
Milo & Otis '89
Mrs. Brown, You've Got a Lovely Daughter '68
Mr. Superinvisible '73
Mom, the Wolfman and Me '80
Mongrel '83
Monster Dog '82
Monster-in-Law '05
More Dogs Than Bones '00
Murder She Purred: A Mrs. Murphy Mystery '98
Must Love Dogs '05
My Dog Shep '46
My Dog Skip '99 ▶
My Dog, the Thief '69
My Magic Dog '97
Napoleon '96
The Night Cry '26
Nikki, the Wild Dog of the North '61
Nutty Professor 2: The Klumps '00
Obsession '49
Oh, Heavenly Dog! '80
Old Yeller '57 ▶
Oliver & Company '88
101 Dalmatians '61 ▶
101 Dalmatians '96
The Pack '77
The Painted Hills '51
Ping! '99
The Plague Dogs '82
Play Dead '81
Poco '77
The Pooch and the Pauper '99
Pound Puppies and the Legend of Big Paw '88
Princess O'Rourke '43
Quigley '03
The Return of Grey Wolf '22
Reuben, Reuben '83 ▶
Rin Tin Tin, Hero of the West '55
Rough Magic '95
Rover Dangerfield '91
Rugrats Go Wild! '03
Rusty's Birthday '49
The Sandlot '93 ▶
Santa Buddies '09
Savage Sam '63
Saving Shiloh '06
Scooby-Doo '02
Screwed '00
Shadow of the Thin Man '41 ▶
The Shaggy D.A. '76
The Shaggy Dog '59
The Shaggy Dog '06
Shep Comes Home '49
Sherlock: Undercover Dog '94
Shiloh '97
Shiloh 2: Shiloh Season '99
Silver Stallion '41
Six of a Kind '34 ▶
Skeezer '82
Skull & Crown '35
Sleeping Dogs Lie '06
Smoke '70
Snow Buddies '08
Snow Dogs '02
Soccer Dog: The Movie '98
Son of Lassie '45
Son of Rusty '47
Song of the Thin Man '47
Space Buddies '08
Sputnik '61
Spy with a Cold Nose '66
Station Jim '01
Storm in a Teacup '37
Summerdog '78
Sweet November '01
Teddy at the Throttle '16
The Tender Years '47
There's Something about Mary '98 ▶
They Only Kill Their Masters '72
The Thin Man '34 ▶
The Thin Man Goes Home '44
Three Wishes '95
To Dance with the White Dog '93 ▶
Toby McTeague '87
Tom and Jerry: The Movie '93
Top Dog '95
Tracked '98
The Triplets of Belleville '02 ▶
The Truth about Cats and Dogs '96 ▶
Turner and Hooch '89
The Twelve Dogs of Christmas '05
Twin Town '97
The Ugly Dachshund '65
Umberto D '55 ▶
The Undercover Kid '95
The Underdog '43
Up '09 ▶
Watchers '88
Watchers 2 '90
Watchers Reborn '98
We Think the World of You '88 ▶
Wendy and Lucy '08 ▶
When Lightning Strikes '34
Where the Red Fern Grows '74
Where the Red Fern Grows: Part 2 '92
White Dog '82
White Fang 2: The Myth of the White Wolf '94
White Fang and the Hunter '85
Whitewater Sam '78
The Wizard of Oz '39 ▶
Wolf Dog '33
Wolfheart's Revenge '25
Wonder Boys '00 ▶
Zeus and Roxanne '96
Zoltan... Hound of Dracula '78

Kings

see *Royalty; Royalty, British; Royalty, French; Royalty, Russian*

Korean War

All the Young Men '60 ▶
American Gun '02 ▶
Battle Circus '53
Battle Hymn '57
Big Fish '03 ▶
The Bridges at Toko-Ri '55 ▶
Dragonfly Squadron '54
Field of Honor '86
Fixed Bayonets! '51 ▶
For the Boys '91
The Hunters '58
I Want You '51
Iron Angel '64
Korea Patrol '47
The Last Picture Show '71 ▶
MacArthur '77
The Manchurian Candidate '62 ▶
M*A*S*H '70 ▶
M*A*S*H: Goodbye, Farewell & Amen '83 ▶
Men in War '57
Men of the Fighting Lady '54 ▶
Mr. Walkie Talkie '52
One Minute to Zero '52
Operation Dames '59
Pork Chop Hill '59 ▶
Retreat, Hell! '52
Sabre Jet '53
Sayonara '57 ▶
Sergeant Ryker '68
The Steel Helmet '51 ▶
Tae Guk Gi: The Brotherhood of War '04 ▶
Torpedo Alley '53
Wonsan Operation '78

Kung Fu

see *Martial Arts*

L.A.

see also *Earthquakes*

Abbott and Costello in Hollywood '45
Act of Violence '48
Against the Law '98
Agent of Death '99
Akeelah and the Bee '06
An Alan Smithee Film: Burn, Hollywood, Burn '97
The Alarmist '98
All About You '01
All Over the Guy '01
Alvin and the Chipmunks '07
Always Outnumbered Always Outgunned '98 ▶
American East '07
An American Rhapsody '01 ▶
American Virgin '98
Amy's O '02
Angel's Dance '99
The Anniversary Party '01 ▶
Apartment Complex '98
Arc '06
Armored '09
Asian Stories '06
Ask the Dust '06
Assault on Precinct 13 '76 ▶
At Any Cost '00
The Aviator '04 ▶
Baby Boy '01
Bad Influence '90
Bandits '01
Bang '95
Bar Hopping '00
Bark! '02
Barton Fink '91 ▶
Be Cool '05
Bean '97 ▶
Beefcake '99
Bellyfruit '99
Best of the Best: Without Warning '98
The Beverly Hillbillies '93
Beverly Hills Bodysnatchers '89
Beverly Hills Brats '89
Beverly Hills Ninja '96
Beyond Suspicion '00
The Big Fall '96
Big Fat Liar '02
The Big Lebowski '97 ▶
Big Momma's House 2 '06
The Big Picture '89
The Big Tease '99
Biker Boyz '03
Billy's Hollywood Screen Kiss '98
The Black Dahlia '06
Black Gunn '72
Black Scorpion 2: Ground Zero '96
Blast from the Past '98
Bloodstream '00
Blow '01
Blue Streak '99
Body Double '84 ▶
Border Blues '03
Born to Lose '99
Bottoms Up '06
Bowfinger '99 ▶
A Boy Called Hate '95
The Boys Next Door '85
Bram Stoker's Way of the Vampire '05
Bread and Roses '00
Break of Dawn '88
The Breaks '99
The Broken Hearts Club '00 ▶
Broken Vessels '98 ▶
Brown's Requiem '98
Bruno '09
Bulletproof '96
Call Me: The Rise and Fall of Heidi Fleiss '04
Candyman 3: Day of the Dead '98
Carolina '03
Carpool Guy '05
Celebrity '98 ▶
Cement '99
Chain of Souls '00
Changeling '08 ▶
Charlotte Sometimes '02
Chasing Papi '03
A Cinderella Story '04
Circuit '02
City of Angels '98
City of Industry '96
Cleopatra's Second Husband '00
Collateral '04 ▶
Collateral Damage '02
Color of a Brisk and Leaping Day '95
Come See the Paradise '90 ▶
Confidence '03
Constantine '05
Cool Blue '88
Cover Me '95
Cradle 2 the Grave '03
The Craft '96
Crank '06
Crank: High Voltage '09
Crash '05 ▶
crazy/beautiful '01
Crimes of Passion '84 ▶
Criminal '04
The Crimson Kimono '59
Crocodile Dundee in Los Angeles '01
Crossing Over '09
The Crow 2: City of Angels '96
Crystal's Diary '99
Cursed '04
Cyxork 7 '06
Dark Blue '03 ▶
Dark Justice '00
Dark World '08
Darkwolf '03
The Day After Tomorrow '04
The Day of the Locust '75 ▶
A Day Without a Mexican '04
Daybreak '01
Dead Again '91 ▶
Dead Bang '89
The Dead Girl '06
Dead Lenny '06
Dead Sexy '01
Dear God '96
Death Wish 2 '82
Defying Gravity '99
Delta Heat '92
The Dentist '96
The Destiny of Marty Fine '96
Devil in a Blue Dress '95 ▶
Devil's Knight '03
Die Hard '88 ▶
Dinner and Driving '97
Dirty '05
The Disappearance of Kevin Johnson '95
Disney's The Kid '00
Doc Hollywood '91
The Dog Problem '06
Domino '05
Don't Be a Menace to South Central While Drinking Your Juice in the Hood '95
The Doom Generation '95 ▶
Double Down '01
Down in the Valley '05
Drag Me to Hell '09
Drift '00
Dunston Checks In '95
East Side Story '07
Eastside '99
8mm '98
The Elder Son '06
Ellie Parker '05 ▶
Encino Man '92
The End of Violence '97
Escape from L.A. '96
ESL: English as a Second Language '05
The Exiles '61
Face/Off '97 ▶
The Fall '06
Falling Down '93
Fast & Furious '09
The Fast and the Furious '01
Fast Sofa '01
Fast Times at Ridgemont High '82 ▶
Female Perversions '96
52 Pick-Up '86
Final Combination '93
(500) Days of Summer '09
Flashbacks of a Fool '08
The Fluffer '01
Forfeit '07
44 Minutes: The North Hollywood Shootout '03
Four Dogs Playing Poker '00
Four Rooms '95
Fracture '07
Fragments '08
Free Enterprise '98
Freeway '88
French Exit '97
Friends with Money '06
Frisk '95
Full Contact '93
Full Frontal '02
Funny People '09
Gang Boys '97
Garden Party '08
Get Him to the Greek '10
Get On the Bus '96 ▶
Get Shorty '95 ▶
Get Smart '08
Glam '97
The Glass House '01
The Glimmer Man '96
Go '99 ▶
Goal! The Dream Begins '06
Gods and Monsters '98 ▶
Going Shopping '05
Goodbye, Lover '99
Grand Canyon '91 ▶
Grand Theft Parsons '03
Greenberg '10
Gridiron Gang '06
Grindin' '07
The Guardian '00
Guarding Eddy '04
Hair Show '04
Hancock '08
Hanging Up '99
Happy Endings '05
Hard As Nails '01
Hard Candy '06
Harsh Times '05
He Walked by Night '48 ▶
Heart of Stone '01

Heat '95 ▶
Henry Poole Is Here '08 ▶
Hijacking Hollywood '97
The Hillside Strangler '04
Hindsight '97
Holding Trevor '07
The Holiday '06
Hollywood Homicide '03
Hollywood, Je T'Aime '09
Hollywoodland '06
Hostage '05
Hot Tamale '06
The Hottie and the Nottie '08
How to Kill Your Neighbor's Dog '01
How to Lose Your Lover '04
Hugo Pool '97
Hurlyburly '98
Hustler White '96
I Am Omega '07
I Love You, Alice B. Toklas! '68
I Love You, Don't Touch Me! '97
I Love Your Work '03
In God We Trust '80
The Informers '09
Internal Affairs '90
Intolerable Cruelty '03
The Italian Job '03 ▶
It's My Party '95
Jackie Brown '97 ▶
Jack's Back '87 ▶
Jimmy Hollywood '94
johns '96
The Journey of Jared Price '00
Julia '08
Just Write '97
K-911 '99
Kate's Addiction '99
The Kid and I '05
The Kids Are All Right '10
Kill Bill Vol. 1 '03 ▶
Killer of Sheep '77 ▶
Kiss & Tell '99
Kiss Kiss Bang Bang '05 ▶
Kiss Tomorrow Goodbye '00
Kitchen Privileges '00
L.A. Bad '85
L.A. Bounty '89
L.A. Confidential '97 ▶
L.A. Crackdown '87
L.A. Crackdown 2 '88
L.A. Dicks '05
L.A. Goddess '92
L.A. Law '86 ▶
L.A. Rules: The Pros and Cons of Breathing '94
L.A. Story '91 ▶
L.A. Twister '04
L.A. Vice '89
Lady Jayne Killer '03
Lakeview Terrace '08 ▶
Land of Plenty '04
L.A.P.D.: To Protect and Serve '01
Last Call: The Final Chapter of F. Scott Fitzgerald '02
The Last Days of Frankie the Fly '96
Late Last Night '99
Latin Dragon '03
Laurel Canyon '02
Lawnmower Man 2: Beyond Cyberspace '95
The Learning Curve '01
Let the Devil Wear Black '99
Lethal Weapon 4 '98
Liberty Stands Still '02
Lies & Alibis '06
Lime Salted Love '06
The Limey '99 ▶
Living in Peril '97
The Lodger '09
Long-Term Relationship '06
Lost Angels '89
Love Don't Cost a Thing '03
The Loved One '65
Loveless in Los Angeles '07
Lover Girl '97
The Low Life '95
Luminarias '99
Luster '02
MacArthur Park '01
The Man from Elysian Fields '01 ▶
Maneater '09
Manpower '41
Marshal Law '96
Matter of Trust '98
Mayor of the Sunset Strip '03 ▶
Meet Market '08
Memento '00 ▶
Men '97
The Mexican '01
Mexican Gangster '08
Michael Jackson's This Is It '09
Midnight Blue '96
Million Dollar Baby '04 ▶
The Mod Squad '99
Model Shop '69
Modern Vampires '98
Mommie Dearest '81
More Dogs Than Bones '00
Mortal Challenge '97
Mother and Child '09
Mulholland Drive '01 ▶
Murder by Contract '58
The Muse '99
My Uncle: The Alien '96
Nails '92
Nancy Drew '07
National Lampoon Presents Cattle Call '06
National Security '03
Neil Simon's The Odd Couple 2 '98
Never Die Alone '04
Never Say Macbeth '07
The New Age '94
Next '07
The Next Best Thing '00
Nick of Time '95
The Nickel Children '05
Night at the Golden Eagle '02
A Night at the Roxbury '98
Night Hunter '95
Night on Earth '91 ▶
Nightstalker '02
The Nines '07 ▶
1941 '79
Nowhere '96
On the Doll '07
187 '97
100 Mile Rule '02
One Last Ride '03
Overnight '03 ▶
Pandemic '07
Paparazzi '04
Paper Bullets '99
Parental Guidance '98
Paulie '98
Perfect Strangers '50
Permanent Midnight '98
Phat Beach '96
Pie in the Sky '95
The Player '92 ▶
Point Blank '67
Powder Blue '09
Predator 2 '90
Prey for Rock and Roll '03 ▶
P.S. Your Cat is Dead! '02
Pursuit of Happiness '01
Quarantine '08
Quiet Days in Hollywood '97
Quinceanera '06 ▶
Race '99
Raging Angels '95
Raise Your Voice '04
Rampage: The Hillside Strangler Murders '04
Rave Review '95
Real Women Have Curves '02 ▶
Recoil '97
Redbelt '08 ▶
Relax.. It's Just Sex! '98
Relentless '89
The Replacement Killers '98
Repo Man '83 ▶
Revenge Quest '96
Right at Your Door '06
Riot '96
Riot in the Streets '96
Rize '05 ▶
Roman Polanski: Wanted and Desired '08
Rumor Has It.. '05
Rumpelstiltskin '96
Running Mates '00
Running Woman '98
Rush Hour '98
Ruthless People '86 ▶
Safe House '99
Save the Tiger '73 ▶
Scandal Sheet '85
Scorcher '02
Scream 3 '00
Seamless '00
Seed of Chucky '04
Serpent's Lair '95
Set It Off '96
Shadow Dancer '96
Shadow of Doubt '98
Shakedown '02
Sherrybaby '06
Shopgirl '05 ▶
Short Cuts '93 ▶
The Shot '96
Showtime '02
Shrink '09
The Singing Detective '03
A Single Man '09 ▶
Sink or Swim '97
S.I.S. '08
Sister Aimee: The Aimee Semple McPherson Story '06
Skyscraper '95
Slaves of Hollywood '99
Sleeper Cell '05
Smiley Face '07
Smiling Fish & Goat on Fire '99
Sol Goode '01
Sold for Marriage '16
Soldier's Fortune '91
The Soloist '09
Somebody to Love '94
Something New '06
Somewhere in the Night '46
The Souler Opposite '97
South of Pico '07
Southland Tales '06
Spanglish '04
Spanish Judges '99
Special '06
Speed '94 ▶
Spent '00
Splendor '99
Splinter '06
Spread '09
Spun '02
Stand and Deliver '88 ▶
Stand-Ins '97
Standing on Fishes '99
Standing Still '05
Star Maps '97
Starry Night '99
Steel '97
Sticks '98
Still Breathing '97
Storm Tracker '99
Strange Days '95 ▶
Street Corner Justice '96
The Street King '02
Street Kings '08
The Streets of L.A. '79
Strictly Sexual '08
Stuntmen '09
Sueno '05
Sugar Town '99
Sunset Boulevard '50 ▶
Sunset Strip '99
S.W.A.T. '03
Swimming with Sharks '94 ▶
Swingers '96 ▶
Swordfish '01
The Take '07
The Talent Given Us '04 ▶
Talking about Sex '94
Telling You '98
10 Items or Less '06
The Terrorist Next Door '08
Testosterone '03
They Call Me Sirr '00
Thicker than Water '99
This Christmas '07
This World, Then the Fireworks '97
Three Strikes '00
Time Code '00
Tinseltown '97
To Live & Die in L.A. '85
Too Fast, Too Young '96
Tortilla Soup '01
Totally F***ed Up '94
Touch '96
The Towering Inferno '74
Training Day '01
The Trigger Effect '96
The Trip '02
20 Dates '99
Twilight '98 ▶
Two Days in the Valley '96 ▶
The Two Jakes '90
Under the Same Moon '07
The Underground '97
Undiscovered '05
Unlawful Entry '92
Valentina's Tango '07
Valentine's Day '10
Vampire Night '00
Virtuosity '95
Volcano '97
Waist Deep '06
The Wash '01
Wassup Rockers '06
Welcome Says the Angel '01
What Just Happened '08
What We Do Is Secret '07
Whatever It Takes '00
What's Up, Scarlet? '05
Where the Truth Lies '05
Where's Marlowe? '98
Whirlpool '49
Who Made the Potatoe Salad? '05
The Whole Ten Yards '04
Witchcraft 9: Bitter Flesh '96
With Friends Like These '98 ▶
Wonderland '03
Yellow '98
Yes Man '08
You Got Served '04

Labor & Unions

***see also** Miners & Mining*

Act of Vengeance '86
Black Fury '35 ▶
Blue Collar '78 ▶
Boxcar Bertha '72
Bread and Roses '00
Brother John '70 ▶
The Burning Season '94 ▶
Canada's Sweetheart: The Saga of Hal C. Banks '85
Daens '92
Deadly Stranger '88
The Devil & Miss Jones '41 ▶
The End of St. Petersburg '27 ▶
End of the Line '88
Fame Is the Spur '47
F.I.S.T. '78
The $5.20 an Hour Dream '80
The Garment Jungle '57
Gung Ho '85
Harlan County, U.S.A. '76 ▶
Harlan County War '00
Hoffa '92 ▶
I Was a Communist for the FBI '51
I'm All Right Jack '59 ▶
Joyride '77
Keeping On '81
Killing Floor '85
Land of Promise '74
Last Exit to Brooklyn '90 ▶
Liam '00
Long Road Home '91
Mac '93 ▶
Man of Iron '81 ▶
Man of Marble '76 ▶
Matewan '87 ▶
Molly Maguires '70
Moonlighting '82 ▶
Never Steal Anything Small '59
New in Town '09
Newsies '92
Norma Rae '79 ▶
North Dallas Forty '79 ▶
On the Waterfront '54 ▶
The Organizer '64
The Pajama Game '57 ▶
Riff Raff '92 ▶
Salt of the Earth '54 ▶
The Seafarers '53
Silkwood '83 ▶
Singleton's Pluck '84 ▶
Sons of Steel '35
Strike '24 ▶
Take This Job & Shove It '81
Teamster Boss: The Jackie Presser Story '92 ▶
The Triangle Factory Fire Scandal '79
Waterfront '83
Which Way Is Up? '77
The Woman on Pier 13 '50

Las Vegas

***see** Viva Las Vegas!*

Late Bloomin' Love

***see also** Growing Older*

Adorable Julia '62
The African Queen '51 ▶
Ali: Fear Eats the Soul '74 ▶
Atlantic City '81 ▶
Autumn Sun '98 ▶
Bed & Breakfast '92
Breakfast in Paris '81
The Bridges of Madison County '95 ▶
Brief Encounter '46 ▶
Camilla '94
Cass Timberlane '47
Charly '68 ▶
Children of Nature '91
The Christmas Wife '88
Circle of Two '80
Cold Sassy Tree '89 ▶
Crazy from the Heart '91 ▶
Devil in the Flesh '46 ▶
Digger '94
Doctor in Distress '63
End of August '82
A Fine Romance '92
Finnegan Begin Again '84
Forbidden Love '82
Foreign Affairs '93 ▶
Forty Carats '73
Gal Young 'Un '79 ▶
Gin Game '84 ▶
Grumpier Old Men '95
Grumpy Old Men '93 ▶
Harold and Maude '71 ▶
If Ever I See You Again '78
Innocence '00 ▶
La Symphonie Pastorale '46 ▶
Ladies in Lavender '04
The Last Winters '71
Lonely Hearts '82 ▶
The Lonely Passion of Judith Hearne '87 ▶
Love Among the Ruins '75 ▶
Macaroni '85
A Majority of One '56
A Man and a Woman '66 ▶
Mrs. 'Arris Goes to Paris '92
A Month by the Lake '95
The Night of the Iguana '64 ▶
One Special Night '99
Other People's Money '91
The Pamela Principle '91
Players '79
Queen of the Stardust Ballroom '75 ▶
The Rainmaker '56 ▶
Roman Spring of Mrs. Stone '61 ▶
San Antonio '45
Shadowlands '93 ▶
Shirley Valentine '89 ▶
The Shock '23
The Shop Around the Corner '40 ▶
Shore Leave '25 ▶
A Small Killing '81
Something in Common '86
Stay As You Are '78
Stormy Waters '41
Stroszek '77 ▶
Summertime '55 ▶
To Love Again '80
Travelling North '87
24 Hours in a Woman's Life '61
Twice in a Lifetime '85 ▶
Used People '92
With Six You Get Eggroll '68

Law & Lawyers

***see also** Order in the Court*

Adam's Rib '50 ▶
The Advocate '93 ▶
After Innocence '05 ▶
Afterburn '92 ▶
Afterwards '08
American Tragedy '00
American Violet '09
Amistad '97 ▶
Anatomy of a Murder '59 ▶
And Justice for All '79
Angel on My Shoulder '80
Assault at West Point: The Court-Martial of Johnson Whittaker '94
Before and After '95
Better Off Dead '94
Beyond a Reasonable Doubt '56
Beyond a Reasonable Doubt '09
Beyond the Silhouette '90
Big Daddy '99
Bleak House '85
Bleak House '05
Blind Faith '98
Blood Brothers '74
Body Chemistry 4: Full Exposure '95
Body Language '95
Boomerang '47 ▶
Brain Donors '92
Breaking Point '09
Bringing Down the House '03
Brothers in Law '57
Brother's Keeper '92 ▶
The Candidate '72 ▶
Cape Fear '61 ▶
Cape Fear '91 ▶
Carlito's Way '93 ▶
A Case for Murder '93
A Case of Libel '83
Castle on the Hudson '40 ▶
Cause of Death '00
A Certain Justice '99
The Chamber '96
Changeling '08 ▶
Changing Lanes '02 ▶
Character '97
Chase '85
Cherish '02
Chicago '02 ▶
A Christmas Proposal '08
Circonstances Attenuantes '36
Citizen Cohn '92
A Civil Action '98
Class Action '91 ▶
The Client '94
Color of Justice '97
Compulsion '59 ▶
The Confession '98
Confusion of Genders '00
The Conqueror Worm '68 ▶
Conspiracy Theory '97 ▶
Convicted '04
Cop-Out '67
The Coroner '98
Counsellor-at-Law '33 ▶
Criminal Justice '08
Criminal Law '89
Critical Care '97
Daddy's Little Girls '07
Dark Justice '91
Dawg '02
Death and the Maiden '94 ▶
Death Benefit '96
Death of a Soldier '85
Defenders of the Law '31
The Defenders: Payback '97
The Defenders: Taking the First '98
Degree of Guilt '95
Deliberate Intent '01
Destination Vegas '95
The Devil's Advocate '97
Dirty Mary Crazy Larry '74 ▶
Disorganized Crime '89
The Divorce of Lady X '38
Dr. Dolittle 2 '01
Dr. Jekyll and Mr. Hyde '08
Down the Drain '89
Dragons Forever '88
Ebbtide '94
El Paso '49
Enemy of the State '98
The Enforcer '51
Erin Brockovich '00 ▶
Evelyn '02 ▶
Evelyn Prentice '34
The Exorcism of Emily Rose '05 ▶
Eye Witness '49
Fair Game '95
False Witness '89
Father's Day '96
Fear and Loathing in Las Vegas '98
Female Perversions '96
Fever '91

▶ = *rated three bones or higher*

A Few Good Men '92 ▸
Final Appeal '93
Final Justice '98
Final Verdict '91
Find Me Guilty '06 ▸
The Firm '93 ▸
First Monday in October '81
The First Texan '56
The Fixer '97
For Roseanna '96
Forbidden Sins '99
Force of Evil '49 ▸
Fracture '07
The Franchise Affair '52
Frank McKlusky, C.I. '02
A Free Soul '31
From the Hip '86
Genealogies of a Crime '97
Georgia '87
Getting Gotti '94
The Ghost of Spoon River '00
Ghosts of Mississippi '96
Gideon's Trumpet '80
The Girl From Monaco '08
The Girl in the News '41
The Girl on the Train '09
The Glass Shield '95
The Good Fight '92
The Great American Sex Scandal '94
The Guilty '99
Guilty as Sin '93
Guilty Conscience '85 ▸
The Hard Word '02
Having Wonderful Crime '45
Heaven Is a Playground '91
Heavens Fall '06
High Crimes '02
Honor Thy Father and Mother: The True Story of the Menendez Brothers '94
I Am Sam '01
I Am the Law '38 ▸
I Love You, Alice B. Toklas! '68
I Now Pronounce You Chuck and Larry '07
The Ice Harvest '05
Illegal '55
Illegal Affairs '96
I'm No Angel '33 ▸
In Pursuit '00
In the Name of the Father '93 ▸
The Incident '89 ▸
Inherit the Wind '99
Intolerable Cruelty '03
The Island of Dr. Moreau '96
It Runs in the Family '03
It's the Rage '99
JAG '95
The Jagged Edge '85
John Grisham's The Rainmaker '97
The Judge '49
Judge Dredd '95
Judge Priest '34 ▸
Judicial Consent '94
The Juror '96
Jury Duty '95
Just Cause '94
The Killing Yard '01
King and Country '64 ▸
L.A. Law '86 ▸
Lansdown '01
Last Dance '96
The Last Innocent Man '87
Laws of Attraction '04
Laws of Deception '97
Legal Deceit '95
Legal Eagles '86
Legalese '98
Legally Blonde '01
Legally Blonde 2: Red White & Blonde '03
Legend of Billie Jean '85
Lemon Tree '08
Let Freedom Ring '39
Let's Kill All the Lawyers '93
Liar Liar '97
Life & Times of Judge Roy Bean '72
Losing Isaiah '94 ▸
Love Among the Ruins '75 ▸
Love Crimes '92
Love Letters '99 ▸
Love Stinks '99
Loved '97
Lucky Seven '03
Luminarias '99
Madame X '66
The Magnificent Yankee '50 ▸
Man from Colorado '49
Man From Galveston '63
Man of the House '95
The Man Who Shot Liberty Valance '62 ▸
Manhattan Melodrama '34 ▸
Marked Woman '37 ▸
Marriage on the Rocks '65
Matter of Trust '98
Melanie Darrow '97
The Merchant of Venice '04 ▸
Michael Clayton '07 ▸
Minbo—Or the Gentle Art of Japanese Extortion '92
Misbehaving Husbands '41
Mr. & Mrs. Loving '96 ▸
Moonlight Mile '02 ▸
Move Over, Darling '63
Murder in the First '95
A Murder of Crows '99
My Cousin Vinny '92 ▸
My Sister's Keeper '09
The Narrow Margin '52 ▸
National Lampoon Presents RoboDoc '08
Night and the City '92 ▸
Night Falls on Manhattan '96 ▸
Nixon '95 ▸
North '94
North Country '05
Nothing But the Truth '08 ▸
Nuremberg '00
One Night at McCool's '01
Ordeal by Innocence '84
Original Intent '91
Our Mutual Friend '98
The Paper Chase '73 ▸
Party Girl '58 ▸
The Pelican Brief '93
Penthouse '33 ▸
The People vs. Larry Flynt '96 ▸
Perfect Witness '89
Perry Mason Returns '85 ▸
Philadelphia '93 ▸
Physical Evidence '89
Picture Windows '95
Pillow of Death '45
Pinocchio's Revenge '96
Plain Dirty '04
Plain Truth '04
Poor White Trash '00
Portraits of a Killer '95
Power of Attorney '94
Presumed Innocent '90 ▸
Primal Fear '96
Prom Queen '04
Promised a Miracle '88
Psychopath '97
The Reader '08
Red Corner '97
Reet, Petite and Gone '47 ▸
Regarding Henry '91 ▸
Restraining Order '99
Return to Paradise '98 ▸
R.I.C.C.O. '02
Rio Rita '29
Road Agent '26
Roman Polanski: Wanted and Desired '08
Rounders '98
Roxie Hart '42
Runaway Father '91
Runaway Jury '03 ▸
Rustler's Valley '37
Scandal '50
Scott Turow's The Burden of Proof '92
The Sea Inside '04 ▸
Shadow of Doubt '98
The Shaggy Dog '06
Shakedown '88
Shall We Dance? '04
Sharon's Secret '95
Shoot to Kill '47
A Simple Twist of Fate '94
The Skeleton Key '05
Sleepers '96
The Sleepy Time Gal '01
Slightly Honorable '40
Smart Woman '48
Split Second '99
The Star Chamber '83
State's Attorney '31
Steel Toes '06
Stephen King's Thinner '96
A Stranger in the Kingdom '98
Street Law '95
The Summer of Ben Tyler '96
The Sun Shines Bright '53
The Sweet Hereafter '96 ▸
Swoon '91 ▸
They Call It Murder '71
A Time to Kill '96 ▸
To Kill a Mockingbird '62 ▸
Too Young to Die '90
Town without Pity '61
The Trial '93
Trial & Error '62
Trial and Error '92
Trial and Error '96
Trial by Jury '94
The Trial of Old Drum '00
Trois Couleurs: Rouge '94 ▸
True Believer '89
True Colors '91
Truth or Die '86
Twelve Angry Men '57 ▸
Twelve Angry Men '97
Undermind '03
Up for Grabs '05
The Verdict '82 ▸
Victim '61 ▸
Web of Deceit '90
Where the Truth Lies '99
Whitewash: The Clarence Brandley Story '02
Wild Things '98
The Winslow Boy '48 ▸
The Winslow Boy '98 ▸
The Wistful Widow of Wagon Gap '47
Witness for the Prosecution '57 ▸
Woman of Desire '93
The World's Oldest Living Bridesmaid '92
The Young Philadelphians '59 ▸

Leprechauns

Darby O'Gill & the Little People '59 ▸
Finian's Rainbow '68 ▸
Leprechaun '93
Leprechaun 2 '94
Leprechaun 3 '95
Leprechaun 4: In Space '96
Leprechaun 5: In the Hood '99
Leprechaun 6: Back 2 Tha Hood '03
The Luck of the Irish '48
The Magical Legend of the Leprechauns '99
Spellbreaker: Secret of the Leprechauns '96

Lesbians

see also Bisexuality; Gays; Gender Bending

Affinity '08
Aimee & Jaguar '98
Alien Prey '78
All Over Me '96 ▸
The Alley Cats '65
And Then Came Lola '09
Another Way '82 ▸
April's Shower '03
Bam Bam & Celeste '05 ▸
Bar Girls '95
The Berlin Affair '85
Better Than Chocolate '99
The Bitter Tears of Petra von Kant '72
Black Cobra '83
The Black Dahlia '06
The Blood Spattered Bride '72
Blow Dry '00
Bobbie's Girl '02
Bound '96
Boys on the Side '94
Bug '06
But I'm a Cheerleader '99
Butterfly Kiss '94
The Celluloid Closet '95 ▸
Chasing Amy '97
The Children's Hour '61
Chuck & Buck '00
Chutney Popcorn '99
Claire of the Moon '92
Common Ground '00
Crocodiles in Amsterdam '89
Daphne '07
Dark Town '04
Daughters of Darkness '71 ▸
D.E.B.S. '04
Desert Hearts '86 ▸
Desperate Remedies '93
Devotion '95
Different Story '78
Do I Love You? '02
Double Face '70
The Edge of Heaven '07 ▸
Entre-Nous '83 ▸
Eternal '04
Eulogy '04
Even Cowgirls Get the Blues '94
Everything Relative '96
Extramuros '85
A Family Affair '01
Fanci's Persuasion '95
Fine Dead Girls '02
Fire '96
Fish Without a Bicycle '03
The Fourth Sex '61
Foxfire '96
French Twist '95
Gaudi Afternoon '01
The Gay Bed and Breakfast of Terror '07
Ghosted '09
Gia '98
Gigli '03
The Girl '01
Girl Play '04
Gray Matters '06
The Gymnast '06
Happy Endings '05
Hardcore '04
He Died With a Felafel in His Hand '01
Head in the Clouds '04
Her and She and Him '69
High Art '98
Higher Learning '94
The Hours '02 ▸
The Hunger '83
If These Walls Could Talk 2 '00
Imagine Me & You '06
In Her Line of Fire '06
The Incredibly True Adventure of Two Girls in Love '95
It's In the Water '96
Itty Bitty Titty Committee '07
I've Heard the Mermaids Singing '87 ▸
The Jane Austen Book Club '07 ▸
Just One Time '00
Kamikaze Hearts '91
The Kids Are All Right '10
The Killing of Sister George '69
Kissing Jessica Stein '02
Late Bloomers '95
L'Auberge Espagnole '02 ▸
Law of Desire '86 ▸
Le Jupon Rouge '87
Les Voleurs '96 ▸
Lianna '83 ▸
Listen '96
Little City '97
Lost and Delirious '01
Love and Other Catastrophes '95
Love on the Side '04
A Love to Keep '07
Loving Annabelle '06
Maedchen in Uniform '31 ▸
May '02
Memento Mori '00
The Monkey's Mask '00
My Baby's Daddy '04
My Father Is Coming '91
My Mother Likes Women '02
My Sister, My Love '78
My Summer of Love '05
Nadja '95 ▸
Nina's Heavenly Delights '06
November Moon '85
Nowhere '96
On the Other Hand, Death '08
101 Reykjavik '00
Only the Brave '94
Oranges Are Not the Only Fruit '89
Out at the Wedding '07
Personal Best '82 ▸
Possession '02
Pretty Persuasion '05
Prey for Rock and Roll '03 ▸
A Question of Love '78 ▸
The Rainbow '89 ▸
Relax... It's Just Sex! '98
Rent '05
Robin's Hood '03
Russian Dolls '05
Saving Face '04
The Scorpion Woman '89
The Secrets '07
Seducers '77
Serving in Silence: The Margarethe Cammermeyer Story '95 ▸
Set It Off '96
Shades of Black '93
She Hate Me '04
She Must Be Seeing Things '87
Shelter Island '03
Show Me Love '99
The Silence '63 ▸
Simone Barbes '80
Skin Deep '94
Slaves to the Underground '96
Some Prefer Cake '97
The Souler Opposite '97
Spider Lilies '06
Standing Still '05
The Sticky Fingers of Time '97
Sugar Cookies '77
Sugar Sweet '02
Tell No One '06 ▸
Therese & Isabelle '67
These Three '36 ▸
Things You Can Tell Just by Looking at Her '00
Three of Hearts '93
Three Times '05
Tick Tock '00 ▸
Tick Tock Lullaby '07
Tipping the Velvet '02
Tokyo Cowboy '94
Totally F***ed Up '94
Trapped '06
The Truth About Jane '00
The Twilight Girls '57
Under the Tuscan Sun '03
Unveiled '05
Vampire Killers '09
The Vampire Lovers '70
Vampyres '74
A Village Affair '95
Virgin Machine '88
Walk on the Wild Side '62
The Watermelon Woman '97
What's Up, Scarlet? '05
When Love Comes '98
When Night Is Falling '95 ▸
Wicked Lake '08
Wild Side '95
Windows '80
A Woman's a Helluva Thing '01
The Women on the Roof '89
X, Y & Zee '72

Libraries and Librarians

Adventure '45
Black Mask '96
The Breakfast Club '85 ▸
City of Angels '98
Desk Set '57 ▸
Foul Play '78 ▸
Fright Night 2 '88
Ghostbusters '84 ▸
Good News '47
Goodbye Columbus '69 ▸
The Gun in Betty Lou's Handbag '92
Hard-Boiled '92
It's a Wonderful Life '46 ▸
Kicking and Screaming '95 ▸
Last Life in the Universe '03
The Librarian: Curse of the Judas Chalice '08
The Librarian: Quest for the Spear '04
The Librarian: Return to King Solomon's Mines '06
Mr. Sycamore '74
The Mummy '99
The Music Man '62 ▸
The Name of the Rose '86
No Man of Her Own '32
Off Beat '86
Only Two Can Play '62 ▸
The Pagemaster '94
Party Girl '94
7 Faces of Dr. Lao '63 ▸
The Shawshank Redemption '94 ▸
Shooting the Past '99
Something Wicked This Way Comes '83
The Time Traveler's Wife '09
Where the Heart Is '00
With Honors '94

Lifeguards

see also Beach Blanket Bingo; Swimming

Baywatch the Movie: Forbidden Paradise '95
Caddyshack '80 ▸
Fun in Acapulco '63
Lifeguard '76
The Sandlot '93 ▸
That Summer of White Roses '90
Wet and Wild Summer '92

Little People

Bad Santa '03
The Chronicles of Narnia: Prince Caspian '08
Foul Play '78 ▸
Fred Claus '07
The Hobbit '78 ▸
In Bruges '08
Little Man '06
The Lord of the Rings '78
Lord of the Rings: The Fellowship of the Ring '01 ▸
Lord of the Rings: The Two Towers '02 ▸
Lord of the Rings: The Return of the King '03 ▸
Poltergeist '82 ▸
Poltergeist 2: The Other Side '86
Poltergeist 3 '88
Santa Baby '06
Snow White and the Seven Dwarfs '37 ▸
Snow White and the Seven Dwarfs '83 ▸
Snow White: The Fairest of Them All '02
Time Bandits '81
Under the Rainbow '81
Willow '88
The Wizard of Oz '25
The Wizard of Oz '39 ▸

London

see also Great Britain; Royalty

Abbott and Costello Meet Dr. Jekyll and Mr. Hyde '52
About a Boy '02 ▸
Agatha Christie's Murder is Easy '82
Agent Cody Banks 2: Destination London '04
AKA '02
Alfie '66 ▸
All or Nothing '02
Almost Strangers '01 ▸
Amazing Grace '06 ▸
American Roulette '88
An American Werewolf in London '81 ▸
Annie: A Royal Adventure '95
Another Life '01
The Assassination Bureau '69 ▸
Atonement '07 ▸
Austin Powers: International Man of Mystery '97 ▸
Autobiography of a Princess '75
The Avengers '98
B. Monkey '97
Bad Behavior '92

▸ = rated three bones or higher

Ballet Shoes '07
The Bank Job '08 ▶
Basic Instinct 2 '06
Beat Girl '60
Beautiful People '99
Beautiful Thing '95 ▶
Bedlam '45 ▶
Bedrooms and Hallways '98
Being Julia '04 ▶
Bend It Like Beckham '02 ▶
Berkeley Square '98
Betrayal '83
Beyond Borders '03
Born Romantic '00
The Bourne Ultimatum '07 ▶
Breaking and Entering '06
Bridget Jones: The Edge of Reason '04
Bridget Jones's Diary '01 ▶
Bright Star '09
Bright Young Things '03
The Broken '08
Broken Blossoms '19 ▶
The Buddha of Suburbia '92 ▶
Caffeine '06
Call It a Day '37
Carpet of Horror '64
Cassandra's Dream '07
Century '94
A Certain Justice '99
Charlie '04
Charlie Chan in London '34
Charlie White '04
Chicago Joe & the Showgirl '90
The Chronicles of Narnia: The Lion, the Witch and the Wardrobe '05
Claudia '85
Clean '04
Close My Eyes '91
Closer '04 ▶
Color Me Kubrick '05
Comic Act '98 ▶
Contraband '40
The Contractor '07
The Criminal '00
Croupier '97 ▶
Curse of the Yellow Snake '63
Danger UXB '81
Dead Cool '04
Dead Fish '04
Dead Gorgeous '02
Deadlier Than the Male '67
Death on the Set '35
Dick Barton, Special Agent '48
Die Another Day '02
Different for Girls '96 ▶
Dirty Pretty Things '03 ▶
The Disappeared '08
Disraeli '79 ▶
Do I Love You? '02
Dot the I '03
Double Vision '92
Dracula's Daughter '36 ▶
Dream Street '21
The Duchess '08 ▶
The Duchess of Duke Street '78 ▶
Eagles Over London '69
Eastern Promises '07 ▶
An Education '09 ▶
An Egyptian Story '82
84 Charing Cross Road '86 ▶
The Elephant Man '80 ▶
11 Harrowhouse '74 ▶
Elizabeth '98 ▶
End of the Affair '55
The End of the Affair '99 ▶
Endgame '01
Entrapment '99
Esther Kahn '00
Eurotrip '04
Expresso Bongo '59
Extraordinary Rendition '07
Face '97
Faith '94
Fanny Hill '07
Fanny Hill: Memoirs of a Woman of Pleasure '64
Fever Pitch '96
Fierce Creatures '96
Filth '08
Filth and Wisdom '08
Flawless '07
Flood '07
Flushed Away '06 ▶
Fool's Gold: The Story of the Brink's-Mat Robbery '92
Foreign Affairs '93 ▶
Foreign Correspondent '40 ▶
Forever and a Day '43 ▶
Forgive and Forget '99
The Fourth Angel '01
Frenzy '72 ▶
Friends & Crocodiles '05
The Frightened City '61
The Frightened Man '52
From Hell '01 ▶
Full Moon in Paris '84
The Gambler & the Lady '52
Gangster No. 1 '00
Gaslight '40 ▶
The Gathering Storm '02 ▶
The Gay Lady '49
Gentlemen's Relish '01
Get Him to the Greek '10
Gideon's Daughter '05
The Golden Bowl '72 ▶
The Golden Bowl '00
Great Expectations '81
Great Expectations '99
The Great Muppet Caper '81 ▶
The Green Cockatoo '37
Green Street Hooligans '05 ▶
Hands of a Murderer '90
Hangover Square '45
Happy-Go-Lucky '08 ▶
A Harlot's Progress '06
The Heart of Me '02
Heaven's a Drag '94
High Heels and Low Lifes '01
Hope and Glory '87 ▶
The Horse's Mouth '58 ▶
The House of Eliott '92
How to Be '08
Husbands '70
I, Monster '71 ▶
I Really Hate My Job '07
An Ideal Husband '47
An Ideal Husband '99 ▶
If Only '04
I'll Never Forget You '51
I'll Sleep When I'm Dead '03 ▶
Imagine Me & You '06
Immortality '98
In a Day '06
In Bruges '08
In the Loop '09
In the Name of the Father '93 ▶
Incendiary '08
Incognito '97
The Innocent Sleep '95
Intimacy '00
Irina Palm '07
It Always Rains on Sunday '47
Janice Beard '99
John and Julie '55
Johnny Was '05
Journey for Margaret '42 ▶
Just Like a Woman '95
Killing Me Softly '01
Kings '07
The Knack '65 ▶
The Krays '90 ▶
The L-Shaped Room '62 ▶
Lady L '65
Lamb '85
Last Chance Harvey '08
The Last Enemy '08
Last Orders '01 ▶
Layer Cake '05 ▶
The Leading Man '96
The League of Extraordinary Gentlemen '03
Like It Is '98 ▶
The Line of Beauty '06
The Little Princess '39 ▶
London Voodoo '04
The Long Good Friday '80 ▶
The Lost Boys '78 ▶
Lost in Austen '08
The Lost Language of Cranes '92 ▶
The Lost Son '98
Love Actually '03
Love Among the Ruins '75 ▶
Love and Death on Long Island '97
Love and Other Disasters '06
Love Is the Devil '98 ▶
The Low Down '00
Lured '47
The Magician '93
Man Hunt '41 ▶
Man in the Attic '53
The Man Who Knew Too Little '97
The Man Who Made Husbands Jealous '98
Mary Poppins '64 ▶
Mary Reilly '95
Match Point '05 ▶
Maybe Baby '99
Me & Mrs. Jones '02
Me Without You '01
Meantime '81
A Merry War '97 ▶
Metroland '97
Midnight Lace '60
Ministry of Fear '44 ▶
Miranda '01
Miss Conception '08
Miss Pettigrew Lives for a Day '08 ▶
Mission: Impossible '96 ▶
The Missionary '82
Mrs. 'Arris Goes to Paris '92
Mrs. Dalloway '97
Mrs. Henderson Presents '05
Mrs. Palfrey at the Claremont '05
Mr. Right '06
Moll Flanders '96
Moonlighting '82 ▶
The Mother '03 ▶
The Mummy Returns '01
The Murder of Stephen Lawrence '99 ▶
Murder on Line One '90
My Beautiful Laundrette '85 ▶
My Friend Walter '93
My Wife is an Actress '01
The Mysterious Dr. Fu Manchu '29
The Mysterious Magician '65
Mysterious Mr. Moto '38
Naked '93 ▶
National Lampoon's European Vacation '85
Neil Gaiman's NeverWhere '96
Nicholas Nickleby '02 ▶
Night and the City '50 ▶
Night Junkies '07
Nighthawks '78
Nil by Mouth '96
Notes on a Scandal '06 ▶
The Notorious Landlady '62
Notting Hill '99 ▶
The Old Curiosity Shop '94
Oliver Twist '85
Oliver Twist '97
Oliver Twist '00 ▶
Oliver Twist '05 ▶
Oliver Twist '07
101 Dalmatians '96
One Wish Too Many '55
Othello '01 ▶
Our Mutual Friend '98
The Painted Lady '97 ▶
The Parent Trap '98
P.D. James: The Murder Room '04
Penelope '06
Phantom Fiend '35
The Phantom of the Opera '62
Photographing Fairies '97
Pinochet's Last Stand '06
Plain Jane '01
Played '06
Plunkett & Macleane '98
Poldark '96
Possession '02
Postman's Knock '62
Preaching to the Perverted '97
Priest '94
Pure '02 ▶
Quatermass and the Pit '58
Radio Cab Murder '54
Rancid Aluminium '00
Raw Meat '72
Razor Blade Smile '98
Red Mercury '05
Reign of Fire '02
The Return of Dr. Fu Manchu '30
Return to Never Land '02
The Riddle '07
The Ripper '97
Robert Louis Stevenson's The Game of Death '99
RocknRolla '08
Romance and Rejection '96
Rough Cut '80
Royal Wedding '51 ▶
Ruby in the Smoke '06
Run, Fatboy, Run '07
Russian Dolls '05
Sabotage '36 ▶
The Saint in London '39
Salt & Pepper '68
Sammy & Rosie Get Laid '87 ▶
Say Hello to Yesterday '71
Scenes of a Sexual Nature '06
The Search for John Gissing '01
The Secret Agent '96
The Secret Life of Mrs. Beeton '06
Secrets and Lies '95
Seeing Red '99
Seven Days to Noon '50
Sexy Beast '00 ▶
The Shadow in the North '07
Shakespeare in Love '98 ▶
Shanghai Knights '03
Shaun of the Dead '04 ▶
She Wolf of London '46
Sherlock: Case of Evil '02
Sherlock Holmes '09
Shine '95 ▶
Shooters '00
Shooting Fish '98
Shooting the Past '99
The Siege of Sidney Street '60
Sirens '02
Sliding Doors '97
Snatch '00 ▶
Soho Square '00
Solitaire for 2 '94
Sorted '04
Spice World: The Movie '97
Spider '02 ▶
Split Second '92
Stage Beauty '04
Stella Does Tricks '96
Strange Bedfellows '65
Strapless '90
Success Is the Best Revenge '84
Sugarhouse '07
Sunday, Bloody Sunday '71 ▶
Surveillance 24/7 '07
Sweeney Todd: The Demon Barber of Fleet Street '07
Tale of a Vampire '92
The Tall Guy '89 ▶
These Foolish Things '06
They Made Me a Fugitive '47
This Above All '42
The Three Penny Opera '62
Tick Tock Lullaby '07
Time After Time '79 ▶
Tinker, Tailor, Soldier, Spy '80 ▶
Tipping the Velvet '02
To Each His Own '46 ▶
To Sir, with Love '67
Topsy Turvy '99 ▶
Touch of Pink '04
Touching Evil '97 ▶
Trauma '04
Turtle Diary '86 ▶
23 Paces to Baker Street '56
24 Hours in London '00
28 Days Later '02
28 Weeks Later '07
Twice upon a Yesterday '98
Twinkletoes '26
Ultraviolet '98
Unknown White Male '05 ▶
The Upturned Glass '47
V for Vendetta '06
Vanity Fair '99
Venus '06 ▶
Vera Drake '04 ▶
The Verdict '46
The Very Thought of You '98
Virtual Sexuality '99
Water Babies '79
Waterloo Bridge '40 ▶
Waterloo Road '44
The Way We Live Now '02
The Wedding Date '05
Werewolf of London '35
What a Girl Wants '03
Wild West '93
Wilde '97
Wimbledon '04
The Wings of the Dove '97 ▶
The Winslow Boy '98 ▶
Witchcraft 10: Mistress of the Craft '98
A Woman's Guide to Adultery '93
Wonderland '99
The Young Americans '93
The Young Poisoner's Handbook '94 ▶
Young Sherlock Holmes '85

Loneliness

see *Only the Lonely*

Loner Cops

see also *Cops*

Above the Law '88
Action Jackson '88
Bad Attitude '93
Bad Lieutenant '92 ▶
The Blue Knight '75
The Breed '01
Code of Silence '85
The Cop & the Girl '86
Cop in Blue Jeans '78
Dead Bang '89
The Dead Pool '88
Deadly Dancer '90
Die Hard '88 ▶
Die Hard 2: Die Harder '90 ▶
Die Hard: With a Vengeance '95
Dirty Harry '71 ▶
The Enforcer '76
Excessive Force '93
Exit Wounds '01
Force of One '79
The Gauntlet '77
Hard-Boiled '92
Heat '87
Heat '95 ▶
In the Heat of the Night '67 ▶
Judge Dredd '95
Klute '71 ▶
Live Free or Die Hard '07
Magnum Force '73
Martial Outlaw '93
McQ '74
Minority Report '02 ▶
Mission of Death '97
Murder by Numbers '02
Navajo Blues '97
Nightstick '87
Northwest Trail '46
One Good Cop '91
One Man Jury '78
The Pledge '00 ▶
Rent-A-Cop '88
RoboCop '87 ▶
Serpico '73 ▶
Sharky's Machine '81
SnakeEater '89
SnakeEater 2: The Drug Buster '89
SnakeEater 3: His Law '92
Soho Square '00
Speed '94 ▶
Stick '85
Stone Cold '91
The Street King '02
Striking Distance '93
Sudden Impact '83
Ten to Midnight '83
Top Dog '95
Year of the Dragon '85

Look Ma! I'm on TV!

see also *Mass Media*

Almost Heaven '06
Are You Scared? '06
At Home with the Webbers '94
Auto Focus '02 ▶
Carolina '03
The Condemned '07
Confessions of a Dangerous Mind '02
Cruel World '05
Death to Smoochy '02
Dr. Dolittle: Million Dollar Mutts '09
Eat Your Heart Out '96
EDtv '99
15 Minutes '01
Gale Force '01
Hairspray '07 ▶
Halloween: Resurrection '02
I-See-You.Com '06
Killer Movie '08
Love or Money '01
Loveless in Los Angeles '07
Magnolia '99 ▶
Monday Night Mayhem '02
My Best Friend '06
The New Gladiators '83
The Nines '07 ▶
Paul Bartel's The Secret Cinema '69
Pleasantville '98 ▶
Series 7: The Contenders '01
Showtime '02
Sink or Swim '97
Slumdog Millionaire '08 ▶
Starter for Ten '06
Stay Tuned '92
Strange Wilderness '08
Stuck On You '03
Sugar Sweet '02
The Truman Show '98 ▶
The TV Set '06
The 24 Hour Woman '99
War Tapes '06 ▶
Whatever You Say '02
Woman on Top '00
Wrong Turn 2: Dead End '07

Lost Worlds

see also *Parallel Universe*

At the Earth's Core '76
Beyond Atlantis '73
Brigadoon '54 ▶
Creatures the World Forgot '70
Gold of the Amazon Women '79
Jane & the Lost City '87
Journey to the Center of the Earth '59 ▶
Journey to the Center of the Earth '99
Journey to the Center of the Earth '08
Jumanji '95
The Land That Time Forgot '75
The Land That Time Forgot '09
The Land Unknown '57
The Lost Continent '51
Lost Horizon '37 ▶
The Lost World '25
Mysterious Island '61 ▶
Mysterious Island of Beautiful Women '79
The People That Time Forgot '77
She '65
Warriors of Virtue '97
What Waits Below '83
When Dinosaurs Ruled the Earth '70
Where Time Began '77

Lottery Winners

Antoine et Antoinette '47
Babette's Feast '87 ▶
Dual Alibi '47
Everything's Gone Green '06
Finder's Fee '01
Fox and His Friends '75 ▶
How Much Do You Love Me? '05
It Could Happen to You '94
Just Your Luck '96
Le Million '31 ▶
Loco Love '03
Lots of Luck '85
Lottery Bride '30
The Lottery Ticket '10
Lucky Numbers '00
Lucky Partners '40
The Million Dollar Kid '99

Next Friday '00
The Squeeze '87
The Ticket '97
29th Street '91
Uptown Saturday Night '74
Waking Ned Devine '98 ▸
The Wrong Box '66 ▸

Louisiana

see also American South; New Orleans; Southern Belles
All the King's Men '49 ▸
The Apostle '97 ▸
As Summers Die '86
Bayou Romance '86
Blaze '89
Divine Secrets of the Ya-Ya Sisterhood '02
The Drowning Pool '75
Eve's Bayou '97 ▸
Fletch Lives '89
Frankenfish '04
Heaven's Prisoners '95
House of Wax '05
JFK '91 ▸
Kingfish: A Story of Huey P. Long '95
Louisiana '87
Louisiana Purchase '41
Louisiana Story '48 ▸
Mammoth '06
No Mercy '86
Passion Fish '92 ▸
Road House 2: Last Call '06
The Skeleton Key '05
A Soldier's Story '84 ▸
Sounder '72 ▸
Stay Alive '06
Steel Magnolias '89 ▸
Tigerland '00 ▸
Venom '05
Way Down South '39

Lovable Loonies

see also Shrinks
Bean '97 ▸
Benny & Joon '93
Best in Show '00 ▸
Beyond Therapy '86
Box of Moonlight '96
The Couch Trip '87
Crazy People '90
Crazylove '05
David and Lisa '62 ▸
The Eighth Day '95
The Fisher King '91 ▸
Ghost World '01 ▸
Gridlock'd '96 ▸
Julian Po '97
King of California '07
The King of Hearts '66 ▸
Lars and the Real Girl '07
Meet Wally Sparks '97
The Ninth Configuration '79 ▸
One Flew Over the Cuckoo's Nest '75 ▸
Patch Adams '98
The Ruling Class '72 ▸
Sing and Like It '34
Superstar '99
What about Bob? '91 ▸

Lovers on the Lam

see also Fugitives
Badlands '74 ▸
Blood & Wine '96
Bobby Z '07
Bonnie & Clyde '67 ▸
Boys '95
Criminal Lovers '99
Feeling Minnesota '96
The Getaway '72
The Getaway '93
Ghost of a Chance '01
Gun Crazy '49 ▸
Guncrazy '92
Heaven's Burning '97
Helen of Troy '03
Hide '08
The Island '05
Jailbreakers '94
Jimmy & Judy '06
Kalifornia '93
Kill Me Later '01
Kiss or Kill '97
Le Choc '82
Love and a .45 '94
Love Lies Bleeding '07
Mad Love '95
Man Who Loved Cat Dancing '73
Natural Born Killers '94
Niagara, Niagara '97
On the Run '73
Perfect Hideout '08
River of Grass '94
The Road '00
Rough Magic '95
Shark Skin Man and Peach Hip Girl '98
Shockproof '49
The Sugarland Express '74 ▸
Trojan Eddie '96 ▸
True Romance '93
Two If by Sea '95
Underworld: Evolution '05
When Brendan Met Trudy '00 ▸
Where Danger Lives '50
Wild at Heart '90 ▸

Mad Scientists

see also Inventors & Inventions; Science & Scientists
Alien Terminator '95
Alone in the Dark '05
The Amazing Transparent Man '60
The Animal '01
The Ape '40
The Ape Man '43
Atom Age Vampire '61
Attack of the Puppet People '58
Attack of the 60-Foot Centerfold '95
Attack of the Swamp Creature '75
The Avengers '98
Before I Hang '40 ▸
Bela Lugosi Meets a Brooklyn Gorilla '52
Beverly Hills Bodysnatchers '89
Beyond Re-Animator '03
The Black Sleep '56
Bloodbath at the House of Death '85
Bloodlust '59
Bloodstorm: Subspecies 4 '98
Body Armor '96
The Body Shop '72
The Boogie Man Will Get You '42
Bowery Boys Meet the Monsters '54
The Brain that Wouldn't Die '63
Brenda Starr '86
Bride of Re-Animator '89
Bride of the Monster '55
Bug Buster '99
Captain America '44
Captive Wild Woman '43
The Cars That Ate Paris '74 ▸
Castle of Evil '66
Castle of the Creeping Flesh '68
The City of Lost Children '95 ▸
Clockstoppers '02
The Cobweb '55
The Corpse Vanishes '42
Creator '85
Creature of the Walking Dead '60
The Creeper '48
The Creeping Flesh '72
The Creeps '97
The Crime of Dr. Crespi '35
Crimes of Dr. Mabuse '32 ▸
The Curse of the Aztec Mummy '59
Cyborg Cop '93
Darkman '90 ▸
Darkman 2: The Return of Durant '94
Darkman 3: Die Darkman Die '95
The Dead Next Door '89
Dead Pit '89
Dead Sleep '91
Death Warmed Up '85
Deep Red '94
Devil Doll '36 ▸
Dr. Black, Mr. Hyde '76
Doctor Blood's Coffin '62
Doctor Butcher M.D. '80
Dr. Caligari '89
Dr. Cyclops '40
Dr. Death, Seeker of Souls '73
Dr. Frankenstein's Castle of Freaks '74
Dr. Goldfoot and the Bikini Machine '66
Dr. Jekyll and Mr. Hyde '20 ▸
Dr. Jekyll and Mr. Hyde '32 ▸
Dr. Jekyll and Mr. Hyde '41 ▸
Dr. Jekyll and Mr. Hyde '68
Dr. Jekyll and Mr. Hyde '73
Dr. Jekyll and Sister Hyde '71
Dr. Jekyll and the Wolfman '71
Dr. Jekyll's Dungeon of Death '82
Dr. No '62 ▸
Dr. Orloff's Monster '64
Dr. Renault's Secret '42
Doctor X '32
Donovan's Brain '53 ▸
The Double O Kid '92
Dracula 2: Ascension '03
Embryo '76
Evil Town '87
Faceless '88
The Fear Chamber '68
Firestarter 2: Rekindled '02
The Flesh Eaters '64
Frankenhooker '90
Frankenstein '31 ▸
Frankenstein '73
Frankenstein '82
Frankenstein '93
Frankenstein and the Monster from Hell '74
Frankenstein '80 '79
Frankenstein General Hospital '88
Frankenstein Must Be Destroyed '69
Frankenstein Reborn '98
Frankenstein Unbound '90 ▸
Frankenstein's Daughter '58
Freaked '93
The Freakmaker '73
Geisha Girl '52
The Gene Generation '07
The Giant Spider Invasion '75
Girl in His Pocket '57
The Glass Trap '04
Godsend '04
The Head '59
Hellmaster '92
Hideous Sun Demon '59
Hollow Man '00
Horrors of Malformed Men '69
House of Frankenstein '44
Hyena of London '62
I, Monster '71 ▸
Igor '08
The Immortalizer '89
The Incredible Two-Headed Transplant '71
The Indestructible Man '56
Invasion! '99
Invasion of the Zombies '61
The Invisible Dr. Mabuse '62 ▸
The Invisible Man '33 ▸
The Invisible Ray '36
The Invisible Terror '63
The Island of Dr. Moreau '77
The Island of Dr. Moreau '96
Island of Lost Souls '32 ▸
Jekyll and Hyde '90
Jungle Captive '45
Jungle Woman '44
Jurassic Park '93 ▸
Kids in the Hall: Brain Candy '96
The Killing Device '92
King Kong Escapes '67
King of Kong Island '78
King of the Zombies '41
Lady Frankenstein '72
The Lawnmower Man '92
Lawnmower Man 2: Beyond Cyberspace '95
Lightblast '85
The Living Dead '33
The Lost City '34
The Mad Ghoul '43
Man Made Monster '41
The Man They Could Not Hang '39
The Man Who Lived Again '36
The Man with Two Lives '42
Mandroid '93
Maniac '34
The Manster '59
Marrionnier '05
Mary Shelley's Frankenstein '94
Master Minds '49
Metamorphosis '90
Miami Horror '87
Mr. Stitch '95
Mom's Outta Sight '01
The Monster '25 ▸
The Monster Maker '44
Monsters Crash the Pajama Party '65
The Mosaic Project '95
The Munsters' Revenge '81
Murders in the Rue Morgue '32
Mystery Science Theater 3000: The Movie '96
Naked Souls '95
Nightmare Castle '65
Nightmare Weekend '86
Orloff and the Invisible Man '70
The Outer Limits: Sandkings '95 ▸
Philadelphia Experiment 2 '93
Piano Tuner of Earthquakes '05
The Pink Panther Strikes Again '76 ▸
Proteus '95
Puzzlehead '05
The Rage '07
Re-Animator '84 ▸
Red Blooded American Girl '90
Repo! The Genetic Opera '08
Retroactive '97
Return of the Killer Tomatoes! '88
Revenge of the Zombies '43
Revolt of the Zombies '36
Rites of Frankenstein '72
The Robot vs. the Aztec Mummy '59
Rubber's Lover '97
Sabretooth '01
Samson in the Wax Museum '63
Savage '96
Scanner Cop '94
Science Crazed '90
Screamers '80
Seven Days to Noon '50
Severed Ties '92
Shadow Creature '96
Shadow of Chinatown '36
She Demons '58
Shock Waves '77
Sky Captain and the World of Tomorrow '04
Species 3 '04
Spider-Man '02 ▸
Spider-Man 2 '04 ▸
Spy Kids 3-D: Game Over '03
Star Trek: Generations '94 ▸
Strange Behavior '81
Strange Case of Dr. Jekyll & Mr. Hyde '68
Superargo '67
Supersonic Man '78
Tammy and the T-Rex '94
Teenage Zombies '58
Terror Is a Man '59
Testament of Dr. Mabuse '62
The Tingler '59 ▸
Torture Ship '39
Transmutations '85
Underdog '07
The Unearthly '57
The Vampire Bat '32
Vile 21 '99
Virtual Seduction '96
Vulture '67
The Wasp Woman '96
Werewolf of London '35
Wes Craven Presents Mind Ripper '95
Wild Wild West '99
Woman Condemned '33

Madrid

see also Barcelona; Spain
All About My Mother '99 ▸
The Barefoot Contessa '54 ▸
Boystown '07
Chef's Special '08
Goal 2: Living the Dream '07
Km. 0 '00
Labyrinth of Passion '82
Live Flesh '97 ▸
Martin (Hache) '97
The Method '05 ▸
Pepi, Luci, Bom and Other Girls on the Heap '80
What Have I Done to Deserve This? '85 ▸
Women on the Verge of a Nervous Breakdown '88 ▸

Mafia

see Organized Crime

Magic

see also Genies; Magic Carpet Rides; Occult
Alabama's Ghost '72
The Alchemist '81
Arabian Nights '00
Balloon Farm '97
Bedknobs and Broomsticks '71
Bewitched '05
The Black Cauldron '85
Black Magic Terror '79
Bogus '96
The Brothers Grimm '05
The Butcher's Wife '91
Celine and Julie Go Boating '74
Chandu on the Magic Island '34
Chandu the Magician '32
The Chronicles of Narnia: The Lion, the Witch and the Wardrobe '05
The Color of Magic '08
The Craft '96
Cthulhu Mansion '91
The Day the Earth Froze '59
Death Defying Acts '07
Death Magic '92
Deathstalker 3 '89
Doctor Mordrid: Master of the Unknown '90
Don't Torture a Duckling '72
Doogal '05
Dream a Little Dream 2 '94
Dungeons and Dragons '00
Ella Enchanted '04 ▸
Enchanted '07
Escape to Witch Mountain '75 ▸
Eternally Yours '39
FairyTale: A True Story '97
The Geisha Boy '58
Get to Know Your Rabbit '72
The Great Buck Howard '09
Gryphon '88
Happily N'Ever After '07
Harry Potter and the Chamber of Secrets '02 ▸
Harry Potter and the Goblet of Fire '05 ▸
Harry Potter and the Half-Blood Prince '09
Harry Potter and the Order of the Phoenix '07
Harry Potter and the Prisoner of Azkaban '04
Harry Potter and the Sorcerer's Stone '01 ▸
Houdini '53
Houdini '99
The Illusionist '06
Is Anybody There? '08
Kids of the Round Table '96
Killing Grandpa '91
Knights of Bloodsteel '09
Lady in Distress '39
The Linguini Incident '92
Long Life, Happiness and Prosperity '02
Lord of Illusions '95
Lord of the Rings: The Fellowship of the Ring '01 ▸
Lord of the Rings: The Two Towers '02 ▸
Lord of the Rings: The Return of the King '03 ▸
Luna e L'Altra '96
Magic Moments '89
Magic Serpent '66 ▸
The Magician '58 ▸
The Magician of Lublin '79
The Man in the Santa Claus Suit '79
Mary, My Dearest '83
Merlin '92
Merlin '98 ▸
Merlin's Apprentice '06
Mr. Magorium's Wonder Emporium '07
The Mistress of Spices '05
My Chauffeur '86
The Mysterious Stranger '82
Nanny McPhee '06
Next '07
Penelope '06
Penn and Teller Get Killed '90
Pick a Card '97
Practical Magic '98
The Prestige '06 ▸
Prospero's Books '91 ▸
Pufnstuf '70
Quicker Than the Eye '88
Ratz '99
Rough Magic '95
Scoop '06
The Seeker: The Dark Is Rising '07
7 Faces of Dr. Lao '63 ▸
Shorts: The Adventures of the Wishing Rock '09
Simon the Magician '99
A Simple Wish '97
The Sorcerer's Apprentice '10
Stardust '07 ▸
Stephen King's Thinner '96
The Swan Princess 2: Escape from Castle Mountain '97
Sword & the Sorcerer '82
Teen Witch '89
The Tempest '99
13 Going on 30 '04
Three ... Extremes '04
Tooth Fairy '10
Turnaround '87
Tut & Tuttle '81
Wedding Band '89
Willow '88
The Wizard of Gore '70
The Wizard of Gore '07
Wizards of the Demon Sword '94
The Wizards of Waverly Place: The Movie '09
Zotz! '62

Magic Carpet Rides

see also Genies
Aladdin '92 ▸
Aladdin and the King of Thieves '96
Arabian Nights '00
Golden Voyage of Sinbad '73
1001 Arabian Nights '59
The Seventh Voyage of Sinbad '58 ▸
Sinbad and the Eye of the Tiger '77
Sinbad of the Seven Seas '89
Sinbad, the Sailor '47 ▸
The Thief of Bagdad '40 ▸
The Thief of Baghdad '24 ▸
Thief of Baghdad '61
The Thief of Baghdad '78

Mail-Order Brides

see also Marriage; Wedding Bells
Birthday Girl '02
Mail Order Bride '63
Mail Order Bride '08
Mail Order Wife '04
Mississippi Mermaid '69 ▸
Naked Jungle '54 ▸
Naughty Marietta '35

▸ = rated three bones or higher

Original Sin '01
Prairie Fever '08
The Purchase Price '32
Sweet Land '05
2 Brothers & a Bride '03
Zandy's Bride '74

Makeovers

Another Cinderella Story '08
The Church Mouse '34
Cinderella '50 ▶
A Cinderella Story '04
Clueless '95 ▶
Enchanted '07
Ever After: A Cinderella Story '98 ▶
Gigi '58 ▶
Grease '78 ▶
Lady for a Day '33 ▶
Let Us Be Gay '30
The Mirror Has Two Faces '96
Miss Congeniality '00
Miss Pettigrew Lives for a Day '08 ▶
Muriel's Wedding '94 ▶
My Big Fat Greek Wedding '02
My Fair Lady '64 ▶
The Princess Diaries '01
Pygmalion '38 ▶
Sabrina '54 ▶
Sabrina '95
She's All That '99
Union Depot '32
Vertigo '58 ▶

Making Friends

***see also** Mad Scientists; Renegade Body Parts*
Andy Warhol's Frankenstein '74
Bill & Ted's Bogus Journey '91
Deadly Friend '86
Frankenhooker '90
Frankenstein '31 ▶
Frankenstein '73
Frankenstein '82
Frankenstein '93
Frankenstein Created Woman '66 ▶
Frankenstein Must Be Destroyed '69
Frankenstein Reborn '98
Frankenstein Unbound '90 ▶
Frankenstein's Daughter '58
Lost in Space '98
Making Mr. Right '86
Mary Shelley's Frankenstein '94
Multiplicity '96
Repli-Kate '01
The Vindicator '85
Young Frankenstein '74 ▶

Marriage

***see also** Divorce; In-Laws; Killer Spouses; Marriage Hell; Marriages of Convenience; Otherwise Engaged; War Between the Sexes; Wedding Bells; Wedding Hell*
ABCD '99
Above Suspicion '00
Abraham's Valley '93
Absent Without Leave '95
Accused '36
Across the Wide Missouri '51
The Adjuster '91
The Adultress '77
The Adventures of Mark Twain '44 ▶
An Affair in Mind '89
Affairs of Anatol '21
After Sex '97
Afterglow '97
The Age of Innocence '93 ▶
Alfredo, Alfredo '72
All Things Fair '95
All This and Heaven Too '40 ▶
Almost You '85
Always '85 ▶
Amelia '09
American Beauty '99 ▶
American Matchmaker '40
America's Sweethearts '01
Amnesia '96
Angel '37
Angels in America '03 ▶
The Anniversary Party '01 ▶
Antoine et Antoinette '47
Any Wednesday '66
April's Shower '03
Arabian Nights '00
The Aristocrats '99
Arnold '73
Arrivederci, Baby! '66
As You Desire Me '32 ▶
Ash Wednesday '73
Ask Any Girl '59
Assault and Matrimony '87
The Astronaut's Wife '99
Asunder '99
Attack of the 50 Ft. Woman '93
Auto Focus '02 ▶
Autumn Leaves '56
Autumn Marathon '79
Awake '07
Away From Her '06 ▶
Away We Go '09
Baby Doll '56 ▶
The Baby Maker '70
Baby on Board '08
Bachelor in Paradise '69
Bachelor Party '84
Back to the Wall '56
Backstreet Dreams '90
Bad Behavior '92
Bad Girl '31
Bad Manners '98
Barefoot in the Park '67 ▶
Barjo '93
Bark! '02
The Barkleys of Broadway '49 ▶
Battle of the Sexes '28
A Beautiful Mind '01 ▶
Because of You '52
Becky Sharp '35
Bed and Board '70 ▶
Bedelia '46 ▶
Bedroom Eyes 2 '89
Being John Malkovich '99 ▶
The Beneficiary '97
Best Enemies '86
Best Friends '82
The Best Intentions '92 ▶
The Best Man '97
Betrayal '83
Betsy's Wedding '90
Beyond the Rocks '22
Big Business Girl '31
Big Fish '03 ▶
The Big Squeeze '96
A Black Veil for Lisa '68
Blanche Fury '48
Blindfold: Acts of Obsession '94
Bliss '96
The Bliss of Mrs. Blossom '68 ▶
Blonde Venus '32 ▶
Blondie '38
Blondie Hits the Jackpot '49
Blondie in Society '41
Blondie Knows Best '46
Blondie Plays Cupid '40
Blood of Jesus '41
The Blood Oranges '97
Blood Wedding '81 ▶
Bloom '03
Blue Heaven '84
Blue in the Face '95
Blue Moon '00
Blue Sky '91 ▶
Bluebeard's Eighth Wife '38
Blume in Love '73 ▶
Body Chemistry '90
Body Strokes '95
Book of Love '04
Boulevard of Broken Dreams '88
Brand New Life '72
Bread and Tulips '01 ▶
Breaking the Waves '95 ▶
Breaking Up '97
Breathing Lessons '94 ▶
Bride & Prejudice '04
The Bride & the Beast '58
Bride of the Wind '01
The Bride Walks Out '36
Broken Glass '96
Brothers '04 ▶
Brothers '09
Brown Sugar '02
The Browning Version '94
The Buccaneers '95 ▶
Bullwhip '58
Burn Witch, Burn! '62 ▶
The Burning Bed '85 ▶
A Business Affair '93
The Butcher's Wife '91
By Love Possessed '61
By the Light of the Silvery Moon '53
Cairo Time '09
Calendar '93 ▶
Captain's Paradise '53 ▶
Car Trouble '86
Casanova Brown '44
Cast a Dark Shadow '55 ▶
Catherine Cookson's Colour Blind '98
Catherine Cookson's The Man Who Cried '93
Catherine Cookson's The Round Tower '98
Caught '96
Cause for Alarm '51
Chained '34
Change of Heart '98
A Change of Seasons '80
Changing Times '04
Chaos '01
Chaos Theory '08
Charles & Diana: A Palace Divided '93
Charulata '64
Cheaper by the Dozen 2 '05
Cheaters '84
Cheatin' Hearts '93
Child Bride of Short Creek '81
China Moon '91
Chinese Roulette '86
Chloe '09
Chloe in the Afternoon '72 ▶
The Chocolate Soldier '41
Choices '86
Christina '74
A Christmas Tale '08 ▶
Cinderella Man '05 ▶
Circumstances Unknown '95
Circus '00
Claire's Knee '71 ▶
Clash by Night '52 ▶
The Clearing '04 ▶
Click '06
Close My Eyes '91
Coast to Coast '80
Coast to Coast '04
Cold Heaven '92
Come Back, Little Sheba '52 ▶
The Comfort of Strangers '91 ▶
Coming to America '88 ▶
Committed '99
Common Law Wife '63
Company Man '00
Conflict '45 ▶
Consenting Adults '92
Consolation Marriage '31
Conspiracy of Terror '75
The Convent '95
Cool and the Crazy '94
Cosmic Slop '94
Cotton Mary '99
Country Girl '54 ▶
Country Girl '82
The Cowboy and the Lady '38
Crash '95
Crazy in Love '92
Creation '09
Creation of Adam '93
Crime & Passion '75
Critic's Choice '63
A Cry in the Night '93
The Crying Child '96
Cul de Sac '66 ▶
Damage '92 ▶
Dancing in the Dark '86
Dangerous Game '93
Dangerous Liaisons '60
Daniel Deronda '02
Danielle Steel's Changes '91
Darlings of the Gods '90
Darwin's Darkest Hour '09
Date Night '10
Days and Clouds '07
The Daytrippers '96
De-Lovely '04
De Mayerling a Sarajevo '40
The Dead '87 ▶
Dead Husbands '98
Dead in the Water '91
Dead Mate '88
Dead On '93
Death Kiss '74
Deception '92
Deep in the Heart (of Texas) '98
Deja Vu '98
Designing Woman '57 ▶
Desire and Hell at Sunset Motel '92
Desire Under the Elms '58
Desperate Characters '71 ▶
Desperate Hours '90
Desperate Remedies '93
The Devil in Silk '56
The Devil's Advocate '97
Diabolically Yours '67
Dial "M" for Murder '54 ▶
Diary of a Mad Black Woman '05
Diary of a Mad Housewife '70 ▶
The Diary of Ellen Rimbauer '03
Diary of the Dead '76
Dinner with Friends '01
The Disappearance of Christina '93
The Disciple '15
Divided We Fall '00
Divorce American Style '67
Divorce—Italian Style '62 ▶
The Divorce of Lady X '38
Do Not Disturb '65
Doctor Zhivago '65 ▶
Doctor Zhivago '03
Doctors' Wives '70
Dodsworth '36 ▶
Doing Time on Maple Drive '92
Dollar '38
A Doll's House '59
A Doll's House '73
A Doll's House '73 ▶
Dominique Is Dead '79
Don Juan DeMarco '94
Dona Flor and Her Two Husbands '78 ▶
Donkey Skin '70 ▶
Don't Raise the Bridge, Lower the River '68
Don't Say a Word '01
Don't Talk to Strangers '94
Doomsday '28
The Door in the Floor '04 ▶
Dot the I '03
Double Deal '84
Double Exposure '93
Double Harness '33
Double Indemnity '44 ▶
Double Standard '88
Doubting Thomas '35
Dream Lover '93
Dressmaker '56
Drifting Souls '32
Drowning by Numbers '87 ▶
Drums Along the Mohawk '39 ▶
Dry Cleaning '97
Duane Hopwood '05 ▶
Duplex '03
East Is East '99 ▶
East Side, West Side '49
East-West '99
Easy Living '37 ▶
Easy Living '49
Easy Money '83
Eat a Bowl of Tea '89 ▶
Ecstasy '33
Edward and Mrs. Simpson '80
Effi Briest '74 ▶
Egg and I '47 ▶
El '52
El Cantante '06
El Crimen Perfecto '04
Elective Affinities '96
Element of Doubt '96
Elizabeth of Ladymead '48 ▶
Ellie '84
Elvis and Me '88
Emissary '89
Emma '09
Emmanuelle '74
Emmanuelle, the Queen '79
Encore '52 ▶
End of Desire '62
The End of the Affair '99 ▶
End of the Road '70
Enemies, a Love Story '89 ▶
Enormous Changes '83 ▶
Enough '02
The Entertainer '60 ▶
Entre-Nous '83 ▶
Ernie Kovacs: Between the Laughter '84
Erotic Images '85
Escapade '55 ▶
Escape Clause '96
Estate of Insanity '64
Eternally Yours '39
Ethan Frome '92
Eureka! '81
Evelyn Prentice '34
Every Breath '93
Every Girl Should Be Married '48
Everybody's All American '88
Everyone Says I Love You '96 ▶
Everything I Have is Yours '52
Eve's Bayou '97 ▶
The Ex '96
Ex-Lady '33
Experiment Perilous '45 ▶
The Eyes of Youth '19
Eyes Wide Shut '99
Faces '68 ▶
Facing Windows '03
The Facts of Life '60
Faithful '95
Faithless '00 ▶
Falling for a Dancer '98
Falling from Grace '92
The Family Man '79
Family Man '00
The Family Stone '05
Family Upside Down '78 ▶
Far Cry from Home '81
Far from Heaven '02 ▶
The Farmer's Wife '28
Fatal Attraction '87 ▶
Father of the Bride '50 ▶
Fear of Fear '75
Fearless '93 ▶
Feast of Love '07
Femme Fatale '90
Fergie & Andrew: Behind Palace Doors '93
Fever '88
Fictitious Marriage '88
Fiddler on the Roof '71 ▶
A Fine Romance '92
Fireproof '08
Fireworks '97
First Affair '83
5x2 '04
Flannel Pajamas '06
Flirt '95
Flower & Snake 2 '05
The Flower of My Secret '95 ▶
Flying By '09
Follow the Boys '44 ▶
Fools '70
Fools Rush In '97
The Foot Fist Way '08
For Keeps '88
For Love or Country: The Arturo Sandoval Story '00
For Love or Money '63
For Pete's Sake '74
Forbidden Fruit '52 ▶
Forever Love '98
Forget Paris '95
Fortune's Fool '21
Fortunes of War '87 ▶
Four Daughters '38 ▶
Four Days in July '85
Four Rooms '95
The Four Seasons '81
Fourth Story '90 ▶
Free Money '99
The Freebie '10
French Twist '95
Frida '02
Frieda '47
Friends with Money '06
From the Terrace '60
Fulfillment '89
Full of Life '56
Fun with Dick and Jane '77
Fun With Dick and Jane '05
Funny About Love '90
Fur: An Imaginary Portrait of Diane Arbus '06
Gabbeh '96 ▶
Gabrielle '05
Games '67
Gaslight '40 ▶
Gaslight '44 ▶
A Gathering of Eagles '63
The Gathering Storm '02 ▶
A Gentle Woman '69
George Washington '84
George Washington: The Forging of a Nation '86
Gertrud '64 ▶
Get Out Your Handkerchiefs '78 ▶
Getting Up and Going Home '92
Ghosts Never Sleep '05
Giant '56 ▶
The Gift of Love '90
Girl from Hunan '86 ▶
Girl with a Pearl Earring '03 ▶
Goin' to Town '35
The Golden Bowl '72 ▶
The Golden Bowl '00
The Good Girl '02 ▶
The Good Wife '86
Gore Vidal's Lincoln '88
Gosford Park '01 ▶
Grace of My Heart '96
Grand Isle '92
Grand Theft Auto '77
The Grass Is Greener '61
Greed '24 ▶
The Greek Tycoon '78
Grievous Bodily Harm '89
Group Marriage '72
Grown Ups '80
Grumpier Old Men '95
The Guardsman '31 ▶
Guess Who '05
Guess Who's Coming to Dinner '67 ▶
Guest Wife '45
A Guide for the Married Man '67 ▶
A Guide for the Married Woman '78
The Hairdresser's Husband '92
Halfmoon '95
Hammers over the Anvil '91
Hamsun '96
A Handful of Dust '88
Happily Ever After '04
Happiness '98 ▶
Hard Promises '92
The Hard Word '02
Harlan County War '00
Harriet Craig '50 ▶
Harrison's Flowers '02
The Hawk '93
Head Above Water '96
Head On '04
The Healer '02
The Heart of Me '02
Heartburn '86 ▶
Heaven '99
The Heavenly Body '44
Heaven's Prisoners '95
Heist '01 ▶
Helas pour Moi '94
Hell-Ship Morgan '36
Hello Goodbye '08
Here We Go Again! '42
Hidden '05 ▶
High Crimes '02
High Heels '72
High Society '56 ▶
Highway Patrolman '91
Hilary and Jackie '98 ▶
Hindsight '97
His Secret Life '01 ▶
Hitched '01
Homecoming '28 ▶
Honeymoon Lodge '43
The Honeymooners '05
Hope Floats '98
The Horrible Dr. Hichcock '62
Hostage for a Day '94
Hot Spell '58
Hot Tip '35
Hotel Room '93
Houdini '99

The Hours '02 ►
House of Mirth '00 ►
The Householder '63
How to Be a Woman and Not Die in the Attempt '91
How to Break Up a Happy Divorce '76
How to Commit Marriage '69
How to Kill Your Neighbor's Dog '01
How to Make an American Quilt '95
How to Marry a Millionaire '53
How to Murder Your Wife '64 ►
Howard's End '92 ►
The Howards of Virginia '40
Hurry, Charlie, Hurry '41
Husbands '70
Husbands and Lovers '91
Husbands and Wives '92 ►
Hush '98
I Dood It '43
I Like It Like That '94 ►
I Love My... Wife '70
I Love You Again '40 ►
I Love You, Goodbye '74
I Love You Rosa '72
I Love You to Death '90
I Love Your Work '03
I Married a Vampire '87
I Married a Woman '56
I Only Want You to Love Me '76
I Take This Woman '40
I Think I Love My Wife '07
I Was a Male War Bride '49 ►
I Will, I Will for Now '76
I Wonder Who's Killing Her Now? '76
An Ideal Husband '47
An Ideal Husband '99 ►
Il Bell'Antonio '60
Il Grido '57
I'll See You in My Dreams '51
Illicit '31
Illusions '91
Immortal Bachelor '80
The Imported Bridegroom '89
In a Savage Land '99
In Celebration '75 ►
In Name Only '39
In the Bedroom '01 ►
In the Lake of the Woods '96
In the Mood for Love '00
Indecent Proposal '93
Inevitable Grace '94
Infinity '96
Innocents with Dirty Hands '76
Intersection '93
Intimacy '00
Intimate Story '81
Intimate Strangers '77
Intruso '93
The Invasion of Carol Enders '74
The Invisible Ghost '41
Ira & Abby '06
Iris '01 ►
Isn't She Great '00
It Came from the Sky '98
It Runs in the Family '03
It Started with a Kiss '59
It Takes Two '88
It's a Pleasure '45
It's the Rage '99
Jackie, Ethel, Joan: The Kennedy Women '01
Java Head '35 ►
Jenny '70
The Jeweller's Shop '90
John Adams '08
Josepha '82 ►
Ju Dou '90 ►
Jubal '56
Jubilee Trail '54
Jude '96 ►
Jude the Obscure '71
Julie & Julia '09 ►
Juliet of the Spirits '65 ►
Just a Little Harmless Sex '99
Just Like Weather '86 ►
Kadosh '99
The Keeper '96
Keeper of the Flame '42
Keeping Mum '05
The Kettles on Old MacDonald's Farm '57
The Kill-Off '90
Killers '10
Killing Heat '84
Killing Me Softly '01
A Kind of Loving '62 ►
King's Ransom '05
Kira's Reason—A Love Story '01
Kiss and Be Killed '91
Kuni Lemel in Tel Aviv '77
La Bete Humaine '38 ►
La Chienne '31 ►
La Deroute '98
La Moustache '05
La Mujer de Mi Hermano '06
La Notte '60 ►
La Petite Jerusalem '05
La Vengeance d'une Femme '89
La Vie Continue '82
Lady Audley's Secret '00
Lady Chatterley's Lover '55
Lady Chatterley's Lover '81
Lady Godiva '55
Lady L '65
Lady Windermere's Fan '25
Lantana '01 ►
Last Breath '96
The Last Dance '93
The Last Days of Chez Nous '92
The Last Kiss '06
The Last Married Couple in America '80
Last Night '10
The Last Station '09
L'Atalante '34 ►
Late Spring '49 ►
Laurel & Hardy: Be Big '31
Lawless Heart '01
Le Beau Mariage '82 ►
Le Bonheur '65
Le Bonheur Est Dans le Pre '95
Le Chat '75 ►
Lea '96
The Leather Boys '63
Leaving Metropolis '02
The Legend of Zorro '05
Leila '97
L'Enfer '93 ►
Leo Tolstoy's Anna Karenina '96
Les Destinees '00
Lesson in Love '54
Let's Get Married '60
A Letter to Three Wives '49 ►
Lianna '83 ►
The Liars '64
Liar's Moon '82
Lie Down with Lions '94
Life of Oharu '52 ►
Like It Never Was Before '95
Linda '29
Linda '93
The Lion in Winter '68 ►
Listen, Darling '38
A Little Sex '82
Lonely Wives '31
The Long Haul '57
Lord Love a Duck '66
Losing Chase '96
Lost Highway '96
Lost Honeymoon '47
Lost in Translation '03 ►
The Lotus Eaters '93
Loulou '80 ►
Love, Cheat & Steal '93
A Love Divided '01
Love, etc. '96
Love from a Stranger '37
Love in Pawn '53
Love in the Time of Cholera '07
Love Matters '93
Love Thy Neighbor '02
Love Walked In '97
The Lovers '59 ►
Lovers and Other Strangers '70 ►
Loving Couples '80
Lucia, Lucia '03
Lucie Aubrac '98
Lucy and Desi: Before the Laughter '91
Lured Innocence '97
Lust and Revenge '95
The Luzhin Defence '00
Ma Saison Preferee '93 ►
Maborosi '95 ►
Mad at the Moon '92
Mad Love '01
Madame Bovary '91 ►
Madame Bovary '00
Madame Butterfly '95
Madame Sans-Gene '62
Magnificent Doll '46
Magnolia '99 ►
Mail Order Wife '04
Making Love '82
The Makioka Sisters '83 ►
The Male Animal '42
The Man from Elysian Fields '01 ►
Man from Nowhere '37
The Man of My Life '06
Man of the House '95
The Man Who Made Husbands Jealous '98
The Man Who Wasn't There '01 ►
Manhattan Murder Mystery '93 ►
A Map of the World '99
Maria Chapdelaine '34 ►
Marie Antoinette '06
The Marquise of O '76
The Marriage Circle '24 ►
Marriage Is Alive and Well '80
Marriage Italian Style '64 ►
The Marriage of Maria Braun '79 ►
Marriage on the Rocks '65
Married? '26
Married People, Single Sex 2: For Better or Worse '94
Married to It '93
Married Too Young '62
A Married Woman '65 ►
The Marrying Kind '52
Martha and I '91 ►
Marty '55 ►
Mary, Mary '63
Mary, Queen of Scots '71
Master Spy: The Robert Hanssen Story '02
Matrimaniac '16
A Matter of Dignity '57
Max, Mon Amour '86
Maybe Baby '99
McLintock! '63 ►
Me Myself I '99
Me You Them '00
The Member of the Wedding '83
Memories of a Marriage '90 ►
Memory of Us '74
Men... '85 ►
Merci pour le Chocolat '00 ►
The Merry Widow '52
Metroland '97
Mexican Spitfire at Sea '42
Miami Rhapsody '95
Microwave Massacre '83
Mid-Channel '20
Midnight '39 ►
Midnight Crossing '87
Mighty Aphrodite '95
A Mighty Heart '07 ►
Milk and Honey '03
The Millionairess '60
Miracle of Morgan's Creek '44 ►
The Mirror Has Two Faces '96
Misbehaving Husbands '41
Mrs. Dalloway '97
Mrs. Mike '49
Mr. & Mrs. Smith '41 ►
Mr. & Mrs. Smith '05 ►
Mr. Barrington '03
Mr. Love '86
Mr. Mom '83 ►
Mr. Skeffington '44 ►
Mr. Sycamore '74
Mr. Wonderful '93
Mistress '53 ►
Modern Love '90
Moment to Moment '66
Mona Lisa Smile '03
The Money Pit '86
Mongol '07 ►
Montana '90
Moon over Harlem '39
Moonlight Mile '02 ►
The Moon's Our Home '36
Motherhood '09
Mouth to Mouth '95
Move Over, Darling '63
Multiplicity '96
Murder at 45 R.P.M. '65
Murder Czech Style '66
Murder So Sweet '93
Murders in the Zoo '33
Muriel's Wedding '94 ►
The Music Lovers '71
My Dear Secretary '49
My First Wife '84
My 5 Wives '00
My Foolish Heart '49
My Husband's Double Life '01
My Life So Far '98
My Life Without Me '03
My Little Chickadee '40 ►
My Michael '75 ►
My New Gun '92
My Other Husband '85
My Sweet Victim '85
My Wife is an Actress '01
Naked Jungle '54 ►
The Namesake '06 ►
Nanny Insanity '06
Napoleon '03
Narc '02 ►
Nathalie '03
Never Forever '07
The New Age '94
Night Ride Home '99
Nightkill '80
Nina Takes a Lover '94
Nora '00
Normal '03
Normal Life '96
Not Tonight Darling '72
Notes on a Scandal '06 ►
The Notorious Lady '27
Nouvelle Vague '90
Now and Forever '82
Nowhere in Africa '02
Nudo di Donna '83 ►
Nurse Marjorie '20
O Quatrilho '95
Obsessed '09
Odd Obsession '60
The Oh in Ohio '06
O'Hara's Wife '82
The O.J. Simpson Story '94
Oldest Confederate Widow Tells All '95 ►
On Approval '44 ►
On Golden Pond '81 ►
On Her Majesty's Secret Service '69 ►
On Valentine's Day '86
One Good Turn '95
One Hour Photo '02 ►
One Hour with You '32
One Night in the Tropics '40
One of My Wives Is Missing '76
One Sunday Afternoon '33
One Trick Pony '80
Only with Married Men '74
Orchestra Wives '42 ►
Othello '01 ►
Our Italian Husband '04
Our Town '03
Out of Order '03
The Paint Job '93
Paint Your Wagon '69
The Painted Veil '34
The Painted Veil '06
Pajama Tops '83
The Palm Beach Story '42 ►
Pandaemonium '00
Panic '00
Paper Marriage '88
Paper Marriage '93
Paradise '91 ►
Pardon Mon Affaire '76 ►
Pardon Mon Affaire, Too! '77
Parenthood '89 ►
Paris, France '94
Party '96
Passion in Paradise '89
The Passion of Ayn Rand '99
A Passion to Kill '94
Pavilion of Women '01
Pedale Douce '96
Peggy Sue Got Married '86
The Penitent '88
Pennies from Heaven '81 ►
Perfect Alibi '94
The Perfect Bride '91
Perfect Crime '97
The Perfect Marriage '46
A Perfect Murder '98
Period of Adjustment '62 ►
Persuasion '71
Pete 'n' Tillie '72
Petulia '68 ►
Phaedra '61
Phffft! '54
The Philadelphia Story '40 ►
The Piano '93 ►
Picture Bride '94
A Piece of Pleasure '74 ►
Pipe Dreams '76
Platinum Blonde '31 ►
Playing Dead '15
Pollock '00 ►
Portrait of a Lady '96 ►
Portrait of an Assassin '49
Portrait of Teresa '79 ►
The Postman Always Rings Twice '46 ►
The Postman Always Rings Twice '81
Praying Mantis '93
Premonition '07
Pride and Prejudice '05 ►
Primary Colors '98
The Primitive Lover '16
Prisoner of Second Avenue '74
Prisoners of Inertia '89
Private Confessions '98
Private Life '82
Private Lives '31 ►
The Private Lives of Pippa Lee '09
Promises! Promises! '63
Provincial Actors '79
Prowler '51
The Pumpkin Eater '64 ►
The Purchase Price '32
Pushing Hands '92
Quartet '81 ►
Queen Bee '55
Queen Margot '94 ►
Question of Faith '93
Race for Life '55
Raging Bull '80 ►
Rain '01
Raise the Red Lantern '91 ►
Rally 'Round the Flag, Boys! '58
Range of Motion '00
Rape and Marriage: The Rideout Case '80
Rebecca '40 ►
Rebecca '97 ►
Reckless '97 ►
The Rector's Wife '94
Red Lights '04 ►
Red Rock West '93 ►
Remember Me '85
The Rendering '02
The Republic of Love '03
A Respectable Trade '98
Revenge of the Stepford Wives '80
Reversal of Fortune '90 ►
Rich and Famous '81
Rich and Strange '32
The Rich Man's Wife '96
Rider from Tucson '50
Riptide '34 ►
Risky Business '28
Rocky 2 '79
Romantic Englishwoman '75 ►
The Roof '56
Rose of Washington Square '39
Roseanne: An Unauthorized Biography '94
A Royal Scandal '96
The Royal Tenenbaums '01 ►
Rumor Has It... '05
Runaways '75
Ryan's Daughter '70
Safe Passage '94
The Safety of Objects '01
The Sandy Bottom Orchestra '00
The Santa Clause 2 '02
Santa Fe '97
Saraband '03 ►
Sarah's Child '96
Satan's Black Wedding '75
Saturday Night and Sunday Morning '60 ►
Savage Attraction '83
Say Nothing '01
Say Yes! '86
Scar of Shame '27
Scarlet Dawn '32
Scenes from a Mall '91
Scenes from a Marriage '73 ►
Scorchers '92
Score '72
Scotland, PA '02
Season of Fear '89
Second Chance '80
Second Skin '99
A Secret '07 ►
Secret Beyond the Door '48
The Secret Life of Girls '99
The Secret Life of Mrs. Beeton '06
The Secret Lives of Dentists '02 ►
Secrets of Women '52 ►
Seeing Other People '04
Seems Like Old Times '80
Send Me No Flowers '64 ►
Separate Vacations '86
Separate Ways '82
Seven Chances '25 ►
The Seven Year Itch '55 ►
The Seventeenth Bride '84
Seventh Heaven '98
75 Degrees '00
Sex and the City 2 '10
Sex and the Single Girl '64
The Sex Monster '99
Sexpot '88
Sexual Malice '93
Shadowlands '85 ►
Shadowlands '93 ►
The Shakiest Gun in the West '68
Shall We Dance? '04
The Shame '68 ►
Shattered '72
She and He '63
She-Devil '89
She Waits '71
She's So Lovely '97
She's the One '96
Shoot the Moon '82
Shooting Elizabeth '92
The Show Off '26
Sibling Rivalry '90
Sidewalks of New York '01
Signs & Wonders '00
Silent Tongue '92
Silent Victim '92
Sin and Redemption '94
Sin Takes a Holiday '30
The Singing Blacksmith '38
The Single Standard '29
The Sisters '38 ►
Sketch Artist '92
Skinner's Dress Suit '26
The Slugger's Wife '85
Small Time Crooks '00
Smart Woman '31
Smash Palace '82
Smash-Up: The Story of a Woman '47 ►
The Smiling Lieutenant '31
Smoking/No Smoking '94
Smother '08
Smouldering Fires '25
Snow White: A Tale of Terror '97
So This Is Paris '26 ►
Sofie '92
The Soft Skin '64 ►
Something About Sex '98
Something to Talk About '95
A Song for Martin '01
The Son's Room '00 ►
Soul Food '97
Sound of Murder '82
Splendor '35
The Stationmaster's Wife '77
Steam: A Turkish Bath '96 ►
The Stepford Wives '75 ►
Story of a Love Affair '50
The Story of Boys & Girls '91 ►
The Story of Esther Costello '57

► = rated three bones or higher

The Story of Us '99
The Story of Xinghua '93
Strange Bedfellows '65
Stromboli '50
The Student Affair '97
The Substitute Wife '94
Sudden Fear '52 ▶
Summer Wishes, Winter Dreams '73
Suspicion '41 ▶
Suspicion '03
Sweet Hearts Dance '88
Sweet Home Alabama '02
Sweet Movie '75
Sweet Nothing '96 ▶
Sweet Poison '91
Sweet Revenge '90
Sweethearts '38 ▶
Sylvia '03
The Syrian Bride '04
The Tailor of Panama '00 ▶
Tarnished Angels '57 ▶
The Taste of Others '00 ▶
Tell Me a Riddle '80
Tell Me That You Love Me '84
The Tenant of Wildfell Hall '96
Tender Is the Night '55
Tess of the D'Urbervilles '98
Test Pilot '38 ▶
Thanks for the Memory '38
That Certain Thing '28
That Old Feeling '96
That Uncertain Feeling '41
Thicker Than Water '93
The Third '72
Third Walker '79 ▶
30 Is a Dangerous Age, Cynthia '68
Three Broadway Girls '32 ▶
Three Daring Daughters '48
Three for the Show '55
Three Husbands '50
Three Smart Girls '36 ▶
Thursday's Game '74 ▶
Till Death Do Us Part '72
Till Marriage Do Us Part '74
Till Murder Do Us Part '92
Till the End of the Night '94
Tim Burton's Corpse Bride '05 ▶
The Time Traveler's Wife '09
Tin Men '87
To Joy '50 ▶
Tom & Viv '94 ▶
Too Beautiful for You '88
Too Far to Go '79 ▶
Too Many Husbands '40
Torchlight '85
The Torture of Silence '17
A Touch of Class '73 ▶
Town and Country '01
Trade Off '95
Traps '93
Tricks of the Trade '88
Tristan & Isolde '06
Tropix '02
True Lies '94
True Love '89 ▶
The Truman Show '98 ▶
Trust the Man '06
Tugboat Annie '33 ▶
The Tunnel '89
The Tunnel of Love '58
Turn of the Blade '97
Twice a Woman '79
Twilight '98 ▶
The Twilight of the Golds '97
Two Family House '99
Two for the Road '67 ▶
The Two Mrs. Carrolls '47
Tyler Perry's Why Did I Get Married? '07
Tyler Perry's Why Did I Get Married Too '10
Ulysses '67
The Unchastened Woman '25
Under Capricorn '49
Under Capricorn '82
Under the Lighthouse Dancing '97
Under the Sand '00 ▶
Under the Volcano '84 ▶
Undercover Blues '93
Undercurrent '46
Undertow '10
Une Parisienne '58
Unfaithfully Yours '48 ▶
Unfaithfully Yours '84
Unholy Wife '57
The Unkissed Bride '66
Until September '84
Uptown New York '32
The Van '95 ▶
Vanishing Act '88
Vanity Fair '67
Vanity Fair '99
Vasectomy: A Delicate Matter '86
Velvet Goldmine '98
The Vertical Ray of the Sun '00
Victoria & Albert '01
A Village Affair '95
Violets Are Blue '86
The Virgin of Nuremberg '65
Vivacious Lady '38 ▶
A Vow to Kill '94
Voyage in Italy '53
Vukovar '94 ▶
W '74
Waking Up in Reno '02
A Walk in the Clouds '95
Walk in the Spring Rain '70
Walk the Line '05 ▶
Walking and Talking '96
Waltz of the Toreadors '62 ▶
War Brides '80
The Wash '88 ▶
Waterland '92
Waterloo Road '44
Way Down East '20 ▶
The Wayward Wife '52
We Don't Live Here Anymore '04
A Wedding '78
The Wedding Gift '93 ▶
Wedding in Blood '74 ▶
A Wedding in Galilee '87 ▶
The Weight of Water '00
We're Not Married '52 ▶
What Lies Beneath '00
What's Good for the Goose '69
When a Man Loves a Woman '94
Where Angels Fear to Tread '91 ▶
Where Were You When the Lights Went Out? '68
Whirlpool '49
White Gold '28 ▶
White Mischief '88 ▶
White Noise '05
Who's Afraid of Virginia Woolf? '66 ▶
Who's Got the Action? '63
Why Do Fools Fall in Love? '98
Wicked Ways '99
The Widow of Saint-Pierre '00 ▶
Widow's Kiss '94
The Wife '95
Wife Versus Secretary '36 ▶
Wifemistress '79
Wilde '97
With a Friend Like Harry '00 ▶
With Six You Get Eggroll '68
Without Anesthesia '78
Wolf Trap '57
The Woman in White '97
A Woman Named Jackie '91
The Woman Next Door '81 ▶
Woman of the Year '42 ▶
The Woman on Pier 13 '50
Woman on Top '00
A Woman under the Influence '74 ▶
Woman Undone '95
Woman with a Past '92
A Woman's Guide to Adultery '93
A Woman's World '54 ▶
The Women '39 ▶
Women from the Lake of Scented Souls '94
Women vs. Men '02
The Wooden Man's Bride '94
The World Is Full of Married Men '80
World's Greatest Lover '77
Worth Winning '89
Woyzeck '94
X, Y & Zee '72
A Year in Provence '89 ▶
Yerma '99
You Can't Fool Your Wife '40
You Gotta Stay Happy '48
The Young Pioneers '76
The Young Victoria '09 ▶
Younger & Younger '94
Yours, Mine & Ours '68
Yours, Mine & Ours '05
You've Got to Have Heart '77
Zandy's Bride '74
Zebra Lounge '01
Zombie Honeymoon '04

Marriage Hell

***see also** Divorce; Domestic Abuse; Killer Spouses; Marriages of Convenience*

Abraham's Valley '93
The Adultress '77
An Affair in Mind '89
Affairs of Anatol '21
After Sex '97
Afterglow '97
All Things Fair '95
American Beauty '99 ▶
Amnesia '96
Angel '37
Angels in America '03 ▶
Another Woman '94
Antichrist '09
Arnold '73
Arrivederci, Baby! '66
Assault and Matrimony '87
Attack of the 50 Ft. Woman '93
Autumn Hearts: A New Beginning '07
Autumn Leaves '56
Back to the Wall '56
The Backwoods '06
Bad Manners '98
Bedelia '46 ▶
Behind That Curtain '29
The Best Intentions '92 ▶
Betrayal '83
The Big Squeeze '96
The Bigamist '53
A Black Veil for Lisa '68
Blanche Fury '48
Blind Date '08
Blindfold: Acts of Obsession '94
Blonde Venus '32 ▶
The Blood Oranges '97
Blood Wedding '81 ▶
Blue Valentine '10
Boulevard of Broken Dreams '88
The Box '09
Bright Leaf '50
The Buccaneers '95 ▶
The Burning Bed '85 ▶
The Buttercup Chain '70
Car Trouble '85
Carry On Cabby '63
Cast a Dark Shadow '55 ▶
Catherine Cookson's The Man Who Cried '93
Cause for Alarm '51
Chained '34
A Change of Seasons '80
Charles & Diana: A Palace Divided '93
Charulata '64
Cheaters '84
Cheatin' Hearts '93
Child Bride of Short Creek '81
Chinese Roulette '86
Christina '74
Clash by Night '52 ▶
Cold Heaven '92
Come Back, Little Sheba '52 ▶
The Comfort of Strangers '91 ▶
Committed '99
Conflict '45 ▶
Cool and the Crazy '94
Cotton Mary '99
Country Girl '54 ▶
Country Girl '82
Cover '08
Crazy Love '07 ▶
Crime & Passion '75
A Cry in the Night '93
Cul de Sac '66 ▶
Damage '92 ▶
Dangerous Game '93
Dangerous Liaisons '60
Daniel Deronda '02
Day-Time Wife '39
Dead Husbands '98
Dead in the Water '91
Dead Mate '88
Dead On '93
Deadly Illusion '87
Death Kiss '74
Desire and Hell at Sunset Motel '92
Desire Under the Elms '58
The Devil in Silk '56
Dial "M" for Murder '54 ▶
Diary of a Mad Black Woman '05
Diary of a Mad Housewife '70 ▶
The Diary of Ellen Rimbauer '03
Did You Hear About the Morgans? '09
The Disappearance of Christina '93
The Divorcee '30
A Doll's House '59
A Doll's House '73
A Doll's House '73 ▶
Dominique Is Dead '79
Doomsday '28
The Door in the Floor '04 ▶
Double Deal '84
Double Exposure '93
Double Indemnity '44 ▶
Double Standard '88
Downloading Nancy '08
Dream Lover '93
Drifting Souls '32
Drowning by Numbers '87 ▶
The Duchess '08 ▶
Easy Living '49
The Edge of Love '08
Effi Briest '74 ▶
El '52
Element of Doubt '96
Ellie '84
Emmanuelle, the Queen '79
End of Desire '62
Enough '02
The Entertainer '60 ▶
Ethan Frome '92
Everlasting Moments '08
Faithful '95
Faithless '00 ▶
Falling for a Dancer '98
Far Cry from Home '81
Far from Heaven '02 ▶
Fergie & Andrew: Behind Palace Doors '93
5x2 '04
The Flower of My Secret '95 ▶
Forbidden Fruit '52 ▶
French Twist '95
Gaslight '40 ▶
Gaslight '44 ▶
A Gentle Woman '69
The Girl in the Red Velvet Swing '55
The Golden Bowl '72 ▶
The Golden Bowl '00
Good '08
The Good Wife '86
Greed '24 ▶
Grindstone Road '07
Harriet Craig '50 ▶
The Hawk '93
Haywire '80
Head Above Water '96
The Heart of Me '02
Heartburn '86 ▶
Heaven '99
Hell-Ship Morgan '36
He's Just Not That Into You '09
Hindsight '97
Hitched '01
The Horrible Dr. Hitchcock '62
Hostage for a Day '94
Husbands and Lovers '91
Husbands and Wives '92 ▶
Hush '98
Ice Follies of 1939 '39
Illicit '31
In a Savage Land '99
In Name Only '39
The Innocent '76
Innocents with Dirty Hands '76
The Inveterate Bachelor '58
Invisible '06
The Jane Austen Book Club '07 ▶
Ju Dou '90 ▶
Jude the Obscure '71
The Kill-Off '90
Killing Me Softly '01
La Bete Humaine '38 ▶
La Chienne '31 ▶
Lantana '01 ▶
The Last Dance '93
The Last Days of Chez Nous '92
Le Chat '75 ▶
Lea '96
L'Enfer '93 ▶
Leo Tolstoy's Anna Karenina '96
Life During Wartime '09
Linda '93
Little Devil '07
Loulou '80 ▶
A Love Divided '01
The Love Guru '08
Love Matters '93
The Love Parade '29
The Lovers '59 ▶
Lured Innocence '97
Lymelife '08
Mad Love '01
Madame Bovary '91 ▶
Madame Bovary '00
Madame Butterfly '95
Mail Order Wife '04
Man from Nowhere '37
Maneater '09
Marie and Bruce '04
Married Life '07 ▶
Married People, Single Sex 2: For Better or Worse '94
A Matter of Dignity '57
Merrily We Go to Hell '32
Mid-Channel '20
Moon over Harlem '39
Moscow, Belgium '08
Mouth to Mouth '95
Murder Czech Style '66
Murder So Sweet '93
Murders in the Zoo '33
The Music Lovers '71
My Blueberry Nights '07
My First Wife '84
My Foolish Heart '49
My Husband's Double Life '01
The Nanny Diaries '07
Nature's Grave '08
Nevermore '07
Nightkill '80
Nora '00
Normal Life '96
Not Easily Broken '09
Odd Obsession '60
One Trick Pony '80
Out of Order '84
The Painted Veil '34
The Painted Veil '06
A Passion to Kill '94
Payment on Demand '51
Perfect Alibi '94
A Perfect Murder '98
Petulia '68 ▶
Portrait of a Lady '67
Portrait of an Assassin '49
Praying Mantis '93
Private Confessions '98
The Pumpkin Eater '64 ▶
Queen Bee '55
Raise the Red Lantern '91 ▶
Rape and Marriage: The Rideout Case '80
Reversal of Fortune '90 ▶
Revolutionary Road '08
The Rich Man's Wife '96
Romance & Cigarettes '05
Rose of Washington Square '39
A Royal Scandal '96
Savage Attraction '83
Scar of Shame '27
Scenes from a Mall '91
Scenes from a Marriage '73 ▶
Scorchers '92
Second Skin '99
Secret Beyond the Door '48
The Secret Life of Girls '99
Serious Moonlight '09
Seventh Heaven '98
She-Devil '89
Shoot the Moon '82
Silent Victim '92
Sleeping with the Enemy '91
Slippery Slope '06
Smart Woman '31
Snow Angels '07 ▶
Sound of Murder '82
Spring Fever '09
The Stepford Wives '75 ▶
The Stepford Wives '04
The Stone Angel '07
The Stone Merchant '06
The Stoning of Soraya M. '08
Story of a Love Affair '50
The Story of Xinghua '93
Sudden Fear '52 ▶
Suspicion '41 ▶
Suspicion '87
Sylvia '86
Tension '50
Term of Trial '63
The Third '04
Till Murder Do Us Part '92
Tom & Viv '94 ▶
Too Far to Go '79 ▶
Town and Country '01
Twinkletoes '26
Two for the Road '67 ▶
Under Capricorn '49
Under Capricorn '82
Undercurrent '46
Up the Ladder '25
Vacancy '07
A Vow to Kill '94
The War of the Roses '89 ▶
We Don't Live Here Anymore '04
What Happens in Vegas '08
Who's Afraid of Virginia Woolf? '66 ▶
The Widowing of Mrs. Holroyd '95
With a Song in My Heart '52 ▶
Wolf Trap '57
Wuthering Heights '09

Marriages of Convenience

Angelique '64
Between Love & Goodbye '08
Brokeback Mountain '05 ▶
The Crown Prince '06
De-Lovely '04
Fall Guy '82
Flickers '80
The Great McGinty '40 ▶
Green Card '90
Head On '04
Honeymoon '87
I Now Pronounce You Chuck and Larry '07
Kill the Poor '06
Loco Love '03
Lorna's Silence '08
Love for Rent '05
Love or Money '01
Loving Leah '09
Mail Order Wife '04
Never Say Die '39
A Paper Wedding '89 ▶
The Proposal '09
Rachel and the Stranger '48 ▶
Seducing Maarya '99
Tim Burton's Corpse Bride '05 ▶
2 Brothers & a Bride '03
The Wedding Banquet '93 ▶

Mars

***see also** Space Operas*

Abbott and Costello Go to Mars '53
The Angry Red Planet '59
Buck Rogers in the 25th Century '79
Capricorn One '78 ▶
Crimson Force '05
Doom '05
Escape from Mars '99
Flight to Mars '52

▶ = rated three bones or higher

Frankenstein Meets the Space Monster '65
The Invader '96
It! The Terror from Beyond Space '58
John Carpenter's Ghosts of Mars '01
Mars Attacks! '96
The Martian Chronicles: Part 1 '79
The Martian Chronicles: Part 2 '79
The Martian Chronicles: Part 3 '79
Martians Go Home! '90
Mission to Mars '00
My Favorite Martian '98
Planet of Blood '66
Project Shadowchaser 3000 '95
Red Planet '00
Red Planet Mars '52
RocketMan '97
Rocketship X-M '50
Santa Claus Conquers the Martians '64
Species 2 '98
Total Recall '90 ▸
Zombies of the Stratosphere '52

Martial Arts

***see also** Ninjas; Supernatural Martial Arts*

Above the Law '88
Aeon Flux '05
Alley Cat '84
Aloha Summer '88
American Chinatown '96
American Kickboxer 1 '91
American Kickboxer 2: To the Death '93
American Ninja '85
American Ninja 2: The Confrontation '87
American Ninja 3: Blood Hunt '89
American Ninja 4: The Annihilation '91
American Samurai '92
American Shaolin: King of the Kickboxers 2 '92
American Streetfighter '96
The Amsterdam Connection '78
Angel of Fury '93
Angel Town '89
Ashes of Time '94 ▸
Ashes of Time Redux '08
Azumi '03 ▸
Azumi 2 '05
Back in Action '94
Balance of Power '96
Balls of Fury '07
Bells of Death '68
Best of the Best '89
Best of the Best 2 '93
Best of the Best 3: No Turning Back '95
Best of the Best: Without Warning '98
Beverly Hills Ninja '96
The Big Brawl '80
Big Stan '07
Big Trouble in Little China '86
Bionic Ninja '85
Black Belt '92
Black Belt '07
Black Belt Jones '74
Black Eagle '88
Black Mask '96
Black Mask 2: City of Masks '02
Black Samurai '77
Blackbelt 2: Fatal Force '93
Blind Fury '90
Blind Rage '78
Blood for Blood '95
Blood Ring '93
Blood Stained Tradewind '90
Blood Warriors '93
Bloodfist '89
Bloodfist 2 '90
Bloodfist 3: Forced to Fight '92
Bloodfist 4: Die Trying '92
Bloodfist 5: Human Target '93
Bloodfist 6: Ground Zero '94
Bloodfist 7: Manhunt '95
Bloodfist 8: Hard Way Out '96
Bloodmatch '91
Bloodsport '88
Bloodsport 2: The Next Kumite '95
Bloodsport 3 '97
Bloodsport 4: The Dark Kumite '98
The Bodyguard '76
Born Losers '67
Bounty Tracker '93
Braddock: Missing in Action 3 '88
Brain Smasher... A Love Story '93
Breaker! Breaker! '77
Breathing Fire '91
The Bride with White Hair '93
The Bride with White Hair 2 '93
The Bronx Executioner '86
Bruce Lee: Curse of the Dragon '93 ▸
Bruce Lee Fights Back from the Grave '76
Bulletproof Monk '03
The Bushido Blade '80
Cage 2: The Arena of Death '94
Capital Punishment '96
Catch the Heat '87
The Cave of the Silken Web '67
The Challenge '05
Challenge of the Masters '89
Chandni Chowk to China '09
China O'Brien '88
China O'Brien 2 '89
China White '91
The Chinatown Kid '78
Chinese Connection '73
Chinese Connection 2 '77
Circle of Iron '78
The City of Violence '06
Clash of the Ninja '86
Cleopatra Jones '73
Cleopatra Jones & the Casino of Gold '75
Clones of Bruce Lee '80
The Cobra '68
Come Drink with Me '65 ▸
Counter Attack '84
Crack Shadow Boxers '79
Cradle 2 the Grave '03
Crime Story '93
The Crippled Masters '82
Crouching Tiger, Hidden Dragon '00 ▸
Curse of the Golden Flower '06
Cyber Ninja '94
A Dangerous Place '94
Day of the Panther '88
Deadly Bet '91
Deadly Target '94
Death Challenge '80
Death Machines '76
Death Match '94
Death Ring '93
Death Trance '05
Death Warrant '90
Deathfight '93
Desert Kickboxer '92
The Divine Enforcer '91
DOA: Dead or Alive '06
Dolemite '75
Double Dragon '94
Double Impact '91
Dragon Fury '95
Dragon Lord '82
Dragon: The Bruce Lee Story '93 ▸
Dragons Forever '88
Drunken Monkey '02
Duel of Fists '71
Duel to the Death '82
The Dynamite Brothers '74
Dynasty '77
Eagle's Shadow '84
18 Fingers of Death '05
Elektra '05
The Eliminators '86
Enter the Dragon '73 ▸
Enter the Ninja '81
Equal Impact '96
The Executioners '93
Exorcist Master '93
An Eye for an Eye '81
Fantasy Mission Force '84
Fatal Combat '96
Fearless Tiger '94
Ferocious Female Freedom Fighters '88
The Fighter '95
Fighting Black Kings '76
Final Impact '91
Firecracker '81
Firewall '06
Fist of Fear, Touch of Death '80
Fist of Glory '95
Fist of Legend '94
Fist of Steel '93
Fists of Blood '87
Fists of Fury '73 ▸
Fists of Iron '94
Five Element Ninjas '82
Flash Point '07
The Foot Fist Way '08
The Forbidden Kingdom '08
Force of One '79
Force of the Ninja '88
Forced Vengeance '82
Forgotten Warrior '86
Four Robbers '87
Full Contact '93
Full Metal Ninja '89
Futurekick '91
G2: Mortal Conquest '99
The Gambling Samurai '60
Game of Death '79
Gang Justice '94
Gang Wars '75
Ghostwarrior '86
Gladiator Cop: The Swordsman 2 '95
The Glimmer Man '96
Gods of Wu Tang '83
Golden Swallow '68 ▸
Goldfinger '64 ▸
Good Guys Wear Black '78
The Great Challenge '04
Guardian Angel '94
Gymkata '85
Half a Loaf of Kung Fu '78
Hard to Kill '89
Have Sword, Will Travel '69
Hawk's Vengeance '96
Heart of Dragon '85
Heatseeker '95
Heaven & Hell '78
Hero '03 ▸
Hero and the Terror '88
The Heroic Trio '93
Honor '06
Hot Potato '76
House of Flying Daggers '04 ▸
House of Fury '05
House of Traps '81
Human Lanterns '82
Immortal Combat '94
In Your Face '77
The Instructor '83
Invasion U.S.A. '85
Iron Monkey '93
Iron Thunder '89
Ironheart '92
Jackie Chan's First Strike '96 ▸
Jaguar Lives '79
Jet Li's Fearless '06
Jet Li's The Enforcer '95
Joe Somebody '01
Karate Cop '91
The Karate Kid '84 ▸
The Karate Kid '10
The Karate Kid: Part 2 '86
The Karate Kid: Part 3 '89
Karate Warrior '88
Kentucky Fried Movie '77 ▸
The Kick Fighter '91
Kick of Death: The Prodigal Boxer '73
Kickboxer '89
Kickboxer 2: The Road Back '90
Kickboxer 3: The Art of War '92
Kickboxer 4: The Aggressor '94
Kickboxer the Champion '91
Kill and Kill Again '81
Kill Bill Vol. 1 '03 ▸
Kill Bill Vol. 2 '04 ▸
Kill Line '91
Kill or Be Killed '80
Kill Squad '81
Kill the Golden Goose '79
Killer Elephants '76
King Boxer '72
The King of the Kickboxers '91
Kingfisher the Killer '81
Kiss of the Dragon '01
Knights '93
Knock Off '98
The Kumite '03
Kung Fu '72
Kung Fu Hustle '04
Kung Fu Panda '08 ▸
Kung Fu: The Movie '86
Kung Pow! Enter the Fist '02
Lady Dragon '92
Lady Dragon 2 '93
The Last Dragon '85
Last Hurrah for Chivalry '78
Latin Dragon '03
Legacy of Rage '86
The Legend of Drunken Master '94 ▸
Legend of the Liquid Sword '93
The Legend of the 7 Golden Vampires '73
Lethal Ninja '93
Lethal Panther '90
Life Gamble '04
Lionheart '90
Little Dragons '80
Little Ninjas '92
Lone Wolf and Cub '72
Lone Wolf and Cub: Baby Cart at the River Styx '72
Mafia vs. Ninja '84
Magic Kid '92
Magic Kid 2 '94
Magnum Killers '76
Manchurian Avenger '84
Marked for Death '90
Martial Law '90
Martial Law 2: Undercover '91
Martial Outlaw '93
The Master '80
Master of the Flying Guillotine '75
Master with Cracked Fingers '71
Master's Revenge '71
Maximum Risk '96
The Medallion '03
Meltdown '95
The Millionaire's Express '86
Mission of Justice '92
Mr. Nice Guy '98
Mortal Kombat 1: The Movie '95
Mortal Kombat 2: Annihilation '97
The Mosaic Project '95
Moving Target '00
My Samurai '92
Naked Killer '92
Never Back Down '08
New Fist of Fury '76
New York Cop '94
The Next Karate Kid '94
Night Hunter '95
Night Master '87
Night of the Kickfighters '91
Night of the Warrior '91
9 1/2 Ninjas '90
Nine Deaths of the Ninja '85
Ninja 3: The Domination '84
Ninja Academy '90
Ninja: American Warrior '90
Ninja Assassin '09
Ninja Brothers of Blood '89
Ninja Champion '80
Ninja Commandments '87
Ninja Condors '87
Ninja Connection '90
Ninja Death Squad '87
Ninja Destroyer '70
Ninja Fantasy '86
Ninja Hunt '86
Ninja in the U.S.A. '88
Ninja Masters of Death '85
Ninja Mission '84
Ninja of the Magnificence '89
Ninja Operation: Licensed to Terminate '87
Ninja Phantom Heroes '87
Ninja Powerforce '90
Ninja Showdown '90
Ninja Strike Force '88
Ninja the Battalion '90
Ninja, the Violent Sorcerer '86
Ninja Vengeance '93
No Retreat, No Surrender '86
No Retreat, No Surrender 2 '89
No Retreat, No Surrender 3: Blood Brothers '91
Octagon '80
Omega Cop '90
Once Upon a Time in China '91 ▸
Once Upon a Time in China II '92 ▸
Once Upon a Time in China III '93 ▸
The One '01
One Down, Two to Go! '82
One-Eyed Swordsman '63
One Man Army '93
Ong-Bak '03 ▸
Ong Bak 2 '08
Only the Strong '93
Open Fire '94
Operation Condor '91
Operation Golden Phoenix '94
Operation Orient '78
Opium and Kung-Fu Master '84 ▸
Out for Blood '93
Out for Justice '91
Overkill '86
Pay or Die '83
The Perfect Weapon '91
Pit Fighter '05
The Power of the Ninjitsu '88
The Power Within '95
Pray for Death '85
The Princess Blade '02
The Prisoner '90
The Prodigal Son '82
Project A '83
Project A: Part 2 '87
The Promise '05
Protector '85
The Purifiers '04
Pursuit '90
Pushed to the Limit '92
The Quest '96
Rage and Honor '92
Rage and Honor 2: Hostile Takeover '93
Rage of Honor '87
Ragin' Cajun '90
Rapid Fire '92
Raw Force '81
Raw Target '95
The Rebel '08 ▸
Red Sun Rising '94
Redbelt '08 ▸
Redemption: Kickboxer 5 '95
Remo Williams: The Adventure Begins '85
Retrievers '82
Return of the Dragon '73
Return of the Street Fighter '74
Return of the Tiger '78
Revenge of the Ninja '83
Rica '72
Rica 2: Lonely Wanderer '73
Rica 3: Juvenile's Lullaby '73
Ring of Fire '91
Ring of Fire 2: Blood and Steel '92
Ring of Fire 3: Lion Strike '94
Ring of Steel '94
Riot '96
Roller Blade '85
Romeo Must Die '00
Rumble in the Bronx '96
Running on Karma '03
Sanshiro Sugata '43 ▸
Sci-Fighter '04
Scorpion '86
The Shadow Whip '71
Shanghai Knights '03
Shaolin & Wu Tang '81 ▸
Shaolin Soccer '01
The Shepherd: Border Patrol '08
Shogun's Ninja '83
Shootfighter: Fight to the Death '93
Shootfighter 2: Kill or Be Killed! '96
Showdown '93
Showdown in Little Tokyo '91
Sidekicks '93
Silent Assassins '88
Silent Rage '82
Silver Hawk '04
Sister Street Fighter '76
Slaughter in San Francisco '81
Sleepy Eyes of Death: The Chinese Jade '63
Sloane '84
The Spy Next Door '10
Stickfighter '89
The Stranger and the Gunfighter '76
Stranglehold '94
The Street Fighter '74
Street Fighter: The Legend of Chun-Li '09
The Street Fighter's Last Revenge '74
Street Hunter '90
Street Soldiers '91
Super Inframan '76
Supercop '92
Supercop 2 '93
Surf Ninjas '93
Survival Game '87
Sword Masters: Brothers Five '70
Sword Masters: Two Champions of Shaolin '80
Sword of Doom '67 ▸
Sword of Honor '94
Swords of Death '71
Swordsmen in Double Flag Town '91
Sworn to Justice '97
Taken Alive '95
Talons of the Eagle '92
Teenage Mutant Ninja Turtles: The Movie '90
Teenage Mutant Ninja Turtles 2: The Secret of the Ooze '91
Teenage Mutant Ninja Turtles 3 '93
They Call Me Bruce? '82
They Still Call Me Bruce '86
The 36th Chamber of Shaolin '78 ▸
The Three Avengers '80
3 Ninjas '92
3 Ninjas: High Noon at Mega Mountain '97
3 Ninjas Kick Back '94
3 Ninjas Knuckle Up '95
Throw Down '00
Tiger Claws '91
Tiger Heart '96
Tigershark '87
Timecop '94
Timecop 2: The Berlin Decision '03
TNT Jackson '75
To Be the Best '93
To the Death '93
Tokyo Raiders '00 ▸
Tongs: An American Nightmare '88
Top Dog '95
Tough Guy '70
Trancers 3: Deth Lives '92
Triple Impact '92
Tsui Hark's Vampire Hunters '02
Tube '03
24 Hours to Midnight '92
Twin Dragons '92
Twin Warriors '93
The Two Great Cavaliers '73
Ultraviolet '06
Undefeatable '94
Unleashed '05
Unmasking the Idol '86
Vampire Assassin '05
Vampire Effect '03

▸ = rated three bones or higher

Vampire Raiders—Ninja Queen '89
Vengeance is a Golden Blade '69
Versus '00
The Wandering Swordsman '70
Warrior of Justice '96
Warriors of Heaven and Earth '03
The Water Margin '72
Way of the Black Dragon '81
The Way To Fight '96
When Taekwondo Strikes '83
White Phantom: Enemy of Darkness '87
White Tiger '95
Wing Chun '94
Without Mercy '95
The Young Bruce Lee '80
Young Master '80
Young Tiger '74
Zatoichi: Master Ichi and a Chest of Gold '64
Zatoichi: The Blind Swordsman and the Chess Expert '65
Zatoichi: The Blind Swordsman's Vengeance '66
Zatoichi vs. Yojimbo '70 ▶
Zu Warriors '01

Martyred Pop Icons

see also *Rock Stars on Film*
Beatlemania! The Movie '81
Blue Hawaii '62
The Buddy Holly Story '78 ▶
Bus Stop '56 ▶
Clambake '67
The Doors '91
Elvis and Me '88
Elvis: The Movie '79
Fun in Acapulco '63
Highway '01
I Shot Andy Warhol '96 ▶
John & Yoko: A Love Story '85
King Creole '58
Kissin' Cousins '64
La Bamba '87 ▶
Lenny '74 ▶
Live a Little, Love a Little '68
Love Me Tender '56
Marilyn: The Untold Story '80 ▶
Norma Jean and Marilyn '95
Paradise, Hawaiian Style '66
Rebel without a Cause '55 ▶
The Rose '79 ▶
Roustabout '64
Sgt. Pepper's Lonely Hearts Club Band '78
The Seven Year Itch '55 ▶
Speedway '68
Spinout '66
Stardust Memories '80
Stay Away, Joe '68
This Is Elvis '81
Train to Hollywood '86 ▶
The Trouble with Girls (and How to Get into It) '69 ▶

Mass Media

see also *Front Page; Radio*
Against the Law '98
America '86
American Tragedy '00
And Nothing But the Truth '82
The Answer Man '09
At Home with the Webbers '94
The Barefoot Executive '71
Behind the Rising Sun '43
Bigfoot: The Unforgettable Encounter '94
Blankman '94
Breaking News '04
Broadcast Bombshells '95
The Cable Guy '96
A Case of Libel '83
Chill Factor '90
Color of Justice '97
Confetti '06
Crimetime '96
A Cry in the Dark '88 ▶
Dead Men Don't Die '91
Death Watch '80 ▶
Deep Impact '98
Demonstone '89
E. Nick: A Legend in His Own Mind '84
Eternity '90
Exiled to Shanghai '37
The Gladiators '70
Good Night, and Good Luck '05 ▶
The Groove Tube '72
Hero '92 ▶
Holy Man '98
I Was a Teenage TV Terrorist '87
The Image '89
In and Out '97 ▶
Indictment: The McMartin Trial '95 ▶
Intern '00
International House '33
Interview '07 ▶
Jasper, Texas '03
Jiminy Glick in LaLa Wood '05
King of the Airwaves '94
The Last Minute '01
The Late Shift '96
Lions for Lambs '07
Lipstick Camera '93
Little Black Book '04
Live! From Death Row '92
Livin' Large '91
The Lost Honor of Katharina Blum '75 ▶
Love and a .45 '94
Mad City '97
Mastergate '92 ▶
Medium Cool '69 ▶
Meet Wally Sparks '97
Mrs. Doubtfire '93
Mr. Reliable: A True Story '95
My Favorite Year '82 ▶
Naked City: A Killer Christmas '98
National Lampoon's Attack of the 5 Ft. 2 Women '94
Natural Born Killers '94
Network '76 ▶
No Such Thing '01
Nothing Sacred '37 ▶
Orwell Rolls in His Grave '03
Outfoxed: Rupert Murdoch's War on Journalism '04 ▶
The Passenger '75 ▶
Place of Execution '09
Pleasantville '98 ▶
Pray TV '80
Primary Colors '98
Prime Suspect '82
Prime Time Murder '92
Primeval '07
Private Parts '96
Quiz Show '94 ▶
Raising the Heights '97
Ratings Game '84
Ready to Wear '94
Riders of the Storm '88
RKO 281 '99 ▶
Roman Polanski: Wanted and Desired '08
Scream '96 ▶
Scrooged '88
The Second Civil War '97
The Seduction '82
Serving in Silence: The Margarethe Cammermeyer Story '95 ▶
Sex Through a Window '72
S.F.W. '94
Showtime '02
Soft and Hard '85
Stardom '00
The Story of Esther Costello '57
The Stuff '85
Superstar: The Life and Times of Andy Warhol '90 ▶
Tabloid! '88
This Revolution '05
The Thrill of It All! '63
Tomorrow Never Dies '97
Tootsie '82 ▶
Trial by Media '00
The Truman Show '98 ▶
Tunnelvision '76
24 Hour Party People '01
The Ugly Truth '09
UHF '89
Videodrome '83
Wayne's World '92 ▶
Weapons of Mass Distraction '97
Weather Girl '09
Welcome to Sarajevo '97 ▶
Wild Horses '95
Witness to the Execution '94
Zelig '83 ▶

Masseurs

At First Sight '98
Breathtaking '00
Happy Times '00
Living Out Loud '98
Love Kills '98
The Mystic Masseur '01
Never Say Never Again '83
Winter of Frozen Dreams '08

Mathemagicians

Agatha Christie's Murder is Easy '82
The Bank '01
A Beautiful Mind '01 ▶
Beautiful Ohio '06
Breaking the Code '95
The Computer Wore Tennis Shoes '69
Conceiving Ada '97
Cube '98
Dear Brigitte '65
Enigma '01
Fermat's Room '07
Good Will Hunting '97
The Last Enemy '08
Pi '98
Proof '91 ▶
Proof '05 ▶
Rain Man '88 ▶
Raising Genius '04
Real Genius '85 ▶
Sphere '97
Stand and Deliver '88 ▶
Stand-In '37 ▶
21 '08
21 Grams '03 ▶

May-December Romance

see also *Coming of Age; Growing Older; Romantic Adventures; Romantic Comedy; Romantic Drama*
After Sex '97
Agata and the Storm '04
All That Heaven Allows '55 ▶
Atlantic City '81 ▶
Autumn in New York '00
Cass Timberlane '47
The Cat's Meow '01
Cheri '09
The Color of Evening '95
Crush '02
Elegy '08
Fascination '04
Flirting with Forty '09
Forty Shades of Blue '05
The Gang's All Here '43
Georgy Girl '66 ▶
Girl with Green Eyes '64
Girl's Dormitory '36
Goodbye Again '61
The Graduate '67 ▶
Guinevere '99 ▶
Harold and Maude '71 ▶
The Housekeeper '02
The Human Stain '03
I Heart Huckabees '04
Live Bait '95
Lolita '62 ▶
Lolita '97
Love and Pain and the Whole Damn Thing '73
Love in the Afternoon '57
The Love Letter '99
Lured Innocence '97
The Mother '03 ▶
Nelly et Monsieur Arnaud '95 ▶
Our Lady of the Assassins '01
The Pallbearer '95
Paris in Spring '35
Perfect Love '96
Prime '05
P.S. '04
The Quiet American '02 ▶
Reckless '97 ▶
Reckless: The Sequel '98 ▶
Roman Spring of Mrs. Stone '61 ▶
Rumor Has It... '05
Sabrina '54 ▶
Seducing Maarya '99
Shopgirl '05 ▶
Six Days, Seven Nights '98
Slogan '69
Suburban Girl '07
That Obscure Object of Desire '77 ▶
Tim '79
Trojan Eddie '96 ▶
Venus '06 ▶
Whatever Works '09

The Meaning of Life

The Apostle '97 ▶
At Home with the Webbers '94
Being Human '94
The Blood of Others '84
Breathing Lessons '94 ▶
The Castle '68 ▶
The Designated Mourner '97
End of the Road '70
Field of Dreams '89 ▶
The French Lieutenant's Woman '81 ▶
Full Body Massage '95
Funny Face '57 ▶
Galaxies Are Colliding '92
Gospa '94
Heaven Can Wait '43 ▶
Heaven Can Wait '78 ▶
Here Comes Mr. Jordan '41 ▶
The Hitchhiker's Guide to the Galaxy '05 ▶
Joey Breaker '93 ▶
Julian Po '97
Land and Freedom '95 ▶
Life Upside Down '64
Love and Death '75 ▶
Monty Python's The Meaning of Life '83 ▶
My Life '93
My Own Private Idaho '91 ▶
Off the Lip '04
The Razor's Edge '46 ▶
The Razor's Edge '84
The Remains of the Day '93 ▶
Searching For Wooden Watermelons '01
Shadowlands '93 ▶
The Sheltering Sky '90 ▶
Tattoo, a Love Story '02
The Trial '93
Why Has Bodhi-Darma Left for the East '89
Wings of Desire '88 ▶
A Woman's a Helluva Thing '01
Zabriskie Point '70 ▶

Medieval Romps

see also *Camelot (Old); Historical Drama; Period Piece; Swashbucklers*
The Adventures of Marco Polo '38
The Adventures of Robin Hood '38 ▶
Army of Darkness '92 ▶
Beatrice '88 ▶
Becket '64 ▶
Being Human '94
Black Knight '01
The Black Rose '50
Braveheart '95 ▶
Brothers Lionheart '77
Camelot '67
The Canterbury Tales '71
The Castilian '63
A Challenge for Robin Hood '68
Choice of Weapons '76
Chunhyang '00
The Company of Wolves '85 ▶
Conquest of the Normans '62
Crusade: A March through Time '06
Deathstalker '83
Deathstalker 2: Duel of the Titans '87
The Decameron '70 ▶
Decameron Nights '53
Destiny '97
Diane '55
Don Quixote '57 ▶
Don Quixote '00
Donkey Skin '70 ▶
Dragon Storm '04
Dragonheart '96
Dragonheart: A New Beginning '00
Dragonslayer '81 ▶
El Cid '61 ▶
Excalibur '81 ▶
The Fighting Prince of Donegal '66
Fire and Sword '82
First Knight '95
The Flame & the Arrow '50 ▶
Flesh and Blood '85
Francesco '93
Galgameth '96
Gate of Hell '54 ▶
George and the Dragon '04
Hamlet '90 ▶
Hawk and Castile '67
Hawk the Slayer '81
In the Name of the King: A Dungeon Siege Tale '08
Inquisition '76
Ivanhoe '52 ▶
Ivanhoe '82
Ivanhoe '97 ▶
Jabberwocky '77
Jack the Giant Killer '62 ▶
The Juniper Tree '87
Just Visiting '01
King Arthur, the Young Warlord '75
Kingdom of Heaven '05 ▶
A Knight in Camelot '98
Knights of the Round Table '53
A Knight's Tale '01
Kojiro '67 ▶
Kristin Lavransdatter '95
Ladyhawke '85
The Lady's Not for Burning '87
Lancelot of the Lake '74
Legend '86
Leonor '75
The Lion in Winter '68 ▶
The Lion in Winter '03 ▶
Lionheart '87
Magdalene '88
Magic Serpent '66 ▶
The Magic Stone '95
The Magic Sword '62
Mark of the Devil '69
Mark of the Devil 2 '72
Masque of the Red Death '65 ▶
Masque of the Red Death '89
The Mongols '60
Monty Python and the Holy Grail '75 ▶
The Name of the Rose '86
Naughty Knights '71
The Navigator '88 ▶
Omar Khayyam '57
Onibaba '64 ▶
Passion of Joan of Arc '28 ▶
Perceval '78
Pied Piper '72
Pippin '81 ▶
The Prince of Thieves '48
Prince Valiant '97
Princess of Thieves '01
Quest for Camelot '98
Ran '85 ▶
Rashomon '51 ▶
The Return of Martin Guerre '83 ▶
Richard III '55 ▶
Robin and Marian '76
Robin Hood '22 ▶
Robin Hood '73 ▶
Robin Hood '91 ▶
Robin Hood '10
Robin Hood: Men in Tights '93
Robin Hood: Prince of Thieves '91
Robin Hood... The Legend: Herne's Son '85
Robin Hood... The Legend: Robin Hood and the Sorcerer '83
Robin Hood... The Legend: The Swords of Wayland '83
Robin Hood... The Legend: The Time of the Wolf '85
Ruyblas '48
Sansho the Bailiff '54 ▶
The Scalawag Bunch '75
The Secret of El Zorro '57
Seven Samurai '54 ▶
The Seventh Seal '56 ▶
Skullduggery '79
Sorceress '88 ▶
Star Knight '85
Stealing Heaven '88
Sword & the Dragon '56
Sword & the Sorcerer '82
The Sword in the Stone '63 ▶
Sword of Lancelot '63
Sword of Sherwood Forest '60
Sword of the Valiant '83
Tales of Robin Hood '52
Temptation of a Monk '94
Tharus Son of Attila '62
The 13th Warrior '99
Throne of Blood '57 ▶
Time Bandits '81
Time Trackers '88
Timeline '03
Tor '64
Tristan & Isolde '06
The Undead '57
Unidentified Flying Oddball '79
The Vikings '58
The Warrior & the Sorceress '84
Warriors of Heaven and Earth '03
When Knights Were Bold '36
Wholly Moses! '80
Wizards of the Demon Sword '94
Wizards of the Lost Kingdom '85
Young Ivanhoe '95
Young Warlord '75
The Zany Adventures of Robin Hood '84

Meltdown

see also *Disaster Flicks*
Above and Beyond '53 ▶
Access Code '84
Amazing Grace & Chuck '87
American Meltdown '04
The Atomic Cafe '82 ▶
The Atomic Kid '54
Beneath the Planet of the Apes '70
Black Rain '88 ▶
Bloodfist 6: Ground Zero '94
Bomb Squad '97
Bombs Away! '86
Broken Arrow '95
Chain Reaction '80
The China Syndrome '79 ▶
Cloak and Dagger '46
Control '87
Crimson Tide '95 ▶
Critical Mass '00
Cyclotrode "X" '46
Danger Beneath the Sea '02
The Day After '83 ▶
The Day the Earth Caught Fire '61 ▶
The Death Merchant '91
Desert Bloom '86 ▶
Dick Barton Strikes Back '48
Disaster at Silo 7 '88
Dr. Strangelove, or: How I Learned to Stop Worrying and Love the Bomb '64 ▶
Doomsdayer '99
Doomsdayer '01
Enola Gay: The Men, the Mission, the Atomic Bomb '80
Fail-Safe '64 ▶
Fat Man and Little Boy '89
Final Sanction '89
First Spaceship on Venus '60 ▶
First Strike '85
First Yank into Tokyo '45

▶ = rated three bones or higher

Flight of Black Angel '91
The Fourth Protocol '87 ▸
Freedom Strike '98
Full Fathom Five '90
Future Kill '85
Gangland '00
Geisha Girl '52
Glen and Randa '71
Ground Zero '88 ▸
H-Man '59
Hiroshima '95 ▸
Hiroshima Maiden '88
Hiroshima: Out of the Ashes '90 ▸
I Live in Fear '55 ▸
Interceptor Force 2 '02
Invasion U.S.A. '52
Jackie Chan's First Strike '96 ▸
A Man Called Rage '84
The Manhattan Project '86
Massive Retaliation '85
Miracle Mile '89 ▸
Modern Problems '81
Night Siege Project: Shadowchaser 2 '94
Nuclear Conspiracy '85
A Nymphoid Barbarian in Dinosaur Hell '94
Omega Man '71
On the Beach '59 ▸
On the Beach '00
One Night Stand '84 ▸
Panic in the Year Zero! '62
The Patriot '86
The Peacekeeper '98
The Peacemaker '97
Plutonium Incident '82
Prisoner in the Middle '74
Radioactive Dreams '86
Rats '83
Reactor '78
The Reflecting Skin '91
Rhapsody in August '91
Rocket Attack U.S.A. '58
The Sacrifice '86 ▸
Scorcher '02
Seven Days in May '64 ▸
Seven Days to Noon '50
The Shoes of the Fisherman '68
Silkwood '83 ▸
Slugs '87
Southland Tales '06
Special Bulletin '83 ▸
Split Second '53
The Spy Who Loved Me '77
State of Things '82 ▸
Superman 4: The Quest for Peace '87
TC 2000 '93
Testament '83 ▸
This Is Not a Test '62
Threads '85 ▸
True Lies '94
The 27th Day '57
U.S. Seals 2 '01
Universal Soldier: Regeneration '09
Unknown World '51
Utopia '51
Voyage to the Bottom of the Sea '61 ▸
WarGames '83
Warhead '96
When the Wind Blows '86 ▸
The World Is Not Enough '99
Young Lady Chatterly 2 '85

Memphis

see also *American South; Nashville Narratives*

The Blind Side '09
The Client '94
Elvis and Me '88
Elvis: The Movie '79
Finding Graceland '98
The Firm '93 ▸
Forty Shades of Blue '05
Hustle & Flow '05 ▸
John Grisham's The Rainmaker '97
Kill Switch '08
The Loss of a Teardrop Diamond '08
My Blueberry Nights '07
Mystery Train '89 ▸
The Silence of the Lambs '91 ▸
Walk the Line '05 ▸

Men

see also *Dads; Repressed Men; War Between the Sexes*

Bachelor Apartment '31
Beau Brummell: This Charming Man '06
Beefcake '99
The Bible and Gun Club '96
Blades of Glory '07
Brief Interviews With Hideous Men '09
Carnal Knowledge '71 ▸
City Hall '95 ▸
City Slickers '91 ▸
Escanaba in da Moonlight '01
The Full Monty '96 ▸
Good Luck '96
The Hammer '07
Hurlyburly '98
Hustler White '96
In the Company of Men '96
The Incredible Shrinking Man '57 ▸
The Joe McDoakes Collection '42
The King of Kong: A Fistful of Quarters '07 ▸
Kings '07
La Grande Bouffe '73 ▸
Lakeboat '00
The Men's Club '86
Mr. Mom '83 ▸
My Effortless Brilliance '08
90 Days '86 ▸
Patti Rocks '88 ▸
Planet of the Apes '68 ▸
The Promotion '08
Raging Bull '80 ▸
The Saint of Fort Washington '93
School for Scoundrels '06
Sleuth '07
Solitary Man '10
Swingers '96 ▸
Talk to Her '02 ▸
Three Men and a Baby '87 ▸
Three Men and a Cradle '85 ▸
Thursday's Game '74 ▸
Truth or Die '86
Twelve Angry Men '97
Up to a Certain Point '83
Valentino: The Last Emperor '08
Vince Vaughn's Wild West Comedy Show '06
Watch It '93 ▸
When a Man Falls in the Forest '07
Wild Hogs '07
The Wonderful Ice Cream Suit '98
The Young Poisoner's Handbook '94 ▸

Men in Prison

see also *Fugitives; Great Escapes; POW/MIA; Women in Prison*

After Innocence '05 ▸
Against the Wall '94 ▸
Alias, La Gringa '91
All the Pretty Horses '00
American History X '98
American Me '92 ▸
Andersonville '95 ▸
Angels with Dirty Faces '38 ▸
Animal '05
Animal 2 '07
Animal Factory '00
Appointment with Crime '45
Attica '80 ▸
Baba '73 ▸
Bad Boys '83 ▸
Bait '00
Band of the Hand '86
Beaumarchais the Scoundrel '96
Before Night Falls '00 ▸
Beggar's Opera '54
Behind Prison Walls '43
Beyond Re-Animator '03
Beyond the Call '96
Beyond the Walls '84
Big Stan '07
Birdman of Alcatraz '62 ▸
Black Lemons '70
Blind Faith '89
Bloodsport 2: The Next Kumite '95
Bloodsport 4: The Dark Kumite '98
Blow '01
Blues Brothers 2000 '98
The Boston Strangler: The Untold Story '08
Botany Bay '53
Boy's Reformatory '39
The Break '97
Break of Dawn '88
Breaker Morant '80 ▸
Breakout '75
The Brig '64 ▸
Broken Melody '34
Bronson '09
Brubaker '80 ▸
Brute Force '47 ▸
Bundy: A Legacy of Evil '08
Buried Alive '39
Buy & Cell '89
The Cable Guy '96
Caged Heat 2: Stripped of Freedom '94
Caged in Paradiso '89
Call Northside 777 '48 ▸
Captives '94
Carandiru '03
Castle on the Hudson '40 ▸
Catch a Fire '06
Catch Me If You Can '02
Chain Gang Killings '80
The Chair '87
The Chamber '96
Chopper '00
City Without Men '43
Club Fed '90
Colonel Chabert '94
The Color of Freedom '07
Coming Out of the Ice '82 ▸
Con Air '97 ▸
Con Games '02
Condemned '29
Confusion of Genders '00
Convict Cowboy '95
Conviction '02
Cool Hand Luke '67 ▸
The Count of Monte Cristo '12
The Count of Monte Cristo '34 ▸
The Count of Monte Cristo '74
The Count of Monte Cristo '99
The Count of Monte Cristo '02
Crashout '55
Criminal Code '31
Criminal Justice '08
Cry Danger '51 ▸
Dangerous Relations '93
Dante 01 '08
Dark Blue World '01
Darkdrive '98
Dead Man Out '89 ▸
Dead Right '68
Deadlock '91
Deadlock 2 '94
Death House '88
Death Race '08
Death Warrant '90
Deathrow Gameshow '88
The Defiant Ones '58 ▸
Devil's Canyon '53
The Devil's Cargo '48
The Dirty Dozen '67 ▸
The Dirty Dozen: The Deadly Mission '87
The Dirty Dozen: The Fatal Mission '88
The Dirty Dozen: The Next Mission '85
Doin' Time '85
Doing Time '02
Doing Time for Patsy Cline '97
The Domino Principle '77
Double Team '97
Down by Law '86 ▸
Each Dawn I Die '39
Eagles Attack at Dawn '70
Edmond '05
Embassy '72
Empire of the Sun '87 ▸
Ernest Goes to Jail '90
Escape from Alcatraz '79 ▸
Escape from Death Row '73
Escape from DS-3 '81
Escape from El Diablo '83
Escape from New York '81
Execution of Raymond Graham '85
The Executioner's Song '82
The Experiment '01
Face/Off '97 ▸
Fast Walking '82
Felon '08
The Fence '94
The Fiend Who Walked the West '58
First Time Felon '97
The Fixer '68 ▸
Fled '96
Fortress '93
Fortress 2: Re-Entry '99
Framed '75
Freedom Is Paradise '89 ▸
Gang Busters '55
Gideon's Trumpet '80
The Glass House '72 ▸
The Grave '95
The Green Mile '99
Green Street Hooligans 2 '09
Greenfingers '00
Guantanamero '07
Gulag '85
Half-Baked '97
Half Past Dead '02
Hangfire '91
Hard Frame '70
Hard Justice '95
The Hard Word '02
He Got Game '98
Hellgate '52
The Hill '65
Hold 'Em Jail '32
House Across the Bay '40
The Hurricane '99 ▸
I Am a Fugitive from a Chain Gang '32 ▸
I Killed That Man '42
I Love You Phillip Morris '10
In God's Hands '98
In Hell '03
In Hot Pursuit '77
In the Name of the Father '93 ▸
An Innocent Man '89
Inside '96 ▸
Instinct '99
Invasion '65
The Invisible Strangler '76
Jailbreakin' '72
Jailhouse Rock '57 ▸
The Jericho Mile '79
John Carpenter's Ghosts of Mars '01
Johnny Handsome '89 ▸
Kabei: Our Mother '08
Kansas City Confidential '52 ▸
The Keeper '96
Keillers Park '05
Killer: A Journal of Murder '95
The Killing Yard '01
King of the Damned '36
Kiss of the Spider Woman '85 ▸
L'Addition '85
Land of the Blind '06
The Last Castle '01
The Last Detail '73 ▸
The Last Mile '32
Last Rites '98
Le Trou '59 ▸
Leo '02
Les Miserables '95
Les Miserables '97 ▸
A Lesson Before Dying '99 ▸
Let's Go to Prison '06
Life '95
Life '99
The Life of David Gale '03
The Life of Emile Zola '37 ▸
Lilies '96
The Line '80
Little Red Schoolhouse '36
Live Flesh '97 ▸
Live! From Death Row '92
Lock Up '89
Lockdown '00
The Longest Yard '74 ▸
The Longest Yard '05
Lost Highway '96
Lucie Aubrac '98
Lucky Break '01
A Man Escaped '57 ▸
Man of La Mancha '72
The Man Who Broke 1,000 Chains '87
Maximum Security '87
McKenzie Break '70 ▸
McVicar '80
Mean Frank and Crazy Tony '75
Mean Machine '01
Memron '04
Midnight Express '78 ▸
Mrs. Soffel '84
Mr. Frost '89
Monster's Ball '01 ▸
Monte Cristo '22
Moon 44 '90
Most Wanted '97
Murder in the First '95
Mutiny in the Big House '39
My Boys Are Good Boys '78
My Cousin Vinny '92 ▸
New Crime City: Los Angeles 2020 '94
New Eden '94
The New Guy '02
The Night and the Moment '94
The Night Visitor '70
No Escape '94
Ocean's Eleven '01 ▸
Off the Wall '82
On the Yard '79
One Sunday Afternoon '33
Out in Fifty '99
Out of Sight '98 ▸
Papillon '73 ▸
Pardon Us '31
Payback '94
Penitentiary '79
Penitentiary 2 '82
Penitentiary 3 '87
Phantom Empire '87
Pressure Point '62 ▸
Prison '88
Prison Break '38
Prison on Fire '87
Prison on Fire 2 '91
Prison Planet '92
Prison Train '38
The Prisoner '90
Prisoner '07
The Prisoner of Shark Island '36
The Prisoner of Zenda '22
A Prophet '09 ▸
Pros & Cons '99
Proximity '00
The Pursuit of Happiness '70
The Quare Fellow '62
Real Bullets '90
Red Dragon '02
Redeemer '02
Return to Paradise '98 ▸
Ring of Death '08
Riot '69
Riot in Cell Block 11 '54 ▸
The Road to Guantanamo '06
The Rock '96 ▸
Runaway Train '85 ▸
Sade '00
St. Michael Had a Rooster '72
Samar '62
San Quentin '37
The Santa Trap '02
Say It With Songs '29
Scum '79 ▸
A Sense of Freedom '78 ▸
The Shawshank Redemption '94 ▸
Shoeshine '47 ▸
Shooting Fish '98
Short Eyes '79 ▸
Shot in the Heart '01 ▸
Six: The Mark Unleashed '04
Slam '98
Slaughterhouse Rock '88
A Slipping Down Life '99
Some Mother's Son '96 ▸
Soul Vengeance '75
Space Rage '86
Spy Game '01
Standard Operating Procedure '08 ▸
Steel City '06
Stir Crazy '80
Sullivan's Travels '41 ▸
The Survivor '98
Taking Care of Business '90
Tank '83
Tempest '28
Terminal Island '73
Terror of the Bloodhunters '62
Terror on Alcatraz '86
There Was a Crooked Man '70 ▸
There's Something about Mary '98 ▸
They Never Come Back '32
They Went That-a-Way & That-a-Way '78
Three Monkeys '08
Timelock '99
Tomb of the Undead '72
Torture Ship '39
Tracked '98
Tracks '05
Trading Places '83
Traitor '08
Triumph of the Spirit '89 ▸
The Truce '96 ▸
True Crime '99
Truth or Die '86
20,000 Years in Sing Sing '33
Two-Way Stretch '60
Ulee's Gold '97 ▸
Undisputed '02
Undisputed II: Last Man Standing '06
Unshackled '00
Up the River '30
The Valachi Papers '72
The Visit '00 ▸
Warden of Red Rock '01
Weeds '87 ▸
Who is Cletis Tout? '02
William Faulkner's Old Man '97
Wishmaster 2: Evil Never Dies '98
Without Evidence '96
Women's Prison Massacre '85
XXX: State of the Union '05
Yol '82 ▸

Mental Hospitals

see also *Doctors & Nurses; Sanity Check; Shrinks*

Adam Resurrected '08
Asylum '05
Beyond the Wall of Sleep '06
Boogeyman 2 '07
Choke '08
Crazy as Hell '02
Crazylove '05
Elling '01
Final '01
Frayed '07
Girl, Interrupted '99
Gothika '03
Halloween: Resurrection '02
Happy Hell Night '92
House of Fools '02
Insanitarium '08
The Jacket '05
Killer Instinct '00
Kings and Queen '04 ▸
Kisses in the Dark '97
The Lazarus Project '08
A Light in the Darkness '02
A Love to Keep '07
Madhouse '04
Manic '01
Murder Without Conviction '04
Nothing to Lose '08
On the Edge '00
Opium: Diary of a Madwoman '07
Reprise '06
Revolution 9 '01
Screaming Dead '03
Session 9 '01

▸ = rated three bones or higher

▸ = rated three bones or higher

Ishtar '87
Jarhead '05
The Jewel of the Nile '85
Joseph '95
Kandahar '01
The Keeper: The Legend of Omar Khayyam '05
Khartoum '66
Killing Streets '91
King Richard and the Crusaders '54
The Kingdom '07
Land of Plenty '04
Lawrence of Arabia '62 ▸
Lebanon '09
Legend of the Lost Tomb '97
Leila '97
Lemon Tree '08
Life and Nothing More ... '92
The Lighthorsemen '87 ▸
The Lone Runner '88
Looking for Comedy in the Muslim World '06
Marooned in Iraq '02
A Matter of WHO '62
Mercenary '96
A Mighty Heart '07 ▸
Moses '96
The Nativity Story '06
The Objective '08
Occupation: Dreamland '05 ▸
Orde Wingate '76
Osama '03 ▸
Our Music '04
Paradise '82
Paradise Now '05 ▸
Passion in the Desert '97
The Passion of the Christ '04 ▸
Peace, Propaganda & the Promised Land '04
Raiders of the Lost Ark '81 ▸
The Road to Guantanamo '06
The Road to Morocco '42 ▸
The Robe '53
Rosebud '75
Sadat '83
The Sheik '21 ▸
The Silences of the Palace '94 ▸
Silent Waters '03
Sirocco '51
Son of Ali Baba '52
Spartan '04 ▸
The Spy Who Loved Me '77
Steel Sharks '97
Surface to Air '98
Syriana '05 ▸
Team America: World Police '04 ▸
Through the Olive Trees '94 ▸
The Tiger and the Snow '05
Torn Apart '89
Traitor '08
Trident Force '88
Turtles Can Fly '04 ▸
Uncovered: The War on Iraq '04
Under the Bombs '07
Unveiled '94
Voices of Iraq '04 ▸
Wall '04 ▸
Waltz with Bashir '08 ▸
War, Inc. '08
The War Within '05
Warbirds '88
A Wedding in Galilee '87 ▸
West Beirut '98
Yellow Asphalt '01

Midlife Crisis

***see also** Adultery; Growing Older; Strained Suburbia*

American Beauty '99 ▸
The Babysitters '07
Being Julia '04 ▸
The Black Marble '79 ▸
Bob Funk '09
Box of Moonlight '96
Broken Flowers '05
City Slickers '91 ▸
Cyrus '10
Eat, Pray, Love '10
Edmond '05
Falling in Love Again '80
Fashion Victims '07
Flying By '09
Fortunes '05
Full Moon in Blue Water '88
The Hammer '07
Hello Goodbye '08
I Love You, Alice B. Toklas! '68
I Think I Love My Wife '07
It's Complicated '09
King of the Corner '04 ▸
Kings '07
L'Ennui '98
Loving '70
The Man of My Life '06
The Matador '06 ▸
Meet Bill '07
Milk and Honey '03
Nights in Rodanthe '08
Notre Histoire '84
On a Clear Day '05
The Savages '07 ▸
Shall We Dance? '04
Shirley Valentine '89 ▸
Sideways '04 ▸
States of Control '98
Step Brothers '08
The Tempest '82 ▸
35 Shots of Rum '08
Two Tickets to Paradise '06
Up in the Air '09 ▸
Vincent, Francois, Paul and the Others '76 ▸
The Weather Man '05
When a Man Falls in the Forest '07
When Did You Last See Your Father? '07
Whole New Thing '05
Wild Hogs '07
Wonderful World '09

Military: Air Force

***see also** Airborne*

Afterburn '92 ▸
Air Force '43 ▸
Battle Hymn '57
Black Thunder '98
Bombers B-52 '57
Call to Glory '84
Desert Thunder '99
God is My Co-Pilot '45
The Haunted Airman '06
Hot Shots! '91 ▸
Hot Shots! Part Deux '93
Mach 2 '00
McHale's Navy Joins the Air Force '65
Memphis Belle '90 ▸
Operation Haylift '50
The Pentagon Wars '98
Rally 'Round the Flag, Boys! '58
Rescue Dawn '06 ▸
Sergeant Matlovich vs. the U.S. Air Force '78
Space Cowboys '00 ▸
Starlift '51
Storm Catcher '99
Strategic Air Command '55
Tactical Assault '99
Terminator 3: Rise of the Machines '03 ▸
Terror Street '54
Valiant '05
War Lover '62

Military: Army

Active Stealth '99
After the Rain '99
American Soldiers '05
Band of Brothers '01 ▸
The Base '99
Basic '03
Battle of the Bulge '65
Battle of the Commandos '71
Behind the Lines '97
The Better 'Ole '26
Big Bear '98
The Big Red One '80 ▸
Big Steal '49 ▸
Black Hawk Down '01 ▸
Bloody Sunday '01 ▸
Buffalo Soldiers '97 ▸
Buffalo Soldiers '01
Call Out the Marines '42
Casualties of War '89 ▸
Chaos Factor '00
Combat Killers '68
The Command '54
Courage Under Fire '96 ▸
The Court Martial of Billy Mitchell '55 ▸
The Court Martial of Jackie Robinson '90 ▸
The Crossing '00
Dead Men Can't Dance '97
Deadly Game '77
Dear John '10
D.I. '57
The Dirty Dozen '67 ▸
The Dirty Dozen: The Deadly Mission '87
The Dirty Dozen: The Fatal Mission '88
The Dirty Dozen: The Next Mission '85
A Distant Trumpet '64
Dondi '61
The Duchess of Buffalo '26
Elvira Madigan '67 ▸
Ernest in the Army '97
Evolution '01
Fatal Error '99
Fatal Vision '84
The Fighting Eagle '27
Florence Nightingale '85
Florence Nightingale '08
A Foreign Affair '48 ▸
Francis Joins the WACs '54
The Gay Deceivers '69
The General's Daughter '99
Geronimo: An American Legend '93
Gettysburg '93 ▸
G.I. Blues '60
G.I. Joe: The Rise of Cobra '09
Gods and Generals '03
Godzilla '98
The Good German '06
The Great Raid '05
The Green Berets '68
Hart's War '02
Hellgate '52
Home of the Brave '06
The Hunt for Eagle One: Crash Point '06
The Hunted '03
The Hurt Locker '08 ▸
Ignition '01
In Pursuit of Honor '95
In the Army Now '94
In the Valley of Elah '07 ▸
Independence Day '96 ▸
Invasion of the Star Creatures '63
The Last Castle '01
Lost Battalion '01
The Lucky Ones '08
MacArthur '77
The Major and the Minor '42 ▸
M*A*S*H '70 ▸
M*A*S*H: Goodbye, Farewell & Amen '83 ▸
The Men Who Stare at Goats '09
The Messenger '09 ▸
A Midnight Clear '92 ▸
Military Intelligence and You! '06
The Missing '03 ▸
Never Wave at a WAC '52
New World '95
1915 '82
1941 '79
Occupation: Dreamland '05 ▸
One Little Indian '73
One Man's Hero '98
Only the Brave '06
Operation Dumbo Drop '95
Operation Mad Ball '57
Operation Valkyrie '04
Organizm '08
Pandemic '09
Patton '70 ▸
The Peacemaker '97
The Perfect Furlough '59
Platoon '86 ▸
Platoon Leader '87
Private Benjamin '80
Rage '72
Rangers '00
Ravenous '99
The Red Raiders '27
Red Salute '35
Red Sands '09
Redacted '07
Restrepo '10
Saving Private Ryan '98 ▸
The Sergeant '68
Serving in Silence: The Margarethe Cammermeyer Story '95 ▸
The Siege '98
Slayer '06
Soldier '98
Soldier's Girl '03 ▸
A Soldier's Story '84 ▸
Something for the Boys '44
Special Forces '03
Spirit: Stallion of the Cimarron '02
Spring Parade '40
Standard Operating Procedure '08 ▸
Starship Troopers '97 ▸
Steel '97
Stop-Loss '08 ▸
The Story of a Three Day Pass '68
The Story of G.I. Joe '45 ▸
Stripes '81
Taking Sides '01 ▸
Taxi to the Dark Side '07 ▸
The Thin Red Line '64
The Thin Red Line '98 ▸
Three Kings '99 ▸
Tigerland '00 ▸
The Tillman Story '10
To End All Wars '01
Tomahawk '51
Top Secret Affair '57
Transformers: Revenge of the Fallen '09
The Trench '99
Tunnel Rats '08
28 Days Later '02
28 Weeks Later '07
UKM: The Ultimate Killing Machine '06
Wackiest Ship in the Army '61
The Wall '99 ▸
Waterloo Road '44
We'll Meet Again '82
West Point '27
Westbound '58
When Trumpets Fade '98
When Willie Comes Marching Home '50 ▸
X-Men Origins: Wolverine '09
X2: X-Men United '03 ▸
XXX: State of the Union '05
Yossi & Jagger '02

Military Comedy

***see also** Comedy; War, General*

Abbott and Costello in the Foreign Legion '50
Abroad with Two Yanks '44
Article 99 '92
As You Were '51
At War with the Army '50
The Baby and the Battleship '56
Basic Training '86
Best Defense '84
Best Foot Forward '43
Biloxi Blues '88
Black and White in Color '76 ▸
The Captain from Koepenick '56
Carbide and Sorrel '63
Caught in the Draft '41 ▸
Chesty Anderson USN '76
Clipped Wings '53
Combat Academy '86
Delta Farce '07
Don't Go Near the Water '57
Down Periscope '96
Ensign Pulver '64
Ernest in the Army '97
The Fighting Eagle '27
The Flying Deuces '39 ▸
Follow That Camel '67
Follow the Leader '44
Francis Goes to West Point '52
Francis in the Navy '55
Francis Joins the WACs '54
The Gendarme of Saint-Tropez '64
Getting Wasted '80
G.I. Blues '60
G.I. Jane '51
Going Under '91
Here Come the Marines '52
Hillbilly Blitzkrieg '42
Hot Shots! '91 ▸
Hot Shots! Part Deux '93
In the Army Now '94
Jumping Jacks '52
Leave It to the Marines '51
Major Payne '95
A Man Called Sarge '90
M*A*S*H '70 ▸
M*A*S*H: Goodbye, Farewell & Amen '83 ▸
McHale's Navy '64
McHale's Navy '97
McHale's Navy Joins the Air Force '65
Military Intelligence and You! '06
Miracle of Morgan's Creek '44 ▸
Mr. Walkie Talkie '52
The Mouse That Roared '59 ▸
Never Wave at a WAC '52
1941 '79
No Time for Sergeants '58 ▸
The Odd Squad '86
Off Limits '53
Operation Dames '59
Operation Mad Ball '57
The Perfect Furlough '59
Private Benjamin '80
Private Manoeuvres '83
Private Navy of Sgt. O'Farrell '68
Private Valentine: Blonde & Dangerous '08
The Private War of Major Benson '55
Privates on Parade '84
Renaissance Man '94
The Sad Sack '57
Sgt. Bilko '95
She's in the Army Now '81
Snuffy Smith, Yard Bird '42
Soldier in the Rain '63
The Square Peg '58
Stripes '81
Suppose They Gave a War and Nobody Came? '70
Tanks a Million '41
Three Legionnaires '37
23 1/2 Hours Leave '37
The Virgin Soldiers '69
Viva Max '69
Weekend Pass '84
Weekend Warriors '86
We're in the Legion Now '37
We're in the Navy Now '27
The West Point Story '50

Military Crimes & Trials

***see also** Foreign Intrigue; Military: Air Force; Military: Army; Military Comedy; Military: Foreign; Military: Marines; Military: Navy; Order in the Court*

Buffalo Soldiers '01
The Caine Mutiny '54 ▸
The Caine Mutiny Court Martial '88 ▸
Carrington, V.C. '54 ▸
Casualties of War '89 ▸
The Clay Pigeon '49
The Court Martial of Billy Mitchell '55 ▸
The Court Martial of Jackie Robinson '90 ▸
A Few Good Men '92 ▸
A Glimpse of Hell '01
Hart's War '02
High Crimes '02
The Hill '65
Ignition '01
The Last Castle '01
One Kill '00 ▸
Paths of Glory '57 ▸
Rules of Engagement '00
A Rumor of War '80 ▸
Sergeant Matlovich vs. the U.S. Air Force '78
Sergeant Rutledge '60 ▸
South Sea Woman '53
Under the Flag of the Rising Sun '72 ▸

Military: Foreign

The Adventures of Werner Holt '65
All Quiet on the Western Front '30 ▸
All Quiet on the Western Front '79
All the King's Men '99
Ambush '99 ▸
The Ascent '76 ▸
Atonement '07 ▸
Battle of Britain '69
The Beast '88
Beaufort '07 ▸
Bees in Paradise '44
Black and White in Color '76 ▸
Breaker Morant '80 ▸
The Brylcreem Boys '96
Captain Corelli's Mandolin '01
Captains of the Clouds '42
Captive Heart '47 ▸
Carry On Sergeant '58
Carry On Up the Khyber '68
The Charge of the Light Brigade '36 ▸
The Charge of the Light Brigade '68
The Cuckoo '02
Cup Final '92
Das Boot '81 ▸
Days of Glory '06
The Devil Is a Woman '35 ▸
Devils on the Doorstep '00
Die Another Day '02
Dog Soldiers '01
Doomsday '08
Dresden '06
The Duchess of Langeais '07 ▸
Eagles Over London '69
Enemy at the Gates '00
Escape from Sobibor '87 ▸
The Fighting Rats of Tobruk '44
Five Cartridges '60
Five Graves to Cairo '43 ▸
Flags of Our Fathers '06 ▸
Flanders '06
For the Moment '94
The Four Feathers '02
Gallipoli '81 ▸
The Hasty Heart '86
The Hill '65
Hostile Waters '97
The Hunt for Red October '90 ▸
I Was Nineteen '68
I'll Remember April '99
In Which We Serve '43 ▸
An Indecent Obsession '85
The Indian Tomb '21
The Informant '97 ▸
Katyn '07
King and Country '64 ▸
Kippur '00 ▸
Lagaan: Once upon a Time in India '01
The Last Lieutenant '94
The Last Outpost '35
The Last September '99
Lebanon '09
Lemon Tree '08
Letters from Iwo Jima '06 ▸
The Lighthorsemen '87 ▸
Madame Sans-Gene '62
The Marquise of O '76
The Milky Way '97
Mister Drake's Duck '50
Night of the Generals '67 ▸
No Man's Land '01
100 Days Before the Command '90
The One That Got Away '96
Passion in the Desert '97
Passion of Love '82 ▸
Pretty Village, Pretty Flame '96 ▸
Prisoner of the Mountains '96 ▸
Savior '98 ▸
The Scarlet Tunic '97
Sharpe's Challenge '06
633 Squadron '64
Soldier of Orange '78 ▸
Stairway to Heaven '46 ▸
Stalingrad '94

Story of a Prostitute *'65*
Sword of Honour *'01*
Tempest *'28*
The 300 Spartans *'62*
The 317th Platoon *'65* ▸
Time of Favor *'00*
To End All Wars *'01*
Traffic *'00* ▸
Troubles *'88*
Two Men Went to War *'02*
The Unknown Soldier *'98*
Victory at Entebbe *'76*
Waltz with Bashir *'08* ▸
Warriors *'02*
The Water Horse: Legend of the Deep *'07*
White Badge *'97*
The Widow of Saint-Pierre *'00* ▸
The Wind That Shakes the Barley *'06* ▸
A Woman in Berlin *'08*
Woyzeck *'78* ▸
Wozzeck *'47*
Zafarinas *'94*
Zone 39 *'96*

Military: Marines

American Son *'08*
Annapolis *'06*
Back to Bataan *'45*
Bataan *'43*
Battle Cry *'55* ▸
Black Ops *'07*
Brothers *'09*
Dangerous Evidence: The Lori Jackson Story *'99*
Death Before Dishonor *'87*
Doom *'05*
A Few Good Men *'92* ▸
Flags of Our Fathers *'06* ▸
Flying Leathernecks *'51* ▸
Full Metal Jacket *'87* ▸
Generation Kill *'08* ▸
Guadalcanal Diary *'43*
The Halls of Montezuma *'50*
Heartbreak Ridge *'86* ▸
High Crimes *'02*
Jarhead *'05*
Leprechaun 4: In Space *'96*
The Marine *'06*
The Marine 2 *'09*
Most Wanted *'97*
One Kill *'00* ▸
Perfect Crime *'97*
Platoon *'86* ▸
Pork Chop Hill *'59* ▸
Pride of the Marines *'45* ▸
Purple Heart *'05*
Quicksand *'01*
The Real Glory *'39* ▸
The Rock *'96* ▸
Rules of Engagement *'00*
Sand Serpents *'09*
Sands of Iwo Jima *'49* ▸
Second in Command *'05*
The Siege of Firebase Gloria *'89*
Sniper 2 *'02*
South Sea Woman *'53*
Spartan *'04* ▸
Stateside *'04*
Surface to Air *'98*
Taking Chance *'09*
The Walking Dead *'94*
The Wind and the Lion *'75* ▸
Windtalkers *'02*

Military: Navy

***see also** Sail Away*
Agent Red *'00*
Anchors Aweigh *'45* ▸
Annapolis *'28*
Annapolis *'06*
An Annapolis Story *'55*
Antwone Fisher *'02* ▸
Behind Enemy Lines *'01*
Behind Enemy Lines 2: Axis of Evil *'06*
Behind Enemy Lines 3: Colombia *'08*
Black Ops *'07*
The Bridges at Toko-Ri *'55* ▸
The Caine Mutiny *'54* ▸
Chasers *'94*
Common Ground *'00*
Crimson Tide *'95* ▸
The Crowded Sky *'60*
Danger Beneath the Sea *'02*
David Harding, Counterspy *'50*
Depth Charge *'08*
Dive Bomber *'41* ▸
The Divine Lady *'29*
Down Periscope *'96*
Enemy Below *'57* ▸
A Few Good Men *'92* ▸
Fighting Seabees *'44*
The Fighting Sullivans *'42* ▸
Flags of Our Fathers *'06* ▸
Francis in the Navy *'55*
Freedom Strike *'98*
The Gallant Hours *'60* ▸
G.I. Jane *'97*
A Glimpse of Hell *'01*
Hellcats of the Navy *'57*
Here Come the Waves *'45* ▸
The Honeymoon Machine *'61*
Horatio Hornblower *'99* ▸
Horatio Hornblower: The Adventure Continues *'01* ▸
Hostile Waters *'97*
The Hunt for Red October *'90* ▸
In Love and War *'91*
John Paul Jones *'59*
The King *'05*
The Last Detail *'73* ▸
The Man Without a Country *'73* ▸
Master and Commander: The Far Side of the World *'03* ▸
McHale's Navy *'64*
McHale's Navy *'97*
McHale's Navy Joins the Air Force *'65*
Men of Honor *'00*
Mission of the Shark *'91* ▸
Mister Roberts *'55* ▸
Moment to Moment *'66*
Mutiny *'99*
Navy Blue and Gold *'37*
The Navy Comes Through *'42*
Navy SEALS *'90*
Navy vs. the Night Monsters *'66*
Navy Way *'44*
No Man Is an Island *'62*
No Way Out *'87* ▸
An Officer and a Gentleman *'82* ▸
On the Town *'49* ▸
Operation Bikini *'63*
Operation Petticoat *'59* ▸
The Pacifier *'05*
Pearl *'78*
Pearl Harbor *'01*
Perfect Crime *'97*
Private Navy of Sgt. O'Farrell *'68*
PT 109 *'63*
Rodgers & Hammerstein's South Pacific *'01*
Run Silent, Run Deep *'58* ▸
Sabotage *'96*
Sailor Beware *'52*
Sailor of the King *'53*
The Sand Pebbles *'66* ▸
Seas Beneath *'31*
The Sender *'98*
Shadow Warriors *'97*
Shipmates Forever *'35*
Silent Venom *'08*
Skirts Ahoy! *'52*
South Pacific *'58* ▸
Stateside *'04*
Stealth *'05*
Stealth Fighter *'99*
Steel Sharks *'97*
Submerged *'00*
Surface to Air *'98*
Tears of the Sun *'03*
They Were Expendable *'45* ▸
Three Sailors and a Girl *'53*
Top Gun *'86*
True Vengeance *'97*
U-571 *'00*
Under Siege *'92*
U.S. Navy SEALS: Dead or Alive *'02*
U.S. Seals *'98*
U.S. Seals 2 *'01*
U.S. SEALs: Dead or Alive *'02*
Wolverine *'96*
XXX: State of the Union *'05*
Yankee Buccaneer *'52*

Military School

Child's Play 3 *'91*
Damien: Omen 2 *'78*
Dress Gray *'86* ▸
Dress Parade *'27*
Evilspeak *'82*
Junior Army *'42*
The Long Gray Line *'55* ▸
The Lords of Discipline *'83*
The Major and the Minor *'42* ▸
Major Payne *'95*
The Private War of Major Benson *'55*
Renaissance Man *'94*
Taps *'81*
Toy Soldiers *'84*
Up the Academy *'80*

Military Westerns

***see also** Military: Army; Westerns*
The Alamo *'60* ▸
Bugles in the Afternoon *'52*
Cavalry Charge *'51*
Cavalry Command *'63*
The Command *'54*
A Distant Trumpet *'64*
Escape from Fort Bravo *'53*
The Glory Trail *'36*
Hawmps! *'76*
Hellgate *'52*
Hondo *'53* ▸
The Horse Soldiers *'59*
In Pursuit of Honor *'95*
Pharoah's Army *'95*
The Red Raiders *'27*
Rio Grande *'50* ▸
Sergeant Rutledge *'60* ▸
Sergeants 3 *'62*
She Wore a Yellow Ribbon *'49* ▸
Shenandoah *'65* ▸
Soldier Blue *'70*
They Died with Their Boots On *'41* ▸
Virginia City *'40* ▸
Westbound *'58*

Milwaukee

***see also** Romantic Mystery*
American Movie *'99* ▸
BASEketball *'98*
Dawn of the Dead *'04* ▸
Ed's Next Move *'96*
The Giant Spider Invasion *'75*
Mr. 3000 *'04*

Miners & Mining

Ace in the Hole *'51* ▸
Act of Vengeance *'86*
The Adventures of Bullwhip Griffin *'66*
Angels Die Hard *'70*
Backlash: Oblivion 2 *'95*
The Badlanders *'58*
Ballad of Cable Hogue *'70* ▸
Barricade *'49*
The Big Man: Crossing the Line *'91* ▸
Billy Elliot *'00* ▸
Black Fury *'35* ▸
Blood Diamond *'06*
Brassed Off *'96*
Burning Rage *'84*
Cannibal! The Musical *'96*
Chained Heat 3: Hell Mountain *'98*
Challenge to White Fang *'86*
The Christmas Coal Mine Miracle *'77*
The Claim *'00*
Coal Miner's Daughter *'80* ▸
The Corn Is Green *'79* ▸
Dear Wendy *'05*
The Dude Goes West *'48*
Dudley Do-Right *'99*
Eureka Stockade *'49*
Fighting Cowboy *'33*
Fighting Valley *'43*
Fire Down Below *'97*
Flaming Frontiers *'38*
Gangster's Den *'45*
Gangsters of the Frontier *'44*
Garden of Evil *'54*
Germinal *'93* ▸
Ghost Town Renegades *'47*
Girl Rush *'44*
Goldrush: A Real Life Alaskan Adventure *'98*
Grand Canyon Trail *'48*
Green Fire *'55*
The Hallelujah Trail *'65*
Harlan County, U.S.A. *'76* ▸
Harlan County War *'00*
Haunted Gold *'32*
Hills of Utah *'51*
How Green Was My Valley *'41* ▸
Human Hearts *'22*
Jack London's The Call of the Wild *'97*
The Jackals *'67*
Kameradschaft *'31* ▸
King Solomon's Mines *'85*
Little Church Around the Corner *'23*
Lucky Texan *'34*
The Man from Music Mountain *'38*
Margaret's Museum *'95* ▸
Matewan *'87* ▸
McCabe & Mrs. Miller *'71* ▸
Molly Maguires *'70*
Moon *'09*
Naked Hills *'56*
'Neath Canadian Skies *'46*
No Man's Law *'27*
North Country *'05*
North Star *'96*
North to Alaska *'60* ▸
The Nugget *'02*
October Sky *'99* ▸
Out of the Black *'01*
Paint Your Wagon *'69*
Pale Rider *'85* ▸
Panama Flo *'32*
Phantom Gold *'38*
Picture Windows *'95*
Poldark *'75* ▸
Poldark *'96*
Poldark 2 *'75* ▸
Precious Find *'96*
The Rainbow Gang *'73*
Re-Generation *'04*
Red Earth *'82*
Rider from Tucson *'50*
The Rider of Death Valley *'32*
The Rundown *'03*
The Ruthless Four *'70*
Salt of the Earth *'54* ▸
Sands of Sacrifice *'21*
Silver Bandit *'50*
Smilla's Sense of Snow *'96*
Solomon and Gaenor *'98*
The Spoilers *'42* ▸
The Stars Look Down *'39* ▸
The Strangeness *'85*
The Trail of '98 *'28*
Wanda Nevada *'79*
The War Wagon *'67* ▸
Way Out West *'37* ▸
Where the Green Ants Dream *'84*
Where Trails End *'42*
The Widowing of Mrs. Holroyd *'95*
Wildrose *'85* ▸
Within the Rock *'96*
Xica *'76* ▸

Minnesota

Aurora Borealis *'06*
Beautiful Girls *'96* ▸
D3: The Mighty Ducks *'96*
D2: The Mighty Ducks *'94*
The Emigrants *'72* ▸
Far North *'88*
Fargo *'96* ▸
Feeling Minnesota *'96*
The Good Son *'93*
Grace Is Gone *'07* ▸
Graffiti Bridge *'90*
The Great Northfield Minnesota Raid *'72*
Grumpier Old Men *'95*
Grumpy Old Men *'93* ▸
The Heartbreak Kid *'72* ▸
Ice Castles *'79*
Into Temptation *'09*
Iron Will *'93*
Jingle All the Way *'96*
Joe Somebody *'01*
Leatherheads *'08*
Little Big League *'94*
A Little Trip to Heaven *'05*
The Long Riders *'80* ▸
The Mighty Ducks *'92*
Milwaukee, Minnesota *'03*
New in Town *'09*
The New Land *'73* ▸
North Country *'05*
Patti Rocks *'88* ▸
The Personals *'83*
A Prairie Home Companion *'06*
Purple Rain *'84*
A Serious Man *'09* ▸
A Simple Plan *'98* ▸
Slaughterhouse Five *'72*
That Was Then... This Is Now *'85*
Untamed Heart *'93*
Wildrose *'85* ▸

Missing Persons

***see also** Hostage!; Kidnapped!*
Abandon *'02*
Abandoned *'47*
Adam *'83* ▸
Agatha *'79*
Agatha Christie: A Life in Pictures *'04*
All Good Things *'09*
Almost Human *'79*
American Nightmare *'81*
Anastasia *'56* ▸
Anastasia: The Mystery of Anna *'86*
AngKor: Cambodia Express *'81*
Arc *'06*
Assassination in Rome *'65*
Between *'05*
Big Jake *'71*
Blind Eye *'06*
Bloodstream *'00*
The Bravos *'72*
Breakdown *'96* ▸
Bureau of Missing Persons *'33*
Cavalcade of the West *'36*
Chain of Souls *'00*
Changeling *'08* ▸
Chasing Sleep *'00*
Christina *'74*
Coming Out Alive *'84*
Conspiracy *'08*
The Crow Road *'96*
The Cry: La Llorona *'07*
Curse of the Pink Panther *'83*
Dangerous Crossing *'53*
Dark World *'08*
Direct Contact *'09*
Disappearance *'81*
The Disappeared *'08*
Dying Room Only *'73*
The Emerald Forest *'85* ▸
Empire State *'87*
The Empty Acre *'07*
The Empty Beach *'85*
Equinox *'71* ▸
Escapade in Japan *'57*
Experiment in Terror *'62* ▸
Eye Witness *'49*
Final Cut *'88*
Five Days *'07*
The Flock *'07*
Foxtrap *'85*
Frantic *'88* ▸
Freedomland *'06*
From Hollywood to Deadwood *'89*
Get a Clue *'02*
Girl Hunters *'63*
The Girl With the Dragon Tattoo *'09* ▸
Give Me Your Hand *'09*
Gone Baby Gone *'07* ▸
The Good German *'06*
The Good Student *'08*
Grayeagle *'77*
Green Eyes *'76* ▸
Grievous Bodily Harm *'89*
The Hangover *'09*
Harem *'85*
Harper *'66* ▸
Harrison's Flowers *'02*
Heading for Heaven *'47*
Hell Squad *'85*
Hide in Plain Sight *'80* ▸
High Road to China *'83*
The Hit List *'88*
Hogfather *'06*
Hollywood Chaos *'89*
Home for Christmas *'93*
Home Is Where the Hart Is *'88*
Hoodwinked Too! Hood vs. Evil *'10*
Hurricane Smith *'92*
Imagining Argentina *'04*
In the Mouth of Madness *'95*
Into Thin Air *'85* ▸
The Invisible *'07*
The Iris Effect *'04*
The Island at the Top of the World *'74*
Jesse Stone: Thin Ice *'09*
Journey to the Center of the Earth *'08*
Jungle Goddess *'49*
Just Business *'08*
Katyn *'07*
Keane *'04* ▸
Kentucky Jubilee *'51*
Kidnap Syndicate *'76*
The Lady Vanishes *'38* ▸
The Lady Vanishes *'79*
Larceny in her Heart *'46*
The Last Winter *'84*
Left Bank *'08*
Lies and Illusions *'09*
Long Time Since *'97*
Looking for Kitty *'04*
Lost Treasure of the Maya *'08*
A Low Down Dirty Shame *'94*
Lucky Number Slevin *'06*
The Men Who Stare at Goats *'09*
Mexico City *'00*
Midnight Warning *'32*
Misery *'90* ▸
Miss Tatlock's Millions *'48*
Missing *'82* ▸
Missing Brendan *'03*
The Missing Corpse *'45*
Mr. District Attorney *'41*
Murder, My Sweet *'44* ▸
Nickel & Dime *'92*
Night of the Cyclone *'90*
Nim's Island *'08*
The Norliss Tapes *'73*
Norseman *'78*
Old Gringo *'89*
The Orphanage *'07* ▸
Passengers *'08*
Percy Jackson & The Olympians: The Lightning Thief *'10*
Perfect Assassins *'98*
Picnic at Hanging Rock *'75* ▸
The Port of Missing Girls *'38*
Prisoner of Zenda *'37* ▸
The Professionals *'66* ▸
Psych-Out *'68*
Psycho from Texas *'75*
Pure Luck *'91*
Raising Arizona *'87* ▸
Romancing the Stone *'84* ▸
Scandalous *'88*
Seance on a Wet Afternoon *'64* ▸
The Search for One-Eye Jimmy *'96*
The Searchers *'56* ▸
Short Night of Glass Dolls *'71*
The Shortcut *'09*
Shutter Island *'09* ▸
Sin *'02*
Skull: A Night of Terror *'88*
Snow 2: Brain Freeze *'08*
Stark *'85*
Street Girls *'75*
Street Justice *'89*
Surfacing *'84*
Tarzan the Fearless *'33*
Terminal Force *'88*
The Theory of the Leisure Class *'01*
Thin Air *'00*
Threat of Exposure *'02*
Tokyo Joe *'49*
Tony Rome *'67*
Tower of the Firstborn *'98*
The Tracey Fragments *'07*

▸ *= rated three bones or higher*

Trails of the Wild '35
2 Minutes Later '07
Under the Bombs '07
Vampire Night '00
The Vanishing '88 ▸
Wanted: Babysitter '75
Where Are the Children? '85
Where's Piccone '84 ▸
White Fire '53
Who Saw Her Die? '72
The Wicker Man '75 ▸
The Wicker Man '06
Winter's Bone '10
Without a Trace '83
The Wolfman '09
The X Files: I Want to Believe '08

Missionaries

see also *Nuns & Priests; Religion; Religious Epics*

The African Queen '51 ▸
At Play in the Fields of the Lord '91 ▸
Beyond the Next Mountain '87
Black Robe '91 ▸
End of the Spear '06
Ethan '71
Hawaii '66 ▸
The Inn of the Sixth Happiness '58 ▸
The Keys of the Kingdom '44 ▸
The Mission '86 ▸
Mission to Glory '80
The Missionary '82
The Other Side of Heaven '02
Paradise Road '97
Rambo '08

Mistaken Identity

see also *Amnesia; Gender Bending; Role Reversal*

Across the Bridge '57
The Adventurer '17
The Adventures of Bullwhip Griffin '66
Along Came Jones '45 ▸
Alvin Rides Again '74
American Cop '94
Amore! '93
Amos and Andrew '93
Another You '91
Apres-Vous '03
As Good as Dead '95
As You Desire Me '32 ▸
As You Like It '36
As You Like It '06
As Young As You Feel '51 ▸
The Assignment '97
The Associate '79
The Aura '05 ▸
Bachelor Mother '39 ▸
The Ballad of Little Jo '93
Baran '01
Barocco '76
The Beautician and the Beast '97
The Beautiful Blonde from Bashful Bend '49
Being There '79 ▸
Betrayed '54 ▸
A Better Way to Die '00
Beyond Suspicion '00
The Big Lebowski '97 ▸
Big Mouth '67
Billy the Kid Returns '38
Bittersweet Love '76
Black Glove '54
Blackjack '78
Blame It on the Bellboy '92
Blind Justice '86
Blondie Knows Best '46
Bobby Z '07
Body Snatchers '93
Borderline '50
The Boss of It All '06
Boy's Reformatory '39
Breakin' All The Rules '04
Brighton Strangler '45
Broadway Limited '41
Broken Melody '34
Bullets or Ballots '38 ▸
Bullseye! '90
Bundle of Joy '56
Buona Sera, Mrs. Campbell '68
Bushwhacked '95
Butler's Dilemma '43
Camp Cucamonga: How I Spent My Summer Vacation '90
The Capture '50 ▸
Caroline? '90 ▸
Carry On Admiral '57
A Case of Deadly Force '86 ▸
CB4: The Movie '93
Center of the Web '92
The Challengers '89
Chameleon Street '89 ▸
Chandni Chowk to China '09
Changeling '08 ▸
Charade '63 ▸
Charley's Aunt '25
The Chase '66
Christmas in the Clouds '01
City of Ghosts '03
The Closet '00
Colonel Chabert '94
Company Man '00
Convicted '86
Convicts at Large '38
Cornbread, Earl & Me '75
A Couch in New York '95
The Couch Trip '87
Counterblast '48
Court Jester '56 ▸
Date Night '10
Daughters of the Sun '00
Dave '93 ▸
Deadwood '65
Deconstructing Sarah '94
The Desert Song '53
Dog Gone Love '03
Don Juan DeMarco '94
Don't Tell Her It's Me '90
Double Play '96
Double Take '97
Double Take '01
Double Vision '92
The Drifter '44
The Duchess of Buffalo '26
El Mariachi '93 ▸
Ernest Goes to Jail '90
Erotic Touch of Hot Skin '65
Evergreen '34
Everybody Wants to Be Italian '08
Everyman's Law '36
Execution of Raymond Graham '85
F/X 2: The Deadly Art of Illusion '91
The Family Plan '05
Family Reunion '88
Fargo Express '32
Fatal Exposure '91
Father '90
Feet First '30
Fighting Parson '35
Five Graves to Cairo '43 ▸
The Flame of New Orleans '41 ▸
Flightplan '05
Focus '01
Gangway '37
Garfield: A Tail of Two Kitties '06
The Gay Divorcee '34 ▸
Generale Della Rovere '60 ▸
Gentleman Bandit '81
Get That Man '35
The Glass Bottom Boat '66
Good Neighbor Sam '64 ▸
The Great Dictator '40 ▸
Grosse Fatigue '94 ▸
The Gun in Betty Lou's Handbag '92
Gunfire '50
Gunsmoke Trail '38
Happy Go Lovely '51
Hell on Frisco Bay '55
Her Life as a Man '83
Hero '92 ▸
High & Low '62 ▸
High Lonesome '50
Highway 13 '48
His Brother's Ghost '45
His Wife's Lover '31 ▸
Hittin' the Trail '37
Hollywood Chaos '89
Hometown Boy Makes Good '93
Honolulu '39
A House in the Hills '93
Houseguest '94
I Love You '81
I Want to Live! '58 ▸
I Will, I Will for Now '76
If Looks Could Kill '91
The Imposters '98
The Impostor '84
In Person '35
In Society '44
The Inspector General '49 ▸
Intimate Strangers '04 ▸
Invasion of the Body Snatchers '78 ▸
It Started with Eve '41 ▸
It Takes Two '95
It! The Terror from Beyond Space '58
Jade '95
Johnny Handsome '89 ▸
Johnny Stecchino '92 ▸
Junk Mail '97
Just Write '97
Kansas City Confidential '52 ▸
Keaton's Cop '90
Kid from Spain '32
Killer Dill '47
The Killing Time '87
The King of Masks '99 ▸
A Kiss Before Dying '91
Km. 0 '00
Lady Killer '97
Landslide '92
The Last Contract '77
The Last Winter '84
Laughing at Danger '24
Laurel & Hardy: The Hoose-Gow '29
Law of the Underworld '38
Le Bonheur Est Dans le Pre '95
Life Is a Long Quiet River '88 ▸
Lisa '90
The Little Drummer Girl '84 ▸
Little Man '06
Little Sister '92
The Lizzie McGuire Movie '03
The Lookalike '90
Lost Highway '96
Love at Large '89 ▸
Lucky Cisco Kid '40
Lucky Number Slevin '06
Mad About Music '38 ▸
Made in America '93
The Magnificent Two '67
Maid's Night Out '38
The Majestic '01
Mamma Mia! '08
The Man '05
Man From God's Country '58
The Man in the Raincoat '57
The Man on the Box '25
Man on the Run '49
Man on the Run '74
The Man Who Knew Too Little '97
The Man with One Red Shoe '85
Manhandled '24
The Mark of Zorro '40 ▸
McHale's Navy Joins the Air Force '65
Meet the Deedles '98
Meet the Mob '42
Memento '00 ▸
Miami Hustle '95
Mickey Blue Eyes '99
The Misadventures of Mr. Wilt '90
Mississippi Mermaid '69 ▸
Mistaken Identity '36
Mr. Headmistress '98
Mr. Klein '76 ▸
Monsieur Beaucaire '46 ▸
Monsignor Quixote '91
The Monster '96
Monte Carlo Nights '34
My Geisha '62
My Man Godfrey '36 ▸
My Outlaw Brother '51
My Twentieth Century '90 ▸
Mystery Date '91
Naked Tango '91
Naughty Marietta '35
Never a Dull Moment '68
Next of Kin '84
Nick and Jane '96
The Night We Never Met '93
Nightfall '56 ▸
Nobody's Perfect '90
North by Northwest '59 ▸
The Nutt House '95
The Obsessed '51
Obsession '76
Off Season '01
One Body Too Many '44
Only You '94
Opportunity Knocks '90
Oscar '91
Out of Bounds '86
Out on a Limb '92
The Painted Trail '38
Pale Saints '97
Palmy Days '31
Paper Mask '91
Paperback Hero '99
Pardon My Sarong '42
The Parent Trap '61
The Parent Trap '98
The Passenger '75 ▸
The Perfect Man '05
Phantom Fiend '35
Phantom Killer '42
Picture Perfect '96
Pier 23 '51
The Player '92 ▸
The Pope Must Diet '91
Prelude to a Kiss '92
Priceless '06
Prime '05
The Princess Comes Across '36 ▸
Princess O'Rourke '43
Private Life of Don Juan '34
The Private Secretary '35
Profile '54
Purple Noon '60 ▸
Ranson's Folly '26
Rattler Kid '68
Red Firecracker, Green Firecracker '93
The Red Half-Breed '70
Red Heat '85
Red Rock West '93 ▸
Reindeer Games '00
The Reluctant Agent '89
The Reluctant Astronaut '67
Return of Jesse James '50
The Return of Martin Guerre '83 ▸
Return of the Tall Blond Man with One Black Shoe '74
Riding Wild '35
River Beat '54
The Road to Guantanamo '06
Romance on the High Seas '48 ▸
Running Hot '83
Ruyblas '48
Safe Men '98
St. Benny the Dip '51
The Santa Clause '94
Santa with Muscles '96
Say It Isn't So '01
The Scar '48
Scream of Fear '61 ▸
Seconds '66 ▸
The Secret of My Success '87
A Self-Made Hero '95 ▸
The 7th Commandment '61
Shadows on the Sage '42
She Must Be Seeing Things '87
She's the Man '06
The Sinister Invasion '68
Sister Act '92
Sister Act 2: Back in the Habit '93
Six Gun Gospel '43
Six of a Kind '34 ▸
The Sleepy Time Gal '01
Slightly Terrific '44
Small Kill '93
Smokey and the Bandit, Part 3 '83
Social Error '35
Soldat Duroc... Ca Va Etre Ta Fete! '75
Someone at the Door '50
Something in the Wind '47
Splitting Heirs '93
The Square Peg '58
Stolen Identity '53
A Stolen Life '46
Straight Talk '92
Stray Bullet '98
The Stupids '95
The Suitors '88
Sunday '96
Supergrass '87
Support Your Local Gunfighter '71 ▸
Suture '93
Switched at Birth '91
Taken Alive '95
Tattle Tale '92
10 Rillington Place '71 ▸
The Tenth Man '88
Texas Carnival '51
Texas Cyclone '32
They Knew What They Wanted '40 ▸
The Thin Blue Line '88 ▸
Things Change '88 ▸
Things I Never Told You '96
The 39 Steps '35 ▸
Tombstone Terror '34
Top Hat '35 ▸
Toto le Heros '91 ▸
Trailing Trouble '37
Tropic Thunder '08 ▸
True Identity '91
The Truth about Cats and Dogs '96 ▸
Twelfth Night '96
Twin Dragons '92
Two Much '96
The Unholy Three '30 ▸
The Well '51 ▸
We're No Angels '89
West of the Pecos '45
Westward Bound '30
While You Were Sleeping '95 ▸
Whiskers '96
White Eagle '32
White of the Eye '88 ▸
Who's Harry Crumb? '89
Wings of the Morning '37
Withnail and I '87 ▸
The Worldly Madonna '22
The Wrong Guys '88
Young Master '80
Zertigo Diamond Caper '82

Mockumentary

see also *Documentary; Genre Spoofs*

Acapulco Gold '78
All You Need Is Cash '78 ▸
...And God Spoke '94
Best in Show '00 ▸
Big Man Japan '07
The Blair Witch Project '99
Bob Roberts '92 ▸
Borat: Cultural Learnings of America for Make Benefit Glorious Nation of Kazakhstan '06 ▸
Born to Lose '99
Brothers of the Head '06
Comic Book: The Movie '04 ▸
Confetti '06
CSA: The Confederate States of America '04
Danny Roane: First Time Director '06
A Day Without a Mexican '04
Drop Dead Gorgeous '99
Elvis Meets Nixon '98
Fear of a Black Hat '94
Flyboys '06
For Your Consideration '06
Forgotten Silver '96 ▸
Gamers '06
Glen or Glenda? '53
Grunt! The Wrestling Movie '85
Hard Core Logo '96
Incident at Loch Ness '04 ▸
It's All Gone, Pete Tong '04
Jackie's Back '99
The Last Broadcast '98 ▸
The Last Polka '84 ▸
Lisa Picard Is Famous '01
Mail Order Wife '04
Memron '04
A Mighty Wind '03 ▸
Never Been Thawed '05
On Edge '03
Pittsburgh '06
Real Time: Siege at Lucas Street Market '00
Rescue Dawn '06 ▸
The Return of Spinal Tap '92
Stardom '00
SuperGuy: Behind the Cape '02
This Is Spinal Tap '84 ▸
Tristram Shandy: A Cock and Bull Story '05
Waiting for Guffman '96
Walk Hard: The Dewey Cox Story '07
Zelig '83 ▸

Model Citizens

Abdulla the Great '56
Blackjack '97
The Bride Is Much Too Beautiful '58
Captivity '07
The Case of the Bloody Iris '72
A Change of Place '94
Cover Girl '44 ▸
Cover Girl Models '75
The Cover Girl Murders '93
Covergirl '83
Daniella by Night '61
Darling '65 ▸
Designing Woman '57 ▸
Domino '05
D.R.E.A.M. Team '99
Eight Miles High '07
Eight Miles High '08
The Eighteenth Angel '97
Eyes of Laura Mars '78
Faceless '88
Fall '97
Funny Face '57 ▸
Gia '98
Giving It Up '99
Head Over Heels '01
Human Desires '97
In and Out '97 ▸
Intimate Deception '96
The Invisibles '99
Looker '81
Mahogany '75
Model Behavior '82
Model Behavior '00
Model by Day '94
Model Shop '69
Nothing Underneath '85
Obsession: A Taste for Fear '89
One Last Thing '05
The Pink Jungle '68
Pleasure '31
Portfolio '88
Raising Helen '04
Ready to Wear '94
Screaming Dead '03
Slaves of New York '89
So Fine '81
Stardom '00
Storm Warning '51
Taxi '04
30 Years to Life '01
Tight Spot '55 ▸
The Unbelievable Truth '90
Unzipped '94 ▸
The Valet '06
What a Woman! '56
What's New Pussycat? '65 ▸
When the Cat's Away '96 ▸
Zoolander '01

Modern Cowboys

see also *Western Comedy; Westerns*

All the Pretty Horses '00
Another Pair of Aces: Three of a Kind '91 ▸
Barbarosa '82 ▸
The Big Empty '04
Brokeback Mountain '05 ▸
Bronco Billy '80
By Dawn's Early Light '00
City Slickers '91 ▸
City Slickers 2: The Legend of Curly's Gold '94
Coogan's Bluff '68 ▸
Cowboy Up '00
The Cowboy Way '94
Don't Come Knocking '05
Down in the Valley '05
Dudes '87
8 Seconds '94

▸ = *rated three bones or higher*

The Electric Horseman '79
Fool for Love '86
The Hi-Lo Country '98
Hope Ranch '02
The Horse Whisperer '97
The Last of the Dogmen '95
Lonely Are the Brave '62 ►
My Heroes Have Always Been Cowboys '91
A Prairie Home Companion '06
Rhinestone '84
Ruby Jean and Joe '96
Samurai Cowboy '93
Sweet Creek County War '79
Tears of the Black Tiger '00
Toy Story '95 ►
Toy Story 2 '99 ►
True West '86 ►
An Unfinished Life '05
Wild Horses '84

Moms

see also *Bad Dads; Dads; Monster Moms; Parenthood*

ABCD '99
Above the Rim '94
Agnes Browne '99
Alice Doesn't Live Here Anymore '74
All About My Mother '99 ►
All That Heaven Allows '55 ►
Amazing Grace '74
American Movie '99 ►
Antonia's Line '95
Anywhere But Here '99
Applause '29 ►
Aurora '84
Autumn Sonata '78 ►
Baby '00
Baby Boom '87
Bad Boy '39
The Bad Seed '56
The Bad Seed '85
The Banger Sisters '02
Bastard out of Carolina '96
Beautiful '00
Beautiful Thing '95 ►
Because I Said So '07
Beloved '98
Better Than Chocolate '99
Bogus '96
The Brady Bunch Movie '95 ►
Bridge to Silence '89
A Brivele der Mamen '38 ►
Cadillac Girls '93
A Call to Remember '97
Carnegie Hall '47
Charms for the Easy Life '02
Children of the Revolution '95
Chocolat '00 ►
Choke '08
Cider with Rosie '99
Cinderella Liberty '73 ►
Clean '04
Come Undone '00
Comedy of Innocence '00
Crash Course '00
The Damned Don't Cry '50
Dangerous Beauty '98 ►
Dangerous Child '01
Dark Water '02
Daughter of Keltoum '01
The Daytrippers '96
Dead Ahead '96
The Dead Girl '06
The Deep End '01 ►
The Deep End of the Ocean '98
The Deli '97
Detective Sadie & Son '84
The Devil's Sleep '51
Digging to China '98
Dim Sum: A Little Bit of Heart '85 ►
Do or Die '01
The Dollmaker '84
Dona Herlinda & Her Son '86
Double Jeopardy '99
Double Parked '00
Double Platinum '99
Down in the Delta '98 ►
Driving Lessons '06
Drop Dead Gorgeous '99
Dumbo '41 ►
Edward the King '75
Emma's Wish '98
Evening '07
Every Other Weekend '91 ►
A Family Affair '01
Family of Strangers '93
First Born '84
First Do No Harm '97
First, Last and Deposit '00
Flight of the Red Balloon '08
Food of Love '02
For One More Day '07
Forrest Gump '94 ►
Found Alive '34
Four Sons '28
Frank McKlusky, C.I. '02
Frankie Starlight '95
Freaky Friday '76
Freaky Friday '03 ►
Frisco Jenny '32
Frozen River '08 ►
Garbo Talks '84
Gas Food Lodging '92 ►
Georgia '87
Getting Out '94
Gia '98
The Girl '68 ►
God Said "Ha!" '99 ►
Good Bye, Lenin! '03 ►
Grace '09
Gypsy '62 ►
Gypsy '93
Hairspray '07 ►
Harnessing Peacocks '92
Heartbreakers '01
Heavy '94 ►
Held for Murder '32
High Tide '87 ►
Holiday Affair '96
Homage '95
Home '08
A Home of Our Own '93
Hope Floats '98
The Horse Whisperer '97
The Hours '02 ►
House Arrest '96
House of Cards '92
Hysterical Blindness '02
I Don't Want to Talk About It '94
I Remember Mama '48 ►
Illegal Tender '07
Imitation of Life '34
Imitation of Life '59 ►
In the Gloaming '97 ►
The Incredible Shrinking Woman '81
Indochine '92 ►
Into Thin Air '85 ►
Invisible Mom '96
The Iris Effect '04
Jenny's War '85
The Joy Luck Club '93 ►
Junior's Groove '97
The Juror '96
Kabei: Our Mother '08
King of the Jungle '01
Kissing Jessica Stein '02
La Cicada '83
Ladies of the Chorus '49
Lady by Choice '34
Lady Jayne Killer '03
Lake City '08
Laurel Canyon '02
Leo '02
Let No Man Write My Epitaph '60
Lift '01
The Lion King 1 1/2 '04 ►
Listen, Darling '38
Little Women '94 ►
Lola and Billy the Kid '98
Lost for Words '99 ►
Love Come Down '00
The Love Letter '99
Love Strange Love '82
Lovely & Amazing '02 ►
Loverboy '05
Lucky Seven '03
Lullaby '08
Luminous Motion '00
Mad About Music '38 ►
Madame X '66
Made in America '93
Madeo '09
Mama Flora's Family '98
Mama's Boy '07
Mamma Mia! '08
Mamma Roma '62 ►
Mammoth '09
Manny & Lo '96 ►
Marius and Jeannette '97
Mary, Mother of Jesus '99
Mask '85 ►
Me Myself I '99
Meet the Fockers '04
Mermaids '90 ►
The Midnight Lady '32
The Mighty '98 ►
Mildred Pierce '45 ►
Mrs. Wiggs of the Cabbage Patch '34
Mrs. Winterbourne '96
Mr. Woodcock '07
Mom and Dad Save the World '92
Mom's Outta Sight '01
Moscow, Belgium '08
Mother '96
The Mother '03 ►
Mother and Child '09
Mother and Son '97
Mother of Mine '05 ►
Motherhood '09
A Mother's Prayer '95
Murmur of the Heart '71 ►
My Family Treasure '93
My Life Without Me '03
My Mom's New Boyfriend '08
My Mother Likes Women '02
My Mother's Secret Life '84
My One and Only '09
Nancy Goes to Rio '50
The Natalee Holloway Story '09
Never Met Picasso '96
'night, Mother '86
Night Ride Home '99
Nightmare '91
Nowhere Boy '09
Nowhere to Run '93
The Old Maid '39 ►
On My Own '92
One True Thing '98 ►
101 Reykjavik '00
Only the Lonely '91
Only When I Laugh '81 ►
Or (My Treasure) '04
Oranges Are Not the Only Fruit '89
Our Sons '91
Out of Sight, Out of Her Mind '89
Over the Hill '93
Panic Room '02
Pavilion of Women '01
Pay It Forward '00
The Perfect Man '05
Pharoah's Army '95
Pilgrim, Farewell '82
Places in the Heart '84 ►
Playing by Heart '98
Poor White Trash '00
Postcards from the Edge '90 ►
The Prize Winner of Defiance, Ohio '05 ►
Psycho '98
A Question of Love '78 ►
Rachel, Rachel '68 ►
Rain '01
The Real McCoy '93
Real Women Have Curves '02 ►
The Reception '05
Reckless Moment '49 ►
Relative Values '99
Requiem for a Dream '00 ►
River Queen '05
The River Wild '94
The Road from Coorain '02
The Road Home '01 ►
Robot Stories '03
Rockabye '86
Roses Bloom Twice '77
Rumpelstiltskin '96
Santitos '99
Satan's Little Helper '04
Say Uncle '05
Scandal in a Small Town '88
See How She Runs '78 ►
Shadows '07
She-Devil '89
She's Having a Baby '88
Silent Hill '06
Simon Birch '98
The Sin of Madelon Claudet '31 ►
Since Otar Left... '03
A Sinful Life '89
Skipped Parts '00
Smother '08
Snap Decision '01
So I Married an Axe Murderer '93
Soft Fruit '99
Solas '99
Some Mother's Son '96 ►
Something's Gotta Give '03 ►
Star Wars: Episode 2—Attack of the Clones '02 ►
Stella '89
Stella Dallas '37 ►
Stop! or My Mom Will Shoot '92
The Story of Esther Costello '57
Striptease '96
Tarnation '03
Terms of Endearment '83 ►
Third Walker '79 ►
Thirteen '03 ►
Throw Momma from the Train '87 ►
A Time to Remember '03
To Each His Own '46 ►
To See Paris and Die '93
Trading Mom '94
The Trip to Bountiful '85 ►
Troop Beverly Hills '89
The Truth About Jane '00
Tumbleweeds '98
Turn the River '07
The 24 Hour Woman '99
Two Women '61 ►
Under One Roof '02
Under the Same Moon '07
Under the Skin '97
An Unexpected Life '97
Unhook the Stars '96
A Very Brady Sequel '96
The Visit '00 ►
The Visitor '07 ►
Volver '06 ►
A Walk on the Moon '99
The War at Home '96
The Waterboy '98
What Time Is It There? '01
When a Man Loves a Woman '94
Where's Poppa? '70 ►
Will It Snow for Christmas? '96
The Winter Guest '97 ►
A Woman's a Helluva Thing '01
The Yards '00

Monkeyshines

see also *Jungle Stories; Killer Apes and Monkeys; Wild Kingdom*

Babe: Pig in the City '98
The Barefoot Executive '71
Bedtime for Bonzo '51
Blood Monkey '07
Born to Be Wild '95
The Bride & the Beast '58
Buddy '97
Carry On Up the Jungle '70
Cloudy with a Chance of Meatballs '09
Congo '95
Curious George '06
Curtain at Eight '33
Dr. Dolittle '98
Dr. Renault's Secret '42
Dunston Checks In '95
Ed '96
George of the Jungle '97 ►
Instinct '99
Jay and Silent Bob Strike Back '01
Jungle Captive '45
King Kong '33 ►
King Kong '76
Mom, Can I Keep Her? '98
Monkey Shines '88
Monkey Trouble '94
Monkeybone '01
MVP (Most Valuable Primate) '00
MVP2: Most Vertical Primate '01
MXP: Most Xtreme Primate '03
Outbreak '94 ►
Planet of the Apes '01 ►
The Powerpuff Girls Movie '02 ►
Race to Space '01
The Rundown '03
The Sisters '05
Space Chimps '08
Speed Racer '08
Summer of the Monkeys '98
Tarzan '99 ►
Terror Tract '00
Vanilla Gorilla '09
Who's Your Monkey '07
The Wild Thornberrys Movie '02 ►

Monks

see also *Clergymen; Martial Arts*

The Da Vinci Code '06 ►
The Forbidden Kingdom '08
Hitman '07
The Judgement '04
Kundun '97 ►
Monty Python and the Holy Grail '75 ►
Nacho Libre '06
The Name of the Rose '86
Rasputin '85 ►
Rasputin and the Empress '33 ►
Rasputin: Dark Servant of Destiny '96 ►
The Secret of Kells '09
The 36th Chamber of Shaolin '78 ►
Van Helsing '04 ►

Monster Moms

see also *Bad Dads; Dads; Moms; Parenthood*

Alias Betty '01
Almost Dead '94
The American '01
American Venus '07
The Anniversary '68
The Baby '72
Bad Boy Bubby '93
Bellissima '51 ►
Beowulf '07 ►
Berlinguer I Love You '77
Beyond the Door '75
Big Bad Mama '74
Big Bad Mama 2 '87
Bloody Mama '70
Boystown '07
Brand Upon the Brain! '06 ►
Carrie '76 ►
Carrie '02
Carved '07
Catfish in Black Bean Sauce '00
Chutney Popcorn '99
Cop Au Vin '85
Cora Unashamed '00
Dead Alive '93
Dead Pet '01
Deadly Advice '93
Die! Die! My Darling! '65
Die Mommie Die! '03
Divine Secrets of the Ya-Ya Sisterhood '02
Dolores Claiborne '94 ►
East of Eden '54 ►
East of Eden '80
Ed and His Dead Mother '93
Felicia's Journey '99 ►
Fiona '98
Flesh Eating Mothers '89
From Dusk Till Dawn 3: The Hangman's Daughter '99
A Gentleman After Dark '42
Ghosts Never Sleep '05
Glass House: The Good Mother '06
Gone Baby Gone '07 ►
Gorgo '61
Gracie's Choice '04
The Graveyard '74
The Grifters '90 ►
Hard, Fast and Beautiful '51
Harm's Way '07
His Greatest Gamble '34
Hush '98
Hush Little Baby '93
Ice Princess '05
The Intended '02
Introducing the Dwights '07
Invaders from Mars '53
Invaders from Mars '86
A Light in the Darkness '02
Little Voice '98 ►
The Locusts '97
Ma Barker's Killer Brood '60
Mad Youth '40
The Manchurian Candidate '62 ►
A Matter of Dignity '57
Medea '70
Mom '89
Mommie Dearest '81
Mommy '95
Mommy 2: Mommy's Day '96
Monster-in-Law '05
Monster's Ball '01 ►
Mother '94
Mother's Boys '94
Mother's Day '80
The Nightman '93
Nutcracker: Money, Madness & Murder '87 ►
Parents '89 ►
Passion '99
Picture Mommy Dead '66
Pilgrimage '33
The Positively True Adventures of the Alleged Texas Cheerleader-Murdering Mom '93 ►
Precious: Based on the Novel by Sapphire '09 ►
Psycho '60 ►
Psycho 2 '83
Psycho 3 '86
Public Enemies '96
Rosetta '99
Running with Scissors '06
Santa Sangre '90 ►
Savage Grace '07
Say It Isn't So '01
Serial Mom '94 ►
Six Ways to Sunday '99
Sleepwalkers '92
Sleepwalking '08
Small Sacrifices '89
Sonny '02
Spanglish '04
Spanking the Monkey '94 ►
The Star '52 ►
The Stepmother '71
Sybil '76 ►
Touch of Pink '04
Trilogy of Terror 2 '96
The Ugly '96
White Oleander '02
Wild at Heart '90 ►
Wild Iris '01
Willard '03

Monster Yuks

Abbott and Costello Meet Dr. Jekyll and Mr. Hyde '52
Abbott and Costello Meet Frankenstein '48 ►
Abbott and Costello Meet the Killer, Boris Karloff '49
Abbott and Costello Meet the Mummy '55
The Addams Family '91
Addams Family Values '93
The Calamari Wrestler '04
Drop Dead Fred '91
Little Monsters '89
Monsters, Inc. '01 ►
Munster, Go Home! '66
Pom Poko '94
Scooby-Doo 2: Monsters Unleashed '04
The Water Horse: Legend of the Deep '07

Monsters, General

see *Bigfoot/Yeti; Ghosts, Ghouls, & Goblins; Giants; Killer Beasts; Killer Bugs and Slugs; Killer Plants; Killer Reptiles; Killer Sea Critters; Killer Toys; Mad Scientists; Mummies; Robots & Androids; Vampires; Werewolves; Zombies*

► = rated three bones or higher

Montana

Almost Heroes '97
Always '89
Amazing Grace & Chuck '87
The Ballad of Little Jo '93
Big Eden '00
Bright Angel '91
Bustin' Loose '81 ▸
Cattle Queen of Montana '54
Clay Pigeons '98
Cold Feet '89
Disorganized Crime '89
Evel Knievel '72
Everything That Rises '98
Fear X '03 ▸
Forrest Gump '94 ▸
A Guy Named Joe '44
The Horse Whisperer '97
Jeremiah Johnson '72 ▸
Keep the Change '92
The Killer Inside Me '76
Legends of the Fall '94
Little Big Man '70 ▸
Lonesome Dove '89 ▸
Me & Will '99
Missouri Breaks '76
Montana '90
Montana '97
Montana Belle '52
The Patriot '99
Rancho Deluxe '75 ▸
Return to Lonesome Dove '93
A River Runs Through It '92 ▸
The River Wild '94
Season of Change '94
The Slaughter Rule '01
Stacking '87
Star Trek: First Contact '96 ▸
Stay Away, Joe '68
The Stone Boy '84 ▸
They Died with Their Boots On '41 ▸
Thunderbolt & Lightfoot '74 ▸
Under Siege 2: Dark Territory '95
War Party '89
Winterhawk '76

Monte Carlo/Monaco

Charlie Chan at Monte Carlo '37
The Counterfeiters '07 ▸
Easy Virtue '08
The Garden of Eden '28 ▸
The Girl From Monaco '08
Grand Prix '66
Herbie Goes to Monte Carlo '77
Monaco Forever '83
Monte Carlo '30
Monte Carlo '86
Monte Carlo Nights '34
Priceless '06
Rebecca '40 ▸
Rebecca '97 ▸
The Red Shoes '48 ▸
Seven Thieves '60 ▸
Strike It Rich '90
Those Daring Young Men in Their Jaunty Jalopies '69

Montreal

see also Canada
The Apprentice '71
The Apprenticeship of Duddy Kravitz '74 ▸
The Barbarian Invasions '03 ▸
Because Why? '93
Being at Home with Claude '92
Bon Cop Bad Cop '06
A Bullet for Joey '55
Cafe Ole '00
Eddie and the Cruisers 2: Eddie Lives! '89
Eliza's Horoscope '70
Eternal '04
Familia '05
Jesus of Montreal '89 ▸
Karmina '96
Leolo '92 ▸
L'Escorte '96
Love and Human Remains '93 ▸
Malarek '89
Mambo Italiano '03
Mystery of the Million Dollar Hockey Puck '75
Night Zoo '87
The Pact '99
Pale Saints '97
The Quarrel '93
The Red Violin '98
The Score '01
Seducing Doctor Lewis '03
Seducing Maarya '99
Set Me Free '99
Steel Toes '06
Straight for the Heart '88
Taking Lives '04
2 Seconds '98
The Victory '81
The Whole Nine Yards '00
A Wind from Wyoming '94

Mormons

see also Religion
Angels in America '03 ▸
The Avenging Angel '95
Bonneville '06
Brigham City '01
Brigham Young: Frontiersman '40
Georgia Rule '07
Latter Days '04
Lies & Alibis '06
Messenger of Death '88
A Mormon Maid '17
Orgazmo '98
The Other Side of Heaven '02
September Dawn '07
Wagon Master '50 ▸

Moscow

see also Russia/USSR
American Cop '94
Back in the USSR '92
Black Eyes '39
Botched '07
The Bourne Ultimatum '07 ▸
Command Performance '09
Comrade X '40
Day Watch '06 ▸
An Englishman Abroad '83 ▸
Get Smart '08
Gorky Park '83 ▸
Luna Park '91
Mission to Moscow '43
Moscow Does Not Believe in Tears '80 ▸
Moscow on the Hudson '84 ▸
Moscow Parade '92
Moscow Zero '06
Mute Witness '95
Night Watch '04
Perestroika '09
Police Academy 7: Mission to Moscow '94
PU-239 '06
Red Heat '88
Redline '97
The Russia House '90
The Saint '97
Silent Partner '05
Taxi Blues '90 ▸
12 '07
Very Close Quarters '84

Moscow Mafia

see also Gangs; Organized Crime; Russia/USSR
Birthday Girl '02
Brother '97
City Unplugged '95
The Code '09
Eastern Promises '07 ▸
Goldeneye '95 ▸
Hard As Nails '01
The Jackal '97
Lethal '04
Little Odessa '94
PU-239 '06
Red Heat '88
Ripley's Game '02 ▸
RocknRolla '08
Rounders '98
Ruslan '09
We Own the Night '07

Motor Vehicle Dept.

see also Bikers; Checkered Flag; Killer Cars
Action Jackson '88
The Adventures of Ford Fairlane '90
American Graffiti '73 ▸
Back to the Future '85 ▸
Bail Out '90
Belle Americaine '61
The Betsy '78
Black Cat Run '98
Black Moon Rising '86
Blitz '85
Blood, Guts, Bullets and Octane '99
The Blues Brothers '80 ▸
Cadillac Man '90
Captured '99
The Car '77
Car Babes '06
Car Trouble '85
Car Trouble '86
Car Wash '76
Carpool '96
Carpool Guy '05
The Chase '93
Chitty Chitty Bang Bang '68
Coneheads '93
Corvette Summer '78
Coupe de Ville '90
Crash '95
Cry Panic '74
Dangerous Curves '88
Dark of the Night '85
D.C. Cab '84
Deadline Auto Theft '83
Death Proof '07
Devil's Knight '03
Dream Machine '91
Drive-In '76
Drive-In Massacre '74
The Driver '78
Driving Me Crazy '91
Duel '71 ▸
The Dukes of Hazzard '05
Dumb & Dumber '94
Fast & Furious '09
The Fast and the Furious '01
Ferris Bueller's Day Off '86 ▸
Firebird 2015 A.D. '81
The First Auto '27
Flash of Genius '08
Follow That Car '80
Ford: The Man & the Machine '87
Free Ride '86
Freedom '82
Freeway '88
Gone in 60 Seconds '74
Gone in 60 Seconds '00
The Goods: Live Hard, Sell Hard '09
Gran Torino '08 ▸
Great American Traffic Jam '80
Gung Ho '85
The Hearse '80
Herbie: Fully Loaded '05
Herbie Rides Again '74
High Rolling in a Hot Corvette '77
Highway Patrolman '91
Highwaymen '03
The Hollywood Knights '80
Hometown U.S.A. '79
Hotwire '80
How I Learned to Love Women '66
Jade '95
Joyride '97
The Karate Kid '84 ▸
License to Drive '88
The Love Bug '68
The Love Bug '97
Maximum Overdrive '86
Mr. Toad's Wild Ride '96
Moonshine Highway '96
Motorama '91
Moving Violations '85
My Chauffeur '86
National Lampoon's Vacation '83 ▸
Nick & Norah's Infinite Playlist '08 ▸
Night on Earth '91 ▸
Octane '07
One Deadly Owner '74
Pepper and His Wacky Taxi '72
Pie in the Sky '95
Repo Jake '90
Repo Man '83 ▸
Road to Nhill '97
Roger & Me '89 ▸
R.P.M. '97
Sex Drive '08
Silkwood '83 ▸
Smokey & the Hotwire Gang '79
Steel Arena '72
Stephen King's Thinner '96
Stingray '78
The Sucker '65
Sunset Limousine '83
Superbug Super Agent '76
Tail Lights Fade '99
This Man Must Die '70 ▸
Tomboy '85
Traffic '71
Transporter 3 '08
True Lies '94
Tucker: The Man and His Dream '88 ▸
Two Lane Blacktop '71 ▸
Uncle Buck '89 ▸
Used Cars '80 ▸
The Van '77
Vanishing Point '71
Wheels of Terror '90
Zero to Sixty '78

Mountaineering

The Abominable Snowman '57
Alpine Fire '89
The Ascent '94
Bushwhacked '95
The Challenge '38 ▸
Cliffhanger '93 ▸
The Climb '87
Courage Mountain '89
The Eiger Sanction '75
Extreme Ops '02
Five Days One Summer '82
God's Bloody Acre '75
Heidi '67
Into Thin Air: Death on Everest '97
K2: The Ultimate High '92
The Mountain '56
Mountain Patrol: Kekexili '04
My Side of the Mountain '69
North Face '08 ▸
Seven Years in Tibet '97
Storm and Sorrow '90
Third Man on the Mountain '59
Touch the Top of the World '06
Touching the Void '03
Vertical Limit '00
The White Tower '50 ▸
The Wildest Dream: Conquest of Everest '10

Mummies

see also Zombies
Abbott and Costello Meet the Mummy '55
All New Adventures of Laurel and Hardy: For Love or Mummy '98
Ancient Evil: Scream of the Mummy '00
Attack of the Mayan Mummy '63
The Awakening '80
Belphegar: Phantom of the Louvre '01
Blood from the Mummy's Tomb '71
Bram Stoker's The Mummy '97
Bubba Ho-Tep '03 ▸
Castle of the Living Dead '64
The Creeps '97
The Curse of the Aztec Mummy '59
Dawn of the Mummy '82
The External '99
Legend of the Bog '08
Mad Monster Party '68
The Monster Squad '87
The Mummy '32 ▸
The Mummy '59 ▸
The Mummy '99
Mummy & Curse of the Jackal '67
The Mummy Lives '93
The Mummy Returns '01
The Mummy: Tomb of the Dragon Emperor '08
The Mummy's Curse '44
The Mummy's Ghost '44
The Mummy's Hand '40
The Mummy's Revenge '73
The Mummy's Shroud '67
The Mummy's Tomb '42
The Robot vs. the Aztec Mummy '59
Russell Mulcahy's Tale of the Mummy '99
Sphinx '81
Wrestling Women vs. the Aztec Mummy '59

Museums

Abbott and Costello Meet Frankenstein '48 ▸
After Midnight '04
All New Adventures of Laurel and Hardy: For Love or Mummy '98
Belphegar: Phantom of the Louvre '01
Blood Relic '05
Charlie Chan at the Wax Museum '40
Crucible of Terror '72
Curious George '06
The Da Vinci Code '06 ▸
Dirty Pictures '00
Erotic House of Wax '97
From the Mixed-Up Files of Mrs. Basil E. Frankweiler '95
Ghostbusters 2 '89
The Hideaways '73
House of Wax '53 ▸
House of Wax '05
Mad City '97
The Maiden Heist '08
Mammoth '06
Manticore '05
Midnight at the Wax Museum '36
Mr. Moto Takes a Vacation '39
Mr. Takes a Vacation '39
The Mummy Returns '01
Mystery of the Wax Museum '33 ▸
Night at the Museum '06
Night at the Museum: Battle of the Smithsonian '09
Nightmare in Wax '69
The Outing '87
Paul Bartel's The Secret Cinema '69
P.D. James: The Murder Room '04
The Pick-Up Artist '87
The Relic '96
Scooby-Doo 2: Monsters Unleashed '04
The Shape of Things '03
The Silence '06
Tenacious D in the Pick of Destiny '06
Terror in the Wax Museum '73
The Thomas Crown Affair '99 ▸
Topkapi '64 ▸
Vibes '88
Waxwork '88
Waxwork 2: Lost in Time '91
Waxworks '24 ▸
The Witness '99

Musical Comedy

see also Musicals
Adventures of Power '08
The Adventures of Priscilla, Queen of the Desert '94 ▸
The Affairs of Dobie Gillis '53
Almost Angels '62
Alvin and the Chipmunks: The Squeakuel '09
Amateur Night '85
Andy Hardy Meets Debutante '40
April in Paris '52
Around the World '43
Artists and Models '55
Athena '54
Babes in Arms '39
Babes on Broadway '41
Bathing Beauty '44
Battlefield Baseball '03
Be Yourself '30
Beach Blanket Bingo '65 ▸
Beach Party '63
Because You're Mine '52
Beggar's Opera '54
Bert Rigby, You're a Fool '89
Best Foot Forward '43
The Best Little Whorehouse in Texas '82
The Big Broadcast of 1938 '38
Bikini Beach '64
Billy Rose's Jumbo '62 ▸
Birth of the Blues '41
Blossoms on Broadway '37
The Blues Brothers '80 ▸
Blues Brothers 2000 '98
Boardinghouse Blues '48
The Boy Friend '71 ▸
Boy! What a Girl '45
The Boys and Girl From County Clare '03
Bride & Prejudice '04
Broadway Melody of 1936 '35 ▸
Broadway Rhythm '44
Bundle of Joy '56
Bye, Bye, Birdie '63 ▸
Cairo '42
Call Out the Marines '42
Cannibal! The Musical '96
Captain January '36
Carefree '38 ▸
The Cocoanuts '29
Colleen '36
College Humor '33
College Swing '38
Copacabana '47
Court Jester '56 ▸
Cover Girl '44 ▸
Cry-Baby '90 ▸
Dames '34 ▸
Dance, Girl, Dance '40
Dangerous When Wet '53
Darling Lili '70
Delightfully Dangerous '45
The Devil's Brother '33
Diplomaniacs '33
Disorderlies '87
Dixiana '30
Dixie Jamboree '44
Doll Face '46
Double or Nothing '37
Du Barry Was a Lady '43
The Duchess of Idaho '50
Easy Come, Easy Go '67
Easy to Wed '46
The Eighties '83
Escape to Paradise '39
Evergreen '34
Everybody Sing '38
Everyone Says I Love You '96 ▸
Fashions of 1934 '34
Feel the Motion '86
Femmes de Paris '53
Finian's Rainbow '68 ▸
The First Nudie Musical '75
Flirtation Walk '34
Flower Drum Song '61
Flying High '31
Follow That Dream '61
Follow That Rainbow '79
Four Jacks and a Jill '41
Four Jills in a Jeep '44
Frankie and Johnny '65
The French Line '53
The French Way '40
Frolics on Ice '39
Fun in Acapulco '63
Funny Face '57 ▸
A Funny Thing Happened on the Way to the Forum '66 ▸

▸ = rated three bones or higher

Musical Drama

see also Musicals

▸ = rated three bones or higher

Ziegfeld Girl '41 ▸
Zoot Suit '81 ▸
Zou Zou '34

Musical Fantasy

***see also** Musicals*

Alice '86
Anything But Love '02
Babes in Toyland '61
Bandh Darwaza '90
Bedknobs and Broomsticks '71
Brigadoon '54 ▸
Butterfly Ball '76
Cabin in the Sky '43 ▸
Carousel '56 ▸
Chitty Chitty Bang Bang '68
Cinderella '64
Cinderella '97
Cinderella 2000 '78
Comic Book Kids '82
A Connecticut Yankee in King Arthur's Court '49
Damn Yankees '58 ▸
Dancer in the Dark '99
Doctor Dolittle '67
Down to Earth '47
8 Women '02 ▸
Fairy Tales '76
The 5000 Fingers of Dr. T '53 ▸
Gepetto '00
High School Musical '06
Kismet '55
Labyrinth '86 ▸
The Little Match Girl '84
The Little Prince '74
Magical Mystery Tour '67
March of the Wooden Soldiers '34 ▸
Mary Poppins '64 ▸
Moulin Rouge '01 ▸
Neapolitan Carousel '54
The New Adventures of Pippi Longstocking '88
Once Upon a Brothers Grimm '77
Peter Pan '60 ▸
Purana Mandir '84 ▸
Repo! The Genetic Opera '08
Return to Waterloo '85
Rumpelstiltskin '86
The Singing Detective '03
Sleeping Beauty '89
The Slipper and the Rose '76
Strange Frequency 2 '01
Willy Wonka & the Chocolate Factory '71 ▸
The Wizard of Oz '39 ▸
Wonderwall: The Movie '69
Xanadu '80
Zero Patience '94

Musicals

***see also** Animated Musicals; Contemporary Musicals; Disco Musicals; Musical Comedy; Musical Drama; Musical Fantasy*

Alexander's Ragtime Band '38 ▸
An American in Paris '51 ▸
Anchors Aweigh '45 ▸
Annie '82
Annie '99 ▸
Annie Get Your Gun '50 ▸
Babes in Toyland '86
Balalaika '39
Beat Street '84
Billy's Holiday '95
Bitter Sweet '40
Black Tights '60
Blue Skies '46 ▸
Born to Dance '36
Breaking the Ice '38
Bride & Prejudice '04
Broadway Melody '29
Broadway Melody of 1938 '37
Broadway Melody of 1940 '40
Bugsy Malone '76
By the Light of the Silvery Moon '53
Calamity Jane '53 ▸
Camp '03
Can't Help Singing '45
Charm of La Boheme '36
De-Lovely '04
Deep in My Heart '54
The Desert Song '53
Dogs in Space '87
The Dolly Sisters '46
Easter Parade '48 ▸
Easy to Love '53
Emperor Waltz '48
Every Little Step '08
The Fantasticks '95
Flying Down to Rio '33
Follies Girl '43
Follies in Concert '85
Follow the Fleet '36 ▸
Footlight Parade '33 ▸
Footlight Serenade '42
For Me and My Gal '42
For the First Time '59
Frankenstein Sings... The Movie '95
From Justin to Kelly '03
The Gang's All Here '43
Hair '79 ▸
Half a Sixpence '67
Hands Across the Border '43
Hans Brinker '69
Hans Christian Andersen '52
Happy Landing '38
Harlem on the Prairie '38
Harvest Melody '43
Hats Off '37
Hawaii Calls '38
Hi-De-Ho '35
Higher and Higher '44
Hillbillies in a Haunted House '67
The Hole '98
The Holy Terror '37
Hot Summer '68
Iceland '42
Incident at Channel Q '86
Invitation to the Dance '56
Jack Ahoy '34
Joseph and the Amazing Technicolor Dreamcoat '00 ▸
Junction 88 '47
Killer Diller '48
Krush Groove '85
Let Freedom Ring '39
Let's Sing Again '36
A Little Night Music '77
London Melody '37
Look for the Silver Lining '49
Love's Labour's Lost '00
Madam Satan '30
Man About Town '39
Manhattan Merry-Go-Round '37
The Marriage of Figaro '49
Maytime '37 ▸
Meet Me in St. Louis '44 ▸
Meet the Navy '46
Mrs. Brown, You've Got a Lovely Daughter '68
Mrs. Santa Claus '96
Moon over Harlem '39
Moon over Miami '41 ▸
Music in My Heart '40
My Lucky Star '38
Oh! Calcutta! '72
Oh! What a Lovely War '69
Oklahoma! '55 ▸
On Moonlight Bay '51
On the Town '91
100 Men and a Girl '37 ▸
Pagan Love Song '50
Perhaps Love '05
Pippin '81 ▸
Private Buckaroo '42
Rainbow over Broadway '33
Red Garters '54
Reet, Petite and Gone '47 ▸
Rhapsody '54
Rhythm Parade '43
Rich, Young and Pretty '51
Rodgers & Hammerstein's South Pacific '01
Rosalie '38
Second Chorus '40
Sepia Cinderella '47
The Seven Hills of Rome '58
She Shall Have Music '36
Something in the Wind '47
South Pacific '58 ▸
Spring Parade '40
Square Dance Jubilee '51
Stage Door Canteen '43
Stingaree '34
Stormy Weather '43
The Story of Vernon and Irene Castle '39 ▸
The Student Prince '54
Sweeney Todd: The Demon Barber of Fleet Street '84
Sweet Adeline '35
Swing Parade of 1946 '46
Take It Big '44
Terror of Tiny Town '38
Thank Your Lucky Stars '43 ▸
That Midnight Kiss '49
That's Dancing! '85 ▸
That's Entertainment '74 ▸
That's Entertainment, Part 2 '76
That's Entertainment, Part 3 '93
Thousands Cheer '43
The Threepenny Opera '31
Thrill of a Romance '45
Tin Pan Alley '40
The Toast of New Orleans '50
Tonight and Every Night '45
The Trouble with Girls (and How to Get into It) '69 ▸
Under the Cherry Moon '86
Vagabond Lover '29
The Vampyr '92
Viva Las Vegas '63
Week-End in Havana '41
Welcome Stranger '47
Wigstock: The Movie '95
Window Shopping '86
Wintertime '43
Words and Music '48
Yes, Sir, Mr. Bones '51
The Young Girls of Rochefort '68
Young People '40

Mutiny

***see also** Deep Blue; Sail Away; Sea Disasters; Shipwrecked*

All the Brothers Were Valiant '53
Amistad '97 ▸
The Bounty '84
The Caine Mutiny '54 ▸
The Caine Mutiny Court Martial '88 ▸
Crimson Tide '95 ▸
The Legend of the Sea Wolf '58
Mutiny '52
The Mutiny of the Elsinore '39
Mutiny on the Blackhawk '39
Mutiny on the Bounty '35 ▸
Mutiny on the Bounty '62
Pirate Ship '49
The Sea Wolf '41 ▸
The Sea Wolf '93

Mystery & Suspense

***see also** Contemporary Noir; Crime Drama; Film Noir; Psycho-Thriller; Serial Killers; Spies & Espionage*

Abduction of St. Anne '75
Above Suspicion '43 ▸
Above Suspicion '95
Absolution '81
Accidental Meeting '93
Accidents '89
Accomplice '46
Accused '36
Ace Drummond '36
Ace of Hearts '85
Across the Bridge '57
Across the Pacific '42 ▸
Acting on Impulse '93
Address Unknown '96
Adrift '93
Adventures of a Private Eye '77
The Adventures of Sherlock Holmes '39
An Affair in Mind '89
African Rage '78
After Dark, My Sweet '90 ▸
After Pilkington '88
After the Thin Man '36 ▸
Agatha '79
Agatha Christie's A Caribbean Mystery '83
Agatha Christie's Murder is Easy '82
Agatha Christie's Murder with Mirrors '85
Agatha Christie's Sparkling Cyanide '83
Agatha Christie's The Pale Horse '96
Agatha Christie's Thirteen at Dinner '85
Alias John Preston '56
Alibi for Murder '36
All-American Murder '91
All Good Things '09
All the Kind Strangers '74
Alligator Eyes '90
Almost Partners '87
The Alphabet Murders '65
Alphaville '65 ▸
The Amateur '82
Amazing Mr. Blunden '72
The Amazing Mr. X '48
The Ambassador '84
The American Friend '77 ▸
American Gigolo '79
Amnesia '96
Amsterdamned '88
And Soon the Darkness '70
And Then There Were None '45 ▸
The Anderson Tapes '71 ▸
Android '82
The Andromeda Strain '71
Angel Dust '96
Angel Heart '87
Angels & Demons '09
Animal Instincts '92
Animal Instincts 2 '94
Another Thin Man '39
Any Man's Death '90
Any Number Can Win '63
Apology '86
Appointment with Death '88
Appointment with Fear '85
Apprentice to Murder '88
Arabesque '66
Are You in the House Alone? '78
Arizona Stagecoach '42
The Arsenal Stadium Mystery '39
The Art of Crime '75
As Good as Dead '95
Assassin '86
Assassin '89
The Assassination File '96
The Assassination Run '84
Assault '70
The Atomic City '52
Autopsy '74
The Avenging Hand '36
The Baby Doll Murders '92
The Babysitter '95
Back from Eternity '56
Back to Hannibal: The Return of Tom Sawyer and Huckleberry Finn '90
Back to the Wall '56
Backfire '88
Backstab '90
Backstreet Justice '93
Backtrack '89 ▸
B.A.D. Cats '80
Bad Company '94
Bad Ronald '74 ▸
The Banker '89
The Barcelona Kill '77
Basic Instinct '92
The Bat Whispers '30
Battle Shock '56
Bedford Incident '65
Bedroom Eyes '86
Bedroom Eyes 2 '89
The Bedroom Window '87
Before I Say Goodbye '03
Before Morning '33
Behind Locked Doors '48
Bell from Hell '74
Bellamy '81
The Beneficiary '97
Benefit of the Doubt '93
Berlin Express '48 ▸
Berserk! '67
Best Seller '87 ▸
Betrayal of the Dove '92
Betrayed '88
Beyond a Reasonable Doubt '56
Beyond the Bermuda Triangle '75
Beyond the Silhouette '90
Big Deadly Game '54
The Big Easy '87 ▸
The Big Fall '96
The Big Fix '78 ▸
The Big Heat '53 ▸
The Big Hurt '87
Big News '29
The Big Sleep '46 ▸
The Big Sleep '78
The Big Switch '70
Big Town After Dark '47
Bikini Island '91
The Bird with the Crystal Plumage '70
Birgitt Haas Must Be Killed '83
Bitter Harvest '93
Bitter Vengeance '94
The Black Abbot '63
Black Bird '75
Black Box Affair '66
The Black Camel '31
The Black Cat '81
Black Cobra '83
The Black Doll '38
The Black Gate '95
Black Glove '54
Black Gold '36
The Black Hand '50 ▸
Black Ice '92
Black Limelight '38
Black Magic Woman '91
Black Panther '77
Black Rainbow '91 ▸
The Black Raven '43
Black Sunday '77
Black Tide '58
Black Tower '50
A Black Veil for Lisa '68
Black Water '94
Black Widow '87 ▸
The Black Windmill '74
Blackmail '29 ▸
Blackmail '91 ▸
Blackout '54
Blackout '85
Blackwater Trail '95
Blind Date '84
Blind Fear '89
Blind Horizon '04
Blind Justice '86
Blind Man's Bluff '91
Blind Side '93
Blind Vision '91
Blind Witness '89
Blindfold: Acts of Obsession '94
Blindside '88
Blindsided '93
Blitz '85
Blonde Blackmailer '58
Blood Frenzy '87
Blood on the Sun '45
Blood Rain '05
Blood Relations '87
Blood Relatives '77
Blood Simple '85 ▸
Bloodhounds '96
Bloodhounds 2 '96
Bloody Avenger '80
Bloody Beach '00
Blow Out '81 ▸
Blown Away '93
Blue City '86
Blue Desert '91 ▸
Blue Ice '92
Blue Smoke '07
Blue Steel '90
Blue Tornado '90
Blue Velvet '86 ▸
Blue, White and Perfect '42
Bodily Harm '95
Body Chemistry '90
Body Chemistry 3: Point of Seduction '93
Body Double '84 ▸
Body Heat '81 ▸
The Body in the Library '84
Body Language '92
Body Language '95
Body of Influence '93
Body Parts '94
Body Shot '93
The Body Vanished '39
Boomerang '47 ▸
Borderline '50
B.O.R.N. '88
Born to Kill '47 ▸
The Boston Strangler '68
Bounty Hunters '89
The Bourne Identity '88 ▸
The Boys from Brazil '78
Brass Target '78
Breakdown '96 ▸
Breakheart Pass '76
Breaking All the Rules '85
Brick '06 ▸
The Bride Wore Black '68 ▸
Brighton Strangler '45
Broken Vows '87
Brotherly Love '85
Bubble '06
Bulldog Drummond '29
Bulldog Drummond at Bay '37
Bulldog Drummond Comes Back '37
Bulldog Drummond's Bride '39
Bulldog Drummond's Peril '38
Bulldog Drummond's Revenge '37
Bulldog Drummond's Secret Police '39
Bullet to Beijing '95
Bulletproof Heart '95 ▸
Bums '93
Burndown '89
Buying Time '89
By Dawn's Early Light '89
By the Blood of Others '73 ▸
Calendar Girl Murders '84
The Caller '87
Calling Paul Temple '48
Candles at Nine '44
Caper of the Golden Bulls '67
Cardiac Arrest '74
Caribe '87
Carnival Lady '33
Carolina Moon '07
Caroline at Midnight '93
A Case for Murder '93
The Case of the Lucky Legs '35
Cast a Dark Shadow '55 ▸
Cast a Deadly Spell '91 ▸
Castle in the Desert '42
Cat and Mouse '78 ▸
The Cat and the Canary '27 ▸
The Cat and the Canary '79
Cat Chaser '90
The Cat o' Nine Tails '71
Catacombs '89
The Catamount Killing '74
Catch Me a Spy '71
Catherine's Grove '98
Caught in the Act '93
Cause for Alarm '51
Center of the Web '92
The Centerfold Girls '74
Chain of Desire '93
Challenge of McKenna '70
Charlie Chan and the Curse of the Dragon Queen '81
Charlie Chan at Monte Carlo '37
Charlie Chan at the Circus '36
Charlie Chan at the Olympics '37
Charlie Chan at the Opera '36 ▸
Charlie Chan at the Race Track '36
Charlie Chan at the Wax Museum '40
Charlie Chan in Egypt '35
Charlie Chan in London '34
Charlie Chan in Paris '35
Charlie Chan in Rio '41
Charlie Chan in Shanghai '35
Charlie Chan in the Secret Service '44
Charlie Chan on Broadway '37
Charlie Chan's Murder Cruise '40
Charlie Chan's Secret '35
Charlie McCarthy, Detective '39
Charlie Muffin '79
Child in the Night '90

▸ = rated three bones or higher

► = rated three bones or higher

Hostage '92
Hostages '80
Hot Child in the City '87
Hotel '01
Hotel Colonial '88
Hotel Reserve '44 ►
Hotline '82
The Hound of London '93
The Hound of the Baskervilles '39 ►
The Hound of the Baskervilles '59
The Hound of the Baskervilles '83
Hour of Decision '57
A House in the Hills '93
House of Fear '45
House of Mystery '34
House of Mystery '41
The House of Secrets '37
House of Shadows '76
The House of the Arrow '53 ►
House of the Damned '71
House of the Rising Sun '87
The House on Carroll Street '88
The Housekeeper '86
Human Desires '97
Human Gorilla '48
The Human Monster '39
Hunt the Man Down '50
Hunter '76
The Hunting '92
The Hustle '75
Hysteria '64
I Am the Cheese '83
I Bury the Living '58 ►
I Confess '53
I Killed That Man '42
I, Madman '89
I See a Dark Stranger '46 ►
I Stand Condemned '36
I, the Jury '82
The Ice House '97 ►
I'd Give My Life '36
If It's a Man, Hang Up '75
If Looks Could Kill '86
I'll Get You '53
I'll Name the Murderer '36
Illegal '55
Illegal in Blue '95
Illicit Behavior '91
Illicit Dreams '94
Illusions '91
I'm Not Scared '03
I'm the Girl He Wants to Kill '74
I'm the One You're Looking For '88
Image of Death '77
Impact '49 ►
Improper Conduct '94
Impulse '55
Impulse '84
Impulse '90
In a Lonely Place '50 ►
In a Moment of Passion '93
In a Stranger's Hand '92
In an Old Manor House '84
In Self Defense '93
In the Cold of the Night '89
In the Deep Woods '91
In the Heat of the Night '67 ►
In the Kingdom of the Blind the Man with One Eye Is King '94
In the Line of Fire '93 ►
In the Secret State '85
In the Spirit '90
In the Valley of Elah '07 ►
Indecency '92
Indecent Behavior '93
Indecent Behavior 2 '94
The Indian Scarf '63
Indiscreet '98
Infamous Crimes '47
Inheritance '47 ►
The Inheritor '90
Inland Empire '06
The Inner Circle '46
Inner Sanctum '48
Inner Sanctum '91
Inner Sanctum 2 '94
The Innocent '93
Innocent Lies '95
Innocent Victim '90
Innocents with Dirty Hands '76
The Inquiry '87
Insanity '76
The Inside Man '84
Inspector Lynley Mysteries: A Great Deliverance '01
The Instructor '83
Interface '84
International Crime '37
Internecine Project '73
The Interpreter '05 ►
Interrupted Journey '49
Intimate Stranger '91
Into the Blue '97
Into the Fire '88
Intrigue '90
Intruder '76
Invasion of Privacy '92
Investigation '79
The Invisible '07
The Invisible Avenger '58
The Invisible Killer '40
Invitation to Hell '84
The Ipcress File '65 ►
The Iris Effect '04
Irish Luck '39
Island Monster '53
Istanbul '85
It Could Happen to You '39
It Happened at Nightmare Inn '70
Jack's Back '87 ►
The Jade Mask '45
The Jagged Edge '85
Jane Doe '83
Jaws of Death '76
Jennifer 8 '92
Jenny Lamour '47
Jezebel's Kiss '90
Jigsaw '90
The Jigsaw Man '84
Jigsaw Murders '89
Johnny Angel '45 ►
Johnny Nobody '61
Johnny Skidmarks '97
Journey into Fear '42 ►
Journey into Fear '74
Joy House '64
JSA: Joint Security Area '00 ►
Judicial Consent '94
Juggernaut '74 ►
Jungle Bride '33
The Junkman '82
Just Another Pretty Face '58
Just Cause '94
Just Off Broadway '42
Kafka '91
Keane '04 ►
Kemek '70
The Kennel Murder Case '33
Kentucky Jubilee '51
Keys to Tulsa '96
The KGB: The Secret War '86
Kid '90
Kidnapped '87
The Kidnapping of the President '80
Kill Cruise '90
The Kill-Off '90
Killer Fish '79
Killer Image '92
A Killer in Every Corner '74
Killer Likes Candy '78
Killer Looks '94
Killer with Two Faces '74
The Killers '64
A Killing Affair '85
The Killing Game '87
Killing Hour '84
The Killing Jar '96
The Killing Kind '73
The Killing Mind '90
Killing Obsession '94
Killing Stone '78
The Killing Time '87
Killjoy '81
Killpoint '84
The King Murder '32
A Kiss Before Dying '91
Kiss Daddy Goodnight '87
Kiss Me a Killer '91
Kiss Me, Kill Me '73
Klute '71 ►
La Ceremonie '95 ►
L.A. Confidential '97 ►
L.A. Goddess '92
La Moustache '05
La Passante '83 ►
Lady Audley's Secret '00
Lady Beware '87
The Lady Confesses '45
The Lady from Shanghai '48 ►
Lady in a Cage '64 ►
Lady in Cement '68
The Lady in Question '99
Lady in the Death House '44
The Lady in White '88 ►
Lady of Burlesque '43
Lady Scarface '41
The Lady Vanishes '38 ►
The Lady Vanishes '79
Ladykiller '92
Ladykillers '88
Laguna Heat '87
Last Dance '91
Last Embrace '79 ►
The Last of Philip Banter '87
The Last of Sheila '73
Last Rites '88
Last Song '80
The Late Show '77 ►
The Laughing Policeman '74
Laura '44 ►
Le Corbeau '43 ►
Le Magnifique '76
Le Polygraphe '96
Le Secret '74 ►
Left for Dead '78
Legacy of Lies '92
Legal Deceit '95
Lemming '05
Letter to My Killer '95
The Liars '64
Liar's Edge '92
Lie Down with Lions '94
Liebestraum '91
Lies '83
Lies Before Kisses '92
The Life of David Gale '03
Lifespan '75
The Lift '85
The Lightning Incident '91
Lights! Camera! Murder! '89
Lily Was Here '89
The Limping Man '53
Linda '93
Lipstick Camera '93
Lisa '90
Lisbon '56
The List of Adrian Messenger '63 ►
The Little Drummer Girl '84 ►
The Little Girl Who Lives down the Lane '76
Little Nikita '88
Living to Die '91
The Lodger '26 ►
Lonely Hearts '91
The Long Goodbye '73 ►
Long Time Gone '86
Loose Cannons '90
The Lost Angel '04
Lost Junction '03
The Lost Jungle '34
The Lost Tribe '89
Love '05
Love and Hate: A Marriage Made in Hell '90
Love & Murder '91
Love at Large '89 ►
Love Camp '81
Love from a Stranger '37
Love from a Stranger '47
Love Kills '91
Love on the Run '85
Lower Level '91
Lure of the Islands '42
Lying Lips '39
The Machinist '04
Mackintosh Man '73
The Mad Executioners '65
Madame Sin '71
Madeleine '50
Madigan '68 ►
Magic Moments '89
Malevolence '04
Malibu Express '85
Malice '93
Malicious '95
A Man About the House '47
Man Bait '52
Man from Headquarters '28
The Man from the Pru '89
The Man Inside '90
Man on Fire '87
The Man on the Roof '76
Man on the Run '74
Man Outside '88
The Man Who Haunted Himself '70
The Man Who Knew Too Much '34 ►
The Man Who Knew Too Much '56
The Man Who Would Not Die '75
Man with a Gun '95
The Manchurian Candidate '62 ►
The Mandarin Mystery '37
Manfish '56
The Manhattan Project '86
Manhunter '86 ►
Maniac '63
Marathon Man '76 ►
Margin for Murder '81
Marie Galante '34 ►
Mark of Cain '84
Mark of the Beast '87
Marked for Murder '89
Marlowe '69
Marnie '64 ►
Maroc 7 '67
Mascara '87
Mask of the Dragon '51
Masks of Death '86
Masquerade '88 ►
Master Touch '74
Masters of Horror: Cigarette Burns '05
Masters of Horror: Deer Woman '05
Masters of Horror: Dream Cruise '07
Masters of Horror: Dreams in the Witch House '05
Masters of Horror: Fair Haired Child '06
Masters of Horror: Family '05
Masters of Horror: Homecoming '05
Masters of Horror: Imprint '05
Masters of Horror: Jenifer '05
Masters of Horror: Pelts '06
Masters of Horror: Pro-Life '05
Masters of Horror: Right to Die '07
Masters of Horror: Sick Girl '06
Masters of Horror: Sounds Like '06
Masters of Horror: The Screwfly Solution '06
Masters of Horror: The V Word '05
Masters of Horror: The Washingtonians '07
Masters of Horror: Valerie on the Stairs '06
Masters of Horror: We All Scream for Ice Cream '07
A Matter of WHO '62
Maya '82
The Maze '85 ►
Mazes and Monsters '82
The McGuffin '85
Medusa '74
Meeting at Midnight '44
Memories of Murder '90
Memories of Murder '03
Men at Work '90
Messenger of Death '88
Miami Blues '90
Michael Shayne: Private Detective '40
Midnight '34
Midnight at the Wax Museum '36
Midnight Faces '26
Midnight Girl '25
Midnight Heat '95
Midnight in Saint Petersburg '97
Midnight Limited '40
Midnight Warning '32
Midnight Witness '93
Mike's Murder '84
Million Dollar Mystery '87
Mind, Body & Soul '92
A Mind to Kill '95
A Mind to Murder '96
Mind Twister '93
Mindfield '89
Mirage '66 ►
Mirage '94
The Mirror Crack'd '80
Mirror Images '91
Mirror Images 2 '93
The Missing Gun '02
Missing Pieces '83
Mistaken Identity '41
Mr. Frost '89
Mr. Moto in Danger Island '39
Mr. Moto Takes a Chance '38
Mr. Moto Takes a Vacation '39
Mr. Moto's Gamble '38
Mr. Moto's Last Warning '39 ►
Mr. Reeder in Room 13 '38
Mr. Scarface '77
Mr. Wong, Detective '38
Mr. Wong in Chinatown '39
Money Madness '47
Monique '76
Monsieur N. '03 ►
The Monster Walks '32
Moon in Scorpio '86
Moonlighting '85
The Moonstone '34
The Moonstone '97 ►
The Morning After '86
Mortal Passions '90
The Most Dangerous Game '32 ►
Mother's Boys '94
Motive for Revenge '35
Mr. Takes a Vacation '39
Motor Patrol '50
Motorcycle Squad '41
Murder '30 ►
Murder Ahoy '64
Murder at 45 R.P.M. '65
Murder at Midnight '31
Murder at 1600 '97
Murder at the Baskervilles '37
Murder at the Gallop '63 ►
Murder by Decree '79 ►
Murder by Natural Causes '79 ►
Murder by Night '89
Murder by Numbers '89
Murder by Phone '82
Murder by Television '35
Murder by the Book '87
Murder in a Small Town '99
Murder in Mind '97
Murder in Space '85
Murder in the Footlights '46
A Murder Is Announced '87
Murder Most Foul '65 ►
Murder, My Sweet '44 ►
A Murder of Crows '99
A Murder of Quality '90
Murder on Approval '56
Murder on the Campus '52
Murder on the High Seas '32
Murder on the Midnight Express '74
Murder on the Orient Express '74 ►
Murder Once Removed '71
Murder 101 '91
Murder over New York '40
Murder Rap '87
Murder She Purred: A Mrs. Murphy Mystery '98
Murder She Said '62
Murder So Sweet '93
Murder Story '89
Murder: Ultimate Grounds for Divorce '84
Murder Without Conviction '04
Murdered Innocence '94
Murderers' Row '66
Murderlust '86
Murderous Vision '91
Murders at Lynch Cross '85
Murders in the Doll House '79
Murders in the Rue Morgue '71
The Murders in the Rue Morgue '86 ►
Mute Witness '95
My Man Adam '86
My Sister, My Love '78
My Sweet Victim '85
Mysterious Doctor Satan '40
The Mysterious Magician '65
Mysterious Mr. Moto '38
Mysterious Mr. Wong '35
Mystery in Swing '40
Mystery Liner '34
The Mystery Man '35
Mystery Mansion '83
The Mystery of Edwin Drood '35
The Mystery of Edwin Drood '93
Mystery of Mr. Wong '39
The Mystery of Rampo '94 ►
The Mystery of the Mary Celeste '35
Mystery of the Riverboat '44
Mystery Plane '39
Mystery Woman: Mystery Weekend '05
Mystic Circle Murder '39
The Naked Edge '61
The Naked Face '84
Naked Obsession '91
The Name of the Rose '86
Nancy Drew '07
Nancy Drew and the Hidden Staircase '39
Nancy Drew—Detective '38
Nancy Drew, Reporter '39
Nancy Drew—Trouble Shooter '39
The Narrow Margin '52 ►
Narrow Margin '90
National Treasure: Book of Secrets '07
Natural Causes '94
Natural Enemy '96
Nature's Playmates '62
The Neighbor '93
Nemesis Game '03
Neutron vs. the Maniac '62
Never Say Die '90
New Year's Evil '78
New York Ripper '82
Newman's Law '74
The Next Victim '71
Next Victim '74
Niagara '52
Night and the City '50 ►
Night Angel '90
Night Birds '31
Night Cries '78
Night Eyes '90
Night Eyes 2 '91
Night Eyes 3 '93
Night Fire '94
A Night for Crime '42
The Night Has Eyes '42
The Night Listener '06
Night Moves '75 ►
Night of Terror '33
Night of the Assassin '77
Night of the Cyclone '90
The Night of the Hunter '55 ►
Night of the Juggler '80
Night Rhythms '92
Night School '81
Night Shadow '90
Night Stalker '87
Night Terror '76
A Night to Remember '42 ►
Night Train '09
Night Train to Munich '40 ►
The Night Visitor '70
Night Watch '72
The Nightcomers '72
Nighthawks '81
Nightkill '80
The Nightman '93
Nightmare in Badham County '76
Nightwaves '03
Nightwing '79
No Mercy '86
No Place to Hide '81
No Place to Hide '93
No Problem '75
No Secrets '91
No Way Out '87 ►
No Way to Treat a Lady '68 ►
No Witness '04
Nocturne '46
Non-Stop New York '37
Norman Conquest '53
North by Northwest '59 ►
Nothing Underneath '85
Notorious '46 ►

▸ = rated three bones or higher

Tough Assignment '49
Tough Guys Don't Dance '87
Tourist Trap '79
Tower of Terror '97
Town That Dreaded Sundown '76
Traces of Red '92
Track 16 '02
Track 29 '88
Trade Secrets '86
The Train Killer '83
Transsiberian '08 ▶
The Trap '59
Trapped '89
Trauma '62
Treacherous Crossing '92
Trial and Error '92
Trial by Jury '94
The Triumph of Sherlock Holmes '35
Tropical Heat '93
Tropix '02
The Trouble with Harry '55 ▶
True Believer '89
True Crime '95
True Lies '94
Twenty Dollar Star '91
23 Paces to Baker Street '56
Twilight '98 ▶
Twilight Man '96
Twin Sisters '91
Twisted Obsession '90
Two by Forsyth '86
Two Fathers' Justice '85
The Two Jakes '90
Ultimate Desires '91
The Ultimate Imposter '79
The Ultimate Thrill '74
Ultraviolet '92
Uncovered '94
Under Capricorn '49
Under Capricorn '82
Under Investigation '93
Under Suspicion '92
Undercover '94
Uneasy Terms '48
Unholy Four '54
Unholy Wife '57
Union City '81
Union Station '50
Unsane '82
Unsuitable Job for a Woman '82
Unveiled '94
Up in the Air '40
Urge to Kill '84
The Usual Suspects '95 ▶
Utz '93
The Vagrant '92
Vamping '84
The Vanishing '88 ▶
The Vanishing '93
Vanishing Act '88
Vatican Conspiracy '81
The Vector File '03
Vegas '78
Velvet Touch '48 ▶
Verdict in Blood '02
Vertigo '58 ▶
The Very Edge '63
Vicious '88
The Vicious Circle '57
Victim of Beauty '91
Victim of Desire '94
Victim of Love '91
Video Murders '87
The Village '04
Violette '78 ▶
The Vision '87
Visions '90
Visiting Hours '82
The Voice of Merrill '52
Voices '08
A Vow to Kill '94
Vultures '84
W '74
Waikiki '80
Wallander: Firewall '08
Wallander: One Step Behind '08
Wallander: Sidetracked '08
Wanted: Babysitter '75
Warm Nights on a Slow-Moving Train '87
Warning Sign '85
Watched '73
The Way Out '56
Wayne Murder Case '32 ▶
Weep No More My Lady '93
We'll Meet Again '02
Whatever Happened to Aunt Alice? '69 ▶
When a Stranger Calls '79
When a Stranger Calls Back '93
When I Close My Eyes '93
When the Bough Breaks '86
Where Are the Children? '85
Where Sleeping Dogs Lie '91
Where the Truth Lies '05
Where's the Money, Noreen? '95
A Whisper to a Scream '88
Whispering City '47 ▶
Whispering Shadow '33
Whispers in the Dark '92
The Whistle Blower '87 ▶
White Fire '84
White Hot: The Mysterious Murder of Thelma Todd '91
White Mischief '88 ▶
White Noise '05
White of the Eye '88 ▶
The White Raven '98
White Sands '92
Who Is the Black Dahlia? '75 ▶
Who Killed Baby Azaria? '83
Who Killed Bambi? '03
Who Killed Mary What's 'Er Name? '71
Whodunit '82
Widow Couderc '74 ▶
Widow's Kiss '94
Widow's Nest '77
Wild Cactus '92
Wild Things '98
Wild West '46
Wildcard '92
The Wind '87
The Window '49 ▶
Witch Hunt '94
Witchfire '86
Without Warning '52
Witness for the Prosecution '57 ▶
Woman Condemned '33
Woman Hunt '72
The Woman Hunter '72
Woman in Black '89
The Woman in Green '49
The Woman in Question '50
The Woman in White '97
Woman of Desire '93
Woman Undone '95
The Woman Who Came Back '45
A Woman's Face '38 ▶
A Woman's Face '41 ▶
Wonderland '88 ▶
The Word '78
Writer's Block '91
The Wrong Man '56 ▶
The Wrong Man '93
The Wrong Woman '95
Yellowstone '36
Young and Innocent '37 ▶
Young Sherlock Holmes '85
Z '69 ▶
Zentropa '92
Zero Boys '86
Zertigo Diamond Caper '82
The Zodiac Killer '71

Mythology

***see also** Folklore & Legends*

Atlantis, the Lost Continent '61
Ba'al: The Storm God '08
Beowulf '07 ▶
The Cave of the Silken Web '67
Cerberus '05
Chupacabra Terror '05
Clash of the Titans '81
Colossus and the Amazon Queen '64
Conquest of Mycene '63
Dragon Wars '07
The Fury of Hercules '61
The Gorgon '64
The Great Yokai War '05
Helen of Troy '03
Hercules '58
Hercules '83
Hercules '97 ▶
Hercules against the Moon Men '64
Hercules and the Captive Women '63
Hercules and the Princess of Troy '65
Hercules in New York '70
Hercules in the Haunted World '64
Hercules, Prisoner of Evil '64
Hercules Unchained '59
Hercules vs. the Sons of the Sun '64
Jason and the Argonauts '00
The Loves of Hercules '60
The Maid '05
Medusa Against the Son of Hercules '62
Onmyoji '01
Onmyoji 2 '03
Orochi, the Eight Headed Dragon '94
Sinbad '71
Sinbad and the Eye of the Tiger '77
Sinbad: Legend of the Seven Seas '03
Sinbad of the Seven Seas '89
Sinbad, the Sailor '47 ▶
Son of Hercules in the Land of Darkness '63
Terror of Rome Against the Son of Hercules '64
The Triumph of Hercules '66
Troy '04
Young Aphrodites '63

Nannies & Governesses

***see also** Babysitting; Bringing Up Baby; The Help: Female; Parenthood*

Adam Had Four Sons '41
Addams Family Values '93
All This and Heaven Too '40 ▶
Anna and the King of Siam '46 ▶
At the Midnight Hour '95
Au Pair '99
Au Pair 2: The Fairy Tale Continues '01
Baby Monitor: Sound of Fear '97
Becky Sharp '35
Berkeley Square '98
Big Momma's House 2 '06
Blanche Fury '48
Blue Blood '73
The Chalk Garden '64 ▶
Corrina, Corrina '94
Cousin Bette '97
The Devil's Own '96 ▶
Eloise at the Plaza '03
Emma's Wish '98
The Family Holiday '07
Flame Over India '60 ▶
Flight of the Red Balloon '08
Friend of the Family 2 '96
The Governess '98
The Hand that Rocks the Cradle '92
The Haunting of Morella '91
Heidi '37
The Innocents '61 ▶
Invisible Child '99
Jack and Sarah '95
Jane Eyre '34
Jane Eyre '44 ▶
Jane Eyre '83 ▶
Jane Eyre '96 ▶
Jane Eyre '97
Jane Eyre '06
The King and I '56 ▶
The King and I '99
Lady Audley's Secret '00
Left Luggage '98
Lily in Winter '94
Mammoth '09
Mary Poppins '64 ▶
Midnight's Child '93
Miss Mary '86
Mrs. Doubtfire '93
Mr. Nanny '93
My Daughter's Keeper '93
The Nanny '65
The Nanny Diaries '07
Nanny Insanity '06
Nanny McPhee '06
Nanny McPhee 2 '10
The Nightcomers '72
Perfect Family '92
The Perfect Nanny '00
Peter Pan '53 ▶
Peter Pan '60 ▶
Provocateur '96
Rescuers: Stories of Courage "Two Women" '97 ▶
The Secret Life of Bees '08 ▶
The Sound of Music '65 ▶
The Turn of the Screw '74
The Turn of the Screw '89
The Turn of the Screw '92
The Turn of the Screw '99
Undesirable '92
The Unknown Woman '06
Uptown Girls '03
Vanity Fair '67
Vanity Fair '99

Nashville

***see also** American South; Nashville Narratives*

The Concrete Cowboys '79
Doing Time for Patsy Cline '97
Honkytonk Man '82
Nashville '75 ▶
Nashville Beat '89
Nashville Girl '76
Neil Young: Heart of Gold '06 ▶
The Night the Lights Went Out in Georgia '81
Sweet Country Road '83
The Thing Called Love '93

Nashville Narratives

***see also** American South; Biopics: Musicians; Southern Belles*

Baja Oklahoma '87
Cassie '83
The City '76
Coal Miner's Daughter '80 ▶
The Country Bears '02
Crazy Heart '09
Doing Time for Patsy Cline '97
Falling from Grace '92
Hard Part Begins '73
Honeysuckle Rose '80
Honkytonk Man '82
Honkytonk Nights '78
Jackpot '01
Lady Grey '82
Living Proof: The Hank Williams Jr. Story '83
Nashville '75 ▶
Nashville Girl '76
The Night the Lights Went Out in Georgia '81
Payday '73
Pure Country '92
Rhinestone '84
Rikky and Pete '88
Road to Nashville '67
Saturday Night Special '92
A Smoky Mountain Christmas '86
Songwriter '84
Sweet Dreams '85
Tender Mercies '83 ▶
The Thing Called Love '93
Wild West '93

National Guard

***see also** Military: Army; Persian Gulf/Iraq War*

Attack! '56 ▶
Beginning of the End '57
Between Heaven and Hell '56 ▶
Delta Farce '07
First Blood '82
The Ground Truth '06
The Hills Have Eyes 2 '07
Kent State '81
Night of the Lepus '72
Southern Comfort '81 ▶
Viva Max '69

Native America

The Abduction of Allison Tate '92
Across the Wide Missouri '51
Angry Joe Bass '76
Apache Blood '75
Apache Chief '50
Apache Woman '55
The Avenging '92
Bad Lands '39
The Bears & I '74
Big Bear '98
Big Eden '00
Billy Jack '71
Billy Two Hats '74
Black Cloud '04
Black Fox: Blood Horse '94
Black Fox: The Price of Peace '94
Black Robe '91 ▶
Bone Eater '07
Born Losers '67
Braveheart '25
Broken Arrow '50
The Broken Chain '93
Brother Bear '03
Brother Bear 2 '06
Brotherhood of the Wolf '01
Buck and the Magic Bracelet '97
Buffalo Bill Rides Again '47
Buffalo Soldiers '97 ▶
Bugles in the Afternoon '52
Bury My Heart at Wounded Knee '07
The Business of Fancydancing '02
Canyon Passage '46 ▶
Captain Apache '71
The Captive: The Longest Drive 2 '76
Carry On Columbus '92
Cavalier of the West '31
Cavalry Charge '51
Centennial '78 ▶
Chato's Land '71
Cheyenne Autumn '64
Cheyenne Warrior '94
Christmas in the Clouds '01
Chuka '67
Circle of Death '36
Clearcut '92
Comanche Moon '08
The Comancheros '61 ▶
The Command '54
Conquest of Cochise '53
Cotter '72
Coyote Waits '03
Crazy Horse '96 ▶
Crazy Horse and Custer: "The Untold Story" '90
Crypt of Dark Secrets '76
Custer's Last Fight '12
Dakota Incident '56
Dalva '95
Dan Candy's Law '73
Dance Me Outside '95
Dances with Wolves '90 ▶
The Dark Wind '91
Dead Man '95
Diplomaniacs '33
A Distant Trumpet '64
The Doe Boy '01
The Education of Little Tree '97 ▶
Escape from Fort Bravo '53
The Exiles '61
Eyes of Fire '84
The Far Horizons '55
Fish Hawk '79
Flags of Our Fathers '06 ▶
Flaming Star '60 ▶
Fleshburn '84
Follow the River '95
Four Sheets to the Wind '07
Frozen River '08 ▶
The Gatling Gun '72
Geronimo '62
Geronimo '93 ▶
Geronimo: An American Legend '93
Ghost Dance '83
The Glory Trail '36
A Good Day to Die '95
Grand Avenue '96
Gunman's Walk '58
Hondo '53 ▶
Hybrid '07
I Heard the Owl Call My Name '73
I Will Fight No More Forever '75 ▶
Incident at Oglala: The Leonard Peltier Story '92 ▶
The Indian Fighter '55 ▶
The Indian in the Cupboard '95
Island of the Blue Dolphins '64
Jim Thorpe: All American '51
Joe Panther '76 ▶
Johnny Firecloud '75
Johnny Tiger '66
Journey Through Rosebud '72
Journey to Spirit Island '92
Lakota Woman: Siege at Wounded Knee '94
The Last of His Tribe '92
The Last of the Dogmen '95
The Last of the Mohicans '20 ▶
The Last of the Mohicans '32
The Last of the Mohicans '36
The Last of the Mohicans '85
The Last of the Mohicans '92 ▶
The Last of the Redmen '47
Legend of Walks Far Woman '82
The Legend of Wolf Mountain '92
The Light in the Forest '58
Little Big Man '70 ▶
The Lost Child '00
Lost Colony: The Legend of Roanoke '07
Lost Legacy: A Girl Called Hatter Fox '77
The Magic Stone '95
The Magnificent Seven '98
A Man Called Horse '70 ▶
Man of the House '95
The Manitou '78
Map of the Human Heart '93
Massacre '34
Miracle at Sage Creek '05
The Missing '03 ▶
Mission to Glory '80
A Mormon Maid '17
Naked in the Sun '57
Natas... The Reflection '83
Navajo Blues '97
The New World '05 ▶
Northern Passage '95
On Top of the Whale '82
One Little Indian '73
The Pathfinder '94
Pathfinder '07
Pocahontas '95 ▶
Pocahontas: The Legend '95
Poltergeist 2: The Other Side '86
Powwow Highway '89 ▶
The Prophecy '95
Ravenhawk '95
Rebel Run '94
The Red Fury '84
The Red Half-Breed '70
The Red Raiders '27
Renegades '89
Requiem for a Heavyweight '56 ▶
Requiem for a Heavyweight '62 ▶
Ricochet River '98
Roanoak '86
Running Brave '83
Savage Sam '63
The Savage Seven '68
Savage Wilderness '55
The Secret of Navajo Cave '76
Seminole Uprising '55
Sergeants 3 '62
Shadowhunter '93
Silent Tongue '92
Sioux City '94
Sitting Bull '54
Skins '02
Skinwalker '02
Skipped Parts '00
Smith! '69
Smoke Signals '98
Spirit Rider '93 ▶

▶ = rated three bones or higher

Spirit: Stallion of the Cimarron '02
Spoilers of the North '47
Squanto: A Warrior's Tale '94 ▶
Sunchaser '96
Taking Chances '09
Tecumseh: The Last Warrior '95
Tell Them Willie Boy Is Here '69 ▶
Terror in the Jungle '68
Texas John Slaughter: Geronimo's Revenge '60
A Thief of Time '04
3 Ninjas Knuckle Up '95
Three Warriors '77
Thunder Warrior '85
Thunder Warrior 2 '85
Thunderheart '92 ▶
Tomahawk '51
Tonka '58
Track of the Moonbeast '76
True Heart '97
True Women '97
The Twilight Saga: New Moon '09
Unconquered '47
Undead or Alive '07
Uninvited '93
The Vanishing American '25
The Villain '79
Wagon Wheels '34
Walk the Proud Land '56
War Party '89
Where the Spirit Lives '89
White Fang 2: The Myth of the White Wolf '94
Wind River '98
Windrunner '94
Windtalkers '02
Windwalker '81 ▶
Winterhawk '76
Zoe '01

Nazis & Other Paramilitary Slugs

***see also** Germany; The Holocaust; Judaism; World War II*

Adam Resurrected '08
All the Queen's Men '02
All Through the Night '42 ▶
Amen '02 ▶
Angel of Death '86
Angel with the Trumpet '50
Angry Harvest '85 ▶
Anima '98
Any Man's Death '90
Apt Pupil '97
Ark of the Sun God '82
Army of Shadows '69 ▶
The Assisi Underground '84
Background to Danger '43 ▶
Bedknobs and Broomsticks '71
The Berlin Affair '85
Berlin Express '48 ▶
Betrayed '54 ▶
Black Book '06 ▶
The Black Klansman '66
Blood Creek '09
The Blues Brothers '80 ▶
Bon Voyage '03 ▶
The Boxer and Death '63 ▶
The Boy in the Striped Pajamas '08 ▶
The Boys from Brazil '78
Brady's Escape '84
Brainwashed '60
Broken Glass '96
Bulletproof Monk '03
Cabaret '72 ▶
Cabo Blanco '81
Casablanca '42 ▶
Casablanca Express '89
Charlie Grant's War '80
Clipped Wings '53
Closet Land '90
Cold Days '66
Commandos Strike at Dawn '43
Confessions of a Nazi Spy '39
The Conformist '71 ▶
Conspiracy '01
Contraband '40
Cottage to Let '41
Counterblast '48
The Counterfeit Traitor '62 ▶
The Counterfeiters '07 ▶
The Courageous Heart of Irena Sendler '09 ▶
The Coward '62
The Cut Throats '69
Dam Busters '55 ▶
Dawn Express '42
A Day in October '92
Dead Bang '89
Dead Snow '09
Death Is Called Engelchen '63 ▶
The Death of Adolf Hitler '84
Defiance '08
Descending Angel '90 ▶
Desert Commandos '67
The Desert Fox '51 ▶
Despair '78 ▶
The Devil's Brigade '68
The Diary of Anne Frank '59 ▶
The Dirty Dozen '67 ▶
The Dirty Dozen: The Deadly Mission '87
The Dirty Dozen: The Fatal Mission '88
The Dirty Dozen: The Next Mission '85
Dirty Heroes '71
Divided We Fall '00
Dominion: Prequel to the Exorcist '05
Downfall '04 ▶
Edge of Darkness '43 ▶
Elves '89
The Empty Mirror '99
Enemy at the Gates '00
Enemy of Women '44
Enigma Secret '79
Equalizer 2000 '86
Escape from Sobibor '87 ▶
Europa, Europa '91 ▶
The Execution '85
Eye of the Needle '81
A Face in the Rain '63
The Fallen '05 ▶
The Fallen Sparrow '43 ▶
Fateless '05 ▶
Father '90
Fatherland '94
The Fifth Horseman Is Fear '64
Firewalker '86
Five Fingers '52 ▶
Five Graves to Cairo '43 ▶
The Flesh Eaters '64
Flesh Feast '69
Forbidden '85
Force 10 from Navarone '78
Foreign Correspondent '40 ▶
The Forty-Ninth Parallel '41 ▶
Four Bags Full '56
The Four Horsemen of the Apocalypse '62
A Friendship in Vienna '88
Genghis Cohn '93
Getting Away With Murder '96
Ghost on the Loose '43
The Girl of Your Dreams '99
The Gleiwitz Case '61
The Goebbels Experiment '05
Goldengirl '79
Good '08
Good Evening, Mr. Wallenberg '93
The Great Dictator '40 ▶
The Great Escape '63 ▶
The Grey Zone '01
Hamsun '96
Hangmen Also Die '42
Hanna's War '88
Hanussen '88 ▶
The Harmonists '99
Hart's War '02
He Lives: The Search for the Evil One '67
Head in the Clouds '04
Hearts of War '07
Hell Commandos '69
Hell Hunters '87
Hell River '75
Hell Squad '58
Hellboy '04
Hell's Bloody Devils '70
Heroes in Hell '73
The Heroes of Telemark '65
The Hiding Place '75
Higher Learning '94
Hitler '62
Hitler: Dead or Alive '43
Hitler: The Last Ten Days '73
Hitler: The Rise of Evil '03
Hitler's Children '43 ▶
Hitler's Daughter '90
Holocaust '78 ▶
The Home Front '02
Hornet's Nest '70
Hotel Reserve '44 ▶
The House on Carroll Street '88
The House on Garibaldi Street '79
House on 92nd Street '45 ▶
Ilsa, Harem Keeper of the Oil Sheiks '76
Ilsa, She-Wolf of the SS '74
In a Glass Cage '86
In the Presence of Mine Enemies '97
The Incredible Mr. Limpet '64
Indiana Jones and the Last Crusade '89 ▶
Indiana Jones and the Temple of Doom '84 ▶
The Infiltrator '95
Inglourious Basterds '09 ▶
Inside Out '75
Inside the Third Reich '82
Into the Homeland '87
Invincible '01
Invisible Agent '42
The Island on Bird Street '97
Jack Higgins' The Windsor Protocol '97
Jacob the Liar '74
Jakob the Liar '99 ▶
Jenny's War '85
Jew-Boy Levi '99
Joe and Max '02 ▶
Judgment at Nuremberg '61 ▶
Julia '77 ▶
Jungle Siren '42
Kanal '56 ▶
Kapo '59 ▶
The Keep '83
The Key to Rebecca '85
The Klansman '74
Kojak: The Belarus File '85
Korczak '90 ▶
La Passante '83 ▶
Lassiter '84
The Last Butterfly '92
The Last Drop '05
The Last Five Days '82
The Last Metro '80 ▶
The Last Train '74
Law of the Jungle '42
Les Miserables '95
Les Violons du Bal '74
Life Is Beautiful '98 ▶
Lifeboat '44 ▶
The Longest Day '62 ▶
Lucie Aubrac '98
The Lucifer Complex '78
Madame Rosa '77 ▶
A Man Escaped '57 ▶
Man Hunt '41 ▶
The Man in the Glass Booth '75 ▶
The Man Who Captured Eichmann '96
Marathon Man '76 ▶
Martha and I '91 ▶
Massacre in Rome '73
Master Key '44
The Master Race '44
Me and the Colonel '58
The Mediterranean in Flames '72
Mephisto '81 ▶
Ministry of Fear '44 ▶
Miracle at Midnight '98
Miracle at Moreaux '86
Missiles from Hell '58
Mr. Klein '76 ▶
The Mortal Storm '40 ▶
Mosley '98
Mother Night '96 ▶
Music Box '89
My Fuhrer '07
My Mother's Courage '95
The Nasty Girl '90 ▶
Night Ambush '57
A Night in Casablanca '46 ▶
Night of the Fox '90
Night of the Generals '67 ▶
The Night Porter '74
Night Train to Munich '40 ▶
Night Train to Venice '93
The Ninth Day '04 ▶
No Dead Heroes '87
The North Star '43 ▶
Northern Pursuit '43
Notorious '46 ▶
November Moon '85
Nuremberg '00
Oasis of the Zombies '82
The Odessa File '74
The Ogre '96
Old Gun '76 ▶
Once Upon a Honeymoon '42
One of Our Aircraft Is Missing '41 ▶
The Only Way '70
Open City '45 ▶
O.S.S. '46 ▶
Out of the Ashes '03
Passage to Marseilles '44 ▶
The Pedestrian '73 ▶
The Pianist '02 ▶
Pimpernel Smith '42
Porcile '69
A Prayer for Katarina Horovitzova '69 ▶
Prayer of the Rollerboys '91
Pressure Point '62 ▶
Prisoner of Paradise '02 ▶
Puppet Master 3: Toulon's Revenge '90
The Quiller Memorandum '66 ▶
Raid on Rommel '71
Raiders of the Lost Ark '81 ▶
Rescuers: Stories of Courage "Two Women" '97 ▶
Reunion in France '42
The Revolt of Job '84 ▶
Richard III '95 ▶
Rio Rita '42
River of Death '90
River of Diamonds '90
The Rocketeer '91 ▶
The Rose Garden '89
Rosenstrasse '03 ▶
The Salzburg Connection '72
Savage Attraction '83
The Scarlet & the Black '83
Schindler's List '93 ▶
Schtonk '92
Scream and Scream Again '70
Sea of Sand '58
The Secret Code '42
Secret Mission '42
The Secret War of Harry Frigg '68
The Seventh Cross '44 ▶
Severed Ties '92
She Demons '58
Shining Through '92
Shock Waves '77
Silent Scream '84
633 Squadron '64
Skinheads: The Second Coming of Hate '88
Snow Treasure '67
So Ends Our Night '41 ▶
Soldier of Orange '78 ▶
A Soldier's Tale '91
Son of Lassie '45
Sophie Scholl: The Final Days '05 ▶
The Sorrow and the Pity '71 ▶
The Sound of Music '65 ▶
The Square Peg '58
Stalag 17 '53 ▶
Stalag Luft '93
The Statement '03
The Stranger '46 ▶
Strangers in Paradise '84
Strayed '03 ▶
Sundown '41
Surf Nazis Must Die '87
Sweet Light in a Dark Room '60 ▶
Swing Kids '93
A Taxing Woman's Return '88 ▶
That Summer of White Roses '90
They Saved Hitler's Brain '64
13 Rue Madeleine '46 ▶
'38: Vienna before the Fall '88
This Land Is Mine '43 ▶
Tiger Fangs '43
Tigershark '87
To Be or Not to Be '42 ▶
To Be or Not to Be '83
To Catch a King '84
Tomorrow the World '44
Top Dog '95
Top Secret! '84 ▶
The Tormentors '71
Train of Life '98
Transport from Paradise '65
Triumph of the Spirit '89 ▶
Triumph of the Will '34 ▶
True Colors '87
U-Boat Prisoner '44
Underground '41
Uprising '01 ▶
Uranus '91 ▶
Valkyrie '08
War & Love '84
War & Remembrance '88
War & Remembrance: The Final Chapter '89
Watch on the Rhine '43 ▶
Waterfront '44
Where Eagles Dare '68 ▶
Where Trails End '42
Wild Geese 2 '85
The Winds of War '83
Wings over the Pacific '43
Winter in Wartime '10
Wizards '77
A Woman at War '94
Wooden Horse '50 ▶
Yank in Libya '42
The Yesterday Machine '63
Zelary '03 ▶
Zentropa '92
Zombie Lake '80
Zone Troopers '84

Near-Death Experiences

***see also** Death & the Afterlife*

Dead Zone '83 ▶
Fearless '93 ▶
The Final Destination '09
Flatliners '90
Ghost Town '08 ▶
The Princess and the Warrior '00 ▶
Shadows '07
Urban Ghost Story '98

Negative Utopia

***see also** Paradise Gone Awry; Post-Apocalypse; Technology—Rampant*

Alphaville '65 ▶
Animal Farm '55 ▶
Brazil '85 ▶
Code 46 '03
El Norte '83 ▶
Futureworld '76
Gattaca '97 ▶
The Island '05
Metropolis '26 ▶
Moonraker '79
The Mosquito Coast '86
1984 '56 ▶
1984 '84 ▶
Rollerball '75
Rollerball '02
Soylent Green '73
10th Victim '65 ▶
THX 1138 '71 ▶
V for Vendetta '06
Whodunit '82
Zardoz '73

Netherlands

***see also** Amsterdam*

Antonia's Line '95
The Audrey Hepburn Story '00
Black Book '06 ▶
A Bridge Too Far '77
Dutch Girls '87
For a Lost Soldier '93
The Hiding Place '75
The Last Drop '05
The Red Mill '27
Spetters '80
Turkish Delight '73
Winter in Wartime '10

New Black Cinema

***see also** African America; Blaxploitation*

Bamboozled '00
Belly '98
Boyz N the Hood '91 ▶
Clockers '95 ▶
Crooklyn '94 ▶
Do the Right Thing '89 ▶
The Five Heartbeats '91 ▶
Get On the Bus '96 ▶
Girl 6 '96
Hangin' with the Homeboys '91 ▶
Hollywood Shuffle '87
I'm Gonna Git You Sucka '88 ▶
Joe's Bed-Stuy Barbershop: We Cut Heads '83
Jungle Fever '91 ▶
Just Another Girl on the I.R.T. '93
Livin' Large '91
Menace II Society '93 ▶
The Meteor Man '93
Mo' Better Blues '90
The Players Club '98 ▶
Poetic Justice '93
Posse '93 ▶
A Rage in Harlem '91 ▶
School Daze '88 ▶
Set It Off '96
She's Gotta Have It '86 ▶
Soul Plane '04
Straight out of Brooklyn '91
To Sleep with Anger '90 ▶

New Jersey

***see also** New York, New York*

Above Suspicion '00
Adventures of Power '08
American Gangster '07 ▶
Aqua Teen Hunger Force Colon Movie Film for Theaters '07
Atlantic City '81 ▶
Baby It's You '82 ▶
Bandslam '09
Be Kind Rewind '08
Beer League '06
Blues in the Night '41
Bogus '96
Bought and Sold '03
Cannibal Campout '88
Chasing Amy '97
Cheaper by the Dozen '50 ▶
Cinderella Man '05 ▶
Cleaner '07
Clerks '94 ▶
Clerks 2 '06 ▶
Cold Hearts '99
Confessions of a Teenage Drama Queen '04
The Cookout '04
Cop Land '97 ▶
Coyote Ugly '00
The Day the Earth Stood Still '08
Dogma '99
Eddie and the Cruisers '83
Eversmile New Jersey '89
Family Man '00
Freedomland '06
Garden State '04 ▶
Harold and Kumar Go to White Castle '04
Hysterical Blindness '02
In the Mix '05
Jersey Girl '92
Jersey Girl '04
Just Friends '05
The Last Broadcast '98 ▶
Lean on Me '89 ▶
Mallrats '95
Moving '88
Nearing Grace '05
New Jersey Drive '95
Now You Know '02
On the Outs '05
Palindromes '04 ▶
Paul Blart: Mall Cop '09
The Purple Rose of Cairo '85 ▶

Return of the Secaucus 7 '80 ▶
Rocket Science '07 ▶
Second Best '05
The Station Agent '03 ▶
This Thing of Ours '03
The Toxic Avenger '86
Tracks '05
Trade '07
War of the Worlds '05 ▶
The War Within '05
The Whole Shebang '01
Winter Solstice '04 ▶
Zombie Honeymoon '04

New Orleans

see also *American South*
Albino Alligator '96
American Virgin '09
Angel Heart '87
Anne Rice's The Feast of All Saints '01
Bad Lieutenant: Port of Call New Orleans '09
Band of Angels '57
The Big Easy '87 ▶
Birth of the Blues '41
Blues Brothers 2000 '98
Boxcar Blues '90
Buccaneer's Girl '50
Candyman 2: Farewell to the Flesh '94
Child of Glass '78
The Cincinnati Kid '65
Crazy in Alabama '99
Cry of the Werewolf '44
The Cure '95
The Curious Case of Benjamin Button '08 ▶
The Dangerous '95
The Dark Side of Love '79
Dead Man Walking '95 ▶
Deja Vu '06
Dixie: Changing Habits '85 ▶
Double Jeopardy '99
Dracula 2: Ascension '03
Easy Rider '69 ▶
End of August '82
False Witness '89
The Family '70
The First 9 1/2 Weeks '98
Flakes '07
The Flame of New Orleans '41 ▶
French Quarter '78
French Quarter Undercover '85
French Silk '94
Fuel '08 ▶
The Glass Cage '96
Hard Target '93
Heaven's Prisoners '95
Hotel '67
In the Electric Mist '08
Interview with the Vampire '94
The Invisible Avenger '58
The Iron Mistress '52
It Happened in New Orleans '36
J.D.'s Revenge '76
Judas Kiss '98
King Creole '58
Last Holiday '06
The Librarian: Curse of the Judas Chalice '08
Lords of the Street '08
A Love Song for Bobby Long '04
Lush '01
Mardi Gras for the Devil '93
Mardi Gras Massacre '78
Midnight Bayou '09
Mirrors '78
A Murder of Crows '99
My Forbidden Past '51
New Orleans '47
New Orleans After Dark '58
Night of the Demons '09
Night of the Strangler '73
One Christmas '95
Panic in the Streets '50 ▶
Passing Glory '99 ▶
Pretty Baby '78 ▶
The Princess and the Frog '09 ▶
Ruby Bridges '98
Runaway Jury '03 ▶
A Saintly Switch '99
Saratoga Trunk '45
The Savage Bees '76
Sonny '02
Storyville '74
Storyville '92
A Streetcar Named Desire '51 ▶
A Streetcar Named Desire '84 ▶
A Streetcar Named Desire '95
Streets of Blood '09
Suddenly, Last Summer '59 ▶
Thunderground '89
Tightrope '84 ▶
Toys in the Attic '63
Tune in Tomorrow '90
12 Rounds '09
Undercover Blues '93
The Unholy '88
Vendetta '99
Walk on the Wild Side '62
The World Moves On '34

New Year's Eve

see also *Christmas; Holidays; Horrible Holidays*
About Last Night... '86 ▶
Are We There Yet? '05
The Art of War '00
Assault on Precinct 13 '05
The Best Man '97
Bloodhounds of Broadway '89
Bloody New Year '87
Century '94
Dirty Dancing: Havana Nights '04
Doctor Who '96
End of Days '99
Entrapment '99
Four Rooms '95
The Godfather, Part 2 '74 ▶
Gridlock'd '96 ▶
Happiness Ahead '34
Happy New Year '73 ▶
A Happy New Year! '79
Happy New Year '87
Hav Plenty '97 ▶
Holiday Affair '96
The Hudsucker Proxy '93 ▶
The January Man '89
Long Time Since '97
More about the Children of Noisy Village '87
New Year's Day '89 ▶
New Year's Evil '78
1999 '98
Ocean's Eleven '01 ▶
Peter's Friends '92
Plan B '97
Poseidon '06
The Poseidon Adventure '72
P.S. Your Cat is Dead! '02
The Quickie '01
The Real Thing '97
Strange Days '95 ▶
Strange Planet '99
The Sum of Us '94 ▶
Taboo '02
Trading Places '83
200 Cigarettes '98
Virtual Seduction '96
Waiting to Exhale '95 ▶
When Harry Met Sally... '89 ▶

New York, New York

see also *The Empire State Building*
A Lot Like Love '05
ABCD '99
The Accidental Husband '08
Across 110th Street '72
Across the Universe '07
Adam '09
Adam & Steve '05
Addicted to Love '96
Addicted to Murder 2: Tainted Blood '97
Addicted to Murder 3: Bloodlust '99
The Addiction '95
Adrift in Manhattan '07
Adventures of Power '08
An Affair to Remember '57
After Hours '85 ▶
Aftershock: Earthquake in New York '99
Afterwards '08
Alfie '04
Alice '90 ▶
All About Eve '50 ▶
All Good Things '09
All Over Me '96 ▶
All That Jazz '79 ▶
All the Vermeers in New York '91 ▶
Alphabet City '84
Amarilly of Clothesline Alley '18
American Psycho '99
Analyze That '02
Analyze This '98 ▶
Anamorph '07
The Anderson Tapes '71 ▶
Angel Rodriguez '05
Angelo My Love '83 ▶
Angels with Dirty Faces '38 ▶
Anne of Green Gables: The Continuing Story '99
Annie '82
Annie '99 ▶
Annie Hall '77 ▶
Another Woman '88 ▶
Anything But Love '02
Anything Else '03
The Apartment '60 ▶
The Ape '05
Armageddon '98
The Art of War '00
Art School Confidential '06
Arthur '81 ▶
Arthur 2: On the Rocks '88
As Good As It Gets '97 ▶
Ash Wednesday '02
The Astronaut's Wife '99
At First Sight '98
August '08
August Rush '07
Autumn in New York '00
Awake '07
Awakenings '90 ▶
Babylon A.D. '08
Bad Lieutenant '92 ▶
Bam Bam & Celeste '05 ▶
Barefoot in the Park '67 ▶
The Basketball Diaries '95
Basquiat '96 ▶
The Beautician and the Beast '97
The Beautiful, the Bloody and the Bare '64
Because of Him '45
Because of You '95
Bed of Roses '95
Before Night Falls '00 ▶
Being John Malkovich '99 ▶
The Believer '01
Bella '06
Between Love & Goodbye '08
Big '88 ▶
The Big Bus '76
Big Business '88
Big Daddy '99
Big Fan '09
Big Night '95
Big Street '42
Birth '04
Blackboard Jungle '55 ▶
The Blackout '97
Blade '72
Blast of Silence '61
Bless the Child '00
Blink '93
Blonde Ambition '07
Bloodhounds of Broadway '52
Bloodhounds of Broadway '89
Bloodmoon '97
Blue in the Face '95
Blue Skies '46 ▶
Blue Steel '90
Boiler Room '00 ▶
Bomb the System '05
Bonanno: A Godfather's Story '99
The Bone Collector '99
The Bonfire of the Vanities '90
Booty Call '96
Boricua's Bond '00
Born to Win '71
Boss of Bosses '99
The Bostonians '84
The Bourne Supremacy '04 ▶
The Bourne Ultimatum '07 ▶
The Bowery '33 ▶
The Brave One '07
The Break '97
Breakfast at Tiffany's '61 ▶
The Breakup Artist '04
Breathing Room '96
Breeders '86
Bride Wars '09
Bright Lights, Big City '88
Brighton Beach Memoirs '86
Bringing Out the Dead '99
Broadway '42
Broadway Bound '92
Broadway Damage '98
Broadway Danny Rose '84 ▶
The Broadway Drifter '27
Broadway Limited '41
Broadway Melody '29
Broadway Melody of 1936 '35 ▶
Broadway Melody of 1938 '37
Broadway Melody of 1940 '40
Broadway Rhythm '44
Broadway Serenade '39
Broken English '07
The Bronx Executioner '86
The Bronx Is Burning '07
A Bronx Tale '93 ▶
The Bronx War '90
The Brooklyn Heist '08
Brooklyn Lobster '05
Brooklyn Rules '07
Brooklyn's Finest '09
The Brother from Another Planet '84 ▶
A Brother's Kiss '97
Brown Sugar '02
Bullet '94
Bulletproof Monk '03
Bullets over Broadway '94 ▶
Burnzy's Last Call '95
Bye Bye Braverman '67
Cafe Society '97
Capote '05 ▶
Carlito's Way '93 ▶
Carlito's Way: Rise to Power '05
Carnal Knowledge '71 ▶
Carnegie Hall '47
Cat People '82
The Caveman's Valentine '01
Center Stage '00
Center Stage: Turn It Up '08
Chain of Desire '93
Changing Lanes '02 ▶
Chapter 27 '07
Charlie Chan on Broadway '37
Chasing Papi '03
The Cheetah Girls '03
Chelsea Walls '01
A Chorus Line '85
Chutney Popcorn '99
City by the Sea '02
City Hall '95 ▶
City of Ghosts '03
City Slickers '91 ▶
Claire Dolan '97
The Clique '08
Clockers '95 ▶
Cloverfield '08
Cocktail '88
The Cocoanuts '29
Codename: Jaguar '00
Cold Souls '09
Collected Stories '02 ▶
The Collectors '99
Color of Justice '97
Coming Soon '99
Coming to America '88 ▶
Compromising Positions '85
Confessions of a Nazi Spy '39
Confessions of a Shopaholic '09
Conspiracy Theory '97 ▶
Conversations with Other Women '05
Coogan's Bluff '68 ▶
Corrupt '99
The Corruptor '99 ▶
The Cotton Club '84 ▶
A Couch in New York '95
Counsellor-at-Law '33 ▶
The Cowboy Way '94
Coyote Ugly '00
Cracked Nuts '41
The Cradle Will Rock '99
Crazy Little Thing '02
Crazy Love '07 ▶
Crimes & Misdemeanors '89 ▶
Critic's Choice '63
Crocodile Dundee '86 ▶
Crocodile Dundee 2 '88
Crooklyn '94 ▶
Crossfire '98
Crossing Delancey '88 ▶
Crossroads '86
The Crowd '28 ▶
Crown Heights '02
Cruel Intentions '98
Cruising '80
The Cry: La Llorona '07
Curious George '06
The Curse of the Jade Scorpion '01
Daredevil '03
Daring Daughters '33
Dark Odyssey '57
Date Night '10
Dave Chappelle's Block Party '06 ▶
David Searching '97
The Day After Tomorrow '04
Day at the Beach '98
A Day in the Life '09
Day Night Day Night '06 ▶
Day Zero '07
Daylight '96
The Daytrippers '96
DC 9/11: Time of Crisis '04
Dead Dog '00
Dead Funny '94
Dead Presidents '95
The Deal '05
Death to Smoochy '02
Deception '08
Dedication '07
Definitely, Maybe '08 ▶
The Deli '97
Delirious '06
Desolation Angels '95
Desperate Characters '71 ▶
Desperately Seeking Susan '85
Detective Story '51 ▶
The Devil Is a Sissy '36
The Devil Wears Prada '06
The Devil's Advocate '97
The Devil's Own '96 ▶
Diamond Run '00
Die Hard: With a Vengeance '95
Dinner Rush '00 ▶
Disappearing Acts '00
Do the Right Thing '89 ▶
Dog Day Afternoon '75 ▶
Dondi '61
Donnie Brasco '96 ▶
Don't Say a Word '01
The Doorbell Rang: A Nero Wolfe Mystery '01
Double Edge '97
Doughboys '08
Down to Earth '01
Down to You '00
Down With Love '03
The Dream Team '89
Dressed to Kill '80
Drunks '96
Duplex '03
Dust '01
Easy Living '37 ▶
Eddie '96
Edge of the City '57
Edmond '05
Ed's Next Move '96
84 Charing Cross Road '86 ▶
El Cantante '06
Elf '03 ▶
Empire '02
Enchanted '07
End of Days '99
An Englishman in New York '09
Entertaining Angels: The Dorothy Day Story '96
Escape from New York '81
The Event '03
Every Little Step '08
Everyone Says I Love You '96 ▶
Everyone's Hero '06
Eyes of Laura Mars '78
Eyes Wide Shut '99
Eyewitness '81
F/X '86 ▶
Face Down '97
Factory Girl '06
The Falcon Takes Over '42
Fall '97
Falling in Love '84
Fame '80 ▶
Fame '09
Fantastic Four '05
Fatal Attraction '87 ▶
Fear, Anxiety and Depression '89
Feardotcom '02
Feel the Noise '07
Fever '99
15 Minutes '01
The Fifth Element '97
54 '98
Fighting '09
Finder's Fee '01
Finding Forrester '00
A Fine Madness '66 ▶
Fingers '78 ▶
Fiona '98
First Love '39
The First Wives Club '96
The Fisher King '91 ▶
Flannel Pajamas '06
Flawless '99
Fleshpot on 42nd Street '71
Flirt '95
Focus '01
Food of Love '02
For Love or Money '93
The Foreigner '78
Fort Apache, the Bronx '81 ▶
42nd Street '33 ▶
.45 '06
Four and a Half Women '05
Frankie and Johnny '91 ▶
The French Connection '71 ▶
Frequency '00
The Freshman '90
Friends and Family '01
Frogs for Snakes '98
Fuel '08 ▶
The Funeral '96 ▶
Funny Girl '68 ▶
Funny Valentine '05
Fur: An Imaginary Portrait of Diane Arbus '06
G '02
Game 6 '05
Games '67
Gangs of New York '02 ▶
The Garment Jungle '57
Get a Clue '02
Get Rich or Die Tryin' '05
Get Well Soon '01
Ghost '90 ▶
Ghost Town '08 ▶
Ghostbusters '84 ▶
Ghostbusters 2 '89
Gildersleeve on Broadway '43
The Girl in the Red Velvet Swing '55
The Girlfriend Experience '09
Giuliani Time '05
Giving It Up '99
Glitter '01
Gloria '98
Go Into Your Dance '35
The Godfather '72 ▶
The Godfather, Part 2 '74 ▶
The Godfather, Part 3 '90 ▶
Godspell '73
Godzilla '98
Going the Distance '10
The Golden Spiders: A Nero Wolfe Mystery '00
The Good Guy '10
The Good Night '07
The Goodbye Girl '77 ▶
Goodbye, New York '85
Goodfellas '90 ▶
Gossip '99
Gotti '96
Grace of My Heart '96
Grand Central Murder '42
Gravesend '97
Gray Matters '06
Great Expectations '97
The Great Gatsby '49
The Great Gatsby '74

▶ = rated three bones or higher

▶ = rated three bones or higher

The Tavern '00
Taxi '04
Taxi Driver '76 ▸
The Tenants '06
The Tender Trap '55
The 10th Kingdom '00
Then She Found Me '07
They Call It Sin '32
The Thing About My Folks '05
Thirteen Conversations About One Thing '01 ▸
Thirty Day Princess '34
30 Years to Life '01
This Revolution '05
The Thomas Crown Affair '99 ▸
3 A.M. '01 ▸
Three Days of the Condor '75 ▸
Three Men and a Baby '87 ▸
Three Sailors and a Girl '53
Through the Eyes of a Killer '92
Through the Fire '05 ▸
The Tic Code '99
Timeless '96
Times Square '80
TMNT (Teenage Mutant Ninja Turtles) '07
To Catch a Yeti '95
The Tollbooth '04
Tony n' Tina's Wedding '07
Tootsie '82 ▸
Torch Singer '33
Torch Song Trilogy '88
Town and Country '01
Transamerica '05 ▸
Trash '70
The Treatment '06
A Tree Grows in Brooklyn '45 ▸
Trick '99 ▸
A Troll in Central Park '94
True Blue '01
Trust the Man '06
Turn the River '07
25th Hour '02
The 24 Hour Woman '99
29th Street '91
Twisted '96
2 by 4 '98
Two for the Money '05
Two Girls and a Guy '98 ▸
200 Cigarettes '98
Two Lovers '09 ▸
Two Ninas '00
Two of Us '00
Two Weeks Notice '02
Ultrachrist! '03
Under Hellgate Bridge '99
Underground U.S.A. '84
Unfaithful '02 ▸
Unknown White Male '05 ▸
An Unmarried Woman '78 ▸
Untamed Heart '93
(Untitled) '09
Unzipped '94 ▸
Up in Central Park '48
Uptown Girls '03
Uptown New York '32
Urbania '00
Vampire in Brooklyn '95
Vanilla Sky '01
Vanya on 42nd Street '94 ▸
Variety '83
Varsity Show '37
The Velocity of Gary '98
A Very Natural Thing '73
Visions of Sugarplums '99
The Visitor '07 ▸
The Wackness '08
The Waiting Game '99
Walking and Talking '96
Wall Street '87 ▸
Walls of Glass '85
Wannabes '01
The War Within '05
Washington Heights '02
Washington Square '97 ▸
The Way We Were '73 ▸
The Wedding Party '69
We're Back! A Dinosaur's Story '93
West Side Story '61 ▸
What Happens in Vegas '08
Whatever Works '09
When Harry Met Sally... '89 ▸
When Will I Be Loved '04
Where God Left His Shoes '07
Where Were You When the Lights Went Out? '68
Whipped '00
Whirlygirl '04
Who Gets to Call It Art? '05
Who's That Knocking at My Door? '68 ▸
The Wild '06
Wild Style '83
Winning Girls Through Psychic Mind Control '02
Winter Passing '05
Wirey Spindell '99
Wise Guys '86
Wisegal '08
Wisegirls '02
Witness to the Mob '98
Wolf '94
Wolfen '81 ▸
The Women '08
Wonderful World '09
Working Girl '88 ▸
World Trade Center '06 ▸
X-Men '00
XX/XY '02
The Yards '00
Year of the Dragon '85
Yellow '06
You Belong to Me '07
You Don't Mess with the Zohan '08
You Stupid Man '02
You Tell Me '06
The Young Girl and the Monsoon '99
The Young Savages '61
You've Got Mail '98

New Zealand

see *Down Under*

Newlyweds

see also *Wedding Bells*
Absent Without Leave '95
Are We Done Yet? '07
Barefoot in the Park '67 ▸
Bittersweet Love '76
The Blood Spattered Bride '72
Born in '45 '65
Chunhyang '00
Crossroads '42
Dark Country '09
Devil's Pond '03
Gasoline Alley '51
A Good Woman '04
The Heartbreak Kid '72 ▸
Highball '97 ▸
Honeymoon Academy '90
Honeymoon Horror '82
I Married a Monster from Outer Space '58
Identity '03
Just Married '03
Lakeview Terrace '08 ▸
The Land That Time Forgot '09
The Long, Long Trailer '54
Love Actually '03
Love from a Stranger '47
Made for Each Other '39 ▸
Made in Heaven '52
Mail Order Bride '63
Mail Order Wife '04
Mannequin '37
Mexican Spitfire '40
Mr. & Mrs. Loving '96 ▸
Mister Drake's Duck '50
Move Over, Darling '63
National Lampoon's Gold Diggers '04
A Perfect Getaway '09
The Ponder Heart '01
Prelude to a Kiss '92
The Reception '05
She's Having a Baby '88
Shrek 2 '04 ▸
Snow 2: Brain Freeze '08
So I Married an Axe Murderer '93
10 '79
Voulez-Vous Danser avec Moi? '59
Weird Woman '44
Wide Sargasso Sea '06
The Wyvern Mystery '00
You, Me and Dupree '06
The Young Pioneers '76
Zombie Honeymoon '04

News at 11

see also *Front Page; Look Ma! I'm on TV!; Mass Media*
All About Steve '09
Anchorman: The Legend of Ron Burgundy '04
Broadcast News '87 ▸
Bruce Almighty '03
The China Syndrome '79 ▸
Control Room '04 ▸
The Dead Pool '88
Eyewitness '81
A Face in the Crowd '57 ▸
15 Minutes '01
Good Night, and Good Luck '05 ▸
The Hunting Party '07
The Insider '99 ▸
Life or Something Like It '02
Little Black Book '04
Live from Baghdad '03 ▸
Morning Glory '10
Natural Born Killers '94
Network '76 ▸
News at Eleven '86
The Night We Called It a Day '03
Outfoxed: Rupert Murdoch's War on Journalism '04 ▸
Quarantine '08
Rec '07
Special Bulletin '83 ▸
Switching Channels '88
This Revolution '05
To Die For '95 ▸
Up Close and Personal '96 ▸
Vantage Point '08
Weapons of Mass Distraction '97

Newspapers

see *Front Page*

Niagara Falls

Bruce Almighty '03
Emma '32
I Now Pronounce You Chuck and Larry '07
The Long Kiss Goodnight '96
Niagara '52
Niagara Motel '06
Niagara, Niagara '97
Superman 2 '80 ▸

Nice Mice

see also *Killer Rodents*
An American Tail '86
An American Tail: Fievel Goes West '91
Babe '95 ▸
Babe: Pig in the City '98
Dr. Seuss' Horton Hears a Who! '08 ▸
Escape from Alcatraz '79 ▸
Flowers for Algernon '00
Flushed Away '06 ▸
The Great Mouse Detective '86 ▸
The Green Mile '99
The Hitchhiker's Guide to the Galaxy '05 ▸
The Island on Bird Street '97
Mouse and His Child '77
Mouse Hunt '97 ▸
Ratatouille '07 ▸
A Rat's Tale '98
Ratz '99
The Rescuers '77 ▸
The Rescuers Down Under '90
Road Trip '00
The Secret of NIMH '82 ▸
The Secret of NIMH 2 '98
Sitcom '97
Stuart Little '99
Stuart Little 2 '02 ▸
The Tale of Despereaux '08

Nightclubs

The Adventures of Pluto Nash '02
Amateur Night '85
Animal Instincts '92
Anything But Love '02
Backbeat '94 ▸
The Bamboo Blonde '46
Be Yourself '30
Berlin Blues '89
Better Than Chocolate '99
Birth of the Blues '41
Black Angel '46 ▸
Black Glove '54
Blood Brothers '07
The Blue Angel '30 ▸
Body Shots '99
The Boob '26
Bordertown '35
Born Romantic '00
The Bride Wore Red '37
A Bunny's Tale '85
Bus Stop '56 ▸
Cabaret '72 ▸
Cabaret Balkan '98
Cafe Society '97
Can-Can '60
Carnival Rock '57
Casablanca '42 ▸
CB4: The Movie '93
Chameleon 2: Death Match '99
Charlie Chan on Broadway '37
City of Ghosts '03
Club Havana '46
Copacabana '47
The Cotton Club '84 ▸
Dance, Girl, Dance '40
Dance Hall Racket '58
Dancing at the Blue Iguana '00
Dark Secrets '95
Dark Streets '08
Deadly Revenge '83
Decay '98
Desperate Cargo '41
Dick Tracy '90 ▸
Double or Nothing '37
Dracula Blows His Cool '82
The Dreamlife of Angels '98 ▸
The Fabulous Baker Boys '89 ▸
Fake Out '82
Femmes de Paris '53
54 '98
Flaming Lead '39
Foxstyle '73
Framed '75
French Can-Can '55 ▸
The French Way '40
Fun in Acapulco '63
G.I. Blues '60
The Girl '01
Girls! Girls! Girls! '62
Go Into Your Dance '35
The Green Cockatoo '37
Greenwich Village '44
Hard to Hold '37
Harlem Nights '89
He Found a Star '41
The Helen Morgan Story '57
Honeydripper '07
I Can Do Bad All By Myself '09
I Was an American Spy '51
Idlewild '06
If I Had My Way '40
In the Mix '05
Invincible '01
Irreversible '02
It Started in Naples '60 ▸
It's All Gone, Pete Tong '04
Jive Junction '43
The Killing of a Chinese Bookie '76
King Creole '58
Kings of South Beach '07
La Cage aux Folles '78 ▸
La Cage aux Folles 2 '81
La Cage aux Folles 3: The Wedding '86
Lady on a Train '45 ▸
Lambada '89
The Last Days of Disco '98 ▸
Last Night at the Alamo '83 ▸
Le Samourai '67 ▸
Lenny '74 ▸
Like It Is '98 ▸
Liquid Dreams '92
Little Shots of Happiness '97
The Lost City '05
Love Come Down '00
Love Goggles '99
Love Jones '96 ▸
Lullaby of Broadway '51
Lured '47
Machine Gun Blues '95
Mad Dog and Glory '93 ▸
Madame Sata '02
The Mambo Kings '92 ▸
Manpower '41
Marked Woman '37 ▸
Martial Law 2: Undercover '91
The Mask '94 ▸
Mickey One '65
Midnight Warrior '89
Mighty Joe Young '49
Miracles '89
Miss Pettigrew Lives for a Day '08 ▸
Moonlight Serenade '09
Morocco '30 ▸
Moulin Rouge '01 ▸
New Orleans '47
Night After Night '32
A Night at the Roxbury '98
A Night in Heaven '83
The Night They Raided Minsky's '69 ▸
No Surrender '86 ▸
Nora Prentiss '47
The Nutty Professor '63 ▸
Pandora and the Flying Dutchman '51
A Paradise Under the Stars '99
Party Girl '58 ▸
Party Girl '94
Party Monster '03
Pecker '98
People '04
Pete Kelly's Blues '55
Play Murder for Me '91
Playing by Heart '98
Preaching to the Perverted '97
The Public Eye '92 ▸
Rebel '85
Ripper Man '96
Roger Dodger '02 ▸
Ruby '92
Ruby's Dream '82
Salt & Pepper '68
The Score '01
Sea Racketeers '37
Sex, Drugs, and Rock-n-Roll '84
Shanghai Triad '95 ▸
The Shining Hour '38
Showgirls '95
Smash-Up: The Story of a Woman '47 ▸
So Close to Paradise '98
Somewhere in the Night '46
Sorted '04
Stark Raving Mad '02
Stonewall '95 ▸
Suffering Bastards '90
The Sunset Murder Case '38
Sweet Evil '98
Swindle '02
Swingers '96 ▸
The Talented Mr. Ripley '99
That Naughty Girl '58
They Never Come Back '32
30 Is a Dangerous Age, Cynthia '68
To Catch a King '84
Torch Singer '33
Treasure of the Moon Goddess '88
Trigger Happy '96
24 Hour Party People '01
200 Cigarettes '98
Undercurrent '99
Underground U.S.A. '84
Uptown Saturday Night '74
Valentina's Tango '07
Vamp '86
We Own the Night '07
Whistle Stop '46
Winning Girls Through Psychic Mind Control '02
A Woman Is a Woman '60 ▸
Wonder Bar '34
Wonderland '88 ▸
Woo '97
Xanadu '80
The Zoo Gang '85

9/11

DC 9/11: Time of Crisis '04
A Few Days in September '06
Giuliani Time '05
The Great New Wonderful '06
The Hamburg Cell '04
Hijacking Catastrophe: 9/11, Fear and the Selling of America '04
Protocols of Zion '05 ▸
Reign Over Me '07
United 93 '06 ▸
Where in the World Is Osama Bin Laden? '06
World Trade Center '06 ▸

Ninjas

see also *Martial Arts*
Azumi '03 ▸
Azumi 2 '05
Batman Begins '05 ▸
Bionic Ninja '85
Black Tight Killers '66 ▸
Elektra '05
Five Element Ninjas '82
Ninja: American Warrior '90
Ninja Assassin '09
Ninja in the U.S.A. '88
RoboCop 3 '91
Shinobi '05 ▸
Shinobi no Mono '62 ▸
Shinobi no Mono 2: Vengeance '63 ▸
Shrink '09
3 Ninjas Kick Back '94
TMNT (Teenage Mutant Ninja Turtles) '07

Ninjitsu

see *Martial Arts*

No-Exit Motel

see also *Grand Hotel*
Axe '06
Bug '06
Cheap Shots '91
Dead Simple '01
Eaten Alive '76
Identity '03
Interstate '07
Lake Dead '07
Memento '00 ▸
Motel Hell '80
Mountaintop Motel Massacre '86
The Newlydeads '87
Pink Motel '82
Poor Pretty Eddie '73
Psycho '60 ▸
Psycho '98
Psycho 2 '83
Psycho 3 '86
Psycho 4: The Beginning '90
Slaughter Hotel '71
Tape '01 ▸
Vacancy '07
Vacancy 2: The First Cut '08

Not-So-True Identity

Above Suspicion '00
Adoration '08
AKA '02
Albino Alligator '96
All Night '18
The Amazing Mrs. Holiday '43
Anonymous Rex '04
Apt Pupil '97
Armistead Maupin's Tales of the City '93
The Associate '96
Autumn Sun '98 ▸
Bad Santa '03
Batman Begins '05 ▸
Beggars of Life '28
Big Momma's House '00
Big Momma's House 2 '06
Black Book '06 ▸
Black Like Me '64
Blue Streak '99
Boat Trip '03
A Boyfriend for Christmas '04
Boys Don't Cry '99 ▸
The Breaks '99
Bubba Ho-Tep '03 ▸

▸ = rated three bones or higher

Buccaneer's Girl '50
Cafe Metropole '37
Catch Me If You Can '02
Catherine's Grove '98
The Charlatan '29
Charley's Aunt '41 ►
Charlotte Gray '01
Chasing Liberty '04
The Claim '00
Clancy Street Boys '43
Code Name: The Cleaner '07
Color Me Kubrick '05
Corky Romano '01
The Cotton Club '84 ►
The Count of Monte Cristo '99
Crossroads '42
Daniel Deronda '02
Dear Frankie '04
Deceived '91
Deception '08
Defying Gravity '99
The Departed '06 ►
Desert Nights '29
Devil in the Flesh 2 '00
A Different Loyalty '04 ►
Don't Lose Your Head '66
Easy to Wed '46
The Elder Son '06
Elf '03 ►
The Emperor's New Clothes '01
Empire of the Wolves '05
Europa, Europa '91 ►
Exit Wounds '01
Extasis '96
Face/Off '97 ►
Face the Music '00
Failure to Launch '06
Femme Fatale '02
For Richer or Poorer '97
Forever Mine '99
Freshman Orientation '04
Gattaca '97 ►
Gentleman's Agreement '47 ►
George White's Scandals '45
G.I. War Brides '46
Good Advice '01
The Good Fairy '35 ►
Gosford Park '01 ►
The Governess '98
Grey Owl '99
Gun Shy '00
The Guru '02
The Half Naked Truth '32
Hannah Montana: The Movie '09
Happiness Ahead '34
Happy, Texas '99 ►
Hard to Forget '98
Head Over Heels '01
Hi, Good Lookin'! '44
High Crimes '02
The History of Mr. Polly '07
A History of Violence '05 ►
Homegrown '97
The Human Stain '03
I Married a Dead Man '82
I Now Pronounce You Chuck and Larry '07
If You Could Only Cook '36
If You Only Knew '00
Imitation of Life '34
Imitation of Life '59 ►
The Importance of Being Earnest '02
Impostor '02
Infernal Affairs '02 ►
The Joneses '10
Just Another Love Story '08
Just My Luck '06
Juwanna Mann '02
A Knight's Tale '01
The Lady Eve '41 ►
The Legend of Rita '99
Les Miserables '97 ►
Lip Service '00
Little Man '06
Little Old New York '23
The Long Kiss Goodnight '96
Lost Boundaries '49
The Mad Adventures of Rabbi Jacob '73 ►
Maid in Manhattan '02
The Major and the Minor '42 ►
Malibu's Most Wanted '03
The Man with Two Faces '34
Mask of Death '97
The Mask of Zorro '98 ►
Master of Disguise '02
The Master Race '44
Me & Mrs. Jones '02
Miss Tatlock's Millions '48
Mrs. Palfrey at the Claremont '05
Mrs. Winterbourne '96
Mr. & Mrs. Smith '05 ►
Mister Lonely '07
Model Behavior '00
Monte Carlo '30
Monte Cristo '22
Moon over Miami '41 ►
Mother Night '96 ►
Mulan '98
Mulholland Drive '01 ►
Mumford '99 ►
My First Wedding '04
Never Been Kissed '99
Nevil Shute's The Far Country '85
The Next Big Thing '02
Nora Prentiss '47
Olivier, Olivier '92 ►
One More Time '70
Orlando '92 ►
The Other Man '08
Our Man in Havana '59 ►
Our Mutual Friend '98
Out at the Wedding '07
Out to Sea '97
The Painted Lady '97 ►
Painting the Clouds With Sunshine '51
A Paradise Under the Stars '99
The Parent Trap '98
Perfect Stranger '07
Pinky '49 ►
Pipe Dream '02
The Prince & Me '04
The Prince and the Pauper '07
The Prince and the Surfer '99
Princess of Thieves '01
Princess Protection Program '09
The Principal Takes a Holiday '98
The Prisoner of Zenda '22
The Quarry '98
The Ringer '05
Rock My World '02
The Rowdy Girls '00
The Saint '97
Sally '29
Scaramouche '23
The Scarlet Pimpernel '34 ►
The Scarlet Pimpernel '82 ►
The Scarlet Pimpernel '99
The Scarlet Pimpernel 2: Mademoiselle Guillotine '99
The Scarlet Pimpernel 3: The Kidnapped King '99
The Secret Agent '96
The Secret Invasion '64
Shadows '60 ►
Shallow Hal '01
The Sheepman '58
The Silencer '99
Silver Hawk '04
Sing Me a Love Song '37
Ski Party '65
Soccer Mom '08
Somewhere in the Night '46
Soul Man '86
Strange Bedfellows '04
The Tailor of Panama '00 ►
Taking Care of Business '90
Taking Lives '04
The Talented Mr. Ripley '99
Tartuffe '25
Tension '50
Texas Trouble '41
That Funny Feeling '65
That Night in Rio '41
The Thief '97
Thirty Day Princess '34
Three to Tango '99
Tooth Fairy '10
Train of Life '98
Trial and Error '96
The Triumph of Love '01
True Identity '91
The Truman Show '98 ►
The Truth About Charlie '02
Twin Dragons '92
Two Shades of Blue '98
Uniform '03
Unveiled '05
The Valet '06
Virtual Sexuality '99
What the Deaf Man Heard '98 ►
Who is Cletis Tout? '02
The Witness Files '00
You Don't Mess with the Zohan '08
Youth in Revolt '10

Nuclear Disaster

see Disaster Flicks; Meltdown

Nuclear Energy

The Abyss '89 ►
Choke Canyon '86
The Chosen '77
Class of Nuke 'Em High '86
Class of Nuke 'Em High 2: Subhumanoid Meltdown '91
Class of Nuke 'Em High 3: The Good, the Bad and the Subhumanoid '94
Desert Warrior '88
Devices and Desires '91 ►
Die, Monster, Die! '65
Dirty Games '89
Final Warning '90
Godzilla '98
Ground Zero '88
Journey to the Center of Time '67
Nightbreaker '89 ►
PU-239 '06
Radar Secret Service '50
Red Alert '77
Return from Witch Mountain '78
The Return of Dr. Mabuse '61
Warning from Space '56

Nuns & Priests

***see also** Missionaries; Religion; Religious Epics*

Absolution '81
Agnes of God '85
The Agony and the Ecstasy '65
All About My Mother '99 ►
Amateur '94 ►
Amen '02 ►
The American '01
Angels with Dirty Faces '38 ►
Anna '51
The Apostate '98
The Assisi Underground '84
The Atonement of Gosta Berling '24 ►
Bad Education '04 ►
The Barbarian Invasions '03 ►
Beautiful Hunter '94
Beavis and Butt-Head Do America '96
Becket '64 ►
Behind the Wall '08
The Bells of St. Mary's '45 ►
Black Narcissus '47 ►
Black Robe '91 ►
The Bloodstained Shadow '78
The Blues Brothers '80 ►
Blues Brothers 2000 '98
The Body '01
Body & Soul '93 ►
The Boys of St. Vincent '93 ►
Boys Town '38 ►
Brides of Christ '91
The Bridge of San Luis Rey '44 ►
The Bridge of San Luis Rey '05
Camila '84 ►
The Cardinal '63
Change of Habit '69
Changing Habits '96
Child of Darkness, Child of Light '91
Chocolat '00 ►
The Christmas Choir '08
Cold Justice '89
Come to the Stable '49 ►
The Confession '20
The Confessional '75
The Confessional '95 ►
The Confessor '04
Conspiracy of Hearts '60 ►
Conspiracy of Silence '03
The Crime of Father Amaro '02 ►
The Cross & the Switchblade '72
Cry, the Beloved Country '95 ►
Curse 4: The Ultimate Sacrifice '90
Daens '92
Damien: The Leper Priest '80
The Dangerous Lives of Altar Boys '02 ►
Daredevil '03
The Day of the Beast '95
Dead Man Walking '95 ►
Dead Waters '94
Death of an Angel '86
Demonia '90
The Detective '54 ►
The Devils '71 ►
The Devil's Playground '76 ►
Diary of a Country Priest '50 ►
The Divine Enforcer '91
Dixie: Changing Habits '85 ►
Dominion: Prequel to the Exorcist '05
Doubt '08 ►
Dracula 2: Ascension '03
Dracula 3: Legacy '05
The Duchess of Langeais '07 ►
The Eighteenth Angel '97
Elmer Gantry '60 ►
End of Days '99
The End of the Affair '99 ►
End of the World '76
The Exorcism of Emily Rose '05 ►
The Exorcist '73 ►
The Exorcist 2: The Heretic '77
Exorcist: The Beginning '04
Extramuros '85
The Father Clements Story '87
The Fifth Element '97
Fighting Father Dunne '48
Final Engagement '07
First Legion '51
Flexing with Monty '10
The Fog '78
For Better and for Worse '92
Forever Young '85
40 Days and 40 Nights '02
The Fugitive '48 ►
The Garden of Redemption '97
Gentleman Bandit '81
Going My Way '44 ►
Gospa '94
Goya's Ghosts '06
Happy Hell Night '92
Heaven Knows, Mr. Allison '57 ►
Henry Poole Is Here '08 ►
Hideous Kinky '99
A Home of Our Own '75
The Hoodlum Priest '61 ►
Hot Under the Collar '91
I Confess '53
I Heard the Owl Call My Name '73
I, the Worst of All '90
In the Region of Ice '76 ►
In This House of Brede '75 ►
Into Temptation '09
Jesus of Montreal '89 ►
John Carpenter Presents Vampires: Los Muertos '02
Joshua '02
Joyeux Noel '05 ►
Judgment '90 ►
Keeping the Faith '00
Kid Monk Baroni '52
Knocks at My Door '93
Lamb '85
The Last Don 2 '98
The Last Request '06
Last Rites '88
The Last Templar '09
The Left Hand of God '55 ►
Leon Morin, Priest '61
Liam '00
License to Wed '07
Lilies of the Field '63 ►
Los Locos Posse '97
Loving Annabelle '06
Loyola, the Soldier Saint '52
Madeline '98
The Magdalene Sisters '02 ►
The Maldonado Miracle '03
Manna from Heaven '02
Mass Appeal '84
Massacre in Rome '73
Mission to Glory '80
Mister Lonely '07
Molokai: The Story of Father Damien '99
Monsignor '82
Mortal Sins '92
Most Wanted '76
Mother Joan of the Angels '60 ►
My First Wedding '04
My Mother's Smile '02
Nacho Libre '06
The Name of the Rose '86
Nasty Habits '77
Nazarin '58 ►
Night of the Assassin '77
Night of the Demons 2 '94
Night Sun '90
The Ninth Day '04 ►
Noel '04
Northfork '03
Not of This World '99
The Nun '66
Nuns on the Run '90
The Nun's Story '59 ►
The Omen '76
The Order '03
Oscar and Lucinda '97
Pale Rider '85 ►
Passing Glory '99 ►
Pier 23 '51
Pope John Paul II '84
The Pope Must Diet '91
The Possessed '77
Possessed '00
Prayer for the Dying '87
Priest '94
Primal Fear '96
Prince of Darkness '87
The Prisoner '55 ►
The Private War of Major Benson '55
The Proposition '97
The Ravagers '65
Ready? OK! '08
The Reaping '07
The Reckoning '03 ►
The Red Inn '51
Revenge of the Musketeers '94
Romance '30
The Rosary Murders '87
The Runner Stumbles '79
Salem's Lot '04
Sanctuary '98
Saving Grace '86
The Scarlet & the Black '83
Scary Movie 2 '01
Sea Wife '57
Second Sight '89
Secret Ingredient '92
September Gun '83
Shattered Vows '84
The Shoes of the Fisherman '68
Shooting Dogs '05
Silver Bullet '85
The Singing Nun '66
Sinner '07
Sister Act '92
Sister Act 2: Back in the Habit '93
Sisters of Satan '75
Sleepers '96
Sorceress '88 ►
Soul Survivors '01
The Sound of Music '65 ►
Spirits '90
Stigmata '99
Stolen Summer '02
Therese '86 ►
Therese: The Story of Saint Therese of Lisieux '04
The Third Miracle '99
Thirst '09 ►
To Kill a Priest '89
Trouble along the Way '53
The Trouble with Angels '66
True Confessions '81 ►
Under Satan's Sun '87 ►
Under the Red Robe '36
The Unholy '88
Vatican Conspiracy '81
Wanted '98
We're No Angels '89
Where Angels Go, Trouble Follows '68
The White Sister '23 ►
Wide Awake '97
The Winter Light '62 ►
The X Files: I Want to Believe '08

Nuns with Guns

The Enforcer '76
Girlfriend from Hell '89
Ms. 45 '81 ►
Nuns on the Run '90
Two Mules for Sister Sara '70 ►
We're No Angels '89
Wuthering Heights '09

Nursploitation!

***see also** Doctors & Nurses; Sexploitation*

Born for Hell '76
Candy Stripe Nurses '74
Emmanuelle in the Country '78
Hospital of Terror '78
Inner Sanctum '91
Night Call Nurses '72
Nurse on Call '88
Private Duty Nurses '71
The Sensuous Nurse '76
The Student Nurses '70
Tender Loving Care '73
The Young Nurses '73
Young Nurses in Love '89

Obsessive Love

Aaron Loves Angela '75
Addicted to Love '96
After Sex '97
Against All Odds '84
Alone With Her '07
Anna Karenina '35 ►
Anna Karenina '48
Anna Karenina '85
Anna Karenina '00
The Aviator's Wife '80 ►
The Best Man '97
Betty Blue '86 ►
Beyond the Clouds '95
Borderline '02 ►
The Bridesmaid '04
Brief Encounter '46 ►
Can't Buy Me Love '87
Carmen '03
Cause Celebre '87 ►
The Center of the World '01
Changing Times '04
Chungking Express '95 ►
The Climax '44
Cracker: True Romance '95 ►
Crazy Love '07 ►
Crazy Moon '87
The Crown Prince '06
The Crush '93
Cupid '96
Cyrano de Bergerac '25 ►
Cyrano de Bergerac '50 ►
Cyrano de Bergerac '85
Cyrano de Bergerac '90 ►
Damage '92 ►
Danger of Love '95
Death and Desire '97
Deceptions 2: Edge of Deception '94
Deep Crimson '96
Devil in the Flesh '87
Devil in the Flesh '98
Devil in the Flesh 2 '00
Doctor Zhivago '03
The Duchess of Langeais '07 ►
8 1/2 Women '99
El '52
Emily Bronte's Wuthering Heights '92
End of the Affair '55
The End of the Affair '99 ►

► = rated three bones or higher

- Endless Love '81
- Enduring Love '04
- The English Patient '96 ▸
- Eros '04
- Eva '62
- The Ex '96
- Eye of God '97 ▸
- Eye of the Beholder '99
- Far from the Madding Crowd '97 ▸
- Fatal Attraction '87 ▸
- Fear '96
- Fever Pitch '05
- Film Geek '06
- First Love, Last Rites '98
- For Sale '98
- G '02
- Ghost '90 ▸
- A Girl Cut in Two '07
- Going Postal '98
- The Good Girl '02 ▸
- The Good Night '07
- Goodbye, Dragon Inn '03
- He Loves Me ... He Loves Me Not '02
- The Heartbreak Kid '72 ▸
- Her and She and Him '69
- Homage '95
- Hush '98
- I Want You '98
- Jealousy '99
- Junk Mail '97
- Kama Sutra: A Tale of Love '96
- Last Breath '96
- L'Ennui '98
- Leo Tolstoy's Anna Karenina '96
- Les Biches '68 ▸
- Letters from a Killer '98
- Live Flesh '97 ▸
- Lost and Delirious '01
- Love and Death on Long Island '97
- Love and Rage '99
- Love in the Time of Cholera '07
- Loved '97
- Loverboy '05
- Lust, Caution '07
- Mad Love '95
- Mad Love '01
- Mararia '98
- Midnight Blue '96
- Miss Monday '98
- Mr. Wrong '95
- The Mystery of Edwin Drood '35
- Notre Histoire '84
- Obsessed '09
- Obsession '97
- One Kill '00 ▸
- Only Love '98
- Our Mutual Friend '98
- Perfect Strangers '03
- Phantom '22
- The Phantom of the Opera '25 ▸
- The Phantom of the Opera '43 ▸
- The Phantom of the Opera '62
- The Phantom of the Opera '89
- The Phantom of the Opera '90
- The Phantom of the Opera '98
- A Place in the Sun '51 ▸
- Plain Jane '01
- Punch-Drunk Love '02 ▸
- The Reader '08
- Romeo and Juliet '36 ▸
- Romeo and Juliet '54
- Romeo and Juliet '68 ▸
- Roxanne '87 ▸
- Sabrina '54 ▸
- Sabrina '95
- Say Nothing '01
- Sea of Love '89 ▸
- Shades of Black '93
- Show Boat '36 ▸
- Show Boat '51
- Skin Deep '94
- A Slipping Down Life '99
- Some Kind of Wonderful '87
- The Sterile Cuckoo '69 ▸
- Summer Storm '44
- Swimfan '02
- Sylvia '03
- Temptress Moon '96
- 10 '79
- Testosterone '03
- There's Something about Mary '98 ▸
- A Thin Line Between Love and Hate '96
- XIII '08
- Time '06
- To Gillian on Her 37th Birthday '96
- Truly, Madly, Deeply '91 ▸
- Twisted Love '95
- Twisted Obsession '90
- Valentin '03
- Walk the Line '05 ▸
- West Side Story '61 ▸
- Wicker Park '04
- Wilde '97
- Wuthering Heights '39 ▸
- Wuthering Heights '53
- Wuthering Heights '70
- Wuthering Heights '98

Occult

see also *Demons & Wizards; Satanism; Witchcraft*

- Alabama's Ghost '72
- Alone in the Dark '05
- The Amazing Mr. X '48
- The American Scream '88
- Amityville Dollhouse '96
- Apprentice to Murder '88
- Army of Darkness '92 ▸
- Bad Dreams '88
- Barbarian Queen '85
- Because of the Cats '74
- The Believers '87
- Beyond Dream's Door '88
- Beyond Evil '80
- Beyond the Door 3 '91
- The Black Cat '81
- Black Circle Boys '97
- Black Magic Terror '79
- Black Magic Woman '91
- Blackbeard's Ghost '67
- Bless the Child '00
- Blood Creek '09
- Blood Diner '87
- The Blood on Satan's Claw '71 ▸
- Blood Orgy of the She-Devils '74
- Bloodspell '87
- Born of Fire '87
- The Brainiac '61
- Brimstone & Treacle '82 ▸
- The Brotherhood 3: The Young Demons '02
- The Brotherhood of Satan '71
- Brotherhood of the Wolf '01
- The Burning Court '62
- Cabin in the Sky '43 ▸
- Cat Girl '57
- Cat in the Cage '68
- The Cellar '90
- Chandu on the Magic Island '34
- Child of Glass '78
- Children Shouldn't Play with Dead Things '72
- Chill '06
- Close Your Eyes '02
- Come Along with Me '84
- The Craft '96
- Craze '74
- The Crow: Wicked Prayer '05
- Curse of Nostradamus '60
- The Curse of the Crying Woman '61
- Curse of the Demon '57 ▸
- Curse of the Devil '73
- Damien: Omen 2 '78
- Damn Yankees '58 ▸
- Dance with the Devil '97
- The Dark Secret of Harvest Home '78
- Darkness '02
- Dead Men Don't Die '91
- Deathstalker 4: Match of Titans '92
- Deep Red: Hatchet Murders '75
- Demon Possessed '93
- Demon Rage '82
- Demon Wind '90
- Demonoid, Messenger of Death '81
- Demons 2 '87
- Demons of Ludlow '75
- The Devil & Daniel Webster '41 ▸
- Devil Dog: The Hound of Hell '78
- Devil Doll '64
- The Devils '71 ▸
- The Devil's Daughter '39
- The Devil's Eye '60
- Devil's Gift '84
- The Devil's Hand '61
- Devil's Kiss '75
- The Devil's Mistress '68
- The Devil's Nightmare '71
- Devil's Rain '75
- Devil's Son-in-Law '77
- Diary of a Madman '63
- Dick Tracy, Detective '45
- Doctor Faustus '68
- Dr. Strange '78
- Dominique Is Dead '79
- Dona Flor and Her Two Husbands '78 ▸
- Donovan's Brain '53 ▸
- Don't Be Afraid of the Dark '73
- Dream Man '94
- Dreamscape '84
- The Dunwich Horror '70
- The Dybbuk '37 ▸
- The Dying Truth '86
- Encounter with the Unknown '75
- The Entity '83
- Equinox '71 ▸
- Eternal Evil '87
- The Evictors '79
- The Evil '78
- Evil Altar '89
- Evil Dead '83
- Evil Dead 2: Dead by Dawn '87
- The Evil Mind '34
- Evilspeak '82
- Excalibur '81 ▸
- Exorcism '74
- The Exorcist '73 ▸
- The Exorcist 2: The Heretic '77
- Exorcist 3: Legion '90
- Eye of the Demon '87
- Eyes of Fire '84
- Fallen '97
- Feast for the Devil '71
- The Final Conflict '81
- The First Power '89
- The Fish that Saved Pittsburgh '79
- Fright House '89
- Full Circle '77
- Gates of Hell 2: Dead Awakening '96
- Genie of Darkness '62
- Ghosts That Still Walk '77
- The Girl in a Swing '89
- God Told Me To '76
- Grave Secrets '89
- The Guardian '90
- Half of Heaven '86 ▸
- Hanussen '88 ▸
- Haunted Symphony '94
- Haxan: Witchcraft through the Ages '22 ▸
- The Hearse '80
- Horror Hotel '60
- House of the Yellow Carpet '84
- The House on Skull Mountain '74
- The House that Bled to Death '81
- I Don't Want to Be Born '75
- I'm Dangerous Tonight '90
- Inferno '80
- Inner Sanctum '48
- Into the Badlands '92
- The Invasion of Carol Enders '74
- Invasion of the Blood Farmers '72
- Kill, Baby, Kill '66 ▸
- Killing Hour '84
- The Kingdom '95 ▸
- The Kingdom 2 '97 ▸
- The Kiss '88
- KISS Meets the Phantom of the Park '78
- Lady Terminator '89
- Land of the Minotaur '77
- The Legacy '79
- The Legend of Bloody Mary '08
- The Legend of Hell House '73 ▸
- Leonor '75
- Life-Size '00
- The Living Head '59
- Lost Souls '00
- The Magician '58 ▸
- Making Contact '86
- The Mangler '94
- Manos, the Hands of Fate '66
- Mardi Gras for the Devil '93
- Mardi Gras Massacre '78
- Maxim Xul '91
- Medea '70
- Men of Two Worlds '46
- Midnight '81
- Midnight Cabaret '90
- Mirror, Mirror '90
- Mirror, Mirror 2: Raven Dance '94
- Mirror of Death '87
- Mirrors '78
- Mists of Avalon '01 ▸
- The Monster Demolisher '60
- Moscow Zero '06
- Mystic Circle Murder '39
- Natas... The Reflection '83
- Necromancer: Satan's Servant '88
- Necropolis '87
- The Night Stalker '71
- The Night Strangler '72
- Ninja, the Violent Sorcerer '86
- The Occultist '89
- Omoo Omoo, the Shark God '49
- Only You '94
- The Oracle '85
- Orgy of the Dead '65
- Out on a Limb '87
- Phantasm '79
- Phantasm 2 '88
- Phantasm 3: Lord of the Dead '94
- Poltergeist '82 ▸
- Poltergeist 2: The Other Side '86
- Poltergeist 3 '88
- Possession: Until Death Do You Part '90
- The Power '80
- The Psychic '68
- The Psychic '78
- Psychic '91
- Psychic Killer '75
- Psychomania '73
- Puppet Master '89
- Quest of the Delta Knights '93
- Race with the Devil '75
- The Raven '63 ▸
- A Reflection of Fear '72
- The Reincarnate '71
- Rendez-Moi Ma Peau '81
- Repossessed '90
- Rest in Pieces '87
- Retribution '88
- Return '88
- Return from Witch Mountain '78
- Return of Chandu '34
- Rosemary's Baby '68 ▸
- Ruby '77
- Run If You Can '87
- The Runestone '91
- Sabaka '55
- Satan's Princess '90
- Satan's Touch '84
- Scared Stiff '87
- Season of the Witch '73
- Second Sight '89
- Seduced by Evil '94
- Seizure '74
- Sensation '94
- The Sentinel '76
- The Seventh Sign '88
- The Seventh Victim '43 ▸
- The Shaman '87
- Shock 'Em Dead '90
- Silent Night, Deadly Night 3: Better Watch Out! '89
- Sorceress '82
- The Spaniard's Curse '58
- Speak of the Devil '90
- The Spellbinder '88
- Spellbound '41
- Spiritism '61
- Student of Prague '13 ▸
- Summer of Fear '78
- Supergirl '84
- Teen Witch '89
- The Tempter '74
- Temptress '95
- Terror Beach '75
- Terror Creatures from the Grave '66
- That Darn Sorceress '88
- Three Sovereigns for Sarah '85
- To the Devil, a Daughter '76
- The Torture Chamber of Dr. Sadism '69
- The Touch of Satan '70
- Treasure of the Four Crowns '82
- The Undead '57
- Unknown Powers '80
- Venus in Furs '70
- Vibes '88
- The Visitor '80
- Warlock Moon '73
- Who Killed Doc Robbin? '48
- The Wicker Man '75 ▸
- Wild Man '89
- Wishmaster '97
- Wishmaster 4: The Prophecy Fulfilled '02
- Witch Hunt '94
- Witch Who Came from the Sea '76
- Witchboard '87
- Witchboard 2: The Devil's Doorway '93
- Witchboard 3: The Possession '95
- Witchcraft 2: The Temptress '90
- Witchcraft 4: Virgin Heart '92
- Witchcraft 5: Dance with the Devil '92
- The Witches of Eastwick '87
- The Witching '72
- Witching Time '84
- The Witchmaker '69
- The Witch's Mirror '60
- The Wizard of Oz '39 ▸
- Wizards '77
- The Woman Who Came Back '45
- Zapped Again '89
- The Zodiac Killer '71

Oceans

see *Deep Blue; Go Fish; Killer Sea Critters; Mutiny; Scuba; Shipwrecked; Submarines*

Office Surprise

- Casino '95 ▸
- Daredevil '03
- Dead Again '91 ▸
- Dial "M" for Murder '54 ▸
- Die Hard '88 ▸
- Goldeneye '95 ▸
- Grosse Pointe Blank '97 ▸
- Henry: Portrait of a Serial Killer '90 ▸
- La Femme Nikita '91 ▸
- Misery '90 ▸
- Mission: Impossible '96 ▸
- 9 to 5 '80
- Office Killer '97
- Point of No Return '93
- The Temp '93

Ohio

see also *Cincinnati*

- Against the Ropes '04
- Air Force One '97 ▸
- American Splendor '03 ▸
- Antwone Fisher '02 ▸
- Beautiful Ohio '06
- Beyond Dream's Door '88
- Brubaker '80 ▸
- Bubble '06
- A Christmas Story '83 ▸
- Dahmer '02
- Dirty Pictures '00
- Edge of Seventeen '99
- The Faculty '98
- The Fortune Cookie '66 ▸
- Guarding Tess '94
- Gummo '97
- A Home at the End of the World '04
- Howard the Duck '86
- Kit Kittredge: An American Girl '08 ▸
- Light of Day '87
- Little Man Tate '91 ▸
- Major League '89
- Major League 2 '94
- The Prize Winner of Defiance, Ohio '05 ▸
- Rain Man '88 ▸
- Reckless '97 ▸
- The Rocker '08
- The Shawshank Redemption '94 ▸
- The Silence of the Lambs '91 ▸
- The Soloist '09
- Stranger than Paradise '84 ▸
- Tango and Cash '89
- Teachers '84
- Traffic '00 ▸
- Trick 'r Treat '08 ▸
- Welcome to Collinwood '02

Oil

see *Black Gold*

Oldest Profession

see also *Women in Prison*

- Accatone! '61 ▸
- Alexander: The Other Side of Dawn '77
- Alien Warrior '85
- The Allnighter '87
- American Gigolo '79
- American Heart '92 ▸
- American Justice '86
- American Nightmare '81
- American Psycho '99
- Amor Bandido '79
- The Amsterdam Connection '78
- Angel '82
- Angel '84
- Angel 3: The Final Chapter '88
- Anna Christie '23 ▸
- Anna Christie '30
- Another Lonely Hitman '95
- Armistead Maupin's More Tales of the City '97
- Aroused '66
- Auntie '73
- Avenging Angel '85
- The Babysitters '07
- Back Roads '81
- Bad Girls '94
- Bad Guy '01
- Bad Lieutenant: Port of Call New Orleans '09
- The Balcony '63 ▸
- Band of Gold '95 ▸
- Before I Forget '07
- Being at Home with Claude '92
- Belle de Jour '67 ▸
- Beloved/Friend '99
- The Best Little Whorehouse in Texas '82
- Between Something & Nothing '08
- Beverly Hills Madam '86
- Beverly Hills Vamp '88
- Beyond Desire '94
- Big City Blues '99
- Blood Money: The Story of Clinton and Nadine '88
- Blow Out '81 ▸
- The Blue Hour '91
- Blush '95
- Boiling Point '93
- The Book of Stars '99
- Bordello '79
- Born Into Brothels: Calcutta's Red Light Kids '04
- Boulevard '94
- Broken Mirrors '85
- Broken Trail '06 ▸
- Business is Business '71
- Butterfield 8 '60 ▸
- Cafe Society '97

▸ = rated three bones or higher

Call Me: The Rise and Fall of Heidi Fleiss '04
Candy Tangerine Man '75
Caravaggio '86 ▶
Carmen, Baby '66
Casino '95 ▶
Catherine & Co. '76
Celebrity '98 ▶
Chained Heat 2 '92
Change My Life '01
Cheri '09
The Cheyenne Social Club '70
Children Underground '03 ▶
Chloe '09
Christiane F. '82 ▶
Cinderella Liberty '73 ▶
The Claim '00
Claire Dolan '97
Class of 1984 '82
Club Life '86
Coffy '73
The Confessional '95 ▶
Confessions of a Vice Baron '42
Corporate Affairs '07
Corvette Summer '78
The Courtesans of Bombay '85 ▶
Cracker: Brotherly Love '95 ▶
Crimes of Passion '84 ▶
Cross Country '83
Cry of a Prostitute: Love Kills '72
Cry, the Beloved Country '95 ▶
Cyclo '95
Dagger Eyes '83
Dangerous Beauty '98 ▶
The Dark Side of the Heart '92
Dead End Street '83
Deadly Sanctuary '68
Death Shot '73
Death Target '83
Deceiver '97
Deconstructing Harry '97
Dedee d'Anvers '49
Desperate Crimes '93
The Desperate Trail '94
Deuce Bigalow: European Gigolo '05
Deuce Bigalow: Male Gigolo '99
Diamond Men '01 ▶
Diamonds '99
Diary of a Lost Girl '29 ▶
The Dirty Girls '64
Diva '82 ▶
Dixie: Changing Habits '85 ▶
Doctor Detroit '83
Dr. Jekyll and Sister Hyde '71
Double Cross '92
Dressed to Kill '80
Drying Up the Streets '76
The Edge of Heaven '07 ▶
Edmond '05
8 Million Ways to Die '85
Elmer Gantry '60 ▶
Emily '77
Emmanuelle & Joanna '78
Endgame '01
Erendira '83
Eros '04
Eva '62
Every Man for Himself '79 ▶
Everybody Wins '90
Fall from Innocence '88
Fanny Hill '07
Finding Amanda '08
Fiona '98
Firepower '93
Flesh '68 ▶
Fleshpot on 42nd Street '71
Flowers of Shanghai '98
For Sale '98
Forbidden Fruit '52 ▶
Forever Amber '47
Foxy Brown '74
Frankenhooker '90
Frankie and Johnny '36
French Quarter '78
From Hell '01 ▶
From the Edge of the City '98
Full Exposure: The Sex Tape Scandals '89
Fyre '78
Gardens of the Night '08
Gate of Flesh '64
George A. Romero's Land of the Dead '05 ▶
Get Rita '75
Ghetto Dawg 2: Out of the Pits '05
The Gift '82
Gigi '58 ▶
The Girlfriend Experience '09
Girls of the White Orchid '85
God's Lonely Man '96
The Grasshopper '69
Great Smokey Roadblock '76
Half Moon Street '86
The Happy Hooker '75
The Happy Hooker Goes Hollywood '80
The Happy Hooker Goes to Washington '77
Hard As Nails '01
Hard Bounty '94
Hard Vice '94
Hardcore '04
A Harlot's Progress '06
Harnessing Peacocks '92
He Got Game '98
Heaven or Vegas '98
Help Wanted Female '68
High Stakes '89
Highway '01
Highway Patrolman '91
The Hillside Strangler '04
Hindsight '97
Hitman '07
Holly '07
Hollywood Chainsaw Hookers '88
Hollywood Vice Sqaud '86
Hot Blooded '98
Hotel '01
Hotel Room '93
Hothead '63
How Much Do You Love Me? '05
Hurlyburly '98
The Hustle '75
Hustle & Flow '05 ▶
Hustler Squad '76
Hustler White '96
Hustling '75 ▶
I Am Frigid... Why? '72
I Don't Kiss '91
I Dreamt Under the Water '07
I Want to Live! '58 ▶
The Iceman Cometh '60 ▶
The Iceman Cometh '73
Identity '03
The Immoral One '80
Impulse '90
In the Flesh '97
Intimate Betrayal '96
Into Temptation '09
Irma La Douce '63
Italian Movie '93
Jack's Back '87 ▶
Jade '95
Jamon, Jamon '93
John Carpenter's Vampires '97
johns '96
Journey to the End of the Night '06
Just a Gigolo '79
Justine '69
Katie Tippel '75
The Killer Inside Me '10
Killing Machine '02
Killing Zoe '94
Kinatay '09
Kinjite: Forbidden Subjects '89
Kiss of the Dragon '01
Kiss the Night '87
Kitty and the Bagman '82
Klute '71 ▶
Km. 0 '00
La Chienne '31 ▶
L.A. Confidential '97 ▶
L.A. Crackdown '87
L.A. Crackdown 2 '88
La Vie Promise '02
Ladies of the Lotus '87
Lady in Waiting '94
Lady of the Evening '75
Lady of the House '78
The Last Prostitute '91
The Last Temptation of Christ '88 ▶
Leaving Las Vegas '95 ▶
Les Miserables '97 ▶
Life of Oharu '52 ▶
A Life of Sin '92
The List '99
Little Ladies of the Night '77
Lola Montes '55 ▶
Lolo '92
Love by Appointment '76
Love Strange Love '82
The Machinist '04
The Mack '73
Madame Rosa '77 ▶
Madea Goes to Jail '09
Magdalene '88
Malibu High '79
Mamma Roma '62 ▶
The Man from Elysian Fields '01 ▶
Man Hunt '41 ▶
Man of Flowers '84
The Man Who Knew Too Little '97
Mandragora '97
Manon '50
Manon '68
Marriage Italian Style '64 ▶
Mayflower Madam '87
McCabe & Mrs. Miller '71 ▶
Miami Blues '90
Mid Knight Rider '79
Midnight Auto Supply '78
Midnight Cop '88
Midnight Cowboy '69 ▶
Midnight Dancers '94
Mifune '99
The Million Dollar Hotel '99
Miss Sadie Thompson '53 ▶
The Missionary '82
Mob Queen '98
Moll Flanders '96
Mon Homme '96
Mona Lisa '86 ▶
Monsieur Ibrahim '03 ▶
Monster '03 ▶
Moulin Rouge '01 ▶
Murderlust '86
Murphy's Law '86
My Life to Live '62 ▶
My Mother's Secret Life '84
My Own Private Idaho '91 ▶
My Pleasure Is My Business '74
My Son the Fanatic '97 ▶
Mysterious Skin '04 ▶
Naked Kiss '64
Naked Tango '91
Nana '55 ▶
Nana '82
Never on Sunday '60 ▶
New York's Finest '87
The Nickel Children '05
Night at the Golden Eagle '02
Night Friend '87
Night of the Generals '67 ▶
Night Shift '82
Night Slasher '69
The Night They Robbed Big Bertha's '75
Nightmare in Badham County '76
Nights of Cabiria '57 ▶
Nightwatch '96
No One Cries Forever '85
No Prince for My Cinderella '78
No Vacancy '99
The Nun '66
Nuts '87 ▶
Off Limits '87
Oldest Profession '67
Olivia '83
On the Doll '07
Once Upon a Time in America '84 ▶
100 Mile Rule '02
One Night Only '84
Out of the Dark '88
Padre Nuestro '85
Paid '06
Pandora's Box '28 ▶
Panic in Needle Park '71 ▶
Party Girls '29
The Passing of Evil '70
Pennies from Heaven '81 ▶
Personal Services '87
Pigalle '95
Play for Me '01
The Players Club '98 ▶
Poker Alice '87
The Poker House '09
Postcards from America '95
Pretty Baby '78 ▶
Pretty Woman '90 ▶
Prettykill '87
Prime Cut '72
The Princess & the Call Girl '84
Prison of Secrets '97
The Pyx '73 ▶
Queen Kelly '29 ▶
Quick, Let's Get Married '71
Quiet Days in Clichy '90
Quiet Days in Hollywood '97
Rain '32
Raw Justice '93
Reason to Die '90
Red Kimono '25
The Red Lily '24
Rent-A-Cop '88
The Ripper '97
Risky Business '83 ▶
A River Made to Drown In '97
Road Movie '72
Roman Spring of Mrs. Stone '61 ▶
Room 43 '58
Roots of Evil '91
Running Out of Time '94
Saint Jack '79 ▶
Samaritan Girl '04
Sandakan No. 8 '74 ▶
Sansho the Bailiff '54 ▶
Santitos '99
Scarred '84
Schnelles Geld '84
Scorchers '92
Secret Games '92
Secrets of a Married Man '84
Sessions '83
Sex, Love and Cold Hard Cash '93
Shadow of Angels '76
Sharky's Machine '81
The Silencer '92
Sin City '05
Single Room Furnished '68
Sinner '07
Sketches of a Strangler '78
Skin Art '93
Slaves in Bondage '37
Sonny '02
Speedway Junky '99
Spenser: Ceremony '93
Spider '02 ▶
SS Girls '77
Star Maps '97
State's Attorney '31
Stella Does Tricks '96
Stickmen '01
Stone Cold Dead '80
Story of a Prostitute '65
Storyville '74
Street Girls '75
Street of Forgotten Women '25
Street of Shame '56 ▶
Street Smart '87
Streetwalkin' '85
The Substitute Wife '94
The Sun's Burial '60 ▶
Suspicious River '00
Sweet Charity '69 ▶
Sweet Revenge '87
Sweet Sweetback's Baadasssss Song '71 ▶
Sweet Trash '70
The Sword and the Cross '58
Talons of the Eagle '92
Taxi Driver '76 ▶
They Were So Young '55
Things '93
Things to Do in Denver When You're Dead '95 ▶
Thomas in Love '01
Thousand Pieces of Gold '91 ▶
Three Seasons '98
Tightrope '84 ▶
Time After Time '79 ▶
Tipping the Velvet '02
The Toilers and the Wayfarers '97
Tokyo Decadence '91
Too Young to Die '90
Trading Places '83
Traffic in Souls '13 ▶
Train Station Pickups '79
The Treat '98
Tricks '97
Tricks of the Trade '88
Truck Stop Women '74
Twenty Dollar Star '91
2046 '04
Twin Falls Idaho '99 ▶
Twin Peaks: Fire Walk with Me '92
Twin Sisters '91
Twist '03 ▶
Twisted '96
Two or Three Things I Know about Her '66
Ultimate Desires '91
Uncaged '91
Utamaro and His Five Women '46
The Vampire Hookers '78
Vanessa '07
Via Appia '92
Vice Squad '82
Vicious Circles '97
Virgil Bliss '01
Walk on the Wild Side '62
The Walker '07
Warm Nights on a Slow-Moving Train '87
Warrior Queen '87
Waterloo Bridge '40 ▶
The Wedding Date '05
Whore '91
Whore 2 '94
The Wicked, Wicked West '97
Wild Bill '95
Wild Orchid 2: Two Shades of Blue '92
Wild Side '95
Winter of Frozen Dreams '08
The Winter of Our Dreams '82
A Woman in Flames '84 ▶
A Woman of Rome '56
Working Girls '75
Working Girls '87 ▶
The World of Suzie Wong '60

The Olympics

***see also** Sports Dramas*

Alex '92
American Anthem '86
Best of the Best '89
Blades of Courage '88
Blades of Glory '07
Blast '96
Breaking the Surface: The Greg Louganis Story '96
Chariots of Fire '81 ▶
Charlie Chan at the Olympics '37
Cool Runnings '93
Crossbar '79
The Cutting Edge '92
The First Olympics: Athens 1896 '84
Geordie '55
Going for the Gold: The Bill Johnson Story '85
International Velvet '78
The Jesse Owens Story '84
The Loretta Claiborne Story '00
A Million to One '37
Miracle on Ice '81
Munich '05 ▶
Pentathlon '94
Personal Best '82 ▶
Prefontaine '96
The Ringer '05
Rowing Through '96
Run for the Dream: The Gail Devers Story '96
Running Brave '83
Special Olympics '78
Swimming Upstream '03
Sword of Gideon '86
Tokyo Olympiad '66 ▶
21 Hours at Munich '76 ▶
Walk, Don't Run '66
Wilma '77
Without Limits '97 ▶

On the Rocks

***see also** Drug Use & Abuse*

Abandon '02
Aberdeen '00
Ace in the Hole '51 ▶
Affliction '97 ▶
Almost Heaven '06
An American Affair '09
Angela's Ashes '99
Arthur '81 ▶
Arthur 2: On the Rocks '88
The Bad News Bears '05
Bad Santa '03
Barfly '87 ▶
Beat '00
Betty '92
The Betty Ford Story '87 ▶
The Big Hangover '50
The Big Lebowski '97 ▶
Black Angel '46 ▶
Black Cloud '04
Blackout '54
Blue Heaven '84
Bob Funk '09
Bounce '00
Break of Hearts '35
Brideshead Revisited '08
Burn After Reading '08
The Butcher Boy '97 ▶
Can't Hardly Wait '98
Casino '95 ▶
Cat on a Hot Tin Roof '58 ▶
Cat on a Hot Tin Roof '84
The Chamber '96
Chelsea Walls '01
Clean and Sober '88 ▶
Cocktail '88
Come Back, Little Sheba '52 ▶
Come Early Morning '06
Cop-Out '67
Country Girl '54 ▶
Country Girl '82
Country Life '95
crazy/beautiful '01
Crazy Heart '09
The Crossing Guard '94 ▶
Crutch '04
A Cry for Love '80
Daddy & Them '99
Dance of Life '29
Dancer, Texas—Pop. 81 '98 ▶
Danger in the Skies '79
Dangerous '35
Dash and Lilly '99
Days of Wine and Roses '58
Days of Wine and Roses '62 ▶
Dead Heat '01
Desert Bloom '86 ▶
The Devil at 4 O'Clock '61
The Devil Thumbs a Ride '47 ▶
Divine Secrets of the Ya-Ya Sisterhood '02
Doing Time on Maple Drive '92
Dona Flor and Her Two Husbands '78 ▶
Drunken Angel '48 ▶
Drunks '96
The Edge of Love '08
Educating Rita '83 ▶
8 Heads in a Duffel Bag '96
800 Bullets '02
El Dorado '67 ▶
The Electric Horseman '79
The Entertainer '60 ▶
Evergreen '04
Eye of the Killer '99
Eye See You '01
F. Scott Fitzgerald in Hollywood '76
Factotum '06 ▶
Fat City '72 ▶
The Fire Within '64 ▶
The First Wives Club '96
Fish Hawk '79
The Flaming Teen-Age '56
Flesh and Bone '93 ▶
Floating '97
For One More Day '07
The Fountainhead '49 ▶
Frances '82 ▶
A Free Soul '31
Georgia '95 ▶

▶ = rated three bones or higher

Georgia Rule '07
Gervaise '56 ▶
The Great Man Votes '38 ▶
The Green Man '91 ▶
Hancock '08
Heaven's Prisoners '95
The Helen Morgan Story '57
Honkytonk Man '82
Hot Summer in Barefoot County '74
How About You '07
I Live with Me Dad '86
The Iceman Cometh '60 ▶
The Iceman Cometh '73
I'll Cry Tomorrow '55 ▶
The Informer '35 ▶
Ironweed '87 ▶
It's a Pleasure '45
Izzy & Moe '85
Jack and Sarah '95
Jack the Bear '93
Jesse Stone: Death in Paradise '06
Jesse Stone: Night Passage '06
Jesse Stone: Stone Cold '05
Jesse Stone: Thin Ice '09
Jiminy Glick in LaLa Wood '05
Joe the King '99
Journey Through Rosebud '72
Julia '08
Kill Cruise '90
Killer McCoy '47
La Cucaracha '99
The Last American Hero '73 ▶
Last Call: The Final Chapter of F. Scott Fitzgerald '02
Last Time Out '94
Le Beau Serge '58 ▶
Leaving Las Vegas '95 ▶
Let It Ride '89
License to Kill '84
Little Boy Blue '97
The Little Foxes '41 ▶
Little Voice '98 ▶
Living Proof: The Hank Williams Jr. Story '83
Long Day's Journey into Night '62 ▶
Long Day's Journey into Night '88
Long Day's Journey Into Night '96 ▶
The Lost Weekend '45 ▶
Love on a Pillow '62
A Love Song for Bobby Long '04
Lush '01
M.A.D.D.: Mothers Against Drunk Driving '83
Marvin & Tige '84
Matter of Trust '98
Mean Dog Blues '78
Merrily We Go to Hell '32
Mrs. Parker and the Vicious Circle '94
The Morning After '86
My Favorite Year '82 ▶
My Name Is Joe '98
My Zinc Bed '08
National Lampoon's Animal House '78 ▶
Nightmare Alley '47
No Laughing Matter '97
No Marriage Ties '33
No Such Thing '01
Notre Histoire '84
Once Were Warriors '94 ▶
One for the Road '82
100 Proof '96
One Too Many '51
Only When I Laugh '81 ▶
Orphan '09
Papa's Delicate Condition '63 ▶
The Pick-Up Artist '87
Place Vendome '98 ▶
Police Court '32
Pollock '00 ▶
Prairie Fever '08
Prozac Nation '01
Pushing Tin '99 ▶
Red Lights '04 ▶
Reuben, Reuben '83 ▶
Revenge of the Nerds '84
Rio Bravo '59 ▶
The River is Red '48
The Robe '53
Rosetta '99
Scandal Sheet '85
Scent of a Woman '92 ▶
The Secret Rapture '94
Shakes the Clown '92
She's So Lovely '97
A Shot at Glory '00
Shrink '09
The Sin of Harold Diddlebock '47
The Singing Blacksmith '38
A Single Man '09 ▶
16 Years of Alcohol '03
Skin Deep '89
Skins '02
Sling Blade '96 ▶
Smash-Up: The Story of a Woman '47 ▶
Snow Angels '07 ▶
Somebody Is Waiting '96
Son-in-Law '93
Spent '00
The Star '52 ▶
A Star Is Born '54 ▶
A Star Is Born '76
Straight Up '90
Stranded '87
Strange Brew '83
Street Kings '08
Struggle '31
Stuart Saves His Family '94
Sunset Strip '99
Take Me Home: The John Denver Story '00
Tales of Ordinary Madness '83
Ten Nights in a Bar-Room '31
Ten Nights in a Barroom '13
The Tenant of Wildfell Hall '96
Tennessee '08
Term of Trial '63
Termini Station '89
Thirteen '03 ▶
Tree's Lounge '96
True Crime '99
Tugboat Annie '33 ▶
24-7 '97
28 Days '00
Twisted '04
Under Capricorn '49
Under Capricorn '82
Under the Volcano '84 ▶
Unearthed '07
Unnatural Pursuits '91
The Verdict '82 ▶
Wagons East '94
What Price Hollywood? '32 ▶
When a Man Loves a Woman '94
Whiskey Galore '48 ▶
White Lightning '73
Wild Iris '01
Willa '79
The Winning Team '52
Winter Passing '05
A Winter Tan '88
You Kill Me '07 ▶

One Last Job

***see also** Crime Drama; Heists; Hit Men/Women; Organized Crime; Scams, Stings & Cons*

Action Man '67
Assassins '95
The Brothers Bloom '09
Canvas: The Fine Art of Crime '92
Carnival of Wolves '96
City of Industry '96
City on Fire '87
Columbus Day '08
The Crew '08
Crime Wave '54
Dead or Alive '02
The Debt '03
Dillinger and Capone '95
Entrapment '99
Exiled '06
Ghetto Dawg 2: Out of the Pits '05
Going in Style '79 ▶
Gone in 60 Seconds '00
The Hard Word '02
Heat '95 ▶
Heist '01 ▶
The Job '03
The Killer '90 ▶
Le Choc '82
The Mummy: Tomb of the Dragon Emperor '08
Once a Thief '90
Out of Sight '98 ▶
The Ref '93 ▶
Reindeer Games '00
The Rundown '03
The Score '01
Seven Thieves '60 ▶
Sexy Beast '00 ▶
Sharpshooter '07
Shooters '00
Small Time Crooks '00
Sniper 2 '02
Solo '06
The Squeeze '80
The Star '52 ▶
Takers '10
Thief '81 ▶
Things to Do in Denver When You're Dead '95 ▶
Tough Guys '86
Two If by Sea '95
The Usual Suspects '95 ▶

Only the Lonely

Abducted '86
The Abduction of Kari Swenson '87
Adrift in Manhattan '07
The Adventures of Sharkboy and Lavagirl in 3-D '05
After the Wedding '06 ▶
All or Nothing '02
All That Heaven Allows '55 ▶
Amelie '01 ▶
American Splendor '03 ▶
Audition '99
An Autumn Afternoon '62 ▶
Autumn Tale '98
Avenue Montaigne '06
The Ballad of Little Jo '93
Bed of Roses '95
Besieged '98
Betrayal '74
Birdman of Alcatraz '62 ▶
The Body Shop '72
Born Romantic '00
Bossa Nova '99
Bread and Tulips '01 ▶
Breakfast in Paris '81
Broken English '07
Broken Flowers '05
The Browning Version '51 ▶
Buddy Boy '99
The Business of Strangers '01
The Cemetery Club '93
The Center of the World '01
Central Station '98 ▶
Change My Life '01
Charlotte Sometimes '02
Choose Me '84 ▶
A Chorus of Disapproval '89
A Christmas Without Snow '80
Citizen Kane '41 ▶
The Closet '00
Conversations with Other Women '05
Cotter '72
Cowboys Don't Cry '88
Cyrano de Bergerac '25 ▶
Cyrano de Bergerac '50 ▶
Cyrano de Bergerac '85
Cyrano de Bergerac '90 ▶
Dam Street '05
A Day in the Country '46 ▶
Day Night Day Night '06 ▶
Dead Letter Office '98
Delirious '06
Desperately Seeking Susan '85
Didn't You Hear? '83
Dirty Dishes '78 ▶
Distant Thunder '88
Docks of New York '28 ▶
Doin' Time on Planet Earth '88
The Doll '62
A Doll's House '59
A Doll's House '73
A Doll's House '73 ▶
Eagle vs. Shark '07
Eat Drink Man Woman '94 ▶
The Eclipse '66 ▶
84 Charing Cross Road '86 ▶
El Super '79 ▶
An Empty Bed '90 ▶
The Enchanted Cottage '45
Escapade in Japan '57
E.T.: The Extra-Terrestrial '82 ▶
Every Man for Himself & God Against All '75 ▶
Eye of the Needle '81
Fanatic '82
Felicia's Journey '99 ▶
Fever '99
Fiances '63
The Final Alliance '89
Fire '96
Full Moon in Blue Water '88
Full Moon in Paris '84
The Game of Love '87
Ginger Snaps '01
God's Lonely Man '96
The Gun in Betty Lou's Handbag '92
Half Broken Things '07
Happy Endings '05
Hard Pill '05
Harold and Maude '71 ▶
The Heart Is a Lonely Hunter '68 ▶
Heavy '94 ▶
Hell Hounds of Alaska '73
Henry Poole Is Here '08 ▶
High Country '81
Hiroshima, Mon Amour '59 ▶
Hoffman '70
The Human Stain '03
The Hunchback of Notre Dame '39 ▶
The Hunchback of Notre Dame '57
Husbands and Wives '92 ▶
I Don't Give a Damn '88
I Sent a Letter to My Love '81 ▶
I Take This Woman '40
I Want Someone to Eat Cheese With '06
In the White City '83 ▶
In the Winter Dark '98
Inside Out '91
Internet Dating '08
Is Anybody There? '08
I've Loved You So Long '08 ▶
Kaspar Hauser '93
La Leon '07
La Petite Sirene '80
La Vie Continue '82
Lana in Love '92
Lars and the Real Girl '07
The Last Best Year '90
Last Chance Harvey '08
The Legend of 1900 '98
Les Bons Debarras '81
Les Voleurs '96 ▶
Let the Right One In '08
The Locket '02
The Lonely Guy '84
Lonely Hearts '82 ▶
Lonely Hearts '06
The Lonely Passion of Judith Hearne '87 ▶
Lonelyhearts '58
Looking for Kitty '04
Looking for Mr. Goodbar '77
Lost in Translation '03 ▶
Lulu on the Bridge '98
Lunatics: A Love Story '92 ▶
Luther the Geek '90
Madagascar Skin '95
Man of Flowers '84
Marty '55 ▶
The Match Factory Girl '90 ▶
Men Don't Leave '89
The Merry Gentleman '08
Midnight Clear '06
Miles to Go Before I Sleep '74
Mind the Gap '04
Minnie and Moskowitz '71
Mrs. Palfrey at the Claremont '05
Mr. Kingstreet's War '71
Moon '09
Mouchette '67 ▶
Moving Malcolm '03
My First Mister '01
976-EVIL '88
Ninotchka '39 ▶
The Noah '75
Noel '04
None But the Lonely Heart '44 ▶
Not of This World '99
Notes from Underground '95
O Fantasma '00
Once Around '91
Only the Lonely '91
Only You '92
Our Miss Brooks '56
Panic Station '82
Pan's Labyrinth '06 ▶
The Passion of Anna '70 ▶
Persona '66 ▶
Pi '98
A Price above Rubies '97
Priest of Love '81
Primal Secrets '94
The Prime of Miss Jean Brodie '69 ▶
The Prince of Central Park '77 ▶
Private Fears in Public Places '06
The Pursuit of Happiness '70
Queen of the Stardust Ballroom '75 ▶
The Rachel Papers '89 ▶
Rachel, Rachel '68 ▶
The Red Desert '64 ▶
Red Kimono '25
Restless '72
Return Engagement '78
Rhythm Thief '94
Richie Rich '94
Risk '94 ▶
Robert et Robert '78 ▶
Roman '06
Roseland '77 ▶
Samurai 2: Duel at Ichijoji Temple '55 ▶
Scene of the Crime '87 ▶
The Seagull '71 ▶
The Seagull '75
Secret Life of an American Wife '68
Seize the Day '86 ▶
Separate Tables '58 ▶
Separate Tables '83
September '88
The Sergeant '68
Shadows in the Storm '88
Sherman's March '86 ▶
Single Bars, Single Women '84
A Single Man '09 ▶
Sleepless in Seattle '93 ▶
Slipstream '73
Snow Cake '06
Solas '99
The Solitary Man '82
Someone to Love '87
Somersault '04
South of Reno '87
The Spectator '04
Speed Dating '07
Spider '02 ▶
The Station Agent '03 ▶
Street Heart '98
Stuart Saves His Family '94
Summer '86 ▶
Sunday '96
Sunday, Bloody Sunday '71 ▶
Synecdoche, New York '08 ▶
Tales of the Klondike: The Scorn of Women '87
Tenth Month '79
That Cold Day in the Park '69
That Evening Sun '09 ▶
Thomas in Love '01
Til There Was You '96
Tomorrow '72 ▶
Too Shy to Try '78
Turtle Diary '86 ▶
12 and Holding '05 ▶
Twin Falls Idaho '99 ▶
Under the Skin '97
Vagabond '85 ▶
The Village Barbershop '08
The Visitor '07 ▶
The Walls of Malapaga '49
The War Zone '98
Waterloo Road '44
What Happened Was... '94
When the Cat's Away '96 ▶
When Your Lover Leaves '83
While You Were Sleeping '95 ▶
Who Is Harry Kellerman and Why Is He Saying Those Terrible Things About Me? '71
Wildest Dreams '90
Willard '71
Willard '03
Woman in the Shadows '34
World Traveler '01
The Young in Heart '38 ▶
Zelly & Me '88 ▶

Opera

***see also** Musicals*

Callas Forever '02
The Climax '44
Cosi '95 ▶
Farinelli '94
The Fifth Element '97
Fleeing by Night '00
Foul Play '78 ▶
Interrupted Melody '55 ▶
Joyeux Noel '05 ▶
Madame Butterfly '95
The Man Who Cried '00
Merci Docteur Rey '04 ▶
Musica Proibita '43
Naughty Marietta '35
A Night at the Opera '35 ▶
Opera '88
The Perfect Husband '92
The Phantom of the Opera '62
The Phantom of the Opera '90
The Phantom of the Opera '98
The Phantom of the Opera '04
Piano Tuner of Earthquakes '05
Puccini for Beginners '06
Rhapsody of Spring '98
Riding Alone for Thousands of Miles '05
Romance '30
So This Is Love '53
Stingaree '34
Tonight or Never '31

Order in the Court

***see also** Justice Prevails...?; Law & Lawyers; Military Crimes & Trials*

Absence of Malice '81
The Accused '48
The Accused '88 ▶
Action for Slander '38
Adam's Rib '50 ▶
All God's Children '80
Amazing Dr. Clitterhouse '38 ▶
The Ambush Murders '82
An American Crime '07
An American Tragedy '31
American Tragedy '00
Anatomy of a Murder '59 ▶
And Justice for All '79
The Andersonville Trial '70 ▶
Angel Face '52 ▶
Artemisia '97
As Summers Die '86
Assault at West Point: The Court-Martial of Johnson Whittaker '94
Bamako '06
Bee Movie '07
Beefcake '99
Before and After '95
Beyond a Reasonable Doubt '56
Big Daddy '99
The Black Legion '37 ▶
Blind Faith '98
Body Chemistry 4: Full Exposure '95
Body of Evidence '92
Boomerang '47 ▶
Bordertown '35
Bounce '00
The Bramble Bush '60
Breaker Morant '80 ▶
Broken Trust '95
The Burning Bed '85 ▶
The Caine Mutiny Court Martial '88 ▶
Carrington, V.C. '54 ▶

▶ = rated three bones or higher

A Case of Libel '83
The Castle '97
Cause Celebre '87 ►
The Chamber '96
The Chatterley Affair '06
The Cheat '31
Chicago 10 '07 ►
A Civil Action '98
Class Action '91 ►
Clearcut '92
The Client '94
Cold Days '66
Color of Justice '97
Comedy of Power '06
Compulsion '59 ►
Conduct Unbecoming '75
The Confession '98
Conspiracy: The Trial of the Chicago Eight '87 ►
Convicted '86
The Court Martial of Billy Mitchell '55 ►
Crazy in Alabama '99
Crime Broker '94
Crime of the Century '96
Crimebroker '93
Criminal Court '46
Cross Examination '32
Crossroads '42
The Crucible '96 ►
A Cry in the Dark '88 ►
Dancer in the Dark '99
Dangerous Beauty '98 ►
Dangerous Evidence: The Lori Jackson Story '99
Deacon Brodie '98
Deadlocked '00
Dear God '96
Death of a Soldier '85
Death Sentence '74
The Defenders: Payback '97
The Defenders: Taking the First '98
Defenseless '91
Degree of Guilt '95
Deliberate Intent '01
Delinquent Parents '38
The Devil & Daniel Webster '41 ►
The Devil's Advocate '97
Dirty Pictures '00
Disclosure '94
Dishonored Lady '47
Dr. Jekyll and Mr. Hyde '08
The Drake Case '29
A Dry White Season '89 ►
8-A '92
Emma '32
Ernest Goes to Jail '90
Eureka! '81
Evelyn '02 ►
Evelyn Prentice '34
Execution of Justice '99
The Exorcism of Emily Rose '05 ►
A Few Good Men '92 ►
Final Appeal '93
Final Justice '98
Final Verdict '91
Find Me Guilty '06 ►
Flash of Genius '08
A Free Soul '31
From the Hip '86
Getting Gotti '94
Ghosts of Mississippi '96
Gideon's Trumpet '80
The Gift '00
A Girl Cut in Two '07
The Girl in the News '41
The Girl in the Red Velvet Swing '55
God on Trial '08
The Good Father '87 ►
The Good Fight '92
The Good Mother '88
Gospa '94
The Great American Sex Scandal '94
Guilty as Sin '93
Guilty of Innocence '87
Hard Traveling '85
Heart of the Beholder '05 ►
Hitz '89
Honor Thy Father and Mother: The True Story of the Menendez Brothers '94
A House Divided '00
How Many Miles to Babylon? '82
The Hurricane '99 ►
I Want to Live! '58 ►
Illegally Yours '87
In the Name of the Father '93 ►
InAlienable '08
Indictment: The McMartin Trial '95 ►
Inherit the Wind '60 ►
Inherit the Wind '99
Invasion of Privacy '96
The Inveterate Bachelor '58
It Could Happen to You '37
Jaded '96
The Jagged Edge '85
Jailbait: Betrayed By Innocence '86
Jasper, Texas '03
Jeanne la Pucelle '94
Joan of Arc '99
John Grisham's The Rainmaker '97
The Judge '49
The Judge and the Assassin '75 ►
Judge Horton and the Scottsboro Boys '76
Judgment at Nuremberg '61 ►
Judgment in Berlin '88
Judicial Consent '94
Jungle Woman '44
The Juror '96
Jury Duty '95
The Jury's Secret '38
A Killing in a Small Town '90 ►
The Killing Yard '01
King and Country '64 ►
King of the Pecos '36
Knock on Any Door '49
Knots '05
L.A. Law '86 ►
The Last Innocent Man '87
The Last Letter '04
The Last Wave '77 ►
Legalese '98
Legally Blonde '01
Les Assassins de L'Ordre '71
Liar Liar '97
The List '99
Little Gloria... Happy at Last '84
The Long Dark Hall '51
The Love God? '70
Loved '97
Lucky Partners '40
Lured Innocence '97
Madame X '37
Madame X '66
Madeleine '50
Man From Galveston '63
The Man in the Glass Booth '75 ►
A Map of the World '99
Melanie Darrow '97
The Merchant of Venice '04 ►
Midnight '34
Midnight in the Garden of Good and Evil '97
Midnight Mary '33
Miracle on 34th Street '47 ►
Miracle on 34th Street '94
Mrs. Harris '05
Mrs. R's Daughter '79
Mr. Deeds Goes to Town '36 ►
Mistrial '96
Monsieur Beaucaire '24
Moonlight Mile '02 ►
Move Over, Darling '63
Murder '30 ►
Murder in the First '95
Murder or Mercy '74
Music Box '89
Mutiny '99
My Cousin Vinny '92 ►
My Sister's Keeper '09
Naked Lie '89
Never Forget '91
The Next Best Thing '00
Night Falls on Manhattan '96 ►
The Notorious Landlady '62
Nuremberg '00
Nutcracker: Money, Madness & Murder '87 ►
Nuts '87 ►
One of Her Own '97
One Way '06
Outrage! '86
The Paradine Case '47
Passion of Joan of Arc '28 ►
Penalty Phase '86
The People vs. Larry Flynt '96 ►
Perfect Crime '97
Perfect Strangers '50
Perry Mason Returns '85 ►
Perry Mason: The Case of the Lost Love '87
Philadelphia '93 ►
The Ponder Heart '01
Presumed Innocent '90 ►
Primal Fear '96
Prisoners of the Sun '91 ►
Psychopath '97
Question of Silence '83 ►
Rampage '87
The Reader '08
Red Corner '97
Red Kimono '25
Remember the Night '40 ►
The Respectful Prostitute '52
Return to Paradise '98 ►
Reversal of Fortune '90 ►
The Rite '69
The River is Red '48
Riverbend '89
Roe vs. Wade '89 ►
The Rose Garden '89
Roxie Hart '42
Rules of Engagement '00
Runaway Jury '03 ►
The Runner Stumbles '79
Sacco & Vanzetti '71
The Scorpion Woman '89
The Secret Passion of Robert Clayton '92
See No Evil: The Moors Murders '06
Separate but Equal '91 ►
Sergeant Rutledge '60 ►
Sergeant Ryker '68
Sex & Lies in Sin City: The Ted Binion Scandal '08
Shadow of Doubt '98
The Shaggy Dog '06
Shattered City: The Halifax Explosion '03
Silent Victim '92
A Simple Twist of Fate '94
Skullduggery '70
Sleepers '96
Small Sacrifices '89
Smart Woman '48
Snow Falling on Cedars '99
Souls at Sea '37
Stairway to Heaven '46 ►
The Star Chamber '83
State's Attorney '31
A Stranger in the Kingdom '98
Stranger on Horseback '55
Stuck on You '84
Suspect '87
Swoon '91 ►
Term of Trial '63
They Won't Believe Me '47 ►
A Time to Kill '96 ►
To Kill a Mockingbird '62 ►
Tom and Huck '95 ►
Too Young to Die '90
Town without Pity '61
The Trial '63 ►
The Trial '93
Trial & Error '62
Trial and Error '96
Trial by Jury '94
The Trial of Lee Harvey Oswald '77
The Trial of Old Drum '00
Trial of the Catonsville Nine '72
The Trials of Oscar Wilde '60 ►
12 '07
Twelve Angry Men '57 ►
Twelve Angry Men '97
Two Years before the Mast '46
The Verdict '82 ►
Verdict on Auschwitz: The Frankfurt Auschwitz Trial 1963—1965 '93 ►
The Weight of Water '00
When Every Day Was the Fourth of July '78
When Thief Meets Thief '37
Where Love Has Gone '64
Where the Truth Lies '99
White Mischief '88 ►
White Squall '96
Why Do Fools Fall in Love? '98
Wilde '97
The Winslow Boy '48 ►
Witness for the Prosecution '57 ►
Wives under Suspicion '38
Woman in Brown '48
Woman Undone '95
A Woman's Face '38 ►
A Woman's Face '41 ►
The Young Philadelphians '59 ►
The Young Savages '61

Organ Transplants

see also ***Disease of the Week; Doctors & Nurses; Hospitals & Medicine; Second Chance***

The Awful Dr. Orloff '62
Black Friday '40
Blood Work '02
Bowery Boys Meet the Monsters '54
Brain of Blood '71
The Brain that Wouldn't Die '63
Brainwaves '82
Dead Man's Eyes '44
The Eye '08
Heart '99
Hybrid '07
I'll Bury You Tomorrow '02
The Incredible Two-Headed Transplant '71
The Indian '07
The Intruder '04 ►
John Q '02
The Man with Two Brains '83 ►
New Blood '99
Night of the Bloody Apes '68
Race Against Time '00
Repo Men '10
Repo! The Genetic Opera '08
Return to Me '00
A Stranger's Heart '07
13 Moons '02
21 Grams '03 ►
Untamed Heart '93
Young Frankenstein '74 ►

Organized Crime

see also ***Crimedy; Disorganized Crime; Gangs; Moscow Mafia; Triads; Urban Gangstas; Yakuza***

Absence of Malice '81
Across 110th Street '72
Action U.S.A. '89
Acts of Betrayal '98
Agent on Ice '86
Alibi '29
The Alien Agenda: Under the Skin '97
Almost Human '79
Alphabet City '84
American Born '89
American Chinatown '96
American Cop '94
American Cousins '02
American Justice '86
The American Soldier '70
American Yakuza '94
Analyze That '02
Analyze This '98 ►
Angel's Dance '99
Angels with Dirty Faces '38 ►
Another Stakeout '93
Armed for Action '92
Armed Response '86
As Tears Go By '88 ►
Atlantic City '81 ►
Avenging Disco Godfather '76
Baby Face Nelson '97
Baby on Board '92
Back to Back '96
Backtrack '89 ►
Bad Charleston Charlie '73
Bad Georgia Road '77
Ball of Fire '41 ►
Ballistic '94
The Barber Shop '33 ►
The Barcelona Kill '77
Batman Begins '05 ►
Be Cool '05
The Beast of the City '32
Beautiful Hunter '94
Beautiful Joe '00
Bella Mafia '97
Best of the Best: Without Warning '98
A Better Way to Die '00
Beverly Hills Bodysnatchers '89
Beverly Hills Cop 3 '94
Big Bad Mama 2 '87
Big Boss '77
Big Combo '55 ►
The Big Hit '98
Big News '29
The Big Slice '90
The Big Sweat '90
The Big Switch '70
Big Town After Dark '47
Billy Bathgate '91
Birth of the Blues '41
Bitter Sweet '98
Black Belt Jones '74
Black Caesar '73
Black Godfather '74
Black Gunn '72
Black Hand '73
Black Lemons '70
Black Lizard '68
Black Shampoo '76
Black Snow '89
Blackjack '78
Blank Check '93
Blind Fury '90
Blood Brothers '74
Blood Money '98
Blood Money '99
Blood Ties '87
Blood Vows: The Story of a Mafia Wife '87
Blown Away '90
Blue Money '84
Blues in the Night '41
Boca '94
Body Trouble '92
Bonanno: A Godfather's Story '99
Bookies '03
Boondock Saints '99
Born to Run '93
Boss of Bosses '99
Bought and Sold '03
Bound '96
The Box '03
The Boys '97
Branded to Kill '67
Breach of Trust '95
Breakaway '95
Brighton Rock '47 ►
A Bronx Tale '93 ►
Brooklyn Rules '07
A Brooklyn State of Mind '97
Brother '97
The Brotherhood '68
The Brothers Rico '57
Bugsy '91 ►
Bugsy Malone '76
A Bullet for Joey '55
Bullets over Broadway '94 ►
B.U.S.T.E.D. '99
The Busy Body '67
The Butcher '07
California Casanova '89
Camorra: The Naples Connection '85
Capone '89
Car Crash '80
Car 54, Where Are You? '94
Casino '95 ►
Chasing Ghosts '05
The Chinatown Murders: Man against the Mob '89
Chu Chu & the Philly Flash '81
City Hall '95 ►
City Unplugged '95
The Client '94
Cobra '71
Cohen and Tate '88
Cold Heat '90
Coldblooded '94
The Collectors '99
Comfort and Joy '84 ►
Confessions of a Hit Man '94
Connie and Carla '04
Cookie '89
Cop in Blue Jeans '78
Cops and Robbersons '94
Corky Romano '01
Corleone '79
Corruption '70
The Corruptor '99 ►
The Cotton Club '84 ►
Courier of Death '84
Crazy Six '98
The Crew '00
The Crew '08
Crime Killer '85
Crime Spree '03
The Criminal Mind '93
Crosscut '95
Dagger Eyes '83
Dangerous Charter '62
Darker than Amber '70
Darkman 3: Die Darkman Die '95
Daughter of the Tong '39
Day at the Beach '98
Dead Heat '01
Dead Lenny '06
Dead Pigeon on Beethoven Street '72
Dead Silent '99
Deadly Game '98
Deadly Rivals '92
Deadly Target '94
Deadly Vengeance '81
Deadly Weapons '70
Death Force '78
Death to Smoochy '02
Death Wish 5: The Face of Death '94
The Debt '98
Decay '98
Defendor '09
Deja Vu '89
Delta Fox '77
The Departed '06 ►
Desperate '47
Desperate Crimes '93
The Destiny of Marty Fine '96
Detour '99
Deuces Wild '02
The Devil's Dominoes '07
Dick Tracy '90 ►
Dinner Rush '00 ►
Dirty Deeds '02 ►
Dirty Work '92
District 13: Ultimatum '09
Doctor Detroit '83
The Don Is Dead '73
Donnie Brasco '96 ►
Double Bang '01
Double Deal '39
Double Edge '97
Doughboys '08
Drunken Angel '48 ►
Eastside '99
Elmore Leonard's Gold Coast '97
The Embalmer '03 ►
Empire of the Wolves '05
The Enforcer '51
Ernest Goes to Jail '90
Essex Boys '99
Eureka! '81
Excellent Cadavers '99
Excessive Force '93
The Executioner '78
The Executioner, Part 2: Frozen Scream '84
Exiled '06
Extreme Vengeance '90
Extremely Dangerous '99
An Eye for an Eye '81
Faith '90
Fake Out '82
The Family '70
A Family Matter '91
Family of Cops 2: Breach of Faith '97
Fass Black '77
Fast Money '96
Fatal Chase '77
Fatal Past '94
Fatally Yours '95
Fear in the City '81

Federal Protection '02
The Fighting Rookie '34
Final Justice '84
The Finger Man '55
Fingers '78 ▸
Fireback '78
The Firm '93 ▸
First Degree '95
Fist of Honor '92
The Fixer '97
Fled '96
Flipping '96
For Which He Stands '98
Force of Evil '49 ▸
The Freshman '90
Friends and Family '01
The Frightened City '61
Frogs for Snakes '98
Fugitive Rage '96
The Funeral '96 ▸
Gang War '40
Gangster No. 1 '00
Gangster Wars '81
Gangsters '79
Gangster's Law '86
The Garment Jungle '57
The George Raft Story '61
Get Rita '75
Getting Gotti '94
Ghetto Dawg '02
Ghetto Dawg 2: Out of the Pits '05
Ghost Dog: The Way of the Samurai '99
Gigli '03
Ginostra '02
The Girl Who Had Everything '53
Gloria '80
Gloria '98
Go Into Your Dance '35
The Godfather '72 ▸
The Godfather 1902-1959: The Complete Epic '81 ▸
The Godfather, Part 2 '74 ▸
The Godfather, Part 3 '90 ▸
The Godson '98
Gomorrah '08 ▸
Goodfellas '90 ▸
Gotti '96
Gozu '03
The Great Plane Robbery '40
Gun Shy '00
Gunblast '74
Gunshy '98 ▸
Hail Mafia '65
Hard-Boiled '92
The Harder They Fall '56 ▸
Harlem Nights '89
Harvard Man '01
Hawk's Vengeance '96
He Sees You When You're Sleeping '02
Heat '87
Hell on Frisco Bay '55
Hell Up in Harlem '73
Heroes in Blue '39
Hey! Hey! USA! '38
Hiding Out '87
High Heels and Low Lifes '01
High Stakes '89
High Voltage '98
Highway '01
Hired to Kill '73
A History of Violence '05 ▸
Hit Lady '74
The Hit List '88
Hit Men '73
Hit the Dutchman '92
Hitman's Journal '99
Hitman's Run '99
Hollywood Cop '87
Hollywood Cowboy '37
Hollywood Man '76
The Hollywood Sign '01
Hong Kong Nights '35
Honor Thy Father '73
Hooch '76
Hoodlum '96
Hoodlum & Son '03
Hoods '98
The Hunted Lady '77
Hurricane Smith '92
I Accidentally Domed Your Son '04
I Died a Thousand Times '55
I, Mobster '58

I Promise to Pay '37
I Went Down '97 ▸
Ice '93
The Ice Harvest '05
Il Divo '08
I'll Sleep When I'm Dead '03 ▸
Illegal Tender '07
In Bruges '08
In the Electric Mist '08
In the Kingdom of the Blind the Man with One Eye Is King '94
In the Mix '05
Infernal Affairs '02 ▸
Infernal Affairs 2 '03
Infernal Affairs 3 '03
Innocent Blood '92
Internes Can't Take Money '37
Johnny Stecchino '92 ▸
The Juror '96
Kansas City '95 ▸
Keaton's Cop '90
Keeper of the City '92
The Key Man '57
Kid Monk Baroni '52
Kill Me Again '89
The Kill Reflex '89
The Killer '90 ▸
Killer Instinct '92
The Killers '46 ▸
Killing in the Sun '73
The Killing Man '94
The Killing of a Chinese Bookie '76
Killing Time '97
The King of the Roaring '20s: The Story of Arnold Rothstein '61
Kings of South Beach '07
Kiss of Death '94
Kiss Toledo Goodbye '00
Kiss Tomorrow Goodbye '50
Knockaround Guys '01
The Krays '90 ▸
La Scorta '94 ▸
L.A. Wars '94
Ladies of the Lotus '87
Lady Jayne Killer '03
Lady Mobster '88
Lady of the Evening '75
Lady Scarface '41
Lansky '99
The Last Contract '77
The Last Days of Frankie the Fly '96
The Last Don '97
The Last Don 2 '98
Last Exit to Brooklyn '90 ▸
Last Rites '88
The Last Shot '04
The Last Word '95
Laws of Deception '97
Layer Cake '05 ▸
Legacy of Lies '92
Lepke '75
Lethal Games '90
Lethal Panther '90
Life Tastes Good '99
The Line '08
Little Caesar '30 ▸
Little Odessa '94
Little Vegas '90
Loan Shark '52
The Long Good Friday '80 ▸
Lorna's Silence '08
Lost Highway '96
Love, Honour & Obey '00
Love to Kill '97
Luck of the Draw '00
Lucky Luciano '74
Lucky Number Slevin '06
Ma and Pa Kettle Go to Town '50
Macbeth '06
Machine Gun Blues '95
Mad Dog and Glory '93 ▸
Made '01
Madigan's Millions '67
Mafia! '98
Mafia Princess '86
Mafia vs. Ninja '84
Mafioso '62
Magic Kid '92
Making the Grade '84
Mambo Cafe '00
The Man I Love '46 ▸
Man in the Vault '56

Man on a String '71
Man with a Gun '95
Manderlay '05
The Manhandlers '73
Manhunt '73
Manhunter '83
Married to the Mob '88 ▸
Mauvais Sang '86
The Mayor of Hell '33
Me and the Mob '94
Mean Machine '73
Mean Streets '73 ▸
The Mechanic '72
Meet Danny Wilson '52
Melvin Purvis: G-Man '74
Men of Means '99
Men of Respect '91
The Messenger '87
Mickey Blue Eyes '99
Mickey One '65
Mikey & Nicky '76
Miller's Crossing '90 ▸
Miracles '89
The Mission '99
Mr. Majestyk '74
Mister Mean '77
Mob Boss '90
Mob Queen '98
Mobsters '91
Money Kings '98
The Monster and the Girl '41
Montana '97
Moon over Harlem '39
Movie... In Your Face '90
Moving Target '89
Moving Target '96
Mulholland Falls '95
Murder, Inc. '60
My Blue Heaven '90
My Husband's Secret Life '98
The Mysteries of Pittsburgh '08
The Narrow Margin '52 ▸
National Lampoon's The Don's Analyst '97
Never Steal Anything Small '59
New Blood '99
New Mafia Boss '72
Next of Kin '89
1931: Once Upon a Time in New York '72
Nitti: The Enforcer '88
No Blood No Tears '02 ▸
No Way Back '96
Nowhere Land '98
No. 3 '97
Odd Jobs '85
Once a Thief '96 ▸
Once Upon a Time in America '84 ▸
Opposite Corners '96
Organized Crime & Triad Bureau '93
Our Family Business '81
Out for Justice '91
The Outfit '93
The Outside Man '73
Overkill '86
Palais Royale '88
The Palermo Connection '91
Panic Button '62
Paper Bullets '99
Party Girl '58 ▸
Party 7 '00
Passion for Power '85
Payoff '91
Penthouse '33 ▸
Perfect Killer '77
Perfect Witness '89
The Pick-Up Artist '87
Played '06
Players '03
The Plot Against Harry '69 ▸
Point Blank '67
Police Academy 7: Mission to Moscow '94
Politics '31
The Pope Must Diet '91
Port of New York '49
Portland Expose '57
Power and Beauty '02
Power of Attorney '94
Pray for Death '85
Prime Target '91
Prizzi's Honor '85 ▸
Pronto '97
The Proposal '00

The Public Eye '92 ▸
Pulp Fiction '94 ▸
Quick '93
The Quickie '01
Rancid Aluminium '00
Rapid Fire '92
Raw Deal '86
Recoil '97
Red Heat '88
The Red Light Sting '84
Red Line '96
Remote Control '94
The Replacement Killers '98
The Revenger '90
Ricco '74
Ring of Fire 3: Lion Strike '94
Ring of the Musketeers '93
Ripley's Game '02 ▸
The Rise and Fall of Legs Diamond '60
Road to Perdition '02 ▸
The Roaring Twenties '39 ▸
Rock, Baby, Rock It '57
RocknRolla '08
Romeo Is Bleeding '93
Romeo Must Die '00
Ruby '92
Rude Boy: The Jamaican Don '03
Rulers of the City '76
Run '91
The Runner '99
Running Scared '06
Rush Hour 3 '07
Ruslan '09
Safe Men '98
Savage Hearts '95
Scarface '31 ▸
Scarface Mob '62
Sex, Love and Cold Hard Cash '93
Shade '03
Shaft's Big Score '72
Shoot to Kill '47
Showdown '94
Sicilian Connection '72
The Sicilian Connection '85
Sitting Ducks '80 ▸
Sizzle '81
Slaughter '72
Slaughter's Big Ripoff '73
Sleepers '96
A Slight Case of Murder '38
Sloane '84
Slow Burn '90
Smalltime '96
Smashing the Rackets '38
Smokescreen '90
Smokin' Aces '07
Snatch '00 ▸
Sno-Line '85
Solo '06
Soul Survivor '95
Southie '98
Special Investigator '36
Squizzy Taylor '84
Stand-In '85
Stark '85
Stark Raving Mad '02
State of Grace '90 ▸
State's Attorney '31
Stephen King's Thinner '96
Sticks '98
Stiletto '69
Stiletto '08
Stiletto Dance '01
The Stone Killer '73
Stonebrook '98
Street Gun '96
Street Hero '84
Street People '76
Street War '76
Sugartime '95
Suicide Ride '97
T-Men '47 ▸
The Takeover '94
Taking the Heat '93
Target for Killing '66
The Taxman '98
Temptress Moon '96
10th & Wolf '06
Terminal Force '88
The Terror of the Tongs '61
They Call Me Bruce? '82
They Paid with Bullets: Chicago 1929 '69
Thick as Thieves '99
Thief '81 ▸

Things Change '88 ▸
Third World Cop '99
36 Hours to Die '99
This Could Be the Night '57
The Threepenny Opera '31
Ticket of Leave Man '37
Tight Spot '55 ▸
To Die For '95 ▸
To the Limit '95
Tokyo Drifter '66
Tony Rome '67
Too Hot to Handle '76
Total Western '00
The Trap '59
Trial by Jury '94
Trigger Happy '96
TripleCross '85
Trojan Eddie '96 ▸
True Identity '91
True Romance '93
24 Hours in London '00
Ulterior Motives '92
Under Hellgate Bridge '99
The Undertaker's Wedding '97
Underworld '27 ▸
Underworld '96
Underworld, U.S.A. '60 ▸
Undisputed II: Last Man Standing '06
Unleashed '05
The Untouchables '87 ▸
The Valachi Papers '72
Valentina's Tango '07
Velvet Smooth '76
Vendetta for the Saint '68
Verne Miller '88
Veronica Guerin '03
Wannabes '01
Wanted '98
We're Talkin' Serious Money '92
West New York '96
Whacked! '02
What Doesn't Kill You '08
What! No Beer? '33
What Up? '08
Where the Hot Wind Blows '59
Where the Sidewalk Ends '50
White Cargo '96
White Heat '49 ▸
White Hot: The Mysterious Murder of Thelma Todd '91
White Sands '92
The Whole Ten Yards '04
Who's Got the Action? '63
The Wild Card '03
Wise Guys '86
Wisegal '08
Wisegirls '02
With Friends Like These '98 ▸
Witness Protection '99 ▸
Witness to the Mob '98
Wolves in the Snow '02
The Wrestler '73
Zatoichi: The Life and Opinion of Masseur Ichi '62
Zatoichi: Zatoichi's Flashing Sword '64
Zebra Force '76

Otherwise Engaged

***see also** Romantic Triangles; Wedding Bells; Wedding Hell*

ABCD '99
The Accidental Husband '08
Across to Singapore '28
An Affair to Remember '57
After Tomorrow '32
The Age of Innocence '93 ▸
Aladdin '92 ▸
Alibi Ike '35
American Crude '07
Arthur '81 ▸
Au Pair '99
The Bachelor '99
Ball & Chain '04
The Barbarian '33
The Battle of Shaker Heights '03
The Baxter '05
Bell, Book and Candle '58
The Big Hit '98
The Birdcage '95 ▸
Black Cat, White Cat '98 ▸

Blind Date '87
Blind Dating '06
Breakfast for Two '37
The Breakup Artist '04
The Brothers '01 ▸
Bubble Boy '01
Captain Corelli's Mandolin '01
Catherine Cookson's The Black Candle '92
Catherine Cookson's The Wingless Bird '97
Chicken Tikka Masala '05
Clarissa '91 ▸
Clerks 2 '06 ▸
Come as You Are '05
Come September '61
Coming to America '88 ▸
Cupid & Cate '00
The Dark Angel '35
Dinner and Driving '97
Divine Secrets of the Ya-Ya Sisterhood '02
A Dog's Breakfast '07
Dot the I '03
Dream Wife '53
East Side of Heaven '39
Easy to Wed '46
Emma '97 ▸
Eva '62
Everyone Says I Love You '96 ▸
The Family Stone '05
Fandango '85
Fantastic Four '05
The Fiance '96
Fiances '63
Final Engagement '07
The Finances of the Grand Duke '24
Firefall '94
The First to Go '97
The Florentine '98
Forces of Nature '99
The Four Feathers '02
Four Weddings and a Funeral '94 ▸
Four's a Crowd '38
Frankenhooker '90
French Kiss '95
Friends and Family '01
Gabriela '01
George of the Jungle '97 ▸
George White's Scandals '45
Getting Gertie's Garter '27
Gildersleeve on Broadway '43
Goal 2: Living the Dream '07
Gone with the Wind '39 ▸
The Graduate '67 ▸
Gray Matters '06
Guess Who '05
A Guy Thing '03
Happy Times '00
Heights '04
Held Up '00
Her First Romance '40
High Society '56 ▸
His Girl Friday '40 ▸
Hotel de Love '96
The House of Yes '97
How to Deal '03
I Capture the Castle '02
I Hope They Serve Beer in Hell '09
I Love You, Man '09 ▸
The Illusionist '06
I'm Reed Fish '06
In and Out '97 ▸
The Intended '02
Intimate Betrayal '96
Intimate Lighting '65
I.Q. '94
It Had to Be You '00
It Takes Two '95
Jealousy '99
John Loves Mary '48
The Jolly Boys' Last Stand '00
Just One Night '00
Just One Time '00
The King's Guard '01
Kiss the Bride '07
Kiss Toledo Goodbye '00
Kissing a Fool '98
Kristin Lavransdatter '95
The Last Time '06
Laurel Canyon '02

Out of Order

Out of This World Sex

Pacific Islands

Painting

Paperboys

Parades & Festivals

Paradise Gone Awry

Parallel Universe

Paramedics

Pardners

Parenthood

▸ = rated three bones or higher

Mom '89
Mom & Dad '47
Monkey Grip '82 ▸
Mother & Daughter: A Loving War '80
Mother and Son '31
My Baby's Daddy '04
My Life '93
My Mom's a Werewolf '89
The Namesake '06 ▸
National Lampoon's European Vacation '85
Natural Enemies '79
The Next Best Thing '00
Next of Kin '84
Night Cries '78
No Dessert Dad, 'Til You Mow the Lawn '94
North '94
The Note '07
Nothing in Common '86
On Golden Pond '81 ▸
On the Third Day '83
One Fine Day '96
One Man's War '90
Only the Lonely '91
Only When I Laugh '81 ▸
The Others '01 ▸
The Pacifier '05
Padre Padrone '77 ▸
The Parent Trap '98
Parenthood '89 ▸
Parents '89 ▸
Paris, Texas '83 ▸
Penny Serenade '41 ▸
Perfect Parents '06
A Place for Annie '94
Poil de Carotte '31
Psycho 4: The Beginning '90
The Quiet Room '96
Raising Arizona '87 ▸
Raising Genius '04
Raising Helen '04
Red Doors '05
The Red House '47 ▸
Red River '48 ▸
Relative Strangers '06
The Reluctant Debutante '58 ▸
Rent-A-Kid '95
Revenge '71
The Revolt of Job '84 ▸
Riding in Cars with Boys '01
Rising Son '90 ▸
The River Rat '84
Room for One More '51
Runaway Father '91
Saint Maybe '98 ▸
The Sandy Bottom Orchestra '00
The Santa Clause '94
Sarah's Child '96
Say It With Songs '29
Scream for Help '86
Secret Ceremony '69
Secrets and Lies '95
Sex and the Single Parent '82
The Shaggy D.A. '76
She Hate Me '04
Sherrybaby '06
Silence of the Heart '84 ▸
Silent Witness '99
A Simple Twist of Fate '94
The Singing Fool '28
A Slightly Pregnant Man '79
Somebody Is Waiting '96
Son of Godzilla '66
Special Olympics '78
Speeding Up Time '71
Steel Magnolias '89 ▸
Stella '89
Stella Dallas '37 ▸
The Storm Within '48 ▸
The Strange Love of Molly Louvain '32
Sunstroke '92
Superdad '73
Suzanne '80
Taken Away '89
Target '85
Tea with Mussolini '99
Teenage Bad Girl '59
Tequila Sunrise '88
Terminator 2: Judgment Day '91 ▸
Terms of Endearment '83 ▸
Thank You for Smoking '06
There Will Be Blood '07 ▸
This Property Is Condemned '66
Three Fugitives '89
Three Men and a Baby '87 ▸
Three Men and a Cradle '85 ▸
Throw Momma from the Train '87 ▸
Times Have Been Better '06
Trading Mom '94
Trucker '08
Tumbleweeds '98
The Turning Point '77
Ulee's Gold '97 ▸
The Unborn 2 '94
Undercover Blues '93
An Unexpected Family '96
Unfinished Business '89
The Unstoppable Man '59
Valentin '02
Wanted: The Perfect Guy '86
When Wolves Cry '69
Where Are the Children? '85
Where's Poppa? '70 ▸
With Six You Get Eggroll '68
Without a Trace '83
The Woman Who Willed a Miracle '83
Yours, Mine & Ours '68
The Zodiac '05

Paris

***see also** France*
A la Mode '94
The Accompanist '93
Accused '36
An Affair of Love '99
After Sex '97
AKA '02
Alberto Express '92
Alias Betty '01
Alice et Martin '98
Almost Peaceful '02 ▸
Alphaville '65 ▸
The Ambassador's Daughter '56
Amelie '01 ▸
The American '01
American Dreamer '84
An American in Paris '51 ▸
An American Werewolf in Paris '97
Angel '37
Angel-A '05
Angelique: The Road to Versailles '65
Another 9 1/2 Weeks '96
Antoine et Antoinette '47
Apres-Vous '03
April in Paris '52
Arch of Triumph '48 ▸
Arch of Triumph '85
The Assignment '97
Au Pair '99
Augustin '95
Avenue Montaigne '06
The Aviator's Wife '80 ▸
Baise Moi '00
Ballet Russes '05 ▸
Balzac: A Life of Passion '99 ▸
The Beat My Heart Skipped '05 ▸
Beau Pere '81 ▸
Beaumarchais the Scoundrel '96
Bed and Board '70 ▸
Before I Forget '07
Before Sunset '04 ▸
Belle Americaine '61
Belle Toujours '06 ▸
Belphegar: Phantom of the Louvre '01
Beyond the Clouds '95
Blame It on Fidel '06
Boarding Gate '07
Boeing Boeing '65
Born in 68 '08
Bottle Shock '08
The Bourne Identity '02 ▸
Boy Meets Girl '84 ▸
Breakfast in Paris '81
Breathless '59 ▸
Broken English '07
The Butterfly '02 ▸
The C-Man '49
Cafe Metropole '37
Camille '36 ▸
Cartouche '62 ▸
Casque d'Or '52 ▸
Catacombs '07
Catherine & Co. '76
Celestial Clockwork '94
Change My Life '01
A Change of Place '94
Chaos '01
Charade '63 ▸
Chariots of Fire '81 ▸
Charlie Chan in City of Darkness '39
Charlie Chan in Paris '35
Cheri '09
Children of Paradise '44 ▸
Children of the Century '99
China White '91
Circle of Love '64
Circle of Passion '97
The Class '08
Clean '04
Cleo from 5 to 7 '61 ▸
Clowning Around '92
Code Unknown '00
Comedy of Innocence '00
Confusion of Genders '00
Cousin Bette '97
The Cousins '59 ▸
CQ '01
Crainquebille '23 ▸
The Crazy Ray '22 ▸
Crime Spree '03
Crimson Rivers 2: Angels of the Apocalypse '05
Crossroads '42
The Da Vinci Code '06 ▸
Dad On the Run '00
Dangerous Liaisons '03
A Dangerous Man: Lawrence after Arabia '91 ▸
Daniella by Night '61
Dear Brigitte '65
Delicatessen '92 ▸
Delta of Venus '95
Demonlover '02
The Destructors '74
Detective '85
The Devil, Probably '77
The Devil Wears Prada '06
Diary of a Seducer '95
Dingo '90
The Dirty Girls '64
The Disenchanted '90
District B13 '04
District 13: Ultimatum '09
Diva '82 ▸
Does This Mean We're Married? '90
Dracula and Son '76
The Dreamers '03
The Duchess of Langeais '07 ▸
Elisa '94
The Emperor's New Clothes '01
Empire of the Wolves '05
Entangled '93
Everyone Says I Love You '96 ▸
The Face at the Window '39
Faithless '00 ▸
The Fall '98
The Fantastic Night '42 ▸
Fashions of 1934 '34
The Fatal Image '90
The Favor, the Watch, & the Very Big Fish '92
Fay Grim '06
Femme Fatale '02
A Few Days in September '06
A Fine Romance '92
Flight of the Red Balloon '08
Forget Paris '95
The Fourth Sex '61
Frantic '88 ▸
French Can-Can '55 ▸
French Kiss '95
The French Lesson '86
French Postcards '79
The French Touch '54
The French Way '40
Friday Night '02
From Hell to Victory '79
From Paris With Love '10
Frontier of Dawn '08
Funny Face '57 ▸
Gabrielle '05
Games of Love and Chance '03
Gentlemen Prefer Blondes '53 ▸
G.I. Joe: The Rise of Cobra '09
Gigi '58 ▸
The Girl '01
A Girl on Her Own '76
The Girl on the Bridge '98 ▸
The Girl on the Train '09
Gold Diggers in Paris '38
The Grand Role '04
The Great Garrick '37
The Green House '96
Half-Shot at Sunrise '30
Hannibal Rising '07
Happenstance '00
Happily Ever After '04
Head in the Clouds '04
Heartbeat '46
Heartbeat Detector '07
Henri Langlois: The Phantom of the Cinematheque '04 ▸
Henry & June '90 ▸
Her and She and Him '69
Hidden '05 ▸
The Holes '72
Hollywood, Je T'Aime '09
House of D '04
The Housekeeper '02
How to Steal a Million '66 ▸
The Hunchback '97
The Hunchback of Notre Dame '39 ▸
The Hunchback of Notre Dame '57
The Hunchback of Notre Dame '82 ▸
The Hunchback of Notre Dame '96 ▸
I Am Frigid... Why? '72
I Can't Sleep '93
I Don't Kiss '91
I Dreamt Under the Water '07
I Want to Go Home '89
If I Were King '38 ▸
If Looks Could Kill '91
I'm Going Home '00 ▸
The Immoral One '80
In Praise of Love '01
Incognito '97
Inglourious Basterds '09 ▸
Innocents in Paris '53
Inside Paris '06
Interview with the Vampire '94
Intimate Strangers '04 ▸
Intolerance '16 ▸
Invisible Circus '00
The Invisibles '99
Irma Vep '96
Is Paris Burning? '66 ▸
Jeanne and the Perfect Guy '98
Jefferson in Paris '94
Julie & Julia '09 ▸
Killing Zoe '94
Kiss of the Dragon '01
La Boum '81
La Chinoise '67
La Marseillaise '37 ▸
La Moustache '05
La Petite Jerusalem '05
La Sentinelle '92
La Separation '98 ▸
La Vie de Boheme '93 ▸
La Vie en Rose '07
The Lady and the Duke '01
Lady L '65
The Last Metro '80 ▸
Last Tango in Paris '73 ▸
The Last Time I Saw Paris '54
Le Cercle Rouge '70 ▸
Le Deuxieme Souffle '66
Le Divorce '03
Le Joli Mai '62 ▸
Le Petit Lieutenant '05
Le Samourai '67 ▸
Le Schpountz '38
Le Trou '59 ▸
Les Miserables '95
Les Miserables '97 ▸
Les Vampires '15 ▸
Like a Brother '05
Little Indian, Big City '95
A Little Romance '79 ▸
Look at Me '04 ▸
Love After Love '94
Love Play '60
Love Songs '07
The Lovers on the Bridge '91
Ma and Pa Kettle on Vacation '53
Ma Saison Super 8 '05
Ma Vie en Rose '97 ▸
The Mad Adventures of Rabbi Jacob '73 ▸
Madame X '37
Made in Paris '65
Madeline '98
The Madwoman of Chaillot '69
The Man in the Iron Mask '98 ▸
Man of the World '31
The Man Who Cried '00
Marquis de Sade '96
Mauvaise Graine '33
Max, Mon Amour '86
Melo '86
Mesmer '94
Metroland '97
Mina Tannenbaum '93
Mrs. 'Arris Goes to Paris '92
The Moderns '88 ▸
Modigliani '04
Mon Oncle d'Amerique '80 ▸
Monsieur Ibrahim '03 ▸
Monsieur N. '03 ▸
Mortal Transfer '01
Moulin Rouge '01 ▸
Murders in the Rue Morgue '71
The Murders in the Rue Morgue '86 ▸
My Best Friend '06
My Life and Times with Antonin Artaud '93 ▸
My Sex Life... Or How I Got into an Argument '96
My Wife is an Actress '01
Napoleon '03
Nelly et Monsieur Arnaud '95 ▸
The New Eve '98 ▸
A New Kind of Love '63
Night on Earth '91 ▸
Ninotchka '39 ▸
November Moon '85
Now and Forever '34
Oliver Twist '33
Once in Paris... '79
One Against the Wind '91 ▸
One Day You'll Understand '08
One Hour with You '32
Orpheus '49
Panique '47 ▸
Paris '08
Paris Blues '61
Paris Holiday '57
Paris in Spring '35
Paris, je t'aime '06
Paris 36 '08
Paris When It Sizzles '64
Parisian Love '25
Pedale Douce '96
Peppermint Soda '77 ▸
The Perfect Furlough '59
Perfume: The Story of a Murderer '06
Perfumed Nightmare '89 ▸
Petits Freres '00
The Phantom of Paris '31
The Phantom of the Opera '25 ▸
The Phantom of the Opera '43 ▸
The Phantom of the Opera '90
The Phantom of the Opera '98
The Phantom of the Opera '04
Pigalle '95
The Pink Panther '06
The Pink Panther 2 '09
Place Vendome '98 ▸
Plucking the Daisy '56
Pola X '99
Portraits Chinois '96
The Private Affairs of Bel Ami '47 ▸
Private Fears in Public Places '06
Ratatouille '07 ▸
Ready to Wear '94
Red Kiss '85 ▸
Red Lights '04 ▸
The Red Lily '24
Renaissance '06
Rendez-vous de Juillet '49
Rendezvous in Paris '95
Rich, Young and Pretty '51
Ridicule '96 ▸
Ronin '98
Round Midnight '86 ▸
Rugrats in Paris: The Movie '00 ▸
Rush Hour 3 '07
Russian Dolls '05
Same Old Song '97 ▸
A Scandal in Paris '46
Scaramouche '23
The Science of Sleep '06
A Self-Made Hero '95 ▸
7th Heaven '27
Sex & Mrs. X '00
Shall We Kiss? '07
Shoot the Piano Player '62 ▸
Simon the Magician '99
Simone Barbes '80
The Sin of Madelon Claudet '31 ▸
Sin Takes a Holiday '30
Since Otar Left... '03
A Single Girl '96
Siren of the Tropics '27
Six in Paris '68
Something's Gotta Give '03 ▸
Son of Gascogne '95
Sons '89
The Story of a Three Day Pass '68
The Street '23
Subway '85
Summer '86 ▸
Taken '08
The Tango Lesson '97
Target '85
Team America: World Police '04 ▸
Tell No One '06 ▸
The Temptress '26
The Testament of Dr. Cordelier '59 ▸
Theatre of Death '67
They Had to See Paris '29
13 Rue Madeleine '46 ▸
Time Out for Love '61
To Paris with Love '55
Total Eclipse '95
Transporter 3 '08
Triple Agent '04
The Triplets of Belleville '02 ▸
Tropic of Cancer '70 ▸
The Truth About Charlie '02
2 Days in Paris '07 ▸
Two or Three Things I Know about Her '66
Under the Roofs of Paris '29 ▸
Under the Sand '00 ▸
Until September '84
Up/Down/Fragile '95
Va Savoir '01
The Valet '06
Venus Beauty Institute '98
A Very Long Engagement '04 ▸
Vicious Circles '97
Victor/Victoria '82 ▸
Victory '81
View from the Top '03
What Time Is It There? '01
When the Cat's Away '96 ▸
Window Shopping '86
Wonder Bar '34
Zazie dans le Metro '61 ▸

Party Hell

The Anniversary Party '01 ▸
April Fool's Day '86
Carrie '76 ▸
Carrie '02
The Club '94
Happy Birthday to Me '81
Hell Night '81
Hello Mary Lou: Prom Night 2 '87
Home '05
Killer Party '86

▸ = rated three bones or higher

▸ = rated three bones or higher

Beau Brummell: This Charming Man '06
Beautiful Dreamers '92
Becky Sharp '35
Becoming Colette '92
Belizaire the Cajun '86
Belle of the Nineties '34
The Best Man '97
Beulah Land '80
Big Bear '98
The Blackheath Poisonings '92
Blacksnake! '73
Blanche Fury '48
Bleak House '85
Blood Red '88
The Bostonians '84
The Bowery '33 ►
Boy in Blue '86
Bram Stoker's Dracula '92
Bright Leaf '50
Bright Star '09
Broken Trail '06 ►
The Brontes of Haworth '73
Brother of Sleep '95 ►
The Brothers Grimm '05
The Brothers Karamazov '58 ►
The Buccaneers '95 ►
Buffalo Girls '95
Bury My Heart at Wounded Knee '07
By Way of the Stars '92
Byron '03
Call of the Wild '93
Camille Claudel '89 ►
Captain Boycott '47
Carmen '03
Carry On Jack '63
Carson City '52
Catherine Cookson's The Black Candle '92
Catherine Cookson's The Black Velvet Gown '92
Catherine Cookson's The Dwelling Place '94
Catherine Cookson's The Fifteen Streets '90
Catherine Cookson's The Glass Virgin '95
Catherine Cookson's Tilly Trotter '99
Cattle Town '52
The Chant of Jimmie Blacksmith '78 ►
The Charge of the Light Brigade '36 ►
The Charge of the Light Brigade '68
Children of the Century '99
A Christmas Carol '38 ►
A Christmas Carol '51 ►
A Christmas Carol '54
A Christmas Carol '84 ►
A Christmas Carol '99
The Cisco Kid '94
The Claim '00
Cobra Verde '88
Colonel Chabert '94
Comanche Moon '08
Conceiving Ada '97
Conduct Unbecoming '75
Conquest '37 ►
Conquest of Cochise '53
The Count of Monte Cristo '74
The Count of Monte Cristo '99
The Count of Monte Cristo '02
Cousin Bette '97
The Covered Wagon '23
Creation '09
The Crown Prince '06
Daisy Miller '74
Damn the Defiant '62 ►
Daniel Deronda '02
Dante's Inferno: Life of Dante Gabriel Rossetti '69
The Dark Angel '91 ►
Darwin's Darkest Hour '09
David Copperfield '70
David Copperfield '99
David Harum '34
Dead Man '95
The Deceivers '88
Demons of the Mind '72
Desiree '54
The Desperate Mission '60 ►
Desperate Remedies '93
Disraeli '30 ►
Disraeli '79 ►
A Distant Trumpet '64
Dr. Bell and Mr. Doyle: The Dark Beginnings of Sherlock Holmes '00
A Dog of Flanders '99
A Doll's House '59
A Doll's House '73
A Doll's House '73 ►
Dostoevsky's Crime and Punishment '99
Dragonwyck '46
Drums of Africa '63
The Duchess of Langeais '07 ►
Duel of Hearts '92
Edge of Madness '02
Edvard Munch '74
Effi Briest '74 ►
1860 '33
Eijanaika '81 ►
Elective Affinities '96
The Elegant Criminal '92
The Elephant Man '80 ►
Elvira Madigan '67 ►
Elvira's Haunted Hills '02
The Emigrants '72 ►
Emma '72
Emma '96 ►
Emma '97 ►
Emma '09
The Emperor's New Clothes '01
End of Summer '97
An Enemy of the People '77
Ethan Frome '92
The Europeans '79 ►
Every Day's a Holiday '38
Far and Away '92
Far from the Madding Crowd '67 ►
Far from the Madding Crowd '97 ►
The Far Pavilions '84
The Far Side of Jericho '06
The Farmer Takes a Wife '35
The Farmer Takes a Wife '53
Feast of July '95
The Fighting Eagle '27
The Fighting Kentuckian '49
Finding Neverland '04 ►
Fiorile '93 ►
Firelight '97
The First Olympics: Athens 1896 '84
Five Weeks in a Balloon '62
The Flame of New Orleans '41 ►
The Flesh and the Fiends '60
Flight of the Eagle '82
Florence Nightingale '85
Florence Nightingale '08
Flowers of Reverie '84
Flowers of Shanghai '98
The Four Feathers '39 ►
The Four Feathers '78
The Four Feathers '02
Frankenstein '31 ►
Frankenstein '73
Frankenstein '82
Frankenstein '93
Frankie and Johnny '65
Freedom Road '79
The French Lieutenant's Woman '81 ►
From Hell '01 ►
The Furies '50
The Gambler '97
The Gambler, the Girl and the Gunslinger '09
Gangs of New York '02 ►
Gaslight '40 ►
Gaslight '44 ►
Germinal '93 ►
Geronimo '62
Geronimo '93 ►
Geronimo: An American Legend '93
Gervaise '56 ►
The Getting of Wisdom '77
The Golden Bowl '72 ►
Goldrush: A Real Life Alaskan Adventure '98
The Gorgeous Hussy '36
Gothic '87 ►
The Governess '98
Goya in Bordeaux '99
Great Expectations '34
Great Expectations '46 ►
Great Expectations '81
Great Expectations '89 ►
Great Expectations '99
Great Expectations: The Untold Story '87
The Great Moment '44
The Great Train Robbery '79 ►
Green Dolphin Street '47
Greyfriars Bobby '61
Hamlet '96 ►
Hands of a Murderer '90
Harmony Lane '35
Haunted Summer '88
Hawaii '66 ►
The Heiress '49 ►
Hellgate '52
Hidalgo '04
The Hidden Blade '04
Hip Hip Hurrah! '87 ►
The History of Mr. Polly '07
Hobson's Choice '53 ►
Hobson's Choice '83
Hooded Angels '00
Horatio Hornblower '99 ►
Horatio Hornblower: The Adventure Continues '01 ►
The Horse Soldiers '59
The Hound of the Baskervilles '39 ►
The Hound of the Baskervilles '59
The Hound of the Baskervilles '83
The Hound of the Baskervilles '00
The Hound of the Baskervilles '02 ►
The House of the Seven Gables '40
Hunger '66
I Dream of Jeannie '52
I, Monster '71 ►
An Ideal Husband '47
Immortal Beloved '94
The Importance of Being Earnest '02
Impromptu '90 ►
In Desert and Wilderness '01
In Old Chicago '37 ►
In the Arms of My Enemy '07
The Innocent '76
Interview with the Vampire '94
The Iron Horse '24 ►
The Iron Mistress '52
The Jack Bull '99
Jamaica Inn '39
Jamaica Inn '82
Jane Eyre '34
Jane Eyre '44 ►
Jane Eyre '83 ►
Jane Eyre '96 ►
Jane Eyre '97
Java Head '35 ►
Jericho '01
Jezebel '38 ►
John Adams '08
Johnson County War '02
Joshua '02
The Journey of August King '95
Journey to the Center of the Earth '99
Journey to the Center of the Earth '08
Jude '96 ►
Jude the Obscure '71
Kaspar Hauser '93
Kate & Leopold '01
Katie Tippel '75
Kim '50 ►
Kim '84
The King and I '56 ►
The King and I '99 ►
Kings in Grass Castles '97
The Kissing Bandit '48
La Chartreuse de Parme '48
La Grande Bourgeoise '74
Lady Audley's Secret '00
Lady Caroline Lamb '73
Lady for a Night '42
Lady from Louisiana '42
The Last Samurai '03 ►
The Lawless Breed '52 ►
The League of Extraordinary Gentlemen '03
The Legend of Zorro '05
Leo Tolstoy's Anna Karenina '96
The Leopard '63 ►
The Life and Adventures of Nicholas Nickleby '81 ►
Life with Father '47 ►
Lillian Russell '40
Lisztomania '75
The Little Colonel '35 ►
Little Dorrit '08
Little Dorrit, Film 1: Nobody's Fault '88 ►
Little Dorrit, Film 2: Little Dorrit's Story '88 ►
Little House on the Prairie '74 ►
Little Men '40
Little Men '98
Little Old New York '23
The Little Princess '39 ►
The Little Princess '87
Little Women '33 ►
Little Women '49 ►
Little Women '78
Little Women '94 ►
The Lives of a Bengal Lancer '35 ►
Lloyds of London '36 ►
Lone Rider '08
The Long Ride Home '01
Lost in Austen '08
Love and Death '75 ►
Love and Rage '99
Love Comes Softly '03
Love Finds a Home '09
Love in the Time of Cholera '07
Love Takes Wing '09
Love's Abiding Joy '06
Love's Enduring Promise '04
Love's Long Journey '05
The Loves of Edgar Allen Poe '42
Love's Unending Legacy '07
Love's Unfolding Dream '07
Madame Bovary '34 ►
Madame Bovary '49 ►
Madame Bovary '91 ►
Madame Bovary '00
Mademoiselle Fifi '44
The Magician '58 ►
Magnificent Doll '46
The Magnificent Seven '98
Mail Order Bride '08
The Man from Snowy River '82
The Man in Grey '45 ►
Man in the Attic '53
The Man Who Came Back '08
Mansfield Park '85
Mansfield Park '99
Mansfield Park '07
The Mark of Zorro '40 ►
Mary Reilly '95
Master and Commander: The Far Side of the World '03 ►
Mayerling '36 ►
Mayerling '68
The Mayor of Casterbridge '03
Melody Master '41
Mesmerized '84
Middlemarch '93 ►
The Mill on the Floss '37
The Mill on the Floss '97
Miracle at Sage Creek '05
Miss Austen Regrets '07
Miss Julie '99
The Missing '03 ►
Mississippi '35
Mrs. Brown '97 ►
Modigliani '58
Molokai: The Story of Father Damien '99
Monsieur N. '03 ►
Monte Cristo '22
Monte Walsh '03
The Moonstone '72
The Moonstone '97 ►
Moulin Rouge '01 ►
Mutiny on the Blackhawk '39
My Antonia '94
My Apprenticeship '39 ►
My Childhood '38 ►
My Universities '40 ►
The Mystery of Edwin Drood '35
The Mystery of Edwin Drood '93
Nanny McPhee '06
Napoleon '03
Ned Kelly '03
The New Land '73 ►
Newsies '92
Nicholas Nickleby '46 ►
Nicholas Nickleby '02 ►
Northanger Abbey '87
Northanger Abbey '07
An Old-Fashioned Thanksgiving '08
Oliver! '68 ►
Oliver Twist '22 ►
Oliver Twist '33
Oliver Twist '48 ►
Oliver Twist '82 ►
Oliver Twist '85
Oliver Twist '97
Oliver Twist '00 ►
Oliver Twist '05 ►
Oliver Twist '07
Once Upon a Time in China '91 ►
One Man's Hero '98
Onegin '99
The Organizer '64
Original Sin '01
Orlando '92 ►
Oscar and Lucinda '97
The Outsider '02
The Ox '91
Pandaemonium '00
Pelle the Conqueror '88 ►
The Perfect Husband '92
Persuasion '71
Persuasion '95 ►
Persuasion '07
The Phantom of the Opera '25 ►
The Phantom of the Opera '43 ►
The Phantom of the Opera '62
The Phantom of the Opera '90
The Phantom of the Opera '98
The Phantom of the Opera '04
The Piano '93 ►
Pink String and Sealing Wax '45
Poldark '96
Portrait of a Lady '67
Portrait of a Lady '96 ►
The Possessed '88
Possession '02
The Prestige '06 ►
Pride and Prejudice '40 ►
Pride and Prejudice '85
Pride and Prejudice '95 ►
Pride and Prejudice '05 ►
Prince of Poisoners: The Life and Crimes of William Palmer '98
Princess Caraboo '94
The Private Affairs of Bel Ami '47 ►
The Proposition '05
P.T. Barnum '99
Race to Freedom: The Story of the Underground Railroad '94
Ravenous '99
The Real Charlotte '91
Return of Sabata '71
The Return of the Native '94
Return to Cranford '09
The Right Hand Man '87
The Ripper '97
River Queen '05
Robert Louis Stevenson's The Game of Death '99
The Rover '67
Rowing with the Wind '88
Ruby in the Smoke '06
Sabata '69
St. Ives '98
Saratoga Trunk '45
A Scandal in Paris '46
Scarlett '94
Sea Devils '53
The Secret Garden '49 ►
The Secret Garden '84
The Secret Garden '87 ►
The Secret Garden '93
The Secret Life of Mrs. Beeton '06
Sense & Sensibility '85
Sense and Sensibility '95 ►
Sense & Sensibility '07
Senso '54 ►
September Dawn '07
Sergeant Rutledge '60 ►
The Shadow in the North '07
Shanghai Knights '03
Shanghai Noon '00
Sharpe's Battle '94
Sharpe's Challenge '06
Sharpe's Company '94
Sharpe's Eagle '93
Sharpe's Enemy '94
Sharpe's Gold '94
Sharpe's Honour '94
Sharpe's Justice '97
Sharpe's Legend '97
Sharpe's Mission '96
Sharpe's Regiment '96
Sharpe's Revenge '97
Sharpe's Rifles '93
Sharpe's Siege '96
Sharpe's Sword '94
Sharpe's Waterloo '97
Sherlock: Case of Evil '02
Sherlock Holmes '09
Show Boat '36 ►
Show Boat '51
The Sign of Four '83
The Sign of Four '01
Silas Marner '85 ►
Silk '07
Sister Dora '77
Sitting Bull '54
Skin Game '71 ►
Sofie '92
Sommersby '93
A Song of Innocence '05
A Song to Remember '45 ►
Song Without End '60
Souls at Sea '37
The Sound and the Silence '93
Spirit: Stallion of the Cimarron '02
Spring Symphony '86
Station Jim '01
Steamboy '05
The Story of Alexander Graham Bell '39 ►
The Story of an African Farm '04
The Stranglers of Bombay '60
The Strauss Family '73
The Substitute Wife '94
Sukiyaki Western Django '08
Sweeney Todd: The Demon Barber of Fleet Street '07
Swept from the Sea '97
Taboo '99
Tai-Pan '86
Tamango '59
Tchaikovsky '71
The Tenant of Wildfell Hall '96
Tess '79 ►
Tess of the D'Urbervilles '98
Tess of the D'Urbervilles '08
The Texans '38
Texas Rangers '01
That Forsyte Woman '50
Therese Raquin '80
Therese: The Story of Saint Therese of Lisieux '04
The Thorn Birds: The Missing Years '96 ►
Three Men in a Boat '56
Tim Burton's Corpse Bride '05 ►
Tipping the Velvet '02
Tom and Huck '95 ►
Tom Sawyer '30 ►
Tom Sawyer '73
Topsy Turvy '99 ►
Torrents of Spring '90
Total Eclipse '95
The Trail of '98 '28
Twelfth Night '96
The Twilight Samurai '02 ►

► = rated three bones or higher

Two Years before the Mast '46
Under Capricorn '49
Under Capricorn '82
Under the Greenwood Tree '05
Utamaro and His Five Women '46
Vacas '91
The Valley of Decision '45 ►
Van Gogh '92 ►
Vanity Fair '32
Vanity Fair '67
Vanity Fair '99
Vanity Fair '04
The Verdict '46
Victoria & Albert '01
Victoria Regina '61
The Village '04
Vincent & Theo '90 ►
Waltz King '63
War and Peace '56
War and Peace '68 ►
War and Peace '73
Warlords '08
Washington Square '97 ►
The Way We Live Now '02
The Weight of Water '00
When the Last Sword is Drawn '02 ►
Wide Sargasso Sea '92
Wide Sargasso Sea '06
The Widow of Saint-Pierre '00 ►
Wild Bill '95
Wild Wild West '99
Wilde '97
Wind River '98
Wives and Daughters '01
The Wolf at the Door '87
The Woman in White '97
A Woman Rebels '36
The World in His Arms '52
The World Moves On '34
Wuthering Heights '09
The Wyvern Mystery '00
The Young Pioneers '76
Young Sherlock Holmes '85
The Young Victoria '09 ►
Zatoichi '03 ►

Period Piece: 20th Century

America's Dream '95 ►
The Babe '92
Bride of the Wind '01
Carrington '95
Century '94
Cobb '94 ►
Coco Before Chanel '09
Coco Chanel '08
Coming Through '85
Cranford '08
A Dance to the Music of Time '97
Dash and Lilly '99
Dust '01
Everlasting Moments '08
Frida '02
Gypsy '62 ►
Gypsy '93
Hold the Dream '86
House of Sand '05 ►
Indochine '92 ►
Interview with the Vampire '94
Iris '01 ►
JFK: Reckless Youth '93
Lagaan: Once upon a Time in India '01
Lansky '99
The Last Emperor '87 ►
The Legend of 1900 '98
Legends of the Fall '94
Lillie '79 ►
Love in the Time of Cholera '07
Malcolm X '92 ►
Mama Flora's Family '98
Me Without You '01
Nanny McPhee '06
Nicholas and Alexandra '71
O Pioneers! '91
Orlando '92 ►
Our Town '03
Rasputin '85 ►
Rasputin and the Empress '33 ►
Rasputin: Dark Servant of Destiny '96 ►
Rasputin the Mad Monk '66
Rich Man, Poor Man '76 ►
Savage Grace '07
The Sexual Life of the Belgians '94
The Song of the Lark '01
Star! '68
Sunshine '99
There Will Be Blood '07 ►
Tom & Viv '94 ►
Trahir '93 ►
The Travelling Players '75
Two Brothers '04
Winchell '98
A Woman of Substance '84
The World Moves On '34
Youth Without Youth '07

Period Piece: 1900s

Anne of Green Gables '85 ►
The Bachelor '93 ►
Back Street '41
Berkeley Square '98
The Best Intentions '92 ►
Beyond the Wall of Sleep '06
Call of the Yukon '38
Cheaper by the Dozen '50 ►
Cheri '09
City Boy '93 ►
Cold Sassy Tree '89 ►
Colonel Redl '84 ►
Daens '92
Daughters of the Dust '91 ►
The Dead '87 ►
December Bride '91
The Dolly Sisters '46
Fanny and Alexander '83 ►
Fiddler on the Roof '71 ►
55 Days at Peking '63 ►
Finding Neverland '04 ►
The Flame Is Love '79
The Forbidden Quest '93
Fulfillment '89
Gentlemen's Relish '01
Glory & Honor '98
The Go-Between '71 ►
The Golden Bowl '00
The Golden Boys '08
The Good Old Boys '95
Grand Isle '92
The Guns and the Fury '83
Hamlet '01
Hangover Square '45
The Happy Years '50
Harem '86
Heart of Darkness '93
Hester Street '75 ►
Home at Last '88
House of Mirth '00 ►
I Remember Mama '48 ►
Illuminata '98
The Illusionist '06
The Imported Bridegroom '89
Institue Benjamenta or This Dream People Call Human Life '95
It's a Dog's Life '55
Jet Li's Fearless '06
Klimt '06
La Ronde '51 ►
Lady L '65
Land of Promise '74
Les Destinees '00
Liebelei '32
Like Water for Chocolate '93 ►
The Lost Boys '78 ►
Love Among the Ruins '75 ►
Madame Butterfly '95
The Magician of Lublin '79
The Magnificent Ambersons '42 ►
The Magnificent Ambersons '02
The Man in the Attic '94
Man of Evil '48
Meet Me in St. Louis '44 ►
A Midsummer Night's Sex Comedy '82 ►
Miss Potter '06
Mrs. Mike '49
Mrs. Soffel '84
Mr. Toad's Wild Ride '96
Mother Wore Tights '47 ►
My Fair Lady '64 ►
My Twentieth Century '90 ►
My Uncle Silas '01 ►
Nora '00
Of Freaks and Men '98
Old San Francisco '27
Our Town '40 ►
Our Town '77 ►
Our Town '89
Papa's Delicate Condition '63 ►
Ragtime '81 ►
The Railway Children '70 ►
The Railway Children '00 ►
A River Runs Through It '92 ►
The Road to Wellville '94
A Room with a View '86 ►
A Room With a View '08
San Francisco '36 ►
Secrets '94
Shadow Magic '00
She Creature '01
A Summer Story '88 ►
Tales from the Gimli Hospital '88
Valley of the Kings '54
Viva Zapata! '52 ►
We of the Never Never '82 ►
When the Greeks '81
Where Angels Fear to Tread '91 ►
The Widowing of Mrs. Holroyd '95
William Shakespeare's A Midsummer Night's Dream '99
Yentl '83

Period Piece: 1910s

Abbott and Costello Meet the Keystone Kops '54
The Actress '53
And Starring Pancho Villa as Himself '03 ►
Anne of Avonlea '87 ►
Atlantis: The Lost Empire '01
The Basket '99
Bluebeard '63 ►
Britannic '99
Brutal Glory '89
Catherine Cookson's Colour Blind '98
The Chambermaid on the Titanic '97
Christy '94
Cider with Rosie '99
Country Life '95
Courage Mountain '89
A Death in the Family '02
Doctor Zhivago '65 ►
Eight Men Out '88 ►
The Englishman Who Went up a Hill But Came down a Mountain '95 ►
FairyTale: A True Story '97
The Fall '06
The Fixer '68 ►
Flambards '78
The Flame Trees of Thika '81 ►
Flickers '80
From Dusk Till Dawn 3: The Hangman's Daughter '99
Gabrielle '05
The Girl in the Red Velvet Swing '55
Good Morning, Babylon '87 ►
Goodbye, Miss 4th of July '88
The Greatest Game Ever Played '05
Grizzly Falls '99
Heartland '81 ►
Hole in the Sky '95
Howard's End '92 ►
The Iceman Cometh '60 ►
The Iceman Cometh '73
Iron Will '93
Jet Li's Fearless '06
Klimt '06
Lady Chatterley '92
Lady Chatterley's Lover '55
Lady Chatterley's Lover '81
The Last of His Tribe '92
The Last Place on Earth '85
The Last Station '09
The Lawrenceville Stories '88
Lily Dale '96
A Little Princess '95 ►
The Lost World '02
Max '02
Michael Collins '96 ►
Mrs. Santa Claus '96
Modigliani '04
The Murder of Mary Phagan '87 ►
O Quatrilho '95
Old Gringo '89
On Moonlight Bay '51
On Valentine's Day '86
Opium: Diary of a Madwoman '07
Peg o' My Heart '22
Picture Bride '94
Plain Jane '01
Red Firecracker, Green Firecracker '93
Rosa Luxemburg '86
Sarah, Plain and Tall '91 ►
Sarah, Plain and Tall: Skylark '93
Sarah, Plain and Tall: Winter's End '99 ►
Savage Messiah '72 ►
Seraphine '08 ►
Shackleton '02 ►
Shattered City: The Halifax Explosion '03
She '65
The Shooting Party '85 ►
Shopworn Angel '38 ►
The Siege of Sidney Street '60
Solomon and Gaenor '98
Stiff Upper Lips '96
Summer Storm '44
Sunday's Children '94 ►
They Came to Cordura '59
Three Times '05
Troubles '88
Tuck Everlasting '02
An Unfinished Piece for a Player Piano '77 ►
A Very Long Engagement '04 ►
Victory '95
Warden of Red Rock '01
Weeping Meadow '04
The White Ribbon '09
The Wings of the Dove '97 ►
The Winslow Boy '98 ►
The Women on the Roof '89

Period Piece: 1920s

Agatha Christie: A Life in Pictures '04
Al Capone '59 ►
Amelia '09
Another Life '01
The Aviator '04 ►
Balto '95
Bare Knees '28
Belles on Their Toes '52
Bix '90
Bobby Jones: Stroke of Genius '04
The Bretts '88 ►
Brideshead Revisited '08
Bright Young Things '03
Bullets over Broadway '94 ►
By the Light of the Silvery Moon '53
The Cat's Meow '01
Changeling '08 ►
Character '97
Chicago '02 ►
Coco Chanel & Igor Stravinksy '09
Cold Comfort Farm '71
Cold Comfort Farm '94 ►
The Cotton Club '84 ►
De-Lovely '04
Death Defying Acts '07
Deja Vu '89
The Disappearance of Aimee '76 ►
Dr. Bethune '90 ►
Easy Virtue '08
Ele, My Friend '93
Enchanted April '92
Entertaining Angels: The Dorothy Day Story '96
Forest of Little Bear '87
The Front Page '74
The Great Gatsby '49
The Great Gatsby '74
The Great Gatsby '01
The Great Waldo Pepper '75 ►
Greenwich Village '44
The Grissom Gang '71 ►
The Harmonists '99
Haunted '95
The Hearst and Davies Affair '85
The Helen Morgan Story '57
High Road to China '83
Hit the Dutchman '92
Hollywood Cavalcade '39
The House of Eliott '92
I'll See You in My Dreams '51
Incantato '03
Inherit the Wind '99
The Intended '02
Intimate Affairs '01
The Jazz Singer '80
Jazzman '84 ►
Johnny Dangerously '84
Killer: A Journal of Murder '95
Lady Chatterley '06 ►
The Last September '99
Leatherheads '08
The Legend of Bagger Vance '00
Legend of Valentino '75
Legionnaire '98
Les Destinees '00
Longitude '00 ►
The Loss of a Teardrop Diamond '08
Love for Lydia '79 ►
The Lover '92
The Luzhin Defence '00
Maids of Wilko '79
Man of the Century '99
Mapp & Lucia '85
Melo '86
Memoirs of a Geisha '05
Mrs. Dalloway '97
Mrs. Parker and the Vicious Circle '94
Mister Johnson '91 ►
The Moderns '88 ►
The Mummy '99
My Life So Far '98
Naked Tango '91
The Newton Boys '97
Once Upon a Time in America '84 ►
The Painted Veil '06
Pancho Barnes '88
Party Girl '58 ►
A Passage to India '84 ►
Pictures '81
The Princess and the Frog '09 ►
Private Confessions '98
The Quest '96
The Rebel '08 ►
Red Sorghum '87 ►
Return to Paradise '53
The Roaring Twenties '39 ►
Robin and the 7 Hoods '64
Rosewood '96 ►
Roxie Hart '42
The St. Valentine's Day Massacre '67
Seraphine '08 ►
Shadow of the Vampire '00 ►
Shake Hands with the Devil '59 ►
Sister Aimee: The Aimee Semple McPherson Story '06
The Slingshot '93 ►
Speedy Death '99 ►
Splendor in the Grass '61 ►
The Stationmaster's Wife '77
The Stranger: Kabloonak '95
Studs Lonigan '60
Sweet Land '05
Swoon '91 ►
Temptress Moon '96
Tenderness of the Wolves '73
Theremin: An Electronic Odyssey '95 ►
Thoroughly Modern Millie '67
Those Daring Young Men in Their Jaunty Jalopies '69
The Tigress '93
Twenty-Four Eyes '54 ►
Under the Biltmore Clock '85
Underworld '27 ►
An Unforgettable Summer '94
The Untouchables '87 ►
Valentino '77
Weeping Meadow '04
Where the Rivers Flow North '94
Wild Party '74
The Wind That Shakes the Barley '06 ►
The Wolves '82 ►
Woman in Black '89
The Wooden Man's Bride '94
You Know My Name '99 ►

Period Piece: 1930s

Acla's Descent into Floristella '87
All My Loved Ones '00
Amelia '09
Ask the Dust '06
Atonement '07 ►
The Aviator '04 ►
Ballet Shoes '07
The Bay Boy '85
Before the Rains '07
Being Julia '04 ►
Belle Epoque '92 ►
Black Belt '07
Blood Brothers '07
Blood Creek '09
Borstal Boy '00
Break of Dawn '88
Brideshead Revisited '08
Broken Glass '96
Burnt by the Sun '94 ►
Butterfly '98 ►
Cambridge Spies '03
Captain Calamity '36
Cause Celebre '87 ►
The Charmer '87
Child Star: The Shirley Temple Story '01
The Children of Huang Shi '08
Cora Unashamed '00
Crime of the Century '96
Dancing at Lughnasa '98
Dark Streets '08
The Devil's Backbone '01
Disappearances '06
Dogville '03
Doktor Faustus '82
Drunken Monkey '02
Durango '99
The Education of Little Tree '97 ►
Emma's Shadow '88 ►
Everyone's Hero '06
The Field '90 ►
Fleeing by Night '00
The Gathering Storm '02 ►
Get Low '09
Go Tell It on the Mountain '84
Good '08
A Good Woman '04
Gosford Park '01 ►
The Grass Harp '95
The Great Debaters '07 ►
Grey Gardens '09 ►
The Habitation of Dragons '91
The Harmonists '99
Head in the Clouds '04
The Heart of Me '02
Heat of the Sun '99 ►
Heavens Fall '06
The Helen Morgan Story '57
The Hindenburg '75
Hoodlum & Son '03
Houdini '53
I Capture the Castle '02
I Don't Want to Talk About It '94
I Served the King of England '07 ►
Idlewild '06
The Imposters '98
In Pursuit of Honor '95
In the Realm of the Senses '76 ►
The Inheritors '82
Innocent Lies '95
Invincible '01
Ivan and Abraham '94
Jew-Boy Levi '99

► = rated three bones or higher

Joe and Max '02 ►
The Journey to Kafiristan '01
King Kong '05 ►
Ladies in Lavender '04
Lassie '05
Last Call: The Final Chapter of F. Scott Fitzgerald '02
Liam '00
Love's Labour's Lost '00
Madame Sata '02
The Man from the Pru '89
The Man Who Cried '00
Manderlay '05
Me and Orson Welles '09
Memoirs of a Geisha '05
A Merry War '97 ►
Miracles '89
Miss Pettigrew Lives for a Day '08 ►
Mrs. Henderson Presents '05
The Moon & the Stars '07
The Mummy Returns '01
Murder in a Small Town '99
Murder, Inc. '60
North Face '08 ►
Nowhere in Africa '02
Out of the Cold '99
Pandora and the Flying Dutchman '51
Papa's Angels '00
Paris 36 '08
Pavilion of Women '01
The Phantom Lover '95
The Prime of Miss Jean Brodie '69 ►
The Proposition '97
Public Enemies '09
Purple Butterfly '03 ►
Quiet Days in Clichy '90
Rabbit-Proof Fence '02 ►
Radioland Murders '94
Ray '04 ►
The Remains of the Day '93 ►
Richard III '95 ►
Road to Perdition '02 ►
The Rocketeer '91 ►
The Saddest Music in the World '03
Shadow on the Sun '88
Shanghai Triad '95 ►
Sirens '94
Sky Captain and the World of Tomorrow '04
The Sleeping Dictionary '02
Stargate: Continuum '08
The Stick-Up '77
Swing Kids '93
Tea with Mussolini '99
These Foolish Things '06
The Thirteenth Floor '99
This Is My Father '99
Triple Agent '04
Under the Volcano '84 ►
Up at the Villa '00
Valley of the Heart's Delight '07
Walk on the Wild Side '62
Weeping Meadow '04
The White Countess '05 ►
The Whole Wide World '96 ►
A Woman at Her Window '77
Yellow Earth '89

Period Piece: 1940s

Aimée & Jaguar '98
All the King's Men '06
All the Pretty Horses '00
All Things Fair '95
Almost Peaceful '02 ►
An American Story '92
Australia '08
The Aviator '04 ►
Back Home '90
Back to the Secret Garden '01
Barton Fink '91 ►
Batman: Mask of the Phantasm '93
Before the Fall '04
The Black Dahlia '06
Bon Voyage '03 ►
Broken Silence '01 ►
Buffalo Boy '04
Bugsy '91 ►
Bye Bye Blues '89
The Caller '08
Carry Me Home '04
Catherine Cookson's The Round Tower '98
Charms for the Easy Life '02
Children On Their Birthdays '02
The Chorus '04
The Chosen '81 ►
The Chronicles of Narnia: The Lion, the Witch and the Wardrobe '05
The Cider House Rules '99 ►
Color of a Brisk and Leaping Day '95
The Color of Courage '98
Confessing to Laura '90
The Counterfeiters '07 ►
The Courageous Heart of Irena Sendler '09 ►
The Curse of the Jade Scorpion '01
Daphne '07
A Dark Adapted Eye '93 ►
Dead Gorgeous '02
Deep Crimson '96
Delta of Venus '95
Devil in a Blue Dress '95 ►
The Diary of Anne Frank '08
Doktor Faustus '82
The Dollmaker '84
The Doorbell Rang: A Nero Wolfe Mystery '01
Downfall '04 ►
Earth '98
East of Elephant Rock '76
East-West '99
Exorcist: The Beginning '04
The Fallen '05 ►
Farewell, My Lovely '75 ►
15 Amore '98
The Fifth Horseman Is Fear '64
Focus '01
For a Lost Soldier '93
The Forbidden Quest '93
The Franchise Affair '88
Gate of Flesh '64
The Golden Spiders: A Nero Wolfe Mystery '00
Good Evening, Mr. Wallenberg '93
The Good German '06
The Good Shepherd '06
Goodbye, Mr. Chips '69
Goodnight, Mr. Tom '99
The Grass Harp '95
The Grey Zone '01
Hannibal Rising '07
Head in the Clouds '04
The Heart of Me '02
Hong Kong 1941 '84
The Hours '02 ►
The Human Stain '03
In the Mood '87
Joe Gould's Secret '00
Julie & Julia '09 ►
Kabei: Our Mother '08
Kinsey '04 ►
Kung Fu Hustle '04
La Vie en Rose '07
The Last Time I Committed Suicide '96
A League of Their Own '92 ►
Les Miserables '95
A Lesson Before Dying '99 ►
Lonely Hearts '06
The Lost City '05
Lost in Yonkers '93
Malena '00
The Man Who Wasn't There '01 ►
Mararia '98
Margaret's Museum '95 ►
Married Life '07 ►
The McCullochs '75
The Member of the Wedding '52 ►
The Member of the Wedding '83
The Member of the Wedding '97
Memoirs of a Geisha '05
Miss Rose White '92 ►
Mrs. Henderson Presents '05
Mountbatten: The Last Viceroy '86
The Mummy: Tomb of the Dragon Emperor '08
My Dog Skip '99 ►
My Fuhrer '07
The Mystery of Rampo '94 ►
The Mystic Masseur '01
The Neon Bible '95
The Ninth Day '04 ►
The Notebook '04
Nowhere in Africa '02
Nuremberg '00
O Jerusalem '07
The Old Settler '01
Orde Wingate '76
Other Voices, Other Rooms '95
The Others '01 ►
Pan's Labyrinth '06 ►
Partition '07
Passion in Paradise '89
The Pianist '02 ►
Pizzicata '96
Pollock '00 ►
Possessed '00
The Power of One '92
The Public Eye '92 ►
The Quarrel '93
Racing with the Moon '84 ►
Ray '04 ►
The Return of Eliot Ness '91
Ride the Wild Fields '00
The Rising Place '02
RKO 281 '99 ►
The Road from Coorain '02
The Rocket '05 ►
Rocky Marciano '99
Rosenstrasse '03 ►
The Runaway '00
Salome '85
Season of Change '94
A Secret '07 ►
A Separate Peace '04
The Seventh Dawn '64
Shanghai '09
The Sins of Rachel Cade '61
Snow Falling on Cedars '99
Snow in August '01
Something for Everyone '70
Sophie Scholl: The Final Days '05 ►
Stand-Ins '97
Strayed '03 ►
Sudie & Simpson '90 ►
The Summer of Ben Tyler '96
Surviving Picasso '96
Swing Shift '84
Three Comrades '38 ►
A Time to Live and a Time to Die '85
Torso '01
Trumbo '07 ►
The Two Jakes '90
Under the Piano '95
Village of Dreams '97
The Water Horse: Legend of the Deep '07
A Winner Never Quits '86
With a Song in My Heart '52 ►
Zelary '03 ►

Period Piece: 1950s

Absolute Beginners '86
The Affairs of Dobie Gillis '53
Alex '92
Alien Trespass '09
All the King's Men '06
An American Rhapsody '01 ►
Amongst Women '98
As Summers Die '86
The Audrey Hepburn Story '00
Austin Powers In Goldmember '02
Back to the Future '85 ►
Back to the Future, Part 2 '89
Badlands '74 ►
Bear Ye One Another's Burden... '88
A Beautiful Mind '01 ►
Beefcake '99
Beyond the Sea '04
Big Night '95
Big Town '87
Blind Faith '98
The Blue Kite '93 ►
Book of Love '91
Born Reckless '59
Boycott '02 ►
The Buddy Holly Story '78 ►
Bye, Bye, Birdie '63 ►
Cadillac Records '08 ►
Cafe Society '97
Calendar Girl '93
The California Kid '74
Capote '05 ►
Celia: Child of Terror '89
Che '08
Chicken Run '00 ►
Child Bride of Short Creek '81
Chocolat '00 ►
Circle of Friends '94
The Climb '97
Club Land '01
Common Ground '00
The Company '07
The Confessional '95 ►
Cool and the Crazy '94
Corrina, Corrina '94
Cotton Mary '99
Crazy Love '07 ►
Crazy Mama '75
Cry-Baby '90 ►
Cuban Blood '03
Dance with a Stranger '85 ►
Daniel Takes a Train '83
Dark Blue World '01
Dark of the Sun '68
Dead Poets Society '89 ►
Desire and Hell at Sunset Motel '92
Deuces Wild '02
Devil's Island '96
Diner '82 ►
Dirty Dancing '87 ►
Dirty Dancing: Havana Nights '04
The Door in the Floor '04 ►
Dreaming of Joseph Lees '99
Echoes '88
Elvis: The Movie '79
End of the Spear '06
The Ernest Green Story '93
Eros '04
Evelyn '02 ►
Evening '07
Evil '03 ►
Fall Time '94
Far from Heaven '02 ►
Father of the Bride '50 ►
Fellow Traveler '89 ►
For the Boys '91
The Front '76 ►
Fur: An Imaginary Portrait of Diane Arbus '06
The Game of Their Lives '05
Girls' Town '59
Going All the Way '97
Golden Gate '93
Good Night, and Good Luck '05 ►
The Good Shepherd '06
Grease '78 ►
Grease 2 '82
Ground Zero '88 ►
Guilty by Suspicion '91
A Gun, a Car, a Blonde '97
Hannibal Rising '07
Haywire '80
The Heart of Dixie '89
Hello, Hemingway '90
Her Majesty '01
A Hole in One '04
Hollywoodland '06
Hometown U.S.A. '79
Honeydripper '07
Hounddog '08
The Hours '02 ►
The House on Carroll Street '88
Housekeeping '87 ►
The Hudsucker Proxy '93 ►
I Am David '04
I Served the King of England '07 ►
In His Life: The John Lennon Story '00
Indiana Jones and the Kingdom of the Crystal Skull '08
Intimate Relations '95
Introducing Dorothy Dandridge '99 ►
Inventing the Abbotts '97
I.Q. '94
Jailbreakers '94
James Dean '76
James Dean '01
James Dean: Live Fast, Die Young '97
Julie & Julia '09 ►
Just Looking '99
A King in New York '57
Kinsey '04 ►
Kitchen Stories '03
The Kitchen Toto '87 ►
La Bamba '87 ►
L.A. Confidential '97 ►
La Vie en Rose '07
Last Exit to Brooklyn '90 ►
The Last Picture Show '71 ►
Liberty Heights '99
Lily in Winter '94
Little Richard '00
The Long Day Closes '92 ►
Long Gone '87
The Long Walk Home '89 ►
The Lords of Flatbush '74
The Lost City '05
Lost, Lonely, and Vicious '59
A Love Divided '01
Loveless '83
Lovers: A True Story '90 ►
Mac '93 ►
The Majestic '01
The Mambo Kings '92 ►
The Man in the Moon '91 ►
Mendel '98 ►
Mischief '85
Mrs. 'Arris Goes to Paris '92
Mr. Rock 'n' Roll: The Alan Freed Story '99
Mob Queen '98
Mona Lisa Smile '03
Monaco Forever '83
Moscow Does Not Believe in Tears '80 ►
The Motorcycle Diaries '04 ►
Mulholland Falls '95
My American Cousin '85 ►
My Favorite Year '82 ►
My Louisiana Sky '02
My Michael '75 ►
My One and Only '09
The Mystic Masseur '01
New World '95
Newsfront '78 ►
Nightbreaker '89 ►
Northfork '03
The Notorious Bettie Page '06
Nowhere Boy '09
Oh, What a Night '92
Once Upon a Time ... When We Were Colored '95 ►
One Plus One '61
Ordeal by Innocence '84
OSS 117: Cairo, Nest of Spies '06
The Other Side of Heaven '02
The Other Side of Sunday '96
Our Time '74
Outlaw Trail '06
A Painted House '03
Palais Royale '88
Parents '89 ►
The Passion of Ayn Rand '99
Peggy Sue Got Married '86
Perfect Harmony '91
The Perfume of Yvonne '94
Pillow Talk '59 ►
The Playboys '92 ►
Pollock '00 ►
Porky's '82
The Prize Winner of Defiance, Ohio '05 ►
The Producers '05
The Quiet American '02 ►
Quiz Show '94 ►
A Rage in Harlem '91 ►
A Raisin in the Sun '89 ►
A Raisin in the Sun '08
Ray '04 ►
The Reader '08
Red Hot '95
Red Kiss '85 ►
The Reflecting Skin '91
Relative Values '99
Revolutionary Road '08
The Road Home '01 ►
Roadracers '94
Rock All Night '57
Rock, Baby, Rock It '57
The Rocket '05 ►
Rocky Marciano '99
The Rosa Parks Story '02
Round Midnight '86 ►
Saint Ralph '04
The Scent of Green Papaya '93 ►
School Ties '92 ►
A Secret '07 ►
Shadowlands '85 ►
Shadowlands '93 ►
Shake, Rattle and Rock '57
Shake, Rattle & Rock! '94
Shout '91
Shutter Island '09 ►
The Silence of Neto '94
The Singing Detective '03
Snow Falling on Cedars '99
Sparkle '76
Stacking '87
The Star Maker '95
Starkweather '04
The Sticky Fingers of Time '97
Strange Invaders '83 ►
A Stranger in the Kingdom '98
The Summer House '94
Superdad '73
Suzanne '80
Swimming Upstream '03
Sylvia '03
Tae Guk Gi: The Brotherhood of War '04 ►
The Talented Mr. Ripley '99
Teenage Doll '57
Terranova '91
That'll Be the Day '73
The Thief '97
This Boy's Life '93 ►
This World, Then the Fireworks '97
Though None Go With Me '06
Three Wishes '95
Tito and Me '92 ►
The Tournament '09
Trading Hearts '87
Traps '93
The Trial of Old Drum '00
Trumbo '07 ►
Tune in Tomorrow '90
Two Family House '99
Valentino Returns '88
Vera Drake '04 ►
Visitants '87
Walk the Line '05 ►
Walker Payne '06
The War of the Worlds '53 ►
The Way We Were '73 ►
When Father Was Away on Business '85 ►
Where the Truth Lies '05
Who Shot Pat? '92
The Wild One '54 ►
Witch Hunt '94
Women Without Men '09
The Wooden Gun '79
Wrestling with Alligators '98
You've Ruined Me, Eddie '58

Period Piece: 1960s

see also Boomer Reunions

A la Mode '94
Across the Universe '07
Adam at 6 a.m. '70
Adam Resurrected '08
Agatha Christie: A Life in Pictures '04
Agnes Browne '99
Ali '01
Alice's Restaurant '69
All I Wanna Do '98
An American Affair '09
American Blue Note '89
An American Crime '07
American Gangster '07 ►
American Graffiti '73 ►
Angels Hard As They Come '71
Asylum '05
Austin Powers 2: The Spy Who Shagged Me '99 ►
Auto Focus '02 ►
Awakenings of the Beast '68

► = rated three bones or higher

The Baader Meinhof Complex '08
Backbeat '94 ▸
Bad Education '04 ▸
The Beautiful, the Bloody and the Bare '64
Believe in Me '06
Berkeley '05
Best Enemies '86
Best of Youth '03 ▸
Best Revenge '83
Beyond the Sea '04
The Big Chill '83 ▸
The Big Fix '78 ▸
Blast-Off Girls '67
The Blue Kite '93 ▸
Blue Sky '91 ▸
Bob & Carol & Ted & Alice '69
Bobby '06
Born in 68 '08
Born on the Fourth of July '89 ▸
The Boston Strangler: The Untold Story '08
The Boys and Girl From County Clare '03
The Boys of 2nd Street Park '03 ▸
Brian's Song '01
The Bridges of Madison County '95 ▸
Brokeback Mountain '05 ▸
A Bronx Tale '93 ▸
Burnt Money '00
Capote '05 ▸
Catch Me If You Can '02
Charlie '04
Chasing Christmas '05
The Chatterley Affair '06
Che '08
Chicago 10 '07 ▸
Children Shouldn't Play with Dead Things '72
City of God '02
The Clay Bird '02
The Company '07
Company Man '00
Confessions of a Dangerous Mind '02
Confessions of Sorority Girls '94
Conspiracy: The Trial of the Chicago Eight '87 ▸
CQ '01
Crazy in Alabama '99
The Crimson Cult '68
Dangerous Liaisons '03
Dead Beat '94
Dead Presidents '95
December Boys '07
Digging to China '98
Dirty Deeds '02 ▸
The Dish '00 ▸
Dogfight '91 ▸
The Doors '91
Doubt '08 ▸
Down With Love '03
The Dreamers '03
Dreamgirls '06 ▸
Dynamite Chicken '70
Easy Rider '69 ▸
An Education '09 ▸
Eight Miles High '07
Eight Miles High '08
El Cantante '06
Eros '04
Even Cowgirls Get the Blues '94
The Express '08
Factory Girl '06
Falling Angels '03
Family Prayers '91
Fatherland '94
Filth '08
First Love and Other Pains / One of Them '99
Five Corners '88 ▸
The Flamingo Rising '01
Flash of Genius '08
Flashback '89 ▸
Flawless '07
Four Friends '81 ▸
Free Grass '69
Freedom Song '00 ▸
Fritz the Cat '72 ▸
From the Earth to the Moon '98 ▸
Gangster No. 1 '00
Gimme Shelter '70
Girl, Interrupted '99
Glory Road '06
The Glory Stompers '67
God's Sandbox '02
Godspell '73
The Good Shepherd '06
Grace of My Heart '96
Greetings '68 ▸
Hair '79 ▸
Hairspray '07 ▸
Head '68 ▸
Hearts in Atlantis '01
Help Wanted Female '68
Hendrix '00
Hideous Kinky '99
High Hopes '88 ▸
The Hollywood Knights '80
Hope '97
The Hours and Times '92 ▸
Hula Girls '06
I Drink Your Blood '71
I Love You, Alice B. Toklas! '68
I Shot Andy Warhol '96 ▸
If These Walls Could Talk 2 '00
Imaginary Crimes '94 ▸
In His Father's Shoes '97
In His Life: The John Lennon Story '00
In the Mood for Love '00
Infamous '06
Isn't She Great '00
John John in the Sky '00
K-19: The Widowmaker '02
The Krays '90 ▸
Like A Bride '94 ▸
The Locusts '97
Longford '06
The Lords of Discipline '83
The Lotus Eaters '93
Love Field '91
Lumumba '01 ▸
M. Butterfly '93
Ma Saison Super 8 '05
The Magdalene Sisters '02 ▸
Malevolence '95
The Manson Family '04
Mantis in Lace '68
Married to It '93
Matinee '92
Metroland '97
Middletown '06
The Milky Way '97
Monsieur Ibrahim '03 ▸
More '69
More American Graffiti '79
My Brother Is an Only Child '07
My Little Assassin '99
Odd Birds '85
Off Limits '87
One Crazy Night '93
The Only Thrill '97
Out '82
Pack of Lies '87
Passing Glory '99 ▸
Path to War '02
Peppermint Soda '77 ▸
A Perfect World '93
Petit Con '84
Pirate Radio '09
Place of Execution '09
A Plumm Summer '08
Poodle Springs '98
Power and Beauty '02
The Private Lives of Pippa Lee '09
Psych-Out '68
Psycho Beach Party '00
Race to Space '01
Rainbow Bridge '71
Ray '04 ▸
The Reader '08
The Rebel Set '59
Rescue Dawn '06 ▸
RFK '02
Rhapsody of Spring '98
Riding in Cars with Boys '01
Riding the Bullet '04
Romulus, My Father '07 ▸
R.P.M.* (*Revolutions Per Minute) '70
Ruby Bridges '98
Ruby's Bucket of Blood '01
Rude Awakening '89
Saint Maybe '98 ▸
The Sandlot '93 ▸
The Sandpiper '65
Satan's Sadists '69
Sea Devils '31
Second Thoughts '83
The Secret Life of Bees '08 ▸
See No Evil: The Moors Murders '06
Selma, Lord, Selma '99
A Serious Man '09 ▸
Set Me Free '99
Sex & Drugs & Rock & Roll '10
Shag: The Movie '89 ▸
A Single Man '09 ▸
The '60s '99
61* '01 ▸
'68 '87
Skipped Parts '00
Slashed Dreams '74
A Small Circle of Friends '80
The Snake People '68
Soldiers of Change '06
The Speed Lovers '68
Steal This Movie! '00
Stoned '05
The Stoned Age '94
The Strawberry Statement '70
Sugartime '95
Surfwise '07 ▸
Sweetwater: A True Rock Story '99
Swimming Upstream '03
Sylvia '03
Taking Woodstock '09
Talk to Me '07
Telling Lies in America '96
A Texas Funeral '99
That Night '93
That Thing You Do! '96 ▸
There Goes My Baby '92
There's a Girl in My Soup '70
Thirteen Days '00 ▸
Three Times '05
Thumb Tripping '72
Tin Men '87
The Trip '67
The Tunnel '01 ▸
Tunnel Rats '08
Used People '92
Valentin '02
Wah-Wah '05
Waiting for the Light '90
Walk Hard: The Dewey Cox Story '07
A Walk on the Moon '99
Walk the Line '05 ▸
The Weather Underground '02 ▸
When I Find the Ocean '06
Where Angels Go, Trouble Follows '68
Where the Eagle Flies '72
Where the Truth Lies '05
Who'll Stop the Rain? '78 ▸
Wild in the Streets '68
Wild Reeds '94 ▸
Wondrous Oblivion '06 ▸
The Woods '03
Woodstock '70 ▸
The World's Fastest Indian '05 ▸
Yellow Submarine '68 ▸
The Zodiac '05
Zodiac '07

Period Piece: 1970s

After the Rain '99
Ali '01
Almost Famous '00 ▸
American Gangster '07 ▸
Anchorman: The Legend of Ron Burgundy '04
Armistead Maupin's More Tales of the City '97
Armistead Maupin's Tales of the City '93
The Assassination of Richard Nixon '05
Austin Powers In Goldmember '02
Auto Focus '02 ▸
Baadasssss! '03 ▸
The Baader Meinhof Complex '08
The Backwoods '06
Bad Education '04 ▸
Balzac and the Little Chinese Seamstress '02
The Bank Job '08 ▸
Beautiful Ohio '06
Best of Youth '03 ▸
The Betty Ford Story '87 ▸
Blame It on Fidel '06
Bloody Sunday '01 ▸
Blow '01
Blue Hill Avenue '01
Boogie Nights '97 ▸
Bottle Shock '08
The Bronx Is Burning '07
Brothers of the Head '06
Bundy: A Legacy of Evil '08
Callas Forever '02
Carlito's Way: Rise to Power '05
Casino '95 ▸
Catch Me If You Can '02
Chopper '00
Chronicle of an Escape '06
City of God '02
Common Ground '00
Confessions of a Dangerous Mind '02
Control '07
Creatures from the Pink Lagoon '07
Crooklyn '94 ▸
Crossing the Bridge '92
The Damned United '09
The Dangerous Lives of Altar Boys '02 ▸
Dazed and Confused '93 ▸
A Decade Under the Influence '02 ▸
Detroit Rock City '99
Dick '99 ▸
Diggers '06
Donnie Brasco '96 ▸
Dreamgirls '06 ▸
Drugstore Cowboy '89 ▸
East Is East '99 ▸
El Cantante '06
The Emperor's Club '02
Escape: Human Cargo '98 ▸
Execution of Justice '99
Fear and Loathing in Las Vegas '98
54 '98
Five Minutes of Heaven '09
Flashbacks of a Fool '08
Forever Mine '99
Frailty '02 ▸
From the Earth to the Moon '98 ▸
Frost/Nixon '08 ▸
Gia '98
Good Fences '03
The Good Humor Man '05
Gracie '07
Grand Theft Parsons '03
Green Dragon '01
Green Plaid Shirt '96
Grey Gardens '09 ▸
Heading South '05 ▸
Hedwig and the Angry Inch '00 ▸
Hideous Kinky '99
The Hillside Strangler '04
The Hoax '06
House of D '04
The Ice Storm '97 ▸
If These Walls Could Talk 2 '00
I'm Not Scared '03
Imagining Argentina '04
The Inkwell '94
Invincible '06 ▸
Invisible Circus '00
Isn't She Great '00
Jadup and Boel '81
Jesus' Son '99
Jill the Ripper '00
Joe the King '99
The Killing Beach '92
The Killing Yard '01
Kippur '00 ▸
The Kite Runner '07 ▸
The Ladies Man '00
The Last King of Scotland '06 ▸
The Last of the High Kings '96
Left Luggage '98
The Legend of Rita '99
The Lesser Evil '97
Local Color '06
Long Time Since '97
Lords of Dogtown '05
A Lost Year '93
A Love to Keep '07
The Lovely Bones '09
Man on the Moon '99
Man on Wire '08
Maryam '00
Meat Loaf: To Hell and Back '00
Metroland '97
Milk '08 ▸
Miracle '04 ▸
Moonlight Mile '02 ▸
Munich '05 ▸
Murder in Greenwich '02
Music Within '07
Nearing Grace '05
New Waterford Girl '99
The Night We Called It a Day '03
No '98
North Country '05
Nothing Personal '95 ▸
Of Love and Shadows '94
Off the Map '03 ▸
Persepolis '07 ▸
Pinero '01
The Poker House '09
Prefontaine '96
Pride '07
Protecting the King '07
Radio '03
Rain '01
Rampage: The Hillside Strangler Murders '04
Ratcatcher '99
Rated X '00
Resurrection Man '97
Rhapsody of Spring '98
Riding in Cars with Boys '01
Rise of the Footsoldier '07
Roll Bounce '05 ▸
Roman Polanski: Wanted and Desired '08
The Royal Tenenbaums '01 ▸
The Runaways '10
Running with Scissors '06
The Sandlot 2 '05
The Sandlot 3: Heading Home '07
Scotland, PA '02
Seeing Red '99
Semi-Pro '08
The '70s '00
Sex & Drugs & Rock & Roll '10
Shot in the Heart '01 ▸
Silent Waters '03
Slums of Beverly Hills '98 ▸
Son of Sam '08
Soul Power '08
Spirit of '76 '91
Spy Game '01
Stander '03
Starsky & Hutch '04
Steal This Movie! '00
Stolen Summer '02
Strawberry and Chocolate '93 ▸
Such a Long Journey '98 ▸
Summer of Sam '99
Sunset Strip '99
Surfwise '07 ▸
Take Me Home: The John Denver Story '00
That's the Way I Like It '99
The Thin Blue Lie '00
The Third Miracle '99
Tigerland '00 ▸
Torremolinos 73 '03
The Trip '02
24 Hour Party People '01
Two of Us '00
The U.S. Vs. John Lennon '06
Velvet Goldmine '98
The Virgin Suicides '99
Waking the Dead '00
Walk Hard: The Dewey Cox Story '07
The War '94
Water Drops on Burning Rocks '99
We Are Marshall '06
The Weather Underground '02 ▸
West Beirut '98
What We Do Is Secret '07
Where the Truth Lies '05
Winter of Frozen Dreams '08
Without Limits '97 ▸
Xiu Xiu: The Sent Down Girl '97 ▸
The Year My Parents Went on Vacation '07
Zodiac '07

Period Piece: 1980s

Adventureland '09 ▸
The Adventures of Sebastian Cole '99
All Good Things '09
American Psycho '99
Angela '02
Anvil! The Story of Anvil '09
Apt Pupil '97
Ash Wednesday '02
The Assignment '97
Autumn Hearts: A New Beginning '07
Bad Education '04 ▸
Best of Youth '03 ▸
Beyond Borders '03
Billy Elliot '00 ▸
Blow '01
Born in 68 '08
Brooklyn Rules '07
Buffalo Soldiers '01
The Business '05
Capturing the Friedmans '03 ▸
Catch a Fire '06
Chapter 27 '07
Charlie Wilson's War '07
City of God '02
The Confessional '95 ▸
Dam Street '05
Dangerous Evidence: The Lori Jackson Story '99
The Day Reagan Was Shot '01
District 9 '09 ▸
Donnie Darko '01 ▸
Drug Wars: The Camarena Story '90 ▸
Dumb and Dumberer: When Harry Met Lloyd '03
Edge of Seventeen '99
Endgame '09
An Englishman in New York '09
An Everlasting Piece '00
Fever Pitch '96
Fierce People '05
Fifty Dead Men Walking '08
Find Me Guilty '06 ▸
Fool's Gold: The Story of the Brink's-Mat Robbery '92
Forever Mine '99
4 Months, 3 Weeks and 2 Days '07 ▸
Friday Night Lights '04 ▸
Friends & Crocodiles '05
Game 6 '05
Ghostboat '06
Gifted Hands: The Ben Carson Story '09
Good Bye, Lenin! '03 ▸
Green Plaid Shirt '96
A Guide to Recognizing Your Saints '06
Heart of the Beholder '05 ▸
The History Boys '06
Hollywood North '03
House of Saddam '08
The House of the Devil '09 ▸
Hurlyburly '98
Hustle '04
Hysterical Blindness '02
In America '02 ▸
The Informant '97 ▸
The Informers '09
Innocent Voices '04
Kill the Poor '06
The Killing of John Lennon '07
Lan Yu '01
The Last Days of Disco '98 ▸
The Last Shot '04
Lebanon '09
The Legend of Rita '99
The Line of Beauty '06
The Lives of Others '06 ▸
The Lovers on the Bridge '91
The Magician '93

▸ = rated three bones or higher

Man on the Moon '99
Memories of Murder '03
Miracle '04 ▸
Mrs. Harris '05
The Mistake '91
Monster '03 ▸
The Mysteries of Pittsburgh '08
Nightstalker '02
No Country for Old Men '07 ▸
Noriega: God's Favorite '00
North Country '05
One Day You'll Understand '08
Owning Mahowny '03
Paid in Full '02
Party Monster '03
The Perez Family '94
Persepolis '07 ▸
Pinero '01
Point of Origin '02
Precious: Based on the Novel by Sapphire '09 ▸
The Pursuit of Happyness '06
Rent '05
The Replacements '00
Riding in Cars with Boys '01
Rise of the Footsoldier '07
The Riverman '04
Rock Star '01
Safe Men '98
A Season on the Brink '02
A Secret '07 ▸
Sex & Drugs & Rock & Roll '10
SLC Punk! '99
Son of Rambow '07
Sonny '02
Spider '02 ▸
Spy Game '01
The Squid and the Whale '05 ▸
Stander '03
Starter for Ten '06
Stateside '04
Summer Palace '06 ▸
Summer's End '99
This Is England '06
To Walk with Lions '99
The Trip '02
24 Hour Party People '01
24-7 '97
200 Cigarettes '98
Typhoon '06
Valentine '01
Velvet Goldmine '98
Waking the Dead '00
Watchmen '09
We Own the Night '07
The Wedding Singer '97
Wet Hot American Summer '01 ▸
What Goes Up '09
Whatever '98
The Witnesses '07
Wonderland '03
The Wood '99

Period Piece: 1990s

Amelie '01 ▸
Among Brothers '05
Battle in Seattle '07
Behind the Red Door '02
Beyond Borders '03
Big Shot: Confessions of a Campus Bookie '02
Black Hawk Down '01 ▸
Bully '01
Chasing the Green '09
Closing the Ring '07
Color Me Kubrick '05
Dark Blue '03 ▸
Dark Matter '07
Definitely, Maybe '08 ▸
The Diving Bell and the Butterfly '07 ▸
An Englishman in New York '09
Enough! '06
Exiled '06
Fanboys '09
The Final Season '07
Five Minutes of Heaven '09
44 Minutes: The North Hollywood Shootout '03
Freedom Writers '07
Friends & Crocodiles '05
Go West '05
Hachiko: A Dog's Tale '09
Highway '01
House of Fools '02
The Human Stain '03
The Hunting Party '07
The Informant! '09
Into the Wild '07 ▸
Invictus '09 ▸
Jasper, Texas '03
Kandahar '01
Kings of South Beach '07
The Listening '06
Live from Baghdad '03 ▸
Man of the Century '99
Marooned in Iraq '02
Mountain Patrol: Kekexili '04
The Murder of Stephen Lawrence '99 ▸
The Navigators '01
No Man's Land '01
Notorious '09
One Long Night '07
Our America '02
Party Monster '03
Perestroika '09
Pinochet's Last Stand '06
PU-239 '06
The Queen '06 ▸
'R Xmas '01
Remember the Daze '07
Shattered Glass '03 ▸
Shooting Dogs '05
Spy Game '01
Strange Justice: The Clarence Thomas and Anita Hill Story '99
Summer Palace '06 ▸
10th & Wolf '06
The Terrorist Next Door '08
Three Kings '99 ▸
21 '08
The Wackness '08
Waking Up Wally '05
Wasted '06
When Did You Last See Your Father? '07

Persian Gulf/Iraq War

see also *Desert War/Foreign Legion*

American Soldiers '05
American Son '08
Courage Under Fire '96 ▸
Generation Kill '08 ▸
Grace Is Gone '07 ▸
Green Zone '10 ▸
The Heroes of Desert Storm '91
Home of the Brave '06
House of Saddam '08
The Human Shield '92
The Hurt Locker '08 ▸
The Jacket '05
Jarhead '05
Lions for Lambs '07
Live from Baghdad '03 ▸
The Lucky Ones '08
The Messenger '09 ▸
The One That Got Away '96
Redacted '07
Seal Team '08
The Situation '06
Standard Operating Procedure '08 ▸
Stir of Echoes 2: The Homecoming '07
Stop-Loss '08 ▸
Tactical Assault '99
Taxi to the Dark Side '07 ▸
Three Kings '99 ▸
Time Bomb '08

Philadelphia

The Answer Man '09
Baby Mama '08
Birdy '84 ▸
Blow Out '81 ▸
Cover '08
Downtown '89
Explicit Ills '08
Fat Albert '04
The Garbage-Picking, Field Goal-Kicking Philadelphia Phenomenon '98
Happy Birthday, Gemini '80
A History of Violence '05 ▸
I Don't Buy Kisses Anymore '92
In Her Shoes '05 ▸
Invincible '06 ▸
King of the Corner '04 ▸
Kitty Foyle '40 ▸
Law Abiding Citizen '09
Like Mike '02
Mannequin '87
Mannequin 2: On the Move '91
Marnie '64 ▸
Money for Nothing '93
My Baby's Daddy '04
My Little Girl '87
Nasty Habits '77
National Treasure '04
Next Day Air '09
Philadelphia '93 ▸
The Philadelphia Story '40 ▸
Pride '07
Rock School '05 ▸
Rocky '76 ▸
Rocky 2 '79
Rocky 3 '82
Rocky 4 '85
Rocky 5 '90
Rocky Balboa '06
The Sixth Sense '99 ▸
Snipes '01
State Property 2 '05
Stonewall '95 ▸
The Thin Blue Lie '00
Time at the Top '99
Trading Places '83
12 Monkeys '95 ▸
Two Bits '96
2 Minutes Later '07
Two Plus One '95
Unbreakable '00
Up Close and Personal '96 ▸
Waiting '00
The Watermelon Woman '97
Winter Kills '79 ▸
Witness '85 ▸
The Young Philadelphians '59 ▸

Philanthropy

see *Kindness of Strangers*

Phobias!

Arachnophobia '90
As Good As It Gets '97 ▸
Blackjack '97
Body Double '84 ▸
Copycat '95
GhostWatcher '02
High Anxiety '77
Home Remedy '88
Inside Out '91
Pontiac Moon '94
Pretty Woman '90 ▸
Vertigo '58 ▸
What about Bob? '91 ▸

Phone Sex

see also *Sex & Sexuality; Sexploitation*

Denise Calls Up '95
Girl 6 '96
Happiness '98 ▸
Listen '96
Love in the Time of Money '02
Mouth to Mouth '95
1-900 '94
Punch-Drunk Love '02 ▸
Short Cuts '93 ▸
The Truth about Cats and Dogs '96 ▸
Walking and Talking '96
A Whisper to a Scream '88

Phone Terror

Are You Lonesome Tonight '92
Black Christmas '06
Black Sabbath '64 ▸
Call Me '88
Cavite '05
Cellular '04
Dead Connection '94
Dial Help '88
Don't Answer the Phone '80
Eagle Eye '08
Echelon Conspiracy '09
88 Minutes '08
The Jerky Boys '95
Lady Beware '87
Liberty Stands Still '02
Lisa '90
Listen '96
Midnight Lace '60
The Night Caller '97
976-EVIL '88
976-EVIL 2: The Astral Factor '91
One Missed Call '08
Party Line '88
Phone '02
Phone Booth '02
Red '91 ▸
Scream '96 ▸
Scream 2 '97 ▸
Scream 3 '00
Smooth Talker '90
Sorry, Wrong Number '48 ▸
Sorry, Wrong Number '89
Telefon '77
Thr3e '07
When a Stranger Calls '79
When a Stranger Calls '06
When a Stranger Calls Back '93

Photography

see *Shutterbugs*

Physical Problems

see also *Blindness; Deafness; Mental Retardation; Savants*

Acorn People '82
Act of Violence '48
The Affair '73 ▸
An Affair to Remember '57
Alien: Resurrection '97 ▸
Amy '81
Amy '98
The Aura '05 ▸
Autumn Sonata '78 ▸
Avatar '09 ▸
Beastly '10
The Big Lebowski '97 ▸
Big Street '42
Blankman '94
The Bone Collector '99
Born on the Fourth of July '89 ▸
Breaking the Waves '95 ▸
A Brief History of Time '92 ▸
A Broken Life '07
Broken Strings '40
Brotherhood of the Wolf '01
The Brute Man '46
Catherine Cookson's The Wingless Bird '97
Chained for Life '51
Charlie & Me '08
Chinese Roulette '86
Choices '81
Closer and Closer '96
Coming Home '78 ▸
Cop Au Vin '85
The Craft '96
Cries of Silence '97
The Crippled Masters '82
Crossbar '79
Dance Me to My Song '98
A Day in the Death of Joe Egg '71 ▸
Dead Silent '99
Deuce Bigalow: Male Gigolo '99
Diamonds '99
The Diving Bell and the Butterfly '07 ▸
Don't Say a Word '01
Double Parked '00
Dracula 2: Ascension '03
The Duchess of Langeais '07 ▸
Eden '98
El Cochecito '60 ▸
The Elephant Man '80 ▸
Endgame '85
Even Cowgirls Get the Blues '94
Event Horizon '97
Everything That Rises '98
The Ex '07
The Fall '06
Fallen Angels '95
Fireworks '97
Flawless '99
Floating '97
Follow the Stars Home '01
Four Fast Guns '59
Frankie Starlight '95
Freddy Got Fingered '01
Front of the Class '08
The Fugitive '93 ▸
George Wallace '97
The Glass Menagerie '87 ▸
Go Now '96 ▸
Good Luck '96
Goodbye, Dragon Inn '03
The Goonies '85
Gray's Anatomy '96
A Gun, a Car, a Blonde '97
Harold '08
The Haunted Airman '06
He Was a Quiet Man '07
Hearing Voices '90
High Country '81
Home of the Brave '06
Hugo Pool '97
Humble Pie '07
The Hunchback '97
The Hunchback of Notre Dame '23 ▸
The Hunchback of Notre Dame '39 ▸
The Hunchback of Notre Dame '57
The Hunchback of Notre Dame '96 ▸
I Don't Want to Talk About It '94
I Know Who Killed Me '07
I Want You '98
Inside Moves '80
It Runs in the Family '03
It's Good to Be Alive '74
Jack and Jill vs. the World '08
Joni '79
The Kid and I '05
Kingpin '96
Knife in the Head '78
Lady Chatterley '06 ▸
Lea '96
Lewis and Clark and George '97
Lightning Jack '94
Locked in Silence '99
Long Journey Back '78
Looking for Richard '96 ▸
The Loretta Claiborne Story '00
Love Affair '39 ▸
Love Affair '94
The Lucky Ones '08
Lucky Star '29
Mac and Me '88
The Man with the Golden Arm '55 ▸
The Man Without a Face '93
Mask '85 ▸
The Men '50 ▸
Micmacs '09
Million Dollar Baby '04 ▸
Miracle in Lane Two '00
The Miracle Worker '62 ▸
The Miracle Worker '79 ▸
The Miracle Worker '00
Mrs. Munck '95
Monkey Shines '88
Murderball '05 ▸
Music Within '07
Mute Witness '95
My Left Foot '89 ▸
Next Victim '74
Niagara, Niagara '97
Night Monster '42
Night Must Fall '37 ▸
Of Human Bondage '34 ▸
Off the Mark '87
Once a Thief '90
One-Eyed Swordsman '63
Orphans '97
The Other Side of the Mountain '75
The Other Side of the Mountain, Part 2 '78
Out of the Black '01
Outside Providence '99
Paperback Romance '96
Passion Fish '92 ▸
The Passion of Anna '70 ▸
The Penalty '20
Penelope '06
The People vs. Larry Flynt '96 ▸
Perception '06
Persons Unknown '96
The Phantom of the Opera '25 ▸
The Phantom of the Opera '43 ▸
The Pit '81
Portrait of an Assassin '49
Powder '95
Pumpkin '02
Quid Pro Quo '08
Ratboy '86
Re-Generation '04
Reach for the Sky '56
Rear Window '54 ▸
Rear Window '98
The Red Dwarf '99
Regarding Henry '91 ▸
Revolver '92
Richard III '55 ▸
Ride a Wild Pony '75 ▸
Ripple Effect '07
The River '51 ▸
Rocket Science '07 ▸
Rory O'Shea Was Here '04
Roxanne '87 ▸
Rumble in the Bronx '96
Saved! '04
Scent of a Woman '92 ▸
The Sea Inside '04 ▸
Second Chances '98
The Secret '93
Seizure: The Story of Kathy Morris '80
The Seventh Veil '46 ▸
Sex & Drugs & Rock & Roll '10
Shallow Hal '01
Shiver '08
Short Night of Glass Dolls '71
Silence '73
Silence Like Glass '90
Silent Witness '99
Silver Bullet '85
Sitcom '97
Skag '79 ▸
The Sky Pilot '21
The Small Back Room '49 ▸
The Son of the Bride '01
Sound of Love '78
Speak '04 ▸
Special Olympics '78
The Spiral Staircase '46 ▸
Spiral Staircase '75
The Station Agent '03 ▸
Steel '97
The Steel Claw '61
Stella Maris '18 ▸
The Stone Merchant '06
The Story of Esther Costello '57
The Stratton Story '49 ▸
Suite 16 '94
The Sum of Us '94 ▸
Sweet and Lowdown '99
Synecdoche, New York '08 ▸
Talk to Me '84
Teeth '07
The Terry Fox Story '83 ▸
A Test of Love '84
There's Something about Mary '98 ▸
Things to Do in Denver When You're Dead '95 ▸
39 Pounds of Love '05
To All My Friends on Shore '71 ▸
Touched '05
Twin Falls Idaho '99 ▸
Under the Piano '95
Untamed Heart '93
Very Annie Mary '00
Vibrations '94
Walking on Air '87
The Waterdance '91 ▸
What Ever Happened to Baby Jane? '62 ▸
What the Deaf Man Heard '98 ▸
What's Eating Gilbert Grape '93 ▸
Whose Life Is It Anyway? '81 ▸
Wild Wild West '99
A Winner Never Quits '86
A Woman's Face '38 ▸
A Woman's Face '41 ▸
X-Men '00
X2: X-Men United '03 ▸

▸ = rated three bones or higher

Pigs

***see also** Killer Pigs*
The Advocate '93 ▸
Animal Farm '99
Babe '95 ▸
Babe: Pig in the City '98
The Black Cauldron '85
Charlotte's Web '73
Charlotte's Web '06 ▸
College Road Trip '08
Doc Hollywood '91
Gordy '95
Leon the Pig Farmer '93
A Private Function '84
The Simpsons Movie '07 ▸
Toy Story '95 ▸
Toy Story 2 '99 ▸
Waikiki Wedding '37 ▸

Pirates

***see also** Island Fare; Sail Away; Swashbucklers*
Abbott and Costello Meet Captain Kidd '52
Against All Flags '52 ▸
The Black Pirate '26 ▸
The Black Swan '42 ▸
Blackbeard the Pirate '52
Blackbeard's Ghost '67
The Buccaneer '58
Buccaneer's Girl '50
Captain Blood '35 ▸
Captain Calamity '36
Captain Kidd '45
Captain Ron '92
Carry On Jack '63
Crimson Pirate '52 ▸
Cutthroat Island '95
Dancing Pirate '36
The Devil-Ship Pirates '64
Double Crossbones '51
Frenchman's Creek '44
Frenchman's Creek '98
His Majesty O'Keefe '53
Hook '91
Horror Island '41
Ice Pirates '84
Long John Silver '54
The Master of Ballantrae '53
Morgan the Pirate '60
Muppet Treasure Island '96
Naughty Marietta '35
New Moon '40
Old Ironsides '26 ▸
Peter Pan '53 ▸
Peter Pan '60 ▸
Peter Pan '03
The Phantom '96
The Pirate '48 ▸
Pirate Movie '82
Pirates of Blood River '62
The Pirates of Penzance '83
Pirates of the Caribbean: At World's End '07
Pirates of the Caribbean: Dead Man's Chest '06
Pirates of the Caribbean: The Curse of the Black Pearl '03 ▸
The Pirates Who Don't Do Anything: A VeggieTales Movie '08
The Princess and the Pirate '44 ▸
The Princess Bride '87 ▸
Return to Never Land '02
The Sea Hawk '24
The Sea Hawk '40 ▸
Shipwrecked '90
Six Days, Seven Nights '98
Son of Captain Blood '62
Space Marines '96
Space Truckers '97
The Spanish Main '45
Stardust '07 ▸
Swashbuckler '76
Swashbuckler '84
The Swiss Family Robinson '60 ▸
Tiger of the Seven Seas '62
Treasure Island '34 ▸
Treasure Island '50 ▸
Treasure Island '72
Treasure Island '89
Treasure Island '99
Treasure Planet '02
Untamable Angelique '67
Yankee Buccaneer '52
Yellowbeard '83

Pittsburgh

Alone in the Neon Jungle '87
Angels in the Outfield '51 ▸
Angels in the Outfield '94
Backstreet Justice '93
Bloodsucking Pharoahs of Pittsburgh '90
Bob Roberts '92 ▸
The Bread, My Sweet '01
The Cemetery Club '93
Diabolique '96
Dominick & Eugene '88 ▸
The Fish that Saved Pittsburgh '79
Flashdance '83
Happy Tears '09
Houseguest '94
I Was a Communist for the FBI '51
Innocent Blood '92
Lady Beware '87
Mrs. Soffel '84
The Mysteries of Pittsburgh '08
No Other Woman '33
The Piano Lesson '94 ▸
Pittsburgh '06
Roommates '95
Silent Witness '85
Smart People '08
Stigmata '99
Striking Distance '93
Sudden Death '95
10th & Wolf '06
The Valley of Decision '45 ▸
Wonder Boys '00 ▸
Zack and Miri Make a Porno '08 ▸

Plastic Surgery

Ash Wednesday '73
The Black Dragons '42
Breast Men '97
The Broken Mask '28
Charlie Chan at the Wax Museum '40
Circus of Horrors '60
Dark Passage '47
Death Becomes Her '92 ▸
Face/Off '97 ▸
Faceless '88
Fallen Angel '99
G-Men Never Forget '48
I Accidentally Domed Your Son '04
The Jigsaw Man '84
The Man with Bogart's Face '80
Nora Prentiss '47
The Promise '79
Rabid '77
A Stolen Face '52
Strange Impersonation '46
30 Years to Life '01
Time '06

Poetry

The Barretts of Wimpole Street '34 ▸
Before Night Falls '00 ▸
Blue Car '03 ▸
Bright Star '09
The Business of Fancydancing '02
Byron '03
The Color of Pomegranates '69 ▸
A Fine Madness '66 ▸
Groundhog Day '93 ▸
Hedd Wyn '92
Henry Fool '98 ▸
I Heart Huckabees '04
I, the Worst of All '90
In Custody '94
The Ister '04 ▸
Lady Caroline Lamb '73
My Life and Times with Antonin Artaud '93 ▸
Pinero '01
Poetic Justice '93
Possession '02
The Postman '94 ▸
Satan's Brew '76
So I Married an Axe Murderer '93
Stevie '78
Swann '96
Sylvia '03
Tales of Ordinary Madness '83
Till Human Voices Wake Us '02
Tom & Viv '94 ▸
Total Eclipse '95

Poisons

Agatha Christie's Sparkling Cyanide '83
Arsenic and Old Lace '44 ▸
Barracuda '78
Batman and Robin '97
Color Me Dead '69
The Crazies '73
D.O.A. '49 ▸
D.O.A. '88
Doomwatch '72
The Emperor's New Groove '00 ▸
The Invisible Killer '40
Juggernaut '37
Kiss and Kill '68
Safe '95 ▸
Snow White and the Seven Dwarfs '37 ▸
Surf 2 '84
The Young Poisoner's Handbook '94 ▸

Poker

***see also** Gambling*
Aces and Eights '36
Angels Over Broadway '40 ▸
A Big Hand for the Little Lady '66
Casino Royale '06 ▸
The Cincinnati Kid '65
Cowboy '58 ▸
Deal '08
Destry Rides Again '39 ▸
Ebenezer '97
Finder's Fee '01
The Gambler Returns: The Luck of the Draw '93
Half a Lifetime '86
Havana '90
Hit Me '96
Honeymoon in Vegas '92
House of Games '87 ▸
It Happened at the World's Fair '63
Kenny Rogers as the Gambler '80
Kenny Rogers as the Gambler, Part 2: The Adventure Continues '83
Kenny Rogers as the Gambler, Part 3: The Legend Continues '87
The Killing of a Chinese Bookie '76
Knock Outs '92
Les Biches '68 ▸
Lucky You '07
Maverick '94
Mr. Mom '83 ▸
The Music of Chance '93
Ocean's Eleven '01 ▸
Poker Alice '87
The Poker Club '08
The Poker House '09
Red Shoe Diaries: Strip Poker '96
Rounders '98
Ruggles of Red Gap '35 ▸
Shade '03
Sheriff of Tombstone '41
The Showdown '40
Sink or Swim '97
Smart Money '31
The Stranger from Pecos '45
Thursday's Game '74 ▸
Wanda Nevada '79
Wild Bill '95

Police Detectives

Abandon '02
Abduction of St. Anne '75
Above the Law '88
All-American Murder '91
Along Came a Spider '01
The Alphabet Killer '08
Anamorph '07
Angel of Death '02
Angels Don't Sleep Here '00
Another Stakeout '93
Another Woman '94
B.A.D. Cats '80
Bad Lieutenant: Port of Call New Orleans '09
Batman Begins '05 ▸
Beautiful Creatures '00
Because of the Cats '74
Below the Deadline '29
Belphegar: Phantom of the Louvre '01
Between '05
Between Your Legs '99
Big Brown Eyes '36
The Black Belly of the Tarantula '71
Black Heat '76
Black Widow '54
Blackmail '29 ▸
Blink '93
Blood Relatives '77
Bloodbath '98
Bloody Avenger '80
Bloody Proof '99 ▸
Blossoms on Broadway '37
A Blueprint for Murder '53
Bon Cop Bad Cop '06
Borderline '02 ▸
The Boston Strangler: The Untold Story '08
Bound by Lies '05
The Box '07
The Brave One '07
Brother's Keeper '02
Bubble '06
A Bullet for Joey '55
Bullitt '68 ▸
Butterfly Collectors '99
Carrie '02
Cat and Mouse '78 ▸
Catherine's Grove '98
Catwoman '04
Chain of Fools '00
The Chaos Experiment '09
Charlie Chan at Treasure Island '39
Charlie Chan in Honolulu '38
Chill '06
City by the Sea '02
Cold and Dark '05
Columbo: Murder by the Book '71
Columbo: Prescription Murder '67
Cookie's Fortune '99 ▸
Counterspy Meets Scotland Yard '50
Cover '08
Coyote Waits '03
The Cradle of Courage '20
Crash '05 ▸
Crime and Punishment, USA '59
Crime Wave '54
The Criminal '00
Criminal Justice '08
Criminals Within '41
The Crimson Kimono '59
Crimson Rivers 2: Angels of the Apocalypse '05
The Cry: La Llorona '07
Cure '97 ▸
Curse of the Pink Panther '83
Cyberstalker '96
The Dancer Upstairs '02
Darkwolf '03
Dead Connection '94
Dead in a Heartbeat '02
Dead Sexy '01
Dead Silence '07
Death from a Distance '36
The Deep End of the Ocean '98
The Detective '68 ▸
Detective '85
Detective Story '51 ▸
Dial Red O '55
Diamond Run '00
Dick Tracy '37
Dick Tracy '90 ▸
Dick Tracy, Detective '45
Dick Tracy Meets Gruesome '47
Dick Tracy Returns '38
Dick Tracy: The Spider Strikes '37
Dick Tracy vs. Crime Inc. '41
Dick Tracy vs. Cueball '46
Dick Tracy's Dilemma '47
Dogwatch '97
Dot.Kill '05
Double Vision '02
Double Whammy '01
Dragnet '54
Dragnet '87
Edge of Darkness '86
Edge of Darkness '10
The Element of Crime '84
Empire of the Wolves '05
The Enforcer '76
Escape Clause '96
Eternal '04
Fall Guy '47
Fallen Angel '99
Falling Down '93
Fear X '03 ▸
Feardotcom '02
15 Minutes '01
Final Move '06
Final Notice '89
The First Deadly Sin '80
Five Days '07
Follow Me Quietly '49 ▸
The Force '94
Formula 51 '01
Foul Play '78 ▸
Freedomland '06
The French Detective '75 ▸
From Hell '01 ▸
Fugitive Among Us '92
Gambler's Choice '44
The Girl by the Lake '07
Gone Baby Gone '07 ▸
The Gore-Gore Girls '72
Grand National Night '53
Green Eyes '34
Green for Danger '47
The Guardian '00
Guardian Angel '94
The Gunman '03
Hard As Nails '01
Heat '95 ▸
Hellraiser 5: Inferno '00
Hero Wanted '08
Hitched '01
Hollywood Stadium Mystery '38
Home Room '02 ▸
Hostage '05
House of Mystery '41
The House of the Arrow '53 ▸
The Human Monster '39
The Hunt for the Night Stalker '91
The Hustle '75
Impact Point '08
In the Cut '03
In the Electric Mist '08
In the Valley of Elah '07 ▸
Infernal Affairs '02 ▸
Infernal Affairs 2 '03
Infernal Affairs 3 '03
Innocent Lies '95
Insomnia '97 ▸
Insomnia '02 ▸
The Invisible Killer '40
Jill the Ripper '00
Just Another Pretty Face '58
K-9 '89
K-9 3: P.I. '01
K-911 '99
Karate Dog '04
Kept '01
Kill Switch '08
Killing Emmett Young '02
A Killing Spring '02
Kiss the Girls '97
Kojak: The Belarus File '85
L.A. Confidential '97 ▸
Lantana '01 ▸
Last Hour '08
Laura '44 ▸
Le Petit Lieutenant '05
Lies & Alibis '06
A Lizard in a Woman's Skin '71
The Lodger '09
Lonely Hearts '06
Loose Cannons '90
The Lost Angel '04
Love and Bullets '79
The Mad Bomber '72
The Magician '93
Magnum Force '73
Man on the Eiffel Tower '48 ▸
Max Payne '08
Mean Streak '99
Memories of Murder '03
The Memory of a Killer '03
Mercy '00
Midnight 2: Sex, Death, and Videotape '93
The Million Dollar Hotel '99
Mind Lies '00
A Mind to Murder '96
Mr. Brooks '07
The Money Trap '65
Mortal Transfer '01
Murder at 1600 '97
Murder at the Vanities '34
Murder by Numbers '02
Murder in Greenwich '02
My New Partner '84
Mystery Street '50
Mystic River '03 ▸
Naked City: A Killer Christmas '98
Naked City: Justice with a Bullet '98
The Natalee Holloway Story '09
New Orleans After Dark '58
Newman's Law '74
Nick Knight '89
Night School '81
Night Stalker '87
Nightwatch '96
No One Sleeps '01
No Way to Treat a Lady '68 ▸
Nocturne '46
November '05 ▸
Number One with a Bullet '87
Observe and Report '09
On Dangerous Ground '51 ▸
One Good Cop '91
One Missed Call '08
One Night at McCool's '01
Open Cam '05
Operation Julie '85
The Organization '71 ▸
The Other Guys '10
Out of the Darkness '85 ▸
Out of the Shadows '88
Out of Time '03
Partners in Crime '99
P.D. James: Death in Holy Orders '03
The Phantom Light '35
The Phantom of Soho '64
Phone Booth '02
The Pink Panther '06
The Pink Panther 2 '09
Place of Execution '09
Play Nice '92
Postmark for Danger '56
Practical Magic '98
The Presidio '88
Prettykill '87
Pride and Glory '08
Private Hell 36 '54
The Prophet's Game '99
Pushover '54
Recipe for Revenge '98
Relentless '89
Relentless 2: Dead On '91
Relentless 3 '93
Relentless 4 '94
Resurrection '99
The Return of Dr. Mabuse '61
Revenge Quest '96
Ricochet '91 ▸
Righteous Kill '08
Ring of Death '69
The River King '05
The Riverman '04
Rough Cut '80
Rush Hour 3 '07
Sanctimony '01
Sapphire '59 ▸
Saw 2 '05
Saw 5 '08
Scotland, PA '02
Sea of Love '89 ▸
Second Sight '99 ▸
Seduced: Pretty When You Cry '01
Seeds of Doubt '96
Seven '95 ▸
The Seven-Ups '73
Shadows of the Orient '37
Showtime '02
The Silence '06
Silk '86
Sin City '05

▸ = rated three bones or higher

16 Blocks '06 ▸
Skinwalker '02
Sleepless '01
The Sniper '52
Someone to Watch Over Me '87 ▸
Somewhere in the Night '46
South Seas Massacre '74
Speed Dating '07
The Spider and the Fly '49
Splinter '06
The Squeeze '77
Stakeout '87
Station '81
Stiletto '08
The Strange Case of Dr. Jekyll and Mr. Hyde '06
Stray Dog '49 ▸
Street Kings '08
Streets of Blood '09
Strike a Pose '93
Suicide Club '02
Surrogates '09
Takers '10
Tales from the Crypt Presents Bordello of Blood '96
Tangled '01
Tell No One '06 ▸
Telling Lies '06
Tenderness '08
Tension '50
That Beautiful Somewhere '06
They Call Me Mr. Tibbs! '70
The Third Key '57
Third World Cop '99
The Thomas Crown Affair '99 ▸
Ticker '01
Ticket to a Crime '34
To Catch a Killer '92 ▸
Touching Evil '97 ▸
Transfixed '01
Trauma '04
True Blue '01
True Romance '93
12 Rounds '09
Twisted '04
V for Vendetta '06
Vampire Assassin '05
Vertigo '58 ▸
Video Murders '87
Violated '84
Wallander: Firewall '08
Wallander: One Step Behind '08
Wallander: Sidetracked '08
Wasabi '01
What to Do in Case of Fire '02
What Your Eyes Don't See '99
When the Sky Falls '99
Where the Sidewalk Ends '50
Whirlpool '49
Who Is the Black Dahlia? '75 ▸
Wild Things '98
Wilder '00
Winter of Frozen Dreams '08
Witchcraft 10: Mistress of the Craft '98
Witness '85 ▸
World of the Depraved '67
X Marks the Spot '42
Zodiac '07

Politics

see also Capitol Capers; Presidency; Vote for Me!

Absolute Power '97
The Act '82
Al Franken: God Spoke '07
All the King's Men '06
Amazing Grace '06 ▸
The American President '95 ▸
An American Story '92
The Americano '17
Americathon '79
And the Band Played On '93 ▸
Angels in America '03 ▸
Angi Vera '78 ▸
Animal Instincts '92
Antonio Das Mortes '68
Archangel '05
The Art of War '00
Art of War 2: The Betrayal '08
Article 99 '92
The Assassination of Richard Nixon '05
Attila '01
Baaria '09
Battle in Seattle '07
Bear Ye One Another's Burden... '88
Beggars in Ermine '34
Being There '79 ▸
Beyond Obsession '82
Beyond Rangoon '95
The Big Brass Ring '99
The Big Hurt '87
The Birdcage '95 ▸
Bitter Sugar '96 ▸
Black Ice '92
Black Jesus '68
Black Sheep '96
Blame It on Fidel '06
Blaze '89
Blood Money: The Story of Clinton and Nadine '88
The Blue Kite '93 ▸
Bob Roberts '92 ▸
Bopha! '93 ▸
The Break '97
Break of Dawn '88
Bulworth '98 ▸
Buried Alive '39
The Burning Season '94 ▸
Burnt by the Sun '94 ▸
Bush's Brain '04
Call Him Mr. Shatter '74
Canadian Bacon '94
The Candidate '72 ▸
Cape of Good Hope '04
Carla's Song '97
Carry On Emmanuelle '78
Casino '95 ▸
Caterina in the Big City '03
Chain of Command '95
Charlie Wilson's War '07
Chasing Freedom '04
Chicago 10 '07 ▸
Children of Men '06 ▸
Children of the Revolution '95
China Gate '57 ▸
Choose Connor '07
Citizen Cohn '92
City Hall '95 ▸
Clear and Present Danger '94
Code Name: Chaos '90
The Colombian Connection '91
Colonel Effingham's Raid '45
The Comedians '67
Complex World '92
Confessing to Laura '90
Conspiracy '89
Conspiracy: The Trial of the Chicago Eight '87 ▸
The Contender '00
Corporate Affairs '90
Country '84 ▸
Country Life '95
The Cradle Will Rock '99
crazy/beautiful '01
CSA: The Confederate States of America '04
A Dangerous Man: Lawrence after Arabia '91 ▸
Daniel Takes a Train '83
Dave '93 ▸
A Day Without a Mexican '04
DC 9/11: Time of Crisis '04
Dead Center '94
The Dead Zone '02
Deadly Exposure '93
The Deal '05
Dear Wendy '05
Death and the Maiden '94 ▸
Death of a Bureaucrat '66 ▸
Defense of the Realm '85 ▸
Devil in a Blue Dress '95 ▸
The Devils '71 ▸
Devlin '92
The Disappearance of Garcia Lorca '96
Disraeli '30 ▸
Disraeli '79 ▸
The Distinguished Gentleman '92
Don's Party '76 ▸
Double Cross '92
Double Edge '92
Down Came a Blackbird '94
The Duchess '08 ▸
Earth Entranced '66
The Edukators '04
8-A '92
Eijanaika '81 ▸
Elizabeth '98 ▸
Elizabeth R '72 ▸
Eminent Domain '91
The Emperor and the Assassin '99
The Emperor's New Clothes '01
Endgame '09
The Enemy Within '94
Enron: The Smartest Guys in the Room '05 ▸
An Everlasting Piece '00
Evita '96
Execution of Justice '99
Eye of the Stranger '93
Eyes of a Witness '94
Fahrenheit 9/11 '04 ▸
Faith '94
Fame Is the Spur '47
The Farmer's Daughter '47 ▸
Fatwa '06
Fever Mounts at El Pao '59
Fidel '02 ▸
The Final Cut '95 ▸
The Final Days '89
Fires Within '91
First Daughter '04
First Family '80
First Monday in October '81
A Flash of Green '85
The Fog of War: Eleven Lessons from the Life of Robert S. McNamara '03 ▸
A Foreign Affair '48 ▸
Foreplay '75
Four Days in September '97
The French Detective '75 ▸
The French Woman '79
Friday Foster '75
Friends '95
Gabriel Over the White House '33 ▸
Gangs of New York '02 ▸
George Wallace '97
Germany in Autumn '78
The Ghost Writer '10
G.I. Jane '97
The Girl in the Cafe '05
A Girl on Her Own '76
Giuliani Time '05
Gladiator '00 ▸
Go Further '03
Going Upriver: The Long War of John Kerry '04
A Good Man in Africa '94
Good Night, and Good Luck '05 ▸
The Gorgeous Hussy '36
The Great Man's Lady '42
The Great McGinty '40 ▸
The Great Water '04
Guilty by Suspicion '91
Hangar 18 '80
Hijacking Catastrophe: 9/11, Fear and the Selling of America '04
Hombres Armados '97 ▸
The Home and the World '84 ▸
Hoodlum Empire '52
Hostages '93 ▸
Hour of the Assassin '86
House of Cards '90
The House of the Spirits '93
How to Frame a Figg '71
The Hunting of the President '04
I Am Cuba '64
I Was Framed '42
An Ideal Husband '47
An Ideal Husband '99 ▸
Il Divo '08
In My Country '04
In the Lake of the Woods '96
In the Line of Duty: Ambush in Waco '93
In the Line of Fire '93 ▸
In the Loop '09
In the Name of the Father '93 ▸
An Inconvenient Truth '06 ▸
Indochine '92 ▸
The Interpreter '05 ▸
Jack Higgins' On Dangerous Ground '95
Jack Higgins' The Windsor Protocol '97
Jackie, Ethel, Joan: The Kennedy Women '01
Jefferson in Paris '94
The Jesse Ventura Story '99
JFK '91 ▸
John and the Missus '87
A Joke of Destiny, Lying in Wait Around the Corner Like a Bandit '84
Journeys with George '02
Just Like Weather '86 ▸
Kansas City '95 ▸
The Keeper: The Legend of Omar Khayyam '05
Killer Image '92
The Killing Beach '92
The Killing Device '92
Kingfish: A Story of Huey P. Long '95
Kissinger and Nixon '96
Knife in the Head '78
Knocks at My Door '93
Kundun '97 ▸
Kurt Vonnegut's Harrison Bergeron '95
Lamerica '95 ▸
Land and Freedom '95 ▸
Land of the Blind '06
Land of the Free '98
Larks on a String '68 ▸
The Last Supper '96
Laurel & Hardy: Chickens Come Home '31
Le Complot '73 ▸
Les Miserables '97 ▸
The Life and Assassination of the Kingfish '76
A Lion Is in the Streets '53 ▸
Lions for Lambs '07
A Little Bit of Soul '97
The Little Drummer Girl '84 ▸
Little Mother '71
Lone Star Kid '88
Looking for Comedy in the Muslim World '06
The Lost City '05
Louisiana Purchase '41
Love Actually '03
Love Letters '99 ▸
Lumumba '01 ▸
M. Butterfly '93
Magnificent Doll '46
Malevolence '95
The Man Who Shot Liberty Valance '62 ▸
The Manchurian Candidate '62 ▸
The Manchurian Candidate '04 ▸
Mandela '87 ▸
Mandela and de Klerk '97
Manderlay '05
Marianne and Juliane '82 ▸
Marilyn & Bobby: Her Final Affair '94
Maryam '00
Mastergate '92 ▸
The Matchmaker '97
The Mating Game '59 ▸
Max '02
Mayerling '68
Medium Cool '69 ▸
Meet Wally Sparks '97
Meeting Venus '91
Michael Collins '96 ▸
The Milky Way '97
Mission of Justice '92
Mission to Moscow '43
Mr. Smith Goes to Washington '39 ▸
Mosley '98
Mountbatten: The Last Viceroy '86
My Brother's War '97
My Little Assassin '99
My Universities '40 ▸
The Mystic Masseur '01
Naked Obsession '91
National Lampoon's Senior Trip '95
Nick of Time '95
Nightbreaker '89 ▸
Nixon '95 ▸
No '98
No End in Sight '07 ▸
No Witness '04
Noriega: God's Favorite '00
Northern Extremes '93
The November Men '93
Nurse Marjorie '20
Of Love and Shadows '94
The Omen '06
Open Doors '89 ▸
Orwell Rolls in His Grave '03
Our Brand Is Crisis '05 ▸
Outfoxed: Rupert Murdoch's War on Journalism '04 ▸
Outrage '09
Palombella Rossa '89
Paradise Now '05 ▸
Paris 36 '08
Peace, Propaganda & the Promised Land '04
The Pelican Brief '93
People I Know '02
The Perez Family '94
Pizza Man '91
A Place in the World '92 ▸
Poldark '96
The Possessed '88
Presumed Innocent '90 ▸
Primary Colors '98
Primary Motive '92
The Promise '94
Purple Butterfly '03 ▸
The Queen '06 ▸
Quiet Fire '91
Rage of Angels: The Story Continues '86
Rain Without Thunder '93
Recount '08
Red Hot '95
Red Kiss '85 ▸
Rendition '07
Report to the Commissioner '74 ▸
Rhodes '97
Richard III '12
Richard III '95 ▸
Robert Kennedy and His Times '90
Ronnie and Julie '97
Rosa Luxemburg '86
Running Mates '86 ▸
Running Mates '92 ▸
Running Mates '00
St. Michael Had a Rooster '72
Salt of the Earth '54 ▸
Samaritan: The Mitch Snyder Story '86 ▸
The Sea Inside '04 ▸
The Second Civil War '97
The Secret '93
Seduced '85
The Seduction of Joe Tynan '79
The '70s '00
The Shadow Conspiracy '96
The Silence of Neto '94
Silver City '04
Some Mother's Son '96 ▸
Sophie Scholl: The Final Days '05 ▸
Spartan '04 ▸
Speak Up! It's So Dark '93
Special Police '85
Speechless '94
Stalin '92
Star Wars: Episode 3—Revenge of the Sith '05 ▸
State of Play '03 ▸
State of Play '09 ▸
State of the Union '48 ▸
The State Within '06
Stop-Loss '08 ▸
Storyville '92
Strange Justice: The Clarence Thomas and Anita Hill Story '99
Strawberry and Chocolate '93 ▸
Striptease '96
Superfly T.N.T. '73
Supreme Sanction '99
Syriana '05 ▸
Tanner '88 '88 ▸
Tanner on Tanner '04
Taxi Blues '90 ▸
Temptation of a Monk '94
This Revolution '05
Three Cases of Murder '55 ▸
Timecop '94
Tito and Me '92 ▸
To Live '94 ▸
To Play the King '93 ▸
The Travelling Players '75
Trial by Media '00
The Trojan Horse '08
Truman '95
The Tunnel '01 ▸
Two Deaths '94
Typhoon '06
Uncovered: The War on Iraq '04
Under Western Stars '38
An Unforgettable Summer '94
The U.S. Vs. John Lennon '06
Unnatural Causes '86 ▸
Up at the Villa '00
Up in Central Park '48
The Uppercrust '81
V for Vendetta '06
The Vector File '03
A Very British Coup '88 ▸
The Veteran '06
Viva Villa! '34 ▸
Viva Zapata! '52 ▸
W. '08 ▸
Wag the Dog '97
Wall '04 ▸
The War Room '93 ▸
Washington Mistress '81
The Weather Underground '02 ▸
Wedding Wars '06
Welcome to Mooseport '04
Werewolf of Washington '73
Who Killed the Electric Car? '06
Wild in the Streets '68
Wild Reeds '94 ▸
The Wind That Shakes the Barley '06 ▸
Windhorse '98
A Woman Named Jackie '91
The Worker and the Hairdresser '96
World War II: When Lions Roared '94
XXX: State of the Union '05
The Yes Men '03
Zero Population Growth '72

Polygamy

see also Adultery; Marriage

Brigham Young: Frontiersman '40
Captain's Paradise '53 ▸
Deceived '91
Enemies, a Love Story '89 ▸
Eyes of Fire '84
The Last King of Scotland '06 ▸
Me You Them '00
Monsieur Verdoux '47 ▸
Moolaade '04
My 5 Wives '00
Relative Strangers '99

Pool

see also Gambling

Albino Alligator '96
The American President '95 ▸
The Baltimore Bullet '80
The Baron and the Kid '84
The Color of Money '86 ▸
The Hustler '61 ▸
Kiss Shot '89
The Last Time I Committed Suicide '96
The Music Man '62 ▸
Pool Hustlers '83
Poolhall Junkies '02
Stickmen '01
Think Tank '06
Turn the River '07
Up Against the Eight Ball '04

Pornography

see also Sex & Sexuality; Sexploitation

Amateur '94 ▸
Auto Focus '02 ▸

▸ = rated three bones or higher

Pregnant Pauses

see also *Bringing Up Baby*

Alien 3 '92
All About My Mother '99 ▸
Almost Pregnant '91
Alternative '76
Angel Baby '95 ▸
Angel Rodriguez '05
Angie '94
Are We Done Yet? '07
Armistead Maupin's More Tales of the City '97
The Astronaut's Wife '99
Away We Go '09
The Baby Dance '98 ▸
The Baby Maker '70
Baby Mama '08
Baby of the Bride '91
Baby on Board '08
Babyfever '94
Babylon A.D. '08
The Back-Up Plan '10
Bad Girl '31
Barbershop '02 ▸
Beautiful People '99
Bed and Board '70 ▸
Bella '06
Bellyfruit '99
Beloved/Friend '99
Between Heaven and Earth '93
Billy: Portrait of a Street Kid '77
Black Irish '07
Bleeding Hearts '94
Boys on the Side '94
Brand New Life '72
Brink of Life '57
The Brothers Solomon '07
Butterfly Wings '91
Cafe au Lait '94 ▸
Cafe Lumiere '05
Caged '50 ▸
Cast the First Stone '89
Catherine Cookson's The Dwelling Place '94
Catherine Cookson's The Round Tower '98
Catherine Cookson's The Wingless Bird '97
Cheyenne Warrior '94
Child of Darkness, Child of Light '91
Children of Men '06 ▸
Choices '86
Chutney Popcorn '99
The Circle '00
Citizen Ruth '96
Cocktail '88
Coming Out '89
Conceiving Ada '97
The Confessional '95 ▸
Confusion of Genders '00
The Cooler '03 ▸
The Corner '00
The Crime of Father Amaro '02 ▸
Crossroads '02
Dam Street '05
Dancing at the Blue Iguana '00
Danielle Steel's Heartbeat '93
Dawn of the Dead '04 ▸
Demon Seed '77 ▸
Divided We Fall '00
Do or Die '03
Down, Out and Dangerous '95
Due East '02
Earth & Water '99
Earthly Possessions '99
Earthquake in Chile '74
Eraserhead '78 ▸
Escape from the Planet of the Apes '71 ▸
Everything Put Together '00
The Evil Within '89
The Exiles '61
The Eye 2 '04
Falling for a Dancer '98
False Prophets '06
A Farewell to Arms '57
Fargo '96 ▸
Father of the Bride Part 2 '95
Father's Little Dividend '51 ▸
Felicia's Journey '99 ▸
Five '51
Flickers '80
Fools Rush In '97
Friends '71
Generation '69
The Good Girl '02 ▸
Good Luck Chuck '07
Half Broken Things '07
The Heart of Me '02
Heartburn '86 ▸
Hell Comes to Frogtown '88
Hellboy II: The Golden Army '08 ▸
Help Wanted: Male '82
Hide and Seek '00
Home Fries '98
How to Deal '03
Hush '98
I Married a Dead Man '82
Ice Age: Dawn of the Dinosaurs '09
If These Walls Could Talk '96
Immediate Family '89
In America '02 ▸
The Innocent '76
Interlocked '98
The Invader '96
Invasion of Privacy '96
Jailbait! '00
Julien Donkey-boy '99
Juno '07 ▸
Just Another Girl on the I.R.T. '93
Kill the Poor '06
A Kind of Loving '62 ▸
Knocked Up '07
The L-Shaped Room '62 ▸
La Buche '00
Labor Pains '99
Labor Pains '09
Lars and the Real Girl '07
The Last Kiss '01
The Last Kiss '06
Le Cas du Dr. Laurent '57 ▸
Le Divorce '03
Lethal Weapon 4 '98
Let's Get Married '60
Levitation '97
Lift '01
Lily Was Here '89
Look Both Ways '05
Lost in Beijing '07
Love Child '82
Love Finds a Home '09
Love for Rent '05
Lucie Aubrac '98
Lullaby '08
Makin' Baby '02
Manny & Lo '96 ▸
Margot at the Wedding '07
Maria Full of Grace '04 ▸
The Marquise of O '76
The Match Factory Girl '90 ▸
Maternal Instincts '96
Maybe Baby '99
Maybe... Maybe Not '94
Maze '01
Me You Them '00
Merrily We Go to Hell '32
Micki & Maude '84
The Miracle '48 ▸
Misbegotten '98
Miss Conception '08
Mists of Avalon '01 ▸
A Modern Affair '94
Mom & Dad '47
Morning Glory '93
My Baby's Daddy '04
My Blue Heaven '50
My Foolish Heart '49
My Life '93
My Little Assassin '99
My Wife is an Actress '01
The Nativity Story '06
Nenette and Boni '96 ▸
Never Too Late '65
The New Eve '98 ▸
The Nickel Children '05
Nickel Mountain '85
Nine Lives '05 ▸
Nine Months '95
No Alibi '00
No Laughing Matter '97
North Shore Fish '97
Now and Then '95
The Object of My Affection '98
On the Outs '05
101 Dalmatians '96
One Last Ride '03
101 Reykjavik '00
The Opposite of Sex '98
Our Song '01 ▸
Our Time '74
Outrageous! '77 ▸
Palindromes '04 ▸
Parenthood '89 ▸
Paternity '81
Perception '06
Personal Velocity: Three Portraits '02 ▸
Pilgrimage '33
Polish Wedding '97
Precious: Based on the Novel by Sapphire '09 ▸
The Princess of Nebraska '07
Prison Break: The Final Break '09
Progeny '98
Promises! Promises! '63
The Prophecy 2: Ashtown '97
Pure '02 ▸
Quinceanera '06 ▸
Rendition '07
Riding in Cars with Boys '01
Robin Hood: Prince of Thieves '91
Rosemary's Baby '68 ▸
Runaway Daughters '94
A Saintly Switch '99
The Santa Clause 3: The Escape Clause '06
Saturday Night and Sunday Morning '60 ▸
Saved! '04
Savior '98 ▸
Seducing Maarya '99
Seed of Chucky '04
Series 7: The Contenders '01
The Seventh Sign '88
Sex and the City 2 '10
Sex and the City: The Movie '08
Shadowboxer '06
She's Having a Baby '88
Shrek the Third '07
Side Street '50
A Single Girl '96
The Sins of Rachel Cade '61
Skipped Parts '00
Sliding Doors '97
Slogan '69
A Smile Like Yours '96
Solomon and Gaenor '98
Soul's Midnight '06
Spice World: The Movie '97
Splendor '99
Star Wars: Episode 3—Revenge of the Sith '05 ▸
Steel Magnolias '89 ▸
Stephanie Daley '06
The Stranger Within '74
Sugar & Spice '01 ▸
Sweet Evil '95
Talk to Her '02 ▸
A Taste of Honey '61 ▸
Tenth Month '79
The Terminator '84 ▸
Tess of the Storm Country '22
Then She Found Me '07
3 Women '77 ▸
Time and Tide '00
Tiptoes '03
Tomorrow '72 ▸
Turn It Up '00
20 Years After '08
The 24 Hour Woman '99
The Twilight of the Golds '97
Two Family House '99
Twogether '94
The Unborn '91
Under the Pavement Lies the Strand '75
Under the Skin '97
Under the Tuscan Sun '03
Undertow '10
Une Femme Mariee '64
The Unearthing '93
An Unexpected Life '97
The Unknown Soldier '98
Vernie '04
The Very Edge '63
The Village Barbershop '08
Waitress '07 ▸
Waking Up in Reno '02
A Walk in the Clouds '95
Way of the Gun '00
Wedding Bell Blues '96
A Weekend in the Country '96
What Matters Most '01
What Planet Are You From? '00
Where the Heart Is '00
William Faulkner's Old Man '97
Winter Flight '84
Woman Wanted '98
Women in Trouble '09
Wonder Boys '00 ▸
Wrestling with Alligators '98
Year Zero '04
You'll Like My Mother '72
The Young Pioneers '76
Yours, Mine & Ours '68
You've Ruined Me, Eddie '58
Zero Population Growth '72

Prep School

see also *Hell High School; Teen Angst*

Afterschool '08
Agent Cody Banks '03
Brotherhood 2: The Young Warlocks '01
Chasing Holden '01
The Covenant '06
Cry_Wolf '05
Dead Poets Society '89 ▸
The Emperor's Club '02
The Fraternity '01
The Happy Years '50
Harry Potter and the Chamber of Secrets '02 ▸
Harry Potter and the Goblet of Fire '05 ▸
Harry Potter and the Order of the Phoenix '07
Harry Potter and the Sorcerer's Stone '01 ▸
The Haunting of Molly Hartley '08
The History Boys '06
If... '69 ▸
Lost and Delirious '01
Making the Grade '84
Murderous Intent '06 ▸
Notes on a Scandal '06 ▸
O '01 ▸
Outside Providence '99
The River King '05
St. Trinian's '07
Scent of a Woman '92 ▸
School Ties '92 ▸
A Separate Peace '04
She's the Man '06
The Smokers '00
Tadpole '02
Tart '01
Telling Lies '06
Underclassman '05
Were the World Mine '08
Whirlygirl '04
Wild Child '08
The Woods '03

Presidency

see also *Camelot (New); Politics*

Abe Lincoln in Illinois '40 ▸
Absolute Power '97
Advise and Consent '62 ▸
Agent of Death '99
Air Force One '97 ▸
All the President's Men '76 ▸
An American Affair '09
American Dreamz '06
The American President '95 ▸
Amistad '97 ▸
Assassination '87
The Assassination File '96
The Assassination of Richard Nixon '05
Backstairs at the White House '79 ▸
The Best Man '64 ▸
The Betty Ford Story '87 ▸
Black Dynamite '09
Black Sunday '77
Capitalism: A Love Story '09
Chasing Liberty '04
Dave '93 ▸
The Day Reagan Was Shot '01
DC 9/11: Time of Crisis '04
Deep Impact '98
Depth Charge '08
Deterrence '00
Dick '99 ▸
Dirty Tricks '81
Dr. Dolittle 4: Tail to the Chief '08
Eleanor & Franklin '76 ▸
Eleanor: First Lady of the World '82
Elvis Meets Nixon '98
The Enemy Within '94
Escape from New York '81
Executive Action '73
Executive Target '97
Fahrenheit 9/11 '04 ▸
Fail Safe '00
The Final Days '89
First Daughter '99
First Family '80
First Kid '96
For the Love of Mary '48
Foreplay '75
Forrest Gump '94 ▸
Frost/Nixon '08 ▸
Gabriel Over the White House '33 ▸
Gore Vidal's Lincoln '88
Guarding Tess '94
Hail '73
Hitman '07
The Hunting of the President '04
Imagemaker '86
In the Line of Fire '93 ▸
Independence Day '96 ▸
Invictus '09 ▸
Jefferson in Paris '94
JFK '91 ▸
The JFK Conspiracy '91
John Adams '08
Journeys with George '02
Kennedy '83
The Kennedys of Massachusetts '95
The Kidnapping of the President '80
Kisses for My President '64
Kissinger and Nixon '96
The Last Bastion '84
LBJ: A Biography '91
LBJ: The Early Years '88 ▸
Magnificent Doll '46
Mail to the Chief '00
Man of the Year '06
Mars Attacks! '96
Meteor '79
Missiles of October '74 ▸
Murder at 1600 '97
My Date with the President's Daughter '98
My Fellow Americans '96
My Uncle: The Alien '96
Nixon '95 ▸
Path to War '02
The Pooch and the Pauper '99
Power and Beauty '02
The President's Analyst '67 ▸
President's Mistress '78
The President's Plane Is Missing '71
Primary Colors '98
Prince Jack '83
The Rat Pack '98
The Reagans '04
RFK '02
Ruby '92
Sadat '83
Sally Hemings: An American Scandal '00
The Second Civil War '97
Secret Honor '85 ▸
The Sentinel '06
The Shadow Conspiracy '96
Suddenly '54 ▸
The Sum of All Fears '02
Sunrise at Campobello '60 ▸
Swing Vote '08
XIII '08
Thirteen Days '00 ▸
The Trojan Horse '08
Truman '95
24 : Redemption '08
The Undercover Kid '95
Vantage Point '08
W. '08 ▸
The War Room '93 ▸
Wild in the Streets '68
Wilson '44 ▸
Winter Kills '79 ▸
XXX: State of the Union '05
Young Mr. Lincoln '39 ▸

Price of Fame

see also *Rags to Riches*

Abraham Lincoln '30
All About Eve '50 ▸
All That Jazz '79 ▸
American Blue Note '89
At Any Cost '00
The Bad and the Beautiful '52 ▸
Bank Robber '93
Bert Rigby, You're a Fool '89
Beyond the Valley of the Dolls '70
The Big Knife '55 ▸
Black Starlet '74
The Bodyguard '92
The Buddy Holly Story '78 ▸
By the Sword '93
Byron '03
Call Me: The Rise and Fall of Heidi Fleiss '04
The Cantor's Son '37
Cassie '83
Champion '49 ▸
A Chorus Line '85
Citizen Kane '41 ▸
Coal Miner's Daughter '80 ▸
Comeback '83
The Comic '69 ▸
The Commitments '91 ▸
Control '07
The Cotton Club '84 ▸
Country Girl '82
Covergirl '83
Crossover Dreams '85
Darling '65 ▸
Dead Ringers '88 ▸
Dreamgirls '06 ▸
Echo Park '86
Eddie and the Cruisers '83
Eddie and the Cruisers 2: Eddie Lives! '89
Edie in Ciao! Manhattan '72
EDtv '99
Elmer Gantry '60 ▸
Elvis and Me '88
Elvis: The Movie '79
Eureka! '81
Extra Girl '23
Factory Girl '06
Fame '80 ▸
The Fan '81
Feel the Noise '07
Fellow Traveler '89 ▸
The Five Heartbeats '91 ▸
Flashdance '83
Frances '82 ▸
Gemini Affair '74
The Gene Krupa Story '59
The Goddess '58 ▸
Goodbye, Norma Jean '75
Goodnight, Sweet Marilyn '89
Gore Vidal's Lincoln '88
Grosse Fatigue '94 ▸
The Gunfighter '50 ▸
Hail Caesar '94
A Hard Day's Night '64 ▸
Hard Part Begins '73
Harvest Melody '43
Hero at Large '80
Hollywood Heartbreak '89
I Ought to Be in Pictures '82
Idolmaker '80
I'll Cry Tomorrow '55 ▸
I'm Not There '07 ▸
Imitation of Life '34
Imitation of Life '59 ▸
Inside Daisy Clover '65
Irreconcilable Differences '84
It Could Happen to You '94
It Should Happen to You '54 ▸
The Jacksons: An American Dream '92
Jacqueline Bouvier Kennedy '81
James Dean '76

The Jayne Mansfield Story '80
The Jazz Singer '80
Jimmy Hollywood '94
Jo Jo Dancer, Your Life Is Calling '86
John & Yoko: A Love Story '85
Keep Punching '39
King of Comedy '82 ▸
La Bamba '87 ▸
La Dolce Vita '60 ▸
Ladies and Gentlemen, the Fabulous Stains '82
Lady Grey '82
Lady Jane '85 ▸
Lady Sings the Blues '72
The Lady Without Camelias '53
Lenny '74 ▸
Let It Rock '86
Little Caesar '30 ▸
The Lonely Lady '83
Lords of Dogtown '05
Love Me or Leave Me '55 ▸
Lucy and Desi: Before the Laughter '91
The Magnificent Ambersons '42 ▸
The Magnificent Ambersons '02
Mahogany '75
The Main Event '79
Man in the Mirror: The Michael Jackson Story '04
The Man Who Would Be King '75 ▸
Marilyn: The Untold Story '80 ▸
Meat Loaf: To Hell and Back '00
Mephisto '81 ▸
Miss All-American Beauty '82
Mistress '91
Mommie Dearest '81
Music & Lyrics '07
My Fair Lady '64 ▸
My Favorite Year '82 ▸
Naked in New York '93
Oh, God! You Devil '84
The One and Only '78
One Trick Pony '80
The Oscar '66
Payday '73
Pecker '98
A Perfect Day '06
Police Court '32
Postcards from the Edge '90 ▸
Prisoner of Rio '89
Provincial Actors '79
Pure Country '92
Purple Rain '84
The Queen of Mean '90
Raging Bull '80 ▸
Ransom '96 ▸
Rocky '76 ▸
Rocky 2 '79
Rocky 3 '82
Rocky 4 '85
Rocky 5 '90
The Rose '79 ▸
Scarlet Diva '00
The Seduction '82
Shadow of China '91 ▸
Shakes the Clown '92
Shop Angel '32
Show People '28 ▸
Sins '85
Small Town Boy '37
Smash-Up: The Story of a Woman '47 ▸
Smithereens '82
S.O.B. '81
Soldier in Love '67
Solo Sunny '80
Star 80 '83
A Star Is Born '37 ▸
A Star Is Born '54 ▸
Stardom '00
Stardust Memories '80
Stoned '05
Sunset Boulevard '50 ▸
Svengali '83
Sweet Dreams '85
Sweet Love, Bitter '67
Sweet Perfection '90
Sweethearts '38 ▸
The Thing Called Love '93
The Tiger Woods Story '98
True Colors '91
Tucker: The Man and His Dream '88 ▸
Twenty Dollar Star '91
Two Weeks in Another Town '62
Undiscovered '05
Valley of the Dolls '67
Velvet Goldmine '98
A Very Private Affair '62
What Ever Happened to Baby Jane? '62 ▸
What Price Hollywood? '32 ▸
What's Love Got to Do with It? '93
While the City Sleeps '56 ▸
Winning '69 ▸
Wired '89
A Woman Named Jackie '91
You Light Up My Life '77
Ziegfeld Girl '41 ▸

Princes/Princesses

see *Royalty; Royalty, British; Royalty, French; Royalty, Russian*

Prison

see *Alcatraz; Devil's Island; Escaped Cons; Great Escapes; Men in Prison; POW/MIA; Women in Prison*

Private Eyes

Abbott and Costello Meet the Invisible Man '51 ▸
Accomplice '46
Adventures of a Private Eye '77
Alone in the Dark '05
Alphaville '65 ▸
Angel Heart '87
Anonymous Rex '04
Are You Lonesome Tonight '92
Arrest Bulldog Drummond '38
The Art of Crime '75
Asylum '97
Backstreet Justice '93
Bad Seed '00
Bedelia '46 ▸
Beyond Justice '01
The Big Empty '98 ▸
The Big Fall '96
The Big Sleep '46 ▸
The Big Sleep '78
Big Store '41
Billion Dollar Brain '67
Black Bird '75
The Black Camel '31
The Black Doll '38
Blackout '54
Blade in Hong Kong '85
Blonde for a Day '46
Bloodhounds 2 '96
Blue Blood '07
The Blue Lightning '86
Blue, White and Perfect '42
Bootleg '85
Brown's Requiem '98
Bulldog Drummond '29
Bulldog Drummond at Bay '37
Bulldog Drummond Comes Back '37
Bulldog Drummond Escapes '37
Bulldog Drummond's Bride '39
Bulldog Drummond's Peril '38
Bulldog Drummond's Revenge '37
Bulldog Drummond's Secret Police '39
Bulldog Jack '35 ▸
The Caller '08
Calling Paul Temple '48
Camouflage '00
The Case of the Lucky Legs '35
Cast a Deadly Spell '91 ▸
Charlie Chan and the Curse of the Dragon Queen '81
Charlie Chan at Monte Carlo '37
Charlie Chan at the Circus '36
Charlie Chan at the Olympics '37
Charlie Chan at the Opera '36 ▸
Charlie Chan at the Race Track '36
Charlie Chan at the Wax Museum '40
Charlie Chan in Egypt '35
Charlie Chan in London '34
Charlie Chan in Paris '35
Charlie Chan in Rio '41
Charlie Chan in Shanghai '35
Charlie Chan in the Secret Service '44
Charlie Chan on Broadway '37
Charlie Chan's Secret '35
Chinatown '74 ▸
The Chinese Cat '44
Clean Slate '94
Conspiracy of Terror '75
Counterspy Meets Scotland Yard '50
Cry Uncle '71
The Curse of the Jade Scorpion '01
Curtain at Eight '33
The Dain Curse '78
Dancing with Danger '93
Dark Corner '46 ▸
The Dark Hour '36
Dark Side of Midnight '86
Dead Again '91 ▸
Dead Evidence '00
Dead Men Don't Wear Plaid '82
Dead Pigeon on Beethoven Street '72
Deadly Force '83
Deadly Illusion '87
Deadly Passion '85
Deadly Sins '95
Death Train '79
Deceptions 2: Edge of Deception '94
Detective Sadie & Son '84
Devil in a Blue Dress '95 ▸
The Devil's Cargo '48
Diabolique '96
The Doorbell Rang: A Nero Wolfe Mystery '01
The Drowning Pool '75
8mm '98
The Empty Beach '85
The End of the Affair '99 ▸
Entangled '93
Everybody Wins '90
Eye of the Killer '99
Face Down '97
Faceless '88
The Falcon in Hollywood '44
The Falcon in Mexico '44
The Falcon's Brother '42
False Witness '89
Farewell, My Lovely '75 ▸
Fearless '77
Fiction Makers '67
For Sale '98
Forbidden Games '95
Fourth Story '90 ▸
From Hollywood to Deadwood '89
Ginger '72
Girl Hunters '63
The Golden Spiders: A Nero Wolfe Mystery '00
Gone Baby Gone '07 ▸
Gotham '88 ▸
Grand Central Murder '42
The Great Plane Robbery '40
The Gumshoe Kid '89
A Gun, a Car, a Blonde '97
Gunfight at Comanche Creek '64
Hard to Forget '98
Hard to Hold '37
Hat Box Mystery '47
Hollywood Confidential '97
Hollywoodland '06
House of Mystery '34
Human Desires '97
Hustle '04
I Heart Huckabees '04
I, the Jury '82
In the Deep Woods '91
Indiscreet '98
Infamous Crimes '47
The Inner Circle '46
Intolerable Cruelty '03
The Invisible Avenger '58
The Jade Mask '45
Just Off Broadway '42
The Kennel Murder Case '33
The Kill '73
Kill Me Again '89
The King Murder '32
Kiss Kiss Bang Bang '05 ▸
Kiss Me Deadly '55 ▸
L.A. Dicks '05
La Rupture '70
Lady in Cement '68
Lady in the Lake '46
Larceny in her Heart '46
Last Days '05
The Late Show '77 ▸
The Long Goodbye '73 ▸
The Long Kiss Goodnight '96
Long Time Gone '86
Looking for Kitty '04
Lord of Illusions '95
The Lost Son '98
Love at Large '89 ▸
Love Walked In '97
A Low Down Dirty Shame '94
Magnum P.I.: Don't Eat the Snow in Hawaii '80
The Maltese Falcon '31 ▸
The Maltese Falcon '41 ▸
The Man Who Would Not Die '75
The Man Who Wouldn't Die '42
The Man with Bogart's Face '80
Margin for Murder '81
Marlowe '69
Meet Mr. Callaghan '54
Meet Sexton Blake '44
Meeting at Midnight '44
Michael Shayne: Private Detective '40
Midnight Limited '40
Mindstorm '01
Mirage '94
Missing Pieces '83
Mr. Moto in Danger Island '39
Mr. Moto Takes a Chance '38
Mr. Moto's Gamble '38
Mr. Moto's Last Warning '39 ▸
Mr. Wong, Detective '38
Mr. Wong in Chinatown '39
The Monkey's Mask '00
Moonlighting '85
Mortal Sins '90
Mr. Takes a Vacation '39
Murder by Death '76
Murder Is My Business '46
Murder, My Sweet '44 ▸
Murder over New York '40
Murderous Vision '91
Murders in the Doll House '79
Mysterious Mr. Moto '38
Mystery of Mr. Wong '39
Nature's Playmates '62
The Next Big Thing '02
Night Moves '75 ▸
On the Other Hand, Death '08
One of My Wives Is Missing '76
One Shoe Makes It Murder '82
Out of the Past '47 ▸
The Panther's Claw '42
Pas Tres Catholique '93
Perfect Lies '97
Peter Gunn '89
Phantom of Chinatown '40
Pier 23 '51
Poodle Springs '98
Powder Burn '96
A Prairie Home Companion '06
Radioactive Dreams '86
The Red Raven Kiss-Off '90
The Return of Boston Blackie '27
Return of Frank Cannon '80
The Right Temptation '00
Roaring City '51
Ryder P.I. '86
San Saba '08
Satan Met a Lady '36
Satan's Harvest '65
Scalp Merchant '77
The Scarlet Clue '45
Secret Agent 00-Soul '89
Sexton Blake and the Hooded Terror '38
Shaft '71 ▸
Shaft '00 ▸
Shaft in Africa '73
Shaft's Big Score '72
Shall We Dance? '04
Shamus '73
The Shanghai Cobra '45
Sheba, Baby '75
Shock to the System '06
Silver City '04
Sin City '05
The Singing Detective '86 ▸
The Singing Detective '03
Sleepers West '41
Slow Burn '86
Small Vices: A Spenser Mystery '99
Smile, Jenny, You're Dead '74
The Soft Kill '94
South Beach '92
Speedtrap '78
Spenser: A Savage Place '94
Spenser: Ceremony '93
Spenser: Pale Kings & Princes '94
Spenser: The Judas Goat '94
Stolen Kisses '68 ▸
Story of a Love Affair '50
The Strange Case of Dr. Rx '42
Strange Shadows in an Empty Room '76
Sunset Grill '92
Suspicious Minds '96
Sweet Lies '88
TekWar '94
Thank you, Mr. Moto '37
There's Something about Mary '98 ▸
They All Laughed '81
Thin Air '00
Think Fast, Mr. Moto '37
Third Degree Burn '89
Third Man Out: A Donald Strachey Mystery '05
Tick Tock '00 ▸
Ticket to a Crime '34
The Tiger Woman '45
Time to Kill '42
Tony Rome '67
Trade Secrets '86
TripleCross '85
Trixie '00
Twilight '98 ▸
The Two Jakes '90
2 Minutes Later '07
Ulterior Motives '92
Under Suspicion '92
The Undercover Woman '46
Uneasy Terms '48
Unsuitable Job for a Woman '82
Vegas '78
V.I. Warshawski '91
Victim of Desire '94
Vortex '81
Waikiki '80
Web of Deception '71
Where's Marlowe? '98
Who Framed Roger Rabbit '88 ▸
Witch Hunt '94
Zero Effect '97

Prohibition Gangs

see also *Gangs; Organized Crime; Period Piece: 1920s*

Al Capone '59 ▸
City Heat '84
Corsair '31
Defenders of the Law '31
The King of the Roaring '20s: The Story of Arnold Rothstein '61
Lady Killer '33 ▸
Miller's Crossing '90 ▸
Mobsters '91
Nitti: The Enforcer '88
Once Upon a Time in America '84 ▸
Public Enemy '31 ▸
The Roaring Twenties '39 ▸
Robin and the 7 Hoods '64
The St. Valentine's Day Massacre '67
The Untouchables '87 ▸

Prom

see also *Hell High School; School Daze*

Bart Got a Room '08
Carrie '76 ▸
Carrie '02
The Club '94
Cynthia '47
Drive Me Crazy '99
Footloose '84
Hello Mary Lou: Prom Night 2 '87
High School Musical 3: Senior Year '08
Jawbreaker '98
Never Been Kissed '99
The Night Before '88
Peggy Sue Got Married '86
Pretty in Pink '86
Prom Night '80
Prom Night '08
Prom Night 3: The Last Kiss '89
Prom Night 4: Deliver Us from Evil '91
Prom Queen '04
Queen Sized '08
The Rage: Carrie 2 '99
Rock, Rock, Rock '56
The Rocker '08
Saved! '04
She's All That '99
The Texas Chainsaw Massacre 4: The Next Generation '95
Trippin' '99
Urban Legends: Bloody Mary '05
Whatever It Takes '00

Propaganda

see also *Patriotism & Paranoia; Politics*

Air Force '43 ▸
Arsenal '29 ▸
The Atomic Cafe '82 ▸
Baltic Deputy '37 ▸
Behind the Rising Sun '43
The Black King '32
Blood on the Sun '45
Born American '86
Chapayev '34 ▸
China '43
The Commies Are Coming, the Commies Are Coming '57
Corregidor '43
Dangerous Hours '19
DC 9/11: Time of Crisis '04
Desperate Journey '42
The End of St. Petersburg '27 ▸
Fighting Seabees '44
The General Line '29 ▸
The Green Berets '68
Guadalcanal Diary '43
Hangmen Also Die '42
Invasion U.S.A. '52
Jud Suess '40 ▸
Mrs. Miniver '42 ▸
A Mormon Maid '17
No Greater Love '43
Passage to Marseilles '44 ▸
Que Viva Mexico '32 ▸
The Red Menace '49
Reefer Madness '38
Reunion in France '42
Rocket Attack U.S.A. '58
Shack Out on 101 '55 ▸
Strike '24 ▸
Teenage Devil Dolls '53
Ten Days That Shook the World '27 ▸
Ten Nights in a Bar-Room '31
The Thief '52

Threads '85 ▸
To the Shores of Tripoli '42
Tomorrow's Children '34
Trapped by the Mormons '22
Zvenigora '28 ▸

Prostitutes

see *Oldest Profession*

Protests

see also *Rebel With a Cause*

Born on the Fourth of July '89 ▸
Forrest Gump '94 ▸
Hairspray '88 ▸
In the Name of the Father '93 ▸
Journey Through Rosebud '72
The Long Walk Home '89 ▸
Malcolm X '92 ▸
Matewan '87 ▸
Michael Collins '96 ▸
Norma Rae '79 ▸
Panther '95
Red Kiss '85 ▸
Silkwood '83 ▸

Psychiatry

see *Shrinks*

Psychic Abilities

see also *Mystery & Suspense; Supernatural Comedies; Supernatural Horror*

Affinity '08
After Midnight '89
The Black Camel '31
Blink of an Eye '92
Carolina Moon '07
Carrie '76 ▸
Carrie '02
The Cell 2 '09
Clive Barker's Book of Blood '08
Close Your Eyes '02
The Dark '79
Dark Sanity '82
Dead Zone '83 ▸
The Dead Zone '02
Death Defying Acts '07
Deathtrap '82
Don't Look Now '73 ▸
Dream Man '94
Dreamscape '84
Everybody Says I'm Fine! '06
Fear '90
Final Destination '00
Final Move '06
Firestarter '84
Firestarter 2: Rekindled '02
First Snow '07
Forbidden Games '95
Friday the 13th, Part 7: The New Blood '88
The Frighteners '96
From Hell '01 ▸
Ghost '90 ▸
The Gift '00
The Haunting '63 ▸
Hearts in Atlantis '01
Imagining Argentina '04
In the Blood '06
L.A. Dicks '05
Last Rites '98
The Legend of Hell House '73 ▸
Life Without Dick '01
Love and Human Remains '93 ▸
The Men Who Stare at Goats '09
Mindstorm '01
Momentum '03
Mother of Tears '08
The Mothman Prophecies '02
Next '07
The Orphanage '07 ▸
Over Her Dead Body '08
Poltergeist '82 ▸
Poltergeist 2: The Other Side '86
Poltergeist 3 '88
The Psychic '68
Push '09
Ringu '98 ▸
Running on Karma '03
Scanner Cop '94
Scanner Cop 2: Volkin's Revenge '94
Scanners '81
Scanners 2: The New Order '91
Scanners 3: The Takeover '92
Scanners: The Showdown '94
Seance '00
Seance on a Wet Afternoon '64 ▸
Second Sight '89
Serenity '05 ▸
The Shining '80
The Sixth Sense '99 ▸
The Skeptic '09
Stephen King's Rose Red '02
Sworn to Justice '97
Thicker than Water '99
Trancers '84
Vibes '88
Voodoo Moon '05
What Women Want '00
Winning Girls Through Psychic Mind Control '02
The X Files: I Want to Believe '08

Psycho-Thriller

see also *Mystery & Suspense*

Absolute Power '97
Afraid of the Dark '92
After Darkness '85
After Midnight '89
Alligator Eyes '90
Almanac of Fall '85
Almost Dead '94
Alone With Her '07
Ambition '91
Anamorph '07
Anatomy of a Psycho '61
Apartment Complex '98
Apartment Zero '88 ▸
Apology '86
Are You Lonesome Tonight '92
The Arousers '70
The Art of Dying '90 ▸
The Astronaut's Wife '99
Asunder '99
Asylum '97
Asylum '05
The Attic '80
The Aura '05 ▸
Awakening of Candra '81
Baby Monitor: Sound of Fear '97
The Babysitter '80
The Backwoods '06
Bad Education '04 ▸
Bad Influence '90
The Bad Seed '56
Baffled '72
Banshee '06
Being at Home with Claude '92
Beneath '07
The Berlin Affair '85
Betrayal '74
Beware, My Lovely '52
Beyond Erotica '79
Bird of Prey '95
Birth '04
Bitter Moon '92
Bizarre '87
Black and White As Day and Night '78
Black Cadillac '03
Black Day Blue Night '95
The Black House '00
Black House '07
Blacklight '98
Blackout '07
Blackwoods '02
Bloodknot '95
Blow-Up '66 ▸
Body Chemistry 2: Voice of a Stranger '91
Bone Daddy '97
Boogeyman '05
Born for Hell '76
Bound '96
The Boys Club '96
Breach of Conduct '94
The Break Up '98
Breaking Point '94
The Bridesmaid '04
Bright Future '03 ▸
Brighton Strangler '45
A Brilliant Disguise '93
Brimstone & Treacle '82 ▸
The Broken '08
By the Blood of Others '73 ▸
Call Me '88
Cape Fear '61 ▸
Cape Fear '91 ▸
Captive '97
Captivity '07
The Case of the Frightened Lady '39
Cat's Play '74
Cause for Alarm '51
Cellular '04
Circumstances Unknown '95
Civic Duty '06
The Clearing '04 ▸
Close Your Eyes '02
Closer and Closer '96
Cold Heaven '92
Cold Light of Day '95
Cold Room '84
Collateral '04 ▸
The Collector '65 ▸
The Comfort of Strangers '91 ▸
Conflict '45 ▸
The Corporate Ladder '97
The Courtyard '95
Crescendo '69
The Crew '95
Crimetime '96
Cronicas '04
The Crush '93
Cul de Sac '66 ▸
Cupid '96
Cure '97 ▸
Curse of the Stone Hand '64
Cyberstalker '96
Daddy's Gone A-Hunting '69 ▸
Dangerous Pursuit '89
Dangerous Touch '94
A Dark Adapted Eye '93 ▸
Dark Honeymoon '08
Dark Mirror '46 ▸
The Dark Past '49 ▸
The Dark Ride '78
Dark Water '02
Dark Waters '44
Darkroom '90
Day of Wrath '43 ▸
The Day the Sun Turned Cold '94 ▸
Dead As a Doorman '85
Dead Calm '89 ▸
Deadbolt '92
Deadly Daphne's Revenge '93
Deadly Game '82
Deadly Hero '75 ▸
Deadly Lessons '94
Deadly Sunday '82
Death Benefit '96
Deceit '06
Deceiver '97
Deconstructing Sarah '94
Deep Down '94
Depraved '98
Derailed '05
Deranged '87
Desperate Measures '98
Desperate Prey '94
Devil Doll '36 ▸
Devil in the Flesh '98
Diabolique '55 ▸
Diabolique '96
Diary '06
Diary of a Serial Killer '97
Disturbance '89
Disturbed '90
Disturbia '07
Dogville '03
Dolores Claiborne '94 ▸
Donkey Punch '08
The Donor '94
Don't Answer the Phone '80
Don't Talk to Strangers '94
Doppelganger: The Evil Within '90
Dot.Kill '05
Down, Out and Dangerous '95
Dream Lover '85
Dream Lover '93
Dressed for Death '74
The Drifter '88
Dynasty of Fear '72
8mm '98
Entangled '93
Every Breath '93
Evil Eyes '04
Evil Has a Face '96
Evil Judgment '85
The Ex '96
Exorcist: The Beginning '04
The Experiment '01
Eye of the Beholder '99
Eye of the Storm '91
Eyes of the Beholder '92
Fabled '02
Facade '98
Facing the Enemy '00
Fair Game '89
The Fall '98
Fallen '97
Falling Down '93
The Fan '96
Fatal Attraction '87 ▸
A Fatal Inversion '92
Fatally Yours '95
Fear '46
Fear '96
The Fear Inside '92
Fear X '03 ▸
Final Approach '91
The Final Cut '04
Final Move '06
First Snow '07
The Flaming Urge '53
Flinch '94
Flower & Snake '04
Force of Evil '77
The Forgotten '04
The 4th Floor '99
Fracture '07
Freeway '88
Freeway '95
Freeze Frame '04
Frenchman's Farm '87
Fright '56
Funny Games '97
Funny Games '07 ▸
Gallowglass '95 ▸
The Game '97 ▸
Gaslight '44 ▸
The Gingerbread Man '97
Girl in Black Stockings '57
Girly '70
The Glass House '01
Godsend '04
Gross Misconduct '93
The Grudge '04
Half Broken Things '07
Half Light '05
Hallucination '67
The Hand '60
The Hand that Rocks the Cradle '92
Hard Candy '06
Hate Crime '05
Haunted '95
Headspace '02
Hellbent '88
Hellbent '04
Hidden '05 ▸
Hide and Seek '05
High Tension '03
Highway Hitcher '98
The Hitch-Hiker '53 ▸
The Hitcher '07
The Hole '01
Homecoming '09
Honeymoon '87
House of Darkness '48
House of Games '87 ▸
House of Wax '05
The House on Todville Road '95
Hush '98
Hush, Hush, Sweet Charlotte '65 ▸
I Know Who Killed Me '07
I Love Your Work '03
I Never Promised You a Rose Garden '77 ▸
Identity '03
I'll Sleep When I'm Dead '03 ▸
I'm Not Scared '03
In a Glass Cage '86
In Dreams '98
In the Heat of Passion '91
In the Heat of Passion 2: Unfaithful '94
In the Lake of the Woods '96
In the Winter Dark '98
The Incident '67
Inevitable Grace '94
Innocent Prey '88
Inside '06
Intimate Stranger '91
Intimate Strangers '04 ▸
Invasion of Privacy '96
Investigation '79
The Invisible Ghost '41
Irresistible '06
It's All About Love '03
Jack Be Nimble '94
The Jacket '05
Jacob's Ladder '90
Jade '95
Jealousy '99
Jericho Mansions '03
Joshua '07 ▸
Joy Ride '01 ▸
Joyride '97
Juggernaut '37
Julia and Julia '87
The Juror '96
Kaaterskill Falls '01
Kill by Inches '99
The Killer Inside Me '76
The Killing Floor '06
The Killing Mind '90
King of the Ants '03
A Kiss Goodnight '94
Kiss of a Killer '93
Knife in the Water '62 ▸
Knight Moves '93
Kontroll '03 ▸
La Moustache '05
La Rupture '70
La Vengeance d'une Femme '89
Lady in Waiting '94
Laser Moon '92
Last Breath '96
Last Life in the Universe '03
The Last of Sheila '73
The Last Seduction '94 ▸
Le Boucher '69 ▸
Leave Her to Heaven '45 ▸
Lemming '05
Les Bonnes Femmes '60 ▸
Letters from a Killer '98
The Limbic Region '96
Little Fish '05 ▸
Living Hell: A Japanese Chainsaw Massacre '00
Living in Peril '97
The Lodger '09
Lonely Hearts '06
Love '05
Love, Cheat & Steal '93
Love Crimes '92
Love Is a Gun '94
Love, Lies and Murder '91
The Machine '96
The Maddening '95
Madhouse '04
Magic '78
The Maid '05
Make Haste to Live '54
Man on Fire '04
Man on the Eiffel Tower '48 ▸
The Man Who Haunted Himself '70
The Manchurian Candidate '04 ▸
The Mark '61 ▸
Marnie '64 ▸
Match Point '05 ▸
Maternal Instincts '96
Mayalunta '86
The Meal '75
Mean Season '85
Memories of Murder '90
Merci pour le Chocolat '00 ▸
Midnight Edition '93
Midnight Fear '90
Midnight Lace '60
Midnight Tease '94
The Mind Benders '63
Mind Games '89
Mind Lies '00
Misbegotten '98
Misery '90 ▸
Mrs. Munck '95
Mr. Brooks '07
Mortal Sins '90
Mortal Sins '92
The Most Dangerous Game '32 ▸
Mother '94
Moving Targets '87
Murder by Numbers '02
Murphy's Law '86
My Blood Runs Cold '65
My Brother Has Bad Dreams '72
My Very Best Friend '96
A Name for Evil '70
Nature of the Beast '94
The Net '95
Net Games '03
Never Talk to Strangers '95
The Night Caller '97
The Night of the Following Day '69
Night Train to Venice '93
The Night Walker '64
Nightmare at Bittercreek '91
Nightwatch '96
November '05 ▸
Number One Fan '94
The Number 23 '07
The Offence '73 ▸
The Omen '06
One Good Turn '95
One Night Stand '78
Open Water '03 ▸
Opposing Force '87
Outrage '93
Pacific Heights '90 ▸
The Paint Job '93
Panic Station '82
Paparazzi '04
The Paperboy '94
Paranoia '98
The Passion of Anna '70 ▸
A Passion to Kill '94
Peephole '93
Peeping Tom '60 ▸
The Penthouse '92
Perfect Alibi '94
Perfect Assassins '98
Perfect Stranger '07
Perfect Strangers '03
Perfect Tenant '99
Performance '70 ▸
Play Misty for Me '71 ▸
Playgirl Killer '66
Playmaker '94
Poison Ivy '92
Portrait in Terror '66
Posed for Murder '89
Posers '02
Possessed '05
Postmortem '98
Powder Burn '96
Power 98 '96
Praying Mantis '83
Premonition '07
Pretty Poison '68 ▸
Prey of the Chameleon '91
Primer '04 ▸
Profile for Murder '96
Psycho 3 '86
Psychomania '63
The Punisher '04
A Pure Formality '94
Rage '95
Raising Cain '92
Ransom '96 ▸
Reason to Die '90
Red Lights '04 ▸
Red Riding Hood '03
A Reflection of Fear '72
Reincarnation '05
Relentless '89
Repulsion '65 ▸
Requiem for Murder '99
Retribution '06
Ricochet '91 ▸
Riding the Bullet '04
The Ring 2 '05
Ringu '98 ▸
Ringu 2 '99
Rituals '79
Room to Let '49
Rorret '87 ▸
Sabotage '36 ▸
Savage Abduction '73

Saw '04
Seance '00
Seconds '66 ▸
Secret Beyond the Door '48
Secret Ceremony '69
Secret Games '92
Secret Games 2: The Escort '93
Secret Games 3 '94
Secret Smile '05
Secret Window '04
The Secretary '94
Secrets of Three Hungry Wives '78
Seduced '85
Seduced by Evil '94
The Seduction '82
Sensation '94
Separate Lives '94
Serial Killer '95
Seven '95 ▸
The Seventh Floor '93
Shadow Puppets '07
Shadows in the Storm '88
Shallow Grave '94
Sharon's Secret '95
Shattered Image '98
Shuttle '09
Siesta '87
The Silence of the Lambs '91 ▸
Single White Female '92
Single White Female 2: The Psycho '05
The Sister-in-Law '95
The Sixth Sense '99 ▸
Skinned Alive '08
Sleeping with the Enemy '91
Slow Burn '05
A Small Killing '81
A Snake of June '02
Snapdragon '93
The Soft Kill '94
Someone Behind the Door '71
Someone to Die For '95
Sorry, Haters '05
Sorry, Wrong Number '48 ▸
Sorry, Wrong Number '89
The Soul Guardians '98
Spartan '04 ▸
Spider Forest '04
Spiral '07
The Spiral Staircase '46 ▸
Spiral Staircase '75
Stalked '94
Stalking Laura '93
Stardust Memories '80
Stay '05
The Stepfather '87 ▸
Stepfather 2: Make Room for Daddy '89
Stepfather 3: Father's Day '92
Stigmata '99
Storm '87
Strange Illusion '45
The Stranger '87 ▸
Stranger by Night '94
A Stranger in Town '95
The Strangers '08
Striking Distance '93
Stripteaser '95
Suspect Zero '04
Suspended Animation '02
Suture '93
Svengali '31 ▸
Svengali '83
Sweet Killing '93
Taboo '02
Tails You Live, Heads You're Dead '95
Taking Lives '04
Talking Head '92
Tall, Dark and Deadly '95
A Taste for Killing '92
Tattoo '81
Telling Lies '06
The Temp '93
The Tenant '76 ▸
Terrified '94
Thesis '96
Thicker Than Water '93
36 Hours '64 ▸
Thr3e '07
301/302 '95
The Three Lives of Karen '97
Through a Glass Darkly '61 ▸
Through the Eyes of a Killer '92
The Tie That Binds '95
Till the End of the Night '94
Timebomb '91
To Play or to Die '91
Tortured '08
Tower of Terror '42
Trapped '89
Trapped '02
Trauma '62
Tryst '94
Tunnel Vision '95
Twisted '04
Twisted Love '95
The Two Mrs. Carrolls '47
Undertow '95
Unforgettable '96
Unlawful Entry '92
Unspeakable '02
The Vanishing '88 ▸
Vengeance Is Mine '79 ▸
Vengeance of the Dead '01
Victim of Love '91
Violated '53
Voyage '93
Wait until Dark '67 ▸
Web of Deceit '90
What Ever Happened To... '93
When a Stranger Calls '06
When Hell Was in Session '82 ▸
When the Bough Breaks '93
When the Dark Man Calls '95
Where Are the Children? '85
While I Live '47
Who Killed Bambi? '03
Wicked '98
Wicked Ways '99
Wicker Park '04
Wild Side '95
The Wind '87
A Woman Hunted '03
Woman in the Window '44 ▸
Yella '07 ▸
You'll Like My Mother '72
Young Adam '03 ▸
The Young Poisoner's Handbook '94 ▸

Psychotics/Sociopaths

***see also** Roommates from Hell*
Accidental Meeting '93
Albino Alligator '96
Angel Face '52 ▸
Apartment Zero '88 ▸
The Assassination of Jesse James by the Coward Robert Ford '07 ▸
The Assassination of Richard Nixon '05
The Avenger '60
Bad Ronald '74 ▸
The Bad Seed '56
Badlands '74 ▸
Ball of Wax '03
Bellamy '81
Berserk! '67
Black Eliminator '78
Black Panther '77
Black Pit of Dr. M '47
Blind Side '93
Blind Vision '91
Blue Steel '90
Body Bags '93
Bone Daddy '97
Born for Hell '76
Born Killers '05
The Boston Strangler '68
Boxing Helena '93
The Boys '98 ▸
The Boys Next Door '85
Breakdown '96 ▸
Broken Arrow '95
The Butcher Boy '97 ▸
The Cable Guy '96
Cape Fear '61 ▸
Cape Fear '91 ▸
The Centerfold Girls '74
City Killer '87
Clay Pigeons '98
Cold Creek Manor '03
Cold Eyes of Fear '70
Cold Steel '87
Con Air '97 ▸
Consenting Adults '92
Crimes of Dr. Mabuse '32 ▸
The Crush '93
Damned River '89
Dario Argento's Trauma '93
The Dark Knight '08 ▸
The Dark Past '49 ▸
The Dark Ride '78
Dead As a Doorman '85
Dead Boyz Can't Fly '93
Deadbolt '92
Deadly Daphne's Revenge '93
Deadly Game '82
Death Benefit '96
Death of a Soldier '85
Death Sentence '74
Dee Snider's Strangeland '98
Demolition Man '93
Demon Hunter '88
The Dentist '96
Deranged '74 ▸
Deranged '87
Desperate Measures '98
Desperate Motives '92
Diary '06
Diary of a Teenage Hitchhiker '82
Dr. Giggles '92
Don't Answer the Phone '80
Don't Talk to Strangers '94
Doppelganger: The Evil Within '90
Dot.Kill '05
Down in the Valley '05
Down, Out and Dangerous '95
The Drifter '88
Escape Velocity '99
The Escort '97
Ex-Cop '93
Eye of God '97 ▸
Eyes of the Beholder '92
Fade to Black '80
Fair Game '82
Falling Down '93
The Fan '81
The Fan '96
Fast Gun '93
Fatal Attraction '87 ▸
Fear '88
Fear '96
Fear City '85
The Fear Inside '92
The Fiance '96
The Fiend Who Walked the West '58
The Fool Killer '65
Force of Evil '77
Frayed '07
From Dusk Till Dawn '95
The Front Line '06
Funny Games '07 ▸
Gallowglass '95 ▸
The Gingerbread Man '97
Girl in Black Stockings '57
The Glimmer Man '96
Gloria '98
Guardian Angel '94
Guilty as Sin '93
Halloween: H20 '98 ▸
Headless Body in Topless Bar '96
Heat '95 ▸
Helter Skelter '76
Helter Skelter Murders '71
Hide '08
High Tension '03
Highway Hitcher '98
The Hitcher '07
Homage '95
Homer and Eddie '89
Honeymoon '87
The Hostage '67
Hot Potato '76
Hot Touch '82
House of Terror '72
The Housekeeper '86
Hush '98
I Know What You Did Last Summer '97 ▸
I Still Know What You Did Last Summer '98
Ichi the Killer '01
In Dreams '98
In the Lake of the Woods '96
In the Line of Fire '93 ▸
In the Mouth of Madness '95
Invasion of Privacy '96
The Invisible Terror '63
Joy Ride 2: Dead Ahead '08
Kalifornia '93
Keys to Tulsa '96
The Killer Inside Me '76
The Killer Inside Me '10
Killing Obsession '94
Killing Zoe '94
Killzone '85
The King '05
Kiss the Girls '97
The Last House on the Left '09
Lightning Bolt '67
The Lightship '86
The Little Girl Who Lives down the Lane '76
Live Wire '92
Lonely Hearts '06
Lunatic '91
The Machine '96
The Mad Bomber '72
Mad Dog Killer '77
The Mad Executioners '65
Mademoiselle '66
A Man in Uniform '93
Maniac Warriors '88
Maternal Instincts '96
Meet the Deedles '98
Metro '96
Midnight 2: Sex, Death, and Videotape '93
Midnight Edition '93
Midnight Fear '90
Midnight Ride '92
Misbegotten '98
Mommie Dearest '81
Mondo Balordo '64
Most Wanted '76
Mother's Boys '94
Motor Home Massacre '05
Moving Targets '87
Murder by Numbers '02
Murder Elite '86
Murderlust '86
The Naked Flame '68
Natural Enemy '96
The Neighbor '93
The Neighbor No. Thirteen '05
No Country for Old Men '07 ▸
Office Killer '97
One Good Turn '95
Pacific Heights '90 ▸
The Paperboy '94
Past Midnight '92
Perfect Family '92
Perfect Victims '87
Perfume: The Story of a Murderer '06
Play Nice '92
Playgirl Killer '66
Poison Ivy '92
Pretty Poison '68 ▸
Prime Time Murder '92
Prom Night '08
Psycho '60 ▸
Psycho 2 '83
Psycho 3 '86
Psycho 4: The Beginning '90
Psycho Girls '86
Psychos in Love '87
Pulse '03
Quake '92
The Rage '96
Rampage '87
Relentless '89
Repulsion '65 ▸
Reservoir Dogs '92 ▸
Resurrection Man '97
Retroactive '97
The Rich Man's Wife '96
Ricochet '91 ▸
Ripley's Game '02 ▸
The River Wild '94
The Road Killers '95
Roadkill '89
The Sadist '63
Sarah's Child '96
Savage Abduction '73
Saw 2 '05
Saw 3 '06
Scream '96 ▸
Scream 2 '97 ▸
Scream 3 '00
The Sea Wolf '41 ▸
Secret Smile '05
Secret Window '04
The Secretary '94
The Seduction '82
See No Evil '06
Seven '95 ▸
Seven Hours to Judgment '88
The Seventh Floor '93
Shattered '07
The Shining '80
Shutter Island '09 ▸
Shuttle '09
The Silencer '92
Single White Female '92
Single White Female 2: The Psycho '05
The Sister-in-Law '95
The Sitter '07
Skinner '93
Small Kill '93
Someone Behind the Door '71
Speed '94 ▸
Speed 2: Cruise Control '97
Stalked '94
Starved '97
The Stepfather '87 ▸
The Stepfather '09
Stepfather 2: Make Room for Daddy '89
Stepfather 3: Father's Day '92
Still Life '92
Stripped to Kill '87
Stripteaser '95
Sugarhouse '07
Suspect Zero '04
Suspicious River '00
Sweet Hostage '75
Tainted Blood '93
Taking Lives '04
The Taking of Beverly Hills '91
The Talented Mr. Ripley '99
Tall, Dark and Deadly '95
Ted & Venus '93
The Temp '93
The Tenant '76 ▸
Tetsuo: The Iron Man '92
A Thin Line Between Love and Hate '96
Thirteenth Day of Christmas '85
Three the Hard Way '74
3000 Miles to Graceland '01
Through the Eyes of a Killer '92
To Die For '95 ▸
The Tripper '06
Truth or Consequences, N.M. '97
Turbulence '96
Twin Peaks: Fire Walk with Me '92
The Two Mrs. Carrolls '47
U-Turn '97 ▸
Ultraviolet '91
Unlawful Entry '92
Unspeakable '02
Urban Legend '98
The Vanishing '93
Vice Squad '82
Violence at Noon '66 ▸
Voyage '93
What Ever Happened to Baby Jane? '62 ▸
When a Stranger Calls '06
When a Stranger Calls Back '93
Whispers '89
White Heat '49 ▸
With a Friend Like Harry '00 ▸
The Witness '99
Wolf Creek '05
Writer's Block '91
The Young Poisoner's Handbook '94 ▸
Zero Degrees Kelvin '95
The Zombie Army '93

Publicists

***see also** Behind the Scenes*
Amelia Earhart: The Final Flight '94
America's Sweethearts '01
The Big Circus '59
Breaking News '04
Cursed '04
For Your Consideration '06
Four's a Crowd '38
Gideon's Daughter '05
A Girl Cut in Two '07
Go West, Young Man '36
The Great Buck Howard '09
The Half Naked Truth '32
Hancock '08
The Harder They Fall '56 ▸
Jersey Girl '04
Jiminy Glick in LaLa Wood '05
Loving You '57
Mad About Music '38 ▸
The Nines '07 ▸
The Parent Trap '98
People I Know '02
Phone Booth '02
Sweet Smell of Success '57 ▸
Win a Date with Tad Hamilton! '04

Puerto Rico

The Apostate '98
Assassins '95
D.R.E.A.M. Team '99
Feel the Noise '07
Frankenstein Meets the Space Monster '65
Illegal Tender '07
Nanny McPhee 2 '10
Ship Ahoy '42
Sunstorm '01

Punk Rock

***see also** Rock Flicks*
Battle Heater '89
Born to Lose '99
Control '07
Decline of Western Civilization 1 '81 ▸
End of the Century: The Story of the Ramones '03 ▸
The Filth and the Fury '99
Hard Core Logo '96
Ladies and Gentlemen, the Fabulous Stains '82
Repo Man '83 ▸
Rock 'n' Roll High School '79 ▸
Rock 'n' Roll High School Forever '91
Sex & Drugs & Rock & Roll '10
Sid & Nancy '86 ▸
Times Square '80
24 Hour Party People '01
What We Do Is Secret '07

Puppets

***see also** Killer Toys; Toys*
The Adventures of Pinocchio '96
Alice in Wonderland '50
Along with Ghosts '69
Curse of the Puppet Master: The Human Experiment '98
The Dark Crystal '82 ▸
Devil Doll '64
Dolls '02 ▸
Extreme Movie '08
Gepetto '00
The Great Gabbo '29
The Great Rupert '50 ▸
Lili '53 ▸
Magic '78
Meet the Feebles '89
MirrorMask '05
The Muppets' Wizard of Oz '05
100 Monsters '68
Paper Heart '09
Pinocchio '40 ▸
Pinocchio '02
Puppet Master '89
Puppet Master 2 '90
Puppet Master 4 '93
Puppet Master 5: The Final Chapter '94
A Rat's Tale '98
Retro Puppet Master '99
Saw '04
The Sound of Music '65 ▸
Spook Warfare '68
Team America: World Police '04 ▸
3 Extremes 2 '02

▸ = *rated three bones or higher*

Pure Ego Vehicles

***see also** Big-Budget Bombs; Rock Stars on Film*

The Adventures of Ford Fairlane '90
Air America '90
Assault of the Rebel Girls '59
The Big One '98
Boom! '68
Charade '53
Conan the Destroyer '84
The Dead Pool '88
Dee Snider's Strangeland '98
Dirty Love '05
Fire Down Below '97
Foolish '99
Get Carter '00
Gummo '97
Harlem Nights '89
Hello, Dolly! '69
Hudson Hawk '91
I Got the Hook-Up '98
The Jazz Singer '80
Last Action Hero '93
Le Repos du Guerrier '62
Marie Antoinette '38
Modern Love '90
On Deadly Ground '94
Private Parts '96
Purple Rain '84
Rambo 3 '88
Richard Petty Story '72
Running out of Luck '86
The Scarlet Letter '95
Sidekicks '93
SnakeEater '89
Sophia Loren: Her Own Story '80
Staying Alive '83
Sweet Country Road '83
Tarzan, the Ape Man '81
Thank Your Lucky Stars '43 ►
A Thin Line Between Love and Hate '96
Torch Song '53
200 Motels '71
Under the Cherry Moon '86
Vampire in Brooklyn '95
Waterworld '95
What Comes Around '85
Wildcats '86
The Wizard of Speed and Time '88
Yes, Giorgio '82

Queens

***see** Royalty; Royalty, British; Royalty, French; Royalty, Russian*

Rabbi

***see also** Clergymen; Judaism*

Before the Rain '94 ►
Bulletproof Monk '03
The Chosen '77
The Deal '08
Enemies, a Love Story '89 ►
The Frisco Kid '79
God on Trial '08
Hearts of War '07
Hello Goodbye '08
In the Presence of Mine Enemies '97
Loving Leah '09
Lucky Number Slevin '06
Outside Chance of Maximillian Glick '88
The Quarrel '93
Rasputin '85 ►
Rasputin and the Empress '33 ►
The Secrets '07
A Serious Man '09 ►
Stolen Summer '02
Time of Favor '00
The Unborn '09

Rabbits

Alice '88 ►
Alice in Wonderland '51 ►
Alice in Wonderland '99
Bambi '42 ►
Bunny Whipped '06
Donnie Darko '01 ►
Fatal Attraction '87 ►
The Geisha Boy '58
Get to Know Your Rabbit '72
Hank and Mike '08
Harvey '50 ►
Hoodwinked '05 ►
Igor '08
Inland Empire '06
The Last Mimzy '07
Mona Lisa '86 ►
Monty Python and the Holy Grail '75 ►
Nasty Rabbit '64
Night of the Lepus '72
Phenomenon '96
Roger & Me '89 ►
Space Jam '96
Wallace & Gromit in The Curse of the Were-Rabbit '05 ►
Watership Down '78
Who Framed Roger Rabbit '88 ►

Race Against Time

Acceptable Risks '86
Alien Space Avenger '91
The Andromeda Strain '71
Andromedia '00
Apollo 13 '95 ►
Around the World in 80 Days '04
Balto '95
Bitter Harvest '81 ►
Black Dawn '05
Blown Away '94
The Borrowers '97
Broken Arrow '95
Bronson '09
Cellular '04
Chain Reaction '80
The China Syndrome '79 ►
Collateral '04 ►
Coma '78 ►
Convicted '04
The Corporation '96
Daylight '96
Death Note 3: L, Change the World '08
Death Trance '05
Deja Vu '06
D.O.A. '49 ►
D.O.A. '88
Eagle Eye '08
88 Minutes '08
Escape from L.A. '96
Fail-Safe '64 ►
Free Willy 2: The Adventure Home '95
Free Willy 3: The Rescue '97
Germicide '74
Grand Tour: Disaster in Time '92
Hell Commandos '69
I Wouldn't Be in Your Shoes '48
I'll Be Home for Christmas '98
In Pursuit of Honor '95
Independence Day '96 ►
Jet Over the Atlantic '59
Killer on Board '77
The Killer That Stalked New York '47
Last Dance '96
Last Flight Out: A True Story '90
Lorenzo's Oil '92 ►
Nezulla the Rat Monster '02
Nick of Time '95
Octopussy '83
Once Upon a Forest '93
Outbreak '94 ►
Panic in Echo Park '77
Panic in the Streets '50 ►
The Peacemaker '97
The Princess Diaries 2: Royal Engagement '04
Prisoner in the Middle '74
Pursuit '72 ►
Race Against Time '00
A Rat's Tale '98
Return to Paradise '98 ►
Robot in the Family '94
Saigon '47
Saw '04
Shiri '99
The Silver Streak '34
Somebody Has to Shoot the Picture '90 ►
Sudden Death '95
The Taking of Beverly Hills '91
Terror Street '54
Terror Taxi '04
Things to Do in Denver When You're Dead '95 ►
Time Lock '57
Time Without Pity '57
Too Many Winners '47
Tramp, Tramp, Tramp '26
TripFall '00
True Crime '99
Twister '96
Tycus '98
Unborn but Forgotten '02
WarGames '83

Radio

***see also** Mass Media*

The Accidental Husband '08
The Adventures of Ford Fairlane '90
Airheads '94
Alibi for Murder '36
American Graffiti '73 ►
American Nightmare '00
Amy's O '02
Bad Channels '92
The Brave One '07
Break of Dawn '88
Breakfast in Hollywood '46
Buck Benny Rides Again '40
Bye Bye, Love '94
Cadillac Records '08 ►
Carefree '38 ►
Choose Me '84 ►
Citizens Band '77 ►
City in Panic '86
Comfort and Joy '84 ►
The Couch Trip '87
Danger on the Air '38
The Day Silence Died '98
Dead Air '94
Dirty Mind of Young Sally '72
The Fisher King '91 ►
FM '78
The Fog '78
Freeway '88
Frequency '00
Girls Night Out '83
Good Morning, Vietnam '87 ►
The Great American Broadcast '41 ►
Grosse Pointe Blank '97 ►
Hollywood Hotel '37
The Hucksters '47 ►
I'll Believe You '07
The Jackpot '50
Joe Dirt '01
The Key Man '57
Laser Moon '92
Look Who's Laughing '41
Love Serenade '96
The Man Who Came to Dinner '41 ►
Midnight Confessions '95
Mr. Rock 'n' Roll: The Alan Freed Story '99
My Blue Heaven '50
My Dream Is Yours '49
The Next Voice You Hear '50
The Night Caller '97
The Night Listener '06
Night Rhythms '92
The Night Watchman '02
No Trace '50
Old Barn Dance '38
On the Air '95
On the Air Live with Captain Midnight '79
Once Upon a Honeymoon '42
Open House '86
Our America '02
Outside Ozona '98
People Are Funny '46
People's Choice '46
The Phantom Broadcast '33
Pirate Radio '09
Play Misty for Me '71 ►
Pontypool '09
Pot o' Gold '41
Power 98 '96
A Prairie Home Companion '06
Private Parts '96
Psycho 4: The Beginning '90
Pump Up the Volume '90
Rachel River '87
Radio Days '87 ►
Radioland Murders '94
Rebecca of Sunnybrook Farm '38
The Republic of Love '03
Requiem for Murder '99
Rude '96
Say It With Songs '29
Sexual Response '92
The Singing Kid '36
Sleepless in Seattle '93 ►
The Sleepy Time Gal '01
Straight Talk '92
Strike Up the Band '40
Talk Radio '88 ►
Talk to Me '07
Telling Lies in America '96
There Goes Kelly '45
Torch Singer '33
The Truth about Cats and Dogs '96 ►
Tune in Tomorrow '90
20 Years After '08
The Unsuspected '47
Up in the Air '40
The Warriors '79
When the Dark Man Calls '95
Whistling in Brooklyn '43
Who Done It? '42
Winchell '98

Rags to Riches

***see also** Cinderella Stories; Price of Fame; Wrong Side of the Tracks*

The Abe Lincoln of Ninth Avenue '39
Aladdin '92 ►
All the King's Men '49 ►
The Amorous Adventures of Moll Flanders '65
Annie '82
B.A.P.'s '97
Better Late Than Never '83
The Beverly Hillbillies '93
Blank Check '93
Body Slam '87
Boogie Nights '97 ►
Breaking Glass '80
Brewster's Millions '85
The Buddy Holly Story '78 ►
Callie and Son '81
Can You Hear the Laughter? The Story of Freddie Prinze '79
Christmas in July '40 ►
Cinderella Man '05 ►
Citizen Kane '41 ►
Coal Miner's Daughter '80 ►
The Cookout '04
Covergirl '83
Craig's Wife '36 ►
Daddy Long Legs '55 ►
The Damned Don't Cry '50
Dangerous When Wet '53
Darling '65 ►
Dodsworth '36 ►
Dreamer '79
Drifting Souls '32
EDtv '99
Emperor Jones '33
Envy '04
Evita '96
Fifth Avenue Girl '39
Film Geek '06
Footlight Parade '33 ►
For Richer, for Poorer '92
Forever Amber '47
G '02
Give a Girl a Break '53
Goal! The Dream Begins '06
Great Expectations '97
The Great Rupert '50 ►
Hero '92 ►
Honeyboy '82
The Hudsucker Proxy '93 ►
I Love Melvin '53
It Could Happen to You '94
Jailhouse Rock '57 ►
The Jerk '79
Jimmy Hollywood '94
Joseph Andrews '77
Kept Husbands '31
Kipps '41 ►
La Vie Est Belle '87
Lady for a Day '33 ►
Lady Grey '82
The Last American Hero '73 ►
The Last Laugh '24 ►
Laurel & Hardy: Below Zero '30
Lenny '74 ►
Lili '53 ►
Little Lord Fauntleroy '36 ►
Little Lord Fauntleroy '80
Little Lord Fauntleroy '95
Livin' Large '91
Lots of Luck '85
Love Nest '51
Lucky Partners '40
The Mambo Kings '92 ►
The Manions of America '81
Mannequin '37
Meet John Doe '41 ►
Memoirs of a Geisha '05
Million Dollar Baby '04 ►
A Million to Juan '94
Miss Melody Jones '73
Mrs. Parkington '44
Mrs. Winterbourne '96
Mr. Billion '77
Money for Nothing '93
My Fair Lady '64 ►
New York's Finest '87
The Object of Beauty '91 ►
One in a Million: The Ron LeFlore Story '78
Only One Night '42
Overnight '03 ►
The Patsy '64
The Pearl '48 ►
Peddlin' in Society '47
Possessed '31
Power '34
Pride of the Clan '18
The Prince and the Pauper '37 ►
The Prince and the Pauper '78
The Prince and the Pauper '01
The Prince and the Showgirl '57
Princess Tam Tam '35 ►
Pygmalion '38 ►
Rebecca of Sunnybrook Farm '17
The Return of the Beverly Hillbillies '81
Rocky '76 ►
Rudo y Cursi '09
Scarlet Dawn '32
Scruples '80
The Secret of My Success '87
Sepia Cinderella '47
The Sin of Harold Diddlebock '47
The Sin of Madelon Claudet '31 ►
Sing Your Worries Away '42
Slumdog Millionaire '08 ►
Speak Easily '32
The Stars Fell on Henrietta '94
The Stork Club '45
Straight Talk '92
Striker's Mountain '87
Sweet Adeline '26
Sweet Hearts Dance '88
The Tall Guy '89 ►
Tennessee Stallion '78
There Will Be Blood '07 ►
They Had to See Paris '29
Three Coins in the Fountain '54
The Toast of New Orleans '50
Toast of New York '37 ►
Trading Places '83
Trois Couleurs: Blanc '94 ►
The Unsinkable Molly Brown '64 ►
Up Close and Personal '96 ►
Vanity Fair '04
What Price Hollywood? '32 ►
Willy Wonka & the Chocolate Factory '71 ►
A Woman of Substance '84
Working Girl '88 ►
Ziegfeld Girl '41 ►

Rape

***see also** Sexual Abuse*

The Accused '88 ►
Act of Vengeance '74
The Adventurers '70
All About Lily Chou-Chou '01 ►
American Commandos '84
American Gun '05
And Justice for All '79
Awakening of Candra '81
Backlash '86
Bad Lieutenant '92 ►
Baise Moi '00
Bandit Queen '94
Bastard out of Carolina '96
The Beast Within '82
Because of the Cats '74
Black Heat '76
Blackrock '97
Blind Justice '86
Blue Desert '91 ►
Body Shots '99
Bordertown '06
Born Innocent '74
Boys Don't Cry '99 ►
Broken Badge '85 ►
A Brother's Kiss '97
Bullies '86
Caged Heat 2: Stripped of Freedom '94
Caged Terror '72
Cannibal Holocaust '80
The Casino Job '08
Cast the First Stone '89
Casualties of War '89 ►
The Center of the World '01
Certain Sacrifice '80
Chain Gang Women '72
Chaos '05
Class of 1984 '82
A Clockwork Orange '71 ►
Code of Honor '82
Convicted '86
Coward of the County '81
Cracker: Men Should Weep '94
Cronicas '04
Dead Man Walking '95 ►
Deadline Assault '90
Deadly Daphne's Revenge '93
Deadly Darling '85
Deadly Twins '85
Death and the Maiden '94 ►
Death Blow '87
Death Wish '74
Deep in the Heart '83
Deliverance '72 ►
Demented '80
Demon Seed '77 ►
Derailed '05
Descent '07
Desolation Angels '95
The Desperados '70
Devil Hunter '08
Diary of a Lost Girl '29 ►
Diary of a Teenage Hitchhiker '82
Divided We Stand '00
Dogville '03
Emmanuelle's Daughter '79
The Entity '83
Extremities '86
An Eye for an Eye '95
Female Prisoner: Caged '83
Final Justice '94
Flesh and Blood '85
Forbidden Sun '89
Forced Entry '75
Free, White, and 21 '62
From the Life of the Marionettes '80 ►
Fugitive Among Us '92
The General's Daughter '99
Gentle Savage '73
Girls Town '95
Gonin 2 '96
Gossip '99
Guncrazy '92
Hands of a Stranger '87
Hannie Caulder '72
The Heart Is Deceitful Above All Things '04
Heat of the Flame '76
His Name Was King '71
Home Before Midnight '84
The Hooked Generation '69

► = rated three bones or higher

The Hotel New Hampshire '84
Hounddog '08
I Am Frigid... Why? '72
I Spit on Your Grave '77
Ichi the Killer '01
I'll Sleep When I'm Dead '03 ▸
I'm the One You're Looking For '88
In Trouble '67
Incognito '99
Irreversible '02
It's Alive '74 ▸
Jackson County Jail '76
Jaded '96
Jailbait: Betrayed By Innocence '86
Judge Horton and the Scottsboro Boys '76
Kika '94
Kiss of a Killer '93
The Kite Runner '07 ▸
The Ladies Club '86
Lady Snowblood '73 ▸
Landscape in the Mist '88 ▸
The Last House on the Left '09
Lethal Woman '88
Lipstick '76
Liquid Sky '83 ▸
Lost in Beijing '07
Love and Debate '06
The Marquise of O '76
Memoirs of a Geisha '05
Memories of Murder '03
Ms. 45 '81 ▸
Mrs. R's Daughter '79
Most Wanted '76
Motor Psycho '65
The Mudge Boy '03
Multiple Maniacs '70
Mysterious Skin '04 ▸
Naked Vengeance '85
Necromancer: Satan's Servant '88
Night of the Demon '80
Northville Cemetery Massacre '76
Olivier, Olivier '92 ▸
Once Upon a Time in America '84 ▸
One of Her Own '97
One Tough Cop '98
One Way '06
Open Doors '89 ▸
Open Window '06
The Outrage '64
Outrage '93
Palindromes '04 ▸
A Passage to India '84 ▸
The Phantom of Soho '64
Positive I.D. '87
Postcards from America '95
Precious: Based on the Novel by Sapphire '09 ▸
The Principal '87
Purgatory '89
Quiet Days in Hollywood '97
Rage '80 ▸
Rape and Marriage: The Rideout Case '80
Rape of Love '79
Rashomon '51 ▸
A Reason to Believe '95
The Reckoning '03 ▸
Redacted '07
Rica '72
Rider on the Rain '70 ▸
Rob Roy '95 ▸
Sci-Fighters '96
Screamer '74
Sex Crimes '92
Shame '87
Shame '92
The Shaming '79
She Came on the Bus '69
Short Fuse '88
Showgirls '95
Silent Witness '85
Sin and Redemption '94
Sirens '02
Sketch Artist 2: Hands That See '94
Slashed Dreams '74
Speak '04 ▸
The Story of Esther Costello '57
A Stranger Is Watching '82
Straw Dogs '72 ▸
Streets '90
Studs Lonigan '60
Sudden Death '85
Sudden Impact '83
Suspicious River '00
Tainted '88
Talk to Her '02 ▸
Tarnation '03
The Tenth Circle '08
Things Behind the Sun '01
Time to Kill '89
A Time to Kill '96 ▸
Titus '99
To Kill a Mockingbird '62 ▸
To Kill a Stranger '84
The Tormentors '71
Town without Pity '61
Trade '07
Trespasses '86
Violated '84
Violent Ones '68
The Violent Years '56
Virgin '03
The Virgin Spring '59 ▸
Vukovar '94 ▸
When He's Not a Stranger '89 ▸
When Justice Fails '98
Wild Riders '71
The Wind '28 ▸
A Woman in Berlin '08
Woman, Thou Art Loosed '04
The Young One '61

Rats!

see also *Killer Rodents; Nice Mice*
Ben '72
Beverly Hills Chihuahua '08
Beyond Re-Animator '03
Burial of the Rats '95
Charlotte's Web '73
Charlotte's Web '06 ▸
Chicken Run '00 ▸
Deadly Eyes '82
Enchanted '07
Flushed Away '06 ▸
Food of the Gods '76
Food of the Gods: Part 2 '88
The Great Mouse Detective '86 ▸
Insanitarium '08
Mulberry Street '06
Muppets from Space '99
The Muppets Take Manhattan '84 ▸
Pied Piper '72
The Pied Piper of Hamelin '57
Ratatouille '07 ▸
Rats '83
The Rats '01
The Rats Are Coming! The Werewolves Are Here! '72
The Secret of NIMH '82 ▸
The Secret of NIMH 2 '98
The Tale of Despereaux '08
Teenage Mutant Ninja Turtles: The Movie '90
Teenage Mutant Ninja Turtles 2: The Secret of the Ooze '91
Teenage Mutant Ninja Turtles 3 '93
TMNT (Teenage Mutant Ninja Turtles) '07
Wanted '08 ▸
Willard '71
Willard '03

Real Estate

All Good Things '09
Are We Done Yet? '07
Barbershop 2: Back in Business '04 ▸
*batteries not included '87
Battle of the Sexes '28
The Beat My Heart Skipped '05 ▸
The Big Bounce '04
Boy, Did I Get a Wrong Number! '66
Boys on the Side '94
Boystown '07
A Brooklyn State of Mind '97
Burning Daylight '28
Career Girls '97 ▸
Chasing Butterflies '94
Clean and Sober '88 ▸
Confidentially Yours '83 ▸
Contagion '87
Daughter of Don Q '46
The Deadly Secret '94
Different Story '78
District 13: Ultimatum '09
Duplex '03
Empire of the Ants '77
The Evictors '79
For Love or Money '88
For Love or Money '93
Furry Vengeance '10
Garden Party '08
Glengarry Glen Ross '92 ▸
A Good Year '06
The Haunted Mansion '03
Hollywood Homicide '03
House 4: Home Deadly Home '91
Irresistible Impulse '95
Just Add Water '07
Kill the Poor '06
Killer Instinct '00
Last Call '90
The Last Word '80
Love on the Side '04
The Low Down '00
Make Me an Offer '80
Meatballs 4 '92
Messenger of Death '88
Miranda '01
Moonlight Mile '02 ▸
My 5 Wives '00
Open House '86
Protection '01
Read My Lips '01
Remedy for Riches '40
River Street '95
RocknRolla '08
Rubin & Ed '92
Rude Awakening '81
Rule 3 '93
Same Old Song '97 ▸
Shadow of Angels '76
South Riding '37
Stay Hungry '76 ▸
Stormy Monday '88
The Stranger from Pecos '45
Sunshine State '02 ▸
Teenage Exorcist '93
Terror Tract '00
To Die For '89
The Two Jakes '90
Two Weeks Notice '02
Vive l'Amour '94
Wild Brian Kent '36
Wild Orchid '90

REALLY Bad TV

see also *Technology—Rampant*
Poltergeist '82 ▸
Remote Control '88
The Ring '02
Terrorvision '86
The Video Dead '87
Videodrome '83

Rebel With a Cause

see also *Rebel Without a Cause; The Resistance*
Acceptable Risks '86
The Accused '88 ▸
Ace High '68
Aeon Flux '05
Afterburn '92 ▸
Alice's Restaurant '69
American Tiger '89
And Starring Pancho Villa as Himself '03 ▸
Ann Vickers '33
The Applegates '89
Armageddon: The Final Challenge '94
As Young As You Feel '51 ▸
The Attic: The Hiding of Anne Frank '88
Basquiat '96 ▸
Billy Jack '71
The Blob '58
Blue Collar '78 ▸
Born Losers '67
Boyz N the Hood '91 ▸
Braveheart '95 ▸
Broken Silence '01 ▸
Brubaker '80 ▸
Burglar '87 ▸
The Burmese Harp '56 ▸
The China Syndrome '79 ▸
Courage '86 ▸
Courageous Dr. Christian '40
Crime of Honor '85
Dark Rider '91
Daybreak '93
Dead Poets Society '89 ▸
Deadly Business '86 ▸
Deadly Stranger '88
Demolition High '95
Die Hard '88 ▸
Die Hard 2: Die Harder '90 ▸
Disturbing Behavior '98
Dragon Fury '95
A Dream for Christmas '73 ▸
Dust '85 ▸
East of Eden '54 ▸
East of Eden '80
Easy Wheels '89
The Edukators '04
Exiled in America '90
The Fighter '52 ▸
The Fighter '95
The Final Alliance '89
The Firing Line '91
The $5.20 an Hour Dream '80
Flesh and the Spur '57
Flight of the Intruder '90
Foxfire '96
The Fugitive '48 ▸
The Gambling Samurai '60
Game of Survival '89
Gandhi '82 ▸
Go Further '03
Gorillas in the Mist '88 ▸
Guess Who's Coming to Dinner '67 ▸
Hair '79 ▸
Hardcore '79
Hidden City '87
In the Name of the Father '93 ▸
Iron Horsemen '71
Iron Thunder '89
James Dean: Live Fast, Die Young '97
Jesse '88
Joe Kidd '72
Johnny Firecloud '75
Katherine '75
Kidnapped '95
Killing of Randy Webster '81
Knights of the City '85
Kung Fu '72
La Marseillaise '37 ▸
The Last American Hero '73 ▸
Lawrence of Arabia '62 ▸
Legend of Billie Jean '85
Legend of Earl Durand '74
Legend of the Lone Ranger '81
Light It Up '99
Little Tough Guys '38
Lois Gibbs and the Love Canal '82
The Loneliness of the Long Distance Runner '62 ▸
Lust for Life '56 ▸
Luther '74
Man of Marble '76 ▸
The Manhattan Project '86
Marie '85 ▸
Memories of Underdevelopment '68
Michael Collins '96 ▸
Mr. Smith Goes to Washington '39 ▸
Mountain Man '77
Network '76 ▸
Night of Evil '62
Norma Rae '79 ▸
Northern Lights '79 ▸
Odd Man Out '47 ▸
One-Eyed Jacks '61 ▸
One Man Jury '78
One Man's War '90
Original Intent '91
Outbreak '94 ▸
Overdrawn at the Memory Bank '83
Patch Adams '98
Paths of Glory '57 ▸
Patty Hearst '88
Plutonium Baby '87
Prefontaine '96
The Principal '87
Private Parts '96
Project X '87
Quarantine '89
A Raisin in the Sun '61 ▸
A Raisin in the Sun '89 ▸
The Rebel '08 ▸
Rob Roy '95 ▸
Robin Hood: Prince of Thieves '91
The Rock '96 ▸
Roe vs. Wade '89 ▸
Rooster: Spurs of Death! '83
Runaway Daughters '94
Sakharov '84 ▸
Samaritan: The Mitch Snyder Story '86 ▸
The Sand Pebbles '66 ▸
Sansho the Bailiff '54 ▸
Save the Lady '82
The Scarlet Pimpernel '34 ▸
The Scarlet Pimpernel '82 ▸
The Scarlet Pimpernel '99
The Scarlet Pimpernel 2: Mademoiselle Guillotine '99
The Scarlet Pimpernel 3: The Kidnapped King '99
The Secret Agent '96
Secret of Stamboul '36
Serpico '73 ▸
The Shock '23
Silkwood '83 ▸
Sins of Rome '54
Solo '96
Somebody Has to Shoot the Picture '90 ▸
Stay Away, Joe '68
Steel Frontier '94
The Stranger '95
The Stranger Wore a Gun '53
Sympathy for the Devil '70
Taffin '88
Tank Girl '94
The Texican '66
This Land Is Mine '43 ▸
The Tin Star '57 ▸
To Kill a Priest '89
Trial of the Catonsville Nine '72
True Believer '89
Under Western Stars '38
V: The Final Battle '84
Vengeance '86
WarGames '83
The Westerner '40 ▸
When a Man Rides Alone '33
Wisdom '87
Without Limits '97 ▸

Rebel Without a Cause

see also *Rebel With a Cause*
Across the Tracks '89
All Night Long '81 ▸
Badlands '74 ▸
A Boy and His Dog '75
The Boys Next Door '85
Breathless '59 ▸
Breathless '83
Charlie Bartlett '07 ▸
Cheech and Chong's Up in Smoke '79
A Clockwork Orange '71 ▸
Cool As Ice '91
The Cruel Story of Youth '60 ▸
Dino '57
Easy Rider '69 ▸
The Electric Horseman '79
The Fence '94
Ferris Bueller's Day Off '86 ▸
Five Easy Pieces '70 ▸
The Fugitive Kind '60
Fury to Freedom: The Life Story of Raul Ries '85
Girls' Town '59
Going Places '74 ▸
Gore Vidal's Billy the Kid '89
Great Missouri Raid '51
Guncrazy '92
Heart Beat '80
Hud '63 ▸
I Was a Teenage Werewolf '57
If... '69 ▸
Inventing the Abbotts '97
Just for the Hell of It '68
Kicked in the Head '97
Leather Jackets '90
The Little Valentino '79
Loser '97
Lost Angels '89
Niagara, Niagara '97
Noi '03
On the Edge: The Survival of Dana '79
Over the Edge '79 ▸
Petit Con '84
Presumed Guilty '91
Pump Up the Volume '90
Rambo: First Blood, Part 2 '85
Rambo 3 '88
Rebel High '88
Rebel Rousers '69
Rebel Run '94
Rebel without a Cause '55 ▸
Reckless '84
Road House '89
Roadracers '94
Rocky 4 '85
September 30, 1955 '77
sex, lies and videotape '89 ▸
Shopping '93
SLC Punk! '99
Snow Kill '90
Suburbia '83
Summer Camp Nightmare '86
That Was Then... This Is Now '85
3:15—The Moment of Truth '86
Thunder Road '58 ▸
Top Gun '86
The Violent Years '56
West Side Story '61 ▸
The Wild Angels '66
The Wild One '54 ▸
The Wild Ride '60
Youth in Revolt '10

Red Cross

China Beach '88 ▸
One Against the Wind '91 ▸
So Proudly We Hail '43 ▸
The White Cliffs of Dover '44 ▸

Red Scare

see also *Cold War Spies; Communists & Communism; Foreign Intrigue; Politics; Russia/USSR*
Arsenal '29 ▸
Baltic Deputy '37 ▸
The Bamboo Saucer '68
Battle Beneath the Earth '68
A Beautiful Mind '01 ▸
Big Jim McLain '52
A Bullet for Joey '55
Chapayev '34 ▸
China Cry '91
China, My Sorrow '89
Coming Out of the Ice '82 ▸
Comment Ca Va? '76
The Commies Are Coming, the Commies Are Coming '57
Commissar '68 ▸
Comrade X '40
Conspirator '49
Dash and Lilly '99
Death of a Bureaucrat '66 ▸
Earth '30 ▸
Eminent Domain '91
Fellow Traveler '89 ▸
Golden Gate '93
The Great Armored Car Swindle '64
Guilty by Suspicion '91
Guilty of Treason '50
Hands Up '81 ▸
Hawthorne of the USA '19
I Was a Communist for the FBI '51
Indochine '92 ▸
The Inner Circle '91 ▸
The Interrogation '82 ▸
Invasion U.S.A. '52
Invasion U.S.A. '85
Jet Pilot '57
Little World of Don Camillo '51 ▸
Man of Iron '81 ▸

Man of Marble '76 ►
The Manchurian Candidate '62 ►
Mandela '87 ►
Mother Kusters Goes to Heaven '76 ►
Mother of Kings '82
Never Let Me Go '53
Nicholas and Alexandra '71
Night Crossing '81
Night Flight from Moscow '73
The Oak '93
Oh, Bloody Life! '88
Open Doors '89 ►
Red Dawn '84
The Red Menace '49
Reds '81 ►
Requiem for Dominic '91 ►
Revolution! A Red Comedy '91 ►
The She-Beast '65
Sideburns '91
Strike '24 ►
The Theme '79 ►
Thoughts Are Free '84 ►
Tito and Me '92 ►
Tobor the Great '54
Trahir '93 ►
The Ugly American '63
Uranus '91 ►
When Father Was Away on Business '85 ►
The Woman on Pier 13 '50

Reefer Madness

Alpha Dog '06
Cash Crop '01
Cheech and Chong's Next Movie '80
Cheech and Chong's Nice Dreams '81
Cheech and Chong's Up in Smoke '79
Dead Man on Campus '97
Dealing: Or the Berkeley-to-Boston Forty-Brick Lost-Bag Blues '72
Friday '95
Garden Party '08
The Good Girl '02 ►
Grandma's Boy '06
Half-Baked '97
Harold & Kumar Escape from Guantanamo Bay '08
Harold and Kumar Go to White Castle '04
How High '01
Humboldt County '08
I Love You, Alice B. Toklas! '68
Knocked Up '07
Next Day Air '09
Pineapple Express '08 ►
Police, Adjective '09
Puff, Puff, Pass '06
Reefer Madness '38
Saving Grace '00
Shrink '09
Smiley Face '07
Strange Wilderness '08
Surfer, Dude '08
The Wackness '08
The Wash '01

Reggae

see also Jamaica; Rock Flicks
Dancehall Queen '97
The Harder They Come '72
Rude Boy: The Jamaican Don '03
Soul Survivor '95

Rehab

see also Drug Use & Abuse; On the Rocks
Bounce '00
Clean '04
Clean and Sober '88 ►
Crutch '04
Down to the Bone '04
Eye See You '01
Gridlock'd '96 ►
Jesus' Son '99
Rachel Getting Married '08 ►
Save Me '07
Scandal Sheet '85
Slums of Beverly Hills '98 ►
True Confessions of a Hollywood Starlet '08
28 Days '00
When a Man Loves a Woman '94

Reincarnation

see also Death & the Afterlife
Andromedia '00
Angel on My Shoulder '46 ►
Angel on My Shoulder '80
Audrey Rose '77
Birth '04
Bram Stoker's The Mummy '97
The Calamari Wrestler '04
Chances Are '89 ►
Chandni Chowk to China '09
Cleo/Leo '89
Creature of Destruction '67
Dead Again '91 ►
Devi '60 ►
Down to Earth '01
Fluke '95
Goodbye Charlie '64
Heart and Souls '93
Heaven Can Wait '78 ►
Here Comes Mr. Jordan '41 ►
I Married a Witch '42 ►
Little Buddha '93
The Mummy '99
The Mummy Lives '93
The Mummy Returns '01
My Blood Runs Cold '65
Oh, Heavenly Dog! '80
On a Clear Day You Can See Forever '70
P.S. '04
Quigley '03
Racing Daylight '07
Rapturious '07
Rasen '98
The Reincarnation of Peter Proud '75
The Robot vs. the Aztec Mummy '59
The Search for Bridey Murphy '56
She '65
Special Unit 2002 '01
Switch '91 ►
Tales of the Kama Sutra 2: Monsoon '98
Tequila Body Shots '99
The Unmistaken Child '08
The Vengeance of She '68
Youth Without Youth '07

Religion

see also Buddhism; Islam; Judaism; Missionaries; Nuns & Priests; Religious Epics; Saints
The Abdication '74
Abduction of St. Anne '75
Absolution '81
Adam's Apples '05
The Addiction '95
Alice Sweet Alice '76
Amazing Grace '06 ►
Ancient Relic '02
Androcles and the Lion '52
Angel Baby '61
Angel of Death '02
Angela '94
Angels in America '03 ►
Anna '51
The Apostle '97 ►
Augustine of Hippo '72 ►
The Avenging Angel '95
Bad Education '04 ►
Bear Ye One Another's Burden... '88
Before the Rain '94 ►
Bernadette '90
The Big Squeeze '96
The Birch Interval '78
Blood of Jesus '41
The Body '01
Body and Soul '24
Breaking the Waves '95 ►
Brides of Christ '91
Brigham City '01
Brigham Young: Frontiersman '40
Broken Vows '87
Brother Sun, Sister Moon '73
Brotherhood of the Wolf '01
Brothers in Arms '88
The Butcher Boy '97 ►
Camila '84 ►
Catholics '73 ►
Chariots of Fire '81 ►
Children of Fury '94
Chocolat '00 ►
The Choir '95 ►
The Chronicles of Narnia: The Lion, the Witch and the Wardrobe '05
The Church '98 ►
Citizen Ruth '96
Come to the Stable '49 ►
Commandments '96
Conquest of Space '55
Conspiracy of Silence '03
Contact '97
The Convent '95
Cosmic Slop '94
The Courageous Mr. Penn '41
Cracker: The Big Crunch '94
Creation '09
Crimes of Passion '84 ►
Critical Choices '97
The Crucible '57 ►
A Cry from the Mountain '85
The Da Vinci Code '06 ►
Day of Judgment '81
Day of Triumph '54
Dead Man Walking '95 ►
Def by Temptation '90
Destiny '97
Devi '60 ►
The Devil at 4 O'Clock '61
The Disappearance of Aimee '76 ►
Divided by Hate '96
Dr. Syn '37
Dr. Syn, Alias the Scarecrow '64
Dogma '99
A Dream for Christmas '73 ►
Earth '98
El Cid '61 ►
Elizabeth '98 ►
Emanon '86
The Embezzled Heaven '58
The End of the Affair '99 ►
End of the Spear '06
Enjo '58
Entertaining Angels: The Dorothy Day Story '96
An Everlasting Piece '00
The Exorcism of Emily Rose '05 ►
Extramuros '85
Eye of God '97 ►
False Prophets '06
Father of Lies '07
The Favor, the Watch, & the Very Big Fish '92
The Fiend '71
Final Judgment '92
The Flowers of St. Francis '50 ►
A Fond Kiss '04
A Fool and His Money '88
Francesco '93
Friendly Persuasion '56 ►
From a Far Country: Pope John Paul II '81
The Garden '90
The Gathering '02
The Gaucho '27 ►
The Ghoul '75
Glory! Glory! '90 ►
Go Down Death '41
The Godfather, Part 3 '90 ►
God's Gun '75
Godspell '73
Gospa '94
The Gospel '05 ►
Greaser's Palace '72
The Greatest Story Ever Told '65
Green Pastures '36 ►
The Guyana Tragedy: The Story of Jim Jones '80
Hail Mary '85
Hallelujah! '29 ►
Harvest of Fire '95
Hate Crime '05
Hazel's People '73
The Healer '02
The Heart Is Deceitful Above All Things '04
Heart of the Beholder '05 ►
Heavens Above '63 ►
Helas pour Moi '94
Hellfire '48
Henry Poole Is Here '08 ►
Holy Girl '04 ►
Holy Man '98
Holy Matrimony '94
Household Saints '93 ►
The Hunchback '97
I, the Worst of All '90
I'd Climb the Highest Mountain '51 ►
In God We Trust '80
In the Line of Duty: Ambush in Waco '93
Inherit the Wind '60 ►
The Inquiry '87
Invasion of the Space Preachers '90
Iron Horsemen '71
Jada '08
Jeanne la Pucelle '94
Jerusalem '96
Jesus '79
Jesus Christ, Superstar '73 ►
Jesus Christ Superstar '00
Jesus of Nazareth '28
Jesus of Nazareth '77 ►
The Jesus Trip '71
The Jew '96
Joan of Arc '48
Joan of Arc '99
Joni '79
Joshua '02
The Judas Project: The Ultimate Encounter '94
The Keeper: The Legend of Omar Khayyam '05
Keeping Mum '05
Kingdom of Heaven '05 ►
Klondike Annie '36
Knocks at My Door '93
Kristin Lavransdatter '95
La Chartreuse de Parme '48
La Petite Jerusalem '05
The Last Temptation of Christ '88 ►
Latter Days '04
Laughing Sinners '31
Leap of Faith '92
Leaves from Satan's Book '19
Left Behind: The Movie '00
Les Destinees '00
Levity '03
The Light of Faith '22
Lilies '96
Little Buddha '93
Little Church Around the Corner '23
Little Richard '00
The Littlest Angel '69
Loggerheads '05 ►
Looking for Comedy in the Muslim World '06
The Loss of Sexual Innocence '98
Love and Faith '78 ►
A Love Divided '01
Lust and Revenge '95
Luther '74
Major Barbara '41 ►
The Maldonado Miracle '03
A Man Called Peter '55 ►
A Man for All Seasons '66 ►
A Man for All Seasons '88 ►
Marjoe '72
Martin Luther '53
Mary, Mother of Jesus '99
Mary, Queen of Scots '71
Mayflower: The Pilgrims' Adventure '79
The Message '77
The Milky Way '68 ►
The Milky Way '97
The Miracle '48 ►
Miracle in Rome '88
The Miracle of Marcelino '55
Miracle of Our Lady of Fatima '52
The Miracle Woman '31
Monsieur Vincent '47 ►
Monsignor Quixote '91
Monty Python's Life of Brian '79 ►
A Mormon Maid '17
Mother Joan of the Angels '60 ►
Mother Teresa: In the Name of God's Poor '97
My Mother's Smile '02
The Neon Bible '95
New York Doll '05 ►
The Next Voice You Hear '50
The Night of the Iguana '64 ►
The Ninth Day '04 ►
Nostalghia '83
Oh, God! '77
The Omen '06
One Man's Way '63
Oranges Are Not the Only Fruit '89
Ordet '55 ►
Ordinary Sinner '02
The Other Side of Heaven '02
The Other Side of Sunday '96
Padre Nuestro '85
Paradise Now '05 ►
Partition '07
Pass the Ammo '88
The Passion of Darkly Noon '95
Passion of Joan of Arc '28 ►
The Passover Plot '75
P.D. James: Death in Holy Orders '03
Pearl Diver '04
The Penitent '88
Peter and Paul '81
Pi '98
Picking Up the Pieces '99
Pray TV '80
Pray TV '82
A Prayer in the Dark '97
Preacherman '83
The Preacher's Wife '96
Priest '94
Prisoner of Rio '89
Private Confessions '98
The Private Secretary '35
The Prodigal Planet '88
Promised a Miracle '88
Protocols of Zion '05 ►
The Quarry '98
Queen Margot '94 ►
Quo Vadis '51 ►
Quo Vadis '85
Rain '32
The Rapture '91
The Reckoning '03 ►
The Rector's Wife '94
Red Planet Mars '52
Religulous '08 ►
Resurrection '80 ►
Resurrection '99
Return to Paradise '53
Revelation '00
Rock Haven '07
RoGoPaG '62
Romero '89
The Rook '99
Sacrilege '86
St. Benny the Dip '51
Saint Joan '57
Saint Maybe '98 ►
St. Patrick: The Irish Legend '00
Saint Ralph '04
Saints and Soldiers '03
Salome '85
Salvation! '87
Sanctuary of Fear '79
Saved! '04
The Scarlet Letter '79 ►
Sebastiane '79 ►
The Second Chance '06
Shadowlands '93 ►
The Sky Pilot '21
Son of Rambow '07
The Song of Bernadette '43 ►
Stigmata '99
Stolen Summer '02
A Stranger in the Kingdom '98
Susan and God '40 ►
Tales from the Crypt Presents Bordello of Blood '96
That Eye, the Sky '94
There Will Be Blood '07 ►
The Third Miracle '99
This Stuff'll Kill Ya! '71
Through a Glass Darkly '61 ►
The Tollbooth '04
Touch '96
Tournament '29
Trapped by the Mormons '22
Tribulation '00
21 Grams '03 ►
Ultrachrist! '03
Under the Moonlight '01 ►
Ushpizin '04
Virgin '03
The Vision '87
A Walk to Remember '02
Wall '04 ►
Welcome to Paradise '07
West Beirut '98
When Night Is Falling '95 ►
Where Angels Go, Trouble Follows '68
Whistle down the Wind '61 ►
Whistling in the Dark '41 ►
Whitcomb's War '87
The White Rose '23 ►
Wholly Moses! '80
Why Has Bodhi-Darma Left for the East '89
The Wicker Man '06
Wide Awake '97
The Winter Light '62 ►
Wise Blood '79 ►
Witness '85 ►
Woman, Thou Art Loosed '04
The Word '78
The Worldly Madonna '22

Religious Epics

see also Religion
Abraham '94
A.D. '85
The Agony and the Ecstasy '65
...And God Spoke '94
Barabbas '62
Ben-Hur '26 ►
Ben-Hur '59 ►
The Bible '66
Cleopatra '63
David '97
David and Bathsheba '51 ►
Demetrius and the Gladiators '54
The Egyptian '54
El Cid '61 ►
From the Manger to the Cross '15
The Gospel According to St. Matthew '64 ►
The Gospel of John '03
In the Name of the Pope-King '85 ►
Jacob '94
Jesus '00
Jesus of Nazareth '28
Joseph '95
Judith of Bethulia '14 ►
The King of Kings '61 ►
Kingdom of Heaven '05 ►
The Messiah '75 ►
Moses '76
Moses '96
The Nativity Story '06
Noah's Ark '99
The Passion of the Christ '04 ►
Prince of Egypt '98 ►
The Prodigal '55
The Robe '53
Samson and Delilah '96
The Sign of the Cross '33
Sodom and Gomorrah '62
The Song of Bernadette '43 ►
The Story of David '76 ►
The Story of Jacob & Joseph '74 ►
The Story of Ruth '60
The Sword and the Cross '58
The Ten Commandments '23
The Ten Commandments '56 ►

Renegade Body Parts

see also Killer Brains
The Addams Family '91
Addams Family Values '93
And Now the Screaming Starts '73
The Animal '01
The Beast with Five Fingers '46

Blood of Ghastly Horror '72
Body Parts '91
Body Parts '94
The Brain that Wouldn't Die '63
Careless '07
The Crawling Eye '58
The Crawling Hand '63
Crazy in Alabama '99
Demonoid, Messenger of Death '81
Doctor Butcher M.D. '80
Dr. Terror's House of Horrors '65
8 Heads in a Duffel Bag '96
Evil Dead 2: Dead by Dawn '87
Gravesend '97
The Hand '81 ▶
Hands of a Stranger '62
The Hands of Orlac '25
The Hands of Orlac '60
How to Get Ahead in Advertising '89 ▶
Idle Hands '99
The Incredible Two-Headed Transplant '71
Killer Tongue '96
The Kingdom '95 ▶
The Kingdom 2 '97 ▶
Machined '06
Mad Love '35 ▶
The Man with Two Brains '83 ▶
Mindkiller '87
Picking Up the Pieces '99
Planet Terror '07
Quicksilver Highway '98
Severed Ties '92
The Thing with Two Heads '72
Tomcats '01
Virus '98
Waxwork 2: Lost in Time '91

Rent-a-Cop

Above the Rim '94
Armed and Dangerous '86
The Cookout '04
Critical Mass '00
Cyber-Tracker '93
The Doll '62
Eddie Presley '92
End of Days '99
Fear X '03 ▶
Friday After Next '02
The Heist '89
Hobgoblins '87
Inspector Gadget '99
Light It Up '99
Looney Tunes: Back in Action '03
The Maiden Heist '08
Mannequin '87
Mirrors '08
National Security '03
Night at the Museum '06
Night at the Museum: Battle of the Smithsonian '09
Observe and Report '09
P2 '07
Paul Blart: Mall Cop '09
Rent-A-Cop '88
The Shape of Things '03
Star Spangled Rhythm '42 ▶
Tapeheads '89
Trixie '00
Unbreakable '00
Underdog '07
Urban Legend '98

Repressed Men

see also *Men*
The Age of Innocence '93 ▶
American Beauty '99 ▶
Beloved/Friend '99
Bitter Moon '92
Bleak Moments '71
The Bodyguard '92
Box of Moonlight '96
Changing Times '04
Creation of Adam '93
The Eighth Day '95
El '52
Falling Down '93
Far Side of the Moon '03
Felicia's Journey '99 ▶
Fight Club: ' '99 ▶
The Game '97 ▶
The Good Shepherd '06
The Hawk Is Dying '06
Howard's End '92 ▶
In and Out '97 ▶
Kiss the Sky '98
Last Life in the Universe '03
Like It Never Was Before '95
Little Children '06 ▶
The Little Kidnappers '90
Love and Death on Long Island '97
Maurice '87 ▶
My Best Friend '06
On a Clear Day '05
The Preacher's Wife '96
A Rather English Marriage '98
The Red Dwarf '99
The Remains of the Day '93 ▶
Shadowlands '93 ▶
Sirens '94
Split Second '99
Till Human Voices Wake Us '02
When Did You Last See Your Father? '07
Yi Yi '00
Zero Degrees Kelvin '95

Rescue Missions

see also *Rescue Missions Involving Time Travel*
Agent of Death '99
Air Rage '01
Alaska '96
Alone in the Woods '95
The Amazing Panda Adventure '95
Angelique and the Sultan '68
Any Place But Home '97
Apollo 13 '95 ▶
Balto '95
Beer for My Horses '08
Behind Enemy Lines '96
Behind Enemy Lines '01
Berlin Tunnel 21 '81
Beverly Hills Chihuahua '08
Beyond Borders '03
Bionicle 3: Web of Shadows '05
Black Dawn '05
Black Hawk Down '01 ▶
Blade 2 '02
Blind Heat '00
Bolt '08 ▶
Boomerang '76
Born to Be Wild '95
Breakout '75
A Bug's Life '98 ▶
Caged Fear '92
The Chamber '96
The Children '90
The City of Lost Children '95 ▶
Comanche Station '60
Commando '85 ▶
Con Air '97 ▶
Courage Under Fire '96 ▶
Crossfire '89
Dante's Peak '97
Daredevils of the Red Circle '38
Dark Mountain '44
The Day After Tomorrow '04
Daylight '96
Dead Ahead '96
Desperate Women '78
The Diamond of Jeru '01
Die Hard '88 ▶
Die Hard 2: Die Harder '90 ▶
Die Hard: With a Vengeance '95
The Dirty Dozen: The Deadly Mission '87
Django Strikes Again '87
Dragonworld '94
Eight Below '06
Enough! '06
Ernest Scared Stupid '91
Escape from L.A. '96
Event Horizon '97
The Ewok Adventure '84
Executioner of Venice '63
Executive Decision '96
Expect No Mercy '95
Far from Home: The Adventures of Yellow Dog '94
Fever '91
Finding Nemo '03 ▶
First Daughter '99
Force: Five '81
Free Willy '93
Free Willy 2: The Adventure Home '95
Free Willy 3: The Rescue '97
The Golden Compass '07
The Great Raid '05
Grizzly Mountain '97
The Guardian '06
Hard Ticket to Hawaii '87
The Hidden Fortress '58 ▶
High Velocity '76
The Hills Have Eyes 2 '07
Hired to Kill '91
Honeybaby '74
Hoot '06
Ice Age '02 ▶
Ice Age: Dawn of the Dinosaurs '09
In Her Line of Fire '06
In the Company of Spies '99
Independence Day '96 ▶
Inkheart '09
The Inn of the Sixth Happiness '58 ▶
Island in the Sky '53 ▶
Jenny's War '85
Jeopardy '53
Joey '98
Journey to the Center of the Earth '99
Jurassic Park 3 '01
Kidnapped in Paradise '98
Kids of the Round Table '96
Killing Streets '91
The Last Hard Men '76
Legend of the Lost Tomb '97
Lisbon '56
The Lone Runner '88
The Losers '70
Losing Isaiah '94 ▶
The Lost Treasure of the Grand Canyon '08
Lucie Aubrac '98
The Magnificent Seven '60 ▶
Managua '97
The Marine '06
Master of Disguise '02
The Matrix Revolutions '03 ▶
Mercenary 2: Thick and Thin '97
Mercy Mission '93
Miracle at Midnight '98
Ms. Bear '97
The Missing '03 ▶
Missing in Action '84
Missing in Action 2: The Beginning '85
Mission: Impossible 3 '06 ▶
Mission to Mars '00
Morning Departure '50
Moscow Zero '06
Naked Souls '95
Navy SEALS '90
Oliver & Company '88
One Small Hero '99
Operation Cross Eagles '69
Operation Delta Force 2: Mayday '97
Operation Dumbo Drop '95
Ordeal in the Arctic '93
Outbreak '94 ▶
Pirates of the Caribbean: At World's End '07
Pirates of the Caribbean: The Curse of the Black Pearl '03 ▶
Pray for Death '85
Prince Valiant '97
Raid on Entebbe '77 ▶
Rambo: First Blood, Part 2 '85
Red Planet '00
The Rescue '88
Rescue Me '93
The Rescuers '77 ▶
The Rescuers Down Under '90
Rescuers: Stories of Courage—Two Couples '98 ▶
Return of Chandu '34
Revenge of the Barbarians '60
Revenge of the Musketeers '94
Riot '96
The Rock '96 ▶
Rules of Engagement '00
Sasquatch '02
Saving Private Ryan '98 ▶
Saving Shiloh '06
Screamers: The Hunting '09
The Sea Shall Not Have Them '55
The Searchers '56 ▶
The Secret Agent Club '96
The Secret Invasion '64
The Secret of NIMH 2 '98
Seven Samurai '54 ▶
Seven Seconds '05
Shadow Warriors 2: Hunt for the Death Merchant '97
Shanghai Noon '00
Shrek '01 ▶
Silver Hawk '04
The Slender Thread '65 ▶
Soldier Boyz '95
Soldier of Fortune Inc. '97
Space Marines '96
Special Forces '03
Spy Game '01
Spy Kids '01 ▶
Star Trek: Insurrection '98
Starship Troopers 3: Marauder '08
Steel Sharks '97
The Story of Dr. Wassell '44
Stranglehold '94
Street Fighter '94
Submarine Attack '54
Submerged '00
Sudden Death '95
Supernova '99
Surface to Air '98
The Survivor '98
Taken '08
The Taking of Flight 847: The Uli Derickson Story '88 ▶
The Tale of Despereaux '08
Tears of the Sun '03
A Thousand Heroes '92
Three Bad Men '05
Three Days to a Kill '91
Thunder in Paradise '93
Thunder in Paradise 2 '94
Toy Story '95 ▶
Toy Story 2 '99 ▶
Tugboat Annie '33 ▶
The Tunnel '01 ▶
Two Bits & Pepper '95
2001: A Space Travesty '00
Uncommon Valor '83
Valiant '05
Varian's War '01
Vertical Limit '00
Victory at Entebbe '76
Volcano '97
Waikiki Wedding '37 ▶
Welcome to Sarajevo '97 ▶
The Wild '06
William Faulkner's Old Man '97
Wings in the Dark '35
Wolverine '96
The World in His Arms '52
The World Is Not Enough '99
World Trade Center '06 ▶
X2: X-Men United '03 ▶
The Yakuza '75
Yankee Buccaneer '52
Zathura '05 ▶

Rescue Missions Involving Time Travel

see also *Rescue Missions*
Back to the Future '85 ▶
Back to the Future, Part 2 '89
Back to the Future, Part 3 '90 ▶
Bill & Ted's Excellent Adventure '89
Deja Vu '06
Disney's The Kid '00
Frequency '00
Jumanji '95
Lost in Space '98
Maximum Breakout '91
Millennium '89
The Navigator '88 ▶
Star Trek 4: The Voyage Home '86 ▶
Star Trek: First Contact '96 ▶
Superman: The Movie '78 ▶
The Terminator '84 ▶
Terminator 2: Judgment Day '91 ▶
Terminator 3: Rise of the Machines '03 ▶
Time After Time '79 ▶
Timeline '03
Timemaster '95
Trancers 2: The Return of Jack Deth '90
When Time Expires '97
Yesterday's Target '96
Zathura '05 ▶

The Resistance

see also *World War II; World War II Spies*
Action in the North Atlantic '43
Alien Siege '05
Army of Shadows '69 ▶
Black Book '06 ▶
Carve Her Name with Pride '58
Casablanca '42 ▶
Charlotte Gray '01
The Day and the Hour '63
A Day in October '92
Defiance '08
Edge of Darkness '43 ▶
Equilibrium '02
A Generation '54 ▶
Hangmen Also Die '42
The Heroes of Telemark '65
Holocaust '78 ▶
Johnny Frenchman '46
Julia '77 ▶
The Last Lieutenant '94
The Last Metro '80 ▶
Les Miserables '95
Lucie Aubrac '98
Manon '50
Missiles from Hell '58
One Against the Wind '91 ▶
Passage to Marseilles '44 ▶
Resistance '03
Soldier of Orange '78 ▶
Sophie Scholl: The Final Days '05 ▶
The Square Peg '58
That Summer of White Roses '90
This Land Is Mine '43 ▶
To Be or Not to Be '42 ▶
To Be or Not to Be '83
The Train '65 ▶
Underground '41
Watch on the Rhine '43 ▶
When Willie Comes Marching Home '50 ▶
The White Rose '83 ▶
Winter in Wartime '10
A Woman at War '94

Reunited

see also *Amnesia; I'm Not Dead, Yet!; Island Fare; Missing Persons*
Autumn Hearts: A New Beginning '07
Before Sunset '04 ▶
Cast Away '00 ▶
The Deep End of the Ocean '98
The End of the Affair '99 ▶
Garden State '04 ▶
The Groomsmen '06
Hard to Kill '89
Hired Hand '71
Johnson Family Vacation '04
Keeping Up with the Steins '06
Love '05
Magnolia '99 ▶
Marilyn Hotchkiss' Ballroom Dancing & Charm School '06
Matchstick Men '03 ▶
Mrs. Wiggs of the Cabbage Patch '34
Move Over, Darling '63
My Favorite Wife '40 ▶
The Parent Trap '61
The Parent Trap '98
Pronto '97
Riding Alone for Thousands of Miles '05
Rude '96
Second Honeymoon '37
A Simple Twist of Fate '94
Sin Nombre '09 ▶
Sons '89
Story of a Love Affair '50
The Sunshine Boys '95

Revealing Swimwear

The American Angels: Baptism of Blood '89
Beach Babes from Beyond '93
Beach Girls '82
The Bikini Car Wash Company '90
The Bikini Car Wash Company 2 '92
Bikini Island '91
Bikini Summer '91
Bikini Summer 2 '92
Blood of Dracula's Castle '69
Body Waves '92
Buford's Beach Bunnies '92
California Girls '84
The Cover Girl Murders '93
Dark Tide '93
The Dolls '83
Fit to Kill '93
Frankenstein Island '81
Fun in Acapulco '63
Girls Next Door '79
Great Bikini Off-Road Adventure '94
Hardbodies '84
Hollywood High, Part 2 '81
Hollywood Hot Tubs '84
Hollywood Hot Tubs 2: Educating Crystal '89
Horrors of Spider Island '59
Hot Resort '85
The House that Vanished '73
Island of Lost Girls '68
L'Annee des Meduses '86
Malibu Beach '78
The Malibu Beach Vampires '91
Malibu Bikini Shop '86
Malibu Express '85
Mugsy's Girls '85
Ocean Drive Weekend '85
Pauline at the Beach '83 ▶
Pin-Up Girl '44
Playgirl Killer '66
Private Lessons, Another Story '94
Slumber Party Massacre 2 '87
Sorority House Party '92
Starhops '78
Summer City '77
Summer Fantasy '84
Swimsuit '89
Tarzan, the Ape Man '81
They Were So Young '55
Tintorera... Tiger Shark '78
Vice Academy 3 '91
Welcome to Spring Break '88
When Dinosaurs Ruled the Earth '70

Revenge

see also *Vigilantes*
Act of Aggression '73
Act of Passion: The Lost Honor of Kathryn Beck '83
Act of Vengeance '74
Act of Violence '48
An Actor's Revenge '63
Addicted to Love '96
Adios, Hombre '68
The Adventurers '70
Ajami '09 ▶
The Alchemist '81
Alien Seed '89
All Dogs Go to Heaven '89
Along with Ghosts '69
Already Dead '07
Amazon Warrior '97
Ambush '99 ▶
American Buffalo '95
American Commandos '84
American Eagle '90
American Samurai '92

▶ = rated three bones or higher

Amusement '08
Anatomy of a Psycho '61
Angel and the Badman '47 ▸
Angel of Destruction '94
Angel Square '92
Angels from Hell '68
Appointment with Crime '45
Archer: The Fugitive from the Empire '81
Arizona Terror '31
Ash Wednesday '02
Asylum '72
Attack of the 50 Ft. Woman '93
The Avenging '92
Avenging Angel '85
Avenging Angelo '02
Avenging Force '86
Azumi '03 ▸
Back in Action '94
Back to Back '90
Bad Blood '94
Bad Reputation '05 ▸
The Badlanders '58
Ballad of Cable Hogue '70 ▸
The Ballad of the Sad Cafe '91
Bandits '86
Bang '95
Bangkok Dangerous '00
Banzai Runner '86
The Baron '88
Basket Case '82 ▸
Batman Begins '05 ▸
The Beast with Five Fingers '46
The Beguiled '70 ▸
Behind the Sun '01
Bell from Hell '74
Bella Mafia '97
Benefit of the Doubt '93
Beowulf & Grendel '06
Best of the Best 2 '93
Beyond Forgiveness '94
Big Bully '95
Big Jake '71
Bird of Prey '95
Bitter Sweet '98
Bitter Vengeance '94
Black Arrow '48 ▸
The Black Arrow '84
Black Belt '07
Black Cobra '83
The Black Doll '38
Black Fox: Good Men and Bad '94
Black Gunn '72
The Black Hand '50 ▸
The Black Klansman '66
The Black Pirate '26 ▸
The Black Raven '43
Black Scorpion '95
The Black Six '74
The Black Sleep '56
Black Sunday '60 ▸
A Black Veil for Lisa '68
Blackbelt 2: Fatal Force '93
Blastfighter '85
Blind Vengeance '90
Blind Woman's Curse '70
Blood and Guns '79
Blood Crime '02
Blood for a Silver Dollar '66
Blood on the Mountain '88
Blood Red '88
Blood Ring '93
Bloodfist '89
Bloodknot '95
Bloodmatch '91
BloodRayne '06
Bloody Birthday '80
Blue City '86
The Blue Knight '75
The Blue Lamp '49 ▸
Blue Tiger '94
Body Count '95
Bohachi Bushido: Code of the Forgotten Eight '73
Boiling Point '93
Bone Dry '07
Bones '01
Border Lost '08
Border Rangers '50
Bounty Hunters '89
Bounty Tracker '93
Branded a Coward '35
Breakdown '96 ▸
Bride of Killer Nerd '91
Broken Embraces '09 ▸
Broken Harvest '94
Bronze Buckaroo '39
Brotherhood of Justice '86
Bruiser '00
The Brute Man '46
Bugles in the Afternoon '52
Bulldance '88
Bulldog Courage '35
Bullet '94
Bullet for Sandoval '70
Bullies '86
Buried Alive 2 '97
The Burning '82
Bury Me an Angel '71
The Butcher '07
Cadillac Man '90
Caged Heat 2: Stripped of Freedom '94
Caged Terror '72
The California Kid '74
Cape Fear '61 ▸
Cape Fear '91 ▸
The Caravan Trail '46
Carolina Skeletons '92
Carson City Kid '40
Cartouche '62 ▸
The Casino Job '08
Cellblock Sisters: Banished Behind Bars '95
Certain Sacrifice '80
Chain Gang Women '72
The Chair '87
Challenge '74
Chameleon '95
Chan Is Missing '82 ▸
Changing Lanes '02 ▸
The Chase '46
Chisum '70
The Chosen One: Legend of the Raven '98
Christie's Revenge '07
Chrome and Hot Leather '71
Chrysalis '07
Circumstances Unknown '95
Class of 1984 '82
Clayton County Line '78
Closure '07
Cobra '71
Code Name: Zebra '84
Code of Honor '82
Code of Honor '84
Coffy '73
Cold Eyes of Fear '70
Cold Justice '89
Cold Steel '87
Cold Sweat '71
Cole Justice '89
Collateral Damage '02
Commando Invasion '87
Conflict of Interest '92
The Conqueror & the Empress '64
The Contract '98
Cornered '45 ▸
The Coroner '98
Coroner Creek '48
The Corsican Brothers '42
The Count of Monte Cristo '12
The Count of Monte Cristo '34 ▸
The Count of Monte Cristo '74
The Count of Monte Cristo '99
The Count of Monte Cristo '02
The Count of the Old Town '34
The Courier '88
Cousin Bette '97
Covert Assassin '94
The Cowboys '72 ▸
Crack House '89
The Craft '96
Crank '06
Crazed Cop '88
Creepers '85
Creepshow 2 '87
Crimebusters '79
Crimson Gold '03
The Crippled Masters '82
The Crossing Guard '94 ▸
The Crow '93
The Crow 2: City of Angels '96
The Crow: Salvation '00
The Crow: Wicked Prayer '05
The Crucible '96 ▸
Cry Danger '51 ▸
Cry of the Innocent '80 ▸
The Cry of the Owl '87
Cry Vengeance '54
Curse of the Devil '73
Cybercity '99
Daddy-O '59
Daddy's Gone A-Hunting '69 ▸
Danger Zone 2 '89
Dangerous Obsession '88
Dangerous Orphans '86
Daredevil '03
Dark August '76
Dark River: A Father's Revenge '90
Darkman '90 ▸
Darkness Falls '98
Daughter of the Dragon '31
DaVinci's War '92
Dawn Rider '35
The Day the Women Got Even '80
Dead Boyz Can't Fly '93
Dead Dog '00
Dead Man's Revenge '93
Dead Man's Shoes '04
Dead on the Money '91
Dead Silence '98
Deadly Daphne's Revenge '93
Deadly Darling '85
Deadly Game '91
Deadly Lessons '94
Deadly Reactor '89
The Deadly Secret '94
Deadly Sting '73
The Deadly Trackers '73
Deadly Twins '85
Deadly Vengeance '81
Deadly Weapon '88
Death and the Maiden '94 ▸
Death Blow '87
Death Magic '92
Death Row Diner '88
Death Sentence '07
Death to Smoochy '02
Death Valley: The Revenge of Bloody Bill '04
Death Wish '74
Death Wish 2 '82
Death Wish 3 '85
Deathlands: Homeward Bound '03
Deep in the Heart '83
The Defenders: Payback '97
Delinquent Girl Boss: Blossoming Night Dreams '70
Demented '80
The Demons '74
Demons from Her Past '07
Demonwarp '87
Descent '07
Desert Heat '99
Desolation Angels '95
Desperado '95 ▸
The Desperados '70
Desperate Crimes '93
Devastator '85
Devil Times Five '74
Devil Woman '76
Devil's Canyon '53
Devil's Knight '03
The Devil's Mistress '68
The Devil's Possessed '74
The Devil's Rejects '05
Devonsville Terror '83
The Diabolical Dr. Z '65
Die! Die! My Darling! '65
Die Hard: With a Vengeance '95
Dingaka '65
Dinner at the Ritz '37
Dinner Rush '00 ▸
Diplomatic Immunity '91
Dirty Harry '71 ▸
Dirty Little Secret '98
Dirty Work '97
Disclosure '94
The Divine Enforcer '91
Dixie Dynamite '76
Do or Die '91
Dr. Jekyll & Mr. Hyde '99
Dr. Syn, Alias the Scarecrow '64
Dr. Terror's House of Horrors '65
Dogville '03
Dogwatch '97
Dolemite '75
Double Exposure '93
Double Impact '91
Double Jeopardy '99
The Double Negative '80
Double Revenge '89
Driven to Kill '90
Drop Zone '94
Drums of Jeopardy '31
Dudes '87
Duel at Silver Creek '52
Dynasty '77
Eagle vs. Shark '07
Eagles Attack at Dawn '70
Easy Kill '89
Edge of Darkness '86
The Eiger Sanction '75
El Barbaro '84
Election '99 ▸
Electric Dragon 80,000V '01
The Eliminators '86
Emmanuelle, the Queen '79
The Empire of Passion '76 ▸
Enough '02
Escape '90
The Evil That Men Do '84
Evilspeak '82
The Ex '96
Ex-Cop '93
The Execution '85
The Executioner, Part 2: Frozen Scream '84
Executive Koala '06 ▸
The Expert '95
Exterminator '80
Exterminator 2 '84
Extreme Vengeance '90
Extremely Dangerous '99
Extremities '86
An Eye for an Eye '81
An Eye for an Eye '95
Eye of the Eagle 2 '89
Eye of the Tiger '86
Face/Off '97 ▸
A Face to Kill For '99
Facing the Enemy '00
Fair Game '85
Faithful '95
The Fall of the House of Usher '49
The Fall of the House of Usher '60 ▸
The Fall of the House of Usher '80
Falling Down '93
The Family '70
Far Country '55 ▸
Faust: Love of the Damned '00
Felony '95
Fight for Us '89
Fight for Your Life '77
The Fighter '52 ▸
Fighting Back '82
The Fighting Legion '30
Fighting Mad '76
Final Impact '91
Final Mission '84
Fine Gold '88
Fiorile '93 ▸
Firecracker '81
The First Wives Club '96
Fist Fighter '88
Fist of Honor '92
Fists of Blood '87
Fists of Iron '94
Five Element Ninjas '82
Five Minutes of Heaven '09
Flesh and Blood '22
Flesh and Blood '85
Flesh and the Spur '57
Flesh Feast '69
Fleshburn '84
Fog Island '45
For Which He Stands '98
For Your Eyes Only '81 ▸
The Forbidden Christ '50
Forbidden Sun '89
Force of Evil '77
Forced Vengeance '82
Forfeit '07
Forgotten Warrior '86
Four Brothers '05
The Four Musketeers '75 ▸
The Fourth Angel '01
Frame Up '91
Framed '75
Freaks '32 ▸
Freakshow '95
Freeway '88
Friend of the Family 2 '96
Frightmare '81
Frogs '72
From Hell It Came '57
Fudoh: The New Generation '96
Full Contact '92
Full Contact '93
Full Metal Jacket '87 ▸
Full Metal Ninja '89
The Funeral '96 ▸
Funland '89
Future Kill '85
"G" Men '35 ▸
Galloping Dynamite '37
The Gambling Samurai '60
Gang Boys '97
Gang of Roses '03
Gangs, Inc. '41
Gangs of New York '02 ▸
Garringo '69
Gator Bait 2: Cajun Justice '88
Genghis Cohn '93
Gentleman from Dixie '41
Get Carter '71 ▸
Get Carter '00
Getting Even '92
Ghetto Dawg 2: Out of the Pits '05
The Ghost '63
The Ghost '04
Ghost Dance '83
The Ghost of Yotsuya '58
Ghostriders '87
The Girl with the Hungry Eyes '94
Gladiator '00 ▸
The Godfather '72 ▸
The Godfather 1902-1959: The Complete Epic '81 ▸
The Godfather, Part 2 '74 ▸
God's Gun '75
Golden Swallow '68 ▸
Gone with the West '72
Gonin 2 '96
Goyokin '69 ▸
Grave of the Vampire '72
The Graveyard '74
The Green Cockatoo '37
Green Mansions '59
Gunfighter '98
Gunplay '51
Gunsmoke: Return to Dodge '87
Halloween '78 ▸
Halloween 6: The Curse of Michael Myers '95
Hamlet '48 ▸
Hamlet '90 ▸
Hamlet '96 ▸
Hamlet '01
Hang 'Em High '67
Hannibal '01
Hannibal Rising '07
Hannie Caulder '72
Harakiri '62 ▸
Hard Bounty '94
Hard Candy '06
Hard to Kill '89
Hardcase and Fist '89
Harold Robbins' Body Parts '99
The Haunted Palace '63
HauntedWeen '91
Hawkeye '88
He Who Gets Slapped '24 ▸
Headless Eyes '83
Heat Street '87
Heavy Metal 2000 '00
The Heist '89
Hell Hunters '87
Hell on Frisco Bay '55
Hell Ride '08
Hellbent '88
Hello Mary Lou: Prom Night 2 '87
Hell's Angels '69 '69
Hell's Belles '69
Hell's Kitchen NYC '97
Hennessy '75
Hi-Riders '77
The Hidden Room '49 ▸
High Command '37
High Noon '00
Highlander: Endgame '00
The Highway Man '99
Highwaymen '03
Hired Hand '71
Hit! '73
Hit & Run '82
Hitched '01
Hog Wild '80
Homeboy '75
Hornet's Nest '70
Horror Rises from the Tomb '72
The Horror Show '89
Hostage Hotel '00
Hot Lead '51
Hour of the Gun '67
Hourglass '95
House Across the Bay '40
A House in the Hills '93
House of Horrors '46
House of Strangers '49 ▸
The House of Usher '88
Housewife '72
How to Make a Monster '58
Human Beasts '80
The Human Factor '75
Human Lanterns '82
Hunter '76
I Drink Your Blood '71
I Married a Witch '42 ▸
I Met a Murderer '39
I Spit on Your Grave '77
If I Die Before I Wake '98
Igor & the Lunatics '85
I'll Sleep When I'm Dead '03 ▸
Illicit Behavior '91
Illtown '96
I'm the One You're Looking For '88
In a Glass Cage '86
In the Arms of My Enemy '07
In the Bedroom '01 ▸
In the Line of Duty: A Cop for the Killing '90
In the Presence of Mine Enemies '97
In Your Face '77
The Indestructible Man '56
The Indian Tomb '21
Inglourious Basterds '09 ▸
Inn of the Damned '74
An Innocent Man '89
Innocent Victim '90
Inquisition '76
Instant Justice '86
Instinct to Kill '01
The Invisible Man's Revenge '44
Ironheart '92
Irreversible '02
The Italian Job '03 ▸
Jack Frost 2: Revenge of the Mutant Killer Snowman '00
The Jayhawkers '59
Jenny Lamour '47
Jessi's Girls '75
The Jitters '88
Joe Somebody '01
John Tucker Must Die '06
Johnny Handsome '89 ▸
Joshua '76
Jubal '56
Kansas City Confidential '52 ▸
The Karate Kid: Part 2 '86
Karate Warrior '88
Kemek '70
Keys to Tulsa '96
Kickboxer 2: The Road Back '90
Kickboxer 4: The Aggressor '94
Kid '90
Kid Colter '85
Kid Vengeance '75
Kidnap Syndicate '76
Kill Alex Kill '76
Kill Bill Vol. 1 '03 ▸
Kill Bill Vol. 2 '04 ▸
Kill Line '91
Killcrazy '89
The Killing Kind '73
Killing Machine '02
Killing Time '97
The Killing Zone '90
King Boxer '72
King of the Ants '03

▸ = rated three bones or higher

The King of the Kickboxers '91
King of the Pecos '36
Kingfisher the Killer '81
Kiss Daddy Goodbye '81
Kiss of Death '94
Kuffs '92
L.A. Bounty '89
L.A. Crackdown '87
L.A. Heat '88
La Passante '83 ▸
La Vengeance d'une Femme '89
L.A. Vice '89
The Ladies Club '86
The Ladies of the Bois de Bologne '44
Lady Avenger '89
Lady Dragon '92
Lady Dragon 2 '93
The Lady in White '88 ▸
Lady Mobster '88
Lady Snowblood '73 ▸
Lady Street Fighter '86
Lady Vengeance '05
L'Annee des Meduses '86
Laserblast '78
Last Bullet '50
The Last Days of Dolwyn '49
The Last Don 2 '98
The Last Hard Men '76
The Last Hour '91
Last House on the Left '72
The Last House on the Left '09
Last Hurrah for Chivalry '78
The Last Outlaw '93
The Last Reunion '80
Last Train from Gun Hill '59 ▸
The Late Show '77 ▸
Law Abiding Citizen '09
Law of the Sea '32
Legacy of Rage '86
Legends of the Poisonous Seductress 1: Female Demon Ohyaku '68
Legends of the Poisonous Seductress 2: Quick Draw Okatsu '69
Legends of the Poisonous Seductress 3: Okatsu the Fugitive '69
Let's Go to Prison '06
License to Kill '89 ▸
The Life Aquatic with Steve Zissou '04
Lightnin' Bill Carson '36
The Limey '99 ▸
Lionheart '90
The Lion's Share '79
Lip Service '00
Lipstick '76
Little Boy Blue '97
Little Moon & Jud McGraw '78
Live Flesh '97 ▸
Living Doll '90
Lorna Doone '34
Lorna Doone '90
Lorna Doone '01 ▸
The Losers '10
Lovely... But Deadly '82
Lure of the Sila '49
Lust and Revenge '95
Macbeth '70 ▸
Macbeth '88
The Machine Girl '07
Macho Callahan '70
Mad Dog '84
Mad Max '80 ▸
Madame O '67
Magdalene '88
Make a Million '35
Make Haste to Live '54
Malicious '95
Malicious Intent '99
A Man Apart '03
The Man from Laramie '55 ▸
The Man in the Iron Mask '39 ▸
The Man in the Iron Mask '97
The Man in the Iron Mask '98 ▸
Man in the Wilderness '71
Man on Fire '04
The Man They Could Not Hang '39
The Man Who Came Back '08
The Manhandlers '73
Manhunt '73
Maniac '77
Manon of the Spring '87 ▸
Marathon Man '76 ▸
Mars '96
The Mask '94 ▸
Mask of Death '97
Massacre at Central High '76
The Master '80
The Match Factory Girl '90 ▸
Maternal Instincts '96
Max Payne '08
McBain '91 ▸
McQ '74
Mean Creek '04 ▸
Mean Girls '04 ▸
Mean Machine '73
Medea '88
Memento '00 ▸
Memories of Murder '90
Men... '85 ▸
Mercenary '96
The Merchant of Venice '04 ▸
Merchants of Death '99
Mercy '96
The Messenger '87
Metro '96
Miami Cops '89
Miami Vendetta '87
Micmacs '09
Midnite Spares '85
Millie '31
Mind Trap '91
Mindstorm '01
Ms. 45 '81 ▸
Missing Pieces '83
Mission Kashmir '00
Missionary Man '07
Mrs. Munck '95
Model by Day '94
Molly and Gina '94
The Monster and the Girl '41
Monte Cristo '22
Monte Walsh '70 ▸
Monument Ave. '98
Mooncussers '62
Moonshine County Express '77
Motor Psycho '65
The Mummy '59 ▸
Murder on Lenox Avenue '41
Murdered Innocence '94
The Murderers Are Among Us '46
Murphy's Law '86
Murphy's War '71
The Mysterious Dr. Fu Manchu '29
Nails '92
The Naked Angels '69
Naked Vengeance '85
Narc '02 ▸
Nasty Hero '89
Navajo Joe '67
Necromancer: Satan's Servant '88
The Neighbor No. Thirteen '05
The Nesting '80
Nevada Smith '66
Never Pick Up a Stranger '79
Never Say Die '94
The New Frontier '35
The New Kids '85
The Newlydeads '87
Next of Kin '89
Night Creature '79
Night Hunter '95
Night Train Murders '75
The Night Visitor '70
Nightmare '00
Nightmare Castle '65
Nightmare in Wax '69
9 to 5 '80
No Name on the Bullet '59 ▸
No Safe Haven '87
Nomad Riders '81
Nowhere to Run '88
The Nurse '97
Object of Obsession '95
Obsessed '88
Ocean's Thirteen '07 ▸
Offerings '89
Office Killer '97
Oklahoma Kid '39 ▸
Old Boyfriends '79
Old Gun '76 ▸
Oldboy '03 ▸
Olivia '83
On Dangerous Ground '51 ▸
On Guard! '03 ▸
Once a Thief '90
Once Upon a Time in Mexico '03 ▸
One Arabian Night '21 ▸
One Armed Executioner '80
One Deadly Summer '83 ▸
One-Eyed Jacks '61 ▸
One Man Army '93
One Man's Justice '95
One Man's War '90
One Russian Summer '73
Ong Bak 2 '08
Operation Intercept '95
The Operator '01
Opium and Kung-Fu Master '84 ▸
Orca '77
Original Gangstas '96
Othello '65 ▸
Othello '95 ▸
The Other Side of Midnight '77
Out for Blood '93
Out for Justice '91
Outlaw Force '87
The Outlaw Josey Wales '76 ▸
Outrage! '86
Outrage '93
Overkill '86
The Page Turner '06
Panhandle '48
Paparazzi '04
Paper Bullets '99
Parting Shots '98
Pathfinder '87 ▸
Pathfinder '07
The Patriot '00
Patriot Games '92 ▸
Pay Off '89
Payback '89
Payback '90
Payback '94
Payback '98 ▸
Payoff '91
Pecos Kid '35
The Penalty '20
Pepi, Luci, Bom and Other Girls on the Heap '80
The Perfect Bride '91
The Perfect Weapon '91
The Perfect Wife '00
The Phantom Bullet '26
The Phantom of Soho '64
Phantom of the Paradise '74
The Pit '81
Pit Fighter '05
Platoon the Warriors '88
Play Dead '81
Pledge Night '90
Plutonium Baby '87
Point Blank '67
Poison Ivy 3: The New Seduction '97
Positive I.D. '87
Posse '93 ▸
Possession: Until Death Do You Part '90
The Power of the Ninjitsu '88
Premature Burial '62
President's Target '93
Pretty Persuasion '05
Prey of the Jaguar '96
The Princess Blade '02
Prison '88
The Professional '94
Prom Night '80
The Prowler '81
Psychic Killer '75
Psycho Girls '86
Psychopath '73
Public Enemy '02
Pumpkinhead '88
The Punisher '90
The Punisher '04
Puppet Master 3: Toulon's Revenge '90
Pursued '47 ▸
Pushed to the Limit '92
Quantum of Solace '08
The Quick and the Dead '95
Quiet Cool '86
Quiet Fire '91
Rage '72
Rainbow Ranch '33
Rapid Fire '89
The Raven '35 ▸
Raven '97
Raw Deal '48 ▸
Raw Target '95
Recoil '97
Redline '97
Redline '07
Relentless '89
Remember Me '10
Renegades '89
The Replacement Killers '98
Reservoir Dogs '92 ▸
Rest Stop: Don't Look Back '08
The Restless Breed '58
Retribution '88
The Return of Dr. Fu Manchu '30
Return of Frank James '40 ▸
Return of the Evil Dead '75
Return of the Magnificent Seven '66
The Return of the Musketeers '89
Return of the Vampire '43
Return of Wildfire '48
Return to Macon County '75
Revenge '71
Revenge '86
Revenge '90
Revenge of the Barbarians '85
Revenge of the Nerds '84
Revenge of the Nerds 2: Nerds in Paradise '87
Revenge of the Radioactive Reporter '91
Revenge of the Red Baron '93
The Revenge Rider '35
Revolt of the Zombies '36
Revolver '92
Ricco '74
Ricochet '91 ▸
Ride Clear of Diablo '54
Ride Lonesome '59
Ride to Glory '71
Ride with the Devil '99
Ringside '49
Rio Lobo '70
Rip Roarin' Buckaroo '36
Rise: Blood Hunter '07
Rites of Frankenstein '72
Road to Perdition '02 ▸
Rock House '88
Rolling Thunder '77
Rolling Vengeance '87
Romola '25
Rose of Rio Grande '38
Rosewood '96 ▸
Round Numbers '91
Royal Deceit '94
Ruby Gentry '52
Rulers of the City '76
Runaways '75
Rushmore '98 ▸
Rustler's Paradise '35
Ruyblas '48
Sacrifice '00
Sacrilege '86
Samurai Reincarnation '81
The Satan Killer '93
Savage Drums '51
Savage Instinct '89
Savage Island '03
Savage Justice '88
Savage Run '70 ▸
Savage Streets '83
Scam '93
Scanner Cop 2: Volkin's Revenge '94
Scorned '93
Scorned 2 '96
The Scorpion King 2: Rise of a Warrior '08
Scream Dream '89
Screamer '74
Search and Destroy '81
Second Victory '87
The Secret Four '40
Seed '08
Seraphim Falls '06
Serial Bomber '96
Seven Hours to Judgment '88
The Seven-Ups '73
Severed Ties '92
Sex and Fury '73
Sex Crimes '92
The Shadow Man '53
Shadowheart '09
Shame '87
Shame '92
Sharpe's Eagle '93
The She-Beast '65
She-Devil '89
She Devils in Chains '76
She-Freak '67
Shinobi '05 ▸
Shoot Out '71
Shootfighter 2: Kill or Be Killed! '96
The Shooting '66 ▸
Shooting Fish '98
Short Eyes '79 ▸
Shotgun Stories '07
The Showdown '50
Showdown '93
Shutter '05
Silent Night, Deadly Night 2 '87
Simba '55 ▸
Simple Justice '89
Sin '02
Sin City '05
The Sin of Harold Diddlebock '47
Sirens '02
The Sister-in-Law '95
Sisters of Death '76
Six Shootin' Sheriff '38
Sizzle '81
Slaughter '72
Slaughter's Big Ripoff '73
Slayground '84
Sleep Easy, Hutch Rimes '00
Sleepers '96
Sleeping with the Enemy '91
Sloane '84
A Small Town in Texas '76
Smart Money '88
Smoke in the Wind '75
The Smokers '00
Snake Woman's Curse '68
SnakeEater '89
SnakeEater 3: His Law '92
Soldier Blue '70
Soldier's Fortune '91
Sometimes They Come Back '91
Sons of Katie Elder '65 ▸
Sorority Girl '57
Soul Vengeance '75
Sound of Murder '82
Sour Grapes '98
Special Investigator '36
The Specialist '94
Speed 2: Cruise Control '97
Speeding Up Time '71
Spider-Man 3 '07
The Spoilers '42 ▸
Stanley '72
Star Trek 2: The Wrath of Khan '82 ▸
Star Trek: First Contact '96 ▸
Steel and Lace '90
Steele Justice '87
Stiletto '08
The Sting 2 '83
Straight Shooter '99
Strange Confession '45 ▸
Strange Shadows in an Empty Room '76
Stranger in Paso Bravo '68
Strangler of the Swamp '46
Straw Dogs '72 ▸
Street Hunter '90
Street Law '74
Street Vengeance '95
Street War '76
Street Wars '91
Striker '88
Stuck '07
The Substitute '96
The Substitute 2: School's Out '97
Sudden Death '85
Sudden Impact '83
Sukiyaki Western Django '08
Super Force '90
The Supernaturals '86
Sweeney Todd: The Demon Barber of Fleet Street '07
Sweet Justice '92
Sweet Poison '91
Sweet Revenge '90
Sweet Revenge '98
Swift Justice '88
Sword Masters: Brothers Five '70
Sword Masters: The Battle Wizard '77
Sword Masters: Two Champions of Shaolin '80
Sword of Gideon '86
Sword of Venus '53
Swordsmen in Double Flag Town '91
Sworn Enemies '96
Sympathy for Mr. Vengeance '02 ▸
Tactical Assault '99
Take Two '87
Talion '66
Tarzan's Greatest Adventure '59
Taste the Blood of Dracula '70
Tears of the Black Tiger '00
Terror Creatures from the Grave '66
Terror in a Texas Town '58
Texas Kid '43
Texas Payback '95
The Texican '66
Theatre of Blood '73 ▸
They Made Me a Fugitive '47
Things '89
The 36th Chamber of Shaolin '78 ▸
This Gun for Hire '42 ▸
This Man Must Die '70 ▸
Thou Shalt Not Kill...Except '87
Threat '49
Three Husbands '50
Three in the Cellar '70
The 3 Marias '03
Thunder in the Desert '38
Thunder Warrior 3 '88
Tillie's Punctured Romance '14
A Time of Destiny '88
Time to Die '83
A Time to Kill '96 ▸
Timecop 2: The Berlin Decision '03
Titus '99
To Be the Best '93
Today We Kill, Tomorrow We Die '71
Tombs of the Blind Dead '72
Top of the Heap '72
Tormented '60
The Tormentors '71
The Torture Chamber of Dr. Sadism '69
Toy Soldiers '84
The Trackers '71
Trained to Kill '88
Transformers: Revenge of the Fallen '09
Trapped '02
Trapper County War '89
Trick or Treat '86
Tricks '97
Trigger Tricks '30
Trois Couleurs: Blanc '94 ▸
Truck Turner '74
Tube '03
Turk 182! '85
The 24th Day '04
24 Hours to Midnight '92
Twice a Judas '69
Twilight People '72
Twin Town '97
Twisted Brain '74
Twisted Nightmare '87
Two by Forsyth '86
Two Fathers' Justice '85
2000 Maniacs '64
Unconquered Bandit '35
Undefeatable '94
Under the Gun '88
Underworld '96
Underworld, U.S.A. '60 ▸
Underworld USA '61
Unfaithfully Yours '48 ▸
Unfaithfully Yours '84

▸ = *rated three bones or higher*

Unholy Four '54
Universal Soldier: The Return '99
The Unstoppable Man '59
Until They Get Me '18
Up River '79
Urban Justice '07
The Usual Suspects '95 ►
Utu '83 ►
V for Vendetta '06
Valentine '01
Valmont '89 ►
Vampire Journals '96
Vendetta '85
Vengeance '80
Vengeance is a Golden Blade '69
Vengeance of the Zombies '72
The Vernonia Incident '89
Vietnam, Texas '90
The Vigilantes Are Coming '36
Viper '88
The Virgin Spring '59 ►
Voodoo Black Exorcist '73
Voodoo Dawn '99
Walking Tall '73
Walking Tall: Part 2 '75
Walking the Edge '83
Wanted '08 ►
War '07
The War Wagon '67 ►
Water Rustlers '39
Waterfront '39
Weekend of Shadows '77 ►
The Weirdo '89
West of Zanzibar '28
The Wharf Rat '95
What's the Worst That Could Happen? '01
When Will I Be Loved '04
The White Sheik '52 ►
White Tiger '95
Wicked Lake '08
Wild Bill '95
Wild Gypsies '69
Wild Man '89
Wild Wheels '69
Wired to Kill '86
Witchouse '99
Without Honors '32
Wolf '94
Wolf Lake '79
The Women '39 ►
Wonder Man '45
Wounded '97
Write to Kill '91
Wuthering Heights '09
X Marks the Spot '42
X-Men Origins: Wolverine '09
X2: X-Men United '03 ►
Xtro 3: Watch the Skies '95
Young Warriors '83
Youth of the Beast '63
Yuma '70
Zero Tolerance '93
Zombie Lake '80
Zombie Nightmare '86

Revolutionary War

America '24
The Bastard '78
Benedict Arnold: A Question of Honor '03
The Crossing '00
The Devil's Disciple '59 ►
George Washington '84
The Howards of Virginia '40
John Paul Jones '59
Johnny Tremain & the Sons of Liberty '58
The Patriot '00
The Rebels '79
Revolution '85
The Seekers '79
1776 '72 ►
Sweet Liberty '86
The Time of Their Lives '46

Rio

Amor Bandido '79
Before the Devil Knows You're Dead '07 ►
Black Orpheus '58 ►
Blame It on Rio '84
Boca '94
Bossa Nova '99
Central Station '98 ►
City of God '02
City of Men '07 ►
Exposure '91
Flying Down to Rio '33
Herbie Goes Bananas '80
Kickboxer 3: The Art of War '92
Madame Sata '02
Notorious '46 ►
Orfeu '99
Party Girls for Sale '54
Possible Loves '00 ►
The Road to Rio '47 ►
The Story of Fausta '88
Subway to the Stars '87
That Night in Rio '41
Venus in Furs '70
Via Appia '92
Wild Orchid '90

A River Runs Through the Plot

see also *Sail Away; Whitewater Rafting*

The Adventures of Huck Finn '93 ►
The Adventures of Huckleberry Finn '39 ►
The Adventures of Huckleberry Finn '60
The Adventures of Huckleberry Finn '78
The Adventures of Huckleberry Finn '85
The African Queen '51 ►
Anacondas: The Hunt for the Blood Orchid '04
Apocalypse Now '79 ►
Bend of the River '52 ►
Beyond the Call of Duty '92
The Big Sky '52 ►
The Bridge at Remagen '69
The Bridge on the River Kwai '57 ►
Cape Fear '91 ►
Cold Fever '95
Death on the Nile '78
Delinquent Parents '38
The Edge '97
The Far Horizons '55
Lord of the Rings: The Fellowship of the Ring '01 ►
Lord of the Rings: The Return of the King '03 ►
Mean Creek '04 ►
Missouri Breaks '76
Mystic River '03 ►
The Outlaw Josey Wales '76 ►
The River '51 ►
The River '84
River of No Return '54
A River Runs Through It '92 ►
The River Wild '94
River's Edge '87 ►
Rooster Cogburn '75
Striking Distance '93
White River '99
Without a Paddle '04

Road Trip

see also *Bikers; Checkered Flag; Motor Vehicle Dept.*

Aberdeen '00
About Schmidt '02 ►
The Acid Eaters '67
Across the Great Divide '76
Across the Moon '94
Adrenaline Drive '99
The Adventures of Felix '99
The Adventures of Huck Finn '93 ►
The Adventures of Milo & Otis '89 ►
The Adventures of Priscilla, Queen of the Desert '94 ►
Alice Doesn't Live Here Anymore '74
All About Steve '09
Alligator Eyes '90
Almost Famous '00 ►
Aloha, Bobby and Rose '74
Along for the Ride '00
American Autobahn '84
American Fabulous '92
American Gun '02 ►
American Virgin '09
Another Day in Paradise '98
Are We There Yet? '05
Ariel '89 ►
Armed for Action '92
Around the Bend '04
Around the World in 80 Days '56 ►
Around the World in 80 Days '89 ►
Around the World in 80 Days '04
The Art of Travel '08
As Good As It Gets '97 ►
Ashik Kerib '88 ►
Away We Go '09
Babel '06 ►
Babylon A.D. '08
Bad Company '72 ►
Badland '07
Bam Bam & Celeste '05 ►
Bandwagon '95
The Beautiful Country '04
Beautiful Joe '00
Beavis and Butt-Head Do America '96
Because of You '95
Beethoven's 3rd '00
Beggars of Life '28
Betty '97
The Big Crimewave '86
The Big Empty '04
Big Fish '03 ►
Bingo '91
Bird on a Wire '90
Black Day Blue Night '95
Black Dog '98
The Black Rose '50
Blue De Ville '86
Blue Murder at St. Trinian's '56 ►
Blue State '07
The Blues Brothers '80 ►
Blues Brothers 2000 '98
Bolero '84
Bond of Fear '56
Bonneville '06
Boogie Boy '98
Borat: Cultural Learnings of America for Make Benefit Glorious Nation of Kazakhstan '06 ►
Born to Be Wild '95
Bound for Glory '76 ►
The Bounty Hunter '10
The Bourne Ultimatum '07 ►
Box of Moonlight '96
Boxcar Blues '90
A Boy Called Hate '95
Boys on the Side '94
Breaking the Rules '92
Breathing Lessons '94 ►
Bright Angel '91
Broken Flowers '05
Bronson's Revenge '72
The Brothers Grimm '05
The Brown Bunny '03
Bubble Boy '01
Buck and the Preacher '72
The Bucket List '07
Bustin' Loose '81 ►
Butch Cassidy and the Sundance Kid '69 ►
Butterfly Kiss '94
By Dawn's Early Light '00
Bye Bye Brazil '79
Calendar Girl '93
California Dreaming '07
California Straight Ahead! '37
Camilla '94
Candy Mountain '87
Cannonball '76
Cannonball Run '81
Cannonball Run 2 '84
A Canterbury Tale '44 ►
Carbide and Sorrel '63
Central Station '98 ►
Chandni Chowk to China '09
Changes '69
The Chase '93
Chasers '94
Chasing Liberty '04
Cheech and Chong: Things Are Tough All Over '82
Children of Hannibal '98
The Children of Huang Shi '08
Cirque du Freak: The Vampire's Assistant '09
Clodhopper '17
Coast to Coast '80
Coast to Coast '04
Cold Around the Heart '97
Cold Fever '95
Cold Mountain '03 ►
College Road Trip '08
Committed '99
The Concrete Cowboys '79
Cooperstown '93
Coupe de Ville '90
Crazy in Alabama '99
Crazy Mama '75
Crossroads '86
Crossroads '02
The Cure '95
Cycle Vixens '79
Daddy & Them '99
Damnation Alley '77
Danzon '91 ►
The Darjeeling Limited '07 ►
Dark Country '09
Daughter of Keltoum '01
The Daytrippers '96
The Delivery '99
Delusion '91
Der Purimshpiler '37
Detour '46 ►
The Devil Thumbs a Ride '47 ►
Diamond Men '01 ►
Diamonds '99
Diminished Capacity '08
Disappearances '06
Disney's Teacher's Pet '04 ►
Doctor Chance '97
Dogma '99
Doing Time for Patsy Cline '97
Don't Come Knocking '05
The Doom Generation '95 ►
Down by Law '86 ►
The Dream Catcher '99
Dream with the Fishes '97
Dreaming of Rita '94
Drive '96
Driving Lessons '06
Drowning on Dry Land '00
Dumb & Dumber '94
Dutch '91
Earthly Possessions '99
The Easy Life '63 ►
Easy Rider '69 ►
Eat, Pray, Love '10
El Camino '08
Elvis Has Left the Building '04
End of the Line '88
Endplay '75
Eternity and a Day '97
Eurotrip '04
Every Other Weekend '91 ►
Every Which Way But Loose '78
Everybody's Fine '09
Everything is Illuminated '05 ►
Extremedays '01
Eye of the Beholder '99
Fandango '85
Far Out Man '89
Fast Sofa '01
Father Hood '93
Fear and Loathing in Las Vegas '98
Finders Keepers '84
Finding Graceland '98
Finding North '97
$5 a Day '08
Flash & Firecat '75
Flight of the Innocent '93
Flim-Flam Man '67
Flirting with Disaster '95 ►
Forces of Nature '99
The Forsaken '01
Four Days '99
Free Zone '05
Freeway 2: Confessions of a Trickbaby '99
From Dusk Till Dawn '95
Get On the Bus '96 ►
Girl in the Cadillac '94
Give Me Your Hand '09
Go Further '03
The Go-Getter '07
Goodbye Pork Pie '81
A Goofy Movie '94
Grace Is Gone '07 ►
Grand Theft Parsons '03
The Grapes of Wrath '40 ►
The Great Buck Howard '09
Great Smokey Roadblock '76
The Great Texas Dynamite Chase '76
Greedy Terror '78
Guantanamera '95 ►
Gypsy 83 '01
The Happening '08
Hard Core Logo '96
Hard Luck '01
Harold and Kumar Go to White Castle '04
Harry and Tonto '74 ►
Having Wonderful Crime '45
Heart Beat '80
Heaven's Burning '97
Heck's Way Home '95
Hedwig and the Angry Inch '00 ►
Hell's Angels on Wheels '67
High Rolling in a Hot Corvette '77
Highway '01
Highway Hitcher '98
The Highway Man '99
Highway 61 '91
Highwaymen '03
The Hitcher '86
The Hitcher '07
The Hitcher 2: I've Been Waiting '03
Hitchhikers '72
Hollywood or Bust '56
Hombres Complicados '97
Home of Angels '94
Homecoming '96
Homer and Eddie '89
Homeward Bound 2: Lost in San Francisco '96
Homeward Bound: The Incredible Journey '93 ►
Honkytonk Man '82
Hot Blooded '98
House of Wax '05
Huck and the King of Hearts '93
I Accidentally Domed Your Son '04
I Am David '04
I Got Five on It '05
Ice Age: The Meltdown '06
Il Sorpasso '63
I'll Be Home for Christmas '98
I'll Take You There '99
In This World '03
The Incredible Journey '63
Innocents '00
Interstate '07
Interstate 60 '02
Into the Night '85
Into the West '92 ►
Into the Wild '07 ►
The Intruder '04 ►
Is Anybody There? '08
It Takes Two '88
The Italian '05
It's a Mad, Mad, Mad, Mad World '63
Jackpot '01
Jam '06
James' Journey to Jerusalem '03
Jay and Silent Bob Strike Back '01
Jeepers Creepers '01
Jerome '98 ►
Jiminy Glick in LaLa Wood '05
Joe Dirt '01
Johnson Family Vacation '04
Jon Jost's Frameup '93
Josh and S.A.M. '93
The Journey of Natty Gann '85 ►
The Journey to Kafiristan '01
Joy Ride '01 ►
Joy Ride to Nowhere '78
Joyride '77
The Judge Steps Out '49
Just Like the Son '06
Kalifornia '93
Kandahar '01
Kikujiro '99
Kill Your Darlings '06
Killer Bud '00
Kingpin '96
Kings of the Road—In the Course of Time '76 ►
Kiss My Grits '82
Kiss or Kill '97
La Strada '54 ►
La Vie Promise '02
Ladies and Gentlemen, the Fabulous Stains '82
Ladies on the Rocks '83
Lady Jayne Killer '03
Lamerica '95 ►
Landscape in the Mist '88 ►
Larger Than Life '96
Lassie '05
The Last Legion '07
Last Orders '01 ►
Last Stop for Paul '08
Leap Year '10
Leaving Normal '92
Leningrad Cowboys Go America '89
Les Rendez-vous D'Anna '78
Lewis and Clark and George '97
A Life Less Ordinary '97
The Limits of Control '09
The Lion of Africa '87
Lisboa '99
Little Miss Sunshine '06 ►
The Living End '92
Lolita '97
Loners '72
The Long Haul '57
The Long, Long Trailer '54
Loose Connections '87
Lord of the Rings: The Fellowship of the Ring '01 ►
Lord of the Rings: The Two Towers '02 ►
Lord of the Rings: The Return of the King '03 ►
Los Locos Posse '97
Lost '05
Lost in America '85 ►
Love and a .45 '94
A Loving Father '02
The Lucky Ones '08
Luminous Motion '00
Mad Love '95
Made in USA '88
Marooned in Iraq '02
Me and the Kid '93
Me & Will '99
Me, Myself, and Irene '00 ►
Meet the Fockers '04
The Mexican '01
Michael '96
Midnight Run '88 ►
Mob Story '90
Monsieur Ibrahim '03 ►
Monster Man '03
More '69
The Motorcycle Diaries '04 ►
Moving McAllister '07
The Muppet Movie '79 ►
The Music of Chance '93
My Blueberry Nights '07
My Fellow Americans '96
My Life in Ruins '09
My One and Only '09
My Own Private Idaho '91 ►
National Lampoon's Vacation '83 ►
The National Tree '09
Natural Born Killers '94
Neil Simon's The Odd Couple 2 '98
Neon City '91
Never on Tuesday '88
Niagara, Niagara '97
Night on Earth '91 ►
No Place to Run '72
No Sleep 'Til Madison '02
Nurse Betty '00 ►
The Odyssey '97
Omaha (the movie) '95
One Way Out '95
The Open Road '09
The Opposite of Sex '98
Out '82
Outside Ozona '98
Over the Hill '93
Overnight Delivery '96
Palindromes '04 ►
Paper Heart '09
Paper Moon '73 ►
The Passing of Evil '70
Patti Rocks '88 ►
Paulie '98

Pee-wee's Big Adventure '85 ▸
Phat Beach '96
Pieces of April '03
Pierrot le Fou '65 ▸
Pink Cadillac '89
Pinocchio '02
Planes, Trains & Automobiles '87
Play for Me '01
Play It to the Bone '99
The Pleasure Drivers '05
Pontiac Moon '94
Powwow Highway '89 ▸
Prime Target '91
Prison Train '38
Pulse '03
The Raffle '94
Rain Man '88 ▸
The Rain People '69 ▸
Rainbow Bridge '71
Rat Race '01
Reckless '95
Red Blooded 2 '96
Red Lights '04 ▸
The Reivers '69 ▸
Rescue Me '93
Retroactive '97
Ride '98
Ride in the Whirlwind '66
Riding Alone for Thousands of Miles '05
The Road '00
The Road '09
Road Games '81
Road Kill USA '93
The Road Killers '95
Road Movie '72
The Road to Bali '53 ▸
The Road to El Dorado '00
The Road to Galveston '96 ▸
The Road to Hong Kong '62
The Road to Morocco '42 ▸
Road to Perdition '02 ▸
The Road to Rio '47 ▸
The Road to Singapore '40
The Road to Utopia '46 ▸
The Road to Zanzibar '41 ▸
Road Trip '00
Road Trip: Beer Pong '09
The Road Warrior '82 ▸
Roadie '80
Roadkill '89
Roadside Prophets '92
The Rocker '08
Rockin' Road Trip '85
Rolling Family '04
Rough Magic '95
Round Trip to Heaven '92
Rubin & Ed '92
The Runaway Bus '54
Runaway Daughters '94
Running Hot '83
Running Wild '94
RV '06
Rx '06
The Saragossa Manuscript '65
Sawdust & Tinsel '53 ▸
Say It Isn't So '01
Scarecrow '73
Schultze Gets the Blues '03
Searching for Bobby D '05
Secret Ballot '01 ▸
September Gun '83
Serving Sara '02
Sesame Street Presents: Follow That Bird '85
Sex Drive '08
A Shadow You Soon Will Be '94
Sherman's March '86 ▸
Sherman's Way '08
Shrek the Third '07
Siddhartha '72
Sideways '04 ▸
Silk '07
The Simpsons Movie '07 ▸
Sin Nombre '09 ▸
Sincerely Charlotte '86 ▸
Six of a Kind '34 ▸
Six-String Samurai '98
Slither '73 ▸
Smoke Signals '98
Something Wild '86
Sorcerer '77
Soul Men '08
Spare Me '92
Sparkler '99
Speed Racer '08
Spies Like Us '85
Starlight Hotel '90
Starman '84 ▸
Stay As You Are '78
Stealth '06
Stir Crazy '80
Stop-Loss '08 ▸
The Straight Story '99 ▸
Strawberry Fields '97
Summer City '77
Sunchaser '96
The Sure Thing '85 ▸
Surfwise '07 ▸
The Sweetest Thing '02
Taking Chance '09
The Talent Given Us '04 ▸
Tenacious D in the Pick of Destiny '06
Tennessee '08
Testosterone '03
Thelma & Louise '91 ▸
Then Came Bronson '68
The Thing About My Folks '05
39 Pounds of Love '05
Those Magnificent Men in Their Flying Machines '65 ▸
The Three Burials of Melquiades Estrada '05 ▸
Three Days to Vegas '07
Three for the Road '87
Thumb Tripping '72
Tilt '78
Time of the Wolf '03 ▸
Time Out '01
To Wong Foo, Thanks for Everything, Julie Newmar '95
Tokyo Pop '88
Tommy Boy '95
Torque '04
Tourist Trap '98
Trading Favors '97
Transamerica '05 ▸
Traveling Man '89
Trouble Bound '92
The Truce '96 ▸
True Romance '93
Truth or Consequences, N.M. '97
Twentieth Century '34 ▸
28 Days Later '02
Twentynine Palms '03
Twins '88
Two for the Road '67 ▸
Two Tickets to Paradise '06
Under the Same Moon '07
Until the End of the World '91 ▸
Vince Vaughn's Wild West Comedy Show '06
Voyage in Italy '53
Wagons East '94
Waking Up in Reno '02
The Way West '67
Wedding Bell Blues '96
Weekend '67 ▸
West of Here '02
Western '96
Where the Eagle Flies '72
Where the Heart Is '00
White Line Fever '75
White River '99
Wieners '08
Wild America '97 ▸
Wild at Heart '90 ▸
Wild Boys of the Road '33
Wild Hogs '07
Wild Horses '95
The Wizard '89
The Wizard of Oz '39 ▸
World Traveler '01
Wristcutters: A Love Story '06
The Wrong Man '93
Y Tu Mama Tambien '01
The Yellow Handkerchief '08 ▸
Zoe '01
Zombieland '09 ▸

Robots & Androids

see also *Technology—Rampant*

A. I.: Artificial Intelligence '01
Alien '79 ▸
Alien Chaser '96
Alien: Resurrection '97 ▸
Aliens '86 ▸
American Cyborg: Steel Warrior '94
And You Thought Your Parents Were Weird! '91
Android '82
The Android Affair '95
A.P.E.X. '94
Assassin '86
Astro Boy '09
The Astro-Zombies '67
Automatic '94
Battlestar Galactica: The Plan '09
Bicentennial Man '99
Bill & Ted's Bogus Journey '91
The Black Hole '79
Blade Runner '82 ▸
Caprica '09
Carver's Gate '96
The Chess Player '27
Chicken Little '05
Chopping Mall '86
Circuitry Man '90
Class of 1999 '90
Class of 1999 2: The Substitute '93
The Companion '94
The Creation of the Humanoids '62
Cyber-Tracker '93
Cyber-Tracker 2 '95
Cyberzone '95
Cyborg '89
Cyborg 2 '93
Cyborg 3: The Recycler '95
Cyborg Cop '93
Cyborg Soldier '94
Cyborg Soldier '08
Daleks—Invasion Earth 2150 A.D. '66
D.A.R.Y.L. '85
The Day the Earth Stood Still '51 ▸
Devil Girl from Mars '54
Digital Man '94
Dr. Goldfoot and the Bikini Machine '66
Doctor of Doom '62
Doctor Satan's Robot '40
Downdraft '96
Edward Scissorhands '90 ▸
The Eliminators '86
The Empire Strikes Back '80 ▸
Eve of Destruction '90
Evolver '94
The Fifth Element '97
Forbidden Planet '56 ▸
Future Cop '76
G-Force '09
Ghost in the Shell '95 ▸
Heartbeeps '81
Heatseeker '95
The Hitchhiker's Guide to the Galaxy '81 ▸
The Hitchhiker's Guide to the Galaxy '05 ▸
How to Make a Doll '68
The Human Duplicators '64
Humanoid Defender '85
I, Robot '04
Inhumanoid '96
The Invisible Boy '57
The Iron Giant '99 ▸
K-9000 '89
Killing Machine '02
King Kong Escapes '67
Knights '93
Kronos '57
Light Years '88
Lost in Space '98
Mac and Me '88
Mandroid '93
Marebito '04
Meet Dave '08
Megaville '91
Metropolis '26 ▸
Monsters vs. Aliens '09
Moon '09
Mortal Challenge '97
Mystery Science Theater 3000: The Movie '96
National Lampoon Presents RoboDoc '08
Natural City '03
Negadon: The Monster from Mars '05
Nemesis '93
Nemesis 2: Nebula '94
Nemesis 3: Time Lapse '96
Night Siege Project: Shadowchaser 2 '94
Not Quite Human '87
Not Quite Human 2 '89
Omega Doom '96
Piano Tuner of Earthquakes '05
Planets Against Us '61
Plughead Rewired: Circuitry Man 2 '94
Programmed to Kill '86
Project: Shadowchaser '92
Project Shadowchaser 3000 '95
Prototype '83 ▸
Prototype X29A '92
Puzzlehead '05
Return of the Jedi '83 ▸
Robo Warriors '96
RoboCop '87 ▸
RoboCop 2 '90
RoboCop 3 '91
Roboman '75
Robot Holocaust '87
Robot in the Family '94
Robot Jox '90
Robot Monster '53
Robot Stories '03
The Robot vs. the Aztec Mummy '59
Robot Wars '93
Robots '05
R.O.T.O.R. '88
Runaway '84
Running Delilah '93
Serenity '05 ▸
Shadow Warriors '95
Short Circuit '86
Short Circuit 2 '88
Silent Running '71 ▸
Sky Captain and the World of Tomorrow '04
Solo '96
Space Truckers '97
Star Crash '78
Star Trek: First Contact '96 ▸
Star Trek: Generations '94 ▸
Star Trek: Nemesis '02
Star Wars '77 ▸
Star Wars: Episode 1—The Phantom Menace '99 ▸
Star Wars: Episode 2—Attack of the Clones '02 ▸
Star Wars: Episode 3—Revenge of the Sith '05 ▸
Star Wars: The Clone Wars '08
Starship '87
Steel and Lace '90
The Stepford Wives '04
Still Not Quite Human '92
Storm Trooper '98
Surrogates '09
Suspect Device '95
T-Force '94
TC 2000 '93
The Terminator '84 ▸
Terminator 2: Judgment Day '91 ▸
Terminator 3: Rise of the Machines '03 ▸
Terminator Salvation '09
Terror of Mechagodzilla '78
Tetsujin 28 '04
Tobor the Great '54
Total Recall 2070: Machine Dreams '99
Transformers '07
Transformers: Revenge of the Fallen '09
Treasure Planet '02
Universal Soldier: The Return '99
The Vindicator '85
Virus '98
Voyage of the Rock Aliens '87
WALL-E '08 ▸
Westworld '73 ▸
Zathura '05 ▸

Rock Flicks

The Adventures of Buckaroo Banzai Across the Eighth Dimension '84 ▸
Almost Famous '00 ▸
Alvin and the Chipmunks '07
American Pop '81
Anvil! The Story of Anvil '09
At Any Cost '00
Awesome! I F***in' Shot That! '06 ▸
Backbeat '94 ▸
Beat Street '84
Beyond the Valley of the Dolls '70
Blame It on the Night '84
The Blues Brothers '80 ▸
Blues Brothers 2000 '98
Born to Boogie '72
Brothers of the Head '06
Bummer '73
Burglar '87 ▸
Chuck Berry: Hail! Hail! Rock 'n' Roll '87 ▸
The Commitments '91 ▸
Confessions of a Teenage Drama Queen '04
The Courier '88
Cry-Baby '90 ▸
Dead Girls '90
Decline of Western Civilization 1 '81 ▸
Decline of Western Civilization 2: The Metal Years '88 ▸
Detroit Rock City '99
DIG! '04 ▸
Disorderlies '87
The Doors '91
Double Trouble '67
Eddie and the Cruisers '83
Eddie and the Cruisers 2: Eddie Lives! '89
Elvis and Me '88
Elvis: The Movie '79
End of the Century: The Story of the Ramones '03 ▸
Face the Music '00
Festival Express '03 ▸
The Filth and the Fury '99
The Five Heartbeats '91 ▸
FM '78
Follow That Dream '61
Frankie and Johnny '65
Garage Days '03
Get Crazy '83
Get Him to the Greek '10
Gimme Shelter '70
The Girl Can't Help It '56
Give My Regards to Broad Street '84
Grace of My Heart '96
Grand Theft Parsons '03
Great Balls of Fire '89
Gypsy 83 '01
Hail Caesar '94
Hard Core Logo '96
A Hard Day's Night '64 ▸
The Harder They Come '72
Head '68 ▸
Heaven Tonight '93
Hedwig and the Angry Inch '00 ▸
Help! '65 ▸
Horsey '99
I'll Be There '03
In His Life: The John Lennon Story '00
Incident at Channel Q '86
It Couldn't Happen Here '88
It Might Get Loud '09
The Jacksons: An American Dream '92
Jailhouse Rock '57 ▸
Johnny Suede '92
Jonas Brothers: The 3D Concert Experience '09
Josie and the Pussycats '01
The Kids Are Alright '79 ▸
KISS Meets the Phantom of the Park '78
La Bamba '87 ▸
Last Days '05
The Last Waltz '78 ▸
Laurel Canyon '02
Leningrad Cowboys Go America '89
Let It Be '70
Light of Day '87
Lip Service '00
Little Richard '00
Loving You '57
Masked and Anonymous '03
A Matter of Degrees '90
Mayor of the Sunset Strip '03 ▸
Meat Loaf: To Hell and Back '00
Metallica: Some Kind of Monster '04 ▸
Monterey Pop '68 ▸
Music & Lyrics '07
Neil Young: Heart of Gold '06 ▸
Netherworld '90
Nico Icon '95 ▸
1991: The Year Punk Broke '92
Nowhere Boy '09
Party! Party! '83
Prey for Rock and Roll '03 ▸
Privilege '67
Quadrophenia '79 ▸
Queen of the Damned '02
Red Hot '95
The Return of Spinal Tap '92
Rock & Roll Cowboys '92
Rock & Rule '83
Rock, Baby, Rock It '57
Rock My World '02
Rock 'n' Roll High School '79 ▸
Rock 'n' Roll High School Forever '91
Rock 'n' Roll Nightmare '85
Rock, Pretty Baby '56
Rock Star '01
The Rocker '08
Rocktober Blood '85
The Runaways '10
Running out of Luck '86
Satisfaction '88
Scenes from the Goldmine '87
School of Rock '03 ▸
Sex & Drugs & Rock & Roll '10
Shock 'Em Dead '90
Shooting Livien '05
Shout '91
Sid & Nancy '86 ▸
Six-String Samurai '98
Spellcaster '91
Spice World: The Movie '97
Still Crazy '98 ▸
Streets of Fire '84
The Suburbans '99
Suck '09
Sugar Town '99
Sunset Strip '85
Sunset Strip '99
Sweetwater: A True Rock Story '99
Taking Woodstock '09
The T.A.M.I. Show '64 ▸
Tapeheads '89
Tenacious D in the Pick of Destiny '06
Terror on Tour '83
That Thing You Do! '96 ▸
Theremin: An Electronic Odyssey '95 ▸
This Is Elvis '81
This Is Spinal Tap '84 ▸
Thunder Alley '85
Thunder & Mud '89
Tokyo Pop '88
Tommy '75
Trick or Treat '86
24 Hour Party People '01
U2: Rattle and Hum '88
Velvet Goldmine '98
Vibrations '94
Voyage of the Rock Aliens '87
Walk Hard: The Dewey Cox Story '07
What We Do Is Secret '07
When Love Comes '98
Wild Guitar '62
Woodstock '70 ▸
Yellow Submarine '68 ▸
Zombie and the Ghost Train '91

Rock Stars on Film

see also *Concert Films; Martyred Pop Icons; Pure Ego Vehicles*

Absolute Beginners '86
All You Need Is Cash '78 ▸

▸ = rated three bones or higher

Backbeat '94 ▸
Bill & Ted's Excellent Adventure '89
Black Dog '98
Blow-Up '66 ▸
Blue Hawaii '62
The Blues Brothers '80 ▸
Blues Brothers 2000 '98
The Bodyguard '92
Breaking Glass '80
The Bride '85
B.U.S.T.E.D. '99
Carny '80 ▸
Caveman '81
Charro! '69
Chuck Berry: Hail! Hail! Rock 'n' Roll '87 ▸
Cinderella '97
Clambake '67
Coal Miner's Daughter '80 ▸
The Crossing Guard '94 ▸
Crossroads '86
Detroit Rock City '99
DIG! '04 ▸
Double Trouble '67
Dune '84
Easy Come, Easy Go '67
Elvis: The Movie '79
End of the Century: The Story of the Ramones '03 ▸
End of the Line '88
Festival Express '03 ▸
Fire Down Below '97
Flaming Star '60 ▸
Follow That Dream '61
Frankie and Johnny '65
Freddy's Dead: The Final Nightmare '91
Fun in Acapulco '63
G.I. Blues '60
The Girl Can't Help It '56
Girl Happy '65
Girls! Girls! Girls! '62
Give My Regards to Broad Street '84
Go, Johnny Go! '59
Gypsy 83 '01
A Hard Day's Night '64 ▸
The Harder They Come '72
Harum Scarum '65
Head '68 ▸
Heat '95 ▸
Help! '65 ▸
How I Won the War '67
The Hunger '83
I Still Know What You Did Last Summer '98
It Happened at the World's Fair '63
Jailhouse Rock '57 ▸
Jawbreaker '98
Johnny Mnemonic '95
Kid Galahad '62
King Creole '58
KISS Meets the Phantom of the Park '78
Kissin' Cousins '64
La Bamba '87 ▸
Labyrinth '86 ▸
The Last Temptation of Christ '88 ▸
The Leading Man '96
The Legacy '79
Let It Be '70
Lisztomania '75
Live a Little, Love a Little '68
Lock, Stock and 2 Smoking Barrels '98 ▸
Love Me Tender '56
Loving You '57
The Magic Christian '69 ▸
Magical Mystery Tour '67
The Man Who Fell to Earth '76 ▸
Mayor of the Sunset Strip '03 ▸
McVicar '80
Merry Christmas, Mr. Lawrence '83 ▸
Metallica: Some Kind of Monster '04 ▸
Mrs. Brown, You've Got a Lovely Daughter '68
Monster Dog '82
Moonlight and Valentino '95
My Life '93
Neil Young: Heart of Gold '06 ▸
No Looking Back '98
Nomads '86
One Trick Pony '80
Paradise, Hawaiian Style '66
Pat Garrett & Billy the Kid '73 ▸
Performance '70 ▸
Pied Piper '72
Pink Floyd: The Wall '82
The Players Club '98 ▸
Poetic Justice '93
The Postman '97
The Preacher's Wife '96
Privilege '67
Quadrophenia '79 ▸
Return to Waterloo '85
Rock 'n' Roll High School '79 ▸
Roustabout '64
Row Your Boat '98
Runaway '84
The Running Man '87
Sgt. Pepper's Lonely Hearts Club Band '78
Sextette '78
Speedway '68
Spice World: The Movie '97
Spinout '66
Stay Away, Joe '68
That'll Be the Day '73
This Is Elvis '81
Tickle Me '65
Tommy '75
Traveller '96 ▸
The Trouble with Girls (and How to Get into It) '69 ▸
Under the Cherry Moon '86
Viva Las Vegas '63
Waiting to Exhale '95 ▸
The Wedding Singer '97
Wild in the Country '61
Wild Zero '00
Woodstock '70 ▸
Yellow Submarine '68 ▸

Rodeos

***see also** Westerns*

The Adventures of Gallant Bess '48
Arizona Cowboy '49
Bells of Capistrano '42
Born Reckless '59
Convict Cowboy '95
Cowboy Up '00
The Cowboy Way '94
Desert Trail '35
8 Seconds '94
Every Second Counts '08
Feud of the West '35
Girl from Calgary '32
Goldenrod '77
Junior Bonner '72 ▸
Kid from Gower Gulch '50
Lady Takes a Chance '43 ▸
The Last Ride '94
Lights of Old Santa Fe '47
The Lusty Men '52 ▸
Luzia '88
Man from Utah '34
The Misfits '61 ▸
My Heroes Have Always Been Cowboys '91
Never a Dull Moment '50
Oklahoma Cyclone '30
Painted Hero '95
Pee-wee's Big Adventure '85 ▸
Rhythm on the Range '36
Rider from Tucson '50
Rodeo Girl '80
Rodeo King and the Senorita '51
Rodeo Rhythm '42
Rolling Home '48
Ruby Jean and Joe '96
The Saddle Buster '32
Stir Crazy '80
Trouble in Texas '37
Wild Horse '31
Wild Horse Rodeo '37

Rogue Cops

***see also** Crime Drama; Organized Crime*

Armed and Dangerous '86
Assault on Precinct 13 '05
Back in Business '96
Bad Lieutenant '92 ▸
Bad Lieutenant: Port of Call New Orleans '09
Badge of the Assassin '85
Big Momma's House 2 '06
Blastfighter '85
Changeling '08 ▸
Chasing Ghosts '05
Cop Land '97 ▸
Corrupt '84 ▸
Dark Blue '03 ▸
Dealing: Or the Berkeley-to-Boston Forty-Brick Lost-Bag Blues '72
Dirty '05
District 13: Ultimatum '09
Dogwatch '97
Double Bang '01
Endgame '01
Enough '02
Eraser '96
Exit Wounds '01
Final Payback '99
Fish in a Barrel '01
Flashfire '94
Gang Related '96
The Gauntlet '77
The Glass Shield '95
Goodbye South, Goodbye '96
Hard to Kill '89
Harsh Times '05
Heaven '01
Internal Affairs '90
Kiss of the Dragon '01
L.A. Confidential '97 ▸
Lakeview Terrace '08 ▸
L.A.P.D.: To Protect and Serve '01
Last Man Standing '96
Lethal Force '00
Lethal Weapon 3 '92
Lone Star '95 ▸
Magnum Force '73
The Mod Squad '99
The Money Trap '65
Narc '02 ▸
The Negotiator '98
New Jersey Drive '95
Night Falls on Manhattan '96 ▸
One of Her Own '97
One Way Out '02
Our Man in Havana '59 ▸
Payback '98 ▸
Pressure '02
Pride and Glory '08
The Professional '94
Rent-A-Cop '88
Rip It Off '02
Romeo Is Bleeding '93
The Salton Sea '02
Samaritan Girl '04
Serpico '73 ▸
Shaft '00 ▸
Shakedown '88
Sin City '05
16 Blocks '06 ▸
The Spree '96
Stander '03
The Stickup '01
Stiletto '08
Striking Distance '93
Super Troopers '01
S.W.A.T. '03
Tales from the Hood '95
The Thin Blue Lie '00
Things to Do in Denver When You're Dead '95 ▸
Touch of Evil '58 ▸
Training Day '01
2 Fast 2 Furious '03
Unlawful Entry '92
Violent Cop '89
Witness '85 ▸

Role Reversal

***see also** Gender Bending*

Age Isn't Everything '91
All of Me '84
Anastasia '56 ▸
Anastasia: The Mystery of Anna '86
Angel '84
Angel on My Shoulder '46 ▸
Angel on My Shoulder '80
Babe '95 ▸
Bad Manners '84
The Bank Dick '40 ▸
Before Morning '33
Belfast Assassin '84
Big '88 ▸
Biggles '85
Billy Madison '94
Blood of Dracula '57
Bloodlink '86
The Captain from Koepenick '56
Captive Heart '47 ▸
Cheech and Chong's The Corsican Brothers '84
Christmas in Connecticut '45 ▸
Cinderfella '60
Clambake '67
Class Act '91
Cleo/Leo '89
Coming to America '88 ▸
Condorman '81
The Couch Trip '87
Courage '86 ▸
Dating the Enemy '95
Dave '93 ▸
The Deputy Drummer '35
Desperately Seeking Susan '85
Devil's Canyon '53
Dr. Black, Mr. Hyde '76
Doctor Detroit '83
Doctor Dolittle '67
Dr. Heckyl and Mr. Hype '80
Dr. Jekyll and Mr. Hyde '20 ▸
Dr. Jekyll and Mr. Hyde '32 ▸
Dr. Jekyll and Mr. Hyde '41 ▸
Dr. Jekyll and Mr. Hyde '68
Dr. Jekyll and Mr. Hyde '73
Doctors and Nurses '82
Down and Out in Beverly Hills '86
Dream a Little Dream '89
A Dream of Passion '78
18 Again! '88
Extremities '86
The $5.20 an Hour Dream '80
For Ladies Only '81
48 Hrs. '82 ▸
Freaky Friday '76
Freaky Friday '03 ▸
Garfield: A Tail of Two Kitties '06
The Gladiator '38 ▸
The Grand Duchess and the Waiter '26 ▸
The Great Gabbo '29
Greystoke: The Legend of Tarzan, Lord of the Apes '84
Guest Wife '45
Gunfire '50
Heart Like a Wheel '83
Her Life as a Man '83
Hero '92 ▸
Hiding Out '87
The Hot Chick '02
Identity Crisis '90
The Incredible Mr. Limpet '64
Iron Maze '91
It's a Boy Girl Thing '06
Jekyll and Hyde '90
Johnny Guitar '53 ▸
Junior '94
Just One of the Guys '85
Kagemusha '80 ▸
Kim '50 ▸
Kings and Desperate Men '83
La Femme Nikita '91 ▸
La Ronde '51 ▸
The Lady Vanishes '38 ▸
The Lady Vanishes '79
Ladybugs '92
Law and Order '42
Liane, Jungle Goddess '56
Like Father, Like Son '87
Liquid Sky '83 ▸
Lonely Wives '31
Maid to Order '87
Male and Female '19 ▸
The Man Who Haunted Himself '70
The Man Who Wagged His Tail '57
Man with Two Heads '72
Mrs. Winterbourne '96
Mr. Fix It '06
Monkey Business '52 ▸
Moon over Parador '88
My Blue Heaven '90
My Fair Lady '64 ▸
Naked Souls '95
Now, Voyager '42 ▸
Opportunity Knocks '90
Overboard '87
Panamint's Bad Man '38
Paris When It Sizzles '64
People's Choice '46
Performance '70 ▸
Persona '66 ▸
Pocketful of Miracles '61 ▸
Point of No Return '93
Posse '75 ▸
The Prince and the Pauper '37 ▸
The Prince and the Pauper '62
The Prince and the Pauper '78
The Prince and the Pauper '01
Prisoner of Zenda '37 ▸
Prisoner of Zenda '52
Prisoner of Zenda '79
Psycho '60 ▸
Quicksilver '86
Rabbit Test '78
The Raggedy Rawney '90
Raid on Rommel '71
Red Lion '69
Red Rock Outlaw '47
Rendez-Moi Ma Peau '81
Rider of the Law '35
The Road to Yesterday '25
Roman Holiday '53 ▸
A Saintly Switch '99
Satanik '69
Savages '72
Scalpel '76
The Scarlet Pimpernel '82 ▸
The Secret '07
September Affair '50
The Shaggy D.A. '76
The Shaggy Dog '59
Showdown in Little Tokyo '91
Silent Night, Deadly Night '84
Slapstick of Another Kind '84
A Slightly Pregnant Man '79
Small Town Boy '37
Something Special '86
Sommersby '93
Song of Texas '43
A Stolen Face '52
Stoogemania '85
Straight Talk '92
Summer Night with Greek Profile, Almond Eyes & Scent of Basil '87
Sweet Revenge '90
Switch '91 ▸
Sylvia Scarlett '35
Taking Care of Business '90
A Tale of Two Cities '89 ▸
The Tango Lesson '97
That's My Baby! '88
Tomboy '40
Tootsie '82 ▸
Trading Places '83
Triple Echo '77
The Two Faces of Dr. Jekyll '60
Ultimate Desires '91
Vice Versa '88 ▸
Victor/Victoria '82 ▸
Wait Till Your Mother Gets Home '83
Watermelon Man '70
White Man's Burden '95
White Sands '92
Wish upon a Star '96
Wonder Man '45
Yankee Zulu '95
Yentl '83
Yidl Mitn Fidl '36

Romance

***see** Late Bloomin' Love; Lovers on the Lam; Romantic Adventures; Romantic Comedy; Romantic Drama; Romantic Triangles; Teen Romance*

Romance

***see** Late Bloomin' Love; Lovers on the Lam; Romantic Adventures; Romantic Comedy; Romantic Drama; Romantic Triangles; Teen Romance*

Forbidden Valley '38

Romantic Adventures

Above Suspicion '43 ▸
The African Queen '51 ▸
Antz '98 ▸
Arabian Nights '42
Arabian Nights '00
As You Like It '06
The Awakening '95
Away We Go '09
Baby... Secret of the Lost Legend '85
Bagdad '49
The Barbarian '33
The Bounty Hunter '10
Brigham Young: Frontiersman '40
Broken Lullaby '94
Caprice '67
Captain Calamity '36
Captain from Castile '47 ▸
Casanova '05
Casanova '05 ▸
Chasing Liberty '04
China Seas '35 ▸
Crouching Tiger, Hidden Dragon '00 ▸
Destiny Turns on the Radio '95
Down Argentine Way '40 ▸
Duplicity '09
Durango '99
Ever After: A Cinderella Story '98 ▸
Fanfan la Tulipe '51 ▸
Flame of Araby '51
Fool's Gold '08
Frenchman's Creek '44
Frenchman's Creek '98
Gun Crazy '49 ▸
Guncrazy '92
Gypsy Angels '94
If I Were King '38 ▸
The Indian Fighter '55 ▸
Invisible Agent '42
The Jewel of the Nile '85
Joe Versus the Volcano '90
A Knight's Tale '01
The Last of the Mohicans '92 ▸
The Last Templar '09
Lie Down with Lions '94
The Mask of Zorro '98 ▸
Mogambo '53 ▸
Oscar and Lucinda '97
Pocahontas '95 ▸
The Proposition '96
Red Dust '32 ▸
Robot Pilot '41
The Rocketeer '91 ▸
Romancing the Stone '84 ▸
Rough Magic '95
Russian Dolls '05
The Seventh Dawn '64
Sideways '04 ▸
Six Days, Seven Nights '98
Son of Ali Baba '52
Spider-Man 3 '07
The Thomas Crown Affair '99 ▸
A Thousand and One Nights '45
The Truth About Charlie '02

Romantic Comedy

A Lot Like Love '05
Abdulla the Great '56
About Adam '00
About Last Night... '86 ▸
The Accidental Husband '08
Acqua e Sapone '83
Adam & Steve '05
Adam's Rib '50 ▸
Addicted to Love '96
The Admiral Was a Lady '50
Adorable Julia '62
Adrenaline Drive '99
The Adventures of Sadie '55
Advertising Rules! '01
After Midnight '04
Aggie Appleby, Maker of Men '33
Alchemy '05
Alex & Emma '03
Alfredo, Alfredo '72
All About Steve '09

▸ = *rated three bones or higher*

Just Write '97
Kate & Leopold '01
Keeping the Faith '00
Kettle of Fish '06
Key Exchange '85
Key to the City '50
Kill Me Later '01
The King on Main Street '25
King Ralph '91
A Kiss for Mary Pickford '27
Kiss Me Goodbye '82
Kiss Shot '89
Kiss the Bride '07
Kissing a Fool '98
Kissing Jessica Stein '02
Km. 0 '00
Knocked Up '07
Kuni Lemel in Tel Aviv '77
La Collectionneuse '67
La Lectrice '88
L.A. Story '91 ►
La Vie de Boheme '93 ►
Labor Pains '99
The Lady Eve '41 ►
The Lady Is Willing '42
Lady L '65
Lady on a Train '45 ►
Lady Takes a Chance '43 ►
The Lady's Not for Burning '87
L'Annee des Meduses '86
Lassie from Lancashire '38
The Last Fling '86
The Last Kiss '01
The Last Married Couple in America '80
The Last of the High Kings '96
Late Bloomers '95
Late for Dinner '91
Latter Days '04
L'Auberge Espagnole '02 ►
Laws of Attraction '04
Le Beau Mariage '82 ►
Le Magnifique '76
The Leading Man '96
Leap Year '10
Legal Eagles '86
Lena's Holiday '90
Les Grandes Manoeuvres '55 ►
Let It Snow '99
Let Us Be Gay '30
Let's Make It Legal '51
Let's Make Love '60
License to Wed '07
Lt. Robin Crusoe, U.S.N. '66
Life in the Fast Lane '00
Life or Something Like It '02
Life Without Dick '01
The Linguini Incident '92
Listen to Your Heart '83
Little Black Book '04
Little City '97
Little Manhattan '05
Little Noises '91
A Little Romance '79 ►
Little Sister '92
A Little Stiff '91
Little White Lies '89
Live Bait '95
Living on Love '37
Loco Love '03
The Lonely Guy '84
Lonely Hearts '82 ►
Lonely in America '90
Long-Term Relationship '06
Look Who's Talking '89 ►
Look Who's Talking, Too '90
Loose in New York '74
Lost and Found '79
Lost in Yonkers '93
Love Actually '03
The Love Affair, or The Case of the Missing Switch-board Operator '67 ►
Love Among the Ruins '75 ►
Love and Mary '07
Love and Other Disasters '06
Love and Other Four Letter Words '07
Love & Sex '00
Love at First Sight '76
Love by Appointment '76
Love Can Seriously Damage Your Health '96
Love Don't Cost a Thing '03
Love for Rent '05
Love Happens '09
Love Hurts '91
Love in the Afternoon '57
Love Is All There Is '96
Love Is Better Than Ever '52
Love Jones '96 ►
Love Laughs at Andy Hardy '46
Love, Ludlow '05
Love Me if You Dare '03
Love on the Run '36
Love Potion #9 '92
Love Stinks '99
The Love Trap '29
Loveless in Los Angeles '07
Lovelife '97
Lovelines '84
Lover Come Back '61
Loverboy '89
Lovers and Liars '81
Lover's Knot '96
Lovers Like Us '75
Lovers' Lovers '94
Loves & Times of Scar-amouche '76
Love's Labour's Lost '00
Loving Couples '80
Loving Jezebel '99
Loving Leah '09
The Low Down '00
Lucky Seven '03
Luminarias '99
The Lunatic '92
Lunatics: A Love Story '92 ►
Luster '02
Made in America '93
Made in Heaven '52
Made of Honor '08
Magic on Love Island '80
The Magnificent Dope '42
The Maid '90
Maid in Manhattan '02
Maid's Night Out '38
The Main Event '79
Main Street to Broadway '53
A Majority of One '56
Making Mr. Right '86
Male and Female '19 ►
The Male Animal '42
Mama, There's a Man in Your Bed '89 ►
Mambo Italiano '03
A Man, a Woman, and a Bank '79
Man Trouble '92
The Man Who Loved Women '77 ►
The Man Who Loved Women '83
The Man Who Made Hus-bands Jealous '98
Management '09
Manhattan '79 ►
Manhattan Merenque! '95
Mannequin '87
Marius and Jeannette '97
Marriage Italian Style '64 ►
The Marriage of Figaro '49
Married? '26
Married to the Mob '88 ►
The Marrying Man '91
The Matchmaker '58 ►
The Matchmaker '97
The Mating Habits of the Earthbound Human '99
Matrimaniac '16
May Wine '90
Me and You and Everyone We Know '05 ►
Me, Myself & I '92
Me, Myself, and Irene '00 ►
Meet Market '08
Meeting Daddy '98
Meeting Venus '91
Miami Rhapsody '95
Michael '96
Mickey Blue Eyes '99
Micki & Maude '84
A Midsummer Night's Dream '35 ►
A Midsummer Night's Dream '68
A Midsummer Night's Dream '96
Milk Money '94
The Millionairess '60
Minnie and Moskowitz '71
Miracle Beach '92
The Mirror Has Two Faces '96
The Misadventures of Merlin Jones '63
Miss Right '81
Mrs. Winterbourne '96
Mr. Boggs Steps Out '38
Mr. Fix It '06
Mr. Jealousy '98
Mr. Love '86
Mr. Lucky '43 ►
Mr. Peabody & the Mermaid '48
Mr. Right '06
Mr. Wonderful '93
Mr. Write '92
A Modern Affair '94
Modern Love '90
Modern Romance '81 ►
Monaco Forever '83
Money Buys Happiness '99
Monsoon Wedding '01 ►
A Month by the Lake '95
The Moon Is Blue '53
Moon Pilot '62
Moonstruck '87 ►
Morgan: A Suitable Case for Treatment '66
Mostly Martha '01 ►
Mouth to Mouth '95
Move Over, Darling '63
Much Ado about Nothing '93 ►
Murphy's Romance '85 ►
Music & Lyrics '07
Music from Another Room '97
Must Love Dogs '05
My Best Friend's Girl '84
My Best Friend's Girl '08
My Best Friend's Wedding '97
My Boss's Daughter '03
My Brother's Wife '89
My Dear Secretary '49
My Faraway Bride '06
My First Wedding '04
My Girl 2 '94
My Life in Ruins '09
My Love For Yours '39
My Man Godfrey '57
My Night at Maud's '69 ►
My Sassy Girl '08
My Sex Life... Or How I Got into an Argument '96
My Stepmother Is an Alien '88
My Tutor '82
Mystery Date '91
The Mystery Man '35
Naked in New York '93
Never Again '01
Never Been Kissed '99
Never Met Picasso '96
Never on Sunday '60 ►
The New Eve '98 ►
New in Town '09
A New Kind of Love '63
A New Leaf '71
Next Stop, Wonderland '98
Next Time I Marry '38
Next Year If All Goes Well '83
Nice Girl Like Me '69
Nice Girls Don't Explode '87
Nice Guys Sleep Alone '99 ►
Nick and Jane '96
Night and Day '91 ►
The Night Club '25
The Night We Never Met '93
Nina Takes a Lover '94
Ninotchka '39 ►
No Reservations '07
Nobody's Fool '86
The Norman Conquests, Part 1: Table Manners '78 ►
The Norman Conquests, Part 2: Living Together '78 ►
The Norman Conquests, Part 3: Round and Round the Garden '78 ►
North to Alaska '60 ►
Nothin' 2 Lose '00
Nothing Personal '80
Notting Hill '99 ►
Novel Romance '06
Off Beat '86
Okoge '93
On Approval '44 ►
On the Line '01
On the Sunny Side '62
Once Around '91
Once Upon a Wedding '05
One Fine Day '96
One Rainy Afternoon '36
One, Two, Three '61 ►
One Wild Moment '78
Only the Lonely '91
Only with Married Men '74
Only You '92
Only You '94
The Opposite Sex and How to Live With Them '93
The Other Brother '02
The Other End of the Line '08
The Other Side of the Bed '03
The Other Sister '98
Our Miss Brooks '56
Out at the Wedding '07
Outrageous Fortune '87
Outsourced '06
Over Her Dead Body '08
Overboard '87
Overnight Delivery '96
The Owl and the Pussycat '70 ►
The Pallbearer '95
Panama Lady '39
Pantaloons '57
Paper Marriage '88
Paper Marriage '93
Paperback Hero '99
Paperback Romance '96
A Paradise Under the Stars '99
Pardon Mon Affaire '76 ►
Paris Holiday '57
Party '96
Pat and Mike '52 ►
The Patsy '28
Pedale Douce '96
Peggy Sue Got Married '86
Penelope '06
The Perfect Gift '95
The Perfect Holiday '07
The Perfect Man '05
Perfect Match '88
Perfectly Normal '91
Personal Property '37
The Personals '83
The Personals '98
Personals '00
Phffft! '54
Pick a Card '97
The Pick-Up Artist '87
Picture Perfect '96
Pie in the Sky '95
Pillow Talk '59 ►
Pirate Radio '09
Pizza '05
Play It Again, Sam '72 ►
Playing Mona Lisa '00
Playmates '72
Please Not Now! '61
The Pompatus of Love '95
Pool Hustlers '83
Pool Sharks '15
Pop Always Pays '40
Possible Loves '00 ►
Practical Magic '98
Preaching to the Perverted '97
Prelude to a Kiss '92
Pretty Woman '90 ►
The Price of Milk '00
Priceless '06
Priceless Beauty '90
Prime '05
The Prince & Me '04
The Prince and the Showgirl '57
The Princess and the Pirate '44 ►
The Princess Diaries 2: Royal Engagement '04
Princess O'Rourke '43
Prisoner of Zenda '79
Private Lives '31 ►
Probation '32
Promise Her Anything '66
Promises! Promises! '63
The Proposal '09
Protocol '84
Puccini for Beginners '06
The Purple Rose of Cairo '85 ►
Pursuit of Happiness '01
A Pyromaniac's Love Story '95
Quackser Fortune Has a Cousin in the Bronx '70 ►
Queens Logic '91
Quick Change '90
The Quiet Man '52 ►
The Raffle '94
Rafter Romance '34
The Rage of Paris '38 ►
The Ranch '88
The Rat Race '60 ►
Rattle of a Simple Man '64
Reaching for the Moon '31
Reality Bites '94
Regular Guys '96
Relative Values '99
Relax... It's Just Sex! '98
The Reluctant Debutante '58 ►
Remember the Night '40 ►
Rendez-vous de Juillet '49
Return to Me '00
Rich in Love '93
The Ritz '76 ►
River Street '95
Road to Ruin '91
Roads to the South '78
The Roaring Road '19
Roman Holiday '53 ►
Romance and Rejection '96
Romantic Comedy '83
Roses Bloom Twice '77
Round Numbers '91
Roxanne '87 ►
Roxie Hart '42
Rumor Has It... '05
Run, Fatboy, Run '07
Runaway Bride '99 ►
Running Mates '92 ►
Russian Dolls '05
Sabrina '54 ►
Sabrina '95
St. Ives '98
Saratoga '37
Saving Face '04
Scorchers '92
Seaside Swingers '65
Second Honeymoon '37
Secret Admirer '85
Secret Ingredient '92
Secret Life of an American Wife '68
The Secret of My Success '87
See You in the Morning '89
Seeing Other People '04
Seems Like Old Times '80
Send Me No Flowers '64 ►
The Sensual Man '74
The Sensuous Nurse '76
Separate Vacations '86
Serendipity '01
Service De Luxe '38
Seven Days Ashore '44
Seven Girlfriends '00
Seven Minutes in Heaven '86
The Seven Year Itch '55 ►
Sex and the Single Girl '64
Sex and the Single Parent '82
Sex is Comedy '02
The Sex Monster '99
Shadow of the Thin Man '41 ►
Shakespeare in Love '98 ►
Shall We Dance? '04
Shall We Kiss? '07
Shall We Kiss '09
Shallow Hal '01
Shanghai Surprise '86
She Done Him Wrong '33 ►
She Wouldn't Say Yes '45
She's All That '99
She's Gotta Have It '86 ►
She's Having a Baby '88
She's Out of My League '10
She's the One '96
The Shop Around the Cor-ner '40 ►
Shopgirl '05 ►
Shore Leave '25 ►
Short Circuit '86
The Shrimp on the Barbie '90
Shut Up and Kiss Me '05
Sibling Rivalry '90
Sidewalks of New York '01
Silver Streak '76 ►
Simply Irresistible '99
Singles '92 ►
Sixteen Candles '84 ►
Skin Deep '89
Sleepless in Seattle '93 ►
A Smile Like Yours '96
Smiles of a Summer Night '55 ►
Smiling Fish & Goat on Fire '99
Smokescreen '90
Snapshots '02
Snow: The Movie '83
Snowballin' '71
So This Is Paris '26 ►
Soapdish '91 ►
The Social Secretary '16
Sol Goode '01
Soldat Duroc... Ca Va Etre Ta Fete! '75
Solitaire for 2 '94
Some Prefer Cake '97
Someone Like You '01
Something About Sex '98
Something More '99
Something New '06
Something Short of Paradise '79
Something's Gotta Give '03 ►
Son of Gascogne '95
The Souler Opposite '97
Soup for One '82
Southern Belles '05
Spanglish '04
Special Unit 2002 '01
Speechless '94
Speed Dating '07
Spite Marriage '29 ►
Splash '84
Splendor '99
Sprung '96
Stand-In '37 ►
Standing on Fishes '99
Starter for Ten '06
State of the Union '48 ►
The Station '92
The Sterile Cuckoo '69 ►
Still Breathing '97
Stolen Kisses '68 ►
The Story of Boys & Girls '91 ►
The Story of Us '99
Straight Talk '92
Strange Bedfellows '65
Strange Planet '99
Strictly Ballroom '92 ►
Strictly Business '91
Stroke of Midnight '90
The Student Affair '97
Suburban Girl '07
Sugar Sweet '02
Summer School '77
A Summer's Tale '96
Sunday in New York '63
Sunset Limousine '83
Surf Party '64
Surrender '87
Surviving Desire '91 ►
Suzy '36
The Swan '25
The Swan '56 ►
Sweet Home Alabama '02
Sweet Lies '88
Sweet Talker '91
The Sweetest Thing '02
Table for Three '09
Tadpole '02
The Tall Guy '89 ►
The Taming of the Shrew '29
The Taming of the Shrew '67 ►
Tammy and the Bachelor '57
Tammy and the Doctor '63
The Tao of Steve '00 ►
Tattoo, a Love Story '02
The Teahouse of the August Moon '56
Ted & Venus '93
The Tender Trap '55
The Terminal '04
Thanks for the Memory '38
That Certain Thing '28
That Funny Feeling '65
That Lucky Touch '75
That Old Feeling '96

► *= rated three bones or higher*

That Touch of Mink '62
That Uncertain Feeling '41
Theodora Goes Wild '36 ▶
There's a Girl in My Soup '70
There's Something about Mary '98 ▶
They All Kissed the Bride '42
They All Laughed '81
They Got Me Covered '43
The Thing Called Love '93
The Things of Life '70 ▶
The Third Wheel '02
13 Going on 30 '04
Thirty Day Princess '34
30 Is a Dangerous Age, Cynthia '68
30 Years to Life '01
This Could Be the Night '57
This Happy Feeling '58
Thomas Graal's Best Film '17 ▶
Thomas Graal's First Child '18 ▶
Those Endearing Young Charms '45
Three Broadway Girls '32 ▶
Three Can Play That Game '07
Three Coins in the Fountain '54
Three for Bedroom C '52
Three Guys Named Mike '51
Three Husbands '50
Three of Hearts '93
Three Smart Girls Grow Up '39 ▶
Three to Tango '99
Three Way Weekend '81
Threesome '94
Tieta of Agreste '96
Tiger and the Pussycat '67
Til There Was You '96
Till Marriage Do Us Part '74
Tillie's Punctured Romance '14
Time of the Gypsies '90 ▶
Tin Cup '96 ▶
To Cross the Rubicon '91
To Paris with Love '55
Togetherness '70
Tokyo Cowboy '94
Tom, Dick, and Harry '41
Tom Jones '63 ▶
Tomboy '40
Tomboy '85
Too Beautiful for You '88
Too Smooth '98
Topsy Turvy '84
Totally Blonde '01
A Touch of Class '73 ▶
Touch of Pink '04
Town and Country '01
Train Man: Densha Otoko '05
The Treatment '06
Trick '99 ▶
Trippin' '99
The Triumph of Love '01
Trojan War '97
Trouble in Paradise '32 ▶
The Truth about Cats and Dogs '96 ▶
The Truth About Love '04
Tulips '81
Tune in Tomorrow '90
Twelfth Night '96
24 Nights '99
27 Dresses '08
Twice upon a Yesterday '98
2 Brothers & a Bride '03
2 Days in Paris '07 ▶
Two-Faced Woman '41 ▶
Two If by Sea '95
Two Much '96
Two Nights with Cleopatra '54
Two Ninas '00
Two of a Kind '83
Two Weeks Notice '02
The Ugly Truth '09
Under One Roof '02
Undercover Angel '99
Underground Aces '80
The Undertaker's Wedding '97
Une Parisienne '58
The Unkissed Bride '66
Up Your Alley '89
Utilities '83
The Vacillations of Poppy Carew '94
Valley Girl '83
Venus Beauty Institute '98
The Very Thought of You '98
Vicky Cristina Barcelona '08
Victor/Victoria '82 ▶
Vivacious Lady '38 ▶
Waiting for the Light '90
Walk, Don't Run '66
Warm Summer Rain '89
Watch It '93 ▶
Watching the Detectives '07
Wavelength '96
We All Loved Each Other So Much '77 ▶
We Were Dancing '42
The Wedding Banquet '93 ▶
Wedding Bell Blues '96
The Wedding Date '05
Wedding Daze '06
The Wedding Party '69
The Wedding Party '97
The Wedding Planner '01
The Wedding Singer '97
A Weekend in the Country '96
We're Not Married '52 ▶
What a Woman! '56
What Happened to Rosa? '21 ▶
What Happens in Vegas '08
What Women Want '00
Whatever It Takes '00
What's Good for the Goose '69
What's New Pussycat? '65 ▶
When Brendan Met Trudy '00 ▶
When Harry Met Sally... '89 ▶
When in Rome '09
When Ladies Meet '41
While You Were Sleeping '95 ▶
Whipped '00
Who Am I This Time? '82 ▶
The Whole Shebang '01
Why Change Your Wife? '20
Wilderness Love '02
Wildest Dreams '90
William Shakespeare's A Midsummer Night's Dream '99
Wimbledon '04
Wimps '87
Win a Date with Tad Hamilton! '04
A Wind from Wyoming '94
Wishful Thinking '92
Wishful Thinking '96
With Six You Get Eggroll '68
Without Love '45
Without Reservations '46
Woman Hater '49
The Woman in Red '84
Woman of the Year '42 ▶
Woman on Top '00
A Woman's a Helluva Thing '01
The Women '68
Working Girl '88 ▶
World and Time Enough '95
The World's Oldest Living Bridesmaid '92
Worth Winning '89
You Can't Fool Your Wife '40
You Gotta Stay Happy '48
You, Me and Dupree '06
You Stupid Man '02
You Tell Me '06
Younger & Younger '94
Your Place or Mine '83
You've Got Mail '98
You've Got to Have Heart '77
Zack & Reba '98
Zeus and Roxanne '96
Zus & Zo '01

Romantic Drama

A Coeur Joie '67
Aaron Loves Angela '75
Absent Without Leave '95
The Accidental Tourist '88 ▶
The Accompanist '93
Across to Singapore '28
Adam '09
Addicted '02
Adelheid '69
The Adorable Cheat '28
The Affair '73 ▶
The Affair '95
An Affair of Love '99
An Affair to Remember '57
The African Queen '51 ▶
After Julius '78
After Midnight '33
After Sex '97
Afterglow '97
Against All Odds '84
Against the Wind '90
The Age of Innocence '93 ▶
Aimee & Jaguar '98
Algiers '38 ▶
Ali: Fear Eats the Soul '74 ▶
Alice '90 ▶
Alice Adams '35
Alice et Martin '98
Alive and Kicking '96
All About You '01
All That Heaven Allows '55 ▶
All the Pretty Horses '00
All the Real Girls '03 ▶
All the Vermeers in New York '91 ▶
All This and Heaven Too '40 ▶
Almost Blue '93
Always '89
The American '01
Anatomy of a Seduction '79
And a Nightingale Sang '91
And Now My Love '74
Angel '37
Angel Baby '95 ▶
Angel Eyes '01
Angel Square '92
Angels and Insects '95 ▶
The Animal Kingdom '32 ▶
Ann Vickers '33
Anna '51
Anna Christie '23 ▶
Anna Karenina '48
Anna Karenina '85
Anna Karenina '00
Annapolis '28
An Annapolis Story '55
Anne of Avonlea '87 ▶
Another Time, Another Place '83 ▶
Another Way '82 ▶
Anthony Adverse '36
Apart from Hugh '94
The Apprentice '71
Arch of Triumph '48 ▶
Arch of Triumph '85
Arizona Sky '08
As Is '85
Ask the Dust '06
Aspen Extreme '93
Asylum '05
At First Sight '98
Atalia '85
Atonement '07 ▶
The Atonement of Gosta Berling '24 ▶
Audrey's Rain '03
Australia '08
Autumn Moon '92
The Average Woman '24
Back Street '41
Back Street '61
Backstreet Dreams '90
Bad Girl '31
Bad Love '95
The Ballad of the Sad Cafe '91
Balzac and the Little Chinese Seamstress '02
Band of Angels '57
Bandh Darwaza '90
Barbarian and the Geisha '58
The Barretts of Wimpole Street '34 ▶
Basil '98
Bayou Romance '86
The Beast '75
Beau Revel '21 ▶
Beauty and the Beast '46 ▶
Because of You '52
Becoming Jane '07
Bed of Roses '95
Before Sunrise '94
Before Sunset '04 ▶
Before the Rain '94 ▶
Beloved Enemy '36 ▶
Beloved Infidel '59
The Bengali Night '88
Berlin Blues '89
Besieged '98
The Best Intentions '92 ▶
The Best of Everything '59 ▶
Betty Blue '86 ▶
Beware of Pity '46
Beyond Borders '03
Beyond the Clouds '95
Beyond the Rocks '22
The Big Parade '25 ▶
Big Street '42
The Bigamist '53
Bird of Paradise '32
Bitter Sugar '96 ▶
Bitter Sweet '33
The Bitter Tea of General Yen '33 ▶
The Bitter Tears of Petra von Kant '72
The Black Marble '79 ▶
Black Orchid '59
Bleeding Hearts '94
Blind Husbands '19 ▶
The Blonde '92
Blonde Comet '41
Blood and Sand '22
Blood and Sand '89
Blood Feud '79
The Blood of Others '84
Bloom '03
The Blue Hour '91
The Blue Light '32 ▶
Blue Smoke '07
Blue Valentine '10
Blush '95
Bolero '84
Bombay Talkie '70
Born to Be Bad '50
Born Under Libra '01
The Boss Is Served '76
Bounce '00
The Boxer '97
Boy Takes Girl '83
Boys '95
Boys Love '06
Breakfast in Paris '81
Breaking and Entering '06
Breathless '59 ▶
Bride of the Wind '01
The Bride Wore Red '37
The Bridge '00 ▶
The Bridges of Madison County '95 ▶
Brief Encounter '46 ▶
Bright Star '09
Brokeback Mountain '05 ▶
Broken English '07
Broken Silence '01 ▶
The Brylcreem Boys '96
Buffalo Jump '90 ▶
Bullfighter & the Lady '50
Burning Secret '89
Buster and Billie '74
The Buttercup Chain '70
By Love Possessed '61
Bye Bye Blues '89
Cabiria '14
Cabo Blanco '81
Cactus '86
Cactus in the Snow '72
Caddie '76
Calendar '93 ▶
Camila '84 ▶
Camille '36 ▶
Camille Claudel '89 ▶
Captive Hearts '87
Captives '94
Carla's Song '97
Carmen '83 ▶
Carnival Story '54
Carolina Moon '07
The Carpetbaggers '64
Carrington '95
Casablanca '42 ▶
Cash McCall '60
Casino '80
Cass Timberlane '47
Castaway '87
The Castaway Cowboy '74
Catch and Release '07
Catherine Cookson's The Fifteen Streets '90
Catherine Cookson's The Moth '96
Catherine Cookson's The Secret '00 ▶
Catherine Cookson's The Wingless Bird '97
Catherine Cookson's Tilly Trotter '99
Caught '49 ▶
Chain Lightning '50
Chained '34
The Chambermaid on the Titanic '97
Chanel Solitaire '81
Changing Times '04
Chapter Two '79
Charles & Diana: A Palace Divided '93
Charlotte Gray '01
Charulata '64
Cheri '09
The Children '90
Children of a Lesser God '86 ▶
Children of the Century '99
The Christmas Card '06
Christopher Strong '33
Chunhyang '00
Cinderella Liberty '73 ▶
Circle of Friends '94
Circle of Love '64
Circle of Passion '97
Circle of Two '80
Circus World '64
City for Conquest '40 ▶
City Girl '30
Claire of the Moon '92
Clash by Night '52 ▶
Climates '06 ▶
Close My Eyes '91
Closer '04 ▶
Closing the Ring '07
Cloud Waltzing '87
Cobra '25
Cocktail '88
Code 46 '03
Cold Sassy Tree '89 ▶
Collector's Item '89 ▶
The Color of Evening '95
Come and Get It '36 ▶
Come See the Paradise '90 ▶
Coming Home '98
The Coming of Amos '25 ▶
Coming Through '85
The Competition '80 ▶
Condemned '29
Conquest '37 ▶
Consolation Marriage '31
The Constant Gardener '05 ▶
The Cooler '03 ▶
Corregidor '43
Corrina, Corrina '94
The Courage to Love '00
The Cousins '59 ▶
The Cowboy & the Ballerina '84
The Cranes Are Flying '57 ▶
crazy/beautiful '01
Crazylove '05
The Crossing '92
Crystal Heart '87
Cupid's Mistake '01
The Curious Case of Benjamin Button '08 ▶
The Cutting Edge '92
The Cutting Edge: Going for the Gold '05
Cyrano de Bergerac '25 ▶
Cyrano de Bergerac '50 ▶
Daddy Long Legs '19
Daisy Kenyon '47
Dalva '95
Damage '92 ▶
Dance '90
Dancers '87
Dangerous Beauty '98 ▶
Dangerous Liaisons '88 ▶
Dangerous Liaisons '03
Daniel Deronda '02
Danielle Steel's Changes '91
Danielle Steel's Daddy '91
Danielle Steel's Heartbeat '93
Danielle Steel's Palomino '91
Danielle Steel's Star '93
The Dark Angel '35
Dark Eyes '87 ▶
Dark Journey '37 ▶
Dark Odyssey '57
The Dark Side of the Sun '88
Dash and Lilly '99
The Dawning '88
A Day in October '92
Day-Time Wife '39
Daybreak '93
Days and Nights in the Forest '70
Dead Beat '94
Deadly Desire '91
Dear John '10
Death Takes a Holiday '34 ▶
December Bride '91
Deception '46 ▶
A Dedicated Man '86
Deja Vu '84
Deja Vu '98
The Delta '97
The Deluge '73
Desert Hearts '86 ▶
Desert Winds '95
Desire '36 ▶
Desire '93
Desperate Remedies '93
Devdas '55 ▶
Devdas '02 ▶
Devil in the Flesh '46 ▶
Devil in the Flesh '87
The Devil Is a Woman '35 ▶
Devil's Wanton '49
Devotion '31
Devotion '95
Diamond Girl '98
Die Grosse Freiheit Nr. 7 '45
Disappearing Acts '00
Divided Heaven '64
The Divine Lady '29
The Divorcee '30
Doctor Zhivago '65 ▶
Doctor Zhivago '03
Dogfight '91 ▶
Dogtown '97
The Dolls '83
Dolls '02 ▶
The Dolphin '87
Don Juan DeMarco '94
Doomsday '28
Dot the I '03
Down in the Valley '05
A Dream of Kings '69 ▶
The Dreamers '03
Dreams Lost, Dreams Found '87
Dresden '06
The Dressmaker '89
Dubarry '30
The Duchess of Langeais '07 ▶
Duel of Hearts '92
The Dying Gaul '05 ▶
Dying Young '91
Dynasty '76
The Eagle Has Two Heads '48 ▶
Earth & Water '99
Earthquake in Chile '74
The Easiest Way '31
East Side, West Side '49
Echoes '88
Ecstasy '33
The Edge of Love '08
Edward and Mrs. Simpson '80
Effi Briest '74 ▶
8 Seconds '94
84 Charing Cross Road '86 ▶
El Diputado '78 ▶
Elective Affinities '96
Elegy '08
Elena and Her Men '56 ▶
Elephant Walk '54
Elizabeth I '05 ▶
Elizabethtown '05
Eliza's Horoscope '70
Emily Bronte's Wuthering Heights '92
Emma '72
Emma '96 ▶
Emma '97 ▶
Empty Canvas '64
Enchanted April '92
End of August '82
End of Summer '97
End of the Affair '55
The End of the Affair '99 ▶
Endless Love '81
The English Patient '96 ▶
Entropy '99
Escape to Love '82
Eternal Sunshine of the Spotless Mind '04 ▶

▶ = rated three bones or higher

Ethan '71
Ethan Frome '92
Evangeline '29
Every Time We Say Goodbye '86
Everybody's All American '88
Everything Happens at Night '39 ▸
Ex-Lady '33
The Eyes, the Mouth '83
The Fable of the Beautiful Pigeon Fancier '88
Facing Windows '03
Faithless '00 ▸
Falling for a Dancer '98
Falling in Love '84
The Family Man '79
Fanny '32 ▸
Fanny '61 ▸
The Fantastic Night '42 ▸
Far and Away '92
Far from Heaven '02 ▸
Far from the Madding Crowd '67 ▸
Far from the Madding Crowd '97 ▸
The Far Pavilions '84
A Farewell to Arms '32 ▸
A Farewell to Arms '57
The Farmer Takes a Wife '35
Fascination '04
Fatal Attraction '80
Feast of July '95
Feast of Love '07
Fergie & Andrew: Behind Palace Doors '93
Fiances '63
Fire '96
Fire and Ice '87
Fire and Sword '82
Fire with Fire '86
Firelight '97
Fires Within '91
First Affair '83
First Knight '95
First Love '70
First Love '77
First Love and Other Pains / One of Them '99
First Love, Last Rites '98
Five Days One Summer '82
5x2 '04
The Flame Is Love '79
Flannel Pajamas '06
Fling '08
Flor Silvestre '58
The Flying Fool '29
A Fond Kiss '04
Food of Love '02
Fool for Love '86
Fools '70
For Love Alone '86
For Love or Money '88
For Sale '98
For the Love of Angela '82
For the Moment '94
Forbidden '85
Forbidden Fruit '52 ▸
Foreign Affairs '93 ▸
Foreign Student '94
Forever '78
Forever: A Ghost of a Love Story '92
Forever Emmanuelle '75
Foxfire Light '82
Franz '72
The French Lieutenant's Woman '81 ▸
French Postcards '79
Fresh Cut Grass '04
Fresh Horses '88
The Fugitive Kind '60
Fulfillment '89
Full Moon in Paris '84
G '02
Gabriela '01
Gal Young 'Un '79 ▸
Gamble on Love '86
The Game of Love '87
A Gentle Woman '69
Georgia, Georgia '72
Ghost '90 ▸
G.I. War Brides '46
The Gift of Love '90
Girl in Black '56
The Girl in Blue '74
The Girl in the Cafe '05
The Girl on the Bridge '98 ▸
The Girl with a Suitcase '60
Girl with Green Eyes '64
Girl's Dormitory '36
Glitter '01
The Go-Between '71 ▸
Going Shopping '05
Golden Demon '53
Golden Gate '93
Gone with the Wind '39 ▸
The Good German '06
Goodbye Again '61
The Gorgeous Hussy '36
The Governess '98
Grand Isle '92
The Great Gatsby '01
The Great Lie '41 ▸
Green Dolphin Street '47
Green Fields '37
Green Fire '55
Green Mansions '59
Greenberg '10
Griffin & Phoenix '06
Griffin and Phoenix: A Love Story '76
Guinevere '99 ▸
The Gymnast '06
The Hairdresser's Husband '92
Hammers over the Anvil '91
Hanover Street '79
Harem '85
Harem '86
Harnessing Peacocks '92
Havana '90
Head On '04
Head Over Heels '67 ▸
Hearing Voices '90
The Hearst and Davies Affair '85
Heart of Humanity '18
Heartbreakers '84 ▸
Hearts of War '07
Heartwood '98
Heat and Dust '82 ▸
The Heiress '49 ▸
Henry Hill '00
Here on Earth '00
Heroes '77
He's Just Not That Into You '09
The Hidden Blade '04
Hide-Out '34
High Art '98
His Private Secretary '33
History Is Made at Night '37 ▸
H.M. Pulham Esquire '41
Hold the Dream '86
Holding Trevor '07
Holiday Affair '49
Holiday Affair '96
Hollywood Cavalcade '39
Holocaust Survivors... Remembrance of Love '83
The Home and the World '84 ▸
Home Before Midnight '84
Home Sweet Home '14
Homecoming '48
Hong Kong 1941 '84
Honky '71
Hope Floats '98
The Horse Whisperer '97
Horsey '99
Hotel America '81
Hotel Room '93
The Hottest State '06
The Human Contract '08
Humoresque '46 ▸
Hurricane '79
Husbands and Wives '92 ▸
I Can't Escape '34
I Capture the Castle '02
I Conquer the Sea '36
I Live in Grosvenor Square '46
I Love N.Y. '87
I Love You '81
I Love You All '80
I Never Sang for My Father '70 ▸
Ice Castles '79
If Only '04
Iguana '89
I'll Be Seeing You '44
I'll Never Forget You '51
Image of Passion '86
In a Shallow Grave '88
In Dangerous Company '88
In Love and War '96
In Love and War '01
In Search of Anna '79
In the Mood for Love '00
In the Shadows '98
In Too Deep '90
Incantato '03
An Indecent Obsession '85
Indecent Proposal '93
Independence Day '83
Indiscretion of an American Wife '54
Indochine '92 ▸
Infinity '96
Innocence '00 ▸
Interval '73
Intimate Strangers '04 ▸
Intrigue and Love '59
Intruso '93
Inventing the Abbotts '97
Invisible Circus '00
Invitation '51
Iron Cowboy '68
Island of Desire '52
Isle of Secret Passion '82
Istanbul '57
It's All About Love '03
It's My Party '95
I've Always Loved You '46
Jacko & Lise '82
Jailbreakers '94
The Jane Austen Book Club '07 ▸
Jane Doe '96
Jane Eyre '34
Jane Eyre '44 ▸
Jane Eyre '83 ▸
Jane Eyre '96 ▸
Jane Eyre '97
Jane Eyre '06
Japanese Story '03 ▸
Jason's Lyric '94
Jenny '70
Jewels '92
Johnny Frenchman '46
Jon Jost's Frameup '93
Josepha '82 ▸
Jude '96 ▸
Jude the Obscure '71
Jules and Jim '62 ▸
Jungle Fever '91 ▸
Just Between Friends '86
Kept Husbands '31
The Key '58
Killing Heat '84
King Kong '05 ▸
Kings Go Forth '58
The King's Rhapsody '55
The King's Whore '90
Kipperbang '82
Kiss of Fire '98
Kissed '96
Kitty Foyle '40 ▸
Knight Without Armour '37 ▸
Knights of the Round Table '53
Kristin Lavransdatter '95
The L-Shaped Room '62 ▸
La Chartreuse de Parme '48
La Grande Bourgeoise '74
La Mujer de Mi Hermano '06
La Notte '60 ▸
La Petite Jerusalem '05
La Petite Lili '03
La Petite Sirene '80
La Separation '98 ▸
La Strada '54 ▸
Ladies in Lavender '04
The Ladies of the Bois de Bologne '44
Lady Chatterley '92
Lady Chatterley '06 ▸
Lady Chatterley's Lover '81
Lady from Louisiana '42
The Lady in Question '40
The Lady Refuses '31
The Lady with the Dog '59 ▸
Lagaan: Once upon a Time in India '01
The Lake House '06
L'Amour en Herbe '77
Lana in Love '92
The Land Girls '98
Landscape After Battle '70
Last Chance Harvey '08
The Last Confederate: The Story of Robert Adams '05
The Last Kiss '06
The Last Prostitute '91
The Last Ride '94
The Last Time I Saw Paris '54
The Last Train '74
The Last Winters '71
Lazybones '25
Le Bonheur '65
Le Jupon Rouge '87
Le Petit Soldat '60 ▸
Le Repos du Guerrier '62
A Legacy for Leonette '85
The Legend of Paul and Paula '73
Legends of the Fall '94
Leo Tolstoy's Anna Karenina '96
Leon Morin, Priest '61
The Leopard '63 ▸
Leopard in the Snow '78
Letters from the Park '88 ▸
Lianna '83 ▸
Liebelei '32
Lies and Whispers '98
Lies of the Twins '91
The Life and Loves of Mozart '59
Life and Nothing But '89 ▸
A Life of Her Own '50
Light of My Eyes '01
Lighthouse Hill '04
Lilith '64 ▸
Limbo '99
Linda '29
Listen to Me '89
The Little American '17
Little Dorrit, Film 2: Little Dorrit's Story '88 ▸
Little Minister '34 ▸
Lola '61 ▸
Lola '69
Long Ago Tomorrow '71
The Long, Hot Summer '58 ▸
The Long, Hot Summer '86 ▸
Lorna Doone '34
Lorna Doone '90
Lorna Doone '01 ▸
Louisiana '87
Loulou '80 ▸
Love Affair '39 ▸
Love Affair '94
Love Affair: The Eleanor & Lou Gehrig Story '77 ▸
Love After Love '94
Love and Basketball '00 ▸
Love and Faith '78 ▸
Love and the Frenchwoman '60 ▸
Love at the Top '86
Love Goggles '99
Love in Bloom '35
A Love in Germany '84
Love in the Time of Cholera '07
Love Is a Many-Splendored Thing '55
The Love Letter '98
Love Letters '45
Love Letters '83 ▸
Love Letters '99 ▸
The Love Light '21
The Love of Jeanne Ney '27
The Love of Three Queens '54
Love on a Pillow '62
Love on the Run '78 ▸
Love Play '60
Love Songs '84
Love Songs '99
Love Songs '07
Love Streams '84
Love with a Perfect Stranger '86
Love with the Proper Stranger '63 ▸
Love Without Pity '91
The Lover '92
The Lovers '59 ▸
Lovers: A True Story '90 ▸
Lovers of the Arctic Circle '98
The Lovers on the Bridge '91
The Loves of Carmen '48
Love's Savage Fury '79
Love's Unfolding Dream '07
Lovespell '79
Lucky Star '29
Lulu on the Bridge '98
Lust, Caution '07
The Luzhin Defence '00
Lydia '41 ▸
Machine Gun Blues '95
Mad Bull '77
Mad Love '95
Madagascar Skin '95
Madame Bovary '34 ▸
Madame Bovary '49 ▸
Madame Bovary '91 ▸
Madame Bovary '00
Maelstrom '00
Magenta '96
The Magnificent Matador '55
Magnificent Obsession '35
Maids of Wilko '79
Mambo '55
A Man and a Woman '66 ▸
The Man in Grey '45 ▸
The Man in the Moon '91 ▸
Man Is Not a Bird '65
The Man Who Cried '00
The Man Who Guards the Greenhouse '88
Mannequin '37
Manon '50
Mansfield Park '99
Mansfield Park '07
Map of the Human Heart '93
Margaret's Museum '95 ▸
Maria Chapdelaine '34 ▸
Maria Chapdelaine '84
Marigold '07
Marilyn & Bobby: Her Final Affair '94
Marjorie Morningstar '58
Martha and I '91 ▸
Marty '55 ▸
Match Point '05 ▸
A Matter of Love '78
Mayerling '36 ▸
Mayerling '68
Medicine Man '92
Melo '86
Melody '71
Memoirs of a Geisha '05
Men '97
Merry-Go-Round '23 ▸
Message in a Bottle '98
Middlemarch '93 ▸
The Mill on the Floss '37
The Mill on the Floss '97
The Million Dollar Hotel '99
A Million to One '37
Minna von Barnhelm or The Soldier's Fortune '62
Mirrors '85
Mississippi Masala '92 ▸
Mississippi Mermaid '69 ▸
Mrs. Mike '49
Mrs. Soffel '84
The Mistake '91
Mr. & Mrs. Loving '96 ▸
Mr. Jones '93
The Mistress of Spices '05
Model Behavior '82
Mogambo '53 ▸
Monsoon '97
Moondance '95
Moonlight Sonata '38
Moonlight Whispers '99
Morgan's Ferry '99
Morning Glory '93
Morocco '30 ▸
The Mother '03 ▸
Mouvements du Desir '94
Mozart and the Whale '05
My Antonia '94
My Brother Tom '86
My Forbidden Past '51
My Man Adam '86
My Name Is Joe '98
My Reputation '46
Mysteries '84
Nairobi Affair '88
Nais '45 ▸
Naked Tango '91
Nativity '78
Nelly et Monsieur Arnaud '95 ▸
The Nest '80
Nevil Shute's The Far Country '85
New York Nights '84
Next Time '99
Next Time We Love '36
Nicole '72
The Night and the Moment '94
A Night Full of Rain '78
Night Games '80
A Night in Heaven '83
Night Is My Future '47
Nights in Rodanthe '08
No Looking Back '98
No One Man '32
North Shore '87
Northanger Abbey '87
Northanger Abbey '07
Not Easily Broken '09
Not Quite Paradise '86
The Note 2: Taking a Chance on Love '09
The Notebook '04
Notorious '46 ▸
Nouvelle Vague '90
November Moon '85
Now and Forever '82
Now & Forever '02
O Pioneers! '91
O Quatrilho '95
Obsession '97
Of Human Bondage '34 ▸
Of Love and Shadows '94
Of Mice and Men '39 ▸
An Officer and a Gentleman '82 ▸
Old Gringo '89
Oliver's Story '78
Once in Paris... '79
One Brief Summer '70
One Summer Love '76
Only Love '98
Only Once in a Lifetime '79
The Only Thrill '97
Operator 13 '34
The Other Boleyn Girl '03
The Other Boleyn Girl '08
The Other Side of the Mountain '75
The Other Side of the Mountain, Part 2 '78
Our Modern Maidens '29
Our Mutual Friend '98
Our Time '74
Out of Season '75
Outcasts of the City '58
Over the Summer '85
Oxford Blues '84
The Painted Veil '06
Panama Flo '32
A Paper Wedding '89 ▸
Parrish '61
Partition '07
Passion of Love '82 ▸
A Patch of Blue '65
Paul and Michelle '74
Pay It Forward '00
Pepe Le Moko '37 ▸
The Perfect Husband '92
Perfect Love '96
Perfect Strangers '50
The Perfume of Yvonne '94
Personal Maid '31
Persuasion '71
Persuasion '95 ▸
Persuasion '07
Peter and Vandy '09
Petty Crimes '02
The Phantom of the Opera '90
The Pianist '91
The Piano '93 ▸
Picnic '55 ▸
Pittsburgh '42
Pizzicata '96
The Playboys '92 ▸
Playing Around '30
Playing by Heart '98
Pleasure '31
Poetic Justice '93
Poor White Trash '57
Port of Call '48 ▸
Portrait of Jennie '48 ▸
Portraits Chinois '96
Possessed '31
Possession '02
Pride and Prejudice '95 ▸
Pride and Prejudice '05 ▸
Pride of the Clan '18
Princess Yang Kwei Fei '55 ▸
Private Confessions '98
Private Fears in Public Places '06
The Private Lives of Elizabeth & Essex '39 ▸
The Prizefighter and the Lady '33 ▸
The Promise '79

▸ *= rated three bones or higher*

The Promise '94
Proof of Life '00
The Proposition '96
The Proud Ones '53
P.S. '04
P.S. I Love You '07
The Public Eye '92 ▸
Purana Mandir '84 ▸
Pure Country '92
Purple Hearts '84
The Purple Taxi '77
Purple Violets '07
Quality Street '37
Quatorze Juliet '32
Queen Bee '55
Queen Christina '33 ▸
Queen of the Stardust Ballroom '75 ▸
Rachel, Rachel '68 ▸
Rachel's Man '75
Racing with the Moon '84 ▸
Raffles '30 ▸
Rage of Angels '83
Rage of Angels: The Story Continues '86
The Railway Station Man '92 ▸
The Rainmaker '56 ▸
Raise Your Voice '04
Random Hearts '99
Reach the Rock '98
The Real Charlotte '91
Rebel '85
Rebel Love '85
Reckless '84
Reconstruction '03
Red Firecracker, Green Firecracker '93
Red Headed Woman '32 ▸
Red Kiss '85 ▸
The Red Lily '24
Red Sorghum '87 ▸
The Red Squirrel '93
Redwoods '09
Regeneration '15
Remember Me '10
Rendezvous in Paris '95
The Republic of Love '03
Resistance '03
The Restless '06
Return Engagement '78
The Return of Martin Guerre '83 ▸
The Return of the Native '94
Return of the Soldier '82 ▸
Return to Paradise '53
Return to the Blue Lagoon '91
Return to Two Moon Junction '93
Reunion in France '42
The Ring '27
Risk '94 ▸
The Road Home '01 ▸
The Road to Yesterday '25
Rob Roy '95 ▸
Rock Haven '07
Roman Spring of Mrs. Stone '61 ▸
The Roman Spring of Mrs. Stone '03
Romance '30
Romance in Manhattan '34
The Romance of Astrea and Celadon '07
Romance on the Orient Express '89
Romantic Englishwoman '75 ▸
Rome Adventure '62
Romeo and Juliet '36 ▸
Romeo and Juliet '54
Romeo and Juliet '68 ▸
Romper Stomper '92
Room at the Top '59 ▸
Room 314 '07
A Room with a View '86 ▸
A Room With a View '08
The Rose Tattoo '55 ▸
The Rover '67
Rowing with the Wind '88
Ruby's Bucket of Blood '01
The Run of the Country '95 ▸
Running Away '89
Running Out of Time '94
Ruyblas '48
Ryan's Daughter '70
Sadie Thompson '28 ▸
The Sailor Who Fell from Grace with the Sea '76
Sally Hemings: An American Scandal '00
Sam & Janet '02
Same Time, Next Year '78 ▸
San Francisco '36 ▸
Sand and Blood '87
The Sandpiper '65
Santa Fe '97
Sarah, Plain and Tall '91 ▸
Saratoga Trunk '45
Savage Capitalism '93
Savage Messiah '72 ▸
Saving Face '04
Say Hello to Yesterday '71
Sayonara '57 ▸
Scarlet Dawn '32
Scarlett '94
Scenes from the Goldmine '87
Scenes of a Sexual Nature '06
The Sea is Watching '02 ▸
Sea Wife '57
Second Wind '76
Secret Obsession '88
Secret of Yolanda '82
Secret Passions '87
The Secrets '07
Sense & Sensibility '85
Sense and Sensibility '95 ▸
Sense & Sensibility '07
The Separation '94
September Affair '50
The Serpent's Kiss '97
Seven Pounds '08
7th Heaven '27
The Seventh Stream '01
Shadow of China '91 ▸
Shadowlands '85 ▸
The Shape of Things '03
Shelter '07
The Shining Hour '38
Shining Through '92
Shinobi '05 ▸
Shoot the Piano Player '62 ▸
Shop Angel '32
Shopworn Angel '38 ▸
Silver City '84
The Silver Horde '30
Silver Strand '95
A Simple Promise '07
Sin Takes a Holiday '30
Sincerely Charlotte '86 ▸
Singapore '47
Sinners in the Sun '32
The Sins of Rachel Cade '61
Siren of the Tropics '27
Sister Dora '77
A Slave of Love '78 ▸
Sleep with Me '94
The Sleeping Dictionary '02
A Slipping Down Life '99
Slipstream '73
Smart Woman '48
Smilin' Through '33 ▸
Snow Country '57
The Soft Skin '64 ▸
Sold for Marriage '16
A Soldier's Tale '91
Solomon and Gaenor '98
Somewhere I'll Find You '42 ▸
Somewhere in Time '80
Somewhere Tomorrow '85
Sommersby '93
A Song for Martin '01
The Song of Songs '33
A Song to Remember '45 ▸
Sooner or Later '78
The Sorrows of Satan '26 ▸
South Riding '37
Souvenir '88
A Special Day '77 ▸
The Spider and the Fly '49
Splendor '35
Stage Beauty '04
Stanley and Iris '90
Stateside '04
Stealing Heaven '88
Stella '55
The Stilts '84 ▸
Stolen Hours '63
Stormy Waters '41
The Story of a Three Day Pass '68
The Story of Marie and Julien '03
The Story of the Late Chrysanthemum '39 ▸
The Story of Three Loves '53
The Story of Xinghua '93
The Strange Love of Molly Louvain '32
Strangers Kiss '83
Strangers When We Meet '60
Strapless '90
Strayed '03 ▸
Street Angel '28
Street Scene '31 ▸
The Student Prince in Old Heidelberg '27
Sugartime '95
Summer Affair '71
Summer Lovers '82
Summer Palace '06 ▸
Summer Storm '44
A Summer Story '88 ▸
Summertime '55 ▸
Susan Slade '61
Suspicious River '00
Sweet Bird of Youth '89
Sweet Land '05
Sweet Light in a Dark Room '60 ▸
Sweet November '68
Swept from the Sea '97
Swimming Pool '70
A Tale of Two Cities '80
A Tale of Winter '92
Talk of Angels '96
Talk to Me '84
Tango '98
Tango Bar '88
Tarzan Escapes '36 ▸
Tears in the Rain '88
The Tempest '63
The Temptress '26
The Tenant of Wildfell Hall '96
Tender Mercies '83 ▸
Tess '79 ▸
Tess of the D'Urbervilles '98
Tess of the D'Urbervilles '08
Tess of the Storm Country '22
Test Pilot '38 ▸
That Long Night in '43 '60
That Night '93
That Summer of White Roses '90
The Theory of Flight '98
Therese Raquin '80
They Call It Sin '32
36 Fillete '88 ▸
This Above All '42
This Is My Father '99
This Is the Sea '96
This Matter of Marriage '98
The Thorn Birds: The Missing Years '96 ▸
Three Comrades '38 ▸
Three Times '05
Through the Olive Trees '94 ▸
The Tiger and the Snow '05
Tilai '90
Till Human Voices Wake Us '02
Tim '79
Time Out for Love '61
A Time to Love & a Time to Die '58
The Time Traveler's Wife '09
Timeless '96
Tiptoes '03
To Have & Have Not '44 ▸
To Love Again '80
Today We Live '33
Together? '79
Tomorrow '72 ▸
Tomorrow Is Forever '46
Tonight or Never '31
The Torch '50
Torn Apart '89
Torn Between Two Lovers '79
Torrents of Spring '90
The Torture of Silence '17
The Touch '71
Touched '05
A Town Like Alice '85
Trapeze '56 ▸
Tristan & Isolde '06
Tristana '70 ▸
Tropical Malady '04
Trouble in Mind '86 ▸
True Heart Susie '19
True Romance '93
Trust the Man '06
The Tsar's Bride '66 ▸
The Tunnel '89
21 Days '37
24 Hours in a Woman's Life '61
2046 '04
Twin Falls Idaho '99 ▸
Twist & Shout '84 ▸
Two Daughters '61 ▸
Two English Girls '72 ▸
Two Lovers '09 ▸
Two Moon Junction '88
Two Plus One '95
Un Coeur en Hiver '93
The Unbearable Lightness of Being '88 ▸
Under the Greenwood Tree '05
Under the Lighthouse Dancing '97
Under the Sun '98
Undertow '30
The Unknown Soldier '98
An Unremarkable Life '89
Untamed Heart '93
Up Close and Personal '96 ▸
The Upside of Anger '05 ▸
The Valley of Decision '45 ▸
Vanity Fair '32
Vanity Fair '04
Verboten! '59
A Very Long Engagement '04 ▸
Vibrations '94
The Victory '81
The Virgin and the Gypsy '70
Virgin Machine '88
Vive l'Amour '94
Voyage of the Heart '90
Voyager '91 ▸
A Walk in the Clouds '95
Walk in the Spring Rain '70
A Walk on the Moon '99
Walk Softly, Stranger '50
A Walk to Remember '02
The Walls of Malapaga '49
Waltz across Texas '83
The Wanderer '67
War & Love '84
War and Peace '56
War and Peace '68 ▸
War and Peace '73
War Lover '62
Washington Mistress '81
Waterfront '83
The Way We Were '73 ▸
We the Living '42
Weather in the Streets '84
Wedding in Blood '74 ▸
The Wedding March '28 ▸
Weeping Meadow '04
We'll Meet Again '82
West Side Story '61 ▸
What Dreams May Come '98
When a Man Loves '27
When I Close My Eyes '95
When Love Comes '98
When Night Is Falling '95 ▸
When the Time Comes '91
When Thief Meets Thief '37
Where the Boys Are '60
Which Way Home '90
Whistle Stop '46
White Cargo '42
The White Countess '05 ▸
White Light '90
White Nights '57 ▸
White Palace '90
The White Sister '23 ▸
Wicker Park '04
Wide Sargasso Sea '92
Wide Sargasso Sea '06
Wife Versus Secretary '36 ▸
Wild at Heart '90 ▸
Wild Hearts Can't Be Broken '91 ▸
Wildfire '88
William Shakespeare's Romeo and Juliet '96 ▸
Wind '92
The Wind and the Lion '75 ▸
Windmills of the Gods '88
Windrider '86
The Winds of Jarrah '83
Wings '27
Wings of Desire '88 ▸
The Wings of the Dove '97 ▸
Wings of the Morning '37
Winter Flight '84
Winter People '89
Without Orders '36
Wives and Daughters '01
A Woman at Her Window '77
A Woman at War '94
The Woman He Loved '88
Woman Is the Future of Man '04 ▸
The Woman Next Door '81 ▸
A Woman of Substance '84
A Woman Without Love '51 ▸
A Woman's Guide to Adultery '93
The Women on the Roof '89
The World of Suzie Wong '60
The Wrath of the Gods '14
Wuthering Heights '39 ▸
Wuthering Heights '53
Wuthering Heights '70
Wuthering Heights '98
Wuthering Heights '09
Yanks '79
Year of the Quiet Sun '84 ▸
Yes '04
Yesterday's Hero '79
You and Me '38
You Light Up My Life '77
The Young and the Guilty '58
Young Lady Chatterly 2 '85
The Young Victoria '09 ▸
Youth on Parole '37
Zelary '03 ▸
Zhou Yu's Train '02

Romantic Mystery

see also *Mystery & Suspense; Psycho-Thriller; Romantic Drama*

American Dreamer '84
Angels Fall '07
Another Woman '94
At the Midnight Hour '95
The Black Widow '05
Blue Smoke '07
Carolina Moon '07
A Change of Place '94
Charade '63 ▸
Every Woman Knows a Secret '99
Hard to Forget '98
High Noon '09
Laura '44 ▸
Loving Evangeline '98
Married Life '07 ▸
Midnight Bayou '09
Montana Sky '07
The Moon-Spinners '64
Moontide '42
Murder Is My Business '46
Notorious '46 ▸
Rear Window '54 ▸
Recipe for Revenge '98
Rough Cut '80
Secret Smile '05
The Thin Man '34 ▸
To Catch a Thief '55 ▸
To Have & Have Not '44 ▸
Treacherous Beauties '94
Tribute '09
The Undercover Woman '46
The Waiting Game '98

Romantic Triangles

see also *Otherwise Engaged*

A Coeur Joie '67
Across to Singapore '28
After Midnight '04
The Age of Innocence '93 ▸
Aladdin '92 ▸
All the Brothers Were Valiant '53
All Things Fair '95
The Alley Cats '65
Amateur '94 ▸
Amnesia '96
Among Giants '98
Amores Perros '00 ▸
Angie '94
Anna '51
Another Woman's Husband '00
Anything But Love '02
The Apprentice '71
Apres-Vous '03
The Art of Murder '99
Ash Wednesday '02
Autopsy: A Love Story '02
The Aviator's Wife '80 ▸
Baby Monitor: Sound of Fear '97
Baja '95
Balzac and the Little Chinese Seamstress '02
Bandits '01
Baton Rouge '88
The Baxter '05
The Best Man '97
A Better Tomorrow, Part 3 '89
Beyond the Rocks '22
The Big Bounce '69
Bitter Moon '92
The Black Dahlia '06
Black Day Blue Night '95
Blue Skies '46 ▸
Blush '95
Body Heat '81 ▸
Bon Voyage '03 ▸
Book of Love '04
Boom Town '40
Bordertown '35
The Boys and Girl From County Clare '03
Bread, Love and Dreams '53
Breakin' All The Rules '04
Bride of the Wind '01
Bridget Jones: The Edge of Reason '04
Broadcast News '87 ▸
Brothers '04 ▸
Brothers '09
The Brylcreem Boys '96
Bubble '06
Bugles in the Afternoon '52
Bull Durham '88 ▸
A Business Affair '93
Business for Pleasure '96
Cactus Flower '69
Cafe au Lait '94 ▸
Cake '05
Calendar '93 ▸
Call of the Yukon '38
Call Out the Marines '42
Canyon Passage '46 ▸
Captain Corelli's Mandolin '01
Carnal Knowledge '71 ▸
Carny '80 ▸
Carried Away '95
Carrington '95
Casablanca '42 ▸
Casino '95 ▸
Caught '96
Celine and Julie Go Boating '74
Children of the Century '99
Circle of Passion '97
Circus Girl '37
Cleopatra's Second Husband '00
Closer '04 ▸
Coastlines '02
Coco Before Chanel '09
The Color of Evening '95
Coming Out '89
Condition Red '95
The Cook, the Thief, His Wife & Her Lover '90 ▸
Country Life '95
Cowboy Up '00
Cowboys and Angels '00
Crashing '07
The Crucible '96 ▸
Cruel Intentions 3 '04
The Cuckoo '02
Daisy Kenyon '47
Dalva '95
Damage '92 ▸
The Dangerous '95
Dangerous Indiscretion '94
Dangerous Passion '95
A Dangerous Woman '93
The Dark Angel '35
Dark Blue World '01
Dark Harbor '98
Days '02
Days of Being Wild '91 ▸
Dead Beat '94

▸ = rated three bones or higher

Dead in the Water '01
Dead Ringers '88 ▸
Dear John '10
Dear Wendy '05
Death in Brunswick '90
Deceit '06
December Bride '91
The Devil Is a Woman '35 ▸
Devotion '95
Diabolique '96
Dinner and Driving '97
The Doom Generation '95 ▸
Dot the I '03
The Dreamers '03
Dreaming of Joseph Lees '99
Dreamland '06 ▸
Drift '00
Driven '01
Dry Cleaning '97
The Dying Gaul '05 ▸
East Side Story '07
The Edge of Love '08
The Edukators '04
Elephant Walk '54
The Embalmer '03 ▸
Emma '96 ▸
End of the Affair '55
The End of the Affair '99 ▸
Enduring Love '04
The English Patient '96 ▸
Eros '04
Ethan Frome '92
Everyone Says I Love You '96 ▸
Evil Dead Trap 2: Hideki '91
The Ex '96
Facing Windows '03
Faithless '00 ▸
A Family Affair '01
Far from Heaven '02 ▸
Far North '07
The Favor '92
Feast of July '95
Feast of Love '07
Fever '91
First Knight '95
The First Wives Club '96
The Flame of New Orleans '41 ▸
Fleeing by Night '00
Flirt '95
The Fluffer '01
A Foreign Affair '48 ▸
Forever Mine '99
Forty Shades of Blue '05
Foxfire Light '82
French Kiss '95
French Twist '95
Frontier of Dawn '08
Full Time Killer '01
G '02
Garage Days '03
Gay in Amsterdam '04
The Getaway '72
The Getaway '93
A Girl Cut in Two '07
The Girl with a Suitcase '60
Girl's Dormitory '36
Gloomy Sunday '02 ▸
The Golden Bowl '72 ▸
The Golden Bowl '00
The Good Guy '10
Goodbye, Lover '99
Goodbye My Fancy '51
Gray Matters '06
The Great Gatsby '49
The Great Gatsby '74
Grind '96
Gunshy '98 ▸
Hana & Alice '04 ▸
Happily Ever After '04
Hard Evidence '94
The Hard Truth '94
Head in the Clouds '04
The Heart of Me '02
Hearts of War '07
Henry & June '90 ▸
Here on Earth '00
Hero '03 ▸
The Hi-Lo Country '98
High Art '98
High Society '56 ▸
Hilary and Jackie '98 ▸
Hindsight '97
Hollywoodland '06
Homage '95
A Home at the End of the World '04
Hong Kong 1941 '84
Hot Saturday '32
I Love You Baby '01
I Take This Woman '40
Imagine Me & You '06
In the Shadows '98
Indecent Proposal '93
Indiscreet '98
Interlocked '98
Intersection '93
Intimate Betrayal '96
Intimate Relations '95
Intruso '93
Irreversible '02
Is Money Everything? '23
It Could Happen to You '94
It's Complicated '09
J'accuse! '19 ▸
Jason's Lyric '94
Journey Through Rosebud '72
Jules and Jim '62 ▸
Just Another Love Story '08
Kaaterskill Falls '01
The Keeper: The Legend of Omar Khayyam '05
Keeping the Faith '00
Kid Sister '45
Killer Looks '94
Kiss the Sky '98
Kissing a Fool '98
La Mujer de Mi Hermano '06
La Petite Lili '03
La Piscine '69
La Roue '23 ▸
Ladies in Lavender '04
The Ladies of the Bois de Bologne '44
Lady Chatterley '92
The Last Days of Chez Nous '92
The Last Kiss '01
The Last Man '00
The Last of the Mohicans '92 ▸
The Last Outpost '35
The Last Time '06
Le Jupon Rouge '87
The Leading Man '96
Leaving Metropolis '02
Legends of the Fall '94
Les Biches '68 ▸
Les Voleurs '96 ▸
L'Escorte '96
Liebelei '32
Lloyds of London '36 ▸
Love Actually '03
Love, etc. '96
Love Play '60
Love Serenade '96
Love Songs '07
Love Thy Neighbor '02
Love Walked In '97
The Lovers '59 ▸
Lucky Seven '03
Lucky Star '29
Lured Innocence '97
Made in Paris '65
Made of Honor '08
Magenta '96
Making Love '82
The Man I Love '97
The Man in the Attic '94
Man in the Saddle '51
Manpower '41
Mararia '98
Married Life '07 ▸
The Married Virgin '18
Match Point '05 ▸
Matter of Trust '98
Maybe... Maybe Not '94
Maze '01
Melinda and Melinda '05
Melo '86
Mildred Pierce '45 ▸
Miller's Crossing '90 ▸
Mr. Jealousy '98
Mists of Avalon '01 ▸
Mo' Better Blues '90
Mogambo '53 ▸
Mojave Moon '96
Moment to Moment '66
Mon Homme '96
Money Train '95
Moondance '95
Moonlight Whispers '99
Moonshine Highway '96
Moscow, Belgium '08
The Mother '03 ▸
The Mother and the Whore '73 ▸
Mouth to Mouth '95
Murder Czech Style '66
My Best Friend's Girl '08
My Best Friend's Wedding '97
My Brother Is an Only Child '07
My Favorite Wife '40 ▸
My Husband's Secret Life '98
My Zinc Bed '08
The Mysteries of Pittsburgh '08
Never Say Die '39
The New Twenty '08
Next Time We Love '36
Nick and Jane '96
No One Man '32
No Way Home '96
Obsession '97
On the Beach '00
Once a Thief '96 ▸
Once Upon a Time in the Midlands '02
One Night Stand '97 ▸
One Sunday Afternoon '33
Only You '94
The Opposite of Sex '98
Ordinary Sinner '02
The Other Boleyn Girl '08
Other Men's Women '31
Out of Africa '85 ▸
The Pallbearer '95
Palmetto '98
The Patsy '28
Pearl Harbor '01
Pedale Douce '96
The Perfect Gift '95
Perhaps Love '05
The Philadelphia Story '40 ▸
The Pianist '91
Plain Dirty '04
Play It to the Bone '99
Playing by Heart '98
Polish Wedding '97
Portrait in Black '60
Portraits Chinois '96
Possessed by the Night '93
Power and Beauty '02
Power Dive '41
A Price above Rubies '97
Private Confessions '98
The Promise '05
Puccini for Beginners '06
Pushing Tin '99 ▸
Puzzlehead '05
Queer Duck: The Movie '06
The Quiet American '02 ▸
Quiet Days in Hollywood '97
Radio Inside '94
Rancid '04
Reality Bites '94
Reckless '97 ▸
Reckless: The Sequel '98 ▸
Reducing '31
Restoration '94 ▸
Revenge '90
Riders '88
Rift '96
Risk '00
Road House '48
Road to Riches '01 ▸
Robin Hood: Prince of Thieves '91
A Room with a View '86 ▸
Rory O'Shea Was Here '04
Rumor Has It... '05
Sabrina '54 ▸
Sabrina '95
Samurai Banners '69
Sand and Blood '87
Saturday Night and Sunday Morning '60 ▸
Saturday Night Special '92
Savage Capitalism '93
Scorned 2 '96
The Second Front '05
Second Skin '99
The Separation '94
The Serpent's Kiss '97
Sex and the Other Man '95
The Sex Monster '99
She's Gotta Have It '86 ▸
She's So Lovely '97
Shopgirl '05 ▸
Silk '07
Simpatico '99
The Situation '06
Six Days, Six Nights '94
Sky Captain and the World of Tomorrow '04
Slaves to the Underground '96
Sleep with Me '94
Sleepless in Seattle '93 ▸
Sliding Doors '97
Slogan '69
The Smiling Lieutenant '31
Something More '99
Something's Gotta Give '03 ▸
Sommersby '93
The Song of Songs '33
The Spectator '04
Splendor '99
Spring Fever '09
Stella '55
Stella Maris '18 ▸
Stonewall '95 ▸
Stormy Nights '97
Story of a Prostitute '65
The Story of Xinghua '93
The Student Affair '97
Sueno '05
Summer Catch '01
Summer Lovers '82
Superman Returns '06
Susan Slade '61
Sweet Home Alabama '02
A Tale of Winter '92
Talk of Angels '96
Tangled '01
Tango '98
Tape '01 ▸
Tempted '01
The Tenant of Wildfell Hall '96
The Tenants '06
Tequila Sunrise '88
Tess '79 ▸
Tess of the D'Urbervilles '98
There's Something about Mary '98 ▸
These Foolish Things '06
A Thin Line Between Love and Hate '96
The Third '04
Though None Go With Me '06
Three for the Show '55
Three of Hearts '93
Three to Tango '99
3-Way '04
Threesome '94
Thunder Birds '42
Tiger of Eschnapur '59
Tilai '90
Time of Favor '00
Tin Cup '96 ▸
Tollbooth '94
Torrents of Spring '90
Torrid Zone '40
Totally Blonde '01
Town and Country '01
Trace of Stones '66
The Trio '97
Triplecross '95
Trojan War '97
Trouble in Paradise '32 ▸
The Truth about Cats and Dogs '96 ▸
Twice upon a Yesterday '98
The Twilight Saga: New Moon '09
Twister '96
Two Girls and a Guy '98 ▸
Two Lovers '09 ▸
Two Much '96
Two Ninas '00
Two Plus One '95
Two Shades of Blue '98
U-Turn '97
The Unbearable Lightness of Being '88 ▸
Under Hellgate Bridge '99
The Underneath '95 ▸
Undertow '30
Undertow '10
Unfaithful '02 ▸
The Unknown Soldier '98
Untold Scandal '03
The Valet '06
Valley of the Kings '54
The Velocity of Gary '98
Vicky Cristina Barcelona '08
The Viking '28
A Village Affair '95
Vive l'Amour '94
Waiting to Exhale '95 ▸
A Walk on the Moon '99
Warlords '08
Wavelength '96
We All Fall Down '00
We Don't Live Here Anymore '04
The Wedding Banquet '93 ▸
The Wedding Singer '97
Welcome to Mooseport '04
The West Wittering Affair '05
What a Woman! '56
When Will I Be Loved '04
While You Were Sleeping '95 ▸
White Mischief '88 ▸
The Whole Nine Yards '00
Wild Things '98
Willie & Phil '80
A Wind from Wyoming '94
The Wings of the Dove '97 ▸
The Winning of Barbara Worth '26
Wishful Thinking '96
Without Orders '36
Wolf Trap '57
The Woman and the Stranger '84
A Woman at Her Window '77
Woman Is the Future of Man '04 ▸
Woman Wanted '98
A Woman's a Helluva Thing '01
The Women on the Roof '89
Wonder Bar '34
X, Y & Zee '72
XX/XY '02
Yes '04
You and Me '06
You Gotta Stay Happy '48
You Stupid Man '02
Zhou Yu's Train '02

Rome—Ancient

***see also** Historical Drama; Italy*

A.D. '85
Alone Against Rome '62
Amazons and Gladiators '01
Attila '54
Attila '01
Battle of Valiant '63
Ben-Hur '26 ▸
Ben-Hur '59 ▸
Caesar and Cleopatra '46
Caligula '80
Cleopatra '34
Cleopatra '63
Cleopatra '99
Cyclops '08
Demetrius and the Gladiators '54
Druids '01
Duel of Champions '61
Fabiola '48 ▸
The Fall of the Roman Empire '64 ▸
Fellini Satyricon '69 ▸
A Funny Thing Happened on the Way to the Forum '66 ▸
Gladiator '00 ▸
Julius Caesar '53 ▸
Julius Caesar '70
King Arthur '04
Last Days of Pompeii '35
The Last Days of Pompeii '60
The Last Legion '07
Quo Vadis '12
Quo Vadis '51 ▸
Quo Vadis '85
The Robe '53
Roman Scandals '33
Rome '78 '78
The Sign of the Cross '33
Spartacus '60 ▸
Three Ages '23 ▸
Titus '99
Troy '04
Two Gladiators '64

Rome—Modern

***see also** Italy*

The Abdication '74
And the Wild, Wild Women '59
Angels & Demons '09
Artemisia '97
Assassination in Rome '65
Bellissima '51 ▸
The Belly of an Architect '91 ▸
Besieged '98
Camille 2000 '69
Caterina in the Big City '03
Daniella by Night '61
Days '02
Don't Tell '05
Facing Windows '03
Fellini's Roma '72
Four Flies on Grey Velvet '72
The Frightened Woman '71
Ginger & Fred '86 ▸
The Godfather, Part 3 '90 ▸
Hudson Hawk '91
Indiscretion of an American Wife '54
La Dolce Vita '60 ▸
The Last Kiss '01
The Listening '06
The Moon & the Stars '07
My Own Private Idaho '91 ▸
National Lampoon's European Vacation '85
Night on Earth '91 ▸
Ocean's Twelve '04
The Omen '06
The Order '03
Portrait of a Lady '96 ▸
Quiet Chaos '08
Red Riding Hood '03
Roman Holiday '53 ▸
Roman Spring of Mrs. Stone '61 ▸
The Scarlet & the Black '83
A Special Day '77 ▸
The Spectator '04
Steam: A Turkish Bath '96 ▸
The Stendahl Syndrome '95
The Talented Mr. Ripley '99
Ten Thousand Bedrooms '57
Traveling Companion '96
The Unfaithfuls '60
Valentino: The Last Emperor '08
When in Rome '09
The White Sheik '52 ▸

Roommates from Hell

***see also** Psychotics/Sociopaths*

Deadbolt '92
The Fear Inside '92
He Died With a Felafel in His Hand '01
The Last Supper '96
Lip Service '00
Malice '93
Man in the Attic '53
The Night We Never Met '93
Pacific Heights '90 ▸
Perfect Tenant '99
Shallow Grave '94
Single White Female '92
Single White Female 2: The Psycho '05
Sweet Murder '93
Table for Three '09
Zero Degrees Kelvin '95

Royalty

***see also** Historical Drama; Medieval Romps; Period Piece; Royalty, British; Royalty, Russian*

Abdulla the Great '56
The Adventures of Marco Polo '38
Aladdin '92 ▸
Ali Baba and the Forty Thieves '43
Ali Baba and the 40 Thieves '54 ▸
Alice '09
Alice in Wonderland '10
Angelique and the Sultan '68
Anna and the King '99
Anna and the King of Siam '46 ▸
Annie: A Royal Adventure '95
Arabian Nights '42
Arabian Nights '00

▸ = *rated three bones or higher*

▶ = rated three bones or higher

Commissar '68 ▶
Comrade X '40
Creation of Adam '93
Crimson Tide '95 ▶
Days of Glory '43
The Deal '05
The Death of Mr. Lazarescu '05
Dersu Uzala '75 ▶
A Different Loyalty '04 ▶
Direct Contact '09
Doctor Zhivago '65 ▶
Doctor Zhivago '03
Don't Drink the Water '69
Dostoevsky's Crime and Punishment '99
Drums of Jeopardy '31
The Duchess of Buffalo '26
The Eagle '25 ▶
East-West '99
The End of St. Petersburg '27 ▶
Enemy at the Gates '00
The Extraordinary Adventures of Mr. West in the Land of the Bolsheviks '24
Final Assignment '80
Final Warning '90
First Strike '85
The Fixer '68 ▶
Frederick Forsyth's Icon '05
Freeze-Die-Come to Life '90 ▶
The Gambler '97
The Girl from Petrovka '74
Goldeneye '95 ▶
Gorky Park '83 ▶
Gulag '85
Hitman '07
House of Fools '02
The Hunt for Red October '90 ▶
I Killed Rasputin '67
The Ice Runner '93
In Hell '03
In Tranzit '07
The Inner Circle '91 ▶
The Ister '04 ▶
The Italian '05
Ivan the Terrible, Part 1 '44 ▶
Ivan the Terrible, Part 2 '46 ▶
The Jackal '97
K-19: The Widowmaker '02
Kindergarten '84 ▶
Laser Mission '90
Last Command '28 ▶
The Last Station '09
The Light Ahead '39
Little Vera '88 ▶
Love and Death '75 ▶
The Man with the Movie Camera '29 ▶
The Mirror '75 ▶
Moscow Does Not Believe in Tears '80 ▶
Mother '26 ▶
Mother and Son '97
Mute Witness '95
My Family Treasure '93
My Name Is Ivan '62 ▶
Never Let Me Go '53
Nicholas and Alexandra '71
Night Watch '04
Nostalghia '83
One Day in the Life of Ivan Denisovich '71 ▶
100 Days Before the Command '90
One Russian Summer '73
The Peacemaker '97
Peter the Great '86 ▶
The Possessed '88
Prisoner of the Mountains '96 ▶
Rasputin '85 ▶
Rasputin and the Empress '33 ▶
Rasputin the Mad Monk '66
The Red and the White '68 ▶
Red Cherry '95
Red Heat '88
Red Hot '95
Reds '81 ▶
The Road to Life '31
The Russia House '90
Russian Dolls '05
Russian Roulette '93
The Saint '97
Sakharov '84 ▶
Scarlet Dawn '32
Scarlet Empress '34 ▶
Schizo '04
The Seagull '71 ▶
Siberiade '79 ▶
Sideburns '91
Since Otar Left... '03
A Slave of Love '78 ▶
Solo Voyage: The Revenge '90
Stalin '92
Stalingrad '94
Summer Storm '44
Taxi Blues '90 ▶
Terminal Velocity '94
Theremin: An Electronic Odyssey '95 ▶
The Thief '97
Three Legionnaires '37
The Three Sisters '65
Torrents of Spring '90
The Truce '96 ▶
2 Brothers & a Bride '03
The Ultimate Imposter '79
War and Peace '56
War and Peace '68 ▶
War and Peace '73
We the Living '42
White Nights '85
Window to Paris '95
The Winter War '89 ▶
World War III '86
Young Catherine '91 ▶

Russian Revolution

***see also** Red Scare; Russia/USSR; World War I*
Anastasia '56 ▶
Anastasia '97
Anastasia: The Mystery of Anna '86
The Battleship Potemkin '25 ▶
Doctor Zhivago '65 ▶
Doctor Zhivago '03
Nicholas and Alexandra '71
Rasputin '85 ▶
Rasputin and the Empress '33 ▶
Rasputin the Mad Monk '66
Reds '81 ▶
Scarlet Dawn '32
Tempest '28
Ten Days That Shook the World '27 ▶
Three Legionnaires '37

Rwanda

***see also** Africa*
Gorillas in the Mist '88 ▶
Hotel Rwanda '04
Shake Hands With the Devil: The Journey of Romeo Dallaire '04 ▶
Shooting Dogs '05
Sometimes in April '05 ▶

Sail Away

***see also** Deep Blue; Go Fish; Killer Sea Critters; Mutiny; Scuba; Shipwrecked; Submarines*
Abandon Ship '57
Across to Singapore '28
Adrift '93
Adventure Island '47
The Adventures of Huckleberry Finn '39 ▶
An Affair to Remember '57
The African Queen '51 ▶
All the Brothers Were Valiant '53
And the Ship Sails On '83 ▶
Anna Christie '30
Annapolis '28
Assault on a Queen '66
Away All Boats '56
The Baby and the Battleship '56
The Battleship Potemkin '25 ▶
Beat the Devil '53 ▶
Beyond the Poseidon Adventure '79
The Big Broadcast of 1938 '38
The Big Game '72
Billy Budd '62 ▶
Bitter Moon '92
Black Ops '07
Blast '04
Blondie Goes Latin '42
Blood Voyage '77
Blood Work '02
Blue, White and Perfect '42
A Blueprint for Murder '53
Boat Trip '03
The Boatniks '70
Botany Bay '53
The Bounty '84
Boy in Blue '86
Breakfast for Two '37
Brideshead Revisited '08
Britannic '99
Brittanic '00
Cabin Boy '94
The Caine Mutiny Court Martial '88 ▶
Captain Caution '40
Captain Horatio Hornblower '51 ▶
Captain Jack '98
Captain Ron '92
Captains Courageous '37 ▶
Captains Courageous '95
Captain's Paradise '53 ▶
The Captain's Table '60
Carry On Admiral '57
Carry On Cruising '62
Carry On Jack '63
The Cat's Meow '01
Charlie Chan in Honolulu '38
Charlie Chan's Murder Cruise '40
China Seas '35 ▶
Christopher Columbus '85
Chupacabra Terror '05
The Coast Patrol '25
Colleen '36
Convoy '40
Counterstrike '03
A Countess from Hong Kong '67
The Crew '95
Crimson Tide '95 ▶
Cruise into Terror '78
The Curious Case of Benjamin Button '08 ▶
Damn the Defiant '62 ▶
Danger Beneath the Sea '02
Dangerous Charter '62
Dangerous Crossing '53
Dangerous Passage '44
Dark Tide '93
Das Boot '81 ▶
Day of the Assassin '81
The Day Will Dawn '42 ▶
Dead Ahead: The Exxon Valdez Disaster '92 ▶
Dead Calm '89 ▶
Dead in the Water '01
Dead Reckoning '89
Dead Tides '97
Deadly Voyage '96
Death Cruise '74
Death Ship '80
Death Tide '58
The Deep '77
Deep Rising '98
Destroyer '43 ▶
Diary of a Suicide '73
Die Hard: With a Vengeance '95
Dixie Jamboree '44
Doctor at Sea '56
Don Winslow of the Coast Guard '43
Donkey Punch '08
The Dove '74
Down Periscope '96
Down to the Sea in Ships '22
The Ebb-Tide '97
Ensign Pulver '64
Erik, the Viking '65
Escape from Atlantis '97
Escape under Pressure '00
The Evil Below '87
Failure to Launch '06
Far from Home: The Adventures of Yellow Dog '94
Feet First '30
Ferry to Hong Kong '59
The Fighting Sullivans '42 ▶
The Final Countdown '80 ▶
Final Voyage '99
Flat Top '52
Flight of the Intruder '90
Flipper '96 ▶
Fool's Gold '08
Francis in the Navy '55
Friday the 13th, Part 8: Jason Takes Manhattan '89
Gambling Ship '33
Gangway '37
Geheimakte WB1 '42
The Ghost Ship '43
Ghost Ship '53
Ghost Ship '02
The Gift Horse '52
A Girl in Every Port '28
A Girl in Every Port '52
Give Me a Sailor '38
Going Overboard '89
Going Under '91
Golden Rendezvous '77
Goliath Awaits '81
Gone Fishin' '97
Gray Lady Down '77
The Great Lover '49
Gun Cargo '49
The Hairy Ape '44
Haunted Harbor '44
The Haunted Sea '97
Hawaii Calls '38
He Is My Brother '75
Hell-Ship Morgan '36
Hey! Hey! USA! '38
History Is Made at Night '37 ▶
Horatio Hornblower '99 ▶
Horatio Hornblower: The Adventure Continues '01 ▶
Horror of the Zombies '74
The Hunt for Red October '90 ▶
I Conquer the Sea '36
The Imposters '98
In Which We Serve '43 ▶
The Incredible Mr. Limpet '64
The Incredible Petrified World '58
Ironclads '90
Isle of Forgotten Sins '43
JAG '95
Jason and the Argonauts '00
Jaws '75 ▶
Jaws 2 '78
The Jewel of the Nile '85
Johnny Angel '45 ▶
Juggernaut '74 ▶
Kill Cruise '90
Killer on Board '77
King Kelly of the U.S.A. '34
King of Alcatraz '38
Knife in the Water '62 ▶
Lakeboat '00
The Last of Sheila '73
The Last Voyage '60
Law of the Sea '32
Le Crabe Tambour '77 ▶
The Legend of 1900 '98
The Legend of Sea Wolf '75
The Legend of the Sea Wolf '58
Lifeboat '44 ▶
Light at the Edge of the World '71
The Lightship '86
Live and Let Die '73
Loch Ness '95
Long John Silver '54
The Long Ships '64
The Long Voyage Home '40 ▶
Longitude '00 ▶
Lord Jim '65 ▶
Lost in the Bermuda Triangle '98
Lost Voyage '01
Love Affair '39 ▶
Luxury Liner '48
Madison '01
The Magic Stone '95
Maiden Voyage: Ocean Hijack '04
A Majority of One '56
Manfish '56
Master and Commander: The Far Side of the World '03 ▶
Mayflower: The Pilgrims' Adventure '79
McHale's Navy '64
Mean Creek '04 ▶
The Mermaids of Tiburon '62
Message in a Bottle '98
Mister Roberts '55 ▶
Monkey Business '31 ▶
Moon in Scorpio '86
Moran of the Lady Letty '22
Morituri '65 ▶
Morning Light '08
Muppet Treasure Island '96
Murder on the High Seas '32
Mutiny '52
The Mutiny of the Elsinore '39
Mutiny on the Blackhawk '39
Mutiny on the Bounty '35 ▶
Mutiny on the Bounty '62
Mystery Liner '34
The Mystery of the Mary Celeste '35
The Navigator '24 ▶
The Navy Comes Through '42
New Moon '40
A Night to Remember '58 ▶
No More Women '34
The Odyssey '97
Old Ironsides '26 ▶
One Crazy Summer '86
One Way Passage '32
Operation Petticoat '59 ▶
Out to Sea '97
Oxford Blues '84
Passenger '61 ▶
The Perfect Storm '00
Pirate Radio '09
Pirate Ship '49
Pirates of the Caribbean: At World's End '07
Pirates of the Caribbean: The Curse of the Black Pearl '03 ▶
The Port of Missing Girls '38
The Poseidon Adventure '72
The Princess Comes Across '36 ▶
Pueblo Affair '73 ▶
Pursuit of the Graf Spee '57
Rainbow Warrior '94
Reaching for the Moon '31
Reap the Wild Wind '42
Red Ensign '34
Rich and Strange '32
Roaring Speedboats '37
Romancing the Stone '84 ▶
Run Silent, Run Deep '58 ▶
The Sand Pebbles '66 ▶
Save the Lady '82
Sea Chase '55
Sea Devils '31
Sea Racketeers '37
The Sea Wolf '41 ▶
The Sea Wolf '93
The Seafarers '53
Seven Days Ashore '44
Seven Were Saved '47
Shades of Fear '93
Sharks' Treasure '75
She Creature '01
She Shall Have Music '36
Ship Ahoy '42
Ship of Fools '65 ▶
Ships in the Night '28
Shout at the Devil '76
Sinbad: Legend of the Seven Seas '03
Sinbad, the Sailor '47 ▶
Sink the Bismarck '60 ▶
Souls at Sea '37
South Seas Massacre '74
Speed 2: Cruise Control '97
Spiders 2: Breeding Ground '01
Stargate: Continuum '08
Steamboat Bill, Jr. '28 ▶
Steamboat Round the Bend '35
The Story of Three Loves '53
Submarine Seahawk '59
Swashbuckler '76
The Talented Mr. Ripley '99
Tamango '59
Task Force '49
Temptation '94
Tentacles of the North '26
They Were Expendable '45 ▶
Think Fast, Mr. Moto '37
The Third '04
The 13th Warrior '99
Three Daring Daughters '48
Three Men in a Boat '56
Thunder in Paradise '93
Tiger Shark '32
Till There Was You '91
Titanic '53 ▶
Titanic '96
Titanic '97 ▶
To Gillian on Her 37th Birthday '96
To Have & Have Not '44 ▶
Today We Live '33
Torpedo Run '58
Transatlantic Merry-Go-Round '34
Treacherous Crossing '92
The Treasure of Jamaica Reef '74
Treasure Planet '02
The Triangle '01
Tugboat Annie '33 ▶
2103: Deadly Wake '97
Two Years before the Mast '46
U-Boat Prisoner '44
Under Siege '92
The Unsinkable Molly Brown '64 ▶
Up the Creek '58
Up the Creek '84
Valhalla Rising '09
The Viking '28
Virus '98
Visitors '03
Voyage '93
Voyage of Terror: The Achille Lauro Affair '90
Voyage of the Damned '76 ▶
Wake of the Red Witch '49
Waterworld '95
The Weight of Water '00
We're Not Dressing '34 ▶
Wetbacks '56
White Squall '96
Wild Orchids '28
Wind '92
Windjammer '37
Windrider '86
Winds of Terror '01
Witch Who Came from the Sea '76
Woman of Desire '93
Wonderland Cove '75
The World in His Arms '52
The Wreck of the Mary Deare '59
Yankee Clipper '27

St. Peterburg (Russia)

***see also** Russia/USSR*
Anastasia '97
Anna Karenina '35 ▶
Anna Karenina '48
Anna Karenina '85
Anna Karenina '00
Brother '97
Bullet to Beijing '95
Cold Souls '09
The Iris Effect '04
Leo Tolstoy's Anna Karenina '96
Midnight in Saint Petersburg '97
The Music Lovers '71
Of Freaks and Men '98
Onegin '99
2 Brothers & a Bride '03
Water '05

Saints

***see also** Religion*
Augustine of Hippo '72 ▶
Bernadette '90
Brother Sun, Sister Moon '73
The Flowers of St. Francis '50 ▶
Francesco '93
Joan of Arc '48
Millions '05 ▶
Miracle in Rome '88
Miracle of Our Lady of Fatima '52
My Mother's Smile '02
Passion of Joan of Arc '28 ▶
The Proprietor '96
Saint Joan '57
St. Patrick: The Irish Legend '00
Sebastiane '79 ▶
The Song of Bernadette '43 ▶
Therese '86 ▶

▶ = *rated three bones or higher*

Therese: The Story of Saint Therese of Lisieux '04
A Time for Miracles '80

Salespeople

***see also** Corporate Shenanigans*

Adventures in Babysitting '87
Agata and the Storm '04
The Alarmist '98
Alien Trespass '09
The Assassination of Richard Nixon '05
The Bible and Gun Club '96
Big Fish '03 ▸
The Big Kahuna '00
Breakfast of Champions '98
Cadillac Man '90
Car Babes '06
Death of a Salesman '51 ▸
Death of a Salesman '86 ▸
Diamond Men '01 ▸
El Crimen Perfecto '04
Failure to Launch '06
The Fan '96
Fashion Victims '07
First Snow '07
Foul Play '78 ▸
Gigantic '08
Glengarry Glen Ross '92 ▸
A Good Baby '99
The Good Girl '02 ▸
The Goods: Live Hard, Sell Hard '09
Great World of Sound '07
Grilled '06
Happily Ever After '04
The Iceman Cometh '60 ▸
The Iceman Cometh '73
Jingle All the Way '96
Last Holiday '06
Lisboa '99
The Magnificent Two '67
The Man '05
Me and You and Everyone We Know '05 ▸
Meet Bill '07
Miss Rose White '92 ▸
Moscow on the Hudson '84 ▸
The Music Man '62 ▸
My First Mister '01
Nathalie Granger '72
100 Mile Rule '02
Our Man in Havana '59 ▸
Pennies from Heaven '81 ▸
Phat Girlz '06
Pretty Woman '90 ▸
The Rainmaker '56 ▸
Re-Generation '04
Risk '00
Role Models '08 ▸
The Sensation of Sight '06
Side Effects '05
Sing Me a Love Song '37
Suckerfish '99
Super Sucker '03
Terror Tract '00
Tin Men '87
Torremolinos 73 '03
The Traveling Saleswoman '50
Trojan Eddie '96 ▸

Samurai

***see also** Japan*

The Adventures of Buckaroo Banzai Across the Eighth Dimension '84 ▸
American Samurai '92
Azumi '03 ▸
Blind Fury '90
Blood: The Last Vampire '09
The Bushido Blade '80
The Challenge '82
Cyber Ninja '94
Daimajin '66
Dororo '07
47 Ronin, Part 1 '42 ▸
47 Ronin, Part 2 '42 ▸
The Gambling Samurai '60
Ghost Dog: The Way of the Samurai '99
Ghostwarrior '86
Gonza the Spearman '86
Goyokin '69 ▸
Harakiri '62 ▸
Heaven & Earth '90 ▸
The Hidden Blade '04
House Where Evil Dwells '82
Hunter in the Dark '80
Kibakichi '04
Kibakichi 2 '04
Kill Bill Vol. 1 '03 ▸
The Last Samurai '03 ▸
Lone Wolf and Cub '72
Lone Wolf and Cub: Baby Cart to Hades '72
Moon over Tao '97 ▸
One-Eyed Swordsman '63
The Princess Blade '02
Rashomon '51 ▸
Red Sun '71
Return of Daimajin '66
Ronin Gai '90
Samurai Banners '69
Samurai Fiction '99 ▸
Sanjuro '62 ▸
The Sea is Watching '02 ▸
Seven Samurai '54 ▸
Shinobi '05 ▸
Shogun '80 ▸
Shogun Assassin '80
Shogun Assassin 2: Lightning Swords of Death '73 ▸
Shogun's Samurai—The Yagyu Clan Conspiracy '78
Sukiyaki Western Django '08
Sword of Doom '67 ▸
Taboo '99
Throne of Blood '57 ▸
The Twilight Samurai '02 ▸
When the Last Sword is Drawn '02 ▸
Wrath of Daimajin '66
Yojimbo '61 ▸
Zatoichi '03 ▸
Zatoichi: Master Ichi and a Chest of Gold '64
Zatoichi: The Blind Swordsman and the Chess Expert '65
Zatoichi: The Blind Swordsman's Vengeance '66
Zatoichi: The Life and Opinion of Masseur Ichi '62
Zatoichi vs. Yojimbo '70 ▸

San Diego

Anchorman: The Legend of Ron Burgundy '04
Antwone Fisher '02 ▸
The Cat's Meow '01
Devil Dogs of the Air '35
Dive Bomber '41 ▸
Flirting with Disaster '95 ▸
Gardens of the Night '08
In the Navy '41
My Blue Heaven '90
Ready? OK! '08
Sideways '04 ▸
Tiger Shark '32
Top Gun '86
Traffic '00 ▸
Tumbleweeds '98
29th & Gay '05

San Francisco

***see also** Earthquakes*

After the Shock '90
Against the Wall '04
All About You '01
All Dogs Go to Heaven 2 '95
The Amazing Mrs. Holiday '43
And Then Came Lola '09
Armistead Maupin's More Tales of the City '97
Armistead Maupin's Tales of the City '93
Aussie and Ted's Great Adventure '09
The Bachelor '99
Barbary Coast '35 ▸
The Barbary Coast '74
Basic Instinct '92
Behind That Curtain '29
Beyond the Door '75
Big Trouble in Little China '86
Bullitt '68 ▸
Cardiac Arrest '74
Chan Is Missing '82 ▸
Charlie Chan at Treasure Island '39
Cherish '02
The Chinatown Kid '78
Clowning Around 2 '93
Confessions of a Sociopathic Social Climber '05
The Conversation '74 ▸
Copycat '95
The Cradle of Courage '20
Days of Wine and Roses '62 ▸
The Dead Pool '88
Dealing: Or the Berkeley-to-Boston Forty-Brick Lost-Bag Blues '72
Desperate Measures '98
Desperate Moves '86
Dim Sum: A Little Bit of Heart '85 ▸
Dirty Harry '71 ▸
Dr. Dolittle '98
Dr. Jekyll's Dungeon of Death '82
Doctor Who '96
Dogfight '91 ▸
Dogwatch '97
Dopamine '03
Dream for an Insomniac '96
Dream with the Fishes '97
Dying to Remember '93
The Enforcer '76
Execution of Justice '99
An Eye for an Eye '81
The Fan '96
Fanci's Persuasion '95
Final Analysis '92
Fisherman's Wharf '39
Flame of the Barbary Coast '45
Flower Drum Song '61
Fools '70
40 Days and 40 Nights '02
48 Hrs. '82 ▸
Foul Play '78 ▸
Four Christmases '08
Freebie & the Bean '74
Frisco Jenny '32
The Frisco Kid '79
The Game '97 ▸
George of the Jungle '97 ▸
Going the Distance '10
Golden Gate '93
Groove '00 ▸
Ground Zero '88
Guinevere '99 ▸
Haiku Tunnel '00
Hello, Frisco, Hello '43
Homeward Bound 2: Lost in San Francisco '96
I Remember Mama '48 ▸
Invasion of the Body Snatchers '78 ▸
It Came from Beneath the Sea '55 ▸
Jade '95
Just like Heaven '05
Just One Night '00
Key to the City '50
Kicks '85
Kuffs '92
Lady from Louisiana '42
Lady of the House '78
The Laughing Policeman '74
Life Tastes Good '99
Lightblast '85
The Lineup '58
Little City '97
Magnum Force '73
The Maltese Falcon '41 ▸
Medicine for Melancholy '08
Mega Shark Vs. Giant Octopus '09
Memoirs of an Invisible Man '92
The Men's Club '86
Metro '96
Milk '08 ▸
Mission '00
Mr. Moto Takes a Vacation '39
The Mistress of Spices '05
Monster in the Closet '86
Mysterious Mr. Wong '35
Nightmare in Blood '75
Nim's Island '08
Nina Takes a Lover '94
Nine Months '95
No One Sleeps '01
Nora Prentiss '47
Old San Francisco '27
The Other End of the Line '08
Pacific Heights '90 ▸
Playing Mona Lisa '00
Poltergeist: The Legacy '96
The Presidio '88
The Princess Diaries '01
The Princess of Nebraska '07
The Pursuit of Happyness '06
Rated X '00
The Rock '96 ▸
The Saint Strikes Back '39
Salome, Where She Danced '45
San Francisco '36 ▸
San Franpsycho '06
Serendipity '01
Serial '80 ▸
Seven Days Ashore '44
The Shock '23
The Single Standard '29
The Sisters '38 ▸
'68 '87
A Smile Like Yours '96
The Sniper '52
So I Married an Axe Murderer '93
Some Prefer Cake '97
Starlift '51
Stealing Heaven '88
Sucker Free City '05 ▸
Sudden Impact '83
Sweet November '01
The Sweetest Thing '02
Ticker '01
Time After Time '79 ▸
Times of Harvey Milk '83 ▸
True Crime '99
Tweek City '05
Twisted '04
Under One Roof '02
Up for Grabs '05
Vertigo '58 ▸
War '07
Waterfront '44
The Wedding Planner '01
West Is West '87
What's Up, Doc? '72 ▸
The Wild Parrots of Telegraph Hill '03 ▸
Wild West '93
Wildflowers '99
The Woman on Pier 13 '50
Woman on Top '00
You Kill Me '07 ▸
The Zodiac '05
Zodiac '07
The Zodiac Killer '71

Sanity Check

***see also** Doctors & Nurses; Hospitals & Medicine; Shrinks*

Adam Resurrected '08
Affliction '97 ▸
Aguirre, the Wrath of God '72 ▸
All the Little Animals '98
Alone in the Dark '82
Along for the Ride '00
The Alphabet Killer '08
The Amazing Howard Hughes '77
American Eagle '90
American Psycho '99
American Psycho 2: All American Girl '02
American Venus '07
Amos '85
An Angel at My Table '89 ▸
Angels Fall '07
Anger Management '03
Anguish '88
Another Time, Another Place '58
Antichrist '09
Apartment Complex '98
Appointment with Fear '85
Arabian Nights '00
Arsenic and Old Lace '44 ▸
The Astronaut's Wife '99
Asylum '72
Asylum '97
Asylum of Satan '72
Bad Dreams '88
Bark! '02
Bartleby '01
Batman Forever '95 ▸
Battle Shock '56
Beautiful Dreamers '92
A Beautiful Mind '01 ▸
Beauty on the Beach '61
Bedlam '45 ▸
Behind Locked Doors '48
Behind the Lines '97
Being John Malkovich '99 ▸
The Bell Jar '79
The Bells '26 ▸
Beloved '98
Beneath '07
Beyond Therapy '86
Big Fan '09
Birds of America '08
Black Snake Moan '07
Blackwoods '02
A Blade in the Dark '83
Blood Frenzy '87
Blood Salvage '90
Blood Song '82
Bloody Wednesday '87
Body Chemistry '90
Borderline '02 ▸
Boxing Helena '93
The Boys Next Door '96
Brain Dead '89 ▸
Bringing Out the Dead '99
Bug '06
Buried Alive '89
Burnt Money '00
The Butcher Boy '97 ▸
The Butterfly Effect '04
Cabaret Balkan '98
Camille Claudel '89 ▸
Cannibal Man '71
Canvas '06
Captain Newman, M.D. '63
Captive '97
The Carpenter '89
Cat in the Cage '68
Cause for Alarm '51
The Caveman's Valentine '01
Cecil B. Demented '00
The Cell '00
Cello '05
The Chaos Experiment '09
Chapter 27 '07
Charles: Dead or Alive '69
Charming Billy '98
Chasing Holden '01
Chasing Sleep '00
Chattahoochee '89
Choke '08
Clockwise '86
Close Encounters of the Third Kind '77 ▸
Coast to Coast '80
Cobra Verde '88
The Cobweb '55
The Collector '65 ▸
Come Undone '00
Comedy of Innocence '00
Committed '91
The Confession '98
Conjurer '08
Conspiracy Theory '97 ▸
Cotton Mary '99
The Couch Trip '87
The Cracker Factory '79
The Craft '96
Cravings '06
Crazed '82
The Crazies '09
Crazy as Hell '02
Crazy Fat Ethel II '85
Crazy in Alabama '99
Crazy Like a Fox '04
Crazy People '90
Crime and Punishment '35 ▸
Crime and Punishment '70
The Crime of Dr. Crespi '35
Criminally Insane '75
Crow Hollow '52
Cry Wolf '47
Cthulhu '08
Cutting Class '89
The Dark Knight '08 ▸
Dark Mirror '07
Dark Obsession '90
Dark Places '73
Dark Sanity '82
Dark Water '02
Dark Waters '44
Darkness Falls '03
Darkroom '90
A Day at the Races '37 ▸
Dead Man Out '89 ▸
Dead of Night '45 ▸
Dead Pit '89
Deadline '09
Deadly Innocence '88
Deadly Intruder '84
Deadly Strangers '82
The Deadly Trap '71
Death Kiss '74
Death Nurse '87
Death to Smoochy '02
Dee Snider's Strangeland '98
Defendor '09
Dementia 13 '63
A Demon in My View '92
Demons of the Mind '72
Deranged '87
Despair '78 ▸
Desperate Living '77
Deutschland im Jahre Null '47 ▸
Devi '60 ▸
The Devil and the Deep '32
The Devil Bat '41
The Devil Bat's Daughter '46
Devil Doll '36 ▸
The Devil in Silk '56
Devil in the Flesh '87
Devil in the Flesh 2 '00
Devil Times Five '74
Devil Wears White '86
The Devil's Advocate '97
Devil's Pond '03
Diary of a Mad Housewife '70 ▸
Diary of a Madman '63
Diary of a Young Comic '79
Diary of Forbidden Dreams '73 ▸
Dick Barton, Special Agent '48
Die! Die! My Darling! '65
Die Screaming, Marianne '73
Diminished Capacity '08
The Disappeared '08
Disorder '06
Disturbance '89
Disturbed '90
The Doctor and the Devils '85
Doctor Blood's Coffin '62
Doctor Butcher M.D. '80
Dr. Caligari '89
Dr. Frankenstein's Castle of Freaks '74
Dr. Hackenstein '88
Dr. Jekyll and Mr. Hyde '20 ▸
Dr. Jekyll and Mr. Hyde '32 ▸
Dr. Jekyll and Mr. Hyde '41 ▸
Dr. Jekyll and Mr. Hyde '68
Dr. Jekyll and Mr. Hyde '73
Dr. Jekyll and the Wolfman '71
Dr. Mabuse, The Gambler '22 ▸
Dr. Mabuse vs. Scotland Yard '64
Dr. Strangelove, or: How I Learned to Stop Worrying and Love the Bomb '64 ▸
Dr. T & the Women '00 ▸
Dr. Tarr's Torture Dungeon '75
Doctor X '32
Dog Day Afternoon '75 ▸
Doktor Faustus '82
The Doll '62
Dominique Is Dead '79
Don Quixote '00
Donnie Darko '01 ▸
Don't Go in the House '80
Don't Go in the Woods '81
Don't Look in the Basement '73
Don't Look Now '73 ▸
Don't Mess with My Sister! '85
Don't Open Till Christmas '84
Don't Say a Word '01
Doom Asylum '88
Dostoevsky's Crime and Punishment '99
A Double Life '47 ▸
Dream Lover '85
Dream No Evil '70
The Dream Team '89

Easy Rider '69 ►
Eaten Alive '76
Echoes '83
Ed Gein '01
Eddie Presley '92
Edge of Sanity '89
Elling '01
The Empty Acre '07
The Empty Mirror '99
The End of Innocence '90
End of the Road '70
Endless Love '81
Endless Night '71
Enigma '01
Equus '77
Escape from Safehaven '88
Estate of Insanity '64
Europa '51 '52
Evan Almighty '07
Event Horizon '97
Everything Put Together '00
Evil Eyes '04
Exorcism's Daughter '74
The Eye '02
Eye of the Beholder '99
Eye of the Storm '98
Eyeball '78
The Eyes of the Amaryllis '82
Fabled '02
Facade '98
The Fall of the House of Usher '49
The Fall of the House of Usher '60 ►
The Fall of the House of Usher '80
False Identity '90
Family Life '71
The Fan '96
Far Harbor '96
Fat Guy Goes Nutzoid '86
Fear of Fear '75
Fear Strikes Out '57 ►
Fever '99
The Fiend Who Walked the West '58
The Fifth Floor '80
Fight Club: ' '99 ►
Final '01
The Fisher King '91 ►
5 Against the House '55
The Five of Me '81
The Flying Scotsman '06
Follow Me Quietly '49 ►
Forced March '90
Forfeit '07
Four Flies on Grey Velvet '72
1408 '07
The 4th Dimension '06
The Fourth Kind '09
The 4th Man '79 ►
Frailty '02 ►
Frances '82 ►
Fright '71
From Noon Till Three '76
From the Life of the Marionettes '80 ►
Frontier of Dawn '08
Games '67
Genealogies of a Crime '97
Get Well Soon '01
The Ghost Ship '43
The Gift '00
The Girl in Room 2A '76
Girl, Interrupted '99
A Girl Thing '01
Gloria '98
The Goalie's Anxiety at the Penalty Kick '71 ►
Going Postal '98
Gothika '03
Great Expectations '97
Grindstone Road '07
Gulliver's Travels '95
The Hairdresser's Husband '92
Halloween '07
Halloween II '09
Hamlet '90 ►
Hamlet '96 ►
Hamlet '01
Hammersmith Is Out '72
Hannibal '01
Happy Accidents '00
Hard Candy '06
Hard Luck '01
Harsh Times '05
Harvey '50 ►
The Haunting '63 ►
The Haunting '99
The Haunting of Molly Hartley '08
Haunting of Sarah Hardy '89
Haunts '77
He Loves Me ... He Loves Me Not '02
Heart '99
Heart of Midnight '89
Heat and Sunlight '87
Heavenly Creatures '94 ►
Hell's Gate '01
Henry IV '85
Heroes '77
Hey, Happy! '01
Hider in the House '90
Hip Hip Hurrah! '87 ►
Hollywood Kills '06
Homecoming '09
The Horrible Dr. Hichcock '62
The Horror Chamber of Dr. Faustus '59 ►
Horror Hospital '73
Horror House on Highway 5 '86
The Hospital '71 ►
Hotline '82
The Hours '02 ►
House of Darkness '48
House of Fools '02
House of 1000 Corpses '03
The House of Usher '88
The House of Yes '97
The Housekeeper '86
How to Get Ahead in Advertising '89 ►
How to Make a Monster '58
Hush '98
Hush, Hush, Sweet Charlotte '65 ►
Hysteria '64
I Am the Cheese '83
I Dismember Mama '74
I Know Who Killed Me '07
I Never Promised You a Rose Garden '77 ►
I Stand Alone '98
Ichi the Killer '01
Icy Breasts '75 ►
The Idiots '99
If Things Were Different '79
I'll Be Seeing You '44
I'll Take You There '99
Illusions '91
Images '72
Impulse '84
In Dreams '98
In the Mouth of Madness '95
The Incredible Two-Headed Transplant '71
The Informant! '09
Innocent Victim '90
Innocents '00
Insanitarium '08
Insanity '76
Inside Paris '06
Instinct '99
Interiors '78 ►
Invisible '06
The Invisible Ghost '41
Irma Vep '96
It Happened at Nightmare Inn '70
It's Alive! '68
J'accuse! '19 ►
The Jacket '05
Jekyll and Hyde '90
Joe Gould's Secret '00
Juggernaut '37
Julien Donkey-boy '99
K-PAX '01
Keane '04 ►
Keeper '76
Kill Your Darlings '06
The Killing of John Lennon '07
The Killing Room '09
King Lear '98 ►
King of California '07
The King of Hearts '66 ►
Kira's Reason—A Love Story '01
Kitchen Privileges '00
Lassie from Lancashire '38
The Last Don 2 '98
The Last of Philip Banter '87
The Last Ride '91
The Last Seduction '94 ►
The Lazarus Project '08
Leave Her to Heaven '45 ►
Lethal Weapon '87 ►
Let's Scare Jessica to Death '71
Life Upside Down '64
A Light in the Darkness '02
Lilian's Story '95
Lilith '64 ►
Little Boy Blue '97
Living Doll '90
The Locusts '97
The Lonely Sex '59
Los Locos Posse '97
Lost Angels '89
A Love to Keep '07
Lower Level '91
Ludwig '72
Lunatics: A Love Story '92 ►
Luther the Geek '90
Macabre '80
The Machinist '04
Mad Cowgirl '06
Mad Love '35 ►
Mad Love '95
Mad Love '01
Man Facing Southeast '86 ►
Manhunter '86 ►
Manic '01
Mary, My Dearest '83
May '02
Michael Clayton '07 ►
Midnight Warning '32
Mind Games '89
Mine Own Executioner '47 ►
Ministry of Fear '44 ►
Mr. Deeds Goes to Town '36 ►
Mr. Jingles '06
Mr. Jones '93
Mixed Nuts '94
Morgan: A Suitable Case for Treatment '66
Mother Kusters Goes to Heaven '76 ►
Murder in Mind '97
Murder in the First '95
My Blood Runs Cold '65
My First Wife '84
My Sister's Keeper '02
My Very Best Friend '96
Neither the Sea Nor the Sand '73
Network '76 ►
Nevermore '07
Night of Bloody Horror '69
Night of Terror '87
The Night Visitor '70
Night Wars '88
Night Watch '72
Nijinsky '80
1941 '79
The Ninth Configuration '79 ►
The Noah '75
Nobody's Perfekt '79
Nothing to Lose '08
The Number 23 '07
Nurse Betty '00 ►
Nutcracker: Money, Madness & Murder '87 ►
Nuts '87 ►
Obsessed '09
Obsession '49
The October Man '48 ►
Offerings '89
Office Killer '97
One Flew Over the Cuckoo's Nest '75 ►
One Hour Photo '02 ►
125 Rooms of Comfort '83
One Summer Love '76
The Onion Field '79 ►
Open Your Eyes '97 ►
Opium: Diary of a Madwoman '07
The Order '03
Orphan '09
The Others '01 ►
Out of Sight, Out of Her Mind '89
Overexposed '90
Pale Blood '91
Paperback Hero '73
Passion of Mind '00
Pay Off '89
Pecker '98
Peeping Tom '60 ►
The Perfect Nanny '00
Performance '70 ►
Peril '00
Phoebe in Wonderland '08
A Piano for Mrs. Cimino '82 ►
The Piano Teacher '01
Picture Mommy Dead '66
Pigs '73
Pink Floyd: The Wall '82
The Pink Panther Strikes Again '76 ►
The Pit and the Pendulum '61 ►
The Pit & the Pendulum '91
Play Misty for Me '71 ►
Poison '91 ►
Poison '01
The Possessed '47 ►
Post Concussion '99 ►
Premonition '07
The President's Analyst '67 ►
Prettykill '87
Prime Suspect '88
Private Parts '72
Psychic Killer '75
Psycho '60 ►
Psycho '98
Psycho 2 '83
Psycho Cop '88
Psycho Cop 2 '94
Psychos in Love '87
Purple Heart '05
Question of Silence '83 ►
Raising Cain '92
Rasputin '85 ►
The Red Desert '64 ►
Reign Over Me '07
The Rejuvenator '88
Remember Me '85
Rescue Dawn '06 ►
Respiro '02
Return of the Ape Man '44
Return to Cabin by the Lake '01
Return to Waterloo '85
Revenge in the House of Usher '82
Revolt of the Zombies '36
Revolution 9 '01
Revolutionary Road '08
Richard III '55 ►
Romulus, My Father '07 ►
Room to Let '49
The Ruling Class '72 ►
Running with Scissors '06
Savage Grace '07
Scarlet Empress '34 ►
Scissors '91
The Scout '94
Scream Bloody Murder '72
Scream for Help '86
Screamer '74
Screw Loose '99
Seance on a Wet Afternoon '64 ►
Secret Beyond the Door '48
Secretary '02 ►
The Sender '82
Session 9 '01
Sessions '83
Seven Days in May '64 ►
Seventh Heaven '98
Shades of Black '93
Shadow Play '86
Shattered '72
Shattered Image '98
Shattered Silence '71
Shattered Spirits '86
The Shining '80
Shock Corridor '63 ►
The Silence of the Lambs '91 ►
Silent Night, Bloody Night '73
Sisters '73 ►
Sisters, Or the Balance of Happiness '79
Skeletons in the Closet '00
Sketches of a Strangler '78
Slaughter Hotel '71
Sledgehammer '83
Sling Blade '96 ►
A Snake of June '02
The Sniper '52
Sniper '75 ►
Solaris '72
Solaris '02
Some Folks Call It a Sling Blade '94 ►
Sophie's Choice '82 ►
Sordid Lives '00
Soul Survivors '01
Soundman '99
South of Reno '87
Spectre of the Rose '46
Spellbound '45 ►
Spider '02 ►
Star Maps '97
States of Control '98
The Stepfather '09
The Story of Adele H. '75 ►
Strait-Jacket '64
Strange Illusion '45
Stranger Than Fiction '06
Strangers on a Train '51 ►
Street Asylum '90
A Streetcar Named Desire '51 ►
A Streetcar Named Desire '84 ►
Strong Medicine '84
Stuart Bliss '98
Stuart Saves His Family '94
The Substance of Fire '96
The Survivalist '87
Suspended Animation '02
Svengali '55
Sweeney Todd: The Demon Barber of Fleet Street '07
Sweethearts '97
Sybil '76 ►
Sylvia '03
Synecdoche, New York '08 ►
Tainted Image '91
Teenage Frankenstein '58
The Tenant '76 ►
The Testament of Dr. Cordelier '59 ►
They Might Be Giants '71 ►
The Thin Red Line '64
Thomas in Love '01
3 Extremes 2 '02
The Three Faces of Eve '57
The 300 Year Weekend '71
Three Nuts in Search of a Bolt '64
Tideland '05
Time Out '01
Titus '99
Torture Train '75
Touched '82
Tracks '76
Trapped in Silence '86
Trauma '04
The Turn of the Screw '74
The Turn of the Screw '92
The Turn of the Screw '99
12 Monkeys '95 ►
Twilight Man '96
Twin Peaks: Fire Walk with Me '92
Twinsanity '70
Twister '89
Two Drifters '05
The Two Faces of Dr. Jekyll '60
The Ugly '96
Under the Sand '00 ►
Under the Skin '97
The Unsaid '01
Urge to Kill '84
Vampire's Kiss '88 ►
Vengeance Is Mine '79 ►
Vincent & Theo '90 ►
Violated '53
Virtual Seduction '96
Visitor Q '01
Walter and Henry '01 ►
Ward Six '78
Watched '73
What about Bob? '91 ►
What Ever Happened to Baby Jane? '62 ►
What's the Matter with Helen? '71
Where Danger Lives '50
While I Live '47
White Badge '97
White Heat '49 ►
Wide Sargasso Sea '06
The Wind '87
Witchfire '86
The Wizard of Gore '07
Woman in Black '89
The Woman in White '97
A Woman under the Influence '74 ►
Woyzeck '94
Year of the Dog '07
Yerma '99
You Belong to Me '07

Satanism

***see also** Demons & Wizards; Devils; Occult*

Alison's Birthday '79
Amazon Jail '85
Angel on My Shoulder '80
Asylum of Satan '72
Bad Dreams '88
Beast of the Yellow Night '70
Beyond the Door 3 '91
The Black Cat '34 ►
Black Roses '88
Black Sunday '60 ►
Bless the Child '00
The Blood on Satan's Claw '71 ►
Blood Orgy of the She-Devils '74
The Bloodsuckers '70
The Brotherhood of Satan '71
Child of Darkness, Child of Light '91
The Chosen '77
The Convent '00
The Crimson Cult '68
The Crow: Wicked Prayer '05
Damien: Omen 2 '78
The Day of the Beast '95
The Demon Lover '77
Demonoid, Messenger of Death '81
The Devil & Daniel Webster '41 ►
The Devil Rides Out '68 ►
The Devils '71 ►
The Devil's Daughter '91
The Devil's Eye '60
The Devil's Mistress '68
The Devil's Nightmare '71
The Devil's Partner '58
The Devil's Possessed '74
The Devil's Prey '01
Devil's Rain '75
Devil's Son-in-Law '77
The Devil's Web '74
Disciple of Death '72
Doctor Faustus '68
Dominion: Prequel to the Exorcist '05
Equinox '71 ►
Eternal Evil '87
Evil Altar '89
Evilspeak '82
Exorcism '74
The Exorcist '73 ►
The Exorcist 2: The Heretic '77
Eye of the Demon '87
Family Reunion '79
Fear No Evil '80
The Final Conflict '81
Ghoulies 4 '93
Guardian of the Abyss '82
Hack O'Lantern '87
Halloween Night '90
Highway to Hell '92
House of the Black Death '65
I Don't Want to Be Born '75
I Drink Your Blood '71
Inferno '80
Invitation to Hell '82
Invitation to Hell '84
Jaws of Satan '81
Land of the Minotaur '77
Leaves from Satan's Book '19
The Legend of Hillbilly John '73
Leonor '75
A Little Bit of Soul '97
Lost Souls '00
The Man and the Monster '65
The Mangler '94
Maxim Xul '91
The Mephisto Waltz '71 ►
Merchants of Death '99
Midnight '81
Midnight Cabaret '90
Midnight's Child '93
Mind, Body & Soul '92
Mysterious Doctor Satan '40

Necromancer: Satan's Servant '88
Night Visitor '89
976-EVIL '88
976-EVIL 2: The Astral Factor '91
The Ninth Gate '99
The Occultist '89
Oh, God! You Devil '84
The Omen '76
One of Them '03
Other Hell '85
Prime Evil '88
Prince of Darkness '87
The Pyx '73 ▶
Race with the Devil '75
Raging Angels '95
The Relic '96
Rest in Pieces '87
Revenge '86
Rosemary's Baby '68 ▶
The Satanic Rites of Dracula '73
Satan's Black Wedding '75
Satan's Blood '77
Satan's Cheerleaders '77
Satan's Princess '90
Satan's School for Girls '73
Satan's Touch '84
Satanwar '79
The Sentinel '76
Servants of Twilight '91
The Seventh Victim '43 ▶
Sheitan '06
Shock 'Em Dead '90
Sisters of Satan '75
The Soul Guardians '98
Speak of the Devil '90
Specters '87
The Spellbinder '88
Sugar Cookies '77
The Tempter '74
Terror Beach '75
To the Devil, a Daughter '76
Tombs of the Blind Dead '72
The Visitor '80
Warlock '91
Warlock: The Armageddon '93
Weirdsville '07
Witchcraft '88
Witchcraft 3: The Kiss of Death '90
Witchcraft 5: Dance with the Devil '92
Witchcraft 6: The Devil's Mistress '94
Witchcraft 10: Mistress of the Craft '98
WitchTrap '89

Satire & Parody

***see also** Black Comedy; Comedy; Genre Spoofs*

A Propos de Nice '29 ▶
Abbott and Costello Go to Mars '53
Abduction '75
The Act '82
The Adventures of Picasso '80
Adventures of Power '08
The Adventures of Sherlock Holmes' Smarter Brother '78 ▶
The Affairs of Annabel '38
Aftershock '88
Airplane! '80 ▶
Airplane 2: The Sequel '82
An Alan Smithee Film: Burn, Hollywood, Burn '97
Alex in Wonderland '70
Alien Trespass '09
All Through the Night '42 ▶
All You Need Is Cash '78 ▶
The Alphabet Murders '65
Amazing Dr. Clitterhouse '38 ▶
Amazon Women on the Moon '87
America 3000 '86
An American Carol '08
American Dreamz '06
American Psycho '99
American Tickler '76
America's Deadliest Home Video '91
Americathon '79
...And God Spoke '94
Andy Warhol's Dracula '74 ▶
Andy Warhol's Frankenstein '74
Animal Farm '55 ▶
Animal Farm '99
Any Wednesday '66
The Apartment '60 ▶
As Young As You Feel '51 ▶
The Associate '79
Attack of the Robots '66
Attack the Gas Station '99
Auntie Mame '58 ▶
Austin Powers: International Man of Mystery '97 ▶
Austin Powers 2: The Spy Who Shagged Me '99 ▶
Backfire! '94
Bad Manners '84
Bad Medicine '85
Bamboozled '00
Bananas '71 ▶
Bank Robber '93
Barjo '93
Barry McKenzie Holds His Own '74
Based on an Untrue Story '93
Basic Training '86
The Bawdy Adventures of Tom Jones '76
Beautiful '00
Being There '79 ▶
Best in Show '00 ▶
The Best Man '64 ▶
Beyond the Valley of the Dolls '70
Beyond Therapy '86
The Big Bus '76
Big Deal on Madonna Street '58 ▶
The Big Picture '89
The Big Tease '99
Big Trouble in Little China '86
Black and White in Color '76 ▶
Black Bird '75
Bob & Carol & Ted & Alice '69
Bob Roberts '92 ▶
The Bogus Witch Project '00
The Bonfire of the Vanities '90
Born in East L.A. '87
Boss '74
Boy Meets Girl '38 ▶
The Brady Bunch Movie '95 ▶
Bread and Chocolate '73 ▶
Breakfast of Champions '98
Bring It On '00
Britannia Hospital '82
Buffalo Soldiers '01
Bullshot '83
Bulworth '98 ▶
The 'Burbs '89
But I'm a Cheerleader '99
Camera Buff '79
Canadian Bacon '94
The Candidate '72 ▶
Candy '68
Carry On Cleo '65
Carry On Dick '75
Casino Royale '67
Caveman '81
CB4: The Movie '93
Cecil B. Demented '00
Champagne for Caesar '50 ▶
Chaos Theory '08
The Cheap Detective '78 ▶
Cherry Falls '00
Children of the Revolution '95
Chronically Unfeasible '00
Citizen Ruth '96
Clockwise '86
A Clockwork Orange '71 ▶
Club Dread '04
The Coca-Cola Kid '84 ▶
Code Name: Chaos '90
Cold Turkey '71 ▶
Contract '80 ▶
Coup de Grace '78
Crainquebille '23 ▶
Creature from the Haunted Sea '60
Crimewave '85
Curtain Up '53
Dark Habits '84
Dark Star '74 ▶
Darktown Strutters '74
Darling Lili '70
Date Movie '06
A Day Without a Mexican '04
Dead Men Don't Die '91
Dead Men Don't Wear Plaid '82
The Deal '08
Deal of the Century '83
Death of a Bureaucrat '66 ▶
Deathrow Gameshow '88
Diary of a Chambermaid '64 ▶
Dick '99 ▶
Dirty Dishes '78 ▶
The Disappearance of Kevin Johnson '95
The Discreet Charm of the Bourgeoisie '72 ▶
Dr. Heckyl and Mr. Hype '80
Doctors and Nurses '82
Don't Be a Menace to South Central While Drinking Your Juice in the Hood '95
Down & Dirty '76 ▶
Down and Out in Beverly Hills '86
Down to Earth '47
Down Under '86
Dracula: Dead and Loving It '95
Dracula Sucks '79
Dragnet '87
Drop Dead Gorgeous '99
E. Nick: A Legend in His Own Mind '84
Easy Wheels '89
EDtv '99
Election '99 ▶
11 Harrowhouse '74 ▶
Ella Cinders '26 ▶
Erik the Viking '89
Evil Roy Slade '71 ▶
Executive Koala '06 ▶
Exposed '03
The Extraordinary Adventures of Mr. West in the Land of the Bolsheviks '24
The Family Game '83 ▶
The Fat Spy '66
Fatal Instinct '93
Fay Grim '06
Fear of a Black Hat '94
Ferocious Female Freedom Fighters '88
Fido '06
First Family '80
The Flaming Teen-Age '56
Flesh Gordon '72
Flicks '85
Floundering '94
Forgotten Silver '96 ▶
The Fortune Cookie '66 ▶
Frankenstein General Hospital '88
Frankenstein Sings... The Movie '95
Frankenweenie '84
The French Touch '54
The Freshman '90
From Here to Maternity '85
The Front '76 ▶
Funny Money '82
Fuse '03
Gabriel Over the White House '33 ▶
Galactic Gigolo '87
Galaxina '80
Ganjasaurus Rex '87
Gas '81
Geek Maggot Bingo '83
Genevieve '53 ▶
Gentlemen Prefer Blondes '53 ▶
Get to Know Your Rabbit '72
Girls in Prison '94
Glory! Glory! '90 ▶
Go for Zucker '05
Going Berserk '83
Going Places '74 ▶
Going Postal '98
Gosford Park '01 ▶
Greaser's Palace '72
Great American Traffic Jam '80
The Great Dictator '40 ▶
The Great Madcap '49
Great McGonagall '75
The Great White Hype '96
The Groove Tube '72
Grunt! The Wrestling Movie '85
Gulliver's Travels '95
Gumshoe '72
Gypsy '75
Hail '73
Hail the Conquering Hero '44 ▶
Hairspray '88 ▶
Half a Sixpence '67
Hamlet 2 '08 ▶
Happiness '32
Hard Core Logo '96
Heaven Can Wait '43 ▶
Heavens Above '63 ▶
Heckler '08
Hexed '93
High Anxiety '77
High Hopes '88 ▶
High School High '96
High Season '88
Hijacking Hollywood '97
History of the World: Part 1 '81
Hollywood Harry '86
Hollywood North '03
Home Movies '79
The Horror of Frankenstein '70
The Hospital '71 ▶
Hot Shots! '91 ▶
Hot Shots! Part Deux '93
The Hound of the Baskervilles '77
How I Got into College '89
I Love You, Alice B. Toklas! '68
I Married a Vampire '87
I Was a Zombie for the FBI '82
I Was Born But... '32 ▶
The Icicle Thief '89 ▶
Idiocracy '06
I'll Do Anything '93
I'm All Right Jack '59 ▶
I'm Gonna Git You Sucka '88 ▶
In the Loop '09
The Incredible Shrinking Woman '81
Incredibly Strange Creatures Who Stopped Living and Became Mixed-Up Zombies '63
The Inspector General '52
Intern '00
Invasion Earth: The Aliens Are Here! '87
Irma Vep '96
Is There Sex After Death? '71 ▶
It Couldn't Happen Here '88
J-Men Forever! '79 ▶
Jabberwocky '77
Jack and His Friends '92
Jail Party '04
Jailbait! '00
Jamon, Jamon '93
Jay and Silent Bob Strike Back '01
Jekyll & Hyde... Together Again '82
Jet Benny Show '86
Johnny Dangerously '84
A Joke of Destiny, Lying in Wait Around the Corner Like a Bandit '84
The Kaiser's Lackey '51
Kentucky Fried Movie '77 ▶
Kids in the Hall: Brain Candy '96
The King of Hearts '66 ▶
Kurt Vonnegut's Harrison Bergeron '95
The Ladies' Man '61
L'Age D'Or '30 ▶
The Last Polka '84 ▶
Lawn Dogs '96
Le Schpountz '38
Legalese '98
Leon the Pig Farmer '93
Let's Kill All the Lawyers '93
Lip Service '88 ▶
Look Out Sister '48 ▶
Lord Love a Duck '66
Love and a .45 '94
Love and Death '75 ▶
Love at Stake '87
The Loved One '65
Mad City '97
Mad Mission 3 '84
Mad Monster Party '68
Malibu's Most Wanted '03
Man Bites Dog '91
The Man in the White Suit '51 ▶
The Man Who Came to Dinner '41 ▶
Man Who Had Power Over Women '70
The Man with Bogart's Face '80
The Man with Two Brains '83 ▶
Mapp & Lucia '85
Mars Attacks! '96
Mastergate '92 ▶
Me and the Colonel '58
Men... '85 ▶
The Men Who Stare at Goats '09
The Meteor Man '93
Mickey '17
A Mighty Wind '03 ▶
The Milky Way '68 ▶
Minbo—Or the Gentle Art of Japanese Extortion '92
Miss Cast Away '04
The Missionary '82
Mister Drake's Duck '50
Mr. Write '92
Mob Boss '90
Modern Times '36 ▶
Monster in a Box '92 ▶
Monty Python and the Holy Grail '75 ▶
Monty Python's Life of Brian '79 ▶
Monty Python's The Meaning of Life '83 ▶
More Wild, Wild West '80
The Mouse on the Moon '62 ▶
The Mouse That Roared '59 ▶
Movers and Shakers '85
Movie, Movie '78
Murder by Death '76
Mutant on the Bounty '89
My Best Friend Is a Vampire '88
My Best Girl '27 ▶
My Fuhrer '07
Myra Breckinridge '70
Mystery Science Theater 3000: The Movie '96
The Naked Gun: From the Files of Police Squad '88 ▶
Naked in New York '93
Nasty Habits '77
National Lampoon Goes to the Movies '81
National Lampoon's Animal House '78 ▶
National Lampoon's Attack of the 5 Ft. 2 Women '94
National Lampoon's Loaded Weapon 1 '93
Natural Born Killers '94
Night Patrol '85
99 & 44/100 Dead '74
No News from God '01
Nocturna '79
Northanger Abbey '87
No. 3 '97
The Nutty Professor '63 ▶
Office Space '98
On the Avenue '37 ▶
Open Season '95
Orchestra Rehearsal '78
Oscar '91
Overdrawn at the Memory Bank '83
Padre Nuestro '85
Pajama Tops '83
Pandemonium '82
Paramedics '88
Pardners '56
Partners '82
Pass the Ammo '88
P.C.U. '94
The Pentagon Wars '98
Personal Services '87
Phantom of Liberty '74 ▶
Pictures '81
The Pink Chiquitas '86
Pipe Dream '02
Plan 10 from Outer Space '95
The Player '92 ▶
Polyester '81
The Positively True Adventures of the Alleged Texas Cheerleader-Murdering Mom '93 ▶
Pray TV '80
The President's Analyst '67 ▶
Primary Colors '98
Prime Time '77
The Princess Bride '87 ▶
Prisoner of Rio '89
A Private Function '84
Prize of Peril '84
The Producers '68 ▶
Purana Mandir '84 ▶
Putney Swope '69 ▶
Rat Pfink a Boo-Boo '66
Ready to Wear '94
Real Men '87
Really Weird Tales '86
Red Desert Penitentiary '83
Red Earth '82
Red Garters '54
Reno 911! Miami '07
Rentadick '72
Repentance '87 ▶
The Report on the Party and the Guests '66 ▶
Repossessed '90
Return of Captain Invincible '83
The Return of Spinal Tap '92
Revolution! A Red Comedy '91 ▶
Ricky 1 '88
Ring of the Musketeers '93
Robin Hood: Men in Tights '93
The Rocky Horror Picture Show '75 ▶
Romeo Is Bleeding '93
Rosalie Goes Shopping '89 ▶
The Royal Bed '31
Rude Awakening '89
The Rug Cop '06
The Ruling Class '72 ▶
Running Mates '92 ▶
Running Mates '00
Sallah '63 ▶
Salvation! '87
Sammy & Rosie Get Laid '87 ▶
Samurai Fiction '99 ▶
Save the Green Planet '03
Saved! '04
Scary Movie '00
Scary Movie 4 '06
Scenes from the Class Struggle in Beverly Hills '89
Schizopolis '97
School for Scoundrels '60 ▶
Scream '96 ▶
Scream 2 '97 ▶
Scream 3 '00
Scrooged '88
Search and Destroy '94
The Second Civil War '97
Second Time Lucky '84
Secret Agent 00-Soul '89
The Secret Diary of Sigmund Freud '84
Seduction of Mimi '72 ▶
The Senator Was Indiscreet '47 ▶
Serial '80 ▶
Serial Mom '94 ▶
Series 7: The Contenders '01
A Session with The Committee '68
Sex Adventures of the Three Musketeers '71
Sex with a Smile '76
Shame of the Jungle '75
Shampoo '75
A Shock to the System '90 ▶
Shoot or Be Shot '02
Shriek If You Know What I Did Last Friday the 13th '00
Sideburns '91
Silence of the Hams '93
Silent Movie '76
Silver City '04
Simon of the Desert '66 ▶

▶ = rated three bones or higher

Sink or Swim '97
Slammer Girls '87
Slap Her, She's French '02
Sleeper '73 ▸
Smile '75 ▸
S.O.B. '81
Soul Plane '04
Spaceballs '87
Spaced Out '80
Spaceship '81
Spare Me '92
The Specials '00 ▸
Spirit of '76 '91
Spy Hard '96
Stan Helsing '09
Starsky & Hutch '04
State of Things '82 ▸
Stay Tuned '92
Stiff Upper Lips '96
Straight to Hell '87
Strange Invaders '83 ▸
Streetfight '75
Sullivan's Travels '41 ▸
Sunset '88
SuperGuy: Behind the Cape '02
Suppose They Gave a War and Nobody Came? '70
Surf Nazis Must Die '87
Swimming with Sharks '94 ▸
Sympathy for the Devil '70
Tanner '88 '88 ▸
Tanner on Tanner '04
Tapeheads '89
Tartuffe '84
A Taste for Flesh and Blood '90
Team America: World Police '04 ▸
Terror 2000 '92
Thank You for Smoking '06
That's Adequate '90
They Call Me Bruce? '82
They Live '88
They Still Call Me Bruce '86
This Is Spinal Tap '84 ▸
The Thorn '74
Three Ages '23 ▸
The Thrill of It All! '63
To Be or Not to Be '83
Tokyo Gore Police '08
Tom and Francie '05 ▸
Too Many Crooks '59
Top Secret! '84 ▸
Trailer, the Movie '99
Transylvania 6-5000 '85
Trash '70
Traxx '87
Trial & Error '62
Tropic Thunder '08 ▸
True Stories '86 ▸
Trust Me '89
Tunnelvision '76
Turumba '84 ▸
The TV Set '06
2001: A Space Travesty '00
Uforia '81
UHF '89
Ultrachrist! '03
Undercover Brother '02
Unmasking the Idol '86
(Untitled) '09
Up from the Depths '79
Up the Academy '80
Vacuuming Completely Nude in Paradise '01
Vanity Fair '67
Vanity Fair '99
A Very Brady Sequel '96
A Very Curious Girl '69
Very Important Person '61
The Villain Still Pursued Her '41
Virgin High '90
Voyage of the Rock Aliens '87
Waiting for Guffman '96
Walker '87
War, Inc. '08
Watermelon Man '70
Way He Was '76
Weapons of Mass Distraction '97
What to Do in Case of Fire '02
What's Up, Tiger Lily? '66 ▸
The Wheeler Dealers '63 ▸
When Nature Calls '85
When Willie Comes Marching Home '50 ▸
Where in the World Is Osama Bin Laden? '06
Where the Buffalo Roam '80
Where the Bullets Fly '66
Where's Marlowe? '98
The White Sheik '52 ▸
Wholly Moses! '80
Who's Who '78
Wild, Wild West Revisited '79
Will Success Spoil Rock Hunter? '57
Window to Paris '95
Without a Clue '88
World Gone Wild '88
The World Sinks Except Japan '06
The Worm Eaters '77
The Would-Be Gentleman '58
Xala '75 ▸
Yin & Yang of Mr. Go '71
You'll Find Out '40
Young Doctors in Love '82
Young Frankenstein '74 ▸
Young Nurses in Love '89
Zachariah '70
The Zany Adventures of Robin Hood '84
Zarkorr! The Invader '96
Zelig '83 ▸
Zeta One '69
Zoolander '01
Zorro, the Gay Blade '81

Savannah

***see also** American South*
Crime and Punishment in Suburbia '00
Forces of Nature '99
The Gingerbread Man '97
The Legend of Bagger Vance '00
Midnight in the Garden of Good and Evil '97
Scarlett '94

Savants

***see also** Mental Retardation*
Being There '79 ▸
Champagne for Caesar '50 ▸
Charly '68 ▸
Doctor Dolittle '67
Forrest Gump '94 ▸
King Lear '71 ▸
Malcolm '86
Mercury Rising '98
Rain Man '88 ▸
Tony Draws a Horse '51

Scams, Stings & Cons

***see also** Heists*
Abbott and Costello Meet the Keystone Kops '54
Adios Amigo '75
After the Fox '66
Alien Fury: Countdown to Invasion '00
The Amazing Mr. X '48
American Buffalo '95
Angel-A '05
Another You '91
Anton, the Magician '78
Argentine Nights '40
Assault on a Queen '66
Back in Business '06
Backflash '01
Bad Company '02
Bad Guy '01
Barnaby and Me '77
Beautiful Joe '00
Bedtime Story '63
Best Laid Plans '99
Best of the Badmen '50
Beyond a Reasonable Doubt '56
The Big Bounce '04
The Big Lebowski '97 ▸
The Big Squeeze '96
Big Trouble '86
Billionaire Boys Club '87
Birds & the Bees '56
Birthday Girl '02
Black Cat, White Cat '98 ▸
Black Oak Conspiracy '77
Blackheart '98
Blackmail '91 ▸
Blackout '54
Blonde Crazy '31
Blood on the Moon '48
Blossoms on Broadway '37
Blue Murder at St. Trinian's '56 ▸
Border Phantom '37
Border Saddlemates '52
Bottle Rocket '95
The Brothers Bloom '09
The Brothers Grimm '05
Brown's Requiem '98
Buffalo Stampede '33
Buona Sera, Mrs. Campbell '68
Burning Down the House '01
Butterfly Affair '71
Came a Hot Friday '85
Candleshoe '78
Caper of the Golden Bulls '67
Capricorn One '78 ▸
The Captain from Koepenick '56
Cartier Affair '84
Casino '95 ▸
Catch Me a Spy '71
Catch Me If You Can '02
Cause for Alarm '51
Chameleon Street '89 ▸
The Charmer '87
Cheap Shots '91
Cheech and Chong: Things Are Tough All Over '82
Children On Their Birthdays '02
Chinatown '74 ▸
Choke '08
Circus '00
City of Ghosts '03
Club Fed '90
Cold Justice '89
Color Me Kubrick '05
The Color of Money '86 ▸
The Con '98
The Con Artists '80
Confidence '03
Consenting Adults '92
The Conversation '74 ▸
Convicts at Large '38
Cops and Robbers '73
Cotton Comes to Harlem '70 ▸
Country Gentlemen '36
Crack-Up '46
Cracked Nuts '41
Criminal '04
Croupier '97 ▸
Curly Sue '91
The Curse of Inferno '96
Dangerous Summer '82
Dead Heat on a Merry-Go-Round '66 ▸
The Dead Pool '88
Deadfall '93
The Deal '05
The Deal '08
Dear God '96
Death Defying Acts '07
Deception '92
Deception '08
Deep Crimson '96
Dennis the Menace Strikes Again '98
The Desperate Trail '94
Destiny Turns on the Radio '95
Diggstown '92
Dirty Rotten Scoundrels '88 ▸
The Distinguished Gentleman '92
Dr. Christian Meets the Women '40
Dollar '38
Dudley Do-Right '99
Elmer Gantry '60 ▸
The Embezzled Heaven '58
Every Day's a Holiday '38
Everything's Gone Green '06
F/X '86 ▸
F/X 2: The Deadly Art of Illusion '91
Fakers '04
The Family Holiday '07
Fargo '96 ▸
Federal Agents vs. Underworld, Inc. '49
Fierce Creatures '96
A Fish Called Wanda '88 ▸
$5 a Day '08
Flim-Flam Man '67
For Better or Worse '95
Forger of London '61
Formula for a Murder '85
The Fortune Cookie '66 ▸
The Fourth Protocol '87 ▸
The 4th Tenor '02
Framed '90
Frauds '93
Freelance '71
The Frighteners '96
Gang Related '96
The Gang's All Here '40
Get Shorty '95 ▸
A Girl in Every Port '52
Girl Under the Sheet '61
Glengarry Glen Ross '92 ▸
Glory! Glory! '90 ▸
Goin' to Town '44
Gone Fishin' '97
Good Neighbor Sam '64 ▸
Goodbye, Lover '99
Great Bank Hoax '78
The Great Impostor '61
The Great White Hype '96
Great World of Sound '07
Green Card '90
The Grifters '90 ▸
Gun Smoke '31
Harlem Rides the Range '39
Harry & Walter Go to New York '76
Heartbreakers '01
The Heat's On '43
Hi Diddle Diddle '43
The Hoax '06
Hold Your Man '33 ▸
The Honeymoon Machine '61
Hopscotch '80 ▸
The Hot Rock '70 ▸
House of Errors '42
House of Games '87 ▸
Housesitter '92
I Got the Hook-Up '98
I Love Melvin '53
I Love You Again '40 ▸
I Love You Phillip Morris '10
If I Were Rich '33
Il Bidone '55
In the Soup '92
The Infernal Trio '74
The Inspectors 2: A Shred of Evidence '00
Invasion of the Space Preachers '90
Irish Jam '05
Irresistible Impulse '95
Jackie Brown '97 ▸
Just the Ticket '98
Kid from Not-So-Big '78
Killer '73
The Killing '56 ▸
Kind Hearts and Coronets '49 ▸
The King and Four Queens '56
The King of Marvin Gardens '72
King's Ransom '05
Kiss or Kill '97
The Lady Eve '41 ▸
A Lady of Chance '28
The Ladykillers '04
Lamerica '95 ▸
The Last Adventure '67
The Last of Mrs. Cheyney '37 ▸
The Last Seduction 2 '98
Law and Order '42
Le Gentleman D'Epsom '62
Leap of Faith '92
The Learning Curve '01
The Lemon Drop Kid '51
Let's Do It Again '75
The Liars '64
Lies '83
Life Stinks '91
Like a Fish Out of Water '99
The Little Giant '33
Lock, Stock and 2 Smoking Barrels '98 ▸
Lonely Hearts '91
Lonely Hearts '06
Louisiana Hayride '44
The Lovable Cheat '49
Love Kills '98
Love the Hard Way '01
Lovers: A True Story '90 ▸
The Madwoman of Chaillot '69
The Magician of Lublin '79
Mail Order Bride '08
Malone '87
The Man '05
Man of the World '31
Manhattan Melodrama '34 ▸
Marshal of Cedar Rock '53
The Mask of Diijon '46
Matchstick Men '03 ▸
Maverick '94
McHale's Navy '64
McHale's Navy '97
Me and the Kid '93
Medicine Man '30
Mexican Hayride '48
Mexican Spitfire at Sea '42
Miami Hustle '95
Millions '90
Milwaukee, Minnesota '03
The Miracle Woman '31
Miranda '01
Mistaken Identity '36
Mr. Boggs Steps Out '38
Mr. Lucky '43 ▸
Mo' Money '92
The Monster '96
Murder for Sale '68
Murder on Approval '56
Murder on the Yukon '40
The Music Man '62 ▸
National Lampoon Presents Cattle Call '06
National Lampoon's Gold Diggers '04
Never Give a Sucker an Even Break '41 ▸
Never Say Never Again '83
The Next Big Thing '02
Nickel & Dime '92
Night and the City '50 ▸
Night and the City '92 ▸
Nightmare Alley '47
Nine Queens '00
No Way Out '87 ▸
None But the Lonely Heart '44 ▸
Nothing Sacred '37 ▸
Now and Forever '34
Ocean's Thirteen '07 ▸
Office Space '98
The Old Lady Who Walked in the Sea '91
Old Spanish Custom '36
On the Fiddle '61
One Christmas '95
100 Mile Rule '02
One of My Wives Is Missing '76
One Way Passage '32
Opportunity Knocks '90
Ossessione '42 ▸
Out to Sea '97
Pale Saints '97
Palmetto '98
Panic Button '62
Paper Man '71
Paper Moon '73 ▸
The Parallax View '74 ▸
Parole, Inc. '49
Pass the Ammo '88
The Pest '96
Phantom Gold '38
Piece of the Action '77
The Pope Must Diet '91
Popi '69 ▸
Portrait of a Lady '96 ▸
The President's Plane Is Missing '71
The Prime Gig '00
Prisoner of Rio '89
The Producers '68 ▸
The Producers '05
The Promoter '52 ▸
Purlie Victorious '63
The Quest '96
Quiz Show '94 ▸
Reborn '81
The Red Light Sting '84
Remedy for Riches '40
The Ringer '05
Risk '00
Risky Business '83 ▸
The Road to El Dorado '00
The Road to Zanzibar '41 ▸
Roaring Speedboats '37
Rule 3 '93
Ruthless People '86 ▸
Sands of Sacrifice '21
Save the Tiger '73 ▸
Scam '93
Scandalous '84
Schemes '95
Schtonk '92
Seance '00
Search for Beauty '34
Sgt. Bilko '95
The Settlement '99
Sexual Intent '94
Shade '03
Shattered Image '93
Shooting Fish '98
Silk 'n' Sabotage '94
Silver Bears '78
Simpatico '99
Sinner '07
Six Degrees of Separation '93
Skin Game '71 ▸
Sky Hei$t '75
Slackers '02
Slither '73 ▸
Small Hotel '57
Something for Everyone '70
South Riding '37
Southern Belles '05
The Spanish Prisoner '97 ▸
Spenser: A Savage Place '94
The Squeeze '80
The Squeeze '87
Stacy's Knights '83
Stagecoach to Denver '46
The Star Maker '95
Stavisky '74 ▸
Still Breathing '97
The Sting '73 ▸
The Sting 2 '83
Stolen Hearts '95
The Story of a Cheat '36 ▸
The Story of Esther Costello '57
The Stranger from Pecos '45
Sucker Money '34
Suicide Kings '97
Sunburn '79
Support Your Local Gunfighter '71 ▸
Sweet Talker '91
Swindle '92
The Swindle '97
Swindled '04
The Switch '76
Tall in the Saddle '44
A Taste for Killing '92
Tax Season '90
The Taxman '98
The Ten Million Dollar Getaway '91
Tequila Sunrise '88
Things Change '88 ▸
Things to Do in Denver When You're Dead '95 ▸
The Third Key '57
36 Hours '64 ▸
This Is a Hijack '73
This World, Then the Fireworks '97
365 Nights in Hollywood '34
Thrilled to Death '88
Ticket of Leave Man '37
The Tigress '93
Title Shot '81
Too Bad She's Bad '54
Too Pretty to Be Honest '72
Tootsie '82 ▸
Touch '96
Train Robbers '73
Traveller '96 ▸
Tricheurs '84
Trojan Eddie '96 ▸
Trouble in Paradise '32 ▸
Trust Me '89
Two Much '96
Underworld Scandal '47
The Unholy Three '30 ▸
Union Depot '32
Walpurgis Night '41 ▸
The Warrior & the Sorceress '84
Watch the Birdie '50
We Were Dancing '42
The Wendell Baker Story '05

We're Talkin' Serious Money '92
Whacked! '02
The Wharf Rat '95
When Will I Be Loved '04
Where the Money Is '00
White Men Can't Jump '92
White River '99
Why Me? '90
Wild Things '98
The Winner '96
Wish You Were Dead '00
Write to Kill '91
Yonkers Joe '08

Scared 'Chuteless

see also *Airborne; Skydiving*
Con Air '97 ▶
Double Team '97
Eraser '96
Firehouse Dog '07
Goldeneye '95 ▶
Point Break '91
Terminal Velocity '94

School Daze

see also *Campus Capers; Hell High School*
Absolution '81
Accident '67
The Adventures of Sebastian Cole '99
All God's Children '80
All I Wanna Do '98
All Things Fair '95
Alley Cats Strike '00
American Friends '91
Amy '81
Angels in the Endzone '98
Anna and the King of Siam '46 ▶
Around the Fire '98
Art School Confidential '06
Au Revoir les Enfants '87 ▶
Back to School '86
Backfield in Motion '91
The Basket '99
Before the Fall '04
The Beguiled '70 ▶
The Belles of St. Trinian's '53 ▶
The Bells of St. Mary's '45 ▶
Big and Hairy '98
Big Bully '95
Billy Madison '94
Black Narcissus '47 ▶
Blood Pledge '09
Blue Jeans '78
Blue Ridge Fall '99
Bluffing It '87
Boarding School '83
Boys '95
The Broadway Drifter '27
The Browning Version '51 ▶
The Browning Version '94
Brutal Fury '92
Buried Alive '89
Cheaters '00
Cheers for Miss Bishop '41
Children of a Lesser God '86 ▶
The Children's Hour '61
The Chocolate War '88 ▶
Christy '94
Ciao, Professore! '94
Clueless '95 ▶
Common Ground '00
The Convent '00
The Corn Is Green '45 ▶
crazy/beautiful '01
Crazy for Love '52
Crazy from the Heart '91 ▶
Cruel Intentions '98
The Dangerous Lives of Altar Boys '02 ▶
Dead Poets Society '89 ▶
Deadly Sins '95
Death Tunnel '05
The Devil's Backbone '01
The Devil's Playground '76 ▶
Diabolique '96
Diary of a Wimpy Kid '10
Doctor Dolittle '67
Dream to Believe '85
Dress Gray '86 ▶
Drive Me Crazy '99
D3: The Mighty Ducks '96
Eden '98
Educating Rita '83 ▶
The Elementary School '91
The Ernest Green Story '93
Europa, Europa '91 ▶
Eyes Right! '26
The Faculty '98
Fame '80 ▶
Fast Times at Ridgemont High '82 ▶
Final Exam '98
Finding Forrester '00
Flirting '89 ▶
Flubber '97
Forever Mary '89 ▶
Free of Eden '98
The French Lesson '86
French Postcards '79
Frog and Wombat '98
Games Girls Play '75
Get Real '99
Getting It On '83
The Getting of Wisdom '77
Getting Straight '70
Getting Wasted '80
The Girl, the Body and the Pill '67
The Girl Who Spelled Freedom '86 ▶
The Girls of Huntington House '73
The Goodbye Bird '93
Goodbye, Mr. Chips '39 ▶
Goodbye, Mr. Chips '69
The Gospel According to Vic '87
Grown Ups '80
Guess What We Learned in School Today? '70
The Guinea Pig '48
Half Nelson '06 ▶
The Halfback of Notre Dame '96
The Happiest Days of Your Life '50 ▶
Hard Knox '83
Hard Lessons '86
Harry Potter and the Half-Blood Prince '09
Heavenly Creatures '94 ▶
Here Come the Co-Eds '45
The History Boys '06
Homework '82
Horsemasters '61
How I Got into College '89
How to Eat Fried Worms '06
Idle Hands '99
Impure Thoughts '86
In a Class of His Own '99
Iron & Silk '91
Is There Life Out There? '94
Jack '96
Johnny Holiday '49
Johnny Tiger '66
Judy Berlin '99
The Kid with the 200 I.Q. '83
Kindergarten Cop '90
Kurt Vonnegut's Harrison Bergeron '95
Lambada '89
Last Time Out '94
Late Bloomers '95
Leader of the Band '87
Liberty Heights '99
Little Men '98
The Little Princess '39 ▶
A Little Princess '95 ▶
Little Red Schoolhouse '36
Lloyd '00
The Long Gray Line '55 ▶
The Lords of Discipline '83
Love Me if You Dare '03
Luna e L'Altra '96
Maedchen in Uniform '31 ▶
The Major and the Minor '42 ▶
Major Payne '95
Married to It '93
Masterminds '96
Matilda '96 ▶
Max Keeble's Big Move '01
Mean Girls '04 ▶
Memento Mori '00
A Minor Miracle '83
Mr. Headmistress '98
A Murder of Quality '90
Murder 101 '91
Music of the Heart '99
My Teacher Ate My Homework '98
My Teacher's Wife '95
National Lampoon's Class Reunion '82
National Lampoon's Senior Trip '95
The NeverEnding Story '84 ▶
Nighthawks '78
Not Quite Human 2 '89
Old Mother Riley, Headmistress '50
Oleanna '94
Our Time '74
Outside Providence '99
Oxford Blues '84
Passing Glory '99 ▶
Passion for Life '48
The People '71
Perfect Harmony '91
Porky's '82
The Possessed '77
Powder '95
Prep School '81
Pride of Jesse Hallum '81
The Prime of Miss Jean Brodie '69 ▶
The Principal Takes a Holiday '98
The Private War of Major Benson '55
The Pure Hell of St. Trinian's '61
Rachel, Rachel '68 ▶
The Rage: Carrie 2 '99
The Rascals '81
Real Genius '85 ▶
Rebel '70
Remember the Daze '07
Renaissance Man '94
Ricochet River '98
Robin of Locksley '95
Ruby Bridges '98
Sabrina the Teenage Witch '96
Safety Patrol '98
The St. Tammany Miracle '94
The Sandpiper '65
Satan's School for Girls '73
School for Scoundrels '60 ▶
School of Life '06
Secret Places '85
A Separate Peace '73
September Gun '83
Shout '91
Sing '89
The Sixth Sense '99 ▶
Stanley and Iris '90
Star Kid '97 ▶
The Strange One '57
Student Confidential '87
The Student Teachers '73
The Substitute '93
The Substitute 2: School's Out '97
The Substitute 4: Failure is Not an Option '00
Summer School Teachers '75
Tea and Sympathy '56 ▶
To Sir, with Love '67
Tom Brown's School Days '40
Tom Brown's School Days '51 ▶
Tommy Boy '95
Topaze '33 ▶
Topaze '51 ▶
Toy Soldiers '91
Treehouse Hostage '99
Trippin' '99
The Trouble with Angels '66
Twenty-Four Eyes '54 ▶
The Twilight Girls '57
The Underachievers '88
Undergrads '85 ▶
Up the Academy '80
Up the Down Staircase '67 ▶
Virgin Queen of St. Francis High '88
Vital Signs '90
Waiting for Superman '10
Waterland '92
Whatever It Takes '00
Where Is My Friend's House? '87 ▶
Whispering Corridors '98
Why Shoot the Teacher '79 ▶
Wild Reeds '94 ▶
The Winslow Boy '48 ▶
The Wishing Stairs '03
With Honors '94
The Worst Witch '86
Yentl '83
You Are Not Alone '78
Zebrahead '92 ▶

Sci Fi

see also *Alien Babes; Alien Beings—Benign; Alien Beings—Vicious; Alien Cops; Aliens Are People, Too; Animated Sci-Fi; Cloning Around; Comedy Sci-Fi; Fantasy; Future Cop; Future Shock; Out of This World Sex; Sci-Fi Westerns; Space Operas*
A. I.: Artificial Intelligence '01
Abbott and Costello Go to Mars '53
Abraxas: Guardian of the Universe '90
The Abyss '89 ▶
Acceptable Risk '01
Access Code '84
Adrenalin: Fear the Rush '96
Aelita: Queen of Mars '24
Aeon Flux '05
After the Fall of New York '85
Aftermath '85
Aftershock '88
Akira '89
The Alchemists '99
Alice '09
Alien '79 ▶
Alien 3 '92
The Alien Agenda: Out of the Darkness '96
Alien Agent '07
Alien Chaser '96
Alien Contamination '81
The Alien Factor '78
Alien from L.A. '87
Alien Intruder '93
Alien Nation '88
Alien Nation: Body and Soul '95
Alien Nation: Dark Horizon '94
Alien Nation: Millennium '96
Alien Nation: The Enemy Within '96
Alien Predators '80
Alien Private Eye '87
Alien: Resurrection '97 ▶
Alien Space Avenger '91
Alien Terminator '95
Alien vs. Predator '04
Alien Warrior '85
Alienator '89
Aliens '86 ▶
Aliens Are Coming '80
Aliens from Spaceship Earth '77
Aliens vs. Predator: Requiem '07
Allegro '05
The Alpha Incident '76
Alphaville '65 ▶
Altered States '80 ▶
The Amazing Colossal Man '57
Amazing Stories '85
American Cyborg: Steel Warrior '94
Android '82
The Android Affair '95
Andromedia '00
The Angry Red Planet '59
Anna to the Infinite Power '84
A.P.E.X. '94
The Apocalypse '96
Arcade '93
Arena '89
Armageddon: The Final Challenge '94
Around the World Under the Sea '65
The Arrival '90
The Arrival '96
The Arrival 2 '98
Artifacts '08
The Asphyx '72 ▶
Assassin '86
Assignment Outer Space '61
The Astounding She-Monster '58
The Astro-Zombies '67
At the Earth's Core '76
Atom Man vs. Superman '50
The Atomic Brain '64
The Atomic Man '56
Atomic Submarine '59
Attack from Mars '88
Attack of the 50 Foot Woman '58
Attack of the 50 Ft. Woman '93
Attack of the Giant Leeches '59
Attack of the Killer Tomatoes '77
Attack of the Mushroom People '63
The Aurora Encounter '85
Automatic '94
Avatar '09 ▶
Ba'al: The Storm God '08
Babylon A.D. '08
Backlash: Oblivion 2 '95
Bad Channels '92
Bad Girls from Mars '90
The Bamboo Saucer '68
Barb Wire '96
Barbarella '68
*batteries not included '87
Battle Beneath the Earth '68
Battle Beyond the Stars '80
Battle Beyond the Sun '63
Battle for the Planet of the Apes '73
Battle of the Worlds '61
Battle Queen 2020 '99
Battlestar Galactica '78
Battlestar Galactica: The Plan '09
The Beast from 20,000 Fathoms '53
The Beast of Yucca Flats '61
The Bees '78
Beginning of the End '57
Beneath the Bermuda Triangle '98
Beneath the Planet of the Apes '70
Beware! The Blob '72
Beyond Sherwood Forest '09
Beyond the Stars '89
Beyond the Time Barrier '60
Bicentennial Man '99
Biohazard: The Alien Force '95
The Black Hole '79
Black Mask 2: City of Masks '02
Black Scorpion '95
Blade Runner '82 ▶
Blake of Scotland Yard '36
The Blob '58
The Blob '88 ▶
The Blood of Heroes '89
Blue Flame '93
Blue Monkey '87
Body Melt '93
Body Snatchers '93
Bog '84
Bombshell '97
The Book of Eli '10
Boom in the Moon '46
Bounty Hunter 2002 '94
A Boy and His Dog '75
The Brain Eaters '58
The Brain from Planet Arous '57
Brainstorm '83
Brainwaves '82
Breeders '86
The Bronx Executioner '86
The Brother from Another Planet '84 ▶
Buck Rogers Conquers the Universe '39
Buck Rogers in the 25th Century '79
Bug '75
Bugs '03
Caged Heat 3000 '95
Caprica '09
Capricorn One '78 ▶
Captive Planet '78
Carver's Gate '96
The Castle of Fu Manchu '68
Cat Women of the Moon '53
The Cave '05
Chameleon '98
Chameleon 2: Death Match '99
Chameleon 3: Dark Angel '00
Charly '68 ▶
Cherry 2000 '88
Children of Dune '03
Children of the Damned '63
The Chronicles of Riddick '04
Chrysalis '07
Cinderella 2000 '78
Circuitry Man '90
City Limits '85
City of Ember '08
Class of 1999 '90
Class of 1999 2: The Substitute '93
The Clones '73
The Clonus Horror '79
Close Encounters of the Third Kind '77 ▶
Cloverfield '08
Club Extinction '89
Cocoon '85 ▶
Code 46 '03
The Colony '98
Colossus: The Forbin Project '70 ▶
Communion '89
The Companion '94
Conquest of Space '55
Conquest of the Planet of the Apes '72
Contact '97 ▶
Convict 762 '98
The Cosmic Man '59
The Cosmic Monsters '58
Cosmic Slop '94
Cosmos: War of the Planets '80
Crash and Burn '90
The Crazies '73
The Creation of the Humanoids '62
Creature '85
Creatures the World Forgot '70
Crime Zone '88
Crimson Force '05
Cube '98
Cube 2: Hypercube '02
Cube: Zero '04
Cyber Bandits '94
Cyber Ninja '94
Cyber-Tracker '93
Cyber-Tracker 2 '95
Cybercity '99
Cyberzone '95
Cyborg '89
Cyborg 2 '93
Cyborg 3: The Recycler '95
Cypher '02 ▶
Cyxork 7 '06
D-Day on Mars '45
Dagora, the Space Monster '65
Daleks—Invasion Earth 2150 A.D. '66
Damnation Alley '77
Dante 01 '08
Dark Breed '96
Dark City '97
Dark Planet '97
Dark Side of the Moon '90
Dark Universe '93
Darkdrive '98
Darkman '90 ▶
D.A.R.Y.L. '85
The Day It Came to Earth '77
Day of the Triffids '63 ▶
The Day the Earth Caught Fire '61 ▶
The Day the Earth Stood Still '51 ▶
The Day the Earth Stood Still '08
The Day the Sky Exploded '57
Day Time Ended '80
Day Watch '06 ▶
Dead End Drive-In '86
Dead Fire '98
Dead Man Walking '88
Dead Space '90
Dead Weekend '95
Deadly Harvest '72

▶ = rated three bones or higher

The Deadly Mantis '57
Deadly Weapon '88
Death Machine '95
Death Race '08
Death Sport '78
Death Watch '80 ►
Deathlands: Homeward Bound '03
Decoys '04
Decoys: The Second Seduction '07
Deep Red '94
Deep Space '87
Deepstar Six '89
Def-Con 4 '85
Deja Vu '06
Deluge '33
Demolition Man '93
Demon Seed '77 ►
Destination Moon '50
Destination Moonbase Alpha '75
Destination Saturn '39
Destroy All Monsters '68
Destroy All Planets '68
Devil Girl from Mars '54
Digital Man '94
Dinosaurus! '60
Do or Die '03
Doc Savage '75
Dr. Alien '88
Dr. Cyclops '40
Dr. Goldfoot and the Bikini Machine '66
Doctor Mordrid: Master of the Unknown '90
Doctor Satan's Robot '40
Doctor Who '96
Donovan's Brain '53 ►
Doom Runners '97
Doomsday '08
Dragon Fury '95
Dragon Fury 2 '96
Dragon Storm '04
Dune '84
Dune '00
Dune Warriors '91
Duplicates '92
Earth vs. the Flying Saucers '56
Earth vs. the Spider '58
Electra '95
Electric Dragon 80,000V '01
The Electronic Monster '57
The Element of Crime '84
The Eliminators '86
Embryo '76
Empire of the Ants '77
The Empire Strikes Back '80 ►
Encounter at Raven's Gate '88
Encrypt '03
End of the World '76
Endangered Species '02
Endgame '85
Endless Descent '90
Enemy Mine '85
Epoch '00
Epoch: Evolution '03
Equalizer 2000 '86
Equilibrium '02
Escape from Galaxy Three '81
Escape from L.A. '96
Escape from New York '81
Escape from Planet Earth '67
Escape from the Bronx '85
Escape from the Planet of the Apes '71 ►
Escape 2000 '81
Escapes '86
E.S.P. '83
E.T.: The Extra-Terrestrial '82 ►
Eternal Sunshine of the Spotless Mind '04 ►
Eve of Destruction '90
Event Horizon '97
Evil Alien Conquerors '02
eXistenZ '99
Expect No Mercy '95
Experiment '05
Explorers '85
Exterminators in the Year 3000 '83
The Eye Creatures '65
Eyes Behind the Stars '72
The Faculty '98
Fahrenheit 451 '66 ►
Falling Fire '97
Fangs '75
Fantastic Four: Rise of the Silver Surfer '07
Fantastic Planet '73 ►
Fantastic Voyage '66 ►
Feeders '96
Femalien '96
Femalien 2 '98
Fiend without a Face '58
The Fifth Element '97
The Final Cut '04
Final Encounter '00
Final Equinox '95
The Final Executioner '83
The Final Programme '73
Fire in the Sky '93
Fire Maidens from Outer Space '56
The Fire Next Time '93
Fire Serpent '07
Firebird 2015 A.D. '81
First Encounter '97
First Man into Space '59
First Men in the Moon '64
First Spaceship on Venus '60 ►
Five '51
Flash Gordon '80
Flash Gordon Conquers the Universe '40
Flash Gordon: Mars Attacks the World '39
Flash Gordon: Rocketship '40
The Flesh Eaters '64
Flesh Gordon '72
Flesh Gordon 2: Flesh Gordon Meets the Cosmic Cheerleaders '90
Flight to Mars '52
The Fly '58 ►
The Fly '86 ►
The Fly 2 '89
The Flying Saucer '50
Forbidden Planet '56 ►
Forbidden World '82
Forbidden Zone '80
Forbidden Zone: Alien Abduction '96
Force on Thunder Mountain '77
The Forgotten '04
Fortress '93
Fortress 2: Re-Entry '99
Fortress of Amerikka '89
Four Sided Triangle '53
The 4D Man '59
Frankenfish '04
Frankenstein Conquers the World '64
Frankenstein Meets the Space Monster '65
Freejack '92
Frequency '00
From the Earth to the Moon '58
Frozen Alive '64
Fugitive Mind '99
Future Force '89
Future Hunters '88
Future Zone '90
Futurekick '91
Futuresport '98
Futureworld '76
G2: Mortal Conquest '99
Galactic Gigolo '87
Galaxis '95
Galaxy Invader '85
Galaxy of Terror '81
Game of Survival '89
Gamer '09
Gamera, the Invincible '66
Gamera vs. Barugon '66
Gamera vs. Gaos '67
Gamera vs. Guiron '69
Gamera vs. Zigra '71
The Gamma People '56
Gangster World '98
Gappa the Trifibian Monster '67
Gattaca '97 ►
Geisha Girl '52
The Gene Generation '07
Ghidrah the Three Headed Monster '65
Ghost Patrol '36
The Giant Claw '57
The Giant Gila Monster '59
The Giant Spider Invasion '75
The Gladiators '70
Glen and Randa '71
Godzilla '98
Godzilla, King of the Monsters '56
Godzilla 1985 '85
Godzilla on Monster Island '72
Godzilla Raids Again '55
Godzilla vs. Biollante '89
Godzilla vs. King Ghidora '91
Godzilla vs. Megalon '76
Godzilla vs. Monster Zero '68
Godzilla vs. Mothra '64
Godzilla vs. the Cosmic Monster '74
Godzilla vs. the Sea Monster '66
Godzilla vs. the Smog Monster '72
Godzilla's Revenge '69
Gorath '62
Gorgo '61
Grand Tour: Disaster in Time '92
The Green Slime '68
Groom Lake '02
The Groundstar Conspiracy '72 ►
The Guyver '91
Guyver 2: Dark Hero '94
H-Man '59
Habitat '97
Half Human '58
The Handmaid's Tale '90
Hands of Steel '86
Hangar 18 '80
Hardware '90
Hardwired '09
Headspace '02
Heatseeker '95
Heavy Metal 2000 '00
The Hidden '87 ►
The Hidden 2 '94
Hide and Seek '77
Hideous Sun Demon '59
The High Crusade '92
High Desert Kill '90
Highlander 2: The Quickening '91
Highlander: The Source '07
The Hitchhiker's Guide to the Galaxy '81 ►
The Hitchhiker's Guide to the Galaxy '05 ►
The Hole '98
Hollow Man 2 '06
Hollywood Boulevard 2 '89
Hologram Man '95
Homewrecker '92
Horrors of the Red Planet '64
Howl's Moving Castle '04
The Human Duplicators '64
Humanoid Defender '85
Hybrid '97
Hyper-Sapien: People from Another Star '86
Hyper Space '89
I Am Legend '07 ►
I Come in Peace '90
I Married a Monster '98
I Married a Monster from Outer Space '58
I, Robot '04
Iceman '84 ►
Idaho Transfer '73
The Illustrated Man '69 ►
Immortal '04
In the Aftermath: Angels Never Sleep '87
In the Cold of the Night '89
In the Dead of Space '99
InAlienable '08
Inception '10
The Incredible Hulk '08
Incredible Melting Man '77
The Incredible Petrified World '58
The Incredible Shrinking Man '57 ►
Independence Day '96 ►
Infra-Man '76
Inhumanoid '96
Innerspace '87
Inseminoid '80
Interceptor Force 2 '02
Interzone '88
Intruder Within '81
Intruders '92
Invader '91
The Invader '96
The Invaders '95
Invaders from Mars '53
Invaders from Mars '86
Invasion '65
Invasion: Earth '98
Invasion Earth: The Aliens Are Here! '87
Invasion of the Animal People '62
Invasion of the Bee Girls '73 ►
Invasion of the Body Snatchers '56 ►
Invasion of the Body Snatchers '78 ►
Invasion of the Body Stealers '69
Invasion of the Girl Snatchers '73
Invasion of the Space Preachers '90
Invisible Adversaries '77
The Invisible Boy '57
Invisible Invaders '59
The Invisible Man Returns '40 ►
The Invisible Terror '63
Invisible: The Chronicles of Benjamin Knight '93
Isaac Asimov's Nightfall '00
The Island '05
Island of Terror '66 ►
Island of the Burning Doomed '67
Island of the Lost '68
It Came from Beneath the Sea '55 ►
It Came from Outer Space '53 ►
It Came from Outer Space 2 '95
It Conquered the World '56
It! The Terror from Beyond Space '58
It's All About Love '03
Jason X '01
John Carpenter's Ghosts of Mars '01
Johnny 2.0 '99
Josh Kirby... Time Warrior: Chapter 6, Last Battle for the Universe '96
Journey Beneath the Desert '61
Journey to the Center of the Earth '59 ►
Journey to the Center of the Earth '88
Journey to the Center of Time '67
Journey to the Far Side of the Sun '69 ►
Jumper '08
Kaena: The Prophecy '03
Killers from Space '54
The Killing Edge '86
Killing Machine '02
Killings at Outpost Zeta '80
King Dinosaur '55
King Kong '05 ►
King Kong vs. Godzilla '63
The Kirlian Witness '78
Knights '93
Kronos '57
Krull '83
Kurt Vonnegut's Harrison Bergeron '95
Laboratory '80
The Land That Time Forgot '75
The Land Unknown '57
Laserblast '78
Last Chase '81
Last Exit to Earth '96
Last Lives '98
The Last Mimzy '07
The Last Sentinel '07
The Last Starfighter '84
Last War '68
The Last Woman on Earth '61
The Lathe of Heaven '80
The Lathe of Heaven '02
Latitude Zero '69
The Lawless Land '88
The Lawnmower Man '92
Lawnmower Man 2: Beyond Cyberspace '95
Legend of the Dinosaurs and Monster Birds '77
Legion '98
Leprechaun 4: In Space '96
Lethal Dose '03
Leviathan '89
Lifeforce '85
Lifeform '96
Lifepod '80
Lifepod '93
Light Years '88
Liquid Sky '83 ►
The Living Dead '33
Lobster Man from Mars '89
Lock 'n' Load '90
Locusts: The 8th Plague '05
Logan's Run '76
Lolida 2000 '97
Looker '81
Lords of the Deep '89
The Lost Empire '83
Lost in Space '98
The Lost Missile '58
Lost Planet Airmen '49
The Lucifer Complex '78
Making Mr. Right '86
A Man Called Rage '84
The Man from Atlantis '77
The Man from Planet X '51
The Man Who Fell to Earth '76 ►
Mandroid '93
Manhunt of Mystery Island '45
Maniac Warriors '88
The Manster '59
Marooned '69
Mars '96
Mars Attacks! '96
Mars Needs Women '66
The Martian Chronicles: Part 1 '79
The Martian Chronicles: Part 2 '79
The Martian Chronicles: Part 3 '79
Masked Rider—The First '05
Masters of Venus '62
Matango '63
The Matrix '99 ►
The Matrix Reloaded '03
The Matrix Revolutions '03 ►
Meet Dave '08
Meet the Hollowheads '89
Meet the Robinsons '07
Megaforce '82
Megalodon '03
Megaville '91
Mesa of Lost Women '52
Metallica '85
Metalstorm: The Destruction of Jared Syn '83
Metamorphosis '90
Metropolis '26 ►
Millennium '89
Mimic '97
The Mind Benders '63
Mind Snatchers '72
Mind Trap '91
Mind Warp '72
Mindwarp '91
Minority Report '02 ►
Minutemen '08
Misfits of Science '85
Missile to the Moon '59
Mission Galactica: The Cylon Attack '78
Mission Mars '67
Mission Stardust '68
Mistress of the World '59
The Mole People '56
Momentum '03
Monkey Boy '90
Monolith '93
The Monolith Monsters '57
Monster a Go-Go! '65
Monster from Green Hell '58
Monster from the Ocean Floor '54
The Monster Maker '44
The Monster of Piedras Blancas '57
Monster on the Campus '59
The Monster That Challenged the World '57
Moon '09
Moon 44 '90
Moon Pilot '62
Moonbase '97
Moontrap '89
Mortal Challenge '97
Mosquito '95
Mothra '62 ►
Murder by Moonlight '91
Murder in Space '85
Mutant Chronicles '08
Mutant Hunt '87
Mutant Species '95
Mutator '90
The Mysterians '58
Mysterious Island '61 ►
Mysterious Two '82
Mystery Science Theater 3000: The Movie '96
Naked Souls '95
Natural City '03
Navy vs. the Night Monsters '66
Negadon: The Monster from Mars '05
Nemesis '93
Nemesis 2: Nebula '94
Nemesis 3: Time Lapse '96
Nemesis 4: Cry of Angels '97
Neon City '91
The Nest '88
Neutron and the Black Mask '61
Neutron vs. the Amazing Dr. Caronte '61
Neutron vs. the Death Robots '62
New Crime City: Los Angeles 2020 '94
New Eden '94
The New Gladiators '83
The New Invisible Man '58
Next One '84
Nezulla the Rat Monster '02
Night Beast '83
Night Caller from Outer Space '66
Night of the Blood Beast '58
Night of the Lepus '72
Night Skies '07
Nightfall '88
Nightflyers '87
1984 '56 ►
1984 '84 ►
No Survivors, Please '63
Norman's Awesome Experience '88
Not Like Us '96
Not of This Earth '88
Not of This Earth '96
Nude on the Moon '61
Oblivion '94
Octaman '71
Official Denial '93
Omega Doom '96
Omega Man '71
On the Comet '68 ►
One Million B.C. '40
Organizm '08
The Original Fabulous Adventures of Baron Munchausen '61
The Outer Limits: Sandkings '95 ►
Outland '81
Outlander '08
The P.A.C.K. '96
Pandorum '09
Paprika '06
Parasite '82
Parasite '03
Parasite Eve '97 ►
Past Perfect '98
Peacemaker '90
The People '71
The People That Time Forgot '77
People Who Own the Dark '75
The Phantom Empire '35
Phantom from Space '53
The Phantom from 10,000 Leagues '56

► = rated three bones or higher

Sci-Fi Romance

Sci-Fi Westerns

Science & Scientists

Android '82
The Andromeda Strain '71
The Andromeda Strain '08
Around the World Under the Sea '65
Arrowsmith '32
Assassin '86
Astro Boy '09
The Atomic City '52
The Atomic Man '56
Attack of the Robots '66
Beach Party '63
A Beautiful Mind '01 ▸
The Big Game '72
Black Swarm '07
Bombshell '97
A Brief History of Time '92 ▸
Brotherhood of the Wolf '01
A Bullet for Joey '55
Caravan to Vaccares '74
Chain Reaction '96
Children of the Damned '63
Chill Factor '99
Contact '97
The Core '03
Corn '02
Creation '09
Cybermutt '02
The Dallas Connection '94
Dam Busters '55 ▸
Dark Matter '07
Dark Star '74 ▸
Darkman '90 ▸
The Darwin Conspiracy '99
Darwin's Darkest Hour '09
The Day After Tomorrow '04
The Day of the Dolphin '73
Day One '89 ▸
The Day the Earth Stood Still '08
Dead Men Don't Wear Plaid '82
The Dead Next Door '89
Deadly Friend '86
Deadly Outbreak '96
Deep Blue Sea '99
Deep Core '00
The Defector '66
Demon Seed '77 ▸
Dick Barton, Special Agent '48
Die Laughing '80
Die, Monster, Die! '65
Dirty Games '89
The Dish '00 ▸
Dr. Alien '88
Doctor Dolittle '67
Dr. Ehrlich's Magic Bullet '40
Dr. Jekyll and Ms. Hyde '95
Dragon Fury 2 '96
Earth II '71
Eight Below '06
Electra '95
The Eliminators '86
Encounters at the End of the World '07 ▸
Evolution '01
Eye of the Beast '07
Fantastic Voyage '66 ▸
Fat Man and Little Boy '89
The Fly '58 ▸
The Fly '86 ▸
The Fly 2 '89
Forbidden World '82
Forever Darling '56
Four Sided Triangle '53
The 4D Man '59
From Hell It Came '57
From the Earth to the Moon '58
Gattaca '97 ▸
Geheimakte WB1 '42
The Gene Generation '07
Genesis II '73
Glory Enough for All: The Discovery of Insulin '92
Habitat '97
The Henderson Monster '80
How to Make a Doll '68
Hulk '03
Human Gorilla '48
Human Nature '02
Humanoid Defender '85
Illegal Entry: Formula for Fear '93
Illumination '73
An Inconvenient Truth '06 ▸
The Incredible Hulk '08
The Incredible Hulk Returns '88
Infinity '96
International House '33
The Invisible Man Returns '40 ▸
I.Q. '94
The Ister '04 ▸
Journey to the Center of the Earth '08
Junior '94
Jurassic Park '93 ▸
Kate & Leopold '01
Killer Wave '07
The Killing Room '09
Kinsey '04 ▸
Kitchen Stories '03
Land of the Lost '09
Last Day of the War '69
Laughing at Danger '24
Lifeform '96
Link '86
A Little Bit of Soul '97
The Lost World '92
The Lost World: Jurassic Park 2 '97
Love Potion #9 '92
Magma: Volcanic Disaster '06
The Man with Two Brains '83 ▸
Mary Reilly '95
Medicine Man '92
Meteor '09
Mimic '97
The Mind Benders '63
Miracle Mile '89 ▸
Mr. Superinvisible '73
Monkey Boy '90
Monkey Business '52 ▸
Monkey's Uncle '65
Mosquitoman '05
My Science Project '85
My Stepmother Is an Alien '88
Nautilus '99
Neptune Factor '73
No Smoking '55
October Sky '99 ▸
Outbreak '94 ▸
Perestroika '09
Pete's Meteor '98
Phantom Empire '87
Project X '87
Prototype X29A '92
The Quiet Earth '85 ▸
Re-Generation '04
Real Genius '85 ▸
The Reaping '07
The Relic '96
Return of Captain Invincible '83
Return of the Ape Man '44
Return of the Fly '59
The Rocky Horror Picture Show '75 ▸
The Saint '97
The Secret of the Telegian '61
Senseless '98
The Sex Machine '75
Shaker Run '85
Shakma '89
Simon '80
Sir Arthur Conan Doyle's The Lost World '98
Smilla's Sense of Snow '96
Son of Flubber '63
A Sound of Thunder '05
Space Master X-7 '58
Spaceways '53
Species '95
Sphere '97
Splice '09
Stephen King's Golden Years '91
The Story of Louis Pasteur '36 ▸
The Structure of Crystals '69
Sub Down '97
Sunshine '07
Surf 2 '84
Swamp Thing '82
Tarantula '55 ▸
Termination Point '07
The Thing '82
Things to Come '36 ▸
This Island Earth '55
Threshold '83
Threshold '03
Tidal Wave '75
Time Trackers '88
The Time Travelers '64
Timecrimes '07
Timeline '03
Tomcat: Dangerous Desires '93
12:01 '93
Ultraviolet '98
Unforgettable '96
Unknown Island '48
Unknown World '51
Virus '98
The Void '01
What the $*! Do We Know? '04
Where Time Began '77
The Wild and the Free '80
Woman in the Dunes '64 ▸
Yes '04
The Yesterday Machine '63

Scotland

***see also** Edinburgh; Glasgow*

Aberdeen '00
The Acid House '98
Almost Heaven '06
Another Time, Another Place '83 ▸
Behind the Lines '97
Beneath Loch Ness '01
The Big Man: Crossing the Line '91 ▸
Blood Clan '91
Bonnie Prince Charlie '48
Bonnie Scotland '35
Braveheart '95 ▸
Breaking the Waves '95 ▸
Brigadoon '54 ▸
The Bruce '96
Challenge to Lassie '49
Chasing the Deer '94
Deacon Brodie '98
Dear Frankie '04
Devil Girl from Mars '54
The Devil's Undead '75
Dr. Bell and Mr. Doyle: The Dark Beginnings of Sherlock Holmes '00
Dog Soldiers '01
Dragonworld '94
Dreams Lost, Dreams Found '87
Entrapment '99
Escape '90
The Flying Scotsman '06
Geordie '55
The Gospel According to Vic '87
The Governess '98
Gregory's Girl '80 ▸
Greystoke: The Legend of Tarzan, Lord of the Apes '84
Happy Go Lovely '51
Highlander: Endgame '00
I Know Where I'm Going '45 ▸
Incident at Loch Ness '04 ▸
Joyeux Noel '05 ▸
Kidnapped '48
Kidnapped '95
Kidnapped '05 ▸
Lady of the Lake '28
The Last Musketeer '00
Little Minister '34 ▸
Local Hero '83 ▸
Loch Ness '95
Made of Honor '08
Madeleine '50
Mary of Scotland '36 ▸
Mary, Queen of Scots '71
The Master of Ballantrae '53
The Match '99
Mister Lonely '07
Morvern Callar '02
My Life So Far '98
One More Kiss '99
The Pointsman '86
Pride of the Clan '18
Ratcatcher '99
Ring of Bright Water '69 ▸
Rob Roy '95 ▸
Rob Roy—The Highland Rogue '53
St. Ives '98
The Secret of the Loch '34
A Shot at Glory '00
Sweet Sixteen '02 ▸
This Is Not a Love Song '02
The Three Lives of Thomasina '63 ▸
The Tournament '09
Tragedy of Flight 103: The Inside Story '91 ▸
Trouble in the Glen '54
Urban Ghost Story '98
The Water Horse: Legend of the Deep '07
When Eight Bells Toll '71
Whiskey Galore '48 ▸
Wilbur Wants to Kill Himself '02 ▸
Wild Country '05
Year of the Comet '92
Young Adam '03 ▸

Scotland Yard

***see also** Foreign Cops*

Across the Bridge '57
The Adventures of Sherlock Holmes '39
Agatha Christie's Murder is Easy '82
Agent Cody Banks 2: Destination London '04
The Arsenal Stadium Mystery '39
Basic Instinct 2 '06
Behind That Curtain '29
The Black Cat '81
The Black Sleep '56
Blackmail '29 ▸
Brides of Fu Manchu '66
Bulldog Drummond's Bride '39
Bulldog Drummond's Peril '38
Bulldog Drummond's Revenge '37
A Certain Justice '99
Charlie Chan's Murder Cruise '40
Circus of Fear '67
Close Your Eyes '02
Cottage to Let '41
The Day of the Jackal '73 ▸
Dick Barton Strikes Back '48
Dr. Mabuse vs. Scotland Yard '64
Don't Open Till Christmas '84
Dracula's Daughter '36 ▸
Dressed to Kill '46
Drums of Fu Manchu '40 ▸
Eastern Promises '07 ▸
The Fiendish Plot of Dr. Fu Manchu '80
Foreign Correspondent '40 ▸
The Fourth Angel '01
Frenzy '72 ▸
From Hell '01 ▸
Gallery of Horrors '67
Gaslight '44 ▸
Green for Danger '47
Hangover Square '45
The Hound of the Baskervilles '39 ▸
The Hound of the Baskervilles '59
The Hound of the Baskervilles '77
The Hound of the Baskervilles '83
The Hound of the Baskervilles '00
The Hound of the Baskervilles '02 ▸
The House of Secrets '37
The House that Dripped Blood '71
International Lady '41
The Invisible Man Returns '40 ▸
Kaleidoscope '66
Kill Me Tomorrow '57
The Lavender Hill Mob '51 ▸
The Man from Planet X '51
The Man Who Knew Too Much '34 ▸
The Medusa Touch '78
Midnight Lace '60
A Mind to Murder '96
Ministry of Fear '44 ▸
The Moonstone '34
The Moonstone '72
The Moonstone '97 ▸
Obsession '49
P.D. James: Death in Holy Orders '03
A Pocketful of Rye '87
Raw Meat '72
Razor Blade Smile '98
Return of the Vampire '43
Rough Cut '80
The Runaway Bus '54
Sabotage '36 ▸
The Saint in London '39
The Satanic Rites of Dracula '73
Shadows on the Stairs '41
Shanghai Knights '03
She Wolf of London '46
Sherlock Holmes and the Secret Weapon '42 ▸
Shiner '00
The Squeaker '37
The Strange Case of the End of Civilization As We Know It '93
Terror by Night '46
The 39 Steps '35 ▸
The Trygon Factor '66
The Vengeance of Fu Manchu '67
The Verdict '46
The Voice of Merrill '52
The Wolfman '09
The Woman in Green '49

Screwball Comedy

***see also** Comedy; Romantic Comedy; Slapstick Comedy*

All in a Night's Work '61
Amazing Adventure '37
Ambassador Bill '31
America '86
And Baby Makes Six '79
Antonio '73
Argentine Nights '40
As You Like It '36
As You Were '51
Assault of the Party Nerds '89
Attention Shoppers '99
Auntie '73
The Awful Truth '37 ▸
The Baby and the Battleship '56
The Bachelor and the Bobby-Soxer '47 ▸
Bachelor Mother '39 ▸
Bachelor of Hearts '58
Back to School '86
Bank Shot '74 ▸
Bedazzled '68 ▸
Bedtime Story '63
Beer '85
Big Brown Eyes '36
Big Business '88
Blame It on the Bellboy '92
The Bliss of Mrs. Blossom '68 ▸
Blue Murder at St. Trinian's '56 ▸
Boeing Boeing '65
The Break-Up '06
Breakfast for Two '37
The Bride Came C.O.D. '41
Bringing Down the House '03
Bringing Up Baby '38 ▸
Bullseye! '90
Buona Sera, Mrs. Campbell '68
The Calamari Wrestler '04
Camp Cucamonga: How I Spent My Summer Vacation '90
Carry On Admiral '57
The Chaplin Revue '58
Charlie Chaplin: Night at the Show '15
Charlie Chaplin ... Our Hero! '15 ▸
Christmas in the Clouds '01
The Circus '19 ▸
Combat Academy '86
Connie and Carla '04
The Couch Trip '87
The Count '16
Crackers '84
Days of Thrills and Laughter '61 ▸
Doctor in the House '53 ▸
Dr. Otto & the Riddle of the Gloom Beam '86
Doctor Takes a Wife '40 ▸
Don Juan, My Love '90 ▸
Double Wedding '37 ▸
Doubting Thomas '35
Down Among the Z Men '52
Down the Drain '89
Easy Living '37 ▸
Easy Money '83
Easy Street '16 ▸
Egg and I '47 ▸
El Matador '03
Everything You Always Wanted to Know about Sex (But Were Afraid to Ask) '72 ▸
The Family Stone '05
The Favor, the Watch, & the Very Big Fish '92
Fireballs '90
The Fireman '16
Fit for a King '37
The Floorwalker '17 ▸
Forces of Nature '99
Forever Darling '56
Forsaking All Others '35
Four's a Crowd '38
The Gay Deceivers '69
The Geisha Boy '58
Get Crazy '83
Gray Matters '06
Hands Across the Table '35 ▸
A Hard Day's Night '64 ▸
Hard to Get '38
Harvey '50 ▸
Her Husband's Affairs '47
He's My Girl '87
Holiday '38 ▸
How Sweet It Is! '68
I Heart Huckabees '04
I Love My... Wife '70
I Love You Again '40 ▸
If You Could Only Cook '36
Inspector Hornleigh '39
Intolerable Cruelty '03
Italian Straw Hat '27 ▸
It's the Old Army Game '26
Joy of Living '38 ▸
La Chevre '81 ▸
Labyrinth of Passion '82
The Ladies Man '00
The Lady Eve '41 ▸
Laws of Attraction '04
Leatherheads '08
Libeled Lady '36 ▸
A Life Less Ordinary '97
Life Stinks '91
Lobster Man from Mars '89
The Long, Long Trailer '54
Lots of Luck '85
The Love Bug '68
Love Crazy '41 ▸
Love Is News '37 ▸
Lucky Partners '40
Lunatics & Lovers '76
Madhouse '90
The Major and the Minor '42 ▸
Make Mine Mink '60 ▸
Malibu Beach '78
Malibu Bikini Shop '86
The Marriage Circle '24 ▸
Marriage on the Rocks '65
The Marx Brothers in a Nutshell '90 ▸
The Mating Game '59 ▸
Me and Him '89
Meatballs 2 '84
Meet the Parents '00 ▸
A Midsummer Night's Sex Comedy '82 ▸
Miracle of Morgan's Creek '44 ▸
Miss Tatlock's Millions '48
Mr. & Mrs. Smith '41 ▸
Modern Girls '86
The Money Pit '86
Monkey Business '52 ▸
Monkeys, Go Home! '66
The Moon's Our Home '36
The More the Merrier '43 ▸
Morons from Outer Space '85
Mugsy's Girls '85
The Munsters' Revenge '81
My American Cousin '85 ▸
My Chauffeur '86
My Favorite Brunette '47

▸ = *rated three bones or higher*

Nightmare Detective '06
A Nightmare on Elm Street '10
Nightscare '93
Nightstalker '02
Nightwatch '96
No One Sleeps '01
No Way to Treat a Lady '68 ▸
Office Killer '97
Open Cam '05
Outside Ozona '98
The Paint Job '93
Pale Blood '91
The Perfect Witness '07
Piano Man '96
Pillow of Death '45
The Pledge '00 ▸
Portraits of a Killer '95
Postmortem '98
Power 98 '96
Prey of the Chameleon '91
Prime Suspect '92 ▸
Probable Cause '95
Profile for Murder '96
The Prophet's Game '99
Psychic '91
Psychopath '97
The Rain Killer '90
Rampage: The Hillside Strangler Murders '04
Ravenous '99
The Reaper '97
Red Dragon '02
Relentless '89
Relentless 3 '93
Relentless 4 '94
Replicant '01
Rest Stop '06
Resurrection '99
Retribution '98
Retribution '06
Return to Cabin by the Lake '01
Revenge Quest '96
Righteous Kill '08
Rites of Frankenstein '72
The Riverman '04
Roman de Gare '07
The Rosary Murders '87
Sacrifice '00
San Franpsycho '06
Sanctimony '01
The Satan Killer '93
Satan's Little Helper '04
Saw '04
Saw 2 '05
Saw 4 '07
Saw 6 '09
Scary Movie '00
Scoop '06
Scream '96 ▸
Scream 2 '97 ▸
Scream 3 '00
Serial Killer '95
Serial Killing 101 '04
Serial Mom '94 ▸
Serial Slayer '03
Seven '95 ▸
Shadow of a Scream '97
Shallow Ground '04
The Silence of the Lambs '91 ▸
Skeleton Crew '09
Skinned Alive '08
Slaughter of the Innocents '93
Sleepless '01
Sleepstalker: The Sandman's Last Rites '94
Snapdragon '93
So I Married an Axe Murderer '93
Soho Square '00
Son of Sam '08
Split Second '92
Stagefright '87
Stamp of a Killer '87
Star Time '92
Starkweather '04
The Stendahl Syndrome '95
Still Life '92
The Strange Case of Dr. Jekyll and Mr. Hyde '06
The Strange Case of Dr. Rx '42
Stranger by Night '94
Strangler of Blackmoor Castle '63
Striking Distance '93
Summer of Sam '99
Surveillance '08
Suspect Zero '04
Sweeney Todd: The Demon Barber of Fleet Street '07
Switchback '97
Tails You Live, Heads You're Dead '95
Taking Lives '04
Talking Head '92
10 Rillington Place '71 ▸
Ten to Midnight '83
Tenderness of the Wolves '73
Terror at London Bridge '85
There's Something about Mary '98 ▸
Things 2 '97
Thirst '09 ▸
Thr3e '07
3 A.M. '01 ▸
Tinseltown '97
To Catch a Killer '92 ▸
The Todd Killings '71
Trail of a Serial Killer '98
Transfixed '01
True Crime '95
Tunnel Vision '95
Turbulence '96
Twisted '04
The Ugly '96
Unconditional Love '03
Uncovered '94
Undefeatable '94
Unspeakable '02
Untraceable '08
Urban Menace '99
Vacancy 2: The First Cut '08
Valentine '01
Vegas Vice '94
Vice Girls '96
The Watcher '00
When a Stranger Calls '06
When the Bough Breaks '93
While the City Sleeps '56 ▸
White River '99
Winter Kill '74
Witchcraft 10: Mistress of the Craft '98
Without Warning '52
Wolf Creek '05
Writer's Block '91
Zipperface '92
The Zodiac '05
Zodiac '07

Serials

Ace Drummond '36
The Adventures of Captain Marvel '41
The Adventures of Frank and Jesse James '48
Adventures of Red Ryder '40
Adventures of Smilin' Jack '43
The Adventures of Tarzan '21
Amazing Stories '85
Atom Man vs. Superman '50
Battling with Buffalo Bill '31
The Black Widow '47
Blake of Scotland Yard '36
Captain America '44
Cheyenne Rides Again '38
The Clutching Hand '36
Curse of Nostradamus '60
Custer's Last Stand '36
Cyclotrode "X" '46
D-Day on Mars '45
Daredevils of the Red Circle '38
Darkest Africa '36
Daughter of Don Q '46
Destination Saturn '39
Devil Horse '32
Dick Tracy '37
Dick Tracy Returns '38
Dick Tracy vs. Crime Inc. '41
Doctor Satan's Robot '40
Don Daredevil Rides Again '51
Don Winslow of the Coast Guard '43
Don Winslow of the Navy '43
Drums of Fu Manchu '40 ▸
Federal Agents vs. Underworld, Inc. '49
Federal Operator 99 '45
Fighting Devil Dogs '43
Fighting Marines '36
Fighting with Kit Carson '33
Flaming Frontiers '38
Flash Gordon Conquers the Universe '40
Flash Gordon: Mars Attacks the World '39
Flash Gordon: Rocketship '40
G-Men Never Forget '48
G-Men vs. the Black Dragon '43
The Galloping Ghost '31
Genie of Darkness '62
Government Agents vs. Phantom Legion '51
Green Archer '40
The Green Hornet '39
Haunted Harbor '44
Hawk of the Wilderness '38
Holt of the Secret Service '42
The Houdini Serial '20
Hurricane Express '32
The Invisible Monster '50
The Ivory Handled Gun '35
Jesse James Rides Again '47
Judex '16
Jungle Drums of Africa '53
Junior G-Men '40
Junior G-Men of the Air '42
King of the Congo '52
King of the Forest Rangers '46
King of the Kongo '29
King of the Rocketmen '49
King of the Texas Rangers '41
Last Frontier '32
The Last of the Mohicans '32
Law for Tombstone '35
Law of the Wild '34
A Lawman Is Born '37 ▸
Les Vampires '15 ▸
Lightning Hutch '26
Lightning Warrior '31
The Lone Defender '32
The Lone Ranger '38
Lone Ranger '56
The Lost City '34
Lost City of the Jungle '45
The Lost Jungle '34
Lost Planet Airmen '49
Manhunt in the African Jungles '43
Manhunt of Mystery Island '45
The Masked Marvel '43
Master Key '44
Masters of Venus '62
The Miracle Rider '35
The Monster Demolisher '60
Mysterious Doctor Satan '40
Mystery Mountain '34
Mystery of the Riverboat '44
Mystery Squadron '33
Mystery Trooper '32
The New Adventures of Tarzan '35
Nyoka and the Tigermen '42
Overland Mail '42
The Painted Stallion '37
The Perils of Pauline '34
Perils of the Darkest Jungle '44
The Phantom Creeps '39
The Phantom Empire '35
Phantom of the Air '33
Phantom of the West '31
The Phantom Rider '36
The Phantom Rider '46
Pirates of the High Seas '50
The Purple Monster Strikes '45
Queen of the Jungle '35
Radar Men from the Moon '52
Radar Patrol vs. Spy King '49
Radio Patrol '37
Raiders of Ghost City '44
Red Barry '38
Return of Chandu '34
Riders of Death Valley '41
Robinson Crusoe of Clipper Island '36
Robinson Crusoe of Mystery Island '36
Rustlers of Red Dog '35
Savage Fury '35
Sea Hound '47
The Secret Code '42
Shadow of Chinatown '36
Shadow of the Eagle '32
Son of Zorro '47
S.O.S. Coast Guard '37
Space Soldiers Conquer the Universe '40
The Spider Returns '41
The Spider's Web '38
Spy Smasher '42
Spy Smasher Returns '42
Stone Cold Dead '80
Stone of Silver Creek '35
Sunset on the Desert '42
Tailspin Tommy '34
Tarzan the Fearless '33
Tarzan the Tiger '29
Texas to Bataan '42
The Three Musketeers '33
Tim Tyler's Luck '37
Trader Tom of the China Seas '54
Trail of the Silver Spurs '41
Trail Riders '42
Tumbledown Ranch in Arizona '41
Undersea Kingdom '36
Vanishing Legion '31
The Vigilantes Are Coming '36
Whispering Shadow '33
Winners of the West '40
Wolf Dog '33
A Woman in Grey '20
Zombies of the Stratosphere '52
Zorro Rides Again '37
Zorro's Black Whip '44
Zorro's Fighting Legion '39

Sex & Sexuality

see also *Crimes of Passion; Erotic Thrillers; Pornography; Sex on the Beach; Sexploitation*

About Adam '00
Accident '67
Acting on Impulse '93
The Adjuster '91
The Adultress '77
Adventures of a Private Eye '77
Adventures of a Taxi Driver '76
The Adventures of Sadie '55
The Advocate '93 ▸
An Affair of Love '99
Affairs of Anatol '21
After Tomorrow '32
Afterglow '97
Alfie '66 ▸
Alfie '04
Alien Nation: Body and Soul '95
All Things Fair '95
The Alley Cats '65
The Allnighter '87
Almost Pregnant '91
Alpine Fire '89
Alvin Purple '73
Alvin Rides Again '74
The Amazing Transplant '70
American Beauty '99 ▸
American Gigolo '79
American Pie '99 ▸
American Pie 2 '01
American Virgin '98
The Amorous Adventures of Moll Flanders '65
The Amy Fisher Story '93
Anatomy of Hell '04
And God Created Woman '57
And God Created Woman '88
Angel Blue '97
Angel of H.E.A.T. '82
Angels and Insects '95 ▸
Angels in America '03 ▸
Animal Instincts '92
Animal Instincts 2 '94
Animal Instincts 3: The Seductress '95
Anne Rice's The Feast of All Saints '01
Any Wednesday '66
The Apartment '60 ▸
Armistead Maupin's More Tales of the City '97
Armistead Maupin's Tales of the City '93
The Arousers '70
Arrivederci, Baby! '66
Art for Teachers of Children '95
Assault '70
Asylum '05
Baby Doll '56 ▸
The Baby Doll Murders '92
Baby Face '33
Baby Love '69
The Baby Maker '70
The Bachelor '93 ▸
Bachelor in Paradise '69
Bachelor Party '84
Bad Company '94
Bad Company '99
Bad Girls from Mars '90
The Banger Sisters '02
Bank Robber '93
Barbarella '68
Basic Instinct 2 '06
Basic Training '86
Baton Rouge '88
Battle in Heaven '05
Battle of the Sexes '28
The Bawdy Adventures of Tom Jones '76
Beach Girls '82
The Beast '75
Beau Pere '81 ▸
Becoming Colette '92
Bedroom Eyes '86
Bedroom Eyes 2 '89
Before Sunrise '94
Belle Epoque '92 ▸
Belle of the Nineties '34
Beneath the Valley of the Ultra-Vixens '79
Bent '97
The Best Little Whorehouse in Texas '82
Betrayal '78
Better Than Chocolate '99
Better Than Sex '00
Beverly Hills Madam '86
Beyond Erotica '79
Beyond the Silhouette '90
The Big Bet '85
The Big Dis '89
Bikini House Calls '96
Bikini Med School '98
Bilitis '77
The Bitch '78
Bitter Harvest '93
Bitter Rice '49 ▸
Black & White '99
Black Book '06 ▸
The Black Room '82
Black Starlet '74
Blind Vision '91
Blindfold: Acts of Obsession '94
Bliss '96
Blood and Sand '41 ▸
The Blood Oranges '97
Bloodbath '76
Bloodbath '98
Blown Away '93
The Blue Angel '30 ▸
Blue Jeans '78
The Blue Lagoon '80
Blue Movies '88
Boarding School '83
Bob & Carol & Ted & Alice '69
Boccaccio '70 '62
Bodily Harm '95
Body Chemistry '90
Body Chemistry 2: Voice of a Stranger '91
Body Chemistry 3: Point of Seduction '93
Body Double '84 ▸
Body Language '95
Body of Influence 2 '96
Body Shots '99
Body Waves '92
Boeing Boeing '65
Bonjour Tristesse '57 ▸
Booty Call '96
Born Romantic '00
The Boss' Wife '86
Bound by Lies '05
Boxing Helena '93
A Boy and His Dog '75
Boys' Night Out '62 ▸
The Boys of 2nd Street Park '03 ▸
Bram Stoker's Dracula '92
Breaking the Waves '95 ▸
Breathless '83
The Bride Is Much Too Beautiful '58
Brides of the Beast '68
Broken Flowers '05
Broken Trust '93
The Brown Bunny '03
Buford's Beach Bunnies '92
Bully '01
Business As Usual '88
Business for Pleasure '96
Butterfield 8 '60 ▸
Butterfly '82
Bye Bye Baby '88
Cactus in the Snow '72
Cal '84 ▸
Camille 2000 '69
Can I Do It... Till I Need Glasses? '77
Can't Hardly Wait '98
The Canterbury Tales '71
Captives '94
Caresses '97
Carmen, Baby '66
Carnal Crimes '91
Carnal Knowledge '71 ▸
Carnival in Flanders '35 ▸
Carried Away '95
Carry On Camping '71
Carry On Emmanuelle '78
Carry On Henry VIII '71
Casanova '87
Casanova '70 '65
Casual Sex? '88
Cat on a Hot Tin Roof '58 ▸
Cat on a Hot Tin Roof '84
Cat People '82
Cave Girl '85
Cesar & Rosalie '72 ▸
Chain of Desire '93
Champagne for Breakfast '35
Chasing Amy '97
Chatterbox '76
The Chatterley Affair '06
Cheaters '84
Cheech and Chong's Up in Smoke '79
Cherry Falls '00
Cherry 2000 '88
The Chicken Chronicles '77
Chinese Roulette '86
Choose Me '84 ▸
Chuck & Buck '00
Cinderella 2000 '78
Claire's Knee '71 ▸
Class '83
Class of '63 '73
Class Reunion '72
Cleo/Leo '89
Cleopatra '99
Closely Watched Trains '66 ▸
Cock & Bull Story '03
Cold Sweat '93
Collector's Item '89 ▸
Color of Night '94
Come Early Morning '06
Come Undone '00
Coming Apart '69
Coming Soon '99
Compromising Positions '85
Conspiracy '89
Contagion '87
Conversations with Other Women '05
The Cool Surface '92
Cool World '92
The Cooler '03 ▸
Corruption '70
The Courtesans of Bombay '85 ▸
The Crime of Father Amaro '02 ▸
Cruel Intentions '98
Cruel Intentions 2 '99
Cruel Intentions 3 '04
The Cruel Story of Youth '60 ▸

▸ = rated three bones or higher

▸ = rated three bones or higher

Passion '82
Passion '99
The Passion of Ayn Rand '99
The Passion of Darkly Noon '95
Pauline at the Beach '83 ▸
Payback '94
The Penitent '88
Pepi, Luci, Bom and Other Girls on the Heap '80
The Perfect Gift '95
Performance '70 ▸
The Perils of Gwendoline '84
Peyton Place '57 ▸
Picnic '55 ▸
Pigalle '95
Pinero '01
A Place Called Truth '98
Play Time '94
Playback '95
Playgirl Killer '66
Playmaker '94
A Pleasure Doing Business '79
Point of Terror '71
Poison Ivy '92
Poison Ivy 2: Lily '95
Poison Ivy 3: The New Seduction '97
The Pornographers '66 ▸
Portnoy's Complaint '72
Possessed by the Night '93
The Postman Always Rings Twice '46 ▸
The Postman Always Rings Twice '81
Power, Passion & Murder '83
Praise '98 ▸
Preacherman '83
Prep School '81
Pretty Baby '78 ▸
Pretty Woman '90 ▸
The Princess & the Call Girl '84
Private Lessons '75
Private Lessons, Another Story '94
Quartier Mozart '92
Quid Pro Quo '08
Quiet Days in Hollywood '97
Rain '32
Rain '01
Raising Cain '92
Rambling Rose '91 ▸
Rattle of a Simple Man '64
The Razor: Sword of Justice '72
A Real Young Girl '75
Reckless '97 ▸
Reckless: The Sequel '98 ▸
Red Blooded 2 '96
Red Kiss '85 ▸
Red Meat '98
Red Shoe Diaries '92
Red Shoe Diaries 2: Double Dare '92
Red Shoe Diaries 3: Another Woman's Lipstick '93
Red Shoe Diaries 4: Auto Erotica '93
Red Shoe Diaries 5: Weekend Pass '95
Red Shoe Diaries 6: How I Met My Husband '95
Red Shoe Diaries 7: Burning Up '96
Red Shoe Diaries 8: Night of Abandon '97
Red Shoe Diaries: Four on the Floor '96
Red Shoe Diaries: Luscious Lola '00
Red Shoe Diaries: Strip Poker '96
Red Shoe Diaries: Swimming Naked '00
The Red Violin '98
The Reincarnation of Golden Lotus '89 ▸
Rendez-vous '85 ▸
Repo Jake '90
Repulsion '65 ▸
Restless '72
Return to Peyton Place '61
Riders '88
The Right Temptation '00
Ripe '97
Rita, Sue & Bob Too '87 ▸
Rites of Frankenstein '72
The Road to Wellville '94
The Rocky Horror Picture Show '75 ▸
Roger Dodger '02 ▸
Romance '99
Rosebud Beach Hotel '85
The Rowdy Girls '00
R.S.V.P. '84
Rubdown '93
The Rue Morgue Massacres '73
Russian Dolls '05
The Sailor Who Fell from Grace with the Sea '76
Saints and Sinners '95
Salmonberries '91
Salome '85
Sammy & Rosie Get Laid '87 ▸
Save Me '93
The Scarlet Letter '79 ▸
Scene of the Crime '87 ▸
Scenes from the Class Struggle in Beverly Hills '89
Scorchy '76
Score '72
Scorned '93
Scorned 2 '96
Screwball Academy '86
Scrubbers '82
Sea of Love '89 ▸
Secret Games 2: The Escort '93
Secret Games 3 '94
Secret Life of an American Wife '68
Secrets '71
Secrets '77
Secrets of Three Hungry Wives '78
Seduce Me: Pamela Principle 2 '94
The Seduction of Joe Tynan '79
Seduction: The Cruel Woman '89
The Seductress '00
Seeing Other People '04
The Seniors '78
Sensations '87
Sensuous Summer '93
Separate Vacations '86
Serpent's Lair '95
The '70s '00
Sex '20
Sex and Breakfast '07
Sex and Lucia '01
Sex & Mrs. X '00
Sex and the Other Man '95
Sex and Zen '93
Sex Crimes '92
Sex is Comedy '02
Sex on the Run '78
Sextette '78
Sexual Intent '94
The Sexual Life of the Belgians '94
Sexual Malice '93
Sexual Response '92
Sexual Roulette '96
Sexus '64
Shadow Dancer '96
Shadow of a Scream '97
Shame, Shame, Shame '98
The Shaming '79
Shampoo '75
Shattered '21 ▸
Sherrybaby '06
She's Gotta Have It '86 ▸
Shopgirl '05 ▸
Showgirls '95
Sibling Rivalry '90
Siddhartha '72
Silk 'n' Sabotage '94
Silver Strand '95
Sinbad '71
Single Bars, Single Women '84
Sins of the Mind '97
Sirens '94
The Sister-in-Law '74
Sisters '97
Sisters of Satan '75
Six Days, Six Nights '94
Ski School '91
Skin Deep '89
The Slap '76
Sleeping with Strangers '94
Sliver '93
Smooth Talker '90
Snapdragon '93
Somersault '04
Something About Sex '98
Somewhere in the City '97
Sooner or Later '78
Sous Sol '96
Species 3 '04
Spirit Lost '96
Splendor in the Grass '61 ▸
Sprung '96
Star 80 '83
The Stationmaster's Wife '77
The Statue '71
Stiff Upper Lips '96
The Stilts '84 ▸
The Storm Within '48 ▸
Stormswept '95
Storyville '92
Strangers '91
The Strangers '98
Strictly Sexual '08
Strike a Pose '93
Stripped to Kill '87
The Stripper '63
The Stud '78
Sugarbaby '85 ▸
Summer Heat '87
Summer Lovers '82
Summer of '04 '06
Summer School Teachers '75
Super Bitch '73
Superbad '07 ▸
Supervixens '75
Surfacing '84
Susan Slept Here '54
Susana '51 ▸
Sweet Ecstasy '62
Sweet Evil '98
Sweet Lies '88
Sweet Movie '75
Sweet Poison '91
Sweet Spirits '71
Swimming Pool '70
Swimming Pool '03 ▸
Swindle '92
Swingers '96 ▸
Sylvia '03
Tale of Two Sisters '89
Tales of Erotica '93
Tales of the Kama Sutra: The Perfumed Garden '98
Talkin' Dirty after Dark '91
Talking about Sex '94
Talking Walls '85
The Taste of Others '00 ▸
Tattoo '81
Tea and Sympathy '56 ▸
Tea for Three '84
Teach Me '97
Temptation '94
Tempted '01
Temptress Moon '96
Teorema '68
Terrified '94
The Terror Within '88
Test Tube Babies '48
Texasville '90
That Obscure Object of Desire '77 ▸
Therese & Isabelle '67
Thief of Hearts '84
Things You Can Tell Just by Looking at Her '00
Thirteen '03 ▸
36 Fillete '88 ▸
This Property Is Condemned '66
This Sweet Sickness '77
Three in the Attic '68
Three in the Cellar '70
3-Way '04
Tigers in Lipstick '80
The Tigress '93
'Tis a Pity She's a Whore '73
To Sleep with a Vampire '92
Together? '79
Tom Jones '63 ▸
Tom Jones '98 ▸
Tonight for Sure '61
Too Good to Be True '98
Trash '70
Trojan War '97
Tropic of Cancer '70 ▸
Tropical Heat '93
Truth about Women '58
Tryst '94
Turkish Delight '73
Twenty-One '91
Twentynine Palms '03
Twin Peaks: Fire Walk with Me '92
Twins of Evil '71
Twist '76
2 by 4 '98
2 Days in Paris '07 ▸
Two Days in the Valley '96 ▸
Two Deaths '94
Twogether '94
The Ultimate Thrill '74
The Unbearable Lightness of Being '88 ▸
Under Investigation '93
Under Suspicion '92
Under the Skin '97
Under the Yum-Yum Tree '63
The Underachievers '88
Untold Scandal '03
Up in the Air '09 ▸
Vacuuming Completely Nude in Paradise '01
The Valley Obscured by the Clouds '70
Valmont '89 ▸
Vanilla Sky '01
Variety '83
A Very Curious Girl '69
Via Appia '92
Vibration '68
Vicious Circles '97
The Vicious Kind '09
A View to a Kill '85
Virgin Queen of St. Francis High '88
The Virgin Soldiers '69
Virtual Encounters '96
Virtual Girl '00
Virtual Sexuality '99
The Voyeur '94
Wager of Love '90
Waiting '05
Watch Me '96
Water Drops on Burning Rocks '99
We Don't Live Here Anymore '04
Wedding in Blood '74 ▸
Weekend Pass '84
Welcome to L.A. '77 ▸
What Planet Are You From? '00
Whatever You Say '02
What's Good for the Goose '69
What's Up Front '63
When Will I Be Loved '04
When Women Had Tails '70
Where '90
Where the Boys Are '84 '84
Where the Hot Wind Blows '59
Where the Truth Lies '05
A Whisper to a Scream '88
Whispers in the Dark '92
Wide Sargasso Sea '92
Wild at Heart '90 ▸
Wild Things '98
Winter Sleepers '97
A Winter Tan '88
Wish Me Luck '95
Wish You Were Here '87 ▸
The Witches of Eastwick '87
A Woman, Her Men and Her Futon '92
A Woman in Flames '84 ▸
The Woman Next Door '81 ▸
Woman of Desire '93
Woman Times Seven '67
Women in Love '70 ▸
Women on the Verge of a Nervous Breakdown '88 ▸
Women's Club '87
The Worker and the Hairdresser '96
Working Girls '75
Working Girls '87 ▸
The World Is Full of Married Men '80
The Wrong Man '93
X, Y & Zee '72
Xica '76 ▸
Yanks '79
Yesterday, Today and Tomorrow '64 ▸
You Don't Mess with the Zohan '08
Young Adam '03 ▸
Young Aphrodites '63
Young Lady Chatterly 2 '85
Young Love, First Love '79
Young Nurses in Love '89
Your Friends & Neighbors '98 ▸
Your Ticket Is No Longer Valid '84
Youth in Revolt '10
You've Got to Have Heart '77
The Yum-Yum Girls '78
Zabriskie Point '70 ▸
Zandalee '91
Zapped! '82
Zombie Island Massacre '84

Sex on the Beach

***see also** Island Fare*

Against All Odds '84
Airplane! '80 ▸
The Beach '00
The Blue Lagoon '80
Come Undone '00
Cote d'Azur '05
The Firm '93 ▸
From Here to Eternity '53 ▸
Heading South '05 ▸
Kiss Tomorrow Goodbye '00
Maslin Beach '97
Memoirs of an Invisible Man '92
Mixed Nuts '94
Phat Beach '96
Sweet Ecstasy '62
Swept Away... '75 ▸
Swept from the Sea '97
Tales of the Kama Sutra 2: Monsoon '98
Vibration '68
Young Adam '03 ▸

Sexcapades

Agnes and His Brothers '04
Alfie '04
American Crude '07
American Pie Presents: The Naked Mile '06
American Virgin '09
American Wedding '03
Andy Warhol's Dracula '74 ▸
Andy Warhol's Frankenstein '74
Angel Heart '87
Another 9 1/2 Weeks '96
Audition '99
Auto Focus '02 ▸
Bad Lieutenant '92 ▸
Basic Instinct '92
Being at Home with Claude '92
Belle de Jour '67 ▸
Betty Blue '86 ▸
Between Your Legs '99
Bitter Moon '92
Black Snake Moan '07
The Blackout '97
Blue Velvet '86 ▸
Boarding Gate '07
Body of Evidence '92
Bruno '09
Byron '03
Caligula '80
The Camomile Lawn '92
Candy '68
The Center of the World '01
Chloe '09
Choke '08
Circuit '02
Cleopatra's Second Husband '00
The Comfort of Strangers '91 ▸
Confusion of Genders '00
The Cook, the Thief, His Wife & Her Lover '90 ▸
Cougar Club '07
Crash '95
Crazy Little Thing '02
Crimes of Passion '84 ▸
Cruising '80
Dare '09
Dark Side '02
Deception '08
Delta of Venus '95
Devil in the Flesh '87
A Dirty Shame '04
Dona Herlinda & Her Son '86
Donkey Punch '08
Don't Let Me Die on a Sunday '98
Downloading Nancy '08
Eating Out 3: All You Can Eat '09
8 1/2 Women '99
8mm '98
El Crimen Perfecto '04
En la Cama '05
Exit to Eden '94
Exotica '94 ▸
Extreme Movie '08
Fellini Satyricon '69 ▸
Filth and Wisdom '08
Fired Up! '09
The First 9 1/2 Weeks '98
First Turn On '83
Forbidden Homework '92
Four Times That Night '69
French Fried Vacation '79
Frida '02
The Frightened Woman '71
Frisk '95
Geek Mythology '08
Getting It '06
The Girl From Monaco '08
Girls Can't Swim '99
Giving It Up '99
God's Comedy '95
The Guitar '08
Harvard Man '01
Havoc 2: Normal Adolescent Behavior '07
Henry & June '90 ▸
Hey, Happy! '01
Homework '90
Humpday '09
Husbands and Lovers '91
I Am Frigid... Why? '72
Ice Men '04
In the Cut '03
In the Realm of the Senses '76 ▸
The Informers '09
Irreversible '02
The Isle '01
Jade '95
Jill the Ripper '00
Just Before Nightfall '71
Just One Time '00
Kama Sutra: A Tale of Love '96
Kill Me Tomorrow '99
Killing Me Softly '01
Kiss the Sky '98
Kissed '96
Lady Chatterley '06 ▸
Lake Consequence '92
Laurel Canyon '02
Little Shots of Happiness '97
The Long Weekend '05
Love and Human Remains '93 ▸
Love and Rage '99
Love Is the Devil '98 ▸
Lust, Caution '07
Mad Cowgirl '06
Maitresse '76
Mango Yellow '02
Marquis de Sade '96
Men Cry Bullets '00
Miranda '01
Miss March '09
Mister Foe '07
The Monkey's Mask '00
Naked Lunch '91 ▸
Never Again '01
The New Eve '98 ▸
The Night Porter '74
9 1/2 Weeks '86
Not Tonight Darling '72
The Oh in Ohio '06
One Night at McCool's '01
On_Line '01
Opium: Diary of a Madwoman '07
The Other Side of the Bed '03
Paris, France '94
Payback '98 ▸
Peeping Tom '60 ▸
Perfect Stranger '07

▸ = rated three bones or higher

The Piano Teacher '01
Pigs '07
The Pillow Book '95
Preaching to the Perverted '97
Priceless '06
Raging Hormones '99
Return to Two Moon Junction '93
The Ring Finger '05
Road Trip: Beer Pong '09
The Rough and the Smooth '59
The Rules of Attraction '02
Secretary '02 ▶
Seduced: Pretty When You Cry '01
Sex and Death 101 '07
Sex and the City: The Movie '08
sex, lies and videotape '89 ▶
The Sex Machine '75
The Shadows '07
Simone Barbes '80
Sitcom '97
Sleeping Dogs Lie '06
Spider Lilies '06
Spread '09
The Story of O '75
The Story of O, Part 2 '87
Suite 16 '94
The Sweetest Thing '02
Take Me '01
Teenage Caveman '01
Teeth '07
The Ten '07
These Girls '05
Thirst '09 ▶
Tie Me Up! Tie Me Down! '90
Tokyo Decadence '91
Tomcats '01
Torremolinos 73 '03
The Trio '97
Two Moon Junction '88
Unfaithful '02 ▶
Van Wilder: Freshman Year '08
Visitor Q '01
When Will I Be Loved '04
Whipped '00
White Mischief '88 ▶
Whore '91
Why Do They Call It Love When They Mean Sex? '92
Wild Orchid '90
Wild Orchid 2: Two Shades of Blue '92
Y Tu Mama Tambien '01
Zebra Lounge '01

Sexploitation

***see also** Erotic Thrillers; Exploitation*

The Abductors '72
The Acid Eaters '67
Agony of Love '66
Amazon Jail '85
Angel 3: The Final Chapter '88
Aroused '66
Attack Girls' Swim Team vs. the Undead '07
Au Pair Girls '72
Baby Love '69
Bad Girls Do Cry '54
Bad Girls Go to Hell '65
Barbarian Queen 2: The Empress Strikes Back '89
The Bawdy Adventures of Tom Jones '76
Beach Babes 2: Cave Girl Island '95
Beach Babes from Beyond '93
The Beast That Killed Women '65
Bedroom Eyes '86
The Bellboy and the Playgirls '62
Beneath the Valley of the Ultra-Vixens '79
The Big Bust Out '73
The Big Doll House '71
The Bikini Car Wash Company '90
The Bikini Car Wash Company 2 '92
Black Venus '83
Blazing Stewardesses '75
Blood Gnome '02
Bolero '84
Broadcast Bombshells '95
Caged Fury '90
Candy Stripe Nurses '74
Candy Tangerine Man '75
Carnal Crimes '91
Chain Gang Women '72
Champagne for Breakfast '35
Cheering Section '73
The Cheerleaders '72
Cheerleaders' Wild Weekend '85
Cherry Hill High '76
Chesty Anderson USN '76
Class Reunion '72
Cleo/Leo '89
Corruption '70
Cruel Restaurant '08
The Curious Dr. Humpp '70
Dandelions '74
Deadly Embrace '88
Death Row Girls '08
Def Jam's How to Be a Player '97
Delinquent School Girls '84
Devil's Wedding Night '73
Dinosaur Island '93
Dirty Mind of Young Sally '72
Domino '88
Dracula Sucks '79
Eastern Promises '07 ▶
Ecstasy '84
Emily '77
Emmanuelle '74
Emmanuelle 4 '84
Emmanuelle 5 '87
Emmanuelle 6 '88
Emmanuelle & Joanna '78
Emmanuelle in the Country '78
Emmanuelle on Taboo Island '76
Emmanuelle, the Joys of a Woman '76
Erotic Escape '72
Erotic Touch of Hot Skin '65
Fanny Hill: Memoirs of a Woman of Pleasure '64
Fantasies '73
Feelin' Up '76
Female Prisoner: Caged '83
Female Prisoner Sigma '06
Firehouse '87
The First Nudie Musical '75
Flesh Gordon '72
Flesh Gordon 2: Flesh Gordon Meets the Cosmic Cheerleaders '90
Fleshpot on 42nd Street '71
Flower & Snake '04
Flower & Snake 2 '05
Flower & Snake '74 '74
Forever Emmanuelle '75
The French Woman '79
Ghosts Can't Do It '90
Gimme an F '85
Ginger '72
The Girl, the Body and the Pill '67
Good-bye, Emmanuelle '77
Great Bikini Off-Road Adventure '94
The Happy Hooker '75
The Happy Hooker Goes to Washington '77
Hard Ticket to Hawaii '87
Hard to Die '90
Hardbodies '84
Help Wanted Female '68
Hollywood Boulevard 2 '89
Hollywood High '77
Hollywood High, Part 2 '81
Hollywood Hot Tubs '84
Hollywood Hot Tubs 2: Educating Crystal '89
Homework '82
Honkytonk Nights '78
Hot Moves '84
Hot T-Shirts '79
H.O.T.S. '79
How to Make a Doll '68
Human Trafficking '05
Ilsa, She-Wolf of the SS '74
Ilsa, the Tigress of Siberia '79
Ilsa, the Wicked Warden '78
Inferno in Paradise '88
Inhibition '76
Inn of Temptation '73
Invasion of the Girl Snatchers '73
The Invisible Maniac '90
Joy of Sex '84
Kandyland '87
Killing Machine '02
Knock Outs '92
Lady Godiva Rides '68
Last Dance '91
Liane, Jungle Goddess '56
Lips of Blood '75
Liquid Dreams '92
Little Miss Innocence '73
The Living Dead Girl '82
Love Desperados '68
Love Notes '88
Lust for Dracula '04
Lust for Freedom '87
Madame O '67
Mistress Pamela '74
Modern Girls '86
Mondo Balordo '64
My Pleasure Is My Business '74
My Therapist '84
Mysterious Jane '81
Naked Killer '92
Naked Venus '58
Naked Weapon '03
Nature's Playmates '62
Naughty Knights '71
Night Call Nurses '72
The Night Evelyn Came Out of the Grave '71
Nine Ages of Nakedness '69
Nude on the Moon '61
Nurse on Call '88
Olga's Girls '64
On the Doll '07
Orgy of the Dead '65
Pagan Island '60
Paranoia '69
Party Favors '89
Party Plane '90
Perfect Timing '84
The Perverse Countess '73
Please Don't Eat My Mother '72
Prehistoric Bimbos in Armageddon City '93
Preppies '82
The Prime Time '60
Private Duty Nurses '71
Private Passions '85
Profile for Murder '96
Rebel Vixens '69
Red Shoe Diaries 2: Double Dare '92
Return to the Blue Lagoon '91
Revenge of the Cheerleaders '76
Revenge of the Virgins '62
Sacrilege '86
Screen Test '85
Scum of the Earth '63
Sea of Dreams '90
The Seducers '70
Sensual Partners '87
The Sensuous Teenager '70
Sex Adventures of the Three Musketeers '71
Sex and Buttered Popcorn '91
Sex and Fury '73
Sex and Zen '93
Sex Is Crazy '79
Sex Through a Window '72
Shanty Tramp '67
She Came on the Bus '69
She Devils in Chains '76
Slammer Girls '87
Slumber Party Massacre 3 '90
Snapshot '77
Snowballing '85
Sorority Babes in the Slimeball Bowl-A-Rama '87
Sorority House Party '92
Spaced Out '80
The Speed Lovers '68
Strange World of Coffin Joe '68
The Student Nurses '70
The Student Teachers '73
Submission '77
Suburban Roulette '67
Sugar Cookies '77
Superchick '71
Supervixens '75
Sweater Girls '78
Sweet Georgia '72
Sweet Young Thing '79
The Swinging Cheerleaders '74
Tarzana, the Wild Girl '69
Tender Flesh '97
Tender Loving Care '73
Test Tube Teens from the Year 2000 '93
Thinkin' Big '87
Tomcat: Dangerous Desires '93
Train Station Pickups '79
Truck Stop '78
Truck Stop Women '74
2069: A Sex Odyssey '78
Ultimate Desires '91
The Vampire Hookers '78
Venus in Furs '70
Vice Academy '88
Vice Academy 2 '90
Vice Academy 3 '91
Wanda, the Sadistic Hypnotist '67
The Watcher in the Attic '76
Wham-Bam, Thank You Spaceman '75
Witchcraft 2: The Temptress '90
Witchcraft 3: The Kiss of Death '90
Witchcraft 5: Dance with the Devil '92
World of the Depraved '67
The Young Nurses '73
The Zombie Army '93

Sexual Abuse

***see also** Domestic Abuse; Rape*

The Accused '88 ▶
All About Lily Chou-Chou '01 ▶
Bad Education '04 ▶
The Bed You Sleep In '93
Boxing Helena '93
The Boys of St. Vincent '93 ▶
Breathtaking '00
The Devils '71 ▶
Fall from Innocence '88
Fortune and Men's Eyes '71
Hard Candy '06
Heart of the Stag '84
Ilsa, Harem Keeper of the Oil Sheiks '76
Loved '97
Man of Ashes '86
Mesmerized '84
Mysterious Skin '04 ▶
Mystic River '03 ▶
The Night Porter '74
The Notorious Bettie Page '06
Priest '94
Romper Stomper '92
Southern Man '99
Trade '07
Twin Peaks: Fire Walk with Me '92
Whatever '98
Woman, Thou Art Loosed '04

Sexual Harrassment

Brilliant Lies '96
Disclosure '94
Foxfire '96
G.I. Jane '97
Improper Conduct '94
9 to 5 '80
North Country '05
Oleanna '94
Strange Justice: The Clarence Thomas and Anita Hill Story '99

Ships

***see** Deep Blue; Mutiny; Sail Away; Shipwrecked; Submarines*

Shipwrecked

***see also** Sea Disasters*

Adventures of Eliza Fraser '76
Benji the Hunted '87
The Black Pirate '26 ▶
The Black Stallion '79 ▶
Blue Fin '78
The Blue Lagoon '80
Cabeza de Vaca '90 ▶
Dead of Night '99
Dungeon of Harrow '64
Eye of the Needle '81
Far from Home: The Adventures of Yellow Dog '94
Greystoke: The Legend of Tarzan, Lord of the Apes '84
Hawk of the Wilderness '38
He Is My Brother '75
Humongous '82
The Island of Dr. Moreau '77
Island of Lost Souls '32 ▶
Island of the Lost '68
Jungle Bride '33
Kilma, Queen of the Amazons '75
The Last Templar '09
The Legend of the Sea Wolf '58
Light at the Edge of the World '71
Madagascar '05
Male and Female '19 ▶
Matango '63
Mongol '07 ▶
The Most Dangerous Game '32 ▶
Mutiny on the Bounty '35 ▶
Mutiny on the Bounty '62
My Favorite Wife '40 ▶
Pardon My Sarong '42
Princess Caraboo '94
Project: Genesis '93
Rich and Strange '32
Robby '68
Robinson Crusoe '36
Robinson Crusoe '96
Robinson Crusoe & the Tiger '72
Sea Gypsies '78
The Sea Wolf '41 ▶
The Sea Wolf '93
She Gods of Shark Reef '56
Shogun '80 ▶
Summer Affair '71
Swept Away... '75 ▶
Swept from the Sea '97
The Swiss Family Robinson '60 ▶
Trader Tom of the China Seas '54
20,000 Leagues under the Sea '54 ▶
Two Lost Worlds '50

Shops & Shopping

The American Mall '08
Attention Shoppers '99
Bad Santa '03
Bride Wars '09
Christmas in Wonderland '07
Clueless '95 ▶
Dawn of the Dead '04 ▶
Department Store '35
Elf '03 ▶
The 40 Year Old Virgin '05 ▶
Going Shopping '05
Heater '99
Holy Man '98
Lost Embrace '04
Meet Market '08
Mr. Magorium's Wonder Emporium '07
Observe and Report '09
Paul Blart: Mall Cop '09
Pretty Woman '90 ▶
Priceless '06
Scenes from a Mall '91
Seven Doors to Death '44
Sex and the City: The Movie '08
Shopgirl '05 ▶
Shopping '93
Wal-Mart: The High Cost of Low Price '05 ▶
Washington Heights '02
Where the Heart Is '00
Who's Minding the Store? '63

Showbiz Comedies

Adaptation '02 ▶
Alex in Wonderland '70
Alvin and the Chipmunks '07
American Dreamz '06
America's Sweethearts '01
Art House '98
Bamboozled '00
Be Cool '05
Because of Him '45
Being John Malkovich '99 ▶
Betty '97
Bewitched '05
The Big Broadcast of 1938 '38
Big Fat Liar '02
The Big Picture '89
Blazing Saddles '74 ▶
Bloodhounds of Broadway '89
Boardinghouse Blues '48
Bollywood Hero '09
Bowfinger '99 ▶
The Boy Friend '71 ▶
Broadway Melody '29
Broadway Melody of 1936 '35 ▶
Broadway Melody of 1938 '37
Broadway Melody of 1940 '40
Brutal Massacre: A Comedy '07
Bullets over Broadway '94 ▶
Burning Down the House '01
Camp '03
Cannes Man '96
Cats Don't Dance '97
Celebrity '98 ▶
The Comic '69 ▶
Comic Act '98 ▶
Crazy House '43
Criminal Ways '03
Critic's Choice '63
The Dark Backward '91
The Day the Women Got Even '80
The Deal '08
Delirious '91
Dickie Roberts: Former Child Star '03
Die Mommie Die! '03
Dog Pound Shuffle '75 ▶
EDtv '99
Ella Cinders '26 ▶
Ellie Parker '05 ▶
Enemies of Laughter '00
The Errand Boy '61
Everybody Sing '38
Everybody's Famous! '00
Exposed '03
Extra Girl '23
Fall Guy '82
The Final Hit '02
Fish Without a Bicycle '03
Forever Female '53 ▶
Free and Easy '30
Funny Bones '94 ▶
Funny People '09
Galaxy Quest '99
Ganked '05
Get Shorty '95 ▶
Glam '97
Good Times '67
Goodbye Charlie '64
The Grand Role '04
Grave Secrets '89
Grindin' '07
Gypsy '62 ▶
Gypsy '93
The Hard Way '91 ▶
Havana Widows '33
Hear My Song '91 ▶
Here Comes Cookie '35
Hit and Runway '01
Hollywood Boulevard 2 '89
Hollywood Chaos '89
Hollywood Ending '02
Hollywood in Trouble '87
Hollywood North '03
Hollywood Party '34
Hollywood Shuffle '87
The Hollywood Sign '01
Hooper '78
How to Lose Friends & Alienate People '08

▶ = rated three bones or higher

I'll Do Anything '93
In the Doghouse '98
The Independent '00
Introducing the Dwights '07
It's a Date '40
It's a Great Feeling '49
Jackie's Back '99
Jay and Silent Bob Strike Back '01
Jiminy Glick in LaLa Wood '05
Joey Breaker '93 ▶
Josie and the Pussycats '01
Just Write '97
The Kid and I '05
Killer Movie '08
L.A. Twister '04
Lady Killer '33 ▶
The Last Shot '04
Let's Make Love '60
Life with Mikey '93
Lisa Picard Is Famous '01
Looney Tunes: Back in Action '03
Louisiana Hayride '44
Mad About Music '38 ▶
Main Street to Broadway '53
Man About Town '39
Marci X '03
Merci Docteur Rey '04 ▶
Merton of the Movies '47
A Midwinter's Tale '95
Misleading Lady '32
Mr. Saturday Night '92
Movies Money Murder '96
The Muppet Movie '79 ▶
The Muppets Take Manhattan '84 ▶
The Muse '99
Music & Lyrics '07
My Blue Heaven '50
My Date With Drew '05 ▶
My Dream Is Yours '49
My Favorite Year '82 ▶
Nancy Goes to Rio '50
The Night They Raided Minsky's '69 ▶
Notting Hill '99 ▶
Nudity Required '90
Panama Hattie '42
Panic Button '62
The Party '68 ▶
Pick a Star '37
Pipe Dream '02
Postcards from the Edge '90 ▶
The Prince and the Showgirl '57
The Producers '68 ▶
The Producers '05
Ratings Game '84
The Real Blonde '97
Rock-A-Bye Baby '57
Rubberface '81
Salut l'Artiste '74 ▶
Searching for Bobby D '05
Second Fiddle '39
Seed of Chucky '04
Shoot or Be Shot '02
The Shot '96
Silent Movie '76
Sing and Like It '34
The Singing Kid '36
Sink or Swim '97
Soapdish '91 ▶
S.O.B. '81
The Souler Opposite '97
Soundman '99
Stage Struck '36
Star Spangled Rhythm '42 ▶
Still Crazy '98 ▶
Stuntmen '09
Sullivan's Travels '41 ▶
The Sunshine Boys '95
Swingers '96 ▶
Tapeheads '89
There's No Business Like Show Business '54 ▶
These Old Broads '01
13 Moons '02
365 Nights in Hollywood '34
Tinseltown '97
Tom and Francie '05 ▶
Too Smooth '98
Tropic Thunder '08 ▶
True Confessions of a Hollywood Starlet '08
Tune in Tomorrow '90
The 24 Hour Woman '99
Wag the Dog '97
Waiting for Guffman '96
Walk Hard: The Dewey Cox Story '07
Who Framed Roger Rabbit '88 ▶
Win a Date with Tad Hamilton! '04
Winning Girls Through Psychic Mind Control '02
With Friends Like These '98 ▶
The Wizard of Speed and Time '88
World's Greatest Lover '77
Young and Willing '42
Young People '40

Showbiz Dramas

Actors and Sin '52
Agatha Christie's Thirteen at Dinner '85
All About Eve '50 ▶
American Blue Note '89
The Ann Jillian Story '88
Anna '87 ▶
The Anniversary Party '01 ▶
The Audrey Hepburn Story '00
The Aviator '04 ▶
Baadasssss! '03 ▶
The Barefoot Contessa '54 ▶
The Beatniks '60
Being Julia '04 ▶
The Big Knife '55 ▶
Blast-Off Girls '67
Blonde '01
Blues in the Night '41
The Bodyguard '92
Boogie Nights '97 ▶
Can You Hear the Laughter? The Story of Freddie Prinze '79
Cassie '83
The Cat's Meow '01
Celine '08
Child Star: The Shirley Temple Story '01
A Chorus Line '85
Clean '04
Club Land '01
The Comic '85
Concrete Angels '87
Control '07
The Cradle Will Rock '99
Crazy Heart '09
Dancing in September '00
Dangerous '35
Day for Night '73 ▶
The Day of the Locust '75 ▶
Delirious '06
Doll Face '46
Double Platinum '99
Dragon: The Bruce Lee Story '93 ▶
The Dresser '83 ▶
The Dying Gaul '05 ▶
Eddie Presley '92
Eight Miles High '08
El Cantante '06
Entropy '99
Ernie Kovacs: Between the Laughter '84
Everything for Sale '68
F. Scott Fitzgerald in Hollywood '76
The Fabulous Dorseys '47
Fame '80 ▶
Flynn '96
For Ever Mozart '96
For the Boys '91
Frances '82 ▶
From the Journals of Jean Seberg '95
Funny Girl '68 ▶
Funny Lady '75
The George Raft Story '61
The Girl Said No '37
The Goddess '58 ▶
Gods and Monsters '98 ▶
Goodbye, Norma Jean '75
Goodnight, Sweet Marilyn '89
Grace of My Heart '96
The Great Buck Howard '09
Happily Ever After '82
Hard Part Begins '73
Harlow '65
Haywire '80
He Found a Star '41
The Hit '06
Hollywood Cavalcade '39
Hollywood Dreams '94
Hollywood Heartbreak '89
Hollywood Mystery '34
Hollywoodland '06
Honey '03
Honeydripper '07
Hughes & Harlow: Angels in Hell '77
I'm Losing You '98
The Incredible Sarah '76
The Informers '09
Introducing Dorothy Dandridge '99 ▶
Isn't She Great '00
It Happened in Hollywood '37
The Jacksons: An American Dream '92
James Dean '01
James Dean: Live Fast, Die Young '97
King Kong '05 ▶
King of Comedy '82 ▶
La Dolce Vita '60 ▶
La Vie en Rose '07
Ladies and Gentlemen, the Fabulous Stains '82
Last Call: The Final Chapter of F. Scott Fitzgerald '02
Last Days '05
The Last Metro '80 ▶
Last Summer In the Hamptons '96 ▶
The Last Tycoon '76 ▶
Lenny '74 ▶
Lillian Russell '40
Little Voice '98 ▶
Livin' for Love: The Natalie Cole Story '00
The Lonely Lady '83
Lucky Devils '33
Lucy and Desi: Before the Laughter '91
Madonna: Innocence Lost '95
Mae West '84
A Man Called Adam '66
Man in the Mirror: The Michael Jackson Story '04
Man of a Thousand Faces '57 ▶
Man on the Moon '99
Maneater '09
The Marc Pease Experience '09
Marilyn: The Untold Story '80 ▶
Me and Orson Welles '09
Mickey One '65
Mr. Imperium '51
Mommie Dearest '81
My Wicked, Wicked Ways '84
Network '76 ▶
The Next Step '95
Night and Day '46
The Night of Nights '39
Norma Jean and Marilyn '95
Once in Paris... '79
Out of Order '03
Out of the Cold '99
Paparazzi '04
Payday '73
Perhaps Love '05
Permanent Midnight '98
The Player '92 ▶
Postcards from the Edge '90 ▶
Protecting the King '07
Pure Country '92
Rainbow over Broadway '33
Rhapsody in Blue '45 ▶
Rita Hayworth: The Love Goddess '83
RKO 281 '99 ▶
The Runaways '10
Sam's Son '84
Scandal Sheet '85
Searching for Paradise '02
Second Coming of Suzanne '80
Sex is Comedy '02
Shadow of the Vampire '00 ▶
Shakespeare Wallah '65 ▶
Show Girl in Hollywood '30
Sidewalks of London '38 ▶
Simone '02
Sinatra '92
The Singing Fool '28
Smash-Up: The Story of a Woman '47 ▶
Somebody to Love '94
Something to Sing About '36
Souls for Sale '23
Sparkle '76
Stage Struck '57
Stand-Ins '97
The Star '52 ▶
Star! '68
Star 80 '83
A Star Is Born '37 ▶
A Star Is Born '54 ▶
A Star Is Born '76
The Starter Wife '07
State and Main '00 ▶
Stoned '05
Sugar Town '99
Sunset Boulevard '50 ▶
Targets '68 ▶
They Call It Sin '32
Time Code '00
Topsy Turvy '99 ▶
Undiscovered '05
What's Love Got to Do with It? '93
Where the Truth Lies '05
Who Is Harry Kellerman and Why Is He Saying Those Terrible Things About Me? '71
Why Do Fools Fall in Love? '98
Wired '89
With a Song in My Heart '52 ▶

Showbiz Horror

***see also** Behind the Scenes; Showbiz Dramas; Showbiz Thrillers*
Audition '99
A Blade in the Dark '83
Cut '00
Hollywood Kills '06
Madhouse '74
Popcorn '89
Prisoner '07
Scream 2 '97 ▶
Shadow of the Vampire '00 ▶
Skeleton Crew '09
Theatre of Blood '73 ▶

Showbiz Musicals

***see also** Musical Fantasy; Musicals; Showbiz Comedies*
All That Jazz '79 ▶
Bloodhounds of Broadway '89
Broadway Serenade '39
Bye Bye Birdie '95
Cats Don't Dance '97
Chicago '02 ▶
A Chorus Line '85
George White's Scandals '45
Glitter '01
Gold Diggers in Paris '38
Greenwich Village '44
Hedwig and the Angry Inch '00 ▶
The Helen Morgan Story '57
Hollywood Hotel '37
Idlewild '06
If I'm Lucky '46
It's a Great Life '29
Kiss Me Kate '53 ▶
Ladies of the Chorus '49
Moulin Rouge '01 ▶
Nine '09
Noises Off '92
On with the Show '29
Sally '29
Sing and Like It '34
Singin' in the Rain '52 ▶
Something for the Boys '44
Step Lively '44
The Suburbans '99
Swingtime Johnny '43
The Temptations '98
There's No Business Like Show Business '54 ▶
Three for the Show '55
Three Little Words '50
Till the Clouds Roll By '46
Variety Girl '47
Varsity Show '37
Wonder Bar '34
Yankee Doodle Dandy '42 ▶

Showbiz Thrillers

Broken Embraces '09 ▶
Children Shouldn't Play with Dead Things '72
Dead of Winter '87 ▶
The Dead Pool '88
Death on the Set '35
Destroyer '88
F/X '86 ▶
F/X 2: The Deadly Art of Illusion '91
The House of Seven Corpses '73
I Wake Up Screaming '41 ▶
Kiss Tomorrow Goodbye '00
Lady of Burlesque '43
Number One Fan '94
Reincarnation '05
Return to Cabin by the Lake '01
Return to Horror High '87
Satan in High Heels '61
Stage Fright '83
Strangers Kiss '83
The Stunt Man '80 ▶
The Sunset Murder Case '38
Up in the Air '40
What Ever Happened To... '93
What Ever Happened to Baby Jane? '62 ▶
The Wizard of Speed and Time '88

Shrinkage

***see also** Metamorphosis*
The Ant Bully '06
Arthur and the Invisibles '06
Attack of the Puppet People '58
Bad Channels '92
Dr. Cyclops '40
Honey, I Shrunk the Kids '89
Honey, We Shrunk Ourselves '97
The Incredible Shrinking Man '57 ▶
The Incredible Shrinking Woman '81
Meet Dave '08
Phantasm '79
The Seventh Voyage of Sinbad '58 ▶

Shrinks

***see also** Doctors & Nurses*
The Accidental Husband '08
Agnes of God '85
Almost Dead '94
America '09
Analyze That '02
Analyze This '98 ▶
Angel Dust '96
Anger Management '03
Antwone Fisher '02 ▶
Assault on Precinct 13 '05
Bark! '02
Basic Instinct 2 '06
Batman Forever '95 ▶
Baton Rouge '88
A Beautiful Mind '01 ▶
Beauty on the Beach '61
Behind the Lines '97
Betrayal '78
Betty '97
Beyond Reason '77
Beyond Therapy '86
Big Jim McLain '52
Bliss '96
Blood Frenzy '87
Body Chemistry 2: Voice of a Stranger '91
Body of Influence '93
Body of Influence 2 '96
Borderline '02 ▶
The Brain '88
Breathtaking '00
A Brilliant Disguise '93
Captain Newman, M.D. '63
The Cell '00
Charlie Bartlett '07 ▶
The Cobweb '55
Color of Night '94
Coming Apart '69
Conspiracy Theory '97 ▶
A Couch in New York '95
The Couch Trip '87
Couples Retreat '09
Cracker: Best Boys '95 ▶
Cracker: Brotherly Love '95 ▶
Cracker: Men Should Weep '94
Cracker: The Big Crunch '94
Cracker: To Be a Somebody '94
Cracker: True Romance '95 ▶
Cravings '06
Crazy as Hell '02
Cruel Intentions '98
Dallas 362 '03
Dark Asylum '01
Dark Mirror '46 ▶
The Day the World Ended '01
Dead Man Out '89 ▶
Deconstructing Harry '97
Disney's The Kid '00
Disturbing Behavior '98
The Dog Problem '06
Don Juan DeMarco '94
Don't Look Down '98
Don't Say a Word '01
Downloading Nancy '08
The Dream Team '89
88 Minutes '08
Eros '04
The Evening Star '96
Exit in Red '97
The Eye '02
Face to Face '76 ▶
Faithful '95
Fear '90
The Fear '94
Female Perversions '96
Final '01
Final Analysis '92
Final Approach '91
A Fine Madness '66 ▶
The Fourth Kind '09
Future Shock '93
Genealogies of a Crime '97
A Girl Thing '01
Good Will Hunting '97
Gothika '03
Grosse Pointe Blank '97 ▶
The Grudge 3 '09
Gun Shy '00
Halloween '78 ▶
Halloween II '09
Hangman '00
Happiness '98 ▶
Heaven '99
Hell's Gate '01
High Anxiety '77
The Hole '01
Home Movie '08
Home Movies '79
Hometown Boy Makes Good '93
House of Games '87 ▶
Human Experiments '79
I Don't Buy Kisses Anymore '92
I Never Promised You a Rose Garden '77 ▶
I, Robot '04
I Was a Teenage Werewolf '57
If Lucy Fell '95
The Impossible Years '68
Indecent Behavior 2 '94
Inevitable Grace '94
Inside Out '05
Instinct '99
Intimate Strangers '04 ▶
The Invasion '07
Jade '95
K-PAX '01
Karla '06
Kill Your Darlings '06
Lantana '01 ▶
Last Rites '98
Lies and Whispers '98
Lies of the Twins '91
A Lizard in a Woman's Skin '71
Locked in Silence '99
Lovesick '83
Lovey: A Circle of Children 2 '82
The Machine '96
The Man Who Loved Women '83

▶ = rated three bones or higher

Judex '16
Judith of Bethulia '14 ▸
Just Suppose '26
The Kid '21 ▸
The Kid Brother '27 ▸
King of Kings '27
King of the Kongo '29
King of the Rodeo '28
King of the Wild Horses '24 ▸
King of the Wild Stallions '59
The King on Main Street '25
Kismet '20 ▸
The Kiss '29 ▸
Kriemhilde's Revenge '24 ▸
La Chute de la Maison Usher '28 ▸
La Roue '23 ▸
A Lady of Chance '28
Lady of the Lake '28
Lady Windermere's Fan '25
The Lamb '15
Last Command '28 ▸
The Last Laugh '24 ▸
The Last of the Mohicans '20 ▸
The Last Outlaw '27
Laughing at Danger '24
Lazybones '25
Leap Year '21
The Leatherneck '28
Leaves from Satan's Book '19
The Leopard Woman '20
Let 'er Go Gallegher '28
Let's Go! '23
The Light of Faith '22
Lightning Hutch '26
Linda '29
The Little American '17
Little Annie Rooney '25
Little Church Around the Corner '23
Little Old New York '23
The Lodger '26 ▸
Long Pants '27 ▸
The Lost World '25
Love 'Em and Leave 'Em '26 ▸
The Love Flower '20
The Love of Jeanne Ney '27
Lucky Devil '25
Mabel & Fatty '16
Mack & Carole '28
The Mad Whirl '25
Male and Female '19 ▸
The Man from Beyond '22
The Man From Oklahoma '26
The Man from Painted Post '17
Man in the Silk Hat '15
Man in the Silk Hat '83 ▸
The Man on the Box '25
The Man Who Laughs '27 ▸
The Man with the Movie Camera '29 ▸
Manhandled '24
Mantrap '26
The Manxman '29
Mark of Zorro '20 ▸
Marked Money '28
The Marriage Circle '24 ▸
Married? '26
Master of the House '25 ▸
Matrimaniac '16
Merry-Go-Round '23 ▸
Metropolis '26 ▸
The Michigan Kid '28
Mickey '17
Mid-Channel '20
Midnight Faces '26
Moana, a Romance of the Golden Age '26 ▸
Modern Times '36 ▸
The Mollycoddle '20
Monsieur Beaucaire '24
Moran of the Lady Letty '22
A Mormon Maid '17
Mother '26 ▸
My Best Girl '27 ▸
My Boy '21
My Lady of Whims '25
The Mysterious Lady '28
Napoleon '27 ▸
Narrow Trail '17 ▸
The Navigator '24 ▸
The Nervous Wreck '26 ▸
Nevada '27
The Night Club '25
The Night Cry '26
The Night Patrol '26
No Man's Law '27
Nomads of the North '20
Nosferatu '22 ▸
The Notorious Lady '27
Nurse Marjorie '20
The Nut '21
Old Ironsides '26 ▸
Oliver Twist '22 ▸
On the Night Stage '15
One A.M. '16
One Arabian Night '21 ▸
One-Punch O'Day '26
Orphans of the Storm '21 ▸
Othello '22
Our Dancing Daughters '28
Our Hospitality '23 ▸
The Outlaw and His Wife '17
Outside the Law '21
Pace That Kills '28
Pandora's Box '28 ▸
Passion '19
Passion of Joan of Arc '28 ▸
Patchwork Girl of Oz '14
Paths to Paradise '25 ▸
The Patsy '28
Pawnshop '16
The Peacock Fan '29
Peck's Bad Boy '21
Peg o' My Heart '22
The Perfect Clown '25
Peter Pan '24
Phantom '22
The Phantom Chariot '20
The Phantom Flyer '28
The Phantom of the Opera '25 ▸
The Plastic Age '25
Playing Dead '15
The Plunderers '60
Pollyanna '20
The Pony Express '25
Pool Sharks '15
A Poor Little Rich Girl '17 ▸
Power '28
The Prairie King '27
The Prairie Pirate '25
Pride of the Clan '18
The Primitive Lover '16
The Prisoner of Zenda '22
Q Ships '28
Queen Kelly '29 ▸
Quo Vadis '12
Ranson's Folly '26
The Raven '15
Reaching for the Moon '17
Rebecca of Sunnybrook Farm '17
Red Kimono '25
The Red Lily '24
The Red Mill '27
The Red Raiders '27
Red Signals '27
Regeneration '15
Reggie Mixes In '16 ▸
Renoir Shorts '27 ▸
The Return of Boston Blackie '27
Return of Draw Egan '16
The Return of Grey Wolf '22
Riders of the Purple Sage '25
Riders of the Range '24
The Ring '27
The Rink '16 ▸
Risky Business '28
The Road to Ruin '28
The Road to Yesterday '25
The Roaring Road '19
Robin Hood '22 ▸
Robinson Crusoe '36
Romola '25
Rounding Up the Law '22
Running Wild '27
Sadie Thompson '28 ▸
Safety Last '23 ▸
Salammbo '14
Sally of the Sawdust '25
Salome '22
Sands of Sacrifice '21
The Saphead '21
Scar of Shame '27
Scaramouche '23
The Scarlet Car '17
The Sea Lion '21
Secrets of a Soul '25
Seven Chances '25 ▸
Seven Years Bad Luck '21 ▸
7th Heaven '27
Sex '20
Shadows '22
Shattered '21 ▸
She '25
The Sheik '21 ▸
Sherlock Holmes '22
Shifting Sands '18
Ships in the Night '28
The Shock '23
Show People '28 ▸
Siegfried '24 ▸
The Silent Mr. Sherlock Holmes '12
Silent Movie '76
The Single Standard '29
Siren of the Tropics '27
Skinner's Dress Suit '26
Sky High '22
The Smart Set '28
So This Is Paris '26 ▸
The Social Secretary '16
Sold for Marriage '16
Son of a Gun '19
The Sorrows of Satan '26 ▸
Soul-Fire '25
Soul of the Beast '23
Souls for Sale '23
Spangles '26
Sparrows '26 ▸
The Speed Spook '24
Speedway '29
Spiders '18 ▸
Spies '28 ▸
Spite Marriage '29 ▸
The Spoilers '14
Spring Fever '27
Square Shoulders '29
Stand and Deliver '28
Steamboat Bill, Jr. '28 ▸
Stella Maris '18 ▸
Storm over Asia '28 ▸
Straight Shootin' '17
The Street '23
Street Angel '28
Street of Forgotten Women '25
Strike '24 ▸
Student of Prague '13 ▸
The Student Prince in Old Heidelberg '27
Suds '20
Sunny Side Up '28
Sunrise '27 ▸
The Swan '25
Sweet Adeline '26
Tabu: A Story of the South Seas '31 ▸
Tartuffe '25
Tarzan of the Apes '17
Tarzan the Tiger '29
The Taxi Mystery '26
Teddy at the Throttle '16
Tempest '28
The Temptress '26
The Ten Commandments '23
Ten Days That Shook the World '27 ▸
Ten Nights in a Barroom '13
Tentacles of the North '26
Tess of the Storm Country '22
Test of Donald Norton '26
That Certain Thing '28
The Thief '52
The Thief of Baghdad '24 ▸
Thomas Graal's Best Film '17 ▸
Thomas Graal's First Child '18 ▸
Three Ages '23 ▸
Three Charlies and One Phoney! '18
The Three Musketeers '16
The Three Musketeers '21 ▸
Three Word Brand '21
Through the Breakers '28
Tillie Wakes Up '17
Tillie's Punctured Romance '14
Tol'able David '21
The Toll Gate '20
The Tomboy '24
The Tong Man '19
Too Wise Wives '21
The Torture of Silence '17
Tournament '29
Traffic in Souls '13 ▸
The Trail of '98 '28
Trailin' '21
Tramp, Tramp, Tramp '26
The Trap '22
Trapped by the Mormons '22
Treasure of Arne '19
True Heart Susie '19
20,000 Leagues under the Sea '16 ▸
Twinkletoes '26
Two Men & a Wardrobe '58
Un Chien Andalou '28 ▸
The Unchastened Woman '25
Uncle Tom's Cabin '14
Uncle Tom's Cabin '27
Underworld '27 ▸
The Unholy Three '25 ▸
The Unknown '27 ▸
The Untamable '23
Until They Get Me '18
Up the Ladder '25
The Vagabond '16
The Vanishing American '25
Variety '25 ▸
The Viking '28
The Virginian '23
Virtue's Revolt '24
Wagon Tracks '19
Walking Back '26
The Walloping Kid '26
Warning Shadows '23 ▸
Waxworks '24 ▸
Way Down East '20 ▸
The Wedding March '28 ▸
We're in the Navy Now '27
West-Bound Limited '23
West of Zanzibar '28
West Point '27
What Happened to Rosa? '21 ▸
When a Man Loves '27
When the Clouds Roll By '19 ▸
Where East Is East '29
White Gold '28 ▸
The White Rose '23 ▸
The White Sin '24
The White Sister '23 ▸
White Tiger '23
Why Change Your Wife? '20
Wild Horse Canyon '25
Wild Orchids '28
The Wind '28 ▸
Wings '27
The Wishing Ring '14 ▸
With Kit Carson over the Great Divide '25
The Wizard of Oz '25
Wolf Blood '25
Wolfheart's Revenge '25
A Woman in Grey '20
Woman in the Moon '29
A Woman of Affairs '28
A Woman of the World '25
The Worldly Madonna '22
The Wrath of the Gods '14
Yankee Clipper '27
Yankee Doodle in Berlin '19
Zvenigora '28 ▸

Silent Horror/Fantasy Classics

***see also** Silent Films*

Aelita: Queen of Mars '24
The Cabinet of Dr. Caligari '19 ▸
Dante's Inferno '24 ▸
Dr. Jekyll and Mr. Hyde '20 ▸
The Golem '20 ▸
The Hunchback of Notre Dame '23 ▸
La Chute de la Maison Usher '28 ▸
Les Vampires '15 ▸
Metropolis '26 ▸
The Monster '25 ▸
Nosferatu '22 ▸
The Penalty '20
The Phantom of the Opera '25 ▸
The Thief of Baghdad '24 ▸
20,000 Leagues under the Sea '16 ▸
Vampyr '31 ▸
The Wizard of Oz '25

Single Parents

***see also** Bringing Up Baby; Parenthood*

About a Boy '02 ▸
Air Bud 2: Golden Receiver '98
Akeelah and the Bee '06
Alias Betty '01
All About My Mother '99 ▸
An American Crime '07
American Gun '05
American History X '98
American Violet '09
Amreeka '09 ▸
And Then Came Love '07
The Answer Man '09
Anywhere But Here '99
Are We There Yet? '05
As Good As It Gets '97 ▸
Baby Boom '87
Bandslam '09
Beautiful '00
Because I Said So '07
Because of Winn-Dixie '05
Blue Car '03 ▸
Bogus '96
Bon Cop Bad Cop '06
Boricua's Bond '00
The Boys Are Back '09
Brave New Girl '04
Broken Wings '02 ▸
Bye Bye, Love '94
Cape of Good Hope '04
Casper '95 ▸
Catch and Release '07
Changeling '08 ▸
Chicken Little '05
Chitty Chitty Bang Bang '68
Christmas Town '08
Crazy on the Outside '10
Crows '94
The Cry: La Llorona '07
Cybermutt '02
Cyrus '10
Daddy's Little Girls '07
Daltry Calhoun '05
Dancehall Queen '97
Dancer in the Dark '99
Dark Water '02
Dear Frankie '04
Double Parked '00
Enchanted '07
Erin Brockovich '00 ▸
E.T.: The Extra-Terrestrial '82 ▸
Evelyn '02 ▸
Evergreen '04
Father and Son '03
Fay Grim '06
Fierce People '05
First, Last and Deposit '00
Fish Tank '09 ▸
Flight of the Red Balloon '08
Flightplan '05
Flirting with Forty '09
Free Style '09
Gifted Hands: The Ben Carson Story '09
The Girl Next Door '53
Girlfight '99 ▸
The Goodbye Girl '77 ▸
Grbavica: The Land of My Dreams '06
The Green Promise '49
Hearts in Atlantis '01
Hide and Seek '05
Hideous Kinky '99
High Noon '09
House of D '04
How I Killed My Father '03 ▸
How Stella Got Her Groove Back '98
Hysterical Blindness '02
I Am Sam '01
I Could Never Be Your Woman '06
I Now Pronounce You Chuck and Larry '07
Ice Princess '05
I'll Be There '03
In the Valley of Elah '07 ▸
Introducing the Dwights '07
Jerry Maguire '96 ▸
Jersey Girl '04
The Karate Kid '84 ▸
Knowing '09
Kramer vs. Kramer '79 ▸
Leaving Barstow '08
Life According to Muriel '97
Limbo '99
A Little Inside '01
Long Life, Happiness and Prosperity '02
Loverboy '05
Maid in Manhattan '02
Margarita Happy Hour '01
Martian Child '07
Me and You and Everyone We Know '05 ▸
Meet Dave '08
Message in a Bottle '98
The Mighty Celt '05
Millions '05 ▸
Mind the Gap '04
Mrs. Wiggs of the Cabbage Patch '34
The Most Wonderful Time of the Year '08
The Mother '03 ▸
The Mudge Boy '03
Music of the Heart '99
Must Love Dogs '05
My Baby's Daddy '04
Nanny McPhee '06
Never Back Down '08
No Reservations '07
Novel Romance '06
One Fine Day '96
The Pacifier '05
Paul Blart: Mall Cop '09
Pay It Forward '00
The Perfect Holiday '07
The Perfect Man '05
The Players Club '98 ▸
The Principal '87
Private Property '06
Pure '02 ▸
Quiet Chaos '08
Ready? OK! '08
The Ring '02
Row Your Boat '98
Rugrats in Paris: The Movie '00 ▸
Sabotage '96
Scandal Sheet '85
The Shipping News '01
The Sixth Sense '99 ▸
Skeletons in the Closet '00
Sleepless in Seattle '93 ▸
Sleepwalking '08
Something Like Happiness '05
Son of Rambow '07
The Spiderwick Chronicles '08 ▸
The Spring '00
Sunshine Cleaning '09 ▸
Sweet Sixteen '02 ▸
The Sweetest Gift '98
Swing Vote '08
Ten Things I Hate about You '99 ▸
Things You Can Tell Just by Looking at Her '00
Thirteen '03 ▸
The Tic Code '99
Time to Leave '05 ▸
The Town Is Quiet '00
Trucker '08
Twilight '08
Tyler Perry's Meet the Browns '08
The Ultimate Gift '07
Undertow '04
An Unfinished Life '05
Untraceable '08
Waist Deep '06
A Walk to Remember '02
Welcome to Paradise '07
What a Girl Wants '03
Where the Heart Is '00
Where the Wild Things Are '09
The White Countess '05 ▸
Wilbur Wants to Kill Himself '02 ▸
Wilderness Love '02
Wildflowers '99
Winter Solstice '04 ▸
World's Greatest Dad '09 ▸
You Can Count On Me '99 ▸
Yours, Mine & Ours '05
Zeus and Roxanne '96

▸ = rated three bones or higher

Singles

see also Dates from Hell

About a Boy '02 ►
About Last Night... '86 ►
Bar Hopping '00
Beautiful Girls '96 ►
Before Sunrise '94
Boys' Night Out '62 ►
Breakfast at Tiffany's '61 ►
Bridal Fever '08
Bridget Jones's Diary '01 ►
Bye Bye, Love '94
Crossing Delancey '88 ►
Ed's Next Move '96
Everyone Says I Love You '96 ►
Everything Relative '96
Extreme Dating '04
Forget Paris '95
Funny Valentine '05
He Said, She Said '91
He's Just Not That Into You '09
Kicking and Screaming '95 ►
Love & Sex '00
Management '09
Meet Market '08
Metropolitan '90 ►
Mr. Wonderful '93
Mr. Wrong '95
Mystic Pizza '88 ►
The Opposite Sex and How to Live With Them '93
The Personals '98
Pillow Talk '59 ►
Pirate Radio '09
Reality Bites '94
St. Elmo's Fire '85
Singles '92 ►
Sleepless in Seattle '93 ►
Sliding Doors '97
Speed Dating '07
That Touch of Mink '62
The Thing Called Love '93
Trial and Error '96
Wedding Bell Blues '96
When Harry Met Sally... '89 ►
When the Cat's Away '96 ►
The Wild Life '84

Sixties

see Period Piece: 1960s

Skateboarding

Above and Beyond '53 ►
Back to the Future '85 ►
Boxboarders! '07
Clueless '95 ►
Dishdogz '05
Gleaming the Cube '89
Grind '03
Gummo '97
Kids '95
The Last Drop '05
Lords of Dogtown '05
MVP2: Most Vertical Primate '01
Paranoid Park '07
Skateboard '77
The Skateboard Kid 2 '94
Wassup Rockers '06

Skating

see also Hockey

Airborne '93
American Venus '07
ATL '06
Blades of Courage '88
Blades of Glory '07
Breaking the Ice '38
Brink '98
The Cutting Edge '92
The Cutting Edge 3: Chasing the Dream '08
The Cutting Edge: Going for the Gold '05
Death to Smoochy '02
Derby '71 ►
Everything Happens at Night '39 ►
Frolics on Ice '39
Hans Brinker '69
Happy Landing '38
Ice Castles '79
Ice Follies of 1939 '39
Ice Pawn '92
Ice Princess '05
The Ice Rink '99
Iceland '42
It's a Pleasure '45
It's All About Love '03
My Life on Ice '02
My Lucky Star '38
On Edge '03
One in a Million '36 ►
Prayer of the Rollerboys '91
Roll Bounce '05 ►
Roller Boogie '79
Schizo '77
Sun Valley Serenade '41
Unholy Rollers '72
Whip It '09 ►
Wintertime '43
Xanadu '80

Skiing

Aspen Extreme '93
Avalanche '78
Better Off Dead '85
Christmas in the Clouds '01
Club Med '83
Deep Winter '08
Downhill Racer '69
Downhill Willie '96
Dumb & Dumber '94
Extreme Ops '02
Fire and Ice '87
Fire, Ice and Dynamite '91
For Your Eyes Only '81 ►
Going for the Gold: The Bill Johnson Story '85
Hot Dog... The Movie! '83
Ice Spiders '07
Iced '88
Lost and Found '79
On Her Majesty's Secret Service '69 ►
One Last Run '89
The Other Side of the Mountain '75
The Other Side of the Mountain, Part 2 '78
Out Cold '01
Red Snow '91
Reno and the Doc '84
Ski Bum '75
Ski Party '65
Ski Patrol '89
Ski School '91
Ski School 2 '94
Ski Troop Attack '60
Skier's Dream '88
Snow: The Movie '83
Snowball Express '72
Snowballin' '71
Snowballing '85
Snowblind '78
Striker's Mountain '87
True Lies '94

Skinheads

see also Nazis & Other Paramilitary Slugs

Adam's Apples '05
American History X '98
An American Werewolf in Paris '97
The Believer '01
Brotherhood of Murder '99
Cracker: To Be a Somebody '94
The Infiltrator '95
Lola and Billy the Kid '98
Luna Park '91
Meantime '81
The Murder of Stephen Lawrence '99 ►
Red Scorpion 2 '94
Romper Stomper '92
Skin '89
Speak Up! It's So Dark '93
Steel Toes '06
The Substitute 4: Failure is Not an Option '00
Surf Nazis Must Die '87
Terror 2000 '92
This Is England '06
The Turning '92
White Lies '98

Skydiving

Cutaway '00
Drop Zone '94
Fandango '85
The Gypsy Moths '69
Honeymoon in Vegas '92
Point Break '91
Terminal Velocity '94

Slapstick Comedy

see also Comedy; Screwball Comedy

Abbott and Costello Go to Mars '53
Abbott and Costello in Hollywood '45
Abbott and Costello in the Foreign Legion '50
Abbott and Costello Meet Captain Kidd '52
Abbott and Costello Meet Dr. Jekyll and Mr. Hyde '52
Abbott and Costello Meet Frankenstein '48 ►
Abbott and Costello Meet the Invisible Man '51 ►
Abbott and Costello Meet the Keystone Kops '54
Abbott and Costello Meet the Killer, Boris Karloff '49
Abbott and Costello Meet the Mummy '55
Abroad with Two Yanks '44
Ace Ventura: Pet Detective '93
Ace Ventura: When Nature Calls '95
The Adventurer '17
The Adventures of Buckaroo Banzai Across the Eighth Dimension '84 ►
Africa Screams '49
After the Fox '66
Air Raid Wardens '43
All New Adventures of Laurel and Hardy: For Love or Mummy '98
All of Me '84
All Over Town '37
Alvin Purple '73
Alvin Rides Again '74
American Aristocracy '17
American Pluck '25
Amos and Andrew '93
Animal Crackers '30 ►
Any Which Way You Can '80
Armed and Dangerous '86
Around the World in 80 Ways '86
Around the World in a Daze '63
Assault and Matrimony '87
At the Circus '39
At War with the Army '50
Baby's Day Out '94
The Bad News Bears '76 ►
The Bad News Bears Go to Japan '78
The Bad News Bears in Breaking Training '77
The Bank Dick '40 ►
The Barber Shop '33 ►
The Barefoot Executive '71
The Battle of the Sexes '60 ►
Bean '97 ►
Bedtime for Bonzo '51
Beethoven '92
Beethoven's 2nd '93
The Bellboy '60
Big Mouth '67
Big Store '41
Black Cat, White Cat '98 ►
Block-heads '38 ►
Bohemian Girl '36 ►
Bonnie Scotland '35
Bowery Boys Meet the Monsters '54
Boy, Did I Get a Wrong Number! '66
Boys Will Be Boys '97
Brain Donors '92
Buck Privates '41
Buck Privates Come Home '47 ►
Bullfighters '45
The Caddy '53
Candleshoe '78
Carolina Cannonball '55
Carry On Abroad '72
Carry On at Your Convenience '71
Carry On Behind '75
Carry On Cabby '63
Carry On Camping '71
Carry On Columbus '92
Carry On Constable '60
Carry On Cruising '62
Carry On Doctor '68 ►
Carry On Emmanuelle '78
Carry On England '76
Carry On Henry VIII '71
Carry On Jack '63
Carry On Loving '70
Carry On Matron '72
Carry On Nurse '59
Carry On Regardless '61
Carry On Spying '64
Carry On Up the Jungle '70
Carry On Up the Khyber '68
Casanova's Big Night '54
Cheech and Chong: Still Smokin' '83
Cheech and Chong: Things Are Tough All Over '82
Cheech and Chong's Next Movie '80
Cheech and Chong's The Corsican Brothers '84
Cheech and Chong's Up in Smoke '79
Christmas in July '40 ►
A Chump at Oxford '40
Cinderfella '60
Cockeyed Cavaliers '34
College '27 ►
Comin' Round the Mountain '51
Corky Romano '01
Cracking Up '83
The Cure '17
Dance with Me, Henry '56
Date Movie '06
A Day at the Races '37 ►
The Delicate Delinquent '56
The Dentist '32 ►
Detective School Dropouts '85
Disorderly Orderly '64
Don't Lose Your Head '66
Don't Raise the Bridge, Lower the River '68
Double Trouble '41
Doughboys '30
Dragons Forever '88
Duck Soup '33 ►
Ernest Goes to Africa '97
Ernest Goes to Camp '87
Ernest Goes to Jail '90
Ernest Goes to School '94
Ernest Rides Again '93
Ernest Scared Stupid '91
The Errand Boy '61
Family Jewels '65
The Feud '90
Finders Keepers '84
A Fine Mess '86
Flim-Flam Man '67
Flubber '97
The Flying Deuces '39 ►
Folks! '92
Follow That Camel '67
The Foot Fist Way '08
Francis Covers the Big Town '53
Francis Goes to the Races '51
Francis Goes to West Point '52
Francis in the Haunted House '56
Francis in the Navy '55
Francis Joins the WACs '54
Francis the Talking Mule '49 ►
Freddy Got Fingered '01
Free and Easy '30
The Fuller Brush Girl '50
The Fuller Brush Man '48
Funny Farm '88
George Washington Slept Here '42 ►
Get Smart, Again! '89
The Ghost and Mr. Chicken '66
Ghost in the Noonday Sun '74
Ghost on the Loose '43
A Girl in Every Port '52
The Gods Must Be Crazy '84 ►
The Gods Must Be Crazy 2 '89
Going Bananas '88
The Gorilla '39
Great Guns '41
The Great Lover '49
The Great Race '65
A Guide for the Married Man '67 ►
Gus '76
Half-Shot at Sunrise '30
Hands Up '26
Hardly Working '81
Have Rocket Will Travel '59
Here Come the Co-Eds '45
Hold That Ghost '41 ►
Hollywood or Bust '56
Home Alone '90 ►
Home Alone 2: Lost in New York '92
Home Alone 3 '97
The Horn Blows at Midnight '45 ►
Horse Feathers '32 ►
Hot Lead & Cold Feet '78
I Hate Blondes '83
The Imposters '98
In Society '44
Ishtar '87
It Seemed Like a Good Idea at the Time '75
It's a Mad, Mad, Mad, Mad World '63
Jack & the Beanstalk '52
Jackass: The Movie '02
The Jerk '79
Jingle All the Way '96
Johnson Family Vacation '04
Jour de Fete '48 ►
Julia Misbehaves '48 ►
Jumping Jacks '52
Kentucky Kernels '34
The Kettles in the Ozarks '56
The Kettles on Old MacDonald's Farm '57
The Klutz '73
The Last Remake of Beau Geste '77
Laurel & Hardy and the Family '33
Laurel & Hardy: Another Fine Mess '30
Laurel & Hardy: At Work '32
Laurel & Hardy: Be Big '31
Laurel & Hardy: Below Zero '30
Laurel & Hardy: Berth Marks '29
Laurel & Hardy: Blotto '30
Laurel & Hardy: Brats '30
Laurel & Hardy: Chickens Come Home '31
Laurel & Hardy: Hog Wild '30
Laurel & Hardy: Laughing Gravy '31
Laurel & Hardy: Men O'War '29
Laurel & Hardy: Night Owls '30
Laurel & Hardy On the Lam '30
Laurel & Hardy: Perfect Day '29
Laurel & Hardy Spooktacular '34
Laurel & Hardy: Stan "Helps" Ollie '33
Laurel & Hardy: The Hoose-Gow '29
Let's Go! '23
Little Giant '46
Long Pants '27 ►
Lost in a Harem '44
Lost in Alaska '52
The Lost Stooges '33
Love Happy '50
Ma and Pa Kettle '49
Ma and Pa Kettle at the Fair '52
Ma and Pa Kettle at Waikiki '55
Ma and Pa Kettle Back On the Farm '51
Ma and Pa Kettle Go to Town '50
The Mad Adventures of Rabbi Jacob '73 ►
Man of the House '95
Man's Favorite Sport? '63
Matilda '78
Meatballs 3 '87
Meatballs 4 '92
Menage '86 ►
Mexican Hayride '48
Milky Way '36
Mr. Bean's Holiday '07
Mr. Hulot's Holiday '53 ►
Mr. Magoo '97
Monkey Business '31 ►
Monkey Trouble '94
The Monster '96
My Friend Irma '49
The Naughty Nineties '45
The Navigator '24 ►
Never Give a Sucker an Even Break '41 ►
A Night at the Opera '35 ►
A Night in Casablanca '46 ►
The Noose Hangs High '48 ►
Norbit '07
The North Avenue Irregulars '79
Not Quite Human '87
Not Quite Human 2 '89
Nothing But Trouble '44
Nuns on the Run '90
Odd Jobs '85
Off Limits '53
Off the Wall '82
One A.M. '16
Our Relations '36 ►
Out of the Blue '47
The Out-of-Towners '99
The Outlaws Is Coming! '65
Pack Up Your Troubles '32
Pardon My Sarong '42
Pardon My Trunk '52
Pardon Us '31
The Party '68 ►
The Patsy '64
Pawnshop '16
Pharmacist '32
The Pink Panther '06
Playtime '67 ►
Police Academy 2: Their First Assignment '85
Police Academy 4: Citizens on Patrol '87
Police Academy 5: Assignment Miami Beach '88
Police Academy 6: City under Siege '89
Police Academy 7: Mission to Moscow '94
Pom Poko '94
Problem Child 2 '91
Purple Violets '07
Quick, Let's Get Married '71
Railrodder '65 ►
Rally 'Round the Flag, Boys! '58
Reckless Kelly '93
Red Salute '35
The Red Spectacles '87
Rescue from Gilligan's Island '78
Rio Rita '42
The Road to Hong Kong '62
Robin Hood: Men in Tights '93
RocketMan '97
Rockin' Road Trip '85
Room Service '38
Sailor Beware '52
Saps at Sea '40
Say It Isn't So '01
Seducing Doctor Lewis '03
Serving Sara '02
Seven Years Bad Luck '21 ►
Show People '28 ►
Sidewalks of New York '31
Slapstick of Another Kind '84
Snow White and the Three Stooges '61
So This Is Africa '33
Son of the Pink Panther '93
Sons of the Desert '33 ►
The Speed Spook '24
Strangers with Candy '06
The Strongest Man in the World '75
The Stupids '95
Sundance and the Kid '69
Superstar '99
Surviving Christmas '04
Swiss Miss '38
Take the Money and Run '69 ►
Tanks a Million '41
The 30-Foot Bride of Candy Rock '59

► = rated three bones or higher

Three Charlies and One Phoney! '18
Three Stooges in Orbit '62
The Three Stooges Meet Hercules '61
Tillie Wakes Up '17
Too Shy to Try '78
Tramp, Tramp, Tramp '26
Trial and Error '96
Two-Way Stretch '60
Up the Creek '58
Utopia '51
Voyage Suprise '46 ▸
Walk Like a Man '87
Weekend at Bernie's '89
Weekend at Bernie's 2 '93
What! No Beer? '33
Who Done It? '42
Who Killed Doc Robbin? '48
The Whole Nine Yards '00
Who's Minding the Store? '63
Why Me? '90
Wide Open Faces '38
A Woman of Distinction '50 ▸
The Wonders of Aladdin '61
Yankee Doodle in Berlin '19
The Yellow Cab Man '50
Yellowbeard '83
Yours, Mine & Ours '05

Slasher Flicks

***see also** Bloody Messages; Horror Comedy; Serial Killers; Supernatural Horror; Teen Horror*

The Amityville Horror '79
Amityville 2: The Possession '82
Amityville 3: The Demon '83
Amityville 4: The Evil Escapes '89
Amityville: A New Generation '93
The Amityville Curse '90
Amityville Dollhouse '96
Amityville 1992: It's About Time '92
Are You Scared? '06
Bad Dreams '88
Bad Reputation '05 ▸
Black Christmas '06
Bloody Beach '00
Boogeyman 2 '07
Boogeyman 3 '08
Born for Hell '76
Chaos '05
Cry_Wolf '05
Cult '07
Death Proof '07
The Descent '05
Devon's Ghost: Legend of the Bloody Boy '05
Evil Dead '83
Evil Dead 2: Dead by Dawn '87
Frayed '07
Freddy vs. Jason '03
Freddy's Dead: The Final Nightmare '91
Friday the 13th '09
Friday the 13th '80
Friday the 13th, Part 2 '81
Friday the 13th, Part 3 '82
Friday the 13th, Part 4: The Final Chapter '84
Friday the 13th, Part 5: A New Beginning '85
Friday the 13th, Part 6: Jason Lives '86
Friday the 13th, Part 7: The New Blood '88
Friday the 13th, Part 8: Jason Takes Manhattan '89
The Gay Bed and Breakfast of Terror '07
Hack! '07
Hallowed '05
Halloween '78 ▸
Halloween 2: The Nightmare Isn't Over! '81
Halloween 3: Season of the Witch '82
Halloween 4: The Return of Michael Myers '88
Halloween 5: The Revenge of Michael Myers '89
Halloween 6: The Curse of Michael Myers '95
Halloween: H20 '98 ▸
Halloween: Resurrection '02
Hangman's Curse '03
Happy Birthday to Me '81
Happy Hell Night '92
He Knows You're Alone '80
Hellbent '04
Hello Mary Lou: Prom Night 2 '87
High Tension '03
The Hills Have Eyes '06
Home Sick '08
Hostel '06
House of Wax '05
I Know What You Did Last Summer '97 ▸
I Still Know What You Did Last Summer '98
Incubus '05
Jack Frost '97
Jason Goes to Hell: The Final Friday '93
Lake Dead '07
Last Resort '09
Living Hell: A Japanese Chainsaw Massacre '00
The Morgue '07
Motel Hell '80
Motor Home Massacre '05
My Bloody Roommates '06
My Bloody Valentine 3D '09
Night Screams '87
Nightmare '00
Nightmare Man '06
A Nightmare on Elm Street '84
A Nightmare on Elm Street 2: Freddy's Revenge '85
A Nightmare on Elm Street 3: Dream Warriors '87
A Nightmare on Elm Street 4: Dream Master '88
A Nightmare on Elm Street 5: Dream Child '89
P2 '07
Prom Night '80
Prom Night 3: The Last Kiss '89
Prom Night 4: Deliver Us from Evil '91
The Raven '07
Rest Stop '06
Rest Stop: Don't Look Back '08
Rooms for Tourists '04
School's Out '99
Scream '96 ▸
Scream 2 '97 ▸
Scream 3 '00
Seance '06
See No Evil '06
Seed '08
Shriek If You Know What I Did Last Friday the 13th '00
Shrooms '07
Simon Says '07
Slaughter High '86
Sorority Row '09
Sweet Insanity '06
Terror Train '80
The Texas Chainsaw Massacre: The Beginning '06
Tourist Trap '79
Vacancy '07
Vacancy 2: The First Cut '08
Valentine '01
Wes Craven's New Nightmare '94 ▸
Wishmaster '97
Wishmaster 2: Evil Never Dies '98
Wishmaster 3: Beyond the Gates of Hell '01
Wishmaster 4: The Prophecy Fulfilled '02

Slavery

***see also** Civil Rights*

The Abductors '72
Acla's Descent into Floristella '87
The Adventures of Huckleberry Finn '85
Amazing Grace '06 ▸
Amistad '97 ▸
Angel City '80
The Arena '73
Band of Angels '57
Being Human '94
Beloved '98
The Big Bust Out '73
Black Fox: The Price of Peace '94
Black Girl '66 ▸
Blacksnake! '73
Brother Future '91
Buck and the Preacher '72
Burn! '70 ▸
Candyman 2: Farewell to the Flesh '94
Cobra Verde '88
The Colombian Connection '91
CSA: The Confederate States of America '04
Dragonard '88
Drums of Africa '63
Gladiator '00 ▸
Gone Are the Days '63
Half Slave, Half Free '85
A House Divided '00
The House of Dies Drear '88
The House of 1000 Dolls '67
Intimate Power '89
Island of Lost Girls '68
Jefferson in Paris '94
Joseph '95
The Journey of August King '95
The King and I '56 ▸
Kull the Conqueror '97
The Last Supper '76 ▸
Lust for Freedom '87
The Magic Stone '95
Man Friday '75
Man from Deep River '77
Manderlay '05
Mandinga '77
Mandingo '75
Moses '96
Mutiny on the Blackhawk '39
Naked in the Sun '57
Nightjohn '96
Olga's Girls '64
Once Upon a Time in China '91 ▸
Ong Bak 2 '08
Planet of the Apes '01 ▸
The Promise '05
Pudd'nhead Wilson '84
Queen '93 ▸
Quilombo '84
Race to Freedom: The Story of the Underground Railroad '94
A Respectable Trade '98
Ride with the Devil '99
The Road to Morocco '42 ▸
The Robe '53
Roots '77 ▸
Roots: The Gift '88
St. Patrick: The Irish Legend '00
Sally Hemings: An American Scandal '00
Sansho the Bailiff '54 ▸
Shadrach '98
Shaft in Africa '73
The Silencer '92
Skin Game '71 ▸
Slavers '77
Souls at Sea '37
Spartacus '60 ▸
Stolen Childhoods '05
Sunshine Run '79
Tamango '59
Traffic in Souls '13 ▸
True Women '97
Uncle Tom's Cabin '14
Uncle Tom's Cabin '27
Uncle Tom's Cabin '69
Uncle Tom's Cabin '87
Wanda, the Sadistic Hypnotist '67
White Slave '86
A Woman Called Moses '78
Xica '76 ▸

Slob Comedy

***see also** Slapstick Comedy; Stupid Is...*

Accepted '06
Airheads '94
Anger Management '03
The Animal '01
Bachelor Party '84
Bait Shop '08
Beer League '06
Beerfest '06
The Benchwarmers '06
Better Off Dead '85
Beverly Hills Ninja '96
Big Daddy '99
Bill & Ted's Bogus Journey '91
Bill & Ted's Excellent Adventure '89
Billy Madison '94
Bio-Dome '96
Black Sheep '96
The Blues Brothers '80 ▸
Blues Brothers 2000 '98
Bob the Butler '05
Caddyshack '80 ▸
Caddyshack 2 '88
Dead Man on Campus '97
Delta Farce '07
Deuce Bigalow: Male Gigolo '99
Dirty Work '97
Dodgeball: A True Underdog Story '04
Dude, Where's My Car? '00
Dumb & Dumber '94
Employee of the Month '06
Friday '95
Friday After Next '02
Grandma's Boy '06
Grind '03
Half-Baked '97
Happy Gilmore '96
Harold and Kumar Go to White Castle '04
The Hollywood Knights '80
The Hot Chick '02
How High '01
Idiocracy '06
In the Army Now '94
Jackass Number Two '06
Jackass: The Movie '02
Joe Dirt '01
Kangaroo Jack '02
Knocked Up '07
Let's Go to Prison '06
Little Athens '05
Little Nicky '00
Making the Grade '84
Malibu's Most Wanted '03
Meatballs '79
Mr. Deeds '02
The Moguls '05
My Baby's Daddy '04
Nacho Libre '06
National Lampoon's Animal House '78 ▸
National Lampoon's Holiday Reunion '03
National Lampoon's Van Wilder '02
National Lampoon's Van Wilder 2: The Rise of Taj '06
The New Guy '02
Next Friday '00
Night Shift '82
The Nugget '02
Old School '03
One Crazy Summer '86
P.C.U. '94
Police Academy '84
Porky's '82
Porky's 2: The Next Day '83
Porky's Revenge '85
Postal '07
Road Trip '00
School of Rock '03 ▸
Screwed '00
Shakes the Clown '92
Son-in-Law '93
Sorority Boys '02
Spies Like Us '85
Step Brothers '08
Strange Brew '83
Strange Wilderness '08
Stripes '81
Super Troopers '01
Tomcats '01
Tommy Boy '95
Waiting '05
The Wash '01
The Waterboy '98
Wayne's World '92 ▸
Wayne's World 2 '93
The Wedding Singer '97
White Coats '04
The Whoopee Boys '86
Wieners '08
Without a Paddle '04

Small-Town Sheriffs

Ace in the Hole '51 ▸
Angels Fall '07
The Badge '02
Beer for My Horses '08
Best Men '98
Black Cadillac '03
Black Swarm '07
Blood Crime '02
Blue Ridge Fall '99
Bone Eater '07
Brigham City '01
Bubble '06
The California Kid '74
Cash Crop '01
Cherry Falls '00
Children On Their Birthdays '02
Christmas Caper '07
Coastlines '02
Cop Land '97 ▸
The Dawn Trail '30
The Day of the Wolves '71
Deadly Game '77
Dear Wendy '05
Death of a Gunfighter '69
The Desperadoes '43
The Devil's Dominoes '07
The Devil's Rejects '05
Down in the Valley '05
The Dukes of Hazzard '05
Eight Legged Freaks '02
El Dorado '67 ▸
El Paso '49
Exiled in America '90
Eye of the Storm '98
Forty Guns '57
Frayed '07
The Good Witch '08
Gospel Hill '08
The Gunfight at Dodge City '59
Halloween II '09
Happy, Texas '99 ▸
Hard Luck '01
Hard Rain '97
A History of Violence '05 ▸
I Walk the Line '70
In the Heat of the Night '67 ▸
Jesse Stone: Death in Paradise '06
Jesse Stone: Night Passage '06
Jesse Stone: Sea Change '07
Jesse Stone: Stone Cold '05
Jesse Stone: Thin Ice '09
The Killer Inside Me '10
Knockaround Guys '01
The Last Hard Men '76
Little Chenier: A Cajun Story '06
A Lobster Tale '06
Lone Star '95 ▸
Maneater '07
The Mothman Prophecies '02
My Bloody Valentine 3D '09
No Country for Old Men '07 ▸
Pardners '56
Piranha 3D '10
Planet Terror '07
A Real American Hero '78
Red Rock West '93 ▸
Retribution Road '07
Rio Bravo '59 ▸
Rustin '01
Shallow Ground '04
The Sheriff of Fractured Jaw '59
Silverado '85 ▸
Slither '06 ▸
A Small Town in Texas '76
Snakehead Terror '04
Strange Fruit '04
Sudden Impact '83
Sundown: The Vampire in Retreat '08
Swamp Devil '08
Switchback '97
Taking Chances '09
The Texas Chainsaw Massacre '03
The Texas Chainsaw Massacre: The Beginning '06
30 Days of Night '07
Twilight '08
Unearthed '07
An Unfinished Life '05
Valley of the Heart's Delight '07
Walking Tall '73
Walking Tall '04
Walking Tall: Lone Justice '07
Walking Tall: Part 2 '75
Walking Tall: The Final Chapter '77
Water's Edge '03
Winter Kill '74
Witless Protection '08

Smuggler's Blues

***see also** Crime & Criminals; Drug Use & Abuse*

Acapulco Gold '78
Afterschool '08
American Gangster '07 ▸
Arc '06
Bad Boys 2 '03
Bad Lieutenant: Port of Call New Orleans '09
Better Luck Tomorrow '02 ▸
The Big Turnaround '88
The Blonde '92
Blow '01
Blue, White and Perfect '42
Boarding Gate '07
Bobby Z '07
Breaking Point '09
The Bribe '48
Brick '06 ▸
Brooklyn's Finest '09
Brother '00 ▸
The Business '05
Charlie Bartlett '07 ▸
Charlie Chan in Shanghai '35
Chip of the Flying U '39
City of God '02
Codename: Wildgeese '84
The Corner '00
The Crew '08
Cutaway '00
Dealing: Or the Berkeley-to-Boston Forty-Brick Lost-Bag Blues '72
Detention '03
Deuces Wild '02
Drug Wars: The Camarena Story '90 ▸
Drug Wars 2: The Cocaine Cartel '92
Drunken Monkey '02
Empire '02
Erik '90
Essex Boys '99
Exit Wounds '01
Fast & Furious '09
Final Engagement '07
Finish Line '08
Formula 51 '01
Frozen River '08 ▸
Gone Baby Gone '07 ▸
The Guardian '00
Half-Baked '97
High School Confidential '58
Humboldt County '08
In Too Deep '99
The Informers '09
Jimmy Zip '00
Journey to the End of the Night '06
Just Add Water '07
The Last Minute '01
Lethal Weapon 2 '89 ▸
Lies and Illusions '09
The Line '08
The Lineup '58
Linewatch '08
The Living Daylights '87 ▸
Loaded '08
Mad Bad '07
A Man Apart '03
Maria Full of Grace '04 ▸
Martial Outlaw '93
Memento '00 ▸
Mexican Blow '02
Mexican Gangster '08
Miami Vice '06
The Money Trap '65
Next Day Air '09
On the Edge '02
Once in the Life '00
Operation Orient '78

▸ = rated three bones or higher

Our Lady of the Assassins '01
Outta Time '01
Paid '06
Paid in Full '02
Party Monster '03
Pineapple Express '08 ▸
Rare Birds '01
Requiem for a Dream '00 ▸
Return of the Living Dead: Rave to the Grave '05
Rise of the Footsoldier '07
Rude Boy: The Jamaican Don '03
The Rules of Attraction '02
Shaft '00 ▸
The Shepherd: Border Patrol '08
Sherlock: Case of Evil '02
Spun '02
Starsky & Hutch '04
The Street Fighter's Last Revenge '74
Street Vengeance '95
Subterfuge '98
Sugar Hill '94
Sunstorm '01
Super Troopers '01
Sweet Sixteen '02 ▸
Tarzan's Greatest Adventure '59
The Taste of Others '00 ▸
Tequila Sunrise '88
Time and Tide '00
Torque '04
Training Day '01
Transsiberian '08 ▸
True Romance '93
Tweek City '05
Twelve '10
25th Hour '02
Under Hellgate Bridge '99
Up and Down '04
Veronica Guerin '03
Vice '08
Viva Knievel '77
The Wackness '08
We Own the Night '07
Weirdsville '07
Winter's Bone '10

Snakes

see also *Killer Reptiles; Wild Kingdom*

Anaconda '96
Anacondas: The Hunt for the Blood Orchid '04
Anacondas: Trail of Blood '09
Black Cobra '83
Boa '02
Copperhead '84
The Craft '96
Curse 2: The Bite '88
Fer-De-Lance '74
Fools Rush In '97
Foul Play '78 ▸
Green Snake '93
Halfmoon '95
Harry Potter and the Chamber of Secrets '02 ▸
Hounddog '08
Hydra '09
Indiana Jones and the Last Crusade '89 ▸
Indiana Jones and the Temple of Doom '84 ▸
Jennifer '78
Journey to the Lost City '58
The Jungle Book '67 ▸
Kill Bill Vol. 2 '04 ▸
King Cobra '98
Lewis and Clark and George '97
Megasnake '07
Natural Born Killers '94
Python '00
Python 2 '02
Raiders of the Lost Ark '81 ▸
Rattled '96
Rattlers '76
The Reptile '66
The Road Warrior '82 ▸
Silent Predators '99
Silent Venom '08
Silver Stallion '41
The Snake People '68
Snakeman '05
Snakes on a Plane '06
Spasms '82
Sssssss '73
Stanley '72
Venom '05
Venomous '01
The Wild '06
Women's Prison Escape '74

Sniper

see also *Crime Sprees; Hit Men/Women; Military: Army*

Bone Dry '07
Conspiracy '08
Dirty Harry '71 ▸
Enemy at the Gates '00
Jarhead '05
Liberty Stands Still '02
The Manchurian Candidate '04 ▸
The Marine 2 '09
The Musketeer '01
Phone Booth '02
Point Break '91
Purple Heart '05
Sharpshooter '07
Shooter '07
Shot Through the Heart '98 ▸
The Sniper '52
Sniper '75 ▸
The Sniper '78
Sniper '92
Sniper 2 '02
Two Minute Warning '76
Winter Kills '79 ▸

Snowboarding

see also *Skiing*

Agent Cody Banks '03
Extreme Ops '02
First Descent '05
Frozen '10
Out Cold '01

Soccer

Air Bud 3: World Pup '00
Bend It Like Beckham '02 ▸
Big Brother Trouble '00
The Big Green '95
Bossa Nova '99
The Club '81 ▸
Cracker: To Be a Somebody '94
The Cup '99
Cup Final '92
The Damned United '09
Eleven Men Out '05
Fever Pitch '96
The Final Goal '94
The Game of Their Lives '05
Go Now '96 ▸
Goal 2: Living the Dream '07
Goal! The Dream Begins '06
The Goalie's Anxiety at the Penalty Kick '71 ▸
Gracie '07
Green Street Hooligans '05 ▸
Gregory's Girl '80 ▸
Guys and Balls '04
Her Best Move '07
The Hero '71
Home Team '98
Hot Shot '86
Hothead '78
Joyeux Noel '05 ▸
Kicking & Screaming '05
Kicking It '08
Ladybugs '92
Long Shot Kids '81
Looking for Eric '09
The Match '99
Mean Machine '01
One Fine Day '96
The Other Half '06
The Pink Panther '06
Rudo y Cursi '09
Shaolin Soccer '01
She's the Man '06
A Shot at Glory '00
Soccer Dog: The Movie '98
Soccer Mom '08
Stuart Little 2 '02 ▸
Those Glory, Glory Days '83
Victory '81
When Saturday Comes '95
Yesterday's Hero '79

South America

see also *Central America*

Aguirre, the Wrath of God '72 ▸
Amazon '90
The Americano '17
Americano '55
Anacondas: The Hunt for the Blood Orchid '04
Apartment Zero '88 ▸
Argentine Nights '40
Assassination Tango '03 ▸
At Play in the Fields of the Lord '91 ▸
Bananas '71 ▸
Behind Enemy Lines 3: Colombia '08
Behind the Sun '01
Black Orpheus '58 ▸
Boca '94
The Bridge of San Luis Rey '05
Burden of Dreams '82 ▸
The Burning Season '94 ▸
Burnt Money '00
Butch Cassidy and the Sundance Kid '69 ▸
Bye Bye Brazil '79
Carandiru '03
Casa de los Babys '03 ▸
Catch the Heat '87
The Celestine Prophecy '06
Che '08
Chronically Unfeasible '00
Chronicle of an Escape '06
Chronicle of the Raven '04
Clear and Present Danger '94
Cobra Verde '88
Collateral Damage '02
The Colombian Connection '91
Crisis '50
Cronicas '04
The Dancer Upstairs '02
The Dark Side of the Heart '92
Death and the Maiden '94 ▸
Death in the Garden '56
Diplomatic Immunity '91
Doctor Chance '97
Down Argentine Way '40 ▸
Earthquake in Chile '74
800 Leagues Down the Amazon '93
El Carro '04
El Muerto '75
The Emerald Forest '85 ▸
End of the Spear '06
Evita '96
The Expendables '10
Far Away and Long Ago '74
Felicidades '00
Fitzcarraldo '82 ▸
Five Came Back '39
Four Days in September '97
The Fugitive '48 ▸
Funny, Dirty Little War '83
Fury '78
Green Fire '55
Green Mansions '59
Happy Together '96
Hercules vs. the Sons of the Sun '64
Holy Girl '04 ▸
The Hour of the Star '85 ▸
House of Sand '05 ▸
The House of the Spirits '93
I Don't Want to Talk About It '94
Imagining Argentina '04
Indiana Jones and the Kingdom of the Crystal Skull '08
Innocent Voices '04
It's All True '93
Johnny 100 Pesos '93
Journey to the End of the Night '06
Knocks at My Door '93
La Leon '07
Last Flight to Hell '91
The Last Movie '71
Latin Lovers '53
Let's Get Harry '87
Little Mother '71
Lost Embrace '04
Lost Treasure of the Maya '08
Love in the Time of Cholera '07
The Magnificent Two '67
Managua '97
Maria Full of Grace '04 ▸
Max Is Missing '95
Me You Them '00
Mighty Jungle '64
Miracles '86
Miss Mary '86
Missing '82 ▸
The Mission '86 ▸
Mission... Kill '85
Monster '78
Moon over Parador '88
The Motorcycle Diaries '04 ▸
The Muthers '76
Naked Jungle '54 ▸
Naked Tango '91
Nancy Goes to Rio '50
Night Flight '33
Night Gallery '69 ▸
Nine Queens '00
Nostromo '96
O Quatrilho '95
Of Love and Shadows '94
One Man Out '89
Only Angels Have Wings '39 ▸
Oriana '85
Our Brand Is Crisis '05 ▸
Our Lady of the Assassins '01
Overkill '96
The Pink Jungle '68
A Place in the World '92 ▸
The Plague '92
Play for Me '01
Quilombo '84
Ratas, Ratones, Rateros '99
Rodrigo D.: No Future '91
Rolling Family '04
Romancing the Stone '84 ▸
The Savage '75
Secre of the Andes '98
The Secret in Their Eyes '09
A Shadow You Soon Will Be '94
Shoot to Kill '90
Simon Bolivar '69
Slayer '06
The Son of the Bride '01
The Story of Fausta '88
Sweet Country '87
Tango '98
The Temptress '26
Terranova '91
Terror in the Jungle '68
Testosterone '03
Tetro '09
The Three Caballeros '45
To Kill a Stranger '84
Towards Darkness '07
Turistas '06
Under the Pampas Moon '35
Undertow '10
Up '09 ▸
Valentin '02
Veronico Cruz '87
What Your Eyes Don't See '99
The White Diamond '04 ▸
Wild Orchid '90
Xica '76 ▸
The Year My Parents Went on Vacation '07
A Year Without Love '05
You Were Never Lovelier '42 ▸

Southern Belles

see also *American South; Nashville Narratives*

Blaze '89
Cat on a Hot Tin Roof '58 ▸
Cat on a Hot Tin Roof '84
Children On Their Birthdays '02
Crimes of the Heart '86
Dear Dead Delilah '72
Driving Miss Daisy '89 ▸
The Glass Menagerie '87 ▸
Gone with the Wind '39 ▸
Hush, Hush, Sweet Charlotte '65 ▸
Jezebel '38 ▸
The Little Foxes '41 ▸
Miss Firecracker '89 ▸
Nashville '75 ▸
North and South Book 1 '85 ▸
North and South Book 2 '86 ▸
The Notebook '04
Other Voices, Other Rooms '95
Queen Bee '55
Rich in Love '93
Scarlett '94
Scorchers '92
Southern Belles '05
Steel Magnolias '89 ▸
A Streetcar Named Desire '51 ▸
A Streetcar Named Desire '84 ▸
A Streetcar Named Desire '95
The Trip to Bountiful '85 ▸

Space Operas

see also *Alien Beings—Benign; Alien Beings—Vicious*

Alien '79 ▸
Alien Cargo '99
The Apocalypse '96
Apollo 13 '95 ▸
Assignment Outer Space '61
Avatar '09 ▸
Battle Beyond the Stars '80
Battle Beyond the Sun '63
Battlestar Galactica '78
Battlestar Galactica: The Plan '09
The Black Hole '79
Black Horizon '01
Buck Rogers Conquers the Universe '39
Capricorn One '78 ▸
Cat Women of the Moon '53
Conquest of Space '55
Contact '97
Countdown '68
Creature '85
Crimson Force '05
Dante 01 '08
Dark Breed '96
Dark Side of the Moon '90
Dark Star '74 ▸
The Day the Sky Exploded '57
Dead Fire '98
Destination Moon '50
Destination Moonbase Alpha '75
Destination Saturn '39
The Dish '00 ▸
Earth II '71
Earthstorm '06
Escape from Mars '99
Escape from Planet Earth '67
Escape Velocity '99
Event Horizon '97
Explorers '85
Fire Maidens from Outer Space '56
First Encounter '97
First Men in the Moon '64
First Spaceship on Venus '60 ▸
Flight to Mars '52
Fly Me to the Moon '08
Forbidden Planet '56 ▸
From the Earth to the Moon '58
From the Earth to the Moon '98 ▸
Galaxy of Terror '81
Gattaca '97 ▸
The Green Slime '68
Hangar 18 '80
Have Rocket Will Travel '59
Heavens Above '63 ▸
Hellraiser 4: Bloodline '95
Horrors of the Red Planet '64
In the Dead of Space '99
In the Shadow of the Moon '07 ▸
Inseminoid '80
John Carpenter's Ghosts of Mars '01
Journey to the Far Side of the Sun '69 ▸
Killings at Outpost Zeta '80
Laser Mission '90
The Last Starfighter '84
Lifepod '80
Lifepod '93
Lost in Space '98
Marooned '69
Megaforce '82
Mission Galactica: The Cylon Attack '78
Mission Mars '67
Mission to Mars '00
Mom and Dad Save the World '92
Moon 44 '90
Moonraker '79
Moontrap '89
The Mouse on the Moon '62 ▸
Murder in Space '85
Mutant on the Bounty '89
Mystery Science Theater 3000: The Movie '96
Nude on the Moon '61
Outland '81
Pandorum '09
Planet Burg '62
Planet of the Apes '68 ▸
Planet of the Apes '01 ▸
Planet of the Dinosaurs '80
Planet of the Vampires '65
Precious Find '96
Project Moon Base '53
PSI Factor '80
Race to Space '01
Red Planet '00
The Reluctant Astronaut '67
Return of the Jedi '83 ▸
Return to Earth '76
The Right Stuff '83 ▸
Robinson Crusoe on Mars '64
RocketMan '97
Rocketship X-M '50
Scorpio One '97
Serenity '05 ▸
Silent Running '71 ▸
Solar Crisis '92
Solaris '72
Solaris '02
Space Buddies '08
Space Chimps '08
Space Cowboys '00 ▸
Space Mutiny '88
Space Rage '86
Space Raiders '83
Spaceballs '87
SpaceCamp '86
Spacejacked '98
Star Crash '78
Star Slammer '87
Star Trek '09 ▸
Star Trek: The Motion Picture '79
Star Trek 2: The Wrath of Khan '82 ▸
Star Trek 3: The Search for Spock '84
Star Trek 4: The Voyage Home '86 ▸
Star Trek 5: The Final Frontier '89
Star Trek 6: The Undiscovered Country '91
Star Trek: First Contact '96 ▸
Star Trek: Generations '94 ▸
Star Trek: Insurrection '98
Star Trek: Nemesis '02
Star Wars '77 ▸
Star Wars: Episode 2—Attack of the Clones '02 ▸
Star Wars: Episode 3—Revenge of the Sith '05 ▸
Star Wars: The Clone Wars '08
Stargate: The Ark of Truth '08
Starship '87
Sunshine '07
Supernova '99
Tales from a Parallel Universe: Eating Pattern '97
Tales from a Parallel Universe: Giga Shadow '97
The Terrornauts '67
Three Stooges in Orbit '62
Titan A.E. '00
Transformations '88
Trapped in Space '94

Treasure Planet '02
2001: A Space Odyssey '68 ▸
2001: A Space Travesty '00
2010: The Year We Make Contact '84 ▸
Vegas in Space '94
Velocity Trap '99
Voyage to the Planet of Prehistoric Women '68
Voyage to the Prehistoric Planet '65
Walking on Air '87
WALL-E '08 ▸
Warlords of the 21st Century '82
Wing Commander '99
Woman in the Moon '29
Women of the Prehistoric Planet '66

Spaghetti Western

see also ***Western Comedy; Westerns***

Ace High '68
Adios, Hombre '68
Adios, Sabata '71
And God Said to Cain '69
Any Gun Can Play '67
Apache's Last Battle '64
Belle Starr '79
Beyond the Law '68
Blood for a Silver Dollar '66
The Boldest Job in the West '71
Boot Hill '69
Bullet for Sandoval '70
A Bullet for the General '68
Chino '75
Cjamango '67
Dead Man's Bounty '06
Django Shoots First '74
800 Bullets '02
Fistful of Death '71
A Fistful of Dollars '64 ▸
A Fistful of Dynamite '72 ▸
Fistful of Lead '70
Five Giants from Texas '66
For a Few Dollars More '65
Fort Yuma Gold '66
Four Dollars of Revenge '66
Garringo '69
The Good, the Bad and the Ugly '67 ▸
The Grand Duel '73
Gunfight at Red Sands '63
Gunfire '78
Gunslinger '70
Hang 'Em High '67
Hellbenders '67
His Name Was King '71
The Last Tomahawk '65
A Long Ride From Hell '68
Minnesota Clay '65
A Minute to Pray, a Second to Die '67
My Name Is Nobody '74
Navajo Joe '67
Once Upon a Time in the West '68 ▸
Red Sun '71
Return of Sabata '71
Rough Justice '70
The Ruthless Four '70
Sabata '69
Shoot the Living, Pray for the Dead '70
Spaghetti Western '75
The Stranger and the Gunfighter '76
Stranger in Paso Bravo '68
Sukiyaki Western Django '08
Sundance and the Kid '69
Take a Hard Ride '75
Tramplers '66
Trinity Is Still My Name '75
Twice a Judas '69
You're Jinxed, Friend, You've Met Sacramento '70

Spain

see also ***Barcelona; Madrid; Spanish Civil War***

Against the Wind '90
Americano '05
Angel of Death '02
Ay, Carmela! '90 ▸
The Backwoods '06
Bad Education '04 ▸
Barcelona '94 ▸
The Barcelona Kill '77
Behold a Pale Horse '64
Belle Epoque '92 ▸
Blood and Sand '41 ▸
Broken Silence '01 ▸
The Business '05
Butterfly '98 ▸
Caper of the Golden Bulls '67
Carmen, Baby '66
Carnage '02
Carry On Abroad '72
The Castilian '63
Day of Wrath '06
Desire '36 ▸
Destiny '97
The Devil Is a Woman '35 ▸
The Devil's Backbone '01
The Disappearance of Garcia Lorca '96
Donkey Punch '08
800 Bullets '02
El Crimen Perfecto '04
Extramuros '85
Fiesta '95
Food of Love '02
For Whom the Bell Tolls '43 ▸
Gaudi Afternoon '01
The Grandfather '98
Honeymoon Academy '90
I'm the One You're Looking For '88
Intacto '01
It's All Gone, Pete Tong '04
Kevin & Perry Go Large '00
Km. 0 '00
Land and Freedom '95 ▸
The Last Seduction 2 '98
L'Auberge Espagnole '02 ▸
Lazarillo '59
Letters from Alou '90
The Limits of Control '09
Live Flesh '97 ▸
Love and Pain and the Whole Damn Thing '73
Love Can Seriously Damage Your Health '96
A Love to Keep '07
Mad Love '01
Marbella '85
Mondays in the Sun '02
Morvern Callar '02
My Mother Likes Women '02
The Naked Maja '59
Nico and Dani '00
The Orphanage '07 ▸
The Other Side of the Bed '03
Pandora and the Flying Dutchman '51
Pan's Labyrinth '06 ▸
The Pride and the Passion '57
Running Out of Time '94
Sand and Blood '87
The Sea Inside '04 ▸
Second Skin '99
7 Virgins '05
Sexy Beast '00 ▸
Siesta '87
Solas '99
The Spanish Gardener '57 ▸
Surprise Attack '70
The Sword of El Cid '62
Take My Eyes '03
Talk of Angels '96
Talk to Her '02 ▸
Tierra '95
Timecrimes '07
Torremolinos 73 '03
A Touch of Class '73 ▸
Vacas '91
Vantage Point '08
Volver '06 ▸
Warriors '02

Spanish Civil War

Behold a Pale Horse '64
Broken Silence '01 ▸
The Devil's Backbone '01
The Disappearance of Garcia Lorca '96
The Fallen Sparrow '43 ▸
For Whom the Bell Tolls '43 ▸
The Girl of Your Dreams '99
Head in the Clouds '04
If They Tell You I Fell '89
Land and Freedom '95 ▸
The Night Has Eyes '42
Vacas '91

Spiders

see also ***Killer Bugs and Slugs***

The Amazing Spider-Man '77
The Angry Red Planet '59
Arachnophobia '90
Blade Master '84
Charlotte's Web '73
Charlotte's Web '06 ▸
Cirque du Freak: The Vampire's Assistant '09
The Covenant '06
Curse of the Black Widow '77
Earth vs. the Spider '58
Eight Legged Freaks '02
The Giant Spider Invasion '75
Hell Hunters '87
Ice Spiders '07
In the Spider's Web '07
Infestation '09
James and the Giant Peach '96 ▸
Kingdom of the Spiders '77
Kiss of the Tarantula '75
Lord of the Rings: The Return of the King '03 ▸
Lost in Space '98
Microcosmos '96 ▸
Tarantulas: The Deadly Cargo '77
Webs '03

Spies & Espionage

see also ***CIA/NSA; Cold War Spies; Foreign Intrigue; Joke and Dagger; Spy Kids; Terrorism; World War I Spies; World War II Spies***

Above Suspicion '43 ▸
Access Code '84
The Accidental Spy '01
The Adventures of Rocky & Bullwinkle '00
The Adventures of Tartu '43
Aeon Flux '05
Agent Cody Banks 2: Destination London '04
Agent on Ice '86
The Apocalypse Watch '97
Arabesque '66
The Art of War '00
Artists and Models '55
As If It Were Raining '63
Assassin '89
The Assassination Game '92
The Assassination Run '84
The Atomic Kid '54
Attack of the Robots '66
Austin Powers: International Man of Mystery '97 ▸
Austin Powers 2: The Spy Who Shagged Me '99 ▸
Austin Powers In Goldmember '02
The Avengers '98
Bad Company '94
Ballistic: Ecks vs. Sever '02
Balls of Fury '07
The Bank Job '08 ▸
Beaumarchais the Scoundrel '96
Behind Enemy Lines '85
Big Deadly Game '54
The Big Game '72
The Big Lift '50
Billion Dollar Brain '67
Black Brigade '69
Black Eagle '88
The Black Windmill '74
Blue Ice '92
Blue, White and Perfect '42
The Bourne Identity '88 ▸
The Bourne Identity '02 ▸
The Bourne Supremacy '04 ▸
The Bourne Ultimatum '07 ▸
Breach '07
British Intelligence '40
Bulldog Drummond at Bay '37
Bulldog Drummond Escapes '37
Bulletproof '88
Cambridge Spies '03
Carolina Cannonball '55
Carry On Spying '64
Casablanca '42 ▸
Casino Royale '67
Casino Royale '06 ▸
A Casualty of War '90
Cats & Dogs: The Revenge of Kitty Galore '10
Charge of the Model T's '76
Charlie Chan at the Olympics '37
Clear and Present Danger '94
Code Name: Chaos '90
Code Name: Diamond Head '77
Codename: Foxfire '85
Codename: Icarus '85
Codename: Wildgeese '84
Comrades in Arms '91
Confessions of a Nazi Spy '39
Contraband '40
Cradle 2 the Grave '03
Criminals Within '41
Dandy in Aspic '68
Daniel '83
Daniella by Night '61
Dark Journey '37 ▸
Darling Lili '70
The Day and the Hour '63
The Day of the Dolphin '73
The Day of the Jackal '73 ▸
Deadly Currents '93
Deadly Rivals '92
Deadly Spygames '89
The Deadly Trap '71
Death Ray 2000 '81
Deathcheaters '76
Delta Force Commando 2 '90
Derailed '02
Desperate Cargo '41
Diamonds Are Forever '71 ▸
Die Another Day '02
A Different Loyalty '04 ▸
Dishonored '31
Dr. No '62 ▸
The Doll Squad '73
Don't Drink the Water '69
Doomsday Gun '94
Double Agents '59
Double Deal '50
Down Among the Z Men '52
The Dunera Boys '85 ▸
Edge of Darkness '86
Elizabeth '98 ▸
Embassy '85
Enforcer from Death Row '78
Erik '90
Escape from Fort Bravo '53
Espionage in Tangiers '65
The Executioner '70
Extremely Dangerous '99
Eyewitness '81
The Falcon's Brother '42
False Faces '18
Fathom '67
Fay Grim '06
Federal Agent '36
A Few Days in September '06
The Final Option '82
Fire Over England '37 ▸
Firefall '94
Flight to Nowhere '46
Flying Blind '41
The Foreigner '78
The Formula '80
French Intrigue '70
From Paris With Love '10
The General Died at Dawn '36 ▸
Get Smart '08
Get Smart, Again! '89
Girls Are for Loving '73
The Glass Bottom Boat '66
Golden Earrings '47
Goldeneye '95 ▸
Goldeneye: The Secret Life of Ian Fleming '89
Goldfinger '64 ▸
The Groundstar Conspiracy '72 ▸
Gunpowder '87
The Hades Factor '06
Hanky Panky '82
Hard Ticket to Hawaii '87
Head Over Heels '01
Heroes Stand Alone '89
Hidden Agenda '99
Hillbillies in a Haunted House '67
The Holcroft Covenant '85
The Holy Terror '37
Honeymoon Academy '90
Hostage '92
Hour of the Assassin '86
The House on Garibaldi Street '79
House on 92nd Street '45 ▸
The Hunt for Red October '90 ▸
Hunter '73
I Stand Condemned '36
The Impossible Spy '87 ▸
In the Secret State '85
Inside the Lines '30
Internecine Project '73
It Means That to Me '60
J-Men Forever! '79 ▸
Jack Higgins' The Windsor Protocol '97
Jack Higgins' Thunder Point '97
Jackie Chan's First Strike '96 ▸
Jakarta '88
Joan of Paris '42 ▸
Johnny English '03
Journey into Fear '74
Jungle Drums of Africa '53
Keep Talking Baby '61
Kill Factor '78
Kim '50 ▸
Kiss Me Deadly '08
Knight and Day '10
Koroshi '67
La Cage aux Folles 2 '81
Ladies' Man '62
Last Embrace '79 ▸
Last Run '01
Le Magnifique '76
Le Professionnel '81 ▸
License to Kill '64
License to Kill '89 ▸
Lie Down with Lions '94
Lightning Bolt '67
Lipstick Camera '93
The Little Drummer Girl '84 ▸
Live and Let Die '73
The Lives of Others '06 ▸
Loaded Guns '75
Lost Diamond '86
The Love Light '21
Love on the Run '36
Ma and Pa Kettle on Vacation '53
Mad Mission 3 '84
Madame Sin '71
Make Your Bets Ladies '65
Malone '87
Man from Headquarters '28
Man Hunt '41 ▸
The Man on the Box '25
The Man Outside '68
The Man Who Wasn't There '83
The Man with the Golden Gun '74
Marie Galante '34 ▸
Maroc 7 '67
The Mask of Dimitrios '44 ▸
Master Spy: The Robert Hanssen Story '02
Mata Hari '32 ▸
Mata Hari '85
The Medallion '03
Midnight in Saint Petersburg '97
The Mind Benders '63
Mind Trap '91
Mindfield '89
Mission: Impossible '96 ▸
Mission: Impossible 2 '00 ▸
Mission: Impossible 3 '06 ▸
Mission to Venice '63
Mr. Moto Takes a Chance '38
Mr. Superinvisible '73
Modesty Blaise '66
The Monocle '64
Moonraker '79
Murder for Sale '68
Murder on the Midnight Express '74
Murderers' Row '66
The Mysterious Lady '28
Mystery Plane '39
Never Say Never Again '83
Never Too Young to Die '86
Ninja Champion '80
North by Northwest '59 ▸
Number 1 of the Secret Service '77
The Odessa File '74
Old Mother Riley's Ghosts '41
On Her Majesty's Secret Service '69 ▸
One Armed Executioner '80
One of Our Dinosaurs Is Missing '75
Operator 13 '34
OSS 117: Cairo, Nest of Spies '06
Pack of Lies '87
Panama Patrol '39
Paper Tiger '74
Paradisio '61
Pascali's Island '88 ▸
Patriot Games '92 ▸
Permission To Kill '75
Picasso Trigger '89
President's Mistress '78
Prime Risk '84
Protocol '84
Quantum of Solace '08
The Quiller Memorandum '66 ▸
Rebel Love '85
The Recruit '03
Reilly: Ace of Spies '87 ▸
Rescue from Gilligan's Island '78
Retrievers '82
Return of the Man from U.N.C.L.E. '83
Return to Savage Beach '97
Robinson Crusoe of Mystery Island '36
Ronin '98
Running Blind '78
Running Delilah '93
Running Scared '79
Sabotage '36 ▸
The Saint '97
Salt & Pepper '68
S.A.S. San Salvador '84
Sea Devils '53
The Secret Agent '36 ▸
The Secret Agent '96
Secret Agent 00 '67
Secret Agent Super Dragon '66
Secret Weapon '90
Seoul Raiders '05
Shadows over Shanghai '38
S*H*E '79
A Show of Force '90
The Silencers '66
Sky Parade '36
Smiley's People '82
Sneakers '92
The Soldier '82
A Southern Yankee '48
The Spanish Prisoner '97 ▸
Spartan '04 ▸
Spies '28 ▸
Spies, Lies and Naked Thighs '91
Spitfire '94
Spy '89
Spy Game '01
Spy in Black '39 ▸
The Spy Next Door '10
Spy of Napoleon '36
The Spy Ring '38
Spy Train '43
The Spy Who Loved Me '77
Spy with a Cold Nose '66
The Spy Within '94
Spymaker: The Secret Life of Ian Fleming '90
State Department File 649 '49
Strike Commando '87
Subterfuge '68
Swordfish '01
Syriana '05 ▸
The Tailor of Panama '00 ▸
Taken '08
The Tall Blond Man with One Black Shoe '72 ▸
Tangiers '83
Target for Killing '66

▸ = rated three bones or higher

Target of Opportunity *'04*
Terminal Entry *'87*
Terminal Velocity *'94*
Texas to Bataan *'42*
There Goes Barder *'54*
They Got Me Covered *'43*
The Third Man *'49* ►
XIII *'08*
The 39 Steps *'35* ►
The Thirty-Nine Steps *'79*
Three Days of the Condor *'75* ►
Three Kinds of Heat *'87*
Thunderball *'65*
Tiffany Jones *'75*
Tinker, Tailor, Soldier, Spy *'80* ►
To Live and Die in Hong Kong *'89*
Tokyo Joe *'49*
Tomorrow Never Dies *'97*
Trader Tom of the China Seas *'54*
Traitor *'08*
Trenchcoat *'83*
Trident Force *'88*
Triple Agent *'04*
Tripwire *'89*
The Tuxedo *'02*
Undeclared War *'91*
Under the Rainbow *'81*
Undercover Blues *'93*
Undercover Brother *'02*
The Uranium Conspiracy *'78*
A View to a Kill *'85*
Viper *'88*
Virginia City *'40* ►
The Waiting Time *'99*
Wanted Dead or Alive *'86*
When Eight Bells Toll *'71*
Where the Bullets Fly *'66*
White Ghost *'88*
WhiteForce *'88*
Wild Wild West *'99*
The Wrecking Crew *'68*
XXX *'02*
Yin & Yang of Mr. Go *'71*
You Only Live Twice *'67*
Young Nurses in Love *'89*
Your Turn Darling *'63*
Zeppelin *'71*
Zeta One *'69*
Zotz! *'62*

Sports

see ***Baseball; Basketball; Bicycling; Boxing; Football; Golf; Hockey; The Olympics; Running; Scuba; Skating; Skiing; Skydiving; Soccer; Sports Comedies; Sports Dramas; Surfing; Swimming; Tennis; Volleyball***

Sports Comedies

Air Bud *'97*
Air Bud 2: Golden Receiver *'98*
Air Bud 3: World Pup *'00*
Air Bud 4: Seventh Inning Fetch *'02*
Air Bud 5: Buddy Spikes Back *'03*
The Air Up There *'94*
Alibi Ike *'35*
Angels in the Infield *'00*
Angels in the Outfield *'94*
The Bad News Bears *'76* ►
The Bad News Bears *'05*
The Bad News Bears Go to Japan *'78*
The Bad News Bears in Breaking Training *'77*
Balls of Fury *'07*
Balls Out: Gary the Tennis Coach *'09*
BASEketball *'98*
Battlefield Baseball *'03*
Beer League *'06*
The Benchwarmers *'06*
Bend It Like Beckham *'02* ►
The Best of Times *'86*
Big and Hairy *'98*
The Big Green *'95*
Billie *'65*
Bingo Long Traveling All-Stars & Motor Kings *'76* ►
Blades of Glory *'07*
Blue Juice *'95*
Blue Skies Again *'83*
Body Slam *'87*
Bowery Blitzkrieg *'41*
Boxboarders! *'07*
The Boys *'97*
Bring It On: Fight to the Finish *'09*
Bull Durham *'88* ►
Cars *'06* ►
Celtic Pride *'96*
Comeback Kid *'80*
The Comebacks *'07*
The Comrades of Summer *'92*
Cool Runnings *'93*
The Cup *'99*
Day the Bookies Wept *'39*
Diggstown *'92*
Dodgeball: A True Underdog Story *'04*
Downhill Willie *'96*
D3: The Mighty Ducks *'96*
D2: The Mighty Ducks *'94*
Ed *'96*
Eddie *'96*
Eleven Men Out *'05*
Fast Break *'79*
Fever Pitch *'96*
Fever Pitch *'05*
First & Ten: The Team Scores Again *'85*
The Fish that Saved Pittsburgh *'79*
For Heaven's Sake *'79*
The Foul King *'00*
The Freshman *'25* ►
The Game Plan *'07*
Game 6 *'05*
Geordie *'55*
Goof Balls *'87*
The Great White Hype *'96*
Gus *'76*
Guys and Balls *'04*
Gym Teacher: The Movie *'08*
The Hammer *'07*
Happy Gilmore *'96*
Her Best Move *'07*
Hold 'Em Jail *'32*
Home Team *'98*
Hot Dog.. The Movie! *'83*
Hothead *'78*
The Iron Ladies *'00*
The Iron Ladies 2 *'03*
It Happens Every Spring *'49* ►
Jerry Maguire *'96* ►
Jocks *'87*
Johnny Be Good *'88*
Kicking & Screaming *'05*
Kill the Umpire *'50*
Kingpin *'96*
Ladybugs *'92*
A League of Their Own *'92* ►
Leatherheads *'08*
Little Big League *'94*
Little Giants *'94*
The Longest Yard *'74* ►
The Longshot *'86*
The Longshots *'08*
Major League *'89*
Major League 2 *'94*
Major League 3: Back to the Minors *'98*
The Man with the Perfect Swing *'95*
The Match *'99*
Men with Brooms *'02*
The Mighty Ducks *'92*
Mr. Baseball *'92*
Mr. 3000 *'04*
Monty Python's The Meaning of Life *'83* ►
MVP (Most Valuable Primate) *'00*
Mystery, Alaska *'99*
Nacho Libre *'06*
National Lampoon's Golf Punks *'99*
Necessary Roughness *'91*
North Dallas Forty *'79* ►
Off the Mark *'87*
The One and Only *'78*
One-Punch O'Day *'26*
Paper Lion *'68*
Pat and Mike *'52* ►
Perfect Game *'00*
Ping Pong *'02* ►
Possums *'99*
Prehysteria 3 *'95*
Prize Fighter *'79*
Rebound *'05*
The Replacements *'00*
Rhubarb *'51*
The Ringer *'05*
Rookie of the Year *'93*
Rudo y Cursi *'09*
Run, Fatboy, Run *'07*
The St. Tammany Miracle *'94*
The Sandlot *'93* ►
The Sandlot 2 *'05*
The Sandlot 3: Heading Home *'07*
The Scout *'94*
Semi-Pro *'08*
Semi-Tough *'77*
Shaolin Soccer *'01*
The Sixth Man *'97*
Ski School *'91*
Slam Dunk Ernest *'95*
Slap Shot *'77* ►
Slap Shot 2: Breaking the Ice *'02*
The Smart Set *'28*
Soccer Dog: The Movie *'98*
Soccer Mom *'08*
Space Jam *'96*
Speedway *'29*
Splitz *'84*
Spring Fever *'27*
Spring Fever *'81*
Squeeze Play *'79*
Stick It *'06*
Sunset Park *'96*
Swim Team *'79*
Tin Cup *'96* ►
Trading Hearts *'87*
The Waterboy *'98*
White Men Can't Jump *'92*
Who's Your Caddy? *'07*
Wildcats *'86*
Wimbledon *'04*
The World's Greatest Athlete *'73*

Sports Documentaries

Bigger Stronger Faster *'08*
The First Saturday in May *'08*
Hank Aaron: Chasing the Dream *'95* ►
The Heart of the Game *'05*
Hoop Dreams *'94* ►
The Life and Times of Hank Greenberg *'99* ►
More Than a Game *'08*
Morning Light *'08*
Murderball *'05* ►
Through the Fire *'05* ►
Tyson *'08*
Up for Grabs *'05*
When We Were Kings *'96* ►

Sports Dramas

Above the Rim *'94*
Airborne *'93*
Alex *'92*
All the Right Moves *'83*
American Anthem *'86*
American Flyers *'85*
American Kickboxer 1 *'91*
Annapolis *'06*
Any Given Sunday *'99* ►
Babe! *'75* ►
The Babe *'92*
Babe Ruth Story *'48*
Ball of Wax *'03*
Bang the Drum Slowly *'56*
Bang the Drum Slowly *'73* ►
Beach Kings *'08*
Believe in Me *'06*
The Big Blue *'88*
Big Mo *'73*
Black Cloud *'04*
Blades of Courage *'88*
The Blind Side *'09*
Blonde Comet *'41*
Blue Chips *'94*
Bobby Jones: Stroke of Genius *'04*
Body and Soul *'47* ►
Body & Soul *'81*
Boy in Blue *'86*
The Break *'95*
Breaking Away *'79* ►
Breaking Free *'95*
Brian's Song *'71* ►
The Bronx Is Burning *'07*
Brutal Glory *'89*
Camera: The Walking Mountain *'08*
Challenge of a Lifetime *'85*
Champion *'49* ►
Champions *'84*
Chariots of Fire *'81* ►
Chasing Dreams *'81*
The Club *'81* ►
Coach *'78*
Coach Carter *'05* ►
Cobb *'94* ►
The Color of Money *'86* ►
Crossbar *'79*
Crossover *'06*
The Cutting Edge *'92*
The Damned United *'09*
Dawn! *'83*
Days of Thunder *'90*
Deep Winter *'08*
Dempsey *'83*
Diving In *'90*
Don't Look Back: The Story of Leroy "Satchel" Paige *'81*
Downhill Racer *'69*
Dream to Believe *'85*
Dreamer *'79*
Dreamer: Inspired by a True Story *'05*
Dynamite Dan *'24*
Eight Men Out *'88* ►
8 Seconds *'94*
The Express *'08*
The Fan *'96*
Fat City *'72* ►
Field of Dreams *'89* ►
Fight for the Title *'57*
The Final Season *'07*
Final Shot: The Hank Gathers Story *'92*
Finish Line *'89*
The First Olympics: Athens 1896 *'84*
The Flying Scotsman *'06*
Follow the Sun *'51*
For Love of the Game *'99*
Forever Strong *'08*
The Four Minute Mile *'88*
Free Style *'09*
Friday Night Lights *'04* ►
Full Ride *'02*
Futuresport *'98*
The Game of Their Lives *'05*
Game 6 *'05*
Gentleman Jim *'42* ►
Girlfight *'99* ►
Gladiator *'92*
Glory Road *'06*
Go for the Gold *'84*
Goal 2: Living the Dream *'07*
Goal! The Dream Begins *'06*
Going for the Gold: The Bill Johnson Story *'85*
The Gold & Glory *'88*
Goldengirl *'79*
Gracie *'07*
Grambling's White Tiger *'81*
The Greatest Game Ever Played *'05*
Green Street Hooligans *'05* ►
Gridiron Gang *'06*
Guarding Eddy *'04*
Hard, Fast and Beautiful *'51*
He Got Game *'98*
Heart Like a Wheel *'83*
Heaven Is a Playground *'91*
The Hero *'71*
Hockey Night *'84*
Honeyboy *'82*
Hoosiers *'86* ►
Hot Shot *'86*
Hurricane Season *'08*
The Hustler *'61* ►
Ice Castles *'79*
Ice Pawn *'92*
Ice Princess *'05*
International Velvet *'78*
Invictus *'09* ►
Invincible *'06* ►
The Jericho Mile *'79*
The Jesse Owens Story *'84*
Jim Thorpe: All American *'51*
The Joe Louis Story *'53*
Joe Torre: Curveballs Along the Way *'97*
The Kid From Cleveland *'49*
Kid Galahad *'37* ►
Kid Monk Baroni *'52*
Knute Rockne: All American *'40* ►
Lagaan: Once upon a Time in India *'01*
The Last American Hero *'73* ►
The Last Fight *'82*
Last Time Out *'94*
The Legend of Bagger Vance *'00*
The Loneliest Runner *'76*
Long Gone *'87*
The Longshots *'08*
Love and Basketball *'00* ►
Madison *'01*
Maker of Men *'31*
Marciano *'79*
A Matter of Honor *'95*
Miracle *'04* ►
Miracle on Ice *'81*
My Champion *'81*
Nadia *'84*
The Natural *'84* ►
O *'01* ►
On the Edge *'86*
One in a Million: The Ron LeFlore Story *'78*
One Last Run *'89*
One on One *'77*
Opposite Corners *'96*
Over the Top *'86*
Paperback Hero *'73*
Passing Glory *'99* ►
Pastime *'91* ►
Peaceful Warrior *'06*
Personal Best *'82* ►
Ping Pong *'02* ►
Pistol: The Birth of a Legend *'90*
Players *'79*
Prefontaine *'96*
Price of Glory *'00*
Pride *'07*
Pride of St. Louis *'52*
The Pride of the Yankees *'42* ►
The Program *'93*
Pulsebeat *'85*
Radio *'03*
Raging Bull *'80* ►
Rebound: The Legend of Earl "The Goat" Manigault *'96*
Red Line 7000 *'65*
Red Surf *'90*
Remember the Titans *'00* ►
Requiem for a Heavyweight *'56* ►
Requiem for a Heavyweight *'62* ►
Resurrecting the Champ *'07*
Rock the Paint *'05*
The Rocket *'05* ►
Rocky *'76* ►
Rocky 2 *'79*
Rocky 3 *'82*
Rocky 4 *'85*
Rocky 5 *'90*
Rocky Marciano *'99*
Rollerball *'02*
Rowing Through *'96*
Rudy *'93*
Run for the Dream: The Gail Devers Story *'96*
Running Brave *'83*
Saint Ralph *'04*
School Ties *'92* ►
A Season on the Brink *'02*
Shiner *'00*
A Shot at Glory *'00*
Side Out *'90*
61* *'01* ►
Skier's Dream *'88*
Soul of the Game *'96* ►
The Spirit of West Point *'47*
The Sprinter *'84*
The Spy Ring *'38*
Sticks and Stones *'08*
The Stratton Story *'49* ►
Sugar *'09* ►
Summer Catch *'01*
Supercross: The Movie *'05*
Swimming Upstream *'03*
Talent for the Game *'91*
That Championship Season *'82*
They Call Me Sirr *'00*
This Sporting Life *'63* ►
Tiger Town *'83*
The Tiger Woods Story *'98*
Touch and Go *'86*
Touchdown *'31*
21 Hours at Munich *'76* ►
Two for the Money *'05*
Varsity Blues *'98*
Victory *'81*
Vision Quest *'85*
We Are Marshall *'06*
When Saturday Comes *'95*
Wilma *'77*
Wind *'92*
A Winner Never Quits *'86*
The Winning Team *'52*
Without Limits *'97* ►
Wondrous Oblivion *'06* ►
The World's Fastest Indian *'05* ►
The Wrestler *'08* ►
Youngblood *'86*

Spring Break

see also ***Vacations***

From Justin to Kelly *'03*
Lauderdale *'89*
Palm Springs Weekend *'63*
Spring Break *'83*
Spring Breakdown *'08*
Teresa's Tattoo *'94*
There's Nothing out There *'90*
Where the Boys Are *'60*

Spy Kids

see also ***Childhood Visions; Spies & Espionage; Teen Angst***

Adventures in Spying *'92*
Agent Cody Banks *'03*
Agent Cody Banks 2: Destination London *'04*
Alex Rider: Operation Stormbreaker *'06*
Cloak & Dagger *'84*
Codename: Icarus *'85*
The Day Will Dawn *'42* ►
Defense Play *'88*
The Double O Kid *'92*
The Fantastic World of D.C. Collins *'84*
Hangman's Curse *'03*
Harriet the Spy *'96*
If Looks Could Kill *'91*
The Kid with the X-Ray Eyes *'99*
Kim *'84*
Max Rules *'05*
My Name Is Ivan *'62* ►
The Secret Agent Club *'96*
Spy Kids *'01* ►
Spy Kids 2: The Island of Lost Dreams *'02* ►
Spy Kids 3-D: Game Over *'03*
Spy School *'08*
Spy Trap *'88*
Thunderbirds *'04*

Stagestruck

see also ***Showbiz Comedies; Showbiz Dramas; Showbiz Thrillers***

The Actress *'53*
All About Eve *'50* ►
Applause *'29* ►
Because of Him *'45*
Being Julia *'04* ►
Bigger Than the Sky *'05*
Black Widow *'54*
Bloodhounds of Broadway *'52*
Bloodhounds of Broadway *'89*
Broadway Damage *'98*
Broadway Danny Rose *'84* ►
Broadway Limited *'41*
Broadway Melody *'29*
Broadway Melody of 1938 *'37*
Broadway Rhythm *'44*
Bullets over Broadway *'94* ►
Cain and Mabel *'36*
Carnegie Hall *'47*
Cold Souls *'09*
The Cradle Will Rock *'99*
Critic's Choice *'63*
Curtain at Eight *'33*
Dames *'34* ►
Dancing Lady *'33*

► = rated three bones or higher

Dare '09
The Dolly Sisters '46
An Englishman in New York '09
Esther Kahn '00
Every Little Step '08
Everything I Have is Yours '52
Exit Smiling '26
Fame '80 ▶
First a Girl '35
Fish Without a Bicycle '03
Frogs for Snakes '98
George White's Scandals '45
Go Into Your Dance '35
Gold Diggers of 1937 '36
The Great Garrick '37
The Great Ziegfeld '36 ▶
Gypsy '62 ▶
Gypsy '93
The Half Naked Truth '32
Hamlet 2 '08 ▶
Haunted '98
Heights '04
The Helen Morgan Story '57
Illuminata '98
I'm Going Home '00 ▶
Interview with the Vampire '94
Introducing the Dwights '07
Jesus of Montreal '89 ▶
The King of Masks '99 ▶
Kiss Me, Guido '97
The Lady in Question '99
The Last Metro '80 ▶
The Leading Man '96
Let's Make Love '60
Lillian Russell '40
Lillie '79 ▶
Look for the Silver Lining '49
Lucky Break '01
The Man with Two Faces '34
Me and Orson Welles '09
Meet the People '44
A Midwinter's Tale '95
Mrs. Henderson Presents '05
Moon over Broadway '98 ▶
Morning Glory '33
Mother Wore Tights '47 ▶
Myrt and Marge '33
Never Say Macbeth '07
The Next Step '95
Next Time We Love '36
Nicholas Nickleby '02 ▶
No '98
On with the Show '29
Paris 36 '08
The Phantom Lover '95
The Producers '05
The Reckoning '03 ▶
Sally '29
Shakespeare in Love '98 ▶
The Singing Fool '28
The Singing Kid '36
Slightly Terrific '44
Slings & Arrows: Season 2 '05 ▶
Stage Door '37 ▶
Stage Struck '57
Stagefright '87
Star! '68
Success Is the Best Revenge '84
Synecdoche, New York '08 ▶
Tea for Two '50 ▶
These Foolish Things '06
Three Sailors and a Girl '53
Tipping the Velvet '02
Topsy Turvy '99 ▶
Va Savoir '01
Valentin '03
Vanya on 42nd Street '94 ▶
Varsity Show '37
William Shakespeare's A Midsummer Night's Dream '99
Witchcraft 11: Sisters in Blood '00
Yankee Doodle Dandy '42 ▶

Stalked!

see also *Obsessive Love*

Addicted to Love '96
Alone With Her '07
Backwoods '87
Baghead '08
Blood Trails '06
The Bottom of the Sea '03 ▶
Breach of Conduct '94
Buddy Boy '99
The Cable Guy '96
The Case of the Bloody Iris '72
Cherish '02
Christina's House '99
Chuck & Buck '00
Copycat '95
Dying Game '94
Enduring Love '04
Evil Obsession '96
The Fan '81
The Fan '96
Fatal Attraction '87 ▶
The Gingerbread Man '97
He Loves Me ... He Loves Me Not '02
Hoot '06
I Love Your Work '03
Impulse '08
Incognito '99
Irresistible '06
The Killing Floor '06
The Killing of John Lennon '07
A Kiss Goodnight '94
Klute '71 ▶
Living in Peril '97
Mr. Wrong '95
Number One Fan '94
O Fantasma '00
Obsessed '09
P2 '07
A Perfect Getaway '09
Perfect Strangers '03
Prom Night '08
Raw Summer '06 ▶
Red Road '06
The Rendering '02
Secret Window '04
The Seduction '82
Stalked '99
Stalker '98
Stalking Laura '93
Taxi Driver '76 ▶
Turn of the Blade '97
Twilight Man '96
Wicker Park '04
Yella '07 ▶

Star Gazing

The Arrival '96
Deep Impact '98
Eliza's Horoscope '70
The Fish that Saved Pittsburgh '79
The Heavenly Body '44
How Come Nobody's On Our Side? '73
Lamp at Midnight '66
Local Hero '83 ▶
My Stepmother Is an Alien '88
Roxanne '87 ▶

Stay-at-Home Dads

see also *Dads; Doofus Dads*

The Ballad of Jack and Rose '05 ▶
Daddy Day Care '03
Kramer vs. Kramer '79 ▶
Mr. Mom '83 ▶
Signs '02 ▶

Stepparents

see also *Family Ties; Parenthood*

The Adventures of Rusty '45
The Adventures of Sebastian Cole '99
All the Little Animals '98
The Amityville Horror '05
Angel Face '52 ▶
Another Cinderella Story '08
Ararat '02 ▶
Are We Done Yet? '07
Beat Girl '60
Beau Pere '81 ▶
Benji: Off the Leash! '04
Big Girls Don't Cry... They Get Even '92
A Blueprint for Murder '53
Cafe Lumiere '05
Cinderella '50 ▶
Cinderella '84 ▶
A Cinderella Story '04
The Day the Earth Stood Still '08
Dead Cool '04
Deathlands: Homeward Bound '03
Domestic Disturbance '01
Electra '95
Ellie '84
Enchanted '07
Ever After: A Cinderella Story '98 ▶
Everyone Says I Love You '96 ▶
Fascination '04
Fear '96
The Furies '50
Georgia Rule '07
Happily N'Ever After '07
Happy Times '00
Hard Frame '70
Home for Christmas '93
Hot Rod '07
House of Darkness '48
I Capture the Castle '02
I-See-You.Com '06
The Judgement '04
Kangaroo Jack '02
Lassie '94
Look at Me '04 ▶
Lost '83
Love Actually '03
Merci pour le Chocolat '00 ▶
Night of the Twisters '95
The Orphan '79
Out on a Limb '92
Pan's Labyrinth '06 ▶
Petits Freres '00
Place of Execution '09
Private Passions '85
Rivals '72
Running Scared '06
Second Sight '99 ▶
Shadowboxer '06
Siblings '04
Snow White: A Tale of Terror '97
Snow White: The Fairest of Them All '02
Step Brothers '08
The Stepdaughter '00
The Stepfather '87 ▶
The Stepfather '09
Stepfather 2: Make Room for Daddy '89
Stepfather 3: Father's Day '92
Stepmom '98 ▶
The Stepmother '71
The Stepsister '97
A Summer to Remember '61 ▶
Tadpole '02
A Tale of Two Sisters '03 ▶
This Boy's Life '93 ▶
Time Regained '99
Transamerica '05 ▶
Unleashed '05
The Wackness '08
Wah-Wah '05
Yours, Mine & Ours '05

Stewardesses

see also *Airborne*

Airplane! '80 ▶
Black Tight Killers '66 ▶
Blazing Stewardesses '75
Boeing Boeing '65
Elizabethtown '05
Executive Decision '96
Jackie Brown '97 ▶
Passenger 57 '92
Stewardess School '86
The Terminal '04
Three Guys Named Mike '51
Turbulence '96
View from the Top '03
Zero Hour! '57

Stolen from Asia

Dark Water '02
The Departed '06 ▶
The Eye '08
A Fistful of Dollars '64 ▶
The Grudge 2 '06
Last Man Standing '96
The Magnificent Seven '60 ▶
Mirrors '08
My Sassy Girl '08
One Missed Call '08
The Outrage '64
Possession '09
Pulse '06
Reservoir Dogs '92 ▶
The Ring '02
The Secret '07
Shall We Dance? '04
Shutter '08
Speed Racer '08
Star Wars '77 ▶
Tortilla Soup '01
The Uninvited '09

Stolen from Europe

Babycakes '89
Blind Date '08
Catch That Kid '04
Dirty Rotten Scoundrels '88 ▶
Head Above Water '96
Insomnia '02 ▶
Interview '07 ▶
The Invisible '07
Jakob the Liar '99 ▶
Kiss Me Goodbye '82
Last House on the Left '72
The Last Kiss '06
Nightwatch '96
No Reservations '07
Pathfinder '07
Quarantine '08
Scent of a Woman '92 ▶
Solaris '02
Swept Away '02
Vanilla Sky '01
The Vanishing '93
A Walk in the Clouds '95
Welcome to Collinwood '02

Stolen from France

The Associate '96
The Birdcage '95 ▶
Blame It on Rio '84
Breathless '83
Buddy Buddy '81
Cactus Flower '69
Casbah '48 ▶
Chloe '09
Cousins '89 ▶
Crossroads '42
Diabolique '96
Down and Out in Beverly Hills '86
Father's Day '96
The Good Thief '03 ▶
Happy New Year '87
I Think I Love My Wife '07
Intersection '93
Jungle 2 Jungle '96
Just Visiting '01
The Long Night '47
The Man Who Loved Women '83
The Man with One Red Shoe '85
Men Don't Leave '89
The Mirror Has Two Faces '96
Mixed Nuts '94
My Father the Hero '93
Nine Months '95
Paradise '91 ▶
Point of No Return '93
Pure Luck '91
Quick Change '90
Return to Paradise '98 ▶
Scenes from the Class Struggle in Beverly Hills '89
Sommersby '93
Sorcerer '77
Taxi '04
Three Fugitives '89
Three Men and a Baby '87 ▶
The Toy '82
12 Monkeys '95 ▶
Under Suspicion '00
Unfaithful '02 ▶
The Woman in Red '84

Storytelling

Babyfever '94
Big Fish '03 ▶
The Company of Wolves '85 ▶
Grim Prairie Tales '89
Lakeboat '00
Little Orphan Annie '18
Monster in a Box '92 ▶
My Dinner with Andre '81 ▶
The NeverEnding Story 3: Escape from Fantasia '94
Paper Tiger '74
The Princess Bride '87 ▶
The Story Lady '93
The Willies '90
Windwalker '81 ▶

Strained Suburbia

see also *Yuppie Nightmares*

Adventures in Spying '92
Alpha Dog '06
American Beauty '99 ▶
The Amityville Horror '79
Amongst Friends '93
Amos and Andrew '93
Arlington Road '99
Beavis and Butt-Head Do America '96
Blue Velvet '86 ▶
The Brady Bunch Movie '95 ▶
The 'Burbs '89
Catch Me If You Can '02
Christmas With the Kranks '04
The Chumscrubber '05
Civic Duty '06
Clownhouse '88
Cold Turkey '71 ▶
Coneheads '93
Consenting Adults '92
The Cookout '04
Crime and Punishment in Suburbia '00
The Crude Oasis '95
Deadly Neighbor '91
Deck the Halls '06
Dennis the Menace '93
Dennis the Menace Strikes Again '98
Desperate Hours '55 ▶
Desperate Hours '90
Disturbia '07
Don't Talk to Strangers '94
Don't Tell Mom the Babysitter's Dead '91
Down to the Bone '04
Edward Scissorhands '90 ▶
Elephant '03 ▶
11:14 '03
Envy '04
Faithful '95
Fatal Fix '80
The Girl Next Door '04
Godmoney '97
Good Fences '03
The Graduate '67 ▶
Grand Canyon '91 ▶
The Grass Is Always Greener Over the Septic Tank '78
Gummo '97
Hidden '05 ▶
Hocus Pocus '93
Home Alone '90 ▶
Home Alone 3 '97
House '86 ▶
How to Beat the High Cost of Living '80
Hugo Pool '97
I Love My... Wife '70
Imaginary Heroes '05
Inside Out '05
Jaws '75 ▶
Jaws 2 '78
Just Before Nightfall '71
Killers '10
Krippendorf's Tribe '98
Little Children '06 ▶
Little Man '06
Loving '70
Madhouse '90
Marked for Death '90
The Meal '75
Mr. & Mrs. Smith '05 ▶
Mr. Blandings Builds His Dream House '48 ▶
The Money Pit '86
Monster House '06 ▶
My Blue Heaven '90
My New Gun '92
Neighbors '81
Next Friday '00
1941 '79
101 Ways (The Things a Girl Will Do to Keep Her Volvo) '00
Opportunity Knocks '90
The Osterman Weekend '83
Over the Edge '79 ▶
Over the Hedge '06 ▶
Palindromes '04 ▶
Parents '89 ▶
The People Next Door '70
Please Don't Eat the Daisies '60
Polyester '81
The Positively True Adventures of the Alleged Texas Cheerleader-Murdering Mom '93 ▶
Premonition '07
The Prize Winner of Defiance, Ohio '05 ▶
Rally 'Round the Flag, Boys! '58
Red Doors '05
Return of the Living Dead 2 '88
Revenge of the Stepford Wives '80
Revolutionary Road '08
Serial Mom '94 ▶
Serial Slayer '03
Shattered Spirits '86
Short Cuts '93 ▶
The Stepford Wives '75 ▶
The Stepford Wives '04
The Stranger '46 ▶
The Swimmer '68 ▶
Terrorvision '86
Three Wishes '95
The Trigger Effect '96
12 and Holding '05 ▶
Twice in a Lifetime '85 ▶
The Underworld Story '50
A Very Brady Sequel '96
The Virgin Suicides '99
The War of the Roses '89 ▶
When Every Day Was the Fourth of July '78
The Whole Nine Yards '00
Winter Solstice '04 ▶
Your Friends & Neighbors '98 ▶

Strippers

American Wedding '03
The Badge '02
Blaze '89
Blood Money '98
Body Language '95
The Box '03
Breakdown '96 ▶
Cadillac Ranch '96
The Casino Job '08
The Center of the World '01
Choke '08
Closer '04 ▶
Club Vampire '98
Crystal's Diary '99
Dance of the Damned '88
Dancing at the Blue Iguana '00
Dangerous Ground '96
The Dark Dancer '95
Day of the Warrior '96
Decay '98
Devil's Den '06
A Dirty Shame '04
Doctor in Love '60
The Dog Problem '06
Dogma '99
ESL: English as a Second Language '05
Exit '95
Exotica '94 ▶
The Fluffer '01
For Ladies Only '81
From Dusk Till Dawn '95
The Full Monty '96 ▶
The Glass Cage '96
Gypsy '62 ▶
Gypsy '93
The Hangover '09
Hard As Nails '01
Headless Body in Topless Bar '96
The Heart Is Deceitful Above All Things '04
Heaven '99
Hustle & Flow '05 ▶
I Hope They Serve Beer in Hell '09
I Know Who Killed Me '07
Keys to Tulsa '96
Kiss of Death '94
Kiss of Fire '98
Lady of Burlesque '43
Lap Dancing '95

▶ = rated three bones or higher

The Last Word '95
Laws of Deception '97
Lenny '74 ▸
Love and Other Four Letter Words '07
Made '01
Master Spy: The Robert Hanssen Story '02
Miami Hustle '95
Midnight Tease '94
Midnight Tease 2 '95
Mrs. Henderson Presents '05
A Night in Heaven '83
Night Junkies '07
Overnight Delivery '96
Pecker '98
Pigalle '95
Planet Terror '07
The Players Club '98 ▸
Plucking the Daisy '56
Powder Blue '09
Seven Thieves '60 ▸
Sex & Lies in Sin City: The Ted Binion Scandal '08
Shadow Dancer '96
The Showgirl Murders '95
Showgirls '95
Sin City '05
Sins of the Night '93
Sparkler '99
Stag '97
Strip Search '97
The Stripper '63
Stripper '86
Stripshow '95
Striptease '96
Stripteaser '95
Studs Lonigan '60
Sweet Evil '98
13 Moons '02
Time Served '99
Tin Cup '96 ▸
True Lies '94
Tully '00 ▸
Under Siege '92
Vacuuming Completely Nude in Paradise '01
Whirlygirl '04
Working Girls '75
The Wrestler '08 ▸
Yellow '06
Zombie Strippers '08

Struggling Artists

***see also** Art & Artists; Biopics: Artists*

Apartment 12 '06
Art School Confidential '06
Basquiat '96 ▸
Before Night Falls '00 ▸
Brother to Brother '04
Heights '04
In the Realms of the Unreal '04 ▸
Love in Pawn '53
Love Letters '99 ▸
Shopgirl '05 ▸
A Simple Promise '07
Standing on Fishes '99
The Tollbooth '04
Vincent & Theo '90 ▸

Struggling Musicians

The Adventures of Buckaroo Banzai Across the Eighth Dimension '84 ▸
All You Need Is Cash '78 ▸
American Blue Note '89
Backbeat '94 ▸
The Beat My Heart Skipped '05 ▸
Beyond the Valley of the Dolls '70
Bikini Summer '91
Billy's Holiday '95
Blast-Off Girls '67
Blues in the Night '41
The Brady Bunch Movie '95 ▸
Breaking Glass '80
Bye Bye Blues '89
Cheech and Chong's Up in Smoke '79
The Competition '80 ▸
Cotton Candy '82
Crossover Dreams '85
Crossroads '86
Dangerous Holiday '37
Dangerous Moonlight '41 ▸
Departures '08
Dogs in Space '87
Doing Time for Patsy Cline '97
Eddie and the Cruisers '83
Eddie and the Cruisers 2: Eddie Lives! '89
The Eternal Waltz '54
The Fabulous Dorseys '47
Falling from Grace '92
Fear of a Black Hat '94
The Five Heartbeats '91 ▸
Ganked '05
Garden Party '08
Gridlock'd '96 ▸
Heaven Tonight '93
Hustle & Flow '05 ▸
Jack Frost '98
Killing 'Em Softly '85
Knights of the City '85
Light of Day '87
Love Song '00
A Man Called Adam '66
Mo' Better Blues '90
Murder Rap '87
Oh, God! You Devil '84
One Trick Pony '80
The Pacific and Eddy '07
Punk Love '06
Purple Rain '84
The Return of Spinal Tap '92
Rhinestone '84
Rock & Rule '83
Rock School '05 ▸
Rock Star '01
The Rose '79 ▸
Satisfaction '88
School of Rock '03 ▸
A Simple Promise '07
A Slipping Down Life '99
Sparkle '76
A Star Is Born '76
Streets of Fire '84
subUrbia '96
Sueno '05
Sunset Strip '99
Tender Mercies '83 ▸
This Is Spinal Tap '84 ▸
Vamping '84
Vibrations '94
Winning Girls Through Psychic Mind Control '02
You Light Up My Life '77

Stuntmen

Death Proof '07
800 Bullets '02
The Fall '06
Fantastic Seven '79
Ghost Rider '07
Hooper '78
Hot Rod '07
Looney Tunes: Back in Action '03
Lucky Devils '33
Miss Tatlock's Millions '48
Movie Stuntmen '53
Slogan '69
The Stunt Man '80 ▸
Stuntmen '09
Vendetta '85

Stupid Is...

American Pie Presents Band Camp '05
Be Kind Rewind '08
Bean '97 ▸
Beavis and Butt-Head Do America '96
Being There '79 ▸
The Benchwarmers '06
Big Top Pee-wee '88
Bill & Ted's Bogus Journey '91
Bill & Ted's Excellent Adventure '89
Billy Madison '94
Bio-Dome '96
Black Sheep '96
Blonde and Blonder '07
Caddyshack '80 ▸
Chairman of the Board '97
The Curse of Inferno '96
The Dinner Game '98
Drowning Mona '00
Dudley Do-Right '99
Dumb & Dumber '94
Dumb and Dumberer: When Harry Met Lloyd '03
Employee of the Month '06
The Extreme Adventures of Super Dave '98
Fast Times at Ridgemont High '82 ▸
Forrest Gump '94 ▸
Frank McKlusky, C.I. '02
Get Smart '08
Half-Baked '97
Happy Gilmore '96
Hot Rod '07
Idiot Box '97
Idle Hands '99
In God We Trust '80
Jackass Number Two '06
The Jerk '79
The Jerky Boys '95
Joe Dirt '01
Kickin' It Old Skool '07
Killer Bud '00
Let's Go to Prison '06
The Life of Lucky Cucumber '08
Little Nicky '00
Lock, Stock and 2 Smoking Barrels '98 ▸
Meet the Deedles '98
Mr. Accident '99
Mr. Bean's Holiday '07
National Lampoon's Animal House '78 ▸
The Nutty Professor '63 ▸
Orgazmo '98
Pee-wee's Big Adventure '85 ▸
The Pink Panther 2 '09
Ready to Rumble '00
Road Trip '00
Romy and Michele's High School Reunion '97
The Sasquatch Gang '06
Scary Movie 4 '06
Son-in-Law '93
Stealing Harvard '02
Step Brothers '08
Strange Wilderness '08
The Stupids '95
Tommy Boy '95
The Waterboy '98
Wayne's World '92 ▸
What Up? '08
White Mile '94
Witless Protection '08
Young Einstein '89
Zoolander '01

Submarines

***see also** Deep Blue*

Above Us the Waves '56 ▸
The Abyss '89 ▸
Action in the North Atlantic '43
Agent Red '00
Assault on a Queen '66
Atlantis: The Lost Empire '01
Atomic Submarine '59
Bear Island '80
Below '02
Beneath the Bermuda Triangle '98
Captain Nemo and the Underwater City '69
Counter Measures '99
Crash Dive '43
Crash Dive '96
Crimson Tide '95 ▸
Danger Beneath the Sea '02
Das Boot '81 ▸
The Day Will Dawn '42 ▸
Depth Charge '08
Destination Tokyo '43
The Devil and the Deep '32
Down Periscope '96
Enemy Below '57 ▸
Fer-De-Lance '74
First Strike '85
For Your Eyes Only '81 ▸
Full Fathom Five '90
Ghostboat '06
Going Under '91
Hostile Waters '97
The Hunley '99
The Hunt for Red October '90 ▸
Ice Station Zebra '68
In Enemy Hands '04
The Incredible Mr. Limpet '64
The Inside Man '84
K-19: The Widowmaker '02
Latitude Zero '69
The League of Extraordinary Gentlemen '03
Leviathan '89
Magma: Volcanic Disaster '06
Mega Shark Vs. Giant Octopus '09
Morning Departure '50
Mysterious Island '61 ▸
Nautilus '99
1941 '79
Octopus '00
On the Beach '00
Operation Bikini '63
Operation Delta Force 2: Mayday '97
Operation Delta Force 3: Clear Target '98
Operation Petticoat '59 ▸
Q Ships '28
Raise the Titanic '80
Run Silent, Run Deep '58 ▸
Sailor Beware '52
Silent Venom '08
The Spy Who Loved Me '77
Stargate: Continuum '08
Steel Sharks '97
Sub Down '97
Submarine Attack '54
Submarine Seahawk '59
Submerged '05
Three Sailors and a Girl '53
Torpedo Alley '53
Torpedo Attack '72
Torpedo Run '58
20,000 Leagues under the Sea '16 ▸
20,000 Leagues under the Sea '54 ▸
20,000 Leagues Under the Sea '97
U-571 '00
Up Periscope '59
Voyage to the Bottom of the Sea '61 ▸
We Dive at Dawn '43 ▸
Yellow Submarine '68 ▸
You Only Live Twice '67

Subways

***see also** Trains*

Adventures in Babysitting '87
Angel Dust '96
Bugs '03
Bulletproof Monk '03
Carlito's Way '93 ▸
Daybreak '01
Die Hard: With a Vengeance '95
Dutchman '67 ▸
Eve of Destruction '90
The French Connection '71 ▸
The Fugitive '93 ▸
Highlander 2: The Quickening '91
The Incident '67
The Italian Job '03 ▸
The Jackal '97
Kontroll '03 ▸
Lethal Weapon 3 '92
Man Hunt '41 ▸
The Midnight Meat Train '08
Mimic '97
Money Train '95
Next Stop, Wonderland '98
On the Line '01
Predator 2 '90
Pretty Baby '50
Quatermass and the Pit '58
Raw Meat '72
Reconstruction '03
Risky Business '83 ▸
ShadowZone: The Undead Express '96
Sliding Doors '97
Speed '94 ▸
Subway '85
Subway Stories '97
The Taking of Pelham One Two Three '74 ▸
The Taking of Pelham 123 '09
Train Man: Densha Otoko '05
Trick '99 ▸
Tube '03
The Warriors '79
Zazie dans le Metro '61 ▸

Suicide

***see also** Death & the Afterlife*

Absence of Malice '81
According to Greta '08
Alien 3 '92
All About Lily Chou-Chou '01 ▸
All My Sons '48 ▸
American Strays '96
Angels Over Broadway '40 ▸
The Apartment '60 ▸
Apartment 1303 '07
Apres-Vous '03
Ararat '02 ▸
The Arrangement '69
Asylum '97
Attack Squadron '63
Autopsy '74
Bad Girls Dormitory '84
Ballast '08
Bedazzled '68 ▸
Believers '07
The Bell Jar '79
Better Off Dead '85
The Big Chill '83 ▸
The Black House '00
Blacklight '98
Blood Pledge '09
Body & Soul '93 ▸
Boogeyman 3 '08
A Broken Life '07
Brute Force '47 ▸
Buddy Buddy '81
Can You Hear the Laughter? The Story of Freddie Prinze '79
Cause Celebre '87 ▸
Change My Life '01
Christie's Revenge '07
The Chumscrubber '05
Club Extinction '89
Come Undone '00
The Confessor '04
Conspiracy of Silence '03
Control '07
Cookie's Fortune '99 ▸
Courage Under Fire '96 ▸
Crimes of the Heart '86
The Crown Prince '06
The Crude Oasis '95
Crumb '94 ▸
The Curve '97
Dangerous Corner '34 ▸
Dark Remains '05
Dark Side '02
Dead Man on Campus '97
Dead Poets Society '89 ▸
Death Wish Club '83
Delicatessen '92 ▸
Delinquent Daughters '44
Der Todesking '89
Deutschland im Jahre Null '47 ▸
The Devil in Silk '56
Divine '90
Docks of New York '28 ▸
Dolls '02 ▸
Dominique Is Dead '79
Double Suicide '69 ▸
Downloading Nancy '08
Dream with the Fishes '97
The Eagle and the Hawk '33 ▸
Elisa '94
Elizabethtown '05
The End '78 ▸
Europa '51 '52
Eva '62
The Event '03
Event Horizon '97
The Eye 2 '04
The Eyes, the Mouth '83
Faithful '95
Father's Day '96
The Fire Within '64 ▸
The First Wives Club '96
For One More Day '07
From the Journals of Jean Seberg '95
Frontier of Dawn '08
Frozen '98
Full Metal Jacket '87 ▸
Fuzz '72
A Gentle Woman '69
The Girl on the Bridge '98 ▸
Golden Gate '93
Gonin 2 '96
Goodbye Cruel World '82
Goodbye Solo '08
The Guyana Tragedy: The Story of Jim Jones '80
Hamlet '96 ▸
The Hanging Garden '97
Hangman's Curse '03
The Happening '08
Harold and Maude '71 ▸
Haywire '80
Head On '04
Heading for Heaven '47
Heat '95 ▸
Heathers '89 ▸
Hide and Seek '05
Hollywoodland '06
The Hours '02 ▸
The Hudsucker Proxy '93 ▸
The Hustle '75
The Iceman Cometh '73
Imaginary Heroes '05
Iris '89
The Isle '01
It's a Wonderful Life '46 ▸
Julian Po '97
Junk Mail '97
Kill Me Later '01
Kill Your Darlings '06
Kings and Queen '04 ▸
The Kovak Box '06
Last Cry for Help '79
Last Days '05
Last Life in the Universe '03
Last Tango in Paris '73 ▸
The Last Time I Committed Suicide '96
The Last Word '08
Law of the Sea '32
Le Corbeau '43 ▸
Leaving Las Vegas '95 ▸
Love Liza '02
Love on a Pillow '62
Maborosi '95 ▸
Madame Bovary '00
Maedchen in Uniform '31 ▸
Marebito '04
M*A*S*H '70 ▸
Melo '86
Memorial Day '83
Missing Pieces '00
Mrs. Dalloway '97
Mixed Nuts '94
Monster's Ball '01 ▸
Mortal Danger '94
Morvern Callar '02
Mother Kusters Goes to Heaven '76 ▸
Mouchette '67 ▸
My Sweet Suicide '98
Nais '45 ▸
Natural Enemies '79
'night, Mother '86
The Night Watchman '02
Nightmare Detective '06
Now & Forever '02
The Odd Job '78
Ode to Billy Joe '76
On the Edge '00
One Flew Over the Cuckoo's Nest '75 ▸
Ordinary People '80 ▸
Pain in the A— '77 ▸
The Pallbearer '95
Paradise Now '05 ▸
Peeping Tom '60 ▸
Permanent Record '88
Possession '02
Primary Colors '98
Prozac Nation '01
Pulse '01
Pulse '06
Purgatory House '04
Remolino de Pasiones '68
Retribution '88
Return of Frank Cannon '80
Reuben, Reuben '83 ▸
Riding the Bullet '04
Right of Way '84
Robert Louis Stevenson's The Game of Death '99
Romeo and Juliet '36 ▸
Romeo and Juliet '54
Romeo and Juliet '68 ▸
Romulus, My Father '07 ▸
The Rules of Attraction '02
Samaritan Girl '04
Scent of a Woman '92 ▸

▸ = rated three bones or higher

The Sea Inside '04 ▸
The Sergeant '68
Seven Pounds '08
Show Girl in Hollywood '30
Shrink '09
Silence of the Heart '84 ▸
Sisters, Or the Balance of Happiness '79
The Slender Thread '65 ▸
Solo Sunny '80
Stay '05
Stealing Home '88
Stella Maris '18 ▸
Suicide Club '02
Sylvia '03
A Tale of Two Sisters '03 ▸
Talk to Her '02 ▸
The Taste of Cherry '96
The Tenant '76 ▸
Then Came Bronson '68
Things I Never Told You '96
To Save a Life '10
Two Days '03
Unholy '07
The Unknown Soldier '98
The Unsaid '01
Village Tale '35
The Virgin Suicides '99
Warm Summer Rain '89
Wetherby '85 ▸
Whale Music '94
What Dreams May Come '98
What We Do Is Secret '07
Where the Truth Lies '05
Whose Life Is It Anyway? '81 ▸
Wilbur Wants to Kill Himself '02 ▸
Women Without Men '09
World's Greatest Dad '09 ▸
Wristcutters: A Love Story '06

Summer Camp

Addams Family Values '93
American Pie Presents Band Camp '05
Arizona Summer '03
Backwoods '87
Berserker '87
The Best Way '76
Bloody Murder '99
Bloody Murder 2 '03
The Burning '82
Bushwhacked '95
But I'm a Cheerleader '99
Camp '03
Camp Cucamonga: How I Spent My Summer Vacation '90
Camp Nowhere '94
Camp Rock '08
Cannibal Campout '88
A Cry from the Mountain '85
Daddy Day Camp '07
Deliverance '72 ▸
Dishdogz '05
Don't Go in the Woods '81
Ernest Goes to Camp '87
Escanaba in da Moonlight '01
Evil Dead '83
Evils of the Night '85
Father and Scout '94
The Final Terror '83
Fired Up! '09
First Turn On '83
Forever Evil '87
Friday the 13th '09
Friday the 13th '80
Friday the 13th, Part 2 '81
Friday the 13th, Part 3 '82
Friday the 13th, Part 4: The Final Chapter '84
Gimme an F '85
Gorp '80
The Great Outdoors '88
Grim Prairie Tales '89
Grizzly '76
Happy Campers '01
Having a Wonderful Time '38
Heavyweights '94
The Hills Have Eyes '77
Hot Resort '85
Indian Summer '93
Little Bigfoot 2: The Journey Home '97
Little Darlings '80
Man of the House '95
Meatballs '79
Meatballs 2 '84
Meatballs 3 '87
Meatballs 4 '92
Memorial Valley Massacre '88
Mr. Troop Mom '09
Mother's Day '80
Nature's Grave '08
No Kidding '60
Nuts in May '76
Oddballs '84
One Small Hero '99
The Parent Trap '61
The Parent Trap '98
Party Camp '87
A Pig's Tale '94
Poison Ivy '85
The Prey '80
Princes in Exile '90
Race for Your Life, Charlie Brown '77
Race with the Devil '75
Raise Your Voice '04
Redwood Forest Trail '50
Rituals '79
The River Wild '94
Sleepaway Camp '83
Sleepaway Camp 2: Unhappy Campers '88
Sleepaway Camp 3: Teenage Wasteland '89
Storm '87
Stuckey's Last Stand '80
Summer Camp Nightmare '86
There's Nothing out There '90
Three Way Weekend '81
Ticks '93
Troop Beverly Hills '89
Wet Hot American Summer '01 ▸
The Willies '90

Super Heroes

The Adventures of Sharkboy and Lavagirl in 3-D '05
The Amazing Spider-Man '77
Batman '66
Batman '89 ▸
Batman and Robin '97
Batman Begins '05 ▸
Batman Forever '95 ▸
Batman: Mask of the Phantasm '93
Batman Returns '92
Big Man Japan '07
Black Mask '96
Black Scorpion '95
Blade: Trinity '04
Blankman '94
Captain America '79
Captain America '89
Captain America 2: Death Too Soon '79
Catwoman '04
Chinese Web '78
The Chosen One: Legend of the Raven '98
Cloak & Dagger '84
Comic Book: The Movie '04 ▸
Condorman '81
Constantine '05
Daredevil '03
Dark Justice '00
The Dark Knight '08 ▸
Death of the Incredible Hulk '90
Defendor '09
Dr. Strange '78
Electric Dragon 80,000V '01
Elektra '05
Fantastic Four '05
Fantastic Four: Rise of the Silver Surfer '07
The Flash '90
Flash Gordon '80
Freddie the Frog '92
Hancock '08
Hellboy II: The Golden Army '08 ▸
Howard the Duck '86
The Incredible Hulk '77
The Incredible Hulk Returns '88
The Incredibles '04 ▸
Infra-Man '76
Iron Man '08 ▸
Iron Man 2 '10
Kick-Ass '10
The League of Extraordinary Gentlemen '03
The Legend of Zorro '05
The Mask '94 ▸
Masked Rider—The First '05
The Meteor Man '93
Mighty Morphin Power Rangers: The Movie '95
My Super Ex-Girlfriend '06
Mystery Men '99
Orgazmo '98
The Phantom '96
Phantom 2040 Movie: The Ghost Who Walks '95
Pootie Tang '01
Prey of the Jaguar '96
The Puma Man '80
The Punisher '90
The Punisher '04
Rat Pfink a Boo-Boo '66
Return of Captain Invincible '83
Sgt. Kabukiman N.Y.P.D. '94
The Shadow '94
Silver Hawk '04
Sky High '05 ▸
Spawn '97 ▸
Special '06
The Specials '00 ▸
Spider-Man '02 ▸
Spider-Man 2 '04 ▸
Spider-Man 3 '07
Spiderman: The Deadly Dust '78
The Spirit '08
Steel '97
The Strongest Man in the World '75
Super Capers '09
Super Fuzz '81
Super Inframan '76
Supergirl '84
SuperGuy: Behind the Cape '02
Superhero Movie '08
Superman: The Movie '78 ▸
Superman 2 '80 ▸
Superman 3 '83
Superman 4: The Quest for Peace '87
Superman & the Mole Men '51
Superman Returns '06
Supersonic Man '78
3 Ninjas: High Noon at Mega Mountain '97
TMNT (Teenage Mutant Ninja Turtles) '07
Todd McFarlane's Spawn '97 ▸
The Toxic Avenger, Part 2 '89
The Trial of the Incredible Hulk '89
Turbo: A Power Rangers Movie '96
Unbreakable '00
Underdog '07
VIP, My Brother Superman '90
Watchmen '09
The Wild World of Batwoman '66
X-Men '00
X-Men: The Last Stand '06
X2: X-Men United '03 ▸
Zebraman '04
Zoom '06
Zorro '74

Supernatural Comedies

see also Comedy

Angels in the Outfield '94
Bedazzled '00
Beetlejuice '88 ▸
Bell, Book and Candle '58
Bernard and the Genie '91
Blackbeard's Ghost '67
The Craft '96
Dead Heat '88
The Devil & Max Devlin '81
Fridays of Eternity '81
The Frighteners '96
Ghost Chasers '51
Ghost Dad '90
Ghost Fever '87
The Ghost Goes West '36 ▸
Ghost Writer '89
Ghostbusters '84 ▸
Ghostbusters 2 '89
Ghosts Can Do It '87
Ghosts of Berkeley Square '47
Haunted Honeymoon '86
Heart and Souls '93
High Spirits '88
Hillbillies in a Haunted House '67
Hocus Pocus '93
Just like Heaven '05
Just My Luck '06
Limit Up '89
Love at Stake '87
The Man in the Santa Claus Suit '79
Matilda '96 ▸
Michael '96
My Best Friend Is a Vampire '88
Oh, God! '77
Oh, God! Book 2 '80
Oh, God! You Devil '84
Over Her Dead Body '08
Quigley '03
Rockula '90
Saturday the 14th '81
Saturday the 14th Strikes Back '88
She-Devil '89
The Sixth Man '97
Son of the Mask '05
Spook Busters '48
Spooks Run Wild '41
Teen Wolf '85
Teen Wolf Too '87
Terror Taxi '04
Topper '37 ▸
Topper Returns '41 ▸
Topper Takes a Trip '39 ▸
When Pigs Fly '93
Who Killed Doc Robbin? '48
Wicked Stepmother '89
Winning Girls Through Psychic Mind Control '02
Wishful Thinking '92
A Witch Without a Broom '68

Supernatural Horror

see also Classic Horror

The Abandoned '06
Afghan Knights '07
Alabama's Ghost '72
Alison's Birthday '79
All Souls Day '05
Alone in the Dark '05
Along with Ghosts '69
An American Haunting '05
The Amityville Horror '79
Amityville 2: The Possession '82
Amityville 3: The Demon '83
Amityville 4: The Evil Escapes '89
Amityville: A New Generation '93
The Amityville Horror '05
Amityville 1992: It's About Time '92
Apartment 1303 '07
The Appointment '82
Asylum of the Damned '03
Attack of the Puppet People '58
Audrey Rose '77
Bachelor Party in the Bungalow of the Damned '08
Bad Dreams '88
Bandh Darwaza '90
The Believers '87
Beyond Evil '80
The Black Cat '81
Blade: Trinity '04
Bless the Child '00
Blood from the Mummy's Tomb '71
Blood Gnome '02
Blood Orgy of the She-Devils '74
Blood Pledge '09
Blood Relic '05
Bloodbeat '85
Bloodlust '59
BloodRayne '06
Bones '01
Boogeyman '05
Boogeyman 3 '08
Book of Shadows: Blair Witch 2 '00
Border Patrol '01
Born of Fire '87
The Brainiac '61
Bruiser '00
The Butterfly Effect 2 '06
Candyman '92
Carved '07
Cassandra '87
Cerberus '05
Charlie Boy '81
The Child '76
Children of the Night '92
Chill '06
Christine '84
Chupacabra Terror '05
Cirque du Freak: The Vampire's Assistant '09
Clive Barker's Book of Blood '08
Close Your Eyes '02
Conjurer '08
Constantine '05
The Covenant '06
Crimes of Dr. Mabuse '32 ▸
The Crow: Salvation '00
Crypt of Dark Secrets '76
Cthulhu '08
Cult '07
Curse of the Black Widow '77
Curse of the Blue Lights '88
The Curse of the Crying Woman '61
Curse of the Demon '57 ▸
Curse of the Headless Horseman '72
Curse of the Living Corpse '64
Curse of the Stone Hand '64
The Curse of the Werewolf '61
Cursed '04
The Cursed Mountain Mystery '93
Daimajin '66
Damien: Omen 2 '78
Dance of Death '68
The Dark '79
Dark Places '73
Dark Remains '05
The Dark Secret of Harvest Home '78
Dark Tower '87
Dark Water '02
Darklight '04
Darkness Falls '03
The Daughter of Dr. Jekyll '57
Daughters of Satan '72
Dawn of the Mummy '82
Day Watch '06 ▸
Dead and Buried '81
Dead Are Alive '72
The Dead Don't Die '75
The Death Curse of Tartu '66
Death Mask '98
Death Ship '80
Death Tunnel '05
Death Valley: The Revenge of Bloody Bill '04
Deathdream '72
Deathhead Virgin '74
Deathmoon '78
Deathwatch '02
Deep Red: Hatchet Murders '75
Def by Temptation '90
The Demon Lover '77
Demon of Paradise '87
Demon Rage '82
Demon Wind '90
Demonia '90
Demonoid, Messenger of Death '81
The Demons '74
Demons '86
Demons 2 '87
Demons of Ludlow '75
Demonstone '89
Demonwarp '87
Destroyer '88
Devil Dog: The Hound of Hell '78
Devil Doll '64
The Devil Rides Out '68 ▸
Devil Woman '76
The Devil's Daughter '39
The Devil's Daughter '91
Devil's Gift '84
The Devil's Hand '61
The Devil's Nightmare '71
The Devil's Partner '58
The Devil's Possessed '74
Devil's Rain '75
The Devil's Web '74
Devil's Wedding Night '73
Devonsville Terror '83
Devour '05
The Diabolical Dr. Z '65
Diary of a Madman '63
Diary of the Dead '76
Die, Monster, Die! '65
Diecovery '03
Disciple of Death '72
The Doctor and the Devils '85
Doctor Butcher M.D. '80
Dr. Frankenstein's Castle of Freaks '74
Doctor Phibes Rises Again '72
Dr. Tarr's Torture Dungeon '75
Dr. Terror's House of Horrors '65
Dominion: Prequel to the Exorcist '05
Don't Be Afraid of the Dark '73
Don't Go to Sleep '82
Drag Me to Hell '09
The Drop '06
The Dunwich Horror '70
Dust Devil '93
Edge of Sanity '89
The Eighteenth Angel '97
Embrace of the Vampire '95
Endangered Species '02
Equinox '71 ▸
The Evil '78
Evil Altar '89
Evil Dead Trap '88 ▸
Evil Dead Trap 2: Hideki '91
Evil Town '87
Evilspeak '82
Exorcism '74
The Exorcism of Emily Rose '05 ▸
The Exorcist '73 ▸
The Exorcist 2: The Heretic '77
The Eye '08
The Eye 2 '04
Fallen '97
Farmhouse '08
Feast for the Devil '71
Female Prisoner Sigma '06
Female Vampire '73
The Final Conflict '81
Firestarter '84
The First Power '89
The Fog '05
1408 '07
The Fourth Kind '09
Fright House '89
From Beyond the Grave '73
From Dusk Till Dawn '95
The Fury Within '98
The Gate '87
Gate 2 '92
Gates of Hell 2: Dead Awakening '96
George A. Romero's Land of the Dead '05 ▸
The Ghastly Ones '68
The Ghost '63
The Ghost '04
The Ghost Brigade '93
Ghost Dance '83
Ghost Keeper '80
The Ghost of Rashmon Hall '47
The Ghost of Yotsuya '58
Ghost Rider '07
Ghost Story '81
Ghosthouse '88
Ghostriders '87
The Ghosts of Hanley House '68
Ghosts That Still Walk '77

▸ = rated three bones or higher

GhostWatcher '02
Ghouls '07
Giant from the Unknown '58
Ginger Snaps Back: The Beginning '04
Ginger Snaps: Unleashed '04
God Told Me To '76
Godsend '04
Grave Secrets: The Legacy of Hilltop Drive '92
The Grudge '04
Half-Caste '04
Half Light '05
The Happiness of the Katakuris '01
Haunted Highway '05
The Haunted Palace '63
The Haunting in Connecticut '09
The Haunting of Molly Hartley '08
The Hazing '04
Headspace '02
The Hearse '80
Heaven & Hell '78
Hellbound: Hellraiser 2 '88
Hellraiser '87
Hellraiser 3: Hell on Earth '92
Hellraiser 4: Bloodline '95
Hellraiser: Deader '05
Hellraiser: Hellseeker '02
Hellraiser: Hellworld '05
Hidden Floor '06
Hide and Seek '05
Home Sick '08
The Horrible Dr. Bones '00
The Horrible Dr. Hichcock '62
Horror Express '72
Horror Hotel '60
Horror of the Blood Monsters '70
Horror Rises from the Tomb '72
The House by the Cemetery '83
The House in Marsh Road '60
The House of Seven Corpses '73
House of the Dead '03
House of the Yellow Carpet '84
The House on Skull Mountain '74
The House that Bled to Death '81
House Where Evil Dwells '82
The Howling '81 ▶
Howling 2: Your Sister Is a Werewolf '85
Howling 3: The Marsupials '87
Howling 4: The Original Nightmare '88
Howling 5: The Rebirth '89
Howling 6: The Freaks '90
Immortal Sins '91
The Indestructible Man '56
Inferno '80
Initiation of Sarah '78
The Innocents '61 ▶
Inquisition '76
Inugami '01 ▶
Invasion of the Blood Farmers '72
Invasion of the Zombies '61
The Invisible '07
Invitation to Hell '82
It's Alive! '68
Jack O'Lantern '04
Jaws of Satan '81
J.D.'s Revenge '76
Jennifer '78
Jennifer's Body '09
Ju-On 2 '00
Ju-On: The Grudge '03
Ju-Rei: The Uncanny '04
Judgment Day '88
Kill, Baby, Kill '66 ▶
The Kiss '88
Kiss Daddy Goodbye '81
Knocking on Death's Door '99
Kwaidan '64 ▶
Land of the Minotaur '77
The Last Broadcast '98 ▶
The Last Gasp '94
The Last Man on Earth '64
Left Bank '08
Left in Darkness '06
The Legacy '79
The Legend of Bloody Mary '08
The Legend of Hell House '73 ▶
The Legend of Lucy Keyes '06
Lethal Dose '03
Let's Scare Jessica to Death '71
Lisa and the Devil '75
Living Doll '90
The Living Head '59
Lord of Illusions '95
Lost Colony: The Legend of Roanoke '07
Lost Souls '00
Lurkers '88
Lust for a Vampire '71
The Maid '05
The Man and the Monster '65
Manhattan Baby '82
Maniac '34
The Manitou '78
Manos, the Hands of Fate '66
Manticore '05
Mardi Gras for the Devil '93
Mardi Gras Massacre '78
Mark of the Devil '69
Mark of the Devil 2 '72
Marrionnier '05
Mary, Mary, Bloody Mary '76
Maxim Xul '91
The Medusa Touch '78
Megalodon '03
Memento Mori '00
The Mephisto Waltz '71 ▶
Meridian: Kiss of the Beast '90
The Messengers '07
Messengers 2: The Scarecrow '09
Messiah of Evil '74
Midnight '81
Midnight Cabaret '90
Midnight's Child '93
Mirror, Mirror '90
Mirror of Death '87
Mirrors '08
The Mist '07 ▶
The Monster Demolisher '60
The Morgue '07
Mother of Tears '08
The Mummy's Revenge '73
The Mummy's Shroud '67
Necromancer: Satan's Servant '88
Necropolis '87
Neon Maniacs '86
The Nesting '80
Netherworld '90
The Night Evelyn Came Out of the Grave '71
Night Life '90
Night Nurse '77
Night of Horror '78
Night of the Death Cult '75
Night of the Demons '88
Night of the Demons '09
Night of the Demons 2 '94
Night of the Ghouls '59
Night of the Sorcerers '70
Night Orchid '97 ▶
The Night Stalker '71
The Night Strangler '72
Night Vision '87
Night Visitor '89
Night Watch '04
Nightmare '00
Nightmare Castle '65
Nightmare Detective '06
Nightmare in Blood '75
Nightmare Sisters '87
Nightmare Weekend '86
Nightstalker '81
Nightwish '89
Nomads '86
The Norliss Tapes '73
Nothing But the Night '72
The Objective '08
The Occultist '89
Of Unknown Origin '83
The Offspring '87
The Omen '76
The Omen '06
Omen 4: The Awakening '91
100 Feet '08
100 Monsters '68
One Missed Call '03 ▶
One Missed Call 2 '05
One Missed Call 3: Final '06
Onmyoji '01
Onmyoji 2 '03
The Oracle '85
The Order '03
Orgy of the Dead '65
Orgy of the Vampires '73
The Orphanage '07 ▶
The Other '72 ▶
Other Hell '85
The Others '01 ▶
Out of the Body '88
The Outing '87
P '04
Pan's Labyrinth '06 ▶
Paranormal Activity '09 ▶
Parasite '03
Patrick '78
Pet Sematary '89
Pet Sematary 2 '92
Phantasm '79
Phantasm 2 '88
Phantom of the Ritz '88
Phantoms '97
Phone '02
Poltergeist '82 ▶
Poltergeist 2: The Other Side '86
Poltergeist 3 '88
Poltergeist: The Legacy '96
The Possessed '77
Possession '09
The Possession of Joel Delaney '72
Pray '05
The Premonition '75
Premonition '98
Premonition '04
The Prophecy '95
The Psychic '68
Psychomania '73
Pulse '01
Pulse '06
Pumpkinhead '88
Pumpkinhead 3: Ashes to Ashes '06
Pumpkinhead 4: Blood Feud '07
Purana Mandir '84 ▶
Quarantine '08
R-Point '04
Rapturious '07
Rasen '98
Rawhead Rex '87
Re-Cycle '06
The Reaping '07
Red Sands '09
The Red Shoes '05
Reincarnation '05
The Relic '96
Rest Stop: Don't Look Back '08
Return of Daimajin '66
Return to House on Haunted Hill '07
Revolt of the Zombies '36
The Ring '02
The Ring 2 '05
The Ring Virus '99
Ringu '98 ▶
Ringu 0 '01
Ringu 2 '99
Route 666 '01
Salem's Lot '04
Sarah's Child '96
Sauna '08
Savage Harvest 2: October Blood '06
Scream of the Wolf '74
Seance '00
Seance '06
Session 9 '01
Shadows '07
Shallow Ground '04
Shock 'Em Dead '90
Shutter '08
Signs '02 ▶
Silent Hill '06
The Skeleton Key '05
The Skeptic '09
The Skull '65
The Sleeping Car '90
Sleepstalker: The Sandman's Last Rites '94
Snake Woman's Curse '68
Sorceress '94
Sorum '01
The Soul Guardians '98
Soul Survivors '01
Space Master X-7 '58
Specters '87
Spider Forest '04
Spook Warfare '68
Spooky Encounters '80
Stephen King's Rose Red '02
Stephen King's The Storm of the Century '99
Stephen King's Thinner '96
Stir of Echoes '99
Sundown: The Vampire in Retreat '08
Supernatural '33
The Supernaturals '86
A Tale of Two Sisters '03 ▶
Terror Creatures from the Grave '66
They Watch '93
13 Ghosts '60
13 Ghosts '01
3 Extremes 2 '02
The Tooth Fairy '06
The Turn of the Screw '74
The Turn of the Screw '89
The Turn of the Screw '92
The Turn of the Screw '99
The Unborn '09
Unborn but Forgotten '02
The Uninvited '09
Unseen Evil '99
Unspeakable '00
Urban Ghost Story '98
Uzumaki '00
The Vault '00
Versus '00
The Village '04
The Visitors '89
Vlad '03
Voices from Beyond '90
Voodoo Academy '00
Vulture's Eye '04
Wendigo '01
Wes Craven Presents: They '02
The Whip and the Body '63
Whispering Corridors '98
White Noise '05
White Noise 2: The Light '07
Wicked Lake '08
Wind Chill '07
The Wishing Stairs '03
Witchcraft 4: Virgin Heart '92
Witchcraft 10: Mistress of the Craft '98
The Witches '66
The Wraith '87
Wrath of Daimajin '66

Supernatural Martial Arts

The Crow '93
Hellbound '94
The Heroic Trio '93
The Legend of the 7 Golden Vampires '73
Lone Wolf and Cub: Baby Cart at the River Styx '72
Lone Wolf and Cub: Baby Cart to Hades '72
The Mummy: Tomb of the Dragon Emperor '08
Ninja, the Violent Sorcerer '86
Remo Williams: The Adventure Begins '85
Sgt. Kabukiman N.Y.P.D. '94
Sword Masters: The Battle Wizard '77
TMNT (Teenage Mutant Ninja Turtles) '07
Vampire Raiders—Ninja Queen '89
Wind and Cloud: The Storm Riders '04
Zu: Warriors from the Magic Mountain '83

Supernatural Westerns

Billy the Kid Versus Dracula '66
BloodRayne 2: Deliverance '07
Curse of the Undead '59
Dead Birds '04
The Devil's Mistress '68
Ghostriders '87
Grim Prairie Tales '89
The Hitcher '86
Into the Badlands '92
Jesse James Meets Frankenstein's Daughter '65
John Carpenter's Vampires '97
Jonah Hex '10
Mad at the Moon '92
Near Dark '87 ▶
Sundown '91
Sundown: The Vampire in Retreat '08
Timerider '83

Surfing

***see also** Beach Blanket Bingo*

Aloha Summer '88
Beach Blanket Bingo '65 ▶
Beach Party '63
Big Wednesday '78
Bikini Beach '64
Blackrock '97
Blood Surf '00
Blue Crush '02 ▶
Blue Juice '95
Bra Boys '07
California Dreaming '79
Chairman of the Board '97
Computer Beach Party '88
The Endless Summer '66 ▶
The Endless Summer 2 '94 ▶
Escape from L.A. '96
Fantastic Four: Rise of the Silver Surfer '07
Flirting with Forty '09
Follow Me '69
Gidget '59
How to Stuff a Wild Bikini '65
In God's Hands '98
Lauderdale '89
Lilo & Stitch '02 ▶
Local Boys '02
Mad Wax: The Surf Movie '90
Meet the Deedles '98
Muscle Beach Party '64
Newcastle '08
North Shore '87
Off the Lip '04
Point Break '91
Psycho Beach Party '00
Puberty Blues '81
Red Surf '90
Ride the Wild Surf '64
Riding Giants '04
Shelter '07
South Beach Academy '96
Step Into Liquid '03 ▶
Summer City '77
Surf Nazis Must Die '87
Surf Party '64
Surf 2 '84
Surfer, Dude '08
Surf's Up '07
Surfwise '07 ▶

Survival

***see also** Hunted!; Negative Utopia; Post-Apocalypse*

Abandon Ship '57
Adam Resurrected '08
The Admirable Crichton '57
Adrift '93
Adventure in Sahara '38
Adventure Island '47
Adventures of Eliza Fraser '76
Alive '93
Alpine Fire '89
Amusement '08
And I Alone Survived '78
Antarctica '84
Arctic Blue '93
Arctic Tale '07
Attack of the Beast Creatures '85
The Aviator '85
Back from Eternity '56
Bat 21 '88
Battle for Terra '09 ▶
Battlefield Earth '00
Beverly Hills Family Robinson '97
Black Book '06 ▶
Black Rain '88 ▶
The Book of Eli '10
Born Killer '89
Born Wild '95
The Bridge on the River Kwai '57 ▶
Buffalo Rider '78
A Bullet Is Waiting '54
Cage 2: The Arena of Death '94
Caged in Paradiso '89
Captain January '36
A Captive in the Land '91
Carriers '09
Cast Away '00 ▶
Challenge To Be Free '76
Cheyenne Warrior '94
City of Ember '08
Clearcut '92
Cliffhanger '93 ▶
Clown '53
Cold Mountain '03 ▶
Cold River '81
The Colony '98
Cool Hand Luke '67 ▶
The Core '03
Courage Under Fire '96 ▶
Damned River '89
Das Boot '81 ▶
The Dawson Patrol '78
The Day After '83 ▶
Daylight '96
Dead Calm '89 ▶
Deadly Harvest '72
Deadly Prey '87
Death Hunt '81
Death Valley '04
Def-Con 4 '85
Deliverance '72 ▶
Delos Adventure '86
Delusion '91
The Descent '05
Desert Nights '29
Desperate Target '80
The Devil at 4 O'Clock '61
Diamonds of the Night '64 ▶
The Dive '89
Dust Devil '93
Earthling '80
Edge of Honor '91
Eight Below '06
Empire of the Sun '87 ▶
Endangered '94
Endgame '85
Enemy Mine '85
Enemy Territory '87
Erendira '83
Eric '75 ▶
Escape from Hell '79
Escape from Mars '99
Escape from Wildcat Canyon '99
Escapist '83
Exit Speed '08
Far from Home: The Adventures of Yellow Dog '94
Far North '07
Fateless '05 ▶
Fight for Your Life '77
The Final Destination '09
Firehawk '92
Five '51
Five Came Back '39
Fixed Bayonets! '51 ▶
Flags of Our Fathers '06 ▶
Flight from Glory '37
Flight from Singapore '62
Flight of the Eagle '82
The Flight of the Phoenix '65 ▶
Flight of the Phoenix '04
The Forbidden Quest '93
Fortress '85
Found Alive '34
Fragments '08
Gangland '00
Gas-s-s-s! '70
Germany, Pale Mother '80
Gerry '02
Grave of the Fireflies '88 ▶
He Is My Brother '75
Heaven and Earth '93
Heaven Knows, Mr. Allison '57 ▶
Heck's Way Home '95

▶ = rated three bones or higher

Heroes for Sale '33 ▶
High Ice '80
High Noon '52 ▶
High Noon '00
House of 9 '05
House of Sand '05 ▶
Hunter's Blood '87
I Am Legend '07 ▶
I Am Omega '07
In Desert and Wilderness '01
The Incredible Journey '63
Intacto '01
The Interrogation '82 ▶
Into Thin Air: Death on Everest '97
The Island '61 ▶
The Island at the Top of the World '74
Island of the Blue Dolphins '64
Island of the Lost '68
The Island on Bird Street '97
Jeremiah Johnson '72 ▶
Jungle Inferno '72
Just Before Dawn '80
Kameradschaft '31 ▶
Killing at Hell's Gate '81
The Killing Fields '84 ▶
King Rat '65 ▶
The Land That Time Forgot '75
The Last Chance '45 ▶
Last Exit to Brooklyn '90 ▶
The Last Flight of Noah's Ark '80
The Last of the Dogmen '95
Le Dernier Combat '84 ▶
Legend of Alfred Packer '80
The Legend of Wolf Mountain '92
Legion '10
Legionnaire '98
L'Enfant d'Eau '95
The Leopard Son '96 ▶
The Life and Death of Colonel Blimp '43 ▶
Lifeboat '44 ▶
Lily Was Here '89
Limbo '99
Little Dorrit, Film 1: Nobody's Fault '88 ▶
Little Dorrit, Film 2: Little Dorrit's Story '88 ▶
Lord of the Flies '63 ▶
Lord of the Flies '90
Lost '83
Lost '86
Love on the Dole '41 ▶
Male and Female '19 ▶
Man in the Wilderness '71
Manon '50
Marooned in Iraq '02
Melody '71
Merry Christmas, Mr. Lawrence '83 ▶
Mr. Robinson Crusoe '32
Morning Departure '50
The Mosquito Coast '86
The Most Dangerous Game '32 ▶
My Side of the Mountain '69
Mysterious Island '61 ▶
The Naked Prey '66 ▶
Nightmare at Bittercreek '91
Nightmare at Noon '87
9 '09 ▶
North Face '08 ▶
Objective, Burma! '45 ▶
On the Beach '59 ▶
On the Beach '00
Once Before I Die '65
Ordeal in the Arctic '93
Osa '85
Out of Control '85
Packin' It In '83
Pagan Island '60
Panic in the Year Zero! '62
Panic Room '02
Paradise '82
Passion in the Desert '97
Perfect Witness '89
Phone Call from a Stranger '52
The Pianist '02 ▶
Pioneer Woman '73
Pitch Black '00 ▶
Poseidon '06
The Poseidon Adventure '72
A Prophet '09 ▶
Proteus '95
Pulse 2: Afterlife '08
Quest for Fire '82 ▶
Ravager '97
Resident Evil: Apocalypse '04
Resident Evil: Extinction '07
The Return of Grey Wolf '22
Return of the Jedi '83 ▶
The Revolt of Job '84 ▶
The Ride Back '57
The Road '09
Robby '68
Robinson Crusoe '36
Sahara '43 ▶
Savage Hunger '84
Savage Is Loose '74
Sea Gypsies '78
The Sea Shall Not Have Them '55
Sea Wife '57
Seven Days in May '64 ▶
Seven Were Saved '47
Severed Ways '09
Shackleton '02 ▶
Shadow of the Wolf '92
She'll Be Wearing Pink Pajamas '84
Silence '73
Silence of the North '81
Six Days, Seven Nights '98
Skyline '84 ▶
Sniper '92
The Snow Walker '03
Snowbound: The Jim and Jennifer Stolpa Story '94
S.O.S. Pacific '60
Sourdough '77
SpaceCamp '86
Stagecoach '39 ▶
Standoff '97
Starbird and Sweet William '73
Storm and Sorrow '90
The Strangers '08
Sub Down '97
Survival Quest '89
Survival Run '80
The Survivalist '87
Sweet Sweetback's Baadasssss Song '71 ▶
Swept Away '02
The Swiss Family Robinson '60 ▶
The Terror '63
Testament '83 ▶
Thief '81 ▶
Three Came Home '50 ▶
The Ticket '97
Titanic '96
Tooth and Nail '07
Touching the Void '03
The Trail of '98 '28
Trouble in Paradise '88
Trucks '97
True Heart '97
Tundra '36
20 Years After '08
28 Days Later '02
Two Women '61 ▶
Unsettled Land '88
Voyage '93
The Voyage of the Yes '72
Vukovar '94 ▶
Wagon Master '50 ▶
Walkabout '71 ▶
Walking Thunder '94
Warriors of the Apocalypse '85
Waterworld '95
When Trumpets Fade '98
The White Dawn '75
White Fang and the Hunter '85
White Water Summer '87
White Wolves 3: Cry of the White Wolf '98
Wild America '97 ▶
World Trade Center '06 ▶
Zarkorr! The Invader '96
Zombieland '09 ▶

Suspended Animation

Alien 3 '92
Aliens '86 ▶
Austin Powers: International Man of Mystery '97 ▶
Batman and Robin '97
Buck Rogers in the 25th Century '79
Chances Are '89 ▶
Coma '78 ▶
Demolition Man '93
Dragon Fury 2 '96
Encino Man '92
Forever Young '92
Genesis II '73
Late for Dinner '91
Planet of the Apes '68 ▶

Suspense

***see also** Mystery & Suspense*

Almost Strangers '01 ▶
Arlington Road '99
Black Book '06 ▶
Bound by Lies '05
Breach '07
Dead Dog '00
The Devil's Advocate '97
Disturbia '07
Gone Dark '03
The Good Shepherd '06
The Gunman '03
Half Light '05
I'm Not Scared '03
Incubus '05
King of the Ants '03
Lady Killer '97
The Lives of Others '06 ▶
The Lookout '07 ▶
Man in the Attic '53
The Mapmaker '01
Marebito '04
Mr. Brooks '07
Next '07
The Night Watchman '02
Panic Room '02
Perfect Stranger '07
Pulse '03
Red Road '06
Rx '06
Savage Island '03
Shelter Island '03
Sphere '97
The Strangers '08
Ten 'Til Noon '06
The Tesseract '03
That Beautiful Somewhere '06
Trail of a Serial Killer '98
The 24th Day '04
Urban Ghost Story '98
The Well '97
The Wild Card '03
Your Vice is a Closed Room and Only I Have the Key '72
Zeder '83

Swashbucklers

***see also** Action-Adventure; Fencing; Medieval Romps*

Abbott and Costello Meet Captain Kidd '52
Adventures of Captain Fabian '51
Adventures of Don Juan '49 ▶
The Adventures of Robin Hood '38 ▶
Against All Flags '52 ▶
Ali Baba and the Forty Thieves '43
Ali Baba and the 40 Thieves '54 ▶
Anthony Adverse '36
Arabian Nights '42
At Sword's Point '51
Bardelys the Magnificent '26
The Beloved Rogue '27 ▶
The Black Pirate '26 ▶
The Black Rose '50
The Black Shield of Falworth '54
The Black Swan '42 ▶
Blackbeard the Pirate '52
Blackbeard's Ghost '67
Bluebeard '72
The Bold Caballero '36
The Buccaneer '58
Buccaneer's Girl '50
Captain Blood '35 ▶
Captain Calamity '36
Captain Horatio Hornblower '51 ▶
Captain Kidd '45
Captain Kronos: Vampire Hunter '74 ▶
Captain Ron '92
Carry On Jack '63
Cartouche '62 ▶
Casanova '05
The Challenge '82
Cheech and Chong's The Corsican Brothers '84
China Seas '35 ▶
The Conqueror & the Empress '64
Corsair '31
The Corsican Brothers '42
The Count of Monte Cristo '12
The Count of Monte Cristo '34 ▶
The Count of Monte Cristo '74
The Count of Monte Cristo '99
The Count of Monte Cristo '02
Court Jester '56 ▶
Crimson Pirate '52 ▶
Cutthroat Island '95
Dancing Pirate '36
The Devil-Ship Pirates '64
Dr. Syn '37
Dr. Syn, Alias the Scarecrow '64
Don Juan DeMarco '94
Don Q., Son of Zorro '25
Double Crossbones '51
The Elusive Pimpernel '50
Executioner of Venice '63
Fanfan la Tulipe '51 ▶
The Fencing Master '92
The Fifth Musketeer '79
Fighting Marines '36
The Fighting Prince of Donegal '66
The Flame & the Arrow '50 ▶
The Four Musketeers '75 ▶
The 4 Musketeers '05
Frenchman's Creek '44
Frenchman's Creek '98
Ghost in the Noonday Sun '74
Gypsy '75
Hawk of the Wilderness '38
Hell Ship Mutiny '57
Highlander: The Gathering '92
His Majesty O'Keefe '53
Hook '91
If I Were King '38 ▶
The Iron Mask '29
The Island '80
Island Trader '71
Kidnapped '05 ▶
The King's Guard '01
The King's Thief '55
Kojiro '67 ▶
The Lady and the Highwayman '89
The Lamb '15
The Legend of Zorro '05
The Lives of a Bengal Lancer '35 ▶
Long John Silver '54
Magic Island '95
The Man in the Iron Mask '39 ▶
The Man in the Iron Mask '77 ▶
The Man in the Iron Mask '97
The Man in the Iron Mask '98 ▶
Marauder '65
Mark of Zorro '20 ▶
The Mark of Zorro '40 ▶
The Mask of Zorro '98 ▶
The Master of Ballantrae '53
Master of Dragonard Hill '89
Monty Python's The Meaning of Life '83 ▶
Mooncussers '62
Moonfleet '55
Moran of the Lady Letty '22
Morgan the Pirate '60
Muppet Treasure Island '96
The Musketeer '01
My Favorite Year '82 ▶
My Wicked, Wicked Ways '84
Nate and Hayes '83
Naughty Marietta '35
New Moon '40
Old Ironsides '26 ▶
On Guard! '03 ▶
The Phantom '96
The Pirate '48 ▶
Pirate Movie '82
Pirate Warrior '64
Pirates '86
Pirates of Blood River '62
The Pirates of Penzance '83
Pirates of the Caribbean: At World's End '07
Pirates of the Caribbean: The Curse of the Black Pearl '03 ▶
Pirates of the Coast '61
Pirates of the Seven Seas '62
Prince of Foxes '49
The Princess and the Pirate '44 ▶
The Princess Bride '87 ▶
Princess of Thieves '01
Prisoner of Zenda '37 ▶
Prisoner of Zenda '52
Prisoner of Zenda '79
Project A '83
Project A: Part 2 '87
Quentin Durward '55
Quest of the Delta Knights '93
The Return of the Musketeers '89
Revenge of the Musketeers '63
Revenge of the Musketeers '94
Ring of the Musketeers '93
Robin Hood '73 ▶
Romola '25
Royal Flash '75 ▶
Scaramouche '52 ▶
The Scarlet Pimpernel '34 ▶
The Scarlet Pimpernel '82 ▶
The Scarlet Pimpernel '99
The Scarlet Pimpernel 2: Mademoiselle Guillotine '99
The Scarlet Pimpernel 3: The Kidnapped King '99
The Sea Hawk '24
The Sea Hawk '40 ▶
Sea Hound '47
The Secret of El Zorro '57
Shipwrecked '90
The Sign of Zorro '60
Sinbad and the Eye of the Tiger '77
Sinbad, the Sailor '47 ▶
Son of Ali Baba '52
Son of Captain Blood '62
Son of Fury '42 ▶
The Son of Monte Cristo '40
Son of Zorro '47
South of Pago Pago '40
South Seas Massacre '74
The Spanish Main '45
The Story of Robin Hood & His Merrie Men '52 ▶
Swashbuckler '76
Swashbuckler '84
The Swiss Family Robinson '60 ▶
Sword & the Sorcerer '82
Sword of Sherwood Forest '60
The Swordsman '92
Tharus Son of Attila '62
Three Amigos '86
The Three Musketeers '16
The Three Musketeers '21 ▶
The Three Musketeers '33
The Three Musketeers '35
The Three Musketeers '39
The Three Musketeers '48
The Three Musketeers '74 ▶
The Three Musketeers '93
Tiger of the Seven Seas '62
Treasure Island '34 ▶
Treasure Island '50 ▶
Treasure Island '72
Treasure Island '89
Treasure Island '99
Treasure of the Golden Condor '53
Treasure of the Moon Goddess '88
Two Lost Worlds '50
Under the Red Robe '36
Virgin Territory '07
Wallaby Jim of the Islands '37
The Warriors '55
The Wicked Lady '83
Yankee Buccaneer '52
Yellowbeard '83
Zorro '74
Zorro, the Gay Blade '81

Swimming

***see also** Deep Blue; Go Fish; Island Fare; Killer Sea Critters; Lifeguards; Pacific Islands*

Alex '92
Back to School '86
Barracuda '78
Bathing Beauty '44
The Big Bad Swim '06
The Bridges at Toko-Ri '55 ▶
Cocoon '85 ▶
Dangerous When Wet '53
Dawn! '83
Easy to Love '53
Fast Times at Ridgemont High '82 ▶
Gremlins '84 ▶
The Guardian '06
Imaginary Heroes '05
Jaws '75 ▶
The Man from Atlantis '77
Million Dollar Mermaid '52
Neptune's Daughter '49
Off the Mark '87
On a Clear Day '05
Pride '07
Sea People '00
Sleeping with the Enemy '91
Splash '84
Swim Team '79
Swimfan '02
The Swimmer '68 ▶
Swimming Upstream '03
Thrill of a Romance '45
The Tunnel '01 ▶
Unbreakable '00
Water Lilies '07

Swingers

Barfly '87 ▶
Bob & Carol & Ted & Alice '69
A Change of Seasons '80
Eating Raoul '82 ▶
Group Marriage '72
Invasion of the Bee Girls '73 ▶
Looking for Mr. Goodbar '77
9 1/2 Weeks '86
The Other Side of the Bed '03
The Party '68 ▶
The Swap '71
The Swinging Cheerleaders '74
The Unfaithfuls '60
Your Friends & Neighbors '98 ▶

Sword & Sandal

Alexander '04
Ali Baba and the Forty Thieves '43
Ali Baba and the 40 Thieves '54 ▶
Ali Baba and the Seven Saracens '64
Alone Against Rome '62
Amazons and Gladiators '01
Arabian Nights '42
Ashes of Time '94 ▶
The Avenger '62
Battle of Valiant '63
The Beast of Babylon Against the Son of Hercules '63
Caesar the Conqueror '63
Challenge of the Gladiator '65
Colossus and the Amazon Queen '64
Colossus of the Arena '62
Coriolanus, Man without a Country '64
Cyclops '08
Duel of Champions '61
Fabiola '48 ▶
Fire Monsters Against the Son of Hercules '62

▶ = rated three bones or higher

Giants of Rome '63
Gladiator '00 ▸
Gladiator of Rome '63
Gladiators 7 '62
Goliath Against the Giants '63
Goliath and the Barbarians '60
Goliath and the Dragon '61
Goliath and the Sins of Babylon '64
Gor '88
Hercules '58
Hercules against the Moon Men '64
Hercules and the Captive Women '63
Hercules and the Princess of Troy '65
Hercules in the Haunted World '64
Hercules, Prisoner of Evil '64
Hercules Unchained '59
Hercules vs. the Sons of the Sun '64
Hero of Rome '63
The Invincible Gladiator '62
The Invincible Gladiator '63
The Last Days of Pompeii '60
Revak the Rebel '60
Revenge of the Barbarians '60
Revolt of the Barbarians '64
Roland the Mighty '56
Samson '61
Samson Against the Sheik '62
Samson and His Mighty Challenge '64
Samson and the 7 Miracles of the World '62
The Scorpion King '02
The Scorpion King 2: Rise of a Warrior '08
Sins of Rome '54
Son of Ali Baba '52
Son of Hercules in the Land of Darkness '63
Sword of Venus '53
Terror of the Steppes '64
Thor and the Amazon Women '60
300 '07
The 300 Spartans '62
Tristan & Isolde '06
The Triumph of Hercules '66
The Trojan Horse '62
Troy '04
Two Gladiators '64
Warriors of Heaven and Earth '03

Sydney

see also ***Down Under***
Better Than Sex '00
Bra Boys '07
Cosi '95 ▸
Danny Deckchair '03
Dirty Deeds '02 ▸
Doing Time for Patsy Cline '97
Don's Party '76 ▸
Floating Life '95
He Died With a Felafel in His Hand '01
Introducing the Dwights '07
Joey '98
The Last Wave '77 ▸
Lilian's Story '95
Little Fish '05 ▸
Me Myself I '99
Napoleon '96
$9.99 '08
Out of the Body '88
Over the Hill '93
Paperback Hero '99
The Road from Coorain '02
The Silence '06
Solo '06
The Sum of Us '94 ▸
Young Einstein '89

Tale of the Tape

see also ***Sexcapades***
Afterschool '08
Alone With Her '07
American Virgin '09
Auto Focus '02 ▸
Be Kind Rewind '08
Benny's Video '92
The Big Hit '98
The Blair Witch Project '99
A Broken Life '07
Capturing the Friedmans '03 ▸
Cloverfield '08
Comedy of Innocence '00
The Darwin Awards '06
Deadline '09
Diary of the Dead '07
Donkey Punch '08
Enemy of the State '98
The Fantastic World of D.C. Collins '84
Felony '95
Final Assignment '80
Final Cut '98
Forbidden Homework '92
The Fourth Kind '09
Freeze Frame '04
Hard to Kill '89
Home Movie '08
Homework '90
I'm Reed Fish '06
Interview with the Assassin '02
Janice Beard '99
Jimmy & Judy '06
The Jolly Boys' Last Stand '00
Love or Money '01
My Life on Ice '02
100 Mile Rule '02
The Perfect Witness '07
Prisoner '07
Quarantine '08
Rasen '98
Red Road '06
Red Roses and Petrol '03
The Ring Virus '99
Ringu '98 ▸
Ringu 0 '01
Ringu 2 '99
Road Trip '00
The Rutanga Tapes '90
Savage Harvest 2: October Blood '06
sex, lies and videotape '89 ▸
Shredderman Rules '07
Sky High '84
Sliver '93
Son of Rambow '07
Spy Games '99
Two Weeks '06
Vacancy '07
Vacancy 2: The First Cut '08
Video Murders '87
Video Violence '87
Warm Blooded Killers '01
The Wedding Bros. '08

Talking Animals

see also ***Wild Kingdom***
Air Bud 6: Air Buddies '06
Alice in Wonderland '10
Animal Farm '99
The Ape '05
Aussie and Ted's Great Adventure '09
Babe '95 ▸
Babe: Pig in the City '98
Barnyard '06
Beverly Hills Chihuahua '08
Big Top Pee-wee '88
Brother Bear 2 '06
Cats & Dogs '01
Charlotte's Web '06 ▸
Chicken Little '05
The Chronicles of Narnia: The Lion, the Witch and the Wardrobe '05
Clifford's Really Big Movie '04
Cloudy with a Chance of Meatballs '09
Dead Men Tell '41
Dinotopia '02
Doctor Dolittle '67
Dr. Dolittle '98
Dr. Dolittle 2 '01
Dr. Dolittle 3 '06
Dr. Dolittle 4: Tail to the Chief '08
Dr. Dolittle: Million Dollar Mutts '09
Dr. Seuss' Horton Hears a Who! '08 ▸
Flushed Away '06 ▸
Francis Covers the Big Town '53
Francis Goes to the Races '51
Francis Goes to West Point '52
Francis in the Haunted House '56
Francis in the Navy '55
Francis Joins the WACs '54
Francis the Talking Mule '49 ▸
G-Force '09
Garfield: A Tail of Two Kitties '06
George of the Jungle '97 ▸
The Golden Compass '07
Good Boy! '03
Harvey '50 ▸
Home on the Range '04
Homeward Bound 2: Lost in San Francisco '96
Homeward Bound: The Incredible Journey '93 ▸
Hoodwinked '05 ▸
Inland Empire '06
Karate Dog '04
Kung Fu Panda '08 ▸
Little Nicky '00
Madagascar '05
Madagascar: Escape 2 Africa '08
Malibu's Most Wanted '03
Marmaduke '10
Men in Black '97 ▸
Men in Black 2 '02
Over the Hedge '06 ▸
Paulie '98
Pooh's Heffalump Movie '05
The Princess and the Frog '09 ▸
Racing Stripes '05
The Real Macaw '98
Santa Buddies '09
Sherlock: Undercover Dog '94
Shrek the Third '07
The SpongeBob SquarePants Movie '04
Stuart Little '99
The Undercover Kid '95
Up '09 ▸

Tattoos

Blue Tiger '94
Cape Fear '91 ▸
The Crow 2: City of Angels '96
Cyber Bandits '94
Double Team '97
Down Periscope '96
Eastern Promises '07 ▸
Escape from L.A. '96
Foxfire '96
The Girl With the Dragon Tattoo '09 ▸
Hesher '10
Hitman '07
Horsemen '09
Houseguest '94
The Illustrated Man '69 ▸
In the Cut '03
Lust in the Dust '85 ▸
Memento '00 ▸
The Night of the Hunter '55 ▸
Prey for Rock and Roll '03 ▸
Skin Deep '94
Son-in-Law '93
Spider Lilies '06
Starship Troopers '97 ▸
Stir Crazy '80
The Taking of Pelham 123 '09
Tattoo '81
Tattoo, a Love Story '02
The Tattooist '07
Teresa's Tattoo '94
XIII '08
Waterworld '95
The Yakuza '75

Taxing Situations

The Brady Bunch Movie '95 ▸
Dinner for Schmucks '10
Exotica '94 ▸
Hair Show '04
Lagaan: Once upon a Time in India '01
Mary, Mary '63
The Mating Game '59 ▸
Off the Map '03 ▸
Seven Pounds '08
Speedway '68
Strange Bedfellows '04
Stranger Than Fiction '06
A Taxing Woman '87 ▸
A Taxing Woman's Return '88 ▸
The Taxman '98

Team Efforts

The Alamo '60 ▸
The Bad News Bears '05
The Bad News Bears Go to Japan '78
The Bad News Bears in Breaking Training '77
Beerfest '06
Breaking Away '79 ▸
The Club '81 ▸
Coach '78
Codename: Foxfire '85
Codename: Wildgeese '84
The Comebacks '07
Crossfire '89
The Cutting Edge '92
The Dirty Dozen '67 ▸
The Dirty Dozen: The Deadly Mission '87
The Dirty Dozen: The Fatal Mission '88
The Dirty Dozen: The Next Mission '85
The Doll Squad '73
D3: The Mighty Ducks '96
D2: The Mighty Ducks '94
Eddie '96
Fantastic Four '05
The Final Season '07
Finger on the Trigger '65
Force Five '75
Force 10 from Navarone '78
Forever Strong '08
Full Ride '02
The Game of Their Lives '05
The Game Plan '07
The Guns of Navarone '61 ▸
Hoosiers '86 ▸
Innocents with Dirty Hands '76
Invictus '09 ▸
Kicking & Screaming '05
Kill and Kill Again '81
Ladybugs '92
Let's Get Harry '87
The Longest Yard '05
The Losers '70
The Magnificent Seven '60 ▸
Major League 3: Back to the Minors '98
Memphis Belle '90 ▸
The Mighty Ducks '92
Miracle '04 ▸
Miracle on Ice '81
The Mod Squad '99
More Than a Game '08
Necessary Roughness '91
Ocean's 11 '60
Ocean's Eleven '01 ▸
Ocean's Twelve '04
Pride '07
Race the Sun '96
Radio '03
Rebound '05
Recipe for Disaster '03
Remember the Titans '00 ▸
Renaissance Man '94
The Sandlot 2 '05
The Sandlot 3: Heading Home '07
School of Rock '03 ▸
Seven Magnificent Gladiators '84
Seven Samurai '54 ▸
Silverado '85 ▸
The Sixth Man '97
Soldier Boyz '95
Space Jam '96
Steel '97
Sunset Park '96
Sunstorm '01
S.W.A.T. '03
Team America: World Police '04 ▸
That Thing You Do! '96 ▸
Three the Hard Way '74
The Tunnel '01 ▸
Twister '96
Uncommon Valor '83
The Untouchables '87 ▸
Varsity Blues '98
Victory '81
White Squall '96
Wild Geese '78
Wild Geese 2 '85
Wind '92

Tearjerkers

Acorn People '82
An Affair to Remember '57
After the Promise '87
All About My Mother '99 ▸
All Dogs Go to Heaven '89
All Fall Down '62
All Mine to Give '56
Angels in America '03 ▸
Another Time, Another Place '58
Autumn in New York '00
Baby Face '33
Back Street '61
Balboa '82
Ballad in Blue '66
Bang the Drum Slowly '56
Bang the Drum Slowly '73 ▸
Beaches '88 ▸
Because of You '52
Big Bluff '55
Bittersweet Love '76
Black Eyes '39
Black Peter '63
Blind Spot '93
Blood of Jesus '41
Blossoms in the Dust '41
Bonjour Tristesse '57 ▸
Bouquet of Barbed Wire '76
Breaking the Rules '92
Brian's Song '71 ▸
The Cabin in the Cotton '32
Camille '21
Carrie '52 ▸
Carry On Cruising '62
Cast the First Stone '89
The Champ '32 ▸
The Champ '79
Change of Heart '98
Chantilly Lace '93
The Cheat '15 ▸
Chinatown After Dark '31
Choices '81
Christmas Comes to Willow Creek '87
City That Never Sleeps '53
City Without Men '43
Claudia '85
Clown '53
Coquette '29
The Country Kid '23 ▸
The Courtney Affair '47
Craig's Wife '36 ▸
Crawlspace '86
Curly Sue '91
Dance Fools Dance '31 ▸
Danielle Steel's Fine Things '90
Dead Wrong '83
Death Be Not Proud '75 ▸
Dedee d'Anvers '49
Delinquent Parents '38
A Dog of Flanders '59
Dog Pound Shuffle '75 ▸
An Early Frost '85 ▸
Easy Virtue '27
The Eddy Duchin Story '56
Eric '75 ▸
Escape Me Never '47
The Evening Star '96
The Event '03
Fire Down Below '57
Flamingo Road '49 ▸
The Forbidden City '18
Forever Love '98
Fortune's Fool '21
Found Alive '34
Fourth Wish '75
Fulfillment '89
Gangs, Inc. '41
The Garden of Allah '36 ▸
The Gathering '77
The Gathering: Part 2 '79
Ghost '90 ▸
Gideon '99
Girl from Chicago '32
The Girl Who Had Everything '53
Goodbye, Mr. Chips '39 ▸
Goodbye, My Lady '56
Great Day '46
The Greatest Question '19
Griffin & Phoenix '06
Griffin and Phoenix: A Love Story '76
Hachiko: A Dog's Tale '09
Harlow '65
The Healer '02
Hearts of Humanity '32
Heaven and Earth '93
Heaven's a Drag '94
Hell-Ship Morgan '36
Her Silent Sacrifice '18
Here on Earth '00
High Gear '33
A Home of Our Own '93
Home Room '02 ▸
Honky Tonk '41 ▸
Hot Spell '58
Human Desire '54
Human Hearts '22
I Conquer the Sea '36
I Sent a Letter to My Love '81 ▸
Ice Castles '79
If Ever I See You Again '78
Imitation of Life '34
In This Our Life '42
Inside Daisy Clover '65
Intermezzo '36 ▸
Intermezzo '39 ▸
Introducing Dorothy Dandridge '99 ▸
Jack the Bear '93
Johnny Belinda '48 ▸
Johnny Belinda '82
Johnny Eager '42 ▸
Journey for Margaret '42 ▸
Keep Punching '39
The Kid with the Broken Halo '82
La Bete Humaine '38 ▸
La Chienne '31 ▸
Lady Caroline Lamb '73
The Lady Without Camelias '53
The Last Best Year '90
Le Jour Se Leve '39 ▸
Legends of the Fall '94
Leo '02
Leopard in the Snow '78
Leper '76
Letter from an Unknown Woman '48 ▸
The Little Match Girl '84
The Little Princess '39 ▸
A Little Princess '95 ▸
Look Who's Talking Now '93
Looking for an Echo '99
Love Affair '39 ▸
Love Affair '94
Love Affair: The Eleanor & Lou Gehrig Story '77 ▸
Love Butcher '82
The Love Flower '20
Love Has Many Faces '65
The Love Light '21
Love Songs '85
Love Story '70 ▸
Lovers of Their Time '85
Loving '84
Lure of the Sila '49
Madame Butterfly '95
Madame X '37
Magnificent Obsession '54
Man of Evil '48
The Manxman '29
Marvin's Room '96
Matters of the Heart '90
Mayerling '68
Mildred Pierce '45 ▸
Miles to Go '86
Millie '31
Mimi '35
The Miniver Story '50
Miss Julie '50
Missing Brendan '03
Mrs. Silly '85
Mr. Holland's Opus '95 ▸
Mr. Skeffington '44 ▸
Mistress '87
Moon over Harlem '39
A Mormon Maid '17
Mother and Son '31
Murder on Lenox Avenue '41

▸ = rated three bones or higher

My Foolish Heart *'49*
My Girl *'91*
My Life Without Me *'03*
The Nest *'80*
The Night Cry *'26*
Night Life in Reno *'31*
Nomads of the North *'20*
Now, Voyager *'42* ▸
Old Yeller *'57* ▸
One More Kiss *'99*
One True Thing *'98* ▸
Only Angels Have Wings *'39* ▸
An Orphan Boy of Vienna *'37*
The Other Side of the Mountain *'75*
The Other Side of the Mountain, Part 2 *'78*
Our Sons *'91*
Our Time *'74*
Paradise Road *'97*
The Passing of the Third Floor Back *'36*
Pattes Blanches *'49*
Peg o' My Heart *'22*
Penny Serenade *'41* ▸
A Place in the Sun *'51* ▸
The Pride of the Yankees *'42* ▸
The Promise *'79*
Question of Faith *'93*
A Question of Guilt *'78*
Quicksand *'50*
The Racket *'51* ▸
Rage of Angels *'83*
Rain Man *'88* ▸
The Rains Came *'39*
Random Harvest *'42* ▸
Rebecca of Sunnybrook Farm *'17*
Red Kimono *'25*
Remolino de Pasiones *'68*
Rikisha-Man *'58* ▸
The Road to Ruin *'28*
Romola *'25*
Scar of Shame *'27*
Secrets of a Married Man *'84*
Seizure: The Story of Kathy Morris *'80*
Sex *'20*
Shadowlands *'93* ▸
She Goes to War *'29*
A Shining Season *'79* ▸
The Shock *'23*
Shopworn Angel *'38* ▸
Silent Night, Lonely Night *'69*
The Sin of Madelon Claudet *'31* ▸
Since You Went Away *'44* ▸
Six Weeks *'82*
Smilin' Through *'33* ▸
Sommersby *'93*
Sooner or Later *'78*
Sparrows *'26* ▸
Steel Magnolias *'89* ▸
Stella *'89*
Stella Dallas *'37* ▸
Stella Maris *'18* ▸
Stolen Hours *'63*
The Story of Esther Costello *'57*
Strangers: The Story of a Mother and Daughter *'79* ▸
Stromboli *'50*
Struggle *'31*
Suds *'20*
Summer and Smoke *'61*
A Summer Place *'59*
Sunny *'41*
Sunny Skies *'30*
Susan Lenox: Her Fall and Rise *'31*
Sweet November *'68*
Sweet November *'01*
Tango *'36*
Tell Me That You Love Me *'84*
Tender Comrade *'43*
Terms of Endearment *'83* ▸
Test Tube Babies *'48*
That Certain Woman *'37*
They Drive by Night *'40* ▸
Things in Their Season *'74*
This Boy's Life *'93* ▸
Three Secrets *'50*
Thursday's Child *'43*
Tiefland *'44*
A Time for Dancing *'00*
A Time to Live *'85*
To Gillian on Her 37th Birthday *'96*
Tomorrow's Children *'34*
The Tong Man *'19*
Torch Song *'53*
Toute Une Nuit *'82* ▸
Traffic in Souls *'13* ▸
Trapped by the Mormons *'22*
Two Drifters *'05*
Under the Roofs of Paris *'29* ▸
The Underdog *'43*
The Unholy Three *'25* ▸
The Unholy Three *'30* ▸
Untamed Heart *'93*
Uptown New York *'32*
Valentin *'02*
The Visit *'00* ▸
Walk on the Wild Side *'62*
Walpurgis Night *'41* ▸
Waterfront *'39*
Waterloo Bridge *'40* ▸
Waterproof *'99* ▸
Way Down East *'20* ▸
The Weaker Sex *'49*
Welcome Home *'89*
West-Bound Limited *'23*
West of Zanzibar *'28*
When Wolves Cry *'69*
Where East Is East *'29*
Where the Red Fern Grows *'74*
The White Cliffs of Dover *'44* ▸
The White Rose *'23* ▸
Wide Sargasso Sea *'92*
Winter Meeting *'48*
Without a Trace *'83*
A Woman of Affairs *'28*
The World Accuses *'35*
The World Is Full of Married Men *'80*
The World Owes Me a Living *'47*
Written on the Wind *'56* ▸
X, Y & Zee *'72*
The Yarn Princess *'94*
The Yearling *'46* ▸

Technicolor Yawn

Ace Ventura: When Nature Calls *'95*
Anaconda *'96*
BASEketball *'98*
Blood Simple *'85* ▸
Boat Trip *'03*
Car Wash *'76*
The Crying Game *'92* ▸
The Cutting Edge *'92*
Dogfight *'91* ▸
Eating Raoul *'82* ▸
The Exorcist *'73* ▸
Fear and Loathing in Las Vegas *'98*
52 Pick-Up *'86*
Heathers *'89* ▸
Jackass Number Two *'06*
Jaws *'75* ▸
Kingpin *'96*
Larry the Cable Guy: Health Inspector *'06*
Monty Python's The Meaning of Life *'83* ▸
My Giant *'98*
National Lampoon's Animal House *'78* ▸
Osmosis Jones *'01*
Parenthood *'89* ▸
Pinocchio 964 *'92*
Poltergeist 2: The Other Side *'86*
The Sandlot *'93* ▸
Sirens *'94*
Stand by Me *'86* ▸
This Is Spinal Tap *'84* ▸
The Verdict *'82* ▸
The Witches of Eastwick *'87*

Technology—Rampant

see also ***Computers; Killer Appliances; Robots & Androids***

A Nous la Liberte *'31* ▸
The Android Affair *'95*
Armageddon: The Final Challenge *'94*
Assassin *'86*
Attack of the Robots *'66*
Baby Girl Scott *'87*
Back to the Future *'85* ▸
Batman Forever *'95* ▸
Best Defense *'84*
Bicentennial Man *'99*
Billion Dollar Brain *'67*
The Bionic Woman *'75*
Black Cobra 3: The Manila Connection *'90*
The Black Hole *'79*
Black Mask 2: City of Masks *'02*
Blade Runner *'82* ▸
Blades *'89*
Bloodlust *'59*
Brainscan *'94*
Breakout *'98*
Bullet to Beijing *'95*
Chameleon *'98*
Chameleon 2: Death Match *'99*
Chameleon 3: Dark Angel *'00*
Chandu the Magician *'32*
Charly *'68* ▸
Chopping Mall *'86*
Circuitry Man *'90*
Colossus: The Forbin Project *'70* ▸
The Companion *'94*
Computer Beach Party *'88*
Computer Wizard *'77*
Confess *'05*
The Corporation *'96*
Crash and Burn *'90*
The Creation of the Humanoids *'62*
Cyber Bandits *'94*
Cyber-Tracker 2 *'95*
Dean Koontz's Black River *'01*
Dean Koontz's Mr. Murder *'98*
Death Ray 2000 *'81*
Defense Play *'88*
Demon Seed *'77* ▸
Demonlover *'02*
Denise Calls Up *'95*
Detonator 2: Night Watch *'95*
Devour *'05*
Diamonds Are Forever *'71* ▸
Digital Man *'94*
Dr. Goldfoot and the Bikini Machine *'66*
Doctor of Doom *'62*
Doomsdayer *'99*
Downdraft *'96*
Dream House *'98*
Dungeonmaster *'83*
Duplicates *'92*
Electric Dreams *'84*
The Eliminators *'86*
Encrypt *'03*
Enemy of the State *'98*
Eve of Destruction *'90*
Evolver *'94*
Fail-Safe *'64* ▸
Fair Game *'95*
Family Viewing *'87* ▸
Fatal Error *'99*
Feardotcom *'02*
The Fifth Element *'97*
Final Mission *'93*
The Final Programme *'73*
The Fly *'58* ▸
The Fly *'86* ▸
The Fly 2 *'89*
Fugitive Mind *'99*
Future Cop *'76*
Futureworld *'76*
Geheimakte WB1 *'42*
Ghost in the Machine *'93*
Goldeneye *'95* ▸
Hackers *'95*
Hide and Seek *'77*
Hologram Man *'95*
Hostile Intent *'97*
How to Make a Monster *'01*
I, Robot *'04*
Improper Channels *'82*
iMurders *'08*
Interface *'84*
The Invisible Boy *'57*
Johnny Mnemonic *'95*
Johnny 2.0 *'99*
A Joke of Destiny, Lying in Wait Around the Corner Like a Bandit *'84*
Judge Dredd *'95*
A King in New York *'57*
Lawnmower Man 2: Beyond Cyberspace *'95*
The Lift *'85*
Live Free or Die Hard *'07*
Live Wire: Human Timebomb *'95*
Lost in Space *'98*
Lost Legacy: A Girl Called Hatter Fox *'77*
The Matrix *'99* ▸
The Matrix Reloaded *'03*
The Matrix Revolutions *'03* ▸
Maximum Overdrive *'86*
Metropolis *'26* ▸
Microwave Massacre *'83*
Mr. Toad's Wild Ride *'96*
Modern Times *'36* ▸
Mon Oncle *'58* ▸
Moonraker *'79*
The Mosaic Project *'95*
The Munsters' Revenge *'81*
Murder by Phone *'82*
Murder by Television *'35*
Mutant Hunt *'87*
Mutant Species *'95*
Natural City *'03*
The Net *'95*
Net Games *'03*
New Crime City: Los Angeles 2020 *'94*
Night of the Kickfighters *'91*
Nightflyers *'87*
One Deadly Owner *'74*
On_Line *'01*
Out of Order *'84*
Panique *'47* ▸
Perfect Stranger *'07*
The Philadelphia Experiment *'84*
The Pirates of Silicon Valley *'99*
Plughead Rewired: Circuitry Man 2 *'94*
The Power Within *'79*
Project: Eliminator *'91*
Project: Shadowchaser *'92*
Pulse *'06*
Pulse 2: Afterlife *'08*
The Quiet Earth *'85* ▸
R-Point *'04*
Rage *'95*
Ravager *'97*
Redline *'97*
Remote *'93*
Replikator: Cloned to Kill *'94*
Resident Evil *'02*
RoboCop *'87* ▸
RoboCop 2 *'90*
RoboCop 3 *'91*
Robot Holocaust *'87*
Robot Jox *'90*
Rock & Roll Cowboys *'92*
R.O.T.O.R. *'88*
Runaway *'84*
Screamers *'96*
Search and Destroy *'88*
The Seventh Floor *'93*
Shadowzone *'89*
Shaker Run *'85*
Shocker *'89*
Short Circuit *'86*
Short Circuit 2 *'88*
Simone *'02*
Small Soldiers *'98*
Smart House *'00*
Sneakers *'92*
Soldier *'98*
Solo *'96*
Speaking Parts *'89* ▸
Speed 2: Cruise Control *'97*
The Spy Who Loved Me *'77*
Stay Tuned *'92*
Stealth *'05*
Steel and Lace *'90*
Strange New World *'75*
Subliminal Seduction *'96*
Terminal Choice *'85*
Terminal Entry *'87*
Terminal Impact *'95*
The Terminal Man *'74*
The Terminator *'84* ▸
Terminator 2: Judgment Day *'91* ▸
Terminator 3: Rise of the Machines *'03* ▸
Terrorvision *'86*
Things to Come *'36* ▸
The Thirteenth Floor *'99*
Three Blind Mice *'02*
Thrillkill *'84*
Tom Clancy's Netforce *'98*
Touki Bouki *'73*
Tron *'82*
12:01 *'93*
Twisted *'86*
2001: A Space Odyssey *'68* ▸
The Ultimate Imposter *'79*
The Unborn *'91*
Under Siege 2: Dark Territory *'95*
The Vindicator *'85*
Virtual Sexuality *'99*
Virtuosity *'95*
WarGames *'83*
WarGames 2: The Dead Code *'08*
Warning Sign *'85*
Webmaster *'98*
Weird Science *'85*
Westworld *'73* ▸
Wild Palms *'93*
Wired to Kill *'86*
Zardoz *'73*
Zombie Strippers *'08*

Teen Angst

see also ***Coming of Age; Hell High School; Teen Comedy; Teen Drama; Teen Horror; Teen Romance***

Above the Rim *'94*
Abuse *'82*
Across the Tracks *'89*
Address Unknown *'96*
Adoration *'08*
Adventures in Dinosaur City *'92*
The Adventures of Sebastian Cole *'99*
The Adventures of Werner Holt *'65*
Afterschool *'08*
Age Isn't Everything *'91*
Ah, Wilderness! *'35* ▸
Airborne *'93*
Alex *'92*
Alice Upside Down *'07*
All Over Me *'96* ▸
All the Real Girls *'03* ▸
All Things Fair *'95*
Always Will *'06*
American Beauty *'99* ▸
American Graffiti *'73* ▸
American Pie 2 *'01*
An American Rhapsody *'01* ▸
An American Summer *'90*
American Teen *'08*
American Virgin *'98*
Amor Bandido *'79*
Andy Hardy Gets Spring Fever *'39*
Andy Hardy Meets Debutante *'40*
Andy Hardy's Double Life *'42*
Andy Hardy's Private Secretary *'41*
Angel *'84*
Angel Rodriguez *'05*
Angels with Dirty Faces *'38* ▸
Angus *'95*
Annie O *'95*
Anything for Love *'93*
Anywhere But Here *'99*
Apt Pupil *'97*
Around the Fire *'98*
Art for Teachers of Children *'95*
Arthur's Quest *'99*
Autumn Moon *'92*
Baby It's You *'82* ▸
The Baby-Sitters' Club *'95*
The Bachelor and the Bobby-Soxer *'47* ▸
Backstreet Dreams *'90*
Bad Company *'99*
Bad Ronald *'74* ▸
The Banger Sisters *'02*
The Battle of Shaker Heights *'03*
The Bay Boy *'85*
Beach Blanket Bingo *'65* ▸
Beach House *'82*
Beach Party *'63*
The Beat *'88*
Beau Pere *'81* ▸
Beautiful Thing *'95* ▸
Beavis and Butt-Head Do America *'96*
Before and After *'95*
Beijing Bicycle *'01*
Bellyfruit *'99*
Bend It Like Beckham *'02* ▸
The Beniker Gang *'83*
Benny's Video *'92*
Berserker *'87*
The Best Little Girl in the World *'81* ▸
Better Luck Tomorrow *'02* ▸
Beyond Innocence *'87*
The Big Bet *'85*
Big Bully *'95*
Big Fat Liar *'02*
Big Girls Don't Cry... They Get Even *'92*
Big Town *'87*
Bikini Beach *'64*
Bill & Ted's Excellent Adventure *'89*
The Black Balloon *'09*
Black Irish *'07*
Blackboard Jungle *'55* ▸
Bleeding Hearts *'94*
Blue Car *'03* ▸
BMX Bandits *'83*
Body Snatchers *'93*
Bonjour Monsieur Shlomi *'03* ▸
Book of Love *'91*
Born Bad *'97*
Born Innocent *'74*
Born to Be Wild *'95*
Borstal Boy *'00*
Boston Kickout *'95*
A Boy Called Hate *'95*
Boys *'95*
The Boys Club *'96*
Boys Life *'94*
Boy's Reformatory *'39*
Boyz N the Hood *'91* ▸
Brainscan *'94*
Bratz *'07*
Brave New Girl *'04*
The Break *'95*
The Breakfast Club *'85* ▸
Breaking All the Rules *'85*
Breaking Away *'79* ▸
Breaking Free *'95*
The Bridge *'59*
Brotherhood of Justice *'86*
Buck and the Magic Bracelet *'97*
Buffy the Vampire Slayer *'92* ▸
Bully *'01*
The Bumblebee Flies Anyway *'98*
Burglar *'87* ▸
Buster and Billie *'74*
But I'm a Cheerleader *'99*
Buying Time *'89*
By Dawn's Early Light *'00*
Bye, Bye, Birdie *'63* ▸
Cadillac Girls *'93*
Can You Feel Me Dancing? *'85*
Candy *'68*
Can't Buy Me Love *'87*
Can't Hardly Wait *'98*
The Canterville Ghost *'96*
Captain Nuke and the Bomber Boys *'95*
Career Opportunities *'91*
Carrie *'76* ▸
Carrie *'02*
Carried Away *'95*
Catch Me If You Can *'02*
Cave Girl *'85*
The Cement Garden *'93*
The Chalk Garden *'64* ▸
Cherry Falls *'00*
The Chicken Chronicles *'77*
Children of the Corn 2: The Final Sacrifice *'92*
China, My Sorrow *'89*
Choices *'81*
Choose Connor *'07*
The Choppers *'61*
The Chosen *'81* ▸
Christine *'84*
City of Ember *'08*

▸ = rated three bones or higher

► = *rated three bones or higher*

Ruby Jean and Joe '96
The Run of the Country '95 ▶
Running Mates '86 ▶
Rushmore '98 ▶
Sabrina the Teenage Witch '96
Save the Last Dance '01
Saved! '04
Scarred '84
Scary Movie '00
Schizo '04
Scream for Help '86
Screen Test '85
Screwballs '83
Seamless '00
Season of Change '94
Secret Admirer '85
The Secret Life of Girls '99
Secrets of Sweet Sixteen '74
Seizure: The Story of Kathy Morris '80
Senior Trip '81
Serial Killing 101 '04
Set Me Free '99
Seven Minutes in Heaven '86
Seventeen Again '00
The Seventh Coin '92
S.F.W. '94
ShadowZone: The Undead Express '96
Shag: The Movie '89 ▶
Shake, Rattle and Rock '57
Shake, Rattle & Rock! '94
Sharma & Beyond '84
Sharon's Secret '95
She's All That '99
She's Out of Control '89
Shine '95 ▶
Shooting '82
Shout '91
Show Me Love '99
Shriek If You Know What I Did Last Friday the 13th '00
The Silent One '86
Sing '89
Skateboard '77
Skeletons in the Closet '00
Skipped Parts '00
SLC Punk! '99
Sleepers '96
Slumdog Millionaire '08 ▶
Small Soldiers '98
Smart People '08
Smokey Bites the Dust '81
Smugglers' Cove '48 ▶
Snowballing '85
Social Misfits '00
Solarbabies '86
Some Kind of Wonderful '87
Somebody Is Waiting '96
Something Special '86
Sooner or Later '78
The Spell '77
Spetters '80
Spirit Rider '93 ▶
Splendor in the Grass '61 ▶
Spring Fever '81
Squeeze '97
Stand and Deliver '88 ▶
Starchaser: The Legend of Orin '85
State and Main '00 ▶
Stealing Beauty '96
Stella Does Tricks '96
Sticks and Stones '96
Sticky Fingers '88
Still Not Quite Human '92
Stones of Death '88
Straight out of Brooklyn '91
Straight Up '90
Strange Illusion '45
Strawberry Fields '97
Streets '90
The Stripper '63
Suburbia '83
Sugar & Spice '01 ▶
Suicide Club '02
Summer Camp Nightmare '86
Summer Holiday '48
Summer of '42 '71 ▶
The Summer of My German Soldier '78 ▶
Summer School '77
Summer School '87
Sunchaser '96
Sunnyside '79
Swap Meet '79
Sweet Jane '98
Sweet 16 '81
Sweet Sixteen '02 ▶
Swim Team '79
Swimming Pool '03 ▶
Swing Kids '93
A Swingin' Summer '65
Tadpole '02
Tainted Blood '93
Take It to the Limit '00
Talisman '98
Tammy and the T-Rex '94
Tearaway '87
Teen Wolf '85
Teenage '44
Teenage Bad Girl '59
Teenage Bonnie & Klepto Clyde '93
Teenage Caveman '58
Teenage Caveman '01
Teenage Crime Wave '55
Teenage Doll '57
Teenage Mother '67
Teenage Strangler '64
Teenage Wolfpack '57
Teenager '74
Teenagers from Outer Space '59
Telling Lies '06
Telling Lies in America '96
The Tender Age '84
The Tenth Circle '08
Terminal Bliss '91
Tex '82
That Certain Age '38
That Darn Cat '96
That Night '93
That Thing You Do! '96 ▶
That Was Then... This Is Now '85
There Goes My Baby '92
Therese & Isabelle '67
They Made Me a Criminal '39
Thirteen '03 ▶
13 Going on 30 '04
36 Fillete '88 ▶
This Boy's Life '93 ▶
This Special Friendship '67
Thrashin' '86
3:15—The Moment of Truth '86
Three o'Clock High '87
Tiger Heart '96
Time at the Top '99
Time Stands Still '82 ▶
Timeless '96
Times Square '80
To Die For '95 ▶
To Gillian on Her 37th Birthday '96
To Play or to Die '91
Together '02
The Toilers and the Wayfarers '97
Tom Brown's School Days '51 ▶
Too Young to Die '90
Totally F***ed Up '94
Toughlove '85
Toy Soldiers '91
The Tracey Fragments '07
Trading Favors '97
Treasure Island '72
Trojan War '97
Troop Beverly Hills '89
The Trouble with Angels '66
Trust '91
The Truth About Jane '00
Tuck Everlasting '02
12 and Holding '05 ▶
24-7 '97
Twilight '08
Twirl '81
Twist & Shout '84 ▶
Twisted '86
Twisted Love '95
Two Friends '86
Two Hands '98 ▶
Uncle Buck '89 ▶
Under the Boardwalk '89
Under the Domim Tree '95
Unfinished Business '89
United States of Leland '03
The Unsaid '01
Unstrung Heroes '95
Up Against the Wall '91
Uptown Angel '90
Valley Girl '83
The Vals '85
The Van '77
Varsity Blues '98
A Very Brady Sequel '96
Village of the Giants '65
Virgin High '90
The Virgin Suicides '99
Virtual Sexuality '99
Vision Quest '85
The Voyage of the Yes '72
A Walk to Remember '02
Walking Back '26
Wanderers '79 ▶
The War Zone '98
Warriors of Virtue '97
Weird Science '85
Welcome Home, Roxy Carmichael '90
Welcome to 18 '87
Welcome to the Dollhouse '95
West Beirut '98
What a Girl Wants '03
What Goes Up '09
Whatever '98
Whatever It Takes '00
Where Angels Go, Trouble Follows '68
Where the Boys Are '84 '84
Where the Day Takes You '92
Whip It '09 ▶
White Oleander '02
White Wolves 2: Legend of the Wild '94
White Wolves 3: Cry of the White Wolf '98
Wild Iris '01
The Wild Life '84
Wild Ones on Wheels '62
Wild Pony '83
Wild Things 2 '04
Wildflowers '99
William Shakespeare's Romeo and Juliet '96 ▶
Windrunner '94
Winter in Wartime '10
Winter's Bone '10
Wish upon a Star '96
Wish You Were Here '87 ▶
The Wooden Gun '79
The Wounds '98
The Wraith '87
X-Men '00
X2: X-Men United '03 ▶
Xiu Xiu: The Sent Down Girl '97 ▶
The Year My Voice Broke '87 ▶
Yellow '98
You'll Get Over It '02
A Young Connecticut Yankee in King Arthur's Court '95
The Young Girl and the Monsoon '99
The Young Graduates '71
Young Guns '88
Young Hercules '97
Young Love, First Love '79
The Young Poisoner's Handbook '94 ▶
Youngblood '86
Youth Aflame '44
Youth on Parole '37
You've Ruined Me, Eddie '58
Zebrahead '92 ▶
Zero Boys '86
Zoe '01
Zombie Nightmare '86
The Zoo Gang '85

Teen Comedy

see also High School

Agent Cody Banks '03
Agent Cody Banks 2: Destination London '04
Ah, Wilderness! '35 ▶
American Pie '99 ▶
American Pie Presents: The Naked Mile '06
Angus '95
Angus, Thongs and Perfect Snogging '08
Aquamarine '06
The Baby-Sitters' Club '95
Balls Out: Gary the Tennis Coach '09
Bart Got a Room '08
Better Off Dead '85
Big Fat Liar '02
The Biggest Fan '02
Bill & Ted's Bogus Journey '91
Bill & Ted's Excellent Adventure '89
Book of Love '91
Boxboarders! '07
The Brady Bunch Movie '95 ▶
Bring It On '00
Bring It On: Fight to the Finish '09
Calendar Girl '93
Camp '03
Can't Hardly Wait '98
Charlie Bartlett '07 ▶
Clueless '95 ▶
College '08
Confessions of a Teenage Drama Queen '04
Cow Belles '06
The Curiosity of Chance '06
D.E.B.S. '04
Don't Tell Mom the Babysitter's Dead '91
Drillbit Taylor '08
Duck Season '04 ▶
Extreme Movie '08
Fast Times at Ridgemont High '82 ▶
Fat Albert '04
Ferris Bueller's Day Off '86 ▶
Fired Up! '09
First Daughter '04
Foreign Exchange '08
Full of It '07
Getting It '06
The Ghost of Dragstrip Hollow '59
The Girl Next Door '04
Hannah Montana: The Movie '09
Happy Campers '01
Harold '08
Heavyweights '94
Her Best Move '07
Hoot '06
Hot Summer '68
House Party '90 ▶
I Love You, Beth Cooper '09
It's a Boy Girl Thing '06
John Tucker Must Die '06
Jump In! '07
Just One of the Girls '93
Kamikaze Girls '04
Kevin & Perry Go Large '00
Kick-Ass '10
Kids in America '05
Linda Linda Linda '05 ▶
The Lizzie McGuire Movie '03
Love Laughs at Andy Hardy '46
Mean Girls '04 ▶
Minutemen '08
Modern Girls '86
My Father the Hero '93
New Waterford Girl '99
New York Minute '04
Nick & Norah's Infinite Playlist '08 ▶
Not Another Teen Movie '01
One Crazy Night '93
One Crazy Summer '86
One Last Thing '05
Orange County '02
The Perfect Man '05
The Perfect Score '04
Picture This! '08
Ping Pong '02 ▶
Porky's '82
Porky's 2: The Next Day '83
Porky's Revenge '85
Quarterback Princess '85
Raging Hormones '99
Raising Genius '04
The Red Sneakers '01
Remember the Daze '07
Risky Business '83 ▶
Rock 'n' Roll High School '79 ▶
Rock 'n' Roll High School Forever '91
Rock, Rock, Rock '56
Senior Skip Day '08
17 Again '09
Sex Drive '08
She's All That '99
Shredderman Rules '07
Sisterhood of the Traveling Pants '05
Sixteen Candles '84 ▶
Sky High '05 ▶
Sleepover '04
Stick It '06
Sugar & Spice '01 ▶
Superbad '07 ▶
Sydney White '07
These Girls '05
Thumbsucker '05 ▶
Too Cool for Christmas '04
True Confessions of a Hollywood Starlet '08
Unaccompanied Minors '06
Wassup Rockers '06
Wild Child '08
Youth in Revolt '10

Teen Drama

see also Hell High School; High School; Teen Comedy; Teen Horror; Teen Romance

Alex Rider: Operation Stormbreaker '06
All About Lily Chou-Chou '01 ▶
America '09
An American Affair '09
Angel Rodriguez '05
ATL '06
Ben X '07
Bomb the System '05
Brick '06 ▶
The Chumscrubber '05
The Class '08
Crusade: A March through Time '06
Dare '09
The Disappeared '08
800 Bullets '02
Every Second Counts '08
Evil '03 ▶
The Fast and the Furious: Tokyo Drift '06
Fish Tank '09 ▶
Fly with the Hawk '85
The Forbidden Kingdom '08
Freedom Writers '07
Freeway '95
Full Count '06
Gardens of the Night '08
The Good Humor Man '05
Gracie '07
Graduation '07
Hard Candy '06
Hardcore '04
Havoc 2: Normal Adolescent Behavior '07
Heart of America '03
The History Boys '06
Holy Girl '04 ▶
If... '69 ▶
Japan Japan '07
Keith '08
Ladies and Gentlemen, the Fabulous Stains '82
The Last Song '10
Linda Linda Linda '05 ▶
Love Under Pressure '78
Murderous Intent '06 ▶
Never Back Down '08
The Nickel Children '05
On the Outs '05
One Last Thing '05
Our America '02
Palo Alto '07
Paranoid Park '07
Ping Pong '02 ▶
Pretty Persuasion '05
Prom Queen '04
Queen Sized '08
The Quiet '05
Quinceanera '06 ▶
Rebels of the Neon God '92
River's End '05
Rock the Paint '05
Rocket Science '07 ▶
Running with Scissors '06
Ryna '05
Samaritan Girl '04
Say Anything '89 ▶
7 Virgins '05
Silence of the Heart '84 ▶
Sin Nombre '09 ▶
Somersault '04
Stephanie Daley '06
Still Green '07
Take the Lead '06
Teenage Mutant Ninja Turtles 2: The Secret of the Ooze '91
To Save a Life '10
Towelhead '07
True Crime '95
Wah-Wah '05
Wassup Rockers '06
Water Lilies '07
White Squall '96
Wild Boys of the Road '33
The Witness '99

Teen Horror

see also Hell High School; Horror Comedy; Teen Angst

Alien Trespass '09
Automaton Transfusion '06
Blood & Chocolate '07
Boogeyman 3 '08
Boogiepop and Others '00
The Brotherhood 3: The Young Demons '02
Centipede '05
Chaos '05
Cherry Falls '00
Cry_Wolf '05
Cursed '04
Dance of the Dead '08
Dead Silence '98
Decoys '04
Decoys: The Second Seduction '07
Devon's Ghost: Legend of the Bloody Boy '05
Devour '05
Disturbing Behavior '98
The Eye 3 '05
Fear of the Dark '02
Final Destination 3 '06
Flu Birds '08
Freddy vs. Jason '03
Ginger Snaps '01
The Glass House '01
Grizzly Rage '07
Hangman's Curse '03
Happy Hell Night '92
The Haunting of Molly Hartley '08
The Hitcher '07
The Hollow '04
Home Sick '08
Hostel '06
I Know What You Did Last Summer '97 ▶
I Still Know What You Did Last Summer '98
The Initiation of Sarah '06
The Invisible '07
Jennifer's Body '09
Killer Instinct '00
Never Cry Werewolf '08
One Missed Call 3: Final '06
One of Them '03
Predator Island '05
Prom Night '08
Pulse '01
Red Riding Hood '03
School's Out '99
Scream '96 ▶
Serial Killing 101 '04
The Shortcut '09
Spliced '03
Stay Alive '06
Student Bodies '81
Superhero Movie '08
Sweet Insanity '06
Swimfan '02
Teeth '07
Venom '05
When a Stranger Calls '06
When Evil Calls '06
Wild Country '05
Wishmaster 3: Beyond the Gates of Hell '01
Witches of the Caribbean '05

Teen Musicals

Absolute Beginners '86
The American Mall '08
Another Cinderella Story '08
Bandslam '09
Camp Rock '08

▶ = rated three bones or higher

The Cheetah Girls *'03*
The Cheetah Girls 2 *'06*
The Cheetah Girls: One World *'08*
Cry-Baby *'90* ►
Fame *'80* ►
Fame *'09*
Grease *'78* ►
Grease 2 *'82*
Hairspray *'88* ►
High School Musical *'06*
High School Musical 2 *'07*
High School Musical 3: Senior Year *'08*
How She Move *'08*
Josie and the Pussycats *'01*
Rock 'n' Roll High School *'79* ►
Rock 'n' Roll High School Forever *'91*
Rock, Pretty Baby *'56*
Spectacular *'09*
Step Up 2 the Streets *'08*
Untamed Youth *'57*
Were the World Mine *'08*

Teen Romance

see also *Cinderella Stories; High School; Teen Angst; Teen Comedy*

Aaron Loves Angela *'75*
According to Greta *'08*
Aloha Summer *'88*
The American Mall *'08*
Another Cinderella Story *'08*
Aquamarine *'06*
Beautiful Thing *'95* ►
The Biggest Fan *'02*
The Blue Lagoon *'80*
Book of Love *'04*
Boys *'95*
Boys and Girls *'00*
Buster and Billie *'74*
Can't Buy Me Love *'87*
Cherry Crush *'07*
Cold Showers *'05*
crazy/beautiful *'01*
Cynthia *'47*
Down in the Valley *'05*
Dreaming About You *'92*
Drive Me Crazy *'99*
An Education *'09* ►
Ella Enchanted *'04* ►
Endless Love *'81*
First Daughter *'04*
Flirting *'89* ►
Forever *'78*
Full Ride *'02*
Games of Love and Chance *'03*
Get Over It! *'01*
Gregory's Girl *'80* ►
Harry Potter and the Half-Blood Prince *'09*
Here on Earth *'00*
High School Musical *'06*
High School Musical 2 *'07*
High School Musical 3: Senior Year *'08*
I Love You, I Love You Not *'97*
The Incredibly True Adventure of Two Girls in Love *'95*
Jacob Have I Loved *'88*
John Tucker Must Die *'06*
Keith *'08*
Kids in America *'05*
Like a Brother *'05*
Lila Says *'04*
The Man in the Moon *'91* ►
Marking Time *'03*
My Summer of Love *'05*
O *'01* ►
Ode to Billy Joe *'76*
Pizza *'05*
Pope Dreams *'06*
Pretty in Pink *'86*
Punk Love *'06*
Raise Your Voice *'04*
Romeo and Juliet *'68* ►
Ronnie and Julie *'97*
Sixteen Candles *'84* ►
Snow Angels *'07* ►
Some Kind of Wonderful *'87*
Step Up *'06*
Ten Things I Hate about You *'99* ►
This Is the Sea *'96*
Twilight *'08*
The Twilight Saga: Eclipse *'10*
The Twilight Saga: New Moon *'09*
Valley Girl *'83*
The Wackness *'08*
What Matters Most *'01*
Whatever It Takes *'00*
William Shakespeare's Romeo and Juliet *'96* ►
Zebrahead *'92* ►

Televangelists

see also *Look Ma! I'm on TV!; Mass Media; Religion*

Almost an Angel *'90*
Devil in the Flesh *'98*
The Eyes of Tammy Faye *'00*
Fletch Lives *'89*
Forfeit *'07*
Glory! Glory! *'90* ►
Jesus Camp *'06*
License to Kill *'89* ►
Lost *'05*
Mortal Sins *'90*
Repo Man *'83* ►
Repossessed *'90*
Tales from the Crypt Presents Bordello of Blood *'96*

Television

see *Look Ma! I'm on TV!; Mass Media; TV Pilot Movies*

Tennis

Balls Out: Gary the Tennis Coach *'09*
The Break *'95*
Fletch *'85*
Hard, Fast and Beautiful *'51*
Jocks *'87*
Match Point *'05* ►
Nobody's Perfect *'90*
Players *'79*
Racquet *'79*
Spring Fever *'81*
The Squid and the Whale *'05* ►
Wimbledon *'04*
The Witches of Eastwick *'87*

Terminal Confusion

Beavis and Butt-Head Do America *'96*
Big Trouble *'02*
Dumb & Dumber *'94*
8 Heads in a Duffel Bag *'96*
Home Alone 2: Lost in New York *'92*
Home Alone 3 *'97*
Jet Lag *'02*
Knockaround Guys *'01*
More Dogs Than Bones *'00*
The Out-of-Towners *'99*
Stray Bullet *'98*
Terminal Invasion *'02*
Unaccompanied Minors *'06*
Up in the Air *'09* ►
Wait until Dark *'67* ►
What's Up, Doc? *'72* ►

Terminal Illness

see also *Disease of the Week*

Ba'al: The Storm God *'08*
The Barbarian Invasions *'03* ►
Beaches *'88* ►
Because of You *'95*
Behind the Red Door *'02*
Big Bad Love *'02*
Big Fish *'03* ►
Blow Dry *'00*
The Blue Butterfly *'04*
Boom! *'68*
The Bread, My Sweet *'01*
Break *'09*
Bright Star *'09*
The Bucket List *'07*
The Bumblebee Flies Anyway *'98*
The Cake Eaters *'07*
Cherry Blossoms *'08*
Chinese Box *'97*
The Christmas Shoes *'02*
A Christmas Tale *'08* ►
The Claim *'00*
Crank *'06*
Cria Cuervos *'76* ►
Cries and Whispers *'72* ►
The Dark Side of the Sun *'88*
Death Be Not Proud *'75* ►
The Death of Mr. Lazarescu *'05*
Dying Young *'91*
The End of the Affair *'99* ►
Evening *'07*
Fanboys *'09*
48 Angels *'06*
The Fountain *'06*
Funny People *'09*
Gabriel & Me *'01*
Girls' Night *'97*
The Grand Role *'04*
Griffin & Phoenix *'06*
Groom Lake *'02*
The Guitar *'08*
Hard Luck *'01*
Henry Poole Is Here *'08* ►
Here on Earth *'00*
Hong Kong 1941 *'84*
Igby Goes Down *'02* ►
In America *'02* ►
In Love We Trust *'07*
In the Shadows *'98*
Juncture *'07*
Keith *'08*
Klimt *'06*
The Last Hit Man *'08*
Last Holiday *'06*
The Last Request *'06*
Late August, Early September *'98*
Life as a House *'01*
The Line *'08*
Love and Pain and the Whole Damn Thing *'73*
Magnolia *'99* ►
Marion Bridge *'02*
The Medicine Show *'01*
Missing Brendan *'03*
Mrs. Wiggs of the Cabbage Patch *'34*
Mr. Rice's Secret *'00*
Moulin Rouge *'01* ►
My Brother *'06*
My First Mister *'01*
My Life Without Me *'03*
Never Say Die *'39*
Next Time We Love *'36*
The Night Listener *'06*
One Last Thing *'05*
One More Kiss *'99*
One True Thing *'98* ►
One Way Passage *'32*
Parting Shots *'98*
The Perfect Son *'00*
Perfume *'01*
Pieces of April *'03*
Pope Dreams *'06*
Pride and Glory *'08*
Rage *'72*
Rails & Ties *'07*
Red Meat *'98*
Ripley's Game *'02* ►
The Secret of Dr. Kildare *'39*
The Secrets *'07*
The Settlement *'99*
Seven Pounds *'08*
Shadowboxer *'06*
The Singing Fool *'28*
The Sleepy Time Gal *'01*
Soft Fruit *'99*
Speed of Life *'99*
Stealing Beauty *'96*
Stepmom *'98* ►
Sweet November *'68*
Sweet November *'01*
Tennessee *'08*
Terms of Endearment *'83* ►
The Theory of Flight *'98*
Things You Can Tell Just by Looking at Her *'00*
13 Moons *'02*
Time to Leave *'05* ►
Tuesdays with Morrie *'99*
21 Grams *'03* ►
Two Weeks *'06*
The Ultimate Gift *'07*
Under the Lighthouse Dancing *'97*
Vernie *'04*
A Very Serious Person *'06*
Vintage Model *'92*
The Visit *'00* ►
A Walk to Remember *'02*
When Did You Last See Your Father? *'07*
The Wings of the Dove *'97* ►
Wit *'01* ►
With Honors *'94*

Terror in Tall Buildings

see also *Elevators; Mystery & Suspense*

Blackout *'78*
Botched *'07*
Die Hard *'88* ►
Firetrap *'01*
George A. Romero's Land of the Dead *'05* ►
The Glass Trap *'04*
Hard to Die *'90*
Poltergeist 3 *'88*
Project: Shadowchaser *'92*
Skyscraper *'95*
Speed *'94* ►
Terror on the 40th Floor *'74*
Tower of Terror *'42*
The Towering Inferno *'74*
World Trade Center *'06* ►

Terrorism

see also *Crime & Criminals; Foreign Intrigue; Spies & Espionage*

Act of Passion: The Lost Honor of Kathryn Beck *'83*
Act of Piracy *'89*
Act of War *'96*
Active Stealth *'99*
Agent Red *'00*
Air Force One *'97* ►
Airborne *'98*
Airboss *'97*
The Amateur *'82*
American Dreamz *'06*
American Meltdown *'04*
Angel of Fury *'93*
Antibody *'02*
The Applegates *'89*
Arlington Road *'99*
The Art of War 3: Retribution *'08*
The Assassination Run *'84*
The Assignment *'97*
The Baader Meinhof Complex *'08*
Bad Company *'02*
Barcelona *'94* ►
Belfast Assassin *'84*
Black Cobra 2 *'89*
Black Cobra 3: The Manila Connection *'90*
Black Dawn *'05*
Black Sunday *'77*
Black Terrorist *'85*
Blast *'96*
Blast *'04*
Blink of an Eye *'92*
Blood on the Badge *'92*
Bloodfist 6: Ground Zero *'94*
Blown Away *'94*
Body of Lies *'08*
Bomb Squad *'97*
Bombshell *'97*
Buried *'10*
Captain America 2: Death Too Soon *'79*
Captive *'87*
Captive Rage *'88*
The Cassandra Crossing *'76*
Cavite *'05*
Chasing Freedom *'04*
Children of Men *'06* ►
Children of Rage *'75*
C.I.A. 2: Target Alexa *'94*
Circle of Deceit *'94*
Civic Duty *'06*
Codename: Vengeance *'87*
Collateral Damage *'02*
Command Performance *'09*
Commando *'85* ►
Could It Happen Here? *'77*
Counter Measures *'99*
Counterstrike *'03*
Cover-Up *'91*
Covert Assassin *'94*
Crackerjack 2 *'97*
Crash and Burn *'90*
Crash & Byrnes *'99*
Crash Dive *'96*
Critical Mass *'00*
Crossfire *'98*
Cry of the Innocent *'80* ►
The Crying Game *'92* ►
The Dancer Upstairs *'02*
Dark Rider *'91*
Day Night Day Night *'06* ►
DC 9/11: Time of Crisis *'04*
Dead in a Heartbeat *'02*
Dead or Alive *'02*
Deadline *'87*
Deadly Heroes *'96*
Deadly Outbreak *'96*
Death Before Dishonor *'87*
The Death Merchant *'91*
Death Note 3: L, Change the World *'08*
Death of the Incredible Hulk *'90*
Death Ray *'67*
Death Row Girls *'08*
Delta Force *'86*
Delta Force 3: The Killing Game *'91*
Delta Force Commando *'87*
Delta Force Commando 2 *'90*
Demolition High *'95*
Desert Thunder *'99*
The Devil's Own *'96* ►
Dick Barton, Special Agent *'48*
Die Hard *'88* ►
Die Hard 2: Die Harder *'90* ►
Die Hard: With a Vengeance *'95*
Diplomatic Siege *'99*
Dirty Games *'89*
Dr. Otto & the Riddle of the Gloom Beam *'86*
Dog Day Afternoon *'75* ►
The Dogfighters *'95*
Doomsdayer *'01*
Double Team *'97*
D.R.E.A.M. Team *'99*
The Enforcer *'76*
Eraser *'96*
Escape under Pressure *'00*
The Evil That Men Do *'84*
Executive Decision *'96*
Exposed *'83*
Extreme Limits *'01*
Extreme Ops *'02*
Face/Off *'97* ►
Fahrenheit 9/11 *'04* ►
Falling Fire *'97*
Fast Kill *'73*
A Father's Revenge *'88*
Fatwa *'06*
ffolkes *'80*
The Final Cut *'96*
The Final Option *'82*
Final Voyage *'99*
Five Fingers *'06*
Flashpoint Africa *'84*
Fortress of Amerikka *'89*
48 Hours to Live *'60*
The Fourth Angel *'01*
Freedom Strike *'98*
French Quarter Undercover *'85*
From Paris With Love *'10*
Full Disclosure *'00*
Full Fathom Five *'90*
Futuresport *'98*
Galyon *'77*
Germicide *'74*
G.I. Joe: The Rise of Cobra *'09*
The Glass Jungle *'88*
The Glory Boys *'84*
The Great New Wonderful *'06*
Harold & Kumar Escape from Guantanamo Bay *'08*
Heaven *'01*
Held Hostage *'91*
Hell Squad *'85*
Hidden Agenda *'90*
Hologram Man *'95*
Hostage *'87*
Human Bomb *'97*
The Hunt for Eagle One: Crash Point *'06*
In the Name of the Father *'93* ►
Incendiary *'08*
The Insurgents *'06*
Invasion Force *'90*
Invasion U.S.A. *'85*
Invisible Circus *'00*
Iran: Days of Crisis *'91*
Iron Man *'08* ►
Jericho Fever *'93*
Judgment in Berlin *'88*
Juggernaut *'74* ►
July Group *'81*
Jungle Assault *'89*
Kamikaze *'89* *'83* ►
Katherine *'75*
The Kidnapping of the President *'80*
The Kingdom *'07*
Kings and Desperate Men *'83*
Knock Off *'98*
Land of Plenty *'04*
Land of the Blind *'06*
Land of the Free *'98*
L'Annee Sainte *'76*
The Legend of Rita *'99*
Lethal Tender *'96*
The Little Drummer Girl *'84* ►
Live Free or Die Hard *'07*
Live Wire *'92*
The Lost Command *'66*
The Mad Bomber *'72*
Maiden Voyage: Ocean Hijack *'04*
The Man Who Knew Too Little *'97*
Marianne and Juliane *'82* ►
The Marine 2 *'09*
McHale's Navy *'97*
Memorial Day *'98*
Merchants of War *'90*
Michael Collins *'96* ►
Midnight in Saint Petersburg *'97*
Molly Maguires *'70*
Munich *'05* ►
Murder on Flight 502 *'75*
My Brother's War *'97*
Naked Gun 33 1/3: The Final Insult *'94*
Navy SEALS *'90*
Next *'07*
Night of the Assassin *'77*
Nighthawks *'81*
Nightstick *'87*
Ninja Connection *'90*
Ninja the Battalion *'90*
No *'98*
No Contest *'94*
No Dead Heroes *'87*
Odd Man Out *'47* ►
Omega Syndrome *'87*
Once Upon a Time in China II *'92* ►
Open Fire *'94*
Operation Thunderbolt *'77*
Panic in the Streets *'50* ►
Panic on the 5:22 *'74*
Paradise Now *'05* ►
The Passenger *'75* ►
Passenger 57 *'92*
Path to Paradise *'97*
The Patriot *'86*
Patriot Games *'92* ►
Patty Hearst *'88*
The Peacekeeper *'98*
The Peacemaker *'97*
Postal *'07*
Programmed to Kill *'86*
Project: Alien *'89*
Protocols of Zion *'05* ►
Pursuit *'72* ►
Python Wolf *'88*
Rachida *'05* ►
Raid on Entebbe *'77* ►
The Railway Station Man *'92* ►
Rangers *'00*
Rapid Assault *'99*
Rebel *'70*
Red Mercury *'05*
Rendition *'07*
Riot *'96*
The Rock *'96* ►
Rollercoaster *'77*
Rosebud *'75*
Royal Warriors *'86*
The Rug Cop *'06*
Running Delilah *'93*
Running Out of Time *'94*
The Rutanga Tapes *'90*
The Secret Agent *'96*
Secret Agent 00 *'67*
Secret Agent Super Dragon *'66*

► = *rated three bones or higher*

Shakedown '02
The Siege '98
Silk Degrees '94
Skeleton Coast '89
Skull: A Night of Terror '88
Sleeper Cell '05
Sniper 3 '04
Special Bulletin '83 ▶
Stalking Danger '86
Standard Operating Procedure '08 ▶
The State Within '06
The Stone Merchant '06
Submerged '00
Sudden Death '95
The Sum of All Fears '02
Surface to Air '98
Sweepers '99
Swordfish '01
Syriana '05 ▶
The Taking of Flight 847: The Uli Derickson Story '88 ▶
The Taking of Pelham One Two Three '74 ▶
Team America: World Police '04 ▶
Terminal Entry '87
Terminal Rush '96
Termination Man '97
Terror in Beverly Hills '90
Terror in Paradise '90
Terror Squad '87
The Terrorist '98
The Terrorist Next Door '08
The Terrorists '74
Terrorists '88
Thunder Run '86
Thunderball '65
Time of Favor '00
A Town Called Hell '72
Toy Soldiers '91
The Tragedy of a Ridiculous Man '81
Tragedy of Flight 103: The Inside Story '91 ▶
Trained to Kill, U.S.A. '75
Traitor '08
Treasure of the Lost Desert '83
Trident Force '88
Troma's War '88
True Lies '94
Tube '03
Turbulence 2: Fear of Flying '99
Turk 182! '85
21 Hours at Munich '76 ▶
Typhoon '06
Undeclared War '91
Under Siege '92
United 93 '06 ▶
U.S. Navy SEALS: Dead or Alive '02
U.S. SEALs: Dead or Alive '02
Universal Soldier: Regeneration '09
V for Vendetta '06
The Vector File '03
The Vernonia Incident '89
Victory at Entebbe '76
Viper '88
Voyage of Terror: The Achille Lauro Affair '90
Wanted Dead or Alive '86
The War Within '05
The Way of War '08
The Weather Underground '02 ▶
Where in the World Is Osama Bin Laden? '06
The White Lioness '96
Winds of Terror '01
Women on the Verge of a Nervous Breakdown '88 ▶
The World Is Not Enough '99
World Trade Center '06 ▶
Wrong Is Right '82
Year of the Gun '91
You Don't Mess with the Zohan '08
You Only Live Twice '67

Texas

***see also** American South; Dallas; Houston; Westerns*

The Alamo '60 ▶
The Alamo '04
Alamo Bay '85
All the Pretty Horses '00
American Violet '09
The Astronaut Farmer '07
Blood Simple '85 ▶
Boom Town '40
Cattle Town '52
Christmas Child '03
The Comebacks '07
Dancer, Texas—Pop. 81 '98 ▶
Days of Heaven '78 ▶
Dazed and Confused '93 ▶
The Deadbeat Club '04
Dr. T & the Women '00 ▶
Drop Dead Sexy '05
Duel in the Sun '46 ▶
Exit Speed '08
The First Texan '56
$5 a Day '08
Friday Night Lights '04 ▶
Giant '56 ▶
Glory Road '06
The Great Debaters '07 ▶
Happy, Texas '99 ▶
Hope Floats '98
The Hot Spot '90
I'll Be Seeing You '44
It's a Big Country '51
JFK '91 ▶
The Keeper '09
Kill the Umpire '50
The Killer Inside Me '10
The King '05
Larry McMurtry's Streets of Laredo '95 ▶
The Last Picture Show '71 ▶
The Life of David Gale '03
Little Boy Blue '97
Lonesome Dove '89 ▶
Man From Galveston '63
Man of the House '05
Nadine '87
No Country for Old Men '07 ▶
Paradise, Texas '05
Paris, Texas '83 ▶
A Perfect World '93
Places in the Heart '84 ▶
Planet Terror '07
The Positively True Adventures of the Alleged Texas Cheerleader-Murdering Mom '93 ▶
Raggedy Man '81 ▶
Retribution Road '07
The Return '06
Return to Lonesome Dove '93
Rio Lobo '70
River's End '05
The Road to Galveston '96 ▶
The Searchers '56 ▶
75 Degrees '00
Sons of Katie Elder '65 ▶
Soul's Midnight '06
Spring Breakdown '08
The Stars Fell on Henrietta '94
Stop-Loss '08 ▶
The Sugarland Express '74 ▶
Tarnation '03
Terror in a Texas Town '58
There Will Be Blood '07 ▶
39 Pounds of Love '05
The Three Burials of Melquiades Estrada '05 ▶
Three Texas Steers '39
Thunder Over Texas '34
Tin Cup '96 ▶
The Trip to Bountiful '85 ▶
True Stories '86 ▶
Varsity Blues '98
Vietnam, Texas '90
The Wendell Baker Story '05
What Matters Most '01
Whip It '09 ▶
The Wild Man of the Navidad '08

Thanksgiving

***see also** Holidays*

American Son '08
Avalon '90 ▶
Breathing Room '96
A Day for Thanks on Walton's Mountain '82
Familiar Strangers '08
Hannah and Her Sisters '86 ▶
Home for the Holidays '95
The House of Yes '97
The Ice Storm '97 ▶
Mrs. Wiggs of the Cabbage Patch '34
The Myth of Fingerprints '97
National Lampoon's Holiday Reunion '03
An Old-Fashioned Thanksgiving '08
Palo Alto '07
Peter and Vandy '09
Pieces of April '03
Planes, Trains & Automobiles '87
Squanto: A Warrior's Tale '94 ▶
Tadpole '02
A Time to Remember '03
The Vicious Kind '09
The War at Home '96
What's Cooking? '00 ▶
Who Made the Potatoe Salad? '05

There Goes the Neighborhood

***see also** Apartments & Apartment Buildings; Real Estate; Strained Suburbia; Yuppie Nightmares*

American Beauty '99 ▶
The Applegates '89
Arlington Road '99
The 'Burbs '89
Civic Duty '06
The Damned '06
Despicable Me '10
Disturbia '07
Fright Night '85
Jack the Bear '93
The Joneses '10
Lakeview Terrace '08 ▶
Neighbors '81
Never Cry Werewolf '08
Rear Window '54 ▶
Rear Window '98
Revenge of the Stepford Wives '80
Rosemary's Baby '68 ▶
Serial Mom '94 ▶
Sliver '93
Sorum '01
The Stepford Wives '75 ▶
The Stepford Wives '04
The Town That Banned Christmas '06
The Whole Nine Yards '00

The 3rd Degree

Antibodies '05
Being at Home with Claude '92
The Box '07
Brainwashed '60
Chronicle of an Escape '06
Cover '08
Deceiver '97
East Palace, West Palace '96
Extraordinary Rendition '07
Guantanamero '07
The Informant '97 ▶
The Interview '98 ▶
Jadup and Boel '81
Murderous Intent '06 ▶
A Pure Formality '94
Roman de Gare '07
Seduced: Pretty When You Cry '01
Standard Operating Procedure '08 ▶
Surveillance '08
Taxi to the Dark Side '07 ▶
Transsiberian '08 ▶
Under Suspicion '00

This Is My Life

***see also** This Is Your Life*

The Ann Jillian Story '88
The Flying Irishman '39
The Greatest '77
A Guide to Recognizing Your Saints '06
The Island on Bird Street '97
The Jackie Robinson Story '50 ▶
Jo Jo Dancer, Your Life Is Calling '86
The Kid Stays in the Picture '02 ▶
Livin' for Love: The Natalie Cole Story '00
Of Time and the City '08
Persepolis '07 ▶
Private Parts '96
Richard Petty Story '72
Running with Scissors '06
Searching For Wooden Watermelons '01
Sophia Loren: Her Own Story '80
To Hell and Back '55

This Is Your Life

***see also** Biopics: Artists; Biopics: Cops & Robbers; Biopics: Military; Biopics: Musicians; Biopics: Politics; Biopics: Religious; Biopics: Royalty; Biopics: Royalty; Biopics: Science/ Medical; Biopics: Showbiz; Biopics: Sports; Biopics: Writers; Camelot (New); Nashville Narratives*

Amarcord '74 ▶
Amelia '09
American Graffiti '73 ▶
American Splendor '03 ▶
Anita, Dances of Vice '87
Anne Frank: The Whole Story '01 ▶
Annie Oakley '35 ▶
Antony and Cleopatra '73
Au Revoir les Enfants '87 ▶
The Autobiography of Miss Jane Pittman '74 ▶
Barnum '86
Beau Brummell: This Charming Man '06
Beaumarchais the Scoundrel '96
Bernard and Doris '08 ▶
The Best Intentions '92 ▶
Blades of Courage '88
Blossoms in the Dust '41
Blow '01
Born Again '78
Born on the Fourth of July '89 ▶
Borstal Boy '00
Cabeza de Vaca '90 ▶
Caddie '76
Calamity Jane '82
Canada's Sweetheart: The Saga of Hal C. Banks '85
Caro Diario '93 ▶
Casanova '87
Chain Lightning '50
Chanel Solitaire '81
A Chef in Love '96
Child Star: The Shirley Temple Story '01
Christopher Columbus '49
Christopher Columbus: The Discovery '92
Coco Chanel '08
The Color of Pomegranates '69 ▶
Conrack '74 ▶
The Courageous Heart of Irena Sendler '09 ▶
Cowboy '58 ▶
Crazy Horse '96 ▶
Crime Lords '91
Damien: The Leper Priest '80
Dance with a Stranger '85 ▶
Daniel Boone '34
Dawn! '83
Destiny '97
Diary of a Rebel '68
The Diary of Anne Frank '59 ▶
The Disappearance of Aimee '76 ▶
Double Exposure: The Story of Margaret Bourke-White '89
Dracula: The Dark Prince '01
Dreamchild '85 ▶
Edie in Ciao! Manhattan '72
Edison the Man '40
The Education of Sonny Carson '74
8 Seconds '94
Eleni '85
Europa, Europa '91 ▶
Evel Knievel '72
Evita '96
Fanny and Alexander '83 ▶
Fidel '02 ▶
For Us, the Living '88 ▶
Ford: The Man & the Machine '87
The Fountainhead '49 ▶
1492: Conquest of Paradise '92
Francesco '93
Gia '98
Gifted Hands: The Ben Carson Story '09
The Gorgeous Hussy '36
Gorillas in the Mist '88 ▶
The Great Impostor '61
The Great Wallendas '78
The Greatest Story Ever Told '65
The Greek Tycoon '78
Grey Owl '99
Hamsun '96
Hank Aaron: Chasing the Dream '95 ▶
The Happy Hooker Goes Hollywood '80
Having Our Say: The Delany Sisters' First 100 Years '99
Heaven and Earth '93
Hoffa '92 ▶
Home Sweet Home '14
Hoodoo Ann '16
Houdini '99
Hugh Hefner: Once Upon a Time '92 ▶
The Hunter '80
I, the Worst of All '90
I'll Cry Tomorrow '55 ▶
In Love and War '91
In Love and War '96
The Inn of the Sixth Happiness '58 ▶
The Iron Mistress '52
Jacqueline Bouvier Kennedy '81
The Jayne Mansfield Story '80
Jeanne la Pucelle '94
Jesse James Under the Black Flag '21
Jesus '79
Jesus '00
Jesus Christ, Superstar '73 ▶
The Jew '96
Joni '79
Judith of Bethulia '14 ▶
Kennedy '83
King '78 ▶
The King of Kings '61 ▶
La Signora di Tutti '34 ▶
Lakota Woman: Siege at Wounded Knee '94
The Last of Mrs. Lincoln '76
The Late Shift '96
The Learning Tree '69
Lepke '75
The Life and Times of Hank Greenberg '99 ▶
The Life of Emile Zola '37 ▶
The Light in the Jungle '91
The Lost Child '00
Love Affair: The Eleanor & Lou Gehrig Story '77 ▶
Madman '79
Malcolm X '92 ▶
Malcolm X: Make It Plain '95 ▶
A Man Called Peter '55 ▶
Man on Wire '08
Marco '73
Marie '85 ▶
Marjoe '72
Martin Luther '53
Mary, Mother of Jesus '99
Mary White '77
Mesmer '94
Mr. Rock 'n' Roll: The Alan Freed Story '99
Molokai: The Story of Father Damien '99
Monsieur Vincent '47 ▶
Mother Teresa: In the Name of God's Poor '97
Murderers Among Us: The Simon Wiesenthal Story '89 ▶
Murrow '86
My Father's Glory '91 ▶
Nadia '84
The Naked Civil Servant '75 ▶
Nostradamus '93
October Sky '99 ▶
Onassis '88
One Man's Way '63
Padre Padrone '77 ▶
Pancho Barnes '88
Pancho Villa '72
Patty Hearst '88
The People vs. Larry Flynt '96 ▶
Perfumed Nightmare '89 ▶
Personal Services '87
Peter and Paul '81
The Pirates of Silicon Valley '99
Poor Little Rich Girl: The Barbara Hutton Story '87
Pope John Paul II '84
Portrait of a Rebel: Margaret Sanger '82
Power and Beauty '02
Prick Up Your Ears '87 ▶
Priest of Love '81
Private Parts '96
P.T. Barnum '99
Queen '93 ▶
The Queen of Mean '90
Queenie '87
Rainbow '78
Rasputin '85 ▶
Rasputin: Dark Servant of Destiny '96 ▶
Rasputin the Mad Monk '66
Rated X '00
The Raven '15
Reilly: Ace of Spies '87 ▶
Return to Earth '76
Rhodes '36
Rhodes '97
Riel '79
Ring of Bright Water '69 ▶
Rodeo Girl '80
Romero '89
Rosa Luxemburg '86
The Rosa Parks Story '02
Rowing with the Wind '88
Ruby '92
Rush '91 ▶
Sade '00
Samaritan: The Mitch Snyder Story '86 ▶
A Scandal in Paris '46
Schindler's List '93 ▶
A Sense of Freedom '78 ▶
Seven Years in Tibet '97
The Sexual Life of the Belgians '94
Shadow on the Sun '88
Silent Victory: The Kitty O'Neil Story '79 ▶
Sister Kenny '46 ▶
Soldier in Love '67
Spirit of St. Louis '57 ▶
Squizzy Taylor '84
Stars and Stripes Forever '52 ▶
Steal This Movie! '00
The Story of Adele H. '75 ▶
The Stratton Story '49 ▶
Striker's Mountain '87
Sunday's Children '94 ▶
Sylvia '86
Teamster Boss: The Jackie Presser Story '92 ▶
The Ten Commandments '56 ▶
The Testament of Orpheus '59 ▶
Testament of Youth '79
That Hamilton Woman '41 ▶
This Boy's Life '93 ▶
Three Came Home '50 ▶
To Kill a Priest '89
To Race the Wind '80
To Walk with Lions '99
Tom Horn '80
24 Hour Party People '01
An Unreasonable Man '06 ▶
Veronika Voss '82 ▶
Victoria & Albert '01

▶ = rated three bones or higher

The Virginia Hill Story *'76*
Viva Villa! *'34* ▸
Wagner: The Movie *'85*
Wait until Spring, Bandini *'90*
Waiting for the Moon *'87*
Walk the Proud Land *'56*
Wild America *'97* ▸
Wild Hearts Can't Be Broken *'91* ▸
Winchell *'98*
The Winds of Kitty Hawk *'78*
Wings of Eagles *'57*
Wittgenstein *'93*
A Woman Called Moses *'78*
A Woman Named Jackie *'91*
Young Bill Hickok *'40*
The Young Bruce Lee *'80*
Young Buffalo Bill *'40*
Young Winston *'72* ▸

3-D Flicks

Alice in Wonderland *'10*
Amityville 3: The Demon *'83*
Andy Warhol's Frankenstein *'74*
Avatar *'09* ▸
Battle for Terra *'09* ▸
The Bellboy and the Playgirls *'62*
Cat Women of the Moon *'53*
Cats & Dogs: The Revenge of Kitty Galore *'10*
A Christmas Carol *'09*
Cloudy with a Chance of Meatballs *'09*
Coraline *'09* ▸
Creature from the Black Lagoon *'54* ▸
The Creature Walks among Us *'56*
Devil's Canyon *'53*
Dogs of Hell *'83*
Dynasty *'77*
The Final Destination *'09*
Flesh and Blood Show *'73*
Fly Me to the Moon *'08*
The French Line *'54*
Friday the 13th, Part 3 *'82*
G-Force *'09*
Gun Fury *'53*
House of Wax *'53* ▸
Ice Age: Dawn of the Dinosaurs *'09*
It Came from Outer Space *'53* ▸
Jaws 3 *'83*
Jonas Brothers: The 3D Concert Experience *'09*
Kaena: The Prophecy *'03*
Kiss Me Kate *'53* ▸
The Man Who Wasn't There *'83*
The Mask *'61*
Miss Sadie Thompson *'53* ▸
Monsters vs. Aliens *'09*
My Bloody Valentine 3D *'09*
Paradisio *'61*
Parasite *'82*
Piranha 3D *'10*
Revenge of the Creature *'55*
Robot Monster *'53*
Shrek Forever After *'10*
Spacehunter: Adventures in the Forbidden Zone *'83*
Spy Kids 3-D: Game Over *'03*
Starchaser: The Legend of Orin *'85*
Step Up 3D *'10*
The Stranger Wore a Gun *'53*
Toy Story 3 *'10*
Up *'09* ▸

Thumbs Up

The Adventures of Felix *'99*
Alligator Eyes *'90*
Black Day Blue Night *'95*
Blood Simple *'85* ▸
Bonneville *'06*
Cold Around the Heart *'97*
Creepshow 2 *'87*
Diary of a Teenage Hitchhiker *'82*
Doing Time for Patsy Cline *'97*
The Dream Catcher *'99*
The Drifter *'88*
Easy Rider *'69* ▸
Even Cowgirls Get the Blues *'94*
Fear and Loathing in Las Vegas *'98*
Finding Graceland *'98*
The Forsaken *'01*
The Hitcher *'86*
The Hitcher *'07*
The Hitcher 2: I've Been Waiting *'03*
Hitchhikers *'72*
The Hitchhiker's Guide to the Galaxy *'81* ▸
The Hitchhiker's Guide to the Galaxy *'05* ▸
I Love You, Alice B. Toklas! *'68*
Interstate *'07*
Invitation au Voyage *'82*
Jerome *'98* ▸
Josh and S.A.M. *'93*
Kaaterskill Falls *'01*
Kalifornia *'93*
Larger Than Life *'96*
Lost Junction *'03*
Melvin and Howard *'80* ▸
Moving McAllister *'07*
My Own Private Idaho *'91* ▸
Pee-wee's Big Adventure *'85* ▸
A Perfect Getaway *'09*
Personal Velocity: Three Portraits *'02* ▸
Pink Flamingos *'72*
Riding the Bullet *'04*
Road Games *'81*
Ruby Jean and Joe *'96*
Save the Tiger *'73* ▸
Score *'95*
The Sure Thing *'85* ▸
The Texas Chainsaw Massacre *'74*
Thelma & Louise *'91* ▸
There's Something about Mary *'98* ▸
Track 29 *'88*
Transamerica *'05* ▸
Vagabond *'85* ▸
Vanishing Point *'71*
Western *'96*
World Traveler *'01*
The Yellow Handkerchief *'08* ▸

Tibet

The Cup *'99*
Himalaya *'99* ▸
Kundun *'97* ▸
Mountain Patrol: Kekexili *'04*
Seven Years in Tibet *'97*

Tijuana

***see also** Mexico*
Kitten with a Whip *'64*
The Long Goodbye *'73* ▸
Losin' It *'82*

Time Travel

***see also** Rescue Missions Involving Time Travel*
Adventures in Dinosaur City *'92*
The Alien Agenda: Out of the Darkness *'96*
Amazing Mr. Blunden *'72*
Ancient Relic *'02*
A.P.E.X. *'94*
Army of Darkness *'92* ▸
The Arrival *'90*
Arthur's Quest *'99*
Austin Powers In Goldmember *'02*
Back to the Future *'85* ▸
Back to the Future, Part 2 *'89*
Back to the Future, Part 3 *'90* ▸
Battle for the Planet of the Apes *'73*
Beastmaster 2: Through the Portal of Time *'91*
Being Human *'94*
Beneath the Bermuda Triangle *'98*
Beneath the Planet of the Apes *'70*
Beyond the Time Barrier *'60*
Biggles *'85*
Bill & Ted's Bogus Journey *'91*
Bill & Ted's Excellent Adventure *'89*
Blue Flame *'93*
The Blue Yonder *'86*
Brother Future *'91*
Buck Rogers in the 25th Century *'79*
The Butterfly Effect *'04*
The Butterfly Effect 2 *'06*
The Butterfly Effect 3: Revelation *'09*
Chasing Christmas *'05*
A Connecticut Yankee *'31* ▸
A Connecticut Yankee in King Arthur's Court *'49*
A Connecticut Yankee in King Arthur's Court *'89*
Conquest of the Planet of the Apes *'72*
Crusade: A March through Time *'06*
Day Time Ended *'80*
The Devil's Arithmetic *'99*
Dinosaur Valley Girls *'96*
Doctor Mordrid: Master of the Unknown *'90*
Doctor Who *'96*
The Eliminators *'86*
Escape from the Planet of the Apes *'71* ▸
Escapes *'86*
The Final Countdown *'80* ▸
The Forbidden Kingdom *'08*
Frankenstein Unbound *'90* ▸
Freejack *'92*
Future Zone *'90*
Galaxis *'95*
Godzilla vs. King Ghidora *'91*
Grand Tour: Disaster in Time *'92*
Grizzly Mountain *'97*
Harry Potter and the Prisoner of Azkaban *'04*
Hercules in New York *'70*
Highlander 2: The Quickening *'91*
Highlander: The Final Dimension *'94*
Hocus Pocus *'93*
Hot Tub Time Machine *'10*
Idaho Transfer *'73*
I'll Never Forget You *'51*
In His Father's Shoes *'97*
The Indian in the Cupboard *'95*
The Jacket *'05*
Josh Kirby. . .Time Warrior: Chapter 1, Planet of the Dino-Knights *'95*
Josh Kirby... Time Warrior: Chapter 2, The Human Pets *'95*
Josh Kirby... Time Warrior: Chapter 3, Trapped on Toyworld *'95*
Josh Kirby... Time Warrior: Chapter 4, Eggs from 70 Million B.C. *'95*
Josh Kirby... Time Warrior: Chapter 5, Journey to the Magic Cavern *'96*
Josh Kirby... Time Warrior: Chapter 6, Last Battle for the Universe *'96*
Journey to the Center of Time *'67*
Just Visiting *'01*
A Kid in Aladdin's Palace *'97*
A Knight in Camelot *'98*
The Lake House *'06*
Lords of Magick *'88*
Lost in Austen *'08*
Lost in Space *'98*
The Love Letter *'98*
Mannequin 2: On the Move *'91*
Meet the Robinsons *'07*
Millennium *'89*
Minutemen *'08*
Nautilus *'99*
The Navigator *'88* ▸
Next One *'84*
Night of Dark Shadows *'71* ▸
Past Perfect *'98*
Peggy Sue Got Married *'86*
Phantasm 4: Oblivion *'98*
The Philadelphia Experiment *'84*
Philadelphia Experiment 2 *'93*
Planet of the Apes *'68* ▸
Primer *'04* ▸
Returner *'02*
Roman Scandals *'33*
Running Against Time *'90*
The Seeker: The Dark Is Rising *'07*
Somewhere in Time *'80*
A Sound of Thunder *'05*
Spirit of '76 *'91*
Star Trek *'09* ▸
Star Trek 4: The Voyage Home *'86* ▸
Star Trek: First Contact *'96* ▸
Stargate *'94*
Stargate: Continuum *'08*
The Sticky Fingers of Time *'97*
The Swordsman *'92*
Teenage Mutant Ninja Turtles 3 *'93*
Termination Point *'07*
The Terminator *'84* ▸
Terminator 2: Judgment Day *'91* ▸
Terminator 3: Rise of the Machines *'03* ▸
Test Tube Teens from the Year 2000 *'93*
The Thirteenth Floor *'99*
The Three Stooges Meet Hercules *'61*
Thrill Seekers *'99*
Time After Time *'79* ▸
Time at the Top *'99*
Time Bandits *'81*
Time Chasers *'95*
The Time Guardian *'87*
The Time Machine *'60* ▸
Time Machine *'78*
The Time Machine *'02*
Time Runner *'92*
Time Tracers *'97*
Time Trackers *'88*
The Time Travelers *'64*
The Time Traveler's Wife *'09*
Timecop *'94*
Timecop 2: The Berlin Decision *'03*
Timeline *'03*
Timemaster *'95*
Timerider *'83*
Timestalkers *'87*
The Tomorrow Man *'01*
Total Reality *'97*
Trancers *'84*
Trancers 2: The Return of Jack Deth *'90*
Trancers 3: Deth Lives *'92*
Trancers 4: Jack of Swords *'93*
Trancers 5: Sudden Deth *'94*
12 Monkeys *'95* ▸
12:01 *'93*
Twice upon a Yesterday *'98*
Unidentified Flying Oddball *'79*
The Visitors *'95*
Vlad *'03*
Warlock *'91*
Waxwork 2: Lost in Time *'91*
When Time Expires *'97*
A Witch Without a Broom *'68*
Yor, the Hunter from the Future *'83*
A Young Connecticut Yankee in King Arthur's Court *'95*

Time Warped

Austin Powers: International Man of Mystery *'97* ▸
Austin Powers 2: The Spy Who Shagged Me *'99* ▸
Black Knight *'01*
Blast from the Past *'98*
The Brady Bunch Movie *'95* ▸
Demolition Man *'93*
Disney's The Kid *'00*
Encino Man *'92*
Forever Young *'92*
Genesis II *'73*
Groundhog Day *'93* ▸
Kate & Leopold *'01*
Kickin' It Old Skool *'07*
La Vie en Rose *'07*
Late for Dinner *'91*
Leave It to Beaver *'97*
Paycheck *'03*
Peggy Sue Got Married *'86*
Pleasantville *'98* ▸
Retroactive *'97*
13 Going on 30 *'04*
Timecrimes *'07*
The Two Worlds of Jenny Logan *'79*
A Very Brady Sequel *'96*
Zathura *'05* ▸

Titanic

The Chambermaid on the Titanic *'97*
A Night to Remember *'58* ▸
Raise the Titanic *'80*
S.O.S. Titanic *'79*
Titanic *'53* ▸
Titanic *'96*
Titanic *'97* ▸
The Unsinkable Molly Brown *'64* ▸

To the Moon!

***see also** Space Operas*
The Adventures of Baron Munchausen *'89* ▸
The Adventures of Pluto Nash *'02*
Alien Fury: Countdown to Invasion *'00*
Apollo 13 *'95* ▸
Beyond the Stars *'89*
Cat Women of the Moon *'53*
Countdown *'68*
Dark Side of the Moon *'90*
Despicable Me *'10*
Destination Moon *'50*
Destination Moonbase Alpha *'75*
The Dish *'00* ▸
First Men in the Moon *'64*
Fly Me to the Moon *'08*
From the Earth to the Moon *'58*
From the Earth to the Moon *'98* ▸
In the Shadow of the Moon *'07* ▸
Missile to the Moon *'59*
Moon *'09*
Moon Pilot *'62*
The Mouse on the Moon *'62* ▸
Project Moon Base *'53*
Quatermass 2 *'57* ▸
Radar Men from the Moon *'52*
They Came from Beyond Space *'67*

Tokyo

***see also** Japan*
Akira *'89*
Angel Dust *'96*
Austin Powers In Goldmember *'02*
An Autumn Afternoon *'62* ▸
Babel *'06* ▸
The Bad News Bears Go to Japan *'78*
Big Man Japan *'07*
Black Lizard *'68*
Black Rain *'89*
Boys Love *'06*
Bright Future *'03* ▸
Cafe Lumiere *'05*
Cherry Blossoms *'08*
Dodes 'ka-den *'70* ▸
The Dragon Painter *'19*
Escapade in Japan *'57*
The Fast and the Furious: Tokyo Drift *'06*
First Yank into Tokyo *'45*
Gamera vs. Barugon *'66*
Gappa the Trifibian Monster *'67*
Ghidrah the Three Headed Monster *'65*
Godzilla, King of the Monsters *'56*
Godzilla 2000 *'99* ▸
Godzilla vs. King Ghidora *'91*
Godzilla vs. Megalon *'76*
The Grudge 2 *'06*
H-Man *'59*
House of Bamboo *'55*
Ju-On: The Grudge *'03*
Kabei: Our Mother *'08*
Kill Bill Vol. 1 *'03* ▸
Marebito *'04*
Mega Shark Vs. Giant Octopus *'09*
Mothra *'62* ▸
Nobody Knows *'04*
Okoge *'93*
One Wonderful Sunday *'47*
Otaku No Video *'91* ▸
Proof of the Man *'77*
Pulse *'01*
The Ramen Girl *'08*
Running Brave *'83*
Shutter *'08*
Stopover Tokyo *'57*
Street of Shame *'56* ▸
Suicide Club *'02*
A Taxing Woman's Return *'88* ▸
Thirty Seconds Over Tokyo *'44* ▸
Tokyo! *'09*
Tokyo Decadence *'91*
Tokyo-Ga *'85* ▸
Tokyo Joe *'49*
Tokyo Pop *'88*
Tokyo Sonata *'09* ▸
Tokyo Story *'53* ▸
War of the Gargantuas *'70*
Wasabi *'01*

Torn in Two (or More)

Abbott and Costello Meet Dr. Jekyll and Mr. Hyde *'52*
Ashes of Time *'94* ▸
Batman Forever *'95* ▸
Carbon Copy *'69*
Color of Night *'94*
The Dark Knight *'08* ▸
Dr. Heckyl and Mr. Hype *'80*
Dr. Jekyll and Ms. Hyde *'95*
Dr. Jekyll and Mr. Hyde *'20* ▸
Dr. Jekyll and Mr. Hyde *'32* ▸
Dr. Jekyll and Mr. Hyde *'41* ▸
Dr. Jekyll and Mr. Hyde *'68*
Dr. Jekyll and Mr. Hyde *'73*
Dr. Jekyll and Sister Hyde *'71*
Edge of Sanity *'89*
Exorcist 3: Legion *'90*
Fight Club: ' *'99* ▸
The Five of Me *'81*
Hulk *'03*
I, Monster *'71* ▸
The Incredible Hulk *'08*
Jekyll *'07*
Jekyll and Hyde *'90*
Jekyll & Hyde... Together Again *'82*
The League of Extraordinary Gentlemen *'03*
Luna e L'Altra *'96*
Mary Reilly *'95*
Me, Myself, and Irene *'00* ▸
Mirage *'94*
Multiplicity *'96*
Never Talk to Strangers *'95*
The Nutty Professor *'63* ▸
The Nutty Professor *'96* ▸
Nutty Professor 2: The Klumps *'00*
Passion of Mind *'00*
Primal Fear *'96*
Psycho Beach Party *'00*
Raising Cain *'92*
A Scanner Darkly *'06*
Separate Lives *'94*
Shattered Image *'98*
Spider-Man *'02* ▸
The Strange Case of Dr. Jekyll and Mr. Hyde *'06*
Sybil *'76* ▸
The Three Faces of Eve *'57*
Three Lives and Only One Death *'96*
The Three Lives of Karen *'97*
Tierra *'95*
Voices from a Locked Room *'95*

Toronto

***see also** Canada*
Anvil! The Story of Anvil *'09*
Ararat *'02* ▸
Between Strangers *'02*

▸ = rated three bones or higher

Bon Cop Bad Cop '06
Chloe '09
Exotica '94 ▸
Hollywood North '03
How She Move '08
Jiminy Glick in LaLa Wood '05
Last Night '98 ▸
The Life Before This '99
The Newton Boys '97
Owning Mahowny '03
Paris, France '94
Picture Claire '01
The Republic of Love '03
Rude '96
Siblings '04
Skin Deep '94
Soul Survivor '95
Spenser: A Savage Place '94
Twist '03 ▸

Torrid Love Scenes

***see also** Sex & Sexuality; Sex on the Beach; Sexploitation*

The Adventurers '70
Against All Odds '84
Alien Prey '78
Angel Heart '87
Atlantic City '81 ▸
Basic Instinct '92
The Berlin Affair '85
Betty Blue '86 ▸
The Big Easy '87 ▸
Bitter Moon '92
Black Ice '92
Blue Velvet '86 ▸
Body Double '84 ▸
Body Heat '81 ▸
Body of Evidence '92
Bram Stoker's Dracula '92
Breathless '83
Broken English '96
Bull Durham '88 ▸
Cat Chaser '90
Cat on a Hot Tin Roof '58 ▸
Close My Eyes '91
Color of Night '94
The Cook, the Thief, His Wife & Her Lover '90 ▸
Crimes of Passion '84 ▸
Dark Obsession '90
Deadly Desire '91
The Dolphin '87
Dona Flor and Her Two Husbands '78 ▸
Don't Look Now '73 ▸
Everything Relative '96
The Executioner's Song '82
Exit to Eden '94
The Fabulous Baker Boys '89 ▸
Fatal Attraction '87 ▸
Five Easy Pieces '70 ▸
From Here to Eternity '53 ▸
Green Fire '55
The Harvest '92
Heat of Desire '84
Henry & June '90 ▸
The Hunting '92
In the Realm of the Senses '76 ▸
Jason's Lyric '94
Kiss Me a Killer '91
La Mujer de Mi Hermano '06
Lady Godiva Rides '68
Last Tango in Paris '73 ▸
Law of Desire '86 ▸
The Lawnmower Man '92
Live Flesh '97 ▸
The Lover '92
The Lovers '59 ▸
Lust, Caution '07
Mad Dog and Glory '93 ▸
The Mambo Kings '92 ▸
Men in Love '90
Moon in the Gutter '83
Moonstruck '87 ▸
Night Eyes 2 '91
Night Eyes 3 '93
9 1/2 Weeks '86
1900 '76 ▸
An Officer and a Gentleman '82 ▸
The Pamela Principle '91
The Postman Always Rings Twice '81
Prizzi's Honor '85 ▸
Pyrates '91
Rage of Angels '83
Revenge '90
Risky Business '83 ▸
Sea of Love '89 ▸
Secrets '71
Sexual Response '92
Siesta '87
Skeleton Key 2: 667, the Neighbor of the Beast '08
Sliver '93
Something Wild '86
The Story of O '75
Summer of '04 '06
Summer Palace '06 ▸
Swept Away... '75 ▸
Tattoo '81
Tequila Sunrise '88
Threesome '94
The Unbearable Lightness of Being '88 ▸
White Palace '90
Wide Sargasso Sea '92
Wild at Heart '90 ▸
Wild Orchid '90
Wild Orchid 2: Two Shades of Blue '92
The Woman Next Door '81 ▸
Women & Men: In Love There Are No Rules '91
Women in Love '70 ▸
Year of the Gun '91
Yeti: A Love Story '08
Zandalee '91

Toys

***see also** Killer Toys*

Aussie and Ted's Great Adventure '09
Babes in Toyland '61
Big '88 ▸
Child's Play '88
Child's Play 2 '90
Dance of Death '68
Demonic Toys '90
Dolls '87
Dolly Dearest '92
Home Alone 3 '97
Jingle All the Way '96
Josh Kirby... Time Warrior: Chapter 3, Trapped on Toyworld '95
Life-Size '00
Mr. Magorium's Wonder Emporium '07
9 '09 ▸
Not Quite Human '87
Postal '07
Silent Night, Deadly Night 5: The Toymaker '91
The Toy '82
Toy Story '95 ▸
Toy Story 2 '99 ▸
Toy Story 3 '10
Toys '92
Wired to Kill '86
Zathura '05 ▸

Tragedy

***see also** Drama; Tearjerkers*

After the Deluge '03 ▸
Against the Wind '90
All the King's Men '99
An American Tragedy '31
Angel with the Trumpet '50
Anna Karenina '35 ▸
Baba '73 ▸
Babel '06 ▸
Bangkok Dangerous '00
Battle in Heaven '05
Bitter Sweet '33
Blind Woman's Curse '70
Boutique '04
Brothers '04 ▸
Camille '21
Camille '36 ▸
Catherine Cookson's The Fifteen Streets '90
Celebrity '85
Charly '68 ▸
The Crucified Lovers '54 ▸
Damage '92 ▸
Danielle Steel's Palomino '91
Dark Odyssey '57
Deadman's Curve '78
Death Sentence '07
Deep End '70 ▸
Devdas '55 ▸
Devdas '02 ▸
The Discovery Program '89
Doktor Faustus '82
The Door in the Floor '04 ▸
Dream Lovers '86
Dreaming of Joseph Lees '99
Dying Young '91
East of Eden '54 ▸
East of Eden '80
Effi Briest '74 ▸
El Amor Brujo '86 ▸
El Bruto '52
The Embalmer '03 ▸
End of the Road '70
Enduring Love '04
Enemies, a Love Story '89 ▸
Ernie Kovacs: Between the Laughter '84
Ethan Frome '92
Evangeline '29
Everybody's All American '88
The Fighting Sullivans '42 ▸
First Knight '95
Flowers of Reverie '84
Forbidden Choices '94
Franz '72
The French Lieutenant's Woman '81 ▸
From the Journals of Jean Seberg '95
Gate of Hell '54 ▸
Girl in Black '56
Golden Boy '39 ▸
A Good Day to Die '95
Hamlet '48 ▸
Hamlet '69
Hamlet '96 ▸
Hamlet '01
Harmony Lane '35
Heaven '01
Henry IV '85
Hong Kong 1941 '84
House of Cards '92
House of Sand and Fog '03 ▸
Howard's End '92 ▸
The Hunchback of Notre Dame '57
I Dreamed of Africa '00
I Walk the Line '70
Il Grido '57
In Memoriam '76
In the Bedroom '01 ▸
Into the Wild '07 ▸
Intrigue and Love '59
Jalsaghar '58
Jude '96 ▸
Jude the Obscure '71
Jules and Jim '62 ▸
Julius Caesar '53 ▸
Julius Caesar '70
King Lear '71 ▸
King Lear '87
King Lear '98 ▸
La Roue '23 ▸
Landscape After Battle '70
Law of Desire '86 ▸
Leo Tolstoy's Anna Karenina '96
The Life Before Her Eyes '07
Lime Salted Love '06
Love Is a Many-Splendored Thing '55
Love Story '70 ▸
Lovespell '79
Lush Life '94 ▸
Macbeth '48 ▸
Macbeth '70 ▸
Macbeth '71 ▸
Macbeth '88
Madame Bovary '49 ▸
Madame Bovary '91 ▸
Madame Butterfly '95
A Map of the World '99
Margaret's Museum '95 ▸
Maria Candelaria '46
Marilyn & Bobby: Her Final Affair '94
Martha and I '91 ▸
Mary of Scotland '36 ▸
The Merchant of Venice '73 ▸
A Mighty Heart '07 ▸
Mother Night '96 ▸
The Mummy '59 ▸
Mystic River '03 ▸
The Nest '80
Night Ride Home '99
9 Souls '03
Nothing Personal '95 ▸
The Notorious Lady '27
O '01 ▸
Oedipus Rex '67 ▸
The Old Curiosity Shop '07
Onegin '99
Othello '22
Othello '52 ▸
Othello '65 ▸
Othello '95 ▸
Our Time '74
Pennies from Heaven '81 ▸
The Perfect Storm '00
Personal Effects '09
Phaedra '61
Piece of Cake '88
A Place in the Sun '51 ▸
The Prestige '06 ▸
Princess Yang Kwei Fei '55 ▸
Queen Bee '55
Ran '85 ▸
The Red Spectacles '87
The Red Violin '98
Reign Over Me '07
Reservation Road '07
The Return of the Native '94
Romeo and Juliet '36 ▸
Romeo and Juliet '54
Romeo and Juliet '68 ▸
Savior '98 ▸
The Scarlet Tunic '97
The Secret Agent '96
Selena '96
Shadowlands '93 ▸
Shadows of Forgotten Ancestors '64 ▸
Shattered '21 ▸
The Shooting Party '77
Silent Tongue '92
16 Years of Alcohol '03
Solomon and Gaenor '98
The Son's Room '00 ▸
South of Pico '07
Stag '97
Stella '55
Stephanie Daley '06
The Stoning of Soraya M. '08
Sure Fire '90
The Sweet Hereafter '96 ▸
Swept from the Sea '97
Tess '79 ▸
Tess of the D'Urbervilles '98
Tess of the D'Urbervilles '08
Three Comrades '38 ▸
Throne of Blood '57 ▸
Tilai '90
Titanic '53 ▸
Tragedy of Flight 103: The Inside Story '91 ▸
Trois Couleurs: Bleu '93 ▸
Trojan Women '71
Turkish Delight '73
The Unknown Soldier '98
Variety '25 ▸
A Very Private Affair '62
The Virgin Spring '59 ▸
Voyager '91 ▸
The Walls of Malapaga '49
The War Zone '98
The Wedding Gift '93 ▸
Where Angels Fear to Tread '91 ▸
The White Cliffs of Dover '44 ▸
White Mile '94
The White Sister '23 ▸
William Shakespeare's Romeo and Juliet '96 ▸
A Woman at Her Window '77
The Woman Next Door '81 ▸
The Wooden Man's Bride '94
The World According to Garp '82 ▸
Wuthering Heights '70
Wuthering Heights '98
Wuthering Heights '09

Trains

***see also** Heists: Trains; Subways*

Across the Bridge '57
Agatha Christie's Murder is Easy '82
Alberto Express '92
Around the World in 80 Days '04
Atomic Train '99
Avalanche Express '79
Back to the Future, Part 3 '90 ▸
Before Sunrise '94
Berlin Express '48 ▸
Blood and Steel '25
Bombay Mail '34
Boxcar Bertha '72
The Brain '69
Breakheart Pass '76
Broken Arrow '95
Bullet to Beijing '95
Cafe Express '83
Cafe Lumiere '05
California Straight Ahead! '37
Carson City '52
The Cassandra Crossing '76
Chattanooga Choo Choo '84
Closely Watched Trains '66 ▸
Color of a Brisk and Leaping Day '95
Courage Under Fire '96 ▸
Crackerjack 2 '97
Dakota '45
Danger Lights '30
Daniel Takes a Train '83
The Darjeeling Limited '07 ▸
Death Train '79
The Denver & Rio Grande '51
Derailed '02
Detonator '93
The Dirty Dozen: The Fatal Mission '88
Emperor of the North Pole '73 ▸
End of the Line '88
Eurotrip '04
Express to Terror '79
Finders Keepers '84
Flame Over India '60 ▸
The Flying Scotsman '29
Free Money '99
From Russia with Love '63 ▸
The Fugitive '93 ▸
Gambling Ship '33
The General '26 ▸
The Ghost and the Darkness '96
The Ghost Train '41
The Girl on the Train '09
The Glory Trail '36
Go Kill and Come Back '68
Grand Central Murder '42
Great K & A Train Robbery '26
The Great Locomotive Chase '56
The Great Train Robbery '79 ▸
The Greatest Show on Earth '52 ▸
The Grey Fox '83 ▸
Hachiko: A Dog's Tale '09
The Harvey Girls '46 ▸
Horror Express '72
Hot Lead & Cold Feet '78
The Illusion Travels by Streetcar '53 ▸
Indiscretion of an American Wife '54
The Inglorious Bastards '78
Inner Sanctum '48
Interrupted Journey '49
The Iron Horse '24 ▸
It's a Big Country '51
Jesse James at Bay '41
The Journey of Natty Gann '85 ▸
La Bete Humaine '38 ▸
La Roue '23 ▸
The Lady Eve '41 ▸
Lady on a Train '45 ▸
The Lady Vanishes '38 ▸
The Lady Vanishes '79
The Legend of Zorro '05
The Major and the Minor '42 ▸
Malcolm '86
Man Who Loved Cat Dancing '73
Man Without a Star '55 ▸
Midnight Limited '40
The Millionaire's Express '86
Mission: Impossible '96 ▸
Mrs. Winterbourne '96
Mouvements du Desir '94
Murder on the Midnight Express '74
Murder on the Orient Express '74 ▸
My House in Umbria '03 ▸
My Twentieth Century '90 ▸
Mystery Mountain '34
Narrow Margin '90
The Navigators '01
The Newton Boys '97
Night Passage '57
Night Train '09
Night Train Murders '75
Night Train to Munich '40 ▸
Night Train to Terror '84
Night Train to Venice '93
No. 17 '32 ▸
The Odyssey of the Pacific '82
Oh, Mr. Porter '37
Once Upon a Time in the West '68 ▸
Other Men's Women '31
The Out-of-Towners '99
Panic on the 5:22 '74
Paris Express '53
The Peacemaker '97
Phantom Express '32
Plunder Road '57
The Polar Express '04
Prison Train '38
Railrodder '65 ▸
Rails & Ties '07
Red Lights '04 ▸
Red Signals '27
The Return of Casey Jones '34
Return to Cranford '09
Return to Waterloo '85
Rhythm on the Range '36
The Road Home '95
The Road to Yesterday '25
Robbery '67
Romance on the Orient Express '89
Runaway Train '85 ▸
Running Scared '86
Saratoga Trunk '45
Shanghai Express '32 ▸
The Silver Streak '34
Silver Streak '76 ▸
Sleepers West '41
The Sleeping Car '90
Sleeping Car to Trieste '45
Some Like It Hot '59 ▸
Spy Train '43
Starman '84 ▸
The Station Agent '03 ▸
Station Jim '01
Strangers on a Train '51 ▸
Subway '85
Switchback '97
A Tale of Winter '92
Terror Train '80
Thomas and the Magic Railroad '00
Those Who Love Me Can Take the Train '98
Three for Bedroom C '52
3:10 to Yuma '57 ▸
Throw Momma from the Train '87 ▸
Thunder Over Texas '34
Ticket to Tomahawk '50
Torture Train '75
Tough Guys '86
Tracks '76
Trading Places '83
The Trail of the Lonesome Pine '36 ▸
The Train '65 ▸
The Train Killer '83
Train of Life '98
Train Robbers '73
Train to Tombstone '50
Transsiberian '08 ▸
The Truce '96 ▸
Tube '03
Two Weeks to Live '43
Unbreakable '00
Under Siege 2: Dark Territory '95
Union Depot '32
Union Pacific '39 ▸
Von Ryan's Express '65 ▸
Warm Nights on a Slow-Moving Train '87

▸ = rated three bones or higher

Which Way Home '09
While You Were Sleeping '95 ▸
Without Reservations '46
Zentropa '92
Zhou Yu's Train '02

Transvestites & Transsexuals

see Gender Bending

Trapped with a Killer!

see also Psychotics/ Sociopaths

Adrift '93
Air Force One '97 ▸
Alien Terminator '95
Blackout '07
Blind Witness '89
Blink '93
Blood at Sundown '88
Blood Bride '80
The Butcher '07
Clue '85
Con Air '97 ▸
Copycat '95
Dead Calm '89 ▸
Deadbolt '92
Extremities '86
Eye of the Needle '81
Eyes of the Beholder '92
Fatal Attraction '87 ▸
Fever '91
Final Justice '94
Headless Body in Topless Bar '96
Hider in the House '90
High Tension '03
The Hills Have Eyes '06
Kalifornia '93
The Killing Room '09
Kiss the Girls '97
Last Hour '08
Lifepod '93
Living Hell: A Japanese Chainsaw Massacre '00
The Maddening '95
Malevolence '04
Manhunter '86 ▸
Mindhunters '05
Misery '90 ▸
Mute Witness '95
Narrow Margin '90
No Way Back '90
Pacific Heights '90 ▸
The Penthouse '92
Perfect Hideout '08
Rest Stop '06
Saw '04
See No Evil '06
Serial Slayer '03
The Shining '80
The Silence of the Lambs '91 ▸
Slaughter of the Innocents '93
Ten Little Indians '75
Ten Little Indians '89
The Terror '63
Terror Train '80
The Texas Chainsaw Massacre: The Beginning '06
Through the Eyes of a Killer '92
The Tie That Binds '95
Tracks of a Killer '95
Turbulence '96
Undertow '95
Unveiled '94
Virus '98
Voyage '93
Wait until Dark '67 ▸
What's the Matter with Helen? '71
When a Stranger Calls '79
When a Stranger Calls '06
When a Stranger Calls Back '93
Whiteout '09

Treasure Hunt

Abbott and Costello Meet the Mummy '55
Adventure of the Action Hunters '87
The Adventurers '51
After the Storm '01
All the Brothers Were Valiant '53
Arthur and the Invisibles '06
Beethoven's 5th '03
Big Mouth '67
Blue Jeans and Dynamite '76
Cabo Blanco '81
Call of the Wild '93
Captain Calamity '36
City Slickers 2: The Legend of Curly's Gold '94
Coast of Skeletons '63
Comin' Round the Mountain '51
Curse of the Crystal Eye '93
Cutthroat Island '95
Dead Men Tell '41
Diamond Dogs '07
The Diamond of Jeru '01
Diamonds '99
Double Trouble '41
Enemy Gold '93
Ernest Rides Again '93
Escape under Pressure '00
The Fat Spy '66
The Fiend Who Walked the West '58
Finger on the Trigger '65
Fool's Gold '08
Forgotten City '98
Girls in Prison '56
Gold Diggers: The Secret of Bear Mountain '95
The Goonies '85
The Grave '95
Greedy '94
Green Fire '55
The Haunted Sea '97
Hear No Evil '93
Holes '03 ▸
Hunters of the Golden Cobra '82
Inside Out '75
Into the Blue '05
Into the Blue 2: The Reef '09
It's a Mad, Mad, Mad, Mad World '63
The Jewel of the Nile '85
Jupiter's Thigh '81
Kelly's Heroes '70
The Killing Grounds '97
King of California '07
Klondike Fever '79
Kraken: Tentacles of the Deep '06
Kull the Conqueror '97
Lara Croft: Tomb Raider '01
Lara Croft Tomb Raider: The Cradle of Life '03
The Last Adventure '67
The Last Templar '09
Legends of the North '95
Lewis and Clark and George '97
The Librarian: Curse of the Judas Chalice '08
The Librarian: Quest for the Spear '04
The Librarian: Return to King Solomon's Mines '06
The Lost Treasure of the Grand Canyon '08
Lost Treasure of the Maya '08
Lust in the Dust '85 ▸
Max Is Missing '95
The Mermaids of Tiburon '62
Million Dollar Mystery '87
Missing Pieces '91
The Mummy '99
Muppet Treasure Island '96
My Family Treasure '93
Naked Hills '56
National Treasure '04
National Treasure: Book of Secrets '07
Old Mother Riley's Jungle Treasure '51
One-Eyed Soldiers '67
Operation Condor '91
Operation Golden Phoenix '94
Outlaw Trail '06
Pattern for Plunder '62
Payback '94
The Phantom of the Range '38
The Pink Jungle '68
Pirates of Blood River '62
Rat Race '01
The Ravagers '65
The Real Macaw '98
Red Water '01
Romancing the Stone '84 ▸
Rudyard Kipling's The Jungle Book '94
The Rundown '03
Russell Mulcahy's Tale of the Mummy '99
Sahara '05
The Sea God '30
Secre of the Andes '98
The Secret of the Golden Eagle '91
Secret of the Ice Cave '89
Shadow of Chikara '77
Sleepover '04
Slow Burn '00
Tarzan's Secret Treasure '41
Terror on Alcatraz '86
Thank you, Mr. Moto '37
That Man from Rio '64
There Goes the Neighborhood '92
Thieves of Fortune '89
Tom and Huck '95 ▸
Treasure Island '34 ▸
Treasure Island '50 ▸
Treasure Island '72
Treasure Island '89
Treasure Island '99
The Treasure of Jamaica Reef '74
The Treasure of Matecumbe '76
The Treasure of the Amazon '84
Treasure of the Four Crowns '82
Treasure of the Golden Condor '53
Treasure of the Sierra Madre '48 ▸
Treasure of the Yankee Zephyr '83
Treasure Planet '02
The Treasure Seekers '79
Trespass '92
The Triangle '01
Undertow '04
Uninvited '93
Warrior Spirit '94
Whistling in Dixie '42
Wild Ones on Wheels '62
Without a Paddle '04
The Wrong Road '37

Trees & Forests

see also Wilderness

Adam's Apples '05
The Adventures of Robin Hood '38 ▸
Alien 3000 '04
Antichrist '09
As You Like It '06
Avatar '09 ▸
The Backwoods '06
Backwoods '08
Bambi II '06
Big Trees '52 ▸
Blackwoods '02
Blood Crime '02
Blood Trails '06
The Brothers Grimm '05
The Burning Season '94 ▸
Charisma '99
The Contract '07
A Crack in the Floor '00
Criminal Lovers '99
Crosscut '95
Dead in the Water '06
Dead Snow '09
Defiance '08
Dr. Dolittle 2 '01
Dr. Tarr's Torture Dungeon '75
Equinox '71 ▸
Evil Dead '83
Family Tree '00
Fatal Passion '94
Fear Runs Silent '99
Ferngully: The Last Rain Forest '92
5 Dark Souls '96
Flu Birds '08
Fly with the Hawk '85
Forest Warrior '95
Frayed '07
Furry Vengeance '10
Grizzly Rage '07
Heartwood '98
Himatsuri '85 ▸
Hole in the Sky '95
Hoodwinked '05 ▸
The Hunted '03
The Ice Flood '26
Inferno '01
Invisible '06
It Waits '05
Jailbird's Vacation '65
King of the Forest Rangers '46
Lassie: Adventures of Neeka '68
The Last Broadcast '98 ▸
Lemon Tree '08
Lunatic '91
The Many Adventures of Winnie the Pooh '77
Mrs. Mike '49
Mr. Sycamore '74
Motor Home Massacre '05
Murder at Devil's Glen '99
The National Tree '09
The Night Brings Charlie '90
Nightmare Man '06
Old Joy '06 ▸
Open Season '06
Out of Time '00
The Passion of Darkly Noon '95
Piglet's Big Movie '03
Poltergeist 2: The Other Side '86
Redwood Curtain '95
Redwood Forest Trail '50
Return of the Jedi '83 ▸
Robin Hood: Prince of Thieves '91
The Romance of Astrea and Celadon '07
Sasquatch '02
The Secret of Kells '09
Severance '06
Shrooms '07
Simon Says '07
Smoke Jumpers '08
Soft for Digging '01
SuperFire '02
Surfacing '84
Surviving the Game '94
Tell No One '06 ▸
The Tripper '06
Vertigo '58 ▸
The Village '04
The Watcher in the Woods '81
Where the Rivers Flow North '94
Where the Wild Things Are '09
William Shakespeare's A Midsummer Night's Dream '99
Without a Paddle: Nature's Calling '09
The Wizard of Oz '39 ▸
The Woods '03
Wounded '97
Wrong Turn '03

Triads

see also China; Gangs

The Art of War '00
Blood Stained Tradewind '90
The Corruptor '99 ▸
Dogwatch '97
Hard-Boiled '92
Infernal Affairs '02 ▸
The Killer '90 ▸
Lethal Weapon 4 '98
Robin-B-Hood '06
Rush Hour 2 '01
Time and Tide '00
War '07

True Crime

see also Crime & Criminals; This Is Your Life; True Stories

Aileen: Life and Death of a Serial Killer '03 ▸
Alpha Dog '06
An American Crime '07
American Gangster '07 ▸
American Tragedy '00
Among Brothers '05
Angela '02
Another Life '01
The Assassination of Richard Nixon '05
At Close Range '86 ▸
Awakening of Candra '81
Ballad of Gregorio Cortez '83 ▸
The Bank Job '08 ▸
Beyond Reasonable Doubt '80
Big Shot: Confessions of a Campus Bookie '02
Billionaire Boys Club '87
The Black Dahlia '06
Black Oak Conspiracy '77
Black Panther '77
Blackrock '97
Blanche Fury '48
Bluebeard '63 ▸
Boomerang '47 ▸
Borderland '07
Bordertown '06
The Boston Strangler '68
The Boston Strangler: The Untold Story '08
Boys Don't Cry '99 ▸
BTK Killer '06
Bully '01
Burnt Money '00
Capote '05 ▸
Capturing the Friedmans '03 ▸
Catch Me If You Can '02
The Cat's Meow '01
Cause Celebre '87 ▸
Changeling '08 ▸
Chapter 27 '07
Chicago Joe & the Showgirl '90
Chopper '00
Citizen X '95 ▸
City by the Sea '02
City of God '02
Color Me Kubrick '05
Compulsion '59 ▸
Confessions of a Nazi Spy '39
Crazy Love '07 ▸
Crime of the Century '96
Crimson Gold '03
Dahmer '02
Danger of Love '95
Deadly Voyage '96
Death Scream '75
Deep Crimson '96
The Deliberate Stranger '86 ▸
Dick Turpin '25
Dillinger '73
Dr. Petiot '90
Double-Crossed '91
Drug Wars: The Camarena Story '90 ▸
Echo of Murder '00
Echoes in the Darkness '87
Ed Gein '01
The Elegant Criminal '92
Essex Boys '99
Excellent Cadavers '99
Execution of Justice '99
The Executioner's Song '82
The Falcon and the Snowman '85 ▸
Final Appeal '93
Fool's Gold: The Story of the Brink's-Mat Robbery '92
44 Minutes: The North Hollywood Shootout '03
From Hell '01 ▸
The General '98 ▸
Getting Gotti '94
The Girl in the Red Velvet Swing '55
Gotti '96
Great Gold Swindle '84
The Great St. Louis Bank Robbery '59
The Happy Face Murders '99
Headless Body in Topless Bar '96
Heavens Fall '06
Helter Skelter '76
Helter Skelter Murders '71
The Hillside Strangler '89
The Hillside Strangler '04
Hollywoodland '06
Honor Thy Father and Mother: The True Story of the Menendez Brothers '94
I Can't Sleep '93 ▸
In Cold Blood '96
Jasper, Texas '03
Johnny 100 Pesos '93
Karla '06
Keillers Park '05
Killer: A Journal of Murder '95
Kings of South Beach '07
L'Appat '94
The Laramie Project '02 ▸
Let Him Have It '91 ▸
The Life Before This '99
Lonely Hearts '06
Mad Dog Morgan '76
The Magician '93
The Man from the Pru '89
The Man in the Attic '94
The Manson Family '04
Master Spy: The Robert Hanssen Story '02
McVicar '80
Midnight in the Garden of Good and Evil '97
Milk '08 ▸
Mrs. Harris '05
Mrs. Soffel '84
Money Movers '78
Monster '03 ▸
Murder in Coweta County '83
Murder in Greenwich '02
Murder in New Hampshire: The Pamela Smart Story '91
Murder in Texas '81 ▸
Murder, Inc. '60
The Murder of Stephen Lawrence '99 ▸
Murder So Sweet '93
Murph the Surf '75
The Natalee Holloway Story '09
The Newton Boys '97
Nightstalker '02
Normal Life '96
Nowhere to Run '88
Nutcracker: Money, Madness & Murder '87 ▸
The O.J. Simpson Story '94
100 Proof '96
One Kill '00 ▸
One of Her Own '97
The Onion Field '79 ▸
Our Mother's Murder '97
Owning Mahowny '03
Party Monster '03
Path to Paradise '97
The People vs. Jean Harris '81 ▸
Perfect Crime '97
Perfect Murder, Perfect Town '00
Point of Origin '02
The Preppie Murder '89
Prince of Poisoners: The Life and Crimes of William Palmer '98
Prince of the City '81 ▸
The Pursuit of D.B. Cooper '81
Rainbow Warrior '94
Rampage '87
Rampage: The Hillside Strangler Murders '04
Rise of the Footsoldier '07
The Riverman '04
Rule 3 '93
Savage Grace '07
See No Evil: The Moors Murders '06
Sex & Lies in Sin City: The Ted Binion Scandal '08
Sister My Sister '94
Soldier's Girl '03 ▸
Son of Sam '08
Squizzy Taylor '84
Stalking Laura '93
Stand Off '93
Stander '03
Starkweather '04
Summer of Sam '99
Swoon '91 ▸
The Terrorist Next Door '08
The Theory of the Leisure Class '01
Till Murder Do Us Part '92

Too Young to Die '90
Tracks '05
Triple Agent '04
Triple Cross '67 ▶
Under the Pear Tree '73
Undercover Cop '94
The Untold Story of Emmett Louis Till '05 ▶
Valley of the Heart's Delight '07
Verdict on Auschwitz: The Frankfurt Auschwitz Trial 1963—1965 '93 ▶
Verne Miller '88
Veronica Guerin '03
When the Sky Falls '99
Winter of Frozen Dreams '08
A Winter Tan '88
Wisegal '08
Without Evidence '96
Witness to the Mob '98
Wolf Creek '05
Wonderland '03
The Zodiac '05
Zodiac '07
The Zodiac Killer '71

True Stories

***see also** This Is Your Life; True Crime*
The Abduction '96
The Abduction of Kari Swenson '87
Above and Beyond '53 ▶
The Accused '88 ▶
Act of Vengeance '86
Adam '83 ▶
The Adventures of Nellie Bly '81
The Affair of the Necklace '01
After the Promise '87
After the Shock '90
Afterburn '92 ▶
Against the Wall '94 ▶
Aileen: Life and Death of a Serial Killer '03 ▶
Aimee & Jaguar '98
AKA '02
Al Capone '59 ▶
The Alamo '60 ▶
Alamo Bay '85
Aldrich Ames: Traitor Within '98
Alive '93
All Mine to Give '56
All My Loved Ones '00
All the King's Men '99
All the President's Men '76 ▶
Alvarez Kelly '66
Amazing Grace '06 ▶
The Ambush Murders '82
Amelia Earhart: The Final Flight '94
An American Haunting '05
An American Story '92
American Violet '09
The Amityville Horror '79
Amor Bandido '79
The Amy Fisher Story '93
And I Alone Survived '78
And the Band Played On '93 ▶
Andersonville '95 ▶
Andre '94
Angel '82
The Ann Jillian Story '88
Anna and the King of Siam '46 ▶
Antwone Fisher '02 ▶
Apollo 13 '95 ▶
Apprentice to Murder '88
Archer's Adventure '85
The Aristocrats '99
Art for Teachers of Children '95
Artemisia '97
The Ascent '94
The Assassination of Richard Nixon '05
Assault at West Point: The Court-Martial of Johnson Whittaker '94
The Assisi Underground '84
The Attic: The Hiding of Anne Frank '88
Attica '80 ▶
Au Revoir les Enfants '87 ▶
The Aviator '04 ▶
Awakening of Candra '81
Awakenings '90 ▶
Away All Boats '56
Baadasssss! '03 ▶
The Baader Meinhof Complex '08
Backbeat '94 ▶
Bad Blood '81
Badge of the Assassin '85
Badlands '74 ▶
Ballad in Blue '66
Ballad of Gregorio Cortez '83 ▶
The Ballad of Little Jo '93
Balto '95
The Basketball Diaries '95
Bataan '43
Battle Hell '56
Battle Hymn '57
Battle in Seattle '07
Battle of the Eagles '79
Beaufort '07 ▶
Beautiful Dreamers '92
Behind the Mask '99
Believe in Me '06
The Believer '01
Beloved Infidel '59
Ben X '07
The Bengali Night '88
Bernard and Doris '08 ▶
The Betty Ford Story '87 ▶
Beyond Reasonable Doubt '80
Beyond the Next Mountain '87
Beyond the Sea '04
Big Mo '73
The Big Red One '80 ▶
Bill '81 ▶
Bill: On His Own '83 ▶
Bitter Harvest '81 ▶
Black Hawk Down '01 ▶
Black Oak Conspiracy '77
Black Panther '77
Blind Ambition '79
The Blind Side '09
Blood Clan '91
Bloody Sunday '01 ▶
Blow '01
The Blue Butterfly '04
Bonanno: A Godfather's Story '99
Bonnie & Clyde '67 ▶
The Boston Strangler '68
Bottle Shock '08
The Bounty '84
The Boys of St. Vincent '93 ▶
Breach '07
Breast Men '97
Brian's Song '71 ▶
The Bridge '59
The Bridge at Remagen '69
Brink's Job '78 ▶
Britannic '99
Brittanic '00
The Bronx Is Burning '07
Brotherhood of Murder '99
Brutal Glory '89
Buddy '97
Burke & Wills '85
The Burning Bed '85 ▶
The Burning Season '94 ▶
Cabeza de Vaca '90 ▶
Cafe Society '97
Calendar Girls '03
Call Me: The Rise and Fall of Heidi Fleiss '04
Call Northside 777 '48 ▶
Cambridge Spies '03
Camel Boy '84
Camila '84 ▶
Can You Hear the Laughter? The Story of Freddie Prinze '79
Canada's Sweetheart: The Saga of Hal C. Banks '85
The Cantor's Son '37
The Captain from Koepenick '56
Carandiru '03
Carve Her Name with Pride '58
A Case of Deadly Force '86 ▶
Cast the First Stone '89
Castaway '87
Casualties of Love: The "Long Island Lolita" Story '93
Casualties of War '89 ▶
Catch a Fire '06
Chameleon Street '89 ▶
Champions '84
Chariots of Fire '81 ▶
Charlie Grant's War '80
Charlie Wilson's War '07
Charlotte Forten's Mission: Experiment in Freedom '85 ▶
The Chase '91
Chasing the Green '09
Chattahoochee '89
Cheaper by the Dozen '50 ▶
Cheaters '00
Cheyenne Autumn '64
The Children of An Lac '80
Children of Fury '94
The Children of Huang Shi '08
China Cry '91
Christabel '89
Christian the Lion '76
Christiane F. '82 ▶
Chronicle of an Escape '06
Churchill and the Generals '81
Cinderella Man '05 ▶
Circle of Power '83
Citizen X '95 ▶
A Civil Action '98
The Climb '87
Coach Carter '05 ▶
The Color of Courage '98
Coming Out of the Ice '82 ▶
Coming Through '85
Communion '89
Confessions of a Serial Killer '87
Confessions of Tom Harris '72
Conrack '74 ▶
Convicted '86
Conviction '02
Cool Runnings '93
The Counterfeit Traitor '62 ▶
The Counterfeiters '07 ▶
Courage '86 ▶
The Courage to Love '00
The Courageous Heart of Irena Sendler '09 ▶
The Court Martial of Billy Mitchell '55 ▶
The Court Martial of Jackie Robinson '90 ▶
Cowboy '58 ▶
The Cradle Will Rock '99
Crash Course '00
The Crash of Flight 401 '78
Crime of Honor '85
Crimson Gold '03
The Crossing '00
The Crown Prince '06
Cry Freedom '87
A Cry in the Dark '88 ▶
Dance with a Stranger '85 ▶
Dangerous Life '89
Dangerous Minds '95
Dark Matter '07
David and Lisa '62 ▶
Dawn! '83
Day One '89 ▶
The Day Reagan Was Shot '01
Days of Glory '06
DC 9/11: Time of Crisis '04
Dead Ahead: The Exxon Valdez Disaster '92 ▶
Dead Ringers '88 ▶
Deadly Business '86 ▶
Death of a Centerfold '81
Death of a Soldier '85
The Death of Adolf Hitler '84
The Death of Richie '76
Death Scream '75
Defiance '08
The Deliberate Stranger '86 ▶
Delta Force '86
Deranged '74 ▶
The Diary of Anne Frank '59 ▶
The Diary of Anne Frank '08
A Different Loyalty '04 ▶
Dillinger '45 ▶
Dillinger '73
Dirty Pictures '00
The Dish '00 ▶
Divided by Hate '96
The Diving Bell and the Butterfly '07 ▶
The Doctor '91
Dr. Bethune '90 ▶
Dr. Ehrlich's Magic Bullet '40
Dog Day Afternoon '75 ▶
Domino '05
Donner Pass: The Road to Survival '84
Donnie Brasco '96 ▶
Don't Cry, It's Only Thunder '82
Doomsday Gun '94
Double-Crossed '91
Double Exposure: The Story of Margaret Bourke-White '89
The Dove '74
Dreamer: Inspired by a True Story '05
Drugstore Cowboy '89 ▶
Drum Beat '54
The Duchess '08 ▶
Duma '05 ▶
East-West '99
Echoes in the Darkness '87
Eddie Macon's Run '83
Edie in Ciao! Manhattan '72
Edison the Man '40
The Education of Sonny Carson '74
Edward and Mrs. Simpson '80
Egg and I '47 ▶
8-A '92
Eight Below '06
Eight Men Out '88 ▶
8 Seconds '94
84 Charing Cross Road '86 ▶
Eleni '85
The Elephant Man '80 ▶
Elvira Madigan '67 ▶
Elvis and Me '88
Elvis Meets Nixon '98
Elvis: The Movie '79
The Emerald Forest '85 ▶
Eminent Domain '91
Empire of the Sun '87 ▶
Encounter with the Unknown '75
End of the Spear '06
Endangered Species '82
Enemy at the Gates '00
Enemy of Women '44
The Enforcer '51
An Englishman Abroad '83 ▶
Enigma Secret '79
Enjo '58
Enola Gay: The Men, the Mission, the Atomic Bomb '80
Enter Laughing '67
Entertaining Angels: The Dorothy Day Story '96
The Entity '83
Eric '75 ▶
Erin Brockovich '00 ▶
The Ernest Green Story '93
Escape from Sobibor '87 ▶
Escape: Human Cargo '98 ▶
Europa, Europa '91 ▶
Evel Knievel '72
Evelyn '02 ▶
Every Man for Himself & God Against All '75 ▶
Evil '03 ▶
The Execution of Private Slovik '74 ▶
Execution of Raymond Graham '85
The Executioner's Song '82
Exodus '60 ▶
The Express '08
Extraordinary Measures '10
Extreme Justice '93
Eye on the Sparrow '91
The Falcon and the Snowman '85 ▶
False Arrest '92
Farinelli '94
Fast Company '78
Fat Man and Little Boy '89
Fatal Vision '84
The Father Clements Story '87
The FBI Story '59 ▶
Fear Strikes Out '57 ▶
Fifth Day of Peace '72
Fifty Dead Men Walking '08
Fighting Father Dunne '48
Fighting Seabees '44
The Fighting Sullivans '42 ▶
Filth '08
The Final Days '89
The Final Season '07
Final Warning '90
Find Me Guilty '06 ▶
Fire and Rain '89
Fire in the Sky '93
First Time Felon '97
Fitzcarraldo '82 ▶
Five Minutes of Heaven '09
The Fixer '68 ▶
Flash of Genius '08
Flight of the Eagle '82
Florence Nightingale '85
Florence Nightingale '08
Flyboys '06
The Flying Scotsman '06
For Love or Country: The Arturo Sandoval Story '00
The Forbidden Christ '50
Forever Love '98
Forever Strong '08
Forty Days of Musa Dagh '85
Foul Play '76
Four Days in September '97
Frances '82 ▶
Francis Gary Powers: The True Story of the U-2 Spy '76
Freedom Writers '07
Friday Night Lights '04 ▶
Front of the Class '08
Frost/Nixon '08 ▶
Gaby: A True Story '87 ▶
The Game of Their Lives '05
Gentleman Bandit '81
George Wallace '97
Geronimo '93 ▶
Get Rich or Die Tryin' '05
The Ghost and the Darkness '96
Ghosts of Mississippi '96
Gia '98
Gideon's Trumpet '80
Gifted Hands: The Ben Carson Story '09
The Girl on the Train '09
The Girl Who Spelled Freedom '86 ▶
Girls of the White Orchid '85
The Gleiwitz Case '61
Glory Enough for All: The Discovery of Insulin '92
Glory Road '06
Going for the Gold: The Bill Johnson Story '85
Going Home '86
Goldrush: A Real Life Alaskan Adventure '98
Good Evening, Mr. Wallenberg '93
Good Night, and Good Luck '05 ▶
Goodbye, Miss 4th of July '88
Goodfellas '90 ▶
Gospa '94
Gracie '07
Gracie's Choice '04
Grain of Sand '84 ▶
Grambling's White Tiger '81
Grand Theft Parsons '03
Grave Secrets: The Legacy of Hilltop Drive '92
The Great Debaters '07 ▶
The Great Escape '63 ▶
Great Gold Swindle '84
The Great Impostor '61
The Great Locomotive Chase '56
The Great Raid '05
The Great Riviera Bank Robbery '79
The Great Train Robbery '79 ▶
The Great Wallendas '78
The Greatest Game Ever Played '05
The Greek Tycoon '78
Greenfingers '00
The Grey Fox '83 ▶
Grey Gardens '09 ▶
Grey Owl '99
The Grey Zone '01
Gridiron Gang '06
Gross Misconduct '93
Guarding Eddy '04
Guilty of Innocence '87
The Guyana Tragedy: The Story of Jim Jones '80
The Guys '02 ▶
Hachiko: A Dog's Tale '09
Hanna's War '88
Hard Choices '84 ▶
Hard Lessons '86
Harlan County War '00
The Harmonists '99
The Hatfields & the McCoys '75
The Haunting in Connecticut '09
He Walked by Night '48 ▶
He Who Walks Alone '78
The Heart Is Deceitful Above All Things '04
Heart Like a Wheel '83
Heart of the Beholder '05 ▶
Heartland '81 ▶
Heavenly Creatures '94 ▶
Hedd Wyn '92
Held Hostage '91
Hell to Eternity '60
Hellcats of the Navy '57
Helter Skelter '76
Helter Skelter Murders '71
Henry & June '90 ▶
Henry: Portrait of a Serial Killer '90 ▶
Hide in Plain Sight '80 ▶
The Hiding Place '75
The Highest Honor '84
Hilary and Jackie '98 ▶
The Hindenburg '75
The Hoax '06
Holy Terror '65
A Home of Our Own '75
A Home of Our Own '93
Honeymoon Killers '70 ▶
Honor Thy Father '73
Honor Thy Father and Mother: The True Story of the Menendez Brothers '94
Hoodlum Empire '52
The Hoodlum Priest '61 ▶
The Horse Soldiers '59
Hostage High '97
Hostages '93 ▶
Hostile Waters '97
Hotel Rwanda '04
A House Divided '00
The House on Garibaldi Street '79
The House on Todville Road '95
How to Lose Friends & Alienate People '08
Hula Girls '06
The Hunley '99
The Hunt for the Night Stalker '91
The Hunter '80
The Hurricane '99 ▶
I Am a Fugitive from a Chain Gang '32 ▶
I Dreamed of Africa '00
I Love You Phillip Morris '10
I Love You to Death '90
I Only Want You to Love Me '76
I Shot Andy Warhol '96 ▶
I, the Worst of All '90
I Was an American Spy '51
I Will Fight No More Forever '75 ▶
If You Could See What I Hear '82
Il Divo '08
I'm Dancing as Fast as I Can '82
The Impossible Spy '87 ▶
In a Class of His Own '99
In Cold Blood '67 ▶
In Love and War '01
In Pursuit of Honor '95
In the Line of Duty: Ambush in Waco '93
In the Line of Duty: The FBI Murders '88 ▶
In the Mood '87
In the Name of the Father '93 ▶
In the Time of the Butterflies '01

▶ = *rated three bones or higher*

In Which We Serve '43 ▶
The Incredible Journey of Mary Bryant '05
Indictment: The McMartin Trial '95 ▶
The Infernal Trio '74
The Infiltrator '95
Infinity '96
The Informant! '09
Inherit the Wind '60 ▶
Inherit the Wind '99
The Inn of the Sixth Happiness '58 ▶
The Inner Circle '91 ▶
Inside the Third Reich '82
The Insider '99 ▶
Interrupted Melody '55 ▶
Intimate Relations '95
Into the Wild '07 ▶
Into Thin Air: Death on Everest '97
Invictus '09 ▶
Invincible '01
Invincible '06 ▶
Iron Will '93
Ironclads '90
Island of the Blue Dolphins '64
It's Good to Be Alive '74
It's My Party '95
Izzy & Moe '85
The Jayne Mansfield Story '80
Jenny's War '85
Jerusalem '96
The Jesse Owens Story '84
The Jesse Ventura Story '99
Jesus Christ, Superstar '73 ▶
The Jew '96
JFK '91 ▶
Jo Jo Dancer, Your Life Is Calling '86
Joe Torre: Curveballs Along the Way '97
Johnson County War '02
Joni '79
Journey of Hope '90 ▶
The Journey to Kafiristan '01
Joyeux Noel '05 ▶
Judge Horton and the Scottsboro Boys '76
Judgment in Berlin '88
Julia '77 ▶
Julie & Julia '09 ▶
Justin Morgan Had a Horse '81
K-19: The Widowmaker '02
Kaspar Hauser '93
Katyn '07
The Kid and I '05
Kidco '83
Killer: A Journal of Murder '95
The Killing Fields '84 ▶
A Killing in a Small Town '90 ▶
The Killing Yard '01
King of the Wind '93
Kinky Boots '06
Knights of the South Bronx '05
Knute Rockne: All American '40 ▶
Korczak '90 ▶
The Krays '90 ▶
Kundun '97 ▶
Ladies They Talk About '33
Lady Jane '85 ▶
Lady of the House '78
Ladybird, Ladybird '93 ▶
Larry '74
The Last American Hero '73 ▶
Last Call: The Final Chapter of F. Scott Fitzgerald '02
The Last Days of Dolwyn '49
The Last Five Days '82
Last Flight Out: A True Story '90
The Last Place on Earth '85
The Last Shot '04
The Last Supper '76 ▶
The Late Shift '96
Lean on Me '89 ▶
The Legend of Blood Castle '72
Legend of Boggy Creek '75
Let Him Have It '91 ▶

Lethal Lolita—Amy Fisher: My Story '92
The Libertine '05
Life & Times of Grizzly Adams '74
Life Support '07 ▶
Little Boy Lost '78
Little Gloria... Happy at Last '84
Little Heroes '91
Little Laura & Big John '73
A Little Stiff '91
Live from Baghdad '03 ▶
Living Proof '08
Locked in Silence '99
Lone Star Kid '88
Longford '06
Longitude '00 ▶
The Longshots '08
Lords of Dogtown '05
Lorenzo's Oil '92 ▶
The Loretta Claiborne Story '00
Lost '86
Lost Battalion '01
Lost Boundaries '49
The Lost Boys '78 ▶
The Lost Child '00
The Lost One '51
Love and Rage '99
A Love Divided '01
Love Leads the Way '84
Love, Lies and Murder '91
Lovey: A Circle of Children 2 '82
Lucie Aubrac '98
Lumumba '01 ▶
Luna: Spirit of the Whale '07
M. Butterfly '93
Ma Barker's Killer Brood '60
Machine Gun Kelly '58
Mad Dog Morgan '76
M.A.D.D.: Mothers Against Drunk Driving '83
Madeleine '50
Madison '01
Madman '79
The Magdalene Sisters '02 ▶
Malaya '49
A Man Escaped '57 ▶
The Man Who Captured Eichmann '96
The Man Who Never Was '55 ▶
Mandela and de Klerk '97
Manhunt for Claude Dallas '86
The Manson Family '04
Marciano '79
Marianne and Juliane '82 ▶
Marie '85 ▶
Mark Twain and Me '91
Marked Woman '37 ▶
Mary White '77
Mask '85 ▶
Massacre in Rome '73
Mata Hari '32 ▶
Matewan '87 ▶
A Matter of Life and Death '81
Mayerling '36 ▶
Mayerling '68
The McConnell Story '55
Melvin and Howard '80 ▶
Memphis Belle '90 ▶
Men of Honor '00
Michael Collins '96 ▶
Midnight Express '78 ▶
A Mighty Heart '07 ▶
Miracle '04 ▶
Miracle in Lane Two '00
Miracle of Our Lady of Fatima '52
The Miracle Worker '62 ▶
The Miracle Worker '79 ▶
The Miracle Worker '00
Miss Evers' Boys '97
Missing '82 ▶
Mission of the Shark '91 ▶
Mrs. R's Daughter '79
Mrs. Soffel '84
Mr. & Mrs. Loving '96 ▶
Mr. Horn '79
Mr. Reliable: A True Story '95
Mockingbird Don't Sing '01
Molly Maguires '70
Molokai: The Story of Father Damien '99

Money for Nothing '93
Money Movers '78
Mother Joan of the Angels '60 ▶
Mother of Mine '05 ▶
Mother Teresa: In the Name of God's Poor '97
A Mother's Prayer '95
The Mothman Prophecies '02
Mountain Man '77
Mountain Patrol: Kekexili '04
Mozart and the Whale '05
Murder in Coweta County '83
Murder in the First '95
Murder in the Old Red Barn '36
The Murder of Mary Phagan '87 ▶
Murder One '88
Murder Ordained '87
Murph the Surf '75
Music of the Heart '99
Music Within '07
Mutiny '99
Mutiny on the Bounty '35 ▶
Mutiny on the Bounty '62
My Darling Clementine '46 ▶
My Husband's Double Life '01
My Left Foot '89 ▶
My Mother's Courage '95
My Name Is Bill W. '89 ▶
My Own Country '98
My Pleasure Is My Business '74
My Sister's Keeper '02
The Mystery of Alexina '86
The Mystery of the Mary Celeste '35
Naked in the Sun '57
The Nasty Girl '90 ▶
Ned Kelly '03
The Neon Empire '89
The New World '05 ▶
The Newton Boys '97
Night Ambush '57
Night Crossing '81
A Night to Remember '58 ▶
The Night We Called It a Day '03
Nightmare at 43 Hillcrest '74
The Ninth Day '04 ▶
Nitti: The Enforcer '88
No Man Is an Island '62
Norma Rae '79 ▶
Normal Life '96
North Country '05
North Face '08 ▶
Not in This Town '97
Not Without My Daughter '90
Nowhere to Run '88
Nuremberg '00
Nurse Edith Cavell '39 ▶
October Sky '99 ▶
Old Gringo '89
Olivier, Olivier '92 ▶
On the Outs '05
On Wings of Eagles '86
One Against the Wind '91 ▶
One in a Million: The Ron LeFlore Story '78
One Man's Hero '98
One That Got Away '57 ▶
The One That Got Away '96
The Onion Field '79 ▶
Only the Brave '06
Operation Haylift '50
Operation Thunderbolt '77
Operation Valkyrie '04
Opposing Force '87
The Ordeal of Dr. Mudd '80 ▶
The Other Side of the Mountain '75
The Other Side of the Mountain, Part 2 '78
Our America '02
Out of the Ashes '03
The Ox '91
Pack of Lies '87
Pancho Barnes '88
Passion in Paradise '89
Passion of Joan of Arc '28 ▶
Pat Garrett & Billy the Kid '73 ▶
Paths of Glory '57 ▶
Patton '70 ▶

Patty Hearst '88
The Pentagon Wars '98
The People vs. Larry Flynt '96 ▶
The Perfect Storm '00
Phar Lap '84
Philby, Burgess and MacLean: Spy Scandal of the Century '84
The Pianist '02 ▶
Pinochet's Last Stand '06
A Place for Annie '94
Playing for Time '80 ▶
Portrait of a Rebel: Margaret Sanger '82
The Positively True Adventures of the Alleged Texas Cheerleader-Murdering Mom '93 ▶
Possessed '00
The Preppie Murder '89
Pressure Point '62 ▶
Pretty Village, Pretty Flame '96 ▶
Prick Up Your Ears '87 ▶
Pride '07
Pride of the Marines '45 ▶
Primeval '07
Prince of the City '81 ▶
Princess Caraboo '94
The Prisoner of Shark Island '36
A Private Matter '92 ▶
The Prize Pulitzer '89
The Prize Winner of Defiance, Ohio '05 ▶
Prom Queen '04
Promised a Miracle '88
Protecting the King '07
PT 109 '63
The Pursuit of Happyness '06
Quarterback Princess '85
The Queen '06 ▶
A Question of Attribution '91
Question of Faith '93
Question of Honor '80
Qui Etes Vous, Mr. Sorge? '61
Quilombo '84
Rabbit-Proof Fence '02 ▶
Radio '03
Raid on Entebbe '77 ▶
Rainbow Drive '90
Rape and Marriage: The Rideout Case '80
Rasputin: Dark Servant of Destiny '96 ▶
Rated X '00
Reach for the Sky '56
A Real American Hero '78
Rebound: The Legend of Earl "The Goat" Manigault '96
Reckless Disregard '84
Recount '08
Red Cherry '95
Red Cliff '08 ▶
Redacted '07
Reds '81 ▶
Reilly: Ace of Spies '87 ▶
Rescue Dawn '06 ▶
Rescuers: Stories of Courage—Two Couples '98 ▶
Rescuers: Stories of Courage "Two Women" '97 ▶
The Return of Martin Guerre '83 ▶
Reversal of Fortune '90 ▶
Rhodes '97
Riding in Cars with Boys '01
Ring of Bright Water '69 ▶
Ring of Terror '62
Riot in Cell Block 11 '54 ▶
Riot in the Streets '96
River's Edge '87 ▶
The Road to Galveston '96 ▶
Rodeo Girl '80
Roe vs. Wade '89 ▶
Rogue Trader '98
Room for One More '51
Rosewood '96 ▶
Roswell: The U.F.O. Cover-Up '94
Rough Riders '97
A Royal Scandal '96
Ruby '92
Ruby Bridges '98

Rudy '93
The Rumor Mill '86
A Rumor of War '80 ▶
Run for the Dream: The Gail Devers Story '96
Runaway Father '91
The Runaways '10
The Runner Stumbles '79
Running Brave '83
Sacco & Vanzetti '71
Sadat '83
St. Helen's, Killer Volcano '82
The St. Valentine's Day Massacre '67
Sakharov '84 ▶
Samaritan: The Mitch Snyder Story '86 ▶
Samurai 1: Musashi Miyamoto '55 ▶
Samurai 2: Duel at Ichijoji Temple '55 ▶
Samurai 3: Duel at Ganryu Island '56 ▶
Savage Attraction '83
Savage Messiah '02
Saved by the Light '95
Scandal '89 ▶
A Scandal in Paris '46
The Scarlet & the Black '83
Schindler's List '93 ▶
Sea Gypsies '78
The Sea Inside '04 ▶
Sea Wolves '81
The Search for Bridey Murphy '56
Searching for Bobby Fischer '93 ▶
Secret Weapon '90
Seeing Red '99
Seizure: The Story of Kathy Morris '80
Selena '96
Selma, Lord, Selma '99
Separate but Equal '91 ▶
Sergeant Matlovich vs. the U.S. Air Force '78
Sergeant York '41 ▶
Serpico '73 ▶
Serving in Silence: The Margarethe Cammermeyer Story '95 ▶
Seven Years in Tibet '97
Sexual Intent '94
Shackleton '02 ▶
Shadow on the Sun '88
Shadowlands '93 ▶
Shake Hands With the Devil: The Journey of Romeo Dallaire '04 ▶
Shattered City: The Halifax Explosion '03
Shattered Dreams '90
Shattered Glass '03 ▶
Shattered Vows '84
Shine '95 ▶
A Shining Season '79 ▶
Shooting Dogs '05
Shot in the Heart '01 ▶
Shot Through the Heart '98 ▶
Shout at the Devil '76
The Sicilian '87
Sid & Nancy '86 ▶
The Siege of Sidney Street '60
Silence of the North '81
Silent Victim '92
Silent Victory: The Kitty O'Neil Story '79 ▶
Silkwood '83 ▶
The Singing Nun '66
Sins of the Father '01 ▶
Sister Aimee: The Aimee Semple McPherson Story '06
Six Degrees of Separation '93
633 Squadron '64
Skeezer '82
Skin '89
The Slender Thread '65 ▶
Small Sacrifices '89
Smile '05
Snap Decision '01
Sniper '75 ▶
Snowbound: The Jim and Jennifer Stolpa Story '94
So Proudly We Hail '43 ▶
Soldier Blue '70

The Soloist '09
The Son of the Shark '93
Sophie Scholl: The Final Days '05 ▶
Soul of the Game '96 ▶
The Sound of Music '65 ▶
Spartacus '60 ▶
Spirit of St. Louis '57 ▶
The Spirit of West Point '47
Springfield Rifle '52
Squizzy Taylor '84
Stand and Deliver '88 ▶
Star 80 '83
Starved '97
Stealing Heaven '88
Stonewall '95 ▶
The Stoning of Soraya M. '08
Storm and Sorrow '90
The Story of Dr. Wassell '44
The Straight Story '99 ▶
Strange Justice: The Clarence Thomas and Anita Hill Story '99
The Stratton Story '49 ▶
Street Smart '87
Stuck '07
The Sugarland Express '74 ▶
Sugartime '95
Sweetwater: A True Rock Story '99
Swimming Upstream '03
Switched at Birth '91
Take the Lead '06
Taking Chance '09
The Taking of Flight 847: The Uli Derickson Story '88 ▶
Taking Sides '01 ▶
Talk to Me '07
Teamster Boss: The Jackie Presser Story '92 ▶
The Ten Million Dollar Getaway '91
10 Rillington Place '71 ▶
Ten Who Dared '60
Tenderness of the Wolves '73
The Terry Fox Story '83 ▶
They Call Me Sirr '00
The Thin Blue Lie '00
The Thin Blue Line '88 ▶
Thirteen Days '00 ▶
Thirty Seconds Over Tokyo '44 ▶
A Thousand Heroes '92
Thousand Pieces of Gold '91 ▶
Three Came Home '50 ▶
The Three Faces of Eve '57
The 300 Spartans '62
The Tiger Woods Story '98
Till Death Do Us Part '92
Time Out '01
Titanic '53 ▶
Titanic '96
Titanic '97 ▶
To Catch a Killer '92 ▶
To End All Wars '01
To Heal a Nation '88
To Kill a Priest '89
Toast of New York '37 ▶
Torso '01
Touch the Top of the World '06
Touched by Love '80
Touching the Void '03
Town That Dreaded Sundown '76
Tragedy of Flight 103: The Inside Story '91 ▶
The Trial of Old Drum '00
The Triangle Factory Fire Scandal '79
Triple Cross '67 ▶
Triumph of the Spirit '89 ▶
True Confessions '81 ▶
The Truth About Jane '00
Tuesdays with Morrie '99
The Tunnel '01 ▶
The Tuskegee Airmen '95 ▶
21 '08
24 Hour Party People '01
29th Street '91
Two Men Went to War '02
Tyson '95
Under the Lighthouse Dancing '97
United 93 '06 ▶

▶ = rated three bones or higher

Unknown White Male '05 ▶
Unshackled '00
The Untold Story of Emmett Louis Till '05 ▶
Valentin '02
Valkyrie '08
Varian's War '01
Vendetta '99
Vengeance Is Mine '79 ▶
Victory at Entebbe '76
Video Voyeur: The Susan Wilson Story '02
Violette '78 ▶
Voyage of Terror: The Achille Lauro Affair '90
Voyage of the Damned '76 ▶
Waking Up Wally '05
Walk the Proud Land '56
Walking Tall '73
Walking Tall: Part 2 '75
Walking Tall: The Final Chapter '77
Walking Through the Fire '80
The Wall '83 ▶
The Wannsee Conference '84 ▶
We Are Marshall '06
The Wedding Gift '93 ▶
Wedding in Blood '74 ▶
Weeds '87 ▶
Welcome to Sarajevo '97 ▶
What's Love Got to Do with It? '93
When Hell Was in Session '82 ▶
Whirlygirl '04
White Mile '94
White Mischief '88 ▶
The White Rose '83 ▶
Whitewash: The Clarence Brandley Story '02
The Whole Wide World '96 ▶
Wild America '97 ▶
The Wild Child '70 ▶
Wild Hearts Can't Be Broken '91 ▶
Will: G. Gordon Liddy '82
A Winner Never Quits '86
With a Song in My Heart '52 ▶
Without a Trace '83
A Woman at War '94
A Woman Called Golda '82 ▶
The Woman He Loved '88
Woman with a Past '92
Wooden Horse '50 ▶
A World Apart '88 ▶
World Trade Center '06 ▶
The World's Fastest Indian '05 ▶
The Wrong Man '56 ▶
You Know My Name '99 ▶
The Young Poisoner's Handbook '94 ▶
Yours, Mine & Ours '68
Yuri Nosenko, KGB '86
The Zodiac Killer '71
Zoot Suit '81 ▶
Zulu '64

TV Pilot Movies

Africa Texas Style '67
The Alice '04
American Dream '81 ▶
Anti-Terrorist Cell: Manhunt '01
The Art of Crime '75
Balboa '82
Battlestar Galactica '78
The Bionic Woman '75
Blade in Hong Kong '85
Blue De Ville '86
Brass '85
Buck Rogers in the 25th Century '79
Call to Glory '84
Caprica '09
China Beach '88 ▶
Christy '94
City Beneath the Sea '71
Columbo: Prescription Murder '67
The Concrete Cowboys '79
Conspiracy of Terror '75
Cruel Intentions 2 '99
Daring Game '68
The Dead Zone '02
Death Ray 2000 '81
Destination Moonbase Alpha '75
Dr. Strange '78
Evil Roy Slade '71 ▶
Express to Terror '79
Fantasy Island '76
The Flash '90
Force Five '75
Genesis II '73
The Gunfighters '87
The Hanged Man '74
Hercules and the Princess of Troy '65
Hercules the Legendary Journeys, Vol. 1: And the Amazon Women '94
Highlander: The Gathering '92
The Hunted Lady '77
Hunter '73
The Immortal '01
The Incredible Hulk '77
JAG '95
Jigsaw '71
The Kid with the Broken Halo '82
Kung Fu '72
L.A. Law '86 ▶
The Lazarus Man '96
The Legend of Butch & Sundance '04
Little House on the Prairie '74 ▶
Loving '84
The Magnificent Seven '98
Magnum P.I.: Don't Eat the Snow in Hawaii '80
Miami Vice '84
Misfits of Science '85
Moonlighting '85
Nick Knight '89
Night Gallery '69 ▶
The Night Stalker '71
Our Family Business '81
Out of Order '03
Poltergeist: The Legacy '96
Probe '72
Rags to Riches '87
Riding with Death '76
Sabrina the Teenage Witch '96
Sanctuary of Fear '79
Scarface Mob '62
Search for the Gods '75
She's in the Army Now '81
Skag '79 ▶
Smile, Jenny, You're Dead '74
Soldier of Fortune Inc. '97
Space: 1999—Alien Attack '79 ▶
Spraggue '84
Stalk the Wild Child '76
Star Wars: The Clone Wars '08
Stark '85
Strange New World '75
The Streets of San Francisco '72 ▶
Strike Force '75
Superman & the Mole Men '51
TekWar '94
Terraces '77
Then Came Bronson '68
Thunder in Paradise '93
Tour of Duty '87
V '83 ▶
Vegas '78
Waikiki '80
Walker: Texas Ranger: One Riot, One Ranger '93
White Dwarf '95
Winter Kill '74
The Women of Brewster Place '89 ▶
The Young Pioneers '76

TV Series

Aeon Flux '05
And Now for Something Completely Different '72 ▶
Dark Justice '91
Davy Crockett and the River Pirates '56
Davy Crockett, King of the Wild Frontier '55 ▶
Queen for a Day '51
Requiem for a Heavyweight '56 ▶
Robin Hood: The Movie '55
Rocky Jones, Space Ranger: Renegade Satellite '54
Serenity '05 ▶
Tanner on Tanner '04
Thunderbirds '04
Wild, Wild West Revisited '79

Twins

see also *Brothers & Sisters; Family Ties*

The Abandoned '06
Adaptation '02 ▶
After Darkness '85
Angels Don't Sleep Here '00
The Attic '06
Bad Company '02
Basket Case '82 ▶
Basket Case 2 '90
Basket Case 3: The Progeny '92
Big Business '88
Billboard Dad '98
Bloodlink '86
The Bride with White Hair '93
Brotherly Love '85
Brothers of the Head '06
Campus Knights '29
Chained for Life '51
A Change of Place '94
Children of Dune '03
A Cinderella Story '04
Citizen Toxie: The Toxic Avenger 4 '01
City of Shadows '86
Class of Nuke 'Em High 3: The Good, the Bad and the Subhumanoid '94
Cobra Woman '44
Coffee and Cigarettes '03 ▶
The Corsican Brothers '42
The Crazysitter '94
Crescendo '69
Dark Side '02
Dead Men Walk '43
Dead Ringer '64
Dead Ringers '88 ▶
Deadly Twins '85
Decay '98
Devil's Wedding Night '73
Double Double Toil and Trouble '94
Double Impact '91
The Double Life of Veronique '91
Double Trouble '91
Double Vision '92
The Dreamers '03
Dual Alibi '47
Equal Impact '96
Equinox '93
The Eyes, the Mouth '83
The Fat Spy '66
The Fifth Musketeer '79
Freaks '32 ▶
Give Me Your Hand '09
The Good Thief '03 ▶
Hangman's Curse '03
Here Come the Waves '45 ▶
Hotel de Love '96
House of Wax '05
How the West Was Fun '95
Into the Fire '05
Invitation au Voyage '82
It Takes Two '95
Jack's Back '87 ▶
Killer with Two Faces '74
The Krays '90 ▶
Lies of the Twins '91
Looney Tunes: Back in Action '03
Lost Honeymoon '47
Love and Mary '07
Love! Valour! Compassion! '96
Madhouse '87
Major League 3: Back to the Minors '98
The Man in the Iron Mask '39 ▶
The Man in the Iron Mask '77 ▶
The Man in the Iron Mask '97
The Man in the Iron Mask '98 ▶
Man with a Gun '95
Maximum Risk '96
Mercy Streets '00
Mirror Images '91
Mirror Images 2 '93
Mother Lode '82
New York Minute '04
Newcastle '08
Nukie '93
The Nutt House '95
One More Time '70
The Other '72 ▶
Out on a Limb '92
The Parent Trap '61
The Parent Trap '98
Preaching to the Choir '05
The Prince and the Pauper '07
The Prince and the Surfer '99
Private Property '06
Raising Cain '92
Rebirth of Mothra '96
Rebirth of Mothra 2 '97
The Reluctant Agent '89
Ripe '97
Schizopolis '97
Second Sight '99 ▶
Seed of Chucky '04
Simon Says '07
Sisters '73 ▶
Slightly Terrific '44
The Sphinx '33
The Spiderwick Chronicles '08 ▶
Spy Smasher '42
Spy Smasher Returns '42
Start the Revolution without Me '70 ▶
Steal Big, Steal Little '95
A Stolen Life '46
Strangers in Love '32
Stuck On You '03
Thicker Than Water '93
This World, Then the Fireworks '97
Three ... Extremes '04
Thunder Trail '37
The Tiger's Tale '06
To Grandmother's House We Go '94
Trail of the Mounties '47
12 and Holding '05 ▶
Twin Dragons '92
Twin Falls Idaho '99 ▶
Twin Sisters '91
Twin Town '97
Twins '88
Twins of Evil '71
Twinsanity '70
Twinsitters '95
Twitches '05
Twitches Too '07
2 Minutes Later '07
Two Much '96
Urban Legends 2: Final Cut '00
Vampire Effect '03
Village of Dreams '97
Wagons Westward '40
Woman Condemned '33
Wonder Man '45
The Worldly Madonna '22
The Young Girls of Rochefort '68

Twister!

see also *Disaster Flicks*

Category 7 : The End of the World '05
Category 6 : Day of Destruction '04
The Day After Tomorrow '04
Eye of the Storm '98
Night of the Twisters '95
Places in the Heart '84 ▶
Storm Cell '08
Storm Chasers: Revenge of the Twister '98
Storm Tracker '99
Tornado! '96
Twister '96
Where the Heart Is '00
The Wizard of Oz '25
The Wizard of Oz '39 ▶

UFOs

see *Alien Beings—Benign; Alien Beings—Vicious; Space Operas*

Under My Skin

Antibody '02
Fantastic Voyage '66 ▶
Innerspace '87
Osmosis Jones '01

Undercover Cops

see also *Crime Drama; Organized Crime*

Angel of Destruction '94
Assault on Precinct 13 '05
Bad Boys 2 '03
Ballistic '94
Beyond Suspicion '00
Beyond the Law '92
Big Momma's House '00
Big Momma's House 2 '06
The Boob '26
Border Incident '49
Boss of Boomtown '44
Break a Leg '03
Brooklyn's Finest '09
Bullets or Ballots '38 ▶
City on Fire '87
The Code '09
Con Games '02
Cruising '80
Cutaway '00
Dead Pigeon on Beethoven Street '72
Death Rides the Range '40
The Departed '06 ▶
District B13 '04
Donnie Brasco '96 ▶
Drop Zone '94
Drug Wars: The Camarena Story '90 ▶
The Finishing Touch '92
Force Five '75
Get Christie Love! '74
Hard-Boiled '92
Hellcats '68
Hell's Bloody Devils '70
Hot Stuff '80
House of Bamboo '55
Idiot Box '97
Impulse '90
In the Flesh '97
In the Line of Duty: A Cop for the Killing '90
In the Shadows '01
In Too Deep '99
Infernal Affairs '02 ▶
Infernal Affairs 2 '03
Infernal Affairs 3 '03
Kindergarten Cop '90
Kings of South Beach '07
Kiss of Death '94
The Last Shot '04
Miami Vice '06
Miss Congeniality 2: Armed and Fabulous '05
The Mod Squad '99
Motor Patrol '50
The Naked Gun: From the Files of Police Squad '88 ▶
Narc '02 ▶
No Man's Land '87
Plain Clothes '88
Police, Adjective '09
Protector '97
Raw Deal '86
Reservoir Dogs '92 ▶
Ring of Death '08
Running Scared '06
Rush '91 ▶
Saints and Sinners '95
A Scanner Darkly '06
Serpico '73 ▶
Sharky's Machine '81
Small Kill '93
Stiletto Dance '01
Stone Cold '91
A Stranger Among Us '92
The Substitute 4: Failure is Not an Option '00
The Sweeper '95
Swindle '02
TekWar '94
Threat of Exposure '02
Tortured '08
Traffic '00 ▶
Training Day '01
Tube '03
2 Fast 2 Furious '03
Underclassman '05
White Chicks '04
Wisegirls '02
Witness '85 ▶

Unexplained Phenomena

The Amityville Curse '90
Angel Baby '61
Beyond the Bermuda Triangle '75
The Birds '63 ▶
Black Rainbow '91 ▶
Blue Tornado '90
Book of Shadows: Blair Witch 2 '00
The Carpathian Eagle '81
The Carpenter '89
Carrie '76 ▶
Carrie '02*
Catacombs '89
Cube '98
Cube 2: Hypercube '02
A Day Without a Mexican '04
Dead Again '91 ▶
Dead Zone '83 ▶
Delusion '80
Destiny Turns on the Radio '95
Die, Monster, Die! '65
Dream a Little Dream 2 '94
Dying to Remember '93
Encounter with the Unknown '75
Endgame '85
The Entity '83
Escapes '86
E.S.P. '83
Eternal Evil '87
The Evil Mind '34
Eyes of Laura Mars '78
Fallen '97
Fire in the Sky '93
Firestarter '84
The 4D Man '59
The Fury '78
Ghost Chasers '51
Ghost Town '88
The Ghosts of Hanley House '68
Grandma's House '88
Hangar 18 '80
The Haunting Passion '83
The House of Seven Corpses '73
In Dreams '98
Lisa and the Devil '75
Lost Voyage '01
Lurkers '88
Maximum Overdrive '86
Michael '96
Miracle in Rome '88
Miracle of Our Lady of Fatima '52
Mondo Balordo '64
Murphy's Fault '88
A Name for Evil '70
Nomads '86
Out There '95
Paranormal Activity '09 ▶
Phenomenon '96
Psychic '91
The Psychotronic Man '91
Race to Witch Mountain '09
The Rage: Carrie 2 '99
The Reaping '07
Retribution '88
Return from Witch Mountain '78
Roswell: The U.F.O. Cover-Up '94
Salem's Lot '79
Scared Stiff '53 ▶
Shattered Silence '71
The Sleeping Car '90
Spook Busters '48
The Stranger '73
Things Happen at Night '48
The Three Lives of Thomasina '63 ▶
The Tin Drum '79 ▶
Truly, Madly, Deeply '91 ▶
Unbreakable '00
The Undead '57
Visions '90
Visions of Evil '75

▶ = rated three bones or higher

Head Above Water *'96*
Heading South *'05* ►
The Hills Have Eyes *'06*
The Hills Have Eyes *'77*
Hollywood, Je T'Aime *'09*
Home Alone *'90* ►
Home Alone 2: Lost in New York *'92*
Hot Pursuit *'87*
Hot Summer *'68*
The Hours and Times *'92* ►
The Housekeeper *'02*
How Stella Got Her Groove Back *'98*
The Inkwell *'94*
Jack Frost 2: Revenge of the Mutant Killer Snowman *'00*
Judgment Day *'88*
Just Looking *'99*
Kevin & Perry Go Large *'00*
Killing at Hell's Gate *'81*
The King Is Alive *'00*
La Collectionneuse *'67*
La Piscine *'69*
Last Holiday *'06*
The Last of the High Kings *'96*
Last Summer In the Hamptons *'96* ►
Lena's Holiday *'90*
Lie Down with Dogs *'95*
Like It Never Was Before *'95*
Little Bigfoot *'96*
The Long, Long Trailer *'54*
Love and Pain and the Whole Damn Thing *'73*
Love! Valour! Compassion! *'96*
The Lunatic *'92*
Mafioso *'62*
Magic in the Water *'95*
Magic Kid *'92*
The Man of My Life *'06*
The Man Who Knew Too Much *'34* ►
The Man Who Knew Too Much *'56*
The Mask of Dimitrios *'44* ►
Mr. Hobbs Takes a Vacation *'62* ►
Mr. Hulot's Holiday *'53* ►
A Month by the Lake *'95*
Morvern Callar *'02*
My Father, My Mother, My Brothers and My Sisters *'99*
My Father the Hero *'93*
My Grandpa Is a Vampire *'92*
My Life in Ruins *'09*
My Uncle Silas *'01* ►
National Lampoon's Christmas Vacation *'89*
National Lampoon's Dad's Week Off *'97*
National Lampoon's European Vacation *'85*
National Lampoon's Vacation *'83* ►
Nico and Dani *'00*
Nightmare at Bittercreek *'91*
Nights in Rodanthe *'08*
Off Season *'01*
Ollie Hopnoodle's Haven of Bliss *'88*
Open Water *'03* ►
The Out-of-Towners *'70* ►
Overkill *'96*
Pauline at the Beach *'83* ►
Phat Girlz *'06*
Poor White Trash 2 *'75*
Rain *'01*
Raising Victor Vargas *'03*
Red Lights *'04* ►
Red Salute *'35*
Ring of Fire 3: Lion Strike *'94*
The River Wild *'94*
Rugrats Go Wild! *'03*
Russian Roulette *'93*
RV *'06*
Shark Attack 3: Megalodon *'02*
Siam Sunset *'99*
Sisterhood of the Traveling Pants *'05*
The Sisterhood of the Traveling Pants 2 *'08*
Six Days, Seven Nights *'98*
Spellbreaker: Secret of the Leprechauns *'96*
Spring Break *'83*
Spring Breakdown *'08*
Stealing Beauty *'96*
Still Green *'07*
The Sucker *'65*
Summer of '04 *'06*
Summer Rental *'85*
A Summer's Tale *'96*
Swimming Pool *'03* ►
A Tale of Winter *'92*
Target *'85*
Terror at Red Wolf Inn *'72*
Terror at Tenkiller *'86*
The Third *'04*
Tourist Trap *'98*
Tracks of a Killer *'95*
TripFall *'00*
Twitch of the Death Nerve *'71*
2 Days in Paris *'07* ►
The Two Faces of Evil *'82*
Two for the Road *'67* ►
Two If by Sea *'95*
Tyler Perry's Why Did I Get Married? *'07*
Tyler Perry's Why Did I Get Married Too *'10*
Uncivilized *'94*
Unlawful Passage *'94*
Vegas Vacation *'96*
Vibration *'68*
Vicky Cristina Barcelona *'08*
The Wailer *'06*
A Walk on the Moon *'99*
Week-End in Havana *'41*
Weekend at Bernie's *'89*
A Weekend in the Country *'96*
Welcome to Spring Break *'88*
Where the Boys Are *'60*
Where the Boys Are '84 *'84*
Wild Cactus *'92*
The Wild Life *'84*
Witchery *'88*
With a Friend Like Harry *'00* ►
The Wizards of Waverly Place: The Movie *'09*

Vampire Babes

see also *Up All Night; Vampires*

Addicted to Murder *'95*
Addicted to Murder 2: Tainted Blood *'97*
Addicted to Murder 3: Bloodlust *'99*
The Addiction *'95*
American Vampire *'97*
Blade 2 *'02*
Blood Angels *'05*
The Blood Spattered Bride *'72*
Blood: The Last Vampire *'09*
BloodRayne *'06*
The Brides of Dracula *'60*
Buffy the Vampire Slayer *'92* ►
Captain Kronos: Vampire Hunter *'74* ►
Cold Hearts *'99*
Count Dracula *'77*
The Craving *'80*
Crypt of the Living Dead *'73*
Daughters of Darkness *'71* ►
Demon Queen *'80*
Dracula's Daughter *'36* ►
Elvira's Haunted Hills *'02*
Eternal *'04*
Fangs of the Living Dead *'68*
The Fearless Vampire Killers *'67* ►
The Forsaken *'01*
Fright Night *'85*
From Dusk Till Dawn *'95*
From Dusk Till Dawn 3: The Hangman's Daughter *'99*
The Girl with the Hungry Eyes *'94*
Habit *'97*
The Insatiable *'06*
Interview with the Vampire *'94*
John Carpenter Presents Vampires: Los Muertos *'02*
John Carpenter's Vampires *'97*
Karmina *'96*
The Kiss *'88*
The League of Extraordinary Gentlemen *'03*
Lemora; Lady Dracula *'73*
The Librarian: Curse of the Judas Chalice *'08*
Lips of Blood *'75*
Lust for a Vampire *'71*
Lust for Dracula *'04*
Mary, Mary, Bloody Mary *'76*
The Midnight Hour *'86*
Nadja *'95* ►
Night Junkies *'07*
Night of the Sorcerers *'70*
Night Shade *'97*
Nightlife *'90*
Once Bitten *'85*
Queen of the Damned *'02*
Razor Blade Smile *'98*
Rise: Blood Hunter *'07*
Samson vs. the Vampire Women *'61*
Saturday the 14th Strikes Back *'88*
Sergio Lapel's Drawing Blood *'99*
Sorority House Vampires *'95*
Stephen King's The Night Flier *'96*
Suck *'09*
Tales from the Crypt Presents Bordello of Blood *'96*
The Thirst *'06*
Twins of Evil *'71*
Ultraviolet *'06*
Underworld: Evolution *'05*
Vamp *'86*
Vampire Centerfolds *'98*
Vampire Killers *'09*
The Vampire Lovers *'70*
Vampire Night *'00*
Vampires of Sorority Row: Kickboxers From Hell *'99*
Vampyres *'74*
Van Helsing *'04* ►
The Velvet Vampire *'71*
Witchcraft 10: Mistress of the Craft *'98*
The Witches Hammer *'06*

Vampire Spoof

see also *Horror Comedy; Vampires*

Andy Warhol's Dracula *'74* ►
Beverly Hills Vamp *'88*
Buffy the Vampire Slayer *'92* ►
Dracula and Son *'76*
Dracula Blows His Cool *'82*
Dracula: Dead and Loving It *'95*
Dracula Sucks *'79*
Dracula vs. Frankenstein *'71*
Elvira's Haunted Hills *'02*
The Fearless Vampire Killers *'67* ►
Gore-Met Zombie Chef from Hell *'87*
I Married a Vampire *'87*
Karmina *'96*
The Little Vampire *'00*
Love at First Bite *'79*
The Malibu Beach Vampires *'91*
Mr. Vampire *'86*
My Best Friend Is a Vampire *'88*
My Grandpa Is a Vampire *'92*
Near Dark *'87* ►
Netherbeast Incorporated *'07*
Once Bitten *'85*
A Polish Vampire in Burbank *'80*
Rockula *'90*
Skeleton Key 2: 667, the Neighbor of the Beast *'08*
Suck *'09*
Sundown: The Vampire in Retreat *'08*
Teen Vamp *'88*
Transylmania *'09*
Vamp *'86*
The Vampire Happening *'71*
Vampire Killers *'09*

Vampires

see also *Up All Night; Vampire Babes; Vampire Spoof*

Addicted to Murder *'95*
Addicted to Murder 2: Tainted Blood *'97*
Addicted to Murder 3: Bloodlust *'99*
The Addiction *'95*
Against the Dark *'08*
Alien Massacre *'67*
Angel of the Night *'98*
Attack from Mars *'88*
Bandh Darwaza *'90*
The Bat People *'74*
Beast of Morocco *'66*
Billy the Kid Versus Dracula *'66*
The Black Room *'82*
Black Sabbath *'64* ►
Blacula *'72*
Blade *'98*
Blade 2 *'02*
Blade: Trinity *'04*
Blood & Donuts *'95*
Blood and Roses *'61*
Blood Freak *'72*
Blood of Dracula's Castle *'69*
Blood of the Vampire *'58*
The Blood Spattered Bride *'72*
Blood Thirst *'65*
Blood Ties *'92*
Bloodbath *'98*
Bloodlust: Subspecies 3 *'93*
BloodRayne *'06*
BloodRayne 2: Deliverance *'07*
Bloodstone: Subspecies 2 *'92*
Bloodstorm: Subspecies 4 *'98*
The Bloodsuckers *'70*
Bloodsuckers from Outer Space *'83*
Body Snatcher from Hell *'69*
Bram Stoker's Dracula *'92*
The Breed *'01*
The Brides of Dracula *'60*
Brotherhood of Blood *'08*
Buffy the Vampire Slayer *'92* ►
Captain Kronos: Vampire Hunter *'74* ►
Cave of the Living Dead *'65*
Children of the Night *'92*
Cirque du Freak: The Vampire's Assistant *'09*
Club Vampire *'98*
Condemned to Live *'35*
Count Dracula *'71*
Count Dracula *'77*
Count Yorga, Vampire *'70*
The Craving *'80*
Cronos *'94*
Crypt of the Living Dead *'73*
Curse of Nostradamus *'60*
Curse of the Undead *'59*
The Damned *'06*
Dance of the Damned *'88*
Dark Town *'04*
Daughter of Darkness *'89*
Daughters of Darkness *'71* ►
Day Watch *'06* ►
Daybreakers *'09*
Dead Men Walk *'43*
Demon Queen *'80*
The Devil Bat *'41*
The Devil Bat's Daughter *'46*
Devil's Wedding Night *'73*
Dr. Terror's House of Horrors *'65*
Dracula (Spanish Version) *'31*
Dracula *'31* ►
Dracula *'73*
Dracula *'79*
Dracula A.D. 1972 *'72*
Dracula: Dead and Loving It *'95*
Dracula Has Risen from the Grave *'68*
Dracula Rising *'93*
Dracula 2000 *'00*
Dracula vs. Frankenstein *'69*
Dracula's Daughter *'36* ►
Dracula's Great Love *'72*
Dracula's Last Rites *'79*
Dracula's Widow *'88*
Elvira, Mistress of the Dark *'88*
Embrace of the Vampire *'95*
Evils of the Night *'85*
Fangs of the Living Dead *'68*
Female Vampire *'73*
The Forsaken *'01*
Fright Night *'85*
Fright Night 2 *'88*
From Dusk Till Dawn *'95*
From Dusk Till Dawn 2: Texas Blood Money *'98*
Ganja and Hess *'73*
Genie of Darkness *'62*
Grave of the Vampire *'72*
Graveyard Shift *'87*
Habit *'97*
Heartstopper *'92*
The Horror of Dracula *'58* ►
Horror of the Blood Monsters *'70*
House of Dark Shadows *'70* ►
House of Dracula *'45*
House of Frankenstein *'44*
The House that Dripped Blood *'71*
Howling 6: The Freaks *'90*
The Hunger *'83*
I Like Bats *'85*
I, Vampiri *'56*
Immortality *'98*
Innocent Blood *'92*
Interview with the Vampire *'94*
Invasion of the Vampires *'61*
Isle of the Dead *'45*
John Carpenter's Vampires *'97*
Karmina *'96*
Kiss of the Vampire *'62*
The Last Man on Earth *'64*
Legend of the Liquid Sword *'93*
The Legend of the 7 Golden Vampires *'73*
Lemora, Lady Dracula *'73*
Les Vampires *'15* ►
Let the Right One In *'08*
Let's Scare Jessica to Death *'71*
Lifeforce *'85*
Lips of Blood *'75*
The Lost Boys *'87*
Lost Boys: The Tribe *'08*
The Lost Platoon *'89*
Lust for a Vampire *'71*
Mark of the Vampire *'35* ►
Martin *'77* ►
Mary, Mary, Bloody Mary *'76*
The Midnight Hour *'86*
Midnight Kiss *'93*
Modern Vampires *'98*
The Monster Club *'85*
The Monster Demolisher *'60*
The Monster Squad *'87*
My Grandpa Is a Vampire *'92*
My Son, the Vampire *'52*
Nadja *'95* ►
Near Dark *'87* ►
Nick Knight *'89*
Night Hunter *'95*
Night Junkies *'07*
Night of Dark Shadows *'71* ►
Night of the Sorcerers *'70*
The Night Stalker *'71*
Night Watch *'04*
Nightlife *'90*
Nightmare in Blood *'75*
Ninja, the Violent Sorcerer *'86*
Nocturna *'79*
Nosferatu *'22* ►
Nosferatu the Vampyre *'79*
Not of This Earth *'88*
Not of This Earth *'96*
Once Bitten *'85*
Orgy of the Vampires *'73*
Pale Blood *'91*
Planet of Blood *'66*
Planet of the Vampires *'65*
Project Vampire *'93*
Pulse *'03*
Queen of the Damned *'02*
Rabid *'77*
Red Blooded American Girl *'90*
The Reflecting Skin *'91*
The Return of Count Yorga *'71*
Return of the Vampire *'43*
Return to Salem's Lot *'87*
Rise: Blood Hunter *'07*
The Saga of the Draculas *'72*
Salem's Lot *'79*
Salem's Lot *'04*
Samson vs. the Vampire Women *'61*
The Satanic Rites of Dracula *'73*
The Scars of Dracula *'70*
Scream Blacula Scream *'73*
Shadow of the Vampire *'00* ►
ShadowZone: The Undead Express *'96*
The Slaughter of the Vampires *'62*
Slayer *'06*
Sleepwalkers *'92*
Son of Dracula *'43* ►
Sorority House Vampires *'95*
Stephen King's The Night Flier *'96*
Subspecies *'90*
Suck *'09*
Sundown *'91*
Tainted *'98*
Tale of a Vampire *'92*
Tales from the Crypt Presents Bordello of Blood *'96*
A Taste of Blood *'67*
Taste the Blood of Dracula *'70*
Theatre of Death *'67*
Thirst *'79*
The Thirst *'06*
Thirst *'09* ►
The Thirsty Dead *'74*
30 Days of Night *'07*
To Die For *'89*
To Die For 2: Son of Darkness *'91*
To Sleep with a Vampire *'92*
Track of the Vampire *'66*
Transylvania Twist *'89*
Tsui Hark's Vampire Hunters *'02*
Twilight *'08*
The Twilight Saga: Eclipse *'10*
The Twilight Saga: New Moon *'09*
Twins of Evil *'71*
Ultraviolet *'98*
Uncle Was a Vampire *'59*
Understudy: The Graveyard Shift 2 *'88*
Underworld *'03*
Underworld: Evolution *'05*
Underworld: Rise of the Lycans *'09*
The Unearthing *'93*
Vamp *'86*
The Vampire *'57*
Vampire Assassin *'05*
Vampire at Midnight *'88*
The Vampire Bat *'32*
Vampire Circus *'71*
Vampire Cop *'90*
Vampire Effect *'03*
The Vampire Happening *'71*
The Vampire Hookers *'78*
Vampire in Brooklyn *'95*
Vampire Journals *'96*
The Vampire Lovers *'70*
The Vampire People *'66*
Vampire Time Travelers *'98*
Vampirella *'96*
The Vampire's Coffin *'58*
The Vampire's Ghost *'45*
Vampire's Kiss *'88* ►
Vampyr *'31* ►
The Vampyr *'92*
Vampyres *'74*
Van Helsing *'04* ►
The Velvet Vampire *'71*
Vlad *'03*
The Werewolf vs. the Vampire Woman *'70*

► = rated three bones or higher

Feeling Minnesota '96
Finding Amanda '08
The Flintstones in Viva Rock Vegas '00
Fools Rush In '97
For Which He Stands '98
Gamble on Love '86
Get Shorty '95 ▸
The Girl Next Door '04
Girls' Night '97
Go '99 ▸
The Grasshopper '69
The Great Buck Howard '09
The Great White Hype '96
The Hangover '09
Happily Ever After '82
Hard Vice '94
Heat '87
Heaven or Vegas '98
Hell Squad '85
High Stakes '93
Honey, I Blew Up the Kid '92
Honeymoon in Vegas '92
I Shot a Man in Vegas '96
Indecent Proposal '93
Jinxed '82
Jocks '87
Kingpin '96
Kiss Me, Stupid! '64
Lady Cocoa '75
Las Vegas Hillbillys '66
Las Vegas Lady '76
Las Vegas Serial Killer '86
The Las Vegas Story '52
Las Vegas Weekend '85
Leaving Las Vegas '95 ▸
Leprechaun 3 '95
Looney Tunes: Back in Action '03
The Lucky Ones '08
Lucky You '07
Luckytown '00
The Marrying Man '91
Meet Me in Las Vegas '56
The Mexican '01
Miss Congeniality 2: Armed and Fabulous '05
My Blueberry Nights '07
Nature of the Beast '94
The Night Stalker '71
Ocean's 11 '60
Ocean's Eleven '01 ▸
Painting the Clouds With Sunshine '51
Play It to the Bone '99
Player 5150 '08
Rain Man '88 ▸
The Rat Pack '98
Rat Race '01
Rock-a-Doodle '92
R.S.V.P. '02
The Runner '99
Rush Hour 2 '01
Saint John of Las Vegas '09
Sex & Lies in Sin City: The Ted Binion Scandal '08
The Showgirl Murders '95
Showgirls '95
Sister Act '92
Six-String Samurai '98
Sparkler '99
Speedway Junky '99
Starman '84 ▸
Stripshow '95
Sugartime '95
Swingers '96 ▸
Sword of Honor '94
Texas Payback '95
Three Days to Vegas '07
3000 Miles to Graceland '01
Tomcats '01
Tricks '97
21 '08
Two for the Money '05
Up Against the Eight Ball '04
Vampirella '96
The Vegas Strip Wars '84
Vegas Vacation '96
Vegas Vice '94
Very Bad Things '98
Viva Las Vegas '63
Wedding Bell Blues '96
What Happens in Vegas '08
The Wild Card '03
The Winner '96
Yonkers Joe '08

Volcanos

see also *Disaster Flicks*

Dante's Peak '97
The Devil at 4 O'Clock '61
Ginostra '02
The Happiness of the Katakuris '01
Joe Versus the Volcano '90
Krakatoa East of Java '69
Last Days of Pompeii '35
The Last Days of Pompeii '60
Magma: Volcanic Disaster '06
Nutcase '83
St. Helen's, Killer Volcano '82
Volcano '97
Volcano: Fire on the Mountain '97
Waikiki Wedding '37 ▸
When Time Ran Out '80
The Wrath of the Gods '14

Volleyball

Air Bud 5: Buddy Spikes Back '03
Beach Kings '08
Cast Away '00 ▸
Impact Point '08
The Iron Ladies '00
The Iron Ladies 2 '03
Meet the Parents '00 ▸
Side Out '90
South Beach Academy '96
Superdad '73
Top Gun '86

Voodoo

see also *Occult*

Angel Heart '87
Asylum '72
Black Devil Doll from Hell '84
Black Magic Woman '91
Blues Brothers 2000 '98
Caribe '87
Curse 3: Blood Sacrifice '90
Curtis's Charm '96
The Devil's Daughter '39
Dr. Terror's House of Horrors '65
Eve's Bayou '97 ▸
Headhunter '89
The House on Skull Mountain '74
Household Saints '93 ▸
How to Stuff a Wild Bikini '65
I Eat Your Skin '64
I Walked with a Zombie '43 ▸
Jonah Hex '10
Jungle Drums of Africa '53
Live and Let Die '73
London Voodoo '04
Macumba Love '60
Marked for Death '90
Naked Evil '66
The Offspring '87
Plague of the Zombies '66
The Possession of Joel Delaney '72
Scared Stiff '87
Scream Blacula Scream '73
The Serpent and the Rainbow '87
Shrunken Heads '94
The Snake People '68
Tales from the Hood '95
Theatre of Death '67
Venom '05
Voodoo '95
Voodoo Academy '00
Voodoo Black Exorcist '73
Voodoo Dawn '89
Voodoo Dawn '99
Weekend at Bernie's 2 '93

Vote for Me!

see also *Capitol Capers*

The Adjustment Bureau '10
All the King's Men '06
The Big Brass Ring '99
Bobby '06
Bulworth '98 ▸
The Candidate '72 ▸
Choose Connor '07
The Contract '98
Definitely, Maybe '08 ▸
Deterrence '00
Election '99 ▸
Goodbye My Fancy '51
Hard to Kill '89
Head of State '03
Homicide: The Movie '00
If I'm Lucky '46
JFK: Reckless Youth '93
The Last Debate '00
Life Begins at Forty '35
A Lion in the Streets '53
Maid in Manhattan '02
Mail to the Chief '00
Malibu's Most Wanted '03
Man of the Year '06
The Manchurian Candidate '62 ▸
Me & Mrs. Jones '02
Menno's Mind '96
My Date with the President's Daughter '98
The Palermo Connection '91
Politics '31
Poster Boy '04
Primary Colors '98
Race '99
Random Hearts '99
Recount '08
Running Mates '00
The Seduction of Joe Tynan '79
Slow Burn '05
Southland Tales '06
Swing Vote '08
The Trojan Horse '08
An Unreasonable Man '06 ▸
Waking the Dead '00

Wagon Train

see also *Military Westerns; Westerns*

Across the Plains '39
Bend of the River '52 ▸
Big Trail '30 ▸
The Command '54
Covered Wagon Trails '40
Dawn on the Great Divide '42
Donner Pass: The Road to Survival '84
Doomed Caravan '41 ▸
Fighting Caravans '31
The Forty-Niners '32
The Hallelujah Trail '65
The Indian Fighter '55 ▸
Lawless Plainsmen '42
The Painted Stallion '37
The Paleface '48 ▸
Roll, Wagons, Roll '39
September Dawn '07
Seven Alone '75
Silverado '85 ▸
Solaris '02
Thunder Trail '37
Wackiest Wagon Train in the West '77
Wagon Master '50 ▸
Wagon Wheels '34
Wagons East '94
Westward Ho '35

Waiters & Waitresses

About Adam '00
According to Greta '08
Alice Doesn't Live Here Anymore '74
Alien Trespass '09
Along Came Polly '04
Amelie '01 ▸
Anything But Love '02
Apres-Vous '03
Arthur '81 ▸
As Good As It Gets '97 ▸
Ask the Dust '06
Atlantic City '81 ▸
Avenue Montaigne '06
Battle Shock '56
Bikini Bistro '94
Broken English '96
Bug '06
Cafe Romeo '91
Caffeine '06
Celebrity '98 ▸
Code Name: The Cleaner '07
Coffee and Cigarettes '03 ▸
Come Back to the Five & Dime Jimmy Dean, Jimmy Dean '82 ▸
The Cooler '03 ▸
Coyote Ugly '00
Dancer, Texas—Pop. 81 '98 ▸
Dream for an Insomniac '96
Duets '00
East Side Story '07
Edmond '05
The Embalmer '03 ▸
Exiled in America '90
Eye of God '97 ▸
Fear and Loathing in Las Vegas '98
Feeling Minnesota '96
Five Easy Pieces '70 ▸
The 4th Tenor '02
Fragments '08
Frankie and Johnny '91 ▸
Gloomy Sunday '02 ▸
Hard Eight '96 ▸
Having a Wonderful Time '38
Heavy '94 ▸
Highway Hitcher '98
Holiday in Handcuffs '07
Hysterical Blindness '02
I Served the King of England '07 ▸
In the Weeds '00
It Could Happen to You '94
Joey Breaker '93 ▸
Jon Jost's Frameup '93
Just a Kiss '02
Just Your Luck '96
Love on the Side '04
The Machinist '04
Million Dollar Baby '04 ▸
Monster's Ball '01 ▸
Moon over Miami '41 ▸
Moontide '42
The Muppets Take Manhattan '84 ▸
My Blueberry Nights '07
Mystic Pizza '88 ▸
No Looking Back '98
Nurse Betty '00 ▸
Office Space '98
The Postman Always Rings Twice '46 ▸
The Postman Always Rings Twice '81
Protocol '84
Pure Danger '96
The Purple Rose of Cairo '85 ▸
Quiet Days in Hollywood '97
The Red Mill '27
Restaurant '98
Return to Me '00
The Runner '99
Salem's Lot '04
A Season for Miracles '99
Sex and Lucia '01
Shaft '00 ▸
Skipped Parts '00
Sliding Doors '97
Spare Me '92
The Spitfire Grill '95
Still Waiting '08
A Summer's Tale '96
Swimming '00
Tennessee '08
Thelma & Louise '91 ▸
Time to Leave '05 ▸
Untamed Heart '93
Waiting '00
Waiting '05
The Waiting Game '99
Waitress '81
Waitress '07 ▸
Weather Girl '09
Wedding Daze '06
The Wedding Singer '97
White Palace '90
Willa '79
Wisegirls '02

Wall Street

see also *Corporate Shenanigans*

American Psycho '99
Boiler Room '00 ▸
The Bonfire of the Vanities '90
The Cheat '15 ▸
Family Man '00
From the Terrace '60
The Good Guy '10
Toast of New York '37 ▸
Trading Places '83
Wall Street '87 ▸
Wall Street 2: Money Never Sleeps '10
The Wheeler Dealers '63 ▸
Working Girl '88 ▸

War Between the Sexes

see also *Divorce; Marriage; Singles*

About Last Night... '86 ▸
Adam's Rib '50 ▸
Addicted to Love '96
The African Queen '51 ▸
All of Me '84
All Tied Up '92
All's Fair '89
Alternative '76
Always '85 ▸
America 3000 '86
Anchorman: The Legend of Ron Burgundy '04
Annie Hall '77 ▸
Around the World Under the Sea '65
Autumn Marathon '79
The Awful Truth '37 ▸
Baby on Board '08
The Ballad of the Sad Cafe '91
Bare Essentials '91
Basic Training '86
Battle of the Sexes '28
Behind Office Doors '31
The Best Intentions '92 ▸
Beware of Pity '46
The Bigamist '53
Blood and Sand '41 ▸
The Bodyguard '92
Bonnie's Kids '73
Boomerang '92
The Bride Walks Out '36
Brief Interviews With Hideous Men '09
Bringing Up Baby '38 ▸
Buffalo Jump '90 ▸
Bull Durham '88 ▸
Cannibal Women in the Avocado Jungle of Death '89
Carmen '83 ▸
Carmen Jones '54 ▸
Carrington, V.C. '54 ▸
Carry On Cabby '63
Carry On Nurse '59
Casablanca '42 ▸
Casanova's Big Night '54
Castaway '87
Casual Sex? '88
Chained '34
Cold Heat '90
Concrete Beat '84
Cruel Intentions '98
The Cry of the Owl '87
The Cutting Edge '92
Dangerous Liaisons '60
Dating the Enemy '95
Dear Murderer '47
Dear Wife '49
Def Jam's How to Be a Player '97
Designing Woman '57 ▸
Disclosure '94
Divorce His, Divorce Hers '72
Divorce—Italian Style '62 ▸
Dogfight '91 ▸
Don Juan, My Love '90 ▸
Dream Wife '53
Easy Wheels '89
Far and Away '92
The Favor '92
The Female Bunch '69
Fever '91
The Fighting Sheriff '31
First Monday in October '81
The First to Go '97
The First Wives Club '96
Forever Darling '56
Forget Paris '95
Frankie and Johnny '91 ▸
A Girl in a Million '46
Gone with the Wind '39 ▸
The Good Father '87 ▸
Goodbye Love '34
Guarding Tess '94
The Happy Ending '69
Hardhat & Legs '80
Having It All '82
He Said, She Said '91
Hearing Voices '90
Heartburn '86 ▸
His Girl Friday '40 ▸
Hot Summer '68
Hotel Room '93
Housesitter '92
I Live My Life '35
I Love My... Wife '70
I Love Trouble '94
I Love You '81
I Love You All '80
In the Good Old Summertime '49 ▸
In the Line of Fire '93 ▸
Intimate Story '81
Irreconcilable Differences '84
It Happened One Night '34 ▸
The Jewel of the Nile '85
Juliet of the Spirits '65 ▸
June Bride '48 ▸
Just Tell Me What You Want '80
Key Exchange '85
The King and I '56 ▸
Kiss Me Kate '53 ▸
Kramer vs. Kramer '79 ▸
La Discrete '90 ▸
L.A. Story '91 ▸
The Lady Says No '51
The Last Woman on Earth '61
Le Chat '75 ▸
Legion of Iron '90
Letters to an Unknown Lover '84
Lily in Love '85
The Lion in Winter '68 ▸
Love Crazy '41 ▸
Love in the Afternoon '57
Love Nest '51
Lover Come Back '61
Loyalties '86
Lucky Partners '40
Man of Destiny '73
The Man Who Guards the Greenhouse '88
Manhattan '79 ▸
Many Rivers to Cross '55
Maria's Lovers '84
The Marriage of Maria Braun '79 ▸
The Marrying Man '91
A Matter of Love '78
Maverick '94
McLintock! '63 ▸
Men... '85 ▸
A Midsummer Night's Dream '35 ▸
A Midsummer Night's Dream '96
Moonlighting '85
Moonstruck '87 ▸
Mortal Thoughts '91
Much Ado about Nothing '93 ▸
Murphy's Law '86
My Brilliant Career '79 ▸
Near Misses '91
A New Leaf '71
9 to 5 '80
Nothing in Common '86
One Woman or Two '85
The Opposite Sex and How to Live With Them '93
Pajama Tops '83
Pat and Mike '52 ▸
Patti Rocks '88 ▸
Pauline at the Beach '83 ▸
A Piece of Pleasure '74 ▸
Pillow Talk '59 ▸
Places in the Heart '84 ▸
Portrait of Teresa '79 ▸
The Practice of Love '84
Private Lives '31 ▸
Prizzi's Honor '85 ▸
Public Enemy '31 ▸
Queen of Outer Space '58
Question of Silence '83 ▸
The Quiet Man '52 ▸
Ramrod '47
The Ref '93 ▸
Romancing the Stone '84 ▸
Rooster Cogburn '75
Running Mates '92 ▸
Sabrina '54 ▸
Sabrina '95

▸ = rated three bones or higher

Scenes from a Mall '91
Seance on a Wet Afternoon '64 ▶
The Sensual Man '74
Serious Moonlight '09
Sex and the College Girl '64
She-Devil '89
Shore Leave '25 ▶
Siberian Lady Macbeth '61 ▶
The Single Standard '29
The Social Secretary '16
Solitaire for 2 '94
Someone Like You '01
Sotto, Sotto '85
Speechless '94
Speedtrap '78
Spies, Lies and Naked Thighs '91
Star 80 '83
The Story of Fausta '88
Summer Night with Greek Profile, Almond Eyes & Scent of Basil '87
Swept Away '02
Switch '91 ▶
Switching Channels '88
The Taming of the Shrew '29
The Taming of the Shrew '67 ▶
A Taxing Woman '87 ▶
Teacher's Pet '58 ▶
Ted & Venus '93
That Old Feeling '96
That's My Baby! '88
Thelma & Louise '91 ▶
The Thing '51 ▶
Thor and the Amazon Women '60
Three of Hearts '93
Thunder in the Pines '49
Tiger and the Pussycat '67
To Have & Have Not '44 ▶
To Wong Foo, Thanks for Everything, Julie Newmar '95
Tony Draws a Horse '51
True Love '89 ▶
Two-Faced Woman '41 ▶
Two Weeks Notice '02
The Ugly Truth '09
Vasectomy: A Delicate Matter '86
War Between the Tates '76
The War of the Roses '89 ▶
When Harry Met Sally... '89 ▶
When Ladies Meet '41
When Women Lost Their Tails '75
Who's Afraid of Virginia Woolf? '66 ▶
Wife Versus Secretary '36 ▶
The Witches of Eastwick '87
Without Love '45
A Woman of Distinction '50 ▶
Woman of the Year '42 ▶
Women & Men: In Love There Are No Rules '91
Women & Men: Stories of Seduction '90
Women on the Verge of a Nervous Breakdown '88 ▶
Women vs. Men '02
The World According to Garp '82 ▶
Year of the Comet '92
Yesterday, Today and Tomorrow '64 ▶
Your Friends & Neighbors '98 ▶
You're a Big Boy Now '66 ▶

War Brides

see also *Marriage; Marriages of Convenience; Vietnam War; World War I; World War II*
G.I. War Brides '46
Heaven and Earth '93
I Was a Male War Bride '49 ▶
John Loves Mary '48
Sayonara '57 ▶
The War Bride '01

War, General

see also *Anti-War War Movies; Big Battles; Civil War; Korean War; Persian Gulf/Iraq War; Postwar; POW/MIA; Revolutionary War; Terrorism; Veterans; Vietnam War; World War I; World War II*
The Alamo '60 ▶
The Alamo: Thirteen Days to Glory '87
Alexander '04
Alexander Nevsky '38 ▶
Alexander the Great '55
Alone Against Rome '62
Alsino and the Condor '82 ▶
And Starring Pancho Villa as Himself '03 ▶
Anna Karenina '48
Atlas '60
The Avenger '62
Ay, Carmela! '90 ▶
Ballad of a Soldier '60 ▶
Bang Rajan '00 ▶
Barb Wire '96
Battle Hell '56
The Battle of Algiers '66 ▶
The Battle of Austerlitz '60
The Beast '88
Beau Geste '39 ▶
Before the Rain '94 ▶
Behind the Front '26
The Bitter Tea of General Yen '33 ▶
Blood Diamond '06
Braveheart '95 ▶
Brothers '04 ▶
The Buccaneer '58
A Bullet for the General '68
By Dawn's Early Light '89
Captain Caution '40
Captain Horatio Hornblower '51 ▶
Carthage in Flames '60
Cast a Giant Shadow '66
Cavalry Command '63
Chapayev '34 ▶
The Charge of the Light Brigade '36 ▶
The Charge of the Light Brigade '68
Civilization '16 ▶
Codename: Terminate '90
Colonel Chabert '94
Colonel Wolodyjowski '69
The Conqueror '56
Conquest of the Normans '62
Control Room '04 ▶
Coup de Grace '78
The Court Martial of Billy Mitchell '55 ▶
Cromwell '70
Cup Final '92
Danton '82 ▶
Days of Hell '84
Deadline '87
The Deluge '73
The Desert of the Tartars '76
The Devil Came on Horseback '07
Devil Wears White '86
Distant Drums '51
Dragon Seed '44
Eagles Attack at Dawn '70
1860 '33
El Cid '61 ▶
El Paso Stampede '53
Elizabeth of Ladymead '48 ▶
Emissary '89
The Enchanted Cottage '45
The End of St. Petersburg '27 ▶
The Expendables '89
Fahrenheit 9/11 '04 ▶
The Fall of the Roman Empire '64 ▶
Field of Honor '87
Fiesta '95
The Fighter '52 ▶
Fighting Marines '36
Fighting Pilot '35
The Fighting Prince of Donegal '66
The Finest Hour '91
Fire Over England '37 ▶
The Firing Line '91
Flor Silvestre '58
Flowers of Reverie '84
Forever and a Day '43 ▶
Fort Apache '48 ▶
Forty Days of Musa Dagh '85
The Four Feathers '39 ▶
The Four Feathers '78
F.P. 1 '33
Funny, Dirty Little War '83
Guerilla Brigade '39
Gunga Din '39 ▶
Gunner Palace '04 ▶
Guns at Batasi '64
Hail the Conquering Hero '44 ▶
Harry's War '84
Heart of a Nation '43 ▶
Heartbreak Ridge '86 ▶
Hearts & Armour '83
Heaven & Earth '90 ▶
Hell in the Pacific '69 ▶
Hell on the Battleground '88
Hell Raiders '68
Henry V '89 ▶
Hero Bunker '71
The Hidden Fortress '58 ▶
Hijacking Catastrophe: 9/11, Fear and the Selling of America '04
Hill 24 Doesn't Answer '55 ▶
Hollow City '04
The Holy Terror '37
Holy Terror '65
Hombres Armados '97 ▶
Homecoming '28 ▶
Hotel Rwanda '04
House of Fools '02
How I Won the War '67
Howl's Moving Castle '04
In the Name of the Pope-King '85 ▶
The Informer '35 ▶
Innocent Voices '04
The Invincible Gladiator '63
Jarhead '05
Johnny Got His Gun '71 ▶
Judith of Bethulia '14 ▶
Khartoum '66
Killers '88
King Arthur '04
Kingdom of Heaven '05 ▶
Kippur '00 ▶
Kolberg '45
Korea Patrol '47
La Marseillaise '37 ▶
La Nuit de Varennes '82 ▶
The Last Command '55
The Last of the Mohicans '20 ▶
The Last of the Mohicans '32
The Last of the Mohicans '36
The Last of the Mohicans '85
The Last of the Mohicans '92 ▶
The Last Valley '71
Late Summer Blues '87
Latino '85
Laughing at Life '33
Le Petit Soldat '60 ▶
The Legend of Suriyothai '02
Legion of Missing Men '37
The Life and Death of Colonel Blimp '43 ▶
Lion of the Desert '81 ▶
Lipstick on Your Collar '94
The Longest Day '62 ▶
The Lost Command '66
Mademoiselle Fifi '44
Man from the Alamo '53 ▶
Man with a Cross '43
Massive Retaliation '85
Megaforce '82
Mercenary Fighters '88
Mission Kashmir '00
Mission to Glory '80
The Mongols '60
The Moonraker '58
Mother '26 ▶
The Mouse That Roared '59 ▶
Mulan '98
Napoleon '27 ▶
No Man's Land '01
Occupation: Dreamland '05 ▶
An Occurrence at Owl Creek Bridge/Coup de Grace '62
Old Gringo '89
One Night Stand '84 ▶
Orphans of the Storm '21 ▶
Our Music '04
Peace, Propaganda & the Promised Land '04
The Phantom Planet '61
Planet of the Apes '01 ▶
Prehistoric Bimbos in Armageddon City '93
The Pride and the Passion '57
Prisoner of the Mountains '96 ▶
Project: Alien '89
Purple Butterfly '03 ▶
Rage to Kill '88
The Rape of the Sabines '61
The Real Glory '39 ▶
A Reason to Live, a Reason to Die '73
The Red and the Black '57 ▶
The Red and the White '68 ▶
Red Dawn '84
Reed: Insurgent Mexico '73
Reign of Terror '49
Revenge of the Barbarians '60
Rhodes '36
Richard III '12
Richard III '95 ▶
Ride to Glory '71
River of Unrest '36
The Road to Guantanamo '06
Rough Riders '97
Ryan's Daughter '70
Saga of the Vagabond '59
Salome, Where She Danced '45
Sanders of the River '35 ▶
Seminole Uprising '55
Senso '54 ▶
The Seventeenth Bride '84
Shake Hands with the Devil '59 ▶
Shake Hands With the Devil: The Journey of Romeo Dallaire '04 ▶
The Shame '68 ▶
Sharpe's Battle '94
Sharpe's Company '94
Sharpe's Eagle '93
Sharpe's Enemy '94
Sharpe's Gold '94
Sharpe's Honour '94
Sharpe's Justice '97
Sharpe's Legend '97
Sharpe's Mission '96
Sharpe's Regiment '96
Sharpe's Revenge '97
Sharpe's Rifles '93
Sharpe's Siege '96
Sharpe's Sword '94
Sharpe's Waterloo '97
Shot Through the Heart '98 ▶
Simon Bolivar '69
Sinai Commandos '68
Smugglers '75
Something of Value '57 ▶
South Park: Bigger, Longer and Uncut '99
Starship Troopers '97 ▶
Storm over Asia '28 ▶
Striker '88
Surprise Attack '70
Taras Bulba '62
This England '42
This Island Earth '55
The 317th Platoon '65 ▶
Tiger Joe '85
Time to Kill '89
The Torch '50
Treasure of the Lost Desert '83
Tristan & Isolde '06
The Troubles We've Seen '94
Troy '04
Turtles Can Fly '04 ▶
The Ugly American '63
Ulysses' Gaze '95
Uncovered: The War on Iraq '04
Under Fire '83 ▶
The Uprising '81 ▶
Vera Cruz '53
Villa Rides '68
Voices of Iraq '04 ▶
Walker '87
War and Peace '56
War and Peace '68 ▶
War and Peace '73
War Bus Commando '89
Warbirds '88
Warlords '08
The Warrior '01 ▶
Warriors '02
Waterloo '71
Weekend War '88
Welcome to Sarajevo '97 ▶
White Dwarf '95
Wild Geese 2 '85
Wing Commander '99
The World Owes Me a Living '47
World War III '86
Yank in Libya '42
Young Winston '72 ▶
Zulu Dawn '79 ▶

Washington, DC

see *Capitol Capers*

Weathermen

see also *News at 11*
The 4th Floor '99
Groundhog Day '93 ▶
L.A. Story '91 ▶
Lucky Numbers '00
The Perfect Storm '00
Twister '96
The Weather Man '05

Wedding Bells

see also *Marriage; Otherwise Engaged; Wedding Hell*
About Schmidt '02 ▶
After the Wedding '06 ▶
Aladdin and the King of Thieves '96
American Wedding '03
Anne of Green Gables: The Continuing Story '99
April's Shower '03
The Arrangement '99 ▶
The Bachelor '99
The Baxter '05
Because I Said So '07
Bend It Like Beckham '02 ▶
The Best Man '99 ▶
Betsy's Wedding '90
Blind Date '87
The Bread, My Sweet '01
Bridal Fever '08
The Bride Came C.O.D. '41
The Bride Walks Out '36
Bride Wars '09
Buying the Cow '02
Cake '05
Chaos Theory '08
Common Ground '00
Confusion of Genders '00
Conversations with Other Women '05
Cowboys and Angels '00
The Cruise of the Jasper B '26
Dan in Real Life '07
Date Bait '60
The Duke '99
Easy Money '83
Easy Virtue '08
8 Seconds '94
Emma '96 ▶
Emma '97 ▶
Esmeralda Comes by Night '98
Evening '07
Everyone Says I Love You '96 ▶
Fanci's Persuasion '95
Fandango '85
Fantastic Four: Rise of the Silver Surfer '07
Father of the Bride '50 ▶
Father of the Bride '91
Fiddler on the Roof '71 ▶
Foolin' Around '80
For Better and for Worse '92
Forget Paris '95
Four Weddings and a Funeral '94 ▶
Freaky Friday '03 ▶
Full of Life '56
Ghosts of Girlfriends Past '09
Give Me a Sailor '38
The Godfather '72 ▶
Good Luck Chuck '07
The Groomsmen '06
Hard Promises '92
Heartbreakers '01
Holy Matrimony '94
Honeymoon in Vegas '92
House Party 3 '94
Housesitter '92
I Do '06
I'm with Lucy '02
Imagine Me & You '06
Intolerable Cruelty '03
Invitation '51
It Started with Eve '41 ▶
Jack and Sarah '95
Jerry Maguire '96 ▶
The Jewel of the Nile '85
John Loves Mary '48
Kissing a Fool '98
Knight and Day '10
Love and Other Four Letter Words '07
Love, etc. '96
Lovers and Other Strangers '70 ▶
Ma Vie en Rose '97 ▶
Mamma Mia! '08
Margot at the Wedding '07
The Marriage of Figaro '49
The Marrying Man '91
Meet the Fockers '04
The Member of the Wedding '97
Miami Rhapsody '95
Mickey Blue Eyes '99
Minnie and Moskowitz '71
The Mirror Has Two Faces '96
Mrs. Winterbourne '96
Monsoon Wedding '01 ▶
Moonstruck '87 ▶
Murders in the Rue Morgue '32
Muriel's Wedding '94 ▶
My Best Friend's Wedding '97
My Big Fat Greek Wedding '02
My Favorite Wife '40 ▶
My First Wedding '04
Nanny McPhee '06
The Neighbor '07
Neil Simon's The Odd Couple 2 '98
Nine Months '95
Noah's Arc: Jumping the Broom '08
Notting Hill '99 ▶
Nutty Professor 2: The Klumps '00
Only You '94
Our Family Wedding '10
Out at the Wedding '07
Painting the Clouds With Sunshine '51
The Philadelphia Story '40 ▶
Pirates of the Caribbean: Dead Man's Chest '06
Polish Wedding '97
Prelude to a Kiss '92
The Prince & Me 2: Royal Wedding '06
Princess O'Rourke '43
The Proposal '09
Reckless: The Sequel '98 ▶
Revenge of the Nerds 4: Nerds in Love '94
Rhythm on the Range '36
Ride with the Devil '99
Roommates '95
The Roundup '41
Royal Wedding '51 ▶
Sex and the City 2 '10
Sex and the City: The Movie '08
She's Having a Baby '88

Sixteen Candles '84 ►
The Son of the Bride '01
The Sound of Music '65 ►
Splendor '99
Standing Still '05
Star Trek: Nemesis '02
Steel Magnolias '89 ►
The Summer House '94
The Tender Trap '55
That Old Feeling '96
The 30-Foot Bride of Candy Rock '59
Three Men and a Little Lady '90
Three Smart Girls Grow Up '39 ►
Tim Burton's Corpse Bride '05 ►
To Each His Own '46 ►
27 Dresses '08
Two Moon Junction '88
Two Weeks Notice '02
Up in the Air '09 ►
Waikiki Wedding '37 ►
A Wedding '78
Wedding Band '89
Wedding Bell Blues '96
The Wedding Bros. '08
Wedding Crashers '05 ►
The Wedding Date '05
The Wedding March '28 ►
The Wedding Party '69
The Wedding Party '97
Wedding Present '36
Wedding Rehearsal '32
Wedding Wars '06
West Is West '87
When Harry Met Sally... '89 ►
Where the Heart Is '00
Where There's Life '47
The Wood '99
The World's Oldest Living Bridesmaid '92

Wedding Hell

see also *Marriage; Marriage Hell; Otherwise Engaged; Wedding Bells*

Analyze This '98 ►
Arthur '81 ►
The Best Man '97
Best Men '98
The Big Day '99
Blood Bride '80
The Blood Spattered Bride '72
The Bride '85
The Bride of Frankenstein '35 ►
Bride of Killer Nerd '91
Bride of Re-Animator '89
Bride of the Gorilla '51
Bride of the Monster '55
The Bride with White Hair '93
The Bride Wore Black '68 ►
Brides of the Beast '68
Captive '97
The Catered Affair '56 ►
Cheatin' Hearts '93
Confetti '06
Contract '80 ►
Dr. T & the Women '00 ►
Feeling Minnesota '96
The Flame of New Orleans '41 ►
Forces of Nature '99
Ganja and Hess '73
A Girl Cut in Two '07
The Graduate '67 ►
The Hanging Garden '97
Hangman's House '28
He Knows You're Alone '80
Highway to Hell '92
Honeymoon '87
Honeymoon Killers '70 ►
I Married a Monster from Outer Space '58
I Think I Do '97
In and Out '97 ►
The In-Laws '03
Kill Bill Vol. 1 '03 ►
Kill Bill Vol. 2 '04 ►
Last Chance Harvey '08
Last Lives '98
Late Marriage '01
Love Stinks '99
Meet the Parents '00 ►
Monster-in-Law '05
My New Gun '92
Niagara '52
Norbit '07
Old School '03
The Perfect Bride '91
Riding in Cars with Boys '01
River Street '95
Runaway Bride '99 ►
Saving Silverman '01
The Sweetest Thing '02
That Old Feeling '96
Tim Burton's Corpse Bride '05 ►
Tomcats '01
Tony n' Tina's Wedding '07
Trojan Eddie '96 ►
True Love '89 ►
28 Days '00
The Undertaker's Wedding '97
Very Bad Things '98
The Wedding Banquet '93 ►
Wedding in Blood '74 ►
Wedding in White '72
The Wedding Planner '01
The Wedding Singer '97
You and Me '38

Werewolves

see also *Metamorphosis*

An American Werewolf in London '81 ►
An American Werewolf in Paris '97
Bad Moon '96
The Beast Must Die '75
Big Fish '03 ►
Blood & Chocolate '07
Blood of Dracula's Castle '69
Bride of the Gorilla '51
Children of the Full Moon '84
The Company of Wolves '85 ►
The Craving '80
The Creeps '97
Cry of the Werewolf '44
Curse of the Devil '73
Curse of the Queerwolf '87
The Curse of the Werewolf '61
Cursed '04
Darkwolf '03
Deathmoon '78
Dr. Jekyll and the Wolfman '71
Dr. Terror's House of Horrors '65
Dog Soldiers '01
Dracula vs. Frankenstein '69
Face of the Screaming Werewolf '59
Frankenstein Meets the Wolfman '42 ►
Full Eclipse '93
The Fury of the Wolfman '70
Ginger Snaps '01
Ginger Snaps Back: The Beginning '04
Ginger Snaps: Unleashed '04
Harry Potter and the Prisoner of Azkaban '04
Hercules, Prisoner of Evil '64
House of Dracula '45
House of Frankenstein '44
The Howling '81 ►
Howling 2: Your Sister Is a Werewolf '85
Howling 3: The Marsupials '87
Howling 4: The Original Nightmare '88
Howling 6: The Freaks '90
The Howling: New Moon Rising '95
I Was a Teenage Werewolf '57
Kibakichi '04
Kibakichi 2 '04
Legend of the Werewolf '75
The Legend of the Wolf Woman '77
Lone Wolf '88
Mad at the Moon '92
The Mad Monster '42
Mating Dance '08
Meridian: Kiss of the Beast '90
Monster Dog '82
The Monster Squad '87
Moon of the Wolf '72
My Mom's a Werewolf '89
Nature of the Beast '07
Never Cry Werewolf '08
Night of the Howling Beast '75
Orgy of the Dead '65
Project Metalbeast: DNA Overload '94
Rage of the Werewolf '99
The Rats Are Coming! The Werewolves Are Here! '72
Return of the Vampire '43
Scream of the Wolf '74
She Wolf of London '46
Silver Bullet '85
Skinwalkers '07
The Strangers '98
Teen Wolf '85
Teen Wolf Too '87
The Twilight Saga: Eclipse '10
The Twilight Saga: New Moon '09
Underworld '03
Underworld: Evolution '05
Underworld: Rise of the Lycans '09
The Undying Monster '42
Van Helsing '04 ►
Waxwork '88
Werewolf '95
Werewolf in a Girl's Dormitory '61
Werewolf of London '35
Werewolf of Washington '73
The Werewolf vs. the Vampire Woman '70
Werewolves on Wheels '71
Wilderness '96
Wolf '94
Wolf Blood '25
The Wolf Man '41 ►
Wolfen '81 ►
The Wolfman '82
The Wolfman '09
The Wolves of Kromer '98

Western Comedy

see also *Comedy; Westerns*

Adios Amigo '75
Alias Jesse James '59
Along Came Jones '45 ►
The Apple Dumpling Gang '75
The Apple Dumpling Gang Rides Again '79
Bad Man's River '72
Ballad of Cable Hogue '70 ►
Bang Bang Kid '67
The Beautiful Blonde from Bashful Bend '49
Beyond the Trail '26 ►
Blazing Saddles '74 ►
Bordello '79
Border Phantom '37
Boss '74
Bowery Buckaroos '47
Branded Men '31
Bronco Billy '80
Brothers O'Toole '73
Buck Benny Rides Again '40
Bus Stop '56 ►
Carry On Cowboy '66
Cat Ballou '65 ►
Catlow '71
Check & Double Check '30
The Cherokee Kid '96
The Cheyenne Social Club '70
The Cisco Kid '94
City Slickers '91 ►
City Slickers 2: The Legend of Curly's Gold '94
Cold Feet '89
Companeros '70
The Cowboy Way '94
Desperate Women '78
Destry Rides Again '39 ►
The Duchess and the Dirtwater Fox '76
The Dude Goes West '48
Ebenezer '97
800 Bullets '02
El Diablo Rides '39
Evil Roy Slade '71 ►
Four Eyes and Six Guns '93
Four for Texas '63
The Frisco Kid '79
From Noon Till Three '76
Go West '40
Goin' South '78 ►
Gold Raiders '51
The Good Guys and the Bad Guys '69
Greaser's Palace '72
Great Scout & Cathouse Thursday '76
Gun Crazy '69
The Hallelujah Trail '65
Hangman's Knot '52
Hawmps! '76
Hearts of the West '75 ►
Home on the Range '04
How the West Was Fun '95
I'm from Arkansas '44
The Incredible Rocky Mountain Race '77
The Kid Brother '27 ►
Lemonade Joe '64
Life & Times of Judge Roy Bean '72
Lightning Jack '94
Local Badman '32
Lucky Luke '94
Mail Order Bride '63
Many Rivers to Cross '55
Maverick '94
McLintock! '63 ►
More Wild, Wild West '80
The Nervous Wreck '26 ►
Oklahoma Kid '39 ►
The Outlaws Is Coming! '65
Over the Hill Gang '69
The Paleface '48 ►
Pardners '56
Pocket Money '72
Rachel and the Stranger '48 ►
Rancho Deluxe '75 ►
Red Garters '54
Rhythm on the Range '36
Ride 'Em Cowboy '42
The Rounders '65
Rustler's Rhapsody '85
Sam Whiskey '69
Samurai Cowboy '93
The Scalphunters '68
Scandalous John '71
September Gun '83
Sergeants 3 '62
The Shakiest Gun in the West '68
Shame, Shame on the Bixby Boys '82
Shanghai Knights '03
Shanghai Noon '00
The Sheepman '58
The Sheriff of Fractured Jaw '59
Sodbusters '94
Son of Paleface '52 ►
Sons of Trinity '95
Sting of the West '72
Straight to Hell '87
Sundance and the Kid '69
Sunset '88
Support Your Local Gunfighter '71 ►
Support Your Local Sheriff '69 ►
Take Me Back to Oklahoma '40
Texas '41 ►
Texas Across the River '66
There Was a Crooked Man '70 ►
They Call Me Trinity '72
Three Godfathers '48 ►
Ticket to Tomahawk '50
The Traveling Saleswoman '50
Trinity Is Still My Name '75
Troublemakers '94
Undead or Alive '07
Under Montana Skies '30
The Villain '79
Wackiest Wagon Train in the West '77
Wagons East '94
Waterhole Number 3 '67
Way Out West '37 ►
Wild & Wooly '78
Wild Horse Phantom '44
Wild Rovers '71
Wild, Wild West Revisited '79
The Wistful Widow of Wagon Gap '47
Yellow Hair & the Fortress of Gold '84
Zachariah '70

Westerns

see also *Sci-Fi Westerns; Spaghetti Western; Supernatural Westerns; Western Comedy; Westrogens*

Abilene Town '46 ►
Aces and Eights '36
Aces 'n Eights '08
Aces Wild '37
Across the Line '00
Across the Plains '39
The Adventures of Gallant Bess '48
Adventures of Red Ryder '40
Against a Crooked Sky '75
The Alamo '60 ►
The Alamo '04
Alias Billy the Kid '46
Alias John Law '35
All the Pretty Horses '00
Allegheny Uprising '39
Along the Great Divide '51
Along the Navaho Trail '45
Along the Sundown Trail '42
Alvarez Kelly '66
Ambush at Tomahawk Gap '53
Ambush Trail '46
American Empire '42
American Outlaws '01
Americano '55
Angel and the Badman '47 ►
Angel and the Badman '09
Animal Called Man '72
Another Man, Another Chance '77
Another Pair of Aces: Three of a Kind '91 ►
Apache '54
Apache Blood '75
Apache Chief '50
Apache Kid's Escape '30
Apache Rose '47
Apache Uprising '66
Apache Woman '55
The Appaloosa '66
Appaloosa '08 ►
Arizona '40
Arizona Bound '41
Arizona Bushwackers '67
Arizona Cowboy '49
Arizona Cyclone '41
Arizona Days '37
Arizona Gangbusters '40
Arizona Gunfighter '37
Arizona Kid '39
Arizona Mahoney '36
Arizona Raiders '65
Arizona Roundup '42
Arizona Stagecoach '42
Arizona Terror '31
Arizona Whirlwind '44
Arrowhead '53
The Assassination of Jesse James by the Coward Robert Ford '07 ►
At Gunpoint '55
The Avenging '92
The Avenging Angel '95
Avenging Angel '07
Back in the Saddle '41
Backfire '22
Bad Company '72 ►
Bad Day at Black Rock '54 ►
Bad Guys '79
Bad Jim '89
Bad Lands '39
Bad Man of Deadwood '41
Bad Men of the Border '45
The Badlanders '58
Badman's Territory '46 ►
Badmen of Nevada '33
Ballad of a Gunfighter '64
Ballad of Gregorio Cortez '83 ►
Bandit King of Texas '49
Bandit Queen '51
The Bandits '67
Bandolero! '68
Banjo Hackett '76
Barbarosa '82 ►
The Bargain '15
Baron of Arizona '51 ►
Barricade '49
Battle of Elderbush Gulch '13
Battling Marshal '48
Battling with Buffalo Bill '31
Bells of Capistrano '42
Bells of Coronado '50
Bells of Rosarita '45
Bells of San Angelo '47
Bells of San Fernando '47
Below the Border '42
Bend of the River '52 ►
Best of the Badmen '50
Between Fighting Men '32
Between God, the Devil & a Winchester '72
Between Men '35
Beyond the Rockies '32
Big Calibre '35
The Big Cat '49
The Big Country '58
A Big Hand for the Little Lady '66
Big Jake '71
Big Show '37
The Big Sky '52 ►
The Big Sombrero '49
Big Stakes '22
The Big Stampede '32
Big Trail '30 ►
Billy the Kid '41
Billy the Kid in Santa Fe '41
Billy the Kid in Texas '40
Billy the Kid Returns '38
Billy the Kid Trapped '42
Billy Two Hats '74
Bite the Bullet '75 ►
Black Fox: Blood Horse '94
Black Fox: Good Men and Bad '94
Black Fox: The Price of Peace '94
Black Hills '48
The Black Lash '52
Black Market Rustlers '43
Black Patch '57
Blazing Across the Pecos '48
Blazing Guns '50
Blind Justice '94
Blood at Sundown '88
Blood on the Moon '48
Bloody Trail '72
Blue '68
Blue Canadian Rockies '52
Blue Steel '34
Boiling Point '32
Bonanza: The Return '93
Bonanza Town '51
Boot Hill Bandits '42
Boothill Brigade '37
Boots & Saddles '37
Boots of Destiny '37
Border Badmen '45
Border Bandits '46
Border Caballero '36
Border Devils '32
Border Feud '47
Border Law '31
The Border Legion '40
Border Patrol '43
Border Rangers '50
Border River '47
Border Romance '30
Border Roundup '41
Border Saddlemates '52
Border Shootout '90
Border Vengeance '35
Border Vigilantes '41
Borderland '37
Bordertown Gunfighters '43
Born in America '90
Boss Cowboy '35
Boss of Boomtown '44
Boss of Bullion City '41
Boss of Rawhide '44
The Bounty Man '72
Brand of Fear '49
Brand of Hate '34
Brand of the Outlaws '36
Branded '50
Branded a Bandit '24
Branded a Coward '35
The Bravados '58 ►

▸ = rated three bones or higher

Westerns

Last of the Pony Riders '53
Last of the Warrens '36
Last of the Wild Horses '49
The Last Outlaw '27
Last Outlaw '36
The Last Outlaw '93
The Last Ride of the Dalton Gang '79
Last Stand at Saber River '96
Last Train from Gun Hill '59 ►
The Law and Jake Wade '58
Law and Lawless '33
Law and Order '40
Law and Order '42
Law and Order '53
Law for Tombstone '35
Law of the Land '76
Law of the Lash '47
Law of the Pampas '39
Law of the Saddle '43
Law of the Texan '38
The Law Rides '36
The Law Rides Again '43
Law West of Tombstone '38
The Lawless Breed '52 ►
Lawless Frontier '35
Lawless Plainsmen '42
Lawless Range '35
A Lawless Street '55
Lawman '71 ►
A Lawman Is Born '37 ►
Lawmen '44
The Lazarus Man '96
Leather Burners '43
The Left-Handed Gun '58 ►
Legend of Alfred Packer '80
The Legend of Butch & Sundance '04
Legend of Earl Durand '74
The Legend of Frank Woods '77
Legend of Frenchie King '71
The Legend of Jedediah Carver '76
Legend of the Lone Ranger '81
Legend of Tom Dooley '59
The Legend of Zorro '05
Legion of the Lawless '40
The Light of Western Stars '30
The Light of Western Stars '40
Lightnin' Bill Carson '36
Lightnin' Carson Rides Again '38
Lightning Bill '35
Lightning Bill Crandall '37
Lightning Raiders '45
Lightning Range '33
Lightning Strikes West '40
Lightning Warrior '31
Lights of Old Santa Fe '47
Lion's Den '36
Little Big Horn '51
Little Big Man '70 ►
Little Moon & Jud McGraw '78
Loaded Pistols '48
The Lone Avenger '33
Lone Bandit '33
The Lone Defender '32
Lone Justice '93
Lone Justice 2 '93
Lone Justice 3: Showdown at Plum Creek '96
The Lone Ranger '38
Lone Ranger '56
Lone Rider '08
The Lone Rider Crosses the Rio '41
The Lone Rider in Cheyenne '42
The Lone Rider in Frontier Fury '41
The Lone Rider in Ghost Town '41
Lone Star '52
Lone Star '95 ►
Lone Star Law Men '42
The Lone Star Ranger '30
The Lone Star Trail '43
Lone Wolf McQuade '83
Lonely Are the Brave '62 ►
Lonely Man '57
Lonesome Dove '89 ►
Lonesome Trail '55
The Long Ride Home '01
The Long Riders '80 ►
The Longest Drive '76
Los Locos Posse '97
Lost Canyon '43
Love Comes Softly '03
Love Desperados '68
Love's Abiding Joy '06
Love's Enduring Promise '04
Love's Long Journey '05
Lucky Cisco Kid '40
Lucky Terror '36
Lucky Texan '34
Lust for Gold '49
The Lusty Men '52 ►
Macho Callahan '70
MacKenna's Gold '69
Madron '70
The Magnificent Seven '60 ►
Mail Order Bride '08
Major Dundee '65
A Man Alone '55
Man & Boy '71
A Man Called Horse '70 ►
A Man Called Sledge '71
Man from Button Willow '65
Man from Cheyenne '42
Man from Colorado '49
Man From God's Country '58
The Man from Gun Town '36
The Man from Hell '34
Man from Hell's Edges '32
The Man from Laramie '55 ►
Man from Montana '41
Man from Monterey '33
The Man from Music Mountain '38
The Man From Oklahoma '26
The Man from Painted Post '17
The Man from Snowy River '82
Man from Texas '39
Man from the Alamo '53 ►
Man from Thunder River '43
Man from Utah '34
Man in the Saddle '51
Man in the Shadow '57
Man of Action '33
Man of the Forest '33
Man of the West '58
Man or Gun '58
The Man Who Came Back '08
Man Who Loved Cat Dancing '73
The Man Who Shot Liberty Valance '62 ►
Man Without a Star '55 ►
Manchurian Avenger '84
The Manhunt '86
Man's Country '38
Man's Land '32
Mark of the Spur '32
Marked for Murder '45
Marked Trails '44
Marshal of Cedar Rock '53
Marshal of Heldorado '50
The Marshal's Daughter '53
The Masked Rider '41
Mason of the Mounted '32
Massacre '56
McCabe & Mrs. Miller '71 ►
The McMasters '70
The Meanest Men in the West '67
Melody of the Plains '37
Melody Ranch '40
Melody Trail '35
Men of America '32
Mesquite Buckaroo '39
Miracle at Sage Creek '05
Miracle in the Wilderness '91
The Miracle Rider '35
The Missing '03 ►
Missouri Breaks '76
Missourians '50
Mr. Horn '79
Mohawk '56
Molly & Lawless John '72
Montana '50
Montana '90
Montana Belle '52
Monte Walsh '70 ►
Monte Walsh '03
The Moonlighter '53
More Dead Than Alive '68
Mosby's Marauders '66
Mountain Justice '30
The Mountain Men '80
My Darling Clementine '46 ►
My Heroes Have Always Been Cowboys '91
My Outlaw Brother '51
My Pal, the King '32
My Pal Trigger '46
Mysterious Desperado '49
The Mysterious Rider '33
The Mysterious Rider '38
The Mysterious Rider '42
Mystery Man '44
Mystery Mountain '34
Mystery of the Hooded Horseman '37
Mystery Ranch '34
Mystery Trooper '32
Naked Hills '56
Naked in the Sun '57
The Naked Spur '53 ►
Narrow Trail '17 ►
Near the Rainbow's End '30
'Neath the Arizona Skies '34
Ned Kelly '70
Nevada '27
Nevada '44
The Nevada Buckaroo '31
Nevada City '41
Nevada Smith '66
The Nevadan '50
The New Frontier '35
Night of the Grizzly '66
Night Passage '57
Night Rider '32
Night Riders of Montana '50
Night Stage to Galveston '52
Night Time in Nevada '48
The Nine Lives of Elfego Baca '58
No Man's Law '27
No Man's Range '35
No Name on the Bullet '59 ►
North of the Great Divide '50
Northern Passage '95
Oath of Vengeance '44
Oh Susannah '38
Oklahoma Annie '51
Oklahoma Badlands '48
Oklahoma Cyclone '30
Oklahoma Frontier '39
Oklahoma Renegades '40
The Oklahoman '56
Old Barn Dance '38
Old Corral '36
On the Night Stage '15
On the Old Spanish Trail '47
On Top of Old Smoky '53
One-Eyed Jacks '61 ►
100 Rifles '69
One Little Indian '73
Only the Valiant '50
Open Range '03 ►
The Outcast '54
Outcasts of the Trail '49
The Outlaw '43
Outlaw Country '49
The Outlaw Deputy '35
Outlaw Express '38
Outlaw Fury '50
Outlaw Gang '49
The Outlaw Josey Wales '76 ►
Outlaw Justice '32
Outlaw Justice '98
Outlaw of the Plains '46
Outlaw Roundup '44
Outlaw Rule '36
The Outlaw Tamer '33
Outlaw Trail '44
Outlaw Women '52
Outlaws of Sonora '38
Outlaws of the Cherokee Trail '41
Outlaws of the Desert '41
Outlaws of the Range '36
Outlaws of the Rio Grande '41
Outlaw's Paradise '39
The Outrage '64
The Outsider '02
Overland Mail '42
Overland Stage Raiders '38 ►
The Ox-Bow Incident '43 ►
Painted Desert '31
The Painted Trail '38
Pair of Aces '90
Pale Rider '85 ►
Pals of the Range '35
Pals of the Saddle '38
Panamint's Bad Man '38
Pancho Villa '72
Pancho Villa Returns '50
Panhandle '48
Pardon My Gun '30
Paroled to Die '37
Partners of the Trail '44
Passion '54
Pat Garrett & Billy the Kid '73 ►
Pecos Kid '35
Peter Lundy and the Medicine Hat Stallion '77
The Phantom Bullet '26
Phantom Gold '38
The Phantom of the Range '38
Phantom of the West '31
Phantom Patrol '36
The Phantom Pinto '41
Phantom Rancher '39
Phantom Ranger '38
The Phantom Rider '36
The Phantom Rider '46
Phantom Stallion '54
Phantom Thunderbolt '33
Pinto Canyon '40
Pinto Rustlers '36
Pioneer Marshal '49
Pioneer Woman '73
The Pioneers '41
Pioneers of the West '40
Pistoleros Asesinos '87
A Place Called Glory '66
The Plainsman '37
The Pledge '08
The Pocatello Kid '31
The Pony Express '25
Pony Express '53 ►
Pony Express Rider '76 ►
Pony Post '40
Posse '75 ►
Posse '93 ►
Powdersmoke Range '35
The Prairie King '27
Prairie Moon '38
Prairie Pals '42
The Prairie Pirate '25
Prescott Kid '36
The Professionals '66 ►
The Proposition '05
The Proud and the Damned '72
Proud Men '87
Proud Rebel '58 ►
Public Cowboy No. 1 '37
Purgatory '99
Purple Vigilantes '38
Pursued '47 ►
Quick Trigger Lee '31
Quigley Down Under '90
Racketeers of the Range '39
Rage at Dawn '55
Raiders of Red Gap '43
Raiders of the Border '44
Rainbow over Texas '46
Rainbow Ranch '33
Rainbow's End '35
Rancho Notorious '52 ►
Randy Rides Alone '34
Range Busters '40
Range Feud '31
Range Law '31
Range Law '44
Range Renegades '48
Range Riders '35
Rangeland Empire '50
Ranger and the Lady '40
The Rangers' Roundup '38
The Rangers Step In '37
Rangers Take Over '42
The Rare Breed '66
Rattler Kid '68
Rawhide '38
Rawhide '50 ►
Rawhide Romance '34
A Reason to Live, a Reason to Die '73
Red Desert '50
Red Headed Stranger '87
Red River '48 ►
Red River Valley '36
Red River Valley '41
Red Rock Outlaw '47
The Red Rope '37
The Redhead from Wyoming '53
Redwood Forest Trail '50
Renegade Girl '46
Renegade Trail '39
The Restless Breed '58
Retribution Road '07
The Return of a Man Called Horse '76
Return of Draw Egan '16
Return of Frank James '40 ►
Return of Jesse James '50
The Return of Josey Wales '86
Return of the Bad Men '48
Return of the Frontiersman '50
Return of the Lash '47
Return of the Magnificent Seven '66
The Return of the Rangers '43
Return of Wildfire '48
Return to Lonesome Dove '93
Return to Snowy River '88 ►
Revenge of the Virgins '62
The Revenge Rider '35
The Ride Back '57
Ride Clear of Diablo '54
Ride 'Em Cowgirl '41
Ride Him, Cowboy '32 ►
Ride in the Whirlwind '66
Ride Lonesome '59
Ride, Ranger, Ride '36
Ride the High Country '62 ►
Ride the Man Down '53
Ride to Glory '71
Rider from Tucson '50
The Rider of Death Valley '32
Rider of the Law '35
Riders of Death Valley '41
Riders of Destiny '33
Riders of Pasco Basin '40
Riders of the Desert '32
Riders of the Purple Sage '25
Riders of the Purple Sage '96
Riders of the Range '24
Riders of the Range '50
Riders of the Rio Grande '43
Riders of the Rockies '37
Riders of the Timberline '41
Riders of the West '42
Riders of the Whistling Pines '49
Riders of the Whistling Skull '37
Ridin' Down the Canyon '42
The Ridin' Fool '31
Ridin' for Justice '32
Ridin' on a Rainbow '41
Ridin' the Lone Trail '37
Ridin' the Trail '40
Ridin' Thru '35
The Riding Avenger '36
Riding On '37
Riding Speed '35
Riding the California Trail '47
Riding the Sunset Trail '41 ►
The Riding Tornado '32
Riding Wild '35
Rim of the Canyon '49
Rimfire '49
Rin Tin Tin, Hero of the West '55
Rio Bravo '59 ►
Rio Conchos '64 ►
Rio Diablo '93
Rio Grande '50 ►
Rio Grande Raiders '46
Rio Grande Ranger '37
Rio Lobo '70
Rio Rattler '35
River of No Return '54
Road Agent '26
The Roamin' Cowboy '37
Roarin' Lead '37
Roaring Guns '36
Roaring Ranch '30
Roaring Six Guns '37
Robbery under Arms '57
Robin Hood of Texas '47
Robin Hood of the Pecos '41
Rock River Renegades '42
Rockwell: A Legend of the Wild West '93
Rocky Mountain '50
Rocky Mountain Rangers '40
Rodeo Girl '80
Rodeo King and the Senorita '51
Rodeo Rhythm '42
Rogue of the Range '36
Rogue of the Rio Grande '30
Roll Along Cowboy '37
Roll on Texas Moon '46
Rollin' Plains '38
Romance on the Range '42
Rooster Cogburn '75
Rootin' Tootin' Rhythm '38
Rose Hill '97
Rose of Rio Grande '38
Rough Night in Jericho '67
Rough Riders of Cheyenne '45
Rough Riders' Roundup '39
Rough Ridin' Rhythm '37
Rough Riding Ranger '35
Round-Up Time in Texas '37
Rounding Up the Law '22
The Roundup '41
Run of the Arrow '56
Running Wild '73
Rustler's Hideout '44
Rustlers of Red Dog '35
Rustler's Paradise '35
Rustler's Roundup '33
Rustler's Valley '37
The Sacketts '79
Sacred Ground '83
Saddle Aces '35
The Saddle Buster '32
Saddle Mountain Roundup '41
Saddle the Wind '58
Saddle Tramp '47
Saga of Death Valley '39
Sagebrush Law '43
Sagebrush Trail '33 ►
San Antonio '45
San Fernando Valley '44
Sandflow '37
Santa Fe '51
Santa Fe Bound '37
Santa Fe Marshal '40
Santa Fe Stampede '38
Santa Fe Trail '40
Santa Fe Uprising '46
Santee '73
Sartana's Here... Trade Your Pistol for a Coffin '70
Savage Journey '83
Savage Land '94
Savage Wilderness '55
Scalps '83
The Searchers '56 ►
Seminole Uprising '55
September Dawn '07
Seraphim Falls '06
Seven Cities of Gold '55
Seventh Cavalry '56
The Shadow Riders '82
Shadowheart '09
Shadows of Death '45
Shadows of Tombstone '53
Shadows on the Sage '42
Shalako '68
Shane '53 ►
Sheriff of Tombstone '41
Shine on, Harvest Moon '38
Shoot Out '71
Shoot the Sun Down '81
The Shooter '97
The Shooting '66 ►
The Shootist '76 ►
Shotgun '55
The Showdown '40
The Showdown '50
Showdown '73
Showdown at Boot Hill '58
Showdown at Williams Creek '91
Silent Tongue '92
Silent Valley '35
Silver Bandit '50
The Silver Bullet '34
The Silver Bullet '42
Silver City Bonanza '51
Silver City Kid '45
Silver Lode '54
Silver Queen '42
Silver River '48
Silver Spurs '43

► = rated three bones or higher

Silver Stallion '41
Silver Star '55
Silverado '85 ▶
Sing, Cowboy, Sing '37
Singing Buckaroo '37
The Singing Cowgirl '39
Single Handed Sanders '32
Siringo '94
Sitting Bull '54
Six Gun Gospel '43
Six Gun Rhythm '39
Six Gun Trail '38
Six Shootin' Sheriff '38
Sky High '22
Slaughter Trail '51
Smoke in the Wind '75
Smokey Smith '36
The Sombrero Kid '42
Somewhere in Sonora '33
Son of a Gun '19
Son of God's Country '48
Son of the Morning Star '91 ▶
Song of Arizona '46
Song of Nevada '44
Song of Old Wyoming '45
Song of Texas '43
Song of the Gringo '36
Song of the Trail '36
Songs and Bullets '38
Sonora Stagecoach '44
Sons of Katie Elder '65 ▶
Sons of the Pioneers '42
South of Heaven, West of Hell '00
South of Monterey '47
South of St. Louis '48
South of Santa Fe '32
South of Santa Fe '42
South of the Border '39
South of the Rio Grande '45
Southward Ho! '39
Spirit of the West '32
Springfield Rifle '52
Springtime in the Rockies '37
Springtime in the Sierras '47
Spurs '30
Square Dance Jubilee '51
Square Shooter '35
Stage to Mesa City '48
Stagecoach '39 ▶
Stagecoach '86
Stagecoach Buckaroo '42
Stagecoach to Denver '46
The Stalking Moon '69
Standing Tall '78
The Star Packer '34
Station West '48 ▶
Stingaree '34
Stone of Silver Creek '35
Storm over Wyoming '50
Storm Rider '57
Stormy Trails '36
Straight Shootin' '17
The Stranger from Arizona '38
The Stranger from Pecos '45
Stranger on Horseback '55
The Stranger Wore a Gun '53
Strawberry Roan '33
Sudden Death '50
Sundown Fury '42
Sundown Kid '43
Sundown Riders '48
Sundown Saunders '36
Sunrise Trail '31
Sunset in El Dorado '45
Sunset in the West '50
Sunset on the Desert '42
Sunset Range '35
Sunset Serenade '42
Sunset Trail '32
Susanna Pass '49
Sweet Georgia '72
Swifty '35
Talion '66
Tall in the Saddle '44
The Tall Men '55
The Tall T '57
Tall Tale: The Unbelievable Adventures of Pecos Bill '95
Taste of Death '68
Tears of the Black Tiger '00
Telegraph Trail '33
Tell Them Willie Boy Is Here '69 ▶
Ten Wanted Men '54
Tennessee's Partner '55
Tension at Table Rock '56
Terror in a Texas Town '58
Terror of Tiny Town '38
Terror Trail '33
Test of Donald Norton '26
Tex Rides with the Boy Scouts '37
The Texans '38
Texas '94
Texas, Adios '66
Texas Bad Man '32
Texas Buddies '32
Texas Cyclone '32
Texas Gunfighter '32
Texas Guns '90
Texas Jack '35
Texas John Slaughter: Geronimo's Revenge '60
Texas John Slaughter: Stampede at Bitter Creek '62
Texas Justice '42
Texas Kid '43
Texas Legionnaires '43
Texas Masquerade '44
Texas Pioneers '32
The Texas Rangers '36
The Texas Rangers '51
The Texas Rangers Ride Again '40
Texas Terror '35
Texas to Bataan '42
Texas Trouble '41
Texas Wildcats '39
The Texican '66
Thousand Pieces of Gold '91 ▶
Three Bad Men '05
Three Bullets for a Long Gun '73
The Three Burials of Melquiades Estrada '05 ▶
Three Desperate Men '50
Three Faces West '40
Three in the Saddle '45
The Three Mesquiteers '36
Three on the Trail '36 ▶
3:10 to Yuma '57 ▶
3:10 to Yuma '07 ▶
Three Texas Steers '39
Three Violent People '57
Three Word Brand '21
The Throwback '35
Thunder in God's Country '51
Thunder in the Desert '38
Thunder Mountain '35
Thunder Over Texas '34
Thunder Pass '37
Thunder Pass '54
Thunder River Feud '42
Thundering Gunslingers '44
Thundering Trail '51
The Tin Star '57 ▶
The Tioga Kid '48
To the Last Man '33
Today We Kill, Tomorrow We Die '71
The Toll Gate '20
Toll of the Desert '35
Tom Horn '80
Tomahawk '51
Tombstone '93 ▶
Tombstone Canyon '32
Tombstone Terror '34
Tonto Basin Outlaws '41
The Tonto Kid '35
The Topeka Terror '45
The Tracker '88
The Trackers '71
Trail Beyond '34
Trail Drive '33
Trail of Robin Hood '50
Trail of Terror '35
Trail of the Hawk '37
Trail of the Mounties '47
Trail of the Silver Spurs '41
Trail Riders '42
Trail Street '47
Trail to San Antone '47
Trailin' '21
Trailing Double Trouble '40
Trailing Trouble '30
Trailing Trouble '37
Trails of the Wild '35
Train Robbers '73
Train to Tombstone '50
The Traitor '36
Treason '33
Treasure of Pancho Villa '55
Tribute to a Bad Man '56 ▶
Trigger, Jr. '50
Trigger Men '41
Trigger Pals '39
Trigger Tricks '30
The Trigger Trio '37
Triumphs of a Man Called Horse '83
Trouble Busters '33
Trouble in Texas '37
True Grit '69 ▶
Tumbledown Ranch in Arizona '41
Tumbleweed Trail '42
Tumbleweeds '25 ▶
Twilight in the Sierras '50
Twilight on the Rio Grande '41
Twilight on the Trail '41
Two Fisted Justice '31
Two-Fisted Justice '43
Two-Fisted Law '32
Two for Texas '97
Two Gun Man '31
Two-Gun Man from Harlem '38
Two-Gun Troubador '37
Two Mules for Sister Sara '70 ▶
Two Rode Together '61
Ulzana's Raid '72 ▶
Unconquered Bandit '35
The Undefeated '69
Under California Stars '48
Under Colorado Skies '47
Under Nevada Skies '46
Under Western Stars '38
Undercover Man '36
Underground Rustlers '41
An Unfinished Life '05
The Unforgiven '60 ▶
Unforgiven '92 ▶
Uninvited '93
Union Pacific '39 ▶
The Unknown Ranger '36
Up River '79
Utah '45
Utah Trail '38
Valdez Is Coming '71
Valley of Fire '51
Valley of Terror '38
Valley of the Lawless '36
Valley of the Sun '42 ▶
The Vanishing American '25
Vanishing Legion '31
The Vanishing Westerner '50
Vengeance Valley '51
Vigilantes of Boom Town '46
Villa Rides '68
The Violent Men '55
The Virginian '23
The Virginian '29 ▶
The Virginian '46
The Virginian '99
Wagon Tracks '19
Wagon Trail '35
Wagons Westward '40
Walk the Proud Land '56
Walking Thunder '94
Wall Street Cowboy '39
The Walloping Kid '26
Wanda Nevada '79
War Arrow '53
War of the Wildcats '43
The War Wagon '67 ▶
Warden of Red Rock '01
Warlock '59 ▶
Water Rustlers '39
Way of the West '35
The Way West '67
West of Cimarron '41
West of Nevada '36
West of Pinto Basin '40
West of the Divide '33
West of the Law '42
West of the Pecos '45
West to Glory '47
Western Courage '35
Western Frontier '35
Western Gold '37
Western Justice '35
Western Mail '42
Western Pacific Agent '51
Western Trails '38
Western Union '41 ▶
The Westerner '40 ▶
Westward Bound '30
Westward Bound '44
Westward Ho, the Wagons! '56
Westward the Women '51 ▶
When a Man Rides Alone '33
When a Man Sees Red '34
When a Man's a Man '35
When the Legends Die '72 ▶
When the West Was Young '32
Where Trails Divide '37
Where Trails End '42
Whirlwind Horseman '38
Whistlin' Dan '32
Whistling Bullets '36
The White Buffalo '77
White Comanche '67
White Eagle '32
White Gold '28 ▶
Wild Bill '95
The Wild Bunch '69 ▶
Wild Country '47
The Wild Country '71
Wild Frontier '47
Wild Horse '31
Wild Horse Canyon '25
Wild Horse Canyon '39
Wild Horse Rodeo '37
Wild Horse Valley '40
Wild Mustang '35
Wild Times '79
Wild West '46
Wild Wild West '99
The Wildcat '26
Wildfire '45
Will Penny '67 ▶
Winchester '73 '50 ▶
The Wind '28 ▶
Wind River '98
Winds of the Wasteland '36
Winners of the West '40
The Winning of Barbara Worth '26
Winning of the West '53
With Kit Carson over the Great Divide '25
Without Honors '32
Wolf Call '39
Wolfheart's Revenge '25
The Woman of the Town '44
Wrangler '88
Wyatt Earp '94
Wyatt Earp: Return to Tombstone '94
Wyoming Outlaw '39
Yellow Dust '36
The Yellow Rose of Texas '44
Yodelin' Kid from Pine Ridge '37
You Know My Name '99 ▶
Young Bill Hickok '40
Young Blood '33
Young Buffalo Bill '40
Young Guns '88
Young Guns 2 '90
The Young Land '59
The Young Pioneers '76
Yuma '70
Zandy's Bride '74
Zorro Rides Again '37
Zorro's Fighting Legion '39

Westrogens

see also *Westerns; Wonder Women*

Angel and the Badman '47 ▶
Annie Get Your Gun '50 ▶
Annie Oakley '35 ▶
Bad Girls '94
The Ballad of Little Jo '93
The Beautiful Blonde from Bashful Bend '49
Belle Starr '79
A Big Hand for the Little Lady '66
Buffalo Girls '95
Calamity Jane '53 ▶
Calamity Jane '82
Cat Ballou '65 ▶
Comes a Horseman '78
Even Cowgirls Get the Blues '94
The Far Side of Jericho '06
Gang of Roses '03
Girl from Calgary '32
The Gunslinger '56
Hannie Caulder '72
Heartland '81 ▶
Hooded Angels '00
Johnny Guitar '53 ▶
The Maverick Queen '55
McCabe & Mrs. Miller '71 ▶
Nevada '97
Poker Alice '87
Prairie Fever '08
The Quick and the Dead '95
Raiders of Sunset Pass '43
Ramrod '47
Riders of the Purple Sage '96
The Rowdy Girls '00
Texas Lady '56
Tulsa '49 ▶
Two Mules for Sister Sara '70 ▶
The Wicked, Wicked West '97
Wild Women '70
Zorro's Black Whip '44

Whales

see also *Deep Blue; Wild Kingdom*

The Adventures of Baron Munchausen '89 ▶
The Adventures of Pinocchio '96
Deep Blue '03 ▶
Earth '07
Free Willy '93
Free Willy 2: The Adventure Home '95
Free Willy 3: The Rescue '97
Luna: Spirit of the Whale '07
Moby Dick '56 ▶
Moby Dick '98
Namu, the Killer Whale '66
Orca '77
Pinocchio '40 ▶
Star Trek 4: The Voyage Home '86 ▶
Whale for the Killing '81
Whale Music '94
Whale of a Tale '76
The Whales of August '87 ▶
When the Whales Came '89
The White Dawn '75

Whitewater Rafting

A Cry from the Mountain '85
Deliverance '72 ▶
Good Luck '96
Race for Your Life, Charlie Brown '77
The River Wild '94
Same River Twice '97
Scream '83
White Water Summer '87

Widows & Widowers

see also *Single Parents; Stepparents*

ABCD '99
About Schmidt '02 ▶
Akeelah and the Bee '06
Alice Upside Down '07
All I Want for Christmas '07
Alpha Male '06
Amongst Women '98
Appaloosa '08 ▶
At the Midnight Hour '95
Au Pair '99
Audition '99
Belles on Their Toes '52
Beyond Justice '01
Birth '04
A Blueprint for Murder '53
Bonneville '06
The Boynton Beach Club '05
Bye Bye Braverman '67
Cafe Ole '00
Caged '50 ▶
Calendar Girls '03
Cape of Good Hope '04
The Cemetery Club '93
Charlie & Me '08
Cherry Blossoms '08
Children On Their Birthdays '02
The Christmas Miracle of Jonathan Toomey '07
The Clay Pigeon '49
Cop Au Vin '85
Cravings '06
Crescendo '69
Dan in Real Life '07
Dancing in Twilight '05
Dead Ringer '64
Doctor Bull '33
Dragonfly '02
Dreamland '06 ▶
Due East '02
Edge of Darkness '10
Emma '32
The Emperor's New Clothes '01
Everybody's Fine '09
The Far Side of Jericho '06
Fascination '04
Final Cut '98
Finding Neverland '04 ▶
First Degree '98
Fishtales '07
Frailty '02 ▶
The Gambler, the Girl and the Gunslinger '09
Georgia Rule '07
Ghost Town '08 ▶
The Girl Next Door '53
The Girl on the Train '09
The Golden Boys '08
Good Will Hunting '97
Grace Is Gone '07 ▶
Gran Torino '08 ▶
The Green Promise '49
The Gunman '03
Heaven '01
Hidden Places '06
His Secret Life '01 ▶
The Home Front '02
Hondo '53 ▶
Hoodlum & Son '03
Horsemen '09
House of D '04
House of Sand '05 ▶
The Human Stain '03
Hurt '09
I Downloaded a Ghost '04
I Now Pronounce You Chuck and Larry '07
Illegal Tender '07
Incendiary '08
Innocence '00 ▶
The Intended '02
Jada '08
Kill Me Tomorrow '57
King of the Wild Stallions '59
Kings and Queen '04 ▶
La Petite Jerusalem '05
La Roue '23 ▶
Lemon Tree '08
Lethal Weapon '87 ▶
Local Boys '02
Love and Rage '99
Love Comes Softly '03
Love Happens '09
Love Liza '02
Love's Unending Legacy '07
Loving Leah '09
Lucky Star '29
Luxury Liner '48
Madeo '09
Mail Order Bride '63
A Man Apart '03
Manderlay '05
Marilyn Hotchkiss' Ballroom Dancing & Charm School '06
Married Life '07 ▶
The Merchant of Venice '04 ▶
Message in a Bottle '98
The Messenger '09 ▶
A Mighty Heart '07 ▶
Mrs. Henderson Presents '05
Monster's Ball '01 ▶
The Mother '03 ▶
The Mothman Prophecies '02
Move Over, Darling '63
The Mudge Boy '03
My Life in Ruins '09
My Reputation '46
Nanny McPhee '06
The National Tree '09
Nightmare Alley '47
Nightwaves '03
No Turning Back '01
The Note '07
An Old-Fashioned Thanksgiving '08
One Last Thing '05
The Passion of Anna '70 ▶

▶ = rated three bones or higher

The Pilot's Wife '01
The Pledge '08
Politics '31
Private Benjamin '80
P.S. I Love You '07
Pure '02 ▸
Quiet Chaos '08
Race to Space '01
The Reading Room '05
Red Roses and Petrol '03
Relative Strangers '99
Renegade Trail '39
Return to Me '00
Rick '03
The Road Home '01 ▸
Rocky Balboa '06
The Roman Spring of Mrs. Stone '03
Ruby Blue '07
Safe Harbour '07
St. Patrick's Day '99
The Salton Sea '02
Sam Whiskey '69
Satin Rouge '02
Schizo '04
The Secret '07
7 Faces of Dr. Lao '63 ▸
The Shipping News '01
Signs '02 ▸
Silent Waters '03
Skinwalkers '07
Sleepless in Seattle '93 ▸
Smart People '08
Song of Love '47 ▸
Starman '84 ▸
Strayed '03 ▸
That Evening Sun '09 ▸
Things We Lost in the Fire '07
35 Shots of Rum '08
This Revolution '05
A Thousand Years of Good Prayers '07
Time of the Wolf '03 ▸
To Gillian on Her 37th Birthday '96
Together Again '43
The Treatment '06
The Trial of Old Drum '00
Trouble in Paradise '32 ▸
The Truth About Charlie '02
21 Grams '03 ▸
The Twilight Samurai '02 ▸
Under the Flag of the Rising Sun '72 ▸
Undertow '04
Up '09 ▸
Used People '92
The Visitor '07 ▸
Volver '06 ▸
Water '05
We'll Meet Again '02
What Time Is It There? '01
Where the Sidewalk Ends '50
White Noise '05
The Whole Shebang '01
The Widowing of Mrs. Holroyd '95
Widows '02
Winter Solstice '04 ▸
Wisegal '08
Witness '85 ▸
Yours, Mine & Ours '68
Yours, Mine & Ours '05

Wild Kingdom

***see also** Bears; Birds; Cats; Dinosaurs; Elephants; Killer Apes and Monkeys; Killer Beasts; Killer Bugs and Slugs; Killer Dogs; Killer Kats; Killer Pigs; Killer Sea Critters; King of Beasts (Dogs); Monkeyshines; Nice Mice; Pigs; Rabbits; Talking Animals; Whales; Wilderness*

Ace Ventura: When Nature Calls '95
The Adventures of Ford Fairlane '90
The Adventures of Tarzan '21
Africa Texas Style '67
Alaska '96
All Creatures Great and Small '74 ▸
All Dogs Go to Heaven 2 '95
All Roads Lead Home '08
The Amazing Panda Adventure '95
An American Tail '86
Andre '94
The Animal '01
Animal Farm '55 ▸
Arctic Tale '07
Attack of the Sabretooth '05
Ava's Magical Adventure '94
Bambi '42 ▸
Bambi II '06
The Barefoot Executive '71
The Bear '89 ▸
The Bears & I '74
The Beast That Killed Women '65
Beastmaster '82
Beastmaster 2: Through the Portal of Time '91
Beasts '83
Bedtime for Bonzo '51
The Belstone Fox '73
Black Cobra '83
Bless the Beasts and Children '71
Born Free '66 ▸
Born to Be Wild '95
Born Wild '95
The Brave One '56 ▸
A Breed Apart '84
Bringing Up Baby '38 ▸
Brother Bear 2 '06
Brotherhood of the Wolf '01
Buddy '97
Buffalo Rider '78
Call of the Wild '72
Captive Wild Woman '43
Carnage '02
Catch as Catch Can '68
Cheetah '89
Christian the Lion '76
The Chronicles of Narnia '89
Clarence, the Cross-eyed Lion '65 ▸
Courage of the North '35
The Crocodile Hunter: Collision Course '02
A Cry in the Dark '88 ▸
A Cry in the Wild '90 ▸
Dark Age '88
Darkest Africa '36
Day of the Animals '77
The Day of the Dolphin '73
Doctor Dolittle '67
Dr. Dolittle '98
Dr. Dolittle 2 '01
Duma '05 ▸
Dumbo '41 ▸
Dunston Checks In '95
Eaten Alive '76
Ed '96
The Edge '97
Ele, My Friend '93
The Electric Horseman '79
Elephant Boy '37 ▸
An Elephant Called Slowly '69
The Emperor's New Groove '00 ▸
Every Which Way But Loose '78
Eye of the Wolf '95
Eyes of the Panther '90
Fantastic Mr. Fox '09 ▸
Far from Home: The Adventures of Yellow Dog '94
Fierce Creatures '96
The Fifth Monkey '90
50 First Dates '04
Flight of the Grey Wolf "76
Flipper '63 ▸
Flipper '96 ▸
Fly Away Home '96 ▸
The Fox and the Hound '81 ▸
Francis Covers the Big Town '53
Francis Goes to the Races '51
Francis Goes to West Point '52
Francis in the Haunted House '56
Francis in the Navy '55
Francis Joins the WACs '54
Francis the Talking Mule '49 ▸
Frasier the Sensuous Lion '73
Furry Vengeance '10
Futz '69
Gentle Giant '67
George of the Jungle '97 ▸
The Ghost and the Darkness '96
Gladiator '00 ▸
Going Ape! '81
Going Bananas '88
The Golden Seal '83
Gordy '95
Gorilla '56
Gorillas in the Mist '88 ▸
The Great Adventure '53 ▸
The Great Elephant Escape '95
The Great Rupert '50 ▸
Grizzly Adams: The Legend Continues '90
Grizzly Man '05 ▸
Groundhog Day '93 ▸
Gus '76
Harry and the Hendersons '87
Hatari! '62 ▸
Hawmps! '76
Hollywood Safari '96
Homeward Bound 2: Lost in San Francisco '96
Hoot '06
I Dreamed of Africa '00
Ice Age '02 ▸
In the Shadow of Kilimanjaro '86
The Island of Dr. Moreau '96
Island of Lost Souls '32 ▸
Island of the Blue Dolphins '64
Joey '98
Jumanji '95
Jungle '52
The Jungle Book '67 ▸
The Jungle Book 2 '03
Jungle Boy '96
Jungle Drums of Africa '53
King Kung Fu '87
King of the Grizzlies '69
Lassie, Come Home '43
The Last Safari '67
Legend of Lobo '62
Leonard Part 6 '87
The Leopard Son '96 ▸
The Lion King '94 ▸
The Lion King 1 1/2 '04 ▸
The Lion King: Simba's Pride '98
Living Free '72
Madagascar: Escape 2 Africa '08
The Many Adventures of Winnie the Pooh '77
March of the Penguins '05 ▸
Matilda '78
Max, Mon Amour '86
The Mighty Peking Man '77
The Misadventures of Merlin Jones '63
Mr. Kingstreet's War '71
Mr. Toad's Wild Ride '96
Monkey Trouble '94
Monkeys, Go Home! '66
Monkey's Uncle '65
The Monster and the Girl '41
Mountain Family Robinson '79
Mountain Man '77
Murders in the Rue Morgue '32
My Sister, My Love '78
Napoleon '96
Napoleon and Samantha '72 ▸
Never Cry Wolf '83 ▸
Night of the Grizzly '66
Nikki, the Wild Dog of the North '61
Noah's Ark '99
Once Upon a Forest '93
Operation Dumbo Drop '95
Operation Haylift '50
Pardon My Trunk '52
Passion in the Desert '97
Paulie '98
Pet Sematary 2 '92
Piglet's Big Movie '03
Pippi Longstocking '69
Planet of the Apes '68 ▸
Project X '87
Razorback '84
Red Earth '82
The Rescuers '77 ▸
The Rescuers Down Under '90
Ring of Bright Water '69 ▸
Rock-a-Doodle '92
Rudyard Kipling's The Jungle Book '94
Rudyard Kipling's the Second Jungle Book: Mowgli and Baloo '97
The Runaways '75
Running Free '94
Running Wild '99
Sabretooth '01
Sammy, the Way-Out Seal '62
The Secret of NIMH '82 ▸
Shakma '89
Silver Streak '76 ▸
Slappy and the Stinkers '97
Soul of the Beast '23
Stalk the Wild Child '76
The Story of the Weeping Camel '03 ▸
A Summer to Remember '84
Super Seal '77
The Tender Warrior '71
Those Calloways '65
Thumbelina '82 ▸
A Tiger Walks '64
To Walk with Lions '99
Tomboy & the Champ '58
Trap on Cougar Mountain '72
Two Brothers '04
Vampire Circus '71
The Wagons Roll at Night '41
Walk Like a Man '87
Waltz with Bashir '08 ▸
Watership Down '78
When the North Wind Blows '74
Whispers: An Elephant's Tale '00
The White Buffalo '77
White Pongo '45
White Wolves 2: Legend of the Wild '94
The Wild '06
Wild America '97 ▸
Wild Horses '82
The Wild Thornberrys Movie '02 ▸
The Yearling '46 ▸
The Yearling '94
Zebra in the Kitchen '65
Zeus and Roxanne '96

Wilderness

***see also** Trees & Forests*

Abducted '86
Across the Great Divide '76
The Adventures of Frontier Fremont '75
The Adventures of the Wilderness Family '76
Alaska '96
All Mine to Give '56
Almost Heroes '97
Arctic Blue '93
Backwoods '87
The Bear '89 ▸
Beyond Fear '93
Black Robe '91 ▸
Blood of the Hunter '94
The Bridge to Nowhere '86
Brother Bear '03
Bullies '86
Bushwhacked '95
Call of the Wild '04
Call of the Yukon '38
Cannibal! The Musical '96
The Capture of Grizzly Adams '82
Charlie the Lonesome Cougar '67
Claws '77
Clearcut '92
Cold River '81
Continental Divide '81
The Cowboys '72 ▸
Cross Creek '83
Davy Crockett and the River Pirates '56
Davy Crockett, King of the Wild Frontier '55 ▸
Dead Ahead '96
Death Hunt '81
Decoy '95
Dominion '94
Duma '05 ▸
Earthling '80
The Edge '97
Edge of Honor '91
Edge of Madness '02
Endangered '94
Eyes of Fire '84
Far from Home: The Adventures of Yellow Dog '94
Father and Scout '94
Ferngully: The Last Rain Forest '92
Flight from Glory '37
Further Adventures of the Wilderness Family, Part 2 '77
Gerry '02
God's Country '46
Great Adventure '75
The Great Outdoors '88
Grizzly '76
Grizzly Adams: The Legend Continues '90
Grizzly Falls '99
Grizzly Man '05 ▸
Grizzly Mountain '97
Heaven on Earth '89
Hunter's Blood '87
Ice Palace '60
Into the Wild '07 ▸
Jeremiah Johnson '72 ▸
Just Before Dawn '80
Kid Colter '85
The Last of the Dogmen '95
The Legend of Wolf Mountain '92
Life & Times of Grizzly Adams '74
Little Bigfoot '96
Lost '83
Lost in the Barrens '91
Man in the Wilderness '71
Man of the House '95
The Many Adventures of Winnie the Pooh '77
March of the Penguins '05 ▸
Mountain Charlie '80
Mountain Family Robinson '79
Mountain Man '77
Napoleon '96
Napoleon and Samantha '72 ▸
Never Cry Wolf '83 ▸
Northwest Passage '40 ▸
Northwest Trail '46
Orphans of the North '40
The Parent Trap '61
Quest for Fire '82 ▸
River's End '05
Shoot to Kill '88 ▸
Silence '73
Silence of the North '81
Silver Wolf '98
Slashed Dreams '74
Sourdough '77
Spirit of the Eagle '90
Starbird and Sweet William '73
Strange Wilderness '08
The Tale of Ruby Rose '87 ▸
Tales of the Klondike: In a Far Country '87
Tales of the Klondike: Race for Number One '87
Tales of the Klondike: The Scorn of Women '87
Tales of the Klondike: The Unexpected '87
The Ticket '97
Timber Queen '44
True Heart '97
Tundra '36
Violent Zone '89
Warrior Spirit '94
White Fang '91 ▸
White Fang and the Hunter '85
The White Tower '50 ▸
White Water Summer '87
White Wolves 2: Legend of the Wild '94
White Wolves 3: Cry of the White Wolf '98
Whitewater Sam '78
The Wolves '95
Young & Free '78
Zero Degrees Kelvin '95

Wine & Vinyards

Bottle Shock '08
Cloud Waltzing '87
Diamond Girl '98
A Good Year '06
I Am David '04
May Fools '90 ▸
Mondovino '04
The Parent Trap '98
Sideways '04 ▸
The Vineyard '89
A Walk in the Clouds '95

Wisconsin

All Mine to Give '56
American Movie '99 ▸
BASEketball '98
Citizen Cohn '92
Critical Choices '97
Deranged '74 ▸
Dogma '99
Ed's Next Move '96
Fear X '03 ▸
The Giant Spider Invasion '75
Love Actually '03
A Map of the World '99
Mr. 3000 '04
No Sleep 'Til Madison '02
Our Vines Have Tender Grapes '45 ▸
The Prince & Me '04
The Smokers '00
Things in Their Season '74
Wayne's World '92 ▸

Witchcraft

***see also** Demons & Wizards; Occult*

Beastly '10
Bell, Book and Candle '58
Bewitched '05
Beyond Darkness '92
Black Magic '92
Black Sunday '60 ▸
Book of Shadows: Blair Witch 2 '00
The Bride with White Hair '93
The Bride with White Hair 2 '93
Brotherhood 2: The Young Warlocks '01
The Brothers Grimm '05
Burn Witch, Burn! '62 ▸
Cast a Deadly Spell '91 ▸
The Conqueror Worm '68 ▸
The Covenant '06
The Craft '96
The Crucible '57 ▸
The Crucible '96 ▸
Cry of the Banshee '70
The Curse of the Crying Woman '61
Curse of the Devil '73
Daughters of Satan '72
Day of Wrath '43 ▸
The Day the Earth Froze '59
The Demons '74
The Devil Rides Out '68 ▸
The Devils '71 ▸
Devonsville Terror '83
Dr. Strange '78
Double Double Toil and Trouble '94
The Eternal '99
Eye of the Demon '87
Eyes of Fire '84
Final Encounter '00
The Forbidden Kingdom '08
Four Rooms '95
Fright House '89
The Golden Compass '07
The Good Witch '08
Halloweentown '98
Halloweentown 2: Kalabar's Revenge '01
Halloweentown High '04
Harry Potter and the Prisoner of Azkaban '04
The Haunted Palace '63
The Haunting of Morella '91
Hellblock 13 '97
Hercules, Prisoner of Evil '64
Hocus Pocus '93

▸ = rated three bones or higher

Horror Hotel '60
Horror Rises from the Tomb '72
The Hospital '71 ▶
House of the Black Death '65
Howl's Moving Castle '04
I Married a Witch '42 ▶
The Initiation of Sarah '06
Inquisition '76
I've Been Waiting for You '98
The Juniper Tree '87
Kiki's Delivery Service '98
Kill, Baby, Kill '66 ▶
Kill Me Tomorrow '99
The Lady's Not for Burning '87
Lisa and the Devil '75
Little Witches '96
Lost Legacy: A Girl Called Hatter Fox '77
Love at Stake '87
Maciste in Hell '60
Mark of the Devil '69
Mark of the Devil 2 '72
Mother of Tears '08
The Muppets' Wizard of Oz '05
Nanny McPhee '06
Netherworld '90
Night of the Scarecrow '95
P '04
The Polar Bear King '94
Practical Magic '98
Pufnstuf '70
Pumpkinhead 3: Ashes to Ashes '06
Pumpkinhead 4: Blood Feud '07
Quartier Mozart '92
Rendez-Moi Ma Peau '81
The Resurrected '91
Return to Halloweentown '06
Return to Oz '85
Ruddigore '82
Sabrina the Teenage Witch '96
Season of the Witch '73
Season of the Witch '10
The She-Beast '65
The Shrieking '73
Silent Hill '06
Sleepy Hollow '99 ▶
Snow White: A Tale of Terror '97
Snow White: The Fairest of Them All '02
Something Weird '68
Sorceress '88 ▶
Sorceress '94
Spellbreaker: Secret of the Leprechauns '96
Stardust '07 ▶
The Story of Three Loves '53
Summer of Fear '78
The Terror '79
Terror Beach '75
That Darn Sorceress '88
Three Sovereigns for Sarah '85
The Touch of Satan '70
Troll 2 '92
Twitches '05
Twitches Too '07
The Undead '57
The Virgin Witch '70
Warlock '91
Warlock 3: The End of Innocence '98
Warlock Moon '73
Warlock: The Armageddon '93
The Werewolf vs. the Vampire Woman '70
Whispering Corridors '98
Wicked Lake '08
Wicked Stepmother '89
The Witch '66
Witch Who Came from the Sea '76
A Witch Without a Broom '68
Witchcraft '88
Witchcraft 3: The Kiss of Death '90
Witchcraft 4: Virgin Heart '92
Witchcraft 7: Judgement Hour '95
Witchcraft 8: Salem's Ghost '95
Witchcraft 9: Bitter Flesh '96
Witchcraft 10: Mistress of the Craft '98
Witchcraft 11: Sisters in Blood '00
Witchery '88
The Witches '66
The Witches '90 ▶
Witches' Brew '79
Witches' Mountain '71
The Witches of Eastwick '87
Witches of the Caribbean '05
The Witching of Ben Wagner '95
The Witchmaker '69
Witchouse '99
Witchouse 2: Blood Coven '00
Witchouse 3: Demon Fire '01
The Witch's Mirror '60
WitchTrap '89
The Wizard of Oz '39 ▶
The Woman Who Came Back '45
The Woods '03
The Worst Witch '86
Yaaba '89 ▶

Witness Protection Program

***see also** Organized Crime; U.S. Marshals*

Acts of Betrayal '98
Ballistic '94
Bird on a Wire '90
Charlie's Angels: Full Throttle '03
Did You Hear About the Morgans? '09
Drop Zone '94
Eraser '96
Federal Protection '02
Forget About It '06
The Godfather, Part 2 '74 ▶
Goodfellas '90 ▶
Hide in Plain Sight '80 ▶
Lethal Weapon 2 '89 ▶
My Blue Heaven '90
Navajo Blues '97
Nowhere Land '98
The Pact '99
Protection '01
Romeo Is Bleeding '93
See Spot Run '01
Shadowboxer '06
Sister Act '92
Trapped '06
The Whole Nine Yards '00
Witless Protection '08
Witness Protection '99 ▶

Women

***see also** Dream Girls; Femme Fatale; Moms; Westrogens; Women in Prison; Wonder Women*

Absolutely Fabulous: The Last Shout '96
Accidental Meeting '93
Acts of Worship '01
Alice Doesn't Live Here Anymore '74
Amelia Earhart: The Final Flight '94
Anatomy of Hell '04
Anna '87 ▶
Another Way '82 ▶
Another Woman '88 ▶
Antonia and Jane '91 ▶
Arizona '40
Artemisia '97
The Astounding She-Monster '58
Babyfever '94
Bachelor Mother '39 ▶
Backstreet Justice '93
Bandit Queen '94
Bang '95
Bar Girls '95
Beaches '88 ▶
Beauty Shop '05 ▶
Becoming Jane '07
Bella Mafia '97
Betty '92
The Betty Ford Story '87 ▶
Bhaji on the Beach '94
The Big City '63
Black Day Blue Night '95
Black Girl '66 ▶
Black Scorpion '95
Blood and Sand '41 ▶
Blood Games '90
Blue De Ville '86
The Bostonians '84
Boulevard '94
Boys on the Side '94
Bridget Jones: The Edge of Reason '04
The Buccaneers '95 ▶
A Bunny's Tale '85
Business As Usual '88
Camilla '94
Cape of Good Hope '04
Certain Fury '85
Challenge of a Lifetime '85
Chantilly Lace '93
The Children's Hour '61
China Beach '88 ▶
The Circle '00
Citizen Ruth '96
City Without Men '43
Claire of the Moon '92
The Color Purple '85 ▶
Come Back to the Five & Dime Jimmy Dean, Jimmy Dean '82 ▶
Come Early Morning '06
Comedy of Power '06
Commissar '68 ▶
Conceiving Ada '97
The Courage to Love '00
Courage Under Fire '96 ▶
Crazy Mama '75
Cry of the Werewolf '44
Daisy Miller '74
The Dallas Connection '94
Dames Ahoy '30
The Damned Don't Cry '50
Dangerous Prey '95
A Dangerous Woman '93
Darktown Strutters '74
The Day the Women Got Even '80
The Dead Girl '06
Dead Men Can't Dance '97
Deconstructing Harry '97
Defenseless '91
The Descent '05
The Desperate Trail '94
The Devil Wears Prada '06
Dirty Dishes '78 ▶
Dogs: The Rise and Fall of an All-Girl Bookie Joint '96
Dogville '03
A Doll's House '59
A Doll's House '73
A Doll's House '73 ▶
Double Obsession '93
The Dreamlife of Angels '98 ▶
Dreams '55
The Duchess of Duke Street '78 ▶
Early Summer '51 ▶
Easy Virtue '27
Eat, Pray, Love '10
Eating '90
Eddie '96
8 1/2 Women '99
Eleanor: First Lady of the World '82
Elizabeth R '72 ▶
Enchanted April '92
Enid Is Sleeping '90
Enormous Changes '83 ▶
Entertaining Angels: The Dorothy Day Story '96
Erotique '94
Even Cowgirls Get the Blues '94
Evita '96
The Execution '85
An Eye for an Eye '95
Faces of Women '85
Family Secrets '84
Feast of July '95
Feds '88
Female Perversions '96
Fire '96
Fire in the Night '85
The First Wives Club '96
Fish Without a Bicycle '03
Flatbed Annie and Sweetiepie: Lady Truckers '79
Florence Nightingale '85
Florence Nightingale '08
The Flower of My Secret '95 ▶
Follow the River '95
Fran '85
Free Zone '05
Fried Green Tomatoes '91 ▶
Friends '95
From the Journals of Jean Seberg '95
Fur: An Imaginary Portrait of Diane Arbus '06
Gangs, Inc. '41
A Geisha '53 ▶
Gentlemen Prefer Blondes '53 ▶
G.I. Jane '97
Girl 6 '96
A Girl Thing '01
Girlfriends '78 ▶
Going Shopping '05
Good Girls Don't '95
Grace of My Heart '96
The Great Man's Lady '42
The Group '66
Guardian Angel '94
The Happy Ending '69
Hard Country '81
Harvest of Fire '95
Head of the Family '71
Heading South '05 ▶
The Headless Woman '08
Heat and Dust '82 ▶
Heaven and Earth '93
The Heidi Chronicles '95
Hellcats '68
The Heroic Trio '93
Hidden Assassin '94
Honey & Ashes '96
Horror of the Zombies '74
The Hours '02 ▶
House of Whipcord '75
Household Saints '93 ▶
How the Garcia Girls Spent Their Summer '05
How to Be a Woman and Not Die in the Attempt '91
How to Make an American Quilt '95
How to Marry a Millionaire '53
I Dreamed of Africa '00
I Like It Like That '94 ▶
I Really Hate My Job '07
If These Walls Could Talk '96
In the Land of Women '06
In This House of Brede '75 ▶
The Insect Woman '63 ▶
Introducing Dorothy Dandridge '99 ▶
Is There Life Out There? '94
Island of Lost Girls '68
Isn't She Great '00
Jaded '96
James Joyce's Women '85 ▶
Jamon, Jamon '93
Je Tu Il Elle '74
Joan Rivers: A Piece of Work '10
The Journey to Kafiristan '01
The Joy Luck Club '93 ▶
Joy Ride to Nowhere '78
Judicial Consent '94
Juliet of the Spirits '65 ▶
Just Another Girl on the I.R.T. '93
Kamikaze Hearts '91
Kandahar '01
Katie Tippel '75
The Ladies Club '86
Ladies on the Rocks '83
Ladybird, Ladybird '93 ▶
The Last Best Year '90
Late Chrysanthemums '54
A League of Their Own '92 ▶
Leaving Normal '92
The Legend of Blood Castle '72
Les Bonnes Femmes '60 ▶
Little Mother '71
Little Women '33 ▶
Little Women '49 ▶
Little Women '78
Little Women '94 ▶
Live Nude Girls '95
Living Proof '08
Lola Montes '55 ▶
Losing Isaiah '94 ▶
Love After Love '94
Love and Basketball '00 ▶
The Love Goddesses '65 ▶
Lucia, Lucia '03
Lumiere '76
Madame Bovary '34 ▶
Madame Bovary '91 ▶
Madame Bovary '00
Madonna: Innocence Lost '95
Maedchen in Uniform '31 ▶
The Magic Bubble '93
Magnificent Doll '46
Malou '83
Mapp & Lucia '85
Marianne and Juliane '82 ▶
Marilyn: The Untold Story '80 ▶
Mars Needs Women '66
Mary, Queen of Scots '71
Memoirs of a Geisha '05
Memories of Murder '90
Messidor '77
Mi Vida Loca '94
Miles to Go '86
The Milk of Sorrow '09
Mina Tannenbaum '93
Miss Firecracker '89 ▶
Moll Flanders '96
Monkey Grip '82 ▶
Monster '03 ▶
Moolaade '04
Moonlight and Valentino '95
Mortal Thoughts '91
Moscow Does Not Believe in Tears '80 ▶
Mother and Child '09
Mother & Daughter: A Loving War '80
Mother Teresa: In the Name of God's Poor '97
My Brilliant Career '79 ▶
My Twentieth Century '90 ▶
Nathalie Granger '72
Nine '09
Nine Lives '05 ▶
9 to 5 '80
Nomugi Pass '79
Nora's Hair Salon '04
Norma Jean and Marilyn '95
North Country '05
Now and Then '95
The Nun '66
One Sings, the Other Doesn't '77
One True Thing '98 ▶
The Opposite Sex '56
Osaka Elegy '36
Overseas: Three Women with Man Trouble '90 ▶
Pancho Barnes '88
Passenger '61 ▶
Passion Fish '92 ▶
Patti Rocks '88 ▶
Perfume '91
Persepolis '07 ▶
Personal Velocity: Three Portraits '02 ▶
The Pillow Book '95
Poetic Justice '93
Poor Little Rich Girl: The Barbara Hutton Story '87
Portrait of a Lady '96 ▶
Portrait of a Showgirl '82
Portrait of Teresa '79 ▶
Posers '02
A Price above Rubies '97
Prime Suspect '92 ▶
Private Valentine: Blonde & Dangerous '08
Quartier Mozart '92
Queen of Diamonds '91
The Queen's Sister '05
Question of Silence '83 ▶
The Rector's Wife '94
Rescuers: Stories of Courage "Two Women" '97 ▶
Revenge of the Teenage Vixens from Outer Space '86
Rich and Famous '81
Rosa Luxemburg '86
The Rosa Parks Story '02
Roseanne: An Unauthorized Biography '94
Rosenstrasse '03 ▶
Ruby in Paradise '93 ▶
Run for the Dream: The Gail Devers Story '96
Running Mates '00
Salmonberries '91
Samson vs. the Vampire Women '61
Sandra of a Thousand Delights '65
The Scent of Green Papaya '93 ▶
Searching For Wooden Watermelons '01
The September Issue '09
Set It Off '96
The '70s '00
Sexual Intent '94
Shadow on the Sun '88
She-Devil '89
Sherman's March '86 ▶
The Silences of the Palace '94 ▶
A Single Girl '96
Sister Aimee: The Aimee Semple McPherson Story '06
Sister Street Fighter '76
The Sisterhood '88
Sisters of the Gion '36
Sisters, Or the Balance of Happiness '79
Slander House '38
Snapdragon '93
Sorceress '88 ▶
Spices '86 ▶
The Spitfire Grill '95
Stage Door '37 ▶
Star! '68
Steaming '86
Steel and Lace '90
Steel Magnolias '89 ▶
The Stoning of Soraya M. '08
The Story of Qiu Ju '91 ▶
The Story of Women '88 ▶
The Stranger '95
Strangers in Good Company '91 ▶
Strangers: The Story of a Mother and Daughter '79 ▶
Street of Shame '56 ▶
Stripper '86
Sudden Death '85
Sunset Strip '91
Swann '96
Synecdoche, New York '08 ▶
Take Care of My Cat '01
Talk '94
Talking about Sex '94
The Tango Lesson '97
Tara Road '05
The Taxi Mystery '26
Tell Me Where It Hurts '74
Tender Comrade '43
The Terrorist '98
Testament of Youth '79
30 Years to Life '01
The 3 Marias '03
301, 302 '94
Three Secrets '50
3 Women '77 ▶
Tomorrow's Children '34
Trojan Women '71
True Women '97
Trumps '83
Twenty-One '91
Unhook the Stars '96
An Unmarried Woman '78 ▶
Unnatural '52
Untraceable '08
Up/Down/Fragile '95
Utamaro and His Five Women '46
Veronica Guerin '03
Visiting Hours '82
Viva Maria! '65
Volver '06 ▶
Voyage en Douce '81
Waiting to Exhale '95 ▶
Walpurgis Night '41 ▶
Warrior Queen '03
Washington Square '97 ▶
The Weight of Water '00
We'll Meet Again '02
Westward the Women '51 ▶
What's Love Got to Do with It? '93
When a Woman Ascends the Stairs '60

▶ = rated three bones or higher

Whose Child Am I? '75
The Wicker Man '06
Widow's Peak '94
Wildrose '85 ▶
Wing Chun '94
Witchfire '86
A Woman and a Woman '80
A Woman Named Jackie '91
A Woman Rebels '36
Woman, Thou Art Loosed '04
The Women '39 ▶
The Women '08
Women from the Lake of Scented Souls '94
Women in Prison '49
The Women of Brewster Place '89 ▶
Women on the Verge of a Nervous Breakdown '88 ▶
Women Without Men '09
Working Girl '88 ▶
Working Girls '87 ▶
Wrestling with Alligators '98
The Wrong Woman '95
Yella '07 ▶

Women Cops

***see also** Cops*
Arizona Heat '87
Black Widow '87 ▶
Blue Steel '90
China O'Brien '88
Copycat '95
Corky Romano '01
Dear Detective '77
Dear Detective '78
The Deep End of the Ocean '98
Do or Die '91
The Enforcer '76
Fargo '96 ▶
Fatal Beauty '87
Get Christie Love! '74
Impulse '90
L.A. Crackdown '87
L.A. Crackdown 2 '88
Miss Congeniality '00
The Mod Squad '99
One of Her Own '97
Policewoman Centerfold '83
Policewomen '73
Prey of the Chameleon '91
Scorchy '76
The Silence of the Lambs '91 ▶
Silk 2 '89
A Stranger Among Us '92
Tereza '61 ▶
Twisted '04
V.I. Warshawski '91
Vice Girls '96

Women in Prison

***see also** Exploitation; Men in Prison; Sexploitation*
Affinity '08
Alien 3 '92
Amazon Jail '85
And the Wild, Wild Women '59
Bad Girls Dormitory '84
Bandits '99
Better Off Dead '94
The Big Bird Cage '72
The Big Bust Out '73
The Big Doll House '71
Born Innocent '74
Bridget Jones: The Edge of Reason '04
Brokedown Palace '99
Caged '50 ▶
Caged Fear '92
Caged Fury '80
Caged Fury '90
Caged Hearts '95
Caged Heat '74
Caged Heat 2: Stripped of Freedom '94
Caged Heat 3000 '95
Caged in Paradiso '89
Caged Women '84
Cellblock Sisters: Banished Behind Bars '95
Chain Gang Girls '08
Chained Heat '83
Chained Heat 2 '92
Chasers '94
Chicago '02 ▶
The Circle '00
Civil Brand '02
The Concrete Jungle '82
Condemned to Hell '84
Condition Red '95
Convicted '04
Convicted: A Mother's Story '87
Deadlock '91
Deadlock 2 '94
Death Row Girls '08
Desperate Women '78
Diary of a Suicide '73
East-West '99
Escape from Cell Block 3 '74
Escape from Hell '79
False Arrest '92
Female Prisoner: Caged '83
Female Prisoner Sigma '06
Fugitive Rage '96
Fun '94
Getting Out '94
Girl on a Chain Gang '65
Girls in Chains '43
Girls in Prison '56
Girls in Prison '94
Girls Riot '88
Hellblock 13 '97
Hot Box '72
Human Experiments '79
I Want to Live! '58 ▶
I'll Be Seeing You '44
Ilsa, the Wicked Warden '78
Jailbird Rock '88
Ladies They Talk About '33
Lady in the Death House '44
Last Dance '96
Lion's Den '08
Longford '06
Love Child '82
Lust for Freedom '87
Madea Goes to Jail '09
A Map of the World '99
Me & Veronica '93
Midnight '34
Mommy 2: Mommy's Day '96
The Muthers '76
Naked Cage '86
Nightmare in Badham County '76
99 Women '69
Nothing But the Truth '08 ▶
Off the Wall '82
Outside Chance '78
Paradise Road '97
Playing for Time '80 ▶
Prison Break: The Final Break '09
Prison of Secrets '97
Prison Stories: Women on the Inside '91 ▶
Purgatory '89
Red Heat '85
Red Letters '00
Reflections in the Dark '94
Reform School Girl '57
Reform School Girls '86
Savage Island '85
Scrubbers '82
Slammer Girls '87
Star Slammer '87
Sweet Sugar '72
10 Violent Women '79
Terminal Island '73
Time Served '99
Untamed Youth '57
V for Vendetta '06
Vendetta '85
Vera Drake '04 ▶
Violent Women '59
White Oleander '02
Why Must I Die? '60
Women in Cell Block 7 '77
Women in Fury '84
Women Unchained '72
Women's Prison Escape '74
Women's Prison Massacre '85

Women in War

***see also** Doctors & Nurses; Korean War; Vietnam War; Women; Wonder Women; World War I; World War II*
China Beach '88 ▶
Courage Under Fire '96 ▶
The English Patient '96 ▶
A Farewell to Arms '32 ▶
G.I. Jane '97
A Guy Named Joe '44
Hanna's War '88
In Love and War '96
Nurse Edith Cavell '39 ▶
Paradise Road '97
Purple Hearts '84
Rodgers & Hammerstein's South Pacific '01
She Goes to War '29
So Proudly We Hail '43 ▶
South Pacific '58 ▶
A Town Like Alice '85
A Woman in Berlin '08

Wonder Women

***see also** Dream Girls*
The Abductors '72
Act of Vengeance '74
Against the Ropes '04
Alien '79 ▶
Alien 3 '92
Alien: Resurrection '97 ▶
Aliens '86 ▶
Alley Cat '84
Amazon Warrior '97
The Amazons '84
Amazons '86
Amazons and Gladiators '01
The American Angels: Baptism of Blood '89
Angel's Brigade '79
Angel's Dance '99
The Associate '96
Attack of the 50 Foot Woman '58
Attack of the 50 Ft. Woman '93
Attack of the 60-Foot Centerfold '95
Azumi '03 ▶
Bad Georgia Road '77
Barbarian Queen '85
Barbarian Queen 2: The Empress Strikes Back '89
Basic Training '86
Batman and Robin '97
Batman Returns '92
Battle Queen 2020 '99
Beauty for the Asking '39
Bees in Paradise '44
Big Bad Mama 2 '87
The Big Bust Out '73
Billie '65
Bimini Code '84
The Bionic Woman '75
Black Scorpion 2: Ground Zero '96
Blonde in Black Leather '77
Blonde Savage '47
Blue Tiger '94
Buffy the Vampire Slayer '92 ▶
Bury Me an Angel '71
Business As Usual '88
Chameleon '98
Chameleon 2: Death Match '99
Chameleon 3: Dark Angel '00
Charlie's Angels '00
Charlie's Angels: Full Throttle '03
China O'Brien 2 '89
Chopper Chicks in Zombietown '91
Circadian Rhythm '05
The Clan of the Cave Bear '86
Cleopatra '34
Cleopatra '63
Cleopatra Jones '73
Coffy '73
Colossus and the Amazon Queen '64
Crouching Tiger, Hidden Dragon '00 ▶
Cutthroat Island '95
Danger Zone '87
The Deadly and the Beautiful '73
Deadly Weapons '70
Death Proof '07
The Demolitionist '95
Do or Die '91
DOA: Dead or Alive '06
Doctor of Doom '62
Doomsday '08
Dragon Fury 2 '96
Elektra '05
Evita '96
The Executioners '93
The $5.20 an Hour Dream '80
Fugitive Rage '96
Galaxis '95
Get Christie Love! '74
G.I. Jane '97
God Said "Ha!" '99 ▶
Golden Lady '79
The Great Texas Dynamite Chase '76
Heartland '81 ▶
Heavy Metal 2000 '00
Hercules the Legendary Journeys, Vol. 1: And the Amazon Women '94
Hot Box '72
Hundra '85
I Spit on Your Grave '77
Invincible Barbarian '83
Kill Bill Vol. 1 '03 ▶
Kill Bill Vol. 2 '04 ▶
Kilma, Queen of the Amazons '75
Kisses for My President '64
L.A. Crackdown '87
La Femme Nikita '91 ▶
Lady Scarface '41
Lara Croft: Tomb Raider '01
Lara Croft Tomb Raider: The Cradle of Life '03
Lethal Panther '90
Lethal Woman '88
The Long Kiss Goodnight '96
The Lost Empire '83
Mame '74
Mankillers '87
Marie '85 ▶
The Messenger: The Story of Joan of Arc '99
Mind Trap '91
Mission of Justice '92
Mistress of the Apes '79
Moonshine County Express '77
My Name is Modesty: A Modesty Blaise Adventure '04
My Super Ex-Girlfriend '06
Nancy Drew, Reporter '39
Night Partners '83
Not Without My Daughter '90
Nyoka and the Tigermen '42
One Million Years B.C. '66
Panther Squad '84
The Perils of Pauline '34
Phoenix the Warrior '88
Pocahontas '95 ▶
Point of No Return '93
Prehistoric Women '50
Queen of the Road '84
Ravenhawk '95
Resurrection '80 ▶
The River Wild '94
Roller Blade '85
Runaway Nightmare '84
Running Delilah '93
Sara Dane '81
Savage Beach '89
The Savage Girl '32
Savage Streets '83
See How She Runs '78 ▶
S*H*E '79
Sheena '84
She'll Be Wearing Pink Pajamas '84
She's in the Army Now '81
The Silence of the Lambs '91 ▶
Silver Hawk '04
Sister Kenny '46 ▶
Skyscraper '95
Speed 2: Cruise Control '97
Spice World: The Movie '97
Stormquest '87
Sunstorm '01
Superchick '71
Supergirl '84
Sweet Revenge '87
Switchblade Sisters '75
Terminal Velocity '94
Thor and the Amazon Women '60
Tiffany Jones '75
Trapped '89
Tulsa '49 ▶
The 24 Hour Woman '99
Uncaged '91
Velvet Smooth '76
Waiting to Exhale '95 ▶
Wanted '08 ▶
The Wild World of Batwoman '66
The Wind and the Lion '75 ▶
A Woman Rebels '36
The World Is Not Enough '99
Wrestling Women vs. the Aztec Mummy '59
Zorro's Black Whip '44

Words Come to Life

***see also** Parallel Universe; Writers*
Adaptation '02 ▶
Alex & Emma '03
American Dreamer '84
Cashback '06
The Crow Road '96
Final Draft '07
Lost in Austen '08
Love Comes Lately '07
Lovely by Surprise '07
Nim's Island '08
The Number 23 '07
P.S. I Love You '07
Sex and Lucia '01
Something's Gotta Give '03 ▶
Stranger Than Fiction '06
You and Me '06

Workin' for a Livin'

Adventureland '09 ▶
All or Nothing '02
Astoria '00
Bartleby '01
Bee Movie '07
Belles on Their Toes '52
The Black House '00
Blonde Ambition '07
Bob Funk '09
Brown Sugar '02
Bubble '06
Caffeine '06
Car Babes '06
Carry On Regardless '61
The Church Mouse '34
Clerks 2 '06 ▶
Clockwatchers '97
Close My Eyes '91
Colleen '36
Come Early Morning '06
Confessions of a Shopaholic '09
Cow Belles '06
Cursed '04
Dancehall Queen '97
Day-Time Wife '39
Days and Clouds '07
Dear Me: A Blogger's Tale '08
Departures '08
Diggers '06
Dirty Pretty Things '03 ▶
Edge of the City '57
Employee of the Month '06
Entry Level '07
Everything's Gone Green '06
The Ex '07
Extract '09
Factotum '06 ▶
The Family Plan '05
Far from Heaven '02 ▶
Fashion Victims '07
Flakes '07
Flawless '07
The Foot Fist Way '08
Friday After Next '02
Friends & Crocodiles '05
Frozen River '08 ▶
The Girlfriend Experience '09
Going the Distance '10
The Good Girl '02 ▶
The Good Guy '10
Grocer's Son '07
Happiness Ahead '34
Happy Times '00
Hard to Get '38
High School Musical 2 '07
The Human Stain '03
Humble Pie '07
I Hate Valentine's Day '09
I Promise to Pay '37
I Really Hate My Job '07
Imagine That '09
Irina Palm '07
Janice Beard '99
Ju-Rei: The Uncanny '04
Juke Girl '42
Just Add Water '07
Killer of Sheep '77 ▶
Kinky Boots '06
A Lobster Tale '06
Mad Money '08
Maid in Manhattan '02
The Man Without a Past '02 ▶
Manpower '41
Meet the People '44
Memron '04
The Method '05 ▶
Mondays in the Sun '02
Moonlight & Mistletoe '08
Morning Glory '10
Moscow, Belgium '08
My Boss's Daughter '03
The Mystic Masseur '01
The Nanny Diaries '07
The Navigators '01
Netherbeast Incorporated '07
New in Town '09
9 to 5 '80
No Other Woman '33
North Country '05
Not So Dusty '56
Office Space '98
One Hour Photo '02 ▶
101 Ways (The Things a Girl Will Do to Keep Her Volvo) '00
Outsourced '06
Post Grad '09
Pretty Baby '50
Punch-Drunk Love '02 ▶
The Pursuit of Happyness '06
Read My Lips '01
Real Women Have Curves '02 ▶
Revolution 9 '01
The Ring Finger '05
Saturday Night at the Baths '75
The Search for John Gissing '01
Shorts: The Adventures of the Wishing Rock '09
A Simple Curve '05
Soul Kitchen '09
Spiral '07
Spring Forward '99
Sunshine Cleaning '09 ▶
10 Items or Less '06
Time Out '01
Traveling Companion '96
Up in the Air '09 ▶
Vacuuming Completely Nude in Paradise '01
Very Annie Mary '00
The Wedding Bros. '08
Wendy and Lucy '08 ▶
Wine, Women and Horses '37
Wonderful World '09
Working Girl '88 ▶
You Kill Me '07 ▶

World War I

Ace of Aces '33
The African Queen '51 ▶
All Quiet on the Western Front '30 ▶
All Quiet on the Western Front '79
All the King's Men '99
Anne of Green Gables: The Continuing Story '99
Anzacs: The War Down Under '85 ▶
Arsenal '29 ▶
Behind the Lines '97
The Better 'Ole '26
The Big Parade '25 ▶
Biggles '85
The Blue Max '66
Capitaine Conan '96 ▶
Catherine Cookson's The Cinder Path '94
Catherine Cookson's The Wingless Bird '97

The Chaplin Revue '58
Charge of the Model T's '76
Crimson Romance '34
The Dark Angel '35
Dark Journey '37 ▶
Darling Lili '70
Dawn Patrol '38 ▶
The Day That Shook the World '78
Deathwatch '02
Devil in the Flesh '46 ▶
Dishonored '31
Dr. Mabuse, The Gambler '22 ▶
Doctor Zhivago '65 ▶
Doctor Zhivago '03
Doughboys '30
The Eagle and the Hawk '33 ▶
Elizabeth of Ladymead '48 ▶
The End of St. Petersburg '27 ▶
FairyTale: A True Story '97
False Faces '18
A Farewell to Arms '32 ▶
A Farewell to Arms '57
Fifth Day of Peace '72
The Fighting 69th '40 ▶
Finding Rin Tin Tin '07
Flambards '78
Flyboys '06
For Me and My Gal '42
Fort Saganne '84
The Four Horsemen of the Apocalypse '21 ▶
Four Sons '28
Gallipoli '81 ▶
Gods and Monsters '98 ▶
Going Home '86
Golden Dawn '30
Grand Illusion '37 ▶
The Great War '59
Half-Shot at Sunrise '30
Heart of Humanity '18
Hearts of the World '18 ▶
Hedd Wyn '92
Hell's Angels '30 ▶
Hotel Imperial '27
How Many Miles to Babylon? '82
In Love and War '96
An Indecent Obsession '85
Inside the Lines '30
The Iron Major '43
Isn't Life Wonderful '24 ▶
J'accuse! '19 ▶
Jericho '38
Joyeux Noel '05 ▶
Killing Floor '85
King and Country '64 ▶
The King of Hearts '66 ▶
Lafayette Escadrille '58
The Land That Time Forgot '75
The Last Outpost '35
Lawrence of Arabia '62 ▶
The Legend of Bagger Vance '00
Legends of the Fall '94
Les Destinees '00
The Life and Death of Colonel Blimp '43 ▶
Life and Nothing But '89 ▶
The Lighthorsemen '87 ▶
The Little American '17
Lost Battalion '01
The Lost Patrol '34 ▶
The Love Light '21
Man of Legend '71
Mata Hari '32 ▶
Mata Hari '85
Miracle of Our Lady of Fatima '52
My Boy Jack '07
My Son, My Son '40
Nicholas and Alexandra '71
1915 '82
1918 '85
Nurse Edith Cavell '39 ▶
Oh! What a Lovely War '69
Paths of Glory '57 ▶
The Patriots '33 ▶
Photographing Fairies '97
Pilgrimage '33
Q Ships '28
Return of the Soldier '82 ▶
Revolt of the Zombies '36
7th Heaven '27
She Goes to War '29
Shopworn Angel '38 ▶
Shout at the Devil '76
Spy in Black '39 ▶
Suicide Fleet '31
Suzy '36
Testament of Youth '79
Three Legionnaires '37
Tin Pan Alley '40
Today We Live '33
Tomorrow Is Forever '46
The Trench '99
The Unknown Soldier '98
A Very Long Engagement '04 ▶
Waterloo Bridge '40 ▶
Weeping Meadow '04
Westfront 1918 '30 ▶
What Price Glory? '52 ▶
When the Whales Came '89
The White Cliffs of Dover '44 ▶
Wilson '44 ▶
Wings '27
Wings of Eagles '57
The Woman and the Stranger '84
Women of All Nations '31
Yankee Doodle in Berlin '19
Zeppelin '71

World War I Spies

see also *Spies & Espionage; World War I*

Charge of the Model T's '76
Dark Journey '37 ▶
Darling Lili '70
Dishonored '31
False Faces '18
Heart of Humanity '18
Hotel Imperial '27
Inside the Lines '30
The Love Light '21
Mata Hari '32 ▶
Mata Hari '85
Seas Beneath '31
Spy in Black '39 ▶
Zeppelin '71

World War II

see also *Biopics: Military; The Holocaust; The Homefront: England; The Homefront: U.S./Canada; Nazis & Other Paramilitary Slugs; Postwar; POW/MIA; The Resistance; World War II Spies*

Above and Beyond '53 ▶
Above Suspicion '43 ▶
Above Us the Waves '56 ▶
Abroad with Two Yanks '44
Absent Without Leave '95
The Accompanist '93
Action in the North Atlantic '43
Adventures of Smilin' Jack '43
The Adventures of Werner Holt '65
The Affair '95
After the Deluge '03 ▶
Air Force '43 ▶
Alan & Naomi '92
Alexandria... Why? '78
All the Queen's Men '02
Ambush '99 ▶
The Americanization of Emily '64 ▶
And a Nightingale Sang '91
Angels One Five '54
Angry Harvest '85 ▶
An Annapolis Story '55
Anne Frank: The Whole Story '01 ▶
Another Time, Another Place '58
Another Time, Another Place '83 ▶
Anzio '68
Arch of Triumph '48 ▶
Arch of Triumph '85
Army of Shadows '69 ▶
Around the World '43
The Ascent '76 ▶
The Ascent '94
Ashes and Diamonds '58 ▶
The Assault '86 ▶
Assault on Agathon '75
The Assisi Underground '84
Atonement '07 ▶
Attack! '56 ▶
Attack Force Z '84
Attack Squadron '63
The Attic: The Hiding of Anne Frank '88
Au Revoir les Enfants '87 ▶
The Audrey Hepburn Story '00
Away All Boats '56
Baaria '09
Back Home '90
Back to Bataan '45
The Bamboo Blonde '46
Band of Brothers '01 ▶
Bataan '43
Battle Cry '55 ▶
The Battle of Blood Island '60
Battle of Britain '69
The Battle of El Alamein '68
Battle of Neretva '69
Battle of the Bulge '65
Battle of the Commandos '71
Battle of the Eagles '79
The Battle of the Japan Sea '70
Battle of the Rails '46 ▶
Battleforce '78
Battleground '49 ▶
Bedknobs and Broomsticks '71
Behind Enemy Lines '85
Below '02
The Best Years of Our Lives '46 ▶
Betrayal from the East '44
Between Heaven and Hell '56 ▶
The Big Lift '50
The Big Red One '80 ▶
Black Brigade '69
Black Rain '88 ▶
Blockhouse '73
The Blood of Others '84
Blood on the Sun '45
The Boat Is Full '81 ▶
Bomb at 10:10 '67
Bombardier '43
Bon Voyage '03 ▶
The Boxer and Death '63 ▶
The Boy in the Striped Pajamas '08 ▶
Brady's Escape '84
Brainwashed '60
Brass Target '78
The Brave Bunch '70
Breaking the Code '95
Breakthrough '78
Brideshead Revisited '08
The Bridge '59
The Bridge at Remagen '69
The Bridge on the River Kwai '57 ▶
Bridge to Hell '87
A Bridge Too Far '77
Brief Encounter '46 ▶
The Brylcreem Boys '96
Burma Convoy '41
The Burmese Harp '56 ▶
The Caine Mutiny '54 ▶
The Camomile Lawn '92
A Canterbury Tale '44 ▶
The Canterville Ghost '44
Captain Corelli's Mandolin '01
Captain Newman, M.D. '63
Captains of the Clouds '42
Captive Heart '47 ▶
Captive Hearts '87
Carrie's War '04
Carry Me Home '04
Carry On England '76
Casablanca '42 ▶
Casablanca Express '89
Castle Keep '69 ▶
Catch-22 '70 ▶
Caught in the Draft '41 ▶
Chain Lightning '50
Charlie Grant's War '80
Charlotte Gray '01
Chicago Joe & the Showgirl '90
China '43
China Sky '44
Chips, the War Dog '90
Christ Stopped at Eboli '79 ▶
Christabel '89
The Chronicles of Narnia: The Lion, the Witch and the Wardrobe '05
Churchill and the Generals '81
Class of '44 '73
The Clock '45 ▶
Closely Watched Trains '66 ▶
Closing the Ring '07
Cold Days '66
The Colditz Story '55
Combat Killers '68
Come and See '85 ▶
Come See the Paradise '90 ▶
Coming Home '98
Command Decision '48
Commando Attack '67
Commando Squad '76
Commandos '73
Commandos Strike at Dawn '43
Conspiracy '01
Conspiracy of Hearts '60 ▶
Contraband '40
Convoy '40
Cornered '45 ▶
Corregidor '43
Cottage to Let '41
The Coward '62
The Cranes Are Flying '57 ▶
Crash Dive '43
Cross of Iron '76
The Cruel Sea '53 ▶
Cry of Battle '63
The Cuckoo '02
D-Day, the Sixth of June '56 ▶
Dam Busters '55 ▶
Danger UXB '81
Dangerous Moonlight '41 ▶
Darby's Rangers '58
Dark Blue World '01
Das Boot '81 ▶
David '79 ▶
The Day and the Hour '63
A Day in October '92
Day One '89 ▶
Days of Glory '43
Days of Glory '06
Deadly Mission '78
Death Is Called Engelchen '63 ▶
Death of a Soldier '85
The Death of Adolf Hitler '84
December '91
December 7th: The Movie '91
Deep Six '58
Defiance '08
Desert Commandos '67
The Desert Fox '51 ▶
The Desert Rats '53 ▶
Despair '78 ▶
Desperate Journey '42
Destination Tokyo '43
Destroyer '43 ▶
The Devil's Brigade '68
Devils on the Doorstep '00
Diamonds of the Night '64 ▶
The Diary of Anne Frank '59 ▶
The Dirty Dozen '67 ▶
The Dirty Dozen: The Deadly Mission '87
The Dirty Dozen: The Fatal Mission '88
The Dirty Dozen: The Next Mission '85
Dirty Heroes '71
Distant Thunder '73 ▶
Distant Voices, Still Lives '88 ▶
Dive Bomber '41 ▶
Divided We Fall '00
Dr. Akagi '98
Dr. Petiot '90
Dominion: Prequel to the Exorcist '05
Dondi '61
Downfall '04 ▶
Dresden '06
The Dresser '83 ▶
The Dressmaker '89
The Dunera Boys '85 ▶
The Eagle Has Landed '77 ▶
Eagles Over London '69
Edge of Darkness '43 ▶
Eighteen '04
Elizabeth of Ladymead '48 ▶
The Elusive Corporal '62 ▶
Empire of the Sun '87 ▶
The Empty Mirror '99
End of the Affair '55
The End of the Affair '99 ▶
Enemy at the Gates '00
Enemy Below '57 ▶
Enemy of Women '44
The English Patient '96 ▶
Enigma '01
Enigma Secret '79
Enola Gay: The Men, the Mission, the Atomic Bomb '80
Ensign Pulver '64
Era Notte a Roma '60 ▶
Escape from Sobibor '87 ▶
Escape to Athena '79
Europa, Europa '91 ▶
Every Time We Say Goodbye '86
Everything is Illuminated '05 ▶
The Execution '85
The Execution of Private Slovik '74 ▶
A Face in the Rain '63
Fall from Grace '94
The Fallen '05 ▶
Farewell to the King '89
Fat Man and Little Boy '89
Fateless '05 ▶
Father '67 ▶
Father Goose '64
Father of the Kamikaze '74
The Fifth Seal '76
Fight for the Title '57
Fighter Attack '53
The Fighting Rats of Tobruk '44
Fighting Seabees '44
The Fighting Sullivans '42 ▶
The Final Countdown '80 ▶
Fireball Forward '72
Fires on the Plain '59 ▶
First Yank into Tokyo '45
Fist of Legend '94
Five Fingers '52 ▶
Five for Hell '67
Flags of Our Fathers '06 ▶
Flame to the Phoenix '85
Flat Top '52
Flying Leathernecks '51 ▶
Flying Tigers '42
Follow the Boys '44 ▶
For the Boys '91
For the Moment '94
Forbidden '85
Forbidden Games '52 ▶
Force 10 from Navarone '78
Foreign Correspondent '40 ▶
A Foreign Field '93
The Foreman Went to France '42
Fortunes of War '87 ▶
The Forty-Ninth Parallel '41 ▶
Forty Thousand Horsemen '41
Four Bags Full '56
The Four Horsemen of the Apocalypse '62
Four in a Jeep '51
Four Jills in a Jeep '44
Foxtrot '76
Frieda '47
A Friendship in Vienna '88
From Hell to Victory '79
From Here to Eternity '53 ▶
From Here to Eternity '79
G-Men vs. the Black Dragon '43
The Gallant Hours '60 ▶
The Gang's All Here '43
The Garden of Redemption '97
The Garden of the Finzi-Continis '71 ▶
Geheimakte WB1 '42
Generale Della Rovere '60 ▶
A Generation '54 ▶
Germany, Pale Mother '80
The Gift Horse '52
The Girl of Your Dreams '99
The Gleiwitz Case '61
Gloomy Sunday '02 ▶
Go for Broke! '51
God is My Co-Pilot '45
The Goebbels Experiment '05
Golden Earrings '47
Great Day '46
The Great Escape '63 ▶
The Great Escape 2: The Untold Story '88
The Great Raid '05
The Great Water '04
Green for Danger '47
The Green Glove '52
The Green House '96
Greta '86 ▶
Guadalcanal Diary '43
Gung Ho! '43
The Guns of Navarone '61 ▶
A Guy Named Joe '44
The Gypsy Warriors '78
The Halls of Montezuma '50
Hamsun '96
The Hand '60
Hanna's War '88
Hanover Street '79
Hart's War '02
The Hasty Heart '86 ▶
Head in the Clouds '04
The Heat of the Day '91
Heaven Knows, Mr. Allison '57 ▶
Hell Commandos '69
Hell Is for Heroes '62 ▶
Hell River '75
Hell Squad '58
Hell to Eternity '60
Hellcats of the Navy '57
Hell's Brigade: The Final Assault '80
Heroes Die Young '60
The Heroes of Telemark '65
The Hiding Place '75
The Highest Honor '84
The Hill '65
Hillbilly Blitzkrieg '42
Hiroshima '95 ▶
Hiroshima Maiden '88
Hiroshima: Out of the Ashes '90 ▶
Hitler '62
Hitler: The Last Ten Days '73
Hitler's Children '43 ▶
Hollywood Canteen '44 ▶
Holocaust '78 ▶
The Home Front '02
Home of the Brave '49 ▶
Homecoming '48
Hope and Glory '87 ▶
The Horizontal Lieutenant '62
Hornet's Nest '70
The Human Comedy '43 ▶
The Human Condition: A Soldier's Prayer '61 ▶
The Human Condition: No Greater Love '58 ▶
The Human Condition: Road to Eternity '59 ▶
Hunted '88
Hunters of the Golden Cobra '82
Hustler Squad '76
I Bombed Pearl Harbor '60
I Was a Male War Bride '49 ▶
I Was Nineteen '68
Identity Unknown '45
Ike '79
Ike: Countdown to D-Day '04
I'll Remember April '99
Immortal Battalion '44 ▶
Immortal Sergeant '43
The Imperial Japanese Empire '85
In a Shallow Grave '88
In Enemy Hands '04
In Harm's Way '65
In Love and War '01
In Tranzit '07
In Which We Serve '43 ▶
The Incident '89 ▶
The Incredible Mr. Limpet '64
Infinity '96
The Inglorious Bastards '78
Inglourious Basterds '09 ▶
The Inheritors '82
Inside the Third Reich '82
Is Paris Burning? '66 ▶
The Island on Bird Street '97
Jacob the Liar '74
Jadup and Boel '81
Jenny's War '85
Jive Junction '43

▶ = rated three bones or higher

Joan of Paris '42 ►
Johnny Frenchman '46
Journey for Margaret '42 ►
Judgment at Nuremberg '61 ►
Julia '77 ►
Jungle Patrol '48
Kanal '56 ►
Kapo '59 ►
Katyn '07
Kelly's Heroes '70
The Key '58
The Key to Rebecca '85
Kindergarten '84 ►
King Rat '65 ►
Kings Go Forth '58
Korczak '90 ►
La Grande Vadrouille '66 ►
La Silence de la Mer '47 ►
The Land Girls '98
Landscape After Battle '70
Lassiter '84
The Last Bastion '84
The Last Bridge '54
The Last Butterfly '92
The Last Chance '45 ►
Last Day of the War '69
The Last Days of Patton '86
The Last Drop '05
The Last Five Days '82
The Last Lieutenant '94
The Last Metro '80 ►
The Last of the Blonde Bombshells '00
The Last Train '74
The Last Warrior '89
Law of the Jungle '42
A League of Their Own '92 ►
Leon Morin, Priest '61
Les Miserables '95
Les Violons du Bal '74
Letters from Iwo Jima '06 ►
Letters to an Unknown Lover '84
The Life and Death of Colonel Blimp '43 ►
Life Is Beautiful '98 ►
Lifeboat '44 ►
The Lion Has Wings '40
The Little Thief '89 ►
The Longest Day '62 ►
Lotna '64
A Love in Germany '84
Love Letters '45
Lucie Aubrac '98
MacArthur '77
MacArthur's Children '85 ►
Malaya '49
Malta Story '53
A Man Called Sarge '90
A Man Escaped '57 ►
Manhunt in the African Jungles '43
Manon '50
Map of the Human Heart '93
Maria's Lovers '84
Marine Raiders '43
Massacre in Rome '73
The Master Race '44
Max and Helen '90
The McConnell Story '55
McHale's Navy '64
McKenzie Break '70 ►
Me and the Colonel '58
Mediterraneo '91 ►
Meet Sexton Blake '44
Memoirs of a Geisha '05
Memphis Belle '90 ►
The Men '50 ►
Mephisto '81 ►
Merrill's Marauders '62
Merry Christmas, Mr. Lawrence '83 ►
A Midnight Clear '92 ►
Midway '76
Military Intelligence and You! '06
Miracle at Midnight '98
Miracle at Moreaux '86
Miracle at St. Anna '08
The Miracle of the White Stallions '63
The Mirror '75 ►
The Misfit Brigade '87
Missiles from Hell '58
Mission Batangas '69
Mission of the Shark '91 ►
Mission to Death '66
Mrs. Henderson Presents '05
Mrs. Miniver '42 ►
Mr. Kingstreet's War '71
Mr. Klein '76 ►
Mister Roberts '55 ►
Mr. Skeffington '44 ►
Mr. Winkle Goes to War '44
The More the Merrier '43 ►
The Mortal Storm '40 ►
Moscow Parade '92
Mosley '98
Mother of Kings '82
Mother of Mine '05 ►
The Mountain Road '60
Murderers Among Us: The Simon Wiesenthal Story '89 ►
Murphy's War '71
Music Box '89
Mussolini & I '85
Mutiny '99
My Brother Tom '86
The Naked and the Dead '58
The Nasty Girl '90 ►
The Navy Comes Through '42
Navy Way '44
Never So Few '59
Never Wave at a WAC '52
Night Ambush '57
Night of the Fox '90
The Night of the Shooting Stars '82 ►
The Nightmare Years '89
Nine Men '43
1941 '79
The Ninth Day '04 ►
No Greater Love '43
No Man Is an Island '62
No Regrets for Our Youth '46 ►
None But the Brave '65
The North Star '43 ►
The Notebook '04
Nous N'Irons Plus au Bois '69
November Moon '85
The Nun's Story '59 ►
Objective, Burma! '45 ►
The Odd Squad '86
The Ogre '96
On the Fiddle '61
Once Before I Die '65
One Against the Wind '91 ►
One Day You'll Understand '08
One of Our Aircraft Is Missing '41 ►
One That Got Away '57 ►
Only the Brave '06
The Only Way '70
Open City '45 ►
Operation Bikini '63
Operation Valkyrie '04
The Oppermann Family '82
Overlanders '46 ►
Pacific Inferno '85
Paisan '46 ►
Paradise Road '97
Passage to Marseilles '44 ►
Patton '70 ►
The Pawnbroker '65 ►
Pearl '78
Pearl Harbor '01
The Philadelphia Experiment '84
Piece of Cake '88
Pimpernel Smith '42
Pin-Up Girl '44
Place in Hell '69
Playing for Time '80 ►
Prelude to War '42
Pride of the Marines '45 ►
Prisoners of the Sun '91 ►
Private Buckaroo '42
Private Contentment '83
Private Navy of Sgt. O'Farrell '68
PT 109 '63
The Purple Heart '44
Pursuit of the Graf Spee '57
Raggedy Man '81 ►
Raid on Rommel '71
Raiders of Leyte Gulf '63
Raiders of Sunset Pass '43
The Ravagers '65
Reach for the Sky '56
Rebel '85
Red Ball Express '52
Red Cherry '95
The Reflecting Skin '91
Rescuers: Stories of Courage "Two Women" '97 ►
Resistance '03
Return to Never Land '02
Reunion '88 ►
Reunion in France '42
The Revolt of Job '84 ►
Rodgers & Hammerstein's South Pacific '01
Rosenstrasse '03 ►
Run Silent, Run Deep '58 ►
Running Away '89
Sahara '43 ►
Saigon '47
Sailor of the King '53
Saint-Ex: The Story of the Storyteller '95
Saints and Soldiers '03
Salo, or the 120 Days of Sodom '75
Salute John Citizen '42 ►
San Demetrio, London '47
Sands of Iwo Jima '49 ►
Saving Private Ryan '98 ►
The Scarlet & the Black '83
Schindler's List '93 ►
Sea Chase '55
Sea of Sand '58
The Sea Shall Not Have Them '55
Sea Wife '57
Sea Wolves '81
The Search '48 ►
Second Victory '87
The Secret Invasion '64
The Secret of Santa Vittoria '69
The Secret War of Harry Frigg '68
Seven Beauties '76 ►
Seven Days' Leave '42
Seven Years in Tibet '97
The Seventh Cross '44 ►
Shadows over Shanghai '38
Shell Shock '63
Sherlock Holmes and the Secret Weapon '42 ►
Sherlock Holmes: The Voice of Terror '42
Ship of Fools '65 ►
The Shop on Main Street '65 ►
Signs of Life '68
The Silent Enemy '58
Silent Raiders '54
Since You Went Away '44 ►
Sink the Bismarck '60 ►
633 Squadron '64
Ski Troop Attack '60
The Sky Is Falling '00
Slaughterhouse Five '72
The Small Back Room '49 ►
Snow Treasure '67
So Proudly We Hail '43 ►
So This Is Washington '43
Soldat Duroc... Ca Va Etre Ta Fete! '75
Soldier of Orange '78 ►
A Soldier's Story '84 ►
A Soldier's Tale '91
Somewhere I'll Find You '42 ►
Son of Lassie '45
Sophie Scholl: The Final Days '05 ►
The Sorrow and the Pity '71 ►
The Sound of Music '65 ►
South Pacific '58 ►
South Sea Woman '53
Special Forces '68
Spitfire '42 ►
The Square Peg '58
SS Girls '77
Stage Door Canteen '43
Stairway to Heaven '46 ►
Stalag Luft '93
Stalingrad '94
Star Spangled Rhythm '42 ►
The Steel Claw '61
Story of a Prostitute '65
The Story of Dr. Wassell '44
The Story of G.I. Joe '45 ►
Straight into Darkness '04
Strayed '03 ►
Strictly G.I. '44
Submarine Attack '54
Submarine Seahawk '59
The Summer of My German Soldier '78 ►
Sundown '41
Surviving Picasso '96
Sweet Light in a Dark Room '60 ►
Sword of Honour '01
Taking Sides '01 ►
Tank Commando '59
Task Force '49
A Taste of Hell '73
Tea with Mussolini '99
The Teahouse of the August Moon '56
Tender Comrade '43
The Tenth Man '88
Thank Your Lucky Stars '43 ►
That Long Night in '43 '60
That Summer of White Roses '90
They Were Expendable '45 ►
The Thin Red Line '64
The Thin Red Line '98 ►
Thirty Seconds Over Tokyo '44 ►
36 Hours '64 ►
Thirty-Six Hours of Hell '77
This Is the Army '43
This Land Is Mine '43 ►
Those People Next Door '52
Thousands Cheer '43
Three Came Home '50 ►
Thunder Birds '42
Tides of War '90
Tiger Fangs '43
A Time of Destiny '88
A Time to Love & a Time to Die '58
The Tin Drum '79 ►
To Be or Not to Be '42 ►
To Be or Not to Be '83
To Each His Own '46 ►
To End All Wars '01
To Have & Have Not '44 ►
To Hell and Back '55
To the Shores of Tripoli '42
Tobruk '66
Tomorrow Is Forever '46
Tonight and Every Night '45
Too Late the Hero '70 ►
Tora! Tora! Tora! '70
Torpedo Attack '72
Torpedo Run '58
Tower of Terror '42
A Town Like Alice '85
The Train '65 ►
Transport from Paradise '65
Treasure Island '99
Triple Echo '77
Triumph of the Spirit '89 ►
Triumph of the Will '34 ►
The Truce '96 ►
True Colors '87
The Tuskegee Airmen '95 ►
Twelve o'Clock High '49 ►
25 Fireman's Street '73 ►
Two Girls and a Sailor '44 ►
Two Men Went to War '02
The Two of Us '68 ►
Two Women '61 ►
U-Boat Prisoner '44
U-571 '00
Uncertain Glory '44
Under the Earth '86 ►
Under the Flag of the Rising Sun '72 ►
The Underdog '43
Underground '41
Underground '95 ►
Until They Sail '57
Up in Arms '44
Uprising '01 ►
Valiant '05
Valkyrie '08
Varian's War '01
Very Important Person '61
The Victors '63
Victory '81
Von Ryan's Express '65 ►
Voyage of the Damned '76 ►
Wackiest Ship in the Army '61
Wake Island '42 ►
A Walk in the Sun '46 ►
The Walls of Hell '64
The Wannsee Conference '84 ►
War & Love '84
War & Remembrance '88
War & Remembrance: The Final Chapter '89
The War Boy '85
War Lover '62
Warbirds '08
Warkill '65
We Dive at Dawn '43 ►
We Were One Man '80
We Will Not Enter the Forest '79 ►
The Weaker Sex '49
Wedding in White '72
Weeping Meadow '04
Well-Digger's Daughter '46 ►
We'll Meet Again '82
What Did You Do in the War, Daddy? '66
When Hell Broke Loose '58
When Taekwondo Strikes '83
When Trumpets Fade '98
When Willie Comes Marching Home '50 ►
The White Cliffs of Dover '44 ►
The White Rose '83 ►
The Winds of War '83
Windtalkers '02
A Wing and a Prayer '44 ►
Wings over the Pacific '43
Winter in Wartime '10
The Wizard of Loneliness '88
A Woman at War '94
A Woman in Berlin '08
Women of Valor '86
Wooden Horse '50 ►
World War II: When Lions Roared '94
A Yank in Australia '43
A Yank in the R.A.F. '41
Yanks '79
You'll Never Get Rich '41 ►
The Young Lions '58 ►
Zelary '03 ►
Zero '84
Zone Troopers '84

World War II Spies

see also ***Nazis & Other Paramilitary Slugs; Spies & Espionage; World War II***

Above Suspicion '43 ►
Across the Pacific '42 ►
Action in Arabia '44
Against the Wind '48
Air Raid Wardens '43
All the Queen's Men '02
All Through the Night '42 ►
Armored Command '61
Background to Danger '43 ►
Bear Island '80
Berlin Express '48 ►
Betrayed '54 ►
Black Book '06 ►
The Black Dragons '42
Bon Voyage '03 ►
Cairo '42
Call Out the Marines '42
Carve Her Name with Pride '58
Charlotte Gray '01
Clipped Wings '53
Cloak and Dagger '46
Code Name: Emerald '85
Confessions of a Nazi Spy '39
Counterblast '48
The Counterfeit Traitor '62 ►
Cowboy Commandos '43
David Harding, Counterspy '50
Dawn Express '42
The Day Will Dawn '42 ►
Enigma '01
Eye of the Needle '81
A Face in the Rain '63
Fall from Grace '94
The Fallen Sparrow '43 ►
Five Fingers '52 ►
Five for Hell '67
Five Graves to Cairo '43 ►
Foreign Correspondent '40 ►
Head in the Clouds '04
The Heat of the Day '91
Heroes in Hell '73
Hidden Enemy '40
Holt of the Secret Service '42
Hotel Reserve '44 ►
I See a Dark Stranger '46 ►
I Was an American Spy '51
International Lady '41
Invisible Agent '42
Journey into Fear '42 ►
The Lost One '51
Lust, Caution '07
The Man Who Never Was '55 ►
The Master Race '44
The Mediterranean in Flames '72
Ministry of Fear '44 ►
Monte Carlo '86
Morituri '65 ►
Mother Night '96 ►
My Favorite Blonde '42 ►
My Name Is Ivan '62 ►
Night Train to Munich '40 ►
Notorious '46 ►
Once Upon a Honeymoon '42
Operation Amsterdam '60
Operation Cross Eagles '69
Operation Crossbow '65 ►
O.S.S. '46 ►
Panama Hattie '42
Panama Menace '41
Qui Etes Vous, Mr. Sorge? '61
Rio Rita '42
Robot Pilot '41
The Rocketeer '91 ►
Saboteur '42 ►
The Second Front '05
The Secret Code '42
Secret Mission '42
Shining Through '92
Ship Ahoy '42
Spy Smasher '42
Spy Smasher Returns '42
Stalag 17 '53 ►
The Stranger '46 ►
13 Rue Madeleine '46 ►
36 Hours '64 ►
Triple Cross '67 ►
Under the Rainbow '81
Underground Agent '42
Up Periscope '59
Watch on the Rhine '43 ►
Waterfront '44
Where Eagles Dare '68 ►

Wrestling

...All the Marbles '81
The American Angels: Baptism of Blood '89
Bad Guys '86
Below the Belt '80
Body Slam '87
The Calamari Wrestler '04
Doctor of Doom '62
The Foul King '00
Grunt! The Wrestling Movie '85
Hadley's Rebellion '84
Invasion of the Zombies '61
The Jesse Ventura Story '99
Mad Bull '77
Man on the Moon '99
Mugsy's Girls '85
Nacho Libre '06
The Naked Man '98
No Holds Barred '89
Oh! My Zombie Mermaid '04
The One and Only '78
Paradise Alley '78
Park Avenue Logger '37
Pin Down Girls '51
Ready to Rumble '00
Samson in the Wax Museum '63
Secret Society '00
Spider-Man '02 ►
Superargo '67
Take Down '79
Think Big '90
Thunder & Mud '89
Vision Quest '85
Women in Love '70 ►
The World According to Garp '82 ►
The Wrestler '73
The Wrestler '08 ►
Wrestling Women vs. the Aztec Mummy '59

Writers

see also This Is Your Life

Adaptation '02 ►
The Adventures of Mark Twain '44 ►
Agatha '79
Agatha Christie: A Life in Pictures '04
Alex & Emma '03
Alias Betty '01
All the Wrong Places '00
Ambition '91
American Dreamer '84
American Splendor '03 ►
Amuck! '71
Amy's O '02
An Angel at My Table '89 ►
Anne of Green Gables: The Continuing Story '99
Another Man's Poison '52
The Answer Man '09
Anything Else '03
The Ape '05
As Good As It Gets '97 ►
Ask the Dust '06
Atonement '07 ►
Author! Author! '82
Balzac: A Life of Passion '99 ►
Bamboozled '00
Barton Fink '91 ►
Basic Instinct 2 '06
The Basketball Diaries '95
Beat '00
Beau Brummell: This Charming Man '06
Beautiful Dreamers '92
Becoming Colette '92
Becoming Jane '07
Before Night Falls '00 ►
Before Sunset '04 ►
Behind the Lines '97
Beloved Infidel '59
The Best Man '99 ►
Best Seller '87 ►
Big Bad Love '02
The Big Slice '90
Bloodhounds '96
Bloodhounds 2 '96
The Blue Tooth Virgin '09
Bone Daddy '97
Boom! '68
Borstal Boy '00
Breakfast at Tiffany's '61 ►
Breakfast of Champions '98
Breakin' All The Rules '04
Bridal Fever '08
Bright Young Things '03
The Brontes of Haworth '73
Burial of the Rats '95
A Business Affair '93
Bye Bye Braverman '67
Cabin by the Lake '00
Capote '05 ►
Casanova '05 ►
Celebrity '98 ►
Celeste '81 ►
Chaos Theory '08
Chapter Two '79
Cheaper by the Dozen '03
Chelsea Walls '01
Closer '04 ►
Closer and Closer '96
Collected Stories '02 ►
Coming Through '85
Crashing '07
Cross Creek '83
Croupier '97 ►
Dante's Inferno: Life of Dante Gabriel Rossetti '69
The Dark Half '91
The Dark Side of the Heart '92
Dash and Lilly '99
Dead Cool '04
Dead Husbands '98
Dean Koontz's Mr. Murder '98
Deathtrap '82
Deconstructing Harry '97
Dedication '07
Delirious '91
Dinner and Driving '97
The Disappearance of Garcia Lorca '96
Divine Secrets of the Ya-Ya Sisterhood '02
Doctor Zhivago '65 ►
Doctor Zhivago '03
The Dog Problem '06
The Door in the Floor '04 ►
Double Whammy '01
Down With Love '03
Duplex '03
The End of the Affair '99 ►
Enemies of Laughter '00
Eternity and a Day '97
Eva '62
Evidence of Blood '97
Evil Eyes '04
Evil Lives '92
F. Scott Fitzgerald in Hollywood '76
Factotum '06 ►
Faithless '00 ►
Fall '97
Father's Day '96
Fear and Loathing in Las Vegas '98
Final Draft '07
Finding Forrester '00
A Fine Madness '66 ►
The Flower of My Secret '95 ►
Footsteps '03
For Hire '98
Forbidden Passion: The Oscar Wilde Movie '85
1408 '07
Freedom Writers '07
Fresh Cut Grass '04
From Noon Till Three '76
Full Speed '96
The Gambler '97
Game 6 '05
Gentlemen Broncos '09
The Ghost Writer '10
Ghosts Never Sleep '05
Ghostwriter '84
A Girl Cut in Two '07
Glam '97
Goldeneye: The Secret Life of Ian Fleming '89
Gothic '87 ►
Hamsun '96
Happy Hour '03
Harriet the Spy '96
Haunted Summer '88
Hav Plenty '97 ►
Heart Beat '80
Heartburn '86 ►
Heat Wave '54
Henry & June '90 ►
Her Alibi '88
Hit and Runway '01
The Hoax '06
The Hours '02 ►
House of the Long Shadows '82
How to Be '08
How to Kill Your Neighbor's Dog '01
How to Lose Your Lover '04
The Human Stain '03
Hustler White '96
I Capture the Castle '02
Impromptu '90 ►
In Praise of Love '01
In the Cut '03
In the Deep Woods '91
In the Mouth of Madness '95
In the Realms of the Unreal '04 ►
Infamous '06
Iris '01 ►
Isn't She Great '00
Jack London '44
James Joyce: A Portrait of the Artist as a Young Man '77 ►
James Joyce's Women '85 ►
Jane Doe '96
The Jew '96
Joe Gould's Secret '00
Joshua Then and Now '85 ►
Just Write '97
Kafka '91
The Keeper: The Legend of Omar Khayyam '05
Kissing a Fool '98
The Kovak Box '06
Lady in the Water '06
Lady on a Train '45 ►
The Last Days of Chez Nous '92
The Last Station '09
The Last Word '08
Late August, Early September '98
Letters from a Killer '98
Lies and Whispers '98
The Life of Emile Zola '37 ►
The Lonely Lady '83
Long Day's Journey Into Night '96 ►
Look at Me '04 ►
The Lost Boys '78 ►
Love and Death on Long Island '97
Love Comes Lately '07
A Love Song for Bobby Long '04
Lovely by Surprise '07
The Loves of Edgar Allen Poe '42
A Loving Father '02
Lucia, Lucia '03
The Majestic '01
Mambo Italiano '03
The Man from Elysian Fields '01 ►
Margot at the Wedding '07
Martian Child '07
The Mask of Dimitrios '44 ►
Maybe Baby '99
Melissa '97
Men Cry Bullets '00
A Merry War '97 ►
Meteor & Shadow '85
Misery '90 ►
Miss Monday '98
Mission '00
Mrs. Palfrey at the Claremont '05
Mrs. Parker and the Vicious Circle '94
Mr. Jealousy '98
Mr. Woodcock '07
Mixing Nia '98
Moliere '07
The Moon's Our Home '36
Mother '96
Motherhood '09
Moulin Rouge '01 ►
Murder by the Book '87
A Murder of Crows '99
The Muse '99
My Apprenticeship '39 ►
My Boy Jack '07
My Brilliant Career '79 ►
My Childhood '38 ►
My Effortless Brilliance '08
My House in Umbria '03 ►
My Left Foot '89 ►
My Sister Eileen '42
My Universities '40 ►
The Mystery of Rampo '94 ►
Mystery Woman: Mystery Weekend '05
The Mystic Masseur '01
Naked Lunch '91 ►
Nerolio '96
The Night and the Moment '94
Nim's Island '08
Novel Romance '06
101 Ways (The Things a Girl Will Do to Keep Her Volvo) '00
Our Lady of the Assassins '01
Out of Africa '85 ►
Out of Order '03
Pandaemonium '00
Paperback Hero '99
Paperback Romance '96
The Passion of Ayn Rand '99
A Perfect Day '06
Personal Velocity: Three Portraits '02 ►
Personals '00
Petrified Forest '36 ►
The Pillow Book '95
Pleasure '31
Portraits Chinois '96
Possession '02
Postmortem '98
The Prize '63 ►
The Proprietor '96
Pulp '72
Purple Violets '07
Quills '00
Re-Cycle '06
The Real Howard Spitz '98
The Reaper '97
Redeemer '02
Reds '81 ►
Reprise '06
Restaurant '98
The Riddle '07
Roman de Gare '07
Romancing the Stone '84 ►
Romantic Comedy '83
Route 30 '08
Rowing with the Wind '88
The Royal Tenenbaums '01 ►
Ruslan '09
Russian Dolls '05
Saint-Ex: The Story of the Storyteller '95
Salem's Lot '04
The Savages '07 ►
The Sculptress '97
Second Best '05
The Secret in Their Eyes '09
Secret Window '04
Sex and Lucia '01
Sex and the City: The Movie '08
Shadowlands '85 ►
Shadowlands '93 ►
The Shadows '07
Shakespeare in Love '98 ►
The Shining '80
The Singing Detective '03
Sink or Swim '97
Sitting Pretty '48 ►
Slam '98
The Sleepy Time Gal '01
Sleuth '07
Slipstream '07
The Snows of Kilimanjaro '52 ►
Something's Gotta Give '03 ►
Spymaker: The Secret Life of Ian Fleming '90
The Squid and the Whale '05 ►
Stand by Me '86 ►
Starting Out in the Evening '07
The Sticky Fingers of Time '97
Stone Reader '02 ►
Storytelling '01 ►
Stranger Than Fiction '06
Street Smart '87
Swann '96
Sweet and Lowdown '99
Swimming Pool '03 ►
Sylvia '03
Teach Me '97
The Tenants '06
Thanks for the Memory '38
Theodora Goes Wild '36 ►
Things 2 '97
The Third Man '49 ►
301, 302 '94
Time Regained '99
Tom & Viv '94 ►
The Town That Banned Christmas '06
The Trials of Oscar Wilde '60 ►
The Trip '02
The TV Set '06
2046 '04
Two Ninas '00
Two Shades of Blue '98
Under the Tuscan Sun '03
Undercover Angel '99
United States of Leland '03
Unsane '82
The Voice of Merrill '52
The Weather Man '05
White Badge '97
The Whole Wide World '96 ►
Wilde '97
Winter Passing '05
The Witnesses '07
The Women '68
Wonder Boys '00 ►
The Wonderful World of the Brothers Grimm '62
The World According to Garp '82 ►
World's Greatest Dad '09 ►
A Year Without Love '05
You and Me '06
You Stupid Man '02
Your Vice is a Closed Room and Only I Have the Key '72
Zeder '83
Zora Is My Name! '90
Zorba the Greek '64 ►

The Wrong Man

see also Frame-Ups; Mistaken Identity

Absolute Power '97
After Innocence '05 ►
And the Wild, Wild Women '59
Bad Seed '00
The Bedroom Window '87
The Big Hit '98
Big Steal '49 ►
Black Angel '46 ►
Bloodfist 7: Manhunt '95
Body Heat '81 ►
The Butterfly Effect 3: Revelation '09
Catherine Cookson's The Black Candle '92
Chain Reaction '96
Charlie Chan in London '34
Cherish '02
Codename: Jaguar '00
The Confessor '04
Consenting Adults '92
The Contractor '07
Cookie's Fortune '99 ►
Cop-Out '67
The Criminal '00
Criminal Justice '08
The Crow: Salvation '00
Dangerous Evidence: The Lori Jackson Story '99
Dead End '98
Deadline '00
Deadlocked '00
Delivered '98
Disorder '06
Double Jeopardy '99
Double Take '01
Exit Smiling '26
Extremely Dangerous '99
Fall Guy '47
Fallen '97
Frenzy '72 ►
The Fugitive '93 ►
Girls in Prison '94
High Lonesome '50
The House of the Seven Gables '40
I Confess '53
In Pursuit '00
In the Name of the Father '93 ►
The Jacket '05
Jack's Back '87 ►
Jennifer 8 '92
The Jury's Secret '38
Kansas City Confidential '52 ►
Kept '01
Kick of Death: The Prodigal Boxer '73
Kiss of the Dragon '01
The Last Musketeer '00
Life '99
Life & Times of Grizzly Adams '74
The Lone Rider in Frontier Fury '41
A Long Ride From Hell '68
The Long Ride Home '01
The Loss of a Teardrop Diamond '08
Madeo '09
The Man Who Knew Too Much '34 ►
The Man Who Knew Too Much '56 ►
Marked Man '96
Melissa '97
Men of America '32
The Midnight Lady '32
Ministry of Fear '44 ►
Minority Report '02 ►
Mission of Death '97
Most Wanted '97
Murder in Greenwich Village '37
Mysterious Mr. Nicholson '47
Mystery Street '50
The Negotiator '98
Night of January 16th '41
One Way '06
One Way Out '02
Partners in Crime '99
Perfect Target '98
Phantom Lady '44 ►
Plato's Run '96
Pressure '02
Presumed Innocent '90 ►
Pros & Cons '99
Rancid '04
Red Corner '97
The Ridin' Fool '31
Ridin' for Justice '32
Running Woman '98
Saddle Aces '35
Salt '10
Saving Shiloh '06
Secret Window '04
The Sentinel '06
Seven Doors to Death '44
The Shadow Whip '71
Shooter '07
Small Vices: A Spenser Mystery '99
Spoiler '98
Steamboat Round the Bend '35
Storm Catcher '99
A Stranger in the Kingdom '98
The Sun Sets at Dawn '50
Swamp Devil '08
Tell No One '06 ►
Terror Street '54
They Made Me a Criminal '39
The 39 Steps '35 ►
Three Days of the Condor '75 ►
Ticket of Leave Man '37
Time Served '99
Under Suspicion '92
U.S. Marshals '98
The Verdict '46
We'll Meet Again '02
When Danger Follows You Home '97
Where the Sidewalk Ends '50
Whirlpool '49
Whitewash: The Clarence Brandley Story '02
The Whole Town's Talking '35 ►
Why Must I Die? '60
The Winslow Boy '98 ►
Winterset '36
The Wrong Guy '96
The Wrong Man '56 ►
The Wrong Man '93
Wrongfully Accused '98

Wrong Side of the Tracks

see also Rags to Riches

Aaron Loves Angela '75
Algiers '38 ►
Alice Adams '35
All Good Things '09
Amarilly of Clothesline Alley '18
Angel and the Badman '47 ►
Angels with Dirty Faces '38 ►
Anna Christie '30
Bachelor Party '84
Back Door to Heaven '39 ►
Breaking Away '79 ►
The Bride of Frank '96
The Bride Wore Red '37
Camille '36 ►
Cannery Row '82
Captains Courageous '37 ►
Captives '94
Carbon Copy '81
Careful, He Might Hear You '84 ►
Carrie '52 ►
Cat Ballou '65 ►
Chains '89
Cherry Crush '07
China Girl '87
Claudia '85
Cool and the Crazy '94
Cool As Ice '91
The Courtney Affair '47
Courtship '87 ►
crazy/beautiful '01
The Crucified Lovers '54 ►
Cry-Baby '90 ►
The Dark Side of Love '79
Diary of a Chambermaid '46 ►
Dirty Dancing '87 ►

► = rated three bones or higher

Dragstrip Girl '94
Eegah! '62
Far and Away '92
Federal Hill '94
The Fence '94
Fire with Fire '86
The Flamingo Kid '84 ▶
Foxfire Light '82
Fresh Horses '88
Future Kill '85
Grease '78 ▶
Great Expectations '97
The Great Gatsby '49
The Great Gatsby '74
The Hairy Ape '44
Hearts of Humanity '32
Here on Earth '00
Hush '98
Iron Maze '91
It '27
It Could Happen to You '37
It Happened One Night '34 ▶
Jailbait! '00
Jersey Girl '92
Jungle Fever '91 ▶
King Ralph '91
The Lacemaker '77 ▶
Last Exit to Brooklyn '90 ▶
Liar's Moon '82
Little Minister '34 ▶
The Loves of Carmen '48
Luzia '88
Mad About Mambo '00
The Man from Snowy River '82
Manhattan Melodrama '34 ▶
Masquerade '88 ▶
A Million to One '37
Min & Bill '30
My Forbidden Past '51
My Man Godfrey '36 ▶
Naked Youth '59
Night Beat '48
Off Beat '86
Outpost in Morocco '49
Over the Brooklyn Bridge '83
The Phantom in the House '29
The Phantom of the Opera '25 ▶
Picnic on the Grass '59
A Place in the Sun '51 ▶
The Pope of Greenwich Village '84
Port of New York '49
Pretty in Pink '86
Primrose Path '40
Princess Tam Tam '35 ▶
Probation '32
Pygmalion '38 ▶
The Rage: Carrie 2 '99
Reckless '84
Reform School Girl '57
Return to Snowy River '88 ▶
Rich Girl '91
Riff Raff '92 ▶
Rocky '76 ▶
Room at the Top '59 ▶
Rosewood '96 ▶
Ruby Gentry '52
Rumble Fish '83 ▶
San Francisco '36 ▶
The Second Chance '06
The Servant '63 ▶
Set It Off '96
sex, lies and videotape '89 ▶
She's All That '99
Show People '28 ▶
Small Faces '95 ▶
Snow Country '57
Some Kind of Wonderful '87
Somebody Up There Likes Me '56 ▶
Starter for Ten '06
Stay Hungry '76 ▶
Step Up '06
Step Up 2 the Streets '08
Stomp the Yard '07
The Story of the Late Chrysanthemum '39 ▶
Suburbia '83
The Swan '25
The Swan '56 ▶
Sweet Light in a Dark Room '60 ▶
The Tamarind Seed '74
Tango '36
That Night '93
This Sporting Life '63 ▶
Those People Next Door '52
Tortilla Flat '42 ▶
A Tree Grows in Brooklyn '45 ▶
Under the Boardwalk '89
Uptown Angel '90
Valley Girl '83
The Valley of Decision '45 ▶
Virtue's Revolt '24
Vivacious Lady '38 ▶
Waterloo Bridge '40 ▶
White Palace '90
The White Sin '24
The World of Suzie Wong '60
The Young Philadelphians '59 ▶

Yakuza

***see also** Crime & Criminals; Japan; Organized Crime*

Adrenaline Drive '99
American Yakuza '94
Another Lonely Hitman '95
Beautiful Beast '95
Black Rain '89
Blind Woman's Curse '70
The Bodyguard '76
Boiling Point '90
Brother '00 ▶
Delinquent Girl Boss: Blossoming Night Dreams '70
Dolls '02 ▶
Double Edge '97
Fudoh: The New Generation '96
Girls of the White Orchid '85
Gonin 2 '96
Gozu '03
Graveyard of Honor '02
Hard As Nails '01
Ichi the Killer '01
Johnny Mnemonic '95
Kill Bill Vol. 1 '03 ▶
Minbo—Or the Gentle Art of Japanese Extortion '92
No Way Back '96
Organized Crime & Triad Bureau '93
Overkill '86
Sex and Fury '73
Showdown in Little Tokyo '91
Sonatine '96 ▶
The Street Fighter's Last Revenge '74
Sympathy for the Underdog '71
Tokyo Drifter '66
War '07
Wasabi '01
Wicked City '92
The Wolves '82 ▶
The Yakuza '75
Youth of the Beast '63
Zatoichi: The Life and Opinion of Masseur Ichi '62
Zatoichi: Zatoichi's Flashing Sword '64

Yoga

The Crippled Masters '82
Hollywood Homicide '03
The Next Best Thing '00
What Women Want '00

You are Getting Sleepy!

The Angry Red Planet '59
Blood of Dracula '57
Brainscan '94
Carefree '38 ▶
The Curse of the Jade Scorpion '01
Dead Again '91 ▶
Devil Doll '36 ▶
Devour '05
The Exorcist 2: The Heretic '77
The Fourth Kind '09
The Great Buck Howard '09
Haunting Fear '91
A Killing in a Small Town '90 ▶
The Mask of Diijon '46
The Misadventures of Merlin Jones '63
On a Clear Day You Can See Forever '70
Scared to Death '46
Shallow Hal '01
She Creature '01
Somewhere in Time '80
Stir of Echoes '99
Telefon '77
Threat of Exposure '02
The Three Faces of Eve '57
Thumbsucker '05 ▶
A Wind from Wyoming '94

You Big Dummy!

***see also** Killer Toys*

Charlie McCarthy, Detective '39
Dead Silence '07
Devil Doll '64
Dummy '02
The Dummy Talks '43
The Great Gabbo '29
Magic '78
1941 '79
The Ten '07
The Unholy Three '25 ▶

You Lose, You Die

***see also** Post-Apocalypse*

Alien vs. Predator '04
Arcade '93
Are You Scared? '06
The Arena '73
Arena '89
Blade Boxer '97
Bloodsport 4: The Dark Kumite '98
The Condemned '07
Cruel World '05
Death Race '08
Death Race 2000 '75
Deathrow Gameshow '88
DOA: Dead or Alive '06
Dominion '94
80 Minutes '08
Fatal Combat '96
Futuresport '98
The Game '97 ▶
Gamebox 1.0 '04
Gamer '09
Hostel: Part 2 '07
Last Resort '09
Mad Max: Beyond Thunderdome '85
Mean Guns '97
Mortal Challenge '97
Nemesis Game '03
Prayer of the Rollerboys '91
Robot Jox '90
Roller Blade '85
Roller Blade Warriors: Taken By Force '90
Rollerball '75
Rollerball '02
The Running Man '87
Sci-Fighter '04
Smokin' Aces 2: Assassins' Ball '10
Solarbabies '86
Star Hunter '95
Stay Alive '06
10th Victim '65 ▶
Thr3e '07
The Tournament '09
Tron '82
Vacancy '07
Webmaster '98
Wrong Turn 2: Dead End '07

Yuppie Nightmares

***see also** Strained Suburbia*

Addams Family Values '93
Alice '90 ▶
Almost You '85
Amos and Andrew '93
Baby Boom '87
Bad Influence '90
Barbarians at the Gate '93 ▶
Bare Essentials '91
Bedroom Eyes '86
Beetlejuice '88 ▶
The Big Chill '83 ▶
Blind Date '87
Blind Side '93
Boiler Room '00 ▶
The Bonfire of the Vanities '90
The Boost '88
Bright Lights, Big City '88
Cape Fear '91 ▶
City of Hope '91 ▶
Clara's Heart '88
Clean and Sober '88 ▶
Cold Creek Manor '03
Cold Fever '95
Coma '78 ▶
Consenting Adults '92
Curly Sue '91
Dead Calm '89 ▶
Denise Calls Up '95
Desperately Seeking Susan '85
Diary of a Mad Housewife '70 ▶
Down and Out in Beverly Hills '86
Drop Dead Fred '91
Edge of Honor '91
The End of Innocence '90
Eye of the Demon '87
Fatal Attraction '87 ▶
The First Wives Club '96
The Fisher King '91 ▶
Folks! '92
Fun with Dick and Jane '77
The Further Adventures of Tennessee Buck '88
The Game '97 ▶
Goodbye, New York '85
The Guardian '90
The Hand that Rocks the Cradle '92
Happiness '98 ▶
The Hard Way '91 ▶
He Said, She Said '91
Heartburn '86 ▶
Hiding Out '87
In the Company of Men '96
In the Spirit '90
Indian Summer '93
Jungle Fever '91 ▶
Key Exchange '85
Kicks '85
L.A. Story '91 ▶
Let's Kill All the Lawyers '93
Limit Up '89
Looking for Mr. Goodbar '77
Lost in America '85 ▶
Madhouse '90
Maid to Order '87
The Malibu Beach Vampires '91
Maniac '77
Micki & Maude '84
Mifune '99
The Mighty Ducks '92
The Money Pit '86
Mother's Boys '94
Moving '88
My Daughter's Keeper '93
My New Gun '92
Neighbors '81
New Year's Day '89 ▶
Next Door '94
Night of the Living Babes '87
Nothing But Trouble '91
Nothing in Common '86
Oasis of the Zombies '82
The Object of Beauty '91 ▶
Pacific Heights '90 ▶
Perfect Family '92
Permanent Vacation '84
Preppies '82
Private Benjamin '80
Quicksilver '86
The Quiet '05
Reversal of Fortune '90 ▶
Roadhouse 66 '84
Rude Awakening '89
Ruthless People '86 ▶
The Safety of Objects '01
St. Elmo's Fire '85
The Secret of My Success '87
The Secretary '94
September '88
sex, lies and videotape '89 ▶
Shattered '91
A Shock to the System '90 ▶
Six Degrees of Separation '93
A Smile Like Yours '96
Something Wild '86
Stay Tuned '92
Straw Dogs '72 ▶
Summer Rental '85
Taking Care of Business '90
Taking the Heat '93
The Temp '93
Three Men and a Little Lady '90
Through the Eyes of a Killer '92
The Tie That Binds '95
The Toxic Avenger, Part 3: The Last Temptation of Toxie '89
Trading Places '83
Trapped '89
The Trigger Effect '96
Truth or Consequences, N.M. '97
Under Pressure '98
Unlawful Entry '92
The Vagrant '92
Voodoo Dawn '89
Wall Street '87 ▶
The War of the Roses '89 ▶
Westworld '73 ▶
What about Bob? '91 ▶
When a Man Loves a Woman '94
Windy City '84
Wolf '94
Your Friends & Neighbors '98 ▶

Zombie Soldiers

***see also** Zombies*

Akira Kurosawa's Dreams '90
Army of Darkness '92 ▶
The Dark Power '85
Dead Snow '09
Deathdream '72
Hard Rock Zombies '85
House '86 ▶
Jonah Hex '10
Oasis of the Zombies '82
Revenge of the Zombies '43
Revolt of the Zombies '36
Scream and Scream Again '70
She Demons '58
Shock Waves '77
The Supernaturals '86
They Saved Hitler's Brain '64
The Zombie Army '93
Zombie Lake '80

Zombies

***see also** Death & the Afterlife; Ghosts, Ghouls, & Goblins; Zombie Soldiers*

The Alchemist '81
Alice '09
Alien Dead '79
Alien Massacre '67
All Souls Day '05
Almost Dead '94
The Astro-Zombies '67
Automaton Transfusion '06
Battlefield Baseball '03
Beast Within '08
The Beyond '82
Beyond Re-Animator '03
Biozombie '98
Bowery at Midnight '42
Bride of Re-Animator '89
Cabin Fever '03
Carnival of Souls '62 ▶
Cast a Deadly Spell '91 ▶
Cemetery Man '95
Children of the Living Dead '00
Children Shouldn't Play with Dead Things '72
The Chilling '89
Chopper Chicks in Zombietown '91
C.H.U.D. 2: Bud the Chud '89
City of the Walking Dead '80
Creature of the Walking Dead '60
Creatures from the Pink Lagoon '07
The Curse of the Aztec Mummy '59
Dance of the Dead '08
Dawn of the Dead '78 ▶
Dawn of the Dead '04 ▶
Dawn of the Mummy '82
Day of the Dead '85
Dead Alive '93
Dead Creatures '01
The Dead Don't Die '75
The Dead Hate the Living '99
Dead Heat '88
Dead Heist '07
Dead in the Water '06
Dead Men Don't Die '91
The Dead Next Door '89
The Dead One '07
Dead Pit '89
Dead Snow '09
Death Becomes Her '92 ▶
The Death Curse of Tartu '66
Death Valley: The Revenge of Bloody Bill '04
Deathdream '72
Demon Wind '90
Destroyer '88
Devil's Kiss '75
Diary of the Dead '07
Ed and His Dead Mother '93
Evil Town '87
Fido '06
Flight of the Living Dead: Outbreak on a Plane '07
George A. Romero's Land of the Dead '05 ▶
The Ghost Brigade '93
The Ghoul '75
The Granny '94
The Hanging Woman '72
Haunting Fear '91
Hellgate '89
Horror of the Zombies '74
Horror Rises from the Tomb '72
The House of Seven Corpses '73
House of the Dead '78
House of the Dead '03
House of the Dead 2: Dead Aim '05
I Am Legend '07 ▶
I Eat Your Skin '64
I Walked with a Zombie '43 ▶
I Was a Teenage Zombie '87
Infested: Invasion of the Killer Bugs '02
Invisible Invaders '59
Isle of the Dead '45
The Jitters '88
John Carpenter's Ghosts of Mars '01
King of the Zombies '41
Kiss Daddy Goodbye '81
The Legend of the 7 Golden Vampires '73
Let Sleeping Corpses Lie '74
The Mad Ghoul '43
Messiah of Evil '74
Mortuary '05
Mulberry Street '06
The Mummy '32 ▶
The Mummy '59 ▶
The Mummy '99
Mummy & Curse of the Jackal '67
The Mummy's Revenge '73
Mutant Chronicles '08
Mutants '08
My Boyfriend's Back '93
Neon Maniacs '86
Night Life '90
Night of Horror '78
Night of the Comet '84
Night of the Creeps '86
Night of the Death Cult '75
Night of the Ghouls '59
Night of the Living Babes '87
Night of the Living Dead '68 ▶
Night of the Living Dead '90
Night of the Living Dead, 25th Anniversary Documentary '93
Nightmare Weekend '86
Oasis of the Zombies '82
Oh! My Zombie Mermaid '04
Orgy of the Dead '65
Otto: Or, Up with Dead People '08
The Outing '87
Pet Sematary 2 '92
Phantasm 3: Lord of the Dead '94
Plague of the Zombies '66

▶ = rated three bones or higher

► = *rated three bones or higher*

Kibbles and Series List

The **Kibbles** and **Series** indexes have been combined into one index. This is where you'll find info on where your favorite movies came from—literary, theatrical, cartoon, and television adaptations to name a few, as well as the behind the scenes talents that make movies possible, such as producers and special effects wizards. Another important feature of this index is the quality check it provides with categories like **Woofs!**, **4 Bones**, and **Top Grossing Films** by year. This index also provides information on recurring characters like James Bond, Jack Ryan, or Mike Hammer, as well as notable screen partnerships. Some examples include Abbott & Costello, Hope & Crosby, and De Niro & Scorsese. **A tipped triangle denotes a three-bone or higher rating** The categories are as follows, with an asterisk (*) denoting a new category:

* = new to this edition

Allen & Johansson
Almodovar & Banderas
Altman & Gould
Altman & Murphy
Anderson & Murray
Bergman & Ullmann
Bergman & von Sydow
Boetticher & Scott
Bunuel & F. Rey
Burton & Depp
Capra & Stewart
Carpenter & Russell
Chabrol & Audran
Chabrol & Huppert
Coraci & Sandler
Cukor & Hepburn
Donner & Gibson
Dugan & Sandler
*Fincher & Pitt
Ford & Wayne
Frankeneheimer & Lancaster
Hawks & Wayne
Herzog & Kinski
Hill & Newman
Hitchcock & Stewart
Holofcener & Keener
Howard & Hanks
Howard & Keaton
Huston & Bogart
Jordan & Rea
King & Peck
Kurosawa & Mifune
LaBute & Eckart
Lee & Washington
Linklater & Hawke
Lynch & Nance
Mann & Stewart
McKay & Ferrell
Needham & Reynolds
Newman & Woodward
Poitier & Cosby
Pollack & Redford
Rafelson & Nicholson
Raimi & Campbell
Raimi & 1973 Oldsmobile Delta 88
Reiner & Martin
Ritt & Newman
Rodriguez & Banderas
Sayles & Clapp
Sayles & Cooper
Sayles & Strathairn
Scorsese & De Niro
Scorsese & Keitel
Scott (Ridley) & Crowe
Scott (Tony) & Washington
Shadyac & Carrey
Sheridan & Day-Lewis
Siegel & Eastwood
Sirk & Hudson
Soderburgh & Clooney
Soderburgh & Roberts
Spielberg & Dreyfuss
Spielberg & Hanks
*Sturges & McCrea
Techine & Deneuve
Truffault & Leaud
Verhoeven & R. Hauer
von Sternberg & Dietrich
Walsh & Bogart
Woo & Fat
Zemeckis & Hanks

Dirty Harry

Disney Animated Movies

Disney Family Movies

Doc Holliday

Dr. Christian

Dr. Mabuse

Dr. Seuss

Dracula

Dreamworks Animated Movies

Elvisfilm

The Falcon

4 Bones

Francis the Talking Mule

Frankenstein

Fu Manchu

Godzilla and Friends

Hallmark Hall of Fame

Hammer Films: Horror

Hammer Films: Sci Fi & Fantasy

Hercule Poirot

Hercules

Highest Grossing Films of All Time

Hopalong Cassidy

Indiana Jones

Inspector Clouseau

Jack Ryan

Jack the Ripper

James Bond

James Bond Spoofs

Jason Bourne

Jesse James

John McClane

Lassie

Live Action/Animation Combos

The Lone Rider

Ma & Pa Kettle

The Marx Brothers

MGM Musicals

Mike Hammer

Miss Marple

Mister Moto

Mr. Wong

Modern Shakespeare

Modern Updates

Monty Python

The Muppets

National Lampoon

Our Gang

Philip Marlowe

Pixar Animated Movies

The Planet of the Apes

Plays to Film:

Maxwell Anderson
James M. Barrie
Anton Chekov
Noel Coward
Horton Foote
Beth Henley
David Mamet
Arthur Miller
Eugene O'Neill
Rodgers & Hammerstein
Arthur Schnitzler
William Shakespeare
George Bernard Shaw
Sam Shepard
Robert E. Sherwood
Neil Simon
Tom Stoppard
Tennessee Williams

Producers:

Robert Altman
Judd Apatow
Bruckheimer/Simpson
William Castle
Coppola/American Zoetrope
Roger Corman/New World
Val Lewton
George Lucas
Merchant Ivory
George Pal
Steven Spielberg
Andy Warhol

Rambo

The Rangebusters

Recycled Footage/Redubbed Dialogue

Renfrew of the Mounties

Restored Footage

***Rin Tin Tin**

The Ritz Brothers

Robin Hood

The Rough Riders

Rusty the Dog

The Saint

Sinbad

Screen Teams:

Abbott & Costello
Allen & Farrow
Allen & Keaton
Astaire & Rogers
Ball & Arnaz
Belushi & Aykroyd
Bogart & Bacall
Bronson & Ireland
Burton & Taylor
Cagney & O'Brien
Cheech & Chong
Cusack & Piven
Cusack & Robbins
Damon & B. Affleck
De Niro & Keitel
De Niro & Pesci
Depardieu & Deneuve
Douglas & Lancaster
Eastwood & Locke
Eddy & McDonald
Farley & Spade
Favreau & Vaughn
Flynn & de Havilland
Gable & Crawford
*Gable & Loy
*Gable & Turner
Garland & Rooney
Garson & Pidgeon
*Gaynor & Farrell
Gibson & Glover
Hawn & Russell
Hepburn & Grant
Hepburn & Tracy
Hope & Crosby
Ladd & Lake
Laurel & Hardy
Lee & Cushing
Lemmon & Matthau
Loy & Powell
Martin & Lewis
Newman & Woodward
*Powell & Keeler
Power & Tierney
Power & L. Young
Redford & Newman
Reynolds & DeLuise
Reynolds & Field
Rogers & Evans
Snipes & Harrelson
Stewart & Sullavan
Stiller & O. Wilson
Turner & Douglas
Wayne & O'Hara
Wilder & Pryor

Scrooge

Sexton Blake

Sherlock Holmes

Special FX Extravaganzas

Special FX Extravaganzas: Make-Up

Special FX Wizards:

Rick Baker
Rob Bottin
Anton Furst
Ray Harryhausen
Herschell Gordon Lewis
Tom Savini
Dick Smith
Douglas Trumball

Star Wars

Tarzan

The Texas Rangers

The Thin Man

The Three Mesquiteers

The Three Musketeers

Three Stooges

Tom Ripley

Top Grossing Films: 1939-2009

The Trail Blazers

Trash

Troma Films

Universal Studios' Classic Horror

Wild Bill Hickok

The Wolfman

Wyatt Earp

Zorro

Zucker/Abrahams/Zucker

** = new to this edition*

Kibbles and Series Index

Recurrent characters, cinematic collaborations, various adaptations, and important behind-the-scenes personnel information is the focus of the **Kibbles and Series Index**. These categories are listed alphabetically. **A tipped triangle indicates a video rated three bones or higher**.

Adapted from a Cartoon

The Addams Family *'91*
Addams Family Values *'93*
The Adventures of Captain Marvel *'41*
Adventures of Red Ryder *'40*
Adventures of Smilin' Jack *'43*
Aeon Flux *'05*
Alvin and the Chipmunks *'07*
The Amazing Spider-Man *'77*
Barbarella *'68*
The Belles of St. Trinian's *'53* ▸
Big Zapper *'73*
Blondie *'38*
Blondie Brings Up Baby *'39*
Blondie for Victory *'42*
Blondie Goes Latin *'42*
Blondie Goes to College *'42*
Blondie Has Trouble *'40*
Blondie Hits the Jackpot *'49*
Blondie in Society *'41*
Blondie Knows Best *'46*
Blondie Meets the Boss *'39*
Blondie On a Budget *'40*
Blondie Plays Cupid *'40*
Blondie Takes a Vacation *'39*
Blondie's Blessed Event *'42*
Bratz *'07*
Casper *'95* ▸
Cool World *'92*
Crimewave *'85*
Death Note *'06* ▸
Death Note 2: The Last Name *'07*
Death Note 3: L, Change the World *'08*
Dennis the Menace *'93*
Dennis the Menace: Dinosaur Hunter *'93*
Dennis the Menace Strikes Again *'98*
Dick Tracy *'37*
Dick Tracy vs. Cueball *'46*
Dick Tracy's Dilemma *'47*
Disney's Teacher's Pet *'04* ▸
Dr. Strange *'78*
Doogal *'05*
Dudley Do-Right *'99*
Edward Scissorhands *'90* ▸
Elvira, Mistress of the Dark *'88*
Fat Albert *'04*
Fatty Finn *'84*
The Fighting Redhead *'50*
The Flash *'90*
Flash Gordon *'80*
Flesh Gordon 2: Flesh Gordon Meets the Cosmic Cheerleaders *'90*
The Flintstones *'94*
The Flintstones in Viva Rock Vegas *'00*
Footlight Glamour *'43*
Friday Foster *'75*
Frostbiter: Wrath of the Wendigo *'94*
George of the Jungle *'97* ▸
The Great St. Trinian's Train Robbery *'66*
The Guyver *'91*
Guyver 2: Dark Hero *'94*
Heavy Metal *'81* ▸
Hillbilly Blitzkrieg *'42*
Inspector Gadget *'99*
It's a Great Life *'43*
Jane & the Lost City *'87*
Josie and the Pussycats *'01*
Li'l Abner *'40*
Little Nemo: Adventures in Slumberland *'92*
Little Orphan Annie *'32*
The Mask *'94* ▸
Masters of the Universe *'87*
Maybe... Maybe Not *'94*
Mighty Morphin Power Rangers: The Movie *'95*
Mr. Magoo *'97*
Office Space *'98*
The Perils of Gwendoline *'84*
Petit Con *'84*
Phantom 2040 Movie: The Ghost Who Walks *'95*
The Pink Panther *'64* ▸
The Pink Panther Strikes Again *'76* ▸
Prince Valiant *'54*
The Pure Hell of St. Trinian's *'61*
Queer Duck: The Movie *'06*
Reg'lar Fellers *'41*
The Return of Swamp Thing *'89*
Richie Rich *'94*
The Sad Sack *'57*
Scooby-Doo *'02*
Scooby-Doo 2: Monsters Unleashed *'04*
The SpongeBob SquarePants Movie *'04*
Supergirl *'84*
Superman 2 *'80* ▸
Tank Girl *'94*
Teenage Mutant Ninja Turtles: The Movie *'90*
Teenage Mutant Ninja Turtles 2: The Secret of the Ooze *'91*
Teenage Mutant Ninja Turtles 3 *'93*
Tetsujin 28 *'04*
Timecop *'94*
Tom and Jerry: The Movie *'93*
Transformers *'07*
Turbo: A Power Rangers Movie *'96*
The Villain *'79*
Wild Palms *'93*
The Wild World of Batwoman *'66*
Yu-Gi-Oh! The Movie: Pyramid of Light *'04*

Adapted from a Disney Amusement Park Ride

The Country Bears *'02*
The Haunted Mansion *'03*
Pirates of the Caribbean: Dead Man's Chest *'06*
Pirates of the Caribbean: The Curse of the Black Pearl *'03* ▸

Adapted from a Fairy Tale

The Adventures of Pinocchio *'96*
Aladdin *'86*
Aladdin *'92* ▸
Aladdin and His Wonderful Lamp *'84*
Alice in Wonderland *'50*
Beanstalk *'94*
Beauty and the Beast *'46* ▸
Beauty and the Beast *'83* ▸
Beauty and the Beast *'91* ▸
The Blue Light *'32* ▸
The Boy Who Left Home to Find Out About the Shivers *'81*
The Brothers Grimm *'05*
Butterfly Ball *'76*
Chicken Little *'05*
Cinderella *'50* ▸
Cinderella *'64*
Cinderella *'84* ▸
Cinderella *'97*
A Cinderella Story *'04*
Cinderella 2000 *'78*
Cinderfella *'60*
The Company of Wolves *'85* ▸
The Dancing Princesses *'84* ▸
Deadtime Stories *'86*
Donkey Skin *'70* ▸
Ella Enchanted *'04* ▸
The Emperor's New Clothes *'84* ▸
Enchanted *'07*
Ever After: A Cinderella Story *'98* ▸
Fairy Tales *'76*
Freeway *'95*
Fun & Fancy Free *'47* ▸
George Balanchine's The Nutcracker *'93*
The Glass Slipper *'55*
Goldilocks & the Three Bears *'83*
Green Snake *'93*
Hans Christian Andersen *'52*
Hansel and Gretel *'82*
Happily Ever After *'93*
Happily N'Ever After *'07*
Hoodwinked *'05* ▸
A Hungarian Fairy Tale *'87* ▸
Irish Cinderella *'22*
Jack & the Beanstalk *'52*
Jack & the Beanstalk *'83* ▸
Jack and the Beanstalk: The Real Story *'01*
La Petite Sirene *'80*
Lady in the Water *'06*
Les Visiteurs du Soir *'42* ▸
The Little Match Girl *'84*
The Little Match Girl *'87*
The Little Mermaid *'75*
The Little Mermaid *'89* ▸
Little Red Riding Hood *'83* ▸
The Magic Fountain *'61*
The Magic Sword *'62*
March of the Wooden Soldiers *'34* ▸
Mother Goose Rock 'n' Rhyme *'90*
The Muppets' Wizard of Oz *'05*
The NeverEnding Story *'84* ▸
The NeverEnding Story 3: Escape from Fantasia *'94*
The Nightingale *'83* ▸
The Nutcracker Prince *'91*
Nutcracker: The Motion Picture *'86*
Once Upon a Brothers Grimm *'77*
Peau D'Ane *'71* ▸
Peter Pan *'53* ▸
Peter Pan *'60* ▸
The Pied Piper of Hamelin *'57*
The Pied Piper of Hamelin *'84*
Pin... *'88*
Pinocchio *'83* ▸
Pinocchio's Revenge *'96*
The Princess and the Pea *'83* ▸
The Princess Bride *'87* ▸
The Princess Who Never Laughed *'84* ▸
Puss 'n Boots *'84* ▸
Rapunzel *'82*
Red Riding Hood *'88*
The Red Shoes *'05*
Rip van Winkle *'85*
Rumpelstiltskin *'82* ▸
Rumpelstiltskin *'86*
The Scalawag Bunch *'75*
Shrek 2 *'04* ▸
The Singing Princess *'49*
Sleeping Beauty *'59* ▸
Sleeping Beauty *'83* ▸
Sleeping Beauty *'89*
The Slipper and the Rose *'76*
The Snow Queen *'83*
The Snow Queen *'02*
Snow White *'89*
Snow White: A Tale of Terror *'97*
Snow White and the Seven Dwarfs *'83* ▸
Snow White and the Three Stooges *'61*
Snow White: The Fairest of Them All *'02*
The Swan *'56* ▸
The Swan Princess *'94*
Sydney White *'07*
The Tale of the Frog Prince *'83* ▸
The Three Little Pigs *'84*
Thumbelina *'82* ▸
Thumbelina *'94*
The Tin Soldier *'95*
Tom Thumb *'58* ▸
Who Slew Auntie Roo? *'71*
The Witches *'90* ▸
The Wonderful World of the Brothers Grimm *'62*
The Wonders of Aladdin *'61*

Adapted from a Game

Alien vs. Predator *'04*
Aliens vs. Predator: Requiem *'07*
Alone in the Dark *'05*
BloodRayne *'06*
BloodRayne 2: Deliverance *'07*

▸ = *rated three bones or higher*

Clue '85
DOA: Dead or Alive '06
Doom '05
Double Dragon '94
Dungeons and Dragons '00
Final Encounter '00
Final Fantasy: The Spirits Within '01
Hitman '07
House of the Dead '03
In the Name of the King: A Dungeon Siege Tale '08
The King of Kong: A Fistful of Quarters '07 ▸
Lara Croft: Tomb Raider '01
Lara Croft Tomb Raider: The Cradle of Life '03
Max Payne '08
Mortal Kombat 1: The Movie '95
Mortal Kombat 2: Annihilation '97
Postal '07
Prince of Persia: The Sands of Time '10
Resident Evil '02
Resident Evil: Apocalypse '04
Resident Evil: Extinction '07
Silent Hill '06
Street Fighter '94
Street Fighter: The Legend of Chun-Li '09
Super Mario Bros. '93
Tag: The Assassination Game '82
Wing Commander '99
Yu-Gi-Oh! The Movie: Pyramid of Light '04

Adapted from a Musical

Annie '82
Annie '99 ▸
Babes in Arms '39
Babes in Toyland '61
Beatlemania! The Movie '81
Bells Are Ringing '60 ▸
Best Foot Forward '43
The Best Little Whorehouse in Texas '82
Brigadoon '54 ▸
Bye, Bye, Birdie '63 ▸
Bye Bye Birdie '95
Cabaret '72 ▸
Can-Can '60
Charm of La Boheme '36
Chicago '02 ▸
A Chorus Line '85
Cool Mikado '63
Damn Yankees '58 ▸
Dark Streets '08
The Desert Song '53
Dreamgirls '06 ▸
Evita '96
The Fantasticks '95
Fiddler on the Roof '71 ▸
Finian's Rainbow '68 ▸
Flower Drum Song '61
Flying High '31
Follies in Concert '85
Footlight Serenade '42
A Funny Thing Happened on the Way to the Forum '66 ▸
The Gay Divorcee '34 ▸
Gentlemen Prefer Blondes '53 ▸
Godspell '73
Grease '78 ▸
Grease 2 '82
The Guardsman '31 ▸
Gypsy '62 ▸
Gypsy '93
Hair '79 ▸
Hairspray '07 ▸
Hello, Dolly! '69
Irma La Douce '63
The King and I '56 ▸
Kiss Me Kate '53 ▸
Lady Be Good '41
A Little Night Music '77
Mame '74
Maytime '37 ▸
The Merry Widow '34 ▸
The Merry Widow '52
The Music Man '62 ▸
My Fair Lady '64 ▸
Nine '09
Oh! Calcutta! '72
On a Clear Day You Can See Forever '70
Opera do Malandro '87
Paint Your Wagon '69
The Pajama Game '57 ▸
The Phantom of the Opera '04
The Producers '05
Sally '29
1776 '72 ▸
Show Boat '36 ▸
Show Boat '51
Sweeney Todd: The Demon Barber of Fleet Street '84
Sweeney Todd: The Demon Barber of Fleet Street '07
Sweet Charity '69 ▸
The Threepenny Opera '31
West Side Story '61 ▸
The Wiz '78

Adapted from a Play

Abe Lincoln in Illinois '40 ▸
The Actress '53
The Admirable Crichton '57
Aelita: Queen of Mars '24
Age Old Friends '89 ▸
Agnes of God '85
Ah, Wilderness! '35 ▸
Alfie '66 ▸
Alice '86
All My Sons '48 ▸
All My Sons '86 ▸
All Over the Guy '01
Amadeus '84 ▸
Amen '02 ▸
American Buffalo '95
Anastasia '56 ▸
Animal Crackers '30 ▸
The Animal Kingdom '32 ▸
Anna Christie '23 ▸
Anna Christie '30
Annie Get Your Gun '50 ▸
The Anniversary '68
Another Country '84
Another Man's Poison '52
Any Wednesday '66
The Architect '06
Arsenic and Old Lace '44 ▸
As Is '85
As You Desire Me '32 ▸
The Avenger '62
The Awful Truth '37 ▸
Babes in Toyland '86
The Baby Dance '98 ▸
Baby Doll '56 ▸
Baby, the Rain Must Fall '64
The Bacchantes '63
Bad Manners '98
The Balcony '63 ▸
The Ballad of the Sad Cafe '91
Bar Girls '95
The Barbarian '33
Barefoot in the Park '67 ▸
Beau Brummel '24
Beau Brummel '54 ▸
Beautiful Thing '95 ▸
Becket '64 ▸
Becky Sharp '35
Being at Home with Claude '92
The Bells '26 ▸
Bent '97
The Best Man '64 ▸
Betrayal '83
Beyond Therapy '86
Big Boy '30
The Big Kahuna '00
The Big Knife '55 ▸
Big News '29
Billie '65
Biloxi Blues '88
The Birth of a Nation '15 ▸
Bitter Sweet '40
Black Limelight '38
Black Lizard '68
Black Orpheus '58 ▸
Blessed Event '32 ▸
Blithe Spirit '45 ▸
Blood Wedding '81 ▸
Bluebeard's Eighth Wife '38
Bodies, Rest & Motion '93
Boesman & Lena '00
Bopha! '93 ▸
Born Yesterday '50 ▸
Born Yesterday '93
Boy Meets Girl '38 ▸
The Boys '98 ▸
The Boys in the Band '70
The Boys Next Door '96
Breaking the Code '95
Breaking Up '97
Breath of Scandal '60
The Brig '64 ▸
Brighton Beach Memoirs '86
Brilliant Lies '96
Broadway Bound '92
Broken Glass '96
A Bronx Tale '93 ▸
A Brother's Kiss '97
The Browning Version '51 ▸
The Browning Version '94
Bug '06
Bus Stop '56 ▸
Butterflies Are Free '72 ▸
Cabaret Balkan '98
Cactus Flower '69
Caesar and Cleopatra '46
California Suite '78 ▸
Can-Can '60
Caresses '97
Casablanca '42 ▸
Casanova Brown '44
Cast a Dark Shadow '55 ▸
Casual Sex? '88
The Cat and the Canary '79
The Cat's Meow '01
Cavalcade '33 ▸
Cease Fire '85
Ceiling Zero '35 ▸
The Chalk Garden '64 ▸
Chapter Two '79
Charley's Aunt '41 ▸
The Chase '66
The Cheap Detective '78 ▸
Chelsea Walls '01
Children of a Lesser God '86 ▸
The Children's Hour '61
Chimes at Midnight '67 ▸
China '43
A Chorus of Disapproval '89
Clarence, the Cross-eyed Lion '65 ▸
Clash by Night '52 ▸
The Climax '44
Closer '04 ▸
Cock & Bull Story '03
Cold Comfort '90
Collected Stories '02 ▸
Columbo: Prescription Murder '67
Come Back, Little Sheba '52 ▸
Come Back to the Five & Dime Jimmy Dean, Jimmy Dean '82 ▸
Come Blow Your Horn '63 ▸
Command Decision '48
Conduct Unbecoming '75
The Connection '61 ▸
Coquette '29
The Corn Is Green '45 ▸
The Corn Is Green '79 ▸
Cosi '95 ▸
Counsellor-at-Law '33 ▸
The Count of the Old Town '34
Country Girl '54 ▸
County Fair '20
Craig's Wife '36 ▸
Crimes of the Heart '86
Critic's Choice '63
The Crucible '57 ▸
The Crucible '96 ▸
Curse of the Golden Flower '06
Curse of the Starving Class '94
Cyrano de Bergerac '85
Cyrano de Bergerac '90 ▸
Da '88
Daddy Long Legs '19
Daddy's Dyin'... Who's Got the Will? '90
Dancing at Lughnasa '98
Dangerous Liaisons '88 ▸
A Day in the Death of Joe Egg '71 ▸
Day of Wrath '43 ▸
Daybreak '93
Dead End '37 ▸
Dead Heart '96 ▸
Death and the Maiden '94 ▸
Death of a Salesman '51 ▸
Death of a Salesman '86 ▸
Death Takes a Holiday '34 ▸
Deathtrap '82
The Designated Mourner '97
Desire Under the Elms '58
Desk Set '57 ▸
Desperate Hours '55 ▸
Detective Story '51 ▸
Devil Girl from Mars '54
The Devils '71 ▸
The Devil's Brother '33
Dial "M" for Murder '54 ▸
Diary of a Hitman '91
Diary of a Mad Black Woman '05
Die Mommie Die! '03
The Dining Room '86
Dinner at Eight '33 ▸
Dinner with Friends '01
Disco Pigs '01
Disraeli '30 ▸
The Divorce of Lady X '38
The Doctor and the Devils '85
Doctor X '32
Doll Face '46
A Doll's House '59
A Doll's House '73
A Doll's House '73 ▸
Don't Drink the Water '69
Double Wedding '37 ▸
Doubt '08 ▸
Dracula '31 ▸
The Dresser '83 ▸
Driving Miss Daisy '89 ▸
Drunks '96
Du Barry Was a Lady '43
Duet for One '86
Dumb Waiter '87
Dutchman '67 ▸
The Eagle Has Two Heads '48 ▸
Early Days '81
East Is East '99 ▸
Easy Virtue '27
Easy Virtue '08
Edge of the City '57
Educating Rita '83 ▸
Edward II '92
The Effect of Gamma Rays on Man-in-the-Moon Marigolds '73 ▸
84 Charing Cross Road '86 ▸
Emperor Jones '33
Employees' Entrance '33 ▸
The Enchanted Cottage '45
An Enemy of the People '77
Ensign Pulver '64
The Entertainer '60 ▸
Entertaining Mr. Sloane '70
Equus '77
Escanaba in da Moonlight '01
Escapade '55 ▸
Escape Me Never '47
Execution of Justice '99
Extremities '86
Eye of the Storm '98
Faithful '95
Far Side of the Moon '03
The Farmer Takes a Wife '53
The Farmer's Wife '28
The Fever '04
A Few Good Men '92 ▸
The Field '90 ▸
Finding Neverland '04 ▸
A Fine Romance '92
Five Graves to Cairo '43 ▸
Fog Island '45
Fool for Love '86
Footsteps in the Dark '41
Forbidden Planet '56 ▸
Forever Female '53 ▸
Fortune and Men's Eyes '71
Forty Carats '73
Foxfire '87 ▸
Frankenstein Sings... The Movie '95
Frankie and Johnny '91 ▸
The Front Page '31 ▸
The Fugitive Kind '60
Fun '94
Futz '69
Gabriel & Me '01
Gangster No. 1 '00
Gaslight '40 ▸
Gaslight '44 ▸
The Gazebo '59 ▸
Generation '69
George Washington Slept Here '42 ▸
Get Real '99
Getting Gertie's Garter '45
Getting Out '94
The Ghost Breakers '40 ▸
The Girl on the Train '09
Girl Play '04
Give Me a Sailor '38
The Glass Menagerie '87 ▸
Glengarry Glen Ross '92 ▸
God Said "Ha!" '99 ▸
Golden Boy '39 ▸
The Golden Coach '52 ▸
Gone Are the Days '63
Good '08
The Good Fairy '35 ▸
Goodbye Charlie '64
The Goodbye Girl '77 ▸
Goodbye My Fancy '51
The Gorilla '39
Grace & Glorie '98
The Great White Hope '70
Green Pastures '36 ▸
The Grey Zone '01
Grown Ups '86
The Guys '02 ▸
The Hairy Ape '44
Hamlet '48 ▸
Hamlet '69
Hamlet '90 ▸
Hamlet '96 ▸
The Happiest Days of Your Life '50 ▸
Happy Birthday, Gemini '80
Harriet Craig '50 ▸
Having a Wonderful Time '38
Having Our Say: The Delany Sisters' First 100 Years '99
He Who Gets Slapped '24 ▸
Heartbreak House '86
Heaven Can Wait '43 ▸
Heaven Can Wait '78 ▸
Hedda '75
The Heidi Chronicles '95
Henry IV '85
Henry V '44 ▸
Henry V '89 ▸
His Double Life '33
His Girl Friday '40 ▸
The History Boys '06
Hit the Deck '55
Holiday '38 ▸
Holiday Heart '00
Homage '95
Home of the Brave '49 ▸
The Honey Pot '67
Hoopla '33
Hotel Paradiso '66
The Hound of London '93
House of the Long Shadows '82
The House of Yes '97
Hurlyburly '98
Hysterical Blindness '02
I Confess '53
I Love You, I Love You Not '97
I Married an Angel '42
I Never Sang for My Father '70 ▸
I Ought to Be in Pictures '82
I Remember Mama '48 ▸
An Ideal Husband '47
An Ideal Husband '99 ▸
Idiot's Delight '39 ▸
I'll Be Seeing You '44
I'll Be Yours '47
I'll Never Forget You '51
Illicit '31
Illuminata '98
Illusions '91
I'm Not Rappaport '96
The Importance of Being Earnest '02
The Impossible Years '68
In Celebration '75 ▸
In Search of the Castaways '62 ▸
In the Good Old Summertime '49 ▸
Indiscreet '88
Inherit the Wind '60 ▸
Inherit the Wind '99
Intrigue and Love '59
Iphigenia '77 ▸
Italian Straw Hat '27 ▸
It's the Rage '99
Jacknife '89 ▸
Jeffrey '95
Jesus Christ, Superstar '73 ▸
Johnny Belinda '82
Jubal '56
Julius Caesar '53 ▸
Julius Caesar '70
Key Exchange '85
The Killing of Sister George '69
King and Country '64 ▸
The King and I '99
King Lear '71 ▸
King Lear '87
King Lear '98 ▸
The King on Main Street '25
Kingdom Come '01
Kings '07
Kiss Me, Stupid! '64
The Knack '65 ▸
Knocks at My Door '93
K2: The Ultimate High '92
La Cage aux Folles '78 ▸
La Cage aux Folles 2 '81
La Cage aux Folles 3: The Wedding '86
Ladies They Talk About '33
The Lady's Not for Burning '87
Lantana '01 ▸
The Laramie Project '02 ▸
Last Night '10
The Last of Mrs. Cheyney '37 ▸
Last of the Red Hot Lovers '72
Laughing Sinners '31
Leaving Metropolis '02
Lenny '74 ▸
Les Enfants Terrible '50 ▸
The Libertine '05
Life '95
A Life in the Theater '93
Life Tastes Good '99
Li'l Abner '59
Lilies '96
Lily Dale '96
The Lion in Winter '68 ▸
The Lion in Winter '03 ▸
The Little Foxes '41 ▸
Little Murders '71 ▸
Little Shop of Horrors '86 ▸
Little Voice '98 ▸
Long Day's Journey into Night '62 ▸
Long Day's Journey into Night '88
Long Day's Journey Into Night '96 ▸
The Long Voyage Home '40 ▸
Look Back in Anger '58 ▸
Look Back in Anger '80
Look Back in Anger '89 ▸
Looking for Richard '96 ▸
Loot... Give Me Money, Honey! '70
The Loss of a Teardrop Diamond '08
Lost in Yonkers '93
Louisiana Purchase '41
The Lovable Cheat '49
Love and Human Remains '93 ▸
Love, Ludlow '05
Love! Valour! Compassion! '96
Loving Leah '09
The Lower Depths '36 ▸
The Lower Depths '57 ▸
M. Butterfly '93
Macbeth '48 ▸
Macbeth '70 ▸
Macbeth '71 ▸
Macbeth '88
Madame X '37
Madame X '66
The Madwoman of Chaillot '69
The Magnificent Yankee '50 ▸
The Mahabharata '89
Major Barbara '41 ▸
A Majority of One '56
Male and Female '19 ▸
The Male Animal '42
Mambo Italiano '03
A Man for All Seasons '66 ▸
A Man for All Seasons '88 ▸

The Man in the Glass Booth '75 ▶
Man of La Mancha '72
The Man Who Came to Dinner '41 ▶
The Man with Two Faces '34
Marie and Bruce '04
Marion Bridge '02
Marius '31 ▶
Marriage Italian Style '64 ▶
Marvin's Room '96
Mary, Mary '63
Mass Appeal '84
Master Harold and the Boys '84 ▶
The Matchmaker '58 ▶
Me and the Colonel '58
Medea '70
Medea '88
Men in White '34
Merton of the Movies '47
The Method '05 ▶
Mexican Hayride '48
Midnight Lace '60
A Midsummer Night's Dream '35 ▶
A Midsummer Night's Dream '68
The Migrants '74 ▶
The Millionairess '60
Minna von Barnhelm or The Soldier's Fortune '62
The Miracle Woman '31
The Miracle Worker '62 ▶
The Miracle Worker '79 ▶
The Miracle Worker '00
Miss Evers' Boys '97
Miss Firecracker '89 ▶
Miss Julie '50
Miss Julie '99
Miss Rose White '92 ▶
Mississippi '35
Mister Drake's Duck '50
Mr. Music '50
Mister Roberts '55 ▶
Mr. Write '92
Mogambo '53 ▶
Monster in a Box '92 ▶
Morning Glory '33
Move Over, Darling '63
Much Ado about Nothing '93 ▶
Murder '30 ▶
Murder at the Vanities '34
Murder by Death '76
My Big Fat Greek Wedding '02
My Boy Jack '07
My Brother's Wife '89
My Sister Eileen '42
My Sister Eileen '55 ▶
My Zinc Bed '08
Nell '94
Never Say Die '39
Never Steal Anything Small '59
Never Too Late to Mend '37
New Faces of 1952 '54
New Moon '40
Nico and Dani '00
Night Must Fall '37 ▶
Night of January 16th '41
The Night of the Iguana '64 ▶
No '98
No, No Nanette '40
No Other Woman '33
No Sex Please—We're British '73
No Time for Sergeants '58 ▶
Noises Off '92
Normal '03
The Norman Conquests, Part 1: Table Manners '78 ▶
The Norman Conquests, Part 2: Living Together '78 ▶
The Norman Conquests, Part 3: Round and Round the Garden '78 ▶
Norman, Is That You? '76
North Shore Fish '97
No. 17 '32 ▶
Nurse Marjorie '20
The Obsessed '51
The Odd Couple '68 ▶
Oedipus Rex '67 ▶
Off the Map '03 ▶
Oh Dad, Poor Dad (Momma's Hung You in the Closet & I'm Feeling So Sad) '67
Oh! What a Lovely War '69
Oklahoma! '55 ▶
The Old Settler '01
Oleanna '94
On Approval '44 ▶
On Borrowed Time '39 ▶
On Golden Pond '81 ▶
On the Town '49 ▶
Once in the Life '00
One Night Stand '78
1-900 '94
One of My Wives Is Missing '76
One Touch of Venus '48
One Trick Pony '80
The Only Thrill '97
Only When I Laugh '81 ▶
Ordet '55 ▶
Orfeu '99
Orphans '87 ▶
Orphans of the Storm '21 ▶
Orpheus Descending '91
Oscar '91
Othello '22
Othello '52 ▶
Othello '65 ▶
Othello '95 ▶
Other People's Money '91
Our Town '40 ▶
Our Town '77 ▶
Our Town '89
Our Town '03
Out of Season '75
Out of the Fog '41
The Owl and the Pussycat '70 ▶
Panama Hattie '42
The Passing of the Third Floor Back '36
Patterns '56 ▶
Peephole '93
People Will Talk '51 ▶
The Perfect Marriage '46
A Perfect Murder '98
Period of Adjustment '62 ▶
Personal Property '37
Peter and Vandy '09
Petrified Forest '36 ▶
Phaedra '61
The Phantom of the Opera '90
The Phantom of the Opera '98
Phantom of the Paradise '74
The Philadelphia Story '40 ▶
The Piano Lesson '94 ▶
Pippin '81 ▶
The Pirates of Penzance '83
Play It Again, Sam '72 ▶
Playboy of the Western World '62
Plaza Suite '71 ▶
Plenty '85
The Portrait '93 ▶
Portrait in Black '60
Prelude to a Kiss '92
The Prime of Miss Jean Brodie '69 ▶
Prince of Central Park '00
Princess Tam Tam '35 ▶
Prisoner of Second Avenue '74
Private Fears in Public Places '06
Private Lives '31 ▶
The Private Secretary '35
Privates on Parade '84
The Producers '05
P.S. Your Cat is Dead! '02
Psycho Beach Party '00
Purlie Victorious '63
Pygmalion '38 ▶
The Quare Fellow '62
A Question of Attribution '91
Quiet Day in Belfast '74 ▶
A Quiet Duel '49
Quills '00
Radiance '98
The Rainmaker '56 ▶
A Raisin in the Sun '61 ▶
A Raisin in the Sun '89 ▶
A Raisin in the Sun '08
Ran '85 ▶
Real Women Have Curves '02 ▶
Reckless '95
Red Planet Mars '52
Red Roses and Petrol '03
Redwood Curtain '95
Rent '05
The Return of Peter Grimm '35
Rhythm Romance '39
Richard III '55 ▶
Ride the Wild Fields '00
Riders to the Sea '88
The Right to Remain Silent '95
The Ritz '76 ▶
The River is Red '48
Rodgers & Hammerstein's South Pacific '01
Roman Spring of Mrs. Stone '61 ▶
Romance '30
Romantic Comedy '83
Romeo and Juliet '36 ▶
Romeo and Juliet '54
Romeo and Juliet '68 ▶
Romy and Michele's High School Reunion '97
The Room '87
Room 314 '07
Roosters '95
Rope '48 ▶
Rosencrantz & Guildenstern Are Dead '90 ▶
Roxie Hart '42
Ruby '92
The Runner Stumbles '79
Sabrina '54 ▶
Sabrina '95
Saint Joan '57
Same Time, Next Year '78 ▶
The Saphead '21
Sarafina! '92 ▶
Scorchers '92
Scum '79 ▶
The Seagull '71 ▶
The Seagull '75
Search and Destroy '94
Secret Honor '85 ▶
The Secret Rapture '94
Separate Tables '58 ▶
Separate Tables '83
Serious Charge '59
Seven Chances '25 ▶
Sex and the Other Man '95
Sextette '78
The Shadow Box '80 ▶
Shadow of Angels '76
Shadowlands '93 ▶
The Shanghai Gesture '42
The Shape of Things '03
Shirley Valentine '89 ▶
The Shop Around the Corner '40 ▶
Short Eyes '79 ▶
The Shot '96
The Show-Off '46
Siberian Lady Macbeth '61 ▶
The Sicilian '87
The Sign of the Cross '33
Silent Night, Lonely Night '69
Silk Stockings '57 ▶
A Sinful Life '89
The Singing Blacksmith '38
The Sisters '05
Six Degrees of Separation '93
Skin Game '31
Sleuth '72 ▶
Sleuth '07
A Slight Case of Murder '38
Small Hotel '57
Smart Woman '31
Smoking/No Smoking '94
So Ends Our Night '41 ▶
A Soldier's Story '84 ▶
Solid Gold Cadillac '56 ▶
The Song of Songs '33
Sordid Lives '00
Sorrento Beach '95
South Pacific '58 ▶
Spring Fever '27
Stage Door '37 ▶
Stand-Ins '97
Star Spangled Girl '71
State of the Union '48 ▶
Stevie '78
Stolen Hours '63
The Storm Within '48 ▶
Strange Interlude '32 ▶
Strange Interlude '90
The Strange Love of Molly Louvain '32
Streamers '83
Street Scene '31 ▶
A Streetcar Named Desire '51 ▶
A Streetcar Named Desire '84 ▶
A Streetcar Named Desire '95
The Stripper '63
The Student Affair '97
The Subject Was Roses '68 ▶
The Substance of Fire '96
subUrbia '96
Suddenly, Last Summer '59 ▶
Sugarhouse '07
The Sum of Us '94 ▶
Summer and Smoke '61
Summertime '55 ▶
Summertree '71
Sunday in New York '63
Sunday in the Park with George '86 ▶
Sunrise at Campobello '60 ▶
The Sunshine Boys '75 ▶
The Sunshine Boys '95
Susan Slept Here '54
Sweet Bird of Youth '62 ▶
Sweet Bird of Youth '89
Sweet Nothing in My Ear '08
Sweet Revenge '98
Sylvia and the Phantom '45 ▶
Taking Sides '01 ▶
Talk Radio '88 ▶
Tall Story '60
The Taming of the Shrew '29
The Taming of the Shrew '67 ▶
Tape '01 ▶
Tartuffe '25
Tartuffe '84
Tartuffe '90
A Taste of Honey '61 ▶
Tea and Sympathy '56 ▶
Tea for Two '50 ▶
The Teahouse of the August Moon '56
The Tempest '63
The Tempest '82 ▶
The Terror '38
That Championship Season '82
That Championship Season '99
There's a Girl in My Soup '70
These Girls '05
These Three '36 ▶
They Knew What They Wanted '40 ▶
Thin Ice '37 ▶
This Happy Breed '47 ▶
This Is the Army '43
This Property Is Condemned '66
Thoroughly Modern Millie '67
Those Endearing Young Charms '45
Those People Next Door '52
A Thousand Clowns '65 ▶
Three Daring Daughters '48
Three for the Show '55
Three Men on a Horse '36 ▶
Throne of Blood '57 ▶
Tidy Endings '88
Time Lock '57
The Time of Your Life '48 ▶
Time Without Pity '57
Tom & Viv '94 ▶
Tomorrow the World '44
Tonight or Never '31
Tony n' Tina's Wedding '07
Too Many Girls '40
Topaze '33 ▶
Topaze '51 ▶
Torch Song Trilogy '88
Tough Guy '53
Toys in the Attic '63
Trial & Error '62
Trial by Media '00
The Trials of Oscar Wilde '60 ▶
The Trip to Bountiful '85 ▶
The Triumph of Love '01
Trojan Women '71
Trouble in Paradise '32 ▶
True West '86 ▶
Trumbo '07 ▶
The Tunnel of Love '58
The Turning '92
Twelfth Night '96
Twelve Angry Men '57 ▶
Twelve Angry Men '97
21 Days '37
The Twilight of the Golds '97
Twin Beds '42
Twisted '86
Two Alone '34
Two for the Seesaw '62 ▶
Two Small Bodies '93
Tyler Perry's Why Did I Get Married? '07
Un Air de Famille '96
The Unapproachable '82
Under Milk Wood '73
Under the Yum-Yum Tree '63
Up in Central Park '48
Urbania '00
The Visit '00 ▶
Volpone '39 ▶
A Voyage 'Round My Father '89 ▶
Wait until Dark '67 ▶
The War at Home '96
The War Lord '65 ▶
Watch on the Rhine '43 ▶
Water Drops on Burning Rocks '99
The Water Engine '92
Waterfront '39
Waterloo Bridge '40 ▶
Weekend at the Waldorf '45 ▶
We're No Angels '55 ▶
We're No Angels '89
We're Not Dressing '34 ▶
The Whales of August '87 ▶
What a Girl Wants '03
Where Were You When the Lights Went Out? '68
Whoopee! '30
Who's Afraid of Virginia Woolf? '66 ▶
Whose Life Is It Anyway? '81 ▶
The Widowing of Mrs. Holroyd '95
Wild Bill '95
The Wild Duck '84
Will Success Spoil Rock Hunter? '57
William Shakespeare's Romeo and Juliet '96 ▶
Window Shopping '86
The Winner '96
The Winslow Boy '48 ▶
The Winslow Boy '98 ▶
The Winter Guest '97 ▶
Wit '01 ▶
Without Love '45
The Wolves of Kromer '98
The Women '39 ▶
Woyzeck '78 ▶
Woyzeck '94
Wozzeck '47
Yellow Dust '36
Yerma '99
You Can't Take It with You '38 ▶
Young and Willing '42
Zalmen or the Madness of God '75
Zemsta '02
Zooman '95 ▶
Zoot Suit '81 ▶

Adapted from a Play Adapted from a Movie

The Abdication '74
Hairspray '07 ▶
Little Shop of Horrors '86 ▶
Nine '09
The Producers '05

Adapted from a Poem

The Bells '26 ▶
Beowulf '98
Beowulf '07 ▶
Beowulf & Grendel '06
Braveheart '95 ▶
The Castilian '63
The Charge of the Light Brigade '36 ▶
The Charge of the Light Brigade '68
Evangeline '29
Gunga Din '39 ▶
The Man from Snowy River '82
The Odyssey '97
Old Ironsides '26 ▶
Perceval '78
The Set-Up '49 ▶
Troy '04
Ulysses '55
The White Cliffs of Dover '44 ▶
Wild Party '74

Adapted from a Radio Show

Behind the Mask '46
Big Town '47
Buck Benny Rides Again '40
Calling Dr. Death '43
Check & Double Check '30
Counterspy Meets Scotland Yard '50
Dead Man's Eyes '44
The Devil's Eye '60
Dreaming Out Loud '40
Gang Busters '42
Gang Busters '55
Gildersleeve on Broadway '43
Goin' to Town '44
Goon Movie '52
The Great Gildersleeve '43
Here Come the Nelsons '52
Here We Go Again! '42
Inner Sanctum '48
International Crime '37
The Invisible Avenger '58
Mr. Arkadin '55 ▶
Mr. District Attorney '41
My Friend Irma '49
Myrt and Marge '33
A Prairie Home Companion '06
Queen for a Day '51
Renfrew of the Royal Mounted '37
The Shadow '94
The Shadow Strikes '37
Sorry, Wrong Number '48 ▶
Treacherous Crossing '92
The War of the Worlds '53 ▶
Weird Woman '44

Adapted from a Song

Alice's Restaurant '69
The Baron and the Kid '84
Beer for My Horses '08
Beyond the Wall of Sleep '06
Born in East L.A. '87
Convoy '78
Coward of the County '81
Elisa '94
Frankie and Johnny '36
Frankie and Johnny '65
The Gambler Returns: The Luck of the Draw '93
Girls Just Want to Have Fun '85
The Indian Runner '91
Is There Life Out There? '94
Kenny Rogers as the Gambler '80
Kenny Rogers as the Gambler, Part 2: The Adventure Continues '83
Kenny Rogers as the Gambler, Part 3: The Legend Continues '87
Legend of Tom Dooley '59
Love Potion #9 '92
My Boyfriend's Back '93
The Night the Lights Went Out in Georgia '81
Ode to Billy Joe '76
Purple People Eater '88
Single Bars, Single Women '84
Take This Job & Shove It '81
Yellow Submarine '68 ▶
You Light Up My Life '77

Adapted from a Story

A. I.: Artificial Intelligence '01
ABC Stage 67: Truman Capote's A Christmas Memory '66
The Adventures of Ichabod and Mr. Toad '49 ▶

Alibi Ike '35
Alice in Wonderland '51 ▸
Alice in Wonderland '99
Amanda and the Alien '95
Ambassador Bill '31
America's Dream '95 ▸
Androcles and the Lion '52
The Android Affair '95
The Angel Levine '70
Angels in the Outfield '51 ▸
Angels with Dirty Faces '38 ▸
Appointment with Crime '45
Arizona Bushwackers '67
As Young As You Feel '51 ▸
Ashik Kerib '88 ▸
The Assassination Bureau '69 ▸
Ava's Magical Adventure '94
Away From Her '06 ▸
Babette's Feast '87 ▸
The Babysitter '95
The Ballad of the Sad Cafe '91
Bartleby '70
The Beast from 20,000 Fathoms '53
Benefit of the Doubt '93
Big Business Girl '31
The Big Stampede '32
Billy the Kid '41
The Birds '63 ▸
The Black Abbot '63
Blackmail '91 ▸
Blood and Roses '61
The Blood Spattered Bride '72
Bloodhounds of Broadway '52
Boots of Destiny '37
Border Caballero '36
Boss of Bullion City '41
The Box '09
A Boy and His Dog '75
Boys '95
Boys' Night Out '62 ▸
Bram Stoker's Shadow-builder '98
Breakfast at Tiffany's '61 ▸
Brief Encounter '46 ▸
Brigham Young: Frontiersman '40
Bright Angel '91
Bubba Ho-Tep '03 ▸
Burial of the Rats '95
Burning Daylight '28
Bury Me Not on the Lone Prairie '41
By the Light of the Silvery Moon '53
Call of the Wild '72
Candyman '92
Candyman 2: Farewell to the Flesh '94
The Canterville Ghost '44
The Canterville Ghost '96
Casanova's Big Night '54
Cat's Eye '85
Caught in the Draft '41 ▸
Celine and Julie Go Boating '74
Charade '63 ▸
The Children of Noisy Village '86
Children of the Corn '84
Children On Their Birthdays '02
Christmas Child '03
Cinderella 2000 '78
The Cisco Kid '94
College Swing '38
Comanche Territory '50
Come to the Stable '49 ▸
Comrade X '40
Cora Unashamed '00
Cosmic Slop '94
Crash Dive '43
Creature from the Black Lagoon '54 ▸
Creature with the Blue Hand '70
Cricket on the Hearth '23
Cult of the Cobra '55
The Curious Case of Benjamin Button '08 ▸
Curse of the Demon '57 ▸
Curtis's Charm '96
Dark Eyes '87 ▸
Daughter of the Dragon '31
A Day in the Country '46 ▸
The Day the Earth Stood Still '51 ▸
The Dead '87 ▸
The Decameron '70 ▸
Decameron Nights '53
Department Store '35
Detonator 2: Night Watch '95
The Devil & Daniel Webster '41 ▸
Diary of a Madman '63
Die, Monster, Die! '65
Dive Bomber '41 ▸
Doomed at Sundown '37
Door with the Seven Locks '62
Double Trouble '67
Double Vision '92
D.P. '85
Drift Fence '36
DROP Squad '94
The Dropkick '27 ▸
Eat a Bowl of Tea '89 ▸
The Emperor's Club '02
Esther Kahn '00
The Eyes of the Amaryllis '82
Eyes of the Panther '90
A Face in the Crowd '57 ▸
Face to Face '52
Fall Guy '47
Fallen Angels 1 '93 ▸
Fallen Angels 2 '93 ▸
Feud Maker '38
The Fig Tree '87
The Fighter '52 ▸
Fighting Caravans '31
First Love '77
First Love, Last Rites '98
Five Days One Summer '82
The 5000 Fingers of Dr. T '53 ▸
Flirtation Walk '34
Forger of London '61
Frankenstein Conquers the World '64
Freaks '32 ▸
From Beyond '86 ▸
Frontier Uprising '61
Gabrielle '05
Galloping Romeo '33
Gangway '37
A Gentle Woman '69
The Ghost of Frankenstein '42
Ghost Valley '32
The Gift of Love '90
The Girl with the Hungry Eyes '94
The Glass House '72 ▸
The Go-Between '71 ▸
Great Adventure '75
The Great Man's Lady '42
Gunfight at the O.K. Corral '57 ▸
Halfmoon '95
Hands Across the Table '35 ▸
The Happy Years '50
The Hard Way '91 ▸
Haunting Fear '91
The Haunting of Hell House '99
The Haunting of Morella '91
Highlander '86 ▸
Hills of Oklahoma '50
Hole in the Sky '95
Home for the Holidays '95
Homecoming '48
Hondo '53 ▸
Hostile Guns '67
The House of Usher '88
How About You '07
How to Steal a Million '66 ▸
H.P. Lovecraft's Necronomicon: Book of the Dead '93
I Don't Want to Talk About It '94
I'm the One You're Looking For '88
The Importance of Being Earnest '52 ▸
Impostor '02
In Memoriam '76
In Old Chicago '37 ▸
In the Gloaming '97 ▸
The Incredible Sarah '76
The Indian Scarf '63
Internes Can't Take Money '37
Into the Badlands '92
Invasion U.S.A. '52
The Invisible Boy '57
The Invisible Woman '40 ▸
Isaac Asimov's Nightfall '00
Isle of Forgotten Sins '43
It Came from Outer Space 2 '95
It Started with Eve '41 ▸
It's a Date '40
It's a Dog's Life '55
Jigsaw '49 ▸
Jindabyne '06
Johnny Eager '42 ▸
Johnny Mnemonic '95
Johnny Reno '66
Jonathan Livingston Seagull '73
Judgment Night '93
The Jungle Book '42
The Juniper Tree '87
Kaos '85 ▸
Key to the City '50
The Kill-Off '90
The Killers '46 ▸
Kim '50 ▸
Kissed '96
Kull the Conqueror '97
Kurt Vonnegut's Harrison Bergeron '95
Kurt Vonnegut's Monkey House '91
La Chute de la Maison Usher '28 ▸
La Merveilleuse Visite '74
The Ladies of the Bois de Bologne '44
The Lady Eve '41 ▸
Lady Killer '33 ▸
Lady on a Train '45 ▸
The Lady with the Dog '59 ▸
The Land Unknown '57
Landscape After Battle '70
The Last Mimzy '07
Late Chrysanthemums '54
The Lawnmower Man '92
The Lawrenceville Stories '88
Le Plaisir '52
The Leech Woman '59
The Legend of Johnny Lingo '03
Legends of the North '95
L'Eleve '95
Life is Hot in Cracktown '08
Life on a String '90
The Little Prince '74
Lone Star '52
Lord of Illusions '95
The Lost World '25
The Lost World '92
The Love Letter '98
Love on the Run '36
Love Play '60
Loyalties '86
Lurking Fear '94
Lust, Caution '07
Maborosi '95 ▸
The Magic Fountain '61
The Magnificent Dope '42
Main Street to Broadway '53
The Man Without a Country '73 ▸
Manfish '56
The Mangler '94
Mapp & Lucia '85
Margaret's Museum '95 ▸
The Masked Rider '41
Masque of the Red Death '65 ▸
Masque of the Red Death '89
Masque of the Red Death '90
Matango '63
Maximum Overdrive '86
Menace II Society '93 ▸
Midnight '39 ▸
A Million to Juan '94
Miracle in Rome '88
Mr. Deeds Goes to Town '36 ▸
A Month by the Lake '95
More about the Children of Noisy Village '87
The Most Dangerous Game '32 ▸
The Mummy's Curse '44
The Mummy's Tomb '42
Murders in the Rue Morgue '71
The Murders in the Rue Morgue '86 ▸
My Apprenticeship '39 ▸
My Childhood '38 ▸
My Favorite Blonde '42 ▸
My Foolish Heart '49
My Lucky Star '38
My Mother's Castle '91 ▸
My Sister Eileen '55 ▸
My Uncle Silas '01 ▸
My Universities '40 ▸
The Mysterious Magician '65
Mystic Circle Murder '39
Naked Jungle '54 ▸
The Naked Maja '59
Ned Kelly '03
Nevada '44
Never Say Goodbye '46
New Rose Hotel '98
Night Sun '90
Nightfall '88
Nightflyers '87
Noir et Blanc '86
Noon Wine '84 ▸
Now and Forever '34
Objective, Burma! '45 ▸
The Oblong Box '69
O.C. and Stiggs '87
An Occurrence at Owl Creek Bridge/Coup de Grace '62
Of Human Hearts '38
An Old-Fashioned Thanksgiving '08
Old Joy '06 ▸
On Moonlight Bay '51
One Christmas '95
100 Men and a Girl '37 ▸
Our Modern Maidens '29
Our Relations '36 ▸
The Outlaw Deputy '35
The Oval Portrait '88
Peck's Bad Boy '21
Personal Velocity: Three Portraits '02 ▸
The Pied Piper of Hamelin '84
The Pit and the Pendulum '61 ▸
The Pit & the Pendulum '91
Pittsburgh '42
Play Misty for Me '71 ▸
The Possessed '47 ▸
Premature Burial '62
The Prince and the Pauper '62
Pudd'nhead Wilson '84
The Purchase Price '32
The Quarrel '93
The Queen of Spades '49 ▸
Quest for Love '71
Quicksilver Highway '98
Rasen '98
Rawhead Rex '87
Re-Animator '84 ▸
Rear Window '54 ▸
The Red Shoes '48 ▸
The Redhead from Wyoming '53
The Report on the Party and the Guests '66 ▸
Return to Paradise '53
Return to the Lost World '93
Revenge of the Creature '55
Rica '72
Rica 2: Lonely Wanderer '73
Rica 3: Juvenile's Lullaby '73
Ride Him, Cowboy '32 ▸
Ridin' Down the Canyon '42
Ridin' the Lone Trail '37
Robbers of the Sacred Mountain '83
Robert Louis Stevenson's The Game of Death '99
Rocket to the Moon '86
The Rocking Horse Winner '49
Roman Holiday '53 ▸
The Roman Spring of Mrs. Stone '03
Roommate '84
Rough Ridin' Rhythm '37
Ruggles of Red Gap '35 ▸
Rumpelstiltskin '86
The Safety of Objects '01
St. Michael Had a Rooster '72
Santa Fe '51
Saturday Night Fever '77
The Scarlet Tunic '97
Screamers '96
Secret of the Black Trunk '62
Secretary '02 ▸
Seven Brides for Seven Brothers '54 ▸
The Seven Hills of Rome '58
Sex and Fury '73
Shadow of a Doubt '43 ▸
Shadrach '98
Shanghai Express '32 ▸
The Shawshank Redemption '94 ▸
Shinbone Alley '70
The Shooting Party '77
Shopworn Angel '38 ▸
Short Cuts '93 ▸
The Skull '65
Sleep of Death '79
Sleeping Car to Trieste '45
Smooth Talk '85 ▸
The Snow Queen '83
The Snow Walker '03
Snow White and the Seven Dwarfs '37 ▸
The Snows of Kilimanjaro '52 ▸
A Soldier's Sweetheart '98
Sometimes They Come Back... Again '96
Somewhere I'll Find You '42 ▸
Sorrows of Gin '79
Sorry, Wrong Number '89
The Southerner '45 ▸
The Spectre of Edgar Allen Poe '73
Stagecoach '39 ▸
Station West '48 ▸
Stephen King's The Night Flier '96
The Strange Countess '61
The Strange Door '51
Strawberry and Chocolate '93 ▸
Suicide Kings '97
Summer Storm '44
A Summer Story '88 ▸
A Summer to Remember '84
Sunset Boulevard '50 ▸
Swept from the Sea '97
The Swimmer '68 ▸
The Switch '10
Tails You Live, Heads You're Dead '95
Taking Lives '04
Tales from the Darkside: The Movie '90
Tales of Terror '62
Tales of the Klondike: In a Far Country '87
Tales of the Klondike: Race for Number One '87
Tales of the Klondike: The Scorn of Women '87
Tales of the Klondike: The Unexpected '87
The Tell-Tale Heart '60
Tennessee's Partner '55
That Evening Sun '09 ▸
They Met in Bombay '41
They Watch '93
The Thing '82
This World, Then the Fireworks '97
Three Brothers '80 ▸
Three Cases of Murder '55 ▸
The Three Little Pigs '84
Three Smart Girls '36 ▸
3:10 to Yuma '07 ▸
Through the Eyes of a Killer '92
Thunder Pass '54
The Tin Soldier '95
Today We Live '33
Tomb of Ligeia '64 ▸
Tomorrow '72 ▸
Tonto Basin Outlaws '41
Too Far to Go '79 ▸
The Topeka Terror '45
Torrents of Spring '90
Torture Garden '67
Torture Ship '39
Transmutations '85
Trapped in Space '94
Tribute to a Bad Man '56 ▸
Trio '50 ▸
Tropical Heat '93
Trucks '97
Trumps '83
Tugboat Annie '33 ▸
Tully '00 ▸
The Twelve Chairs '70 ▸
12:01 '93
Two by Forsyth '86
Two Daughters '61 ▸
Two Evil Eyes '90
Uncertain Glory '44
Under the Biltmore Clock '85
An Unforgettable Summer '94
The Vampire Lovers '70
Vampyr '31 ▸
Vanina Vanini '61 ▸
Ward Six '78
Wee Willie Winkie '37 ▸
Who Am I This Time? '82 ▸
Who Slew Auntie Roo? '71
Who's the Man? '93
The Window '49 ▸
Wintertime '43
A Woman Without Love '51 ▸
A Woman's World '54 ▸
Women & Men: In Love There Are No Rules '91
Women & Men: Stories of Seduction '90
The Wonderful Ice Cream Suit '98
The Yellow Handkerchief '08 ▸
Young at Heart '54
The Young Land '59
The Young One '61
Youth Aflame '44

Adapted from an Article

All Mine to Give '56
American Gangster '07 ▸
Biker Boyz '03
Blue Crush '02 ▸
Christiane F. '82 ▸
City by the Sea '02
Coyote Ugly '00
The Hunting Party '07
I Was a Communist for the FBI '51
The Insider '99 ▸
Isn't She Great '00
Joe Gould's Secret '00
The Last American Hero '73 ▸
The Last Shot '04
My Sister Eileen '42
New Jersey Drive '95
Olivier, Olivier '92 ▸
Pushing Tin '99 ▸
Resurrecting the Champ '07
Shattered Glass '03 ▸
Streetwise '84 ▸
Trade '07
Two or Three Things I Know about Her '66
Witness Protection '99 ▸

Adapted from an Opera

Aria '88
Balalaika '39
Baritone '85
Beggar's Opera '54
Broken Melody '34
Burlesque on Carmen '16
Carmen '83 ▸
Carmen: A Hip Hopera '01
Carmen, Baby '66
Carmen Jones '54 ▸
The Chocolate Soldier '41
Farewell My Concubine '93
Fitzcarraldo '82 ▸
For the First Time '59
The Great Caruso '51
The Great Waltz '38 ▸
Gypsy Blood '18
I Dream Too Much '35
Jesus Christ, Superstar '73 ▸
La Grande Vadrouille '66 ▸
Life of Verdi '82
The Magic Flute '73 ▸
The Marriage of Figaro '49
The Medium '51
Meeting Venus '91
Midnight Girl '25
The Mozart Brothers '86 ▸
Otello '86 ▸
The Panther's Claw '42

The Phantom of the Opera '25 ▶
The Phantom of the Opera '43 ▶
The Red Mill '27
Rick '03
Rose Marie '36 ▶
Ruddigore '82
The Tales of Hoffmann '51
The Three Penny Opera '62
The Toast of New Orleans '50
The Tsar's Bride '66 ▶
The Vampyr '92
Verdi '53
Wagner: The Complete Epic '85
Wagner: The Movie '85

Adapted from Comics

American Splendor '03 ▶
Annie '82
Archie: Return to Riverdale '90
Art School Confidential '06
Astro Boy '09
Azumi '03 ▶
Azumi 2 '05
Barb Wire '96
Batman '66
Batman '89 ▶
Batman and Robin '97
Batman Begins '05 ▶
Batman Forever '95 ▶
Batman Returns '92
Battlefield Baseball '03
Black Mask '96
Blade '98
Blade 2 '02
Blade: Trinity '04
Bohachi Bushido: Code of the Forgotten Eight '73
Boogiepop and Others '00
Brenda Starr '86
Bulletproof Monk '03
Captain America '44
Captain America '79
Captain America '89
Captain America 2: Death Too Soon '79
Casper '95 ▶
Catwoman '04
Constantine '05
Corky of Gasoline Alley '51
Creepshow '82
The Crow '93
The Crow 2: City of Angels '96
The Crow: Salvation '00
The Crow: Wicked Prayer '05
Daredevil '03
Dark Water '02
The Dead One '07
Death Note '06 ▶
Death Note 2: The Last Name '07
Death Note 3: L, Change the World '08
Dennis the Menace '93
Dennis the Menace Strikes Again '98
Dick Tracy '90 ▶
Doing Time '02
Dondi '61
Dororo '07
Elektra '05
Fantastic Four '05
Fantastic Four: Rise of the Silver Surfer '07
Faust: Love of the Damned '00
Fist of the North Star '95
Fudoh: The New Generation '96
Garfield: A Tail of Two Kitties '06
Garfield: The Movie '04
Gasoline Alley '51
Ghost in the Shell '95 ▶
Ghost Rider '07
Ghost World '01 ▶
Hellboy '04
A History of Violence '05 ▶
Howard the Duck '86
Hulk '03
Ichi the Killer '01
Immortal '04
The Incredible Hulk '77
The Incredible Hulk Returns '88
Josie and the Pussycats '01
Judge Dredd '95
Kick-Ass '10
Killer Condom '95
Kull the Conqueror '97
Lady Snowblood '73 ▶
The League of Extraordinary Gentlemen '03
Marmaduke '10
The Mask '94 ▶
Masked Rider—The First '05
Men in Black '97 ▶
Modesty Blaise '66
Monkeybone '01
Moonlight Whispers '99
My Name is Modesty: A Modesty Blaise Adventure '04
Mystery Men '99
Over the Hedge '06 ▶
Persepolis '07 ▶
The Phantom '96
Ping Pong '02 ▶
Premonition '04
Prince Valiant '97
The Princess Blade '02
The Punisher '90
The Punisher '04
The Red Spectacles '87
Richie Rich '94
Ringu '98 ▶
Ringu 0 '01
Ringu 2 '99
Sabrina the Teenage Witch '96
St. Trinian's '07
Scott Pilgrim vs. the World '10
Shark Skin Man and Peach Hip Girl '98
Shogun Assassin 2: Lightning Swords of Death '73 ▶
Sin City '05
Spawn '97 ▶
Spider-Man '02 ▶
Spider-Man 2 '04 ▶
Spider-Man 3 '07
The Spirit '08
Spriggan '98
Steel '97
Stray Dog '91
Superman: The Movie '78 ▶
Superman 2 '80 ▶
Superman 3 '83
Superman 4: The Quest for Peace '87
Superman & the Mole Men '51
Superman Returns '06
Surrogates '09
Swamp Thing '82
Tales from the Crypt '72 ▶
Tales from the Crypt '89
Tales from the Crypt Presents Bordello of Blood '96
Tales from the Crypt Presents Demon Knight '94
Tetsujin 28 '04
XIII '08
30 Days of Night '07
300 '07
TMNT (Teenage Mutant Ninja Turtles) '07
Todd McFarlane's Spawn '97 ▶
Tomie '99
Uzumaki '00
V for Vendetta '06
Vampirella '96
Vault of Horror '73
Virus '98
Voices '08
Wanted '08 ▶
Wicked City '92
X-Men '00
X2: X-Men United '03 ▶
Yu-Gi-Oh! The Movie: Pyramid of Light '04
Zoom '06

Adapted from DC/Vertigo Comics

The Adventures of Captain Marvel '41
Batman '89 ▶
Batman and Robin '97
Batman Begins '05 ▶
Batman Forever '95 ▶
Batman Returns '92
Catwoman '04
The Dark Knight '08 ▶
The Flash '90
Jonah Hex '10
The League of Extraordinary Gentlemen '03
Superman: The Movie '78 ▶
Superman 2 '80 ▶
Superman 3 '83
Superman 4: The Quest for Peace '87
Superman & the Mole Men '51
Superman Returns '06
Swamp Thing '82
V for Vendetta '06
Watchmen '09

Adapted from Marvel Comics

Blade '72
Blade 2 '02
Blade: Trinity '04
Captain America '44
Captain America '79
Captain America '89
Captain America 2: Death Too Soon '79
Daredevil '03
Fantastic Four '05
Fantastic Four: Rise of the Silver Surfer '07
Ghost Rider '35
Hellboy II: The Golden Army '08 ▶
Hulk '03
The Incredible Hulk '08
Iron Man '08 ▶
Iron Man 2 '10
Men in Black '97 ▶
Men in Black 2 '02
The Punisher '04
Punisher: War Zone '08
Spider-Man '02 ▶
Spider-Man 2 '04 ▶
Spider-Man 3 '07
X-Men '00
X-Men Origins: Wolverine '09
X-Men: The Last Stand '06
X2: X-Men United '03 ▶

Adapted from Memoirs or Diaries

Angela's Ashes '99
Anna and the King '99
Anne Frank: The Whole Story '01 ▶
At First Sight '98
Bandit Queen '94
The Basketball Diaries '95
Belles on Their Toes '52
The Boys Are Back '09
A Business Affair '93
Caro Diario '93 ▶
Celeste '81 ▶
Churchill and the Generals '81
The Color of Freedom '07
Control '07
The Counterfeiters '07 ▶
Cowboy '58 ▶
Danger UXB '81
Daphne '07
The Diary of Anne Frank '59 ▶
The Diary of Anne Frank '08
The Diving Bell and the Butterfly '07 ▶
Doing Time '02
Downfall '04 ▶
Eat, Pray, Love '10
An Education '09 ▶
Edvard Munch '74
The Elegant Criminal '92
The Flame Trees of Thika '81 ▶
A Free Soul '31
The Gathering Storm '74
Girl, Interrupted '99
God is My Co-Pilot '45
Goodbye, Miss 4th of July '88
Gypsy '62 ▶
The Happy Hooker '75
The Happy Hooker Goes Hollywood '80
The Happy Hooker Goes to Washington '77
Haywire '80
Heart Beat '80
Heartland '81 ▶
Henry & June '90 ▶
How to Lose Friends & Alienate People '08
I Remember Mama '48 ▶
I Was Nineteen '68
I'll Cry Tomorrow '55 ▶
I'm Dancing as Fast as I Can '82
In Love and War '96
In Love and War '01
In the Name of the Father '93 ▶
Inside the Third Reich '82
Iris '01 ▶
Jacquot '91
Julia '77 ▶
Julie & Julia '09 ▶
Just Like a Woman '95
The Kid Stays in the Picture '02 ▶
Kings in Grass Castles '97
The Lady and the Duke '01
Last Call: The Final Chapter of F. Scott Fitzgerald '02
The Lawless Breed '52 ▶
Lost for Words '99 ▶
Maids of Wilko '79
Man on Wire '08
Marley & Me '08
Meetings with Remarkable Men '79
A Mighty Heart '07 ▶
Mommie Dearest '81
The Motorcycle Diaries '04 ▶
My Life and Times with Antonin Artaud '93 ▶
My Own Country '98
My Sister's Keeper '02
October Sky '99 ▶
Opium: Diary of a Madwoman '07
The Other Side of Heaven '02
Our Lady of the Assassins '01
Papa's Delicate Condition '63 ▶
The Passion of Ayn Rand '99
The Pianist '02 ▶
The Pillow Book '95
The Road from Coorain '02
Romulus, My Father '07 ▶
Seven Years in Tibet '97
Shot in the Heart '01 ▶
Sister Kenny '46 ▶
Stars and Stripes Forever '52 ▶
The Summer of Aviya '88
Sweet Nothing '96 ▶
Taking Woodstock '09
This Boy's Life '93 ▶
Touch the Top of the World '06
Under the Domim Tree '95
Village of Dreams '97
What's Love Got to Do with It? '93
When Did You Last See Your Father? '07
The Whole Wide World '96 ▶
Wish You Were Here '87 ▶
A Woman in Berlin '08
Yes Man '08

Adapted from Saturday Night Live

The Blues Brothers '80 ▶
Blues Brothers 2000 '98
Coneheads '93
It's Pat: The Movie '94
The Ladies Man '00
MacGruber '10
A Night at the Roxbury '98
Stuart Saves His Family '94
Superstar '99
Wayne's World '92 ▶
Wayne's World 2 '93

Adapted from Television

The A-Team '10
Absolutely Fabulous: The Last Shout '96
The Addams Family '91
Addams Family Values '93
The Adventures of Rocky & Bullwinkle '00
Aeon Flux '05
Alien Nation: Dark Horizon '94
Aqua Teen Hunger Force Colon Movie Film for Theaters '07
Astro Boy '09
The Avengers '98
Batman '66
Batman: Mask of the Phantasm '93
Baywatch the Movie: Forbidden Paradise '95
Bean '97 ▶
Beavis and Butt-Head Do America '96
The Beverly Hillbillies '93
Bewitched '05
Big Top Pee-wee '88
Bonanza: The Return '93
Boris and Natasha: The Movie '92
The Brady Bunch Movie '95 ▶
Car 54, Where Are You? '94
Charlie's Angels '00
Charlie's Angels: Full Throttle '03
Clifford's Really Big Movie '04
Coneheads '93
The Crawling Eye '58
Days of Wine and Roses '62 ▶
The Defenders: Payback '97
Dennis the Menace '93
Dennis the Menace Strikes Again '98
Doctor Who '96
Doogal '05
Dragnet '87
Dragonball: Evolution '09
Dudley Do-Right '99
The Dukes of Hazzard '05
The Extreme Adventures of Super Dave '98
Fat Albert '04
The Flintstones '94
The Flintstones in Viva Rock Vegas '00
Flipper '96 ▶
The Fugitive '93 ▶
Gargoyles, The Movie: The Heroes Awaken '94
George of the Jungle '97 ▶
Get Smart, Again! '89
Good Burger '97
Hannah Montana: The Movie '09
Here Come the Littles: The Movie '85
The Honeymooners '05
I Spy '02
The Invaders '95
Jackass: The Movie '02
Jetsons: The Movie '90
Jiminy Glick in LaLa Wood '05
Joe's Apartment '96
Kevin & Perry Go Large '00
The Key to Rebecca '85
Kids in the Hall: Brain Candy '96
Land of the Lost '09
Lassie '94
The Last Airbender '10
Leave It to Beaver '97
The Left-Handed Gun '58 ▶
The Lizzie McGuire Movie '03
Lost in Space '98
Maverick '94
McHale's Navy '64
McHale's Navy '97
McHale's Navy Joins the Air Force '65
Miami Vice '06
Mission: Impossible '96 ▶
Mission: Impossible 2 '00 ▶
The Mod Squad '99
Munster, Go Home! '66
My Favorite Martian '98
Mystery Science Theater 3000: The Movie '96
The Naked Gun: From the Files of Police Squad '88 ▶
Naked Gun 33 1/3: The Final Insult '94
Naked Gun 2 1/2: The Smell of Fear '91
Noah's Arc: Jumping the Broom '08
The Nude Bomb '80
Our Miss Brooks '56
Pee-wee's Big Adventure '85 ▶
Pennies from Heaven '81 ▶
The People Next Door '70
Phantom 2040 Movie: The Ghost Who Walks '95
Pokemon: The First Movie '99
Pootie Tang '01
Pufnstuf '70
Queen for a Day '51
Reno 911! Miami '07
Requiem for a Heavyweight '62 ▶
Rescue from Gilligan's Island '78
The Return of the Beverly Hillbillies '81
Ringmaster '98
Rugrats Go Wild! '03
Rugrats in Paris: The Movie '00 ▶
The Rugrats Movie '98 ▶
The Saint '68
Serenity '05 ▶
Sgt. Bilko '95
Sergeant Ryker '68
Sex and the City: The Movie '08
The Simpsons Movie '07 ▶
The Singing Detective '03
South Park: Bigger, Longer and Uncut '99
Speed Racer '08
Star Trek: The Motion Picture '79
Star Trek 2: The Wrath of Khan '82 ▶
Star Trek 3: The Search for Spock '84
Star Trek 4: The Voyage Home '86 ▶
Star Trek 5: The Final Frontier '89
Star Trek 6: The Undiscovered Country '91
Star Trek: First Contact '96 ▶
Star Trek: Generations '94 ▶
Star Trek: Insurrection '98
Star Trek: Nemesis '02
Stargate: Continuum '08
Starsky & Hutch '04
State of Play '09 ▶
Strange Frequency 2 '01
Strangers with Candy '06
S.W.A.T. '03
Tales from the Crypt Presents Bordello of Blood '96
Tales from the Crypt Presents Demon Knight '94
Thomas and the Magic Railroad '00
Thunder in Paradise 2 '94
Thunder in Paradise 3 '94
Twin Peaks: Fire Walk with Me '92
Underdog '07
The Untouchables '87 ▶
A Very Brady Sequel '96
Wackiest Wagon Train in the West '77
The Wild Thornberrys Movie '02 ▶
Wild Wild West '99
The X-Files '98
The X Files: I Want to Believe '08

Adapted from the Bible

Abraham '94
A.D. '85
The Bible '66
David '97
David and Bathsheba '51 ▶
The Decalogue '88 ▶
Esther '98
Godspell '73

▶ = rated three bones or higher

The Gospel According to St. Matthew '64 ▸
The Gospel of John '03
Jacob '94
Jeremiah '98
Jesus '00
Jesus Christ, Superstar '73 ▸
Jesus Christ Superstar '00
Joseph '95
Joseph and the Amazing Technicolor Dreamcoat '00 ▸
King David '85
King of Kings '27
The King of Kings '61 ▸
The Last Supper '76 ▸
Mary and Joseph: A Story of Faith '79
Mary, Mother of Jesus '99
The Messiah '75 ▸
The Miracle Maker: The Story of Jesus '00
Moses '76
Moses '96
Noah '98
Noah's Ark '99
The Passion of the Christ '04 ▸
Peter and Paul '81
Prince of Egypt '98 ▸
Salome '22
Salome '53
Salome '85
Samson and Delilah '50 ▸
Samson and Delilah '84
Samson and Delilah '96
Saul and David '64
Sins of Jezebel '54
Solomon '98
The Story of Jacob & Joseph '74 ▸
The Ten Commandments '23
The Ten Commandments '56 ▸

Andy Hardy

Andy Hardy Gets Spring Fever '39
Andy Hardy Meets Debutante '40
Andy Hardy's Double Life '42
Andy Hardy's Private Secretary '41
Life Begins for Andy Hardy '41 ▸
Love Finds Andy Hardy '38 ▸
Love Laughs at Andy Hardy '46

Angelique

Angelique '64
Angelique and the King '66
Angelique and the Sultan '68
Angelique: The Road to Versailles '65
Untamable Angelique '67

B/W & Color Combos

Amazon Women on the Moon '87
And Now My Love '74
Andrei Rublev '66 ▸
Antichrist '09
Awakenings of the Beast '68
The Blue Bird '40 ▸
Dead Again '91 ▸
Dixiana '30
D.O.A. '88
The 4th Dimension '06
Gods and Monsters '98 ▸
Hollywood, Je T'Aime '09
Hollywood Revue of 1929 '29
Ice Follies of 1939 '39
If... '69 ▸
I'll Never Forget You '51
It's a Great Life '29
JFK '91 ▸
Kafka '91
Kiss of the Spider Woman '85 ▸
Made in Heaven '87
A Man and a Woman '66 ▸
Martin '77 ▸
Mishima: A Life in Four Chapters '85 ▸
The Moon and Sixpence '43 ▸
Movie, Movie '78
Natural Born Killers '94
A Nightmare on Elm Street 4: Dream Master '88
Nixon '95 ▸
Portrait of Jennie '48 ▸
Rio Rita '29
Rumble Fish '83 ▸
Sally '29
Schindler's List '93 ▸
She's Gotta Have It '86 ▸
Stalker '79 ▸
Tetro '09
Transylvania Twist '89
Truth or Dare '91
Unzipped '94 ▸
Wings of Desire '88 ▸
The Wizard of Oz '39 ▸
The Women '39 ▸
Zelig '83 ▸

Batman

Batman '66
Batman '89 ▸
Batman and Robin '97
Batman Forever '95 ▸
Batman: Mask of the Phantasm '93
Batman Returns '92
The Dark Knight '08 ▸

Beach Party

Back to the Beach '87
Beach Blanket Bingo '65 ▸
Beach Party '63
Bikini Beach '64
Ghost in the Invisible Bikini '66
How to Stuff a Wild Bikini '65
Muscle Beach Party '64
Pajama Party '64

Beatlesfilm

Across the Universe '07
All You Need Is Cash '78 ▸
Backbeat '94 ▸
A Hard Day's Night '64 ▸
Help! '65 ▸
The Hours and Times '92 ▸
I Wanna Hold Your Hand '78
John & Yoko: A Love Story '85
Let It Be '70
Magical Mystery Tour '67
Yellow Submarine '68 ▸

Billy the Kid

Battling Outlaw '40
Billy the Kid '41
Billy the Kid in Santa Fe '41
Billy the Kid in Texas '40
Billy the Kid Returns '38
Billy the Kid Trapped '42
Billy the Kid Versus Dracula '66
BloodRayne 2: Deliverance '07
Border Badmen '45
Deadwood '65
Devil Riders '44
Frontier Outlaws '44
Gangster's Den '45
Gore Vidal's Billy the Kid '89
I Shot Billy the Kid '50
Law and Order '42
The Left-Handed Gun '58 ▸
The Mysterious Rider '42
Oath of Vengeance '44
The Outlaw '43
Outlaw of the Plains '46
Pat Garrett & Billy the Kid '73 ▸
Rustler's Hideout '44
Shadows of Death '45
Texas Trouble '41
Thundering Gunslingers '44
Trigger Men '41
Wild Horse Phantom '44
Young Guns '88
Young Guns 2 '90

Blondie

Blondie '38
Blondie Brings Up Baby '39
Blondie for Victory '42
Blondie Goes Latin '42
Blondie Goes to College '42
Blondie Has Trouble '40
Blondie Hits the Jackpot '49
Blondie in Society '41
Blondie Knows Best '46
Blondie Meets the Boss '39
Blondie On a Budget '40
Blondie Plays Cupid '40
Blondie Takes a Vacation '39
Blondie's Blessed Event '42
Footlight Glamour '43
It's a Great Life '43

Books to Film: Richard Adams

The Girl in a Swing '89
The Plague Dogs '82
Watership Down '78

Books to Film: Louisa May Alcott

Little Men '40
Little Men '98
Little Women '33 ▸
Little Women '49 ▸
Little Women '78
Little Women '94 ▸
An Old-Fashioned Thanksgiving '08

Books to Film: Nelson Algren

The Man with the Golden Arm '55 ▸
Walk on the Wild Side '62

Books to Film: Eric Ambler

Background to Danger '43 ▸
Hotel Reserve '44 ▸
Journey into Fear '42 ▸
The Mask of Dimitrios '44 ▸

Books to Film: Kingsley Amis

Lucky Jim '58
That Uncertain Feeling '41

Books to Film: Martin Amis

The Rachel Papers '89 ▸

Books to Film: Hans Christian Andersen

The Red Shoes '48 ▸
The Snow Queen '02

Books to Film: Maya Angelou

Georgia, Georgia '72
I Know Why the Caged Bird Sings '79 ▸

Books to Film: Isaac Asimov

Bicentennial Man '99
I, Robot '04
Isaac Asimov's Nightfall '00
Nightfall '88

Books to Film: Eliot Asinof

Breakout '75
Eight Men Out '88 ▸

Books to Film: Jane Austen

Bride & Prejudice '04
Emma '72
Emma '96 ▸
Emma '97 ▸
Emma '09
Lost in Austen '08
Mansfield Park '85
Mansfield Park '99
Mansfield Park '07
Northanger Abbey '87
Northanger Abbey '07
Persuasion '71
Persuasion '95 ▸
Persuasion '07
Pride and Prejudice '40 ▸
Pride and Prejudice '85
Pride and Prejudice '95 ▸
Pride and Prejudice '05 ▸
Sense and Sensibility '85
Sense and Sensibility '95 ▸
Sense & Sensibility '07

Books to Film: Honore de Balzac

Colonel Chabert '94
Cousin Bette '97
The Duchess of Langeais '07 ▸
Passion in the Desert '97
The True and the False '55

Books to Film: Russell Banks

Affliction '97 ▸
Sunshine '07
The Sweet Hereafter '96 ▸

Books to Film: Clive Barker

Candyman '92
Candyman 2: Farewell to the Flesh '94
Clive Barker's Book of Blood '08
Hellbound: Hellraiser 2 '88
Hellraiser '87
Hellraiser '09
Hellraiser 3: Hell on Earth '92
Hellraiser 4: Bloodline '95
Lord of Illusions '95
The Midnight Meat Train '08
Nightbreed '90
Rawhead Rex '87
Transmutations '85

Books to Film: Peter Benchley

The Beast '96
The Deep '77
Jaws '75 ▸

Books to Film: Thomas Berger

The Feud '90
Little Big Man '70 ▸
Neighbors '81

Books to Film: Ambrose Bierce

Eyes of the Panther '90
An Occurrence at Owl Creek Bridge/Coup de Grace '62

Books to Film: Maeve Binchy

Circle of Friends '94
How About You '07
Tara Road '05

Books to Film: Robert Bloch

The Skull '65
Torture Garden '67

Books to Film: Judy Blume

Forever '78

Books to Film: Ray Bradbury

The Beast from 20,000 Fathoms '53
Fahrenheit 451 '66 ▸
The Illustrated Man '69 ▸
It Came from Outer Space '53 ▸
The Martian Chronicles: Part 1 '79
The Martian Chronicles: Part 2 '79
The Martian Chronicles: Part 3 '79
Something Wicked This Way Comes '83
A Sound of Thunder '05
Walking on Air '87

Books to Film: Barbara Taylor Bradford

Hold the Dream '86
A Woman of Substance '84

Books to Film: Max Brand

Branded '50
The Desperadoes '43
Destry Rides Again '39 ▸
Justice Rides Again '32
My Outlaw Brother '51
Trailin' '21

Books to Film: The Brontes

Emily Bronte's Wuthering Heights '92
Jane Eyre '34
Jane Eyre '44 ▸
Jane Eyre '83 ▸
Jane Eyre '96 ▸
Jane Eyre '97
Jane Eyre '06
MTV's Wuthering Heights '03
The Tenant of Wildfell Hall '96
Wuthering Heights '39 ▸
Wuthering Heights '53
Wuthering Heights '70
Wuthering Heights '98
Wuthering Heights '09

Books to Film: Pearl S. Buck

China Sky '44
Dragon Seed '44
The Good Earth '37 ▸
Pavilion of Women '01

Books to Film: Charles Bukowski

Factotum '06 ▸
My Old Man '79

Books to Film: Frances Hodgson Burnett

Little Lord Fauntleroy '36 ▸
Little Lord Fauntleroy '80
Little Lord Fauntleroy '95
The Little Princess '39 ▸
The Little Princess '87
A Little Princess '95 ▸
The Secret Garden '49 ▸
The Secret Garden '84
The Secret Garden '87 ▸
The Secret Garden '93

Books to Film: W.R. Burnett

Arrowhead '53
The Badlanders '58
Dance Hall '41
Dark Command '40 ▸
High Sierra '41 ▸
I Died a Thousand Times '55
Law and Order '40
Law and Order '53
Little Caesar '30 ▸
The Whole Town's Talking '35 ▸
Wine, Women and Horses '37

Books to Film: Edgar Rice Burroughs

At the Earth's Core '76
Greystoke: The Legend of Tarzan, Lord of the Apes '84
The Land That Time Forgot '75
The Land That Time Forgot '09
The People That Time Forgot '77
Tarzan '99 ▸
Tarzan and His Mate '34 ▸
Tarzan and the Green Goddess '38
Tarzan and the Lost Safari '57
Tarzan and the She-Devil '53
Tarzan and the Slave Girl '50
Tarzan and the Trappers '58
Tarzan Escapes '36 ▸
Tarzan Finds a Son '39 ▸
Tarzan, the Ape Man '32 ▸
Tarzan, the Ape Man '81
Tarzan the Fearless '33
Tarzan the Magnificent '60
Tarzan's Fight for Life '58
Tarzan's Greatest Adventure '59
Tarzan's Hidden Jungle '55
Tarzan's Magic Fountain '48
Tarzan's New York Adventure '42
Tarzan's Peril '51
Tarzan's Revenge '38
Tarzan's Savage Fury '52
Tarzan's Secret Treasure '41

Books to Film: William Burroughs

Naked Lunch '91 ▸

Books to Film: James M. Cain

Butterfly '82
Double Indemnity '44 ▸
Girl in the Cadillac '94
Mildred Pierce '45 ▸
The Postman Always Rings Twice '46 ▸
The Postman Always Rings Twice '81
Slightly Scarlet '56

Books to Film: Truman Capote

ABC Stage 67: Truman Capote's A Christmas Memory '66
Breakfast at Tiffany's '61 ▸
Children On Their Birthdays '02
The Glass House '72 ▸
The Grass Harp '95
In Cold Blood '67 ▸
In Cold Blood '96
Other Voices, Other Rooms '95

Books to Film: Forrest Carter

The Education of Little Tree '97 ▸
The Outlaw Josey Wales '76 ▸

Books to Film: Barbara Cartland

Duel of Hearts '92
The Flame Is Love '79
The Lady and the Highwayman '89
Love Comes Lately '07

Books to Film: Willa Cather

My Antonia '94
O Pioneers! '91
The Song of the Lark '01

Books to Film: Raymond Chandler

The Big Sleep '46 ▸
The Big Sleep '78
The Falcon Takes Over '42
Farewell, My Lovely '75 ▸
The Finger Man '55
Lady in the Lake '46
The Long Goodbye '73 ▸
Marlowe '69
Murder, My Sweet '44 ▸

Books to Film: Paddy Chayefsky

Altered States '80 ▸
As Young As You Feel '51 ▸
The Catered Affair '56 ▸

Books to Film: John Cheever

Sorrows of Gin '79
The Swimmer '68 ▸

Books to Film: Agatha Christie

Agatha Christie's A Caribbean Mystery '83
Agatha Christie's Murder is Easy '82
Agatha Christie's Murder with Mirrors '85
Agatha Christie's Sparkling Cyanide '83
Agatha Christie's The Pale Horse '96
Agatha Christie's Thirteen at Dinner '85

▸ = rated three bones or higher

The Alphabet Murders *'65*
And Then There Were None *'45* ►
Appointment with Death *'88*
The Body in the Library *'84*
Death on the Nile *'78*
Endless Night *'71*
Evil under the Sun *'82*
Love from a Stranger *'37*
Love from a Stranger *'47*
The Mirror Crack'd *'80*
Murder Ahoy *'64*
Murder at the Gallop *'63* ►
A Murder Is Announced *'87*
Murder Most Foul *'65* ►
Murder on the Orient Express *'74* ►
Murder She Said *'62*
Ordeal by Innocence *'84*
A Pocketful of Rye *'87*
Ten Little Indians *'75*
Ten Little Indians *'89*
Witness for the Prosecution *'57* ►

Books to Film: Tom Clancy

Clear and Present Danger *'94*
The Hunt for Red October *'90* ►
Patriot Games *'92* ►
The Sum of All Fears *'02*

Books to Film: Mary Higgins Clark

Before I Say Goodbye *'03*
The Cradle Will Fall *'83*
A Cry in the Night *'93*
Double Vision *'92*
He Sees You When You're Sleeping *'02*
Terror Stalks the Class Reunion *'93*
We'll Meet Again *'02*

Books to Film: Arthur C. Clarke

Trapped in Space *'94*
2001: A Space Odyssey *'68* ►
2010: The Year We Make Contact *'84* ►

Books to Film: James Clavell

King Rat *'65* ►
Noble House *'88*
Shogun *'80* ►
Tai-Pan *'86*

Books to Film: Jackie Collins

The Bitch *'78*
The World Is Full of Married Men *'80*
Yesterday's Hero *'79*

Books to Film: Wilkie Collins

Basil *'98*
The Moonstone *'34*
The Moonstone *'72*
The Moonstone *'97* ►
The Woman in White *'97*

Books to Film: Richard Condon

Gun Crazy *'69*
The Manchurian Candidate *'62* ►
The Manchurian Candidate *'04* ►
Prizzi's Honor *'85* ►
Winter Kills *'79* ►

Books to Film: Joseph Conrad

Apocalypse Now *'79* ►
The Duellists *'77* ►
Face to Face *'52*
Gabrielle *'05*
Heart of Darkness *'93*
Lord Jim *'65* ►
Nostromo *'96*
The Rover *'67*
Sabotage *'36* ►
The Secret Agent *'96*
Swept from the Sea *'97*
Victory *'95*

Books to Film: Pat Conroy

Conrack *'74* ►
The Great Santini *'80* ►
The Lords of Discipline *'83*
The Prince of Tides *'91* ►

Books to Film: Robin Cook

Coma *'78* ►
Robin Cook's Invasion *'97*
Robin Cook's Terminal *'96*
Sphinx *'81*

Books to Film: Catherine Cookson

Catherine Cookson's Colour Blind *'98*
Catherine Cookson's The Black Candle *'92*
Catherine Cookson's The Black Velvet Gown *'92*
Catherine Cookson's The Cinder Path *'94*
Catherine Cookson's The Dwelling Place *'94*
Catherine Cookson's The Fifteen Streets *'90*
Catherine Cookson's The Gambling Man *'98*
Catherine Cookson's The Girl *'96*
Catherine Cookson's The Glass Virgin *'95*
Catherine Cookson's The Man Who Cried *'93*
Catherine Cookson's The Moth *'96*
Catherine Cookson's The Rag Nymph *'96*
Catherine Cookson's The Round Tower *'98*
Catherine Cookson's The Secret *'00* ►
Catherine Cookson's The Tide of Life *'96*
Catherine Cookson's The Wingless Bird *'97*
Catherine Cookson's Tilly Trotter *'99*

Books to Film: James Fenimore Cooper

The Deerslayer *'78*
The Last of the Mohicans *'20* ►
The Last of the Mohicans *'32*
The Last of the Mohicans *'36*
The Last of the Mohicans *'85*
The Last of the Mohicans *'92* ►
The Last of the Redmen *'47*
The Pathfinder *'94*
The Pioneers *'41*

Books to Film: Stephen Crane

Face to Face *'52*
The Red Badge of Courage *'51* ►

Books to Film: Michael Crichton

The Andromeda Strain *'71*
The Andromeda Strain *'08*
Congo *'95*
The Great Train Robbery *'79* ►
Jurassic Park *'93* ►
The Lost World: Jurassic Park 2 *'97*
Rising Sun *'93* ►
Sphere *'97*
The Terminal Man *'74*
The 13th Warrior *'99*
Timeline *'03*
Westworld *'73* ►

Books to Film: Michael Cunningham

A Home at the End of the World *'04*
The Hours *'02* ►

Books to Film: Clive Cussler

Raise the Titanic *'80*
Sahara *'05*

Books to Film: Roald Dahl

Charlie and the Chocolate Factory *'05* ►
Fantastic Mr. Fox *'09* ►
James and the Giant Peach *'96* ►
Matilda *'96* ►
Willy Wonka & the Chocolate Factory *'71* ►
The Witches *'90* ►

Books to Film: Miguel de Cervantes

Don Quixote *'35* ►
Man of La Mancha *'72*

Books to Film: Guy de Maupassant

A Day in the Country *'46* ►
Diary of a Madman *'63*
Le Plaisir *'52*
The Private Affairs of Bel Ami *'47* ►
The True and the False *'55*
A Woman Without Love *'51* ►

Books to Film: Daniel Defoe

The Amorous Adventures of Moll Flanders *'65*
Crusoe *'89*
Man Friday *'75*
Moll Flanders *'96*
Robinson Crusoe *'36*
Robinson Crusoe *'96*
Robinson Crusoe on Mars *'64*

Books to Film: Len Deighton

Bullet to Beijing *'95*
Funeral in Berlin *'66* ►
The Ipcress File *'65* ►
Midnight in Saint Petersburg *'97*

Books to Film: Phillip K. Dick

The Adjustment Bureau *'10*
Barjo *'93*
Blade Runner *'82* ►
Impostor *'02*
Minority Report *'02* ►
Next *'07*
Paycheck *'03*
A Scanner Darkly *'06*
Screamers *'96*
Screamers: The Hunting *'09*
Total Recall *'90* ►
Total Recall 2070: Machine Dreams *'99*

Books to Film: Charles Dickens

An American Carol *'08*
An American Christmas Carol *'79*
Bleak House *'85*
Bleak House *'05*
A Christmas Carol *'38* ►
A Christmas Carol *'51* ►
A Christmas Carol *'54*
A Christmas Carol *'84* ►
A Christmas Carol *'99*
A Christmas Carol *'09*
Cricket on the Hearth *'23*
David Copperfield *'35* ►
David Copperfield *'70*
David Copperfield *'99*
Great Expectations *'34*
Great Expectations *'46* ►
Great Expectations *'81*
Great Expectations *'89* ►
Great Expectations *'97*
Great Expectations *'99*
Great Expectations: The Untold Story *'87*
The Life and Adventures of Nicholas Nickleby *'81* ►
Little Dorrit *'08*
Little Dorrit, Film 1: Nobody's Fault *'88* ►
Little Dorrit, Film 2: Little Dorrit's Story *'88* ►
Martin Chuzzlewit *'94*
Ms. Scrooge *'97*
The Muppet Christmas Carol *'92*
The Mystery of Edwin Drood *'35*
The Mystery of Edwin Drood *'93*
Nicholas Nickleby *'46* ►
Nicholas Nickleby *'02* ►
The Old Curiosity Shop *'35*
The Old Curiosity Shop *'75*
The Old Curiosity Shop *'94*
The Old Curiosity Shop *'07*
Oliver! *'68* ►
Oliver & Company *'88*
Oliver Twist *'22* ►
Oliver Twist *'33*
Oliver Twist *'48* ►
Oliver Twist *'82* ►
Oliver Twist *'85*
Oliver Twist *'97*
Oliver Twist *'00* ►
Oliver Twist *'05* ►
Oliver Twist *'07*
Our Mutual Friend *'98*
The Pickwick Papers *'54*
Scrooge *'35* ►
Scrooge *'70*
A Tale of Two Cities *'36* ►
A Tale of Two Cities *'58* ►
A Tale of Two Cities *'80*
A Tale of Two Cities *'89* ►
Twist *'03* ►
Twisted *'96*

Books to Film: William Diehl

Primal Fear *'96*
Sharky's Machine *'81*

Books to Film: E.L. Doctorow

Billy Bathgate *'91*
Daniel *'83*
Ragtime *'81* ►

Books to Film: Fyodor Dostoyevski

The Brothers Karamazov *'58* ►
Crime and Punishment *'35* ►
Crime and Punishment *'70*
Crime and Punishment in Suburbia *'00*
Crime and Punishment, USA *'59*
Dostoevsky's Crime and Punishment *'99*
The Gambler *'97*
A Gentle Woman *'69*
La Vengeance d'une Femme *'89*
L'Idiot *'46*
Notes from Underground *'95*
The Possessed *'88*
White Nights *'57* ►

Books to Film: Sir Arthur Conan Doyle

The Adventures of Sherlock Holmes *'39*
The Crucifer of Blood *'91*
Dressed to Kill *'46*
The Fighting Eagle *'27*
The Hound of the Baskervilles *'39* ►
The Hound of the Baskervilles *'59*
The Hound of the Baskervilles *'77*
The Hound of the Baskervilles *'83*
The Hound of the Baskervilles *'00*
The Hound of the Baskervilles *'02* ►
House of Fear *'45*
The Lost World *'25*
The Lost World *'92*
The Lost World *'02*
Masks of Death *'86*
Murder at the Baskervilles *'37*
The Pearl of Death *'44*
Return to the Lost World *'93*
Robbers of the Sacred Mountain *'83*
Scarlet Claw *'44* ►
Sherlock Holmes *'22*
Sherlock Holmes *'09*
Sherlock Holmes and the Deadly Necklace *'62*
Sherlock Holmes and the Secret Weapon *'42* ►
The Sign of Four *'83*
The Sign of Four *'01*
The Silent Mr. Sherlock Holmes *'12*
Tales from the Darkside: The Movie *'90*
The Triumph of Sherlock Holmes *'35*
The Woman in Green *'49*

Books to Film: Daphne Du Maurier

The Birds *'63* ►
Don't Look Now *'73* ►
Frenchman's Creek *'44*
Frenchman's Creek *'98*
Jamaica Inn *'39*
Jamaica Inn *'82*
Rebecca *'40* ►
Rebecca *'97* ►

Books to Film: Alexandre Dumas

At Sword's Point *'51*
Black Magic *'49*
Camille *'21*
Camille *'36* ►
Camille 2000 *'69*
The Corsican Brothers *'42*
The Count of Monte Cristo *'12*
The Count of Monte Cristo *'34* ►
The Count of Monte Cristo *'74*
The Count of Monte Cristo *'99*
The Count of Monte Cristo *'02*
The Four Musketeers *'75* ►
The 4 Musketeers *'05*
The Iron Mask *'29*
The Man in the Iron Mask *'39* ►
The Man in the Iron Mask *'77* ►
The Man in the Iron Mask *'97*
The Man in the Iron Mask *'98* ►
Monte Cristo *'22*
The Musketeer *'01*
The Prince of Thieves *'48*
Queen Margot *'94* ►
The Return of the Musketeers *'89*
Robin Hood *'22* ►
Sword of Monte Cristo *'51*
The Three Musketeers *'16*
The Three Musketeers *'21* ►
The Three Musketeers *'33*
The Three Musketeers *'35*
The Three Musketeers *'39* ►
The Three Musketeers *'48*
The Three Musketeers *'74* ►

Books to Film: Lois Duncan

I Know What You Did Last Summer *'97* ►
I've Been Waiting for You *'98*
Killing Mr. Griffin *'97*
Summer of Fear *'78*

Books to Film: Dominick Dunne

An Inconvenient Woman *'91*

Books to Film: George Eliot

Daniel Deronda *'02*
Middlemarch *'93* ►
The Mill on the Floss *'37*
The Mill on the Floss *'97*
Silas Marner *'85* ►
A Simple Twist of Fate *'94*

Books to Film: Bret Easton Ellis

American Psycho *'99*
The Informers *'09*
Less Than Zero *'87*
The Rules of Attraction *'02*

Books to Film: James Ellroy

The Black Dahlia *'06*
Brown's Requiem *'98*
Cop *'88*
Dark Blue *'03* ►
L.A. Confidential *'97* ►
Street Kings *'08*

Books to Film: Howard Fast

The Crossing *'00*
Freedom Road *'79*

Books to Film: William Faulkner

Intruder in the Dust *'49* ►
Land of the Pharaohs *'55*
The Long, Hot Summer *'58* ►
The Long, Hot Summer *'86* ►
The Reivers *'69* ►
Tarnished Angels *'57* ►
Today We Live *'33*
Tomorrow *'72* ►
William Faulkner's Old Man *'97*

Books to Film: Edna Ferber

Cimarron *'31*
Cimarron *'60*
Come and Get It *'36* ►
Dinner at Eight *'33* ►
Dinner at Eight *'89*
Giant *'56* ►
Saratoga Trunk *'45*
Show Boat *'36* ►
Show Boat *'51*
Stage Door *'37* ►

Books to Film: Henry Fielding

Joseph Andrews *'77*
Tom Jones *'63* ►
Tom Jones *'98* ►

Books to Film: F. Scott Fitzgerald

The Curious Case of Benjamin Button *'08* ►
G *'02*
The Great Gatsby *'49*
The Great Gatsby *'74*
The Great Gatsby *'01*
The Last Time I Saw Paris *'54*
The Last Tycoon *'76* ►
Tender Is the Night *'55*

Books to Film: Gustov Flaubert

Madame Bovary *'34* ►
Madame Bovary *'49* ►
Madame Bovary *'91* ►
Madame Bovary *'00*
Salammbo *'14*

Books to Film: Ian Fleming

Casino Royale *'67*
Casino Royale *'06* ►
Chitty Chitty Bang Bang *'68*
Diamonds Are Forever *'71* ►
Dr. No *'62* ►
For Your Eyes Only *'81* ►
From Russia with Love *'63* ►
Goldfinger *'64* ►
License to Kill *'89* ►
Live and Let Die *'73*
The Living Daylights *'87* ►
The Man with the Golden Gun *'74*
Moonraker *'79*
Never Say Never Again *'83*
Octopussy *'83*
On Her Majesty's Secret Service *'69* ►
The Poppy Is Also a Flower *'66*
The Spy Who Loved Me *'77*

Thunderball '65
A View to a Kill '85
You Only Live Twice '67

Books to Film: Ken Follett

Capricorn One '78 ▸
Eye of the Needle '81
The Key to Rebecca '85
Lie Down with Lions '94

Books to Film: E.M. Forster

Howard's End '92 ▸
Maurice '87 ▸
A Passage to India '84 ▸
A Room with a View '86 ▸
A Room With a View '08
Where Angels Fear to Tread '91 ▸

Books to Film: Frederick Forsyth

The Day of the Jackal '73 ▸
The Dogs of War '81
The Fourth Protocol '87 ▸
The Odessa File '74
Two by Forsyth '86
Wolverine '96

Books to Film: John Fowles

The Collector '65 ▸
Ebony Tower '86
The French Lieutenant's Woman '81 ▸

Books to Film: Rumer Godden

Black Narcissus '47 ▸
In This House of Brede '75 ▸
The River '51 ▸

Books to Film: Nikolai Gogol

The Overcoat '59 ▸
Taras Bulba '62

Books to Film: William Goldman

Heat '87
Magic '78
Marathon Man '76 ▸
The Princess Bride '87 ▸

Books to Film: David Goodis

Dark Passage '47
Moon in the Gutter '83
Nightfall '56 ▸
Shoot the Piano Player '62 ▸

Books to Film: Elizabeth Goudge

Green Dolphin Street '47

Books to Film: Kenneth Grahame

The Adventures of Ichabod and Mr. Toad '49 ▸

Books to Film: Graham Greene

Across the Bridge '57
Beyond the Limit '83
Brighton Rock '47 ▸
The Comedians '67
End of the Affair '55
The End of the Affair '99 ▸
The Fallen Idol '49 ▸
The Fugitive '48 ▸
The Green Cockatoo '37
The Human Factor '79
Ministry of Fear '44 ▸
Monsignor Quixote '91
Our Man in Havana '59 ▸
The Quiet American '02 ▸
Strike It Rich '90
The Tenth Man '88
The Third Man '49 ▸
This Gun for Hire '42 ▸
This Gun for Hire '90
Travels with My Aunt '72

Books to Film: Zane Grey

Arizona Mahoney '36
The Border Legion '40
Desert Gold '36
Drift Fence '36
Dude Ranger '34
Fighting Caravans '31
Forlorn River '37
Helltown '38
The Light of Western Stars '30
Man of the Forest '33
Nevada '27
Nevada '44
Riders of the Purple Sage '25
Riders of the Purple Sage '96
Roll Along Cowboy '37
Thunder Mountain '35
Thunder Pass '37
To the Last Man '33
The Vanishing American '25
Wagon Wheels '34
West of the Pecos '45
When the West Was Young '32

Books to Film: John Grisham

The Chamber '96
Christmas With the Kranks '04
The Client '94
The Firm '93 ▸
John Grisham's The Rainmaker '97
A Painted House '03
The Pelican Brief '93
Runaway Jury '03 ▸
A Time to Kill '96 ▸

Books to Film: H. Rider Haggard

Allan Quatermain and the Lost City of Gold '86
King Solomon's Mines '37 ▸
King Solomon's Mines '50 ▸
King Solomon's Mines '85
She '25
She '35
She '65

Books to Film: Arthur Hailey

Airport '70 ▸
Hotel '67
Time Lock '57
Zero Hour! '57

Books to Film: Alex Haley

Malcolm X '92 ▸
Mama Flora's Family '98
Queen '93 ▸
Roots '77 ▸
Roots: The Gift '88
Roots: The Next Generation '79 ▸

Books to Film: Dashiell Hammett

After the Thin Man '36 ▸
Another Thin Man '39
The Dain Curse '78
The Glass Key '42 ▸
Hammett '82
The Maltese Falcon '31 ▸
The Maltese Falcon '41 ▸
No Good Deed '02
Satan Met a Lady '36
Shadow of the Thin Man '41 ▸
Song of the Thin Man '47
The Thin Man '34 ▸
The Thin Man Goes Home '44
Woman in the Shadows '34

Books to Film: Thomas Hardy

The Claim '00
Far from the Madding Crowd '67 ▸
Far from the Madding Crowd '97 ▸
Jude '96 ▸
Jude the Obscure '71
The Mayor of Casterbridge '03
The Return of the Native '94
The Scarlet Tunic '97
Tess '79 ▸
Tess of the D'Urbervilles '98
Tess of the D'Urbervilles '08
Under the Greenwood Tree '05

Books to Film: Harlequin Romances

Another Woman '94
At the Midnight Hour '95
The Awakening '95
Broken Lullaby '94
A Change of Place '94
Diamond Girl '98
Dreams Lost, Dreams Found '87
Hard to Forget '98
Love with a Perfect Stranger '86
Loving Evangeline '98
Recipe for Revenge '98
This Matter of Marriage '98
Treacherous Beauties '94
The Waiting Game '98
The Winds of Jarrah '83

Books to Film: Thomas Harris

Black Sunday '77
Hannibal '01
Manhunter '86 ▸
Red Dragon '02
The Silence of the Lambs '91 ▸

Books to Film: Jim Harrison

Carried Away '95
Dalva '95
Legends of the Fall '94
Revenge '90
Wolf '94

Books to Film: Nathaniel Hawthorne

The House of the Seven Gables '40
The Scarlet Letter '34
The Scarlet Letter '73 ▸
The Scarlet Letter '79 ▸
The Scarlet Letter '95
Twice-Told Tales '63 ▸

Books to Film: Ernest Hemingway

After the Storm '01
A Farewell to Arms '32 ▸
A Farewell to Arms '57
For Whom the Bell Tolls '43 ▸
Islands in the Stream '77
The Killers '46 ▸
The Killers '64
My Old Man '79
The Old Man and the Sea '58 ▸
The Old Man and the Sea '90
The Snows of Kilimanjaro '52 ▸
To Have & Have Not '44 ▸
Women & Men: Stories of Seduction '90

Books to Film: O. Henry

The Cisco Kid '94
The Gift of Love '90
Ruthless People '86 ▸

Books to Film: Patricia Highsmith

The American Friend '77 ▸
Purple Noon '60 ▸
Ripley's Game '02 ▸
Strangers on a Train '51 ▸
The Talented Mr. Ripley '99

Books to Film: Tony Hillerman

Coyote Waits '03
The Dark Wind '91
Skinwalker '02
A Thief of Time '04

Books to Film: James Hilton

Goodbye, Mr. Chips '02
Lost Horizon '37 ▸
Random Harvest '42 ▸
The Story of Dr. Wassell '44

Books to Film: S.E. Hinton

The Outsiders '83
Rumble Fish '83 ▸
Tex '82
That Was Then... This Is Now '85

Books to Film: Nick Hornby

About a Boy '02 ▸
An Education '09 ▸
Fever Pitch '96
Fever Pitch '05
High Fidelity '00 ▸

Books to Film: Victor Hugo

Delusions of Grandeur '76
The Halfback of Notre Dame '96
The Hunchback '97
The Hunchback of Notre Dame '23 ▸
The Hunchback of Notre Dame '39 ▸
The Hunchback of Notre Dame '57
The Hunchback of Notre Dame '82 ▸
The Hunchback of Notre Dame '96 ▸
Les Miserables '35 ▸
Les Miserables '52
Les Miserables '57 ▸
Les Miserables '78 ▸
Les Miserables '95
Les Miserables '97 ▸
Ruyblas '48

Books to Film: Evan Hunter (aka Ed McBain)

Blackboard Jungle '55 ▸
Blood Relatives '77
The Chisholms '79
Fuzz '72
High & Low '62 ▸
Last Summer '69
Strangers When We Meet '60
Stray Dog '49 ▸
The Young Savages '61

Books to Film: Fanny Hurst

Back Street '41
Back Street '61
Four Daughters '38 ▸
Imitation of Life '34
Imitation of Life '59 ▸
Young at Heart '54

Books to Film: John Irving

The Cider House Rules '99 ▸
The Door in the Floor '04 ▸
The Hotel New Hampshire '84
The World According to Garp '82 ▸

Books to Film: Washington Irving

The Adventures of Ichabod and Mr. Toad '49 ▸
The Legend of Sleepy Hollow '49
The Legend of Sleepy Hollow '79
The Legend of Sleepy Hollow '86 ▸
Rip van Winkle '85
Sleepy Hollow '99 ▸

Books to Film: Susan Isaacs

Compromising Positions '85
Shining Through '92

Books to Film: Rona Jaffe

Mazes and Monsters '82

Books to Film: John Jakes

The Bastard '78
Killer Elephants '76
North and South Book 1 '85 ▸
North and South Book 2 '86 ▸
The Rebels '79
The Seekers '79

Books to Film: Henry James

The American '01
The Bostonians '84
Celine and Julie Go Boating '74
Daisy Miller '74
The Europeans '79 ▸
The Golden Bowl '72 ▸
The Golden Bowl '00
The Green Room '78
The Haunting of Hell House '99
The Heiress '49 ▸
In the Shadows '98
The Innocents '61 ▸
L'Eleve '95
Lost Moment '47
The Nightcomers '72
P.D. James: The Murder Room '04
Portrait of a Lady '67
Portrait of a Lady '96 ▸
The Turn of the Screw '74
The Turn of the Screw '89
The Turn of the Screw '92
The Turn of the Screw '99
Washington Square '97 ▸
The Wings of the Dove '97 ▸

Books to Film: P.D. James

A Certain Justice '99
Children of Men '06 ▸
Devices and Desires '91 ▸
A Mind to Murder '96
P.D. James: Death in Holy Orders '03
Unsuitable Job for a Woman '82

Books to Film: Janette Oke

Love Comes Softly '03
Love Finds a Home '09
Love Takes Wing '09
Love's Abiding Joy '06
Love's Enduring Promise '04
Love's Long Journey '05
Love's Unending Legacy '07
Love's Unfolding Dream '07

Books to Film: James Jones

From Here to Eternity '53 ▸
From Here to Eternity '79
Some Came Running '58 ▸
The Thin Red Line '64
The Thin Red Line '98 ▸

Books to Film: James Joyce

Bloom '03
The Dead '87 ▸
Finnegan's Wake '65
James Joyce: A Portrait of the Artist as a Young Man '77 ▸
Ulysses '67

Books to Film: Franz Kafka

The Castle '68 ▸
The Trial '63 ▸
The Trial '93

Books to Film: Stephen King

Apt Pupil '97
Carrie '76 ▸
Carrie '02
Cat's Eye '85
Children of the Corn '84
Christine '84
Creepshow '82
Creepshow 2 '87
Cujo '83
The Dark Half '91
Dead Zone '83 ▸
The Dead Zone '02
Dolores Claiborne '94 ▸
Dreamcatcher '03
Firestarter '84
1408 '07
Graveyard Shift '90
The Green Mile '99
Hearts in Atlantis '01
The Lawnmower Man '92
The Mangler '94
Maximum Overdrive '86
Misery '90 ▸
The Mist '07 ▸
Needful Things '93
Pet Sematary '89
Return to Salem's Lot '87
Riding the Bullet '04
The Running Man '87
Salem's Lot '79
Salem's Lot '04
Secret Window '04
The Shawshank Redemption '94 ▸
The Shining '80
Silver Bullet '85
Sleepwalkers '92
Sometimes They Come Back '91
Sometimes They Come Back... Again '96
Stand by Me '86 ▸
Stephen King's Golden Years '91
Stephen King's It '90
Stephen King's Rose Red '02
Stephen King's The Langoliers '95
Stephen King's The Night Flier '96
Stephen King's The Stand '94
Stephen King's The Storm of the Century '99
Stephen King's The Tommyknockers '93
Stephen King's Thinner '96
Tales from the Darkside: The Movie '90
Trucks '97

Books to Film: W.P. Kinsella

Dance Me Outside '95
Field of Dreams '89 ▸

Books to Film: Rudyard Kipling

Captains Courageous '37 ▸
Captains Courageous '95
A Fool There Was '14
Gunga Din '39 ▸
The Jungle Book '42
Kim '50 ▸
Kim '84
The Man Who Would Be King '75 ▸
Rudyard Kipling's The Jungle Book '94
Rudyard Kipling's the Second Jungle Book: Mowgli and Baloo '97
They Watch '93
Wee Willie Winkie '37 ▸

Books to Film: Andrew Klavan

Don't Say a Word '01
True Crime '99
White of the Eye '88 ▸

Books to Film: Dean R. Koontz

Dean Koontz's Black River '01
Dean Koontz's Mr. Murder '98
Demon Seed '77 ▸
Hideaway '94
Intruder '76
Phantoms '97
Servants of Twilight '91
Watchers '88
Watchers Reborn '98
Whispers '89

▸ = rated three bones or higher

Books to Film: Judith Krantz

Mistral's Daughter *'84*
Princess Daisy *'83*
Scruples *'80*

Books to Film: Louis L'Amour

The Burning Hills *'56*
Cancel My Reservation *'72*
Conagher *'91*
Crossfire Trail *'01* ►
The Diamond of Jeru *'01*
Heller in Pink Tights *'60*
Hondo *'53* ►
The Quick and the Dead *'87*
The Sacketts *'79*
The Shadow Riders *'82*
Shalako *'68*
Stranger on Horseback *'55*

Books to Film: Ring Lardner

Alibi Ike *'35*
Champion *'49* ►

Books to Film: D.H. Lawrence

Kangaroo *'86* ►
Lady Chatterley *'92*
Lady Chatterley *'06* ►
Lady Chatterley's Lover *'55*
Lady Chatterley's Lover *'81*
The Rainbow *'89* ►
The Rocking Horse Winner *'49*
Trespasser *'81*
The Virgin and the Gypsy *'70*
The Widowing of Mrs. Holroyd *'95*
Women in Love *'70* ►
Young Lady Chatterly 2 *'85*

Books to Film: John Le Carre

The Constant Gardener *'05* ►
The Little Drummer Girl *'84* ►
The Looking Glass War *'69*
A Murder of Quality *'90*
A Perfect Spy *'88*
The Russia House *'90*
Smiley's People *'82*
The Spy Who Came in from the Cold *'65* ►
The Tailor of Panama *'00* ►
Tinker, Tailor, Soldier, Spy *'80* ►

Books to Film: Harper Lee

To Kill a Mockingbird *'62* ►

Books to Film: Dennis Lehane

Shutter Island *'09* ►

Books to Film: Elmore Leonard

The Ambassador *'84*
Be Cool *'05*
The Big Bounce *'69*
The Big Bounce *'04*
Cat Chaser *'90*
Elmore Leonard's Gold Coast *'97*
52 Pick-Up *'86*
Get Shorty *'95* ►
Glitz *'88*
Hombre *'67* ►
Jackie Brown *'97* ►
Killshot *'09*
Last Stand at Saber River *'96*
Mr. Majestyk *'74*
Out of Sight *'98* ►
Pronto *'97*
Stick *'85*
3:10 to Yuma *'57* ►
3:10 to Yuma *'07* ►
Touch *'96*
Valdez Is Coming *'71*

Books to Film: Ira Levin

The Boys from Brazil *'78*
A Kiss Before Dying *'91*
Rosemary's Baby *'68* ►
Sliver *'93*
The Stepford Wives *'75* ►
The Stepford Wives *'04*

Books to Film: Sinclair Lewis

Ann Vickers *'33*
Arrowsmith *'32*
Dodsworth *'36* ►
Elmer Gantry *'60* ►
There Will Be Blood *'07* ►

Books to Film: C.S. Lewis

The Chronicles of Narnia *'89*
The Chronicles of Narnia: Prince Caspian *'08*
The Chronicles of Narnia: The Lion, the Witch and the Wardrobe *'05*

Books to Film: Astrid Lindgren

Brothers Lionheart *'77*
The Children of Noisy Village *'86*
The Land of Faraway *'87*
More about the Children of Noisy Village *'87*
The New Adventures of Pippi Longstocking *'88*
Pippi Goes on Board *'69*
Pippi in the South Seas *'70*
Pippi Longstocking *'69*
Pippi on the Run *'70*

Books to Film: Jack London

The Assassination Bureau *'69* ►
Barricade *'49*
Burning Daylight *'28*
Call of the Wild *'72*
Call of the Wild *'93*
The Fighter *'52* ►
Great Adventure *'75*
Jack London's The Call of the Wild *'97*
The Legend of Sea Wolf *'75*
The Legend of the Sea Wolf *'58*
Legends of the North *'95*
The Mutiny of the Elsinore *'39*
The Sea Wolf *'41* ►
The Sea Wolf *'93*
Tales of the Klondike: In a Far Country *'87*
Tales of the Klondike: Race for Number One *'87*
Tales of the Klondike: The Scorn of Women *'87*
Tales of the Klondike: The Unexpected *'87*
Torture Ship *'39*
White Fang *'91* ►
White Fang and the Hunter *'85*
Wolf Call *'39*

Books to Film: H.P. Lovecraft

Beyond the Wall of Sleep *'06*
Blood Island *'68*
Bride of Re-Animator *'89*
Chill *'06*
Cthulhu *'08*
Cthulhu Mansion *'91*
The Curse *'87*
Die, Monster, Die! *'65*
The Dunwich Horror *'70*
From Beyond *'86* ►
The Haunted Palace *'63*
H.P. Lovecraft's Necronomicon: Book of the Dead *'93*
Lurking Fear *'94*
Re-Animator *'84* ►
The Resurrected *'91*
The Sinister Invasion *'68*
The Unnamable *'88*
The Unnamable 2: The Statement of Randolph Carter *'92*

Books to Film: Robert Ludlum

The Apocalypse Watch *'97*
The Bourne Identity *'88* ►
The Bourne Identity *'02* ►
The Bourne Supremacy *'04* ►
The Bourne Ultimatum *'07* ►
The Hades Factor *'06*
The Holcroft Covenant *'85*
The Osterman Weekend *'83*

Books to Film: Peter Maas

King of the Gypsies *'78*
Marie *'85* ►
Serpico *'73* ►
Vipers *'08*

Books to Film: Alistair MacLean

Bear Island *'80*
Breakheart Pass *'76*
Caravan to Vaccares *'74*
Detonator *'93*
Detonator 2: Night Watch *'95*
Force 10 from Navarone *'78*
Golden Rendezvous *'77*
The Guns of Navarone *'61* ►
Ice Station Zebra *'68*
Puppet on a Chain *'72*
River of Death *'90*
When Eight Bells Toll *'71*
Where Eagles Dare *'68* ►

Books to Film: Norman Mailer

The Executioner's Song *'82*
Marilyn: The Untold Story *'80* ►
The Naked and the Dead *'58*
Pursuit *'72* ►
Tough Guys Don't Dance *'87*

Books to Film: Bernard Malamud

The Angel Levine *'70*
The Assistant *'97*
The Fixer *'68* ►
The Natural *'84* ►
Shrek Forever After *'10*
The Tenants *'06*

Books to Film: Richard Matheson

The Box *'09*
Cold Sweat *'71*
Duel *'71* ►
I Am Legend *'07* ►
Icy Breasts *'75* ►
The Incredible Shrinking Man *'57* ►
The Last Man on Earth *'64*
The Legend of Hell House *'73* ►
Omega Man *'71*
Somewhere in Time *'80*
Stir of Echoes *'99*
What Dreams May Come *'98*
Young Warriors *'83*

Books to Film: W. Somerset Maugham

Adorable Julia *'62*
Beachcomber *'38* ►
Being Julia *'04* ►
Dirty Gertie from Harlem U.S.A. *'46*
Encore *'52* ►
The Letter *'40* ►
Miss Sadie Thompson *'53* ►
The Moon and Sixpence *'43* ►
Of Human Bondage *'34* ►
Of Human Bondage *'64*
The Painted Veil *'34*
The Painted Veil *'06*
Rain *'32*
The Razor's Edge *'46* ►
The Razor's Edge *'84*
Sadie Thompson *'28* ►
Trio *'50* ►
Up at the Villa *'00*

Books to Film: Cormac McCarthy

All the Pretty Horses *'00*
No Country for Old Men *'07* ►
The Road *'09*

Books to Film: Colleen McCullough

An Indecent Obsession *'85*
The Thorn Birds *'83* ►
Tim *'79*

Books to Film: Ian McEwan

Atonement *'07* ►
The Cement Garden *'93*
The Comfort of Strangers *'91* ►
The Innocent *'93*

Books to Film: Terry McMillan

Disappearing Acts *'00*
How Stella Got Her Groove Back *'98*
Waiting to Exhale *'95* ►

Books to Film: Larry McMurtry

The Best Little Whorehouse in Texas *'82*
Comanche Moon *'08*
Hud *'63* ►
Larry McMurtry's Dead Man's Walk *'96*
The Last Picture Show *'71* ►
Lonesome Dove *'89* ►
Terms of Endearment *'83* ►
Texasville *'90*

Books to Film: Herman Melville

Bartleby *'70*
Bartleby *'01*
Enchanted Island *'58*
Moby Dick *'56* ►
Moby Dick *'98*
Pola X *'99*

Books to Film: James Michener

The Bridges at Toko-Ri *'55* ►
Centennial *'78* ►
Dynasty *'76*
Hawaii *'66* ►
Return to Paradise *'53*
Sayonara *'57* ►
Texas *'94*
Until They Sail *'57*

Books to Film: Sue Miller

Family Pictures *'93* ►
The Good Mother *'88*
Inventing the Abbotts *'97*

Books to Film: L.M. Montgomery

Anne of Avonlea *'87* ►
Anne of Green Gables *'34* ►
Anne of Green Gables *'85* ►
Lantern Hill *'90*

Books to Film: Brian Moore

Black Robe *'91* ►
Catholics *'73* ►
Cold Heaven *'92*
The Lonely Passion of Judith Hearne *'87* ►

Books to Film: Vladimir Nabokov

Despair *'78* ►
Lolita *'62* ►
Lolita *'97*
The Luzhin Defence *'00*

Books to Film: John Nichols

The Milagro Beanfield War *'88* ►
The Sterile Cuckoo *'69* ►
The Wizard of Loneliness *'88*

Books to Film: Joyce Carol Oates

Blonde *'01*
Foxfire *'96*
Smooth Talk *'85* ►

Books to Film: John O'Hara

Butterfield 8 *'60* ►
From the Terrace *'60*
Pal Joey *'57* ►
Ten North Frederick *'58*

Books to Film: George Orwell

Animal Farm *'99*
A Merry War *'97* ►
1984 *'56* ►
1984 *'84* ►

Books to Film: Marcel Pagnol

The Baker's Wife *'33* ►
Fanny *'32* ►
Jean de Florette *'87* ►
Manon of the Spring *'87* ►
Marius *'31* ►
My Father's Glory *'91* ►
My Mother's Castle *'91* ►
Topaze *'33* ►

Books to Film: Chuck Palahniuk

Choke *'08*
Fight Club: *' '99* ►

Books to Film: Robert B. Parker

Appaloosa *'08* ►
Jesse Stone: Death in Paradise *'06*
Jesse Stone: Night Passage *'06*
Jesse Stone: Sea Change *'07*
Jesse Stone: Stone Cold *'05*
Jesse Stone: Thin Ice *'09*
Monte Walsh *'03*
Poodle Springs *'98*
Small Vices: A Spenser Mystery *'99*
Spenser: A Savage Place *'94*
Spenser: Ceremony *'93*
Spenser: Pale Kings & Princes *'94*
Spenser: The Judas Goat *'94*
Thin Air *'00*

Books to Film: James Patterson

Along Came a Spider *'01*
Child of Darkness, Child of Light *'91*
Kiss the Girls *'97*

Books to Film: Jodi Picoult

My Sister's Keeper *'09*
Plain Truth *'04*
The Tenth Circle *'08*

Books to Film: Nicholas Pileggi

Casino *'95* ►
Goodfellas *'90* ►

Books to Film: Edgar Allan Poe

The Bells *'26* ►
The Black Cat *'34* ►
The Black Cat *'81*
Dr. Tarr's Torture Dungeon *'75*
The Fall of the House of Usher *'49*
The Fall of the House of Usher *'60* ►
The Fall of the House of Usher *'80*
The Haunted Palace *'63*
Haunting Fear *'91*
The Haunting of Morella *'91*
The House of Usher *'88*
The House of Usher *'06*
Jaws of Justice *'33*
La Chute de la Maison Usher *'28* ►
The Living Coffin *'58*
Manfish *'56*
Masque of the Red Death *'65* ►
Masque of the Red Death *'89*
Masque of the Red Death *'90*
Murders in the Rue Morgue *'32*
Murders in the Rue Morgue *'71*
The Murders in the Rue Morgue *'86* ►
The Oblong Box *'69*
The Oval Portrait *'88*
The Pit and the Pendulum *'61* ►
The Pit & the Pendulum *'91*
Premature Burial *'62*
The Raven *'15*
The Raven *'63* ►
The Raven *'07*
The Spectre of Edgar Allen Poe *'73*
Spirits of the Dead *'68* ►
Tales of Terror *'62*
The Tell-Tale Heart *'60*
Tomb of Ligeia *'64* ►
The Torture Chamber of Dr. Sadism *'69*
Two Evil Eyes *'90*
Web of the Spider *'70*

Books to Film: Katherine Anne Porter

Noon Wine *'84* ►
Ship of Fools *'65* ►

Books to Film: Richard Price

Bloodbrothers *'78*
Clockers *'95* ►
Freedomland *'06*
Wanderers *'79* ►

Books to Film: Mario Puzo

The Godfather *'72* ►
The Godfather, Part 2 *'74* ►
The Godfather, Part 3 *'90* ►
The Last Don *'97*
The Sicilian *'87*

Books to Film: Ruth Rendell

Alias Betty *'01*
The Bridesmaid *'04*
A Dark Adapted Eye *'93* ►
A Demon in My View *'92*
A Fatal Inversion *'92*
Gallowglass *'95* ►
La Ceremonie *'95* ►
Live Flesh *'97* ►

Books to Film: Anne Rice

Anne Rice's The Feast of All Saints *'01*
Exit to Eden *'94*
Interview with the Vampire *'94*
Queen of the Damned *'02*

Books to Film: Mordecai Richler

The Apprenticeship of Duddy Kravitz *'74* ►
Jacob Two Two Meets the Hooded Fang *'99*
Joshua Then and Now *'85* ►

Books to Film: Harold Robbins

The Adventurers *'70*
The Betsy *'78*
The Carpetbaggers *'64*
King Creole *'58*
The Lonely Lady *'83*
Nevada Smith *'66*
Never Love a Stranger *'58*
Stiletto *'69*
Where Love Has Gone *'64*

Books to Film: Nora Roberts

Angels Fall *'07*
Blue Smoke *'07*
Carolina Moon *'07*
High Noon *'09*
Magic Moments *'89*
Midnight Bayou *'09*

► = rated three bones or higher

Montana Sky '07
Tribute '09

Books to Film: Sax Rohmer
Brides of Fu Manchu '66
The Castle of Fu Manchu '68
Daughter of the Dragon '31
The Fiendish Plot of Dr. Fu Manchu '80
Kiss and Kill '68
The Mask of Fu Manchu '32
The Mysterious Dr. Fu Manchu '29
The Return of Dr. Fu Manchu '30
The Vengeance of Fu Manchu '67

Books to Film: Philip Roth
Elegy '08
Goodbye Columbus '69 ▸
The Human Stain '03
Portnoy's Complaint '72

Books to Film: J.K. Rowling
Harry Potter and the Chamber of Secrets '02 ▸
Harry Potter and the Goblet of Fire '05 ▸
Harry Potter and the Half-Blood Prince '09
Harry Potter and the Order of the Phoenix '07
Harry Potter and the Prisoner of Azkaban '04
Harry Potter and the Sorcerer's Stone '01 ▸

Books to Film: Damon Runyon
Big Street '42
Bloodhounds of Broadway '52
Bloodhounds of Broadway '89
40 Pounds of Trouble '62
Guys and Dolls '55 ▸
It Ain't Hay '43
Lady for a Day '33 ▸
The Lemon Drop Kid '51
Little Miss Marker '34 ▸
Little Miss Marker '80
Money from Home '53
Pocketful of Miracles '61 ▸
Sorrowful Jones '49

Books to Film: Rafael Sabatini
Bardelys the Magnificent '26
The Black Swan '42 ▸
Captain Blood '35 ▸
Christopher Columbus '49
Scaramouche '23
Scaramouche '52 ▸

Books to Film: Sir Walter Scott
Ivanhoe '52 ▸
Ivanhoe '82
Ivanhoe '97 ▸
King Richard and the Crusaders '54
Quentin Durward '55

Books to Film: Erich Segal
Love Story '70 ▸
Man, Woman & Child '83
Oliver's Story '78
Only Love '98

Books to Film: Hubert Selby, Jr.
Last Exit to Brooklyn '90 ▸
Requiem for a Dream '00 ▸

Books to Film: Irwin Shaw
Easy Living '49
Two Weeks in Another Town '62
The Young Lions '58 ▸

Books to Film: Sidney Sheldon
The Naked Face '84
The Other Side of Midnight '77
Rage of Angels '83
Rage of Angels: The Story Continues '86
Sidney Sheldon's Bloodline '79
Windmills of the Gods '88

Books to Film: Mary Shelley
The Bride of Frankenstein '35 ▸
Frankenstein '31 ▸
Frankenstein '73
Frankenstein '82
Frankenstein '93
Frankenstein Unbound '90 ▸
Mary Shelley's Frankenstein '94

Books to Film: Jean Shepherd
A Christmas Story '83 ▸
My Summer Story '94
Ollie Hopnoodle's Haven of Bliss '88

Books to Film: Georges Simenon
All Good Things '09
Betty '92
The Brothers Rico '57
Cop-Out '67
Man on the Eiffel Tower '48 ▸
Monsieur Hire '89 ▸
Paris Express '53
Red Lights '04 ▸

Books to Film: Nicholas Sparks
Dear John '10
The Last Song '10
Message in a Bottle '98
The Notebook '04
A Walk to Remember '02

Books to Film: Mickey Spillane
Girl Hunters '63
I, the Jury '82
Margin for Murder '81

Books to Film: Danielle Steel
Danielle Steel's Changes '91
Danielle Steel's Daddy '91
Danielle Steel's Fine Things '90
Danielle Steel's Heartbeat '93
Danielle Steel's Kaleidoscope '90
Danielle Steel's Palomino '91
Danielle Steel's Star '93
Now and Forever '82
The Promise '79
Safe Harbour '07

Books to Film: John Steinbeck
Cannery Row '82
East of Eden '54 ▸
East of Eden '80
The Grapes of Wrath '40 ▸
Lifeboat '44 ▸
Of Mice and Men '39 ▸
Of Mice and Men '81 ▸
Of Mice and Men '92 ▸
The Pearl '48 ▸
The Red Pony '49 ▸
The Red Pony '76 ▸
Tortilla Flat '42 ▸

Books to Film: Stendhal
La Chartreuse de Parme '48
The Red and the Black '57 ▸
Vanina Vanini '61 ▸

Books to Film: Robert Louis Stevenson
Abbott and Costello Meet Dr. Jekyll and Mr. Hyde '52
Adventure Island '47
Black Arrow '48 ▸
The Body Snatcher '45 ▸
Dr. Jekyll and Mr. Hyde '20 ▸
Dr. Jekyll and Mr. Hyde '32 ▸
Dr. Jekyll and Mr. Hyde '41 ▸
Dr. Jekyll and Mr. Hyde '68
Dr. Jekyll and Mr. Hyde '73
Dr. Jekyll and Mr. Hyde '08
Dr. Jekyll and Sister Hyde '71
The Ebb-Tide '97
I, Monster '71 ▸
Jekyll '07
Jekyll and Hyde '90
Jekyll & Hyde... Together Again '82
Kidnapped '48
Kidnapped '60
Kidnapped '95
Kidnapped '05 ▸
Man with Two Heads '72
The Master of Ballantrae '53
Muppet Treasure Island '96
Robert Louis Stevenson's The Game of Death '99
St. Ives '98
Strange Case of Dr. Jekyll & Mr. Hyde '68
Strange Case of Dr. Jekyll & Mr. Hyde '89
The Strange Case of Dr. Jekyll and Mr. Hyde '06
The Strange Door '51
Treasure Island '34 ▸
Treasure Island '50 ▸
Treasure Island '72
Treasure Island '89
Treasure Island '99
Treasure Planet '02
The Wrong Box '66 ▸

Books to Film: Bram Stoker
Blood from the Mummy's Tomb '71
Bram Stoker's Dracula '92
Bram Stoker's Shadowbuilder '98
Bram Stoker's The Mummy '97
Burial of the Rats '95
Count Dracula '71
Count Dracula '77
Dracula (Spanish Version) '31
Dracula '31 ▸
Dracula '73
Dracula '79
Dracula '06
The Horror of Dracula '58 ▸
The Lair of the White Worm '88 ▸
Nosferatu '22 ▸
Nosferatu the Vampyre '79
Tomb '86
Van Helsing '04 ▸

Books to Film: Harriet Beecher Stowe
Uncle Tom's Cabin '14
Uncle Tom's Cabin '27
Uncle Tom's Cabin '69
Uncle Tom's Cabin '87

Books to Film: Jacqueline Susann
The Love Machine '71
Once Is Not Enough '75

Books to Film: Jonathan Swift
Gulliver's Travels '39
Gulliver's Travels '77
Gulliver's Travels '95
The Three Worlds of Gulliver '59

Books to Film: William Makepeace Thackeray
Barry Lyndon '75 ▸
Becky Sharp '35
Vanity Fair '32
Vanity Fair '67
Vanity Fair '99
Vanity Fair '04

Books to Film: Paul Theroux
Half Moon Street '86
The Mosquito Coast '86
Saint Jack '79 ▸

Books to Film: Jim Thompson
After Dark, My Sweet '90 ▸
Coup de Torchon '81 ▸
The Getaway '72
The Getaway '93
The Grifters '90 ▸
Hit Me '96
The Kill-Off '90
The Killer Inside Me '10
This World, Then the Fireworks '97

Books to Film: Roderick Thorp
The Detective '68 ▸
Devlin '92
Die Hard '88 ▸
Rainbow Drive '90

Books to Film: James Thurber
The Battle of the Sexes '60 ▸
Billy Liar '63 ▸
The Secret Life of Walter Mitty '47 ▸

Books to Film: J.R.R. Tolkien
The Hobbit '78 ▸
The Lord of the Rings '78
Lord of the Rings: The Fellowship of the Ring '01 ▸
Lord of the Rings: The Two Towers '02 ▸
Lord of the Rings: The Return of the King '03 ▸
The Return of the King '80

Books to Film: Leo Tolstoy
Anna Karenina '35 ▸
Anna Karenina '48
Anna Karenina '85
Anna Karenina '00
The Kreutzer Sonata '08
The Last Gangster '37
Leo Tolstoy's Anna Karenina '96
Night Sun '90
Prisoner of the Mountains '96 ▸
War and Peace '56
War and Peace '68 ▸
War and Peace '73

Books to Film: Scott Turow
Presumed Innocent '90 ▸

Books to Film: Mark Twain
The Adventures of Huck Finn '93 ▸
The Adventures of Huckleberry Finn '39 ▸
The Adventures of Huckleberry Finn '60
The Adventures of Huckleberry Finn '78
The Adventures of Huckleberry Finn '85
The Adventures of Tom Sawyer '38 ▸
The Adventures of Tom Sawyer '73
Arthur's Quest '99
Ava's Magical Adventure '94
A Connecticut Yankee '31 ▸
A Connecticut Yankee in King Arthur's Court '49
A Connecticut Yankee in King Arthur's Court '89
Huck and the King of Hearts '93
Huckleberry Finn '74
Huckleberry Finn '75
Huckleberry Finn '81
The Innocents Abroad '84
A Kid in King Arthur's Court '95
A Knight in Camelot '98
A Million to Juan '94
The Modern Adventures of Tom Sawyer '99
The Mysterious Stranger '82
The Prince and the Pauper '37 ▸
The Prince and the Pauper '62
The Prince and the Pauper '78
The Prince and the Pauper '01
The Prince and the Pauper '07
The Prince and the Surfer '99
The Private History of a Campaign That Failed '81
Pudd'nhead Wilson '84
Tom and Huck '95 ▸
Tom Sawyer '30 ▸
Tom Sawyer '73
Unidentified Flying Oddball '79
A Young Connecticut Yankee in King Arthur's Court '95

Books to Film: Anne Tyler
The Accidental Tourist '88 ▸
Breathing Lessons '94 ▸
Earthly Possessions '99
Saint Maybe '98 ▸

Books to Film: John Updike
Roommate '84
Too Far to Go '79 ▸
The Witches of Eastwick '87

Books to Film: Leon Uris
Battle Cry '55 ▸
Exodus '60 ▸
QB VII '74 ▸
Topaz '69 ▸

Books to Film: Jules Verne
Around the World in 80 Days '56 ▸
Around the World in 80 Days '89
Around the World in 80 Days '04
Around the World in a Daze '63
Captain Nemo and the Underwater City '69
800 Leagues Down the Amazon '93
Five Weeks in a Balloon '62
From the Earth to the Moon '58
In Search of the Castaways '62 ▸
Journey to the Center of the Earth '59 ▸
Journey to the Center of the Earth '88
Journey to the Center of the Earth '99
Journey to the Center of the Earth '08
Light at the Edge of the World '71
Master of the World '61
Mysterious Island '61 ▸
On the Comet '68 ▸
Those Fantastic Flying Fools '67
20,000 Leagues under the Sea '16 ▸
20,000 Leagues under the Sea '54 ▸
20,000 Leagues Under the Sea '97
Where Time Began '77

Books to Film: Kurt Vonnegut
Breakfast of Champions '98
D.P. '85
Kurt Vonnegut's Harrison Bergeron '95
Mother Night '96 ▸
Slapstick of Another Kind '84
Slaughterhouse Five '72
Who Am I This Time? '82 ▸

Books to Film: Alice Walker
The Color Purple '85 ▸

Books to Film: Edgar Wallace
The Black Abbot '63
Chamber of Horrors '40
Creature with the Blue Hand '70
Curse of the Yellow Snake '63
Dead Eyes of London '61
Door with the Seven Locks '62
Forger of London '61
The Human Monster '39
The Indian Scarf '63
Mr. Reeder in Room 13 '38
The Mysterious Magician '65
The Secret Four '40
Secret of the Black Trunk '62
The Squeaker '37
The Squeaker '65
The Strange Countess '61
The Terror '38

Books to Film: Joseph Wambaugh
The Black Marble '79 ▸
The Choirboys '77
Echoes in the Darkness '87
The Glitter Dome '84
The New Centurions '72
The Onion Field '79 ▸

Books to Film: Evelyn Waugh
Brideshead Revisited '81 ▸
Brideshead Revisited '08
Bright Young Things '03
A Handful of Dust '88
The Loved One '65
Sword of Honour '01

Books to Film: H.G. Wells
Empire of the Ants '77
First Men in the Moon '64
Food of the Gods '76
Food of the Gods: Part 2 '88
Half a Sixpence '67
The History of Mr. Polly '07
The Invisible Man '33 ▸
The Invisible Man's Revenge '44
The Island of Dr. Moreau '77
The Island of Dr. Moreau '96
Island of Lost Souls '32 ▸
Kipps '41 ▸
La Merveilleuse Visite '74
The Man Who Could Work Miracles '37 ▸
The New Invisible Man '58
Terror Is a Man '59
Things to Come '36 ▸
The Time Machine '60 ▸
Time Machine '78
The Time Machine '02
Village of the Giants '65
The War of the Worlds '53 ▸
War of the Worlds '05 ▸

Books to Film: Donald Westlake (aka Richard Stark)
Bank Shot '74 ▸
The Busy Body '67
Cops and Robbers '73
The Hot Rock '70 ▸
Made in USA '88
Payback '98 ▸
Point Blank '67
Slayground '84
A Slight Case of Murder '99
Two Much '96
What's the Worst That Could Happen? '01
Why Me? '90

Books to Film: Edith Wharton
The Age of Innocence '93 ▸
The Buccaneers '95 ▸
The Children '90
Ethan Frome '92
House of Mirth '00 ▸
The Old Maid '39 ▸

▸ = rated three bones or higher

Books to Film: William Wharton

Birdy '84 ▸
Dad '89
A Midnight Clear '92 ▸

Books to Film: E(lwyn) B(rooks) White

Charlotte's Web '73
Charlotte's Web '06 ▸
Stuart Little '99
Stuart Little 2 '02 ▸
The Trumpet of the Swan '01

Books to Film: Oscar Wilde

The Canterville Ghost '44
The Canterville Ghost '96
Dorian Gray '70
A Good Woman '04
An Ideal Husband '47
An Ideal Husband '99 ▸
The Importance of Being Earnest '52 ▸
The Importance of Being Earnest '02
Lady Windermere's Fan '25
Picture of Dorian Gray '45 ▸
Salome '22
Salome '53
Salome '85
The Sins of Dorian Gray '82

Books to Film: Thornton Wilder

The Bridge of San Luis Rey '44 ▸
The Bridge of San Luis Rey '05
Hello, Dolly! '69
The Matchmaker '58 ▸
Mr. North '88
Our Town '40 ▸
Our Town '77 ▸
Our Town '89

Books to Film: Ben Ames Williams

All the Brothers Were Valiant '53
Leave Her to Heaven '45 ▸
The Strange Woman '46

Books to Film: Virginia Woolf

Mrs. Dalloway '97
To the Lighthouse '83

Books to Film: Cornell Woolrich

Black Angel '46 ▸
The Bride Wore Black '68 ▸
The Chase '46
Deadline at Dawn '46
Fall Guy '47
Fear in the Night '47 ▸
I Married a Dead Man '82
The Leopard Man '43
Mississippi Mermaid '69 ▸
Mrs. Winterbourne '96
Original Sin '01
Phantom Lady '44 ▸
Rear Window '54 ▸
Rear Window '98
The Window '49 ▸

Books to Film: Herman Wouk

The Caine Mutiny '54 ▸
The Caine Mutiny Court Martial '88 ▸
Marjorie Morningstar '58
War & Remembrance '88
War & Remembrance: The Final Chapter '89
The Winds of War '83

Books to Film: Emile Zola

The Game Is Over '66
Germinal '93 ▸
Gervaise '56 ▸
Human Desire '54
La Bete Humaine '38 ▸
Nana '55 ▸
Nana '82
Therese Raquin '80

The Bowery Boys

Angels with Dirty Faces '38 ▸
Blues Busters '50
Bowery Blitzkrieg '41
Bowery Boys Meet the Monsters '54
Bowery Buckaroos '47
Boys of the City '40
Clancy Street Boys '43
Clipped Wings '53
Dead End '37 ▸
East Side Kids '40
Flying Wild '41
Follow the Leader '44
Ghost Chasers '51
Ghost on the Loose '43
Hard-Boiled Mahoney '47
Here Come the Marines '52
Kid Dynamite '43
Let's Get Tough '42
Little Tough Guys '38
Master Minds '49
Million Dollar Kid '44
Mr. Muggs Rides Again '45
Mr. Wise Guy '42
'Neath Brooklyn Bridge '42
Pride of the Bowery '41
Smart Alecks '42
Smugglers' Cove '48 ▸
Spook Busters '48
Spooks Run Wild '41
That Gang of Mine '40
They Made Me a Criminal '39

Broken Lizard

Beerfest '06
Club Dread '04
The Dukes of Hazzard '05
Super Troopers '01

Buffalo Bill Cody

Annie Oakley '35 ▸
Buffalo Bill '44
Buffalo Bill & the Indians '76 ▸
Buffalo Bill Rides Again '47
The Plainsman '37
Pony Express '53 ▸
Young Buffalo Bill '40

Bulldog Drummond

Arrest Bulldog Drummond '38
Bulldog Drummond '29
Bulldog Drummond at Bay '37
Bulldog Drummond Comes Back '37
Bulldog Drummond Escapes '37
Bulldog Drummond's Bride '39
Bulldog Drummond's Peril '38
Bulldog Drummond's Revenge '37
Bulldog Drummond's Secret Police '39
Bulldog Jack '35 ▸
Deadlier Than the Male '67

Carry On

Carry On Abroad '72
Carry On Again Doctor '69
Carry On at Your Convenience '71
Carry On Behind '75
Carry On Cabby '63
Carry On Camping '71
Carry On Cleo '65
Carry On Columbus '92
Carry On Constable '60
Carry On Cowboy '66
Carry On Cruising '62
Carry On Dick '75
Carry On Doctor '68 ▸
Carry On Emmanuelle '78
Carry On England '76
Carry On Henry VIII '71
Carry On Jack '63
Carry On Loving '70
Carry On Matron '72
Carry On Nurse '59
Carry On Regardless '61
Carry On Screaming '66
Carry On Sergeant '58
Carry On Spying '64
Carry On Up the Jungle '70
Carry On Up the Khyber '68
Don't Lose Your Head '66
Follow That Camel '67

Charlie Brown and the Peanuts Gang

Bon Voyage, Charlie Brown '80
Race for Your Life, Charlie Brown '77

Charlie Chan

Behind That Curtain '29
The Black Camel '31
Castle in the Desert '42
Charlie Chan and the Curse of the Dragon Queen '81
Charlie Chan at Monte Carlo '37
Charlie Chan at the Circus '36
Charlie Chan at the Olympics '37
Charlie Chan at the Opera '36 ▸
Charlie Chan at the Race Track '36
Charlie Chan at the Wax Museum '40
Charlie Chan at Treasure Island '39
Charlie Chan in City of Darkness '39
Charlie Chan in Egypt '35
Charlie Chan in Honolulu '38
Charlie Chan in London '34
Charlie Chan in Paris '35
Charlie Chan in Rio '41
Charlie Chan in Shanghai '35
Charlie Chan in the Secret Service '44
Charlie Chan on Broadway '37
Charlie Chan's Murder Cruise '40
Charlie Chan's Secret '35
The Chinese Cat '44
Dead Men Tell '41
The Jade Mask '45
Meeting at Midnight '44
Murder over New York '40
The Scarlet Clue '45
The Shanghai Cobra '45

Cisco Kid

The Cisco Kid '94
Guns of Fury '49
In Old New Mexico '45
Lucky Cisco Kid '40
Riding the California Trail '47
South of Monterey '47
South of the Rio Grande '45

Corman's Mama

Big Bad Mama '74
Big Bad Mama 2 '87
Bloody Mama '70
Crazy Mama '75

Dead End Kids

Angels with Dirty Faces '38 ▸
Crime School '38
Dead End '37 ▸
Little Tough Guys '38
They Made Me a Criminal '39

Director/Star Teams: Allen & Johansson

Match Point '05 ▸
Vicky Cristina Barcelona '08

Director/Star Teams: Almodovar & Banderas

Labyrinth of Passion '82
Law of Desire '86 ▸
Matador '86
Tie Me Up! Tie Me Down! '90

Director/Star Teams: Altman & Gould

The Long Goodbye '73 ▸
M*A*S*H '70 ▸
Nashville '75 ▸
The Player '92 ▸

Director/Star Teams: Altman & Murphy

Brewster McCloud '70 ▸
The Caine Mutiny Court Martial '88 ▸
Countdown '68
Kansas City '95 ▸
M*A*S*H '70 ▸
McCabe & Mrs. Miller '71 ▸
Nashville '75 ▸
Tanner '88 '88 ▸
Tanner on Tanner '04
That Cold Day in the Park '69

Director/Star Teams: W. Anderson & Murray

The Life Aquatic with Steve Zissou '04
The Royal Tenenbaums '01 ▸
Rushmore '98 ▸

Director/Star Teams: Bergman & Ullmann

Cries and Whispers '72 ▸
Face to Face '76 ▸
Hour of the Wolf '68 ▸
The Passion of Anna '70 ▸
Persona '66 ▸
Saraband '03 ▸
Scenes from a Marriage '73 ▸
The Serpent's Egg '78
The Shame '68 ▸

Director/Star Teams: Bergman & von Sydow

Brink of Life '57
Hour of the Wolf '68 ▸
The Magician '58 ▸
The Passion of Anna '70 ▸
The Seventh Seal '56 ▸
The Shame '68 ▸
Through a Glass Darkly '61 ▸
The Touch '71
The Virgin Spring '59 ▸
Wild Strawberries '57 ▸
The Winter Light '62 ▸

Director/Star Teams: Boetticher & Scott

Buchanan Rides Alone '58
Comanche Station '60
Decision at Sundown '57
Ride Lonesome '59
The Tall T '57
Westbound '58

Director/Star Teams: Bunuel & F. Rey

The Discreet Charm of the Bourgeoisie '72 ▸
That Obscure Object of Desire '77 ▸
Tristana '70 ▸
Viridiana '61 ▸

Director/Star Teams: Burton & Depp

Ed Wood '94 ▸
Edward Scissorhands '90 ▸
Sleepy Hollow '99 ▸
Sweeney Todd: The Demon Barber of Fleet Street '07
Tim Burton's Corpse Bride '05 ▸

Director/Star Teams: Capra & Stewart

It's a Wonderful Life '46 ▸
Mr. Smith Goes to Washington '39 ▸
You Can't Take It with You '38 ▸

Director/Star Teams: Carpenter & Russell

Big Trouble in Little China '86
Elvis: The Movie '79
Escape from L.A. '96
Escape from New York '81
The Thing '82

Director/Star Teams: Chabrol & Audran

Betty '92
The Blood of Others '84
Blood Relatives '77
Bluebeard '63 ▸
Cop Au Vin '85
Just Before Nightfall '71
La Femme Infidele '69 ▸
La Rupture '70
Le Boucher '69 ▸
Les Biches '68 ▸
Les Bonnes Femmes '60 ▸
Love Laughs at Andy Hardy '46
National Lampoon's Van Wilder 2: The Rise of Taj '06
Quiet Days in Clichy '90
Six in Paris '68
Twist '76
Violette '78 ▸
Wedding in Blood '74 ▸

Director/Star Teams: Chabrol & Huppert

Comedy of Power '06
Il Bidone '55
La Ceremonie '95 ▸
Madame Bovary '91 ▸
Merci pour le Chocolat '00 ▸
The Story of Women '88 ▸

Director/Star Teams: Coraci & Sandler

Click '06
The Waterboy '98
The Wedding Singer '97

Director/Star Teams: Cukor & Hepburn

Adam's Rib '50 ▸
A Bill of Divorcement '32
The Corn Is Green '79 ▸
Holiday '38 ▸
Keeper of the Flame '42
Little Women '33 ▸
Love Among the Ruins '75 ▸
Pat and Mike '52 ▸
The Philadelphia Story '40 ▸
Sylvia Scarlett '35

Director/Star Teams: Donner & Gibson

Conspiracy Theory '97 ▸
Lethal Weapon '87 ▸
Lethal Weapon 2 '89 ▸
Lethal Weapon 3 '92
Lethal Weapon 4 '98
Maverick '94

Director/Star Teams: Dugan & Sandler

Big Daddy '99
Grown Ups '10
Happy Gilmore '96

Director/Star Teams: Fincher & Pitt

The Curious Case of Benjamin Button '08 ▸
Fight Club: ' '99 ▸
Seven '95 ▸

Director/Star Teams: Ford & Wayne

Donovan's Reef '63 ▸
Fort Apache '48 ▸
The Horse Soldiers '59
How the West Was Won '63 ▸
The Long Voyage Home '40 ▸
The Man Who Shot Liberty Valance '62 ▸
The Quiet Man '52 ▸
Rio Grande '50 ▸
The Searchers '56 ▸
She Wore a Yellow Ribbon '49 ▸
Stagecoach '39 ▸
They Were Expendable '45 ▸
Three Godfathers '48 ▸
Wings of Eagles '57

Director/Star Teams: Frankenheimer & Lancaster

Birdman of Alcatraz '62 ▸
The Gypsy Moths '69
The Savage Bees '76
Seven Days in May '64 ▸
Terror Out of the Sky '78
The Train '65 ▸
The Young Savages '61

Director/Star Teams: Hawks & Wayne

El Dorado '67 ▸
Hatari! '62 ▸
Red River '48 ▸
Rio Bravo '59 ▸
Rio Lobo '70

Director/Star Teams: Herzog & Kinski

Aguirre, the Wrath of God '72 ▸
Cobra Verde '88
Fitzcarraldo '82 ▸
Nosferatu the Vampyre '79
Woyzeck '78 ▸

Director/Star Teams: Hill & Newman

Butch Cassidy and the Sundance Kid '69 ▸
Slap Shot '77 ▸
The Sting '73 ▸

Director/Star Teams: Hitchcock & Stewart

The Man Who Knew Too Much '56
Rear Window '54 ▸
Rope '48 ▸
Vertigo '58 ▸

Director/Star Teams: Holofcener & Keener

Friends with Money '06
Lovely & Amazing '02 ▸
Walking and Talking '96

Director/Star Teams: Howard & Hanks

Apollo 13 '95 ▸
The Da Vinci Code '06 ▸

Director/Star Teams: Howard & Keaton

Gung Ho! '43
Night Shift '82

Director/Star Teams: Huston & Bogart

Across the Pacific '42 ▸
The African Queen '51 ▸
Beat the Devil '53 ▸
Key Largo '48 ▸
The Maltese Falcon '41 ▸
Treasure of the Sierra Madre '48 ▸

Director/Star Teams: Jordan & Rea

The Butcher Boy '97 ▸
The Company of Wolves '85 ▸
The Crying Game '92 ▸
Danny Boy '82 ▸
The End of the Affair '99 ▸
In Dreams '98
Interview with the Vampire '94
Michael Collins '96 ▸

Director/Star Teams: King & Peck

Beloved Infidel '59
The Bravados '58 ▸
The Gunfighter '50 ▸
The Snows of Kilimanjaro '52 ▸
Twelve o'Clock High '49 ▸

Director/Star Teams: Kurosawa & Mifune

The Bad Sleep Well '60 ▸
Drunken Angel '48 ▸
The Hidden Fortress '58 ▸
High & Low '62 ▸
A Quiet Duel '49
Rashomon '51 ▸
Red Beard '65 ▸
Sanjuro '62 ▸
Scandal '50
Seven Samurai '54 ▸
Stray Dog '49 ▸
Throne of Blood '57 ▸
Yojimbo '61 ▸

▸ = rated three bones or higher

Director/Star Teams: LaBute & Eckhart

In the Company of Men '96
Nurse Betty '00 ▸
Possession '02
Your Friends & Neighbors '98 ▸

Director/Star Teams: Lee & Washington

He Got Game '98
Inside Man '06 ▸
Malcolm X '92 ▸
Mo' Better Blues '90

Director/Star Teams: Linklater & Hawke

Before Sunrise '94
Before Sunset '04 ▸
The Newton Boys '97
Tape '01 ▸
Waking Life '01

Director/Star Teams: Lynch & Nance

Blue Velvet '86 ▸
Dune '84
Eraserhead '78 ▸
Lost Highway '96
Twin Peaks: Fire Walk with Me '92
Wild at Heart '90 ▸

Director/Star Teams: Mann & Stewart

Bend of the River '52 ▸
Far Country '55 ▸
The Man from Laramie '55 ▸
The Naked Spur '53 ▸
Winchester '73 '50 ▸

Director/Star Teams: McKay & Ferrell

Anchorman: The Legend of Ron Burgundy '04
The Other Guys '10
Step Brothers '08
Talladega Nights: The Ballad of Ricky Bobby '06

Director/Star Teams: Needham & Reynolds

Cannonball Run '81
Cannonball Run 2 '84
Hooper '78
Smokey and the Bandit '77
Smokey and the Bandit 2 '80
Stroker Ace '83

Director/Star Teams: Newman & Woodward

The Effect of Gamma Rays on Man-in-the-Moon Marigolds '73 ▸
The Glass Menagerie '87 ▸
Harry & Son '84
Rachel, Rachel '68 ▸
The Shadow Box '80 ▸

Director/Star Teams: Poitier & Cosby

Ghost Dad '90
Let's Do It Again '75
Piece of the Action '77
Uptown Saturday Night '74

Director/Star Teams: Pollack & Redford

The Electric Horseman '79
Havana '90
Jeremiah Johnson '72 ▸
Out of Africa '85 ▸
This Property Is Condemned '66
Three Days of the Condor '75 ▸
The Way We Were '73 ▸

Director/Star Teams: R. Rodriguez & Banderas

Desperado '95 ▸
Four Rooms '95
Spy Kids '01 ▸
Spy Kids 2: The Island of Lost Dreams '02 ▸

Director/Star Teams: Rafelson & Nicholson

Blood & Wine '96
Five Easy Pieces '70 ▸
Head '68 ▸
The King of Marvin Gardens '72
Man Trouble '92
The Postman Always Rings Twice '81

Director/Star Teams: Raimi & Campbell

Army of Darkness '92 ▸
Crimewave '85
Darkman '90 ▸
Evil Dead '83
Evil Dead 2: Dead by Dawn '87
Spider-Man '02 ▸
Spider-Man 2 '04 ▸
Spider-Man 3 '07

Director/Star Teams: Raimi & 1973 Oldsmobile Delta 88

Army of Darkness '92 ▸
Crimewave '85
Darkman '90 ▸
Evil Dead '83
Evil Dead 2: Dead by Dawn '87
For Love of the Game '99
The Gift '00
A Simple Plan '98 ▸
Spider-Man '02 ▸
Spider-Man 2 '04 ▸
Spider-Man 3 '07

Director/Star Teams: Reiner & Martin

All of Me '84
Dead Men Don't Wear Plaid '82
The Jerk '79
The Man with Two Brains '83 ▸

Director/Star Teams: Ritt & Newman

Hombre '67 ▸
Hud '63 ▸
The Long, Hot Summer '58 ▸
Paris Blues '61

Director/Star Teams: Sayles & Clapp

Eight Men Out '88 ▸
Matewan '87 ▸
Return of the Secaucus 7 '80 ▸
Sunshine State '02 ▸

Director/Star Teams: Sayles & Cooper

City of Hope '91 ▸
Lone Star '95 ▸
Matewan '87 ▸
Silver City '04

Director/Star Teams: Sayles & Strathairn

The Brother from Another Planet '84 ▸
City of Hope '91 ▸
Eight Men Out '88 ▸
Limbo '99
Matewan '87 ▸
Passion Fish '92 ▸
Return of the Secaucus 7 '80 ▸

Director/Star Teams: Scorsese & De Niro

Cape Fear '91 ▸
Casino '95 ▸
Goodfellas '90 ▸
King of Comedy '82 ▸
Mean Streets '73 ▸
New York, New York '77 ▸
Raging Bull '80 ▸
Taxi Driver '76 ▸

Director/Star Teams: Scorsese & DiCaprio

The Aviator '85
The Departed '06 ▸
Gangs of New York '02 ▸
Shutter Island '09 ▸

Director/Star Teams: Scorsese & Keitel

Alice Doesn't Live Here Anymore '74
The Last Temptation of Christ '88 ▸
Mean Streets '73 ▸
Taxi Driver '76 ▸
Who's That Knocking at My Door? '68 ▸

Director/Star Teams: R. Scott & Crowe

American Gangster '07 ▸
Body of Lies '08
Gladiator '00 ▸
A Good Year '06
Robin Hood '10

Director/Star Teams: T. Scott & Washington

Crimson Tide '95 ▸
Deja Vu '06
Man on Fire '04
The Taking of Pelham 123 '09

Director/Star Teams: Shadyac & Carrey

Ace Ventura: Pet Detective '93
Bruce Almighty '03
Liar Liar '97

Director/Star Teams: Sheridan & Day-Lewis

The Boxer '97
In the Name of the Father '93 ▸
My Left Foot '89 ▸

Director/Star Teams: Siegel & Eastwood

The Beguiled '70 ▸
Coogan's Bluff '68 ▸
Dirty Harry '71 ▸
Escape from Alcatraz '79 ▸
Two Mules for Sister Sara '70 ▸

Director/Star Teams: Sirk & Hudson

All That Heaven Allows '55 ▸
Battle Hymn '57
Tarnished Angels '57 ▸
Written on the Wind '56 ▸

Director/Star Teams: Smith & Affleck

Chasing Amy '97
Clerks 2 '06 ▸
Dogma '99
Jay and Silent Bob Strike Back '01
Jersey Girl '04
Mallrats '95

Director/Star Teams: Soderbergh & Clooney

The Good German '06
The Limey '99 ▸
Ocean's Eleven '01 ▸
Ocean's Twelve '04
Out of Sight '98 ▸
Solaris '02

Director/Star Teams: Soderburgh & Roberts

Erin Brockovich '00 ▸
Full Frontal '02
Ocean's Eleven '01 ▸
Ocean's Twelve '04

Director/Star Teams: Spielberg & Dreyfuss

Always '89
Close Encounters of the Third Kind '77 ▸
Jaws '75 ▸

Director/Star Teams: Spielberg & Hanks

Catch Me If You Can '02
Saving Private Ryan '98 ▸
The Terminal '04

Director/Star Teams: Sturges & McCrea

The Great Moment '44
The Palm Beach Story '42 ▸
Sullivan's Travels '41 ▸

Director/Star Teams: Techine & Deneuve

Ma Saison Preferee '93 ▸

Director/Star Teams: Truffaut & Leaud

Bed and Board '70 ▸
Day for Night '73 ▸
The 400 Blows '59 ▸
Hotel America '81
Stolen Kisses '68 ▸
Two English Girls '72 ▸

Director/Star Teams: Verhoeven & Hauer

Flesh and Blood '85
Katie Tippel '75
Soldier of Orange '78 ▸
Spetters '80
Turkish Delight '73

Director/Star Teams: von Sternberg & Dietrich

Blonde Venus '32 ▸
The Blue Angel '30 ▸
Dishonored '31
Morocco '30 ▸
Scarlet Empress '34 ▸
Shanghai Express '32 ▸

Director/Star Teams: Walsh & Bogart

The Enforcer '51
High Sierra '41 ▸
The Roaring Twenties '39 ▸
They Drive by Night '40 ▸

Director/Star Teams: Woo & Fat

A Better Tomorrow, Part 1 '86
A Better Tomorrow, Part 2 '88
A Bullet in the Head '90 ▸
Hard-Boiled '92
The Killer '90 ▸

Director/Star Teams: Zemeckis & Hanks

Cast Away '00 ▸
Forrest Gump '94 ▸
The Polar Express '04

Dirty Harry

The Dead Pool '88
Dirty Harry '71 ▸
The Enforcer '76
Magnum Force '73
Sudden Impact '83

Disney Animated Movies

Aladdin '92 ▸
Aladdin and the King of Thieves '96
Alice in Wonderland '51 ▸
The Aristocats '70 ▸
Bambi '42 ▸
Bambi II '06
Beauty and the Beast '91 ▸
Bionicle 3: Web of Shadows '05
The Black Cauldron '85
Bolt '08 ▸
Brother Bear '03
Brother Bear 2 '06
Cars '06 ▸
Chicken Little '05
A Christmas Carol '09
Cinderella '50 ▸
Dinosaur '00
Doug's 1st Movie '99 ▸
DuckTales the Movie: Treasure of the Lost Lamp '90
Dumbo '41 ▸
The Emperor's New Groove '00 ▸
Fantasia '40 ▸
Fantasia/2000 '00
The Fox and the Hound '81 ▸
The Fox and the Hound 2 '06
A Goofy Movie '94
The Great Mouse Detective '86 ▸
Hercules '97 ▸
The Hunchback of Notre Dame '96 ▸
The Incredibles '04 ▸
The Jungle Book '67 ▸
The Jungle Book 2 '03
Lady and the Tramp '55 ▸
Lilo & Stitch '02 ▸
The Lion King '94 ▸
The Lion King 1 1/2 '04 ▸
The Lion King: Simba's Pride '98
The Little Mermaid '89 ▸
The Many Adventures of Winnie the Pooh '77
Meet the Robinsons '07
Melody Time '48 ▸
Mulan '98
The Nightmare Before Christmas '93 ▸
Oliver & Company '88
101 Dalmatians '61 ▸
Peter Pan '53 ▸
Piglet's Big Movie '03
Pinocchio '40 ▸
Pocahontas '95 ▸
Pooh's Heffalump Movie '05
The Princess and the Frog '09 ▸
The Rescuers '77 ▸
The Rescuers Down Under '90
The Return of Jafar '94
Return to Never Land '02
Robin Hood '73 ▸
Sleeping Beauty '59 ▸
Snow White and the Seven Dwarfs '37 ▸
The Sword in the Stone '63 ▸
Tarzan '99 ▸
Tarzan 2 '05
The Three Caballeros '45
Treasure Planet '02
Up '09 ▸
Valiant '05
The Wild '06

Disney Family Movies

The Absent-Minded Professor '61 ▸
The Adventures of Bullwhip Griffin '66
The Adventures of Huck Finn '93 ▸
The Adventures of Ichabod and Mr. Toad '49 ▸
The Air Up There '94
Almost Angels '62
Amy '81
Angels in the Endzone '98
Angels in the Outfield '94
The Apple Dumpling Gang '75
The Apple Dumpling Gang Rides Again '79
Babes in Toyland '61
The Barefoot Executive '71
The Bears & I '74
Bedknobs and Broomsticks '71
Bedtime Stories '08
Benji the Hunted '87
Beverly Hills Chihuahua '08
Big Red '62
Black Arrow '48 ▸
The Black Arrow '84
The Black Hole '79
Blackbeard's Ghost '67
Blank Check '93
The Blue Yonder '86
Bon Voyage! '62
Breakin' Through '84
Bridge to Terabithia '07
Candleshoe '78
The Castaway Cowboy '74
The Cat from Outer Space '78
Charley and the Angel '73
Charlie the Lonesome Cougar '67
Cheetah '89
The Cheetah Girls: One World '08
Child of Glass '78
The Chronicles of Narnia: Prince Caspian '08
The Chronicles of Narnia: The Lion, the Witch and the Wardrobe '05
College Road Trip '08
The Computer Wore Tennis Shoes '69
Condorman '81
The Country Bears '02
Darby O'Gill & the Little People '59 ▸
Davy Crockett and the River Pirates '56
Davy Crockett, King of the Wild Frontier '55 ▸
The Devil & Max Devlin '81
Dr. Syn, Alias the Scarecrow '64
D3: The Mighty Ducks '96
Emil and the Detectives '64
Enchanted '07
Escapade in Florence '62
Escape to Witch Mountain '75 ▸
A Far Off Place '93
The Fighting Prince of Donegal '66
Flight of the Grey Wolf '76
Flight of the Navigator '86
Flubber '97
Freaky Friday '76
Freaky Friday '03 ▸
Fun & Fancy Free '47 ▸
The Girl Who Spelled Freedom '86 ▸
The Gnome-Mobile '67
Goal! The Dream Begins '06
Gone Are the Days '84
A Goofy Movie '94
The Great Locomotive Chase '56
Greyfriars Bobby '61
Gus '76
Halloweentown '98
Halloweentown 2: Kalabar's Revenge '01
Halloweentown High '04
Heavyweights '94
Herbie: Fully Loaded '05
Herbie Goes Bananas '80
Herbie Goes to Monte Carlo '77
Herbie Rides Again '74
High School Musical '06
Homeward Bound: The Incredible Journey '93 ▸
Honey, I Blew Up the Kid '92
Honey, I Shrunk the Kids '89
Honey, We Shrunk Ourselves '97
The Horse in the Gray Flannel Suit '68
The Horse Without a Head '63
Horsemasters '61
Hot Lead & Cold Feet '78
The Hunchback of Notre Dame '96 ▸
In Search of the Castaways '62 ▸
The Incredible Journey '63
The Incredibles '04 ▸
Invincible '06 ▸
Iron Will '93
The Island at the Top of the World '74
Johnny Shiloh '63
Johnny Tremain & the Sons of Liberty '58
The Journey of Natty Gann '85 ▸
Jump In! '07
Justin Morgan Had a Horse '81
King of the Grizzlies '69
The Last Flight of Noah's Ark '80
The Last Song '10
Lt. Robin Crusoe, U.S.N. '66
The Light in the Forest '58
The Littlest Horse Thieves '76
The Littlest Outlaw '54
Lots of Luck '85
The Love Bug '68

▸ = rated three bones or higher

Love Leads the Way '84
Mary Poppins '64 ▶
Menace on the Mountain '70
Million Dollar Duck '71
Miracle Down Under '87
The Miracle of the White Stallions '63
The Misadventures of Merlin Jones '63
Monkeys, Go Home! '66
Monkey's Uncle '65
Moon Pilot '62
The Moon-Spinners '64
Mooncussers '62
Mosby's Marauders '66
My Dog, the Thief '69
My Favorite Martian '98
Napoleon and Samantha '72 ▶
Never a Dull Moment '68
Newsies '92
Night Crossing '81
Nikki, the Wild Dog of the North '61
The Nine Lives of Elfego Baca '58
No Deposit, No Return '76
The North Avenue Irregulars '79
Now You See Him, Now You Don't '72
Old Dogs '09
Old Yeller '57 ▶
The One and Only, Genuine, Original Family Band '68 ▶
101 Dalmatians '96
102 Dalmatians '00
One Little Indian '73
One Magic Christmas '85
One of Our Dinosaurs Is Missing '75
The Parent Trap '61
Pete's Dragon '77
Pocahontas '95 ▶
Pollyanna '60 ▶
Princess Protection Program '09
Race to Witch Mountain '09
Return from Witch Mountain '78
Return to Halloweentown '06
Return to Oz '85
Ride a Wild Pony '75 ▶
Rob Roy—The Highland Rogue '53
The Rocketeer '91 ▶
Sammy, the Way-Out Seal '62
Savage Sam '63
Scandalous John '71
The Secret of El Zorro '57
The Shaggy D.A. '76
The Shaggy Dog '59
The Shaggy Dog '06
The Sign of Zorro '60
Sky High '05 ▶
Smith! '69
Smoke '70
Snow Dogs '02
Snowball Express '72
So Dear to My Heart '49 ▶
Son of Flubber '63
The Sorcerer's Apprentice '10
The Story of Robin Hood & His Merrie Men '52 ▶
The Strongest Man in the World '75
Summer Magic '63
Summer of the Monkeys '98
Superdad '73
The Swiss Family Robinson '60 ▶
The Sword & the Rose '53
Tall Tale: The Unbelievable Adventures of Pecos Bill '95
Ten Who Dared '60
That Darn Cat '65
That Darn Cat '96
Third Man on the Mountain '59
Those Calloways '65
The Three Lives of Thomasina '63 ▶
3 Ninjas '92
3 Ninjas Kick Back '94
A Tiger Walks '64
Toby Tyler '59 ▶
Tom and Huck '95 ▶
Tonka '58
Toothless '97
Toy Story '95 ▶
Treasure Island '50 ▶
The Treasure of Matecumbe '76
20,000 Leagues under the Sea '54 ▶
The Ugly Dachshund '65
Underdog '07
Undergrads '85 ▶
Unidentified Flying Oddball '79
Waltz King '63
The Watcher in the Woods '81
Westward Ho, the Wagons! '56
White Fang '91 ▶
White Fang 2: The Myth of the White Wolf '94
The Wild Country '71
Wild Hearts Can't Be Broken '91 ▶
The World's Greatest Athlete '73

Doc Holliday

Cheyenne Autumn '64
Gunfight at the O.K. Corral '57 ▶
Hour of the Gun '67
My Darling Clementine '46 ▶
Tombstone '93 ▶
Wyatt Earp '94

Dr. Christian

Courageous Dr. Christian '40
Dr. Christian Meets the Women '40
Meet Dr. Christian '39
Melody for Three '41
Remedy for Riches '40
They Meet Again '41

Dr. Mabuse

Dr. Mabuse, The Gambler '22 ▶
Dr. Mabuse vs. Scotland Yard '64
The Invisible Dr. Mabuse '62 ▶
The Return of Dr. Mabuse '61
The Thousand Eyes of Dr. Mabuse '60

Dr. Seuss

Dr. Seuss' Horton Hears a Who! '08 ▶
Dr. Seuss' How the Grinch Stole Christmas '00
Dr. Seuss' The Cat in the Hat '03
The 5000 Fingers of Dr. T '53 ▶

Dracula

Abbott and Costello Meet Frankenstein '48 ▶
Blood of Dracula '57
Blood of Dracula's Castle '69
Bram Stoker's Dracula '92
Bram Stoker's Way of the Vampire '05
The Brides of Dracula '60
Count Dracula '71
Count Dracula '77
The Creeps '97
Dracula (Spanish Version) '31
Dracula '31 ▶
Dracula '73
Dracula '79
Dracula '06
Dracula 2: Ascension '03
Dracula 3: Legacy '05
Dracula A.D. 1972 '72
Dracula and Son '76
Dracula: Dead and Loving It '95
Dracula Has Risen from the Grave '68
Dracula, Prince of Darkness '66
Dracula Rising '93
Dracula Sucks '79
Dracula: The Dark Prince '01
Dracula 2000 '00
Dracula vs. Frankenstein '69
Dracula vs. Frankenstein '71
Dracula's Daughter '36 ▶
Dracula's Great Love '72
Dracula's Last Rites '79
Dracula's Widow '88
Gallery of Horrors '67
The Horror of Dracula '58 ▶
House of Dracula '45
House of Frankenstein '44
Hysterical '83
The Legend of the 7 Golden Vampires '73
Love at First Bite '79
Lust for Dracula '04
Mad Monster Party '68
The Monster Squad '87
Nocturna '79
Return of Dracula '58
Return of the Vampire '43
The Satanic Rites of Dracula '73
The Scars of Dracula '70
The Screaming Dead '72
Son of Dracula '43 ▶
Taste the Blood of Dracula '70
To Die For '89
Transylvania 6-5000 '85
Vampire Circus '71
Van Helsing '04 ▶
Waxwork '88
Zoltan... Hound of Dracula '78

Dreamworks Animated Movies

Antz '98 ▶
Bee Movie '07
Chicken Run '00 ▶
How to Train Your Dragon '10
Kung Fu Panda '08 ▶
Madagascar '05
Madagascar: Escape 2 Africa '08
Monsters vs. Aliens '09
Over the Hedge '06 ▶
Prince of Egypt '98 ▶
The Road to El Dorado '00
Shark Tale '04
Shrek '01 ▶
Shrek 2 '04 ▶
Sinbad: Legend of the Seven Seas '03
Spirit: Stallion of the Cimarron '02
Wallace & Gromit in The Curse of the Were-Rabbit '05 ▶

East End Kids

Bowery Blitzkrieg '41
Boys of the City '40
East Side Kids '40
Flying Wild '41
Kid Dynamite '43
Let's Get Tough '42
Million Dollar Kid '44
Mr. Wise Guy '42
'Neath Brooklyn Bridge '42
Pride of the Bowery '41
Smart Alecks '42
Spooks Run Wild '41
That Gang of Mine '40

Elvisfilm

Blue Hawaii '62
Bubba Ho-Tep '03 ▶
Change of Habit '69
Charro! '69
Clambake '67
Double Trouble '67
Easy Come, Easy Go '67
Eddie Presley '92
Elvis and Me '88
Elvis Has Left the Building '04
Elvis in Hollywood '93 ▶
Elvis Meets Nixon '98
Elvis: The Movie '79
Finding Graceland '98
Flaming Star '60 ▶
Follow That Dream '61
Frankie and Johnny '65
Fun in Acapulco '63
G.I. Blues '60
Girl Happy '65
Girls! Girls! Girls! '62
Harum Scarum '65
Heartbreak Hotel '88
Honeymoon in Vegas '92
Hounddog '08
It Happened at the World's Fair '63
Jailhouse Rock '57 ▶
Kid Galahad '62
King Creole '58
Kissin' Cousins '64
Live a Little, Love a Little '68
Love Me Tender '56
Loving You '57
Paradise, Hawaiian Style '66
Protecting the King '07
Rock-a-Doodle '92
Roustabout '64
Six-String Samurai '98
Speedway '68
Spinout '66
Stay Away, Joe '68
This Is Elvis '81
3000 Miles to Graceland '01
Tickle Me '65
Top Secret! '84 ▶
The Trouble with Girls (and How to Get into It) '69 ▶
True Romance '93
Viva Las Vegas '63
Wild in the Country '61
The Woman Who Loved Elvis '93

The Falcon

The Amityville Curse '90
The Devil's Cargo '48
The Falcon in Hollywood '44
The Falcon in Mexico '44
The Falcon Takes Over '42
The Falcon's Brother '42

4 Bones

A Nous la Liberte '31 ▶
Abe Lincoln in Illinois '40 ▶
Adam's Rib '50 ▶
The Adventures of Robin Hood '38 ▶
The African Queen '51 ▶
All About Eve '50 ▶
All Quiet on the Western Front '30 ▶
All the King's Men '49 ▶
An American in Paris '51 ▶
Anatomy of a Murder '59 ▶
Andrei Rublev '66 ▶
An Angel at My Table '89 ▶
Angels with Dirty Faces '38 ▶
Angi Vera '78 ▶
Annie Hall '77 ▶
Apocalypse Now '79 ▶
The Asphalt Jungle '50 ▶
Au Revoir les Enfants '87 ▶
The Awful Truth '37 ▶
The Ballad of Narayama '83 ▶
Bambi '42 ▶
The Bank Dick '40 ▶
The Battleship Potemkin '25 ▶
Beauty and the Beast '46 ▶
Beauty and the Beast '91 ▶
Ben-Hur '26 ▶
Ben-Hur '59 ▶
Best of Youth '03 ▶
The Best Years of Our Lives '46 ▶
The Bicycle Thief '48 ▶
The Big Parade '25 ▶
The Big Sleep '46 ▶
The Birth of a Nation '15 ▶
The Blue Angel '30 ▶
The Boys of St. Vincent '93 ▶
Breathless '59 ▶
Brian's Song '71 ▶
The Bride of Frankenstein '35 ▶
The Bridge on the River Kwai '57 ▶
Brief Encounter '46 ▶
Bringing Up Baby '38 ▶
The Burmese Harp '56 ▶
Butch Cassidy and the Sundance Kid '69 ▶
The Cabinet of Dr. Caligari '19 ▶
The Caine Mutiny '54 ▶
The Cameraman '28 ▶
Casablanca '42 ▶
Cesar '36 ▶
Children of Paradise '44 ▶
Chimes at Midnight '67 ▶
Chinatown '74 ▶
Christ Stopped at Eboli '79 ▶
A Christmas Carol '51 ▶
A Christmas Story '83 ▶
Citizen Kane '41 ▶
City Lights '31 ▶
A Clockwork Orange '71 ▶
Close Encounters of the Third Kind '77 ▶
Colonel Redl '84 ▶
Come and See '85 ▶
Commissar '68 ▶
The Conformist '71 ▶
Crime and Punishment '35 ▶
The Crowd '28 ▶
Cyrano de Bergerac '50 ▶
Cyrano de Bergerac '90 ▶
Danton '82 ▶
The Dark Knight '08 ▶
Das Boot '81 ▶
David Copperfield '35 ▶
Day for Night '73 ▶
Day of Wrath '43 ▶
Dead of Night '45 ▶
The Deer Hunter '78 ▶
Deliverance '72 ▶
Destry Rides Again '39 ▶
Diamonds of the Night '64 ▶
Dinner at Eight '33 ▶
The Discreet Charm of the Bourgeoisie '72 ▶
Dr. Strangelove, or: How I Learned to Stop Worrying and Love the Bomb '64 ▶
Don Quixote '35 ▶
Double Indemnity '44 ▶
Duck Soup '33 ▶
Dumbo '41 ▶
The Earrings of Madame De... '54 ▶
Earth '30 ▶
East of Eden '54 ▶
8 1/2 '63 ▶
El Norte '83 ▶
The Elephant Man '80 ▶
The Empire Strikes Back '80 ▶
The English Patient '96 ▶
E.T.: The Extra-Terrestrial '82 ▶
Every Man for Himself & God Against All '75 ▶
Fanny '32 ▶
Fanny and Alexander '83 ▶
Fantasia '40 ▶
Festival Express '03 ▶
Finding Nemo '03 ▶
Fitzcarraldo '82 ▶
Five Easy Pieces '70 ▶
Forbidden Games '52 ▶
Foreign Correspondent '40 ▶
Forever and a Day '43 ▶
42nd Street '33 ▶
The Four Feathers '39 ▶
The 400 Blows '59 ▶
Frankenstein '31 ▶
The Freshman '25 ▶
From Here to Eternity '53 ▶
The Fugitive '48 ▶
Gallipoli '81 ▶
The Garden of the Finzi-Continis '71 ▶
The General '26 ▶
The General Line '29 ▶
Gigi '58 ▶
The Godfather '72 ▶
The Godfather 1902-1959: The Complete Epic '81 ▶
The Godfather, Part 2 '74 ▶
The Gold Rush '25 ▶
Gone with the Wind '39 ▶
Goodfellas '90 ▶
The Gospel According to St. Matthew '64 ▶
The Graduate '67 ▶
Grand Illusion '37 ▶
The Great Dictator '40 ▶
Great Expectations '46 ▶
Greed '24 ▶
Gunga Din '39 ▶
Hamlet '48 ▶
Hamlet '96 ▶
Harlan County, U.S.A. '76 ▶
Harold and Maude '71 ▶
Harvest '37 ▶
Hearts of Darkness: A Filmmaker's Apocalypse '91 ▶
Henry V '44 ▶
Henry V '89 ▶
Henry: Portrait of a Serial Killer '90 ▶
Here Comes Mr. Jordan '41 ▶
High Noon '52 ▶
Hiroshima, Mon Amour '59 ▶
His Girl Friday '40 ▶
Hollywood Canteen '44 ▶
Hoop Dreams '94 ▶
How Green Was My Valley '41 ▶
Howard's End '92 ▶
Hud '63 ▶
The Hunchback of Notre Dame '39 ▶
The Hustler '61 ▶
I Am a Fugitive from a Chain Gang '32 ▶
The Idiot '51 ▶
If... '69 ▶
Ikiru '52 ▶
The Informer '35 ▶
Intolerance '16 ▶
The Invisible Man '33 ▶
Isn't Life Wonderful '24 ▶
It Happened One Night '34 ▶
It's a Wonderful Life '46 ▶
Ivan the Terrible, Part 1 '44 ▶
James Joyce: A Portrait of the Artist as a Young Man '77 ▶
Ju Dou '90 ▶
Judgment at Nuremberg '61 ▶
Jules and Jim '62 ▶
The Killers '46 ▶
The King and I '56 ▶
King Kong '33 ▶
Knife in the Water '62 ▶
Koyaanisqatsi '83 ▶
Kriemhilde's Revenge '24 ▶
Kwaidan '64 ▶
La Chienne '31 ▶
L.A. Confidential '97 ▶
La Dolce Vita '60 ▶
La Notte '60 ▶
La Strada '54 ▶
Lady and the Tramp '55 ▶
The Lady Eve '41 ▶
The Lady Vanishes '38 ▶
L'Age D'Or '30 ▶
Last Command '28 ▶
The Last Detail '73 ▶
The Last Emperor '87 ▶
The Last Picture Show '71 ▶
The Last Seduction '94 ▶
Late Spring '49 ▶
Laura '44 ▶
Lawrence of Arabia '62 ▶
Le Trou '59 ▶
Les Miserables '35 ▶
The Letter '40 ▶
A Letter to Three Wives '49 ▶
Letters from Iwo Jima '06 ▶
The Life and Death of Colonel Blimp '43 ▶
The Life and Times of Hank Greenberg '99 ▶
Life Is Beautiful '98 ▶
The Lion in Winter '68 ▶
The Lion King '94 ▶
Little Women '33 ▶
Little Women '94 ▶
The Lives of a Bengal Lancer '35 ▶
Local Hero '83 ▶
Lola Montes '55 ▶
Long Day's Journey into Night '62 ▶
Lord of the Rings: The Two Towers '02 ▶
Lord of the Rings: The Return of the King '03 ▶
Lost Horizon '37 ▶
The Lost Weekend '45 ▶
M '31 ▶
The Magnificent Ambersons '42 ▶
The Magnificent Seven '60 ▶
Male and Female '19 ▶
The Maltese Falcon '41 ▶
A Man for All Seasons '66 ▶
The Man Who Would Be King '75 ▶
The Manchurian Candidate '62 ▶
Manhattan '79 ▶

Marius '31 ▸
The Marriage of Maria Braun '79 ▸
M*A*S*H '70 ▸
Master and Commander: The Far Side of the World '03 ▸
McCabe & Mrs. Miller '71 ▸
Mean Streets '73 ▸
Metropolis '26 ▸
Miracle of Morgan's Creek '44 ▸
Miracle on 34th Street '47 ▸
Mrs. Miniver '42 ▸
Mr. & Mrs. Bridge '90 ▸
Mister Roberts '55 ▸
Mr. Smith Goes to Washington '39 ▸
Modern Times '36 ▸
Mon Oncle '58 ▸
Monster's Ball '01 ▸
The Mother and the Whore '73 ▸
Murderball '05 ▸
The Music Man '62 ▸
Mutiny on the Bounty '35 ▸
My Left Foot '89 ▸
My Life As a Dog '85 ▸
My Life to Live '62 ▸
My Man Godfrey '36 ▸
Napoleon '27 ▸
Nashville '75 ▸
National Velvet '44 ▸
The New World '05 ▸
A Night at the Opera '35 ▸
The Night of the Hunter '55 ▸
The Night of the Shooting Stars '82 ▸
No Country for Old Men '07 ▸
North by Northwest '59 ▸
Nosferatu '22 ▸
Notorious '46 ▸
O Lucky Man! '73 ▸
Objective, Burma! '45 ▸
Of Mice and Men '39 ▸
Oldboy '03 ▸
Oliver Twist '48 ▸
On the Waterfront '54 ▸
One Flew Over the Cuckoo's Nest '75 ▸
Only Angels Have Wings '39 ▸
Open City '45 ▸
Osama '03 ▸
Our Hospitality '23 ▸
The Outlaw Josey Wales '76 ▸
The Ox-Bow Incident '43 ▸
Pandora's Box '28 ▸
Pan's Labyrinth '06 ▸
Passion of Joan of Arc '28 ▸
Pather Panchali '54 ▸
Paths of Glory '57 ▸
Pelle the Conqueror '88 ▸
Persona '66 ▸
Petulia '68 ▸
The Philadelphia Story '40 ▸
Pinocchio '40 ▸
Pixote '81 ▸
Poltergeist '82 ▸
The Private Life of Henry VIII '33 ▸
Psycho '60 ▸
Pulp Fiction '94 ▸
The Quiet Man '52 ▸
Quiz Show '94 ▸
Raging Bull '80 ▸
Raiders of the Lost Ark '81 ▸
A Raisin in the Sun '61 ▸
Ran '85 ▸
Rashomon '51 ▸
Rear Window '54 ▸
Rebecca '40 ▸
Rebel without a Cause '55 ▸
Red River '48 ▸
The Red Shoes '48 ▸
The Reincarnation of Golden Lotus '89 ▸
The Report on the Party and the Guests '66 ▸
Ride the High Country '62 ▸
The River '51 ▸
Road to Perdition '02 ▸
A Room with a View '86 ▸
Roots '77 ▸
Rosemary's Baby '68 ▸
Ruggles of Red Gap '35 ▸
The Rules of the Game '39 ▸
S21: The Khmer Rouge Killing Machine '03 ▸
Sansho the Bailiff '54 ▸
Saving Private Ryan '98 ▸
Scenes from a Marriage '73 ▸
Schindler's List '93 ▸
The Searchers '56 ▸
Sergeant York '41 ▸
Seven Beauties '76 ▸
Seven Samurai '54 ▸
The Seventh Seal '56 ▸
Shakespeare in Love '98 ▸
Shane '53 ▸
Shin Heike Monogatari '55 ▸
Shoeshine '47 ▸
Shoot the Piano Player '62 ▸
The Shop on Main Street '65 ▸
Show Boat '36 ▸
Siegfried '24 ▸
Singin' in the Rain '52 ▸
Small Change '76 ▸
Snow White and the Seven Dwarfs '37 ▸
Some Like It Hot '59 ▸
The Sound of Music '65 ▸
Sounder '72 ▸
The Southerner '45 ▸
Spartacus '60 ▸
Spider '02 ▸
Stagecoach '39 ▸
Stalag 17 '53 ▸
Star Wars '77 ▸
Storm over Asia '28 ▸
Strangers on a Train '51 ▸
A Streetcar Named Desire '51 ▸
The Stunt Man '80 ▸
Sullivan's Travels '41 ▸
Sunrise '27 ▸
A Tale of Two Cities '36 ▸
The Third Man '49 ▸
The 39 Steps '35 ▸
The Three Burials of Melquiades Estrada '05 ▸
Throne of Blood '57 ▸
The Tin Drum '79 ▸
To Kill a Mockingbird '62 ▸
To Live '94 ▸
Tokyo Story '53 ▸
Tom Jones '63 ▸
Tootsie '82 ▸
Top Hat '35 ▸
Touch of Evil '58 ▸
Toy Story '95 ▸
Toy Story 2 '99 ▸
The Train '65 ▸
Treasure of the Sierra Madre '48 ▸
The Triplets of Belleville '02 ▸
Tristana '70 ▸
Tropic Thunder '08 ▸
The Truman Show '98 ▸
Twelve Angry Men '57 ▸
Twentieth Century '34 ▸
2001: A Space Odyssey '68 ▸
Two Women '61 ▸
Umberto D '55 ▸
Un Chien Andalou '28 ▸
Under the Flag of the Rising Sun '72 ▸
Vampyr '31 ▸
Variety '25 ▸
Vertigo '58 ▸
Viridiana '61 ▸
Viva Zapata! '52 ▸
Wages of Fear '55 ▸
The Wedding March '28 ▸
Who's Afraid of Virginia Woolf? '66 ▸
The Wild Bunch '69 ▸
Wild Strawberries '57 ▸
The Wind '28 ▸
The Wizard of Oz '39 ▸
Woman in the Dunes '64 ▸
Woman of the Year '42 ▸
Woodstock '70 ▸
The World of Apu '59 ▸
Wuthering Heights '39 ▸
Yankee Doodle Dandy '42 ▸
Yojimbo '61 ▸
Young Frankenstein '74 ▸
Z '69 ▸
Zero for Conduct '33 ▸
Zvenigora '28 ▸

Francis the Talking Mule

Francis Covers the Big Town '53
Francis Goes to the Races '51
Francis Goes to West Point '52
Francis in the Haunted House '56
Francis in the Navy '55
Francis Joins the WACs '54
Francis the Talking Mule '49 ▸

Frankenstein

Abbott and Costello Meet Frankenstein '48 ▸
Andy Warhol's Frankenstein '74
Blackenstein '73
Boltneck '98
The Bride '85
The Bride of Frankenstein '35 ▸
The Creeps '97
The Curse of Frankenstein '57
Dr. Frankenstein's Castle of Freaks '74
Dracula vs. Frankenstein '69
Dracula vs. Frankenstein '71
The Evil of Frankenstein '64
Frankenstein '31 ▸
Frankenstein '73
Frankenstein '82
Frankenstein '93
Frankenstein 1970 '58
Frankenstein and Me '96
Frankenstein and the Monster from Hell '74
Frankenstein Conquers the World '64
Frankenstein Created Woman '66 ▸
Frankenstein '80 '79
Frankenstein General Hospital '88
Frankenstein Island '81
Frankenstein Meets the Space Monster '65
Frankenstein Meets the Wolfman '42 ▸
Frankenstein Must Be Destroyed '69
Frankenstein Reborn '98
Frankenstein Sings.. The Movie '95
Frankenstein Unbound '90 ▸
Frankenstein's Daughter '58
Frankenstein's Great Aunt Tillie '83
Frankenweenie '84
The Ghost of Frankenstein '42
Gothic '87 ▸
The Horror of Frankenstein '70
House of Dracula '45
House of Frankenstein '44
Jesse James Meets Frankenstein's Daughter '65
Lady Frankenstein '72
Mad Monster Party '68
Mary Shelley's Frankenstein '94
Mr. Stitch '95
The Munsters' Revenge '81
Nosferatu '22 ▸
Prototype '83 ▸
The Revenge of Frankenstein '58
Rites of Frankenstein '72
The Screaming Dead '72
Son of Frankenstein '39 ▸
Subject Two '06
Teenage Frankenstein '58
Van Helsing '04 ▸
The Vindicator '85
Young Frankenstein '74 ▸

Fu Manchu

Brides of Fu Manchu '66
The Castle of Fu Manchu '68
Daughter of the Dragon '31
The Fiendish Plot of Dr. Fu Manchu '80
Kiss and Kill '68
The Mask of Fu Manchu '32
The Mysterious Dr. Fu Manchu '29
The Return of Dr. Fu Manchu '30
The Vengeance of Fu Manchu '67

Gamera

Gamera the Brave '06

Godzilla and Friends

Dagora, the Space Monster '65
Destroy All Monsters '68
Destroy All Planets '68
Frankenstein Conquers the World '64
Gamera vs. Barugon '66
Gamera vs. Gaos '67
Gamera vs. Guiron '69
Gamera vs. Zigra '71
Gappa the Trifibian Monster '67
Ghidrah the Three Headed Monster '65
Godzilla '98
Godzilla, King of the Monsters '56
Godzilla 1985 '85
Godzilla on Monster Island '72
Godzilla Raids Again '55
Godzilla 2000 '99 ▸
Godzilla vs. Biollante '89
Godzilla vs. King Ghidora '91
Godzilla vs. Mechagodzilla II '93
Godzilla vs. Megalon '76
Godzilla vs. Monster Zero '68
Godzilla vs. Mothra '64
Godzilla vs. the Cosmic Monster '74
Godzilla vs. the Sea Monster '66
Godzilla vs. the Smog Monster '72
Godzilla's Revenge '69
King Kong Escapes '67
King Kong vs. Godzilla '63
Mothra '62 ▸
Rebirth of Mothra '96
Rebirth of Mothra 2 '97
Rodan '56
Son of Godzilla '66
Terror of Mechagodzilla '78
Varan the Unbelievable '61
War of the Gargantuas '70
X from Outer Space '67
Yog, Monster from Space '71
Yongkari Monster of the Deep '67

Hallmark Hall of Fame

An American Story '92
Blind Spot '93
The Boys Next Door '96
Breathing Lessons '94 ▸
Calm at Sunset '96
Caroline? '90 ▸
Cupid & Cate '00
Decoration Day '90 ▸
A Dog Named Christmas '09
Durango '99
The Echo of Thunder '98
Ellen Foster '97
Fallen Angel '03
The Flamingo Rising '01
Follow the Stars Home '01
Foxfire '87 ▸
Front of the Class '08
Grace & Glorie '98
Harvest of Fire '95
In Love and War '01
Journey '95
Little John '02
The Locket '02
The Lost Child '00
The Love Letter '98
Miss Rose White '92 ▸
Missing Pieces '00
My Sister's Keeper '02
Night Ride Home '99
O Pioneers! '91
One Against the Wind '91 ▸
A Painted House '03
The Piano Lesson '94 ▸
Pictures of Hollis Woods '07
A Place for Annie '94
Redwood Curtain '95
The Return of the Native '94
Rose Hill '97
The Runaway '00
Saint Maybe '98 ▸
Sarah, Plain and Tall '91 ▸
Sarah, Plain and Tall: Skylark '93
Sarah, Plain and Tall: Winter's End '99 ▸
A Season for Miracles '99
The Secret Garden '87 ▸
The Seventh Stream '01
The Shell Seekers '89
The Summer of Ben Tyler '96
Sweet Nothing in My Ear '08
That Russell Girl '08
To Dance with the White Dog '93 ▸
20,000 Leagues Under the Sea '97
What the Deaf Man Heard '98 ▸
William Faulkner's Old Man '97

Hammer Films: Horror

The Abominable Snowman '57
Asylum '72
Blood of the Vampire '58
The Blood on Satan's Claw '71 ▸
The Brides of Dracula '60
Captain Kronos: Vampire Hunter '74 ▸
The Creeping Flesh '72
Crescendo '69
The Curse of Frankenstein '57
The Curse of the Werewolf '61
The Devil Rides Out '68 ▸
Die Screaming, Marianne '73
Dr. Jekyll and Sister Hyde '71
Dr. Terror's House of Horrors '65
Dracula A.D. 1972 '72
Dracula Has Risen from the Grave '68
Dracula, Prince of Darkness '66
Dynasty of Fear '72
The Evil of Frankenstein '64
Frankenstein and the Monster from Hell '74
Frankenstein Created Woman '66 ▸
Frankenstein Must Be Destroyed '69
The Ghoul '75
The Gorgon '64
Hands of the Ripper '71
The Horror of Dracula '58 ▸
The Horror of Frankenstein '70
The Hound of the Baskervilles '59
Hysteria '64
Kiss of the Vampire '62
The Legend of the 7 Golden Vampires '73
Lust for a Vampire '71
Maniac '63
The Mummy '59 ▸
The Mummy's Shroud '67
The Nanny '65
Nightmare '63
Paranoiac '62
The Phantom of the Opera '62
Plague of the Zombies '66
Rasputin the Mad Monk '66
The Reptile '66
The Revenge of Frankenstein '58
The Satanic Rites of Dracula '73
The Scars of Dracula '70
Tales from the Crypt '72 ▸
Tales That Witness Madness '73
Taste the Blood of Dracula '70
Theatre of Blood '73 ▸
To the Devil, a Daughter '76
Twins of Evil '71
The Two Faces of Dr. Jekyll '60
Vampire Circus '71
The Vampire Lovers '70
Vault of Horror '73
The Witches '66

Hammer Films: Sci Fi & Fantasy

Creatures the World Forgot '70
Four Sided Triangle '53
Men of Sherwood Forest '57
One Million Years B.C. '66
Prehistoric Women '67
Quatermass 2 '57 ▸
Quatermass and the Pit '58
The Quatermass Experiment '56 ▸
She '65
Spaceways '53
Sword of Sherwood Forest '60
The Vengeance of She '68
The Viking Queen '67
When Dinosaurs Ruled the Earth '70
X The Unknown '56

Hercule Poirot

Agatha Christie's Thirteen at Dinner '85
The Alphabet Murders '65
Appointment with Death '88
Death on the Nile '78
Murder on the Orient Express '74 ▸

Hercules

Conquest of Mycene '63
The Fury of Hercules '61
Hercules '58
Hercules '97 ▸
Hercules 2 '85
Hercules against the Moon Men '64
Hercules and the Captive Women '63
Hercules in New York '70
Hercules in the Haunted World '64
Hercules, Prisoner of Evil '64
Hercules the Legendary Journeys, Vol. 1: And the Amazon Women '94
Hercules the Legendary Journeys, Vol. 2: The Lost Kingdom '94
Hercules the Legendary Journeys, Vol. 3: The Circle of Fire '94
Hercules the Legendary Journeys, Vol. 4: In the Underworld '94
Hercules Unchained '59
Hercules vs. the Sons of the Sun '64
Jason and the Argonauts '63 ▸
The Loves of Hercules '60
Samson and His Mighty Challenge '64
The Three Stooges Meet Hercules '61
The Triumph of Hercules '66
Young Hercules '97

Highest Grossing Films of All Time

Avatar '09 ▸
The Dark Knight '08 ▸
E.T.: The Extra-Terrestrial '82 ▸
Finding Nemo '03 ▸
Forrest Gump '94 ▸
Jurassic Park '93 ▸
The Lion King '94 ▸
Lord of the Rings: The Two Towers '02 ▸
Lord of the Rings: The Return of the King '03 ▸
The Passion of the Christ '04 ▸
Pirates of the Caribbean: Dead Man's Chest '06

▸ = rated three bones or higher

The Strange Case of Dr. Jekyll and Mr. Hyde '06
Sydney White '07
Ten Things I Hate about You '99 ▸
Twisted '96
Whatever It Takes '00
William Shakespeare's Romeo and Juliet '96 ▸

Monty Python

The Adventures of Baron Munchausen '89 ▸
All You Need Is Cash '78 ▸
And Now for Something Completely Different '72 ▸
Brazil '85 ▸
Clockwise '86
Consuming Passions '88
Down Among the Z Men '52
Erik the Viking '89
A Fish Called Wanda '88 ▸
The Fisher King '91 ▸
Jabberwocky '77
The Missionary '82
Monty Python and the Holy Grail '75 ▸
Monty Python's Life of Brian '79 ▸
Monty Python's The Meaning of Life '83 ▸
Nuns on the Run '90
The Odd Job '78
Personal Services '87
A Private Function '84
Privates on Parade '84
Rentadick '72
Romance with a Double Bass '74 ▸
The Secret Policeman's Other Ball '82 ▸
Secret Policeman's Private Parts '81
Time Bandits '81
Yellowbeard '83

The Muppets

The Adventures of a Gnome Named Gnorm '93
The Great Muppet Caper '81 ▸
Labyrinth '86 ▸
The Muppet Christmas Carol '92
The Muppet Movie '79 ▸
Muppet Treasure Island '96
Muppets from Space '99
The Muppets Take Manhattan '84 ▸
Sesame Street Presents: Follow That Bird '85

National Lampoon

National Lampoon Presents Cattle Call '06
National Lampoon Presents RoboDoc '08
National Lampoon's Adam & Eve '05
National Lampoon's Animal House '78 ▸
National Lampoon's Attack of the 5 Ft. 2 Women '94
National Lampoon's Christmas Vacation '89
National Lampoon's Christmas Vacation 2: Cousin Eddie's Big Island Adventure '03
National Lampoon's Class of '86 '86
National Lampoon's Class Reunion '82
National Lampoon's European Vacation '85
National Lampoon's Favorite Deadly Sins '95
National Lampoon's Gold Diggers '04
National Lampoon's Golf Punks '99
National Lampoon's Holiday Reunion '03
National Lampoon's Last Resort '94
National Lampoon's Loaded Weapon 1 '93
National Lampoon's Senior Trip '95
National Lampoon's The Don's Analyst '97
National Lampoon's The Stoned Aged '07
National Lampoon's Vacation '83 ▸
National Lampoon's Van Wilder '02

Our Gang

General Spanky '36
The Little Rascals '94

Philip Marlowe

The Big Sleep '46 ▸
Farewell, My Lovely '75 ▸
Lady in the Lake '46
The Long Goodbye '73 ▸
Marlowe '69
Murder, My Sweet '44 ▸
Poodle Springs '98

Pixar Animated Movies

A Bug's Life '98 ▸
Cars '06 ▸
Finding Nemo '03 ▸
The Incredibles '04 ▸
Monsters, Inc. '01 ▸
Ratatouille '07 ▸
Toy Story '95 ▸
Toy Story 2 '99 ▸
Toy Story 3 '10
Up '09 ▸
WALL-E '08 ▸

The Planet of the Apes

Battle for the Planet of the Apes '73
Beneath the Planet of the Apes '70
Conquest of the Planet of the Apes '72
Escape from the Planet of the Apes '71 ▸
Planet of the Apes '68 ▸

Plays to Film: Maxwell Anderson

Anne of the Thousand Days '69 ▸
The Bad Seed '56
The Bad Seed '85
The Guardsman '31 ▸
Joan of Arc '48
Key Largo '48 ▸
Mary of Scotland '36 ▸
Meet Joe Black '98
The Private Lives of Elizabeth & Essex '39 ▸
What Price Glory? '52 ▸
Winterset '36

Plays to Film: James M. Barrie

The Admirable Crichton '57
Hook '91
Little Minister '34 ▸
Peter Pan '24
Peter Pan '53 ▸
Peter Pan '60 ▸
Peter Pan '03
Quality Street '37
Seven Days' Leave '42

Plays to Film: Anton Chekhov

August '95
Country Life '95
La Petite Lili '03
The Lady with the Dog '59 ▸
The Seagull '71 ▸
The Seagull '75
The Shooting Party '77
The Three Sisters '65
An Unfinished Piece for a Player Piano '77 ▸
Vanya on 42nd Street '94 ▸
Ward Six '78

Plays to Film: Noel Coward

Bitter Sweet '33
Bitter Sweet '40
Blithe Spirit '45 ▸
Brief Encounter '46 ▸
Cavalcade '33 ▸
Easy Virtue '08
Private Lives '31 ▸
Relative Values '99
This Happy Breed '47 ▸
We Were Dancing '42

Plays to Film: Horton Foote

Baby, the Rain Must Fall '64
The Chase '66
Courtship '87 ▸
Lily Dale '96
1918 '85
The Trip to Bountiful '85 ▸

Plays to Film: Beth Henley

Crimes of the Heart '86
Miss Firecracker '89 ▸
Nobody's Fool '86
True Stories '86 ▸

Plays to Film: David Mamet

About Last Night... '86 ▸
American Buffalo '95
Edmond '05
Glengarry Glen Ross '92 ▸
Lakeboat '00
Oleanna '94

Plays to Film: Arthur Miller

All My Sons '48 ▸
All My Sons '86 ▸
Broken Glass '96
The Crucible '57 ▸
The Crucible '96 ▸
Death of a Salesman '86 ▸
Everybody Wins '90
Focus '01

Plays to Film: Eugene O'Neill

Ah, Wilderness! '35 ▸
Anna Christie '23 ▸
Anna Christie '30
Desire Under the Elms '58
Emperor Jones '33
The Hairy Ape '44
The Iceman Cometh '60 ▸
The Iceman Cometh '73
Long Day's Journey into Night '62 ▸
Long Day's Journey into Night '88
Long Day's Journey Into Night '96 ▸
The Long Voyage Home '40 ▸
On Borrowed Time '39 ▸
Strange Interlude '32 ▸
Strange Interlude '90
Summer Holiday '48

Plays to Film: Rodgers & Hammerstein

Carousel '56 ▸
Cinderella '64
Flower Drum Song '61
The King and I '56 ▸
Oklahoma! '55 ▸
Rodgers & Hammerstein's South Pacific '01
The Sound of Music '65 ▸
South Pacific '58 ▸

Plays to Film: Arthur Schnitzler

Affairs of Anatol '21
Circle of Love '64
Eyes Wide Shut '99
La Ronde '51 ▸
Liebelei '32

Plays to Film: William Shakespeare

Antony and Cleopatra '73
As You Like It '36
As You Like It '06
Carry On Cleo '65
Hamlet '48 ▸
Hamlet '69
Hamlet '90 ▸
Hamlet '96 ▸
Hamlet '00 ▸
Hamlet '01
Henry V '44 ▸
Henry V '89 ▸
Julius Caesar '53 ▸
Julius Caesar '70
King Lear '71 ▸
King Lear '87
King Lear '98 ▸
King of Texas '02 ▸
Looking for Richard '96 ▸
Love's Labour's Lost '00
Macbeth '48 ▸
Macbeth '70 ▸
Macbeth '71 ▸
Macbeth '88
Macbeth '06
The Merchant of Venice '73 ▸
The Merchant of Venice '04 ▸
The Merry Wives of Windsor '50
A Midsummer Night's Dream '35 ▸
A Midsummer Night's Dream '68
A Midsummer Night's Dream '96
Much Ado about Nothing '93 ▸
Othello '22
Othello '52 ▸
Othello '65 ▸
Othello '95 ▸
Othello '01 ▸
Prospero's Books '91 ▸
Ran '85 ▸
Richard III '12
Richard III '55 ▸
Richard III '95 ▸
Romeo and Juliet '36 ▸
Romeo and Juliet '54
Romeo and Juliet '68 ▸
Shakespeare in Love '98 ▸
The Taming of the Shrew '29
The Taming of the Shrew '67 ▸
The Tempest '63
The Tempest '82 ▸
The Tempest '99
Ten Things I Hate about You '99 ▸
Titus '99
Tromeo & Juliet '95
Twelfth Night '96
Were the World Mine '08
William Shakespeare's A Midsummer Night's Dream '99
William Shakespeare's Romeo and Juliet '96 ▸

Plays to Film: George Bernard Shaw

Androcles and the Lion '52
Caesar and Cleopatra '46
The Devil's Disciple '59 ▸
Heartbreak House '86
Major Barbara '41 ▸
The Millionairess '60
Pygmalion '38 ▸
Saint Joan '57

Plays to Film: Sam Shepard

Curse of the Starving Class '94
Fool for Love '86
Simpatico '99
True West '86 ▸

Plays to Film: Robert E. Sherwood

Abe Lincoln in Illinois '40 ▸
Idiot's Delight '39 ▸
Jupiter's Darling '55
Main Street to Broadway '53
Petrified Forest '36 ▸
Rebecca '40 ▸
The Royal Bed '31
Waterloo Bridge '40 ▸

Plays to Film: Neil Simon

Barefoot in the Park '67 ▸
Biloxi Blues '88
Brighton Beach Memoirs '86
Broadway Bound '92
California Suite '78 ▸
Chapter Two '79
The Cheap Detective '78 ▸
Come Blow Your Horn '63 ▸
The Goodbye Girl '77 ▸
The Heartbreak Kid '72 ▸
I Ought to Be in Pictures '82
Last of the Red Hot Lovers '72
Lost in Yonkers '93
The Marrying Man '91
Max Dugan Returns '83
Murder by Death '76
The Odd Couple '68 ▸
One Trick Pony '80
Only When I Laugh '81 ▸
The Out-of-Towners '70 ▸
Plaza Suite '71 ▸
Prisoner of Second Avenue '74
Seems Like Old Times '80
The Slugger's Wife '85
Star Spangled Girl '71
The Sunshine Boys '75 ▸
Sweet Charity '69 ▸

Plays to Film: Tom Stoppard

Rosencrantz & Guildenstern Are Dead '90 ▸

Plays to Film: Tennessee Williams

Baby Doll '56 ▸
Boom! '68
Cat on a Hot Tin Roof '58 ▸
Cat on a Hot Tin Roof '84
The Fugitive Kind '60
The Glass Menagerie '87 ▸
The Loss of a Teardrop Diamond '08
The Migrants '74 ▸
The Night of the Iguana '64 ▸
Orpheus Descending '91
Period of Adjustment '62 ▸
Roman Spring of Mrs. Stone '61 ▸
The Rose Tattoo '55 ▸
A Streetcar Named Desire '51 ▸
A Streetcar Named Desire '84 ▸
A Streetcar Named Desire '95
Suddenly, Last Summer '59 ▸
Summer and Smoke '61
Sweet Bird of Youth '62 ▸
Sweet Bird of Youth '89
This Property Is Condemned '66

Producers: Robert Altman

Buffalo Bill & the Indians '76 ▸
Kansas City '95 ▸
The Late Show '77 ▸
Nashville '75 ▸
Quintet '79
Rich Kids '79
A Wedding '78
Welcome to L.A. '77 ▸

Producers: Bruckheimer/Simpson

Bad Boys '95
Beverly Hills Cop '84
Beverly Hills Cop 2 '87
Crimson Tide '95 ▸
Dangerous Minds '95
Days of Thunder '90
Flashdance '83
The Ref '93 ▸
The Rock '96 ▸
Thief of Hearts '84
Top Gun '86

Producers: William Castle

Bug '75
House on Haunted Hill '58
Macabre '69
Riot '69
Rosemary's Baby '68 ▸
Strait-Jacket '64
13 Ghosts '60
Zotz! '62

Producers: Coppola/American Zoetrope

American Graffiti '73 ▸
The Black Stallion '79 ▸
The Conversation '74 ▸
The Escape Artist '82 ▸
The Godfather, Part 2 '74 ▸
Hammett '82

Producers: Roger Corman/New World

Atlas '60
Attack of the Giant Leeches '59
Avalanche '78
Battle Beyond the Stars '80
Battle Beyond the Sun '63
Beyond the Call of Duty '92
Big Bad Mama '74
Big Bad Mama 2 '87
The Big Bird Cage '72
The Big Doll House '71
Bloodfist '89
Bloodfist 2 '90
Bloody Mama '70
Body Waves '92
Boxcar Bertha '72
A Bucket of Blood '59 ▸
Caged Heat '74
Candy Stripe Nurses '74
Carnival Rock '57
Cocaine Wars '86
Cockfighter '74 ▸
The Corporation '96
Crazy Mama '75
Daddy's Boys '87
Day the World Ended '55
Death Race 2000 '75
Death Sport '78
Dementia 13 '63
Dinosaur Island '93
The Dunwich Horror '70
Eat My Dust '76
Eye of the Eagle 3 '91
The Fall of the House of Usher '60 ▸
Field of Fire '92
Fighting Mad '76
Firehawk '92
Forbidden World '82
Futurekick '91
Galaxy of Terror '81
Gas-s-s-s! '70
Grand Theft Auto '77
The Gunslinger '56
The Haunted Palace '63
Humanoids from the Deep '80
I, Mobster '58
I Never Promised You a Rose Garden '77 ▸
In the Heat of Passion '91
It Conquered the World '56
Jackson County Jail '76
Lady in Red '79
The Last Woman on Earth '61
Little Shop of Horrors '60 ▸
Lords of the Deep '89
Lumiere '76
Machine Gun Kelly '58
Masque of the Red Death '65 ▸
Masque of the Red Death '89
Monster from the Ocean Floor '54
Munchies '87
Nam Angels '88
Night of the Blood Beast '58
Not of This Earth '96
Piranha '78
The Pit and the Pendulum '61 ▸
Premature Burial '62
Primary Target '89
Private Duty Nurses '71
Raiders of the Sun '92
The Raven '63 ▸
Rock 'n' Roll High School Forever '91
The St. Valentine's Day Massacre '67
Ski Troop Attack '60
Small Change '76 ▸
Smokey Bites the Dust '81
Stripped to Kill '87
The Student Nurses '70
T-Bird Gang '59
Tales of Terror '62
Targets '68 ▸
Teenage Caveman '58
The Terror '63
Thunder and Lightning '77
Time Trackers '88
Tomb of Ligeia '64 ▸

▸ = rated three bones or higher

Too Hot to Handle *'76*
The Trip *'67*
The Undead *'57*
Unholy Rollers *'72*
Voyage to the Planet of Prehistoric Women *'68*
The Wasp Woman *'59*
The Wasp Woman *'96*
The Wild Angels *'66*
The Wild Ride *'60*
X: The Man with X-Ray Eyes *'63* ▸
The Young Nurses *'73*

Producers: Judd Apatow

Anchorman: The Legend of Ron Burgundy *'04*
The Cable Guy *'96*
Celtic Pride *'96*
Drillbit Taylor *'08*
Forgetting Sarah Marshall *'08*
The 40 Year Old Virgin *'05* ▸
Funny People *'09*
Get Him to the Greek *'10*
Heavyweights *'94*
Kicking & Screaming *'05*
Knocked Up *'07*
Pineapple Express *'08* ▸
Step Brothers *'08*
Superbad *'07* ▸
Talladega Nights: The Ballad of Ricky Bobby *'06*
The TV Set *'06*
Walk Hard: The Dewey Cox Story *'07*
Year One *'09*

Producers: Val Lewton

Bedlam *'45* ▸
The Body Snatcher *'45* ▸
Cat People *'42* ▸
Isle of the Dead *'45*
The Leopard Man *'43*

Producers: George Lucas

The Empire Strikes Back *'80* ▸
The Ewok Adventure *'84*
More American Graffiti *'79*
Raiders of the Lost Ark *'81* ▸
Return of the Jedi *'83* ▸

Producers: Merchant Ivory

Autobiography of a Princess *'75*
The Ballad of the Sad Cafe *'91*
Bombay Talkie *'70*
The Courtesans of Bombay *'85* ▸
The Europeans *'79* ▸
Fast Talking *'86*
Feast of July *'95*
The Golden Bowl *'00*
Howard's End *'92* ▸
Hullabaloo over Georgie & Bonnie's Pictures *'78*
Jane Austen in Manhattan *'80*
Jefferson in Paris *'94*
Maurice *'87* ▸
Mr. & Mrs. Bridge *'90* ▸
The Remains of the Day *'93* ▸
A Room with a View *'86* ▸
Roseland *'77* ▸
Shakespeare Wallah *'65* ▸
A Soldier's Daughter Never Cries *'98*
Surviving Picasso *'96*
The White Countess *'05* ▸

Producers: George Pal

Atlantis, the Lost Continent *'61*
Conquest of Space *'55*
Destination Moon *'50*
Doc Savage *'75*
The Great Rupert *'50* ▸
Naked Jungle *'54* ▸
7 Faces of Dr. Lao *'63* ▸
Time Machine *'78*
The War of the Worlds *'53* ▸
When Worlds Collide *'51*

Producers: Steven Spielberg

Amazing Stories *'85*
An American Tail *'86*
An American Tail: Fievel Goes West *'91*
Back to the Future *'85* ▸
The Color Purple *'85* ▸
Empire of the Sun *'87* ▸
The Goonies *'85*
Gremlins *'84* ▸
Honey, I Shrunk the Kids *'89*
Innerspace *'87*
Jurassic Park *'93* ▸
Poltergeist *'82* ▸
The Terminal *'04*
Twilight Zone: The Movie *'83*
Who Framed Roger Rabbit *'88* ▸
Young Sherlock Holmes *'85*

Producers: Andy Warhol

Andy Warhol's Bad *'77* ▸
Cocaine Cowboys *'79*
Flesh *'68* ▸
Heat *'72* ▸
Trash *'70*

Rambo

First Blood *'82*
Rambo: First Blood, Part 2 *'85*
Rambo 3 *'88*

The Rangebusters

Arizona Stagecoach *'42*
Black Market Rustlers *'43*
Boot Hill Bandits *'42*
Cowboy Commandos *'43*
Fugitive Valley *'41*
Haunted Ranch *'43*
Kid's Last Ride *'41*
Land of Hunted Men *'43*
Range Busters *'40*
Rock River Renegades *'42*
Saddle Mountain Roundup *'41*
Texas to Bataan *'42*
Thunder River Feud *'42*
Tonto Basin Outlaws *'41*
Trail of the Silver Spurs *'41*
Trail Riders *'42*
Trailing Double Trouble *'40*
Tumbledown Ranch in Arizona *'41*
Two-Fisted Justice *'43*
Underground Rustlers *'41*
West of Pinto Basin *'40*

Recycled Footage/ Redubbed Dialogue

Battle Beyond the Sun *'63*
Contact *'97*
Dead Men Don't Wear Plaid *'82*
Fast, Cheap & Out of Control *'97* ▸
Ferocious Female Freedom Fighters *'88*
Forrest Gump *'94* ▸
Good Night, and Good Luck *'05* ▸
J-Men Forever! *'79* ▸
Last Action Hero *'93*
The Legend of Drunken Master *'94* ▸
Mystery Science Theater 3000: The Movie *'96*
Planet of Blood *'66*
Twin Dragons *'92*
Voyage to the Planet of Prehistoric Women *'68*
Voyage to the Prehistoric Planet *'65*
What's Up, Tiger Lily? *'66* ▸
Zelig *'83* ▸

Renfrew of the Mounties

Danger Ahead *'40*
Fighting Mad *'39*
Murder on the Yukon *'40*
Renfrew of the Royal Mounted *'37*
Renfrew on the Great White Trail *'38*
Sky Bandits *'40*
Yukon Flight *'40*

Restored Footage

Army of Shadows *'69* ▸
Ashes of Time Redux *'08*
Beau Revel *'21* ▸
Crimes of Passion *'84* ▸
Dr. Jekyll and Mr. Hyde *'32* ▸
Foolish Wives *'22* ▸
Frankenstein *'31* ▸
Isadora *'68* ▸
Lawrence of Arabia *'62* ▸
The Leopard *'63* ▸
Lost Horizon *'37* ▸
The Lost World *'25*
New York, New York *'77* ▸
Othello *'52* ▸
Que Viva Mexico *'32* ▸
Red River *'48* ▸
The Rules of the Game *'39* ▸
Sadie Thompson *'28* ▸
Spartacus *'60* ▸
Spiders *'18* ▸
A Star Is Born *'54* ▸
Star Trek: The Motion Picture *'79*
Sunny Side Up *'28*
Tarzan and His Mate *'34* ▸
Twelve o'Clock High *'49* ▸
Two English Girls *'72* ▸
Wages of Fear *'55* ▸
When Time Ran Out *'80*

Rin Tin Tin

Lightning Warrior *'31*
The Lone Defender *'32*
The Night Cry *'26*

The Ritz Brothers

Argentine Nights *'40*
Blazing Stewardesses *'75*
The Goldwyn Follies *'38*
The Gorilla *'39*

Robin Hood

The Adventures of Robin Hood *'38* ▸
Beyond Sherwood Forest *'09*
A Challenge for Robin Hood *'68*
Men of Sherwood Forest *'57*
The Prince of Thieves *'48*
Princess of Thieves *'01*
Robin and Marian *'76*
Robin Hood *'22* ▸
Robin Hood *'73* ▸
Robin Hood *'91* ▸
Robin Hood *'10*
Robin Hood: Men in Tights *'93*
Robin Hood: Prince of Thieves *'91*
Robin Hood... The Legend: Herne's Son *'85*
Robin Hood... The Legend: Robin Hood and the Sorcerer *'83*
Robin Hood... The Legend: The Swords of Wayland *'83*
Robin Hood... The Legend: The Time of the Wolf *'85*
Robin Hood: The Movie *'55*
Robin of Locksley *'95*
The Story of Robin Hood & His Merrie Men *'52* ▸
Sword of Sherwood Forest *'60*
Tales of Robin Hood *'52*
Time Bandits *'81*
Young Ivanhoe *'95*
The Zany Adventures of Robin Hood *'84*

The Rough Riders

Arizona Bound *'41*
Below the Border *'42*
Dead Man *'95*
Down Texas Way *'42*
Forbidden Trails *'41*
Ghost Town Law *'42*
Gunman from Bodie *'41*
Riders of the West *'42*

Rusty the Dog

The Adventures of Rusty *'45*
Rusty's Birthday *'49*
Son of Rusty *'47*

The Saint

Fiction Makers *'67*
The Saint *'68*
The Saint *'97*
The Saint in London *'39*
The Saint in New York *'38*
The Saint Strikes Back *'39*
The Saint Takes Over *'40*
The Saint's Double Trouble *'40*
Vendetta for the Saint *'68*

Screen Teams: Abbott & Costello

Abbott and Costello Go to Mars *'53*
Abbott and Costello in Hollywood *'45*
Abbott and Costello in the Foreign Legion *'50*
Abbott and Costello Meet Captain Kidd *'52*
Abbott and Costello Meet Dr. Jekyll and Mr. Hyde *'52*
Abbott and Costello Meet Frankenstein *'48* ▸
Abbott and Costello Meet the Invisible Man *'51* ▸
Abbott and Costello Meet the Keystone Kops *'54*
Abbott and Costello Meet the Killer, Boris Karloff *'49*
Abbott and Costello Meet the Mummy *'55*
Africa Screams *'49*
Buck Privates *'41*
Buck Privates Come Home *'47* ▸
Comin' Round the Mountain *'51*
Dance with Me, Henry *'56*
Here Come the Co-Eds *'45*
Hit the Ice *'43*
Hold That Ghost *'41* ▸
In Society *'44*
In the Navy *'41*
It Ain't Hay *'43*
Jack & the Beanstalk *'52*
Keep 'Em Flying *'41*
Little Giant *'46*
Lost in a Harem *'44*
Lost in Alaska *'52*
Mexican Hayride *'48*
The Naughty Nineties *'45*
The Noose Hangs High *'48* ▸
One Night in the Tropics *'40*
Pardon My Sarong *'42*
Ride 'Em Cowboy *'42*
Rio Rita *'42*
The 30-Foot Bride of Candy Rock *'59*
The Time of Their Lives *'46*
Who Done It? *'42*
The Wistful Widow of Wagon Gap *'47*

Screen Teams: Allen & Farrow

Alice *'90* ▸
Another Woman *'88* ▸
Broadway Danny Rose *'84* ▸
Crimes & Misdemeanors *'89* ▸
Hannah and Her Sisters *'86* ▸
Husbands and Wives *'92* ▸
A Midsummer Night's Sex Comedy *'82* ▸
New York Stories *'89* ▸
The Purple Rose of Cairo *'85* ▸
Radio Days *'87* ▸
September *'88*
Shadows and Fog *'92*
Zelig *'83* ▸

Screen Teams: Allen & Keaton

Annie Hall *'77* ▸
Interiors *'78* ▸
Love and Death *'75* ▸
Manhattan *'79* ▸
Manhattan Murder Mystery *'93* ▸
Play It Again, Sam *'72* ▸
Sleeper *'73* ▸

Screen Teams: Astaire & Rogers

The Barkleys of Broadway *'49* ▸
Carefree *'38* ▸
Flying Down to Rio *'33*
Follow the Fleet *'36* ▸
The Gay Divorcee *'34* ▸
Roberta *'35* ▸
Shall We Dance *'37* ▸
The Story of Vernon and Irene Castle *'39* ▸
Swing Time *'36* ▸
Top Hat *'35* ▸

Screen Teams: Ball & Arnaz

The Long, Long Trailer *'54*

Screen Teams: Belushi & Aykroyd

The Blues Brothers *'80* ▸
Neighbors *'81*
1941 *'79*

Screen Teams: Bogart & Bacall

The Big Sleep *'46* ▸
Dark Passage *'47*
To Have & Have Not *'44* ▸

Screen Teams: Bronson & Ireland

Breakheart Pass *'76*
Breakout *'75*
Chino *'75*
Cold Sweat *'71*
Death Wish 2 *'82*
The Family *'70*
From Noon Till Three *'76*
Hard Times *'75* ▸
Love and Bullets *'79*
The Mechanic *'72*
Rider on the Rain *'70* ▸
Someone Behind the Door *'71*
The Valachi Papers *'72*
Villa Rides *'68*

Screen Teams: Burton & Taylor

Boom! *'68*
Cleopatra *'63*
The Comedians *'67*
Divorce His, Divorce Hers *'72*
Doctor Faustus *'68*
Hammersmith Is Out *'72*
The Sandpiper *'65*
The Taming of the Shrew *'67* ▸
Under Milk Wood *'73*
The V.I.P.'s *'63* ▸
Who's Afraid of Virginia Woolf? *'66* ▸

Screen Teams: Cagney & O'Brien

Angels with Dirty Faces *'38* ▸
Boy Meets Girl *'38* ▸
Ceiling Zero *'35* ▸
The Fighting 69th *'40* ▸
Ragtime *'81* ▸
Torrid Zone *'40*

Screen Teams: Cheech & Chong

After Hours *'85* ▸
Cheech and Chong: Still Smokin' *'83*
Cheech and Chong: Things Are Tough All Over *'82*
Cheech and Chong's Next Movie *'80*
Cheech and Chong's Nice Dreams *'81*
Cheech and Chong's The Corsican Brothers *'84*
Cheech and Chong's Up in Smoke *'79*

Screen Teams: Cusack & Piven

Bob Roberts *'92* ▸
Floundering *'94*
The Grifters *'90* ▸
Grosse Pointe Blank *'97* ▸
One Crazy Summer *'86*
The Player *'92* ▸
Runaway Jury *'03* ▸
Say Anything *'89* ▸
Serendipity *'01*

Screen Teams: Cusack & Robbins

Bob Roberts *'92* ▸
The Cradle Will Rock *'99*
High Fidelity *'00* ▸
The Player *'92* ▸
The Sure Thing *'85* ▸
Tapeheads *'89*

Screen Teams: Damon & Affleck

Chasing Amy *'97*
Dogma *'99*
Good Will Hunting *'97*
Jay and Silent Bob Strike Back *'01*
Jersey Girl *'04*
School Ties *'92* ▸

Screen Teams: De Niro & Keitel

The Bridge of San Luis Rey *'05*
Cop Land *'97* ▸
Falling in Love *'84*
Mean Streets *'73* ▸
Taxi Driver *'76* ▸

Screen Teams: De Niro & Pesci

A Bronx Tale *'93* ▸
Casino *'95* ▸
Goodfellas *'90* ▸
Once Upon a Time in America *'84* ▸
Raging Bull *'80* ▸

Screen Teams: Depardieu & Deneuve

Changing Times *'04*
Choice of Arms *'83*
Fort Saganne *'84*
The Last Metro *'80* ▸

Screen Teams: Eastwood & Locke

Any Which Way You Can *'80*
Bronco Billy *'80*
Every Which Way But Loose *'78*
The Gauntlet *'77*
The Outlaw Josey Wales *'76* ▸
Sudden Impact *'83*

Screen Teams: Eddy & McDonald

Bitter Sweet *'40*
Girl of the Golden West *'38*
I Married an Angel *'42*
Maytime *'37* ▸
Naughty Marietta *'35*
New Moon *'40*
Rose Marie *'36* ▸
Sweethearts *'38* ▸

Screen Teams: Farley & Spade

Black Sheep *'96*
Coneheads *'93*
Tommy Boy *'95*

Screen Teams: Favreau & Vaughn

The Break Up *'98*
Four Christmases *'08*
Made *'01*
Rudy *'93*
Swingers *'96* ▸

Screen Teams: Flynn & de Havilland

Captain Blood *'35* ▸
The Charge of the Light Brigade *'36* ▸
Dodge City *'39* ▸
Four's a Crowd *'38*
The Private Lives of Elizabeth & Essex *'39* ▸
Santa Fe Trail *'40*
They Died with Their Boots On *'41* ▸

▸ *= rated three bones or higher*

Screen Teams: Gable & Crawford

Chained '34
Dance Fools Dance '31 ►
Dancing Lady '33
Forsaking All Others '35
Laughing Sinners '31
Love on the Run '36
Possessed '31
Strange Cargo '40

Screen Teams: Gable & Loy

Manhattan Melodrama '34 ►
Men in White '34
Test Pilot '38 ►
Too Hot to Handle '38 ►
Wife Versus Secretary '36 ►

Screen Teams: Gable & Turner

Betrayed '54 ►
Homecoming '48
Honky Tonk '41 ►
Somewhere I'll Find You '42 ►

Screen Teams: Garland & Rooney

Andy Hardy Meets Debutante '40
Babes in Arms '39
Babes on Broadway '41
Girl Crazy '43 ►
Life Begins for Andy Hardy '41 ►
Love Finds Andy Hardy '38 ►
Strike Up the Band '40
Thoroughbreds Don't Cry '37
Thousands Cheer '43
Words and Music '48

Screen Teams: Garson & Pidgeon

Blossoms in the Dust '41
Julia Misbehaves '48 ►
Madame Curie '43 ►
The Miniver Story '50
Mrs. Miniver '42 ►
Mrs. Parkington '44
That Forsyte Woman '50

Screen Teams: J. Gaynor & C. Farrell

Lucky Star '29
The Man Who Came Back '08
7th Heaven '27
Street Angel '28
Tess of the Storm Country '22

Screen Teams: Gibson & Glover

Lethal Weapon '87 ►
Lethal Weapon 2 '89 ►
Lethal Weapon 3 '92
Lethal Weapon 4 '98
Maverick '94

Screen Teams: Hepburn & Grant

Bringing Up Baby '38 ►
Holiday '38 ►
The Philadelphia Story '40 ►
Sylvia Scarlett '35

Screen Teams: Hepburn & Tracy

Adam's Rib '50 ►
Desk Set '57 ►
Guess Who's Coming to Dinner '67 ►
Pat and Mike '52 ►
State of the Union '48 ►
Without Love '45
Woman of the Year '42 ►

Screen Teams: Hope & Crosby

Cancel My Reservation '72
My Favorite Blonde '42 ►
My Favorite Brunette '47
The Princess and the Pirate '44 ►
The Road to Bali '53 ►
The Road to Hong Kong '62
The Road to Morocco '42 ►
The Road to Rio '47 ►
The Road to Singapore '40
The Road to Utopia '46 ►
The Road to Zanzibar '41 ►
Scared Stiff '53 ►
Star Spangled Rhythm '42 ►

Screen Teams: Ladd & Lake

The Blue Dahlia '46 ►
The Glass Key '42 ►
This Gun for Hire '42 ►

Screen Teams: Lancaster & Douglas

The Devil's Disciple '59 ►
Gunfight at the O.K. Corral '57 ►
The List of Adrian Messenger '63 ►
Seven Days in May '64 ►
Tough Guys '86
Victory at Entebbe '76

Screen Teams: Laurel & Hardy

Air Raid Wardens '43
Block-heads '38 ►
Bohemian Girl '36 ►
Bonnie Scotland '35
Bullfighters '45
A Chump at Oxford '40
The Devil's Brother '33
The Flying Deuces '39 ►
Great Guns '41
Hollywood Party '34
Laurel & Hardy and the Family '33
Laurel & Hardy: Another Fine Mess '30
Laurel & Hardy: At Work '32
Laurel & Hardy: Be Big '31
Laurel & Hardy: Below Zero '30
Laurel & Hardy: Berth Marks '29
Laurel & Hardy: Blotto '30
Laurel & Hardy: Brats '30
Laurel & Hardy: Chickens Come Home '31
Laurel & Hardy: Hog Wild '30
Laurel & Hardy: Laughing Gravy '31
Laurel & Hardy: Men O'War '29
Laurel & Hardy: Night Owls '30
Laurel & Hardy On the Lam '30
Laurel & Hardy: Perfect Day '29
Laurel & Hardy Spooktacular '34
Laurel & Hardy: Stan "Helps" Ollie '33
Laurel & Hardy: The Hoose-Gow '29
Nothing But Trouble '44
Our Relations '36 ►
Pack Up Your Troubles '32
Pardon Us '31
Pick a Star '37
Saps at Sea '40
Sons of the Desert '33 ►
Swiss Miss '38
Utopia '51
Way Out West '37 ►
The Young Victoria '09 ►

Screen Teams: Lee & Cushing

The Creeping Flesh '72
The Curse of Frankenstein '57
The Devil's Undead '75
Dr. Terror's House of Horrors '65
Dracula A.D. 1972 '72
The Gorgon '64
Hamlet '48 ►
Horror Express '72
The Horror of Dracula '58 ►
The Hound of the Baskervilles '59
The House that Dripped Blood '71
Island of the Burning Doomed '67
Moulin Rouge '52 ►
The Mummy '59 ►
Nothing But the Night '72
The Satanic Rites of Dracula '73
Scream and Scream Again '70
The Skull '65

Screen Teams: Lemmon & Matthau

Buddy Buddy '81
The Fortune Cookie '66 ►
The Front Page '74
The Grass Harp '95
Grumpier Old Men '95
Grumpy Old Men '93 ►
JFK '91 ►
Neil Simon's The Odd Couple 2 '98
The Odd Couple '68 ►
Out to Sea '97

Screen Teams: Loy & Powell

After the Thin Man '36 ►
Another Thin Man '39
Double Wedding '37 ►
Evelyn Prentice '34
The Great Ziegfeld '36 ►
I Love You Again '40 ►
Libeled Lady '36 ►
Love Crazy '41 ►
Manhattan Melodrama '34 ►
Shadow of the Thin Man '41 ►
Song of the Thin Man '47
The Thin Man '34 ►
The Thin Man Goes Home '44

Screen Teams: Martin & Lewis

Artists and Models '55
At War with the Army '50
The Caddy '53
Hollywood or Bust '56
Jumping Jacks '52
Money from Home '53
My Friend Irma '49
Pardners '56
The Road to Bali '53 ►
Sailor Beware '52
Scared Stiff '53 ►
The Stooge '51

Screen Teams: Newman & Woodward

The Drowning Pool '75
From the Terrace '60
The Long, Hot Summer '58 ►
Mr. & Mrs. Bridge '90 ►
A New Kind of Love '63
Paris Blues '61
Rally 'Round the Flag, Boys! '58

Screen Teams: Powell & Keeler

Colleen '36
Dames '34 ►
Flirtation Walk '34
Footlight Parade '33 ►
42nd Street '33 ►
Gold Diggers of 1933 '33 ►
Shipmates Forever '35

Screen Teams: Power & Tierney

The Nevada Buckaroo '31
The Razor's Edge '46 ►
Return of Frank James '40 ►
Son of Fury '42 ►
That Wonderful Urge '48

Screen Teams: Power & Young

Cafe Metropole '37
Love Is News '37 ►
Second Honeymoon '37

Screen Teams: Redford & Newman

Butch Cassidy and the Sundance Kid '69 ►
The Sting '73 ►

Screen Teams: Reynolds & DeLuise

The Best Little Whorehouse in Texas '82
Cannonball Run '81
Cannonball Run 2 '84
The End '78 ►
Smokey and the Bandit 2 '80

Screen Teams: Reynolds & Field

The End '78 ►
Hooper '78
Smokey and the Bandit '77
Smokey and the Bandit 2 '80

Screen Teams: Rogers & Evans

Along the Navaho Trail '45
Apache Rose '47
Bells of Coronado '50
Bells of Rosarita '45
Bells of San Angelo '47
Cowboy & the Senorita '44
Don't Fence Me In '45
Down Dakota Way '49
The Golden Stallion '49
Helldorado '46
Home in Oklahoma '47
My Pal Trigger '46
Rainbow over Texas '46
Roll on Texas Moon '46
Song of Arizona '46
Sunset in El Dorado '45
Susanna Pass '49
Trigger, Jr. '50
Twilight in the Sierras '50
Under Nevada Skies '46
Utah '45

Screen Teams: Snipes & Harrelson

Money Train '95
White Men Can't Jump '92
Wildcats '86

Screen Teams: Stewart & Sullavan

The Mortal Storm '40 ►
The Shop Around the Corner '40 ►
Shopworn Angel '38 ►

Screen Teams: Stiller & O. Wilson

Meet the Fockers '04
Meet the Parents '00 ►
Permanent Midnight '98
The Royal Tenenbaums '01 ►
Starsky & Hutch '04
Zoolander '01

Screen Teams: Turner & Douglas

The Jewel of the Nile '85
Romancing the Stone '84 ►
The War of the Roses '89 ►

Screen Teams: Wayne & O'Hara

Big Jake '71
McLintock! '63 ►
The Quiet Man '52 ►
Rio Grande '50 ►
Wings of Eagles '57

Screen Teams: Wilder & Pryor

Another You '91
See No Evil, Hear No Evil '89
Silver Streak '76 ►
Stir Crazy '80

Scrooge

An American Christmas Carol '79
A Christmas Carol '38 ►
A Christmas Carol '51 ►
A Christmas Carol '54
A Christmas Carol '84 ►
A Christmas Carol '99
Ms. Scrooge '97
Scrooged '88

Sexton Blake

Echo Murders '45
Meet Sexton Blake '44
Sexton Blake and the Hooded Terror '38
Stage Struck '57

Sherlock Holmes

The Adventures of Sherlock Holmes '39
The Adventures of Sherlock Holmes' Smarter Brother '78 ►
The Crucifer of Blood '91
Dr. Bell and Mr. Doyle: The Dark Beginnings of Sherlock Holmes '00
Dressed to Kill '46
Hands of a Murderer '90
The Hound of London '93
The Hound of the Baskervilles '39 ►
The Hound of the Baskervilles '59
The Hound of the Baskervilles '77
The Hound of the Baskervilles '83
The Hound of the Baskervilles '00
The Hound of the Baskervilles '02 ►
House of Fear '45
Masks of Death '86
Murder at the Baskervilles '37
Murder by Decree '79 ►
The Pearl of Death '44
The Private Life of Sherlock Holmes '70 ►
Pursuit to Algiers '45
Scarlet Claw '44 ►
The Seven-Per-Cent Solution '76 ►
Sherlock: Case of Evil '02
Sherlock Holmes '22
Sherlock Holmes '09
Sherlock Holmes and the Deadly Necklace '62
Sherlock Holmes and the Incident at Victoria Falls '91
Sherlock Holmes and the Secret Weapon '42 ►
Sherlock Holmes Faces Death '43 ►
Sherlock Holmes in Washington '43
Sherlock Holmes: The Voice of Terror '42
The Sign of Four '83
The Sign of Four '01
The Silent Mr. Sherlock Holmes '12
The Speckled Band '31 ►
Spider Woman '44 ►
The Strange Case of the End of Civilization As We Know It '93
A Study in Scarlet '33
A Study in Terror '66 ►
Terror by Night '46
They Might Be Giants '71 ►
The Triumph of Sherlock Holmes '35
Without a Clue '88
The Woman in Green '49
Young Sherlock Holmes '85

Sinbad

Captain Sinbad '63
Golden Voyage of Sinbad '73
Invitation to the Dance '56
The Magic Voyage of Sinbad '52
The Seventh Voyage of Sinbad '58 ►
Sinbad and the Eye of the Tiger '77
Sinbad: Legend of the Seven Seas '03
Son of Sinbad '55
What the Moon Saw '90

Special FX Extravaganzas

The Abyss '89 ►
Alice in Wonderland '85
Alien: Resurrection '97 ►
Aliens '86 ►
An American Werewolf in Paris '97
Anaconda '96
The Arrival '96
Baby Geniuses '98
Batman '89 ►
Batman and Robin '97
Batman Forever '95 ►
Beetlejuice '88 ►
Big Trouble in Little China '86
The Black Hole '79
Blithe Spirit '45 ►
The Borrowers '97
Captain Sinbad '63
The Chronicles of Riddick '04
Crash Dive '43
Dante's Peak '97
Daylight '96
Dragonheart '96
Event Horizon '97
The Ewok Adventure '84
The Exorcist '73 ►
The Exorcist 2: The Heretic '77
FairyTale: A True Story '97
Fantastic Voyage '66 ►
The Fifth Element '97
Forbidden Planet '56 ►
Hideaway '94
Highlander: The Final Dimension '94
Independence Day '96 ►
Innerspace '87
Judge Dredd '95
Jumanji '95
Jurassic Park '93 ►
Lifeforce '85
The Lost World: Jurassic Park 2 '97
Mars Attacks! '96
Mary Shelley's Frankenstein '94
The Mask '94 ►
My Favorite Martian '98
Poltergeist '82 ►
The Rains Came '39
Return of the Jedi '83 ►
The Shadow '94
Small Soldiers '98
Solar Crisis '92
Spawn '97 ►
Species '95
Species 2 '98
Star Trek 2: The Wrath of Khan '82 ►
Star Trek 4: The Voyage Home '86 ►
Star Trek: Generations '94 ►
Superman 2 '80 ►
The Terminator '84 ►
Terminator 2: Judgment Day '91 ►
The Thing '82
Total Recall '90 ►
Twister '96
2001: A Space Odyssey '68 ►
2010: The Year We Make Contact '84 ►
Virtuosity '95
Virus '98
Volcano '97
Who Framed Roger Rabbit '88 ►
Wolfen '81 ►

Special FX Extravaganzas: Make-Up

An American Werewolf in London '81 ►
The Associate '96
Bad Moon '96
Batman and Robin '97
Battle for the Planet of the Apes '73
Beetlejuice '88 ►
Beneath the Planet of the Apes '70
Body Melt '93
Conquest of the Planet of the Apes '72
Darkman 2: The Return of Durant '94
Darkman 3: Die Darkman Die '95
Dawn of the Dead '78 ►
Day of the Dead '85

Escape from the Planet of the Apes '71 ►
The Exorcist '73 ►
The Fly '86 ►
The Fly 2 '89
Freaked '93
Hocus Pocus '93
The Howling '81 ►
The Island of Dr. Moreau '96
The Man Without a Face '93
Mary Shelley's Frankenstein '94
The Nutty Professor '96 ►
Nutty Professor 2: The Klumps '00
Planet of the Apes '68 ►
Planet of the Apes '01 ►
Scanner Cop '94
Scanners '81
Sssssss '73
The Thing '82
Vampire in Brooklyn '95
Warriors of Virtue '97
Wolf '94

Special FX Wizards: Rick Baker

An American Werewolf in London '81 ►
Food of the Gods '76
The Funhouse '81
The Fury '78
Greystoke: The Legend of Tarzan, Lord of the Apes '84
Harry and the Hendersons '87
Incredible Melting Man '77
The Incredible Shrinking Woman '81
It's Alive '74 ►
King Kong '76
Men in Black '97 ►
Mighty Joe Young '98
The Nutty Professor '96 ►
Octaman '71
Planet of the Apes '01 ►
Schlock '73
Squirm '76
Star Wars '77 ►
Tanya's Island '81
Track of the Moonbeast '76
Videodrome '83
Wolf '94

Special FX Wizards: Rob Bottin

Bugsy '91 ►
Explorers '85
Fear and Loathing in Las Vegas '98
The Fog '78
The Howling '81 ►
Humanoids from the Deep '80
Innerspace '87
Legend '86
Mission: Impossible '96 ►
RoboCop '87 ►
Tanya's Island '81
The Thing '82
Total Recall '90 ►
Twilight Zone: The Movie '83
The Witches of Eastwick '87

Special FX Wizards: Anton Furst

Alien '79 ►
Batman '89 ►
The Company of Wolves '85 ►
Full Metal Jacket '87 ►
Moonraker '79
Star Wars '77 ►

Special FX Wizards: Ray Harryhausen

The Beast from 20,000 Fathoms '53
Clash of the Titans '81
Earth vs. the Flying Saucers '56
First Men in the Moon '64
Golden Voyage of Sinbad '73
It Came from Beneath the Sea '55 ►
Jason and the Argonauts '63 ►
Mighty Joe Young '49
Mysterious Island '61 ►
One Million Years B.C. '66
The Seventh Voyage of Sinbad '58 ►
Sinbad and the Eye of the Tiger '77
The Three Worlds of Gulliver '59
20 Million Miles to Earth '57
The Valley of Gwangi '69 ►

Special FX Wizards: Herschell Gordon Lewis

Blood Feast '63
Color Me Blood Red '64
Gruesome Twosome '67
Just for the Hell of It '68
Moonshine Mountain '64
The Psychic '68
She-Devils on Wheels '68
Suburban Roulette '67
This Stuff'll Kill Ya! '71
2000 Maniacs '64
The Wizard of Gore '70

Special FX Wizards: Tom Savini

Creepshow '82
Dawn of the Dead '78 ►
Day of the Dead '85
Deathdream '72
Deranged '74 ►
Friday the 13th '80
Friday the 13th, Part 4: The Final Chapter '84
Knightriders '81
Maniac '80
Martin '77 ►
Midnight '81
Monkey Shines '88
The Prowler '81
The Ripper '86
The Texas Chainsaw Massacre 2 '86

Special FX Wizards: Dick Smith

Altered States '80 ►
Amadeus '84 ►
The Exorcist '73 ►
Ghost Story '81
The Godfather '72 ►
House of Dark Shadows '70 ►
Little Big Man '70 ►
Marathon Man '76 ►
Midnight Cowboy '69 ►
Scanners '81
The Sentinel '76
Spasms '82
The Stepford Wives '75 ►
The Sunshine Boys '75 ►
Taxi Driver '76 ►
The World of Henry Orient '64 ►

Special FX Wizards: Douglas Trumball

The Andromeda Strain '71
Blade Runner '82 ►
Brainstorm '83
Close Encounters of the Third Kind '77 ►
Silent Running '71 ►
Star Trek: The Motion Picture '79
2001: A Space Odyssey '68 ►

Star Wars

The Empire Strikes Back '80 ►
The Ewok Adventure '84
The Ewoks: Battle for Endor '85
Fanboys '09
Return of the Jedi '83 ►
Star Wars '77 ►
Star Wars: Episode 1—The Phantom Menace '99 ►
Star Wars: Episode 2—Attack of the Clones '02 ►
Star Wars: Episode 3—Revenge of the Sith '05 ►
Star Wars: The Clone Wars '08

Tarzan

Greystoke: The Legend of Tarzan, Lord of the Apes '84
The New Adventures of Tarzan '35
Tarzan '99 ►
Tarzan 2 '05
Tarzan and His Mate '34 ►
Tarzan and the Green Goddess '38
Tarzan and the Lost City '98
Tarzan and the Lost Safari '57
Tarzan and the She-Devil '53
Tarzan and the Slave Girl '50
Tarzan and the Trappers '58
Tarzan Escapes '36 ►
Tarzan Finds a Son '39 ►
Tarzan of the Apes '17
Tarzan, the Ape Man '32 ►
Tarzan, the Ape Man '81
Tarzan the Fearless '33
Tarzan the Magnificent '60
Tarzan the Tiger '29
Tarzan's Fight for Life '58
Tarzan's Greatest Adventure '59
Tarzan's Hidden Jungle '55
Tarzan's Magic Fountain '48
Tarzan's New York Adventure '42
Tarzan's Peril '51
Tarzan's Revenge '38
Tarzan's Savage Fury '52
Tarzan's Secret Treasure '41
Walk Like a Man '87

The Texas Rangers

Boss of Rawhide '44
Comanche Moon '08
Dead or Alive '44
Enemy of the Law '45
Fighting Valley '43
Flaming Bullets '45
Frontier Fugitives '45
Gangsters of the Frontier '44
Guns of the Law '44
Hello Trouble '32
Man of the House '05
Marked for Murder '45
Outlaw Roundup '44
Outlaws of the Cherokee Trail '41
The Rangers' Roundup '38
Rangers Take Over '42
The Return of the Rangers '43
Rio Grande Ranger '37
Rio Rita '29
Three in the Saddle '45
Trade '07
Wild West '46

The Thin Man

After the Thin Man '36 ►
Another Thin Man '39
Shadow of the Thin Man '41 ►
Song of the Thin Man '47
The Thin Man '34 ►
The Thin Man Goes Home '44

3.5 Bones

Cure '97 ►
J'accuse! '19 ►
JSA: Joint Security Area '00 ►
The Leopard '63 ►
There Will Be Blood '07 ►
Up '09 ►
WALL-E '08 ►

The Three Mesquiteers

Call the Mesquiteers '38
Code of the Outlaw '42
Come on, Cowboys '37
Covered Wagon Days '40
Cowboys from Texas '39
Frontier Horizon '39
Gangs of Sonora '41
Gauchos of El Dorado '41
Ghost Town Gold '36
Heart of the Rockies '37
Heroes of the Hills '38
Heroes of the Saddle '40
Hit the Saddle '37
The Kansas Terrors '39
Oklahoma Renegades '40
Outlaws of Sonora '38
Outlaws of the Cherokee Trail '41
Overland Stage Raiders '38 ►
Pals of the Saddle '38
Pioneers of the West '40
Powdersmoke Range '35
Purple Vigilantes '38
Riders of the Rio Grande '43
Riders of the Whistling Skull '37
Roarin' Lead '37
Rocky Mountain Rangers '40
Santa Fe Stampede '38
Shadows on the Sage '42
The Three Mesquiteers '36
Three Texas Steers '39
The Trigger Trio '37
West of Cimarron '41
Wild Horse Rodeo '37
Wyoming Outlaw '39

The Three Musketeers

The Four Musketeers '75 ►
The 4 Musketeers '05
The Man in the Iron Mask '98 ►
The Musketeer '01
Revenge of the Musketeers '63
Ring of the Musketeers '93
The Three Musketeers '16
The Three Musketeers '21 ►
The Three Musketeers '33
The Three Musketeers '35
The Three Musketeers '39
The Three Musketeers '48
The Three Musketeers '74 ►
The Three Musketeers '93

3 Stooges

Around the World in a Daze '63
Dancing Lady '33
Gold Raiders '51
Have Rocket Will Travel '59
Hollywood Party '34
It's a Mad, Mad, Mad, Mad World '63
The Lost Stooges '33
The Outlaws Is Coming! '65
Snow White and the Three Stooges '61
Stoogemania '85
Three Stooges in Orbit '62
The Three Stooges Meet Hercules '61

Tom Ripley

The American Friend '77 ►
Purple Noon '60 ►
Ripley's Game '02 ►
The Talented Mr. Ripley '99

Top Grossing Films of 1939

Gone with the Wind '39 ►
The Hunchback of Notre Dame '39 ►
Jesse James '39 ►
Mr. Smith Goes to Washington '39 ►
The Wizard of Oz '39 ►

Top Grossing Films of 1940

Boom Town '40
Fantasia '40 ►
Pinocchio '40 ►
Rebecca '40 ►
Santa Fe Trail '40

Top Grossing Films of 1941

Honky Tonk '41 ►
The Philadelphia Story '40 ►
Sergeant York '41 ►
A Yank in the R.A.F. '41

Top Grossing Films of 1942

Bambi '42 ►
Casablanca '42 ►
Mrs. Miniver '42 ►
Random Harvest '42 ►
Yankee Doodle Dandy '42 ►

Top Grossing Films of 1943

The Outlaw '43
The Song of Bernadette '43 ►
Stage Door Canteen '43
This Is the Army '43

Top Grossing Films of 1944

Going My Way '44 ►
Meet Me in St. Louis '44 ►
Since You Went Away '44 ►
Thirty Seconds Over Tokyo '44 ►

Top Grossing Films of 1945

Anchors Aweigh '45 ►
The Bells of St. Mary's '45 ►
Spellbound '45 ►
Weekend at the Waldorf '45 ►

Top Grossing Films of 1946

The Best Years of Our Lives '46 ►
Duel in the Sun '46 ►
The Jolson Story '46 ►

Top Grossing Films of 1947

Egg and I '47 ►
Life with Father '47 ►

Top Grossing Films of 1948

Johnny Belinda '48 ►
On an Island with You '48
The Paleface '48 ►
Red River '48 ►
The Red Shoes '48 ►
The Three Musketeers '48

Top Grossing Films of 1949

Battleground '49 ►
Jolson Sings Again '49
Samson and Delilah '50 ►
Sands of Iwo Jima '49 ►

Top Grossing Films of 1950

Annie Get Your Gun '50 ►
Cinderella '50 ►
Father of the Bride '50 ►
King Solomon's Mines '50 ►

Top Grossing Films of 1951

Alice in Wonderland '51 ►
David and Bathsheba '51 ►
The Great Caruso '51
Quo Vadis '51 ►
Show Boat '51

Top Grossing Films of 1952

The Greatest Show on Earth '52 ►
Hans Christian Andersen '52
Ivanhoe '52 ►
The Snows of Kilimanjaro '52 ►

Top Grossing Films of 1953

From Here to Eternity '53 ►
How to Marry a Millionaire '53
Peter Pan '53 ►
The Robe '53
Shane '53 ►

Top Grossing Films of 1954

The Caine Mutiny '54 ►
The Glenn Miller Story '54 ►
Rear Window '54 ►
20,000 Leagues under the Sea '54 ►
White Christmas '54 ►

Top Grossing Films of 1955

Battle Cry '55 ►
Lady and the Tramp '55 ►
Mister Roberts '55 ►
Oklahoma! '55 ►

Top Grossing Films of 1956

Around the World in 80 Days '56 ►
Giant '56 ►
The King and I '56 ►
The Ten Commandments '56 ►

Top Grossing Films of 1957

The Bridge on the River Kwai '57 ►
Old Yeller '57 ►
Peyton Place '57 ►
Raintree County '57
Sayonara '57 ►

Top Grossing Films of 1958

Auntie Mame '58 ►
Cat on a Hot Tin Roof '58 ►
Gigi '58 ►
No Time for Sergeants '58 ►
South Pacific '58 ►

Top Grossing Films of 1959

Ben-Hur '59 ►
Darby O'Gill & the Little People '59 ►
Operation Petticoat '59 ►
The Shaggy Dog '59
Sleeping Beauty '59 ►

Top Grossing Films of 1960

The Alamo '60 ►
Exodus '60 ►
Psycho '60 ►
Spartacus '60 ►
The Swiss Family Robinson '60 ►

Top Grossing Films of 1961

The Absent-Minded Professor '61 ►
El Cid '61 ►
The Guns of Navarone '61 ►
West Side Story '61 ►

Top Grossing Films of 1962

How the West Was Won '63 ►
In Search of the Castaways '62 ►
Lawrence of Arabia '62 ►
The Longest Day '62 ►
The Music Man '62 ►

Top Grossing Films of 1963

Cleopatra '63
Irma La Douce '63
It's a Mad, Mad, Mad, Mad World '63
The Sword in the Stone '63 ►
Tom Jones '63 ►

Top Grossing Films of 1964

The Carpetbaggers '64
From Russia with Love '63 ►
Goldfinger '64 ►
Mary Poppins '64 ►
My Fair Lady '64 ►

Top Grossing Films of 1965

Doctor Zhivago '65 ►
The Sound of Music '65 ►
That Darn Cat '65
Those Magnificent Men in Their Flying Machines '65 ►
Thunderball '65

Top Grossing Films of 1966

Hawaii '66 ►
Lt. Robin Crusoe, U.S.N. '66
A Man for All Seasons '66 ►
Who's Afraid of Virginia Woolf? '66 ►

► = rated three bones or higher

Top Grossing Films of 1967

Bonnie & Clyde '67 ▸
The Dirty Dozen '67 ▸
The Graduate '67 ▸
Guess Who's Coming to Dinner '67 ▸
The Jungle Book '67 ▸

Top Grossing Films of 1968

Bullitt '68 ▸
Funny Girl '68 ▸
The Odd Couple '68 ▸
Romeo and Juliet '68 ▸
2001: A Space Odyssey '68 ▸

Top Grossing Films of 1969

Butch Cassidy and the Sundance Kid '69 ▸
Easy Rider '69 ▸
Hello, Dolly! '69
The Love Bug '68
Midnight Cowboy '69 ▸

Top Grossing Films of 1970

Airport '70 ▸
Love Story '70 ▸
M*A*S*H '70 ▸
Patton '70 ▸

Top Grossing Films of 1971

Billy Jack '71
Diamonds Are Forever '71 ▸
Fiddler on the Roof '71 ▸
The French Connection '71 ▸
Summer of '42 '71 ▸

Top Grossing Films of 1972

Deliverance '72 ▸
The Godfather '72 ▸
Jeremiah Johnson '72 ▸
The Poseidon Adventure '72
What's Up, Doc? '72 ▸

Top Grossing Films of 1973

American Graffiti '73 ▸
The Exorcist '73 ▸
Papillon '73 ▸
The Sting '73 ▸
The Way We Were '73 ▸

Top Grossing Films of 1974

Blazing Saddles '74 ▸
Earthquake '74
The Towering Inferno '74
The Trial of Billy Jack '74
Young Frankenstein '74 ▸

Top Grossing Films of 1975

Dog Day Afternoon '75 ▸
Jaws '75 ▸
One Flew Over the Cuckoo's Nest '75 ▸

Top Grossing Films of 1976

All the President's Men '76 ▸
King Kong '76
Rocky '76 ▸
Silver Streak '76 ▸
A Star Is Born '76

Top Grossing Films of 1977

Close Encounters of the Third Kind '77 ▸
The Goodbye Girl '77 ▸
Saturday Night Fever '77
Smokey and the Bandit '77
Star Wars '77 ▸

Top Grossing Films of 1978

Every Which Way But Loose '78
Grease '78 ▸
Jaws 2 '78
National Lampoon's Animal House '78 ▸
Superman: The Movie '78 ▸

Top Grossing Films of 1979

Alien '79 ▸
The Jerk '79
Kramer vs. Kramer '79 ▸
Rocky 2 '79
Star Trek: The Motion Picture '79

Top Grossing Films of 1980

Airplane! '80 ▸
Any Which Way You Can '80
The Empire Strikes Back '80 ▸
9 to 5 '80
Stir Crazy '80

Top Grossing Films of 1981

Arthur '81 ▸
Cannonball Run '81
On Golden Pond '81 ▸
Raiders of the Lost Ark '81 ▸
Stripes '81
Superman 2 '80 ▸

Top Grossing Films of 1982

E.T.: The Extra-Terrestrial '82 ▸
An Officer and a Gentleman '82 ▸
Porky's '82
Rocky 3 '82

Top Grossing Films of 1983

Return of the Jedi '83 ▸
Superman 3 '83
Terms of Endearment '83 ▸
Trading Places '83
WarGames '83

Top Grossing Films of 1984

Beverly Hills Cop '84
Ghostbusters '84 ▸
Gremlins '84 ▸
Indiana Jones and the Temple of Doom '84 ▸
The Karate Kid '84 ▸

Top Grossing Films of 1985

Back to the Future '85 ▸
The Color Purple '85 ▸
Out of Africa '85 ▸
Rambo: First Blood, Part 2 '85
Rocky 4 '85

Top Grossing Films of 1986

Crocodile Dundee '86 ▸
The Karate Kid: Part 2 '86
Platoon '86 ▸
Star Trek 4: The Voyage Home '86 ▸
Top Gun '86

Top Grossing Films of 1987

Beverly Hills Cop 2 '87
Fatal Attraction '87 ▸
Good Morning, Vietnam '87 ▸
Lethal Weapon '87 ▸
Three Men and a Baby '87 ▸
The Untouchables '87 ▸

Top Grossing Films of 1988

Coming to America '88 ▸
Crocodile Dundee 2 '88
Die Hard '88 ▸
Rain Man '88 ▸
Twins '88
Who Framed Roger Rabbit '88 ▸

Top Grossing Films of 1989

Batman '89 ▸
Driving Miss Daisy '89 ▸
Ghostbusters 2 '89
Honey, I Shrunk the Kids '89
Indiana Jones and the Last Crusade '89 ▸
Lethal Weapon 2 '89 ▸

Top Grossing Films of 1990

Dances with Wolves '90 ▸
Dick Tracy '90 ▸
Die Hard 2: Die Harder '90 ▸
Ghost '90 ▸
Home Alone '90 ▸
The Hunt for Red October '90 ▸
Pretty Woman '90 ▸
Teenage Mutant Ninja Turtles: The Movie '90
Total Recall '90 ▸

Top Grossing Films of 1991

The Addams Family '91
Backdraft '91
Boyz N the Hood '91 ▸
City Slickers '91 ▸
Doc Hollywood '91
Dying Young '91
Hot Shots! '91 ▸
Naked Gun 2 1/2: The Smell of Fear '91
New Jack City '91
101 Dalmatians '61 ▸
Robin Hood: Prince of Thieves '91
The Rocketeer '91 ▸
The Silence of the Lambs '91 ▸
Sleeping with the Enemy '91
Teenage Mutant Ninja Turtles 2: The Secret of the Ooze '91
Terminator 2: Judgment Day '91 ▸
What about Bob? '91 ▸

Top Grossing Films of 1992

Aladdin '92 ▸
Alien 3 '92
Basic Instinct '92
Batman Returns '92
The Bodyguard '92
Boomerang '92
Bram Stoker's Dracula '92
Fried Green Tomatoes '91 ▸
The Hand that Rocks the Cradle '92
Home Alone 2: Lost in New York '92
The Last of the Mohicans '92 ▸
A League of Their Own '92 ▸
Lethal Weapon 3 '92
Patriot Games '92 ▸
Sister Act '92
Under Siege '92
Unforgiven '92 ▸
Wayne's World '92 ▸
White Men Can't Jump '92

Top Grossing Films of 1993

Aladdin '92 ▸
Cliffhanger '93 ▸
A Few Good Men '92 ▸
The Firm '93 ▸
Free Willy '93
The Fugitive '93 ▸
In the Line of Fire '93 ▸
Indecent Proposal '93
Jurassic Park '93 ▸
Sleepless in Seattle '93 ▸

Top Grossing Films of 1994

Ace Ventura: Pet Detective '93
Clear and Present Danger '94
The Client '94
The Flintstones '94
Forrest Gump '94 ▸
The Lion King '94 ▸
The Mask '94 ▸
Maverick '94
Speed '94 ▸
True Lies '94

Top Grossing Films of 1995

Ace Ventura: When Nature Calls '95
Apollo 13 '95 ▸
Batman Forever '95 ▸
Casper '95 ▸
Die Hard: With a Vengeance '95
Goldeneye '95 ▸
Jumanji '95
Pocahontas '95 ▸
Seven '95 ▸
Toy Story '95 ▸

Top Grossing Films of 1996

The Birdcage '95 ▸
Broken Arrow '95
The Cable Guy '96
Courage Under Fire '96 ▸
Eraser '96
The First Wives Club '96
The Hunchback of Notre Dame '96 ▸
Independence Day '96 ▸
Jack '96
Jerry Maguire '96 ▸
Mission: Impossible '96 ▸
The Nutty Professor '96 ▸
101 Dalmatians '96
Phenomenon '96
Ransom '96 ▸
The Rock '96 ▸
Space Jam '96
Star Trek: First Contact '96 ▸
A Time to Kill '96 ▸
Twister '96

Top Grossing Films of 1997

Air Force One '97 ▸
Batman and Robin '97
Con Air '97 ▸
Conspiracy Theory '97 ▸
Contact '97
Face/Off '97 ▸
Flubber '97
George of the Jungle '97 ▸
Hercules '97 ▸
I Know What You Did Last Summer '97 ▸
Jerry Maguire '96 ▸
Liar Liar '97
The Lost World: Jurassic Park 2 '97
Men in Black '97 ▸
My Best Friend's Wedding '97
Scream '96 ▸
Scream 2 '97 ▸
Star Wars '77 ▸
Titanic '97 ▸
Tomorrow Never Dies '97

Top Grossing Films of 1998

Antz '98 ▸
Armageddon '98
As Good As It Gets '97 ▸
A Bug's Life '98 ▸
Deep Impact '98
Dr. Dolittle '98
Enemy of the State '98
Godzilla '98
Good Will Hunting '97
Lethal Weapon 4 '98
The Mask of Zorro '98 ▸
Mulan '98
The Rugrats Movie '98 ▸
Saving Private Ryan '98 ▸
There's Something about Mary '98 ▸
Titanic '97 ▸
The Truman Show '98 ▸
The Waterboy '98
The X-Files '98

Top Grossing Films of 1999

American Pie '99 ▸
Analyze This '98 ▸
Austin Powers 2: The Spy Who Shagged Me '99 ▸
Big Daddy '99
The Blair Witch Project '99
A Bug's Life '98 ▸
Entrapment '99
The Matrix '99 ▸
The Mummy '99
Notting Hill '99 ▸
Runaway Bride '99 ▸
Shakespeare in Love '98 ▸
The Sixth Sense '99 ▸
Star Wars: Episode 1—The Phantom Menace '99 ▸
Tarzan '99 ▸
Toy Story 2 '99 ▸
Wild Wild West '99
The World Is Not Enough '99
You've Got Mail '98

Top Grossing Films of 2000

Big Momma's House '00
Cast Away '00 ▸
Charlie's Angels '00
Chicken Run '00 ▸
Dinosaur '00
Dr. Seuss' How the Grinch Stole Christmas '00
Erin Brockovich '00 ▸
George Wallace '97
Gladiator '00 ▸
Gone in 60 Seconds '00
Me, Myself, and Irene '00 ▸
Meet the Parents '00 ▸
Mission: Impossible 2 '00 ▸
Nutty Professor 2: The Klumps '00
The Patriot '00
The Perfect Storm '00
Remember the Titans '00 ▸
Scary Movie '00
What Women Want '00
X-Men '00

Top Grossing Films of 2001

American Pie 2 '01
Cast Away '00 ▸
Crouching Tiger, Hidden Dragon '00 ▸
Dr. Dolittle 2 '01
The Fast and the Furious '01
Hannibal '01
Harry Potter and the Sorcerer's Stone '01 ▸
Jurassic Park 3 '01
Lara Croft: Tomb Raider '01
Lord of the Rings: The Fellowship of the Ring '01 ▸
The Matrix Revolutions '03 ▸
Monsters, Inc. '01 ▸
The Mummy Returns '01
Pearl Harbor '01
Planet of the Apes '01 ▸
Rush Hour 2 '01
Shrek '01 ▸
Traffic '00 ▸

Top Grossing Films of 2002

Austin Powers In Goldmember '02
Die Another Day '02
Harry Potter and the Chamber of Secrets '02 ▸
Ice Age '02 ▸
Lilo & Stitch '02 ▸
Lord of the Rings: The Fellowship of the Ring '01 ▸
Lord of the Rings: The Two Towers '02 ▸
Men in Black 2 '02
Minority Report '02 ▸
Mr. Deeds '02
My Big Fat Greek Wedding '02
The Ring '02
The Santa Clause 2 '02
Scooby-Doo '02
Signs '02 ▸
Spider-Man '02 ▸
Star Wars: Episode 2—Attack of the Clones '02 ▸
Sweet Home Alabama '02

Top Grossing Films of 2003

Anger Management '03
Bad Boys 2 '03
Bringing Down the House '03
Bruce Almighty '03
Chicago '02 ▸
Elf '03 ▸
Finding Nemo '03 ▸
Hulk '03
Lord of the Rings: The Return of the King '03 ▸
The Matrix Reloaded '03
Pirates of the Caribbean: The Curse of the Black Pearl '03 ▸
Terminator 3: Rise of the Machines '03 ▸
2 Fast 2 Furious '03
X2: X-Men United '03 ▸

Top Grossing Films of 2004

The Bourne Supremacy '04 ▸
The Day After Tomorrow '04
Dodgeball: A True Underdog Story '04
Fahrenheit 9/11 '04 ▸
50 First Dates '04
Harry Potter and the Prisoner of Azkaban '04
I, Robot '04
The Incredibles '04 ▸
Lord of the Rings: The Return of the King '03 ▸
Meet the Fockers '04
National Treasure '04
Ocean's Twelve '04
The Passion of the Christ '04 ▸
The Polar Express '04
Shark Tale '04
Shrek 2 '04 ▸
Spider-Man 2 '04 ▸
Surfwise '07 ▸
Troy '04
Van Helsing '04 ▸
The Village '04

Top Grossing Films of 2005

Batman Begins '05 ▸
Charlie and the Chocolate Factory '05 ▸
Chicken Little '05
The Chronicles of Narnia: The Lion, the Witch and the Wardrobe '05
Fantastic Four '05
The 40 Year Old Virgin '05 ▸
Harry Potter and the Goblet of Fire '05 ▸
Hitch '05
King Kong '05 ▸
The Longest Yard '05
Madagascar '05
Meet the Fockers '04
Million Dollar Baby '04 ▸
The Pacifier '05
Robots '05
Star Wars: Episode 3—Revenge of the Sith '05 ▸
Walk the Line '05 ▸
War of the Worlds '05 ▸
Wedding Crashers '05 ▸

Top Grossing Films of 2006

Borat: Cultural Learnings of America for Make Benefit Glorious Nation of Kazakhstan '06 ▸
The Break-Up '06
Cars '06 ▸
Casino Royale '06 ▸
Click '06
The Da Vinci Code '06 ▸
The Departed '06 ▸
The Devil Wears Prada '06
Failure to Launch '06
Happy Feet '06 ▸
Ice Age: The Meltdown '06
Mission: Impossible 3 '06 ▸
Night at the Museum '06
Over the Hedge '06 ▸
Pirates of the Caribbean: Dead Man's Chest '06
The Pursuit of Happyness '06
Scary Movie 4 '06
Superman Returns '06
Talladega Nights: The Ballad of Ricky Bobby '06

▸ = *rated three bones or higher*

X-Men: The Last Stand *'06*

Top Grossing Films of 2007

Alvin and the Chipmunks *'07*
American Gangster *'07* ▸
Bee Movie *'07*
Blades of Glory *'07*
The Bourne Ultimatum *'07* ▸
Enchanted *'07*
Fantastic Four: Rise of the Silver Surfer *'07*
Hairspray *'07* ▸
Harry Potter and the Order of the Phoenix *'07*
I Am Legend *'07* ▸
I Now Pronounce You Chuck and Larry *'07*
Knocked Up *'07*
Live Free or Die Hard *'07*
National Treasure: Book of Secrets *'07*
Ocean's Thirteen *'07* ▸
Ratatouille *'07* ▸
Rush Hour 3 *'07*
Shrek the Third *'07*
The Simpsons Movie *'07* ▸
Spider-Man 3 *'07*
Superbad *'07* ▸
300 *'07*
Transformers *'07*
Wild Hogs *'07*

Top Grossing Films of 2008

Bolt *'08* ▸
The Chronicles of Narnia: Prince Caspian *'08*
The Dark Knight *'08* ▸
Dr. Seuss' Horton Hears a Who! *'08* ▸
Four Christmases *'08*
Get Smart *'08*
Hancock *'08*
The Incredible Hulk *'08*
Indiana Jones and the Kingdom of the Crystal Skull *'08*
Iron Man *'08* ▸
Juno *'07* ▸
Kung Fu Panda *'08* ▸
Madagascar: Escape 2 Africa *'08*
Mamma Mia! *'08*
Quantum of Solace *'08*
Sex and the City: The Movie *'08*
Tropic Thunder *'08* ▸
Twilight *'08*
WALL-E *'08* ▸
Wanted *'08* ▸

Top Grossing Films of 2009

Alvin and the Chipmunks: The Squeakuel *'09*
Avatar *'09* ▸
The Blind Side *'09*
Fast & Furious *'09*
G.I. Joe: The Rise of Cobra *'09*
The Hangover *'09*
Harry Potter and the Half-Blood Prince *'09*
Ice Age: Dawn of the Dinosaurs *'09*
Monsters vs. Aliens *'09*
Night at the Museum: Battle of the Smithsonian *'09*
Paul Blart: Mall Cop *'09*
The Proposal *'09*
Sherlock Holmes *'09*
Star Trek *'09* ▸
Taken *'08*
Transformers: Revenge of the Fallen *'09*
2012 *'09*
The Twilight Saga: New Moon *'09*
Up *'09* ▸
X-Men Origins: Wolverine *'09*

The Trail Blazers

Arizona Whirlwind *'44*
Death Valley Rangers *'44*
The Law Rides Again *'43*
Outlaw Trail *'44*
Westward Bound *'44*

Troma Films

Beware! Children at Play *'95*
Blades *'89*
Blondes Have More Guns *'95*
Bloodsucking Freaks *'75*
Bugged! *'96*
Cannibal! The Musical *'96*
Chopper Chicks in Zombietown *'91*
The Chosen One: Legend of the Raven *'98*
Christmas Evil *'80*
Citizen Toxie: The Toxic Avenger 4 *'01*
Class of Nuke 'Em High *'86*
Class of Nuke 'Em High 2: Subhumanoid Meltdown *'91*
Class of Nuke 'Em High 3: The Good, the Bad and the Subhumanoid *'94*
Combat Shock *'84*
Cry Uncle *'71*
Cyxork 7 *'06*
Deadly Daphne's Revenge *'93*
Escape from Hell *'79*
Evil Clutch *'89*
Fat Guy Goes Nutzoid *'86*
Ferocious Female Freedom Fighters *'88*
Frostbiter: Wrath of the Wendigo *'94*
Girls School Screamers *'86*
I Married a Vampire *'87*
I Was a Teenage TV Terrorist *'87*
Invasion of the Space Preachers *'90*
Maniac Nurses Find Ecstasy *'94*
A Nymphoid Barbarian in Dinosaur Hell *'94*
Preacherman *'83*
Rabid Grannies *'89*
Redneck Zombies *'88*
Sgt. Kabukiman N.Y.P.D. *'94*
Sergio Lapel's Drawing Blood *'99*
Sizzle Beach U.S.A. *'74*
Splatter University *'84*
Squeeze Play *'79*
Stuck on You *'84*
Student Confidential *'87*
Surf Nazis Must Die *'87*
Teenage Catgirls in Heat *'00*
The Toxic Avenger *'86*
The Toxic Avenger, Part 2 *'89*
The Toxic Avenger, Part 3: The Last Temptation of Toxie *'89*
Troma's War *'88*
Tromeo & Juliet *'95*
Unspeakable *'00*
Vegas in Space *'94*
Wizards of the Demon Sword *'94*
Zombie Island Massacre *'84*

Universal Studios' Classic Horror

Abbott and Costello Meet Dr. Jekyll and Mr. Hyde *'52*
Abbott and Costello Meet Frankenstein *'48* ▸
Abbott and Costello Meet the Killer, Boris Karloff *'49*
The Black Cat *'34* ▸
The Bride of Frankenstein *'35* ▸
Creature from the Black Lagoon *'54* ▸
The Creature Walks among Us *'56*
Dracula (Spanish Version) *'31*
Dracula *'31* ▸
Dracula's Daughter *'36* ▸
Frankenstein *'31* ▸
Frankenstein Meets the Wolfman *'42* ▸
The Ghost of Frankenstein *'42*
House of Dracula *'45*
House of Frankenstein *'44*
The Hunchback of Notre Dame *'23* ▸
Invisible Agent *'42*
The Invisible Man *'33* ▸
The Invisible Man Returns *'40* ▸
The Invisible Woman *'40* ▸
Island of Lost Souls *'32* ▸
The Mummy *'32* ▸
The Mummy's Curse *'44*
The Mummy's Ghost *'44*
The Mummy's Hand *'40*
The Mummy's Tomb *'42*
Murders in the Rue Morgue *'32*
The Phantom of the Opera *'25* ▸
The Phantom of the Opera *'43* ▸
The Raven *'35* ▸
Revenge of the Creature *'55*
Son of Dracula *'43* ▸
Son of Frankenstein *'39* ▸
Van Helsing *'04* ▸
Werewolf of London *'35*
The Wolf Man *'41* ▸

Wild Bill Hickok

Buffalo Girls *'95*
Calamity Jane *'53* ▸
Calamity Jane *'82*
Little Big Man *'70* ▸
The Plainsman *'37*
Pony Express *'53* ▸
The White Buffalo *'77*
Wild Bill *'95*
Young Bill Hickok *'40*

The Wolfman

Frankenstein Meets the Wolfman *'42* ▸
House of Dracula *'45*
House of Frankenstein *'44*
Mad Monster Party *'68*
The Monster Squad *'87*
Van Helsing *'04* ▸
The Wolf Man *'41* ▸
The Wolfman *'82*

Woofs!

The Adventurers *'70*
Adventures of a Taxi Driver *'76*
The Adventures of Ford Fairlane *'90*
The Adventures of Pluto Nash *'02*
The Adventurous Knights *'35*
After the Fall of New York *'85*
Albino *'76*
The Alchemist *'81*
The Alien Agenda: Out of the Darkness *'96*
Alien Contamination *'81*
Alien from L.A. *'87*
Alien Massacre *'67*
Alien Predators *'80*
Alien Warrior *'85*
Almost Human *'79*
Alone in the Dark *'05*
The Amazing Transparent Man *'60*
The Amazing Transplant *'70*
The Ambushers *'67*
American Gothic *'88*
American Ninja 3: Blood Hunt *'89*
American Ninja 4: The Annihilation *'91*
American Soldiers *'05*
Americathon *'79*
Amin: The Rise and Fall *'82*
Amityville 2: The Possession *'82*
The Amityville Curse *'90*
Anatomy of Hell *'04*
Angel 3: The Final Chapter *'88*
Angel of Death *'86*
Angel of H.E.A.T. *'82*
Angels' Wild Women *'72*
The Annihilators *'85*
Another 9 1/2 Weeks *'96*
A*P*E* *'76*
The Appointment *'82*
April Fool's Day *'08*
Are You Scared? *'06*
The Astounding She-Monster *'58*
The Astro-Zombies *'67*
Atlas in the Land of the Cyclops *'61*
Atom Age Vampire *'61*
The Atomic Brain *'64*
Ator the Fighting Eagle *'83*
Attack Force *'06*
Attack of the Beast Creatures *'85*
Attack of the Killer Tomatoes *'77*
Attack of the Mayan Mummy *'63*
Attack of the Swamp Creature *'75*
Auntie *'73*
Automaton Transfusion *'06*
Avenging Angel *'85*
Awakening of Candra *'81*
Axe *'06*
Ba'al: The Storm God *'08*
Baby Love *'69*
Baby Love *'83*
Bachelor Party Vegas *'05*
Bad Charleston Charlie *'73*
Bad Girls Do Cry *'54*
Bad Girls from Mars *'90*
Bad Girls Go to Hell *'65*
Bad Medicine *'85*
Baise Moi *'00*
Balboa *'82*
Bananas Boat *'78*
Bar-B-Q *'00*
Barn of the Naked Dead *'73*
Barracuda *'78*
Basic Training *'86*
Battlefield Earth *'00*
Beaks: The Movie *'87*
Beast of the Yellow Night *'70*
The Beast of Yucca Flats *'61*
The Bees *'78*
Bela Lugosi Meets a Brooklyn Gorilla *'52*
The Bellboy and the Playgirls *'62*
Beware! Children at Play *'95*
Beyond Atlantis *'73*
Beyond Evil *'80*
Beyond the Door *'75*
Beyond the Door 3 *'91*
The Big Bust Out *'73*
Big Foot *'72*
The Bikini Car Wash Company *'90*
The Birds 2: Land's End *'94*
The Bitch *'78*
The Black Cat *'81*
Black Cobra *'83*
The Black Cobra *'87*
Black Gestapo *'75*
Black Magic Woman *'91*
Black Shampoo *'76*
Black Venus *'83*
Blackenstein *'73*
Blacksnake! *'73*
Blackwoods *'02*
Blade of the Ripper *'70*
Blastfighter *'85*
Blazing Stewardesses *'75*
Bleeders *'97*
Blockhouse *'73*
Blood Beach *'81*
Blood Diner *'87*
Blood Freak *'72*
Blood Games *'90*
Blood of Ghastly Horror *'72*
Blood Orgy of the She-Devils *'74*
Blood Rage *'87*
Blood Screams *'88*
Blood Sisters *'86*
Blood Voyage *'77*
Bloodmoon *'90*
BloodRayne *'06*
BloodRayne 2: Deliverance *'07*
Bloodstalkers *'76*
Bloodstream *'00*
Bloodsuckers from Outer Space *'83*
Bloodsucking Freaks *'75*
Bloodsucking Pharoahs of Pittsburgh *'90*
The Bloody Brood *'59*
Bloody Moon *'83*
Bloody Murder *'99*
Bloody Murder 2 *'03*
The Blue Lagoon *'80*
Blue Movies *'88*
Boat Trip *'03*
The Body Beneath *'70*
Body of Evidence *'92*
Body Rock *'84*
The Body Shop *'72*
Bolero *'84*
Bomb the System *'05*
Boogey Man 2 *'83*
Boom in the Moon *'46*
Border Radio *'88*
Bottoms Up *'06*
Brain of Blood *'71*
Breeders *'97*
The Bride & the Beast *'58*
Bride of the Monster *'55*
Brides of the Beast *'68*
Brotherhood 2: The Young Warlocks *'01*
The Brotherhood 3: The Young Demons *'02*
BTK Killer *'06*
Bug *'75*
Bullies *'86*
Bummer *'73*
Bundy: A Legacy of Evil *'08*
Cabin Boy *'94*
Caged Terror *'72*
The Calamari Wrestler *'04*
California Casanova *'89*
Caligula *'80*
Can I Do It.. Till I Need Glasses? *'77*
Cannibal Apocalypse *'80*
Can't Stop the Music *'80*
Carnival of Souls *'98*
Cartel *'90*
Castle of Evil *'66*
Castle of the Creeping Flesh *'68*
Cave Girl *'85*
Cave of the Living Dead *'65*
Cellar Dweller *'87*
The Centerfold Girls *'74*
Centipede *'05*
Chain Gang Women *'72*
Chain of Souls *'00*
Chained for Life *'51*
Chairman of the Board *'97*
Challenge *'74*
Chaos *'05*
Charlie McCarthy, Detective *'39*
Charlie White *'04*
Cheaper to Keep Her *'80*
Cheech and Chong's The Corsican Brothers *'84*
Cheering Section *'73*
Cheerleader Camp *'88*
The Cheerleaders *'72*
Cheerleaders' Wild Weekend *'85*
Cherry Hill High *'76*
The Children *'80*
Children of the Living Dead *'00*
Child's Play 2 *'90*
The Chilling *'89*
Chilly Dogs *'01*
The Chosen *'77*
Chu Chu & the Philly Flash *'81*
C.H.U.D. *'84*
C.H.U.D. 2: Bud the Chud *'89*
Citizen Toxie: The Toxic Avenger 4 *'01*
City on Fire *'78*
Clash of the Titans *'81*
Class of 1984 *'82*
Class of Nuke 'Em High 3: The Good, the Bad and the Subhumanoid *'94*
Class Reunion *'72*
Class Reunion Massacre *'77*
Claws *'85*
Clifford *'92*
Closure *'07*
Color Me Blood Red *'64*
Condemned to Hell *'84*
Confidential *'86*
The Conqueror *'56*
The Conqueror & the Empress *'64*
Cop Killers *'73*
The Corpse Grinders *'71*
Corruption *'70*
Cosh Boy *'52*
Cosmos: War of the Planets *'80*
The Cradle Will Fall *'83*
The Crater Lake Monster *'77*
The Crawling Hand *'63*
Crazed *'82*
Crazy Fat Ethel II *'85*
The Creation of the Humanoids *'62*
Creatures the World Forgot *'70*
Creeping Terror *'64*
The Cremators *'72*
Crocodile *'81*
Crocodile 2: Death Swamp *'01*
Crucible of Terror *'72*
Cruel World *'05*
Cruise into Terror *'78*
Crypt of the Living Dead *'73*
Cthulhu Mansion *'91*
The Curse of the Aztec Mummy *'59*
Curse of the Blue Lights *'88*
Curse of the Stone Hand *'64*
Curtains *'83*
Cycle Psycho *'72*
Cycle Vixens *'79*
Dagora, the Space Monster *'65*
Dance of Death *'68*
Danger Zone *'87*
Dangerous Love *'87*
Dark Sanity *'82*
Dawn of the Mummy *'82*
The Day It Came to Earth *'77*
Dead Aim *'87*
Dead Pit *'89*
Dead Women in Lingerie *'90*
Deadly Darling *'85*
Deadly Embrace *'88*
Deadly Prey *'87*
Deadly Sanctuary *'68*
Deadly Twins *'85*
The Death Curse of Tartu *'66*
Death Ray *'67*
Death Spa *'87*
Death Wish 2 *'82*
Death Wish 5: The Face of Death *'94*
Deathstalker *'83*
Decay *'98*
Dee Snider's Strangeland *'98*
Delinquent School Girls *'84*
Delirium *'77*
The Demon Lover *'77*
Demon of Paradise *'87*
Demonia *'90*
Demonwarp *'87*
Detour to Danger *'45*
Deuce Bigalow: European Gigolo *'05*
Devil Woman *'76*
Devil's Gift *'84*
The Devil's Rejects *'05*
Devil's Son-in-Law *'77*
Devil's Wedding Night *'73*
Die Laughing *'80*
Digging Up Business *'91*
Dirty Laundry *'87*
Dirty Love *'05*
Dirty Mind of Young Sally *'72*
Doctor Butcher M.D. *'80*
Doctor of Doom *'62*
Dr. Orloff's Monster *'64*
Dr. Tarr's Torture Dungeon *'75*
The Dolls *'83*
Don't Go in the Woods *'81*
Don't Look in the Attic *'81*
Don't Open the Door! *'74*
Don't Open Till Christmas *'84*
Doom Asylum *'88*
Dorm That Dripped Blood *'82*
Dracula: Dead and Loving It *'95*
Dracula vs. Frankenstein *'71*
Dracula's Great Love *'72*
Dracula's Last Rites *'79*
Driller Killer *'79*
Drive-In *'76*
Drive-In Massacre *'74*
Driver's Seat *'73*

▸ = *rated three bones or higher*

Drop Dead Fred '91
Drum '76
Drums O'Voodoo '34
Dutch Girls '87
Eating Out 3: All You Can Eat '09
Ecstasy '84
Ed '96
Eegah! '62
Emily '77
End of the World '76
Endless Descent '90
Equilibrium '02
Erotic Images '85
Escape from Hell '79
Escape from Safehaven '88
Escape from the KGB '87
Escape 2000 '81
Escapist '83
Eve of Destruction '90
The Evictors '79
Evil Laugh '86
The Evil Within '89
Evilspeak '82
Executive Koala '06 ►
Expose '97
Exterminators in the Year 3000 '83
Eyeball '78
Eyes of a Stranger '81
Fade to Black '80
Fair Game '82
Fair Game '85
Fair Game '89
Fanatic '82
Fanny Hill: Memoirs of a Woman of Pleasure '64
Fantasies '73
Far Out Man '89
Farmhouse '08
Fascination '04
Fat Guy Goes Nutzoid '86
The Fat Spy '66
Fatal Pulse '88
The Fear Chamber '68
Feed '05
Feeders '96
Feelin' Up '76
The Female Bunch '69
Femme Fontaine: Killer Babe for the C.I.A. '95
Fever Pitch '85
Fiend '83
The Fiendish Plot of Dr. Fu Manchu '80
The Fifth Floor '80
Final Exam '81
Final Payback '99
Fire Serpent '07
The First 9 1/2 Weeks '98
Flesh Feast '69
Flight to Nowhere '46
Flu Birds '08
Food of the Gods '76
Food of the Gods: Part 2 '88
Foolish '99
The Forbidden Dance '90
Forbidden World '82
Foreplay '75
Fowl Play '75
Frankenstein '80 '79
Frankenstein General Hospital '88
Frankenstein Island '81
Frankenstein Meets the Space Monster '65
Frankenstein's Great Aunt Tillie '83
Freddy Got Fingered '01
Friday the 13th, Part 2 '81
Friday the 13th, Part 3 '82
Friday the 13th, Part 4: The Final Chapter '84
Friday the 13th, Part 5: A New Beginning '85
Friday the 13th, Part 6: Jason Lives '86
Friday the 13th, Part 7: The New Blood '88
From Hell It Came '57
From Justin to Kelly '03
Fun Down There '88
Galactic Gigolo '87
The Gamma People '56
Gangster's Law '86
The Garbage Pail Kids Movie '87
Gas '81
Gates of Hell '80
Getting Away With Murder '96
The Ghastly Ones '68
Ghost Fever '87
Ghost in the Noonday Sun '74
Ghoulies 3: Ghoulies Go to College '91
Giant from the Unknown '58
Giants of Rome '63
Gimme an F '85
The Girl in Room 2A '76
Girl on a Chain Gang '65
Glen or Glenda? '53
Glitter '01
The Glory Stompers '67
Goblin '93
God's Bloody Acre '75
Gods of Wu Tang '83
Godzilla vs. the Sea Monster '66
Goliath and the Dragon '61
Gone Fishin' '97
Goof Balls '87
Gore-Met Zombie Chef from Hell '87
Gorp '80
The Green Berets '68
The Green Slime '68
Grotesque '87
Grunt! The Wrestling Movie '85
Guess What We Learned in School Today? '70
Gummo '97
H-Bomb '71
H-Man '59
Hallowed '05
Halloween with the Addams Family '79
Hallucination '67
Hands of Steel '86
Hangmen '87
Hardbodies 2 '86
Hawmps! '76
The Hearse '80
Heart of America '03
Heavenly Bodies '84
Hell Night '81
Hell of the Living Dead '83
Hell Up in Harlem '73
Hellcats '68
Hellgate '89
Hellriders '84
Hell's Belles '95
Hell's Brigade: The Final Assault '80
Helter Skelter Murders '71
High Tension '03
Hillbillies in a Haunted House '67
The Hills Have Eyes '77
His Name Was King '71
Hitchhikers '72
The Hollywood Strangler Meets the Skid Row Slasher '79
Hollywood Zap '86
Hometown U.S.A. '79
Horror House on Highway 5 '86
Horror of Party Beach '64
Horror of the Blood Monsters '70
Hospital Massacre '81
Hot Box '72
Hot T-Shirts '79
Hot Touch '82
The Hound of the Baskervilles '77
House of 1000 Corpses '03
House of Psychotic Women '73
House of the Dead '03
House of Whipcord '75
House on the Edge of the Park '84
How to Seduce a Woman '74
Humanoids from the Deep '80
Humongous '82
Hurricane '79
I Dismember Mama '74
I Eat Your Skin '64
I Spit on Your Corpse '74
I Spit on Your Grave '77
I Was a Communist for the FBI '51
I Was a Teenage TV Terrorist '87
Icebox Murders '82
Idaho Transfer '73
If I Die Before I Wake '98
Ilsa, Harem Keeper of the Oil Sheiks '76
Ilsa, She-Wolf of the SS '74
Ilsa, the Tigress of Siberia '79
Ilsa, the Wicked Warden '78
Impulse '74
In God We Trust '80
In Search of Anna '79
In the Mix '05
In the Shadow of Kilimanjaro '86
In Trouble '67
Incredible Melting Man '77
The Incredible Petrified World '58
The Incredible Two-Headed Transplant '71
Incredibly Strange Creatures Who Stopped Living and Became Mixed-Up Zombies '63
Incubus '82
Infra-Man '76
Inhumanoid '96
Inner Sanctum '91
Inseminoid '80
Invasion of the Animal People '62
Invasion of the Blood Farmers '72
Invasion of the Body Stealers '69
Invasion of the Girl Snatchers '73
Invasion of the Star Creatures '63
Invincible Barbarian '83
Invincible Gladiators '64
The Invisible Maniac '90
Invitation to Hell '82
The Island '80
Island Claw '80
Island of Lost Girls '68
It Waits '05
It's Alive 2: It Lives Again '78
It's All Gone, Pete Tong '04
It's Not the Size That Counts '74
It's Pat: The Movie '94
Jack Frost 2: Revenge of the Mutant Killer Snowman '00
Jason Goes to Hell: The Final Friday '93
Jaws of Satan '81
The Jazz Singer '80
The Jerky Boys '95
Joy Sticks '83
Junior '86
Just for the Hell of It '68
Kidnapped '87
Kill Alex Kill '76
Kill Factor '78
Killer Party '86
Killers from Space '54
Killing Moon '00
Kilma, Queen of the Amazons '75
King Kong Escapes '67
King of Kong Island '78
The King of the Kickboxers '91
King of the Zombies '41
King's Ransom '91
Lake Placid 2 '07
Lap Dancing '95
Larry the Cable Guy: Health Inspector '06
Las Vegas Serial Killer '86
The Las Vegas Story '52
Laserblast '78
Last Days of Planet Earth '74
Last Hour '08
Last House on Dead End Street '77
Last Mercenary '84
The Last Season '87
The Last Slumber Party '87
The Last Woman on Earth '61
Lauderdale '89
A Legacy for Leonette '85
Legacy of Horror '78
Legend of the Dinosaurs and Monster Birds '77
Legend of the Liquid Sword '93
Leprechaun '93
Leprechaun 4: In Space '96
Leprechaun 5: In the Hood '99
Leprechaun 6: Back 2 Tha Hood '03
Lethal '04
The Life of Lucky Cucumber '08
The Lifetaker '89
Link '86
Lipstick '76
Lisa and the Devil '75
Lisztomania '75
Little Darlings '80
Loaded Guns '75
The Loch Ness Horror '82
The Lone Runner '88
The Lonely Lady '83
The Long Weekend '05
The Longshot '86
Lords of the Deep '89
Lost Boys: The Tribe '08
Love Thrill Murders '71
The Loves of Hercules '60
Love's Savage Fury '79
Lurkers '88
Lust for Dracula '04
Luther the Geek '90
Machined '06
Mack the Knife '89
Mad About You '90
The Mad Bomber '72
Mad Doctor of Blood Island '68
Mad Dog '84
Mad Youth '40
Madigan's Millions '67
Mama Dracula '80
A Man Called Rage '84
Man from Deep River '77
Maniac '34
Maniac '80
Maniac Nurses Find Ecstasy '94
Mannequin 2: On the Move '91
Manos, the Hands of Fate '66
Mardi Gras Massacre '78
Maslin Beach '97
A Matter of Time '76
Maxim Xul '91
Maximum Thrust '88
Maya '82
Meatballs 3 '87
The Meateater '79
Megaforce '82
Memron '04
Mesa of Lost Women '52
Meteor '79
Midnight Cabaret '90
The Mighty Peking Man '77
Mindhunters '05
Mirror Wars: Reflection One '05
Miss March '09
Mr. Jingles '06
Mistress of the Apes '79
Mom '89
Mondo Trasho '69
Mongrel '83
Monsignor '82
Monster a Go-Go! '65
Monster Dog '82
The Monster of Piedras Blancas '57
Moonshine Mountain '64
Mortuary '05
Moscow Zero '06
Moses '76
Motor Psycho '65
Mountain of the Cannibal God '79
Mountaintop Motel Massacre '86
Mummy & Curse of the Jackal '67
Murderer's Keep '70
Murderlust '86
Mutant Hunt '87
Mutants '08
Mutants In Paradise '84
The Mutilator '85
My African Adventure '87
My First Wedding '04
My Therapist '84
Myra Breckinridge '70
Nail Gun Massacre '86
Naked Cage '86
The Naked Flame '68
Naked Vengeance '85
Naked Youth '59
The Narcotics Story '58
National Lampoon Presents Cattle Call '06
National Lampoon's Class Reunion '82
National Lampoon's Gold Diggers '04
National Lampoon's The Stoned Aged '07
National Lampoon's Van Wilder 2: The Rise of Taj '06
Navy vs. the Night Monsters '66
Neon Maniacs '86
The New Gladiators '83
New Year's Evil '78
New York Ripper '82
The Night God Screamed '71
A Night in Heaven '83
Night of the Bloody Apes '68
Night of the Bloody Transplant '86
Night of the Demon '80
Night of the Demons 3 '97
Night of the Ghouls '59
Night of the Living Babes '87
Night of the Sharks '87
Night of the Sorcerers '70
Night Patrol '85
Night Train Murders '75
Night Train to Terror '84
Nightmare '82
Nightmare Sisters '87
Nightstalker '81
Nine Deaths of the Ninja '85
1990: The Bronx Warriors '83
Ninja Champion '80
Ninja Fantasy '86
Ninja Hunt '86
No One Cries Forever '85
No Way Back '90
Nobody's Perfekt '79
Nocturna '79
Norman's Awesome Experience '88
Nude on the Moon '61
A Nymphoid Barbarian in Dinosaur Hell '94
The Occultist '89
Ocean Drive Weekend '85
Oddballs '84
On Deadly Ground '94
One Brief Summer '70
One Down, Two to Go! '82
One of Them '03
One Russian Summer '73
Orca '77
Orgy of the Dead '65
The Other Side of Midnight '77
Parasite '82
Party Favors '89
People Who Own the Dark '75
Perfect Timing '84
Phobia '80
Pieces '83
Pink Motel '82
Plan 9 from Outer Space '56
Please Don't Eat My Mother '72
Police Academy 5: Assignment Miami Beach '88
Prehistoric Bimbos in Armageddon City '93
Prehistoric Women '50
Pretty Smart '87
Prettykill '87
The Prime Time '60
Private Manoeuvres '83
The Psychic '68
Psychos in Love '87
Puff, Puff, Pass '06
Pulsebeat '85
The Puma Man '80
Python 2 '02
Queen of Outer Space '58
Quick, Let's Get Married '71
Rabid Grannies '89
Raise the Titanic '80
The Rape of the Sabines '61
Rat Pfink a Boo-Boo '66
The Rats Are Coming! The Werewolves Are Here! '72
Razorteeth '05
Rebel Vixens '69
The Red Menace '49
The Return '80
Return to Frogtown '92
Revenge '86
Ridin' the Lone Trail '37
Ring of Darkness '04
Ringmaster '98
The Ripper '86
The Robot vs. the Aztec Mummy '59
Rocket Attack U.S.A. '58
Roller Boogie '79
The Room '03
Rooster: Spurs of Death! '83
The Rug Cop '06
Rumpelstiltskin '96
Sabretooth '01
Sahara '83
Sanctimony '01
Santa Claus '59
Sasquatch '76
Satan's Cheerleaders '77
Satan's Touch '84
Satanwar '79
Savage! '73
Savage Is Loose '74
Savage Weekend '80
The Scarlet Letter '95
Scarlet Spear '54
Score '95
Scream Bloody Murder '72
Scream of the Demon Lover '71
Screen Test '85
Screwed '00
Secrets of Sweet Sixteen '74
See Spot Run '01
Senior Week '88
Sensual Partners '87
The Sensuous Teenager '70
Sgt. Kabukiman N.Y.P.D. '94
Sgt. Pepper's Lonely Hearts Club Band '78
The Serpent and the Rainbow '87
The Severed Arm '73
Sex Adventures of the Three Musketeers '71
Sex, Drugs, and Rock-n-Roll '84
The Sex Machine '75
Sex on the Run '78
Sextette '78
She Came on the Bus '69
She Demons '58
She-Devils on Wheels '68
Sheena '84
Showgirls '95
Shriek of the Mutilated '74
Sidney Sheldon's Bloodline '79
Sincerely Yours '56
Single White Female 2: The Psycho '05
The Sinister Urge '60
Sinner's Blood '70
Skinned Alive '89
Skullduggery '79
Sky Pirates '87
Slashdance '89
The Slasher '72
The Slaughter of the Vampires '62
Slaughterhouse '87
Slaughterhouse Rock '88
The Slayer '82
Sledgehammer '83
Sleepaway Camp 3: Teenage Wasteland '89
The Slime People '63
Slithis '78
Sloane '84
Slugs '87
Slumber Party Massacre 2 '87
Slumber Party Massacre 3 '90
Smashing Time '67

► = rated three bones or higher

Wyatt Earp

Zorro

Zucker/Abrahams/Zucker

▸ = rated three bones or higher

The **Awards Index** lists films honored (or dishonored, in some cases) by nine national and international award bodies, representing over 100 categories of recognition. This information can also be found in the reviews, following the credits. **Only features available on video and reviewed in the main section are listed in this index; movies not yet released on video are not covered here.** As award-winning and nominated films find their way to video, they will be added to the review section and covered in this index. **Nominations are once again covered in this index; they are not covered in the individual reviews.** The awards covered include:

Academy Awards
British Academy of Film and Television Arts
Directors Guild of America
Golden Globe
Golden Raspberries
Independent Spirit Awards
National Film Registry
Screen Actors Guild Awards
Writers Guild of America

ACADEMY AWARDS

ACTOR

1928

★Emil Jannings/*Last Command*

Charlie Chaplin/*The Circus*

1929

Chester Morris/*Alibi*

1930

★George Arliss/*Disraeli*

Wallace Beery/*The Big House*

Ronald Colman/*Bulldog Drummond*

Ronald Colman/*Condemned*

1931

★Lionel Barrymore/*A Free Soul*

Richard Dix/*Cimarron*

Adolphe Menjou/*The Front Page*

1932

★Wallace Beery/*The Champ*

★Fredric March/*Dr. Jekyll and Mr. Hyde*

Alfred Lunt/*The Guardsman*

1933

★Charles Laughton/*The Private Life of Henry VIII*

Paul Muni/*I Am a Fugitive from a Chain Gang*

1934

★Clark Gable/*It Happened One Night*

William Powell/*The Thin Man*

1935

★Victor McLaglen/*The Informer*

Clark Gable/*Mutiny on the Bounty*

Charles Laughton/*Mutiny on the Bounty*

Franchot Tone/*Mutiny on the Bounty*

1936

★Paul Muni/*The Story of Louis Pasteur*

Gary Cooper/*Mr. Deeds Goes to Town*

Walter Huston/*Dodsworth*

William Powell/*My Man Godfrey*

Spencer Tracy/*San Francisco*

1937

★Spencer Tracy/*Captains Courageous*

Charles Boyer/*Conquest*

Fredric March/*A Star Is Born*

Robert Montgomery/*Night Must Fall*

Paul Muni/*The Life of Emile Zola*

1938

★Spencer Tracy/*Boys Town*

Charles Boyer/*Algiers*

James Cagney/*Angels with Dirty Faces*

Robert Donat/*The Citadel*

Leslie Howard/*Pygmalion*

1939

★Robert Donat/*Goodbye, Mr. Chips*

Clark Gable/*Gone with the Wind*

Laurence Olivier/*Wuthering Heights*

Mickey Rooney/*Babes in Arms*

James Stewart/*Mr. Smith Goes to Washington*

1940

★James Stewart/*The Philadelphia Story*

Charlie Chaplin/*The Great Dictator*

Henry Fonda/*The Grapes of Wrath*

Raymond Massey/*Abe Lincoln in Illinois*

Laurence Olivier/*Rebecca*

1941

★Gary Cooper/*Sergeant York*

Cary Grant/*Penny Serenade*

Walter Huston/*The Devil & Daniel Webster*

Robert Montgomery/*Here Comes Mr. Jordan*

Orson Welles/*Citizen Kane*

1942

★James Cagney/*Yankee Doodle Dandy*

Ronald Colman/*Random Harvest*

Gary Cooper/*The Pride of the Yankees*

Walter Pidgeon/*Mrs. Miniver*

1943

★Paul Lukas/*Watch on the Rhine*

Humphrey Bogart/*Casablanca*

Gary Cooper/*For Whom the Bell Tolls*

Walter Pidgeon/*Madame Curie*

Mickey Rooney/*The Human Comedy*

1944

★Bing Crosby/*Going My Way*

Charles Boyer/*Gaslight*

Barry Fitzgerald/*Going My Way*

Cary Grant/*None But the Lonely Heart*

Alexander Knox/*Wilson*

1945

★Ray Milland/*The Lost Weekend*

Bing Crosby/*The Bells of St. Mary's*

Gene Kelly/*Anchors Aweigh*

Gregory Peck/*The Keys of the Kingdom*

Cornel Wilde/*A Song to Remember*

1946

★Fredric March/*The Best Years of Our Lives*

Laurence Olivier/*Henry V*

Larry Parks/*The Jolson Story*

Gregory Peck/*The Yearling*

James Stewart/*It's a Wonderful Life*

1947

★Ronald Colman/*A Double Life*

John Garfield/*Body and Soul*

Gregory Peck/*Gentleman's Agreement*

William Powell/*Life with Father*

1948

★Laurence Olivier/*Hamlet*

Lew Ayres/*Johnny Belinda*

Montgomery Clift/*The Search*

Clifton Webb/*Sitting Pretty*

1949

★Broderick Crawford/*All the King's Men*

Kirk Douglas/*Champion*

Gregory Peck/*Twelve o'Clock High*

John Wayne/*Sands of Iwo Jima*

1950

★Jose Ferrer/*Cyrano de Bergerac*

Louis Calhern/*The Magnificent Yankee*

William Holden/*Sunset Boulevard*

James Stewart/*Harvey*

Spencer Tracy/*Father of the Bride*

1951

★Humphrey Bogart/*The African Queen*

Marlon Brando/*A Streetcar Named Desire*

Montgomery Clift/*A Place in the Sun*

1952

★Gary Cooper/*High Noon*

Marlon Brando/*Viva Zapata!*

Kirk Douglas/*The Bad and the Beautiful*

Jose Ferrer/*Moulin Rouge*

Alec Guinness/*The Lavender Hill Mob*

1953

★William Holden/*Stalag 17*

Marlon Brando/*Julius Caesar*

Richard Burton/*The Robe*

Montgomery Clift/*From Here to Eternity*

Burt Lancaster/*From Here to Eternity*

1954

★Marlon Brando/*On the Waterfront*

Humphrey Bogart/*The Caine Mutiny*

Bing Crosby/*Country Girl*

James Mason/*A Star Is Born*

1955

★Ernest Borgnine/*Marty*

James Cagney/*Love Me or Leave Me*

James Dean/*East of Eden*

Frank Sinatra/*The Man with the Golden Arm*

Spencer Tracy/*Bad Day at Black Rock*

1956

★Yul Brynner/*The King and I*

James Dean/*Giant*

Kirk Douglas/*Lust for Life*

Rock Hudson/*Giant*

Laurence Olivier/*Richard III*

1957

★Alec Guinness/*The Bridge on the River Kwai*

Marlon Brando/*Sayonara*

Charles Laughton/*Witness for the Prosecution*

1958

★David Niven/*Separate Tables*

Tony Curtis/*The Defiant Ones*

Paul Newman/*Cat on a Hot Tin Roof*

Sidney Poitier/*The Defiant Ones*

1959

★Charlton Heston/*Ben-Hur*

Laurence Harvey/*Room at the Top*

Jack Lemmon/*Some Like It Hot*

Paul Muni/*The Last Angry Man*

James Stewart/*Anatomy of a Murder*

Spencer Tracy/*The Old Man and the Sea*

1960

★Burt Lancaster/*Elmer Gantry*

★ = winner

Jack Lemmon/*The Apartment*

Laurence Olivier/*The Entertainer*

Spencer Tracy/*Inherit the Wind*

1961

★Maximilian Schell/*Judgment at Nuremberg*

Charles Boyer/*Fanny*

Paul Newman/*The Hustler*

Spencer Tracy/*Judgment at Nuremberg*

Stuart Whitman/*The Mark*

1962

★Gregory Peck/*To Kill a Mockingbird*

Burt Lancaster/*Birdman of Alcatraz*

Jack Lemmon/*Days of Wine and Roses*

Marcello Mastroianni/*Divorce—Italian Style*

Peter O'Toole/*Lawrence of Arabia*

1963

★Sidney Poitier/*Lilies of the Field*

Albert Finney/*Tom Jones*

Richard Harris/*This Sporting Life*

Rex Harrison/*Cleopatra*

Paul Newman/*Hud*

1964

★Rex Harrison/*My Fair Lady*

Richard Burton/*Becket*

Peter O'Toole/*Becket*

Anthony Quinn/*Zorba the Greek*

Peter Sellers/*Dr. Strangelove, or: How I Learned to Stop Worrying and Love the Bomb*

1965

★Lee Marvin/*Cat Ballou*

Richard Burton/*The Spy Who Came in from the Cold*

Laurence Olivier/*Othello*

Rod Steiger/*The Pawnbroker*

Oskar Werner/*Ship of Fools*

1966

★Paul Scofield/*A Man for All Seasons*

Alan Arkin/*The Russians Are Coming, the Russians Are Coming*

Richard Burton/*Who's Afraid of Virginia Woolf?*

Michael Caine/*Alfie*

Steve McQueen/*The Sand Pebbles*

1967

★Rod Steiger/*In the Heat of the Night*

Warren Beatty/*Bonnie & Clyde*

Dustin Hoffman/*The Graduate*

Paul Newman/*Cool Hand Luke*

Spencer Tracy/*Guess Who's Coming to Dinner*

1968

★Cliff Robertson/*Charly*

Alan Arkin/*The Heart Is a Lonely Hunter*

Alan Bates/*The Fixer*

Ron Moody/*Oliver!*

Peter O'Toole/*The Lion in Winter*

1969

★John Wayne/*True Grit*

Richard Burton/*Anne of the Thousand Days*

Dustin Hoffman/*Midnight Cowboy*

Peter O'Toole/*Goodbye, Mr. Chips*

Jon Voight/*Midnight Cowboy*

1970

★George C. Scott/*Patton*

Melvyn Douglas/*I Never Sang for My Father*

James Earl Jones/*The Great White Hope*

Jack Nicholson/*Five Easy Pieces*

Ryan O'Neal/*Love Story*

1971

★Gene Hackman/*The French Connection*

Peter Finch/*Sunday, Bloody Sunday*

Walter Matthau/*Kotch*

George C. Scott/*The Hospital*

Chaim Topol/*Fiddler on the Roof*

1972

★Marlon Brando/*The Godfather*

Michael Caine/*Sleuth*

Peter O'Toole/*The Ruling Class*

Laurence Olivier/*Sleuth*

Paul Winfield/*Sounder*

1973

★Jack Lemmon/*Save the Tiger*

Marlon Brando/*Last Tango in Paris*

Jack Nicholson/*The Last Detail*

Al Pacino/*Serpico*

Robert Redford/*The Sting*

1974

★Art Carney/*Harry and Tonto*

Albert Finney/*Murder on the Orient Express*

Dustin Hoffman/*Lenny*

Jack Nicholson/*Chinatown*

Al Pacino/*The Godfather, Part 2*

1975

★Jack Nicholson/*One Flew Over the Cuckoo's Nest*

Walter Matthau/*The Sunshine Boys*

Al Pacino/*Dog Day Afternoon*

Maximilian Schell/*The Man in the Glass Booth*

James Whitmore/*Give 'Em Hell, Harry!*

1976

★Peter Finch/*Network*

Robert De Niro/*Taxi Driver*

Giancarlo Giannini/*Seven Beauties*

William Holden/*Network*

Sylvester Stallone/*Rocky*

1977

★Richard Dreyfuss/*The Goodbye Girl*

Woody Allen/*Annie Hall*

Richard Burton/*Equus*

Marcello Mastroianni/*A Special Day*

John Travolta/*Saturday Night Fever*

1978

★Jon Voight/*Coming Home*

Warren Beatty/*Heaven Can Wait*

Gary Busey/*The Buddy Holly Story*

Robert De Niro/*The Deer Hunter*

Laurence Olivier/*The Boys from Brazil*

1979

★Dustin Hoffman/*Kramer vs. Kramer*

Jack Lemmon/*The China Syndrome*

Al Pacino/*And Justice for All*

Roy Scheider/*All That Jazz*

Peter Sellers/*Being There*

1980

★Robert De Niro/*Raging Bull*

Robert Duvall/*The Great Santini*

John Hurt/*The Elephant Man*

Jack Lemmon/*Tribute*

Peter O'Toole/*The Stunt Man*

1981

★Henry Fonda/*On Golden Pond*

Warren Beatty/*Reds*

Burt Lancaster/*Atlantic City*

Dudley Moore/*Arthur*

Paul Newman/*Absence of Malice*

1982

★Ben Kingsley/*Gandhi*

Dustin Hoffman/*Tootsie*

Jack Lemmon/*Missing*

Paul Newman/*The Verdict*

Peter O'Toole/*My Favorite Year*

1983

★Robert Duvall/*Tender Mercies*

Michael Caine/*Educating Rita*

Tom Conti/*Reuben, Reuben*

Tom Courtenay/*The Dresser*

Albert Finney/*The Dresser*

1984

★F. Murray Abraham/*Amadeus*

Jeff Bridges/*Starman*

Albert Finney/*Under the Volcano*

Tom Hulce/*Amadeus*

Sam Waterston/*The Killing Fields*

1985

★William Hurt/*Kiss of the Spider Woman*

Harrison Ford/*Witness*

James Garner/*Murphy's Romance*

Jack Nicholson/*Prizzi's Honor*

Jon Voight/*Runaway Train*

1986

★Paul Newman/*The Color of Money*

Dexter Gordon/*Round Midnight*

Bob Hoskins/*Mona Lisa*

William Hurt/*Children of a Lesser God*

James Woods/*Salvador*

1987

★Michael Douglas/*Wall Street*

William Hurt/*Broadcast News*

Marcello Mastroianni/*Dark Eyes*

Jack Nicholson/*Ironweed*

Robin Williams/*Good Morning, Vietnam*

1988

★Dustin Hoffman/*Rain Man*

Gene Hackman/*Mississippi Burning*

Tom Hanks/*Big*

Edward James Olmos/*Stand and Deliver*

Max von Sydow/*Pelle the Conqueror*

1989

★Daniel Day-Lewis/*My Left Foot*

Kenneth Branagh/*Henry V*

Tom Cruise/*Born on the Fourth of July*

Morgan Freeman/*Driving Miss Daisy*

Robin Williams/*Dead Poets Society*

1990

★Jeremy Irons/*Reversal of Fortune*

Kevin Costner/*Dances with Wolves*

Robert De Niro/*Awakenings*

Gerard Depardieu/*Cyrano de Bergerac*

Richard Harris/*The Field*

1991

★Anthony Hopkins/*The Silence of the Lambs*

Warren Beatty/*Bugsy*

Robert De Niro/*Cape Fear*

Nick Nolte/*The Prince of Tides*

Robin Williams/*The Fisher King*

1992

★Al Pacino/*Scent of a Woman*

Robert Downey, Jr./*Chaplin*

Clint Eastwood/*Unforgiven*

Stephen Rea/*The Crying Game*

Denzel Washington/*Malcolm X*

1993

★Tom Hanks/*Philadelphia*

Daniel Day-Lewis/*In the Name of the Father*

Laurence Fishburne/*What's Love Got to Do with It?*

Anthony Hopkins/*The Remains of the Day*

Liam Neeson/*Schindler's List*

1994

★Tom Hanks/*Forrest Gump*

Morgan Freeman/*The Shawshank Redemption*

Nigel Hawthorne/*The Madness of King George*

Paul Newman/*Nobody's Fool*

John Travolta/*Pulp Fiction*

1995

★Nicolas Cage/*Leaving Las Vegas*

Richard Dreyfuss/*Mr. Holland's Opus*

Anthony Hopkins/*Nixon*

Sean Penn/*Dead Man Walking*

Massimo Troisi/*The Postman*

1996

★Geoffrey Rush/*Shine*

Tom Cruise/*Jerry Maguire*

Ralph Fiennes/*The English Patient*

Woody Harrelson/*The People vs. Larry Flynt*

Billy Bob Thornton/*Sling Blade*

1997

★Jack Nicholson/*As Good As It Gets*

Matt Damon/*Good Will Hunting*

Robert Duvall/*The Apostle*

Peter Fonda/*Ulee's Gold*

Dustin Hoffman/*Wag the Dog*

1998

★Roberto Benigni/*Life Is Beautiful*

Tom Hanks/*Saving Private Ryan*

Ian McKellen/*Gods and Monsters*

Nick Nolte/*Affliction*

Edward Norton/*American History X*

1999

★Kevin Spacey/*American Beauty*

Russell Crowe/*The Insider*

Richard Farnsworth/*The Straight Story*

Sean Penn/*Sweet and Lowdown*

Denzel Washington/*The Hurricane*

2000

★Russell Crowe/*Gladiator*

Javier Bardem/*Before Night Falls*

Tom Hanks/*Cast Away*

Ed Harris/*Pollock*

Geoffrey Rush/*Quills*

2001

★Denzel Washington/*Tràining Day*

Russell Crowe/*A Beautiful Mind*

Sean Penn/*I Am Sam*

Will Smith/*Ali*

Tom Wilkinson/*In the Bedroom*

2002

★Adrien Brody/*The Pianist*

Nicolas Cage/*Adaptation*

Michael Caine/*The Quiet American*

Daniel Day-Lewis/*Gangs of New York*

Jack Nicholson/*About Schmidt*

2003

★Sean Penn/*Mystic River*

Johnny Depp/*Pirates of the Caribbean: The Curse of the Black Pearl*

Ben Kingsley/*House of Sand and Fog*

Jude Law/*Cold Mountain*

Bill Murray/*Lost in Translation*

2004

★Jamie Foxx/*Ray*

Don Cheadle/*Hotel Rwanda*

Johnny Depp/*Finding Neverland*

Leonardo DiCaprio/*The Aviator*

Clint Eastwood/*Million Dollar Baby*

2005

★Philip Seymour Hoffman/*Capote*

Terrence Howard/*Hustle & Flow*

Heath Ledger/*Brokeback Mountain*

Joaquin Rafael (Leaf) Phoenix/*Walk the Line*

David Strathairn/*Good Night, and Good Luck*

2006

★Forest Whitaker/*The Last King of Scotland*

Leonardo DiCaprio/*Blood Diamond*

Ryan Gosling/*Half Nelson*

Peter O'Toole/*Venus*

Will Smith/*The Pursuit of Happyness*

2007

★Daniel Day-Lewis/*There Will Be Blood*

George Clooney/*Michael Clayton*

Johnny Depp/*Sweeney Todd: The Demon Barber of Fleet Street*

Tommy Lee Jones/*In the Valley of Elah*

Viggo Mortensen/*Eastern Promises*

2008

★Sean Penn/*Milk*

Richard Jenkins/*The Visitor*

Frank Langella/*Frost/Nixon*

Brad Pitt/*The Curious Case of Benjamin Button*

Mickey Rourke/*The Wrestler*

2009

★Jeff Bridges/*Crazy Heart*

George Clooney/*Up in the Air*

Colin Firth/*A Single Man*

Morgan Freeman/*Invictus*

Jeremy Renner/*The Hurt Locker*

ACTOR—SUPPORTING

1936

★Walter Brennan/*Come and Get It*

Mischa Auer/*My Man Godfrey*

Stuart Erwin/*Pigskin Parade*

Basil Rathbone/*Romeo and Juliet*

Akim Tamiroff/*The General Died at Dawn*

1937

★Joseph Schildkraut/*The Life of Emile Zola*

Ralph Bellamy/*The Awful Truth*

Thomas Mitchell/*The Hurricane*

H.B. Warner/*Lost Horizon*

Roland Young/*Topper*

1938

John Garfield/*Four Daughters*

Gene Lockhart/*Algiers*

Robert Morley/*Marie Antoinette*

1939

★Thomas Mitchell/*Stagecoach*

Brian Aherne/*Juarez*

Harry Carey, Sr./*Mr. Smith Goes to Washington*

Brian Donlevy/*Beau Geste*

Claude Rains/*Mr. Smith Goes to Washington*

1940

★Walter Brennan/*The Westerner*

Albert Bassermann/*Foreign Correspondent*

William Gargan/*They Knew What They Wanted*

Jack Oakie/*The Great Dictator*

James Stephenson/*The Letter*

1941

★Donald Crisp/*How Green Was My Valley*

Walter Brennan/*Sergeant York*

Charles Coburn/*The Devil & Miss Jones*

James Gleason/*Here Comes Mr. Jordan*

Sydney Greenstreet/*The Maltese Falcon*

1942

★Van Heflin/*Johnny Eager*

William Bendix/*Wake Island*

Walter Huston/*Yankee Doodle Dandy*

Frank Morgan/*Tortilla Flat*

Henry Travers/*Mrs. Miniver*

★ = winner

1943

★Charles Coburn/*The More the Merrier*

Charles Bickford/*The Song of Bernadette*

J. Carrol Naish/*Sahara*

Claude Rains/*Casablanca*

Akim Tamiroff/*For Whom the Bell Tolls*

1944

★Barry Fitzgerald/*Going My Way*

Hume Cronyn/*The Seventh Cross*

Claude Rains/*Mr. Skeffington*

Clifton Webb/*Laura*

Monty Woolley/*Since You Went Away*

1945

★James Dunn/*A Tree Grows in Brooklyn*

Michael Chekhov/*Spellbound*

John Dall/*The Corn Is Green*

1946

★Harold Russell/*The Best Years of Our Lives*

William Demarest/*The Jolson Story*

Claude Rains/*Notorious*

Clifton Webb/*The Razor's Edge*

1947

★Edmund Gwenn/*Miracle on 34th Street*

Charles Bickford/*The Farmer's Daughter*

Robert Ryan/*Crossfire*

Richard Widmark/*Kiss of Death*

1948

★Walter Huston/*Treasure of the Sierra Madre*

Charles Bickford/*Johnny Belinda*

Jose Ferrer/*Joan of Arc*

Oscar Homolka/*I Remember Mama*

1949

★Dean Jagger/*Twelve o'Clock High*

John Ireland/*All the King's Men*

Cecil Kellaway/*The Luck of the Irish*

Arthur Kennedy/*Champion*

Ralph Richardson/*The Heiress*

James Whitmore/*Battleground*

1950

★George Sanders/*All About Eve*

Jeff Chandler/*Broken Arrow*

Sam Jaffe/*The Asphalt Jungle*

Erich von Stroheim/*Sunset Boulevard*

1951

★Karl Malden/*A Streetcar Named Desire*

Leo Genn/*Quo Vadis*

Peter Ustinov/*Quo Vadis*

1952

★Anthony Quinn/*Viva Zapata!*

Arthur Hunnicutt/*The Big Sky*

Victor McLaglen/*The Quiet Man*

Jack Palance/*Sudden Fear*

1953

★Frank Sinatra/*From Here to Eternity*

Eddie Albert/*Roman Holiday*

Jack Palance/*Shane*

Robert Strauss/*Stalag 17*

Brandon de Wilde/*Shane*

1954

★Edmond O'Brien/*The Barefoot Contessa*

Lee J. Cobb/*On the Waterfront*

Karl Malden/*On the Waterfront*

Rod Steiger/*On the Waterfront*

Tom Tully/*The Caine Mutiny*

1955

★Jack Lemmon/*Mister Roberts*

Joe Mantell/*Marty*

Sal Mineo/*Rebel without a Cause*

Arthur O'Connell/*Picnic*

1956

★Anthony Quinn/*Lust for Life*

Don Murray/*Bus Stop*

Anthony Perkins/*Friendly Persuasion*

Robert Stack/*Written on the Wind*

1957

★Red Buttons/*Sayonara*

Sessue Hayakawa/*The Bridge on the River Kwai*

Arthur Kennedy/*Peyton Place*

Russ Tamblyn/*Peyton Place*

1958

★Burl Ives/*The Big Country*

Theodore Bikel/*The Defiant Ones*

Lee J. Cobb/*The Brothers Karamazov*

Vittorio De Sica/*A Farewell to Arms*

Arthur Kennedy/*Some Came Running*

Gig Young/*Teacher's Pet*

1959

★Hugh Griffith/*Ben-Hur*

Arthur O'Connell/*Anatomy of a Murder*

George C. Scott/*Anatomy of a Murder*

Robert Vaughn/*The Young Philadelphians*

Ed Wynn/*The Diary of Anne Frank*

1960

★Peter Ustinov/*Spartacus*

Jack Kruschen/*The Apartment*

Sal Mineo/*Exodus*

Chill Wills/*The Alamo*

1961

★George Chakiris/*West Side Story*

Montgomery Clift/*Judgment at Nuremberg*

Peter Falk/*Murder, Inc.*

Peter Falk/*Pocketful of Miracles*

Jackie Gleason/*The Hustler*

George C. Scott/*The Hustler*

1962

★Ed Begley, Sr./*Sweet Bird of Youth*

Victor Buono/*What Ever Happened to Baby Jane?*

Telly Savalas/*Birdman of Alcatraz*

Omar Sharif/*Lawrence of Arabia*

Terence Stamp/*Billy Budd*

1963

★Melvyn Douglas/*Hud*

Bobby Darin/*Captain Newman, M.D.*

Hugh Griffith/*Tom Jones*

John Huston/*The Cardinal*

1964

★Peter Ustinov/*Topkapi*

John Gielgud/*Becket*

Stanley Holloway/*My Fair Lady*

Edmond O'Brien/*Seven Days in May*

Lee Tracy/*The Best Man*

1965

★Martin Balsam/*A Thousand Clowns*

Ian Bannen/*The Flight of the Phoenix*

Tom Courtenay/*Doctor Zhivago*

Michael Dunn/*Ship of Fools*

Frank Finlay/*Othello*

1966

★Walter Matthau/*The Fortune Cookie*

Mako/*The Sand Pebbles*

James Mason/*Georgy Girl*

George Segal/*Who's Afraid of Virginia Woolf?*

Robert Shaw/*A Man for All Seasons*

1967

★George Kennedy/*Cool Hand Luke*

John Cassavetes/*The Dirty Dozen*

Gene Hackman/*Bonnie & Clyde*

Cecil Kellaway/*Guess Who's Coming to Dinner*

Michael J. Pollard/*Bonnie & Clyde*

1968

★Jack Albertson/*The Subject Was Roses*

Seymour Cassel/*Faces*

Daniel Massey/*Star!*

Jack Wild/*Oliver!*

Gene Wilder/*The Producers*

1969

★Gig Young/*They Shoot Horses, Don't They?*

Rupert Crosse/*The Reivers*

Elliott Gould/*Bob & Carol & Ted & Alice*

Jack Nicholson/*Easy Rider*

Anthony Quayle/*Anne of the Thousand Days*

1970

★John Mills/*Ryan's Daughter*

Richard S. Castellano/*Lovers and Other Strangers*

Chief Dan George/*Little Big Man*

Gene Hackman/*I Never Sang for My Father*

John Marley/*Love Story*

1971

★Ben Johnson/*The Last Picture Show*

Jeff Bridges/*The Last Picture Show*

Leonard Frey/*Fiddler on the Roof*

Richard Jaeckel/*Sometimes a Great Notion*

Roy Scheider/*The French Connection*

1972

★Joel Grey/*Cabaret*

Eddie Albert/*The Heartbreak Kid*

James Caan/*The Godfather*

Robert Duvall/*The Godfather*

Al Pacino/*The Godfather*

1973

★John Houseman/*The Paper Chase*

Vincent Gardenia/*Bang the Drum Slowly*

Jack Gilford/*Save the Tiger*

Jason Miller/*The Exorcist*

Randy Quaid/*The Last Detail*

1974

★Robert De Niro/*The Godfather, Part 2*

Fred Astaire/*The Towering Inferno*

Jeff Bridges/*Thunderbolt & Lightfoot*

Michael V. Gazzo/*The Godfather, Part 2*

Lee Strasberg/*The Godfather, Part 2*

1975

★George Burns/*The Sunshine Boys*

Brad Dourif/*One Flew Over the Cuckoo's Nest*

Burgess Meredith/*The Day of the Locust*

Chris Sarandon/*Dog Day Afternoon*

Jack Warden/*Shampoo*

1976

★Jason Robards, Jr./*All the President's Men*

Ned Beatty/*Network*

Burgess Meredith/*Rocky*

Laurence Olivier/*Marathon Man*

Burt Young/*Rocky*

1977

★Jason Robards, Jr./*Julia*

Mikhail Baryshnikov/*The Turning Point*

Peter Firth/*Equus*

Alec Guinness/*Star Wars*

Maximilian Schell/*Julia*

1978

★Christopher Walken/*The Deer Hunter*

Bruce Dern/*Coming Home*

Richard Farnsworth/*Comes a Horseman*

John Hurt/*Midnight Express*

Jack Warden/*Heaven Can Wait*

1979

★Melvyn Douglas/*Being There*

Robert Duvall/*Apocalypse Now*

Frederic Forrest/*The Rose*

Justin Henry/*Kramer vs. Kramer*

Mickey Rooney/*The Black Stallion*

1980

★Timothy Hutton/*Ordinary People*

Judd Hirsch/*Ordinary People*

Michael O'Keefe/*The Great Santini*

Joe Pesci/*Raging Bull*

Jason Robards, Jr./*Melvin and Howard*

1981

★John Gielgud/*Arthur*

James Coco/*Only When I Laugh*

Ian Holm/*Chariots of Fire*

Jack Nicholson/*Reds*

Howard E. Rollins, Jr./*Ragtime*

1982

★Louis Gossett, Jr./*An Officer and a Gentleman*

Charles Durning/*The Best Little Whorehouse in Texas*

John Lithgow/*The World According to Garp*

James Mason/*The Verdict*

Robert Preston/*Victor/Victoria*

1983

★Jack Nicholson/*Terms of Endearment*

Charles Durning/*To Be or Not to Be*

John Lithgow/*Terms of Endearment*

Sam Shepard/*The Right Stuff*

Rip Torn/*Cross Creek*

1984

★Haing S. Ngor/*The Killing Fields*

Adolph Caesar/*A Soldier's Story*

John Malkovich/*Places in the Heart*

Noriyuki "Pat" Morita/*The Karate Kid*

Ralph Richardson/*Greystoke: The Legend of Tarzan, Lord of the Apes*

1985

★Don Ameche/*Cocoon*

Klaus Maria Brandauer/*Out of Africa*

William Hickey/*Prizzi's Honor*

Robert Loggia/*The Jagged Edge*

Eric Roberts/*Runaway Train*

1986

★Michael Caine/*Hannah and Her Sisters*

Tom Berenger/*Platoon*

Willem Dafoe/*Platoon*

Denholm Elliott/*A Room with a View*

Dennis Hopper/*Hoosiers*

1987

★Sean Connery/*The Untouchables*

Albert Brooks/*Broadcast News*

Morgan Freeman/*Street Smart*

Vincent Gardenia/*Moonstruck*

Denzel Washington/*Cry Freedom*

1988

★Kevin Kline/*A Fish Called Wanda*

Alec Guinness/*Little Dorrit, Film 1: Nobody's Fault*

Martin Landau/*Tucker: The Man and His Dream*

River Phoenix/*Running on Empty*

Dean Stockwell/*Married to the Mob*

1989

★Denzel Washington/*Glory*

Danny Aiello/*Do the Right Thing*

Dan Aykroyd/*Driving Miss Daisy*

Marlon Brando/*A Dry White Season*

Martin Landau/*Crimes & Misdemeanors*

1990

★Joe Pesci/*Goodfellas*

Bruce Davison/*Longtime Companion*

Andy Garcia/*The Godfather, Part 3*

Graham Greene/*Dances with Wolves*

Al Pacino/*Dick Tracy*

1991

★Jack Palance/*City Slickers*

Tommy Lee Jones/*JFK*

Harvey Keitel/*Bugsy*

Ben Kingsley/*Bugsy*

Michael Lerner/*Barton Fink*

1992

★Gene Hackman/*Unforgiven*

Jaye Davidson/*The Crying Game*

Jack Nicholson/*A Few Good Men*

Al Pacino/*Glengarry Glen Ross*

David Paymer/*Mr. Saturday Night*

1993

★Tommy Lee Jones/*The Fugitive*

Leonardo DiCaprio/*What's Eating Gilbert Grape*

Ralph Fiennes/*Schindler's List*

John Malkovich/*In the Line of Fire*

Pete Postlethwaite/*In the Name of the Father*

1994

★Martin Landau/*Ed Wood*

Samuel L. Jackson/*Pulp Fiction*

Chazz Palminteri/*Bullets over Broadway*

Paul Scofield/*Quiz Show*

Gary Sinise/*Forrest Gump*

1995

★Kevin Spacey/*The Usual Suspects*

James Cromwell/*Babe*

Ed Harris/*Apollo 13*

Brad Pitt/*12 Monkeys*

Tim Roth/*Rob Roy*

1996

★Cuba Gooding, Jr./*Jerry Maguire*

William H. Macy/*Fargo*

Armin Mueller-Stahl/*Shine*

Edward Norton/*Primal Fear*

James Woods/*Ghosts of Mississippi*

1997

★Robin Williams/*Good Will Hunting*

Robert Forster/*Jackie Brown*

Anthony Hopkins/*Amistad*

Greg Kinnear/*As Good As It Gets*

Burt Reynolds/*Boogie Nights*

1998

★James Coburn/*Affliction*

Robert Duvall/*A Civil Action*

Ed Harris/*The Truman Show*

Geoffrey Rush/*Shakespeare in Love*

Billy Bob Thornton/*A Simple Plan*

1999

★Michael Caine/*The Cider House Rules*

Tom Cruise/*Magnolia*

Michael Clarke Duncan/*The Green Mile*

Jude Law/*The Talented Mr. Ripley*

Haley Joel Osment/*The Sixth Sense*

2000

★Benicio Del Toro/*Traffic*

Jeff Bridges/*The Contender*

Willem Dafoe/*Shadow of the Vampire*

Albert Finney/*Erin Brockovich*

Joaquin Rafael (Leaf) Phoenix/*Gladiator*

2001

★Jim Broadbent/*Iris*

Ethan Hawke/*Training Day*

Ben Kingsley/*Sexy Beast*

★ = *winner*

Ian McKellen/*Lord of the Rings: The Fellowship of the Ring*
Jon Voight/*Ali*

2002
★Chris Cooper/*Adaptation*
Ed Harris/*The Hours*
Paul Newman/*Road to Perdition*
John C. Reilly/*Chicago*
Christopher Walken/*Catch Me If You Can*

2003
★Tim Robbins/*Mystic River*
Alec Baldwin/*The Cooler*
Benicio Del Toro/*21 Grams*
Djimon Hounsou/*In America*
Ken(saku) Watanabe/*The Last Samurai*

2004
★Morgan Freeman/*Million Dollar Baby*
Alan Alda/*The Aviator*
Thomas Haden Church/*Sideways*
Jamie Foxx/*Collateral*
Clive Owen/*Closer*

2005
★George Clooney/*Syriana*
Matt Dillon/*Crash*
Paul Giamatti/*Cinderella Man*
Jake Gyllenhaal/*Brokeback Mountain*
William Hurt/*A History of Violence*

2006
★Alan Arkin/*Little Miss Sunshine*
Jackie Earle Haley/*Little Children*
Djimon Hounsou/*Blood Diamond*
Eddie Murphy/*Dreamgirls*
Mark Wahlberg/*The Departed*

2007
★Javier Bardem/*No Country for Old Men*
Casey Affleck/*The Assassination of Jesse James by the Coward Robert Ford*
Philip Seymour Hoffman/*Charlie Wilson's War*
Hal Holbrook/*Into the Wild*
Tom Wilkinson/*Michael Clayton*

2008
★Heath Ledger/*The Dark Knight*
Josh Brolin/*Milk*
Robert Downey, Jr./*Tropic Thunder*
Philip Seymour Hoffman/*Doubt*
Michael Shannon/*Revolutionary Road*

2009
★Christoph Waltz/*Inglourious Basterds*
Matt Damon/*Invictus*
Woody Harrelson/*The Messenger*
Christopher Plummer/*The Last Station*
Stanley Tucci/*The Lovely Bones*

ACTRESS

1928
★Janet Gaynor/*Sunrise*
Gloria Swanson/*Sadie Thompson*

1929
★Mary Pickford/*Coquette*
Bessie Love/*Broadway Melody*

1930
★Norma Shearer/*The Divorcee*
Greta Garbo/*Anna Christie*
Greta Garbo/*Romance*

1931
★Marie Dressler/*Min & Bill*
Marlene Dietrich/*Morocco*
Irene Dunne/*Cimarron*
Norma Shearer/*A Free Soul*

1932
★Helen Hayes/*The Sin of Madelon Claudet*
Lynn Fontanne/*The Guardsman*

1933
★Katharine Hepburn/*Morning Glory*
May Robson/*Lady for a Day*
Diana Wynyard/*Cavalcade*

1934
★Claudette Colbert/*It Happened One Night*
Grace Moore/*One Night of Love*
Norma Shearer/*The Barretts of Wimpole Street*

1935
★Bette Davis/*Dangerous*
Katharine Hepburn/*Alice Adams*
Miriam Hopkins/*Becky Sharp*

1936
★Luise Rainer/*The Great Ziegfeld*
Irene Dunne/*Theodora Goes Wild*
Carole Lombard/*My Man Godfrey*
Merle Oberon/*The Dark Angel*
Norma Shearer/*Romeo and Juliet*

1937
★Luise Rainer/*The Good Earth*
Irene Dunne/*The Awful Truth*
Greta Garbo/*Camille*
Janet Gaynor/*A Star Is Born*
Barbara Stanwyck/*Stella Dallas*

1938
★Bette Davis/*Jezebel*
Wendy Hiller/*Pygmalion*
Norma Shearer/*Marie Antoinette*
Margaret Sullavan/*Three Comrades*

1939
★Vivien Leigh/*Gone with the Wind*
Bette Davis/*Dark Victory*
Irene Dunne/*Love Affair*
Greta Garbo/*Ninotchka*
Greer Garson/*Goodbye, Mr. Chips*

1940
★Ginger Rogers/*Kitty Foyle*
Bette Davis/*The Letter*
Joan Fontaine/*Rebecca*
Katharine Hepburn/*The Philadelphia Story*
Martha Scott/*Our Town*

1941
★Joan Fontaine/*Suspicion*
Bette Davis/*The Little Foxes*
Greer Garson/*Blossoms in the Dust*
Barbara Stanwyck/*Ball of Fire*

1942
★Greer Garson/*Mrs. Miniver*
Bette Davis/*Now, Voyager*
Katharine Hepburn/*Woman of the Year*
Teresa Wright/*The Pride of the Yankees*

1943
★Jennifer Jones/*The Song of Bernadette*
Jean Arthur/*The More the Merrier*
Ingrid Bergman/*For Whom the Bell Tolls*
Greer Garson/*Madame Curie*
Jane Russell/*My Sister Eileen*

1944
★Ingrid Bergman/*Gaslight*
Claudette Colbert/*Since You Went Away*
Bette Davis/*Mr. Skeffington*
Greer Garson/*Mrs. Parkington*
Barbara Stanwyck/*Double Indemnity*

1945
★Joan Crawford/*Mildred Pierce*
Ingrid Bergman/*The Bells of St. Mary's*
Greer Garson/*The Valley of Decision*
Gene Tierney/*Leave Her to Heaven*

1946
★Olivia de Havilland/*To Each His Own*
Celia Johnson/*Brief Encounter*
Jennifer Jones/*Duel in the Sun*
Rosalind Russell/*Sister Kenny*
Jane Wyman/*The Yearling*

1947
★Loretta Young/*The Farmer's Daughter*
Joan Crawford/*The Possessed*
Susan Hayward/*Smash-Up: The Story of a Woman*
Dorothy McGuire/*Gentleman's Agreement*

1948
★Jane Wyman/*Johnny Belinda*
Ingrid Bergman/*Joan of Arc*
Irene Dunne/*I Remember Mama*
Barbara Stanwyck/*Sorry, Wrong Number*
Olivia de Havilland/*The Snake Pit*

1949
★Olivia de Havilland/*The Heiress*
Jeanne Crain/*Pinky*
Susan Hayward/*My Foolish Heart*
Loretta Young/*Come to the Stable*

1950
★Judy Holliday/*Born Yesterday*
Anne Baxter/*All About Eve*
Bette Davis/*All About Eve*
Eleanor Parker/*Caged*
Gloria Swanson/*Sunset Boulevard*

1951
★Vivien Leigh/*A Streetcar Named Desire*
Katharine Hepburn/*The African Queen*
Eleanor Parker/*Detective Story*
Shelley Winters/*A Place in the Sun*

1952
★Shirley Booth/*Come Back, Little Sheba*
Joan Crawford/*Sudden Fear*
Julie Harris/*The Member of the Wedding*

1953
★Audrey Hepburn/*Roman Holiday*
Leslie Caron/*Lili*
Bette Davis/*The Star*
Ava Gardner/*Mogambo*
Susan Hayward/*With a Song in My Heart*
Deborah Kerr/*From Here to Eternity*
Maggie McNamara/*The Moon Is Blue*

1954
★Grace Kelly/*Country Girl*
Dorothy Dandridge/*Carmen Jones*
Judy Garland/*A Star Is Born*
Audrey Hepburn/*Sabrina*
Jane Wyman/*Magnificent Obsession*

1955
★Anna Magnani/*The Rose Tattoo*
Susan Hayward/*I'll Cry Tomorrow*
Katharine Hepburn/*Summertime*
Jennifer Jones/*Love Is a Many-Splendored Thing*
Eleanor Parker/*Interrupted Melody*

1956
★Ingrid Bergman/*Anastasia*
Carroll Baker/*Baby Doll*
Katharine Hepburn/*The Rainmaker*
Nancy Kelly/*The Bad Seed*
Deborah Kerr/*The King and I*

1957
★Joanne Woodward/*The Three Faces of Eve*
Deborah Kerr/*Heaven Knows, Mr. Allison*
Elizabeth Taylor/*Raintree County*
Lana Turner/*Peyton Place*

1958
★Susan Hayward/*I Want to Live!*
Deborah Kerr/*Separate Tables*
Shirley MacLaine/*Some Came Running*
Rosalind Russell/*Auntie Mame*
Elizabeth Taylor/*Cat on a Hot Tin Roof*

1959
★Simone Signoret/*Room at the Top*
Doris Day/*Pillow Talk*
Audrey Hepburn/*The Nun's Story*
Katharine Hepburn/*Suddenly, Last Summer*
Elizabeth Taylor/*Suddenly, Last Summer*

1960
★Elizabeth Taylor/*Butterfield 8*
Greer Garson/*Sunrise at Campobello*
Deborah Kerr/*The Sundowners*
Shirley MacLaine/*The Apartment*
Melina Mercouri/*Never on Sunday*

1961
★Sophia Loren/*Two Women*
Audrey Hepburn/*Breakfast at Tiffany's*
Piper Laurie/*The Hustler*
Geraldine Page/*Summer and Smoke*
Natalie Wood/*Splendor in the Grass*

1962
★Anne Bancroft/*The Miracle Worker*
Bette Davis/*What Ever Happened to Baby Jane?*
Katharine Hepburn/*Long Day's Journey into Night*
Geraldine Page/*Sweet Bird of Youth*
Lee Remick/*Days of Wine and Roses*

1963
★Patricia Neal/*Hud*
Shirley MacLaine/*Irma La Douce*
Rachel Roberts/*This Sporting Life*
Natalie Wood/*Love with the Proper Stranger*

1964
★Julie Andrews/*Mary Poppins*
Anne Bancroft/*The Pumpkin Eater*
Sophia Loren/*Marriage Italian Style*
Debbie Reynolds/*The Unsinkable Molly Brown*
Kim Stanley/*Seance on a Wet Afternoon*

1965
★Julie Christie/*Darling*
Julie Andrews/*The Sound of Music*
Samantha Eggar/*The Collector*
Elizabeth Hartman/*A Patch of Blue*
Simone Signoret/*Ship of Fools*

1966
★Elizabeth Taylor/*Who's Afraid of Virginia Woolf?*
Anouk Aimee/*A Man and a Woman*
Ida Kaminska/*The Shop on Main Street*
Lynn Redgrave/*Georgy Girl*
Vanessa Redgrave/*Morgan: A Suitable Case for Treatment*

1967
★Katharine Hepburn/*Guess Who's Coming to Dinner*
Anne Bancroft/*The Graduate*
Faye Dunaway/*Bonnie & Clyde*
Audrey Hepburn/*Wait until Dark*

1968
★Katharine Hepburn/*The Lion in Winter*
★Barbra Streisand/*Funny Girl*
Patricia Neal/*The Subject Was Roses*
Vanessa Redgrave/*Isadora*
Joanne Woodward/*Rachel, Rachel*

1969
★Maggie Smith/*The Prime of Miss Jean Brodie*
Genevieve Bujold/*Anne of the Thousand Days*
Jane Fonda/*They Shoot Horses, Don't They?*
Liza Minnelli/*The Sterile Cuckoo*
Jean Simmons/*The Happy Ending*

1970
★Glenda Jackson/*Women in Love*
Jane Alexander/*The Great White Hope*
Ali MacGraw/*Love Story*
Sarah Miles/*Ryan's Daughter*
Carrie Snodgress/*Diary of a Mad Housewife*

1971
★Jane Fonda/*Klute*
Julie Christie/*McCabe & Mrs. Miller*
Glenda Jackson/*Sunday, Bloody Sunday*
Vanessa Redgrave/*Mary, Queen of Scots*
Janet Suzman/*Nicholas and Alexandra*

1972
★Liza Minnelli/*Cabaret*
Diana Ross/*Lady Sings the Blues*
Maggie Smith/*Travels with My Aunt*
Cicely Tyson/*Sounder*
Liv Ullmann/*The Emigrants*

1973
★Glenda Jackson/*A Touch of Class*
Ellen Burstyn/*The Exorcist*
Marsha Mason/*Cinderella Liberty*
Barbra Streisand/*The Way We Were*
Joanne Woodward/*Summer Wishes, Winter Dreams*

1974
★Ellen Burstyn/*Alice Doesn't Live Here Anymore*
Faye Dunaway/*Chinatown*
Valerie Perrine/*Lenny*
Gena Rowlands/*A Woman under the Influence*

1975
★Louise Fletcher/*One Flew Over the Cuckoo's Nest*
Isabelle Adjani/*The Story of Adele H.*
Ann-Margret/*Tommy*
Glenda Jackson/*Hedda*
Carol Kane/*Hester Street*

1976
★Faye Dunaway/*Network*
Marie-Christine Barrault/*Cousin, Cousine*
Talia Shire/*Rocky*
Sissy Spacek/*Carrie*
Liv Ullmann/*Face to Face*

1977
★Diane Keaton/*Annie Hall*
Anne Bancroft/*The Turning Point*
Jane Fonda/*Julia*
Shirley MacLaine/*The Turning Point*
Marsha Mason/*The Goodbye Girl*

1978
★Jane Fonda/*Coming Home*
Ingrid Bergman/*Autumn Sonata*
Ellen Burstyn/*Same Time, Next Year*
Jill Clayburgh/*An Unmarried Woman*
Geraldine Page/*Interiors*

1979
★Sally Field/*Norma Rae*
Jill Clayburgh/*Starting Over*
Jane Fonda/*The China Syndrome*
Marsha Mason/*Chapter Two*

★ = winner

Bette Midler/*The Rose*

1980

★Sissy Spacek/*Coal Miner's Daughter*

Ellen Burstyn/*Resurrection*

Goldie Hawn/*Private Benjamin*

Mary Tyler Moore/*Ordinary People*

Gena Rowlands/*Gloria*

1981

★Katharine Hepburn/*On Golden Pond*

Diane Keaton/*Reds*

Marsha Mason/*Only When I Laugh*

Susan Sarandon/*Atlantic City*

Meryl Streep/*The French Lieutenant's Woman*

1982

★Meryl Streep/*Sophie's Choice*

Julie Andrews/*Victor/Victoria*

Jessica Lange/*Frances*

Sissy Spacek/*Missing*

Debra Winger/*An Officer and a Gentleman*

1983

★Shirley MacLaine/*Terms of Endearment*

Jane Alexander/*Testament*

Meryl Streep/*Silkwood*

Julie Walters/*Educating Rita*

Debra Winger/*Terms of Endearment*

1984

★Sally Field/*Places in the Heart*

Judy Davis/*A Passage to India*

Jessica Lange/*Country*

Vanessa Redgrave/*The Bostonians*

Sissy Spacek/*The River*

1985

★Geraldine Page/*The Trip to Bountiful*

Anne Bancroft/*Agnes of God*

Whoopi Goldberg/*The Color Purple*

Jessica Lange/*Sweet Dreams*

Meryl Streep/*Out of Africa*

1986

★Marlee Matlin/*Children of a Lesser God*

Jane Fonda/*The Morning After*

Sissy Spacek/*Crimes of the Heart*

Kathleen Turner/*Peggy Sue Got Married*

Sigourney Weaver/*Aliens*

1987

★Cher/*Moonstruck*

Glenn Close/*Fatal Attraction*

Holly Hunter/*Broadcast News*

Sally Kirkland/*Anna*

Meryl Streep/*Ironweed*

1988

★Jodie Foster/*The Accused*

Glenn Close/*Dangerous Liaisons*

Melanie Griffith/*Working Girl*

Meryl Streep/*A Cry in the Dark*

Sigourney Weaver/*Gorillas in the Mist*

1989

★Jessica Tandy/*Driving Miss Daisy*

Isabelle Adjani/*Camille Claudel*

Pauline Collins/*Shirley Valentine*

Jessica Lange/*Music Box*

Michelle Pfeiffer/*The Fabulous Baker Boys*

1990

★Kathy Bates/*Misery*

Anjelica Huston/*The Grifters*

Julia Roberts/*Pretty Woman*

Meryl Streep/*Postcards from the Edge*

Joanne Woodward/*Mr. & Mrs. Bridge*

1991

★Jodie Foster/*The Silence of the Lambs*

Geena Davis/*Thelma & Louise*

Laura Dern/*Rambling Rose*

Bette Midler/*For the Boys*

Susan Sarandon/*Thelma & Louise*

1992

★Emma Thompson/*Howard's End*

Catherine Deneuve/*Indochine*

Mary McDonnell/*Passion Fish*

Michelle Pfeiffer/*Love Field*

Susan Sarandon/*Lorenzo's Oil*

1993

★Holly Hunter/*The Piano*

Angela Bassett/*What's Love Got to Do with It?*

Stockard Channing/*Six Degrees of Separation*

Emma Thompson/*The Remains of the Day*

Debra Winger/*Shadowlands*

1994

★Jessica Lange/*Blue Sky*

Jodie Foster/*Nell*

Miranda Richardson/*Tom & Viv*

Winona Ryder/*Little Women*

Susan Sarandon/*The Client*

1995

★Susan Sarandon/*Dead Man Walking*

Elisabeth Shue/*Leaving Las Vegas*

Sharon Stone/*Casino*

Meryl Streep/*The Bridges of Madison County*

Emma Thompson/*Sense and Sensibility*

1996

★Frances McDormand/*Fargo*

Brenda Blethyn/*Secrets and Lies*

Diane Keaton/*Marvin's Room*

Kristin Scott Thomas/*The English Patient*

Emily Watson/*Breaking the Waves*

1997

★Helen Hunt/*As Good As It Gets*

Helena Bonham Carter/*The Wings of the Dove*

Julie Christie/*Afterglow*

Judi Dench/*Mrs. Brown*

Kate Winslet/*Titanic*

1998

★Gwyneth Paltrow/*Shakespeare in Love*

Cate Blanchett/*Elizabeth*

Fernanda Montenegro/*Central Station*

Meryl Streep/*One True Thing*

Emily Watson/*Hilary and Jackie*

1999

★Hilary Swank/*Boys Don't Cry*

Annette Bening/*American Beauty*

Janet McTeer/*Tumbleweeds*

Julianne Moore/*The End of the Affair*

Meryl Streep/*Music of the Heart*

2000

★Julia Roberts/*Erin Brockovich*

Joan Allen/*The Contender*

Juliette Binoche/*Chocolat*

Ellen Burstyn/*Requiem for a Dream*

Laura Linney/*You Can Count On Me*

2001

★Halle Berry/*Monster's Ball*

Judi Dench/*Iris*

Nicole Kidman/*Moulin Rouge*

Sissy Spacek/*In the Bedroom*

Renee Zellweger/*Bridget Jones's Diary*

2002

★Nicole Kidman/*The Hours*

Salma Hayek/*Frida*

Diane Lane/*Unfaithful*

Julianne Moore/*Far from Heaven*

Renee Zellweger/*Chicago*

2003

★Charlize Theron/*Monster*

Keisha Castle-Hughes/*Whale Rider*

Diane Keaton/*Something's Gotta Give*

Naomi Watts/*21 Grams*

2004

★Hilary Swank/*Million Dollar Baby*

Annette Bening/*Being Julia*

Catalina Sandino Moreno/*Maria Full of Grace*

Imelda Staunton/*Vera Drake*

Kate Winslet/*Eternal Sunshine of the Spotless Mind*

2005

★Reese Witherspoon/*Walk the Line*

Judi Dench/*Mrs. Henderson Presents*

Felicity Huffman/*Transamerica*

Keira Knightley/*Pride and Prejudice*

Charlize Theron/*North Country*

2006

★Helen Mirren/*The Queen*

Penelope Cruz/*Volver*

Judi Dench/*Notes on a Scandal*

Meryl Streep/*The Devil Wears Prada*

Kate Winslet/*Little Children*

2007

★Marion Cotillard/*La Vie en Rose*

Cate Blanchett/*Elizabeth: The Golden Age*

Julie Christie/*Away From Her*

Laura Linney/*The Savages*

Ellen Page/*Juno*

2008

★Kate Winslet/*The Reader*

Anne Hathaway/*Rachel Getting Married*

Angelina Jolie/*Changeling*

Melissa Leo/*Frozen River*

Meryl Streep/*Doubt*

2009

★Sandra Bullock/*The Blind Side*

Helen Mirren/*The Last Station*

Carey Mulligan/*An Education*

Gabourney "Gabby" Sidibe/*Precious: Based on the Novel by Sapphire*

Meryl Streep/*Julie & Julia*

ACTRESS—SUPPORTING

1936

★Gale Sondergaard/*Anthony Adverse*

Beulah Bondi/*The Gorgeous Hussy*

Alice Brady/*My Man Godfrey*

Bonita Granville/*These Three*

Maria Ouspenskaya/*Dodsworth*

1937

★Alice Brady/*In Old Chicago*

Andrea Leeds/*Stage Door*

Anne Shirley/*Stella Dallas*

Claire Trevor/*Dead End*

May Whitty/*Night Must Fall*

1938

★Fay Bainter/*Jezebel*

Beulah Bondi/*Of Human Hearts*

Spring Byington/*You Can't Take It with You*

Milza Korjus/*The Great Waltz*

1939

★Hattie McDaniel/*Gone with the Wind*

Geraldine Fitzgerald/*Wuthering Heights*

Edna May Oliver/*Drums Along the Mohawk*

Maria Ouspenskaya/*Love Affair*

Olivia de Havilland/*Gone with the Wind*

1940

★Jane Darwell/*The Grapes of Wrath*

Judith Anderson/*Rebecca*

Ruth Hussey/*The Philadelphia Story*

Barbara O'Neil/*All This and Heaven Too*

Marjorie Rambeau/*Primrose Path*

1941

★Mary Astor/*The Great Lie*

Sara Allgood/*How Green Was My Valley*

Patricia Collinge/*The Little Foxes*

Teresa Wright/*The Little Foxes*

Margaret Wycherly/*Sergeant York*

1942

★Teresa Wright/*Mrs. Miniver*

Gladys Cooper/*Now, Voyager*

Agnes Moorehead/*The Magnificent Ambersons*

Susan Peters/*Random Harvest*

May Whitty/*Mrs. Miniver*

1943

★Katina Paxinou/*For Whom the Bell Tolls*

Gladys Cooper/*The Song of Bernadette*

Paulette Goddard/*So Proudly We Hail*

Anne Revere/*The Song of Bernadette*

Lucile Watson/*Watch on the Rhine*

1944

★Ethel Barrymore/*None But the Lonely Heart*

Jennifer Jones/*Since You Went Away*

Angela Lansbury/*Gaslight*

Aline MacMahon/*Dragon Seed*

Agnes Moorehead/*Mrs. Parkington*

1945

★Anne Revere/*National Velvet*

Eve Arden/*Mildred Pierce*

Ann Blyth/*Mildred Pierce*

Angela Lansbury/*Picture of Dorian Gray*

Joan Lorring/*The Corn Is Green*

1946

★Anne Baxter/*The Razor's Edge*

Ethel Barrymore/*The Spiral Staircase*

Lillian Gish/*Duel in the Sun*

Flora Robson/*Saratoga Trunk*

Gale Sondergaard/*Anna and the King of Siam*

1947

★Celeste Holm/*Gentleman's Agreement*

Ethel Barrymore/*The Paradine Case*

Gloria Grahame/*Crossfire*

Marjorie Main/*Egg and I*

Anne Revere/*Gentleman's Agreement*

1948

★Claire Trevor/*Key Largo*

Barbara Bel Geddes/*I Remember Mama*

Ellen Corby/*I Remember Mama*

Agnes Moorehead/*Johnny Belinda*

Jean Simmons/*Hamlet*

1949

★Mercedes McCambridge/*All the King's Men*

Ethel Barrymore/*Pinky*

Celeste Holm/*Come to the Stable*

Elsa Lanchester/*Come to the Stable*

Ethel Waters/*Pinky*

1950

★Josephine Hull/*Harvey*

Hope Emerson/*Caged*

Celeste Holm/*All About Eve*

Nancy Olson/*Sunset Boulevard*

Thelma Ritter/*All About Eve*

1951

★Kim Hunter/*A Streetcar Named Desire*

Lee Grant/*Detective Story*

1952

★Gloria Grahame/*The Bad and the Beautiful*

Jean Hagen/*Singin' in the Rain*

Colette Marchand/*Moulin Rouge*

Terry Moore/*Come Back, Little Sheba*

1953

★Donna Reed/*From Here to Eternity*

Grace Kelly/*Mogambo*

Marjorie Rambeau/*Torch Song*

Thelma Ritter/*Pickup on South Street*

Thelma Ritter/*With a Song in My Heart*

1954

★Eva Marie Saint/*On the Waterfront*

Nina Foch/*Executive Suite*

Katy Jurado/*Broken Lance*

1955

★Jo Van Fleet/*East of Eden*

Betsy Blair/*Marty*

Peggy Lee/*Pete Kelly's Blues*

Marisa Pavan/*The Rose Tattoo*

Jan Sterling/*The High and the Mighty*

Claire Trevor/*The High and the Mighty*

Natalie Wood/*Rebel without a Cause*

1956

★Dorothy Malone/*Written on the Wind*

Mildred Dunnock/*Baby Doll*

Eileen Heckart/*The Bad Seed*

Mercedes McCambridge/*Giant*

Patty McCormack/*The Bad Seed*

1957

★Miyoshi Umeki/*Sayonara*

Elsa Lanchester/*Witness for the Prosecution*

Hope Lange/*Peyton Place*

Diane Varsi/*Peyton Place*

1958

★Wendy Hiller/*Separate Tables*

Peggy Cass/*Auntie Mame*

Martha Hyer/*Some Came Running*

Maureen Stapleton/*Lonelyhearts*

Cara Williams/*The Defiant Ones*

1959

★Shelley Winters/*The Diary of Anne Frank*

Hermione Baddeley/*Room at the Top*

Susan Kohner/*Imitation of Life*

Juanita Moore/*Imitation of Life*

Thelma Ritter/*Pillow Talk*

1960

★Shirley Jones/*Elmer Gantry*

Glynis Johns/*The Sundowners*

Janet Leigh/*Psycho*

1961

★Rita Moreno/*West Side Story*

Fay Bainter/*The Children's Hour*

Judy Garland/*Judgment at Nuremberg*

Lotte Lenya/*Roman Spring of Mrs. Stone*

Una Merkel/*Summer and Smoke*

1962

★Patty Duke/*The Miracle Worker*

Mary Badham/*To Kill a Mockingbird*

Shirley Knight/*Sweet Bird of Youth*

Angela Lansbury/*The Manchurian Candidate*

Thelma Ritter/*Birdman of Alcatraz*

★ = winner

1963

★Margaret Rutherford/*The V.I.P.'s*

Diane Cilento/*Tom Jones*

Edith Evans/*Tom Jones*

Joyce Redman/*Tom Jones*

Lilia Skala/*Lilies of the Field*

1964

★Lila Kedrova/*Zorba the Greek*

Gladys Cooper/*My Fair Lady*

Edith Evans/*The Chalk Garden*

Grayson Hall/*The Night of the Iguana*

Agnes Moorehead/*Hush, Hush, Sweet Charlotte*

1965

★Shelley Winters/*A Patch of Blue*

Ruth Gordon/*Inside Daisy Clover*

Joyce Redman/*Othello*

Maggie Smith/*Othello*

Peggy Wood/*The Sound of Music*

1966

★Sandy Dennis/*Who's Afraid of Virginia Woolf?*

Wendy Hiller/*A Man for All Seasons*

Jocelyn Lagarde/*Hawaii*

Vivien Merchant/*Alfie*

Geraldine Page/*You're a Big Boy Now*

1967

★Estelle Parsons/*Bonnie & Clyde*

Carol Channing/*Thoroughly Modern Millie*

Mildred Natwick/*Barefoot in the Park*

Beah Richards/*Guess Who's Coming to Dinner*

Katharine Ross/*The Graduate*

1968

★Ruth Gordon/*Rosemary's Baby*

Lynn Carlin/*Faces*

Sondra Locke/*The Heart Is a Lonely Hunter*

Kay Medford/*Funny Girl*

Estelle Parsons/*Rachel, Rachel*

1969

★Goldie Hawn/*Cactus Flower*

Cathy Burns/*Last Summer*

Dyan Cannon/*Bob & Carol & Ted & Alice*

Sylvia Miles/*Midnight Cowboy*

Susannah York/*They Shoot Horses, Don't They?*

1970

★Helen Hayes/*Airport*

Karen Black/*Five Easy Pieces*

Sally Kellerman/*M*A*S*H*

Maureen Stapleton/*Airport*

1971

★Cloris Leachman/*The Last Picture Show*

Ann-Margret/*Carnal Knowledge*

Ellen Burstyn/*The Last Picture Show*

Margaret Leighton/*The Go-Between*

1972

★Eileen Heckart/*Butterflies Are Free*

Jeannie Berlin/*The Heartbreak Kid*

Geraldine Page/*Pete 'n' Tillie*

Susan Tyrrell/*Fat City*

Shelley Winters/*The Poseidon Adventure*

1973

★Tatum O'Neal/*Paper Moon*

Linda Blair/*The Exorcist*

Candy Clark/*American Graffiti*

Madeline Kahn/*Paper Moon*

Sylvia Sidney/*Summer Wishes, Winter Dreams*

1974

★Ingrid Bergman/*Murder on the Orient Express*

Valentina Cortese/*Day for Night*

Madeline Kahn/*Blazing Saddles*

Diane Ladd/*Alice Doesn't Live Here Anymore*

Talia Shire/*The Godfather, Part 2*

1975

★Lee Grant/*Shampoo*

Ronee Blakley/*Nashville*

Sylvia Miles/*Farewell, My Lovely*

Lily Tomlin/*Nashville*

Brenda Vaccaro/*Once Is Not Enough*

1976

★Beatrice Straight/*Network*

Jane Alexander/*All the President's Men*

Jodie Foster/*Taxi Driver*

Lee Grant/*Voyage of the Damned*

Piper Laurie/*Carrie*

1977

★Vanessa Redgrave/*Julia*

Leslie Browne/*The Turning Point*

Quinn Cummings/*The Goodbye Girl*

Melinda Dillon/*Close Encounters of the Third Kind*

Tuesday Weld/*Looking for Mr. Goodbar*

1978

★Maggie Smith/*California Suite*

Dyan Cannon/*Heaven Can Wait*

Penelope Milford/*Coming Home*

Maureen Stapleton/*Interiors*

Meryl Streep/*The Deer Hunter*

1979

★Meryl Streep/*Kramer vs. Kramer*

Jane Alexander/*Kramer vs. Kramer*

Barbara Barrie/*Breaking Away*

Candice Bergen/*Starting Over*

Mariel Hemingway/*Manhattan*

1980

★Mary Steenburgen/*Melvin and Howard*

Eileen Brennan/*Private Benjamin*

Eva LeGallienne/*Resurrection*

Cathy Moriarty/*Raging Bull*

Diana Scarwid/*Inside Moves*

1981

★Maureen Stapleton/*Reds*

Melinda Dillon/*Absence of Malice*

Jane Fonda/*On Golden Pond*

Joan Hackett/*Only When I Laugh*

Elizabeth McGovern/*Ragtime*

1982

★Jessica Lange/*Tootsie*

Glenn Close/*The World According to Garp*

Teri Garr/*Tootsie*

Kim Stanley/*Frances*

Lesley Ann Warren/*Victor/Victoria*

1983

★Linda Hunt/*The Year of Living Dangerously*

Cher/*Silkwood*

Glenn Close/*The Big Chill*

Amy Irving/*Yentl*

Alfre Woodard/*Cross Creek*

1984

★Peggy Ashcroft/*A Passage to India*

Glenn Close/*The Natural*

Lindsay Crouse/*Places in the Heart*

Christine Lahti/*Swing Shift*

Geraldine Page/*The Pope of Greenwich Village*

1985

★Anjelica Huston/*Prizzi's Honor*

Margaret Avery/*The Color Purple*

Amy Madigan/*Twice in a Lifetime*

Meg Tilly/*Agnes of God*

Oprah Winfrey/*The Color Purple*

1986

★Dianne Wiest/*Hannah and Her Sisters*

Tess Harper/*Crimes of the Heart*

Piper Laurie/*Children of a Lesser God*

Mary Elizabeth Mastrantonio/*The Color of Money*

Maggie Smith/*A Room with a View*

1987

★Olympia Dukakis/*Moonstruck*

Norma Aleandro/*Gaby: A True Story*

Anne Archer/*Fatal Attraction*

Anne Ramsey/*Throw Momma from the Train*

Ann Sothern/*The Whales of August*

1988

★Geena Davis/*The Accidental Tourist*

Joan Cusack/*Working Girl*

Frances McDormand/*Mississippi Burning*

Michelle Pfeiffer/*Dangerous Liaisons*

Sigourney Weaver/*Working Girl*

1989

★Brenda Fricker/*My Left Foot*

Anjelica Huston/*Enemies, a Love Story*

Lena Olin/*Enemies, a Love Story*

Julia Roberts/*Steel Magnolias*

Dianne Wiest/*Parenthood*

1990

★Whoopi Goldberg/*Ghost*

Annette Bening/*The Grifters*

Lorraine Bracco/*Goodfellas*

Diane Ladd/*Wild at Heart*

Mary McDonnell/*Dances with Wolves*

1991

★Mercedes Ruehl/*The Fisher King*

Diane Ladd/*Rambling Rose*

Juliette Lewis/*Cape Fear*

Kate Nelligan/*The Prince of Tides*

Jessica Tandy/*Fried Green Tomatoes*

1992

★Marisa Tomei/*My Cousin Vinny*

Judy Davis/*Husbands and Wives*

Joan Plowright/*Enchanted April*

Vanessa Redgrave/*Howard's End*

Miranda Richardson/*Damage*

1993

★Anna Paquin/*The Piano*

Holly Hunter/*The Firm*

Rosie Perez/*Fearless*

Winona Ryder/*The Age of Innocence*

Emma Thompson/*In the Name of the Father*

1994

★Dianne Wiest/*Bullets over Broadway*

Rosemary Harris/*Tom & Viv*

Helen Mirren/*The Madness of King George*

Uma Thurman/*Pulp Fiction*

Jennifer Tilly/*Bullets over Broadway*

1995

★Mira Sorvino/*Mighty Aphrodite*

Joan Allen/*Nixon*

Kathleen Quinlan/*Apollo 13*

Mare Winningham/*Georgia*

Kate Winslet/*Sense and Sensibility*

1996

★Juliette Binoche/*The English Patient*

Joan Allen/*The Crucible*

Lauren Bacall/*The Mirror Has Two Faces*

Barbara Hershey/*Portrait of a Lady*

Marianne Jean-Baptiste/*Secrets and Lies*

1997

★Kim Basinger/*L.A. Confidential*

Joan Cusack/*In and Out*

Minnie Driver/*Good Will Hunting*

Julianne Moore/*Boogie Nights*

Gloria Stuart/*Titanic*

1998

★Judi Dench/*Shakespeare in Love*

Kathy Bates/*Primary Colors*

Brenda Blethyn/*Little Voice*

Rachel Griffiths/*Hilary and Jackie*

Lynn Redgrave/*Gods and Monsters*

1999

★Angelina Jolie/*Girl, Interrupted*

Toni Collette/*The Sixth Sense*

Catherine Keener/*Being John Malkovich*

Samantha Morton/*Sweet and Lowdown*

Chloe Sevigny/*Boys Don't Cry*

2000

★Marcia Gay Harden/*Pollock*

Judi Dench/*Chocolat*

Kate Hudson/*Almost Famous*

Frances McDormand/*Almost Famous*

Julie Walters/*Billy Elliot*

2001

★Jennifer Connelly/*A Beautiful Mind*

Helen Mirren/*Gosford Park*

Maggie Smith/*Gosford Park*

Marisa Tomei/*In the Bedroom*

Kate Winslet/*Iris*

2002

★Catherine Zeta-Jones/*Chicago*

Kathy Bates/*About Schmidt*

Julianne Moore/*The Hours*

Queen Latifah/*Chicago*

Meryl Streep/*Adaptation*

2003

★Renee Zellweger/*Cold Mountain*

Shohreh Aghdashloo/*House of Sand and Fog*

Patricia Clarkson/*Pieces of April*

Marcia Gay Harden/*Mystic River*

Holly Hunter/*Thirteen*

Samantha Morton/*In America*

2004

★Cate Blanchett/*The Aviator*

Laura Linney/*Kinsey*

Virginia Madsen/*Sideways*

Sophie Okonedo/*Hotel Rwanda*

Natalie Portman/*Closer*

2005

★Rachel Weisz/*The Constant Gardener*

Amy Adams/*Junebug*

Catherine Keener/*Capote*

Frances McDormand/*North Country*

Michelle Williams/*Brokeback Mountain*

2006

★Jennifer Hudson/*Dreamgirls*

Adriana Barraza/*Babel*

Cate Blanchett/*Notes on a Scandal*

Abigail Breslin/*Little Miss Sunshine*

Rinko Kikuchi/*Babel*

2007

★Tilda Swinton/*Michael Clayton*

Cate Blanchett/*I'm Not There*

Ruby Dee/*American Gangster*

Saoirse Ronan/*Atonement*

Amy Ryan/*Gone Baby Gone*

2008

★Penelope Cruz/*Vicky Cristina Barcelona*

Amy Adams/*Doubt*

Viola Davis/*Doubt*

Taraji P. Henson/*The Curious Case of Benjamin Button*

Marisa Tomei/*The Wrestler*

2009

★Mo'Nique/*Precious: Based on the Novel by Sapphire*

Penelope Cruz/*Nine*

Vera Farmiga/*Up in the Air*

Maggie Gyllenhaal/*Crazy Heart*

Anna Kendrick/*Up in the Air*

ART DIRECTION

1936

★*The Dark Angel*

1957

★*Sayonara*

Funny Face

Les Girls

Pal Joey

Raintree County

1958

★*Gigi*

Auntie Mame

Bell, Book and Candle

Vertigo

1967

★*Camelot*

Doctor Dolittle

Guess Who's Coming to Dinner

The Taming of the Shrew

Thoroughly Modern Millie

1968

★*Oliver!*

The Shoes of the Fisherman

Star!

2001: A Space Odyssey

War and Peace

1969

★*Hello, Dolly!*

Anne of the Thousand Days

Sweet Charity

They Shoot Horses, Don't They?

1970

★*Patton*

Airport

Molly Maguires

Scrooge

Tora! Tora! Tora!

1971

★*Nicholas and Alexandra*

The Andromeda Strain

Bedknobs and Broomsticks

Fiddler on the Roof

Mary, Queen of Scots

1972

★*Cabaret*

Lady Sings the Blues

The Poseidon Adventure

Travels with My Aunt

Young Winston

1973

★*The Sting*

Brother Sun, Sister Moon

The Exorcist

Tom Sawyer

The Way We Were

1974

★*The Godfather, Part 2*

Chinatown

Earthquake

The Island at the Top of the World

The Towering Inferno

1975

★*Barry Lyndon*

The Hindenburg

The Man Who Would Be King

Shampoo

The Sunshine Boys

1976

★*All the President's Men*

The Incredible Sarah

The Last Tycoon

Logan's Run

The Shootist

1977

★*Star Wars*

Airport '77

★ = winner

Close Encounters of the Third Kind
The Spy Who Loved Me
The Turning Point
1978
★Heaven Can Wait
Brink's Job
California Suite
Interiors
The Wiz
1979
★All That Jazz
Alien
Apocalypse Now
The China Syndrome
Star Trek: The Motion Picture
1980
★Tess
Altered States
Coal Miner's Daughter
The Elephant Man
The Empire Strikes Back
Kagemusha
1981
★Raiders of the Lost Ark
The French Lieutenant's Woman
Heaven's Gate
Ragtime
Reds
1982
★Gandhi
Annie
Blade Runner
Victor/Victoria
1983
★Fanny and Alexander
Return of the Jedi
The Right Stuff
Terms of Endearment
Yentl
1984
★Amadeus
The Cotton Club
The Natural
A Passage to India
2010: The Year We Make Contact
1985
★Out of Africa
Brazil
The Color Purple
Ran
Witness
1986
★A Room with a View
Aliens
The Color of Money
Hannah and Her Sisters
The Mission
1987
★The Last Emperor
Empire of the Sun
Hope and Glory
Radio Days
The Untouchables
1988
★Dangerous Liaisons
Beaches
Rain Man
Tucker: The Man and His Dream
Who Framed Roger Rabbit
1989
★Batman
The Abyss
The Adventures of Baron Munchausen
Driving Miss Daisy
Glory
1990
★Dick Tracy
Cyrano de Bergerac
Dances with Wolves
The Godfather, Part 3
Hamlet
1991
★Bugsy
Barton Fink
The Fisher King
Hook
The Prince of Tides
1992
★Howard's End
Bram Stoker's Dracula
Chaplin
Toys
Unforgiven
1993
★Schindler's List
Addams Family Values
The Age of Innocence
Orlando
The Remains of the Day
1994
★The Madness of King George
Bullets over Broadway
Forrest Gump
Interview with the Vampire
Legends of the Fall
1995
★Restoration
Apollo 13
Babe
A Little Princess
Richard III
1996
★The English Patient
The Birdcage
Evita
Hamlet
William Shakespeare's Romeo and Juliet
1997
★Titanic
Gattaca
Kundun
L.A. Confidential
Men in Black
1998
★Shakespeare in Love
Elizabeth
Pleasantville
Saving Private Ryan
What Dreams May Come
1999
★Sleepy Hollow
Anna and the King
The Cider House Rules
The Talented Mr. Ripley
Topsy Turvy
2000
★Crouching Tiger, Hidden Dragon
Dr. Seuss' How the Grinch Stole Christmas
Gladiator
Quills
2001
★Moulin Rouge
Amelie
Gosford Park
Harry Potter and the Sorcerer's Stone
Lord of the Rings: The Fellowship of the Ring
2002
★Chicago
Frida
Gangs of New York
Lord of the Rings: The Two Towers
Road to Perdition
2003
★Lord of the Rings: The Return of the King
Girl with a Pearl Earring
The Last Samurai
Lord of the Rings: The Return of the King
Master and Commander: The Far Side of the World
Seabiscuit
2004
★The Aviator
Finding Neverland
Lemony Snicket's A Series of Unfortunate Events
The Phantom of the Opera
A Very Long Engagement
2005
★Memoirs of a Geisha
Good Night, and Good Luck
Harry Potter and the Goblet of Fire
King Kong
Pride and Prejudice
2006
★Pan's Labyrinth
Dreamgirls
The Good Shepherd
Pirates of the Caribbean: Dead Man's Chest
The Prestige
2007
★Sweeney Todd: The Demon Barber of Fleet Street
American Gangster
Atonement
The Golden Compass
There Will Be Blood
2008
★The Curious Case of Benjamin Button
Changeling
The Dark Knight
The Duchess
Revolutionary Road
2009
★Avatar
The Imaginarium of Doctor Parnassus
Nine
Sherlock Holmes
The Young Victoria

ART DIRECTION (B&W)

1943
★This Above All
This Above All
1946
★Anna and the King of Siam
1947
★Great Expectations
1948
★Hamlet
Johnny Belinda
1949
★The Heiress
Come to the Stable
Madame Bovary
1950
★Sunset Boulevard
All About Eve
1951
★A Streetcar Named Desire
La Ronde
1952
★The Bad and the Beautiful
Carrie
Rashomon
Viva Zapata!
1953
★Julius Caesar
Martin Luther
Roman Holiday
Titanic
1954
★On the Waterfront
Country Girl
Executive Suite
Le Plaisir
Sabrina
1955
★The Rose Tattoo
Blackboard Jungle
I'll Cry Tomorrow
The Man with the Golden Arm
Marty
1956
★Somebody Up There Likes Me
Seven Samurai
Solid Gold Cadillac
1959
★The Diary of Anne Frank
Career
The Last Angry Man
Some Like It Hot
Suddenly, Last Summer
1960
★The Apartment
The Facts of Life
Psycho
1961
★The Hustler
The Absent-Minded Professor
The Children's Hour
Judgment at Nuremberg
La Dolce Vita
1962
★To Kill a Mockingbird
Days of Wine and Roses
The Longest Day
Period of Adjustment
1963
8 1/2
Hud
Love with the Proper Stranger
1964
★Zorba the Greek
The Americanization of Emily
Hush, Hush, Sweet Charlotte
The Night of the Iguana
Seven Days in May
1965
★Ship of Fools
King Rat
A Patch of Blue
The Slender Thread
The Spy Who Came in from the Cold
1966
★Who's Afraid of Virginia Woolf?
The Fortune Cookie
The Gospel According to St. Matthew
Is Paris Burning?

ART DIRECTION (COLOR)

1947
★Black Narcissus
Life with Father
1948
★The Red Shoes
Joan of Arc
1949
★Little Women
Adventures of Don Juan
1950
★Samson and Delilah
Annie Get Your Gun
Destination Moon
1951
★An American in Paris
David and Bathsheba
Quo Vadis
The Tales of Hoffmann
1952
★Moulin Rouge
Hans Christian Andersen
The Merry Widow
The Quiet Man
The Snows of Kilimanjaro
1953
★The Robe
Knights of the Round Table
Lili
Young Bess
1954
★20,000 Leagues under the Sea
Brigadoon
Desiree
Red Garters
A Star Is Born
1955
★Picnic
Daddy Long Legs
Guys and Dolls
Love Is a Many-Splendored Thing
To Catch a Thief
1956
★The King and I
Around the World in 80 Days
Giant
Lust for Life
The Ten Commandments
1959
★Ben-Hur
Journey to the Center of the Earth
North by Northwest
Pillow Talk
1960
★Spartacus
Cimarron
It Started in Naples
Sunrise at Campobello
1961
★West Side Story
Breakfast at Tiffany's
El Cid
Flower Drum Song
Summer and Smoke
1962
★Lawrence of Arabia
The Music Man
Mutiny on the Bounty
That Touch of Mink
The Wonderful World of the Brothers Grimm
1963
★Cleopatra
The Cardinal
Come Blow Your Horn
How the West Was Won
Tom Jones
1964
★My Fair Lady
Becket
Mary Poppins
The Unsinkable Molly Brown
1965
★Doctor Zhivago
The Agony and the Ecstasy
The Greatest Story Ever Told
Inside Daisy Clover
The Sound of Music
1966
★Fantastic Voyage
Gambit
Juliet of the Spirits
The Oscar
The Sand Pebbles

CINEMATOGRAPHY

1928
★Sunrise
My Best Girl
Sadie Thompson
Tempest
1929
★White Shadows in the South Seas
Our Dancing Daughters
1930
All Quiet on the Western Front
Anna Christie
Hell's Angels
1931
★Tabu: A Story of the South Seas
Cimarron
Morocco
Svengali
1932
★Shanghai Express
Arrowsmith
Dr. Jekyll and Mr. Hyde
1933
★A Farewell to Arms
The Sign of the Cross
1934
★Cleopatra
1935
★A Midsummer Night's Dream
Barbary Coast
The Crusades
Les Miserables
1936
★Anthony Adverse
The General Died at Dawn
The Gorgeous Hussy
1937
★The Good Earth
Dead End
1938
★The Great Waltz
Algiers
Jezebel
Mad About Music
Vivacious Lady
You Can't Take It with You
The Young in Heart
1957
★The Bridge on the River Kwai
An Affair to Remember
Funny Face
Peyton Place
Sayonara
1959
James Wong Howe/The Old Man and the Sea
1967
★Bonnie & Clyde
Camelot
Doctor Dolittle
The Graduate
In Cold Blood

★ = winner

1968
★Romeo and Juliet
Funny Girl
Ice Station Zebra
Oliver!
Star!
1969
★Butch Cassidy and the Sundance Kid
Anne of the Thousand Days
Bob & Carol & Ted & Alice
Hello, Dolly!
Marooned
1970
★Ryan's Daughter
Airport
Patton
Tora! Tora! Tora!
Women in Love
1971
★Fiddler on the Roof
The French Connection
The Last Picture Show
Nicholas and Alexandra
Summer of '42
1972
★Cabaret
Butterflies Are Free
The Poseidon Adventure
1776
Travels with My Aunt
1973
★Cries and Whispers
The Exorcist
Jonathan Livingston Seagull
The Sting
The Way We Were
1974
★The Towering Inferno
Chinatown
Earthquake
Lenny
Murder on the Orient Express
1975
★Barry Lyndon
The Day of the Locust
Funny Lady
The Hindenburg
One Flew Over the Cuckoo's Nest
1976
★Bound for Glory
King Kong
Logan's Run
Network
A Star Is Born
1977
★Close Encounters of the Third Kind
Islands in the Stream
Julia
Looking for Mr. Goodbar
The Turning Point
1978
★Days of Heaven
The Deer Hunter
Heaven Can Wait
Same Time, Next Year
The Wiz
1979
★Apocalypse Now
All That Jazz
The Black Hole
Kramer vs. Kramer
1941
1980
★Tess
The Blue Lagoon
Coal Miner's Daughter
The Formula
Raging Bull
1981
★Reds
Excalibur
On Golden Pond
Ragtime
Raiders of the Lost Ark
1982
★Gandhi
Das Boot
E.T.: The Extra-Terrestrial
Sophie's Choice
Tootsie
1983
★Fanny and Alexander
Flashdance
The Right Stuff
WarGames
Zelig
1984
★The Killing Fields
Amadeus
The Natural
A Passage to India
The River
1985
★Out of Africa
The Color Purple
Murphy's Romance
Ran
Witness
1986
★The Mission
Peggy Sue Got Married
Platoon
A Room with a View
Star Trek 4: The Voyage Home
1987
★The Last Emperor
Broadcast News
Empire of the Sun
Hope and Glory
Matewan
1988
★Mississippi Burning
Rain Man
Tequila Sunrise
The Unbearable Lightness of Being
Who Framed Roger Rabbit
1989
★Glory
The Abyss
Blaze
Born on the Fourth of July
The Fabulous Baker Boys
1990
★Dances with Wolves
Avalon
Dick Tracy
The Godfather, Part 3
Henry & June
1991
★JFK
Bugsy
The Prince of Tides
Terminator 2: Judgment Day
Thelma & Louise
1992
★A River Runs Through It
Hoffa
Howard's End
The Lover
Unforgiven
1993
★Schindler's List
Farewell My Concubine
The Fugitive
The Piano
Searching for Bobby Fischer
1994
★Legends of the Fall
Forrest Gump
The Shawshank Redemption
Trois Couleurs: Rouge
Wyatt Earp
1995
★Braveheart
Batman Forever
A Little Princess
Sense and Sensibility
Shanghai Triad
1996
★The English Patient
Evita
Fargo
Fly Away Home
Michael Collins
1997
★Titanic
Amistad
Kundun
L.A. Confidential
The Wings of the Dove
1998
★Saving Private Ryan
A Civil Action
Elizabeth
The Thin Red Line
1999
★American Beauty
The End of the Affair
The Insider
Sleepy Hollow
Snow Falling on Cedars
2000
★Crouching Tiger, Hidden Dragon
Gladiator
O Brother Where Art Thou?
The Patriot
2001
★Lord of the Rings: The Fellowship of the Ring
Amelie
Black Hawk Down
The Man Who Wasn't There
Moulin Rouge
2002
★Road to Perdition
Chicago
Far from Heaven
Gangs of New York
The Pianist
2003
★Master and Commander: The Far Side of the World
City of God
Cold Mountain
Girl with a Pearl Earring
Seabiscuit
2004
★The Aviator
House of Flying Daggers
The Passion of the Christ
The Phantom of the Opera
A Very Long Engagement
2005
★Memoirs of a Geisha
Batman Begins
Brokeback Mountain
Good Night, and Good Luck
The New World
2006
★Pan's Labyrinth
The Black Dahlia
Children of Men
The Illusionist
The Prestige
2007
★There Will Be Blood
The Assassination of Jesse James by the Coward Robert Ford
Atonement
The Diving Bell and the Butterfly
No Country for Old Men
2008
★Slumdog Millionaire
Changeling
The Curious Case of Benjamin Button
The Dark Knight
The Reader
2009
★Avatar
Harry Potter and the Half-Blood Prince
The Hurt Locker
Inglourious Basterds
The White Ribbon

CINEMATOGRAPHY (B&W)

1939
★Wuthering Heights
First Love
Gunga Din
Intermezzo
Juarez
Only Angels Have Wings
The Rains Came
Stagecoach
1940
★Rebecca
Abe Lincoln in Illinois
All This and Heaven Too
Boom Town
Foreign Correspondent
The Letter
The Long Voyage Home
Waterloo Bridge
1941
★How Green Was My Valley
The Chocolate Soldier
Citizen Kane
Dr. Jekyll and Mr. Hyde
Here Comes Mr. Jordan
Sergeant York
Sun Valley Serenade
Sundown
That Hamilton Woman
1942
★Mrs. Miniver
Kings Row
The Magnificent Ambersons
The Pride of the Yankees
Talk of the Town
1943
★The Song of Bernadette
Air Force
Casablanca
Five Graves to Cairo
The Human Comedy
Madame Curie
The North Star
Sahara
So Proudly We Hail
This Above All
This Above All
1944
★Laura
Double Indemnity
Dragon Seed
Gaslight
Going My Way
Lifeboat
Since You Went Away
Thirty Seconds Over Tokyo
The Uninvited
The White Cliffs of Dover
1945
★Picture of Dorian Gray
The Keys of the Kingdom
The Lost Weekend
Mildred Pierce
Spellbound
1946
★Anna and the King of Siam
1947
★Great Expectations
The Ghost and Mrs. Muir
Green Dolphin Street
1948
★The Naked City
I Remember Mama
Johnny Belinda
Portrait of Jennie
1949
★Battleground
Champion
Come to the Stable
The Heiress
1950
★The Third Man
All About Eve
The Asphalt Jungle
Prince of Foxes
Sunset Boulevard
1951
★A Place in the Sun
The Furies
Strangers on a Train
A Streetcar Named Desire
1952
★The Bad and the Beautiful
The Big Sky
Sudden Fear
1953
★From Here to Eternity
Julius Caesar
Martin Luther
Roman Holiday
1954
★On the Waterfront
Country Girl
Executive Suite
Sabrina
1955
★The Rose Tattoo
Blackboard Jungle
I'll Cry Tomorrow
Marty
Queen Bee
1956
★Somebody Up There Likes Me
Baby Doll
The Bad Seed
The Harder They Fall
1958
★The Defiant Ones
Desire Under the Elms
I Want to Live!
Separate Tables
The Young Lions
1959
★The Diary of Anne Frank
Anatomy of a Murder
Career
The Gazebo
Some Like It Hot
The Young Philadelphians
1960
The Apartment
The Facts of Life
Inherit the Wind
Psycho
1961
★The Hustler
The Absent-Minded Professor
The Children's Hour
Judgment at Nuremberg
One, Two, Three
1962
★The Longest Day
Birdman of Alcatraz
To Kill a Mockingbird
Two for the Seesaw
What Ever Happened to Baby Jane?
1963
★Hud
The Balcony
Lilies of the Field
Love with the Proper Stranger
1964
★Zorba the Greek
The Americanization of Emily
Hush, Hush, Sweet Charlotte
The Night of the Iguana
1965
★Ship of Fools
In Harm's Way
King Rat
Morituri
A Patch of Blue
1966
★Who's Afraid of Virginia Woolf?
The Fortune Cookie
Georgy Girl
Is Paris Burning?
Seconds

CINEMATOGRAPHY (COLOR)

1939
★Gone with the Wind
Drums Along the Mohawk
The Four Feathers
The Private Lives of Elizabeth & Essex
The Wizard of Oz
1940
★The Thief of Bagdad
Bitter Sweet
The Blue Bird
Down Argentine Way
Northwest Passage
1941
★Blood and Sand
Billy the Kid
Blossoms in the Dust
Dive Bomber
Louisiana Purchase
1942
★The Black Swan
Arabian Nights
Captains of the Clouds
The Jungle Book
Reap the Wild Wind
To the Shores of Tripoli
1943
★The Phantom of the Opera
For Whom the Bell Tolls
Heaven Can Wait
Hello, Frisco, Hello
Lassie, Come Home
Thousands Cheer
1944
★Wilson
Cover Girl
Meet Me in St. Louis

★ = winner

1945
★Leave Her to Heaven
Anchors Aweigh
National Velvet
A Song to Remember
The Spanish Main
1946
★The Yearling
The Jolson Story
1947
★Black Narcissus
Life with Father
Mother Wore Tights
1948
★Joan of Arc
The Loves of Carmen
The Three Musketeers
1949
★She Wore a Yellow Ribbon
The Barkleys of Broadway
Jolson Sings Again
Little Women
1950
★King Solomon's Mines
Annie Get Your Gun
Broken Arrow
The Flame & the Arrow
Samson and Delilah
1951
★An American in Paris
David and Bathsheba
Quo Vadis
Show Boat
When Worlds Collide
1952
★The Quiet Man
Hans Christian Andersen
Ivanhoe
Million Dollar Mermaid
The Snows of Kilimanjaro
1953
★Shane
All the Brothers Were Valiant
Beneath the 12-Mile Reef
Lili
The Robe
1954
★Three Coins in the Fountain
The Egyptian
Rear Window
Seven Brides for Seven Brothers
The Silver Chalice
1955
★To Catch a Thief
Guys and Dolls
Love Is a Many-Splendored Thing
A Man Called Peter
Oklahoma!
1956
★Around the World in 80 Days
The Eddy Duchin Story
The King and I
The Ten Commandments
War and Peace
1958
★Gigi
Auntie Mame
Cat on a Hot Tin Roof
South Pacific
1959
★Ben-Hur
The Five Pennies
The Nun's Story
1960
★Spartacus
The Alamo
Butterfield 8
Exodus
1961
★West Side Story
Fanny
Flower Drum Song
One-Eyed Jacks
1962
★Lawrence of Arabia
Gypsy
Hatari!
Mutiny on the Bounty
The Wonderful World of the Brothers Grimm
1963
★Cleopatra
The Cardinal
How the West Was Won
Irma La Douce
It's a Mad, Mad, Mad, Mad World
1964
★My Fair Lady
Becket
Cheyenne Autumn
Mary Poppins
The Unsinkable Molly Brown
1965
★Doctor Zhivago
The Agony and the Ecstasy
The Great Race
The Greatest Story Ever Told
The Sound of Music
1966
★A Man for All Seasons
Fantastic Voyage
Hawaii
The Professionals
The Sand Pebbles

COSTUME DESIGN

1951
The Black Rose
1957
★Les Girls
An Affair to Remember
Funny Face
Pal Joey
Raintree County
1958
★Gigi
Bell, Book and Candle
The Buccaneer
Some Came Running
1967
★Camelot
Bonnie & Clyde
The Happiest Millionaire
The Taming of the Shrew
Thoroughly Modern Millie
1968
★Romeo and Juliet
The Lion in Winter
Oliver!
Planet of the Apes
Star!
1969
★Anne of the Thousand Days
Hello, Dolly!
Sweet Charity
They Shoot Horses, Don't They?
1970
★Cromwell
Airport
Darling Lili
Scrooge
1971
★Nicholas and Alexandra
Bedknobs and Broomsticks
Death in Venice
Mary, Queen of Scots
What's the Matter with Helen?
1972
★Travels with My Aunt
The Godfather
Lady Sings the Blues
The Poseidon Adventure
Young Winston
1973
★The Sting
Cries and Whispers
Tom Sawyer
The Way We Were
1974
★The Great Gatsby
Chinatown
Daisy Miller
The Godfather, Part 2
Murder on the Orient Express
1975
★Barry Lyndon
The Four Musketeers
Funny Lady
The Magic Flute
The Man Who Would Be King
1976
Bound for Glory
The Incredible Sarah
The Passover Plot
The Seven-Per-Cent Solution
1977
★Star Wars
Airport '77
Julia
A Little Night Music
The Other Side of Midnight
1978
★Death on the Nile
Days of Heaven
The Swarm
The Wiz
1979
★All That Jazz
Agatha
Butch and Sundance: The Early Days
The Europeans
La Cage aux Folles
1980
★Tess
The Elephant Man
My Brilliant Career
Somewhere in Time
When Time Ran Out
1981
★Chariots of Fire
The French Lieutenant's Woman
Pennies from Heaven
Ragtime
Reds
1982
★Gandhi
Sophie's Choice
Tron
Victor/Victoria
1983
★Fanny and Alexander
Cross Creek
Heart Like a Wheel
The Return of Martin Guerre
Zelig
1984
★Amadeus
The Bostonians
A Passage to India
Places in the Heart
2010: The Year We Make Contact
1985
★Ran
The Color Purple
The Journey of Natty Gann
Out of Africa
Prizzi's Honor
1986
★A Room with a View
The Mission
Otello
Peggy Sue Got Married
Pirates
1987
★The Last Emperor
The Dead
Empire of the Sun
Maurice
The Untouchables
1988
★Dangerous Liaisons
Coming to America
A Handful of Dust
Sunset
Tucker: The Man and His Dream
1989
★Henry V
The Adventures of Baron Munchausen
Driving Miss Daisy
Harlem Nights
Valmont
1990
★Cyrano de Bergerac
Avalon
Dances with Wolves
Dick Tracy
Hamlet
1991
★Bugsy
The Addams Family
Barton Fink
Hook
Madame Bovary
1992
★Bram Stoker's Dracula
Enchanted April
Howard's End
Malcolm X
Toys
1993
★The Age of Innocence
Orlando
The Piano
The Remains of the Day
Schindler's List
1994
★The Adventures of Priscilla, Queen of the Desert
Bullets over Broadway
Little Women
Maverick
Queen Margot
1995
★Restoration
Braveheart
Richard III
Sense and Sensibility
12 Monkeys
1996
★The English Patient
Angels and Insects
Emma
Hamlet
Portrait of a Lady
1997
★Titanic
Amistad
Kundun
Oscar and Lucinda
The Wings of the Dove
1998
★Shakespeare in Love
Beloved
Elizabeth
Pleasantville
Velvet Goldmine
1999
★Topsy Turvy
Anna and the King
The Talented Mr. Ripley
Titus
2000
★Gladiator
Crouching Tiger, Hidden Dragon
Dr. Seuss' How the Grinch Stole Christmas
102 Dalmatians
Quills
2001
★Moulin Rouge
The Affair of the Necklace
Gosford Park
Harry Potter and the Sorcerer's Stone
Lord of the Rings: The Fellowship of the Ring
2002
★Chicago
Frida
Gangs of New York
The Pianist
2003
★Lord of the Rings: The Return of the King
Girl with a Pearl Earring
The Last Samurai
Master and Commander: The Far Side of the World
Seabiscuit
2004
★The Aviator
Finding Neverland
Lemony Snicket's A Series of Unfortunate Events
Ray
2005
★Memoirs of a Geisha
Charlie and the Chocolate Factory
Mrs. Henderson Presents
Pride and Prejudice
Walk the Line
2006
★Marie Antoinette
Curse of the Golden Flower
The Devil Wears Prada
Dreamgirls
The Queen
2007
★Elizabeth: The Golden Age
Across the Universe
Atonement
La Vie en Rose
Sweeney Todd: The Demon Barber of Fleet Street
2008
★The Duchess
Australia
The Curious Case of Benjamin Button
Milk
Revolutionary Road
2009
★The Young Victoria
Bright Star
Coco Before Chanel
The Imaginarium of Doctor Parnassus
Nine

COSTUME DESIGN (B&W)

1948
★Hamlet
1949
★The Heiress
1950
★All About Eve
Born Yesterday
The Magnificent Yankee
Prince of Foxes
1951
★A Place in the Sun
A Streetcar Named Desire
1952
★The Bad and the Beautiful
Affair in Trinidad
Carrie
Sudden Fear
1953
★Roman Holiday
From Here to Eternity
1954
★Sabrina
The Earrings of Madame De...
Executive Suite
Indiscretion of an American Wife
It Should Happen to You
1955
★I'll Cry Tomorrow
The Pickwick Papers
Queen Bee
The Rose Tattoo
Ugetsu
1956
★Solid Gold Cadillac
Seven Samurai
1959
★Some Like It Hot
Career
The Diary of Anne Frank
The Young Philadelphians
1960
★The Facts of Life
Never on Sunday
The Rise and Fall of Legs Diamond
Seven Thieves
The Virgin Spring
1961
★La Dolce Vita
The Children's Hour
Judgment at Nuremberg
Yojimbo
1962
Days of Wine and Roses
The Man Who Shot Liberty Valance
The Miracle Worker
Phaedra
What Ever Happened to Baby Jane?
1963
★8 1/2
Love with the Proper Stranger
The Stripper
Toys in the Attic
1964
★The Night of the Iguana
Hush, Hush, Sweet Charlotte

★ = winner

Kisses for My President

1965

★*Darling*

Morituri

Ship of Fools

The Slender Thread

1966

★*Who's Afraid of Virginia Woolf?*

The Gospel According to St. Matthew

Morgan: A Suitable Case for Treatment

COSTUME DESIGN (COLOR)

1948

★*Joan of Arc*

1949

★*Adventures of Don Juan*

1950

★*Samson and Delilah*

That Forsyte Woman

1951

★*An American in Paris*

David and Bathsheba

The Great Caruso

Quo Vadis

The Tales of Hoffmann

1952

★*Moulin Rouge*

The Greatest Show on Earth

Hans Christian Andersen

The Merry Widow

1953

★*The Robe*

The Band Wagon

How to Marry a Millionaire

With a Song in My Heart

Young Bess

1954

★*Gate of Hell*

Brigadoon

Desiree

A Star Is Born

There's No Business Like Show Business

1955

★*Love Is a Many-Splendored Thing*

Guys and Dolls

Interrupted Melody

To Catch a Thief

The Virgin Queen

1956

★*The King and I*

Around the World in 80 Days

Giant

The Ten Commandments

War and Peace

1959

★*Ben-Hur*

The Best of Everything

The Five Pennies

1960

★*Spartacus*

Can-Can

Midnight Lace

Sunrise at Campobello

1961

★*West Side Story*

Babes in Toyland

Back Street

Flower Drum Song

Pocketful of Miracles

1962

★*The Wonderful World of the Brothers Grimm*

Bon Voyage!

Gypsy

The Music Man

My Geisha

1963

★*Cleopatra*

The Cardinal

How the West Was Won

A New Kind of Love

1964

★*My Fair Lady*

Becket

Mary Poppins

The Unsinkable Molly Brown

1965

★*Doctor Zhivago*

The Agony and the Ecstasy

The Greatest Story Ever Told

Inside Daisy Clover

The Sound of Music

1966

★*A Man for All Seasons*

Gambit

Hawaii

Juliet of the Spirits

The Oscar

DIRECTOR

1928

Charlie Chaplin/*The Circus*

King Vidor/*The Crowd*

Ted Wilde/*Speedy*

1929

Harry Beaumont/*Broadway Melody*

1930

★Lewis Milestone/*All Quiet on the Western Front*

Clarence Brown/*Anna Christie*

Clarence Brown/*Romance*

Robert Z. Leonard/*The Divorcee*

King Vidor/*Hallelujah!*

1931

Clarence Brown/*A Free Soul*

Lewis Milestone/*The Front Page*

Wesley Ruggles/*Cimarron*

Josef von Sternberg/*Morocco*

1932

King Vidor/*The Champ*

Josef von Sternberg/*Shanghai Express*

1933

★Frank Lloyd/*Cavalcade*

Frank Capra/*Lady for a Day*

George Cukor/*Little Women*

1934

★Frank Capra/*It Happened One Night*

Victor Schertzinger/*One Night of Love*

Woodbridge S. Van Dyke/*The Thin Man*

1935

★John Ford/*The Informer*

Henry Hathaway/*The Lives of a Bengal Lancer*

Frank Lloyd/*Mutiny on the Bounty*

1936

★Frank Capra/*Mr. Deeds Goes to Town*

Gregory La Cava/*My Man Godfrey*

Robert Z. Leonard/*The Great Ziegfeld*

Woodbridge S. Van Dyke/*San Francisco*

William Wyler/*Dodsworth*

1937

★Leo McCarey/*The Awful Truth*

William Dieterle/*The Life of Emile Zola*

Sidney Franklin/*The Good Earth*

Gregory La Cava/*Stage Door*

William A. Wellman/*A Star Is Born*

1938

★Frank Capra/*You Can't Take It with You*

Michael Curtiz/*Angels with Dirty Faces*

Michael Curtiz/*Four Daughters*

Norman Taurog/*Boys Town*

King Vidor/*The Citadel*

1939

★Victor Fleming/*Gone with the Wind*

Frank Capra/*Mr. Smith Goes to Washington*

John Ford/*Stagecoach*

Sam Wood/*Goodbye, Mr. Chips*

William Wyler/*Wuthering Heights*

1940

★John Ford/*The Grapes of Wrath*

George Cukor/*The Philadelphia Story*

Alfred Hitchcock/*Rebecca*

Sam Wood/*Kitty Foyle*

William Wyler/*The Letter*

1941

★John Ford/*How Green Was My Valley*

Alexander Hall/*Here Comes Mr. Jordan*

Howard Hawks/*Sergeant York*

Orson Welles/*Citizen Kane*

William Wyler/*The Little Foxes*

1942

★William Wyler/*Mrs. Miniver*

Michael Curtiz/*Yankee Doodle Dandy*

John Farrow/*Wake Island*

Mervyn LeRoy/*Random Harvest*

Sam Wood/*Kings Row*

1943

★Michael Curtiz/*Casablanca*

Clarence Brown/*The Human Comedy*

Henry King/*The Song of Bernadette*

Ernst Lubitsch/*Heaven Can Wait*

George Stevens/*The More the Merrier*

1944

★Leo McCarey/*Going My Way*

Alfred Hitchcock/*Lifeboat*

Henry King/*Wilson*

Otto Preminger/*Laura*

Billy Wilder/*Double Indemnity*

1945

★Billy Wilder/*The Lost Weekend*

Clarence Brown/*National Velvet*

Alfred Hitchcock/*Spellbound*

Leo McCarey/*The Bells of St. Mary's*

Jean Renoir/*The Southerner*

1946

★William Wyler/*The Best Years of Our Lives*

Clarence Brown/*The Yearling*

Frank Capra/*It's a Wonderful Life*

David Lean/*Brief Encounter*

Robert Siodmak/*The Killers*

1947

★Elia Kazan/*Gentleman's Agreement*

George Cukor/*A Double Life*

Edward Dmytryk/*Crossfire*

Henry Koster/*The Bishop's Wife*

David Lean/*Great Expectations*

1948

★John Huston/*Treasure of the Sierra Madre*

Anatole Litvak/*The Snake Pit*

Jean Negulesco/*Johnny Belinda*

Laurence Olivier/*Hamlet*

Fred Zinnemann/*The Search*

1949

★Joseph L. Mankiewicz/*A Letter to Three Wives*

Carol Reed/*The Fallen Idol*

Robert Rossen/*All the King's Men*

William A. Wellman/*Battleground*

William Wyler/*The Heiress*

1950

★Joseph L. Mankiewicz/*All About Eve*

George Cukor/*Born Yesterday*

John Huston/*The Asphalt Jungle*

Carol Reed/*The Third Man*

Billy Wilder/*Sunset Boulevard*

1951

★George Stevens/*A Place in the Sun*

John Huston/*The African Queen*

Elia Kazan/*A Streetcar Named Desire*

Vincente Minnelli/*An American in Paris*

William Wyler/*Detective Story*

1952

★John Ford/*The Quiet Man*

Cecil B. DeMille/*The Greatest Show on Earth*

John Huston/*Moulin Rouge*

Joseph L. Mankiewicz/*Five Fingers*

Fred Zinnemann/*High Noon*

1953

★Fred Zinnemann/*From Here to Eternity*

George Stevens/*Shane*

Charles Walters/*Lili*

Billy Wilder/*Stalag 17*

William Wyler/*Roman Holiday*

1954

★Elia Kazan/*On the Waterfront*

Alfred Hitchcock/*Rear Window*

George Seaton/*Country Girl*

Billy Wilder/*Sabrina*

1955

★Delbert Mann/*Marty*

Elia Kazan/*East of Eden*

David Lean/*Summertime*

Joshua Logan/*Picnic*

John Sturges/*Bad Day at Black Rock*

William A. Wellman/*The High and the Mighty*

1956

★George Stevens/*Giant*

Michael Anderson, Sr./*Around the World in 80 Days*

Walter Lang/*The King and I*

King Vidor/*War and Peace*

William Wyler/*Friendly Persuasion*

1957

★David Lean/*The Bridge on the River Kwai*

Joshua Logan/*Sayonara*

Sidney Lumet/*Twelve Angry Men*

Mark Robson/*Peyton Place*

Billy Wilder/*Witness for the Prosecution*

1958

★Vincente Minnelli/*Gigi*

Richard Brooks/*Cat on a Hot Tin Roof*

Stanley Kramer/*The Defiant Ones*

Mark Robson/*The Inn of the Sixth Happiness*

Robert Wise/*I Want to Live!*

1959

★William Wyler/*Ben-Hur*

Jack Clayton/*Room at the Top*

George Stevens/*The Diary of Anne Frank*

Billy Wilder/*Some Like It Hot*

Fred Zinnemann/*The Nun's Story*

1960

★Billy Wilder/*The Apartment*

Jules Dassin/*Never on Sunday*

Alfred Hitchcock/*Psycho*

Fred Zinnemann/*The Sundowners*

1961

★Robert Wise/*West Side Story*

Federico Fellini/*La Dolce Vita*

Stanley Kramer/*Judgment at Nuremberg*

Robert Rossen/*The Hustler*

J. Lee Thompson/*The Guns of Navarone*

1962

★David Lean/*Lawrence of Arabia*

Pietro Germi/*Divorce—Italian Style*

Robert Mulligan/*To Kill a Mockingbird*

Arthur Penn/*The Miracle Worker*

Frank Perry/*David and Lisa*

1963

★Tony Richardson/*Tom Jones*

Federico Fellini/*8 1/2*

Otto Preminger/*The Cardinal*

Martin Ritt/*Hud*

1964

★George Cukor/*My Fair Lady*

Michael Cacoyannis/*Zorba the Greek*

Peter Glenville/*Becket*

Stanley Kubrick/*Dr. Strangelove, or: How I Learned to Stop Worrying and Love the Bomb*

Robert Stevenson/*Mary Poppins*

1965

★Robert Wise/*The Sound of Music*

David Lean/*Doctor Zhivago*

John Schlesinger/*Darling*

Hiroshi Teshigahara/*Woman in the Dunes*

William Wyler/*The Collector*

1966

★Fred Zinnemann/*A Man for All Seasons*

Michelangelo Antonioni/*Blow-Up*

Richard Brooks/*The Professionals*

Claude Lelouch/*A Man and a Woman*

Mike Nichols/*Who's Afraid of Virginia Woolf?*

1967

★Mike Nichols/*The Graduate*

Richard Brooks/*In Cold Blood*

Norman Jewison/*In the Heat of the Night*

Stanley Kramer/*Guess Who's Coming to Dinner*

Arthur Penn/*Bonnie & Clyde*

1968

★Carol Reed/*Oliver!*

Anthony Harvey/*The Lion in Winter*

Stanley Kubrick/*2001: A Space Odyssey*

Gillo Pontecorvo/*The Battle of Algiers*

Franco Zeffirelli/*Romeo and Juliet*

1969

★John Schlesinger/*Midnight Cowboy*

Constantin Costa-Gavras/*Z*

George Roy Hill/*Butch Cassidy and the Sundance Kid*

Arthur Penn/*Alice's Restaurant*

Sydney Pollack/*They Shoot Horses, Don't They?*

1970

★Franklin J. Schaffner/*Patton*

Robert Altman/*M*A*S*H*

Federico Fellini/*Fellini Satyricon*

Arthur Hiller/*Love Story*

Ken Russell/*Women in Love*

1971

★William Friedkin/*The French Connection*

Peter Bogdanovich/*The Last Picture Show*

Norman Jewison/*Fiddler on the Roof*

Stanley Kubrick/*A Clockwork Orange*

John Schlesinger/*Sunday, Bloody Sunday*

1972

★Bob Fosse/*Cabaret*

John Boorman/*Deliverance*

Francis Ford Coppola/*The Godfather*

Joseph L. Mankiewicz/*Sleuth*

Jan Troell/*The Emigrants*

1973

★George Roy Hill/*The Sting*

Ingmar Bergman/*Cries and Whispers*

Bernardo Bertolucci/*Last Tango in Paris*

William Friedkin/*The Exorcist*

George Lucas/*American Graffiti*

1974

★Francis Ford Coppola/*The Godfather, Part 2*

John Cassavetes/*A Woman under the Influence*

Bob Fosse/*Lenny*

Roman Polanski/*Chinatown*

Francois Truffaut/*Day for Night*

1975

★Milos Forman/*One Flew Over the Cuckoo's Nest*

★ = *winner*

Robert Altman/*Nashville*
Federico Fellini/*Amarcord*
Stanley Kubrick/*Barry Lyndon*
Sidney Lumet/*Dog Day Afternoon*

1976

★John G. Avildsen/*Rocky*
Ingmar Bergman/*Face to Face*
Sidney Lumet/*Network*
Alan J. Pakula/*All the President's Men*
Lina Wertmuller/*Seven Beauties*

1977

★Woody Allen/*Annie Hall*
George Lucas/*Star Wars*
Herbert Ross/*The Turning Point*
Steven Spielberg/*Close Encounters of the Third Kind*
Fred Zinnemann/*Julia*

1978

★Michael Cimino/*The Deer Hunter*
Woody Allen/*Interiors*
Hal Ashby/*Coming Home*
Warren Beatty/*Heaven Can Wait*
Buck Henry/*Heaven Can Wait*
Alan Parker/*Midnight Express*

1979

★Robert Benton/*Kramer vs. Kramer*
Francis Ford Coppola/*Apocalypse Now*
Bob Fosse/*All That Jazz*
Edouard Molinaro/*La Cage aux Folles*
Peter Yates/*Breaking Away*

1980

★Robert Redford/*Ordinary People*
David Lynch/*The Elephant Man*
Roman Polanski/*Tess*
Richard Rush/*The Stunt Man*
Martin Scorsese/*Raging Bull*

1981

★Warren Beatty/*Reds*
Hugh Hudson/*Chariots of Fire*
Louis Malle/*Atlantic City*
Mark Rydell/*On Golden Pond*
Steven Spielberg/*Raiders of the Lost Ark*

1982

★Richard Attenborough/*Gandhi*
Sidney Lumet/*The Verdict*
Wolfgang Petersen/*Das Boot*
Sydney Pollack/*Tootsie*
Steven Spielberg/*E.T.: The Extra-Terrestrial*

1983

★James L. Brooks/*Terms of Endearment*
Bruce Beresford/*Tender Mercies*
Ingmar Bergman/*Fanny and Alexander*
Mike Nichols/*Silkwood*
Peter Yates/*The Dresser*

1984

★Milos Forman/*Amadeus*
Woody Allen/*Broadway Danny Rose*
Robert Benton/*Places in the Heart*
Roland Joffe/*The Killing Fields*
David Lean/*A Passage to India*

1985

★Sydney Pollack/*Out of Africa*
Hector Babenco/*Kiss of the Spider Woman*
John Huston/*Prizzi's Honor*
Akira Kurosawa/*Ran*
Peter Weir/*Witness*

1986

★Oliver Stone/*Platoon*
Woody Allen/*Hannah and Her Sisters*
James Ivory/*A Room with a View*
Roland Joffe/*The Mission*
David Lynch/*Blue Velvet*

1987

★Bernardo Bertolucci/*The Last Emperor*
John Boorman/*Hope and Glory*
Lasse Hallstrom/*My Life As a Dog*
Norman Jewison/*Moonstruck*
Adrian Lyne/*Fatal Attraction*

1988

★Barry Levinson/*Rain Man*
Charles Crichton/*A Fish Called Wanda*
Mike Nichols/*Working Girl*
Alan Parker/*Mississippi Burning*
Martin Scorsese/*The Last Temptation of Christ*

1989

★Oliver Stone/*Born on the Fourth of July*
Woody Allen/*Crimes & Misdemeanors*
Kenneth Branagh/*Henry V*
Jim Sheridan/*My Left Foot*
Peter Weir/*Dead Poets Society*

1990

★Kevin Costner/*Dances with Wolves*
Francis Ford Coppola/*The Godfather, Part 3*
Stephen Frears/*The Grifters*
Barbet Schroeder/*Reversal of Fortune*
Martin Scorsese/*Goodfellas*

1991

★Jonathan Demme/*The Silence of the Lambs*
Barry Levinson/*Bugsy*
Ridley Scott/*Thelma & Louise*
John Singleton/*Boyz N the Hood*
Oliver Stone/*JFK*

1992

★Clint Eastwood/*Unforgiven*
Robert Altman/*The Player*
Martin Brest/*Scent of a Woman*
James Ivory/*Howard's End*
Neil Jordan/*The Crying Game*

1993

★Steven Spielberg/*Schindler's List*
Robert Altman/*Short Cuts*
Jane Campion/*The Piano*
James Ivory/*The Remains of the Day*
Jim Sheridan/*In the Name of the Father*

1994

★Robert Zemeckis/*Forrest Gump*
Woody Allen/*Bullets over Broadway*
Krzysztof Kieslowski/*Trois Couleurs: Rouge*
Robert Redford/*Quiz Show*
Quentin Tarantino/*Pulp Fiction*

1995

★Mel Gibson/*Braveheart*
Mike Figgis/*Leaving Las Vegas*
Chris Noonan/*Babe*
Michael Radford/*The Postman*
Tim Robbins/*Dead Man Walking*

1996

★Anthony Minghella/*The English Patient*
Joel Coen/*Fargo*
Milos Forman/*The People vs. Larry Flynt*
Scott Hicks/*Shine*
Mike Leigh/*Secrets and Lies*

1997

★James Cameron/*Titanic*
Peter Cattaneo/*The Full Monty*
Atom Egoyan/*The Sweet Hereafter*
Curtis Hanson/*L.A. Confidential*
Gus Van Sant/*Good Will Hunting*

1998

★Steven Spielberg/*Saving Private Ryan*
Roberto Benigni/*Life Is Beautiful*
John Madden/*Shakespeare in Love*
Terrence Malick/*The Thin Red Line*
Peter Weir/*The Truman Show*

1999

★Sam Mendes/*American Beauty*
Lasse Hallstrom/*The Cider House Rules*
Spike Jonze/*Being John Malkovich*
Michael Mann/*The Insider*
M. Night Shyamalan/*The Sixth Sense*

2000

★Steven Soderbergh/*Traffic*
Stephen Daldry/*Billy Elliot*
Ang Lee/*Crouching Tiger, Hidden Dragon*
Ridley Scott/*Gladiator*
Steven Soderbergh/*Erin Brockovich*

2001

★Ron Howard/*A Beautiful Mind*
Robert Altman/*Gosford Park*
Peter Jackson/*Lord of the Rings: The Fellowship of the Ring*
David Lynch/*Mulholland Drive*
Ridley Scott/*Black Hawk Down*

2002

★Roman Polanski/*The Pianist*
Pedro Almodovar/*Talk to Her*
Stephen Daldry/*The Hours*
Rob Marshall/*Chicago*
Martin Scorsese/*Gangs of New York*

2003

★Peter Jackson/*Lord of the Rings: The Return of the King*
Sofia Coppola/*Lost in Translation*
Clint Eastwood/*Mystic River*
Fernando Meirelles/*City of God*
Peter Weir/*Master and Commander: The Far Side of the World*

2004

★Clint Eastwood/*Million Dollar Baby*
Taylor Hackford/*Ray*
Mike Leigh/*Vera Drake*
Alexander Payne/*Sideways*
Martin Scorsese/*The Aviator*

2005

★Ang Lee/*Brokeback Mountain*
George Clooney/*Good Night, and Good Luck*
Paul Haggis/*Crash*
Bennett Miller/*Capote*
Steven Spielberg/*Munich*

2006

★Martin Scorsese/*The Departed*
Clint Eastwood/*Letters from Iwo Jima*
Stephen Frears/*The Queen*
Paul Greengrass/*United 93*
Alejandro Gonzalez Inarritu/*Babel*

2007

★Ethan Coen/*No Country for Old Men*
★Joel Coen/*No Country for Old Men*
Paul Thomas Anderson/*There Will Be Blood*
Tony Gilroy/*Michael Clayton*
Jason Reitman/*Juno*
Julian Schnabel/*The Diving Bell and the Butterfly*

2008

★Danny Boyle/*Slumdog Millionaire*
Stephen Daldry/*The Reader*
David Fincher/*The Curious Case of Benjamin Button*
Ron Howard/*Frost/Nixon*
Gus Van Sant/*Milk*

2009

★Kathryn Bigelow/*The Hurt Locker*
James Cameron/*Avatar*
Lee Daniels/*Precious: Based on the Novel by Sapphire*
Jason Reitman/*Up in the Air*
Quentin Tarantino/*Inglourious Basterds*

FILM

1928

★*Wings*
Last Command

1929

★*Broadway Melody*
Alibi

1930

★*All Quiet on the Western Front*
The Big House
Disraeli
The Divorcee

1931

★*Cimarron*
The Front Page
Trader Horn

1932

★*Grand Hotel*
Arrowsmith
The Champ
Shanghai Express

1933

★*Cavalcade*
A Farewell to Arms
42nd Street
I Am a Fugitive from a Chain Gang
Lady for a Day
Little Women
The Private Life of Henry VIII
She Done Him Wrong
Smilin' Through

1934

★*It Happened One Night*
The Barretts of Wimpole Street
Cleopatra
Flirtation Walk
The Gay Divorcee
Imitation of Life
One Night of Love
The Thin Man
Viva Villa!

1935

★*Mutiny on the Bounty*
Alice Adams
Broadway Melody of 1936
Captain Blood
David Copperfield
The Informer
Les Miserables
The Lives of a Bengal Lancer
A Midsummer Night's Dream
Naughty Marietta
Ruggles of Red Gap
Top Hat

1936

★*The Great Ziegfeld*
Anthony Adverse
Dodsworth
Libeled Lady
Mr. Deeds Goes to Town
Romeo and Juliet
San Francisco
The Story of Louis Pasteur
A Tale of Two Cities
Three Smart Girls

1937

★*The Life of Emile Zola*
The Awful Truth
Captains Courageous
Dead End
The Good Earth
In Old Chicago
Lost Horizon
100 Men and a Girl
Stage Door
A Star Is Born

1938

★*You Can't Take It with You*
Alexander's Ragtime Band
Boys Town
The Citadel
Four Daughters
Grand Illusion
Jezebel
Pygmalion
Test Pilot

1939

★*Gone with the Wind*
Dark Victory
Goodbye, Mr. Chips
Love Affair
Mr. Smith Goes to Washington
Ninotchka
Of Mice and Men
Stagecoach
The Wizard of Oz
Wuthering Heights

1940

★*Rebecca*
All This and Heaven Too
Foreign Correspondent
The Grapes of Wrath
The Great Dictator
Kitty Foyle
The Letter
The Long Voyage Home
Our Town
The Philadelphia Story

1941

★*How Green Was My Valley*
Blossoms in the Dust
Citizen Kane
Here Comes Mr. Jordan
The Little Foxes
The Maltese Falcon
Sergeant York
Suspicion

1942

★*Mrs. Miniver*
Kings Row
The Magnificent Ambersons
The Pride of the Yankees
Random Harvest
Talk of the Town
Wake Island
Yankee Doodle Dandy

1943

★*Casablanca*
For Whom the Bell Tolls
Heaven Can Wait
The Human Comedy
In Which We Serve
Madame Curie
The More the Merrier
The Ox-Bow Incident
The Song of Bernadette
Watch on the Rhine

1944

★*Going My Way*
Double Indemnity
Gaslight
Since You Went Away
Wilson

1945

★*The Lost Weekend*
Anchors Aweigh
The Bells of St. Mary's
Mildred Pierce
Spellbound

1946

★*The Best Years of Our Lives*
Henry V
It's a Wonderful Life
The Razor's Edge
The Yearling

1947

★*Gentleman's Agreement*
The Bishop's Wife
Crossfire
Great Expectations
Miracle on 34th Street

1948

★*Hamlet*
Johnny Belinda
The Red Shoes
The Snake Pit
Treasure of the Sierra Madre

1949

★*All the King's Men*
Battleground
The Heiress
A Letter to Three Wives
Twelve o'Clock High

1950

★*All About Eve*
Born Yesterday
Father of the Bride
King Solomon's Mines

★ = *winner*

Sunset Boulevard
1951
★An American in Paris
A Place in the Sun
Quo Vadis
A Streetcar Named Desire
1952
★The Greatest Show on Earth
High Noon
Ivanhoe
Moulin Rouge
The Quiet Man
1953
★From Here to Eternity
Julius Caesar
The Robe
Roman Holiday
Shane
1954
★On the Waterfront
The Caine Mutiny
Country Girl
Seven Brides for Seven Brothers
Three Coins in the Fountain
1955
★Marty
Love Is a Many-Splendored Thing
Mister Roberts
Picnic
The Rose Tattoo
1956
★Around the World in 80 Days
Friendly Persuasion
Giant
The King and I
The Ten Commandments
1957
★The Bridge on the River Kwai
Peyton Place
Sayonara
Twelve Angry Men
Witness for the Prosecution
1958
★Gigi
Auntie Mame
Cat on a Hot Tin Roof
The Defiant Ones
Separate Tables
1959
★Ben-Hur
Anatomy of a Murder
The Diary of Anne Frank
The Nun's Story
Room at the Top
1960
★The Apartment
The Alamo
Elmer Gantry
The Sundowners
1961
★West Side Story
Fanny
The Guns of Navarone
The Hustler
Judgment at Nuremberg
1962
★Lawrence of Arabia
The Longest Day
The Music Man
Mutiny on the Bounty
To Kill a Mockingbird
1963
★Tom Jones
Cleopatra
How the West Was Won
Lilies of the Field
1964
★My Fair Lady
Becket
Dr. Strangelove, or: How I Learned to Stop Worrying and Love the Bomb
Mary Poppins
Zorba the Greek
1965
★The Sound of Music
Darling
Doctor Zhivago
Ship of Fools
A Thousand Clowns
1966
★A Man for All Seasons
Alfie
The Russians Are Coming, the Russians Are Coming
The Sand Pebbles
Who's Afraid of Virginia Woolf?
1967
★In the Heat of the Night
Bonnie & Clyde
Doctor Dolittle
The Graduate
Guess Who's Coming to Dinner
1968
★Oliver!
Funny Girl
The Lion in Winter
Rachel, Rachel
Romeo and Juliet
1969
★Midnight Cowboy
Anne of the Thousand Days
Butch Cassidy and the Sundance Kid
Hello, Dolly!
Z
1970
★Patton
Airport
Five Easy Pieces
Love Story
M*A*S*H
1971
★The French Connection
A Clockwork Orange
Fiddler on the Roof
The Last Picture Show
Nicholas and Alexandra
1972
★The Godfather
Cabaret
Deliverance
The Emigrants
Sounder
1973
★The Sting
American Graffiti
Cries and Whispers
The Exorcist
A Touch of Class
1974
★The Godfather, Part 2
Chinatown
The Conversation
Lenny
The Towering Inferno
1975
★One Flew Over the Cuckoo's Nest
Barry Lyndon
Dog Day Afternoon
Jaws
Nashville
1976
★Rocky
All the President's Men
Bound for Glory
Network
Taxi Driver
1977
★Annie Hall
The Goodbye Girl
Julia
Star Wars
The Turning Point
1978
★The Deer Hunter
Coming Home
Heaven Can Wait
Midnight Express
An Unmarried Woman
1979
★Kramer vs. Kramer
All That Jazz
Apocalypse Now
Breaking Away
Norma Rae
1980
★Ordinary People
Coal Miner's Daughter
The Elephant Man
Raging Bull
Tess
1981
★Chariots of Fire
Atlantic City
On Golden Pond
Raiders of the Lost Ark
Reds
1982
★Gandhi
E.T.: The Extra-Terrestrial
Missing
Tootsie
The Verdict
1983
★Terms of Endearment
The Big Chill
The Dresser
The Right Stuff
Tender Mercies
1984
★Amadeus
The Killing Fields
A Passage to India
Places in the Heart
A Soldier's Story
1985
★Out of Africa
The Color Purple
Kiss of the Spider Woman
Prizzi's Honor
Witness
1986
★Platoon
Children of a Lesser God
Hannah and Her Sisters
The Mission
A Room with a View
1987
★The Last Emperor
Broadcast News
Fatal Attraction
Hope and Glory
Moonstruck
1988
★Rain Man
The Accidental Tourist
Dangerous Liaisons
Mississippi Burning
Working Girl
1989
★Driving Miss Daisy
Born on the Fourth of July
Dead Poets Society
Field of Dreams
My Left Foot
1990
★Dances with Wolves
Awakenings
Ghost
The Godfather, Part 3
Goodfellas
1991
★The Silence of the Lambs
Beauty and the Beast
Bugsy
JFK
The Prince of Tides
1992
★Unforgiven
The Crying Game
A Few Good Men
Howard's End
Scent of a Woman
1993
★Schindler's List
The Fugitive
In the Name of the Father
The Piano
The Remains of the Day
1994
★Forrest Gump
Four Weddings and a Funeral
Pulp Fiction
Quiz Show
The Shawshank Redemption
1995
★Braveheart
Apollo 13
Babe
The Postman
Sense and Sensibility
1996
★The English Patient
Fargo
Jerry Maguire
Secrets and Lies
Shine
1997
★Titanic
As Good As It Gets
The Full Monty
Good Will Hunting
L.A. Confidential
1998
★Shakespeare in Love
Elizabeth
Life Is Beautiful
Saving Private Ryan
The Thin Red Line
1999
★American Beauty
The Cider House Rules
The Green Mile
The Insider
The Sixth Sense
2000
★Gladiator
Chocolat
Crouching Tiger, Hidden Dragon
Erin Brockovich
Traffic
2001
★A Beautiful Mind
Gosford Park
In the Bedroom
Lord of the Rings: The Fellowship of the Ring
Moulin Rouge
2002
★Chicago
Gangs of New York
The Hours
Lord of the Rings: The Two Towers
The Pianist
2003
★Lord of the Rings: The Return of the King
Lost in Translation
Master and Commander: The Far Side of the World
Mystic River
Seabiscuit
2004
★Million Dollar Baby
The Aviator
Finding Neverland
Ray
Sideways
2005
★Crash
Brokeback Mountain
Capote
Good Night, and Good Luck
Munich
2006
★The Departed
Babel
Letters from Iwo Jima
Little Miss Sunshine
The Queen
2007
★No Country for Old Men
Atonement
Juno
Michael Clayton
There Will Be Blood
2008
★Slumdog Millionaire
The Curious Case of Benjamin Button
Frost/Nixon
Milk
The Reader
2009
★The Hurt Locker
Avatar
The Blind Side
District 9
An Education
Inglourious Basterds
Precious: Based on the Novel by Sapphire
A Serious Man
Up
Up in the Air

FEATURE DOCUMENTARY

1942
★Prelude to War
1961
★The Sky Above, the Mud Below
1970
★Woodstock
1971
★The Hellstrom Chronicle
1972
★Marjoe
1976
★Harlan County, U.S.A.
1977
The Children of Theatre Street
1983
★Times of Harvey Milk
1988
Let's Get Lost
1989
★Common Threads: Stories from the Quilt
1993
The War Room
1996
★When We Were Kings
1999
Buena Vista Social Club
2002
★Bowling for Columbine
Children Underground
Winged Migration
2003
★The Fog of War: Eleven Lessons from the Life of Robert S. McNamara
Capturing the Friedmans
My Architect: A Son's Journey
The Weather Underground
2004
★Born Into Brothels: Calcutta's Red Light Kids
The Story of the Weeping Camel
Super Size Me
2005
★March of the Penguins
Enron: The Smartest Guys in the Room
2006
★An Inconvenient Truth
2007
★Taxi to the Dark Side
No End in Sight
Sicko
2008
★Man on Wire
Encounters at the End of the World
2009
★The Cove
Food, Inc.
Which Way Home

FILM EDITING

1934
Cleopatra
One Night of Love
1935
★A Midsummer Night's Dream
David Copperfield
The Informer
Les Miserables
The Lives of a Bengal Lancer
Mutiny on the Bounty
1936
★Anthony Adverse
Come and Get It
The Great Ziegfeld
Lloyds of London
A Tale of Two Cities
Theodora Goes Wild
1937
★Lost Horizon
The Awful Truth
Captains Courageous
The Good Earth
100 Men and a Girl
1938
★The Adventures of Robin Hood
Alexander's Ragtime Band
The Great Waltz
Test Pilot
You Can't Take It with You
1939
★Gone with the Wind
Goodbye, Mr. Chips

★ = winner

Mr. Smith Goes to Washington
The Rains Came
Stagecoach
1940
The Grapes of Wrath
The Letter
The Long Voyage Home
Rebecca
1941
★Sergeant York
Citizen Kane
Dr. Jekyll and Mr. Hyde
How Green Was My Valley
The Little Foxes
1942
★The Pride of the Yankees
Mrs. Miniver
Talk of the Town
This Above All
Yankee Doodle Dandy
1943
★Air Force
Casablanca
Five Graves to Cairo
For Whom the Bell Tolls
The Song of Bernadette
This Above All
1944
★Wilson
Going My Way
None But the Lonely Heart
Since You Went Away
1945
★National Velvet
The Bells of St. Mary's
The Lost Weekend
Objective, Burma!
A Song to Remember
1946
★The Best Years of Our Lives
It's a Wonderful Life
The Jolson Story
The Killers
The Yearling
1947
★Body and Soul
The Bishop's Wife
Gentleman's Agreement
Green Dolphin Street
Odd Man Out
1948
★The Naked City
Joan of Arc
Johnny Belinda
Red River
The Red Shoes
1949
★Champion
All the King's Men
Battleground
Sands of Iwo Jima
The Window
1950
★King Solomon's Mines
Annie Get Your Gun
Sunset Boulevard
The Third Man
1951
★A Place in the Sun
An American in Paris
Quo Vadis
The Well
1952
★High Noon
Come Back, Little Sheba
Flat Top
The Greatest Show on Earth
Moulin Rouge

1953
★From Here to Eternity
The Moon Is Blue
Roman Holiday
The War of the Worlds
1954
★On the Waterfront
The Caine Mutiny
Seven Brides for Seven Brothers
20,000 Leagues under the Sea
1955
★Picnic
Blackboard Jungle
The Bridges at Toko-Ri
Oklahoma!
The Rose Tattoo
1956
★Around the World in 80 Days
The Brave One
Giant
Somebody Up There Likes Me
The Ten Commandments
1957
★The Bridge on the River Kwai
Gunfight at the O.K. Corral
Pal Joey
Sayonara
Witness for the Prosecution
1958
★Gigi
Auntie Mame
Cowboy
The Defiant Ones
I Want to Live!
1959
★Ben-Hur
Anatomy of a Murder
North by Northwest
The Nun's Story
On the Beach
1960
★The Apartment
The Alamo
Inherit the Wind
Spartacus
1961
★West Side Story
Fanny
The Guns of Navarone
Judgment at Nuremberg
The Parent Trap
1962
★Lawrence of Arabia
The Longest Day
The Manchurian Candidate
The Music Man
Mutiny on the Bounty
1963
★How the West Was Won
The Cardinal
Cleopatra
The Great Escape
It's a Mad, Mad, Mad World
1964
★Mary Poppins
Becket
Father Goose
Hush, Hush, Sweet Charlotte
My Fair Lady
1965
★The Sound of Music
Cat Ballou
Doctor Zhivago
The Flight of the Phoenix

The Great Race
1966
★Grand Prix
Fantastic Voyage
The Russians Are Coming, the Russians Are Coming
The Sand Pebbles
Who's Afraid of Virginia Woolf?
1967
★In the Heat of the Night
The Dirty Dozen
Doctor Dolittle
Guess Who's Coming to Dinner
1968
★Bullitt
Funny Girl
The Odd Couple
Oliver!
Wild in the Streets
1969
★Z
Hello, Dolly!
Midnight Cowboy
They Shoot Horses, Don't They?
1970
★Patton
Airport
M*A*S*H
Tora! Tora! Tora!
Woodstock
1971
★The French Connection
The Andromeda Strain
A Clockwork Orange
Kotch
Summer of '42
1972
★Cabaret
Deliverance
The Godfather
The Hot Rock
The Poseidon Adventure
1973
★The Sting
American Graffiti
The Day of the Jackal
The Exorcist
Jonathan Livingston Seagull
1974
★The Towering Inferno
Blazing Saddles
Chinatown
Earthquake
The Longest Yard
1975
★Jaws
Dog Day Afternoon
The Man Who Would Be King
One Flew Over the Cuckoo's Nest
Three Days of the Condor
1976
★Rocky
All the President's Men
Bound for Glory
Network
Two Minute Warning
1977
★Star Wars
Close Encounters of the Third Kind
Julia
Smokey and the Bandit
The Turning Point
1978
★The Deer Hunter
The Boys from Brazil

Coming Home
Midnight Express
Superman: The Movie
1979
★All That Jazz
Apocalypse Now
The Black Stallion
Kramer vs. Kramer
The Rose
1980
★Raging Bull
Coal Miner's Daughter
The Competition
The Elephant Man
Fame
1981
★Raiders of the Lost Ark
Chariots of Fire
The French Lieutenant's Woman
On Golden Pond
Reds
1982
★Gandhi
Das Boot
E.T.: The Extra-Terrestrial
An Officer and a Gentleman
Tootsie
1983
★The Right Stuff
Blue Thunder
Flashdance
Silkwood
Terms of Endearment
1984
★The Killing Fields
Amadeus
The Cotton Club
A Passage to India
Romancing the Stone
1985
★Witness
A Chorus Line
Out of Africa
Prizzi's Honor
Runaway Train
1986
★Platoon
Aliens
Hannah and Her Sisters
The Mission
Top Gun
1987
★The Last Emperor
Broadcast News
Empire of the Sun
Fatal Attraction
RoboCop
1988
★Who Framed Roger Rabbit
Die Hard
Gorillas in the Mist
Mississippi Burning
Rain Man
1989
★Born on the Fourth of July
The Bear
Driving Miss Daisy
The Fabulous Baker Boys
Glory
1990
★Dances with Wolves
Ghost
The Godfather, Part 3
Goodfellas
The Hunt for Red October
1991
★JFK
The Commitments

The Silence of the Lambs
Terminator 2: Judgment Day
Thelma & Louise
1992
★Unforgiven
Basic Instinct
The Crying Game
A Few Good Men
The Player
1993
★Schindler's List
The Fugitive
In the Line of Fire
In the Name of the Father
The Piano
1994
★Forrest Gump
Hoop Dreams
Pulp Fiction
The Shawshank Redemption
Speed
1995
★Apollo 13
Babe
Braveheart
Crimson Tide
Seven
1996
★The English Patient
Evita
Fargo
Jerry Maguire
Shine
1997
★Titanic
Air Force One
As Good As It Gets
Good Will Hunting
L.A. Confidential
1998
★Saving Private Ryan
Life Is Beautiful
Out of Sight
Shakespeare in Love
The Thin Red Line
1999
★The Matrix
American Beauty
The Cider House Rules
The Insider
The Sixth Sense
2000
★Traffic
Almost Famous
Crouching Tiger, Hidden Dragon
Gladiator
Wonder Boys
2001
★Black Hawk Down
A Beautiful Mind
Lord of the Rings: The Fellowship of the Ring
Memento
Moulin Rouge
2002
★Chicago
Gangs of New York
The Hours
Lord of the Rings: The Two Towers
The Pianist
2003
★Lord of the Rings: The Return of the King
City of God
Cold Mountain
Master and Commander: The Far Side of the World
Seabiscuit

2004
★The Aviator
Collateral
Finding Neverland
Million Dollar Baby
Ray
2005
★Crash
Cinderella Man
The Constant Gardener
Munich
Walk the Line
2006
★The Departed
Babel
Blood Diamond
Children of Men
United 93
2007
★The Bourne Ultimatum
The Diving Bell and the Butterfly
Into the Wild
No Country for Old Men
There Will Be Blood
2008
★Slumdog Millionaire
The Curious Case of Benjamin Button
The Dark Knight
Frost/Nixon
Milk
2009
★The Hurt Locker
Avatar
District 9
Inglourious Basterds
Precious: Based on the Novel by Sapphire

MAKEUP

1981
★An American Werewolf in London
1982
★Quest for Fire
Gandhi
1984
★Amadeus
Greystoke: The Legend of Tarzan, Lord of the Apes
2010: The Year We Make Contact
1985
★Mask
The Color Purple
Remo Williams: The Adventure Begins
1986
★The Fly
The Clan of the Cave Bear
Legend
1987
★Harry and the Hendersons
Happy New Year
1988
★Beetlejuice
1989
★Driving Miss Daisy
The Adventures of Baron Munchausen
Dad
1990
★Dick Tracy
Cyrano de Bergerac
Edward Scissorhands
1991
★Terminator 2: Judgment Day
Hook
Star Trek 6: The Undiscovered Country

★ = winner

1992
★*Bram Stoker's Dracula*
Batman Returns
Hoffa
1993
★*Mrs. Doubtfire*
Philadelphia
Schindler's List
1994
★*Ed Wood*
Forrest Gump
Mary Shelley's Frankenstein
1995
★*Braveheart*
My Family
Roommates
1996
★*The Nutty Professor*
Ghosts of Mississippi
Star Trek: First Contact
1997
★*Men in Black*
Mrs. Brown
Titanic
1998
★*Elizabeth*
Saving Private Ryan
Shakespeare in Love
1999
★*Topsy Turvy*
Austin Powers 2: The Spy Who Shagged Me
Bicentennial Man
Life
2000
The Cell
Dr. Seuss' How the Grinch Stole Christmas
Shadow of the Vampire
2001
A Beautiful Mind
Lord of the Rings: The Fellowship of the Ring
Moulin Rouge
2002
★*Frida*
The Time Machine
2003
★*Lord of the Rings: The Return of the King*
Master and Commander: The Far Side of the World
Pirates of the Caribbean: The Curse of the Black Pearl
2004
★*Lemony Snicket's A Series of Unfortunate Events*
The Passion of the Christ
The Sea Inside
2005
★*The Chronicles of Narnia: The Lion, the Witch and the Wardrobe*
Cinderella Man
Star Wars: Episode 3—Revenge of the Sith
2006
★*Pan's Labyrinth*
Apocalypto
Click
2007
★*La Vie en Rose*
Norbit
Pirates of the Caribbean: At World's End
2008
★*The Curious Case of Benjamin Button*
The Dark Knight
Hellboy II: The Golden Army
2009
★*Star Trek*
Il Divo
Star Trek
The Young Victoria

ADAPTED SCORE

1962
★*The Music Man*
Billy Rose's Jumbo
Gypsy
The Wonderful World of the Brothers Grimm
1963
★*Irma La Douce*
Bye, Bye, Birdie
A New Kind of Love
Sundays & Cybele
The Sword in the Stone
1964
★*My Fair Lady*
A Hard Day's Night
Robin and the 7 Hoods
The Unsinkable Molly Brown
1965
★*The Sound of Music*
Cat Ballou
A Thousand Clowns
1966
★*A Funny Thing Happened on the Way to the Forum*
The Gospel According to St. Matthew
Return of the Magnificent Seven
The Singing Nun
1967
★*Camelot*
Guess Who's Coming to Dinner
Valley of the Dolls
1968
★*Oliver!*
Star!

ORIGINAL DRAMATIC SCORE

1941
★*The Devil & Daniel Webster*
Ball of Fire
Cheers for Miss Bishop
Citizen Kane
Dr. Jekyll and Mr. Hyde
How Green Was My Valley
King of the Zombies
The Little Foxes
Lydia
Sergeant York
So Ends Our Night
Sundown
Suspicion
Tanks a Million
That Uncertain Feeling
1942
★*Now, Voyager*
Arabian Nights
Bambi
The Black Swan
The Corsican Brothers
Flying Tigers
I Married a Witch
Joan of Paris
The Jungle Book
The Pride of the Yankees
Random Harvest
The Shanghai Gesture
Silver Queen
Talk of the Town
To Be or Not to Be
1943
★*The Song of Bernadette*
The Amazing Mrs. Holiday
Casablanca
Commandos Strike at Dawn
The Fallen Sparrow
For Whom the Bell Tolls
Hangmen Also Die
Hi Diddle Diddle
Johnny Come Lately
The Kansan
Lady of Burlesque
Madame Curie
The Moon and Sixpence
The North Star
War of the Wildcats
1944
★*Cover Girl*
★*Since You Went Away*
The Adventures of Mark Twain
The Bridge of San Luis Rey
Casanova Brown
Double Indemnity
Fighting Seabees
The Hairy Ape
Higher and Higher
Jack London
None But the Lonely Heart
The Princess and the Pirate
Wilson
The Woman of the Town
1945
★*Spellbound*
The Bells of St. Mary's
Brewster's Millions
Captain Kidd
The Enchanted Cottage
Flame of the Barbary Coast
Guest in the House
Guest Wife
The Keys of the Kingdom
The Lost Weekend
Objective, Burma!
A Song to Remember
The Southerner
The Valley of Decision
Woman in the Window
1946
★*The Best Years of Our Lives*
Anna and the King of Siam
Henry V
Humoresque
The Killers
1947
★*A Double Life*
The Bishop's Wife
Captain from Castile
Forever Amber
Life with Father
The Road to Rio
1948
★*The Red Shoes*
Hamlet
Joan of Arc
Johnny Belinda
The Snake Pit
1949
★*The Heiress*
Beyond the Forest
Champion
1950
★*Sunset Boulevard*
All About Eve
The Flame & the Arrow
Samson and Delilah
1951
★*A Place in the Sun*
David and Bathsheba
Quo Vadis
A Streetcar Named Desire
1952
★*High Noon*
Ivanhoe
Miracle of Our Lady of Fatima
The Thief
Viva Zapata!
1953
★*Lili*
Above and Beyond
From Here to Eternity
Julius Caesar
1954
★*The High and the Mighty*
The Caine Mutiny
Genevieve
On the Waterfront
The Silver Chalice
1955
★*Love Is a Many-Splendored Thing*
Battle Cry
The Man with the Golden Arm
Picnic
The Rose Tattoo
1956
★*Around the World in 80 Days*
Anastasia
Between Heaven and Hell
Giant
The Rainmaker
1958
★*The Old Man and the Sea*
The Big Country
Separate Tables
The Young Lions
1959
★*Ben-Hur*
The Diary of Anne Frank
The Nun's Story
On the Beach
Pillow Talk
1960
★*Exodus*
The Alamo
Elmer Gantry
The Magnificent Seven
Spartacus
1961
★*Breakfast at Tiffany's*
El Cid
Fanny
The Guns of Navarone
Summer and Smoke
1971
★*Summer of '42*
Mary, Queen of Scots
Nicholas and Alexandra
Shaft
Straw Dogs
1972
Napoleon and Samantha
The Poseidon Adventure
Sleuth
1973
★*The Way We Were*
Cinderella Liberty
The Day of the Dolphin
Papillon
A Touch of Class
1974
★*The Godfather, Part 2*
Chinatown
Murder on the Orient Express
The Towering Inferno
1995
★*The Postman*
Apollo 13
Braveheart
Nixon
Sense and Sensibility
1996
★*The English Patient*
Hamlet
Michael Collins
Shine
Sleepers
1998
★*Life Is Beautiful*
Elizabeth
Pleasantville
Saving Private Ryan

ORIGINAL MUSICAL/ COMEDY SCORE

1997
★*The Full Monty*
Anastasia
As Good As It Gets
Men in Black
My Best Friend's Wedding
1998
★*Shakespeare in Love*
A Bug's Life
Mulan
Patch Adams
Prince of Egypt

ORIGINAL SONG SCORE AND/OR ADAPTATION

1957
★*The Bridge on the River Kwai*
1970
★*Let It Be*
The Baby Maker
Darling Lili
Scrooge
1971
★*Fiddler on the Roof*
Bedknobs and Broomsticks
The Boy Friend
Tchaikovsky
Willy Wonka & the Chocolate Factory
1972
★*Cabaret*
Lady Sings the Blues
Man of La Mancha
1973
★*The Sting*
Jesus Christ, Superstar
Tom Sawyer
1974
★*The Great Gatsby*
The Little Prince
Phantom of the Paradise
1975
★*Barry Lyndon*
Funny Lady
1976
★*Bound for Glory*
A Star Is Born
1977
★*A Little Night Music*
Pete's Dragon
1978
★*The Buddy Holly Story*
Pretty Baby
The Wiz
1979
★*All That Jazz*
Breaking Away
The Muppet Movie
1982
★*Victor/Victoria*
Annie
One from the Heart
1983
★*Yentl*
The Sting 2
Trading Places
1984
★*Purple Rain*
The Muppets Take Manhattan
Songwriter

SCORE

1934
★*One Night of Love*
The Gay Divorcee
The Lost Patrol
1935
★*The Informer*
Mutiny on the Bounty
1936
★*Anthony Adverse*
The Charge of the Light Brigade
The Garden of Allah
The General Died at Dawn
Winterset
1937
★*100 Men and a Girl*
The Hurricane
In Old Chicago
The Life of Emile Zola
Lost Horizon
Make a Wish
Maytime
Prisoner of Zenda
Quality Street
Snow White and the Seven Dwarfs
Something to Sing About
Souls at Sea
Way Out West
1938
★*Alexander's Ragtime Band*
Carefree
The Goldwyn Follies
Jezebel
Mad About Music
Sweethearts
1939
★*Stagecoach*
Babes in Arms
First Love
The Hunchback of Notre Dame
Intermezzo
Mr. Smith Goes to Washington
The Private Lives of Elizabeth & Essex
They Shall Have Music
Way Down South
1940
★*Tin Pan Alley*
Our Town
The Sea Hawk
Second Chorus
Strike Up the Band
1957
An Affair to Remember
An Affair to Remember
Raintree County
2001
A. I.: Artificial Intelligence
A Beautiful Mind
Harry Potter and the Sorcerer's Stone
Lord of the Rings: The Fellowship of the Ring
Monsters, Inc.

★ = *winner*

2002
★*Frida*
Catch Me If You Can
Far from Heaven
The Hours
Road to Perdition

SCORING OF A MUSICAL

1941
★*Dumbo*
Birth of the Blues
Buck Privates
The Chocolate Soldier
Strawberry Blonde
Sun Valley Serenade
Sunny
You'll Never Get Rich
1942
★*Yankee Doodle Dandy*
For Me and My Gal
Holiday Inn
It Started with Eve
You Were Never Lovelier
1943
★*This Is the Army*
The Phantom of the Opera
The Sky's the Limit
Stage Door Canteen
Star Spangled Rhythm
Thousands Cheer
1944
Hollywood Canteen
Meet Me in St. Louis
Sensations of 1945
Up in Arms
1945
★*Anchors Aweigh*
Can't Help Singing
Rhapsody in Blue
State Fair
The Three Caballeros
Tonight and Every Night
Wonder Man
1946
★*The Jolson Story*
Blue Skies
The Harvey Girls
Night and Day
1947
★*Mother Wore Tights*
1948
★*Easter Parade*
Emperor Waltz
The Pirate
Romance on the High Seas
1949
★*On the Town*
Jolson Sings Again
Look for the Silver Lining
1950
★*Annie Get Your Gun*
Cinderella
Three Little Words
The West Point Story
1951
★*An American in Paris*
Alice in Wonderland
The Great Caruso
Show Boat
1952
Hans Christian Andersen
The Medium
Singin' in the Rain
1953
The Band Wagon
Calamity Jane
The 5000 Fingers of Dr. T
Kiss Me Kate
1954
★*Seven Brides for Seven Brothers*
Carmen Jones
The Glenn Miller Story
A Star Is Born
There's No Business Like Show Business
1955
★*Oklahoma!*
Daddy Long Legs
Guys and Dolls
It's Always Fair Weather
Love Me or Leave Me
1956
★*The King and I*
The Eddy Duchin Story
High Society
Meet Me in Las Vegas
1958
★*Gigi*
Damn Yankees
South Pacific
1959
The Five Pennies
Li'l Abner
Sleeping Beauty
1960
★*Song Without End*
Bells Are Ringing
Can-Can
Let's Make Love
1961
★*West Side Story*
Babes in Toyland
Flower Drum Song
Paris Blues
1968
Finian's Rainbow
Funny Girl
1969
★*Hello, Dolly!*
Goodbye, Mr. Chips
Paint Your Wagon
Sweet Charity
They Shoot Horses, Don't They?

ORIGINAL SCORE

1938
★*The Adventures of Robin Hood*
Breaking the Ice
The Cowboy and the Lady
Marie Antoinette
The Young in Heart
1939
★*The Wizard of Oz*
Dark Victory
Eternally Yours
Golden Boy
Gone with the Wind
Gulliver's Travels
The Man in the Iron Mask
Nurse Edith Cavell
Of Mice and Men
The Rains Came
Wuthering Heights
1940
★*Pinocchio*
Arizona
Dark Command
The Grapes of Wrath
The Great Dictator
The Howards of Virginia
The Letter
The Long Voyage Home
The Mark of Zorro
My Favorite Wife
One Million B.C.
Rebecca
The Thief of Bagdad
Waterloo Bridge
1953
★*With a Song in My Heart*
1962
★*Lawrence of Arabia*
Mutiny on the Bounty
Taras Bulba
To Kill a Mockingbird
1963
★*Tom Jones*
Cleopatra
55 Days at Peking
How the West Was Won
It's a Mad, Mad, Mad, Mad World
1964
★*Mary Poppins*
Becket
The Fall of the Roman Empire
Hush, Hush, Sweet Charlotte
Mary Poppins
The Pink Panther
1965
★*Doctor Zhivago*
The Agony and the Ecstasy
The Greatest Story Ever Told
A Patch of Blue
Umbrellas of Cherbourg
1966
★*Born Free*
The Bible
Cool Hand Luke
Hawaii
The Sand Pebbles
Who's Afraid of Virginia Woolf?
1967
★*Thoroughly Modern Millie*
Doctor Dolittle
Far from the Madding Crowd
In Cold Blood
Thoroughly Modern Millie
1968
★*The Lion in Winter*
Planet of the Apes
The Shoes of the Fisherman
The Thomas Crown Affair
1969
★*Butch Cassidy and the Sundance Kid*
Anne of the Thousand Days
The Reivers
The Wild Bunch
1970
★*Love Story*
Airport
Cromwell
Patton
1975
★*Jaws*
Bite the Bullet
One Flew Over the Cuckoo's Nest
Tommy
The Wind and the Lion
1976
★*The Omen*
Bugsy Malone
Obsession
The Outlaw Josey Wales
Taxi Driver
Voyage of the Damned
1977
★*Star Wars*
Close Encounters of the Third Kind
Julia
The Message
The Spy Who Loved Me
1978
★*Midnight Express*
The Boys from Brazil
Days of Heaven
Heaven Can Wait
Superman: The Movie
1979
★*A Little Romance*
The Amityville Horror
The Champ
Star Trek: The Motion Picture
10
1980
★*Fame*
Altered States
The Elephant Man
The Empire Strikes Back
Tess
1981
★*Chariots of Fire*
Dragonslayer
On Golden Pond
Ragtime
Raiders of the Lost Ark
1982
★*E.T.: The Extra-Terrestrial*
Gandhi
An Officer and a Gentleman
Poltergeist
Sophie's Choice
1983
★*The Right Stuff*
Cross Creek
Return of the Jedi
Terms of Endearment
Under Fire
1984
★*A Passage to India*
Indiana Jones and the Temple of Doom
The Natural
The River
Under the Volcano
1985
★*Out of Africa*
Agnes of God
The Color Purple
Silverado
Witness
1986
★*Round Midnight*
Aliens
Hoosiers
The Mission
Star Trek 4: The Voyage Home
1987
★*The Last Emperor*
Cry Freedom
Empire of the Sun
The Untouchables
The Witches of Eastwick
1988
★*The Milagro Beanfield War*
The Accidental Tourist
Dangerous Liaisons
Gorillas in the Mist
Rain Man
1989
★*The Little Mermaid*
Born on the Fourth of July
The Fabulous Baker Boys
Field of Dreams
Indiana Jones and the Last Crusade
1990
★*Dances with Wolves*
Avalon
Ghost
Havana
Home Alone
1991
★*Beauty and the Beast*
Bugsy
The Fisher King
JFK
The Prince of Tides
1992
★*Aladdin*
Basic Instinct
Chaplin
Howard's End
A River Runs Through It
1993
★*Schindler's List*
The Age of Innocence
The Firm
The Fugitive
The Remains of the Day
1994
★*The Lion King*
Forrest Gump
Interview with the Vampire
Little Women
The Shawshank Redemption
1995
★*Pocahontas*
The American President
Sabrina
Toy Story
Unstrung Heroes
1996
★*Emma*
The First Wives Club
The Hunchback of Notre Dame
James and the Giant Peach
The Preacher's Wife
1997
★*Titanic*
Amistad
Good Will Hunting
Kundun
L.A. Confidential
1999
★*The Red Violin*
American Beauty
Angela's Ashes
The Cider House Rules
The Talented Mr. Ripley
2000
★*Crouching Tiger, Hidden Dragon*
Chocolat
The Patriot
2003
★*Lord of the Rings: The Return of the King*
Big Fish
Cold Mountain
Finding Nemo
House of Sand and Fog
2004
★*Finding Neverland*
Harry Potter and the Prisoner of Azkaban
Lemony Snicket's A Series of Unfortunate Events
The Passion of the Christ
The Village
2005
★*Brokeback Mountain*
The Constant Gardener
Memoirs of a Geisha
Munich
Pride and Prejudice
2006
★*Babel*
The Good German
Notes on a Scandal
Pan's Labyrinth
The Queen
2007
★*Atonement*
The Kite Runner
Michael Clayton
Ratatouille
3:10 to Yuma
2008
★*Slumdog Millionaire*
The Curious Case of Benjamin Button
Defiance
Milk
WALL-E
2009
★*Up*
Avatar
Fantastic Mr. Fox
The Hurt Locker
Sherlock Holmes

SONG

1934
★"The Continental"/*The Gay Divorcee*
"Carioca"/*Flying Down to Rio*
1935
★"Lullaby of Broadway"/*Gold Diggers of 1935*
"Cheek to Cheek"/*Top Hat*
"Lovely to Look At"/*Roberta*
1936
★"Pennies from Heaven"/*Pennies from Heaven*
★"The Way You Look Tonight"/*Swing Time*
"A Melody from the Sky"/*The Trail of the Lonesome Pine*
"Did I Remember"/*Suzy*
"I've Got You Under My Skin"/*Born to Dance*
"My Own"/*That Certain Age*
1937
★"Sweet Leilani"/*Waikiki Wedding*
"That Old Feeling"/*Vogues of 1938*
"They Can't Take That Away From Me"/*Shall We Dance*
1938
★"Thanks for the Memories"/*The Big Broadcast of 1938*
"Always and Always"/*Mannequin*
"Change Partners and Dance with Me"/*Carefree*
"Now It Can Be Told"/*Alexander's Ragtime Band*
"The Cowboy and the Lady"/*The Cowboy and the Lady*
1939
★"Over the Rainbow"/*The Wizard of Oz*
"Faithful Forever"/*Gulliver's Travels*
"I Poured My Heart Into Song"/*Second Fiddle*
"Wishing"/*Love Affair*
1940
★"When You Wish Upon a Star"/*Pinocchio*
"Down Argentine Way"/*Down Argentine Way*
"I'd Know You Anywhere"/*You'll Find Out*
"It's a Blue World"/*Music in My Heart*
"Love of My Life"/*Second Chorus*
"Only Forever"/*Rhythm on the River*

★ = *winner*

"Our Love Affair"/*Strike Up the Band*

1941

★"The Last Time I Saw Paris"/*Lady Be Good*

"Baby Mine"/*Dumbo*

"Be Honest With Me"/*Ridin' on a Rainbow*

"Blues In the Night"/*Blues in the Night*

"Boogie Woogie Bugle Boy of Company B"/*Buck Privates*

"Chattanooga Choo Choo"/*Sun Valley Serenade*

"Since I Kissed My Baby Goodbye"/*You'll Never Get Rich*

1942

★"White Christmas"/*Holiday Inn*

"Dearly Beloved"/*You Were Never Lovelier*

"How About You?"/*Babes on Broadway*

"I've Got a Gal in Kalamazoo"/*Orchestra Wives*

"Love Is a Song"/*Bambi*

1943

★"You'll Never Know"/*Hello, Frisco, Hello*

"Happiness Is a Thing Called Joe"/*Cabin in the Sky*

"My Shining Hour"/*The Sky's the Limit*

"That Old Black Magic"/*Star Spangled Rhythm*

"They're Either Too Young or Too Old"/*Thank Your Lucky Stars*

"We Mustn't Say Goodbye"/*Stage Door Canteen*

1944

★"Swinging on a Star"/*Going My Way*

"I Couldn't Sleep A Wink Last Night"/*Higher and Higher*

"I'll Walk Alone"/*Follow the Boys*

"Long Ago and Far Away"/*Cover Girl*

"Now I Know"/*Up in Arms*

"Sweet Dreams Sweetheart"/*Hollywood Canteen*

"The Trolley Song"/*Meet Me in St. Louis*

1945

★"It Might as Well Be Spring"/*State Fair*

"Accentuate the Positive"/*Here Come the Waves*

"Anywhere"/*Tonight and Every Night*

"Aren't You Glad You're You"/*The Bells of St. Mary's*

"I Fall in Love Too Easily"/*Anchors Aweigh*

"More and More"/*Can't Help Singing*

"So in Love"/*Wonder Man*

"Some Sunday Morning"/*San Antonio*

1946

★"On the Atchison, Topeka and Santa Fe"/*The Harvey Girls*

"I Can't Begin to Tell You"/*The Dolly Sisters*

"You Keep Coming Back Like a Song"/*Blue Skies*

1947

"I Wish I Didn't Love You So"/*The Perils of Pauline*

"Pass That Peace Pipe"/*Good News*

"You Do"/*Mother Wore Tights*

1948

★"Buttons and Bows"/*The Paleface*

"For Every Man There's a Woman"/*Casbah*

"It's Magic"/*Romance on the High Seas*

1949

★"Baby It's Cold Outside"/*Neptune's Daughter*

"It's a Great Feeling"/*It's a Great Feeling*

"Lavender Blue"/*So Dear to My Heart*

"My Foolish Heart"/*My Foolish Heart*

"Through a Long and Sleepless Night"/*Come to the Stable*

1950

"Be My Love"/*The Toast of New Orleans*

"Bibbidy-Bobbidi-Boo"/*Cinderella*

1951

★"In the Cool, Cool, Cool of the Evening"/*Here Comes the Groom*

"Too Late Now"/*Royal Wedding*

"Wonder Why"/*Rich, Young and Pretty*

1952

★"High Noon (Do Not Forsake Me, Oh My Darlin')"/*High Noon*

"Am I in Love"/*Son of Paleface*

"Because You're Mine"/*Because You're Mine*

"Thumbelina"/*Hans Christian Andersen*

"Zing a Little Zong"/*Just for You*

1953

★"Secret Love"/*Calamity Jane*

"My Flaming Heart"/*Small Town Girl*

"Sadie Thompson's Song (Blue Pacific Blues)"/*Miss Sadie Thompson*

"That's Amore"/*The Caddy*

"The Moon is Blue"/*The Moon Is Blue*

1954

★"Three Coins in the Fountain"/*Three Coins in the Fountain*

"Count Your Blessings Instead of Sheep"/*White Christmas*

"Hold My Hand"/*Susan Slept Here*

"The Man That Got Away"/*A Star Is Born*

1955

★"Love Is a Many-Splendored Thing"/*Love Is a Many-Splendored Thing*

"(Love Is) The Tender Trap"/*The Tender Trap*

"I'll Never Stop Loving You"/*Love Me or Leave Me*

"Something's Gotta Give"/*Daddy Long Legs*

"The High and the Mighty"/*The High and the Mighty*

1956

★"Que Sera, Sera"/*The Man Who Knew Too Much*

"Friendly Persuasion (Thee I Love)"/*Friendly Persuasion*

"True Love"/*High Society*

"Written on the Wind"/*Written on the Wind*

1957

"An Affair to Remember"/*An Affair to Remember*

"Tammy"/*Tammy and the Bachelor*

1958

★"Gigi"/*Gigi*

"A Very Precious Love"/*Marjorie Morningstar*

"Almost in Your Arms (Love Song from Houseboat)"/*Houseboat*

"To Love and Be Loved"/*Some Came Running*

1959

★"High Hopes"/*A Hole in the Head*

"Strange Are the Ways of Love"/*The Young Land*

"The Best of Everything"/*The Best of Everything*

"The Five Pennies"/*The Five Pennies*

"The Hanging Tree"/*The Hanging Tree*

1960

★"Never on Sunday"/*Never on Sunday*

"The Facts of Life"/*The Facts of Life*

"The Green Leaves of Summer"/*The Alamo*

1961

★"Moon River"/*Breakfast at Tiffany's*

"Bachelor in Paradise"/*Bachelor in Paradise*

"Love Theme (The Falcon and the Dove)"/*El Cid*

"Pocketful of Miracles"/*Pocketful of Miracles*

"Town without Pity"/*Town without Pity*

1962

★"Days of Wine and Roses"/*Days of Wine and Roses*

"Love Song (Follow Me)"/*Mutiny on the Bounty*

"Song fromm Two for the Seesaw (Second Chance)"/*Two for the Seesaw*

"Walk on the Wild Side"/*Walk on the Wild Side*

1963

★"Call Me Irresponsible"/*Papa's Delicate Condition*

"Charade"/*Charade*

"It's a Mad, Mad, Mad, Mad World"/*It's a Mad, Mad, Mad, Mad World*

"More"/*Mondo Cane*

"So Little Time"/*55 Days at Peking*

1964

★"Chim Chim Cher-ee"/*Mary Poppins*

"Hush, Hush, Sweet Charlotte"/*Hush, Hush, Sweet Charlotte*

"My Kind of Town"/*Robin and the 7 Hoods*

"Where Love Has Gone"/*Where Love Has Gone*

1965

★"The Shadow of Your Smile"/*The Sandpiper*

"I Will Wait for You"/*Umbrellas of Cherbourg*

"The Ballad of Cat Ballou"/*Cat Ballou*

"The Sweetheart Tree"/*The Great Race*

"What's New Pussycat?"/*What's New Pussycat?*

1966

★"Born Free"/*Born Free*

"Alfie"/*Alfie*

"Georgy Girl"/*Georgy Girl*

"My Wishing Doll"/*Hawaii*

1967

★"Talk to the Animals"/*Doctor Dolittle*

"The Bare Necessities"/*The Jungle Book*

"The Look of Love"/*Casino Royale*

"Thoroughly Modern Millie"/*Thoroughly Modern Millie*

1968

★"The Windmills of Your Mind"/*The Thomas Crown Affair*

"Chitty Chitty Bang Bang"/*Chitty Chitty Bang Bang*

"For Love of Ivy"/*For Love of Ivy*

"Funny Girl"/*Funny Girl*

"Star!"/*Star!*

1969

★"Raindrops Keep Fallin' on My Head"/*Butch Cassidy and the Sundance Kid*

"Come Saturday Morning"/*The Sterile Cuckoo*

"Jean"/*The Prime of Miss Jean Brodie*

"True Grit"/*True Grit*

"What Are You Doing the Rest of Your Life?"/*The Happy Ending*

1970

★"For All We Know"/*Lovers and Other Strangers*

"Thank You Very Much"/*Scrooge*

"Till Love Touches Your Life"/*Madron*

"Whistling Away the Dark"/*Darling Lili*

1971

★"Theme from Shaft"/*Shaft*

"All His Children"/*Sometimes a Great Notion*

"Bless the Beasts and the Children"/*Bless the Beasts and Children*

"Life Is What You MaKe It"/*Kotch*

"The Age of Not Believing"/*Bedknobs and Broomsticks*

1972

★"The Morning After"/*The Poseidon Adventure*

"Ben"/*Ben*

"Marmalade, Molasses & Honey"/*Life & Times of Judge Roy Bean*

"Strange Are the Ways of Love"/*The Stepmother*

1973

★"The Way We Were"/*The Way We Were*

"All That Love Went to Waste"/*A Touch of Class*

"Live and Let Die"/*Live and Let Die*

"Love"/*Robin Hood*

"You're So Nice to Be Around"/*Cinderella Liberty*

1974

★"We May Never Love Like This Again"/*The Towering Inferno*

"Benji's Theme (I Feel Love)"/*Benji*

"Blazing Saddles"/*Blazing Saddles*

"Little Prince"/*The Little Prince*

1975

★"I'm Easy"/*Nashville*

"How Lucky Can You Get"/*Funny Lady*

"Now That We're in Love"/*Whiffs*

"Richard's Window"/*The Other Side of the Mountain*

"Theme from Mahogany"/*Mahogany*

1976

★"Evergreen"/*A Star Is Born*

"Ave Satani"/*The Omen*

"Come to Me"/*The Pink Panther Strikes Again*

"Gonna Fly Now"/*Rocky*

1977

★"You Light Up My Life"/*You Light Up My Life*

"Candle on the Water"/*Pete's Dragon*

"Nobody Does It Better"/*The Spy Who Loved Me*

"Someone's Waiting for You"/*The Rescuers*

1978

★"Last Dance"/*Thank God It's Friday*

"Hopelessly Devoted to You"/*Grease*

"Ready to Take a Chance Again"/*Foul Play*

"The Last Time I Felt Like This"/*Same Time, Next Year*

"When You're Loved"/*Magic of Lassie*

1979

★"It Goes Like It Goes"/*Norma Rae*

"Song from 10 (It's Easy to Say)"/*10*

"The Rainbow Connection"/*The Muppet Movie*

"Theme from Ice Castles-Through the Eyes of Love"/*Ice Castles*

"Theme from The Promise: I'll Never Say Goodbye"/*The Promise*

1980

★"Fame"/*Fame*

"Nine to Five"/*9 to 5*

"On the Road Again"/*Honeysuckle Rose*

"Out Here on My Own"/*Fame*

"People Alone"/*The Competition*

1981

★"Arthur's Theme"/*Arthur*

"Endless Love"/*Endless Love*

"For Your Eyes Only"/*For Your Eyes Only*

"One More Hour"/*Ragtime*

"The First Time It Happens"/*The Great Muppet Caper*

1982

★"Up Where We Belong"/*An Officer and a Gentleman*

"Eye of the Tiger"/*Rocky 3*

"How Do You Keep the Music Playing?"/*Best Friends*

"If We Were in Love"/*Yes, Giorgio*

"It Might Be You"/*Tootsie*

1983

★"Flashdance...What a Feeling"/*Flashdance*

"Maniac"/*Flashdance*

"Over You"/*Tender Mercies*

"Papa, Can You Hear Me?"/*Yentl*

"The Way He Makes Me Feel"/*Yentl*

1984

★"I Just Called to Say I Love You"/*The Woman in Red*

"Against All Odds (Take a Look at Me Now)"/*Against All Odds*

"Footloose"/*Footloose*

"Ghostbusters"/*Ghostbusters*

"Let's Hear It for the Boy"/*Footloose*

1985

★"Say You, Say Me"/*White Nights*

"Miss Celie's Blues (Sister)"/*The Color Purple*

"Separate Lives (Love Theme from White Nights)"/*White Nights*

"Surprise, Surprise"/*A Chorus Line*

"The Power of Love"/*Back to the Future*

1986

★"Take My Breath Away"/*Top Gun*

"Glory of Love"/*The Karate Kid: Part 2*

"Life in a Looking Glass"/*That's Life!*

"Mean Green Mother from Outer Space"/*Little Shop of Horrors*

"Somewhere Out There"/*An American Tail*

1987

★"(I've Had) the Time of My Life"/*Dirty Dancing*

"Cry Freedom"/*Cry Freedom*

"Nothing's Gonna Stop Us Now"/*Mannequin*

"Shakedown"/*Beverly Hills Cop 2*

"Storybook Love"/*The Princess Bride*

1988

★"Let the River Run"/*Working Girl*

"Calling You"/*Bagdad Cafe*

"Two Hearts"/*Buster*

1989

★"Under the Sea"/*The Little Mermaid*

"After All"/*Chances Are*

"I Love to See You Smile"/*Parenthood*

"Kiss the Girl"/*The Little Mermaid*

"The Girl Who Used to Be Me"/*Shirley Valentine*

1990

★"Sooner or Later"/*Dick Tracy*

"Blaze of Glory"/*Young Guns 2*

"I'm Checkin' Out"/*Postcards from the Edge*

"Promise Me You'll Remember"/*The Godfather, Part 3*

"Somewhere in My Memory"/*Home Alone*

1991

★"Beauty and the Beast"/*Beauty and the Beast*

"(Everything I Do) I Do It for You"/*Robin Hood: Prince of Thieves*

"Be Our Guest"/*Beauty and the Beast*

"Belle"/*Beauty and the Beast*

"When You're Alone"/*Hook*

1992

★"A Whole New World"/*Aladdin*

"Beautiful Maria of My Soul"/*The Mambo Kings*

★ = *winner*

"Friend Like Me"/*Aladdin*
"I Have Nothing"/*The Bodyguard*
"Run to You"/*The Bodyguard*
1993
★"Streets of Philadelphia"/*Philadelphia*
"A Wink and a Smile"/*Sleepless in Seattle*
"Again"/*Poetic Justice*
"Philadelphia"/*Philadelphia*
"The Day I Fall in Love"/*Beethoven's 2nd*
1994
★"Can You Feel the Love Tonight"/*The Lion King*
"Circle of Life"/*The Lion King*
"Hakuna Matata"/*The Lion King*
"Look What Love Has Done"/*Junior*
"Make Up Your Mind"/*The Paper*
1995
★"Colors of the Wind"/*Pocahontas*
"Dead Man Walking"/*Dead Man Walking*
"Have You Ever Really Loved a Woman?"/*Don Juan DeMarco*
"Moonlight"/*Sabrina*
"You've Got a Friend"/*Toy Story*
1996
★"You Must Love Me"/*Evita*
"Because You Loved Me"/*Up Close and Personal*
"For the First Time"/*One Fine Day*
"I've Finally Found Someone"/*The Mirror Has Two Faces*
"That Thing You Do!"/*That Thing You Do!*
1997
★"My Heart Will Go On"/*Titanic*
"Go the Distance"/*Hercules*
"How Do I Live"/*Con Air*
"Journey to the Past"/*Anastasia*
"Miss Misery"/*Good Will Hunting*
1998
★"When You Believe"/*Prince of Egypt*
"A Soft Place to Fall"/*The Horse Whisperer*
"I Don't Want to Miss a Thing"/*Armageddon*
"That'll Do"/*Babe: Pig in the City*
"The Prayer"/*Quest for Camelot*
1999
★"You'll Be In My Heart"/*Tarzan*
"Blame Canada"/*South Park: Bigger, Longer and Uncut*
"Music of My Heart"/*Music of the Heart*
"Save Me"/*Magnolia*
"When She Loved Me"/*Toy Story 2*
2000
★"Things Have Changed"/*Wonder Boys*
"A Fool in Love"/*Meet the Parents*
"A Love Before Time"/*Crouching Tiger, Hidden Dragon*
"I've Seen It All"/*Dancer in the Dark*
"My Funny Friend and Me"/*The Emperor's New Groove*
2001
★"If I Didn't Have You"/*Monsters, Inc.*
"May It Be"/*Lord of the Rings: The Fellowship of the Ring*
"There You'll Be"/*Pearl Harbor*
"Until"/*Kate & Leopold*
"Vanilla Sky"/*Vanilla Sky*
2002
★"Lose Yourself"/*8 Mile*
"Burn It Blue"/*Frida*
"Father and Daughter"/*The Wild Thornberrys Movie*
"I Move On"/*Chicago*
"The Hands That Built America"/*Gangs of New York*
2003
★"Into the West"/*Lord of the Rings: The Return of the King*
"A Kiss at the End of the Rainbow"/*A Mighty Wind*
"Belleville Rendez-Vous"/*The Triplets of Belleville*
"Scarlet Tide"/*Cold Mountain*
2004
★"Al Otro Lado Del Rio"/*The Motorcycle Diaries*
"Accidently in Love"/*Shrek 2*
"Believe"/*The Polar Express*
"Learn to be Lonely"/*The Phantom of the Opera*
2005
★"It's Hard Out Here for a Pimp"/*Hustle & Flow*
"In the Deep"/*Crash*
"Travelin' Thru"/*Transamerica*
2006
★"I Need to Wake Up"/*An Inconvenient Truth*
"Listen"/*Dreamgirls*
"Love You I Do"/*Dreamgirls*
"Our Town"/*Cars*
"Patience"/*Dreamgirls*
2007
★"Falling Slowly"/*Once*
"Happy Working Song"/*Enchanted*
"Raise It Up"/*August Rush*
"So Close"/*Enchanted*
"That's How You Know"/*Enchanted*
2008
★"Jai Ho"/*Slumdog Millionaire*
"Down to Earth"/*WALL-E*
"O Saya"/*Slumdog Millionaire*
2009
★"The Weary Kind"/*Crazy Heart*
"Almost There"/*The Princess and the Frog*
"Down in New Orleans"/*The Princess and the Frog*
"Loin de Paname"/*Paris 36*
"Take It All"/*Nine*

SOUND

1933
★*A Farewell to Arms*
42nd Street
Gold Diggers of 1933
I Am a Fugitive from a Chain Gang
1934
★*One Night of Love*
Cleopatra
The Gay Divorcee
Imitation of Life
Viva Villa!
1935
★*Naughty Marietta*
The Bride of Frankenstein
Captain Blood
I Dream Too Much
The Lives of a Bengal Lancer
1936
★*San Francisco*
The Charge of the Light Brigade
The Dark Angel
Dodsworth
General Spanky
Mr. Deeds Goes to Town
The Texas Rangers
That Girl from Paris
Three Smart Girls
1937
★*The Hurricane*
The Girl Said No
In Old Chicago
The Life of Emile Zola
Lost Horizon
Maytime
100 Men and a Girl
Topper
1938
★*The Cowboy and the Lady*
Four Daughters
Sweethearts
That Certain Age
Vivacious Lady
You Can't Take It with You
1939
Balalaika
Gone with the Wind
Goodbye, Mr. Chips
The Hunchback of Notre Dame
Mr. Smith Goes to Washington
Of Mice and Men
The Private Lives of Elizabeth & Essex
The Rains Came
1940
★*Strike Up the Band*
Captain Caution
The Grapes of Wrath
The Howards of Virginia
Kitty Foyle
Our Town
The Sea Hawk
1941
★*That Hamilton Woman*
Ball of Fire
The Chocolate Soldier
Citizen Kane
How Green Was My Valley
Sergeant York
Too Many Husbands
Topper Returns
1942
★*Yankee Doodle Dandy*
Arabian Nights
Bambi
Flying Tigers
Mrs. Miniver
Once Upon a Honeymoon
The Pride of the Yankees
The Road to Morocco
You Were Never Lovelier
1943
★*This Land Is Mine*
Madame Curie
The North Star
The Phantom of the Opera
Sahara
So This Is Washington
The Song of Bernadette
This Above All
This Above All
This Is the Army
War of the Wildcats
1944
★*Wilson*
Casanova Brown
Cover Girl
Double Indemnity
His Butler's Sister
Hollywood Canteen
1945
★*The Bells of St. Mary's*
Flame of the Barbary Coast
Lady on a Train
Leave Her to Heaven
Rhapsody in Blue
A Song to Remember
The Southerner
They Were Expendable
The Three Caballeros
Wonder Man
1946
★*The Jolson Story*
The Best Years of Our Lives
It's a Wonderful Life
1947
★*The Bishop's Wife*
Green Dolphin Street
T-Men
1948
★*The Snake Pit*
Johnny Belinda
The Smallest Show on Earth
1949
★*Twelve o'Clock High*
Sands of Iwo Jima
1950
★*All About Eve*
Cinderella
Trio
1951
★*The Great Caruso*
A Streetcar Named Desire
Two Tickets to Broadway
1952
Hans Christian Andersen
The Promoter
The Quiet Man
1953
★*From Here to Eternity*
Calamity Jane
Knights of the Round Table
The War of the Worlds
With a Song in My Heart
1954
★*The Glenn Miller Story*
Brigadoon
The Caine Mutiny
Rear Window
Susan Slept Here
1955
★*Oklahoma!*
Love Is a Many-Splendored Thing
Love Me or Leave Me
Mister Roberts
Not as a Stranger
1956
★*The King and I*
The Brave One
The Eddy Duchin Story
Friendly Persuasion
The Ten Commandments
1957
★*Sayonara*
Gunfight at the O.K. Corral
Les Girls
Pal Joey
Witness for the Prosecution
1958
★*South Pacific*
I Want to Live!
A Time to Love & a Time to Die
Vertigo
The Young Lions
1959
★*Ben-Hur*
Journey to the Center of the Earth
The Nun's Story
1960
★*The Alamo*
The Apartment
Cimarron
Sunrise at Campobello
1961
★*West Side Story*
The Children's Hour
Flower Drum Song
The Guns of Navarone
The Parent Trap
1962
★*Lawrence of Arabia*
Bon Voyage!
The Music Man
That Touch of Mink
What Ever Happened to Baby Jane?
1963
★*How the West Was Won*
Bye, Bye, Birdie
Captain Newman, M.D.
Cleopatra
It's a Mad, Mad, Mad, Mad World
1964
★*My Fair Lady*
Becket
Father Goose
Mary Poppins
The Unsinkable Molly Brown
1965
★*The Sound of Music*
The Agony and the Ecstasy
Doctor Zhivago
The Great Race
Shenandoah
1966
★*Grand Prix*
Gambit
Hawaii
The Sand Pebbles
Who's Afraid of Virginia Woolf?
1967
★*In the Heat of the Night*
Camelot
The Dirty Dozen
Doctor Dolittle
Thoroughly Modern Millie
1968
★*Oliver!*
Bullitt
Finian's Rainbow
Funny Girl
Star!
1969
★*Hello, Dolly!*
Anne of the Thousand Days
Butch Cassidy and the Sundance Kid
Marooned
1970
★*Patton*
Airport
Ryan's Daughter
Tora! Tora! Tora!
Woodstock
1971
★*Fiddler on the Roof*
Diamonds Are Forever
The French Connection
Kotch
Mary, Queen of Scots
1972
★*Cabaret*
Butterflies Are Free
The Candidate
The Godfather
The Poseidon Adventure
1973
★*The Exorcist*
The Day of the Dolphin
The Paper Chase
Paper Moon
The Sting
1974
★*Earthquake*
Chinatown
The Conversation
The Towering Inferno
Young Frankenstein
1975
★*Jaws*
Bite the Bullet
Funny Lady
The Hindenburg
The Wind and the Lion
1976
★*All the President's Men*
King Kong
Rocky
Silver Streak
A Star Is Born
1977
★*Star Wars*
Close Encounters of the Third Kind
The Deep
Sorcerer
The Turning Point
1978
★*The Deer Hunter*
The Buddy Holly Story
Days of Heaven
Hooper
Superman: The Movie
1979
★*Apocalypse Now*
The Electric Horseman
Meteor
1941
The Rose
1980
★*The Empire Strikes Back*
Coal Miner's Daughter
Fame
Raging Bull
1981
★*Raiders of the Lost Ark*
On Golden Pond
Outland
Pennies from Heaven
Reds
1982
★*Gandhi*
Das Boot
E.T.: The Extra-Terrestrial
Tootsie
Tron
1983
★*The Right Stuff*
Never Cry Wolf
Return of the Jedi
Terms of Endearment
WarGames

★ = *winner*

1984
★Amadeus
Dune
A Passage to India
The River
2010: The Year We Make Contact
1985
★Out of Africa
Back to the Future
A Chorus Line
Ladyhawke
Silverado
1986
★Platoon
Aliens
Heartbreak Ridge
Star Trek 4: The Voyage Home
Top Gun
1987
★The Last Emperor
Empire of the Sun
Lethal Weapon
RoboCop
The Witches of Eastwick
1988
★Bird
Die Hard
Gorillas in the Mist
Mississippi Burning
Who Framed Roger Rabbit
1989
★Glory
The Abyss
Black Rain
Born on the Fourth of July
Indiana Jones and the Last Crusade
1990
★Dances with Wolves
Days of Thunder
Dick Tracy
The Hunt for Red October
Total Recall
1991
★Terminator 2: Judgment Day
Backdraft
Beauty and the Beast
JFK
The Silence of the Lambs
1992
★The Last of the Mohicans
Aladdin
A Few Good Men
Under Siege
Unforgiven
1993
★Jurassic Park
Cliffhanger
The Fugitive
Geronimo: An American Legend
Schindler's List
1994
★Speed
Clear and Present Danger
Forrest Gump
Legends of the Fall
The Shawshank Redemption
1995
★Apollo 13
Batman Forever
Braveheart
Crimson Tide
Waterworld
1996
★The English Patient
Evita
Independence Day
The Rock
Twister
1997
★Titanic
Air Force One
Con Air
Contact
L.A. Confidential
1998
★Saving Private Ryan
Armageddon
The Mask of Zorro
Shakespeare in Love
The Thin Red Line
1999
★The Matrix
The Green Mile
The Insider
The Mummy
Star Wars: Episode 1—The Phantom Menace
2000
★Gladiator
The Patriot
The Perfect Storm
U-571
2001
★Black Hawk Down
Amelie
Lord of the Rings: The Fellowship of the Ring
Moulin Rouge
Pearl Harbor
2002
★Chicago
Gangs of New York
Lord of the Rings: The Two Towers
Road to Perdition
Spider-Man
2003
★Lord of the Rings: The Return of the King
The Last Samurai
Lord of the Rings: The Return of the King
Master and Commander: The Far Side of the World
Pirates of the Caribbean: The Curse of the Black Pearl
Seabiscuit
2004
★Ray
The Aviator
The Incredibles
The Polar Express
Spider-Man 2
2005
★King Kong
The Chronicles of Narnia: The Lion, the Witch and the Wardrobe
Memoirs of a Geisha
Walk the Line
War of the Worlds
2006
★Dreamgirls
Apocalypto
Blood Diamond
Flags of Our Fathers
Pirates of the Caribbean: Dead Man's Chest
2007
★The Bourne Ultimatum
No Country for Old Men
Ratatouille
3:10 to Yuma
Transformers
2008
★Slumdog Millionaire
The Curious Case of Benjamin Button
The Dark Knight
WALL-E
Wanted
2009
★The Hurt Locker
Avatar
Inglourious Basterds
Star Trek
Transformers: Revenge of the Fallen

SOUND EFFECTS EDITING

1963
★It's a Mad, Mad, Mad, Mad World
1964
★Goldfinger
1965
★The Great Race
1966
★Grand Prix
1967
★The Dirty Dozen
1975
★The Hindenburg
1977
★Close Encounters of the Third Kind
1979
★The Black Stallion
1986
★Aliens
1990
★The Hunt for Red October
1991
★Terminator 2: Judgment Day
1992
★Bram Stoker's Dracula
Aladdin
Under Siege
1993
★Jurassic Park
Cliffhanger
The Fugitive
1996
★The Ghost and the Darkness
Daylight
The English Patient
1997
★Titanic
Face/Off
The Fifth Element
1998
★Saving Private Ryan
Armageddon
The Mask of Zorro
2000
★U-571
Space Cowboys
2003
★Master and Commander: The Far Side of the World
Finding Nemo
Master and Commander: The Far Side of the World
2004
★The Incredibles
The Polar Express
Spider-Man 2
2006
★Letters from Iwo Jima
Apocalypto
Blood Diamond
Flags of Our Fathers
Pirates of the Caribbean: Dead Man's Chest
2007
★The Bourne Ultimatum
No Country for Old Men
Ratatouille
There Will Be Blood
Transformers
2008
★The Dark Knight
Iron Man
Slumdog Millionaire
WALL-E
Wanted
2009
★The Hurt Locker
Avatar
Inglourious Basterds
Star Trek
Up

ADAPTED SCREENPLAY

1928
The Jazz Singer
1931
★Cimarron
Criminal Code
Little Caesar
1932
Arrowsmith
Dr. Jekyll and Mr. Hyde
1933
★Little Women
Lady for a Day
1934
★It Happened One Night
The Thin Man
Viva Villa!
1956
★Around the World in 80 Days
Baby Doll
Friendly Persuasion
Giant
Lust for Life
1957
★The Bridge on the River Kwai
Heaven Knows, Mr. Allison
Peyton Place
Sayonara
Twelve Angry Men
1958
★Gigi
Cat on a Hot Tin Roof
The Horse's Mouth
I Want to Live!
Separate Tables
1959
★Room at the Top
Anatomy of a Murder
Ben-Hur
The Nun's Story
Some Like It Hot
1960
★Elmer Gantry
Inherit the Wind
The Sundowners
Tunes of Glory
1961
★Judgment at Nuremberg
Breakfast at Tiffany's
The Guns of Navarone
The Hustler
West Side Story
1962
★To Kill a Mockingbird
David and Lisa
Lawrence of Arabia
Lolita
The Miracle Worker
1963
★Tom Jones
Captain Newman, M.D.
Hud
Lilies of the Field
Sundays & Cybele
1964
★Becket
Dr. Strangelove, or: How I Learned to Stop Worrying and Love the Bomb
Mary Poppins
My Fair Lady
Zorba the Greek
1965
★Doctor Zhivago
Cat Ballou
The Collector
Ship of Fools
A Thousand Clowns
1966
★A Man for All Seasons
Alfie
Cool Hand Luke
The Professionals
The Russians Are Coming, the Russians Are Coming
Who's Afraid of Virginia Woolf?
1967
★In the Heat of the Night
The Graduate
In Cold Blood
Ulysses
1968
★The Lion in Winter
The Odd Couple
Oliver!
Rachel, Rachel
Rosemary's Baby
1969
★Midnight Cowboy
Anne of the Thousand Days
Goodbye Columbus
They Shoot Horses, Don't They?
Z
1970
★M*A*S*H
Airport
I Never Sang for My Father
Lovers and Other Strangers
Women in Love
1971
★The French Connection
A Clockwork Orange
The Conformist
The Garden of the Finzi-Continis
The Last Picture Show
1972
★The Godfather
Cabaret
The Emigrants
Pete 'n' Tillie
Sounder
1973
★The Exorcist
The Last Detail
The Paper Chase
Paper Moon
Serpico
1974
★The Godfather, Part 2
The Apprenticeship of Duddy Kravitz
Lenny
Murder on the Orient Express
Young Frankenstein
1975
★One Flew Over the Cuckoo's Nest
Barry Lyndon
The Man Who Would Be King
The Scent of a Woman
The Sunshine Boys
1976
★All the President's Men
Bound for Glory
The Seven-Per-Cent Solution
Voyage of the Damned
1977
★Julia
Equus
I Never Promised You a Rose Garden
Oh, God!
That Obscure Object of Desire
1978
★Midnight Express
Bloodbrothers
California Suite
Heaven Can Wait
Same Time, Next Year
1979
★Kramer vs. Kramer
Apocalypse Now
La Cage aux Folles
A Little Romance
Norma Rae
1980
★Ordinary People
Breaker Morant
Coal Miner's Daughter
The Elephant Man
The Stunt Man
1981
★On Golden Pond
The French Lieutenant's Woman
Pennies from Heaven
Prince of the City
Ragtime
1982
★Missing
Das Boot
Sophie's Choice
The Verdict
Victor/Victoria
1983
★Terms of Endearment
Betrayal
The Dresser
Educating Rita
Reuben, Reuben
1984
★Amadeus
Greystoke: The Legend of Tarzan, Lord of the Apes
The Killing Fields
A Passage to India
A Soldier's Story
1985
★Out of Africa
The Color Purple
Kiss of the Spider Woman
Prizzi's Honor
The Trip to Bountiful
1986
★A Room with a View
Children of a Lesser God
The Color of Money
Crimes of the Heart
Stand by Me
1987
★The Last Emperor
The Dead
Fatal Attraction
Full Metal Jacket
My Life As a Dog
1988
★Dangerous Liaisons
The Accidental Tourist

★ = winner

Gorillas in the Mist
Little Dorrit, Film 1: Nobody's Fault
The Unbearable Lightness of Being

1989
★Driving Miss Daisy
Born on the Fourth of July
Enemies, a Love Story
Field of Dreams
My Left Foot

1990
★Dances with Wolves
Awakenings
Goodfellas
The Grifters
Reversal of Fortune

1991
★The Silence of the Lambs
Europa, Europa
Fried Green Tomatoes
JFK
The Prince of Tides

1992
★Howard's End
Enchanted April
The Player
A River Runs Through It
Scent of a Woman

1993
★Schindler's List
The Age of Innocence
In the Name of the Father
The Remains of the Day
Shadowlands

1994
★Forrest Gump
The Madness of King George
Nobody's Fool
Quiz Show
The Shawshank Redemption

1995
★Sense and Sensibility
Apollo 13
Babe
Leaving Las Vegas
The Postman

1996
★Sling Blade
The Crucible
The English Patient
Hamlet
Trainspotting

1997
★L.A. Confidential
Donnie Brasco
The Sweet Hereafter
Wag the Dog
The Wings of the Dove

1998
★Gods and Monsters
Out of Sight
Primary Colors
A Simple Plan
The Thin Red Line

1999
★The Cider House Rules
Election
The Green Mile
The Insider
The Talented Mr. Ripley

2000
★Traffic
Chocolat
Crouching Tiger, Hidden Dragon
O Brother Where Art Thou?
Wonder Boys

2001
★A Beautiful Mind
Ghost World
In the Bedroom
Lord of the Rings: The Fellowship of the Ring
Shrek

2002
★The Pianist
About a Boy
Adaptation
Chicago
The Hours

2003
★Lord of the Rings: The Return of the King
American Splendor
City of God
Mystic River
Seabiscuit

2004
★Sideways
Before Sunset
Finding Neverland
Million Dollar Baby
The Motorcycle Diaries

2005
★Brokeback Mountain
Capote
The Constant Gardener
A History of Violence
Munich

2006
★The Departed
Borat: Cultural Learnings of America for Make Benefit Glorious Nation of Kazakhstan
Children of Men
Little Children
Notes on a Scandal

2007
★No Country for Old Men
Atonement
Away From Her
The Diving Bell and the Butterfly
There Will Be Blood

2008
★Slumdog Millionaire
The Curious Case of Benjamin Button
Doubt
Frost/Nixon
The Reader

2009
★Precious: Based on the Novel by Sapphire
District 9
An Education
In the Loop
Up in the Air

ORIGINAL SCREENPLAY

1940
★The Great McGinty
Angels Over Broadway
Foreign Correspondent
The Great Dictator

1941
★Citizen Kane
The Devil & Miss Jones
Sergeant York

1942
★Woman of the Year
One of Our Aircraft Is Missing
The Road to Morocco
Wake Island

1943
Air Force
In Which We Serve
The North Star
So Proudly We Hail

1944
★Wilson
Hail the Conquering Hero
Miracle of Morgan's Creek
Two Girls and a Sailor
A Wing and a Prayer

1945
Dillinger

1946
★The Seventh Veil
The Blue Dahlia
Children of Paradise
Notorious
The Road to Utopia
To Each His Own

1947
★The Bachelor and the Bobby-Soxer
Body and Soul
A Double Life
Monsieur Verdoux
Shoeshine

1956
★The Red Balloon
La Strada
The Ladykillers

1974
★Chinatown
Alice Doesn't Live Here Anymore
The Conversation
Day for Night
Harry and Tonto

1975
★Dog Day Afternoon
Amarcord
And Now My Love
Lies My Father Told Me
Shampoo

1976
★Network
Cousin, Cousine
The Front
Rocky
Seven Beauties

1977
★Annie Hall
The Goodbye Girl
The Late Show
Star Wars
The Turning Point

1978
★Coming Home
Autumn Sonata
The Deer Hunter
Interiors
An Unmarried Woman

1979
★Breaking Away
All That Jazz
And Justice for All
The China Syndrome
Manhattan

1980
★Melvin and Howard
Brubaker
Fame
Mon Oncle d'Amerique
Private Benjamin

1981
★Chariots of Fire
Absence of Malice
Arthur
Atlantic City
Reds

1982
★Gandhi
Diner
E.T.: The Extra-Terrestrial
An Officer and a Gentleman
Tootsie

1983
★Tender Mercies
The Big Chill
Fanny and Alexander
Silkwood
WarGames

1984
★Places in the Heart
Beverly Hills Cop
Broadway Danny Rose
El Norte
Splash

1985
★Witness
Back to the Future
Brazil
The Official Story
The Purple Rose of Cairo

1986
★Hannah and Her Sisters
Crocodile Dundee
My Beautiful Laundrette
Platoon
Salvador

1987
★Moonstruck
Au Revoir les Enfants
Broadcast News
Hope and Glory
Radio Days

1988
★Rain Man
Big
Bull Durham
A Fish Called Wanda
Running on Empty

1989
★Dead Poets Society
Crimes & Misdemeanors
Do the Right Thing
sex, lies and videotape
When Harry Met Sally...

1990
★Ghost
Alice
Avalon
Green Card
Metropolitan

1991
★Thelma & Louise
Boyz N the Hood
Bugsy
The Fisher King
Grand Canyon

1992
★The Crying Game
Husbands and Wives
Lorenzo's Oil
Passion Fish
Unforgiven

1993
★The Piano
Dave
In the Line of Fire
Philadelphia
Sleepless in Seattle

1994
★Pulp Fiction
Bullets over Broadway
Four Weddings and a Funeral
Heavenly Creatures
Trois Couleurs: Rouge

1995
★The Usual Suspects
Braveheart
Mighty Aphrodite
Nixon
Toy Story

1996
★Fargo
Jerry Maguire
Lone Star
Secrets and Lies
Shine

1997
★Good Will Hunting
As Good As It Gets
Boogie Nights
Deconstructing Harry
The Full Monty

1998
★Shakespeare in Love
Bulworth
Life Is Beautiful
Saving Private Ryan
The Truman Show

1999
★American Beauty
Being John Malkovich
Magnolia
The Sixth Sense
Topsy Turvy

2000
★Almost Famous
Billy Elliot
Erin Brockovich
Gladiator
You Can Count On Me

2001
★Gosford Park
Amelie
Memento
Monster's Ball
The Royal Tenenbaums

2002
★Talk to Her
Far from Heaven
Gangs of New York
My Big Fat Greek Wedding
Y Tu Mama Tambien

2003
★Lost in Translation
The Barbarian Invasions
Dirty Pretty Things
Finding Nemo
In America

2004
★Eternal Sunshine of the Spotless Mind
The Aviator
Hotel Rwanda
The Incredibles
Vera Drake

2005
★Crash
Good Night, and Good Luck
Match Point
The Squid and the Whale
Syriana

2006
★Little Miss Sunshine
Babel
Letters from Iwo Jima
Pan's Labyrinth
The Queen

2007
★Juno
Lars and the Real Girl
Michael Clayton
Ratatouille
The Savages

2008
★Milk
Frozen River
Happy-Go-Lucky
In Bruges
Milk
WALL-E

2009
★The Hurt Locker
Inglourious Basterds
The Messenger
A Serious Man
Up

SCREENPLAY

1935
★The Informer
The Lives of a Bengal Lancer
Mutiny on the Bounty

1936
After the Thin Man
Dodsworth
Mr. Deeds Goes to Town
My Man Godfrey

1937
★The Life of Emile Zola
The Awful Truth
Captains Courageous
Stage Door

1938
★Pygmalion
The Citadel
Four Daughters
You Can't Take It with You

1939
★Gone with the Wind
Goodbye, Mr. Chips
Wuthering Heights

1940
★The Philadelphia Story
The Grapes of Wrath
Kitty Foyle
The Long Voyage Home
Rebecca

1941
★Here Comes Mr. Jordan
How Green Was My Valley
The Little Foxes
The Maltese Falcon

1942
★Mrs. Miniver
The Forty-Ninth Parallel
The Pride of the Yankees
Random Harvest
Talk of the Town

1943
★Casablanca
The More the Merrier
The Song of Bernadette
Watch on the Rhine

1944
★Going My Way
Double Indemnity
Gaslight
Laura
Meet Me in St. Louis

1945
★The Lost Weekend
Mildred Pierce
A Tree Grows in Brooklyn

1946
★The Best Years of Our Lives
Anna and the King of Siam
Brief Encounter
The Killers
Open City

1947
★Miracle on 34th Street
Boomerang

★ = winner

Crossfire
Gentleman's Agreement
Great Expectations
1948
★Treasure of the Sierra Madre
Johnny Belinda
The Search
The Snake Pit
1949
★A Letter to Three Wives
All the King's Men
The Bicycle Thief
Champion
The Fallen Idol
1950
★All About Eve
The Asphalt Jungle
Born Yesterday
Broken Arrow
Father of the Bride
1951
★A Place in the Sun
The African Queen
Detective Story
La Ronde
A Streetcar Named Desire
1952
★The Bad and the Beautiful
Five Fingers
High Noon
The Man in the White Suit
The Quiet Man
1953
★From Here to Eternity
The Cruel Sea
Lili
Roman Holiday
Shane
Titanic
1954
★Country Girl
The Caine Mutiny
Rear Window
Sabrina
Seven Brides for Seven Brothers
1955
★Marty
Bad Day at Black Rock
Blackboard Jungle
East of Eden
Interrupted Melody
Love Me or Leave Me

STORY

1928
★Underworld
Last Command
1931
Public Enemy
Smart Money
1932
★The Champ
What Price Hollywood?
1933
The Prizefighter and the Lady
Rasputin and the Empress
1934
★Manhattan Melodrama
Hide-Out
1935
Broadway Melody of 1936
1936
★The Story of Louis Pasteur
Fury
The Great Ziegfeld
San Francisco
Three Smart Girls
1937
★A Star Is Born
In Old Chicago
100 Men and a Girl
1938
★Boys Town
Alexander's Ragtime Band
Angels with Dirty Faces
The Black Legion
Mad About Music
Test Pilot
1939
★Mr. Smith Goes to Washington
Bachelor Mother
Love Affair
Ninotchka
Young Mr. Lincoln
1940
Comrade X
Edison the Man
My Favorite Wife
The Westerner
1941
★Here Comes Mr. Jordan
Ball of Fire
The Lady Eve
Meet John Doe
Tom, Dick, and Harry
1942
★The Forty-Ninth Parallel
Holiday Inn
The Pride of the Yankees
Talk of the Town
Yankee Doodle Dandy
1943
★The Human Comedy
Action in the North Atlantic
Destination Tokyo
The More the Merrier
Shadow of a Doubt
1944
★Going My Way
A Guy Named Joe
Lifeboat
1945
★House on 92nd Street
Objective, Burma!
A Song to Remember
1946
Dark Mirror
The Strange Love of Martha Ivers
The Stranger
1947
★Miracle on 34th Street
Kiss of Death
Smash-Up: The Story of a Woman
1948
★The Search
Louisiana Story
The Naked City
Red River
The Red Shoes
1949
★The Stratton Story
Come to the Stable
It Happens Every Spring
Sands of Iwo Jima
White Heat
1950
★Panic in the Streets
Bitter Rice
The Gunfighter
1951
Bullfighter & the Lady
Here Comes the Groom
When Willie Comes Marching Home
1952
★The Greatest Show on Earth
The Narrow Margin
Pride of St. Louis
1953
★Roman Holiday
Above and Beyond
Captain's Paradise
Hondo
Titanic
1954
★Broken Lance
Forbidden Games
There's No Business Like Show Business
1955
★Love Me or Leave Me
The Private War of Major Benson
Rebel without a Cause
The Sheep Has Five Legs
Strategic Air Command
1956
★The Brave One
The Eddy Duchin Story
High Society
The Proud Ones
Umberto D

STORY & SCREENPLAY

1949
★Battleground
Jolson Sings Again
Paisan
Passport to Pimlico
1950
★Sunset Boulevard
Adam's Rib
Caged
The Men
No Way Out
1951
★An American in Paris
David and Bathsheba
Go for Broke!
The Well
1952
★The Lavender Hill Mob
The Atomic City
Pat and Mike
Viva Zapata!
1953
★Titanic
The Band Wagon
The Desert Rats
The Naked Spur
1954
★On the Waterfront
The Barefoot Contessa
Genevieve
The Glenn Miller Story
1955
★Interrupted Melody
The Court Martial of Billy Mitchell
It's Always Fair Weather
Mr. Hulot's Holiday
The Seven Little Foys
1957
★Designing Woman
Funny Face
I Vitelloni
Man of a Thousand Faces
The Tin Star
1958
★The Defiant Ones
The Goddess
Houseboat
Teacher's Pet
1959
★Pillow Talk
The 400 Blows
North by Northwest
Operation Petticoat
Wild Strawberries
1960
★The Apartment
The Facts of Life
Hiroshima, Mon Amour
Never on Sunday
1961
★Splendor in the Grass
Ballad of a Soldier
La Dolce Vita
Lover Come Back
1962
★Divorce—Italian Style
Last Year at Marienbad
That Touch of Mink
Through a Glass Darkly
1963
★How the West Was Won
8 1/2
Love with the Proper Stranger
1964
★Father Goose
That Man from Rio
Alun Owen/A Hard Day's Night
1965
★Darling
Casanova '70
Those Magnificent Men in Their Flying Machines
The Train
Umbrellas of Cherbourg
1966
★A Man and a Woman
Blow-Up
The Fortune Cookie
Khartoum
The Naked Prey
1967
★Guess Who's Coming to Dinner
Bonnie & Clyde
Divorce American Style
Two for the Road
1968
★The Producers
The Battle of Algiers
Faces
Hot Millions
2001: A Space Odyssey
1969
★Butch Cassidy and the Sundance Kid
Bob & Carol & Ted & Alice
The Damned
Easy Rider
The Wild Bunch
1970
★Patton
Five Easy Pieces
Joe
Love Story
My Night at Maud's
1971
★The Hospital
Klute
Summer of '42
Sunday, Bloody Sunday
1972
★The Candidate
The Discreet Charm of the Bourgeoisie
Lady Sings the Blues
Murmur of the Heart
Young Winston
1973
★The Sting
American Graffiti
Cries and Whispers
Save the Tiger
A Touch of Class

WRITING

1929
The Leatherneck
Our Dancing Daughters
1930
All Quiet on the Western Front
Disraeli
The Divorcee
1931
Smart Money
1938
The Black Legion

FILM—FOREIGN LANGUAGE

1948
★Monsieur Vincent
1949
★The Bicycle Thief
1950
★The Walls of Malapaga
1951
★Rashomon
1952
★Forbidden Games
1954
★Gate of Hell
1955
★Samurai 1: Musashi Miyamoto
1956
★La Strada
The Burmese Harp
Gervaise
1957
★Nights of Cabiria
1958
★Mon Oncle
Big Deal on Madonna Street
1959
★Black Orpheus
The Bridge
The Great War
1960
★The Virgin Spring
Kapo
1961
★Through a Glass Darkly
1962
★Sundays & Cybele
1963
★8 1/2
Knife in the Water
1964
★Yesterday, Today and Tomorrow
Sallah
1965
★The Shop on Main Street
Kwaidan
Umbrellas of Cherbourg
Woman in the Dunes
1966
★A Man and a Woman
The Battle of Algiers
Loves of a Blonde
1967
★Closely Watched Trains
1968
★War and Peace
The Firemen's Ball
Stolen Kisses
1969
★Z
Battle of Neretva
1970
First Love
My Night at Maud's
Tristana
1971
★The Garden of the Finzi-Continis
Dodes 'ka-den
Tchaikovsky
1972
★The Discreet Charm of the Bourgeoisie
I Love You Rosa
1973
★Day for Night
The Deluge
The House on Chelouche Street
The Pedestrian
Turkish Delight
1974
★Amarcord
Cat's Play
1975
★Dersu Uzala
Land of Promise
Sandakan No. 8
The Scent of a Woman
1976
★Black and White in Color
Cousin, Cousine
Jacob the Liar
Nights and Days
Seven Beauties
1977
★Madame Rosa
Iphigenia
Operation Thunderbolt
A Special Day
That Obscure Object of Desire
1978
★Get Out Your Handkerchiefs
1979
★The Tin Drum
Maids of Wilko
Mama Turns a Hundred
A Simple Story
To Forget Venice
1980
★Moscow Does Not Believe in Tears
Kagemusha
The Last Metro
The Nest
1981
★Mephisto
The Boat Is Full
Man of Iron
Three Brothers
1982
Alsino and the Condor
Coup de Torchon
Flight of the Eagle
Private Life
1983
★Fanny and Alexander
Carmen
Entre-Nous
Le Bal
1984
★Dangerous Moves
Beyond the Walls
Camila
1985
★The Official Story
Angry Harvest

★ = winner

Colonel Redl
Three Men and a Cradle
When Father Was Away on Business
1986
★*The Assault*
Betty Blue
The Decline of the American Empire
My Sweet Little Village
1987
★*Babette's Feast*
Au Revoir les Enfants
The Family
Pathfinder
1988
★*Pelle the Conqueror*
Hanussen
The Music Teacher
Salaam Bombay!
Women on the Verge of a Nervous Breakdown
1989
★*Cinema Paradiso*
Camille Claudel
Jesus of Montreal
1990
★*Journey of Hope*
Cyrano de Bergerac
Ju Dou
The Nasty Girl
Open Doors
1991
★*Mediterraneo*
The Elementary School
The Ox
Raise the Red Lantern
Sweetie
1992
★*Indochine*
Children of Nature
Close to Eden
Daens
Schtonk
1993
★*Belle Epoque*
Farewell My Concubine
Hedd Wyn
The Scent of Green Papaya
The Wedding Banquet
1994
★*Burnt by the Sun*
Before the Rain
Eat Drink Man Woman
Farinelli
Strawberry and Chocolate
1995
★*Antonia's Line*
All Things Fair
Lamerica
O Quatrilho
The Star Maker
1996
★*Kolya*
★*Ridicule*
A Chef in Love
The Other Side of Sunday
Prisoner of the Mountains
Ridicule
1997
★*Character*
Beyond Silence
Four Days in September
Secrets of the Heart
The Thief
1998
★*Life Is Beautiful*
Central Station
The Grandfather
Tango

1999
★*All About My Mother*
East-West
Himalaya
Solomon and Gaenor
Under the Sun
2000
★*Crouching Tiger, Hidden Dragon*
Amores Perros
Divided We Fall
Everybody's Famous!
2001
★*No Man's Land*
Amelie
2002
★*Nowhere in Africa*
The Crime of Father Amaro
Elling
Lagaan: Once upon a Time in India
The Man Without a Past
Mondays in the Sun
The Son of the Bride
Zus & Zo
2003
★*The Barbarian Invasions*
2004
★*The Sea Inside*
2005
★*Tsotsi*
Paradise Now
2006
★*The Lives of Others*
Don't Tell
Pan's Labyrinth
2007
★*The Counterfeiters*
Beaufort
Katyn
2008
★*Departures*
The Class
12
Waltz with Bashir
2009
★*The Secret in Their Eyes*
Ajami
The Milk of Sorrow
A Prophet
The White Ribbon

VISUAL EFFECTS

1963
★*Cleopatra*
1964
★*Mary Poppins*
1965
★*Thunderball*
1966
★*Fantastic Voyage*
1967
★*Doctor Dolittle*
1968
★*2001: A Space Odyssey*
1969
★*Marooned*
1970
★*Tora! Tora! Tora!*
1971
★*Bedknobs and Broomsticks*
1972
★*The Poseidon Adventure*
1974
★*Earthquake*
1975
★*The Hindenburg*
1976
★*King Kong*
★*Logan's Run*
1977
★*Star Wars*
1978
★*Superman: The Movie*
1979
★*Alien*
1980
★*The Empire Strikes Back*
1981
★*Raiders of the Lost Ark*
1982
★*E.T.: The Extra-Terrestrial*
1983
★*Return of the Jedi*
1984
★*Indiana Jones and the Temple of Doom*
1985
★*Cocoon*
1986
★*Aliens*
1987
★*Innerspace*
1988
★*Who Framed Roger Rabbit*
1989
★*The Abyss*
1990
★*Total Recall*
1991
★*Terminator 2: Judgment Day*
Backdraft
Hook
1992
★*Death Becomes Her*
Alien 3
Batman Returns
1993
★*Jurassic Park*
Cliffhanger
The Nightmare Before Christmas
1994
★*Forrest Gump*
The Mask
True Lies
1995
★*Babe*
1996
★*Independence Day*
Dragonheart
Twister
1997
★*Titanic*
The Lost World: Jurassic Park 2
Starship Troopers
1998
★*What Dreams May Come*
Armageddon
Mighty Joe Young
1999
★*The Matrix*
Star Wars: Episode 1—The Phantom Menace
Stuart Little
2000
★*Gladiator*
Hollow Man
The Perfect Storm
2001
A. I.: Artificial Intelligence
Lord of the Rings: The Fellowship of the Ring
Pearl Harbor
2002
★*Lord of the Rings: The Two Towers*
Spider-Man
Star Wars: Episode 2—Attack of the Clones
2003
★*Lord of the Rings: The Return of the King*
Master and Commander: The Far Side of the World
Pirates of the Caribbean: The Curse of the Black Pearl
2004
★*Spider-Man 2*
Harry Potter and the Prisoner of Azkaban
I, Robot
2005
★*King Kong*
The Chronicles of Narnia: The Lion, the Witch and the Wardrobe
War of the Worlds
2006
★*Pirates of the Caribbean: Dead Man's Chest*
Poseidon
Superman Returns
2007
★*The Golden Compass*
Pirates of the Caribbean: At World's End
Transformers
2008
★*The Curious Case of Benjamin Button*
The Dark Knight
Iron Man
2009
★*Avatar*
District 9
Star Trek

ANIMATED FILM

2001
★*Shrek*
Jimmy Neutron: Boy Genius
Monsters, Inc.
2002
★*Spirited Away*
Ice Age
Lilo & Stitch
Spirit: Stallion of the Cimarron
Treasure Planet
2003
★*Finding Nemo*
Brother Bear
The Triplets of Belleville
2004
★*The Incredibles*
Shark Tale
Shrek 2
2005
★*Wallace & Gromit in The Curse of the Were-Rabbit*
Howl's Moving Castle
2006
★*Happy Feet*
Cars
Monster House
2007
★*Ratatouille*
Persepolis
Surf's Up
2008
★*WALL-E*
Bolt
Kung Fu Panda
2009
★*Up*
Coraline
Fantastic Mr. Fox
The Princess and the Frog
The Secret of Kells

BRITISH ACADEMY OF FILM AND TELEVISION ARTS

ACTOR

1952
★Marlon Brando/*Viva Zapata!*
1953
★Marlon Brando/*Julius Caesar*
★John Gielgud/*Julius Caesar*
1954
★Marlon Brando/*On the Waterfront*
★Kenneth More/*Doctor in the House*
1955
★Ernest Borgnine/*Marty*
★Laurence Olivier/*Richard III*
1956
★Francois Perier/*Gervaise*
1957
★Henry Fonda/*Twelve Angry Men*
★Alec Guinness/*The Bridge on the River Kwai*
1958
★Trevor Howard/*The Key*
★Sidney Poitier/*The Defiant Ones*
1959
★Jack Lemmon/*Some Like It Hot*
★Peter Sellers/*I'm All Right Jack*
1960
★Jack Lemmon/*The Apartment*
1961
★Peter Finch/*No Love for Johnnie*
★Paul Newman/*The Hustler*
1962
★Burt Lancaster/*Birdman of Alcatraz*
★Peter O'Toole/*Lawrence of Arabia*
1963
★Dirk Bogarde/*The Servant*
★Marcello Mastroianni/*Divorce—Italian Style*
1964
★Richard Attenborough/*Seance on a Wet Afternoon*
★Marcello Mastroianni/*Yesterday, Today and Tomorrow*
1965
★Dirk Bogarde/*Darling*
★Lee Marvin/*Cat Ballou*
1966
★Richard Burton/*Who's Afraid of Virginia Woolf?*
★Rod Steiger/*The Pawnbroker*
1967
★Paul Scofield/*A Man for All Seasons*
★Rod Steiger/*In the Heat of the Night*
1968
★Spencer Tracy/*Guess Who's Coming to Dinner*
1969
★Dustin Hoffman/*Midnight Cowboy*
1970
★Robert Redford/*Butch Cassidy and the Sundance Kid*
1971
★Peter Finch/*Sunday, Bloody Sunday*
1972
★Gene Hackman/*The French Connection*
1973
★Walter Matthau/*Pete 'n' Tillie*
1974
★Jack Nicholson/*Chinatown*
★Jack Nicholson/*The Last Detail*
1975
★Al Pacino/*Dog Day Afternoon*
1976
★Jack Nicholson/*One Flew Over the Cuckoo's Nest*
1977
★Peter Finch/*Network*
1978
★Richard Dreyfuss/*The Goodbye Girl*
1979
★Jack Lemmon/*The China Syndrome*
1980
★John Hurt/*The Elephant Man*
1981
★Burt Lancaster/*Atlantic City*
1982
★Ben Kingsley/*Gandhi*
1983
★Michael Caine/*Educating Rita*
★Dustin Hoffman/*Tootsie*
1984
★Haing S. Ngor/*The Killing Fields*
1985
★William Hurt/*Kiss of the Spider Woman*
1986
★Bob Hoskins/*Mona Lisa*
1987
★Sean Connery/*The Name of the Rose*
1988
★John Cleese/*A Fish Called Wanda*
1989
★Daniel Day-Lewis/*My Left Foot*
1990
★Philippe Noiret/*Cinema Paradiso*
1991
★Anthony Hopkins/*The Silence of the Lambs*
1992
★Robert Downey, Jr./*Chaplin*
1993
★Anthony Hopkins/*The Remains of the Day*
Daniel Day-Lewis/*In the Name of the Father*
1994
★Hugh Grant/*Four Weddings and a Funeral*
Anthony Hopkins/*Shadowlands*
Liam Neeson/*Schindler's List*

★ = *winner*

1995

★Nigel Hawthorne/*The Madness of King George*

Nicolas Cage/*Leaving Las Vegas*

Jonathan Pryce/*Carrington*

Massimo Troisi/*The Postman*

1996

★Geoffrey Rush/*Shine*

Ralph Fiennes/*The English Patient*

Ian McKellen/*Richard III*

Timothy Spall/*Secrets and Lies*

1997

★Robert Carlyle/*The Full Monty*

Billy Connolly/*Mrs. Brown*

Kevin Spacey/*L.A. Confidential*

Ray Winstone/*Nil by Mouth*

1998

★Roberto Benigni/*Life Is Beautiful*

Michael Caine/*Little Voice*

Joseph Fiennes/*Shakespeare in Love*

Tom Hanks/*Saving Private Ryan*

1999

★Kevin Spacey/*American Beauty*

Jim Broadbent/*Topsy Turvy*

Russell Crowe/*The Insider*

Ralph Fiennes/*The End of the Affair*

Om Puri/*East Is East*

2000

★Jamie Bell/*Billy Elliot*

2001

★Russell Crowe/*A Beautiful Mind*

Jim Broadbent/*Iris*

Ian McKellen/*Lord of the Rings: The Fellowship of the Ring*

Kevin Spacey/*The Shipping News*

Tom Wilkinson/*In the Bedroom*

2002

★Daniel Day-Lewis/*Gangs of New York*

Adrien Brody/*The Pianist*

Nicolas Cage/*Adaptation*

Michael Caine/*The Quiet American*

Jack Nicholson/*About Schmidt*

2003

★Johnny Depp/*Pirates of the Caribbean: The Curse of the Black Pearl*

★Bill Murray/*Lost in Translation*

Benicio Del Toro/*21 Grams*

Jude Law/*Cold Mountain*

Sean Penn/*Mystic River*

Sean Penn/*21 Grams*

2004

★Jamie Foxx/*Ray*

Gael Garcia Bernal/*The Motorcycle Diaries*

Jim Carrey/*Eternal Sunshine of the Spotless Mind*

Johnny Depp/*Finding Neverland*

Leonardo DiCaprio/*The Aviator*

2005

★Philip Seymour Hoffman/*Capote*

Ralph Fiennes/*The Constant Gardener*

Terrence Howard/*Hustle & Flow*

Heath Ledger/*Brokeback Mountain*

Joaquin Rafael (Leaf) Phoenix/*Walk the Line*

David Strathairn/*Good Night, and Good Luck*

2006

★Forest Whitaker/*The Last King of Scotland*

Daniel Craig/*Casino Royale*

Leonardo DiCaprio/*The Departed*

Richard Griffiths/*The History Boys*

Peter O'Toole/*Venus*

2007

★Daniel Day-Lewis/*There Will Be Blood*

George Clooney/*Michael Clayton*

James McAvoy/*Atonement*

Viggo Mortensen/*Eastern Promises*

Ulrich Muehe/*The Lives of Others*

2008

★Mickey Rourke/*The Wrestler*

Frank Langella/*Frost/Nixon*

Dev Patel/*Slumdog Millionaire*

Sean Penn/*Milk*

Brad Pitt/*The Curious Case of Benjamin Button*

2009

★Colin Firth/*A Single Man*

Jeff Bridges/*Crazy Heart*

George Clooney/*Up in the Air*

Jeremy Renner/*The Hurt Locker*

Andy Serkis/*Sex & Drugs & Rock & Roll*

ACTOR—SUPPORTING

1969

★Laurence Olivier/*Oh! What a Lovely War*

1971

★Edward Fox/*The Go-Between*

1972

★Ben Johnson/*The Last Picture Show*

1973

★Arthur Lowe/*O Lucky Man!*

1974

★John Gielgud/*Murder on the Orient Express*

1975

★Fred Astaire/*The Towering Inferno*

1976

★Brad Dourif/*One Flew Over the Cuckoo's Nest*

1977

★Edward Fox/*A Bridge Too Far*

1978

★John Hurt/*Midnight Express*

1979

★Robert Duvall/*Apocalypse Now*

1981

★Ian Holm/*Chariots of Fire*

1982

★Jack Nicholson/*Reds*

1983

★Denholm Elliott/*Trading Places*

1984

★Denholm Elliott/*A Private Function*

1985

★Denholm Elliott/*Defense of the Realm*

1986

★Ray McAnally/*The Mission*

1987

★Daniel Auteuil/*Jean de Florette*

1988

★Michael Palin/*A Fish Called Wanda*

1989

★Ray McAnally/*My Left Foot*

1990

★Salvatore Cascio/*Cinema Paradiso*

1991

★Alan Rickman/*Robin Hood: Prince of Thieves*

1992

★Gene Hackman/*Unforgiven*

1993

★Ralph Fiennes/*Schindler's List*

Tommy Lee Jones/*The Fugitive*

John Malkovich/*In the Line of Fire*

1994

★Samuel L. Jackson/*Pulp Fiction*

Ben Kingsley/*Schindler's List*

1995

★Tim Roth/*Rob Roy*

Ian Holm/*The Madness of King George*

Martin Landau/*Ed Wood*

Alan Rickman/*Sense and Sensibility*

1996

★Paul Scofield/*The Crucible*

John Gielgud/*Shine*

Edward Norton/*Primal Fear*

Alan Rickman/*Michael Collins*

1997

★Tom Wilkinson/*The Full Monty*

Mark Addy/*The Full Monty*

Rupert Everett/*My Best Friend's Wedding*

Burt Reynolds/*Boogie Nights*

1998

★Geoffrey Rush/*Shakespeare in Love*

Ed Harris/*The Truman Show*

Geoffrey Rush/*Elizabeth*

Tom Wilkinson/*Shakespeare in Love*

1999

★Jude Law/*The Talented Mr. Ripley*

Wes Bentley/*American Beauty*

Michael Caine/*The Cider House Rules*

Rhys Ifans/*Notting Hill*

Timothy Spall/*Topsy Turvy*

2000

★Benicio Del Toro/*Traffic*

2001

★Jim Broadbent/*Moulin Rouge*

Hugh Bonneville/*Iris*

Robbie Coltrane/*Harry Potter and the Sorcerer's Stone*

Colin Firth/*Bridget Jones's Diary*

Eddie Murphy/*Shrek*

2002

★Christopher Walken/*Catch Me If You Can*

Chris Cooper/*Adaptation*

Ed Harris/*The Hours*

Alfred Molina/*Frida*

Paul Newman/*Road to Perdition*

2003

★Bill Nighy/*Love Actually*

Paul Bettany/*Master and Commander: The Far Side of the World*

Albert Finney/*Big Fish*

Ian McKellen/*Lord of the Rings: The Return of the King*

Tim Robbins/*Mystic River*

2004

★Clive Owen/*Closer*

Alan Alda/*The Aviator*

Philip Davis/*Vera Drake*

Jamie Foxx/*Collateral*

Rodrigo de la Serna/*The Motorcycle Diaries*

2005

★Jake Gyllenhaal/*Brokeback Mountain*

Don Cheadle/*Crash*

George Clooney/*Good Night, and Good Luck*

George Clooney/*Syriana*

Matt Dillon/*Crash*

2006

★Alan Arkin/*Little Miss Sunshine*

James McAvoy/*The Last King of Scotland*

Jack Nicholson/*The Departed*

Leslie Phillips/*Venus*

Brad Pitt/*Burn After Reading*

Michael Sheen/*The Queen*

2007

★Javier Bardem/*No Country for Old Men*

Paul Franklin Dano/*There Will Be Blood*

Philip Seymour Hoffman/*Charlie Wilson's War*

Tommy Lee Jones/*No Country for Old Men*

Tom Wilkinson/*Michael Clayton*

2008

★Heath Ledger/*The Dark Knight*

Robert Downey, Jr./*Tropic Thunder*

Brendan Gleeson/*In Bruges*

Philip Seymour Hoffman/*Doubt*

2009

★Christoph Waltz/*Inglourious Basterds*

Alec Baldwin/*It's Complicated*

Christian McKay/*Me and Orson Welles*

Alfred Molina/*An Education*

Stanley Tucci/*The Lovely Bones*

ACTRESS

1952

★Vivien Leigh/*A Streetcar Named Desire*

1953

★Leslie Caron/*Lili*

★Audrey Hepburn/*Roman Holiday*

1955

★Betsy Blair/*Marty*

★Katie Johnson/*The Ladykillers*

1956

★Anna Magnani/*The Rose Tattoo*

1958

★Simone Signoret/*Room at the Top*

1959

★Audrey Hepburn/*The Nun's Story*

★Shirley MacLaine/*Ask Any Girl*

1960

★Shirley MacLaine/*The Apartment*

★Rachel Roberts/*Saturday Night and Sunday Morning*

1961

★Sophia Loren/*Two Women*

1962

★Anne Bancroft/*The Miracle Worker*

1963

★Patricia Neal/*Hud*

★Rachel Roberts/*This Sporting Life*

1964

★Audrey Hepburn/*Charade*

1965

★Julie Christie/*Darling*

★Patricia Neal/*In Harm's Way*

1966

★Elizabeth Taylor/*Who's Afraid of Virginia Woolf?*

1967

★Anouk Aimee/*A Man and a Woman*

1968

★Katharine Hepburn/*Guess Who's Coming to Dinner*

1969

★Maggie Smith/*The Prime of Miss Jean Brodie*

1970

★Katharine Ross/*Butch Cassidy and the Sundance Kid*

1971

★Glenda Jackson/*Sunday, Bloody Sunday*

1972

★Liza Minnelli/*Cabaret*

1973

★Delphine Seyrig/*The Discreet Charm of the Bourgeoisie*

1974

★Joanne Woodward/*Summer Wishes, Winter Dreams*

1975

★Ellen Burstyn/*Alice Doesn't Live Here Anymore*

1976

★Louise Fletcher/*One Flew Over the Cuckoo's Nest*

1977

★Diane Keaton/*Annie Hall*

1978

★Jane Fonda/*Julia*

1979

★Jane Fonda/*The China Syndrome*

1980

★Judy Davis/*My Brilliant Career*

1981

★Meryl Streep/*The French Lieutenant's Woman*

1982

★Katharine Hepburn/*On Golden Pond*

1983

★Julie Walters/*Educating Rita*

1984

★Maggie Smith/*A Private Function*

1985

★Peggy Ashcroft/*A Passage to India*

1986

★Maggie Smith/*A Room with a View*

1987

★Anne Bancroft/*84 Charing Cross Road*

1988

★Maggie Smith/*The Lonely Passion of Judith Hearne*

1989

★Pauline Collins/*Shirley Valentine*

1990

★Jessica Tandy/*Driving Miss Daisy*

1991

★Jodie Foster/*The Silence of the Lambs*

1992

★Emma Thompson/*Howard's End*

1993

★Holly Hunter/*The Piano*

Miranda Richardson/*Tom & Viv*

1994

★Susan Sarandon/*The Client*

Emma Thompson/*The Remains of the Day*

Debra Winger/*Shadowlands*

1995

★Emma Thompson/*Sense and Sensibility*

Nicole Kidman/*To Die For*

Helen Mirren/*The Madness of King George*

Elisabeth Shue/*Leaving Las Vegas*

1996

★Brenda Blethyn/*Secrets and Lies*

Frances McDormand/*Fargo*

Kristin Scott Thomas/*The English Patient*

Emily Watson/*Breaking the Waves*

1997

★Judi Dench/*Mrs. Brown*

Kim Basinger/*L.A. Confidential*

Helena Bonham Carter/*The Wings of the Dove*

Kathy Burke/*Nil by Mouth*

1998

★Cate Blanchett/*Elizabeth*

Jane Horrocks/*Little Voice*

Gwyneth Paltrow/*Shakespeare in Love*

Emily Watson/*Hilary and Jackie*

1999

★Annette Bening/*American Beauty*

Linda Bassett/*East Is East*

Julianne Moore/*The End of the Affair*

Emily Watson/*Angela's Ashes*

2000

★Julia Roberts/*Erin Brockovich*

2001

★Judi Dench/*Iris*

Nicole Kidman/*The Others*

Sissy Spacek/*In the Bedroom*

Audrey Tautou/*Amelie*

Renee Zellweger/*Bridget Jones's Diary*

★ = *winner*

2002
★Nicole Kidman/*The Hours*
Halle Berry/*Monster's Ball*
Salma Hayek/*Frida*
Meryl Streep/*The Hours*
Renee Zellweger/*Chicago*
2003
★Scarlett Johansson/*Lost in Translation*
Scarlett Johansson/*Girl with a Pearl Earring*
Uma Thurman/*Kill Bill Vol. 1*
Naomi Watts/*21 Grams*
2004
★Imelda Staunton/*Vera Drake*
Charlize Theron/*Monster*
Kate Winslet/*Eternal Sunshine of the Spotless Mind*
Kate Winslet/*Finding Neverland*
Zhang Ziyi/*House of Flying Daggers*
2005
★Reese Witherspoon/*Walk the Line*
Judi Dench/*Mrs. Henderson Presents*
Keira Knightley/*Pride and Prejudice*
Charlize Theron/*North Country*
Rachel Weisz/*The Constant Gardener*
Zhang Ziyi/*Memoirs of a Geisha*
2006
★Helen Mirren/*The Queen*
Penelope Cruz/*Volver*
Judi Dench/*Notes on a Scandal*
Meryl Streep/*The Devil Wears Prada*
Kate Winslet/*Little Children*
2007
★Marion Cotillard/*La Vie en Rose*
Cate Blanchett/*Elizabeth: The Golden Age*
Julie Christie/*Away From Her*
Keira Knightley/*Atonement*
Ellen Page/*Juno*
2008
★Kate Winslet/*The Reader*
Angelina Jolie/*Changeling*
Kristin Scott Thomas/*I've Loved You So Long*
Meryl Streep/*Doubt*
Kate Winslet/*Revolutionary Road*
Kate Winslet/*Revolutionary Road*
2009
★Carey Mulligan/*An Education*
Saoirse Ronan/*The Lovely Bones*
Gabourney "Gabby" Sidibe/*Precious: Based on the Novel by Sapphire*
Meryl Streep/*Julie & Julia*
Audrey Tautou/*Coco Before Chanel*

ACTRESS—SUPPORTING

1961
★Dora Bryan/*A Taste of Honey*
1969
★Celia Johnson/*The Prime of Miss Jean Brodie*
Mary Wimbush/*Oh! What a Lovely War*
1970
★Susannah York/*They Shoot Horses, Don't They?*
1971
★Margaret Leighton/*The Go-Between*
1972
★Cloris Leachman/*The Last Picture Show*
1973
★Valentina Cortese/*Day for Night*
1974
★Ingrid Bergman/*Murder on the Orient Express*
1975
★Diane Ladd/*Alice Doesn't Live Here Anymore*
1976
★Jodie Foster/*Taxi Driver*
1977
★Jenny Agutter/*Equus*
1978
★Geraldine Page/*Interiors*
★Vanessa Redgrave/*Julia*
1979
★Rachel Roberts/*Yanks*
1982
★Rohini Hattangady/*Gandhi*
★Maureen Stapleton/*Reds*
1983
★Jamie Lee Curtis/*Trading Places*
1984
★Liz Smith/*A Private Function*
Tuesday Weld/*Once Upon a Time in America*
1985
★Rosanna Arquette/*Desperately Seeking Susan*
1986
★Judi Dench/*A Room with a View*
1987
★Susan Wooldridge/*Hope and Glory*
1988
★Judi Dench/*A Handful of Dust*
1989
★Michelle Pfeiffer/*Dangerous Liaisons*
1990
★Whoopi Goldberg/*Ghost*
1991
★Kate Nelligan/*Frankie and Johnny*
1992
★Miranda Richardson/*Damage*
1993
★Miriam Margolyes/*The Age of Innocence*
Holly Hunter/*The Firm*
Maggie Smith/*The Secret Garden*
1994
★Kristin Scott Thomas/*Four Weddings and a Funeral*
Winona Ryder/*The Age of Innocence*
1995
★Kate Winslet/*Sense and Sensibility*
Joan Allen/*Nixon*
Mira Sorvino/*Mighty Aphrodite*
Elizabeth Spriggs/*Sense and Sensibility*
1996
★Juliette Binoche/*The English Patient*
Lauren Bacall/*The Mirror Has Two Faces*
Marianne Jean-Baptiste/*Secrets and Lies*
Lynn Redgrave/*Shine*
1997
★Sigourney Weaver/*The Ice Storm*
Jennifer Ehle/*Wilde*
Lesley Sharp/*The Full Monty*
Zoe Wanamaker/*Wilde*
1998
★Judi Dench/*Shakespeare in Love*
Kathy Bates/*Primary Colors*
Brenda Blethyn/*Little Voice*
Lynn Redgrave/*Gods and Monsters*
1999
★Maggie Smith/*Tea with Mussolini*
Thora Birch/*American Beauty*
Cate Blanchett/*The Talented Mr. Ripley*
Cameron Diaz/*Being John Malkovich*
Mena Suvari/*American Beauty*
2000
★Julie Walters/*Billy Elliot*
2001
★Jennifer Connelly/*A Beautiful Mind*
Judi Dench/*The Shipping News*
Helen Mirren/*Gosford Park*
Maggie Smith/*Gosford Park*
Kate Winslet/*Iris*
2002
★Catherine Zeta-Jones/*Chicago*
Toni Collette/*About a Boy*
Julianne Moore/*The Hours*
Queen Latifah/*Chicago*
Meryl Streep/*Adaptation*
2003
★Renee Zellweger/*Cold Mountain*
Holly Hunter/*Thirteen*
Laura Linney/*Mystic River*
Judy Parfitt/*Girl with a Pearl Earring*
Emma Thompson/*Love Actually*
2004
★Cate Blanchett/*The Aviator*
Julie Christie/*Finding Neverland*
Heather Craney/*Vera Drake*
Natalie Portman/*Closer*
Meryl Streep/*The Manchurian Candidate*
2005
★Thandie Newton/*Crash*
Brenda Blethyn/*Pride and Prejudice*
Catherine Keener/*Capote*
Frances McDormand/*North Country*
Michelle Williams/*Brokeback Mountain*
2006
★Jennifer Hudson/*Dreamgirls*
Emily Blunt/*The Devil Wears Prada*
Abigail Breslin/*Little Miss Sunshine*
Toni Collette/*Little Miss Sunshine*
2007
Tilda Swinton/*Burn After Reading*
Frances de la Tour/*The History Boys*
2007
★Tilda Swinton/*Michael Clayton*
Cate Blanchett/*I'm Not There*
Kelly Macdonald/*No Country for Old Men*
Samantha Morton/*Control*
Saoirse Ronan/*Atonement*
2008
★Penelope Cruz/*Vicky Cristina Barcelona*
Amy Adams/*Doubt*
Penelope Cruz/*Vicky Cristina Barcelona*
Freida Pinto/*Slumdog Millionaire*
Marisa Tomei/*The Wrestler*
2009
★Mo'Nique/*Precious: Based on the Novel by Sapphire*
Anne-Marie Duff/*Nowhere Boy*
Vera Farmiga/*Up in the Air*
Anna Kendrick/*Up in the Air*
Kristin Scott Thomas/*Nowhere Boy*

ART DIRECTION

1969
★*Oh! What a Lovely War*
1997
★*William Shakespeare's Romeo and Juliet*
1999
★*Sleepy Hollow*
American Beauty
Angela's Ashes
The End of the Affair
The Matrix

CINEMATOGRAPHY

1969
★*Oh! What a Lovely War*
1984
Once Upon a Time in America
1995
★*Braveheart*
Apollo 13
The Madness of King George
Sense and Sensibility
1996
★*The English Patient*
1997
★*The Wings of the Dove*
L.A. Confidential
Titanic
William Shakespeare's Romeo and Juliet
1998
★*Elizabeth*
Saving Private Ryan
Shakespeare in Love
The Truman Show
1999
★*American Beauty*
Angela's Ashes
The End of the Affair
The Matrix
The Talented Mr. Ripley
2000
★*Gladiator*
2001
Black Hawk Down
Lord of the Rings: The Fellowship of the Ring
Moulin Rouge
2002
★*Road to Perdition*
Chicago
Gangs of New York
Lord of the Rings: The Two Towers
The Pianist
2003
★*Lord of the Rings: The Return of the King*
Cold Mountain
Girl with a Pearl Earring
Lost in Translation
Master and Commander: The Far Side of the World
2004
★*Collateral*
The Aviator
Finding Neverland
House of Flying Daggers
The Motorcycle Diaries
2005
★*Memoirs of a Geisha*
Brokeback Mountain
The Constant Gardener
Crash
March of the Penguins
2006
★*Children of Men*
Babel
Casino Royale
Pan's Labyrinth
United 93
2007
★*No Country for Old Men*
American Gangster
Atonement
The Bourne Ultimatum
There Will Be Blood
2008
★*Slumdog Millionaire*
Changeling
The Curious Case of Benjamin Button
The Dark Knight
The Reader
2009
★*The Hurt Locker*
Avatar
District 9
Inglourious Basterds
The Road

COSTUME DESIGN

1969
★*Oh! What a Lovely War*
1984
★*Once Upon a Time in America*
1997
★*Mrs. Brown*
L.A. Confidential
Titanic
The Wings of the Dove
1998
★*Velvet Goldmine*
Elizabeth
The Mask of Zorro
Shakespeare in Love
1999
★*Sleepy Hollow*
The End of the Affair
An Ideal Husband
Tea with Mussolini
2001
★*Gosford Park*
Harry Potter and the Sorcerer's Stone
Lord of the Rings: The Fellowship of the Ring
Moulin Rouge
Planet of the Apes
2002
★*Lord of the Rings: The Two Towers*
Catch Me If You Can
Chicago
Gangs of New York
2003
★*Master and Commander: The Far Side of the World*
Cold Mountain
Girl with a Pearl Earring
Lord of the Rings: The Return of the King
Pirates of the Caribbean: The Curse of the Black Pearl
2004
★*Vera Drake*
The Aviator
Finding Neverland
House of Flying Daggers
2005
★*Memoirs of a Geisha*
Charlie and the Chocolate Factory
The Chronicles of Narnia: The Lion, the Witch and the Wardrobe
Mrs. Henderson Presents
Pride and Prejudice
2006
★*Pan's Labyrinth*
The Devil Wears Prada
Marie Antoinette
Pirates of the Caribbean: Dead Man's Chest
The Queen
2007
★*La Vie en Rose*
Elizabeth: The Golden Age
Lust, Caution
Sweeney Todd: The Demon Barber of Fleet Street
2008
★*The Duchess*
Changeling
The Curious Case of Benjamin Button
The Dark Knight
Revolutionary Road
2009
★*The Young Victoria*
Bright Star
Coco Before Chanel
An Education
A Single Man

DIRECTOR

1955
★Laurence Olivier/*Richard III*
1968
★Mike Nichols/*The Graduate*
1969
★John Schlesinger/*Midnight Cowboy*
Richard Attenborough/*Oh! What a Lovely War*
1970
★George Roy Hill/*Butch Cassidy and the Sundance Kid*
1971
★John Schlesinger/*Sunday, Bloody Sunday*
1972
★Bob Fosse/*Cabaret*
1973
★Francois Truffaut/*Day for Night*
1974
★Roman Polanski/*Chinatown*
1975
★Stanley Kubrick/*Barry Lyndon*
1976
★Milos Forman/*One Flew Over the Cuckoo's Nest*
1977
★Woody Allen/*Annie Hall*
1978
★Alan Parker/*Midnight Express*

British Academy Awards

1979

★Francis Ford Coppola/*Apocalypse Now*

1980

★Akira Kurosawa/*Kagemusha*

1981

★Louis Malle/*Atlantic City*

1982

★Richard Attenborough/*Gandhi*

1983

★Bill Forsyth/*Local Hero*

1984

★Wim Wenders/*Paris, Texas*

Sergio Leone/*Once Upon a Time in America*

1986

★Woody Allen/*Hannah and Her Sisters*

1987

★Oliver Stone/*Platoon*

1988

★Louis Malle/*Au Revoir les Enfants*

1989

★Kenneth Branagh/*Henry V*

1990

★Martin Scorsese/*Goodfellas*

1991

★Alan Parker/*The Commitments*

1992

★Clint Eastwood/*Unforgiven*

1993

★Steven Spielberg/*Schindler's List*

1994

★Mike Newell/*Four Weddings and a Funeral*

Richard Attenborough/*Shadowlands*

Jane Campion/*The Piano*

James Ivory/*The Remains of the Day*

1995

★Michael Radford/*The Postman*

Mel Gibson/*Braveheart*

Nicholas Hytner/*The Madness of King George*

Ang Lee/*Sense and Sensibility*

1996

★Joel Coen/*Fargo*

Scott Hicks/*Shine*

Mike Leigh/*Secrets and Lies*

Anthony Minghella/*The English Patient*

1997

★Baz Luhrmann/*William Shakespeare's Romeo and Juliet*

James Cameron/*Titanic*

Peter Cattaneo/*The Full Monty*

Curtis Hanson/*L.A. Confidential*

1998

★Peter Weir/*The Truman Show*

Shekhar Kapur/*Elizabeth*

John Madden/*Shakespeare in Love*

Steven Spielberg/*Saving Private Ryan*

1999

★Pedro Almodovar/*All About My Mother*

Neil Jordan/*The End of the Affair*

Sam Mendes/*American Beauty*

Anthony Minghella/*The Talented Mr. Ripley*

M. Night Shyamalan/*The Sixth Sense*

2000

★Ang Lee/*Crouching Tiger, Hidden Dragon*

2001

★Peter Jackson/*Lord of the Rings: The Fellowship of the Ring*

Robert Altman/*Gosford Park*

Ron Howard/*A Beautiful Mind*

Jean-Pierre Jeunet/*Amelie*

Baz Luhrmann/*Moulin Rouge*

2002

★Roman Polanski/*The Pianist*

Stephen Daldry/*The Hours*

Peter Jackson/*Lord of the Rings: The Two Towers*

Rob Marshall/*Chicago*

Martin Scorsese/*Gangs of New York*

2003

★Peter Weir/*Master and Commander: The Far Side of the World*

Tim Burton/*Big Fish*

Sofia Coppola/*Lost in Translation*

Peter Jackson/*Lord of the Rings: The Return of the King*

Anthony Minghella/*Cold Mountain*

2004

★Mike Leigh/*Vera Drake*

Marc Forster/*Finding Neverland*

Michel Gondry/*Eternal Sunshine of the Spotless Mind*

Michael Mann/*Collateral*

Martin Scorsese/*The Aviator*

2005

George Clooney/*Good Night, and Good Luck*

Fernando Meirelles/*The Constant Gardener*

Bennett Miller/*Capote*

2006

★Paul Greengrass/*United 93*

Jonathan Dayton/*Little Miss Sunshine*

Valerie Faris/*Little Miss Sunshine*

Stephen Frears/*The Queen*

Alejandro Gonzalez Inarritu/*Babel*

Martin Scorsese/*The Departed*

2007

★Ethan Coen/*No Country for Old Men*

★Joel Coen/*No Country for Old Men*

Paul Thomas Anderson/*There Will Be Blood*

Paul Greengrass/*The Bourne Ultimatum*

Joe Wright/*Atonement*

Florian Henskel von Donnersmarck/*The Lives of Others*

2008

★Danny Boyle/*Slumdog Millionaire*

Stephen Daldry/*The Reader*

Clint Eastwood/*Changeling*

David Fincher/*The Curious Case of Benjamin Button*

Ron Howard/*Frost/Nixon*

2009

★Kathryn Bigelow/*The Hurt Locker*

Neil Blomkamp/*District 9*

James Cameron/*Avatar*

Lone Scherfig/*An Education*

Quentin Tarantino/*Inglourious Basterds*

FILM

1947

★*The Best Years of Our Lives*

★*Odd Man Out*

1948

★*The Fallen Idol*

★*Hamlet*

1949

★*The Bicycle Thief*

★*The Third Man*

1950

★*All About Eve*

★*The Blue Lamp*

1951

★*La Ronde*

★*The Lavender Hill Mob*

1953

★*Forbidden Games*

★*Genevieve*

1954

★*Hobson's Choice*

★*Wages of Fear*

1955

★*Richard III*

1956

★*Gervaise*

★*Reach for the Sky*

1957

★*The Bridge on the River Kwai*

1958

★*Room at the Top*

1959

★*Ben-Hur*

★*Sapphire*

1960

★*The Apartment*

★*Saturday Night and Sunday Morning*

1961

★*Ballad of a Soldier*

★*The Hustler*

★*A Taste of Honey*

1962

★*Lawrence of Arabia*

1963

★*Tom Jones*

1964

★*Dr. Strangelove, or: How I Learned to Stop Worrying and Love the Bomb*

★*King and Country*

1965

★*The Ipcress File*

★*My Fair Lady*

1966

★*The Spy Who Came in from the Cold*

★*Who's Afraid of Virginia Woolf?*

1967

★*A Man for All Seasons*

1968

★*The Graduate*

1969

★*Midnight Cowboy*

Oh! What a Lovely War

1970

★*Butch Cassidy and the Sundance Kid*

1971

★*Sunday, Bloody Sunday*

1972

★*Cabaret*

1973

★*Day for Night*

1975

★*Alice Doesn't Live Here Anymore*

1976

★*One Flew Over the Cuckoo's Nest*

1977

★*Annie Hall*

1978

★*Julia*

1979

★*Manhattan*

1980

★*The Elephant Man*

1981

★*Chariots of Fire*

1982

★*Gandhi*

1983

★*Educating Rita*

1984

★*The Killing Fields*

1985

★*The Purple Rose of Cairo*

1986

★*A Room with a View*

1987

★*Hope and Glory*

★*Jean de Florette*

1988

★*The Last Emperor*

1989

★*Dead Poets Society*

1990

★*Goodfellas*

1991

★*The Commitments*

1992

★*Unforgiven*

1993

★*Schindler's List*

★*Shadowlands*

Naked

Raining Stones

Tom & Viv

1994

★*Four Weddings and a Funeral*

The Piano

The Remains of the Day

1995

★*Sense and Sensibility*

Babe

Carrington

Land and Freedom

The Madness of King George

Trainspotting

The Usual Suspects

1996

★*The English Patient*

Fargo

Secrets and Lies

Shine

1997

★*The Full Monty*

★*Nil by Mouth*

Behind the Lines

The Borrowers

L.A. Confidential

Mrs. Brown

Titanic

24-7

1998

★*Elizabeth*

★*Shakespeare in Love*

Hilary and Jackie

Little Voice

Lock, Stock and 2 Smoking Barrels

My Name Is Joe

Saving Private Ryan

Sliding Doors

The Truman Show

1999

★*American Beauty*

★*East Is East*

The End of the Affair

Notting Hill

Onegin

Ratcatcher

The Sixth Sense

The Talented Mr. Ripley

Topsy Turvy

Wonderland

2000

★*Billy Elliot*

★*Gladiator*

2001

★*Gosford Park*

★*Lord of the Rings: The Fellowship of the Ring*

Amelie

A Beautiful Mind

Bridget Jones's Diary

Harry Potter and the Sorcerer's Stone

Iris

Moulin Rouge

Shrek

2002

★*The Pianist*

Chicago

Gangs of New York

The Hours

Lord of the Rings: The Two Towers

2003

★*Lord of the Rings: The Return of the King*

Big Fish

Cold Mountain

Lost in Translation

The Magdalene Sisters

Master and Commander: The Far Side of the World

2004

★*The Aviator*

Eternal Sunshine of the Spotless Mind

The Motorcycle Diaries

Vera Drake

2005

★*Brokeback Mountain*

Capote

The Constant Gardener

Crash

Good Night, and Good Luck

2006

★*The Queen*

Babel

The Departed

The Last King of Scotland

Little Miss Sunshine

2007

★*Atonement*

American Gangster

The Lives of Others

No Country for Old Men

There Will Be Blood

2008

★*Slumdog Millionaire*

The Curious Case of Benjamin Button

Frost/Nixon

Milk

The Reader

2009

★*The Hurt Locker*

Avatar

An Education

Precious: Based on the Novel by Sapphire

Up in the Air

FILM EDITING

1969

Oh! What a Lovely War

1997

★*L.A. Confidential*

The Full Monty

Titanic

William Shakespeare's Romeo and Juliet

1998

★*Shakespeare in Love*

Elizabeth

Lock, Stock and 2 Smoking Barrels

Saving Private Ryan

1999

★*American Beauty*

Being John Malkovich

The Matrix

The Sixth Sense

2001

Amelie

Black Hawk Down

Lord of the Rings: The Fellowship of the Ring

Moulin Rouge

2002

Chicago

Gangs of New York

The Hours

Lord of the Rings: The Two Towers

2003

★*Lost in Translation*

Cold Mountain

Kill Bill Vol. 1

Lord of the Rings: The Return of the King

21 Grams

2004

★*Eternal Sunshine of the Spotless Mind*

The Aviator

Collateral

House of Flying Daggers

Vera Drake

2005

★*The Constant Gardener*

Brokeback Mountain

Crash

Good Night, and Good Luck

March of the Penguins

2006

★*United 93*

Babel

Casino Royale

The Departed

The Queen

2007

★*The Bourne Ultimatum*

American Gangster

Atonement

Michael Clayton

No Country for Old Men

2008

★*Slumdog Millionaire*

Changeling

The Curious Case of Benjamin Button

The Dark Knight

Frost/Nixon

In Bruges

★ = *winner*

2009
Avatar
District 9
Inglourious Basterds
Up in the Air

MAKEUP

1997
★The Wings of the Dove
1999
★Topsy Turvy
American Beauty
The End of the Affair
An Ideal Husband
2002
★Frida
Chicago
The Hours
Lord of the Rings: The Two Towers
2003
★Pirates of the Caribbean: The Curse of the Black Pearl
Big Fish
Cold Mountain
Girl with a Pearl Earring
Lord of the Rings: The Return of the King
2004
★The Aviator
Finding Neverland
Harry Potter and the Prisoner of Azkaban
House of Flying Daggers
Vera Drake
2005
★The Chronicles of Narnia: The Lion, the Witch and the Wardrobe
Charlie and the Chocolate Factory
Harry Potter and the Goblet of Fire
Memoirs of a Geisha
Pride and Prejudice
2006
★Pan's Labyrinth
The Devil Wears Prada
Marie Antoinette
Pirates of the Caribbean: Dead Man's Chest
The Queen
2007
★La Vie en Rose
Atonement
Elizabeth: The Golden Age
Hairspray
Sweeney Todd: The Demon Barber of Fleet Street
2008
★The Curious Case of Benjamin Button
The Dark Knight
The Duchess
Frost/Nixon
Milk
2009
★The Young Victoria
Coco Before Chanel
An Education
The Imaginarium of Doctor Parnassus
Nine

SCORE

1993
Sleepless in Seattle
1994
The Piano
Schindler's List
1995
★The Postman
Braveheart
The Madness of King George
Sense and Sensibility
1996
★The English Patient
1997
★William Shakespeare's Romeo and Juliet
The Full Monty
L.A. Confidential
Titanic
1998
★Elizabeth
Hilary and Jackie
Saving Private Ryan
Shakespeare in Love
1999
★American Beauty
2000
★Crouching Tiger, Hidden Dragon
2001
★Moulin Rouge
Amelie
Lord of the Rings: The Fellowship of the Ring
Mulholland Drive
Shrek
2002
★The Hours
Catch Me If You Can
Chicago
Gangs of New York
The Pianist
2003
★Cold Mountain

ORIGINAL SCORE

1984
★Once Upon a Time in America
1999
Buena Vista Social Club
The End of the Affair
The Talented Mr. Ripley
2003
Girl with a Pearl Earring
Kill Bill Vol. 1
Lord of the Rings: The Return of the King
Lost in Translation
2004
The Aviator
Finding Neverland
Ray
2005
★Memoirs of a Geisha
★The Motorcycle Diaries
The Constant Gardener
Mrs. Henderson Presents
2006
★Babel
Casino Royale
Dreamgirls
Happy Feet
The Queen
2007
★La Vie en Rose
American Gangster
Atonement
The Kite Runner
There Will Be Blood
2008
★Slumdog Millionaire
The Curious Case of Benjamin Button
The Dark Knight
Mamma Mia!
WALL-E
2009
★Up
Avatar
Crazy Heart
Fantastic Mr. Fox
Sex & Drugs & Rock & Roll

SOUND

1997
★L.A. Confidential
The Full Monty
Titanic
William Shakespeare's Romeo and Juliet
1998
★Saving Private Ryan
Hilary and Jackie
Little Voice
Shakespeare in Love
1999
★The Matrix
American Beauty
Buena Vista Social Club
2001
★Moulin Rouge
Black Hawk Down
Harry Potter and the Sorcerer's Stone
Lord of the Rings: The Fellowship of the Ring
Shrek
2002
Gangs of New York
Harry Potter and the Chamber of Secrets
Lord of the Rings: The Two Towers
The Pianist
2003
★Chicago
★Master and Commander: The Far Side of the World
Cold Mountain
Kill Bill Vol. 1
Lord of the Rings: The Return of the King
Pirates of the Caribbean: The Curse of the Black Pearl
2004
★Ray
The Aviator
Collateral
House of Flying Daggers
Spider-Man 2
2005
★Walk the Line
Batman Begins
The Constant Gardener
Crash
King Kong
2006
★Casino Royale
Babel
Pan's Labyrinth
Pirates of the Caribbean: Dead Man's Chest
United 93
2007
★The Bourne Ultimatum
La Vie en Rose
No Country for Old Men
There Will Be Blood
2008
★Slumdog Millionaire
Changeling
The Dark Knight
Quantum of Solace
WALL-E
2009
★The Hurt Locker
Avatar
District 9
Star Trek
Up

ADAPTED SCREENPLAY

1983
★Heat and Dust
1984
★The Killing Fields
1985
★Prizzi's Honor
1986
★Out of Africa
1987
★Jean de Florette
1988
★The Unbearable Lightness of Being
1989
★Dangerous Liaisons
1990
★Goodfellas
1991
★The Commitments
1992
★The Player
1993
★Schindler's List
In the Name of the Father
Scent of a Woman
1994
★Quiz Show
The Remains of the Day
Schindler's List
Shadowlands
1995
★Trainspotting
Babe
Leaving Las Vegas
The Madness of King George
The Postman
Sense and Sensibility
1996
★The English Patient
The Crucible
Evita
Richard III
1997
★William Shakespeare's Romeo and Juliet
The Ice Storm
L.A. Confidential
The Wings of the Dove
1998
★Primary Colors
Hilary and Jackie
Little Voice
Wag the Dog
1999
★The End of the Affair
East Is East
An Ideal Husband
The Talented Mr. Ripley
2000
★Traffic
2001
★Shrek
A Beautiful Mind
Bridget Jones's Diary
Iris
Lord of the Rings: The Fellowship of the Ring
2002
★Adaptation
About a Boy
Catch Me If You Can
The Hours
The Pianist
2003
★Lord of the Rings: The Return of the King
Big Fish
Cold Mountain
Girl with a Pearl Earring
Mystic River
2004
★Sideways
Closer
Finding Neverland
The Motorcycle Diaries
2005
★Brokeback Mountain
Capote
The Constant Gardener
A History of Violence
Pride and Prejudice
2006
★The Last King of Scotland
Casino Royale
The Departed
The Devil Wears Prada
Notes on a Scandal
2007
★The Diving Bell and the Butterfly
Atonement
The Kite Runner
No Country for Old Men
There Will Be Blood
2008
★Slumdog Millionaire
The Curious Case of Benjamin Button
Frost/Nixon
The Reader
Revolutionary Road
2009
★Up in the Air
District 9
An Education
In the Loop
Precious: Based on the Novel by Sapphire

ORIGINAL SCREENPLAY

1983
★King of Comedy
1984
★Broadway Danny Rose
1985
★The Purple Rose of Cairo
1986
★Hannah and Her Sisters
1987
★Wish You Were Here
1988
★A World Apart
1989
★When Harry Met Sally...
1990
★Cinema Paradiso
1991
★Truly, Madly, Deeply
1992
★Husbands and Wives
1993
★Groundhog Day
In the Line of Fire
Sleepless in Seattle
1994
★Pulp Fiction
The Piano
1995
★The Usual Suspects
Bullets over Broadway
Muriel's Wedding
Seven
1996
★Secrets and Lies
Brassed Off
Fargo
Lone Star
Shine
1997
★Nil by Mouth
Boogie Nights
The Full Monty
Mrs. Brown
1998
★The Truman Show
Elizabeth
Life Is Beautiful
Shakespeare in Love
1999
★Being John Malkovich
All About My Mother
American Beauty
The Sixth Sense
Topsy Turvy
2001
★Amelie
Gosford Park
Moulin Rouge
The Others
The Royal Tenenbaums
2002
★Talk to Her
Gangs of New York
Y Tu Mama Tambien
2003
★The Barbarian Invasions
★The Station Agent
Finding Nemo
Lost in Translation
21 Grams
2004
★Eternal Sunshine of the Spotless Mind
The Aviator
Collateral
Ray
Vera Drake
2005
★Crash
Cinderella Man
Good Night, and Good Luck
Mrs. Henderson Presents
2006
★Little Miss Sunshine
Babel
Pan's Labyrinth
The Queen
United 93
2007
★Juno
American Gangster
The Lives of Others
Michael Clayton
This Is England
2008
★In Bruges
Burn After Reading
Changeling
I've Loved You So Long
Milk
2009
★The Hurt Locker
The Hangover
Inglourious Basterds
A Serious Man
Up

SCREENPLAY

1955
★The Ladykillers
1956
★The Man Who Never Was
1957
★The Bridge on the River Kwai
1959
★I'm All Right Jack

★ = winner

1961

★*The Day the Earth Caught Fire*

1962

★*Lawrence of Arabia*

★*A Taste of Honey*

1963

★*Tom Jones*

1964

★*The Pumpkin Eater*

1965

★*Darling*

1966

★*Morgan: A Suitable Case for Treatment*

1967

★*A Man for All Seasons*

1968

★*The Graduate*

1969

★*Midnight Cowboy*

1970

★*Butch Cassidy and the Sundance Kid*

1971

★*The Go-Between*

1972

★*The Hospital*

★*The Last Picture Show*

1973

★*The Discreet Charm of the Bourgeoisie*

1974

★*Chinatown*

★*The Last Detail*

1975

★*Alice Doesn't Live Here Anymore*

1976

★*Bugsy Malone*

1977

★*Annie Hall*

1978

★*Julia*

1979

★*Manhattan*

1981

★*Gregory's Girl*

1982

★*Missing*

2003

The Magdalene Sisters

FILM—FOREIGN LANGUAGE

1982

★*Christ Stopped at Eboli*

1983

★*Danton*

1984

★*Carmen*

1985

★*Colonel Redl*

1986

★*Ran*

1987

★*The Sacrifice*

1988

★*Babette's Feast*

1989

★*Life and Nothing But*

1990

★*Cinema Paradiso*

1991

★*The Nasty Girl*

1992

★*Raise the Red Lantern*

1993

★*Farewell My Concubine*

Indochine

Like Water for Chocolate

Un Coeur en Hiver

1994

★*To Live*

1995

★*The Postman*

Burnt by the Sun

Les Miserables

Queen Margot

1996

Antonia's Line

Kolya

Nelly et Monsieur Arnaud

1997

Ma Vie en Rose

The Tango Lesson

1998

★*Central Station*

Life Is Beautiful

Live Flesh

1999

★*All About My Mother*

Buena Vista Social Club

The Celebration

Run Lola Run

2000

★*Crouching Tiger, Hidden Dragon*

2001

★*Amores Perros*

★*Behind the Sun*

Amelie

Monsoon Wedding

2002

★*Talk to Her*

Y Tu Mama Tambien

2003

★*In This World*

The Barbarian Invasions

Good Bye, Lenin!

Spirited Away

The Triplets of Belleville

2004

★*The Motorcycle Diaries*

Bad Education

House of Flying Daggers

A Very Long Engagement

2005

★*The Beat My Heart Skipped*

Tsotsi

2006

★*Pan's Labyrinth*

Apocalypto

Volver

2007

★*The Lives of Others*

The Diving Bell and the Butterfly

The Kite Runner

La Vie en Rose

Lust, Caution

2008

Persepolis

Waltz with Bashir

2009

★*I've Loved You So Long*

★*A Prophet*

Broken Embraces

Coco Before Chanel

Let the Right One In

The White Ribbon

VISUAL EFFECTS

1997

★*The Fifth Element*

1999

★*The Matrix*

Sleepy Hollow

2001

★*Lord of the Rings: The Fellowship of the Ring*

A. I.: Artificial Intelligence

Harry Potter and the Sorcerer's Stone

Moulin Rouge

Shrek

2002

★*Lord of the Rings: The Two Towers*

Gangs of New York

Gangs of New York

Harry Potter and the Chamber of Secrets

Minority Report

Spider-Man

2003

★*Lord of the Rings: The Return of the King*

Big Fish

Kill Bill Vol. 1

Master and Commander: The Far Side of the World

Pirates of the Caribbean: The Curse of the Black Pearl

2004

★*The Day After Tomorrow*

The Aviator

Harry Potter and the Prisoner of Azkaban

House of Flying Daggers

Spider-Man 2

2005

★*King Kong*

Batman Begins

Charlie and the Chocolate Factory

The Chronicles of Narnia: The Lion, the Witch and the Wardrobe

Harry Potter and the Goblet of Fire

2006

★*Pirates of the Caribbean: Dead Man's Chest*

Casino Royale

Children of Men

Pan's Labyrinth

Superman Returns

2007

★*The Golden Compass*

The Bourne Ultimatum

Harry Potter and the Order of the Phoenix

Pirates of the Caribbean: At World's End

Spider-Man 3

2008

★*The Curious Case of Benjamin Button*

The Dark Knight

Indiana Jones and the Kingdom of the Crystal Skull

Iron Man

Quantum of Solace

2009

★*Avatar*

District 9

Harry Potter and the Half-Blood Prince

The Hurt Locker

Star Trek

ANIMATED FILM

2006

★*Happy Feet*

Cars

Flushed Away

2007

★*Ratatouille*

Shrek the Third

The Simpsons Movie

2008

★*WALL-E*

Persepolis

Waltz with Bashir

2009

★*Up*

Coraline

Fantastic Mr. Fox

DIRECTORS GUILD OF AMERICA

DIRECTOR

1948

★Joseph L. Mankiewicz/*A Letter to Three Wives*

1949

★Carol Reed/*The Third Man*

1950

★Joseph L. Mankiewicz/*All About Eve*

1951

★George Stevens/*A Place in the Sun*

1952

★John Ford/*The Quiet Man*

1953

★Fred Zinnemann/*From Here to Eternity*

1954

★Elia Kazan/*On the Waterfront*

★Billy Wilder/*Sabrina*

1955

★Delbert Mann/*Marty*

1956

★George Stevens/*Giant*

1957

★David Lean/*The Bridge on the River Kwai*

1958

★Vincente Minnelli/*Gigi*

1959

★William Wyler/*Ben-Hur*

1960

★Billy Wilder/*The Apartment*

1961

★Jerome Robbins/*West Side Story*

★Robert Wise/*West Side Story*

1962

★David Lean/*Lawrence of Arabia*

1963

★Tony Richardson/*Tom Jones*

1964

★George Cukor/*My Fair Lady*

1965

★Robert Wise/*The Sound of Music*

1966

★Fred Zinnemann/*A Man for All Seasons*

1967

★Mike Nichols/*The Graduate*

1968

★Anthony Harvey/*The Lion in Winter*

1969

★John Schlesinger/*Midnight Cowboy*

1970

★Charles Jarrott/*Anne of the Thousand Days*

★Franklin J. Schaffner/*Patton*

Richard Attenborough/*Oh! What a Lovely War*

1971

★William Friedkin/*The French Connection*

1972

★Francis Ford Coppola/*The Godfather*

1973

★George Roy Hill/*The Sting*

1974

★Francis Ford Coppola/*The Godfather, Part 2*

1975

★Milos Forman/*One Flew Over the Cuckoo's Nest*

1976

★John G. Avildsen/*Rocky*

1977

★Woody Allen/*Annie Hall*

1978

★Michael Cimino/*The Deer Hunter*

1979

★Robert Benton/*Kramer vs. Kramer*

1980

★Robert Redford/*Ordinary People*

1981

★Warren Beatty/*Reds*

1982

★Richard Attenborough/*Gandhi*

1983

★James L. Brooks/*Terms of Endearment*

1984

★Milos Forman/*Amadeus*

1985

★Steven Spielberg/*The Color Purple*

1986

★Oliver Stone/*Platoon*

1987

★Bernardo Bertolucci/*The Last Emperor*

1988

★Barry Levinson/*Rain Man*

1989

★Oliver Stone/*Born on the Fourth of July*

1990

★Kevin Costner/*Dances with Wolves*

1991

★Jonathan Demme/*The Silence of the Lambs*

1992

★Clint Eastwood/*Unforgiven*

1993

★Steven Spielberg/*Schindler's List*

Jane Campion/*The Piano*

Andrew Davis/*The Fugitive*

James Ivory/*The Remains of the Day*

Martin Scorsese/*The Age of Innocence*

1994

★Robert Zemeckis/*Forrest Gump*

Frank Darabont/*The Shawshank Redemption*

Mike Newell/*Four Weddings and a Funeral*

Robert Redford/*Quiz Show*

Quentin Tarantino/*Pulp Fiction*

1995

★Ron Howard/*Apollo 13*

Mike Figgis/*Leaving Las Vegas*

Mel Gibson/*Braveheart*

Ang Lee/*Sense and Sensibility*

Michael Radford/*The Postman*

1996

★Anthony Minghella/*The English Patient*

Joel Coen/*Fargo*

Cameron Crowe/*Jerry Maguire*

Scott Hicks/*Shine*

Mike Leigh/*Secrets and Lies*

1997

★James Cameron/*Titanic*

James L. Brooks/*As Good As It Gets*

Curtis Hanson/*L.A. Confidential*

Steven Spielberg/*Amistad*

Gus Van Sant/*Good Will Hunting*

1998

★Steven Spielberg/*Saving Private Ryan*

Roberto Benigni/*Life Is Beautiful*

John Madden/*Shakespeare in Love*

Terrence Malick/*The Thin Red Line*

Peter Weir/*The Truman Show*

1999

★Sam Mendes/*American Beauty*

Frank Darabont/*The Green Mile*

Spike Jonze/*Being John Malkovich*

Michael Mann/*The Insider*

M. Night Shyamalan/*The Sixth Sense*

2000

★Ang Lee/*Crouching Tiger, Hidden Dragon*

Cameron Crowe/*Almost Famous*

Ridley Scott/*Gladiator*

Steven Soderbergh/*Erin Brockovich*

Steven Soderbergh/*Traffic*

2001

★Ron Howard/*A Beautiful Mind*

Peter Jackson/*Lord of the Rings: The Fellowship of the Ring*

Baz Luhrmann/*Moulin Rouge*

Christopher Nolan/*Memento*

Ridley Scott/*Black Hawk Down*

2002

★Rob Marshall/*Chicago*

Stephen Daldry/*The Hours*

Peter Jackson/*Lord of the Rings: The Two Towers*

Roman Polanski/*The Pianist*

Martin Scorsese/*Gangs of New York*

2003

★Peter Jackson/*Lord of the Rings: The Return of the King*

Sofia Coppola/*Lost in Translation*

Clint Eastwood/*Mystic River*

Gary Ross/*Seabiscuit*

Peter Weir/*Master and Commander: The Far Side of the World*

2004

★Clint Eastwood/*Million Dollar Baby*

Marc Forster/*Finding Neverland*

Taylor Hackford/*Ray*

Alexander Payne/*Sideways*

Martin Scorsese/*The Aviator*

2005

★Ang Lee/*Brokeback Mountain*

George Clooney/*Good Night, and Good Luck*

Paul Haggis/*Crash*

★ = *winner*

Bennett Miller/*Capote*
Steven Spielberg/*Munich*
2006
★Martin Scorsese/*The Departed*
Bill Condon/*Dreamgirls*
Jonathan Dayton/*Little Miss Sunshine*
Valerie Faris/*Little Miss Sunshine*
Stephen Frears/*The Queen*
Alejandro Gonzalez Inarritu/*Babel*
2007
★Ethan Coen/*No Country for Old Men*
★Joel Coen/*No Country for Old Men*
Paul Thomas Anderson/*There Will Be Blood*
Tony Gilroy/*Michael Clayton*
Sean Penn/*Into the Wild*
Julian Schnabel/*The Diving Bell and the Butterfly*
2008
★Danny Boyle/*Slumdog Millionaire*
David Fincher/*The Curious Case of Benjamin Button*
Ron Howard/*Frost/Nixon*
Christopher Nolan/*The Dark Knight*
Gus Van Sant/*Milk*
2009
★Kathryn Bigelow/*The Hurt Locker*
James Cameron/*Avatar*
Lee Daniels/*Precious: Based on the Novel by Sapphire*
Jason Reitman/*Up in the Air*
Quentin Tarantino/*Inglourious Basterds*

FEATURE DOCUMENTARY

1992
★Joe Berlinger/*Brother's Keeper*
★Bruce Sinofsky/*Brother's Keeper*
1995
★Steve James/*Hoop Dreams*
★Terry Zwigoff/*Crumb*
1996
★Al Pacino/*Looking for Richard*
2003
The Weather Underground
Andrew Jarecki/*Capturing the Friedmans*
Errol Morris/*The Fog of War: Eleven Lessons from the Life of Robert S. McNamara*
2004
★*The Story of the Weeping Camel*
Born Into Brothels: Calcutta's Red Light Kids
Control Room
Fahrenheit 9/11
2005
★Werner Herzog/*Grizzly Man*
2008
★*Waltz with Bashir*

GOLDEN GLOBE AWARDS

ACTOR—DRAMA

1944
★Paul Lukas/*Watch on the Rhine*
1945
★Alexander Knox/*Wilson*
1946
★Ray Milland/*The Lost Weekend*
1947
★Gregory Peck/*The Yearling*
1948
★Ronald Colman/*A Double Life*
1949
★Laurence Olivier/*Hamlet*
1950
★Broderick Crawford/*All the King's Men*
1951
★Jose Ferrer/*Cyrano de Bergerac*
1953
★Gary Cooper/*High Noon*
1955
★Marlon Brando/*On the Waterfront*
1956
★Ernest Borgnine/*Marty*
1957
★Kirk Douglas/*Lust for Life*
1958
★Alec Guinness/*The Bridge on the River Kwai*
1959
★David Niven/*Separate Tables*
1960
★Anthony (Tony) Franciosa/*Career*
1961
★Burt Lancaster/*Elmer Gantry*
1962
★Maximilian Schell/*Judgment at Nuremberg*
1963
★Gregory Peck/*To Kill a Mockingbird*
1964
★Sidney Poitier/*Lilies of the Field*
1965
★Peter O'Toole/*Becket*
1966
★Omar Sharif/*Doctor Zhivago*
1967
★Paul Scofield/*A Man for All Seasons*
1968
★Rod Steiger/*In the Heat of the Night*
1969
★Peter O'Toole/*The Lion in Winter*
1970
★John Wayne/*True Grit*
1971
★George C. Scott/*Patton*
1972
★Gene Hackman/*The French Connection*
1973
★Marlon Brando/*The Godfather*
1974
★Al Pacino/*Serpico*
1975
★Jack Nicholson/*Chinatown*
1976
★Jack Nicholson/*One Flew Over the Cuckoo's Nest*
1977
★Peter Finch/*Network*
1978
★Richard Burton/*Equus*
1979
★Jon Voight/*Coming Home*
1980
★Dustin Hoffman/*Kramer vs. Kramer*
1981
★Robert De Niro/*Raging Bull*
1982
★Henry Fonda/*On Golden Pond*
1983
★Robert Duvall/*Tender Mercies*
★Ben Kingsley/*Gandhi*
1984
★Tom Courtenay/*The Dresser*
1985
★F. Murray Abraham/*Amadeus*
1986
★Jon Voight/*Runaway Train*
1987
★Bob Hoskins/*Mona Lisa*
1988
★Michael Douglas/*Wall Street*
1989
★Dustin Hoffman/*Rain Man*
1990
★Tom Cruise/*Born on the Fourth of July*
1991
★Jeremy Irons/*Reversal of Fortune*
1992
★Nick Nolte/*The Prince of Tides*
1993
★Al Pacino/*Scent of a Woman*
1994
★Tom Hanks/*Philadelphia*
Daniel Day-Lewis/*In the Name of the Father*
Harrison Ford/*The Fugitive*
Anthony Hopkins/*The Remains of the Day*
Liam Neeson/*Schindler's List*
1995
★Tom Hanks/*Forrest Gump*
Richard Dreyfuss/*Mr. Holland's Opus*
Morgan Freeman/*The Shawshank Redemption*
Paul Newman/*Nobody's Fool*
Brad Pitt/*Legends of the Fall*
John Travolta/*Pulp Fiction*
1996
★Nicolas Cage/*Leaving Las Vegas*
Anthony Hopkins/*Nixon*
Ian McKellen/*Richard III*
Sean Penn/*Dead Man Walking*
1997
★Geoffrey Rush/*Shine*
Ralph Fiennes/*The English Patient*
Mel Gibson/*Ransom*
Woody Harrelson/*The People vs. Larry Flynt*
Liam Neeson/*Michael Collins*
1998
★Peter Fonda/*Ulee's Gold*
Matt Damon/*Good Will Hunting*
Daniel Day-Lewis/*The Boxer*
Leonardo DiCaprio/*Titanic*
Djimon Hounsou/*Amistad*
Ian McKellen/*Gods and Monsters*
1999
★Jim Carrey/*The Truman Show*
Stephen Fry/*Wilde*
Tom Hanks/*Saving Private Ryan*
Nick Nolte/*Affliction*
2000
★Denzel Washington/*The Hurricane*
Russell Crowe/*The Insider*
Matt Damon/*The Talented Mr. Ripley*
Richard Farnsworth/*The Straight Story*
Kevin Spacey/*American Beauty*
2002
★Russell Crowe/*A Beautiful Mind*
Will Smith/*Ali*
Kevin Spacey/*The Shipping News*
Billy Bob Thornton/*The Man Who Wasn't There*
Denzel Washington/*Training Day*
2003
★Jack Nicholson/*About Schmidt*
Adrien Brody/*The Pianist*
Michael Caine/*The Quiet American*
Daniel Day-Lewis/*Gangs of New York*
Leonardo DiCaprio/*Catch Me If You Can*
2004
★Sean Penn/*Mystic River*
Russell Crowe/*Master and Commander: The Far Side of the World*
Tom Cruise/*The Last Samurai*
Ben Kingsley/*House of Sand and Fog*
Jude Law/*Cold Mountain*
2005
★Leonardo DiCaprio/*The Aviator*
Javier Bardem/*The Sea Inside*
Don Cheadle/*Hotel Rwanda*
Liam Neeson/*Kinsey*
2006
★Philip Seymour Hoffman/*Capote*
Russell Crowe/*Cinderella Man*
Terrence Howard/*Hustle & Flow*
Heath Ledger/*Brokeback Mountain*
David Strathairn/*Good Night, and Good Luck*
2007
★Forest Whitaker/*The Last King of Scotland*
Leonardo DiCaprio/*Blood Diamond*
Leonardo DiCaprio/*The Departed*
Peter O'Toole/*Venus*
Will Smith/*The Pursuit of Happyness*
2008
★Daniel Day-Lewis/*There Will Be Blood*
George Clooney/*Michael Clayton*
James McAvoy/*Atonement*
Viggo Mortensen/*Eastern Promises*
Denzel Washington/*American Gangster*
2009
★Mickey Rourke/*The Wrestler*
Leonardo DiCaprio/*Revolutionary Road*
Frank Langella/*Frost/Nixon*
Sean Penn/*Milk*
Brad Pitt/*The Curious Case of Benjamin Button*
2010
★Jeff Bridges/*Crazy Heart*
George Clooney/*Up in the Air*
Colin Firth/*A Single Man*
Morgan Freeman/*Invictus*
Tobey Maguire/*Brothers*

ACTOR—MUSICAL/COMEDY

1951
★Fred Astaire/*Three Little Words*
1953
★Donald O'Connor/*Singin' in the Rain*
1954
★David Niven/*The Moon Is Blue*
1955
★James Mason/*A Star Is Born*
1956
★Tom Ewell/*The Seven Year Itch*
1957
★Cantinflas/*Around the World in 80 Days*
1958
★Frank Sinatra/*Pal Joey*
1960
★Jack Lemmon/*Some Like It Hot*
1961
★Jack Lemmon/*The Apartment*
1962
★Glenn Ford/*Pocketful of Miracles*
1963
★Marcello Mastroianni/*Divorce—Italian Style*
1965
★Rex Harrison/*My Fair Lady*
1966
★Lee Marvin/*Cat Ballou*
1967
★Alan Arkin/*The Russians Are Coming, the Russians Are Coming*
1968
★Richard Harris/*Camelot*
1969
★Ron Moody/*Oliver!*
1970
★Peter O'Toole/*Goodbye, Mr. Chips*
1971
★Albert Finney/*Scrooge*
1972
★Chaim Topol/*Fiddler on the Roof*
1974
★George Segal/*A Touch of Class*
1975
★Art Carney/*Harry and Tonto*
1976
★Walter Matthau/*The Sunshine Boys*
1977
★Kris Kristofferson/*A Star Is Born*
1978
★Richard Dreyfuss/*The Goodbye Girl*
1979
★Warren Beatty/*Heaven Can Wait*
1980
★Peter Sellers/*Being There*
1981
★Ray Sharkey/*Idolmaker*
1982
★Dudley Moore/*Arthur*
1983
★Dustin Hoffman/*Tootsie*
1984
★Michael Caine/*Educating Rita*
1985
★Dudley Moore/*Micki & Maude*
1986
★Jack Nicholson/*Prizzi's Honor*
1987
★Paul Hogan/*Crocodile Dundee*
1988
★Robin Williams/*Good Morning, Vietnam*
1989
★Tom Hanks/*Big*
1990
★Morgan Freeman/*Driving Miss Daisy*
1991
★Gerard Depardieu/*Green Card*
1992
★Robin Williams/*The Fisher King*
1993
★Tim Robbins/*The Player*
1994
★Robin Williams/*Mrs. Doubtfire*
Johnny Depp/*Benny & Joon*
Tom Hanks/*Sleepless in Seattle*
Kevin Kline/*Dave*
Colm Meaney/*The Snapper*
1995
★Hugh Grant/*Four Weddings and a Funeral*
Jim Carrey/*The Mask*
Johnny Depp/*Ed Wood*
Arnold Schwarzenegger/*Junior*
Terence Stamp/*The Adventures of Priscilla, Queen of the Desert*
1996
★John Travolta/*Get Shorty*
Michael Douglas/*The American President*
Harrison Ford/*Sabrina*
Steve Martin/*Father of the Bride Part 2*
Patrick Swayze/*To Wong Foo, Thanks for Everything, Julie Newmar*
1997
★Tom Cruise/*Jerry Maguire*
Antonio Banderas/*Evita*
Kevin Costner/*Tin Cup*
Tom Cruise/*Jerry Maguire*
Nathan Lane/*The Birdcage*
Eddie Murphy/*The Nutty Professor*
1998
★Jack Nicholson/*As Good As It Gets*
Antonio Banderas/*The Mask of Zorro*
Jim Carrey/*Liar Liar*

★ = *winner*

Dustin Hoffman/*Wag the Dog*
Samuel L. Jackson/*Jackie Brown*
Kevin Kline/*In and Out*

1999
★Michael Caine/*Little Voice*
John Travolta/*Primary Colors*
Robin Williams/*Patch Adams*

2000
★Jim Carrey/*Man on the Moon*
Robert De Niro/*Analyze This*
Rupert Everett/*An Ideal Husband*
Hugh Grant/*Notting Hill*
Sean Penn/*Sweet and Lowdown*

2001
★George Clooney/*O Brother Where Art Thou?*

2002
★*Moulin Rouge*
★Gene Hackman/*The Royal Tenenbaums*
Hugh Jackman/*Kate & Leopold*
Ewan McGregor/*Moulin Rouge*
John Cameron Mitchell/*Hedwig and the Angry Inch*
Billy Bob Thornton/*Bandits*

2003
★Richard Gere/*Chicago*
Nicolas Cage/*Adaptation*
Kieran Culkin/*Igby Goes Down*
Hugh Grant/*About a Boy*
Adam Sandler/*Punch-Drunk Love*

2004
★Bill Murray/*Lost in Translation*
Jack Black/*School of Rock*
Johnny Depp/*Pirates of the Caribbean: The Curse of the Black Pearl*
Jack Nicholson/*Something's Gotta Give*
Billy Bob Thornton/*Bad Santa*

2005
★Jamie Foxx/*Ray*
Jim Carrey/*Eternal Sunshine of the Spotless Mind*
Paul Giamatti/*Sideways*
Kevin Kline/*De-Lovely*
Kevin Spacey/*Beyond the Sea*

2006
★Joaquin Rafael (Leaf) Phoenix/*Walk the Line*
Jeff Daniels/*The Squid and the Whale*
Johnny Depp/*Charlie and the Chocolate Factory*
Nathan Lane/*The Producers*

2007
★Sacha Baron Cohen/*Borat: Cultural Learnings of America for Make Benefit Glorious Nation of Kazakhstan*
Johnny Depp/*Pirates of the Caribbean: Dead Man's Chest*
Aaron Eckhart/*Thank You for Smoking*
Chiwetel Ejiofor/*Kinky Boots*
Will Ferrell/*Stranger Than Fiction*

2008
★Johnny Depp/*Sweeney Todd: The Demon Barber of Fleet Street*
Ryan Gosling/*Lars and the Real Girl*
Tom Hanks/*Charlie Wilson's War*
Philip Seymour Hoffman/*The Savages*
John C. Reilly/*Walk Hard: The Dewey Cox Story*

2009
★Colin Farrell/*In Bruges*
Mamma Mia!
Javier Bardem/*Vicky Cristina Barcelona*
James Franco/*Pineapple Express*
Brendan Gleeson/*In Bruges*
Dustin Hoffman/*Last Chance Harvey*

2010
★Robert Downey, Jr./*Sherlock Holmes*
Matt Damon/*The Informant!*
Daniel Day-Lewis/*Nine*
Joseph Gordon-Levitt/*(500) Days of Summer*
Michael Stuhlbarg/*A Serious Man*

ACTOR—SUPPORTING

1945
★Barry Fitzgerald/*Going My Way*

1947
★Clifton Webb/*The Razor's Edge*

1948
★Edmund Gwenn/*Miracle on 34th Street*

1949
★Walter Huston/*Treasure of the Sierra Madre*

1950
★James Whitmore/*Battleground*

1952
★Peter Ustinov/*Quo Vadis*

1954
★Frank Sinatra/*From Here to Eternity*

1955
★Edmond O'Brien/*The Barefoot Contessa*

1957
★Earl Holliman/*The Rainmaker*

1958
★Red Buttons/*Sayonara*

1959
★Burl Ives/*The Big Country*

1960
★Stephen Boyd/*Ben-Hur*

1961
★Sal Mineo/*Exodus*

1962
★George Chakiris/*West Side Story*

1963
★Omar Sharif/*Lawrence of Arabia*

1964
★John Huston/*The Cardinal*

1965
★Edmond O'Brien/*Seven Days in May*

1966
★Oskar Werner/*The Spy Who Came in from the Cold*

1967
★Richard Attenborough/*The Sand Pebbles*

1968
★David Attenborough/*Doctor Dolittle*

1970
★Gig Young/*They Shoot Horses, Don't They?*

1971
★John Mills/*Ryan's Daughter*

1972
★Ben Johnson/*The Last Picture Show*

1973
★Joel Grey/*Cabaret*

1974
★John Houseman/*The Paper Chase*

1975
★Fred Astaire/*The Towering Inferno*

1976
★Richard Benjamin/*The Sunshine Boys*

1977
★Laurence Olivier/*Marathon Man*

1978
★Peter Firth/*Equus*

1979
★John Hurt/*Midnight Express*

1980
★Melvyn Douglas/*Being There*
★Robert Duvall/*Apocalypse Now*

1981
★Timothy Hutton/*Ordinary People*

1982
★John Gielgud/*Arthur*

1983
★Louis Gossett, Jr./*An Officer and a Gentleman*

1984
★Jack Nicholson/*Terms of Endearment*

1985
★Haing S. Ngor/*The Killing Fields*

1986
★Klaus Maria Brandauer/*Out of Africa*

1987
★Tom Berenger/*Platoon*

1988
★Sean Connery/*The Untouchables*

1989
★Martin Landau/*Tucker: The Man and His Dream*

1990
★Denzel Washington/*Glory*
Joe Pesci/*Goodfellas*

1991
★Bruce Davison/*Longtime Companion*

1992
★Jack Palance/*City Slickers*

1993
★Gene Hackman/*Unforgiven*

1994
★Tommy Lee Jones/*The Fugitive*
Leonardo DiCaprio/*What's Eating Gilbert Grape*
Ralph Fiennes/*Schindler's List*
John Malkovich/*In the Line of Fire*
Sean Penn/*Carlito's Way*

1995
★Martin Landau/*Ed Wood*
Kevin Bacon/*The River Wild*
Samuel L. Jackson/*Pulp Fiction*
Gary Sinise/*Forrest Gump*
John Turturro/*Quiz Show*

1996
★Brad Pitt/*12 Monkeys*
Ed Harris/*Apollo 13*
John Leguizamo/*To Wong Foo, Thanks for Everything, Julie Newmar*
Tim Roth/*Rob Roy*
Kevin Spacey/*The Usual Suspects*

1997
★Edward Norton/*Primal Fear*
Cuba Gooding, Jr./*Jerry Maguire*
Samuel L. Jackson/*A Time to Kill*
Paul Scofield/*The Crucible*
James Woods/*Ghosts of Mississippi*

1998
★Burt Reynolds/*Boogie Nights*
Rupert Everett/*My Best Friend's Wedding*
Anthony Hopkins/*Amistad*
Burt Reynolds/*Boogie Nights*
Jon Voight/*John Grisham's The Rainmaker*
Robin Williams/*Good Will Hunting*

1999
★Ed Harris/*The Truman Show*
Robert Duvall/*A Civil Action*
Bill Murray/*Rushmore*
Geoffrey Rush/*Shakespeare in Love*
Donald Sutherland/*Without Limits*
Billy Bob Thornton/*A Simple Plan*

2000
★Tom Cruise/*Magnolia*
Michael Caine/*The Cider House Rules*
Michael Clarke Duncan/*The Green Mile*
Jude Law/*The Talented Mr. Ripley*
Haley Joel Osment/*The Sixth Sense*

2001
★Benicio Del Toro/*Traffic*

2002
★Jim Broadbent/*Iris*
Steve Buscemi/*Ghost World*
Hayden Christensen/*Life as a House*
Ben Kingsley/*Sexy Beast*
Jude Law/*A. I.: Artificial Intelligence*
Jon Voight/*Ali*

2003
★Chris Cooper/*Adaptation*
Ed Harris/*The Hours*
Paul Newman/*Road to Perdition*
Dennis Quaid/*Far from Heaven*
John C. Reilly/*Chicago*

2004
★Tim Robbins/*Mystic River*
Alec Baldwin/*The Cooler*
Albert Finney/*Big Fish*
William H. Macy/*Seabiscuit*
Peter Sarsgaard/*Shattered Glass*
Ken(saku) Watanabe/*The Last Samurai*

2005
★Clive Owen/*Closer*
David Carradine/*Kill Bill Vol. 2*
Thomas Haden Church/*Sideways*
Jamie Foxx/*Collateral*
Morgan Freeman/*Million Dollar Baby*

2006
★George Clooney/*Syriana*
Matt Dillon/*Crash*
Bob Hoskins/*Mrs. Henderson Presents*

2007
★Eddie Murphy/*Dreamgirls*
Ben Affleck/*Hollywoodland*
Jack Nicholson/*The Departed*
Brad Pitt/*Babel*
Mark Wahlberg/*The Departed*

2008
★Javier Bardem/*No Country for Old Men*
Casey Affleck/*The Assassination of Jesse James by the Coward Robert Ford*
Philip Seymour Hoffman/*Charlie Wilson's War*
John Travolta/*Hairspray*
Tom Wilkinson/*Michael Clayton*

2009
Tom Cruise/*Tropic Thunder*
Robert Downey, Jr./*Tropic Thunder*
Ralph Fiennes/*The Duchess*
Philip Seymour Hoffman/*Doubt*

2010
★Christoph Waltz/*Inglourious Basterds*
Matt Damon/*Invictus*
Woody Harrelson/*The Messenger*
Stanley Tucci/*The Lovely Bones*

ACTRESS—DRAMA

1944
★Jennifer Jones/*The Song of Bernadette*

1945
★Ingrid Bergman/*Gaslight*

1946
★Ingrid Bergman/*The Bells of St. Mary's*

1947
★Rosalind Russell/*Sister Kenny*

1949
★Jane Wyman/*Johnny Belinda*

1950
★Olivia de Havilland/*The Heiress*

1951
★Gloria Swanson/*Sunset Boulevard*

1953
★Shirley Booth/*Come Back, Little Sheba*

1954
★Audrey Hepburn/*Roman Holiday*

1955
★Grace Kelly/*Country Girl*

1956
★Anna Magnani/*The Rose Tattoo*

1957
★Ingrid Bergman/*Anastasia*

1958
★Joanne Woodward/*The Three Faces of Eve*

1959
★Susan Hayward/*I Want to Live!*

1960
★Elizabeth Taylor/*Suddenly, Last Summer*

1961
★Greer Garson/*Sunrise at Campobello*

1962
★Geraldine Page/*Summer and Smoke*

1963
★Geraldine Page/*Sweet Bird of Youth*

1966
★Samantha Eggar/*The Collector*

1967
★Anouk Aimee/*A Man and a Woman*

1969
★Joanne Woodward/*Rachel, Rachel*

1970
★Genevieve Bujold/*Anne of the Thousand Days*

1971
★Ali MacGraw/*Love Story*

1972
★Jane Fonda/*Klute*

1974
★Marsha Mason/*Cinderella Liberty*

1975
★Gena Rowlands/*A Woman under the Influence*

1976
★Louise Fletcher/*One Flew Over the Cuckoo's Nest*

1977
★Faye Dunaway/*Network*

1978
★Jane Fonda/*Julia*

1979
★Jane Fonda/*Coming Home*

1980
★Sally Field/*Norma Rae*

1981
★Mary Tyler Moore/*Ordinary People*

1982
★Meryl Streep/*The French Lieutenant's Woman*

1983
★Meryl Streep/*Sophie's Choice*

1984
★Shirley MacLaine/*Terms of Endearment*

1985
★Sally Field/*Places in the Heart*

1986
★Whoopi Goldberg/*The Color Purple*

1987
★Marlee Matlin/*Children of a Lesser God*

1988
★Sally Kirkland/*Anna*
★Sigourney Weaver/*Gorillas in the Mist*

1989
★Jodie Foster/*The Accused*
★Shirley MacLaine/*Madame Sousatzka*

1990
★Michelle Pfeiffer/*The Fabulous Baker Boys*

1991
★Kathy Bates/*Misery*

1992
★Jodie Foster/*The Silence of the Lambs*

1993
★Emma Thompson/*Howard's End*

1994
★Holly Hunter/*The Piano*

★ = *winner*

Juliette Binoche/*Trois Couleurs: Bleu*
Michelle Pfeiffer/*The Age of Innocence*
Emma Thompson/*The Remains of the Day*
Debra Winger/*A Dangerous Woman*

1995
★Jessica Lange/*Blue Sky*
Jodie Foster/*Nell*
Jennifer Jason Leigh/*Mrs. Parker and the Vicious Circle*
Miranda Richardson/*Tom & Viv*
Meryl Streep/*The River Wild*

1996
★Sharon Stone/*Casino*
Susan Sarandon/*Dead Man Walking*
Elisabeth Shue/*Leaving Las Vegas*
Meryl Streep/*The Bridges of Madison County*
Emma Thompson/*Sense and Sensibility*

1997
★Brenda Blethyn/*Secrets and Lies*
Courtney Love/*The People vs. Larry Flynt*
Kristin Scott Thomas/*The English Patient*
Meryl Streep/*Marvin's Room*
Emily Watson/*Breaking the Waves*

1998
★Judi Dench/*Mrs. Brown*
Helena Bonham Carter/*The Wings of the Dove*
Jodie Foster/*Contact*
Jessica Lange/*A Thousand Acres*
Emily Watson/*Hilary and Jackie*
Kate Winslet/*Titanic*

1999
★Cate Blanchett/*Elizabeth*
Fernanda Montenegro/*Central Station*
Susan Sarandon/*Stepmom*
Meryl Streep/*One True Thing*

2000
★Hilary Swank/*Boys Don't Cry*
Annette Bening/*American Beauty*
Julianne Moore/*The End of the Affair*
Meryl Streep/*Music of the Heart*
Sigourney Weaver/*A Map of the World*

2001
★Julia Roberts/*Erin Brockovich*

2002
★Sissy Spacek/*In the Bedroom*
Halle Berry/*Monster's Ball*
Judi Dench/*Iris*
Nicole Kidman/*The Others*
Tilda Swinton/*The Deep End*

2003
★Nicole Kidman/*The Hours*
Salma Hayek/*Frida*
Diane Lane/*Unfaithful*
Julianne Moore/*Far from Heaven*
Meryl Streep/*The Hours*

2004
★Charlize Theron/*Monster*
Cate Blanchett/*Veronica Guerin*
Scarlett Johansson/*Girl with a Pearl Earring*
Nicole Kidman/*Cold Mountain*
Imelda Staunton/*Vera Drake*
Uma Thurman/*Kill Bill Vol. 1*
Evan Rachel Wood/*Thirteen*

2005
★Hilary Swank/*Million Dollar Baby*
Nicole Kidman/*Birth*
Uma Thurman/*Kill Bill Vol. 2*

2006
★Felicity Huffman/*Transamerica*
Maria Bello/*A History of Violence*
Gwyneth Paltrow/*Proof*
Charlize Theron/*North Country*
Zhang Ziyi/*Memoirs of a Geisha*

2007
★Helen Mirren/*The Queen*
Penelope Cruz/*Volver*
Judi Dench/*Notes on a Scandal*
Maggie Gyllenhaal/*Sherrybaby*
Kate Winslet/*Little Children*

2008
★Julie Christie/*Away From Her*
Cate Blanchett/*Elizabeth: The Golden Age*
Jodie Foster/*The Brave One*
Angelina Jolie/*A Mighty Heart*
Keira Knightley/*Atonement*

2009
★Kate Winslet/*Revolutionary Road*
Anne Hathaway/*Rachel Getting Married*
Angelina Jolie/*Changeling*
Kristin Scott Thomas/*I've Loved You So Long*
Meryl Streep/*Doubt*

2010
★Sandra Bullock/*The Blind Side*
Emily Blunt/*The Young Victoria*
Helen Mirren/*The Last Station*
Carey Mulligan/*An Education*
Gabourney "Gabby" Sidibe/*Precious: Based on the Novel by Sapphire*

ACTRESS—MUSICAL/COMEDY

1951
★Judy Holliday/*Born Yesterday*

1955
★Judy Garland/*A Star Is Born*

1956
★Jean Simmons/*Guys and Dolls*

1957
★Deborah Kerr/*The King and I*

1958
★Kay Kendall/*Les Girls*

1959
★Rosalind Russell/*Auntie Mame*

1960
★Marilyn Monroe/*Some Like It Hot*

1961
★Shirley MacLaine/*The Apartment*

1963
★Doris Day/*Move Over, Darling*
★Rosalind Russell/*Gypsy*

1964
★Shirley MacLaine/*Irma La Douce*

1965
★Julie Andrews/*Mary Poppins*

1966
★Julie Andrews/*The Sound of Music*

1967
★Lynn Redgrave/*Georgy Girl*

1968
★Anne Bancroft/*The Graduate*

1969
★Barbra Streisand/*Funny Girl*

1971
★Carrie Snodgress/*Diary of a Mad Housewife*

1972
★Twiggy/*The Boy Friend*

1973
★Liza Minnelli/*Cabaret*

1974
★Glenda Jackson/*A Touch of Class*

1975
★Raquel Welch/*The Three Musketeers*

1976
★Ann-Margret/*Tommy*

1977
★Barbra Streisand/*A Star Is Born*

1978
★Diane Keaton/*Annie Hall*
★Marsha Mason/*The Goodbye Girl*

1979
★Ellen Burstyn/*Same Time, Next Year*
★Maggie Smith/*California Suite*

1980
★Bette Midler/*The Rose*

1981
★Sissy Spacek/*Coal Miner's Daughter*

1982
★Bernadette Peters/*Pennies from Heaven*

1983
★Julie Andrews/*Victor/Victoria*

1984
★Julie Walters/*Educating Rita*

1985
★Kathleen Turner/*Romancing the Stone*

1986
★Kathleen Turner/*Prizzi's Honor*

1987
★Sissy Spacek/*Crimes of the Heart*

1988
★Cher/*Moonstruck*

1989
★Melanie Griffith/*Working Girl*

1990
★Jessica Tandy/*Driving Miss Daisy*

1991
★Julia Roberts/*Pretty Woman*
Andie MacDowell/*Green Card*

1992
★Bette Midler/*For the Boys*

1993
★Miranda Richardson/*Enchanted April*

1994
★Angela Bassett/*What's Love Got to Do with It?*
Stockard Channing/*Six Degrees of Separation*
Anjelica Huston/*Addams Family Values*
Diane Keaton/*Manhattan Murder Mystery*
Meg Ryan/*Sleepless in Seattle*

1995
★Jamie Lee Curtis/*True Lies*
Geena Davis/*Speechless*
Andie MacDowell/*Four Weddings and a Funeral*
Shirley MacLaine/*Guarding Tess*
Emma Thompson/*Junior*

1996
★Nicole Kidman/*To Die For*
Annette Bening/*The American President*
Sandra Bullock/*While You Were Sleeping*
Toni Collette/*Muriel's Wedding*
Vanessa Redgrave/*A Month by the Lake*

1997
★Madonna/*Evita*
Glenn Close/*101 Dalmatians*
Frances McDormand/*Fargo*
Debbie Reynolds/*Mother*
Barbra Streisand/*The Mirror Has Two Faces*

1998
★Helen Hunt/*As Good As It Gets*
Joey Lauren Adams/*Chasing Amy*
Pam Grier/*Jackie Brown*
Jennifer Lopez/*Selena*
Julia Roberts/*My Best Friend's Wedding*

1999
★Gwyneth Paltrow/*Shakespeare in Love*
Cameron Diaz/*There's Something about Mary*
Jane Horrocks/*Little Voice*
Christina Ricci/*The Opposite of Sex*
Meg Ryan/*You've Got Mail*

2000
★Janet McTeer/*Tumbleweeds*
Julianne Moore/*An Ideal Husband*
Julia Roberts/*Notting Hill*
Sharon Stone/*The Muse*
Reese Witherspoon/*Election*

2001
★Renee Zellweger/*Nurse Betty*

2002
★Nicole Kidman/*Moulin Rouge*
Thora Birch/*Ghost World*
Cate Blanchett/*Bandits*
Reese Witherspoon/*Legally Blonde*
Renee Zellweger/*Bridget Jones's Diary*

2003
★Renee Zellweger/*Chicago*
Maggie Gyllenhaal/*Secretary*
Goldie Hawn/*The Banger Sisters*
Nia Vardalos/*My Big Fat Greek Wedding*
Catherine Zeta-Jones/*Chicago*

2004
★Diane Keaton/*Something's Gotta Give*
Jamie Lee Curtis/*Freaky Friday*
Scarlett Johansson/*Lost in Translation*
Diane Lane/*Under the Tuscan Sun*
Helen Mirren/*Calendar Girls*

2005
★Annette Bening/*Being Julia*
Ashley Judd/*De-Lovely*
Emmy Rossum/*The Phantom of the Opera*
Kate Winslet/*Eternal Sunshine of the Spotless Mind*
Renee Zellweger/*Bridget Jones: The Edge of Reason*

2006
★Reese Witherspoon/*Walk the Line*
Judi Dench/*Mrs. Henderson Presents*
Keira Knightley/*Pride and Prejudice*
Laura Linney/*The Squid and the Whale*
Sarah Jessica Parker/*The Family Stone*

2007
★Meryl Streep/*The Devil Wears Prada*
Annette Bening/*Running with Scissors*
Toni Collette/*Little Miss Sunshine*
Beyonce Knowles/*Dreamgirls*
Renee Zellweger/*Miss Potter*

2008
★Marion Cotillard/*La Vie en Rose*
Amy Adams/*Enchanted*
Nicole Blonsky/*Hairspray*
Helena Bonham Carter/*Sweeney Todd: The Demon Barber of Fleet Street*
Ellen Page/*Juno*

2009
★Sally Hawkins/*Happy-Go-Lucky*
Rebecca Hall/*Vicky Cristina Barcelona*
Frances McDormand/*Burn After Reading*
Meryl Streep/*Mamma Mia!*
Emma Thompson/*Last Chance Harvey*

2010
★Meryl Streep/*Julie & Julia*
Sandra Bullock/*The Proposal*
Marion Cotillard/*Nine*
Julia Roberts/*Duplicity*
Meryl Streep/*It's Complicated*

ACTRESS—SUPPORTING

1945
★Agnes Moorehead/*Mrs. Parkington*

1946
★Angela Lansbury/*Picture of Dorian Gray*

1947
★Anne Baxter/*The Razor's Edge*

1948
★Celeste Holm/*Gentleman's Agreement*

1949
★Ellen Corby/*I Remember Mama*

1950
★Mercedes McCambridge/*All the King's Men*

1951
★Josephine Hull/*Harvey*

1952
★Kim Hunter/*A Streetcar Named Desire*

1953
★Katy Jurado/*High Noon*

1954
★Grace Kelly/*Mogambo*

1955
★Jan Sterling/*The High and the Mighty*

1956
★Marisa Pavan/*The Rose Tattoo*

1957
★Eileen Heckart/*The Bad Seed*

1958
★Elsa Lanchester/*Witness for the Prosecution*

1959
★Hermione Gingold/*Gigi*

1960
★Susan Kohner/*Imitation of Life*

1961
★Janet Leigh/*Psycho*

1962
★Rita Moreno/*West Side Story*

1963
★Angela Lansbury/*The Manchurian Candidate*

1964
★Margaret Rutherford/*The V.I.P.'s*

1965
★Agnes Moorehead/*Hush, Hush, Sweet Charlotte*

1966
★Ruth Gordon/*Inside Daisy Clover*

1967
★Jocelyn Lagarde/*Hawaii*

1968
★Carol Channing/*Thoroughly Modern Millie*

1969
★Ruth Gordon/*Rosemary's Baby*

1970
★Goldie Hawn/*Cactus Flower*

1971
★Karen Black/*Five Easy Pieces*
★Maureen Stapleton/*Airport*

1972
★Ann-Margret/*Carnal Knowledge*

1973
★Shelley Winters/*The Poseidon Adventure*

1974
★Linda Blair/*The Exorcist*

1975
★Karen Black/*The Great Gatsby*

1976
★Brenda Vaccaro/*Once Is Not Enough*

1977
★Katharine Ross/*Voyage of the Damned*

★ = winner

1978

★Vanessa Redgrave/*Julia*

1979

★Dyan Cannon/*Heaven Can Wait*

1980

★Meryl Streep/*Kramer vs. Kramer*

1981

★Mary Steenburgen/*Melvin and Howard*

1982

★Joan Hackett/*Only When I Laugh*

1983

★Jessica Lange/*Tootsie*

1984

★Cher/*Silkwood*

1985

★Peggy Ashcroft/*A Passage to India*

1986

★Meg Tilly/*Agnes of God*

1987

★Maggie Smith/*A Room with a View*

1988

★Olympia Dukakis/*Moonstruck*

1989

★Sigourney Weaver/*Working Girl*

1990

★Julia Roberts/*Steel Magnolias*

Lorraine Bracco/*Goodfellas*

1991

★Whoopi Goldberg/*Ghost*

Nicole Kidman/*Billy Bathgate*

1992

★Mercedes Ruehl/*The Fisher King*

1993

★Joan Plowright/*Enchanted April*

1994

★Winona Ryder/*The Age of Innocence*

Penelope Ann Miller/*Carlito's Way*

Anna Paquin/*The Piano*

Rosie Perez/*Fearless*

Emma Thompson/*In the Name of the Father*

1995

★Dianne Wiest/*Bullets over Broadway*

Kirsten Dunst/*Interview with the Vampire*

Sophia Loren/*Ready to Wear*

Uma Thurman/*Pulp Fiction*

Robin Wright Penn/*Forrest Gump*

1996

★Mira Sorvino/*Mighty Aphrodite*

Anjelica Huston/*The Crossing Guard*

Kathleen Quinlan/*Apollo 13*

Kyra Sedgwick/*Something to Talk About*

Kate Winslet/*Sense and Sensibility*

1997

★Lauren Bacall/*The Mirror Has Two Faces*

Joan Allen/*The Crucible*

Juliette Binoche/*The English Patient*

Barbara Hershey/*Portrait of a Lady*

Marianne Jean-Baptiste/*Secrets and Lies*

Marion Ross/*The Evening Star*

1998

★Kim Basinger/*L.A. Confidential*

Joan Cusack/*In and Out*

Julianne Moore/*Boogie Nights*

Gloria Stuart/*Titanic*

Sigourney Weaver/*The Ice Storm*

1999

★Lynn Redgrave/*Gods and Monsters*

Kathy Bates/*Primary Colors*

Brenda Blethyn/*Little Voice*

Judi Dench/*Shakespeare in Love*

Sharon Stone/*The Mighty*

2000

★Angelina Jolie/*Girl, Interrupted*

Cameron Diaz/*Being John Malkovich*

Catherine Keener/*Being John Malkovich*

Samantha Morton/*Sweet and Lowdown*

Natalie Portman/*Anywhere But Here*

Chloe Sevigny/*Boys Don't Cry*

2001

★Kate Hudson/*Almost Famous*

2002

★Jennifer Connelly/*A Beautiful Mind*

Cameron Diaz/*Vanilla Sky*

Helen Mirren/*Gosford Park*

Maggie Smith/*Gosford Park*

Marisa Tomei/*In the Bedroom*

Kate Winslet/*Iris*

2003

★Meryl Streep/*Adaptation*

Kathy Bates/*About Schmidt*

Cameron Diaz/*Gangs of New York*

Queen Latifah/*Chicago*

Susan Sarandon/*Igby Goes Down*

2004

★Renee Zellweger/*Cold Mountain*

Maria Bello/*The Cooler*

Patricia Clarkson/*Pieces of April*

Hope Davis/*American Splendor*

Holly Hunter/*Thirteen*

2005

★Natalie Portman/*Closer*

Cate Blanchett/*The Aviator*

Laura Linney/*Kinsey*

Virginia Madsen/*Sideways*

Meryl Streep/*The Manchurian Candidate*

2006

★Rachel Weisz/*The Constant Gardener*

Will Ferrell/*The Producers*

Scarlett Johansson/*Match Point*

Shirley MacLaine/*In Her Shoes*

Frances McDormand/*North Country*

Michelle Williams/*Brokeback Mountain*

2007

★Jennifer Hudson/*Dreamgirls*

Adriana Barraza/*Babel*

Cate Blanchett/*Notes on a Scandal*

Emily Blunt/*The Devil Wears Prada*

Rinko Kikuchi/*Babel*

2008

★Cate Blanchett/*I'm Not There*

Julia Roberts/*Charlie Wilson's War*

Saoirse Ronan/*Atonement*

Amy Ryan/*Gone Baby Gone*

Tilda Swinton/*Michael Clayton*

2009

★Kate Winslet/*The Reader*

Amy Adams/*Doubt*

Penelope Cruz/*Vicky Cristina Barcelona*

Viola Davis/*Doubt*

Marisa Tomei/*The Wrestler*

2010

★Mo'Nique/*Precious: Based on the Novel by Sapphire*

Penelope Cruz/*Nine*

Vera Farmiga/*Up in the Air*

Anna Kendrick/*Up in the Air*

Julianne Moore/*A Single Man*

Christopher Plummer/*The Last Station*

BEST FILM—DRAMA

1944

★*The Song of Bernadette*

1945

★*Going My Way*

1946

★*The Lost Weekend*

1947

★*The Best Years of Our Lives*

1948

★*Gentleman's Agreement*

1949

★*Johnny Belinda*

★*Treasure of the Sierra Madre*

1950

★*All the King's Men*

1951

★*Sunset Boulevard*

1952

★*A Place in the Sun*

1953

★*The Greatest Show on Earth*

1954

★*The Robe*

1955

★*On the Waterfront*

1956

★*East of Eden*

1957

★*Around the World in 80 Days*

1958

★*The Bridge on the River Kwai*

1959

★*The Defiant Ones*

1960

★*Ben-Hur*

1961

★*Spartacus*

1962

★*The Guns of Navarone*

1963

★*Lawrence of Arabia*

1964

★*The Cardinal*

1965

★*Becket*

1966

★*Doctor Zhivago*

1967

★*A Man for All Seasons*

1968

★*In the Heat of the Night*

1969

★*The Lion in Winter*

1970

★*Anne of the Thousand Days*

1971

★*Love Story*

1972

★*The French Connection*

1973

★*The Godfather*

1974

★*The Exorcist*

1975

★*Chinatown*

1976

★*One Flew Over the Cuckoo's Nest*

1977

★*Rocky*

1978

★*The Turning Point*

1979

★*Midnight Express*

1980

★*Kramer vs. Kramer*

1981

★*Ordinary People*

1982

★*On Golden Pond*

1983

★*E.T.: The Extra-Terrestrial*

1984

★*Terms of Endearment*

1985

★*Amadeus*

1986

★*Out of Africa*

1987

★*Platoon*

1988

★*The Last Emperor*

1989

★*Rain Man*

1990

★*Born on the Fourth of July*

Goodfellas

1991

★*Dances with Wolves*

1992

★*Bugsy*

1993

★*Scent of a Woman*

1994

★*Schindler's List*

The Age of Innocence

In the Name of the Father

The Piano

The Remains of the Day

1995

★*Forrest Gump*

Legends of the Fall

Nell

Pulp Fiction

Quiz Show

1996

★*Sense and Sensibility*

Apollo 13

Braveheart

The Bridges of Madison County

Leaving Las Vegas

1997

★*The English Patient*

Breaking the Waves

The People vs. Larry Flynt

Secrets and Lies

Shine

1998

★*Titanic*

Amistad

The Boxer

Good Will Hunting

The Horse Whisperer

L.A. Confidential

The Truman Show

1999

★*Saving Private Ryan*

Elizabeth

Gods and Monsters

2000

★*American Beauty*

The End of the Affair

The Hurricane

The Insider

The Talented Mr. Ripley

2001

★*Gladiator*

2002

★*A Beautiful Mind*

In the Bedroom

Lord of the Rings: The Fellowship of the Ring

The Man Who Wasn't There

Mulholland Drive

2003

★*The Hours*

About Schmidt

Gangs of New York

Lord of the Rings: The Two Towers

The Pianist

2004

★*Lord of the Rings: The Return of the King*

Cold Mountain

Master and Commander: The Far Side of the World

Mystic River

Seabiscuit

2005

★*The Aviator*

Closer

Finding Neverland

Hotel Rwanda

Kinsey

Million Dollar Baby

2006

★*Brokeback Mountain*

The Constant Gardener

Good Night, and Good Luck

A History of Violence

Match Point

2007

★*Babel*

Bobby

The Departed

Little Children

The Queen

2008

★*Atonement*

American Gangster

Eastern Promises

The Great Debaters

Michael Clayton

No Country for Old Men

There Will Be Blood

2009

★*Slumdog Millionaire*

The Curious Case of Benjamin Button

Frost/Nixon

The Reader

Revolutionary Road

2010

★*Avatar*

★*The Hangover*

The Hurt Locker

Inglourious Basterds

Precious: Based on the Novel by Sapphire

Up in the Air

BEST FILM—MUSICAL/ COMEDY

1952

★*An American in Paris*

1955

★*Carmen Jones*

1956

★*Guys and Dolls*

1957

★*The King and I*

1958

★*Les Girls*

1959

★*Gigi*

1960

★*Some Like It Hot*

1961

★*The Apartment*

★*Song Without End*

1962

★*West Side Story*

1963

★*The Music Man*

★*That Touch of Mink*

1964

★*Tom Jones*

1965

★*My Fair Lady*

1966

★*The Sound of Music*

1967

★*The Russians Are Coming, the Russians Are Coming*

1968

★*The Graduate*

1969

★*Oliver!*

1971

★*M*A*S*H*

1972

★*Fiddler on the Roof*

1973

★*Cabaret*

1974

★*American Graffiti*

1975

★*The Longest Yard*

1976

★*The Sunshine Boys*

1977

★*A Star Is Born*

1978

★*The Goodbye Girl*

1979

★*Heaven Can Wait*

1980

★*Breaking Away*

1981

★*Coal Miner's Daughter*

1982

★*Arthur*

1983

★*Tootsie*

1984

★*Yentl*

1985

★*Romancing the Stone*

1986

★*Prizzi's Honor*

1987

★*Hannah and Her Sisters*

1988

★*Hope and Glory*

★ = winner

1989

★*Working Girl*

1990

★*Driving Miss Daisy*

1991

★*Green Card*

1992

★*Beauty and the Beast*

1993

★*The Player*

1994

★*Mrs. Doubtfire*

Dave

Much Ado about Nothing

Sleepless in Seattle

Strictly Ballroom

1995

★*The Lion King*

The Adventures of Priscilla, Queen of the Desert

Ed Wood

Four Weddings and a Funeral

Ready to Wear

1996

★*Babe*

The American President

Get Shorty

Sabrina

Toy Story

1997

★*Evita*

The Birdcage

Everyone Says I Love You

Fargo

Jerry Maguire

1998

★*As Good As It Gets*

The Full Monty

The Mask of Zorro

Men in Black

My Best Friend's Wedding

Wag the Dog

1999

★*Shakespeare in Love*

Bulworth

Patch Adams

Still Crazy

There's Something about Mary

Warren Beatty/*Bulworth*

2000

★*Toy Story 2*

Analyze This

Being John Malkovich

Man on the Moon

Notting Hill

2001

★*Almost Famous*

2002

★*Moulin Rouge*

Bridget Jones's Diary

Gosford Park

Legally Blonde

Shrek

2003

★*Chicago*

About a Boy

Adaptation

My Big Fat Greek Wedding

Nicholas Nickleby

2004

★*Lost in Translation*

Bend It Like Beckham

Big Fish

Finding Nemo

Love Actually

2005

★*Sideways*

Eternal Sunshine of the Spotless Mind

The Incredibles

The Phantom of the Opera

Ray

2006

★*Walk the Line*

Mrs. Henderson Presents

Pride and Prejudice

The Producers

The Squid and the Whale

2007

★*Dreamgirls*

Borat: Cultural Learnings of America for Make Benefit Glorious Nation of Kazakhstan

The Devil Wears Prada

Little Miss Sunshine

Thank You for Smoking

2008

★*Sweeney Todd: The Demon Barber of Fleet Street*

Across the Universe

Charlie Wilson's War

Hairspray

Juno

2009

★*Vicky Cristina Barcelona*

Burn After Reading

Happy-Go-Lucky

In Bruges

2010

(500) Days of Summer

It's Complicated

Julie & Julia

Nine

DIRECTOR

1944

★Henry King/*The Song of Bernadette*

1945

★Leo McCarey/*Going My Way*

1946

★Billy Wilder/*The Lost Weekend*

1947

★Frank Capra/*It's a Wonderful Life*

1948

★Elia Kazan/*Gentleman's Agreement*

1949

★John Huston/*Treasure of the Sierra Madre*

1950

★Robert Rossen/*All the King's Men*

1951

★Billy Wilder/*Sunset Boulevard*

1953

★Cecil B. DeMille/*The Greatest Show on Earth*

1954

Fred Zinnemann/*From Here to Eternity*

1955

★Elia Kazan/*On the Waterfront*

1956

★Joshua Logan/*Picnic*

1957

★Elia Kazan/*Baby Doll*

1958

★David Lean/*The Bridge on the River Kwai*

1959

★Vincente Minnelli/*Gigi*

1960

★William Wyler/*Ben-Hur*

1962

★Stanley Kramer/*Judgment at Nuremberg*

1963

★David Lean/*Lawrence of Arabia*

1965

★George Cukor/*My Fair Lady*

1966

★David Lean/*Doctor Zhivago*

1967

★Fred Zinnemann/*A Man for All Seasons*

1968

★Mike Nichols/*The Graduate*

1969

★Paul Newman/*Rachel, Rachel*

1970

★Charles Jarrott/*Anne of the Thousand Days*

1971

★Arthur Hiller/*Love Story*

1972

★William Friedkin/*The French Connection*

1973

★Francis Ford Coppola/*The Godfather*

1974

★William Friedkin/*The Exorcist*

1975

★Roman Polanski/*Chinatown*

1976

★Milos Forman/*One Flew Over the Cuckoo's Nest*

1977

★Sidney Lumet/*Network*

1978

★Herbert Ross/*The Turning Point*

1979

★Michael Cimino/*The Deer Hunter*

1980

★Francis Ford Coppola/*Apocalypse Now*

1981

★Robert Redford/*Ordinary People*

1982

★Warren Beatty/*Reds*

1983

★Richard Attenborough/*Gandhi*

1984

★Barbra Streisand/*Yentl*

1985

★Milos Forman/*Amadeus*

Sergio Leone/*Once Upon a Time in America*

1986

★John Huston/*Prizzi's Honor*

1987

★Oliver Stone/*Platoon*

1988

★Bernardo Bertolucci/*The Last Emperor*

1989

★Clint Eastwood/*Bird*

1990

★Oliver Stone/*Born on the Fourth of July*

Martin Scorsese/*Goodfellas*

1991

★Kevin Costner/*Dances with Wolves*

1992

★Oliver Stone/*JFK*

1993

★Clint Eastwood/*Unforgiven*

1994

★Steven Spielberg/*Schindler's List*

Jane Campion/*The Piano*

Andrew Davis/*The Fugitive*

James Ivory/*The Remains of the Day*

Martin Scorsese/*The Age of Innocence*

1995

★Robert Zemeckis/*Forrest Gump*

Robert Redford/*Quiz Show*

Oliver Stone/*Natural Born Killers*

Quentin Tarantino/*Pulp Fiction*

Edward Zwick/*Legends of the Fall*

1996

★Mel Gibson/*Braveheart*

Mike Figgis/*Leaving Las Vegas*

Ron Howard/*Apollo 13*

Ang Lee/*Sense and Sensibility*

Rob Reiner/*The American President*

Martin Scorsese/*Casino*

1997

★Milos Forman/*The People vs. Larry Flynt*

Joel Coen/*Fargo*

Scott Hicks/*Shine*

Anthony Minghella/*The English Patient*

Alan Parker/*Evita*

1998

★James Cameron/*Titanic*

James L. Brooks/*As Good As It Gets*

Curtis Hanson/*L.A. Confidential*

Jim Sheridan/*The Boxer*

Steven Spielberg/*Amistad*

1999

★Steven Spielberg/*Saving Private Ryan*

Shekhar Kapur/*Elizabeth*

John Madden/*Shakespeare in Love*

Robert Redford/*The Horse Whisperer*

Peter Weir/*The Truman Show*

2000

★Sam Mendes/*American Beauty*

Norman Jewison/*The Hurricane*

Neil Jordan/*The End of the Affair*

Michael Mann/*The Insider*

Anthony Minghella/*The Talented Mr. Ripley*

2001

★Ang Lee/*Crouching Tiger, Hidden Dragon*

2002

★Robert Altman/*Gosford Park*

Ron Howard/*A Beautiful Mind*

Peter Jackson/*Lord of the Rings: The Fellowship of the Ring*

Baz Luhrmann/*Moulin Rouge*

David Lynch/*Mulholland Drive*

David Spielberg/*A. I.: Artificial Intelligence*

2003

★Martin Scorsese/*Gangs of New York*

Stephen Daldry/*The Hours*

Peter Jackson/*Lord of the Rings: The Two Towers*

Spike Jonze/*Adaptation*

Rob Marshall/*Chicago*

Alexander Payne/*About Schmidt*

2004

★Peter Jackson/*Lord of the Rings: The Return of the King*

Sofia Coppola/*Lost in Translation*

Clint Eastwood/*Mystic River*

Anthony Minghella/*Cold Mountain*

Peter Weir/*Master and Commander: The Far Side of the World*

2005

★Clint Eastwood/*Million Dollar Baby*

Woody Allen/*Match Point*

Marc Forster/*Finding Neverland*

Mike Nichols/*Closer*

Alexander Payne/*Sideways*

Martin Scorsese/*The Aviator*

2006

★Ang Lee/*Brokeback Mountain*

George Clooney/*Good Night, and Good Luck*

Peter Jackson/*King Kong*

Fernando Meirelles/*The Constant Gardener*

Steven Spielberg/*Munich*

2007

★Martin Scorsese/*The Departed*

Clint Eastwood/*Flags of Our Fathers*

Clint Eastwood/*Letters from Iwo Jima*

Stephen Frears/*The Queen*

Alejandro Gonzalez Inarritu/*Babel*

2008

★Julian Schnabel/*The Diving Bell and the Butterfly*

Tim Burton/*Sweeney Todd: The Demon Barber of Fleet Street*

Ethan Coen/*No Country for Old Men*

Joel Coen/*No Country for Old Men*

Ridley Scott/*American Gangster*

Joe Wright/*Atonement*

2009

★David Amann/*Slumdog Millionaire*

Stephen Daldry/*The Reader*

David Fincher/*The Curious Case of Benjamin Button*

Ron Howard/*Frost/Nixon*

Sam Mendes/*Revolutionary Road*

2010

★*Avatar*

Kathryn Bigelow/*The Hurt Locker*

Clint Eastwood/*Invictus*

Jason Reitman/*Up in the Air*

Quentin Tarantino/*Inglourious Basterds*

SCORE

1948

★*Life with Father*

1949

★*The Red Shoes*

1950

★*The Inspector General*

1951

★*Sunset Boulevard*

1952

★*September Affair*

1953

★*High Noon*

1960

★*On the Beach*

1961

★*The Alamo*

1962

★*The Guns of Navarone*

1963

★*To Kill a Mockingbird*

1965

★*The Fall of the Roman Empire*

1966

★*Doctor Zhivago*

1967

★*Hawaii*

1968

★*Camelot*

1969

★*The Shoes of the Fisherman*

1970

★*Butch Cassidy and the Sundance Kid*

1971

★*Love Story*

1972

★*Shaft*

1973

★*The Godfather*

1974

★*Jonathan Livingston Seagull*

1975

★*The Little Prince*

1976

★*Jaws*

1977

★*A Star Is Born*

1978

★*Star Wars*

1979

★*Midnight Express*

1980

★*Apocalypse Now*

1981

★*The Stunt Man*

1983

★*E.T.: The Extra-Terrestrial*

1984

★*Flashdance*

1985

★*A Passage to India*

1986

★*Out of Africa*

1987

★*The Mission*

1988

★*The Last Emperor*

1989

★*Gorillas in the Mist*

1990

★*The Little Mermaid*

1991

★*The Sheltering Sky*

1993

★*Aladdin*

1994

★*Heaven and Earth*

The Nightmare Before Christmas

The Piano

Schindler's List

★ = winner

Trois Couleurs: Bleu

1995

★*The Lion King*

Forrest Gump

Interview with the Vampire

Legends of the Fall

Nell

1996

★*A Walk in the Clouds*

Braveheart

Don Juan DeMarco

Pocahontas

Sense and Sensibility

1997

★*The English Patient*

The Hunchback of Notre Dame

Michael Collins

The Mirror Has Two Faces

Shine

1998

★*Titanic*

Gattaca

Kundun

L.A. Confidential

Seven Years in Tibet

1999

★*The Truman Show*

A Bug's Life

Mulan

Prince of Egypt

Saving Private Ryan

2000

★*The Legend of 1900*

2001

★*Gladiator*

2002

★*Moulin Rouge*

A. I.: Artificial Intelligence

Ali

A Beautiful Mind

Lord of the Rings: The Fellowship of the Ring

Mulholland Drive

Pearl Harbor

The Shipping News

2003

★*Frida*

★*25th Hour*

Far from Heaven

The Hours

Rabbit-Proof Fence

ORIGINAL SCORE

1985

Once Upon a Time in America

2000

American Beauty

Angela's Ashes

Anna and the King

The End of the Affair

Eyes Wide Shut

The Insider

The Straight Story

The Talented Mr. Ripley

2004

★*Lord of the Rings: The Return of the King*

Big Fish

Cold Mountain

Girl with a Pearl Earring

The Last Samurai

2005

★*The Aviator*

Finding Neverland

Million Dollar Baby

Sideways

Spanglish

2006

★*Memoirs of a Geisha*

Brokeback Mountain

The Chronicles of Narnia: The Lion, the Witch and the Wardrobe

King Kong

Syriana

2007

★*The Painted Veil*

Babel

The Da Vinci Code

The Fountain

2008

★*Atonement*

Eastern Promises

Grace Is Gone

Into the Wild

The Kite Runner

2009

★*Slumdog Millionaire*

Changeling

The Curious Case of Benjamin Button

Defiance

Frost/Nixon

2010

★*Up*

Avatar

The Informant!

A Single Man

Where the Wild Things Are

SONG

1961

★"Town without Pity"/*Town without Pity*

1965

★"Circus World"/*Circus World*

1968

★"If Ever I Should Leave You"/*Camelot*

1969

★"The Windmills of Your Mind"/*The Thomas Crown Affair*

1970

★"Jean"/*The Prime of Miss Jean Brodie*

1971

★"Whistling Away the Dark"/*Darling Lili*

1972

★"Life Is What You Make It"/*Kotch*

1973

★"Ben"/*Ben*

1974

★"The Way We Were"/*The Way We Were*

1975

★"I Feel Love"/*Benji*

1976

★"I'm Easy"/*Nashville*

1977

★"Evergreen"/*A Star Is Born*

1978

★"You Light Up My Life"/*You Light Up My Life*

1980

★"The Rose"/*The Rose*

1981

★"Fame"/*Fame*

1982

★"Arthur's Theme"/*Arthur*

1983

★"Up Where We Belong"/*An Officer and a Gentleman*

1984

★"Flashdance...What a Feeling"/*Flashdance*

1985

★"I Just Called to Say I Love You"/*The Woman in Red*

1986

★"Say You, Say Me"/*White Nights*

1987

★"Take My Breath Away"/*Top Gun*

1988

★"(I've Had) the Time of My Life"/*Dirty Dancing*

1989

★"Let the River Run"/*Working Girl*

1990

★"Under the Sea"/*The Little Mermaid*

1991

★"Blaze of Glory"/*Young Guns 2*

1993

★"A Whole New World"/*Aladdin*

1994

★"Streets of Philadelphia"/*Philadelphia*

"(You Made Me the) Thief of Your Heart"/*In the Name of the Father*

"Again"/*Poetic Justice*

"Stay"/*Faraway, So Close!*

"The Day I Fall in Love"/*Beethoven's 2nd*

1995

★"Can You Feel the Love Tonight?"/*The Lion King*

"Circle of Life"/*The Lion King*

"Far Longer than Forever"/*The Swan Princess*

"I'll Remember"/*With Honors*

"Look What Love Has Done"/*Junior*

"The Color of the Night"/*Color of Night*

1996

★"Colors of the Wind"/*Pocahontas*

"Have You Ever Really Loved a Woman?"/*Don Juan DeMarco*

"Hold Me, Thrill Me, Kiss Me, Kill Me"/*Batman Forever*

"Moonlight"/*Sabrina*

"You Got a Friend in Me"/*Toy Story*

1997

★"You Must Love Me"/*Evita*

"Because You Loved Me"/*Up Close and Personal*

"For the First Time"/*One Fine Day*

"I've Finally Found Someone"/*The Mirror Has Two Faces*

"That Thing You Do!"/*That Thing You Do!*

1998

★"My Heart Will Go On"/*Titanic*

"Go the Distance"/*Hercules*

"Journey to the Past"/*Anastasia*

"Once Upon a December"/*Anastasia*

"Tomorrow Never Dies"/*Tomorrow Never Dies*

1999

★"The Prayer"/*Quest for Camelot*

"Reflection"/*Mulan*

"The Flame Still Burns"/*Still Crazy*

"The Magic Sword"/*Quest for Camelot*

"The Mighty"/*The Mighty*

"Uninvited"/*City of Angels*

"When You Believe"/*Prince of Egypt*

2000

★"You'll Be In My Heart"/*Tarzan*

"Beautiful Stranger"/*Austin Powers 2: The Spy Who Shagged Me*

"How Can I Not Love You"/*Anna and the King*

"Save Me"/*Magnolia*

"When She Loved Me"/*Toy Story 2*

2001

★"Things Have Changed"/*Wonder Boys*

2002

★"Until"/*Kate & Leopold*

"Come What May"/*Moulin Rouge*

"May It Be"/*Lord of the Rings: The Fellowship of the Ring*

"There You'll Be"/*Pearl Harbor*

"Vanilla Sky"/*Vanilla Sky*

2003

★"The Hands That Built America"/*Gangs of New York*

"Die Another Day"/*Die Another Day*

"Father and Daughter"/*The Wild Thornberrys Movie*

"Here I Am"/*Spirit: Stallion of the Cimarron*

"Lose Yourself"/*8 Mile*

2004

★"Into the West"/*Lord of the Rings: The Return of the King*

"Man of the Hour"/*Big Fish*

"The Heart of Every Girl"/*Mona Lisa Smile*

"Time Enough for Tears"/*In America*

"You Will Be My Ain True Love"/*Cold Mountain*

2005

★"Old Habits Die Hard"/*Alfie*

"Accidently in Love"/*Shrek 2*

"Believe"/*The Polar Express*

"Learn to be Lonely"/*The Phantom of the Opera*

"Million Voices"/*Hotel Rwanda*

2006

★"A Love That Will Never Grow Old"/*Brokeback Mountain*

"There's Nothing Like a Show on Broadway"/*The Producers*

"Travelin' Thru"/*Transamerica*

"Wunderkind"/*The Chronicles of Narnia: The Lion, the Witch and the Wardrobe*

2007

★"The Song of the Heart"/*Happy Feet*

"A Father's Way"/*The Pursuit of Happyness*

"Listen"/*Dreamgirls*

"Never Gonna Break My Faith"/*Bobby*

2008

★"Guaranteed"/*Into the Wild*

"Despedida"/*Love in the Time of Cholera*

"Grace is Gone"/*Grace Is Gone*

"That's How You Know"/*Enchanted*

"Walk Hard"/*Walk Hard: The Dewey Cox Story*

2009

★"The Wrestler"/*The Wrestler*

"Down to Earth"/*WALL-E*

"Gran Torino"/*Gran Torino*

"I Thought I Lost You"/*Bolt*

"Once in a Lifetime"/*Cadillac Records*

2010

★"The Weary Kind"/*Crazy Heart*

"(I Want to) Come Home"/*Everybody's Fine*

"Cinema Italiano"/*Nine*

"I See You"/*Avatar*

"Winter"/*Brothers*

SCREENPLAY

1948

★*Miracle on 34th Street*

1949

★*The Search*

1950

★*Battleground*

1951

★*All About Eve*

1953

★*Five Fingers*

1954

★*Lili*

1955

★*Sabrina*

1966

★*Doctor Zhivago*

1967

★*A Man for All Seasons*

1968

★*In the Heat of the Night*

1969

★*Charly*

1970

★*Anne of the Thousand Days*

1971

★*Love Story*

1972

★*The Hospital*

1973

★*The Godfather*

1974

★*The Exorcist*

1975

★*Chinatown*

1976

★*One Flew Over the Cuckoo's Nest*

1977

★*Network*

1978

★*The Goodbye Girl*

1979

★*Midnight Express*

1980

★*Kramer vs. Kramer*

1981

★*The Ninth Configuration*

1982

★*On Golden Pond*

1983

★*Gandhi*

1984

★*Terms of Endearment*

1985

★*Amadeus*

1986

★*The Purple Rose of Cairo*

1987

★*The Mission*

1988

★*The Last Emperor*

1989

★*Running on Empty*

1990

★*Born on the Fourth of July*

Goodfellas

1991

★*Dances with Wolves*

1993

★*Scent of a Woman*

1994

★*Schindler's List*

Philadelphia

The Piano

The Remains of the Day

Short Cuts

1995

★*Pulp Fiction*

Forrest Gump

Four Weddings and a Funeral

Mr. Holland's Opus

Quiz Show

The Shawshank Redemption

1996

★*Sense and Sensibility*

The American President

Braveheart

Dead Man Walking

Get Shorty

1997

★*The People vs. Larry Flynt*

The English Patient

Fargo

Lone Star

Shine

1998

★*Good Will Hunting*

As Good As It Gets

L.A. Confidential

Titanic

Wag the Dog

1999

★*Shakespeare in Love*

Bulworth

Happiness

Saving Private Ryan

The Truman Show

2000

★*American Beauty*

Being John Malkovich

The Cider House Rules

The Insider

The Sixth Sense

2001

★*Traffic*

2002

★*A Beautiful Mind*

Gosford Park

The Man Who Wasn't There

Memento

Mulholland Drive

2003

★*About Schmidt*

Adaptation

Chicago

Far from Heaven

The Hours

2004

★*Lost in Translation*

Cold Mountain

In America

Love Actually

Mystic River

2005

★*Sideways*

The Aviator

Closer

Eternal Sunshine of the Spotless Mind

Finding Neverland

★ = winner

2006
★Brokeback Mountain
Crash
Good Night, and Good Luck
Match Point
Munich
2007
★The Queen
Babel
The Departed
Little Children
Notes on a Scandal
2008
★No Country for Old Men
Atonement
Charlie Wilson's War
The Diving Bell and the Butterfly
Juno
2009
★Slumdog Millionaire
The Curious Case of Benjamin Button
Doubt
Frost/Nixon
The Reader
2010
★Up in the Air
District 9
The Hurt Locker
Inglourious Basterds
It's Complicated

FILM—FOREIGN LANGUAGE

1950
★The Bicycle Thief
1955
★Genevieve
1956
★Ordet
1957
★Richard III
★War and Peace
1959
★A Night to Remember
1960
★Black Orpheus
★Odd Obsession
★Wild Strawberries
1961
★The Virgin Spring
1962
★Two Women
1963
★Divorce—Italian Style
1964
★Tom Jones
1965
★Marriage Italian Style
★Sallah
1966
★Darling
1967
★Alfie
★A Man and a Woman
1969
★Romeo and Juliet
★War and Peace
1970
★Oh! What a Lovely War
★Z
1971
★Rider on the Rain
★Women in Love
1972
★Sunday, Bloody Sunday
1973
★Young Winston
1974
★The Pedestrian
1975
★Scenes from a Marriage
1976
★Lies My Father Told Me
1977
★Face to Face
1978
★A Special Day
1979
★Autumn Sonata
1980
★La Cage aux Folles
1981
★Tess
1982
★Chariots of Fire
1983
★Gandhi
1984
★Fanny and Alexander
1985
★A Passage to India
1986
★The Official Story
1987
★The Assault
1988
★My Life As a Dog
1989
★Pelle the Conqueror
1990
★Cinema Paradiso
1991
★Cyrano de Bergerac
1992
★Europa, Europa
1993
★Indochine
1994
★Farewell My Concubine
Flight of the Innocent
Trois Couleurs: Bleu
The Wedding Banquet
1995
★Farinelli
Eat Drink Man Woman
Queen Margot
To Live
Trois Couleurs: Rouge
1996
★Les Miserables
Brother of Sleep
French Twist
Shanghai Triad
1997
★Kolya
The Eighth Day
Luna e L'Altra
Prisoner of the Mountains
Ridicule
1998
★Ma Vie en Rose
Artemisia
The Best Man
Lea
The Thief
1999
★Central Station
The Celebration
Hombres Armados
2000
★All About My Mother
The Red Violin
2001
★Crouching Tiger, Hidden Dragon
Amores Perros
The Widow of Saint-Pierre
2002
Amelie
Monsoon Wedding
2003
★Talk to Her
City of God
The Crime of Father Amaro
2004
The Barbarian Invasions
2005
★The Sea Inside
House of Flying Daggers
The Motorcycle Diaries
A Very Long Engagement
2006
★Paradise Now
Tsotsi
2007
★Letters from Iwo Jima
Apocalypto
Pan's Labyrinth
Volver
2008
★The Diving Bell and the Butterfly
The Kite Runner
Lust, Caution
2009
★Waltz with Bashir
I've Loved You So Long
2010
★The White Ribbon
Baaria
Broken Embraces
The Maid
A Prophet

ANIMATED FILM

2007
★Cars
Happy Feet
Monster House
2008
★Ratatouille
Bee Movie
The Simpsons Movie
2009
★WALL-E
Bolt
Kung Fu Panda
2010
★Up
Cloudy with a Chance of Meatballs
Coraline
Fantastic Mr. Fox
The Princess and the Frog

INDEPENDENT SPIRIT AWARDS

ACTOR

1986
★M. Emmet Walsh/Blood Simple
1987
★James Woods/Salvador
1988
★Dennis Quaid/The Big Easy
1989
★Edward James Olmos/Stand and Deliver
1990
★Matt Dillon/Drugstore Cowboy
1991
★Danny Glover/To Sleep with Anger
1992
★River Phoenix/My Own Private Idaho
1993
★Harvey Keitel/Bad Lieutenant
1994
★Jeff Bridges/American Heart
Vincent D'Onofrio/Household Saints
Mitchell Lichtenstein/The Wedding Banquet
Matthew Modine/Equinox
Tyrin Turner/Menace II Society
1995
★Samuel L. Jackson/Pulp Fiction
Sihung Lung/Eat Drink Man Woman
William H. Macy/Oleanna
Campbell Scott/Mrs. Parker and the Vicious Circle
Jon Seda/I Like It Like That
1996
★Sean Penn/Dead Man Walking
Nicolas Cage/Leaving Las Vegas
Tim Roth/Little Odessa
Jimmy Smits/My Family
Kevin Spacey/Swimming with Sharks
1997
★William H. Macy/Fargo
Chris Cooper/Lone Star
Christopher Penn/The Funeral
1998
★Robert Duvall/The Apostle
Peter Fonda/Ulee's Gold
Christopher Guest/Waiting for Guffman
Philip Baker Hall/Hard Eight
John Turturro/Box of Moonlight
1999
★Ian McKellen/Gods and Monsters
Dylan Baker/Happiness
Nick Nolte/Affliction
Sean Penn/Hurlyburly
Courtney B. Vance/Blind Faith
2000
★Richard Farnsworth/The Straight Story
John Cusack/Being John Malkovich
Terence Stamp/The Limey
David Strathairn/Limbo
2001
★Javier Bardem/Before Night Falls
Adrien Brody/Restaurant
Billy Crudup/Jesus' Son
Mark Ruffalo/You Can Count On Me
2002
★Tom Wilkinson/In the Bedroom
Brian Cox/L.I.E.
Jake Gyllenhaal/Donnie Darko
John Cameron Mitchell/Hedwig and the Angry Inch
2003
★Derek Luke/Antwone Fisher
Graham Greene/Skins
Jeremy Renner/Dahmer
Campbell Scott/Roger Dodger
2004
★Bill Murray/Lost in Translation
Peter Dinklage/The Station Agent
Paul Giamatti/American Splendor
Ben Kingsley/House of Sand and Fog
Lee Pace/Soldier's Girl
2005
★Paul Giamatti/Sideways
Kevin Bacon/The Woodsman
Jeff Bridges/The Door in the Floor
Liam Neeson/Kinsey
2006
★Philip Seymour Hoffman/Capote
Jeff Daniels/The Squid and the Whale
Terrence Howard/Hustle & Flow
Heath Ledger/Brokeback Mountain
David Strathairn/Good Night, and Good Luck
2007
★Ryan Gosling/Half Nelson
Aaron Eckhart/Thank You for Smoking
Edward Norton/The Painted Veil
Forest Whitaker/American Gun
2008
★Philip Seymour Hoffman/The Savages
Don Cheadle/Talk to Me
Tony Leung Chiu-Wai/Lust, Caution
2009
★Mickey Rourke/The Wrestler
Javier Bardem/Vicky Cristina Barcelona
Richard Jenkins/The Visitor
Sean Penn/Milk
Jeremy Renner/The Hurt Locker
Jeremy Renner/The Hurt Locker
JimMyron Ross/Ballast
2010
★Jeff Bridges/Crazy Heart
Colin Firth/A Single Man
Joseph Gordon-Levitt/(500) Days of Summer
Souleymane Sy Savane/Goodbye Solo
Adam Scott/The Vicious Kind

ACTOR—SUPPORTING

1988
★Morgan Freeman/Street Smart
1989
★Lou Diamond Phillips/Stand and Deliver
1990
★Max Perlich/Drugstore Cowboy
1991
★Bruce Davison/Longtime Companion
1992
★David Strathairn/City of Hope
1993
★Steve Buscemi/Reservoir Dogs
1994
★Christopher Lloyd/Twenty Bucks
David Chung/Combination Platter
Tate Donovan/Inside Monkey Zetterland
Todd Field/Ruby in Paradise
Edward Furlong/American Heart
1995
★Chazz Palminteri/Bullets over Broadway
Giancarlo Esposito/Fresh
Larry Pine/Vanya on 42nd Street
Eric Stoltz/Pulp Fiction
Nicholas Turturro/Federal Hill
1996
★Benicio Del Toro/The Usual Suspects
James LeGros/Living in Oblivion
David Morse/The Crossing Guard
Max Perlich/Georgia
Harold Perrineau, Jr./Smoke
1997
★Benicio Del Toro/Basquiat
★Jason Lee/Chasing Amy
Kevin Corrigan/Walking and Talking
Matthew Faber/Welcome to the Dollhouse
Gary Farmer/Dead Man
Richard Jenkins/Flirting with Disaster
1998
Efrain Figueroa/Star Maps
Samuel L. Jackson/Hard Eight
Ajay Naidu/subUrbia
Roy Scheider/The Myth of Fingerprints
1999
★Bill Murray/Rushmore
James Coburn/Affliction
Charles S. Dutton/Blind Faith
Gary Farmer/Smoke Signals
Philip Seymour Hoffman/Happiness
2000
★Steve Zahn/Happy, Texas
Charles S. Dutton/Cookie's Fortune
Clark Gregg/The Adventures of Sebastian Cole
Luis Guzman/The Limey
Terrence Howard/The Best Man
2001
Cole Hauser/Tigerland
Gary Oldman/The Contender
Giovanni Ribisi/The Gift
2002
★Steve Buscemi/Ghost World
Billy Kay/L.I.E.
Garrett Morris/Jackpot
John C. Reilly/The Anniversary Party
2003
★Dennis Quaid/Far from Heaven
Alan Arkin/Thirteen Conversations About One Thing
Ray Liotta/Narc
John C. Reilly/The Good Girl
2004
★Djimon Hounsou/In America
Judah Friedlander/American Splendor
Troy Garity/Soldier's Girl
Alessandro Nivola/Laurel Canyon
Peter Sarsgaard/Shattered Glass

★ = winner

2005

★Thomas Haden Church/*Sideways*

Jon(athan) Gries/*Napoleon Dynamite*

Roger Robinson/*Brother to Brother*

Peter Sarsgaard/*Kinsey*

2006

★Matt Dillon/*Crash*

Jesse Eisenberg/*The Squid and the Whale*

2007

★Alan Arkin/*Little Miss Sunshine*

Daniel Craig/*Infamous*

Paul Franklin Dano/*Little Miss Sunshine*

Channing Tatum/*A Guide to Recognizing Your Saints*

2008

★Chiwetel Ejiofor/*Talk to Me*

Marcus Carl Franklin/*I'm Not There*

Kene Holliday/*Great World of Sound*

Irfan Khan/*The Namesake*

Steve Zahn/*Rescue Dawn*

2009

★James Franco/*Milk*

Anthony Mackie/*The Hurt Locker*

Anthony Mackie/*The Hurt Locker*

Charlie McDermott/*Frozen River*

Haaz Sleiman/*The Visitor*

2010

★Woody Harrelson/*The Messenger*

Jemaine Clement/*Gentlemen Broncos*

Christian McKay/*Me and Orson Welles*

Ray McKinnon/*That Evening Sun*

Christopher Plummer/*The Last Station*

ACTRESS

1986

★Geraldine Page/*The Trip to Bountiful*

1987

★Isabella Rossellini/*Blue Velvet*

1988

★Sally Kirkland/*Anna*

1989

★Jodie Foster/*Five Corners*

1990

★Andie MacDowell/*sex, lies and videotape*

1991

★Anjelica Huston/*The Grifters*

1992

★Judy Davis/*Impromptu*

1993

★Fairuza Balk/*Gas Food Lodging*

1994

★Ashley Judd/*Ruby in Paradise*

Suzy Amis/*The Ballad of Little Jo*

May Chin/*The Wedding Banquet*

Ariyan Johnson/*Just Another Girl on the I.R.T.*

Emma Thompson/*Much Ado about Nothing*

1995

★Linda Fiorentino/*The Last Seduction*

Jennifer Jason Leigh/*Mrs. Parker and the Vicious Circle*

Karen Sillas/*What Happened Was...*

Lauren Velez/*I Like It Like That*

Chien-Lien Wu/*Eat Drink Man Woman*

1996

★Elisabeth Shue/*Leaving Las Vegas*

Jennifer Jason Leigh/*Georgia*

Elina Lowensohn/*Nadja*

Julianne Moore/*Safe*

Lili Taylor/*The Addiction*

1997

★Frances McDormand/*Fargo*

Maria Conchita Alonso/*Caught*

Scarlett Johansson/*Manny & Lo*

Catherine Keener/*Walking and Talking*

Renee Zellweger/*The Whole Wide World*

1998

★Julie Christie/*Afterglow*

Stacy Edwards/*In the Company of Men*

Alison Folland/*All Over Me*

Lisa Harrow/*Sunday*

Robin Wright Penn/*Loved*

1999

★Ally Sheedy/*High Art*

Katrin Cartlidge/*Claire Dolan*

Christina Ricci/*The Opposite of Sex*

Robin Tunney/*Niagara, Niagara*

Alfre Woodard/*Down in the Delta*

2000

★Hilary Swank/*Boys Don't Cry*

Diane Lane/*A Walk on the Moon*

Janet McTeer/*Tumbleweeds*

Reese Witherspoon/*Election*

2001

★Ellen Burstyn/*Requiem for a Dream*

Joan Allen/*The Contender*

Sanaa Lathan/*Love and Basketball*

Laura Linney/*You Can Count On Me*

Kelly Macdonald/*Two Family House*

2002

★Sissy Spacek/*In the Bedroom*

Molly Parker/*The Center of the World*

Tilda Swinton/*The Deep End*

Kerry Washington/*Lift*

2003

★Julianne Moore/*Far from Heaven*

Jennifer Aniston/*The Good Girl*

Maggie Gyllenhaal/*Secretary*

Catherine Keener/*Lovely & Amazing*

Parker Posey/*Personal Velocity: Three Portraits*

2004

★Charlize Theron/*Monster*

Agnes Bruckner/*Blue Car*

Zooey Deschanel/*All the Real Girls*

Samantha Morton/*In America*

2005

★Catalina Sandino Moreno/*Maria Full of Grace*

Kimberly Elise/*Woman, Thou Art Loosed*

2006

★Felicity Huffman/*Transamerica*

Vera Farmiga/*Down to the Bone*

Angelina Jolie/*A Mighty Heart*

Laura Linney/*The Squid and the Whale*

Sienna Miller/*Interview*

2007

★Shareeka Epps/*Half Nelson*

Catherine O'Hara/*For Your Consideration*

Michelle Williams/*Land of Plenty*

Robin Wright Penn/*Sorry, Haters*

2008

★*Juno*

Parker Posey/*Broken English*

Tang Wei/*Lust, Caution*

2009

★Melissa Leo/*Frozen River*

Summer Bishil/*Towelhead*

Anne Hathaway/*Rachel Getting Married*

Melissa Leo/*Frozen River*

Tarra Riggs/*Ballast*

Michelle Williams/*Wendy and Lucy*

2010

★Gabourney "Gabby" Sidibe/*Precious: Based on the Novel by Sapphire*

Maria Bello/*Downloading Nancy*

Nisreen Faour/*Amreeka*

Helen Mirren/*The Last Station*

Gwyneth Paltrow/*Two Lovers*

ACTRESS—SUPPORTING

1988

★Anjelica Huston/*The Dead*

1989

★Rosanna Desoto/*Stand and Deliver*

1990

★Laura San Giacomo/*sex, lies and videotape*

1991

★Sheryl Lee Ralph/*To Sleep with Anger*

1992

★Diane Ladd/*Rambling Rose*

1993

★Alfre Woodard/*Passion Fish*

1994

★Lili Taylor/*Household Saints*

Lara Flynn Boyle/*Equinox*

Ah-Leh Gua/*The Wedding Banquet*

Lucinda Jenney/*American Heart*

Julianne Moore/*Short Cuts*

1995

★Dianne Wiest/*Bullets over Broadway*

V.S. Brodie/*Go Fish*

Carla Gallo/*Spanking the Monkey*

Kelly Lynch/*Forbidden Choices*

Brooke Smith/*Vanya on 42nd Street*

1996

★Mare Winningham/*Georgia*

Jennifer Lopez/*My Family*

Vanessa Redgrave/*Little Odessa*

Chloe Sevigny/*Kids*

Celia Weston/*Dead Man Walking*

1997

★Elizabeth Pena/*Lone Star*

Mary Kay Place/*Manny & Lo*

Queen Latifah/*Set It Off*

Lili Taylor/*Girls Town*

Lily Tomlin/*Flirting with Disaster*

1998

★Debbi (Deborah) Morgan/*Eve's Bayou*

Farrah Fawcett/*The Apostle*

Amy Madigan/*Loved*

Miranda Richardson/*The Apostle*

Patricia Richardson/*Ulee's Gold*

1999

★Lynn Redgrave/*Gods and Monsters*

Stockard Channing/*The Baby Dance*

Patricia Clarkson/*High Art*

Lisa Kudrow/*The Opposite of Sex*

Joely Richardson/*In the Shadows*

2000

★Chloe Sevigny/*Boys Don't Cry*

Barbara Barrie/*Judy Berlin*

Vanessa Martinez/*Limbo*

Julianne Nicholson/*Tully*

Sarah Polley/*Go*

Jean Smart/*Guinevere*

2001

★Zhang Ziyi/*Crouching Tiger, Hidden Dragon*

Pat Carroll/*Songcatcher*

Jennifer Connelly/*Requiem for a Dream*

Marcia Gay Harden/*Pollock*

Lupe Ontiveros/*Chuck & Buck*

2002

★Carrie-Anne Moss/*Memento*

Uma Thurman/*Tape*

Tamara Tunie/*The Caveman's Valentine*

2003

★Emily Mortimer/*Lovely & Amazing*

Viola Davis/*Antwone Fisher*

2004

★Shohreh Aghdashloo/*House of Sand and Fog*

★Hope Davis/*The Secret Lives of Dentists*

Sarah Bolger/*In America*

Patricia Clarkson/*Pieces of April*

Frances McDormand/*Laurel Canyon*

2005

★Virginia Madsen/*Sideways*

Cate Blanchett/*Coffee and Cigarettes*

Loretta Devine/*Woman, Thou Art Loosed*

Yenny Paola Vega/*Maria Full of Grace*

2006

★Amy Adams/*Junebug*

Maggie Gyllenhaal/*Happy Endings*

Michelle Williams/*Brokeback Mountain*

2007

★Frances McDormand/*Friends with Money*

Melonie Diaz/*A Guide to Recognizing Your Saints*

Marcia Gay Harden/*American Gun*

2008

★Cate Blanchett/*I'm Not There*

Anna Kendrick/*Rocket Science*

Jennifer Jason Leigh/*Margot at the Wedding*

Tamara Podemski/*Four Sheets to the Wind*

Marisa Tomei/*Before the Devil Knows You're Dead*

2009

★Penelope Cruz/*Vicky Cristina Barcelona*

Rosemarie DeWitt/*Rachel Getting Married*

Rosie Perez/*The Take*

Misty Upham/*Frozen River*

Debra Winger/*Rachel Getting Married*

2010

★Mo'Nique/*Precious: Based on the Novel by Sapphire*

Dina Korzun/*Cold Souls*

Samantha Morton/*The Messenger*

Nathalie Press/*Fifty Dead Men Walking*

Mia Wasikowska/*That Evening Sun*

CINEMATOGRAPHY

1986

★*Trouble in Mind*

1987

★*Platoon*

1988

★*Matewan*

1989

★*The Unbearable Lightness of Being*

1990

★*Drugstore Cowboy*

1991

★*Wild at Heart*

1992

★*Kafka*

1993

★*Night on Earth*

1994

★*Menace II Society*

American Heart

Chain of Desire

Equinox

Ruby in Paradise

1995

★*Barcelona*

Eat Drink Man Woman

Forbidden Choices

I Like It Like That

Suture

1996

★*Leaving Las Vegas*

Little Odessa

Nadja

The Underneath

The Usual Suspects

1997

★*Fargo*

Bound

Color of a Brisk and Leaping Day

Dead Man

The Funeral

1998

★*Kama Sutra: A Tale of Love*

The Bible and Gun Club

Habit

Hard Eight

Sunday

1999

★*Velvet Goldmine*

Affliction

Belly

High Art

2000

★*Three Seasons*

Judy Berlin

Julien Donkey-boy

Twin Falls Idaho

2001

★*Requiem for a Dream*

Before Night Falls

Hamlet

Shadow of the Vampire

2002

★*Mulholland Drive*

The Deep End

Hedwig and the Angry Inch

Memento

2003

★*Far from Heaven*

Narc

Personal Velocity: Three Portraits

2004

★*In America*

Elephant

Northfork

Shattered Glass

2005

★*The Motorcycle Diaries*

Saints and Soldiers

We Don't Live Here Anymore

2006

★*Good Night, and Good Luck*

Capote

Youth Without Youth

2007

★*Pan's Labyrinth*

Brothers of the Head

2008

★*The Diving Bell and the Butterfly*

Lust, Caution

The Savages

2009

★*The Wrestler*

Ballast

Milk

2010

★*A Serious Man*

Bad Lieutenant: Port of Call New Orleans

Cold Souls

Sin Nombre

DIRECTOR

1986

★Joel Coen/*Blood Simple*

★Martin Scorsese/*After Hours*

1987

★Oliver Stone/*Platoon*

1988

★John Huston/*The Dead*

1989

★Ramon Menendez/*Stand and Deliver*

1990

★Steven Soderbergh/*sex, lies and videotape*

1991

★Charles Burnett/*To Sleep with Anger*

★ = winner

1992

★Martha Coolidge/*Rambling Rose*

1993

★Carl Franklin/*One False Move*

1994

★Robert Altman/*Short Cuts*

Ang Lee/*The Wedding Banquet*

Victor Nunez/*Ruby in Paradise*

Robert Rodriguez/*El Mariachi*

John Turturro/*Mac*

1995

★Quentin Tarantino/*Pulp Fiction*

John Dahl/*Red Rock West*

Ang Lee/*Eat Drink Man Woman*

Roman Polanski/*Death and the Maiden*

Alan Rudolph/*Mrs. Parker and the Vicious Circle*

1996

★Mike Figgis/*Leaving Las Vegas*

Michael Almereyda/*Nadja*

Ulu Grosbard/*Georgia*

Todd Haynes/*Safe*

John Sayles/*The Secret of Roan Inish*

1997

★Joel Coen/*Fargo*

Abel Ferrara/*The Funeral*

David O. Russell/*Flirting with Disaster*

Todd Solondz/*Welcome to the Dollhouse*

Robert M. Young/*Caught*

1998

★Robert Duvall/*The Apostle*

Larry Fessenden/*Habit*

Victor Nunez/*Ulee's Gold*

Paul Schrader/*Touch*

Wim Wenders/*The End of Violence*

1999

★Wes Anderson/*Rushmore*

Todd Haynes/*Velvet Goldmine*

Lodge Kerrigan/*Claire Dolan*

Paul Schrader/*Affliction*

Todd Solondz/*Happiness*

2000

★Alexander Payne/*Election*

Harmony Korine/*Julien Donkey-boy*

Doug Liman/*Go*

David Lynch/*The Straight Story*

Steven Soderbergh/*The Limey*

2001

★Ang Lee/*Crouching Tiger, Hidden Dragon*

★Christopher Nolan/*Memento*

Darren Aronofsky/*Requiem for a Dream*

Miguel Arteta/*Chuck & Buck*

Christopher Guest/*Best in Show*

Julian Schnabel/*Before Night Falls*

2002

Michael Cuesta/*L.I.E.*

Richard Linklater/*Waking Life*

John Cameron Mitchell/*Hedwig and the Angry Inch*

2003

★Todd Haynes/*Far from Heaven*

Joe Carnahan/*Narc*

Nicole Holofcener/*Lovely & Amazing*

2004

★Sofia Coppola/*Lost in Translation*

Shari Springer Berman/*American Splendor*

Robert Pulcini/*American Splendor*

Jim Sheridan/*In America*

Peter Sollett/*Raising Victor Vargas*

Gus Van Sant/*Elephant*

2005

★Alexander Payne/*Sideways*

Shane Carruth/*Primer*

Joshua Marston/*Maria Full of Grace*

Walter Salles/*The Motorcycle Diaries*

Mario Van Peebles/*Baadasssss!*

2006

★Ang Lee/*Brokeback Mountain*

Noah Baumbach/*The Squid and the Whale*

George Clooney/*Good Night, and Good Luck*

2007

★Jonathan Dayton/*Little Miss Sunshine*

★Valerie Faris/*Little Miss Sunshine*

Robert Altman/*A Prairie Home Companion*

Ryan Fleck/*Half Nelson*

Steven Soderbergh/*Bubble*

2008

★Julian Schnabel/*The Diving Bell and the Butterfly*

Todd Haynes/*I'm Not There*

Tamara Jenkins/*The Savages*

Jason Reitman/*Juno*

2009

★Thomas (Tom) McCarthy/*The Visitor*

Jonathan Demme/*Rachel Getting Married*

Lance Hammer/*Ballast*

Courtney Hunt/*Frozen River*

2010

★Lee Daniels/*Precious: Based on the Novel by Sapphire*

Ethan Coen/*A Serious Man*

Joel Coen/*A Serious Man*

Cary Fukunaga/*Sin Nombre*

James Gray/*Two Lovers*

Michael Hoffman/*The Last Station*

FILM

1986

★*After Hours*

1987

★*Platoon*

1988

★*River's Edge*

1989

★*Stand and Deliver*

1990

★*sex, lies and videotape*

1991

★*The Grifters*

1992

★*Rambling Rose*

1993

★*The Player*

1994

★*Short Cuts*

Equinox

Much Ado about Nothing

Ruby in Paradise

The Wedding Banquet

1995

★*Pulp Fiction*

Bullets over Broadway

Eat Drink Man Woman

Mrs. Parker and the Vicious Circle

Wes Craven's New Nightmare

1996

★*Leaving Las Vegas*

The Addiction

Living in Oblivion

Safe

The Secret of Roan Inish

1997

★*Fargo*

Dead Man

The Funeral

Lone Star

Welcome to the Dollhouse

1998

★*The Apostle*

Chasing Amy

Loved

Ulee's Gold

Waiting for Guffman

1999

★*Gods and Monsters*

Affliction

Claire Dolan

A Soldier's Daughter Never Cries

Velvet Goldmine

2000

★*Election*

Cookie's Fortune

The Limey

The Straight Story

Sugar Town

Tully

2001

★*Crouching Tiger, Hidden Dragon*

Before Night Falls

Ghost Dog: The Way of the Samurai

Requiem for a Dream

2002

★*Memento*

Hedwig and the Angry Inch

L.I.E.

Waking Life

2003

★*Far from Heaven*

The Good Girl

Lovely & Amazing

Secretary

2004

★*Lost in Translation*

American Splendor

In America

Raising Victor Vargas

Shattered Glass

2005

★*Sideways*

Baadasssss!

Kinsey

Maria Full of Grace

Primer

2006

★*Brokeback Mountain*

Capote

Good Night, and Good Luck

The Squid and the Whale

2007

★*Little Miss Sunshine*

American Gun

Half Nelson

Pan's Labyrinth

2008

★*Juno*

The Diving Bell and the Butterfly

I'm Not There

A Mighty Heart

2009

★*The Wrestler*

Ballast

Frozen River

Rachel Getting Married

Wendy and Lucy

2010

★*Precious: Based on the Novel by Sapphire*

Amreeka

(500) Days of Summer

The Last Station

Sin Nombre

FEATURE DOCUMENTARY

2003

★*Bowling for Columbine*

2004

★*The Fog of War: Eleven Lessons from the Life of Robert S. McNamara*

My Architect: A Son's Journey

2005

★*Metallica: Some Kind of Monster*

Tarnation

2006

★*Enron: The Smartest Guys in the Room*

Grizzly Man

2007

★*The Road to Guantanamo*

2008

★*Crazy Love*

2010

★*Anvil! The Story of Anvil*

Food, Inc.

More Than a Game

FIRST FEATURE

1987

★*She's Gotta Have It*

1988

★*Dirty Dancing*

1989

★*Mystic Pizza*

1990

★*Heathers*

1991

★*Metropolitan*

1992

★*Straight out of Brooklyn*

1993

★*The Waterdance*

1994

★*El Mariachi*

American Heart

Combination Platter

Mac

Menace II Society

1995

★*Spanking the Monkey*

Clean, Shaven

Clerks

I Like It Like That

Suture

1996

★*The Brothers McMullen*

Kids

Little Odessa

Picture Bride

River of Grass

1997

★*Sling Blade*

Big Night

I Shot Andy Warhol

Manny & Lo

Tree's Lounge

Tony Shalhoub/*Big Night*

Stanley Tucci/*Big Night*

1998

★*Eve's Bayou*

The Bible and Gun Club

Hard Eight

In the Company of Men

Star Maps

1999

★*The Opposite of Sex*

Buffalo 66

High Art

Pi

Slums of Beverly Hills

2000

★*Being John Malkovich*

The Blair Witch Project

Boys Don't Cry

Judy Berlin

Three Seasons

Twin Falls Idaho

Xiu Xiu: The Sent Down Girl

2001

★*You Can Count On Me*

Boiler Room

Girlfight

Love and Basketball

2002

★*In the Bedroom*

The Anniversary Party

Donnie Darko

Ghost World

2003

★*The Dangerous Lives of Altar Boys*

Paid in Full

Roger Dodger

2004

★*Monster*

House of Sand and Fog

Pieces of April

2005

★*Garden State*

Brother to Brother

Napoleon Dynamite

Saints and Soldiers

The Woodsman

2006

★*Crash*

Transamerica

2008

★*The Lookout*

Rocket Science

2 Days in Paris

2009

★*Synecdoche, New York*

2010

★*Crazy Heart*

The Messenger

Paranormal Activity

A Single Man

SCREENPLAY

1986

★*The Trip to Bountiful*

1987

★*Platoon*

1988

★*River's Edge*

1989

★*Stand and Deliver*

1990

★*Drugstore Cowboy*

1991

★*To Sleep with Anger*

1992

★*My Own Private Idaho*

1993

★*The Waterdance*

1994

★*Short Cuts*

Combination Platter

Household Saints

Ruby in Paradise

The Wedding Banquet

1995

★*Pulp Fiction*

Bullets over Broadway

Eat Drink Man Woman

Mrs. Parker and the Vicious Circle

Red Rock West

1996

★*The Usual Suspects*

Leaving Las Vegas

Living in Oblivion

Safe

The Secret of Roan Inish

1997

★*Chasing Amy*

★*Fargo*

Dead Man

Flirting with Disaster

The Funeral

Lone Star

1998

The Apostle

Touch

Ulee's Gold

Waiting for Guffman

1999

★*The Opposite of Sex*

Affliction

Blind Faith

Gods and Monsters

The Spanish Prisoner

2000

★*Election*

Dogma

Guinevere

The Limey

SLC Punk!

Tully

2001

★*Memento*

★*You Can Count On Me*

Chuck & Buck

Love & Sex

Two Family House

Waking the Dead

2002

In the Bedroom

Monster's Ball

Waking Life

2003

★*The Good Girl*

Roger Dodger

Thirteen Conversations About One Thing

2004

★*Lost in Translation*

American Splendor

A Mighty Wind

Pieces of April

Shattered Glass

2005

★*Sideways*

Baadasssss!

Before Sunset

The Door in the Floor

Kinsey

★ = winner

2006

★*Capote*

The Squid and the Whale

2007

★*Thank You for Smoking*

Friends with Money

The Illusionist

Sorry, Haters

2008

★*The Savages*

The Diving Bell and the Butterfly

Waitress

Year of the Dog

2009

★*Vicky Cristina Barcelona*

Savage Grace

Synecdoche, New York

2010

★*(500) Days of Summer*

Adventureland

The Last Station

The Messenger

The Vicious Kind

DEBUT PERFORMANCE

1995

★Sean Nelson/*Fresh*

Jeff Anderson/*Clerks*

Jeremy Davies/*Spanking the Monkey*

Alicia Witt/*Fun*

Renee Zellweger/*Love and a .45*

1996

★Justin Pierce/*Kids*

Jason Andrews/*Rhythm Thief*

Lisa Bowman/*River of Grass*

Gabriel Casseus/*New Jersey Drive*

Rose McGowan/*The Doom Generation*

1997

★Heather Matarazzo/*Welcome to the Dollhouse*

Jena Malone/*Bastard out of Carolina*

Brendan Sexton, III/*Welcome to the Dollhouse*

Arie Verveen/*Caught*

Jeffrey Wright/*Basquiat*

1998

★Aaron Eckhart/*In the Company of Men*

Tyrone Burton/*Squeeze*

Eddie Cutanda/*Squeeze*

Phuong Duong/*Squeeze*

Lysa Flores/*Star Maps*

Darling Narita/*Bang*

Douglas Spain/*Star Maps*

1999

★Evan Adams/*Smoke Signals*

Anthony Roth Costanzo/*A Soldier's Daughter Never Cries*

Andrea Hart/*Miss Monday*

Sonja Sohn/*Slam*

Saul Williams/*Slam*

2000

★Kimberly J. Brown/*Tumbleweeds*

Bob Burrus/*Tully*

Jessica Campbell/*Election*

Chris Stafford/*Edge of Seventeen*

2001

★Michelle Rodriguez/*Girlfight*

Rory Culkin/*You Can Count On Me*

Emmy Rossum/*Songcatcher*

Mike White/*Chuck & Buck*

2002

★Paul Franklin Dano/*L.I.E.*

2003

★Nia Vardalos/*My Big Fat Greek Wedding*

America Ferrera/*Real Women Have Curves*

Raven Goodwin/*Lovely & Amazing*

Artel Kayaru/*Dahmer*

2004

★Nikki Reed/*Thirteen*

Anna Kendrick/*Camp*

Judy Marte/*Raising Victor Vargas*

Victor Rasuk/*Raising Victor Vargas*

2005

★Rodrigo de la Serna/*The Motorcycle Diaries*

The Woodsman

Anthony Mackie/*Brother to Brother*

David Sullivan/*Primer*

FIRST SCREENPLAY

1995

★*Spanking the Monkey*

Blessing

Clerks

Fun

What Happened Was...

1996

Kids

Little Odessa

Postcards from America

River of Grass

Smoke

1997

★*Big Night*

Girl 6

Manny & Lo

Tree's Lounge

The Whole Wide World

1998

The Bible and Gun Club

Critical Care

Hard Eight

Star Maps

1999

★*In the Company of Men*

★*Pi*

High Art

Niagara, Niagara

Slums of Beverly Hills

Smoke Signals

2000

★*Being John Malkovich*

The Adventures of Sebastian Cole

Boys Don't Cry

Cookie's Fortune

The Straight Story

2004

★*The Station Agent*

Blue Car

Monster

Raising Victor Vargas

Thirteen

2005

★*Maria Full of Grace*

Brother to Brother

Garden State

Primer

2006

★*Transamerica*

Junebug

2007

★*Little Miss Sunshine*

Conversations with Other Women

A Guide to Recognizing Your Saints

Half Nelson

The Painted Veil

2008

★*Juno*

Before the Devil Knows You're Dead

Broken English

A Mighty Heart

Rocket Science

2009

★*Milk*

Ballast

Frozen River

Rachel Getting Married

The Wackness

2010

★*Precious: Based on the Novel by Sapphire*

Amreeka

Cold Souls

Crazy Heart

A Single Man

FILM—FOREIGN LANGUAGE

1986

★*Kiss of the Spider Woman*

1987

★*A Room with a View*

1988

★*My Life As a Dog*

1989

★*Wings of Desire*

1990

★*My Left Foot*

1992

★*An Angel at My Table*

1993

★*The Crying Game*

1994

★*The Piano*

Like Water for Chocolate

Naked

Orlando

The Story of Qiu Ju

1995

★*Trois Couleurs: Rouge*

The Blue Kite

The Boys of St. Vincent

Ladybird, Ladybird

32 Short Films about Glenn Gould

1996

★*Before the Rain*

The City of Lost Children

Exotica

I Am Cuba

Through the Olive Trees

1997

Breaking the Waves

Chungking Express

Lamerica

Secrets and Lies

Trainspotting

1998

★*The Sweet Hereafter*

Happy Together

Mouth to Mouth

Nenette and Boni

Underground

1999

★*The Celebration*

Central Station

The Eel

Fireworks

The General

2000

★*Run Lola Run*

All About My Mother

My Son the Fanatic

Rosetta

Topsy Turvy

2001

★*Dancer in the Dark*

In the Mood for Love

The Terrorist

The War Zone

2002

Amelie

Amores Perros

Lumumba

Sexy Beast

2003

★*Y Tu Mama Tambien*

Bloody Sunday

The Fast Runner

The Piano Teacher

Time Out

2004

★*Whale Rider*

City of God

The Magdalene Sisters

The Triplets of Belleville

2005

★*The Sea Inside*

Bad Education

Red Lights

2006

★*Paradise Now*

2008

★*Once*

Persepolis

2009

★*The Class*

2010

★*An Education*

Everlasting Moments

Madeo

The Maid

A Prophet

NATIONAL FILM REGISTRY

1989

★*The Best Years of Our Lives*

★*Casablanca*

★*Citizen Kane*

★*The Crowd*

★*Dr. Strangelove, or: How I Learned to Stop Worrying and Love the Bomb*

★*The General*

★*Gone with the Wind*

★*The Grapes of Wrath*

★*High Noon*

★*Intolerance*

★*The Learning Tree*

★*The Maltese Falcon*

★*Mr. Smith Goes to Washington*

★*Modern Times*

★*On the Waterfront*

★*The Searchers*

★*Singin' in the Rain*

★*Snow White and the Seven Dwarfs*

★*Some Like It Hot*

★*Star Wars*

★*Sunrise*

★*Sunset Boulevard*

★*Vertigo*

★*The Wizard of Oz*

1990

★*All About Eve*

★*All Quiet on the Western Front*

★*Bringing Up Baby*

★*Dodsworth*

★*Duck Soup*

★*Fantasia*

★*The Freshman*

★*The Godfather*

★*Harlan County, U.S.A.*

★*How Green Was My Valley*

★*It's a Wonderful Life*

★*Killer of Sheep*

★*Ninotchka*

★*Raging Bull*

★*Rebel without a Cause*

★*Red River*

★*Sullivan's Travels*

★*Top Hat*

★*Treasure of the Sierra Madre*

★*A Woman under the Influence*

1991

★*Blood of Jesus*

★*Chinatown*

★*City Lights*

★*David Holzman's Diary*

★*Frankenstein*

★*Gigi*

★*Greed*

★*I Am a Fugitive from a Chain Gang*

★*The Italian*

★*King Kong*

★*Lawrence of Arabia*

★*The Magnificent Ambersons*

★*My Darling Clementine*

★*Out of the Past*

★*A Place in the Sun*

★*A Poor Little Rich Girl*

★*Prisoner of Zenda*

★*Shadow of a Doubt*

★*Sherlock, Jr.*

★*Tevye*

★*2001: A Space Odyssey*

1992

★*Adam's Rib*

★*Annie Hall*

★*The Bank Dick*

★*The Big Parade*

★*The Birth of a Nation*

★*Bonnie & Clyde*

★*Carmen Jones*

★*Detour*

★*Dog Star Man*

★*Double Indemnity*

★*Footlight Parade*

★*The Gold Rush*

★*Letter from an Unknown Woman*

★*Morocco*

★*Nashville*

★*The Night of the Hunter*

★*Paths of Glory*

★*Psycho*

★*Ride the High Country*

★*Salt of the Earth*

1993

★*An American in Paris*

★*Badlands*

★*The Black Pirate*

★*Blade Runner*

★*Cat People*

★*The Cheat*

★*The Godfather, Part 2*

★*His Girl Friday*

★*It Happened One Night*

★*Lassie, Come Home*

★*A Night at the Opera*

★*Nothing but a Man*

★*One Flew Over the Cuckoo's Nest*

★*Shadows*

★*Shane*

★*Sweet Smell of Success*

★*Touch of Evil*

★*The Wind*

★*Yankee Doodle Dandy*

1994

★*The African Queen*

★*The Apartment*

★*The Cool World*

★*E.T.: The Extra-Terrestrial*

★*Force of Evil*

★*Freaks*

★*Hell's Hinges*

★*Invasion of the Body Snatchers*

★*The Lady Eve*

★*Louisiana Story*

★*The Manchurian Candidate*

★*Marty*

★*Meet Me in St. Louis*

★*Midnight Cowboy*

★*Pinocchio*

★*Safety Last*

★*Scarface*

★*Tabu: A Story of the South Seas*

★*Taxi Driver*

1995

★*The Adventures of Robin Hood*

★*All That Heaven Allows*

★*American Graffiti*

★*The Band Wagon*

★*Cabaret*

★*Chan Is Missing*

★*The Conversation*

★*The Day the Earth Stood Still*

★*El Norte*

★*The Four Horsemen of the Apocalypse*

★*Fury*

★*The Hospital*

★*The Last of the Mohicans*

★*North by Northwest*

★*The Philadelphia Story*

★*Stagecoach*

★*To Kill a Mockingbird*

1996

★*The Awful Truth*

★*Broken Blossoms*

★*The Deer Hunter*

★*Destry Rides Again*

★*The Graduate*

★*The Heiress*

★*The Jazz Singer*

★*M*A*S*H*

★*Mildred Pierce*

★*The Outlaw Josey Wales*

★*The Producers*

★*The Road to Morocco*

★*She Done Him Wrong*

★*Shock Corridor*

★*Show Boat*

★*The Thief of Baghdad*

★*To Be or Not to Be*

★*Woodstock*

1997

★*Ben-Hur*

★*The Big Sleep*

★*The Bridge on the River Kwai*

★*The Great Dictator*

★*Harold and Maude*

★*How the West Was Won*

★*The Hustler*

★*Knute Rockne: All American*

★*Little Fugitive*

★*Mean Streets*

★*The Naked Spur*

★*Rear Window*

★*Return of the Secaucus 7*

★*The Thin Man*

★ = winner

★West Side Story
★Wings
1998
★The Bride of Frankenstein
★Easy Rider
★42nd Street
★From the Manger to the Cross
★Gun Crazy
★The Hitch-Hiker
★The Immigrant
★The Last Picture Show
★Little Miss Marker
★The Lost World
★The Ox-Bow Incident
★The Phantom of the Opera
★Public Enemy
★Sky High
★Tootsie
★Twelve o'Clock High
1999
★Civilization
★Do the Right Thing
★Docks of New York
★Emperor Jones
★Gunga Din
★Kiss Me Deadly
★Laura
★My Man Godfrey
★Night of the Living Dead
★Raiders of the Lost Ark
★Roman Holiday
★The Shop Around the Corner
★A Streetcar Named Desire
★The Ten Commandments
★The Wild Bunch
★Woman of the Year
2000
★Apocalypse Now
★Dracula
★Five Easy Pieces
★Goodfellas
★Koyaanisqatsi
★La Chute de la Maison Usher
★The Life of Emile Zola
★Little Caesar
★Love Finds Andy Hardy
★Network
★Peter Pan
★Regeneration
★Salome
★Shaft
★A Star Is Born
★The Tall T
★Will Success Spoil Rock Hunter?
2001
★Abbott and Costello Meet Frankenstein
★All That Jazz
★All the King's Men
★Hoosiers
★It
★Jaws
★Manhattan
★Miracle of Morgan's Creek
★National Lampoon's Animal House
★Planet of the Apes
★The Sound of Music
★Stormy Weather
★The Thin Blue Line
★The Thing
2002
★Alien
★The Bad and the Beautiful
★Beauty and the Beast
★The Black Stallion
★Boyz N the Hood
★The Endless Summer
★From Here to Eternity
★In the Heat of the Night
★Lady Windermere's Fan
★Melody Ranch
★The Pearl
★Sabrina
★Stranger than Paradise
★This Is Spinal Tap
2003
★Atlantic City
★Butch Cassidy and the Sundance Kid
★Gold Diggers of 1933
★The Hunters
★Medium Cool
★National Velvet
★Naughty Marietta
★Patton
★Show People
★Son of the Sheik
★Tarzan and His Mate
★The Wedding March
★White Heat
★Young Frankenstein
★Young Mr. Lincoln
2004
★Ben-Hur
★Court Jester
★Daughters of the Dust
★D.O.A.
★Enter the Dragon
★Eraserhead
★Going My Way
★Jailhouse Rock
★The Nutty Professor
★Schindler's List
★Seven Brides for Seven Brothers
★Swing Time
2005
★Baby Face
★The Cameraman
★Cool Hand Luke
★The Fall of the House of Usher
★Fast Times at Ridgemont High
★The French Connection
★Giant
★Hands Up
★Hoop Dreams
★Imitation of Life
★Miracle on 34th Street
★The Music Man
★A Raisin in the Sun
★The Rocky Horror Picture Show
★The Sting
★Toy Story
2006
★Applause
★Big Trail
★Blazing Saddles
★Fargo
★The Flesh and the Devil
★Groundhog Day
★Halloween
★Last Command
★Notorious
★Red Dust
★Rocky
★sex, lies and videotape
★The T.A.M.I. Show
★Traffic in Souls
2007
★Back to the Future
★Bullitt
★Close Encounters of the Third Kind
★Dance, Girl, Dance
★Dances with Wolves
★Days of Heaven
★Grand Hotel
★In a Lonely Place
★The Man Who Shot Liberty Valance
★The Naked City
★Now, Voyager
★Oklahoma!
★Strong Man
★Tol'able David
★Twelve Angry Men
★The Women
★Wuthering Heights
2008
★The Asphalt Jungle
★Deliverance
★A Face in the Crowd
★Flower Drum Song
★Foolish Wives
★Hallelujah!
★In Cold Blood
★The Invisible Man
★Johnny Guitar
★The Killers
★The Pawnbroker
★Sergeant York
★The Seventh Voyage of Sinbad
★The Terminator
2009
★Dog Day Afternoon
★The Exiles
★The Incredible Shrinking Man
★Jezebel
★The Mark of Zorro
★Mrs. Miniver
★The Muppet Movie
★Once Upon a Time in the West
★Pillow Talk
★The Story of G.I. Joe
★Under Western Stars

SCREEN ACTORS GUILD AWARDS

ACTOR

1994
★Tom Hanks/Forrest Gump
Morgan Freeman/The Shawshank Redemption
Paul Newman/Nobody's Fool
Tim Robbins/The Shawshank Redemption
John Travolta/Pulp Fiction
1995
★Nicolas Cage/Leaving Las Vegas
Anthony Hopkins/Nixon
James Earl Jones/Cry, the Beloved Country
Sean Penn/Dead Man Walking
Massimo Troisi/The Postman
1996
★Geoffrey Rush/Shine
Tom Cruise/Jerry Maguire
Ralph Fiennes/The English Patient
Woody Harrelson/The People vs. Larry Flynt
Billy Bob Thornton/Sling Blade
1997
★Jack Nicholson/As Good As It Gets
Matt Damon/Good Will Hunting
Robert Duvall/The Apostle
Peter Fonda/Ulee's Gold
Dustin Hoffman/Wag the Dog
1998
★Roberto Benigni/Life Is Beautiful
Joseph Fiennes/Shakespeare in Love
Tom Hanks/Saving Private Ryan
Ian McKellen/Gods and Monsters
Nick Nolte/Affliction
1999
★Kevin Spacey/American Beauty
Jim Carrey/Man on the Moon
Russell Crowe/The Insider
Philip Seymour Hoffman/Flawless
Denzel Washington/The Hurricane
2000
★Benicio Del Toro/Traffic
Jamie Bell/Billy Elliot
Russell Crowe/Gladiator
Geoffrey Rush/Quills
2001
★Russell Crowe/A Beautiful Mind
Kevin Kline/Life as a House
Sean Penn/I Am Sam
Denzel Washington/Training Day
Tom Wilkinson/In the Bedroom
2002
★Daniel Day-Lewis/Gangs of New York
Adrien Brody/The Pianist
Nicolas Cage/Adaptation
Richard Gere/Chicago
Jack Nicholson/About Schmidt
2003
★Johnny Depp/Pirates of the Caribbean: The Curse of the Black Pearl
Peter Dinklage/The Station Agent
Ben Kingsley/House of Sand and Fog
Bill Murray/Lost in Translation
Sean Penn/Mystic River
2004
★Jamie Foxx/Ray
Don Cheadle/Hotel Rwanda
Johnny Depp/Finding Neverland
Leonardo DiCaprio/The Aviator
Paul Giamatti/Sideways
2005
★Philip Seymour Hoffman/Capote
Russell Crowe/Cinderella Man
Heath Ledger/Brokeback Mountain
Joaquin Rafael (Leaf) Phoenix/Walk the Line
David Strathairn/Good Night, and Good Luck
2006
★Forest Whitaker/The Last King of Scotland
Leonardo DiCaprio/Blood Diamond
Ryan Gosling/Half Nelson
Peter O'Toole/Venus
Will Smith/The Pursuit of Happyness
2007
★Daniel Day-Lewis/There Will Be Blood
George Clooney/Michael Clayton
Ryan Gosling/Lars and the Real Girl
Emile Hirsch/Into the Wild
Viggo Mortensen/Eastern Promises
2008
★Sean Penn/Milk
Richard Jenkins/The Visitor
Frank Langella/Frost/Nixon
Brad Pitt/The Curious Case of Benjamin Button
Mickey Rourke/The Wrestler
2009
★Jeff Bridges/Crazy Heart
George Clooney/Up in the Air
Colin Firth/A Single Man
Morgan Freeman/Invictus
Jeremy Renner/The Hurt Locker

ACTOR—SUPPORTING

1994
★Martin Landau/Ed Wood
Gary Sinise/Forrest Gump
1995
★Ed Harris/Apollo 13
Kevin Bacon/Murder in the First
Kenneth Branagh/Othello
Don Cheadle/Devil in a Blue Dress
Kevin Spacey/The Usual Suspects
1996
★Cuba Gooding, Jr./Jerry Maguire
Hank Azaria/The Birdcage
Nathan Lane/The Birdcage
William H. Macy/Fargo
Noah Taylor/Shine
1997
★Robin Williams/Good Will Hunting
Billy Connolly/Mrs. Brown
Anthony Hopkins/Amistad
Greg Kinnear/As Good As It Gets
Burt Reynolds/Boogie Nights
1998
★Robert Duvall/A Civil Action
James Coburn/Affliction
David Kelly/Waking Ned Devine
Geoffrey Rush/Shakespeare in Love
Billy Bob Thornton/A Simple Plan
1999
★Michael Caine/The Cider House Rules
Chris Cooper/American Beauty
Tom Cruise/Magnolia
Michael Clarke Duncan/The Green Mile
Haley Joel Osment/The Sixth Sense
2000
★Albert Finney/Erin Brockovich
Jeff Bridges/The Contender
Willem Dafoe/Shadow of the Vampire
Gary Oldman/The Contender
Joaquin Rafael (Leaf) Phoenix/Gladiator
2001
★Ian McKellen/Lord of the Rings: The Fellowship of the Ring
Jim Broadbent/Iris
Hayden Christensen/Life as a House
Ethan Hawke/Training Day
Ben Kingsley/Sexy Beast
2002
★Christopher Walken/Catch Me If You Can
Chris Cooper/Adaptation
Ed Harris/The Hours
Alfred Molina/Frida
Dennis Quaid/Far from Heaven
2003
★Tim Robbins/Mystic River
Alec Baldwin/The Cooler
Chris Cooper/Seabiscuit
Benicio Del Toro/21 Grams
2004
★Morgan Freeman/Million Dollar Baby
Thomas Haden Church/Sideways
Jamie Foxx/Collateral
James Garner/The Notebook
Freddie Highmore/Finding Neverland
2005
★Paul Giamatti/Cinderella Man
Don Cheadle/Crash
George Clooney/Syriana
Matt Dillon/Crash
Jake Gyllenhaal/Brokeback Mountain
2006
★Eddie Murphy/Dreamgirls
Alan Arkin/Little Miss Sunshine
Leonardo DiCaprio/The Departed
Jackie Earle Haley/Little Children
Djimon Hounsou/Blood Diamond
2007
★Javier Bardem/No Country for Old Men
Casey Affleck/The Assassination of Jesse James by the Coward Robert Ford
Hal Holbrook/Into the Wild
Tommy Lee Jones/No Country for Old Men
Tom Wilkinson/Michael Clayton
2008
★Heath Ledger/The Dark Knight
Josh Brolin/Milk
Robert Downey, Jr./Tropic Thunder
Philip Seymour Hoffman/Doubt
Dev Patel/Slumdog Millionaire
2009
★Christoph Waltz/Inglourious Basterds
Matt Damon/Invictus
Woody Harrelson/The Messenger
Christopher Plummer/The Last Station
Stanley Tucci/The Lovely Bones

ACTRESS

1994
★Jodie Foster/Nell
Jessica Lange/Blue Sky
Meg Ryan/When a Man Loves a Woman
Susan Sarandon/The Client
Meryl Streep/The River Wild

★ = winner

1995

★Susan Sarandon/*Dead Man Walking*

Joan Allen/*Nixon*

Elisabeth Shue/*Leaving Las Vegas*

Meryl Streep/*The Bridges of Madison County*

Emma Thompson/*Sense and Sensibility*

1996

★Frances McDormand/*Fargo*

Brenda Blethyn/*Secrets and Lies*

Diane Keaton/*Marvin's Room*

Gena Rowlands/*Unhook the Stars*

Kristin Scott Thomas/*The English Patient*

1997

★Helen Hunt/*As Good As It Gets*

Helena Bonham Carter/*The Wings of the Dove*

Judi Dench/*Mrs. Brown*

Pam Grier/*Jackie Brown*

Kate Winslet/*Titanic*

Robin Wright Penn/*She's So Lovely*

1998

★Gwyneth Paltrow/*Shakespeare in Love*

Cate Blanchett/*Elizabeth*

Jane Horrocks/*Little Voice*

Meryl Streep/*One True Thing*

Emily Watson/*Hilary and Jackie*

1999

★Annette Bening/*American Beauty*

Janet McTeer/*Tumbleweeds*

Julianne Moore/*The End of the Affair*

Meryl Streep/*Music of the Heart*

Hilary Swank/*Boys Don't Cry*

2000

★Julia Roberts/*Erin Brockovich*

Joan Allen/*The Contender*

Juliette Binoche/*Chocolat*

Ellen Burstyn/*Requiem for a Dream*

Laura Linney/*You Can Count On Me*

2001

★Halle Berry/*Monster's Ball*

Jennifer Connelly/*A Beautiful Mind*

Judi Dench/*Iris*

Sissy Spacek/*In the Bedroom*

Renee Zellweger/*Bridget Jones's Diary*

2002

★Renee Zellweger/*Chicago*

Salma Hayek/*Frida*

Nicole Kidman/*The Hours*

Diane Lane/*Unfaithful*

Julianne Moore/*Far from Heaven*

2003

★Charlize Theron/*Monster*

Patricia Clarkson/*The Station Agent*

Diane Keaton/*Something's Gotta Give*

Naomi Watts/*21 Grams*

Evan Rachel Wood/*Thirteen*

2004

★Hilary Swank/*Million Dollar Baby*

Annette Bening/*Being Julia*

Cloris Leachman/*Spanglish*

Catalina Sandino Moreno/*Maria Full of Grace*

Imelda Staunton/*Vera Drake*

Kate Winslet/*Eternal Sunshine of the Spotless Mind*

2005

★Reese Witherspoon/*Walk the Line*

Judi Dench/*Mrs. Henderson Presents*

Felicity Huffman/*Transamerica*

Charlize Theron/*North Country*

Zhang Ziyi/*Memoirs of a Geisha*

2006

★Helen Mirren/*The Queen*

Penelope Cruz/*Volver*

Judi Dench/*Notes on a Scandal*

Meryl Streep/*The Devil Wears Prada*

Kate Winslet/*Little Children*

2007

★Julie Christie/*Away From Her*

Cate Blanchett/*Elizabeth: The Golden Age*

Marion Cotillard/*La Vie en Rose*

Angelina Jolie/*A Mighty Heart*

Ellen Page/*Juno*

2008

★Meryl Streep/*Doubt*

Anne Hathaway/*Rachel Getting Married*

Angelina Jolie/*Changeling*

Melissa Leo/*Frozen River*

2009

★Sandra Bullock/*The Blind Side*

Vera Farmiga/*Up in the Air*

Anna Kendrick/*Up in the Air*

Helen Mirren/*The Last Station*

Carey Mulligan/*An Education*

Gabourney "Gabby" Sidibe/*Precious: Based on the Novel by Sapphire*

Meryl Streep/*Julie & Julia*

ACTRESS—SUPPORTING

1994

★Dianne Wiest/*Bullets over Broadway*

Sally Field/*Forrest Gump*

Robin Wright Penn/*Forrest Gump*

1995

★Kate Winslet/*Sense and Sensibility*

Stockard Channing/*Smoke*

Anjelica Huston/*The Crossing Guard*

Mira Sorvino/*Mighty Aphrodite*

Mare Winningham/*Georgia*

1996

★Lauren Bacall/*The Mirror Has Two Faces*

Juliette Binoche/*The English Patient*

Marisa Tomei/*Unhook the Stars*

Gwen Verdon/*Marvin's Room*

Renee Zellweger/*Jerry Maguire*

1997

★Kim Basinger/*L.A. Confidential*

★Gloria Stuart/*Titanic*

Minnie Driver/*Good Will Hunting*

Alison Elliott/*The Wings of the Dove*

Julianne Moore/*Boogie Nights*

1998

★Kathy Bates/*Primary Colors*

Brenda Blethyn/*Little Voice*

Judi Dench/*Shakespeare in Love*

Rachel Griffiths/*Hilary and Jackie*

Lynn Redgrave/*Gods and Monsters*

1999

★Angelina Jolie/*Girl, Interrupted*

Cameron Diaz/*Being John Malkovich*

Angelina Jolie/*Girl, Interrupted*

Catherine Keener/*Being John Malkovich*

Julianne Moore/*Magnolia*

Chloe Sevigny/*Boys Don't Cry*

2000

★Judi Dench/*Chocolat*

Kate Hudson/*Almost Famous*

Frances McDormand/*Almost Famous*

Julie Walters/*Billy Elliot*

Kate Winslet/*Quills*

2001

★Helen Mirren/*Gosford Park*

Cate Blanchett/*Bandits*

Judi Dench/*The Shipping News*

Cameron Diaz/*Vanilla Sky*

Dakota Fanning/*I Am Sam*

2002

★Catherine Zeta-Jones/*Chicago*

Kathy Bates/*About Schmidt*

Julianne Moore/*The Hours*

Michelle Pfeiffer/*White Oleander*

Queen Latifah/*Chicago*

2003

★Renee Zellweger/*Cold Mountain*

Maria Bello/*The Cooler*

Keisha Castle-Hughes/*Whale Rider*

Patricia Clarkson/*Pieces of April*

Holly Hunter/*Thirteen*

Ken(saku) Watanabe/*The Last Samurai*

2004

★Cate Blanchett/*The Aviator*

Laura Linney/*Kinsey*

Virginia Madsen/*Sideways*

Sophie Okonedo/*Hotel Rwanda*

2005

★Rachel Weisz/*The Constant Gardener*

Amy Adams/*Junebug*

Catherine Keener/*Capote*

Frances McDormand/*North Country*

Michelle Williams/*Brokeback Mountain*

2006

★Jennifer Hudson/*Dreamgirls*

Adriana Barraza/*Babel*

Cate Blanchett/*Notes on a Scandal*

Abigail Breslin/*Little Miss Sunshine*

Rinko Kikuchi/*Babel*

2007

★Ruby Dee/*American Gangster*

Cate Blanchett/*I'm Not There*

Catherine Keener/*Into the Wild*

Amy Ryan/*Gone Baby Gone*

Tilda Swinton/*Michael Clayton*

2008

★Kate Winslet/*The Reader*

Amy Adams/*Doubt*

Penelope Cruz/*Vicky Cristina Barcelona*

Viola Davis/*Doubt*

Taraji P. Henson/*The Curious Case of Benjamin Button*

2009

★Mo'Nique/*Precious: Based on the Novel by Sapphire*

★Mo'Nique/*Precious: Based on the Novel by Sapphire*

Penelope Cruz/*Nine*

Diane Kruger/*Inglourious Basterds*

CAST

1995

★*Apollo 13*

Get Shorty

How to Make an American Quilt

Nixon

Sense and Sensibility

1996

★*The Birdcage*

The English Patient

Marvin's Room

Shine

Sling Blade

1997

★*The Full Monty*

Boogie Nights

Good Will Hunting

L.A. Confidential

Titanic

1998

★*Shakespeare in Love*

Life Is Beautiful

Little Voice

Saving Private Ryan

Waking Ned Devine

1999

★*American Beauty*

Being John Malkovich

The Cider House Rules

The Green Mile

Magnolia

2000

★*Traffic*

Almost Famous

Billy Elliot

Chocolat

Gladiator

2001

★*Gosford Park*

A Beautiful Mind

In the Bedroom

Lord of the Rings: The Fellowship of the Ring

Moulin Rouge

2002

★*Chicago*

Adaptation

The Hours

Lord of the Rings: The Two Towers

My Big Fat Greek Wedding

2003

★*Lord of the Rings: The Return of the King*

In America

Mystic River

Seabiscuit

The Station Agent

2004

★*Sideways*

The Aviator

Finding Neverland

Hotel Rwanda

Million Dollar Baby

Ray

2005

★*Crash*

Brokeback Mountain

Capote

Good Night, and Good Luck

Hustle & Flow

2006

★*Little Miss Sunshine*

Babel

Bobby

The Departed

Dreamgirls

2007

★*No Country for Old Men*

American Gangster

Hairspray

Into the Wild

3:10 to Yuma

2008

★*Slumdog Millionaire*

The Curious Case of Benjamin Button

Doubt

Frost/Nixon

Milk

2009

★*Inglourious Basterds*

An Education

The Hurt Locker

Nine

Precious: Based on the Novel by Sapphire

WRITERS GUILD OF AMERICA

FEATURE DOCUMENTARY

2005

★*Enron: The Smartest Guys in the Room*

2009

★*The Cove*

ADAPTED SCREENPLAY

1968

★*Goodbye Columbus*

1969

★*Butch Cassidy and the Sundance Kid*

★*Midnight Cowboy*

1970

★*I Never Sang for My Father*

★*M*A*S*H*

1971

★*The French Connection*

★*Kotch*

1972

★*Cabaret*

★*The Godfather*

1973

★*Paper Moon*

★*Serpico*

1974

★*The Apprenticeship of Duddy Kravitz*

★*The Godfather, Part 2*

1975

★*One Flew Over the Cuckoo's Nest*

★*The Sunshine Boys*

1976

★*All the President's Men*

★*The Pink Panther Strikes Again*

1977

★*Julia*

★*Oh, God!*

1978

★*Heaven Can Wait*

★*Midnight Express*

1979

★*Being There*

★*Kramer vs. Kramer*

1980

★*Airplane!*

★*Ordinary People*

1981

★*On Golden Pond*

★*Rich and Famous*

1982

★*Missing*

★*Victor/Victoria*

1983

★*Reuben, Reuben*

★*Terms of Endearment*

1984

★*The Killing Fields*

1985

★*Prizzi's Honor*

1986

★*A Room with a View*

1987

★*Roxanne*

1988

★*Dangerous Liaisons*

1989

★*Driving Miss Daisy*

1990

★*Dances with Wolves*

1991

★*The Silence of the Lambs*

1992

★*The Player*

1993

★*Schindler's List*

The Fugitive

In the Name of the Father

The Joy Luck Club

The Remains of the Day

1994

★*Forrest Gump*

Little Women

The Madness of King George

Quiz Show

The Shawshank Redemption

1995

★*Sense and Sensibility*

Apollo 13

Babe

Get Shorty

Leaving Las Vegas

1996

★*Sling Blade*

The Birdcage

Emma

The English Patient

Trainspotting

1997

★*L.A. Confidential*

Donnie Brasco

The Ice Storm

Wag the Dog

The Wings of the Dove

1998

★*Out of Sight*

A Civil Action

Gods and Monsters

Primary Colors

A Simple Plan

★ = winner

1999
★*Election*
The Cider House Rules
The Insider
October Sky
The Talented Mr. Ripley
2000
★*Traffic*
Chocolat
Crouching Tiger, Hidden Dragon
High Fidelity
Wonder Boys
2001
★*A Beautiful Mind*
Black Hawk Down
Bridget Jones's Diary
Ghost World
Lord of the Rings: The Fellowship of the Ring
2002
★*The Hours*
About a Boy
About Schmidt
Adaptation
Chicago
2003
★*American Splendor*
Cold Mountain
Lord of the Rings: The Return of the King
Mystic River
Seabiscuit
2004
★*Sideways*
Before Sunset
Mean Girls
Million Dollar Baby
The Motorcycle Diaries
2005
★*Brokeback Mountain*
Capote
The Constant Gardener
A History of Violence
Syriana
2006
★*The Departed*
The Devil Wears Prada
Little Children
Thank You for Smoking
2007
★*No Country for Old Men*
The Diving Bell and the Butterfly
Into the Wild
There Will Be Blood
Zodiac
2008
★*Slumdog Millionaire*
The Curious Case of Benjamin Button
The Dark Knight
Doubt
Frost/Nixon
2009
★*Up in the Air*
Crazy Heart
Julie & Julia
Precious: Based on the Novel by Sapphire
Star Trek

ORIGINAL SCREENPLAY

1967
★*Bonnie & Clyde*
1968
★*The Producers*
1969
★*Bob & Carol & Ted & Alice*
1970
★*The Out-of-Towners*
★*Patton*
1971
★*The Hospital*
★*Sunday, Bloody Sunday*
1972
★*The Candidate*
★*What's Up, Doc?*
1973
★*Save the Tiger*
★*A Touch of Class*
1974
★*Blazing Saddles*
★*Chinatown*
1975
★*Dog Day Afternoon*
★*Shampoo*
1976
★*The Bad News Bears*
★*Network*
1977
★*Annie Hall*
★*The Turning Point*
1978
★*Coming Home*
★*Movie, Movie*
1979
★*Breaking Away*
★*The China Syndrome*
1980
★*Melvin and Howard*
★*Private Benjamin*
1981
★*Arthur*
★*Reds*
1982
★*E.T.: The Extra-Terrestrial*
★*Tootsie*
1983
★*The Big Chill*
★*Tender Mercies*
1984
★*Broadway Danny Rose*
1985
★*Witness*
1986
★*Hannah and Her Sisters*
1987
★*Moonstruck*
1988
★*Bull Durham*
1989
★*Crimes & Misdemeanors*
1990
★*Avalon*
1991
★*Thelma & Louise*
1992
★*The Crying Game*
1993
★*The Piano*
Dave
In the Line of Fire
Philadelphia
Sleepless in Seattle
1994
★*Four Weddings and a Funeral*
The Adventures of Priscilla, Queen of the Desert
Bullets over Broadway
Ed Wood
Heavenly Creatures
1995
★*Braveheart*
The American President
Clueless
Mighty Aphrodite
Muriel's Wedding
1996
★*Fargo*
Jerry Maguire
Lone Star
Secrets and Lies
Shine
1997
★*As Good As It Gets*
Boogie Nights
The Full Monty
Good Will Hunting
Titanic
1998
★*Shakespeare in Love*
Bulworth
The Opposite of Sex
Saving Private Ryan
The Truman Show
1999
★*American Beauty*
Being John Malkovich
Magnolia
The Sixth Sense
Three Kings
2000
★*You Can Count On Me*
Almost Famous
Best in Show
Billy Elliot
Erin Brockovich
2001
★*Gosford Park*
The Man Who Wasn't There
Monster's Ball
Moulin Rouge
The Royal Tenenbaums
2002
★*Bowling for Columbine*
Antwone Fisher
Far from Heaven
Gangs of New York
My Big Fat Greek Wedding
2003
★*Lost in Translation*
Bend It Like Beckham
Dirty Pretty Things
In America
The Station Agent
2004
★*Eternal Sunshine of the Spotless Mind*
The Aviator
Garden State
Hotel Rwanda
Kinsey
2005
★*Crash*
Cinderella Man
The 40 Year Old Virgin
Good Night, and Good Luck
The Squid and the Whale
2006
★*Little Miss Sunshine*
Babel
The Queen
Stranger Than Fiction
United 93
2007
★*Juno*
Knocked Up
Lars and the Real Girl
Michael Clayton
The Savages
2008
★*Milk*
Burn After Reading
Vicky Cristina Barcelona
The Wrestler
2009
★*The Hurt Locker*
Avatar
(500) Days of Summer
The Hangover
A Serious Man

GOLDEN RASPBERRY AWARDS

DIRECTOR

2008
Jason Friedberg/*Disaster Movie*
Aaron Seltzer/*Disaster Movie*

WORST PICTURE

1980
★*Can't Stop the Music*
1981
★*Mommie Dearest*
1983
★*The Lonely Lady*
1984
★*Bolero*
1985
★*Rambo: First Blood, Part 2*
1986
★*Howard the Duck*
★*Under the Cherry Moon*
1987
★*Leonard Part 6*
1988
★*Cocktail*
1989
★*Star Trek 5: The Final Frontier*
1990
★*The Adventures of Ford Fairlane*
★*Ghosts Can't Do It*
1991
★*Hudson Hawk*
1992
★*Shining Through*
1993
★*Indecent Proposal*
1994
★*Color of Night*
North
On Deadly Ground
The Specialist
Wyatt Earp
1995
★*Showgirls*
Congo
It's Pat: The Movie
Waterworld
1996
★*Striptease*
Barb Wire
Ed
The Island of Dr. Moreau
The Stupids
1997
★*The Postman*
Anaconda
Batman and Robin
Fire Down Below
Speed 2: Cruise Control
1998
★*An Alan Smithee Film: Burn, Hollywood, Burn*
Armageddon
The Avengers
Godzilla
Spice World: The Movie
1999
★*Wild Wild West*
Big Daddy
The Blair Witch Project
The Haunting
Star Wars: Episode 1—The Phantom Menace
2000
★*Battlefield Earth*
Book of Shadows: Blair Witch 2
The Flintstones in Viva Rock Vegas
Little Nicky
The Next Best Thing
2001
★*Freddy Got Fingered*
2002
★*Swept Away*
2003
★*Gigli*
Charlie's Angels: Full Throttle
Dr. Seuss' The Cat in the Hat
From Justin to Kelly
2004
★*Catwoman*
Alexander
Superbabies: Baby Geniuses 2
Surviving Christmas
White Chicks
2005
★*Dirty Love*
Deuce Bigalow: European Gigolo
The Dukes of Hazzard
House of Wax
Son of the Mask
2006
★*Basic Instinct 2*
BloodRayne
Lady in the Water
Little Man
The Wicker Man
2007
★*I Know Who Killed Me*
Bratz
Daddy Day Camp
I Now Pronounce You Chuck and Larry
Norbit
2008
★*The Love Guru*
Disaster Movie
The Happening
The Hottie and the Nottie
In the Name of the King: A Dungeon Siege Tale
Meet the Spartans
2009
★*Transformers: Revenge of the Fallen*
All About Steve
G.I. Joe: The Rise of Cobra
Land of the Lost
Old Dogs

Worst Remake

2006
★*Little Man*
The Pink Panther
Poseidon
The Shaggy Dog
The Wicker Man
2007
★*I Know Who Killed Me*
Are We Done Yet?
Bratz
Epic Movie
Who's Your Caddy?
2009
★*Land of the Lost*
G.I. Joe: The Rise of Cobra
The Pink Panther 2

Worst Sequel/Prequel

2006
★*Basic Instinct 2*
Big Momma's House 2
Garfield: A Tail of Two Kitties
The Santa Clause 3: The Escape Clause
The Texas Chainsaw Massacre: The Beginning
2007
★*Daddy Day Camp*
Aliens vs. Predator: Requiem
Evan Almighty
Hannibal Rising
Hostel: Part 2
2008
★*Indiana Jones and the Kingdom of the Crystal Skull*
The Day the Earth Stood Still
Disaster Movie
Meet the Spartans
Speed Racer
Star Wars: The Clone Wars
2009
The Pink Panther 2
Transformers: Revenge of the Fallen
The Twilight Saga: New Moon

WORST REMAKE/SEQUEL

1994
★*Wyatt Earp*
The Flintstones
1995
★*The Scarlet Letter*
1997
★*Speed 2: Cruise Control*
Batman and Robin
Home Alone 3
The Lost World: Jurassic Park 2
McHale's Navy
1998
★*The Avengers*
★*Godzilla*
★*Psycho*
Godzilla
Lost in Space
Meet Joe Black
Psycho
2000
★*Book of Shadows: Blair Witch 2*
Dr. Seuss' How the Grinch Stole Christmas
The Flintstones in Viva Rock Vegas
Get Carter
Mission: Impossible 2
2001
★*Planet of the Apes*
2003
★*Charlie's Angels: Full Throttle*
Dumb and Dumberer: When Harry Met Lloyd
From Justin to Kelly
The Texas Chainsaw Massacre
2 Fast 2 Furious
2004
★*Scooby-Doo 2: Monsters Unleashed*
Alien vs. Predator
Anacondas: The Hunt for the Blood Orchid
Around the World in 80 Days
Exorcist: The Beginning

★ = *winner*

2005

★*Son of the Mask*

Bewitched

Deuce Bigalow: European Gigolo

The Dukes of Hazzard

House of Wax

WORST ACTOR

1980

★Neil Diamond/*The Jazz Singer*

1981

★Klinton Spilsbury/*Legend of the Lone Ranger*

1983

★Christopher Atkins/*A Night in Heaven*

1984

★Sylvester Stallone/*Rhinestone*

1985

★Sylvester Stallone/*Rambo: First Blood, Part 2*

★Sylvester Stallone/*Rocky 4*

1986

★Prince/*Under the Cherry Moon*

1987

★Bill Cosby/*Leonard Part 6*

1988

★Sylvester Stallone/*Rambo 3*

1989

★William Shatner/*Star Trek 5: The Final Frontier*

1990

★Andrew (Dice Clay) Silverstein/*The Adventures of Ford Fairlane*

1991

★Kevin Costner/*Robin Hood: Prince of Thieves*

1992

★Sylvester Stallone/*Stop! or My Mom Will Shoot*

1993

★Burt Reynolds/*Cop and a Half*

1994

★Kevin Costner/*Wyatt Earp*

Macaulay Culkin/*Getting Even with Dad*

Macaulay Culkin/*The Pagemaster*

Macaulay Culkin/*Richie Rich*

Bruce Willis/*Color of Night*

Bruce Willis/*North*

1995

★Pauly Shore/*Jury Duty*

Kevin Costner/*Waterworld*

Kyle MacLachlan/*Showgirls*

Sylvester Stallone/*Assassins*

Sylvester Stallone/*Judge Dredd*

1996

★Tom Arnold/*Big Bully*

★Tom Arnold/*Carpool*

★Tom Arnold/*The Stupids*

★Pauly Shore/*Bio-Dome*

Keanu Reeves/*Chain Reaction*

Adam Sandler/*Bulletproof*

Adam Sandler/*Happy Gilmore*

Sylvester Stallone/*Daylight*

1997

★Kevin Costner/*The Postman*

Val Kilmer/*The Saint*

Shaquille O'Neal/*Steel*

Steven Seagal/*Fire Down Below*

Jon Voight/*Anaconda*

1998

★Bruce Willis/*Armageddon*

★Bruce Willis/*Mercury Rising*

★Bruce Willis/*The Siege*

Ralph Fiennes/*The Avengers*

Ryan O'Neal/*An Alan Smithee Film: Burn, Hollywood, Burn*

Ryan Phillippe/*54*

Adam Sandler/*The Waterboy*

1999

★Adam Sandler/*Big Daddy*

Kevin Costner/*For Love of the Game*

Kevin Costner/*Message in a Bottle*

Kevin Kline/*Wild Wild West*

Arnold Schwarzenegger/*End of Days*

Robin Williams/*Bicentennial Man*

Robin Williams/*Jakob the Liar*

2000

★John Travolta/*Battlefield Earth*

Leonardo DiCaprio/*The Beach*

Adam Sandler/*Little Nicky*

Arnold Schwarzenegger/*The 6th Day*

Sylvester Stallone/*Get Carter*

2001

★Tom Green/*Freddy Got Fingered*

2002

★Roberto Benigni/*Pinocchio*

2003

★Ben Affleck/*Daredevil*

★Ben Affleck/*Gigli*

★Ben Affleck/*Paycheck*

Cuba Gooding, Jr./*Boat Trip*

Cuba Gooding, Jr./*The Fighting Temptations*

Cuba Gooding, Jr./*Radio*

Justin Guarini/*From Justin to Kelly*

Ashton Kutcher/*Cheaper by the Dozen*

Ashton Kutcher/*Just Married*

Ashton Kutcher/*My Boss's Daughter*

Mike Myers/*Dr. Seuss' The Cat in the Hat*

2004

★George W. Bush/*Fahrenheit 9/11*

Ben Affleck/*Jersey Girl*

Ben Affleck/*Surviving Christmas*

Vin Diesel/*The Chronicles of Riddick*

Colin Farrell/*Alexander*

Ben Stiller/*Along Came Polly*

Ben Stiller/*Anchorman: The Legend of Ron Burgundy*

Ben Stiller/*Dodgeball: A True Underdog Story*

Ben Stiller/*Envy*

Ben Stiller/*Starsky & Hutch*

2005

★Rob Schneider/*Deuce Bigalow: European Gigolo*

Tom Cruise/*War of the Worlds*

Will Ferrell/*Bewitched*

Dwayne "The Rock" Johnson/*Doom*

Jamie Kennedy/*Son of the Mask*

2006

★M. Night Shyamalan/*Lady in the Water*

★Marlon Wayans/*Little Man*

★Shawn Wayans/*Little Man*

Tim Allen/*The Santa Clause 3: The Escape Clause*

Tim Allen/*The Shaggy Dog*

Tim Allen/*Zoom*

Nicolas Cage/*The Wicker Man*

Larry the Cable Guy/*Larry the Cable Guy: Health Inspector*

Rob Schneider/*The Benchwarmers*

Rob Schneider/*Little Man*

David Thewlis/*Basic Instinct 2*

2007

★Eddie Murphy/*Norbit*

Nicolas Cage/*Ghost Rider*

Jim Carrey/*The Number 23*

Cuba Gooding, Jr./*Daddy Day Camp*

Adam Sandler/*I Now Pronounce You Chuck and Larry*

2008

★Mike Myers/*The Love Guru*

Larry the Cable Guy/*Witless Protection*

Eddie Murphy/*Meet Dave*

Al Pacino/*88 Minutes*

Al Pacino/*Righteous Kill*

Mark Wahlberg/*The Happening*

Mark Wahlberg/*Max Payne*

2009

★Joe Jonas/*Jonas Brothers: The 3D Concert Experience*

★Kevin Jonas/*Jonas Brothers: The 3D Concert Experience*

★Nick Jonas/*Jonas Brothers: The 3D Concert Experience*

Will Ferrell/*Land of the Lost*

Steve Martin/*The Pink Panther 2*

Eddie Murphy/*Imagine That*

John Travolta/*Old Dogs*

WORST ACTRESS

1980

★Brooke Shields/*The Blue Lagoon*

1981

★Bo Derek/*Tarzan, the Ape Man*

★Faye Dunaway/*Mommie Dearest*

1982

★Pia Zadora/*Butterfly*

1983

★Pia Zadora/*The Lonely Lady*

1984

★Bo Derek/*Bolero*

1985

★Linda Blair/*Night Patrol*

★Linda Blair/*Savage Island*

★Linda Blair/*Savage Streets*

1986

★Madonna/*Shanghai Surprise*

1987

★Madonna/*Who's That Girl?*

★Liza Minnelli/*Arthur 2: On the Rocks*

1988

★Liza Minnelli/*Rent-A-Cop*

1990

★Bo Derek/*Ghosts Can't Do It*

1991

★Sean Young/*A Kiss Before Dying*

1992

★Melanie Griffith/*Shining Through*

★Melanie Griffith/*A Stranger Among Us*

1993

★Madonna/*Body of Evidence*

1994

★Sharon Stone/*Intersection*

★Sharon Stone/*The Specialist*

Uma Thurman/*Even Cowgirls Get the Blues*

1995

★Elizabeth Berkley/*Showgirls*

1996

★Demi Moore/*Striptease*

Whoopi Goldberg/*Bogus*

Whoopi Goldberg/*Eddie*

Whoopi Goldberg/*Theodore Rex*

Melanie Griffith/*Two Much*

Demi Moore/*The Juror*

Julia Roberts/*Mary Reilly*

1997

★Demi Moore/*G.I. Jane*

Sandra Bullock/*Speed 2: Cruise Control*

Fran Drescher/*The Beautician and the Beast*

Lauren Holly/*A Smile Like Yours*

Lauren Holly/*Turbulence*

Alicia Silverstone/*Excess Baggage*

1998

★Victoria (Posh Spice) Beckham/*Spice World: The Movie*

★Melanie (Scary Spice) Brown/*Spice World: The Movie*

★Emma (Baby Spice) Bunton/*Spice World: The Movie*

★Melanie (Sporty Spice) Chisholm/*Spice World: The Movie*

★Geri (Ginger Spice) Halliwell/*Spice World: The Movie*

Yasmine Bleeth/*BASEketball*

Anne Heche/*Psycho*

Jessica Lange/*Hush*

Uma Thurman/*The Avengers*

1999

★Heather Donahue/*The Blair Witch Project*

Melanie Griffith/*Crazy in Alabama*

Milla Jovovich/*The Messenger: The Story of Joan of Arc*

Sharon Stone/*Gloria*

Catherine Zeta-Jones/*Entrapment*

Catherine Zeta-Jones/*The Haunting*

2000

★Madonna/*The Next Best Thing*

Kim Basinger/*Bless the Child*

Kim Basinger/*I Dreamed of Africa*

Melanie Griffith/*Cecil B. Demented*

Bette Midler/*Isn't She Great*

Demi Moore/*Passion of Mind*

2001

★Mariah Carey/*Glitter*

2002

★Madonna/*Swept Away*

★Britney Spears/*Crossroads*

2003

★Jennifer Lopez/*Gigli*

Drew Barrymore/*Charlie's Angels: Full Throttle*

Kelly Clarkson/*From Justin to Kelly*

Cameron Diaz/*Charlie's Angels: Full Throttle*

Angelina Jolie/*Beyond Borders*

Angelina Jolie/*Lara Croft Tomb Raider: The Cradle of Life*

2004

★Halle Berry/*Catwoman*

Hilary Duff/*A Cinderella Story*

Hilary Duff/*Raise Your Voice*

Angelina Jolie/*Alexander*

Angelina Jolie/*Taking Lives*

Ashley (Fuller) Olsen/*New York Minute*

Mary-Kate Olsen/*New York Minute*

Marlon Wayans/*White Chicks*

Shawn Wayans/*White Chicks*

2005

★Jenny McCarthy/*Dirty Love*

Jessica Alba/*Fantastic Four*

Jessica Alba/*Into the Blue*

Hilary Duff/*Cheaper by the Dozen 2*

Hilary Duff/*The Perfect Man*

Jennifer Lopez/*Monster-in-Law*

Tara Reid/*Alone in the Dark*

2006

★Sharon Stone/*Basic Instinct 2*

Haylie Duff/*Material Girls*

Hilary Duff/*Material Girls*

Lindsay Lohan/*Just My Luck*

Kristanna Loken/*BloodRayne*

Jessica Simpson/*Employee of the Month*

2007

★Lindsay Lohan/*I Know Who Killed Me*

Jessica Alba/*Awake*

Logan Browning/*Bratz*

Elisha Cuthbert/*Captivity*

Diane Keaton/*Because I Said So*

Janel Parrish/*Bratz*

Nathalia Ramos/*Bratz*

Skyler Shaye/*Bratz*

2008

★Paris Hilton/*The Hottie and the Nottie*

Jessica Alba/*The Eye*

Jessica Alba/*The Love Guru*

Annette Bening/*The Women*

Cameron Diaz/*What Happens in Vegas*

Kate Hudson/*Fool's Gold*

Kate Hudson/*My Best Friend's Girl*

Eva Mendes/*The Women*

Debra Messing/*The Women*

Jada Pinkett Smith/*The Women*

Meg Ryan/*The Women*

2009

★Sandra Bullock/*All About Steve*

Miley Cyrus/*Hannah Montana: The Movie*

Megan Fox/*Jennifer's Body*

Megan Fox/*Transformers: Revenge of the Fallen*

Beyonce Knowles/*Obsessed*

Sarah Jessica Parker/*Did You Hear About the Morgans?*

Kelly Preston/*Old Dogs*

WORST SUPPORTING ACTOR

1980

★John Adams/*Gloria*

★Laurence Olivier/*The Jazz Singer*

1981

★Steve Forrest/*Mommie Dearest*

1982

★Ed McMahon/*Butterfly*

1983

★Jim Nabors/*Stroker Ace*

1985

★Rob Lowe/*St. Elmo's Fire*

1986

★Jerome Benton/*Under the Cherry Moon*

1987

★David Mendenhall/*Over the Top*

1988

★Dan Aykroyd/*Caddyshack 2*

1989

★Christopher Atkins/*Listen to Me*

1991

★Dan Aykroyd/*Nothing But Trouble*

1992

★Tom Selleck/*Christopher Columbus: The Discovery*

1993

★Woody Harrelson/*Indecent Proposal*

1994

★O.J. Simpson/*Naked Gun 33 1/3: The Final Insult*

1995

★Dennis Hopper/*Waterworld*

Robert Davi/*Showgirls*

1996

Marlon Brando/*The Island of Dr. Moreau*

Val Kilmer/*The Ghost and the Darkness*

Val Kilmer/*The Island of Dr. Moreau*

Burt Reynolds/*Striptease*

Steven Seagal/*Executive Decision*

Quentin Tarantino/*From Dusk Till Dawn*

1997

★Dennis Rodman/*Double Team*

Willem Dafoe/*Speed 2: Cruise Control*

Chris O'Donnell/*Batman and Robin*

Arnold Schwarzenegger/*Batman and Robin*

Jon Voight/*Most Wanted*

Jon Voight/*U-Turn*

1998

★Joe Eszterhas/*An Alan Smithee Film: Burn, Hollywood, Burn*

Sean Connery/*The Avengers*

Joe Pesci/*Lethal Weapon 4*

Sylvester Stallone/*An Alan Smithee Film: Burn, Hollywood, Burn*

1999

Kenneth Branagh/*Wild Wild West*

Gabriel Byrne/*End of Days*

Gabriel Byrne/*Stigmata*

★ = *winner*

Jake Lloyd/*Star Wars: Episode 1—The Phantom Menace*

Rob Schneider/*Big Daddy*

2000

★Barry Pepper/*Battlefield Earth*

Stephen Baldwin/*The Flintstones in Viva Rock Vegas*

Keanu Reeves/*The Watcher*

Forest Whitaker/*Battlefield Earth*

2001

★Charlton Heston/*Planet of the Apes*

2002

★Hayden Christensen/*Star Wars: Episode 2—Attack of the Clones*

2003

★Sylvester Stallone/*Spy Kids 3-D: Game Over*

Anthony Anderson/*Kangaroo Jack*

Alec Baldwin/*Dr. Seuss' The Cat in the Hat*

Al Pacino/*Gigli*

Christopher Walken/*Gigli*

Christopher Walken/*Kangaroo Jack*

2004

★Donald Rumsfeld/*Fahrenheit 9/11*

Val Kilmer/*Alexander*

Arnold Schwarzenegger/*Around the World in 80 Days*

Jon Voight/*Superbabies: Baby Geniuses 2*

Lambert Wilson/*Catwoman*

2005

★Hayden Christensen/*Star Wars: Episode 3—Revenge of the Sith*

Alan Cumming/*Son of the Mask*

Will Ferrell/*Kicking & Screaming*

Bob Hoskins/*Son of the Mask*

Eugene Levy/*Cheaper by the Dozen 2*

Burt Reynolds/*The Dukes of Hazzard*

Burt Reynolds/*The Longest Yard*

2006

Danny DeVito/*Deck the Halls*

Ben Kingsley/*BloodRayne*

Martin Short/*The Santa Clause 3: The Escape Clause*

2007

★Eddie Murphy/*Norbit*

Orlando Bloom/*Pirates of the Caribbean: At World's End*

Kevin James/*I Now Pronounce You Chuck and Larry*

Rob Schneider/*I Now Pronounce You Chuck and Larry*

Jon Voight/*Bratz*

2008

★Pierce Brosnan/*Mamma Mia!*

Uwe Boll/*Postal*

Myron Goble/*Postal*

Ben Kingsley/*The Love Guru*

Ben Kingsley/*The Wackness*

Ben Kingsley/*War, Inc.*

Burt Reynolds/*Deal*

Burt Reynolds/*In the Name of the King: A Dungeon Siege Tale*

Verne Troyer/*The Love Guru*

2009

★Billy Ray Cyrus/*Hannah Montana: The Movie*

Hugh Hefner/*Miss March*

Robert Pattinson/*The Twilight Saga: New Moon*

Jorma Taccone/*Land of the Lost*

Marlon Wayans/*G.I. Joe: The Rise of Cobra*

WORST SUPPORTING ACTRESS

1980

★Amy Irving/*Honeysuckle Rose*

1981

★Diana Scarwid/*Mommie Dearest*

1982

★Aileen Quinn/*Annie*

1983

★Sybil Danning/*Chained Heat*

★Sybil Danning/*Hercules*

1984

★Lynn-Holly Johnson/*Where the Boys Are '84*

1985

★Brigitte Nielsen/*Rocky 4*

1987

★Daryl Hannah/*Wall Street*

1988

★Kristy McNichol/*Two Moon Junction*

1989

★Brooke Shields/*Speed Zone*

1990

★Sofia Coppola/*The Godfather, Part 3*

1991

★Sean Young/*A Kiss Before Dying*

1992

★Estelle Getty/*Stop! or My Mom Will Shoot*

1993

★Faye Dunaway/*The Temp*

1994

★Rosie O'Donnell/*Car 54, Where Are You?*

★Rosie O'Donnell/*Exit to Eden*

★Rosie O'Donnell/*The Flintstones*

Elizabeth Taylor/*The Flintstones*

1995

★Madonna/*Four Rooms*

Gina Gershon/*Showgirls*

1996

★Melanie Griffith/*Mulholland Falls*

Faye Dunaway/*The Chamber*

Faye Dunaway/*Dunston Checks In*

Jami Gertz/*Twister*

Daryl Hannah/*Two Much*

Teri Hatcher/*Heaven's Prisoners*

Teri Hatcher/*Two Days in the Valley*

1997

★Alicia Silverstone/*Batman and Robin*

Faye Dunaway/*Albino Alligator*

Milla Jovovich/*The Fifth Element*

Julia Louis-Dreyfus/*Father's Day*

Demi Moore/*G.I. Jane*

Uma Thurman/*Batman and Robin*

1998

★Maria Pitillo/*Godzilla*

Ellen A. Dow/*54*

Jenny McCarthy/*BASEketball*

Roger Moore/*Spice World: The Movie*

Liv Tyler/*Armageddon*

Raquel Welch/*Chairman of the Board*

1999

★Denise Richards/*The World Is Not Enough*

Sofia Coppola/*Star Wars: Episode 1—The Phantom Menace*

Salma Hayek/*Dogma*

Salma Hayek/*Wild Wild West*

Juliette Lewis/*The Other Sister*

2000

★Kelly Preston/*Battlefield Earth*

Patricia Arquette/*Little Nicky*

Joan Collins/*The Flintstones in Viva Rock Vegas*

Thandie Newton/*Mission: Impossible 2*

Rene Russo/*The Adventures of Rocky & Bullwinkle*

2001

★Estella Warren/*Planet of the Apes*

2002

★Madonna/*Die Another Day*

2003

★Demi Moore/*Charlie's Angels: Full Throttle*

Lainie Kazan/*Gigli*

Brittany Murphy/*Just Married*

Kelly Preston/*Dr. Seuss' The Cat in the Hat*

Tara Reid/*My Boss's Daughter*

2004

★Britney Spears/*Fahrenheit 9/11*

Carmen Electra/*Starsky & Hutch*

Jennifer Lopez/*Jersey Girl*

Condoleeza Rice/*Fahrenheit 9/11*

Sharon Stone/*Catwoman*

2005

★Paris Hilton/*House of Wax*

Carmen Electra/*Dirty Love*

Katie Holmes/*Batman Begins*

Jessica Simpson/*The Dukes of Hazzard*

2006

★Carmen Electra/*Date Movie*

Kate (Catherine) Bosworth/*Superman Returns*

Kristin Chenoweth/*Deck the Halls*

Kristin Chenoweth/*The Pink Panther*

Kristin Chenoweth/*RV*

Jenny McCarthy/*John Tucker Must Die*

Michelle Rodriguez/*BloodRayne*

2007

★Eddie Murphy/*Norbit*

Jessica Biel/*I Now Pronounce You Chuck and Larry*

Carmen Electra/*Epic Movie*

Julia Ormond/*I Know Who Killed Me*

Nicolette Sheridan/*Code Name: The Cleaner*

2008

★Paris Hilton/*Repo! The Genetic Opera*

Carmen Electra/*Disaster Movie*

Carmen Electra/*Meet the Spartans*

Kim Kardashian/*Disaster Movie*

Jenny McCarthy/*Witless Protection*

Leelee Sobieski/*88 Minutes*

Leelee Sobieski/*In the Name of the King: A Dungeon Siege Tale*

2009

★Sienna Miller/*G.I. Joe: The Rise of Cobra*

Candice Bergen/*Bride Wars*

Ali Larter/*Obsessed*

Julie White/*Transformers: Revenge of the Fallen*

WORST DIRECTOR

1980

★Robert Greenwald/*Xanadu*

1981

★Michael Cimino/*Heaven's Gate*

1982

★Ken Annakin/*Pirate Movie*

1983

★Peter Sasdy/*The Lonely Lady*

1984

★John Derek/*Bolero*

1985

★Sylvester Stallone/*Rocky 4*

1986

★Prince/*Under the Cherry Moon*

1987

★Norman Mailer/*Tough Guys Don't Dance*

★Elaine May/*Ishtar*

1988

★Blake Edwards/*Sunset*

★Stewart Raffill/*Mac and Me*

1989

★William Shatner/*Star Trek 5: The Final Frontier*

1990

★John Derek/*Ghosts Can't Do It*

1991

★Michael Lehmann/*Hudson Hawk*

1992

★David Seltzer/*Shining Through*

1993

★Jennifer Lynch/*Boxing Helena*

1994

★Steven Seagal/*On Deadly Ground*

1995

★Paul Verhoeven/*Showgirls*

1996

★Andrew Bergman/*Striptease*

John Frankenheimer/*The Island of Dr. Moreau*

Stephen Frears/*Mary Reilly*

John Landis/*The Stupids*

Brian Levant/*Jingle All the Way*

1997

★Kevin Costner/*The Postman*

Jan De Bont/*Speed 2: Cruise Control*

Luis Llosa/*Anaconda*

Joel Schumacher/*Batman and Robin*

Oliver Stone/*U-Turn*

1998

★Gus Van Sant/*Psycho*

Michael Bay/*Armageddon*

Jeremiah S. Chechik/*The Avengers*

Roland Emmerich/*Godzilla*

Arthur Hiller/*An Alan Smithee Film: Burn, Hollywood, Burn*

1999

★Barry Sonnenfeld/*Wild Wild West*

Jan De Bont/*The Haunting*

Dennis Dugan/*Big Daddy*

Peter Hyams/*End of Days*

George Lucas/*Star Wars: Episode 1—The Phantom Menace*

2000

★Roger Christian/*Battlefield Earth*

Brian De Palma/*Mission to Mars*

John Schlesinger/*The Next Best Thing*

2001

★Tom Green/*Freddy Got Fingered*

2002

★Guy Ritchie/*Swept Away*

2003

★Martin Brest/*Gigli*

Robert Iscove/*From Justin to Kelly*

Mort Nathan/*Boat Trip*

Andy Wachowski/*The Matrix Reloaded*

Andy Wachowski/*The Matrix Revolutions*

Larry Wachowski/*The Matrix Reloaded*

Larry Wachowski/*The Matrix Revolutions*

Bo Welch/*Dr. Seuss' The Cat in the Hat*

2004

★Pitof/*Catwoman*

Bob (Benjamin) Clark/*Superbabies: Baby Geniuses 2*

Renny Harlin/*Exorcist: The Beginning*

Oliver Stone/*Alexander*

Keenen Ivory Wayans/*White Chicks*

2005

★John Mallory Asher/*Dirty Love*

Uwe Boll/*Alone in the Dark*

Jay Chandrasekhar/*The Dukes of Hazzard*

Nora Ephron/*Bewitched*

Lawrence (Larry) Guterman/*Son of the Mask*

2006

★M. Night Shyamalan/*Lady in the Water*

Uwe Boll/*BloodRayne*

Michael Caton-Jones/*Basic Instinct 2*

Ron Howard/*The Da Vinci Code*

Keenen Ivory Wayans/*Little Man*

2007

★Chris Sivertson/*I Know Who Killed Me*

Dennis Dugan/*I Now Pronounce You Chuck and Larry*

Roland Joffe/*Captivity*

Brian Robbins/*Norbit*

Fred Savage/*Daddy Day Camp*

2008

★Uwe Boll/*In the Name of the King: A Dungeon Siege Tale*

★Uwe Boll/*Postal*

Jason Friedberg/*Meet the Spartans*

Tom Putnam/*The Hottie and the Nottie*

Marco Schnabel/*The Love Guru*

Aaron Seltzer/*Meet the Spartans*

M. Night Shyamalan/*The Happening*

2009

★Michael Bay/*Transformers: Revenge of the Fallen*

Walt Becker/*Old Dogs*

Brad Silberling/*Land of the Lost*

Stephen Sommers/*G.I. Joe: The Rise of Cobra*

Phil Traill/*All About Steve*

WORST SCREENPLAY

1980

★*Can't Stop the Music*

1981

★*Mommie Dearest*

1983

★*The Lonely Lady*

1984

★*Bolero*

1985

★*Rambo: First Blood, Part 2*

★*Rocky 4*

1986

★*Howard the Duck*

1987

★*Leonard Part 6*

1988

★*Cocktail*

1989

★*Harlem Nights*

1990

★*The Adventures of Ford Fairlane*

1991

★*Hudson Hawk*

1992

★*Stop! or My Mom Will Shoot*

1993

★*Indecent Proposal*

1994

★*The Flintstones*

1995

★*Showgirls*

1996

★*Striptease*

Barb Wire

Ed

The Island of Dr. Moreau

The Stupids

1997

★*The Postman*

Anaconda

Batman and Robin

The Lost World: Jurassic Park 2

Speed 2: Cruise Control

1998

★*An Alan Smithee Film: Burn, Hollywood, Burn*

Armageddon

The Avengers

Godzilla

Spice World: The Movie

1999

★*Wild Wild West*

Big Daddy

The Haunting

★ = *winner*

The Mod Squad

Star Wars: Episode 1—The Phantom Menace

2000

★*Battlefield Earth*

Book of Shadows: Blair Witch 2

Dr. Seuss' How the Grinch Stole Christmas

Little Nicky

The Next Best Thing

2001

★*Freddy Got Fingered*

2003

★*Gigli*

Charlie's Angels: Full Throttle

Dr. Seuss' The Cat in the Hat

Dumb and Dumberer: When Harry Met Lloyd

From Justin to Kelly

2004

★*Catwoman*

Alexander

Superbabies: Baby Geniuses 2

Surviving Christmas

White Chicks

2005

★*Dirty Love*

Bewitched

Deuce Bigalow: European Gigolo

The Dukes of Hazzard

Son of the Mask

2006

★*Basic Instinct 2*

BloodRayne

Lady in the Water

Little Man

The Wicker Man

2007

★*I Know Who Killed Me*

Daddy Day Camp

Epic Movie

I Now Pronounce You Chuck and Larry

Norbit

2008

★*The Love Guru*

The Happening

The Hottie and the Nottie

In the Name of the King: A Dungeon Siege Tale

Meet the Spartans

2009

★*Transformers: Revenge of the Fallen*

All About Steve

G.I. Joe: The Rise of Cobra

Land of the Lost

The Twilight Saga: New Moon

WORST SONG

1980

★"The Man with Bogart's Face"/*The Man with Bogart's Face*

1981

★"Baby Talk"/*Paternity*

1982

★"Pumpin' and Blowin'"/*Pirate Movie*

1983

★"The Way You Do It"/*The Lonely Lady*

1984

★"Drinkenstein"/*Rhinestone*

1985

★"Peace In Our Life"/*Rambo: First Blood, Part 2*

1986

★"Love or Money"/*Under the Cherry Moon*

1987

★"I Want Your Sex"/*Beverly Hills Cop 2*

1988

★"Jack Fresh"/*Caddyshack 2*

1989

★"Bring Your Daughter to the Slaughter"/*A Nightmare on Elm Street 5: Dream Child*

1990

★"He's Comin' Back (The Devil!)"/*Repossessed*

1991

★"Addams Groove"/*The Addams Family*

1992

★"High Times, Hard Times"/*Newsies*

1993

★"WHOOMP! There It Is"/*Addams Family Values*

1994

★"Marry the Mole"/*Thumbelina*

1995

★"Walk into the Wind"/*Showgirls*

1996

★"Pussy, Pussy, Pussy (Whose Kitty Cat Are You?)"/*Striptease*

"Welcome to Planet Boom!"/*Barb Wire*

"Whenever There is Love"/*Daylight*

1997

★Entire Song Score/*The Postman*

"Fire Down Below"/*Fire Down Below*

"How Do I Live"/*Con Air*

"My Dream"/*Speed 2: Cruise Control*

"The End is The Beginning is The End"/*Batman and Robin*

1998

★"I Wanna Be Mike Ovitz!"/*An Alan Smithee Film: Burn, Hollywood, Burn*

"Barney, The Song"/*Barney's Great Adventure*

"I Don't Want to Miss a Thing"/*Armageddon*

"Storm"/*The Avengers*

"Too Much"/*Spice World: The Movie*

1999

★"Wild Wild West"/*Wild Wild West*

2002

★"I'm Not a Girl, Not Yet a Woman"/*Crossroads*

WORST NEW STAR

1981

★Klinton Spilsbury/*Legend of the Lone Ranger*

1982

★Pia Zadora/*Butterfly*

1983

★Lou Ferrigno/*Hercules*

1984

★Olivia D'Abo/*Bolero*

★Olivia D'Abo/*Conan the Destroyer*

1985

★Brigitte Nielsen/*Red Sonja*

★Brigitte Nielsen/*Rocky 4*

1987

★David Mendenhall/*Over the Top*

1990

★Sofia Coppola/*The Godfather, Part 3*

1991

★Vanilla Ice/*Cool As Ice*

1992

★Pauly Shore/*Encino Man*

1993

★Janet Jackson/*Poetic Justice*

1994

★Anna Nicole Smith/*Naked Gun 33 1/3: The Final Insult*

1995

★Elizabeth Berkley/*Showgirls*

David Caruso/*Kiss of Death*

Cindy Crawford/*Fair Game*

Julia Sweeney/*It's Pat: The Movie*

1996

★Pamela Anderson/*Barb Wire*

Ellen DeGeneres/*Mr. Wrong*

1997

★Dennis Rodman/*Double Team*

Tori Spelling/*The House of Yes*

Howard Stern/*Private Parts*

Chris Tucker/*The Fifth Element*

Chris Tucker/*Money Talks*

1998

★Joe Eszterhas/*An Alan Smithee Film: Burn, Hollywood, Burn*

★Jerry Springer/*Ringmaster*

Barney/*Barney's Great Adventure*

The Spice Girls/*Spice World: The Movie*

Carrot Top/*Chairman of the Board*

★ = winner

The Cast Index provides a complete videography for cast members with more than one appearance on video. The listings for the actor names follow an alphabetical sort by last name (although the names appear in a first name-last name format). The videographies are listed chronologically, from most recent film to earliest appearance, making it easier to trace the development of your favorite actor's career. When a cast member appears in more than one film in the same year, these movies are listed alphabetically within the year. A (V) beside a movie title indicates voice-only work, while an (N) indicates narrator duties.

Beverly Aadland (1943-)
Assault of the Rebel Girls *'59*
Raiders of Sunset Pass *'43*

Lee Aaker (1943-)
Courage of Rin Tin Tin *'57*
Rin Tin Tin, Hero of the West *'55*
Hondo *'53*
Jeopardy *'53*
The Atomic City *'52*

Aaliyah (1979-2001)
Queen of the Damned *'02*
Romeo Must Die *'00*

Angela Aames (1956-88)
Basic Training *'86*
Bachelor Party *'84*
The Lost Empire *'83*

Willie Aames (1960-)
Cut and Run *'85*
Paradise *'82*
Zapped! *'82*
Scavenger Hunt *'79*
Frankenstein *'73*

Caroline Aaron (1952-)
Love Comes Lately *'07*
Nancy Drew *'07*
Grilled *'06*
Beyond the Sea *'04*
Cellular *'04*
A Day Without a Mexican *'04*
Two Days *'03*
Amy's O *'02*
Pumpkin *'02*
Joe Dirt *'01*
Never Again *'01*
Running Mates *'00*
What Planet Are You From? *'00*
Anywhere But Here *'99*
Tuesdays with Morrie *'99*
Primary Colors *'98*
Deconstructing Harry *'97*
Weapons of Mass Distraction *'97*
House Arrest *'96*
A Modern Affair *'94*
Alice *'90*
Edward Scissorhands *'90*
Crimes & Misdemeanors *'89*
Heartburn *'86*

Judith Abarbanel
American Matchmaker *'40*
The Cantor's Son *'37*
Uncle Moses *'32*

Silvia Abascal (1979-)
My Mother Likes Women *'02*
The Yellow Fountain *'99*

Diego Abatantuono (1955-)
I'm Not Scared *'03*
Children of Hannibal *'98*
The Best Man *'97*
Nirvana *'97*
Mediterraneo *'91*

Sean Abbananto
Bikini Med School *'98*
Bikini House Calls *'96*

Hiam Abbass (1960-)
Amreeka *'09*
Lemon Tree *'08*
The Visitor *'07*
The Nativity Story *'06*
Free Zone *'05*
Munich *'05*
Paradise Now *'05*
The Syrian Bride *'04*
Satin Rouge *'02*

Bruce Abbott (1954-)
Melanie Darrow *'97*
The Prophecy 2: Ashtown *'97*
The Demolitionist *'95*
Dillinger *'91*
Bride of Re-Animator *'89*
Trapped *'89*
Bad Dreams *'88*
Interzone *'88*
Summer Heat *'87*
Re-Animator *'84*

Bud Abbott (1895-1974)
Dance with Me, Henry *'56*
Abbott and Costello Meet the Mummy *'55*
Abbott and Costello Meet the Keystone Kops *'54*
Abbott and Costello Go to Mars *'53*
Abbott and Costello Meet Captain Kidd *'52*
Abbott and Costello Meet Dr. Jekyll and Mr. Hyde *'52*
Jack & the Beanstalk *'52*
Lost in Alaska *'52*
Abbott and Costello Meet the Invisible Man *'51*
Comin' Round the Mountain *'51*
Abbott and Costello in the Foreign Legion *'50*
Abbott and Costello Meet the Killer, Boris Karloff *'49*
Africa Screams *'49*
Abbott and Costello Meet Frankenstein *'48*
Mexican Hayride *'48*
The Noose Hangs High *'48*
Buck Privates Come Home *'47*
The Wistful Widow of Wagon Gap *'47*
Little Giant *'46*
The Time of Their Lives *'46*
Abbott and Costello in Hollywood *'45*
Here Come the Co-Eds *'45*
The Naughty Nineties *'45*
In Society *'44*
Lost in a Harem *'44*
Hit the Ice *'43*
It Ain't Hay *'43*
Pardon My Sarong *'42*
Ride 'Em Cowboy *'42*
Rio Rita *'42*
Who Done It? *'42*
Buck Privates *'41*
Hold That Ghost *'41*
In the Navy *'41*
Keep 'Em Flying *'41*
One Night in the Tropics *'40*

Diahnne Abbott (1945-)
Jo Jo Dancer, Your Life Is Calling *'86*
Love Streams *'84*
King of Comedy *'82*
New York, New York *'77*

John Abbott (1905-96)
The Merry Widow *'52*
Adventure Island *'47*
Anna and the King of Siam *'46*
Deception *'46*
Humoresque *'46*
Pursuit to Algiers *'45*
The Vampire's Ghost *'45*
Cry of the Werewolf *'44*
End of the Road *'44*
The Falcon in Hollywood *'44*
U-Boat Prisoner *'44*
Mrs. Miniver *'42*

Philip Abbott (1923-98)
The Fantastic World of D.C. Collins *'84*
Hangar 18 *'80*
The Invisible Boy *'57*

Khalid Abdalla
The Kite Runner *'07*
United 93 *'06*

Nassim Abdi
Secret Ballot *'01*
Guns of Fury *'49*

Paula Abdul (1962-)
Robots *'05 (V)*
Mr. Rock 'n' Roll: The Alan Freed Story *'99*
The Waiting Game *'98*

Kareem Abdul-Jabbar (1947-)
BASEketball *'98*
Rebound: The Legend of Earl "The Goat" Manigault *'96*
Slam Dunk Ernest *'95*
D2: The Mighty Ducks *'94*
Stephen King's The Stand *'94*
Purple People Eater *'88*
Chuck Berry: Hail! Hail! Rock 'n' Roll *'87*
Fletch *'85*
Airplane! *'80*
The Fish that Saved Pittsburgh *'79*
Game of Death *'79*

Hiroshi Abe (1964-)
Tokyo Raiders *'00*
Godzilla 2000 *'99*
Moon over Tao *'97*
Orochi, the Eight Headed Dragon *'94*

Sadao Abe
The Great Yokai War *'05*
Kamikaze Girls *'04*
Uzumaki *'00*

Toru Abe
Blind Woman's Curse *'70*
The Human Condition: No Greater Love *'58*

Alfred Abel (1879-1937)
Metropolis *'26*
The Finances of the Grand Duke *'24*
Dr. Mabuse, The Gambler *'22*
Phantom *'22*

Jake Abel (1987-)
Angel of Death *'09*
Flash of Genius *'08*

Walter Abel (1898-1987)
Grace Quigley *'84*
The Man Without a Country *'73*
Silent Night, Bloody Night *'73*
Quick, Let's Get Married *'71*
Mirage *'66*
Raintree County *'57*
The Indian Fighter *'55*
Island in the Sky *'53*
So This Is Love *'53*
Curley *'47*
Fabulous Joe *'47*
Kid from Brooklyn *'46*
13 Rue Madeleine *'46*
Mr. Skeffington *'44*
So Proudly We Hail *'43*
Holiday Inn *'42*
Wake Island *'42*
Dance, Girl, Dance *'40*
Michael Shayne: Private Detective *'40*
Law of the Underworld *'38*
Fury *'36*
The Three Musketeers *'35*

Lionel Abelanski (1964-)
The Grand Role *'04*
My Wife is an Actress *'01*
Train of Life *'98*

Jim Abele (1960-)
Model Behavior *'00*
Student Affairs *'88*
Wimps *'87*

Tim Abell (1968-)
Miracle at Sage Creek *'05*
Special Forces *'03*
Dead Simple *'01*
Instinct to Kill *'01*
The Substitute 4: Failure is Not an Option *'00*
The Base *'99*
Rapid Assault *'99*
Death and Desire *'97*
Hybrid *'97*
Night Shade *'97*
Soldier of Fortune Inc. *'97*
Steel Sharks *'97*
Sexual Roulette *'96*
Attack of the 60-Foot Centerfold *'95*
Masseuse *'95*

Over the Wire '95

Ian Abercrombie (1933-)

Star Wars: The Clone Wars '08 (V)
Garfield: A Tail of Two Kitties '06
Inland Empire '06
Marilyn Hotchkiss' Ballroom Dancing & Charm School '06
Scooby-Doo 2: Monsters Unleashed '04 (V)
Rattled '96
Test Tube Teens from the Year 2000 '93
Army of Darkness '92
Zandalee '91
Curse 4: The Ultimate Sacrifice '90
Puppet Master 3: Toulon's Revenge '90
Catacombs '89
Kicks '85
Backstairs at the White House '79

Keith Aberdein (1943-)

Smash Palace '82
Wild Horses '82

Sivi Aberg (1944-)

Dr. Death, Seeker of Souls '73
The Killing of Sister George '69

Abigail (1945-)

Breaking Loose '90
Adventures of Eliza Fraser '76

Simon Abkarian (1962-)

Persepolis '07 (V)
Casino Royale '06
Yes '04
Almost Peaceful '02
Ararat '02

Whitney Able

Love and Mary '07
Dead Lenny '06

F. Murray Abraham (1939-)

Perestroika '09
Camera: The Walking Mountain '08
Shark Swarm '08
Blood Monkey '07
The Stone Merchant '06
The Bridge of San Luis Rey '05
Joshua '02
13 Ghosts '01
Finding Forrester '00
Excellent Cadavers '99
Muppets from Space '99
Noah's Ark '99
All New Adventures of Laurel and Hardy: For Love or Mummy '98
Esther '98
Star Trek: Insurrection '98
Baby Face Nelson '97
Color of Justice '97
Mimic '97
Larry McMurtry's Dead Man's Walk '96
Looking for Richard '96
Children of the Revolution '95
Dillinger and Capone '95
Mighty Aphrodite '95
Surviving the Game '94
By the Sword '93
Last Action Hero '93
National Lampoon's Loaded Weapon 1 '93
Nostradamus '93
Sweet Killing '93
Mobsters '91
The Bonfire of the Vanities '90
Beyond the Stars '89
An Innocent Man '89
Intimate Power '89
Slipstream '89
Third Solution '89
The Name of the Rose '86
Amadeus '84
Scarface '83
Madman '79
The Big Fix '78
All the President's Men '76
The Ritz '76
The Sunshine Boys '75
Prisoner of Second Avenue '74
Serpico '73
They Might Be Giants '71

Ken Abraham

Marked for Murder '89
Deadly Embrace '88
Vice Academy '88
Creepozoids '87

Jim Abrahams (1944-)

Airplane! '80
Kentucky Fried Movie '77

Jon Abrahams (1977-)

Bottoms Up '06
Deceit '06
House of Wax '05
Prime '05
Standing Still '05
My Boss's Daughter '03
Wes Craven Presents: They '02
Texas Rangers '01
Boiler Room '00
Meet the Parents '00
Scary Movie '00
Bringing Out the Dead '99
Outside Providence '99
The Faculty '98
Masterminds '96
Dead Man Walking '95
Kids '95

Michele Abrams

Buffy the Vampire Slayer '92
Cool World '92

Josef Abrham (1939-)

I Served the King of England '07
All My Loved Ones '00

Andrei Abrikosov (1906-73)

Sword & the Dragon '56
Alexander Nevsky '38

Victoria Abril (1959-)

Swindled '04
No News from God '01
101 Reykjavik '00
Between Your Legs '99
My Father, My Mother, My Brothers and My Sisters '99
French Twist '95
Jimmy Hollywood '94
Kika '94
Intruso '93
High Heels '91
Lovers: A True Story '90
Tie Me Up! Tie Me Down! '90
If They Tell You I Fell '89
Baton Rouge '88
Max, Mon Amour '86
After Darkness '85
L'Addition '85
Padre Nuestro '85
Moon in the Gutter '83
On the Line '83
I Married a Dead Man '82

Omid Abtahi

The Mysteries of Pittsburgh '08
Space Chimps '08 (V)
You Don't Mess with the Zohan '08

Yussef Abu-Warda

Amreeka '09
Kadosh '99
The Milky Way '97

Stefano Accorsi (1971-)

Saturn in Opposition '07
Shall We Kiss? '07
Blame It on Fidel '06
His Secret Life '01
The Last Kiss '01
The Son's Room '00

Kirk Acevedo (1974-)

Invincible '06
Band of Brothers '01
Bait '00
Boiler Room '00
Dinner Rush '00
In the Weeds '00
The Thin Red Line '98
Witness to the Mob '98
The Sunshine Boys '95

James Acheson

The Garden of Redemption '97
Kazaam '96
Body Language '92

Sharon Acker (1935-)

Happy Birthday to Me '81
Off Your Rocker '80
The Hanged Man '74
The Stranger '73
Lucky Jim '58

Forrest J Ackerman (1916-2008)

Attack of the 60-Foot Centerfold '95
Dead Alive '93
Innocent Blood '92
Hard to Die '90
The Wizard of Speed and Time '88
Amazon Women on the Moon '87
Curse of the Queerwolf '87
Evil Spawn '87
Aftermath '85
The Howling '81
Kentucky Fried Movie '77
Schlock '73
Dracula vs. Frankenstein '71
Planet of Blood '66

Leslie Ackerman (1956-)

Blame It on the Night '84
Shattered Vows '84
Skag '79
Young Love, First Love '79
Joy Ride to Nowhere '78
The First Nudie Musical '75
Law and Disorder '74

Joss Ackland (1928-)

Flawless '07
How About You '07
Hogfather '06
Moscow Zero '06
These Foolish Things '06
Asylum '05
Frederick Forsyth's Icon '05
A Different Loyalty '04
I'll Be There '03
K-19: The Widowmaker '02
No Good Deed '02
Passion of Mind '00
Heat of the Sun '99
Firelight '97
Swept from the Sea '97
Deadly Voyage '96
D3: The Mighty Ducks '96
Surviving Picasso '96
Citizen X '95
A Kid in King Arthur's Court '95
Jacob '94
Miracle on 34th Street '94
Mother's Boys '94
Shameless '94
Nowhere to Run '93
The Strange Case of the End of Civilization As We Know It '93
The Mighty Ducks '92
Once Upon a Crime '92
Project: Shadowchaser '92
Bill & Ted's Bogus Journey '91
Codename Kyril '91
The Object of Beauty '91
The Palermo Connection '91
A Woman Named Jackie '91
The Hunt for Red October '90
Jekyll and Hyde '90
A Murder of Quality '90
Spymaker: The Secret Life of Ian Fleming '90
Lethal Weapon 2 '89
To Kill a Priest '89
It Couldn't Happen Here '88
White Mischief '88
A Zed & Two Noughts '88
Queenie '87
The Sicilian '87
Lady Jane '85
Shadowlands '85
The Apple '80
Rough Cut '80
Tinker, Tailor, Soldier, Spy '80
The Big Scam '79
Saint Jack '79
Silver Bears '78
Watership Down '78 (V)
Who Is Killing the Great Chefs of Europe? '78
Royal Flash '75
The Little Prince '74
S*P*Y*S '74
Hitler: The Last Ten Days '73
Mind Snatchers '72
Cry of the Penguins '71
The House that Dripped Blood '71
Crescendo '69

Jensen Ackles (1978-)

My Bloody Valentine 3D '09
Devour '05
Blonde '01

Bill Ackridge

Voyage of the Heart '90
Signal 7 '83

David Ackroyd (1940-)

Raven '97
Against the Wall '94
Dead On '93
Love, Cheat & Steal '93
The Fear Inside '92
Memories of Me '88
Windmills of the Gods '88
Poor Little Rich Girl: The Barbara Hutton Story '87
The Children of Times Square '86
A Smoky Mountain Christmas '86
Cocaine: One Man's Seduction '83
When Your Lover Leaves '83
Sound of Murder '82
A Gun in the House '81
And I Alone Survived '78
The Dark Secret of Harvest Home '78

Jack Ackroyd (1890-)

The Better 'Ole '26
The Cruise of the Jasper B '26

Rodolfo Acosta (1920-74)

Savage Run '70
Flaming Star '60
Let No Man Write My Epitaph '60
Drum Beat '54
Hondo '53
Yankee Buccaneer '52
Pancho Villa Returns '50

Jay Acovone (1955-)

InAlienable '08
Rancid '04
Crash Dive '96
Opposite Corners '96
Showdown '94
Born to Run '93
The Magician '93
Quicksand: No Escape '91
Doctor Mordrid: Master of the Unknown '90

Acquanetta (1921-2004)

Grizzly Adams: The Legend Continues '90
The Lost Continent '51
Dead Man's Eyes '44
Jungle Woman '44
Captive Wild Woman '43

Eddie Acuff (1908-56)

G-Men Never Forget '48
It Happened Tomorrow '44
Guadalcanal Diary '43
They Died with Their Boots On '41
Law of the Underworld '38
The Black Legion '37
Shipmates Forever '35

Deborah Adair (1952-)

Endless Descent '90
Gore Vidal's Lincoln '88

Dick Adair

Pay or Die '83
Blind Rage '78

Phyllis Adair

Land of Hunted Men '43
Trigger Men '41
Wild Horse Valley '40

Robert Adair (1900-54)

Norman Conquest '53
The Face at the Window '39
Ticket of Leave Man '37

Ronald Adam (1896-1979)

Tomb of Ligeia '64
The Obsessed '51
Seven Days to Noon '50
The Foreman Went to France '42

Jiri Adamira (1926-93)

Flowers of Reverie '84
A Prayer for Katarina Horovitzova '69
The Fifth Horseman Is Fear '64

Amy Adams (1974-)

Leap Year '10
Julie & Julia '09
Moonlight Serenade '09
Night at the Museum: Battle of the Smithsonian '09
Sunshine Cleaning '09
Doubt '08
Miss Pettigrew Lives for a Day '08
Charlie Wilson's War '07
Enchanted '07
The Ex '07
Underdog '07 (V)
Talladega Nights: The Ballad of Ricky Bobby '06
Tenacious D in the Pick of Destiny '06
Junebug '05
Standing Still '05
The Wedding Date '05
Catch Me If You Can '02
Pumpkin '02
Serving Sara '02
The Slaughter Rule '01
Psycho Beach Party '00
Cruel Intentions 2 '99
Drop Dead Gorgeous '99

Beverly Adams (1945-)

The Ambushers '67
Devil's Angels '67
Torture Garden '67
Murderers' Row '66
How to Stuff a Wild Bikini '65
Roustabout '64

Brandon Adams (1979-)

MacArthur Park '01
Ghost in the Machine '93
The Sandlot '93
The People under the Stairs '91

Brooke Adams (1949-)

The Legend of Lucy Keyes '06
The Baby-Sitters' Club '95
The Last Hit '93
The Sandlot '93
Gas Food Lodging '92
Sometimes They Come Back '91
The Unborn '91
The Lion of Africa '87
Man on Fire '87
Almost You '85
Key Exchange '85
The Stuff '85
The Innocents Abroad '84
Dead Zone '83
Utilities '83
Tell Me a Riddle '80
Cuba '79
A Man, a Woman, and a Bank '79
Days of Heaven '78
Invasion of the Body Snatchers '78
Shock Waves '77
James Dean '76

Catlin Adams (1950-)

The Jazz Singer '80
The Jerk '79
Panic in Echo Park '77

Christine Adams

Eye of the Dolphin '06
Submerged '05

Claire Adams (1898-1978)

The Big Parade '25
Heart's Haven '22
The Penalty '20

Don Adams (1923-2005)

Inspector Gadget '99 (V)
Get Smart, Again! '89
Back to the Beach '87
Jimmy the Kid '82
The Nude Bomb '80

Donald Adams

Merlin and the Book of Beasts '09
The Betrayed '08

Dorothy Adams (1899-1988)

The Prodigal '55
Streets of Sin '49
The Best Years of Our Lives '46
Laura '44
So Proudly We Hail '43

Edie Adams (1929-2008)

Armistead Maupin's Tales of the City '93
Adventures Beyond Belief '87
Shooting Stars '85
Ernie Kovacs: Between the Laughter '84
Haunting of Harrington House '82
Cheech and Chong's Up in Smoke '79
Racquet '79
The Seekers '79
Evil Roy Slade '71
The Honey Pot '67
The Oscar '66
Made in Paris '65
The Best Man '64
Call Me Bwana '63
It's a Mad, Mad, Mad, Mad World '63
Love with the Proper Stranger '63
Under the Yum-Yum Tree '63
Lover Come Back '61
The Apartment '60

Ernie Adams (1885-1946)

Son of Zorro '47
Sagebrush Law '43
Wings over the Pacific '43
Stagecoach Buckaroo '42
Arizona Gunfighter '37
Gun Lords of Stirrup Basin '37
Lightning Bill Crandall '37
Ridin' the Lone Trail '37
The Gun Ranger '34
Breed of the Border '33
Galloping Romeo '33
Beyond the Rockies '32
The Tip-Off '31
The Fighting Legion '30

Nevada '27

Evan Adams (1966-)
The Business of Fancydancing '02
Smoke Signals '98
Lost in the Barrens '91

Jane Adams (1921-)
The Brute Man '46
House of Dracula '45
Lost City of the Jungle '45

Jane Adams (1965-)
The Wackness '08
Last Holiday '06
The Sensation of Sight '06
Jesse Stone: Stone Cold '05
Eternal Sunshine of the Spotless Mind '04
Orange County '02
The Anniversary Party '01
Wonder Boys '00
Mumford '99
Songcatcher '99
A Texas Funeral '99
Day at the Beach '98
Happiness '98
Music from Another Room '97
Father of the Bride Part 2 '95
Kansas City '95
I Love Trouble '94
Rising Son '90
Vital Signs '90

Joey Lauren Adams (1971-)
Trucker '08
The Break-Up '06
Bunny Whipped '06
The Big Empty '04
The Gunman '03
Dr. Dolittle 2 '01 (V)
Harvard Man '01
In the Shadows '01
Jay and Silent Bob Strike Back '01
Beautiful '00
Big Daddy '99
The Dress Code '99
A Cool, Dry Place '98
Chasing Amy '97
Bio-Dome '96
Mallrats '95
L.A. Rules: The Pros and Cons of Breathing '94
S.F.W. '94
Sleep with Me '94
Dazed and Confused '93
The Program '93

Julie Adams (1926-)
Backtrack '89
Black Roses '88
The Killer Inside Me '76
The McCullochs '75
Psychic Killer '75
McQ '74
The Last Movie '71
The Trackers '71
Tickle Me '65
The Gunfight at Dodge City '59
Away All Boats '56
The Private War of Major Benson '55
Creature from the Black Lagoon '54
Francis Joins the WACs '54
Man from the Alamo '53
Horizons West '52
The Lawless Breed '52
Blazing Guns '50
Last Bullet '50
Outlaw Fury '50
Sudden Death '50

Kathryn Adams (1920-)
One Missed Call 2 '05
Blonde for a Day '46
Arizona Cyclone '41

Kristin Adams (1982-)
Where the Truth Lies '05
Falling Angels '03

Lynne Adams
Dangerous Liaisons '03
Requiem for Murder '99

Time at the Top '99
Psychopath '97
The Ultimate Weapon '97
Silent Hunter '94
The Carpenter '89
Blood Relations '87
Night Zoo '87

Mason Adams (1919-2005)
From the Earth to the Moon '98
The Lesser Evil '97
Touch '96
Houseguest '94
Son-in-Law '93
F/X '86
Rage of Angels: The Story Continues '86
Half Slave, Half Free '85
Adam '83
The Kid with the Broken Halo '82
The Final Conflict '81
Revenge of the Stepford Wives '80
A Shining Season '79

Maud Adams (1945-)
Silent Night, Deadly Night 4: Initiation '90
Intimate Power '89
The Kill Reflex '89
Angel 3: The Final Chapter '88
Deadly Intent '88
A Man of Passion '88
Nairobi Affair '88
Hell Hunters '87
Jane & the Lost City '87
Women's Club '87
Target Eagle '84
Octopussy '83
Tattoo '81
The Hostage Tower '80
Playing for Time '80
Killer Force '75
Rollerball '75
The Girl in Blue '74
The Man with the Golden Gun '74

Nick Adams (1931-68)
Godzilla vs. Monster Zero '68
Mission Mars '67
Mosby's Marauders '66
Die, Monster, Die! '65
Frankenstein Conquers the World '64
Hell Is for Heroes '62
The Interns '62
The FBI Story '59
Pillow Talk '59
No Time for Sergeants '58
Teacher's Pet '58
Our Miss Brooks '56
Mister Roberts '55
Picnic '55
Rebel without a Cause '55

Polly Adams
United 93 '06
Uptown Girls '03
People I Know '02
Celebrity '98
The Juror '96

Polly Adams (1939-)
Element of Doubt '96
A Dark Adapted Eye '93

Stanley Adams (1915-77)
The Passing of Evil '70
Thunder Alley '67
Lilies of the Field '63
Requiem for a Heavyweight '62
Hell Ship Mutiny '57

Steve Adams (1939-)
The Blue Butterfly '04
Strange Fits of Passion '99
Whiskers '96

Ted Adams (1890-1973)
Outlaw Country '49
Billy the Kid '41
The Lone Rider in Frontier Fury '41

Law and Order '40
Pinto Canyon '40
Wild Horse Valley '40
El Diablo Rides '39
Fighting Renegade '39
Outlaw's Paradise '39
Phantom Rancher '39
Six Gun Rhythm '39
Texas Wildcats '39
Gunsmoke Trail '38
Lightnin' Carson Rides Again '38
Pals of the Saddle '38
Six Gun Trail '38
Arizona Gunfighter '37
Border Caballero '36
Desert Phantom '36
The Lion Man '36
Undercover Man '36
His Fighting Blood '35
Social Error '35
Toll of the Desert '35
Ghost Valley '32
The Savage Girl '32
The Ridin' Fool '31

Tom Adams (1938-)
License to Kill '89
Fast Kill '73
The House that Dripped Blood '71
Subterfuge '68
Fathom '67
The Fighting Prince of Donegal '66
Where the Bullets Fly '66
Second Best Secret Agent in the Whole Wide World '65
The Great Escape '63

Tracey Adams
See Deborah Blaisdell

Chris(topher) Adamson
Dead of Night '99
Razor Blade Smile '98
Shameless '94

George Adamson (1906-89)
Christian the Lion '76
An Elephant Called Slowly '69

Meat Loaf Aday (1948-)
BloodRayne '06
Masters of Horror: Pelts '06
Tenacious D in the Pick of Destiny '06
Chasing Ghosts '05
Crazylove '05
The Pleasure Drivers '05
Extreme Dating '04
A Hole in One '04
The Salton Sea '02
Focus '01
Formula 51 '01
Rustin '01
Crazy in Alabama '99
Fight Club '99
Black Dog '98
Everything That Rises '98
Gunshy '98
The Mighty '98
Outside Ozona '98
Spice World: The Movie '97
To Catch a Yeti '95
Leap of Faith '92
Wayne's World '92
Motorama '91
The Squeeze '87
Feel the Motion '86
Roadie '80
Americathon '79
The Rocky Horror Picture Show '75

Anthony Addabbo (1960-)
A Place Called Truth '98
Red Shoe Diaries 5: Weekend Pass '95
The Gunfighters '87

Dawn Addams (1930-85)
Vault of Horror '73
The Vampire Lovers '70
Zeta One '69

Ballad in Blue '66
Where the Bullets Fly '66
The Liars '64
The Thousand Eyes of Dr. Mabuse '60
The Two Faces of Dr. Jekyll '60
Voulez-Vous Danser avec Moi? '59
The Silent Enemy '58
A King in New York '57
The Robe '53

Milo Addica
The King '05
Birth '04
Monster's Ball '01

Robert Addie (1960-2003)
Captain Jack '98
A Knight in Camelot '98
Another Country '84
Excalibur '81

Nancy Addison (1948-2002)
Somewhere Tomorrow '85
The Dain Curse '78

Mark Addy (1963-)
Robin Hood '10
Around the World in 80 Days '04
The Order '03
The Time Machine '02
Down to Earth '01
A Knight's Tale '01
The Flintstones in Viva Rock Vegas '00
Jack Frost '98
The Full Monty '96

Wesley Addy (1913-96)
Hiroshima '95
A Modern Affair '94
The Bostonians '84
The Verdict '82
The Europeans '79
Network '76
The Grissom Gang '71
Tora! Tora! Tora! '70
Seconds '66
The Big Knife '55
Kiss Me Deadly '55

Paul Adelstein (1969-)
Be Cool '05
Intolerable Cruelty '03

Isabelle Adjani (1955-)
Bon Voyage '03
Monsieur Ibrahim '03
Diabolique '96
Queen Margot '94
Camille Claudel '89
Ishtar '87
Subway '85
Next Year If All Goes Well '83
One Deadly Summer '83
Possession '81
Quartet '81
Nosferatu the Vampyre '79
The Driver '78
Barocco '76
The Slap '76
The Tenant '76
The Story of Adele H. '75

Scott Adkins
The Tournament '09
The Shepherd: Border Patrol '08
Undisputed II: Last Man Standing '06
Special Forces '03
Black Mask 2: City of Masks '02

Seth Adkins (1989-)
Gepetto '00
Stir '98
First Do No Harm '97

Bill Adler
Van Nuys Blvd. '79
Blue Sunshine '78
Pom Pom Girls '76
Switchblade Sisters '75

Charles Adler
Transformers: Revenge of the Fallen '09 (V)
Tiny Toon Adventures: How I Spent My Vacation '91 (V)
Stage Struck '36

Jay Adler (1896-1978)
Grave of the Vampire '72
Curse of the Undead '59
Crime of Passion '57
The Killing '56

Jerry Adler (1929-)
Find Me Guilty '06
In Her Shoes '05
Six Ways to Sunday '99
Manhattan Murder Mystery '93
The Public Eye '92

Joanna Adler
The Big Bad Swim '06
Book of Love '04
The Event '03

Luther Adler (1903-84)
Absence of Malice '81
Voyage of the Damned '76
The Man in the Glass Booth '75
Mean Johnny Barrows '75
Murph the Surf '75
The Brotherhood '68
The Three Sisters '65
The Last Angry Man '59
Crashout '55
The Girl in the Red Velvet Swing '55
Hoodlum Empire '52
The Desert Fox '51
Kiss Tomorrow Goodbye '50
South Sea Sinner '50
D.O.A. '49
House of Strangers '49
Wake of the Red Witch '49
The Loves of Carmen '48
Saigon '47
Cornered '45

Matt Adler (1966-)
Diving In '90
Doin' Time on Planet Earth '88
North Shore '87
White Water Summer '87
Flight of the Navigator '86

Sarah Adler
Our Music '04
Year Zero '04

Edvin Adolphson (1893-1979)
Boy of Two Worlds '59
Only One Night '42
Dollar '38
The Count of the Old Town '34

Frank Adonis (1935-)
Suicide Ride '97
True Romance '93

Renee Adoree (1898-1933)
The Michigan Kid '28
The Big Parade '25

Mario Adorf (1930-)
Smilla's Sense of Snow '96
The Holcroft Covenant '85
Invitation au Voyage '82
Milo Milo '79
The Tin Drum '79
The Lost Honor of Katharina Blum '75
Hired to Kill '73
Hit Men '73
Manhunt '73
Short Night of Glass Dolls '71
The Bird with the Crystal Plumage '70
Brainwashed '60

Raz Adoti
Cover '08
Doom '05
Haven '04
Resident Evil: Apocalypse '04

Iris Adrian (1912-94)
Blue Hawaii '62
Carnival Rock '57
The Fast and the Furious '54
G.I. Jane '51
Stop That Cab '51
Hi-Jacked '50
The Lovable Cheat '49
The Paleface '48
Infamous Crimes '47
The Bamboo Blonde '46
The Stork Club '45
I'm from Arkansas '44
Million Dollar Kid '44
Shake Hands with Murder '44
Action in the North Atlantic '43
I Killed That Man '42
The Road to Zanzibar '41

Max Adrian (1903-73)
The Boy Friend '71
The Devils '71
The Music Lovers '71
Dr. Terror's House of Horrors '65
Henry V '44

Patricia Adriani (1958-)
I'm the One You're Looking For '88
The Nest '80

Ljubica Adzovic
Black Cat, White Cat '98
Time of the Gypsies '90

Sean Michael Afable (1988-)
To Save a Life '10
Akeelah and the Bee '06

Ben Affleck (1972-)
Extract '09
He's Just Not That Into You '09
State of Play '09
Smokin' Aces '07
Clerks 2 '06
Hollywoodland '06
Jersey Girl '04
Surviving Christmas '04
Daredevil '03
Gigli '03
Paycheck '03
Changing Lanes '02
The Sum of All Fears '02
The Third Wheel '02
Jay and Silent Bob Strike Back '01
Pearl Harbor '01
Boiler Room '00
Bounce '00
Reindeer Games '00
Daddy & Them '99
Dogma '99
Forces of Nature '99
Armageddon '98
Shakespeare in Love '98
200 Cigarettes '98
Chasing Amy '97
Going All the Way '97
Good Will Hunting '97
Phantoms '97
Glory Daze '96
Mallrats '95
Dazed and Confused '93
Buffy the Vampire Slayer '92
School Ties '92
Wanted: The Perfect Guy '86

Casey Affleck (1975-)
The Killer Inside Me '10
The Assassination of Jesse James by the Coward Robert Ford '07
Gone Baby Gone '07
Ocean's Thirteen '07
The Last Kiss '06
Lonesome Jim '06
Ocean's Twelve '04
Gerry '02
American Pie 2 '01
Ocean's Eleven '01
Soul Survivors '01
Drowning Mona '00
Hamlet '00

American Pie '99
Attention Shoppers '99
Committed '99
Desert Blue '98
200 Cigarettes '98
Good Will Hunting '97
Race the Sun '96
To Die For '95

John Agar (1921-2002)
Body Bags '93
Invasion of Privacy '92
The Perfect Bride '91
Fear '90
Miracle Mile '89
Perfect Victims '87
King Kong '76
Big Jake '71
Chisum '70
The Undefeated '69
Hell Raiders '68
The St. Valentine's Day Massacre '67
Curse of the Swamp Creature '66
Johnny Reno '66
Women of the Prehistoric Planet '66
Zontar, the Thing from Venus '66
Cavalry Command '63
Invisible Invaders '59
Attack of the Puppet People '58
The Brain from Planet Arous '57
The Daughter of Dr. Jekyll '57
Flesh and the Spur '57
The Mole People '56
Lonesome Trail '55
Revenge of the Creature '55
Tarantula '55
Along the Great Divide '51
The Woman on Pier 13 '50
Sands of Iwo Jima '49
She Wore a Yellow Ribbon '49
Fort Apache '48

Tetchie Agbayani
Deathfight '93
Rikky and Pete '88
Mission Manila '87
Gymkata '85
The Dolls '83

Suzanne Ager
Fatal Justice '93
Evil Toons '90

Shohreh Aghdashloo (1952-)
The Adjustment Bureau '10
House of Saddam '08
The Sisterhood of the Traveling Pants 2 '08
The Stoning of Soraya M. '08
American Dreamz '06
The Lake House '06
The Nativity Story '06
X-Men: The Last Stand '06
The Exorcism of Emily Rose '05
House of Sand and Fog '03
Maryam '00

Pierre Agostino
Las Vegas Serial Killer '86
The Hollywood Strangler Meets the Skid Row Slasher '79

Janet Agren (1949-)
Karate Warrior '88
Magdalene '88
Night of the Sharks '87
Aladdin '86
Hands of Steel '86
Emerald Jungle '80
Gates of Hell '80
Perfect Crime '79
The Uranium Conspiracy '78
Panic '76

George Aguilar
Lunatics: A Love Story '92
The Trial of Billy Jack '74

Kris Aguilar
Fist of Steel '93
Bloodfist 2 '90
Bloodfist '89

Jenny Agutter (1952-)
Irina Palm '07
The Railway Children '00
The Buccaneers '95
Freddie the Frog '92 (V)
Child's Play 2 '90
Darkman '90
Dark Tower '87
Secret Places '85
Silas Marner '85
An American Werewolf in London '81
Amy '81
Survivor '80
Dominique Is Dead '79
Mayflower: The Pilgrims' Adventure '79
The Riddle of the Sands '79
Sweet William '79
Gunfire '78
The Eagle Has Landed '77
Equus '77
The Man in the Iron Mask '77
Logan's Run '76
Walkabout '71
The Railway Children '70
Star! '68

Brian Aherne (1902-86)
Sword of Lancelot '63
Waltz King '63
Susan Slade '61
The Best of Everything '59
The Swan '56
A Bullet Is Waiting '54
Prince Valiant '54
I Confess '53
Titanic '53
Smart Woman '48
Forever and a Day '43
My Sister Eileen '42
A Night to Remember '42
Smilin' Through '41
The Lady in Question '40
My Son, My Son '40
The Great Garrick '37
Beloved Enemy '36
I Live My Life '35
Sylvia Scarlett '35
The Song of Songs '33

Borje Ahlstedt (1939-)
Saraband '03
Sunday's Children '94
Emma's Shadow '88
I Am Curious (Yellow) '67

Ahmed Ahmed
Iron Man '08
Vince Vaughn's Wild West Comedy Show '06

Philip Ahn (1911-78)
Paradise, Hawaiian Style '66
Shock Corridor '63
Battle Hymn '57
Battle Circus '53
His Majesty O'Keefe '53
I Was an American Spy '51
Impact '49
Back to Bataan '45
They Were Expendable '45
Betrayal from the East '44
China Sky '44
The Story of Dr. Wassell '44
China '43
Across the Pacific '42
Drums of Fu Manchu '40
Hawaii Calls '38
Thank you, Mr. Moto '37
The General Died at Dawn '36

Sung-kee Ahn
The Warrior '01
The Soul Guardians '98

Sung-Ki Ahn (1952-)
White Badge '97
White Badge '92

Charles Aidman (1925-93)
Prime Suspect '82
Zoot Suit '81

House of the Dead '78
Zone of the Dead '78
The Barbary Coast '74
The Invasion of Carol Enders '74
Picture of Dorian Gray '74
Adam at 6 a.m. '70
Menace on the Mountain '70
Countdown '68
Hour of the Gun '67
Pork Chop Hill '59

Danny Aiello (1933-)
The Last Request '06
Lucky Number Slevin '06
Brooklyn Lobster '05
Dinner Rush '00
Mambo Cafe '00
Prince of Central Park '00
Hitman's Journal '99
Dead Silence '98
The Last Don 2 '98
A Brooklyn State of Mind '97
The Last Don '97
Mojave Moon '96
Two Days in the Valley '96
Two Much '96
City Hall '95
The Road Home '95
Power of Attorney '94
The Professional '94
Ready to Wear '94
The Cemetery Club '93
Me and the Kid '93
The Pickle '93
Ruby '92
The Closer '91
Hudson Hawk '91
Mistress '91
Once Around '91
29th Street '91
Jacob's Ladder '90
Do the Right Thing '89
Harlem Nights '89
The January Man '89
The Preppie Murder '89
Third Solution '89
White Hot '88
Alone in the Neon Jungle '87
Man on Fire '87
Moonstruck '87
The Pick-Up Artist '87
Radio Days '87
Key Exchange '85
Protector '85
The Purple Rose of Cairo '85
The Stuff '85
Old Enough '84
Once Upon a Time in America '84
Chu Chu & the Philly Flash '81
Fort Apache, the Bronx '81
Hide in Plain Sight '80
Question of Honor '80
Defiance '79
Bloodbrothers '78
Fingers '78
The Front '76
Hooch '76
The Godfather, Part 2 '74
Bang the Drum Slowly '73
Deathmask '69

Rick Aiello (1958-)
Brooklyn Lobster '05
Hollywood Confidential '97
Endangered '94
Uncivilized '94
The Closer '91
Jungle Fever '91
29th Street '91

Sho Aikawa
Zebraman '04
Gozu '03

Elaine Aiken (1927-98)
Caddyshack '80
Lonely Man '57

Liam Aiken (1990-)
The Killer Inside Me '10
Fay Grim '06
Lemony Snicket's A Series of Unfortunate Events '04
Good Boy! '03
Road to Perdition '02
Sweet November '01

I Dreamed of Africa '00
Stepmom '98

Anouk Aimee (1932-)
Happily Ever After '04
Napoleon '03
Festival at Cannes '02
Solomon '98
Ready to Wear '94
Dr. Bethune '90
A Man and a Woman: 20 Years Later '86
Success Is the Best Revenge '84
The Tragedy of a Ridiculous Man '81
Justine '69
Model Shop '69
A Man and a Woman '66
8 1/2 '63
Sodom and Gomorrah '62
Lola '61
La Dolce Vita '60
Modigliani '58
Paris Express '53
The Golden Salamander '51

Anthony Ainley (1932-2004)
The Land That Time Forgot '75
Inspector Clouseau '68
Naked Evil '66

Richard Ainley (1910-67)
Above Suspicion '43
I Dood It '43
White Cargo '42

Mary Ainslee (1919-91)
The Spider Returns '41
Mad Youth '40
Desert Nights '29

Holly Aird (1969-)
Scenes of a Sexual Nature '06
Possession '02
The Criminal '00
Dreaming of Joseph Lees '99
The Theory of Flight '98
Fever Pitch '96
Intimate Relations '95
Over Indulgence '87
The Flame Trees of Thika '81

Andrew Airlie
Storm Cell '08
Normal '07
Common Ground '00
Hard Evidence '94

Maria Aitken (1945-)
Grave Indiscretions '96
A Fish Called Wanda '88

Spottiswoode Aitken (1868-1933)
Monte Cristo '22
The Americano '17
The Birth of a Nation '15

Michael Aitkens (1947-)
Moving Targets '87
The Highest Honor '84

Franklin Ajaye (1949-)
American Yakuza '94
The Wrong Guys '88
Fraternity Vacation '85
Get Crazy '83
The Jazz Singer '80
Convoy '78
Car Wash '76

Denis Akayama
My Baby's Daddy '04
Killing Moon '00
Johnny Mnemonic '95

Chantal Akerman (1950-)
News from Home '76 (N)
Je Tu Il Elle '74

Malin Akerman (1978-)
Couples Retreat '09
The Proposal '09
Watchmen '09

27 Dresses '08
The Brothers Solomon '07
The Heartbreak Kid '07
Heavy Petting '07
The Invasion '07
The Utopian Society '03

Andra Akers (1944-2002)
Desert Hearts '86
E. Nick: A Legend in His Own Mind '84

Karen Akers (1945-)
Heartburn '86
The Purple Rose of Cairo '85

Lucy Akhurst (1975-)
Don't Tell '05
The Land Girls '98

Hano Aki
Rebirth of Mothra 2 '97
Rebirth of Mothra '96

Adewale Akinnuoye-Agbaje (1967-)
G.I. Joe: The Rise of Cobra '09
Get Rich or Die Tryin' '05
The Mistress of Spices '05
Preaching to the Choir '05
The Bourne Identity '02
The Mummy Returns '01
Lip Service '00
Legionnaire '98

Claude Akins (1918-94)
The Gambler Returns: The Luck of the Draw '93
Falling from Grace '92
The Curse '87
Manhunt for Claude Dallas '86
Monster in the Closet '86
Pecos Bill '86
The Concrete Cowboys '79
Killer on Board '77
Tarantulas: The Deadly Cargo '77
Tentacles '77
The Big Push '75
Eric '75
Battle for the Planet of the Apes '73
The Death Squad '73
The Norliss Tapes '73
A Man Called Sledge '71
The Night Stalker '71
The Devil's Brigade '68
Waterhole Number 3 '67
Return of the Magnificent Seven '66
A Distant Trumpet '64
The Killers '64
Merrill's Marauders '62
Comanche Station '60
Inherit the Wind '60
Rio Bravo '59
The Kettles on Old MacDonald's Farm '57
Sea Chase '55
The Caine Mutiny '54
From Here to Eternity '53

Carl Alacchi
Taken '99
The Pianist '91

Marc Alaimo (1942-)
The Fence '94
Quicksand: No Escape '91
Arena '89
Tango and Cash '89
Archer: The Fugitive from the Empire '81

Steve Alaimo (1939-)
Alligator Alley '72
Wild Rebels '71
The Hooked Generation '69

Craig Alan
Endangered '94
Sex Crimes '92

Nelly Alard
Venice, Venice '92
Eating '90

Joe Alaskey (1949-)
Looney Tunes: Back in Action '03 (V)
The Rugrats Movie '98 (V)
Casper '95 (V)
Bank Robber '93
Tiny Toon Adventures: How I Spent My Vacation '91 (V)
Lucky Stiff '88

Carlos Alazraqui
Reno 911! Miami '07
I Downloaded a Ghost '04

Jessica Alba (1981-)
The Killer Inside Me '10
Valentine's Day '10
The Eye '08
The Love Guru '08
Awake '07
Fantastic Four: Rise of the Silver Surfer '07
Good Luck Chuck '07
Meet Bill '07
The Ten '07
Fantastic Four '05
Into the Blue '05
Sin City '05
Honey '03
The Sleeping Dictionary '02
Idle Hands '99
Never Been Kissed '99
Camp Nowhere '94

Maria Alba (1910-99)
Chandu on the Magic Island '34
Return of Chandu '34
Mr. Robinson Crusoe '32

Javier Albala (1969-)
Between Your Legs '99
Second Skin '99
Zafarinas '94

Carlo Alban (1979-)
Strangers with Candy '06
The Tavern '00

Captain Lou Albano (1933-)
Complex World '92
Body Slam '87
Wise Guys '86

John Albasiny
Have No Fear: The Life of Pope John Paul II '05
Kipperbang '82

Josh Albee
The Runaways '75
The Adventures of Tom Sawyer '73
Jeremiah Johnson '72

Kevin Alber (1963-)
Alien Terminator '95
Burial of the Rats '95
The Showgirl Murders '95

Anna Maria Alberghetti (1936-)
Friends and Family '01
The Whole Shebang '01
Cinderfella '60
Ten Thousand Bedrooms '57
The Last Command '55
Here Comes the Groom '51
The Medium '51

Luis Alberni (1887-1962)
Harvest Melody '43
The Great Man Votes '38
The Great Garrick '37
Hats Off '37
Dancing Pirate '36
Goodbye Love '34
One Night of Love '34
The California Trail '33
Man from Monterey '33
The Sphinx '33
The Big Stampede '32

Hans Albers (1892-1960)
Die Grosse Freiheit Nr. 7 '45
Baron Munchausen '43
F.P. 1 Doesn't Answer '33
The Blue Angel '30

Eddie Albert (1906-2005)
The Big Picture '89
Out of Sight, Out of Her Mind '89
Turnaround '87
Brenda Starr '86
Dress Gray '86
Head Office '86
Stitches '85
Burning Rage '84
Dreamscape '84
The Act '82
Yes, Giorgio '82
Goliath Awaits '81
Peter and Paul '81
Take This Job & Shove It '81
The Victory '81
Beulah Land '80
Foolin' Around '80
How to Beat the High Cost of Living '80
The Concorde: Airport '79 '79
The Birch Interval '78
The Crash of Flight 401 '78
The Word '78
Moving Violation '76
Devil's Rain '75
Escape to Witch Mountain '75
Whiffs '75
The Longest Yard '74
McQ '74
Fireball Forward '72
The Heartbreak Kid '72
Captain Newman, M.D. '63
The Miracle of the White Stallions '63
Who's Got the Action? '63
The Longest Day '62
Beloved Infidel '59
Attack! '56
The Teahouse of the August Moon '56
I'll Cry Tomorrow '55
Oklahoma! '55
Roman Holiday '53
Actors and Sin '52
Carrie '52
The Fuller Brush Girl '50
The Dude Goes West '48
You Gotta Stay Happy '48
Smash-Up: The Story of a Woman '47
The Perfect Marriage '46
Bombardier '43
Out of the Fog '41
The Wagons Roll at Night '41

Edward Albert (1951-2006)
Extreme Honor '01
Mimic 2 '01
Ablaze '00
The Man in the Iron Mask '97
The Secret Agent Club '96
Space Marines '96
Guarding Tess '94
Hard Drive '94
Red Sun Rising '94
Sorceress '94
Broken Trust '93
The Ice Runner '93
Sexual Malice '93
Shootfighter: Fight to the Death '93
Body Language '92
Exiled in America '90
Accidents '89
Mind Games '89
Wild Zone '89
Fist Fighter '88
The Rescue '88
The Underachievers '88
Distortions '87
Terminal Entry '87
Getting Even '86
Ellie '84
Time to Die '83
Butterfly '82
House Where Evil Dwells '82
Galaxy of Terror '81
The Squeeze '80
When Time Ran Out '80
Silent Victory: The Kitty O'Neil Story '79
The Greek Tycoon '78
The Rip Off '78
The Domino Principle '77
The Purple Taxi '77
Death Cruise '74
Forty Carats '73
Butterflies Are Free '72
The Fool Killer '65

Laura Albert
Blood Games '90
Dr. Caligari '89
Death by Dialogue '88
The Unnamable '88

Marv Albert (1941-)
The Cookout '04
Remo Williams: The Adventure Begins '85

Shari Albert (1971-)
The Groomsmen '06
The Brothers McMullen '94

Giorgio Albertazzi (1923-)
Eva '62
Last Year at Marienbad '61

Guido Alberti (1909-96)
Ten Days Wonder '72
Casanova '70 '65

Giampiero Albertini (1927-91)
Life of Verdi '82
Zorro '74
Commandos '73
The Case of the Bloody Iris '72
Return of Sabata '71
Burn! '70

Frank Albertson (1909-64)
Psycho '60
Nightfall '56
Killer Dill '47
It's a Wonderful Life '46
Junior G-Men of the Air '42
Underground Agent '42
Wake Island '42
Burma Convoy '41
Louisiana Purchase '41
Man Made Monster '41
Room Service '38
Navy Blue and Gold '37
Fury '36
Ah, Wilderness! '35
Alice Adams '35
Hollywood Mystery '34
Rainbow over Broadway '33
Way Back Home '32
Big Business Girl '31
A Connecticut Yankee '31 •

Jack Albertson (1907-81)
Charlie and the Great Balloon Chase '82
Dead and Buried '81
The Fox and the Hound '81 (V)
Marriage Is Alive and Well '80
The Poseidon Adventure '72
Where the Eagle Flies '72
Willy Wonka & the Chocolate Factory '71
Changes '69
Justine '69
The Subject Was Roses '68
Flim-Flam Man '67
How to Murder Your Wife '64
Kissin' Cousins '64
The Patsy '64
Roustabout '64
Who's Got the Action? '63
Days of Wine and Roses '62
Period of Adjustment '62
Lover Come Back '61
Never Steal Anything Small '59
Teacher's Pet '58
Miracle on 34th Street '47

Mabel Albertson (1901-82)
Barefoot in the Park '67
Ma and Pa Kettle at Waikiki '55

Karl Otto Alberty (1933-)
Battle of the Bulge '65
The Great Escape '63

Jens Albinus
The Boss of It All '06
The Idiots '99

Ariauna Albright (1969-)
Mom's Outta Sight '01
Ancient Evil: Scream of the Mummy '00
Witchouse 2: Blood Coven '00
Witchouse '99

Dan Albright
Bobby Jones: Stroke of Genius '04
I Know What You Did Last Summer '97
To Dance with the White Dog '93

Hardie Albright (1903-75)
Mom & Dad '47
The Jade Mask '45
Sunset in El Dorado '45
Bambi '42 (V)
Champagne for Breakfast '35
Red Salute '35
Sing Sing Nights '35
The Scarlet Letter '34
The Song of Songs '33
The Purchase Price '32

Lola Albright (1924-)
The Impossible Years '68
Where Were You When the Lights Went Out? '68
The Way West '67
Lord Love a Duck '66
Joy House '64
Kid Galahad '62
The Monolith Monsters '57
The Tender Trap '55
Champion '49
The Killer That Stalked New York '47

Wally Albright (1925-99)
Vengeance '37
Law of the Sea '32

Chris Alcaide (1923-2004)
Rock All Night '57
Jupiter's Darling '55

Damian Alcazar (1953-)
Cronicas '04
And Starring Pancho Villa as Himself '03
The Crime of Father Amaro '02
Hombres Armados '97

Victor Alcocer (1917-84)
Pistoleros Asesinos '87
It Happened at Nightmare Inn '70

Alan Alda (1936-)
Diminished Capacity '08
Flash of Genius '08
Nothing But the Truth '08
Resurrecting the Champ '07
The Aviator '04
Club Land '01
The Killing Yard '01
What Women Want '00
The Object of My Affection '98
Mad City '97
Murder at 1600 '97
Everyone Says I Love You '96
Flirting with Disaster '95
Canadian Bacon '94
White Mile '94
And the Band Played On '93
Manhattan Murder Mystery '93
Whispers in the Dark '92
Betsy's Wedding '90
Crimes & Misdemeanors '89
A New Life '88
Sweet Liberty '86
M*A*S*H: Goodbye, Farewell & Amen '83
The Four Seasons '81
The Seduction of Joe Tynan '79
California Suite '78
Same Time, Next Year '78
The Glass House '72
Playmates '72
To Kill a Clown '72
The Mephisto Waltz '71
Jenny '70
Paper Lion '68
Gone Are the Days '63
Purlie Victorious '63

Antony Alda (1956-)
The Killing Device '92
Homeboy '88
Movie Maker '86

Robert Alda (1914-86)
The Squeeze '80
Express to Terror '79
Every Girl Should Have One '78
The Rip Off '78
Bittersweet Love '76
I Will, I Will for Now '76
Love by Appointment '76
Lisa and the Devil '75
Night Flight from Moscow '73
The Devil's Hand '61
Force of Impulse '60
Revenge of the Barbarians '60
Tarzan and the Slave Girl '50
Nora Prentiss '47
The Beast with Five Fingers '46
Cloak and Dagger '46
The Man I Love '46
Rhapsody in Blue '45

Rutanya Alda (1945-)
Murder Without Conviction '04
The Souler Opposite '97
The Ref '93
Article 99 '92
Leaving Normal '92
The Dark Half '91
Rainbow Drive '90
Prancer '89
Black Widow '87
Racing with the Moon '84
Girls Night Out '83
Vigilante '83
Amityville 2: The Possession '82
Mommie Dearest '81
Christmas Evil '80
When a Stranger Calls '79
The Deer Hunter '78
The Fury '78
Scarecrow '73

Mary Alden (1883-1946)
Strange Interlude '32
April Fool '26
The Plastic Age '25
The Birth of a Nation '15

Norman Alden (1924-)
Ben '72
Tora! Tora! Tora! '70
The Devil's Brigade '68
Good Times '67
The Patsy '64
The Nutty Professor '63
The Sword in the Stone '63 (V)

Priscilla Alden (1939-2007)
Death Nurse '87
Crazy Fat Ethel II '85
Criminally Insane '75

John Alderman (1933-87)
The Alpha Incident '76
Little Miss Innocence '73
Love Desperados '68

Eddie Alderson
Changeling '08
Reservation Road '07

Erville Alderson (1882-1957)
Objective, Burma! '45
Sergeant York '41
Square Shooter '35
The Dawn Trail '30
Sally of the Sawdust '25
America '24

John Alderton (1940-)
Calendar Girls '03
Speedy Death '99
Zardoz '73
Macbeth '70
The Girl Getters '66

Mari Aldon (1925-2004)
Race for Life '55
Summertime '55
This Woman Is Dangerous '52
Distant Drums '51

Tom Aldredge (1928-)
The Assassination of Jesse James by the Coward Robert Ford '07
Game 6 '05
Cold Mountain '03
Intolerable Cruelty '03
Message in a Bottle '98
Rounders '98
A Stranger in the Kingdom '98
Commandments '96
Lawn Dogs '96
Andersonville '95
Harvest of Fire '95
The Adventures of Huck Finn '93
O Pioneers! '91
Other People's Money '91
What about Bob? '91
Pudd'nhead Wilson '84
Gentleman Bandit '81
The Rain People '69

Rhonda Aldrich
Jailbird Rock '88
Saturday the 14th Strikes Back '88

Kay Aldridge (1917-95)
The Phantom of 42nd Street '45
Haunted Harbor '44
Nyoka and the Tigermen '42
Down Argentine Way '40

Kitty Aldridge (1962-)
The Ice House '97
To Play the King '93
An African Dream '90
Slipstream '89
American Roulette '88

Michael Aldridge (1920-94)
Bullshot '83
Tinker, Tailor, Soldier, Spy '80
Love for Lydia '79

Sabrina Aldridge
April Fool's Day '08
Deck the Halls '06

Norma Aleandro (1936-)
Live-In Maid '04
The Son of the Bride '01
Autumn Sun '98
One Man's War '90
Vital Signs '90
Cousins '89
Gaby: A True Story '87
The Official Story '85

Julio Aleman (1933-)
The Green Wall '70
Neutron vs. the Death Robots '62
Neutron and the Black Mask '61
Neutron vs. the Amazing Dr. Caronte '61
The Monster Demolisher '60

Aki Aleong (1934-)
Sci-Fighter '04
Missing Brendan '03
Perfect Assassins '98
Lewis and Clark and George '97
The Quest '96
Farewell to the King '89
Braddock: Missing in Action 3 '88
Hanoi Hilton '87

Yassmin Alers
The American Mall '08
Chain Link '08

John Ales (1969-)
Dragon Wars '07
Life of the Party '05
Burning Down the House '01
Uprising '01
Nutty Professor 2: The Klumps '00
Ride with the Devil '99

Raquel Alessi
Miss March '09
Ghost Rider '07

Barbara Lee (Niven) Alexander (1953-)
Psycho Cop 2 '94
Illegal Entry: Formula for Fear '93
Hired to Kill '91

Ben Alexander (1911-69)
Man in the Shadow '57
Dragnet '54
Criminals Within '41
Legion of Missing Men '37
Western Gold '37
Red Lights Ahead '36
All Quiet on the Western Front '30
Hearts of the World '18
Little Orphan Annie '18
The Little American '17

Elizabeth (Liz) Alexander (1952-)
Salem's Lot '04
Alien Cargo '99
Killing of Angel Street '81
The Chant of Jimmie Blacksmith '78
Scalp Merchant '77

Erika Alexander (1969-)
Deja Vu '06
Love Liza '02
30 Years to Life '01

Flex Alexander (1970-)
The Hills Have Eyes 2 '07
Love and Other Four Letter Words '07
Poor Man's Game '06
Snakes on a Plane '06
Man in the Mirror: The Michael Jackson Story '04
Santa and Pete '99
She's All That '99

Jace Alexander (1964-)
Love and a .45 '94
City of Hope '91
Mistress '91
Crocodile Dundee 2 '88
Eight Men Out '88
Matewan '87

Jaimie Alexander
Rest Stop '06
Evil Dead Trap 2: Hideki '91

Jane Alexander (1939-)
Terminator Salvation '09
The Unborn '09
Gigantic '08
Feast of Love '07
Fur: An Imaginary Portrait of Diane Arbus '06
Carry Me Home '04
The Ring '02
Sunshine State '02
The Cider House Rules '99
In Love and War '91
Glory '89

A Friendship in Vienna '88
Square Dance '87
Sweet Country '87
The Rumor Mill '86
City Heat '84
Testament '83
Calamity Jane '82
In the Custody of Strangers '82
Lovey: A Circle of Children 2 '82
Night Crossing '81
Brubaker '80
Playing for Time '80
Kramer vs. Kramer '79
The Betsy '78
A Question of Love '78
All the President's Men '76
Eleanor & Franklin '76
Death Be Not Proud '75
The New Centurions '72
A Gunfight '71
The Great White Hope '70

Jason Alexander (1959-)
Hachiko: A Dog's Tale '09
Meteor '09
How to Go Out on a Date in Queens '06
Ira & Abby '06
On Edge '03
Shallow Hal '01
The Trumpet of the Swan '01 (V)
The Adventures of Rocky & Bullwinkle '00
Love and Action in Chicago '99
Something About Sex '98
Cinderella '97
The Hunchback of Notre Dame '96 (V)
The Last Supper '96
Love! Valour! Compassion! '96
Bye Bye Birdie '95
Dunston Checks In '95
For Better or Worse '95
Blankman '94
North '94
The Paper '94
The Return of Jafar '94 (V)
Coneheads '93
I Don't Buy Kisses Anymore '92
Jacob's Ladder '90
Pretty Woman '90
White Palace '90
Brighton Beach Memoirs '86
The Mosquito Coast '86
Rockabye '86
The Burning '82

Jeff Alexander (1910-89)
Twisted Brain '74
Curse of the Swamp Creature '66

John Alexander (1897-1982)
The Marrying Kind '52
Fancy Pants '50
Where There's Life '47
The Jolson Story '46
The Horn Blows at Midnight '45
A Tree Grows in Brooklyn '45
Arsenic and Old Lace '44
Mr. Skeffington '44

Katherine Alexander (1898-1981)
John Loves Mary '48
On the Sunny Side '42
Dance, Girl, Dance '40
The Great Man Votes '38
That Certain Woman '37
The Devil Is a Sissy '36
Splendor '35
The Barretts of Wimpole Street '34
Death Takes a Holiday '34
Operator 13 '34

Khandi Alexander (1957-)
Rain '06
Dark Blue '03
Killing Emmett Young '02
The Corner '00
Thick as Thieves '99
There's Something about Mary '98
Robin Cook's Terminal '96
Greedy '94
Sugar Hill '94
CB4: The Movie '93
What's Love Got to Do with It? '93

Peter Alexander
Seamless '00
Color of a Brisk and Leaping Day '95

Richard Alexander (1902-89)
The Kansas Terrors '39
Renfrew on the Great White Trail '38
S.O.S. Coast Guard '37
Riding Wild '35
Daring Danger '32
Scarlet Dawn '32
Texas Bad Man '32
All Quiet on the Western Front '30
The Mysterious Lady '28

Ross Alexander (1907-37)
Captain Blood '35
A Midsummer Night's Dream '35
Shipmates Forever '35
Flirtation Walk '34

Sarah Alexander (1971-)
Stardust '07
I Could Never Be Your Woman '06

Sasha Alexander (1973-)
Love Happens '09
Yes Man '08
Mission: Impossible 3 '06
All Over the Guy '01

Tad Alexander (1922-)
Rasputin and the Empress '33
Ambassador Bill '31

Terence Alexander (1923-)
Waterloo '71
What's Good for the Goose '69
The Mind Benders '63
The Square Peg '58
The Runaway Bus '54

Terry Alexander (1947-)
Conspiracy Theory '97
Hurricane Streets '96
Amateur '94
The Horror Show '89
Day of the Dead '85
Flashpoint '84

Charlotta Alexandra
Good-bye, Emmanuelle '77
A Real Young Girl '75

Tiana Alexandra
Catch the Heat '87
Pearl '78

Manuel Alexandre (1917-)
Swindled '04
Two Tough Guys '03

Victor Alfieri
I-See-You.Com '06
The Roman Spring of Mrs. Stone '03

Lidia Alfonsi (1928-)
Life Is Beautiful '98
Open Doors '89
Black Sabbath '64
The Trojan Horse '62

Kristian Alfonso (1964-)
Army of One '94
Blindfold: Acts of Obsession '94

Chuck Alford
The Hollywood Strangler Meets the Skid Row Slasher '79
Commando Squad '76

David Alford
The Second Chance '06
A Death in the Family '02

Phillip Alford (1948-)
Shenandoah '65
To Kill a Mockingbird '62

Mark Alfred
Rhythm Thief '94
Spare Me '92

Hans Alfredson (1931-)
The Adventures of Picasso '80
The New Land '73
Pippi on the Run '70
The Shame '68

Mahershalhashbaz Ali
Predators '10
The Curious Case of Benjamin Button '08

Muhammad Ali (1942-)
Soul Power '08
Doin' Time '85
Body & Soul '81
Freedom Road '79
The Greatest '77
Requiem for a Heavyweight '62

Tatyana Ali (1979-)
Nora's Hair Salon 2: A Cut Above '08
Back in the Day '05
Nora's Hair Salon '04
The Brothers '01

Grant Alianak
Pontypool '09
One Night Only '84

Mary Alice (1941-)
The Matrix Revolutions '03
Sunshine State '02
Catfish in Black Bean Sauce '00
Down in the Delta '98
Laurel Avenue '93
To Sleep with Anger '90
The Women of Brewster Place '89
Charlotte Forten's Mission: Experiment in Freedom '85
Killing Floor '85
He Who Walks Alone '78
Sparkle '76

Ana Alicia (1956-)
Romero '89
Coward of the County '81

Lisa Aliff (1960-)
Playroom '90
Damned River '89
Trained to Kill '88

Dean Alioto
Shadowheart '09
L.A. Dicks '05

Roger Allam (1953-)
Speed Racer '08
V for Vendetta '06
The Roman Spring of Mrs. Stone '03

Elizabeth Allan (1908-90)
The Haunted Strangler '58
No Highway in the Sky '51
Camille '36
The Shadow '36
A Tale of Two Cities '36
A Woman Rebels '36
Java Head '35
Mark of the Vampire '35
Phantom Fiend '35
Men in White '34
Ace of Aces '33
No Marriage Ties '33

Harris Allan
Masters of Horror: Jenifer '05
A Home at the End of the World '04

Hugh Allan (1903-)
Annapolis '28
Dress Parade '27

Jed Allan (1937-)
Suspect Device '95
Lethal Charm '90
Lassie: Adventures of Neeka '68

Louise Allbritton (1920-79)
The Doolins of Oklahoma '49
Sitting Pretty '48
Egg and I '47
Son of Dracula '43
Pittsburgh '42
Who Done It? '42

Michael Alldredge
Robot Jox '90
About Last Night... '86

Catherine Allegret (1946-)
La Vie en Rose '07
Paul and Michelle '74
Last Tango in Paris '73

Aleisha Allen (1991-)
Are We Done Yet? '07
Are We There Yet? '05
School of Rock '03

Bambi Allen (1938-73)
Outlaw Riders '72
Satan's Sadists '69

Barbara Jo Allen (1905-74)
The Sword in the Stone '63 (V)
Sleeping Beauty '59 (V)
Girl Rush '44

Bill Allen (1962-)
Sioux City '94
Born on the Fourth of July '89
Rad '86
Streamers '83
Maniac '77

Chad Allen (1974-)
Hollywood, Je T'Aime '09
On the Other Hand, Death '08
Save Me '07
End of the Spear '06
Shock to the System '06
Third Man Out: A Donald Strachey Mystery '05
What Matters Most '01
Praying Mantis '93
Murder in New Hampshire: The Pamela Smart Story '91
Camp Cucamonga: How I Spent My Summer Vacation '90
Straight Up '90
The Bad Seed '85

Christa B. Allen (1991-)
The Town That Banned Christmas '06
13 Going on 30 '04

Corey Allen (1934-)
Darby's Rangers '58
Party Girl '58
The Night of the Hunter '55
Rebel without a Cause '55

Crystal Allen (1978-)
Anacondas: Trail of Blood '09
Anaconda 3: The Offspring '08

Debbie Allen (1950-)
Fame '09
Next Day Air '09
All About You '01
The Old Settler '01
Jo Jo Dancer, Your Life Is Calling '86
Ragtime '81
The Fish that Saved Pittsburgh '79
Roots: The Next Generation '79

Elizabeth Allen (1929-2006)
Star Spangled Girl '71
Donovan's Reef '63

Fred Allen (1894-1956)
We're Not Married '52
It's in the Bag '45

Gary Allen
Alice Sweet Alice '76
The Night They Robbed Big Bertha's '75

Ginger Lynn Allen (1962-)
The Independent '00
Bound and Gagged: A Love Story '93
Mind, Body & Soul '92
Vice Academy 3 '91
Leather Jackets '90
Vice Academy 2 '90
Young Guns 2 '90
Buried Alive '89
Cleo/Leo '89
Hollywood Boulevard 2 '89
Wild Man '89
Vice Academy '88

Gracie Allen (1902-64)
Two Girls and a Sailor '44
The Gracie Allen Murder Case '39
Honolulu '39
College Swing '38
A Damsel in Distress '37
Here Comes Cookie '35
Love in Bloom '35
Six of a Kind '34
We're Not Dressing '34
International House '33

India Allen (1965-)
Tattoo, a Love Story '02
Seduce Me: Pamela Principle 2 '94
Wild Cactus '92

Jack Allen (1908-95)
Radio Cab Murder '54
The Four Feathers '39

Jeffrey Allen (1910-79)
This Stuff'll Kill Ya! '71
Something Weird '68
Moonshine Mountain '64
2000 Maniacs '64

Jo Harvey Allen
The Wendell Baker Story '05
Checking Out '89
Tapeheads '89
True Stories '86

Joan Allen (1956-)
Hachiko: A Dog's Tale '09
Death Race '08
The Bourne Ultimatum '07
Bonneville '06
The Upside of Anger '05
The Bourne Supremacy '04
The Notebook '04
Yes '04
Off the Map '03
Mists of Avalon '01
The Contender '00
It's the Rage '99
When the Sky Falls '99
Pleasantville '98
Face/Off '97
The Ice Storm '97
The Crucible '96
Mad Love '95
Nixon '95
Josh and S.A.M. '93
Searching for Bobby Fischer '93
Ethan Frome '92
Without Warning: The James Brady Story '91
In Country '89
Tucker: The Man and His Dream '88
All My Sons '86
Fat Guy Goes Nutzoid '86
Manhunter '86
Peggy Sue Got Married '86

John Allen (1944-)
The Odd Angry Shot '79
Roses Bloom Twice '77

Jonelle Allen (1944-)
Mr. Barrington '03
Next Time '99
Grave Secrets: The Legacy of Hilltop Drive '92
The Midnight Hour '86
Penalty Phase '86
The River Niger '76

Judith Allen (1911-96)
Train to Tombstone '50
Tough Kid '39
The Port of Missing Girls '38
Boots & Saddles '37
Git Along Little Dogies '37
Healer '36
Bright Eyes '34
Night Alarm '34
Buffalo Stampede '33
Dancing Man '33

Karen Allen (1951-)
Indiana Jones and the Kingdom of the Crystal Skull '08
Plain Dirty '04
Poster Boy '04
When Will I Be Loved '04
In the Bedroom '01
World Traveler '01
The Perfect Storm '00
The Basket '99
Wind River '98
Til There Was You '96
Ghost in the Machine '93
King of the Hill '93
The Sandlot '93
Voyage '93
Malcolm X '92
The Turning '92
Sweet Talker '91
Secret Weapon '90
Animal Behavior '89
Backfire '88
Scrooged '88
The Glass Menagerie '87
Starman '84
Until September '84
Lovey: A Circle of Children 2 '82
Shoot the Moon '82
Split Image '82
Raiders of the Lost Ark '81
Cruising '80
East of Eden '80
A Small Circle of Friends '80
Manhattan '79
Wanderers '79
National Lampoon's Animal House '78

Keith Allen (1953-)
Agent Cody Banks 2: Destination London '04
De-Lovely '04
My Wife is an Actress '01
24 Hour Party People '01
Rancid Aluminium '00
Prince of Poisoners: The Life and Crimes of William Palmer '98
Loch Ness '95
Captives '94
Second Best '94
Shallow Grave '94
Nightscare '93
The Young Americans '93
Kafka '91
Small Time '91
Chicago Joe & the Showgirl '90
A Very British Coup '88

Krista Allen (1972-)
The Final Destination '09
Meet Market '08
Silent Venom '08
Tony n' Tina's Wedding '07
Feast '06

Shut Up and Kiss Me *'05*
Anger Management *'03*
Totally Blonde *'01*
Sunset Strip *'99*
The Haunted Sea *'97*
Raven *'97*

Laura Allen (1974-)
Old Dogs *'09*
How You Look to Me *'05*
Sucker Free City *'05*

Marty Allen (1922-)
Whale of a Tale *'76*
Harrad Summer *'74*
Jailbreakin' *'72*

Mike Allen
Death Driver *'78*
Hooch *'76*

Nancy Allen (1950-)
Kiss Toledo Goodbye *'00*
Children of the Corn 666: Isaac's Return *'99*
Against the Law *'98*
Highway Hitcher *'98*
Out of Sight *'98*
Secre of the Andes *'98*
The Last Assassins *'96*
Acting on Impulse *'93*
RoboCop 3 *'91*
Memories of Murder *'90*
RoboCop 2 *'90*
Limit Up *'89*
Poltergeist 3 *'88*
RoboCop *'87*
Sweet Revenge *'87*
The Gladiator *'86*
Not for Publication *'84*
The Philadelphia Experiment *'84*
The Buddy System *'83*
Strange Invaders *'83*
Blow Out *'81*
Dressed to Kill *'80*
Home Movies *'79*
1941 *'79*
I Wanna Hold Your Hand *'78*
Carrie *'76*
Forced Entry *'75*
The Last Detail *'73*

Parry Allen
See Parry Shen

Patrick Allen (1927-2206)
Bullet to Beijing *'95*
Body & Soul *'93*
Full Metal Ninja *'89*
Thirteenth Day of Christmas *'85*
Agatha Christie's Murder is Easy *'82*
Puppet on a Chain *'72*
When Dinosaurs Ruled the Earth *'70*
Invasion of the Body Stealers *'69*
Island of the Burning Doomed *'67*
Flight from Singapore *'62*
Tread Softly Stranger *'58*
The Long Haul *'57*

Penelope Allen (1943-)
The Thin Red Line *'98*
Looking for Richard *'96*
Scarecrow *'73*
Oh! What a Lovely War *'69*

Ray Allen (1975-)
Harvard Man *'01*
He Got Game *'98*

Rex Allen (1921-99)
Me, Myself, and Irene *'00 (V)*
The Secret of Navajo Cave *'76 (N)*
Charlie the Lonesome Cougar *'67 (N)*
Legend of Lobo *'62 (N)*
Phantom Stallion *'54*
Iron Mountain Trail *'53*
Shadows of Tombstone *'53*
Border Saddlemates *'52*
Colorado Sundown *'52*
I Dream of Jeannie *'52*
Rodeo King and the Senorita *'51*
Silver City Bonanza *'51*
Thunder in God's Country *'51*
Hills of Oklahoma *'50*
Redwood Forest Trail *'50*
Trail of Robin Hood *'50*
Arizona Cowboy *'49*

Robert "Tex" Allen (1906-98)
The Awful Truth *'37*
The Rangers Step In *'37*
Rio Grande Ranger *'37*
The Unknown Ranger *'36*
The Black Room *'35*
Crime and Punishment *'35*
Fighting Shadows *'35*
The Revenge Rider *'35*
The Perils of Pauline *'34*

Ronald Allen (1930-91)
Eat the Rich *'87*
Supergrass *'87*

Rosalind Allen (1957-)
Pinocchio's Revenge *'96*
Ticks *'93*
Children of the Corn 2: The Final Sacrifice *'92*
To Die For 2: Son of Darkness *'91*

Sage Allen
Suspended Animation *'02*
Mr. Saturday Night *'92*

Sheila Allen (1932-)
Pascali's Island *'88*
Bouquet of Barbed Wire *'76*
The Alphabet Murders *'65*
Children of the Damned *'63*

Sian Barbara Allen (1946-)
Eric *'75*
Billy Two Hats *'74*
You'll Like My Mother *'72*

Steve Allen (1921-2000)
Casino *'95*
The St. Tammany Miracle *'94*
The Player *'92*
Great Balls of Fire *'89*
Amazon Women on the Moon *'87*
Alice in Wonderland *'85*
Ratings Game *'84*
Heart Beat *'80*
Where Were You When the Lights Went Out? *'68*
The Benny Goodman Story *'55*

Tanya Allen (1975-)
Silent Hill *'06*
Lone Hero *'02*
Tail Lights Fade *'99*
White Lies *'98*
Behind the Lines *'97*
Spenser: Ceremony *'93*

Tim Allen (1953-)
Crazy on the Outside *'10*
Toy Story 3 *'10 (V)*
Redbelt *'08*
Wild Hogs *'07*
The Santa Clause 3: The Escape Clause *'06*
The Shaggy Dog *'06*
Zoom *'06*
Christmas With the Kranks *'04*
Big Trouble *'02*
The Santa Clause 2 *'02*
Who is Cletis Tout? *'02*
Joe Somebody *'01*
Galaxy Quest *'99*
Toy Story 2 *'99 (V)*
For Richer or Poorer *'97*
Jungle 2 Jungle *'96*
Toy Story *'95 (V)*
The Santa Clause *'94*

Todd Allen (1960-)
The Apostle *'97*
The Postman *'97*
Pinocchio's Revenge *'96*
Tall, Dark and Deadly *'95*
Wyatt Earp *'94*
Storm and Sorrow *'90*
Brothers in Arms *'88*
Witchboard *'87*

Tom Allen
Clash of the Ninja *'86*
Shadows *'60*

Woody Allen (1935-)
Scoop *'06*
Anything Else *'03*
Hollywood Ending *'02*
The Curse of the Jade Scorpion *'01*
Company Man *'00*
Small Time Crooks *'00*
Picking Up the Pieces *'99*
Sweet and Lowdown *'99*
Antz *'98 (V)*
The Imposters *'98*
Deconstructing Harry *'97*
Everyone Says I Love You *'96*
Mighty Aphrodite *'95*
The Sunshine Boys *'95*
Manhattan Murder Mystery *'93*
Husbands and Wives *'92*
Shadows and Fog *'92*
Scenes from a Mall *'91*
Crimes & Misdemeanors *'89*
New York Stories *'89*
King Lear *'87*
Radio Days *'87 (N)*
Hannah and Her Sisters *'86*
Broadway Danny Rose *'84*
Zelig *'83*
A Midsummer Night's Sex Comedy *'82*
Stardust Memories *'80*
Manhattan *'79*
Annie Hall *'77*
The Front *'76*
Love and Death *'75*
Sleeper *'73*
Everything You Always Wanted to Know about Sex (But Were Afraid to Ask) *'72*
Play It Again, Sam *'72*
Bananas *'71*
Take the Money and Run *'69*
Casino Royale *'67*
What's Up, Tiger Lily? *'66 (N)*
What's New Pussycat? *'65*

Fernando Allende (1954-)
Naked Lies *'98*
Heartbreaker *'83*

Kirstie Alley (1951-)
Blonde *'01*
Drop Dead Gorgeous *'99*
The Last Don 2 *'98*
Deconstructing Harry *'97*
For Richer or Poorer *'97*
The Last Don *'97*
Nevada *'97*
Toothless *'97*
Sticks and Stones *'96*
It Takes Two *'95*
Village of the Damned *'95*
Look Who's Talking Now *'93*
Look Who's Talking, Too *'90*
Madhouse *'90*
One More Chance *'90*
Sibling Rivalry *'90*
Look Who's Talking *'89*
Loverboy *'89*
Shoot to Kill *'88*
Prince of Bel Air *'87*
Summer School *'87*
North and South Book 2 *'86*
A Bunny's Tale *'85*
North and South Book 1 *'85*
Blind Date *'84*
Champions *'84*
Runaway *'84*
Star Trek 2: The Wrath of Khan *'82*

Sara Allgood (1883-1950)
Cheaper by the Dozen *'50*
Challenge to Lassie *'49*
The Accused *'48*
The Fabulous Dorseys *'47*
Mother Wore Tights *'47*
The Spiral Staircase *'46*
The Strange Affair of Uncle Harry *'45*
Jane Eyre *'44*
The Keys of the Kingdom *'44*
City Without Men *'43*
Roxie Hart *'42*
Dr. Jekyll and Mr. Hyde *'41*
How Green Was My Valley *'41*
That Hamilton Woman *'41*
Storm in a Teacup *'37*
Juno and the Paycock *'30*
Blackmail *'29*

Jeff Allin
A Matter of Love *'78*
American Tickler *'76*

Dorothy Allison (1949-)
Rikky and Pete *'88*
See No Evil *'71*
The Scamp *'57*
The Third Key *'57*

Claud Allister (1888-1970)
Lillian Russell *'40*
Bulldog Drummond at Bay *'37*
The Dark Angel *'35*
The Private Life of Henry VIII *'33*
Monte Carlo *'30*
Bulldog Drummond *'29*

Gregg Allman (1947-)
Rush *'91*
Rush Week *'88*

Jamie Anne Allman
Farmhouse *'08*
Prairie Fever *'08*

Marshall Allman
Dishdogz *'05*
Hostage *'05*

James Allodi (1967-)
Snow Cake *'06*
Men with Brooms *'02*
Invasion! *'99*

Christopher Allport
Garden Party *'08*
Though None Go With Me *'06*
Jack Frost 2: Revenge of the Mutant Killer Snowman *'00*
Jack Frost *'97*
News at Eleven *'86*
Circle of Power *'83*
Special Bulletin *'83*
Savage Weekend *'80*

Corbin Allred (1979-)
Saints and Soldiers *'03*
Diamonds *'99*
Address Unknown *'96*
Josh Kirby... Time Warrior: Chapter 5, Journey to the Magic Cavern *'96*
Josh Kirby... Time Warrior: Chapter 6, Last Battle for the Universe *'96*
Josh Kirby. . .Time Warrior: Chapter 1, Planet of the Dino-Knights *'95*
Josh Kirby... Time Warrior: Chapter 2, The Human Pets *'95*
Josh Kirby... Time Warrior: Chapter 3, Trapped on Toyworld *'95*
Josh Kirby... Time Warrior: Chapter 4, Eggs from 70 Million B.C. *'95*
Quest of the Delta Knights *'93*

Astrid Allwyn (1905-78)
Cracked Nuts *'41*
Love Affair *'39*
International Crime *'37*
It Could Happen to You *'37*
Stowaway *'36*
Charlie Chan's Secret *'35*
Hands Across the Table *'35*
Beggars in Ermine *'34*
Monte Carlo Nights *'34*
Mystery Liner *'34*

June Allyson (1917-2006)
The Kid with the Broken Halo *'82*
Blackout *'78*
Vegas *'78*
Curse of the Black Widow *'77*
They Only Kill Their Masters *'72*
My Man Godfrey *'57*
The Opposite Sex *'56*
The McConnell Story *'55*
Strategic Air Command *'55*
Executive Suite *'54*
The Glenn Miller Story *'54*
A Woman's World *'54*
Battle Circus *'53*
Little Women *'49*
The Stratton Story *'49*
The Three Musketeers *'48*
Words and Music *'48*
Good News *'47*
Till the Clouds Roll By *'46*
Meet the People *'44*
Two Girls and a Sailor *'44*
Best Foot Forward *'43*
Girl Crazy *'43*
Thousands Cheer *'43*

Mario Almada (1922-)
Blood Screams *'88*
357 Magnum *'79*

Gila Almagor (1939-)
Munich *'05*
Under the Domim Tree *'95*
The Summer of Aviya *'88*
Every Time We Say Goodbye *'86*
Hide and Seek *'80*
The House on Chelouche Street *'73*
Sallah *'63*

Joaquim Almeida
Bobby Z *'07*
The Celestine Prophecy *'06*

Susan Almgren
The Witness *'99*
Deadly Surveillance *'91*
Twin Sisters *'91*

Adrian Alonso
Under the Same Moon *'07*
The Legend of Zorro *'05*

Chelo Alonso (1933-)
The Good, the Bad and the Ugly *'67*
Son of Samson *'62*
Atlas in the Land of the Cyclops *'61*
Girl Under the Sheet *'61*

Daniella Alonso
The Hills Have Eyes 2 *'07*
Wrong Turn 2: Dead End *'07*

Ernesto Alonso (1917-2007)
The Criminal Life of Archibaldo de la Cruz *'55*
Wuthering Heights *'53*

Jose Alonso
Homework *'90*
El Diputado *'78*

Laz Alonso
Avatar *'09*
Fast & Furious *'09*
Miracle at St. Anna *'08*
Captivity *'07*
Stomp the Yard *'07*
This Christmas *'07*
Bunny Whipped *'06*
The Tenants *'06*
All Souls Day *'05*
Jarhead *'05*
G *'02*

Maria Conchita Alonso (1957-)
Maneater *'09*
Spread *'09*
The Art of Travel *'08*
The Dead One *'07*
Material Girls *'06*
ESL: English as a Second Language *'05*
Chasing Papi *'03*
Heart of America *'03*
Blind Heat *'00*
Chain of Command *'00*
High Noon *'00*
Acts of Betrayal *'98*
Blackheart *'98*
Catherine's Grove *'98*
Footsteps *'98*
For Which He Stands *'98*
My Husband's Secret Life *'98*
Caught *'96*
Roosters *'95*
Texas *'94*
The House of the Spirits *'93*
Teamster Boss: The Jackie Presser Story *'92*
McBain *'91*
Predator 2 *'90*
Colors *'88*
Vampire's Kiss *'88*
Blood Ties *'87*
Extreme Prejudice *'87*
The Running Man *'87*
A Fine Mess *'86*
Touch and Go *'86*
Fear City *'85*
Moscow on the Hudson *'84*

Ryan Alosio (1973-)
Darkwolf *'03*
Something About Sex *'98*

David Alpay
All Hat *'07*
Closing the Ring *'07*
Ararat *'02*

Corinne Alphen (1953-)
New York Nights *'84*
C.O.D. *'83*
Spring Break *'83*
Hot T-Shirts *'79*

Catherine Alric (1954-)
Jupiter's Thigh *'81*
The Associate *'79*
Dear Detective *'77*

Carol Alt (1960-)
The Man Who Came Back *'08*
The Town That Banned Christmas *'06*
Snakehead Terror *'04*
Revelation *'00*
Deadly Game *'98*
Storm Trooper *'98*
Crackerjack 2 *'97*
Body Armor *'96*
Private Parts *'96*
Deadly Past *'95*
Ring of Steel *'94*
Thunder in Paradise 2 *'94*
Thunder in Paradise 3 *'94*
Thunder in Paradise *'93*
Beyond Justice *'92*
A Family Matter *'91*
Millions *'90*
My Wonderful Life *'90*
Bye Bye Baby *'88*
Portfolio *'88*

John Altamura
Bikini Bistro *'94*
The Toxic Avenger, Part 2 *'89*
The Toxic Avenger, Part 3: The Last Temptation of Toxie *'89*
New York's Finest *'87*

Ernesto Alterio (1970-)
The Method *'05*
Swindled *'04*
The Other Side of the Bed *'03*

Hector Alterio (1929-)
The Son of the Bride *'01*
Wild Horses *'95*
I, the Worst of All *'90*
The Official Story *'85*
Camila *'84*
Basileus Quartet *'82*
Fridays of Eternity *'81*

The Nest *'80*
Cria Cuervos *'76*

Bruce Altman (1955-)
Bride Wars *'09*
Peter and Vandy *'09*
The Skeptic *'09*
Recount *'08*
Running Scared *'06*
Matchstick Men *'03*
L.I.E. *'01*
To Gillian on Her 37th Birthday *'96*
Vibrations *'94*
White Mile *'94*
Mr. Jones *'93*
Mr. Wonderful *'93*
The Favor, the Watch, & the Very Big Fish *'92*
Glengarry Glen Ross *'92*
My New Gun *'92*

Jeff Altman (1951-)
Russian Roulette *'93*
Doin' Time *'85*
In Love with an Older Woman *'82*

Marnie Alton
Shadowheart *'09*
In Hell *'03*

Walter George Alton (1941-)
Heavenly Bodies *'84*
The Puma Man *'80*

Angela Alvarado
Lone Rider *'08*
Boss of Bosses *'99*
Hollywood Confidential *'97*

Crox Alvarado (1911-84)
The Curse of the Aztec Mummy *'59*
The Robot vs. the Aztec Mummy *'59*

Dan Alvarado
Shoot to Kill *'90*
Federal Agent *'36*

Don Alvarado (1904-67)
Big Steal *'49*
Demon for Trouble *'34*
Rio Rita *'29*
Battle of the Sexes *'28*

Magali Alvarado
Mi Vida Loca *'94*
Salsa *'88*

Trini Alvarado (1967-)
All Good Things *'09*
Paulie *'98*
The Frighteners *'96*
Little Women *'94*
The Perez Family *'94*
The Babe *'92*
American Friends *'91*
American Blue Note *'89*
Stella *'89*
Nitti: The Enforcer *'88*
Satisfaction *'88*
The Chair *'87*
Sweet Lorraine *'87*
Mrs. Soffel *'84*
Private Contentment *'83*
Times Square *'80*
Rich Kids *'79*

Enrique Garcia Alvarez
The Exterminating Angel *'62*
Invasion of the Vampires *'61*

Carlos Alvarez-Novoa (1940-)
Lucia, Lucia *'03*
Solas *'99*

John Alvin (1917-)
Objective, Burma! *'45*
The Fighting Sullivans *'42*

Anicee Alvina (1953-2006)
Paul and Michelle *'74*
Friends *'71*

Kirk Alyn (1910-99)
Atom Man vs. Superman *'50*
Federal Agents vs. Underworld, Inc. *'49*
Radar Patrol vs. Spy King *'49*
Daughter of Don Q *'46*

Lyle Alzado (1949-92)
Comrades in Arms *'91*
Hangfire *'91*
Neon City *'91*
Club Fed *'90*
Tapeheads *'89*
Who's Harry Crumb? *'89*
Zapped Again *'89*
Destroyer *'88*
Ernest Goes to Camp *'87*
Oceans of Fire *'86*

Shigeru Amachi (1931-85)
Zatoichi: The Blind Swordsman's Vengeance *'66*
Zatoichi: The Life and Opinion of Masseur Ichi *'62*
The Ghost of Yotsuya *'58*

Magali Amadei
House of D *'04*
Taxi *'04*

Said Amadia
A Few Days in September *'06*
The Situation *'06*

Chisco Amado (1962-)
My Mother Likes Women *'02*
Nico and Dani *'00*

Mathieu Amalric (1965-)
A Christmas Tale *'08*
Quantum of Solace *'08*
The Diving Bell and the Butterfly *'07*
Heartbeat Detector *'07*
A Secret *'07*
La Moustache *'05*
Munich *'05*
Kings and Queen *'04*
Alice et Martin *'98*
Late August, Early September *'98*
My Sex Life... Or How I Got into an Argument *'96*
Diary of a Seducer *'95*

Yuki Amami
Inugami *'01*
Serial Bomber *'96*

Eisei Amamoto (1926-2003)
Masked Rider—The First *'05*
The Red Spectacles *'87*
Godzilla's Revenge *'69*
King Kong Escapes *'67*
What's Up, Tiger Lily? *'66*
Attack of the Mushroom People *'63*

Tom Amandes (1956-)
Bonneville *'06*
Live from Baghdad *'03*
When Good Ghouls Go Bad *'01*
Brokedown Palace *'99*
Billboard Dad *'98*
From the Earth to the Moon *'98*
Second Chances *'98*
The Long Kiss Goodnight *'96*

Betty Amann (1906-90)
Nancy Drew, Reporter *'39*
Rich and Strange *'32*

Audrey Amber
See Andriana Ambesi

Andriana Ambesi
Fangs of the Living Dead *'68*
Stranger in Paso Bravo *'68*
Secret Agent Super Dragon *'66*

Lauren Ambrose (1978-)
Cold Souls *'09*
Loving Leah *'09*
Where the Wild Things Are *'09 (V)*
Starting Out in the Evening *'07*
Diggers *'06*
Psycho Beach Party *'00*
Swimming *'00*
Can't Hardly Wait *'98*
In and Out *'97*

Tangie Ambrose
Jackie's Back *'99*
Ringmaster *'98*

Don Ameche (1908-93)
Corrina, Corrina *'94*
Homeward Bound: The Incredible Journey *'93 (V)*
Folks! *'92*
Sunstroke *'92*
Oddball Hall *'91*
Oscar *'91*
Cocoon: The Return *'88*
Coming to America *'88*
Things Change *'88*
Harry and the Hendersons *'87*
Pals *'87*
Cocoon *'85*
Trading Places *'83*
The Boatniks *'70*
Suppose They Gave a War and Nobody Came? *'70*
Picture Mommy Dead *'66*
Guest Wife *'45*
It's in the Bag *'45*
Greenwich Village *'44*
A Wing and a Prayer *'44*
Heaven Can Wait *'43*
The Magnificent Dope *'42*
Moon over Miami *'41*
That Night in Rio *'41*
Down Argentine Way *'40*
Lillian Russell *'40*
Hollywood Cavalcade *'39*
Midnight *'39*
The Story of Alexander Graham Bell *'39*
The Three Musketeers *'39*
Alexander's Ragtime Band *'38*
Happy Landing *'38*
In Old Chicago *'37*
Love Is News *'37*
One in a Million *'36*

John Patrick Amedori (1987-)
Stick It *'06*
Little Athens *'05*
The Butterfly Effect *'04*

Claudio Amendola (1963-)
Caterina in the Big City *'03*
Jesus *'00*
Nostromo *'96*
The Horseman on the Roof *'95*
La Scorta *'94*
Queen Margot *'94*

Tony Amendola
The Perfect Sleep *'08*
The Dead One *'07*
Crimson Force *'05*
Dragon Storm *'04*
The Mask of Zorro *'98*
Three of Hearts *'93*

George American Horse (1944-)
Son of the Morning Star *'91*
Kenny Rogers as the Gambler, Part 3: The Legend Continues *'87*

Adrienne Ames (1907-47)
Panama Patrol *'39*
Slander House *'38*
Harmony Lane *'35*
The Death Kiss *'33*
Sinners in the Sun *'32*

Heather Ames
How to Make a Monster *'58*
Blood of Dracula *'57*

Leon Ames (1902-93)
Peggy Sue Got Married *'86*
Testament *'83*
Claws *'77*
The Big Push *'75*
The Meal *'75*
Tora! Tora! Tora! *'70*
Monkey's Uncle *'65*
The Misadventures of Merlin Jones *'63*
Son of Flubber *'63*
The Absent-Minded Professor *'61*
From the Terrace *'60*
Peyton Place *'57*
By the Light of the Silvery Moon *'53*
Angel Face *'52*
On Moonlight Bay *'51*
The Big Hangover *'50*
Crisis *'50*
The Happy Years *'50*
Watch the Birdie *'50*
Battleground *'49*
A Date with Judy *'48*
On an Island with You *'48*
Velvet Touch *'48*
Merton of the Movies *'47*
Song of the Thin Man *'47*
Lady in the Lake *'46*
The Postman Always Rings Twice *'46*
The Show-Off *'46*
Anchors Aweigh *'45*
Son of Lassie *'45*
They Were Expendable *'45*
Weekend at the Waldorf *'45*
Yolanda and the Thief *'45*
Thirty Seconds Over Tokyo *'44*
The Iron Major *'43*
East Side Kids *'40*
Mr. Moto in Danger Island *'39*
Panama Patrol *'39*
Mysterious Mr. Moto *'38*
The Spy Ring *'38*
Charlie Chan on Broadway *'37*
Murder in Greenwich Village *'37*
Get That Man *'35*
Murders in the Rue Morgue *'32*
Uptown New York *'32*
State's Attorney *'31*

Ramsay Ames (1919-98)
G-Men Never Forget *'48*
The Mummy's Ghost *'44*
Calling Dr. Death *'43*

Robert Ames (1889-1931)
Behind Office Doors *'31*
Millie *'31*
Smart Woman *'31*

Madchen Amick (1970-)
The Rats *'01*
Hangman *'00*
The List *'99*
Mr. Rock 'n' Roll: The Alan Freed Story *'99*
The Hunted *'98*
Bombshell *'97*
French Exit *'97*
Psychopath *'97*
Wounded *'97*
The Courtyard *'95*
The Great American Sex Scandal *'94*
Trapped in Paradise *'94*
Dream Lover *'93*
Love, Cheat & Steal *'93*
Sleepwalkers *'92*
Twin Peaks: Fire Walk with Me *'92*
Don't Tell Her It's Me *'90*
I'm Dangerous Tonight *'90*

Amidou (1942-)
And Now Ladies and Gentlemen *'02*
Hot Chocolate *'92*

Soudad Amidou (1959-)
Petit Con *'84*
Sorcerer *'77*

Suzy Amis (1962-)
Judgment Day *'99*
The Beneficiary *'97*
Firestorm *'97*
Titanic *'97*
Cadillac Ranch *'96*
The Ex *'96*
Last Stand at Saber River *'96*
Nadja *'95*
One Good Turn *'95*
The Usual Suspects *'95*
Blown Away *'94*
The Ballad of Little Jo *'93*
Rich in Love *'93*
Two Small Bodies *'93*
Watch It *'93*
Where the Heart Is *'90*
Twister *'89*
Plain Clothes *'88*
Rocket Gibraltar *'88*
Big Town *'87*
Fandango *'85*

Christopher Amitrano
Jam *'06*

Renee Ammann
See Renee Griffin

Luigi Amodeo
Art House *'98*
B.A.P.'s *'97*
Red Shoe Diaries 6: How I Met My Husband *'95*

Christine Amor (1952-)
Bloodmoon *'90*
Now and Forever *'82*

David Amos
Flipping *'96*
The Takeover *'94*

John Amos (1941-)
Dr. Dolittle 3 *'06*
Voodoo Moon *'05*
My Baby's Daddy *'04*
Disappearing Acts *'00*
The Players Club *'98*
For Better or Worse *'95*
Hologram Man *'95*
Mac *'93*
Mardi Gras for the Devil *'93*
Ricochet *'91*
Die Hard 2: Die Harder *'90*
Two Evil Eyes *'90*
Lock Up *'89*
Coming to America *'88*
American Flyers *'85*
Beastmaster *'82*
Touched by Love *'80*
Willa *'79*
Roots *'77*
Future Cop *'76*
Let's Do It Again *'75*
The World's Greatest Athlete *'73*
Sweet Sweetback's Baadasssss Song *'71*

John Amplas (1949-)
Creepshow *'82*
Midnight *'81*
Martin *'77*

Morey Amsterdam (1908-96)
Sooner or Later *'78*
Muscle Beach Party *'64*
Beach Party *'63*
Murder, Inc. *'60*
Machine Gun Kelly *'58*

Roland Amstutz
Nouvelle Vague *'90*
Every Man for Himself *'79*

Niki Amuka-Bird
The Disappeared *'08*
Five Days *'07*

Eva Amurri (1985-)
The Life Before Her Eyes *'07*
Saved! *'04*
The Banger Sisters *'02*

Susie Amy (1981-)
House of 9 *'05*
Modigliani *'04*

Kristina Anapau (1979-)
Cruel Intentions 3 *'04*
Cursed *'04*
Madison *'01*

Elena Anaya (1975-)
Cairo Time *'09*
Savage Grace *'07*
In the Land of Women *'06*
Dead Fish *'04*
Van Helsing *'04*
Two Tough Guys *'03*
Sex and Lucia *'01*

Leo Anchoriz
Spaghetti Western *'75*
The Invincible Gladiator *'62*

Dominic Anciano (1959-)
Love, Honour & Obey *'00*
Final Cut *'98*

Richard Anconina (1953-)
Police *'85*
Love Songs *'84*
Tchao Pantin *'84*

Avalon Anders
The Portrait *'99*
Wish Me Luck *'95*
Great Bikini Off-Road Adventure *'94*
Bikini Summer 2 *'92*
Sorority House Party *'92*

David Anders
Into the Blue 2: The Reef *'09*
Left in Darkness *'06*
Circadian Rhythm *'05*

Glenn Anders (1889-1981)
Tarzan's Peril *'51*
Nancy Goes to Rio *'50*
The Lady from Shanghai *'48*

Luana Anders (1938-96)
Limit Up *'89*
Border Radio *'88*
Movers and Shakers *'85*
Irreconcilable Differences *'84*
Goin' South *'78*
The Killing Kind *'73*
Greaser's Palace *'72*
Manipulator *'71*
Easy Rider *'69*
Games *'67*
The Trip *'67*
Sex and the College Girl *'64*
Dementia 13 *'63*
Night Tide *'63*
The Pit and the Pendulum *'61*
Reform School Girl *'57*

Merry Anders (1932-)
Blood Legacy *'73*
Women of the Prehistoric Planet *'66*
The Time Travelers *'64*
Desk Set *'57*
Phffft! *'54*
The Farmer Takes a Wife *'53*

Rudolph Anders (1895-1987)
36 Hours *'64*
She Demons *'58*
Phantom from Space *'53*
Actors and Sin *'52*
Under Nevada Skies *'46*
Junior Army *'42*
We're in the Legion Now *'37*

Bridgette Andersen (1975-)
Between Two Women *'86*
Fever Pitch *'85*
A Summer to Remember *'84*
Hansel and Gretel *'82*
Savannah Smiles *'82*

Elga Andersen (1939-94)
Night Flight from Moscow *'73*

Le Mans '71
Coast of Skeletons '63
Your Turn Darling '63
The Twilight Girls '57

Susy Andersen

Gangster's Law '86
Black Sabbath '64
Thor and the Amazon Women '60

Andy Anderson (1947-)

Salem's Lot '04
Garage Days '03
The Junction Boys '02

Anthony Anderson (1970-)

Transformers '07
Arthur and the Invisibles '06 (V)
The Departed '06
Scary Movie 4 '06
Hoodwinked '05 (V)
Hustle & Flow '05
King's Ransom '05
Agent Cody Banks 2: Destination London '04
Harold and Kumar Go to White Castle '04
My Baby's Daddy '04
Cradle 2 the Grave '03
Malibu's Most Wanted '03
Scary Movie 3 '03
Barbershop '02
Kangaroo Jack '02
Exit Wounds '01
Kingdom Come '01
See Spot Run '01
Two Can Play That Game '01
Big Momma's House '00
Me, Myself, and Irene '00
Romeo Must Die '00
Urban Legends 2: Final Cut '00
Liberty Heights '99
Life '99

Cheryl Anderson

Writer's Block '91
Acorn People '82
Rosie: The Rosemary Clooney Story '82

David Anderson

The Siege of Firebase Gloria '89
Bon Voyage, Charlie Brown '80 (V)

Deke Anderson

Balls Out: Gary the Tennis Coach '09
White Fury '90

Donna Anderson (1925-)

Inherit the Wind '60
On the Beach '59

Eddie Anderson (1905-77)

It's a Mad, Mad, Mad, Mad World '63
The Show-Off '46
Brewster's Millions '45
I Love a Bandleader '45
Broadway Rhythm '44
Cabin in the Sky '43
Star Spangled Rhythm '42
Tales of Manhattan '42
Birth of the Blues '41
Topper Returns '41
Buck Benny Rides Again '40
Gone with the Wind '39
Honolulu '39
You Can't Cheat an Honest Man '39
Jezebel '38
Thanks for the Memory '38
You Can't Take It with You '38
Green Pastures '36
False Faces '32

Erich Anderson

Due East '02
Love Kills '91
Bat 21 '88
Friday the 13th, Part 4: The Final Chapter '84

Erika Anderson (1965-)

Red Shoe Diaries 8: Night of Abandon '97
Object of Obsession '95
Quake '92
Zandalee '91
A Nightmare on Elm Street 5: Dream Child '89

Gillian Anderson (1968-)

How to Lose Friends & Alienate People '08
The X Files: I Want to Believe '08
Closure '07
The Last King of Scotland '06
Bleak House '05
The Mighty Celt '05
Tristram Shandy: A Cock and Bull Story '05
House of Mirth '00
Chicago Cab '98
The Mighty '98
Playing by Heart '98
Princess Mononoke '98 (V)
The X-Files '98
The Turning '92

Harry Anderson (1952-)

Spies, Lies and Naked Thighs '91
Mother Goose Rock 'n' Rhyme '90
Stephen King's It '90

Herbert Anderson (1917-94)

I Bury the Living '58
Night Passage '57
Battleground '49
The Male Animal '42
Dive Bomber '41
The Fighting 69th '40

James Anderson (1872-1953)

Five '51
Sergeant York '41
The Freshman '25

James Anderson (1921-69)

Take the Money and Run '69
The Connection '61
Hellgate '52

Jean Anderson (1907-2001)

Prince Brat and the Whipping Boy '95
Back Home '90
Death by Prescription '86
Screamtime '83
Lucky Jim '58

Jeff Anderson (1970-)

Zack and Miri Make a Porno '08
Clerks 2 '06
Now You Know '02
Dogma '99
Clerks '94

Jo Anderson (1958-)

From the Earth to the Moon '98
Daylight '96
Season of Change '94
Decoration Day '90
Suspicion '87

Joe Anderson

Amelia '09
The Ruins '08
Across the Universe '07
Becoming Jane '07
Control '07

John Anderson (1922-92)

Eight Men Out '88
Firehouse '87
Donner Pass: The Road to Survival '84
Ashes and Embers '82
Zoot Suit '81
Smokey and the Bandit 2 '80

Backstairs at the White House '79
The Deerslayer '78
The Specialist '75
Smile, Jenny, You're Dead '74
Executive Action '73
The Stepmother '71
Cotton Comes to Harlem '70
The Desperados '70
Five Card Stud '68
Namu, the Killer Whale '66
Geronimo '62
Ride the High Country '62
Psycho '60

Judith Anderson (1898-1992)

Star Trek 3: The Search for Spock '84
Inn of the Damned '74
A Man Called Horse '70
Elizabeth, the Queen '68
Cinderfella '60
Cat on a Hot Tin Roof '58
The Ten Commandments '56
Salome '53
The Furies '50
Pursued '47
The Red House '47
Tycoon '47
Diary of a Chambermaid '46
Spectre of the Rose '46
The Strange Love of Martha Ivers '46
And Then There Were None '45
Laura '44
Edge of Darkness '43
Stage Door Canteen '43
All Through the Night '42
Kings Row '41
Lady Scarface '41
Rebecca '40

Kenneth Anderson

Behind Enemy Lines 3: Colombia '08
Feast of July '95

Kevin Anderson (1960-)

Charlotte's Web '06
Carry Me Home '04
Monday Night Mayhem '02
Power and Beauty '02
The Doe Boy '01
Ruby's Bucket of Blood '01
Eye of God '97
Firelight '97
A Thousand Acres '97
The Night We Never Met '93
Rising Sun '93
The Wrong Man '93
Hoffa '92
Liebestraum '91
Orpheus Descending '91
Sleeping with the Enemy '91
In Country '89
Miles from Home '88
Orphans '87
Pink Nights '87
Risky Business '83

Lindsay Anderson (1923-94)

Blame It on the Bellboy '92
Prisoner of Honor '91
Chariots of Fire '81

Lisa Arrindell Anderson (1969-)

Big Momma's House 2 '06
Madea's Family Reunion '06
The Second Chance '06
Disappearing Acts '00
Having Our Say: The Delany Sisters' First 100 Years '99
A Lesson Before Dying '99
Clockers '95
Trial by Jury '94
Livin' Large '91
One Good Cop '91

Loni Anderson (1945-)

A Night at the Roxbury '98
3 Ninjas: High Noon at Mega Mountain '97
Munchie '92

White Hot: The Mysterious Murder of Thelma Todd '91
Blown Away '90
All Dogs Go to Heaven '89 (V)
Sorry, Wrong Number '89
My Mother's Secret Life '84
Stroker Ace '83
Sizzle '81
The Jayne Mansfield Story '80

Louie Anderson (1953-)

Coming to America '88
The Wrong Guys '88
Ferris Bueller's Day Off '86
Quicksilver '86

Mary Anderson

Dangerous Crossing '53
False Faces '18

Mary Anderson (1921-)

The Underworld Story '50
Whispering City '47
To Each His Own '46
Lifeboat '44
Wilson '44
Bahama Passage '42
Gone with the Wind '39

Melissa Sue Anderson (1962-)

Chattanooga Choo Choo '84
First Affair '83
Happy Birthday to Me '81
On the Edge: The Survival of Dana '79
The Loneliest Runner '76
Little House on the Prairie '74

Melody Anderson (1955-)

Marilyn & Bobby: Her Final Affair '94
Landslide '92
Hitler's Daughter '90
Final Notice '89
Speed Zone '88
Beverly Hills Madam '86
Boy in Blue '86
Firewalker '86
Ernie Kovacs: Between the Laughter '84
Policewoman Centerfold '83
Dead and Buried '81
Flash Gordon '80

Michael Anderson, Jr. (1943-)

Sunset Grill '92
The Great Land of Small '86
A Legacy for Leonette '85
Sons of Katie Elder '65
In Search of the Castaways '62
The Sundowners '60
Tiger Bay '59

Michael J. Anderson (1953-)

Snow White: The Fairest of Them All '02
Mulholland Drive '01
Club Vampire '98

Miles Anderson (1947-)

The King Is Alive '00
A Certain Justice '99
Into the Blue '97
The Rector's Wife '94
A Far Off Place '93
House of Cards '90

Mitchell Anderson (1961-)

If These Walls Could Talk 2 '00
Relax... It's Just Sex! '98
Is There Life Out There? '94
Back to Hannibal: The Return of Tom Sawyer and Huckleberry Finn '90
Deadly Dreams '88
Goodbye, Miss 4th of July '88

Myrtle Anderson

Follow the Sun '51
Green Pastures '36

Nathan Anderson

Alien Siege '05
Tequila Body Shots '99

Pamela Anderson (1967-)

Blonde and Blonder '07
Borat: Cultural Learnings of America for Make Benefit Glorious Nation of Kazakhstan '06
Scary Movie 3 '03
Barb Wire '96
Baywatch the Movie: Forbidden Paradise '95
Naked Souls '95
Raw Justice '93
Snapdragon '93

Pat Anderson

Cover Girl Models '75
Summer School Teachers '75
TNT Jackson '75

Richard Anderson (1926-)

In the Lake of the Woods '96
The Glass Shield '95
Gettysburg '93
The Player '92
Perry Mason Returns '85
Retrievers '82
Murder by Natural Causes '79
Pearl '78
The Bionic Woman '75
The Night Strangler '72
Tora! Tora! Tora! '70
Seconds '66
Kitten with a Whip '64
Seven Days in May '64
Compulsion '59
The Gunfight at Dodge City '59
The Long, Hot Summer '58
Paths of Glory '57
Forbidden Planet '56
The Search for Bridey Murphy '56
Hit the Deck '55
Dream Wife '53
Escape from Fort Bravo '53
Give a Girl a Break '53
I Love Melvin '53
The Story of Three Loves '53
Scaramouche '52
Payment on Demand '51
Rich, Young and Pretty '51
The Magnificent Yankee '50
The Vanishing Westerner '50

Richard Dean Anderson (1950-)

Stargate: Continuum '08
Pandora's Clock '96
Past the Bleachers '95
Through the Eyes of a Killer '92
Ordinary Heroes '85

Robert Anderson (1890-1963)

White Shadows in the South Seas '29
The Temptress '26

Shedrack Anderson, III

Fat Albert '04
Gracie's Choice '04

Stanley Anderson (1945-)

Runaway Jury '03
40 Days and 40 Nights '02
Red Dragon '02
Simone '02
Spider-Man '02
Proof of Life '00
Trial by Media '00
Arlington Road '99
Primal Fear '96
The Shadow Conspiracy '96
He Said, She Said '91

Son of the Morning Star '91

Warner Anderson (1911-76)

Armored Command '61
The Lineup '58
Blackboard Jungle '55
A Lawless Street '55
The Caine Mutiny '54
Drum Beat '54
A Lion in the Streets '53
A Lion Is in the Streets '53
The Star '52
Detective Story '51
Go for Broke! '51
Santa Fe '51
Destination Moon '50
Command Decision '48
Song of the Thin Man '47
My Reputation '46
Abbott and Costello in Hollywood '45
Objective, Burma! '45
Weekend at the Waldorf '45
Destination Tokyo '43

Whitney Anderson

Zombie Strippers '08
Prehysteria 3 '95

Bibi Andersson (1935-)

Babette's Feast '87
Law of Desire '86
Exposed '83
The Concorde: Airport '79 '79
Quintet '79
Twice a Woman '79
An Enemy of the People '77
I Never Promised You a Rose Garden '77
Germicide '74
Scenes from a Marriage '73
The Touch '71
The Passion of Anna '70
Duel at Diablo '66
Persona '66
The Devil's Eye '60
The Magician '58
Brink of Life '57
Wild Strawberries '57
The Seventh Seal '56

Harriet Andersson (1932-)

Dogville '03
Fanny and Alexander '83
Cries and Whispers '72
Through a Glass Darkly '61
Dreams '55
Smiles of a Summer Night '55
Lesson in Love '54
Sawdust & Tinsel '53
Monika '52

Peter Andersson (1953-)

Flickering Lights '01
The Last Dance '93

Keith Andes (1920-2005)

The Ultimate Imposter '79
Hell's Bloody Devils '70
Tora! Tora! Tora! '70
Away All Boats '56
Back from Eternity '56
Blackbeard the Pirate '52

Eiko Ando

Paper Tiger '74
Barbarian and the Geisha '58

Mansanobu Ando

Sukiyaki Western Django '08
Nightmare Detective '06
Adrenaline Drive '99

Noboru Ando

The Wolves '82
Sympathy for the Underdog '71

Paul Andor (1901-91)

Union City '81
Enemy of Women '44

Peter Andorai (1948-)

Simon the Magician '99
My Twentieth Century '90

Mephisto *'81*

Gaby Andre (1920-72)

Goliath and the Dragon *'61*
The Cosmic Monsters *'58*
East of Kilimanjaro *'57*
Verdi *'53*
The Green Glove *'52*

Lona Andre (1915-92)

Slaves in Bondage *'37*
Trailing Trouble *'37*
Custer's Last Stand *'36*
Lucky Terror *'36*
Badmen of Nevada *'33*
The Mysterious Rider *'33*

Marcel Andre (1885-1974)

The Storm Within *'48*
Beauty and the Beast *'46*
Maniac *'34*

Andre 3000

See Andre Benjamin

Andre the Giant (1946-93)

The Princess Bride *'87*
Micki & Maude *'84*

Starr Andreeff (1964-)

Club Vampire *'98*
Amityville Dollhouse *'96*
Vampire Journals *'96*
Syngenor *'90*
Dance of the Damned *'88*
Out of the Dark *'88*
The Terror Within *'88*

Damir Andrei

A Different Loyalty *'04*
Soft Deceit *'94*

Natasha Andreichenko (1956-)

Modern Vampires *'98*
Operation Intercept *'95*
Little Odessa *'94*

Ursula Andress (1936-)

The Chinatown Murders: Man against the Mob *'89*
Peter the Great *'86*
Clash of the Titans *'81*
Tigers in Lipstick *'80*
The Fifth Musketeer *'79*
Mountain of the Cannibal God *'79*
Loves & Times of Scaramouche *'76*
The Sensuous Nurse *'76*
Loaded Guns *'75*
Stateline Motel *'75*
Red Sun *'71*
Casino Royale *'67*
The Blue Max *'66*
Once Before I Die *'65*
She *'65*
10th Victim *'65*
What's New Pussycat? *'65*
Four for Texas *'63*
Fun in Acapulco *'63*
Dr. No *'62*

Simon Andreu (1941-)

Art Heist *'05*
Beyond Re-Animator *'03*
Hidden Assassin *'94*
Sharpe's Rifles *'93*
Blood and Sand *'89*
Fist Fighter *'88*
The Barcelona Kill *'77*
Blue Jeans and Dynamite *'76*
The Blood Spattered Bride *'72*
Night of the Sorcerers *'70*
Surprise Attack *'70*

Anthony Andrews (1948-)

Cambridge Spies *'03*
Haunted *'95*
Jewels *'92*
Hands of a Murderer *'90*
Strange Case of Dr. Jekyll & Mr. Hyde *'89*
Hanna's War *'88*
The Woman He Loved *'88*
The Lighthorsemen *'87*
Second Victory *'87*
Suspicion *'87*
A.D. *'85*
The Holcroft Covenant *'85*
Under the Volcano *'84*
Agatha Christie's Sparkling Cyanide *'83*
Ivanhoe *'82*
The Scarlet Pimpernel *'82*
Brideshead Revisited *'81*
Danger UXB *'81*

Barry Andrews (1944-)

The Blood on Satan's Claw *'71*
Dracula Has Risen from the Grave *'68*

Dana Andrews (1909-92)

Prince Jack *'83*
Danger in the Skies *'79*
Ike *'79*
Born Again *'78*
The Last Tycoon *'76*
Airport '75 *'75*
The Cobra *'68*
The Devil's Brigade *'68*
Johnny Reno *'66*
Battle of the Bulge *'65*
In Harm's Way *'65*
The Loved One *'65*
The Crowded Sky *'60*
Enchanted Island *'58*
Curse of the Demon *'57*
Zero Hour! *'57*
Beyond a Reasonable Doubt *'56*
While the City Sleeps *'56*
Elephant Walk *'54*
I Want You *'51*
Where the Sidewalk Ends *'50*
My Foolish Heart *'49*
Boomerang *'47*
Daisy Kenyon *'47*
The Best Years of Our Lives *'46*
Canyon Passage *'46*
A Walk in the Sun *'46*
State Fair *'45*
Laura *'44*
The Purple Heart *'44*
Up in Arms *'44*
A Wing and a Prayer *'44*
Crash Dive *'43*
The North Star *'43*
The Ox-Bow Incident *'43*
Ball of Fire *'41*
Kit Carson *'40*
Lucky Cisco Kid *'40*
The Westerner *'40*

David Andrews (1952-)

Terminator 3: Rise of the Machines *'03*
Hannibal *'01*
From the Earth to the Moon *'98*
Under Pressure *'98*
Apollo 13 *'95*
Deconstructing Sarah *'94*
Wyatt Earp *'94*
Graveyard Shift *'90*
Cherry 2000 *'88*
Wild Horses *'84*

Dean Andrews

My Summer of Love *'05*
The Navigators *'01*

Edward Andrews (1914-85)

Sixteen Candles *'84*
Avanti! *'72*
How to Frame a Figg *'71*
Tora! Tora! Tora! *'70*
Over the Hill Gang *'69*
The Trouble with Girls (and How to Get into It) *'69*
The Glass Bottom Boat *'66*
Good Neighbor Sam *'64*
Kisses for My President *'64*
A Tiger Walks *'64*
The Brass Bottle *'63*
Man From Galveston *'63*
The Thrill of It All! *'63*
Advise and Consent *'62*
40 Pounds of Trouble *'62*
The Absent-Minded Professor *'61*
The Young Savages *'61*
Elmer Gantry *'60*
The Fiend Who Walked the West *'58*
Tea and Sympathy *'56*

Giuseppe Andrews (1979-)

Tweek City *'05*
Cabin Fever *'03*
Local Boys *'02*
Detroit Rock City *'99*
American History X *'98*
Independence Day *'96*

Harry Andrews (1911-89)

Cause Celebre *'87*
Mesmerized *'84*
Hawk the Slayer *'81*
The Curse of King Tut's Tomb *'80*
S.O.S. Titanic *'79*
The Big Sleep *'78*
Death on the Nile *'78*
The Four Feathers *'78*
The Medusa Touch *'78*
Watership Down *'78 (V)*
Equus *'77*
Sky Riders *'76*
The Passover Plot *'75*
The Story of Jacob & Joseph *'74*
The Final Programme *'73*
Internecine Project *'73*
Mackintosh Man *'73*
Theatre of Blood *'73*
I Want What I Want *'72*
Man of La Mancha *'72*
The Nightcomers *'72*
The Ruling Class *'72*
What the Peeper Saw *'72*
Horrors of Burke & Hare *'71*
Nicholas and Alexandra *'71*
Entertaining Mr. Sloane *'70*
Too Late the Hero *'70*
Wuthering Heights *'70*
Battle of Britain *'69*
Nice Girl Like Me *'69*
The Charge of the Light Brigade *'68*
Dandy in Aspic *'68*
The Girl Getters *'66*
Modesty Blaise *'66*
The Agony and the Ecstasy *'65*
The Hill *'65*
633 Squadron *'64*
The Devil's Disciple *'59*
Saint Joan *'57*
Helen of Troy *'56*
Moby Dick *'56*
Alexander the Great *'55*

Jason Andrews

Federal Hill *'94*
Rhythm Thief *'94*

Julie Andrews (1935-)

Despicable Me *'10 (V)*
Shrek Forever After *'10 (V)*
Tooth Fairy *'10*
Enchanted *'07 (N)*
Shrek the Third *'07 (V)*
The Princess Diaries 2: Royal Engagement *'04*
Shrek 2 *'04 (V)*
Eloise at the Plaza *'03*
The Princess Diaries *'01*
One Special Night *'99*
Relative Values *'99*
A Fine Romance *'92*
Our Sons *'91*
Duet for One *'86*
That's Life! *'86*
The Man Who Loved Women *'83*
Victor/Victoria *'82*
S.O.B. *'81*
Little Miss Marker *'80*
10 *'79*
The Tamarind Seed *'74*
Darling Lili *'70*
Star! *'68*
Thoroughly Modern Millie *'67*
Hawaii *'66*
Torn Curtain *'66*
The Sound of Music *'65*
The Americanization of Emily *'64*
Mary Poppins *'64*
The Singing Princess *'49*

Naveen Andrews (1971-)

The Brave One *'07*
Planet Terror *'07*
Bride & Prejudice *'04*
Rollerball *'02*
Drowning on Dry Land *'00*
My Own Country *'98*
The English Patient *'96*
Kama Sutra: A Tale of Love *'96*
Wild West *'93*
The Buddha of Suburbia *'92*

Peter Andrews

See Steven Soderbergh

Real Andrews (1963-)

Family of Cops 2: Breach of Faith *'97*
Soldier of Fortune Inc. *'97*
Expect No Mercy *'95*
Red Scorpion 2 *'94*
Showdown *'94*
Circle Man *'87*

Russell Andrews

The Punisher *'04*
The In-Laws *'03*

Slim Andrews (1906-92)

The Driftin' Kid *'41*
The Pioneers *'41*
Riding the Sunset Trail *'41*

Stanley Andrews (1891-1969)

The Adventures of Frank and Jesse James *'48*
Return of Wildfire *'48*
Crash Dive *'43*
In Old Colorado *'41*
Brigham Young: Frontiersman *'40*
Beau Geste *'39*
Blondie *'38*
Shine on, Harvest Moon *'38*
Wild Brian Kent *'36*

Tod Andrews (1914-72)

In Harm's Way *'65*
She Demons *'58*
Between Heaven and Hell *'56*
I Was Framed *'42*
Dive Bomber *'41*
They Died with Their Boots On *'41*

The Andrews Sisters

Melody Time *'48 (V)*
The Road to Rio *'47*
Swingtime Johnny *'43*
Private Buckaroo *'42*
Buck Privates *'41*
Hold That Ghost *'41*
In the Navy *'41*
Argentine Nights *'40*

James Andronica (1945-)

First Degree *'98*
Mirage *'94*
The November Men *'93*

Anemone (1950-)

A Song of Innocence *'05*
Son of Gascogne *'95*
Pas Tres Catholique *'93*
Twisted Obsession *'90*
Le Grand Chemin *'87*

Michael Angarano (1987-)

Gentlemen Broncos *'09*
The Forbidden Kingdom *'08*
Black Irish *'07*
The Final Season *'07*
Snow Angels *'07*
Dear Wendy *'05*
Lords of Dogtown *'05*
One Last Thing *'05*
Sky High *'05*
Speak *'04*
Little Secrets *'02*

Julie Ange (1940-)

Teenage Mother *'67*
Girl on a Chain Gang *'65*

Heather Angel (1909-86)

Backstairs at the White House *'79*
Premature Burial *'62*
Peter Pan *'53 (V)*
Lifeboat *'44*
Time to Kill *'42*
The Undying Monster *'42*
Shadows on the Stairs *'41*
Suspicion *'41*
Half a Soldier *'40*
Bulldog Drummond's Bride *'39*
Bulldog Drummond's Secret Police *'39*
Arrest Bulldog Drummond *'38*
Bulldog Drummond Escapes *'37*
Western Gold *'37*
The Bold Caballero *'36*
The Last of the Mohicans *'36*
Headline Woman *'35*
The Informer *'35*
The Mystery of Edwin Drood *'35*
The Three Musketeers *'35*
Daniel Boone *'34*
Pilgrimage *'33*

Mikel Angel

Evil Spirits *'91*
Grotesque *'87*
The Black Six *'74*

Vanessa Angel (1963-)

The Perfect Score *'04*
Superbabies: Baby Geniuses 2 *'04*
Firetrap *'01*
Sabretooth *'01*
Camouflage *'00*
Enemies of Laughter *'00*
Made Men *'99*
Partners *'99*
Kissing a Fool *'98*
Kingpin *'96*
The Cover Girl Murders *'93*
Homicidal Impulse *'92*

Pier Angeli (1932-71)

Octaman *'71*
One Step to Hell *'67*
Battle of the Bulge *'65*
Sodom and Gomorrah *'62*
S.O.S. Pacific *'60*
Somebody Up There Likes Me *'56*
The Silver Chalice *'54*
The Story of Three Loves *'53*

Chris Angelo

The Damned *'06*
San Franpsycho *'06*
I Got Five on It *'05*

Maya Angelou (1928-)

Madea's Family Reunion *'06*
The Runaway *'00*
How to Make an American Quilt *'95*
Roots *'77*

Muriel Angelus (1909-2004)

The Great McGinty *'40*
Night Birds *'31*

Angelyne (1958-)

The Malibu Beach Vampires *'91*
Earth Girls Are Easy *'89*

Luciana Angiolillo (1925-)

The Easy Life *'63*
The Trojan Horse *'62*
The Girl with a Suitcase *'60*

Jean-Hugues Anglade (1955-)

Taking Lives *'04*
Mortal Transfer *'01*
Innocents *'00*
Elective Affinities *'96*
Maximum Risk *'96*
Nelly et Monsieur Arnaud *'95*
Killing Zoe *'94*
Queen Margot *'94*
La Femme Nikita *'91*
Betty Blue *'86*
Subway *'85*
L'Homme Blesse *'83*

Philip Anglim (1953-)

Deadly Currents *'93*
Haunted Summer *'88*
Testament *'83*

Sally Anglim

Thundering Trail *'51*
Yes, Sir, Mr. Bones *'51*

Alex Angulo (1953-)

Pan's Labyrinth *'06*
My Mother Likes Women *'02*
Live Flesh *'97*
The Day of the Beast *'95*

Christien Anholt (1971-)

Dark Corners *'06*
Flyboys *'06*
The Waiting Time *'99*
Appetite *'98*
Preaching to the Perverted *'97*
The Blackheath Poisonings *'92*
Class of '61 *'92*
One Against the Wind *'91*
Reunion *'88*

Jennifer Aniston (1969-)

The Bounty Hunter *'10*
The Switch *'10*
He's Just Not That Into You *'09*
Love Happens *'09*
Management *'09*
Marley & Me *'08*
The Break-Up *'06*
Friends with Money *'06*
Derailed *'05*
Rumor Has It... *'05*
Along Came Polly *'04*
Bruce Almighty *'03*
The Good Girl *'02*
Rock Star *'01*
The Iron Giant *'99 (V)*
The Object of My Affection *'98*
Office Space *'98*
Dream for an Insomniac *'96*
Picture Perfect *'96*
She's the One *'96*
Til There Was You *'96*
Leprechaun *'93*

Paul Anka (1941-)

Shake, Rattle & Rock! *'94*
Ordinary Magic *'93*
The Return of Spinal Tap *'92*
The Longest Day *'62*
Girls' Town *'59*

Evelyn Ankers (1918-85)

Parole, Inc. *'49*
Tarzan's Magic Fountain *'48*
The Last of the Redmen *'47*
Spoilers of the North *'47*
Black Beauty *'46*
Flight to Nowhere *'46*
His Butler's Sister *'44*
The Invisible Man's Revenge *'44*
Jungle Woman *'44*
The Pearl of Death *'44*
Weird Woman *'44*
Captive Wild Woman *'43*
The Mad Ghoul *'43*
Son of Dracula *'43*
The Ghost of Frankenstein *'42*
Sherlock Holmes: The Voice of Terror *'42*
Burma Convoy *'41*
Hold That Ghost *'41*
The Wolf Man *'41*

Morris Ankrum (1898-1964)
X: The Man with X-Ray Eyes *'63*
Giant from the Unknown *'58*
Half Human *'58*
How to Make a Monster *'58*
Beginning of the End *'57*
The Giant Claw *'57*
Earth vs. the Flying Saucers *'56*
Crashout *'55*
Silver Star *'55*
Invaders from Mars *'53*
Borderline *'50*
The Damned Don't Cry *'50*
Colorado Territory *'49*
The Lion Hunters *'47*
Border Vigilantes *'41*
Doomed Caravan *'41*
I Wake Up Screaming *'41*
In Old Colorado *'41*
The Light of Western Stars *'40*
The Showdown *'40*
Borderland *'37*
Hopalong Cassidy Returns *'36*

Ann-Margret (1941-)
Old Dogs *'09*
The Loss of a Teardrop Diamond *'08*
The Break-Up *'06*
Memory *'06*
Taxi *'04*
Interstate 60 *'02*
Blonde *'01*
A Woman's a Helluva Thing *'01*
Perfect Murder, Perfect Town *'00*
The 10th Kingdom *'00*
Any Given Sunday *'99*
The Happy Face Murders *'99*
Grumpier Old Men *'95*
Scarlett *'94*
Grumpy Old Men *'93*
Queen *'93*
Newsies *'92*
Our Sons *'91*
A New Life *'88*
A Tiger's Tale *'87*
52 Pick-Up *'86*
Twice in a Lifetime *'85*
A Streetcar Named Desire *'84*
I Ought to Be in Pictures *'82*
Lookin' to Get Out *'82*
Return of the Soldier *'82*
Middle Age Crazy *'80*
The Villain *'79*
The Cheap Detective *'78*
Magic *'78*
Joseph Andrews *'77*
The Last Remake of Beau Geste *'77*
Twist *'76*
Tommy *'75*
The Outside Man *'73*
Train Robbers *'73*
Carnal Knowledge *'71*
C.C. & Company *'70*
R.P.M.* (*Revolutions Per Minute) *'70*
Tiger and the Pussycat *'67*
Murderers' Row *'66*
The Cincinnati Kid *'65*
Made in Paris *'65*
Kitten with a Whip *'64*
Bye, Bye, Birdie *'63*
Viva Las Vegas *'63*
State Fair *'62*
Pocketful of Miracles *'61*

Annabella (1909-96)
13 Rue Madeleine *'46*
Dinner at the Ritz *'37*
Wings of the Morning *'37*
Under the Red Robe *'36*
Le Million *'31*
Napoleon *'27*

Amina Annabi (1962-)
Mr. Average *'06*
The Advocate *'93*
The Sheltering Sky *'90*

Glory Annen
Spaced Out *'80*
Alien Prey *'78*

Frank Annese (1950-)
Another Chance *'88*
House of the Rising Sun *'87*

Francesca Annis (1944-)
Return to Cranford *'09*
Cranford *'08*
Jane Eyre *'06*
The Libertine *'05*
Revolver *'05*
Wives and Daughters *'01*
Onegin *'99*
Reckless: The Sequel *'98*
Reckless *'97*
Doomsday Gun *'94*
Onassis *'88*
Under the Cherry Moon *'86*
The Maze *'85*
Dune *'84*
Krull *'83*
Coming Out of the Ice *'82*
Lillie *'79*
Edward the King *'75*
Macbeth *'71*
Murder Most Foul *'65*
Flipper's New Adventure *'64*

Michael Ansara (1922-)
Border Shootout *'90*
Assassination *'87*
Bayou Romance *'86*
The KGB: The Secret War *'86*
Knights of the City *'85*
Access Code *'84*
The Fantastic World of D.C. Collins *'84*
The Guns and the Fury *'83*
Mission to Glory *'80*
Centennial *'78*
The Manitou *'78*
Day of the Animals *'77*
The Message *'77*
The Barbary Coast *'74*
The Bears & I *'74*
It's Alive *'74*
The Doll Squad *'73*
Dear Dead Delilah *'72*
Quick, Let's Get Married *'71*
Powder Keg *'70*
Guns of the Magnificent Seven *'69*
Daring Game *'68*
The Pink Jungle *'68*
And Now Miguel *'66*
Texas Across the River *'66*
Harum Scarum *'65*
Voyage to the Bottom of the Sea *'61*
Abbott and Costello Meet the Mummy *'55*
Diane *'55*
Jupiter's Darling *'55*
The Lawless Breed *'52*
Hill Number One *'51*
Action in Arabia *'44*

Zachary Ansley (1972-)
The Spring *'00*
This Boy's Life *'93*
Princes in Exile *'90*
Christmas Comes to Willow Creek *'87*

Susan Anspach (1939-)
Back to Back *'90*
The Rutanga Tapes *'90*
Blood Red *'88*
Into the Fire *'88*
Blue Monkey *'87*
Gone Are the Days *'84*
Misunderstood *'84*
The Devil & Max Devlin *'81*
Gas *'81*
Montenegro *'81*
The Big Fix *'78*
Mad Bull *'77*
Blume in Love *'73*
Deadly Encounter *'72*
Play It Again, Sam *'72*
Five Easy Pieces *'70*

Norman Anstey
Queen's Messenger II *'01*
Scavengers *'87*

Adam Ant (1954-)
Face Down *'97*
Lover's Knot *'96*
Desert Winds *'95*
Cyber Bandits *'94*
Acting on Impulse *'93*
Last Action Hero *'93*
Sunset Heat *'92*
Spellcaster *'91*
Trust Me *'89*
World Gone Wild *'88*
Cold Steel *'87*
Slamdance *'87*
Nomads *'86*

Carl Anthony
The Sinister Urge *'60*
Plan 9 from Outer Space *'56*

Gerald Anthony (1951-)
To Die Standing *'91*
Secret of the Ice Cave *'89*

Lysette Anthony (1963-)
Beneath Loch Ness *'01*
Russell Mulcahy's Tale of the Mummy *'99*
Misbegotten *'98*
Dead Cold *'96*
The Fiance *'96*
Robinson Crusoe *'96*
Trilogy of Terror 2 *'96*
Dr. Jekyll and Ms. Hyde *'95*
Dracula: Dead and Loving It *'95*
The Hard Truth *'94*
The Advocate *'93*
A Brilliant Disguise *'93*
Look Who's Talking Now *'93*
Save Me *'93*
Face the Music *'92*
Husbands and Wives *'92*
The Lady and the Highwayman *'89*
The Bretts *'88*
Without a Clue *'88*
Krull *'83*
Ivanhoe *'82*
Oliver Twist *'82*

Marc Anthony (1969-)
El Cantante *'06*
Man on Fire *'04*
In the Time of the Butterflies *'01*
Bringing Out the Dead *'99*
The Substitute *'96*
Big Night *'95*

Paul Anthony (1975-)
Suck *'09*
Blade: Trinity *'04*
Eighteen *'04*
House Party *'90*

Ray Anthony (1922-)
Girls' Town *'59*
High School Confidential *'58*
The Girl Can't Help It *'56*

Tony Anthony (1937-)
Treasure of the Four Crowns *'82*
1931: Once Upon a Time in New York *'72*
Force of Impulse *'60*

Steve Antin (1956-)
Inside Monkey Zetterland *'93*
Survival Quest *'89*
The Accused *'88*
Penitentiary 3 *'87*
Last American Virgin *'82*

Susan Anton (1950-)
Lena's Holiday *'90*
Options *'88*
Making Mr. Right *'86*
The Boy Who Loved Trolls *'84*
Cannonball Run 2 *'84*
Spring Fever *'81*
Goldengirl *'79*

Laura Antonelli (1941-)
Collector's Item *'89*
Swashbuckler *'84*
Passion of Love *'82*
Tigers in Lipstick *'80*
Wifemistress *'79*
How Funny Can Sex Be? *'76*
The Innocent *'76*
Malicious *'74*
Till Marriage Do Us Part *'74*
High Heels *'72*
Divine Nymph *'71*
A Man Called Sledge *'71*

Gabriele Antonini
Hero of Rome *'63*
Samson and the 7 Miracles of the World *'62*

Jose Antonio
See Anthony (Jose, J. Antonio, J.A.) Mayans

Alexander Antonov
The Battleship Potemkin *'25*
Strike *'24*

Omero Antonutti (1935-)
Farinelli *'94*
The Fencing Master *'92*
Good Morning, Babylon *'87*
Kaos *'85*
Basileus Quartet *'82*
Life of Verdi *'82*
The Night of the Shooting Stars *'82*
Padre Padrone *'77*

Scott Antony (1950-)
The Freakmaker *'73*
Savage Messiah *'72*

Cas Anvar
Dr. Jekyll and Mr. Hyde *'08*
Shattered Glass *'03*
Seducing Maarya *'99*
Psychopath *'97*

Gabrielle Anwar (1971-)
iMurders *'08*
Crazy Eights *'06*
The Librarian: Return to King Solomon's Mines *'06*
Sherlock: Case of Evil *'02*
If You Only Knew *'00*
Turbulence 3: Heavy Metal *'00*
The Guilty *'99*
My Little Assassin *'99*
Nevada *'97*
The Ripper *'97*
Sub Down *'97*
The Grave *'95*
In Pursuit of Honor *'95*
Innocent Lies *'95*
Things to Do in Denver When You're Dead *'95*
Body Snatchers *'93*
Fallen Angels 2 *'93*
For Love or Money *'93*
The Three Musketeers *'93*
Scent of a Woman *'92*
If Looks Could Kill *'91*
Wild Hearts Can't Be Broken *'91*
A Night of Love *'87*

Anya
Naked Weapon *'03*
Special Unit 2002 *'01*

Perry Anzilotti
Air Bud 2: Golden Receiver *'98*
Kiss of Fire *'98*

Yu Aoi
Tokyo! *'09*
Hula Girls *'06*
Hana & Alice *'04*
Tetsujin 28 *'04*
All About Lily Chou-Chou *'01*

Devon Aoki (1982-)
Mutant Chronicles *'08*
War *'07*
DOA: Dead or Alive *'06*
Sin City *'05*
D.E.B.S. *'04*
2 Fast 2 Furious *'03*

Rika Aoki
Rica 2: Lonely Wanderer *'73*
Rica 3: Juvenile's Lullaby *'73*
Rica *'72*

Rocky Aoki
That's Adequate *'90*
For Us, the Living *'88*

Tsuru Aoki
The Dragon Painter *'19*
The Wrath of the Gods *'14*

Yoshihiko Aoyama
Spook Warfare *'68*
Daimajin *'66*

Magda Apanowicz
Caprica *'09*
Every Second Counts *'08*

Oscar Apfel (1878-1939)
Shadows of the Orient *'37*
Bulldog Edition *'36*
Rainbow's End *'35*

Apollonia (1961-)
Black Magic Woman *'91*
Back to Back *'90*
Ministry of Vengeance *'89*
Tricks of the Trade *'88*
Purple Rain *'84*
Heartbreaker *'83*

Peter Appel (1959-)
Tadpole *'02*
Six Ways to Sunday *'99*
Extreme Measures *'96*
Man of the House *'95*

Noel Appleby
My Grandpa Is a Vampire *'92*
The Navigator *'88*

Shiri Appleby (1978-)
What Love Is *'07*
I-See-You.Com *'06*
I'm Reed Fish *'06*
The Killing Floor *'06*
Everything You Want *'05*
When Do We Eat? *'05*
Darklight *'04*
Undertow *'04*
The Battle of Shaker Heights *'03*
Swimfan *'02*
A Time for Dancing *'00*
Deal of a Lifetime *'99*
Perfect Family *'92*

Christina Applegate (1971-)
Going the Distance *'10*
Alvin and the Chipmunks: The Squeakuel *'09 (V)*
The Rocker *'08*
Anchorman: The Legend of Ron Burgundy *'04*
Surviving Christmas *'04*
Grand Theft Parsons *'03*
View from the Top *'03*
Wonderland *'03*
The Sweetest Thing *'02*
Just Visiting *'01*
The Brutal Truth *'99*
Out in Fifty *'99*
The Big Hit *'98*
Kiss of Fire *'98*
Mafia! *'98*
Nowhere *'96*
Wild Bill *'95*
Across the Moon *'94*
Vibrations *'94*
Don't Tell Mom the Babysitter's Dead *'91*
Streets *'90*
Jaws of Satan *'81*

Royce D. Applegate (1939-2003)
Gods and Generals *'03*
Intolerable Cruelty *'03*
Seabiscuit *'03*
The Rookie *'02*
O Brother Where Art Thou? *'00*
Inherit the Wind *'99*
Gettysburg *'93*
Outside Chance *'78*

Hale Appleman (1986-)
Teeth *'07*
Beautiful Ohio *'06*

John Aprea (1940-)
Dead Man on Campus *'97*
To the Limit *'95*
Cyber-Tracker *'93*
Direct Hit *'93*
Picasso Trigger *'89*
Savage Beach *'89*
Idolmaker *'80*
Caged Heat *'74*
The Godfather, Part 2 *'74*
The Arousers *'70*

Annabelle Apsion
From Hell *'01*
My Uncle Silas *'01*
The War Zone *'98*
Framed *'93*

Amy Aquino
A Lot Like Love *'05*
In Good Company *'04*
Undisputed *'02*
White Oleander *'02*
My Brother's Keeper *'95*
Alan & Naomi *'92*
Descending Angel *'90*

Angelica Aragon (1953-)
Bella *'06*
La Mujer de Mi Hermano *'06*
The Crime of Father Amaro *'02*
Optic Fiber *'97*
On the Air *'95*
A Walk in the Clouds *'95*
Like A Bride *'94*

Art Aragon (1927-)
To Hell and Back *'55*
The Ring *'52*

Julian (Sonny) Arahanga (1972-)
The Matrix *'99*
Broken English *'96*
Once Were Warriors *'94*

Hirofumi Arai (1979-)
The Neighbor No. Thirteen *'05*
Captive *'87*

Tomas Arana (1959-)
Defiance *'08*
Bats: Human Harvest *'07*
The Bourne Supremacy *'04*
Frankenfish *'04*
Rampage: The Hillside Strangler Murders *'04*
This Girl's Life *'03*
Derailed *'02*
Pearl Harbor *'01*
Gladiator *'00*
Wildflowers *'99*
The Church *'98*
The Bodyguard *'92*
The Devil's Daughter *'91*
Domino *'88*
The Last Temptation of Christ *'88*

Angel Aranda (1934-)
Satan's Blood *'77*
Planet of the Vampires *'65*

Manuel Aranguiz (1945-)
Levity *'03*
Eclipse *'94*
A Paper Wedding *'89*

Ray Aranha (1939-)
The Kid *'97*
City of Hope *'91*

Yoshisaburo Arashi
47 Ronin, Part 1 *'42*
47 Ronin, Part 2 *'42*

Julie Araskog
Seven *'95*
In a Moment of Passion *'93*

Arata
Ping Pong *'02*
After Life *'98*

Michiyo Aratama (1930-2001)
Kwaidan *'64*

The Human Condition: A Soldier's Prayer '61
The Gambling Samurai '60
The Human Condition: Road to Eternity '59
Saga of the Vagabond '59
The Human Condition: No Greater Love '58

Alfonso Arau (1932-)
Committed '99
Picking Up the Pieces '99
Dynamite and Gold '88
Three Amigos '86
Romancing the Stone '84
Posse '75
Scandalous John '71

Fatty Arbuckle (1887-1933)
Leap Year '21
Mabel & Fatty '16

Allan Arbus (1918-)
M*A*S*H: Goodbye, Farewell & Amen '83
Americathon '79
Damien: Omen 2 '78
Cinderella Liberty '73
Coffy '73
The Young Nurses '73
Greaser's Palace '72

Gabriel Arcand (1949-)
Post Mortem '99
Blood of the Hunter '94
Suzanne '80

Nathaniel Arcand (1971-)
Montana Sky '07
Clawed: The Legend of Sasquatch '05
Black Cloud '04
Ginger Snaps Back: The Beginning '04
Skins '02
American Outlaws '01
Grey Owl '99

Bernard Archard (1922-)
The Horror of Frankenstein '70
Village of the Damned '60

Anne Archer (1947-)
Ghosts of Girlfriends Past '09
Felon '08
End Game '06
Man of the House '05
November '05
The Iris Effect '04
Uncle Nino '03
The Art of War '00
Innocents '00
Rules of Engagement '00
Whispers: An Elephant's Tale '00 (V)
My Husband's Secret Life '98
Mojave Moon '96
Clear and Present Danger '94
The Man in the Attic '94
Question of Faith '93
Short Cuts '93
Body of Evidence '92
The Last of His Tribe '92
Nails '92
Patriot Games '92
Eminent Domain '91
Family Prayers '91
Narrow Margin '90
Love at Large '89
Fatal Attraction '87
Check Is in the Mail '85
Too Scared to Scream '85
The Naked Face '84
Waltz across Texas '83
Green Ice '81
Hero at Large '80
Raise the Titanic '80
Good Guys Wear Black '78
Paradise Alley '78
Lifeguard '76
Cancel My Reservation '72

John Archer (1915-99)
Blue Hawaii '62
City of Fear '59
Decision at Sundown '57
Santa Fe '51
Best of the Badmen '50
High Lonesome '50
Colorado Territory '49
White Heat '49
Crash Dive '43
Guadalcanal Diary '43
Hello, Frisco, Hello '43
Sherlock Holmes in Washington '43
Gangs, Inc. '41
King of the Zombies '41
Overland Stage Raiders '38

Leila Arcieri (1973-)
Mammoth '06
King's Ransom '05
Wild Things 2 '04

Fanny Ardant (1949-)
Hello Goodbye '08
Roman de Gare '07
The Secrets '07
Paris, je t'aime '06
Nathalie '03
Callas Forever '02
8 Women '02
Change My Life '01
No News from God '01
Balzac: A Life of Passion '99
Elizabeth '98
Pedale Douce '96
Ridicule '96
Beyond the Clouds '95
Sabrina '95
Colonel Chabert '94
Afraid of the Dark '92
The Family '87
Conseil de Famille '86
Melo '86
Love Unto Death '84
Next Summer '84
Swann in Love '84
Confidentially Yours '83
Life Is a Bed of Roses '83
The Woman Next Door '81

Eve Arden (1907-90)
Cinderella '84
Grease 2 '82
Pandemonium '82
Under the Rainbow '81
Grease '78
A Guide for the Married Woman '78
The Strongest Man in the World '75
Anatomy of a Murder '59
Our Miss Brooks '56
Phone Call from a Stranger '52
We're Not Married '52
Goodbye My Fancy '51
Tea for Two '50
Three Husbands '50
My Dream Is Yours '49
One Touch of Venus '48
Song of Scheherazade '47
Kid from Brooklyn '46
My Reputation '46
Night and Day '46
Mildred Pierce '45
Cover Girl '44
Manpower '41
That Uncertain Feeling '41
Whistling in the Dark '41
Ziegfeld Girl '41
Comrade X '40
No, No Nanette '40
Slightly Honorable '40
At the Circus '39
Eternally Yours '39
Having a Wonderful Time '38
Having Wonderful Time '38
Letter of Introduction '38
Stage Door '37
Dancing Lady '33

Robert Arden (1922-2004)
The Final Conflict '81
Mr. Arkadin '55

George Ardisson (1931-)
Hercules in the Haunted World '64
The Invaders '63

Pierre Arditti (1944-)
Private Fears in Public Places '06
The Count of Monte Cristo '99
Same Old Song '97
The Horseman on the Roof '95
Smoking/No Smoking '94
Melo '86
Love Unto Death '84
Life Is a Bed of Roses '83
Blaise Pascal '71

Rosita (Rosa) Arenas (1933-)
Neutron vs. the Death Robots '62
The Curse of the Crying Woman '61
Neutron and the Black Mask '61
Neutron vs. the Amazing Dr. Caronte '61
The Witch's Mirror '60
The Curse of the Aztec Mummy '59
The Robot vs. the Aztec Mummy '59
El Bruto '52

Lee Arenberg (1962-)
Pirates of the Caribbean: At World's End '07
Pirates of the Caribbean: Dead Man's Chest '06
Pirates of the Caribbean: The Curse of the Black Pearl '03
Dungeons and Dragons '00
The Cradle Will Rock '99
Waterworld '95
Bob Roberts '92
Brain Dead '89
Tapeheads '89

Geoffrey Arend (1978-)
(500) Days of Summer '09
Loveless in Los Angeles '07
The Ringer '05
It Runs in the Family '03

Eddi Arent (1925-)
Circus of Fear '67
The Trygon Factor '66
The Mysterious Magician '65
The Squeaker '65
Door with the Seven Locks '62
Dead Eyes of London '61
Forger of London '61

Joey Aresco
Circle of Fear '89
Primary Target '89

Niels Arestrup (1949-)
A Prophet '09
The Diving Bell and the Butterfly '07
The Beat My Heart Skipped '05
Meeting Venus '91
Sincerely Charlotte '86
Lumiere '76
Je Tu Il Elle '74

Robert Arevalo
The Siege of Firebase Gloria '89
The Ravagers '65

Asia Argento (1975-)
Mother of Tears '08
Boarding Gate '07
Marie Antoinette '06
George A. Romero's Land of the Dead '05
Last Days '05
The Heart Is Deceitful Above All Things '04
XXX '02
Scarlet Diva '00
The Church '98
New Rose Hotel '98
The Phantom of the Opera '98
B. Monkey '97
Traveling Companion '96
The Stendahl Syndrome '95
Queen Margot '94
Dario Argento's Trauma '93
Palombella Rossa '89
Demons 2 '87

Dario Argento (1940-)
Innocent Blood '92
The Bird with the Crystal Plumage '70

Fiore Argento (1970-)
Demons '86
Creepers '85

Carmen Argenziano (1943-)
Identity '03
Warm Blooded Killers '01
Andersonville '95
The Burning Season '94
Final Combination '93
Unlawful Entry '92
Red Scorpion '89
The Accused '88
Starchaser: The Legend of Orin '85 (V)
When a Stranger Calls '79
Death Force '78

Allison Argo (1953-)
A Cry from the Mountain '85
Return of Frank Cannon '80

Victor Argo (1934-2004)
Anything But Love '02
Angel Eyes '01
Don't Say a Word '01
Double Whammy '01
'R Xmas '01
Blue Moon '00
The Yards '00
Ghost Dog: The Way of the Samurai '99
Lulu on the Bridge '98
Next Stop, Wonderland '98
Blue in the Face '95
Smoke '95
Household Saints '93
True Romance '93
Bad Lieutenant '92
King of New York '90
Quick Change '90
The Pick-Up Artist '87
After Hours '85
Force Five '75
Mean Streets '73
Boxcar Bertha '72

David Argue (1959-)
Napoleon '96 (V)
Backlash '86
Razorback '84
BMX Bandits '83
Snow: The Movie '83
Gallipoli '81

Imanol Arias (1956-)
The Flower of My Secret '95
Intruso '93
Camila '84
Demons in the Garden '82
Labyrinth of Passion '82

Moises Arias
Hannah Montana: The Movie '09
Beethoven's Big Break '08
Nacho Libre '06

Yancey Arias (1971-)
Behind Enemy Lines 3: Colombia '08
Live Free or Die Hard '07
The Time Machine '02
Crossfire '98

Anna Aries
Invasion of the Bee Girls '73
Omega Man '71

Ineko Arima (1932-)
Equinox Flower '58
The Human Condition: No Greater Love '58

Ben Aris (1937-2003)
Tommy '75
If... '69
The Charge of the Light Brigade '68

Yareli Arizmendi
A Day Without a Mexican '04
Bloody Proof '99
The Big Green '95
Like Water for Chocolate '93

Adam Arkin (1956-)
A Serious Man '09
Graduation '07
Marilyn Hotchkiss' Ballroom Dancing & Charm School '06
Hitch '05
Kids in America '05
Stark Raving Mad '02
Off Season '01
Mission '00
Hanging Up '99
A Slight Case of Murder '99
Halloween: H20 '98
With Friends Like These '98
Not in This Town '97
The Doctor '91
Heat Wave '90
Necessary Parties '88
Fourth Wise Man '85
Pearl '78

Alan Arkin (1934-)
The Private Lives of Pippa Lee '09
Sunshine Cleaning '09
Get Smart '08
Marley & Me '08
Rendition '07
Firewall '06
Little Miss Sunshine '06
Raising Flagg '06
The Santa Clause 3: The Escape Clause '06
Eros '04
Noel '04
And Starring Pancho Villa as Himself '03
Thirteen Conversations About One Thing '01
Varian's War '01
Blood Money '99
Jakob the Liar '99
Slums of Beverly Hills '98
Four Days in September '97
Gattaca '97
Grosse Pointe Blank '97
Mother Night '96
Heck's Way Home '95
The Jerky Boys '95
Steal Big, Steal Little '95
Doomsday Gun '94
North '94
Cooperstown '93
Indian Summer '93
So I Married an Axe Murderer '93
Taking the Heat '93
Glengarry Glen Ross '92
The Rocketeer '91
Coupe de Ville '90
Edward Scissorhands '90
Havana '90
Necessary Parties '88
Escape from Sobibor '87
Big Trouble '86
Deadly Business '86
Bad Medicine '85
Fourth Wise Man '85
Joshua Then and Now '85
The Emperor's New Clothes '84
A Matter of Principle '83
Return of Captain Invincible '83
Improper Channels '82
The Last Unicorn '82 (V)
Chu Chu & the Philly Flash '81
Simon '80
The In-Laws '79
The Magician of Lublin '79
The Seven-Per-Cent Solution '76
Hearts of the West '75
Rafferty & the Gold Dust Twins '75
Freebie & the Bean '74
Last of the Red Hot Lovers '72
Little Murders '71
Catch-22 '70
Popi '69
The Heart Is a Lonely Hunter '68
Inspector Clouseau '68
Wait until Dark '67
Woman Times Seven '67
The Russians Are Coming, the Russians Are Coming '66

David Arkin (1941-90)
All the President's Men '76
Nashville '75
The Long Goodbye '73
M*A*S*H '70
I Love You, Alice B. Toklas! '68

Matthew Arkin
Raising Flagg '06
Second Best '05

Allen Arkus
A Matter of Honor '95
Brutal Fury '92

John Arledge
Campus Confessions '38
Shipmates Forever '35

Elizabeth Arlen (1964-)
In the Company of Spies '99
Separate Lives '94
The First Power '89
Lucky Stiff '88
The Whoopee Boys '86

Richard Arlen (1898-1976)
Hostile Guns '67
Road to Nashville '67
Apache Uprising '66
Johnny Reno '66
To the Shores of Hell '65
The Human Duplicators '64
Sex and the College Girl '64
Cavalry Command '63
The Crawling Hand '63
Warlock '59
Blonde Blackmailer '58
Hidden Guns '56
The Mountain '56
Return of Wildfire '48
Buffalo Bill Rides Again '47
Accomplice '46
Identity Unknown '45
That's My Baby! '44
Timber Queen '44
Wildcat '42
Flying Blind '41
Power Dive '41
Mutiny on the Blackhawk '39
Call of the Yukon '38
Murder in Greenwich Village '37
Let 'Em Have It '35
College Humor '33
Island of Lost Souls '32
Tiger Shark '32
Gun Smoke '31
Touchdown '31
The Light of Western Stars '30
The Sea God '30
The Virginian '29
Beggars of Life '28
Feel My Pulse '28
Wings '27
Behind the Front '26

Arletty (1898-1992)
The Longest Day '62
Portrait of an Assassin '49
Children of Paradise '44
Les Visiteurs du Soir '42
Le Jour Se Leve '39
Circonstances Attenuantes '36

Dimitra Arliss (1932-)
Eleni '85
Ski Bum '75
The Sting '73

George Arliss (1868-1946)
Dr. Syn '37
Transatlantic Tunnel '35
The Iron Duke '34
Disraeli '30

Jillian Armenante (1968-)
Prairie Fever '08
North Country '05

Delivered *'98*

Pedro Armendariz, Sr. (1912-63)
Captain Sinbad *'63*
From Russia with Love *'63*
Flor Silvestre *'58*
The Conqueror *'56*
Diane *'55*
The Littlest Outlaw *'54*
El Bruto *'52*
The Torch *'50*
Tulsa *'49*
Fort Apache *'48*
The Fugitive *'48*
The Pearl *'48*
Three Godfathers *'48*
Border River *'47*
Maria Candelaria *'46*

Pedro Armendariz, Jr. (1930-)
And Starring Pancho Villa as Himself *'03*
Once Upon a Time in Mexico *'03*
The Crime of Father Amaro *'02*
Original Sin *'01*
Esmeralda Comes by Night *'98*
The Mask of Zorro *'98*
Like A Bride *'94*
Tombstone *'93*
Old Gringo *'89*
La Chevre *'81*
A Home of Our Own *'75*
The Deadly Trackers *'73*
Don't Be Afraid of the Dark *'73*

Henry Armetta (1888-1945)
Colonel Effingham's Raid *'45*
Big Store *'41*
Fisherman's Wharf *'39*
Let's Sing Again *'36*
The Black Cat *'34*
The Cat and the Fiddle *'34*
The Merry Widow *'34*
What! No Beer? *'33*
Speak Easily *'32*
Street Angel *'28*

Armida (1911-89)
Jungle Goddess *'49*
Bad Men of the Border *'45*
Border Romance *'30*

Fred Armisen (1966-)
Confessions of a Shopaholic *'09*
Post Grad *'09*
The Promotion *'08*
The Rocker *'08*
The Ex *'07*
Tenacious D in the Pick of Destiny *'06*
Deuce Bigalow: European Gigolo *'05*
Anchorman: The Legend of Ron Burgundy *'04*
Eurotrip *'04*

Russell Arms (1922-)
By the Light of the Silvery Moon *'53*
Stage to Mesa City *'48*
Fighting Vigilantes *'47*
Captains of the Clouds *'42*

Alun Armstrong (1946-)
Filth *'08*
Little Dorrit *'08*
Eragon *'06*
Millions *'05*
Oliver Twist *'05*
Carrie's War *'04*
Van Helsing *'04*
It's All About Love *'03*
Harrison's Flowers *'02*
The Mummy Returns *'01*
Strictly Sinatra *'01*
Proof of Life *'00*
The Aristocrats *'99*
David Copperfield *'99*
Onegin *'99*
Sleepy Hollow *'99*
The Saint *'97*
Braveheart *'95*
An Awfully Big Adventure *'94*
Black Beauty *'94*
Split Second *'92*
White Hunter, Black Heart *'90*
Get Carter *'71*

Bess Armstrong (1953-)
Corporate Affairs *'07*
Diamond Men *'01*
Forever Love *'98*
Pecker *'98*
The Perfect Daughter *'96*
That Darn Cat *'96*
Dream Lover *'93*
The Skateboard Kid *'93*
Second Sight *'89*
Nothing in Common *'86*
High Road to China *'83*
Jaws 3 *'83*
Jekyll & Hyde... Together Again *'82*
The Four Seasons *'81*
Walking Through the Fire *'80*
How to Pick Up Girls *'78*

Curtis Armstrong (1953-)
Foreign Exchange *'08*
Route 30 *'08*
Moola *'07*
Shredderman Rules *'07*
Akeelah and the Bee *'06*
Southland Tales *'06*
Man of the House *'05*
Ray *'04*
Quigley *'03*
National Lampoon's Van Wilder *'02*
Gale Force *'01*
Elvis Meets Nixon *'98*
Safety Patrol *'98*
Big Bully *'95*
Revenge of the Nerds 4: Nerds in Love *'94*
The Adventures of Huck Finn *'93*
Revenge of the Nerds 3: The Next Generation *'92*
Revenge of the Nerds 2: Nerds in Paradise *'87*
One Crazy Summer *'86*
Bad Medicine *'85*
Better Off Dead *'85*
Revenge of the Nerds *'84*
Risky Business *'83*

Jack Armstrong (1958-)
Eden *'93*
Eden 2 *'93*
Eden 3 *'93*
Eden 4 *'93*

Katherine Armstrong
Ambition *'91*
Street Soldiers *'91*

Kerry Armstrong (1958-)
Lantana *'01*
Amy *'98*
The Hunting *'92*

Lee Armstrong (1970-)
Leprechaun 3 *'95*
Magic Island *'95*

Louis Armstrong (1900-71)
Hello, Dolly! *'69*
A Man Called Adam *'66*
Paris Blues *'61*
The Five Pennies *'59*
High Society *'56*
The Glenn Miller Story *'54*
Here Comes the Groom *'51*
New Orleans *'47*
Cabin in the Sky *'43*
Pennies from Heaven *'36*

Melinda Armstrong
Bikini Summer 2 *'92*
Bikini Summer *'91*

R.G. Armstrong (1917-)
Invasion of Privacy *'96*
Payback *'94*
Warlock: The Armageddon *'93*
Dick Tracy *'90*
Ghetto Blaster *'89*
Bulletproof *'88*
Predator *'87*
Children of the Corn *'84*
The Beast Within *'82*
Evilspeak *'82*
The Shadow Riders *'82*
Steel *'80*
Where the Buffalo Roam *'80*
Dear Detective *'78*
Devil Dog: The Hound of Hell *'78*
The Car *'77*
The Pack *'77*
Texas Detour *'77*
Dixie Dynamite *'76*
Race with the Devil *'75*
Boss *'74*
My Name Is Nobody *'74*
Reflections of Murder *'74*
Final Comedown *'72*
The Great Northfield Minnesota Raid *'72*
Angels Die Hard *'70*
The Great White Hope *'70*
El Dorado *'67*
Ride the High Country *'62*
The Fugitive Kind *'60*
No Name on the Bullet *'59*

R.L. Armstrong (1924-78)
Slumber Party '57 *'76*
The Hard Ride *'71*

Robert Armstrong (1890-1973)
Mighty Joe Young *'49*
The Fugitive *'48*
The Paleface *'48*
Fall Guy *'47*
Criminal Court *'46*
Decoy *'46*
G.I. War Brides *'46*
Blood on the Sun *'45*
Action in Arabia *'44*
Mr. Winkle Goes to War *'44*
Navy Way *'44*
The Kansan *'43*
The Mad Ghoul *'43*
Wings over the Pacific *'43*
Baby Face Morgan *'42*
Gang Busters *'42*
Dive Bomber *'41*
The Flying Irishman *'39*
The Girl Said No *'37*
Three Legionnaires *'37*
Ex-Mrs. Bradford *'36*
Without Orders *'36*
"G" Men *'35*
The Mystery Man *'35*
Palooka *'34*
Search for Beauty *'34*
King Kong *'33*
Son of Kong *'33*
Lost Squadron *'32*
The Most Dangerous Game *'32*
Panama Flo *'32*
Suicide Fleet *'31*
The Tip-Off *'31*
Be Yourself *'30*
Danger Lights *'30*
Big News *'29*
The Racketeer *'29*
A Girl in Every Port *'28*

Samaire Armstrong (1980-)
It's a Boy Girl Thing *'06*
Just My Luck *'06*
Stay Alive *'06*
Darkwolf *'03*

Todd Armstrong (1939-93)
Dead Heat on a Merry-Go-Round *'66*
King Rat *'65*
Jason and the Argonauts *'63*

John Arnatt (1917-99)
Crucible of Terror *'72*
A Challenge for Robin Hood *'68*
Second Best Secret Agent in the Whole Wide World *'65*

Desi Arnaz, Sr. (1917-86)
The Escape Artist *'82*
Forever Darling *'56*
The Long, Long Trailer *'54*
Holiday in Havana *'49*
Bataan *'43*
The Navy Comes Through *'42*
Four Jacks and a Jill *'41*
Too Many Girls *'40*

Desi Arnaz, Jr. (1953-)
The Mambo Kings *'92*
Fake Out *'82*
House of the Long Shadows *'82*
Great American Traffic Jam *'80*
How to Pick Up Girls *'78*
A Wedding *'78*
Joyride *'77*
Billy Two Hats *'74*
Marco *'73*
The Voyage of the Yes *'72*

Lucie Arnaz (1951-)
Down to You *'00*
Second Thoughts *'83*
Mating Season *'81*
Washington Mistress *'81*
The Jazz Singer *'80*
Death Scream *'75*
Who Is the Black Dahlia? *'75*

Adelheid Arndt (1952-)
Rosa Luxemburg *'86*
Chinese Boxes *'84*

Denis Arndt (1939-)
Behind Enemy Lines 2: Axis of Evil *'06*
Anacondas: The Hunt for the Blood Orchid *'04*
Sniper 3 *'04*
Undisputed *'02*
Asteroid *'97*
The Beast *'96*
Metro *'96*
Amelia Earhart: The Final Flight *'94*
Basic Instinct *'92*

Peter Arne (1920-83)
Victor/Victoria *'82*
Straw Dogs *'72*
The Oblong Box *'69*
Battle Beneath the Earth *'68*
Pirates of Blood River *'62*
The Hellfire Club *'61*
The Moonraker *'58*
Tarzan and the Lost Safari *'57*
The Atomic Man *'56*
Tarzan's Hidden Jungle *'55*

James Arness (1923-)
The Alamo: Thirteen Days to Glory *'87*
Gunsmoke: Return to Dodge *'87*
Alias Jesse James *'59*
Flame of the Islands *'55*
Many Rivers to Cross *'55*
Sea Chase *'55*
Them! *'54*
Hondo *'53*
Island in the Sky *'53*
Big Jim McLain *'52*
Hellgate *'52*
Horizons West *'52*
The Thing *'51*
Stars in My Crown *'50*
Two Lost Worlds *'50*
Wagon Master *'50*
Battleground *'49*
The Farmer's Daughter *'47*

Will Arnett (1970-)
Despicable Me *'10 (V)*
Jonah Hex *'10*
Brief Interviews With Hideous Men *'09*
G-Force *'09*
Monsters vs. Aliens *'09 (V)*
When in Rome *'09*
Dr. Seuss' Horton Hears a Who! *'08 (V)*
The Rocker *'08*
Semi-Pro *'08*
Blades of Glory *'07*
The Brothers Solomon *'07*
The Comebacks *'07*
Hot Rod *'07*
Ratatouille *'07 (V)*
The Great New Wonderful *'06*
Ice Age: The Meltdown *'06 (V)*
Let's Go to Prison *'06*
RV *'06*
Wristcutters: A Love Story *'06*
Monster-in-Law *'05*
Series 7: The Contenders *'01 (N)*
The Waiting Game *'99*

Jeanetta Arnette (1954-)
Snow Angels *'07*
Sniper 3 *'04*
The Shipping News *'01*
The '70s *'00*
Boys Don't Cry *'99*
Ladybugs *'92*
The Shadow Riders *'82*
Class Reunion Massacre *'77*

Stefan Arngrim (1955-)
Misbegotten *'98*
Class of 1984 *'82*
Fear No Evil *'80*
Getting Wasted *'80*

Alice Arno (1946-)
Female Vampire *'73*
The Perverse Countess *'73*

Edward Arnold (1890-1956)
The Ambassador's Daughter *'56*
City That Never Sleeps *'53*
Belles on Their Toes *'52*
Annie Get Your Gun *'50*
The Yellow Cab Man *'50*
Dear Wife *'49*
Take Me Out to the Ball Game *'49*
John Loves Mary *'48*
Three Daring Daughters *'48*
The Hucksters *'47*
Ziegfeld Follies *'46*
Weekend at the Waldorf *'45*
Mrs. Parkington *'44*
Johnny Eager *'42*
The Devil & Daniel Webster *'41*
Meet John Doe *'41*
Johnny Apollo *'40*
Lillian Russell *'40*
Slightly Honorable *'40*
Idiot's Delight *'39*
Let Freedom Ring *'39*
Man About Town *'39*
Mr. Smith Goes to Washington *'39*
You Can't Take It with You *'38*
Blossoms on Broadway *'37*
Easy Living *'37*
Toast of New York *'37*
Come and Get It *'36*
Crime and Punishment *'35*
Hide-Out *'34*
Sadie McKee *'34*
Thirty Day Princess *'34*
The Barbarian *'33*
I'm No Angel *'33*
Rasputin and the Empress *'33*
Roman Scandals *'33*

Jack Arnold (1916-92)
The Favor, the Watch, & the Very Big Fish *'92*
Into the Night *'85*
The Mummy's Tomb *'42*

Mal Arnold
Blood Feast *'63*
Scum of the Earth *'63*

Mark Arnold (1957-)
Threesome *'94*
Trancers 5: Sudden Deth *'94*
Trancers 4: Jack of Swords *'93*

Tichina Arnold (1971-)
Wild Hogs *'07*
Preaching to the Choir *'05*
Civil Brand *'02*
Little Shop of Horrors *'86*

Tom Arnold (1959-)
The Great Buck Howard *'09*
The Skeptic *'09*
A Christmas Proposal *'08*
Gardens of the Night *'08*
The Final Season *'07*
Palo Alto *'07*
Pride *'07*
Chasing Christmas *'05*
Happy Endings *'05*
The Kid and I *'05*
Mr. 3000 *'04*
Soul Plane *'04*
Cradle 2 the Grave *'03*
Children On Their Birthdays *'02*
Exit Wounds *'01*
Ablaze *'00*
Animal Factory *'00*
Bar Hopping *'00*
Lloyd *'00*
Shriek If You Know What I Did Last Friday the 13th *'00*
Blue Ridge Fall *'99*
Jackie's Back *'99*
Malicious Intent *'99*
National Lampoon's Golf Punks *'99*
Austin Powers: International Man of Mystery *'97*
McHale's Navy *'97*
Sink or Swim *'97*
Carpool *'96*
Touch *'96*
Big Bully *'95*
Nine Months *'95*
The Stupids *'95*
True Lies *'94*
Undercover Blues *'93*
The Woman Who Loved Elvis *'93*
Hero *'92*
Backfield in Motion *'91*
Freddy's Dead: The Final Nightmare *'91*

Victor Arnold (1936-)
The Yards *'00*
Shaft *'71*
The Incident *'67*

David Arnott (1976-)
The Last Man *'00*
Crisscross *'92*

Mark Arnott (1950-)
Not Quite Human 2 *'89*
Return of the Secaucus 7 *'80*

Francoise Arnoul (1931-)
After Sex *'97*
The Little Theatre of Jean Renoir *'71*
French Can-Can *'55*
Forbidden Fruit *'52*

Charles Arnt (1908-90)
Big Town *'47*
Big Town After Dark *'47*
Fall Guy *'47*
That Brennan Girl *'46*
Strange Illusion *'45*
Dangerous Passage *'44*
Gambler's Choice *'44*
The Great Gildersleeve *'43*
Twin Beds *'42*
It Happened in Hollywood *'37*

Michael J. Aronin (1944-)
Getting Even *'92*
Miami Cops *'89*
The Lone Runner *'88*

Judie Aronson (1964-)
Desert Kickboxer *'92*
The Sleeping Car *'90*
After Midnight *'89*
American Ninja *'85*
Friday the 13th, Part 4: The Final Chapter *'84*

Alexis Arquette (1969-)
Spun *'02*
The Trip *'02*
Cleopatra's Second Husband *'00*
She's All That *'99*
Bride of Chucky *'98*
Children of the Corn 5: Fields of Terror *'98*
Love Kills *'98*
I Think I Do *'97*
The Wedding Singer *'97*
Never Met Picasso *'96*
Sometimes They Come Back... Again *'96*
Things I Never Told You *'96*
Dead Weekend *'95*
Frisk *'95*
Wigstock: The Movie *'95*
Don't Do It *'94*
Frank and Jesse *'94*
Grief *'94*
Jack Be Nimble *'94*
Pulp Fiction *'94*
Threesome *'94*
The Ghost Brigade *'93*
Jumpin' at the Boneyard *'92*
Miracle Beach *'92*
Terminal Bliss *'91*
Down and Out in Beverly Hills *'86*

David Arquette (1971-)
Hamlet 2 *'08*
The Darwin Awards *'06*
The Tripper *'06*
The Adventures of Sharkboy and Lavagirl in 3-D *'05*
Never Die Alone *'04*
Riding the Bullet *'04*
Stealing Sinatra *'04*
2 Brothers & a Bride *'03*
Eight Legged Freaks *'02*
The Grey Zone *'01*
See Spot Run *'01*
3000 Miles to Graceland *'01*
Ready to Rumble *'00*
Scream 3 *'00*
Free Money *'99*
Muppets from Space *'99*
Never Been Kissed *'99*
Ravenous *'99*
The Alarmist *'98*
Dream with the Fishes *'97*
R.P.M. *'97*
Scream 2 *'97*
Beautiful Girls *'96*
johns *'96*
Larry McMurtry's Dead Man's Walk *'96*
Scream *'96*
Wild Bill *'95*
Airheads *'94*
At Home with the Webbers *'94*
Fall Time *'94*
Roadracers *'94*
The Ghost Brigade *'93*
Buffy the Vampire Slayer *'92*
Where the Day Takes You *'92*

Lewis Arquette (1935-2001)
Little Nicky *'00*
Ready to Rumble *'00*
Get a Clue! *'98*
Kiki's Delivery Service *'98* (V)
Almost Heroes *'97*
A River Made to Drown In *'97*
Scream 2 *'97*
Waiting for Guffman *'96*
Sleep with Me *'94*
Attack of the 50 Ft. Woman *'93*
The Linguini Incident *'92*
Book of Love *'91*
Rock 'n' Roll High School Forever *'91*
Syngenor *'90*
Tango and Cash *'89*
Nobody's Fool *'86*

Patricia Arquette (1968-)
Fast Food Nation *'06*
Holes *'03*
Tiptoes *'03*
The Badge *'02*
Human Nature *'02*
Little Nicky *'00*
Bringing Out the Dead *'99*
Goodbye, Lover *'99*
Stigmata *'99*
The Hi-Lo Country *'98*
Infinity *'96*
Lost Highway *'96*
Nightwatch *'96*
The Secret Agent *'96*
Beyond Rangoon *'95*
Flirting with Disaster *'95*
Ed Wood *'94*
Holy Matrimony *'94*
Inside Monkey Zetterland *'93*
True Romance *'93*
Ethan Frome *'92*
Trouble Bound *'92*
Dillinger *'91*
The Indian Runner *'91*
Prayer of the Rollerboys *'91*
Wildflower *'91*
Far North *'88*
A Nightmare on Elm Street 3: Dream Warriors *'87*
Pretty Smart *'87*

Richmond Arquette (1964-)
Made of Honor *'08*
The Tripper *'06*
Spent *'00*
Kiss & Tell *'99*
Sugar Town *'99*
The Treat *'98*
Love to Kill *'97*
Girls in Prison *'94*

Rosanna Arquette (1959-)
I-See-You.Com *'06*
Iowa *'05*
Kids in America *'05*
Dead Cool *'04*
Big Bad Love *'02*
Good Advice *'01*
Things Behind the Sun *'01*
The Whole Nine Yards *'00*
The '60s *'99*
Sugar Town *'99*
Voodoo Dawn *'99*
Hope Floats *'98*
I'm Losing You *'98*
Buffalo 66 *'97*
Deceiver *'97*
Gone Fishin' *'97*
Hell's Kitchen NYC *'97*
Trading Favors *'97*
Crash *'95*
Pulp Fiction *'94*
Search and Destroy *'94*
Nowhere to Run *'93*
The Wrong Man *'93*
Fathers and Sons *'92*
The Linguini Incident *'92*
Black Rainbow *'91*
In the Deep Woods *'91*
Son of the Morning Star *'91*
...Almost *'90*
Don't Hang Up *'90*
Flight of the Intruder *'90*
Sweet Revenge *'90*
New York Stories *'89*
The Big Blue *'88*
Promised a Miracle *'88*
Amazon Women on the Moon *'87*
Nobody's Fool *'86*
After Hours *'85*
The Aviator *'85*
Desperately Seeking Susan *'85*
8 Million Ways to Die *'85*
Silverado *'85*
One Cooks, the Other Doesn't *'83*
Baby It's You *'82*
The Executioner's Song *'82*
Johnny Belinda *'82*
Off the Wall *'82*
A Long Way Home *'81*
S.O.B. *'81*
Gorp *'80*
More American Graffiti *'79*
The Dark Secret of Harvest Home *'78*

Rod Arrants (1944-)
Vamping *'84*
A*P*E* *'76*

Jeri Arredondo
Four Sheets to the Wind *'07*
The Doe Boy *'01*
Color of a Brisk and Leaping Day *'95*
Tecumseh: The Last Warrior *'95*
Silent Tongue *'92*
Spirit of the Eagle *'90*

Lisa Arrindell
See Lisa Arrindell Anderson

Carlos Arruza (1920-66)
The Alamo *'60*
Torero *'56*

Antonin Artaud (1896-1948)
Passion of Joan of Arc *'28*
Napoleon *'27*

Gemma Arterton (1986-)
Prince of Persia: The Sands of Time *'10*
Lost in Austen *'08*
Quantum of Solace *'08*
Tess of the D'Urbervilles *'08*
St. Trinian's *'07*

Bea Arthur (1923-2009)
Enemies of Laughter *'00*
For Better or Worse *'95*
History of the World: Part 1 *'81*
Mame *'74*
Lovers and Other Strangers *'70*
How to Commit Marriage *'69*

George K. Arthur
Spring Fever *'27*
The Boob *'26*

Indus Arthur (1941-84)
M*A*S*H *'70*
Alvarez Kelly *'66*

Jean Arthur (1900-91)
Shane *'53*
A Foreign Affair *'48*
Lady Takes a Chance *'43*
The More the Merrier *'43*
Talk of the Town *'42*
The Devil & Miss Jones *'41*
Arizona *'40*
Too Many Husbands *'40*
Mr. Smith Goes to Washington *'39*
Only Angels Have Wings *'39*
You Can't Take It with You *'38*
Easy Living *'37*
History Is Made at Night *'37*
The Plainsman *'37*
Ex-Mrs. Bradford *'36*
If You Could Only Cook *'36*
Mr. Deeds Goes to Town *'36*
The Whole Town's Talking *'35*
Danger Lights *'30*
The Return of Dr. Fu Manchu *'30*
The Silver Horde *'30*
The Mysterious Dr. Fu Manchu *'29*

Johnny Arthur (1883-1951)
The Masked Marvel *'43*
The Road to Singapore *'40*
Danger on the Air *'38*
The Ghost Walks *'34*
The Monster *'25*

Maureen Arthur (1934-)
The Love Machine *'71*
The Love God? *'70*
How to Succeed in Business without Really Trying *'67*

Robert Arthur (1925-)
Naked Youth *'59*
Hellcats of the Navy *'57*
Belles on Their Toes *'52*
Just for You *'52*
The Ring *'52*
Ace in the Hole *'51*
September Affair *'50*
Twelve o'Clock High *'49*
Mother Wore Tights *'47*

Douglas Arthurs (1959-)
Act of War *'96*
Dead Ahead *'96*

Michael Artura
Apt Pupil *'97*
Money Train *'95*
Killer Looks *'94*
Kiss of Death *'94*
Amongst Friends *'93*

Lisa Arturo
Insanitarium *'08*
18 Fingers of Death *'05*

Tadanobu Asano (1973-)
Kabei: Our Mother *'08*
Mongol *'07*
Funky Forest: The First Contact *'06*
The Taste of Tea *'04*
Bright Future *'03*
Last Life in the Universe *'03*
Zatoichi *'03*
Electric Dragon 80,000V *'01*
Ichi the Killer *'01*
Party 7 *'00*
Taboo *'99*
Shark Skin Man and Peach Hip Girl *'98*
Maborosi *'95*

Ariane Ascaride (1954-)
My Life on Ice *'02*
The Town Is Quiet *'00*
The Adventures of Felix *'99*
Marius and Jeannette *'97*

Oscar Asche (1871-1936)
Don Quixote *'35*
The Private Secretary *'35*
Scrooge *'35*

Neus Asensi (1965-)
Arachnid *'01*
The Girl of Your Dreams *'99*

Leslie Ash (1960-)
Shadey *'87*
Murder: Ultimate Grounds for Divorce *'84*
Curse of the Pink Panther *'83*
Quadrophenia *'79*

William Ash (1977-)
Mad About Mambo *'00*
All the King's Men *'99*

Ashanti (1980-)
Resident Evil: Extinction *'07*
John Tucker Must Die *'06*
Coach Carter *'05*
The Muppets' Wizard of Oz *'05*

Jayne Ashbourne (1969-)
Prince of Poisoners: The Life and Crimes of William Palmer *'98*
Sharpe's Gold *'94*

Lorraine Ashbourne (1961-)
Fever Pitch *'96*
Distant Voices, Still Lives *'88*

Dana Ashbrook (1967-)
Sundown: The Vampire in Retreat *'08*
Python 2 *'02*
Angels Don't Sleep Here *'00*
Kisses in the Dark *'97*
Twin Peaks: Fire Walk with Me *'92*
Ghost Dad *'90*
Girlfriend from Hell *'89*
She's Out of Control *'89*
Return of the Living Dead 2 *'88*
Waxwork *'88*

Daphne Ashbrook (1966-)
The Love Letter *'98*
Doctor Who *'96*
Automatic *'94*
Murder So Sweet *'93*
Intruders *'92*
Sunset Heat *'92*
Quiet Cool *'86*

Linden Ashby (1960-)
Anacondas: Trail of Blood *'09*
Against the Dark *'08*
Impact Point *'08*
Resident Evil: Extinction *'07*
Wild Things 2 *'04*
A Woman Hunted *'03*
Sniper 2 *'02*
Facing the Enemy *'00*
Tick Tock *'00*
Where the Truth Lies *'99*
Murder She Purred: A Mrs. Murphy Mystery *'98*
Shelter *'98*
The Beneficiary *'97*
Blast *'96*
Cadillac Ranch *'96*
Wyatt Earp *'94*
The Perfect Bride *'91*

Peggy Ashcroft (1907-91)
The Heat of the Day *'91*
Madame Sousatzka *'88*
When the Wind Blows *'86* (V)
The Jewel in the Crown *'84*
A Passage to India *'84*
Hullabaloo over Georgie & Bonnie's Pictures *'78*
The Pedestrian *'73*
Sunday, Bloody Sunday *'71*
Secret Ceremony *'69*
The Nun's Story *'59*
Rhodes *'36*
The 39 Steps *'35*

Eve Brent Ashe
See Eve Brent

Jane Asher (1946-)
Death at a Funeral *'07*
The Choir *'95*
A Voyage 'Round My Father *'89*
Dreamchild *'85*
The Buttercup Chain *'70*
Deep End *'70*
Alfie *'66*
Masque of the Red Death *'65*
The Prince and the Pauper *'62*

Renee Asherson (1920-)
The Others *'01*
Grey Owl *'99*
Harnessing Peacocks *'92*
Edwin *'84*
Rasputin the Mad Monk *'66*
Henry V *'44*
Immortal Battalion *'44*

Ron Asheton (1948-)
Mosquito *'95*
Frostbiter: Wrath of the Wendigo *'94*

Kate Ashfield (1972-)
The Diary of Anne Frank *'08*
Secret Smile *'05*
Fakers *'04*
Shaun of the Dead *'04*
Beyond Borders *'03*
Pure *'02*
Do or Die *'01*
The Last Minute *'01*
The Low Down *'00*
The War Zone *'98*

Makoto Ashikawa
Ju-On 2 *'00*
Violent Cop *'89*

Lior Loui Ashkenazi
Hello Goodbye *'08*
Late Marriage *'01*

Edward Ashley (1904-2000)
Beyond the Next Mountain *'87*
Dick Tracy Meets Gruesome *'47*
Nocturne *'46*
The Black Swan *'42*
Bitter Sweet *'40*

Elizabeth Ashley (1939-)
The Cake Eaters *'07*
Happiness *'98*
Just the Ticket *'98*
The Buccaneers *'95*
Dangerous Curves *'88*
A Man of Passion *'88*
Vampire's Kiss *'88*
Dragnet *'87*
Stagecoach *'86*
Svengali *'83*
Paternity *'81*
Windows *'80*
Coma *'78*
Great Scout & Cathouse Thursday *'76*
One of My Wives Is Missing *'76*
War Between the Tates *'76*
Rancho Deluxe *'75*
Paperback Hero *'73*
Shattered Silence *'71*
Ship of Fools *'65*
The Carpetbaggers *'64*

Jennifer Ashley
Inseminoid *'80*
Tintorera... Tiger Shark *'78*
Pom Pom Girls *'76*
Barn of the Naked Dead *'73*
Hell on Wheels *'67*

John Ashley (1934-97)
Smoke in the Wind *'75*
Beyond Atlantis *'73*
Twilight People *'72*
Woman Hunt *'72*
Beast of the Yellow Night *'70*
Brides of the Beast *'68*
Mad Doctor of Blood Island *'68*
Hell on Wheels *'67*
Beach Blanket Bingo *'65*
The Eye Creatures *'65*
How to Stuff a Wild Bikini *'65*
Bikini Beach *'64*
Muscle Beach Party *'64*
Beach Party *'63*
Hud *'63*
High School Caesar *'60*
Frankenstein's Daughter *'58*
How to Make a Monster *'58*
Dragstrip Girl *'57*
Motorcycle Gang *'57*

Aaron Ashmore (1979-)
The Thaw *'09*
The Christmas Cottage *'08*
Palo Alto *'07*
The Stone Angel *'07*
Brave New Girl *'04*
Prom Queen *'04*
A Separate Peace *'04*
The Skulls 2 *'02*
My Husband's Double Life *'01*

Shawn Ashmore (1979-)
Frozen *'10*
The Ruins *'08*
X-Men: The Last Stand *'06*
The Quiet *'05*
Underclassman *'05*
X2: X-Men United *'03*
X-Men *'00*
Melanie Darrow *'97*
Guitarman *'95*

John Ashton (1948-)
Gone Baby Gone *'07*
Avalanche *'99*
Instinct *'99*
For Which He Stands *'98*
Meet the Deedles *'98*
Fast Money *'96*
Hidden Assassin *'94*
Little Big League *'94*

Trapped in Paradise *'94*
Stephen King's The Tommyknockers *'93*
Dirty Work *'92*
Love, Lies and Murder *'91*
L.A. Gangs Rising *'89*
Midnight Run *'88*
She's Having a Baby *'88*
Beverly Hills Cop 2 *'87*
Some Kind of Wonderful *'87*
The Deliberate Stranger *'86*
King Kong Lives *'86*
The Adventures of Buckaroo Banzai Across the Eighth Dimension *'84*
Beverly Hills Cop *'84*

Joseph Ashton (1986-)
The Education of Little Tree *'97*
Slappy and the Stinkers *'97*

Roger Ashton-Griffiths (1957-)
Gangs of New York *'02*
Princess of Thieves *'01*
Vanity Fair *'99*
Haunted Honeymoon *'86*

Tom Ashworth
Killer Tomatoes Eat France *'91*
Killer Tomatoes Strike Back *'90*

Desmond Askew (1972-)
The Hills Have Eyes *'06*
Turistas *'06*
Fabled *'02*
Repli-Kate *'01*
Go *'99*

Luke Askew (1937-)
The Greatest Game Ever Played *'05*
Frailty *'02*
Traveller *'96*
Dune Warriors *'91*
Back to Back *'90*
Kung Fu: The Movie *'86*
The Warrior & the Sorceress *'84*
Wanda Nevada *'79*
The Longest Drive *'76*
Posse *'75*
Slipstream *'73*
The Great Northfield Minnesota Raid *'72*
Angel Unchained *'70*
Easy Rider *'69*
The Devil's Brigade *'68*
The Green Berets *'68*
Cool Hand Luke *'67*

Arthur Askey
Bees in Paradise *'44*
The Ghost Train *'41*

Leon Askin (1907-2005)
Savage Island *'85*
Dr. Death, Seeker of Souls *'73*
Sherlock Holmes and the Deadly Necklace *'62*
Valley of the Kings *'54*
South Sea Woman *'53*

Robin Askwith (1950-)
Flesh and Blood Show *'73*
Horror Hospital *'73*
Hans Brinker *'69*

Gregoire Aslan (1908-82)
Golden Voyage of Sinbad *'73*
Moment to Moment *'66*
Paris When It Sizzles *'64*
Our Man in Havana *'59*
The Red Inn *'51*

Ed Asner (1929-)
Up *'09 (V)*
Gigantic *'08*
The Christmas Card *'06*
Elf *'03*
Missing Brendan *'03*
National Lampoon's Christmas Vacation 2: Cousin Eddie's Big Island Adventure *'03*
The Animal *'01*
Above Suspicion *'00*
Common Ground *'00*
Perfect Game *'00*
The Bachelor *'99*
Love and Action in Chicago *'99*
Armistead Maupin's More Tales of the City *'97*
Hard Rain *'97*
Gargoyles, The Movie: The Heroes Awaken *'94 (V)*
Gypsy *'93*
Happily Ever After *'93 (V)*
Heads *'93*
JFK *'91*
Silent Motive *'91*
Switched at Birth *'91*
A Friendship in Vienna *'88*
Moon over Parador *'88*
A Case of Libel *'83*
Daniel *'83*
O'Hara's Wife *'82*
Fort Apache, the Bronx *'81*
A Small Killing *'81*
The Family Man *'79*
The Gathering *'77*
Roots *'77*
Gus *'76*
The Life and Assassination of the Kingfish *'76*
Rich Man, Poor Man *'76*
Death Scream *'75*
The Wrestler *'73*
Haunts of the Very Rich *'72*
Skin Game *'71*
The Todd Killings *'71*
They Call Me Mr. Tibbs! *'70*
Change of Habit *'69*
El Dorado *'67*
The Doomsday Flight *'66*
Kid Galahad *'62*

Kumiko Aso (1978-)
Black House *'07*
Pulse *'01*
Ringu 0 *'01*
Dr. Akagi *'98*

Fred Asparagus (1947-98)
Just the Ticket *'98*
Colors *'88*

Armand Assante (1949-)
Breaking Point *'09*
The Chaos Experiment *'09*
The Line *'08*
The Man Who Came Back *'08*
Shark Swarm *'08*
American Gangster *'07*
Dead Lenny *'06*
Soul's Midnight *'06*
Confessions of a Pit Fighter *'05*
Dot.Kill *'05*
Mirror Wars: Reflection One *'05*
Two for the Money *'05*
Federal Protection *'02*
After the Storm *'01*
Last Run *'01*
On the Beach *'00*
The Road to El Dorado *'00 (V)*
The Hunley *'99*
Looking for an Echo *'99*
The Odyssey *'97*
Gotti *'96*
Striptease *'96*
Judge Dredd *'95*
Kidnapped *'95*
Blind Justice *'94*
Trial by Jury *'94*
Fatal Instinct *'93*
1492: Conquest of Paradise *'92*
Hoffa *'92*
The Mambo Kings *'92*
Fever *'91*
The Marrying Man *'91*
Eternity *'90*
Q & A *'90*
Animal Behavior *'89*
Passion in Paradise *'89*
Jack the Ripper *'88*
The Penitent *'88*
Hands of a Stranger *'87*
Belizaire the Cajun *'86*
Deadly Business *'86*
Unfaithfully Yours *'84*
Rage of Angels *'83*
I, the Jury *'82*
Little Darlings *'80*
Private Benjamin *'80*
Sophia Loren: Her Own Story *'80*
Prophecy *'79*
Lady of the House *'78*
Paradise Alley *'78*
The Lords of Flatbush *'74*

Pat Ast (1942-2001)
Reform School Girls *'86*
Heat *'72*

Fred Astaire (1899-1987)
That's Dancing! *'85*
Ghost Story *'81*
The Man in the Santa Claus Suit *'79*
Family Upside Down *'78*
The Purple Taxi *'77*
The Amazing Dobermans *'76*
That's Entertainment, Part 2 *'76 (N)*
That's Entertainment *'74*
The Towering Inferno *'74*
Finian's Rainbow *'68*
Paris When It Sizzles *'64*
The Notorious Landlady *'62*
On the Beach *'59*
Funny Face *'57*
Silk Stockings *'57*
Daddy Long Legs *'55*
The Band Wagon *'53*
The Belle of New York *'52*
Royal Wedding *'51*
Let's Dance *'50*
Three Little Words *'50*
The Barkleys of Broadway *'49*
Easter Parade *'48*
Blue Skies *'46*
Ziegfeld Follies *'46*
Yolanda and the Thief *'45*
The Sky's the Limit *'43*
Holiday Inn *'42*
You Were Never Lovelier *'42*
You'll Never Get Rich *'41*
Broadway Melody of 1940 *'40*
Second Chorus *'40*
The Story of Vernon and Irene Castle *'39*
Carefree *'38*
A Damsel in Distress *'37*
Shall We Dance *'37*
Follow the Fleet *'36*
Swing Time *'36*
Roberta *'35*
Top Hat *'35*
The Gay Divorcee *'34*
Dancing Lady *'33*
Flying Down to Rio *'33*

Nils Asther (1897-1981)
Son of Lassie *'45*
Bluebeard *'44*
Night Monster *'42*
Flying Blind *'41*
Make-Up *'37*
The Bitter Tea of General Yen *'33*
The Single Standard *'29*
Our Dancing Daughters *'28*
Wild Orchids *'28*

Adriana Asti (1933-)
Best of Youth *'03*
Caligula *'80*
The Sex Machine *'75*
Phantom of Liberty *'74*
Zorro *'74*
Before the Revolution *'65*
Accatone! *'61*

John Astin (1930-)
School of Life *'06*
The Frighteners *'96*
Huck and the King of Hearts *'93*
Silence of the Hams *'93*
Stepmonster *'92*
Killer Tomatoes Eat France *'91*
Gremlins 2: The New Batch *'90*
Killer Tomatoes Strike Back *'90*
Night Life *'90*
Return of the Killer Tomatoes! *'88*
Adventures Beyond Belief *'87*
Body Slam *'87*
Teen Wolf Too *'87*
National Lampoon's European Vacation *'85*
Halloween with the Addams Family *'79*
The Barcelona Kill *'77*
Freaky Friday *'76*
Only with Married Men *'74*
Brothers O'Toole *'73*
Get to Know Your Rabbit *'72*
Pepper and His Wacky Taxi *'72*
Evil Roy Slade *'71*
Viva Max *'69*
Candy *'68*
Move Over, Darling *'63*
The Wheeler Dealers *'63*
That Touch of Mink *'62*

MacKenzie Astin (1973-)
Military Intelligence and You! *'06*
Love's Enduring Promise *'04*
Off the Lip *'04*
How to Deal *'03*
Two Days *'03*
The Mating Habits of the Earthbound Human *'99*
Stranger than Fiction *'99*
The Last Days of Disco *'98*
Dream for an Insomniac *'96*
The Evening Star *'96*
In Love and War *'96*
Widow's Kiss *'94*
Wyatt Earp *'94*
Iron Will *'93*
The Garbage Pail Kids Movie *'87*

Sean Astin (1971-)
The Color of Magic *'08*
Forever Strong *'08*
Borderland *'07*
The Final Season *'07*
What Love Is *'07*
Click *'06*
Love and Debate *'06*
Marilyn Hotchkiss' Ballroom Dancing & Charm School *'06*
Bigger Than the Sky *'05*
Smile *'05*
Elvis Has Left the Building *'04*
50 First Dates *'04*
Lord of the Rings: The Return of the King *'03*
The Final Hit *'02*
Lord of the Rings: The Two Towers *'02*
Lord of the Rings: The Fellowship of the Ring *'01*
Deterrence *'00*
Bulworth *'98*
Dish Dogs *'98*
Courage Under Fire *'96*
Kurt Vonnegut's Harrison Bergeron *'95*
The Low Life *'95*
Safe Passage *'94*
Rudy *'93*
Encino Man *'92*
Where the Day Takes You *'92*
Toy Soldiers *'91*
Memphis Belle *'90*
The Willies *'90*
Staying Together *'89*
The War of the Roses *'89*
Like Father, Like Son *'87*
White Water Summer *'87*
The Goonies *'85*

John Aston
I Want to Go Home *'89*
Last Resort *'86*

Gertrude Astor (1887-1977)
After Midnight *'33*
Carnival Lady *'33*
They Never Come Back *'32*
Be Yourself *'30*
Dames Ahoy *'30*
The Cat and the Canary *'27*
The Cheerful Fraud *'27*
Strong Man *'26*
Beyond the Rocks *'22*

Mary Astor (1906-87)
Hush, Hush, Sweet Charlotte *'65*
Return to Peyton Place *'61*
This Happy Feeling *'58*
Any Number Can Play *'49*
Little Women *'49*
Act of Violence *'48*
Cass Timberlane *'47*
Cynthia *'47*
Meet Me in St. Louis *'44*
Thousands Cheer *'43*
Across the Pacific *'42*
The Palm Beach Story *'42*
The Great Lie *'41*
The Maltese Falcon *'41*
Brigham Young: Frontiersman *'40*
Midnight *'39*
Listen, Darling *'38*
The Hurricane *'37*
Prisoner of Zenda *'37*
Dodsworth *'36*
Lady from Nowhere *'36*
The Man with Two Faces *'34*
The Kennel Murder Case *'33*
The Little Giant *'33*
Lost Squadron *'32*
Red Dust *'32*
Behind Office Doors *'31*
Other Men's Women *'31*
The Royal Bed *'31*
Smart Woman *'31*
Don Juan *'26*
Don Q., Son of Zorro *'25*
Beau Brummel *'24*
The Fighting American *'24*
Mark of Zorro *'20*

Patti Astor
Assault of the Killer Bimbos *'88*
Underground U.S.A. *'84*
The Foreigner *'78*

Nancy Moore Atchison
The Yearling *'94*
Midnight Edition *'93*

Hooper Atchley (1887-1943)
Roarin' Lead *'37*
Prescott Kid *'36*
I Can't Escape *'34*
The Dude Bandit *'33*
Local Badman *'32*
Midnight Warning *'32*
Spirit of the West *'32*
Arizona Terror *'31*
Clearing the Range *'31*

Roscoe Ates (1892-1962)
Hills of Oklahoma *'50*
Thunder in the Pines *'49*
Black Hills *'48*
Check Your Guns *'48*
The Hawk of Powder River *'48*
The Tioga Kid *'48*
West to Glory *'47*
Wild Country *'47*
Colorado Serenade *'46*
Driftin' River *'46*
Wild West *'46*
Reg'lar Fellers *'41*
Robin Hood of the Pecos *'41*
Three Texas Steers *'39*
Woman in the Shadows *'34*
Cheyenne Kid *'33*
Lucky Devils *'33*
What! No Beer? *'33*
The Champ *'32*
Come on Danger! *'32*
Freaks *'32*
Cimarron *'31*
Politics *'31*

Ted Atherton
Max Payne *'08*
An Old-Fashioned Thanksgiving *'08*
XIII *'08*
The Company *'07*
The Stone Angel *'07*

William Atherton (1947-)
Aces 'n Eights *'08*
Ghouls *'07*
Towards Darkness *'07*
The Last Samurai *'03*
Headspace *'02*
Burning Down the House *'01*
Race to Space *'01*
The Crow: Salvation *'00*
Introducing Dorothy Dandridge *'99*
Executive Power *'98*
Mad City *'97*
Bio-Dome *'96*
Hoodlum *'96*
Broken Trust *'95*
Ravenhawk *'95*
Saints and Sinners *'95*
Frank and Jesse *'94*
The Pelican Brief *'93*
Chrome Soldiers *'92*
Buried Alive *'90*
Die Hard 2: Die Harder *'90*
A Fight for Jenny *'90*
Intrigue *'90*
Grim Prairie Tales *'89*
Die Hard *'88*
No Mercy *'86*
Real Genius *'85*
Ghostbusters *'84*
Tomorrow's Child *'82*
Centennial *'78*
Looking for Mr. Goodbar *'77*
The Day of the Locust *'75*
The Hindenburg *'75*
The Sugarland Express *'74*
Class of '44 *'73*

Harvey Atkin (1942-)
Critical Care *'97*
SnakeEater 2: The Drug Buster *'89*
Meatballs *'79*
War Between the Tates *'76*

Feodor Atkine (1948-)
Alexander *'04*
Angel of Death *'02*
Carnage *'02*
Vatel *'00*
Spy Games *'99*
Ronin *'98*
Doctor Chance *'97*
Sharpe's Revenge *'97*
Sharpe's Siege *'96*
Three Lives and Only One Death *'96*
High Heels *'91*
Sorceress *'88*
Pauline at the Beach *'83*
Le Beau Mariage *'82*
Le Choc *'82*

Christopher Atkins (1961-)
Quigley *'03*
Malicious Intent *'99*
Mutual Needs *'97*
Red Shoe Diaries: Four on the Floor *'96*
It's My Party *'95*
Project Shadowchaser 3000 *'95*
Bullet Down Under *'94*
Die Watching *'93*
Dracula Rising *'93*
Fatal Charm *'92*
Shoot *'92*
Wet and Wild Summer *'92*
King's Ransom *'91*
Mortuary Academy *'91*
Listen to Me *'89*
Shakma *'89*
Beaks: The Movie *'87*
Secret Weapons *'85*
A Night in Heaven *'83*
Pirate Movie *'82*
Child Bride of Short Creek *'81*

The Blue Lagoon '80

Dave Atkins

The Last Seduction 2 '98
Plunkett & Macleane '98
The Advocate '93
London Kills Me '91
Hellraiser '87
Personal Services '87
Prick Up Your Ears '87
Britannia Hospital '82
Bury Me an Angel '71

Eileen Atkins (1934-)

Robin Hood '10
Cranford '08
Last Chance Harvey '08
Ballet Shoes '07
Evening '07
Ask the Dust '06
Scenes of a Sexual Nature '06
Vanity Fair '04
Cold Mountain '03
What a Girl Wants '03
The Hours '02
Gosford Park '01
Wit '01
The Avengers '98
A Dance to the Music of Time '97
Jack and Sarah '95
Cold Comfort Farm '94
Wolf '94
The Lost Language of Cranes '92
Let Him Have It '91
The Vision '87
The Dresser '83
Oliver Twist '82
Smiley's People '82
I Don't Want to Be Born '75

Essence Atkins (1972-)

Dance Flick '09
Love and Other Four Letter Words '07
Deliver Us from Eva '03
How High '01
Love Song '00

Tom Atkins (1938-)

My Bloody Valentine 3D '09
Out of the Black '01
Bruiser '00
Bob Roberts '92
Two Evil Eyes '90
Dead Man Out '89
The Heist '89
Maniac Cop '88
Lethal Weapon '87
Blind Justice '86
Night of the Creeps '86
Desperate Lives '82
Halloween 3: Season of the Witch '82
Skeezer '82
Escape from New York '81
The Fog '78
Tarantulas: The Deadly Cargo '77
Special Delivery '76
The Detective '68

Beverly Hope Atkinson (1935-2001)

Uforia '81
Heavy Traffic '73

Frank Atkinson (1893-1963)

Pygmalion '38
The Green Cockatoo '37
Young and Innocent '37

Jayne Atkinson (1959-)

12 and Holding '05
The Village '04
Our Town '03
Free Willy 2: The Adventure Home '95
Free Willy '93
Capone '89

Rowan Atkinson (1955-)

Mr. Bean's Holiday '07
Keeping Mum '05
Johnny English '03
Love Actually '03
Scooby-Doo '02
Rat Race '01
Maybe Baby '99
Bean '97
Four Weddings and a Funeral '94
The Lion King '94 (V)
Hot Shots! Part Deux '93
Bernard and the Genie '91
The Witches '90
The Tall Guy '89
Never Say Never Again '83

Yvan Attal (1965-)

Rush Hour 3 '07
The Interpreter '05
Munich '05
Happily Ever After '04
Bon Voyage '03
And Now Ladies and Gentlemen '02
My Wife is an Actress '01
The Criminal '00
Love, etc. '96
Portraits Chinois '96

Dave Attell (1965-)

Scary Movie 4 '06
Pootie Tang '01

Richard Attenborough (1923-)

Jack and the Beanstalk: The Real Story '01
Joseph and the Amazing Technicolor Dreamcoat '00
The Railway Children '00
Elizabeth '98
The Lost World: Jurassic Park 2 '97
Hamlet '96
Wavelength '96
Miracle on 34th Street '94
Jurassic Park '93
The Human Factor '79
Brannigan '75
Conduct Unbecoming '75
Rosebud '75
Ten Little Indians '75
10 Rillington Place '71
David Copperfield '70
Loot.. Give Me Money, Honey! '70
The Magic Christian '69
The Bliss of Mrs. Blossom '68
Doctor Dolittle '67
The Sand Pebbles '66
The Flight of the Phoenix '65
Guns at Batasi '64
Seance on a Wet Afternoon '64
The Great Escape '63
Only Two Can Play '62
Trial & Error '62
The League of Gentlemen '60
S.O.S. Pacific '60
Sea of Sand '58
Brothers in Law '57
The Scamp '57
The Baby and the Battleship '56
The Gift Horse '52
Morning Departure '50
The Guinea Pig '48
Brighton Rock '47
Stairway to Heaven '46
In Which We Serve '43

Malcolm Atterbury (1907-92)

Emperor of the North Pole '73
How to Make a Monster '58
Blood of Dracula '57
Crime of Passion '57
I Was a Teenage Werewolf '57

Edward Atterton (1962-)

Carolina '03
Children of Dune '03
Mists of Avalon '01
Brittanic '00
Britannic '99
Relative Values '99
The Man in the Iron Mask '98
Catherine Cookson's The Wingless Bird '97
The Hunchback '97
Far Harbor '96
The Vacillations of Poppy Carew '94

Michael Attwell (1943-)

Poldark '96
Joseph '95

Barry Atwater (1918-78)

The Night Stalker '71
Night Gallery '69
Pork Chop Hill '59

Edith Atwater (1911-86)

Family Plot '76
Die Sister, Die! '74
Our Time '74
The Love Machine '71
True Grit '69
Strait-Jacket '64
It Happened at the World's Fair '63
The Body Snatcher '45

Hayley Atwell

The Prisoner '09
Brideshead Revisited '08
The Duchess '08
Cassandra's Dream '07
How About You '07
Mansfield Park '07
The Shadow in the North '07
The Line of Beauty '06
Ruby in the Smoke '06

Lionel Atwill (1885-1946)

Fog Island '45
House of Dracula '45
Lost City of the Jungle '45
Captain America '44
House of Frankenstein '44
Lady in the Death House '44
Raiders of Ghost City '44
Cairo '42
Frankenstein Meets the Wolfman '42
The Ghost of Frankenstein '42
Junior G-Men of the Air '42
Night Monster '42
Pardon My Sarong '42
Sherlock Holmes and the Secret Weapon '42
The Strange Case of Dr. Rx '42
To Be or Not to Be '42
Man Made Monster '41
Boom Town '40
Charlie Chan's Murder Cruise '40
Johnny Apollo '40
Balalaika '39
The Gorilla '39
The Hound of the Baskervilles '39
Mr. Moto Takes a Vacation '39
Mr. Takes a Vacation '39
The Secret of Dr. Kildare '39
Son of Frankenstein '39
The Three Musketeers '39
The Great Waltz '38
Three Comrades '38
The Great Garrick '37
High Command '37
The Wrong Road '37
Captain Blood '35
The Devil Is a Woman '35
Mark of the Vampire '35
Beggars in Ermine '34
Murders in the Zoo '33
Mystery of the Wax Museum '33
The Song of Songs '33
The Sphinx '33
Doctor X '32
The Vampire Bat '32

Anat Atzmon (1958-)

Double Edge '92
Every Time We Say Goodbye '86
Dead End Street '83
Shell Shock '63

Robert Atzorn (1945-)

The Wannsee Conference '84
From the Life of the Marionettes '80

Brigitte Auber (1928-)

To Catch a Thief '55
Femmes de Paris '53
Rendez-vous de Juillet '49

Rene Auberjonois (1940-)

Eulogy '04
Burning Down the House '01
Gepetto '00
The Patriot '00
Sally Hemings: An American Scandal '00
We All Fall Down '00
Inspector Gadget '99
Cats Don't Dance '97 (V)
Los Locos Posse '97
Batman Forever '95
The Ballad of Little Jo '93
Lone Justice '93
Little Nemo: Adventures in Slumberland '92 (V)
The Lost Language of Cranes '92
The Player '92
Wildcard '92
The Feud '90
Once Upon a Midnight Scary '90
A Connecticut Yankee in King Arthur's Court '89
Gore Vidal's Billy the Kid '89
The Little Mermaid '89 (V)
My Best Friend Is a Vampire '88
Police Academy 5: Assignment Miami Beach '88
Walker '87
A Smoky Mountain Christmas '86
3:15—The Moment of Truth '86
Where the Buffalo Roam '80
Wild, Wild West Revisited '79
The Dark Secret of Harvest Home '78
Eyes of Laura Mars '78
The Big Bus '76
King Kong '76
Images '72
Pete 'n' Tillie '72
McCabe & Mrs. Miller '71
Brewster McCloud '70
M*A*S*H '70
Petulia '68
Lilith '64

K.D. Aubert (1978-)

In the Mix '05
Frankenfish '04
Soul Plane '04
Friday After Next '02

Lenore Aubert (1913-93)

Abbott and Costello Meet the Killer, Boris Karloff '49
Abbott and Costello Meet Frankenstein '48
Having Wonderful Crime '45
Action in Arabia '44

James Aubrey (1947-)

Buddy's Song '91
Riders of the Storm '88
Forever Young '85
Home Before Midnight '84
The Hunger '83
The Terror '79
Bouquet of Barbed Wire '76
Lord of the Flies '63

Jimmy Aubrey (1887-1983)

The Drifter '44
Wild Horse Valley '40
Legion of Missing Men '37
Aces and Eights '36
Fast Bullets '36
Stormy Trails '36
Courage of the North '35
Go-Get-'Em-Haines '35

Juliet Aubrey (1969-)

The Constant Gardener '05
The Mayor of Casterbridge '03
Iris '01
Extremely Dangerous '99
Still Crazy '98
The Unknown Soldier '98
Welcome to Sarajevo '97
Catherine Cookson's The Moth '96
Go Now '96
Jacob '94
Middlemarch '93

Cecile Aubry

The Black Rose '50
Manon '50

Danielle Aubry

Operation C.I.A. '65
Bikini Beach '64

Jacques Aubuchon (1924-91)

Thunder Road '58
Gun Glory '57

Michel Auclair (1922-88)

Swashbuckler '84
The Story of a Love Story '73
Murder at 45 R.P.M. '65
Manon '50
Beauty and the Beast '46

Maxine Audley (1923-92)

Frankenstein Must Be Destroyed '69
Peeping Tom '60
The Trials of Oscar Wilde '60
A King in New York '57

Stephane Audran (1932-)

The Girl From Monaco '08
Madeline '98
Maximum Risk '96
Son of Gascogne '95
Betty '92
The Turn of the Screw '92
Quiet Days in Clichy '90
Sons '89
Faceless '88
Babette's Feast '87
Poor Little Rich Girl: The Barbara Hutton Story '87
La Cage aux Folles 3: The Wedding '86
Cop Au Vin '85
The Blood of Others '84
Le Choc '82
Brideshead Revisited '81
Coup de Torchon '81
The Big Red One '80
Eagle's Wing '79
Silver Bears '78
Violette '78
Blood Relatives '77
Twist '76
Vincent, Francois, Paul and the Others '76
Black Bird '75
Ten Little Indians '75
Wedding in Blood '74
The Discreet Charm of the Bourgeoisie '72
Just Before Nightfall '71
La Rupture '70
La Femme Infidele '69
Le Boucher '69
Les Biches '68
Six in Paris '68
Bluebeard '63
Les Bonnes Femmes '60
The Cousins '59

Mischa Auer (1905-67)

Arrivederci, Baby! '66
The Christmas That Almost Wasn't '66
Sputnik '61
Mr. Arkadin '55
And Then There Were None '45
Brewster's Millions '45
Around the World '43
Twin Beds '42
Cracked Nuts '41
The Flame of New Orleans '41
Hold That Ghost '41
Seven Sinners '40
Spring Parade '40
Destry Rides Again '39
East Side of Heaven '39
The Rage of Paris '38
Service De Luxe '38
Sweethearts '38
You Can't Take It with You '38
100 Men and a Girl '37
Pick a Star '37
Vogues of 1938 '37
The Gay Desperado '36
My Man Godfrey '36
The Princess Comes Across '36
That Girl from Paris '36
Three Smart Girls '36
Condemned to Live '35
The Crusades '35
I Dream Too Much '35
The Lives of a Bengal Lancer '35
Sucker Money '34
Flaming Signal '33
Woman Condemned '33
The Monster Walks '32
Drums of Jeopardy '31
Inside the Lines '30

Claudine Auger (1942-)

Secret Places '85
Lobster for Breakfast '82
The Associate '79
Ricco '74
The Black Belly of the Tarantula '71
Head of the Family '71
Twitch of the Death Nerve '71
The Killing Game '67
Triple Cross '67
Thunderball '65

Lance August (1961-)

Stripteaser '95
Terror Eyes '87

Pernilla August (1958-)

Star Wars: Episode 2—Attack of the Clones '02
Mary, Mother of Jesus '99
Star Wars: Episode 1—The Phantom Menace '99
Private Confessions '98
Jerusalem '96
The Best Intentions '92

Robert August (1945-)

The Endless Summer 2 '94
The Endless Summer '66

Sherman Augustus (1959-)

The Foreigner '03
ZigZag '02
Virus '98
Colors '88

Ewa Aulin (1949-)

The Legend of Blood Castle '72
Start the Revolution without Me '70
Candy '68

Jean-Pierre Aumont (1913-2001)

The Proprietor '96
Jefferson in Paris '94
Becoming Colette '92
A Tale of Two Cities '89
Windmills of the Gods '88
Sweet Country '87
The Blood of Others '84
Nana '82
Don't Look in the Attic '81
A Time for Miracles '80
Something Short of Paradise '79
Blackout '78
Cat and Mouse '78
Catherine & Co. '76
The Happy Hooker '75
Mahogany '75

Henry V '44
Mr. Emmanuel '44
The Demi-Paradise '43
Thursday's Child '43
The Girl in the News '41
Spellbound '41
Night Train to Munich '40
The Case of the Frightened Lady '39
Action for Slander '38
Dreaming Lips '37
As You Like It '36
Nine Days a Queen '36
The Shadow '36
The Evil Mind '34
The Iron Duke '34

John Aylward (1946-)

Down With Love '03
Path to War '02
Just Visiting '01
Instinct '99
From the Earth to the Moon '98
Three Fugitives '89

Agnes Ayres (1898-1940)

Son of the Sheik '26
Affairs of Anatol '21
The Sheik '21

Fraser Ayres

Wide Sargasso Sea '06
Intimacy '00

Leah Ayres (1957-)

Bloodsport '88
Eddie Macon's Run '83
The Burning '82

Lew Ayres

Ice Follies of 1939 '39
Murder With Pictures '36

Lew Ayres (1908-96)

Cast the First Stone '89
Of Mice and Men '81
Salem's Lot '79
Damien: Omen 2 '78
End of the World '76
Francis Gary Powers: The True Story of the U-2 Spy '76
Battle for the Planet of the Apes '73
The Stranger '73
Earth II '71
The Carpetbaggers '64
Advise and Consent '62
Donovan's Brain '53
The Capture '50
Johnny Belinda '48
Dark Mirror '46
Dr. Kildare's Strange Case '40
Broadway Serenade '39
The Secret of Dr. Kildare '39
Holiday '38
All Quiet on the Western Front '30
Big News '29
The Kiss '29

Robert Ayres (1914-68)

Battle Beneath the Earth '68
Cat Girl '57
Time Lock '57
River Beat '54

Rosalind Ayres (1946-)

Christmas in the Clouds '01
Beautiful People '99
Gods and Monsters '98
The Slipper and the Rose '76
That'll Be the Day '73

Rochelle Aytes (1976-)

Madea's Family Reunion '06
White Chicks '04

Lubna Azabal

Paradise Now '05
Changing Times '04
Almost Peaceful '02

Hank Azaria (1964-)

Night at the Museum: Battle of the Smithsonian '09
Year One '09
Chicago 10 '07 (V)
Run, Fatboy, Run '07
The Simpsons Movie '07 (V)
Along Came Polly '04
Dodgeball: A True Underdog Story '04
Eulogy '04
Shattered Glass '03
Bark! '02
America's Sweethearts '01
Uprising '01
Fail Safe '00
The Cradle Will Rock '99
Mystery, Alaska '99
Mystery Men '99
Tuesdays with Morrie '99
Celebrity '98
Godzilla '98
Anastasia '97 (V)
Great Expectations '97
Grosse Pointe Blank '97
Homegrown '97
The Birdcage '95
Heat '95
Quiz Show '94
Cool Blue '88

Sabine Azema (1955-)

La Buche '00
Same Old Song '97
Le Bonheur Est Dans le Pre '95
Smoking/No Smoking '94
Life and Nothing But '89
Melo '86
Love Unto Death '84
A Sunday in the Country '84
Life Is a Bed of Roses '83

Ayu Azhari (1970-)

Without Mercy '95
Diamond Run '90

Tony Azito (1949-95)

Bloodhounds of Broadway '89
Chattanooga Choo Choo '84
Private Resort '84
Union City '81

Anthony Azizi

Eagle Eye '08
American East '07

Shabana Azmi (1948-)

Fire '96
In Custody '94
Son of the Pink Panther '93
City of Joy '92
The Bengali Night '88
Madame Sousatzka '88

Charles Aznavour (1924-)

Ararat '02
The Truth About Charlie '02
Edith & Marcel '83
The Tin Drum '79
Sky Riders '76
Twist '76
Ten Little Indians '75
Blockhouse '73
The Adventurers '70
Carbon Copy '69
Candy '68
Shoot the Piano Player '62
The Testament of Orpheus '59

Eloy Azorin (1977-)

Warriors '02
Mad Love '01
All About My Mother '99

Candice Azzara (1945-)

In Her Shoes '05
Doin' Time on Planet Earth '88
Easy Money '83
Fatso '80
House Calls '78

Lisa B

See Lisa Barbuscia

B-Real

See Louis Freese

Karin Baal (1940-)

Berlin Alexanderplatz '80
Dead Eyes of London '61
Teenage Wolfpack '57

Obba Babatunde (1951-)

Black Dynamite '09
Cover '08
The Eye '08
The Celestine Prophecy '06
Material Girls '06
After the Sunset '04
The Manchurian Candidate '04
John Q '02
Redeemer '02
The Wild Thornberrys Movie '02 (V)
How High '01
The Visit '00
Introducing Dorothy Dandridge '99
Life '99
Apartment Complex '98
The Temptations '98
Miss Evers' Boys '97
Multiplicity '96
Soul of the Game '96
That Thing You Do! '96
A Reason to Believe '95
Philadelphia '93
Undercover Blues '93
The Silence of the Lambs '91
Miami Blues '90
God Bless the Child '88

Barbara Babcock (1937-)

Space Cowboys '00
Far and Away '92
Happy Together '89
The Heart of Dixie '89
News at Eleven '86
Quarterback Princess '85
That Was Then... This Is Now '85
The Lords of Discipline '83
The Black Marble '79
On the Edge: The Survival of Dana '79
The Christmas Coal Mine Miracle '77

Fabienne Babe (1962-)

La Vie Promise '02
Les Voleurs '96
Singing the Blues in Red '87

Lauren Bacall (1924-)

The Walker '07
These Foolish Things '06
Manderlay '05
Birth '04
Howl's Moving Castle '04 (V)
Dogville '03
Gone Dark '03
Diamonds '99
The Mirror Has Two Faces '96
My Fellow Americans '96
From the Mixed-Up Files of Mrs. Basil E. Frankweiler '95
Ready to Wear '94
A Foreign Field '93
The Portrait '93
All I Want for Christmas '91
Innocent Victim '90
Misery '90
Dinner at Eight '89
Appointment with Death '88
Mr. North '88
The Fan '81
The Shootist '76
Murder on the Orient Express '74
Harper '66
Sex and the Single Girl '64
Flame Over India '60
Designing Woman '57
Written on the Wind '56
Blood Alley '55
The Cobweb '55
A Woman's World '54
How to Marry a Millionaire '53
Bright Leaf '50
Young Man with a Horn '50
Key Largo '48
Dark Passage '47
The Big Sleep '46
To Have & Have Not '44

Michael Bacall

Inglourious Basterds '09
Death Proof '07
Manic '01
Urban Legends 2: Final Cut '00
Wait until Spring, Bandini '90

Salvatore Baccaloni (1900-69)

Rock-A-Bye Baby '57
Full of Life '56

Morena Baccarin

Stargate: The Ark of Truth '08
Serenity '05

Barbara Bach (1947-)

Give My Regards to Broad Street '84
Princess Daisy '83
Caveman '81
The Great Alligator '81
Screamers '80
The Unseen '80
Up the Academy '80
Jaguar Lives '79
Force 10 from Navarone '78
The Spy Who Loved Me '77
The Legend of Sea Wolf '75
Stateline Motel '75
Street Law '74
The Black Belly of the Tarantula '71
Short Night of Glass Dolls '71

Catherine Bach (1954-)

The Nutt House '95
Rage and Honor '92
The Masters of Menace '90
Street Justice '89
Criminal Act '88
Driving Force '88
Cannonball Run 2 '84
Strange New World '75
Nicole '72

John Bach (1946-)

Kidnapped '05
Ike: Countdown to D-Day '04
Crimebroker '93
The Sound and the Silence '93
Iris '89
The Lost Tribe '89
Georgia '87
Wild Horses '82

Dian Bachar (1971-)

The Life of Lucky Cucumber '08
The Adventures of Rocky & Bullwinkle '00
BASEketball '98
Orgazmo '98

Burt Bacharach (1928-)

Austin Powers In Goldmember '02
Austin Powers 2: The Spy Who Shagged Me '99

Stephanie Bachelor (1912-96)

Springtime in the Sierras '47
G.I. War Brides '46
The Undercover Woman '46

Alicja Bachleda-Curus

Trade '07
Stealth '06

Hans Bachman

Invader '91
Star Quest '89

Steve Bacic (1965-)

Afghan Knights '07
The Tooth Fairy '06
Encrypt '03
Firefight '03
Threshold '03
Ballistic: Ecks vs. Sever '02
The 6th Day '00
Bounty Hunters 2: Hardball '97

George Back

The Comebacks '07
Sam & Janet '02

Brian Backer (1956-)

The Money Pit '86
Moving Violations '85
Talk to Me '84
The Burning '82
Fast Times at Ridgemont High '82

Jim Backus (1913-89)

Slapstick of Another Kind '84
Angel's Brigade '79
C.H.O.M.P.S. '79
The Rebels '79
Rescue from Gilligan's Island '78
Pete's Dragon '77
Crazy Mama '75
Now You See Him, Now You Don't '72
Myra Breckinridge '70
Hello Down There '69
Where Were You When the Lights Went Out? '68
Billie '65
Critic's Choice '63
It's a Mad, Mad, Mad, Mad World '63
Operation Bikini '63
Sunday in New York '63
The Wheeler Dealers '63
The Horizontal Lieutenant '62
The Wonderful World of the Brothers Grimm '62
Zotz! '62
Ice Palace '60
Ask Any Girl '59
1001 Arabian Nights '59 (V)
Man of a Thousand Faces '57
The Pied Piper of Hamelin '57
Top Secret Affair '57
Meet Me in Las Vegas '56
Naked Hills '56
Francis in the Navy '55
Rebel without a Cause '55
Above and Beyond '53
I Love Melvin '53
Don't Bother to Knock '52
Here Come the Nelsons '52
Pat and Mike '52
His Kind of Woman '51
I Want You '51
I'll See You in My Dreams '51
Father Was a Fullback '49
The Great Lover '49

Olga Baclanova (1899-1974)

Freaks '32
Docks of New York '28
The Man Who Laughs '27

Irving Bacon (1893-1965)

Ma and Pa Kettle at Home '54
Cause for Alarm '51
Dynamite '49
The Green Promise '49
Monsieur Verdoux '47
Footlight Glamour '43
It's a Great Life '43
Two Weeks to Live '43
The Bashful Bachelor '42
Blondie for Victory '42
Blondie Goes Latin '42
Blondie's Blessed Event '42
Caught in the Draft '41
Western Union '41
Blondie Has Trouble '40
Blondie On a Budget '40
Blondie Plays Cupid '40
Dreaming Out Loud '40
The Howards of Virginia '40
Blondie Brings Up Baby '39
Blondie Meets the Boss '39
Blondie Takes a Vacation '39
Internes Can't Take Money '37
Branded Men '31

Kevin Bacon (1958-)

My One and Only '09
Taking Chance '09
Frost/Nixon '08
The Air I Breathe '07
Death Sentence '07
Rails & Ties '07
Beauty Shop '05
Loverboy '05
Where the Truth Lies '05
The Woodsman '04
In the Cut '03
Mystic River '03
Trapped '02
Novocaine '01
Hollow Man '00
My Dog Skip '99
Stir of Echoes '99
Digging to China '98
Wild Things '98
Picture Perfect '96
Sleepers '96
Telling Lies in America '96
Apollo 13 '95
Balto '95 (V)
Murder in the First '95
The Air Up There '94
The River Wild '94
A Few Good Men '92
He Said, She Said '91
JFK '91
Pyrates '91
Queens Logic '91
Flatliners '90
The Big Picture '89
Criminal Law '89
Tremors '89
End of the Line '88
She's Having a Baby '88
Planes, Trains & Automobiles '87
White Water Summer '87
Quicksilver '86
Footloose '84
Enormous Changes '83
Trumps '83
Diner '82
Only When I Laugh '81
Friday the 13th '80
Hero at Large '80
Starting Over '79
National Lampoon's Animal House '78

Lloyd Bacon (1890-1955)

Wagon Tracks '19
Charlie Chaplin ... Our Hero! '15

Max Bacon

Privilege '67
Bees in Paradise '44

Jean-Pierre Bacri (1951-)

Look at Me '04
The Housekeeper '02
The Taste of Others '00
Place Vendome '98
Same Old Song '97
Un Air de Famille '96
Entre-Nous '83

Marco Bacuzzi

Borderland '07
Species 4: The Awakening '07

Angelo Badalamenti (1937-)

Mulholland Drive '01
Blue Velvet '86

Michael Badalucco (1954-)

Bewitched '05
2B Perfectly Honest '04
13 Moons '02
The Man Who Wasn't There '01
O Brother Where Art Thou? '00
Summer of Sam '99
You've Got Mail '98
Love Walked In '97
The Search for One-Eye Jimmy '96
Blue in the Face '95
The Sunshine Boys '95

Two If by Sea *'95*
The Professional *'94*
Mac *'93*
Night and the City *'92*
Jungle Fever *'91*

Hermione Baddeley (1906-86)
The Aristocats *'70 (V)*
Do Not Disturb *'65*
Marriage on the Rocks *'65*
Mary Poppins *'64*
The Unsinkable Molly Brown *'64*
Let's Get Married *'60*
Room at the Top *'59*
The Pickwick Papers *'54*
The Belles of St. Trinian's *'53*
Cosh Boy *'52*
A Christmas Carol *'51*
The Woman in Question *'50*
Passport to Pimlico *'49*
Brighton Rock *'47*

Alan Badel (1923-82)
Nijinsky *'80*
The Riddle of the Sands *'79*
The Medusa Touch *'78*
Luther *'74*
The Day of the Jackal *'73*
The Adventurers *'70*
Arabesque *'66*
Children of the Damned *'63*
This Sporting Life *'63*
Three Cases of Murder *'55*

Sarah Badel (1943-)
Just Visiting *'01*
Cotton Mary *'99*
Mrs. Dalloway *'97*
Not Without My Daughter *'90*
Cold Comfort Farm *'71*

Diedrich Bader (1966-)
Meet the Spartans *'08*
Space Buddies *'08*
Balls of Fury *'07*
Surf's Up *'07 (V)*
National Lampoon Presents Cattle Call *'06*
Miss Congeniality 2: Armed and Fabulous *'05*
Eurotrip *'04*
Napoleon Dynamite *'04*
The Country Bears *'02 (V)*
Evil Alien Conquerors *'02*
Ice Age *'02 (V)*
Jay and Silent Bob Strike Back *'01*
Office Space *'98*
The Assassination File *'96*
Teresa's Tattoo *'94*
The Beverly Hillbillies *'93*

Rupert Baderman
Shadowlands *'85*
1984 *'84*

Russ Badger
Shanghai Noon *'00*
The Gore-Gore Girls *'72*

Penn Badgley (1986-)
The Stepfather *'09*
Forever Strong *'08*
John Tucker Must Die *'06*

Mary Badham (1952-)
This Property Is Condemned *'66*
To Kill a Mockingbird *'62*

Mina (Badiyi) Badie
Touched *'05*
Laws of Attraction *'04*
Mind the Gap *'04*
Road to Perdition *'02*
Roger Dodger *'02*
The Anniversary Party *'01*
Georgia *'95*
Mrs. Parker and the Vicious Circle *'94*
War Between the Tates *'76*

Annette Badland (1950-)
The Kovak Box *'06*
Secret Society *'00*
Little Voice *'98*
Angels and Insects *'95*
Hollow Reed *'95*
Captives *'94*
Pictures *'81*
Jabberwocky *'77*

Jane Badler (1953-)
Under the Gun *'95*
Black Snow *'89*
Easy Kill *'89*
Fine Gold *'88*
V *'83*

Sayed Badreya
Iron Man *'08*
W. *'08*
American East *'07*

Erykah Badu (1971-)
House of D *'04*
The Cider House Rules *'99*
Blues Brothers 2000 *'98*
Deep Red: Hatchet Murders *'75*

Du-na Bae
The Host *'06*
Linda Linda Linda *'05*
Tube *'03*
Sympathy for Mr. Vengeance *'02*
Take Care of My Cat *'01*
The Ring Virus *'99*

Buddy Baer (1915-86)
Giant from the Unknown *'58*
Dream Wife *'53*
The Big Sky *'52*
Jack & the Beanstalk *'52*
Flame of Araby *'51*
Quo Vadis *'51*

Edouard Baer
Moliere *'07*
Alias Betty *'01*

Harry Baer (1947-)
Big Boss *'77*
Mr. Scarface *'77*
Rulers of the City *'76*
Fox and His Friends *'75*
Whity *'70*

John Baer (1925-)
Night of the Blood Beast *'58*
We're No Angels *'55*
Above and Beyond *'53*
Indian Uprising *'51*

Max Baer, Sr. (1909-59)
The Harder They Fall *'56*
Riding High *'50*
Africa Screams *'49*
Buckskin Frontier *'43*
The Navy Comes Through *'42*
The Prizefighter and the Lady *'33*

Max Baer, Jr. (1937-)
The McCullochs *'75*
Macon County Line *'74*

Meridith Baer (1945-)
The Chicken Chronicles *'77*
The Sister-in-Law *'74*

Parley Baer (1914-2002)
Dave *'93*
Almost an Angel *'90*
Time Trackers *'88*
Rodeo Girl *'80*
The Amazing Dobermans *'76*
Sixteen *'72*
The Ugly Dachshund *'65*
The Brass Bottle *'63*
Gypsy *'62*
The Adventures of Huckleberry Finn *'60*
Cash McCall *'60*
The FBI Story *'59*
The Young Lions *'58*

Rafael Baez
Shanghai Noon *'00*
Went to Coney Island on a Mission from God... Be Back by Five *'98*

Paloma Baeza (1974-)
The Way We Live Now *'02*
Anna Karenina *'00*
A Knight in Camelot *'98*
Far from the Madding Crowd *'97*
The Odyssey *'97*
A Kid in King Arthur's Court *'95*

Regina Baff
Below the Belt *'80*
Road Movie *'72*

Larry Bagby (1974-)
Forever Strong *'08*
Walk the Line *'05*
Saints and Soldiers *'03*

William Bagdad (1920-75)
Blood Orgy of the She-Devils *'74*
The Doll Squad *'73*
The Astro-Zombies *'67*

Carol Bagdasarian
The Aurora Encounter *'85*
Charge of the Model T's *'76*

Vladas Bagdonas
House of Fools *'02*
Come and See *'85*

Lorri Bagley (1973-)
Ice Age *'02 (V)*
Trick *'99*

Tim Bagley
Knocked Up *'07*
Employee of the Month *'06*
Memron *'04*
The Fluffer *'01*

Vernel Bagneris (1949-)
Down by Law *'86*
Pennies from Heaven *'81*

Marcus Bagwell (1970-)
Terror Tract *'00*
Day of the Warrior *'96*

Blake Bahner (1959-)
Cyberstalker *'96*
Wizards of the Demon Sword *'94*
Blackbelt 2: Fatal Force *'93*
Fatal Exposure *'90*
Deadly Breed *'89*
Thrilled to Death *'88*
Sensations *'87*

Maxine Bahns (1971-)
Conjurer *'08*
Cutaway *'00*
Dangerous Curves *'99*
She's the One *'96*
The Brothers McMullen *'94*

Wu Bai (1968-)
Time and Tide *'00*
The Personals *'98*

Charles "Chuck" Bail
L.A. Bad *'85*
The Stunt Man *'80*

Bill Bailey (1964-)
Heat and Sunlight *'87*
On the Edge *'86*

Blake Bailey
Head of the Family *'96*
Lurking Fear *'94*

Bunty Bailey
Spellcaster *'91*
Dolls *'87*

Eion Bailey (1976-)
(Untitled) *'09*
Life of the Party *'05*
Mindhunters *'05*
And Starring Pancho Villa as Himself *'03*
The Home Front *'02*
Band of Brothers *'01*
Almost Famous *'00*
Center Stage *'00*
Fight Club *'99*

Fred Bailey
Nam Angels *'88*
Silk *'86*

G.W. Bailey (1945-)
Home on the Range *'04 (V)*
Scorcher *'02*
Jesus *'00*
The Thin Blue Lie *'00*
Police Academy 7: Mission to Moscow *'94*
An American Story *'92*
Double-Crossed *'91*
Held Hostage *'91*
Write to Kill *'91*
Police Academy 6: City under Siege *'89*
Burglar *'87*
Mannequin *'87*
A Winner Never Quits *'86*
Rustler's Rhapsody *'85*
M*A*S*H: Goodbye, Farewell & Amen *'83*
The Capture of Grizzly Adams *'82*

Jim Bailey (1948-)
Penitentiary 3 *'87*
Vultures *'84*

Mark Bailey
Simple Men *'92*
The Unbelievable Truth *'90*

Pearl Bailey (1918-90)
Peter Gunn *'89*
The Member of the Wedding *'83*
The Fox and the Hound *'81 (V)*
Norman, Is That You? *'76*
Carmen Jones *'54*

Raymond Bailey (1904-80)
The Gallant Hours *'60*
Vertigo *'58*
The Incredible Shrinking Man *'57*
Picnic *'55*

Richard Bailey
Forever Amber *'47*
Manhunt of Mystery Island *'45*
That's My Baby! *'44*

Robert Bailey, Jr.
To Save a Life *'10*
Coraline *'09 (V)*
The Happening *'08*
What the #$*! Do We Know? *'04*
Dragonfly *'02*
Little John *'02*

Robin Bailey (1919-99)
Screamtime *'83*
See No Evil *'71*

William Bailey (1886-1962)
Thunder Mountain *'35*
The Lone Avenger *'33*
Is Money Everything? *'23*

David Bailie (1937-)
Pirates of the Caribbean: Dead Man's Chest *'06*
Pirates of the Caribbean: The Curse of the Black Pearl *'03*

Nick Baillie
All the Good Ones Are Married *'07*
Eternal *'04*

Adrienne Bailon (1983-)
The Cheetah Girls: One World *'08*
The Cheetah Girls 2 *'06*
The Cheetah Girls *'03*

Kirk Baily (1952-)
The Sixth Man *'97*
3 Ninjas: High Noon at Mega Mountain *'97*
Voodoo Dawn *'89*

Barbara Bain (1931-)
Trapped *'06*
American Gun *'02*
Panic *'00*
Gideon *'99*
Spirit of '76 *'91*
Trust Me *'89*
Skinheads: The Second Coming of Hate *'88*
Space: 1999—Alien Attack *'79*
Destination Moonbase Alpha *'75*
Murder Once Removed *'71*

Conrad Bain (1923-)
Postcards from the Edge *'90*
Child Bride of Short Creek *'81*
C.H.O.M.P.S. *'79*
A Pleasure Doing Business *'79*
The Anderson Tapes *'71*
Bananas *'71*
Fury on Wheels *'71*
Who Killed Mary What's 'Er Name? *'71*

Cynthia Bain (1963-)
Hometown Boy Makes Good *'93*
Danielle Steel's Changes *'91*
Spontaneous Combustion *'89*
Pumpkinhead *'88*

Sherry Bain (1947-)
Wild & Wooly *'78*
Pipe Dreams *'76*
Jailbreakin' *'72*
The Hard Ride *'71*
Wild Riders *'71*

Fay Bainter (1892-1968)
The Children's Hour *'61*
Close to My Heart *'51*
June Bride *'48*
The Secret Life of Walter Mitty *'47*
Kid from Brooklyn *'46*
The Virginian *'46*
State Fair *'45*
Dark Waters *'44*
The Heavenly Body *'44*
The Human Comedy *'43*
Presenting Lily Mars *'43*
Journey for Margaret *'42*
Woman of the Year *'42*
Babes on Broadway *'41*
Our Town *'40*
Young Tom Edison *'40*
Jezebel *'38*
The Shining Hour *'38*
Make Way for Tomorrow *'37*
Quality Street *'37*

Jimmy Baio (1962-)
Kiss and Be Killed *'91*
Playing for Keeps *'86*
Brass *'85*
The Bad News Bears in Breaking Training *'77*

Scott Baio (1961-)
Finish Line *'08*
Cursed *'04*
Superbabies: Baby Geniuses 2 *'04*
The Bread, My Sweet *'01*
Bar Hopping *'00*
I Love N.Y. *'87*
Alice in Wonderland *'85*
Zapped! *'82*
Senior Trip *'81*
Foxes *'80*
Bugsy Malone *'76*

Antony Baird (1920-)
The Ghost of Rashmon Hall *'47*
Dead of Night *'45*

Diora Baird (1983-)
Night of the Demons *'09*
Stan Helsing *'09*
My Best Friend's Girl *'08*
Accepted *'06*
Hot Tamale *'06*
The Texas Chainsaw Massacre: The Beginning *'06*
Bachelor Party Vegas *'05*
Wedding Crashers *'05*

Harry Baird (1931-2005)
Castle Keep *'69*
The Oblong Box *'69*
The Story of a Three Day Pass *'68*
Tor *'64*
Thor and the Amazon Women *'60*

Jimmy Baird (1948-)
Black Orchid *'59*
Return of Dracula *'58*

Scott Bairstow (1970-)
New Best Friend *'02*
Tuck Everlasting *'02*
Dead in the Water *'01*
Delivered *'98*
Black Circle Boys *'97*
Killing Mr. Griffin *'97*
The Postman *'97*
Two for Texas *'97*
Wild America *'97*
White Fang 2: The Myth of the White Wolf *'94*

Mitsuko Baisho (1946-)
The Eel *'96*
Akira Kurosawa's Dreams *'90*
Vengeance Is Mine *'79*

Jon Robin Baitz (1961-)
Last Summer In the Hamptons *'96*
One Fine Day *'96*

Sidiki Bakaba (1949-)
Faces of Women *'85*
Le Professionnel *'81*

Helmut Bakaitis (1944-)
The Matrix Reloaded *'03*
The Matrix Revolutions *'03*

Richard Bakalyan (1931-)
The Fox and the Hound *'81 (V)*
The Strongest Man in the World *'75*
The Computer Wore Tennis Shoes *'69*
The St. Valentine's Day Massacre *'67*
Von Ryan's Express *'65*
Panic in the Year Zero! *'62*
Up Periscope *'59*

Ariyon Bakare (1971-)
After the Rain *'99*
A Respectable Trade *'98*

Art Baker (1898-1966)
The Underworld Story *'50*
Impact *'49*
Task Force *'49*
Homecoming *'48*
A Southern Yankee *'48*

Benny Baker (1907-94)
Loan Shark *'52*
Drift Fence *'36*
Murder With Pictures *'36*

Blanche Baker (1956-)
Dead Funny *'94*
Livin' Large *'91*
The Handmaid's Tale *'90*
Shakedown *'88*
Embassy *'85*
Cold Feet *'84*
Sixteen Candles *'84*
Awakening of Candra *'81*
French Postcards *'79*
Mary and Joseph: A Story of Faith *'79*

Bob Baker (1910-75)
Overland Mail *'42*
Riders of Pasco Basin *'40*
Chip of the Flying U *'39*
Oklahoma Frontier *'39*
Ghost Town Riders *'38*
Outlaw Express *'38*
Western Trails *'38*

Carroll Baker (1931-)
The Game *'97*
North Shore Fish *'97*

Just Your Luck '96
Dalva '95
Kindergarten Cop '90
Ironweed '87
Native Son '86
The Secret Diary of Sigmund Freud '84
Star 80 '83
The Watcher in the Woods '81
The World Is Full of Married Men '80
Andy Warhol's Bad '77
You've Got to Have Heart '77
Bloodbath '76
Next Victim '74
Kiss Me, Kill Me '73
Captain Apache '71
Paranoia '69
The Greatest Story Ever Told '65
Harlow '65
The Carpetbaggers '64
Cheyenne Autumn '64
How the West Was Won '63
But Not for Me '59
The Big Country '58
Baby Doll '56
Giant '56
Easy to Love '53

Christopher Baker

The Condemned '07
Ike: Countdown to D-Day '04

Colin Baker (1943-)

The Waiting Time '99
War and Peace '73
The Moonstone '72

David Aaron Baker (1963-)

Kissing Jessica Stein '02
Kate & Leopold '01
The Tao of Steve '00

Dee Bradley Baker

The Trumpet of the Swan '01 (V)
A Rat's Tale '98 (V)

Diane Baker (1938-)

The Keeper: The Legend of Omar Khayyam '05
Harrison's Flowers '02
Murder at 1600 '97
The Cable Guy '96
The Net '95
Imaginary Crimes '94
The Joy Luck Club '93
Twenty Bucks '93
The Closer '91
The Silence of the Lambs '91
A Woman of Substance '84
Danger in the Skies '79
Baker's Hawk '76
Krakatoa East of Java '69
The Horse in the Gray Flannel Suit '68
Mirage '66
Marnie '64
Strait-Jacket '64
The Prize '63
Stolen Hours '63
The 300 Spartans '62
The Best of Everything '59
The Diary of Anne Frank '59
Journey to the Center of the Earth '59

Dylan Baker (1958-)

Diminished Capacity '08
Revolutionary Road '08
Trick 'r Treat '08
Chicago 10 '07 (V)
The Hunting Party '07
Spider-Man 3 '07
The Stone Angel '07
When a Man Falls in the Forest '07
Fido '06
Let's Go to Prison '06
The Matador '06
Hide and Seek '05
Kinsey '04
Spider-Man 2 '04
Head of State '03
How to Deal '03
Rick '03
Changing Lanes '02
Road to Perdition '02
Along Came a Spider '01
A Gentleman's Game '01
The Cell '00
Thirteen Days '00
Oxygen '99
Random Hearts '99
Simply Irresistible '99
Celebrity '98
From the Earth to the Moon '98
Happiness '98
Disclosure '94
The Last of the Mohicans '92
Love Potion #9 '92
Delirious '91
The Long Walk Home '89
The Wizard of Loneliness '88
Planes, Trains & Automobiles '87

Fay Baker (1917-87)

Sorority Girl '57
The Star '52

Frank Baker (1892-1980)

Run of the Arrow '56
Tarzan and the Green Goddess '38
The New Adventures of Tarzan '35

George Baker (1931-)

Little Lord Fauntleroy '95
The Charmer '87
Robin Hood... The Legend: Herne's Son '85
A Woman of Substance '84
Goodbye, Mr. Chips '69
Sword of Lancelot '63
Dangerous Youth '58
The Moonraker '58
Tread Softly Stranger '58

Jay Baker (1961-)

Naked Lies '98
Storm and Sorrow '90
April Fool's Day '86

Jill Baker (1952-)

Secret Smile '05
Catherine Cookson's The Girl '96
Hope and Glory '87

Joby Baker (1934-)

Blackbeard's Ghost '67
Gidget '59

Joe Don Baker (1936-)

Strange Wilderness '08
The Dukes of Hazzard '05
Poodle Springs '98
George Wallace '97
Tomorrow Never Dies '97
Mars Attacks! '96
Congo '95
Felony '95
Goldeneye '95
The Grass Harp '95
Panther '95
The Underneath '95
Reality Bites '94
Ring of Steel '94
Citizen Cohn '92
The Distinguished Gentleman '92
Cape Fear '91
The Children '90
Criminal Law '89
The Abduction of Kari Swenson '87
The Killing Time '87
Leonard Part 6 '87
The Living Daylights '87
Edge of Darkness '86
Getting Even '86
Fletch '85
Final Justice '84
The Natural '84
Joy Sticks '83
Wacko '83
Speedtrap '78
The Pack '77
Shadow of Chikara '77
Framed '75
Mitchell '75
Charley Varrick '73
Walking Tall '73
Junior Bonner '72
Wild Rovers '71
Adam at 6 a.m. '70
Guns of the Magnificent Seven '69
Cool Hand Luke '67

Jolyon Baker

Out of the Ashes '03
Attila '01
Duel of Hearts '92
Final Analysis '92

Jonathan Baker

Great World of Sound '07
Savage Harvest 2: October Blood '06

Josephine Baker (1906-75)

The French Way '40
Princess Tam Tam '35
Zou Zou '34
Siren of the Tropics '27

Kai Baker

American Eagle '90
Stormquest '87

Kathy Baker (1950-)

Jesse Stone: Thin Ice '09
Last Chance Harvey '08
The Jane Austen Book Club '07
Jesse Stone: Sea Change '07
All the King's Men '06
Nine Lives '05
Sucker Free City '05
13 Going on 30 '04
Assassination Tango '03
Cold Mountain '03
The Glass House '01
A Little Inside '01
Things You Can Tell Just by Looking at Her '00
The Cider House Rules '99
Ratz '99
A Season for Miracles '99
Inventing the Abbotts '97
Not in This Town '97
Weapons of Mass Distraction '97
To Gillian on Her 37th Birthday '96
Lush Life '94
Mad Dog and Glory '93
Article 99 '92
Jennifer 8 '92
Edward Scissorhands '90
Dad '89
The Image '89
Jacknife '89
Mr. Frost '89
Clean and Sober '88
Permanent Record '88
Street Smart '87
A Killing Affair '85
The Right Stuff '83

Kenny Baker (1934-)

Star Wars: Episode 3—Revenge of the Sith '05
Star Wars: Episode 2—Attack of the Clones '02
Sleeping Beauty '89
Amadeus '84
Return of the Jedi '83
Time Bandits '81
The Elephant Man '80
The Empire Strikes Back '80
Star Wars '77

Kenny L. Baker (1912-85)

The Harvey Girls '46
At the Circus '39

Kirsten Baker (1962-)

Friday the 13th, Part 2 '81
Gas Pump Girls '79
Girls Next Door '79

Max Baker

Bailey's Billion$ '05
Constantine '05
The Island '05
Looking for Kitty '04

Phil Baker (1896-1963)

The Gang's All Here '43
The Goldwyn Follies '38

Ray Baker (1948-)

Without a Paddle '04
44 Minutes: The North Hollywood Shootout '03
The Trip '02
Anywhere But Here '99
The Final Cut '96
Camp Nowhere '94
The Hard Truth '94
Speechless '94
Heart Condition '90
Everybody's All American '88
Rockabye '86
Places in the Heart '84

Rick Baker (1950-)

Kentucky Fried Movie '77
King Kong '76
The Thing with Two Heads '72

Robert Baker (1979-)

Save Me '07
Seraphim Falls '06
Special '06
Out of Time '03
Chinese Connection '73

Scott Thompson Baker (1961-)

The Cutting Edge: Going for the Gold '05
Cleo/Leo '89
New York's Finest '87
Rest in Pieces '87

Simon Baker (1969-)

The Killer Inside Me '10
The Lodger '09
Women in Trouble '09
Sex and Death 101 '07
The Devil Wears Prada '06
Something New '06
George A. Romero's Land of the Dead '05
The Ring 2 '05
Book of Love '04
The Missing '03
The Affair of the Necklace '01
Red Planet '00
Ride with the Devil '99
Sunset Strip '99
Judas Kiss '98
Restaurant '98
Smoke Signals '98
L.A. Confidential '97
Most Wanted '97

Stanley Baker (1928-76)

Zorro '74
Butterfly Affair '71
A Lizard in a Woman's Skin '71
Queen of Diamonds '70
Accident '67
Robbery '67
Dingaka '65
Zulu '64
Eva '62
Sodom and Gomorrah '62
The Guns of Navarone '61
Very Important Person '61
Helen of Troy '56
Richard III '55
The Cruel Sea '53
Knights of the Round Table '53
Home to Danger '51
The Hidden Room '49

Stephen Baker

Dead Lenny '06
Little Marines '90

Susan Baker

A Wind Named Amnesia '93 (V)
Tommy '75

Timothy Baker

Out for Blood '93
Bloodfist 2 '90

Tom Baker (1934-)

Doogal '05 (V)
Dungeons and Dragons '00
The Chronicles of Narnia '89
The Zany Adventures of Robin Hood '84
Fyre '78
Candy Stripe Nurses '74
The Freakmaker '73
Golden Voyage of Sinbad '73
Vault of Horror '73
Nicholas and Alexandra '71
Angels Die Hard '70

Edward Baker-Duly

Botched '07
De-Lovely '04

Gary Bakewell

Neil Gaiman's NeverWhere '96
Backbeat '94

William "Billy" Bakewell (1908-93)

Davy Crockett, King of the Wild Frontier '55
Lucky Me '54
Radar Men from the Moon '52
The Capture '50
Romance on the High Seas '48
You Gotta Stay Happy '48
Dawn Express '42
Gone with the Wind '39
The Duke of West Point '38
Exiled to Shanghai '37
Roaring Speedboats '37
Sons of Steel '35
Lucky Devils '33
Dance Fools Dance '31
Politics '31
Reducing '31
All Quiet on the Western Front '30
Playing Around '30
The Iron Mask '29
On with the Show '29
Annapolis '28
Battle of the Sexes '28
West Point '27

Brenda Bakke (1963-)

The Quickie '01
Shelter '98
The Fixer '97
Trucks '97
Lone Justice 3: Showdown at Plum Creek '96
Under Siege 2: Dark Territory '95
Star Quest '94
Tales from the Crypt Presents Demon Knight '94
Twogether '94
Fast Gun '93
Hot Shots! Part Deux '93
Lone Justice 2 '93
Fist Fighter '88
Dangerous Love '87
Death Spa '87
Scavengers '87
Hardbodies 2 '86

Brigitte Bako (1967-)

Paranoia '98
Dinner and Driving '97
Double Take '97
The Escape '95
Strange Days '95
Replikator: Cloned to Kill '94
Dark Tide '93
A Man in Uniform '93
Red Shoe Diaries '92

Muhamad Bakri

The Milky Way '97
The Mummy Lives '93
Cup Final '92
Double Edge '92
Beyond the Walls '84
Hanna K. '83

Scott Bakula (1955-)

The Informant! '09
Blue Smoke '07
A Girl Thing '01
Life as a House '01
Above Suspicion '00
Papa's Angels '00
The Trial of Old Drum '00
American Beauty '99
Luminarias '99
Mean Streak '99
Major League 3: Back to the Minors '98
Tom Clancy's Netforce '98
Cats Don't Dance '97 (V)
The Invaders '95
Lord of Illusions '95
Color of Night '94
My Family '94
A Passion to Kill '94
Mercy Mission '93
Necessary Roughness '91
Sibling Rivalry '90
The Last Fling '86

Bob Balaban (1945-)

Recount '08
Dedication '07
No Reservations '07
For Your Consideration '06
Lady in the Water '06
Capote '05
Marie and Bruce '04
A Mighty Wind '03
Ghost World '01
Gosford Park '01
The Majestic '01
The Mexican '01
Best in Show '00
The Cradle Will Rock '99
Jakob the Liar '99
Three to Tango '99
Clockwatchers '97
Deconstructing Harry '97
No Money Down '97
The Late Shift '96
Waiting for Guffman '96
Pie in the Sky '95
Greedy '94
Amos and Andrew '93
For Love or Money '93
Bob Roberts '92
Unnatural Pursuits '91
Alice '90
Dead Bang '89
End of the Line '88
2010: The Year We Make Contact '84
Absence of Malice '81
Whose Life Is It Anyway? '81
Altered States '80
Girlfriends '78
Close Encounters of the Third Kind '77
Bank Shot '74
Catch-22 '70
The Strawberry Statement '70
Midnight Cowboy '69

Liane Balaban (1980-)

Definitely, Maybe '08
Last Chance Harvey '08
Eternal '04
Spliced '03
World Traveler '01
New Waterford Girl '99

Belinda Balaski (1947-)

Runaway Daughters '94
Gremlins 2: The New Batch '90
Proud Men '87
The Howling '81
Cannonball '76

Josiane Balasko (1952-)

Ruby Blue '07
French Twist '95
Grosse Fatigue '94
Too Beautiful for You '88
Hotel America '81
French Fried Vacation '79
This Sweet Sickness '77

Anna Baldaccini

Boy Meets Girl '84
Every Man for Himself '79

Leonor Baldaque

Belle Toujours '06
I'm Going Home '00

Nick Baldasare
They Bite '95
Beyond Dream's Door '88

Rebecca Balding
Silent Scream '80
Deadly Game '77

Renato Baldini (1921-)
Four Ways Out '57
Submarine Attack '54
The Wayward Wife '52

A. Michael Baldwin (1965-)
Phantasm 4: Oblivion '98
Vice Girls '96
Phantasm 3: Lord of the Dead '94

Adam Baldwin (1962-)
Gospel Hill '08
The Thirst '06
Serenity '05
Evil Eyes '04
Lady Jayne Killer '03
Double Bang '01
Jackpot '01
Pursuit of Happiness '01
The Patriot '00
The Right Temptation '00
Dr. Jekyll & Mr. Hyde '99
From the Earth to the Moon '98
Gargantua '98
Indiscreet '98
Independence Day '96
Lover's Knot '96
Sawbones '95
Trade Off '95
Blind Justice '94
Digital Man '94
Wyatt Earp '94
Bitter Harvest '93
Cold Sweat '93
800 Leagues Down the Amazon '93
Deadbolt '92
Radio Flyer '92
Where the Day Takes You '92
Guilty by Suspicion '91
Predator 2 '90
Next of Kin '89
The Chocolate War '88
Cohen and Tate '88
Full Metal Jacket '87
Bad Guys '86
3:15—The Moment of Truth '86
D.C. Cab '84
Hadley's Rebellion '84
Reckless '84
My Bodyguard '80
Ordinary People '80

Alec Baldwin (1958-)
Cats & Dogs: The Revenge of Kitty Galore '10 (V)
It's Complicated '09
My Sister's Keeper '09
Lymelife '08
Madagascar: Escape 2 Africa '08 (V)
My Best Friend's Girl '08
Brooklyn Rules '07
Suburban Girl '07
The Departed '06
The Good Shepherd '06
Running with Scissors '06
Elizabethtown '05
Fun With Dick and Jane '05
Along Came Polly '04
The Aviator '04
The Last Shot '04
The SpongeBob SquarePants Movie '04 (V)
The Cooler '03
Dr. Seuss' The Cat in the Hat '03
Path to War '02
Cats & Dogs '01 (V)
Final Fantasy: The Spirits Within '01 (V)
Pearl Harbor '01
The Royal Tenenbaums '01 (N)
Nuremberg '00
State and Main '00
Thomas and the Magic Railroad '00
Outside Providence '99
Thick as Thieves '99
The Confession '98
Mercury Rising '98
The Edge '97
Ghosts of Mississippi '96
The Juror '96
Looking for Richard '96
Two Bits '96 (V)
Heaven's Prisoners '95
A Streetcar Named Desire '95
The Shadow '94
The Getaway '93
Malice '93
Glengarry Glen Ross '92
Prelude to a Kiss '92
The Marrying Man '91
Alice '90
The Hunt for Red October '90
Miami Blues '90
Great Balls of Fire '89
Beetlejuice '88
Married to the Mob '88
She's Having a Baby '88
Talk Radio '88
Working Girl '88
The Alamo: Thirteen Days to Glory '87
Forever, Lulu '87
Dress Gray '86
Love on the Run '85
Code of Honor '84

Daniel Baldwin (1960-)
Grey Gardens '09
The Devil's Dominoes '07
Moola '07
Final Move '06
Anonymous Rex '04
Paparazzi '04
Stealing Candy '04
King of the Ants '03
Water's Edge '03
Homicide: The Movie '00
In Pursuit '00
Killing Moon '00
Active Stealth '99
Desert Thunder '99
Silicon Towers '99
Wild Grizzly '99
Love Kills '98
On the Border '98
Phoenix '98
The Treat '98
John Carpenter's Vampires '97
The Invader '96
Tree's Lounge '96
Yesterday's Target '96
Bodily Harm '95
Family of Cops '95
Mulholland Falls '95
Car 54, Where Are You? '94
Dead on Sight '94
Attack of the 50 Ft. Woman '93
Knight Moves '93
Lone Justice '93
Harley Davidson and the Marlboro Man '91
The Heroes of Desert Storm '91
Born on the Fourth of July '89

Janit Baldwin (1955-)
Humongous '82
Ruby '77
Born Innocent '74
The California Kid '74
Gator Bait '73

Peter Baldwin (1929-)
The Ghost '63
Era Notte a Roma '60

Robert Baldwin (1904-96)
Courageous Dr. Christian '40
Meet Dr. Christian '39

Stephen Baldwin (1966-)
Earthstorm '06
Jesse Stone: Night Passage '06
Midnight Clear '06
Bound by Lies '05
Snakeman '05
Six: The Mark Unleashed '04
Firefight '03
Shelter Island '03
Slap Shot 2: Breaking the Ice '02
Greenmail '01
Protection '01
Spider's Web '01
Zebra Lounge '01
Cutaway '00
The Flintstones in Viva Rock Vegas '00
Mercy '00
Table One '00
Xchange '00
Absence of the Good '99
Friends & Lovers '99
The Sex Monster '99
Dean Koontz's Mr. Murder '98
One Tough Cop '98
Scarred City '98
Half-Baked '97
Sub Down '97
Bio-Dome '96
Crimetime '96
Fled '96
Dead Weekend '95
Under the Hula Moon '95
The Usual Suspects '95
8 Seconds '94
Fall Time '94
The Great American Sex Scandal '94
New Eden '94
A Simple Twist of Fate '94
Threesome '94
Bitter Harvest '93
Posse '93
Crossing the Bridge '92
Last Exit to Brooklyn '90
Born on the Fourth of July '89
The Beast '88
The Lawrenceville Stories '88

Walter Baldwin (1889-1977)
Interrupted Melody '55
The Long, Long Trailer '54
I Want You '51
Winter Meeting '48
The Best Years of Our Lives '46
Mr. Winkle Goes to War '44

William Baldwin (1963-)
Forgetting Sarah Marshall '08
A Plumm Summer '08
Adrift in Manhattan '07
Humble Pie '07
Noise '07
Full Count '06
Art Heist '05
The Squid and the Whale '05
You Stupid Man '02
Double Bang '01
Say Nothing '01
Brotherhood of Murder '99
Relative Values '99
Shattered Image '98
Virus '98
Curdled '95
Fair Game '95
A Pyromaniac's Love Story '95
Sliver '93
Three of Hearts '93
Backdraft '91
Flatliners '90
Internal Affairs '90
Born on the Fourth of July '89
The Preppie Murder '89

Christian Bale (1974-)
Public Enemies '09
Terminator Salvation '09
The Dark Knight '08
I'm Not There '07
3:10 to Yuma '07
The Prestige '06
Rescue Dawn '06
Batman Begins '05
Harsh Times '05
The New World '05
Howl's Moving Castle '04 (V)
The Machinist '04
Equilibrium '02
Laurel Canyon '02
Reign of Fire '02
Captain Corelli's Mandolin '01
Shaft '00
American Psycho '99
Mary, Mother of Jesus '99
William Shakespeare's A Midsummer Night's Dream '99
All the Little Animals '98
Velvet Goldmine '98
Metroland '97
Portrait of a Lady '96
The Secret Agent '96
Pocahontas '95 (V)
Little Women '94
Royal Deceit '94
Swing Kids '93
Newsies '92
A Murder of Quality '90
Henry V '89
Treasure Island '89
Empire of the Sun '87
The Land of Faraway '87

Carla Balenda (1925-)
Phantom Stallion '54
Outlaw Women '52

Betty Balfour (1903-78)
Evergreen '34
Champagne '28

Eric Balfour
Horsemen '09
Hell Ride '08
The Spirit '08
The Elder Son '06
Rx '06
The Texas Chainsaw Massacre '03
What Women Want '00

Michael Balfour (1918-97)
The Canterbury Tales '71
The Private Life of Sherlock Holmes '70
The Flesh and the Fiends '60
Fiend without a Face '58
Quatermass 2 '57
Murder on Approval '56
Genevieve '53
Moulin Rouge '52

Jennifer Balgobin
Roadside Prophets '92
Dr. Caligari '89
City Limits '85
Repo Man '83

Jeanne Balibar (1968-)
The Girl From Monaco '08
The Duchess of Langeais '07
Clean '04
Code 46 '03
Va Savoir '01
Comedy of Innocence '00
Sade '00
Late August, Early September '98
My Sex Life... Or How I Got into an Argument '96

Ina Balin (1937-90)
Vasectomy: A Delicate Matter '86
The Children of An Lac '80
Galyon '77
Panic on the 5:22 '74
The Don Is Dead '73
The Projectionist '71
Charro! '69
The Patsy '64
The Comancheros '61
From the Terrace '60
Black Orchid '59

Andras Balint (1943-)
The Moon & the Stars '07
Citizen X '95
Stalin '92
Colonel Redl '84
A Happy New Year! '79
25 Fireman's Street '73
Love Film '70
Father '67

Eszter Balint (1966-)
Tree's Lounge '96
The Linguini Incident '92
Bail Jumper '89
Stranger than Paradise '84

Fairuza Balk (1974-)
Bad Lieutenant: Port of Call New Orleans '09
Humboldt County '08
Grindstone Road '07
Wild Tigers I Have Known '06
Don't Come Knocking '05
Deuces Wild '02
Personal Velocity: Three Portraits '02
Almost Famous '00
Life in the Fast Lane '00
Red Letters '00
American History X '98
The Maker '98
The Waterboy '98
The Craft '96
The Island of Dr. Moreau '96
Danger of Love '95
Things to Do in Denver When You're Dead '95
Imaginary Crimes '94
Tollbooth '94
Gas Food Lodging '92
Shame '92
Valmont '89
Outside Chance of Maximilian Glick '88
The Worst Witch '86
Return to Oz '85

Angeline Ball (1969-)
Bloom '03
Bait '02
Kitchen Privileges '00
The General '98
The Gambler '97
Trojan Eddie '96
Brothers in Trouble '95
The Commitments '91

Frank Ball (1876-1968)
Feud Maker '38
Boothill Brigade '37
Gun Lords of Stirrup Basin '37
Galloping Romeo '33
When a Man Rides Alone '33
The Forty-Niners '32

Jonas Ball
The Objective '08
The Killing of John Lennon '07

Lucille Ball (1911-89)
Mame '74
Yours, Mine & Ours '68
A Guide for the Married Man '67
Critic's Choice '63
The Facts of Life '60
Forever Darling '56
The Long, Long Trailer '54
Fancy Pants '50
The Fuller Brush Girl '50
A Woman of Distinction '50
Easy Living '49
Miss Grant Takes Richmond '49
Sorrowful Jones '49
Her Husband's Affairs '47
Lured '47
Dark Corner '46
Easy to Wed '46
Ziegfeld Follies '46
Without Love '45
Meet the People '44
Best Foot Forward '43
Du Barry Was a Lady '43
Thousands Cheer '43
Big Street '42
Seven Days' Leave '42
Valley of the Sun '42
A Girl, a Guy and a Gob '41
Look Who's Laughing '41
Dance, Girl, Dance '40
Too Many Girls '40
You Can't Fool Your Wife '40
Beauty for the Asking '39
Five Came Back '39
Panama Lady '39
The Affairs of Annabel '38
Having a Wonderful Time '38
Having Wonderful Time '38
Joy of Living '38
Next Time I Marry '38
Room Service '38
Stage Door '37
Follow the Fleet '36
That Girl from Paris '36
I Dream Too Much '35
Roberta '35
Top Hat '35
Murder at the Vanities '34
Roman Scandals '33

Nicholas Ball (1946-)
Croupier '97
Claudia '85
Lifeforce '85
The House that Bled to Death '81

Samuel Ball (1973-)
Net Games '03
Pumpkin '02
The Last Castle '01
Urbania '00

Suzan Ball
War Arrow '53
Yankee Buccaneer '52

Vincent Ball (1924-)
Sirens '94
Breaker Morant '80
Demolition '77
Not Tonight Darling '72
Oh! What a Lovely War '69
Where Eagles Dare '68
A Matter of WHO '62
Dead Lucky '60
Blonde Blackmailer '58
Blood of the Vampire '58
Sea of Sand '58
John and Julie '55
Terror Ship '54

Carl Ballantine (1917-2009)
Dying to Get Rich '98
Mr. Saturday Night '92
Hollywood Chaos '89
World's Greatest Lover '77
Revenge of the Cheerleaders '76
Speedway '68

Jeff(rey) Ballard (1987-)
Dead in a Heartbeat '02
Children of the Corn: Revelation '01

Kaye Ballard (1926-)
Ava's Magical Adventure '94
Eternity '90
Fate '90
Modern Love '90
Tiger Warsaw '87
Freaky Friday '76
The Ritz '76
The Girl Most Likely '57

Edoardo Ballerini (1970-)
Dinner Rush '00
Romeo Must Die '00
Looking for an Echo '99
I Shot Andy Warhol '96
The Pest '96

Juan Jose Ballesta
7 Virgins '05
El Bola '00

Smith Ballew (1902-84)
Gun Cargo '49
Hawaiian Buckaroo '38
Panamint's Bad Man '38
Rawhide '38

Roll Along Cowboy *'37*
Western Gold *'37*

Timothy Balme

The Vector File *'03*
Jack Brown, Genius *'94*
Dead Alive *'93*

Jean-Francois Balmer (1946-)

Tokyo! *'09*
Comedy of Power *'06*
Belphegar: Phantom of the Louvre *'01*
Time Regained *'99*
The Swindle *'97*
Beaumarchais the Scoundrel *'96*
Madame Bovary *'91*
Window Shopping *'86*

Martin Balsam (1919-96)

Silence of the Hams *'93*
Cape Fear *'91*
Two Evil Eyes *'90*
Innocent Prey *'88*
P.I. Private Investigations *'87*
Queenie *'87*
Delta Force *'86*
Grown Ups *'86*
Death Wish 3 *'85*
Murder in Space *'85*
St. Elmo's Fire *'85*
Little Gloria... Happy at Last *'84*
The Goodbye People *'83*
The Salamander *'82*
The People vs. Jean Harris *'81*
The Warning *'80*
The House on Garibaldi Street *'79*
Silver Bears *'78*
Death Rage *'77*
Raid on Entebbe *'77*
All the President's Men *'76*
The Lindbergh Kidnapping Case *'76*
Two Minute Warning *'76*
Mitchell *'75*
Spaghetti Western *'75*
Miles to Go Before I Sleep *'74*
Murder on the Orient Express *'74*
The Taking of Pelham One Two Three *'74*
The Stone Killer *'73*
Summer Wishes, Winter Dreams *'73*
Brand New Life *'72*
Confessions of a Police Captain *'72*
Eyes Behind the Stars *'72*
The Anderson Tapes *'71*
Season for Assassins *'71*
Catch-22 *'70*
Hard Frame *'70*
Little Big Man *'70*
Tora! Tora! Tora! *'70*
The Good Guys and the Bad Guys *'69*
Hombre *'67*
After the Fox *'66*
Bedford Incident *'65*
Harlow *'65*
A Thousand Clowns *'65*
The Carpetbaggers *'64*
Seven Days in May *'64*
Breakfast at Tiffany's *'61*
Cape Fear *'61*
Psycho *'60*
Al Capone *'59*
Marjorie Morningstar *'58*
Twelve Angry Men *'57*

Talia Balsam (1960-)

The Wackness *'08*
The Cake Eaters *'07*
All the King's Men *'06*
Into the Fire *'05*
Coldblooded *'94*
The Companion *'94*
Homicidal Impulse *'92*
Trust Me *'89*
In the Mood *'87*
The Kindred *'87*
P.I. Private Investigations *'87*
Private Investigations *'87*
Crawlspace *'86*
Consenting Adult *'85*
Mass Appeal *'84*
Nadia *'84*
Calamity Jane *'82*
Kent State *'81*
On the Edge: The Survival of Dana *'79*
Sunnyside *'79*

Humbert Balsan (1954-)

I Married a Dead Man *'82*
Lancelot of the Lake *'74*

Kirk Baltz (1959-)

Forfeit *'07*
Bloodhounds *'96*
Kingfish: A Story of Huey P. Long *'95*
Probable Cause *'95*
Natural Born Killers *'94*
Skin Art *'93*
Reservoir Dogs *'92*

Alexander Baluyev (1958-)

Deep Impact *'98*
The Peacemaker *'97*

David Bamber (1954-)

Valkyrie *'08*
Miss Potter *'06*
Daniel Deronda *'02*
The Railway Children *'00*
Pride and Prejudice *'95*
Stalag Luft *'93*
The Buddha of Suburbia *'92*
High Hopes *'88*

Jamie Bamber (1973-)

Pulse 2: Afterlife *'08*
Daniel Deronda *'02*
Band of Brothers *'01*
Horatio Hornblower: The Adventure Continues *'01*
Lady Audley's Secret *'00*

Judy Bamber (1936-)

The Atomic Brain *'64*
A Bucket of Blood *'59*

Firdous Bamji (1966-)

The War Within *'05*

Gerry Bamman (1941-)

Runaway Jury *'03*
Home Alone 2: Lost in New York *'92*
Lorenzo's Oil *'92*
The Chase *'91*
The Ten Million Dollar Getaway *'91*

Daisuke Ban

Ringu 0 *'01*
Ringu 2 *'99*
Ringu *'98*

Janos Ban (1955-)

Fateless *'05*
My Sweet Little Village *'86*

Junzaburo Ban

Dodes 'ka-den *'70*
Snake Woman's Curse *'68*

Eric Bana (1968-)

Funny People *'09*
Mary and Max *'09*
Star Trek *'09*
The Time Traveler's Wife *'09*
The Other Boleyn Girl *'08*
Lucky You *'07*
Romulus, My Father *'07*
Munich *'05*
Troy *'04*
Finding Nemo *'03 (V)*
Hulk *'03*
The Nugget *'02*
Black Hawk Down *'01*
Chopper *'00*
The Castle *'97*

Anne Bancroft (1931-2005)

Delgo *'08 (V)*
The Roman Spring of Mrs. Stone *'03*
Heartbreakers *'01*
Keeping the Faith *'00*
Up at the Villa *'00*
Antz *'98 (V)*
Critical Care *'97*
G.I. Jane *'97*
Great Expectations *'97*
Homecoming *'96*
Sunchaser *'96*
Dracula: Dead and Loving It *'95*
Home for the Holidays *'95*
How to Make an American Quilt *'95*
Oldest Confederate Widow Tells All *'95*
Malice *'93*
Mr. Jones *'93*
Point of No Return *'93*
Broadway Bound *'92*
Honeymoon in Vegas *'92*
Love Potion #9 *'92*
Bert Rigby, You're a Fool *'89*
Torch Song Trilogy *'88*
84 Charing Cross Road *'86*
'night, Mother *'86*
Agnes of God *'85*
Garbo Talks *'84*
To Be or Not to Be *'83*
The Elephant Man *'80*
Fatso *'80*
The Bell Jar *'79*
Jesus of Nazareth *'77*
The Turning Point *'77*
Lipstick *'76*
Silent Movie *'76*
The Hindenburg *'75*
Prisoner of Second Avenue *'74*
Young Winston *'72*
The Graduate *'67*
The Slender Thread *'65*
The Pumpkin Eater *'64*
The Miracle Worker *'62*
The Restless Breed *'58*
Girl in Black Stockings *'57*
Nightfall *'56*
Walk the Proud Land *'56*
Savage Wilderness *'55*
Demetrius and the Gladiators *'54*
Treasure of the Golden Condor *'53*
Don't Bother to Knock *'52*

Bradford Bancroft

A Time to Die *'91*
Damned River *'89*
Bachelor Party *'84*

Cameron Bancroft (1967-)

Flirting with Forty *'09*
Mail Order Bride *'08*
Anything But Love *'02*
He Sees You When You're Sleeping *'02*
MVP2: Most Vertical Primate *'01*
Anything for Love *'93*
Just One of the Girls *'93*
Love and Human Remains *'93*

George Bancroft (1882-1956)

Whistling in Dixie *'42*
Texas *'41*
Little Men *'40*
Young Tom Edison *'40*
Each Dawn I Die *'39*
Stagecoach *'39*
Angels with Dirty Faces *'38*
Hell-Ship Morgan *'36*
Mr. Deeds Goes to Town *'36*
Docks of New York *'28*
White Gold *'28*
Underworld *'27*
Old Ironsides *'26*
The Pony Express *'25*

Antonio Banderas (1960-)

Shrek Forever After *'10 (V)*
The Code *'09*
My Mom's New Boyfriend *'08*
The Other Man *'08*
Shrek the Third *'07 (V)*
Bordertown *'06*
Take the Lead *'06*
The Legend of Zorro *'05*
Imagining Argentina *'04*
Shrek 2 *'04 (V)*
And Starring Pancho Villa as Himself *'03*
Once Upon a Time in Mexico *'03*
Spy Kids 3-D: Game Over *'03*
Ballistic: Ecks vs. Sever *'02*
Femme Fatale *'02*
Frida *'02*
Spy Kids 2: The Island of Lost Dreams *'02*
The Body *'01*
Original Sin *'01*
Spy Kids *'01*
Play It to the Bone *'99*
The 13th Warrior *'99*
White River *'99*
The Mask of Zorro *'98*
Evita *'96*
Two Much *'96*
Assassins *'95*
Desperado *'95*
Four Rooms *'95*
Miami Rhapsody *'95*
Never Talk to Strangers *'95*
Interview with the Vampire *'94*
Of Love and Shadows *'94*
The House of the Spirits *'93*
Outrage *'93*
Philadelphia *'93*
The Mambo Kings *'92*
Terranova *'91*
Against the Wind *'90*
Tie Me Up! Tie Me Down! *'90*
If They Tell You I Fell *'89*
Baton Rouge *'88*
Women on the Verge of a Nervous Breakdown *'88*
Law of Desire *'86*
Matador *'86*
Labyrinth of Passion *'82*

Holly (Mike Ragan) Bane (1918-95)

Ride Clear of Diablo *'54*
Storm over Wyoming *'50*
Far Frontier *'48*
Return of Wildfire *'48*

Victor Banerjee (1946-)

Bitter Moon *'92*
Foreign Body *'86*
The Home and the World *'84*
A Passage to India *'84*
Hullabaloo over Georgie & Bonnie's Pictures *'78*

Lisa Banes (1955-)

Dragonfly *'02*
Pumpkin *'02*
Last Exit to Earth *'96*
Cocktail *'88*
Marie *'85*
The Hotel New Hampshire *'84*
Look Back in Anger *'80*

Eun-Jin Bang

301/302 *'95*
301, 302 *'94*

Joy Bang (1947-)

Messiah of Evil *'74*
Night of the Cobra Woman *'72*
Play It Again, Sam *'72*

Donatas Banionis

Solaris *'72*
Adomas Nori Buti Zmogumi *'59*

Tallulah Bankhead (1902-68)

Die! Die! My Darling! *'65*
Main Street to Broadway *'53*
Lifeboat *'44*
Stage Door Canteen *'43*
The Devil and the Deep *'32*
The Cheat *'31*

Aaron Banks

Fist of Fear, Touch of Death *'80*
The Bodyguard *'76*

Boyd Banks (1964-)

George A. Romero's Land of the Dead *'05*
Dawn of the Dead *'04*

Dennis Banks (1937-)

The Last of the Mohicans *'92*
Thunderheart *'92*

Elizabeth Banks (1974-)

The Uninvited *'09*
Comanche Moon *'08*
Definitely, Maybe *'08*
Meet Dave *'08*
Role Models *'08*
W. *'08*
Zack and Miri Make a Porno *'08*
Fred Claus *'07*
Meet Bill *'07*
Spider-Man 3 *'07*
Invincible *'06*
Slither *'06*
The Baxter *'05*
Daltry Calhoun *'05*
The 40 Year Old Virgin *'05*
The Sisters *'05*
Heights *'04*
Spider-Man 2 *'04*
Seabiscuit *'03*
Ordinary Sinner *'02*
Swept Away *'02*
Wet Hot American Summer *'01*

Ernie Banks

Finding Buck McHenry *'00*
Red Shoe Diaries: Luscious Lola *'00*
Pastime *'91*
King *'78*

Jonathan Banks (1947-)

Reign Over Me *'07*
R.S.V.P. *'02*
Crocodile Dundee in Los Angeles *'01*
Foolish *'99*
Let the Devil Wear Black *'99*
Melanie Darrow *'97*
Dark Breed *'96*
Flipper *'96*
Last Man Standing *'95*
Marilyn & Bobby: Her Final Affair *'94*
Body Shot *'93*
Boiling Point *'93*
Freejack *'92*
There Goes the Neighborhood *'92*
Nightmare *'91*
Honeymoon Academy *'90*
Cold Steel *'87*
Armed and Dangerous *'86*
Assassin *'86*
The Adventures of Buckaroo Banzai Across the Eighth Dimension *'84*
Beverly Hills Cop *'84*
Nadia *'84*

Leslie Banks (1890-1952)

Madeleine *'50*
Eye Witness *'49*
Henry V *'44*
Cottage to Let *'41*
Chamber of Horrors *'40*
The Arsenal Stadium Mystery *'39*
Jamaica Inn *'39*
Fire Over England *'37*
21 Days *'37*
Wings of the Morning *'37*
Sanders of the River *'35*
Transatlantic Tunnel *'35*
The Man Who Knew Too Much *'34*
Red Ensign *'34*
The Most Dangerous Game *'32*

Tyra Banks (1973-)

Tropic Thunder *'08*
Halloween: Resurrection *'02*
Coyote Ugly *'00*
Life-Size *'00*
Love Stinks *'99*
Higher Learning *'94*

Vilma Banky (1903-91)

Son of the Sheik *'26*
The Winning of Barbara Worth *'26*
The Eagle *'25*

Ian Bannen (1928-99)

To Walk with Lions *'99*
Waking Ned Devine *'98*
Braveheart *'95*
The Sound and the Silence *'93*
Blue Ice *'92*
Damage *'92*
The Big Man: Crossing the Line *'91*
George's Island *'91*
Catherine Cookson's The Fifteen Streets *'90*
Ghost Dad *'90*
The Courier *'88*
Hope and Glory *'87*
Defense of the Realm *'85*
Lamb *'85*
The Prodigal *'83*
Gandhi *'82*
Eye of the Needle *'81*
The Watcher in the Woods *'81*
Tinker, Tailor, Soldier, Spy *'80*
The Inglorious Bastards *'78*
Bite the Bullet *'75*
The Gathering Storm *'74*
Driver's Seat *'73*
From Beyond the Grave *'73*
Mackintosh Man *'73*
The Offence *'73*
Doomwatch *'72*
Fright *'71*
Ride to Glory *'71*
Too Late the Hero *'70*
The Flight of the Phoenix *'65*
The Hill *'65*
Carlton Browne of the F.O. *'59*
A Tale of Two Cities *'58*
The Third Key *'57*

Jill Banner (1946-82)

Hard Frame *'70*
The President's Analyst *'67*
Spider Baby *'64*

John Banner (1910-73)

Togetherness *'70*
36 Hours *'64*
Guilty of Treason *'50*
The Fallen Sparrow *'43*
Immortal Sergeant *'43*

Kanu Bannerjee (1905-85)

Aparajito *'58*
Pather Panchali *'54*

Karuna Bannerjee (1919-2001)

Aparajito *'58*
Pather Panchali *'54*

Reggie Bannister (1945-)

The Rage *'07*
Bubba Ho-Tep *'03*
Phantasm 4: Oblivion *'98*
Phantasm 3: Lord of the Dead *'94*
Silent Night, Deadly Night 4: Initiation *'90*
Survival Quest *'89*
Phantasm 2 *'88*
Phantasm *'79*

Maya Banno

Funky Forest: The First Contact *'06*
The Taste of Tea *'04*

Jack Bannon (1940-)

DaVinci's War *'92*
Miracle of the Heart: A Boys Town Story *'86*
Take Your Best Shot *'82*

Jim Bannon (1911-86)

Unknown World *'51*
The Fighting Redhead *'50*

Man from Colorado *'49*

Ildiko Bansagi (1947-)
Meeting Venus *'91*
Mephisto *'81*

Chen Baoguo
Robin-B-Hood *'06*
Women from the Lake of Scented Souls *'94*

Nina Bara (1920-90)
Missile to the Moon *'59*
Black Hills *'48*

Theda Bara (1890-1955)
The Love Goddesses *'65*
The Unchastened Woman *'25*
A Fool There Was *'14*

John Baragrey (1918-75)
Gamera, the Invincible *'66*
Pardners *'56*
Shockproof *'49*

Ari Barak
Waterworld *'95*
Jericho Fever *'93*

Angelika Baran
The Art of Travel *'08*
My 5 Wives *'00*

Christine Baranski (1952-)
The Bounty Hunter *'10*
Mamma Mia! *'08*
Bonneville *'06*
Relative Strangers *'06*
Welcome to Mooseport *'04*
Eloise at the Plaza *'03*
Marci X *'03*
Chicago *'02*
The Guru *'02*
Dr. Seuss' How the Grinch Stole Christmas *'00*
Bowfinger *'99*
Bulworth *'98*
Cruel Intentions *'98*
Neil Simon's The Odd Couple 2 *'98*
The Birdcage *'95*
Jeffrey *'95*
New Jersey Drive *'95*
The War *'94*
Addams Family Values *'93*
The Night We Never Met *'93*
The Ref *'93*
To Dance with the White Dog *'93*
Reversal of Fortune *'90*
The Pick-Up Artist *'87*
9 1/2 Weeks *'86*
Crackers *'84*

Phil Barantini (1980-)
The Boys and Girl From County Clare *'03*
Ned Kelly *'03*

Olivia Barash (1965-)
Grave Secrets *'89*
Dr. Alien *'88*
Tuff Turf *'85*
Repo Man *'83*
Tut & Tuttle *'81*
Child of Glass *'78*

Richie Barathy
Body Trouble *'92*
Caged Fury *'90*

Luca Barbareschi (1956-)
Private Affairs *'89*
Bye Bye Baby *'88*
Cannibal Holocaust *'80*

Marc Barbe
The Ring Finger *'05*
My Life and Times with Antonin Artaud *'93*

Adrienne Barbeau (1945-)
Unholy *'07*
Christmas Do-Over *'06*
Ring of Darkness *'04*
Across the Line *'00*
The Convent *'00*
Jack Frost 2: Revenge of the Mutant Killer Snowman *'00*
Burial of the Rats *'95*
Jailbreakers *'94*
Silk Degrees *'94*
Scott Turow's The Burden of Proof *'92*
Double-Crossed *'91*
Two Evil Eyes *'90*
Cannibal Women in the Avocado Jungle of Death *'89*
Back to School *'86*
Open House *'86*
Seduced *'85*
Terror at London Bridge *'85*
Next One *'84*
Charlie and the Great Balloon Chase *'82*
Creepshow *'82*
Swamp Thing *'82*
Cannonball Run *'81*
Escape from New York *'81*
Magic on Love Island *'80*
The Crash of Flight 401 *'78*
The Fog *'78*
Red Alert *'77*
Return to Fantasy Island *'77*

Ellen Barber
Born Beautiful *'82*
Blood Bride *'80*
The Premonition *'75*
Dealing: Or the Berkeley-to-Boston Forty-Brick Lost-Bag Blues *'72*

Frances Barber (1958-)
Goal 2: Living the Dream *'07*
Goal! The Dream Begins *'06*
Esther Kahn *'00*
Shiner *'00*
Still Crazy *'98*
The Ice House *'97*
Photographing Fairies *'97*
Rhodes *'97*
A Royal Scandal *'96*
We Think the World of You *'88*
A Zed & Two Noughts *'88*
Castaway *'87*
Prick Up Your Ears *'87*
Sammy & Rosie Get Laid *'87*
Home Sweet Home *'82*

Gillian Barber (1957-)
Stealing Sinatra *'04*
Suspicious River *'00*
Double Jeopardy *'99*
In Cold Blood *'96*
Maternal Instincts *'96*

Glynis Barber (1955-)
Deja Vu *'98*
Edge of Sanity *'89*
Tangiers *'83*
The Wicked Lady *'83*
The Terror *'79*
Yesterday's Hero *'79*

Paul Barber (1952-)
The Full Monty *'96*
The Long Good Friday *'80*

Katie Barberi (1972-)
Not Quite Human 2 *'89*
The Garbage Pail Kids Movie *'87*

Urbano Barberini (1962-)
Torrents of Spring *'90*
Gor *'88*
Opera *'88*
Outlaw of Gor *'87*
Demons *'86*

Vincent Barbi (1912-98)
Runaways *'75*
Lady Godiva Rides *'68*
The Astro-Zombies *'67*
The Blob *'58*

Christian Barbier (1924-)
Germicide *'74*
Army of Shadows *'69*

George Barbier (1864-1945)
Thunder Birds *'42*
The Man Who Came to Dinner *'41*
Week-End in Havana *'41*
The Adventures of Marco Polo *'38*
Little Miss Broadway *'38*
My Lucky Star *'38*
Thanks for Everything *'38*
On the Avenue *'37*
Waikiki Wedding *'37*
The Princess Comes Across *'36*
Wife Versus Secretary *'36*
The Crusades *'35*
Here Comes Cookie *'35*
Life Begins at Forty *'35*
The Merry Widow *'34*
No Man of Her Own *'32*
No One Man *'32*
One Hour with You *'32*
Strangers in Love *'32*
The Smiling Lieutenant *'31*
Touchdown *'31*

Paula Barbieri (1966-)
The Dangerous *'95*
Night Eyes 4: Fatal Passion *'95*
Red Shoe Diaries 5: Weekend Pass *'95*

Luis Barboo (1927-2001)
The Demons *'74*
Rites of Frankenstein *'72*

Richard Barboza
Tales of Erotica *'93*
Small Time *'91*

Lisa Barbuscia (1971-)
Bridget Jones's Diary *'01*
Highlander: Endgame *'00*
Almost Heroes *'97*
Serpent's Lair *'95*

Artur Barcis (1956-)
The Decalogue *'88*
No End *'84*

Caroline Barclay
Within the Rock *'96*
American Gothic *'88*

Don Barclay (1892-1975)
Outlaw Express *'38*
Thunder in the Desert *'38*
Border Phantom *'37*
Sweetheart of the Navy *'37*
Lion's Den *'36*

Joan Barclay (1914-2002)
The Shanghai Cobra *'45*
Sagebrush Law *'43*
The Black Dragons *'42*
The Corpse Vanishes *'42*
Flying Wild *'41*
Texas Trouble *'41*
Outlaw's Paradise *'39*
Six Gun Rhythm *'39*
Texas Wildcats *'39*
Lightnin' Carson Rides Again *'38*
Purple Vigilantes *'38*
Whirlwind Horseman *'38*
Blake of Scotland Yard *'36*
The Glory Trail *'36*
Phantom Patrol *'36*
Prison Shadows *'36*
Shadow of Chinatown *'36*
West of Nevada *'36*
Feud of the West *'35*
Finishing School *'33*

Roy Barcroft (1902-69)
Billy the Kid Versus Dracula *'66*
The Kettles on Old MacDonald's Farm *'57*
The Last Hunt *'56*
Iron Mountain Trail *'53*
Marshal of Cedar Rock *'53*
Shadows of Tombstone *'53*
Border Saddlemates *'52*
Hoodlum Empire *'52*
Radar Men from the Moon *'52*
Don Daredevil Rides Again *'51*
Rodeo King and the Senorita *'51*
Missourians *'50*
Night Riders of Montana *'50*
North of the Great Divide *'50*
The Vanishing Westerner *'50*
Arizona Cowboy *'49*
Down Dakota Way *'49*
Federal Agents vs. Underworld, Inc. *'49*
Outcasts of the Trail *'49*
Pioneer Marshal *'49*
Eyes of Texas *'48*
Far Frontier *'48*
G-Men Never Forget *'48*
Jesse James Rides Again *'47*
Lights of Old Santa Fe *'47*
Son of Zorro *'47*
Spoilers of the North *'47*
Wild Frontier *'47*
Alias Billy the Kid *'46*
Stagecoach to Denver *'46*
Vigilantes of Boom Town *'46*
Bells of Rosarita *'45*
D-Day on Mars *'45*
Manhunt of Mystery Island *'45*
The Purple Monster Strikes *'45*
Sunset in El Dorado *'45*
The Topeka Terror *'45*
Haunted Harbor *'44*
Bordertown Gunfighters *'43*
Calling Wild Bill Elliott *'43*
Hoppy Serves a Writ *'43*
Raiders of Sunset Pass *'43*
Riders of the Rio Grande *'43*
Sagebrush Law *'43*
Six Gun Gospel *'43*
Below the Border *'42*
Dawn on the Great Divide *'42*
Sunset on the Desert *'42*
Outlaws of the Cherokee Trail *'41*
West of Cimarron *'41*
The Showdown *'40*
Yukon Flight *'40*
Hopalong Cassidy: Renegade Trail *'39*
Renegade Trail *'39*
The Frontiersmen *'38*
Heroes of the Hills *'38*
The Stranger from Arizona *'38*

Ben Bard (1893-1974)
The Ghost Ship *'43*
7th Heaven *'27*

Carlos Bardem
Che *'08*
Dance with the Devil *'97*

Javier Bardem (1969-)
Eat, Pray, Love *'10*
Vicky Cristina Barcelona *'08*
Love in the Time of Cholera *'07*
No Country for Old Men *'07*
Goya's Ghosts *'06*
Collateral *'04*
The Sea Inside *'04*
The Dancer Upstairs *'02*
Mondays in the Sun *'02*
Before Night Falls *'00*
Between Your Legs *'99*
Second Skin *'99*
Dance with the Devil *'97*
Live Flesh *'97*
Extasis *'96*
Mouth to Mouth *'95*
Running Out of Time *'94*
Jamon, Jamon *'93*

Pilar Bardem (1939-)
Live Flesh *'97*
Vacas *'91*

Trevor Bardette (1902-77)
Papa's Delicate Condition *'63*
Thunder Road *'58*
The Monolith Monsters *'57*
Hills of Oklahoma *'50*
Gun Crazy *'49*
Omoo Omoo, the Shark God *'49*
The Secret Code *'42*
Doomed Caravan *'41*
Red River Valley *'41*

Aleksander Bardini (1913-95)
The Silent Touch *'94*
Trois Couleurs: Blanc *'94*
The Double Life of Veronique *'91*
The Decalogue *'88*
No End *'84*

Brigitte Bardot (1934-)
Don Juan (Or If Don Juan Were a Woman) *'73*
Legend of Frenchie King *'71*
Shalako *'68*
Spirits of the Dead *'68*
The Women *'68*
A Coeur Joie *'67*
Head Over Heels *'67*
Dear Brigitte *'65*
Viva Maria! *'65*
Contempt *'64*
Ravishing Idiot *'64*
Le Repos du Guerrier *'62*
Love on a Pillow *'62*
A Very Private Affair *'62*
Please Not Now! *'61*
Voulez-Vous Danser avec Moi? *'59*
The Bride Is Much Too Beautiful *'58*
Mam'zelle Pigalle *'58*
That Naughty Girl *'58*
Une Parisienne *'58*
And God Created Woman *'57*
The Night Heaven Fell *'57*
Doctor at Sea *'56*
Helen of Troy *'56*
Plucking the Daisy *'56*
Les Grandes Manoeuvres *'55*
Crazy for Love *'52*

Edda Barends (1942-)
Broken Mirrors *'85*
Question of Silence *'83*

Sonny Barger (1938-)
Hell's Angels '69 *'69*
Hell's Angels on Wheels *'67*

Ashraf Barhoum
The Kingdom *'07*
Paradise Now *'05*
The Syrian Bride *'04*

Lynn Bari (1913-89)
Trauma *'62*
Abbott and Costello Meet the Keystone Kops *'54*
Francis Joins the WACs *'54*
I Dream of Jeannie *'52*
I'd Climb the Highest Mountain *'51*
The Kid From Cleveland *'49*
The Amazing Mr. X *'48*
Nocturne *'46*
Shock! *'46*
The Bridge of San Luis Rey *'44*
Hello, Frisco, Hello *'43*
The Falcon Takes Over *'42*
The Magnificent Dope *'42*
Orchestra Wives *'42*
Sleepers West *'41*
Sun Valley Serenade *'41*
Kit Carson *'40*
Lillian Russell *'40*
Charlie Chan in City of Darkness *'39*
Mr. Moto's Gamble *'38*

Natalie Barish
Lost and Found *'99*
Round Numbers *'91*

Sophie Barjac (1957-)
Alice *'86*
Holiday Hotel *'77*

Yehuda Barkan (1945-)
The Big Gag *'87*
Eagles Attack at Dawn *'70*
Lupo *'70*

Clive Barker (1952-)
Quicksilver Highway *'98*
Sleepwalkers *'92*

Eric Barker
Carry On Spying *'64*
Carry On Constable *'60*
Dentist In the Chair *'60*
Carry On Sergeant *'58*

Jess Barker (1912-2000)
Kentucky Rifle *'55*
Shack Out on 101 *'55*
Dragonfly Squadron *'54*

Lex Barker (1919-73)
The Torture Chamber of Dr. Sadism *'69*
Woman Times Seven *'67*
A Place Called Glory *'66*
Apache's Last Battle *'64*
Executioner of Venice *'63*
The Invisible Dr. Mabuse *'62*
Pirates of the Coast *'61*
The Return of Dr. Mabuse *'61*
La Dolce Vita *'60*
Mission in Morocco *'59*
Strange Awakening *'58*
Girl in Black Stockings *'57*
Away All Boats *'56*
The Black Devils of Kali *'55*
Tarzan and the She-Devil *'53*
Tarzan's Savage Fury *'52*
Tarzan's Peril *'51*
Tarzan and the Slave Girl *'50*
Mr. Blandings Builds His Dream House *'48*
Tarzan's Magic Fountain *'48*
Velvet Touch *'48*
The Farmer's Daughter *'47*

Ronnie Barker (1929-2005)
My House in Umbria *'03*
The Gathering Storm *'02*
Porridge *'91*
Robin and Marian *'76*
The Man Outside *'68*

Steve Barkett (1950-)
Bikini Drive-In *'94*
Dark Universe *'93*
Dinosaur Island *'93*
Aftermath *'85*

Ellen Barkin (1954-)
Brooklyn's Finest *'09*
Happy Tears *'09*
Ocean's Thirteen *'07*
Trust the Man *'06*
Palindromes *'04*
She Hate Me *'04*
Someone Like You *'01*
Crime and Punishment in Suburbia *'00*
Mercy *'00*
Drop Dead Gorgeous *'99*
White River *'99*
Fear and Loathing in Las Vegas *'98*
The Fan *'96*
Trigger Happy *'96*
Wild Bill *'95*
Bad Company *'94*
Mac *'93*
This Boy's Life *'93*
Into the West *'92*
Man Trouble *'92*
Switch *'91*
Johnny Handsome *'89*
Sea of Love *'89*
Blood Money: The Story of Clinton and Nadine *'88*
The Big Easy *'87*
Made in Heaven *'87*
Siesta *'87*
Act of Vengeance *'86*
Desert Bloom *'86*
Down by Law *'86*
Terminal Choice *'85*
The Adventures of Buckaroo Banzai Across the Eighth Dimension *'84*
Harry & Son *'84*

The Princess Who Never Laughed '84
Daniel '83
Eddie and the Cruisers '83
Enormous Changes '83
Tender Mercies '83
Trumps '83
Diner '82
Kent State '81

Marcie Barkin
Fade to Black '80
Chesty Anderson USN '76

Peter Barkworth (1929-2006)
Champions '84
The Littlest Horse Thieves '76
Where Eagles Dare '68

Pat Barlow
Nanny McPhee '06
April Fool's Day '86

Ivor Barnard (1887-1953)
Beat the Devil '53
Madeleine '50

Barry Barnes
Kings '07
Veronica Guerin '03
Bedelia '46
The Girl in the News '41

Ben Barnes
The Chronicles of Narnia: Prince Caspian '08
Easy Virtue '08

Binnie Barnes (1903-98)
Forty Carats '73
Where Angels Go, Trouble Follows '68
The Trouble with Angels '66
Decameron Nights '53
The Dude Goes West '48
The Time of Their Lives '46
Getting Gertie's Garter '45
It's in the Bag '45
The Spanish Main '45
Call Out the Marines '42
I Married an Angel '42
In Old California '42
Melody Master '41
Day-Time Wife '39
Man About Town '39
The Three Musketeers '39
The Adventures of Marco Polo '38
The Divorce of Lady X '38
Holiday '38
Thanks for Everything '38
Broadway Melody of 1938 '37
The Last of the Mohicans '36
Three Smart Girls '36
Private Life of Don Juan '34
The Private Life of Henry VIII '33

Chris Barnes (1965-)
Tut & Tuttle '81
The Bad News Bears in Breaking Training '77
The Bad News Bears '76

Christopher Daniel Barnes (1972-)
Shut Up and Kiss Me '05
A Very Brady Sequel '96
The Brady Bunch Movie '95
Murder Without Motive '92
The Little Mermaid '89 (V)

Joanna Barnes (1934-)
The Parent Trap '98
I Wonder Who's Killing Her Now? '76
The War Wagon '67
Goodbye Charlie '64
The Parent Trap '61
Spartacus '60

Priscilla Barnes (1955-)
Thr3e '07
The Devil's Rejects '05
Alien 3000 '04
Alone with a Stranger '99
Final Payback '99
Catherine's Grove '98
Implicated '98
The Killing Grounds '97
Mallrats '95
Ava's Magical Adventure '94
The Crossing Guard '94
Erotique '94
National Lampoon's Attack of the 5 Ft. 2 Women '94
Body Trouble '92
Stepfather 3: Father's Day '92
Talons of the Eagle '92
License to Kill '89
Lords of the Deep '89
Traxx '87
The Last Married Couple in America '80
The Seniors '78
Time Machine '78
Beyond Reason '77
Delta Fox '77
Texas Detour '77

Rayford Barnes (1920-2000)
Jesse James Meets Frankenstein's Daughter '65
Sunday in New York '63

Richard Barnes
Lensman '84 (V)
Count Dracula '77

Susan Barnes
Nurse Betty '00
Where the Money Is '00
Lover Girl '97
One Night Stand '97
Nothing to Lose '96
Freeway '95
Serving in Silence: The Margarethe Cammermeyer Story '95
The Applegates '89

T. Roy Barnes (1880-1937)
Sally '29
Seven Chances '25

Walter Barnes
Smokey Bites the Dust '81
Escape to Witch Mountain '75
Challenge of the Gladiator '65
Revenge of the Musketeers '63

Charlie Barnett (1954-)
They Bite '95
My Man Adam '86
Nobody's Fool '86
D.C. Cab '84

Chester Barnett (1885-1947)
Trilby '17
The Wishing Ring '14

Griff Barnett (1884-1958)
Holiday Affair '49
The Millerson Case '47
Shadows on the Sage '42
Frontier Vengeance '40

Tom Barnett
Niagara Motel '06
The Reagans '04

Vince Barnett (1902-77)
Charade '53
Red Planet Mars '52
Kentucky Jubilee '51
Thunder in the Pines '49
Big Town After Dark '47
Shoot to Kill '47
Captive Wild Woman '43
Baby Face Morgan '42
The Corpse Vanishes '42
I Killed That Man '42
X Marks the Spot '42
Blonde Comet '41
Gangs, Inc. '41
Ride 'Em Cowgirl '41
The Singing Cowgirl '39
Boots of Destiny '37
We're in the Legion Now '37
Captain Calamity '36
Yellow Cargo '36
I Live My Life '35
Crimson Romance '34
Thirty Day Princess '34
The Death Kiss '33
The Prizefighter and the Lady '33

Jean Marie Barnwell
Blue River '95
Born to Be Wild '95
From the Mixed-Up Files of Mrs. Basil E. Frankweiler '95

Bruce Baron (1949-)
Ninja Hunt '86
Ninja Champion '80
Fireback '78
Ninja Destroyer '70

Joanne Baron
iMurders '08
The Perfect Witness '07
The Prince & Me '04
Burning Down the House '01
Hard Luck '01
Perfume '01
St. Patrick's Day '99
Allie & Me '97
Pet Shop '94
Crazy in Love '92

Sandy Baron (1937-2001)
Leprechaun 2 '94
Motorama '91
Vamp '86
Birdy '84
Broadway Danny Rose '84
The Out-of-Towners '70
If It's Tuesday, This Must Be Belgium '69
Sweet November '68
Targets '68

Elizabeth Barondes
Love to Kill '97
Adrenalin: Fear the Rush '96
Not of This Earth '96
Full Body Massage '95
Night of the Scarecrow '95

Byron Barr (1917-66)
Down Dakota Way '49
Pitfall '48
Big Town '47
Love Letters '45
Double Indemnity '44

Douglas Barr (1949-)
Spaced Invaders '90
Deadly Blessing '81

Jean-Marc Barr (1960-)
Cote d'Azur '05
Manderlay '05
Tara Road '05
Dogville '03
Le Divorce '03
Dancer in the Dark '99
Don't Let Me Die on a Sunday '98
St. Ives '98
The Scarlet Tunic '97
Breaking the Waves '95
The Favorite Son '94
The Plague '92
Zentropa '92
The Big Blue '88
Hope and Glory '87

Patrick Barr (1908-85)
The Godsend '79
House of Whipcord '75
Flesh and Blood Show '73
The Satanic Rites of Dracula '73
The Case of the Frightened Lady '39
Sailing Along '38

Sharon Barr
The Reluctant Agent '89
Spittin' Image '83
Archer: The Fugitive from the Empire '81

Gianfranco Barra (1940-)
Screw Loose '99
Avanti! '72

Maria Barranco (1961-)
Gaudi Afternoon '01
The Girl of Your Dreams '99
Mouth to Mouth '95
Zafarinas '94
The Red Squirrel '93
Don Juan, My Love '90
Tie Me Up! Tie Me Down! '90
Women on the Verge of a Nervous Breakdown '88

Robert Barrat (1889-1970)
Distant Drums '51
Riders of the Range '50
Magnificent Doll '46
The Road to Utopia '46
Strangler of the Swamp '46
They Were Expendable '45
The Adventures of Mark Twain '44
Captain Caution '40
Go West '40
Northwest Passage '40
Bad Lands '39
Union Pacific '39
Charlie Chan in Honolulu '38
Shadows over Shanghai '38
The Texans '38
The Black Legion '37
The Charge of the Light Brigade '36
Mary of Scotland '36
The Trail of the Lonesome Pine '36
Devil Dogs of the Air '35
Village Tale '35
Massacre '34
Heroes for Sale '33
King of the Jungle '33
Wild Boys of the Road '33

Jean-Louis Barrault (1910-94)
La Nuit de Varennes '82
The Longest Day '62
The Testament of Dr. Cordelier '59
La Ronde '51
Children of Paradise '44
Beethoven '36

Marie-Christine Barrault (1944-)
Obsession '97
Jesus of Montreal '89
Le Jupon Rouge '87
Swann in Love '84
Table for Five '83
Stardust Memories '80
L'Etat Sauvage '78
The Medusa Touch '78
Perceval '78
Cousin, Cousine '76
The Daydreamer '75
Chloe in the Afternoon '72
My Night at Maud's '69

Adriana Barraza (1956-)
Drag Me to Hell '09
Henry Poole Is Here '08
Babel '06
Amores Perros '00

Amy Barrett
House Where Evil Dwells '82
Caged Heat '74

Claudia Barrett
Robot Monster '53
The Happy Years '50
Night Riders of Montana '50

Edith Barrett (1907-77)
Jane Eyre '44
The Ghost Ship '43
I Walked with a Zombie '43
Lady for a Night '42

Jacinda Barrett (1972-)
The Last Kiss '06
The Namesake '06
Poseidon '06
School for Scoundrels '06
Bridget Jones: The Edge of Reason '04
Ladder 49 '04
The Human Stain '03

Jane Barrett (1923-69)
Bond of Fear '56
The Sword & the Rose '53
Eureka Stockade '49

John Barrett (1952-)
To the Death '93
American Kickboxer 1 '91
Lights! Camera! Murder! '89

Judith Barrett (1914-2000)
The Road to Singapore '40
Yellowstone '36

Majel Barrett (1932-2008)
Star Trek '09 (V)
Star Trek: Nemesis '02 (V)
Mommy '95
Star Trek: Generations '94 (V)
Teresa's Tattoo '94
Star Trek 4: The Voyage Home '86
Star Trek: The Motion Picture '79
Westworld '73

Nancy Barrett (1941-)
Belizaire the Cajun '86
Night of Dark Shadows '71
House of Dark Shadows '70

Nitchie Barrett
A Time to Die '91
Preppies '82

Ray Barrett (1927-)
After the Deluge '03
Visitors '03
In the Winter Dark '98
Heaven's Burning '97
Brilliant Lies '96
Hotel de Love '96
Sorrento Beach '95
Rebel '85
The Last Bastion '84
Where the Green Ants Dream '84
Waterfront '83
The Chant of Jimmie Blacksmith '78
Don's Party '76
Revenge '71
The Reptile '66

Sean Barrett (1940-)
Sink the Bismarck '60
War and Peace '56

Tony Barrett (1916-74)
Impact '49
Dick Tracy Meets Gruesome '47

Barbara Barrie (1931-)
Second Best '05
Spent '00
Judy Berlin '99
Hercules '97 (V)
Scarlett '94
End of the Line '88
Real Men '87
The Execution '85
Two of a Kind '82
Private Benjamin '80
To Race the Wind '80
Backstairs at the White House '79
The Bell Jar '79
Breaking Away '79
Child of Glass '78

Chris Barrie
Back in Business '06
When Evil Calls '06

Chris (Christopher) Barrie (1960-)
When Evil Calls '06
Lara Croft Tomb Raider: The Cradle of Life '03
Lara Croft: Tomb Raider '01

Judith Barrie
Hidden Gold '33
Party Girls '29

Mona Barrie (1909-64)
Cass Timberlane '47
Dawn on the Great Divide '42
The Strange Case of Dr. Rx '42
Today I Hang '42
I Take This Woman '40
Charlie Chan in London '34
One Night of Love '34

Wendy Barrie (1912-78)
The Saint Strikes Back: Criminal Court '46
Follies Girl '43
The Saint Takes Over '40
Day-Time Wife '39
Five Came Back '39
The Hound of the Baskervilles '39
The Saint Strikes Back '39
I Am the Law '38
Dead End '37
Vengeance '37
If I Were Rich '33
The Private Life of Henry VIII '33
Wedding Rehearsal '32

Edgar Barrier (1907-64)
The Giant Claw '57
Cobra Woman '44
The Phantom of the Opera '43
Arabian Nights '42

Pat (Barringer) Barrington (1941-)
Mantis in Lace '68
The Acid Eaters '67
Agony of Love '66
Orgy of the Dead '65

Phyllis Barrington
Sucker Money '34
The Drifter '32

Chuck Barris (1929-)
Confessions of a Dangerous Mind '02
Hugo Pool '97

Desmond Barrit (1944-)
Northanger Abbey '07
A Christmas Carol '99
A Midsummer Night's Dream '96

Bob (Robert) Barron (1922-2002)
Ballad of a Gunfighter '64
Tank Commando '59
Sea Hound '47
The Caravan Trail '46
Song of Old Wyoming '45
Guns of the Law '44

Dana Barron (1968-)
National Lampoon's Christmas Vacation 2: Cousin Eddie's Big Island Adventure '03
The Perfect Nanny '00
The Man in the Iron Mask '97
City of Industry '96
National Lampoon's Vacation '83

John Barron (1920-2004)
Agatha Christie's Thirteen at Dinner '85
Whoops Apocalypse '83
Hitler: The Last Ten Days '73

Keith Barron (1936-)
Take Me '01
Madame Bovary '00
Catherine Cookson's The Round Tower '98
At the Earth's Core '76
Nothing But the Night '72
Freelance '71
Baby Love '69

Robert V. Barron (1932-2000)
Bill & Ted's Excellent Adventure *'89*
The Big Turnaround *'88*
Daddy's Boys *'87*
Boss of Boomtown *'44*
The Return of the Rangers *'43*

George Barrows (1913-94)
Hillbillies in a Haunted House *'67*
Robot Monster *'53*

Barta Barry (1911-)
Dr. Jekyll and the Wolfman *'71*
Gladiators 7 *'62*

Bruce Barry (1934-)
The Good Wife *'86*
Plunge Into Darkness *'77*

Donald (Don "Red") Barry (1912-80)
Blazing Stewardesses *'75*
Johnny Got His Gun *'71*
Hard Frame *'70*
The Shakiest Gun in the West *'68*
Hostile Guns *'67*
Iron Angel *'64*
Born Reckless *'59*
Frankenstein 1970 *'58*
Square Dance Jubilee *'51*
Border Rangers *'50*
Gunfire *'50*
I Shot Billy the Kid *'50*
Red Desert *'50*
Train to Tombstone *'50*
Outlaw Gang *'49*
Ringside *'49*
Tough Assignment *'49*
The Purple Heart *'44*
California Joe *'43*
Sundown Kid *'43*
The Sombrero Kid *'42*
Sundown Fury *'42*
Adventures of Red Ryder *'40*
Frontier Vengeance *'40*
Days of Jesse James *'39*
Panama Patrol *'39*
Saga of Death Valley *'39*
Wyoming Outlaw *'39*
The Duke of West Point *'38*
Sinners in Paradise *'38*

Gene Barry (1921-2009)
War of the Worlds *'05*
These Old Broads *'01*
The Gambler Returns: The Luck of the Draw *'93*
Perry Mason: The Case of the Lost Love *'87*
The Adventures of Nellie Bly *'81*
A Cry for Love *'80*
Second Coming of Suzanne *'80*
Subterfuge *'68*
Columbo: Prescription Murder *'67*
Maroc 7 *'67*
Thunder Road *'58*
China Gate *'57*
Forty Guns *'57*
The 27th Day *'57*
Back from Eternity *'56*
Soldier of Fortune *'55*
Red Garters *'54*
The War of the Worlds *'53*
The Atomic City *'52*

Jason Barry (1975-)
Legend of the Bog *'08*
The Still Life *'07*
Honor *'06*
MirrorMask *'05*
Beyond Re-Animator *'03*
Conspiracy of Silence *'03*
When the Sky Falls *'99*
Monument Ave. *'98*
The Last of the High Kings *'96*

Neill Barry (1965-)
Friends & Lovers *'99*
O.C. and Stiggs *'87*
Joey *'85*
Old Enough *'84*

Patricia Barry (1930-)
Twilight Zone: The Movie *'83*
Bogie: The Last Hero *'80*
Kitten with a Whip *'64*
Sammy, the Way-Out Seal *'62*
Riders of the Whistling Pines *'49*
Cry Wolf *'47*

Phyllis Barry (1908-54)
Goodbye Love *'34*
The Moonstone *'34*
What! No Beer? *'33*

Raymond J. Barry (1939-)
The Shortcut *'09*
American Crude *'07*
Flight of the Living Dead: Outbreak on a Plane *'07*
Walk Hard: The Dewey Cox Story *'07*
Steel City *'06*
Just Married *'03*
Interview with the Assassin *'02*
The Deep End *'01*
Training Day *'01*
Best Men *'98*
Flubber *'97*
The Chamber *'96*
Headless Body in Topless Bar *'96*
Dead Man Walking *'95*
Sudden Death *'95*
Cool Runnings *'93*
Falling Down *'93*
The Ref *'93*
K2: The Ultimate High *'92*
Rapid Fire *'92*
The Turning *'92*
Drug Wars: The Camarena Story *'90*
Born on the Fourth of July *'89*
Cop *'88*
Daddy's Boys *'87*
Year of the Dragon *'85*
Christmas Evil *'80*

Roukietou Barry
Tilai *'90*
Yaaba *'89*

Thom Barry
2 Fast 2 Furious *'03*
The Fast and the Furious *'01*
Major League 3: Back to the Minors *'98*
Steel *'97*

Toni Barry
Endgame *'01*
Proteus *'95*
A House in the Hills *'93*

Tony Barry (1941-)
Solo *'06*
Paperback Hero *'99*
Doing Time for Patsy Cline *'97*
Road to Nhill *'97*
Shame *'87*
The Quest *'86*
We of the Never Never *'82*
Goodbye Pork Pie *'81*
Hard Knocks *'80*
The Odd Angry Shot *'79*
Little Boy Lost *'78*

Wendy Barry
Evil Lives *'92*
Knights of the City *'85*

Wesley Barry (1907-94)
Blind Fools *'40*
Sunny Skies *'30*
Battling Bunyon *'24*
The Country Kid *'23*

Deborah Barrymore
See Deborah Maria Moore

Drew Barrymore (1975-)
Going the Distance *'10*
Everybody's Fine *'09*
Grey Gardens *'09*
He's Just Not That Into You *'09*
Whip It *'09*
Beverly Hills Chihuahua *'08 (V)*
Lucky You *'07*
Music & Lyrics *'07*
Curious George *'06 (V)*
Fever Pitch *'05*
50 First Dates *'04*
Charlie's Angels: Full Throttle *'03*
Duplex *'03*
Confessions of a Dangerous Mind *'02*
Donnie Darko *'01*
Riding in Cars with Boys *'01*
Charlie's Angels *'00*
Skipped Parts *'00*
Titan A.E. *'00 (V)*
Never Been Kissed *'99*
Best Men *'98*
Ever After: A Cinderella Story *'98*
Home Fries *'98*
The Wedding Singer *'97*
Everyone Says I Love You *'96*
Scream *'96*
Wishful Thinking *'96*
Batman Forever *'95*
Mad Love *'95*
Bad Girls *'94*
Boys on the Side *'94*
The Amy Fisher Story *'93*
No Place to Hide *'93*
Wayne's World 2 *'93*
Guncrazy *'92*
Poison Ivy *'92*
Sketch Artist *'92*
Motorama *'91*
Waxwork 2: Lost in Time *'91*
Doppelganger: The Evil Within *'90*
Far from Home *'89*
See You in the Morning *'89*
A Conspiracy of Love *'87*
Babes in Toyland *'86*
Cat's Eye *'85*
Firestarter *'84*
Irreconcilable Differences *'84*
E.T.: The Extra-Terrestrial *'82*
Altered States *'80*

Ethel Barrymore (1879-1959)
Young at Heart *'54*
Main Street to Broadway *'53*
The Story of Three Loves *'53*
Just for You *'52*
It's a Big Country *'51*
Pinky *'49*
That Midnight Kiss *'49*
Portrait of Jennie *'48*
The Smallest Show on Earth *'48*
The Farmer's Daughter *'47*
The Paradine Case *'47*
The Spiral Staircase *'46*
None But the Lonely Heart *'44*
Rasputin and the Empress *'33*

John Barrymore (1882-1942)
Playmates *'41*
The Invisible Woman *'40*
Midnight *'39*
Bulldog Drummond's Peril *'38*
The Great Man Votes *'38*
Marie Antoinette *'38*
Spawn of the North *'38*
Bulldog Drummond Comes Back *'37*
Bulldog Drummond's Revenge *'37*
Maytime *'37*
Romeo and Juliet *'36*
Twentieth Century *'34*
Counsellor-at-Law *'33*
Dinner at Eight *'33*
Night Flight *'33*
Rasputin and the Empress *'33*
Topaze *'33*
A Bill of Divorcement *'32*
Grand Hotel *'32*
State's Attorney *'31*
Svengali *'31*
Tempest *'28*
The Beloved Rogue *'27*
When a Man Loves *'27*
Don Juan *'26*
Beau Brummel *'24*
Sherlock Holmes *'22*
Dr. Jekyll and Mr. Hyde *'20*

John Drew (Blythe) Barrymore, Jr. (1932-2004)
Americana *'81*
Smokey Bites the Dust *'81*
The Trojan Horse *'62*
High School Confidential *'58*
Never Love a Stranger *'58*
High Lonesome *'50*

Lionel Barrymore (1878-1954)
Main Street to Broadway *'53*
Lone Star *'52*
Malaya *'49*
Key Largo *'48*
Duel in the Sun *'46*
It's a Wonderful Life *'46*
The Valley of Decision *'45*
A Guy Named Joe *'44*
Since You Went Away *'44*
Thousands Cheer *'43*
Lady Be Good *'41*
Dr. Kildare's Strange Case *'40*
Let Freedom Ring *'39*
On Borrowed Time *'39*
The Secret of Dr. Kildare *'39*
Test Pilot *'38*
You Can't Take It with You *'38*
Captains Courageous *'37*
Navy Blue and Gold *'37*
Saratoga *'37*
Camille *'36*
Devil Doll *'36*
The Gorgeous Hussy *'36*
Ah, Wilderness! *'35*
David Copperfield *'35*
The Little Colonel *'35*
Mark of the Vampire *'35*
The Return of Peter Grimm *'35*
The Girl from Missouri *'34*
Treasure Island *'34*
Dinner at Eight *'33*
Night Flight *'33*
One Man's Journey *'33*
Rasputin and the Empress *'33*
Grand Hotel *'32*
Mata Hari *'32*
A Free Soul *'31*
Free and Easy *'30*
Sadie Thompson *'28*
West of Zanzibar *'28*
The Bells *'26*
The Temptress *'26*
America *'24*
Battle of Elderbush Gulch *'13*

Judith Barsi (1977-88)
All Dogs Go to Heaven *'89 (V)*
The Land Before Time *'88 (V)*
Jaws: The Revenge *'87*
Eye of the Tiger *'86*

Roger Bart (1962-)
Harold & Kumar Escape from Guantanamo Bay *'08*
The Midnight Meat Train *'08*
Spy School *'08*
American Gangster *'07*
Hostel: Part 2 *'07*
The Producers *'05*
The Stepford Wives *'04*

Paul Bartel (1938-2000)
Hamlet *'00*
Billy's Hollywood Screen Kiss *'98*
Armistead Maupin's More Tales of the City *'97*
Lewis and Clark and George *'97*
Basquiat *'96*
Skeletons *'96*
The Death Artist *'95*
The Jerky Boys *'95*
The Usual Suspects *'95*
Grief *'94*
Number One Fan *'94*
Acting on Impulse *'93*
Armistead Maupin's Tales of the City *'93*
Posse *'93*
Desire and Hell at Sunset Motel *'92*
Evil Lives *'92*
Liquid Dreams *'92*
Mortuary Academy *'91*
The Pope Must Diet *'91*
Gremlins 2: The New Batch *'90*
Far Out Man *'89*
Pucker Up and Bark Like a Dog *'89*
Scenes from the Class Struggle in Beverly Hills *'89*
Out of the Dark *'88*
Amazon Women on the Moon *'87*
Munchies *'87*
Chopping Mall *'86*
Killer Party *'86*
Into the Night *'85*
Frankenweenie *'84*
Get Crazy *'83*
Eating Raoul *'82*
Trick or Treats *'82*
Heartbeeps *'81*
Rock 'n' Roll High School *'79*
Piranha *'78*
Grand Theft Auto *'77*
Cannonball *'76*
Eat My Dust *'76*
Hollywood Boulevard *'76*

Eddie Barth (1931-)
Mr. Write *'92*
Twenty Dollar Star *'91*
Thunder and Lightning *'77*

Isolde Barth
Rosenstrasse *'03*
Quiet Days in Clichy *'90*
Club Extinction *'89*

Justin Bartha (1978-)
The Hangover *'09*
National Treasure: Book of Secrets *'07*
Failure to Launch *'06*
Trust the Man *'06*
National Treasure *'04*
Gigli *'03*

Richard Barthelmess (1895-1963)
The Spoilers *'42*
Only Angels Have Wings *'39*
Spy of Napoleon *'36*
Massacre *'34*
Heroes for Sale *'33*
The Cabin in the Cotton *'32*
The Dropkick *'27*
Just Suppose *'26*
Ranson's Folly *'26*
Shore Leave *'25*
Soul-Fire *'25*
Tol'able David *'21*
The Idol Dancer *'20*
The Love Flower *'20*
Way Down East *'20*
Broken Blossoms *'19*

Freddie Bartholomew (1924-92)
St. Benny the Dip *'51*
Sepia Cinderella *'47*
Junior Army *'42*
Tom Brown's School Days *'40*
Listen, Darling *'38*
Captains Courageous *'37*
The Devil Is a Sissy *'36*
Little Lord Fauntleroy *'36*
Lloyds of London *'36*
Anna Karenina *'35*
David Copperfield *'35*

Logan Bartholomew (1984-)
Love's Abiding Joy *'06*
Love's Long Journey *'05*
Nearing Grace *'05*
Love's Enduring Promise *'04*

Lynsey Bartilson (1983-)
A Rat's Tale *'98 (V)*
Mrs. Santa Claus *'96*

Bennie Bartlett (1924-99)
Bowery Boys Meet the Monsters *'54*
Clipped Wings *'53*
Master Minds *'49*
Clancy Street Boys *'43*
Code of the Outlaw *'42*

Bonnie Bartlett (1929-)
Shiloh 2: Shiloh Season *'99*
Tuesdays with Morrie *'99*
Primary Colors *'98*
Shiloh *'97*
Ghosts of Mississippi *'96*
Dave *'93*
Dead to Rights *'93*
Twins *'88*
The Deliberate Stranger *'86*
Dempsey *'83*
Love Letters *'83*
A Long Way Home *'81*
Rape and Marriage: The Rideout Case *'80*

Jamie Bartlett
Beyond Borders *'03*
Ernest Goes to Africa *'97*

Martine Bartlett (1925-2006)
Sybil *'76*
Lord Love a Duck *'66*

Richard Bartlett (1922-94)
Lonesome Trail *'55*
Silver Star *'55*
Silent Raiders *'54*

Robin Bartlett (1951-)
City of Angels *'98*
Honey, We Shrunk Ourselves *'97*
Dangerous Minds *'95*
Fallen Angels 1 *'93*
Deceived *'91*
If Looks Could Kill *'91*
Regarding Henry *'91*
Alice *'90*
Postcards from the Edge *'90*
Lean on Me *'89*
Baby Boom *'87*

Eva Bartok (1926-98)
Blood and Black Lace *'64*
Operation Amsterdam *'60*
S.O.S. Pacific *'60*
Naked in the Night *'58*
Ten Thousand Bedrooms *'57*
The Gamma People *'56*
Norman Conquest *'53*
Spaceways *'53*
Crimson Pirate *'52*

Jayce Bartok (1974-)
The Cake Eaters *'07*
Red Doors *'05*
The Tollbooth *'04*
Murder at Devil's Glen *'99*
subUrbia *'96*

Luciano Bartoli
Bizarre *'87*
Henry IV *'85*

Buzz Barton (1913-90)
Wild Horse Valley *'40*
The Riding Avenger *'36*
Feud of the West *'35*
Powdersmoke Range *'35*
Saddle Aces *'35*
The Tonto Kid *'35*
The Lone Defender *'32*
Mystery Trooper *'32*

Apache Kid's Escape *'30*

Charles T. Barton (1902-81)

Beau Geste *'39*
The Fighting Westerner *'35*

Diana Barton (1966-)

Body of Influence *'93*
Sexual Malice *'93*

Gregg Barton (1912-2000)

Man From God's Country *'58*
Silver City Bonanza *'51*
West to Glory *'47*

J Barton

A Separate Peace *'04*
Legally Blonde 2: Red White & Blonde *'03*

James Barton (1890-1962)

The Misfits *'61*
Naked Hills *'56*
Here Comes the Groom *'51*
The Time of Your Life *'48*
The Shepherd of the Hills *'41*

Margaret Barton

The Gay Dog *'54*
Brief Encounter *'46*

Mischa Barton (1986-)

Homecoming *'09*
Closing the Ring *'07*
St. Trinian's *'07*
Virgin Territory *'07*
The Oh in Ohio *'06*
Pulse *'03*
Lost and Delirious *'01*
Tart *'01*
Skipped Parts *'00*
Pups *'99*
The Sixth Sense *'99*
Lawn Dogs *'96*

Peter Barton (1956-)

Friday the 13th, Part 4: The Final Chapter *'84*
Hell Night *'81*

Skye McCole Bartusiak (1992-)

Kill Your Darlings *'06*
Boogeyman *'05*
Love Comes Softly *'03*
Firestarter 2: Rekindled *'02*
Blonde *'01*
Don't Say a Word *'01*
Riding in Cars with Boys *'01*
The Patriot *'00*

Billy Barty (1924-2000)

Wishful Thinking *'92*
Digging Up Business *'91*
Life Stinks *'91*
Lobster Man from Mars *'89*
Snow White *'89*
UHF *'89*
Willow *'88*
Body Slam *'87*
Masters of the Universe *'87*
Legend *'86*
Rumpelstiltskin *'86*
Tough Guys *'86*
Night Patrol *'85*
Comic Book Kids *'82*
Under the Rainbow *'81*
Foul Play *'78*
The Amazing Dobermans *'76*
The Day of the Locust *'75*
Pufnstuf *'70*
Harum Scarum *'65*
Roustabout *'64*
The Undead *'57*
Mickey the Great *'39*
The Bride of Frankenstein *'35*
A Midsummer Night's Dream *'35*

Siri Baruc (1978-)

Megasnake *'07*
Unholy *'07*
The Foursome *'06*
Blood Angels *'05*

The Glass Trap *'04*

Jay Baruchel (1982-)

How to Train Your Dragon *'10 (V)*
She's Out of My League *'10*
The Sorcerer's Apprentice *'10*
Fanboys *'09*
Nick & Norah's Infinite Playlist *'08*
Real Time *'08*
Tropic Thunder *'08*
Just Buried *'07*
Knocked Up *'07*
I'm Reed Fish *'06*
Million Dollar Baby *'04*
Nemesis Game *'03*

Leon Bary (1880-1954)

King of the Wild Horses *'24*
The Three Musketeers *'21*

Mikhail Baryshnikov (1948-)

Company Business *'91*
Dancers *'87*
That's Dancing! *'85*
White Nights *'85*
The Turning Point *'77*

Gary Basaraba (1959-)

Charlotte's Web *'06*
Jesse Stone: Death in Paradise *'06*
Unfaithful *'02*
K-9 3: P.I. *'01*
Dead Silence *'96*
A Horse for Danny *'95*
The War *'94*
Fried Green Tomatoes *'91*
Midnight Murders *'91*
One Magic Christmas *'85*
Sweet Dreams *'85*

David Alan Basche (1968-)

The Adjustment Bureau *'10*
I'll Believe You *'07*
United 93 *'06*
Crazylove *'05*
War of the Worlds *'05*
Carry Me Home *'04*

Dante Basco (1975-)

Take the Lead *'06*
Extremedays *'01*
Riot in the Streets *'96*
Hook *'91*

Richard Basehart (1914-84)

Marilyn: The Untold Story *'80*
Being There *'79*
The Rebels *'79*
Great Bank Hoax *'78*
The Island of Dr. Moreau *'77*
Flood! *'76*
The Bounty Man *'72*
Rage *'72*
Chato's Land *'71*
City Beneath the Sea *'71*
The Andersonville Trial *'70*
Hans Brinker *'69*
Kings of the Sun *'63*
Hitler *'62*
Portrait in Black *'60*
The Brothers Karamazov *'58*
Moby Dick *'56*
Il Bidone *'55*
La Strada *'54*
Titanic *'53*
Fixed Bayonets! *'51*
Tension *'50*
Reign of Terror *'49*
He Walked by Night *'48*
Cry Wolf *'47*

Blake Bashoff (1981-)

Together Again for the First Time *'08*
Big Bully *'95*

Alain Bashung (1947-)

Confusion of Genders *'00*
My Father, My Mother, My Brothers and My Sisters *'99*

Count Basie (1904-84)

Blazing Saddles *'74*
Sex and the Single Girl *'64*
Cinderfella *'60*
Stage Door Canteen *'43*

Toni Basil (1948-)

Eating *'90*
Rockula *'90*
Angel 3: The Final Chapter *'88*
Slaughterhouse Rock *'88*
Mother, Jugs and Speed *'76*
Easy Rider *'69*
Village of the Giants *'65*
Pajama Party *'64*

Salvatore Basile

Cobra Verde *'88*
Cannibal Holocaust *'80*

Kim Basinger (1953-)

The Informers *'09*
The Burning Plain *'08*
While She Was Out *'08*
Even Money *'06*
The Sentinel *'06*
Cellular *'04*
The Door in the Floor *'04*
Elvis Has Left the Building *'04*
8 Mile *'02*
People I Know *'02*
Bless the Child *'00*
I Dreamed of Africa *'00*
L.A. Confidential *'97*
Ready to Wear *'94*
The Getaway *'93*
The Real McCoy *'93*
Wayne's World 2 *'93*
Cool World *'92*
Final Analysis *'92*
The Marrying Man *'91*
Batman *'89*
My Stepmother Is an Alien *'88*
Blind Date *'87*
Nadine *'87*
Fool for Love *'86*
9 1/2 Weeks *'86*
No Mercy *'86*
The Natural *'84*
The Man Who Loved Women *'83*
Never Say Never Again *'83*
Mother Lode *'82*
Hard Country *'81*
Killjoy *'81*
From Here to Eternity *'79*

Austin Basis

My Sassy Girl *'08*
The Other End of the Line *'08*
Boxboarders! *'07*

Elya Baskin (1951-)

Thirteen Days *'00*
Running Red *'99*
Air Force One *'97*
Deepstar Six *'89*
Enemies, a Love Story *'89*
Spy Trap *'88*
The Name of the Rose *'86*
Moscow on the Hudson *'84*

Antoine Basler

A Prophet *'09*
Irma Vep *'96*
Rendezvous in Paris *'95*

Marianne Basler (1964-)

Va Savoir *'01*
A Soldier's Tale *'91*
Overseas: Three Women with Man Trouble *'90*

Lena Basquette (1907-94)

Heroes of the Heart *'94*
A Night for Crime *'42*
Rose of Rio Grande *'38*
Hello Trouble *'32*
The Midnight Lady *'32*
Arizona Terror *'31*
Hard Hombre *'31*
Pleasure *'31*

Alfie Bass (1921-87)

The Fearless Vampire Killers *'67*
Alfie *'66*
Help! *'65*
Blackout *'54*
Made in Heaven *'52*
The Lavender Hill Mob *'51*
Man on the Run *'49*
It Always Rains on Sunday *'47*

Bobby Bass (1936-2001)

The Squeeze *'87*
Blood Beach *'81*

Tamara La Seon Bass (1978-)

Baby Boy *'01*
Bellyfruit *'99*

Albert Bassermann (1862-1952)

The Red Shoes *'48*
The Private Affairs of Bel Ami *'47*
Rhapsody in Blue *'45*
Since You Went Away *'44*
Madame Curie *'43*
The Moon and Sixpence *'43*
Invisible Agent *'42*
Reunion in France *'42*
The Shanghai Gesture *'42*
Melody Master *'41*
A Woman's Face *'41*
Dr. Ehrlich's Magic Bullet *'40*
Foreign Correspondent *'40*

Angela Bassett (1958-)

Notorious *'09*
Gospel Hill *'08*
Nothing But the Truth *'08*
Tyler Perry's Meet the Browns *'08*
Meet the Robinsons *'07 (V)*
Akeelah and the Bee *'06*
Mr. & Mrs. Smith *'05 (V)*
Mr. 3000 *'04*
Masked and Anonymous *'03*
The Rosa Parks Story *'02*
Sunshine State *'02*
Ruby's Bucket of Blood *'01*
The Score *'01*
Boesman & Lena *'00*
Whispers: An Elephant's Tale *'00 (V)*
Music of the Heart *'99*
Supernova *'99*
How Stella Got Her Groove Back *'98*
Contact *'97*
Strange Days *'95*
Vampire in Brooklyn *'95*
Waiting to Exhale *'95*
What's Love Got to Do with It? *'93*
Innocent Blood *'92*
The Jacksons: An American Dream *'92*
Malcolm X *'92*
Passion Fish *'92*
Boyz N the Hood *'91*
City of Hope *'91*
Critters 4 *'91*
The Heroes of Desert Storm *'91*
F/X *'86*

Linda Bassett (1950-)

Kinky Boots *'06*
Calendar Girls *'03*
The Hours *'02*
Beautiful People *'99*
East Is East *'99*
Oscar and Lucinda *'97*
Mary Reilly *'95*
Waiting for the Moon *'87*

Steve Bassett (1955-)

The Jackal *'97*
Spring Break *'83*

Alexandra Bastedo (1946-)

Draw! *'81*
Find the Lady *'76*
The Ghoul *'75*
The Blood Spattered Bride *'72*
Kashmiri Run *'69*

Billy Bastiani

Blood & Concrete: A Love Story *'90*
Salvation! *'87*

Steve Bastoni (1966-)

Macbeth *'06*
The Crocodile Hunter: Collision Course *'02*
Rodgers & Hammerstein's South Pacific *'01*
Dr. Jekyll & Mr. Hyde *'99*
15 Amore *'98*

Othon Bastos (1933-)

Behind the Sun *'01*
Central Station *'98*
Antonio Das Mortes *'68*
Black God, White Devil *'64*

Michal Bat-Adam

The Impossible Spy *'87*
Atalia *'85*
Madame Rosa *'77*
Rachel's Man *'75*
The House on Chelouche Street *'73*
I Love You Rosa *'72*

Sylvia Bataille (1908-93)

A Day in the Country *'46*
The Crime of Monsieur Lange *'36*

Alexei Batalov (1928-)

Moscow Does Not Believe in Tears *'80*
The Lady with the Dog *'59*
The Cranes Are Flying *'57*

Nikolai Batalov (1899-1937)

The Road to Life *'31*
Bed and Sofa *'27*
Mother *'26*
Aelita: Queen of Mars *'24*

Pierre Batcheff (1901-32)

Un Chien Andalou *'28*
The Chess Player *'27*
Napoleon *'27*
Siren of the Tropics *'27*

Anthony Bate (1929-)

Philby, Burgess and MacLean: Spy Scandal of the Century *'84*
Smiley's People *'82*
Tinker, Tailor, Soldier, Spy *'80*
Madhouse Mansion *'74*

Geoffrey Bateman

Manderlay *'05*
Another Country *'84*

Jason Bateman (1969-)

The Switch *'10*
Couples Retreat *'09*
Extract *'09*
The Invention of Lying *'09*
State of Play *'09*
Up in the Air *'09*
Forgetting Sarah Marshall *'08*
Hancock *'08*
The Ex *'07*
Juno *'07*
The Kingdom *'07*
Mr. Magorium's Wonder Emporium *'07*
Smokin' Aces *'07*
Arthur and the Invisibles *'06 (V)*
The Break-Up *'06*
Dodgeball: A True Underdog Story *'04*
Starsky & Hutch *'04*
One Way Out *'02*
The Sweetest Thing *'02*
Sol Goode *'01*
Love Stinks *'99*
Breaking the Rules *'92*
A Taste for Killing *'92*
Necessary Roughness *'91*
Teen Wolf Too *'87*
Can You Feel Me Dancing? *'85*

Justine Bateman (1966-)

Hybrid *'07*
The TV Set *'06*
Out of Order *'03*
Kiss & Tell *'99*
Highball *'97*
God's Lonely Man *'96*
Another Woman *'94*
The Night We Never Met *'93*
Deadbolt *'92*
Primary Motive *'92*
The Closer *'91*
The Fatal Image *'90*
Satisfaction *'88*
Can You Feel Me Dancing? *'85*

Alan Bates (1934-2003)

Hollywood North *'03*
The Statement *'03*
Evelyn *'02*
The Mothman Prophecies *'02*
The Sum of All Fears *'02*
Gosford Park *'01*
The Prince and the Pauper *'01*
Arabian Nights *'00*
St. Patrick: The Irish Legend *'00*
Grave Indiscretions *'96*
Silent Tongue *'92*
Unnatural Pursuits *'91*
Hamlet *'90*
Club Extinction *'89*
Mr. Frost *'89*
A Voyage 'Round My Father *'89*
We Think the World of You *'88*
Pack of Lies *'87*
Prayer for the Dying *'87*
Duet for One *'86*
An Englishman Abroad *'83*
Separate Tables *'83*
The Wicked Lady *'83*
Britannia Hospital *'82*
Return of the Soldier *'82*
Hands Up *'81*
Quartet *'81*
Trespasser *'81*
Nijinsky *'80*
The Rose *'79*
The Shout *'78*
An Unmarried Woman *'78*
In Celebration *'75*
Royal Flash *'75*
The Story of Jacob & Joseph *'74 (N)*
The Story of a Love Story *'73*
A Day in the Death of Joe Egg *'71*
The Go-Between *'71*
Women in Love *'70*
The Fixer *'68*
Far from the Madding Crowd *'67*
Georgy Girl *'66*
The King of Hearts *'66*
Zorba the Greek *'64*
A Kind of Loving *'62*
Whistle down the Wind *'61*
The Entertainer *'60*

Barbara Bates (1925-69)

Rhapsody *'54*
The Caddy *'53*
Belles on Their Toes *'52*
I'd Climb the Highest Mountain *'51*
Let's Make It Legal *'51*
Cheaper by the Dozen *'50*
The Inspector General *'49*
June Bride *'48*

Florence Bates (1888-1954)

Lullaby of Broadway *'51*
The Judge Steps Out *'49*
A Letter to Three Wives *'49*
My Dear Secretary *'49*
I Remember Mama *'48*
Portrait of Jennie *'48*
Winter Meeting *'48*
The Secret Life of Walter Mitty *'47*

Asylum '72
The Bushbaby '70
Casino Royale '67
King Rat '65

Hal Baylor (1918-98)
A Boy and His Dog '75
Emperor of the North Pole '73
The Young Lions '58
Island in the Sky '53
Sands of Iwo Jima '49

Jordan Bayne
Under Hellgate Bridge '99
A Stranger in the Kingdom '98
Poltergeist: The Legacy '96

Lawrence Bayne
Getting Gotti '94
Lakota Woman: Siege at Wounded Knee '94
Black Robe '91
A Whisper to a Scream '88

Adam Beach (1972-)
Comanche Moon '08
Bury My Heart at Wounded Knee '07
Luna: Spirit of the Whale '07
Flags of Our Fathers '06
The Big Empty '04
A Thief of Time '04
Coyote Waits '03
Now & Forever '02
Posers '02
Skinwalker '02
Windtalkers '02
Joe Dirt '01
The Last Stop '99
Smoke Signals '98
Coyote Summer '96
A Boy Called Hate '95
Dance Me Outside '95
Squanto: A Warrior's Tale '94
Cadillac Girls '93
Spirit Rider '93

Michael Beach (1963-)
First Sunday '08
Stargate: The Ark of Truth '08
Full Count '06
Crazy as Hell '02
Asunder '99
Made Men '99
Ruby Bridges '98
Casualties '97
Ms. Scrooge '97
Soul Food '97
A Family Thing '96
Rebound: The Legend of Earl "The Goat" Manigault '96
Waiting to Exhale '95
Bad Company '94
Sketch Artist 2: Hands That See '94
Final Appeal '93
True Romance '93
One False Move '91
Internal Affairs '90
Cadence '89
Lean on Me '89
In a Shallow Grave '88
Weekend War '88

Stephanie Beacham (1947-)
Love and Other Disasters '06
Seven Days of Grace '06
The Witches Hammer '06
Unconditional Love '03
Wedding Bell Blues '96
A Change of Place '94
Foreign Affairs '93
Troop Beverly Hills '89
Riders '88
The Dying Truth '86
Inseminoid '80
Schizo '77
The Confessional '75
And Now the Screaming Starts '73
Super Bitch '73
Dracula A.D. 1972 '72
The Nightcomers '72

Kate Beahan (1969-)
The Return '06
The Wicker Man '06
Flightplan '05
After the Deluge '03
The Crocodile Hunter: Collision Course '02
Chopper '00

John Beal (1909-97)
The Firm '93
The Kid Who Loved Christmas '90
Amityville 3: The Demon '83
Ten Who Dared '60
Edge of Darkness '43
The Great Commandment '41
I Am the Law '38
Double Wedding '37
Madame X '37
Break of Hearts '35
Les Miserables '35
Little Minister '34

Simon Russell Beale (1961-)
The Gathering '02
A Dance to the Music of Time '97
Hamlet '96
Persuasion '95

Jennifer Beals (1963-)
The Book of Eli '10
The Grudge 2 '06
Catch That Kid '04
Break a Leg '03
Runaway Jury '03
Roger Dodger '02
13 Moons '02
Anne Rice's The Feast of All Saints '01
The Anniversary Party '01
A House Divided '00
Militia '99
Something More '99
Turbulence 2: Fear of Flying '99
Body and Soul '98
The Last Days of Disco '98
The Prophecy 2: Ashtown '97
The Twilight of the Golds '97
The Spree '96
The Thief and the Cobbler '96 (V)
Wishful Thinking '96
Devil in a Blue Dress '95
Four Rooms '95
Dead on Sight '94
Mrs. Parker and the Vicious Circle '94
Day of Atonement '93
Terror Stalks the Class Reunion '93
In the Soup '92
Indecency '92
Blood & Concrete: A Love Story '90
Club Extinction '89
Sons '89
The Gamble '88
Split Decisions '88
Vampire's Kiss '88
The Bride '85
That's Dancing! '85
Cinderella '84
Flashdance '83
My Bodyguard '80

Lee Ann Beaman
Starved '97
Improper Conduct '94
Tropical Heat '93
The Other Woman '92

Orson Bean (1928-)
Frank McKlusky, C.I. '02
Burning Down the House '01
Being John Malkovich '99
Final Judgment '92
Instant Karma '90
Innerspace '87
Movie Maker '86
The Return of the King '80 (V)
The Hobbit '78 (V)
Lola '69
Anatomy of a Murder '59

Robert Bean
Creature from the Haunted Sea '60
The Wild Ride '60

Sean Bean (1959-)
Percy Jackson & The Olympians: The Lightning Thief '10
Far North '07
The Hitcher '07
Outlaw '07
Sharpe's Challenge '06
Silent Hill '06
Flightplan '05
The Island '05
North Country '05
The Big Empty '04
National Treasure '04
Troy '04
Lord of the Rings: The Return of the King '03
Equilibrium '02
Don't Say a Word '01
Lord of the Rings: The Fellowship of the Ring '01
Essex Boys '99
Extremely Dangerous '99
Airborne '98
Ronin '98
Sharpe's Justice '97
Sharpe's Legend '97
Sharpe's Revenge '97
Sharpe's Waterloo '97
Leo Tolstoy's Anna Karenina '96
Sharpe's Mission '96
Sharpe's Regiment '96
Sharpe's Siege '96
Goldeneye '95
When Saturday Comes '95
Black Beauty '94
Jacob '94
Scarlett '94
Sharpe's Battle '94
Sharpe's Company '94
Sharpe's Enemy '94
Sharpe's Gold '94
Sharpe's Honour '94
Sharpe's Sword '94
Sharpe's Eagle '93
Sharpe's Rifles '93
Shopping '93
A Woman's Guide to Adultery '93
Fool's Gold: The Story of the Brink's-Mat Robbery '92
Lady Chatterley '92
Patriot Games '92
Clarissa '91
Catherine Cookson's The Fifteen Streets '90
The Field '90
Lorna Doone '90
Stormy Monday '88
Troubles '88
Caravaggio '86

Matthew "Stymie" Beard (1925-81)
When Did You Last See Your Father? '07
Sophisticated Gents '81
East of Eden '80
Backstairs at the White House '79
Dead Reckoning '47
Broken Strings '40
Way Down South '39
Two-Gun Man from Harlem '38

Tom Beard
Wallander: Firewall '08
Wallander: One Step Behind '08
Wallander: Sidetracked '08

Amanda Bearse (1958-)
Fraternity Vacation '85
Fright Night '85
Protocol '84

Emmanuelle Beart (1965-)
The Witnesses '07
The 4 Musketeers '05
Nathalie '03
The Story of Marie and Julien '03
Strayed '03
8 Women '02
La Buche '00
Les Destinees '00
Time Regained '99
Mission: Impossible '96
Nelly et Monsieur Arnaud '95
L'Enfer '93
Un Coeur en Hiver '93
I Don't Kiss '91
La Belle Noiseuse '90
Date with an Angel '87
Manon of the Spring '87

Allyce Beasley (1954-)
2 Brothers & a Bride '03
Dream with the Fishes '97
Entertaining Angels: The Dorothy Day Story '96
Rumpelstiltskin '96
National Lampoon's Loaded Weapon 1 '93
Stephen King's The Tommyknockers '93
Motorama '91
Silent Night, Deadly Night 4: Initiation '90
Moonlighting '85
Ratings Game '84

John Beasley (1943-)
Walking Tall '04
The Sum of All Fears '02
Freedom Song '00
The Gift '00
Lost Souls '00
Crazy in Alabama '99
The General's Daughter '99
The Apostle '97

Norman Beaton (1934-94)
The Mighty Quinn '89
Playing Away '87

Stephanie Beaton (1972-)
Blood Gnome '02
Witchcraft 11: Sisters in Blood '00
Witchcraft 10: Mistress of the Craft '98
Witchcraft 9: Bitter Flesh '96

Ian Beattie
Alexander '04
Stray Bullet '98

Clyde Beatty (1903-65)
Africa Screams '49
Darkest Africa '36
The Lost Jungle '34

Debra Beatty
Caged Heat 3000 '95
Hollywood Dreams '94

May (Mae) Beatty (1880-1945)
I Wake Up Screaming '41
Mad Love '35

Nancy Beatty
Lars and the Real Girl '07
The Confessor '04
Eye '96
Henry & Verlin '94

Ned Beatty (1937-)
The Killer Inside Me '10
Toy Story 3 '10 (V)
In the Electric Mist '08
Charlie Wilson's War '07
Shooter '07
The Walker '07
Sweet Land '05
Homicide: The Movie '00
Cookie's Fortune '99
Life '99
Spring Forward '99
He Got Game '98
Crazy Horse '96
The Curse of Inferno '96
The Affair '95
Gulliver's Travels '95
Larry McMurtry's Streets of Laredo '95
Black Water '94
Just Cause '94
Radioland Murders '94
Replikator: Cloned to Kill '94
Ed and His Dead Mother '93
Rudy '93
Angel Square '92
Prelude to a Kiss '92
T Bone N Weasel '92
Blind Vision '91
Going Under '91
Hear My Song '91
Illusions '91
Tragedy of Flight 103: The Inside Story '91
Back to Hannibal: The Return of Tom Sawyer and Huckleberry Finn '90
Big Bad John '90
A Cry in the Wild '90
Repossessed '90
Robert Kennedy and His Times '90
Captain America '89
Chattahoochee '89
Ministry of Vengeance '89
Physical Evidence '89
Spy '89
Purple People Eater '88
Shadows in the Storm '88
Switching Channels '88
Time Trackers '88
The Unholy '88
The Big Easy '87
The Fourth Protocol '87
Midnight Crossing '87
Rolling Vengeance '87
The Trouble with Spies '87
Back to School '86
Charlotte Forten's Mission: Experiment in Freedom '85
Konrad '85
Stroker Ace '83
Pray TV '82
Rumpelstiltskin '82
Touched '82
The Toy '82
A Woman Called Golda '82
The Incredible Shrinking Woman '81
All God's Children '80
The Guyana Tragedy: The Story of Jim Jones '80
Hopscotch '80
Superman 2 '80
Friendly Fire '79
1941 '79
Promises in the Dark '79
Wise Blood '79
Great Bank Hoax '78
A Question of Love '78
Superman: The Movie '78
The Exorcist 2: The Heretic '77
Gray Lady Down '77
Our Town '77
All the President's Men '76
The Big Bus '76
Hunter '76
Mikey & Nicky '76
Network '76
Silver Streak '76
Nashville '75
Sniper '75
The Execution of Private Slovik '74
Dying Room Only '73
The Last American Hero '73
The Thief Who Came to Dinner '73
White Lightning '73
Deliverance '72

Robert Beatty (1909-92)
2001: A Space Odyssey '68
Where Eagles Dare '68
Tarzan and the Lost Safari '57
Time Lock '57
Postmark for Danger '56
Tarzan's Hidden Jungle '55
The Love of Three Queens '54
Wings of Danger '52
Captain Horatio Hornblower '51
Against the Wind '48
Counterblast '48
San Demetrio, London '47
Appointment with Crime '45

Warren Beatty (1937-)
Town and Country '01
Bulworth '98
Love Affair '94
Bugsy '91
Dick Tracy '90
Ishtar '87
Reds '81
Heaven Can Wait '78
Shampoo '75
The Parallax View '74
Dollars '71
McCabe & Mrs. Miller '71
Bonnie & Clyde '67
Kaleidoscope '66
Promise Her Anything '66
Mickey One '65
Lilith '64
All Fall Down '62
Roman Spring of Mrs. Stone '61
Splendor in the Grass '61

Madisen Beaty
Bedtime Stories '08
The Curious Case of Benjamin Button '08

Michelle Beaudoin (1975-)
Escape Velocity '99
Sabrina the Teenage Witch '96
Live Bait '95

Hugh Beaumont (1909-82)
The Human Duplicators '64
Night Passage '57
The Mole People '56
Bugles in the Afternoon '52
Phone Call from a Stranger '52
Cavalry Charge '51
Danger Zone '51
The Lost Continent '51
Pier 23 '51
Roaring City '51
Savage Drums '51
Money Madness '47
Railroaded '47
Three on a Ticket '47
Too Many Winners '47
Blonde for a Day '46
The Blue Dahlia '46
Larceny in her Heart '46
Murder Is My Business '46
The Lady Confesses '45
Objective, Burma! '45
Mr. Winkle Goes to War '44
The Fallen Sparrow '43
The Seventh Victim '43
To the Shores of Tripoli '42
Wake Island '42
Panama Menace '41

Kathryn Beaumont (1937-)
Peter Pan '53 (V)
Alice in Wonderland '51 (V)

Lucy Beaumont (1873-1937)
Devil Doll '36
Condemned to Live '35
A Free Soul '31
The Crowd '28

Garcelle Beauvais (1966-)
Maneater '09
I Know Who Killed Me '07
American Gun '05
Barbershop 2: Back in Business '04
Bad Company '02
Double Take '01
Wild Wild West '99
Manhunter '86

Nicolas Beauvy (1958-)
Take Down '79
The Toolbox Murders '78
The Cowboys '72
Rage '72
Shoot Out '71

Jim Beaver (1950-)
Next *'07*
The Life of David Gale *'03*
Bad Girls *'94*
Twogether *'94*
In Country *'89*

Terry Beaver (1948-)
To Dance with the White Dog *'93*
Impure Thoughts *'86*

Louise Beavers (1902-62)
Tammy and the Bachelor *'57*
Goodbye, My Lady *'56*
The Jackie Robinson Story *'50*
My Blue Heaven *'50*
Tell It to the Judge *'49*
Mr. Blandings Builds His Dream House *'48*
Delightfully Dangerous *'45*
Dixie Jamboree *'44*
Du Barry Was a Lady *'43*
Big Street *'42*
Reap the Wild Wind *'42*
Bullets or Ballots *'38*
General Spanky *'36*
It Happened in New Orleans *'36*
Imitation of Life *'34*
In the Money *'34*
She Done Him Wrong *'33*
Woman Condemned *'33*
Too Busy to Work *'32*
Coquette *'29*

Davide Bechini (1962-)
Days *'02*
The Story of Boys & Girls *'91*

Damian Bechir (1963-)
No News from God *'01*
Solo *'96*

Jennifer Beck (1974-)
Gypsy *'93*
Troll *'86*
Tightrope *'84*

John Beck (1943-)
Timecop 2: The Berlin Decision *'03*
Extreme Limits *'01*
Agent of Death *'99*
Militia *'99*
Black Day Blue Night *'95*
Suspect Device *'95*
Honor Thy Father and Mother: The True Story of the Menendez Brothers *'94*
Last Time Out *'94*
A Climate for Killing *'91*
Fire and Rain *'89*
In the Cold of the Night *'89*
Deadly Illusion *'87*
Great American Traffic Jam *'80*
Time Machine *'78*
Audrey Rose *'77*
The Other Side of Midnight *'77*
The Big Bus *'76*
Sky Riders *'76*
Rollerball *'75*
Paperback Hero *'73*
Sleeper *'73*
Lawman *'71*
Three in the Attic *'68*

John (Jack) Beck
Everyman's Law *'36*
King of the Pecos *'36*

Julian Beck (1925-85)
Poltergeist 2: The Other Side *'86*
Oedipus Rex *'67*

Kimberly Beck (1956-)
In the Deep Woods *'91*
Private War *'90*
Nightmare at Noon *'87*
Friday the 13th, Part 4: The Final Chapter *'84*
Roller Boogie *'79*
Massacre at Central High *'76*

Michael Beck (1949-)
Fade to Black *'93*
Deadly Game *'91*
Blackout *'85*
Celebrity *'85*
The Golden Seal *'83*
Megaforce *'82*
Warlords of the 21st Century *'82*
Xanadu *'80*
Madman *'79*
Mayflower: The Pilgrims' Adventure *'79*
The Warriors *'79*
Holocaust *'78*

Thomas Beck (1909-95)
Thank you, Mr. Moto *'37*
Think Fast, Mr. Moto *'37*
Charlie Chan at the Opera *'36*
Charlie Chan at the Race Track *'36*
Charlie Chan in Egypt *'35*
Charlie Chan in Paris *'35*
Life Begins at Forty *'35*

Graham Beckel (1955-)
Bachelor Party Vegas *'05*
Brokeback Mountain *'05*
Northfork *'03*
Two Days *'03*
Hardball *'01*
Pearl Harbor *'01*
The '70s *'00*
Blue Streak *'99*
No Vacancy *'99*
True Crime *'99*
Black Dog *'98*
Bulworth *'98*
Lost in the Bermuda Triangle *'98*
L.A. Confidential *'97*
Jennifer 8 *'92*
O Pioneers! *'91*
Separate but Equal *'91*
Rising Son *'90*
Lost Angels *'89*
The Money *'75*
Hazel's People *'73*
The Paper Chase *'73*

Ben Becker (1964-)
Gloomy Sunday *'02*
The Harmonists *'99*
Samson and Delilah *'96*
Brother of Sleep *'95*

Gerry Becker (1950-)
Blood Work *'02*
Spider-Man *'02*
Mickey Blue Eyes *'99*
Donnie Brasco *'96*
Eraser *'96*
Legacy of Lies *'92*
The Public Eye *'92*

Gretchen Becker
Huck and the King of Hearts *'93*
Maniac Cop 3: Badge of Silence *'93*
Firehead *'90*

Hartmut Becker (1948-)
The Waiting Time *'99*
Escape from Sobibor *'87*
Jenny's War *'85*

Jacques Becker (1906-60)
Grand Illusion *'37*
Boudu Saved from Drowning *'32*

Josh Becker (1958-)
Army of Darkness *'92*
Evil Dead 2: Dead by Dawn *'87*

Kuno Becker (1978-)
Goal 2: Living the Dream *'07*
Sex and Breakfast *'07*
Goal! The Dream Begins *'06*
ESL: English as a Second Language *'05*
Once Upon a Wedding *'05*
Lucia, Lucia *'03*

Meret Becker (1969-)
Munich *'05*
The Harmonists *'99*
The Wicked, Wicked West *'97*
The Promise *'94*

Randy Becker (1970-)
American Adobo *'02*
Love! Valour! Compassion! *'96*
Lie Down with Dogs *'95*

Tony Becker (1963-)
Agent Red *'00*
Cody *'77*

Scotty Beckett (1929-68)
The Oklahoman *'56*
Corky of Gasoline Alley *'51*
Gasoline Alley *'51*
The Happy Years *'50*
Nancy Goes to Rio *'50*
Battleground *'49*
The Jolson Story *'46*
The Climax *'44*
Ali Baba and the Forty Thieves *'43*
Heaven Can Wait *'43*
Kings Row *'41*
My Favorite Wife *'40*
My Son, My Son *'40*
Love Affair *'39*
Devil's Party *'38*
Listen, Darling *'38*
Marie Antoinette *'38*
Conquest *'37*
The Charge of the Light Brigade *'36*
I Dream Too Much *'35*
Stand Up and Cheer *'34*

Tyson Beckford (1970-)
Into the Blue *'05*
Searching for Bobby D *'05*
Biker Boyz *'03*

David Beckham (1975-)
Goal 2: Living the Dream *'07*
Goal! The Dream Begins *'06*

Kate Beckinsale (1973-)
Everybody's Fine *'09*
Underworld: Rise of the Lycans *'09*
Whiteout *'09*
Fragments *'08*
Nothing But the Truth *'08*
Snow Angels *'07*
Vacancy *'07*
Click *'06*
Underworld: Evolution *'05*
The Aviator *'04*
Van Helsing *'04*
Tiptoes *'03*
Underworld *'03*
Laurel Canyon *'02*
Pearl Harbor *'01*
Serendipity *'01*
The Golden Bowl *'00*
Brokedown Palace *'99*
The Last Days of Disco *'98*
Shooting Fish *'98*
Emma *'97*
Haunted *'95*
Cold Comfort Farm *'94*
Royal Deceit *'94*
Uncovered *'94*
Much Ado about Nothing *'93*
One Against the Wind *'91*

Tony Beckley (1927-80)
When a Stranger Calls *'79*
The Fiend *'71*
Get Carter *'71*
Assault *'70*
The Italian Job *'69*

William Beckley (1930-)
Too Late the Hero *'70*
The Killing of Sister George *'69*

Claire Beckman (1961-)
The Thing About My Folks *'05*
Fallout *'01*

Henry Beckman (1925-)
The Man Upstairs *'93*
Family Reunion *'88*
Marnie *'64*

Reginald Beckwith (1908-65)
Burn Witch, Burn! *'62*
Doctor in Love *'60*
Lucky Jim *'58*
Curse of the Demon *'57*
Men of Sherwood Forest *'57*
The Runaway Bus *'54*
Genevieve *'53*
Another Man's Poison *'52*
Mister Drake's Duck *'50*

William Beckwith
Escape from Safehaven *'88*
Prime Evil *'88*

Irene Bedard (1967-)
Tortilla Heaven *'07*
Love's Long Journey *'05*
Miracle at Sage Creek *'05*
The New World *'05*
The Lost Child *'00*
Wildflowers *'99*
Smoke Signals *'98*
Navajo Blues *'97*
True Women *'97*
Two for Texas *'97*
Crazy Horse *'96*
Grand Avenue *'96*
Pocahontas *'95 (V)*
Lakota Woman: Siege at Wounded Knee *'94*
Squanto: A Warrior's Tale *'94*

Don Beddoe (1891-1991)
Nickel Mountain *'85*
Papa's Delicate Condition *'63*
Jack the Giant Killer *'62*
The Night of the Hunter *'55*
Loophole *'54*
Carson City *'52*
The Narrow Margin *'52*
Corky of Gasoline Alley *'51*
The Enforcer *'51*
Gasoline Alley *'51*
Caged *'50*
Gun Crazy *'49*
Buck Privates Come Home *'47*
Welcome Stranger *'47*
The Best Years of Our Lives *'46*
O.S.S. *'46*
Junior Army *'42*
Before I Hang *'40*
Blondie On a Budget *'40*
Charlie Chan's Murder Cruise *'40*
Blondie Meets the Boss *'39*
Golden Boy *'39*

Bonnie Bedelia (1950-)
Berkeley *'05*
Flowers for Algernon *'00*
Sordid Lives *'00*
Anywhere But Here *'99*
Locked in Silence *'99*
Bad Manners *'98*
Gloria *'98*
Homecoming *'96*
Judicial Consent *'94*
Speechless *'94*
Fallen Angels 2 *'93*
The Fire Next Time *'93*
Needful Things *'93*
Switched at Birth *'91*
When the Time Comes *'91*
Die Hard 2: Die Harder *'90*
Presumed Innocent *'90*
Somebody Has to Shoot the Picture *'90*
Fat Man and Little Boy *'89*
Die Hard *'88*
Prince of Pennsylvania *'88*
The Stranger *'87*
The Boy Who Could Fly *'86*
Death of an Angel *'86*
Violets Are Blue *'86*
Lady from Yesterday *'85*
Heart Like a Wheel *'83*
Memorial Day *'83*

Walking Through the Fire *'80*
Salem's Lot *'79*
The Big Fix *'78*
A Question of Love *'78*
Lovers and Other Strangers *'70*
The Gypsy Moths *'69*
They Shoot Horses, Don't They? *'69*
Then Came Bronson *'68*

Rodney Bedell
Just for the Hell of It *'68*
Gruesome Twosome *'67*

Barbara Bedford (1903-81)
The Midnight Phantom *'35*
Found Alive *'34*
The Broken Mask *'28*
Mockery *'27*
The Notorious Lady *'27*
The Mad Whirl *'25*
Tumbleweeds *'25*
The Last of the Mohicans *'20*

Brian Bedford (1935-)
Mr. St. Nick *'02*
Armistead Maupin's More Tales of the City *'97*
Nixon *'95*
Scarlett *'94*
The Last Best Year *'90*
Robin Hood *'73 (V)*
Grand Prix *'66*

Kabir Bedi (1945-)
The Lost Empire *'01*
Lie Down with Lions *'94*
Beyond Justice *'92*
The Beast *'88*
Terminal Entry *'87*
Forty Days of Musa Dagh *'85*
Octopussy *'83*
Demon Rage *'82*
Archer: The Fugitive from the Empire *'81*

Gerry Bednob
Zack and Miri Make a Porno *'08*
Brutal Massacre: A Comedy *'07*

Guy Bedos (1934-)
Pardon Mon Affaire, Too! *'77*
Pardon Mon Affaire *'76*

Alfonso Bedoya (1904-57)
The Stranger Wore a Gun *'53*
Border Incident *'49*
Treasure of the Sierra Madre *'48*
Border River *'47*

Janet Beecher (1884-1955)
The Mark of Zorro *'40*
I'd Give My Life *'36*
The Dark Angel *'35*
Village Tale *'35*

David Beecroft (1956-)
Octopus *'00*
Kidnapped in Paradise *'98*
The Awakening *'95*
The Rain Killer *'90*
Shadowzone *'89*

Daniel Beer
The Last Best Sunday *'98*
Talking about Sex *'94*
Point Break *'91*
Creepshow 2 *'87*

Noah Beery, Sr. (1884-1945)
Overland Mail *'42*
Adventures of Red Ryder *'40*
Pioneers of the West *'40*
Panamint's Bad Man *'38*
Zorro Rides Again *'37*
King of the Damned *'36*
David Harum *'34*
Kentucky Kernels *'34*

Mystery Liner *'34*
Trail Beyond *'34*
Buffalo Stampede *'33*
Fighting with Kit Carson *'33*
Flaming Signal *'33*
Man of the Forest *'33*
She Done Him Wrong *'33*
To the Last Man *'33*
The Big Stampede *'32*
Cornered *'32*
Devil Horse *'32*
The Drifter *'32*
Kid from Spain *'32*
Golden Dawn *'30*
Linda *'29*
The Coming of Amos *'25*
The Vanishing American *'25*
Soul of the Beast *'23*
Mark of Zorro *'20*
A Mormon Maid *'17*

Noah Beery, Jr. (1913-94)
The Capture of Grizzly Adams *'82*
Mysterious Two *'82*
Great American Traffic Jam *'80*
The Bastard *'78*
Francis Gary Powers: The True Story of the U-2 Spy *'76*
Savages *'75*
Walking Tall: Part 2 *'75*
Walking Tall *'73*
Richard Petty Story *'72*
7 Faces of Dr. Lao *'63*
Inherit the Wind *'60*
Decision at Sundown *'57*
Fastest Gun Alive *'56*
Jubal *'56*
War Arrow *'53*
Cavalry Charge *'51*
The Texas Rangers *'51*
Rocketship X-M *'50*
The Doolins of Oklahoma *'49*
Red River *'48*
Million Dollar Kid *'44*
Gung Ho! *'43*
'Neath Brooklyn Bridge *'42*
Overland Mail *'42*
Sergeant York *'41*
Tanks a Million *'41*
Carson City Kid *'40*
Bad Lands *'39*
Of Mice and Men *'39*
Only Angels Have Wings *'39*
Forbidden Valley *'38*
Ace Drummond *'36*
The Avenging Hand *'36*
Savage Fury *'35*
Tailspin Tommy *'34*
Trail Beyond *'34*
Fighting with Kit Carson *'33*
Rustler's Roundup *'33*
The Three Musketeers *'33*
Mark of Zorro *'20*

Wallace Beery (1885-1949)
A Date with Judy *'48*
Ah, Wilderness! *'35*
China Seas *'35*
Treasure Island *'34*
Viva Villa! *'34*
The Bowery *'33*
Dinner at Eight *'33*
Tugboat Annie *'33*
The Champ *'32*
Grand Hotel *'32*
The Big House *'30*
Min & Bill *'30*
Beggars of Life *'28*
We're in the Navy Now *'27*
Behind the Front *'26*
Old Ironsides *'26*
The Lost World *'25*
The Night Club *'25*
The Pony Express *'25*
The Red Lily *'24*
The Sea Hawk *'24*
Three Ages *'23*
White Tiger *'23*
Robin Hood *'22*
The Four Horsemen of the Apocalypse *'21*
The Last of the Mohicans *'20*

The Mollycoddle '20
Teddy at the Throttle '16

Max Beesley (1971-)
The Last Enemy '08
Bloodlines '05
Red Roses and Petrol '03
Glitter '01
Hotel '01
Kill Me Later '01
The Last Minute '01
The Match '99
Tom Jones '98

Chris Beetem (1969-)
Black Hawk Down '01
Grace & Glorie '98

Jason Beghe (1960-)
One Missed Call '08
Baby Monitor: Sound of Fear '97
G.I. Jane '97
The Chinatown Murders: Man against the Mob '89
Monkey Shines '88

Bibiana Beglau (1971-)
The Ninth Day '04
The Legend of Rita '99

Ed Begley, Sr. (1901-70)
The Dunwich Horror '70
Firecreek '68
Road to Salina '68
Wild in the Streets '68
Hang 'Em High '67
The Oscar '66
The Unsinkable Molly Brown '64
Sweet Bird of Youth '62
Odds Against Tomorrow '59
Twelve Angry Men '57
Patterns '56
Boots Malone '52
Lone Star '52
On Dangerous Ground '51
Stars in My Crown '50
The Great Gatsby '49
It Happens Every Spring '49
Tulsa '49
Sitting Pretty '48
Sorry, Wrong Number '48
The Street with No Name '48
Boomerang '47
Saddle Tramp '47

Ed Begley, Jr. (1949-)
Whatever Works '09
Pineapple Express '08
Recount '08
One Long Night '07
The Elder Son '06
For Your Consideration '06
Pittsburgh '06
Relative Strangers '06
Stateside '04
A Mighty Wind '03
Net Games '03
Auto Focus '02
Get Over It! '01
Best in Show '00
I'm Losing You '98
Joey '98
Murder She Purred: A Mrs. Murphy Mystery '98
Horton Foote's Alone '97
Ms. Bear '97
Not in This Town '97
The Student Affair '97
The Late Shift '96
Santa with Muscles '96
Batman Forever '95
Hourglass '95
Rave Review '95
Children of Fury '94
The Crazysitter '94
Even Cowgirls Get the Blues '94
Greedy '94
Incident at Deception Ridge '94
The Pagemaster '94
Renaissance Man '94
Sensation '94
World War II: When Lions Roared '94
Cooperstown '93
The Story Lady '93
Dark Horse '92
Mastergate '92
Running Mates '92
The Great Los Angeles Earthquake '91
Spies, Lies and Naked Thighs '91
The Applegates '89
Scenes from the Class Struggle in Beverly Hills '89
She-Devil '89
The Accidental Tourist '88
Amazon Women on the Moon '87
The Legend of Sleepy Hollow '86
Transylvania 6-5000 '85
Protocol '84
Streets of Fire '84
This Is Spinal Tap '84
Get Crazy '83
Cat People '82
Eating Raoul '82
Elvis: The Movie '79
The In-Laws '79
A Shining Season '79
Blue Collar '78
Goin' South '78
Citizens Band '77
Dead of Night '77
Private Lessons '75
Cockfighter '74
Showdown '73
Billion Dollar Brain '67

Briony Behets (1951-)
Cassandra '87
Alvin Rides Again '74

Dani Behr (1970-)
Rancid Aluminium '00
Like It Is '98

Jason Behr (1973-)
Dragon Wars '07
Skinwalkers '07
The Tattooist '07
Shooting Livien '05
The Grudge '04
The Shipping News '01
Rites of Passage '99

Melissa Behr
Me & Will '99
Perfect Tenant '99
The Landlady '98
Dollman vs Demonic Toys '93

Bernard Behrens
Invasion! '99
Mother Night '96
The Man with Two Brains '83
Galaxy of Terror '81

Sam Behrens (1950-)
Alive '93
And You Thought Your Parents Were Weird! '91
American Blue Note '89
Murder by Numbers '89

Yerye Beirut
The Fear Chamber '68
The Sinister Invasion '68
Battle Shock '56

Brendan Beiser (1970-)
Something Beneath '07
Savage Island '03
The Fear: Halloween Night '99

Berenice Bejo
OSS 117: Cairo, Nest of Spies '06
The Grand Role '04

Leila Bekhti
Paris, je t'aime '06
Sheitan '06

Richard Bekins (1954-)
United 93 '06
George Washington: The Forging of a Nation '86
Model Behavior '82

Barbara Bel Geddes (1922-)
Summertree '71
The Todd Killings '71
The Five Pennies '59
Vertigo '58
Panic in the Streets '50
Caught '49
Blood on the Moon '48
I Remember Mama '48
The Long Night '47

Doris Belack
Doug's 1st Movie '99 (V)
Krippendorf's Tribe '98
Neil Simon's The Odd Couple 2 '98
What about Bob? '91
Opportunity Knocks '90

Harry Belafonte (1927-)
Bobby '06
Kansas City '95
White Man's Burden '95
Ready to Wear '94
The Player '92
Grambling's White Tiger '81
Uptown Saturday Night '74
Buck and the Preacher '72
The Angel Levine '70
Odds Against Tomorrow '59
Island in the Sun '57
Carmen Jones '54

Shari Belafonte (1954-)
Loving Evangeline '98
Mars '96
The Heidi Chronicles '95
French Silk '94
The Player '92
Fire, Ice and Dynamite '91
Murder by Numbers '89
Speed Zone '88
The Midnight Hour '86
If You Could See What I Hear '82

Leon Belasco (1902-88)
Can-Can '60
Abbott and Costello in the Foreign Legion '50
Infamous Crimes '47
It's a Date '40
Fisherman's Wharf '39

Charles Belcher (1872-1943)
King of Kings '27
The Thief of Baghdad '24

Ana Belen (1951-)
Love Can Seriously Damage Your Health '96
The Perfect Husband '92
Demons in the Garden '82

Christine Belford (1949-)
Christine '84
Agatha Christie's Sparkling Cyanide '83
Kenny Rogers as the Gambler '80
The Groundstar Conspiracy '72
Pocket Money '72

Ann Bell (1940-)
When Saturday Comes '95
Christabel '89
Champions '84
The Lost Boys '78
The Statue '71
Fahrenheit 451 '66
The Witches '66
Dr. Terror's House of Horrors '65

Cassandra Bell
Goal! The Dream Begins '06
Cold and Dark '05

Catherine Bell (1968-)
The Good Witch '08
Bruce Almighty '03
Thrill Seekers '99

Christopher Bell (1983-)
Sarah, Plain and Tall: Winter's End '99
Sarah, Plain and Tall: Skylark '93
Sarah, Plain and Tall '91
Without Warning: The James Brady Story '91

Dan Bell
The Shot '96
Terror Eyes '87

Darryl M. Bell (1963-)
Mr. Write '92
School Daze '88

Drake Bell (1986-)
College '08
Superhero Movie '08
Yours, Mine & Ours '05
The Jack Bull '99
The Neon Bible '95

Drew Tyler Bell
Her Best Move '07
Love's Abiding Joy '06
Jeepers Creepers 2 '03

Edward Bell
Image of Passion '86
The Premonition '75
Earth II '71

E.E. Bell (1955-)
Grizzly Mountain '97
800 Leagues Down the Amazon '93

Geoff Bell (1963-)
The Business '05
Green Street Hooligans '05
I'll Sleep When I'm Dead '03
AKA '02

Hank Bell (1892-1950)
Valley of the Sun '42
Border Vengeance '35
The Fiddlin' Buckaroo '33
Beyond the Rockies '32
The Big Stampede '32
South of Santa Fe '32
Whistlin' Dan '32

James Bell (1891-1973)
Tribute to a Bad Man '56
A Lawless Street '55
Teenage Crime Wave '55
Flying Leathernecks '51
The Millerson Case '47
The Leopard Man '43
My Friend Flicka '43
So Proudly We Hail '43

Jamie Bell (1986-)
Defiance '08
Jumper '08
Mister Foe '07
Flags of Our Fathers '06
The Chumscrubber '05
Dear Wendy '05
King Kong '05
Undertow '04
Deathwatch '02
Nicholas Nickleby '02
Billy Elliot '00

Jeannie Bell (1944-)
Fass Black '77
The Muthers '76
TNT Jackson '75
Policewomen '73

Kristen Bell (1980-)
Astro Boy '09 (V)
Couples Retreat '09
Fanboys '09
When in Rome '09
Forgetting Sarah Marshall '08
Pulse '06
Roman '06
Deepwater '05
Gracie's Choice '04
Spartan '04
Pootie Tang '01
Polish Wedding '97

Lake Bell
It's Complicated '09
Over Her Dead Body '08
Pride and Glory '08
What Happens in Vegas '08
Rampage: The Hillside Strangler Murders '04

Marie Bell (1900-85)
Phedre '68
Hotel Paradiso '66
Sandra of a Thousand Delights '65

Marshall Bell (1944-)
Hamlet 2 '08
The Final Season '07
Nancy Drew '07
Rescue Dawn '06
Identity '03
Northfork '03
Mercy '00
Sand '00
Black & White '99
A Slipping Down Life '99
Virus '98
The End of Violence '97
Starship Troopers '97
Too Fast, Too Young '96
Things to Do in Denver When You're Dead '95
Airheads '94
Payback '94
The Vagrant '92
The Heroes of Desert Storm '91
Air America '90
Leather Jackets '90
Total Recall '90
Johnny Be Good '88
Tucker: The Man and His Dream '88
Twins '88
Wildfire '88
No Way Out '87
A Nightmare on Elm Street 2: Freddy's Revenge '85

Michael Bell (1938-)
Rugrats Go Wild! '03 (V)
Hip Hop 4 Life '02
Rugrats in Paris: The Movie '00 (V)
The Rugrats Movie '98 (V)

Nicholas Bell
Attack of the Sabretooth '05
Dead Letter Office '98
Sorrento Beach '95

Rex Bell (1905-62)
Stormy Trails '36
West of Nevada '36
Saddle Aces '35
The Tonto Kid '35
Diamond Trail '33
Fighting Texans '33
Rainbow Ranch '33
Broadway to Cheyenne '32
Law of the Sea '32
Battling with Buffalo Bill '31
They Had to See Paris '29

Rini Bell (1981-)
The Terminal '04
Bring It On '00

Tobin Bell (1942-)
Saw 6 '09
Saw 5 '08
Boogeyman 2 '07
Decoys: The Second Seduction '07
Saw 4 '07
Saw 3 '06
Saw 2 '05
Saw '04
Black Mask 2: City of Masks '02
Power Play '02
The 4th Floor '99
Best of the Best: Without Warning '98
Brown's Requiem '98
Overnight Delivery '96
Serial Killer '95
New Eden '94
The Firm '93
In the Line of Fire '93
Sex, Love and Cold Hard Cash '93
Ruby '92
False Identity '90

Tom Bell (1932-)
The Last Minute '01
Swing '98
The Boxer '97
Preaching to the Perverted '97
Swept from the Sea '97
Feast of July '95
Catherine Cookson's The Cinder Path '94
Prime Suspect '92
Let Him Have It '91
Prospero's Books '91
The Krays '90
Wish You Were Here '87
Royal Flash '75
Dressed for Death '74
Quest for Love '71
Ballad in Blue '66
The L-Shaped Room '62

Zoe Bell (1978-)
Angel of Death '09
Gamer '09
Whip It '09
Death Proof '07

Rachael Bella (1984-)
Jimmy & Judy '06
The Ring '02
The Blood Oranges '97
Household Saints '93
When Pigs Fly '93

Bill Bellamy (1965-)
The Lottery Ticket '10
Getting Played '05
Buying the Cow '02
The Brothers '01
Any Given Sunday '99
Love Stinks '99
Def Jam's How to Be a Player '97
Love Jones '96
Who's the Man? '93

Diana Bellamy (1944-2001)
Amelia Earhart: The Final Flight '94
The Nest '88
Stripped to Kill '87

Madge Bellamy (1899-1990)
Northwest Trail '46
The Ivory Handled Gun '35
Law for Tombstone '35
Stone of Silver Creek '35
The White Zombie '32
Lazybones '25
The Iron Horse '24
The White Sin '24
Soul of the Beast '23
Lorna Doone '22

Ned Bellamy (1960-)
War, Inc. '08
The Contract '07
Wind Chill '07
Tenacious D in the Pick of Destiny '06
Two Tickets to Paradise '06
Saw '04
Angel's Dance '99
Ed Wood '94
Carnosaur '93
Bob Roberts '92
Writer's Block '91

Ralph Bellamy (1904-91)
Pretty Woman '90
War & Remembrance: The Final Chapter '89
The Good Mother '88
War & Remembrance '88
Amazon Women on the Moon '87
Disorderlies '87
Fourth Wise Man '85
Love Leads the Way '84
Trading Places '83
The Winds of War '83
Oh, God! '77
The Boy in the Plastic Bubble '76
Nightmare in Badham County '76
Return to Earth '76
Murder on Flight 502 '75
Search for the Gods '75
Missiles of October '74
Cancel My Reservation '72
Doctors' Wives '70
Rosemary's Baby '68
The Professionals '66
Sunrise at Campobello '60

The Court Martial of Billy Mitchell '55
Delightfully Dangerous '45
Lady on a Train '45
Guest in the House '44
The Ghost of Frankenstein '42
Dive Bomber '41
Footsteps in the Dark '41
The Wolf Man '41
Brother Orchid '40
Dance, Girl, Dance '40
His Girl Friday '40
Boy Meets Girl '38
Carefree '38
The Awful Truth '37
Healer '36
Wild Brian Kent '36
Hands Across the Table '35
Spitfire '34
Woman in the Shadows '34
Ace of Aces '33
Picture Snatcher '33
Young America '32

Clara Bellar

Kill the Poor '06
Dominion: Prequel to the Exorcist '05
A. I.: Artificial Intelligence '01
The First 9 1/2 Weeks '98
David '97
Romance and Rejection '96
Rendezvous in Paris '95

Harry Bellaver (1905-93)

The Old Man and the Sea '58
From Here to Eternity '53
The Lemon Drop Kid '51
No Way Out '50
House on 92nd Street '45

Annie Belle (1956-)

House on the Edge of the Park '84
Naked Paradise '78
Forever Emmanuelle '75
Lips of Blood '75

Camilla Belle (1986-)

Push '09
10,000 B.C. '08
When a Stranger Calls '06
The Ballad of Jack and Rose '05
The Chumscrubber '05
The Quiet '05
Back to the Secret Garden '01
Secre of the Andes '98
Annie: A Royal Adventure '95

David Belle

District 13: Ultimatum '09
District B13 '04

Kathleen Beller (1955-)

Time Trackers '88
Cloud Waltzing '87
Surfacing '84
Sword & the Sorcerer '82
Touched '82
Fort Apache, the Bronx '81
The Manions of America '81
No Place to Hide '81
Mother & Daughter: A Loving War '80
Promises in the Dark '79
Are You in the House Alone? '78
The Betsy '78
Mary White '77
The Godfather, Part 2 '74

Agostina Belli (1949-)

The Chosen '77
The Scent of a Woman '75
The Sex Machine '75
Seduction of Mimi '72

Melvin Belli (1907-96)

Ground Zero '88
Gimme Shelter '70

Cynthia Belliveau

The Dark '94
The Spider and the Fly '94
The Dream Team '89

A New Life '88

Gina Bellman (1966-)

Jekyll '07
Seven Days to Live '01
David '97
Silent Trigger '97
Leon the Pig Farmer '93

Maria Bello (1967-)

Grown Ups '10
The Private Lives of Pippa Lee '09
Downloading Nancy '08
The Mummy: Tomb of the Dragon Emperor '08
The Yellow Handkerchief '08
The Jane Austen Book Club '07
Shattered '07
Towelhead '07
Flicka '06
Thank You for Smoking '06
World Trade Center '06
Assault on Precinct 13 '05
A History of Violence '05
The Sisters '05
Secret Window '04
Silver City '04
The Cooler '03
Auto Focus '02
100 Mile Rule '02
Coyote Ugly '00
Duets '00
Payback '98
Permanent Midnight '98

Sara Bellomo (1974-)

Beach Babes 2: Cave Girl Island '95
Bikini Drive-In '94
Beach Babes from Beyond '93

Gil Bellows (1967-)

Infected '08
The Promotion '08
24 : Redemption '08
The Weather Man '05
Blind Horizon '04
Whitewash: The Clarence Brandley Story '02
She Creature '01
Beautiful Joe '00
Chasing Sleep '00
The Courage to Love '00
Judas Kiss '98
The Assistant '97
Snow White: A Tale of Terror '97
The Substance of Fire '96
Black Day Blue Night '95
Miami Rhapsody '95
Silver Strand '95
Love and a .45 '94
The Shawshank Redemption '94

Monica Bellucci (1968-)

The Sorcerer's Apprentice '10
The Private Lives of Pippa Lee '09
Shoot 'Em Up '07
The Brothers Grimm '05
How Much Do You Love Me? '05
The Passion of the Christ '04
She Hate Me '04
The Matrix Reloaded '03
The Matrix Revolutions '03
Tears of the Sun '03
Irreversible '02
Brotherhood of the Wolf '01
Malena '00
Under Suspicion '00
Like a Fish Out of Water '99
Bram Stoker's Dracula '92

Pamela Bellwood (1951-)

Going Shopping '05
Double Standard '88
Cellar Dweller '87
Agatha Christie's Sparkling Cyanide '83
Cocaine: One Man's Seduction '83

Hangar 18 '80
Deadman's Curve '78

Jean-Paul Belmondo (1933-)

Les Miserables '95
Swashbuckler '84
Le Professionnel '81
Stuntwoman '81
Le Magnifique '76
Stavisky '74
High Heels '72
La Scoumoune '72
Borsalino '70
The Brain '69
Mississippi Mermaid '69
Casino Royale '67
The Thief of Paris '67
Is Paris Burning? '66
Pierrot le Fou '65
That Man from Rio '64
Cartouche '62
Un Singe en Hiver '62
Le Doulos '61
Leon Morin, Priest '61
Two Women '61
Classe Tous Risque '60
Love and the Frenchwoman '60
A Woman Is a Woman '60
Breathless '59
Sois Belle et Tais-Toi '58

Lionel Belmore (1867-1953)

My Son, My Son '40
Son of Frankenstein '39
Police Court '32
Frankenstein '31
Monte Carlo '30
The Love Parade '29
Bardelys the Magnificent '26
Oliver Twist '22

Robert Beltran (1953-)

Taking Chances '09
Fire Serpent '07
Manticore '05
Luminarias '99
Managua '97
Bugsy '91
The Chase '91
Kiss Me a Killer '91
To Die Standing '91
El Diablo '90
Scenes from the Class Struggle in Beverly Hills '89
Gaby: A True Story '87
Latino '85
Night of the Comet '84
Eating Raoul '82

Mark Beltzman (1960-)

Billy Madison '94
Mo' Money '92

James Belushi (1954-)

The Ghost Writer '10
Snow Buddies '08 (V)
Underdog '07
The Wild '06 (V)
Hoodwinked '05 (V)
One Way Out '02
Joe Somebody '01
K-9 3: P.I. '01
Echo of Murder '00
Return to Me '00
Angel's Dance '99
Backlash '99
K-911 '99
Made Men '99
The Florentine '98
Living in Peril '97
Retroactive '97
Gang Related '96
Jingle All the Way '96
Race the Sun '96
Destiny Turns on the Radio '95
Canadian Bacon '94
Parallel Lives '94
The Pebble and the Penguin '94 (V)
Separate Lives '94
Last Action Hero '93
Royce '93
Wild Palms '93
Once Upon a Crime '92
Traces of Red '92

Curly Sue '91
Diary of a Hitman '91
Only the Lonely '91
The Palermo Connection '91
Abraxas: Guardian of the Universe '90
The Masters of Menace '90
Mr. Destiny '90
Taking Care of Business '90
Homer and Eddie '89
K-9 '89
Wedding Band '89
Who's Harry Crumb? '89
Red Heat '88
The Principal '87
Real Men '87
About Last Night... '86
Jumpin' Jack Flash '86
Little Shop of Horrors '86
Salvador '86
Birthday Boy '85
The Man with One Red Shoe '85
Pinocchio '83
Trading Places '83
Thief '81
The Fury '78

John Belushi (1949-82)

Continental Divide '81
Neighbors '81
The Blues Brothers '80
1941 '79
Old Boyfriends '79
All You Need Is Cash '78
Goin' South '78
National Lampoon's Animal House '78
Shame of the Jungle '75 (V)

Lucas Belvaux

Joyeux Noel '05
Cop Au Vin '85

Richard Belzer (1944-)

Homicide: The Movie '00
Get On the Bus '96
Girl 6 '96
Not of This Earth '96
A Very Brady Sequel '96
The Invaders '95
The Puppet Masters '94
Mad Dog and Glory '93
Off and Running '90
The Big Picture '89
Fletch Lives '89
Freeway '88
The Wrong Guys '88
America '86
Flicks '85
Scarface '83
Night Shift '82
Student Bodies '81
Fame '80
The Groove Tube '72

Cliff Bemis

Au Pair 2: The Fairy Tale Continues '01
Modern Love '90

Paul Ben-Victor (1965-)

On the Doll '07
Daredevil '03
Drowning Mona '00
Gun Shy '00
Kiss Toledo Goodbye '00
The Corruptor '99
Crazy in Alabama '99
Maximum Risk '96
Metro '96
Houseguest '94
True Romance '93
Body Parts '91

Jordy Benattar

Charlie & Me '08
Fallen Angel '03

Brian Benben (1956-)

Surf's Up '07 (V)
The Flamingo Rising '01
Radioland Murders '94
I Come in Peace '90
Mortal Sins '90
Clean and Sober '88
Gangster Wars '81

Robert Benchley (1889-1945)

The Road to Utopia '46
It's in the Bag '45

The Stork Club '45
Weekend at the Waldorf '45
The Sky's the Limit '43
I Married a Witch '42
The Major and the Minor '42
Young and Willing '42
Nice Girl? '41
You'll Never Get Rich '41
Foreign Correspondent '40
China Seas '35
The Robert Benchley Miniatures Collection '35
Rafter Romance '34
Dancing Lady '33

Russ Bender (1910-69)

Navy vs. the Night Monsters '66
Space Monster '64
Anatomy of a Psycho '61
The Ghost of Dragstrip Hollow '59
I Bury the Living '58
The War of the Colossal Beast '58
The Amazing Colossal Man '57
Invasion of the Saucer Men '57
It Conquered the World '56

Michael C. Bendetti (1967-)

Red Shoe Diaries: Luscious Lola '00
Amanda and the Alien '95
Netherworld '90

William Bendix (1906-64)

For Love or Money '63
Johnny Nobody '61
The Rough and the Smooth '59
Deep Six '58
Crashout '55
Dangerous Mission '54
Blackbeard the Pirate '52
A Girl in Every Port '52
Macao '52
Detective Story '51
Kill the Umpire '50
Big Steal '49
A Connecticut Yankee in King Arthur's Court '49
Johnny Holiday '49
Babe Ruth Story '48
The Time of Your Life '48
Calcutta '47
I'll Be Yours '47
Where There's Life '47
The Blue Dahlia '46
Dark Corner '46
Two Years before the Mast '46
It's in the Bag '45
Abroad with Two Yanks '44
Greenwich Village '44
The Hairy Ape '44
Lifeboat '44
China '43
Guadalcanal Diary '43
The Glass Key '42
Star Spangled Rhythm '42
Wake Island '42
Who Done It? '42
Woman of the Year '42

Nelly Benedetti

Make Your Bets Ladies '65
The Soft Skin '64

Leonor Benedetto (1941-)

A Place in the World '92
Condemned to Hell '84

Brooks Benedict (1896-1968)

Gun Smoke '31
The Dropkick '27
Ranson's Folly '26
The Freshman '25

Dirk Benedict (1945-)

The A-Team '10
Earthstorm '06
Alaska '96
November Conspiracy '96
The Feminine Touch '95

Official Denial '93
Shadow Force '92
Blue Tornado '90
Body Slam '87
Ruckus '81
Follow That Car '80
Underground Aces '80
Scavenger Hunt '79
Battlestar Galactica '78
Cruise into Terror '78
Mission Galactica: The Cylon Attack '78
W '74
Ssssss '73
Georgia, Georgia '72

Jay Benedict (1951-)

Mosquitoman '05
Carmen '03
Double Team '97

Paul Benedict (1938-2008)

Waiting for Guffman '96
Attack of the 50 Ft. Woman '93
The Addams Family '91
The Freshman '90
Babycakes '89
Cocktail '88
The Chair '87
Desperate Moves '86
This Is Spinal Tap '84
The Man with Two Brains '83
Mandingo '75
Jeremiah Johnson '72

Richard Benedict (1916-84)

Beginning of the End '57
Breakdown '53
Ace in the Hole '51
Omoo Omoo, the Shark God '49
O.S.S. '46
A Walk in the Sun '46

William Benedict (1917-99)

Bride of the Monster '55
Ghost Chasers '51
Master Minds '49
Spook Busters '48
Bowery Buckaroos '47
Hard-Boiled Mahoney '47
Mr. Muggs Rides Again '45
The Story of G.I. Joe '45
Follow the Leader '44
On the Sunny Side '42
Wildcat '42
Legion of the Lawless '40

Yves Beneyton (1946-)

Rogue Trader '98
Letters to an Unknown Lover '84
The Lacemaker '77
By the Blood of Others '73
Weekend '67

John Benfield

Speed Racer '08
Cassandra's Dream '07
Endgame '01
In the Name of the Father '93
Hidden Agenda '90

Wilson Benge (1875-1955)

Queen of the Amazons '47
The Shadow Strikes '37
The Bat Whispers '30
Bulldog Drummond '29
Robin Hood '22

Norma Bengell (1935-)

Hellbenders '67
Planet of the Vampires '65
Mafioso '62

Jean Benguigui

Hello Goodbye '08
Control '87
Buffet Froid '79

Maurice Benichou (1943-)

Hidden '05
Time of the Wolf '03

Amelie '01
The Adventures of Felix '99

Murilo Benicio (1972-)
Paid '06
Possible Loves '00
Woman on Top '00
Orfeu '99

Roberto Benigni (1952-)
The Tiger and the Snow '05
Coffee and Cigarettes '03
Fellini: I'm a Born Liar '03
Pinocchio '02
Life Is Beautiful '98
The Monster '96
Son of the Pink Panther '93
Johnny Stecchino '92
Night on Earth '91
Down by Law '86
Berlinguer I Love You '77

Annette Bening (1958-)
The Kids Are All Right '10
Mother and Child '09
The Women '08
Running with Scissors '06
Mrs. Harris '05
Being Julia '04
Open Range '03
What Planet Are You From? '00
American Beauty '99
In Dreams '98
The Siege '98
Mars Attacks! '96
The American President '95
Richard III '95
Love Affair '94
Bugsy '91
Guilty by Suspicion '91
Regarding Henry '91
The Grifters '90
Postcards from the Edge '90
Valmont '89
The Great Outdoors '88

Andre Benjamin (1975-)
Semi-Pro '08
Battle in Seattle '07
Charlotte's Web '06 (V)
Idlewild '06
Be Cool '05
Four Brothers '05
Revolver '05

Christopher Benjamin (1934-)
The Plague Dogs '82 (V)
Baffled '72

Paul Benjamin (1938-)
The Station Agent '03
Hoodlum '96
Rosewood '96
The Fence '94
The Five Heartbeats '91
Some Kind of Hero '82
Escape from Alcatraz '79
I Know Why the Caged Bird Sings '79
The Education of Sonny Carson '74
The Deadly Trackers '73
Across 110th Street '72
The Anderson Tapes '71

Richard Benjamin (1938-)
Henry Poole Is Here '08
Keeping Up with the Steins '06
Marci X '03
The Pentagon Wars '98
Deconstructing Harry '97
Packin' It In '83
Saturday the 14th '81
First Family '80
How to Beat the High Cost of Living '80
The Last Married Couple in America '80
Love at First Bite '79
Scavenger Hunt '79
Witches' Brew '79
House Calls '78
No Room to Run '78
The Sunshine Boys '75
The Last of Sheila '73
Westworld '73
Portnoy's Complaint '72
The Steagle '71
Catch-22 '70
Diary of a Mad Housewife '70
Goodbye Columbus '69

Kokkorn Benjathikoon (1969-)
The Iron Ladies 2 '03
The Iron Ladies '00

Benji
Benji the Hunted '87
For the Love of Benji '77
Benji '74

Anne Bennent
Seraphine '08
Schnelles Geld '84

David Bennent (1966-)
Legend '86
The Tin Drum '79

Heinz Bennent (1921-)
Possession '81
From the Life of the Marionettes '80
The Last Metro '80
The Tin Drum '79
Nea '78

John Bennes
Stephen King's The Night Flier '96
Black Rainbow '91

Alan Bennett (1934-)
A Dance to the Music of Time '97
Fortunes of War '87

Bruce Bennett (1906-2007)
Lassie: Well of Love '70
The Cosmic Man '59
Three Violent People '57
Daniel Boone: Trail Blazer '56
Hidden Guns '56
Dragonfly Squadron '54
Dream Wife '53
Sudden Fear '52
Angels in the Outfield '51
Cavalry Charge '51
Mystery Street '50
Task Force '49
Silver River '48
Treasure of the Sierra Madre '48
Dark Passage '47
Nora Prentiss '47
The Man I Love '46
A Stolen Life '46
Mildred Pierce '45
I'm from Arkansas '44
U-Boat Prisoner '44
Fighting Devil Dogs '43
The More the Merrier '43
Sahara '43
Underground Agent '42
Before I Hang '40
Daredevils of the Red Circle '38
Hawk of the Wilderness '38
Tarzan and the Green Goddess '38
A Million to One '37
Shadow of Chinatown '36
The New Adventures of Tarzan '35

Constance Bennett (1904-65)
Madame X '66
As Young As You Feel '51
Smart Woman '48
The Unsuspected '47
Two-Faced Woman '41
Topper Takes a Trip '39
Service De Luxe '38
Topper '37
What Price Hollywood? '32
The Easiest Way '31
Sin Takes a Holiday '30
Married? '26

Darlene Bennett
Bad Girls Go to Hell '65
The Beast That Killed Women '65

Eliza Bennett (1992-)
Inkheart '09
The Contractor '07
Nanny McPhee '06
The Prince & Me '04

Elizabeth Bennett
Military Intelligence and You! '06
Soul's Midnight '06
The Duchess of Duke Street '78

Enid Bennett (1893-1969)
The Red Lily '24
The Sea Hawk '24
Robin Hood '22

Frank Bennett
Reggie Mixes In '16
Sold for Marriage '16

Haley Bennett
College '08
The Haunting of Molly Hartley '08
Marley & Me '08
Music & Lyrics '07

Hywel Bennett (1944-)
Vatel '00
Mary, Mother of Jesus '99
Neil Gaiman's NeverWhere '96
A Mind to Kill '95
Deadline '87
Murder Elite '86
Tinker, Tailor, Soldier, Spy '80
Endless Night '71
The Buttercup Chain '70
Loot... Give Me Money, Honey! '70
The Virgin Soldiers '69

Jeff Glenn Bennett (1962-)
Looney Tunes: Back in Action '03 (V)
Return to Never Land '02 (V)
Land Before Time 7: The Stone of Cold Fire '00 (V)
Kiki's Delivery Service '98 (V)
The Land Before Time 6: The Secret of Saurus Rock '98 (V)
The Land Before Time 5: The Mysterious Island '97 (V)
The Land Before Time 4: Journey Through the Mists '96 (V)
The Land Before Time 3: The Time of the Great Giving '95 (V)
Gargoyles, The Movie: The Heroes Awaken '94 (V)
The Land Before Time 2: The Great Valley Adventure '94 (V)

Jill Bennett (1931-90)
And Then Came Lola '09
In Her Line of Fire '06
The Pleasure Drivers '05
The Sheltering Sky '90
Hawks '89
Murders at Lynch Cross '85
For Your Eyes Only '81
Full Circle '77
The Old Curiosity Shop '75
I Want What I Want '72
The Charge of the Light Brigade '68
The Nanny '65
The Skull '65
Lust for Life '56
Moulin Rouge '52

Jimmy Bennett (1996-)
Orphan '09
Shorts: The Adventures of the Wishing Rock '09
Diminished Capacity '08
Snow Buddies '08 (V)
Trucker '08
Evan Almighty '07
South of Pico '07
Firewall '06
Poseidon '06
The Amityville Horror '05
Hostage '05
The Heart Is Deceitful Above All Things '04
The Polar Express '04

Joan Bennett (1910-90)
Suspiria '77
House of Dark Shadows '70
We're No Angels '55
Father's Little Dividend '51
Father of the Bride '50
Reckless Moment '49
The Scar '48
Secret Beyond the Door '48
Colonel Effingham's Raid '45
Scarlet Street '45
Woman in the Window '44
Twin Beds '42
Man Hunt '41
House Across the Bay '40
The Son of Monte Cristo '40
The Man in the Iron Mask '39
The Texans '38
Vogues of 1938 '37
Big Brown Eyes '36
Wedding Present '36
Mississippi '35
Little Women '33
Disraeli '30
Bulldog Drummond '29
Power '28

John Bennett (1928-2005)
Chaos & Cadavers '03
Priest '94
Antonia and Jane '91
Eye of the Needle '81
Hitler: The Last Ten Days '73
The House that Dripped Blood '71
Postman's Knock '62
Victim '61
It Takes a Thief '59

Jonathan Bennett (1981-)
Van Wilder: Freshman Year '08
Bachelor Party Vegas '05
Cheaper by the Dozen 2 '05
Mean Girls '04

Leila Bennett (1890-1965)
No Other Woman '33
Doctor X '32
Tiger Shark '32

Marjorie Bennett (1896-1982)
Stacey '73
The Love God? '70
Games '67
36 Hours '64
Promises! Promises! '63
Kiss Me Deadly '55
Abbott and Costello Meet Dr. Jekyll and Mr. Hyde '52

Nigel Bennett (1949-)
Bridal Fever '08
The Summit '08
Jesse Stone: Sea Change '07
Just Buried '07
The State Within '06
Do or Die '03
Cypher '02
Interceptor Force 2 '02
Widows '02
The Pilot's Wife '01
Anne of Green Gables: The Continuing Story '99
Invasion! '99
Naked City: A Killer Christmas '98
Rescuers: Stories of Courage—Two Couples '98
Gotti '96
Darkman 3: Die Darkman Die '95
Degree of Guilt '95
Kurt Vonnegut's Harrison Bergeron '95
Madonna: Innocence Lost '95
Where's the Money, Noreen? '95
Back in Action '94
Soft Deceit '94

Ray Bennett (1895-1957)
Thundering Trail '51
Border Badmen '45
Death Rides the Plains '44
Lawless Plainsmen '42

Skye Bennett
Against the Dark '08
Shadow Man '06

Sonja Bennett (1980-)
A Dog Named Christmas '09
Elegy '08
Fido '06
Where the Truth Lies '05

Tony Bennett (1926-)
The Scout '94
The Oscar '66

Zachary Bennett (1980-)
Just Business '08
Hearts of War '07
Stir of Echoes 2: The Homecoming '07
Cube: Zero '04
Shattered City: The Halifax Explosion '03
Verdict in Blood '02
Bonanno: A Godfather's Story '99
By Way of the Stars '92
Looking for Miracles '90

Jack Benny (1894-1974)
A Guide for the Married Man '67
It's a Mad, Mad, Mad, Mad World '63
The Great Lover '49
Without Reservations '46
The Horn Blows at Midnight '45
It's in the Bag '45
Hollywood Canteen '44
George Washington Slept Here '42
To Be or Not to Be '42
Charley's Aunt '41
Buck Benny Rides Again '40
Man About Town '39
Broadway Melody of 1936 '35
Transatlantic Merry-Go-Round '34
Medicine Man '30

Martin Benrath (1926-2000)
The White Rose '83
From the Life of the Marionettes '80

Abraham Benrubi (1969-)
Charlotte's Web '06 (V)
Wristcutters: A Love Story '06
Miss Congeniality 2: Armed and Fabulous '05
Without a Paddle '04
Open Range '03
George of the Jungle '97
U-Turn '97
Under Oath '97
Twister '96
Magic Island '95
The Shadow '94
The Program '93

Amber Benson (1977-)
The Blue Tooth Virgin '09
Strictly Sexual '08
Kiss the Bride '07
Latter Days '04
Taboo '02
Bye Bye, Love '94
The Crush '93
King of the Hill '93

Ashley Benson
Bart Got a Room '08
Bring It On: In It to Win It '07

Deborah Benson
Danger of Love '95
Mutant on the Bounty '89
Just Before Dawn '80
September 30, 1955 '77

George Benson (1911-83)
The Creeping Flesh '72
Convoy '40

Jodi Benson (1961-)
Toy Story 3 '10 (V)
Toy Story 2 '99 (V)
Thumbelina '94 (V)
The Little Mermaid '89 (V)

Lucille Benson (1914-84)
1941 '79
Huckleberry Finn '74
Mame '74
Reflections of Murder '74
Cactus in the Snow '72
Private Parts '72
Duel '71

Martin Benson (1918-)
The Omen '76
Tiffany Jones '75
A Matter of WHO '62
Exodus '60
The Cosmic Monsters '58
Istanbul '57
The King and I '56
Recoil '53

Robby Benson (1956-)
MXP: Most Xtreme Primate '03
Dragonheart: A New Beginning '00 (V)
At Home with the Webbers '94
Deadly Exposure '93
Homewrecker '92
Invasion of Privacy '92
Beauty and the Beast '91 (V)
Modern Love '90
Rent-A-Cop '88
White Hot '88
City Limits '85
Harry & Son '84
Running Brave '83
Two of a Kind '82
The Chosen '81
National Lampoon Goes to the Movies '81
Die Laughing '80
Tribute '80
Ice Castles '79
The End '78
One on One '77
Our Town '77
The Death of Richie '76
The Last of Mrs. Lincoln '76
Ode to Billy Joe '76
The Virginia Hill Story '76
Death Be Not Proud '75
All the Kind Strangers '74
Jory '72

Wendy Benson (1971-)
Luck of the Draw '00
Wishmaster '97

Lyriq Bent
Guns '08
Saw 4 '07
Saw 3 '06

Timothy Bentinck (1953-)
Sharpe's Rifles '93
Year of the Comet '92

Michael Bentine (1922-96)
Rentadick '72
Down Among the Z Men '52
Goon Movie '52

Fabrizio Bentivoglio (1957-)
Eternity and a Day '97
The Real Thing '97
Elective Affinities '96
Apartment Zero '88
Vatican Conspiracy '81

Dana Bentley
Sorority House Massacre 2: Nighty Nightmare '92
Karate Cop '91
Bad Girls from Mars '90

John Bentley (1916-)
Submarine Seahawk '59
Istanbul '57
White Huntress '57
Flight from Vienna '56
The Way Out '56
Profile '54
River Beat '54
Scarlet Spear '54
The Happiest Days of Your Life '50
Calling Paul Temple '48

Lamont Bentley (1973-)
The Wash '01
Tales from the Hood '95

Wes Bentley (1978-)
The Last Word '08
Ghost Rider '07
P2 '07
The Perfect Witness '07
Weirdsville '07
The Game of Their Lives '05
The Four Feathers '02
Soul Survivors '01
The Claim '00
American Beauty '99
White River '99

Barbi Benton (1950-)
Deathstalker '83
Hospital Massacre '81
For the Love of It '80

Dean Benton
Cocaine Fiends '36
Thunder Mountain '35

Eddie Benton
Prom Night '80
Dr. Strange '78

Jerome Benton
Graffiti Bridge '90
Under the Cherry Moon '86

Mark Benton (1965-)
Topsy Turvy '99
Career Girls '97
Catherine Cookson's The Girl '96

Susanne Benton (1948-)
A Boy and His Dog '75
Catch-22 '70
That Cold Day in the Park '69

Michael Bentt (1965-)
State Property 2 '05
Ali '01

Femi Benussi (1948-)
Hit Men '73
M'Lady's Court '73
The Slasher '72
Hatchet for the Honeymoon '70
Rattler Kid '68
The Hawks & the Sparrows '67

Luke Benward (1995-)
Dog Gone '08
Minutemen '08
How to Eat Fried Worms '06
Because of Winn-Dixie '05

Julie Benz (1972-)
The Boondock Saints II: All Saints Day '09
Punisher: War Zone '08
Rambo '08
Saw 5 '08
Kill Your Darlings '06
Locusts: The 8th Plague '05
Taken '02
The Brothers '01
Shriek If You Know What I Did Last Friday the 13th '00
Darkdrive '98
Jawbreaker '98

A.J. Benza (1962-)
Rocky Balboa '06
P.S. Your Cat is Dead! '02

Daniel Benzali (1950-)
Believers '07
Dead Heat '01
The Grey Zone '01
Screwed '00
Boss of Bosses '99
All the Little Animals '98
The End of Violence '97
Murder at 1600 '97
A Day in October '92
The Last of His Tribe '92
Messenger of Death '88
Pack of Lies '87

John Beradino (1917-96)
Don't Look Back: The Story of Leroy "Satchel" Paige '81
Moon of the Wolf '72
Seven Thieves '60

George Beranger (1893-1973)
Flirting with Fate '16
The Birth of a Nation '15

Iris Berben (1950-)
Killer Condom '95
Tea for Three '84
Companeros '70

Ady Berber (1913-66)
Door with the Seven Locks '62
Dead Eyes of London '61

Marcel Berbert
The Green Room '78
Mississippi Mermaid '69

Luca Bercovici (1957-)
Burning Down the House '01
Dirt Boy '01
Hard Luck '01
The Big Squeeze '96
Drop Zone '94
Scanner Cop '94
Inside Monkey Zetterland '93
Mirror Images 2 '93
K2: The Ultimate High '92
Mission of Justice '92
Mortal Passions '90
Pacific Heights '90
Clean and Sober '88
American Flyers '85
Parasite '82
Frightmare '81

Blaze Berdahl (1980-)
We're Back! A Dinosaur's Story '93 (V)
Pet Sematary '89

Omar Berdouni
Extraordinary Rendition '07
The Hamburg Cell '04

Tom Berenger (1950-)
Inception '10
Smokin' Aces 2: Assassins' Ball '10
Breaking Point '09
Silent Venom '08
Stiletto '08
The Christmas Miracle of Jonathan Toomey '07
Sniper 3 '04
Johnson County War '02
The Junction Boys '02
Sniper 2 '02
Cruel and Unusual '01
Eye See You '01
The Hollywood Sign '01
Training Day '01
True Blue '01
Cutaway '00
Diplomatic Siege '99
In the Company of Spies '99
A Murder of Crows '99
Turbulence 2: Fear of Flying '99
One Man's Hero '98
Shadow of Doubt '98
The Gingerbread Man '97
Rough Riders '97
An Occasional Hell '96
The Substitute '96
The Avenging Angel '95
Body Language '95
The Last of the Dogmen '95
Chasers '94
Major League 2 '94
Gettysburg '93
Sliver '93
Sniper '92
At Play in the Fields of the Lord '91
Shattered '91
The Field '90
Born on the Fourth of July '89
Love at Large '89
Major League '89
Betrayed '88
Last Rites '88
Shoot to Kill '88
Someone to Watch Over Me '87
Platoon '86
Fear City '85
Rustler's Rhapsody '85
The Big Chill '83
Eddie and the Cruisers '83
Beyond Obsession '82
The Dogs of War '81
Butch and Sundance: The Early Days '79
In Praise of Older Women '78
Johnny We Hardly Knew Ye '77
Looking for Mr. Goodbar '77
Rush It '77
The Sentinel '76

Marisa Berenson (1948-)
People '04
Women '97
Night of the Cyclone '90
White Hunter, Black Heart '90
Trade Secrets '86
The Secret Diary of Sigmund Freud '84
S.O.B. '81
Killer Fish '79
Sex on the Run '78
Barry Lyndon '75
Cabaret '72
Death in Venice '71

Harry Beresford (1864-1944)
Klondike Annie '36
Murders in the Zoo '33
The Sign of the Cross '33

Justin Berfield (1986-)
Max Keeble's Big Move '01
Invisible Mom 2 '99
The Kid with the X-Ray Eyes '99
Mom, Can I Keep Her? '98
Invisible Mom '96

Peter Berg (1964-)
Lions for Lambs '07
Smokin' Aces '07
Collateral '04
Corky Romano '01
Cop Land '97
Sisters '97
Girl 6 '96
The Great White Hype '96
Across the Moon '94
The Last Ride '94
The Last Seduction '94
Aspen Extreme '93
A Case for Murder '93
Fire in the Sky '93
A Midnight Clear '92
Crooked Hearts '91
Late for Dinner '91
Genuine Risk '89
Going Overboard '89
Race for Glory '89
Shocker '89
Tale of Two Sisters '89
Never on Tuesday '88

Judith-Marie Bergan
Never Pick Up a Stranger '79
Abduction '75

Francine Berge (1940-)
The Nun '66
Circle of Love '64
Judex '64

Candice Bergen (1946-)
Bride Wars '09
Sex and the City: The Movie '08
The Women '08
Footsteps '03
The In-Laws '03
View from the Top '03
Sweet Home Alabama '02
Miss Congeniality '00
Mayflower Madam '87
Merlin and the Sword '85
My Sweet Victim '85
Stick '85
2010: The Year We Make Contact '84 (V)
Gandhi '82
Rich and Famous '81
Starting Over '79
A Night Full of Rain '78
Oliver's Story '78
The Domino Principle '77
Bite the Bullet '75
The Wind and the Lion '75
11 Harrowhouse '74
Carnal Knowledge '71
The Adventurers '70
Getting Straight '70
Soldier Blue '70
The Group '66
The Sand Pebbles '66

Edgar Bergen (1903-78)
The Muppet Movie '79
Homecoming: A Christmas Story '71
I Remember Mama '48
Fun & Fancy Free '47 (N)
Stage Door Canteen '43
Here We Go Again! '42
Look Who's Laughing '41
Charlie McCarthy, Detective '39
You Can't Cheat an Honest Man '39
The Goldwyn Follies '38
Letter of Introduction '38

Frances Bergen (1922-2006)
Eating '90
The Morning After '86

Polly Bergen (1930-)
A Very Serious Person '06
Paradise, Texas '05
Dr. Jekyll and Ms. Hyde '95
Once Upon a Time ... When We Were Colored '95
The Lightning Incident '91
Cry-Baby '90
Haunting of Sarah Hardy '89
My Brother's Wife '89
War & Remembrance: The Final Chapter '89
War & Remembrance '88
Making Mr. Right '86
The Winds of War '83
Born Beautiful '82
How to Pick Up Girls '78
Murder on Flight 502 '75
Anatomy of Terror '74
Death Cruise '74
A Guide for the Married Man '67
Kisses for My President '64
Move Over, Darling '63
Cape Fear '61
Escape from Fort Bravo '53
The Stooge '51
At War with the Army '50

Tushka Bergen (1969-)
Invisible Child '99
Journey to the Center of the Earth '99
Lovelife '97
Voices from a Locked Room '95
Barcelona '94
Swing Kids '93
Wrangler '88

Deborah Berger
Rosebud '75
La Merveilleuse Visite '74

Harris Berger (1921-83)
East Side Kids '40
Junior G-Men '40

Helmut Berger (1944-)
The Godfather, Part 3 '90
Faceless '88
Code Name: Emerald '85
Mad Dog '84
Deadly Game '83
Fatal Fix '80
Battleforce '78
Mad Dog Killer '77
Victory at Entebbe '76
Conversation Piece '75
Romantic Englishwoman '75
Ash Wednesday '73
Order to Kill '73
Ludwig '72
The Garden of the Finzi-Continis '71
Dorian Gray '70
The Damned '69

Katya Berger (1964-)
Tales of Ordinary Madness '83
Nana '82

Michael Berger
Sarah's Child '96
Allonsanfan '73

Nicole Berger (1935-67)
The Story of a Three Day Pass '68
Shoot the Piano Player '62
The Siege of Sidney Street '60

Sarah Berger (1960-)
Element of Doubt '96
The Green Man '91

Senta Berger (1947-)
Blitz '85
Swiss Conspiracy '77
The Boss Is Served '76
Cross of Iron '76
Smugglers '75
When Women Lost Their Tails '75
The Scarlet Letter '73
Cobra '71
When Women Had Tails '70
The Ambushers '67
Diabolically Yours '67
Cast a Giant Shadow '66
The Quiller Memorandum '66
Full Hearts & Empty Pockets '63
The Victors '63
Waltz King '63
Secret of the Black Trunk '62
Sherlock Holmes and the Deadly Necklace '62
Testament of Dr. Mabuse '62

Sidney Berger (1936-)
Carnival of Souls '98
Carnival of Souls '62

William Berger (1928-93)
I'm Dangerous Tonight '90
Dial Help '88
Django Strikes Again '87
Hell Hunters '87
Hercules 2 '85
Day of the Cobra '84
Devilfish '84
Hercules '83
Oil '78
Slaughterday '77
Superfly T.N.T. '73
Today We Kill, Tomorrow We Die '71
Five Dolls for an August Moon '70
What a Way to Die '70
Sabata '69

Thommy Berggren (1937-)
Sunday's Children '94
The Adventurers '70
Elvira Madigan '67

Herbert Berghof (1909-90)
Harry and Tonto '74
Master Mind '73
Five Fingers '52
Red Planet Mars '52

Patrick Bergin (1954-)
False Prophets '06
The Far Side of Jericho '06
Played '06
Secret of the Cave '06
Frederick Forsyth's Icon '05
Johnny Was '05
Ella Enchanted '04
The Boys and Girl From County Clare '03
Brush with Fate '03
King of Texas '02
Amazons and Gladiators '01
Beneath Loch Ness '01
The Devil's Prey '01
Cause of Death '00
Deadline '00
Invisible Circus '00
St. Patrick: The Irish Legend '00
Durango '99
Escape Velocity '99
Eye of the Beholder '99
Treasure Island '99
When the Sky Falls '99
One Man's Hero '98
Sir Arthur Conan Doyle's The Lost World '98
The Apocalypse Watch '97
The Island on Bird Street '97
The Ripper '97
The Proposition '96
Suspicious Minds '96
Lawnmower Man 2: Beyond Cyberspace '95
Triplecross '95
Double Cross '94
Soft Deceit '94
Frankenstein '93
Map of the Human Heart '93
They Watch '93
Highway to Hell '92
Love Crimes '92
Patriot Games '92
The Real Charlotte '91
Robin Hood '91
Sleeping with the Enemy '91
Mountains of the Moon '90
The Courier '88
Taffin '88

Emily Bergl (1975-)
Taken '02
Happy Campers '01
Chasing Sleep '00
The Rage: Carrie 2 '99

Erik "Bullen" Berglund (1887-1946)
Only One Night '42
Walpurgis Night '41
Intermezzo '36

Henry Bergman (1868-1946)
Modern Times '36
City Lights '31
Pawnshop '16

Ingrid Bergman (1915-82)
A Woman Called Golda '82
Autumn Sonata '78
A Matter of Time '76
Murder on the Orient Express '74
The Hideaways '73
Walk in the Spring Rain '70
Cactus Flower '69
Goodbye Again '61
24 Hours in a Woman's Life '61

Indiscreet '58
The Inn of the Sixth Happiness '58
Anastasia '56
Elena and Her Men '56
Voyage in Italy '53
Europa '51 '52
Stromboli '50
Under Capricorn '49
Arch of Triumph '48
Joan of Arc '48
Notorious '46
The Bells of St. Mary's '45
Saratoga Trunk '45
Spellbound '45
Gaslight '44
For Whom the Bell Tolls '43
Casablanca '42
Only One Night '42
Adam Had Four Sons '41
Dr. Jekyll and Mr. Hyde '41
Walpurgis Night '41
June Night '40
Intermezzo '39
Dollar '38
A Woman's Face '38
Intermezzo '36
Swedenhielms '35
The Count of the Old Town '34

Jaime Bergman (1975-)

Darkwolf '03
Daybreak '01

Peter Bergman (1953-)

Phantom of the Ritz '88
J-Men Forever! '79

Sandahl Bergman (1951-)

The P.A.C.K. '96
Ice Cream Man '95
Inner Sanctum 2 '94
Body of Influence '93
Lipstick Camera '93
Possessed by the Night '93
Raw Nerve '91
Hell Comes to Frogtown '88
Kandyland '87
Programmed to Kill '86
Stewardess School '86
Red Sonja '85
Getting Physical '84
She '83
Airplane 2: The Sequel '82
Conan the Barbarian '82
Xanadu '80

Elisabeth Bergner (1900-86)

The Pedestrian '73
Cry of the Banshee '70
Dreaming Lips '37
As You Like It '36
Catherine the Great '34

Helena Bergstrom (1964-)

Still Crazy '98
Under the Sun '98
The Last Dance '93
House of Angels '92
The Women on the Roof '89

Linda Bergstrom

More about the Children of Noisy Village '87
The Children of Noisy Village '86

Luis Beristain (1918-62)

The Exterminating Angel '62
El '52

Christian Berkel (1957-)

Valkyrie '08
Black Book '06
Downfall '04
Guys and Balls '04
The Experiment '01

Busby Berkeley (1895-1976)

Million Dollar Mermaid '52
Babes on Broadway '41
Dames '34
Fashions of 1934 '34
42nd Street '33
Roman Scandals '33

Xander Berkeley (1958-)

Kick-Ass '10
Taken '08
Fracture '07
Magma: Volcanic Disaster '06
Deepwater '05
Drop Dead Sexy '05
Standing Still '05
In Enemy Hands '04
Quicksand '01
Shanghai Noon '00
Time Code '00
Universal Soldier: The Return '99
Phoenix '98
Winchell '98
Air Force One '97
One Night Stand '97
Barb Wire '96
Bulletproof '96
If These Walls Could Talk '96
The Killing Jar '96
Persons Unknown '96
The Rock '96
Within the Rock '96
Apollo 13 '95
Heat '95
Poison Ivy 2: Lily '95
Safe '95
Roswell: The U.F.O. Cover-Up '94
Attack of the 50 Ft. Woman '93
Dead to Rights '93
Candyman '92
A Few Good Men '92
The Gun in Betty Lou's Handbag '92
Internal Affairs '90
Short Time '90
Assassin '89
Tapeheads '89
Deadly Dreams '88
The Lawless Land '88
Straight to Hell '87
Sid & Nancy '86

Elizabeth Berkley (1972-)

S. Darko: A Donnie Darko Tale '09
Meet Market '08
Moving Malcolm '03
Roger Dodger '02
The Curse of the Jade Scorpion '01
Any Given Sunday '99
Tail Lights Fade '99
Random Encounter '98
The Taxman '98
The Real Blonde '97
The First Wives Club '96
Showgirls '95
White Wolves 2: Legend of the Wild '94
Point Break '91

Steven Berkoff (1937-)

The Flying Scotsman '06
Charlie '04
Head in the Clouds '04
Children of Dune '03
Attila '01
Rancid Aluminium '00
Legionnaire '98
Another 9 1/2 Weeks '96
Flynn '96
Fair Game '95
Intruders '92
The Krays '90
Prisoner of Rio '89
War & Remembrance: The Final Chapter '89
War & Remembrance '88
Rambo: First Blood, Part 2 '85
Revolution '85
Transmutations '85
Beverly Hills Cop '84
Octopussy '83
Outland '81
The Passenger '75
A Clockwork Orange '71

Terri Berland

The Strangeness '85
Pink Motel '82

Milton Berle (1908-2002)

Storybook '95
Driving Me Crazy '91
Side by Side '88
Broadway Danny Rose '84
Cracking Up '83
Off Your Rocker '80
The Muppet Movie '79
Legend of Valentino '75
Lepke '75
Evil Roy Slade '71
Journey Back to Oz '71 (V)
Where Angels Go, Trouble Follows '68
Who's Minding the Mint? '67
The Oscar '66
The Loved One '65
It's a Mad, Mad, Mad, Mad World '63
The Bellboy '60
Let's Make Love '60
Sun Valley Serenade '41
Mark of Zorro '20

Francois Berleand (1952-)

Transporter 3 '08
A Girl Cut in Two '07
Comedy of Power '06
Tell No One '06
Transporter 2 '05
The Chorus '04
The Grand Role '04
A Model Employee '02
The Transporter '02
Whatever You Say '02
Romance '99
Place Vendome '98
Seventh Heaven '98
Capitaine Conan '96
May Fools '90
Au Revoir les Enfants '87

Jeannie Berlin (1932-)

In the Spirit '90
The Heartbreak Kid '72
Housewife '72
Portnoy's Complaint '72
The Baby Maker '70
Getting Straight '70
The Strawberry Statement '70

Charles Berling (1958-)

Summer Hours '08
The Man of My Life '06
How I Killed My Father '03
Demonlover '02
The Bridge '00
Comedy of Innocence '00
Les Destinees '00
Stardom '00
L'Ennui '98
Those Who Love Me Can Take the Train '98
Dry Cleaning '97
Obsession '97
Love, etc. '96
Ridicule '96
Nelly et Monsieur Arnaud '95

Peter Berling (1934-)

Francesco '93
Cobra Verde '88
Hit Men '73
Aguirre, the Wrath of God '72

Warren Berlinger (1937-)

Backlash '99
The Feminine Touch '95
Hero '92
Take Two '87
Sex and the Single Parent '82
The World According to Garp '82
Four Deuces '75
The Long Goodbye '73
Thunder Alley '67
Spinout '66
Billie '65
Platinum High School '60

Marc Berman

The Girl from Paris '02
Noir et Blanc '86

Shelley Berman (1926-)

You Don't Mess with the Zohan '08
The Holiday '06
Meet the Fockers '04
Motorama '91
Rented Lips '88
Beware! The Blob '72
Think Dirty '70
Divorce American Style '67
The Best Man '64
The Wheeler Dealers '63

Susan Berman

Curtain Call '97
Smithereens '82

Gael Garcia Bernal (1978-)

Letters to Juliet '10
The Limits of Control '09
Mammoth '09
Rudo y Cursi '09
Blindness '08
Babel '06
The Science of Sleep '06
The King '05
Bad Education '04
The Motorcycle Diaries '04
Cuban Blood '03
Dot the I '03
The Crime of Father Amaro '02
Fidel '02
I'm with Lucy '02
No News from God '01
Y Tu Mama Tambien '01
Amores Perros '00

Andre Bernard

The Sea Change '98
The Crying Game '92

Crystal Bernard (1961-)

Welcome to Paradise '07
Jackpot '01
A Face to Kill For '99
Gideon '99
As Good as Dead '95
Siringo '94
Slumber Party Massacre 2 '87

Ed Bernard (1939-)

Reflections of Murder '74
Across 110th Street '72

Jason Bernard (1938-96)

Liar Liar '97
Down, Out and Dangerous '95
While You Were Sleeping '95
Cosmic Slop '94
Paint It Black '89
No Way Out '87
The Children of Times Square '86
All of Me '84
Wilma '77

Paul Bernard (1898-1958)

Pattes Blanches '49
The Ladies of the Bois de Bologne '44

Susan Bernard (1948-)

Teenager '74
Faster, Pussycat! Kill! Kill! '65

Herschel Bernardi (1923-86)

Actor: The Paul Muni Story '78
The Front '76
The Story of Jacob & Joseph '74
No Place to Run '72
Journey Back to Oz '71 (V)
Irma La Douce '63
Love with the Proper Stranger '63
The George Raft Story '61
1001 Arabian Nights '59 (V)
Murder by Contract '58
Green Fields '37

Michael Bernardo (1964-)

Shootfighter 2: Kill or Be Killed! '96
Virtual Combat '95
Shootfighter: Fight to the Death '93

Lynn Bernay (1931-)

The Pit and the Pendulum '61
I Bury the Living '58

Sandra Bernhard (1955-)

Dare '09
Dinner Rush '00
Playing Mona Lisa '00
Footsteps '98
Wrongfully Accused '98
An Alan Smithee Film: Burn, Hollywood, Burn '97
Lover Girl '97
Plump Fiction '97
Somewhere in the City '97
The Apocalypse '96
The Late Shift '96
Inside Monkey Zetterland '93
Hudson Hawk '91
Heavy Petting '89
Track 29 '88
Sesame Street Presents: Follow That Bird '85
King of Comedy '82
Cheech and Chong's Nice Dreams '81

Daniel Bernhardt (1965-)

The Matrix Reloaded '03
G2: Mortal Conquest '99
Bloodsport 4: The Dark Kumite '98
Perfect Target '98
Bloodsport 3 '97
True Vengeance '97
Bloodsport 2: The Next Kumite '95

Kevin Bernhardt (1961-)

The Immortals '95
Beauty School '93
Hellraiser 3: Hell on Earth '92
Midnight Warrior '89
Counterforce '87

Mara Berni (1934-)

The Fury of Hercules '61
Samson '61

Collin Bernsen

Hangfire '91
Puppet Master 2 '90

Corbin Bernsen (1954-)

Depth Charge '08
Vipers '08
Masters of Horror: Right to Die '07
Paid '06
Carpool Guy '05
Kiss Kiss Bang Bang '05
Call Me: The Rise and Fall of Heidi Fleiss '04
Love Comes Softly '03
The Santa Trap '02
The Tomorrow Man '01
Killer Instinct '00
Rangers '00
An American Affair '99
Final Payback '99
The Dentist 2: Brace Yourself '98
Major League 3: Back to the Minors '98
Recipe for Revenge '98
Spacejacked '98
Bloodhounds '96
Bloodhounds 2 '96
The Dentist '96
The Great White Hype '96
Inhumanoid '96
Kounterfeit '96
Menno's Mind '96
Baja '95
Cover Me '95
Operation Intercept '95
Someone to Die For '95
Tails You Live, Heads You're Dead '95
Tales from the Hood '95
Temptress '95
Major League 2 '94
The New Age '94
Radioland Murders '94
Savage Land '94
The Soft Kill '94
A Brilliant Disguise '93
Final Mission '93
The Ghost Brigade '93
Ring of the Musketeers '93
Frozen Assets '92
Dead on the Money '91
Shattered '91
Bert Rigby, You're a Fool '89
Disorganized Crime '89
Major League '89
Dead Aim '87
Hello Again '87
L.A. Law '86
Eat My Dust '76
King Kong '76

Jon Bernthal

The Ghost Writer '10
Night at the Museum: Battle of the Smithsonian '09
Day Zero '07

David Beron

East Side Story '07
Honor Thy Father and Mother: The True Story of the Menendez Brothers '94

Olinka (Schoberova) Berova (1943-)

Togetherness '70
The Vengeance of She '68

Claude Berri (1934-)

Happily Ever After '04
Va Savoir '01
Le Sex Shop '73
Marry Me, Marry Me '69
Please Not Now! '61

Robert Berri

Ladies' Man '62
Dishonorable Discharge '57

Elizabeth Berridge (1962-)

Hidalgo '04
When the Party's Over '91
Montana '90
Five Corners '88
Amadeus '84
Silence of the Heart '84
The Funhouse '81

Elizabeth Berrington (1970-)

Fred Claus '07
Tristram Shandy: A Cock and Bull Story '05
Urban Ghost Story '98

Chuck Berry (1926-)

Chuck Berry: Hail! Hail! Rock 'n' Roll '87
Go, Johnny Go! '59
Rock, Rock, Rock '56

Halle Berry (1968-)

Perfect Stranger '07
Things We Lost in the Fire '07
X-Men: The Last Stand '06
Robots '05 (V)
Catwoman '04
Gothika '03
X2: X-Men United '03
Die Another Day '02
Monster's Ball '01
Swordfish '01
X-Men '00
Introducing Dorothy Dandridge '99
Bulworth '98
Why Do Fools Fall in Love? '98
B.A.P.'s '97
Executive Decision '96
Girl 6 '96

Race the Sun '96
The Rich Man's Wife '96
The Flintstones '94
Losing Isaiah '94
Father Hood '93
The Program '93
Queen '93
Boomerang '92
Jungle Fever '91
The Last Boy Scout '91
Strictly Business '91

Jules Berry (1883-1951)
Les Visiteurs du Soir '42
Le Jour Se Leve '39
The Crime of Monsieur Lange '36

Ken Berry (1930-)
The Cat from Outer Space '78
Mountain Man '77
Herbie Rides Again '74
Hello Down There '69

Mark Berry
Blade: Trinity '04
Delivered '98

Michael Berry
Beyond the Law '92
The Touch of Satan '70

Richard Berry (1950-)
The Valet '06
Pedale Douce '96
L'Appat '94
Day of Atonement '93
Honeymoon '87
A Man and a Woman: 20 Years Later '86
L'Addition '85
Special Police '85

Veronica Berry
Lords of the Street '08
Father of Lies '07

Vincent Berry
Baby '00
Sugar Town '99
The Fury Within '98
Free Willy 3: The Rescue '97
Amnesia '96

Dorothee Berryman (1948-)
The Barbarian Invasions '03
Taken '99
Winter Lily '98
The Pianist '91
Scanners 2: The New Order '91
A Paper Wedding '89
The Decline of the American Empire '86

Michael Berryman (1948-)
The Devil's Rejects '05
Wizards of the Demon Sword '94
Teenage Exorcist '93
Auntie Lee's Meat Pies '92
Beastmaster 2: Through the Portal of Time '91
Evil Spirits '91
The Guyver '91
Haunting Fear '91
The Secret of the Golden Eagle '91
Aftershock '88
Saturday the 14th Strikes Back '88
The Barbarians '87
Voyage of the Rock Aliens '87
Star Trek 4: The Voyage Home '86
Cut and Run '85
The Hills Have Eyes, Part 2 '84
Deadly Blessing '81
The Hills Have Eyes '77
One Flew Over the Cuckoo's Nest '75
Gator King '70

Julien Bertheau (1910-95)
That Obscure Object of Desire '77
Phantom of Liberty '74
Madame Sans-Gene '62

Anders W. Berthelsen (1969-)
Just Another Love Story '08
Italian for Beginners '01
The Weight of Water '00
Mifune '99

Jacques Berthier
Ladies' Man '62
The Master of Ballantrae '53

Dehl Berti (1921-91)
Bullies '86
Wolfen '81
Sweet Hostage '75

Marina Berti (1925-2002)
Night Train Murders '75
Torture Train '75
A Face in the Rain '63
Madame Sans-Gene '62
Quo Vadis '51
Prince of Foxes '49

Francoise Bertin
A Christmas Tale '08
Dad On the Run '00
Happenstance '00

Roland Bertin (1930-)
Pas Tres Catholique '93
The Hairdresser's Husband '92
Cyrano de Bergerac '90
L'Homme Blesse '83
Diva '82

Valerie Bertinelli (1960-)
True Confessions of a Hollywood Starlet '08
Saved! '04
Wilderness Love '02
Taken Away '89
Pancho Barnes '88
Number One with a Bullet '87
Rockabye '86
Ordinary Heroes '85
Silent Witness '85
Aladdin and His Wonderful Lamp '84
Shattered Vows '84
C.H.O.M.P.S. '79
Young Love, First Love '79

Jane Bertish
The Roman Spring of Mrs. Stone '03
Dance with a Stranger '85

Suzanne Bertish (1953-)
The Roman Spring of Mrs. Stone '03
The Scarlet Pimpernel 3: The Kidnapped King '99
Venice, Venice '92
The Hunger '83
To the Lighthouse '83

Juliet Berto (1947-90)
Mr. Klein '76
Celine and Julie Go Boating '74
Le Sex Shop '73
La Chinoise '67
The Joy of Knowledge '65

Paul Bertoya
Angels from Hell '68
Cop-Out '67

Gene Bervoets (1956-)
The Memory of a Killer '03
The Vanishing '88

Bibi Besch (1940-96)
Rattled '96
Doing Time on Maple Drive '92
Crazy from the Heart '91
Betsy's Wedding '90

Kill Me Again '89
Tremors '89
Date with an Angel '87
The Lonely Lady '83
The Beast Within '82
Star Trek 2: The Wrath of Khan '82
Death of a Centerfold '81
Sophisticated Gents '81
Backstairs at the White House '79
Peter Lundy and the Medicine Hat Stallion '77

Melchior Beslon
Paris, je t'aime '06
The Princess and the Warrior '00

Dominique Besnehard (1954-)
Beaumarchais the Scoundrel '96
A Nos Amours '84

Ardon Bess
Moving Target '96
Spenser: The Judas Goat '94

Ted Bessell (1935-96)
Acorn People '82
Breaking Up Is Hard to Do '79
Don't Drink the Water '69
Billie '65
McHale's Navy Joins the Air Force '65

Joe Besser (1907-88)
Savage Intruder '68
Sins of Jezebel '54
Africa Screams '49

Matt Besser
Undead or Alive '07
Walk Hard: The Dewey Cox Story '07

Eugenie Besserer (1868-1934)
Speedway '29
A Lady of Chance '28
The Flesh and the Devil '27
The Jazz Singer '27
Anna Christie '23
What Happened to Rosa? '21
The Greatest Question '19
Little Orphan Annie '18

Ahmed Best (1973-)
Mother and Child '09
Star Wars: Episode 3—Revenge of the Sith '05
Star Wars: Episode 2—Attack of the Clones '02 (V)
Star Wars: Episode 1—The Phantom Menace '99 (V)

Edna Best (1900-74)
The Ghost and Mrs. Muir '47
Intermezzo '39
South Riding '37
The Man Who Knew Too Much '34

James Best (1926-)
Moondance Alexander '07
Death Mask '98
Ode to Billy Joe '76
The Savage Bees '76
The Runaway Barge '75
Mind Warp '72
Sounder '72
Savage Run '70
Shenandoah '65
Shock Corridor '63
The Killer Shrews '59
Ride Lonesome '59
Verboten! '59
The Naked and the Dead '58
Ma and Pa Kettle at the Fair '52

Wayne Best
Mean Streak '99
Summer's Children '79

Willie Best (1913-62)
The Kansan '43
High Sierra '41
The Ghost Breakers '40
The Bride Walks Out '36
The Littlest Rebel '35
Kentucky Kernels '34
The Monster Walks '32

Martine Beswick (1941-)
Night of the Scarecrow '95
Wide Sargasso Sea '92
Evil Spirits '91
Miami Blues '90
Trancers 2: The Return of Jack Deth '90
Cyclone '87
The Offspring '87
Balboa '82
The Happy Hooker Goes Hollywood '80
Devil Dog: The Hound of Hell '78
Strange New World '75
Seizure '74
Dr. Jekyll and Sister Hyde '71
A Bullet for the General '68
Prehistoric Women '67
One Million Years B.C. '66
Thunderball '65
From Russia with Love '63

Anne Betancourt
Bless the Child '00
Fools Rush In '97
Seedpeople '92

Wilson Bethel
Generation Kill '08
Tunnel Rats '08

Sabine Bethmann (1931-)
Dr. Mabuse vs. Scotland Yard '64
The Indian Tomb '59
Journey to the Lost City '58

Zena Bethune (1945-)
Who's That Knocking at My Door? '68
Sunrise at Campobello '60

Paul Bettany (1971-)
Iron Man 2 '10 (V)
Legion '10
Creation '09
Inkheart '09
The Young Victoria '09
Iron Man '08 (V)
The Secret Life of Bees '08
The Da Vinci Code '06
Firewall '06
Wimbledon '04
Dogville '03
Master and Commander: The Far Side of the World '03
The Reckoning '03
The Heart of Me '02
A Beautiful Mind '01
A Knight's Tale '01
Gangster No. 1 '00
After the Rain '99
Every Woman Knows a Secret '99
Robert Louis Stevenson's The Game of Death '99
Coming Home '98
The Land Girls '98
Bent '97
Sharpe's Waterloo '97

Lyle Bettger (1915-2003)
Johnny Reno '66
Nevada Smith '66
Lone Ranger '56
Sea Chase '55
Carnival Story '54
All I Desire '53
Union Station '50

Laura Betti (1934-)
Courage Mountain '89
Lovers and Liars '81
1900 '76
Allonsanfan '73

Sonny and Jed '73
The Canterbury Tales '71
Twitch of the Death Nerve '71
Hatchet for the Honeymoon '70
Teorema '68

Val Bettin (1916-)
The Return of Jafar '94 (V)
The Great Mouse Detective '86 (V)

Angela Bettis (1975-)
Masters of Horror: Sick Girl '06
Carrie '02
Coastlines '02
May '02
The Flamingo Rising '01
Perfume '01
The Ponder Heart '01
Bless the Child '00
The Last Best Sunday '98

Robert Bettles (1962-)
Fourth Wish '75
Ride a Wild Pony '75

Franca Bettoya (1936-)
Marauder '65
The Last Man on Earth '64

Daniel Betts (1970-)
Heat of the Sun '99
The Magical Legend of the Leprechauns '99
The Canterville Ghost '96

Jack Betts
Spider-Man '02
Southern Man '99
Gods and Monsters '98
Dead Men Don't Die '91
Fistful of Death '71
The Bloody Brood '59

Carl Betz (1921-78)
The Meal '75
Spinout '66
Dangerous Crossing '53

Matthew Betz (1881-1938)
Little Red Schoolhouse '36
Racing Blood '36
Trails of the Wild '35
The Fighting Rookie '34
Tarzan the Fearless '33
Broadway to Cheyenne '32
The Fighting Marshal '32
The Wedding March '28
The Unholy Three '25

Billy Bevan (1887-1957)
The Woman in Green '49
The Man Who Wouldn't Die '42
Mrs. Miniver '42
Dr. Jekyll and Mr. Hyde '41
Girl of the Golden West '38
The Wrong Road '37
The Last Outpost '35
The Lost Patrol '34
Cavalcade '33
Vanity Fair '32
High Voltage '29
The White Sin '24

Clem Bevans (1879-1963)
Gold Raiders '51
Silver City Bonanza '51
Rim of the Canyon '49
Highway 13 '48
The Millerson Case '47
The Kansan '43
Sergeant York '41
Abe Lincoln in Illinois '40

Helen Beverly
The Master Race '44
Meeting at Midnight '44
Overture to Glory '40
The Light Ahead '39
Green Fields '37

Leslie Bevis (1957-)
The November Men '93
Alien Nation '88

Nathan Bexton (1977-)
The In Crowd '00
Psycho Beach Party '00
Go '99
Nowhere '96

Turhan Bey (1920-)
Virtual Combat '95
Parole, Inc. '49
The Amazing Mr. X '48
Out of the Blue '47
The Climax '44
Dragon Seed '44
Ali Baba and the Forty Thieves '43
Background to Danger '43
The Mad Ghoul '43
Arabian Nights '42
Junior G-Men of the Air '42
The Mummy's Tomb '42
Footsteps in the Dark '41
Shadows on the Stairs '41

Alexander Beyer (1973-)
Good Bye, Lenin! '03
The Legend of Rita '99

Brad Beyer (1973-)
Monday Night Mayhem '02
Sorority Boys '02
Crazy in Alabama '99
The General's Daughter '99
Trick '99

Troy Beyer (1965-)
John Q '02
A Light in the Darkness '02
Let's Talk About Sex '98
B.A.P.'s '97
The Little Death '95
Weekend at Bernie's 2 '93
Rooftops '89

Richard Beymer (1939-)
Elvis Meets Nixon '98
Foxfire '96
The Disappearance of Kevin Johnson '95
The Little Death '95
Under Investigation '93
Black Belt '92
Silent Night, Deadly Night 3: Better Watch Out! '89
Cross Country '83
Free Grass '69
The Stripper '63
The Longest Day '62
West Side Story '61
The Diary of Anne Frank '59
Johnny Tremain & the Sons of Liberty '58
Indiscretion of an American Wife '54

Didier Bezace (1946-)
The Chambermaid on the Titanic '97
Les Voleurs '96
Between Heaven and Earth '93
L.627 '92
The Little Thief '89

Dante Beze
See Mos Def

Raoul Bhaneja
Weirdsville '07
Touch of Pink '04

Bhasker (1930-2003)
Wild West '93
Drachenfutter '87
I Drink Your Blood '71

Daniela Bianchi (1942-)
Dirty Heroes '71
Secret Agent 00 '67
From Russia with Love '63
The Sword of El Cid '62

Rosa Maria Bianchi
Nicotina '03
Amores Perros '00

Yuen Biao (1957-)
Robin-B-Hood '06
Once Upon a Time in China '91

Miracles '89
Dragons Forever '88
Eastern Condors '87
The Millionaire's Express '86
Project A '83
Zu: Warriors from the Magic Mountain '83
The Prodigal Son '82

Leslie Bibb (1974-)
Iron Man 2 '10
Confessions of a Shopaholic '09
Law Abiding Citizen '09
Iron Man '08
The Midnight Meat Train '08
Trick 'r Treat '08
Sex and Death 101 '07
Talladega Nights: The Ballad of Ricky Bobby '06
Wristcutters: A Love Story '06
See Spot Run '01
The Skulls '00

Charles K. Bibby
Order of the Black Eagle '87
Unmasking the Idol '86

Abner Biberman (1909-77)
Elephant Walk '54
Roaring City '51
Betrayal from the East '44
The Keys of the Kingdom '44
The Leopard Man '43
His Girl Friday '40
Gunga Din '39
Panama Patrol '39
The Rains Came '39

Robert Bice (1914-68)
Dial Red O '55
Invasion U.S.A. '52
Loan Shark '52
Tales of Robin Hood '52
Gunplay '51
Bandit King of Texas '49
The Ghost and the Guest '43

Bruno Bichir (1967-)
Julia '08
La Mujer de Mi Hermano '06
No News from God '01
Midaq Alley '95
A Lost Year '93
Highway Patrolman '91

Demian Bichir
Che '08
In the Time of the Butterflies '01

Stewart Bick
The Reagans '04
Danger Beneath the Sea '02
Life with Judy Garland—Me and My Shadows '01
Lip Service '00
Mercy '00
Sex & Mrs. X '00
One Special Night '99
Captive '97

Charles Bickford (1889-1967)
A Big Hand for the Little Lady '66
Fatal Confinement '64
Days of Wine and Roses '62
The Unforgiven '60
The Big Country '58
The Court Martial of Billy Mitchell '55
Not as a Stranger '55
A Star Is Born '54
Jim Thorpe: All American '51
Branded '50
Guilty of Treason '50
Riding High '50
Whirlpool '49
Babe Ruth Story '48
Command Decision '48
Four Faces West '48
Johnny Belinda '48
Brute Force '47
The Farmer's Daughter '47
Duel in the Sun '46
A Wing and a Prayer '44
Mr. Lucky '43
The Song of Bernadette '43
Reap the Wild Wind '42
Tarzan's New York Adventure '42
Burma Convoy '41
Mutiny in the Big House '39
Of Mice and Men '39
The Plainsman '37
Thunder Pass '37
Thunder Trail '37
The Farmer Takes a Wife '35
Little Miss Marker '34
No Other Woman '33
Panama Flo '32
East of Borneo '31
Anna Christie '30

Andrew Bicknell
Attack Force '06
A Dog of Flanders '99
Buffalo Girls '95
Prince Brat and the Whipping Boy '95
Heidi '93

Jean-Luc Bideau (1940-)
The Red Violin '98
Revenge of the Musketeers '94
Rendez-Moi Ma Peau '81
Jonah Who Will Be 25 in the Year 2000 '76
La Salamandre '71

Michael Biehn (1956-)
Streets of Blood '09
Stiletto '08
Planet Terror '07
The Insatiable '06
The Legend of Butch & Sundance '04
Borderline '02
Clockstoppers '02
The Art of War '00
Chain of Command '00
Cherry Falls '00
Dying to Get Rich '98
The Magnificent Seven '98
Silver Wolf '98
Asteroid '97
Dead Men Can't Dance '97
Double Edge '97
Mojave Moon '96
The Rock '96
Breach of Trust '95
Frame by Frame '95
Jade '95
Blood of the Hunter '94
Deep Red '94
In the Kingdom of the Blind the Man with One Eye Is King '94
Deadfall '93
Strapped '93
Tombstone '93
K2: The Ultimate High '92
A Taste for Killing '92
Timebomb '91
Navy SEALS '90
The Abyss '89
In a Shallow Grave '88
The Seventh Sign '88
Rampage '87
Aliens '86
The Terminator '84
The Lords of Discipline '83
The Fan '81
Hog Wild '80
Coach '78
Grease '78

Dick Biel
Slime City '89
Splatter University '84

Jessica Biel (1982-)
The A-Team '10
Valentine's Day '10
Planet 51 '09 (V)
Powder Blue '09
Easy Virtue '08
I Now Pronounce You Chuck and Larry '07
Next '07
Home of the Brave '06
The Illusionist '06
Elizabethtown '05
London '05
Stealth '05
Blade: Trinity '04
Cellular '04
The Texas Chainsaw Massacre '03
The Rules of Attraction '02
Summer Catch '01
I'll Be Home for Christmas '98
Ulee's Gold '97

Josef Bierbichler (1948-)
The White Ribbon '09
Winter Sleepers '97
Woyzeck '78
Heart of Glass '74

Ramon Bieri (1929-2001)
Love, Lies and Murder '91
Grandview U.S.A. '84
A Matter of Life and Death '81
A Christmas Without Snow '80
The Frisco Kid '79
Love Affair: The Eleanor & Lou Gehrig Story '77
Panic in Echo Park '77
Sorcerer '77
Badlands '74
It's Good to Be Alive '74
Nicole '72
The Andromeda Strain '71
The Passing of Evil '70
The Grasshopper '69

Craig Bierko (1965-)
Scary Movie 4 '06
Cinderella Man '05
Dickie Roberts: Former Child Star '03
The Suburbans '99
The Thirteenth Floor '99
Fear and Loathing in Las Vegas '98
Sour Grapes '98
The Long Kiss Goodnight '96
Til There Was You '96
Danielle Steel's Star '93
Victimless Crimes '90

Adam Biesk
Leprechaun 2 '94
The Applegates '89

Big Boi
See Antwan Andre Patton

Big Pun (1971-2000)
Thicker than Water '99
Urban Menace '99

Claudio Bigagli (1955-)
Fiorile '93
Mille Bolle Blu '93
Mediterraneo '91
Kaos '85
The Night of the Shooting Stars '82

Scott "Bam Bam" Bigelow (1961-)
Major Payne '95
SnakeEater 3: His Law '92

Dan Biggers
Elizabethtown '05
Flash '98
Basket Case 3: The Progeny '92

Sean Biggerstaff (1983-)
Cashback '06
Harry Potter and the Sorcerer's Stone '01
The Winter Guest '97

Jason Biggs (1978-)
Lower Learning '08
My Best Friend's Girl '08
Over Her Dead Body '08
Eight Below '06
Wedding Daze '06
Jersey Girl '04
American Wedding '03
Anything Else '03
American Pie 2 '01
Jay and Silent Bob Strike Back '01
Prozac Nation '01
Saving Silverman '01
Boys and Girls '00
Loser '00
American Pie '99

Richard Biggs (1960-2004)
Ablaze '00
Forever Love '98

Roxann Biggs-Dawson (1964-)
Darkman 3: Die Darkman Die '95
Midnight's Child '93
Dirty Work '92
Mortal Sins '92
Guilty by Suspicion '91
Broken Angel '88

Theodore Bikel (1924-)
Second Chances '98
The Shadow Conspiracy '96
Benefit of the Doubt '93
My Family Treasure '93
The Assassination Game '92
Shattered '91
The Final Days '89
See You in the Morning '89
Dark Tower '87
Very Close Quarters '84
The Return of the King '80 (V)
Victory at Entebbe '76
Murder on Flight 502 '75
200 Motels '71
Darker than Amber '70
My Side of the Mountain '69
Sweet November '68
The Russians Are Coming, the Russians Are Coming '66
My Fair Lady '64
A Dog of Flanders '59
The Defiant Ones '58
I Bury the Living '58
I Want to Live! '58
Enemy Below '57
The Pride and the Passion '57
Above Us the Waves '56
Flight from Vienna '56
Never Let Me Go '53
Moulin Rouge '52
The African Queen '51

Vincent Bilancio
Blood Gnome '02
Crystal's Diary '99

Fernando Bilbao
The Screaming Dead '72
Fangs of the Living Dead '68

Nicole Bilderback (1975-)
The New Twenty '08
Bring It On '00
Paper Bullets '99

Leo Bill
Me and Orson Welles '09
Becoming Jane '07
The Fall '06
Lethal Dose '03
Two Men Went to War '02

Tony Bill (1940-)
Naked City: Justice with a Bullet '98
Barb Wire '96
The Killing Mind '90
Pee-wee's Big Adventure '85
Washington Mistress '81
Heart Beat '80
Little Dragons '80
Are You in the House Alone? '78
Initiation of Sarah '78
Shampoo '75
Haunts of the Very Rich '72
Castle Keep '69
Ice Station Zebra '68
Never a Dull Moment '68
You're a Big Boy Now '66
Marriage on the Rocks '65
None But the Brave '65
Come Blow Your Horn '63
Soldier in the Rain '63

Raoul Billerey (1920-)
Revenge of the Musketeers '94
The Little Thief '89
Sorceress '88
Le Grand Chemin '87

Don Billett
Gloria '98
Prince of the City '81

Roy Billing
Aquamarine '06
Strange Bedfellows '04
Siam Sunset '99

Dawn Ann Billings
Human Desires '97
Warlock: The Armageddon '93
Trancers 3: Deth Lives '92

Earl Billings (1945-)
Something New '06
Christmas at Water's Edge '04
Mr. 3000 '04
American Splendor '03
Antwone Fisher '02
One False Move '91
Stakeout '87

Beau Billingslea (1953-)
Vacancy 2: The First Cut '08
Silent Predators '99
Indecent Behavior 3 '95
Final Justice '94

Barbara Billingsley (1922-)
Leave It to Beaver '97
Back to the Beach '87
Eye of the Demon '87
Airplane! '80

Jennifer Billingsley (1942-)
Hollywood Man '76
The Thirsty Dead '74
White Lightning '73
C.C. & Company '70
Lady in a Cage '64

John Billingsley (1960-)
The Man from Earth '07
Ripple Effect '07
The Nickel Children '05
The Twelve Dogs of Christmas '05
Out of Time '03

Peter Billingsley (1971-)
Iron Man '08
The Break-Up '06
Arcade '93
Beverly Hills Brats '89
Russkies '87
Dirt Bike Kid '86
A Christmas Story '83
Death Valley '81

Stephen Billington (1969-)
Dracula 2: Ascension '03
Resident Evil '02
The Man Who Made Husbands Jealous '98
Braveheart '95

Bruno Bilotta
Excellent Cadavers '99
Titus '99
Double Team '97
The Black Cobra '87
Urban Warriors '87

Rachel Bilson (1981-)
New York, I Love You '09
Jumper '08
The Last Kiss '06

Mike Binder (1958-)
Reign Over Me '07
The Upside of Anger '05
Minority Report '02
The Search for John Gissing '01
The Sex Monster '99
The Hollywood Knights '80

Sybilla Binder (1898-1962)
The Golden Salamander '51
Blanche Fury '48
Counterblast '48

John Bindon (1943-93)
Performance '70
Inspector Clouseau '68

Herman Bing (1889-1947)
Dumbo '41 (V)
Bitter Sweet '40
Bluebeard's Eighth Wife '38
Every Day's a Holiday '38
The Great Waltz '38
Maytime '37
Tango '36
That Girl from Paris '36
Crimson Romance '34
The Merry Widow '34
The Guardsman '31

Barbara Bingham
Beyond Darkness '92
Soldier's Fortune '91
Friday the 13th, Part 8: Jason Takes Manhattan '89

S.J. Bingham
Wolfheart's Revenge '25
Three Word Brand '21

Geoffrey Binney
Raw Force '81
Hot Potato '76

Edward Binns (1916-90)
Return to Eden '89
The Verdict '82
Danger in the Skies '79
Oliver's Story '78
Night Moves '75
Hunter '73
Patton '70
The Americanization of Emily '64
A Public Affair '62
Judgment at Nuremberg '61
Compulsion '59
Curse of the Undead '59
Portland Expose '57
Twelve Angry Men '57
Beyond a Reasonable Doubt '56
Without Warning '52

Juliette Binoche (1964-)
Flight of the Red Balloon '08
Summer Hours '08
Dan in Real Life '07
Breaking and Entering '06
A Few Days in September '06
Paris, je t'aime '06
Bee Season '05
Hidden '05
In My Country '04
Jet Lag '02
Chocolat '00
Code Unknown '00
The Widow of Saint-Pierre '00
Children of the Century '99
Alice et Martin '98
The English Patient '96
A Couch in New York '95
The Horseman on the Roof '95
Trois Couleurs: Blanc '94
Trois Couleurs: Rouge '94
Trois Couleurs: Bleu '93
Damage '92
Emily Bronte's Wuthering Heights '92
The Lovers on the Bridge '91
Women & Men: In Love There Are No Rules '91
The Unbearable Lightness of Being '88
Mauvais Sang '86
Hail Mary '85

Rendez-vous '85

Thelma Biral (1941-)
Fridays of Eternity '81
El Muerto '75

Maurice Biraud (1922-82)
A Slightly Pregnant Man '79
The Last Train '74
Any Number Can Win '63

Paul Birch (1913-69)
The Man Who Shot Liberty Valance '62
Queen of Outer Space '58
Apache Woman '55
Day the World Ended '55
Ride Clear of Diablo '54

Thora Birch (1982-)
Deadline '09
Winter of Frozen Dreams '08
Dark Corners '06
Silver City '04
Ghost World '01
The Hole '01
Dungeons and Dragons '00
The Smokers '00
American Beauty '99
Night Ride Home '99
Alaska '96
Now and Then '95
Clear and Present Danger '94
Monkey Trouble '94
Hocus Pocus '93
Patriot Games '92
All I Want for Christmas '91
Paradise '91

Billie Bird (1908-2002)
Dennis the Menace '93
The End of Innocence '90
Home Alone '90
Ernest Saves Christmas '88
Sixteen Candles '84
Rhubarb '51

Brad Bird (1957-)
Ratatouille '07 (V)
The Incredibles '04 (V)

Larry Bird (1956-)
Celtic Pride '96
Blue Chips '94

Norman Bird (1924-2005)
The Slipper and the Rose '76
Hands of the Ripper '71
The Hill '65
The Mind Benders '63
Term of Trial '63
Burn Witch, Burn! '62
Very Important Person '61
Victim '61
Whistle down the Wind '61

Jesse Birdsall (1963-)
Nightscare '93
Getting It Right '89
Wish You Were Here '87

Mary Birdsong (1968-)
Halloween II '09
Reno 911! Miami '07
Pizza '05

Tala Birell (1907-58)
Song of Love '47
The Purple Heart '44
The White Legion '36
Crime and Punishment '35

David Birkin
Sylvia '03
All the Queen's Men '02
Charlotte Gray '01
Le Petit Amour '87

Jane Birkin (1946-)
Merci Docteur Rey '04
The Last September '99
A Soldier's Daughter Never Cries '98
Same Old Song '97
Daddy Nostalgia '90
La Belle Noiseuse '90
Beethoven's Nephew '88
Le Petit Amour '87
Dust '85
Evil under the Sun '82
Make Room for Tomorrow '81
Death on the Nile '78
Catherine & Co. '76
Don Juan (Or If Don Juan Were a Woman) '73
Seven Deaths in the Cat's Eye '72
Too Pretty to Be Honest '72
Romance of a Horsethief '71
French Intrigue '70
Swimming Pool '70
La Piscine '69
Slogan '69
Wonderwall: The Movie '69
Blow-Up '66

Len Birman (1932-)
Web of Deceit '90
Undergrads '85
Captain America '79
Captain America 2: Death Too Soon '79
Lies My Father Told Me '75

Matt Birman
Family of Cops 2: Breach of Faith '97
Back in Action '94

Serafina Birman (1890-1976)
Ivan the Terrible, Part 2 '46
Ivan the Terrible, Part 1 '44
The Girl with the Hat Box '27

Gil Birmingham
The Twilight Saga: Eclipse '10
Twilight '08

David Birney (1939-)
Nightfall '88
Prettykill '87
The Five of Me '81
Mom, the Wolfman and Me '80
Oh, God! Book 2 '80
Choice of Weapons '76
Caravan to Vaccares '74
Murder or Mercy '74
Only with Married Men '74

Reed Birney (1954-)
From the Earth to the Moon '98
Crimewave '85
Four Friends '81

Christopher Birt
A Soldier's Sweetheart '98
The Bodyguard '92

Eva Birthistle
The Last Enemy '08
Imagine Me & You '06
Middletown '06
The State Within '06
A Fond Kiss '04
The American '01
Borstal Boy '00

Olga Bisera
Women in Cell Block 7 '77
Castle Keep '69

Summer Bishil
Crossing Over '09
Towelhead '07
Return to Halloweentown '06

Debbie Bishop
Sid & Nancy '86
Scrubbers '82

Ed Bishop (1932-)
Saturn 3 '80
S.O.S. Titanic '79
Brass Target '78
The Devil's Web '74
Journey to the Far Side of the Sun '69

Jennifer Bishop (1942-)
We Don't Live Here Anymore '04
Jaws of Death '76
Jessi's Girls '75
Impulse '74
House of Terror '72
Horror of the Blood Monsters '70
The Female Bunch '69

Joey Bishop (1918-2007)
Trigger Happy '96
Betsy's Wedding '90
Delta Force '86
Valley of the Dolls '67
Who's Minding the Mint? '67
Texas Across the River '66
Sergeants 3 '62
Ocean's 11 '60
Deep Six '58
The Naked and the Dead '58

Julie Bishop (1914-2001)
The High and the Mighty '54
Westward the Women '51
Sands of Iwo Jima '49
The Last of the Redmen '47
Rhapsody in Blue '45
Action in the North Atlantic '43
Northern Pursuit '43
I Was Framed '42
Her First Romance '40
Young Bill Hickok '40
The Kansas Terrors '39
Torture Ship '39
Hard to Hold '37
Bohemian Girl '36
Square Shooter '35
The Black Cat '34
Tarzan the Fearless '33

Kelly Bishop (1944-)
Private Parts '96
Miami Rhapsody '95
Queens Logic '91
Dirty Dancing '87

Kevin Bishop (1980-)
Irina Palm '07
Russian Dolls '05
Food of Love '02
L'Auberge Espagnole '02
Muppet Treasure Island '96

Kirsten Bishop
Rudy: The Rudy Giulani Story '03
The Little Mermaid '75 (V)

Larry Bishop (1947-)
Hell Ride '08
Kill Bill Vol. 1 '03
Trigger Happy '96
Underworld '96
Soul Hustler '76
How Come Nobody's On Our Side? '73
Angel Unchained '70
The Savage Seven '68

Pat Bishop
Women of Valor '86
Don's Party '76

Stephen Bishop (1951-)
Someone to Love '87
Twilight Zone: The Movie '83
The Blues Brothers '80
National Lampoon's Animal House '78

Wes Bishop (1933-93)
Dixie Dynamite '76
Black Gestapo '75
Chain Gang Women '72
The Thing with Two Heads '72
Chrome and Hot Leather '71
Rebel Vixens '69
Love Desperados '68

William Bishop (1918-59)
Breakdown '53
The Redhead from Wyoming '53
Harriet Craig '50
Coroner Creek '48
The Killer That Stalked New York '47

Thor Bishopric
Breaking All the Rules '85
The Little Mermaid '75 (V)

Claudio Bisio
The Truce '96
Mediterraneo '91

Steve Bisley
Fast Talking '86
The Highest Honor '84
Chain Reaction '80
Mad Max '80

Whit Bissell (1909-96)
Soylent Green '73
City Beneath the Sea '71
Seven Days in May '64
Spencer's Mountain '63
The Manchurian Candidate '62
The Time Machine '60
No Name on the Bullet '59
Teenage Frankenstein '58
I Was a Teenage Werewolf '57
Invasion of the Body Snatchers '56
Shack Out on 101 '55
The Atomic Kid '54
The Caine Mutiny '54
Creature from the Black Lagoon '54
Devil's Canyon '53
Boots Malone '52
Tales of Robin Hood '52
The Lost Continent '51
He Walked by Night '48
Raw Deal '48
Brute Force '47

Jacqueline Bisset (1944-)
An Old-Fashioned Thanksgiving '08
Carolina Moon '07
Domino '05
Fascination '04
Latter Days '04
The Sleepy Time Gal '01
Brittanic '00
Jesus '00
Sex & Mrs. X '00
Britannic '99
Joan of Arc '99
Let the Devil Wear Black '99
Dangerous Beauty '98
End of Summer '97
La Ceremonie '95
Crime Broker '94
Crimebroker '93
The Maid '90
Wild Orchid '90
Scenes from the Class Struggle in Beverly Hills '89
High Season '88
Choices '86
Anna Karenina '85
Forbidden '85
Under the Volcano '84
Class '83
Rich and Famous '81
When Time Ran Out '80
Together? '79
The Greek Tycoon '78
Who Is Killing the Great Chefs of Europe? '78
The Deep '77
Le Magnifique '76
St. Ives '76
Spiral Staircase '75
Murder on the Orient Express '74
Day for Night '73
The Thief Who Came to Dinner '73
Life & Times of Judge Roy Bean '72
The Mephisto Waltz '71
Secrets '71
Airport '70
The Passing of Evil '70
The First Time '69
The Grasshopper '69
Bullitt '68
The Detective '68
Casino Royale '67
Two for the Road '67
Cul de Sac '66

Josie Bissett (1970-)
Baby Monitor: Sound of Fear '97
Mikey '92
All-American Murder '91
Book of Love '91

Chris Bisson
Chicken Tikka Masala '05
East Is East '99

Joel Bissonnette
Suspicious River '00
Boulevard '94

Chhabi Biswas (1900-62)
Devi '60
Jalsaghar '58

Seema Biswas
Water '05
Bandit Queen '94

Bill Bixby (1934-93)
Death of the Incredible Hulk '90
The Trial of the Incredible Hulk '89
The Incredible Hulk Returns '88
Agatha Christie's Murder is Easy '82
The Incredible Hulk '77
Kentucky Fried Movie '77
Fantasy Island '76
The Invasion of Johnson County '76
Rich Man, Poor Man '76
The Apple Dumpling Gang '75
The Barbary Coast '74
Speedway '68
Clambake '67
Under the Yum-Yum Tree '63
Lonely Are the Brave '62

Denise Bixler
The Assassination Game '92
Evil Dead 2: Dead by Dawn '87

Dragan Bjelogric (1963-)
The Wounds '98
Pretty Village, Pretty Flame '96
Hey, Babu Riba '88

Bjork (1965-)
Dancer in the Dark '99
The Juniper Tree '87

Anita Bjork (1923-)
Secrets of Women '52
Miss Julie '50

Halvar Bjork (1928-)
Autumn Sonata '78
The New Land '73

Irina Bjorklund
Lost '05
Ambush '99

Anna Bjorn
Sword & the Sorcerer '82
More American Graffiti '79

Helgi Bjornsson
Eleven Men Out '05
Remote Control '94

Gunnar Bjornstrand (1909-86)
Autumn Sonata '78
Face to Face '76
The Rite '69
The Shame '68
Persona '66
The Winter Light '62
Through a Glass Darkly '61
The Magician '58
Wild Strawberries '57
The Seventh Seal '56
Dreams '55
Smiles of a Summer Night '55
Lesson in Love '54
Torment '44

Tatjana Blacher
Anne Frank: The Whole Story '01
Yellow Asphalt '01

Claudia Black (1973-)
Stargate: Continuum '08
Stargate: The Ark of Truth '08
Queen of the Damned '02
Pitch Black '00

Gerry Black
The Majestic '01
Re-Animator '84
Backstairs at the White House '79

Isobel Black (1943-)
10 Rillington Place '71
Kiss of the Vampire '62

Jack Black (1969-)
Year One '09
Be Kind Rewind '08
Kung Fu Panda '08 (V)
Tropic Thunder '08
Margot at the Wedding '07
Walk Hard: The Dewey Cox Story '07
Danny Roane: First Time Director '06
The Holiday '06
Nacho Libre '06
Tenacious D in the Pick of Destiny '06
King Kong '05
Anchorman: The Legend of Ron Burgundy '04
Envy '04
Shark Tale '04 (V)
School of Rock '03
Ice Age '02 (V)
Orange County '02
Saving Silverman '01
Shallow Hal '01
High Fidelity '00
The Cradle Will Rock '99
Jesus' Son '99
The Love Letter '99
Bongwater '98
Enemy of the State '98
I Still Know What You Did Last Summer '98
The Jackal '97
Johnny Skidmarks '97
Bio-Dome '96
The Cable Guy '96
Crossworlds '96
The Fan '96
Mars Attacks! '96
Dead Man Walking '95
Waterworld '95
Blind Justice '94
Bye Bye, Love '94
The NeverEnding Story 3: Escape from Fantasia '94
Airborne '93
Demolition Man '93
Bob Roberts '92

James Black
Unshackled '00
Standing on Fishes '99
The Substitute 3: Winner Takes All '99
The First 9 1/2 Weeks '98
The Man with the Perfect Swing '95

Johanna Black
Hide and Seek '00
The Contract '98

Karen Black (1942-)
The Blue Tooth Virgin '09
One Long Night '07
House of 1000 Corpses '03
A Light in the Darkness '02
Gypsy 83 '01
Hard Luck '01
The Independent '00
Red Dirt '99
First Degree '98
Stir '98
Angel Blue '97
Conceiving Ada '97
Cries of Silence '97
Dogtown '97
Invisible Dad '97
Men '97

Children of the Corn 4: The Gathering '96
Crimetime '96
Dinosaur Valley Girls '96
Movies Money Murder '96
Plan 10 from Outer Space '95
Armistead Maupin's Tales of the City '93
Bound and Gagged: A Love Story '93
Auntie Lee's Meat Pies '92
Caged Fear '92
Children of the Night '92
The Double O Kid '92
Final Judgment '92
The Player '92
Rubin & Ed '92
Evil Spirits '91
Haunting Fear '91
Quiet Fire '91
The Children '90
Club Fed '90
The Killer's Edge '90
Mirror, Mirror '90
Night Angel '90
Overexposed '90
Hitz '89
Homer and Eddie '89
Twisted Justice '89
Zapped Again '89
Dixie Lanes '88
The Invisible Kid '88
Out of the Dark '88
Eternal Evil '87
Hostage '87
It's Alive 3: Island of the Alive '87
Invaders from Mars '86
Cut and Run '85
Martin's Day '85
Bad Manners '84
Killing Heat '84
Savage Dawn '84
Can She Bake a Cherry Pie? '83
Come Back to the Five & Dime Jimmy Dean, Jimmy Dean '82
Separate Ways '82
Chanel Solitaire '81
Miss Right '81
The Last Word '80
The Squeeze '80
Killer Fish '79
Mr. Horn '79
Capricorn One '78
In Praise of Older Women '78
Love Under Pressure '78
The Rip Off '78
Burnt Offerings '76
Family Plot '76
Airport '75 '75
Crime & Passion '75
The Day of the Locust '75
Nashville '75
Trilogy of Terror '75
The Great Gatsby '74
Law and Disorder '74
Little Laura & Big John '73
The Pyx '73
Portnoy's Complaint '72
Born to Win '71
A Gunfight '71
Five Easy Pieces '70
Easy Rider '69
You're a Big Boy Now '66
The Prime Time '60

Lewis Black (1948-)
Accepted '06
Man of the Year '06
Unaccompanied Minors '06
Joey Breaker '93
The Night We Never Met '93
Jacob's Ladder '90
Hannah and Her Sisters '86
Hard Way '80

Lucas Black (1982-)
Legion '10
Get Low '09
The Fast and the Furious: Tokyo Drift '06
Deepwater '05
Jarhead '05
Friday Night Lights '04
Killer Diller '04
Cold Mountain '03
All the Pretty Horses '00
The Miracle Worker '00
Crazy in Alabama '99
Flash '98
The X-Files '98
Ghosts of Mississippi '96
Sling Blade '96
The War '94

Maurice Black (1891-1938)
Three Legionnaires '37
Sixteen Fathoms Deep '34
Marked Money '28

Michael Ian Black (1971-)
The Baxter '05
Wet Hot American Summer '01
The Bogus Witch Project '00

Ryan Black (1973-)
Eye of the Beast '07
Stryker '04
Dance Me Outside '95
Geronimo '93

Shane Black (1961-)
An Alan Smithee Film: Burn, Hollywood, Burn '97
As Good As It Gets '97
Predator '87

Richard Blackburn
Under the Piano '95
Eating Raoul '82
Lemora, Lady Dracula '73

Richard Blackburn
Blue State '07
Stephen King's The Storm of the Century '99
Down in the Delta '98
Murder at 1600 '97
In Love and War '96
Sugartime '95
A Man in Uniform '93

Stephen Blackehart (1967-)
The Land That Time Forgot '09
Retro Puppet Master '99

Don Blackman
The Old Man and the Sea '58
Serpent Island '54

Honor Blackman (1926-)
Russell Mulcahy's Tale of the Mummy '99
To Walk with Lions '99
The First Olympics: Athens 1896 '84
The Cat and the Canary '79
To the Devil, a Daughter '76
Fright '71
The Virgin and the Gypsy '70
Lola '69
Shalako '68
Moment to Moment '66
Goldfinger '64
Jason and the Argonauts '63
A Matter of WHO '62
A Night to Remember '58
The Square Peg '58
Suspended Alibi '56
Glass Tomb '55
Green Grow the Rushes '51
Conspirator '49

Jeremy Blackman
Crown Heights '02
Magnolia '99

Joan Blackman (1938-)
Macon County Line '74
Daring Game '68
Blue Hawaii '62
Kid Galahad '62
Career '59
Good Day for a Hanging '58

Sidney Blackmer (1895-1973)
Rosemary's Baby '68
How to Murder Your Wife '64
Tammy and the Bachelor '57
Beyond a Reasonable Doubt '56
High Society '56
The High and the Mighty '54
People Will Talk '51
Buffalo Bill '44
Wilson '44
War of the Wildcats '43
The Panther's Claw '42
Love Crazy '41
Law of the Pampas '39
Charlie Chan at Monte Carlo '37
Heidi '37
The House of Secrets '37
In Old Chicago '37
Shadows of the Orient '37
Thank you, Mr. Moto '37
The President's Mystery '36
The Little Colonel '35
The Count of Monte Cristo '34
Goodbye Love '34
Transatlantic Merry-Go-Round '34
Deluge '33
Little Caesar '30

Paul Blackthorne
Special '06
Lagaan: Once upon a Time in India '01

David Blackwell
The Rookie '02
China O'Brien '88

Taurean Blacque (1941-)
Deepstar Six '89
Oliver & Company '88 (V)
The $5.20 an Hour Dream '80

Ruben Blades (1948-)
Imagining Argentina '04
Spin '04
Assassination Tango '03
The Maldonado Miracle '03
Once Upon a Time in Mexico '03
All the Pretty Horses '00
The Cradle Will Rock '99
Chinese Box '97
The Devil's Own '96
Scorpion Spring '96
Color of Night '94
A Million to Juan '94
Life with Mikey '93
Crazy from the Heart '91
The Super '91
The Josephine Baker Story '90
The Lemon Sisters '90
Mo' Better Blues '90
One Man's War '90
Predator 2 '90
The Two Jakes '90
Dead Man Out '89
Disorganized Crime '89
Homeboy '88
The Milagro Beanfield War '88
Fatal Beauty '87
Critical Condition '86
Crossover Dreams '85
The Last Fight '82

Estella Blain (1936-81)
Angelique and the King '66
The Diabolical Dr. Z '65
Pirates of the Coast '61
The Twilight Girls '57

Gerard Blain (1930-2000)
The American Friend '77
Hatari! '62
The Cousins '59
Le Beau Serge '58
Les Mistons '57

Vivian Blaine (1921-95)
Parasite '82
The Cracker Factory '79
The Dark '79
Guys and Dolls '55
Skirts Ahoy! '52
Doll Face '46
If I'm Lucky '46
State Fair '45
Greenwich Village '44
Something for the Boys '44

Betsy Blair (1923-)
Scarlett '94
Suspicion '87
Il Grido '57
Marty '55

David Blair
Wax, or the Discovery of Television among the Bees '93
The Happy Years '50

Isla Blair (1944-)
The Match '99
The Final Cut '95
Taste the Blood of Dracula '70

Janet Blair (1921-2007)
The One and Only, Genuine, Original Family Band '68
Boys' Night Out '62
Burn Witch, Burn! '62
Black Arrow '48
The Fuller Brush Man '48
The Fabulous Dorseys '47
Tonight and Every Night '45
Blondie Goes to College '42
Broadway '42
My Sister Eileen '42

Linda Blair (1959-)
Gang Boys '97
Prey of the Jaguar '96
Scream '96
Sorceress '94
A Woman Obsessed '93
Dead Sleep '91
Fatal Bond '91
Bail Out '90
Repossessed '90
Bedroom Eyes 2 '89
The Chilling '89
Moving Target '89
Up Your Alley '89
Zapped Again '89
Silent Assassins '88
Witchery '88
Grotesque '87
Nightforce '86
Night Patrol '85
Red Heat '85
Savage Island '85
Chained Heat '83
Savage Streets '83
Hell Night '81
Ruckus '81
Roller Boogie '79
Wild Horse Hank '79
Summer of Fear '78
The Exorcist 2: The Heretic '77
Victory at Entebbe '76
Airport '75 '75
Sweet Hostage '75
Born Innocent '74
The Exorcist '73
The Sporting Club '72

Nicky Blair (1926-98)
The Crossing Guard '94
Viva Las Vegas '63

Pamela Blair (1949-)
Beavis and Butt-Head Do America '96 (V)
Svengali '83

Selma Blair (1972-)
The Poker House '09
Hellboy II: The Golden Army '08
My Mom's New Boyfriend '08
Feast of Love '07
The Killing Gene '07
Purple Violets '07
Lies & Alibis '06
The Night of the White Pants '06
The Deal '05
The Fog '05
Pretty Persuasion '05
Coast to Coast '04
A Dirty Shame '04
Hellboy '04
In Good Company '04
Dallas 362 '03
A Guy Thing '03
The Sweetest Thing '02
Highway '01
Kill Me Later '01
Legally Blonde '01
Storytelling '01
Down to You '00
Brown's Requiem '98
Cruel Intentions '98
Girl '98
No Laughing Matter '97

Tom Blair
The Bed You Sleep In '93
Sure Fire '90
The Game '89

Isabelle Blais
Human Trafficking '05
Savage Messiah '02

Deborah Blaisdell (1959-)
Wildest Dreams '90
Student Affairs '88
Wimps '87
Screen Test '85

Nesbitt Blaisdell (1928-)
The Mothman Prophecies '02
Addicted to Love '96
Kennedy '83

Paul Blaisdell (1929-83)
Dragstrip Girl '57
Invasion of the Saucer Men '57
Motorcycle Gang '57
The Undead '57
Voodoo Woman '57
It Conquered the World '56
Day the World Ended '55

Amanda Blake (1929-89)
The Boost '88
B.O.R.N. '88
Gunsmoke: Return to Dodge '87
Betrayal '74
The Glass Slipper '55
Sabre Jet '53
Cattle Town '52
Counterspy Meets Scotland Yard '50
The Duchess of Idaho '50
Stars in My Crown '50

Andre B. Blake
Hair Show '04
The Other Brother '02
Just the Ticket '98
Philadelphia '93
Who's the Man? '93

Ellen Blake
Suspect Zero '04
Last Resort '86

Geoffrey Blake (1962-)
Life Without Dick '01
Cast Away '00
Contact '97
Entertaining Angels: The Dorothy Day Story '96
The War at Home '96
Dominion '94
Forrest Gump '94
Marilyn & Bobby: Her Final Affair '94
Philadelphia Experiment 2 '93
Fatal Exposure '91
The Abduction of Kari Swenson '87

Gladys Blake
Racing Blood '36
Rainbow over Broadway '33

Jon Blake (1958-)
The Lighthorsemen '87
Anzacs: The War Down Under '85
Early Frost '84
Freedom '82

Julia Blake (1936-)
Aquamarine '06
Salem's Lot '04
Innocence '00
Passion '99
Hotel de Love '96
The Thorn Birds: The Missing Years '96
Father '90
Georgia '87
Travelling North '87
Man of Flowers '84
Lonely Hearts '82
Under Capricorn '82
My Brilliant Career '79

Larry J. Blake (1914-82)
Demon Seed '77
Beginning of the End '57
Holiday Affair '49
The Jury's Secret '38

Madge Blake (1899-1969)
Batman '66
The Long, Long Trailer '54
Singin' in the Rain '52
Prowler '51

Marie Blake (1896-1978)
Sensations of 1945 '44
Love Finds Andy Hardy '38

Mia Blake
The Tattooist '07
Visitor Q '01

Noah Blake (1964-)
The Base '99
Class of Fear '91
Trapper County War '89

Oliver Blake (1905-92)
Ma and Pa Kettle at Waikiki '55
Casablanca '42

Pamela Blake (1918-)
Border Rangers '50
Gunfire '50
Sky Liner '49
Highway 13 '48
Rolling Home '48
Son of God's Country '48
Hat Box Mystery '47
Sea Hound '47
Kid Dynamite '43
Pop Always Pays '40
Wyoming Outlaw '39

Rachael Blake
The Prisoner '09
Perfect Strangers '03
Lantana '01

Robert (Bobby) Blake (1933-)
Lost Highway '96
Money Train '95
Heart of a Champion: The Ray Mancini Story '85
Of Mice and Men '81
Coast to Coast '80
Busting '74
Electra Glide in Blue '73
Counter Punch '71
Tell Them Willie Boy Is Here '69
In Cold Blood '67
This Property Is Condemned '66
PT 109 '63
Town without Pity '61
Pork Chop Hill '59
Treasure of the Golden Condor '53
The Black Rose '50
Treasure of the Sierra Madre '48
Homesteaders of Paradise Valley '47
Humoresque '46
Santa Fe Uprising '46
Stagecoach to Denver '46
Vigilantes of Boom Town '46
Woman in the Window '44
Andy Hardy's Double Life '42

Colin Blakely (1930-87)
Operation Julie *'85*
Loophole *'83*
Evil under the Sun *'82*
The Dogs of War *'81*
Little Lord Fauntleroy *'80*
Nijinsky *'80*
The Big Sleep *'78*
Equus *'77*
The Pink Panther Strikes Again *'76*
Love Among the Ruins *'75*
Murder on the Orient Express *'74*
Shattered *'72*
The Private Life of Sherlock Holmes *'70*
The Vengeance of She *'68*
This Sporting Life *'63*

Donald Blakely
In the Shadow of Kilimanjaro *'86*
Vigilante *'83*
Short Eyes *'79*
Strike Force *'75*

James Blakely (1910-)
The Shadow Strikes *'37*
Small Town Boy *'37*
Paris in Spring *'35*

Susan Blakely (1950-)
Mating Dance *'08*
Hate Crime *'05*
L.A. Twister *'04*
Extreme Limits *'01*
The Perfect Nanny *'00*
Honor Thy Father and Mother: The True Story of the Menendez Brothers *'94*
Russian Roulette *'93*
Intruders *'92*
Blackmail *'91*
Wildflower *'91*
Dead Reckoning *'89*
The Incident *'89*
My Mom's a Werewolf *'89*
Out of Sight, Out of Her Mind *'89*
Broken Angel *'88*
Hiroshima Maiden *'88*
Ladykillers *'88*
The Survivalist *'87*
Over the Top *'86*
A Cry for Love *'80*
Make Me an Offer *'80*
The Concorde: Airport '79 *'79*
Dreamer *'79*
Secrets *'77*
Rich Man, Poor Man *'76*
The Lords of Flatbush *'74*
Report to the Commissioner *'74*
The Towering Inferno *'74*
The Way We Were *'73*
Savages *'72*

Michael Blakemore (1928-)
Country Life *'95*
The Last Bastion *'84*

Sean Blakemore
Woman, Thou Art Loosed *'04*
Motives *'03*

Olive Blakeney (1903-59)
Billy the Kid *'41*
Gangway *'37*

Claudie Blakley
Return to Cranford *'09*
Severance *'06*
Pride and Prejudice *'05*
Gosford Park *'01*

Ronee Blakley (1946-)
Murder by Numbers *'89*
Return to Salem's Lot *'87*
Someone to Love *'87*
Student Confidential *'87*
A Nightmare on Elm Street *'84*
The Baltimore Bullet *'80*
Desperate Women *'78*
The Driver *'78*
The Private Files of J. Edgar Hoover *'77*
She Came to the Valley *'77*
Nashville *'75*

Jolene Blalock
Starship Troopers 3: Marauder *'08*
Shadow Puppets *'07*
Slow Burn *'05*
Jason and the Argonauts *'00*

Dominique Blanc (1962-)
One Day You'll Understand *'08*
A Soldier's Daughter Never Cries *'98*
Those Who Love Me Can Take the Train *'98*
Total Eclipse *'95*
Queen Margot *'94*
Indochine *'92*
May Fools *'90*

Erika Blanc (1942-)
His Secret Life *'01*
The Boss Is Served *'76*
Mark of the Devil 2 *'72*
The Devil's Nightmare *'71*
The Night Evelyn Came Out of the Grave *'71*
Sweet Spirits *'71*
Fistful of Lead *'70*
Sartana's Here... Trade Your Pistol for a Coffin *'70*
Special Forces *'68*
Kill, Baby, Kill *'66*

Jennifer Blanc
Fish Without a Bicycle *'03*
Kiss Tomorrow Goodbye *'00*
Cool and the Crazy *'94*

Manuel Blanc
Beaumarchais the Scoundrel *'96*
I Don't Kiss *'91*

Mel Blanc (1908-89)
Jetsons: The Movie *'90 (V)*
Who Framed Roger Rabbit *'88 (V)*
Strange Brew *'83 (V)*
Looney Looney Looney Bugs Bunny Movie *'81 (V)*
Buck Rogers in the 25th Century *'79 (V)*
Phantom Tollbooth *'69 (V)*
Hey There, It's Yogi Bear *'64 (V)*
Kiss Me, Stupid! *'64*
Gay Purr-ee *'62 (V)*
Neptune's Daughter *'49*

Michel Blanc (1952-)
The Girl on the Train *'09*
The Witnesses *'07*
The Monster *'96*
Grosse Fatigue *'94*
Ready to Wear *'94*
The Favor, the Watch, & the Very Big Fish *'92*
Prospero's Books *'91*
Uranus *'91*
Monsieur Hire *'89*
Menage *'86*
French Fried Vacation *'79*
The Tenant *'76*

Bernard Blancan
Days of Glory *'06*
A Song of Innocence *'05*

Jewel Blanch
Against a Crooked Sky *'75*
Baffled *'72*

Pierre Blanchar (1892-1963)
La Symphonie Pastorale *'46*
Man from Nowhere *'37*
Crime and Punishment *'35*
The Chess Player *'27*

Jarred Blanchard
The Boys Club *'96*
The Yearling *'94*

Mari Blanchard (1927-70)
Son of Sinbad *'55*
Abbott and Costello Go to Mars *'53*

Rachel Blanchard (1976-)
Spread *'09*
Adoration *'08*
Careless *'07*
Snakes on a Plane *'06*
Where the Truth Lies *'05*
Without a Paddle *'04*
Chasing Holden *'01*
Sugar & Spice *'01*
Road Trip *'00*
The Rage: Carrie 2 *'99*
Iron Eagle 4 *'95*
Young Ivanhoe *'95*

Susan Blanchard
Prince of Darkness *'87*
She's in the Army Now *'81*
President's Mistress *'78*

Tammy Blanchard (1976-)
Deadline *'09*
Cadillac Records *'08*
Living Proof *'08*
The Ramen Girl *'08*
Bella *'06*
The Good Shepherd *'06*
Stealing Harvard *'02*
Life with Judy Garland—Me and My Shadows *'01*

Francis Blanche
By the Blood of Others *'73*
Scandal Man *'67*

Bruno Blanchet (1964-)
Seducing Doctor Lewis *'03*

Cate Blanchett (1969-)
Robin Hood *'10*
The Curious Case of Benjamin Button *'08*
Indiana Jones and the Kingdom of the Crystal Skull *'08*
Ponyo *'08 (V)*
Elizabeth: The Golden Age *'07*
Hot Fuzz *'07*
I'm Not There *'07*
Babel *'06*
The Good German *'06*
Notes on a Scandal *'06*
Little Fish *'05*
The Aviator *'04*
The Life Aquatic with Steve Zissou *'04*
Coffee and Cigarettes *'03*
Lord of the Rings: The Return of the King *'03*
The Missing *'03*
Veronica Guerin *'03*
Lord of the Rings: The Two Towers *'02*
Bandits *'01*
Charlotte Gray *'01*
Heaven *'01*
Lord of the Rings: The Fellowship of the Ring *'01*
The Shipping News *'01*
The Gift *'00*
The Man Who Cried *'00*
An Ideal Husband *'99*
Pushing Tin *'99*
The Talented Mr. Ripley *'99*
Elizabeth *'98*
Oscar and Lucinda *'97*
Paradise Road *'97*
The Wedding Party *'97*

Dorothee Blanck (1934-)
Umbrellas of Cherbourg *'64*
Cleo from 5 to 7 *'61*

Sandrine Blancke (1978-)
The Son of the Shark *'93*
Toto le Heros *'91*

Joyce Bland (1906-63)
Dreaming Lips *'37*
Spy of Napoleon *'36*

Peter Bland (1983-)
Tearaway *'87*
Dangerous Orphans *'86*
Came a Hot Friday *'85*

Clara Blandick (1880-1962)
Infamous Crimes *'47*
Pillow of Death *'45*
Dead Man's Eyes *'44*
It Started with Eve *'41*
Dreaming Out Loud *'40*
Tomboy *'40*
The Wizard of Oz *'39*
Small Town Boy *'37*
The Girl from Missouri *'34*
The Bitter Tea of General Yen *'33*
The Easiest Way *'31*
Murder at Midnight *'31*
Romance *'30*

Sally Blane (1910-97)
Charlie Chan at Treasure Island *'39*
Fighting Mad *'39*
The Story of Alexander Graham Bell *'39*
Way Down South *'39*
No More Women *'34*
The Silver Streak *'34*
Heritage of the Desert *'33*
Night of Terror *'33*
Cross Examination *'32*
Law of the Sea *'32*
Local Badman *'32*
Phantom Express *'32*
Probation *'32*
When the West Was Young *'32*
Vagabond Lover *'29*

Mark Blankfield (1950-)
Dracula: Dead and Loving It *'95*
The Great American Sex Scandal *'94*
Robin Hood: Men in Tights *'93*
Angel 3: The Final Chapter *'88*
Frankenstein General Hospital *'88*
The Midnight Hour *'86*
Jack & the Beanstalk *'83*
Jekyll & Hyde... Together Again *'82*

Billy Blanks (1956-)
Shadow Warriors *'97*
Balance of Power *'96*
Expect No Mercy *'95*
Back in Action *'94*
Tough and Deadly *'94*
Showdown *'93*
TC 2000 *'93*
Talons of the Eagle *'92*
The King of the Kickboxers *'91*
The Last Boy Scout *'91*
Timebomb *'91*
Bloodfist *'89*

Arell Blanton
Assault of the Killer Bimbos *'88*
House of Terror *'72*
Wild Riders *'71*

Rosa Blasi (1972-)
The Grudge *'04*
Noriega: God's Favorite *'00*

Caio Blat
The Year My Parents Went on Vacation *'07*
Carandiru *'03*

Maddie (Maddeleine) Blaustein (1960-)
Yu-Gi-Oh! The Movie: Pyramid of Light *'04 (V)*
Pokemon 3: The Movie *'01 (V)*

Charles Blavette (1902-67)
The Horror Chamber of Dr. Faustus *'59*
Toni *'34*

Hans-Christian Blech (1915-93)
Colonel Redl *'84*
The Wrong Move *'78*
Innocents with Dirty Hands *'76*
The Scarlet Letter *'73*
Battle of the Bulge *'65*
The Blum Affair *'48*

Jonah Blechman (1975-)
Arc *'06*
Luster *'02*
Treasure Island *'99*
Fall Time *'94*
This Boy's Life *'93*

Alexis Bledel (1981-)
The Good Guy *'10*
Post Grad *'09*
The Sisterhood of the Traveling Pants 2 *'08*
I'm Reed Fish *'06*
Sin City *'05*
Sisterhood of the Traveling Pants *'05*
Tuck Everlasting *'02*

Tempestt Bledsoe (1973-)
Johnny B. *'00*
Santa and Pete *'99*
Dream Date *'93*

Debra Blee (1961-)
Malibu Bikini Shop *'86*
Sloane *'84*
Savage Streets *'83*
Beach Girls *'82*

Yasmine Bleeth (1968-)
Coming Soon *'99*
Undercover Angel *'99*
BASEketball *'98*
Heaven or Vegas *'98*
It Came from the Sky *'98*
Baywatch the Movie: Forbidden Paradise *'95*

Moritz Bleibtreu (1971-)
Soul Kitchen *'09*
Adam Resurrected *'08*
The Baader Meinhof Complex *'08*
Speed Racer *'08*
The Walker *'07*
The Keeper: The Legend of Omar Khayyam *'05*
Munich *'05*
Agnes and His Brothers *'04*
The Experiment *'01*
Taking Sides *'01*
Invisible Circus *'00*
Run Lola Run *'98*

Claudiu Bleont (1959-)
Vlad *'03*
An Unforgettable Summer *'94*

Brian Blessed (1937-)
As You Like It *'06*
Back in Business *'06*
Day of Wrath *'06*
Alexander *'04*
Star Wars: Episode 1—The Phantom Menace *'99*
Tarzan *'99 (V)*
Tom Jones *'98*
The Bruce *'96*
Hamlet *'96*
Catherine the Great *'95*
Kidnapped *'95*
Chasing the Deer *'94*
Much Ado about Nothing *'93*
Back in the USSR *'92*
Freddie the Frog *'92 (V)*
Prisoner of Honor *'91*
Robin Hood: Prince of Thieves *'91*
Henry V *'89*
High Road to China *'83*
The Hound of the Baskervilles *'83*
Flash Gordon *'80*
King Arthur, the Young Warlord *'75*
Young Warlord *'75*
Man of La Mancha *'72*
Cold Comfort Farm *'71*
Trojan Women *'71*

Jack Blessing (1951-)
Above Suspicion *'00*
The Last of His Tribe *'92*
Galaxy of Terror *'81*

Billy Bletcher (1894-1979)
Boss of Rawhide *'44*
God's Country and the Man *'37*
Hollywood Party *'34 (V)*
Boiling Point *'32*
Branded Men *'31*

Brenda Blethyn (1946-)
Atonement *'07*
Introducing the Dwights *'07*
On a Clear Day *'05*
Pooh's Heffalump Movie *'05 (V)*
Pride and Prejudice *'05*
Beyond the Sea *'04*
A Way of Life *'04*
Lovely & Amazing *'02*
Pumpkin *'02*
The Sleeping Dictionary *'02*
Sonny *'02*
The Wild Thornberrys Movie *'02 (V)*
Anne Frank: The Whole Story *'01*
Saving Grace *'00*
Daddy & Them *'99*
RKO 281 *'99*
In the Winter Dark *'98*
Little Voice *'98*
Girls' Night *'97*
Music from Another Room *'97*
Secrets and Lies *'95*
The Buddha of Suburbia *'92*
A River Runs Through It *'92*
The Witches *'90*
Grown Ups *'80*

Corbin Bleu (1989-)
Free Style *'09*
High School Musical 3: Senior Year *'08*
High School Musical 2 *'07*
Jump In! *'07*
High School Musical *'06*
Catch That Kid *'04*

Bill Blewitt
Johnny Frenchman *'46*
Nine Men *'43*
The Foreman Went to France *'42*

Jason Blicker
Earthstorm *'06*
Owning Mahowny *'03*
Crown Heights *'02*
Naked City: A Killer Christmas *'98*
African Journey *'89*
American Boyfriends *'89*

Bernard Blier (1916-89)
The Possessed *'88*
Buffet Froid *'79*
The Daydreamer *'75*
By the Blood of Others *'73*
The Tall Blond Man with One Black Shoe *'72*
Catch Me a Spy *'71*
Casanova '70 *'65*
The Organizer *'64*
Les Miserables *'57*
The Man in the Raincoat *'57*
Dedee d'Anvers *'49*
Passion for Life *'48*
Jenny Lamour *'47*

Boti Ann Bliss
Pulse 2: Afterlife *'08*
Warlock 3: The End of Innocence *'98*

Ian Bliss
Stealth *'05*
The Matrix Reloaded *'03*
The Matrix Revolutions *'03*
Siam Sunset *'99*

Hunt Block (1955-)
The Dirty Dozen: The Fatal Mission *'88*
Secret Weapons *'85*

Larry Block (1943-)
Dead Man Out '89
High Stakes '89
After Hours '85

Dan Blocker (1928-72)
Lady in Cement '68
The Errand Boy '61

Dirk Blocker (1957-)
Inherit the Wind '99
Night of the Scarecrow '95
Bonanza: The Return '93
Prince of Darkness '87
Trouble in Mind '86
Starman '84

Michael Blodgett (1940-2007)
The Ultimate Thrill '74
The Velvet Vampire '71
Beyond the Valley of the Dolls '70
The Trip '67

Sebastian Blomberg (1972-)
Go for Zucker '05
What to Do in Case of Fire '02
Anatomy '00

Susan Blommaert (1947-)
United 93 '06
Henry Hill '00

Joan Blondell (1909-79)
The Baron '88
The Woman Inside '83
The Champ '79
The Rebels '79
The Glove '78
Grease '78
Opening Night '77
The Dead Don't Die '75
Death at Love House '75
Support Your Local Gunfighter '71
Stay Away, Joe '68
Waterhole Number 3 '67
The Cincinnati Kid '65
Angel Baby '61
Desk Set '57
This Could Be the Night '57
Will Success Spoil Rock Hunter? '57
The Opposite Sex '56
Christmas Eve '47
Nightmare Alley '47
Adventure '45
A Tree Grows in Brooklyn '45
Lady for a Night '42
Topper Returns '41
East Side of Heaven '39
Bullets or Ballots '38
Stand-In '37
Colleen '36
Gold Diggers of 1937 '36
Stage Struck '36
Three Men on a Horse '36
Dames '34
Footlight Parade '33
Gold Diggers of 1933 '33
Havana Widows '33
Three Broadway Girls '32
Three on a Match '32
Union Depot '32
Big Business Girl '31
Blonde Crazy '31
Illicit '31
Millie '31
Night Nurse '31
Other Men's Women '31
Public Enemy '31

Nicole Blonsky
Harold '08
Queen Sized '08
Hairspray '07

Moon Bloodgood (1975-)
Moonlight Serenade '09
Street Fighter: The Legend of Chun-Li '09
Terminator Salvation '09
Pathfinder '07
Eight Below '06

Anne Bloom
That's Adequate '90
Dirt Bike Kid '86

Brian Bloom (1970-)
The A-Team '10
Across the Line '00
Blood Money '99
Knocking on Death's Door '99
Extramarital '98
The Sender '98
Escape from Atlantis '97
Melanie Darrow '97
Vampirella '96
At Home with the Webbers '94
Confessions of Sorority Girls '94
Voyage of Terror: The Achille Lauro Affair '90
Walls of Glass '85
Once Upon a Time in America '84

Claire Bloom (1931-)
The Chatterley Affair '06
Imagining Argentina '04
The Lady in Question '99
What the Deaf Man Heard '98
Wrestling with Alligators '98
Daylight '96
Mighty Aphrodite '95
A Village Affair '95
The Princess and the Goblin '94 (V)
Shameless '94
The Camomile Lawn '92
Crimes & Misdemeanors '89
Shadow on the Sun '88
Intimate Contact '87
Queenie '87
Sammy & Rosie Get Laid '87
Anastasia: The Mystery of Anna '86
Hold the Dream '86
Florence Nightingale '85
Shadowlands '85
This Lightning Always Strikes Twice '85
Deja Vu '84
Ghostwriter '84
Separate Tables '83
Brideshead Revisited '81
Clash of the Titans '81
Backstairs at the White House '79
Islands in the Stream '77
A Doll's House '73
The Illustrated Man '69
Charly '68
Soldier in Love '67
The Spy Who Came in from the Cold '65
The Outrage '64
The Haunting '63
The Wonderful World of the Brothers Grimm '62
Brainwashed '60
The Brothers Karamazov '58
The Buccaneer '58
Look Back in Anger '58
Alexander the Great '55
Richard III '55
Innocents in Paris '53
Limelight '52

John Bloom (1945-99)
Frozen Assets '92
The Great Outdoors '88
Harry and the Hendersons '87
Runaway Train '85
Bachelor Party '84
The Hills Have Eyes, Part 2 '84
The Dark '79
Brain of Blood '71
Dracula vs. Frankenstein '71
The Incredible Two-Headed Transplant '71

John (Joe Bob Briggs) Bloom (1953-)
Casino '95
Stephen King's The Stand '94
The Texas Chainsaw Massacre 2 '86

Lindsay Bloom (1952-)
French Quarter '78
Hughes & Harlow: Angels in Hell '77
Texas Detour '77
Cover Girl Models '75

Orlando Bloom (1977-)
New York, I Love You '09
Pirates of the Caribbean: At World's End '07
Pirates of the Caribbean: Dead Man's Chest '06
Elizabethtown '05
Kingdom of Heaven '05
Haven '04
Troy '04
Lord of the Rings: The Return of the King '03
Ned Kelly '03
Pirates of the Caribbean: The Curse of the Black Pearl '03
Lord of the Rings: The Two Towers '02
Black Hawk Down '01
Lord of the Rings: The Fellowship of the Ring '01

Verna Bloom (1939-)
The Last Temptation of Christ '88
After Hours '85
The Journey of Natty Gann '85
Honkytonk Man '82
Playing for Time '80
National Lampoon's Animal House '78
The Blue Knight '75
Where Have All the People Gone? '74
Badge 373 '73
High Plains Drifter '73
Hired Hand '71
Medium Cool '69

Eric Blore (1887-1959)
Fancy Pants '50
Love Happy '50
The Adventures of Ichabod and Mr. Toad '49 (V)
Romance on the High Seas '48
The Moon and Sixpence '43
The Shanghai Gesture '42
The Lady Eve '41
Lady Scarface '41
The Road to Zanzibar '41
Sullivan's Travels '41
Music in My Heart '40
Joy of Living '38
Swiss Miss '38
Breakfast for Two '37
Quality Street '37
Shall We Dance '37
Ex-Mrs. Bradford '36
Swing Time '36
I Dream Too Much '35
I Live My Life '35
Top Hat '35
The Gay Divorcee '34
Flying Down to Rio '33

Roberts Blossom (1924-)
Balloon Farm '97
The Quick and the Dead '95
Doc Hollywood '91
Home Alone '90
Always '89
The Last Temptation of Christ '88
Candy Mountain '87
Vision Quest '85
Christine '84
Flashpoint '84
Reuben, Reuben '83
Johnny Belinda '82
Resurrection '80
Escape from Alcatraz '79
Citizens Band '77
Deranged '74
Slaughterhouse Five '72
The Hospital '71

Lisa Blount (1957-)
Box of Moonlight '96
Judicial Consent '94
Stalked '94
An American Story '92
Blind Fury '90
Femme Fatale '90
Great Balls of Fire '89
Nightflyers '87
Prince of Darkness '87
South of Reno '87
Radioactive Dreams '86
Cease Fire '85
Cut and Run '85
What Waits Below '83
An Officer and a Gentleman '82
Dead and Buried '81
September 30, 1955 '77

Kurtis Blow (1959-)
The Show '95
Krush Groove '85

Marc Blucas (1972-)
Knight and Day '10
Deadline '09
Mother and Child '09
Stuntmen '09
Meet Dave '08
The Jane Austen Book Club '07
Thr3e '07
The Killing Floor '06
The Alamo '04
First Daughter '04
Prey for Rock and Roll '03
I Capture the Castle '02
Sunshine State '02
We Were Soldiers '02
Wes Craven Presents: They '02
Jay and Silent Bob Strike Back '01
Summer Catch '01

Ben Blue (1901-75)
Where Were You When the Lights Went Out? '68
The Busy Body '67
The Russians Are Coming, the Russians Are Coming '66
Easy to Wed '46
Broadway Rhythm '44
Two Girls and a Sailor '44
For Me and My Gal '42
Panama Hattie '42
The Big Broadcast of 1938 '38
College Swing '38

Callum Blue (1977-)
Red Sands '09
Caffeine '06
The Princess Diaries 2: Royal Engagement '04
In Love and War '01

Monte Blue (1890-1963)
Silver River '48
The Mask of Dimitrios '44
Across the Pacific '42
Casablanca '42
Bad Man of Deadwood '41
Young Bill Hickok '40
Helltown '38
Rootin' Tootin' Rhythm '38
A Million to One '37
Thunder Pass '37
Thunder Trail '37
Desert Gold '36
Prison Shadows '36
Ride, Ranger, Ride '36
Song of the Gringo '36
Undersea Kingdom '36
The Lives of a Bengal Lancer '35
Social Error '35
Trails of the Wild '35
Wagon Wheels '34
White Shadows in the South Seas '29
So This Is Paris '26
The Marriage Circle '24
Affairs of Anatol '21
Orphans of the Storm '21
The Man from Painted Post '17

Ralph Bluemke
Invader '91
Kid and the Killers '74

Brady Bluhm (1983-)
Alone in the Woods '95
The Crazysitter '94

Ina Blum
Virgin Machine '88
Anita, Dances of Vice '87

Jack Blum
SnakeEater 2: The Drug Buster '89
Happy Birthday to Me '81

Mark Blum (1950-)
Shattered Glass '03
Indictment: The McMartin Trial '95
Worth Winning '89
The Presidio '88
Blind Date '87
Crocodile Dundee '86
Desperately Seeking Susan '85

Trevor Blumas (1984-)
Ice Princess '05
The Unsaid '01
The Wall '99

Alan Blumenfeld
Righteous Kill '08
Black Belt '92
Problem Child 2 '91
Dark Side of the Moon '90
Instant Karma '90
Night Life '90
Worth Winning '89

Graeme Blundell (1945-)
Marking Time '03
Idiot Box '97
The Year My Voice Broke '87
Doctors and Nurses '82
The Odd Angry Shot '79
Weekend of Shadows '77
Don's Party '76
Alvin Rides Again '74
Alvin Purple '73

Emily Blunt (1983-)
The Adjustment Bureau '10
The Great Buck Howard '09
Sunshine Cleaning '09
The Wolfman '09
The Young Victoria '09
Charlie Wilson's War '07
Dan in Real Life '07
The Jane Austen Book Club '07
Wind Chill '07
The Devil Wears Prada '06
Irresistible '06
Gideon's Daughter '05
My Summer of Love '05
Warrior Queen '03

Erin Blunt (1963-)
The Bad News Bears Go to Japan '78
The Bad News Bears in Breaking Training '77
The Bad News Bears '76

Lothaire Bluteau (1957-)
Snow Buddies '08 (V)
Disappearances '06
The Healer '02
Dead Heat '01
Urbania '00
Restless Spirits '99
Conquest '98
Shot Through the Heart '98
Bent '97
I Shot Andy Warhol '96
Nostromo '96
The Confessional '95
Other Voices, Other Rooms '95
The Silent Touch '94
Mrs. 'Arris Goes to Paris '92
Orlando '92
Black Robe '91
Jesus of Montreal '89

John Bluthal (1929-)
Dark City '97
The Fifth Element '97
Leapin' Leprechauns '95
Help! '65

Margaret Blye (1939-)
Silhouette '91
Mischief '85
Little Darlings '80
Melvin Purvis: G-Man '74
Ash Wednesday '73
The Sporting Club '72
The Italian Job '69
Waterhole Number 3 '67

Stanley Blystone (1894-1956)
Sundown Fury '42
Fighting Parson '35
Saddle Aces '35
Man of Action '33
The Fighting Legion '30

Ann Blyth (1928-)
The Helen Morgan Story '57
The King's Thief '55
Kismet '55
Rose Marie '54
The Student Prince '54
All the Brothers Were Valiant '53
One Minute to Zero '52
The World in His Arms '52
The Great Caruso '51
I'll Never Forget You '51
Our Very Own '50
Mr. Peabody & the Mermaid '48
Brute Force '47
Killer McCoy '47
Mildred Pierce '45

Benedick Blythe
The Apocalypse Watch '97
One Against the Wind '91

Betty Blythe (1893-1972)
They Were Expendable '45
Girls in Chains '43
Dawn on the Great Divide '42
House of Errors '42
Miracle Kid '42
Honky Tonk '41
Misbehaving Husbands '41
Western Courage '35
The Scarlet Letter '34
She '25
Nomads of the North '20

Domini Blythe (1947-)
Affinity '08
Savage Messiah '02
Afterglow '97
Vampire Circus '71

Janus Blythe
Soldier's Fortune '91
The Hills Have Eyes, Part 2 '84
The Hills Have Eyes '77
Eaten Alive '76

John Blythe (1921-93)
The Gay Dog '54
The Frightened Man '52
This Happy Breed '47

Peter Blythe (1934-2004)
The Luzhin Defence '00
Carrington '95
A Challenge for Robin Hood '68
Frankenstein Created Woman '66

Bruce Boa (1930-2004)
The Neighbor '93
White Light '90
Murder Story '89
Full Metal Jacket '87

Eleanor Boardman (1898-1991)
She Goes to War '29
The Crowd '28
Bardelys the Magnificent '26
Souls for Sale '23

Virginia True Boardman (1889-1971)
Brand of the Outlaws '36
Test of Donald Norton '26

Michael Boatman (1964-)
And Then Came Love '07
Woman, Thou Art Loosed '04
The Peacemaker '97
The Glass Shield '95
Urban Crossfire '94
China Beach '88
Hamburger Hill '87

Anne Bobby (1967-)
What the Deaf Man Heard '98
Beautiful Girls '96
Scott Turow's The Burden of Proof '92
Baby of the Bride '91
Nightbreed '90

Jonah Bobo (1997-)
Zathura '05
Around the Bend '04

Barbara Bobulova (1974-)
Coco Chanel '08
The Spectator '04
In Love and War '01

Delia Boccardo (1948-)
Nostalghia '83
Tentacles '77
A Woman at Her Window '77
Ring of Death '69
Inspector Clouseau '68

Hart Bochner (1956-)
Spread '09
Liberty Stands Still '02
Say Nothing '01
Urban Legends 2: Final Cut '00
Anywhere But Here '99
The Break Up '98
A Good Day to Die '95
Batman: Mask of the Phantasm '93 (V)
The Innocent '93
Mad at the Moon '92
Mr. Destiny '90
Fellow Traveler '89
War & Remembrance: The Final Chapter '89
Apartment Zero '88
Die Hard '88
War & Remembrance '88
Making Mr. Right '86
Supergirl '84
The Wild Life '84
Having It All '82
Rich and Famous '81
East of Eden '80
Haywire '80
Terror Train '80

Lloyd Bochner (1924-2005)
Before I Say Goodbye '03
Bram Stoker's The Mummy '97
Morning Glory '93
Landslide '92
Naked Gun 2 1/2: The Smell of Fear '91
Millennium '89
Fine Gold '88
Crystal Heart '87
Louisiana '87
The Lonely Lady '83
Mazes and Monsters '82
Mary and Joseph: A Story of Faith '79
Terraces '77
It Seemed Like a Good Idea at the Time '75
Satan's School for Girls '73
Ulzana's Raid '72
They Call It Murder '71
The Dunwich Horror '70
The Detective '68
The Horse in the Gray Flannel Suit '68
Point Blank '67
Tony Rome '67
The Night Walker '64
Drums of Africa '63

Robert Bockstael
Time Bomb '08
Plain Truth '04
Snap Decision '01
The Golden Spiders: A Nero Wolfe Mystery '00
Invasion! '99
All I Wanna Do '98

Jose Bodalo (1916-85)
Garringo '69
Django '68

Martin Boddey (1908-75)
Black Glove '54
Valley of the Eagles '51

Wolfgang Bodison (1966-)
Most Wanted '97
The Expert '95
Freeway '95
Little Big League '94
A Few Good Men '92

Erika Bodnar (1948-)
Almanac of Fall '85
A Happy New Year! '79

Jenna Bodnar
The Portrait '99
Friend of the Family 2 '96

Sergei Bodrov, Jr. (1971-2002)
The Quickie '01
East-West '99
Brother '97
Prisoner of the Mountains '96

Karl-Heinz Boehm (1928-)
Mother Kusters Goes to Heaven '76
Fox and His Friends '75
The Wonderful World of the Brothers Grimm '62
Peeping Tom '60
Unnatural '52

Earl Boen (1945-)
Clifford's Really Big Movie '04 (V)
Nutty Professor 2: The Klumps '00
Within the Rock '96
Norma Jean and Marilyn '95
Terminator 2: Judgment Day '91
The Terminator '84

Beatrice Boepple (1962-)
A Nightmare on Elm Street 5: Dream Child '89
Quarantine '89

Dirk Bogarde (1920-99)
Daddy Nostalgia '90
The Vision '87
Despair '78
A Bridge Too Far '77
Providence '77
Permission To Kill '75
The Night Porter '74
Night Flight from Moscow '73
Death in Venice '71
The Damned '69
Justine '69
Oh! What a Lovely War '69
The Fixer '68
Sebastian '68
Accident '67
Modesty Blaise '66
Darling '65
King and Country '64
Doctor in Distress '63
I Could Go on Singing '63
The Mind Benders '63
The Servant '63
Damn the Defiant '62
Victim '61
Song Without End '60
A Tale of Two Cities '58
Doctor at Large '57
Night Ambush '57
The Spanish Gardener '57
Doctor at Sea '56
Cast a Dark Shadow '55
The Sea Shall Not Have Them '55
Simba '55
The Sleeping Tiger '54
Doctor in the House '53
The Woman in Question '50
The Blue Lamp '49

Stephen Bogardus (1954-)
States of Control '98
Love! Valour! Compassion! '96

Humphrey Bogart (1899-1957)
The Harder They Fall '56
Desperate Hours '55
The Left Hand of God '55
We're No Angels '55
The Barefoot Contessa '54
The Caine Mutiny '54
Sabrina '54
Battle Circus '53
Beat the Devil '53
The African Queen '51
The Enforcer '51
Sirocco '51
Chain Lightning '50
In a Lonely Place '50
Knock on Any Door '49
Tokyo Joe '49
Key Largo '48
Treasure of the Sierra Madre '48
Dark Passage '47
Dead Reckoning '47
The Two Mrs. Carrolls '47
The Big Sleep '46
Conflict '45
Passage to Marseilles '44
To Have & Have Not '44
Action in the North Atlantic '43
Sahara '43
Thank Your Lucky Stars '43
Across the Pacific '42
All Through the Night '42
Casablanca '42
High Sierra '41
The Maltese Falcon '41
The Wagons Roll at Night '41
Brother Orchid '40
They Drive by Night '40
Virginia City '40
Dark Victory '39
Invisible Stripes '39
Oklahoma Kid '39
The Roaring Twenties '39
Amazing Dr. Clitterhouse '38
Angels with Dirty Faces '38
Bullets or Ballots '38
Crime School '38
The Black Legion '37
Dead End '37
Kid Galahad '37
Marked Woman '37
San Quentin '37
Stand-In '37
Petrified Forest '36
Midnight '34
Three on a Match '32
Up the River '30

Peter Bogdanovich (1939-)
Humboldt County '08
Dedication '07
Infamous '06
Out of Order '03
Festival at Cannes '02
The Independent '00
Rated X '00
Coming Soon '99
Mr. Jealousy '98
Bella Mafia '97
Highball '97
Saint Jack '79
Targets '68
Voyage to the Planet of Prehistoric Women '68 (N)
The Trip '67
The Wild Angels '66

Eric Bogosian (1953-)
Cadillac Records '08
Blade: Trinity '04
Heights '04
King of the Corner '04
Charlie's Angels: Full Throttle '03
Wonderland '03
Ararat '02
Igby Goes Down '02
Blonde '01
Shot in the Heart '01
In the Weeds '00
Gossip '99
A Bright Shining Lie '98
Deconstructing Harry '97
Office Killer '97
Beavis and Butt-Head Do America '96 (V)
The Thief and the Cobbler '96 (V)
Under Siege 2: Dark Territory '95
Witch Hunt '94
Naked in New York '93
Sex, Drugs, Rock & Roll: Eric Bogosian '91
Last Flight Out: A True Story '90
Suffering Bastards '90
The Caine Mutiny Court Martial '88
Talk Radio '88
Special Effects '85

Elizabeth Bogush (1977-)
Believers '07
Jam '06
Tweek City '05
Eastside '99

Ian Bohen (1976-)
Marigold '07
Special '06
Hometown Legend '02
Young Hercules '97
Frankenstein Sings... The Movie '95
Wyatt Earp '94

Hark Bohm (1939-)
Underground '95
The Promise '94

Karlheinz Bohm
See Karl-Heinz Boehm

Marita Bohme (1939-)
Carbide and Sorrel '63
Minna von Barnhelm or The Soldier's Fortune '62
On the Sunny Side '62

Roman Bohnen (1894-1949)
Open Secret '48
Song of Love '47
The Best Years of Our Lives '46
The Hairy Ape '44

Corinne Bohrer (1959-)
Big Eden '00
Kisses in the Dark '97
Star Kid '97
Revenge of the Nerds 4: Nerds in Love '94
Dead Solid Perfect '88
Vice Versa '88
Stewardess School '86
Jekyll & Hyde... Together Again '82

Richard Bohringer (1942-)
Crime Spree '03
Transfixed '01
The Perfume of Yvonne '94
The Accompanist '93
Barjo '93
The Cook, the Thief, His Wife & Her Lover '90
Le Grand Chemin '87
L'Addition '85
Peril '85
Subway '85
Diva '82
I Married a Dead Man '82

Romane Bohringer (1974-)
He Died With a Felafel in His Hand '01
The King Is Alive '00
The Chambermaid on the Titanic '97
Portraits Chinois '96
Total Eclipse '95
The Accompanist '93
Mina Tannenbaum '93
Les Nuits Fauves '92

Jean Boht (1936-)
Heaven's a Drag '94
Arthur's Hallowed Ground '84

Samuel Boidin
Flanders '06
The Life of Jesus '96

Curt Bois (1901-91)
Wings of Desire '88
The Boat Is Full '81
Caught '49
Princess O'Rourke '43
Blue, White and Perfect '42
Casablanca '42
The Tuttles of Tahiti '42
That Night in Rio '41
Bitter Sweet '40
Boom Town '40
The Lady in Question '40
The Hunchback of Notre Dame '39
Amazing Dr. Clitterhouse '38
Gold Diggers in Paris '38
The Great Waltz '38

Christine Boisson (1957-)
I Dreamt Under the Water '07
The Truth About Charlie '02
Pas Tres Catholique '93
Sorceress '88
Unsettled Land '88
Identification of a Woman '82

James Bolam (1938-)
To Kill a King '03
Stella Does Tricks '96
The Maze '85
In Celebration '75
Dressed for Death '74
Crucible of Terror '72
A Kind of Loving '62
The Loneliness of the Long Distance Runner '62

Eamon Boland (1947-)
All the King's Men '99
Business As Usual '88

Joanne Boland (1975-)
George A. Romero's Land of the Dead '05
Brave New Girl '04

Katie Boland
The Note 2: Taking a Chance on Love '09
The Note '07

Mary Boland (1880-1965)
Julia Misbehaves '48
Nothing But Trouble '44
New Moon '40
One Night in the Tropics '40
Pride and Prejudice '40
The Women '39
Ruggles of Red Gap '35
Six of a Kind '34
Stingaree '34
Personal Maid '31

Philip Daniel Bolden (1995-)
Fly Me to the Moon '08
Are We Done Yet? '07
Are We There Yet? '05
Johnson Family Vacation '04

John Boles (1895-1969)
Thousands Cheer '43
Sinners in Paradise '38
Stella Dallas '37
Craig's Wife '36
Curly Top '35
The Littlest Rebel '35
Stand Up and Cheer '34
Frankenstein '31
King of Jazz '30
Rio Rita '29

John Bolger (1954-)
Just Looking '99
Parting Glances '86

Ray Bolger (1904-87)
That's Dancing! '85
For Heaven's Sake '79
The Runner Stumbles '79
Babes in Toyland '61
April in Paris '52
Look for the Silver Lining '49
The Harvey Girls '46
Stage Door Canteen '43
Four Jacks and a Jill '41
Sunny '41
The Wizard of Oz '39
Rosalie '38
Sweethearts '38
The Great Ziegfeld '36

Sarah Bolger (1991-)
The Spiderwick Chronicles '08
Alex Rider: Operation Stormbreaker '06
In America '02
A Love Divided '01

Florinda Bolkan (1941-)
Collector's Item '89
Some Girls '88
Acqua e Sapone '83
The Day That Shook the World '78
The Word '78
Royal Flash '75
Master Touch '74
Primal Impulse '74
Don't Torture a Duckling '72
The Last Valley '71
A Lizard in a Woman's Skin '71
Black Lemons '70
Ring of Death '69

Tiffany Bolling (1947-)
Ecstasy '84
Kingdom of the Spiders '77
The Centerfold Girls '74
Wild Party '74
Bonnie's Kids '73

Ryan Bollman (1972-)
Black Dawn '05
No Vacancy '99
The NeverEnding Story 3: Escape from Fantasia '94
Children of the Corn 2: The Final Sacrifice '92

Joseph Bologna (1938-)
Ice Age: The Meltdown '06 (V)
The Boynton Beach Club '05
Players '03
Big Daddy '99
National Lampoon's The Don's Analyst '97
Heaven Before I Die '96
Love Is All There Is '96
Danger of Love '95
Revenge of the Nerds 4: Nerds in Love '94
Citizen Cohn '92
Deadly Rivals '92
Jersey Girl '92
Alligator 2: The Mutation '90
Coupe de Ville '90
Not Quite Human '87
Rags to Riches '87
Transylvania 6-5000 '85
Blame It on Rio '84
The Woman in Red '84
One Cooks, the Other Doesn't '83
My Favorite Year '82
Chapter Two '79
Torn Between Two Lovers '79
The Big Bus '76
Cops and Robbers '73

Honor Thy Father '73

Christopher Bolton

Killing Moon '00
City Boy '93
Ordeal in the Arctic '93

Jon Bon Jovi (1962-)

Cry_Wolf '05
John Carpenter Presents Vampires: Los Muertos '02
Pay It Forward '00
U-571 '00
No Looking Back '98
Row Your Boat '98
Homegrown '97
Little City '97
The Leading Man '96
Moonlight and Valentino '95
Young Guns 2 '90

Ronaldo Bonacchi (1950-)

Orchestra Rehearsal '78
The Wide Blue Road '57

Paolo Bonacelli (1939-)

The Stendahl Syndrome '95
Francesco '93
Mille Bolle Blu '93
Johnny Stecchino '92
Night on Earth '91
Henry IV '85
Caligula '80
Christ Stopped at Eboli '79
Salo, or the 120 Days of Sodom '75

Danny Bonaduce (1959-)

America's Deadliest Home Video '91
H.O.T.S. '79
Baker's Hawk '76
Charlotte's Web '73 (V)

Anna Bonaiuto

Il Divo '08
The Story of Boys & Girls '91

Louie Bonanno (1961-)

Student Affairs '88
Night of the Living Babes '87
Wimps '87

Fortunio Bonanova (1895-1969)

An Affair to Remember '57
Double Indemnity '44
Ali Baba and the Forty Thieves '43
Five Graves to Cairo '43
For Whom the Bell Tolls '43
The Black Swan '42

Ivan Bonar (1924-88)

The Haunting Passion '83
MacArthur '77

Derek Bond (1920-2006)

When Eight Bells Toll '71
The Hand '60
Black Tide '58
Rogue's Yarn '56
Svengali '55
The Stranger from Venus '54
Tony Draws a Horse '51
The Weaker Sex '49
Scott of the Antarctic '48
Inheritance '47
Nicholas Nickleby '46

James Bond, III

Def by Temptation '90
School Daze '88
Go Tell It on the Mountain '84
The Fish that Saved Pittsburgh '79

Lillian Bond (1908-91)

Man in the Attic '53
The Westerner '40
China Seas '35
Double Harness '33
Hot Saturday '32
The Old Dark House '32

Renee Bond (1950-96)

Class Reunion '72
Please Don't Eat My Mother '72

Samantha Bond (1962-)

Fanny Hill '07
P.D. James: The Murder Room '04
Yes '04
Die Another Day '02
The World Is Not Enough '99
Emma '97
Tomorrow Never Dies '97
Goldeneye '95
Catherine Cookson's The Black Candle '92

Steve Bond (1953-)

Spacejacked '98
Tryst '94
To Die For 2: Son of Darkness '91
L.A. Gangs Rising '89
Picasso Trigger '89
To Die For '89
Magdalene '88
The Prey '80
Gas Pump Girls '79
H.O.T.S. '79
Massacre at Central High '76

Sudie Bond (1928-84)

I Am the Cheese '83
Trumps '83
Come Back to the Five & Dime Jimmy Dean, Jimmy Dean '82
Where the Lilies Bloom '74
Tomorrow '72
Fury on Wheels '71

Ward Bond (1903-60)

Alias Jesse James '59
Rio Bravo '59
Wings of Eagles '57
Dakota Incident '56
The Searchers '56
The Long Gray Line '55
A Man Alone '55
Mister Roberts '55
Blowing Wild '54
Gypsy Colt '54
Hondo '53
Johnny Guitar '53
The Moonlighter '53
Hellgate '52
The Quiet Man '52
Great Missouri Raid '51
On Dangerous Ground '51
Kiss Tomorrow Goodbye '50
Only the Valiant '50
Riding High '50
Wagon Master '50
Fort Apache '48
The Fugitive '48
Three Godfathers '48
The Time of Your Life '48
Unconquered '47
Canyon Passage '46
It's a Wonderful Life '46
My Darling Clementine '46
Dakota '45
They Were Expendable '45
A Guy Named Joe '44
Tall in the Saddle '44
Hello, Frisco, Hello '43
Hitler: Dead or Alive '43
The Falcon Takes Over '42
The Fighting Sullivans '42
Gentleman Jim '42
The Maltese Falcon '41
Manpower '41
Sergeant York '41
The Shepherd of the Hills '41
Wheel of Fortune '41
Kit Carson '40
Drums Along the Mohawk '39
Gone with the Wind '39
Oklahoma Kid '39
Waterfront '39
Young Mr. Lincoln '39
Amazing Dr. Clitterhouse '38
Born to Be Wild '38
Bringing Up Baby '38
Hawaii Calls '38
Mr. Moto's Gamble '38
Prison Break '38
Park Avenue Logger '37
You Only Live Once '37
Without Orders '36
The Crimson Trail '35
Devil Dogs of the Air '35
Fighting Shadows '35
Justice of the Range '35
Western Courage '35
It Happened One Night '34
Heroes for Sale '33
Hello Trouble '32
White Eagle '32
Big Trail '30

Sergei Bondarchuk (1920-94)

Battle of Neretva '69
War and Peace '68
A Summer to Remember '61
Era Notte a Roma '60

Beulah Bondi (1892-1981)

The Wonderful World of the Brothers Grimm '62
A Summer Place '59
Unholy Wife '57
Back from Eternity '56
Latin Lovers '53
Lone Star '52
Baron of Arizona '51
The Furies '50
So Dear to My Heart '49
The Snake Pit '48
Breakfast in Hollywood '46
It's a Wonderful Life '46
Sister Kenny '46
Back to Bataan '45
The Southerner '45
Watch on the Rhine '43
Penny Serenade '41
The Shepherd of the Hills '41
Our Town '40
Remember the Night '40
Mr. Smith Goes to Washington '39
On Borrowed Time '39
Of Human Hearts '38
The Sisters '38
Vivacious Lady '38
Make Way for Tomorrow '37
The Invisible Ray '36
The Moon's Our Home '36
The Trail of the Lonesome Pine '36
The Good Fairy '35
Two Alone '34
Finishing School '33
Rain '32
Street Scene '31

De'Aundre Bonds (1976-)

Lockdown '00
Three Strikes '00
The Wood '99
Get On the Bus '96
Sunset Park '96
Tales from the Hood '95

Christopher Bondy

The Jesse Ventura Story '99
The Dark '94
Deadly Surveillance '91

Peter Bonerz (1938-)

Man on the Moon '99
Your Place or Mine '83
Serial '80
The Bastard '78
How to Break Up a Happy Divorce '76
Catch-22 '70
Medium Cool '69
A Session with The Committee '68

Ken Bones

Perfect Hideout '08
Bellman and True '88
Jack the Ripper '88

Charles Bonet

Way of the Black Dragon '81
Death Promise '78

Lisa Bonet (1967-)

Biker Boyz '03
The Lathe of Heaven '02
High Fidelity '00
Enemy of the State '98
Dead Connection '94
New Eden '94
Bank Robber '93
Final Combination '93
Angel Heart '87

Nai Bonet (1940-)

Gangsters '79
Nocturna '79
Fairy Tales '76
Soul Hustler '76
Devil's Angels '67

Massimo Bonetti (1954-)

The Story of Boys & Girls '91
Terranova '91
Night Sun '90
Kaos '85
The Night of the Shooting Stars '82

Crispin Bonham Carter (1969-)

Ghostboat '06
Wuthering Heights '98
Catherine Cookson's The Rag Nymph '96
Pride and Prejudice '95

Helena Bonham Carter (1966-)

Alice in Wonderland '10
Harry Potter and the Half-Blood Prince '09
Terminator Salvation '09
Harry Potter and the Order of the Phoenix '07
Sweeney Todd: The Demon Barber of Fleet Street '07
Charlie and the Chocolate Factory '05
Conversations with Other Women '05
Tim Burton's Corpse Bride '05 (V)
Wallace & Gromit in The Curse of the Were-Rabbit '05 (V)
Big Fish '03
Live from Baghdad '03
The Heart of Me '02
Till Human Voices Wake Us '02
Novocaine '01
Planet of the Apes '01
Fight Club '99
Merlin '98
Sweet Revenge '98
The Theory of Flight '98
A Merry War '97
The Wings of the Dove '97
Portraits Chinois '96
Twelfth Night '96
Margaret's Museum '95
Mighty Aphrodite '95
Mary Shelley's Frankenstein '94
A Dark Adapted Eye '93
Francesco '93
Howard's End '92
Where Angels Fear to Tread '91
Hamlet '90
Getting It Right '89
Maurice '87
The Vision '87
A Room with a View '86
Lady Jane '85

Alessio Boni (1966-)

Don't Tell '05
Best of Youth '03

Gabrielle Boni (1985-)

Time at the Top '99
Little Men '98
Daddy's Girl '96

Luisella Boni (1935-)

The Invincible Gladiator '62
The Fury of Hercules '61
Samson '61

Evan Bonifant (1985-)

Blues Brothers 2000 '98
Breakout '98
3 Ninjas Kick Back '94

Paul Bonifas (1902-75)

The Train '65
The Foreman Went to France '42

Jacques Bonnaffe (1958-)

Cote d'Azur '05
Lemming '05
Va Savoir '01
Jeanne and the Perfect Guy '98
Venus Beauty Institute '98
First Name: Carmen '83

Sandrine Bonnaire (1967-)

Intimate Strangers '04
Resistance '03
East-West '99
Circle of Passion '97
La Ceremonie '95
Jeanne la Pucelle '94
The Plague '92
Monsieur Hire '89
Under Satan's Sun '87
La Puritaine '86
Police '85
Vagabond '85
A Nos Amours '84

Lee Bonnell (1918-86)

The Navy Comes Through '42
Look Who's Laughing '41

Vivian Bonnell (1924-2003)

Christmas in Connecticut '92
The Josephine Baker Story '90

Beverly Bonner

Basket Case 2 '90
Frankenhooker '90
Brain Damage '88
Basket Case '82

Bill Bonner

Outlaw Riders '72
Satan's Sadists '69

Frank Bonner (1942-)

Shut Up and Kiss Me '05
The Colony '95
You Can't Hurry Love '88
Equinox '71

Priscilla Bonner (1898-1996)

Long Pants '27
Charley's Aunt '25

Tony Bonner (1943-)

Hurricane Smith '92
Dead Sleep '91
Quigley Down Under '90
The Lighthorsemen '87
Money Movers '78
Alternative '76
Inn of the Damned '74
Creatures the World Forgot '70
Eye Witness '70

Valerie Bonneton

Summer Hours '08
Jeanne and the Perfect Guy '98

Dina Bonnevie (1961-)

American Adobo '02
Fight for Us '89

Maria Bonnevie (1973-)

I Am David '04
Reconstruction '03
Insomnia '97
Jerusalem '96
The Polar Bear King '94

Hugh Bonneville (1963-)

Filth '08
Lost in Austen '08
Five Days '07
Miss Austen Regrets '07
Beau Brummell: This Charming Man '06
Four Last Songs '06
Scenes of a Sexual Nature '06
Asylum '05
Underclassman '05
Conspiracy of Silence '03
Daniel Deronda '02
The Gathering Storm '02
Tipping the Velvet '02
The Emperor's New Clothes '01
Iris '01
Blow Dry '00
Madame Bovary '00
Heat of the Sun '99
Mansfield Park '99
Notting Hill '99
The Man Who Made Husbands Jealous '98
Mosley '98
Stalag Luft '93

Celine Bonnier (1965-)

Human Trafficking '05
Far Side of the Moon '03
The Assignment '97
A Wind from Wyoming '94

Sonny Bono (1935-98)

Under the Boardwalk '89
Hairspray '88
Dirty Laundry '87
Troll '86
The Vals '85
Airplane 2: The Sequel '82
Balboa '82
Escape to Athena '79
Murder on Flight 502 '75
Good Times '67

Brian Bonsall (1981-)

Father and Scout '94
Lily in Winter '94
Blank Check '93
Father Hood '93
Desperate Motives '92
Mikey '92

Deanna (Dee) Booher (1951-)

Brain Smasher... A Love Story '93
Home for Christmas '93
Slashdance '89
Deathstalker 2: Duel of the Titans '87

Sorrell Booke (1930-94)

Rock-a-Doodle '92 (V)
The Other Side of Midnight '77
Special Delivery '76
Bank Shot '74
Devil Times Five '74
The Iceman Cometh '73
Bye Bye Braverman '67
Up the Down Staircase '67
A Fine Madness '66
Joy House '64
Gone Are the Days '63
Purlie Victorious '63
The Iceman Cometh '60

Dany Boon (1966-)

Micmacs '09
My Best Friend '06
The Valet '06
Joyeux Noel '05

Debbie Boone (1956-)

Treehouse Hostage '99
Hollywood Safari '96

Mark Boone, Jr. (1955-)

Frozen River '08
Vice '08
30 Days of Night '07
The Legend of Lucy Keyes '06
Lonesome Jim '06
Wristcutters: A Love Story '06
Batman Begins '05
Dead Birds '04
Frankenfish '04
2 Fast 2 Furious '03
Animal Factory '00

Memento '00
Buddy Boy '99
The General's Daughter '99
The Treat '98
John Carpenter's Vampires '97
Rosewood '96
Tree's Lounge '96
Fever '91
Landlord Blues '87

Pat Boone (1934-)
Roger & Me '89
The Cross & the Switchblade '72
The Greatest Story Ever Told '65
Goodbye Charlie '64
State Fair '62
Journey to the Center of the Earth '59

Richard Boone (1916-81)
The Bushido Blade '80
Winter Kills '79
The Big Sleep '78
The Hobbit '78 (V)
The Shootist '76
Against a Crooked Sky '75
God's Gun '75
Big Jake '71
Madron '70
The Arrangement '69
The Night of the Following Day '69
Hombre '67
The War Lord '65
Rio Conchos '64
The Alamo '60
I Bury the Living '58
The Garment Jungle '57
The Tall T '57
Away All Boats '56
Dragnet '54
Ten Wanted Men '54
Beneath the 12-Mile Reef '53
The Robe '53
The Halls of Montezuma '50

Mika Boorem (1987-)
The Initiation of Sarah '06
Smile '05
Dirty Dancing: Havana Nights '04
Sleepover '04
Carolina '03
Blue Crush '02
Along Came a Spider '01
Hearts in Atlantis '01
Riding in Cars with Boys '01
The Patriot '00

Charley Boorman (1966-)
In My Country '04
The Serpent's Kiss '97
Picture Windows '95
Hope and Glory '87
The Emerald Forest '85
Excalibur '81
Deliverance '72

Katrine Boorman (1958-)
Camille Claudel '89
Hope and Glory '87

Elayne Boosler (1952-)
Mother Goose Rock 'n' Rhyme '90
Meatballs 2 '84

Adrian Booth (1918-)
Son of God's Country '48
Under Colorado Skies '47
Daughter of Don Q '46
Captain America '44
So Proudly We Hail '43
Ridin' Down the Canyon '42
The Man They Could Not Hang '39
Adventure in Sahara '38

Connie Booth (1941-)
The Buccaneers '95
Leon the Pig Farmer '93
The Strange Case of the End of Civilization As We Know It '93
American Friends '91
Hawks '89
Nairobi Affair '88
Little Lord Fauntleroy '80
Monty Python and the Holy Grail '75
Romance with a Double Bass '74
And Now for Something Completely Different '72
John Cleese on How to Irritate People '68

Edwina Booth (1909-91)
The Last of the Mohicans '32
Trader Horn '31

Emma Booth
Blood Creek '09
The Boys Are Back '09
Introducing the Dwights '07

James Booth (1927-2005)
Keeping Mum '05
American Ninja 4: The Annihilation '91
Bad Guys '86
Programmed to Kill '86
Pray for Death '85
Hotline '82
Zorro, the Gay Blade '81
Brannigan '75
That'll Be the Day '73
Rentadick '72
Revenge '71
Darker than Amber '70
Man Who Had Power Over Women '70
The Bliss of Mrs. Blossom '68
Robbery '67
Zulu '64
The Trials of Oscar Wilde '60

Karin (Karen, Katharine) Booth (1919-92)
Beloved Infidel '59
Seminole Uprising '55
Tobor the Great '54
My Foolish Heart '49

Lindy Booth (1979-)
Behind the Wall '08
Dark Honeymoon '08
Cry_Wolf '05
Dawn of the Dead '04
Hollywood North '03
Wrong Turn '03
American Psycho 2: All American Girl '02
The Skulls 2 '02

Shirley Booth (1907-92)
Hot Spell '58
The Matchmaker '58
Main Street to Broadway '53
Come Back, Little Sheba '52

Powers Boothe (1949-)
24 : Redemption '08
The Final Season '07
Sin City '05
Frailty '02
Attila '01
Men of Honor '00
Joan of Arc '99
True Women '97
U-Turn '97
The Spree '96
Dalva '95
Mutant Species '95
Nixon '95
Sudden Death '95
Tombstone '93
Rapid Fire '92
Wildcard '92
Blue Sky '91
By Dawn's Early Light '89
Extreme Prejudice '87
Into the Homeland '87
The Emerald Forest '85
A Breed Apart '84
Red Dawn '84
Plutonium Incident '82
Southern Comfort '81
Cruising '80
A Cry for Love '80
The Guyana Tragedy: The Story of Jim Jones '80
Skag '79

Nick Boraine
Cape of Good Hope '04
Queen's Messenger II '01

Caterina Boratto (1916-)
Salo, or the 120 Days of Sodom '75
Castle Keep '69
Juliet of the Spirits '65
8 1/2 '63

Cornell Borchers (1925-)
Istanbul '57
The Big Lift '50

Lynn Borden (1939-)
Hellhole '85
This Is a Hijack '73
Frogs '72

Rene Borden
Kid Courageous '35
Western Justice '35
Fighting Hero '34

David Boreanaz (1971-)
Mr. Fix It '06
The Crow: Wicked Prayer '05
These Girls '05
I'm with Lucy '02
Valentine '01

Carla Borelli (1942-)
Charlotte Forten's Mission: Experiment in Freedom '85
Asylum of Satan '72

Veda Ann Borg (1915-73)
The Alamo '60
Wings of Eagles '57
Guys and Dolls '55
I'll Cry Tomorrow '55
Love Me or Leave Me '55
Three Sailors and a Girl '53
Big Jim McLain '52
Rider from Tucson '50
Julia Misbehaves '48
The Bachelor and the Bobby-Soxer '47
Big Town '47
Blonde Savage '47
Accomplice '46
Fog Island '45
Treasure of Fear '45
The Falcon in Hollywood '44
Marked Trails '44
Isle of Forgotten Sins '43
Revenge of the Zombies '43
The Corsican Brothers '42
I Married an Angel '42
Honky Tonk '41
Dr. Christian Meets the Women '40
I Take This Oath '40
Melody Ranch '40
Kid Galahad '37
San Quentin '37
False Faces '32

Rikke Borge
Amityville 3: The Demon '83
Tattoo '81

Nelly Borgeaud (1931-2004)
The Accompanist '93
The Man Who Loved Women '77
Mississippi Mermaid '69

Alexandre Borges (1966-)
Bossa Nova '99
Foreign Land '95

Sal Borgese (1937-)
Flight of the Innocent '93
Thundersquad '85
Adios, Sabata '71

Paul Borghese
Find Me Guilty '06
61* '01

Ernest Borgnine (1917-)
Aces 'n Eights '08
Strange Wilderness '08
A Grandpa for Christmas '07
The Long Ride Home '01
BASEketball '98
Small Soldiers '98 (V)
Gattaca '97
McHale's Navy '97
All Dogs Go to Heaven 2 '95 (V)
Mistress '91
Any Man's Death '90
Laser Mission '90
Moving Target '89
The Opponent '89
Skeleton Coast '89
The Big Turnaround '88
The Dirty Dozen: The Fatal Mission '88
Spike of Bensonhurst '88
The Dirty Dozen: The Deadly Mission '87
The Manhunt '86
Alice in Wonderland '85
The Dirty Dozen: The Next Mission '85
Codename: Wildgeese '84
Love Leads the Way '84
Young Warriors '83
Deadly Blessing '81
Escape from New York '81
High Risk '81
Super Fuzz '81
When Time Ran Out '80
All Quiet on the Western Front '79
The Black Hole '79
The Double McGuffin '79
Convoy '78
The Prince and the Pauper '78
Fire '77
The Greatest '77
Jesus of Nazareth '77
Future Cop '76
Love by Appointment '76
Shoot '76
Devil's Rain '75
Law and Disorder '74
Vengeance Is Mine '74
Emperor of the North Pole '73
Neptune Factor '73
Hannie Caulder '72
The Poseidon Adventure '72
Counter Punch '71
The Trackers '71
Willard '71
The Adventurers '70
Bullet for Sandoval '70
Suppose They Gave a War and Nobody Came? '70
The Wild Bunch '69
Ice Station Zebra '68
Chuka '67
The Dirty Dozen '67
The Oscar '66
The Flight of the Phoenix '65
McHale's Navy '64
Barabbas '62
The Badlanders '58
Torpedo Run '58
The Vikings '58
The Catered Affair '56
Jubal '56
The Last Command '55
Marty '55
Bad Day at Black Rock '54
Demetrius and the Gladiators '54
From Here to Eternity '53
Johnny Guitar '53
The Stranger Wore a Gun '53
Vera Cruz '53

Hilda Borgstrom
Night Is My Future '47
The Phantom Chariot '20

Bobby Boriello
A Walk on the Moon '99
Enemy of the State '98
Private Parts '96

Angel Boris (1974-)
Dragon Storm '04
Epoch: Evolution '03
Interceptor Force '99
Warlock 3: The End of Innocence '98

Nicoletta Boris
Desperate Crimes '93
Mille Bolle Blu '93

Carroll Borland (1914-94)
Bio Hazard '85
Mark of the Vampire '35

Matt Borlenghi (1967-)
Blood Surf '00
The Crew '00
Kate's Addiction '99
The American Scream '88

Roscoe Born (1950-)
Haunting of Sarah Hardy '89
Lady Mobster '88

Katherine Borowitz
The Man Who Wasn't There '01
Illuminata '98
Mac '93
Men of Respect '91
Fellow Traveler '89

Jesse Borrego (1962-)
The Maldonado Miracle '03
The Maker '98
Con Air '97
Retroactive '97
Tecumseh: The Last Warrior '95
I Like It Like That '94
Mi Vida Loca '94
Blood In ... Blood Out: Bound by Honor '93

Dieter Borsche (1909-82)
The Mad Executioners '65
The Phantom of Soho '64
The Black Abbot '63
Dead Eyes of London '61
A Time to Love & a Time to Die '58
Ali Baba and the 40 Thieves '54

Alex Borstein (1972-)
Killers '10
The Lookout '07
Little Man '06
Good Night, and Good Luck '05
Catwoman '04
Seeing Other People '04
The Lizzie McGuire Movie '03
Dawg '02

Jason Bortz (1970-)
Take It to the Limit '00
Slaves to the Underground '96

Jean-Mark Bory (1934-2001)
Le Repos du Guerrier '62
Love on a Pillow '62
RoGoPaG '62
The Lovers '59

Frank Borzage (1893-1962)
A Mormon Maid '17
The Wrath of the Gods '14

John Yong Bosch (1976-)
Devon's Ghost: Legend of the Bloody Boy '05
Turbo: A Power Rangers Movie '96
Mighty Morphin Power Rangers: The Movie '95

Philip Bosco (1930-)
The Savages '07
Abandon '02
Kate & Leopold '01
Cupid & Cate '00
Shaft '00
Wonder Boys '00
Bonanno: A Godfather's Story '99
Borough of Kings '98
Moon over Broadway '98
Critical Care '97
Deconstructing Harry '97
My Best Friend's Wedding '97
The First Wives Club '96
It Takes Two '95
Against the Wall '94
Angie '94
Milk Money '94
Nobody's Fool '94
Safe Passage '94
Shadows and Fog '92
Straight Talk '92
F/X 2: The Deadly Art of Illusion '91
The Return of Eliot Ness '91
True Colors '91
Blue Steel '90
Quick Change '90
The Dream Team '89
Another Woman '88
Working Girl '88
Suspect '87
Three Men and a Baby '87
Children of a Lesser God '86
The Money Pit '86
Heaven Help Us '85
Walls of Glass '85
The Pope of Greenwich Village '84

Lucia Bose (1931-)
Harem '99
Lumiere '76
The Legend of Blood Castle '72
Nathalie Granger '72
The Lady Without Camelias '53
Story of a Love Affair '50

Miguel Bose (1956-)
Queen Margot '94
High Heels '91

Rahul Bose
Before the Rains '07
Everybody Says I'm Fine! '06

Guilio Bosetti
Il Divo '08
Incantato '03

Andrea Bosic (1919-)
Hornet's Nest '70
Pirates of the Seven Seas '62
Maciste in Hell '60

Todd Bosley (1984-)
Lloyd '00
Treehouse Hostage '99
Jack '96
Little Giants '94

Tom Bosley (1927-)
Charlie & Me '08
Hidden Places '06
Christmas at Water's Edge '04
Little Bigfoot 2: The Journey Home '97
Fire and Rain '89
Wicked Stepmother '89
Million Dollar Mystery '87
The Jesse Owens Story '84
O'Hara's Wife '82
For the Love of It '80
The Rebels '79
The Triangle Factory Fire Scandal '79
The Bastard '78
Gus '76
Death Cruise '74
The Streets of San Francisco '72
Night Gallery '69
The Secret War of Harry Frigg '68
Yours, Mine & Ours '68
Bang Bang Kid '67

Divorce American Style '67
The World of Henry Orient '64
Love with the Proper Stranger '63

Simon Bossell
Better Than Sex '00
Cut '00
Aberration '97
Hotel de Love '96

Barbara Bosson (1939-)
The Great American Sex Scandal '94
Little Sweetheart '90
The Last Starfighter '84
Mame '74
A Session with The Committee '68

Barry Bostwick (1945-)
Depth Charge '08
Evening '07
Nancy Drew '07
Tales from a Parallel Universe: I Worship His Shadow '97
The Secret Agent Club '96
Spy Hard '96
In the Heat of Passion 2: Unfaithful '94
Project Metalbeast: DNA Overload '94
The Secretary '94
800 Leagues Down the Amazon '93
Praying Mantis '93
Russian Roulette '93
Weekend at Bernie's 2 '93
War & Remembrance '88
George Washington: The Forging of a Nation '86
Jailbait: Betrayed By Innocence '86
George Washington '84
A Woman of Substance '84
Megaforce '82
Red Flag: The Ultimate Game '81
Scruples '80
Murder by Natural Causes '79
Movie, Movie '78
The Rocky Horror Picture Show '75
Fantastic Planet '73 (V)
Road Movie '72

Jackson Bostwick
A Matter of Honor '95
Escape from DS-3 '81

Charles Boswell
Dangerous Passion '95
Kiss Me a Killer '91

Brian Bosworth (1965-)
The Longest Yard '05
Mach 2 '00
Back in Business '96
Black Out '96
Virus '96
One Man's Justice '95
Stone Cold '91

Hobart Bosworth (1867-1943)
King of the Sierras '38
Rollin' Plains '38
The Dark Hour '36
The Crusades '35
Steamboat Round the Bend '35
The Last of the Mohicans '32
Phantom Express '32
Abraham Lincoln '30
Dubarry '30
Annapolis '28
Hangman's House '28
The Smart Set '28
A Woman of Affairs '28
My Best Girl '27
The Nervous Wreck '26
Spangles '26
The Big Parade '25
Little Church Around the Corner '23
The Sea Lion '21
The Little American '17
A Mormon Maid '17

Kate (Catherine) Bosworth (1983-)
21 '08
Superman Returns '06
Bee Season '05
Beyond the Sea '04
Win a Date with Tad Hamilton! '04
Wonderland '03
Blue Crush '02
The Rules of Attraction '02
Remember the Titans '00
The Horse Whisperer '97

Wade Boteler (1888-1943)
The Green Hornet '39
Southward Ho! '39
The Mandarin Mystery '37
You Only Live Once '37
Come on Danger! '32
Big News '29
Let 'er Go Gallegher '28

Niki Botelho
No Turning Back '01
The Ewoks: Battle for Endor '85

Rodrigo Botero
True Friends '98
Beach Babes 2: Cave Girl Island '95

Dick Botiller
Riding Wild '35
Fighting Hero '34

Sara Botsford (1951-)
The Fog '05
Jumpin' Jack Flash '86
The Gunrunner '84
By Design '82
Deadly Eyes '82
Murder by Phone '82
Still of the Night '82

Juan Diego Botto (1975-)
The Dancer Upstairs '02
Broken Silence '01
Martin (Hache) '97
If They Tell You I Fell '89

Maria Botto (1974-)
My Life in Ruins '09
Broken Silence '01
Jealousy '99
If They Tell You I Fell '89

Benjamin Bottoms (1960-)
A Shining Season '79
Stalk the Wild Child '76

Joseph Bottoms (1954-)
Liar's Edge '92
Treacherous Crossing '92
Inner Sanctum '91
Born to Race '88
Open House '86
Celebrity '85
Blind Date '84
Surfacing '84
The Sins of Dorian Gray '82
Intruder Within '81
King of the Mountain '81
Cloud Dancer '80
The Black Hole '79
Holocaust '78
Return Engagement '78
High Rolling in a Hot Corvette '77
Stalk the Wild Child '76
Crime & Passion '75
The Dove '74

Sam Bottoms (1955-2008)
Sherrybaby '06
Shopgirl '05
The Unsaid '01
Angel Blue '97
Mercenary 2: Thick and Thin '97
Project Shadowchaser 3000 '95
The Witching of Ben Wagner '95
Dolly Dearest '92
Hearts of Darkness: A Filmmaker's Apocalypse '91
Ragin' Cajun '90
Return to Eden '89
Gardens of Stone '87
Hunter's Blood '87
In 'n Out '86
Prime Risk '84
Desperate Lives '82
Bronco Billy '80
East of Eden '80
Apocalypse Now '79
Up from the Depths '79
The Outlaw Josey Wales '76
Savages '75
Zandy's Bride '74
Class of '44 '73
The Last Picture Show '71

Timothy Bottoms (1950-)
American Girl: Chrissa Stands Strong '09
The Land That Time Forgot '09
Lone Rider '08
Holiday in Handcuffs '07
Shanghai Kiss '07
Paradise, Texas '05
DC 9/11: Time of Crisis '04
The Girl Next Door '04
Ike: Countdown to D-Day '04
Elephant '03
Diamondbacks '99
The Prince and the Surfer '99
Total Force '98
The Man in the Iron Mask '97
Mortal Challenge '97
Ripper Man '96
Uncle Sam '96
Hourglass '95
The Prince '95
Top Dog '95
Ava's Magical Adventure '94
Digger '94
The Gift of Love '90
Istanbul '90
Texasville '90
The Fantasist '89
The Drifter '88
The Land of Faraway '87
Husbands, Wives, Money, and Murder '86
In the Shadow of Kilimanjaro '86
Invaders from Mars '86
The Sea Serpent '85
Hambone & Hillie '84
Love Leads the Way '84
Tin Man '83
What Waits Below '83
High Country '81
East of Eden '80
Hurricane '79
A Shining Season '79
The Other Side of the Mountain, Part 2 '78
Rollercoaster '77
A Small Town in Texas '76
The Story of David '76
The White Dawn '75
Love and Pain and the Whole Damn Thing '73
The Paper Chase '73
Johnny Got His Gun '71
The Last Picture Show '71

Mathew Botuchis
I-See-You.Com '06
3 Ninjas: High Noon at Mega Mountain '97

Sami Bouajila (1966-)
Days of Glory '06
Change My Life '01
The Adventures of Felix '99
The Siege '98
Bye-Bye '96

Savannah Smith Boucher
Last Summer In the Hamptons '96
The Applegates '89

Barbara Bouchet (1943-)
Rogue '76
Surabaya Conspiracy '75
Mean Machine '73
Cry of a Prostitute: Love Kills '72
Don't Torture a Duckling '72
Amuck! '71
The Black Belly of the Tarantula '71
Casino Royale '67
In Harm's Way '65

Willis Bouchey (1907-77)
The Man Who Shot Liberty Valance '62
Panic in the Year Zero! '62
The Horse Soldiers '59
The Sheepman '58
Zero Hour! '57
Battle Cry '55
The Bridges at Toko-Ri '55
Suddenly '54
Dangerous Crossing '53

Elodie Bouchez (1973-)
Apres Lui '07
Sorry, Haters '05
CQ '01
Don't Let Me Die on a Sunday '98
The Dreamlife of Angels '98
Full Speed '96
Wild Reeds '94

Chili Bouchier (1909-99)
Old Mother Riley's New Venture '49
The Ghost Goes West '36

Patrick Bouchitey (1946-)
Life Is a Long Quiet River '88
The Best Way '76

Jacques Boudet
The Town Is Quiet '00
Marius and Jeannette '97
Farinelli '94
Waiting for the Moon '87

Jean Bouise (1929-89)
La Femme Nikita '91
Le Dernier Combat '84
Hothead '78
Old Gun '76
I Am Cuba '64

Michel Boujenah (1952-)
Les Miserables '95
Three Men and a Cradle '85

Daniel Boulanger (1922-)
Bed and Board '70
The Bride Wore Black '68
The King of Hearts '66
Breathless '59

Sam Bould (1985-)
The End of the Affair '99
Hollow Reed '95

Ingrid Boulting (1947-)
Deadly Passion '85
The Last Tycoon '76

Matthew Boulton (1883-1962)
Night Must Fall '37
Sabotage '36

Carole Bouquet (1957-)
Red Lights '04
Wasabi '01
The Bridge '00
Lucie Aubrac '98
Grosse Fatigue '94
A Business Affair '93
New York Stories '89
Too Beautiful for You '88
Special Police '85
Dagger Eyes '83
For Your Eyes Only '81
Buffet Froid '79
That Obscure Object of Desire '77

Michel Bouquet (1926-)
How I Killed My Father '03
Tous les Matins du Monde '92
Toto le Heros '91
Cop Au Vin '85
Le Complot '73
Just Before Nightfall '71
Borsalino '70
La Rupture '70
La Femme Infidele '69
Mississippi Mermaid '69
The Bride Wore Black '68
This Special Friendship '67
Pattes Blanches '49
Monsieur Vincent '47

Sacha Bourdo (1962-)
The Science of Sleep '06
Western '96

John Bourgeois
XIII '08
A Different Loyalty '04
The Prince & Me '04
Rudy: The Rudy Giulani Story '03
Ginger Snaps '01
Ms. Scrooge '97
Dead Silence '96

Stacie Bourgeois
See Stacie Randall

J.R. Bourne (1970-)
The Lost Treasure of the Grand Canyon '08
The Butterfly Effect 2 '06
Everything's Gone Green '06
The Exorcism of Emily Rose '05
Ginger Snaps Back: The Beginning '04
13 Ghosts '01

Whitney Bourne
Flight from Glory '37
Living on Love '37

Andre Bourvil (1917-70)
Le Cercle Rouge '70
The Brain '69
When Wolves Cry '69
La Grande Vadrouille '66
Jailbird's Vacation '65
The Sucker '65
Les Miserables '57
Four Bags Full '56
Crazy for Love '52
Mr. Peek-A-Boo '50

Adam Bousdoukos
Soul Kitchen '09
Head On '04

Joy Boushel (1959-)
The Fly '86
Humongous '82

Nathalie Boutefeu (1968-)
Kings and Queen '04
Irma Vep '96
Barjo '93

Dennis Boutsikaris (1952-)
Cherry Crush '07
They Crawl '01
Perfect Murder, Perfect Town '00
Taken '99
In Dreams '98
The Three Lives of Karen '97
The Yarn Princess '94
The Dream Team '89
*batteries not included '87

Denise Boutte (1982-)
Tyler Perry's Why Did I Get Married? '07
Bram Stoker's Way of the Vampire '05
Death Valley: The Revenge of Bloody Bill '04

Duane Boutte
You Belong to Me '07
Brother to Brother '04
Stonewall '95

Jean-Pierre Bouvier (1948-)
Ma Saison Preferee '93
Good-bye, Emmanuelle '77

Joe (Joseph) Bova (1924-2006)
Roboman '75
Pretty Poison '68

Raoul Bova (1971-)
The Company '07
Alien vs. Predator '04
Facing Windows '03
Under the Tuscan Sun '03
Avenging Angelo '02

Julie Bovasso (1930-91)
Article 99 '92
Betsy's Wedding '90
Moonstruck '87
Wise Guys '86
The Verdict '82
Gentleman Bandit '81
Willie & Phil '80
The Iceman Cometh '60

Brunella Bovo (1932-)
The White Sheik '52
Miracle in Milan '51

Clara Bow (1905-65)
Hoopla '33
Hula '28
It '27
Wings '27
Dancing Mothers '26
Mantrap '26
Free to Love '25
My Lady of Whims '25
Parisian Love '25
The Plastic Age '25
Down to the Sea in Ships '22

Simmy Bow (1922-88)
Zoltan... Hound of Dracula '78
The Doberman Gang '72

Bow Wow (1987-)
The Lottery Ticket '10
Hurricane Season '08
The Fast and the Furious: Tokyo Drift '06
Roll Bounce '05
Johnson Family Vacation '04
All About the Benjamins '02
Like Mike '02
Carmen: A Hip Hopera '01

Katrina Bowden
The Shortcut '09
Sex Drive '08

Dorris Bowdon (1914-2005)
The Grapes of Wrath '40
Drums Along the Mohawk '39

David Bowe
Dark Justice '00
UHF '89
Back to the Beach '87

John Bowe (1950-)
Cranford '08
Secret Smile '05
Tipping the Velvet '02
Cleopatra '99
Split Second '99
Poldark '96
Body & Soul '93
Prime Suspect '92

Andrew Bowen
Conjurer '08
The Haunting of Hell House '99

Christopher Bowen
Gaudi Afternoon '01
Cold Comfort Farm '94
The Shell Seekers '89

Dennis Bowen
Gas Pump Girls '79
Van Nuys Blvd. '79

Julie Bowen (1970-)
Crazy on the Outside *'10*
Sex and Death 101 *'07*
Kids in America *'05*
Joe Somebody *'01*
The Killing Club *'01*
An American Werewolf in Paris *'97*
Happy Gilmore *'96*
Multiplicity *'96*
Runaway Daughters *'94*

Michael Bowen (1953-)
The Last House on the Left *'09*
Dear Me: A Blogger's Tale *'08*
Walking Tall *'04*
Kill Bill Vol. 1 *'03*
Magnolia *'99*
Jackie Brown *'97*
Cupid *'96*
Excess Baggage *'96*
True Crime *'95*
Love and a .45 *'94*
New Eden *'94*
Casualties of Love: The "Long Island Lolita" Story *'93*
The Player *'92*
The Taking of Beverly Hills *'91*
Mortal Passions *'90*
Season of Fear *'89*
The Abduction of Kari Swenson *'87*
Echo Park *'86*
Iron Eagle *'86*
Night of the Comet *'84*
Valley Girl *'83*
Forbidden World *'82*

Roger Bowen (1932-96)
What about Bob? *'91*
Zapped! *'82*
M*A*S*H *'70*
Petulia *'68*

Malick Bowens
Tears of the Sun *'03*
Ali *'01*
Bopha! *'93*
The Believers *'87*
Out of Africa *'85*

Antoinette Bower (1932-)
The Evil That Men Do *'84*
Blood Song *'82*
Prom Night *'80*
Die Sister, Die! *'74*

Jamie Campbell Bower
Winter in Wartime *'10*
Sweeney Todd: The Demon Barber of Fleet Street *'07*

Tom Bower
The Killer Inside Me *'10*
Bad Lieutenant: Port of Call New Orleans *'09*
Crazy Heart *'09*
Appaloosa *'08*
Familiar Strangers *'08*
Gospel Hill *'08*
Thr3e *'07*
Valley of the Heart's Delight *'07*
Flannel Pajamas *'06*
The Hills Have Eyes *'06*
The Badge *'02*
High Crimes *'02*
Hearts in Atlantis *'01*
The Million Dollar Hotel *'99*
A Slipping Down Life *'99*
Buffalo Soldiers *'97*
The Killing Jar *'96*
The Last Time I Committed Suicide *'96*
The Avenging Angel *'95*
Malevolence *'95*
White Man's Burden *'95*
Against the Wall *'94*
Far from Home: The Adventures of Yellow Dog *'94*
Relentless 3 *'93*
Teenage Bonnie & Klepto Clyde *'93*
Raising Cain *'92*
Love, Lies and Murder *'91*
True Believer *'89*
Promised a Miracle *'88*
Family Sins *'87*
River's Edge *'87*
The Lightship *'86*
Massive Retaliation *'85*
Wildrose *'85*
Ballad of Gregorio Cortez *'83*
When Hell Was in Session *'82*

John Bowers (1899-1936)
Say It With Songs *'29*
The White Sin *'24*
Lorna Doone *'22*
The Sky Pilot *'21*

David Bowie (1947-)
Bandslam *'09*
August *'08*
Arthur and the Invisibles *'06 (V)*
The Prestige *'06*
Mr. Rice's Secret *'00*
B.U.S.T.E.D. *'99*
Gunslinger's Revenge *'98*
Basquiat *'96*
The Linguini Incident *'92*
Twin Peaks: Fire Walk with Me *'92*
The Last Temptation of Christ *'88*
Absolute Beginners *'86*
Labyrinth *'86*
Into the Night *'85*
The Hunger *'83*
Merry Christmas, Mr. Lawrence *'83*
Yellowbeard *'83*
Christiane F. *'82*
Just a Gigolo *'79*
The Man Who Fell to Earth *'76*

Aldrich Bowker (1875-1947)
I Married a Witch *'42*
Nancy Drew—Trouble Shooter *'39*

Judi Bowker (1954-)
Anna Karenina *'85*
The Shooting Party *'85*
Clash of the Titans *'81*
Count Dracula *'77*
East of Elephant Rock *'76*
In This House of Brede *'75*
Brother Sun, Sister Moon *'73*

Paul Bowles (1910-99)
Halfmoon *'95 (N)*
The Sheltering Sky *'90*

Peter Bowles (1936-)
Color Me Kubrick *'05*
In Love and War *'01*
The Legend of Hell House *'73*
The Offence *'73*
A Day in the Death of Joe Egg *'71*
Endless Night *'71*
The Charge of the Light Brigade *'68*
Blow-Up *'66*

Jessica Bowman (1980-)
Derailed *'02*
Joy Ride *'01*
Secrets *'94*
Remote *'93*

Laura Bowman (1881-1957)
Son of Ingagi *'40*
Drums O'Voodoo *'34*

Lee Bowman (1914-79)
My Dream Is Yours *'49*
Smash-Up: The Story of a Woman *'47*
She Wouldn't Say Yes *'45*
Tonight and Every Night *'45*
Cover Girl *'44*
Bataan *'43*
We Were Dancing *'42*
Buck Privates *'41*
Love Affair *'39*
A Man to Remember *'39*
Having a Wonderful Time *'38*
Next Time I Marry *'38*
Internes Can't Take Money *'37*

Lisa Bowman
Dead Dog *'00*
River of Grass *'94*

Paul Bown (1957-)
Butterfly Kiss *'94*
Anne of Green Gables *'85*
Morons from Outer Space *'85*
Transmutations *'85*

John Boxer (1909-82)
The Bridge on the River Kwai *'57*
Mister Drake's Duck *'50*
The Woman in Question *'50*

Bruce Boxleitner (1950-)
Aces 'n Eights *'08*
Bone Eater *'07*
Pandemic *'07*
Sharpshooter *'07*
Snakehead Terror *'04*
Gods and Generals *'03*
Hope Ranch *'02*
The Perfect Nanny *'00*
Wyatt Earp: Return to Tombstone *'94*
The Secret *'93*
The Babe *'92*
Double Jeopardy *'92*
Kuffs *'92*
Perfect Family *'92*
Diplomatic Immunity *'91*
Murderous Vision *'91*
From the Dead of Night *'89*
Kenny Rogers as the Gambler, Part 3: The Legend Continues *'87*
Passion Flower *'86*
Kenny Rogers as the Gambler, Part 2: The Adventure Continues *'83*
Tron *'82*
The Baltimore Bullet *'80*
East of Eden *'80*
Kenny Rogers as the Gambler *'80*

Boy George (1961-)
I Love You Baby *'01*
The Wolves of Kromer *'98 (N)*

Sully Boyar (1923-2001)
In the Soup *'92*
The Manhattan Project *'86*
Car Wash *'76*

Alan Boyce (1961-)
Nowhere *'96*
Totally F***ed Up *'94*
Permanent Record *'88*

Brandon Boyce
Milk *'08*
Public Access *'93*

Cameron Boyce
Eagle Eye *'08*
Mirrors *'08*

Todd Boyce
Spy Game *'01*
Jefferson in Paris *'94*
Great Expectations: The Untold Story *'87*

Alexandra Boyd
Karla *'06*
Dog Gone Love *'03*

Beverly Boyd
Ghost Rider *'43*
Jive Junction *'43*

Billy Boyd (1968-)
The Flying Scotsman *'06*
On a Clear Day *'05*
Seed of Chucky *'04 (V)*
Lord of the Rings: The Return of the King *'03*
Master and Commander: The Far Side of the World *'03*
Lord of the Rings: The Two Towers *'02*
Lord of the Rings: The Fellowship of the Ring *'01*

Blake Boyd
First Kid *'96*
Raiders of the Sun *'92*
Dune Warriors *'91*

Cameron Boyd (1984-)
Manny & Lo *'96*
Bye Bye, Love *'94*
King of the Hill *'93*

Darren Boyd (1971-)
Imagine Me & You *'06*
High Heels and Low Lifes *'01*

Guy Boyd (1943-)
Cries of Silence *'97*
Retroactive *'97*
Past Midnight *'92*
Kiss Me a Killer *'91*
Drug Wars: The Camarena Story *'90*
The Last of the Finest *'90*
The Dark Side of the Sun *'88*
Murder Ordained *'87*
The Jagged Edge *'85*
Body Double *'84*
Eyes of Fire *'84*
The Eyes of the Amaryllis *'82*
Keeping On *'81*
Ticket to Heaven *'81*

Jenna Boyd (1993-)
Sisterhood of the Traveling Pants *'05*
Dickie Roberts: Former Child Star *'03*
The Missing *'03*

Lynda Boyd (1965-)
True Confessions of a Hollywood Starlet *'08*
The Fast and the Furious: Tokyo Drift *'06*
Final Destination 2 *'03*
Leaving Metropolis *'02*

Stephen Boyd (1928-77)
The Squeeze *'77*
The Treasure of Jamaica Reef *'74*
The Big Game *'72*
Hannie Caulder *'72*
Black Brigade *'69*
Shalako *'68*
Caper of the Golden Bulls *'67*
The Bible *'66*
Fantastic Voyage *'66*
The Oscar *'66*
The Fall of the Roman Empire *'64*
Imperial Venus *'63*
Billy Rose's Jumbo *'62*
Ben-Hur *'59*
The Best of Everything *'59*
The Bravados *'58*
Abandon Ship *'57*
The Night Heaven Fell *'57*
The Man Who Never Was *'55*

Tanya Boyd (1951-)
Roots *'77*
Black Heat *'76*
Black Shampoo *'76*
Ilsa, Harem Keeper of the Oil Sheiks *'76*

William Boyd (1898-1972)
Hopalong Cassidy: Borrowed Trouble *'48*
Hopalong Cassidy: Dangerous Venture *'48*
Hopalong Cassidy: False Paradise *'48*
Hopalong Cassidy: Silent Conflict *'48*
Hopalong Cassidy: Sinister Journey *'48*
Hopalong Cassidy: The Dead Don't Dream *'48*
Hopalong Cassidy: Hoppy's Holiday *'47*
Hopalong Cassidy: The Marauders *'47*
Hopalong Cassidy: Unexpected Guest *'47*
Hopalong Cassidy: The Devil's Playground *'46*
Mystery Man *'44*
Texas Masquerade *'44*
Border Patrol *'43*
Colt Comrades *'43*
False Colors *'43*
Hopalong Cassidy: Riders of the Deadline *'43*
Hoppy Serves a Writ *'43*
Leather Burners *'43*
Lost Canyon *'43*
Along the Sundown Trail *'42*
Prairie Pals *'42*
Tumbleweed Trail *'42*
Border Vigilantes *'41*
Doomed Caravan *'41*
In Old Colorado *'41*
Outlaws of the Desert *'41*
Riders of the Timberline *'41*
Twilight on the Trail *'41*
Santa Fe Marshal *'40*
The Showdown *'40*
Hopalong Cassidy: Renegade Trail *'39*
Law of the Pampas *'39*
Renegade Trail *'39*
The Frontiersmen *'38*
Borderland *'37*
Rustler's Valley *'37*
Federal Agent *'36*
Hopalong Cassidy Returns *'36*
Three on the Trail *'36*
Go-Get-'Em-Haines *'35*
Hopalong Cassidy *'35*
Racing Luck *'35*
Lucky Devils *'33*
Men of America *'32*
Midnight Warning *'32*
Gun Smoke *'31*
Painted Desert *'31*
Suicide Fleet *'31*
The Flying Fool *'29*
High Voltage *'29*
His First Command *'29*
The Leatherneck *'28*
Power *'28*
Dress Parade *'27*
King of Kings *'27*
Yankee Clipper *'27*
The Road to Yesterday *'25*

William "Stage" Boyd (1889-1935)
The Lost City *'34*
Laughing at Life *'33*
Oliver Twist *'33*
State's Attorney *'31*

Sally Boyden (1965-)
Little Dragons *'80*
Barnaby and Me *'77*

Charles Boyer (1897-1978)
A Matter of Time *'76*
Stavisky *'74*
The Hot Line *'69*
The Madwoman of Chaillot *'69*
Barefoot in the Park *'67*
Casino Royale *'67*
How to Steal a Million *'66*
Is Paris Burning? *'66*
Adorable Julia *'62*
The Four Horsemen of the Apocalypse *'62*
Fanny *'61*
The Buccaneer *'58*
Une Parisienne *'58*
Around the World in 80 Days *'56*
What a Woman! *'56*
The Cobweb *'55*
Nana *'55*
The Earrings of Madame De... *'54*
First Legion *'51*
Arch of Triumph *'48*
Gaslight *'44*
Heart of a Nation *'43 (N)*
Together Again *'43*
Tales of Manhattan *'42*
Back Street *'41*
All This and Heaven Too *'40*
Love Affair *'39*
Algiers *'38*
Conquest *'37*
History Is Made at Night *'37*
The Garden of Allah *'36*
Mayerling *'36*
Break of Hearts *'35*
Liliom *'35*
Red Headed Woman *'32*

Christopher Boyer (1960-)
Levitation *'97*
Uninvited *'93*

Katy Boyer
White Dwarf *'95*
Tapeheads *'89*
Trapped *'89*
Long Gone *'87*

Miriam Boyer (1948-)
Un Coeur en Hiver *'93*
Tous les Matins du Monde *'92*
Window Shopping *'86*
Jonah Who Will Be 25 in the Year 2000 *'76*

William Boyett (1927-2004)
Girls in Prison *'94*
The Hidden *'87*
Sam Whiskey *'69*

Sarain Boylan
Freezer Burn: The Invasion of Laxdale *'08*
Bon Cop Bad Cop *'06*
Posers *'02*

Lara Flynn Boyle (1971-)
Baby on Board *'08*
Life is Hot in Cracktown *'08*
Land of the Blind *'06*
Men in Black 2 *'02*
Chain of Fools *'00*
Dying to Get Rich *'98*
Happiness *'98*
Red Meat *'98*
Afterglow *'97*
Cafe Society *'97*
Since You've Been Gone *'97*
The Big Squeeze *'96*
Farmer & Chase *'96*
Baby's Day Out *'94*
Jacob *'94*
Past Tense *'94*
The Road to Wellville *'94*
Threesome *'94*
Equinox *'93*
Red Rock West *'93*
The Temp *'93*
Wayne's World *'92*
Where the Day Takes You *'92*
The Dark Backward *'91*
Eye of the Storm *'91*
Mobsters *'91*
May Wine *'90*
The Rookie *'90*
Dead Poets Society *'89*
How I Got into College *'89*
The Preppie Murder *'89*
Poltergeist 3 *'88*

Lisa Boyle (1968-)
The Last Marshal *'99*
Intimate Deception *'96*
Lost Highway *'96*
Friend of the Family *'95*
I Like to Play Games *'95*

Peter Boyle (1933-2006)
All Roads Lead Home *'08*
The Santa Clause 3: The Escape Clause *'06*
Scooby-Doo 2: Monsters Unleashed *'04*
The Adventures of Pluto Nash *'02*
Master Spy: The Robert Hanssen Story *'02*
Monster's Ball *'01*
Dr. Dolittle *'98*

In the Lake of the Woods '96
That Darn Cat '96
Born to Be Wild '95
Bulletproof Heart '95
Sweet Evil '95
While You Were Sleeping '95
The Shadow '94
The Surgeon '94
Urban Crossfire '94
Nervous Ticks '93
Royce '93
Taking the Heat '93
Honeymoon in Vegas '92
Malcolm X '92
Solar Crisis '92
Men of Respect '91
Tragedy of Flight 103: The Inside Story '91
Kickboxer 2: The Road Back '90
The Dream Team '89
Disaster at Silo 7 '88
Red Heat '88
Speed Zone '88
Conspiracy: The Trial of the Chicago Eight '87
Echoes in the Darkness '87
Surrender '87
Walker '87
Turk 182! '85
Johnny Dangerously '84
Yellowbeard '83
Hammett '82
Outland '81
In God We Trust '80
Where the Buffalo Roam '80
Beyond the Poseidon Adventure '79
From Here to Eternity '79
Hardcore '79
Brink's Job '78
F.I.S.T. '78
Swashbuckler '76
Taxi Driver '76
Ghost in the Noonday Sun '74
Young Frankenstein '74
Slither '73
Steelyard Blues '73
The Candidate '72
Joe '70
Medium Cool '69

Max Bozyk (1899-1970)

The Jolly Paupers '38
Mamele '38
Yidl Mitn Fidl '36

Marcel Bozzuffi (1929-88)

La Cage aux Folles 2 '81
Le Gitan '75
Images '72
The French Connection '71
Carbon Copy '69
Z '69
Le Deuxieme Souffle '66

Teda Bracci

The Big Bird Cage '72
C.C. & Company '70

Elizabeth Bracco (1959-)

13 Moons '02
Analyze This '98
The Imposters '98
Tree's Lounge '96
Money for Nothing '93
In the Soup '92
Mystery Train '89
Sons '89

Lorraine Bracco (1954-)

Snowglobe '07
Riding in Cars with Boys '01
Tangled '01
The Basketball Diaries '95
Hackers '95
Being Human '94
Even Cowgirls Get the Blues '94
Getting Gotti '94
Scam '93
Medicine Man '92
Radio Flyer '92
Traces of Red '92
Switch '91
Talent for the Game '91
Goodfellas '90
The Dream Team '89
Sing '89
The Pick-Up Artist '87
Someone to Watch Over Me '87
Camorra: The Naples Connection '85

Eddie Bracken (1920-2002)

Home Alone 2: Lost in New York '92
National Lampoon's Vacation '83
Shinbone Alley '70 (V)
We're Not Married '52
Summer Stock '50
Hail the Conquering Hero '44
Miracle of Morgan's Creek '44
Star Spangled Rhythm '42
Young and Willing '42
Caught in the Draft '41
Too Many Girls '40

Sidney Bracy (1877-1942)

Tangled Destinies '32
The Cameraman '28

Kitty Bradbury (1875-1945)

Our Hospitality '23
The Immigrant '17

Lane Bradbury

The Ultimate Warrior '75
Maybe I'll Come Home in the Spring '71
Maybe I'll Be Home in the Spring '70

Johanna Braddy

The Grudge 3 '09
Hurt '09

Kim Braden (1949-)

Bloodsuckers from Outer Space '83
That'll Be the Day '73

Greg Bradford (1955-)

Lovelines '84
Zapped! '82

Jesse Bradford (1979-)

I Hope They Serve Beer in Hell '09
Table for Three '09
My Sassy Girl '08
W. '08
Flags of Our Fathers '06
Happy Endings '05
Eulogy '04
Heights '04
Clockstoppers '02
Swimfan '02
Bring It On '00
Cherry Falls '00
Speedway Junky '99
A Soldier's Daughter Never Cries '98
William Shakespeare's Romeo and Juliet '96
Hackers '95
Far from Home: The Adventures of Yellow Dog '94
King of the Hill '93
Presumed Innocent '90

Lane Bradford (1922-73)

Gun Glory '57
Ride Clear of Diablo '54
The Fighting Redhead '50
The Invisible Monster '50
Missourians '50
Bandit King of Texas '49
Far Frontier '48
The Hawk of Powder River '48

Richard Bradford (1937-)

The Lost City '05
The Man from Elysian Fields '01
Just the Ticket '98
Elmore Leonard's Gold Coast '97
Hoodlum '96
Indictment: The McMartin Trial '95
The Crossing Guard '94
Arctic Blue '93
Cold Heaven '92
Ambition '91
Servants of Twilight '91
Internal Affairs '90
The Chinatown Murders: Man against the Mob '89
The Heart of Dixie '89
Little Nikita '88
The Milagro Beanfield War '88
Permanent Record '88
Sunset '88
The Untouchables '87
Badge of the Assassin '85
Legend of Billie Jean '85
Mean Season '85
The Trip to Bountiful '85
Running Hot '83
A Rumor of War '80
More American Graffiti '79
Goin' South '78

Cathleen Bradley

About Adam '00
American Women '00

Charlotte Bradley

Speed Dating '07
The Boys and Girl From County Clare '03
About Adam '00

Christopher Bradley (1961-)

Sundown: The Vampire in Retreat '08
Leather Jacket Love Story '98
Killer Instinct '92

David Bradley

Total Reality '97
White Cargo '96
Exit '95
Hard Justice '95
Outside the Law '95
Cyborg Soldier '94
Blood Warriors '93
Cyborg Cop '93
American Samurai '92
American Ninja 4: The Annihilation '91
Lower Level '91
American Ninja 3: Blood Hunt '89

David Bradley (1942-)

Harry Potter and the Half-Blood Prince '09
The Color of Magic '08
Harry Potter and the Order of the Phoenix '07
Harry Potter and the Goblet of Fire '05
Red Mercury '05
Exorcist: The Beginning '04
Harry Potter and the Chamber of Secrets '02
The Intended '02
This Is Not a Love Song '02
The Way We Live Now '02
Gabriel & Me '01
Harry Potter and the Sorcerer's Stone '01
The King Is Alive '00
Vanity Fair '99
Our Mutual Friend '98
Reckless: The Sequel '98
Reckless '97
Catherine Cookson's The Moth '96
Kiss and Tell '96
Martin Chuzzlewit '94
The Buddha of Suburbia '92

Doug Bradley (1954-)

Clive Barker's Book of Blood '08
Pumpkinhead 3: Ashes to Ashes '06
Hellraiser: Deader '05
Hellraiser: Hellworld '05
Hellraiser: Hellseeker '02
Hellraiser 5: Inferno '00
Killer Tongue '96
Hellraiser 4: Bloodline '95
Proteus '95
Hellraiser 3: Hell on Earth '92
Hellbound: Hellraiser 2 '88
Hellraiser '87

Grace Bradley (1913-)

The Invisible Killer '40
Larceny On the Air '37

Kellee Bradley

Frayed '07
Fortress of Amerikka '89

Leslie Bradley (1907-74)

Teenage Caveman '58
The Conqueror '56
Lady Godiva '55
Man in the Attic '53

Olympe Bradna (1920-)

The Night of Nights '39
Souls at Sea '37

Carl Bradshaw

Third World Cop '99
The Lunatic '92
The Harder They Come '72

Cathryn Bradshaw

The Mother '03
Bert Rigby, You're a Fool '89
Oranges Are Not the Only Fruit '89

Terry Bradshaw (1948-)

Failure to Launch '06
Robots '05 (V)
Smokey and the Bandit 2 '80

Alice Brady (1892-1939)

Young Mr. Lincoln '39
Joy of Living '38
Call It a Day '37
In Old Chicago '37
100 Men and a Girl '37
Go West, Young Man '36
My Man Godfrey '36
Three Smart Girls '36
Gold Diggers of 1935 '35
The Gay Divorcee '34
Her Silent Sacrifice '18

Orla Brady (1961-)

Wallander: Firewall '08
How About You '07
Jesse Stone: Death in Paradise '06
The Debt '03
A Love Divided '01
The Luzhin Defence '00
The Magical Legend of the Leprechauns '99
Wuthering Heights '98

Pat Brady (1914-72)

Corky of Gasoline Alley '51
Gasoline Alley '51
Bells of Coronado '50
Trigger, Jr. '50
Twilight in the Sierras '50
Down Dakota Way '49
The Golden Stallion '49
Song of Texas '43
Texas Legionnaires '43
Call of the Canyon '42
Sunset on the Desert '42

Scott Brady (1924-85)

Gremlins '84
Strange Behavior '81
The China Syndrome '79
When Every Day Was the Fourth of July '78
Bonnie's Kids '73
Loners '72
Cain's Cutthroats '71
Dollars '71
Hell's Bloody Devils '70
Gun Riders '69
Satan's Sadists '69
Arizona Bushwackers '67
Journey to the Center of Time '67
Castle of Evil '66
Operation Bikini '63
The Restless Breed '58
Storm Rider '57
Mohawk '56
The Maverick Queen '55
They Were So Young '55
Party Girls for Sale '54
Johnny Guitar '53
White Fire '53
Bloodhounds of Broadway '52
Montana Belle '52
Yankee Buccaneer '52
Port of New York '49
He Walked by Night '48

Wayne Brady (1972-)

Crossover '06
Roll Bounce '05
Clifford's Really Big Movie '04 (V)
Gepetto '00

Eric (Hans Gudegast) Braeden (1943-)

The Man Who Came Back '08
Meet the Deedles '98
The Ambulance '90
Happily Ever After '82
Aliens Are Coming '80
The Power Within '79
The Adultress '77
Death Scream '75
The Ultimate Thrill '74
Lady Ice '73
Escape from the Planet of the Apes '71
Colossus: The Forbin Project '70
Dayton's Devils '68

Zach Braff (1975-)

The Ex '07
The Last Kiss '06
Chicken Little '05 (V)
Garden State '04
The Broken Hearts Club '00
Manhattan Murder Mystery '93

Alice Braga (1983-)

Predators '10
Repo Men '10
Crossing Over '09
Blindness '08
Redbelt '08
I Am Legend '07
Journey to the End of the Night '06

Sonia Braga (1951-)

Bordertown '06
The Hottest State '06
Marilyn Hotchkiss' Ballroom Dancing & Charm School '06
Testosterone '03
Empire '02
Angel Eyes '01
Perfume '01
From Dusk Till Dawn 3: The Hangman's Daughter '99
Tieta of Agreste '96
Larry McMurtry's Streets of Laredo '95
Roosters '95
The Burning Season '94
Two Deaths '94
The Last Prostitute '91
The Rookie '90
The Milagro Beanfield War '88
Moon over Parador '88
The Man Who Broke 1,000 Chains '87
Kiss of the Spider Woman '85
Gabriela '84
I Love You '81
Dona Flor and Her Two Husbands '78
Lady on the Bus '78

Richard Brake

Doom '05
Subterfuge '98

Rachida Brakni (1977-)

Enough! '06
Chaos '01

Wilfrid Brambell (1912-85)

Sword of the Valiant '83
The Adventures of Picasso '80
The Conqueror Worm '68
A Hard Day's Night '64
The 39 Steps '35

Virgile Bramly

Four Last Songs '06
Manderlay '05

Francisco (Frank) Brana (1934-)

Cthulhu Mansion '91
Street Warriors '77
Kilma, Queen of the Amazons '75
Crypt of the Living Dead '73
Graveyard of Horror '71
Emerald of Artama '67

Kenneth Branagh (1960-)

Pirate Radio '09
Valkyrie '08
Wallander: Firewall '08
Wallander: One Step Behind '08
Wallander: Sidetracked '08
Harry Potter and the Chamber of Secrets '02
Rabbit-Proof Fence '02
Shackleton '02
Conspiracy '01
How to Kill Your Neighbor's Dog '01
Love's Labour's Lost '00
The Road to El Dorado '00 (V)
Wild Wild West '99
Celebrity '98
The Theory of Flight '98
The Gingerbread Man '97
The Proposition '97
Hamlet '96
Looking for Richard '96
Othello '95
Mary Shelley's Frankenstein '94
Much Ado about Nothing '93
Swing Kids '93
Peter's Friends '92
Dead Again '91
Henry V '89
Look Back in Anger '89
High Season '88
Fortunes of War '87
The Lady's Not for Burning '87
A Month in the Country '87
Coming Through '85
To the Lighthouse '83

Rustam Branaman

Love to Kill '97
Headless Body in Topless Bar '96
Terrified '94
Hard Ticket to Hawaii '87

Lillo Brancato (1976-)

In the Shadows '01
'R Xmas '01
Blue Moon '00
Enemy of the State '98
Sticks '98
Provocateur '96
Crimson Tide '95
Renaissance Man '94
A Bronx Tale '93

Christopher Brand

Dracula: The Dark Prince '01
Voyage to the Prehistoric Planet '65

Neville Brand (1921-92)

Evils of the Night '85
The Return '80
The Ninth Configuration '79
The Seekers '79
Hi-Riders '77
Eaten Alive '76
The Longest Drive '76
Psychic Killer '75
The Barbary Coast '74
Death Stalk '74

Valerie Breiman
Sisters '97
Tale of Two Sisters '89

Hana Brejchova (1940-)
Loves of a Blonde '65
Fabulous Adventures of Baron Munchausen '61
The Original Fabulous Adventures of Baron Munchausen '61

Jacques Brel (1929-78)
Pain in the A— '77
Franz '72
Les Assassins de L'Ordre '71

Lucille Bremer (1917-96)
Behind Locked Doors '48
Human Gorilla '48
Till the Clouds Roll By '46
Ziegfeld Follies '46
Yolanda and the Thief '45
Meet Me in St. Louis '44

Richard Bremmer (1953-)
Half Past Dead '02
Just Visiting '01
Dostoevsky's Crime and Punishment '99
The 13th Warrior '99

Ewen Bremner (1971-)
Fool's Gold '08
Death at a Funeral '07
Mister Foe '07
Match Point '05
Alien vs. Predator '04
Around the World in 80 Days '04
The Reckoning '03
The Rundown '03
16 Years of Alcohol '03
Black Hawk Down '01
Pearl Harbor '01
Snatch '00
Julien Donkey-boy '99
The Acid House '98
Trainspotting '95
Naked '93

El Brendel (1890-1964)
The Beautiful Blonde from Bashful Bend '49
I'm from Arkansas '44
If I Had My Way '40
Happy Landing '38
The Holy Terror '37
Women of All Nations '31
Big Trail '30
Wings '27

Julia Brendler (1975-)
Deeply '99
Moondance '95

Nicholas Brendon (1971-)
Fire Serpent '07
Unholy '07
Survival Island '02
Psycho Beach Party '00

Shirly Brener (1974-)
Streets of Blood '09
Righteous Kill '08
War, Inc. '08

Brid Brennan (1955-)
Felicia's Journey '99
Dancing at Lughnasa '98
Trojan Eddie '96
Cracker: Brotherly Love '95
Saint-Ex: The Story of the Storyteller '95
Four Days in July '85

Eileen Brennan (1935-)
The Hollow '04
Jeepers Creepers '01
Changing Habits '96
If These Walls Could Talk '96
Reckless '95
Murder So Sweet '93
I Don't Buy Kisses Anymore '92
Texasville '90
White Palace '90
Stella '89
The New Adventures of Pippi Longstocking '88
Rented Lips '88
Sticky Fingers '88
Blood Vows: The Story of a Mafia Wife '87
Babes in Toyland '86
Clue '85
Fourth Wise Man '85
The Funny Farm '82
Pandemonium '82
Private Benjamin '80
My Old Man '79
The Cheap Detective '78
FM '78
The Death of Richie '76
Great Smokey Roadblock '76
Murder by Death '76
My Father's House '75
Daisy Miller '74
Scarecrow '73
The Sting '73
Playmates '72
The Last Picture Show '71
Divorce American Style '67

Michael Brennan (1912-82)
Fright '71
No Trace '50

Stephen Brennan
The Boys and Girl From County Clare '03
St. Patrick: The Irish Legend '00
Eat the Peach '86

Walter Brennan (1894-1974)
Smoke in the Wind '75
Home for the Holidays '72
Over the Hill Gang '69
Support Your Local Sheriff '69
The One and Only, Genuine, Original Family Band '68
The Gnome-Mobile '67
Who's Minding the Mint? '67
The Oscar '66
Those Calloways '65
How the West Was Won '63
Rio Bravo '59
Tammy and the Bachelor '57
Glory '56
Goodbye, My Lady '56
At Gunpoint '55
Far Country '55
Bad Day at Black Rock '54
Along the Great Divide '51
Best of the Badmen '50
The Showdown '50
Ticket to Tomahawk '50
The Green Promise '49
Task Force '49
Blood on the Moon '48
Red River '48
My Darling Clementine '46
A Stolen Life '46
Dakota '45
The Princess and the Pirate '44
To Have & Have Not '44
The North Star '43
Hangmen Also Die '42
The Pride of the Yankees '42
Meet John Doe '41
Nice Girl? '41
Sergeant York '41
Northwest Passage '40
The Westerner '40
Stanley and Livingstone '39
The Story of Vernon and Irene Castle '39
They Shall Have Music '39
The Adventures of Tom Sawyer '38
The Cowboy and the Lady '38
The Texans '38
Come and Get It '36
Fury '36
The Moon's Our Home '36
Prescott Kid '36
These Three '36
Barbary Coast '35
The Bride of Frankenstein '35
The Invisible Man '33
Man of Action '33
Phantom of the Air '33
Texas Cyclone '32
Two-Fisted Law '32

Amy Brenneman (1964-)
Mother and Child '09
Downloading Nancy '08
88 Minutes '08
The Jane Austen Book Club '07
Nine Lives '05
Off the Map '03
Things You Can Tell Just by Looking at Her '00
The Suburbans '99
Your Friends & Neighbors '98
Nevada '97
Daylight '96
Fear '96
Casper '95
Heat '95
Bye Bye, Love '94

Dori Brenner (1946-2000)
Infinity '96
Silent Victim '92
For the Boys '91
Baby Boom '87
Sex and the Single Parent '82
Altered States '80
Summer Wishes, Winter Dreams '73

Eve Brenner
The Great Mouse Detective '86 (V)
Torment '85

Lisa Brenner (1974-)
The Pledge '08
The Diary of Ellen Rimbauer '03
Finding Home '03

Eve Brent (1930-)
The Green Mile '99
Brainwaves '82
Fade to Black '80
Stakeout '62
Tarzan and the Trappers '58
Tarzan's Fight for Life '58
Forty Guns '57
Gun Girls '56

Evelyn Brent (1899-1975)
The Payoff '43
The Seventh Victim '43
Spy Train '43
Holt of the Secret Service '42
Robot Pilot '41
Daughter of the Tong '39
Panama Lady '39
Law West of Tombstone '38
Hopalong Cassidy Returns '36
The President's Mystery '36
Song of the Trail '36
The Crusader '32
The Silver Horde '30
Last Command '28
Underworld '27
Love 'Em and Leave 'Em '26
Trapped by the Mormons '22

George Brent (1904-79)
Born Again '78
FBI Girl '52
Man Bait '52
Montana Belle '52
The Kid From Cleveland '49
Luxury Liner '48
Christmas Eve '47
Out of the Blue '47
My Reputation '46
The Spiral Staircase '46
Tomorrow Is Forever '46
Experiment Perilous '45
In This Our Life '42
Silver Queen '42
Twin Beds '42
The Great Lie '41
International Lady '41
The Fighting 69th '40
Dark Victory '39
The Old Maid '39
The Rains Came '39
Jezebel '38
In Person '35
The Painted Veil '34
Baby Face '33
Female '33
42nd Street '33
The Purchase Price '32
They Call It Sin '32
Lightning Warrior '31

Linda Brent
Death Valley Rangers '44
Below the Border '42

Romney Brent (1902-76)
The Sign of Zorro '60
The Virgin Queen '55
Adventures of Don Juan '49
Dreaming Lips '37
Under the Red Robe '36

Roy Brent
Lightning Raiders '45
The Drifter '44

Timothy Brent
See Giancarlo Prete

Amy Brentano
Blood Sisters '86
Breeders '86

Edmund Breon (1882-1951)
Forever Amber '47
Dressed to Kill '46
Casanova Brown '44
Gaslight '44
The White Cliffs of Dover '44
Woman in the Window '44
The Scarlet Pimpernel '34

Bobbie Bresee (1950-)
Pre-Madonnas: Rebels Without a Clue '95
Evil Spawn '87
Surf Nazis Must Die '87
Ghoulies '84
Mausoleum '83

Abigail Breslin (1996-)
My Sister's Keeper '09
Zombieland '09
Definitely, Maybe '08
Kit Kittredge: An American Girl '08
Nim's Island '08
No Reservations '07
The Ultimate Gift '07
Air Bud 6: Air Buddies '06 (V)
Little Miss Sunshine '06
The Family Plan '05
Keane '04
Raising Helen '04
Signs '02

Spencer Breslin (1992-)
The Happening '08
Harold '08
Air Bud 6: Air Buddies '06 (V)
The Santa Clause 3: The Escape Clause '06
The Shaggy Dog '06
Zoom '06
Raising Helen '04
Dr. Seuss' The Cat in the Hat '03
Return to Never Land '02 (V)
The Santa Clause 2 '02
Disney's The Kid '00

Felix Bressart (1895-1949)
Portrait of Jennie '48
A Song Is Born '48
Without Love '45
Greenwich Village '44
The Seventh Cross '44
Crossroads '42
Iceland '42
To Be or Not to Be '42
Blossoms in the Dust '41
Ziegfeld Girl '41
Bitter Sweet '40
Comrade X '40
Edison the Man '40
The Shop Around the Corner '40
Ninotchka '39

Bernard Bresslaw (1934-93)
Carry On Abroad '72
Carry On Matron '72
Carry On Camping '71
Carry On Up the Jungle '70
Carry On Up the Khyber '68
Carry On Cowboy '66
Morgan: A Suitable Case for Treatment '66

Martin Brest (1951-)
Spies Like Us '85
Fast Times at Ridgemont High '82

Geoff Breton
The Diary of Anne Frank '08
The Old Curiosity Shop '07

Jean Bretonniere (1924-2001)
Mam'zelle Pigalle '58
That Naughty Girl '58
The Green Glove '52

Danielle Brett
Road Rage '01
Jill the Ripper '00
Rated X '00

Jeremy Brett (1935-95)
Moll Flanders '96
Shameless '94
Florence Nightingale '85
The Medusa Touch '78
Haunted: The Ferryman '74
One Deadly Owner '74
The Merchant of Venice '73
My Fair Lady '64
The Very Edge '63
War and Peace '56

Jim Breuer (1967-)
Once in the Life '00
Titan A.E. '00 (V)
Dick '99
Half-Baked '97

Marita Breuer (1953-)
The Princess and the Warrior '00
Heimat 1 '84

Betty Brewer
Juke Girl '42
The Roundup '41

Jonathan Brewer
Journey to the Center of the Earth '08
Apocalypto '06

Juliette Brewer
Balto '95 (V)
The Little Rascals '94

Diane Brewster (1931-91)
King of the Wild Stallions '59
Torpedo Run '58
Black Patch '57
Courage of Black Beauty '57
The Invisible Boy '57

Jordana Brewster (1980-)
Fast & Furious '09
Annapolis '06
The Texas Chainsaw Massacre: The Beginning '06
Nearing Grace '05
D.E.B.S. '04
The Fast and the Furious '01
Invisible Circus '00
The '60s '99
The Faculty '98

Paget Brewster (1969-)
Sublime '07
The Big Bad Swim '06
Cyxork 7 '06
A Perfect Day '06
Unaccompanied Minors '06
Man of the House '05
Now You Know '02
The Adventures of Rocky & Bullwinkle '00
The Specials '00
Let's Talk About Sex '98

Maia Brewton (1977-)
Adventures in Babysitting '87
Back to the Future '85

Kevin Breznahan (1968-)
Winter's Bone '10
SLC Punk! '99
I Love Trouble '94
Alive '93

Tom Breznahan (1965-)
Terrified '94
Ski School '91
The Brain '88
Twice Dead '88

Jean-Claude Brialy (1933-2007)
People '04
The Count of Monte Cristo '99
Beaumarchais the Scoundrel '96
The Monster '96
Portraits Chinois '96
Son of Gascogne '95
Queen Margot '94
No Fear, No Die '90
La Nuit de Varennes '82
Robert et Robert '78
Barocco '76
Catherine & Co. '76
L'Annee Sainte '76
The Judge and the Assassin '75
Phantom of Liberty '74
Claire's Knee '71
The Bride Wore Black '68
Manon '68
The King of Hearts '66
Tonio Kroger '65
Circle of Love '64
The Burning Court '62
Cleo from 5 to 7 '61
Paris Belongs to Us '60
A Woman Is a Woman '60
The Cousins '59
The 400 Blows '59
Le Beau Serge '58

David Brian (1914-93)
Confessions of Tom Harris '72
Castle of Evil '66
Pocketful of Miracles '61
The High and the Mighty '54
Ambush at Tomahawk Gap '53
Million Dollar Mermaid '52
Springfield Rifle '52
This Woman Is Dangerous '52
The Damned Don't Cry '50
Beyond the Forest '49
Flamingo Road '49
Intruder in the Dust '49

Mary Brian (1908-2002)
Amazing Adventure '37
Charlie Chan in Paris '35
Monte Carlo Nights '34
Blessed Event '32
Gun Smoke '31
The Light of Western Stars '30
Running Wild '27
Behind the Front '26
Peter Pan '24

Shane Briant (1946-)
Twisted '96
Tunnel Vision '95
Till There Was You '91
Darlings of the Gods '90
Wrangler '88
Cassandra '87
The Lighthorsemen '87
Moving Targets '87
True Colors '87

Agatha Christie's Murder is Easy '82
Lady Chatterley's Lover '81
The Flame Is Love '79
Captain Kronos: Vampire Hunter '74
Dressed for Death '74
Frankenstein and the Monster from Hell '74
Picture of Dorian Gray '74
Demons of the Mind '72

Fanny Brice (1891-1951)
Ziegfeld Follies '46
Everybody Sing '38
The Great Ziegfeld '36
Be Yourself '30

Pierre Brice (1929-)
Lady of the Evening '75
A Place Called Glory '66
Apache's Last Battle '64
The Bacchantes '63
Sweet Ecstasy '62
Mill of the Stone Women '60

Ron Brice
Mulberry Street '06
Ripe '97
Tar '97
A Horse for Danny '95
Fresh '94
Little Odessa '94
Fly by Night '93

Alexander Brickel
Palindromes '04
Satan's Little Helper '04

Beth Brickell (1941-)
Seducers '77
The Only Way Home '72

Alan Bridge (1891-1957)
Miracle of Morgan's Creek '44
Sullivan's Travels '41
Fast Bullets '36
Outlaw Rule '36
The Three Mesquiteers '36
Silent Valley '35
Sucker Money '34
Cheyenne Kid '33
Cowboy Counselor '33
The Lone Avenger '33
When a Man Rides Alone '33
Broadway to Cheyenne '32
The Forty-Niners '32
Man's Land '32
The Ridin' Fool '31

Beau Bridges (1941-)
Max Payne '08
Stargate: Continuum '08
Stargate: The Ark of Truth '08
Charlotte's Web '06
The Good German '06
I-See-You.Com '06
The Ballad of Jack and Rose '05
Smile '05
Out of the Ashes '03
Common Ground '00
Sordid Lives '00
Inherit the Wind '99
P.T. Barnum '99
White River '99
The Defenders: Taking the First '98
Meeting Daddy '98
The Defenders: Payback '97
RocketMan '97
The Second Civil War '97
Hidden in America '96
Kissinger and Nixon '96
Losing Chase '96
Nightjohn '96
The Outer Limits: Sandkings '95
Married to It '93
The Positively True Adventures of the Alleged Texas Cheerleader-Murdering Mom '93
Sidekicks '93
Wildflower '91
Without Warning: The James Brady Story '91
Daddy's Dyin'... Who's Got the Will? '90
Women & Men: Stories of Seduction '90
The Fabulous Baker Boys '89
The Iron Triangle '89
Signs of Life '89
The Wizard '89
Seven Hours to Judgment '88
The Killing Time '87
The Wild Pair '87
Outrage! '86
Alice in Wonderland '85
The Hotel New Hampshire '84
The Red Light Sting '84
Heart Like a Wheel '83
Silver Dream Racer '83
Love Child '82
Honky Tonk Freeway '81
Night Crossing '81
The Fifth Musketeer '79
Norma Rae '79
The Runner Stumbles '79
The Four Feathers '78
President's Mistress '78
Greased Lightning '77
Mutual Respect '77
One Summer Love '76
Swashbuckler '76
Two Minute Warning '76
The Other Side of the Mountain '75
The Stranger Who Looks Like Me '74
The Man Without a Country '73
Hammersmith Is Out '72
For Love of Ivy '68
The Incident '67
Village of the Giants '65
The Red Pony '49

Chris Bridges
See Ludacris
Max Payne '08
RocknRolla '08
Fred Claus '07

Jeff Bridges (1949-)
Crazy Heart '09
The Men Who Stare at Goats '09
The Open Road '09
How to Lose Friends & Alienate People '08
Iron Man '08
Surf's Up '07 (V)
Stick It '06
The Moguls '05
Tideland '05
The Door in the Floor '04
Lost in La Mancha '03 (N)
Masked and Anonymous '03
Seabiscuit '03
K-PAX '01
The Contender '00
Arlington Road '99
The Muse '99
Simpatico '99
The Big Lebowski '97
Hidden in America '96
The Mirror Has Two Faces '96
White Squall '96
Wild Bill '95
Blown Away '94
Fearless '93
The Vanishing '93
American Heart '92
The Fisher King '91
Texasville '90
Cold Feet '89
The Fabulous Baker Boys '89
See You in the Morning '89
Tucker: The Man and His Dream '88
Nadine '87
The Morning After '86
8 Million Ways to Die '85
The Jagged Edge '85
Against All Odds '84
Starman '84
Kiss Me Goodbye '82
The Last Unicorn '82 (V)
Rapunzel '82
Tron '82
Cutter's Way '81
Heaven's Gate '81
Winter Kills '79
King Kong '76
Stay Hungry '76
Hearts of the West '75
Rancho Deluxe '75
Thunderbolt & Lightfoot '74
The Iceman Cometh '73
The Last American Hero '73
Bad Company '72
Fat City '72
The Last Picture Show '71
Yin & Yang of Mr. Go '71
Silent Night, Lonely Night '69

Jordan Bridges (1973-)
Love Finds a Home '09
Love Takes Wing '09
The Family Plan '05
Mona Lisa Smile '03
Happy Campers '01
Frequency '00
P.T. Barnum '99

Krista Bridges
Dr. Jekyll and Mr. Hyde '08
George A. Romero's Land of the Dead '05
Narc '02

Lloyd Bridges (1913-98)
Mafia! '98
Meeting Daddy '98
The Outer Limits: Sandkings '95
Blown Away '94
Hot Shots! Part Deux '93
Devlin '92
Honey, I Blew Up the Kid '92
Hot Shots! '91
Joe Versus the Volcano '90
The Queen of Mean '90
Cousins '89
Winter People '89
Tucker: The Man and His Dream '88
The Wild Pair '87
Dress Gray '86
North and South Book 2 '86
Weekend Warriors '86
Alice in Wonderland '85
George Washington '84
Loving '84
The Grace Kelly Story '83
Airplane 2: The Sequel '82
The Blue and the Gray '82
Airplane! '80
Bear Island '80
East of Eden '80
The Great Wallendas '78
Mission Galactica: The Cylon Attack '78
Force of Evil '77
Mutual Respect '77
Roots '77
Running Wild '73
Haunts of the Very Rich '72
The Tattered Web '71
The Happy Ending '69
Silent Night, Lonely Night '69
Daring Game '68
Around the World Under the Sea '65
The Goddess '58
The Rainmaker '56
Wetbacks '56
Apache Woman '55
Big Deadly Game '54
The Limping Man '53
Tall Texan '53
High Noon '52
Last of the Comanches '52
Little Big Horn '51
Rocketship X-M '50
Try and Get Me '50
The White Tower '50
Home of the Brave '49
Trapped '49
The Smallest Show on Earth '48
Ramrod '47
Abilene Town '46
Canyon Passage '46
A Walk in the Sun '46
Strange Confession '45
Louisiana Hayride '44
The Master Race '44
The Heat's On '43
Sahara '43
Blondie Goes to College '42
Harmon of Michigan '41

Spencir Bridges (1998-)
Daddy Day Camp '07
The Reading Room '05

Todd Bridges (1965-)
The Damned '06
San Franpsycho '06
I Got Five on It '05
Inhumanity '00
Homeboys '92
She's Out of Control '89
Twice Dead '88
Roots '77

Richard Briers (1934-)
Peter Pan '03
Unconditional Love '03
Love's Labour's Lost '00
Spice World: The Movie '97
Hamlet '96
A Midwinter's Tale '95
Mary Shelley's Frankenstein '94
Much Ado about Nothing '93
Peter's Friends '92
A Chorus of Disapproval '89
Henry V '89
The Norman Conquests, Part 1: Table Manners '78
The Norman Conquests, Part 2: Living Together '78
The Norman Conquests, Part 3: Round and Round the Garden '78
Watership Down '78 (V)
Rentadick '72
Fathom '67
A Matter of WHO '62

Bernard Brieux
Petit Con '84
The Rascals '81

Johnny Briggs (1935-)
Au Pair Girls '72
The Leather Boys '63

Julie Briggs
Brotherhood 2: The Young Warlocks '01
Bowery Buckaroos '47

Cameron Bright (1993-)
The Twilight Saga: Eclipse '10
An American Affair '09
The Twilight Saga: New Moon '09
Normal '07
Running Scared '06
Thank You for Smoking '06
Ultraviolet '06
X-Men: The Last Stand '06
Birth '04
Godsend '04

Richard Bright (1937-2006)
Witness to the Mob '98
Beautiful Girls '96
The Ref '93
Who's the Man? '93
The Ambulance '90
The Godfather, Part 3 '90
Red Heat '88
Once Upon a Time in America '84
Vigilante '83
Idolmaker '80
Marathon Man '76
Rancho Deluxe '75
The Godfather '72
Panic in Needle Park '71
Odds Against Tomorrow '59

Susie Bright (1958-)
Bound '96
Virgin Machine '88

Charlie Brill (1938-)
Bail Out '90
Bloodstone '88

Fran Brill (1946-)
What about Bob? '91
Old Enough '84
Look Back in Anger '80

Patti Brill (1923-63)
Hard-Boiled Mahoney '47
Girl Rush '44

Steven Brill (1962-)
The Mighty Ducks '92
sex, lies and videotape '89

Nick Brimble
Submerged '05
Seven Days to Live '01
Fortress 2: Re-Entry '99
Gone Fishin' '97
Ivanhoe '97
The One That Got Away '96
The Final Cut '95
Loch Ness '95
Robin Hood: Prince of Thieves '91
Frankenstein Unbound '90
S.O.S. Titanic '79

Cynthia Brimhall (1964-)
Fit to Kill '93
Hard Hunted '92
Hard Ticket to Hawaii '87

Wilford Brimley (1934-)
Brigham City '01
Crossfire Trail '01
Progeny '98
Summer of the Monkeys '98
In and Out '97
My Fellow Americans '96
The Good Old Boys '95
The Last of the Dogmen '95 (N)
Mutant Species '95
The Firm '93
Hard Target '93
Where the Red Fern Grows: Part 2 '92
Eternity '90
Thompson's Last Run '90
Gore Vidal's Billy the Kid '89
Cocoon: The Return '88
End of the Line '88
Act of Vengeance '86
American Justice '86
Cocoon '85
The Ewoks: Battle for Endor '85
Murder in Space '85
Remo Williams: The Adventure Begins '85
Country '84
Harry & Son '84
The Hotel New Hampshire '84
The Natural '84
The Stone Boy '84
High Road to China '83
Ten to Midnight '83
Tender Mercies '83
Tough Enough '83
Amber Waves '82
The Thing '82
Absence of Malice '81
Death Valley '81
Borderline '80
Rodeo Girl '80
Roughnecks '80
The China Syndrome '79
The Electric Horseman '79
True Grit '69

Michele Brin
Sexual Intent '94
Secret Games '92

Nancy Brinckman (1924-)
Detour to Danger '45
Mr. Muggs Rides Again '45

Adrian Brine (1936-)
Lily Was Here '89
Waterloo '71

Paul Brinegar (1918-95)
Wyatt Earp: Return to Tombstone '94
The Creature Wasn't Nice '81
Charro! '69
How to Make a Monster '58

Mark Bringleson (1957-)
Soldier '98
Dead Man '95
The Lawnmower Man '92

Christie Brinkley (1954-)
Vegas Vacation '96
National Lampoon's Vacation '83

John Brinkley
A Bucket of Blood '59
T-Bird Gang '59
Teenage Doll '57

Ritch Brinkley (1944-)
Breakdown '96
Cabin Boy '94
Silhouette '91

Bo Brinkman (1956-)
Gods and Generals '03
Gettysburg '93
Ice House '89

Charles Brinley (1880-1946)
The Crimson Trail '35
Moran of the Lady Letty '22

Bill Brinsfield
Warbirds '88
Slaughterhouse '87

Vera Briole
A Single Girl '96
Pigalle '95

Francoise Brion (1938-)
Dangerous Liaisons '03
Nelly et Monsieur Arnaud '95
Ladies' Man '62

Syd Brisbane
Dead Letter Office '98
Alien Visitor '95

David Brisbin
Goodbye, Lover '99
From the Earth to the Moon '98
Leaving Las Vegas '95
Forrest Gump '94
Kiss Daddy Goodnight '87

Brent Briscoe (1961-)
The Big Empty '04
Waking Up in Reno '02
Double Take '01
Driven '01
Madison '01
The Majestic '01
Mulholland Drive '01
Say It Isn't So '01
Beautiful '00
Another Day in Paradise '98
A Simple Plan '98
Sling Blade '96

Danielle Brisebois (1969-)
As Good As It Gets '97
Killcrazy '89
Big Bad Mama 2 '87
Mom, the Wolfman and Me '80
The Premonition '75

Virginia Brissac (1894-1979)
Phantom Lady '44
Black Friday '40

Carl Brisson (1893-1958)
Murder at the Vanities '34
The Manxman '29
The Ring '27

May Britt (1936-)
Haunts '77
Murder, Inc. '60
The Unfaithfuls '60
The Hunters '58
The Young Lions '58
War and Peace '56
There Goes Barder '54

Charlotte Brittain
Secret Society '00
Get Real '99

Morgan Brittany (1951-)
Sundown: The Vampire in Retreat '08
The Biggest Fan '02
Body Armor '96
Sundown '91
LBJ: The Early Years '88
The Prodigal '83
Fantastic Seven '79
Initiation of Sarah '78
Yours, Mine & Ours '68
The Birds '63

Aileen Britton (1916-86)
Now and Forever '82
My Brilliant Career '79

Barbara Britton (1919-80)
Dragonfly Squadron '54
Ride the Man Down '53
Bandit Queen '51
Champagne for Caesar '50
I Shot Jesse James '49
Loaded Pistols '48
The Virginian '46
Captain Kidd '45
The Story of Dr. Wassell '44
So Proudly We Hail '43
Reap the Wild Wind '42
Wake Island '42
Young and Willing '42
Louisiana Purchase '41

Connie Britton (1968-)
A Nightmare on Elm Street '10
Women in Trouble '09
The Last Winter '06
The Lather Effect '06
Friday Night Lights '04
Looking for Kitty '04
The Next Big Thing '02
Child Star: The Shirley Temple Story '01
No Looking Back '98
Escape Clause '96
The Brothers McMullen '94

Pamela Britton (1923-74)
If It's Tuesday, This Must Be Belgium '69
D.O.A. '49
Anchors Aweigh '45

Tony Britton (1924-)
Agatha '79
The Day of the Jackal '73
Cry of the Penguins '71
Sunday, Bloody Sunday '71
Dr. Syn, Alias the Scarecrow '64
Horsemasters '61
Operation Amsterdam '60
The Rough and the Smooth '59

Herman Brix
See Bruce Bennett

Nicolas Bro
Adam's Apples '05
The Green Butchers '03

Jim Broadbent (1949-)
The Damned United '09
Harry Potter and the Half-Blood Prince '09
Inkheart '09
The Young Victoria '09
Indiana Jones and the Kingdom of the Crystal Skull '08
Hot Fuzz '07
When Did You Last See Your Father? '07
Art School Confidential '06
Longford '06
The Chronicles of Narnia: The Lion, the Witch and the Wardrobe '05
Doogal '05 (V)
Robots '05 (V)
Valiant '05 (V)
Around the World in 80 Days '04
Bridget Jones: The Edge of Reason '04
Vanity Fair '04
And Starring Pancho Villa as Himself '03
Bright Young Things '03
Gangs of New York '02
The Gathering Storm '02
Nicholas Nickleby '02
Bridget Jones's Diary '01
Iris '01
Moulin Rouge '01
Topsy Turvy '99
The Avengers '98
Little Voice '98
The Borrowers '97
The Secret Agent '96
Smilla's Sense of Snow '96
Richard III '95
Rough Magic '95
Bullets over Broadway '94
Princess Caraboo '94
Widow's Peak '94
The Wedding Gift '93
The Crying Game '92
Enchanted April '92
Life Is Sweet '90
Erik the Viking '89
The Good Father '87

Kent Broadhurst (1940-)
A Couch in New York '95
The Dark Half '91
Silver Bullet '85

Peter Brocco (1903-92)
Jekyll & Hyde... Together Again '82
One Flew Over the Cuckoo's Nest '75
Homebodies '74
Johnny Got His Gun '71
The Balcony '63
Ma and Pa Kettle on Vacation '53

Anne Brochet (1966-)
Intimate Strangers '04
The Story of Marie and Julien '03
Dust '01
Barjo '93
Tous les Matins du Monde '92
Cyrano de Bergerac '90
The Bengali Night '88

Devin Brochu
Hesher '10
Ghosts of Girlfriends Past '09
In the Valley of Elah '07

Phil Brock (1953-)
Mercy '96
L.A. Rules: The Pros and Cons of Breathing '94
Dollman vs Demonic Toys '93
A Climate for Killing '91
Thunder Alley '85

Stan Brock (1931-91)
Return to Africa '89
UHF '89
Tin Men '87
Galyon '77

Roy Brocksmith (1945-2001)
Kull the Conqueror '97
The Road to Wellville '94
Nickel & Dime '92
Bill & Ted's Bogus Journey '91
Arachnophobia '90
Total Recall '90
Big Business '88
Tales of Ordinary Madness '83
Killer Fish '79
King of the Gypsies '78

Gladys Brockwell (1894-1929)
The Drake Case '29
7th Heaven '27
Spangles '26
Twinkletoes '26
Oliver Twist '22

Beth Broderick (1959-)
Mystery Woman: Mystery Weekend '05
Psycho Beach Party '00
French Exit '97
Maternal Instincts '96
Are You Lonesome Tonight '92
Thousand Pieces of Gold '91

Erin Broderick (1985-)
The Flamingo Rising '01
Black Dog '98

Helen Broderick (1891-1959)
Because of Him '45
Nice Girl? '41
The Rage of Paris '38
Service De Luxe '38
The Bride Walks Out '36
Swing Time '36
Top Hat '35

James Broderick (1927-82)
Keeping On '81
The Shadow Box '80
Dog Day Afternoon '75
The Taking of Pelham One Two Three '74
Alice's Restaurant '69
The Group '66
The Iceman Cometh '60

Matthew Broderick (1962-)
Wonderful World '09
Diminished Capacity '08
Finding Amanda '08
The Tale of Despereaux '08 (V)
All the Good Ones Are Married '07
Bee Movie '07 (V)
Then She Found Me '07
Deck the Halls '06
Strangers with Candy '06
The Producers '05
The Last Shot '04
The Lion King 1 1/2 '04 (V)
Marie and Bruce '04
The Stepford Wives '04
Good Boy! '03 (V)
Election '99
Inspector Gadget '99
You Can Count On Me '99
Godzilla '98
The Lion King: Simba's Pride '98 (V)
Addicted to Love '96
The Cable Guy '96
Infinity '96
The Thief and the Cobbler '96 (V)
The Lion King '94 (V)
Mrs. Parker and the Vicious Circle '94
The Road to Wellville '94
A Life in the Theater '93
The Night We Never Met '93
Out on a Limb '92
The Freshman '90
Family Business '89
Glory '89
Biloxi Blues '88
Torch Song Trilogy '88
Project X '87
Ferris Bueller's Day Off '86
On Valentine's Day '86
Ladyhawke '85
1918 '85
Cinderella '84
Master Harold and the Boys '84
Max Dugan Returns '83
WarGames '83

Don Brodie (1899-2001)
Eat My Dust '76
Detour '46
Pinocchio '40 (V)

Helen Brodie
Tales of the Kama Sutra 2: Monsoon '98
Monsoon '97

Steve Brodie (1919-92)
The Wizard of Speed and Time '88
The Giant Spider Invasion '75
The Wild World of Batwoman '66
Roustabout '64
Blue Hawaii '62
The Caine Mutiny '54
The Beast from 20,000 Fathoms '53
Donovan's Brain '53
Three for Bedroom C '52
The Steel Helmet '51
The Admiral Was a Lady '50
Armored Car Robbery '50
Kiss Tomorrow Goodbye '50
Treasure of Monte Cristo '50
Home of the Brave '49
Tough Assignment '49
Desperate '47
Out of the Past '47
Badman's Territory '46
Criminal Court '46
The Saint Strikes Back: Criminal Court '46
A Walk in the Sun '46
Thirty Seconds Over Tokyo '44

Adam Brody (1980-)
Jennifer's Body '09
Smiley Face '07
The Ten '07
In the Land of Women '06
Thank You for Smoking '06
Mr. & Mrs. Smith '05
Grind '03
Missing Brendan '03

Adrien Brody (1973-)
Predators '10
The Brothers Bloom '09
Fantastic Mr. Fox '09 (V)
Splice '09
Cadillac Records '08
The Darjeeling Limited '07
Hollywoodland '06
The Jacket '05
King Kong '05
The Village '04
The Singing Detective '03
Dummy '02
Harrison's Flowers '02
The Pianist '02
The Affair of the Necklace '01
Love the Hard Way '01
Bread and Roses '00
Liberty Heights '99
Oxygen '99
Six Ways to Sunday '99
Summer of Sam '99
Restaurant '98
Ten Benny '98
The Thin Red Line '98
The Undertaker's Wedding '97
The Last Time I Committed Suicide '96
Solo '96
Bullet '94
Jailbreakers '94
King of the Hill '93
Home at Last '88

Harry Brogan (1905-77)
Broth of a Boy '59
Shake Hands with the Devil '59

Giulio Brogi (1935-)
St. Michael Had a Rooster '72
The Spider's Stratagem '70

Tom Brokaw (1940-)
Tanner on Tanner '04
Journeys with George '02

James Brolin (1940-)
The Goods: Live Hard, Sell Hard '09
Last Chance Harvey '08
The Hunting Party '07
Lies & Alibis '06
Wedding Wars '06
Category 7 : The End of the World '05
The Reagans '04
A Guy Thing '03
Catch Me If You Can '02
Master of Disguise '02
Traffic '00
The Haunted Sea '97
Lewis and Clark and George '97
My Brother's War '97
Terminal Virus '96
The Expert '95
The Fighter '95
Relative Fear '95
Tracks of a Killer '95
Final Justice '94
Indecent Behavior 2 '94
Parallel Lives '94
Cheatin' Hearts '93
City Boy '93
Ted & Venus '93
Gas Food Lodging '92
Twin Sisters '91
Backstab '90
Nightmare on the 13th Floor '90
Bad Jim '89
Finish Line '89
Hold the Dream '86
Pee-wee's Big Adventure '85
Mae West '84
The Ambush Murders '82
High Risk '81
Night of the Juggler '80
The Amityville Horror '79
Capricorn One '78
Steel Cowboy '78
The Car '77
Class of '63 '73
Westworld '73
The Boston Strangler '68
Fantastic Voyage '66
Our Man Flint '66
Von Ryan's Express '65

Josh Brolin (1968-)
Jonah Hex '10
The Tillman Story '10 (N)
Wall Street 2: Money Never Sleeps '10
Women in Trouble '09
Milk '08
W. '08
American Gangster '07
In the Valley of Elah '07
No Country for Old Men '07
Planet Terror '07
The Dead Girl '06
Into the Blue '05
Milwaukee, Minnesota '03
Coastlines '02
Hollow Man '00
Slow Burn '00
Best Laid Plans '99
It's the Rage '99
The Mod Squad '99
Mimic '97
My Brother's War '97
Gang in Blue '96
Nightwatch '96
Bed of Roses '95
Flirting with Disaster '95
Prison for Children '93
Finish Line '89
Thrashin' '86
The Goonies '85

Shane Brolly (1970-)
Underworld: Rise of the Lycans '09
48 Angels '06
Underworld: Evolution '05
Underworld '03
Flypaper '97

J. Edward Bromberg (1903-51)
A Song Is Born '48
Queen of the Amazons '47
Cloak and Dagger '46
The Missing Corpse '45
Dead Man's Eyes '44
The Phantom of the Opera '43
Son of Dracula '43
Invisible Agent '42
Reunion in France '42
The Mark of Zorro '40
Return of Frank James '40
Strange Cargo '40
Hollywood Cavalcade '39
Four Men and a Prayer '38
Mr. Moto Takes a Chance '38
Charlie Chan on Broadway '37
Second Honeymoon '37
Girl's Dormitory '36

John Bromfield (1922-)
Manfish '56
Big Bluff '55
Revenge of the Creature '55
Easy to Love '53
Flat Top '52
The Furies '50

Valri Bromfield (1949-)
Nothing But Trouble '91
Who's Harry Crumb? '89
Home Is Where the Hart Is '88
Mr. Mom '83

Sheila Bromley
See Sheila (Manors) Manners
Texas Gunfighter '32

Sydney Bromley (1909-87)
Crystalstone '88
The NeverEnding Story '84
Frankenstein and the Monster from Hell '74

Eleanor Bron (1934-)
Wimbledon '04
The Heart of Me '02
Iris '01
House of Mirth '00
Vanity Fair '99
A Little Princess '95
Saint-Ex: The Story of the Storyteller '95
Black Beauty '94
Intrigue '90
The Attic: The Hiding of Anne Frank '88
Little Dorrit, Film 1: Nobody's Fault '88
Little Dorrit, Film 2: Little Dorrit's Story '88
Turtle Diary '86
Women in Love '70
Bedazzled '68
Two for the Road '67
Alfie '66
Help! '65

William Bronder (1928-)
Return to Me '00
Flush '81

Brick Bronsky
Class of Nuke 'Em High 3: The Good, the Bad and the Subhumanoid '94
Sgt. Kabukiman N.Y.P.D. '94
Class of Nuke 'Em High 2: Subhumanoid Meltdown '91

Betty Bronson (1906-71)
Naked Kiss '64
Yodelin' Kid from Pine Ridge '37
Medicine Man '30
The Singing Fool '28
Ben-Hur '26
Are Parents People? '25
Peter Pan '24

Charles Bronson (1921-2003)
Family of Cops 3 '98
Family of Cops 2: Breach of Faith '97
Family of Cops '95
Death Wish 5: The Face of Death '94

Dead to Rights '93
The Sea Wolf '93
The Indian Runner '91
Kinjite: Forbidden Subjects '89
Messenger of Death '88
Assassination '87
Death Wish 4: The Crackdown '87
Act of Vengeance '86
Murphy's Law '86
Death Wish 3 '85
The Evil That Men Do '84
Ten to Midnight '83
Death Wish 2 '82
Cabo Blanco '81
Death Hunt '81
Borderline '80
Love and Bullets '79
Raid on Entebbe '77
Telefon '77
The White Buffalo '77
Breakheart Pass '76
From Noon Till Three '76
St. Ives '76
Breakout '75
Chino '75
Hard Times '75
Death Wish '74
Mr. Majestyk '74
The Stone Killer '73
The Mechanic '72
The Valachi Papers '72
Bull of the West '71
Chato's Land '71
Cold Sweat '71
Red Sun '71
Someone Behind the Door '71
The Family '70
Rider on the Rain '70
Lola '69
Honor Among Thieves '68
Once Upon a Time in the West '68
Villa Rides '68
The Dirty Dozen '67
The Meanest Men in the West '67
This Property Is Condemned '66
Battle of the Bulge '65
The Sandpiper '65
Guns of Diablo '64
Four for Texas '63
The Great Escape '63
Kid Galahad '62
Master of the World '61
The Magnificent Seven '60
Never So Few '59
Machine Gun Kelly '58
Showdown at Boot Hill '58
When Hell Broke Loose '58
Jubal '56
Run of the Arrow '56
Apache '54
Crime Wave '54
Drum Beat '54
House of Wax '53
Miss Sadie Thompson '53
Vera Cruz '53
Pat and Mike '52

Lillian Bronson (1903-95)
Spencer's Mountain '63
The Next Voice You Hear '50

Claudio Brook (1929-95)
Cronos '94
The Bees '78
Devil's Rain '75
Dr. Tarr's Torture Dungeon '75
Sisters of Satan '75
The Peking Blond '68
Simon of the Desert '66
Viva Maria! '65
Samson in the Wax Museum '63
The Exterminating Angel '62
Neutron and the Black Mask '61
The Young One '61
Daniel Boone: Trail Blazer '56

Clive Brook (1887-1974)
On Approval '44
Convoy '40
Action for Slander '38
Cavalcade '33
Shanghai Express '32
Hula '28
Underworld '27

Faith Brook (1922-)
Eye of the Needle '81
After Julius '78
Bloodbath '76
War and Peace '73
To Sir, with Love '67
Uneasy Terms '48

Irina Brook (1962-)
Captive '87
The Girl in the Picture '86
Transmutations '85

Isabel Brook
About a Boy '02
Faust: Love of the Damned '00

Jayne Brook (1962-)
Gattaca '97
Ed '96
Last Dance '96
Bye Bye, Love '94
Clean Slate '94
Doing Time on Maple Drive '92
Kindergarten Cop '90

Kelly Brook
Fishtales '07
House of 9 '05

Lesley Brook
House of Darkness '48
Murder in the Footlights '46

Lyndon Brook (1926-2004)
Invasion '65
The Spanish Gardener '57
Above Us the Waves '56

Elwyn Brook-Jones (1911-62)
Rogue's Yarn '56
The Gilded Cage '54
Bonnie Prince Charlie '48

Bunny Brooke (1920-2000)
Dawn! '83
Alison's Birthday '79

Hillary Brooke (1914-99)
The Man Who Knew Too Much '56
Heat Wave '54
Invaders from Mars '53
Abbott and Costello Meet Captain Kidd '52
Never Wave at a WAC '52
The Lost Continent '51
Africa Screams '49
The Woman in Green '49
Big Town '47
Big Town After Dark '47
Underworld Scandal '47
The Road to Utopia '46
Strange Impersonation '46
The Strange Woman '46
The Enchanted Cottage '45
Jane Eyre '44
Ministry of Fear '44
Sherlock Holmes Faces Death '43
Sherlock Holmes: The Voice of Terror '42
To the Shores of Tripoli '42
Wake Island '42
The Lone Rider in Frontier Fury '41
The Philadelphia Story '40

Paul Brooke (1944-)
The Affair of the Necklace '01
Dead of Night '99
The Lair of the White Worm '88

Sandy Brooke
Crazed Cop '88
Miami Vendetta '87
Star Slammer '87
Terror on Alcatraz '86

Tyler Brooke
The Divorcee '30
Monte Carlo '30

Walter Brooke (1914-86)
The Return of Count Yorga '71
Tora! Tora! Tora! '70
Conquest of Space '55

Richard Brooker (1955-)
Friday the 13th, Part 4: The Final Chapter '84
Deathstalker '83
Friday the 13th, Part 3 '82

Jacqueline Brookes (1930-)
Naked Gun 2 1/2: The Smell of Fear '91
Silent Witness '85
Hardhat & Legs '80
Rodeo Girl '80
The Gambler '74

Michelle Brookhurst
Recipe for Disaster '03
Can't Hardly Wait '98

Aimee Brooks (1974-)
The Hillside Strangler '04
Monster Man '03
Critters 3 '91
Say Anything '89

Albert Brooks (1947-)
The Simpsons Movie '07 (V)
Looking for Comedy in the Muslim World '06
Finding Nemo '03 (V)
The In-Laws '03
My First Mister '01
The Muse '99
Dr. Dolittle '98 (V)
Out of Sight '98
Critical Care '97
Mother '96
The Scout '94
I'll Do Anything '93
Defending Your Life '91
Broadcast News '87
Lost in America '85
Unfaithfully Yours '84
Twilight Zone: The Movie '83
Modern Romance '81
Private Benjamin '80
Real Life '79
Taxi Driver '76

Amanda Brooks (1981-)
My Best Friend's Girl '08
Stiletto '08
Dragon Wars '07
River's End '05

Angelle Brooks
Blue Hill Avenue '01
The Brothers '01

Avery Brooks (1948-)
15 Minutes '01
American History X '98
The Big Hit '98
Spenser: A Savage Place '94
Spenser: Pale Kings & Princes '94
Spenser: The Judas Goat '94
The Ernest Green Story '93
Spenser: Ceremony '93
Roots: The Gift '88
Uncle Tom's Cabin '87
Half Slave, Half Free '85

Carroll Brooks
Mauvais Sang '86
Boy Meets Girl '84

Clarence Brooks (1896-1969)
Bronze Buckaroo '39
Harlem Rides the Range '39

Conrad Brooks (1931-)
Skeleton Key 2: 667, the Neighbor of the Beast '08
The Alien Agenda: Under the Skin '97
Bikini Drive-In '94
Ed Wood '94
Test Tube Teens from the Year 2000 '93
Curse of the Queerwolf '87
The Beast of Yucca Flats '61
The Sinister Urge '60
Plan 9 from Outer Space '56
Bride of the Monster '55
Jail Bait '54
Glen or Glenda? '53

David Allan Brooks (1947-)
Cast Away '00
Jack Frost 2: Revenge of the Mutant Killer Snowman '00
The Kindred '87
Manhunter '86
Scream for Help '86

Elisabeth Brooks (1951-97)
The Forgotten One '89
The Howling '81

Foster Brooks (1912-2001)
Oddballs '84
Cracking Up '83
The Villain '79
Super Seal '77

Geraldine Brooks (1925-77)
Bull of the West '71
Johnny Tiger '66
The Green Glove '52
Challenge to Lassie '49
Reckless Moment '49
Cry Wolf '47
The Possessed '47

Golden Brooks (1970-)
Something New '06
Beauty Shop '05
Motives '03

Hildy Brooks
Forbidden Love '82
The Chosen '81
The Iceman Cometh '73

Jean Brooks (1916-63)
Boss of Big Town '43
The Leopard Man '43
The Seventh Victim '43
Boot Hill Bandits '42

Jennifer Brooks
See Laurie Rose

Joel Brooks (1949-)
Bound by Lies '05
The Man Who Captured Eichmann '96
Indecent Proposal '93
Are You Lonesome Tonight '92

Leslie Brooks (1922-)
The Cobra Strikes '48
Romance on the High Seas '48
The Scar '48
I Love a Bandleader '45
Tonight and Every Night '45
City Without Men '43
Underground Agent '42
You Were Never Lovelier '42

Louise Brooks (1906-85)
Overland Stage Raiders '38
Prix de Beaute '30
Diary of a Lost Girl '29
Beggars of Life '28
A Girl in Every Port '28
Pandora's Box '28
It's the Old Army Game '26
Love 'Em and Leave 'Em '26
The Show Off '26

Mel Brooks (1926-)
The Producers '05
Robots '05 (V)
Screw Loose '99
Dracula: Dead and Loving It '95
Robin Hood: Men in Tights '93
Silence of the Hams '93
Life Stinks '91
Look Who's Talking, Too '90 (V)
Spaceballs '87
To Be or Not to Be '83
History of the World: Part 1 '81
The Muppet Movie '79
High Anxiety '77
Silent Movie '76
Blazing Saddles '74
The Twelve Chairs '70
Putney Swope '69
The Producers '68

Phyllis Brooks (1915-95)
Dangerous Passage '44
Silver Spurs '43
The Shanghai Gesture '42
Slightly Honorable '40
Charlie Chan in Honolulu '38
Little Miss Broadway '38
Rebecca of Sunnybrook Farm '38
In Old Chicago '37

Rand Brooks (1918-2003)
Comanche Station '60
To Hell and Back '55
The Vanishing Westerner '50
Ladies of the Chorus '49
Hopalong Cassidy: Borrowed Trouble '48
Hopalong Cassidy: Dangerous Venture '48
Hopalong Cassidy: False Paradise '48
Hopalong Cassidy: Silent Conflict '48
Hopalong Cassidy: Sinister Journey '48
Hopalong Cassidy: The Dead Don't Dream '48
Hopalong Cassidy: Hoppy's Holiday '47
Hopalong Cassidy: The Marauders '47
Hopalong Cassidy: Unexpected Guest '47
Hopalong Cassidy: The Devil's Playground '46
The Sombrero Kid '42
Gone with the Wind '39

Randi Brooks (1956-)
Colors '88
Cop '88
Hamburger... The Motion Picture '86
Ratings Game '84
Tightrope '84
The Man with Two Brains '83
Forbidden Love '82

Randy Brooks
Reservoir Dogs '92
Black Snow '89

Ray Brooks (1939-)
Office Romances '86
House of Whipcord '75
Tiffany Jones '75
Flesh and Blood Show '73
Daleks—Invasion Earth 2150 A.D. '66
The Knack '65

Richard Brooks (1962-)
Johnny B. '00
The Crow 2: City of Angels '96
The Substitute '96
Wolverine '96
Chameleon '95
Machine Gun Blues '95
Memphis '91
To Sleep with Anger '90
84 Charlie MoPic '89
Shocker '89
Shakedown '88
Short Fuse '88
The Hidden '87

Terron Brooks (1974-)
All About You '01
The Temptations '98

Van Brooks
Trespasses '86
Blood Simple '85

Anthony Brophy
The Informant '97
The Run of the Country '95

Brian Brophy
Brain Dead '89
Skinheads: The Second Coming of Hate '88

Edward Brophy (1895-1960)
Last Hurrah '58
Pier 23 '51
Roaring City '51
It Happened on 5th Avenue '47
Renegade Girl '46
Swing Parade of 1946 '46
Cover Girl '44
It Happened Tomorrow '44
The Thin Man Goes Home '44
Air Force '43
Destroyer '43
Larceny, Inc. '42
Dumbo '41 (V)
Sleepers West '41
Dance, Girl, Dance '40
The Invisible Woman '40
Gold Diggers in Paris '38
A Slight Case of Murder '38
The Last Gangster '37
Great Guy '36
Kelly the Second '36
China Seas '35
Mad Love '35
Show Them No Mercy '35
Evelyn Prentice '34
Hide-Out '34
What! No Beer? '33
The Champ '32
Speak Easily '32
Doughboys '30
The Cameraman '28

Kevin Brophy (1953-)
Delos Adventure '86
The Seduction '82
Time Walker '82
Hell Night '81

Pierce Brosnan (1953-)
The Ghost Writer '10
Percy Jackson & The Olympians: The Lightning Thief '10
Remember Me '10
Vanilla Gorilla '09
Mamma Mia! '08
Married Life '07
Shattered '07
The Matador '06
Seraphim Falls '06
After the Sunset '04
Laws of Attraction '04
Die Another Day '02
Evelyn '02
The Tailor of Panama '00
Grey Owl '99
The Match '99
The Thomas Crown Affair '99
The World Is Not Enough '99
Quest for Camelot '98 (V)
Dante's Peak '97
The Nephew '97
Tomorrow Never Dies '97
Mars Attacks! '96
The Mirror Has Two Faces '96
Robinson Crusoe '96
Detonator 2: Night Watch '95
The Disappearance of Kevin Johnson '95
Goldeneye '95
Don't Talk to Strangers '94
Love Affair '94
The Broken Chain '93
Detonator '93

Entangled '93
Mrs. Doubtfire '93
The Lawnmower Man '92
Live Wire '92
Mister Johnson '91
Murder 101 '91
Victim of Love '91
Around the World in 80 Days '89
The Heist '89
The Deceivers '88
Noble House '88
Taffin '88
The Fourth Protocol '87
Nomads '86
The Carpathian Eagle '81
The Manions of America '81
The Long Good Friday '80
The Mirror Crack'd '80

Sean Brosnan

Surveillance 24/7 '07
When Evil Calls '06

Dr. Joyce Brothers (1928-)

National Lampoon's Loaded Weapon 1 '93
Age Isn't Everything '91
The Naked Gun: From the Files of Police Squad '88
Love at Stake '87
The Lonely Guy '84
Desperate Lives '82
Embryo '76

Alan Brough

The Nugget '02
Siam Sunset '99

Liliane Brousse

Maniac '63
Paranoiac '62

Ben Browder (1962-)

Stargate: Continuum '08
Stargate: The Ark of Truth '08
Boogie Boy '98
A Kiss Before Dying '91

Jordan Brower (1981-)

Night Ride Home '99
Speedway Junky '99

Amelda Brown

Little Dorrit, Film 1: Nobody's Fault '88
Little Dorrit, Film 2: Little Dorrit's Story '88
Hope and Glory '87

Barbara Brown (1902-75)

The Terror of the Tongs '61
My Sister Eileen '55
Ma and Pa Kettle on Vacation '53
Jack & the Beanstalk '52
Home Town Story '51
Ma and Pa Kettle Back On the Farm '51
Born Yesterday '50
Ma and Pa Kettle Go to Town '50
Hollywood Canteen '44
The Fighting Sullivans '42

Barry Brown (1951-78)

He Who Walks Alone '78
The Disappearance of Aimee '76
The Ultimate Thrill '74
Bad Company '72
The Bravos '72
Flesh '68

Bille Brown (1952-)

The Dish '00
Oscar and Lucinda '97
Fierce Creatures '96

Billy Aaron Brown (1981-)

Attack of the Sabretooth '05
Jeepers Creepers 2 '03

Blair Brown (1948-)

Dark Matter '07
Griffin & Phoenix '06
The Sentinel '06
The Treatment '06
Loverboy '05
Dogville '03
Follow the Stars Home '01
Hamlet '01
In His Life: The John Lennon Story '00
Space Cowboys '00
The Astronaut's Wife '99
The Day My Parents Ran Away '93
Passed Away '92
Strapless '90
Stealing Home '88
Hands of a Stranger '87
The Bad Seed '85
A Flash of Green '85
Kennedy '83
Continental Divide '81
Altered States '80
One Trick Pony '80
And I Alone Survived '78
The Choirboys '77

Bobby Brown (1969-)

Nora's Hair Salon 2: A Cut Above '08
Nora's Hair Salon '04
Gang of Roses '03
Two Can Play That Game '01
A Thin Line Between Love and Hate '96
Mother Goose Rock 'n' Rhyme '90

Bruce Brown (1938-)

The Endless Summer 2 '94 (N)
Zipperface '92
Eddie and the Cruisers '83
The Endless Summer '66 (N)

Bryan Brown (1947-)

Australia '08
Along Came Polly '04
Footsteps '03
Dirty Deeds '02
On the Beach '00
Risk '00
Styx '00
Grizzly Falls '99
Journey to the Center of the Earth '99
On the Border '98
Tracked '98
Two Hands '98
Dead Heart '96
Twisted '96 (N)
Full Body Massage '95
The Last Hit '93
Blame It on the Bellboy '92
Devlin '92
Dead in the Water '91
F/X 2: The Deadly Art of Illusion '91
Prisoners of the Sun '91
Sweet Talker '91
Cocktail '88
Gorillas in the Mist '88
F/X '86
The Good Wife '86
Tai-Pan '86
The Empty Beach '85
Far East '85
Rebel '85
A Town Like Alice '85
Give My Regards to Broad Street '84
Kim '84
Parker '84
The Thorn Birds '83
The Winter of Our Dreams '82
Blood Money '80
Breaker Morant '80
The Odd Angry Shot '79
Palm Beach '79
The Chant of Jimmie Blacksmith '78
The Irishman '78
Money Movers '78
Newsfront '78

Charles D. Brown (1887-1949)

Follow Me Quietly '49
I Wouldn't Be in Your Shoes '48
Merton of the Movies '47
Having Wonderful Crime '45
International Lady '41
Brother Orchid '40
Old Swimmin' Hole '40
Mr. Moto in Danger Island '39
The Duke of West Point '38
Shopworn Angel '38
Gold Diggers of 1937 '36
Dance of Life '29

Chris Brown (1989-)

Takers '10
This Christmas '07

Clancy Brown (1959-)

A Nightmare on Elm Street '10
The Express '08
Pathfinder '07
The Guardian '06
The SpongeBob SquarePants Movie '04 (V)
Normal '03
Snow White: The Fairest of Them All '02
Boss of Bosses '99
The Hurricane '99
In the Company of Spies '99
Vendetta '99
Flubber '97
Starship Troopers '97
Female Perversions '96
Donor Unknown '95
Pom Poko '94 (V)
The Shawshank Redemption '94
Last Light '93
Past Midnight '92
Pet Sematary 2 '92
Ambition '91
Cast a Deadly Spell '91
Love, Lies and Murder '91
Blue Steel '90
Season of Fear '89
Shoot to Kill '88
Extreme Prejudice '87
Highlander '86
The Bride '85
Thunder Alley '85
The Adventures of Buckaroo Banzai Across the Eighth Dimension '84
Bad Boys '83

David Brown

Freezer Burn: The Invasion of Laxdale '08
The Riverman '04

David G. Brown

Chasing Dreams '81
Deadly Harvest '72

Drew "Bundini" Brown (1928-87)

Shaft's Big Score '72
Shaft '71

D.W. Brown

Mischief '85
Weekend Pass '84

Dwier Brown (1959-)

Fast Girl '07
Red Dragon '02
Same River Twice '97
Intimate Betrayal '96
Deconstructing Sarah '94
Lily in Winter '94
Gettysburg '93
The Cutting Edge '92
Galaxies Are Colliding '92
Mom and Dad Save the World '92
The Guardian '90
Field of Dreams '89

Eric Brown (1964-)

Video Murders '87
They're Playing with Fire '84
Private Lessons '75

Erin Brown

See Misty Mundae

Gary Brown

Invasion of the Space Preachers '90
The Glory Boys '84

Gaye Brown (1941-)

An American Haunting '05
Mata Hari '85
Masque of the Red Death '65

Georg Stanford Brown (1943-)

The Reading Room '05
Tyson '95
Ava's Magical Adventure '94
Murder Without Motive '92
House Party 2: The Pajama Jam '91
Alone in the Neon Jungle '87
North and South Book 1 '85
The Jesse Owens Story '84
The Kid with the Broken Halo '82
The Night the City Screamed '80
Stir Crazy '80
Roots: The Next Generation '79
Roots '77
Colossus: The Forbin Project '70
Dayton's Devils '68

Georgia Brown (1933-92)

Victim of Love '91
Love at Stake '87
Actor: The Paul Muni Story '78
Tales That Witness Madness '73
Nothing But the Night '72
Long Ago Tomorrow '71
The Fixer '68

Henry Brown

Sex, Love and Cold Hard Cash '93
Uncaged '91
Stepfather 2: Make Room for Daddy '89
The Man in the Glass Booth '75

James Brown (1920-93)

Adios Amigo '75
Targets '68
Space Monster '64
Courage of Rin Tin Tin '57
Rin Tin Tin, Hero of the West '55
Montana '50
Sands of Iwo Jima '49
Objective, Burma! '45
Air Force '43
Wake Island '42

James Brown (1933-2006)

Soul Power '08
Undercover Brother '02
Blues Brothers 2000 '98
Doctor Detroit '83
The Blues Brothers '80

Jim Brown (1935-)

Animal '05
She Hate Me '04
On the Edge '02
Any Given Sunday '99
He Got Game '98
Small Soldiers '98 (V)
Mars Attacks! '96
Original Gangstas '96
The Divine Enforcer '91
Crack House '89
L.A. Vice '89
Twisted Justice '89
I'm Gonna Git You Sucka '88
L.A. Heat '88
The Running Man '87
Pacific Inferno '85
One Down, Two to Go! '82
Fingers '78
Kid Vengeance '75
Take a Hard Ride '75
Three the Hard Way '74
Slaughter's Big Ripoff '73
Black Gunn '72
Slaughter '72
El Condor '70
The Passing of Evil '70
The Grasshopper '69
100 Rifles '69
Riot '69
Dark of the Sun '68
Ice Station Zebra '68
The Dirty Dozen '67
Rio Conchos '64

Joe E. Brown (1892-1973)

The Comedy of Terrors '64
It's a Mad, Mad, Mad, Mad World '63
Some Like It Hot '59
Around the World in 80 Days '56
Show Boat '51
The Tender Years '47
Pin-Up Girl '44
The Gladiator '38
Wide Open Faces '38
Fit for a King '37
Riding on Air '37
When's Your Birthday? '37
Earthworm Tractors '36
Alibi Ike '35
A Midsummer Night's Dream '35
Lottery Bride '30
On with the Show '29
Sally '29

Johnny Mack Brown (1904-74)

Apache Uprising '66
Border Bandits '46
Gentleman from Texas '46
The Stranger from Pecos '45
Lawmen '44
Partners of the Trail '44
Raiders of the Border '44
Range Law '44
Ghost Rider '43
The Lone Star Trail '43
Six Gun Gospel '43
Texas Kid '43
Ride 'Em Cowboy '42
The Silver Bullet '42
Stagecoach Buckaroo '42
Arizona Cyclone '41
Boss of Bullion City '41
Bury Me Not on the Lone Prairie '41
Man from Montana '41
The Masked Rider '41
Law and Order '40
Pony Post '40
Riders of Pasco Basin '40
Chip of the Flying U '39
Oklahoma Frontier '39
Flaming Frontiers '38
Helltown '38
Boothill Brigade '37
The Gambling Terror '37
Guns in the Dark '37
A Lawman Is Born '37
Crooked Trail '36
Desert Phantom '36
Everyman's Law '36
Rogue of the Range '36
Undercover Man '36
Valley of the Lawless '36
Between Men '35
Branded a Coward '35
Courageous Avenger '35
Rustlers of Red Dog '35
Belle of the Nineties '34
Female '33
Fighting with Kit Carson '33
Fire Alarm '32
Undertow '30
Coquette '29
The Single Standard '29
Annapolis '28
A Lady of Chance '28
Our Dancing Daughters '28
A Woman of Affairs '28

Juanita Brown

Black Starlet '74
Caged Heat '74
Foxy Brown '74

Judy (Judith) Brown (1944-)

The Manhandlers '73
The Big Doll House '71

Julie Brown (1958-)

Boxboarders! '07
Plump Fiction '97
Clueless '95
Fist of the North Star '95
Out There '95
National Lampoon's Attack of the 5 Ft. 2 Women '94
Nervous Ticks '93
The Opposite Sex and How to Live With Them '93
Raining Stones '93
Shakes the Clown '92
Spirit of '76 '91
Earth Girls Are Easy '89
Bloody Birthday '80

Downtown Julie Brown (1963-)

Bug Buster '99
Ride '98

Kimberly J. Brown (1984-)

Halloweentown High '04
Bringing Down the House '03
My Sister's Keeper '02
Stephen King's Rose Red '02
Halloweentown 2: Kalabar's Revenge '01
Halloweentown '98
Tumbleweeds '98

Lou Brown (1952-)

Death Games '80
Alison's Birthday '79
The Irishman '78

Lowell Brown

The Girl in Lover's Lane '60
High School Caesar '60

Marcus Lyle Brown

Mammoth '06
Venom '05

Melanie (Scary Spice) Brown (1975-)

Telling Lies '06
Lethal Dose '03
Spice World: The Movie '97

Murray Brown (1937-)

Vampyres '74
Dracula '73

Olivia Brown

Memories of Murder '90
Streets of Fire '84

Orlando Brown

The Proud Family Movie '05 (V)
Max Keeble's Big Move '01

Pamela Brown (1917-75)

In This House of Brede '75
Dracula '73
Wuthering Heights '70
Secret Ceremony '69
Cleopatra '63
Victoria Regina '61
Lust for Life '56
Alice in Wonderland '50
I Know Where I'm Going '45
One of Our Aircraft Is Missing '41

Pat Crawford Brown (1929-)

Stuck On You '03
Elvira, Mistress of the Dark '88

Peter Brown (1935-)

Three Bad Men '05
Asylum '97
The Aurora Encounter '85
The Concrete Jungle '82
Act of Vengeance '74
Foxy Brown '74
Memory of Us '74
Slashed Dreams '74
Chrome and Hot Leather '71
Eagles Attack at Dawn '70
Hard Frame '70
Kitten with a Whip '64
Ride the Wild Surf '64

A Tiger Walks '64
Merrill's Marauders '62
Darby's Rangers '58
The Commies Are Coming, the Commies Are Coming '57

Phil Brown (1916-2006)
Tropic of Cancer '70
Operation Cross Eagles '69
The Hidden Room '49
Obsession '49
Without Reservations '46
Jungle Captive '45

Philip Brown (1958-)
Wild Zone '89
Eye of the Needle '81
Special Olympics '78

P.J. Brown (1956-)
Rick '03
Double Parked '00

Ralph Brown (1913-90)
Star Wars: Episode 1—The Phantom Menace '99
Ivanhoe '97
Wayne's World 2 '93
Alien 3 '92
The Crying Game '92
Impromptu '90
Christabel '89
Buster '88
Withnail and I '87

Ralph Brown (1960-)
Closure '07
The Contractor '07
I'll Be There '03
Mean Machine '01
Extremely Dangerous '99

Reb Brown (1948-)
Cage 2: The Arena of Death '94
The Firing Line '91
Last Flight to Hell '91
Street Hunter '90
The Cage '89
Mercenary Fighters '88
Space Mutiny '88
White Ghost '88
Strike Commando '87
Death of a Soldier '85
Howling 2: Your Sister Is a Werewolf '85
Uncommon Valor '83
Yor, the Hunter from the Future '83
Captain America '79
Captain America 2: Death Too Soon '79

Ritza Brown
The McGuffin '85
Ator the Fighting Eagle '83

Rob Brown (1984-)
The Express '08
Stop-Loss '08
Take the Lead '06
Coach Carter '05
Finding Forrester '00

Robert Brown (1918-2003)
License to Kill '89
The Living Daylights '87
A View to a Kill '85
Octopussy '83
Pilgrim, Farewell '82
One Million Years B.C. '66
Tower of London '62
It Takes a Thief '59
Shake Hands with the Devil '59
The Abominable Snowman '57

Roger Aaron Brown (1949-)
Miracle in Lane Two '00
Tall Tale: The Unbelievable Adventures of Pecos Bill '95
Undesirable '92
Don't Cry, It's Only Thunder '82

Ron Brown
The Legend of Black Thunder Mountain '79

Charlie the Lonesome Cougar '67

Samantha Brown (1976-)
Lift '01
New Jersey Drive '95

Sara Suzanne Brown
Killer Looks '94
Secret Games 2: The Escort '93
Test Tube Teens from the Year 2000 '93
The Bikini Car Wash Company 2 '92
The Bikini Car Wash Company '90

Sarah Brown
Heart of the Beholder '05
Super Seal '77

Stanley Brown (1914-2001)
Blondie's Blessed Event '42
Lawless Plainsmen '42
Blondie Meets the Boss '39

Stephen Brown (1917-98)
Beyond Darkness '92
Metamorphosis '90

Thomas Wilson Brown (1972-)
Skeletons '96
Diggstown '92
Honey, I Shrunk the Kids '89
Welcome Home '89

Timothy Brown (1937-)
Pacific Inferno '85
Code Name: Zebra '84
Losin' It '82
Black Heat '76
The Dynamite Brothers '74
Girls Are for Loving '73
A Place Called Today '72
Sweet Sugar '72
M*A*S*H '70

Tom Brown (1913-90)
The Choppers '61
Operation Haylift '50
Ringside '49
Buck Privates Come Home '47
Adventures of Smilin' Jack '43
The Payoff '43
The Duke of West Point '38
In Old Chicago '37
Maytime '37
Navy Blue and Gold '37
I'd Give My Life '36
Anne of Green Gables '34
Two Alone '34

Vanessa Brown (1928-99)
Witch Who Came from the Sea '76
The Fighter '52
Tarzan and the Slave Girl '50
Three Husbands '50
The Heiress '49
The Ghost and Mrs. Muir '47
Mother Wore Tights '47

W. Earl Brown (1963-)
The Big White '05
Killer Diller '04
Dancing at the Blue Iguana '00
Lost Souls '00
Meat Loaf: To Hell and Back '00
There's Something about Mary '98
Scream '96
Dead Air '94
Excessive Force '93

Wally Brown (1904-61)
The Absent-Minded Professor '61
Westbound '58
The High and the Mighty '54
Girl Rush '44

Seven Days Ashore '44
Zombies on Broadway '44

Woody Brown (1956-)
Animal Instincts 2 '94
Dominion '94
Secret Games 3 '94
Alligator 2: The Mutation '90
The Rain Killer '90
The Accused '88
Killer Party '86

Wren Brown
Hellbent '04
Crossfire '89

Charles A. Browne
Federal Agent '36
Tailspin Tommy '34

Coral Browne (1913-91)
Dreamchild '85
American Dreamer '84
An Englishman Abroad '83
Eleanor: First Lady of the World '82
Theatre of Blood '73
The Ruling Class '72
The Killing of Sister George '69
Auntie Mame '58
The Courtney Affair '47

Irene Browne
Serious Charge '59
Pygmalion '38

Leslie Browne (1958-)
Dancers '87
Nijinsky '80
The Turning Point '77

Lucille Browne (1907-76)
Cheyenne Rides Again '38
Crooked Trail '36
Texas Terror '35
Western Frontier '35
Brand of Hate '34
Law of the Wild '34
The Devil's Brother '33
Double Harness '33
Mystery Squadron '33
Battling with Buffalo Bill '31

Roger Browne
Jungle Master '72
Venus Against the Son of Hercules '62

Roscoe Lee Browne (1925-2007)
Garfield: A Tail of Two Kitties '06 *(V)*
Treasure Planet '02 *(V)*
Hamlet '01
Morgan's Ferry '99
Babe: Pig in the City '98 *(N)*
Dear God '96
Last Summer In the Hamptons '96
Babe '95 *(N)*
Forest Warrior '95
The Pompatus of Love '95
Naked in New York '93
Eddie Presley '92
The Mambo Kings '92
Moon 44 '90
For Us, the Living '88
Oliver & Company '88 *(V)*
Jumpin' Jack Flash '86
Legal Eagles '86
Haunting of Harrington House '82
Nothing Personal '80
Unknown Powers '80
King '78
Twilight's Last Gleaming '77
Logan's Run '76
Superfly T.N.T. '73
The World's Greatest Athlete '73
The Cowboys '72
The Liberation of L.B. Jones '70
Black Like Me '64
The Connection '61

Suzanne Browne
See Sara Suzanne Brown

Victor Browne
Love's Unending Legacy '07
Love's Unfolding Dream '07

Zachary Browne (1985-)
Shiloh 2: Shiloh Season '99
Man of the House '95

Alistair Browning
Rain '01
Merry Christmas, Mr. Lawrence '83

Chris Browning
Linewatch '08
A Place Called Truth '98

Emily Browning (1988-)
The Uninvited '09
Lemony Snicket's A Series of Unfortunate Events '04
Ned Kelly '03
Ghost Ship '02

Ricou Browning (1930-)
Flipper's New Adventure '64
The Creature Walks among Us '56
Creature from the Black Lagoon '54

Rod Browning (1942-)
The Life & Times of the Chocolate Killer '88
When Hell Was in Session '82

Ryan Browning (1974-)
The Legend of Butch & Sundance '04
Stealing Sinatra '04
Extremedays '01
The Smokers '00

Frank Brownlee (1874-1948)
Sundown Fury '42
Tombstone Canyon '32

Brenda Bruce (1919-96)
The Widowing of Mrs. Holroyd '95
Splitting Heirs '93
Antonia and Jane '91
December Bride '91
Back Home '90
The Tenth Man '88
Mad Death '83
That'll Be the Day '73
Nightmare '63
Peeping Tom '60

Cheryl Lynn Bruce
Daughters of the Dust '91
Victimless Crimes '90
Music Box '89

Colin Bruce
Chicago Joe & the Showgirl '90
Crusoe '89
Gotham '88

David Bruce (1916-76)
Jungle Hell '55
Pier 23 '51
Hi-Jacked '50
Can't Help Singing '45
Lady on a Train '45
Salome, Where She Danced '45
Calling Dr. Death '43
Honeymoon Lodge '43
The Mad Ghoul '43
The Sea Wolf '41
Sergeant York '41

Kate Bruce (1858-1946)
Struggle '31
The Idol Dancer '20
Way Down East '20
Judith of Bethulia '14

Nigel Bruce (1895-1953)
Limelight '52
The Woman in Green '49

Julia Misbehaves '48
The Two Mrs. Carrolls '47
Dressed to Kill '46
Terror by Night '46
The Corn Is Green '45
House of Fear '45
Pursuit to Algiers '45
Son of Lassie '45
Frenchman's Creek '44
The Pearl of Death '44
Scarlet Claw '44
Spider Woman '44
Lassie, Come Home '43
Sherlock Holmes Faces Death '43
Sherlock Holmes in Washington '43
Journey for Margaret '42
Roxie Hart '42
Sherlock Holmes and the Secret Weapon '42
Sherlock Holmes: The Voice of Terror '42
This Above All '42
The Chocolate Soldier '41
Suspicion '41
The Blue Bird '40
Lillian Russell '40
Rebecca '40
Susan and God '40
The Adventures of Sherlock Holmes '39
•The Hound of the Baskervilles '39
The Rains Came '39
The Last of Mrs. Cheyney '37
Thunder in the City '37
The Charge of the Light Brigade '36
The Trail of the Lonesome Pine '36
Becky Sharp '35
She '35
The Scarlet Pimpernel '34
Stand Up and Cheer '34
Treasure Island '34

Virginia Bruce (1910-82)
Strangers When We Meet '60
State Department File 649 '49
Action in Arabia '44
Pardon My Sarong '42
The Invisible Woman '40
Let Freedom Ring '39
Born to Dance '36
The Great Ziegfeld '36
Let 'Em Have It '35
Dangerous Corner '34
Jane Eyre '34

Agnes Bruckner (1985-)
Last Resort '09
Vacancy 2: The First Cut '08
Blood & Chocolate '07
Dreamland '06
Peaceful Warrior '06
Venom '05
Haven '04
The Iris Effect '04
Stateside '04
Blue Car '03
Rick '03
The Woods '03
Home Room '02
Murder by Numbers '02

Amy Bruckner (1991-)
Nancy Drew '07
Rebound '05

Maximilian Bruckner
Cherry Blossoms '08
Guys and Balls '04

Patrick Bruel (1959-)
O Jerusalem '07
A Secret '07
Comedy of Power '06
Lost and Found '99
Sabrina '95
Secret Obsession '88
Bandits '86

Eddie Brugman (1943-)
Broken Mirrors '85
Katie Tippel '75

Alex Bruhanski
Black Point '01
Showdown at Williams Creek '91

Daniel Bruhl (1978-)
Inglourious Basterds '09
The Bourne Ultimatum '07
In Tranzit '07
Joyeux Noel '05
The Edukators '04
Ladies in Lavender '04
Good Bye, Lenin! '03

John Brumpton
Dance Me to My Song '98
Life '95

Bo Brundin (1937-)
Headless Eyes '83
Shoot the Sun Down '81
Russian Roulette '75

Valeria Bruni-Tedeschi (1964-)
Cote d'Azur '05
Munich '05
Time to Leave '05
5x2 '04
Those Who Love Me Can Take the Train '98
Mon Homme '96
Nenette and Boni '96

Robert Bruning
The Night After Halloween '79
Sunday Too Far Away '74

Chris Bruno
The Cell 2 '09
Prison Break: The Final Break '09
The Dead Zone '02

Dylan Bruno (1972-)
Quid Pro Quo '08
Fresh Cut Grass '04
Going Greek '01
The One '01
Where the Heart Is '00
The Rage: Carrie 2 '99
The Simian Line '99
When Trumpets Fade '98

Nando (Fernando) Bruno (1895-1963)
Time Out for Love '61
Two Nights with Cleopatra '54
Open City '45

Philip Bruns (1931-)
The Opposite Sex and How to Live With Them '93
Dead Men Don't Die '91
Return of the Living Dead 2 '88
The Stunt Man '80
Harry and Tonto '74

Keith Brunsmann
Tweek City '05
Tropix '02
Sticks '98

Eric Bruskotter (1966-)
Major League 3: Back to the Minors '98
Starship Troopers '97
The Fan '96
Major League 2 '94
In the Line of Fire '93
Can't Buy Me Love '87

Dora Bryan (1924-)
MirrorMask '05
Apartment Zero '88
Screamtime '83
Hands of the Ripper '71
The Great St. Trinian's Train Robbery '66
A Taste of Honey '61
Small Hotel '57
Made in Heaven '52
My Son, the Vampire '52
No Trace '50
The Fallen Idol '49

Jane Bryan (1918-)
Each Dawn I Die '39
Invisible Stripes '39

The Old Maid '39
The Sisters '38
A Slight Case of Murder '38
Kid Galahad '37
Marked Woman '37

Sabrina Bryan (1984-)
The Cheetah Girls: One World '08
The Cheetah Girls 2 '06
The Cheetah Girls '03

Zachery Ty Bryan (1981-)
Annapolis '06
The Fast and the Furious: Tokyo Drift '06
The Game of Their Lives '05
A Killing Spring '02
Rustin '01
The Rage: Carrie 2 '99
The Principal Takes a Holiday '98
True Heart '97
First Kid '96
Magic Island '95
Bigfoot: The Unforgettable Encounter '94

Bill Bryant
A Bullet for Joey '55
King Dinosaur '55

Clara Bryant
Bone Eater '07
Due East '02

John Bryant (1916-89)
Run Silent, Run Deep '58
Courage of Black Beauty '57
From Here to Eternity '53

Joy Bryant (1976-)
Welcome Home Roscoe Jenkins '08
Bobby '06
Get Rich or Die Tryin' '05
London '05
The Skeleton Key '05
3-Way '04
Baadasssss! '03
Honey '03
Antwone Fisher '02

Joyce Bryant
East Side Kids '40
Across the Plains '39
Fighting Renegade '39

Lee Bryant (1945-)
Alien Nation: Dark Horizon '94
Half Slave, Half Free '85

Michael Bryant (1928-2002)
The Miracle Maker: The Story of Jesus '00 (V)
King Lear '98
Hamlet '96
Sakharov '84
The Ruling Class '72
Girly '70
Goodbye, Mr. Chips '69
The Mind Benders '63

Nana Bryant (1888-1955)
The Private War of Major Benson '55
Follow the Sun '51
Harvey '50
Ladies of the Chorus '49
Eyes of Texas '48
Inner Sanctum '48
Big Town '47
The Possessed '47
If I Had My Way '40
Give Me a Sailor '38
Sinners in Paradise '38
Pennies from Heaven '36

Pamela Bryant (1959-)
Tigershark '87
Lunch Wagon '81

Virginia Bryant
The Barbarians '87
Demons 2 '87

William (Bill) Bryant (1924-2001)
Mountain Family Robinson '79
Corvette Summer '78
The Hanged Man '74

Claudia Bryar (1918-)
Psycho 2 '83
Green Eyes '76

Paul Bryar (1910-85)
The Night of the Hunter '55
Sky High '51
Three on a Ticket '47

Scott Bryce (1958-)
Up Close and Personal '96
Stalking Laura '93

Rob Brydon (1965-)
MirrorMask '05
Tristram Shandy: A Cock and Bull Story '05

Larry Bryggman (1938-)
Spy Game '01
Die Hard: With a Vengeance '95

Greg Bryk
Screamers: The Hunting '09
XIII '08
Grindstone Road '07
Weirdsville '07
Poor Man's Game '06

Andrew Bryniarski (1969-)
The Texas Chainsaw Massacre: The Beginning '06
44 Minutes: The North Hollywood Shootout '03
The Texas Chainsaw Massacre '03
Black Mask 2: City of Masks '02
Cyborg 3: The Recycler '95
The Program '93
Batman Returns '92

Yul Brynner (1915-85)
Death Rage '77
Futureworld '76
The Ultimate Warrior '75
Night Flight from Moscow '73
Westworld '73
Fuzz '72
Adios, Sabata '71
Catlow '71
Light at the Edge of the World '71
Romance of a Horsethief '71
Battle of Neretva '69
The Madwoman of Chaillot '69
The Magic Christian '69
Villa Rides '68
Triple Cross '67
Cast a Giant Shadow '66
The Poppy Is Also a Flower '66
Return of the Magnificent Seven '66
Morituri '65
Invitation to a Gunfighter '64
Kings of the Sun '63
Taras Bulba '62
The Magnificent Seven '60
Solomon and Sheba '59
The Testament of Orpheus '59
The Brothers Karamazov '58
The Buccaneer '58
Anastasia '56
The King and I '56
The Ten Commandments '56
Port of New York '49

Reine Brynolfsson (1953-)
Kitchen Stories '03
A Song for Martin '01
Les Miserables '97
The Last Dance '93
House of Angels '92

Michael Buble (1975-)
The Snow Walker '03
Totally Blonde '01

Flavio Bucci (1947-)
Il Divo '08
Suspiria '77
Night Train Murders '75
Torture Train '75

Colin Buchanan (1967-)
Catherine Cookson's The Secret '00
Moll Flanders '96

Edgar Buchanan (1903-79)
Yuma '70
Over the Hill Gang '69
Man from Button Willow '65 (V)
The Rounders '65
McLintock! '63
Move Over, Darling '63
Ride the High Country '62
Four Fast Guns '59
It Started with a Kiss '59
King of the Wild Stallions '59
The Devil's Partner '58
The Sheepman '58
Lonesome Trail '55
Rage at Dawn '55
Silver Star '55
Human Desire '54
Make Haste to Live '54
Shane '53
Big Trees '52
She Couldn't Say No '52
The Big Hangover '50
Cheaper by the Dozen '50
Rawhide '50
Lust for Gold '49
Man from Colorado '49
Black Arrow '48
Coroner Creek '48
Abilene Town '46
If I'm Lucky '46
Buffalo Bill '44
City Without Men '43
The Desperadoes '43
Destroyer '43
Talk of the Town '42
Penny Serenade '41
Texas '41
Arizona '40
Too Many Husbands '40

Ian Buchanan (1957-)
Make the Yuletide Gay '09
Panic Room '02
Ivory Tower '97
Marilyn & Bobby: Her Final Affair '94
Blue Flame '93
Double Exposure '93
The Cool Surface '92

Jack Buchanan (1891-1957)
The Band Wagon '53
When Knights Were Bold '36
Monte Carlo '30

Robert Buchanan
That Sinking Feeling '79
The Girl Who Knew Too Much '63

Sherry Buchanan
Doctor Butcher M.D. '80
Emmanuelle & Joanna '78
Eyes Behind the Stars '72

Simone Buchanan (1968-)
Shame '87
Run, Rebecca, Run '81

Christopher Buchholz
Eros '04
Operation Valkyrie '04
Covert Assassin '94
No Fear, No Die '90

Horst Buchholz (1932-2003)
The Enemy '01
Life Is Beautiful '98
Faraway, So Close! '93
Aces: Iron Eagle 3 '92
Code Name: Emerald '85
Sahara '83
Berlin Tunnel 21 '81
Avalanche Express '79
From Hell to Victory '79
Raid on Entebbe '77
Return to Fantasy Island '77
The Savage Bees '76
The Catamount Killing '74
Empty Canvas '64
Fanny '61
One, Two, Three '61
The Magnificent Seven '60
Tiger Bay '59
Teenage Wolfpack '57

Buck
Robinson Crusoe of Clipper Island '36
Robinson Crusoe of Mystery Island '36

Samantha Buck (1974-)
Wirey Spindell '99
The Sticky Fingers of Time '97

John Buckler (1906-36)
Tarzan Escapes '36
The Black Room '35

A. J. Buckley (1978-)
The Box '07
Jimmy & Judy '06

A.J. Buckley
Jimmy & Judy '06
Manticore '05
In Enemy Hands '04
Blue Car '03
Extremedays '01

Betty Buckley (1947-)
The Happening '08
Simply Irresistible '99
Critical Choices '97
Last Time Out '94
Wyatt Earp '94
Rain Without Thunder '93
Babycakes '89
Another Woman '88
Frantic '88
Wild Thing '87
Tender Mercies '83
Carrie '76

Keith Buckley (1941-)
Half Moon Street '86
Excalibur '81
The Virgin Witch '70

Susan Buckner (1951-)
Deadly Blessing '81
Grease '78

Robert Budaska
Grizzly Mountain '97
Ice Pawn '92

Helen Buday (1963-)
Dingo '90
For Love Alone '86
Mad Max: Beyond Thunderdome '85

Genevieve Buechner
Vipers '08
Bob the Butler '05

Gustavo Bueno
The Motorcycle Diaries '04
La Boca del Lobo '89
The City and the Dogs '85

Jack Buetel (1915-89)
The Half-Breed '51
Best of the Badmen '50
The Outlaw '43

Marilyn Buferd (1925-90)
Queen of Outer Space '58
Machine to Kill Bad People '48

Buffalo Bill, Jr. (1896-1961)
Lightning Bill '35
Powdersmoke Range '35
Riding Speed '35
Rawhide Romance '34
Deadwood Pass '33
Fighting Cowboy '33
Terror Trail '33

Jimmy Buffett (1946-)
Hoot '06
From the Earth to the Moon '98
FM '78
Rancho Deluxe '75

Monica Bugajski
Shadrach '98
The Three Lives of Karen '97

Celso Bugallo (1947-)
The Sea Inside '04
Mondays in the Sun '02

Niall Buggy (1948-)
The Playboys '92
Zardoz '73

Joe Bugner (1950-)
The Cursed Mountain Mystery '93
Fatal Bond '91

Valerie Buhagiar (1963-)
Highway 61 '91
Roadkill '89

Gerard Buhr (1928-88)
The Night of the Following Day '69
Bob le Flambeur '55

Genevieve Bujold (1942-)
Disappearances '06
Finding Home '03
Jericho Mansions '03
Eye of the Beholder '99
Last Night '98
The House of Yes '97
Eye '96
Mon Amie Max '94
The Dance Goes On '92
Oh, What a Night '92
False Identity '90
A Paper Wedding '89
Dead Ringers '88
The Moderns '88
Trouble in Mind '86
Choose Me '84
Tightrope '84
Monsignor '82
Final Assignment '80
The Last Flight of Noah's Ark '80
Murder by Decree '79
Coma '78
Another Man, Another Chance '77
Obsession '76
Swashbuckler '76
Earthquake '74
Journey '72
Trojan Women '71
Anne of the Thousand Days '69
The Thief of Paris '67
The King of Hearts '66
La Guerre Est Finie '66

Donald Buka (1921-)
Stolen Identity '53
The Street with No Name '48
Watch on the Rhine '43

Raymond Buktenica (1943-)
My Girl '91
Wait Till Your Mother Gets Home '83
The Adventures of Nellie Bly '81
The Jayne Mansfield Story '80

Peter Bull (1912-84)
Doctor Dolittle '67
Second Best Secret Agent in the Whole Wide World '65
Dr. Strangelove, or: How I Learned to Stop Worrying and Love the Bomb '64
Tom Jones '63
The African Queen '51
A Christmas Carol '51
Marie Antoinette '38
Sabotage '36

Richard Bull (1924-)
Sugar '09
Normal '03
Different Story '78
Lawman '71

Amelia Bullmore (1964-)
State of Play '03
Catherine Cookson's Tilly Trotter '99
Mrs. Dalloway '97

Jeremy Bulloch (1945-)
Return of the Jedi '83
The Empire Strikes Back '80
Hoffman '70

Donna Bullock (1955-)
The Girl Next Door '04
Air Force One '97

Sandra Bullock (1964-)
All About Steve '09
The Blind Side '09
The Proposal '09
Premonition '07
Infamous '06
The Lake House '06
Crash '05
Loverboy '05
Miss Congeniality 2: Armed and Fabulous '05
Divine Secrets of the Ya-Ya Sisterhood '02
Murder by Numbers '02
Two Weeks Notice '02
Lisa Picard Is Famous '01
Gun Shy '00
Miss Congeniality '00
28 Days '00
Forces of Nature '99
Hope Floats '98
Practical Magic '98
Prince of Egypt '98 (V)
Speed 2: Cruise Control '97
In Love and War '96
A Time to Kill '96
The Net '95
Two If by Sea '95
While You Were Sleeping '95
Me and the Mob '94
Speed '94
Demolition Man '93
Fire on the Amazon '93
The Thing Called Love '93
The Vanishing '93
Wrestling Ernest Hemingway '93
Love Potion #9 '92
Who Shot Pat? '92
When the Party's Over '91
A Fool and His Money '88
Hangmen '87

William Bumiller (1956-)
Dark Justice '00
The Heroes of Desert Storm '91
Death Spa '87

Rodger Bumpass (1951-)
The SpongeBob SquarePants Movie '04 (V)
National Lampoon's Class of '86 '86
Heavy Metal '81 (V)

Stuart Bunce (1971-)
The Gospel of John '03
All the King's Men '99
Behind the Lines '97

Brooke Bundy (1944-)
Beverly Hills Bodysnatchers '89
A Nightmare on Elm Street 4: Dream Master '88
Twice Dead '88
A Nightmare on Elm Street 3: Dream Warriors '87
Explorers '85
Two Fathers' Justice '85
The Crash of Flight 401 '78
Francis Gary Powers: The True Story of the U-2 Spy '76
The Gay Deceivers '69

Marie Bunel (1964-)
A Girl Cut in Two '07
The Chorus '04

Close to Leo *'02*
Ma Vie en Rose *'97*
La Discrete *'90*

Edward (Eddie) Bunker (1933-2005)
The Longest Yard *'05*
Animal Factory *'00*
Shadrach *'98*
Somebody to Love *'94*
Best of the Best 2 *'93*
Desperate Motives *'92*
Reservoir Dogs *'92*
Best of the Best *'89*
Miracle Mile *'89*
Relentless *'89*
Tango and Cash *'89*
Fear *'88*
The Running Man *'87*
Shy People *'87*
Runaway Train *'85*
Straight Time *'78*

Avis Bunnage (1923-90)
The Krays *'90*
No Surrender *'86*
Forbidden *'85*
The L-Shaped Room *'62*
The Loneliness of the Long Distance Runner *'62*

Herbert Bunston
The Moonstone *'34*
Dracula *'31*

Luis Bunuel (1900-83)
The Discreet Charm of the Bourgeoisie *'72*
Un Chien Andalou *'28*

Cara Buono (1974-)
Cthulhu *'08*
From Other Worlds *'04*
Hulk *'03*
Happy Accidents *'00*
Two Ninas *'00*
Attention Shoppers *'99*
Chutney Popcorn *'99*
In a Class of His Own *'99*
Man of the Century *'99*
Next Stop, Wonderland *'98*
Kicking and Screaming *'95*
Killer: A Journal of Murder *'95*
The Cowboy Way *'94*
Gladiator *'92*
Waterland *'92*
The River is Red *'48*

Victor Buono (1938-82)
Flight of Dragons *'82 (V)*
The Man with Bogart's Face *'80*
More Wild, Wild West *'80*
Backstairs at the White House *'79*
Better Late Than Never *'79*
The Evil *'78*
The Man from Atlantis *'77*
Arnold *'73*
The Mad Butcher *'72*
Northeast of Seoul *'72*
Beneath the Planet of the Apes *'70*
Boot Hill *'69*
The Silencers *'66*
Hush, Hush, Sweet Charlotte *'65*
Robin and the 7 Hoods *'64*
The Strangler *'64*
Four for Texas *'63*
What Ever Happened to Baby Jane? *'62*

Sonny Bupp (1928-2007)
Citizen Kane *'41*
Three Faces West *'40*
Hopalong Cassidy: Renegade Trail *'39*
Renegade Trail *'39*

Tommy Bupp (1924-83)
Hey! Hey! USA! *'38*
Roarin' Lead *'37*
Tex Rides with the Boy Scouts *'37*
It's a Gift *'34*

Hugh Burden (1913-85)
Blood from the Mummy's Tomb *'71*
Funeral in Berlin *'66*
Ghost Ship *'53*
Fame Is the Spur *'47*
Immortal Battalion *'44*

Suzanne Burden (1958-)
A Mind to Murder *'96*
Strapless *'90*
Office Romances *'86*
Sharma & Beyond *'84*

Ray Burdis (1958-)
Love, Honour & Obey *'00*
Final Cut *'98*

Alexander Burejev
Prisoner of the Mountains *'96*
Freedom Is Paradise *'89*

Kim Burfield
Treasure Island *'72*
The Hero *'71*

Michael J. Burg (1968-)
The Audrey Hepburn Story *'00*
Impostors *'80*

Christopher Burgard
Full Body Massage *'95*
84 Charlie MoPic *'89*
Twice Dead *'88*

Gregg Burge (1957-98)
School Daze *'88*
A Chorus Line *'85*

Dorothy Burgess (1907-61)
Girls in Chains *'43*
Village Tale *'35*
Hold Your Man *'33*
Ladies They Talk About *'33*

John Burgess
Rosencrantz & Guildenstern Are Dead *'90*
Christabel *'89*

Scott Burgess
Dead Easy *'82*
1915 *'82*

Gary Burghoff (1943-)
Small Kill *'93*
Casino *'80*
The Man in the Santa Claus Suit *'79*
M*A*S*H *'70*

Richard Burgi (1958-)
The Christmas Cottage *'08*
Hostel: Part 2 *'07*
Fun With Dick and Jane *'05*
In Her Shoes *'05*
Cellular *'04*
Darklight *'04*
Starship Troopers 2: Hero of the Federation *'04*
I Married a Monster *'98*

Zlatko Buric (1953-)
Dirty Pretty Things *'03*
Pusher *'96*

MyAnna Buring
Vampire Killers *'09*
Doomsday *'08*
The Descent *'05*

Alfred Burke (1918-)
The House on Garibaldi Street *'79*
The Brontes of Haworth *'73*
One Day in the Life of Ivan Denisovich *'71*
Night Caller from Outer Space *'66*
The Nanny *'65*
Children of the Damned *'63*
Dead Lucky *'60*

Billie Burke (1885-1970)
Sergeant Rutledge *'60*
The Young Philadelphians *'59*
Small Town Girl *'53*
Father's Little Dividend *'51*
Father of the Bride *'50*
The Barkleys of Broadway *'49*
Breakfast in Hollywood *'46*
The Cheaters *'45*
Gildersleeve on Broadway *'43*
In This Our Life *'42*
They All Kissed the Bride *'42*
The Man Who Came to Dinner *'41*
Topper Returns *'41*
Eternally Yours *'39*
Topper Takes a Trip *'39*
The Wizard of Oz *'39*
Everybody Sing *'38*
The Young in Heart *'38*
The Bride Wore Red *'37*
Navy Blue and Gold *'37*
Topper *'37*
Craig's Wife *'36*
Becky Sharp *'35*
Doubting Thomas *'35*
Forsaking All Others *'35*
Splendor *'35*
Christopher Strong *'33*
Dinner at Eight *'33*
Finishing School *'33*
A Bill of Divorcement *'32*

Billy Burke (1966-)
The Twilight Saga: Eclipse *'10*
The Twilight Saga: New Moon *'09*
Twilight *'08*
Untraceable *'08*
Feast of Love *'07*
Forfeit *'07*
Fracture *'07*
Three Days to Vegas *'07*
Ladder 49 *'04*
Lost Junction *'03*
Along Came a Spider *'01*
The Independent *'00*
Komodo *'99*
Don't Look Down *'98*
Mafia! *'98*
Without Limits *'97*
To Cross the Rubicon *'91*

Brandon Burke
Best Enemies *'86*
The Odd Angry Shot *'79*

David Burke
King Lear *'98*
Vibrations *'94*

Delta Burke (1956-)
Bridal Fever *'08*
Good Boy! *'03 (V)*
Dangerous Child *'01*
Sordid Lives *'00*
What Women Want *'00*
Melanie Darrow *'97*
Maternal Instincts *'96*
Dynamite and Gold *'88*
A Bunny's Tale *'85*
First & Ten: The Team Scores Again *'85*
The Seekers *'79*

J. Frank Burke (1867-1918)
The Bargain *'15*
The Italian *'15*

James Burke (1886-1968)
In Enemy Hands *'04*
Lucky Me *'54*
Cavalry Charge *'51*
Down to Earth *'47*
At the Circus *'39*
Beau Geste *'39*
Dawn Patrol *'38*
Dead End *'37*
Make a Million *'35*
The Mystery Man *'35*
Ruggles of Red Gap *'35*
Lady by Choice *'34*
Ticket to a Crime *'34*

Joe Michael Burke (1973-)
Wild Things 2 *'04*
The Last Warrior *'99*

Kathleen Burke (1913-80)
The Lion Man *'36*
The Last Outpost *'35*
The Lives of a Bengal Lancer *'35*
Murders in the Zoo *'33*
Island of Lost Souls *'32*

Kathy Burke (1964-)
Flushed Away *'06 (V)*
Once Upon a Time in the Midlands *'02*
Kevin & Perry Go Large *'00*
Love, Honour & Obey *'00*
Dancing at Lughnasa *'98*
Elizabeth *'98*
Nil by Mouth *'96*

Marylouise Burke
A Prairie Home Companion *'06*
Pizza *'05*
Sideways *'04*
Series 7: The Contenders *'01*

Michael Reilly Burke (1969-)
The Collector *'09*
Octopus 2: River of Fear *'02*
Red Shoe Diaries: Luscious Lola *'00*

Michelle Burke
See Michelle Rene Thomas

Patricia Burke (1917-2003)
While I Live *'47*
Murder in the Footlights *'46*

Paul Burke (1926-2009)
The Red Light Sting *'84*
Wild & Wooly *'78*
Psychic Killer *'75*
Anatomy of Terror *'74*
Daddy's Gone A-Hunting *'69*
Valley of the Dolls *'67*
Fatal Confinement *'64*
Francis in the Navy *'55*
Francis Goes to West Point *'52*

Robert John Burke (1961-)
Endgame *'09*
Miracle at St. Anna *'08*
Good Night, and Good Luck *'05*
Hide and Seek *'05*
Connie and Carla *'04*
Speak *'04*
No Such Thing *'01*
A Bright Shining Lie *'98*
First Love, Last Rites *'98*
From the Earth to the Moon *'98*
Somewhere in the City *'97*
Fled *'96*
Stephen King's Thinner *'96*
Killer: A Journal of Murder *'95*
Dust Devil *'93*
A Far Off Place *'93*
Tombstone *'93*
Simple Men *'92*
Rambling Rose *'91*
RoboCop 3 *'91*
The Unbelievable Truth *'90*

Robert Karl Burke
The Basket *'99*
Big and Hairy *'98*

Simon Burke (1961-)
The Alice *'04*
After the Deluge *'03*
Rodgers & Hammerstein's South Pacific *'01*
Pitch Black *'00*
Passion *'99*
The One That Got Away *'96*
Slate, Wyn & Me *'87*
The Irishman *'78*
The Devil's Playground *'76*

Tom Burke (1981-)
Donkey Punch *'08*
I Want Candy *'07*
Dracula *'06*

All the King's Men *'99*

Laura Burkett
Daddy's Boys *'87*
Overkill *'86*

Gedeon Burkhard
Inglourious Basterds *'09*
We'll Meet Again *'02*

Scott Burkholder
Sketch Artist 2: Hands That See *'94*
Class of '61 *'92*
House 4: Home Deadly Home *'91*

Dennis Burkley (1945-)
Possums *'99*
The First 9 1/2 Weeks *'98*
Father's Day *'96*
Tin Cup *'96*
Son-in-Law *'93*
Stop! or My Mom Will Shoot *'92*
The Doors *'91*
Lambada *'89*
Pass the Ammo *'88*
Murphy's Romance *'85*
Bummer *'73*

Tom Burlinson (1957-)
Landslide *'92*
Showdown at Williams Creek *'91*
Piece of Cake *'88*
Return to Snowy River *'88*
The Time Guardian *'87*
Windrider *'86*
Flesh and Blood *'85*
Phar Lap *'84*
The Man from Snowy River *'82*

Leo Burmester (1944-)
Carry Me Home *'04*
City by the Sea *'02*
Limbo *'99*
Speed of Life *'99*
Eye of the Storm *'98*
Switchback *'97*
William Faulkner's Old Man *'97*
Mistrial *'96*
The Great Elephant Escape *'95*
The Neon Bible *'95*
Truman *'95*
Fly by Night *'93*
A Perfect World *'93*
Passion Fish *'92*
The Abyss *'89*
The River is Red *'48*

Tam Dean Burn
Longford *'06*
The Acid House *'98*

Caesar Burner
Green Inferno *'72*
Tombs of the Blind Dead *'72*

Carol Burnett (1933-)
Post Grad *'09*
Dr. Seuss' Horton Hears a Who! *'08 (V)*
The Trumpet of the Swan *'01 (V)*
Moon over Broadway *'98*
Noises Off *'92*
Follies in Concert *'85*
Between Friends *'83*
Annie *'82*
Chu Chu & the Philly Flash *'81*
The Four Seasons *'81*
Friendly Fire *'79*
Tenth Month *'79*
The Grass Is Always Greener Over the Septic Tank *'78*
A Wedding *'78*
The Front Page *'74*
Pete 'n' Tillie *'72*

Olivia Burnette (1977-)
Flourish *'06*
The Thorn Birds: The Missing Years *'96*
Final Verdict *'91*

Smiley Burnette (1911-67)
Last of the Pony Riders *'53*
On Top of Old Smoky *'53*
Winning of the West *'53*
Bonanza Town *'51*
Blazing Across the Pecos *'48*
Call of the Rockies *'44*
Idaho *'43*
King of the Cowboys *'43*
Raiders of Sunset Pass *'43*
Silver Spurs *'43*
Bells of Capistrano *'42*
Call of the Canyon *'42*
Heart of the Golden West *'42*
Heart of the Rio Grande *'42*
Back in the Saddle *'41*
Down Mexico Way *'41*
Ridin' on a Rainbow *'41*
Gaucho Serenade *'40*
South of the Border *'39*
Billy the Kid Returns *'38*
Hollywood Stadium Mystery *'38*
The Man from Music Mountain *'38*
Oh Susannah *'38*
Old Barn Dance *'38*
Prairie Moon *'38*
Rootin' Tootin' Rhythm *'38*
Under Western Stars *'38*
Big Show *'37*
Boots & Saddles *'37*
Dick Tracy *'37*
Dick Tracy: The Spider Strikes *'37*
Git Along Little Dogies *'37*
Larceny On the Air *'37*
Public Cowboy No. 1 *'37*
Round-Up Time in Texas *'37*
Springtime in the Rockies *'37*
Yodelin' Kid from Pine Ridge *'37*
Old Corral *'36*
Red River Valley *'36*
Ride, Ranger, Ride *'36*
Undersea Kingdom *'36*
Harmony Lane *'35*
Melody Trail *'35*
The Phantom Empire *'35*
In Old Santa Fe *'34*
Mystery Mountain *'34*

Alex Burns (1977-)
Brother to Brother *'04*
National Lampoon's Van Wilder *'02*
Thirteen Conversations About One Thing *'01*

Bob Burns (1890-1956)
Waikiki Wedding *'37*
Rhythm on the Range *'36*

Brooke Burns (1978-)
The Art of Travel *'08*
The Most Wonderful Time of the Year *'08*
Smoke Jumpers *'08*
The Salon *'05*
Single White Female 2: The Psycho *'05*
Shallow Hal *'01*

Carol Burns (1947-)
Dusty *'85*
Bad Blood *'81*

Catherine Lloyd Burns (1961-)
The Baxter *'05*
Everything Put Together *'00*

David Burns
Hey! Hey! USA! *'38*
Sidewalks of London *'38*

Edmund Burns (1892-1989)
Reform School Girl *'57*
Sea Devils *'31*
Sunny Side Up *'28*
Made for Love *'26*

Edward Burns (1968-)
Echelon Conspiracy *'09*
One Missed Call *'08*

27 Dresses '08
Purple Violets '07
The Groomsmen '06
The Holiday '06
The River King '05
A Sound of Thunder '05
The Breakup Artist '04
Looking for Kitty '04
Confidence '03
Ash Wednesday '02
Life or Something Like It '02
15 Minutes '01
Sidewalks of New York '01
No Looking Back '98
Saving Private Ryan '98
She's the One '96
The Brothers McMullen '94

George Burns (1896-1996)
Radioland Murders '94
18 Again! '88
Oh, God! You Devil '84
Two of a Kind '82
Oh, God! Book 2 '80
Going in Style '79
Sgt. Pepper's Lonely Hearts Club Band '78
Oh, God! '77
The Sunshine Boys '75
Solid Gold Cadillac '56 (N)
Honolulu '39
College Swing '38
A Damsel in Distress '37
Here Comes Cookie '35
Love in Bloom '35
Six of a Kind '34
We're Not Dressing '34
College Humor '33
International House '33

Heather Burns (1974-)
The Groomsmen '06
Kill the Poor '06
Perception '06
Bewitched '05
Brooklyn Lobster '05
Miss Congeniality 2: Armed and Fabulous '05
Two Weeks Notice '02
Miss Congeniality '00
You Are Here * '00
You've Got Mail '98

Helen Burns
Utilities '83
Zorro, the Gay Blade '81

Jennifer Burns
Isaac Asimov's Nightfall '00
Josh Kirby... Time Warrior: Chapter 5, Journey to the Magic Cavern '96
Josh Kirby... Time Warrior: Chapter 6, Last Battle for the Universe '96
Josh Kirby. . .Time Warrior: Chapter 1, Planet of the Dino-Knights '95
Josh Kirby... Time Warrior: Chapter 2, The Human Pets '95
Josh Kirby... Time Warrior: Chapter 3, Trapped on Toyworld '95
Josh Kirby... Time Warrior: Chapter 4, Eggs from 70 Million B.C. '95
Haunted Symphony '94
The Liar's Club '93

Jere Burns (1954-)
What's Up, Scarlet? '05
Crocodile Dundee in Los Angeles '01
Life-Size '00
Santa Fe '97
Greedy '94
The Gambler Returns: The Luck of the Draw '93
Wired '89

Marilyn Burns (1956-)
The Texas Chainsaw Massacre 4: The Next Generation '95
Future Kill '85
Kiss Daddy Goodbye '81
Eaten Alive '76
Helter Skelter '76
The Texas Chainsaw Massacre '74

Marion Burns (1907-93)
Dawn Rider '35
Paradise Canyon '35

Mark Burns (1936-)
Bullseye! '90
Count Dracula '77
House of the Living Dead '73
Death in Venice '71
The Virgin and the Gypsy '70
The Charge of the Light Brigade '68

Martha Burns
The Trojan Horse '08
Slings & Arrows: Season 2 '05
Siblings '04
The Life Before This '99
Long Day's Journey Into Night '96

Megan Burns (1986-)
28 Days Later '02
Liam '00

Michael Burns (1947-)
Santee '73
Thumb Tripping '72
That Cold Day in the Park '69

Robert Burns (1884-1957)
Western Trails '38
Gun Law '33
When a Man Rides Alone '33
South of Santa Fe '32

Tim Burns (1953-)
Freaked '93
Mad Max '80

Raymond Burr (1917-93)
Delirious '91
Showdown at Williams Creek '91
Perry Mason: The Case of the Lost Love '87
Godzilla 1985 '85
Perry Mason Returns '85
Airplane 2: The Sequel '82
Peter and Paul '81
The Curse of King Tut's Tomb '80
The Night the City Screamed '80
Out of the Blue '80
The Return '80
Love's Savage Fury '79
The Bastard '78 (N)
Centennial '78
Tomorrow Never Comes '77
Crime of Passion '57
Godzilla, King of the Monsters '56
Great Day in the Morning '56
A Man Alone '55
They Were So Young '55
Casanova's Big Night '54
Party Girls for Sale '54
Passion '54
Rear Window '54
Thunder Pass '54
The Blue Gardenia '53
Tarzan and the She-Devil '53
FBI Girl '52
Horizons West '52
Meet Danny Wilson '52
Bride of the Gorilla '51
His Kind of Woman '51
A Place in the Sun '51
Borderline '50
Key to the City '50
Love Happy '50
Adventures of Don Juan '49
Black Magic '49
Pitfall '48
Raw Deal '48
Station West '48
Abandoned '47
Desperate '47

Robert Burr (1926-2000)
Netherworld '90
Look Back in Anger '80
The Possession of Joel Delaney '72

Maryedith Burrell (1952-)
Camp Nowhere '94
The Little Match Girl '87

Sheila Burrell (1922-)
Cold Comfort Farm '94
Paranoiac '62

Ty Burrell (1967-)
The Incredible Hulk '08
The Darwin Awards '06
Friends with Money '06
Fur: An Imaginary Portrait of Diane Arbus '06
Dawn of the Dead '04
In Good Company '04
Black Hawk Down '01
Evolution '01

Hedy Burress (1973-)
Valentine '01
Cabin by the Lake '00
Foxfire '96

Bonnie Burroughs
One Small Hero '99
Hard to Kill '89

Jackie Burroughs (1939-)
King's Ransom '05
Re-Generation '04
Snow '04
A Guy Thing '03
The Republic of Love '03
Willard '03
Lost and Delirious '01
Elvis Meets Nixon '98
Last Night '98
Armistead Maupin's More Tales of the City '97
Bleeders '97
Careful '92
Final Notice '89
A Winter Tan '88
John and the Missus '87
The Housekeeper '86
Anne of Green Gables '85
Undergrads '85
The Grey Fox '83
125 Rooms of Comfort '83
Overdrawn at the Memory Bank '83
Heavy Metal '81 (V)

William S. Burroughs (1914-97)
Wax, or the Discovery of Television among the Bees '93
Bloodhounds of Broadway '89
Drugstore Cowboy '89
Twister '89
Haxan: Witchcraft through the Ages '22 (N)

Darren E. Burrows (1966-)
Forty Shades of Blue '05
Sunset Strip '99
The Hi-Lo Country '98
Class of 1999 '90
Cry-Baby '90

Saffron Burrows (1972-)
Shrink '09
The Bank Job '08
The Guitar '08
Reign Over Me '07
Fay Grim '06
Klimt '06
Troy '04
Peter Pan '03 (N)
Frida '02
Enigma '01
Hotel '01
The Seventh Stream '01
Tempted '01
Gangster No. 1 '00
Time Code '00
Deep Blue Sea '99
Miss Julie '99
Wing Commander '99
The Loss of Sexual Innocence '98
Lovelife '97
The Matchmaker '97
Nevada '97
Hotel de Love '96
Welcome II the Terrordome '95
Circle of Friends '94

Luigi Burruano
Luna e L'Altra '96
The Sicilian Connection '85

Ellen Burstyn (1932-)
According to Greta '08
The Loss of a Teardrop Diamond '08
W. '08
For One More Day '07
The Stone Angel '07
The Elephant King '06
The Fountain '06
The Wicker Man '06
Mrs. Harris '05
Brush with Fate '03
Divine Secrets of the Ya-Ya Sisterhood '02
Red Dragon '02 (V)
Dodson's Journey '01
Mermaid '00
Requiem for a Dream '00
The Yards '00
Night Ride Home '99
Flash '98
Playing by Heart '98
Deceiver '97
The Baby-Sitters' Club '95
The Color of Evening '95
Follow the River '95
How to Make an American Quilt '95
My Brother's Keeper '95
Roommates '95
The Spitfire Grill '95
Getting Gotti '94
Getting Out '94
Primal Secrets '94
When a Man Loves a Woman '94
The Cemetery Club '93
Grand Isle '92
Dying Young '91
Hanna's War '88
Pack of Lies '87
Act of Vengeance '86
Something in Common '86
Into Thin Air '85
Twice in a Lifetime '85
The Ambassador '84
The People vs. Jean Harris '81
Silence of the North '81
Resurrection '80
A Dream of Passion '78
Same Time, Next Year '78
Providence '77
Alice Doesn't Live Here Anymore '74
Harry and Tonto '74
Thursday's Game '74
The Exorcist '73
The King of Marvin Gardens '72
The Last Picture Show '71
Alex in Wonderland '70
Tropic of Cancer '70
Pit Stop '67
Goodbye Charlie '64

Benny Burt (1900-80)
Hawaiian Buckaroo '38
Sea Racketeers '37

Clarence Burton (-1933)
The Fighting Eagle '27
The Navigator '24

Corey Burton (1955-)
Star Wars: The Clone Wars '08 (V)
Return to Never Land '02 (V)
Treasure Planet '02 (V)
Atlantis: The Lost Empire '01 (V)
Dudley Do-Right '99 (N)

Frederick Burton
One Way Passage '32
Too Busy to Work '32
An American Tragedy '31

Harry Burton (1961-)
Devices and Desires '91
Fortunes of War '87

Hilarie Burton
The Secret Life of Bees '08
Havoc 2: Normal Adolescent Behavior '07
The List '07

Jennifer Burton
Death and Desire '97
Watch Me '96
Play Time '94
Truck Stop Women '74

John Burton (1904-87)
Mrs. Miniver '42
Lloyds of London '36

Julian Burton (1932-2006)
Masque of the Red Death '65
A Bucket of Blood '59

Kate Burton (1957-)
Max Payne '08
Quid Pro Quo '08
Lovely by Surprise '07
Empire Falls '05
Stay '05
The Diary of Ellen Rimbauer '03
Swimfan '02
Unfaithful '02
Celebrity '98
Ellen Foster '97
The Ice Storm '97
Mistrial '96
August '95
Love Matters '93
Uncle Tom's Cabin '87
Big Trouble in Little China '86

LeVar Burton (1957-)
Star Trek: Nemesis '02
Ali '01
Dancing in September '00
Star Trek: Insurrection '98
Star Trek: First Contact '96
Yesterday's Target '96
Parallel Lives '94
Star Trek: Generations '94
Firestorm: 72 Hours in Oakland '93
Roots: The Gift '88
The Midnight Hour '86
The Supernaturals '86
The Jesse Owens Story '84
Acorn People '82
Grambling's White Tiger '81
The Guyana Tragedy: The Story of Jim Jones '80
The Hunter '80
One in a Million: The Ron LeFlore Story '78
Billy: Portrait of a Street Kid '77
Roots '77

Marie Burton
Outlaws of the Range '36
Pinto Rustlers '36

Norman Burton (1935-)
Bloodsport '88
Bad Guys '86
Crimes of Passion '84
Mausoleum '83
Fade to Black '80
The Terminal Man '74
Save the Tiger '73
Diamonds Are Forever '71
Jud '71
Simon, King of the Witches '71
Attack of the Mayan Mummy '63
Fright '56

Richard Burton (1925-84)
Wagner: The Complete Epic '85
Wagner: The Movie '85
1984 '84
Absolution '81
Circle of Two '80
Lovespell '79
Breakthrough '78
The Medusa Touch '78
Wild Geese '78
Equus '77
The Exorcist 2: The Heretic '77
The Gathering Storm '74
The Klansman '74
Massacre in Rome '73
Under Milk Wood '73
Assassination of Trotsky '72
Bluebeard '72
Divorce His, Divorce Hers '72
Hammersmith Is Out '72
Raid on Rommel '71
Anne of the Thousand Days '69
Boom! '68
Candy '68
Doctor Faustus '68
Where Eagles Dare '68
The Comedians '67
The Taming of the Shrew '67
Who's Afraid of Virginia Woolf? '66
The Sandpiper '65
The Spy Who Came in from the Cold '65
Becket '64
The Night of the Iguana '64
Zulu '64 (N)
Cleopatra '63
The Tempest '63
The V.I.P.'s '63
The Longest Day '62
The Bramble Bush '60
Ice Palace '60
Look Back in Anger '58
Sea Wife '57
Alexander the Great '55
The Desert Rats '53
The Robe '53
Green Grow the Rushes '51
The Last Days of Dolwyn '49

Robert Burton (1895-1962)
The Slime People '63
Invasion of the Animal People '62
The Gallant Hours '60
Compulsion '59
Teenage Frankenstein '58
The Tall T '57
A Man Called Peter '55
Above and Beyond '53
All the Brothers Were Valiant '53
The Girl Who Had Everything '53

Robert (Skip) Burton
Bucktown '75
Trilogy of Terror '75

Steve (Stephen) Burton (1970-)
Taken '02
The Last Castle '01
Cyber-Tracker 2 '95

Tony Burton (1937-)
Hack! '07
Rocky Balboa '06
The Magnificent Seven '98
Flipping '96
Mission of Justice '92
House Party 2: The Pajama Jam '91
Armed and Dangerous '86
Oceans of Fire '86
The Shining '80
Blackjack '78
Assault on Precinct 13 '76
Rocky '76

Warren Burton (1944-)
Bloodfist 8: Hard Way Out '96
Humanoids from the Deep '96
Gettysburg '93

Wendell Burton (1947-)
East of Eden '80
Fortune and Men's Eyes '71
The Sterile Cuckoo '69

Sean Bury (1954-)
Paul and Michelle '74
The Abominable Dr. Phibes '71
Friends '71
If... '69

Steve Buscemi (1957-)
Youth in Revolt '10
G-Force '09
The Messenger '09
Saint John of Las Vegas '09
Igor '08 (V)
I Now Pronounce You Chuck and Larry '07
I Think I Love My Wife '07
Interview '07
Art School Confidential '06
Charlotte's Web '06 (V)
Delirious '06
Monster House '06 (V)
Paris, je t'aime '06
The Island '05
Romance & Cigarettes '05
Home on the Range '04 (V)
Tanner on Tanner '04
Big Fish '03
Coffee and Cigarettes '03
Spy Kids 3-D: Game Over '03
The Laramie Project '02
Love in the Time of Money '02
Mr. Deeds '02
Spy Kids 2: The Island of Lost Dreams '02
13 Moons '02
Domestic Disturbance '01
Double Whammy '01
Final Fantasy: The Spirits Within '01 (V)
Ghost World '01
The Grey Zone '01
Monsters, Inc. '01 (V)
Animal Factory '00
28 Days '00
Big Daddy '99
Armageddon '98
The Imposters '98
The Big Lebowski '97
Con Air '97
The Real Blonde '97
The Wedding Singer '97
Escape from L.A. '96
Fargo '96
The Search for One-Eye Jimmy '96
Tree's Lounge '96
Desperado '95
Kansas City '95
Things to Do in Denver When You're Dead '95
Airheads '94
Billy Madison '94
Floundering '94
Living in Oblivion '94
Me and the Mob '94
Pulp Fiction '94
Somebody to Love '94
Ed and His Dead Mother '93
The Hudsucker Proxy '93
The Last Outlaw '93
Rising Sun '93
Twenty Bucks '93
Crisscross '92
In the Soup '92
Reservoir Dogs '92
Trusting Beatrice '92
Barton Fink '91
Billy Bathgate '91
King of New York '90
Tales from the Darkside: The Movie '90
Mystery Train '89
New York Stories '89
Slaves of New York '89
Heart '87
Parting Glances '86

Charles Busch (1954-)
A Very Serious Person '06
Die Mommie Die! '03
Psycho Beach Party '00

Ernst Busch (1900-80)
Kameradschaft '31
The Threepenny Opera '31

Mae Busch (1897-1946)
The Mad Monster '42
Ziegfeld Girl '41
Marie Antoinette '38
Bohemian Girl '36
The Clutching Hand '36
Sucker Money '34
Sons of the Desert '33
Doctor X '32
The Rider of Death Valley '32
Without Honors '32
Defenders of the Law '31
Alibi '29
The Unholy Three '25
Souls for Sale '23
Foolish Wives '22

Gary Busey (1944-)
Maneater '07
Chasing Ghosts '05
Border Blues '03
Latin Dragon '03
Quigley '03
On the Edge '02
Sam & Janet '02
Slap Shot 2: Breaking the Ice '02
A Crack in the Floor '00
Hooded Angels '00
Tribulation '00
Detour '99
Jacob Two Two Meets the Hooded Fang '99
No Tomorrow '99
Fear and Loathing in Las Vegas '98
The Girl Next Door '98
Soldier '98
Two Shades of Blue '98
Universal Soldier 2: Brothers in Arms '98
Diary of a Serial Killer '97
The Real Thing '97
Rough Riders '97
Steel Sharks '97
Black Sheep '96
Lethal Tender '96
Lost Highway '96
Plato's Run '96
The Rage '96
Sticks and Stones '96
Suspicious Minds '96
Carried Away '95
Man with a Gun '95
Breaking Point '94
Chasers '94
Drop Zone '94
Surviving the Game '94
Warriors '94
Fallen Angels 1 '93
The Firm '93
Rookie of the Year '93
Canvas: The Fine Art of Crime '92
Chrome Soldiers '92
The Player '92
South Beach '92
Under Siege '92
My Heroes Have Always Been Cowboys '91
Point Break '91
Hider in the House '90
Predator 2 '90
Act of Piracy '89
Dangerous Life '89
The Neon Empire '89
Bulletproof '88
Lethal Weapon '87
Let's Get Harry '87
Eye of the Tiger '86
Half a Lifetime '86
Insignificance '85
Silver Bullet '85
D.C. Cab '84
Didn't You Hear? '83
Barbarosa '82
Carny '80
Foolin' Around '80
Big Wednesday '78
The Buddy Holly Story '78
Straight Time '78
Gumball Rally '76
A Star Is Born '76
The Execution of Private Slovik '74
Thunderbolt & Lightfoot '74
The Last American Hero '73
The Shrieking '73
Angels Hard As They Come '71

Jake Busey (1972-)
Comanche Moon '08
Time Bomb '08
Road House 2: Last Call '06
Wristcutters: A Love Story '06
Christmas With the Kranks '04
The Hitcher 2: I've Been Waiting '03
Identity '03
Lost Junction '03
The First $20 Million is Always the Hardest '02
Fast Sofa '01
Tomcats '01
Held Up '00
Tail Lights Fade '99
Black Cat Run '98
Enemy of the State '98
Home Fries '98
Contact '97
Starship Troopers '97
The Frighteners '96
Twister '96
P.C.U. '94
S.F.W. '94
Windrunner '94

Timothy Busfield (1957-)
National Security '03
Dead in a Heartbeat '02
Terminal Error '02
Time at the Top '99
Dream House '98
Wanted '98
Buffalo Soldiers '97
Shadow of a Scream '97
The Souler Opposite '97
Trucks '97
First Kid '96
Little Big League '94
Fade to Black '93
The Skateboard Kid '93
Striking Distance '93
Sneakers '92
Strays '91
Field of Dreams '89
Revenge of the Nerds 2: Nerds in Paradise '87
Revenge of the Nerds '84

Billy Green Bush (1935-)
Jason Goes to Hell: The Final Friday '93
Conagher '91
Elvis and Me '88
Critters '86
The Deliberate Stranger '86
The Hitcher '86
The River '84
Tom Horn '80
The Invasion of Johnson County '76
Alice Doesn't Live Here Anymore '74
Electra Glide in Blue '73
Culpepper Cattle Co. '72
Five Easy Pieces '70

Grand L. Bush (1955-)
Boa '02
Extreme Honor '01
Demolition Man '93
Freejack '92
Blind Vengeance '90
Lethal Weapon 2 '89
Colors '88
Die Hard '88
Brewster's Millions '85
Streets of Fire '84
Stir Crazy '80

James Bush (1907-87)
King of the Cowboys '43
West of Cimarron '41
Children of the Wild '37
The Glory Trail '36
The Return of Peter Grimm '35
A Shot in the Dark '35
Beggars in Ermine '34
Crimson Romance '34

Jovita Bush
Foxstyle '73
The Cheerleaders '72

Shoshana Bush
Dance Flick '09
Fling '08

Sophia Bush (1982-)
Table for Three '09
The Hitcher '07
John Tucker Must Die '06
Stay Alive '06

Anthony Bushell (1904-97)
A Night to Remember '58
Angel with the Trumpet '50
The Miniver Story '50
The Small Back Room '49
The Arsenal Stadium Mystery '39
Dark Journey '37
The Ghoul '34
The Scarlet Pimpernel '34
Vanity Fair '32
The Royal Bed '31
Disraeli '30

Francis X. Bushman (1883-1966)
The Phantom Planet '61
Sabrina '54
David and Bathsheba '51
Honky Tonk '41
Dick Tracy: The Spider Strikes '37
When Lightning Strikes '34
The Three Musketeers '33
Last Frontier '32
Ben-Hur '26
Eyes Right! '26
Midnight Faces '26

Akosua Busia (1968-)
Tears of the Sun '03
Larry McMurtry's Dead Man's Walk '96
Rosewood '96
The Seventh Sign '88
Hard Lessons '86
Native Son '86
The Color Purple '85
The Final Terror '83

Marion Busia
Deadline Auto Theft '83
Gone in 60 Seconds '74

Pascale Bussieres (1968-)
Afterwards '08
The Blue Butterfly '04
Xchange '00
The Five Senses '99
Girls Can't Swim '99
Set Me Free '99
Jack Higgins' Thunder Point '97
The Twilight of the Ice Nymphs '97
When Night Is Falling '95

Raymond Bussieres (1907-82)
Jonah Who Will Be 25 in the Year 2000 '76
Paris When It Sizzles '64
Beauties of the Night '52
Casque d'Or '52

Budd Buster (1891-1965)
Outlaw of the Plains '46
Border Badmen '45
Frontier Outlaws '44
Cowboy Commandos '43
Raiders of Sunset Pass '43
Thunder River Feud '42
The Lone Rider in Frontier Fury '41
The Lone Rider in Ghost Town '41
Trigger Men '41
West of Cimarron '41
Covered Wagon Trails '40
Pinto Canyon '40
Zorro's Fighting Legion '39
Feud Maker '38
Songs and Bullets '38
Thunder in the Desert '38
Roaring Six Guns '37
Gun Grit '36
Texas Jack '35
The Gun Ranger '34

Mitchell Butel
The Bank '01
Strange Fits of Passion '99
Dark City '97

Dick Butkus (1942-)
Spontaneous Combustion '89
Hamburger... The Motion Picture '86
Johnny Dangerously '84
Cracking Up '83
Deadly Games '80
The Legend of Sleepy Hollow '79
Mother, Jugs and Speed '76
Spaghetti Western '75

Brett Butler (1958-)
The Dress Code '99
Militia '99

Cindy Butler
Boggy Creek II '83
Grayeagle '77

Dan E. Butler (1954-)
The First $20 Million is Always the Hardest '02
Sniper 2 '02
Enemy of the State '98
From the Earth to the Moon '98
Armistead Maupin's More Tales of the City '97
The Assassination File '96
The Fan '96
I Love Trouble '94
Dave '93
Rising Sun '93
Captain Ron '92
The Silence of the Lambs '91
Longtime Companion '90
The Long Walk Home '89
The Manhattan Project '86
Manhunter '86

David Butler
Rhodes '97
Prey for the Hunter '92
Crucible of Horror '69

David Butler (1927-2006)
7th Heaven '27
The Man on the Box '25
The Sky Pilot '21
County Fair '20

Daws Butler (1916-88)
The Good, the Bad, and Huckleberry Hound '88 (V)
Hey There, It's Yogi Bear '64 (V)

Dean Butler (1956-)
The Final Goal '94
Desert Hearts '86
The Kid with the 200 I.Q. '83
Forever '78

Frank Butler (1890-1967)
Made for Love '26
King of the Wild Horses '24

Gerard Butler (1969-)
The Bounty Hunter '10
How to Train Your Dragon '10 (V)
Gamer '09
Law Abiding Citizen '09
The Ugly Truth '09
Nim's Island '08
RocknRolla '08
P.S. I Love You '07
Shattered '07
300 '07
Beowulf & Grendel '06
The Game of Their Lives '05
Dear Frankie '04
The Phantom of the Opera '04
Lara Croft Tomb Raider: The Cradle of Life '03
Timeline '03
Harrison's Flowers '02
Reign of Fire '02
Attila '01
Dracula 2000 '00
Shooters '00
One More Kiss '99
Mrs. Brown '97

Jimmy Butler (1921-45)
When a Man's a Man '35
Manhattan Melodrama '34

Lois Butler (1931-89)
High Lonesome '50
Mickey '48

Patrick Butler
Frostbiter: Wrath of the Wendigo '94
The Carrier '87

Paul Butler
A Single Man '09
Romeo Is Bleeding '93
Zebrahead '92
To Sleep with Anger '90

Roy Butler (1893-1973)
My Dinner with Andre '81
House of Errors '42

Tom Butler (1951-)
Everything's Gone Green '06
Freddy vs. Jason '03
Josie and the Pussycats '01
Deadlocked '00
Life-Size '00
Every Mother's Worst Fear '98
Ronnie and Julie '97
Dead Ahead '96
Maternal Instincts '96
Ernest Rides Again '93
Scanners 2: The New Order '91
Tales of the Klondike: The Scorn of Women '87
Confidential '86
July Group '81

William Butler
Blue Hill Avenue '01
Inner Sanctum '91
Night of the Living Dead '90
Leatherface: The Texas Chainsaw Massacre 3 '89

Yancy Butler (1970-)
The Last Letter '04
Thin Air '00
The Witness Files '00
The Treat '98
Ravager '97
The Ex '96
Fast Money '96
Drop Zone '94
Hard Target '93
The Hit List '93

Merritt Butrick (1959-89)
From the Dead of Night '89
Death Spa '87
Shy People '87
When the Bough Breaks '86
Wired to Kill '86
Code of Honor '84
Star Trek 3: The Search for Spock '84
Star Trek 2: The Wrath of Khan '82
Zapped! '82

Johnny Butt (-1930)
Blackmail '29
Q Ships '28

Lawson Butt (1883-1956)
Lady of the Lake '28
The Beloved Rogue '27
Dante's Inferno '24

Asa Butterfield (1997-)
Nanny McPhee 2 '10
The Wolfman '09

Charles Butterworth (1896-1946)
Dixie Jamboree '44
Follow the Boys '44
Road Show '41
Second Chorus '40
Let Freedom Ring '39
Every Day's a Holiday '38
Thanks for the Memory '38
Swing High, Swing Low '37
It Happened in New Orleans '36
The Moon's Our Home '36
Forsaking All Others '35
Magnificent Obsession '35
The Cat and the Fiddle '34
Hollywood Party '34
Penthouse '33
Illicit '31

Donna Butterworth (1956-)
Paradise, Hawaiian Style '66
Family Jewels '65

Peter Butterworth (1919-79)
Carry On Abroad '72
Carry On Up the Khyber '68
Carry On Cowboy '66
Don't Lose Your Head '66

Jorg Buttgereit (1963-)
Der Todesking '89
Nekromantik '87

Stephanie Buttle
Urban Ghost Story '98
A Couch in New York '95

Red Buttons (1919-2006)
The Story of Us '99
It Could Happen to You '94
The Ambulance '90
18 Again! '88
Alice in Wonderland '85
Side Show '84
Leave 'Em Laughing '81
Off Your Rocker '80
When Time Ran Out '80
C.H.O.M.P.S. '79
Movie, Movie '78
Users '78
Pete's Dragon '77
Viva Knievel '77
The Poseidon Adventure '72
Who Killed Mary What's 'Er Name? '71
They Shoot Horses, Don't They? '69
Harlow '65
Five Weeks in a Balloon '62
Gay Purr-ee '62 (V)
Hatari! '62
The Longest Day '62
The Big Circus '59
Sayonara '57
13 Rue Madeleine '46

Pat Buttram (1917-94)
Back to the Future, Part 3 '90
The Fox and the Hound '81 (V)
The Rescuers '77 (V)
Robin Hood '73 (V)
The Gatling Gun '72
Evil Roy Slade '71 (N)
The Aristocats '70 (V)
Roustabout '64
Blue Canadian Rockies '52
Night Stage to Galveston '52
Hills of Utah '51
Valley of Fire '51

Norbert Lee Butz
Dan in Real Life '07
West of Here '02

Sarah Buxton (1972-)
The Climb '97
Listen '96
Fast Getaway 2 '94
Rock 'n' Roll High School Forever '91
Primal Rage '90
Welcome to Spring Break '88

Margherita Buy (1962-)
Days and Clouds '07
Saturn in Opposition '07
Caterina in the Big City '03
His Secret Life '01
Not of This World '99
The Favorite Son '94
The Station '92

Ruth Buzzi (1939-)
Boys Will Be Boys '97
Troublemakers '94
Wishful Thinking '92
Digging Up Business '91
My Mom's a Werewolf '89
Up Your Alley '89
Dixie Lanes '88
Pound Puppies and the Legend of Big Paw '88 (V)
Bad Guys '86
Surf 2 '84
The Being '83
Chu Chu & the Philly Flash '81
The North Avenue Irregulars '79
Scavenger Hunt '79
The Villain '79
Once Upon a Brothers Grimm '77
Freaky Friday '76

Dave Buzzotta
The Prophecy 3: The Ascent '99
She's All That '99
Children of the Corn 5: Fields of Terror '98
Gang Boys '97
The Real Thing '97

Bobbie Byers
Wild Rebels '71
Savages from Hell '68

Kate Byers
The Man Who Made Husbands Jealous '98
Career Girls '97

Spring Byington (1893-1971)
Please Don't Eat the Daisies '60
Because You're Mine '52
Angels in the Outfield '51
Walk Softly, Stranger '50
The Big Wheel '49
In the Good Old Summertime '49
Cynthia '47
Singapore '47
Dragonwyck '46
The Enchanted Cottage '45
Salty O'Rourke '45
Thrill of a Romance '45
The Heavenly Body '44
I'll Be Seeing You '44
Heaven Can Wait '43
Roxie Hart '42
The Devil & Miss Jones '41
Meet John Doe '41
When Ladies Meet '41
The Blue Bird '40
Lucky Partners '40
The Story of Alexander Graham Bell '39
Jezebel '38
You Can't Take It with You '38
The Charge of the Light Brigade '36
Theodora Goes Wild '36
Ah, Wilderness! '35
Mutiny on the Bounty '35
Werewolf of London '35
Little Women '33

Rolan Bykov (1929-98)
Ivan and Abraham '94
Commissar '68
The Overcoat '59

John Byner (1938-)
My 5 Wives '00
The Black Cauldron '85 (V)
Transylvania 6-5000 '85
The Man in the Santa Claus Suit '79
A Pleasure Doing Business '79

Great Smokey Roadblock '76

Amanda Bynes (1986-)
Living Proof '08
Hairspray '07
Sydney White '07
She's the Man '06
Robots '05 (V)
What a Girl Wants '03
Big Fat Liar '02

Dan Byrd (1985-)
The Hills Have Eyes '06
Jam '06
Outlaw Trail '06
Mortuary '05
A Cinderella Story '04
Salem's Lot '04

David Byrd (1933-2001)
Thick as Thieves '99
The Proposition '97

Eugene Byrd (1975-)
Rails & Ties '07
Confess '05
Anacondas: The Hunt for the Blood Orchid '04
Paranoia 1.0 '04
8 Mile '02
Survival Island '02
Lift '01
Color of Justice '97

Ralph Byrd (1909-52)
Radar Secret Service '50
Jungle Goddess '49
Thunder in the Pines '49
Dick Tracy Meets Gruesome '47
Dick Tracy's Dilemma '47
Guadalcanal Diary '43
The Jungle Book '42
Moontide '42
Time to Kill '42
Desperate Cargo '41
Dick Tracy vs. Crime Inc. '41
Life Begins for Andy Hardy '41
Misbehaving Husbands '41
The Howards of Virginia '40
The Son of Monte Cristo '40
Born to Be Wild '38
Dick Tracy Returns '38
Dick Tracy '37
Dick Tracy: The Spider Strikes '37
S.O.S. Coast Guard '37
The Trigger Trio '37
Blake of Scotland Yard '36
Border Caballero '36
Hell-Ship Morgan '36

Thomas Jefferson Byrd (1960-)
Ray '04
MacArthur Park '01
Bamboozled '00
He Got Game '98
Get On the Bus '96
Set It Off '96
Girls of the White Orchid '85

Miriam Byrd-Nethery (1929-2003)
Civil War Diary '90
Leatherface: The Texas Chainsaw Massacre 3 '89

Bill Byrge
Ernest Goes to School '94
Ernest Goes to Jail '90

Anne Byrne (1943-)
Manhattan '79
A Night Full of Rain '78

Antoine Byrne
I Went Down '97
Oliver Twist '97

Antony Byrne
Touching Evil '97
Catherine Cookson's The Cinder Path '94

Barbara Byrne
Sunday in the Park with George '86
Svengali '83

Catherine Byrne (1954-)
Eat the Peach '86
S.O.S. Titanic '79

David Byrne (1952-)
Heavy Petting '89
True Stories '86

Eddie Byrne (1911-81)
The Mummy '59
Dangerous Youth '58
Abandon Ship '57

Gabriel Byrne (1950-)
Autumn Hearts: A New Beginning '07
Jindabyne '06
Played '06
Assault on Precinct 13 '05
The Bridge of San Luis Rey '05
Wah-Wah '05
P.S. '04
Vanity Fair '04
Shade '03
Ghost Ship '02
Killing Emmett Young '02
Spider '02
End of Days '99
Stigmata '99
Enemy of the State '98
The Man in the Iron Mask '98
Quest for Camelot '98 (V)
The End of Violence '97
Polish Wedding '97
Weapons of Mass Distraction '97
The Brylcreem Boys '96
The Last of the High Kings '96
Smilla's Sense of Snow '96
Somebody Is Waiting '96
This Is the Sea '96
Trigger Happy '96
Buffalo Girls '95
Dead Man '95
Frankie Starlight '95
The Usual Suspects '95
Little Women '94
Royal Deceit '94
A Simple Twist of Fate '94
Trial by Jury '94
A Dangerous Woman '93
Point of No Return '93
Cool World '92
Into the West '92
A Soldier's Tale '91
Dark Obsession '90
Miller's Crossing '90
Shipwrecked '90
The Courier '88
Gothic '87
Hello Again '87
Julia and Julia '87
Lionheart '87
Siesta '87
Christopher Columbus '85
Defense of the Realm '85
Hanna K. '83
The Keep '83
Excalibur '81

Jenna Byrne (1970-)
Club Land '01
Lip Service '00

Martha Byrne (1969-)
Anna to the Infinite Power '84
The Eyes of the Amaryllis '82

Michael Byrne (1943-)
The Sum of All Fears '02
Mists of Avalon '01
The Musketeer '01
Battlefield Earth '00
Heat of the Sun '99
Gunshy '98
Apt Pupil '97
The Saint '97
Agatha Christie's The Pale Horse '96
The Infiltrator '95
Sharpe's Enemy '94
Sharpe's Honour '94
Indiana Jones and the Last Crusade '89

The Good Father '87
Over Indulgence '87
Smiley's People '82
Vampyres '74

Rose Byrne (1979-)
Get Him to the Greek '10
Adam '09
Knowing '09
Just Buried '07
Sunshine '07
28 Weeks Later '07
The Dead Girl '06
Marie Antoinette '06
The Tenants '06
Casanova '05
Troy '04
Wicker Park '04
City of Ghosts '03
The Night We Called It a Day '03
I Capture the Castle '02
Star Wars: Episode 2—Attack of the Clones '02
Two Hands '98

David Byrnes (1952-)
Witchcraft 9: Bitter Flesh '96
Witchcraft 7: Judgement Hour '95

Edd Byrnes (1933-)
Troop Beverly Hills '89
Back to the Beach '87
Mankillers '87
Erotic Images '85
Twirl '81
Grease '78
Go Kill and Come Back '68
Any Gun Can Play '67
The Secret Invasion '64
Darby's Rangers '58

Jim Byrnes (1948-)
Highlander: The Source '07
Highlander: Endgame '00
Starlight '97
Bloodhounds 2 '96
Suspicious Agenda '94
Dirty Work '92

Josephine Byrnes (1966-)
Oscar and Lucinda '97
Frauds '93
Brides of Christ '91

Arthur Byron (1872-1943)
The Whole Town's Talking '35
Two Alone '34
Gabriel Over the White House '33
The Mummy '32

David Byron
Fade to Black '93
Doing Time on Maple Drive '92
My Brother's Wife '89

Jeffrey Byron (1955-)
Dungeonmaster '83
Metalstorm: The Destruction of Jared Syn '83
The Seniors '78

Kathleen Byron (1922-)
From a Far Country: Pope John Paul II '81
The Abdication '74
The Golden Bowl '72
The Moonstone '72
Twins of Evil '71
Burn Witch, Burn! '62
Profile '54
Young Bess '53
The Gambler & the Lady '52
I'll Never Forget You '51
The Small Back Room '49
Black Narcissus '47
Stairway to Heaven '46

Marion Byron (1911-85)
Breed of the Border '33
Steamboat Bill, Jr. '28

Walter Byron (1899-1972)
Mr. Boggs Steps Out '38
The Crusader '32

The Savage Girl '32
Vanity Fair '32
Queen Kelly '29

Susan Byun
Deadly Target '94
Sgt. Kabukiman N.Y.P.D. '94
Final Combination '93
Crime Lords '91

James Caan (1939-)
Cloudy with a Chance of Meatballs '09 (V)
New York, I Love You '09
Get Smart '08
Wisegal '08
City of Ghosts '03
Dallas 362 '03
Dogville '03
Elf '03
The Incredible Mrs. Ritchie '03
Jericho Mansions '03
This Thing of Ours '03
Blood Crime '02
The Lathe of Heaven '02
Night at the Golden Eagle '02
Dead Simple '01
A Glimpse of Hell '01
In the Shadows '01
Warden of Red Rock '01
Luckytown '00
Way of the Gun '00
The Yards '00
Mickey Blue Eyes '99
This Is My Father '99
Poodle Springs '98
Bulletproof '96
Eraser '96
North Star '96
Bottle Rocket '95
A Boy Called Hate '95
Flesh and Bone '93
The Program '93
Honeymoon in Vegas '92
The Dark Backward '91
For the Boys '91
Dick Tracy '90
Misery '90
Alien Nation '88
Gardens of Stone '87
Bolero '82
Kiss Me Goodbye '82
The Godfather 1902-1959: The Complete Epic '81
Thief '81
Hide in Plain Sight '80
Chapter Two '79
Comes a Horseman '78
Little Moon & Jud McGraw '78
Another Man, Another Chance '77
A Bridge Too Far '77
Harry & Walter Go to New York '76
Silent Movie '76
Funny Lady '75
The Killer Elite '75
Rollerball '75
Freebie & the Bean '74
The Gambler '74
The Godfather, Part 2 '74
Cinderella Liberty '73
Slither '73
The Godfather '72
Gone with the West '72
Brian's Song '71
The Rain People '69
Countdown '68
El Dorado '67
Games '67
Red Line 7000 '65
Lady in a Cage '64

Scott Caan (1976-)
Meet Dave '08
Brooklyn Rules '07
Ocean's Thirteen '07
The Dog Problem '06
Friends with Money '06
Lonely Hearts '06
Into the Blue '05
In Enemy Hands '04
Ocean's Twelve '04
Dallas 362 '03
Sonny '02
American Outlaws '01
Novocaine '01

Dead Cool *'04*
Sirens *'02*
Inspector Lynley Mysteries: A Great Deliverance *'01*

Don Calfa (1940-)
Terrified *'94*
H.P. Lovecraft's Necronomicon: Book of the Dead *'93*
Me, Myself & I *'92*
Chopper Chicks in Zombietown *'91*
Weekend at Bernie's *'89*
Blue Movies *'88*
Treasure of the Moon Goddess *'88*
Return of the Living Dead *'85*
E. Nick: A Legend in His Own Mind *'84*
Foul Play *'78*
Cinderella Liberty *'73*
The Rainbow Gang *'73*

Nicole Calfan
A Model Employee *'02*
The Four Musketeers *'75*

Louis Calhern (1895-1956)
Forever Darling *'56*
High Society *'56*
Blackboard Jungle *'55*
The Prodigal *'55*
Athena *'54*
Betrayed *'54*
Executive Suite *'54*
Men of the Fighting Lady *'54*
Rhapsody *'54*
The Student Prince *'54*
Julius Caesar *'53*
Latin Lovers *'53*
Prisoner of Zenda *'52*
We're Not Married *'52*
Invitation *'51*
Annie Get Your Gun *'50*
The Asphalt Jungle *'50*
A Life of Her Own *'50*
The Magnificent Yankee *'50*
Nancy Goes to Rio *'50*
Two Weeks with Love *'50*
The Red Pony *'49*
Arch of Triumph *'48*
Notorious *'46*
The Bridge of San Luis Rey *'44*
Up in Arms *'44*
Heaven Can Wait *'43*
I Take This Woman *'40*
Charlie McCarthy, Detective *'39*
The Gorgeous Hussy *'36*
Last Days of Pompeii *'35*
Sweet Adeline *'35*
The Count of Monte Cristo *'34*
The Man with Two Faces *'34*
Duck Soup *'33*
20,000 Years in Sing Sing *'33*
The World Gone Mad *'33*
Frisco Jenny *'32*
Night After Night *'32*
They Call It Sin *'32*
Blonde Crazy *'31*
The Blot *'21*
Too Wise Wives *'21*

Alice Calhoun (1904-66)
Tentacles of the North *'26*
The Man on the Box *'25*

Monica Calhoun (1971-)
The Salon *'05*
Gang of Roses *'03*
Civil Brand *'02*
The Best Man *'99*
The Players Club *'98*
Rebound: The Legend of Earl "The Goat" Manigault *'96*
Bagdad Cafe *'88*

Rory Calhoun (1922-99)
Pure Country *'92*
Roller Blade Warriors: Taken By Force *'90*
Bad Jim *'89*
Hell Comes to Frogtown *'88*
Avenging Angel *'85*
Angel *'84*
Mission to Glory *'80*
Motel Hell *'80*
Smokey & the Judge *'80*
Flatbed Annie and Sweetiepie: Lady Truckers *'79*
The Rebels *'79*
Midnight Auto Supply *'78*
Night of the Lepus *'72*
Operation Cross Eagles *'69*
Dayton's Devils *'68*
Emerald of Artama *'67*
Apache Uprising *'66*
Finger on the Trigger *'65*
A Face in the Rain *'63*
Hard Drivin' *'60*
Treasure of Pancho Villa *'55*
A Bullet Is Waiting *'54*
River of No Return *'54*
With a Song in My Heart *'52*
I'd Climb the Highest Mountain *'51*
Ticket to Tomahawk *'50*
Adventure Island *'47*
The Red House *'47*

Joseph Cali (1950-)
The Lonely Lady *'83*
The Competition *'80*
Saturday Night Fever *'77*

Brandon Call (1976-)
For the Boys *'91*
The Adventures of Ford Fairlane *'90*
Blind Fury *'90*

R.D. Call
Dark Heart *'06*
Murder by Numbers *'02*
Last Man Standing *'96*
Waterworld *'95*
Other People's Money *'91*
Stephen King's Golden Years *'91*
Young Guns 2 *'90*
Colors *'88*
The Children of Times Square *'86*

James Callahan (1930-2007)
Freddy vs. Jason *'03*
Blood for Blood *'95*
Prison for Children *'93*
Outlaw Blues *'77*
Missiles of October *'74*
Lady Sings the Blues *'72*
Tropic of Cancer *'70*

Margaret Callahan (1910-81)
Special Investigator *'36*
Hot Tip *'35*

Mars Callahan (1972-)
What Love Is *'07*
Poolhall Junkies *'02*

K. Callan (1942-)
Midnight Clear *'06*
Crazylove *'05*
Saved by the Light *'95*
Frankie and Johnny *'91*
The Unborn *'91*
American Gigolo *'79*
A Touch of Class *'73*

Michael Callan (1938-)
Leprechaun 3 *'95*
Freeway *'88*
Donner Pass: The Road to Survival *'84*
Double Exposure *'82*
Blind Ambition *'79*
The Cat and the Canary *'79*
Lepke *'75*
Photographer *'75*
Frasier the Sensuous Lion *'73*
Cat Ballou *'65*
The Victors *'63*
Bon Voyage! *'62*
The Interns *'62*
Gidget Goes Hawaiian *'61*
Mysterious Island *'61*

Rebecca Callard (1976-)
The Miracle Maker: The Story of Jesus *'00 (V)*
The Return of the Borrowers *'96*
The Borrowers *'93*

Charlie Callas (1924-)
Vampire Vixens from Venus *'94*
Amazon Women on the Moon *'87*
History of the World: Part 1 *'81*
Pete's Dragon *'77 (V)*
Big Mouth *'67*

Joseph Calleia (1897-1975)
The Alamo *'60*
The Light in the Forest *'58*
Touch of Evil *'58*
The Littlest Outlaw *'54*
The Caddy *'53*
The Iron Mistress *'52*
Yankee Buccaneer *'52*
Branded *'50*
The Noose Hangs High *'48*
Lured *'47*
Deadline at Dawn *'46*
Gilda *'46*
For Whom the Bell Tolls *'43*
The Glass Key *'42*
The Jungle Book *'42*
The Monster and the Girl *'41*
Sundown *'41*
My Little Chickadee *'40*
Five Came Back *'39*
Golden Boy *'39*
Algiers *'38*
Marie Antoinette *'38*
After the Thin Man *'36*
Riff Raff *'35*

Bryan Callen (1967-)
Scary Movie 4 *'06*
Fish Without a Bicycle *'03*

Dayton Callie
Undisputed *'02*
Executive Target *'97*
The Last Days of Frankie the Fly *'96*

Sarah Wayne Callies (1977-)
Prison Break: The Final Break *'09*
Whisper *'07*
The Celestine Prophecy *'06*

James Callis (1971-)
Merlin and the Book of Beasts *'09*
Bridget Jones: The Edge of Reason *'04*
Dead Cool *'04*
Helen of Troy *'03*
Bridget Jones's Diary *'01*
Heat of the Sun *'99*
The Scarlet Pimpernel 2: Mademoiselle Guillotine *'99*

Simon Callow (1949-)
Surveillance 24/7 *'07*
Bob the Butler *'05*
George and the Dragon *'04*
Merci Docteur Rey *'04*
The Phantom of the Opera *'04*
Angels in America *'03*
Bright Young Things *'03*
No Man's Land *'01*
Bedrooms and Hallways *'98*
Shakespeare in Love *'98*
The Scarlet Tunic *'97*
The Woman in White *'97*
James and the Giant Peach *'96 (V)*
Ace Ventura: When Nature Calls *'95*
Victory *'95*
Four Weddings and a Funeral *'94*
Street Fighter *'94*
Howard's End *'92*
The Crucifer of Blood *'91*
Mr. & Mrs. Bridge *'90*
The Good Father *'87*
Maurice *'87*
A Room with a View *'86*
Amadeus *'84*

Cab Calloway (1907-94)
The Blues Brothers *'80*
The Littlest Angel *'69*
The Cincinnati Kid *'65*
Sensations of 1945 *'44*
Stormy Weather *'43*
Manhattan Merry-Go-Round *'37*
Hi-De-Ho *'35*
International House *'33*

Kirk Calloway (1960-)
Cinderella Liberty *'73*
Summertree *'71*

Vanessa Bell Calloway (1957-)
Aussie and Ted's Great Adventure *'09*
Biker Boyz *'03*
Cheaper by the Dozen *'03*
Love Don't Cost a Thing *'03*
Dawg *'02*
All About You *'01*
The Red Sneakers *'01*
Love Song *'00*
The Temptations *'98*
Daylight *'96*
America's Dream *'95*
Crimson Tide *'95*
What's Love Got to Do with It? *'93*
Bebe's Kids *'92 (V)*
Memphis *'91*
Coming to America *'88*
Number One with a Bullet *'87*

Carla Calo
Ali Baba and the Seven Saracens *'64*
Caesar the Conqueror *'63*

Michael Caloz (1985-)
Escape from Wildcat Canyon *'99*
Little Men *'98*
Screamers *'96*
Whiskers *'96*

Donald Calthrop (1888-1940)
The Phantom Light *'35*
Scrooge *'35*
Red Ensign *'34*
No. 17 *'32*
Blackmail *'29*

Bill Calvert (1966-)
Body Waves *'92*
C.H.U.D. 2: Bud the Chud *'89*
Terror Squad *'87*
When Willie Comes Marching Home *'50*

Phyllis Calvert (1915-2002)
The Woman He Loved *'88*
Oh! What a Lovely War *'69*
Indiscreet *'58*
The Young and the Guilty *'58*
Mandy *'53*
Man of Evil *'48*
The Magic Bow *'47*
Men of Two Worlds *'46*
The Man in Grey *'45*
Kipps *'41*

Corinne Calvet (1925-2001)
Dr. Heckyl and Mr. Hype *'80*
Too Hot to Handle *'76*
Apache Uprising *'66*
Far Country *'55*
What Price Glory? *'52*

Henry Calvin (1918-75)
The Sign of Zorro *'60*
Toby Tyler *'59*

John Calvin
Dragonworld *'94*
The Magic Bubble *'93*
Primary Target *'89*
The Siege of Firebase Gloria *'89*
Back to the Beach *'87*
Ghostwarrior *'86*
California Dreaming *'79*
Winter Kill *'74*

Armando Calvo (1919-96)
Satanik *'69*
The Witch's Mirror *'60*

Jose Calvo
Terror Beach *'75*
Twice a Judas *'69*
Fort Yuma Gold *'66*

Pablito Calvo (1949-)
The Man Who Wagged His Tail *'57*
The Miracle of Marcelino *'55*

Art Camacho
Little Bigfoot 2: The Journey Home *'97*
Chinatown Connection *'90*

Mark Camacho (1965-)
Jericho Mansions *'03*
Nowhere in Sight *'01*
Stiletto Dance *'01*
Killing Moon *'00*
Dead Silent *'99*
Stalker *'98*
The Kid *'97*

Javier Camara (1967-)
Chef's Special *'08*
Bad Education *'04*
Torremolinos 73 *'03*
Talk to Her *'02*
Sex and Lucia *'01*

Roberto Camardiel
Guns for Dollars *'73*
Challenge of McKenna *'70*

Christian Camargo (1971-)
Happy Tears *'09*
The Hurt Locker *'08*
K-19: The Widowmaker *'02*
Lip Service *'00*

Danielle Camastra
ESL: English as a Second Language *'05*
Price of Glory *'00*

Godfrey Cambridge (1933-76)
Friday Foster *'75*
Whiffs *'75*
Beware! The Blob *'72*
Cotton Comes to Harlem *'70*
Watermelon Man *'70*
The Busy Body *'67*
Bye Bye Braverman *'67*
The President's Analyst *'67*
Gone Are the Days *'63*
Purlie Victorious *'63*

Joan Camden (1929-2000)
Gunfight at the O.K. Corral *'57*
Stolen Identity *'53*

Juan Jose Camero (1947-)
Veronico Cruz *'87*
El Muerto *'75*
Far Away and Long Ago *'74*

Candace Cameron (1976-)
NightScreams *'97*
Frankenstein Sings... The Movie *'95*
Sharon's Secret *'95*

Dean Cameron (1962-)
Highball *'97*
Ski School 2 *'94*
Sleep with Me *'94*
The Ghost Brigade *'93*
Miracle Beach *'92*
Ski School *'91*
Rockula *'90*
Bad Dreams *'88*
Summer School *'87*

Earl Cameron (1917-)
The Interpreter *'05*
Submarine Attack *'54*

James Cameron (1954-)
The Muse *'99*
Last Action Hero *'93*

Jane Cameron
The Unborn *'91*
Pair of Aces *'90*

Kirk Cameron (1970-)
Fireproof *'08*
Left Behind: The Movie *'00*
Listen to Me *'89*
Like Father, Like Son *'87*
The Best of Times *'86*

Rod Cameron (1910-83)
Midnight Auto Supply *'78*
Psychic Killer *'75*
Evel Knievel *'72*
The Last Movie *'71*
The Electronic Monster *'57*
Ride the Man Down *'53*
Jungle *'52*
Panhandle *'48*
Salome, Where She Danced *'45*
Boss of Boomtown *'44*
G-Men vs. the Black Dragon *'43*
Honeymoon Lodge *'43*
Manhunt in the African Jungles *'43*
Wake Island *'42*
The Monster and the Girl *'41*

Trent Cameron (1979-)
Shot *'01*
The Wood *'99*
The Kid Who Loved Christmas *'90*

Jesse Cameron-Glickenhaus
Timemaster *'95*
Slaughter of the Innocents *'93*

Terry Camillieri (1949-)
The Invisibles *'99*
Bill & Ted's Excellent Adventure *'89*
The Cars That Ate Paris *'74*

Colleen Camp (1953-)
Four Christmases *'08*
Mystery Woman: Mystery Weekend *'05*
In Good Company *'04*
Joshua *'02*
Trapped *'02*
Loser *'00*
Election *'99*
Plump Fiction *'97*
Speed 2: Cruise Control *'97*
Die Hard: With a Vengeance *'95*
Greedy *'94*
The Magic Bubble *'93*
Sliver *'93*
Wayne's World *'92*
Backfield in Motion *'91*
Wicked Stepmother *'89*
Track 29 *'88*
Illegally Yours *'87*
Police Academy 4: Citizens on Patrol *'87*
Walk Like a Man *'87*
Screwball Academy *'86*
Clue *'85*
D.A.R.Y.L. *'85*
Doin' Time *'85*
Police Academy 2: Their First Assignment *'85*
Rosebud Beach Hotel *'85*
Joy of Sex *'84*
Smokey and the Bandit, Part 3 *'83*
Valley Girl *'83*
The Seduction *'82*
They All Laughed *'81*
Cloud Dancer *'80*
Deadly Games *'80*
Apocalypse Now *'79*
Game of Death *'79*

Lady of the House '78
Midnight Auto Supply '78
Seducers '77
She Devils in Chains '76
Smile '75
The Last Porno Flick '74
The Swinging Cheerleaders '74
Cat in the Cage '68

Hamilton Camp (1934-2005)
Almost Heroes '97
All Dogs Go to Heaven 2 '95 (V)
Attack of the 50 Ft. Woman '93
Arena '89
Lots of Luck '85
Rosebud Beach Hotel '85
Meatballs 2 '84
Under Fire '83
Eating Raoul '82

Bernard Campan
The Man of My Life '06
How Much Do You Love Me? '05

Frank Campanella (1919-2006)
Blood Red '88
Chesty Anderson USN '76
The Producers '68

Joseph Campanella (1927-)
James Dean: Live Fast, Die Young '97
The Glass Cage '96
Magic Kid '92
No Retreat, No Surrender 3: Blood Brothers '91
Original Intent '91
Body Chemistry '90
Club Fed '90
Last Call '90
Down the Drain '89
Steele Justice '87
Comic Book Kids '82
Plutonium Incident '82
Hangar 18 '80
Meteor '79
Pearl '78 (N)
Return to Fantasy Island '77
Sky Hei$t '75
Terror on the 40th Floor '74
Ben '72
Murder Once Removed '71
The President's Plane Is Missing '71
The St. Valentine's Day Massacre '67

Adam Campbell
Epic Movie '07
Date Movie '06

Alex Campbell (1984-)
Siblings '04
Verdict in Blood '02

Beatrice Campbell (1922-79)
Grand National Night '53
The Master of Ballantrae '53
I'll Never Forget You '51
Last Holiday '50

Billy Campbell (1959-)
Meteor '09
The Circuit '08
Ghost Town '08
Gods and Generals '03
Enough '02
The Rising Place '02
Armistead Maupin's More Tales of the City '97
Rudyard Kipling's the Second Jungle Book: Mowgli and Baloo '97
The Brylcreem Boys '96
Lover's Knot '96
Menno's Mind '96
Out There '95
Under the Hula Moon '95
Armistead Maupin's Tales of the City '93
Gettysburg '93
The Night We Never Met '93
Bram Stoker's Dracula '92
The Rocketeer '91

Bruce Campbell (1958-)
Cloudy with a Chance of Meatballs '09 (V)
My Name Is Bruce '08
Sundown: The Vampire in Retreat '08
Aqua Teen Hunger Force Colon Movie Film for Theaters '07 (V)
Spider-Man 3 '07
The Ant Bully '06 (V)
Touch the Top of the World '06
Sky High '05
Comic Book: The Movie '04
Spider-Man 2 '04
Bubba Ho-Tep '03
The Woods '03
Serving Sara '02
Spider-Man '02
Terminal Invasion '02
The Majestic '01
The Ice Rink '99
From Dusk Till Dawn 2: Texas Blood Money '98
Goldrush: A Real Life Alaskan Adventure '98
The Love Bug '97
McHale's Navy '97
Escape from L.A. '96
Menno's Mind '96
Tornado! '96
The Hudsucker Proxy '93
Army of Darkness '92
Eddie Presley '92
Lunatics: A Love Story '92
Mindwarp '91
Sundown '91
Waxwork 2: Lost in Time '91
Darkman '90
Maniac Cop 2 '90
Moontrap '89
Maniac Cop '88
Evil Dead 2: Dead by Dawn '87
Thou Shalt Not Kill...Except '87
Crimewave '85
Evil Dead '83
Going Back '83

Cheryl Campbell (1949-)
The Way We Live Now '02
The Mill on the Floss '97
The Shooting Party '85
Greystoke: The Legend of Tarzan, Lord of the Apes '84
Chariots of Fire '81
McVicar '80
Lillie '79
Testament of Youth '79

Christa Campbell (1973-)
Lies and Illusions '09
Hero Wanted '08
Showdown at Area 51 '07

Christian Campbell (1972-)
The Betrayed '08
Banshee '06
Next Time '99
Trick '99
I've Been Waiting for You '98
Too Smooth '98
Born to Run '93
City Boy '93

Colin Campbell (1859-1928)
The Leather Boys '63
Big Boy '30

David James Campbell
Killer Workout '86
Killzone '85

Elizabeth Campbell (1942-)
Doctor of Doom '62
Wrestling Women vs. the Aztec Mummy '59

Emma Campbell (1971-)
Nightwaves '03
The Hound of the Baskervilles '00

Eric Campbell (1879-1917)
The Cure '17
The Immigrant '17
The Fireman '16
The Vagabond '16

Glen Campbell (1936-)
Rock-a-Doodle '92 (V)
Uphill All the Way '85
True Grit '69

J. Kenneth Campbell
U.S. Seals '98
Operation Delta Force 2: Mayday '97
Ulee's Gold '97

Jessica Campbell (1982-)
The Safety of Objects '01
Election '99

Judy Campbell (1916-2004)
Cry of the Penguins '71
Bonnie Prince Charlie '48
The World Owes Me a Living '47
Convoy '40

Julia Campbell (1963-)
Stephen King's Rose Red '02
Bounce '00
A Slight Case of Murder '99
Poodle Springs '98
Diary of a Serial Killer '97
Romy and Michele's High School Reunion '97
Lone Justice '93
Livin' Large '91
Opportunity Knocks '90

Kate Campbell
Monte Carlo Nights '34
Come on Tarzan '32
Ghost Valley '32

Ken Campbell (1941-)
Smart Money '88
Letter to Brezhnev '86
Joshua Then and Now '85
The Big Red One '80

Ken H. Campbell (1963-)
Breakfast of Champions '98
Down Periscope '96

Larry Joe Campbell (1970-)
Jiminy Glick in LaLa Wood '05
Wedding Crashers '05

Louise Campbell (1911-97)
Bulldog Drummond's Peril '38
Bulldog Drummond Comes Back '37
Bulldog Drummond's Revenge '37

Maia Campbell (1976-)
Trippin' '99
Parental Guidance '98

Michael Leydon Campbell
Bob Funk '09
Knots '05
Sidewalks of New York '01

Naomi Campbell (1970-)
Prisoner of Love '99
Girl 6 '96
Invasion of Privacy '96
Miami Rhapsody '95
Cool As Ice '91

Nell Campbell (1953-)
Great Expectations '97
I Wanna Be a Beauty Queen '85
Pink Floyd: The Wall '82
Shock Treatment '81
Lisztomania '75
The Rocky Horror Picture Show '75

Neve Campbell (1973-)
Closing the Ring '07
I Really Hate My Job '07
Partition '07
Relative Strangers '06
When Will I Be Loved '04
The Company '03
Lost Junction '03
Last Call: The Final Chapter of F. Scott Fitzgerald '02
Intimate Affairs '01
Drowning Mona '00
Panic '00
Scream 3 '00
Three to Tango '99
54 '98
The Lion King: Simba's Pride '98 (V)
Too Smooth '98
Wild Things '98
Scream 2 '97
The Canterville Ghost '96
The Craft '96
Scream '96
Northern Passage '95
The Dark '94

Nicholas (Nick) Campbell (1952-)
Cinderella Man '05
Siblings '04
Prozac Nation '01
Full Disclosure '00
We All Fall Down '00
The Happy Face Murders '99
New Waterford Girl '99
Hard to Forget '98
The Boys Club '96
Guitarman '95
No Contest '94
Naked Lunch '91
The Big Slice '90
Rampage '87
Going Home '86
Certain Fury '85
Knights of the City '85
July Group '81
The Victory '81
Fast Company '78
A Bridge Too Far '77

Paul Campbell
The Long Weekend '05
We'll Meet Again '02
Third World Cop '99
Dancehall Queen '97
The Lunatic '92

Peggy Campbell (1912-85)
Big Calibre '35
Stone of Silver Creek '35
When a Man Sees Red '34

Rob Campbell
Hedwig and the Angry Inch '00
Boys Don't Cry '99
Hostile Waters '97
The Crucible '96
Lone Justice 2 '93
Unforgiven '92

Scott Michael Campbell (1971-)
Brothers Three '07
Who's Your Monkey '07
Brokeback Mountain '05
Flight of the Phoenix '04
The Maldonado Miracle '03
Hart's War '02
Radioland Murders '94

Sean Campbell
Blackwoods '02
He Sees You When You're Sleeping '02

Tisha Campbell (1968-)
The Sweetest Gift '98
Sprung '96
House Party 3 '94
Boomerang '92
House Party 2: The Pajama Jam '91
House Party '90
Rooftops '89
School Daze '88
Rags to Riches '87
Little Shop of Horrors '86

Torquil Campbell
Heaven on Earth '89
The Golden Seal '83

William Campbell (1926-)
Portrait in Terror '66
Track of the Vampire '66
The Secret Invasion '64
Dementia 13 '63
Night of Evil '62
The Sheriff of Fractured Jaw '59
Love Me Tender '56
Man in the Vault '56
Battle Cry '55
Man Without a Star '55
The High and the Mighty '54
Battle Circus '53
Escape from Fort Bravo '53

Frank Campeau (1864-1943)
The Painted Trail '38
Everyman's Law '36
Abraham Lincoln '30
The First Auto '27
Battling Bunyon '24
His Majesty, the American '19
When the Clouds Roll By '19
Heart of Texas Ryan '17
The Man from Painted Post '17

Cris Campion (1966-)
Field of Honor '87
Pirates '86

Tom Campitelli
Gates of Hell 2: Dead Awakening '96
Brutal Fury '92

Wally Campo (1923-)
The Beast from Haunted Cave '60
Ski Troop Attack '60
Tank Commando '59
Hell Squad '58
Machine Gun Kelly '58

Bruno Campos (1974-)
The Princess and the Frog '09 (V)
Crazylove '05
Dopamine '03
Mimic 2 '01
O Quatrilho '95

Rafael Campos (1936-85)
The Return of Josey Wales '86
A Streetcar Named Desire '84
V '83
Where the Buffalo Roam '80
Centennial '78
Slumber Party '57 '76
The Hanged Man '74
The Doll Squad '73
The Astro-Zombies '67
Lady in a Cage '64
This Could Be the Night '57

Victor Campos
Scarface '83
Archer: The Fugitive from the Empire '81

Robert Canada
Bob Funk '09
Danger Zone '87

Ron Canada
The Haunting of Molly Hartley '08
Snowglobe '07
Islander '06
Cinderella Man '05
Just like Heaven '05
Wedding Crashers '05
The Human Stain '03
The Hunted '03
United States of Leland '03
Dean Koontz's Black River '01
Apartment Complex '98
Lost in the Bermuda Triangle '98
Pinocchio's Revenge '96
The American President '95
Lone Star '95
Man of the House '95
Play Nice '92

Gianna Maria Canale (1927-)
Marauder '65
Colossus and the Amazon Queen '64
Tiger of the Seven Seas '62
Hercules '58
I, Vampiri '56
Man from Cairo '54
Sins of Rome '54
Go for Broke! '51

Lee Canalito
The Glass Jungle '88
Paradise Alley '78

Maria Canals (1966-)
Imagining Argentina '04
Master of Disguise '02
My Family '94

Maria Canals-Barrera
The Wizards of Waverly Place: The Movie '09
Camp Rock '08

David Canary (1938-)
King of America '80
Johnny Firecloud '75
Posse '75
Sharks' Treasure '75
Melvin Purvis: G-Man '74

John Henry Canavan (1969-)
Torso '01
The Crossing '00

Urbain Cancellier
Intimate Strangers '04
Amelie '01

Stelio Candelli
A Man Called Rage '84
Planet of the Vampires '65

Candy Candido (1913-99)
The Great Mouse Detective '86 (V)
Peter Pan '53 (V)
Rhythm Parade '43

John Candy (1950-94)
Canadian Bacon '94
Hostage for a Day '94
Wagons East '94
Cool Runnings '93
Boris and Natasha: The Movie '92
Once Upon a Crime '92
Career Opportunities '91
Delirious '91
JFK '91
Nothing But Trouble '91
Only the Lonely '91
Home Alone '90
The Masters of Menace '90
The Rescuers Down Under '90 (V)
Uncle Buck '89
Who's Harry Crumb? '89
The Great Outdoors '88
Hot to Trot! '88 (V)
Speed Zone '88
Planes, Trains & Automobiles '87
Spaceballs '87
Tales of the Klondike: The Unexpected '87
Armed and Dangerous '86
Little Shop of Horrors '86
Really Weird Tales '86
Brewster's Millions '85
Sesame Street Presents: Follow That Bird '85

Summer Rental *'85*
Volunteers *'85*
The Last Polka *'84*
Splash *'84*
Clown Murders *'83*
Going Berserk *'83*
National Lampoon's Vacation *'83*
Heavy Metal *'81 (V)*
Stripes *'81*
The Blues Brothers *'80*
The Double Negative *'80*
Lost and Found *'79*
1941 *'79*
The Silent Partner *'78*
Find the Lady *'76*
Tunnelvision *'76*
It Seemed Like a Good Idea at the Time *'75*
Class of '44 *'73*

Charles Cane (1899-1973)

Revenge of the Creature *'55*
Lucky Me *'54*
Native Son *'51*
Dead Reckoning *'47*

Natalie Canerday (1962-)

Shotgun Stories *'07*
Tully *'00*
October Sky *'99*
Gunshy *'98*
Sling Blade *'96*
One False Move *'91*

Guillaume Canet (1973-)

Last Night *'10*
Tell No One *'06*
Joyeux Noel *'05*
Love Me if You Dare *'03*
Whatever You Say *'02*
The Beach *'00*

Ridge Canipe

Pictures of Hollis Woods *'07*
The Bad News Bears *'05*

Bobby Cannavale (1971-)

Brief Interviews With Hideous Men *'09*
Paul Blart: Mall Cop *'09*
Diminished Capacity *'08*
The Merry Gentleman *'08*
100 Feet *'08*
The Promotion *'08*
Dedication *'07*
The Take *'07*
The Ten *'07*
The Night Listener *'06*
Snakes on a Plane *'06*
10 Items or Less *'06*
Happy Endings *'05*
Romance & Cigarettes *'05*
The Breakup Artist *'04*
Fresh Cut Grass *'04*
Haven *'04*
Shall We Dance? *'04*
The Station Agent *'03*
Washington Heights *'02*
3 A.M. *'01*
The Bone Collector *'99*

Stephen J. Cannell (1942-)

Ice Spiders *'07*
Threshold *'03*
Half Past Dead *'02*
Posse *'93*

Dyan Cannon (1937-)

The Boynton Beach Club *'05*
Diamond Girl *'98*
The Sender *'98*
Allie & Me *'97*
Beverly Hills Family Robinson *'97*
Out to Sea *'97*
8 Heads in a Duffel Bag *'96*
That Darn Cat *'96*
Based on an Untrue Story *'93*
The Pickle *'93*
Christmas in Connecticut *'92*
The End of Innocence *'90*
Caddyshack 2 *'88*
Jenny's War *'85*
Merlin and the Sword *'85*
Author! Author! *'82*
Deathtrap *'82*
Having It All *'82*
Coast to Coast *'80*
Honeysuckle Rose *'80*
Heaven Can Wait *'78*
Lady of the House *'78*
Revenge of the Pink Panther *'78*
The Virginia Hill Story *'76*
The Last of Sheila *'73*
Shamus *'73*
The Anderson Tapes *'71*
The Love Machine *'71*
Doctors' Wives *'70*
Bob & Carol & Ted & Alice *'69*

Esma Cannon (1896-1972)

Carry On Cabby *'63*
Carry On Regardless *'61*
Crow Hollow *'52*
I Met a Murderer *'39*

J.D. Cannon (1922-)

Street Justice *'89*
Death Wish 2 *'82*
The Adventures of Nellie Bly *'81*
Pleasure Palace *'80*
Raise the Titanic *'80*
Walking Through the Fire *'80*
Killing Stone *'78*
Scorpio *'73*
Lawman *'71*
Cotton Comes to Harlem *'70*
Krakatoa East of Java *'69*
Cool Hand Luke *'67*

Katherine (Kathy) Cannon (1953-)

Matters of the Heart *'90*
The Red Fury *'84*
Will: G. Gordon Liddy *'82*
High Noon: Part 2 *'80*
Private Duty Nurses *'71*

Nick Cannon (1980-)

The Killing Room *'09*
American Son *'08*
Bobby *'06*
Even Money *'06*
Monster House *'06 (V)*
Roll Bounce *'05*
Underclassman *'05*
Garfield: The Movie *'04 (V)*
Shall We Dance? *'04*
Love Don't Cost a Thing *'03*
Drumline *'02*

Wanda Cannon (1960-)

The Christmas Blessing *'05*
Masters of Horror: Homecoming *'05*
The 6th Day *'00*
For the Moment *'94*
The Last Winter *'89*
Overdrawn at the Memory Bank *'83*

Sibylle Canonica (1957-)

Mostly Martha *'01*
Beyond Silence *'96*

Diana Canova (1953-)

Night Partners *'83*
The First Nudie Musical *'75*

Judy Canova (1913-83)

Cannonball *'76*
The Adventures of Huckleberry Finn *'60*
Carolina Cannonball *'55*
Oklahoma Annie *'51*
Louisiana Hayride *'44*

Anne Canovos

Ready to Wear *'94*
High Frequency *'88*
Zeder *'83*

Antonio Cantafora (1943-)

Intervista *'87*
Gabriela *'84*
Torture Chamber of Baron Blood *'72*
And God Said to Cain *'69*

Aldo Canti

Reactor *'78*
Sabata *'69*
Five for Hell *'67*

Jose Pablo Cantillo (1979-)

Streets of Blood *'09*
Redbelt *'08*
Cleaner *'07*
Disturbia *'07*
Crank *'06*

Marilyne Canto (1963-)

Comedy of Power *'06*
Apres-Vous *'03*

Toni Canto (1965-)

All About My Mother *'99*
I'm the One You're Looking For *'88*

Eric Cantona

Looking for Eric *'09*
Elizabeth *'98*

Mario Cantone (1959-)

Sex and the City 2 *'10*
Sex and the City: The Movie *'08*
Surf's Up *'07 (V)*
Three Days to Vegas *'07*
The Last Request *'06*

Eddie Cantor (1892-1964)

If You Knew Susie *'48*
Hollywood Canteen *'44*
Show Business *'44*
Thank Your Lucky Stars *'43*
Strike Me Pink *'36*
Kid Millions *'34*
Roman Scandals *'33*
Kid from Spain *'32*
Palmy Days *'31*
Glorifying the American Girl *'30*
Whoopee! *'30*

Yakima Canutt (1895-1986)

The Showdown *'50*
Calling Wild Bill Elliott *'43*
For Whom the Bell Tolls *'43*
Shadows on the Sage *'42*
Frontier Vengeance *'40*
Pioneers of the West *'40*
Gone with the Wind *'39*
The Kansas Terrors *'39*
Wyoming Outlaw *'39*
Overland Stage Raiders *'38*
Santa Fe Stampede *'38*
Heart of the Rockies *'37*
Hit the Saddle *'37*
The Painted Stallion *'37*
Riders of the Rockies *'37*
Riders of the Whistling Skull *'37*
Roarin' Lead *'37*
Trouble in Texas *'37*
Circle of Death *'36*
King of the Pecos *'36*
Outlaw Rule *'36*
Winds of the Wasteland *'36*
Branded a Coward *'35*
Cyclone of the Saddle *'35*
Dawn Rider *'35*
Pals of the Range *'35*
Paradise Canyon *'35*
Rough Riding Ranger *'35*
Lucky Texan *'34*
The Man from Hell *'34*
Man from Utah *'34*
The Star Packer *'34*
Law and Lawless *'33*
Sagebrush Trail *'33*
Telegraph Trail *'33*
West of the Divide *'33*
Last Frontier *'32*
Battling with Buffalo Bill *'31*
Two Fisted Justice *'31*
Westward Bound *'30*
The Fighting Stallion *'26*
Wild Horse Canyon *'25*
Branded a Bandit *'24*

Peter Capaldi (1958-)

In the Loop *'09*
Pinochet's Last Stand *'06*
House of 9 *'05*
Wild Country *'05*
Modigliani *'04*
Max *'02*
Shooting Fish *'98*
Bean *'97*
The Crow Road *'96*
Neil Gaiman's NeverWhere *'96*
Smilla's Sense of Snow *'96*
Captives *'94*
Dangerous Liaisons *'88*
The Lair of the White Worm *'88*
John & Yoko: A Love Story *'85*
Local Hero *'83*

Jad Capelja (1964-)

Freedom *'82*
Puberty Blues *'81*

Peter Capell (1912-86)

For the First Time *'59*
Paths of Glory *'57*

Robert Capelli, Jr.

Breaking Point *'09*
Waltzing Anna *'06*

Virginia Capers (1925-2004)

The Feminine Touch *'95*
Ferris Bueller's Day Off *'86*
Jo Jo Dancer, Your Life Is Calling *'86*
White Mama *'80*
The North Avenue Irregulars *'79*

Lizzy Caplan (1982-)

Hot Tub Time Machine *'10*
Cloverfield *'08*
My Best Friend's Girl *'08*
Crashing *'07*
Mean Girls *'04*

Carmine Capobianco (1958-)

Galactic Gigolo *'87*
Psychos in Love *'87*

John Capodice (1938-)

Shut Up and Kiss Me *'05*
Double Bang *'01*
Out of the Black *'01*
Enemy of the State *'98*
Executive Power *'98*
Ringmaster *'98*
True Friends *'98*
Independence Day *'96*
Wedding Bell Blues *'96*
Trial by Jury *'94*
Honeymoon in Vegas *'92*
Fever *'91*
The Hard Way *'91*
Internal Affairs *'90*
Family Business *'89*
The Children of Times Square *'86*

Lino Capolicchio (1943-)

Traveling Companion *'96*
Fiorile *'93*
The Bloodstained Shadow *'78*
The Garden of the Finzi-Continis *'71*

Nadia Capone

First Degree *'95*
Skull: A Night of Terror *'88*
A Whisper to a Scream *'88*

Truman Capote (1924-84)

Murder by Death *'76*
ABC Stage 67: Truman Capote's A Christmas Memory *'66 (N)*

Carl Capotorto (1959-)

Mac *'93*
American Blue Note *'89*

Joolia Cappleman

Who's Who *'78*
Bleak Moments *'71*

Pier Paolo Capponi (1938-)

Man of Legend *'71*
Super Brother *'68*
The King of Hearts *'66*

Francis Capra (1983-)

Black Irish *'07*
A Simple Wish *'97*
Kazaam *'96*
A Bronx Tale *'93*

Jordanna Capra

Watch It *'93*
Hired to Kill *'91*

Tony Caprari

Armageddon: The Final Challenge *'94*
River of Diamonds *'90*

Ahna Capri (1944-)

The Specialist *'75*
Enter the Dragon *'73*
Payday *'73*
The Brotherhood of Satan *'71*
Darker than Amber *'70*

Vittorio Caprioli (1921-89)

Le Magnifique *'76*
Rulers of the City *'76*

Jessica Capshaw (1976-)

The Groomsmen *'06*
Minority Report *'02*
Valentine *'01*
Something About Sex *'98*
The Locusts *'97*

Kate Capshaw (1953-)

Due East *'02*
A Girl Thing *'01*
The Love Letter *'99*
The Alarmist *'98*
The Locusts *'97*
How to Make an American Quilt *'95*
Just Cause *'94*
Love Affair *'94*
Next Door *'94*
My Heroes Have Always Been Cowboys *'91*
Black Rain *'89*
Love at Large *'89*
Private Affairs *'89*
Code Name: Dancer *'87*
The Quick and the Dead *'87*
Power *'86*
SpaceCamp *'86*
Best Defense *'84*
Dreamscape *'84*
Indiana Jones and the Temple of Doom *'84*
Windy City *'84*
A Little Sex *'82*

Capucine (1933-90)

Scandalous *'88*
Curse of the Pink Panther *'83*
Trail of the Pink Panther *'82*
The Con Artists *'80*
From Hell to Victory *'79*
Jaguar Lives *'79*
The Switch *'76*
Fellini Satyricon *'69*
The Honey Pot *'67*
What's New Pussycat? *'65*
The Pink Panther *'64*
The Seventh Dawn *'64*
Walk on the Wild Side *'62*
North to Alaska *'60*
Song Without End *'60*

Irene Cara (1959-)

Happily Ever After *'93 (V)*
The Magic Voyage *'93 (V)*
Caged in Paradiso *'89*
For Us, the Living *'88*
Busted Up *'86*
Certain Fury *'85*
Killing 'Em Softly *'85*
City Heat *'84*
D.C. Cab *'84*
Fame *'80*
Roots: The Next Generation *'79*
Sparkle *'76*
Aaron Loves Angela *'75*

Flora Carabella (1926-99)

A Night Full of Rain *'78*
The Messiah *'75*

Paul Carafotes (1963-)

Journey to the Center of the Earth *'88*
All the Right Moves *'83*
Choices *'81*

Ion Caramitru (1942-)

Amen *'02*
Citizen X *'95*
Two Deaths *'94*

Joseph Carberry (1948-)

The Ten Million Dollar Getaway *'91*
Vigilante *'83*

Antony Carbone (1927-)

Skateboard *'77*
The Last Porno Flick *'74*
Sex Through a Window *'72*
The Last Woman on Earth *'61*
The Pit and the Pendulum *'61*
Creature from the Haunted Sea *'60*
A Bucket of Blood *'59*

Nestor Carbonell (1967-)

The Dark Knight *'08*
Killer Movie *'08*
Smokin' Aces *'07*
The Lost City *'05*
The Laramie Project *'02*
Noriega: God's Favorite *'00*
Attention Shoppers *'99*

Linda Cardellini (1975-)

Comanche Moon *'08*
The Lazarus Project *'08*
Grandma's Boy *'06*
American Gun *'05*
Brokeback Mountain *'05*
Jiminy Glick in LaLa Wood *'05*
Scooby-Doo 2: Monsters Unleashed *'04*
Scooby-Doo *'02*
Legally Blonde *'01*
The Unsaid *'01*
The Prince and the Surfer *'99*
Dee Snider's Strangeland *'98*
Dead Man on Campus *'97*

Stephen Antonio Cardenas (1974-)

Turbo: A Power Rangers Movie *'96*
Mighty Morphin Power Rangers: The Movie *'95*

Pat Cardi (1952-)

Twisted Brain *'74*
And Now Miguel *'66*

Bill "Chilly Billy" Cardille (1928-)

Night of the Living Dead *'90*
Night of the Living Dead *'68*

Ben Cardinal

Megasnake *'07*
Deepwater *'05*
By Dawn's Early Light *'00*
The Wolves *'95*

Tantoo Cardinal (1951-)

Luna: Spirit of the Whale *'07*
Edge of Madness *'02*
Dodson's Journey *'01*
The Lost Child *'00*
Big Bear *'98*
Smoke Signals *'98*
The Education of Little Tree *'97*
Grand Avenue *'96*
Tecumseh: The Last Warrior *'95*

Brotherly Love '85
Fleshburn '84
Wild Horses '84
In Love with an Older Woman '82
American Dream '81
Octagon '80
Black Oak Conspiracy '77
The Candidate '72
The Student Nurses '70

Kelly Carlson (1976-)
Made of Honor '08
Player 5150 '08
The Marine '06
Starship Troopers 2: Hero of the Federation '04

Leslie (Les) Carlson (1933-)
A Christmas Story '83
Deranged '74

Richard Carlson (1912-77)
Change of Habit '69
The Valley of Gwangi '69
The Doomsday Flight '66
Tormented '60
The Helen Morgan Story '57
The Last Command '55
Creature from the Black Lagoon '54
All I Desire '53
It Came from Outer Space '53
Flat Top '52
Retreat, Hell! '52
King Solomon's Mines '50
Try and Get Me '50
The Amazing Mr. X '48
Behind Locked Doors '48
Human Gorilla '48
Presenting Lily Mars '43
White Cargo '42
Back Street '41
Hold That Ghost '41
The Little Foxes '41
Beyond Tomorrow '40
The Ghost Breakers '40
The Howards of Virginia '40
No, No Nanette '40
Too Many Girls '40
The Duke of West Point '38
The Young in Heart '38

Steve Carlson (1943-)
Brothers O'Toole '73
Deadlier Than the Male '67

Steve Carlson (1955-)
Slap Shot 2: Breaking the Ice '02
Slap Shot '77

Veronica Carlson (1945-)
Freakshow '95
The Horror of Frankenstein '70
Frankenstein Must Be Destroyed '69
Dracula Has Risen from the Grave '68

Karin Carlsson (1906-90)
Walpurgis Night '41
A Woman's Face '38

Hope Marie Carlton (1966-)
Bloodmatch '91
Round Numbers '91
Slumber Party Massacre 3 '90
Picasso Trigger '89
Savage Beach '89
Terminal Exposure '89
Slaughterhouse Rock '88
Hard Ticket to Hawaii '87

Richard Carlyle (1879-1942)
The Lion Man '36
Sons of Steel '35
When a Man's a Man '35
Quick Trigger Lee '31
Playing Around '30

Robert Carlyle (1961-)
The Tournament '09
The Last Enemy '08
24 : Redemption '08
Flood '07
28 Weeks Later '07
Eragon '06
Marilyn Hotchkiss' Ballroom Dancing & Charm School '06
Human Trafficking '05
The Mighty Celt '05
Dead Fish '04
Hitler: The Rise of Evil '03
Once Upon a Time in the Midlands '02
Formula 51 '01
To End All Wars '01
The Beach '00
Angela's Ashes '99
Ravenous '99
The World Is Not Enough '99
Plunkett & Macleane '98
Carla's Song '97
Face '97
The Full Monty '96
Go Now '96
Trainspotting '95
Being Human '94
Cracker: To Be a Somebody '94
Priest '94
Riff Raff '92

Chris Carmack (1980-)
The Butterfly Effect 3: Revelation '09
Into the Blue 2: The Reef '09
Suburban Girl '07

Roger C. Carmel (1932-86)
Hardly Working '81
Thunder and Lightning '77
Skullduggery '70
My Dog, the Thief '69
Alvarez Kelly '66
Gambit '66
The Silencers '66
Goodbye Charlie '64

Jeanne Carmen (1930-2007)
The Monster of Piedras Blancas '57
In Old Montana '39

Jewel Carmen (1897-1984)
The Bat '26
American Aristocracy '17
Flirting with Fate '16

Julie Carmen (1960-)
King of the Jungle '01
Gargantua '98
True Women '97
In the Mouth of Madness '95
Seduced by Evil '94
Deadly Currents '93
Drug Wars 2: The Cocaine Cartel '92
The Hunt for the Night Stalker '91
Kiss Me a Killer '91
Gore Vidal's Billy the Kid '89
The Neon Empire '89
Paint It Black '89
Fright Night 2 '88
The Milagro Beanfield War '88
The Penitent '88
Blue City '86
Last Plane Out '83
She's in the Army Now '81
Gloria '80
Night of the Juggler '80
Can You Hear the Laughter? The Story of Freddie Prinze '79

Jean Carmet (1920-94)
Germinal '93
Secret Obsession '88
Sorceress '88
Buffet Froid '79
Violette '78
Black and White in Color '76
Dupont Lajoie '74
Return of the Tall Blond Man with One Black Shoe '74
The Tall Blond Man with One Black Shoe '72
Just Before Nightfall '71
The Little Theatre of Jean Renoir '71
La Rupture '70
Any Number Can Win '63
There Goes Barder '54
Monsieur Vincent '47

Hoagy Carmichael (1899-1981)
Belles on Their Toes '52
The Las Vegas Story '52
Young Man with a Horn '50
The Best Years of Our Lives '46
Canyon Passage '46
Johnny Angel '45
To Have & Have Not '44
Topper '37

Ian Carmichael (1920-)
Wives and Daughters '01
Dark Obsession '90
Smashing Time '67
Heavens Above '63
School for Scoundrels '60
I'm All Right Jack '59
Lucky Jim '58
Brothers in Law '57
The Colditz Story '55
Betrayed '54

Tullio Carminati (1894-1971)
War and Peace '56
Roman Holiday '53
London Melody '37
Paris in Spring '35
One Night of Love '34
The Duchess of Buffalo '26

Michael Carmine (1959-89)
Leviathan '89
*batteries not included '87
Band of the Hand '86

Primo Carnera (1906-67)
Hercules Unchained '59
A Kid for Two Farthings '55
The Iron Crown '41
The Prizefighter and the Lady '33

Alan Carney (1911-73)
Girl Rush '44
Seven Days Ashore '44
Zombies on Broadway '44

Art Carney (1918-2003)
Last Action Hero '93
Night Friend '87
The Night They Saved Christmas '87
The Blue Yonder '86
Miracle of the Heart: A Boys Town Story '86
Izzy & Moe '85
Undergrads '85
The Emperor's New Clothes '84
Firestarter '84
The Muppets Take Manhattan '84
The Naked Face '84
Better Late Than Never '83
St. Helen's, Killer Volcano '82
Bitter Harvest '81
Take This Job & Shove It '81
Roadie '80
Steel '80
Defiance '79
Going in Style '79
Sunburn '79
House Calls '78
Movie, Movie '78
The Late Show '77
Death Scream '75
Katherine '75
Harry and Tonto '74
Pot o' Gold '41

George Carney (1887-1942)
Brighton Rock '47
I Know Where I'm Going '45
Waterloo Road '44
In Which We Serve '43
Love on the Dole '41

Morris Carnovsky (1897-1992)
Joe's Bed-Stuy Barbershop: We Cut Heads '83
Cyrano de Bergerac '50
Gun Crazy '49
Dead Reckoning '47
Saigon '47
Our Vines Have Tender Grapes '45
Rhapsody in Blue '45

Cindy Carol (1944-)
Dear Brigitte '65
Gidget Goes to Rome '63

John Carol (1910-68)
The Spider and the Fly '49
It Always Rains on Sunday '47

Linda Carol (1970-)
Carnal Crimes '91
Future Hunters '88
Reform School Girls '86

Martine Carol (1920-67)
The Battle of Austerlitz '60
Around the World in 80 Days '56
Lola Montes '55
Nana '55
Beauties of the Night '52
Voyage Suprise '46

Sheila Carol
The Beast from Haunted Cave '60
Ski Troop Attack '60

Sue Carol (1907-82)
The Lone Star Ranger '30
Walking Back '26
Captain Swagger '25

Adam Carolla (1964-)
The Hammer '07
Art House '98
Too Smooth '98

Leslie Caron (1931-)
Le Divorce '03
Chocolat '00
The Last of the Blonde Bombshells '00
Funny Bones '94
Damage '92
Courage Mountain '89
Dangerous Moves '84
The Unapproachable '82
Contract '80
Goldengirl '79
The Man Who Loved Women '77
Valentino '77
QB VII '74
Nicole '72
Head of the Family '71
Madron '70
Is Paris Burning? '66
Promise Her Anything '66
Father Goose '64
The L-Shaped Room '62
Fanny '61
Gigi '58
Daddy Long Legs '55
The Glass Slipper '55
Lili '53
The Story of Three Loves '53
An American in Paris '51

Memmo Carotenuto (1908-80)
Big Deal on Madonna Street '58
Too Bad She's Bad '54

Todd Carpent
Razorteeth '05
Feeders '96

Carleton Carpenter (1926-)
Up Periscope '59
Summer Stock '50
Two Weeks with Love '50
Lost Boundaries '49

Charisma Carpenter (1970-)
The Expendables '10
Voodoo Moon '05

David Carpenter
Spiders '00
Amelia Earhart: The Final Flight '94
Gettysburg '93
Warlock '91

Fred Carpenter (1954-)
Murdered Innocence '94
Small Kill '93

Horace Carpenter (1875-1945)
Range Riders '35
Maniac '34
The Dude Bandit '33

Jack Carpenter (1984-)
I Love You, Beth Cooper '09
Sydney White '07

Jennifer Carpenter (1979-)
Quarantine '08
Battle in Seattle '07
The Exorcism of Emily Rose '05
White Chicks '04

John Carpenter (1914-2003)
Night of the Ghouls '59
Song of Old Wyoming '45

John Carpenter (1948-)
Masters of Horror: Pro-Life '05
The Cradle Will Rock '99
Body Bags '93
Silence of the Hams '93

Paul Carpenter (1921-64)
Call Me Bwana '63
Fire Maidens from Outer Space '56
Black Glove '54
Heat Wave '54
Paid to Kill '54
Unholy Four '54
Uneasy Terms '48

Peter Carpenter
Point of Terror '71
Blood Mania '70

Camilla Carr
Making Love '82
Keep My Grave Open '80
Logan's Run '76
Poor White Trash 2 '75
Don't Look in the Basement '73

Carole Carr (1928-97)
Scream Dream '89
Down Among the Z Men '52
Goon Movie '52

Darlene Carr (1950-)
Piranha '95
Death of a Gunfighter '69
The Jungle Book '67 (V)

Jane Carr
The Prime of Miss Jean Brodie '69
The Church Mouse '34

Mary Carr (1874-1973)
The World Accuses '35
Gun Law '33
The Fighting Marshal '32
Kept Husbands '31
The Night Patrol '26
Red Kimono '25

Paul Carr (1934-)
Sisters of Death '76
Sniper '75
The Bat People '74
Truck Stop Women '74
The Severed Arm '73
Ben '72
Dirt Gang '71

Thomas Carr (1907-97)
S.O.S. Coast Guard '37
The Idol Dancer '20

Raffaella Carra
Von Ryan's Express '65
Caesar the Conqueror '63
Mole Men Against the Son of Hercules '61

David Carradine (1936-2009)
Break '09
The Golden Boys '08
Hell Ride '08
Last Hour '08
Sundown: The Vampire in Retreat '08
Big Stan '07
Epic Movie '07
How to Rob a Bank '07
National Lampoon's The Stoned Aged '07
Final Move '06
Miracle at Sage Creek '05
Kill Bill Vol. 2 '04
Kill Bill Vol. 1 '03 (V)
The Outsider '02
Warden of Red Rock '01
By Dawn's Early Light '00
Codename: Jaguar '00
Isaac Asimov's Nightfall '00
Cybercity '99
Dangerous Curves '99
Knocking on Death's Door '99
Children of the Corn 5: Fields of Terror '98
Capital Punishment '96
Last Stand at Saber River '96
The Rage '96
The Gambler Returns: The Luck of the Draw '93
Animal Instincts '92
Distant Justice '92
Field of Fire '92
Night Rhythms '92
Roadside Prophets '92
Deadly Surveillance '91
Double Trouble '91
Dune Warriors '91
Karate Cop '91
Project: Eliminator '91
Sundown '91
Waxwork 2: Lost in Time '91
Bird on a Wire '90
Evil Toons '90
Future Zone '90
Martial Law '90
Midnight Fear '90
Think Big '90
Future Force '89
Night Children '89
Wizards of the Lost Kingdom 2 '89
Crime Zone '88
Nowhere to Run '88
Tropical Snow '88
Warlords '88
The Misfit Brigade '87
Sonny Boy '87
Armed Response '86
The Dying Truth '86
Kung Fu: The Movie '86
Oceans of Fire '86
The P.O.W. Escape '86
The Bad Seed '85
North and South Book 1 '85
Jealousy '84
The Warrior & the Sorceress '84
Lone Wolf McQuade '83
On the Line '83
Q (The Winged Serpent) '82
Safari 3000 '82
Trick or Treats '82
Americana '81
Cloud Dancer '80
High Noon: Part 2 '80
The Long Riders '80
Mr. Horn '79
Circle of Iron '78
Death Sport '78

The Serpent's Egg *'78*
Gray Lady Down *'77*
Thunder and Lightning *'77*
Bound for Glory *'76*
Cannonball *'76*
Death Race 2000 *'75*
The Long Goodbye *'73*
Mean Streets *'73*
Boxcar Bertha *'72*
Kung Fu *'72*
Maybe I'll Come Home in the Spring *'71*
Macho Callahan *'70*
Maybe I'll Be Home in the Spring *'70*
The McMasters *'70*
The Good Guys and the Bad Guys *'69*
Violent Ones *'68*

John Carradine (1906-88)
Jack-O *'95*
Buried Alive *'89*
Evil Spawn *'87*
Star Slammer *'87*
Monster in the Closet *'86*
Peggy Sue Got Married *'86*
Revenge *'86*
Tomb *'86*
Evils of the Night *'85*
The Monster Club *'85*
The Vals *'85*
Ice Pirates *'84*
Boogey Man 2 *'83*
Demon Rage *'82*
House of the Long Shadows *'82*
The Secret of NIMH *'82 (V)*
Frankenstein Island *'81*
Goliath Awaits *'81*
The Howling *'81*
The Boogey Man *'80*
The Nesting *'80*
Nocturna *'79*
The Seekers *'79*
The Bees *'78*
Monster *'78*
The Vampire Hookers *'78*
The Christmas Coal Mine Miracle *'77*
Golden Rendezvous *'77*
Satan's Cheerleaders *'77*
Shock Waves *'77*
The White Buffalo *'77*
The Killer Inside Me *'76*
The Last Tycoon *'76*
Mary, Mary, Bloody Mary *'76*
The Sentinel *'76*
The Shootist *'76*
Death at Love House *'75*
Bad Charleston Charlie *'73*
Blood Legacy *'73*
The House of Seven Corpses *'73*
The Shrieking *'73*
Silent Night, Bloody Night *'73*
Terror in the Wax Museum *'73*
Big Foot *'72*
Blood of Ghastly Horror *'72*
Boxcar Bertha *'72*
Everything You Always Wanted to Know about Sex (But Were Afraid to Ask) *'72*
The Gatling Gun *'72*
The Night Strangler *'72*
Cain's Cutthroats *'71*
Horror of the Blood Monsters *'70*
The McMasters *'70*
Myra Breckinridge *'70*
Shinbone Alley *'70 (V)*
Blood of Dracula's Castle *'69*
The Good Guys and the Bad Guys *'69*
Gun Riders *'69*
The Trouble with Girls (and How to Get into It) *'69*
Alien Massacre *'67*
The Astro-Zombies *'67*
Autopsy of a Ghost *'67*
Gallery of Horrors *'67*
Hillbillies in a Haunted House *'67*
The Hostage *'67*
Mummy & Curse of the Jackal *'67*
Billy the Kid Versus Dracula *'66*
Munster, Go Home! *'66*
House of the Black Death *'65*
Cheyenne Autumn *'64*
Curse of the Stone Hand *'64*
Horrors of the Red Planet *'64*
The Patsy *'64*
Invasion of the Animal People *'62*
The Man Who Shot Liberty Valance *'62*
The Adventures of Huckleberry Finn *'60*
Tarzan the Magnificent *'60*
The Cosmic Man *'59*
Invisible Invaders *'59*
Half Human *'58*
The Incredible Petrified World *'58*
Last Hurrah *'58*
Showdown at Boot Hill *'58*
Hell Ship Mutiny *'57*
The Unearthly *'57*
Around the World in 80 Days *'56*
The Black Sleep *'56*
Court Jester *'56*
The Female Jungle *'56*
Hidden Guns *'56*
The Ten Commandments *'56*
The Kentuckian *'55*
Stranger on Horseback *'55*
Casanova's Big Night *'54*
The Egyptian *'54*
Thunder Pass *'54*
Johnny Guitar *'53*
The C-Man *'49*
The Private Affairs of Bel Ami *'47*
Captain Kidd *'45*
House of Dracula *'45*
The Adventures of Mark Twain *'44*
Bluebeard *'44*
House of Frankenstein *'44*
The Invisible Man's Revenge *'44*
The Mummy's Ghost *'44*
Return of the Ape Man *'44*
Waterfront *'44*
Captive Wild Woman *'43*
Isle of Forgotten Sins *'43*
Revenge of the Zombies *'43*
Silver Spurs *'43*
Reunion in France *'42*
Son of Fury *'42*
Blood and Sand *'41*
Man Hunt *'41*
Western Union *'41*
Brigham Young: Frontiersman *'40*
The Grapes of Wrath *'40*
Return of Frank James *'40*
Drums Along the Mohawk *'39*
Five Came Back *'39*
The Hound of the Baskervilles *'39*
Jesse James *'39*
Mr. Moto's Last Warning *'39*
Stagecoach *'39*
The Three Musketeers *'39*
Alexander's Ragtime Band *'38*
Four Men and a Prayer *'38*
Of Human Hearts *'38*
Captains Courageous *'37*
The Hurricane *'37*
The Last Gangster *'37*
Thank you, Mr. Moto *'37*
Dimples *'36*
The Garden of Allah *'36*
Mary of Scotland *'36*
The Prisoner of Shark Island *'36*
Winterset *'36*
The Bride of Frankenstein *'35*
Les Miserables *'35*
The Black Cat *'34*
Daniel Boone *'34*
The Invisible Man *'33*
To the Last Man *'33*

Keith Carradine (1951-)
Lake City *'08*
Winter of Frozen Dreams *'08*
All Hat *'07*
Bobby Z *'07*
Coyote Waits *'03*
Monte Walsh *'03*
The Outsider *'02*
The Diamond of Jeru *'01*
Baby *'00*
Hostage Hotel *'00*
Night Ride Home *'99*
Out of the Cold *'99*
Sirens *'99*
Hunter's Moon *'97*
Standoff *'97*
A Thousand Acres *'97*
Larry McMurtry's Dead Man's Walk *'96*
Last Stand at Saber River *'96*
Two Days in the Valley *'96*
The Tie That Binds *'95*
Wild Bill *'95*
Andre *'94*
Is There Life Out There? *'94*
The Bachelor *'93*
Crisscross *'92*
The Ballad of the Sad Cafe *'91*
Eye on the Sparrow *'91*
Payoff *'91*
Daddy's Dyin'... Who's Got the Will? *'90*
Judgment *'90*
Capone *'89*
Cold Feet *'89*
The Forgotten *'89*
Backfire *'88*
The Moderns *'88*
The Inquiry *'87*
Murder Ordained *'87*
Half a Lifetime *'86*
Trouble in Mind *'86*
A Winner Never Quits *'86*
Blackout *'85*
Choose Me *'84*
Maria's Lovers *'84*
Chiefs *'83*
Southern Comfort *'81*
The Long Riders *'80*
A Rumor of War *'80*
An Almost Perfect Affair *'79*
Old Boyfriends *'79*
Pretty Baby *'78*
The Duellists *'77*
Welcome to L.A. *'77*
Lumiere *'76*
Nashville *'75*
Thieves Like Us *'74*
Emperor of the North Pole *'73*
Idaho Transfer *'73*
The Shrieking *'73*
Kung Fu *'72*
A Gunfight *'71*
Man on a String *'71*
McCabe & Mrs. Miller *'71*

Robert Carradine (1954-)
Deep Winter *'08*
Tooth and Nail *'07*
Attack of the Sabretooth *'05*
Supercross: The Movie *'05*
The Lizzie McGuire Movie *'03*
Max Keeble's Big Move *'01*
Dangerous Curves *'99*
The Kid with the X-Ray Eyes *'99*
Shepherd *'99*
Breakout *'98*
Gunfighter *'98*
Stray Bullet *'98*
Scorpio One *'97*
Humanoids from the Deep *'96*
Bird of Prey *'95*
Revenge of the Nerds 4: Nerds in Love *'94*
Body Bags *'93*
The Disappearance of Christina *'93*
Stephen King's The Tommyknockers *'93*
The Player *'92*
Revenge of the Nerds 3: The Next Generation *'92*
Clarence *'91*
Double-Crossed *'91*
Illusions *'91*
Somebody Has to Shoot the Picture *'90*
All's Fair *'89*
Buy & Cell *'89*
The Incident *'89*
Rude Awakening *'89*
Conspiracy: The Trial of the Chicago Eight *'87*
Number One with a Bullet *'87*
Revenge of the Nerds 2: Nerds in Paradise *'87*
Tales of the Klondike: In a Far Country *'87*
Monte Carlo *'86*
As Is *'85*
Aladdin and His Wonderful Lamp *'84*
Just the Way You Are *'84*
Revenge of the Nerds *'84*
Wavelength *'83*
Heartaches *'82*
Tag: The Assassination Game *'82*
The Big Red One *'80*
The Long Riders *'80*
On the Edge: The Survival of Dana *'79*
Blackout *'78*
Coming Home *'78*
Joyride *'77*
Orca *'77*
Cannonball *'76*
Jackson County Jail *'76*
Massacre at Central High *'76*
Pom Pom Girls *'76*
Aloha, Bobby and Rose *'74*
Mean Streets *'73*
The Cowboys *'72*

Carlos Carrasco
Double Take *'01*
One Man's Hero *'98*
Speed *'94*

Isabelle Carre (1971-)
Private Fears in Public Places *'06*
He Loves Me ... He Loves Me Not *'02*
Children of the Century *'99*
The Horseman on the Roof *'95*

Dany Carrel (1935-)
The Hands of Orlac *'60*
Mill of the Stone Women *'60*

Barbara Carrera (1945-)
Love Is All There Is *'96*
Sawbones *'95*
Tryst *'94*
Point of Impact *'93*
Loverboy *'89*
Wicked Stepmother *'89*
The Underachievers *'88*
Love at Stake *'87*
Wild Geese 2 *'85*
Lone Wolf McQuade *'83*
Never Say Never Again *'83*
I, the Jury *'82*
Condorman *'81*
Masada *'81*
When Time Ran Out *'80*
Centennial *'78*
The Island of Dr. Moreau *'77*
Embryo *'76*

Tia Carrere (1967-)
Dark Honeymoon *'08*
Back in the Day *'05*
Lilo & Stitch 2: Stitch Has a Glitch *'05 (V)*
Lilo & Stitch *'02 (V)*
Scarred City *'98*
Tracked *'98*
Kull the Conqueror *'97*
Top of the World *'97*
High School High *'96*
Natural Enemy *'96*
Hollow Point *'95*
The Immortals *'95*
Jury Duty *'95*
My Teacher's Wife *'95*
Hostile Intentions *'94*
True Lies *'94*
Quick *'93*
Rising Sun *'93*
Wayne's World 2 *'93*
Wayne's World *'92*
Showdown in Little Tokyo *'91*
Fatal Mission *'89*
Aloha Summer *'88*
Noble House *'88*
Zombie Nightmare *'86*

Jim Carrey (1962-)
I Love You Phillip Morris *'10*
A Christmas Carol *'09 (V)*
Dr. Seuss' Horton Hears a Who! *'08 (V)*
Yes Man *'08*
The Number 23 *'07*
Fun With Dick and Jane *'05*
Eternal Sunshine of the Spotless Mind *'04*
Lemony Snicket's A Series of Unfortunate Events *'04*
Bruce Almighty *'03*
The Majestic *'01*
Dr. Seuss' How the Grinch Stole Christmas *'00*
Me, Myself, and Irene *'00*
Man on the Moon *'99*
Simon Birch *'98 (N)*
The Truman Show *'98*
Liar Liar *'97*
The Cable Guy *'96*
Ace Ventura: When Nature Calls *'95*
Batman Forever *'95*
Dumb & Dumber *'94*
The Mask *'94*
Ace Ventura: Pet Detective *'93*
Doing Time on Maple Drive *'92*
High Strung *'91*
Earth Girls Are Easy *'89*
Pink Cadillac *'89*
The Dead Pool *'88*
Peggy Sue Got Married *'86*
Once Bitten *'85*
Finders Keepers *'84*
Club Med *'83*
Rubberface *'81*

Corey Carrier (1980-)
Savage Land *'94*
After Dark, My Sweet *'90*
Men Don't Leave *'89*

Matthieu Carriere (1950-)
Luther *'03*
Christopher Columbus: The Discovery *'92*
The Bay Boy *'85*
A Woman in Flames *'84*
La Passante *'83*
The Aviator's Wife *'80*
The Associate *'79*
Coup de Grace *'78*
Born for Hell *'76*
Germicide *'74*
Don Juan (Or If Don Juan Were a Woman) *'73*
An Occurrence at Owl Creek Bridge/Coup de Grace *'62*

Elpidia Carrillo (1963-)
Seven Pounds *'08*
Nine Lives *'05*
Bread and Roses *'00*
Dangerous Passion *'95*
My Family *'94*
The Lightning Incident *'91*
Assassin *'89*
Let's Get Harry *'87*
Predator *'87*
Salvador *'86*
Beyond the Limit *'83*
The Border *'82*

Leo Carrillo (1881-1961)
Pancho Villa Returns *'50*
Guns of Fury *'49*
The Fugitive *'48*
The Phantom of the Opera *'43*
American Empire *'42*
Timber! *'42*
Horror Island *'41*
Riders of Death Valley *'41*
Lillian Russell *'40*
One Night in the Tropics *'40*
Fisherman's Wharf *'39*
Girl of the Golden West *'38*
Too Hot to Handle *'38*
Fit for a King *'37*
History Is Made at Night *'37*
I Promise to Pay *'37*
The Gay Desperado *'36*
If You Could Only Cook *'36*
Manhattan Melodrama *'34*
Viva Villa! *'34*
Before Morning *'33*

Debbie Lee Carrington (1959-)
Tiptoes *'03*
Club Fed *'90*
Spaced Invaders *'90*

Regina Carrol (1943-92)
Black Heat *'76*
Blazing Stewardesses *'75*
Jessi's Girls *'75*
Angels' Wild Women *'72*
Blood of Ghastly Horror *'72*
Brain of Blood *'71*
Dracula vs. Frankenstein *'71*
The Female Bunch *'69*
Satan's Sadists *'69*

Barbara Carroll
Goliath Against the Giants *'63*
The Last Days of Pompeii *'60*

Beeson Carroll
Coming Home *'78*
Werewolf of Washington *'73*

Brandon Carroll
Home Sick *'08*
Hell Squad *'58*

Diahann Carroll (1935-)
The Courage to Love *'00*
Livin' for Love: The Natalie Cole Story *'00*
Sally Hemings: An American Scandal *'00*
Having Our Say: The Delany Sisters' First 100 Years *'99*
The Sweetest Gift *'98*
Eve's Bayou *'97*
The Five Heartbeats *'91*
From the Dead of Night *'89*
I Know Why the Caged Bird Sings *'79*
Death Scream *'75*
Goodbye Again *'61*
Paris Blues *'61*
Carmen Jones *'54*

Helen Carroll
The Man Upstairs *'93*
The Dead *'87*
Backstairs at the White House *'79*

James Carroll
DC 9/11: Time of Crisis *'04*
Under the Piano *'95*
Police Academy 4: Citizens on Patrol *'87*
Girls Night Out *'83*
Senior Trip *'81*
He Knows You're Alone *'80*

James Dennis (Jim) Carroll (1950-2009)
The Basketball Diaries *'95*
The Unholy *'88*

Janet Carroll (1940-)
(Untitled) *'09*
Enough *'02*
Forces of Nature *'99*
The Omega Code *'99*
Family Business *'89*
Memories of Me *'88*
Bluffing It *'87*
Risky Business *'83*

Joan Carroll (1932-)
Tomorrow the World *'44*
Primrose Path *'40*

John Carroll (1905-79)
Decision at Sundown *'57*
Rock, Baby, Rock It *'57*
The Farmer Takes a Wife *'53*
Flying Tigers *'42*
Rio Rita *'42*
Lady Be Good *'41*
Sunny *'41*
Go West *'40*
Susan and God *'40*
Only Angels Have Wings *'39*
Wolf Call *'39*
Rose of Rio Grande *'38*
Zorro Rides Again *'37*

Justin Carroll
Dark Secrets *'95*
Stormswept *'95*

Kevin Carroll
The Notorious Bettie Page *'06*
Paid in Full *'02*
Pipe Dream *'02*
The Secret Lives of Dentists *'02*
Ed's Next Move *'96*

Leo G. Carroll (1892-1972)
That Funny Feeling *'65*
The Prize *'63*
One Plus One *'61*
The Parent Trap *'61*
North by Northwest *'59*
Tarantula *'55*
We're No Angels *'55*
Treasure of the Golden Condor *'53*
The Bad and the Beautiful *'52*
The Snows of Kilimanjaro *'52*
First Legion *'51*
Strangers on a Train *'51*
Father of the Bride *'50*
The Happy Years *'50*
Forever Amber *'47*
The Paradine Case *'47*
Song of Love *'47*
House on 92nd Street *'45*
Spellbound *'45*
Bahama Passage *'42*
Suspicion *'41*
Charlie Chan's Murder Cruise *'40*
Rebecca *'40*
Bulldog Drummond's Secret Police *'39*
Charlie Chan in City of Darkness *'39*
The Private Lives of Elizabeth & Essex *'39*
The Tower of London *'39*
Wuthering Heights *'39*
A Christmas Carol *'38*

Madeleine Carroll (1906-87)
When a Stranger Calls *'06*
Bahama Passage *'42*
My Favorite Blonde *'42*
My Son, My Son *'40*
My Love For Yours *'39*
On the Avenue *'37*
Prisoner of Zenda *'37*
The General Died at Dawn *'36*
Lloyds of London *'36*
The Secret Agent *'36*
The 39 Steps *'35*
The World Moves On *'34*

Madeline Carroll (1996-)
The Spy Next Door *'10*
Vanilla Gorilla *'09*
Swing Vote *'08*

Nancy Carroll (1904-65)
That Certain Age *'38*
Transatlantic Merry-Go-Round *'34*
Hot Saturday *'32*
Scarlet Dawn *'32*
Personal Maid *'31*
Dance of Life *'29*

Pat Carroll (1927-)
Freedom Writers *'07*
Redacted *'07*
Songcatcher *'99*
The Little Mermaid *'89 (V)*
My Neighbor Totoro *'88 (V)*
Brothers O'Toole *'73*
With Six You Get Eggroll *'68*

Peter Carroll (1943-)
Who Killed Baby Azaria? *'83*
Cass *'78*
The Chant of Jimmie Blacksmith *'78*
The Last Wave *'77*

Rocky Carroll (1963-)
Best Laid Plans *'99*
The Great White Hype *'96*
Crimson Tide *'95*

Carrot Top (1967-)
Dennis the Menace Strikes Again *'98*
Chairman of the Board *'97*

Ben Carruthers (1936-83)
Riot *'69*
Shadows *'60*

Julius J. Carry, III (1952-)
The New Guy *'02*
The Last Dragon *'85*
Avenging Disco Godfather *'76*

Charles Carson (1886-1977)
Beau Brummel *'54*
Cry, the Beloved Country *'51*
The Courageous Mr. Penn *'41*
Dreaming Lips *'37*
The Secret Agent *'36*
Broken Melody *'34*

Crystal Carson (1967-)
Kiss and Be Killed *'91*
Cartel *'90*
Killer Tomatoes Strike Back *'90*

Glen Carson
Ninja Death Squad *'87*
Ninja Phantom Heroes *'87*

Hunter Carson (1975-)
Mr. North *'88*
Invaders from Mars *'86*
Paris, Texas *'83*

Jack Carson
Blues in the Night *'41*
I Take This Woman *'40*

Jack Carson (1910-63)
The King of the Roaring '20s: The Story of Arnold Rothstein *'61*
The Bramble Bush *'60*
Cat on a Hot Tin Roof *'58*
Rally 'Round the Flag, Boys! *'58*
Tarnished Angels *'57*
Phffft! *'54*
Red Garters *'54*
A Star Is Born *'54*
Dangerous When Wet *'53*
Bright Leaf *'50*
It's a Great Feeling *'49*
My Dream Is Yours *'49*
John Loves Mary *'48*
Romance on the High Seas *'48*
Mildred Pierce *'45*
Roughly Speaking *'45*
Arsenic and Old Lace *'44*
Hollywood Canteen *'44*
Princess O'Rourke *'43*
Thank Your Lucky Stars *'43*
Gentleman Jim *'42*
Larceny, Inc. *'42*
The Male Animal *'42*
The Bride Came C.O.D. *'41*
Love Crazy *'41*
Mr. & Mrs. Smith *'41*
Strawberry Blonde *'41*
Lucky Partners *'40*
Destry Rides Again *'39*
Mr. Smith Goes to Washington *'39*
Carefree *'38*
Having a Wonderful Time *'38*
The Saint in New York *'38*
Vivacious Lady *'38*
Stage Door *'37*
Stand-In *'37*

John Carson (1927-)
An African Dream *'90*
After Julius *'78*
Captain Kronos: Vampire Hunter *'74*
Emma *'72*
Taste the Blood of Dracula *'70*
Plague of the Zombies *'66*

John David Carson (1952-)
Empire of the Ants *'77*
Charge of the Model T's *'76*
Creature from Black Lake *'76*
Savage Is Loose *'74*

Lisa Nicole Carson (1969-)
Aftershock: Earthquake in New York *'99*
Life *'99*
Eve's Bayou *'97*
Love Jones *'96*
Devil in a Blue Dress *'95*

L.M. Kit Carson (1947-)
Hurricane Streets *'96*
Running on Empty *'88*
David Holzman's Diary *'67*

Shawn Carson
Something Wicked This Way Comes *'83*
The Funhouse *'81*

Silas Carson (1965-)
Star Wars: Episode 3—Revenge of the Sith *'05*
Hidalgo *'04*

Sunset Carson (1922-90)
Battling Marshal *'48*
Alias Billy the Kid *'46*
Rio Grande Raiders *'46*
Bells of Rosarita *'45*
Rough Riders of Cheyenne *'45*
Call of the Rockies *'44*
Stage Door Canteen *'43*

Terrence "T.C." Carson
Final Destination 2 *'03*
U-571 *'00*
Relax... It's Just Sex! *'98*
Gang Related *'96*
Livin' Large *'91*

Peter Carsten (1929-)
Zeppelin *'71*
Black Lemons *'70*
Web of the Spider *'70*
And God Said to Cain *'69*
Dark of the Sun *'68*
Secret of the Black Trunk *'62*

Margit Carstensen (1940-)
Terror 2000 *'92*
Chinese Roulette *'86*
Angry Harvest *'85*
Possession *'81*
Berlin Alexanderplatz *'80*
Mother Kusters Goes to Heaven *'76*
Satan's Brew *'76*
Fear of Fear *'75*
Tenderness of the Wolves *'73*
The Bitter Tears of Petra von Kant *'72*

Alex Carter (1964-)
Out of Time *'03*
Hitched *'01*
Recipe for Revenge *'98*
The Man in the Attic *'94*

Alice Carter
Dangerous Heart *'93*
Gross Anatomy *'89*

Ann Carter (1936-)
Song of Love *'47*
The Two Mrs. Carrolls *'47*
Curse of the Cat People *'44*
I Married a Witch *'42*

Ben Carter (1907-46)
Crash Dive *'43*
Sleepers West *'41*

Dixie Carter (1939-)
That Evening Sun *'09*
The Big Day *'99*
Going Berserk *'83*
Killing of Randy Webster *'81*

Finn Carter (1960-)
Missing Pieces *'00*
Sweet Justice *'92*
How I Got into College *'89*
Tremors *'89*

Gary Carter
Late Bloomers *'95*
Ninja Strike Force *'88*

Georgianna Carter
The Wild Ride *'60*
Night of the Blood Beast *'58*

Helena Carter (1923-2000)
Invaders from Mars *'53*
Bugles in the Afternoon *'52*
Double Crossbones *'51*
Kiss Tomorrow Goodbye *'50*
Something in the Wind *'47*

Jack Carter (1923-)
One Last Ride *'03*
Play It to the Bone *'99*
In the Heat of Passion *'91*
Satan's Princess *'90*
Arena *'89*
Robo-Chic *'89*
Deadly Embrace *'88*
Sexpot *'88*
Death Blow *'87*
Red Nights *'87*
Ecstasy *'84*
Hambone & Hillie *'84*
History of the World: Part 1 *'81*
Alligator *'80*
Octagon *'80*
The Glove *'78*
Rainbow *'78*
The Happy Hooker Goes to Washington *'77*
The Amazing Dobermans *'76*
Resurrection of Zachary Wheeler *'71*
Viva Las Vegas *'63*
The Horizontal Lieutenant *'62*

Janis Carter (1913-94)
Flying Leathernecks *'51*
The Half-Breed *'51*
Santa Fe *'51*
The Woman on Pier 13 *'50*
Miss Grant Takes Richmond *'49*
Lady of Burlesque *'43*
I Married an Angel *'42*
Just Off Broadway *'42*

Jason Carter (1960-)
Behind the Red Door *'02*
The Dark Dancer *'95*

Jim Carter (1948-)
Creation *'09*
Return to Cranford *'09*
Cranford *'08*
The Secret Life of Mrs. Beeton *'06*
The Thief Lord *'06*
Bright Young Things *'03*
Dinotopia *'02*
The Way We Live Now *'02*
The Little Vampire *'00*
102 Dalmatians *'00*
Legionnaire *'98*
Shakespeare in Love *'98*
A Merry War *'97*
Brassed Off *'96*
Grave Indiscretions *'96*
Black Beauty *'94*
Cracker: The Big Crunch *'94*
The Madness of King George *'94*
The Advocate *'93*
Stalin *'92*
A Very British Coup *'88*
A Month in the Country *'87*
Haunted Honeymoon *'86*

Joelle Carter (1972-)
Room 314 *'07*
When Will I Be Loved *'04*
High Fidelity *'00*
It Had to Be You *'00*
Just One Time *'00*
Swimming *'00*

Karen Carter
The Legend of the Wolf Woman *'77*
The Big Bust Out *'73*

Lynda Carter (1951-)
Slayer *'06*
The Dukes of Hazzard *'05*
Sky High *'05*
Super Troopers *'01*
A Prayer in the Dark *'97*
Danielle Steel's Daddy *'91*
I Posed for Playboy *'91*
Rita Hayworth: The Love Goddess *'83*
Hotline *'82*
Baby Broker *'81*
Last Song *'80*
Bobbie Jo and the Outlaw *'76*

Nell Carter (1948-2003)
The Proprietor *'96*
The Grass Harp *'95*
The Crazysitter *'94*
Bebe's Kids *'92 (V)*
Final Shot: The Hank Gathers Story *'92*
Modern Problems *'81*
Hair *'79*

Nick Carter
The Hollow *'04*
Class Reunion Massacre *'77*

Sarah Carter (1980-)
DOA: Dead or Alive *'06*
Berkeley *'05*
Final Destination 2 *'03*

Terry Carter (1929-)
Battlestar Galactica *'78*
Black Force 2 *'78*
Mission Galactica: The Cylon Attack *'78*
Foxy Brown *'74*
Man on the Run *'74*

Thomas Carter (1953-)
Whose Life Is It Anyway? *'81*
Monkey Hustle *'77*

T.K. Carter (1956-)
Domino *'05*
Baadasssss! *'03*
The Corner *'00*
Yesterday's Target *'96*
A Rage in Harlem *'91*
Ski Patrol *'89*
Amazon Women on the Moon *'87*
He's My Girl *'87*
Runaway Train *'85*
Doctor Detroit *'83*
The Thing *'82*
Southern Comfort *'81*
The Hollywood Knights *'80*
Seems Like Old Times *'80*

Anna Carteret (1942-)
Mrs. Palfrey at the Claremont *'05*
The Heat of the Day *'91*
The Shell Seekers *'89*

Katrin Cartlidge (1961-2002)
From Hell *'01*
No Man's Land *'01*
Sword of Honour *'01*
The Weight of Water *'00*
Hi-Life *'98*
The Lost Son *'98*
Career Girls *'97*
Claire Dolan *'97*
Breaking the Waves *'95*
Saint-Ex: The Story of the Storyteller *'95*
Before the Rain *'94*
Naked *'93*

Angela Cartwright (1952-)
Lost in Space *'98*
High School USA *'84*
Scout's Honor *'80*
The Sound of Music *'65*

Lynn Cartwright (1928-2004)
The Wasp Woman *'59*
Queen of Outer Space *'58*

Nancy Cartwright (1959-)
The Simpsons Movie *'07 (V)*
Rugrats Go Wild! *'03 (V)*
The Land Before Time 6: The Secret of Saurus Rock *'98 (V)*
The Little Mermaid *'89 (V)*
Pound Puppies and the Legend of Big Paw *'88 (V)*
Not My Kid *'85*
Twilight Zone: The Movie *'83*

Veronica Cartwright (1950-)
The Invasion *'07*
Kinsey *'04*
Just Married *'03*
Scary Movie 2 *'01*
A Slipping Down Life *'99*
Sparkler *'99*
Quicksilver Highway *'98*
Money Talks *'97*
My Brother's Keeper *'95*
Candyman 2: Farewell to the Flesh *'94*
Dead Air *'94*
Mirror, Mirror 2: Raven Dance *'94*
Man Trouble *'92*
Dead in the Water *'91*
False Identity *'90*
Hitler's Daughter *'90*
Robert Kennedy and His Times *'90*
Valentino Returns *'88*
Wisdom *'87*
The Witches of Eastwick *'87*
Flight of the Navigator *'86*
My Man Adam *'86*
Nightmares *'83*
The Right Stuff *'83*
Prime Suspect *'82*
Alien *'79*
Goin' South *'78*
Invasion of the Body Snatchers *'78*
Kid from Not-So-Big *'78*
Inserts *'76*
The Birds *'63*
One Man's Way *'63*
Spencer's Mountain *'63*
The Children's Hour *'61*

Lisa Marie Caruk
Blood Angels *'05*
Call Me: The Rise and Fall of Heidi Fleiss *'04*

Anthony Caruso (1913-2003)
Claws *'77*
Zebra Force *'76*
Legend of Earl Durand *'74*
Never Steal Anything Small *'59*
When Gangland Strikes *'56*
Cattle Queen of Montana *'54*
Drum Beat *'54*
The Iron Mistress *'52*
The Asphalt Jungle *'50*
Objective, Burma! *'45*
Pride of the Marines *'45*
The Ghost and the Guest *'43*
Watch on the Rhine *'43*

David Caruso (1956-)
Black Point '01
Session 9 '01
Deadlocked '00
Proof of Life '00
Body Count '97
Cold Around the Heart '97
Elmore Leonard's Gold Coast '97
Jade '95
Kiss of Death '94
Mad Dog and Glory '93
King of New York '90
Rainbow Drive '90
China Girl '87
Blue City '86
First Blood '82
An Officer and a Gentleman '82
Getting Wasted '80

Brigitte Carva
Dr. Orloff and the Invisible Man '72
Orloff and the Invisible Man '70

Betty Carvalho
Best of the Best 2 '93
Halloween 5: The Revenge of Michael Myers '89

Brent Carver (1952-)
The Event '03
Ararat '02
Deeply '99
Lilies '96
Whiskers '96
Millennium '89
Crossbar '79
One Night Stand '78

Lynne Carver (1909-55)
Bataan '43
Man from Cheyenne '42
Sunset on the Desert '42
The Adventures of Huckleberry Finn '39
A Christmas Carol '38
Everybody Sing '38
The Bride Wore Red '37
Madame X '37
Maytime '37

Dana Carvey (1955-)
Master of Disguise '02
Little Nicky '00
The Shot '96
Clean Slate '94
The Road to Wellville '94
Trapped in Paradise '94
Wayne's World 2 '93
Wayne's World '92
Opportunity Knocks '90
Moving '88
Tough Guys '86
Racing with the Moon '84
This Is Spinal Tap '84

James Carville
The Assassination of Jesse James by the Coward Robert Ford '07
The People vs. Larry Flynt '96

Eloy Casados (1949-)
Grand Avenue '96
A Climate for Killing '91

Alex Casanovas
What It's All About '95
Kika '94

Amira Casar (1971-)
Piano Tuner of Earthquakes '05
Anatomy of Hell '04
How I Killed My Father '03
Sylvia '03

Maria Casares (1922-96)
Someone Else's America '96
La Lectrice '88
Sand and Blood '87
The Testament of Orpheus '59
Orpheus '49
La Chartreuse de Parme '48
Children of Paradise '44
The Ladies of the Bois de Bologne '44

Antonio Casas (1911-82)
Blood at Sundown '88
Tristana '70
Four Dollars of Revenge '66
The Texican '66

Salvatore Cascio (1979-)
The Pope Must Diet '91
Everybody's Fine '90
Cinema Paradiso '88

Kathleen Case (1933-79)
Human Desire '54
Last of the Pony Riders '53

Max Casella (1967-)
Revolutionary Road '08
Dinosaur '00 (V)
Analyze This '98
Trial and Error '96
Sgt. Bilko '95
Ed Wood '94
Windrunner '94
Newsies '92

Chiara Caselli (1967-)
Ripley's Game '02
Sleepless '01
Forgotten City '98
Beyond the Clouds '95
Fiorile '93
My Own Private Idaho '91

Bernie Casey (1939-)
When I Find the Ocean '06
On the Edge '02
Tomcats '01
In the Mouth of Madness '95
The Cemetery Club '93
Street Knight '93
Chains of Gold '92
Another 48 Hrs. '90
Bill & Ted's Excellent Adventure '89
Backfire '88
I'm Gonna Git You Sucka '88
Rent-A-Cop '88
Steele Justice '87
Spies Like Us '85
The Fantastic World of D.C. Collins '84
Revenge of the Nerds '84
Never Say Never Again '83
Sharky's Machine '81
Sophisticated Gents '81
The Martian Chronicles: Part 1 '79
The Martian Chronicles: Part 2 '79
The Martian Chronicles: Part 3 '79
Ants '77
Dr. Black, Mr. Hyde '76
The Man Who Fell to Earth '76
Cornbread, Earl & Me '75
Panic on the 5:22 '74
Big Mo '73
Cleopatra Jones '73
Black Gunn '72
Boxcar Bertha '72
Brian's Song '71
Guns of the Magnificent Seven '69

Lawrence Casey (1941-)
Acapulco Gold '78
The Hunted Lady '77
The Student Nurses '70
The Gay Deceivers '69

Johnny Cash (1932-2003)
Last Days of Frank & Jesse James '86
Stagecoach '86
North and South Book 1 '85
The Baron and the Kid '84
Murder in Coweta County '83
Pride of Jesse Hallum '81
A Gunfight '71
Road to Nashville '67
Door to Door Maniac '61

June Carter Cash (1929-2003)
The Apostle '97
Last Days of Frank & Jesse James '86
The Baron and the Kid '84
Murder in Coweta County '83

Rosalind Cash (1938-95)
Tales from the Hood '95
The Mighty Pawns '87
The Offspring '87
The Adventures of Buckaroo Banzai Across the Eighth Dimension '84
Go Tell It on the Mountain '84
Death Drug '83
Wrong Is Right '82
Keeping On '81
Sophisticated Gents '81
The Class of Miss MacMichael '78
Monkey Hustle '77
Dr. Black, Mr. Hyde '76
Cornbread, Earl & Me '75
Amazing Grace '74
Omega Man '71

Isadore Cashier (1887-1948)
The Light Ahead '39
The Cantor's Son '37
His Wife's Lover '31

Graciela Casillas
American Streetfighter 2: The Full Impact '97
Fire in the Night '85

Stefania Casini (1948-)
The Bloodstained Shadow '78
Andy Warhol's Bad '77
Suspiria '77
Andy Warhol's Dracula '74

Philip Casnoff (1955-)
Kiss Tomorrow Goodbye '00
Chameleon '98
The Defenders: Taking the First '98
Temptation '94
Sinatra '92
Red Wind '91
Ironclads '90
Hands of a Stranger '87
North and South Book 2 '86
Gorp '80
King of America '80

John Cason (1918-61)
From Here to Eternity '53
Jungle Drums of Africa '53
Last Bullet '50
Outlaw Fury '50
Rangeland Empire '50
Red Desert '50
Sudden Death '50
The Traveling Saleswoman '50
Rimfire '49
Ringside '49
Tough Assignment '49
Outlaw of the Plains '46

Katrina Caspary
My Mom's a Werewolf '89
Mac and Me '88
Can't Buy Me Love '87

Maurice Cass (1884-1954)
Rocky Jones, Space Ranger: Renegade Satellite '54
Spook Busters '48
Thin Ice '37

Peggy Cass (1924-99)
Cheaters '84
Paddy '70
If It's Tuesday, This Must Be Belgium '69
Gidget Goes Hawaiian '61
Auntie Mame '58
The Marrying Kind '52

John Cassavetes (1929-89)
Love Streams '84
Marvin & Tige '84
Incubus '82
The Tempest '82
Whose Life Is It Anyway? '81
Brass Target '78
The Fury '78
Opening Night '77
Mikey & Nicky '76
Two Minute Warning '76
Minnie and Moskowitz '71
Husbands '70
Rosemary's Baby '68
Devil's Angels '67
The Dirty Dozen '67
The Killers '64
Saddle the Wind '58
Edge of the City '57

Nick Cassavetes (1959-)
My Sister's Keeper '09
The Independent '00
The Astronaut's Wife '99
Life '99
Face/Off '97
Just Like Dad '96
Machine Gun Blues '95
Mrs. Parker and the Vicious Circle '94
Twogether '94
Body of Influence '93
Broken Trust '93
Class of 1999 2: The Substitute '93
Sins of the Night '93
Sins of Desire '92
Delta Force 3: The Killing Game '91
Backstreet Dreams '90
Blind Fury '90
Assault of the Killer Bimbos '88
The Wraith '87

Jean-Pierre Cassel (1932-2007)
Stuck On You '03
The Crimson Rivers '01
Sade '00
The Ice Rink '99
La Ceremonie '95
Ready to Wear '94
Between Heaven and Earth '93
The Favor, the Watch, & the Very Big Fish '92
The Fatal Image '90
The Maid '90
The Phantom of the Opera '90
Mr. Frost '89
The Return of the Musketeers '89
Alice '86
La Truite '83
Nudo di Donna '83
La Vie Continue '82
From Hell to Victory '79
Les Rendez-vous D'Anna '78
Who Is Killing the Great Chefs of Europe? '78
The Killing of a Chinese Bookie '76
Twist '76
The Four Musketeers '75
That Lucky Touch '75
Murder on the Orient Express '74
The Three Musketeers '74
The Discreet Charm of the Bourgeoisie '72
La Rupture '70
Army of Shadows '69
Oh! What a Lovely War '69
The Killing Game '67
Is Paris Burning? '66
Those Magnificent Men in Their Flying Machines '65
The Elusive Corporal '62

Seymour Cassel (1935-)
Beer League '06
Lonesome Jim '06
The Tenants '06
The Black Widow '05
Circadian Rhythm '05
The Wendell Baker Story '05
The Life Aquatic with Steve Zissou '04
Manna from Heaven '02
Sonny '02
Stealing Harvard '02
Bartleby '01
The Royal Tenenbaums '01
61* '01
The Sleepy Time Gal '01
Animal Factory '00
The Crew '00
Just One Night '00
Me & Will '99
Emma's Wish '98
Motel Blue '98
Relax... It's Just Sex! '98
Rushmore '98
The Treat '98
Obsession '97
This World, Then the Fireworks '97
Cannes Man '96
Dream for an Insomniac '96
Things I Never Told You '96
Tree's Lounge '96
Bad Love '95
Chasers '94
Dark Side of Genius '94
Imaginary Crimes '94
It Could Happen to You '94
Tollbooth '94
Boiling Point '93
Chain of Desire '93
Hand Gun '93
Indecent Proposal '93
When Pigs Fly '93
Adventures in Spying '92
Honeymoon in Vegas '92
In the Soup '92
There Goes My Baby '92
Trouble Bound '92
Diary of a Hitman '91
White Fang '91
Dick Tracy '90
Sweet Bird of Youth '89
Wicked Stepmother '89
Colors '88
Johnny Be Good '88
Plain Clothes '88
Track 29 '88
Best Seller '87
Survival Game '87
Tin Men '87
Eye of the Tiger '86
Love Streams '84
Double Exposure '82
The Mountain Men '80
California Dreaming '79
Black Oak Conspiracy '77
Seducers '77
Valentino '77
Minnie and Moskowitz '71
Faces '68
The Killers '64

Vincent Cassel (1967-)
Eastern Promises '07
Ocean's Thirteen '07
Sheitan '06
Derailed '05
Ocean's Twelve '04
The Reckoning '03
Birthday Girl '02
Irreversible '02
Brotherhood of the Wolf '01
The Crimson Rivers '01
Read My Lips '01
Shrek '01 (V)
The Messenger: The Story of Joan of Arc '99
Elizabeth '98
Hate '95
L'Eleve '95
Cafe au Lait '94
Hot Chocolate '92

Alan Cassell (1932-)
Strange Bedfellows '04
Squizzy Taylor '84
The Club '81
Breaker Morant '80
Money Movers '78

Wally Cassell (1915-)
Until They Sail '57
Breakdown '53
Island in the Sky '53
Law and Order '53
Sands of Iwo Jima '49
White Heat '49
Saigon '47
The Story of G.I. Joe '45

Andrew Cassese (1972-)
Revenge of the Nerds 2: Nerds in Paradise '87
Revenge of the Nerds '84

Gabriel Casseus (1962-)
Black Hawk Down '01
Bedazzled '00
Lockdown '00
Black Dog '98
Modern Vampires '98
Buffalo Soldiers '97
Don King: Only in America '97
Fallen '97
Get On the Bus '96
Nightjohn '96
Lone Star '95
New Jersey Drive '95

David Cassidy (1950-)
Spirit of '76 '91
Instant Karma '90
The Night the City Screamed '80

Edward Cassidy (1893-1968)
Buffalo Bill Rides Again '47
Son of Zorro '47
Boss of Rawhide '44
Devil Riders '44
Frontier Outlaws '44
Rustler's Hideout '44
Wild Horse Phantom '44
Raiders of Red Gap '43
Sagebrush Law '43
Aces Wild '37
Boothill Brigade '37
Boots of Destiny '37
Roaring Six Guns '37
Santa Fe Bound '37
A Face in the Fog '36
Feud of the West '35
Pecos Kid '35
Toll of the Desert '35

Elaine Cassidy (1979-)
A Room With a View '08
When Did You Last See Your Father? '07
The Lost World '02
Disco Pigs '01
The Others '01
Felicia's Journey '99

Jack Cassidy (1927-76)
The Eiger Sanction '75
Columbo: Murder by the Book '71
The Andersonville Trial '70

Joanna Cassidy (1944-)
For Sale by Owner '09
The Human Contract '08
Kiss the Bride '07
Larry the Cable Guy: Health Inspector '06
The Reading Room '05
Witches of the Caribbean '05
John Carpenter's Ghosts of Mars '01
Dangerous Beauty '98
Executive Power '98
Loved '97
The Second Civil War '97
Chain Reaction '96
Barbarians at the Gate '93
Stephen King's The Tommyknockers '93
Landslide '92
Live! From Death Row '92
Perfect Family '92
All-American Murder '91

Don't Tell Mom the Babysitter's Dead *'91*
Lonely Hearts *'91*
Nightmare at Bittercreek *'91*
A Girl of the Limberlost *'90*
May Wine *'90*
Wheels of Terror *'90*
Where the Heart Is *'90*
1969 *'89*
The Package *'89*
A Father's Revenge *'88*
Who Framed Roger Rabbit *'88*
The Fourth Protocol *'87*
The Children of Times Square *'86*
Club Paradise *'86*
Codename: Foxfire *'85*
Invitation to Hell *'84*
Under Fire *'83*
Blade Runner *'82*
Night Games *'80*
The Glove *'78*
The Late Show *'77*
Prime Time *'77*
Stunts *'77*
Bank Shot *'74*

Katie Cassidy (1986-)
A Nightmare on Elm Street *'10*
Taken *'08*
Black Christmas *'06*
Click *'06*
When a Stranger Calls *'06*

Patrick Cassidy (1961-)
The Fiance *'96*
How the West Was Fun *'95*
Hitler's Daughter *'90*
Longtime Companion *'90*
Love at Stake *'87*
Dress Gray *'86*
Something in Common *'86*
Fever Pitch *'85*
Nickel Mountain *'85*
Just the Way You Are *'84*
Off the Wall *'82*

Raquel Cassidy
Tick Tock Lullaby *'07*
Do I Love You? *'02*

Shaun Cassidy (1958-)
Texas Guns *'90*
Roots: The Gift *'88*

Ted Cassidy (1932-79)
Halloween with the Addams Family *'79*
Sunshine Run *'79*
Goin' Coconuts *'78*
Planet Earth *'74*
Thunder County *'74*
Women's Prison Escape *'74*
Genesis II *'73*
Poor Pretty Eddie *'73*
Butch Cassidy and the Sundance Kid *'69*
MacKenna's Gold *'69*

Claudio Cassinelli (1938-85)
Hands of Steel *'86*
Hercules 2 *'85*
The New Gladiators *'83*
Scorpion with Two Tails *'82*
The Great Alligator *'81*
Mountain of the Cannibal God *'79*
Allonsanfan *'73*

John Cassini
Vice *'08*
Catwoman *'04*
Window Theory *'04*
Break a Leg *'03*
Chain of Fools *'00*
Get Carter *'00*
The Spree *'96*
Man's Best Friend *'93*

Nadia Cassini (1949-)
Star Crash *'78*
Pulp *'72*

Carla Cassola (1947-)
The Devil's Daughter *'91*
Demonia *'90*

Jean-Pierre Castaldi (1944-)
George and the Dragon *'04*
Extreme Ops *'02*
The Musketeer *'01*
A Fine Romance *'92*
La Merveilleuse Visite *'74*

France Castel (1943-)
Karmina *'96*
A Wind from Wyoming *'94*

Lou Castel (1943-)
Heartbeat Detector *'07*
Irma Vep *'96*
Three Lives and Only One Death *'96*
Rorret *'87*
The Eyes, the Mouth *'83*
The American Friend *'77*
The Scarlet Letter *'73*
Beware of a Holy Whore *'70*
Paranoia *'69*
A Bullet for the General *'68*

Dan Castellaneta (1958-)
The Simpsons Movie *'07 (V)*
I-See-You.Com *'06*
The Pursuit of Happyness *'06*
Hey Arnold! The Movie *'02 (V)*
The Settlement *'99*
Plump Fiction *'97*
The Return of Jafar *'94 (V)*
The War of the Roses *'89*
Nothing in Common *'86*

Richard S. Castellano (1933-88)
The Godfather 1902-1959: The Complete Epic *'81*
Night of the Juggler *'80*
Honor Thy Father *'73*
The Godfather *'72*
Lovers and Other Strangers *'70*
A Fine Madness *'66*

Vincent Castellanos (1962-)
Mulholland Drive *'01*
K-911 *'99*
The Last Marshal *'99*
Anaconda *'96*
The Crow 2: City of Angels *'96*

Sergio Castellitto (1953-)
The Chronicles of Narnia: Prince Caspian *'08*
Paris, je t'aime *'06*
The Wedding Director *'06*
Caterina in the Big City *'03*
My Mother's Smile *'02*
Mostly Martha *'01*
Va Savoir *'01*
For Sale *'98*
Pronto *'97*
Portraits Chinois *'96*
The Star Maker *'95*
Alberto Express *'92*
The Big Blue *'88*

Willy Castello (1910-53)
Confessions of a Vice Baron *'42*
Mad Youth *'40*
Cocaine Fiends *'36*

Nino Castelnuovo (1936-)
The English Patient *'96*
Camille 2000 *'69*
Umbrellas of Cherbourg *'64*

Jacques Castelot (1914-89)
Dishonorable Discharge *'57*
Nana *'55*
Forbidden Fruit *'52*

Movita Castenada
See Movita

Movita Castendada
See Movita

Movita Casteneda
See Movita

Christopher Castile (1980-)
Beethoven's 2nd *'93*
Beethoven *'92*

Elias Castillo
The Damned *'06*
San Franpsycho *'06*

Enrique Castillo (1949-)
The Hi-Lo Country *'98*
The End of Violence *'97*
My Family *'94*
Blood In ... Blood Out: Bound by Honor *'93*

Gloria Castillo (1933-)
Invasion of the Saucer Men *'57*
Reform School Girl *'57*
Teenage Monster *'57*
The Night of the Hunter *'55*

Don Castle (1917-66)
Motor Patrol *'50*
I Wouldn't Be in Your Shoes *'48*
Who Killed Doc Robbin? *'48*
Seven Were Saved *'47*
Wake Island *'42*
Power Dive *'41*

John Castle (1940-)
A Harlot's Progress *'06*
The Crucifer of Blood *'91*
RoboCop 3 *'91*
The Bretts *'88*
Lillie *'79*
Antony and Cleopatra *'73*
Man of La Mancha *'72*
The Lion in Winter *'68*
Blow-Up *'66*

Maggie Castle (1983-)
Hank and Mike *'08*
Weirdsville *'07*
The Other Side of the Law *'95*

Mary Castle (1931-98)
Gunsmoke *'53*
White Fire *'53*

Nick Castle (1947-)
Halloween *'78*
Artists and Models *'55*

Peggy Castle (1927-73)
The Seven Hills of Rome *'58*
Beginning of the End *'57*
The Finger Man *'55*
The White Orchid *'54*
Invasion U.S.A. *'52*
Payment on Demand *'51*

Robert Castle
The Manchurian Candidate *'04*
Philadelphia *'93*

Roy Castle (1932-94)
Legend of the Werewolf *'75*
Carry On Up the Khyber *'68*
Alice Through the Looking Glass *'66*
Dr. Terror's House of Horrors *'65*

William Castle (1914-77)
Bug *'75*
Shampoo *'75*
Rosemary's Baby *'68*

Keisha Castle-Hughes (1990-)
The Nativity Story *'06*
Star Wars: Episode 3—Revenge of the Sith *'05*
Whale Rider *'02*

David Castro
Where God Left His Shoes *'07*
Little Fugitive *'06*

Raquel Castro (1996-)
America *'09*
Jersey Girl *'04*

Coralina Cataldi-Tassoni (1971-)
Mother of Tears *'08*
Ghost Son *'06*
The Phantom of the Opera *'98*
Evil Clutch *'89*
Opera *'88*
Demons 2 *'87*

Patrick Catalifo
Don't Let Me Die on a Sunday *'98*
Sand and Blood *'87*

Antonio Catania (1952-)
Bread and Tulips *'01*
Mediterraneo *'91*

Field Cate
Santa Buddies *'09 (V)*
Space Buddies *'08 (V)*

Luciano Catenacci (1933-90)
Crime Busters *'78*
La Scoumoune *'72*

John Cater (1932-)
The Duchess of Duke Street *'78*
Captain Kronos: Vampire Hunter *'74*

Georgina Cates (1975-)
Sinner *'07*
Big City Blues *'99*
Clay Pigeons *'98*
Illuminata *'98*
A Soldier's Sweetheart *'98*
The Treat *'98*
Stiff Upper Lips *'96*
Frankie Starlight *'95*
An Awfully Big Adventure *'94*

Helen Cates
The Whole Wide World *'96*
The Underneath *'95*
A Taste for Killing *'92*

Phoebe Cates (1963-)
The Anniversary Party *'01*
My Life's in Turnaround *'94*
Princess Caraboo *'94*
Bodies, Rest & Motion *'93*
Drop Dead Fred *'91*
Gremlins 2: The New Batch *'90*
I Love You to Death *'90*
The Heart of Dixie *'89*
Shag: The Movie *'89*
Bright Lights, Big City *'88*
Date with an Angel *'87*
Gremlins *'84*
Private School *'83*
Fast Times at Ridgemont High *'82*
Paradise *'82*

Emma Catherwood
Against the Dark *'08*
In the Spider's Web *'07*

Reg E. Cathey (1958-)
20 Years After *'08*
The Machinist *'04*
S.W.A.T. *'03*
Boycott *'02*
Pootie Tang *'01*
Seven *'95*
Airheads *'94*
Tank Girl *'94*
Quick Change *'90*

Brigitte Catillon
The Spectator *'04*
The Housekeeper *'02*
Merci pour le Chocolat *'00*
The Taste of Others *'00*
Artemisia *'97*
Un Coeur en Hiver *'93*
La Lectrice *'88*

Mary Jo Catlett (1938-)
The Benchwarmers *'06*
The SpongeBob SquarePants Movie *'04 (V)*
Ablaze *'00*
Bram Stoker's The Mummy *'97*

Trading Favors *'97*
Serial Mom *'94*
Battling for Baby *'92*
Blood Beach *'81*

Walter Catlett (1889-1960)
The Inspector General *'49*
I'll Be Yours *'47*
I Love a Bandleader *'45*
His Butler's Sister *'44*
They Got Me Covered *'43*
Yankee Doodle Dandy *'42*
It Started with Eve *'41*
Manpower *'41*
Pinocchio *'40 (V)*
Pop Always Pays *'40*
Remedy for Riches *'40*
Bringing Up Baby *'38*
Every Day's a Holiday *'38*
Love Is News *'37*
On the Avenue *'37*
Sing Me a Love Song *'37*
Varsity Show *'37*
Cain and Mabel *'36*
Mr. Deeds Goes to Town *'36*
A Tale of Two Cities *'36*
Rain *'32*
The Front Page *'31*
Maker of Men *'31*

Victoria Catlin
Howling 5: The Rebirth *'89*
Mutant on the Bounty *'89*

Juliette Caton (1975-)
Lady Audley's Secret *'00*
Courage Mountain *'89*
The Last Temptation of Christ *'88*

Michael Caton (1943-)
Strange Bedfellows *'04*
The Animal *'01*
The Echo of Thunder *'98*
The Interview *'98*
The Castle *'97*
The Thorn Birds: The Missing Years *'96*

Christine Cattall
Bedroom Eyes *'86*
Screwball Academy *'86*

Kim Cattrall (1956-)
The Ghost Writer *'10*
Sex and the City 2 *'10*
Sex and the City: The Movie *'08*
My Boy Jack *'07*
The Tiger's Tale *'06*
Ice Princess *'05*
Crossroads *'02*
15 Minutes *'01*
36 Hours to Die *'99*
Baby Geniuses *'98*
Modern Vampires *'98*
Robin Cook's Invasion *'97*
Unforgettable *'96*
Where Truth Lies *'96*
Above Suspicion *'95*
The Heidi Chronicles *'95*
Live Nude Girls *'95*
Breaking Point *'94*
Running Delilah *'93*
Wild Palms *'93*
Double Vision *'92*
Split Second *'92*
Miracle in the Wilderness *'91*
Star Trek 6: The Undiscovered Country *'91*
The Bonfire of the Vanities *'90*
Honeymoon Academy *'90*
Smokescreen *'90*
Goodnight, Michelangelo *'89*
The Return of the Musketeers *'89*
Masquerade *'88*
Palais Royale *'88*
Mannequin *'87*
Midnight Crossing *'87*
Big Trouble in Little China *'86*
City Limits *'85*
Turk 182! *'85*
Police Academy *'84*
Porky's *'82*
Ticket to Heaven *'81*
Scruples *'80*

Tribute *'80*
The Rebels *'79*
The Bastard *'78*
Rosebud *'75*
Deadly Harvest *'72*

Philippe Caubere (1950-)
My Father's Glory *'91*
My Mother's Castle *'91*

Daniel Cauchy (1930-)
Bob le Flambeur *'55*
Grisbi *'53*

Lane Caudell (1952-)
Archer: The Fugitive from the Empire *'81*
Hanging on a Star *'78*

Jessica Cauffiel (1976-)
Hoot *'06*
Guess Who *'05*
D.E.B.S. *'04*
White Chicks *'04*
Legally Blonde 2: Red White & Blonde *'03*
You Stupid Man *'02*
Legally Blonde *'01*
Valentine *'01*
Urban Legends 2: Final Cut *'00*

Joan Caulfield (1922-91)
Pony Express Rider *'76*
Daring Dobermans *'73*
Buckskin *'68*
The Lady Says No *'51*
Dear Wife *'49*
The Unsuspected *'47*
Welcome Stranger *'47*
Blue Skies *'46*
Monsieur Beaucaire *'46*

Maxwell Caulfield (1959-)
Sundown: The Vampire in Retreat *'08*
Dragon Storm *'04*
The Hit *'01*
Facing the Enemy *'00*
Missing Pieces *'00*
Submerged *'00*
Perfect Tenant *'99*
The Real Blonde *'97*
Prey of the Jaguar *'96*
Backlash: Oblivion 2 *'95*
Empire Records *'95*
Inevitable Grace *'94*
Alien Intruder *'93*
Gettysburg *'93*
In a Moment of Passion *'93*
Midnight Witness *'93*
No Escape, No Return *'93*
Animal Instincts *'92*
Dance with Death *'91*
Sundown *'91*
Exiled in America *'90*
Mind Games *'89*
Project: Alien *'89*
The Supernaturals *'86*
The Boys Next Door *'85*
Electric Dreams *'84*
Grease 2 *'82*

Tony Caunter (1937-)
S.O.S. Titanic *'79*
The Hill *'65*

Catherine Cavadini (1967-)
Sky Blue *'03 (V)*
The Powerpuff Girls Movie *'02 (V)*
An American Tail: Fievel Goes West *'91 (V)*

Gary Cavagnaro (1963-)
The Bad News Bears *'76*
Drive-In *'76*

Michael Cavalieri
Seduced: Pretty When You Cry *'01*
Marshal Law *'96*

Kristin Cavallari
Beach Kings *'08*
Van Wilder: Freshman Year *'08*

Valeria Cavalli
Mother of Tears *'08*
A Girl Cut in Two *'07*
Double Team *'97*
Joseph *'95*
Everybody's Fine *'90*
A Blade in the Dark *'83*

Victor Cavallo (1963-)
Dial Help *'88*
The Tragedy of a Ridiculous Man *'81*

Megan Cavanagh (1960-)
Jimmy Neutron: Boy Genius *'01 (V)*
Meet the Deedles *'98*
For Richer or Poorer *'97*
Dracula: Dead and Loving It *'95*
I Love Trouble *'94*
Robin Hood: Men in Tights *'93*
A League of Their Own *'92*

Paul Cavanagh (1895-1959)
The Most Wonderful Time of the Year *'08*
Francis in the Haunted House *'56*
The Prodigal *'55*
Charade *'53*
House of Wax *'53*
Tales of Robin Hood *'52*
Bride of the Gorilla *'51*
The Strange Door *'51*
Hi-Jacked *'50*
The Woman in Green *'49*
Black Arrow *'48*
Humoresque *'46*
House of Fear *'45*
Captains of the Clouds *'42*
The Strange Case of Dr. Rx *'42*
Shadows on the Stairs *'41*
I Take This Woman *'40*
Goin' to Town *'35*
Splendor *'35*
Tarzan and His Mate *'34*
Curtain at Eight *'33*
A Bill of Divorcement *'32*

Tom Cavanagh (1963-)
Snow 2: Brain Freeze *'08*
Sublime *'07*
Gray Matters *'06*
How to Eat Fried Worms *'06*
Snow *'04*
Something More *'99*
Bloodhounds 2 *'96*
A Vow to Kill *'94*

Robert Cavanah (1964-)
Wuthering Heights *'98*
Cracker: True Romance *'95*

Christine Cavanaugh (1963-)
Rugrats in Paris: The Movie *'00 (V)*
The Rugrats Movie *'98 (V)*
Babe *'95 (V)*
Down, Out and Dangerous *'95*

Hobart Cavanaugh (1886-1950)
Up in Central Park *'48*
Black Angel *'46*
Gildersleeve on Broadway *'43*
The Kansan *'43*
The Magnificent Dope *'42*
Rose of Washington Square *'39*
Cain and Mabel *'36*
Wife Versus Secretary *'36*
Wings in the Dark *'35*
I Cover the Waterfront *'33*

Michael Cavanaugh (1942-)
Poison *'01*
Dancing in September *'00*
Black Thunder *'98*
Full Fathom Five *'90*

Patrick Cavanaugh
Transylmania *'09*
Gamebox 1.0 *'04*
Bloody Murder *'99*

Elise Cavanna (1902-63)
The Barber Shop *'33*
The Dentist *'32*
Pharmacist *'32*

Lumi Cavazos (1969-)
Exposed *'03*
In the Time of the Butterflies *'01*
Bless the Child *'00*
Sugar Town *'99*
Optic Fiber *'97*
Last Stand at Saber River *'96*
Bottle Rocket *'95*
Manhattan Merenque! *'95*
Like Water for Chocolate *'93*

Ingrid Caven (1943-)
Malou *'83*
In a Year of 13 Moons *'78*
Mother Kusters Goes to Heaven *'76*
Satan's Brew *'76*
Shadow of Angels *'76*
Tenderness of the Wolves *'73*
The American Soldier *'70*
Beware of a Holy Whore *'70*

Glen Cavender
The Nevada Buckaroo *'31*
The General *'26*

Dick Cavett (1936-)
Duane Hopwood *'05*
The Marx Brothers in a Nutshell *'90*
Beetlejuice *'88*
Moon over Parador *'88*
A Nightmare on Elm Street 3: Dream Warriors *'87*
Annie Hall *'77*

James (Jim) Caviezel (1968-)
The Prisoner *'09*
Nature's Grave *'08*
Outlander *'08*
The Stoning of Soraya M. *'08*
Deja Vu *'06*
Bobby Jones: Stroke of Genius *'04*
The Final Cut *'04*
I Am David *'04*
The Passion of the Christ *'04*
Highwaymen *'03*
The Count of Monte Cristo *'02*
High Crimes *'02*
Angel Eyes *'01*
Madison *'01*
Frequency *'00*
Pay It Forward *'00*
Ride with the Devil *'99*
The Thin Red Line *'98*
G.I. Jane *'97*
Ed *'96*
The Rock *'96*
Wyatt Earp *'94*

Henry Cavill (1983-)
Blood Creek *'09*
Whatever Works *'09*
Stardust *'07*
Tristan & Isolde *'06*
Hellraiser: Hellworld *'05*
The Count of Monte Cristo *'02*
I Capture the Castle *'02*

Joseph Cawthorn (1869-1949)
Harmony Lane *'35*
Sweet Adeline *'35*
The Cat and the Fiddle *'34*
They Call It Sin *'32*
The White Zombie *'32*
The Taming of the Shrew *'29*

Laura Cayouette
Pulse 2: Afterlife *'08*
Deranged *'01*

Elizabeth Cayton
See Elizabeth Kaitan

John Cazale (1936-78)
The Godfather 1902-1959: The Complete Epic *'81*
The Deer Hunter *'78*
Dog Day Afternoon *'75*
The Conversation *'74*
The Godfather, Part 2 *'74*
The Godfather *'72*

Christopher Cazenove (1945-)
Johnson County War *'02*
A Knight's Tale *'01*
The Proprietor *'96*
Aces: Iron Eagle 3 *'92*
Three Men and a Little Lady *'90*
The Fantasist *'89*
The Man Who Guards the Greenhouse *'88*
Souvenir *'88*
Tears in the Rain *'88*
Windmills of the Gods *'88*
Jenny's War *'85*
Mata Hari *'85*
Children of the Full Moon *'84*
Until September *'84*
Heat and Dust *'82*
Eye of the Needle *'81*
From a Far Country: Pope John Paul II *'81*
The Duchess of Duke Street *'78*
East of Elephant Rock *'76*
Royal Flash *'75*

Daniel Ceccaldi (1927-2003)
Twisted Obsession *'90*
Charles et Lucie *'79*
Holiday Hotel *'77*
Chloe in the Afternoon *'72*
Bed and Board *'70*
Make Your Bets Ladies *'65*
The Soft Skin *'64*

Sandra Ceccarelli
The Crown Prince *'06*
Light of My Eyes *'01*

Carlo Cecchi (1939-)
The Red Violin *'98*
Stealing Beauty *'96*
Steam: A Turkish Bath *'96*
La Scorta *'94*

Fulvio Cecere (1960-)
John Tucker Must Die *'06*
Assault on Precinct 13 *'05*
The Perfect Score *'04*
Dead in a Heartbeat *'02*
Valentine *'01*

Edward Cecil (1888-1940)
Desert of the Lost *'27*
Wild Horse Canyon *'25*

Jonathan Cecil (1939-)
The Rector's Wife *'94*
Agatha Christie's Thirteen at Dinner *'85*

Jon Cedar (1931-)
Kiss Daddy Goodbye *'81*
The Manitou *'78*
Day of the Animals *'77*

Larry Cedar (1955-)
Constantine *'05*
Boris and Natasha: The Movie *'92*
C.H.U.D. 2: Bud the Chud *'89*
Feds *'88*

Giuseppe Cederna (1957-)
For Roseanna *'96*
Mediterraneo *'91*

Cedric the Entertainer (1964-)
Cadillac Records *'08*
Madagascar: Escape 2 Africa *'08 (V)*
Street Kings *'08*

Welcome Home Roscoe Jenkins *'08*
Code Name: The Cleaner *'07*
Talk to Me *'07*
Charlotte's Web *'06 (V)*
Be Cool *'05*
The Honeymooners *'05*
Madagascar *'05 (V)*
Man of the House *'05*
Barbershop 2: Back in Business *'04*
Johnson Family Vacation *'04*
Intolerable Cruelty *'03*
Barbershop *'02*
Ice Age *'02 (V)*
Serving Sara *'02*
Kingdom Come *'01*
Big Momma's House *'00*
Ride *'98*

Pablo Cedron (1958-)
The Aura *'05*
Felicidades *'00*

Elisa Cegani (1911-96)
Saul and David *'64*
Medusa Against the Son of Hercules *'62*
What a Woman! *'56*
Nana *'55*
The Iron Crown *'41*

Violeta Cela (1959-)
El Barbaro *'84*
Conquest *'83*

Clementine Celarie (1957-)
Lawless Heart *'01*
Les Miserables *'95*
Sand and Blood *'87*
Betty Blue *'86*

Henry Cele (1949-)
The Ghost and the Darkness *'96*
Curse 3: Blood Sacrifice *'90*
The Last Samurai *'90*
The Rutanga Tapes *'90*
Rage to Kill *'88*
Shaka Zulu *'83*

Maria Celedonio
Freeway 2: Confessions of a Trickbaby *'99*
How to Make an American Quilt *'95*

Adriano Celentano (1938-)
The Con Artists *'80*
The Switch *'76*

Adolfo Celi (1922-86)
Cafe Express *'83*
Perfect Crime *'79*
The Arab Conspiracy *'76*
Intruder *'76*
Ten Little Indians *'75*
Phantom of Liberty *'74*
Hired to Kill *'73*
Hit Men *'73*
Hitler: The Last Ten Days *'73*
1931: Once Upon a Time in New York *'72*
Who Saw Her Die? *'72*
Dirty Heroes *'71*
Murders in the Rue Morgue *'71*
Ring of Death *'69*
Danger: Diabolik *'68*
The Bobo *'67*
The Honey Pot *'67*
Secret Agent 00 *'67*
The King of Hearts *'66*
Target for Killing *'66*
The Agony and the Ecstasy *'65*
Thunderball *'65*
Von Ryan's Express *'65*

Stanislawa Celinska (1947-)
Maids of Wilko *'79*
Landscape After Battle *'70*

Teco Celio
The Truce *'96*
Trois Couleurs: Rouge *'94*

Teresa Celli (1924-)
The Asphalt Jungle *'50*
The Black Hand *'50*
Border Incident *'49*

Antoinette Cellier (1913-81)
Bees in Paradise *'44*
River of Unrest *'36*
Late Extra *'35*

Caroline Cellier (1945-)
L'Eleve *'95*
Farinelli *'94*
Cop Au Vin *'85*
Petit Con *'84*
Pain in the A— *'77*
This Man Must Die *'70*

Frank Cellier (1884-1948)
The Magic Bow *'47*
Cottage to Let *'41*
Non-Stop New York *'37*
O.H.M.S. *'37*
The Man Who Lived Again *'36*
Nine Days a Queen *'36*
The Passing of the Third Floor Back *'36*
Rhodes *'36*
The 39 Steps *'35*

Peter Cellier (1928-)
Fergie & Andrew: Behind Palace Doors *'93*
One Against the Wind *'91*
And the Ship Sails On *'83*
Sister Dora *'77*
Man Friday *'75*
Luther *'74*

Nicholas Celozzi
The Lost Angel *'04*
Hidden Obsession *'92*
Slaughterhouse Rock *'88*

John Cena
12 Rounds *'09*
The Marine *'06*

Angie Cepeda (1974-)
The Dead One *'07*
Love for Rent *'05*

Petr Cepek (1940-94)
The Elementary School *'91*
My Sweet Little Village *'86*
Adelheid *'69*

Michael Cera (1988-)
Scott Pilgrim vs. the World *'10*
Youth in Revolt *'10*
Paper Heart *'09*
Year One *'09*
Extreme Movie *'08*
Nick & Norah's Infinite Playlist *'08*
Juno *'07*
Superbad *'07*
My Louisiana Sky *'02*

Daniel Cerny (1981-)
Children of the Corn 3: Urban Harvest *'95*
Demonic Toys *'90*

Mike Cerrone
Me, Myself, and Irene *'00*
Outside Providence *'99*
Kingpin *'96*

Claude Cerval (1921-72)
Any Number Can Win *'63*
Classe Tous Risque *'60*
The Cousins *'59*

Carlos Cervantes
Fugitive Champion *'99*
Wheels of Terror *'90*

Gino Cervi (1901-74)
Full Hearts & Empty Pockets *'63*
Mistress of the World *'59*
The Naked Maja *'59*
The Lady Without Camelias *'53*
Les Miserables *'52*
Little World of Don Camillo *'51*

The Forbidden Christ *'50*
Fabiola *'48*
The Iron Crown *'41*

Valentina Cervi
Miracle at St. Anna *'08*
James Dean *'01*
Children of Hannibal *'98*
Artemisia *'97*

Renzo Cesana (1907-70)
For the First Time *'59*
The Naked Maja *'59*
Stromboli *'50*

Richard Cetrone
Underworld: Evolution *'05*
John Carpenter's Ghosts of Mars *'01*

Michael Ceveris
The Mexican *'01*
A Woman, Her Men and Her Futon *'92*
Rock 'n' Roll High School Forever *'91*

Alain Chabat (1958-)
Night at the Museum: Battle of the Smithsonian *'09*
I Do *'06*
The Science of Sleep *'06*
Happily Ever After *'04*
The Taste of Others *'00*
French Twist *'95*

Lacey Chabert (1982-)
Ghosts of Girlfriends Past *'09*
Sherman's Way *'08*
A New Wave *'07*
Black Christmas *'06*
Fatwa *'06*
The Pleasure Drivers *'05*
Mean Girls *'04*
Daddy Day Care *'03*
Rugrats Go Wild! *'03 (V)*
The Home Front *'02*
Hometown Legend *'02*
The Wild Thornberrys Movie *'02 (V)*
Not Another Teen Movie *'01*
Tart *'01*
Lost in Space *'98*

Amadee Chabot (1945-)
Autopsy of a Ghost *'67*
Muscle Beach Party *'64*

Thomas Chabrol (1963-)
Comedy of Power *'06*
The Rascals *'81*

Tom Chadbon (1946-)
Devices and Desires *'91*
Dance with a Stranger *'85*
The Beast Must Die *'75*

Alexsei Chadov
Day Watch *'06*
Night Watch *'04*

Cyril Chadwick
The Iron Horse *'24*
Peter Pan *'24*

June Chadwick (1950-)
The Return of Spinal Tap *'92*
Rebel Storm *'90*
Headhunter *'89*
The Evil Below *'87*
Quiet Thunder *'87*
This Is Spinal Tap *'84*
Agatha Christie's Sparkling Cyanide *'83*
Forbidden World *'82*
Golden Lady *'79*

Sarah Chadwick (1960-)
Journey to the Center of the Earth *'99*
The Adventures of Priscilla, Queen of the Desert *'94*
Gross Misconduct *'93*

Suzy Chaffee (1946-)
Fire and Ice *'87*
Snowblind *'78*

George Chakiris (1933-)
Pale Blood '91
Return to Fantasy Island '77
The Hot Line '69
The Young Girls of Rochefort '68
Is Paris Burning? '66
633 Squadron '64
Kings of the Sun '63
Diamond Head '62
West Side Story '61

Kathleen Chalfant (1945-)
Duplicity '09
Perfect Stranger '07
Kinsey '04
2B Perfectly Honest '04
A Death in the Family '02
David Searching '97
A Price above Rubies '97
Bob Roberts '92
Jumpin' at the Boneyard '92

Feodor Chaliapin, Jr. (1907-92)
The Church '98
The Inner Circle '91
The King's Whore '90
Stanley and Iris '90
Moonstruck '87
The Name of the Rose '86
Naked Paradise '78

Garry Chalk (1953-)
Christmas Town '08
Popeye's Voyage: The Quest for Pappy '04
Lone Hero '02
Video Voyeur: The Susan Wilson Story '02
Take Me Home: The John Denver Story '00
My Husband's Secret Life '98
The Spree '96

James Chalke
Direct Contact '09
Missionary Man '07

Sarah Chalke (1977-)
Maneater '09
Chaos Theory '08
Mama's Boy '07
Alchemy '05
Cake '05
Y2K '99
I've Been Waiting for You '98
Our Mother's Murder '97
Dead Ahead '96
Robin of Locksley '95
City Boy '93

William Challee (1904-89)
Zachariah '70
Billy the Kid Versus Dracula '66
Desperate '47

Andrew Chalmers
A Home at the End of the World '04
Siblings '04

Georges Chamarat (1901-82)
Fernandel the Dressmaker '57
Diabolique '55
The French Touch '54

Howland Chamberlain (1911-84)
Francis the Talking Mule '49
The Best Years of Our Lives '46

Richard Chamberlain (1935-)
I Now Pronounce You Chuck and Larry '07
A River Made to Drown In '97
The Thorn Birds: The Missing Years '96
Bird of Prey '95
Ordeal in the Arctic '93
The Return of the Musketeers '89
The Bourne Identity '88
Casanova '87
Allan Quatermain and the Lost City of Gold '86
King Solomon's Mines '85
The Thorn Birds '83
Murder by Phone '82
Shogun '80
Centennial '78
The Swarm '78
The Last Wave '77
The Man in the Iron Mask '77
The Slipper and the Rose '76
The Four Musketeers '75
The Count of Monte Cristo '74
The Three Musketeers '74
The Towering Inferno '74
Lady Caroline Lamb '73
The Music Lovers '71
Julius Caesar '70
The Madwoman of Chaillot '69
Petulia '68
Portrait of a Lady '67

Kevin Chamberlin (1963-)
Lucky Number Slevin '06
Bound by Lies '05
Suspect Zero '04

Carrie Chambers
The Divine Enforcer '91
Karate Cop '91

Faune A. Chambers (1976-)
Epic Movie '07
White Chicks '04
Bring It On Again '03

Justin Chambers (1970-)
Southern Belles '05
The Zodiac '05
Hysterical Blindness '02
Leo '02
The Musketeer '01
The Wedding Planner '01
Liberty Heights '99
Rose Hill '97

Marilyn Chambers (1952-2009)
Bikini Bistro '94
Party Incorporated '89
My Therapist '84
Cassie '83
Angel of H.E.A.T. '82
Rabid '77

Michael "Boogaloo Shrimp" Chambers (1967-)
Breakin' '84
Breakin' 2: Electric Boogaloo '84

Wheaton Chambers (1888-1958)
Big Chase '54
Prowler '51

Jo Champa (1969-)
The Whole Shebang '01
Direct Hit '93
Beretta's Island '92
The Family '87
Salome '85

Gower Champion (1921-80)
Jupiter's Darling '55
Three for the Show '55
Give a Girl a Break '53
Everything I Have is Yours '52
Lovely to Look At '52
Show Boat '51
Mr. Music '50

Marge Champion (1921-)
The Party '68
The Swimmer '68
Jupiter's Darling '55
Three for the Show '55
Give a Girl a Break '53
Everything I Have is Yours '52
Lovely to Look At '52
Mr. Music '50

Michael Champion
Dead Cold '96
Operation Intercept '95
Private Wars '93
The Swordsman '92
The Heroes of Desert Storm '91
One Man Out '89

Dennis Chan
Seventh Moon '08
Naked Weapon '03
Kickboxer 3: The Art of War '92
Kickboxer '89

Jackie Chan (1954-)
The Karate Kid '10
The Spy Next Door '10
The Forbidden Kingdom '08
Kung Fu Panda '08 (V)
Rush Hour 3 '07
Robin-B-Hood '06
Around the World in 80 Days '04
New Police Story '04
The Medallion '03
Shanghai Knights '03
Vampire Effect '03
The Tuxedo '02
The Accidental Spy '01
Rush Hour 2 '01
Shanghai Noon '00
Gen-X Cops '99
Gorgeous '99
Jackie Chan's Who Am I '98
Mr. Nice Guy '98
Rush Hour '98
An Alan Smithee Film: Burn, Hollywood, Burn '97
Downdraft '96
Jackie Chan's First Strike '96
Rumble in the Bronx '96
The Legend of Drunken Master '94
Crime Story '93
Supercop 2 '93
Supercop '92
Twin Dragons '92
Operation Condor '91
The Prisoner '90
Miracles '89
Dragons Forever '88
Project A: Part 2 '87
Operation Condor 2: The Armour of the Gods '86
Heart of Dragon '85
Police Story '85
Protector '85
Cannonball Run 2 '84
Eagle's Shadow '84
Fantasy Mission Force '84
Project A '83
Dragon Lord '82
The Big Brawl '80
Young Master '80
Half a Loaf of Kung Fu '78
New Fist of Fury '76
Young Tiger '74
Enter the Dragon '73
Master with Cracked Fingers '71
Come Drink with Me '65

Jacqueline "Jackie" Chan
Krakatoa East of Java '69
The World of Suzie Wong '60

Kim Chan (1917-)
The Honeymooners '05
Shanghai Knights '03
The Corruptor '99
Who's the Man? '93
American Shaolin: King of the Kickboxers 2 '92

Kwok-Kwan Chan
Kung Fu Hustle '04
Tsui Hark's Vampire Hunters '02

Michael Paul Chan (1950-)
Spy Game '01
Once in the Life '00
The Insider '99
Molly '99
U.S. Marshals '98
Falling Down '93
The Joy Luck Club '93
Rapid Fire '92
Thousand Pieces of Gold '91

Philip Chan (1945-)
Hard-Boiled '92
Twin Dragons '92

Shen Chan
Opium and Kung-Fu Master '84
Shaolin & Wu Tang '81
King Boxer '72

Wai-Man Chan
Downdraft '96
Five Element Ninjas '82

Naomi Chance (1930-2003)
Terror Ship '54
Three Stops to Murder '53
The Gambler & the Lady '52
Wings of Danger '52

Anna Chancellor (1965-)
St. Trinian's '07
The Secret Life of Mrs. Beeton '06
The Hitchhiker's Guide to the Galaxy '05
Agent Cody Banks 2: Destination London '04
The Dreamers '03
What a Girl Wants '03
Crush '02
Tipping the Velvet '02
Longitude '00
Heart '99
The Man Who Knew Too Little '97
Pride and Prejudice '95

Norman Chancer
Local Hero '83
Victor/Victoria '82

Chick Chandler (1905-88)
The Lost Continent '51
Seven Doors to Death '44
Action in the North Atlantic '43
Rhythm Parade '43
Spy Train '43
Baby Face Morgan '42
Blondie in Society '41
I Wake Up Screaming '41
Mr. Moto Takes a Chance '38
Mistaken Identity '36
Tango '36
Circumstantial Evidence '35
Melody Cruise '32

David Chandler (1950-)
Hide and Seek '05
The Grey Zone '01

George Chandler (1898-1985)
Dead Ringer '64
The High and the Mighty '54
Island in the Sky '53
Westward the Women '51
The Next Voice You Hear '50
Behind the Mask '46
Strange Impersonation '46
Roxie Hart '42
Arizona '40
Beau Geste '39
Lady Killer '33
The Light of Western Stars '30

Helen Chandler (1906-65)
Mr. Boggs Steps Out '38
Christopher Strong '33
Dracula '31

Jeff Chandler (1918-61)
Merrill's Marauders '62
Return to Peyton Place '61
The Plunderers '60
The Jayhawkers '59
Man in the Shadow '57
Away All Boats '56
War Arrow '53
Because of You '52
Red Ball Express '52
Yankee Buccaneer '52
Flame of Araby '51
Broken Arrow '50
Abandoned '47

John Davis Chandler (1937-)
The Ultimate Thrill '74
Alligator Alley '72
Shoot Out '71
Ride the High Country '62
The Young Savages '61

Kyle Chandler (1965-)
The Day the Earth Stood Still '08
King Kong '05
And Starring Pancho Villa as Himself '03
Angel's Dance '99
The Color of Evening '95
Convict Cowboy '95
Pure Country '92

Lane Chandler (1899-1972)
Border River '47
Money Madness '47
Silver City Kid '45
Laura '44
Rustler's Hideout '44
Wild Horse Phantom '44
Law of the Saddle '43
Sergeant York '41
Pioneers of the West '40
Pony Post '40
Southward Ho! '39
Heroes of the Alamo '37
Sea Racketeers '37
The Lawless Nineties '36
Stormy Trails '36
Winds of the Wasteland '36
Deluge '33
Lone Bandit '33
The Outlaw Tamer '33
Trouble Busters '33
The Single Standard '29

Simon Chandler
Incognito '97
The Man Who Knew Too Little '97
Middlemarch '93
Who's Who '78

Tanis Chandler (1924-)
Spook Busters '48
Lured '47

Jay Chandrasekhar (1968-)
Beerfest '06
Club Dread '04
Super Troopers '01

Helene Chanel (1941-)
Place in Hell '69
Cjamango '67
Samson and the 7 Miracles of the World '62
Maciste in Hell '60

Lon Chaney, Sr. (1883-1930)
The Unholy Three '30
Where East Is East '29
West of Zanzibar '28
Mockery '27
The Unknown '27
The Monster '25
The Phantom of the Opera '25
The Unholy Three '25
He Who Gets Slapped '24
The Hunchback of Notre Dame '23
The Shock '23
Flesh and Blood '22
The Light of Faith '22
Oliver Twist '22
Shadows '22
The Trap '22
Outside the Law '21
Nomads of the North '20
The Penalty '20
False Faces '18
The Scarlet Car '17
Oubliette '14

Lon Chaney, Jr. (1906-73)
Dracula vs. Frankenstein '71
The Female Bunch '69
Buckskin '68
Alien Massacre '67
Gallery of Horrors '67
Hillbillies in a Haunted House '67
Apache Uprising '66
Johnny Reno '66
House of the Black Death '65
Spider Baby '64
The Haunted Palace '63
Face of the Screaming Werewolf '59
The Defiant Ones '58
The Black Sleep '56
Cyclops '56
Daniel Boone: Trail Blazer '56
The Indestructible Man '56
Manfish '56
Pardners '56
I Died a Thousand Times '55
The Indian Fighter '55
Not as a Stranger '55
Silver Star '55
Big Chase '54
Passion '54
A Lion in the Streets '53
A Lion Is in the Streets '53
Behave Yourself! '52
The Black Castle '52
The Bushwackers '52
High Noon '52
Springfield Rifle '52
Bride of the Gorilla '51
Flame of Araby '51
Only the Valiant '50
Abbott and Costello Meet Frankenstein '48
My Favorite Brunette '47
Here Come the Co-Eds '45
House of Dracula '45
Pillow of Death '45
Strange Confession '45
Cobra Woman '44
Dead Man's Eyes '44
House of Frankenstein '44
The Mummy's Curse '44
The Mummy's Ghost '44
Weird Woman '44
Calling Dr. Death '43
Son of Dracula '43
Frankenstein Meets the Wolfman '42
The Ghost of Frankenstein '42
The Mummy's Tomb '42
Overland Mail '42
Billy the Kid '41
Man Made Monster '41
Riders of Death Valley '41
The Wolf Man '41
One Million B.C. '40
Charlie Chan in City of Darkness '39
Of Mice and Men '39
Cheyenne Rides Again '38
Mr. Moto's Gamble '38
Undersea Kingdom '36
Sixteen Fathoms Deep '34
The Three Musketeers '33
Bird of Paradise '32
Last Frontier '32

Jason Chang
The Heirloom '05
Formula 17 '04

Sylvia Chang (1953-)
American Fusion '05
The Red Violin '98
Eat Drink Man Woman '94
Twin Dragons '92
Mad Mission 3 '84

Carol Channing (1921-)
Thumbelina '94 (V)
Happily Ever After '93 (V)
Alice in Wonderland '85
Shinbone Alley '70 (V)
Thoroughly Modern Millie '67

Stockard Channing (1944-)
Must Love Dogs '05
Red Mercury '05
Anything Else '03
Bright Young Things '03
Hitler: The Rise of Evil '03
Le Divorce '03
Behind the Red Door '02
Life or Something Like It '02
The Business of Strangers '01
A Girl Thing '01
Isn't She Great '00
The Truth About Jane '00
Where the Heart Is '00
The Baby Dance '98
Practical Magic '98
Twilight '98
An Unexpected Life '97
The First Wives Club '96
Lily Dale '96
Moll Flanders '96
An Unexpected Family '96
Up Close and Personal '96
Edie & Pen '95
Smoke '95
To Wong Foo, Thanks for Everything, Julie Newmar '95
Married to It '93
Six Degrees of Separation '93
Bitter Moon '92
The Applegates '89
Perfect Witness '89
Staying Together '89
Tidy Endings '88
A Time of Destiny '88
Echoes in the Darkness '87
Heartburn '86
The Men's Club '86
Not My Kid '85
Table Settings '84
Without a Trace '83
Safari 3000 '82
The Fish that Saved Pittsburgh '79
Silent Victory: The Kitty O'Neil Story '79
The Cheap Detective '78
Grease '78
The Big Bus '76
The Hospital '71

Rosalind Chao (1949-)
Just like Heaven '05
Life of the Party '05
Freaky Friday '03
Enemies of Laughter '00
What Dreams May Come '98
The End of Violence '97
The Joy Luck Club '93
Memoirs of an Invisible Man '92
Thousand Pieces of Gold '91
Drug Wars: The Camarena Story '90
White Ghost '88
M*A*S*H: Goodbye, Farewell & Amen '83
The Terry Fox Story '83
Twirl '81
The Big Brawl '80
Chinese Web '78

Vic Chao
Mega Shark Vs. Giant Octopus '09
Mad Cowgirl '06

Winston Chao (1960-)
Eat Drink Man Woman '94
The Wedding Banquet '93

Damian Chapa (1963-)
Mexican Gangster '08
Lady Jayne Killer '03
Hell's Gate '01
U.S. Seals 2 '01
Cypress Edge '99
Hitman's Run '99
Sometimes They Come Back... For More '99
Footsteps '98
Midnight Blue '96
Saints and Sinners '95
Street Fighter '94
Blood In ... Blood Out: Bound by Honor '93
Final Combination '93

Billy Chapin (1943-)
The Night of the Hunter '55
Tobor the Great '54

Jonathan Chapin
Prison for Children '93
Twice Dead '88

Miles Chapin (1954-)
The People vs. Larry Flynt '96
Get Crazy '83
The Funny Farm '82
Pandemonium '82
The Funhouse '81
French Postcards '79
Bless the Beasts and Children '71

Robert Chapin (1964-)
Dragon Fury 2 '96
Dragon Fury '95
Ring of Steel '94

Ben Chaplin (1970-)
Me and Orson Welles '09
The Water Horse: Legend of the Deep '07
Two Weeks '06
Stage Beauty '04
Birthday Girl '02
Murder by Numbers '02
Lost Souls '00
The Thin Red Line '98
Washington Square '97
The Return of the Borrowers '96
The Truth about Cats and Dogs '96
Feast of July '95
A Fatal Inversion '92

Carmen Chaplin
All About the Benjamins '02
Snapshots '02
The Serpent's Kiss '97
Ma Saison Preferee '93

Charles Chaplin, Jr. (1925-68)
Girls' Town '59
High School Confidential '58
Fangs of the Wild '54

Charlie Chaplin (1889-1977)
Man in the Silk Hat '83
Days of Thrills and Laughter '61
The Chaplin Revue '58
A King in New York '57
Limelight '52
Monsieur Verdoux '47
The Great Dictator '40
Modern Times '36
City Lights '31
The Gold Rush '25
The Kid '21
The Circus '19
Three Charlies and One Phoney! '18
The Adventurer '17
The Cure '17
The Floorwalker '17
The Immigrant '17
Burlesque on Carmen '16
The Count '16
Easy Street '16
The Fireman '16
One A.M. '16
Pawnshop '16
The Rink '16
The Vagabond '16
Charlie Chaplin: Night at the Show '15
Charlie Chaplin ... Our Hero! '15
Tillie's Punctured Romance '14

Dolores Chaplin
The Counterfeiters '07
The Ice Rink '99

Geraldine Chaplin (1944-)
The Wolfman '09
The Orphanage '07
BloodRayne '06
The Bridge of San Luis Rey '05
Talk to Her '02
Mary, Mother of Jesus '99
To Walk with Lions '99
Cousin Bette '97
Mother Teresa: In the Name of God's Poor '97
The Odyssey '97
Crimetime '96
Jane Eyre '96
Gulliver's Travels '95
Home for the Holidays '95
The Age of Innocence '93
A Foreign Field '93
Chaplin '92
Duel of Hearts '92
The Children '90
I Want to Go Home '89
The Return of the Musketeers '89
The Moderns '88
White Mischief '88
Life Is a Bed of Roses '83
Bolero '82
Voyage en Douce '81
The Mirror Crack'd '80
Mama Turns a Hundred '79
A Wedding '78
The Word '78
Elisa, Vida Mia '77
Roseland '77
Welcome to L.A. '77
Buffalo Bill & the Indians '76
Cria '76
In Memoriam '76
The Four Musketeers '75
Nashville '75
The Three Musketeers '74
Zero Population Growth '72
Cop-Out '67
I Killed Rasputin '67
Doctor Zhivago '65

Josephine Chaplin (1949-)
Jack the Ripper '76
Shadow Man '75
Escape to the Sun '72
The Canterbury Tales '71
Scandal Man '67
L'Odeur des Fauves '66

Sydney Chaplin (1885-1965)
Cria Cuervos '76
The Chaplin Revue '58
The Better 'Ole '26
Charley's Aunt '25
The Man on the Box '25
Three Charlies and One Phoney! '18

Sydney Chaplin (1926-)
Satan's Cheerleaders '77
The Sibling '72
The Woman Hunter '72
Double Face '70
A Countess from Hong Kong '67
Abdulla the Great '56
Land of the Pharaohs '55
Limelight '52

Alexander Chapman (1976-)
Lilies '96
Princes in Exile '90

Constance Chapman (1912-2003)
My Friend Walter '93
In Celebration '75

Daniel Chapman (1952-94)
Philadelphia '93
Death Collector '89
Exquisite Corpses '88

Edward Chapman (1901-77)
The Square Peg '58
The Young and the Guilty '58
Bhowani Junction '56
X The Unknown '56
Madeleine '50
Man on the Run '49
The October Man '48
It Always Rains on Sunday '47
Convoy '40
The Church Mouse '34
Juno and the Paycock '30

Edythe Chapman (1863-1948)
Lazybones '25
The Ten Commandments '23
Beyond the Rocks '22

Georgina Chapman
Awake '07
The Business '05
Derailed '05

Graham Chapman (1941-89)
Monty Python's The Meaning of Life '83
Yellowbeard '83
The Secret Policeman's Other Ball '82
Secret Policeman's Private Parts '81
Monty Python's Life of Brian '79
The Odd Job '78
Monty Python and the Holy Grail '75
And Now for Something Completely Different '72
The Magic Christian '69
John Cleese on How to Irritate People '68

Helen Chapman
Hopalong Cassidy: Borrowed Trouble '48
My Dog Shep '46
Outlaw Roundup '44

Judith Chapman (1945-)
Scorpio One '97
Fire on the Amazon '93
Dead Space '90
And God Created Woman '88
Scalpel '76

Kevin Chapman
Black Dynamite '09
Sunshine Cleaning '09
Two for the Money '05
In Good Company '04
Mystic River '03

Lonny (Lonnie) Chapman (1920-2007)
The Hunted '03
Nightwatch '96
The China Lake Murders '90
52 Pick-Up '86
He Who Walks Alone '78
Terror Out of the Sky '78
Alexander: The Other Side of Dawn '77
Moving Violation '76
Witch Who Came from the Sea '76
Where the Red Fern Grows '74
I Walk the Line '70
Take the Money and Run '69
The Birds '63

Marguerite Chapman (1918-99)
The Amazing Transparent Man '60
Bloodhounds of Broadway '52
Flight to Mars '52
Man Bait '52
The Green Promise '49
Coroner Creek '48
Destroyer '43
Spy Smasher '42
Spy Smasher Returns '42
Charlie Chan at the Wax Museum '40

Mark Lindsay Chapman (1954-)
Beethoven's 4th '01
Bram Stoker's The Mummy '97
Stephen King's The Langoliers '95
Separate Lives '94
American Gothic '88

Sean Chapman
The Sea Change '98
Hellbound: Hellraiser 2 '88
Hellraiser '87
Party! Party! '83

Dave Chappelle (1973-)
Dave Chappelle's Block Party '06
Undercover Brother '02
Screwed '00
Blue Streak '99
200 Cigarettes '98
You've Got Mail '98
Con Air '97
Half-Baked '97
Woo '97
The Nutty Professor '96
Getting In '94
Robin Hood: Men in Tights '93

Antoine Chappey (1960-)
Le Petit Lieutenant '05
5x2 '04
I'm Going Home '00

Patricia Charbonneau (1959-)
100 Feet '08
One Special Night '99
Kiss the Sky '98
Portraits of a Killer '95
K2: The Ultimate High '92
RoboCop 2 '90
Brain Dead '89
Call Me '88
Disaster at Silo 7 '88
Shakedown '88
Desert Hearts '86
Manhunter '86
Stalking Danger '86

Tara Charendoff
See Tara Strong

Cyd Charisse (1921-2008)
Swimsuit '89
That's Dancing! '85
Maroc 7 '67
The Silencers '66
Assassination in Rome '65
Two Weeks in Another Town '62
Black Tights '60
Party Girl '58
Silk Stockings '57
Meet Me in Las Vegas '56
It's Always Fair Weather '55
Brigadoon '54
Deep in My Heart '54
The Band Wagon '53
Singin' in the Rain '52
Tension '50
On an Island with You '48
Words and Music '48
The Harvey Girls '46

Andre Charles
See RuPaul Charles

Josh Charles (1971-)
Brief Interviews With Hideous Men '09
The Ex '07
Four Brothers '05
Seeing Other People '04
S.W.A.T. '03
Our America '02
Muppets from Space '99
Meeting Daddy '98
Little City '97
Crossworlds '96
The Grave '95
Norma Jean and Marilyn '95
Pie in the Sky '95
Things to Do in Denver When You're Dead '95
Coldblooded '94
Threesome '94
Cooperstown '93
Crossing the Bridge '92
Don't Tell Mom the Babysitter's Dead '91
Dead Poets Society '89

Ray Charles (1930-2004)
Limit Up '89
The Blues Brothers '80
Ballad in Blue '66

RuPaul Charles (1960-)
Skinwalker '02
Who is Cletis Tout? '02
The Eyes of Tammy Faye '00 (N)
The Truth About Jane '00
But I'm a Cheerleader '99
EDtv '99
An Unexpected Life '97
A Very Brady Sequel '96
Blue in the Face '95
The Brady Bunch Movie '95
A Mother's Prayer '95
Smoke '95
To Wong Foo, Thanks for Everything, Julie Newmar '95
Wigstock: The Movie '95
Crooklyn '94

Ian Charleson (1949-90)
Codename Kyril '91
Opera '88
Troubles '88
Louisiana '87
Car Trouble '86
Greystoke: The Legend of Tarzan, Lord of the Apes '84
Gandhi '82
Chariots of Fire '81

Ray Charleson
Dark Corners '06
United 93 '06

Kim Charney
Man From God's Country '58
Suddenly '54

Charo (1942-)
Thumbelina '94 (V)
Moon over Parador '88
The Concorde: Airport '79 '79

Charpin (1887-1944)
Well-Digger's Daughter '46
Le Schpountz '38
Cesar '36
The Baker's Wife '33
Fanny '32
Marius '31

Henri Charriere (1906-73)
Butterfly Affair '71
Queen of Diamonds '70

Spencer Charters (1875-1943)
High Sierra '41
Mr. Boggs Steps Out '38
Three Comrades '38
Lady from Nowhere '36
The Moon's Our Home '36
The Ghost Walks '34
Palmy Days '31
The Bat Whispers '30

Melanie Chartoff (1955-)
Rugrats Go Wild! '03 (V)
Rugrats in Paris: The Movie '00 (V)
The Rugrats Movie '98 (V)
Kenny Rogers as the Gambler, Part 3: The Legend Continues '87
Doin' Time '85
Stoogemania '85

Having It All *'82*

David Charvet (1972-)

Beach Kings *'08*
Baywatch the Movie: Forbidden Paradise *'95*

Alden Chase (1902-82)

Buried Alive *'39*
Six Gun Trail *'38*
Prescott Kid *'36*
Rogue of the Range *'36*
Cowboy Millionaire *'35*

Annazette Chase

Fist *'76*
Truck Turner *'74*

Charley Chase (1893-1940)

Block-heads *'38*
Kelly the Second *'36*
Sons of the Desert *'33*
King of the Wild Horses *'24*
Three Charlies and One Phoney! *'18*

Cheryl Chase

Rugrats Go Wild! *'03 (V)*
Rugrats in Paris: The Movie *'00 (V)*

Chevy Chase (1943-)

Hot Tub Time Machine *'10*
Zoom *'06*
Ellie Parker *'05*
Karate Dog *'04 (V)*
Our Italian Husband *'04*
Orange County *'02*
Snow Day *'00*
Dirty Work *'97*
Vegas Vacation *'96*
Man of the House *'95*
Cops and Robbersons *'94*
Last Action Hero *'93*
Hero *'92*
Memoirs of an Invisible Man *'92*
Nothing But Trouble *'91*
Fletch Lives *'89*
National Lampoon's Christmas Vacation *'89*
Caddyshack 2 *'88*
Funny Farm *'88*
Three Amigos *'86*
Fletch *'85*
National Lampoon's European Vacation *'85*
Sesame Street Presents: Follow That Bird *'85*
Spies Like Us *'85*
Deal of the Century *'83*
National Lampoon's Vacation *'83*
Modern Problems *'81*
Under the Rainbow *'81*
Caddyshack *'80*
Oh, Heavenly Dog! *'80*
Seems Like Old Times *'80*
Foul Play *'78*
Tunnelvision *'76*
The Groove Tube *'72*

Courtney Chase (1988-)

Mean Girls *'04*
13 Going on 30 *'04*
Nick of Time *'95*

Daveigh Chase (1990-)

S. Darko: A Donnie Darko Tale *'09*
The Ring 2 *'05*
Beethoven's 5th *'03*
Lilo & Stitch *'02 (V)*
The Ring *'02*
The Rats *'01*
Spirited Away *'01 (V)*

Frank Chase (1923-2004)

Attack of the 50 Foot Woman *'58*
The Creature Walks among Us *'56*

Ilka Chase (1905-78)

The Big Knife *'55*
Miss Tatlock's Millions *'48*
Now, Voyager *'42*
The Animal Kingdom *'32*

James Chase (1940-)

The Virgin Witch *'70*
The Victors *'63*

Jeffrey Chase (1968-)

Kids in America *'05*
Transporter 2 *'05*
In the Shadows *'01*
Scream of the Demon Lover *'71*

Jennifer Chase

Death Screams *'83*
Balboa *'82*
House of Death *'82*

Stephan Chase (1900-78)

The Dying Truth *'86*
Florence Nightingale *'85*
The Black Arrow *'84*
Macbeth *'71*
Guns of Fury *'49*

Steve Chase

Eden *'93*
Eden 2 *'93*
Eden 3 *'93*
Eden 4 *'93*

Peter Chatel (1943-86)

Fox and His Friends *'75*
Who Saw Her Die? *'72*

Anucha Chatkaew

The Iron Ladies 2 *'03*
The Iron Ladies *'00*

Sorapong Chatree

Ong Bak 2 *'08*
The Legend of Suriyothai *'02*

Anil Chatterjee (1928-66)

The Big City *'63*
Two Daughters *'61*

Soumitra Chatterjee (1934-)

The Bengali Night *'88*
The Home and the World *'84*
Distant Thunder *'73*
Days and Nights in the Forest *'70*
Charulata *'64*
Two Daughters *'61*
Devi *'60*
The World of Apu *'59*

Ruth Chatterton (1893-1961)

Dodsworth *'36*
Girl's Dormitory *'36*
Female *'33*
Frisco Jenny *'32*

Tom Chatterton (1881-1952)

Overland Mail *'42*
Outlaws of the Cherokee Trail *'41*
Drums of Fu Manchu *'40*
Flash Gordon Conquers the Universe *'40*

Daniel Chatto (1957-)

Little Dorrit, Film 1: Nobody's Fault *'88*
Little Dorrit, Film 2: Little Dorrit's Story *'88*

Charlotte Chatton

Stand-Ins *'97*
Hellraiser 4: Bloodline *'95*

Justin Chatwin (1982-)

Dragonball: Evolution *'09*
The Invisible *'07*
The Chumscrubber *'05*
War of the Worlds *'05*
Superbabies: Baby Geniuses 2 *'04*
Taking Lives *'04*
The Incredible Mrs. Ritchie *'03*

Francois Chau (1959-)

Beverly Hills Ninja *'96*
Teenage Mutant Ninja Turtles 2: The Secret of the Ooze *'91*

Anthony Wong Chau-Sang

Exiled *'06*
House of Fury *'05*
Infernal Affairs 2 *'03*
Infernal Affairs 3 *'03*

Emmanuelle Chaulet

All the Vermeers in New York *'91*
Boyfriends & Girlfriends *'88*

Lilyan Chauvin (1931-)

Tyson *'95*
Silent Night, Deadly Night *'84*
Bloodlust *'59*
Lost, Lonely, and Vicious *'59*

Richard Chaves (1951-)

Night Eyes 2 *'91*
Predator *'87*

Ricardo Chavira

Saving God *'08*
Kings of South Beach *'07*

Maury Chaykin (1949-)

Blindness *'08*
Heavens Fall *'06*
It's a Boy Girl Thing *'06*
Where the Truth Lies *'05*
Being Julia *'04*
White Coats *'04*
Owning Mahowny *'03*
Bartleby *'01*
The Doorbell Rang: A Nero Wolfe Mystery *'01*
Varian's War *'01*
The Art of War *'00*
The Golden Spiders: A Nero Wolfe Mystery *'00*
What's Cooking? *'00*
Entrapment *'99*
Jacob Two Two Meets the Hooded Fang *'99*
Joan of Arc *'99*
Let the Devil Wear Black *'99*
Mystery, Alaska *'99*
Jerry and Tom *'98*
The Mask of Zorro *'98*
A Life Less Ordinary *'97*
Love and Death on Long Island *'97*
Mouse Hunt *'97*
Pale Saints *'97*
Strip Search *'97*
The Sweet Hereafter *'96*
Cutthroat Island *'95*
Devil in a Blue Dress *'95*
Sugartime *'95*
Unstrung Heroes *'95*
Camilla *'94*
Whale Music *'94*
Money for Nothing *'93*
Northern Extremes *'93*
Sommersby *'93*
Hero *'92*
Leaving Normal *'92*
The Adjuster *'91*
George's Island *'91*
The Pianist *'91*
Cold Comfort *'90*
Dances with Wolves *'90*
Mr. Destiny *'90*
Where the Heart Is *'90*
Breaking In *'89*
Millennium *'89*
Higher Education *'88*
Iron Eagle 2 *'88*
Stars and Bars *'88*
Wild Thing *'87*
Canada's Sweetheart: The Saga of Hal C. Banks *'85*
Def-Con 4 *'85*
Mrs. Soffel *'84*
Overdrawn at the Memory Bank *'83*
July Group *'81*

Mariann (Marie-Anne) Chazel (1951-)

The Visitors *'95*
Next Year If All Goes Well *'83*
French Fried Vacation *'79*

Suzanne Chazelle

See Dany Carrel

Don Cheadle (1964-)

Iron Man 2 *'10*
Brooklyn's Finest *'09*
Hotel for Dogs *'09*
Traitor *'08*
Ocean's Thirteen *'07*
Reign Over Me *'07*
Talk to Me *'07*
The Dog Problem *'06*
The Assassination of Richard Nixon *'05*
Crash *'05*
After the Sunset *'04*
Hotel Rwanda *'04*
Ocean's Twelve *'04*
United States of Leland *'03*
Manic *'01*
Ocean's Eleven *'01*
Rush Hour 2 *'01*
Swordfish *'01*
Things Behind the Sun *'01*
Fail Safe *'00*
Family Man *'00*
Mission to Mars *'00*
Traffic *'00*
A Lesson Before Dying *'99*
Bulworth *'98*
Out of Sight *'98*
The Rat Pack *'98*
Boogie Nights *'97*
Volcano *'97*
Rebound: The Legend of Earl "The Goat" Manigault *'96*
Rosewood *'96*
Devil in a Blue Dress *'95*
Things to Do in Denver When You're Dead *'95*
Lush Life *'94*
Colors *'88*
Hamburger Hill *'87*

Andrea Checchi (1916-74)

Waterloo *'71*
Diary of a Rebel *'68*
The Invaders *'63*
Black Sunday *'60*
The Hit Man *'60*
The Lady Without Camelias *'53*
The Walls of Malapaga *'49*

Chubby Checker (1941-)

Calendar Girl *'93*
Purple People Eater *'88*

Molly Cheek (1950-)

A Lot Like Love *'05*
American Wedding *'03*
April's Shower *'03*
American Pie 2 *'01*
American Pie *'99*
Smoke Signals *'98*

Derk Cheetwood (1973-)

Frailty *'02*
U-571 *'00*

Micheline Cheirel (1917-2002)

Cornered *'45*
Carnival in Flanders *'35*

Michael Chekhov (1891-1955)

Rhapsody *'54*
Invitation *'51*
Spectre of the Rose *'46*
Spellbound *'45*

Tsilla Chelton (1918-)

Tatie Danielle *'91*
Peppermint Soda *'77*

Chang Chen (1976-)

Red Cliff *'08*
Three Times *'05*
Eros *'04*
2046 *'04*
Crouching Tiger, Hidden Dragon *'00*
Happy Together *'96*

Daoming Chen (1955-)

Silver Hawk *'04*
Hero *'03*
Infernal Affairs 3 *'03*

Edison Chen (1980-)

Dog Bite Dog *'06*
The Grudge 2 *'06*
Infernal Affairs 2 *'03*
Vampire Effect *'03*

Joan Chen (1961-)

Lust, Caution *'07*
Saving Face *'04*
What's Cooking? *'00*
In a Class of His Own *'99*
Precious Find *'96*
Judge Dredd *'95*
Wild Side *'95*
The Hunted *'94*
On Deadly Ground *'94*
Temptation of a Monk *'94*
Golden Gate *'93*
Heaven and Earth *'93*
The Killing Beach *'92*
Deadlock *'91*
Strangers *'91*
The Blood of Heroes *'89*
The Last Emperor *'87*
Night Stalker *'87*
Tai-Pan *'86*
Dim Sum: A Little Bit of Heart *'85*

Kelly Chen

Breaking News *'04*
Infernal Affairs 3 *'03*
Tokyo Raiders *'00*

Kuan Tai Chen

Opium and Kung-Fu Master *'84*
Human Lanterns *'82*
The Master *'80*
The Water Margin *'72*

Moira Chen

See Laura Gemser

Terry Chen

Memory *'06*
Snakes on a Plane *'06*
Ballistic: Ecks vs. Sever *'02*
Stark Raving Mad *'02*
Almost Famous *'00*
Crash & Byrnes *'99*

Tina Chen (1945-)

Lady from Yesterday *'85*
Paper Man *'71*
Alice's Restaurant *'69*

Adam Cheng (1947-)

Painted Skin *'93*
Fantasy Mission Force *'84*
Zu: Warriors from the Magic Mountain *'83*
Shaolin & Wu Tang *'81*

Ekin Cheng (1967-)

Running Out of Time 2 *'06*
Vampire Effect *'03*
Zu Warriors *'01*
Tokyo Raiders *'00*
The Cave of the Silken Web *'67*

Kent Cheng (1951-)

Flash Point *'07*
The Bodyguard from Beijing *'94*
Crime Story *'93*
Sex and Zen *'93*
Once Upon a Time in China *'91*

Pei Pei Cheng

Naked Weapon *'03*
The Shadow Whip *'71*
Sword Masters: Brothers Five *'70*
Golden Swallow *'68*

Sammi Cheng

Infernal Affairs 3 *'03*
Infernal Affairs *'02*

Kristin Chenoweth (1968-)

Into Temptation *'09*
Four Christmases *'08*
Space Chimps *'08 (V)*
Deck the Halls *'06*
The Pink Panther *'06*
Running with Scissors *'06*
RV *'06*
Bewitched *'05*
Annie *'99*

Cher (1946-)

Stuck On You *'03*
Tea with Mussolini *'99*
If These Walls Could Talk *'96*
Faithful *'95*
Ready to Wear *'94*
The Player *'92*
Mermaids *'90*
Moonstruck *'87*
Suspect *'87*
The Witches of Eastwick *'87*
Mask *'85*
Silkwood *'83*
Come Back to the Five & Dime Jimmy Dean, Jimmy Dean *'82*
Good Times *'67*

Patrice Chereau (1944-)

Time of the Wolf *'03*
Time Regained *'99 (V)*
Lucie Aubrac *'98*
The Last of the Mohicans *'92*
Danton *'82*

Nikolai Cherkassov (1903-66)

Don Quixote *'57*
Ivan the Terrible, Part 2 *'46*
Ivan the Terrible, Part 1 *'44*
Alexander Nevsky *'38*
Peter the First: Part 2 *'38*
Baltic Deputy *'37*
Peter the First: Part 1 *'37*
Happiness *'32*

Jonas Chernick (1973-)

Eloise at the Plaza *'03*
Edge of Madness *'02*
A Woman's a Helluva Thing *'01*

Virginia Cherrill (1908-96)

Late Extra *'35*
City Lights *'31*

Jake Cherry (1996-)

Night at the Museum: Battle of the Smithsonian *'09*
Night at the Museum *'06*

Jonathan Cherry

Final Destination 2 *'03*
House of the Dead *'03*

George Chesebro (1888-1959)

Check Your Guns *'48*
Stage to Mesa City *'48*
Cheyenne Takes Over *'47*
Fighting Vigilantes *'47*
Homesteaders of Paradise Valley *'47*
Return of the Lash *'47*
Boss of Rawhide *'44*
Devil Riders *'44*
The Drifter *'44*
Raiders of Red Gap *'43*
Two-Fisted Justice *'43*
Holt of the Secret Service *'42*
Sundown Fury *'42*
Thunder River Feud *'42*
The Pioneers *'41*
Saddle Mountain Roundup *'41*
Trigger Men *'41*
Lightning Strikes West *'40*
West of Pinto Basin *'40*
Wild Horse Valley *'40*
Purple Vigilantes *'38*
Roarin' Lead *'37*
S.O.S. Coast Guard *'37*
Fast Bullets *'36*
Pinto Rustlers *'36*
Red River Valley *'36*
Fighting Caballero *'35*
Laramie Kid *'35*
The Miracle Rider *'35*
Pals of the Range *'35*
Rough Riding Ranger *'35*
Wild Mustang *'35*
Fighting Hero *'34*
In Old Santa Fe *'34*

The Silver Bullet '34
Fighting Champ '33
Wolf Blood '25

Elizabeth Cheshire (1967-)
Awakening of Candra '81
Melvin and Howard '80

Harry Cheshire (1891-1968)
Impact '49
Shoot to Kill '47

Patrick Chesnais (1947-)
The Diving Bell and the Butterfly '07
After Sex '97
La Lectrice '88

Craig Chester (1965-)
Adam & Steve '05
Kiss Me, Guido '97
I Shot Andy Warhol '96
Frisk '95
Grief '94
Swoon '91

Vanessa Lee Chester (1984-)
The Lost World: Jurassic Park 2 '97
Harriet the Spy '96
A Little Princess '95

Morris Chestnut (1969-)
Not Easily Broken '09
The Game Plan '07
The Perfect Holiday '07
The Cave '05
Anacondas: The Hunt for the Blood Orchid '04
Breakin' All The Rules '04
Ladder 49 '04
Confidence '03
Half Past Dead '02
Like Mike '02
The Brothers '01
The Killing Yard '01
Two Can Play That Game '01
The Best Man '99
G.I. Jane '97
Under Siege 2: Dark Territory '95
The Ernest Green Story '93
Boyz N the Hood '91
The Last Boy Scout '91

Cecilia Cheung (1980-)
The Promise '05
Running on Karma '03
Shaolin Soccer '01
Zu Warriors '01
Tokyo Raiders '00

Cindy Cheung
Lady in the Water '06
Robot Stories '03

Daphne Cheung
Jack Higgins' Midnight Man '96
Jack Higgins' On Dangerous Ground '95

George Kee Cheung
Starsky & Hutch '04
High Voltage '98
Opposing Force '87

Jacky Cheung (1961-)
Ashes of Time Redux '08
Perhaps Love '05
Meltdown '95
Ashes of Time '94
Wicked City '92
Days of Being Wild '91
Once Upon a Time in China '91
A Bullet in the Head '90
As Tears Go By '88

Leslie Cheung (1956-2003)
Ashes of Time Redux '08
Happy Together '96
Temptress Moon '96
The Phantom Lover '95
Ashes of Time '94
The Bride with White Hair '93
The Bride with White Hair 2 '93
Farewell My Concubine '93
Days of Being Wild '91
Once a Thief '90
A Better Tomorrow, Part 2 '88
A Better Tomorrow, Part 1 '86

Maggie Cheung (1964-)
Inglourious Basterds '09
Ashes of Time Redux '08
Clean '04
2046 '04
Hero '03
In the Mood for Love '00
Chinese Box '97
Irma Vep '96
Ashes of Time '94
The Executioners '93
Green Snake '93
The Heroic Trio '93
Supercop '92
Twin Dragons '92
Days of Being Wild '91
Song of the Exile '90
As Tears Go By '88
Paper Marriage '88
Project A: Part 2 '87
Police Story '85

Nick Cheung
Exiled '06
Breaking News '04

Roy Cheung (1964-)
Exiled '06
Infernal Affairs 2 '03
The Mission '99
Organized Crime & Triad Bureau '93
Wicked City '92
City on Fire '87

Siu-fai Cheung
Dog Bite Dog '06
Running on Karma '03

Kevin Timothy Chevalia (1986-)
Homeward Bound 2: Lost in San Francisco '96
Homeward Bound: The Incredible Journey '93
Folks! '92

Maurice Chevalier (1888-1972)
The Sorrow and the Pity '71
Monkeys, Go Home! '66
A New Kind of Love '63
In Search of the Castaways '62
Panic Button '62
Fanny '61
Black Tights '60 (N)
Breath of Scandal '60
Can-Can '60
Gigi '58
Love in the Afternoon '57
The Merry Widow '34
One Hour with You '32
The Smiling Lieutenant '31
The Love Parade '29

Richard Chevolleau (1966-)
Narc '02
Who is Cletis Tout? '02
True Blue '01
Flowers for Algernon '00
No Alibi '00
The Wall '99
Tracked '98
Blood Brothers '97
Rude '96
Indian Summer '93

Lita Chevret
Sandflow '37
Daring Daughters '33

Arno Chevrier
Agnes Browne '99
The Red Dwarf '99

Laureen Chew
Dim Sum: A Little Bit of Heart '85
Chan Is Missing '82

Minoru Chiaki (1917-99)
Face of Another '66
The Human Condition: Road to Eternity '59
The Hidden Fortress '58
Throne of Blood '57
Godzilla Raids Again '55
Seven Samurai '54
Rashomon '51

Dominic Chianese (1931-)
Adrift in Manhattan '07
King of the Corner '04
When Will I Be Loved '04
Unfaithful '02
Once in the Life '00
The Cradle Will Rock '99
Under Hellgate Bridge '99
Went to Coney Island on a Mission from God.. Be Back by Five '98
Gotti '96
Looking for Richard '96
Love Is All There Is '96
Night Falls on Manhattan '96
If Lucy Fell '95
The Night We Never Met '93
The Public Eye '92
Out for Justice '91
The Lost Capone '90
Q & A '90
Second Sight '89
And Justice for All '79
Firepower '79
On the Yard '79
All the President's Men '76
Dog Day Afternoon '75
The Godfather, Part 2 '74

David Chiang (1947-)
The Kumite '03
Heaven & Hell '78
The Water Margin '72
Duel of Fists '71
The Wandering Swordsman '70
Have Sword, Will Travel '69

Roy Chiao (1927-99)
Summer Snow '94
Bloodsport '88

Walter Chiari (1924-91)
The Valachi Papers '72
Girl Under the Sheet '61
The Inveterate Bachelor '58
Bonjour Tristesse '57
Nana '55
Bellissima '51

Stephen Chiau
See Stephen (Chiau) Chow

Sofiko Chiaureli (1937-)
Ashik Kerib '88
The Color of Pomegranates '69

Shigeru Chiba
Stray Dog '91
The Red Spectacles '87

Sonny Chiba (1939-)
The Fast and the Furious: Tokyo Drift '06
Kill Bill Vol. 2 '04
Wind and Cloud: The Storm Riders '04
Kill Bill Vol. 1 '03
Body Count '95
Immortal Combat '94
Aces: Iron Eagle 3 '92
Shogun's Ninja '83
Fall Guy '82
Virus '82
Samurai Reincarnation '81
Hunter in the Dark '80
Shogun's Samurai—The Yagyu Clan Conspiracy '78
The Bodyguard '76
Sister Street Fighter '76
Return of the Street Fighter '74
The Street Fighter '74
The Street Fighter's Last Revenge '74
Terror Beneath the Sea '66

Etienne Chicot (1949-)
The Da Vinci Code '06
36 Fillete '88
Osa '85
Le Choc '82
Hotel America '81

Caroline Chikezie (1979-)
Eragon '06
Aeon Flux '05

Michael Chiklis (1963-)
Eagle Eye '08
Fantastic Four: Rise of the Silver Surfer '07
Rise: Blood Hunter '07
Fantastic Four '05
Spirited Away '01 (V)
Silent Witness '99
Body and Soul '98
Soldier '98
The Taxman '98
Wired '89

Jeremy Child (1944-)
Frenchman's Creek '98
Mosley '98
Behind the Lines '97
Sharpe's Enemy '94
Fool's Gold: The Story of the Brink's-Mat Robbery '92
Florence Nightingale '85
Privilege '67

Patricia Childress (1971-)
Larry McMurtry's Dead Man's Walk '96
Shake, Rattle & Rock! '94

Linden Chiles (1933-)
Deadline Assault '90
To Heal a Nation '88
Forbidden World '82
Red Flag: The Ultimate Game '81
Death Be Not Proud '75
Who Is the Black Dahlia? '75
Texas Across the River '66

Lois Chiles (1947-)
Speed 2: Cruise Control '97
Bliss '96
Wish upon a Star '96
The Babysitter '95
Curdled '95
Lush Life '94
Diary of a Hitman '91
Twister '89
Broadcast News '87
Creepshow 2 '87
Raw Courage '84
Moonraker '79
Coma '78
Death on the Nile '78
The Way We Were '73

Simon Chilvers (1939-)
Ground Zero '88
The Big Hurt '87
Windrider '86
The Dunera Boys '85

Andre Chimene
Computer Beach Party '88
The Outing '87

Joey Chin
King of New York '90
China Girl '87

Siu-hou Chin
House of Traps '81
Sword Masters: Two Champions of Shaolin '80

Tsai Chin (1936-)
The Interpreter '05
Memoirs of a Geisha '05
The Diary of Ellen Rimbauer '03
Long Life, Happiness and Prosperity '02
Red Corner '97
The Joy Luck Club '93
Rentadick '72
The Virgin Soldiers '69
The Castle of Fu Manchu '68
Kiss and Kill '68
The Vengeance of Fu Manchu '67
You Only Live Twice '67
Brides of Fu Manchu '66
Invasion '65

Miao Ching
The Water Margin '72
Have Sword, Will Travel '69

William Ching (1913-89)
Terror in the Haunted House '58
Give a Girl a Break '53
The Moonlighter '53
Never Wave at a WAC '52
Pat and Mike '52
D.O.A. '49
The Wistful Widow of Wagon Gap '47

Kieu Chinh (1939-)
Green Dragon '01
Catfish in Black Bean Sauce '00
Riot in the Streets '96
The Joy Luck Club '93
Hamburger Hill '87
The Girl Who Spelled Freedom '86
The Children of An Lac '80
Operation C.I.A. '65

Nicholas Chinlund (1961-)
Wyvern '09
Felon '08
Avenging Angel '07
Sinner '07
Ultraviolet '06
The Legend of Zorro '05
The Chronicles of Riddick '04
Tears of the Sun '03
Amy's O '02
Below '02
100 Mile Rule '02
Training Day '01
Beyond Suspicion '00
Disney's The Kid '00
Once in the Life '00
Chutney Popcorn '99
Frogs for Snakes '98
A Brother's Kiss '97
Con Air '97
Mr. Magoo '97
Rough Riders '97
Eraser '96
Letter to My Killer '95
Bad Girls '94
Unveiled '94
Red Shoe Diaries 4: Auto Erotica '93
Lethal Weapon 3 '92
The Ambulance '90

Jimmy Chisholm (1956-)
Strictly Sinatra '01
Ivanhoe '97

David Chisum
Dark Mirror '07
Flight of the Living Dead: Outbreak on a Plane '07

Erik Chitty (1907-77)
Doctor Zhivago '65
First Men in the Moon '64

Tony Leung Chiu-wai
Seoul Raiders '05
Infernal Affairs '02
Days of Being Wild '91

Anna Chlumsky (1980-)
The Good Guy '10
In the Loop '09
Gold Diggers: The Secret of Bear Mountain '95
My Girl 2 '94
Trading Mom '94
My Girl '91

John Cho (1972-)
Saint John of Las Vegas '09
Star Trek '09
Harold & Kumar Escape from Guantanamo Bay '08
American Dreamz '06
Bickford Shmeckler's Cool Ideas '06
Bam Bam & Celeste '05
Harold and Kumar Go to White Castle '04
Better Luck Tomorrow '02
Earth vs. the Spider '01
Pavilion of Women '01
American Pie '99
Yellow '98

Margaret Cho (1969-)
One Missed Call '08
Bam Bam & Celeste '05
Spent '00
The Tavern '00
Ground Control '98
Face/Off '97
Sweethearts '97
The Doom Generation '95
It's My Party '95

Tim Choate (1954-2004)
Pearl Harbor '01
Live Nude Girls '95
Blind Witness '89
The Discovery Program '89
Spy '89
Def-Con 4 '85
First Time '82

Charlene (Cheuk-Yin) Choi (1982-)
Diary '06
House of Fury '05
New Police Story '04
Vampire Effect '03

Min-Sik Choi (1962-)
Lady Vengeance '05
Oldboy '03
Shiri '99
The Quiet Family '98
No. 3 '97

David Chokachi
Bats: Human Harvest '07
Crimson Force '05
Shadow of a Scream '97

Justin Chon (1981-)
Balls Out: Gary the Tennis Coach '09
Crossing Over '09
The Twilight Saga: New Moon '09
Twilight '08

Jun Chong
Street Soldiers '91
Silent Assassins '88

Marcus Chong (1967-)
The Crow: Wicked Prayer '05
The Matrix '99
Panther '95

Rae Dawn Chong (1962-)
The Visit '00
Highball '97
Mask of Death '97
Protector '97
Starlight '97
Smalltime '96
The Break '95
Boca '94
Boulevard '94
Hideaway '94
Power of Attorney '94
Dangerous Relations '93
Time Runner '92
Common Bonds '91
Denial: The Dark Side of Passion '91
Prison Stories: Women on the Inside '91
When the Party's Over '91
Amazon '90
Curiosity Kills '90
Tales from the Darkside: The Movie '90
The Borrower '89

Far Out Man '89
The Principal '87
The Squeeze '87
Running out of Luck '86
Soul Man '86
American Flyers '85
Badge of the Assassin '85
City Limits '85
The Color Purple '85
Commando '85
Fear City '85
Beat Street '84
Cheech and Chong's The Corsican Brothers '84
Choose Me '84
Quest for Fire '82

Thomas Chong (1938-)
The Wash '01
Half-Baked '97
McHale's Navy '97
National Lampoon's Senior Trip '95
Ferngully: The Last Rain Forest '92 (V)
Spirit of '76 '91
Far Out Man '89
Tripwire '89
After Hours '85
Cheech and Chong's The Corsican Brothers '84
Cheech and Chong: Still Smokin' '83
Yellowbeard '83
Cheech and Chong: Things Are Tough All Over '82
Cheech and Chong's Nice Dreams '81
Cheech and Chong's Next Movie '80
Cheech and Chong's Up in Smoke '79

Yoko Chosokabe
The Princess Blade '02
Ringu 2 '99

Collin Chou (1967-)
The Forbidden Kingdom '08
Flash Point '07
DOA: Dead or Alive '06
Jet Li's Fearless '06
American Fusion '05
The Matrix Reloaded '03
The Matrix Revolutions '03
Jet Li's The Enforcer '95
The Bodyguard from Beijing '94
Exorcist Master '93

Lawrence Chou
Re-Cycle '06
The Eye '02

Sarita Choudhury (1966-)
Lady in the Water '06
The War Within '05
The Breakup Artist '04
It Runs in the Family '03
Just a Kiss '02
3 A.M. '01
A Perfect Murder '98
Subway Stories '97
Kama Sutra: A Tale of Love '96
Down Came a Blackbird '94
The House of the Spirits '93
Wild West '93
Mississippi Masala '92

Etchika Choureau (1923-)
Darby's Rangers '58
Lafayette Escadrille '58

China Chow (1974-)
Frankenfish '04
Head Over Heels '01
Sol Goode '01
The Big Hit '98

Stephen (Chiau) Chow (1962-)
Kung Fu Hustle '04
Shaolin Soccer '01

Valerie Chow (1970-)
Chungking Express '95
Moltdown '95

Yun-Fat Chow
See Chow Yun-Fat
The Children of Huang Shi '08

Navin Chowdhry (1971-)
Red Mercury '05
The Seventh Coin '92
Madame Sousatzka '88

Ranjit (Chaudry) Chowdhry
Last Holiday '06
Fire '96
Bleeding Hearts '94
The Night We Never Met '93
Mississippi Masala '92
Lonely in America '90

Joseph Chrest
Front of the Class '08
The Underneath '95
King of the Hill '93

Emmanuelle Chriqui (1977-)
Saint John of Las Vegas '09
Taking Chances '09
Women in Trouble '09
August '08
Cadillac Records '08
Tortured '08
You Don't Mess with the Zohan '08
Deceit '06
Waltzing Anna '06
The Crow: Wicked Prayer '05
In the Mix '05
National Lampoon's Adam & Eve '05
Waiting '05
Rick '03
Wrong Turn '03
A. I.: Artificial Intelligence '01
On the Line '01
100 Girls '00
Snow Day '00

Marilyn Chris (1938-)
Waltzing Anna '06
Joe Torre: Curveballs Along the Way '97
Backstairs at the White House '79
Honeymoon Killers '70

Chad Christ (1976-)
Jawbreaker '98
No Laughing Matter '97

David Christensen
Turn of the Blade '97
Over the Wire '95

Erika Christensen (1982-)
How to Rob a Bank '07
Flightplan '05
The Sisters '05
The Upside of Anger '05
The Perfect Score '04
Riding the Bullet '04
MTV's Wuthering Heights '03
The Banger Sisters '02
Home Room '02
Swimfan '02
Can of Worms '00
Traffic '00

Hayden Christensen (1981-)
Takers '10
New York, I Love You '09
Jumper '08
Awake '07
Virgin Territory '07
Factory Girl '06
Star Wars: Episode 3—Revenge of the Sith '05
Shattered Glass '03
Star Wars: Episode 2—Attack of the Clones '02
Life as a House '01

Jesper Christensen (1948-)
The Young Victoria '09
Everlasting Moments '08
Quantum of Solace '08
Casino Royale '06
The Interpreter '05
Uprising '01
The White Lioness '96
Sofie '92

Claudia Christian (1965-)
Half Past Dead '02
Atlantis: The Lost Empire '01 (V)
Final Voyage '99
The Haunting of Hell House '99
The Substitute 3: Winner Takes All '99
Mercenary 2: Thick and Thin '97
Sisters '97
The Adventures of a Gnome Named Gnorm '93
Hexed '93
The Dark Backward '91
Strays '91
Mad About You '90
Maniac Cop 2 '90
Arena '89
Mom '89
Tale of Two Sisters '89
Clean and Sober '88
Never on Tuesday '88
The Hidden '87

John Christian (1957-)
Blood Relic '05
Airboss '97
The Outfit '93
Comrades in Arms '91
Covert Action '88
Mob War '88

Linda Christian (1924-)
Full Hearts & Empty Pockets '63
The V.I.P.'s '63
The Devil's Hand '61
Athena '54

Michael Christian (1947-)
Private Obsession '94
Hard Knocks '79
Mid Knight Rider '79
The Legend of Frank Woods '77
Poor Pretty Eddie '73

Shawn Christian
Mating Dance '08
Meet Dave '08
Tremors 3: Back to Perfection '01

Mady Christians (1900-51)
All My Sons '48
Letter from an Unknown Woman '48
Tender Comrade '43
The Finances of the Grand Duke '24

Benjamin Christiansen (1879-1959)
The Only Way '70
Haxan: Witchcraft through the Ages '22

Audrey Christie (1912-89)
Harper Valley P.T.A. '78
Mame '74
Frankie and Johnny '65
Splendor in the Grass '61
Keeper of the Flame '42

Julie Christie (1941-)
New York, I Love You '09
Away From Her '06
Finding Neverland '04
Harry Potter and the Prisoner of Azkaban '04
Troy '04
I'm with Lucy '02
Snapshots '02
Belphegar: Phantom of the Louvre '01
No Such Thing '01
The Miracle Maker: The Story of Jesus '00 (V)
Afterglow '97
Dragonheart '96
Hamlet '96
The Railway Station Man '92
Fools of Fortune '90
Secret Obsession '88
Miss Mary '86
Power '86
Separate Tables '83
Heat and Dust '82
Return of the Soldier '82
Heaven Can Wait '78
Demon Seed '77
Nashville '75
Shampoo '75
Don't Look Now '73
The Go-Between '71
McCabe & Mrs. Miller '71
Petulia '68
Far from the Madding Crowd '67
Fahrenheit 451 '66
Darling '65
Doctor Zhivago '65
Billy Liar '63

Morven Christie
Oliver Twist '07
The Flying Scotsman '06
House of 9 '05

Warren Christie
Bachelor Party 2: The Last Temptation '08
The Most Wonderful Time of the Year '08

Katia Christine (1946-)
Cosmos: War of the Planets '80
Spirits of the Dead '68

Virginia Christine (1920-96)
Billy the Kid Versus Dracula '66
One Man's Way '63
The Cobweb '55
The Inner Circle '46
The Killers '46
The Mummy's Curse '44
Raiders of Ghost City '44

Eric Christmas (1916-2000)
Air Bud '97
Mouse Hunt '97
Child of Darkness, Child of Light '91
The Challengers '89
Home Is Where the Hart Is '88
Porky's Revenge '85
All of Me '84
The Philadelphia Experiment '84
Porky's 2: The Next Day '83
Porky's '82
Middle Age Crazy '80
Attack of the Killer Tomatoes '77
An Enemy of the People '77
Harold and Maude '71
Johnny Got His Gun '71

Debra Christofferson
Jesse Stone: Death in Paradise '06
The Day the World Ended '01
Mouse Hunt '97
Round Numbers '91

Francoise Christophe (1925-)
Borsalino '70
The King of Hearts '66
The Invaders '63
Walk into Hell '57

Bojesse Christopher
Out in Fifty '99
Meatballs 4 '92
Point Break '91

Dennis Christopher (1955-)
Trapped '06
Mind Lies '00
It's My Party '95
Operation Intercept '95
The Silencers '95
Boys Life '94
Plughead Rewired: Circuitry Man 2 '94
H.P. Lovecraft's Necronomicon: Book of the Dead '93
False Arrest '92
Circuitry Man '90
Doppelganger: The Evil Within '90
Stephen King's It '90
A Sinful Life '89
Jake Speed '86
Didn't You Hear? '83
Jack & the Beanstalk '83
Don't Cry, It's Only Thunder '82
Chariots of Fire '81
Alien Predators '80
Fade to Black '80
The Last Word '80
Breaking Away '79
California Dreaming '79
Elvis: The Movie '79
A Wedding '78
September 30, 1955 '77
3 Women '77
The Young Graduates '71

Thom Christopher (1940-)
Jackie, Ethel, Joan: The Kennedy Women '01
Peril '00
Deathstalker 3 '89
Wizards of the Lost Kingdom '85

Tyler Christopher (1972-)
U.S. Navy SEALS: Dead or Alive '02
U.S. SEALs: Dead or Alive '02
Out of the Black '01
Catfish in Black Bean Sauce '00
Face the Music '00

William (Bill) Christopher (1932-)
M*A*S*H: Goodbye, Farewell & Amen '83
For the Love of It '80
With Six You Get Eggroll '68

Kathy Christopherson
Executive Target '97
Guyver 2: Dark Hero '94

Dorothy Christy (1906-77)
Sons of the Desert '33
Convicted '32
Big Business Girl '31
Night Life in Reno '31

Emily Chu (1960-)
A Better Tomorrow, Part 1 '86
Heart of Dragon '85
Gods of Wu Tang '83

Ke Chu
Five Element Ninjas '82
House of Traps '81

Norman Chu
Legend of the Liquid Sword '93
Gods of Wu Tang '83
The 36th Chamber of Shaolin '78

Paul Chubb (1949-2002)
Road to Nhill '97
The Well '97
Cosi '95
Sweet Talker '91

Delphine Chuillot
Heartbeat Detector '07
Pola X '99

Brett Chukerman
The Curiosity of Chance '06
Eating Out 2: Sloppy Seconds '06

Babz Chula (1946-)
Connie and Carla '04
Moving Malcolm '03
Live Bait '95

Christy Chung (1970-)
The Medallion '03
The Bodyguard from Beijing '94
The Bride with White Hair 2 '93

David Chung (1946-2006)
Color of a Brisk and Leaping Day '95
The Ballad of Little Jo '93
Combination Platter '93

Gillian (Yan-Tung) Chung (1981-)
House of Fury '05
Vampire Effect '03

Jamie Chung (1983-)
Grown Ups '10
Princess Protection Program '09
Sorority Row '09

Mok Siu Chung (1960-)
Once Upon a Time in China III '93
Once Upon a Time in China II '92

Fred Church (1888-1983)
Apache Kid's Escape '30
Son of a Gun '19

Thomas Haden Church (1960-)
Aliens in the Attic '09 (V)
All About Steve '09
Imagine That '09
Smart People '08
Spider-Man 3 '07
Broken Trail '06
Charlotte's Web '06 (V)
Idiocracy '06
Over the Hedge '06 (V)
Serial Killing 101 '04
Sideways '04
Spanglish '04
Lone Star State of Mind '02
3000 Miles to Graceland '01
The Specials '00
Free Money '99
Dean Koontz's Mr. Murder '98
Dying to Get Rich '98
George of the Jungle '97
One Night Stand '97
Tales from the Crypt Presents Demon Knight '94
Tombstone '93

Berton Churchill (1876-1940)
Stagecoach '39
Danger on the Air '38
Four Men and a Prayer '38
Wide Open Faces '38
In Old Chicago '37
The Dark Hour '36
Dimples '36
Mistaken Identity '36
Sing Sing Nights '35
Steamboat Round the Bend '35
Bachelor Bait '34
Badmen of Nevada '33
Doctor Bull '33
The Little Giant '33
The Mysterious Rider '33
So This Is Africa '33
The Big Stampede '32
False Faces '32
Frisco Jenny '32
Two Seconds '32

Donald Churchill (1930-91)
The Hound of the Baskervilles '83

Charlie Muffin '79
Victim '61

Marguerite Churchill (1909-2000)
Alibi for Murder '36
Dracula's Daughter '36
Ambassador Bill '31
Big Trail '30
They Had to See Paris '29

Sarah Churchill
Serious Charge '59
Royal Wedding '51
He Found a Star '41

Chyna
See Joanie Laurer

Julien Ciamaca (1978-)
My Father's Glory '91
My Mother's Castle '91

Eduardo Ciannelli (1889-1969)
MacKenna's Gold '69
Houseboat '58
Monster from Green Hell '58
Mambo '55
The Creeper '48
Heartbeat '46
The Mask of Dimitrios '44
Passage to Marseilles '44
They Got Me Covered '43
Cairo '42
They Met in Bombay '41
Doctor Satan's Robot '40
Foreign Correspondent '40
Kitty Foyle '40
The Mummy's Hand '40
Mysterious Doctor Satan '40
Strange Cargo '40
Bulldog Drummond's Bride '39
Gunga Din '39
Law of the Underworld '38
Marked Woman '37

Eddie Cibrian (1973-)
Not Easily Broken '09
The Cave '05
Say It Isn't So '01
But I'm a Cheerleader '99

Robert Cicchini (1966-)
The Watcher '00
Devlin '92
Age Isn't Everything '91

Jude Ciccolella (1947-)
Julia '08
A Perfect Day '06
Sin City '05
The Manchurian Candidate '04
The Terminal '04
Head of State '03
High Crimes '02
Star Trek: Nemesis '02
Washington Heights '02
Beloved '98
Mad Love '95
Glengarry Glen Ross '92
Shakedown '88

Phyllis Cicero
America's Dream '95
Steele's Law '91

Magdalena Cielecka
Katyn '07
The Third '04

Anna Ciepielewska (1936-2006)
Passenger '61
Mother Joan of the Angels '60

Jennifer Ciesar (1968-)
Red Shoe Diaries 7: Burning Up '96
Red Shoe Diaries: Strip Poker '96
Inner Sanctum 2 '94
Lovers' Lovers '94

Enzo Cilenti (1974-)
The Fourth Kind '09
Millions '05

Diane Cilento (1933-)
Winner Takes All '84
The Wicker Man '75

Hitler: The Last Ten Days '73
Zero Population Growth '72
Negatives '68
Hombre '67
The Agony and the Ecstasy '65
Rattle of a Simple Man '64
Tom Jones '63
The Naked Edge '61
The Admirable Crichton '57

Leonardo Cimino
Trusting Beatrice '92
Penn and Teller Get Killed '90

Maria Cina
April's Shower '03
Suspended Animation '02

Kelly Cinnante
Christmas in Connecticut '92
True Love '89

Luis Miguel Cintra (1949-)
The Dancer Upstairs '02
The Convent '95
Abraham's Valley '93

Charles Cioffi (1935-)
Amy's O '02
The Shadow Conspiracy '96
Newsies '92
Used People '92
Peter Gunn '89
Remo Williams: The Adventure Begins '85
All the Right Moves '83
Missing '82
Time After Time '79
The Arab Conspiracy '76
Return to Earth '76
The Don Is Dead '73
The Thief Who Came to Dinner '73
Klute '71
Shaft '71

Augusta Ciolli (1901-67)
Love with the Proper Stranger '63
Marty '55

Greg Cipes (1980-)
Simon Says '07
The Wild '06 (V)
Ring of Darkness '04

Roberto Citran (1955-)
Nora '00
The Truce '96

Franco Citti (1935-)
Watch Me When I Kill '77
Arabian Nights '74
The Decameron '70
Porcile '69
Super Brother '68
Oedipus Rex '67
Mamma Roma '62
Accatone! '61

Louis CK (1967-)
The Invention of Lying '09
Diminished Capacity '08

Jany Clair (1938-)
Hercules against the Moon Men '64
Conquest of Mycene '63
Planets Against Us '61

Cyrielle Claire (1955-)
The Worker and the Hairdresser '96
Control '87
Code Name: Emerald '85
Sword of the Valiant '83
Le Professionnel '81

Ina Claire (1892-1985)
Ninotchka '39
Three Broadway Girls '32

Tom Clancy (1924-90)
Backstairs at the White House '79
Eric '75

Rony Clanton
Def by Temptation '90

The Education of Sonny Carson '74

Gordon Clapp (1948-)
The Game Plan '07
Sunshine State '02
Skeletons in the Closet '00
The Rage: Carrie 2 '99
Family of Strangers '93
Stand Off '93
Fever '91
Kurt Vonnegut's Monkey House '91
Small Sacrifices '89
Termini Station '89
Eight Men Out '88
Matewan '87
Return of the Secaucus 7 '80

Eric Clapton (1945-)
Chuck Berry: Hail! Hail! Rock 'n' Roll '87
Water '85
Tommy '75

Diane Clare (1938-)
Vulture '67
Beast of Morocco '66
Plague of the Zombies '66
The Haunting '63
Whistle down the Wind '61
The Reluctant Debutante '58
Murder on the Campus '52

Mary Clare (1894-1970)
Mambo '55
Beggar's Opera '54
Moulin Rouge '52
The Three Weird Sisters '48
The Night Has Eyes '42
The Challenge '38
The Mill on the Floss '37
Young and Innocent '37
Lorna Doone '34
Power '34

O.B. Clarence (1870-1955)
Great Expectations '46
On Approval '44
The Courageous Mr. Penn '41
Pygmalion '38
The Scarlet Pimpernel '34
A Shot in the Dark '33

Hans Clarin
Pippi Goes on Board '69
Pippi Longstocking '69

Aime Clariond (1894-1960)
Monsieur Vincent '47
De Mayerling a Sarajevo '40
La Marseillaise '37

Anthony Clark (1964-)
Say Uncle '05
Paid in Full '02
Murder She Purred: A Mrs. Murphy Mystery '98 (V)
The Rock '96
Hourglass '95
Teresa's Tattoo '94
The Thing Called Love '93
Dogfight '91

Blake Clark (1946-)
Toy Story 3 '10 (V)
I Now Pronounce You Chuck and Larry '07
The Benchwarmers '06
50 First Dates '04
The Ladykillers '04
Mr. Deeds '02
Critical Mass '00
Little Nicky '00
The Waterboy '98
Grave Secrets: The Legacy of Hilltop Drive '92
Ladybugs '92
Shakes the Clown '92
Johnny Handsome '89

Bob (Benjamin) Clark (1941-2007)
A Christmas Story '83
Porky's '82

Brett (Baxter) Clark
Stormy Nights '97

Deathstalker 4: Match of Titans '92
Inner Sanctum '91
Eye of the Eagle '87
Alien Warrior '85

Buddy Clark (1912-49)
Melody Time '48 (V)
Seven Days' Leave '42

Candy Clark (1947-)
Zodiac '07
Cherry Falls '00
Buffy the Vampire Slayer '92
Cool As Ice '91
Original Intent '91
The Blob '88
At Close Range '86
Cat's Eye '85
Hambone & Hillie '84
Amityville 3: The Demon '83
Blue Thunder '83
Johnny Belinda '82
Q (The Winged Serpent) '82
National Lampoon Goes to the Movies '81
Rodeo Girl '80
More American Graffiti '79
The Big Sleep '78
Citizens Band '77
James Dean '76
The Man Who Fell to Earth '76
American Graffiti '73
Fat City '72

Cliff Clark (1889-1953)
Home of the Brave '49
The Wagons Roll at Night '41

Dane Clark (1913-98)
Last Rites '88
Blood Song '82
James Dean '76
Murder on Flight 502 '75
Say Goodbye, Maggie Cole '72
The McMasters '70
Massacre '56
Blackout '54
Paid to Kill '54
Thunder Pass '54
The Gambler & the Lady '52
Barricade '49
The Smallest Show on Earth '48
A Stolen Life '46
God is My Co-Pilot '45
Pride of the Marines '45
Hollywood Canteen '44
Action in the North Atlantic '43
Destination Tokyo '43
The Glass Key '42

Daniel Clark (1985-)
That Russell Girl '08
Model Behavior '00
Grizzly Falls '99

Davison Clark (1881-1972)
Rogue's Gallery '44
Dishonored '31

Dick Clark (1929-)
Deadman's Curve '78
Wild in the Streets '68

Ernest Clark (1912-94)
Castle Keep '69
Salt & Pepper '68
The Devil-Ship Pirates '64
Sink the Bismarck '60
1984 '56

Eugene Clark (1955-)
George A. Romero's Land of the Dead '05
Man in the Mirror: The Michael Jackson Story '04
Jasper, Texas '03
Turn It Up '00
Wilder '00
TekWar '94
Trial and Error '92

Frank Clark (1857-1945)
Roaring Ranch '30
The Spoilers '14

Fred Clark (1914-68)
The Horse in the Gray Flannel Suit '68
Dr. Goldfoot and the Bikini Machine '66
Move Over, Darling '63
Zotz! '62
Bells Are Ringing '60
Joyful Laughter '60
Passionate Thief '60
It Started with a Kiss '59
The Mating Game '59
Don't Go Near the Water '57
Solid Gold Cadillac '56
The Court Martial of Billy Mitchell '55
Daddy Long Legs '55
Abbott and Costello Meet the Keystone Kops '54
The Caddy '53
Here Come the Girls '53
Three for Bedroom C '52
The Lemon Drop Kid '51
The Jackpot '50
Sunset Boulevard '50
Flamingo Road '49
The Unsuspected '47

Greydon Clark (1943-)
Bad Bunch '76
Satan's Sadists '69

Harvey Clark (1885-1938)
Law for Tombstone '35
Peck's Bad Boy '34
Shriek in the Night '33
Red Headed Woman '32

Jameson Clark
The Battle of the Sexes '60
Bond of Fear '56

Judy Clark
Kid Sister '45
South of Santa Fe '42

Ken Clark (1927-)
Tarzana, the Wild Girl '69
Desert Commandos '67
Attack of the Giant Leeches '59
Between Heaven and Hell '56

Liddy Clark (1953-)
Deadly Possession '88
Kitty and the Bagman '82
The Chant of Jimmie Blacksmith '78

Marlene Clark
The Baron '88
The Beast Must Die '75
Switchblade Sisters '75
Ganja and Hess '73
Night of the Cobra Woman '72
Slaughter '72

Matt Clark (1936-)
Kiss of Fire '98
Homegrown '97
Trilogy of Terror 2 '96
Barbarians at the Gate '93
Frozen Assets '92
The Harvest '92
Class Action '91
Back to the Future, Part 3 '90
Blind Witness '89
The Horror Show '89
Kenny Rogers as the Gambler, Part 3: The Legend Continues '87
Let's Get Harry '87
The Quick and the Dead '87
Out of the Darkness '85
Return to Oz '85
Tuff Turf '85
The Adventures of Buckaroo Banzai Across the Eighth Dimension '84
Country '84
Love Letters '83
In the Custody of Strangers '82
Chasing Dreams '81
An Eye for an Eye '81
Legend of the Lone Ranger '81

Ruckus '81
Brubaker '80
The Driver '78
The Outlaw Josey Wales '76
The Execution of Private Slovik '74
Melvin Purvis: G-Man '74
Emperor of the North Pole '73
The Great Northfield Minnesota Raid '72

Mystro Clark (1966-)
Out at the Wedding '07
Storm Catcher '99
Chairman of the Board '97

Oliver Clark (1939-)
Nightlife '90
Ernest Saves Christmas '88
One Cooks, the Other Doesn't '83
Mikey & Nicky '76
A Star Is Born '76

Petula Clark (1932-)
Goodbye, Mr. Chips '69
Finian's Rainbow '68
The Gay Dog '54
The Runaway Bus '54
Made in Heaven '52
The Promoter '52

Roger Clark (1909-78)
Monster '78
Girls in Chains '43
The Lady Is Willing '42

Spencer (Treat) Clark (1987-)
The Last House on the Left '09
Superheroes '07
Mystic River '03
Minority Report '02
Gladiator '00
Unbreakable '00
Arlington Road '99
Double Jeopardy '99

Steve Clark (1891-1954)
Range Renegades '48
Fighting Vigilantes '47
Border Bandits '46
The Stranger from Pecos '45
Range Law '44
Land of Hunted Men '43
Pinto Canyon '40
Boothill Brigade '37
Gun Lords of Stirrup Basin '37
Paroled to Die '37
West of Nevada '36
No Man's Range '35

Susan Clark (1940-)
Snowbound: The Jim and Jennifer Stolpa Story '94
Porky's '82
The Choice '81
The Double Negative '80
Murder by Decree '79
Nobody's Perfekt '79
The North Avenue Irregulars '79
Promises in the Dark '79
City on Fire '78
Airport '75 '75
The Apple Dumpling Gang '75
Babe! '75
Night Moves '75
Showdown '73
Skin Game '71
Valdez Is Coming '71
Colossus: The Forbin Project '70
Skullduggery '70
Tell Them Willie Boy Is Here '69
Coogan's Bluff '68
Madigan '68

Ted Clark
Wrong Turn '03
Happy Hell Night '92

Wallis (Clarke) Clark (1886-1961)
Penny Serenade *'41*
Star Reporter *'39*
Postal Inspector *'36*

Andrew Clarke (1954-)
Les Patterson Saves the World *'90*
Anzacs: The War Down Under *'85*

Angela Clarke (1969-)
Land and Freedom *'95*
Memories of Me *'88*
Letter to Brezhnev *'86*

Angela (Clark) Clarke (1912-)
Harrad Summer *'74*
The Interns *'62*
The Seven Little Foys *'55*
The Egyptian *'54*
Beneath the 12-Mile Reef *'53*
Houdini *'53*
House of Wax *'53*
Miracle of Our Lady of Fatima *'52*
The Great Caruso *'51*
The Gunfighter *'50*
Mrs. Mike *'49*

Brian Patrick Clarke (1952-)
Ace Ventura Jr.: Pet Detective *'08*
Private Wars *'93*
Sleepaway Camp 2: Unhappy Campers *'88*

Caitlin Clarke (1952-2004)
Penn and Teller Get Killed *'90*
Dragonslayer *'81*

Cam(eron) Clarke (1957-)
The Pirates Who Don't Do Anything: A VeggieTales Movie *'08 (V)*
Clifford's Really Big Movie *'04 (V)*

Gary Clarke (1936-)
Confessions of Tom Harris *'72*
Bull of the West *'71*
Date Bait *'60*
Missile to the Moon *'59*
How to Make a Monster *'58*

Graham Clarke
Armageddon: The Final Challenge *'94*
Laser Mission *'90*
Lights! Camera! Murder! *'89*

Hope Clarke (1943-)
Seventeen Again *'00*
Piece of the Action *'77*

Jason Clarke
Public Enemies *'09*
Death Race *'08*
The Human Contract *'08*
The Outsider *'02*
Rabbit-Proof Fence *'02*
Risk *'00*

Justine Clarke (1971-)
Look Both Ways *'05*
Danny Deckchair *'03*
Japanese Story *'03*

Lenny Clarke (1953-)
What Doesn't Kill You *'08*
Fever Pitch *'05*
What's the Worst That Could Happen? *'01*
Me, Myself, and Irene *'00*
Rounders *'98*
There's Something about Mary *'98*
Two If by Sea *'95*

Mae Clarke (1907-92)
Because of You *'52*
Pat and Mike *'52*
King of the Rocketmen *'49*
Lost Planet Airmen *'49*
Here Come the Waves *'45*
Flying Tigers *'42*
Hats Off *'37*
Great Guy *'36*
Wild Brian Kent *'36*
The Man with Two Faces *'34*
Lady Killer *'33*
Penthouse *'33*
Frankenstein *'31*
The Front Page *'31*
Public Enemy *'31*

Melinda (Mindy) Clarke (1969-)
Soldier of Fortune Inc. *'97*
Spawn *'97*
Killer Tongue *'96*
Return of the Living Dead 3 *'93*
Return to Two Moon Junction *'93*
Hot Under the Collar *'91*

Richard Clarke (1930-2005)
Identity Crisis *'90*
A Night to Remember *'58*
Charlie Chan in City of Darkness *'39*

Robert Clarke (1920-2005)
Alienator *'89*
Attack from Mars *'88*
Secret File of Hollywood *'62*
Terror of the Bloodhunters *'62*
Beyond the Time Barrier *'60*
Hideous Sun Demon *'59*
The Astounding She-Monster *'58*
Sword of Venus *'53*
Tales of Robin Hood *'52*
Hard, Fast and Beautiful *'51*
The Man from Planet X *'51*
Riders of the Range *'50*
Bedlam *'45*
The Enchanted Cottage *'45*

Robin Clarke
White Wolves 3: Cry of the White Wolf *'98*
Cyberzone *'95*
Inseminoid *'80*

Sarah Clarke (1972-)
The Twilight Saga: Eclipse *'10*
Women in Trouble *'09*
The Lather Effect *'06*
Happy Endings *'05*
Thirteen *'03*

Warren Clarke (1947-)
The Debt *'03*
Blow Dry *'00*
Greenfingers *'00*
A Respectable Trade *'98*
Joseph *'95*
Hands of a Murderer *'90*
Mandela *'87*
Gulag *'85*
Cold Room *'84*
Lassiter *'84*
Enigma *'82*
Firefox *'82*
From a Far Country: Pope John Paul II *'81*
Tinker, Tailor, Soldier, Spy *'80*
The Great Riviera Bank Robbery *'79*
S.O.S. Titanic *'79*
Antony and Cleopatra *'73*
O Lucky Man! *'73*
A Clockwork Orange *'71*

D. A. Clarke-Smith (1888-1959)
The Ghoul *'34*
The Man Who Knew Too Much *'34*

Lana Clarkson (1962-2003)
Vice Girls *'96*
The Haunting of Morella *'91*
Barbarian Queen 2: The Empress Strikes Back *'89*
Wizards of the Lost Kingdom 2 *'89*
Barbarian Queen *'85*
Blind Date *'84*
Deathstalker *'83*

Patricia Clarkson (1959-)
Cairo Time *'09*
Shutter Island *'09*
Whatever Works *'09*
Blind Date *'08*
Elegy *'08*
Phoebe in Wonderland *'08*
Vicky Cristina Barcelona *'08*
Lars and the Real Girl *'07*
Married Life *'07*
No Reservations *'07*
All the King's Men *'06*
The Dying Gaul *'05*
Good Night, and Good Luck *'05*
Miracle *'04*
All the Real Girls *'03*
Dogville *'03*
Pieces of April *'03*
The Station Agent *'03*
The Woods *'03*
Carrie *'02*
Far from Heaven *'02*
Welcome to Collinwood *'02*
The Safety of Objects *'01*
Wendigo *'01*
Joe Gould's Secret *'00*
The Pledge *'00*
The Green Mile *'99*
Simply Irresistible *'99*
High Art *'98*
Playing by Heart *'98*
Pharoah's Army *'95*
Caught in the Act *'93*
Four Eyes and Six Guns *'93*
An American Story *'92*
Legacy of Lies *'92*
Blind Man's Bluff *'91*
The Old Man and the Sea *'90*
Tune in Tomorrow *'90*
The Dead Pool *'88*
Rocket Gibraltar *'88*

Charles Clary (1873-1931)
The Sea Lion *'21*
The Penalty *'20*

Robert Clary (1926-)
Holocaust Survivors... Remembrance of Love *'83*
New Faces of 1952 *'54*

Garance Clavel (1973-)
Apres-Vous *'03*
When the Cat's Away *'96*

Kira Clavell
Kickin' It Old Skool *'07*
House of the Dead *'03*

Christian Clavier (1952-)
The Crown Prince *'06*
Napoleon *'03*
Just Visiting *'01*
The Visitors *'95*
French Fried Vacation *'79*
This Sweet Sickness *'77*

Nicholas Clay (1946-2000)
Merlin *'98*
The Odyssey *'97*
Sleeping Beauty *'89*
Lionheart *'87*
The Hound of the Baskervilles *'83*
Evil under the Sun *'82*
Excalibur *'81*
Lady Chatterley's Lover *'81*
Lovespell *'79*

Jill Clayburgh (1944-)
Running with Scissors *'06*
Never Again *'01*
My Little Assassin *'99*
Fools Rush In *'97*
Going All the Way *'97*
Sins of the Mind *'97*
Honor Thy Father and Mother: The True Story of the Menendez Brothers *'94*
Day of Atonement *'93*
Firestorm: 72 Hours in Oakland *'93*
Naked in New York *'93*
Rich in Love *'93*
Whispers in the Dark *'92*
Shy People *'87*
Miles to Go *'86*
Where Are the Children? *'85*
Hanna K. *'83*
I'm Dancing as Fast as I Can *'82*
First Monday in October *'81*
It's My Turn *'80*
Starting Over *'79*
An Unmarried Woman *'78*
Semi-Tough *'77*
Griffin and Phoenix: A Love Story *'76*
Silver Streak *'76*
The Art of Crime *'75*
Hustling *'75*
The Terminal Man *'74*
The Thief Who Came to Dinner *'73*
Portnoy's Complaint *'72*
The Wedding Party *'69*

John Clayton (1940-2003)
Out of the Body *'88*
High Tide *'87*
Warm Nights on a Slow-Moving Train *'87*
Freedom *'82*

June Clayworth (1912-93)
At Sword's Point *'51*
Dick Tracy Meets Gruesome *'47*
Criminal Court *'46*

John Cleese (1939-)
The Pink Panther 2 *'09*
Planet 51 *'09 (V)*
The Day the Earth Stood Still *'08*
Igor *'08 (V)*
Shrek the Third *'07 (V)*
Charlotte's Web *'06 (V)*
Valiant *'05 (V)*
Around the World in 80 Days *'04*
Shrek 2 *'04 (V)*
Charlie's Angels: Full Throttle *'03*
The Adventures of Pluto Nash *'02*
Die Another Day *'02*
Harry Potter and the Chamber of Secrets *'02*
Pinocchio *'02 (V)*
Scorched *'02*
Harry Potter and the Sorcerer's Stone *'01*
Rat Race *'01*
Isn't She Great *'00*
The Out-of-Towners *'99*
The World Is Not Enough *'99*
Parting Shots *'98*
George of the Jungle *'97 (V)*
Fierce Creatures *'96*
Mr. Toad's Wild Ride *'96*
Mary Shelley's Frankenstein *'94*
Rudyard Kipling's The Jungle Book *'94*
The Swan Princess *'94 (V)*
Splitting Heirs *'93*
The Strange Case of the End of Civilization As We Know It *'93*
An American Tail: Fievel Goes West *'91 (V)*
Bullseye! *'90*
The Big Picture *'89*
Erik the Viking *'89*
A Fish Called Wanda *'88*
Clockwise *'86*
Silverado *'85*
Privates on Parade *'84*
Monty Python's The Meaning of Life *'83*
Whoops Apocalypse *'83*
Yellowbeard *'83*
The Secret Policeman's Other Ball *'82*
The Great Muppet Caper *'81*
Secret Policeman's Private Parts *'81*
Time Bandits *'81*
Monty Python's Life of Brian *'79*
Monty Python and the Holy Grail *'75*
Romance with a Double Bass *'74*
And Now for Something Completely Different *'72*
The Statue *'71*
The Magic Christian *'69*
The Bliss of Mrs. Blossom *'68*
John Cleese on How to Irritate People *'68*

Ellen Cleghorne (1965-)
MacArthur Park *'01*
Coyote Ugly *'00*
Little Nicky *'00*
Mr. Wrong *'95*

Jimmy Clem
Town That Dreaded Sundown *'76*
Winterhawk *'76*

Paul Clemens (1958-)
They're Playing with Fire *'84*
The Beast Within *'82*
The Family Man *'79*
Promises in the Dark *'79*

Christian Clemenson (1959-)
United 93 *'06*
Lost and Found *'99*
And the Band Played On *'93*
Hero *'92*
Bad Influence *'90*

Aurore Clement (1945-)
La Petite Jerusalem *'05*
The Bridesmaid *'04*
Bon Voyage *'03*
For Sale *'98*
The Eighties *'83*
Paris, Texas *'83*
Invitation au Voyage *'82*
Toute Une Nuit *'82*
Les Rendez-vous D'Anna *'78*
Le Crabe Tambour *'77*

Clay Clement
Star Reporter *'39*
Whipsaw *'35*

Jemaine Clement (1974-)
Despicable Me *'10 (V)*
Dinner for Schmucks *'10*
Gentlemen Broncos *'09*
Eagle vs. Shark *'07*

Suzanne Clement
2 Seconds *'98*
The Confessional *'95*

Pierre Clementi (1942-99)
Hideous Kinky *'99*
Sweet Movie *'75*
Steppenwolf *'74*
The Conformist *'71*
Porcile *'69*
Partner *'68*
Belle de Jour *'67*
The Leopard *'63*

John Clements (1910-88)
Oh! What a Lovely War *'69*
The Mind Benders *'63*
The Silent Enemy *'58*
Train of Events *'49*
This England *'42*
Convoy *'40*
The Four Feathers *'39*
South Riding *'37*

Stanley Clements (1926-81)
Johnny Holiday *'49*
Underworld Scandal *'47*
Salty O'Rourke *'45*
On the Sunny Side *'42*

Clarence Clemons (1941-)
Swing *'98*
Fatal Instinct *'93*

David Clennon (1943-)
Saving Sarah Cain *'07*
Life of the Party *'05*
Syriana *'05*
Silver City *'04*
The Visit *'00*
From the Earth to the Moon *'98*
Tecumseh: The Last Warrior *'95*
And the Band Played On *'93*
Light Sleeper *'92*
Man Trouble *'92*
Matinee *'92*
The Trouble with Dick *'88*
Conspiracy: The Trial of the Chicago Eight *'87*
The Couch Trip *'87*
Legal Eagles *'86*
Sweet Dreams *'85*
Falling in Love *'84*
Hanna K. *'83*
The Right Stuff *'83*
Star 80 *'83*
Ladies and Gentlemen, the Fabulous Stains *'82*
Missing *'82*
The Thing *'82*
Go Tell the Spartans *'78*

Corinne Clery (1950-)
Dangerous Obsession *'88*
Yor, the Hunter from the Future *'83*
The Con Artists *'80*
Fatal Fix *'80*
Moonraker *'79*
Insanity *'76*
Love by Appointment *'76*
The Switch *'76*
The Story of O *'75*

Carol Cleveland (1942-)
Monty Python's The Meaning of Life *'83*
Monty Python's Life of Brian *'79*
Monty Python and the Holy Grail *'75*
And Now for Something Completely Different *'72*

Chris Cleveland
Border Lost *'08*
Relax... It's Just Sex! *'98*

George Cleveland (1886-1957)
Carson City *'52*
Trigger, Jr. *'50*
Miss Grant Takes Richmond *'49*
Rimfire *'49*
The Wistful Widow of Wagon Gap *'47*
Little Giant *'46*
The Show-Off *'46*
Pillow of Death *'45*
Abroad with Two Yanks *'44*
Dead Man's Eyes *'44*
It Happened Tomorrow *'44*
Texas Legionnaires *'43*
Valley of the Sun *'42*
Nevada City *'41*
Playmates *'41*
Two-Faced Woman *'41*
Drums of Fu Manchu *'40*
Hidden Enemy *'40*
Midnight Limited *'40*
Pioneers of the West *'40*
Tomboy *'40*
The Abe Lincoln of Ninth Avenue *'39*
Mutiny in the Big House *'39*
Ghost Town Riders *'38*
I Conquer the Sea *'36*
Revolt of the Zombies *'36*
Monte Carlo Nights *'34*

Philippe Clevenot (1942-2001)
Place Vendome *'98*

The Hairdresser's Husband *'92*
Celine and Julie Go Boating *'74*

Jimmy Cliff (1948-)
Rude Boy: The Jamaican Don *'03*
Club Paradise *'86*
The Harder They Come *'72*

John Cliff (1918-2001)
The Three Stooges Meet Hercules *'61*
Teenage Frankenstein *'58*
A Bullet for Joey *'55*
The Finger Man *'55*

Jack Clifford (1880-1956)
King of the Pecos *'36*
The Man from Gun Town *'36*
The Revenge Rider *'35*
Law of the Sea *'32*
South of Santa Fe *'32*
Sunrise Trail *'31*
Sweet Adeline *'26*

Richard Clifford
Carrington *'95*
Much Ado about Nothing *'93*
Henry V *'89*

Tommy Clifford
Song o' My Heart *'30*
Song o' My Heart *'29*

Faith Clift
Savage Journey *'83*
Cataclysm *'81*

Montgomery Clift (1920-66)
The Defector *'66*
Judgment at Nuremberg *'61*
The Misfits *'61*
Suddenly, Last Summer *'59*
Lonelyhearts *'58*
The Young Lions *'58*
Raintree County *'57*
Indiscretion of an American Wife *'54*
From Here to Eternity *'53*
I Confess *'53*
A Place in the Sun *'51*
The Big Lift *'50*
The Heiress *'49*
Red River *'48*
The Search *'48*

Elmer Clifton (1892-1949)
Intolerance *'16*
The Birth of a Nation *'15*

Brett Climo (1964-)
Double Vision *'02*
Blackwater Trail *'95*
Archer's Adventure *'85*

Emily Cline (1969-)
Dead Dog *'00*
In the Company of Men *'96*

Renee Cline
Fatal Exposure *'90*
Invasion Force *'90*
Lock 'n' Load *'90*

George Clinton (1941-)
Good Burger *'97*
P.C.U. *'94*
Graffiti Bridge *'90*

Colin Clive (1898-1937)
History Is Made at Night *'37*
The Bride of Frankenstein *'35*
Mad Love *'35*
Jane Eyre *'34*
Christopher Strong *'33*
Frankenstein *'31*

E.E. Clive (1879-1940)
The Adventures of Sherlock Holmes *'39*
Bulldog Drummond's Bride *'39*
Bulldog Drummond's Secret Police *'39*
The Hound of the Baskervilles *'39*
The Little Princess *'39*
Arrest Bulldog Drummond *'38*
Bulldog Drummond's Peril *'38*
Bulldog Drummond Escapes *'37*
Personal Property *'37*
The Charge of the Light Brigade *'36*
The Dark Hour *'36*
Libeled Lady *'36*
The Bride of Frankenstein *'35*
The Mystery of Edwin Drood *'35*
The Invisible Man *'33*

John Clive (1938-)
A Clockwork Orange *'71*
Yellow Submarine *'68 (V)*

Teagan Clive
Vice Academy 2 *'90*
Alienator *'89*
Sinbad of the Seven Seas *'89*
Interzone *'88*

Al Cliver (1951-)
Devil Hunter *'08*
Demonia *'90*
Endgame *'85*
2020 Texas Gladiators *'85*
The Beyond *'82*
Alien Contamination *'81*
The Black Cat *'81*
Zombie *'80*
Naked Paradise *'78*
Big Boss *'77*
Mr. Scarface *'77*
Rulers of the City *'76*
Forever Emmanuelle *'75*

Kristen Cloke (1970-)
Black Christmas *'06*
Final Destination *'00*
The Rage *'96*
Caged Fear *'92*

George Clooney (1961-)
Fantastic Mr. Fox *'09 (V)*
The Men Who Stare at Goats *'09*
Up in the Air *'09*
Burn After Reading *'08*
Leatherheads *'08*
Michael Clayton *'07*
Ocean's Thirteen *'07*
The Good German *'06*
Good Night, and Good Luck *'05*
Syriana *'05*
Ocean's Twelve *'04*
Intolerable Cruelty *'03*
Spy Kids 3-D: Game Over *'03*
Confessions of a Dangerous Mind *'02*
Solaris *'02*
Welcome to Collinwood *'02*
Ocean's Eleven *'01*
Spy Kids *'01*
Fail Safe *'00*
O Brother Where Art Thou? *'00*
The Perfect Storm *'00*
South Park: Bigger, Longer and Uncut *'99 (V)*
Three Kings *'99*
Out of Sight *'98*
The Thin Red Line *'98*
Batman and Robin *'97*
The Peacemaker *'97*
One Fine Day *'96*
From Dusk Till Dawn *'95*
The Magic Bubble *'93*
Red Surf *'90*
Return of the Killer Tomatoes! *'88*
Return to Horror High *'87*
Combat Academy *'86*

Rosemary Clooney (1928-2002)
Deep in My Heart *'54*
Red Garters *'54*
White Christmas *'54*
Here Come the Girls *'53*

Del Close (1935-99)
Mommy 2: Mommy's Day *'96*
Opportunity Knocks *'90*
The Blob *'88*
Big Town *'87*
Ferris Bueller's Day Off *'86*

Eric Close (1967-)
Taken *'02*
Follow the Stars Home *'01*
The Magnificent Seven *'98*

Glenn Close (1947-)
Hoodwinked Too! Hood vs. Evil *'10 (V)*
Evening *'07*
The Chumscrubber *'05*
Hoodwinked *'05 (V)*
Nine Lives *'05*
Tarzan 2 *'05 (V)*
Heights *'04*
The Stepford Wives *'04*
Brush with Fate *'03*
Le Divorce *'03*
The Lion in Winter *'03*
Pinocchio *'02 (V)*
Rodgers & Hammerstein's South Pacific *'01*
The Safety of Objects *'01*
Baby *'00 (N)*
102 Dalmatians *'00*
Things You Can Tell Just by Looking at Her *'00*
Cookie's Fortune *'99*
Sarah, Plain and Tall: Winter's End *'99*
Tarzan *'99 (V)*
Air Force One *'97*
In the Gloaming *'97*
Paradise Road *'97*
Mars Attacks! *'96*
101 Dalmatians *'96*
Mary Reilly *'95*
Serving in Silence: The Margarethe Cammermeyer Story *'95*
The Paper *'94*
The House of the Spirits *'93*
Sarah, Plain and Tall: Skylark *'93*
Hook *'91*
Meeting Venus *'91*
Sarah, Plain and Tall *'91*
Hamlet *'90*
Reversal of Fortune *'90*
Immediate Family *'89*
Dangerous Liaisons *'88*
Light Years *'88 (V)*
Fatal Attraction *'87*
The Jagged Edge *'85*
Maxie *'85*
The Natural *'84*
The Stone Boy *'84*
The Big Chill *'83*
The World According to Garp *'82*

Orphan Train *'79*
Too Far to Go *'79*

John Close (1921-63)
The Slime People *'63*
Beginning of the End *'57*
The Finger Man *'55*
Above and Beyond *'53*

Joshua Close (1981-)
Diary of the Dead *'07*
Full of It *'07*
The Exorcism of Emily Rose *'05*
Twist *'03*

John Scott Clough (1960-)
Phantoms *'97*
What Ever Happened To... *'93*
Gross Anatomy *'89*
Fast Forward *'84*

Raymond Cloutier (1945-)
Karmina *'96*
Riel *'79*

Vera Clouzot (1921-60)
Diabolique *'55*
Wages of Fear *'55*

David Clover
Zipperface *'92*
Ten Speed *'76*

Jennifer Cluff (1956-)
Kiss or Kill *'97*
Death Games *'80*

Martin Clunes (1963-)
Goodbye, Mr. Chips *'02*
Rock My World *'02*
Lorna Doone *'01*
Saving Grace *'00*
The Acid House *'98*
Shakespeare in Love *'98*
Sweet Revenge *'98*

Michelle Clunie
Leaving Barstow *'08*
The Unseen *'05*

George Clutesi (1905-88)
Nightwing *'79*
Prophecy *'79*

Francois Cluzet (1955-)
Paris *'08*
Tell No One *'06*
Late August, Early September *'98*
The Swindle *'97*
French Kiss *'95*
The Horseman on the Roof *'95*
Les Apprentis *'95*
Ready to Wear *'94*
A Wind from Wyoming *'94*
L'Enfer *'93*
Olivier, Olivier *'92*
Chocolat *'88*
The Story of Women *'88*
Too Beautiful for You *'88*
Round Midnight *'86*
Elsa, Elsa *'85*
The Horse of Pride *'80*

Andy Clyde (1892-1967)
Carolina Cannonball *'55*
Hopalong Cassidy: Borrowed Trouble *'48*
Hopalong Cassidy: Dangerous Venture *'48*
Hopalong Cassidy: False Paradise *'48*
Hopalong Cassidy: Silent Conflict *'48*
Hopalong Cassidy: Sinister Journey *'48*
Hopalong Cassidy: The Dead Don't Dream *'48*
Sundown Riders *'48*
Hopalong Cassidy: Hoppy's Holiday *'47*
Hopalong Cassidy: The Marauders *'47*
Hopalong Cassidy: Unexpected Guest *'47*
Hopalong Cassidy: The Devil's Playground *'46*
Mystery Man *'44*
Texas Masquerade *'44*
Border Patrol *'43*
Colt Comrades *'43*
False Colors *'43*
Hopalong Cassidy: Riders of the Deadline *'43*
Hoppy Serves a Writ *'43*
Leather Burners *'43*
Lost Canyon *'43*
Border Vigilantes *'41*
Doomed Caravan *'41*
In Old Colorado *'41*
Outlaws of the Desert *'41*
Riders of the Timberline *'41*
Twilight on the Trail *'41*
Bad Lands *'39*
Red Lights Ahead *'36*
Yellow Dust *'36*
Annie Oakley *'35*
Village Tale *'35*
Ships in the Night *'28*

Jeremy Clyde (1944-)
The Musketeer *'01*
Kaspar Hauser *'93*
Splitting Heirs *'93*

June Clyde (1909-87)
Behind the Mask *'46*
Seven Doors to Death *'44*
Make-Up *'37*
She Shall Have Music *'36*
Hollywood Mystery *'34*
A Study in Scarlet *'33*
Wayne Murder Case *'32*
Branded Men *'31*
Morals for Women *'31*

Conrad Coates
Christmas Caper *'07*
Earthstorm *'06*

Kim Coates (1959-)
Prison Break: The Final Break *'09*
Hero Wanted *'08*
The Pledge *'08*
Alien Agent *'07*
Hearts of War *'07*
Skinwalkers *'07*
Grilled *'06*
Silent Hill *'06*
Assault on Precinct 13 *'05*
Hostage *'05*
The Island *'05*
Hollywood North *'03*
Open Range *'03*
Black Hawk Down *'01*
Pearl Harbor *'01*
Battlefield Earth *'00*
Beyond Suspicion *'00*
Full Disclosure *'00*
Killing Moon *'00*
Xchange *'00*
Carpool *'96*
Dead Silence *'96*
Lethal Tender *'96*
Unforgettable *'96*
Breach of Trust *'95*
The Outer Limits: Sandkings *'95*
Waterworld *'95*
Black Fox: Good Men and Bad *'94*
The Club *'94*
The Spider and the Fly *'94*
Innocent Blood *'92*
The Last Boy Scout *'91*
The Amityville Curse *'90*
Red Blooded American Girl *'90*
Smokescreen *'90*
Blind Fear *'89*
Cold Front *'89*

Phyllis Coates (1927-)
The Incredible Petrified World *'58*
Teenage Frankenstein *'58*
El Paso Stampede *'53*
Jungle Drums of Africa *'53*
Marshal of Cedar Rock *'53*
Invasion U.S.A. *'52*
Superman & the Mole Men *'51*
Blues Busters *'50*
The Joe McDoakes Collection *'42*

Edmund Cobb (1892-1974)
Tales of Terror *'62*
Guns of Fury *'49*
Far Frontier *'48*
Buffalo Bill Rides Again *'47*
Son of Zorro *'47*
Renegade Girl *'46*
Santa Fe Uprising *'46*
Sunset in El Dorado *'45*
Lawmen *'44*
Texas Kid *'43*
Tonto Basin Outlaws *'41*
Zorro's Fighting Legion *'39*
Wild Horse Rodeo *'37*
Darkest Africa *'36*
Lightnin' Bill Carson *'36*
Danger Trails *'35*
Riding Wild *'35*
Rustler's Paradise *'35*
Gunners & Guns *'34*
Gun Law *'33*
Wild Horse *'31*
The Man From Oklahoma *'26*
Riders of the Range *'24*

Irvin S. Cobb
Hawaii Calls *'38*
Steamboat Round the Bend *'35*

Lee J. Cobb (1911-76)
That Lucky Touch *'75*
The Exorcist *'73*
Man Who Loved Cat Dancing *'73*
Bull of the West *'71*
Lawman *'71*
The Liberation of L.B. Jones *'70*
Macho Callahan *'70*
MacKenna's Gold *'69*
Coogan's Bluff *'68*
In Like Flint *'67*
The Meanest Men in the West *'67*
Our Man Flint *'66*
Come Blow Your Horn *'63*
How the West Was Won *'63*
The Four Horsemen of the Apocalypse *'62*
Exodus *'60*
But Not for Me *'59*
Green Mansions *'59*
The Trap *'59*
The Brothers Karamazov *'58*
Man of the West *'58*
Party Girl *'58*
The Garment Jungle *'57*
The Three Faces of Eve *'57*
Twelve Angry Men *'57*
The Man in the Gray Flannel Suit *'56*
The Left Hand of God *'55*
The Racers *'55*
Day of Triumph *'54*
On the Waterfront *'54*
Tall Texan *'53*
The Fighter *'52*
Sirocco *'51*
The Dark Past *'49*
Call Northside 777 *'48*
The Luck of the Irish *'48*
The Miracle of the Bells *'48*
Boomerang *'47*
Captain from Castile *'47*
Anna and the King of Siam *'46*
Buckskin Frontier *'43*
The Song of Bernadette *'43*
Men of Boys Town *'41*
Golden Boy *'39*
Danger on the Air *'38*
Rustler's Valley *'37*

Randall "Tex" Cobb (1950-)
Liar Liar *'97*
Diggstown *'92*
Raw Nerve *'91*
Blind Fury *'90*
Ernest Goes to Jail *'90*
Buy & Cell *'89*
Fletch Lives *'89*
Raising Arizona *'87*
The Golden Child *'86*
Uncommon Valor *'83*

Bill Cobbs (1935-)
Get Low *'09*
The Morgue *'07*
Three Days to Vegas *'07*
The Ultimate Gift *'07*
Night at the Museum *'06*
The Derby Stallion *'05*
Enough *'02*
Sunshine State *'02*
Random Hearts *'99*
Always Outnumbered Always Outgunned *'98*
Hope Floats *'98*
I Still Know What You Did Last Summer *'98*
Paulie *'98*
Air Bud *'97*
Ed *'96*
First Kid *'96*
Ghosts of Mississippi *'96*
Nightjohn *'96*
That Thing You Do! *'96*
Fluke *'95*
Kingfish: A Story of Huey P. Long *'95*
Man with a Gun *'95*
Out There *'95*

Pocahontas *'95 (V)*
Things to Do in Denver When You're Dead *'95*
Demolition Man *'93*
The Hudsucker Proxy *'93*
The Bodyguard *'92*
Carolina Skeletons *'92*
Decoration Day *'90*
Dominick & Eugene *'88*
Trading Places *'83*

Roberto Cobo (1930-2002)

Santitos *'99*
Esmeralda Comes by Night *'98*
Cabeza de Vaca *'90*
Los Olvidados *'50*

German Cobos

Cria Cuervos *'76*
Hawk and Castile *'67*

Charles Coburn (1877-1961)

John Paul Jones *'59*
Around the World in 80 Days *'56*
Gentlemen Prefer Blondes *'53*
Trouble along the Way *'53*
Monkey Business *'52*
Mr. Music *'50*
Impact *'49*
Lured *'47*
The Paradine Case *'47*
Colonel Effingham's Raid *'45*
Rhapsody in Blue *'45*
Wilson *'44*
Heaven Can Wait *'43*
The More the Merrier *'43*
Princess O'Rourke *'43*
Together Again *'43*
George Washington Slept Here *'42*
In This Our Life *'42*
The Devil & Miss Jones *'41*
H.M. Pulham Esquire *'41*
Kings Row *'41*
The Lady Eve *'41*
Edison the Man *'40*
The Road to Singapore *'40*
Three Faces West *'40*
Bachelor Mother *'39*
Idiot's Delight *'39*
In Name Only *'39*
Made for Each Other *'39*
Stanley and Livingstone *'39*
The Story of Alexander Graham Bell *'39*
Of Human Hearts *'38*
Vivacious Lady *'38*

James Coburn (1928-2002)

American Gun *'02*
Snow Dogs *'02*
The Man from Elysian Fields *'01*
Monsters, Inc. *'01 (V)*
Walter and Henry *'01*
Missing Pieces *'00*
Proximity *'00*
Noah's Ark *'99*
Dean Koontz's Mr. Murder *'98*
Payback *'98*
Affliction *'97*
The Second Civil War *'97*
The Cherokee Kid *'96*
Eraser *'96*
Keys to Tulsa *'96*
The Nutty Professor *'96*
Skeletons *'96*
The Avenging Angel *'95*
The Disappearance of Kevin Johnson *'95*
The Set Up *'95*
Maverick *'94*
A Christmas Reunion *'93*
Deadfall *'93*
The Hit List *'93*
Sister Act 2: Back in the Habit *'93*
Hugh Hefner: Once Upon a Time *'92 (N)*
Mastergate *'92*
The Player *'92*
A Thousand Heroes *'92*
Hudson Hawk *'91*
Young Guns 2 *'90*
Death of a Soldier *'85*
Martin's Day *'85*
Pinocchio *'83*
Crossover *'82*
Draw! *'81*
High Risk *'81*
Looker *'81*
The Baltimore Bullet *'80*
Loving Couples *'80*
Firepower *'79*
Goldengirl *'79*
The Muppet Movie *'79*
The Dain Curse *'78*
Cross of Iron *'76*
The Last Hard Men *'76*
Midway *'76*
Sky Riders *'76*
Bite the Bullet *'75*
Hard Times *'75*
Internecine Project *'73*
The Last of Sheila *'73*
Pat Garrett & Billy the Kid *'73*
A Reason to Live, a Reason to Die *'73*
A Fistful of Dynamite *'72*
Candy *'68*
In Like Flint *'67*
The President's Analyst *'67*
Waterhole Number 3 *'67*
Dead Heat on a Merry-Go-Round *'66*
Our Man Flint *'66*
What Did You Do in the War, Daddy? *'66*
The Loved One *'65*
Major Dundee *'65*
The Americanization of Emily *'64*
Charade *'63*
The Great Escape *'63*
Man From Galveston *'63*
Hell Is for Heroes *'62*
The Magnificent Seven *'60*
Ride Lonesome *'59*

Michael Coby (1943-)

The Bitch *'78*
Supersonic Man *'78*

Imogene Coca (1908-2001)

Alice in Wonderland *'85*
National Lampoon's Vacation *'83*
The Return of the Beverly Hillbillies *'81*
Rabbit Test *'78*
Under the Yum-Yum Tree *'63*

Richard Coca

The Truth about Cats and Dogs *'96*
Street Knight *'93*

Eddie Cochran (1938-60)

Go, Johnny Go! *'59*
Untamed Youth *'57*
The Girl Can't Help It *'56*

Robert Cochran

Mr. Reeder in Room 13 *'38*
I Stand Condemned *'36*
Sanders of the River *'35*
Scrooge *'35*

Shannon Cochran (1958-)

The Ring *'02*
Star Trek: Nemesis *'02*

Steve Cochran (1917-65)

Deadly Companions *'61*
I, Mobster *'58*
Il Grido *'57*
Carnival Story *'54*
Private Hell 36 *'54*
The Desert Song *'53*
Shark River *'53*
Jim Thorpe: All American *'51*
Storm Warning *'51*
The Damned Don't Cry *'50*
White Heat *'49*
A Song Is Born *'48*
Copacabana *'47*
The Best Years of Our Lives *'46*
The Chase *'46*
Wonder Man *'45*

Michael Cochrane

Sharpe's Challenge *'06*
A Different Loyalty *'04*
Incognito *'97*
Sharpe's Regiment *'96*
Sharpe's Eagle *'93*

Rory Cochrane (1972-)

Public Enemies *'09*
The Company *'07*
Right at Your Door *'06*
A Scanner Darkly *'06*
Hart's War *'02*
The Prime Gig *'00*
Black & White *'99*
Flawless *'99*
Sunset Strip *'99*
Dogtown *'97*
The Last Don *'97*
Empire Records *'95*
The Low Life *'95*
Love and a .45 *'94*
Dazed and Confused *'93*
Fathers and Sons *'92*

Arlene Cockburn

The Acid House *'98*
The Governess *'98*
The Winter Guest *'97*

Gary Cockrell

Lolita *'62*
War Lover *'62*

James Coco (1929-87)

That's Adequate *'90*
The Chair *'87*
Hunk *'87*
The Muppets Take Manhattan *'84*
You Can't Take It with You *'84*
Only When I Laugh *'81*
Wholly Moses! *'80*
Scavenger Hunt *'79*
The Cheap Detective *'78*
Murder by Death *'76*
Wild Party *'74*
Man of La Mancha *'72*
A New Leaf *'71*
End of the Road *'70*
The Strawberry Statement *'70*
Generation *'69*
Ensign Pulver *'64*

Jean Cocteau (1889-1963)

The Testament of Orpheus *'59*
The Storm Within *'48 (N)*

Camille Coduri (1966-)

King Ralph *'91*
Nuns on the Run *'90*
Strapless *'90*
Hawks *'89*

Bill Cody (1891-1948)

Outlaws of the Range *'36*
Frontier Days *'34*
Ghost City *'32*
Mason of the Mounted *'32*
Texas Pioneers *'32*

Iron Eyes Cody (1904-99)

Spirit of '76 *'91*
Ernest Goes to Camp *'87*
Grayeagle *'77*
The Longest Drive *'76*
El Condor *'70*
Sitting Bull *'54*
Son of Paleface *'52*
Bowery Buckaroos *'47*
Under Nevada Skies *'46*
King of the Stallions *'42*
Texas Pioneers *'32*
Whistlin' Dan *'32*
The Road to Yesterday *'25*

Kathleen (Kathy) Cody (1953-)

Charley and the Angel *'73*
Girls on the Road *'73*
Superdad *'73*

Lew Cody (1884-1934)

The Crusader *'32*
Dishonored *'31*
Souls for Sale *'23*
Mickey *'17*

Barry Coe (1934-)

The Oval Portrait *'88*
Dr. Death, Seeker of Souls *'73*
The Cat *'66*
Fantastic Voyage *'66*
The 300 Spartans *'62*
But Not for Me *'59*
The Bravados *'58*
Peyton Place *'57*
Love Me Tender *'56*
House of Bamboo *'55*

David Allan Coe (1939-)

Lady Grey *'82*
Take This Job & Shove It *'81*

George Coe

Corporate Affairs *'07*
Diamond Men *'01*
Big Eden *'00*
The Omega Code *'99*
Nick and Jane *'96*
The End of Innocence *'90*
The Hollywood Detective *'89*
Best Seller *'87*
Blind Date *'87*
Uncle Tom's Cabin *'87*
A Flash of Green *'85*
Remo Williams: The Adventure Begins *'85*
Rage of Angels *'83*
Sessions *'83*
Bustin' Loose *'81*
Red Flag: The Ultimate Game *'81*

Peter Coe (1918-93)

Hellgate *'52*
Sands of Iwo Jima *'49*
House of Frankenstein *'44*
The Mummy's Curse *'44*

Paul Coeur

White Fang 2: The Myth of the White Wolf *'94*
Cool Runnings *'93*

Colleen T. Coffey

Indecent Behavior 3 *'95*
The Mosaic Project *'95*
Relentless 4 *'94*

David Coffey

Lawless Heart *'01*
Boyfriends *'96*

Denise Coffey (1936-)

Start the Revolution without Me *'70*
Georgy Girl *'66*

Elizabeth Coffey

Female Trouble *'74*
Pink Flamingos *'72*

Scott Coffey (1967-)

Inland Empire *'06 (V)*
Ellie Parker *'05*
Mulholland Drive *'01*
Route 9 *'98*
Lost Highway *'96*
Breaking Free *'95*
Tank Girl *'94*
Dream Lover *'93*
The Temp *'93*
Shout *'91*
Montana *'90*
Shag: The Movie *'89*
Satisfaction *'88*
Zombie High *'87*

Peter Coffield (1945-83)

Times Square *'80*
The Man Without a Country *'73*

Frederick Coffin (1943-2003)

Identity *'03*
The Base *'99*
Andersonville *'95*
A Streetcar Named Desire *'95*
There Goes My Baby *'92*
Hard to Kill *'89*
Shoot to Kill *'88*
The Bedroom Window *'87*
Manhunt for Claude Dallas *'86*
One Summer Love *'76*

Tristram Coffin (1909-90)

Good Neighbor Sam *'64*
Ma Barker's Killer Brood *'60*
Queen for a Day *'51*
Rodeo King and the Senorita *'51*
Pirates of the High Seas *'50*
King of the Rocketmen *'49*
Lost Planet Airmen *'49*
Jesse James Rides Again *'47*
Land of the Lawless *'47*
Where the North Begins *'47*
Under Nevada Skies *'46*
The Corpse Vanishes *'42*
Holt of the Secret Service *'42*
Meet the Mob *'42*
Spy Smasher *'42*
Spy Smasher Returns *'42*
Tonto Basin Outlaws *'41*
Up in the Air *'40*
West of Pinto Basin *'40*

Henri Cogan (1914-2003)

As If It Were Raining *'63*
It Means That to Me *'60*

Nikki Coghill (1964-)

Dark Age *'88*
The Time Guardian *'87*

Frank "Junior" Coghlan (1917-)

The Adventures of Captain Marvel *'41*
The Fighting 69th *'40*
Little Red Schoolhouse *'36*
Red Lights Ahead *'36*
Kentucky Blue Streak *'35*
In the Money *'34*
Drum Taps *'33*
Hell's House *'32*
The Last of the Mohicans *'32*
Square Shoulders *'29*
Let 'er Go Gallegher *'28*
Marked Money *'28*
Yankee Clipper *'27*

Alain Cohen (1958-)

Happily Ever After *'04*
The Two of Us *'68*

Ari Cohen

The Tracey Fragments *'07*
Category 6 : Day of Destruction *'04*

Assi Cohen (1974-)

Colombian Love *'04*
Bonjour Monsieur Shlomi *'03*
Yossi & Jagger *'02*

Emma Cohen (1946-)

Spaghetti Western *'75*
Bronson's Revenge *'72*
Horror Rises from the Tomb *'72*
Cannibal Man *'71*

Gilles Cohen

A Prophet *'09*
The Girl From Monaco *'08*
The Beat My Heart Skipped *'05*

J.J. (Jeffrey Jay) Cohen (1965-)

Back to the Future, Part 3 *'90*
Back to the Future, Part 2 *'89*
976-EVIL *'88*
The Principal *'87*
Back to the Future *'85*

Kaipo Cohen (1978-)

Under the Domim Tree *'95*
The Summer of Aviya *'88*

Lynn Cohen

Eagle Eye *'08*
Sex and the City: The Movie *'08*
Then She Found Me *'07*
Munich *'05*
The Jimmy Show *'01*
Hurricane Streets *'96*
I Shot Andy Warhol *'96*
Walking and Talking *'96*
Vanya on 42nd Street *'94*
Manhattan Murder Mystery *'93*

Michael Cohen (1970-)

Shall We Kiss? *'07*

Oshri Cohen

Lebanon *'09*
Beaufort *'07*
Bonjour Monsieur Shlomi *'03*

Sacha Baron Cohen (1971-)

Bruno *'09*
Madagascar: Escape 2 Africa *'08 (V)*
Sweeney Todd: The Demon Barber of Fleet Street *'07*
Borat: Cultural Learnings of America for Make Benefit Glorious Nation of Kazakhstan *'06*
Talladega Nights: The Ballad of Ricky Bobby *'06*
Madagascar *'05 (V)*
The Jolly Boys' Last Stand *'00*

Sammy Cohen (1902-81)

The Fighting 69th *'40*
The Phantom of the Range *'38*

Scott Cohen (1964-)

Moonlight Serenade *'09*
Winter of Frozen Dreams *'08*
For One More Day *'07*
Fatal Contact: Bird Flu in America *'06*
Knots *'05*
Kissing Jessica Stein *'02*
Perfect Murder, Perfect Town *'00*
The 10th Kingdom *'00*
Gia *'98*
Gotti *'96*
Sweet Evil *'95*
The Wharf Rat *'95*
Vibrations *'94*

Mindy Cohn

Sex and Death 101 *'07*
Alone with a Stranger *'99*

Lucy Cohu

Ballet Shoes *'07*
The Queen's Sister *'05*

Helen Coker

Vera Drake *'04*
All or Nothing *'02*

Enrico Colantoni (1963-)

Celine *'08*
My Mom's New Boyfriend *'08*
Sherman's Way *'08*
The First $20 Million is Always the Hardest *'02*
Full Frontal *'02*
A. I.: Artificial Intelligence *'01*
James Dean *'01*
Galaxy Quest *'99*
Stigmata *'99*
The Member of the Wedding *'97*
The Wrong Guy *'96*
Money Train *'95*

Nicholas Colasanto (1924-85)

Raging Bull *'80*
Mad Bull *'77*
Family Plot *'76*
Fat City *'72*

Catero Colbert

Zombie Strippers *'08*
Up Against the Wall *'91*
Sweet Perfection *'90*

Sunshine Cleaning '09
Little Chenier: A Cajun Story '06
Capote '05
Dirty '05
Life of the Party '05
Mindhunters '05
Rampage: The Hillside Strangler Murders '04
I Witness '03
Undefeated '03
The Rules of Attraction '02
The Last Castle '01
Price of Glory '00
Tigerland '00
Traffic '00
Light It Up '99
The Replacement Killers '98
The Wonderful Ice Cream Suit '98
187 '97

Cora Sue Collins (1927-)
The World Accuses '35
Evelyn Prentice '34
The Scarlet Letter '34

Dean Collins (1990-)
Hoot '06
Yours, Mine & Ours '05

Eddie Collins (1884-1940)
The Blue Bird '40
Drums Along the Mohawk '39
Young Mr. Lincoln '39
Charlie Chan in Honolulu '38

G. Pat Collins (1895-1959)
Above and Beyond '53
All Quiet on the Western Front '30
Be Yourself '30

Gary Collins (1938-)
Beautiful '00
Watchers Reborn '98
Hangar 18 '80
Airport '70

Greg Collins
Operation Delta Force 3: Clear Target '98
U.S. Seals '98

Jessica Collins (1971-)
The Loss of a Teardrop Diamond '08
Dirty Love '05
Best of the Best: Without Warning '98

Joan Collins (1933-)
These Old Broads '01
The Flintstones in Viva Rock Vegas '00
Joseph and the Amazing Technicolor Dreamcoat '00
Annie: A Royal Adventure '95
A Midwinter's Tale '95
Game for Vultures '86
Monte Carlo '86
Sins '85
Cartier Affair '84
Nutcracker Sweet '84
Her Life as a Man '83
Hansel and Gretel '82
Homework '82
Sunburn '79
The Big Sleep '78
The Bitch '78
The Stud '78
Zero to Sixty '78
Empire of the Ants '77
Fearless '77
The Bawdy Adventures of Tom Jones '76
Great Adventure '75
I Don't Want to Be Born '75
Oh, Alfie '75
Dark Places '73
Tales That Witness Madness '73
Dynasty of Fear '72
Tales from the Crypt '72
Quest for Love '71
Revenge '71
The Executioner '70
Three in the Cellar '70
Subterfuge '68
The Road to Hong Kong '62
Esther and the King '60
Seven Thieves '60
The Bravados '58
Rally 'Round the Flag, Boys! '58
Sea Wife '57
Stopover Tokyo '57
The Opposite Sex '56
The Adventures of Sadie '55
The Girl in the Red Velvet Swing '55
Land of the Pharaohs '55
The Virgin Queen '55
Decameron Nights '53
Tough Guy '53
Cosh Boy '52

Joely Collins
Almost Heaven '06
Diamond Girl '98

Judy Collins (1939-)
A Town Has Turned to Dust '98
Junior '94

Karley Scott Collins (1999-)
The Collector '09
Pulse 2: Afterlife '08

K.C. Collins
Animal 2 '07
Poor Man's Game '06

Kevin Collins
Edward II '92
The Garden '90

Lauren Collins
Picture This! '08
Take the Lead '06

Lewis Collins (1946-)
Jack the Ripper '88
Codename: Wildgeese '84
The Final Option '82

Lynn Collins (1979-)
X-Men Origins: Wolverine '09
Numb '07
The Number 23 '07
Towelhead '07
Bug '06
The Dog Problem '06
The Lake House '06
The Merchant of Venice '04

Misha Collins
Karla '06
Finding Home '03

Mo Collins
Danny Roane: First Time Director '06
Jiminy Glick in LaLa Wood '05

Monte (Monty) Collins (1856-1929)
King of Kings '27
Our Hospitality '23

Monte (Monty) Collins, Jr. (1898-1951)
House of Errors '42
Midnight Limited '40

Patricia Collins
Speaking Parts '89
Pin... '88
When Angels Fly '82
Summer's Children '79

Patrick Collins
Friends and Family '01
Dirt Bike Kid '86

Pauline Collins (1940-)
Paradise Road '97
My Mother's Courage '95
City of Joy '92
Shirley Valentine '89

Phil Collins (1951-)
The Jungle Book 2 '03 (V)
Balto '95 (V)
And the Band Played On '93
Frauds '93
Hook '91
Buster '88
Secret Policeman's Private Parts '81

Ray Collins (1889-1965)
Touch of Evil '58
Solid Gold Cadillac '56
Desperate Hours '55
The Go-Getter '54
The Desert Song '53
Ma and Pa Kettle on Vacation '53
I Want You '51
Invitation '51
Ma and Pa Kettle Back On the Farm '51
The Racket '51
Kill the Umpire '50
Ma and Pa Kettle Go to Town '50
Summer Stock '50
The Fountainhead '49
Francis the Talking Mule '49
The Heiress '49
It Happens Every Spring '49
Man from Colorado '49
Command Decision '48
For the Love of Mary '48
Good Sam '48
Homecoming '48
The Bachelor and the Bobby-Soxer '47
A Double Life '47
The Best Years of Our Lives '46
Crack-Up '46
Can't Help Singing '45
Leave Her to Heaven '45
The Seventh Cross '44
Commandos Strike at Dawn '43
The Human Comedy '43
Whistling in Brooklyn '43
The Magnificent Ambersons '42
The Navy Comes Through '42
Citizen Kane '41

Rick Collins
The Toxic Avenger, Part 2 '89
The Toxic Avenger, Part 3: The Last Temptation of Toxie '89

Roberta Collins (1946-)
Hardbodies '84
Whiskey Mountain '77
Eaten Alive '76
Death Race 2000 '75
Caged Heat '74
The Deadly and the Beautiful '73
Unholy Rollers '72
The Big Doll House '71
The Arousers '70

Russell Collins (1897-1965)
The Matchmaker '58
Enemy Below '57
Savage Wilderness '55
Soldier of Fortune '55
Niagara '52
Shockproof '49

Ruth (Coreen) Collins
Dead Boyz Can't Fly '93
Wildest Dreams '90
Cemetery High '89
Death Collector '89
Doom Asylum '88
Exquisite Corpses '88
Sexpot '88
Galactic Gigolo '87
New York's Finest '87

Shanna Collins
The Haunting of Molly Hartley '08
On the Doll '07
Sublime '07

Stephen Collins (1947-)
Every Second Counts '08
Because I Said So '07
Blood Diamond '06
Drive Me Crazy '99
An Unexpected Life '97
The First Wives Club '96
An Unexpected Family '96
Scarlett '94
High Stakes '93
My New Gun '92
Till Murder Do Us Part '92
A Woman Named Jackie '91
The Big Picture '89
Stella '89
Weekend War '88
Choke Canyon '86
Hold the Dream '86
Jumpin' Jack Flash '86
Brewster's Millions '85
Chiefs '83
Inside the Third Reich '82
Summer Solstice '81
The Henderson Monster '80
Loving Couples '80
The Promise '79
Star Trek: The Motion Picture '79
Between the Lines '77
All the President's Men '76

Wayne Collins
Way Past Cool '00
Bebe's Kids '92 (V)

Madeleine Collinson (1952-)
The Love Machine '71
Twins of Evil '71
The Seducer '69

Mary Collinson (1952-)
The Love Machine '71
Twins of Evil '71
The Seducer '69

Frank Collison (1950-)
The Happening '08
Hidalgo '04
The Village '04
The Whole Ten Yards '04
O Brother Where Art Thou? '00
Dollman '90
Wired to Kill '86

Silvia Colloca (1977-)
Vampire Killers '09
The Detonator '06
Van Helsing '04

Roy Collodi
She-Devils on Wheels '68
Something Weird '68
The Girl, the Body and the Pill '67

Mark Collver
Bix '90
There's Nothing out There '90

June Collyer (1907-68)
A Face in the Fog '36
The Ghost Walks '34
Drums of Jeopardy '31
Four Sons '28
Hangman's House '28

Pamela Collyer
The Kiss '88
Evil Judgment '85

Olivia Colman (1974-)
Hot Fuzz '07
Confetti '06

Ronald Colman (1891-1958)
Around the World in 80 Days '56
Champagne for Caesar '50
A Double Life '47
Random Harvest '42
Talk of the Town '42
Lucky Partners '40
If I Were King '38
Lost Horizon '37
Prisoner of Zenda '37
A Tale of Two Cities '36
Arrowsmith '32
Raffles '30
Bulldog Drummond '29
Condemned '29
The Winning of Barbara Worth '26
Lady Windermere's Fan '25
Romola '25
The White Sister '23

Scott Colomby (1952-)
Porky's Revenge '85
Porky's 2: The Next Day '83
Porky's '82
Caddyshack '80
Are You in the House Alone? '78

Alex Colon (1941-95)
Death of an Angel '86
Invasion U.S.A. '85

Miriam Colon (1945-)
The Cry: La Llorona '07
Goal 2: Living the Dream '07
Goal! The Dream Begins '06
All the Pretty Horses '00
Lone Star '95
Sabrina '95
The House of the Spirits '93
A Life of Sin '92

Jerry Colonna (1904-86)
Meet Me in Las Vegas '56
Alice in Wonderland '51 (V)
Kentucky Jubilee '51
Strictly G.I. '44
The Road to Singapore '40
Rosalie '38

Clara Colosimo (1922-94)
Orchestra Rehearsal '78
Alfredo, Alfredo '72

Vince Colosimo (1966-)
Daybreakers '09
Body of Lies '08
Solo '06
After the Deluge '03
The Hard Word '02
Walking on Water '02
Lantana '01
Chopper '00
Street Hero '84
Moving Out '83

Louisa Colpeyn (1918-)
Marry Me, Marry Me '69
Band of Outsiders '64

Marshall Colt (1948-)
To Heal a Nation '88
Guilty of Innocence '87
Beverly Hills Madam '86
The Jagged Edge '85

Mike Colter (1976-)
Million Dollar Baby '04
The Dreamers '03

Jacque Lynn Colton (1939-)
Heartbreak Hotel '88
Big Bad Mama 2 '87

Robbie Coltrane (1950-)
The Brothers Bloom '09
Harry Potter and the Half-Blood Prince '09
The Tale of Despereaux '08 (V)
Harry Potter and the Order of the Phoenix '07
Alex Rider: Operation Stormbreaker '06
Harry Potter and the Goblet of Fire '05
Harry Potter and the Prisoner of Azkaban '04
Ocean's Twelve '04
Van Helsing '04
Harry Potter and the Chamber of Secrets '02
From Hell '01
Harry Potter and the Sorcerer's Stone '01
Alice in Wonderland '99
The World Is Not Enough '99
Frogs for Snakes '98
Message in a Bottle '98
Buddy '97
The Ebb-Tide '97
Montana '97
Cracker: Best Boys '95
Cracker: Brotherly Love '95
Cracker: True Romance '95
Goldeneye '95
Cracker: Men Should Weep '94
Cracker: The Big Crunch '94
Cracker: To Be a Somebody '94
The Adventures of Huck Finn '93
Oh, What a Night '92
Perfectly Normal '91
The Pope Must Diet '91
Nuns on the Run '90
Where the Heart Is '90
Bert Rigby, You're a Fool '89
Henry V '89
Let It Ride '89
Slipstream '89
Wonderland '88
Loose Connections '87
Caravaggio '86
Mona Lisa '86
Defense of the Realm '85
National Lampoon's European Vacation '85
Chinese Boxes '84

Coluche (1944-86)
My Best Friend's Girl '84
Tchao Pantin' '84

Franco (Columbo) Columbu (1941-)
Taken Alive '95
Desperate Crimes '93
Beretta's Island '92
Circle Man '87
Last Man Standing '87

Catherine Colvey
Levity '03
Captive '97

Peter Colvey
Dead Silent '99
Silent Hunter '94

Pinto Colvig (1892-1967)
Sleeping Beauty '59 (V)
Snow White and the Seven Dwarfs '37 (V)

Jack Colvin (1934-2005)
Child's Play '88
The Incredible Hulk Returns '88
The Incredible Hulk '77

Michael Colyar
House Party 3 '94
Hot Shots! Part Deux '93

Roger Coma
To Die (Or Not) '99
Caresses '97

Richard Comar
Ebenezer '97
Kickboxer 3: The Art of War '92

Muriel Combeau
Near Misses '91
Mama, There's a Man in Your Bed '89

Holly Marie Combs (1973-)
Ocean's Eleven '01
Our Mother's Murder '97
Chain of Desire '93
Dr. Giggles '92
Simple Men '92
Born on the Fourth of July '89
Sweet Hearts Dance '88

Jeffrey Combs (1954-)
Return to House on Haunted Hill '07
The Wizard of Gore '07
All Souls Day '05
Edmond '05
Voodoo Moon '05
Beyond Re-Animator '03
Feardotcom '02
Faust: Love of the Damned '00

Skinheads: The Second Coming of Hate *'88*
Trained to Kill *'88*
Terror Squad *'87*
Summer Camp Nightmare *'86*
The Vals *'85*
Target Eagle *'84*
Airplane 2: The Sequel *'82*
Balboa *'82*
The Capture of Grizzly Adams *'82*
Virus *'82*
Day of the Assassin *'81*
Bordello *'79*
Tourist Trap *'79*
Roots *'77*
Nightmare in Badham County *'76*
The Legend of Sea Wolf *'75*
99 & 44/100 Dead *'74*
Soylent Green *'73*
Embassy *'72*
The Mad Bomber *'72*
Pancho Villa *'72*
The Proud and the Damned *'72*
Ride to Glory *'71*
Captain Nemo and the Underwater City *'69*
Flipper *'63*
Move Over, Darling *'63*
Geronimo *'62*
The Big Country *'58*
Designing Woman *'57*
Old Yeller *'57*
Hot Rod Girl *'56*
South Sea Woman *'53*
Pat and Mike *'52*

Mike Connors (1925-)

Gideon *'99*
James Dean: Live Fast, Die Young *'97*
Fist Fighter *'88*
Too Scared to Scream *'85*
Casino *'80*
Nightkill *'80*
Avalanche Express *'79*
Long Journey Back *'78*
Harlow *'65*
Good Neighbor Sam *'64*
Panic Button *'62*
Flesh and the Spur *'57*
Shake, Rattle and Rock *'57*
Voodoo Woman *'57*
Jaguar *'56*
Day the World Ended *'55*
Swamp Women *'55*
Island in the Sky *'53*
Sudden Fear *'52*

Chris Conrad (1971-)

The Promotion *'08*
Young Hercules *'97*
Airborne *'93*

David Conrad (1967-)

Wedding Crashers *'05*
Anything Else *'03*
Men of Honor *'00*
The Weekend *'00*
A Season for Miracles *'99*
Return to Paradise *'98*
The Wizard of Speed and Time *'88*

Michael Conrad (1925-83)

Bordello *'79*
The Longest Yard *'74*
Scream Blacula Scream *'73*
Gone with the West *'72*
Thumb Tripping *'72*
Castle Keep *'69*
They Shoot Horses, Don't They? *'69*
Blackbeard's Ghost *'67*
The War Lord *'65*

Mikel Conrad (1919-82)

The Flying Saucer *'50*
Abbott and Costello Meet the Killer, Boris Karloff *'49*
Check Your Guns *'48*

Robert Conrad (1935-)

Jingle All the Way *'96*
Samurai Cowboy *'93*
Assassin *'86*
Two Fathers' Justice *'85*
Hard Knox *'83*
Will: G. Gordon Liddy *'82*
Wrong Is Right *'82*
More Wild, Wild West *'80*
Breaking Up Is Hard to Do *'79*
Lady in Red *'79*
Wild, Wild West Revisited *'79*
Centennial *'78*
Sudden Death *'77*
Murph the Surf *'75*
The Bandits *'67*
Palm Springs Weekend *'63*
The Commies Are Coming, the Commies Are Coming *'57*

William Conrad (1920-94)

Vengeance *'89*
Blitz *'85*
Return of Frank Cannon *'80*
The Return of the King *'80 (V)*
The Rebels *'79 (N)*
Night Cries *'78*
Moonshine County Express *'77*
The Ride Back *'57*
Zero Hour! *'57 (N)*
The Conqueror *'56*
5 Against the House *'55*
Naked Jungle *'54*
The Desert Song *'53*
Cry Danger *'51*
The Racket *'51*
Tension *'50*
Body and Soul *'47*
The Killers *'46*

Hans Conried (1917-82)

Tut & Tuttle *'81*
Oh, God! Book 2 *'80*
The Hobbit *'78 (V)*
Brothers O'Toole *'73*
Phantom Tollbooth *'69 (V)*
The Patsy *'64*
Robin and the 7 Hoods *'64*
1001 Arabian Nights *'59 (V)*
Jet Pilot *'57*
The Monster That Challenged the World *'57*
Rock-A-Bye Baby *'57*
Birds & the Bees *'56*
Bus Stop *'56*
Davy Crockett, King of the Wild Frontier *'55*
The Affairs of Dobie Gillis *'53*
The 5000 Fingers of Dr. T *'53*
Peter Pan *'53 (V)*
Behave Yourself! *'52*
Three for Bedroom C *'52*
The World in His Arms *'52*
Rich, Young and Pretty *'51*
Nancy Goes to Rio *'50*
Summer Stock *'50*
My Friend Irma *'49*
The Senator Was Indiscreet *'47*
His Butler's Sister *'44*
Hitler's Children *'43*
Blondie's Blessed Event *'42*
Underground Agent *'42*

Frances Conroy (1953-)

New in Town *'09*
Humboldt County *'08*
The Tale of Despereaux *'08 (V)*
The Seeker: The Dark Is Rising *'07*
Ira & Abby *'06*
A Perfect Day *'06*
The Wicker Man *'06*
Broken Flowers *'05*
Shopgirl *'05*
The Aviator *'04*
Catwoman *'04*
Die Mommie Die! *'03*
Maid in Manhattan *'02*
Murder in a Small Town *'99*
The Crucible *'96*
The Neon Bible *'95*
The Adventures of Huck Finn *'93*
Scent of a Woman *'92*
Another Woman *'88*
Rocket Gibraltar *'88*

Frank Conroy (1890-1964)

The Bramble Bush *'60*
The Day the Earth Stood Still *'51*
All My Sons *'48*
Crash Dive *'43*
The Ox-Bow Incident *'43*
I Live My Life *'35*
The Cat and the Fiddle *'34*
Manhattan Melodrama *'34*
Ace of Aces *'33*
Midnight Mary *'33*

Kevin Conroy (1955-)

Batman: Mask of the Phantasm *'93 (V)*
Chain of Desire *'93*
The Secret Passion of Robert Clayton *'92*
Kennedy *'83*

Neili Conroy

Bloom *'03*
The Van *'95*
Family *'94*

Ruaidhri Conroy (1979-)

Deathwatch *'02*
When the Sky Falls *'99*
Moondance *'95*
Nothing Personal *'95*
The Van *'95*
Into the West *'92*

Charlotte Considine

See Charlotte Stewart

John Considine (1938-)

Gia *'98*
Tinseltown *'97*
Breathing Lessons *'94*
Opposing Force *'87*
Trouble in Mind *'86*
Dixie: Changing Habits *'85*
Choose Me *'84*
Circle of Power *'83*
Rita Hayworth: The Love Goddess *'83*
Endangered Species *'82*
Forbidden Love *'82*
The Shadow Box *'80*
See How She Runs *'78*
A Wedding *'78*
The Late Show *'77*
Welcome to L.A. *'77*
The Thirsty Dead *'74*
Dr. Death, Seeker of Souls *'73*
Reunion in France *'42*

Paddy Considine (1974-)

My Zinc Bed *'08*
The Bourne Ultimatum *'07*
Hot Fuzz *'07*
The Backwoods *'06*
PU-239 *'06*
Cinderella Man *'05*
My Summer of Love *'05*
Stoned *'05*
Dead Man's Shoes *'04*
Close Your Eyes *'02*
In America *'02*
24 Hour Party People *'01*
Born Romantic *'00*

Tim Considine (1940-)

Daring Dobermans *'73*
Patton *'70*
Sunrise at Campobello *'60*
The Shaggy Dog *'59*
The Private War of Major Benson *'55*
Clown *'53*

Anne Consigny

A Christmas Tale *'08*
The Diving Bell and the Butterfly *'07*

Michel Constantin (1924-2003)

Beyond Fear *'75*
La Scoumoune *'72*
The Family *'70*
A Very Curious Girl *'69*
Le Deuxieme Souffle *'66*
Le Trou *'59*

Eddie Constantine (1917-93)

Zentropa *'92*
The Long Good Friday *'80*
It's Alive 2: It Lives Again *'78*
Beware of a Holy Whore *'70*
Attack of the Robots *'66*
Alphaville *'65*
Hail Mafia *'65*
Make Your Bets Ladies *'65*
License to Kill *'64*
As If It Were Raining *'63*
Your Turn Darling *'63*
Ladies' Man *'62*
Cleo from 5 to 7 *'61*
Keep Talking Baby *'61*
It Means That to Me *'60*
S.O.S. Pacific *'60*
Room 43 *'58*
Dishonorable Discharge *'57*
There Goes Barder *'54*

Michael Constantine (1927-)

My Big Fat Greek Wedding *'02*
Winds of Terror *'01*
The Juror *'96*
Stephen King's Thinner *'96*
My Life *'93*
Question of Faith *'93*
Prancer *'89*
In the Mood *'87*
Forty Days of Musa Dagh *'85*
Silent Rebellion *'82*
Fear in the City *'81*
The North Avenue Irregulars *'79*
Billy: Portrait of a Street Kid *'77*
Voyage of the Damned *'76*
Conspiracy of Terror *'75*
Death Cruise *'74*
Killing in the Sun *'73*
Say Goodbye, Maggie Cole *'72*
Dirty Heroes *'71*
Don't Drink the Water *'69*
If It's Tuesday, This Must Be Belgium *'69*
Justine *'69*
The Reivers *'69*
The Hustler *'61*

Mark Consuelos (1971-)

My Super Ex-Girlfriend *'06*
Wedding Daze *'06*

John Conte (1915-2006)

Trauma *'62*
The Man with the Golden Arm *'55*
Lost in a Harem *'44*

Richard Conte (1914-75)

The Godfather 1902-1959: The Complete Epic *'81*
Violent Professionals *'73*
The Godfather *'72*
1931: Once Upon a Time in New York *'72*
Explosion *'69*
Operation Cross Eagles *'69*
Lady in Cement *'68*
Hotel *'67*
Tony Rome *'67*
Assault on a Queen *'66*
Circus World *'64*
Ocean's 11 *'60*
They Came to Cordura *'59*
The Brothers Rico *'57*
Full of Life *'56*
Big Combo *'55*
I'll Cry Tomorrow *'55*
Race for Life *'55*
The Blue Gardenia *'53*
The Fighter *'52*
House of Strangers *'49*
Whirlpool *'49*
Call Northside 777 *'48*
Somewhere in the Night *'46*
13 Rue Madeleine *'46*
A Walk in the Sun *'46*
The Purple Heart *'44*
Guadalcanal Diary *'43*

Steve Conte (1920-97)

The Wild World of Batwoman *'66*
Attack of the Mayan Mummy *'63*
Terror of the Bloodhunters *'62*

Albert Conti (1887-1967)

The Black Cat *'34*
State's Attorney *'31*

Tom Conti (1941-)

O Jerusalem *'07*
Almost Heaven *'06*
Paid *'06*
Derailed *'05*
The Enemy *'01*
Sub Down *'97*
Someone Else's America *'96*
That Summer of White Roses *'90*
Shirley Valentine *'89*
Deep Cover *'88*
Dumb Waiter *'87*
The Gospel According to Vic *'87*
The Quick and the Dead *'87*
Beyond Therapy *'86*
Miracles *'86*
Saving Grace *'86*
American Dreamer *'84*
Merry Christmas, Mr. Lawrence *'83*
The Princess and the Pea *'83*
Reuben, Reuben *'83*
The Norman Conquests, Part 1: Table Manners *'78*
The Norman Conquests, Part 2: Living Together *'78*
The Norman Conquests, Part 3: Round and Round the Garden *'78*
The Duellists *'77*
Full Circle *'77*
If It's a Man, Hang Up *'75*

Ugo Conti (1955-)

Children of Hannibal *'98*
Mediterraneo *'91*

Chantal Contouri (1949-)

Goodbye, Miss 4th of July *'88*
The Night After Halloween *'79*
Thirst *'79*
Alvin Rides Again *'74*

Patricio Contreras (1947-)

Of Love and Shadows *'94*
Old Gringo *'89*
The Official Story *'85*

Frank Converse (1938-)

Our Town *'03*
Brother Future *'91*
Tales of the Unexpected *'91*
Everybody Wins *'90*
Home at Last *'88*
Alone in the Neon Jungle *'87*
Anne of Avonlea *'87*
Uncle Tom's Cabin *'87*
Spring Fever *'81*
The Bushido Blade *'80*
Marilyn: The Untold Story *'80*
Danger in the Skies *'79*
Cruise into Terror *'78*
Sergeant Matlovich vs. the U.S. Air Force *'78*
Killer on Board *'77*
The Tattered Web *'71*

William Converse-Roberts

Bandits *'01*
Crazy in Alabama *'99*
Drive Me Crazy *'99*
Kiss the Girls *'97*
Serving in Silence: The Margarethe Cammermeyer Story *'95*
Courtship *'87*
The Fig Tree *'87*
On Valentine's Day *'86*
1918 *'85*

Bert Convy (1933-91)

Help Wanted: Male *'82*
Cannonball Run *'81*
Hero at Large *'80*
The Man in the Santa Claus Suit *'79*
Racquet *'79*
Jennifer *'78*
Semi-Tough *'77*
The Love Bug *'68*
Susan Slade *'61*
A Bucket of Blood *'59*
Gunman's Walk *'58*

Dan Conway

Things Change *'88*
Blast-Off Girls *'67*

Gary Conway (1936-)

Liberty & Bash *'90*
American Ninja 2: The Confrontation *'87*
Black Gunn *'72*
How to Make a Monster *'58*
Teenage Frankenstein *'58*

Kevin Conway (1942-)

The Bronx Is Burning *'07*
Invincible *'06*
Gods and Generals *'03*
Black Knight *'01*
Thirteen Days *'00*
Two Family House *'99*
The Confession *'98*
Mercury Rising *'98*
Calm at Sunset *'96*
Looking for Richard *'96*
Larry McMurtry's Streets of Laredo *'95*
Lawnmower Man 2: Beyond Cyberspace *'95*
Prince Brat and the Whipping Boy *'95*
The Quick and the Dead *'95*
Gettysburg *'93*
Jennifer 8 *'92*
One Good Cop *'91*
Rambling Rose *'91*
Homeboy *'88*
Rage of Angels *'83*
The Funhouse *'81*
The Lathe of Heaven *'80*
The Scarlet Letter *'79*
F.I.S.T. *'78*
Paradise Alley *'78*
Johnny We Hardly Knew Ye *'77*

Morgan Conway (1903-81)

Dick Tracy vs. Cueball *'46*
Dick Tracy, Detective *'45*
The Saint Takes Over *'40*
Sinners in Paradise *'38*

Pat Conway (1931-81)

Brighty of the Grand Canyon *'67*
Geronimo *'62*
The Deadly Mantis *'57*
An Annapolis Story *'55*

Russ Conway (1913-)

The Screaming Skull *'58*
Love Me Tender *'56*
Twelve o'Clock High *'49*

Tim Conway (1933-)

Air Bud 2: Golden Receiver *'98*
Speed 2: Cruise Control *'97*
Dear God *'96*
The Longshot *'86*
Cannonball Run 2 *'84*
The Private Eyes *'80*
The Apple Dumpling Gang Rides Again *'79*
Prize Fighter *'79*
The Billion Dollar Hobo *'78*
They Went That-a-Way & That-a-Way *'78*
Gus *'76*

The Shaggy D.A. *'76*
The Apple Dumpling Gang *'75*
The World's Greatest Athlete *'73*
McHale's Navy Joins the Air Force *'65*
McHale's Navy *'64*

Tom Conway (1904-67)
Atomic Submarine *'59*
Voodoo Woman *'57*
Murder on Approval *'56*
Norman Conquest *'53*
Peter Pan *'53 (N)*
Tarzan and the She-Devil *'53*
Three Stops to Murder *'53*
Bride of the Gorilla *'51*
Painting the Clouds With Sunshine *'51*
One Touch of Venus *'48*
Criminal Court *'46*
The Saint Strikes Back: Criminal Court *'46*
The Falcon in Hollywood *'44*
The Falcon in Mexico *'44*
I Walked with a Zombie *'43*
The Seventh Victim *'43*
Cat People *'42*
The Falcon's Brother *'42*
Mrs. Miniver *'42*
Rio Rita *'42*
Lady Be Good *'41*
Tarzan's Secret Treasure *'41*

Angell Conwell (1982-)
What About Your Friends: Weekend Getaway *'02*
Baby Boy *'01*
The Wash *'01*

Jackie Coogan (1914-84)
The Escape Artist *'82*
Dr. Heckyl and Mr. Hype *'80*
The Prey *'80*
Halloween with the Addams Family *'79*
Human Experiments *'79*
The Shakiest Gun in the West *'68*
A Fine Madness *'66*
Girl Happy *'65*
High School Confidential *'58*
Lonelyhearts *'58*
Mesa of Lost Women *'52*
Outlaw Women *'52*
College Swing *'38*
Free and Easy *'30*
Tom Sawyer *'30*
Oliver Twist *'22*
The Kid *'21*
My Boy *'21*
Peck's Bad Boy *'21*

Keith Coogan (1970-)
Ivory Tower *'97*
Downhill Willie *'96*
Life 101 *'95*
The Power Within *'95*
Forever: A Ghost of a Love Story *'92*
Book of Love *'91*
Don't Tell Mom the Babysitter's Dead *'91*
Toy Soldiers *'91*
Cheetah *'89*
Cousins *'89*
Under the Boardwalk *'89*
Adventures in Babysitting *'87*
Hiding Out *'87*
The Fox and the Hound *'81 (V)*

Steve Coogan (1965-)
Marmaduke *'10 (V)*
The Other Guys *'10*
Percy Jackson & The Olympians: The Lightning Thief *'10*
In the Loop *'09*
Night at the Museum: Battle of the Smithsonian *'09*
What Goes Up *'09*
Finding Amanda *'08*
Hamlet 2 *'08*
Tropic Thunder *'08*
Hot Fuzz *'07*
Lies & Alibis *'06*
Marie Antoinette *'06*
Night at the Museum *'06*
Happy Endings *'05*
Tristram Shandy: A Cock and Bull Story *'05*
Around the World in 80 Days *'04*
Ella Enchanted *'04 (V)*
Coffee and Cigarettes *'03*
24 Hour Party People *'01*
Sweet Revenge *'98*
Mr. Toad's Wild Ride *'96*

A.J. Cook (1978-)
Night Skies *'07*
I'm Reed Fish *'06*
Final Destination 2 *'03*
The House Next Door *'01*
Out Cold *'01*
Ripper: Letter from Hell *'01*
Wishmaster 3: Beyond the Gates of Hell *'01*
The Virgin Suicides *'99*

Ben Cook
Restless Spirits *'99*
Little Men *'98*

Carole Cook (1928-)
Home on the Range *'04 (V)*
Lost and Found *'99*
Fast Money *'96*
Sixteen Candles *'84*
The Incredible Mr. Limpet *'64*

Clyde Cook (1891-1984)
The White Cliffs of Dover *'44*
White Cargo *'42*
Through the Breakers *'28*
White Gold *'28*

Dale "Apollo" Cook (1958-)
Fist of Glory *'95*
Raw Target *'95*
American Kickboxer 2: To the Death *'93*
Blood Ring *'93*
Fist of Steel *'93*
Triple Impact *'92*

Dane Cook (1972-)
My Best Friend's Girl *'08*
Dan in Real Life *'07*
Good Luck Chuck *'07*
Mr. Brooks *'07*
Employee of the Month *'06*
London *'05*
Waiting *'05*
Mystery Men *'99*
Simon Sez *'99*

Donald Cook (1901-61)
Our Very Own *'50*
Here Come the Co-Eds *'45*
Circus Girl *'37*
Show Boat *'36*
Confidential *'35*
Motive for Revenge *'35*
Viva Villa! *'34*
Baby Face *'33*
Frisco Jenny *'32*
Public Enemy *'31*

Doria Cook
Evil Town *'87*
Mame *'74*

Elisha Cook, Jr. (1906-95)
Hammett *'82*
Leave 'Em Laughing *'81*
Carny *'80*
The Champ *'79*
1941 *'79*
Salem's Lot *'79*
St. Ives *'76*
Winterhawk *'76*
Black Bird *'75*
Messiah of Evil *'74*
Electra Glide in Blue *'73*
Emperor of the North Pole *'73*
Blacula *'72*
The Great Northfield Minnesota Raid *'72*
El Condor *'70*
Rosemary's Baby *'68*
The Haunted Palace *'63*
Papa's Delicate Condition *'63*
One-Eyed Jacks *'61*
Platinum High School *'60*
The Day of the Outlaw *'59*
House on Haunted Hill *'58*
Plunder Road *'57*
The Killing *'56*
The Indian Fighter *'55*
Drum Beat *'54*
Shane *'53*
Behave Yourself! *'52*
Don't Bother to Knock *'52*
The Great Gatsby *'49*
Born to Kill *'47*
Fall Guy *'47*
The Long Night *'47*
The Big Sleep *'46*
Dillinger *'45*
Dark Mountain *'44*
Dark Waters *'44*
Phantom Lady *'44*
Wildcat *'42*
I Wake Up Screaming *'41*
The Maltese Falcon *'41*
Sergeant York *'41*
Stranger on the Third Floor *'40*
Tin Pan Alley *'40*
Love Is News *'37*
They Won't Forget *'37*
Pigskin Parade *'36*

Marianne Cook
See Marianne Koch

Peter Cook (1937-95)
Black Beauty *'94*
Getting It Right *'89*
Great Balls of Fire *'89*
Without a Clue *'88*
The Princess Bride *'87*
Yellowbeard *'83*
Secret Policeman's Private Parts *'81*
The Hound of the Baskervilles *'77*
Find the Lady *'76*
Those Daring Young Men in Their Jaunty Jalopies *'69*
Bedazzled *'68*
Dandy in Aspic *'68*
The Wrong Box *'66*

Rachael Leigh Cook (1979-)
Bob Funk *'09*
The Lodger *'09*
All Hat *'07*
Blonde Ambition *'07*
The Final Season *'07*
Nancy Drew *'07*
The Big Empty *'04*
My First Wedding *'04*
Stateside *'04*
Bookies *'03*
11:14 *'03*
Scorched *'02*
Josie and the Pussycats *'01*
Tangled *'01*
Texas Rangers *'01*
Antitrust *'00*
Blow Dry *'00*
Get Carter *'00*
She's All That *'99*
All I Wanna Do *'98*
The Bumblebee Flies Anyway *'98*
The Naked Man *'98*
The Defenders: Payback *'97*
The Eighteenth Angel *'97*
The House of Yes *'97*
True Women *'97*
Carpool *'96*
The Baby-Sitters' Club *'95*
Tom and Huck *'95*

Roderick Cook (1932-90)
9 1/2 Weeks *'86*
Our Time *'74*

Ron Cook (1948-)
The Diary of Anne Frank *'08*
Filth *'08*
On a Clear Day *'05*
The Merchant of Venice *'04*
Thunderbirds *'04*
The Other Boleyn Girl *'03*
Dead Gorgeous *'02*
The Hound of the Baskervilles *'02*
Charlotte Gray *'01*
Lucky Break *'01*
102 Dalmatians *'00*
Topsy Turvy *'99*
The Odyssey *'97*
Secrets and Lies *'95*
Sharpe's Honour *'94*

Tommy Cook (1930-)
Missile to the Moon *'59*
Night Passage *'57*
Battle Cry *'55*
Teenage Crime Wave *'55*
The Kid From Cleveland *'49*
Adventures of Red Ryder *'40*

Tracy Cook
Killing Moon *'00*
SnakeEater 3: His Law *'92*

Alan Cooke
Young Adam *'03*
Defenders of the Law *'31*

Amelia Cooke
Alien Agent *'07*
Species 3 *'04*

Christopher Cooke
Rhythm Thief *'94*
Spare Me *'92*
The Unbelievable Truth *'90*

Jennifer Cooke (1964-)
Friday the 13th, Part 6: Jason Lives *'86*
Gimme an F *'85*

Josh Cooke (1979-)
Bachelor Party 2: The Last Temptation *'08*
Snowglobe *'07*
Wasted *'06*

Keith Cooke (1959-)
Heatseeker *'95*
The King of the Kickboxers *'91*
China O'Brien 2 *'89*
China O'Brien *'88*

Peter Cookson (1913-90)
Black Tower *'50*
Fear *'46*
Swingtime Johnny *'43*

Hallam Cooley
Frisco Jenny *'32*
The Monster *'25*

Spade Cooley (1910-69)
Everybody's Dancin' *'50*
Kid from Gower Gulch *'50*
Silver Bandit *'50*

Jennifer Coolidge (1963-)
Bad Lieutenant: Port of Call New Orleans *'09*
Gentlemen Broncos *'09*
Foreign Exchange *'08*
Igor *'08 (V)*
Living Proof *'08*
Soul Men *'08*
Epic Movie *'07*
American Dreamz *'06*
Click *'06*
Date Movie *'06*
For Your Consideration *'06*
Robots *'05 (V)*
A Cinderella Story *'04*
American Wedding *'03*
Carolina *'03*
Legally Blonde 2: Red White & Blonde *'03*
A Mighty Wind *'03*
Testosterone *'03*
Women vs. Men *'02*
American Pie 2 *'01*
Down to Earth *'01*
Legally Blonde *'01*
Pootie Tang *'01*
Best in Show *'00*
American Pie *'99*
Slappy and the Stinkers *'97*
Trial and Error *'96*

Philip Coolidge (1908-67)
Inherit the Wind *'60*
The Tingler *'59*

Coolio (1963-)
Three Days to Vegas *'07*
Stealing Candy *'04*
Exposed *'03*
Get Over It! *'01*
Perfume *'01*
Red Water *'01*
The Convent *'00*
Dope Case Pending *'00*
Gangland *'00*
In Pursuit *'00*
Shriek If You Know What I Did Last Friday the 13th *'00*
Submerged *'00*
Judgment Day *'99*
Leprechaun 5: In the Hood *'99*
An Alan Smithee Film: Burn, Hollywood, Burn *'97*
Phat Beach *'96*

James Coombes
A Knight in Camelot *'98*
Agatha Christie's Murder with Mirrors *'85*

Norman Coombes
The House of Usher *'88*
Kill or Be Killed *'80*

Kevin Cooney (1945-)
Fragments *'08*
The Haunting of Molly Hartley *'08*
Bring It On Again *'03*
Clockwatchers *'97*
If These Walls Could Talk *'96*
Full Moon in Blue Water *'88*

Alice Cooper (1948-)
Suck *'09*
Wayne's World *'92*
Freddy's Dead: The Final Nightmare *'91*
Decline of Western Civilization 2: The Metal Years *'88*
Prince of Darkness *'87*
Monster Dog *'82*
Roadie *'80*
Sextette *'78*

Ben Cooper (1930-)
Gunfight at Comanche Creek *'64*
The Rose Tattoo *'55*
Johnny Guitar *'53*

Bradley Cooper (1975-)
The A-Team *'10*
Case 39 *'10*
Valentine's Day *'10*
All About Steve *'09*
The Hangover *'09*
He's Just Not That Into You *'09*
New York, I Love You *'09*
The Midnight Meat Train *'08*
The Rocker *'08*
Yes Man *'08*
The Comebacks *'07*
Failure to Launch *'06*
Wedding Crashers *'05*
Wet Hot American Summer *'01*

Camille (Cami) Cooper
Lawnmower Man 2: Beyond Cyberspace *'95*
The Applegates *'89*
Shocker *'89*

Chris Cooper (1951-)
Remember Me *'10*
New York, I Love You *'09*
Breach *'07*
The Kingdom *'07*
Married Life *'07*
Capote *'05*
Jarhead *'05*
Syriana *'05*
Silver City *'04*
My House in Umbria *'03*
Seabiscuit *'03*
Adaptation *'02*
The Bourne Identity *'02*
Interstate 60 *'02*
Me, Myself, and Irene *'00*
The Patriot *'00*
American Beauty *'99*
October Sky *'99*
Breast Men *'97*
Great Expectations *'97*
The Horse Whisperer *'97*
Horton Foote's Alone *'97*
A Time to Kill *'96*
Lone Star *'95*
Money Train *'95*
Pharoah's Army *'95*
Lone Justice *'93*
Return to Lonesome Dove *'93*
This Boy's Life *'93*
City of Hope *'91*
Guilty by Suspicion *'91*
Thousand Pieces of Gold *'91*
Matewan *'87*

Clancy Cooper (1906-75)
Naked Youth *'59*
A Time to Love & a Time to Die *'58*
Girls in Chains *'43*
The Secret Code *'42*

Dominic Cooper (1978-)
Brief Interviews With Hideous Men *'09*
An Education *'09*
The Duchess *'08*
God on Trial *'08*
Mamma Mia! *'08*
Sense & Sensibility *'07*
The History Boys *'06*
Starter for Ten *'06*

Garry Cooper (1955-)
Universal Soldier: Regeneration *'09*
My Beautiful Laundrette *'85*
Quadrophenia *'79*

Gary Cooper
Naked Gun 33 1/3: The Final Insult *'94*
Dark Before Dawn *'89*
Garden of Evil *'54*
The Devil and the Deep *'32*

Gary Cooper (1901-61)
The Naked Edge *'61*
Alias Jesse James *'59*
The Hanging Tree *'59*
They Came to Cordura *'59*
The Wreck of the Mary Deare *'59*
Man of the West *'58*
Ten North Frederick *'58*
Love in the Afternoon *'57*
Friendly Persuasion *'56*
The Court Martial of Billy Mitchell *'55*
Blowing Wild *'54*
Return to Paradise *'53*
Vera Cruz *'53*
High Noon *'52*
Springfield Rifle *'52*
Distant Drums *'51*
It's a Big Country *'51*
Bright Leaf *'50*
The Fountainhead *'49*
It's a Great Feeling *'49*
Task Force *'49*
Good Sam *'48*
Unconquered *'47*
Cloak and Dagger *'46*
Along Came Jones *'45*
Saratoga Trunk *'45*
Casanova Brown *'44*
The Story of Dr. Wassell *'44*
For Whom the Bell Tolls *'43*
The Pride of the Yankees *'42*
Ball of Fire *'41*
Meet John Doe *'41*
Sergeant York *'41*
The Westerner *'40*
Beau Geste *'39*
The Real Glory *'39*
The Adventures of Marco Polo *'38*

Bluebeard's Eighth Wife '38
The Cowboy and the Lady '38
The Plainsman '37
Souls at Sea '37
Desire '36
The General Died at Dawn '36
Mr. Deeds Goes to Town '36
The Lives of a Bengal Lancer '35
Now and Forever '34
Operator 13 '34
One Sunday Afternoon '33
Today We Live '33
A Farewell to Arms '32
Fighting Caravans '31
Morocco '30
The Virginian '29
Doomsday '28
It '27
The Last Outlaw '27
Nevada '27
Wings '27
The Winning of Barbara Worth '26

George Cooper (1892-1943)

Federal Agent '36
The Phantom Rider '36
Uptown New York '32
The Trail of '98 '28
Smouldering Fires '25
Little Church Around the Corner '23

Gladys Cooper (1888-1971)

Nice Girl Like Me '69
My Fair Lady '64
Separate Tables '58
At Sword's Point '51
Madame Bovary '49
The Secret Garden '49
Homecoming '48
The Pirate '48
The Bishop's Wife '47
Beware of Pity '46
Love Letters '45
The Valley of Decision '45
Mrs. Parkington '44
The White Cliffs of Dover '44
Mr. Lucky '43
Princess O'Rourke '43
The Song of Bernadette '43
Now, Voyager '42
This Above All '42
The Black Cat '41
That Hamilton Woman '41
Kitty Foyle '40
Rebecca '40
The Iron Duke '34

Inez Cooper (1922-)

'Neath Canadian Skies '46
Wings over the Pacific '43
I Married an Angel '42

Jackie Cooper (1922-)

Surrender '87
Superman 3 '83
Superman 2 '80
Superman: The Movie '78
The Love Machine '71
Maybe I'll Come Home in the Spring '71
Maybe I'll Be Home in the Spring '70
The Navy Comes Through '42
Ziegfeld Girl '41
Return of Frank James '40
The Abe Lincoln of Ninth Avenue '39
What a Life '39
That Certain Age '38
The Devil Is a Sissy '36
Peck's Bad Boy '34
Treasure Island '34
The Bowery '33
The Champ '32

Jeanne Cooper (1928-)

Carpool Guy '05
Sweet Hostage '75
Shame '61
Let No Man Write My Epitaph '60
The Commies Are Coming, the Commies Are Coming '57
Plunder Road '57
The Redhead from Wyoming '53
Shadows of Tombstone '53

Jeff Cooper

Circle of Iron '78
Fantastic Balloon Voyage '76
The Impossible Years '68
Born Losers '67

Justin Cooper (1988-)

Dennis the Menace Strikes Again '98
Liar Liar '97

Maggie Cooper

Death Ray 2000 '81
An Eye for an Eye '81
And Baby Makes Six '79

Melville Cooper (1896-1973)

Around the World in 80 Days '56
The King's Thief '55
Let's Dance '50
The Underworld Story '50
Heartbeat '46
13 Rue Madeleine '46
Immortal Sergeant '43
The Lady Eve '41
Murder over New York '40
Rebecca '40
Too Many Husbands '40
The Adventures of Robin Hood '38
Dawn Patrol '38
Four's a Crowd '38
Gold Diggers in Paris '38
The Great Garrick '37
Thin Ice '37
Private Life of Don Juan '34
The Scarlet Pimpernel '34

Miriam Cooper (1894-1976)

Is Money Everything? '23
The Birth of a Nation '15

Pat Cooper (1929-)

Analyze That '02
Analyze This '98

Ralph Cooper (1908-92)

Gang War '40
The Duke Is Tops '38

Scott Cooper

For Sale by Owner '09
Get Low '09
Broken Trail '06

Stan Cooper

See Stelvio Rosi

Ted Cooper

The Caine Mutiny '54
Phantom from Space '53

Terence Cooper (1928-97)

Hell's Belles '95
Heart of the Stag '84
Casino Royale '67

Trevor Cooper (1953-)

The History of Mr. Polly '07
Ivanhoe '97
Framed '93

Wendy Cooper

24 Hours in London '00
Witchcraft 10: Mistress of the Craft '98

Robert Coote (1909-82)

Theatre of Blood '73
Alice Through the Looking Glass '66
My Fair Lady '64
The Horse's Mouth '58
The Merry Widow '52
Othello '52
Scaramouche '52
The Elusive Pimpernel '50
Macbeth '48
The Three Musketeers '48
Forever Amber '47
The Ghost and Mrs. Muir '47
Lured '47
Stairway to Heaven '46
Commandos Strike at Dawn '43
You Can't Fool Your Wife '40
Bad Lands '39
Gunga Din '39
Mr. Moto's Last Warning '39
Nurse Edith Cavell '39

Kenneth Cope (1931-)

Carry On Matron '72
Rentadick '72
Carry On at Your Convenience '71

Joan Copeland (1922-)

Brother Bear '03 (V)
The Adventures of Sebastian Cole '99
The Peacemaker '97
The Laserman '90
Her Alibi '88
Happy New Year '87
Roseland '77
The Iceman Cometh '60

Zane R. (Lil' Zane) Copeland, Jr. (1982-)

Dr. Dolittle 2 '01
Finding Forrester '00

Michael Copeman

Focus '01
His Bodyguard '98
Another Woman '94
Circle Man '87

Geoffrey Copleston

The Belly of an Architect '91
The Black Cat '81

Peter Copley (1915-)

Oliver Twist '05
A Dangerous Man: Lawrence after Arabia '91
Help! '65
King and Country '64
The Golden Salamander '51

Sharlto Copley

The A-Team '10
District 9 '09

Teri Copley (1961-)

Brain Donors '92
Frozen Assets '92
Down the Drain '89
Transylvania Twist '89
In the Line of Duty: The FBI Murders '88
I Married a Centerfold '84

Michael Copon (1982-)

Night of the Demons '09
The Scorpion King 2: Rise of a Warrior '08
Bring It On: In It to Win It '07

Alicia Coppola (1968-)

National Treasure: Book of Secrets '07
Fresh Cut Grass '04
Sin '02
Double Down '01
Blood Money '99
Velocity Trap '99

Christopher Coppola (1962-)

BloodRayne 2: Deliverance '07
Loveless in Los Angeles '07
Postal '07
Undead or Alive '07
Dog Gone Love '03

Francis Ford Coppola (1939-)

Hearts of Darkness: A Filmmaker's Apocalypse '91
Apocalypse Now '79

Sofia Coppola (1971-)

Star Wars: Episode 1—The Phantom Menace '99
Inside Monkey Zetterland '93
The Godfather, Part 3 '90
Peggy Sue Got Married '86
The Godfather '72

Vincent Corazza (1972-)

I Downloaded a Ghost '04
The Cheetah Girls '03
Leaving Metropolis '02
Hangman '00

Brady Corbet (1988-)

Funny Games '07
Mysterious Skin '04
Thunderbirds '04
Thirteen '03

Ben (Benny) Corbett (1892-1961)

Fighting Renegade '39
Outlaw's Paradise '39
Texas Wildcats '39
Six Gun Trail '38
Circle of Death '36
Coyote Trails '35
Westward Bound '30

Glenn Corbett (1934-93)

Shadow Force '92
Midway '76
Ride in a Pink Car '74
The Stranger '73
Dead Pigeon on Beethoven Street '72
Chisum '70
Shenandoah '65
Pirates of Blood River '62
Homicidal '61
All the Young Men '60
The Mountain Road '60
The Crimson Kimono '59
The Violent Years '56

Gretchen Corbett (1947-)

Change of Heart '98
Jaws of Satan '81
PSI Factor '80
Secrets of Three Hungry Wives '78
The Savage Bees '76
Let's Scare Jessica to Death '71

Harry H. Corbett (1925-82)

Silver Dream Racer '83
Jabberwocky '77
Carry On Screaming '66
Rattle of a Simple Man '64
Ladies Who Do '63
The Unstoppable Man '59

John Corbett (1962-)

Ramona and Beezus '10
I Hate Valentine's Day '09
Baby on Board '08
The Burning Plain '08
Street Kings '08
The Messengers '07
Montana Sky '07
Dreamland '06
Bigger Than the Sky '05
Elvis Has Left the Building '04
Raise Your Voice '04
Raising Helen '04
My Big Fat Greek Wedding '02
Prancer Returns '01
Serendipity '01
Dinner Rush '00
Volcano '97
Don't Look Back '96
Wedding Bell Blues '96
Tombstone '93

Ronnie Corbett (1930-)

Fierce Creatures '96
No Sex Please—We're British '73

Barry Corbin (1940-)

That Evening Sun '09
Wyvern '09
Beer for My Horses '08
Lake City '08
In the Valley of Elah '07
No Country for Old Men '07
Hidden Places '06
River's End '05
Monte Walsh '03
Hope Ranch '02
Crossfire Trail '01
Race to Space '01
Held Up '00
A Face to Kill For '99
Solo '96
Curdled '95
Career Opportunities '91
The Chase '91
Conagher '91
The Hot Spot '90
Short Time '90
Who's Harry Crumb? '89
Critters 2: The Main Course '88
It Takes Two '88
LBJ: The Early Years '88
Permanent Record '88
Undercover '87
Nothing in Common '86
Hard Traveling '85
My Science Project '85
What Comes Around '85
Fatal Vision '84
Ratings Game '84
Ballad of Gregorio Cortez '83
Prime Suspect '82
Six Pack '82
Bitter Harvest '81
Dead and Buried '81
Any Which Way You Can '80
Stir Crazy '80
Urban Cowboy '80

Ellen Corby (1913-99)

A Day for Thanks on Walton's Mountain '82
Homecoming: A Christmas Story '71
Support Your Local Gunfighter '71
The Glass Bottom Boat '66
The Strangler '64
Vertigo '58
Night Passage '57
All Mine to Give '56
Illegal '55
Angels in the Outfield '51
Goodbye My Fancy '51
On Moonlight Bay '51
Caged '50
Harriet Craig '50
Ma and Pa Kettle Go to Town '50
I Remember Mama '48
Forever Amber '47
It's a Wonderful Life '46
Bedlam '45

Donna Corcoran (1942-)

Gypsy Colt '54
Don't Bother to Knock '52
Angels in the Outfield '51

Kevin Corcoran (1949-)

A Tiger Walks '64
Johnny Shiloh '63
Savage Sam '63
Mooncussers '62
Pollyanna '60
The Swiss Family Robinson '60
The Shaggy Dog '59
Toby Tyler '59
Old Yeller '57

Alex Cord (1931-)

Air Rage '01
To Be the Best '93
C.I.A.: Code Name Alexa '92
Roots of Evil '91
A Girl to Kill For '90
Street Asylum '90
The Dirty Dozen: The Fatal Mission '88
The Uninvited '88
Jungle Warriors '84
Goliath Awaits '81
Fire '77
Grayeagle '77
Sidewinder One '77
Inn of the Damned '74
Genesis II '73
Dead Are Alive '72
Stiletto '69
The Brotherhood '68
A Minute to Pray, a Second to Die '67

Mara Corday (1932-)

The Black Scorpion '57
The Giant Claw '57
Tarantula '55
Francis Joins the WACs '54

Rita (Paula) Corday (1920-92)

Because You're Mine '52
The Black Castle '52
Sword of Monte Cristo '51
Dick Tracy vs. Cueball '46
The Body Snatcher '45
West of the Pecos '45
The Falcon in Hollywood '44
The Leopard Man '43

Nathan Corddry

The Invention of Lying '09
The Ugly Truth '09
The Nanny Diaries '07

Rob Corddry (1971-)

Hot Tub Time Machine '10
Taking Chances '09
Harold & Kumar Escape from Guantanamo Bay '08
Lower Learning '08
Semi-Pro '08
W. '08
What Happens in Vegas '08
The Heartbreak Kid '07
I Now Pronounce You Chuck and Larry '07
The Ten '07
Unaccompanied Minors '06
Wedding Daze '06

James Corden (1980-)

Vampire Killers '09
The History Boys '06
All or Nothing '02

Harry Cording (1891-1954)

Man in the Attic '53
Trail of the Mounties '47
Law and Order '40
The Black Cat '34

Pancho Cordova

A Home of Our Own '75
The Exterminating Angel '62

Allan Corduner (1951-)

Defiance '08
Bigger Than the Sky '05
Friends & Crocodiles '05
The White Countess '05
De-Lovely '04
The Merchant of Venice '04
Daniel Deronda '02
Food of Love '02
Moonlight Mile '02
The Way We Live Now '02
The Grey Zone '01
Me Without You '01
The Search for John Gissing '01
Joe Gould's Secret '00
Topsy Turvy '99
The Imposters '98
Voices from a Locked Room '95
Heart of Darkness '93
Mandela '87
Yentl '83

Annie Cordy (1928-)

Le Chat '75
La Rupture '70

Raymond Cordy (1898-1956)

Beauties of the Night '52
Beauty and the Devil '50
A Nous la Liberte '31

Nick(y) Corello

Lansky '99
The Last Don '97
Devil in a Blue Dress '95
Blankman '94
Sugar Hill '94
Casualties of Love: The "Long Island Lolita" Story '93
Colors '88

Brigitte Corey
See Luisella Boni
The Treasure of Bengal *'53*

Prof. Irwin Corey (1912-)
The Curse of the Jade Scorpion *'01*
Stuck on You *'84*
Fairy Tales *'76*
How to Commit Marriage *'69*

Isabel Corey (1939-)
The Invincible Gladiator *'63*
Bob le Flambeur *'55*

Jeff Corey (1914-2002)
Color of Night *'94*
Surviving the Game *'94*
Deception *'92*
Secret Ingredient *'92*
Sinatra *'92*
Payoff *'91*
Bird on a Wire *'90*
Messenger of Death *'88*
Creator *'85*
Conan the Destroyer *'84*
Sword & the Sorcerer *'82*
Battle Beyond the Stars *'80*
Butch and Sundance: The Early Days *'79*
Up River *'79*
Jennifer *'78*
Wild Geese *'78*
Curse of the Black Widow *'77*
Moonshine County Express *'77*
Oh, God! *'77*
Banjo Hackett *'76*
The Premonition *'75*
Catlow *'71*
Shoot Out *'71*
Beneath the Planet of the Apes *'70*
Getting Straight *'70*
Little Big Man *'70*
They Call Me Mr. Tibbs! *'70*
Butch Cassidy and the Sundance Kid *'69*
True Grit *'69*
The Boston Strangler *'68*
In Cold Blood *'67*
Seconds *'66*
Mickey One *'65*
Lady in a Cage *'64*
The Balcony *'63*
Superman & the Mole Men *'51*
Bright Leaf *'50*
The Nevadan *'50*
The Next Voice You Hear *'50*
Rawhide *'50*
Bagdad *'49*
Follow Me Quietly *'49*
Home of the Brave *'49*
Kidnapped *'48*
A Southern Yankee *'48*
Brute Force *'47*
Hopalong Cassidy: Hoppy's Holiday *'47*
My Friend Flicka *'43*
The Man Who Wouldn't Die *'42*

Wendell Corey (1914-68)
Buckskin *'68*
The Astro-Zombies *'67*
Women of the Prehistoric Planet *'66*
Alias Jesse James *'59*
The Light in the Forest *'58*
Loving You *'57*
The Rainmaker *'56*
The Big Knife *'55*
Rear Window *'54*
Great Missouri Raid *'51*
Rich, Young and Pretty *'51*
The Furies *'50*
Harriet Craig *'50*
Any Number Can Play *'49*
Holiday Affair *'49*
The Accused *'48*
The Search *'48*
Sorry, Wrong Number *'48*

Danny Corkill (1974-)
Between Two Women *'86*
D.A.R.Y.L. *'85*
Mrs. Soffel *'84*

Al Corley (1956-)
Cowboy Up *'00*
A Kiss Goodnight *'94*
Incident at Channel Q *'86*
Torchlight *'85*
Squeeze Play *'79*

Annie Corley
The Lucky Ones *'08*
Monster *'03*
Seabiscuit *'03*
Juwanna Mann *'02*
Along for the Ride *'00*
Here on Earth *'00*
If You Only Knew *'00*
The '60s *'99*
Free Willy 3: The Rescue *'97*
Box of Moonlight *'96*
The Bridges of Madison County *'95*

Pat Corley (1930-2006)
Come Early Morning *'06*
Mr. Destiny *'90*
Poker Alice *'87*
Silent Witness *'85*
Night Shift *'82*
Of Mice and Men *'81*
Nightwing *'79*
The Two Worlds of Jenny Logan *'79*
Coming Home *'78*

Sharron Corley (1971-)
The Substitute *'96*
New Jersey Drive *'95*

Danielle Cormack
Maiden Voyage: Ocean Hijack *'04*
The Price of Milk *'00*
Siam Sunset *'99*

Maddie Corman (1969-)
Mickey Blue Eyes *'99*
I Think I Do *'97*
My New Gun *'92*
The Adventures of Ford Fairlane *'90*
Seven Minutes in Heaven *'86*

Roger Corman (1926-)
The Manchurian Candidate *'04*
The Independent *'00*
Scream 3 *'00*
Body Bags *'93*
Philadelphia *'93*
The Silence of the Lambs *'91*
Lords of the Deep *'89*
Swing Shift *'84*
State of Things *'82*
The Godfather 1902-1959: The Complete Epic *'81*
The Howling *'81*
Cannonball *'76*
The Godfather, Part 2 *'74*
Atlas *'60*
Creature from the Haunted Sea *'60*

Lee Cormie
December Boys *'07*
Darkness Falls *'03*

Michael Cornelison (1952-)
Real Time: Siege at Lucas Street Market *'00*
Mommy 2: Mommy's Day *'96*
Mommy *'95*

Don Cornelius (1936-)
Tapeheads *'89*
No Way Back *'74*

Ellie Cornell (1963-)
All Souls Day *'05*
House of the Dead *'03*
Chips, the War Dog *'90*
Halloween 5: The Revenge of Michael Myers *'89*
Halloween 4: The Return of Michael Myers *'88*

Clovis Cornillac (1967-)
Paris 36 *'08*
A Very Long Engagement *'04*
Carnage *'02*
The Unbearable Lightness of Being *'88*

Abbie Cornish (1982-)
Bright Star *'09*
Stop-Loss *'08*
Elizabeth: The Golden Age *'07*
Candy *'06*
A Good Year *'06*
Somersault *'04*
Marking Time *'03*

Nick Cornish
Dark Honeymoon *'08*
Hometown Legend *'02*

Robert Cornthwaite (1917-2006)
Matinee *'92*
Time Trackers *'88*
The War of the Worlds *'53*
The Thing *'51*

Anne Cornwall (1897-1980)
Laurel & Hardy: Men O'War *'29*
College *'27*

Charlotte Cornwell
Couples Retreat *'09*
The Saint *'97*
The Krays *'90*
White Hunter, Black Heart *'90*

Judy Cornwell (1942-)
Prince of Poisoners: The Life and Crimes of William Palmer *'98*
Persuasion *'95*
Santa Claus: The Movie *'85*
Think Dirty *'70*
Wuthering Heights *'70*
Two for the Road *'67*

Jose Coronado (1957-)
Goya in Bordeaux *'99*
The Disappearance of Garcia Lorca *'96*

Antoni Corone
Reservation Road *'07*
We Own the Night *'07*
Raging Hormones *'99*

Georges Corraface (1953-)
Km. 0 *'00*
Only Love *'98*
Escape from L.A. *'96*
Red Shoe Diaries: Four on the Floor *'96*
Legends of the North *'95*
Christopher Columbus: The Discovery *'92*
Impromptu *'90*
Not Without My Daughter *'90*

Mady Correll (1907-81)
Monsieur Verdoux *'47*
Texas Masquerade *'44*

Adrienne Corri (1930-)
Rosebud *'75*
Madhouse *'74*
A Clockwork Orange *'71*
Vampire Circus *'71*
Africa Texas Style *'67*
The Viking Queen *'67*
Doctor Zhivago *'65*
The Hellfire Club *'61*
The Tell-Tale Heart *'60*
The Rough and the Smooth *'59*
Corridors of Blood *'58*
Three Men in a Boat *'56*
Make Me an Offer *'55*
Devil Girl from Mars *'54*
Meet Mr. Callaghan *'54*
The River *'51*

Nick Corri
See Jsu Garcia

Sergio Corrieri (1939-)
Memories of Underdevelopment *'68*
I Am Cuba *'64*

Emmett Corrigan
The Beast of the City *'32*
An American Tragedy *'31*

Kevin Corrigan (1969-)
Big Fan *'09*
Definitely, Maybe *'08*
Pineapple Express *'08*
American Gangster *'07*
Superbad *'07*
Delirious *'06*
The Departed *'06*
The Dog Problem *'06*
The Last Winter *'06*
Lonesome Jim *'06*
Anchorman: The Legend of Ron Burgundy *'04*
Break a Leg *'03*
Scotland, PA *'02*
Chelsea Walls *'01*
Chain of Fools *'00*
Steal This Movie! *'00*
Brown's Requiem *'98*
Henry Fool *'98*
Lulu on the Bridge *'98*
Slums of Beverly Hills *'98*
Buffalo 66 *'97*
Kicked in the Head *'97*
The Assassination File *'96*
Illtown *'96*
Tree's Lounge *'96*
Walking and Talking *'96*
Bandwagon *'95*
Kiss of Death *'94*
Living in Oblivion *'94*
Rhythm Thief *'94*
True Romance *'93*
Zebrahead *'92*

Lloyd Corrigan (1900-69)
The Manchurian Candidate *'62*
Bowery Boys Meet the Monsters *'54*
Cavalry Charge *'51*
Ghost Chasers *'51*
When Willie Comes Marching Home *'50*
Blondie Hits the Jackpot *'49*
Lights of Old Santa Fe *'47*
The Chase *'46*
She Wolf of London *'46*
Gambler's Choice *'44*
Since You Went Away *'44*
The Thin Man Goes Home *'44*
Captive Wild Woman *'43*
Hitler's Children *'43*
King of the Cowboys *'43*
A Girl, a Guy and a Gob *'41*
The Lady in Question *'40*
Young Tom Edison *'40*

Ray Corrigan (1907-76)
It! The Terror from Beyond Space *'58*
Trail of Robin Hood *'50*
Renegade Girl *'46*
Black Market Rustlers *'43*
Cowboy Commandos *'43*
Land of Hunted Men *'43*
Arizona Stagecoach *'42*
Boot Hill Bandits *'42*
Rock River Renegades *'42*
Thunder River Feud *'42*
Fugitive Valley *'41*
Kid's Last Ride *'41*
Saddle Mountain Roundup *'41*
Tonto Basin Outlaws *'41*
Trail of the Silver Spurs *'41*
Tumbledown Ranch in Arizona *'41*
Underground Rustlers *'41*
Range Busters *'40*
Trailing Double Trouble *'40*
West of Pinto Basin *'40*
Frontier Horizon *'39*
Three Texas Steers *'39*
Wyoming Outlaw *'39*
Call the Mesquiteers *'38*
Heroes of the Hills *'38*
Outlaws of Sonora *'38*
Overland Stage Raiders *'38*
Pals of the Saddle *'38*
Purple Vigilantes *'38*
Santa Fe Stampede *'38*
Come on, Cowboys *'37*
Heart of the Rockies *'37*
Hit the Saddle *'37*
The Painted Stallion *'37*
Riders of the Whistling Skull *'37*
Roarin' Lead *'37*
The Trigger Trio *'37*
Wild Horse Rodeo *'37*
Country Gentlemen *'36*
Ghost Town Gold *'36*
The Three Mesquiteers *'36*
Undersea Kingdom *'36*

Shirley Corrigan
The Devil's Nightmare *'71*
Dr. Jekyll and the Wolfman *'71*

Aneta Corsaut (1933-95)
Return to Mayberry *'85*
The Toolbox Murders *'78*
The Blob *'58*

Silvana Corsini
Mamma Roma *'62*
Accatone! *'61*

Bill Cort
See William Cort

Bud Cort (1950-)
The Big Empty *'04*
The Life Aquatic with Steve Zissou *'04*
Coyote Ugly *'00*
Pollock *'00*
South of Heaven, West of Hell *'00*
But I'm a Cheerleader *'99*
Dogma *'99*
The Million Dollar Hotel *'99*
Sweet Jane *'98*
Heat *'95*
Girl in the Cadillac *'94*
Ted & Venus *'93*
Going Under *'91*
Brain Dead *'89*
The Chocolate War *'88*
Out of the Dark *'88*
Love at Stake *'87*
Invaders from Mars *'86*
Electric Dreams *'84*
Maria's Lovers *'84*
The Secret Diary of Sigmund Freud *'84*
Hysterical *'83*
Love Letters *'83*
The Nightingale *'83*
Rumpelstiltskin *'82*
Die Laughing *'80*
Why Shoot the Teacher *'79*
Harold and Maude *'71*
Brewster McCloud *'70*
Gas-s-s-s! *'70*
M*A*S*H *'70*
The Strawberry Statement *'70*
Sweet Charity *'69*

William Cort (1936-93)
Elvira, Mistress of the Dark *'88*
Wackiest Wagon Train in the West *'77*

Rowena Cortes
To Live and Die in Hong Kong *'89*
Heroes Three *'84*

Dan Cortese (1967-)
Everybody Wants to Be Italian *'08*
Soccer Mom *'08*
Locusts: The 8th Plague *'05*
The Triangle *'01*
Volcano: Fire on the Mountain *'97*
Public Enemies *'96*
A Weekend in the Country *'96*
At First Sight *'95*
Demolition Man *'93*

Joe Cortese (1949-)
Against the Ropes *'04*
American History X *'98*
Malevolence *'95*
Born to Run *'93*
Ruby *'92*
To Protect and Serve *'92*
The Closer *'91*
Python Wolf *'88*
Assault and Matrimony *'87*
Deadly Illusion *'87*
Stalking Danger *'86*
Letting Go *'85*
Evilspeak *'82*
Windows *'80*
Family Enforcer *'76*

Valentina Cortese (1924-)
The Adventures of Baron Munchausen *'89*
When Time Ran Out *'80*
Widow's Nest *'77*
Kidnap Syndicate *'76*
Brother Sun, Sister Moon *'73*
Day for Night *'73*
Assassination of Trotsky *'72*
First Love *'70*
The Secret of Santa Vittoria *'69*
Juliet of the Spirits *'65*
The Girl Who Knew Too Much *'63*
The Barefoot Contessa *'54*
Les Miserables *'52*
Malaya *'49*

Bella Cortez (1944-)
Ali Baba and the Seven Saracens *'64*
Tor *'64*
Vulcan God of Fire *'62*
The Giant of Metropolis *'61*

Ricardo Cortez (1899-1977)
Last Hurrah *'58*
The Inner Circle *'46*
I Killed That Man *'42*
Murder over New York *'40*
Mr. Moto's Last Warning *'39*
The Gentleman from California *'37*
The Man with Two Faces *'34*
Wonder Bar *'34*
Midnight Mary *'33*
Torch Singer *'33*
No One Man *'32*
Behind Office Doors *'31*
Big Business Girl *'31*
Illicit *'31*
The Maltese Falcon *'31*
Lost Zeppelin *'29*
The Phantom in the House *'29*
Mockery *'27*
The Sorrows of Satan *'26*
The Pony Express *'25*
The Swan *'25*

Jesse Corti
Beauty and the Beast *'91 (V)*
Nightlife *'90*
High Stakes *'89*

Bill Cosby (1937-)
Fat Albert *'04*
Jack *'96*
The Meteor Man *'93*
Ghost Dad *'90*
Leonard Part 6 *'87*
The Devil & Max Devlin *'81*
California Suite *'78*
Piece of the Action *'77*
Mother, Jugs and Speed *'76*
Let's Do It Again *'75*
Uptown Saturday Night *'74*
Man & Boy *'71*
To All My Friends on Shore *'71*

Howard Cosell (1920-95)
Broadway Danny Rose *'84*
The World's Greatest Athlete *'73*
Bananas *'71*

Daniel Cosgrove (1970-)

National Lampoon's Van Wilder '02
They Crawl '01
Valentine '01
The Object of My Affection '98
Too Busy to Work '32

Miranda Cosgrove (1993-)

Despicable Me '10 (V)
Keeping Up with the Steins '06
Yours, Mine & Ours '05
School of Rock '03

James Cosmo (1948-)

The Color of Magic '08
The Last Legion '07
The Seeker: The Dark Is Rising '07
The Chronicles of Narnia: The Lion, the Witch and the Wardrobe '05
Troy '04
All the Queen's Men '02
To End All Wars '01
The Match '99
One More Kiss '99
Split Second '99
Babe: Pig in the City '98 (V)
Urban Ghost Story '98
Ivanhoe '97
Emma '96
Braveheart '95
Stormy Monday '88
Orde Wingate '76

Ernest Cossart (1876-1951)

Love from a Stranger '47
Kings Row '41
Kitty Foyle '40
Three Smart Girls Grow Up '39
Desire '36
The Great Ziegfeld '36
Murder With Pictures '36

James Cossins (1933-97)

Dynasty of Fear '72
Wuthering Heights '70
The Anniversary '68

Pierre Cosso (1961-)

An American Werewolf in Paris '97
My Wonderful Life '90

James Costa

L.I.E. '01
Joe the King '99

Marina Costa

Jungle Raiders '85
The Final Executioner '83

Constantin Costa-Gavras (1933-)

The Stupids '95
Spies Like Us '85

Suzanne Costallos

Lotto Land '95
True Love '89

Paulo Costanzo (1978-)

Everything's Gone Green '06
40 Days and 40 Nights '02
Scorched '02
Gypsy 83 '01
Josie and the Pussycats '01
Road Trip '00

Robert Costanzo

In the Mix '05
61* '01
Air Bud 2: Golden Receiver '98
For Which He Stands '98
With Friends Like These '98
Plump Fiction '97
Underworld '96
For Better or Worse '95
Storybook '95
Lady in Waiting '94
Ring of Fire 3: Lion Strike '94
The Cemetery Club '93
Man's Best Friend '93
Relentless 3 '93
Honeymoon in Vegas '92
Delusion '91
Die Hard 2: Die Harder '90
Ratings Game '84
The Vegas Strip Wars '84
Honeyboy '82

Bob Costas (1951-)

Pootie Tang '01
BASEketball '98
The Scout '94

Dolores Costello (1903-79)

The Magnificent Ambersons '42
Breaking the Ice '38
Little Lord Fauntleroy '36
Old San Francisco '27
When a Man Loves '27

Don Costello (1901-45)

The Blue Dahlia '46
Mystery Man '44
Texas Masquerade '44
Sleepers West '41
Whistling in the Dark '41

Elvis Costello (1954-)

De-Lovely '04
I Love Your Work '03
Austin Powers 2: The Spy Who Shagged Me '99
200 Cigarettes '98
Spice World: The Movie '97
Straight to Hell '87
No Surrender '86
Americathon '79

Helene Costello (1903-57)

Don Juan '26
The Man on the Box '25

Lou Costello (1906-59)

The 30-Foot Bride of Candy Rock '59
Dance with Me, Henry '56
Abbott and Costello Meet the Mummy '55
Abbott and Costello Meet the Keystone Kops '54
Abbott and Costello Go to Mars '53
Abbott and Costello Meet Captain Kidd '52
Abbott and Costello Meet Dr. Jekyll and Mr. Hyde '52
Jack & the Beanstalk '52
Lost in Alaska '52
Abbott and Costello Meet the Invisible Man '51
Comin' Round the Mountain '51
Abbott and Costello in the Foreign Legion '50
Abbott and Costello Meet the Killer, Boris Karloff '49
Africa Screams '49
Abbott and Costello Meet Frankenstein '48
Mexican Hayride '48
The Noose Hangs High '48
Buck Privates Come Home '47
The Wistful Widow of Wagon Gap '47
Little Giant '46
The Time of Their Lives '46
Abbott and Costello in Hollywood '45
Here Come the Co-Eds '45
The Naughty Nineties '45
In Society '44
Lost in a Harem '44
Hit the Ice '43
It Ain't Hay '43
Pardon My Sarong '42
Ride 'Em Cowboy '42
Rio Rita '42
Who Done It? '42
Buck Privates '41
Hold That Ghost '41
In the Navy '41
Keep 'Em Flying '41
One Night in the Tropics '40

Mariclare Costello

Heart of a Champion: The Ray Mancini Story '85
Skeezer '82
Coward of the County '81
All God's Children '80
Conspiracy of Terror '75
The Execution of Private Slovik '74

Ward (Edward) Costello (1919-)

MacArthur '77
The City '76
The Gallant Hours '60

John A. Costelloe

Doubt '08
Kazaam '96
Me and the Mob '94
Billy Bathgate '91

Nicolas Coster (1934-)

Betsy's Wedding '90
The Solitary Man '82
Stir Crazy '80
The Electric Horseman '79
MacArthur '77
The Sporting Club '72
My Blood Runs Cold '65

Ritchie Coster

The Dark Knight '08
The Sentinel '06
The Tuxedo '02
Rear Window '98

Nikolaj Coster-Waldau (1970-)

Firewall '06
Kingdom of Heaven '05
Wimbledon '04
Black Hawk Down '01
Bent '97

George Costigan (1947-)

See No Evil: The Moors Murders '06
Calendar Girls '03
Love or Money '01
Girls' Night '97
The Hawk '93
Rita, Sue & Bob Too '87

Kevin Costner (1955-)

Swing Vote '08
Mr. Brooks '07
The Guardian '06
Rumor Has It... '05
The Upside of Anger '05
Open Range '03
Dragonfly '02
3000 Miles to Graceland '01
Thirteen Days '00
For Love of the Game '99
Message in a Bottle '98
The Postman '97
Tin Cup '96
Waterworld '95
The War '94
Wyatt Earp '94
A Perfect World '93
The Bodyguard '92
JFK '91
Robin Hood: Prince of Thieves '91
Dances with Wolves '90
Revenge '90
Field of Dreams '89
Bull Durham '88
No Way Out '87
The Untouchables '87
Amazing Stories '85
American Flyers '85
Fandango '85
Silverado '85
The Gunrunner '84
Shadows Run Black '84
Stacy's Knights '83
Table for Five '83
Testament '83
Night Shift '82
Chasing Dreams '81
Sizzle Beach U.S.A. '74

Laurence Cote (1966-)

Les Voleurs '96
Up/Down/Fragile '95
Nouvelle Vague '90

Tina Cote

Mean Guns '97
Omega Doom '96
Nemesis 2: Nebula '94

John Cothran, Jr. (1947-)

Black Snake Moan '07
Ricochet '91

Marion Cotillard (1975-)

Inception '10
Nine '09
Public Enemies '09
La Vie en Rose '07
A Good Year '06
You and Me '06
A Very Long Engagement '04
Big Fish '03
Love Me if You Dare '03

Kami Cotler (1965-)

A Day for Thanks on Walton's Mountain '82
The Waltons: The Christmas Carol '80

D.J. Cotrona (1981-)

Dear John '10
Venom '05

Jonathon Cott

Above and Beyond '53
Battle Circus '53

Joseph Cotten (1905-94)

Churchill and the Generals '81
Heaven's Gate '81
Casino '80
Delusion '80
The Hearse '80
Screamers '80
Survivor '80
Perfect Crime '79
Airport '77 '77
Return to Fantasy Island '77
Twilight's Last Gleaming '77
The Lindbergh Kidnapping Case '76
The Big Push '75
Soylent Green '73
Lady Frankenstein '72
Torture Chamber of Baron Blood '72
The Abominable Dr. Phibes '71
City Beneath the Sea '71
The Passing of Evil '70
Tora! Tora! Tora! '70
The Grasshopper '69
Petulia '68
Brighty of the Grand Canyon '67
Hellbenders '67
White Comanche '67
The Oscar '66
Tramplers '66
Hush, Hush, Sweet Charlotte '65
The Money Trap '65
From the Earth to the Moon '58
Touch of Evil '58
A Blueprint for Murder '53
Niagara '52
Othello '52
September Affair '50
Walk Softly, Stranger '50
Beyond the Forest '49
The Third Man '49
Under Capricorn '49
Portrait of Jennie '48
The Farmer's Daughter '47
Duel in the Sun '46
Love Letters '45
Gaslight '44
I'll Be Seeing You '44
Since You Went Away '44
Shadow of a Doubt '43
Journey into Fear '42
The Magnificent Ambersons '42
Citizen Kane '41
Lydia '41

Fanny Cottencon (1957-)

Change My Life '01
Window Shopping '86
Special Police '85

Catherine Cotter

See Marie Burton

Chrissie Cotterill (1955-)

Nil by Mouth '96
Scrubbers '82

Ralph Cotterill (1932-)

Bad Boy Bubby '93
Crimebroker '93
Howling 3: The Marsupials '87
Starship '87
Burke & Wills '85

Mia Cottet (1968-)

Dawg '02
The Tuxedo '02
Nine Months '95

Oliver Cotton (1944-)

Shanghai Knights '03
The Dancer Upstairs '02
Beowulf '98
The Camomile Lawn '92
Christopher Columbus: The Discovery '92
Eleni '85
Robin Hood... The Legend: Herne's Son '85

Erin Cottrell

Love Takes Wing '09
Love's Unending Legacy '07
Love's Unfolding Dream '07
Love's Abiding Joy '06
Love's Long Journey '05

Paul Coufos

Mortal Danger '94
Boxcar Blues '90
Dragonfight '90
Thunderground '89
Food of the Gods: Part 2 '88
Busted Up '86
City of Shadows '86
The Lost Empire '83

Marisa Coughlan (1973-)

Already Dead '07
Wasted '06
I Love Your Work '03
Pumpkin '02
Freddy Got Fingered '01
Super Troopers '01
Gossip '99
Teaching Mrs. Tingle '99

Dave Coulier (1959-)

The Family Holiday '07
Shredderman Rules '07

George Coulouris (1903-89)

The Long Good Friday '80
It's Not the Size That Counts '74
Murder on the Orient Express '74
The Tempter '74
Papillon '73
The Stranger '73
Tower of Evil '72
Blood from the Mummy's Tomb '71
Arabesque '66
The Skull '65
The Womaneater '59
Kill Me Tomorrow '57
Tarzan and the Lost Safari '57
Race for Life '55
Tarzan's Hidden Jungle '55
The Runaway Bus '54
Doctor in the House '53
A Southern Yankee '48
Where There's Life '47
The Verdict '46
Lady on a Train '45
A Song to Remember '45
The Master Race '44
Mr. Skeffington '44
None But the Lonely Heart '44
For Whom the Bell Tolls '43
This Land Is Mine '43
Watch on the Rhine '43
Citizen Kane '41
The Lady in Question '40

Keith Coulouris (1967-)

Beastmaster 3: The Eye of Braxus '95
Dead Man's Revenge '93
Take Down '92

Bernie Coulson (1965-)

Cabin by the Lake '00
The Highway Man '99
Hard Core Logo '96
Adventures in Spying '92
Eddie and the Cruisers 2: Eddie Lives! '89
The Accused '88

Clare Coulter (1942-)

Coast to Coast '04
Hollywood North '03

Claudia Coulter

Jane Eyre '06
The Witches Hammer '06

Raymond Coulthard (1968-)

Agatha Christie: A Life in Pictures '04
Emma '97
Rhodes '97

Barbara Couper (1903-92)

Vanity Fair '67
The Last Days of Dolwyn '49

Clotilde Courau (1969-)

La Vie en Rose '07
Almost Peaceful '02
Whatever You Say '02
Deep in the Woods '00
Deterrence '00
Elisa '94
The Pickle '93

Nicole Courcel (1930-)

Sundays & Cybele '62
Le Cas du Dr. Laurent '57
Rendez-vous de Juillet '49

Hazel Court (1926-2008)

Masque of the Red Death '65
The Raven '63
Doctor Blood's Coffin '62
Premature Burial '62
The Curse of Frankenstein '57
Hour of Decision '57
Devil Girl from Mars '54
Ghost Ship '53
Dear Murderer '47

Jason Court

A Night in the Life of Jimmy Reardon '88
Grandview U.S.A. '84

Margaret Courtenay (1923-96)

The Mirror Crack'd '80
Hot Millions '68

Tom Courtenay (1937-)

Little Dorrit '08
Flood '07
The Golden Compass '07
Nicholas Nickleby '02
Last Orders '01
A Rather English Marriage '98
The Old Curiosity Shop '94
The Last Butterfly '92
Let Him Have It '91
Happy New Year '87
Leonard Part 6 '87
The Dresser '83
I Heard the Owl Call My Name '73
Catch Me a Spy '71
One Day in the Life of Ivan Denisovich '71
Dandy in Aspic '68
Night of the Generals '67

Doctor Zhivago *'65*
King Rat *'65*
Operation Crossbow *'65*
King and Country *'64*
Billy Liar *'63*
The Loneliness of the Long Distance Runner *'62*

Jerome Courtland (1926-)
Tharus Son of Attila *'62*
Tonka *'58*
Santa Fe *'51*
The Texas Rangers *'51*
Battleground *'49*
Man from Colorado *'49*
Tokyo Joe *'49*
Together Again *'43*

Alex Courtney (1940-)
And the Band Played On *'93*
Fatal Pulse *'88*
Enter the Ninja *'81*

Chuck Courtney (1931-2000)
Billy the Kid Versus Dracula *'66*
Teenage Monster *'57*

Inez Courtney (1908-75)
The Thirteenth Man *'37*
Let's Sing Again *'36*
The Reckless Way *'36*
Suzy *'36*
Wedding Present *'36*

Jeni Courtney
Nothing Personal *'95*
The Secret of Roan Inish *'94*

Brian Cousins (1959-)
Soldier of Fortune Inc. *'97*
Invisible: The Chronicles of Benjamin Knight *'93*
Mandroid *'93*
Homicidal Impulse *'92*
Longtime Companion *'90*

Christian Cousins (1983-)
Twinsitters *'95*
Danielle Steel's Heartbeat *'93*

Christopher Cousins (1960-)
Final Approach *'08*
The Grudge 2 *'06*
Wicker Park *'04*
Earth vs. the Spider *'01*
Dead Dog *'00*
Hell High *'86*

Randy Couture
The Expendables *'10*
The Scorpion King 2: Rise of a Warrior *'08*

Allen Covert (1964-)
Strange Wilderness *'08*
I Now Pronounce You Chuck and Larry *'07*
Grandma's Boy *'06*
50 First Dates *'04*
Anger Management *'03*
Mr. Deeds *'02*
Little Nicky *'00*
The Wedding Singer *'97*
Bulletproof *'96*
Happy Gilmore *'96*
Airheads *'94*

Elliot Cowan
Lost in Austen *'08*
Love and Other Disasters *'06*
Alexander *'04*

Jerome Cowan (1897-1972)
Critic's Choice *'63*
Have Rocket Will Travel *'59*
The West Point Story *'50*
Blondie Hits the Jackpot *'49*
June Bride *'48*
Cry Wolf *'47*
Riff-Raff *'47*
Blondie Knows Best *'46*
My Reputation *'46*
The Perfect Marriage *'46*
Fog Island *'45*
Getting Gertie's Garter *'45*
Jungle Captive *'45*
Guest in the House *'44*
Silver Spurs *'43*
Moontide *'42*
Who Done It? *'42*
The Great Lie *'41*
High Sierra *'41*
The Maltese Falcon *'41*
Castle on the Hudson *'40*
Torrid Zone *'40*
East Side of Heaven *'39*
The Gracie Allen Murder Case *'39*
The Saint Strikes Back *'39*
You Only Live Once *'37*

Noel Coward (1899-1973)
The Italian Job *'69*
Boom! *'68*
Paris When It Sizzles *'64*
Our Man in Havana *'59*
Around the World in 80 Days *'56*
In Which We Serve *'43*
Hearts of the World *'18*

Jack Cowell
A Face in the Fog *'36*
Kid Courageous *'35*

Bruce Cowling (1919-86)
To Hell and Back *'55*
Cause for Alarm *'51*
The Painted Hills *'51*
Battleground *'49*
The Stratton Story *'49*

Nicola Cowper (1967-)
Devices and Desires *'91*
Journey to the Center of the Earth *'88*
Lionheart *'87*
Dreamchild *'85*
Transmutations *'85*
Winter Flight *'84*

Alan Cox (1970-)
Mrs. Dalloway *'97*
The Odyssey *'97*
An Awfully Big Adventure *'94*
Young Sherlock Holmes *'85*

Alex Cox (1954-)
Dance with the Devil *'97*
Dead Beat *'94*

Beau Cox (1971-)
Nowhere to Hide *'83*
On the Run *'83*

Brian Cox (1946-)
Battle for Terra *'09 (V)*
Fantastic Mr. Fox *'09 (V)*
The Color of Magic *'08 (N)*
Trick 'r Treat *'08*
The Water Horse: Legend of the Deep *'07*
Zodiac *'07*
The Flying Scotsman *'06*
Running with Scissors *'06*
Match Point *'05*
Red Eye *'05*
The Ringer *'05*
The Bourne Supremacy *'04*
Troy *'04*
X2: X-Men United *'03*
Adaptation *'02*
The Bourne Identity *'02*
The Ring *'02*
The Rookie *'02*
Sin *'02*
25th Hour *'02*
The Affair of the Necklace *'01*
L.I.E. *'01*
Strictly Sinatra *'01*
Super Troopers *'01*
Longitude *'00*
Mad About Mambo *'00*
Nuremberg *'00*
A Shot at Glory *'00*
The Corruptor *'99*
For Love of the Game *'99*
The Minus Man *'99*
Desperate Measures *'98*
Poodle Springs *'98*
Retribution *'98*
Rushmore *'98*
The Boxer *'97*
Kiss the Girls *'97*
Chain Reaction *'96*
The Glimmer Man *'96*
The Long Kiss Goodnight *'96*
Braveheart *'95*
Rob Roy *'95*
Royal Deceit *'94*
Sharpe's Eagle *'93*
Sharpe's Rifles *'93*
The Lost Language of Cranes *'92*
Murder by Moonlight *'91*
Hidden Agenda *'90*
Secret Weapon *'90*
Manhunter *'86*
Florence Nightingale *'85*
Pope John Paul II *'84*
Silent Scream *'84*
Therese Raquin *'80*
In Celebration *'75*

Charlie Cox (1982-)
Stardust *'07*
Casanova *'05*
The Merchant of Venice *'04*
Dot the I *'03*

Christina Cox (1971-)
S.I.S. *'08*
Better Than Chocolate *'99*
Street Law *'95*

Claire Cox (1975-)
Luther *'03*
Shooting Fish *'98*
The Choir *'95*

Courteney Cox (1964-)
Bedtime Stories *'08*
Barnyard *'06 (V)*
Zoom *'06*
The Longest Yard *'05*
November *'05*
Get Well Soon *'01*
3000 Miles to Graceland *'01*
Scream 3 *'00*
The Runner *'99*
Scream 2 *'97*
Commandments *'96*
Scream *'96*
Sketch Artist 2: Hands That See *'94*
Ace Ventura: Pet Detective *'93*
The Opposite Sex and How to Live with Them *'93*
Battling for Baby *'92*
Shaking the Tree *'92*
Blue Desert *'91*
Curiosity Kills *'90*
Mr. Destiny *'90*
Down Twisted *'89*
The Prize Pulitzer *'89*
Cocoon: The Return *'88*
Masters of the Universe *'87*
Misfits of Science *'85*

David A. Cox
Extreme Vengeance *'90*
The Last Season *'87*

Jennifer Elise Cox (1973-)
Hard Pill *'05*
EDtv *'99*
Sometimes They Come Back... Again *'96*
A Very Brady Sequel *'96*
A Weekend in the Country *'96*
The Brady Bunch Movie *'95*

Julie Cox (1973-)
The Riddle *'07*
Second in Command *'05*
Byron *'03*
Children of Dune *'03*
King of Texas *'02*
The War Bride *'01*
Dune *'00*
The Scarlet Pimpernel 2: Mademoiselle Guillotine *'99*
20,000 Leagues Under the Sea *'97*

Mitchell Cox
Crossfire *'98*
A.P.E.X. *'94*
Rule #3 *'93*
Red Snow *'91*

Nikki Cox (1978-)
Nutty Professor 2: The Klumps *'00*
The Glimmer Man *'96*

Richard Cox (1948-)
Missing Brendan *'03*
American Tragedy *'00*
Snowbound: The Jim and Jennifer Stolpa Story *'94*
Street Justice *'89*
Zombie High *'87*
The Vindicator *'85*
King of the Mountain *'81*
Cruising *'80*

Ronny Cox (1938-)
Imagine That *'09*
Crazy as Hell *'02*
Point of Origin *'02*
American Outlaws *'01*
Perfect Murder, Perfect Town *'00*
Forces of Nature *'99*
Frog and Wombat *'98*
From the Earth to the Moon *'98*
Murder at 1600 *'97*
Todd McFarlane's Spawn *'97 (V)*
Rebound: The Legend of Earl "The Goat" Manigault *'96*
Scissors *'91*
Loose Cannons *'90*
Martians Go Home! *'90*
Total Recall *'90*
Captain America *'89*
One Man Force *'89*
In the Line of Duty: The FBI Murders *'88*
Scandal in a Small Town *'88*
The Abduction of Kari Swenson *'87*
Beverly Hills Cop 2 *'87*
RoboCop *'87*
Steele Justice *'87*
Target: Favorite Son *'87*
Hollywood Vice Sqaud *'86*
Vision Quest *'85*
Beverly Hills Cop *'84*
Raw Courage *'84*
Reckless Disregard *'84*
Tangiers *'83*
The Beast Within *'82*
Some Kind of Hero *'82*
Two of a Kind *'82*
When Hell Was in Session *'82*
Fallen Angel *'81*
Taps *'81*
Kavik the Wolf Dog *'80*
Last Song *'80*
The Onion Field *'79*
Harper Valley P.T.A. *'78*
The Car *'77*
Gray Lady Down *'77*
Lost Legacy: A Girl Called Hatter Fox *'77*
Our Town *'77*
Bound for Glory *'76*
Who Is the Black Dahlia? *'75*
The Connection *'73*
Deliverance *'72*
Mind Snatchers *'72*

Ruth Cox
The Attic *'80*
Swap Meet *'79*

Tony Cox (1958-)
Date Movie *'06*
I Accidentally Domed Your Son *'04*
Bad Santa *'03*
Me, Myself, and Irene *'00*
Spaced Invaders *'90*
Jekyll & Hyde... Together Again *'82*

Veanne Cox (1963-)
Marci X *'03*
Beethoven's 4th *'01*
Big Eden *'00*
Erin Brockovich *'00*
National Lampoon's Class of '86 *'86*

Wally Cox (1924-73)
The Night Strangler *'72*
The Barefoot Executive *'71*
The Boatniks *'70*
The One and Only, Genuine, Original Family Band *'68*
A Guide for the Married Man *'67*
Bedford Incident *'65*
Morituri *'65*
Spencer's Mountain *'63*
State Fair *'62*

Jonathan Coy (1953-)
Conspiracy *'01*
The Scarlet Pimpernel *'99*
The Scarlet Pimpernel 2: Mademoiselle Guillotine *'99*
The Scarlet Pimpernel 3: The Kidnapped King *'99*
The Rector's Wife *'94*

Brendan Coyle (1963-)
Perfect Parents *'06*
Conspiracy *'01*
The Mapmaker *'01*
Catherine Cookson's The Glass Virgin *'95*

Richard Coyle (1972-)
The History of Mr. Polly *'07*
The Libertine *'05*
Lorna Doone *'01*
Othello *'01*
Prince of Poisoners: The Life and Crimes of William Palmer *'98*

Susan Coyne
Slings & Arrows: Season 2 *'05*
Ebenezer *'97*

Peter Coyote (1942-)
All Roads Lead Home *'08*
Dr. Dolittle 4: Tail to the Chief *'08*
$5 a Day *'08*
Resurrecting the Champ *'07*
Behind Enemy Lines 2: Axis of Evil *'06*
Deepwater *'05*
A Little Trip to Heaven *'05*
Return of the Living Dead: Rave to the Grave *'05*
The Grand Role *'04*
Bon Voyage *'03*
Northfork *'03*
Femme Fatale *'02*
Purpose *'02*
A Walk to Remember *'02*
Erin Brockovich *'00*
More Dogs Than Bones *'00*
Red Letters *'00*
A Time for Dancing *'00*
The Basket *'99*
Execution of Justice *'99*
Random Hearts *'99*
Indiscreet *'98*
Patch Adams *'98*
Road Ends *'98*
Route 9 *'98*
Sphere *'97*
Top of the World *'97*
Two for Texas *'97*
Seeds of Doubt *'96*
Unforgettable *'96*
Buffalo Girls *'95*
Dalva *'95*
Moonlight and Valentino *'95*
Terminal Justice: Cybertech P.D. *'95*
Breach of Conduct *'94*
Kika *'94*
That Eye, the Sky *'94*
Bitter Moon *'92*
Keeper of the City *'92*
Crooked Hearts *'91*
Exposure *'91*
The Man Inside *'90*
Heart of Midnight *'89*
Best Kept Secrets *'88*
Baja Oklahoma *'87*
Echoes in the Darkness *'87*
A Man in Love *'87*
Outrageous Fortune *'87*
Stacking *'87*
The Blue Yonder *'86*
The Jagged Edge *'85*
Legend of Billie Jean *'85*
Heartbreakers *'84*
Slayground *'84*
Cross Creek *'83*
Strangers Kiss *'83*
Timerider *'83*
Endangered Species *'82*
E.T.: The Extra-Terrestrial *'82*
Out *'82*
The People vs. Jean Harris *'81*
Southern Comfort *'81*
Die Laughing *'80*
Tell Me a Riddle *'80*

Cylk Cozart (1957-)
16 Blocks *'06*
Play It to the Bone *'99*
Three to Tango *'99*
Conspiracy Theory *'97*
White Men Can't Jump *'92*

Buster Crabbe (1907-83)
Alien Dead *'79*
Swim Team *'79*
Arizona Raiders *'65*
King of the Congo *'52*
Pirates of the High Seas *'50*
The Last of the Redmen *'47*
Sea Hound *'47*
Outlaw of the Plains *'46*
Swamp Fire *'46*
Border Badmen *'45*
Gangster's Den *'45*
His Brother's Ghost *'45*
Lightning Raiders *'45*
Shadows of Death *'45*
Devil Riders *'44*
The Drifter *'44*
Frontier Outlaws *'44*
Nabonga *'44*
Oath of Vengeance *'44*
Rustler's Hideout *'44*
Thundering Gunslingers *'44*
Wild Horse Phantom *'44*
Billy the Kid Trapped *'42*
Jungle Siren *'42*
Law and Order *'42*
The Mysterious Rider *'42*
Wildcat *'42*
Flash Gordon Conquers the Universe *'40*
Flash Gordon: Rocketship *'40*
Space Soldiers Conquer the Universe *'40*
Buck Rogers Conquers the Universe *'39*
Destination Saturn *'39*
Flash Gordon: Mars Attacks the World *'39*
Red Barry *'38*
Forlorn River *'37*
Desert Gold *'36*
Drift Fence *'36*
Rocketship *'36*
Search for Beauty *'34*
Buffalo Stampede *'33*
King of the Jungle *'33*
Tarzan the Fearless *'33*
To the Last Man *'33*
Island of Lost Souls *'32*

Ruth Cracknell (1925-2002)
Joey *'98*
Lilian's Story *'95*
Alice to Nowhere *'86*
The Chant of Jimmie Blacksmith *'78*
Island Trader *'71*

Carolyn Craig (1934-70)
Studs Lonigan *'60*
House on Haunted Hill *'58*
Portland Expose *'57*

Catherine Craig (1915-2004)
Seven Were Saved *'47*
Here Come the Waves *'45*
Spy Train *'43*

Daniel Craig (1968-)
Defiance '08
Flashbacks of a Fool '08
Quantum of Solace '08
The Golden Compass '07
The Invasion '07
Casino Royale '06
Infamous '06
Renaissance '06 (V)
Archangel '05
Fateless '05
The Jacket '05
Layer Cake '05
Munich '05
Enduring Love '04
The Mother '03
Sylvia '03
Road to Perdition '02
Lara Croft: Tomb Raider '01
Sword of Honour '01
I Dreamed of Africa '00
Love and Rage '99
The Trench '99
Elizabeth '98
Love Is the Devil '98
The Ice House '97
Obsession '97
Kiss and Tell '96
Moll Flanders '96
A Kid in King Arthur's Court '95
The Power of One '92

Diane Craig (1949-)
All the Rivers Run '84
The Mango Tree '77
Roses Bloom Twice '77
Ned Kelly '70

Helen Craig (1912-86)
They Live by Night '49
The Snake Pit '48

James Craig (1912-85)
The Tormentors '71
The Devil's Brigade '68
Four Fast Guns '59
Man or Gun '58
Naked in the Sun '57
Cyclops '56
Massacre '56
Drums in the Deep South '51
Side Street '50
Our Vines Have Tender Grapes '45
The Heavenly Body '44
The Human Comedy '43
Valley of the Sun '42
The Devil & Daniel Webster '41
Black Friday '40
Kitty Foyle '40
Law and Order '40
Winners of the West '40
Thunder Trail '37

Michael Craig (1928-)
Robin Hood.. The Legend: Herne's Son '85
Escape 2000 '81
The Irishman '78
Night of the Assassin '77
Roses Bloom Twice '77
Ride a Wild Pony '75
Inn of the Damned '74
Vault of Horror '73
Lola '69
Star! '68
Modesty Blaise '66
Sandra of a Thousand Delights '65
Stolen Hours '63
Mysterious Island '61
Doctor in Love '60
Sapphire '59
Sea of Sand '58
The Silent Enemy '58

Philip Craig
Behind the Red Door '02
Spider '02

Wendy Craig (1934-)
The Nanny '65
The Mind Benders '63
The Servant '63
Room at the Top '59

Yvonne Craig (1937-)
Digging Up Business '91
How to Frame a Figg '71
Mars Needs Women '66
Ski Party '65
Kissin' Cousins '64
It Happened at the World's Fair '63
The Young Land '59

Jeanne Crain (1925-2003)
The Night God Screamed '71
Nefertiti, Queen of the Nile '64
Fastest Gun Alive '56
Man Without a Star '55
Dangerous Crossing '53
Belles on Their Toes '52
People Will Talk '51
Cheaper by the Dozen '50
A Letter to Three Wives '49
Pinky '49
Leave Her to Heaven '45
State Fair '45

Grant Cramer (1961-)
Addicted to Murder 3: Bloodlust '99
Leapin' Leprechauns '95
Killer Klowns from Outer Space '88
Hardbodies '84
New Year's Evil '78

Joey Cramer (1974-)
Stone Fox '87
Flight of the Navigator '86

Marc Cramer (1910-88)
First Yank into Tokyo '45
Isle of the Dead '45

Richard Cramer (1889-1960)
Saps at Sea '40
Santa Fe Bound '37
Slaves in Bondage '37
Speed Reporter '36
Frontier Justice '35

Barbara Crampton (1962-)
Poison '01
Cold Harvest '98
The Godson '98
Space Truckers '97
Castle Freak '95
Robot Wars '93
Trancers 2: The Return of Jack Deth '90
Puppet Master '89
Kidnapped '87
Chopping Mall '86
From Beyond '86
Fraternity Vacation '85
Body Double '84
Re-Animator '84

Bob Crane (1928-78)
Gus '76
Superdad '73
Return to Peyton Place '61

Norma Crane (1928-73)
Fiddler on the Roof '71
They Call Me Mr. Tibbs! '70
Night Gallery '69
Tea and Sympathy '56

Richard Crane (1918-69)
The Devil's Partner '58
Guns Don't Argue '57
Rocky Jones, Space Ranger: Renegade Satellite '54
Winning of the West '53
Cavalry Charge '51
Dynamite '49

Tony Crane (1972-)
Wishmaster '97
An American Summer '90
In the Line of Duty: A Cop for the Killing '90
The War of the Roses '89

Kenneth Cranham (1944-)
Tess of the D'Urbervilles '08
Valkyrie '08
The Chatterley Affair '06
A Good Year '06
Layer Cake '05
Trauma '04
Two Men Went to War '02
Born Romantic '00
Gangster No. 1 '00
Lady Audley's Secret '00
Shiner '00
The Murder of Stephen Lawrence '99
Deep in the Heart (of Texas) '98
Our Mutual Friend '98
The Boxer '97
Jack Higgins' Midnight Man '96
The Tenant of Wildfell Hall '96
Jack Higgins' On Dangerous Ground '95
Tale of a Vampire '92
Under Suspicion '92
Prospero's Books '91
Monkey Boy '90
Oranges Are Not the Only Fruit '89
Chocolat '88
Hellbound: Hellraiser 2 '88
Stealing Heaven '88
Danger UXB '81
Therese Raquin '80
Brother Sun, Sister Moon '73

Lorcan Cranitch (1959-)
Shackleton '02
Dancing at Lughnasa '98
Deacon Brodie '98
Cracker: Brotherly Love '95
Cracker: Men Should Weep '94
Cracker: To Be a Somebody '94

Patrick Cranshaw (1919-2005)
Air Bud 5: Buddy Spikes Back '03
Bubble Boy '01
Best in Show '00
Broken Vessels '98
Nothing to Lose '96
The Amazing Transparent Man '60

Bryan Cranston (1956-)
Little Miss Sunshine '06
Seeing Other People '04
National Lampoon's Holiday Reunion '03
Terror Tract '00
From the Earth to the Moon '98
Saving Private Ryan '98
That Thing You Do! '96
The Companion '94
Erotique '94
High Stakes '93
Dead Space '90
The Big Turnaround '88

Paul Crauchet (1920-)
Grocer's Son '07
Beyond Fear '75
Army of Shadows '69

Nick Cravat (1911-94)
The Island of Dr. Moreau '77
The Scalphunters '68
Run Silent, Run Deep '58
Crimson Pirate '52
The Flame & the Arrow '50

Noel Cravat (1910-60)
The 5000 Fingers of Dr. T '53
Pirate Ship '49
The Razor's Edge '46
G-Men vs. the Black Dragon '43

Frank Craven (1875-1945)
Colonel Effingham's Raid '45
Jack London '44
Son of Dracula '43
In This Our Life '42
Keeper of the Flame '42
Pittsburgh '42
City for Conquest '40
Dreaming Out Loud '40
Our Town '40

James Craven (1892-1955)
D-Day on Mars '45
Immortal Sergeant '43
Sherlock Holmes and the Secret Weapon '42
Today I Hang '42
Green Archer '40

Matt Craven (1956-)
The Longshots '08
American Venus '07
Assault on Precinct 13 '05
A Simple Curve '05
The Clearing '04
The Life of David Gale '03
The Statement '03
Timeline '03
Dragonfly '02
Varian's War '01
Nuremberg '00
Things You Can Tell Just by Looking at Her '00
From the Earth to the Moon '98
Paulie '98
The Final Cut '96
The Juror '96
Masterminds '96
Breach of Trust '95
Bulletproof Heart '95
Crimson Tide '95
Kingfish: A Story of Huey P. Long '95
White Tiger '95
Double Cross '94
Indian Summer '93
A Few Good Men '92
K2: The Ultimate High '92
Jacob's Ladder '90
Smokescreen '90
Chattahoochee '89
Palais Royale '88
Agent on Ice '86
Happy Birthday to Me '81
Till Death Do Us Part '72

Mimi (Meyer) Craven
Dogwatch '97
Daddy's Girl '96
Midnight Heat '95
The Last Gasp '94
Open Fire '94
Mikey '92

Wes Craven (1939-)
Red Eye '05
Jay and Silent Bob Strike Back '01
Scream '96
ShadowZone: The Undead Express '96
The Fear '94
Wes Craven's New Nightmare '94
Body Bags '93

Andrew Crawford (1917-94)
The Gay Lady '49
Dear Murderer '47

Anne Crawford (1920-56)
Knights of the Round Table '53
Tony Draws a Horse '51
Night Beat '48
Bedelia '46

Broderick Crawford (1911-86)
Dark Forces '83
The Uppercrust '81
Express to Terror '79
A Little Romance '79
The Private Files of J. Edgar Hoover '77
Proof of the Man '77
Hunter '76
Terror in the Wax Museum '73
Embassy '72
The Tattered Web '71
Yin & Yang of Mr. Go '71
Hell's Bloody Devils '70
Ransom Money '70
Vulture '67
The Oscar '66
The Texican '66
The Castilian '63
Goliath and the Dragon '61
Between Heaven and Hell '56
Fastest Gun Alive '56
Il Bidone '55
Not as a Stranger '55
Human Desire '54
Last of the Comanches '52
Lone Star '52
Scandal Sheet '52
Born Yesterday '50
All the King's Men '49
The Time of Your Life '48
Black Angel '46
Broadway '42
Larceny, Inc. '42
The Black Cat '41
Seven Sinners '40
Slightly Honorable '40
The Texas Rangers Ride Again '40
Beau Geste '39
Eternally Yours '39
The Real Glory '39

Chace Crawford (1985-)
Twelve '10
The Haunting of Molly Hartley '08
Loaded '08
The Covenant '06

Cindy Crawford (1966-)
The Simian Line '99
54 '98
Fair Game '95

Clayne Crawford (1978-)
Smokin' Aces 2: Assassins' Ball '10
On the Doll '07
Strike '07
False Prophets '06
Steel City '06
Wristcutters: A Love Story '06
Swimfan '02
A Walk to Remember '02

Daz Crawford
Caffeine '06
Blade 2 '02

Ellen Crawford
The Man from Earth '07
Cries of Silence '97
Ulterior Motives '92

H. Marion Crawford
See Howard Marion-Crawford

Howard Crawford
See Howard Marion-Crawford

Joan Crawford (1904-77)
Night Gallery '69
Berserk! '67
Fatal Confinement '64
Strait-Jacket '64
What Ever Happened to Baby Jane? '62
The Best of Everything '59
The Story of Esther Costello '57
Autumn Leaves '56
Queen Bee '55
Johnny Guitar '53
Torch Song '53
Sudden Fear '52
This Woman Is Dangerous '52
Goodbye My Fancy '51
The Damned Don't Cry '50
Harriet Craig '50
Flamingo Road '49
It's a Great Feeling '49
Daisy Kenyon '47
The Possessed '47
Humoresque '46
Mildred Pierce '45
Hollywood Canteen '44
Above Suspicion '43
Reunion in France '42
They All Kissed the Bride '42
When Ladies Meet '41
A Woman's Face '41
Strange Cargo '40
Susan and God '40
Ice Follies of 1939 '39
The Women '39
The Shining Hour '38
The Bride Wore Red '37
The Last of Mrs. Cheyney '37
Mannequin '37
The Gorgeous Hussy '36
Love on the Run '36
Forsaking All Others '35
I Live My Life '35
Chained '34
Sadie McKee '34
Dancing Lady '33
The Lost Stooges '33
Today We Live '33
Grand Hotel '32
Rain '32
Dance Fools Dance '31
Laughing Sinners '31
Possessed '31
Our Modern Maidens '29
Across to Singapore '28
Our Dancing Daughters '28
Spring Fever '27
The Unknown '27
West Point '27
The Boob '26
Tramp, Tramp, Tramp '26

John Crawford (1926-)
Hard Knocks '79
The Enforcer '76
The Severed Arm '73
John Paul Jones '59
Actors and Sin '52
Zombies of the Stratosphere '52
The Invisible Monster '50

Johnny Crawford (1946-)
The Gambler Returns: The Luck of the Draw '93
Kenny Rogers as the Gambler, Part 2: The Adventure Continues '83
Outlaw Blues '77
The Great Texas Dynamite Chase '76
El Dorado '67
Village of the Giants '65
Indian Paint '64
Courage of Black Beauty '57

Katherine Crawford (1944-)
Riding with Death '76
Walk in the Spring Rain '70
The Doomsday Flight '66

Kathryn Crawford (1908-80)
Emma '32
Flying High '31
The Concentratin' Kid '30
Mountain Justice '30
King of the Rodeo '28

Michael Crawford (1942-)
Once Upon a Forest '93 (V)
Condorman '81
Hello, Dolly! '69
How I Won the War '67
A Funny Thing Happened on the Way to the Forum '66
The Knack '65

Rachael Crawford (1969-)
The Man '05
Love Songs '99
In His Father's Shoes '97
Pale Saints '97
Curtis's Charm '96
Rude '96
When Night Is Falling '95

Sophia Crawford (1966-)
U.S. Seals 2 *'01*
Sword of Honor *'94*

Wayne Crawford
American Cop *'94*
Crime Lords *'91*
Rebel Storm *'90*
Headhunter *'89*
White Ghost *'88*
The Evil Below *'87*
Quiet Thunder *'87*
Jake Speed *'86*
Barracuda *'78*

Charlie Creed-Miles (1972-)
King Arthur *'04*
Station Jim *'01*
Essex Boys *'99*
Nil by Mouth *'96*
The Young Poisoner's Handbook *'94*

Monica Creel (1970-)
Possums *'99*
Rattled *'96*

Laird Cregar (1916-44)
Hangover Square *'45*
Heaven Can Wait *'43*
Hello, Frisco, Hello *'43*
The Black Swan *'42*
Joan of Paris *'42*
This Gun for Hire *'42*
Charley's Aunt *'41*
I Wake Up Screaming *'41*

Joseph Crehan (1886-1966)
Red Desert *'50*
Ringside *'49*
Night Time in Nevada *'48*
O.S.S. *'46*
Meeting at Midnight *'44*
Phantom Lady *'44*
Hands Across the Border *'43*
Junior Army *'42*
Nevada City *'41*
They Died with Their Boots On *'41*
The Fighting 69th *'40*
Music in My Heart *'40*
Stanley and Livingstone *'39*
Star Reporter *'39*

Francis Creighton (1955-2003)
Barcelona *'94*
The Malibu Beach Vampires *'91*

Jack Creley (1926-2004)
The Reincarnate *'71*
Dr. Strangelove, or: How I Learned to Stop Worrying and Love the Bomb *'64*

Bruno Cremer (1929-)
Under the Sand *'00*
Menage *'86*
Josepha *'82*
A Simple Story *'79*
Sorcerer *'77*
Is Paris Burning? *'66*
The 317th Platoon *'65*

Richard Crenna (1926-2003)
Out of the Ashes *'03*
The Day Reagan Was Shot *'01*
By Dawn's Early Light *'00*
Wrongfully Accused *'98*
20,000 Leagues Under the Sea *'97*
Jade *'95*
A Pyromaniac's Love Story *'95*
Sabrina *'95*
Hot Shots! Part Deux *'93*
Intruders *'92*
Last Flight Out: A True Story *'90*
Montana *'90*
The Hillside Strangler *'89*
Leviathan *'89*
Rambo 3 *'88*
A Case of Deadly Force *'86*
On Wings of Eagles *'86*
Broken Badge *'85*
Rambo: First Blood, Part 2 *'85*
Summer Rental *'85*
The Flamingo Kid *'84*
Table for Five *'83*
First Blood *'82*
Body Heat *'81*
Death Ship *'80*
Stone Cold Dead *'80*
Mayflower: The Pilgrims' Adventure *'79*
Wild Horse Hank *'79*
Centennial *'78*
Devil Dog: The Hound of Hell *'78*
The Evil *'78*
Breakheart Pass *'76*
War Between the Tates *'76*
Catlow *'71*
Ride to Glory *'71*
Thief *'71*
Doctors' Wives *'70*
Marooned *'69*
Star! *'68*
Wait until Dark *'67*
The Sand Pebbles *'66*
Made in Paris *'65*
Our Miss Brooks *'56*
Pride of St. Louis *'52*

Pierre Cressoy (1924-80)
Blood for a Silver Dollar *'66*
The Triumph of Hercules *'66*
The Lion of Thebes *'64*
The Unfaithfuls *'60*
Verdi *'53*

Amanda Crew
The Haunting in Connecticut *'09*
Sex Drive *'08*
Final Destination 3 *'06*
Meltdown *'06*

Laura Hope Crews (1879-1942)
The Rain People *'69*
The Flame of New Orleans *'41*
Gone with the Wind *'39*
The Rains Came *'39*
Thanks for the Memory *'38*
Angel *'37*
Camille *'36*
Rafter Romance *'34*

Terry Crews (1968-)
The Expendables *'10*
The Lottery Ticket *'10*
Gamer *'09*
Get Smart *'08*
Street Kings *'08*
Balls of Fury *'07*
How to Rob a Bank *'07*
Norbit *'07*
The Benchwarmers *'06*
Idiocracy *'06*
Harsh Times *'05*
The Longest Yard *'05*
White Chicks *'04*
Baadasssss! *'03*
Friday After Next *'02*
Serving Sara *'02*
The 6th Day *'00*

Wendy Crewson (1956-)
The Summit *'08*
The Seeker: The Dark Is Rising *'07*
Away From Her *'06*
The Covenant *'06*
Eight Below *'06*
Niagara Motel *'06*
The Santa Clause 3: The Escape Clause *'06*
The Clearing *'04*
Between Strangers *'02*
A Killing Spring *'02*
The Santa Clause 2 *'02*
Verdict in Blood *'02*
Mercy *'00*
The 6th Day *'00*
Better Than Chocolate *'99*
Bicentennial Man *'99*
Escape Velocity *'99*
Summer's End *'99*
From the Earth to the Moon *'98*
Air Force One *'97*
The Eighteenth Angel *'97*
Gang Related *'96*
To Gillian on Her 37th Birthday *'96*
Corrina, Corrina *'94*
The Santa Clause *'94*
Spenser: A Savage Place *'94*
Spenser: The Judas Goat *'94*
The Good Son *'93*
Folks! *'92*
The Doctor *'91*
Spies, Lies and Naked Thighs *'91*
Buffalo Jump *'90*
Hobo's Christmas *'87*
My Father, My Rival *'85*
My Sweet Victim *'85*
Mark of Cain *'84*
Mazes and Monsters *'82*
Skullduggery *'79*

Mik Cribben
Beware! Children at Play *'95*
Nightmare *'82*

Bernard Cribbins (1928-)
Carry On Columbus *'92*
The Adventures of Picasso *'80*
Frenzy *'72*
The Railway Children *'70*
She *'65*
Carry On Spying *'64*
Carry On Jack *'63*
The Wrong Arm of the Law *'63*
The Mouse on the Moon *'62*

Ed Crick
Future Hunters *'88*
Eye of the Eagle *'87*

Missy (Melissa) Crider (1974-)
Gigli *'03*
Frailty *'02*
Instinct to Kill *'01*
Mulholland Drive *'01*
Alien Cargo *'99*
The Sex Monster *'99*
Quicksilver Highway *'98*
Sins of the Mind *'97*
Stand-Ins *'97*
The Beast *'96*
A Boy Called Hate *'95*
Powder *'95*
Girls in Prison *'94*

Lawrence Criner (1898-1965)
Miracle in Harlem *'48*
Gang War *'40*
The Duke Is Tops *'38*

Erno Crisa (1924-68)
Purple Noon *'60*
Lady Chatterley's Lover *'55*

Walter Crisham
Love in Pawn *'53*
Moulin Rouge *'52*

Donald Crisp (1880-1974)
Spencer's Mountain *'63*
Greyfriars Bobby *'61*
Pollyanna *'60*
A Dog of Flanders *'59*
Last Hurrah *'58*
Saddle the Wind *'58*
The Long Gray Line *'55*
The Man from Laramie *'55*
Prince Valiant *'54*
Home Town Story *'51*
Bright Leaf *'50*
Challenge to Lassie *'49*
The Hills of Home *'48*
Ramrod *'47*
Son of Lassie *'45*
The Valley of Decision *'45*
The Adventures of Mark Twain *'44*
National Velvet *'44*
The Uninvited *'44*
Lassie, Come Home *'43*
Dr. Jekyll and Mr. Hyde *'41*
How Green Was My Valley *'41*
Brother Orchid *'40*
City for Conquest *'40*
Dr. Ehrlich's Magic Bullet *'40*
Knute Rockne: All American *'40*
The Sea Hawk *'40*
Oklahoma Kid *'39*
The Old Maid *'39*
The Private Lives of Elizabeth & Essex *'39*
Wuthering Heights *'39*
Amazing Dr. Clitterhouse *'38*
Dawn Patrol *'38*
Jezebel *'38*
The Sisters *'38*
That Certain Woman *'37*
Beloved Enemy *'36*
The Charge of the Light Brigade *'36*
A Woman Rebels *'36*
Mutiny on the Bounty *'35*
Little Minister *'34*
Red Dust *'32*
Svengali *'31*
Stand and Deliver *'28*
The Viking *'28*
The Black Pirate *'26*
Don Q., Son of Zorro *'25*
Broken Blossoms *'19*
The Birth of a Nation *'15*
Home Sweet Home *'14*

Quentin Crisp (1908-99)
Naked in New York *'93*
Philadelphia *'93*
Orlando *'92*
The Bride *'85*

Anthony Criss
See Treach
The Art of War 3: Retribution *'08*

Peter Criss (1947-)
Detroit Rock City *'99*
KISS Meets the Phantom of the Park *'78*

Linda Cristal (1934-)
Midnight Auto Supply *'78*
Hughes & Harlow: Angels in Hell *'77*
The Dead Don't Die *'75*
Mr. Majestyk *'74*
Two Rode Together *'61*
The Alamo *'60*
The Perfect Furlough *'59*
The Fiend Who Walked the West *'58*

Perla Cristal (1937-)
The Fury of the Wolfman *'70*
The Christmas Kid *'68*
A Witch Without a Broom *'68*
White Comanche *'67*
Espionage in Tangiers *'65*
The Awful Dr. Orloff *'62*

Michael Cristofer (1945-)
The Little Drummer Girl *'84*
An Enemy of the People *'77*

Criswell (1907-82)
Orgy of the Dead *'65*
Night of the Ghouls *'59*
Plan 9 from Outer Space *'56*

Roark Critchlow
Hydra *'09*
Shark Swarm *'08*
Bone Eater *'07*
18 Fingers of Death *'05*

Anthony Crivello (1955-)
Running Woman *'98*
Star Portal *'97*
Twisted *'96*
Frankenstein Sings... The Movie *'95*
The Lost Capone *'90*

Karlene Crockett
Return *'88*
Massive Retaliation *'85*
Eyes of Fire *'84*
Diary of a Teenage Hitchhiker *'82*

Jamie Croft (1981-)
Joey *'98*
The Real Macaw *'98*
Napoleon *'96 (V)*
That Eye, the Sky *'94*

Peter Croft (1917-)
O.H.M.S. *'37*
King of the Damned *'36*

Dona Croll
The Shadow in the North *'07*
Manderlay *'05*

Jonathan Crombie (1966-)
Anne of Green Gables: The Continuing Story *'99*
The Waiting Game *'98*
The Good Fight *'92*
Cafe Romeo *'91*
Anne of Avonlea *'87*
Bullies *'86*
The Housekeeper *'86*
Anne of Green Gables *'85*

Peter Crombie
Seven *'95*
Rising Sun *'93*
Smooth Talker *'90*

Ben Crompton (1974-)
All or Nothing *'02*
102 Dalmatians *'00*
All the King's Men *'99*

James Cromwell (1940-)
Surrogates *'09*
Tortured *'08*
W. *'08*
Becoming Jane *'07*
Spider-Man 3 *'07*
The Queen *'06*
The Longest Yard *'05*
I, Robot *'04*
Salem's Lot *'04*
Angels in America *'03*
The Snow Walker *'03*
A Death in the Family *'02*
The Magnificent Ambersons *'02*
RFK *'02*
Spirit: Stallion of the Cimarron *'02 (V)*
The Sum of All Fears *'02*
Space Cowboys *'00*
The Bachelor *'99*
The General's Daughter *'99*
The Green Mile *'99*
RKO 281 *'99*
A Slight Case of Murder *'99*
Snow Falling on Cedars *'99*
Babe: Pig in the City *'98*
Deep Impact *'98*
Species 2 *'98*
The Education of Little Tree *'97*
L.A. Confidential *'97*
Eraser *'96*
The People vs. Larry Flynt *'96*
Star Trek: First Contact *'96*
Babe *'95*
Romeo Is Bleeding *'93*
The Babe *'92*
Spraggue *'84*
The Man with Two Brains *'83*
A Christmas Without Snow *'80*
Deadly Game *'77*

John Cromwell (1888-1979)
3 Women *'77*
Top Secret Affair *'57*

Richard Cromwell (1910-60)
Baby Face Morgan *'42*
Riot Squad *'41*
Young Mr. Lincoln *'39*
The Wrong Road *'37*
Life Begins at Forty *'35*
The Lives of a Bengal Lancer *'35*
Hoopla *'33*
Emma *'32*
The Strange Love of Molly Louvain *'32*
Maker of Men *'31*

Claudia Cron
Running Brave *'83*
Hit & Run *'82*

Gail Cronauer
The Newton Boys *'97*
Carried Away *'95*

Neil Crone
Cube 2: Hypercube *'02*
Verdict in Blood *'02*

David Cronenberg (1943-)
Jason X *'01*
Resurrection *'99*
Last Night *'98*
Extreme Measures *'96*
Blood & Donuts *'95*
The Stupids *'95*
Henry & Verlin *'94*
Nightbreed *'90*
Into the Night *'85*

Jeanette Cronin
Danny Deckchair *'03*
Mr. Accident *'99*
The Boys *'98*

Laurel Cronin (1939-92)
Beethoven *'92*
Housesitter *'92*

Hume Cronyn (1911-2003)
A Separate Peace *'04*
Off Season *'01*
Sea People *'00*
Santa and Pete *'99*
Horton Foote's Alone *'97*
Twelve Angry Men *'97*
Marvin's Room *'96*
Camilla *'94*
The Pelican Brief *'93*
To Dance with the White Dog *'93*
Broadway Bound *'92*
Age Old Friends *'89*
Day One *'89*
Cocoon: The Return *'88*
*batteries not included *'87*
Foxfire *'87*
Brewster's Millions *'85*
Cocoon *'85*
Gin Game *'84*
Impulse *'84*
The World According to Garp *'82*
Honky Tonk Freeway *'81*
Rollover *'81*
Conrack *'74*
The Parallax View *'74*
There Was a Crooked Man *'70*
The Arrangement *'69*
Cleopatra *'63*
Sunrise at Campobello *'60*
A Doll's House *'59*
People Will Talk *'51*
Brute Force *'47*
The Postman Always Rings Twice *'46*
Ziegfeld Follies *'46*
Lifeboat *'44*
The Seventh Cross *'44*
The Phantom of the Opera *'43*
Shadow of a Doubt *'43*

Tandy Cronyn (1945-)
Getting Out *'94*
Age Old Friends *'89*
Twisted *'86*
Once Upon a Time in America *'84*

Mackenzie Crook (1971-)
Sex & Drugs & Rock & Roll *'10*
City of Ember *'08*
I Want Candy *'07*
Pirates of the Caribbean: At World's End *'07*

Land of the Blind '06
Pirates of the Caribbean: Dead Man's Chest '06
The Merchant of Venice '04
Pirates of the Caribbean: The Curse of the Black Pearl '03

Peter Crook (1958-)
Clean Slate '94
The Yarn Princess '94
Peephole '93
Chaplin '92
Bird '88

Leland Crooke
Scorchers '92
Dead Man Walking '88

Anna Cropper (1938-2007)
Praying Mantis '83
The Lost Boys '78
The Moonstone '72

Linda Cropper
Passion '99
Blackrock '97
The Seventh Floor '93

Annette Crosbie (1934-)
Calendar Girls '03
Oliver Twist '00
Shooting Fish '98
Solitaire for 2 '94
Ordeal by Innocence '84
The Slipper and the Rose '76
Edward the King '75
Six Wives of Henry VIII '71

Bing Crosby (1904-77)
That's Entertainment '74
Cancel My Reservation '72
Robin and the 7 Hoods '64
The Road to Hong Kong '62
Let's Make Love '60
Alias Jesse James '59
High Society '56
Country Girl '54
White Christmas '54
The Road to Bali '53
Scared Stiff '53
Just for You '52
Here Comes the Groom '51
Mr. Music '50
Riding High '50
The Adventures of Ichabod and Mr. Toad '49 (V)
A Connecticut Yankee in King Arthur's Court '49
The Legend of Sleepy Hollow '49 (N)
Emperor Waltz '48
My Favorite Brunette '47
The Road to Rio '47
Welcome Stranger '47
Blue Skies '46
The Road to Utopia '46
The Bells of St. Mary's '45
Here Come the Waves '45
Going My Way '44
The Princess and the Pirate '44
Strictly G.I. '44
They Got Me Covered '43 (V)
Holiday Inn '42
My Favorite Blonde '42
The Road to Morocco '42
Star Spangled Rhythm '42
Birth of the Blues '41
The Road to Zanzibar '41
If I Had My Way '40
Rhythm on the River '40
The Road to Singapore '40
East Side of Heaven '39
Double or Nothing '37
Waikiki Wedding '37
Pennies from Heaven '36
Rhythm on the Range '36
Mississippi '35
Here is My Heart '34
We're Not Dressing '34
College Humor '33
Going Hollywood '33
Reaching for the Moon '31
King of Jazz '30

Cathy Lee Crosby (1944-)
Ablaze '00
The Big Tease '99
The Real Howard Spitz '98
The Player '92
World War III '86
Roughnecks '80
The Dark '79
Coach '78

David Crosby (1941-)
Thunderheart '92
Backdraft '91
Hook '91
Gimme Shelter '70

Denise Crosby (1957-)
Mortuary '05
Deep Impact '98
Executive Power '98
Red Shoe Diaries: Four on the Floor '96
Mutant Species '95
Relative Fear '95
Black Water '94
Desperate Crimes '93
Dolly Dearest '92
Red Shoe Diaries 2: Double Dare '92
Miracle Mile '89
Pet Sematary '89
Skin Deep '89
Arizona Heat '87
Desert Hearts '86
The Eliminators '86
Curse of the Pink Panther '83
48 Hrs. '82

Gary Crosby (1933-95)
Chill Factor '90
Night Stalker '87
Justin Morgan Had a Horse '81
Girl Happy '65
Operation Bikini '63

Lindsay Crosby (1938-89)
Free Grass '69
The Glory Stompers '67
Sergeants 3 '62

Lucinda Crosby (1952-)
Blue Movies '88
Naked Cage '86

Mary Crosby (1959-)
The Night Caller '97
Cupid '96
Desperate Motives '92
The Berlin Conspiracy '91
Body Chemistry '90
Corporate Affairs '90
Eating '90
Tapeheads '89
Deadly Innocence '88
Quicker Than the Eye '88
Stagecoach '86
Ice Pirates '84
Last Plane Out '83
Pearl '78

Norm Crosby (1927-)
Adam Sandler's 8 Crazy Nights '02 (V)
Amore! '93

Wade Crosby (1905-75)
Invasion U.S.A. '52
Tales of Robin Hood '52
Rough Riders of Cheyenne '45

Henrietta Crosman (1861-1944)
Personal Property '37
The Moon's Our Home '36
Charlie Chan's Secret '35
The Dark Angel '35
Pilgrimage '33

Ben Cross (1947-)
Star Trek '09
Hero Wanted '08
War, Inc. '08
Finding Rin Tin Tin '07
Species 4: The Awakening '07
Behind Enemy Lines 2: Axis of Evil '06
Undisputed II: Last Man Standing '06
Frederick Forsyth's Icon '05
Exorcist: The Beginning '04
Anti-Terrorist Cell: Manhunt '01
Solomon '98
Tower of the Firstborn '98
The Corporate Ladder '97
20,000 Leagues Under the Sea '97
The Invader '96
Turbulence '96
First Knight '95
Temptress '95
The Ascent '94
Haunted Symphony '94
Cold Sweat '93
The Criminal Mind '93
Diamond Fleece '92
Live Wire '92
The Jeweller's Shop '90
Nightlife '90
Paperhouse '89
Steal the Sky '88
The Unholy '88
The Assisi Underground '84
The Far Pavilions '84
Coming Out of the Ice '82
Chariots of Fire '81
The Flame Trees of Thika '81

David Cross (1964-)
Alvin and the Chipmunks: The Squeakuel '09
Battle for Terra '09 (V)
Year One '09
Kung Fu Panda '08 (V)
Alvin and the Chipmunks '07
I'm Not There '07
Curious George '06 (V)
School for Scoundrels '06
She's the Man '06
Eternal Sunshine of the Spotless Mind '04
Men in Black 2 '02
Scary Movie 2 '01
Chain of Fools '00
Small Soldiers '98
The Cable Guy '96

Dennis Cross (1924-)
How to Make a Monster '58
Crime of Passion '57

Flora Cross
Margot at the Wedding '07
Bee Season '05

Harley Cross (1978-)
Shriek If You Know What I Did Last Friday the 13th '00
Dance with the Devil '97
To Dance with the White Dog '93
Stanley and Iris '90
The Fly 2 '89
Cohen and Tate '88
The Believers '87
Where Are the Children? '85

Joseph Cross (1986-)
Milk '08
Untraceable '08
Flags of Our Fathers '06
Running with Scissors '06
Strangers with Candy '06
The Spring '00
Desperate Measures '98
Jack Frost '98
Wide Awake '97

Larry Cross (1913-76)
The Wind and the Lion '75
Time Lock '57

Paul Cross
The Return of the Borrowers '96
The Borrowers '93
Ice Pawn '92

Peter Cross
See Pierre Cressoy

Rebecca Cross
The Bachelor '99
The Last Warrior '99
Leprechaun 4: In Space '96
Wet and Wild Summer '92

Roger R. Cross
Ballistic: Ecks vs. Sever '02
Interceptor Force 2 '02
A Father's Choice '00

TJ Cross
Showtime '02
Gone in 60 Seconds '00

Rupert Crosse (1927-73)
The Reivers '69
Ride in the Whirlwind '66
Shadows '60

Syd Crossley (1885-1960)
Young and Innocent '37
The Deputy Drummer '35
That Certain Thing '28

Scatman Crothers (1910-86)
The Journey of Natty Gann '85
Twilight Zone: The Movie '83
Two of a Kind '83
Deadly Eyes '82
Zapped! '82
Bronco Billy '80
The Shining '80
Scavenger Hunt '79
Mean Dog Blues '78
Chesty Anderson USN '76
The Shootist '76
Silver Streak '76
Stay Hungry '76
One Flew Over the Cuckoo's Nest '75
Streetfight '75
Black Belt Jones '74
Truck Turner '74
Detroit 9000 '73
The King of Marvin Gardens '72
Bloody Mama '70
The Great White Hope '70
Lady in a Cage '64
The Patsy '64
The Sins of Rachel Cade '61
Between Heaven and Hell '56
Yes, Sir, Mr. Bones '51

Brian Croucher
I'll Sleep When I'm Dead '03
Fool's Gold: The Story of the Brink's-Mat Robbery '92
The House that Bled to Death '81

Lindsay Crouse (1948-)
Mr. Brooks '07
Cherish '02
Impostor '02
The Insider '99
Progeny '98
The Arrival '96
If These Walls Could Talk '96
The Juror '96
Prefontaine '96
The Indian in the Cupboard '95
Norma Jean and Marilyn '95
Being Human '94
Bye Bye, Love '94
Parallel Lives '94
Chantilly Lace '93
Final Appeal '93
Desperate Hours '90
Communion '89
House of Games '87
Iceman '84
Places in the Heart '84
Daniel '83
The Verdict '82
Prince of the City '81
Summer Solstice '81
Between the Lines '77
Slap Shot '77
All the President's Men '76
Eleanor & Franklin '76

Roger Crouzet (1927-2000)
Blue Country '77
The Thief of Paris '67
Double Agents '59
Letters from My Windmill '54

Ashley Crow (1960-)
Minority Report '02
Little Big League '94
Final Appeal '93

Emilia Crow
Grand Tour: Disaster in Time '92
Hitz '89

Graham Crowden (1922-)
Calendar Girls '03
Possession '02
I Want You '98
The Innocent Sleep '95
Monsignor Quixote '91
Code Name: Emerald '85
The Company of Wolves '85
Out of Africa '85
Britannia Hospital '82
The Abdication '74
The Little Prince '74
Romance with a Double Bass '74
Naughty Knights '71
If... '69
Morgan: A Suitable Case for Treatment '66

Russell Crowe (1964-)
Robin Hood '10
State of Play '09
Body of Lies '08
Tenderness '08
American Gangster '07
Bra Boys '07 (V)
3:10 to Yuma '07
A Good Year '06
Cinderella Man '05
Master and Commander: The Far Side of the World '03
A Beautiful Mind '01
Gladiator '00
Proof of Life '00
The Insider '99
Mystery, Alaska '99
Breaking Up '97
Heaven's Burning '97
L.A. Confidential '97
No Way Back '96
The Quick and the Dead '95
Rough Magic '95
Virtuosity '95
For the Moment '94
The Sum of Us '94
The Silver Stallion: King of the Wild Brumbies '93
The Crossing '92
The Efficiency Expert '92
Romper Stomper '92
Hammers over the Anvil '91
Proof '91

Josephine Crowell (1849-1932)
The Man Who Laughs '27
The Greatest Question '19
Hearts of the World '18
The Birth of a Nation '15

Dermot Crowley (1947-)
Dead Gorgeous '02
Falling for a Dancer '98
The Sculptress '97
Echoes '88

Donncha Crowley
Kings '07
Bloom '03

Jeananne Crowley (1946-)
The Real Charlotte '91
Reilly: Ace of Spies '87

Kathleen Crowley (1931-)
Curse of the Undead '59
The Rebel Set '59
The Female Jungle '56
Westward Ho, the Wagons! '56
The Farmer Takes a Wife '53

Pat Crowley
Wild Women of Wongo '59
Money from Home '53

Pat(ricia) Crowley (1929-)
61* '01
Force of Evil '77
Return to Fantasy Island '77
Menace on the Mountain '70
Hollywood or Bust '56
Walk the Proud Land '56
Red Garters '54
Forever Female '53

Suzan Crowley
Devices and Desires '91
Christabel '89

Marie Josee Croze (1970-)
The Diving Bell and the Butterfly '07
Tell No One '06
Munich '05
The Barbarian Invasions '03
Ararat '02
Wolves in the Snow '02
Battlefield Earth '00
Maelstrom '00

Billy Crudup (1968-)
Eat, Pray, Love '10
Public Enemies '09
Watchmen '09
Dedication '07
The Good Shepherd '06
Mission: Impossible 3 '06
Trust the Man '06
Stage Beauty '04
Big Fish '03
Charlotte Gray '01
World Traveler '01
Almost Famous '00
Waking the Dead '00
Jesus' Son '99
The Hi-Lo Country '98
Monument Ave. '98
Princess Mononoke '98 (V)
Inventing the Abbotts '97
Without Limits '97
Grind '96
Sleepers '96

Tom Cruise (1962-)
Knight and Day '10
Tropic Thunder '08
Valkyrie '08
Lions for Lambs '07
Mission: Impossible 3 '06
War of the Worlds '05
Collateral '04
The Last Samurai '03
Austin Powers In Goldmember '02
Minority Report '02
Vanilla Sky '01
Mission: Impossible 2 '00
Eyes Wide Shut '99
Magnolia '99
Jerry Maguire '96
Mission: Impossible '96
Interview with the Vampire '94
The Firm '93
Far and Away '92
A Few Good Men '92
Days of Thunder '90
Born on the Fourth of July '89
Cocktail '88
Rain Man '88
The Color of Money '86
Legend '86
Top Gun '86
All the Right Moves '83
The Outsiders '83
Risky Business '83
Losin' It '82
Endless Love '81
Taps '81

Rosalie Crutchley (1920-97)
A Village Affair '95

Four Weddings and a Funeral '94
Monsignor Quixote '91
The Franchise Affair '88
Eleni '85
The Hunchback of Notre Dame '82
Smiley's People '82
Testament of Youth '79
Night of the Laughing Dead '75
And Now the Screaming Starts '73
Elizabeth R '72
Cold Comfort Farm '71
Six Wives of Henry VIII '71
Creatures the World Forgot '70
Wuthering Heights '70
The Haunting '63
Make Me an Offer '55

Abigail Cruttenden (1969-)

Charlotte Gray '01
Hideous Kinky '99
Into the Blue '97
Jane Eyre '97
Sharpe's Justice '97
Sharpe's Revenge '97
Sharpe's Mission '96
Sharpe's Regiment '96
Sharpe's Siege '96
Intimate Contact '87
Kipperbang '82

Greg Cruttwell (1962-)

George of the Jungle '97
Two Days in the Valley '96
Naked '93

Alexis Cruz (1974-)

Tortilla Heaven '07
Slayer '06
Darkwolf '03
Why Do Fools Fall in Love? '98
Hostage High '97
Grand Avenue '96
Riot in the Streets '96
Larry McMurtry's Streets of Laredo '95
Stargate '94
The Old Man and the Sea '90
Gryphon '88

Brandon Cruz (1962-)

Safe '95
The Bad News Bears '76

Celia Cruz (1924-2003)

Soul Power '08
The Perez Family '94
The Mambo Kings '92

Ernesto Cruz

Midaq Alley '95
El Norte '83
Erendira '83

Penelope Cruz (1974-)

Sex and the City 2 '10
Broken Embraces '09
G-Force '09 (V)
Nine '09
Elegy '08
Vicky Cristina Barcelona '08
The Good Night '07
Volver '06
Sahara '05
Head in the Clouds '04
Noel '04
Gothika '03
Masked and Anonymous '03
Waking Up in Reno '02
Blow '01
Captain Corelli's Mandolin '01
No News from God '01
Vanilla Sky '01
All the Pretty Horses '00
Woman on Top '00
All About My Mother '99
The Girl of Your Dreams '99
The Hi-Lo Country '98
Twice upon a Yesterday '98
Live Flesh '97
Open Your Eyes '97
Love Can Seriously Damage Your Health '96

Talk of Angels '96
Framed '93
Jamon, Jamon '93
Belle Epoque '92

Raymond Cruz

Training Day '01
The Last Marshal '99
From Dusk Till Dawn 2: Texas Blood Money '98
Alien: Resurrection '97
The Rock '96
The Substitute '96
Up Close and Personal '96
Clear and Present Danger '94
Dragstrip Girl '94

Valerie Cruz

The Devil's Tomb '09
The Line '08

Vladimir Cruz (1965-)

A Paradise Under the Stars '99
Strawberry and Chocolate '93

Wilson Cruz (1973-)

He's Just Not That Into You '09
Coffee Date '06
Bam Bam & Celeste '05
Party Monster '03
Supernova '99
Joyride '97
All Over Me '96
johns '96

Jon Cryer (1965-)

Shorts: The Adventures of the Wishing Rock '09
Weather Girl '09
Tortured '08
Holy Man '98
Went to Coney Island on a Mission from God... Be Back by Five '98
Glam '97
Plan B '97
The Pompatus of Love '95
Heads '93
Hot Shots! '91
Dudes '87
Hiding Out '87
Morgan Stewart's Coming Home '87
O.C. and Stiggs '87
Superman 4: The Quest for Peace '87
Pretty in Pink '86
No Small Affair '84
Noon Wine '84

Suzanne Cryer (1967-)

Friends & Lovers '99
Dead Silence '98
Wag the Dog '97
Some Folks Call It a Sling Blade '94

Billy Crystal (1947-)

Tooth Fairy '10
Howl's Moving Castle '04 (V)
Analyze That '02
America's Sweethearts '01
Monsters, Inc. '01 (V)
The Adventures of Rocky & Bullwinkle '00
Analyze This '98
My Giant '98
Deconstructing Harry '97
Father's Day '96
Hamlet '96
Forget Paris '95
City Slickers 2: The Legend of Curly's Gold '94
Mr. Saturday Night '92
City Slickers '91
When Harry Met Sally... '89
Memories of Me '88
The Princess Bride '87
Throw Momma from the Train '87
Running Scared '86
This Is Spinal Tap '84
The Three Little Pigs '84
Enola Gay: The Men, the Mission, the Atomic Bomb '80

Breaking Up Is Hard to Do '79
Rabbit Test '78

Jennifer Crystal Foley (1973-)

61* '01
The American President '95

Sandor Csanyi (1975-)

Kontroll '03
I Love Budapest '01

Gyorgy Cserhalmi (1948-)

Flowers of Reverie '84
Mephisto '81
Hungarian Rhapsody '78

Marton Csokas (1966-)

Alice in Wonderland '10
Romulus, My Father '07
Aeon Flux '05
Asylum '05
The Great Raid '05
Kingdom of Heaven '05
The Bourne Supremacy '04
Garage Days '03
Lord of the Rings: The Return of the King '03
Timeline '03
Kangaroo Jack '02
XXX '02
Lord of the Rings: The Fellowship of the Ring '01
Rain '01
The Monkey's Mask '00
Broken English '96
Jack Brown, Genius '94

David Cubitt (1965-)

Ali '01
The Perfect Son '00
I Shot a Man in Vegas '96
Swann '96

Maria Grazia Cucinotta (1969-)

Our Italian Husband '04
Just One Night '00
Picking Up the Pieces '99
The World Is Not Enough '99
Solomon '98
A Brooklyn State of Mind '97
The Day of the Beast '95
The Postman '94

Michael Cudlitz (1964-)

Surrogates '09
Running Scared '06
Live from Baghdad '03
Band of Brothers '01
Grosse Pointe Blank '97
D3: The Mighty Ducks '96
Last Exit to Earth '96
The Liar's Club '93

Daniel Cudmore (1981-)

X-Men: The Last Stand '06
X2: X-Men United '03

Beto Cuevas

Borderland '07
La Mujer de Mi Hermano '06

Xavier Cugat (1900-90)

Neptune's Daughter '49
A Date with Judy '48
Luxury Liner '48
Holiday in Mexico '46
Two Girls and a Sailor '44
Stage Door Canteen '43
You Were Never Lovelier '42

Vladimir Cuk (1975-)

The Sixth Man '97
Celtic Pride '96

Frances Cuka (1936-)

Oliver Twist '05
The Watcher in the Woods '81

Melinda Culea (1955-)

Down, Out and Dangerous '95
Wagons East '94
Through the Eyes of a Killer '92

Kieran Culkin (1982-)

Scott Pilgrim vs. the World '10
Lymelife '08
The Dangerous Lives of Altar Boys '02
Igby Goes Down '02
The Cider House Rules '99
The Magical Legend of the Leprechauns '99
Music of the Heart '99
She's All That '99
The Mighty '98
Father of the Bride Part 2 '95
My Summer Story '94
Nowhere to Run '93
Home Alone 2: Lost in New York '92
Father of the Bride '91
Home Alone '90

Macaulay Culkin (1980-)

Sex and Breakfast '07
Saved! '04
Party Monster '03
Getting Even with Dad '94
The Pagemaster '94
Richie Rich '94
George Balanchine's The Nutcracker '93
The Good Son '93
Home Alone 2: Lost in New York '92
My Girl '91
Only the Lonely '91
Home Alone '90
Jacob's Ladder '90
See You in the Morning '89
Uncle Buck '89
Rocket Gibraltar '88

Michael Culkin

Crusade: A March through Time '06
Cold and Dark '05
Dangerous Beauty '98
Into the Blue '97
Candyman '92

Rory Culkin (1989-)

Twelve '10
Lymelife '08
The Night Listener '06
The Chumscrubber '05
Down in the Valley '05
The Zodiac '05
Mean Creek '04
It Runs in the Family '03
Igby Goes Down '02
Signs '02
Off Season '01
You Can Count On Me '99

Brett Cullen (1956-)

The Runaways '10
The Burning Plain '08
Ghost Rider '07
National Security '03
The Replacements '00
From the Earth to the Moon '98
Levitation '97
The Killing Jar '96
Apollo 13 '95
Something to Talk About '95
A Kiss Goodnight '94
Prehysteria '93
In a Stranger's Hand '92
Leaving Normal '92
Dead Solid Perfect '88

Max Cullen (1940-)

The Nugget '02
Kings in Grass Castles '97
Kiss or Kill '97
Billy's Holiday '95
Lightning Jack '94
Hard Knocks '80
The Odd Angry Shot '79
Sunday Too Far Away '74

Peter Cullen (1941-)

Transformers: Revenge of the Fallen '09 (V)
Transformers '07 (V)
Pooh's Heffalump Movie '05 (V)
Piglet's Big Movie '03 (V)

Frederick Culley (1879-1942)

The Four Feathers '39
The Private Life of Henry VIII '33

John Cullum (1930-)

The Night Listener '06
The Notorious Bettie Page '06
Held Up '00
Inherit the Wind '99
Ricochet River '98
Undesirable '92
Sweet Country '87
Marie '85
The Day After '83
The Prodigal '83
The Man Without a Country '73

John David (J.D.) Cullum (1966-)

Good Night, and Good Luck '05
Forever Young '92
Roadside Prophets '92
Ambition '91
Fever '91
Reversal of Fortune '90
Glory '89
Morgan Stewart's Coming Home '87
The Manhattan Project '86

Joseph Culp (1963-)

Cyxork 7 '06
Baadasssss! '03
Innocents '00
The Arrival '90
Iguana '89
Dream Lover '85

Robert Culp (1930-2010)

Innocents '00
Newsbreak '00
Running Mates '00
Wanted '98
Most Wanted '97
Mercenary '96
Xtro 3: Watch the Skies '95
The Pelican Brief '93
Murderous Vision '91
Timebomb '91
Voyage of Terror: The Achille Lauro Affair '90
Pucker Up and Bark Like a Dog '89
Silent Night, Deadly Night 3: Better Watch Out! '89
Big Bad Mama 2 '87
The Blue Lightning '86
The Gladiator '86
The Key to Rebecca '85
Turk 182! '85
Calendar Girl Murders '84
Her Life as a Man '83
Killjoy '81
The Night the City Screamed '80
Goldengirl '79
Hot Rod '79
Flood! '76
Great Scout & Cathouse Thursday '76
Sky Riders '76
Inside Out '75
The Castaway Cowboy '74
Hannie Caulder '72
A Name for Evil '70
Bob & Carol & Ted & Alice '69
Demon with a Glass Hand '64
PT 109 '63
Sunday in New York '63
Sammy, the Way-Out Seal '62

Steven Culp (1955-)

Leaving Barstow '08
Firehouse Dog '07
The Sisters '05
Spartan '04
The Emperor's Club '02
How to Make a Monster '01
Thirteen Days '00
Norma Jean and Marilyn '95

Jason Goes to Hell: The Final Friday '93

Calvin Culver (1943-87)

Ginger '72
Score '72

Jeffrey Culver

Bad Girls from Mars '90
Hobgoblins '87

Michael Culver (1938-)

The Green Man '91
Alamut Ambush '86
Deadly Recruits '86
Philby, Burgess and MacLean: Spy Scandal of the Century '84
Conduct Unbecoming '75
The Devil's Web '74
Fast Kill '73

Roland Culver (1900-84)

The Legend of Hell House '73
Term of Trial '63
Betrayed '54
Encore '52
The Obsessed '51
The Great Lover '49
Emperor Waltz '48
Down to Earth '47
Singapore '47
To Each His Own '46
Dead of Night '45
On Approval '44
The Day Will Dawn '42
Secret Mission '42
Spitfire '42
Night Train to Munich '40

Benedict Cumberbatch (1977-)

Creation '09
The Last Enemy '08
The Other Boleyn Girl '08
Atonement '07
Amazing Grace '06
Starter for Ten '06

Ji-Tu Cumbuka (1942-)

Midnight Edition '93
Glitch! '88
Mandingo '75

Alan Cumming (1965-)

Dare '09
Tin Man '07
Gray Matters '06
Bam Bam & Celeste '05
Son of the Mask '05
Sweet Land '05
Garfield: The Movie '04 (V)
Spy Kids 3-D: Game Over '03
X2: X-Men United '03
Nicholas Nickleby '02
The Anniversary Party '01
Intimate Affairs '01
Josie and the Pussycats '01
Spy Kids '01
Company Man '00
The Flintstones in Viva Rock Vegas '00
Get Carter '00
Urbania '00
Annie '99
Eyes Wide Shut '99
Titus '99
Plunkett & Macleane '98
Buddy '97
Romy and Michele's High School Reunion '97
Spice World: The Movie '97
Emma '96
Goldeneye '95
Circle of Friends '94
Second Best '94
Bernard and the Genie '91

Dorothy (Dorothy G. Cummings) Cumming (1899-1983)

Applause '29
The Divine Lady '29
The Wind '28
King of Kings '27

Constance Cummings (1910-2005)
The Battle of the Sexes '60
John and Julie '55
Blithe Spirit '45
The Foreman Went to France '42
This England '42
American Madness '32
Night After Night '32
Criminal Code '31

Irving Cummings (1888-1959)
Hollywood Cavalcade '39
The Saphead '21
Sex '20
Uncle Tom's Cabin '14

James (Jimmy) Cummings (1968-)
Southie '98
Ed's Next Move '96

Jim (Jonah) Cummings (1952-)
The Princess and the Frog '09 (V)
Pooh's Heffalump Movie '05 (V)
Comic Book: The Movie '04
The Lion King 1 1/2 '04 (V)
Piglet's Big Movie '03 (V)
Balto '95 (V)
A Goofy Movie '94 (V)
The Lion King '94 (V)

Quinn Cummings (1967-)
The Babysitter '80
The Goodbye Girl '77
Intimate Strangers '77
Night Terror '76

Robert Cummings (1908-90)
Five Golden Dragons '67
Promise Her Anything '66
The Carpetbaggers '64
Beach Party '63
My Geisha '62
Dial "M" for Murder '54
Lucky Me '54
Reign of Terror '49
Tell It to the Judge '49
The Accused '48
Lost Moment '47
The Chase '46
Forever and a Day '43
Princess O'Rourke '43
Saboteur '42
The Devil & Miss Jones '41
It Started with Eve '41
Kings Row '41
Moon over Miami '41
One Night in the Tropics '40
Spring Parade '40
Charlie McCarthy, Detective '39
Everything Happens at Night '39
Three Smart Girls Grow Up '39
The Texans '38
You and Me '38
Souls at Sea '37
Arizona Mahoney '36
Desert Gold '36

Susan Cummings (1930-)
Verboten! '59
Man From God's Country '58
Swamp Women '55

Eli Cummins
Harley '90
Dakota '88

Gregory Scott Cummins (1956-)
Gang Related '96
The Last of the Dogmen '95
Watchers 3 '94
Lone Justice 2 '93
Action U.S.A. '89
Dead End City '88
Hack O'Lantern '87

Juliette Cummins (1964-)
Deadly Dreams '88
Slumber Party Massacre 2 '87
Friday the 13th, Part 5: A New Beginning '85
Running Hot '83

Martin Cummins (1969-)
Devour '05
Ice Men '04
Liberty Stands Still '02
Love Come Down '00
We All Fall Down '00
Poltergeist: The Legacy '96
Born to Run '93
Friday the 13th, Part 8: Jason Takes Manhattan '89

Peggy Cummins (1925-)
The Captain's Table '60
Dentist In the Chair '60
Carry On Admiral '57
Curse of the Demon '57
Gun Crazy '49
Salute John Citizen '42

Peter Cummins (1931-)
Ground Zero '88
Blue Fire Lady '78

Pamela Cundell (1926-)
24-7 '97
The Return of the Borrowers '96

Rusty Cundieff (1965-)
Sprung '96
Tales from the Hood '95
Fear of a Black Hat '94

Liam Cundill
Reason to Die '90
Return of the Family Man '89

Emma Cunniffe (1973-)
Place of Execution '09
Love or Money '01
Plain Jane '01
All the King's Men '99
Great Expectations '99

Cecil Cunningham (1888-1959)
Above Suspicion '43
Twin Beds '42
Hurry, Charlie, Hurry '41
The Awful Truth '37

Colin Cunningham (1967-)
Masters of Horror: We All Scream for Ice Cream '07
Stealing Sinatra '04
The 6th Day '00

Danny Cunningham (1969-)
24 Hour Party People '01
Loaded '94

Jack Cunningham (1882-1941)
The Quare Fellow '62
Time Lock '57

John Cunningham (1932-)
DC 9/11: Time of Crisis '04
States of Control '98
The Jackal '97
Twisted '86
Lost and Found '79

Liam Cunningham (1961-)
Blood: The Last Vampire '09
The Tournament '09
The Mummy: Tomb of the Dragon Emperor '08
Northanger Abbey '07
The Wind That Shakes the Barley '06
Attila '01
Dog Soldiers '01
A Love Divided '01
RKO 281 '99
Shooting the Past '99
When the Sky Falls '99
Falling for a Dancer '98
Jude '96
Cracker: Best Boys '95
First Knight '95
A Little Princess '95
War of the Buttons '95

Peter "Sugarfoot" Cunningham
Bloodfist 3: Forced to Fight '92
Bloodmatch '91

Alain Cuny (1908-94)
Camille Claudel '89
Detective '85
Basileus Quartet '82
Christ Stopped at Eboli '79
Emmanuelle '74
Fellini Satyricon '69
The Milky Way '68
La Dolce Vita '60
The Lovers '59
The Hunchback of Notre Dame '57
The Lady Without Camelias '53
The Forbidden Christ '50
Les Visiteurs du Soir '42

Kaley Cuoco (1985-)
Killer Movie '08
Cougar Club '07
Wasted '06
The Hollow '04
Alley Cats Strike '00

Tran Manh Cuong
The Vertical Ray of the Sun '00
Three Seasons '98

Barbara Cupisti
The Church '98
Opera '88
Stagefright '87

Monique Gabriela Curnen
The Dark Knight '08
Half Nelson '06

Roland Curram (1932-)
Parting Shots '98
Darling '65

Lynette Curran (1945-)
Somersault '04
Japanese Story '03
The Boys '98
Road to Nhill '97
The Year My Voice Broke '87
Bliss '85

Paul Curran (1913-86)
Merlin '98
Poldark '75

Tony Curran (1969-)
The Lazarus Project '08
The Midnight Meat Train '08
Beowulf & Grendel '06
The Good German '06
Red Road '06
Underworld: Evolution '05
Flight of the Phoenix '04
The League of Extraordinary Gentlemen '03
Blade 2 '02
Pearl Harbor '01
Split Second '99
The 13th Warrior '99
Being Human '94

Cherie Currie (1959-)
Rosebud Beach Hotel '85
Twilight Zone: The Movie '83
Wavelength '83
Parasite '82
Foxes '80

Finlay Currie (1878-1968)
Billy Liar '63
The Adventures of Huckleberry Finn '60
Ben-Hur '59
Corridors of Blood '58
Abandon Ship '57
The King's Rhapsody '55
Make Me an Offer '55
Big Deadly Game '54
Ivanhoe '52
Stars and Stripes Forever '52
People Will Talk '51
Quo Vadis '51
The Black Rose '50
Treasure Island '50
Trio '50
Bonnie Prince Charlie '48
Great Expectations '46
Murder in the Footlights '46
I Know Where I'm Going '45
Sleeping Car to Trieste '45
The Day Will Dawn '42
The Forty-Ninth Parallel '41
Edge of the World '37

Gordon Currie (1965-)
Possessed '05
Highwaymen '03
The Fraternity '01
Left Behind: The Movie '00
The Fear: Halloween Night '99
Laserhawk '99
Dog Park '98
Ripe '97
Listen '96
Blood & Donuts '95
Puppet Master 5: The Final Chapter '94
Puppet Master 4 '93

Louise Currie (1913-)
Three on a Ticket '47
Wild West '46
Million Dollar Kid '44
The Ape Man '43
The Masked Marvel '43
The Bashful Bachelor '42
The Adventures of Captain Marvel '41

Michael Currie
The Dead Pool '88
Sudden Impact '83
Halloween 3: Season of the Witch '82
Pray TV '82

Sondra Currie (1952-)
The Concrete Jungle '82
Jessi's Girls '75
Runaways '75
Mama's Dirty Girls '74
Policewomen '73

Frank Currier (1857-1928)
Across to Singapore '28
The Red Lily '24
The Sea Hawk '24

Mary Currier (1904-57)
Return of the Ape Man '44
Frolics on Ice '39

Bernard Curry
The Junction Boys '02
The Road from Coorain '02

Christopher Curry (1948-)
City of Ghosts '03
Home Alone 3 '97
C.H.U.D. '84

Don "DC" Curry
Friday After Next '02
Next Friday '00

Julian Curry (1937-)
Sky Captain and the World of Tomorrow '04
Rasputin: Dark Servant of Destiny '96

Stephen Curry
Rogue '07
Cut '00
The Castle '97

Tim Curry (1946-)
Alice '09
Return to Cranford '09
The Color of Magic '08
Fly Me to the Moon '08 (V)
Christmas in Wonderland '07
Garfield: A Tail of Two Kitties '06 (V)
Queer Duck: The Movie '06 (V)
Bailey's Billion$ '05
Valiant '05 (V)
Kinsey '04
Sorted '04
Rugrats Go Wild! '03 (V)
The Home Front '02
The Wild Thornberrys Movie '02 (V)
Attila '01
Scary Movie 2 '01
Charlie's Angels '00
Four Dogs Playing Poker '00
Jackie's Back '99
Doom Runners '97
McHale's Navy '97
Tales from a Parallel Universe: Super Nova '97
Lover's Knot '96
Muppet Treasure Island '96
Titanic '96
Congo '95
The Pebble and the Penguin '94 (V)
The Shadow '94
National Lampoon's Loaded Weapon 1 '93
The Three Musketeers '93
Ferngully: The Last Rain Forest '92 (V)
Home Alone 2: Lost in New York '92
Passed Away '92
Oscar '91
The Hunt for Red October '90
Stephen King's It '90
Pass the Ammo '88
Legend '86
The Worst Witch '86
Clue '85
Blue Money '84
The Ploughman's Lunch '83
Annie '82
Oliver Twist '82
Times Square '80
The Shout '78
The Rocky Horror Picture Show '75

Jane Curtin (1947-)
I Love You, Man '09
The Librarian: Curse of the Judas Chalice '08
The Librarian: Return to King Solomon's Mines '06
The Shaggy Dog '06
Brooklyn Lobster '05
The Librarian: Quest for the Spear '04
Our Town '03
Antz '98 (V)
Coneheads '93
O.C. and Stiggs '87
Suspicion '87
How to Beat the High Cost of Living '80
Mr. Mike's Mondo Video '79

Peter Curtin
Darkness Falls '03
Till Human Voices Wake Us '02

Valerie Curtin (1945-)
Big Trouble '86
Down and Out in Beverly Hills '86
Maxie '85
A Christmas Without Snow '80
Different Story '78
Great Smokey Roadblock '76

Alan Curtis (1909-53)
Apache Chief '50
Flight to Nowhere '46
Renegade Girl '46
The Naughty Nineties '45
The Invisible Man's Revenge '44
Phantom Lady '44
Gung Ho! '43
Buck Privates '41
High Sierra '41
Melody Master '41
Hollywood Cavalcade '39
The Duke of West Point '38
Shopworn Angel '38
Mannequin '37
Last Outlaw '36

Billy Curtis (1909-88)
Eating Raoul '82
The Incredible Shrinking Man '57
Terror of Tiny Town '38

Clifford Curtis (1968-)
The Last Airbender '10
Crossing Over '09
Push '09
10,000 B.C. '08
Fracture '07
Live Free or Die Hard '07
Sunshine '07
The Fountain '06
River Queen '05
Runaway Jury '03
Collateral Damage '02
Point of Origin '02
Whale Rider '02
Blow '01
The Majestic '01
Training Day '01
Bringing Out the Dead '99
Three Kings '99
Virus '98
Desperate Remedies '93

Dick Curtis
What Waits Below '83
Motel Hell '80

Dick Curtis (1902-52)
Government Agents vs. Phantom Legion '51
Santa Fe Uprising '46
Arizona Cyclone '41
Billy the Kid '41
Adventure in Sahara '38
Valley of Terror '38
Boothill Brigade '37
A Lawman Is Born '37
Racing Luck '35

Donald Curtis (1915-97)
Night Passage '57
Earth vs. the Flying Saucers '56
Seventh Cavalry '56
It Came from Beneath the Sea '55
The Amazing Mr. X '48
Son of Lassie '45
They Were Expendable '45
Thirty Seconds Over Tokyo '44
Bataan '43
Code of the Outlaw '42
Criminals Within '41

Jack Curtis (1880-1956)
Lawless Range '35
The Sea Lion '21
Until They Get Me '18

Jackie Curtis (1947-85)
WR: Mysteries of the Organism '71
Flesh '68

Jamie Lee Curtis (1958-)
Beverly Hills Chihuahua '08 (V)
Christmas With the Kranks '04
Freaky Friday '03
Halloween: Resurrection '02
Drowning Mona '00
The Tailor of Panama '00
Daddy & Them '99
Halloween: H20 '98
Virus '98
Homegrown '97
Fierce Creatures '96
House Arrest '96
The Heidi Chronicles '95
Mother's Boys '94
My Girl 2 '94
True Lies '94
Forever Young '92
The Return of Spinal Tap '92
My Girl '91
Queens Logic '91
Blue Steel '90

Food of the Gods '76
Kid and the Killers '74
Memory of Us '74
Valdez Is Coming '71

Charles Cyphers (1939-)
Major League '89
Big Bad Mama 2 '87
Escape from New York '81
Halloween 2: The Nightmare Isn't Over! '81
Coming Home '78
Halloween '78
Assault on Precinct 13 '76
Missiles of October '74

Isabelle Cyr
Savage Messiah '02
P.T. Barnum '99
Karmina '96

Myriam Cyr (1960-)
Kill by Inches '99
Species 2 '98
Frankenstein and Me '96
I Shot Andy Warhol '96
Savage Hearts '95
Gothic '87

Billy Ray Cyrus (1961-)
The Spy Next Door '10
Flying By '09
Hannah Montana: The Movie '09
Bait Shop '08
Elvis Has Left the Building '04
Mulholland Drive '01
Wish You Were Dead '00

Miley Cyrus (1992-)
The Last Song '10
Hannah Montana: The Movie '09
Bolt '08 (V)

Henry Czerny (1959-)
That Russell Girl '08
Fido '06
The Pink Panther '06
The Exorcism of Emily Rose '05
Gone Dark '03
Klepto '03
Possessed '00
Range of Motion '00
Cement '99
Eye of the Killer '99
P.T. Barnum '99
The Girl Next Door '98
Glory & Honor '98
The Ice Storm '97
Mission: Impossible '96
Notes from Underground '95
When Night Is Falling '95
Clear and Present Danger '94
The Boys of St. Vincent '93
Northern Extremes '93

Zsuzsi Czinkoczi
An American Rhapsody '01
Nobody's Daughter '76

Chris D (1950-)
Border Radio '88
No Way Out '87

Deezer D
Fear of a Black Hat '94
CB4: The Movie '93

Da Brat (1974-)
Civil Brand '02
Carmen: A Hip Hopera '01 (N)
Glitter '01

Eric (DaRe) Da Re (1965-)
Number One Fan '94
The Takeover '94
Twin Peaks: Fire Walk with Me '92
Silent Night, Deadly Night 3: Better Watch Out! '89

Erick Da Silva
Delta of Venus '95
The Son of the Shark '93

Howard da Silva (1909-86)
Garbo Talks '84
Mommie Dearest '81
The Great Gatsby '74
Missiles of October '74
Smile, Jenny, You're Dead '74
1776 '72
Nevada Smith '66
The Outrage '64
David and Lisa '62
Three Husbands '50
The Underworld Story '50
Border Incident '49
The Great Gatsby '49
They Live by Night '49
Unconquered '47
The Blue Dahlia '46
Two Years before the Mast '46
The Lost Weekend '45
Keeper of the Flame '42
Reunion in France '42
The Sea Wolf '41
Sergeant York '41
Abe Lincoln in Illinois '40

Augusta Dabney (1918-)
The Portrait '93
Running on Empty '88
Violets Are Blue '86
Cold River '81

Maryam D'Abo (1960-)
The Prince & Me 2: Royal Wedding '06
Doctor Zhivago '03
Helen of Troy '03
An American Affair '99
Timelock '99
The Sea Change '98
Romance and Rejection '96
Savage Hearts '95
The Browning Version '94
Solitaire for 2 '94
Stalked '94
Double Obsession '93
Leon the Pig Farmer '93
Red Shoe Diaries 3: Another Woman's Lipstick '93
Shootfighter: Fight to the Death '93
Tomcat: Dangerous Desires '93
Tropical Heat '93
Immortal Sins '91
Nightlife '90
The Living Daylights '87
Xtro '83

Olivia D'Abo (1967-)
The Enemy '01
The Triangle '01
It Had to Be You '00
Seven Girlfriends '00
A Texas Funeral '99
Soccer Dog: The Movie '98
The Velocity of Gary '98
National Lampoon's Dad's Week Off '97
Sink or Swim '97
The Big Green '95
Kicking and Screaming '95
Live Nude Girls '95
Clean Slate '94
Greedy '94
The Last Good Time '94
Pom Poko '94 (V)
Bank Robber '93
Midnight's Child '93
Point of No Return '93
Wayne's World 2 '93
Spirit of '76 '91
Beyond the Stars '89
Into the Fire '88
Bullies '86
Really Weird Tales '86
Dream to Believe '85
Mission... Kill '85
Bolero '84
Conan the Destroyer '84

Mark Dacascos (1964-)
Alien Agent '07
Code Name: The Cleaner '07
I Am Omega '07
The Hunt for Eagle One: Crash Point '06
Only the Brave '06
Final Approach '04
Cradle 2 the Grave '03
Scorcher '02
Brotherhood of the Wolf '01
Instinct to Kill '01
The Base '99
Boogie Boy '98
No Code of Conduct '98
Sanctuary '98
DNA '97
Redline '97
Drive '96
Sabotage '96
Deadly Past '95
Redemption: Kickboxer 5 '95
Double Dragon '94
Dragstrip Girl '94
Only the Strong '93
American Samurai '92

Yaya DaCosta
The Kids Are All Right '10
Honeydripper '07
Take the Lead '06

Jacques Dacqmine
Germinal '93
Melo '86
Phedre '68

Andrew Daddo (1967-)
Body Melt '93
A Kink in the Picasso '90

Cameron Daddo (1965-)
The Perfect Sleep '08
Towards Darkness '07
Category 7 : The End of the World '05
Zebra Lounge '01
Anne of Green Gables: The Continuing Story '99

Frances Dade (1910-68)
Dracula '31
Pleasure '31
Raffles '30

Werner Daehn (1965-)
Shadow Man '06
XXX '02

Willem Dafoe (1955-)
Antichrist '09
Cirque du Freak: The Vampire's Assistant '09
Daybreakers '09
Fantastic Mr. Fox '09 (V)
Adam Resurrected '08
Anamorph '07
Mr. Bean's Holiday '07
The Walker '07
American Dreamz '06
Inside Man '06
Paris, je t'aime '06
The Black Widow '05
Manderlay '05
XXX: State of the Union '05
The Aviator '04
The Clearing '04
The Life Aquatic with Steve Zissou '04
Spider-Man 2 '04
Finding Nemo '03 (V)
Once Upon a Time in Mexico '03
The Reckoning '03
Auto Focus '02
Spider-Man '02
Pavilion of Women '01
Animal Factory '00
Shadow of the Vampire '00
American Psycho '99
Boondock Saints '99
eXistenZ '99
Lulu on the Bridge '98
New Rose Hotel '98
Affliction '97
Speed 2: Cruise Control '97
Basquiat '96
The English Patient '96
Victory '95
Clear and Present Danger '94
The Night and the Moment '94
Tom & Viv '94
Faraway, So Close! '93
Body of Evidence '92
Light Sleeper '92
White Sands '92
Cry-Baby '90
Flight of the Intruder '90
Wild at Heart '90
Born on the Fourth of July '89
Triumph of the Spirit '89
The Last Temptation of Christ '88
Mississippi Burning '88
Off Limits '87
Platoon '86
To Live & Die in L.A. '85
New York Nights '84
Roadhouse 66 '84
Streets of Fire '84
The Hunger '83
Loveless '83

Ifan Huw Dafydd
Cravings '06
The Proposition '96

Jensen (Jennifer) Daggett
Major League 3: Back to the Minors '98
Asteroid '97
Friday the 13th, Part 8: Jason Takes Manhattan '89

Jean-Michel Dagory
Clowning Around 2 '93
Clowning Around '92

Nicholas D'Agosto
Fired Up! '09
Rocket Science '07
Inside '06

Lil Dagover (1897-1980)
The Pedestrian '73
The Strange Countess '61
Tartuffe '25
Dr. Mabuse, The Gambler '22
Phantom '22
Destiny '21
The Cabinet of Dr. Caligari '19
Spiders '18

Alice Dahl
When Lightning Strikes '34
Deadwood Pass '33

Arlene Dahl (1924-)
Night of the Warrior '91
Land Raiders '69
Kisses for My President '64
Journey to the Center of the Earth '59
Slightly Scarlet '56
A Woman's World '54
Here Come the Girls '53
Three Little Words '50
Watch the Birdie '50
Reign of Terror '49
A Southern Yankee '48

Eva Dahlbeck (1920-)
The Counterfeit Traitor '62
Brink of Life '57
Dreams '55
Smiles of a Summer Night '55
Lesson in Love '54
Secrets of Women '52

Paul Dahlke (1904-84)
The Head '59
The Third Sex '57

Yuko Daike
Zatoichi '03
Ju-On 2 '00

Dan Dailey (1913-78)
The Private Files of J. Edgar Hoover '77
Wings of Eagles '57
Meet Me in Las Vegas '56
It's Always Fair Weather '55
There's No Business Like Show Business '54
The Girl Next Door '53
Pride of St. Louis '52
What Price Glory? '52
My Blue Heaven '50
Ticket to Tomahawk '50
When Willie Comes Marching Home '50
Mother Wore Tights '47
Panama Hattie '42
Timber! '42
Lady Be Good '41
Ziegfeld Girl '41

Bill Daily (1927-)
Alligator 2: The Mutation '90
Magic on Love Island '80

Elizabeth (E.G. Dailey) Daily (1961-)
Happy Feet '06 (V)
The Devil's Rejects '05
Rugrats Go Wild! '03 (V)
The Powerpuff Girls Movie '02 (V)
Rugrats in Paris: The Movie '00 (V)
Babe: Pig in the City '98 (V)
The Rugrats Movie '98 (V)
Lorenzo's Oil '92
Dogfight '91
Dutch '91
Loverboy '89
Bad Dreams '88
Better Off Dead '85
Fandango '85
Pee-wee's Big Adventure '85
No Small Affair '84
Streets of Fire '84
Valley Girl '83
The Escape Artist '82
Funny Money '82
One Dark Night '82
Street Music '81

Masaki Daimon
Godzilla vs. the Cosmic Monster '74
Lady Snowblood '73

Nadia Dajani (1965-)
Alchemy '05
Game 6 '05
Sidewalks of New York '01
Happy Accidents '00

David Daker (1937-)
Woman in Black '89
The Optimists '73

Robert Dalban (1903-87)
Killer '73
Diabolique '55
The Walls of Malapaga '49

Alberto Dalbes (1922-83)
Bronson's Revenge '72
Rites of Frankenstein '72
The Screaming Dead '72

Cynthia Dale (1961-)
A Broken Life '07
P.T. Barnum '99
At the Midnight Hour '95
Spenser: A Savage Place '94
Boy in Blue '86
Heavenly Bodies '84
My Bloody Valentine '81

Dick Dale (1937-)
Back to the Beach '87
Muscle Beach Party '64
Beach Party '63

Esther Dale (1885-1961)
Ma and Pa Kettle at the Fair '52
On Moonlight Bay '51
Ma and Pa Kettle Go to Town '50
Holiday Affair '49
Ma and Pa Kettle '49
A Stolen Life '46
Back Street '41
Blondie Has Trouble '40
The Awful Truth '37
Curly Top '35
In Old Kentucky '35

Grover Dale (1935-)
The Young Girls of Rochefort '68
Half a Sixpence '67

James Dale
The Departed '06
Federal Agents vs. Underworld, Inc. '49

Janet Dale
The Tenant of Wildfell Hall '96
The Buddha of Suburbia '92
Prick Up Your Ears '87

Jennifer Dale (1955-)
Love Come Down '00
The Life Before This '99
Dream House '98
Trail of a Serial Killer '98
Once a Thief '96
Broken Lullaby '94
Whale Music '94
Cadillac Girls '93
The Adjuster '91
Separate Vacations '86
Of Unknown Origin '83
When Angels Fly '82
Ticket to Heaven '81
Suzanne '80

Jim Dale (1935-)
The Hunchback '97
Carry On Columbus '92
The Adventures of Huckleberry Finn '85
Scandalous '84
Unidentified Flying Oddball '79
Hot Lead & Cold Feet '78
Joseph Andrews '77
Pete's Dragon '77
Digby, the Biggest Dog in the World '73
Carry On Again Doctor '69
Carry On Doctor '68
Follow That Camel '67
Carry On Cowboy '66
Carry On Screaming '66
Don't Lose Your Head '66
Carry On Cleo '65
Carry On Spying '64
Carry On Cabby '63
Carry On Jack '63

Virginia Dale (1917-94)
Danger Zone '51
Fall Guy '47
Holiday Inn '42
Buck Benny Rides Again '40

Fabienne Dali (1941-)
Mayerling '68
Kill, Baby, Kill '66
Erotic Touch of Hot Skin '65

Tracy Dali (1966-)
American Streetfighter '96
Virgin High '90

David DaLie
Mighty Jungle '64
Virgin Sacrifice '59

Marcel Dalio (1900-83)
The Mad Adventures of Rabbi Jacob '73
How Sweet It Is! '68
How to Steal a Million '66
Lady L '65
The Monocle '64
Can-Can '60
Classe Tous Risque '60
The Perfect Furlough '59
Lafayette Escadrille '58
China Gate '57
Lucky Me '54
Sabrina '54
Lovely to Look At '52
The Merry Widow '52
The Snows of Kilimanjaro '52
Captain Blackjack '51
Rich, Young and Pretty '51
Dedee d'Anvers '49
To Have & Have Not '44
Casablanca '42
The Rules of the Game '39
Grand Illusion '37
Beethoven '36

Ewa Dalkowska (1947-)
Korczak '90
Provincial Actors '79

William Shakespeare's Romeo and Juliet '96
Home for the Holidays '95
How to Make an American Quilt '95
Little Women '94

Shera Danese (1950-)
Enemies of Laughter '00
The Ladies Club '86

Jean Danet (1924-2001)
The Hunchback of Notre Dame '57
There Goes Barder '54

Beverly D'Angelo (1953-)
Aussie and Ted's Great Adventure '09
Harold & Kumar Escape from Guantanamo Bay '08
The House Bunny '08
Gamers '06
Relative Strangers '06
King of the Corner '04
Lansky '99
Sugar Town '99
American History X '98
Illuminata '98
A Rat's Tale '98
With Friends Like These '98
Pterodactyl Woman from Beverly Hills '97
Nowhere '96
Vegas Vacation '96
Edie & Pen '95
An Eye for an Eye '95
The Crazysitter '94
Lightning Jack '94
Widow's Kiss '94
Man Trouble '92
Lonely Hearts '91
The Miracle '91
The Pope Must Diet '91
Daddy's Dyin'... Who's Got the Will? '90
Pacific Heights '90
Cold Front '89
National Lampoon's Christmas Vacation '89
Aria '88
High Spirits '88
Hands of a Stranger '87
In the Mood '87
Maid to Order '87
Trading Hearts '87
Big Trouble '86
The Legend of Sleepy Hollow '86
Slow Burn '86
National Lampoon's European Vacation '85
Finders Keepers '84
A Streetcar Named Desire '84
National Lampoon's Vacation '83
Sleeping Beauty '83
Honky Tonk Freeway '81
Paternity '81
Coal Miner's Daughter '80
Highpoint '80
Hair '79
Every Which Way But Loose '78
Annie Hall '77
First Love '77
The Sentinel '76

Carlo D'Angelo (1919-73)
Secret Agent Super Dragon '66
I, Vampiri '56

Laura D'Angelo
Night Train Murders '75
Torture Train '75

Mirella D'Angelo (1956-)
Apartment Zero '88
Unsane '82

Rodney Dangerfield (1921-2004)
The 4th Tenor '02
Little Nicky '00
My 5 Wives '00
The Godson '98
Meet Wally Sparks '97
Casper '95
Natural Born Killers '94
Ladybugs '92
Rover Dangerfield '91 (V)
Moving '88
Back to School '86
Easy Money '83
Caddyshack '80
The Projectionist '71

Dani (1947-)
Avenue Montaigne '06
Day for Night '73

Brittany Daniel (1976-)
Loveless in Los Angeles '07
Little Man '06
Club Dread '04
Rampage: The Hillside Strangler Murders '04
White Chicks '04
Joe Dirt '01

Floriane Daniel
Cherry Blossoms '08
Winter Sleepers '97

Jennifer Daniel (1939-)
The Reptile '66
Kiss of the Vampire '62

Marek Daniel (1971-)
The Country Teacher '08
Something Like Happiness '05
Up and Down '04

Isa Danieli (1937-)
Ciao, Professore! '94
Macaroni '85

Henry Daniell (1894-1963)
Les Girls '57
Witness for the Prosecution '57
Lust for Life '56
The Man in the Gray Flannel Suit '56
Diane '55
The Prodigal '55
The Egyptian '54
Wake of the Red Witch '49
The Woman in Green '49
Song of Love '47
The Body Snatcher '45
Jane Eyre '44
Mission to Moscow '43
Sherlock Holmes in Washington '43
Watch on the Rhine '43
Castle in the Desert '42
Reunion in France '42
A Woman's Face '41
All This and Heaven Too '40
The Great Dictator '40
The Philadelphia Story '40
The Sea Hawk '40
The Firefly '37
Madame X '37
Camille '36

Suzanne Danielle (1957-)
The Carpathian Eagle '81
Golden Lady '79
Carry On Emmanuelle '78

Alex Daniels (1956-)
The Guardian '06
Star Kid '97
Meridian: Kiss of the Beast '90
Cyborg '89

Anthony Daniels (1946-)
Star Wars: The Clone Wars '08 (V)
Star Wars: Episode 3—Revenge of the Sith '05
Star Wars: Episode 2—Attack of the Clones '02
Return of the Jedi '83
The Empire Strikes Back '80
Star Wars '77

Bebe Daniels (1901-71)
Counsellor-at-Law '33
42nd Street '33
The Maltese Falcon '31
Reaching for the Moon '31
Dixiana '30
Rio Rita '29
Feel My Pulse '28
Monsieur Beaucaire '24
Affairs of Anatol '21
Why Change Your Wife? '20
Male and Female '19

Ben Daniels (1964-)
The State Within '06
Doom '05
Conspiracy '01
The Aristocrats '99
Britannic '99
I Want You '98
Madeline '98
David '97
Passion in the Desert '97
Beautiful Thing '95

Erin Daniels (1973-)
House of 1000 Corpses '03
One Hour Photo '02

Gary Daniels (1963-)
The Expendables '10
Queen's Messenger II '01
No Tomorrow '99
Cold Harvest '98
Spoiler '98
American Streetfighter 2: The Full Impact '97
Bloodmoon '97
Recoil '97
American Streetfighter '96
Capital Punishment '96
Hawk's Vengeance '96
Riot '96
Fist of the North Star '95
Heatseeker '95
Rage '95
White Tiger '95
Deadly Target '94
Firepower '93
Knights '93

Harold Daniels (1903-71)
Oklahoma Renegades '40
Doomed at Sundown '37

J.D. Daniels (1980-)
Beanstalk '94
Roswell: The U.F.O. Cover-Up '94
Man's Best Friend '93

Jeff Daniels (1955-)
The Answer Man '09
Away We Go '09
State of Play '09
Space Chimps '08 (V)
Sweet Nothing in My Ear '08
Traitor '08
The Lookout '07
Mama's Boy '07
Infamous '06
RV '06
Because of Winn-Dixie '05
Good Night, and Good Luck '05
Imaginary Heroes '05
The Squid and the Whale '05
Gods and Generals '03
I Witness '03
Super Sucker '03
Blood Work '02
The Hours '02
Escanaba in da Moonlight '01
Chasing Sleep '00
Cheaters '00
The Crossing '00
It's the Rage '99
My Favorite Martian '98
Pleasantville '98
Fly Away Home '96
101 Dalmatians '96
Trial and Error '96
Two Days in the Valley '96
Redwood Curtain '95
Dumb & Dumber '94
Speed '94
Gettysburg '93
Rain Without Thunder '93
Grand Tour: Disaster in Time '92
Teamster Boss: The Jackie Presser Story '92
There Goes the Neighborhood '92
The Butcher's Wife '91
Love Hurts '91
Arachnophobia '90
Welcome Home, Roxy Carmichael '90
Checking Out '89
The Caine Mutiny Court Martial '88
The House on Carroll Street '88
Love Notes '88
Sweet Hearts Dance '88
Radio Days '87
Heartburn '86
Something Wild '86
Marie '85
The Purple Rose of Cairo '85
Terms of Endearment '83
Ragtime '81
A Rumor of War '80

John Daniels
Getting Over '81
Bare Knuckles '77
Black Shampoo '76
Candy Tangerine Man '75

Mark Daniels
Mr. Holland's Opus '95
Candyman '92

Mickey Daniels (1914-70)
The Great Ziegfeld '36
The Adventurous Knights '35
Roaring Roads '35
Social Error '35

Phil Daniels (1958-)
Chicken Run '00 (V)
Still Crazy '98
Bad Behavior '92
The Bride '85
Meantime '81
Breaking Glass '80
Quadrophenia '79
Scum '79

William Daniels (1927-)
Skin '89
Her Alibi '88
Blind Date '87
The Little Match Girl '87
Rehearsal for Murder '82
All Night Long '81
Reds '81
The Blue Lagoon '80
City in Fear '80
Damien: The Leper Priest '80
Blind Ambition '79
The Rebels '79
Sunburn '79
The Bastard '78
The One and Only '78
Sergeant Matlovich vs. the U.S. Air Force '78
Black Sunday '77
Killer on Board '77
Oh, God! '77
The Parallax View '74
1776 '72
Marlowe '69
The Graduate '67
The President's Analyst '67
Two for the Road '67
A Thousand Clowns '65

Lynn Danielson-Rosenthal
Nickel & Dime '92
Mortuary Academy '91
Out of the Dark '88

Eli Danker
My Mom's New Boyfriend '08
Undisputed II: Last Man Standing '06
Special Forces '03
Impulse '90
The Flight '89
The Taking of Flight 847: The Uli Derickson Story '88

Rick Danko (1943-99)
Man Outside '88
The Kids Are Alright '79

Roger Dann (1910-)
Two for the Road '67
I Confess '53

Blythe Danner (1944-)
The Sisterhood of the Traveling Pants 2 '08
The Last Kiss '06
Howl's Moving Castle '04 (V)
Meet the Fockers '04
Sylvia '03
Invisible Circus '00
Meet the Parents '00
Forces of Nature '99
The Love Letter '99
Eye of the Storm '98
From the Earth to the Moon '98
Murder She Purred: A Mrs. Murphy Mystery '98 (V)
No Looking Back '98
Saint Maybe '98
The X-Files '98
A Call to Remember '97
Mad City '97
The Myth of Fingerprints '97
The Proposition '97
Homage '95
Oldest Confederate Widow Tells All '95
To Wong Foo, Thanks for Everything, Julie Newmar '95
Getting Up and Going Home '92
Husbands and Wives '92
Never Forget '91
The Prince of Tides '91
Alice '90
Judgment '90
Mr. & Mrs. Bridge '90
Another Woman '88
Brighton Beach Memoirs '86
Guilty Conscience '85
Man, Woman & Child '83
Inside the Third Reich '82
The Great Santini '80
Too Far to Go '79
Are You in the House Alone? '78
Love Affair: The Eleanor & Lou Gehrig Story '77
Futureworld '76
Hearts of the West '75
The Seagull '75
1776 '72
To Kill a Clown '72

Sybil Danning (1952-)
L.A. Bounty '89
Amazon Women on the Moon '87
Phantom Empire '87
Warrior Queen '87
Reform School Girls '86
Tomb '86
Howling 2: Your Sister Is a Werewolf '85
Malibu Express '85
Private Passions '85
Young Lady Chatterly 2 '85
Day of the Cobra '84
Jungle Warriors '84
Panther Squad '84
S.A.S. San Salvador '84
Seven Magnificent Gladiators '84
They're Playing with Fire '84
Chained Heat '83
Hercules '83
Daughter of Death '82
The Salamander '82
Separate Ways '82
Battle Beyond the Stars '80
Kill Castro '80
The Man with Bogart's Face '80
The Mercenaries '80
Nightkill '80
The Concorde: Airport '79 '79
The Prince and the Pauper '78
Albino '76
God's Gun '75
Bluebeard '72
Cat in the Cage '68

Paul Franklin Dano (1984-)
Knight and Day '10
Taking Woodstock '09
Where the Wild Things Are '09
Explicit Ills '08
Gigantic '08
There Will Be Blood '07
Fast Food Nation '06
Little Miss Sunshine '06
The Ballad of Jack and Rose '05
The King '05
The Girl Next Door '04
Taking Lives '04
The Emperor's Club '02
L.I.E. '01

Royal Dano (1922-94)
The Dark Half '91
Spaced Invaders '90
Texas Guns '90
Killer Klowns from Outer Space '88
Ghoulies 2 '87
House 2: The Second Story '87
Cocaine Wars '86
Teachers '84
The Right Stuff '83
Something Wicked This Way Comes '83
Bad Georgia Road '77
Hughes & Harlow: Angels in Hell '77
The Killer Inside Me '76
The Outlaw Josey Wales '76
Huckleberry Finn '75
Big Bad Mama '74
Messiah of Evil '74
Wild Party '74
Electra Glide in Blue '73
Moon of the Wolf '72
Death of a Gunfighter '69
7 Faces of Dr. Lao '63
The Adventures of Huckleberry Finn '60
Never Steal Anything Small '59
Man of the West '58
Saddle the Wind '58
Crime of Passion '57
Man in the Shadow '57
All Mine to Give '56
Tribute to a Bad Man '56
The Trouble with Harry '55
Johnny Guitar '53
Bend of the River '52
Flame of Araby '51
The Red Badge of Courage '51

Leslie Danon
Hail Caesar '94
The Whispering '94

Cesare Danova (1926-92)
St. Helen's, Killer Volcano '82
National Lampoon's Animal House '78
Tentacles '77
Scorchy '76
Mean Streets '73
Boy, Did I Get a Wrong Number! '66
Gidget Goes to Rome '63
Viva Las Vegas '63

Ted Danson (1947-)
The Open Road '09
The Human Contract '08
Mad Money '08
Nobel Son '08
Knights of the South Bronx '05
The Moguls '05
Mumford '99
Jerry and Tom '98
Saving Private Ryan '98
Homegrown '97

Illegal in Blue '95
Black Water '94
Renaissance Man '94
Mo' Money '92
Moving '88

Jules Dassin (1911-2008)

Phaedra '61
Never on Sunday '60
Rififi '54

Jean Daste (1904-94)

Love Unto Death '84
The Green Room '78
The Wild Child '70
La Guerre Est Finie '66
Grand Illusion '37
The Crime of Monsieur Lange '36
L'Atalante '34
Zero for Conduct '33
Boudu Saved from Drowning '32

Alex Datcher (1962-)

The Expert '95
Body Bags '93
Passenger 57 '92
Rage and Honor '92

Kristin Dattilo-Hayward (1970-)

Child of Darkness, Child of Light '91
Pyrates '91
Mirror, Mirror '90

James Daughton (1950-)

Girlfriend from Hell '89
Blind Date '84
Swim Team '79
Malibu Beach '78

Claude Dauphin (1903-78)

Les Miserables '78
Madame Rosa '77
The Tenant '76
Rosebud '75
The Madwoman of Chaillot '69
Two for the Road '67
Is Paris Burning? '66
Lady L '65
Tiara Tahiti '62
April in Paris '52
Casque d'Or '52
Le Plaisir '52

Alexa Davalos (1982-)

Defiance '08
Feast of Love '07
The Mist '07
The Chronicles of Riddick '04
And Starring Pancho Villa as Himself '03

Dominique Davalos (1965-)

Salvation! '87
Howard the Duck '86

Elyssa Davalos (1959-)

A House in the Hills '93
Jericho Fever '93
Wild & Wooly '78

Richard (Dick) Davalos (1935-)

Something Wicked This Way Comes '83
Blood Legacy '73
Kelly's Heroes '70
Cool Hand Luke '67
Pit Stop '67
All the Young Men '60
Sea Chase '55
East of Eden '54

Harry Davenport (1866-1949)

December 7th: The Movie '91
Riding High '50
That Forsyte Woman '50
Tell It to the Judge '49
For the Love of Mary '48
Three Daring Daughters '48
The Bachelor and the Bobby-Soxer '47
The Farmer's Daughter '47
Courage of Lassie '46
G.I. War Brides '46
The Enchanted Forest '45
She Wouldn't Say Yes '45
Jack London '44
Meet Me in St. Louis '44
The Thin Man Goes Home '44
The Amazing Mrs. Holiday '43
The Ox-Bow Incident '43
Princess O'Rourke '43
Larceny, Inc. '42
Son of Fury '42
The Bride Came C.O.D. '41
Kings Row '41
That Uncertain Feeling '41
All This and Heaven Too '40
Foreign Correspondent '40
Lucky Partners '40
Too Many Husbands '40
Gone with the Wind '39
The Hunchback of Notre Dame '39
The Story of Alexander Graham Bell '39
The Cowboy and the Lady '38
Marie Antoinette '38
You Can't Take It with You '38
Fit for a King '37

Jack Davenport (1973-)

Pirate Radio '09
Pirates of the Caribbean: At World's End '07
Pirates of the Caribbean: Dead Man's Chest '06
The Incredible Journey of Mary Bryant '05
The Libertine '05
The Wedding Date '05
Pirates of the Caribbean: The Curse of the Black Pearl '03
The Wyvern Mystery '00
Russell Mulcahy's Tale of the Mummy '99
The Talented Mr. Ripley '99
Immortality '98
Ultraviolet '98
Catherine Cookson's The Moth '96

Lucy Davenport

If Only '04
Sylvia '03
Soho Square '00

Madison Davenport (1996-)

Humboldt County '08
Kit Kittredge: An American Girl '08
Over the Hedge '06 (V)

Mary Davenport

Home Movies '79
Sisters '73

Milla Davenport (1891-1936)

The Worldly Madonna '22
Daddy Long Legs '19

Nigel Davenport (1928-)

Without a Clue '88
Caravaggio '86
Death by Prescription '86
Mountbatten: The Last Viceroy '86
A Christmas Carol '84
Greystoke: The Legend of Tarzan, Lord of the Apes '84
Chariots of Fire '81
Nighthawks '81
Cry of the Innocent '80
The Ordeal of Dr. Mudd '80
Soul Patrol '80
Zulu Dawn '79
The Island of Dr. Moreau '77
Phase 4 '74
Picture of Dorian Gray '74
Dracula '73
Living Free '72
The Last Valley '71
Mary, Queen of Scots '71
The Virgin Soldiers '69
Sebastian '68
A Man for All Seasons '66
Ladies Who Do '63
Peeping Tom '60

Robert Davi (1951-)

An American Carol '08
The Butcher '07
In the Mix '05
Call Me: The Rise and Fall of Heidi Fleiss '04
One Last Ride '03
The 4th Tenor '02
The Hot Chick '02
Verdict in Blood '02
My Little Assassin '99
The Bad Pack '98
For Which He Stands '98
The Beneficiary '97
Mutual Needs '97
An Occasional Hell '96
Body Count '95
The Dangerous '95
The Dogfighters '95
Showgirls '95
Blind Justice '94
Cops and Robbersons '94
No Contest '94
Maniac Cop 3: Badge of Silence '93
Mardi Gras for the Devil '93
The November Men '93
Quick '93
Son of the Pink Panther '93
Center of the Web '92
Christopher Columbus: The Discovery '92
Wild Orchid 2: Two Shades of Blue '92
Illicit Behavior '91
The Taking of Beverly Hills '91
White Hot: The Mysterious Murder of Thelma Todd '91
Amazon '90
Legal Tender '90
Maniac Cop 2 '90
Peacemaker '90
Predator 2 '90
License to Kill '89
Die Hard '88
Traxx '87
Wild Thing '87
The Goonies '85
Gangster Wars '81
The $5.20 an Hour Dream '80

Angel David

Two Girls and a Guy '98
The Substitute 2: School's Out '97
The Crow '93
Mixed Blood '84

Clifford David (1932-)

Matters of the Heart '90
Agent on Ice '86
Resurrection '80

Eleanor David (1956-)

Topsy Turvy '99
Slipstream '89
84 Charing Cross Road '86
Sylvia '86
Comfort and Joy '84
Pink Floyd: The Wall '82
The Scarlet Pimpernel '82

Ellen David

Dr. Jekyll and Mr. Hyde '08
Random Encounter '98

Joanna David (1947-)

The Way We Live Now '02
Cotton Mary '99
Murders at Lynch Cross '85

Karen Shenaz David

The Color of Magic '08
The Scorpion King 2: Rise of a Warrior '08

Keith David (1954-)

The Lottery Ticket '10
Coraline '09 (V)
Endgame '09
The Princess and the Frog '09 (V)
Against the Dark '08
Behind Enemy Lines 3: Colombia '08
First Sunday '08
Lost Treasure of the Maya '08
S.I.S. '08
The Butcher '07
Delta Farce '07
The Last Sentinel '07
Transformers '07 (V)
ATL '06
Behind Enemy Lines 2: Axis of Evil '06
The Oh in Ohio '06
Crash '05
Mr. & Mrs. Smith '05
Transporter 2 '05
Agent Cody Banks 2: Destination London '04
The Chronicles of Riddick '04
Agent Cody Banks '03
Head of State '03
Hollywood Homicide '03
Kaena: The Prophecy '03 (V)
Barbershop '02
Final Fantasy: The Spirits Within '01 (V)
Novocaine '01
Seduced: Pretty When You Cry '01
Innocents '00
Pitch Black '00
The Replacements '00
Requiem for a Dream '00
Where the Heart Is '00
Armageddon '98
There's Something about Mary '98
The Tiger Woods Story '98
Don King: Only in America '97
Executive Target '97
Todd McFarlane's Spawn '97 (V)
Volcano '97
Flipping '96
johns '96
Larger Than Life '96
Blue in the Face '95
Clockers '95
Dead Presidents '95
An Eye for an Eye '95
The Quick and the Dead '95
Gargoyles, The Movie: The Heroes Awaken '94 (V)
The Puppet Masters '94
The Last Outlaw '93
Article 99 '92
Final Analysis '92
Marked for Death '90
Men at Work '90
Always '89
Bird '88
They Live '88
Off Limits '87
Platoon '86
The Thing '82

Thayer David (1927-78)

The Duchess and the Dirtwater Fox '76
Rocky '76
The Eiger Sanction '75
Save the Tiger '73
Savages '72
Night of Dark Shadows '71
House of Dark Shadows '70
The Story of Ruth '60
Journey to the Center of the Earth '59
The Legend of the Sea Wolf '58
A Time to Love & a Time to Die '58

Lolita (David) Davidovich (1961-)

September Dawn '07
Kill Your Darlings '06
Dark Blue '03
Hollywood Homicide '03
Snow in August '01
Four Days '99
Mystery, Alaska '99
No Vacancy '99
Play It to the Bone '99
Gods and Monsters '98
Santa Fe '97
Dead Silence '96
Jungle 2 Jungle '96
Touch '96
For Better or Worse '95
Harvest of Fire '95
Indictment: The McMartin Trial '95
Now and Then '95
Cobb '94
Younger & Younger '94
Boiling Point '93
Intersection '93
Keep the Change '92
Leap of Faith '92
Raising Cain '92
The Inner Circle '91
JFK '91
The Object of Beauty '91
Prison Stories: Women on the Inside '91
Blaze '89
Blindside '88
Adventures in Babysitting '87
Big Town '87
Recruits '86

Alan Davidson

Frailty '02
Rift '96

Ben Davidson (1940-)

Conan the Barbarian '82
The Black Six '74

Bruce Davidson

The Librarian: Curse of the Judas Chalice '08
Touched '05

Diana Davidson

Around the World in 80 Ways '86
Scared to Death '80

Eileen Davidson (1959-)

Eternity '90
Easy Wheels '89
The House on Sorority Row '83

Jack Davidson (1936-)

You Tell Me '06
Baby It's You '82
Shock Waves '77

Jaye Davidson (1968-)

Stargate '94
The Crying Game '92

John Davidson (1886-1968)

Bombay Mail '34
Tailspin Tommy '34
Monsieur Beaucaire '24

John Davidson (1941-)

Edward Scissorhands '90
The Squeeze '87
The Concorde: Airport '79 '79
The Happiest Millionaire '67

Max Davidson (1875-1950)

Daring Danger '32
Hotel Imperial '27

Tommy Davidson (1965-)

Black Dynamite '09
The Proud Family Movie '05 (V)
Juwanna Mann '02
Bamboozled '00
Pros & Cons '99
Plump Fiction '97
Woo '97
Booty Call '96
Ace Ventura: When Nature Calls '95
Strictly Business '91

William B. Davidson (1888-1947)

They Were Expendable '45
The Singing Kid '36
I'm No Angel '33
Held for Murder '32
Vice Squad '31
The Silver Horde '30

Embeth Davidtz (1965-)

Fragments '08
Fracture '07
Junebug '05
The Emperor's Club '02
Bridget Jones's Diary '01
The Hole '01
13 Ghosts '01
Bicentennial Man '99
Mansfield Park '99
Last Rites '98
Fallen '97
The Garden of Redemption '97
The Gingerbread Man '97
Matilda '96
Feast of July '95
Murder in the First '95
Schindler's List '93
Sweet Murder '93
Army of Darkness '92

Betty Ann Davies (1910-55)

Alias John Preston '56
Blackout '54
The Belles of St. Trinian's '53
Grand National Night '53
The Blue Lamp '49
It Always Rains on Sunday '47

Geraint Wyn Davies

Slings & Arrows: Season 2 '05
Conspiracy of Fear '96

Gwen Ffrangcon Davies (1891-)

The Devil Rides Out '68
The Witches '66

Jackson Davies

Dead Ahead: The Exxon Valdez Disaster '92
Dead Wrong '83
Jane Doe '83

James Davies

Wildest Dreams '90
Young Nurses in Love '89

Jeremy Davies (1969-)

Rescue Dawn '06
Manderlay '05
Dogville '03
The Laramie Project '02
Searching for Paradise '02
Secretary '02
Solaris '02
CQ '01
Intimate Affairs '01
Up at the Villa '00
The Million Dollar Hotel '99
Ravenous '99
Saving Private Ryan '98
Going All the Way '97
The Locusts '97
Twister '96
Spanking the Monkey '94

John Davies (1953-)

Positive I.D. '87
Interface '84

John (Howard) Davies (1939-)

Tom Brown's School Days '51
The Rocking Horse Winner '49
Oliver Twist '48

Kimberly Davies (1973-)

Psycho Beach Party '00
Twisted '96

Lindy Davies (1946-)

Darlings of the Gods '90
Malcolm '86

Marion Davies (1897-1961)

Cain and Mabel '36
Operator 13 '34

Philip Davis (1953-)
Five Days '07
Beau Brummell: This Charming Man '06
Like Father Like Son '05
Vera Drake '04
Still Crazy '98
Face '97
Photographing Fairies '97
Howling 5: The Rebirth '89
High Hopes '88
The Bounty '84
Grown Ups '80
Quadrophenia '79
Who's Who '78

Phyllis E. Davis (1947-)
Terminal Island '73
Sweet Sugar '72
Beyond the Valley of the Dolls '70

Roger Davis (1939-)
Ruby '77
Flash & Firecat '75
House of Dark Shadows '70

Rufe Davis (1908-74)
Code of the Outlaw '42
Gangs of Sonora '41
Gauchos of El Dorado '41
Outlaws of the Cherokee Trail '41
West of Cimarron '41

Sammi Davis (1964-)
Stand-Ins '97
Four Rooms '95
Indecency '92
The Horseplayer '91
The Perfect Bride '91
Shadow of China '91
Final Warning '90
The Rainbow '89
Consuming Passions '88
The Lair of the White Worm '88
Hope and Glory '87
Pack of Lies '87
Prayer for the Dying '87
Mona Lisa '86

Sammy Davis, Jr. (1925-90)
The Kid Who Loved Christmas '90
Tap '89
Moon over Parador '88
Alice in Wonderland '85
That's Dancing! '85
Cannonball Run 2 '84
Cracking Up '83
Cannonball Run '81
Little Moon & Jud McGraw '78
Gone with the West '72
The Trackers '71
One More Time '70
Sweet Charity '69
Salt & Pepper '68
A Man Called Adam '66
Robin and the 7 Hoods '64
Sergeants 3 '62
The Three Penny Opera '62
Ocean's 11 '60

Scott Davis
The Abomination '88
Tabloid! '88

Sonny Carl Davis
Bad Channels '92
Seedpeople '92
Pair of Aces '90
Verne Miller '88
Fast Money '83
Last Night at the Alamo '83
The Whole Shootin' Match '79

Stringer Davis (1896-1973)
Murder at the Gallop '63
The Smallest Show on Earth '57
The Runaway Bus '54

Tom Davis (1952-)
One More Saturday Night '86
Trading Places '83
All You Need Is Cash '78
Tunnelvision '76

Tracy Davis
Nemesis 2: Nebula '94
Star Quest '89

Ursula Davis
An Angel for Satan '66
Battle of Valiant '63

Viola Davis (1952-)
Eat, Pray, Love '10
Knight and Day '10
Law Abiding Citizen '09
Madea Goes to Jail '09
State of Play '09
The Andromeda Strain '08
Doubt '08
Nights in Rodanthe '08
Jesse Stone: Sea Change '07
The Architect '06
Jesse Stone: Death in Paradise '06
Jesse Stone: Night Passage '06
Get Rich or Die Tryin' '05
Jesse Stone: Stone Cold '05
Antwone Fisher '02
Far from Heaven '02
Solaris '02

Viveka Davis
Cast Away '00
Time Code '00
EDtv '99
Message in a Bottle '98
A Dangerous Woman '93
Stalking Laura '93
Man Trouble '92
The End of Innocence '90
Morgan Stewart's Coming Home '87
Not My Kid '85
Shoot the Moon '82

Warwick Davis (1970-)
Harry Potter and the Half-Blood Prince '09
The Chronicles of Narnia: Prince Caspian '08
Harry Potter and the Order of the Phoenix '07
Harry Potter and the Goblet of Fire '05
The Hitchhiker's Guide to the Galaxy '05
Ray '04
Leprechaun 6: Back 2 Tha Hood '03
Harry Potter and the Chamber of Secrets '02
Snow White: The Fairest of Them All '02
Harry Potter and the Sorcerer's Stone '01
The 10th Kingdom '00
Leprechaun 5: In the Hood '99
Prince Valiant '97
Leprechaun 4: In Space '96
Gulliver's Travels '95
Leprechaun 3 '95
Leprechaun 2 '94
Leprechaun '93
Willow '88
The Ewoks: Battle for Endor '85
The Ewok Adventure '84

William B. Davis (1938-)
The Thaw '09
Numb '07
Max Rules '05
Snakehead Terror '04
Mindstorm '01
The Proposal '00
Perpetrators of the Crime '98
The X-Files '98

Bruce Davison (1946-)
The Line '08
Breach '07
The Dead Girl '06
Going Shopping '05
Hate Crime '05
Evergreen '04
Out of the Ashes '03
Runaway Jury '03
X2: X-Men United '03
Dahmer '02
High Crimes '02
crazy/beautiful '01
Off Season '01
Summer Catch '01
The King Is Alive '00
X-Men '00
Locked in Silence '99
Vendetta '99
At First Sight '98
Paulie '98
Apt Pupil '97
Color of Justice '97
Lovelife '97
The Crucible '96
Grace of My Heart '96
Hidden in America '96
The Baby-Sitters' Club '95
The Cure '95
Down, Out and Dangerous '95
Homage '95
It's My Party '95
Far from Home: The Adventures of Yellow Dog '94
The Skateboard Kid 2 '94
Widow's Kiss '94
Short Cuts '93
Six Degrees of Separation '93
Live! From Death Row '92
Longtime Companion '90
Steel and Lace '90
The Misfit Brigade '87
Poor Little Rich Girl: The Barbara Hutton Story '87
The Ladies Club '86
Spies Like Us '85
Crimes of Passion '84
Lies '83
Kiss My Grits '82
Tomorrow's Child '82
High Risk '81
The Lathe of Heaven '80
The Gathering: Part 2 '79
Short Eyes '79
Brass Target '78
Deadman's Curve '78
French Quarter '78
The Summer of My German Soldier '78
The Gathering '77
Mother, Jugs and Speed '76
Mame '74
The Affair '73
Ulzana's Raid '72
Willard '71
The Strawberry Statement '70
Last Summer '69

Davey Davison (1942-)
When the Line Goes Through '73
No Drums, No Bugles '71

Peter Davison (1951-)
Parting Shots '98
Wuthering Heights '98
Black Beauty '94
Harnessing Peacocks '92
Love for Lydia '79

Ken Davitian
Get Smart '08
Meet the Spartans '08
Borat: Cultural Learnings of America for Make Benefit Glorious Nation of Kazakhstan '06

Andrew Davoli (1973-)
Spartan '04
Welcome to Collinwood '02
Knockaround Guys '01
The Yards '00

Ninetto Davoli (1948-)
Arabian Nights '74
The Canterbury Tales '71
The Decameron '70
The Hawks & the Sparrows '67

Evelyn Daw (1912-70)
Panamint's Bad Man '38
Something to Sing About '36

Marjorie Daw (1902-79)
His Majesty, the American '19
Rebecca of Sunnybrook Farm '17

Pam Dawber (1951-)
I'll Remember April '99
Stay Tuned '92
Through Naked Eyes '87
Wild Horses '84
Holocaust Survivors... Remembrance of Love '83
A Wedding '78

Marpessa Dawn (1934-)
The Womaneater '59
Black Orpheus '58

Sugar Dawn (1931-)
Arizona Roundup '42
Lone Star Law Men '42
Dynamite Canyon '41
Riding the Sunset Trail '41

Anthony Dawson (1916-92)
Dr. No '62
The Curse of the Werewolf '61
Tiger Bay '59
The Haunted Strangler '58
Hour of Decision '57
Dial "M" for Murder '54
The Long Dark Hall '51
The Woman in Question '50
The Queen of Spades '49

Kamala Dawson
The Burning Season '94
Lightning Jack '94

Kim (Kimberly Dawn) Dawson (1963-)
Jimmy Zip '00
Bikini Med School '98
Bikini House Calls '96
The Perfect Gift '95
The Voyeur '94

Richard Dawson (1932-)
The Running Man '87
How to Pick Up Girls '78
The Devil's Brigade '68
Munster, Go Home! '66
King Rat '65
War and Peace '56

Rosario Dawson (1979-)
Killshot '09
Eagle Eye '08
Explicit Ills '08
Seven Pounds '08
Death Proof '07
Descent '07
Clerks 2 '06
A Guide to Recognizing Your Saints '06
The Devil's Rejects '05
Rent '05
Sin City '05
This Revolution '05
Alexander '04
The Rundown '03
Shattered Glass '03
This Girl's Life '03
The Adventures of Pluto Nash '02
Ash Wednesday '02
The First $20 Million is Always the Hardest '02
Love in the Time of Money '02
Men in Black 2 '02
25th Hour '02
Chelsea Walls '01
Josie and the Pussycats '01
King of the Jungle '01
Sidewalks of New York '01
Down to You '00
Light It Up '99
He Got Game '98
Kids '95

Vicky Dawson
Carbon Copy '81
The Prowler '81

Micheline Dax (1924-)
A Slightly Pregnant Man '79
Six in Paris '68
Femmes de Paris '53

Alice Day (1905-95)
Murder on the High Seas '32
Two-Fisted Law '32
The Smart Set '28

Dennis Day (1916-88)
The Girl Next Door '53
Melody Time '48 (V)
Buck Benny Rides Again '40

Doris Day (1910-98)
Turf Boy '42
Lady Be Good '41
Saga of Death Valley '39

Doris Day (1922-)
Where Were You When the Lights Went Out? '68
With Six You Get Eggroll '68
Caprice '67
The Glass Bottom Boat '66
Do Not Disturb '65
Send Me No Flowers '64
Move Over, Darling '63
The Thrill of It All! '63
Billy Rose's Jumbo '62
That Touch of Mink '62
Lover Come Back '61
Midnight Lace '60
Please Don't Eat the Daisies '60
Pillow Talk '59
Teacher's Pet '58
The Tunnel of Love '58
The Pajama Game '57
The Man Who Knew Too Much '56
Love Me or Leave Me '55
Lucky Me '54
Young at Heart '54
By the Light of the Silvery Moon '53
Calamity Jane '53
April in Paris '52
The Winning Team '52
I'll See You in My Dreams '51
Lullaby of Broadway '51
On Moonlight Bay '51
Starlift '51
Storm Warning '51
Tea for Two '50
The West Point Story '50
Young Man with a Horn '50
It's a Great Feeling '49
My Dream Is Yours '49
Romance on the High Seas '48
They Got Me Covered '43

Felecia Day
Dear Me: A Blogger's Tale '08
Prairie Fever '08

Gary Day (1941-)
Crime Broker '94
Night Nurse '77

Josette Day (1914-78)
The Storm Within '48
Beauty and the Beast '46
Well-Digger's Daughter '46

Laraine Day (1920-2007)
Return to Fantasy Island '77
Murder on Flight 502 '75
The High and the Mighty '54
The Woman on Pier 13 '50
My Dear Secretary '49
Tycoon '47
Those Endearing Young Charms '45
The Story of Dr. Wassell '44
Mr. Lucky '43
Journey for Margaret '42
Dr. Kildare's Strange Case '40
Foreign Correspondent '40
I Take This Woman '40
My Son, My Son '40
The Secret of Dr. Kildare '39
Doomed at Sundown '37

Larry Day (1963-)
Snakeman '05
Detention '03
Cause of Death '00
Dead Silent '99

Marceline Day (1907-2000)
Fighting Parson '35
Flaming Signal '33
Telegraph Trail '33
Broadway to Cheyenne '32
The Crusader '32
Fighting Fool '32
The King Murder '32
The Pocatello Kid '31
Paradise Island '30
Sunny Skies '30
The Cameraman '28
The Beloved Rogue '27

Matt(hew) Day (1971-)
And Starring Pancho Villa as Himself '03
The Hound of the Baskervilles '02
Shackleton '02
Doing Time for Patsy Cline '97
Kiss or Kill '97
Dating the Enemy '95
Love and Other Catastrophes '95
Muriel's Wedding '94

Morris Day (1957-2000)
The Adventures of Ford Fairlane '90
Graffiti Bridge '90
Purple Rain '84

Patrick Day (1968-)
Hollywood Hot Tubs 2: Educating Crystal '89
The Adventures of Huckleberry Finn '85

Stuart Garrison Day
Covert Action '88
Search and Destroy '88

Vera Day (1939-)
The Riddle '07
The Womaneater '59
The Haunted Strangler '58
Up the Creek '58
Quatermass 2 '57

Daniel Day-Lewis (1957-)
Nine '09
There Will Be Blood '07
The Ballad of Jack and Rose '05
Gangs of New York '02
The Boxer '97
The Crucible '96
The Age of Innocence '93
In the Name of the Father '93
The Last of the Mohicans '92
Eversmile New Jersey '89
My Left Foot '89
Stars and Bars '88
The Unbearable Lightness of Being '88
A Room with a View '86
My Beautiful Laundrette '85
The Bounty '84
Gandhi '82
How Many Miles to Babylon? '82
Sunday, Bloody Sunday '71

Assaf Dayan (1945-)
The Uranium Conspiracy '78
Operation Thunderbolt '77

Gabrielle Daye (1911-2005)
In Celebration '75
10 Rillington Place '71

Margit Dayka (1907-86)
Nice Neighbor '79
Cat's Play '74

William De Acutis (1957-91)
Chattahoochee '89
Trust Me '89

Joaquim de Almeida (1957-)
The Burning Plain '08
Che '08
Love and Debate '06
Moscow Zero '06
Behind Enemy Lines '01
La Cucaracha '99
No Vacancy '99
Vendetta '99
One Man's Hero '98
Women '97
Larry McMurtry's Dead Man's Walk '96
Nostromo '96
Desperado '95
Clear and Present Danger '94
Only You '94
The Fencing Master '92
Priceless Beauty '90
Good Morning, Babylon '87

Maria de Aragon (1942-)
The Deadly and the Beautiful '73
The Cremators '72
Blood Mania '70

Jean De Baer
Broken Vows '87
84 Charing Cross Road '86

Isaach de Bankole (1957-)
The Limits of Control '09
The Guitar '08
Battle in Seattle '07
The Diving Bell and the Butterfly '07
Casino Royale '06
Manderlay '05
From Other Worlds '04
Coffee and Cigarettes '03
3 A.M. '01
Ghost Dog: The Way of the Samurai '99
A Soldier's Daughter Never Cries '98
The Keeper '96
Heart of Darkness '93
Night on Earth '91
No Fear, No Die '90
Chocolat '88

Brenda de Banzie (1915-81)
The Pink Panther '64
Come September '61
The Mark '61
The Entertainer '60
Too Many Crooks '59
The Man Who Knew Too Much '56
A Kid for Two Farthings '55
Hobson's Choice '53

James De Bello
See James DeBello

Burr de Benning (1936-2003)
Incredible Melting Man '77
City Beneath the Sea '71
Iron Horsemen '71
Sweet November '68

Andre de Beranger (1895-1973)
The Bat '26
So This Is Paris '26

Antje De Boeck (1964-)
A Dog of Flanders '99
Daens '92

Nikki de Boer (1970-)
Christmas Town '08
The Dead Zone '02
Rated X '00
Cube '98
Family of Cops 3 '98
JFK: Reckless Youth '93
Prom Night 4: Deliver Us from Evil '91

Koen de Bouw (1964-)
The Memory of a Killer '03

Yvonne de Bray (1889-1954)
The Storm Within '48
Eternal Return '43

Nigel de Brulier (1877-1948)
The Iron Mask '29
Ben-Hur '26
The Four Horsemen of the Apocalypse '21
The Three Musketeers '21

Celia de Burgh (1958-)
Phar Lap '84
Sound of Love '78

Yvonne De Carlo (1922-2007)
Mirror, Mirror '90
American Gothic '88
Cellar Dweller '87
Vultures '84
The Munsters' Revenge '81
Play Dead '81
Silent Scream '80
Nocturna '79
Satan's Cheerleaders '77
House of Shadows '76
Blazing Stewardesses '75
It Seemed Like a Good Idea at the Time '75
Arizona Bushwackers '67
Hostile Guns '67
Munster, Go Home! '66
A Global Affair '63
McLintock! '63
The Sword and the Cross '58
Band of Angels '57
Death of a Scoundrel '56
The Ten Commandments '56
Flame of the Islands '55
Shotgun '55
Passion '54
Captain's Paradise '53
Sea Devils '53
Tomahawk '51
Buccaneer's Girl '50
Casbah '48
Criss Cross '48
Border River '47
Brute Force '47
Song of Scheherazade '47
Salome, Where She Danced '45
For Whom the Bell Tolls '43
Rhythm Parade '43
The Road to Morocco '42
This Gun for Hire '42

Emma de Caunes (1976-)
Mr. Bean's Holiday '07
The Science of Sleep '06

Pedro de Cordoba (1881-1950)
Guns of Fury '49
Omoo Omoo, the Shark God '49
Mexican Hayride '48
Swamp Fire '46
They Were Expendable '45
For Whom the Bell Tolls '43
Son of Fury '42
Before I Hang '40
The Ghost Breakers '40
Law of the Pampas '39
Condemned to Live '35
The Crusades '35

Arturo de Cordova (1908-73)
The New Invisible Man '58
El '52
New Orleans '47
Frenchman's Creek '44
For Whom the Bell Tolls '43

Ted de Corsia (1903-73)
The Outside Man '73
The Conqueror '56
Dance with Me, Henry '56
The Kettles in the Ozarks '56
The Killing '56
Slightly Scarlet '56
Crime Wave '54
The Enforcer '51
It Happens Every Spring '49
Neptune's Daughter '49
The Lady from Shanghai '48
The Naked City '48

Eduardo de Filippo (1900-84)
The Gold of Naples '54
Seven Deadly Sins '53

Peppino de Filippo (1903-80)
Boccaccio '70 '62
Variety Lights '51

Calvert De Forest
See Calvert Deforest

Helene de Fougerolles (1973-)
Va Savoir '01
The Fall '98

Cecile de France (1975-)
A Secret '07
Avenue Montaigne '06
Russian Dolls '05
Around the World in 80 Days '04
High Tension '03
L'Auberge Espagnole '02

Louis de Funes (1914-83)
Delusions of Grandeur '76
The Mad Adventures of Rabbi Jacob '73
La Grande Vadrouille '66
The Sucker '65
The Gendarme of Saint-Tropez '64
Belle Americaine '61
Four Bags Full '56
The Sheep Has Five Legs '54
Seven Deadly Sins '53

Sam De Grasse (1875-1953)
The Fighting Eagle '27
When a Man Loves '27
Robin Hood '22
The Scarlet Car '17
The Birth of a Nation '15

Gianfranco de Grassi
Night Train Murders '75
Torture Train '75

Julio de Grazia (1920-89)
The Stranger '87
Deadly Revenge '83
Funny, Dirty Little War '83
Time for Revenge '82
The Lion's Share '79

Xavier De Guillebon
Bon Voyage '03
L'Auberge Espagnole '02
The Taste of Others '00

Gloria De Haven (1924-)
Out to Sea '97
Bog '84
Banjo Hackett '76
Two Tickets to Broadway '51
Summer Stock '50
Three Little Words '50
The Yellow Cab Man '50
Summer Holiday '48
Broadway Rhythm '44
The Thin Man Goes Home '44
Two Girls and a Sailor '44
Best Foot Forward '43
Susan and God '40
Modern Times '36

Consuelo de Haviland
Barjo '93
The Unbearable Lightness of Being '88
Betty Blue '86

Olivia de Havilland (1916-)
The Woman He Loved '88
Anastasia: The Mystery of Anna '86
Agatha Christie's Murder is Easy '82
The Fifth Musketeer '79
Roots: The Next Generation '79
The Swarm '78
Airport '77 '77
The Adventurers '70
Hush, Hush, Sweet Charlotte '65
Lady in a Cage '64
Proud Rebel '58
The Ambassador's Daughter '56
Not as a Stranger '55
The Heiress '49
The Snake Pit '48
Dark Mirror '46
To Each His Own '46
Princess O'Rourke '43
Thank Your Lucky Stars '43
In This Our Life '42
The Male Animal '42
Strawberry Blonde '41
They Died with Their Boots On '41
Santa Fe Trail '40
Dodge City '39
Gone with the Wind '39
The Private Lives of Elizabeth & Essex '39
The Adventures of Robin Hood '38
Four's a Crowd '38
Hard to Get '38
Call It a Day '37
The Great Garrick '37
Anthony Adverse '36
The Charge of the Light Brigade '36
Alibi Ike '35
Captain Blood '35
A Midsummer Night's Dream '35

Wanda De Jesus (1960-)
Illegal Tender '07
Blood Work '02
Flawless '99
Elmore Leonard's Gold Coast '97

David de Keyser (1927-)
The Statement '03
The Designated Mourner '97
Leon the Pig Farmer '93
Yentl '83
Valentino '77

Frank De Kova (1910-81)
Johnny Firecloud '75
Frasier the Sensuous Lion '73
Heavy Traffic '73
Cat in the Cage '68
Atlantis, the Lost Continent '61
The Jayhawkers '59
Machine Gun Kelly '58
Teenage Caveman '58
Run of the Arrow '56
Shack Out on 101 '55

Viktor de Kowa (1904-73)
Forger of London '61
The Embezzled Heaven '58

Agathe de la Boulaye
Alien vs. Predator '04
The Girl '01

Simon de la Brosse (1965-98)
Strike It Rich '90
The Little Thief '89
Pauline at the Beach '83

Agathe de la Fontaine (1972-)
Train of Life '98
Another 9 1/2 Weeks '96
King of the Airwaves '94

Christian de la Fuente (1974-)
Once Upon a Wedding '05
Basic '03
John Carpenter Presents Vampires: Los Muertos '02
Driven '01

Joel de la Fuente
The Happening '08
From Other Worlds '04
Personal Velocity: Three Portraits '02

Paz de la Huerta (1984-)
The Limits of Control '09
Deception '08
The Guitar '08
The Tripper '06
Rick '03
Luminous Motion '00

Marguerite de la Motte (1902-50)
The Iron Mask '29
The Nut '21
Mark of Zorro '20

Danny De La Paz (1957-)
Picking Up the Pieces '99
American Me '92
Miracle Mile '89
3:15—The Moment of Truth '86
Boulevard Nights '79

Gemmenne de la Pena
Towelhead '07
The Weather Man '05

George de la Pena (1955-)
Brain Donors '92
Kuffs '92
The Cowboy & the Ballerina '84
Nijinsky '80

Rodrigo de la Serna
Chronicle of an Escape '06
The Motorcycle Diaries '04

Antonio de la Torre
Dark Blue Almost Black '06
Volver '06

Frances de la Tour (1944-)
The History Boys '06
Harry Potter and the Goblet of Fire '05
Tom Jones '98
Flickers '80

John de Lancie (1948-)
Pathology '08
Darklight '04
Woman on Top '00
Schemes '95
Deep Red '94
Evolver '94
Arcade '93
Fearless '93
The Hand that Rocks the Cradle '92
The Fisher King '91

Derek de Lint (1950-)
Black Book '06
When a Stranger Calls '06
Soul Assassin '01
The Man Who Made Husbands Jealous '98
Poltergeist: The Legacy '96
The Endless Game '89
Diary of a Mad Old Man '88
Stealing Heaven '88
The Unbearable Lightness of Being '88
Mascara '87
Three Men and a Baby '87
The Assault '86
Soldier of Orange '78

Michael De Lorenzo
See Michael Delorenzo

Kamar De Los Reyes (1967-)
Undefeated '03
Mambo Cafe '00
Nixon '95
DaVinci's War '92
Coldfire '90
East L.A. Warriors '89
Ghetto Blaster '89
Salsa '88

Alvaro de Luna (1935-)
Broken Silence '01
Hawk and Castile '67

Gordon De Main
Single Handed Sanders '32
The Ridin' Fool '31

Donna De Mario
See Donna (Dona Martel) Martell

Terence de Marney (1909-71)
Beast of Morocco '66
Die, Monster, Die! '65
Dual Alibi '47

Drea De Matteo (1972-)
New York, I Love You '09
Lake City '08
Broken English '07
The Good Life '07
Walker Payne '06
Assault on Precinct 13 '05
Prey for Rock and Roll '03
Crazy Little Thing '02
Deuces Wild '02
Made '01
'R Xmas '01
Swordfish '01

Maria De Medeiros (1965-)
My Life Without Me '03
The Saddest Music in the World '03
Le Polygraphe '96
Pulp Fiction '94
Meeting Venus '91
Henry & June '90

Nieve De Medina (1962-)
Mondays in the Sun '02
El Bola '00

Carlo De Mejo (1945-)
Other Hell '85
Alien Contamination '81
Gates of Hell '80
The Outside Man '73

Alberto De Mendoza (1923-)
Bossa Nova '99
Horror Express '72
The Case of the Scorpion's Tail '71
A Lizard in a Woman's Skin '71
Blade of the Ripper '70

Jo de Meyere (1939-)
The Memory of a Killer '03

Laurence De Monaghan
The Story of a Love Story '73
Claire's Knee '71

Rebecca De Mornay (1962-)
American Venus '07
Music Within '07
Lords of Dogtown '05
Wedding Crashers '05
Raise Your Voice '04
Identity '03
A Girl Thing '01
Range of Motion '00
The Right Temptation '00
Night Ride Home '99
Thick as Thieves '99
Wicked Ways '99
The Con '98
The Winner '96
Never Talk to Strangers '95
Getting Out '94
Blind Side '93
Guilty as Sin '93
The Three Musketeers '93
The Hand that Rocks the Cradle '92

Backdraft '91
An Inconvenient Woman '91
By Dawn's Early Light '89
Dealers '89
And God Created Woman '88
Feds '88
The Murders in the Rue Morgue '86
Pecos Bill '86
Runaway Train '85
The Slugger's Wife '85
The Trip to Bountiful '85
Risky Business '83
Testament '83
One from the Heart '82

Drena De Niro

Ghetto Dawg '02
Showtime '02

Robert De Niro (1943-)

Righteous Kill '08
What Just Happened '08
Stardust '07
Arthur and the Invisibles '06 (V)
The Good Shepherd '06
The Bridge of San Luis Rey '05
Hide and Seek '05
Godsend '04
Meet the Fockers '04
Shark Tale '04 (V)
Analyze That '02
City by the Sea '02
Showtime '02
15 Minutes '01
The Score '01
The Adventures of Rocky & Bullwinkle '00
Meet the Parents '00
Men of Honor '00
Flawless '99
Analyze This '98
Ronin '98
Cop Land '97
Great Expectations '97
Jackie Brown '97
Wag the Dog '97
The Fan '96
Marvin's Room '96
Sleepers '96
Casino '95
Heat '95
Mary Shelley's Frankenstein '94
A Bronx Tale '93
Mad Dog and Glory '93
This Boy's Life '93
Night and the City '92
Backdraft '91
Cape Fear '91
Guilty by Suspicion '91
Mistress '91
Awakenings '90
Goodfellas '90
Stanley and Iris '90
Jacknife '89
We're No Angels '89
Midnight Run '88
Angel Heart '87
The Untouchables '87
The Mission '86
Brazil '85
Falling in Love '84
Once Upon a Time in America '84
King of Comedy '82
The Godfather 1902-1959: The Complete Epic '81
True Confessions '81
Raging Bull '80
The Deer Hunter '78
New York, New York '77
America at the Movies '76
The Last Tycoon '76
1900 '76
Taxi Driver '76
The Godfather, Part 2 '74
Bang the Drum Slowly '73
Mean Streets '73
Born to Win '71
The Swap '71
Bloody Mama '70
Hi, Mom! '70
The Wedding Party '69
Greetings '68

Ana Christine de Oliveira (1973-)

Two Drifters '05
Taxi '04

Rossy de Palma (1965-)

People '04
Talk of Angels '96
The Flower of My Secret '95
Kika '94
Ready to Wear '94
Don Juan, My Love '90
Tie Me Up! Tie Me Down! '90
Women on the Verge of a Nervous Breakdown '88

Josse De Pauw (1952-)

Everybody's Famous! '00
Hombres Complicados '97
The Pointsman '86

Miranda de Pencier (1968-)

Anne of Green Gables: The Continuing Story '99
Kurt Vonnegut's Harrison Bergeron '95
Anne of Green Gables '85

Teresa De Priest (1970-)

Hit and Runway '01
The Doorway '00

Lya de Putti (1897-1931)

The Informer '29
The Sorrows of Satan '26
Variety '25
Othello '22
Phantom '22
The Indian Tomb '21

Emilie de Ravin (1981-)

Remember Me '10
Public Enemies '09
Brick '06
The Hills Have Eyes '06
Carrie '02

Chris De Rose (1948-)

Breakaway '95
Aftershock '88

Portia de Rossi (1973-)

Cursed '04
I Witness '03
The Night We Called It a Day '03
Who is Cletis Tout? '02
The Invisibles '99
Stigmata '99
Girl '98
Perfect Assassins '98
Scream 2 '97
Sirens '94

Anna De Sade

Arizona '86
Sorceress '82

Anthony De Sando (1965-)

Beer League '06
Hysterical Blindness '02
Double Parked '00
Cement '99
Kiss Me, Guido '97
Federal Hill '94
Party Girl '94
Whispers of White '93
Grand Isle '92
The Return of Eliot Ness '91

Joe De Santis (1909-89)

It's Good to Be Alive '74
Blue '68
And Now Miguel '66
The George Raft Story '61
Al Capone '59

Lorraine (De Sette) De Selle (1951-)

The Wild Beasts '85
Women's Prison Massacre '85
Caged Women '84

House on the Edge of the Park '84

Christian de Sica (1951-)

Men Men Men '95
Detective School Dropouts '85
An Almost Perfect Affair '79
The Sex Machine '75
Blaise Pascal '71

Vittorio De Sica (1902-74)

We All Loved Each Other So Much '77
Andy Warhol's Dracula '74
12 Plus 1 '70
The Shoes of the Fisherman '68
Scandal Man '67
L'Odeur des Fauves '66
The Amorous Adventures of Moll Flanders '65
The Wonders of Aladdin '61
The Battle of Austerlitz '60
Generale Della Rovere '60
It Started in Naples '60
The Millionairess '60
Angel in a Taxi '59
The Inveterate Bachelor '58
A Farewell to Arms '57
The Earrings of Madame De... '54
The Gold of Naples '54
Too Bad She's Bad '54
Pardon My Trunk '52
Peddlin' in Society '47
Teresa Venerdi '41

Guiliana de Sio (1957-)

Private Affairs '89
Pool Hustlers '83

Werner De Smedt (1970-)

The Memory of a Killer '03
Everybody's Famous! '00

Melissa De Sousa (1967-)

Bats: Human Harvest '07
30 Years to Life '01
Lockdown '00
Miss Congeniality '00
The Best Man '99
Ride '98

Edward De Souza (1933-)

A Question of Attribution '91
Kiss of the Vampire '62
The Phantom of the Opera '62

Jose-Luis De Villalonga (1920-2007)

Blood and Sand '89
Darling '65
Any Number Can Win '63
The Lovers '59

Brandon de Wilde (1942-72)

In Harm's Way '65
Those Calloways '65
Hud '63
All Fall Down '62
Missouri Traveler '58
Night Passage '57
Goodbye, My Lady '56
Shane '53
The Member of the Wedding '52

Jacqueline De Witt

See Jacqueline DeWit

Francis De Wolff (1913-84)

Devil Doll '64
The Two Faces of Dr. Jekyll '60
The Smallest Show on Earth '57
Geordie '55

Luke De Woolfson

Mr. Right '06
Stoned '05

Marie Dea (1912-92)

Orpheus '49
Les Visiteurs du Soir '42

Brian Deacon (1949-)

A Zed & Two Noughts '88
Jesus '79
Triple Echo '77
Vampyres '74

Richard Deacon (1921-84)

Bad Manners '84
Piranha '78
The One and Only, Genuine, Original Family Band '68
Blackbeard's Ghost '67
The Gnome-Mobile '67
Billie '65
The Patsy '64
Critic's Choice '63
Carousel '56
Francis in the Haunted House '56
Invasion of the Body Snatchers '56
The Kettles in the Ozarks '56
Abbott and Costello Meet the Mummy '55
Blackboard Jungle '55
Them! '54

Lucy Deakins (1971-)

There Goes My Baby '92
Cheetah '89
The Great Outdoors '88
Little Nikita '88
The Boy Who Could Fly '86

Sarah Deakins

The Sandlot 3: Heading Home '07
Hollow Man 2 '06
Possessed '05

Allison Dean

Incognito '99
Where's Marlowe? '98
Ruby in Paradise '93
Coming to America '88

Eddie Dean (1907-99)

Black Hills '48
Check Your Guns '48
The Hawk of Powder River '48
The Tioga Kid '48
West to Glory '47
Wild Country '47
The Caravan Trail '46
Colorado Serenade '46
Driftin' River '46
Wild West '46
Song of Old Wyoming '45
Wildfire '45
Knights of the Range '40
Santa Fe Marshal '40
Law of the Pampas '39
Renegade Trail '39

Felicity Dean (1959-)

The Last of the Blonde Bombshells '00
Persuasion '95
The Whistle Blower '87

Howard Dean (1948-)

Tanner on Tanner '04
Journeys with George '02

Isabel Dean (1918-97)

Weather in the Streets '84
Oh! What a Lovely War '69

James Dean (1931-55)

America at the Movies '76
Giant '56
Rebel without a Cause '55
East of Eden '54
Fixed Bayonets! '51
Hill Number One '51

Jeanne Dean (1925-93)

Clipped Wings '53
Radar Patrol vs. Spy King '49

Jimmy Dean (1928-)

Big Bad John '90
The City '76

Diamonds Are Forever '71
The Ballad of Andy Crocker '69

Loren Dean (1969-)

The Poker Club '08
The Bronx Is Burning '07
The War Bride '01
Space Cowboys '00
Mumford '99
Enemy of the State '98
The End of Violence '97
Gattaca '97
Mrs. Winterbourne '96
Rosewood '96
Apollo 13 '95
How to Make an American Quilt '95
The Passion of Darkly Noon '95
JFK: Reckless Youth '93
1492: Conquest of Paradise '92
Billy Bathgate '91
Say Anything '89
Plain Clothes '88

Man Mountain Dean (1891-1953)

The Gladiator '38
Three Legionnaires '37

Margia Dean (1921-)

The Quatermass Experiment '56
Lonesome Trail '55
Fangs of the Wild '54
Sins of Jezebel '54
Loan Shark '52
Mr. Walkie Talkie '52
Tales of Robin Hood '52
Kentucky Jubilee '51
Leave It to the Marines '51
Pier 23 '51
Savage Drums '51
Sky High '51
Red Desert '50
Rimfire '49
Ringside '49
Shep Comes Home '49

Nathaniel Dean

Somersault '04
Walking on Water '02

Priscilla Dean (1896-1987)

Law of the Sea '32
White Tiger '23
Outside the Law '21

Rick Dean (1953-2006)

Carnosaur 3: Primal Species '96
Max Is Missing '95
Stripteaser '95
Cheyenne Warrior '94
Peephole '93
Bloodfist 3: Forced to Fight '92
Raiders of the Sun '92
Saturday Night Special '92
Naked Obsession '91
Heroes Stand Alone '89
Nam Angels '88
Island of Blood '82

Ron Dean

The Dark Knight '08
Wild Things 2 '04
The Wild Card '03
The Client '94
Rudy '93
Legacy of Lies '92
Cold Justice '89
Above the Law '88
Cocktail '88
Big Score '83

Lezlie (Dean) Deane (1964-)

To Protect and Serve '92
Freddy's Dead: The Final Nightmare '91
Girlfriend from Hell '89
976-EVIL '88

Shirley Deane (1913-83)

Prairie Moon '38
Charlie Chan at the Circus '36

Justin Deas (1948-)

iMurders '08
Montana '90
Dream Lover '85

Jamel Debbouze (1975-)

Days of Glory '06
Angel-A '05
She Hate Me '04
Amelie '01

Kristine DeBell (1954-)

Cheerleaders' Wild Weekend '85
Rooster: Spurs of Death! '83
Tag: The Assassination Game '82
Lifepod '80
Willie & Phil '80

James DeBello (1980-)

Transylmania '09
Ghouls '07
Cabin Fever '03
Players '03
Swimfan '02
Crime and Punishment in Suburbia '00
100 Girls '00
Detroit Rock City '99

John DeBello (1952-)

Killer Tomatoes Eat France '91
Killer Tomatoes Strike Back '90
Out of the Dark '88
Attack of the Killer Tomatoes '77

David Deblinger

Club Land '01
Intern '00
Frogs for Snakes '98

Marcia DeBonis (1960-)

12 and Holding '05
L.I.E. '01

Lee DeBroux (1941-)

The Day the World Ended '01
Death Benefit '96
Mars '96
Open Fire '94
Hangfire '91
Sweet Hostage '75

Jean Debucourt (1894-1958)

The Crucible '57
Nana '55
The Earrings of Madame De... '54
Seven Deadly Sins '53
Monsieur Vincent '47
La Chute de la Maison Usher '28

Cathy DeBuono

And Then Came Lola '09
Out at the Wedding '07

Amanda DeCadenet (1972-)

Fall '97
Four Rooms '95

Rosemary DeCamp (1910-2001)

Saturday the 14th '81
13 Ghosts '60
Many Rivers to Cross '55
By the Light of the Silvery Moon '53
Main Street to Broadway '53
So This Is Love '53
Scandal Sheet '52
On Moonlight Bay '51
Look for the Silver Lining '49
The Story of Seabiscuit '49
Nora Prentiss '47
Pride of the Marines '45
Rhapsody in Blue '45
Commandos Strike at Dawn '43
The Jungle Book '42
Yankee Doodle Dandy '42
Cheers for Miss Bishop '41

Mark DeCarlo (1962-)

The Ant Bully '06 (V)

They Made Me a Criminal '39
Angels with Dirty Faces '38
Crime School '38
Little Tough Guys '38
Dead End '37

Myrna Dell (1924-)
Ma Barker's Killer Brood '60
Naked Hills '56
The Bushwackers '52
The Judge Steps Out '49
Fighting Father Dunne '48
Nocturne '46
Raiders of Red Gap '43

Ottaviano Dell'Acqua
Days of Hell '84
Rats '83

Michael DellaFemina
Bloodlust: Subspecies 3 '93
Invisible: The Chronicles of Benjamin Knight '93
Italian Movie '93
Mandroid '93

Erik Todd Dellums (1964-)
Boycott '02
Blackmale '99
She's Gotta Have It '86

Edouard Delmont (1893-1955)
The Sheep Has Five Legs '54
Passion for Life '48
Harvest '37
Angele '34
Toni '34

Nikki Deloach (1979-)
The Net 2.0 '06
Gunfighter's Moon '96
Traveller '96

Genevieve Deloir
The Screaming Dead '72
The Red Half-Breed '70

Alain Delon (1935-)
Nouvelle Vague '90
Notre Histoire '84
Swann in Love '84
Le Choc '82
The Concorde: Airport '79 '79
Boomerang '76
Mr. Klein '76
Gypsy '75
Icy Breasts '75
Le Gitan '75
Widow Couderc '74
Zorro '74
Scorpio '73
Assassination of Trotsky '72
Red Sun '71
Borsalino '70
Le Cercle Rouge '70
Swimming Pool '70
La Piscine '69
The Girl on a Motorcycle '68
Honor Among Thieves '68
Spirits of the Dead '68
Diabolically Yours '67
The Last Adventure '67
Le Samourai '67
The Eclipse '66
Is Paris Burning? '66
The Lost Command '66
Texas Across the River '66
Joy House '64
Any Number Can Win '63
The Leopard '63
Purple Noon '60
Rocco and His Brothers '60
Sois Belle et Tais-Toi '58

Nathalie Delon (1941-)
Game of Seduction '76
Le Sex Shop '73
Bluebeard '72
Eyes Behind the Stars '72
When Eight Bells Toll '71
Le Samourai '67

Jennifer Delora (1962-)
Bedroom Eyes 2 '89
Deranged '87
New York's Finest '87
Robot Holocaust '87
Sensations '87

Michael Delorenzo (1959-)
Border Patrol '01
Gun Shy '00
The Wall '99
My Family '94
Somebody to Love '94
Platoon Leader '87

Daniele Delorme (1926-)
November Moon '85
Pardon Mon Affaire '76
Les Miserables '57

Julie Delpy (1969-)
The Air I Breathe '07
2 Days in Paris '07
The Hoax '06
The Legend of Lucy Keyes '06
Broken Flowers '05
Before Sunset '04
Intimate Affairs '01
MacArthur Park '01
Waking Life '01
Sand '00
But I'm a Cheerleader '99
Dostoevsky's Crime and Punishment '99
The Passion of Ayn Rand '99
The Treat '98
An American Werewolf in Paris '97
Before Sunrise '94
Killing Zoe '94
Trois Couleurs: Blanc '94
Trois Couleurs: Rouge '94
Younger & Younger '94
The Three Musketeers '93
Europa, Europa '91
Voyager '91
Beatrice '88
Mauvais Sang '86

Rene Deltgen (1909-79)
Black and White As Day and Night '78
Journey to the Lost City '58
Tromba, the Tiger Man '52
The Mozart Story '48

Xavier DeLuc
The Other Side of the Law '95
Captive '87

Rudy DeLuca
Life Stinks '91
The Return of Count Yorga '71

Anne Marie Deluise
The Thaw '09
Ace of Hearts '08
Shock to the System '06

David DeLuise (1971-)
The Wizards of Waverly Place: The Movie '09
Bundy: A Legacy of Evil '08
A Christmas Proposal '08
Dear Me: A Blogger's Tale '08
National Lampoon Presents RoboDoc '08
Route 30 '08
Who's Your Monkey '07
Jam '06
BachelorMan '03
Terror Tract '00
Too Smooth '98

Dom DeLuise (1933-2009)
Girl Play '04
Baby Geniuses '98
The Godson '98
The Secret of NIMH 2 '98 (V)
Boys Will Be Boys '97
Red Line '96
All Dogs Go to Heaven 2 '95 (V)
The Tin Soldier '95
A Troll in Central Park '94 (V)
Happily Ever After '93 (V)
The Magic Voyage '93 (V)
Silence of the Hams '93
The Skateboard Kid '93 (V)
Munchie '92 (V)
Almost Pregnant '91
An American Tail: Fievel Goes West '91 (V)
Driving Me Crazy '91
Loose Cannons '90
All Dogs Go to Heaven '89 (V)
Going Bananas '88
Oliver & Company '88 (V)
My African Adventure '87
Spaceballs '87
An American Tail '86 (V)
Haunted Honeymoon '86
Cannonball Run 2 '84
Johnny Dangerously '84
The Best Little Whorehouse in Texas '82
The Secret of NIMH '82 (V)
Cannonball Run '81
History of the World: Part 1 '81
Fatso '80
Hot Stuff '80
The Last Married Couple in America '80
Smokey and the Bandit 2 '80
Wholly Moses! '80
Diary of a Young Comic '79
The Muppet Movie '79
The Adventures of Sherlock Holmes' Smarter Brother '78
The Cheap Detective '78
The End '78
Sextette '78
World's Greatest Lover '77
Silent Movie '76
Blazing Saddles '74
Evil Roy Slade '71
Who Is Harry Kellerman and Why Is He Saying Those Terrible Things About Me? '71
The Twelve Chairs '70
The Busy Body '67
The Glass Bottom Boat '66
Fail-Safe '64

Michael DeLuise (1970-)
Boys Will Be Boys '97
The Shot '96
Midnight Edition '93
Encino Man '92

Peter DeLuise (1966-)
Before I Say Goodbye '03
National Lampoon's Attack of the 5 Ft. 2 Women '94
Rescue Me '93
Children of the Night '92
Free Ride '86
The Midnight Hour '86

Gordon DeMain (1886-1954)
The Mad Monster '42
International Lady '41
Lucky Texan '34
The Dude Bandit '33
Fighting Texans '33
High Gear '33
Rainbow Ranch '33
The Nevada Buckaroo '31

William Demarest (1892-1983)
The McCullochs '75
Don't Be Afraid of the Dark '73
It's a Mad, Mad, Mad, Mad World '63
Viva Las Vegas '63
The Mountain '56
Sincerely Yours '56
The Far Horizons '55
Hell on Frisco Bay '55
Jupiter's Darling '55
The Private War of Major Benson '55
Dangerous When Wet '53
Escape from Fort Bravo '53
Here Come the Girls '53
Behave Yourself! '52
What Price Glory? '52
First Legion '51
Never a Dull Moment '50
Riding High '50
Jolson Sings Again '49
Sorrowful Jones '49
On Our Merry Way '48
The Perils of Pauline '47
The Jolson Story '46
Along Came Jones '45
Salty O'Rourke '45
The Great Moment '44
Hail the Conquering Hero '44
Miracle of Morgan's Creek '44
All Through the Night '42
The Palm Beach Story '42
Pardon My Sarong '42
The Devil & Miss Jones '41
The Lady Eve '41
Sullivan's Travels '41
Christmas in July '40
The Great McGinty '40
The Great Man Votes '38
Rebecca of Sunnybrook Farm '38
Charlie Chan at the Opera '36
The Great Ziegfeld '36
Love on the Run '36
Wedding Present '36
Hands Across the Table '35
The First Auto '27
The Jazz Singer '27

Donna DeMario
See Donna (Dona Martel) Martell

Derrick DeMarney (1906-78)
Meet Mr. Callaghan '54
Inheritance '47
Frenzy '46
Dangerous Moonlight '41
Young and Innocent '37
Things to Come '36

Orane Demazis (1904-91)
Le Schpountz '38
Harvest '37
Cesar '36
Angele '34
Fanny '32
Marius '31

William DeMeo
Searching for Bobby D '05
Wannabes '01

William Demerest
When Willie Comes Marching Home '50
Easy Living '37

Ellem Demerus
More about the Children of Noisy Village '87
The Children of Noisy Village '86

Alla Demidova (1936-)
The Seagull '71
Tchaikovsky '71

Cecil B. DeMille (1881-1959)
Sunset Boulevard '50
Star Spangled Rhythm '42
Free and Easy '30

Katherine DeMille (1911-95)
The Judge '49
Unconquered '47
In Old Caliente '39
Charlie Chan at the Olympics '37
The Gentleman from California '37
Drift Fence '36
Sky Parade '36
The Black Room '35
The Crusades '35
Belle of the Nineties '34
Viva Villa! '34

Jonathan Demme (1944-)
That Thing You Do! '96
Married to the Mob '88
Into the Night '85
Incredible Melting Man '77

Mylene Demongeot (1936-)
12 Plus 1 '70
Uncle Tom's Cabin '69
The Rape of the Sabines '61
The Giant of Marathon '60
Just Another Pretty Face '58
Sois Belle et Tais-Toi '58
Bonjour Tristesse '57
The Crucible '57

Darcy Demoss (1964-)
Forbidden Zone: Alien Abduction '96
The Death Artist '95
Eden '93
Eden 2 '93
Eden 3 '93
Eden 4 '93
Living to Die '91
Pale Blood '91
Can't Buy Me Love '87
Friday the 13th, Part 6: Jason Lives '86

Anais Demoustier
Give Me Your Hand '09
Time of the Wolf '03

Brendan F. Dempsey
About Adam '00
Waking Ned Devine '98

Patrick Dempsey (1966-)
Valentine's Day '10
Made of Honor '08
Enchanted '07
Freedom Writers '07
Brother Bear 2 '06 (V)
Lucky Seven '03
The Emperor's Club '02
Sweet Home Alabama '02
Blonde '01
Life in the Fast Lane '00
Scream 3 '00
Dostoevsky's Crime and Punishment '99
Me & Will '99
Jeremiah '98
Something About Sex '98
The Treat '98
Hugo Pool '97
Bloodknot '95
The Escape '95
The Right to Remain Silent '95
Ava's Magical Adventure '94
With Honors '94
Bank Robber '93
JFK: Reckless Youth '93
Face the Music '92
For Better and for Worse '92
Mobsters '91
Run '91
Coupe de Ville '90
Happy Together '89
Loverboy '89
In a Shallow Grave '88
Some Girls '88
Can't Buy Me Love '87
In the Mood '87
Meatballs 3 '87
Heaven Help Us '85

Richard Dempsey (1974-)
The Aristocrats '99
Catherine Cookson's Tilly Trotter '99
The Chronicles of Narnia '89

Tanya Dempsey (1975-)
Witchouse 3: Demon Fire '01
Shrieker '97

Carol Dempster (1901-91)
The Sorrows of Satan '26
Sally of the Sawdust '25
America '24
Isn't Life Wonderful '24
The White Rose '23
Sherlock Holmes '22
Dream Street '21
The Love Flower '20

Jeffrey DeMunn (1947-)
Burn After Reading '08
The Mist '07
The Hades Factor '06
Hollywoodland '06
Empire Falls '05
Our Town '03
Cash Crop '01
The Majestic '01
Noriega: God's Favorite '00
The Green Mile '99
Stephen King's The Storm of the Century '99
Harvest '98
The X-Files '98
RocketMan '97
Turbulence '96
Citizen X '95
Hiroshima '95
Down Came a Blackbird '94
Barbarians at the Gate '93
Treacherous Crossing '92
Eyes of an Angel '91
Blaze '89
Betrayed '88
The Blob '88
Gore Vidal's Lincoln '88
Windmills of the Gods '88
The Hitcher '86
A Time to Live '85
Windy City '84
Sessions '83
Trumps '83
Frances '82
Ragtime '81
Christmas Evil '80

Mathieu Demy (1972-)
The Girl on the Train '09
A Few Days in September '06
Jeanne and the Perfect Guy '98
The New Yorker '98
One Hundred and One Nights '95
Le Petit Amour '87

Maggie Dence
Look Both Ways '05
Danny Deckchair '03

Judi Dench (1934-)
Nine '09
Cranford '08
Quantum of Solace '08
Casino Royale '06
Notes on a Scandal '06
Mrs. Henderson Presents '05
Pride and Prejudice '05
The Chronicles of Riddick '04
Home on the Range '04 (V)
Ladies in Lavender '04
Die Another Day '02
The Importance of Being Earnest '02
Iris '01
The Shipping News '01
Chocolat '00
The Last of the Blonde Bombshells '00
Tea with Mussolini '99
The World Is Not Enough '99
Shakespeare in Love '98
Mrs. Brown '97
Tomorrow Never Dies '97
Hamlet '96
Goldeneye '95
Jack and Sarah '95
Henry V '89
A Handful of Dust '88
Saigon: Year of the Cat '87
84 Charing Cross Road '86
A Room with a View '86
Wetherby '85
Luther '74
A Midsummer Night's Dream '68
A Study in Terror '66

Denden
Ju-On 2 *'00*
Uzumaki *'00*
Cure *'97*

Catherine Deneuve
Persepolis *'07 (V)*
Manon *'68*

Catherine Deneuve (1943-)
The Girl on the Train *'09*
A Christmas Tale *'08*
Apres Lui *'07*
Changing Times *'04*
Kings and Queen *'04*
Dangerous Liaisons *'03*
8 Women *'02*
The Musketeer *'01*
I'm Going Home *'00*
Dancer in the Dark *'99*
East-West *'99*
Pola X *'99*
Time Regained *'99*
Place Vendome *'98*
Genealogies of a Crime *'97*
Les Voleurs *'96*
The Convent *'95*
Ma Saison Preferee *'93*
Indochine *'92*
Scene of the Crime *'87*
Love Songs *'85*
Fort Saganne *'84*
Love Songs *'84*
Choice of Arms *'83*
The Hunger *'83*
Le Choc *'82*
Hotel America *'81*
I Love You All *'80*
The Last Metro *'80*
A Slightly Pregnant Man *'79*
March or Die *'77*
The Hustle *'75*
Lovers Like Us *'75*
The Savage *'75*
La Grande Bourgeoise *'74*
Act of Aggression *'73*
Peau D'Ane *'71*
Donkey Skin *'70*
Tristana *'70*
April Fools *'69*
Mississippi Mermaid *'69*
Mayerling *'68*
The Young Girls of Rochefort *'68*
Belle de Jour *'67*
Repulsion *'65*
Umbrellas of Cherbourg *'64*
The Twilight Girls *'57*

Jake Dengel (1933-94)
Prayer of the Rollerboys *'91*
Bloodsucking Pharoahs of Pittsburgh *'90*
Ironweed *'87*

Christopher Denham
El Camino *'08*
Headspace *'02*

Maurice Denham (1909-2002)
Monsignor Quixote *'91*
84 Charing Cross Road *'86*
Mr. Love *'86*
From a Far Country: Pope John Paul II *'81*
Luther *'74*
Sunday, Bloody Sunday *'71*
Negatives *'68*
Night Caller from Outer Space *'66*
The Alphabet Murders *'65*
The Nanny *'65*
Hysteria *'64*
The Seventh Dawn *'64*
The Very Edge *'63*
Damn the Defiant *'62*
Paranoiac *'62*
The Mark *'61*
Sink the Bismarck *'60*
Our Man in Havana *'59*
Curse of the Demon *'57*
23 Paces to Baker Street *'56*
Animal Farm *'55 (V)*
Blanche Fury *'48*
Captain Boycott *'47*

Marianne (Cuau) Denicourt (1966-)
Me Without You *'01*
Sade *'00*
The Lost Son *'98*
My Sex Life... Or How I Got into an Argument *'96*
Up/Down/Fragile *'95*
Doomsday Gun *'94*
La Sentinelle *'92*
La Belle Noiseuse *'90*

Lydie Denier (1964-)
White Cargo *'96*
Guardian Angel *'94*
Mardi Gras for the Devil *'93*
Red Shoe Diaries 3: Another Woman's Lipstick *'93*
Under Investigation *'93*
Invasion of Privacy *'92*
Midnight Cabaret *'90*
Satan's Princess *'90*
Blood Relations *'87*

Jacques Denis (1943-)
This Sweet Sickness *'77*
Jonah Who Will Be 25 in the Year 2000 *'76*
The Clockmaker *'73*
La Salamandre *'71*

Alexis Denisof (1966-)
Rip It Off *'02*
Noah's Ark *'99*
Sharpe's Justice *'97*
Sharpe's Revenge *'97*
Sharpe's Waterloo *'97*

Anthony John (Tony) Denison (1950-)
Crash and Burn *'07*
Wild Things 2 *'04*
Now You Know *'02*
Looking for an Echo *'99*
For Which He Stands *'98*
The Corporate Ladder *'97*
Opposite Corners *'96*
Getting Gotti *'94*
Men of War *'94*
The Amy Fisher Story *'93*
A Brilliant Disguise *'93*
Full Eclipse *'93*
Sex, Love and Cold Hard Cash *'93*
The Harvest *'92*
Child of Darkness, Child of Light *'91*
City of Hope *'91*
Little Vegas *'90*
Full Exposure: The Sex Tape Scandals *'89*
The Great Escape 2: The Untold Story *'88*

Leslie Denison (1905-92)
The Snow Creature *'54*
O.S.S. *'46*
Five Graves to Cairo *'43*
Sherlock Holmes and the Secret Weapon *'42*
To Be or Not to Be *'42*

Michael Denison (1915-98)
Shadowlands *'93*
Angels One Five *'54*
The Franchise Affair *'52*
The Importance of Being Earnest *'52*

David Denman (1973-)
Shutter *'08*
When a Stranger Calls *'06*
Big Fish *'03*
The Replacements *'00*

Tony Denman (1979-)
Transylmania *'09*
Sorority Boys *'02*
Poor White Trash *'00*

Marie Denn
Bury Me an Angel *'71*
Wild Guitar *'62*

Brian Dennehy (1939-)
Righteous Kill *'08*
Marco Polo *'07*
Ratatouille *'07 (V)*
The Ultimate Gift *'07*
Welcome to Paradise *'07*
Everyone's Hero *'06 (V)*
10th & Wolf *'06*
Assault on Precinct 13 *'05*
Category 6 : Day of Destruction *'04*
She Hate Me *'04*
The Roman Spring of Mrs. Stone *'03*
A Season on the Brink *'02*
Stolen Summer *'02*
Summer Catch *'01*
Warden of Red Rock *'01*
Fail Safe *'00*
Out of the Cold *'99*
Silicon Towers *'99*
Sirens *'99*
Dish Dogs *'98*
Tom Clancy's Netforce *'98*
Larry McMurtry's Dead Man's Walk *'96*
Nostromo *'96*
William Shakespeare's Romeo and Juliet *'96*
Tommy Boy *'95*
The Stars Fell on Henrietta *'94*
Final Appeal *'93*
Foreign Affairs *'93*
Diamond Fleece *'92*
Gladiator *'92*
Scott Turow's The Burden of Proof *'92*
Teamster Boss: The Jackie Presser Story *'92*
To Catch a Killer *'92*
The Belly of an Architect *'91*
F/X 2: The Deadly Art of Illusion *'91*
Indio *'90*
A Killing in a Small Town *'90*
The Last of the Finest *'90*
Presumed Innocent *'90*
Rising Son *'90*
Day One *'89*
Perfect Witness *'89*
Cocoon: The Return *'88*
A Father's Revenge *'88*
Miles from Home *'88*
Return to Snowy River *'88*
Best Seller *'87*
The Lion of Africa *'87*
Acceptable Risks *'86*
F/X *'86*
Legal Eagles *'86*
Check Is in the Mail *'85*
Cocoon *'85*
Silverado *'85*
Twice in a Lifetime *'85*
Finders Keepers *'84*
The River Rat *'84*
Gorky Park *'83*
Never Cry Wolf *'83*
First Blood *'82*
Split Image *'82*
Little Miss Marker *'80*
A Rumor of War *'80*
To Love Again *'80*
Butch and Sundance: The Early Days *'79*
The Jericho Mile *'79*
Silent Victory: The Kitty O'Neil Story *'79*
10 *'79*
F.I.S.T. *'78*
Foul Play *'78*
Pearl *'78*
A Real American Hero *'78*
Ants *'77*
Johnny We Hardly Knew Ye *'77*
Semi-Tough *'77*

Barry Dennen (1938-)
Liquid Dreams *'92*
The Shining *'80*
Jesus Christ, Superstar *'73*
Paul Bartel's The Secret Cinema *'69*

Charles Denner (1926-95)
Window Shopping *'86*
Robert et Robert *'78*
The Man Who Loved Women *'77*
Mado *'76*
The Holes *'72*
Les Assassins de L'Ordre *'71*
Z *'69*
The Bride Wore Black *'68*
The Two of Us *'68*
The Thief of Paris *'67*
Life Upside Down *'64*
Bluebeard *'63*

Richard Denning (1914-98)
Alice Through the Looking Glass *'66*
Twice-Told Tales *'63*
An Affair to Remember *'57*
The Black Scorpion *'57*
Girls in Prison *'56*
Day the World Ended *'55*
Creature from the Black Lagoon *'54*
Hangman's Knot *'52*
Double Deal *'50*
Unknown Island *'48*
Seven Were Saved *'47*
Black Beauty *'46*
The Glass Key *'42*
Adam Had Four Sons *'41*
Golden Gloves *'40*
Campus Confessions *'38*

Kat Dennings (1986-)
The Answer Man *'09*
Defendor *'09*
Shorts: The Adventures of the Wishing Rock *'09*
The House Bunny *'08*
Nick & Norah's Infinite Playlist *'08*
Charlie Bartlett *'07*
Big Momma's House 2 *'06*
Down in the Valley *'05*
The 40 Year Old Virgin *'05*
Raise Your Voice *'04*

Gabrielle Dennis
Bring It On: Fight to the Finish *'09*
The Marc Pease Experience *'09*

John Dennis (1919-2004)
Tomb of the Undead *'72*
From Here to Eternity *'53*

Sandy Dennis (1937-92)
The Indian Runner *'91*
Parents *'89*
Another Woman *'88*
976-EVIL *'88*
The Execution *'85*
Come Back to the Five & Dime Jimmy Dean, Jimmy Dean *'82*
The Four Seasons *'81*
Nasty Habits *'77*
God Told Me To *'76*
Mr. Sycamore *'74*
The Out-of-Towners *'70*
That Cold Day in the Park *'69*
Sweet November *'68*
Up the Down Staircase *'67*
Who's Afraid of Virginia Woolf? *'66*
The Three Sisters *'65*
Splendor in the Grass *'61*

Leslie Denniston (1950-)
Blue Heaven *'84*
Pippin *'81*

Reginald Denny (1891-1967)
Assault on a Queen *'66*
Batman *'66*
Cat Ballou *'65*
Around the World in 80 Days *'56*
Escape to Burma *'55*
Sabaka *'55*
Abbott and Costello Meet Dr. Jekyll and Mr. Hyde *'52*
Mr. Blandings Builds His Dream House *'48*
Escape Me Never *'47*
My Favorite Brunette *'47*
Love Letters *'45*
Captains of the Clouds *'42*
Sherlock Holmes: The Voice of Terror *'42*
Thunder Birds *'42*
Rebecca *'40*
Spring Parade *'40*
Bulldog Drummond's Bride *'39*
Bulldog Drummond's Secret Police *'39*
Arrest Bulldog Drummond *'38*
Bulldog Drummond's Peril *'38*
Four Men and a Prayer *'38*
Bulldog Drummond Comes Back *'37*
Bulldog Drummond Escapes *'37*
Bulldog Drummond's Revenge *'37*
We're in the Legion Now *'37*
Anna Karenina *'35*
The Midnight Phantom *'35*
The Lost Patrol *'34*
Of Human Bondage *'34*
The World Moves On *'34*
The Barbarian *'33*
Dancing Man *'33*
Parlor, Bedroom and Bath *'31*
Private Lives *'31*
Madam Satan *'30*
The Cheerful Fraud *'27*
Skinner's Dress Suit *'26*
California Straight Ahead *'25*

Catherine Dent (1965-)
The Natalee Holloway Story *'09*
The Unseen *'05*
Taken *'02*
The Majestic *'01*
Replicant *'01*
Someone Like You *'01*
Venomous *'01*

Vernon Dent (1895-1963)
House of Errors *'42*
Texas Cyclone *'32*
The Cameraman *'28*
His First Flame *'26*
Extra Girl *'23*

Christa Denton (1972-)
Scandal in a Small Town *'88*
Convicted: A Mother's Story *'87*
The Gate *'87*
The Bad Seed *'85*

Donna Denton
Slaughterhouse Rock *'88*
Death Blow *'87*
Glory Years *'87*
Outlaw of Gor *'87*

Graham Denton (1914-66)
The Young One *'61*
The Great St. Louis Bank Robbery *'59*

James Denton
Tortured *'08*
Undead or Alive *'07*

Bob Denver (1935-)
Back to the Beach *'87*
High School USA *'84*
Rescue from Gilligan's Island *'78*
Wackiest Wagon Train in the West *'77*
Who's Minding the Mint? *'67*

John Denver (1943-97)
Walking Thunder *'94*
Higher Ground *'88*
Fire and Ice *'87 (N)*
Foxfire *'87*
Oh, God! *'77*

Elisabeth Depardieu (1941-)
Jean de Florette *'87*
Manon of the Spring *'87*
Tartuffe *'84*

Gerard Depardieu (1948-)
Babylon A.D. *'08*
Hello Goodbye *'08*
La Vie en Rose *'07*
Last Holiday *'06*
Paris, je t'aime *'06*
How Much Do You Love Me? *'05*
Changing Times *'04*
Bon Voyage *'03*
City of Ghosts *'03*
Crime Spree *'03*
Napoleon *'03*
Nathalie *'03*
Between Strangers *'02*
A Loving Father *'02*
CQ *'01*
The Bridge *'00*
The Closet *'00*
102 Dalmatians *'00*
Vatel *'00*
Balzac: A Life of Passion *'99*
The Count of Monte Cristo *'99*
The Man in the Iron Mask *'98*
Bogus *'96*
Hamlet *'96*
The Machine *'96*
The Secret Agent *'96*
Unhook the Stars *'96*
The Horseman on the Roof *'95*
Colonel Chabert *'94*
Elisa *'94*
Helas pour Moi *'94*
A Pure Formality *'94*
Germinal *'93*
My Father the Hero *'93*
1492: Conquest of Paradise *'92*
Tous les Matins du Monde *'92*
Uranus *'91*
Cyrano de Bergerac *'90*
Green Card *'90*
Camille Claudel *'89*
I Want to Go Home *'89*
Too Beautiful for You *'88*
Jean de Florette *'87*
Under Satan's Sun *'87*
Menage *'86*
One Woman or Two *'85*
Police *'85*
Fort Saganne *'84*
Tartuffe *'84*
Choice of Arms *'83*
Les Comperes *'83*
Moon in the Gutter *'83*
The Return of Martin Guerre *'83*
Danton *'82*
La Chevre *'81*
The Woman Next Door *'81*
I Love You All *'80*
The Last Metro *'80*
Loulou *'80*
Mon Oncle d'Amerique *'80*
Buffet Froid *'79*
Get Out Your Handkerchiefs *'78*
This Sweet Sickness *'77*
Barocco *'76*
Maitresse *'76*
1900 *'76*
Vincent, Francois, Paul and the Others *'76*
Going Places *'74*
Stavisky *'74*
The Holes *'72*
Nathalie Granger *'72*

Guillaume Depardieu (1971-2008)
The Duchess of Langeais *'07*
Napoleon *'03*
A Loving Father *'02*
The Count of Monte Cristo *'99*
Pola X *'99*
Les Apprentis *'95*
Tous les Matins du Monde *'92*

Julie Depardieu (1973-)
Rush Hour 3 *'07*
A Secret *'07*

The Witnesses *'07*
Blame It on Fidel *'06*
You and Me *'06*
La Petite Lili *'03*
Les Destinees *'00*
The Count of Monte Cristo *'99*

Johnny Depp (1963-)

Alice in Wonderland *'10*
The Imaginarium of Doctor Parnassus *'09*
Public Enemies *'09*
Pirates of the Caribbean: At World's End *'07*
Sweeney Todd: The Demon Barber of Fleet Street *'07*
Pirates of the Caribbean: Dead Man's Chest *'06*
Charlie and the Chocolate Factory *'05*
The Libertine *'05*
Tim Burton's Corpse Bride *'05 (V)*
Finding Neverland *'04*
Happily Ever After *'04*
Secret Window *'04*
Once Upon a Time in Mexico *'03*
Pirates of the Caribbean: The Curse of the Black Pearl *'03*
Blow *'01*
From Hell *'01*
Before Night Falls *'00*
Chocolat *'00*
The Man Who Cried *'00*
The Astronaut's Wife *'99*
The Ninth Gate *'99*
Sleepy Hollow *'99*
Fear and Loathing in Las Vegas *'98*
Donnie Brasco *'96*
Dead Man *'95*
Nick of Time *'95*
Arizona Dream *'94*
Don Juan DeMarco *'94*
Ed Wood *'94*
Benny & Joon *'93*
What's Eating Gilbert Grape *'93*
Freddy's Dead: The Final Nightmare *'91*
Cry-Baby *'90*
Edward Scissorhands *'90*
Platoon *'86*
A Nightmare on Elm Street *'84*
Private Resort *'84*

Emilie Dequenne (1981-)

The Girl on the Train *'09*
The Bridge of San Luis Rey *'05*
A Song of Innocence *'05*
The Housekeeper *'02*
Brotherhood of the Wolf *'01*
Rosetta *'99*

Gregori Derangere

The 4 Musketeers *'05*
Bon Voyage *'03*

Bo Derek (1956-)

Malibu's Most Wanted *'03*
Sunstorm *'01*
Tommy Boy *'95*
Shattered Image *'93*
Woman of Desire *'93*
Hot Chocolate *'92*
Ghosts Can't Do It *'90*
Bolero *'84*
Tarzan, the Ape Man *'81*
A Change of Seasons *'80*
10 *'79*
Orca *'77*
Fantasies *'73*

John Derek (1926-98)

Once Before I Die *'65*
Exodus *'60*
Omar Khayyam *'57*
The Ten Commandments *'56*
An Annapolis Story *'55*
The Outcast *'54*
Ambush at Tomahawk Gap *'53*
Scandal Sheet *'52*
All the King's Men *'49*
Knock on Any Door *'49*
I'll Be Seeing You *'44*

Joe DeRita (1909-93)

The Outlaws Is Coming! *'65*
Around the World in a Daze *'63*
Four for Texas *'63*
It's a Mad, Mad, Mad, Mad World *'63*
Three Stooges in Orbit *'62*
Snow White and the Three Stooges *'61*
The Three Stooges Meet Hercules *'61*
Have Rocket Will Travel *'59*
Coroner Creek *'48*

Edouard Dermithe (1915-95)

The Testament of Orpheus *'59*
Les Enfants Terrible *'50*
Orpheus *'49*

Bruce Dern (1936-)

The Golden Boys *'08*
Swamp Devil *'08*
The Astronaut Farmer *'07*
The Cake Eaters *'07*
Believe in Me *'06*
Walker Payne *'06*
Down in the Valley *'05*
Masked and Anonymous *'03*
Milwaukee, Minnesota *'03*
Monster *'03*
The Glass House *'01*
Madison *'01*
All the Pretty Horses *'00*
The Haunting *'99*
Small Soldiers *'98 (V)*
Down Periscope *'96*
Last Man Standing *'96*
Mrs. Munck *'95*
A Mother's Prayer *'95*
Mulholland Falls *'95*
Wild Bill *'95*
Amelia Earhart: The Final Flight *'94*
Dead Man's Revenge *'93*
Carolina Skeletons *'92*
Diggstown *'92*
Into the Badlands *'92*
After Dark, My Sweet *'90*
The Court Martial of Jackie Robinson *'90*
The 'Burbs *'89*
1969 *'89*
World Gone Wild *'88*
Big Town *'87*
Uncle Tom's Cabin *'87*
On the Edge *'86*
Toughlove *'85*
Harry Tracy *'83*
That Championship Season *'82*
Tattoo *'81*
Middle Age Crazy *'80*
Coming Home *'78*
The Driver *'78*
Black Sunday *'77*
Family Plot *'76*
Twist *'76*
Posse *'75*
Smile *'75*
The Great Gatsby *'74*
The Laughing Policeman *'74*
The Cowboys *'72*
The King of Marvin Gardens *'72*
Thumb Tripping *'72*
The Incredible Two-Headed Transplant *'71*
Silent Running *'71*
Bloody Mama *'70*
Castle Keep *'69*
Rebel Rousers *'69*
Support Your Local Sheriff *'69*
They Shoot Horses, Don't They? *'69*
Psych-Out *'68*
The St. Valentine's Day Massacre *'67*
The Trip *'67*
The War Wagon *'67*
Waterhole Number 3 *'67*
Will Penny *'67*
The Wild Angels *'66*
Hush, Hush, Sweet Charlotte *'65*
Marnie *'64*

Laura Dern (1966-)

Recount *'08*
Tenderness *'08*
Year of the Dog *'07*
Inland Empire *'06*
Lonely Hearts *'06*
Happy Endings *'05*
The Prize Winner of Defiance, Ohio *'05*
We Don't Live Here Anymore *'04*
Focus *'01*
I Am Sam *'01*
Jurassic Park 3 *'01*
Novocaine *'01*
Dr. T & the Women *'00*
Daddy & Them *'99*
October Sky *'99*
A Season for Miracles *'99*
The Baby Dance *'98*
Citizen Ruth *'96*
Down Came a Blackbird *'94*
Fallen Angels 1 *'93*
Jurassic Park *'93*
A Perfect World *'93*
Afterburn *'92*
Rambling Rose *'91*
Wild at Heart *'90*
Fat Man and Little Boy *'89*
Strange Case of Dr. Jekyll & Mr. Hyde *'89*
Haunted Summer *'88*
Blue Velvet *'86*
Mask *'85*
Smooth Talk *'85*
Teachers *'84*
Ladies and Gentlemen, the Fabulous Stains *'82*
Foxes *'80*
Alice Doesn't Live Here Anymore *'74*

Warren DeRosa

The Art of War 3: Retribution *'08*
Black Dawn *'05*

Barbara DeRossi (1960-)

Blood Ties *'87*
Mussolini & I *'85*
Quo Vadis *'85*

Richard Derr (1918-92)

Adam at 6 a.m. *'70*
Terror Is a Man *'59*
The Invisible Avenger *'58*
When Worlds Collide *'51*
Guilty of Treason *'50*
Castle in the Desert *'42*
Just Off Broadway *'42*
The Man Who Wouldn't Die *'42*

Cleavant Derricks (1953-)

World Traveler *'01*
Carnival of Souls *'98*
Bluffing It *'87*
Off Beat *'86*
The Slugger's Wife *'85*
Moscow on the Hudson *'84*

Donna D'Errico (1968-)

Comic Book: The Movie *'04*
Austin Powers In Goldmember *'02*
Candyman 3: Day of the Dead *'98*

Debi Derryberry

Dr. Seuss' Horton Hears a Who! *'08 (V)*
Comic Book: The Movie *'04*
Jimmy Neutron: Boy Genius *'01 (V)*
Whispers: An Elephant's Tale *'00 (V)*
Kiki's Delivery Service *'98 (V)*

Mark Derwin (1960-)

Accepted *'06*
Evil Obsession *'96*

Janos Derzsi (1954-)

Almanac of Fall *'85*
Bad Guys *'79*

Michael Des Barres (1948-)

Catch That Kid *'04*
The Man from Elysian Fields *'01*
Mulholland Drive *'01*
Sugar Town *'99*
Poison Ivy 3: The New Seduction *'97*
Silk Degrees *'94*
A Simple Twist of Fate *'94*
Widow's Kiss *'94*
The High Crusade *'92*
Waxwork 2: Lost in Time *'91*
Midnight Cabaret *'90*
Pink Cadillac *'89*
Nightflyers *'87*
I, Monster *'71*

Jean Desailly (1920-)

Le Professionnel *'81*
Assassination of Trotsky *'72*
The Soft Skin *'64*
Les Grandes Manoeuvres *'55*
La Symphonie Pastorale *'46*

Anne DeSalvo (1949-)

Hi-Life *'98*
National Lampoon's Attack of the 5 Ft. 2 Women *'94*
Casualties of Love: The "Long Island Lolita" Story *'93*
Dead in the Water *'91*
Taking Care of Business *'90*
Spike of Bensonhurst *'88*
Burglar *'87*
Compromising Positions *'85*
Perfect *'85*
Bad Manners *'84*
D.C. Cab *'84*
My Favorite Year *'82*

Jaclyn DeSantis

Bomb the System *'05*
Carlito's Way: Rise to Power *'05*

Stanley DeSantis (1954-)

The Aviator *'04*
Head Over Heels *'01*
I Am Sam *'01*
Lansky *'99*
Heartwood *'98*
Clockwatchers *'97*
Fools Rush In *'97*
The Truth about Cats and Dogs *'96*
Broken Trust *'95*
National Lampoon's Attack of the 5 Ft. 2 Women *'94*
Armistead Maupin's Tales of the City *'93*
Caged Fear *'92*
Candyman *'92*

Gerard Desarthe (1945-)

Daens *'92*
Uranus *'91*

Alex Descas (1958-)

The Limits of Control *'09*
35 Shots of Rum *'08*
Boarding Gate *'07*
Coffee and Cigarettes *'03*
Lumumba *'01*
Harem *'99*
Late August, Early September *'98*
Irma Vep *'96*
Nenette and Boni *'96*
I Can't Sleep *'93*
No Fear, No Die *'90*

Jerome Deschamps

La Separation *'98*
The Separation *'94*

Emily Deschanel (1976-)

Glory Road *'06*
Boogeyman *'05*
The Alamo *'04*

Mary Jo Deschanel (1945-)

Bark! *'02*
The Patriot *'00*
2010: The Year We Make Contact *'84*
The Right Stuff *'83*

Zooey Deschanel (1980-)

(500) Days of Summer *'09*
Gigantic *'08*
The Happening *'08*
Yes Man *'08*
The Assassination of Jesse James by the Coward Robert Ford *'07*
Bridge to Terabithia *'07*
Flakes *'07*
The Go-Getter *'07*
The Good Life *'07*
Surf's Up *'07 (V)*
Tin Man *'07*
Failure to Launch *'06*
The Hitchhiker's Guide to the Galaxy *'05*
Winter Passing *'05*
Eulogy *'04*
All the Real Girls *'03*
Elf *'03*
Abandon *'02*
Big Trouble *'02*
The Good Girl *'02*
The New Guy *'02*
Manic *'01*
Almost Famous *'00*
Mumford *'99*

Sandy Descher (1948-)

The Cobweb *'55*
The Prodigal *'55*
Them! *'54*

Alex Desert (1968-)

Pretty Persuasion *'05*
Swingers *'96*
P.C.U. *'94*

Robert Desiderio (1951-)

No Laughing Matter *'97*
Gross Anatomy *'89*
Maximum Security *'87*
Oh, God! You Devil *'84*

Florence Desmond (1905-93)

Three Came Home *'50*
Accused *'36*

William Desmond (1878-1949)

Courage of the North *'35*
Cowboy & the Bandit *'35*
Cyclone of the Saddle *'35*
Powdersmoke Range *'35*
Rustlers of Red Dog *'35*
Way of the West *'35*
Tailspin Tommy *'34*
When Lightning Strikes *'34*
Phantom of the Air *'33*
Rustler's Roundup *'33*
Battling with Buffalo Bill *'31*
Phantom of the West *'31*
Blood and Steel *'25*

Ivan Desny (1928-2002)

Les Voleurs *'96*
I Don't Kiss *'91*
The Disenchanted *'90*
Quicker Than the Eye *'88*
Escape from the KGB *'87*
The Future of Emily *'85*
Berlin Alexanderplatz *'80*
The Marriage of Maria Braun *'79*
Touch Me Not *'74*
Little Mother *'71*
Mayerling *'68*
The Snake Hunter Strangler *'66*
End of Desire *'62*
Escapade in Florence *'62*
Sherlock Holmes and the Deadly Necklace *'62*
Daniella by Night *'61*
Song Without End *'60*
Anastasia *'56*
Lola Montes *'55*
The Lady Without Camelias *'53*
The Respectful Prostitute *'52*
Madeleine *'50*

Rosanna Desoto (1950-)

Mambo Cafe *'00*
The 24 Hour Woman *'99*
Star Trek 6: The Undiscovered Country *'91*
Family Business *'89*
Stand and Deliver *'88*
La Bamba *'87*
Ballad of Gregorio Cortez *'83*
The In-Laws *'79*

Nada Despotovich (1967-)

Series 7: The Contenders *'01*
Babycakes *'89*
Taken Away *'89*

Natalie Desselle

B.A.P.'s *'97*
Def Jam's How to Be a Player *'97*

Amanda Detmer (1971-)

American Crude *'07*
American East *'07*
Final Move *'06*
Jam *'06*
You, Me and Dupree *'06*
Extreme Dating *'04*
Big Fat Liar *'02*
A Little Inside *'01*
The Majestic *'01*
Saving Silverman *'01*
Boys and Girls *'00*
Final Destination *'00*
Drop Dead Gorgeous *'99*

Maruschka Detmers (1962-)

Hidden Assassin *'94*
The Mambo Kings *'92*
Hanna's War *'88*
Devil in the Flesh *'87*
First Name: Carmen *'83*

Tamara DeTreaux (1959-90)

Ghoulies *'84*
Don't Be Afraid of the Dark *'73*

Geoffrey Deuel (1943-)

Amateur Night *'85*
Chisum *'70*

Ernst Deutsch (1891-1969)

The Third Man *'49*
The Golem *'20*

Patti Deutsch (1945-)

The Emperor's New Groove *'00 (V)*
Jetsons: The Movie *'90 (V)*

William Devane (1939-)

Chasing the Green *'09*
Jesse Stone: Thin Ice *'09*
Stargate: Continuum *'08*
Jesse Stone: Sea Change *'07*
Jesse Stone: Death in Paradise *'06*
Monte Walsh *'03*
The Badge *'02*
Threat of Exposure *'02*
Race to Space *'01*
Hollow Man *'00*
Poor White Trash *'00*
Space Cowboys *'00*
Payback *'98*
Detonator 2: Night Watch *'95*
Lady in Waiting *'94*
Rubdown *'93*
A Woman Named Jackie *'91*
Chips, the War Dog *'90*
Vital Signs *'90*
The Preppie Murder *'89*
Timestalkers *'87*
Hadley's Rebellion *'84*
Urge to Kill *'84*
Jane Doe *'83*
Testament *'83*
Honky Tonk Freeway *'81*
Red Flag: The Ultimate Game *'81*

The Dark '79
From Here to Eternity '79
Yanks '79
The Bad News Bears in Breaking Training '77
Red Alert '77
Rolling Thunder '77
Family Plot '76
Marathon Man '76
Missiles of October '74
McCabe & Mrs. Miller '71
My Old Man's Place '71
The 300 Year Weekend '71

Joanna DeVarona
See Joanna Kerns

Devin Devasquez (1963-)
Society '92
Can't Buy Me Love '87
House 2: The Second Story '87

Alan Deveau
Recruits '86
Loose Screws '85

Nathaniel DeVeaux
In a Class of His Own '99
Outrage '98
The Spree '96
The Escape '95
Hard Evidence '94
Bad Attitude '93

Stuart Devenie
Jack Brown, Genius '94
Dead Alive '93

Ed Devereaux (1925-)
Goldeneye: The Secret Life of Ian Fleming '89
We'll Meet Again '82
Money Movers '78

Marie Devereux (1941-)
Naked Kiss '64
The Mark '61

Kamala Devi
The Brass Bottle '63
Geronimo '62

Paula DeVicq (1965-)
The Breakup Artist '04
Dinner and Driving '97

Renee Devillers (1902-2000)
The French Touch '54
Heart of a Nation '43
J'Accuse '37

Aidan Devine
Everything's Gone Green '06
Brian's Song '01
Life with Judy Garland—Me and My Shadows '01

Andy Devine (1905-77)
Mouse and His Child '77 (V)
Whale of a Tale '76
Robin Hood '73 (V)
Myra Breckinridge '70
Smoke '70
Over the Hill Gang '69
Zebra in the Kitchen '65
How the West Was Won '63
The Man Who Shot Liberty Valance '62
Two Rode Together '61
The Adventures of Huckleberry Finn '60
Around the World in 80 Days '56
Thunder Pass '54
Island in the Sky '53
Montana Belle '52
The Red Badge of Courage '51
Slaughter Trail '51
Never a Dull Moment '50
The Traveling Saleswoman '50
Eyes of Texas '48
Far Frontier '48
Grand Canyon Trail '48
Night Time in Nevada '48
Under California Stars '48
On the Old Spanish Trail '47
Springtime in the Sierras '47
Canyon Passage '46
Ali Baba and the Forty Thieves '43
The Gay Ranchero '42
Timber! '42
The Flame of New Orleans '41
Buck Benny Rides Again '40
Torrid Zone '40
Mutiny on the Blackhawk '39
Never Say Die '39
Stagecoach '39
Double or Nothing '37
In Old Chicago '37
A Star Is Born '37
Yellowstone '36
Stingaree '34
Doctor Bull '33
Midnight Mary '33

George Devine (1910-66)
Tom Jones '63
Look Back in Anger '58
Time Without Pity '57
Beggar's Opera '54

Loretta Devine (1949-)
Death at a Funeral '10
Beverly Hills Chihuahua '08 (V)
First Sunday '08
Cougar Club '07
Dirty Laundry '07
This Christmas '07
Dreamgirls '06
Crash '05
King's Ransom '05
Woman, Thou Art Loosed '04
I Am Sam '01
Kingdom Come '01
Freedom Song '00
Urban Legends 2: Final Cut '00
What Women Want '00
The Breaks '99
Introducing Dorothy Dandridge '99
Down in the Delta '98
Love Kills '98
Urban Legend '98
Don King: Only in America '97
Lover Girl '97
Hoodlum '96
The Preacher's Wife '96
Rebound: The Legend of Earl "The Goat" Manigault '96
Waiting to Exhale '95
Caged Fear '92
Stanley and Iris '90

Sean Devine (1970-)
The Rendering '02
Dead Silent '99
Perpetrators of the Crime '98

Danny DeVito (1944-)
Solitary Man '10
Nobel Son '08
The Good Night '07
Just Add Water '07
Reno 911! Miami '07
Deck the Halls '06
Even Money '06
Marilyn Hotchkiss' Ballroom Dancing & Charm School '06
The Oh in Ohio '06
Relative Strangers '06
10 Items or Less '06
Be Cool '05
Anything Else '03
Big Fish '03
Austin Powers In Goldmember '02
Death to Smoochy '02
Heist '01
What's the Worst That Could Happen? '01
The Big Kahuna '00
Drowning Mona '00
Screwed '00
Man on the Moon '99
The Virgin Suicides '99
Living Out Loud '98
Hercules '97 (V)
John Grisham's The Rainmaker '97
L.A. Confidential '97
Mars Attacks! '96
Matilda '96
Space Jam '96 (V)
Get Shorty '95
Junior '94
Renaissance Man '94
Jack the Bear '93
Look Who's Talking Now '93 (V)
Batman Returns '92
Hoffa '92
Other People's Money '91
The War of the Roses '89
Twins '88
Throw Momma from the Train '87
Tin Men '87
Head Office '86
Ruthless People '86
Wise Guys '86
Amazing Stories '85
The Jewel of the Nile '85
Johnny Dangerously '84
Ratings Game '84
Romancing the Stone '84
Terms of Endearment '83
Going Ape! '81
Goin' South '78
The Van '77
The Money '75
One Flew Over the Cuckoo's Nest '75
Hurry Up or I'll Be Thirty '73

Matthew Devitt
Waking Ned Devine '98
Funnyman '94

Alan Devlin
Bloom '03
The Playboys '92
The Lonely Passion of Judith Hearne '87
Danny Boy '82

Dean Devlin (1962-)
Moon 44 '90
Real Genius '85

Don Devlin (1930-2000)
Operation Dames '59
Blood of Dracula '57

J.G. Devlin (1909-91)
The Miracle '91
The Raggedy Rawney '90

Gordon Devol (1946-)
Killings at Outpost Zeta '80
Harold and Maude '71

Laura Devon (1940-)
Red Line 7000 '65
Goodbye Charlie '64

Richard Devon (1931-)
Magnum Force '73
The Battle of Blood Island '60
Machine Gun Kelly '58
Blood of Dracula '57
Teenage Doll '57
The Undead '57
The Prodigal '55

Felicity Devonshire
Lisztomania '75
Whose Child Am I? '75

Emmanuelle Devos (1964-)
Coco Before Chanel '09
A Christmas Tale '08
One Day You'll Understand '08
The Beat My Heart Skipped '05
La Moustache '05
Kings and Queen '04
Read My Lips '01
Dad On the Run '00
Esther Kahn '00
My Sex Life... Or How I Got into an Argument '96

Jon (John) DeVries (1947-)
Sarah, Plain and Tall: Skylark '93
Grand Isle '92
Sarah, Plain and Tall '91
Rachel River '87
Truth or Die '86
Act of Passion: The Lost Honor of Kathryn Beck '83
Lianna '83
The 4th Man '79

Elaine Devry (1935-)
The Cheyenne Social Club '70
A Guide for the Married Man '67
Diary of a Madman '63

Eddie Dew (1909-72)
Pagan Island '60
Raiders of Sunset Pass '43
Six Gun Gospel '43
The Fighting 69th '40

Patrick Dewaere (1947-82)
Heat of Desire '84
Beau Pere '81
Hotel America '81
Get Out Your Handkerchiefs '78
Hothead '78
The Best Way '76
Catherine & Co. '76
The French Detective '75
Going Places '74

Jenna Dewan (1980-)
American Virgin '09
Love Lies Bleeding '07
Step Up '06
Take the Lead '06

Colleen Dewhurst (1924-93)
Bed & Breakfast '92
Dying Young '91
Danielle Steel's Kaleidoscope '90
Lantern Hill '90
Termini Station '89
Obsessed '88
Anne of Avonlea '87
Between Two Women '86
The Boy Who Could Fly '86
Sword of Gideon '86
A.D. '85
Anne of Green Gables '85
The Glitter Dome '84
You Can't Take It with You '84
Dead Zone '83
The Blue and the Gray '82
Final Assignment '80
The Guyana Tragedy: The Story of Jim Jones '80
And Baby Makes Six '79
Ice Castles '79
Mary and Joseph: A Story of Faith '79
Silent Victory: The Kitty O'Neil Story '79
Third Walker '79
When a Stranger Calls '79
Annie Hall '77
McQ '74
The Story of Jacob & Joseph '74
The Cowboys '72
A Fine Madness '66
The Nun's Story '59

William Dewhurst (1888-1937)
Non-Stop New York '37
Sabotage '36

Jacqueline DeWit (1912-98)
The Damned Don't Cry '50
Little Giant '46
Lady on a Train '45

Rosemarie DeWitt
Rachel Getting Married '08
The Great New Wonderful '06
Cinderella Man '05

Billy DeWolfe (1907-74)
Billie '65
Lullaby of Broadway '51
Tea for Two '50
Dear Wife '49
The Perils of Pauline '47
Blue Skies '46

Noureen DeWulf (1984-)
Pulse 2: Afterlife '08
The Comebacks '07
Ocean's Thirteen '07
American Dreamz '06

Anthony Dexter (1913-2001)
Married Too Young '62
Three Blondes in His Life '61
Fire Maidens from Outer Space '56

Brad Dexter (1917-2002)
Secret Ingredient '92
Winter Kills '79
None But the Brave '65
Von Ryan's Express '65
Kings of the Sun '63
The George Raft Story '61
The Magnificent Seven '60
Last Train from Gun Hill '59
Run Silent, Run Deep '58
Between Heaven and Hell '56
The Oklahoman '56
House of Bamboo '55
The Las Vegas Story '52

Susan Dey (1952-)
Disappearance '02
Blue River '95
That's Adequate '90
The Trouble with Dick '88
Echo Park '86
L.A. Law '86
Love Leads the Way '84
Sunset Limousine '83
Looker '81
Comeback Kid '80
Little Women '78
First Love '77

Cliff DeYoung (1945-)
Path to War '02
Deliberate Intent '01
Gale Force '01
The Runaway '00
Get a Clue! '98
George Wallace '97
The Last Don '97
Suicide Kings '97
The Craft '96
The Substitute '96
Andersonville '95
JAG '95
Carnosaur 2 '94
Star Quest '94
Revenge of the Red Baron '93
Stephen King's The Tommyknockers '93
Dr. Giggles '92
Nails '92
Immortal Sins '91
To Die Standing '91
Fourth Story '90
Robert Kennedy and His Times '90
Flashback '89
Forbidden Sun '89
Glory '89
Rude Awakening '89
Bulldance '88
Fear '88
In Dangerous Company '88
Pulse '88
Code Name: Dancer '87
The Survivalist '87
F/X '86
Flight of the Navigator '86
Secret Admirer '85
Protocol '84
Reckless '84
The Hunger '83
Independence Day '83
Awakening of Candra '81
Shock Treatment '81
Blue Collar '78
Centennial '78
King '78
The Lindbergh Kidnapping Case '76
Harry and Tonto '74

Ayesha Dharker (1977-)
Outsourced '06
The Mistress of Spices '05
The Mystic Masseur '01
The Terrorist '98
City of Joy '92

Caroline Dhavernas (1978-)
Breach '07
Mr. Average '06
Niagara Motel '06
These Girls '05
Edge of Madness '02
Out Cold '01

Bernard Dheran (1926-)
Ridicule '96
Bernadette '90

Dalia di Lazzaro (1953-)
Creepers '85
Lady of the Evening '75
Andy Warhol's Frankenstein '74

Melissa Di Marco (1969-)
Hustle '04
No Alibi '00

Andrea Di Stefano (1972-)
Angela '02
Before Night Falls '00
The Phantom of the Opera '98

Sergio Di Zio
Just Buried '07
The Lookout '07

Rick Dial (1955-)
Beyond the Wall of Sleep '06
The General's Daughter '99
The Apostle '97
Sling Blade '96

Chris Diamantopoulos
The Starter Wife '07
Three Days to Vegas '07
Wedding Daze '06

Don Diamond (1921-)
The Old Man and the Sea '58
Borderline '50

Harold Diamond
Picasso Trigger '89
Trained to Kill '88
Hard Ticket to Hawaii '87

Marcia Diamond (1942-)
Love Letters '99
Deranged '74

Neil Diamond (1941-)
Keeping Up with the Steins '06
Saving Silverman '01
The Jazz Singer '80

Reed Edward Diamond (1964-)
Good Night, and Good Luck '05
S.W.A.T. '03
Madison '01
High Noon '00
Homicide: The Movie '00
Secrets '94
Blind Spot '93
O Pioneers! '91
Ironclads '90
Memphis Belle '90

Selma Diamond (1920-85)
All of Me '84
Ratings Game '84
Twilight Zone: The Movie '83
Bang the Drum Slowly '73

Sheryl Lee Diamond
See Sheryl Lee

John DiAquino (1958-)
Pumpkinhead *'88*
Slipping into Darkness *'88*

Maimouna Helene Diarra
Bamako *'06*
Moolaade *'04*

Cameron Diaz (1972-)
Knight and Day *'10*
Shrek Forever After *'10 (V)*
The Box *'09*
My Sister's Keeper *'09*
What Happens in Vegas *'08*
Shrek the Third *'07 (V)*
The Holiday *'06*
In Her Shoes *'05*
Shrek 2 *'04 (V)*
Charlie's Angels: Full Throttle *'03*
Gangs of New York *'02*
Slackers *'02*
The Sweetest Thing *'02*
Shrek *'01 (V)*
Vanilla Sky *'01*
Charlie's Angels *'00*
Invisible Circus *'00*
Things You Can Tell Just by Looking at Her *'00*
Any Given Sunday *'99*
Being John Malkovich *'99*
Fear and Loathing in Las Vegas *'98*
There's Something about Mary *'98*
Very Bad Things *'98*
A Life Less Ordinary *'97*
My Best Friend's Wedding *'97*
Feeling Minnesota *'96*
Head Above Water *'96*
Keys to Tulsa *'96*
The Last Supper *'96*
She's the One *'96*
The Mask *'94*

Chico Diaz (1959-)
Mango Yellow *'02*
The Fable of the Beautiful Pigeon Fancier *'88*

Guillermo Diaz (1975-)
Tony n' Tina's Wedding *'07*
The Terminal *'04*
Undefeated *'03*
Fidel *'02*
West of Here *'02*
Just One Time *'00*
200 Cigarettes *'98*
Half-Baked *'97*
I Think I Do *'97*
I'm Not Rappaport *'96*
Nowhere *'96*
Freeway *'95*
Girls Town *'95*
Stonewall *'95*
Party Girl *'94*

Maria Isabel Diaz
Volver *'06*
Extramarital *'98*
The Heroes of Desert Storm *'91*

Melonie Diaz (1984-)
American Son *'08*
Be Kind Rewind *'08*
Hamlet 2 *'08*
Nothing Like the Holidays *'08*
Feel the Noise *'07*
Itty Bitty Titty Committee *'07*
Remember the Daze *'07*
A Guide to Recognizing Your Saints *'06*
Raising Victor Vargas *'03*

Vic Diaz (1932-)
Caged Heat 2: Stripped of Freedom *'94*
The Children of An Lac *'80*
Project: Kill! *'77*
Too Hot to Handle *'76*
Deathhead Virgin *'74*
The Deadly and the Beautiful *'73*
Savage! *'73*
The Big Bird Cage *'72*
Night of the Cobra Woman *'72*
Beast of the Yellow Night *'70*
Flight to Fury *'66*
Blood Thirst *'65*

Tony DiBenedetto (1944-)
Gloria *'98*
Dangerous Passion *'95*
Family Business *'89*
Someone to Watch Over Me *'87*
The Pope of Greenwich Village *'84*
Exterminator *'80*

Luigi Diberti (1939-)
Saturn in Opposition *'07*
For Roseanna *'96*
The Stendahl Syndrome *'95*
All Screwed Up *'74*

Leonardo DiCaprio (1974-)
Inception *'10*
Shutter Island *'09*
Body of Lies *'08*
Revolutionary Road *'08*
The 11th Hour *'07 (N)*
Blood Diamond *'06*
The Departed *'06*
The Aviator *'04*
Catch Me If You Can *'02*
Gangs of New York *'02*
The Beach *'00*
Celebrity *'98*
The Man in the Iron Mask *'98*
Titanic *'97*
Marvin's Room *'96*
William Shakespeare's Romeo and Juliet *'96*
The Basketball Diaries *'95*
The Quick and the Dead *'95*
Total Eclipse *'95*
This Boy's Life *'93*
What's Eating Gilbert Grape *'93*
Critters 3 *'91*

George DiCenzo (1940-)
Hustle *'04*
Tempted *'01*
Down, Out and Dangerous *'95*
Exorcist 3: Legion *'90*
Sing *'89*
18 Again! *'88*
The New Adventures of Pippi Longstocking *'88*
Omega Syndrome *'87*
Walk Like a Man *'87*
About Last Night... *'86*
Back to the Future *'85*
The Night the City Screamed *'80*
The Frisco Kid *'79*
The Ninth Configuration *'79*
Helter Skelter *'76*
Las Vegas Lady *'76*

Bobby DiCicco (1955-)
All Dogs Go to Heaven 2 *'95 (V)*
Killing Obsession *'94*
Ghoulies 4 *'93*
Maniac Cop 3: Badge of Silence *'93*
The Baby Doll Murders *'92*
Frame Up *'91*
The Last Hour *'91*
A Man Called Sarge *'90*
Double Revenge *'89*
She's Back *'88*
Number One with a Bullet *'87*
Tiger Warsaw *'87*
The Supernaturals *'86*
The Philadelphia Experiment *'84*
Splash *'84*
Wavelength *'83*
Night Shift *'82*
National Lampoon Goes to the Movies *'81*
The Big Red One *'80*
1941 *'79*
I Wanna Hold Your Hand *'78*

Andy Dick (1965-)
Hoodwinked Too! Hood vs. Evil *'10 (V)*
Blonde Ambition *'07*
The Comebacks *'07*
Happily N'Ever After *'07 (V)*
Danny Roane: First Time Director *'06*
Employee of the Month *'06*
Hoodwinked *'05 (V)*
Old School *'03*
Scotland, PA *'02*
Dr. Dolittle 2 *'01 (V)*
The Independent *'00*
Loser *'00*
Road Trip *'00*
Inspector Gadget *'99*
Picking Up the Pieces *'99*
Best Men *'98*
Bongwater *'98*
The Lion King: Simba's Pride *'98 (V)*
The Cable Guy *'96*
...And God Spoke *'94*
In the Army Now *'94*

Bryan Dick (1978-)
Blood & Chocolate *'07*
The Old Curiosity Shop *'07*
Brothers of the Head *'06*

Douglas Dick (1920-)
Flaming Star *'60*
The Oklahoman *'56*
The Iron Mistress *'52*
The Red Badge of Courage *'51*
Home of the Brave *'49*
The Accused *'48*
Casbah *'48*
Saigon *'47*

William Dick
The Merry Gentleman *'08*
The Company *'03*

Kim Dickens (1965-)
Red *'08*
Thank You for Smoking *'06*
Wild Tigers I Have Known *'06*
House of Sand and Fog *'03*
Out of Order *'03*
Things Behind the Sun *'01*
The Gift *'00*
Hollow Man *'00*
Committed *'99*
White River *'99*
Mercury Rising *'98*
Great Expectations *'97*
Truth or Consequences, N.M. *'97*
Zero Effect *'97*
Palookaville *'95*

Bonnie Dickenson
Bellyfruit *'99*
Little Shots of Happiness *'97*

Beach Dickerson (1924-2005)
The Dunwich Horror *'70*
The Trip *'67*
Creature from the Haunted Sea *'60*
T-Bird Gang *'59*
Teenage Caveman *'58*
Rock All Night *'57*

George Dickerson (1933-)
After Dark, My Sweet *'90*
Death Warrant *'90*
Blue Velvet *'86*
Cutter's Way *'81*

Dale Dickey
Winter's Bone *'10*
The Pledge *'00*

Lucinda Dickey
Cheerleader Camp *'88*
Breakin' *'84*
Breakin' 2: Electric Boogaloo *'84*
Ninja 3: The Domination *'84*

Angie Dickinson (1931-)
Elvis Has Left the Building *'04*
Big Bad Love *'02*
Ocean's Eleven *'01*
Duets *'00*
Pay It Forward *'00*
National Lampoon's The Don's Analyst *'97*
The Maddening *'95*
Sabrina *'95*
Even Cowgirls Get the Blues *'94*
Wild Palms *'93*
Treacherous Crossing *'92*
Texas Guns *'90*
Fire and Rain *'89*
Big Bad Mama 2 *'87*
Jealousy *'84*
One Shoe Makes It Murder *'82*
Charlie Chan and the Curse of the Dragon Queen *'81*
Death Hunt *'81*
Dressed to Kill *'80*
Klondike Fever *'79*
Pearl *'78*
Big Bad Mama *'74*
Pray for the Wildcats *'74*
The Norliss Tapes *'73*
The Outside Man *'73*
Resurrection of Zachary Wheeler *'71*
Thief *'71*
Sam Whiskey *'69*
Point Blank *'67*
Cast a Giant Shadow *'66*
The Chase *'66*
The Poppy Is Also a Flower *'66*
The Killers *'64*
Captain Newman, M.D. *'63*
Rome Adventure *'62*
The Sins of Rachel Cade *'61*
The Bramble Bush *'60*
Ocean's 11 *'60*
Rio Bravo *'59*
China Gate *'57*
Hidden Guns *'56*
I Married a Woman *'56*
Run of the Arrow *'56 (V)*
Lucky Me *'54*

Gloria Dickson (1917-45)
Power of the Press *'43*
Waterfront *'39*
Gold Diggers in Paris *'38*

Neil Dickson
It Couldn't Happen Here *'88*
The Murders in the Rue Morgue *'86*
Biggles *'85*

Bo Diddley (1928-2008)
Rockula *'90*
Eddie and the Cruisers 2: Eddie Lives! *'89*
Chuck Berry: Hail! Hail! Rock 'n' Roll *'87*
Hell's Angels Forever *'83*

Evelyne Didi
Celestial Clockwork *'94*
La Vie de Boheme *'93*

Gabino Diego (1966-)
Love Can Seriously Damage Your Health *'96*
Belle Epoque *'92*
Ay, Carmela! *'90*

Juan Diego (1942-)
Torremolinos 73 *'03*
Between Your Legs *'99*
Yerma *'99*
Jamon, Jamon *'93*
Cabeza de Vaca *'90*

August Diehl (1976-)
Inglourious Basterds *'09*
A Woman in Berlin *'08*
The Counterfeiters *'07*
The Ninth Day *'04*
Love the Hard Way *'01*

Hans Diehl
Ancient Relic *'02*
The Boat Is Full *'81*

John Diehl (1958-)
The Lucky Ones *'08*
The Far Side of Jericho *'06*
Hidden Places *'06*
Jesse Stone: Death in Paradise *'06*
Down in the Valley *'05*
Land of Plenty *'04*
Bookies *'03*
Jurassic Park 3 *'01*
Pearl Harbor *'01*
Fail Safe *'00*
Lost Souls *'00*
Tully *'00*
Anywhere But Here *'99*
The Hi-Lo Country *'98*
Monument Ave. *'98*
Casualties *'97*
The End of Violence *'97*
Managua *'97*
The Destiny of Marty Fine *'96*
Foxfire *'96*
The Lazarus Man *'96*
A Time to Kill *'96*
Buffalo Girls *'95*
Color of a Brisk and Leaping Day *'95*
The Grave *'95*
Three Wishes *'95*
Wes Craven Presents Mind Ripper *'95*
Almost Dead *'94*
Stargate *'94*
Falling Down *'93*
Gettysburg *'93*
Remote *'93*
Mikey *'92*
Mo' Money *'92*
A Climate for Killing *'91*
Motorama *'91*
Dark Side of the Moon *'90*
Kickboxer 2: The Road Back *'90*
Madhouse *'90*
Cool Blue *'88*
Glitz *'88*
Angel *'84*
Miami Vice *'84*
National Lampoon's Vacation *'83*

John Dierkes (1905-75)
Omega Man *'71*
The Haunted Palace *'63*
Premature Burial *'62*
The Alamo *'60*
The Daughter of Dr. Jekyll *'57*
The Moonlighter *'53*
Abbott and Costello Meet Dr. Jekyll and Mr. Hyde *'52*
The Red Badge of Courage *'51*
The Thing *'51*

Charles Dierkop (1936-)
SuperGuy: Behind the Cape *'02*
Invisible Dad *'97*
Roots of Evil *'91*
Banzai Runner *'86*
The Fix *'84*
Angels Hard As They Come *'71*

Vin Diesel (1967-)
Fast & Furious *'09*
Babylon A.D. *'08*
The Fast and the Furious: Tokyo Drift *'06*
Find Me Guilty *'06*
The Pacifier *'05*
The Chronicles of Riddick *'04*
A Man Apart *'03*
XXX *'02*
The Fast and the Furious *'01*
Knockaround Guys *'01*
Boiler Room *'00*
Pitch Black *'00*
The Iron Giant *'99 (V)*
Saving Private Ryan *'98*
Awakenings *'90*

Gustav Diesl (1899-1948)
Crimes of Dr. Mabuse *'32*
Westfront 1918 *'30*
Pandora's Box *'28*

William Dieterle (1893-1972)
Waxworks *'24*
Backstairs *'21*

Daniel Dietrich
Crossfire *'89*
Dawn of the Dead *'78*

Marlene Dietrich (1901-92)
Just a Gigolo *'79*
The Love Goddesses *'65*
Paris When It Sizzles *'64*
Judgment at Nuremberg *'61*
Touch of Evil *'58*
Witness for the Prosecution *'57*
Around the World in 80 Days *'56*
Rancho Notorious *'52*
No Highway in the Sky *'51*
Stage Fright *'50*
Jigsaw *'49*
A Foreign Affair *'48*
Golden Earrings *'47*
The Lady Is Willing *'42*
Pittsburgh *'42*
The Spoilers *'42*
The Flame of New Orleans *'41*
Manpower *'41*
Seven Sinners *'40*
Destry Rides Again *'39*
Angel *'37*
Knight Without Armour *'37*
Desire *'36*
The Garden of Allah *'36*
The Devil Is a Woman *'35*
Scarlet Empress *'34*
The Song of Songs *'33*
Blonde Venus *'32*
Shanghai Express *'32*
Dishonored *'31*
The Blue Angel *'30*
Morocco *'30*

Frank Dietz
The Jitters *'88*
Zombie Nightmare *'86*
Rock 'n' Roll Nightmare *'85*

Nade Dieu
Our Music *'04*
The Butterfly *'02*

Anton Diffring (1918-89)
Faceless *'88*
S.A.S. San Salvador *'84*
The Winds of War *'83*
Valentino *'77*
The Beast Must Die *'75*
Call Him Mr. Shatter *'74*
Dead Pigeon on Beethoven Street *'72*
Mark of the Devil 2 *'72*
Seven Deaths in the Cat's Eye *'72*
Little Mother *'71*
Zeppelin *'71*
Where Eagles Dare *'68*
The Blue Max *'66*
Fahrenheit 451 *'66*
The Heroes of Telemark *'65*
Circus of Horrors *'60*
The Colditz Story *'55*

Uschi Digart (1948-)
Kentucky Fried Movie *'77*
Black Gestapo *'75*
Supervixens *'75*
Ilsa, She-Wolf of the SS *'74*
Superchick *'71*
All the Lovin' Kinfolk *'70*

Dudley Digges (1879-1947)
Son of Fury *'42*
Love Is News *'37*
The General Died at Dawn *'36*
China Seas *'35*
Mutiny on the Bounty *'35*
Massacre *'34*
The World Moves On *'34*
Emperor Jones *'33*
The Invisible Man *'33*
The Mayor of Hell *'33*
Devotion *'31*

The Maltese Falcon *'31*
Condemned *'29*

Robert Diggs
See RZA

Taye Diggs (1972-)
Cake *'05*
Rent *'05*
Slow Burn *'05*
Basic *'03*
Malibu's Most Wanted *'03*
Brown Sugar *'02*
Chicago *'02*
Equilibrium *'02*
Just a Kiss *'02*
New Best Friend *'02*
Way of the Gun *'00*
The Best Man *'99*
Go *'99*
House on Haunted Hill *'99*
The Wood *'99*
How Stella Got Her Groove Back *'98*

Arthur Dignam (1939-)
Gods and Monsters *'98*
The Nostradamus Kid *'92*
The Everlasting Secret Family *'88*
The Right Hand Man *'87*
The Wild Duck *'84*
Grendel, Grendel, Grendel *'82 (V)*
We of the Never Never *'82*
Strange Behavior *'81*
The Chant of Jimmie Blacksmith *'78*
The Devil's Playground *'76*
Between Wars *'74*

Basil Dignam (1905-79)
The Moonstone *'72*
Persuasion *'71*
Naked Evil *'66*

Mark Dignam (1909-89)
Disraeli *'79*
The Charge of the Light Brigade *'68*
Sink the Bismarck *'60*

Bogdan Diklic (1953-)
Grbavica: The Land of My Dreams *'06*
Fuse *'03*
Cabaret Balkan *'98*

Irasema Dilian (1925-96)
Wuthering Heights *'53*
Teresa Venerdi *'41*

Garret Dillahunt
Winter's Bone *'10*
The Last House on the Left *'09*
The Road *'09*
The Assassination of Jesse James by the Coward Robert Ford *'07*
No Country for Old Men *'07*

Richard Dillane (1964-)
De-Lovely *'04*
Solomon *'98*

Stephen (Dillon) Dillane (1956-)
God on Trial *'08*
John Adams *'08*
Goal 2: Living the Dream *'07*
Savage Grace *'07*
Goal! The Dream Begins *'06*
Klimt *'06*
The Greatest Game Ever Played *'05*
Nine Lives *'05*
Haven *'04*
King Arthur *'04*
The Gathering *'02*
The Hours *'02*
The Truth About Charlie *'02*
Spy Game *'01*
Anna Karenina *'00*
Love and Rage *'99*
Ordinary Decent Criminal *'99*
Deja Vu *'98*
Firelight *'97*
Kings in Grass Castles *'97*
Welcome to Sarajevo *'97*
Two If by Sea *'95*
The Widowing of Mrs. Holroyd *'95*
The Rector's Wife *'94*
An Affair in Mind *'89*
Christabel *'89*

Victoria Dillard (1969-)
Ali *'01*
The Best Man *'99*
Out of Sync *'95*
Deep Cover *'92*
Ricochet *'91*

Phyllis Diller (1917-)
Forget About It *'06*
A Bug's Life *'98 (V)*
Happily Ever After *'93 (V)*
Heartstrings *'93*
Silence of the Hams *'93*
The Nutcracker Prince *'91 (V)*
The Bone Yard *'90*
Pink Motel *'82*
A Pleasure Doing Business *'79*
Mad Monster Party *'68 (V)*
Private Navy of Sgt. O'Farrell *'68*
Eight on the Lam *'67*
Boy, Did I Get a Wrong Number! *'66*
The Fat Spy *'66*
Splendor in the Grass *'61*

Bradford Dillman (1930-)
Heroes Stand Alone *'89*
Lords of the Deep *'89*
Man Outside *'88*
The Treasure of the Amazon *'84*
Sudden Impact *'83*
Legend of Walks Far Woman *'82*
Love and Bullets *'79*
Running Scared *'79*
The Amsterdam Kill *'78*
Piranha *'78*
The Swarm *'78*
The Enforcer *'76*
One Away *'76*
The Widow *'76*
Bug *'75*
Force Five *'75*
Death in Deep Water *'74*
Murder or Mercy *'74*
99 & 44/100 Dead *'74*
The Iceman Cometh *'73*
Master Mind *'73*
The Way We Were *'73*
Moon of the Wolf *'72*
Escape from the Planet of the Apes *'71*
The Mephisto Waltz *'71*
Resurrection of Zachary Wheeler *'71*
Brother John *'70*
Suppose They Gave a War and Nobody Came? *'70*
Black Water Gold *'69*
The Bridge at Remagen *'69*
Sergeant Ryker *'68*
Compulsion *'59*

Brendan Dillon, Jr.
Lords of Magick *'88*
Bug *'75*
Premature Burial *'62*

Denny Dillon (1951-)
United 93 *'06*
Roseanne: An Unauthorized Biography *'94*

Hugh Dillon (1963-)
Surveillance *'08*
Assault on Precinct 13 *'05*
Down to the Bone *'04*
Ginger Snaps Back: The Beginning *'04*
Hard Core Logo *'96*

Kevin Dillon (1965-)
Hotel for Dogs *'09*
The Foursome *'06*
Poseidon *'06*
Hidden Agenda *'99*
Misbegotten *'98*
Stag *'97*
Criminal Hearts *'95*
True Crime *'95*
No Escape *'94*
The Pathfinder *'94*
A Midnight Clear *'92*
The Doors *'91*
Immediate Family *'89*
War Party *'89*
When He's Not a Stranger *'89*
The Blob *'88*
Remote Control *'88*
The Rescue *'88*
Platoon *'86*
Heaven Help Us *'85*
No Big Deal *'83*

Matt Dillon (1964-)
Takers *'10*
Armored *'09*
Old Dogs *'09*
Nothing But the Truth *'08*
Factotum *'06*
You, Me and Dupree *'06*
Crash *'05*
Herbie: Fully Loaded *'05*
Loverboy *'05*
City of Ghosts *'03*
Deuces Wild *'02*
One Night at McCool's *'01*
There's Something about Mary *'98*
Wild Things *'98*
In and Out *'97*
Albino Alligator *'96*
Beautiful Girls *'96*
Grace of My Heart *'96*
Frankie Starlight *'95*
To Die For *'95*
Golden Gate *'93*
Mr. Wonderful *'93*
The Saint of Fort Washington *'93*
Singles *'92*
A Kiss Before Dying *'91*
Women & Men: In Love There Are No Rules *'91*
Bloodhounds of Broadway *'89*
Drugstore Cowboy *'89*
Kansas *'88*
Big Town *'87*
Native Son *'86*
Rebel *'85*
Target *'85*
The Flamingo Kid *'84*
The Outsiders *'83*
Rumble Fish *'83*
Liar's Moon *'82*
Tex *'82*
Little Darlings *'80*
My Bodyguard *'80*
Over the Edge *'79*

Melinda Dillon (1939-)
Reign Over Me *'07*
A Painted House *'03*
Cowboy Up *'00*
Magnolia *'99*
Entertaining Angels: The Dorothy Day Story *'96*
How to Make an American Quilt *'95*
To Wong Foo, Thanks for Everything, Julie Newmar *'95*
Sioux City *'94*
The Prince of Tides *'91*
Captain America *'89*
Nightbreaker *'89*
Spontaneous Combustion *'89*
Staying Together *'89*
Harry and the Hendersons *'87*
Shattered Spirits *'86*
Right of Way *'84*
Songwriter *'84*
A Christmas Story *'83*
Absence of Malice *'81*
Fallen Angel *'81*
Marriage Is Alive and Well *'80*
The Shadow Box *'80*
F.I.S.T. *'78*
Close Encounters of the Third Kind *'77*
Slap Shot *'77*
Bound for Glory *'76*
April Fools *'69*

Mia Dillon (1955-)
Gods and Generals *'03*
Our Town *'03*

Paul Dillon
Chicago Cab *'98*
Austin Powers: International Man of Mystery *'97*
Blink *'93*
The Beat *'88*
Kiss Daddy Goodnight *'87*

Tom Dillon (1896-1962)
Night Tide *'63*
Dressed to Kill *'46*

John DiMaggio (1968-)
Extreme Dating *'04*
The Pirates of Silicon Valley *'99*

Victor Dimattia (1979-)
Danielle Steel's Heartbeat *'93*
Dennis the Menace: Dinosaur Hunter *'93*

Alex Dimitriades (1973-)
Ghost Ship *'02*
Subterano *'01*
Head On *'98*

Alan Dinehart (1889-1944)
The Heat's On *'43*
It's a Great Life *'43*
Sweet Rosie O'Grady *'43*
Everything Happens at Night *'39*
Second Fiddle *'39*
Charlie Chan at the Race Track *'36*
In Old Kentucky *'35*
Baby, Take a Bow *'34*
After Midnight *'33*
No Marriage Ties *'33*
A Study in Scarlet *'33*
Supernatural *'33*

Paul Dinello (1962-)
Strangers with Candy *'06*
Plump Fiction *'97*

Yi Ding
Smile *'05*
Pavilion of Women *'01*
The Amazing Panda Adventure *'95*

Charles Dingle (1887-1956)
The Court Martial of Billy Mitchell *'55*
If You Knew Susie *'48*
A Southern Yankee *'48*
The Beast with Five Fingers *'46*
Guest Wife *'45*
Here Come the Co-Eds *'45*
Johnny Eager *'42*
Somewhere I'll Find You *'42*
The Little Foxes *'41*

Ernie Dingo (1956-)
The Echo of Thunder *'98*
Kings in Grass Castles *'97*
Dead Heart *'96*
Clowning Around 2 *'93*
Clowning Around *'92*
Until the End of the World *'91*
Crocodile Dundee 2 *'88*
A Waltz Through the Hills *'88*
The Fringe Dwellers *'86*

Kelly Dingwall
The Custodian *'94*
Around the World in 80 Ways *'86*

Shaun Dingwall (1972-)
On a Clear Day *'05*
Touching Evil *'97*

Joe Dinicol
Diary of the Dead *'07*
Weirdsville *'07*

Peter Dinklage (1969-)
Death at a Funeral *'10*
Saint John of Las Vegas *'09*
The Chronicles of Narnia: Prince Caspian *'08*
Death at a Funeral *'07*
Underdog *'07*
Find Me Guilty *'06*
Little Fugitive *'06*
Penelope *'06*
The Baxter *'05*
Lassie *'05*
Elf *'03*
The Station Agent *'03*
Tiptoes *'03*
Human Nature *'02*
13 Moons *'02*
Living in Oblivion *'94*

Reece Dinsdale (1959-)
Hamlet *'96*
Romance and Rejection *'96*
Young Catherine *'91*
Threads *'85*
Winter Flight *'84*

Bruce Dinsmore
Nightwaves *'03*
Deadline *'00*
Psychopath *'97*
Stranger in the House *'97*

Jake Dinwiddie
Au Pair 3: Adventure in Paradise *'09*
Au Pair 2: The Fairy Tale Continues *'01*
Au Pair *'99*

Madame Rose (Dion) Dione (1875-1936)
Freaks *'32*
The Duchess of Buffalo *'26*
Salome *'22*
Suds *'20*

Stefano Dionisi (1966-)
Ginostra *'02*
Gloomy Sunday *'02*
Sleepless *'01*
Children of the Century *'99*
Kiss of Fire *'98*
The Loss of Sexual Innocence *'98*
The Truce *'96*
Joseph *'95*
Farinelli *'94*
Mille Bolle Blu *'93*

Silvia Dionisio (1951-)
Street War *'76*
The Scalawag Bunch *'75*
Andy Warhol's Dracula *'74*

Dante DiPaolo (1926-)
Blood and Black Lace *'64*
Venus Against the Son of Hercules *'62*

Kim Director (1977-)
Tony n' Tina's Wedding *'07*
Inside Man *'06*
Book of Shadows: Blair Witch 2 *'00*

John DiResta
15 Minutes *'01*
Miss Congeniality *'00*

John Disanti (1938-)
Man of the House *'95*
Eyes of a Stranger *'81*

Catherine Disher
The Good Witch *'08*
Coast to Coast *'04*

Bob (Robert) Dishy (1943-)
The Wackness *'08*
Along Came Polly *'04*
Judy Berlin *'99*
Jungle 2 Jungle *'96*
Don Juan DeMarco *'94*
My Boyfriend's Back *'93*
Used People *'92*
Brighton Beach Memoirs *'86*
The Big Bus *'76*
I Wonder Who's Killing Her Now? *'76*
Lovers and Other Strangers *'70*

Walt Disney (1901-66)
Fun & Fancy Free *'47 (V)*
Fantasia *'40 (V)*
Hollywood Party *'34 (V)*

Harry Ditson
Tragedy of Flight 103: The Inside Story *'91*
The Sender *'82*

Barbara Dittus (1939-2001)
Anton, the Magician *'78*
The Third *'72*

Divine (1945-88)
Divine *'90*
Hairspray *'88*
Out of the Dark *'88*
Trouble in Mind *'86*
I Wanna Be a Beauty Queen *'85*
Lust in the Dust *'85*
Polyester *'81*
Female Trouble *'74*
Pink Flamingos *'72*
Multiple Maniacs *'70*
Mondo Trasho *'69*

Andrew Divoff (1955-)
The Boston Strangler: The Untold Story *'08*
Indiana Jones and the Kingdom of the Crystal Skull *'08*
The Rage *'07*
Blue Hill Avenue *'01*
Faust: Love of the Damned *'00*
Captured *'99*
Stealth Fighter *'99*
Crossfire *'98*
Wishmaster 2: Evil Never Dies *'98*
Nemesis 4: Cry of Angels *'97*
Wishmaster *'97*
Blast *'96*
Deadly Voyage *'96*
Backlash: Oblivion 2 *'95*
Magic Island *'95*
The Stranger *'95*
Xtro 3: Watch the Skies *'95*
A Low Down Dirty Shame *'94*
Oblivion *'94*
Running Cool *'93*
Back in the USSR *'92*
Interceptor *'92*
Toy Soldiers *'91*
Graveyard Shift *'90*

Billy Dix
She Demons *'58*
Red Rock Outlaw *'47*

Dorothy Dix
Drum Taps *'33*
The Nevada Buckaroo *'31*

Richard Dix (1894-1949)
Buckskin Frontier *'43*
The Ghost Ship *'43*
The Kansan *'43*
American Empire *'42*
The Roundup *'41*
It Happened in Hollywood *'37*
Special Investigator *'36*
Yellow Dust *'36*
Transatlantic Tunnel *'35*
His Greatest Gamble *'34*
Stingaree *'34*
Ace of Aces *'33*
No Marriage Ties *'33*
Lost Squadron *'32*
Cimarron *'31*
Seven Keys to Baldpate *'29*
Lucky Devil *'25*
The Vanishing American *'25*
Souls for Sale *'23*
The Ten Commandments *'23*

Robert Dix (1934-)
Killers *'88*
Cain's Cutthroats *'71*
Hell's Bloody Devils *'70*
Horror of the Blood Monsters *'70*
Blood of Dracula's Castle *'69*
Satan's Sadists *'69*
Wild Wheels *'69*

Deadwood '65
Forty Guns '57
Forbidden Planet '56

Donna Dixon (1957-)
Wayne's World '92
Lucky Stiff '88
Speed Zone '88
The Couch Trip '87
Beverly Hills Madam '86
Spies Like Us '85
Doctor Detroit '83
Margin for Murder '81

Ivan Dixon (1931-2008)
Car Wash '76
Fer-De-Lance '74
Suppose They Gave a War and Nobody Came? '70
A Patch of Blue '65
Nothing but a Man '64
A Raisin in the Sun '61

James Dixon
The Ambulance '90
Maniac Cop 2 '90
Wicked Stepmother '89
It's Alive 3: Island of the Alive '87
Return to Salem's Lot '87
The Stuff '85
Q (The Winged Serpent) '82
It's Alive 2: It Lives Again '78
It's Alive '74
Black Caesar '73
Hell Up in Harlem '73

Jean Dixon (1896-1981)
Joy of Living '38
You Only Live Once '37

Joan Dixon (1930-92)
Gunplay '51
Hot Lead '51

Lee Dixon
Hollywood Hotel '37
Varsity Show '37
Gold Diggers of 1937 '36

MacIntyre Dixon (1931-)
Gettysburg '93
Funny Farm '88
Ghostwriter '84

Michael Dixon
The Deaths of Ian Stone '07
Cashback '06
Chains '89

Pamela Dixon
C.I.A. 2: Target Alexa '94
C.I.A.: Code Name Alexa '92
Magic Kid '92
Chance '89
L.A. Crackdown 2 '88
Hollywood in Trouble '87
L.A. Crackdown '87
Mayhem '87

Reg Dixon
No Smoking '55
Love in Pawn '53

Steve Dixon
Mosquito '95
The Carrier '87

Omid Djalili (1965-)
The Love Guru '08
Over the Hedge '06 (V)
Casanova '05
Modigliani '04
Sky Captain and the World of Tomorrow '04
The Mummy '99

Badja (Medu) Djola (1948-2005)
Deterrence '00
Gunshy '98
Rosewood '96
Heaven's Prisoners '95
Who's the Man? '93
A Rage in Harlem '91
An Innocent Man '89
Mississippi Burning '88
The Serpent and the Rainbow '87
Penitentiary '79

Shae D'Lyn (1963-)
Vegas Vacation '96
Secrets '94

DMX (1970-)
Last Hour '08
Lords of the Street '08
Father of Lies '07
Never Die Alone '04
Cradle 2 the Grave '03
Exit Wounds '01
Romeo Must Die '00
Belly '98

Peter J. D'Noto (1947-)
Chain Reaction '96
Killing Floor '85
Monsters Crash the Pajama Party '65

Mauricio Do Valle (1928-94)
Amazon Jail '85
Antonio Das Mortes '68
Black God, White Devil '64

Valeria (Valerie Dobson) D'Obici (1952-)
The Best Man '97
Escape from the Bronx '85
Passion of Love '82

Alan Dobie (1932-)
White Mischief '88
War and Peace '73
The Chairman '69
The Charge of the Light Brigade '68

Lawrence (Larry) Dobkin (1919-2002)
Hotwire '80
Patton '70
Geronimo '62
Portland Expose '57
Above and Beyond '53
Loan Shark '52
Twelve o'Clock High '49

Nina Dobrev
Chloe '09
The American Mall '08
Never Cry Werewolf '08
Hearts of War '07

Gosia Dobrowolska (1958-)
Lust and Revenge '95
The Custodian '94
Careful '92
A Woman's Tale '92
Around the World in 80 Ways '86
Silver City '84

Karel Dobry (1969-)
The Ninth Day '04
The Girl of Your Dreams '99

James Dobson (1920-87)
Impulse '74
Flying Leathernecks '51

Kevin Dobson (1943-)
Mom, Can I Keep Her? '98
Dirty Work '92
Code of Honor '84
All Night Long '81
Margin for Murder '81
Hardhat & Legs '80
Orphan Train '79
Midway '76

Peter Dobson (1964-)
Protecting the King '07
A Stranger's Heart '07
Lady Jayne Killer '03
Players '03
Double Down '01
Drowning Mona '00
Wicked Ways '99
Nowhere Land '98
Quiet Days in Hollywood '97
The Big Squeeze '96
Dead Cold '96
The Frighteners '96
Riot in the Streets '96
Norma Jean and Marilyn '95
Forrest Gump '94

Where the Day Takes You '92
The Marrying Man '91
Sing '89
Plain Clothes '88

Tamara Dobson (1947-2006)
The Amazons '84
Chained Heat '83
Norman, Is That You? '76
Cleopatra Jones & the Casino of Gold '75
Cleopatra Jones '73

Vernon Dobtcheff (1934-)
Priceless '06
Empire of the Wolves '05
The Body '01
Deja Vu '98
Hilary and Jackie '98
M. Butterfly '93
Pascali's Island '88
Nijinsky '80
The Messiah '75
The Savage '75
Murder on the Orient Express '74
Darling Lili '70
The Assassination Bureau '69

Michelle Dockery
The Courageous Heart of Irena Sendler '09
Return to Cranford '09
Hogfather '06

Gina Doctor
Shopgirl '05
Dead Pet '01

Claire Dodd (1908-64)
The Black Cat '41
If I Had My Way '40
Charlie Chan in Honolulu '38
The Singing Kid '36
Massacre '34
Ex-Lady '33

Jimmie Dodd (1910-64)
Too Late for Tears '49
Riders of the Rio Grande '43
Shadows on the Sage '42
Snuffy Smith, Yard Bird '42
Law and Order '40

K.K. Dodds
Soldier '98
A Life Less Ordinary '97

Megan Dodds (1971-)
The Contract '07
Purpose '02
Sword of Honour '01
Bait '00
Urbania '00
Ever After: A Cinderella Story '98
The Rat Pack '98

Anna Dodge (1867-1945)
Until They Get Me '18
Hoodoo Ann '16

Jack Dodson (1931-94)
A Climate for Killing '91
Return to Mayberry '85
The Getaway '72

John Doe (1954-)
Torque '04
MTV's Wuthering Heights '03
Players '03
The Good Girl '02
Gypsy 83 '01
Drowning on Dry Land '00
Brokedown Palace '99
Forces of Nature '99
Knocking on Death's Door '99
The Rage: Carrie 2 '99
Sugar Town '99
Wildflowers '99
Highway Hitcher '98
Black Circle Boys '97
Boogie Nights '97
Scorpion Spring '96

Touch '96
Georgia '95
Shake, Rattle & Rock! '94
Wyatt Earp '94
Liquid Dreams '92
Pure Country '92
Roadside Prophets '92
A Matter of Degrees '90
Great Balls of Fire '89
Slamdance '87

Christian Doermer
Oh! What a Lovely War '69
Teenage Wolfpack '57

Darrick Doerner
Riding Giants '04
In God's Hands '98

Tatiana Dogileva (1957-)
East-West '99
A Forgotten Tune for the Flute '88

Matt Doherty (1977-)
D3: The Mighty Ducks '96
So I Married an Axe Murderer '93
The Mighty Ducks '92

Shannen Doherty (1971-)
Kiss Me Deadly '08
The Lost Treasure of the Grand Canyon '08
Christmas Caper '07
Category 7 : The End of the World '05
The Rendering '02
Jay and Silent Bob Strike Back '01
The Ticket '97
Nowhere '96
Mallrats '95
Almost Dead '94
Blindfold: Acts of Obsession '94
Jailbreakers '94
Freeze Frame '92
Heathers '89
Girls Just Want to Have Fun '85
Night Shift '82

Lexa Doig (1973-)
Ba'al: The Storm God '08
Jason X '01
No Alibi '00

Lou Doillon (1982-)
Bad Company '99
Le Petit Amour '87

Michael Dolan (1965-)
The Hunley '99
The Turning '92
Biloxi Blues '88
Hamburger Hill '87
Light of Day '87

Thomas Dolby (1958-)
Rockula '90
Howard the Duck '86

Guy Doleman (1924-96)
Billion Dollar Brain '67
Funeral in Berlin '66
The Ipcress File '65
Thunderball '65

Ami Dolenz (1969-)
Virtual Seduction '96
Life 101 '95
Mortal Danger '94
Pumpkinhead 2: Blood Wings '94
Rescue Me '93
Ticks '93
Witchboard 2: The Devil's Doorway '93
Children of the Night '92
Miracle Beach '92
Stepmonster '92
Faith '90
She's Out of Control '89
Can't Buy Me Love '87
The Children of Times Square '86

Mickey Dolenz (1945-)
Invisible Mom 2 '99
The Love Bug '97
Invisible Mom '96
The Brady Bunch Movie '95
Night of the Strangler '73
Head '68

Damon D'Oliveira
My Teacher Ate My Homework '98
Back in Action '94

Dora Doll (1922-)
Black and White in Color '76
Boomerang '76
The Young Lions '58

Patrick Dollaghan
The Bad Pack '98
Circle of Fear '89
Kill Slade '89
Murphy's Fault '88

Jason Dolley (1991-)
Minutemen '08
Saving Shiloh '06

John Doman (1945-)
Blue Valentine '10
All Good Things '09
Gracie '07
Fatwa '06
Rock the Paint '05
Sniper 3 '04
City by the Sea '02
Killing Emmett Young '02
The Opponent '01

Larry Domasin (1955-)
Island of the Blue Dolphins '64
Fun in Acapulco '63

Arielle Dombasle (1955-)
Gradiva '06
Vatel '00
Time Regained '99
L'Ennui '98
Three Lives and Only One Death '96
Little Indian, Big City '95
Raging Angels '95
Celestial Clockwork '94
Twisted Obsession '90
Around the World in 80 Days '89
The Boss' Wife '86
Trade Secrets '86
Pauline at the Beach '83
Le Beau Mariage '82
Perceval '78

Faith Domergue (1925-99)
Blood Legacy '73
The House of Seven Corpses '73
The Sibling '72
Voyage to the Prehistoric Planet '65
The Atomic Man '56
Cult of the Cobra '55
It Came from Beneath the Sea '55
This Island Earth '55
Duel at Silver Creek '52
Where Danger Lives '50

Dagmara Dominczyk (1976-)
Prisoner '07
Trust the Man '06
Kinsey '04
The Count of Monte Cristo '02
Wes Craven Presents: They '02
Rock Star '01

Placido Domingo
Beverly Hills Chihuahua '08 (V)
Otello '86

Adriana Dominguez (1976-)
The Cry: La Llorona '07
The Bridge of San Luis Rey '05

Ibiza Dream '02

Wade Dominguez (1966-98)
Shadow of Doubt '98
The Taxman '98
City of Industry '96

Arturo Dominici (1918-92)
The Trojan Horse '62
Black Sunday '60
Hercules '58

Fats Domino (1928-)
The Girl Can't Help It '56
Rock, Rock, Rock '56

Solveig Dommartin (1961-2007)
Faraway, So Close! '93
Until the End of the World '91
No Fear, No Die '90
Wings of Desire '88

Angelica Domrose (1941-)
The Mistake '91
The Scorpion Woman '89
Girls Riot '88
The Legend of Paul and Paula '73
Under the Pear Tree '73

Linda Dona
Delta Heat '92
Final Embrace '92
Futurekick '91

Ron Donachie
The Flying Scotsman '06
Extremely Dangerous '99

Maurizio Donadoni
The Wedding Director '06
My Mother's Smile '02

Elinor Donahue (1937-)
The Princess Diaries 2: Royal Engagement '04
The Invaders '95
Freddy's Dead: The Final Nightmare '91
Pretty Woman '90
High School USA '84
Going Berserk '83
Girls' Town '59
Love Is Better Than Ever '52
My Blue Heaven '50
Three Daring Daughters '48

Heather Donahue (1974-)
The Morgue '07
Manticore '05
Boys and Girls '00
The Blair Witch Project '99

Troy Donahue (1936-2001)
Showdown '93
A Woman Obsessed '93
Deadly Diamonds '91
The Pamela Principle '91
Sounds of Silence '91
Cry-Baby '90
Nudity Required '90
Omega Cop '90
Shock 'Em Dead '90
Assault of the Party Nerds '89
The Chilling '89
Deadly Spygames '89
Dr. Alien '88
Hawkeye '88
Sexpot '88
Terminal Force '88
Cyclone '87
Deadly Prey '87
Hollywood Cop '87
Grandview U.S.A. '84
Tin Man '83
The Godfather 1902-1959: The Complete Epic '81
The Legend of Frank Woods '77
Cockfighter '74
The Godfather, Part 2 '74
Seizure '74
South Seas Massacre '74

Love Thrill Murders ’71
Those Fantastic Flying Fools ’67
My Blood Runs Cold ’65
A Distant Trumpet ’64
Palm Springs Weekend ’63
Rome Adventure ’62
Parrish ’61
Susan Slade ’61
The Crowded Sky ’60
Imitation of Life ’59
Monster on the Campus ’59
A Summer Place ’59
Tarnished Angels ’57

James Donald (1917-93)

The Big Sleep ’78
Cast a Giant Shadow ’66
King Rat ’65
The Great Escape ’63
Victoria Regina ’61
Third Man on the Mountain ’59
The Vikings ’58
The Bridge on the River Kwai ’57
Lust for Life ’56
Beau Brummel ’54
The Pickwick Papers ’54
The Gay Lady ’49
Immortal Battalion ’44
In Which We Serve ’43

Arthur Donaldson (1869-1955)

The Broadway Drifter ’27
America ’24

Lesleh Donaldson (1964-)

Funeral Home ’82
Happy Birthday to Me ’81

Norma Donaldson (1928-94)

Poetic Justice ’93
The Five Heartbeats ’91
Staying Alive ’83
9 to 5 ’80

Peter Donaldson

Invasion! ’99
Escape Clause ’96
Long Day’s Journey Into Night ’96
The Sweet Hereafter ’96

Ted Donaldson (1933-)

The Green Promise ’49
Rusty’s Birthday ’49
The Red Stallion ’47
Son of Rusty ’47
The Adventures of Rusty ’45
A Tree Grows in Brooklyn ’45
Mr. Winkle Goes to War ’44

Peter Donat (1928-)

The Deep End ’01
The Game ’97
Red Corner ’97
The Babe ’92
School Ties ’92
The War of the Roses ’89
Tucker: The Man and His Dream ’88
Honeymoon ’87
The Bay Boy ’85
Massive Retaliation ’85
Ladies and Gentlemen, the Fabulous Stains ’82
Mazes and Monsters ’82
The China Syndrome ’79
Different Story ’78
F.I.S.T. ’78
Mirrors ’78
Return Engagement ’78
The Godfather, Part 2 ’74
Missiles of October ’74

Richard Donat

Shattered City: The Halifax Explosion ’03
My American Cousin ’85

Robert Donat (1905-58)

The Inn of the Sixth Happiness ’58
The Winslow Boy ’48
Captain Boycott ’47
The Adventures of Tartu ’43
Goodbye, Mr. Chips ’39
The Citadel ’38
Knight Without Armour ’37
The Ghost Goes West ’36
The 39 Steps ’35
The Count of Monte Cristo ’34
If I Were Rich ’33
The Private Life of Henry VIII ’33

Ludwig Donath (1900-67)

Sins of Jezebel ’54
The Great Caruso ’51
The Lovable Cheat ’49
The Killer That Stalked New York ’47
The Jolson Story ’46
The Secret Code ’42

Marc Donato (1989-)

The Blue Butterfly ’04
Dangerous Child ’01
Locked in Silence ’99
Pom Poko ’94 (V)

Len Doncheff

Nuremberg ’00
Moving Target ’96
One Night Stand ’78

Manuel Donde

Swamp of the Lost Monster ’65
Savage Wilderness ’55

Chad E. Donella (1978-)

Hate Crime ’05
Shattered Glass ’03
SuperFire ’02
Final Destination ’00
Disturbing Behavior ’98

Yolande Donlan (1920-)

The Adventurers ’70
Expresso Bongo ’59
Tarzan and the Lost Safari ’57
Tarzan’s Hidden Jungle ’55
Mister Drake’s Duck ’50
The Devil Bat ’41

Brian Donlevy (1899-1972)

Arizona Bushwackers ’67
Five Golden Dragons ’67
Hostile Guns ’67
Pit Stop ’67
The Fat Spy ’66
Gamera, the Invincible ’66
How to Stuff a Wild Bikini ’65
The Errand Boy ’61
Cowboy ’58
Quatermass 2 ’57
The Quatermass Experiment ’56
Big Combo ’55
Ride the Man Down ’53
Hoodlum Empire ’52
Slaughter Trail ’51
Impact ’49
Command Decision ’48
A Southern Yankee ’48
Killer McCoy ’47
Kiss of Death ’47
Song of Scheherazade ’47
Canyon Passage ’46
Two Years before the Mast ’46
The Virginian ’46
Miracle of Morgan’s Creek ’44
A Gentleman After Dark ’42
The Glass Key ’42
The Great Man’s Lady ’42
Hangmen Also Die ’42
Wake Island ’42
Billy the Kid ’41
Birth of the Blues ’41
Brigham Young: Frontiersman ’40
The Great McGinty ’40
Allegheny Uprising ’39
Beau Geste ’39
Destry Rides Again ’39
Jesse James ’39
Union Pacific ’39
In Old Chicago ’37
Strike Me Pink ’36
Barbary Coast ’35

Steve Donmyer

Terminal Exposure ’89
Glitch! ’88

Barnard Pierre Donnadieu (1949-)

Paris 36 ’08
Druids ’01
Beatrice ’88
The Vanishing ’88
The Return of Martin Guerre ’83

Connor Donne

In Enemy Hands ’04

Jeff Donnell (1921-88)

Gidget Goes to Rome ’63
My Man Godfrey ’57
The Blue Gardenia ’53
Because You’re Mine ’52
Three Guys Named Mike ’51
The Fuller Brush Girl ’50
In a Lonely Place ’50
Redwood Forest Trail ’50
Walk Softly, Stranger ’50
Outcasts of the Trail ’49
The Boogie Man Will Get You ’42

Donal Donnelly (1931-)

Love and Rage ’99
This Is My Father ’99
Mesmer ’94
Squanto: A Warrior’s Tale ’94
The Godfather, Part 3 ’90
The Dead ’87
Waterloo ’71
The Knack ’65

Ruth Donnelly (1896-1982)

A Lawless Street ’55
I’d Climb the Highest Mountain ’51
Where the Sidewalk Ends ’50
My Little Chickadee ’40
The Affairs of Annabel ’38
Holiday ’38
A Slight Case of Murder ’38
Cain and Mabel ’36
Mr. Deeds Goes to Town ’36
Alibi Ike ’35
Hands Across the Table ’35
Red Salute ’35
Happiness Ahead ’34
Wonder Bar ’34
Bureau of Missing Persons ’33
Female ’33
Footlight Parade ’33
Ladies They Talk About ’33
Blessed Event ’32

Tim Donnelly (1944-)

The Clonus Horror ’79
The Toolbox Murders ’78

Robert Donner (1931-2006)

Undesirable ’92
Under the Rainbow ’81
The Last Hard Men ’76
The Young Pioneers ’76
Man Who Loved Cat Dancing ’73
Vanishing Point ’71
Lassie: Well of Love ’70
Cool Hand Luke ’67

Giulio Donnini

Hercules vs. the Sons of the Sun ’64
Caesar the Conqueror ’63

Joseph (Joe) D’Onofrio

Spider-Man ’02
Wannabes ’01
Astoria ’00
The Deli ’97
Caught ’96
The Pallbearer ’95
I Love Trouble ’94
A Bronx Tale ’93
Night and the City ’92
Jungle Fever ’91
Goodfellas ’90

Vincent D’Onofrio (1959-)

Brooklyn’s Finest ’09
The Break-Up ’06
Thumbsucker ’05
Bark! ’02
The Dangerous Lives of Altar Boys ’02
Impostor ’02
The Salton Sea ’02
Sherlock: Case of Evil ’02
Chelsea Walls ’01
The Red Sneakers ’01
The Cell ’00
Happy Accidents ’00
Steal This Movie! ’00
Spanish Judges ’99
That Championship Season ’99
The Thirteenth Floor ’99
The Velocity of Gary ’98
Claire Dolan ’97
Men in Black ’97
The Newton Boys ’97
Feeling Minnesota ’96
Good Luck ’96
The Whole Wide World ’96
The Winner ’96
Strange Days ’95
Being Human ’94
Ed Wood ’94
Imaginary Crimes ’94
Stuart Saves His Family ’94
Desire ’93
Household Saints ’93
Mr. Wonderful ’93
The Player ’92
Crooked Hearts ’91
Dying Young ’91
Fires Within ’91
JFK ’91
Naked Tango ’91
The Blood of Heroes ’89
Signs of Life ’89
Mystic Pizza ’88
Adventures in Babysitting ’87
Full Metal Jacket ’87
First Turn On ’83

Amanda Donohoe (1962-)

Starship Troopers 3: Marauder ’08
Circus ’00
Hooded Angels ’00
I’m Losing You ’98
A Knight in Camelot ’98
The Real Howard Spitz ’98
Liar Liar ’97
One Night Stand ’97
The Thorn Birds: The Missing Years ’96
The Madness of King George ’94
The Substitute ’93
A Woman’s Guide to Adultery ’93
Double Cross ’92
Shame ’92
Paper Mask ’91
Dark Obsession ’90
An Affair in Mind ’89
The Rainbow ’89
The Lair of the White Worm ’88
Castaway ’87
Foreign Body ’86

Donovan (1946-)

Secret Policeman’s Private Parts ’81
Aliens from Spaceship Earth ’77

Daisy Donovan (1975-)

Wild Child ’08
Death at a Funeral ’07
Millions ’05

Elisa Donovan (1971-)

The Dog Who Saved Christmas ’09
Framed for Murder ’07
Loving Jezebel ’99
A Night at the Roxbury ’98
Clueless ’95

Jeffrey Donovan (1968-)

Changeling ’08
Believe in Me ’06
Come Early Morning ’06
Purpose ’02
Bait ’00
Book of Shadows: Blair Witch 2 ’00
Catherine’s Grove ’98
When Trumpets Fade ’98

King Donovan (1918-87)

The Hanging Tree ’59
The Perfect Furlough ’59
Cowboy ’58
Invasion of the Body Snatchers ’56
Private Hell 36 ’54
Easy to Love ’53
Forever Female ’53
The Merry Widow ’52
Singin’ in the Rain ’52
The Enforcer ’51

Martin Donovan (1957-)

The Haunting in Connecticut ’09
The Alphabet Killer ’08
Masters of Horror: Right to Die ’07
Wind Chill ’07
The Sentinel ’06
The Quiet ’05
Saved! ’04
Agent Cody Banks ’03
United States of Leland ’03
Insomnia ’02
Pipe Dream ’02
RFK ’02
The Great Gatsby ’01
Heaven ’99
In a Savage Land ’99
Onegin ’99
The Rook ’99
Living Out Loud ’98
The Opposite of Sex ’98
Rescuers: Stories of Courage—Two Couples ’98
When Trumpets Fade ’98
Portrait of a Lady ’96
Flirt ’95
Hollow Reed ’95
Nadja ’95
Amateur ’94
Quick ’93
Simple Men ’92
Surviving Desire ’91
Trust ’91

Robert Donovan

The Hazing ’04
Curse of the Puppet Master: The Human Experiment ’98
Shadow Dancer ’96

Tate Donovan (1963-)

Nancy Drew ’07
Shooter ’07
The Lather Effect ’06
Good Night, and Good Luck ’05
The Pacifier ’05
Exposed ’03
West of Here ’02
Get Well Soon ’01
Hercules ’97 (V)
Murder at 1600 ’97
The Only Thrill ’97
America’s Dream ’95
Holy Matrimony ’94
Equinox ’93
Inside Monkey Zetterland ’93
Ethan Frome ’92
Love Potion #9 ’92
Little Noises ’91
Memphis Belle ’90
Dead Bang ’89
Clean and Sober ’88
Dangerous Curves ’88
Nutcracker: Money, Madness & Murder ’87
SpaceCamp ’86
Into Thin Air ’85
Not My Kid ’85

Terence Donovan (1942-)

The Winds of Jarrah ’83
The Man from Snowy River ’82
Breaker Morant ’80
Money Movers ’78

Ryan Donowho (1980-)

Bandslam ’09
Flakes ’07
The Pacific and Eddy ’07
Strangers with Candy ’06
Imaginary Heroes ’05
A Home at the End of the World ’04
The Mudge Boy ’03

Alison Doody (1966-)

Major League 2 ’94
Temptation ’94
Ring of the Musketeers ’93
Duel of Hearts ’92
Indiana Jones and the Last Crusade ’89
Echoes ’88
Taffin ’88
Prayer for the Dying ’87

James Doohan (1920-2005)

Bug Buster ’99
The Duke ’99
Storybook ’95
Star Trek: Generations ’94
Amore! ’93
National Lampoon’s Loaded Weapon 1 ’93
Double Trouble ’91
Star Trek 6: The Undiscovered Country ’91
Star Trek 5: The Final Frontier ’89
Star Trek 4: The Voyage Home ’86
Star Trek 3: The Search for Spock ’84
Star Trek 2: The Wrath of Khan ’82
Star Trek: The Motion Picture ’79
Man in the Wilderness ’71
36 Hours ’64

Paul Dooley (1928-)

Hairspray ’07
Cars ’06 (V)
Crazy Little Thing ’02
Insomnia ’02
Madison ’01
A Woman’s a Helluva Thing ’01
Guinevere ’99
Happy, Texas ’99
I’ll Remember April ’99
Runaway Bride ’99
Angels in the Endzone ’98
Clockwatchers ’97
Loved ’97
God’s Lonely Man ’96
Telling Lies in America ’96
Waiting for Guffman ’96
Out There ’95
The Underneath ’95
Evolver ’94
State of Emergency ’94
Cooperstown ’93
A Dangerous Woman ’93
My Boyfriend’s Back ’93
Shakes the Clown ’92
White Hot: The Mysterious Murder of Thelma Todd ’91
The Court Martial of Jackie Robinson ’90
Flashback ’89
When He’s Not a Stranger ’89
Last Rites ’88
Lip Service ’88
The Murder of Mary Phagan ’87
O.C. and Stiggs ’87
Big Trouble ’86
Monster in the Closet ’86
Sixteen Candles ’84
Going Berserk ’83

Strange Brew '83
Endangered Species '82
Hansel and Gretel '82
Kiss Me Goodbye '82
Rumpelstiltskin '82
Paternity '81
Popeye '80
Breaking Away '79
Rich Kids '79
A Wedding '78
Slap Shot '77

Lucinda Dooling
Lovely... But Deadly '82
The Alchemist '81
Miracle on Ice '81

Omar Doom (1976-)
Inglourious Basterds '09
Death Proof '07

Patric Doonan (1927-58)
John and Julie '55
Blackout '50
The Blue Lamp '49
Train of Events '49

Mike Dopud
Ruslan '09
Ace of Hearts '08
In the Name of the King: A Dungeon Siege Tale '08
Journey to the Center of the Earth '08
Seed '08
White Noise '05

Robert DoQui (1934-)
Glam '97
Original Intent '91
Miracle Mile '89
Short Fuse '88
RoboCop '87
Nashville '75
Coffy '73
A Dream for Christmas '73

Karin Dor (1936-)
Prisoner in the Middle '74
Die Screaming, Marianne '73
Dracula vs. Frankenstein '69
Topaz '69
The Torture Chamber of Dr. Sadism '69
You Only Live Twice '67
The Last Tomahawk '65
Carpet of Horror '64
Strangler of Blackmoor Castle '63
The Bellboy and the Playgirls '62
The Invisible Dr. Mabuse '62
Forger of London '61

Ann Doran (1911-2000)
Backstairs at the White House '79
Kitten with a Whip '64
The Brass Bottle '63
The FBI Story '59
It! The Terror from Beyond Space '58
Rebel without a Cause '55
The High and the Mighty '54
Island in the Sky '53
Love Is Better Than Ever '52
The Painted Hills '51
Tomahawk '51
Never a Dull Moment '50
The Clay Pigeon '49
The Fountainhead '49
Holiday in Havana '49
The Kid From Cleveland '49
Rusty's Birthday '49
The Accused '48
Pitfall '48
Fear in the Night '47
Seven Were Saved '47
Son of Rusty '47
Here Come the Waves '45
Pride of the Marines '45
Roughly Speaking '45
Air Force '43
Gildersleeve on Broadway '43
The More the Merrier '43
So Proudly We Hail '43
Mr. Wise Guy '42
Criminals Within '41
Dive Bomber '41
Meet John Doe '41
Penny Serenade '41
Blondie '38
Little Red Schoolhouse '36

Jesse Doran
Street Asylum '90
Heart '87

Mary Doran (1907-95)
Sing Sing Nights '35
Sunset Range '35
Ridin' for Justice '32
The Strange Love of Molly Louvain '32
Criminal Code '31
The Divorcee '30
Broadway Melody '29

Richard Doran
Hollywood Boulevard '76
Harrad Summer '74

Edna Dore (1922-)
Nil by Mouth '96
High Hopes '88

Johnny Dorelli (1937-)
The Odd Squad '86
Bread and Chocolate '73
How to Kill 400 Duponts '68

Stephen Dorff (1973-)
Public Enemies '09
Felon '08
XIII '08
Botched '07
.45 '06
The Hades Factor '06
Shadowboxer '06
World Trade Center '06
Alone in the Dark '05
Cold Creek Manor '03
Deuces Wild '02
Feardotcom '02
The Last Minute '01
Cecil B. Demented '00
Earthly Possessions '99
Entropy '99
Blade '98
Space Truckers '97
Blood & Wine '96
City of Industry '96
I Shot Andy Warhol '96
Innocent Lies '95
Reckless '95
Backbeat '94
S.F.W. '94
Judgment Night '93
Rescue Me '93
The Power of One '92
The Gate '87

David Dorfman (1993-)
Drillbit Taylor '08
The Ring 2 '05
The Texas Chainsaw Massacre '03
100 Mile Rule '02
The Ring '02
Bounce '00
Panic '00
Invisible Child '99

Diogo Doria (1953-)
Voyage to the Beginning of the World '96
Abraham's Valley '93

Pierre Doris (1919-)
Overseas: Three Women with Man Trouble '90
The Story of a Three Day Pass '68

Francoise Dorleac (1942-67)
The Young Girls of Rochefort '68
Billion Dollar Brain '67
Cul de Sac '66
The Soft Skin '64
That Man from Rio '64

Richard Dormer
Five Minutes of Heaven '09
My Boy Jack '07
Middletown '06

Dolores Dorn (1935-)
Truck Stop Women '74
Underworld USA '61
Underworld, U.S.A. '60
Lucky Me '54

Michael Dorn (1952-)
Night Skies '07
Heart of the Beholder '05
Shade '03
The Santa Clause 2 '02
Star Trek: Nemesis '02
Ali '01
Mach 2 '00
The Prophet's Game '99
Star Trek: Insurrection '98
Menno's Mind '96
Star Trek: First Contact '96
Amanda and the Alien '95
Timemaster '95
Star Trek: Generations '94
Star Trek 6: The Undiscovered Country '91
The Jagged Edge '85
Rocky '76

Philip Dorn (1901-75)
The Fighting Kentuckian '49
I've Always Loved You '46
Random Harvest '42
Reunion in France '42
Tarzan's Secret Treasure '41
Underground '41
Ziegfeld Girl '41

Jamie Dornan
Turn the River '07
Marie Antoinette '06

Robert Dornan (1933-)
Hell on Wheels '67
The Starfighters '63

Sandra Dorne (1925-92)
Eat the Rich '87
Devil Doll '64
The House in Marsh Road '60
Alias John Preston '56
Roadhouse Girl '53
Happy Go Lovely '51

Lester Dorr (1893-1980)
Meet the Mob '42
Panama Menace '41
Red Salute '35

Diana Dors (1931-84)
Steaming '86
Children of the Full Moon '84
Adventures of a Taxi Driver '76
Craze '74
The Devil's Web '74
From Beyond the Grave '73
A Man with a Maid '73
Theatre of Blood '73
Amazing Mr. Blunden '72
Hannie Caulder '72
Nothing But the Night '72
Pied Piper '72
Deep End '70
There's a Girl in My Soup '70
Baby Love '69
Berserk! '67
The King of the Roaring '20s: The Story of Arnold Rothstein '61
Room 43 '58
Tread Softly Stranger '58
The Long Haul '57
Unholy Wife '57
I Married a Woman '56
A Kid for Two Farthings '55
Man Bait '52
Oliver Twist '48

Brooke D'Orsay (1982-)
It's a Boy Girl Thing '06
King's Ransom '05
Harold and Kumar Go to White Castle '04

Fifi d'Orsay (1904-83)
The Gangster '47
Delinquent Daughters '44
Nabonga '44
Three Legionnaires '37
Going Hollywood '33
Girl from Calgary '32
They Had to See Paris '29

Jimmy Dorsey (1904-57)
The Fabulous Dorseys '47
Hollywood Canteen '44

Tommy Dorsey (1905-56)
The Fabulous Dorseys '47
Presenting Lily Mars '43

Adrien Dorval
Ginger Snaps Back: The Beginning '04
Pressure '02

Gabrielle Dorziat (1880-1979)
The Storm Within '48
Monsieur Vincent '47
De Mayerling a Sarajevo '40

Susana Dosamantes (1948-)
Counterforce '87
Target Eagle '84
Remolino de Pasiones '68

John Dossett
Nick and Jane '96
That Night '93
Longtime Companion '90

Angela Dotchin (1974-)
Maiden Voyage: Ocean Hijack '04
Beyond Justice '01
Dead Evidence '00

Karen Dotrice (1955-)
The Thirty-Nine Steps '79
The Gnome-Mobile '67
Mary Poppins '64
The Three Lives of Thomasina '63

Michele Dotrice (1947-)
Vanity Fair '99
The Blood on Satan's Claw '71
And Soon the Darkness '70
The Witches '66

Roy Dotrice (1925-)
Hellboy II: The Golden Army '08
Played '06
The Scarlet Letter '95
The Cutting Edge '92
Suburban Commando '91
The Eliminators '86
Amadeus '84
Cheech and Chong's The Corsican Brothers '84
The Dancing Princesses '84
Space: 1999—Alien Attack '79
The Buttercup Chain '70
The Heroes of Telemark '65

Attilio Dottesio
Jungle Inferno '72
Man with a Cross '43

David Doty
Nancy Drew '07
Full Moon in Blue Water '88

Kaitlin Doubleday
Waiting '05
Freshman Orientation '04

Catherine Doucet (1875-1958)
It Started with Eve '41
These Three '36

Paul Doucet
The Terrorist Next Door '08
Shattered City: The Halifax Explosion '03
America '24

John Doucette (1921-94)
Fighting Mad '76
Patton '70
True Grit '69
Nevada Smith '66
Paradise, Hawaiian Style '66
The Hunters '58
House of Bamboo '55
Seven Cities of Gold '55
Fixed Bayonets! '51

Doug E. Doug (1970-)
Shark Tale '04 (V)
Eight Legged Freaks '02
That Darn Cat '96
Operation Dumbo Drop '95
Cool Runnings '93
Class Act '91
Hangin' with the Homeboys '91
Jungle Fever '91

Doc Dougherty
I'll Believe You '07
Underground Terror '88

Suzi Dougherty
Chameleon 3: Dark Angel '00
Love and Other Catastrophes '95

Kenny Doughty (1975-)
The Crew '08
My First Wedding '04
Crush '02

Angela Douglas (1940-)
Digby, the Biggest Dog in the World '73
Carry On Up the Khyber '68
Carry On Cowboy '66
Carry On Screaming '66

Brandon Douglas (1968-)
Journey to Spirit Island '92
Chips, the War Dog '90
The Children of Times Square '86

Burt Douglas (1930-2000)
High School Confidential '58
The Law and Jake Wade '58

Cameron Douglas (1978-)
National Lampoon's Adam & Eve '05
It Runs in the Family '03

Cullen Douglas
Shuttle '09
Ace Ventura Jr.: Pet Detective '08

Damon Douglas (1954-)
From Noon Till Three '76
Massacre at Central High '76

Diana Douglas (1923-)
It Runs in the Family '03
Loving '70
The Indian Fighter '55

Donald Douglas
A Mind to Murder '96
Diana: Her True Story '93

Donald "Don" Douglas (1905-45)
Club Havana '46
Murder, My Sweet '44
Action in the North Atlantic '43
Behind the Rising Sun '43
On the Sunny Side '42
Dead Men Tell '41
Night of January 16th '41
Sergeant York '41
Sleepers West '41
Whistling in the Dark '41
Law of the Texan '38
The Spider's Web '38
Tomorrow's Children '34
The Great Gabbo '29

Donna Douglas (1939-)
The Return of the Beverly Hillbillies '81
Frankie and Johnny '65
Career '59

Earl Douglas
Tim Tyler's Luck '37
Fighting Caballero '35

Eric Douglas (1958-2004)
Delta Force 3: The Killing Game '91
Student Confidential '87
Tomboy '85

Illeana Douglas (1965-)
Factory Girl '06
Pittsburgh '06
Alchemy '05
Missing Brendan '03
The Adventures of Pluto Nash '02
Dummy '02
The New Guy '02
Point of Origin '02
Ghost World '01
The Next Best Thing '00
Happy, Texas '99
Lansky '99
Stir of Echoes '99
Message in a Bottle '98
Bella Mafia '97
Flypaper '97
Rough Riders '97
Sink or Swim '97
Weapons of Mass Distraction '97
Grace of My Heart '96
Picture Perfect '96
Wedding Bell Blues '96
To Die For '95
Grief '94
Search and Destroy '94
Alive '93
Household Saints '93
Cape Fear '91
Guilty by Suspicion '91
Goodfellas '90
The Last Temptation of Christ '88

James B. Douglas (1933-)
Men with Brooms '02
Boy in Blue '86
The Changeling '80
The Dawson Patrol '78

Jeff Douglas
Webs '03
The Showgirl Murders '95

John Douglas
Violent Zone '89
Hell's Brigade: The Final Assault '80

Kirk Douglas (1916-)
It Runs in the Family '03
Diamonds '99
Greedy '94
The Secret '93
Oscar '91
Queenie '87
Tough Guys '86
Amos '85
Eddie Macon's Run '83
Holocaust Survivors... Remembrance of Love '83
The Man from Snowy River '82
Draw! '81
The Final Countdown '80
Saturn 3 '80
Home Movies '79
The Villain '79
The Fury '78
The Chosen '77
Victory at Entebbe '76
Once Is Not Enough '75
Posse '75
Master Touch '74
Dr. Jekyll and Mr. Hyde '73
Catch Me a Spy '71
A Gunfight '71
Light at the Edge of the World '71
There Was a Crooked Man '70
The Arrangement '69
The Brotherhood '68
The War Wagon '67
The Way West '67
Cast a Giant Shadow '66
Is Paris Burning? '66
The Heroes of Telemark '65
In Harm's Way '65
Seven Days in May '64

Adam Had Four Sons *'41*
Bad Boy *'39*
Pigskin Parade *'36*
March of the Wooden Soldiers *'34*

Denise Dowse (1958-)
Coach Carter *'05*
Guess Who *'05*
Ray *'04*
What About Your Friends: Weekend Getaway *'02*
Killing Mr. Griffin *'97*
Bio-Dome *'96*

David Doyle (1925-97)
Archie: Return to Riverdale *'90*
Ghost Writer *'89*
For Love or Money *'88*
Wait Till Your Mother Gets Home *'83*
The Line *'80*
My Boys Are Good Boys *'78*
Wild & Wooly *'78*
The Comeback *'77*
Who Killed Mary What's 'Er Name? *'71*
Loving *'70*
Paper Lion *'68*

John (Roy Slaven) Doyle (1953-)
Rock & Roll Cowboys *'92*
The Wicked *'89*
Contagion *'87*

Martin Doyle
Daniel's Daughter *'08*
Mail to the Chief *'00*

Maxine Doyle (1915-73)
Come on, Cowboys *'37*
S.O.S. Coast Guard *'37*
Condemned to Live *'35*
The Mystery Man *'35*

Shawn Doyle (1968-)
Whiteout *'09*
Guns *'08*
Do or Die *'03*
A Killing Spring *'02*
Verdict in Blood *'02*
Don't Say a Word *'01*
The Majestic *'01*
Stiletto Dance *'01*
Frequency *'00*

Tony Doyle (1941-2000)
A Love Divided *'01*
Amongst Women *'98*
I Went Down *'97*
Adventures in Dinosaur City *'92*
Eat the Peach *'86*
The Final Option *'82*

Maria Doyle Kennedy (1964-)
Miss Julie *'99*
The General *'98*
The Break *'97*
The Matchmaker *'97*
Nothing Personal *'95*
The Commitments *'91*

Brian Doyle-Murray (1945-)
Daddy Day Camp *'07*
Snow Dogs *'02*
A Gentleman's Game *'01*
Bedazzled *'00*
Stuart Little *'99*
Dennis the Menace Strikes Again *'98*
As Good As It Gets *'97*
Multiplicity *'96*
Waiting for Guffman *'96*
Jury Duty *'95*
My Brother's Keeper *'95*
Cabin Boy *'94*
Groundhog Day *'93*
Wayne's World *'92*
JFK *'91*
The Experts *'89*
Ghostbusters 2 *'89*
How I Got into College *'89*
National Lampoon's Christmas Vacation *'89*
Scrooged *'88*
Club Paradise *'86*
The Razor's Edge *'84*
Sixteen Candles *'84*
National Lampoon's Vacation *'83*
Modern Problems *'81*
Caddyshack *'80*
Shame of the Jungle *'75 (V)*

Pamella D'Pella (1967-)
Caged Heat 2: Stripped of Freedom *'94*
Uncaged *'91*

Heinz Drache (1923-2002)
Circus of Fear *'67*
Brides of Fu Manchu *'66*
The Mysterious Magician *'65*
The Squeaker *'65*
Coast of Skeletons *'63*
The Indian Scarf *'63*
Door with the Seven Locks *'62*
The Avenger *'60*
Naked in the Night *'58*

Billy Drago (1949-)
The Dead One *'07*
The Hills Have Eyes *'06*
Lime Salted Love *'06*
Blood Relic *'05*
Masters of Horror: Imprint *'05*
Mysterious Skin *'04*
Convict 762 *'98*
Shadow Warriors *'97*
Deadly Heroes *'96*
Mirror, Mirror 3: The Voyeur *'96*
Sci-Fighters *'96*
Phoenix *'95*
Never Say Die *'94*
Solar Force *'94*
The Takeover *'94*
Cyborg 2 *'93*
Death Ring *'93*
In Self Defense *'93*
Lady Dragon 2 *'93*
The Outfit *'93*
Guncrazy *'92*
Secret Games *'92*
China White *'91*
Diplomatic Immunity *'91*
Martial Law 2: Undercover *'91*
Delta Force 2: Operation Stranglehold *'90*
Dark Before Dawn *'89*
Freeway *'88*
Hero and the Terror *'88*
Prime Suspect *'88*
The Untouchables *'87*
Vamp *'86*
Invasion U.S.A. *'85*

BeBe Drake
Friday After Next *'02*
Backstairs at the White House *'79*

Betsy Drake (1923-)
Clarence, the Cross-eyed Lion *'65*
Will Success Spoil Rock Hunter? *'57*
Room for One More *'51*
The Second Woman *'51*
Pretty Baby *'50*
Every Girl Should Be Married *'48*

Charles Drake (1914-94)
Hail, Hero! *'69*
Valley of the Dolls *'67*
No Name on the Bullet *'59*
Until They Sail *'57*
Walk the Proud Land *'56*
To Hell and Back *'55*
Tobor the Great *'54*
Gunsmoke *'53*
It Came from Outer Space *'53*
Red Ball Express *'52*
Comanche Territory *'50*
Harvey *'50*
Winchester '73 *'50*
Tarzan's Magic Fountain *'48*
The Tender Years *'47*
A Night in Casablanca *'46*
Conflict *'45*
Air Force *'43*
Dive Bomber *'41*

Claudia Drake (1918-97)
Detour *'46*
Gentleman from Texas *'46*
Renegade Girl *'46*
The Lady Confesses *'45*
Enemy of Women *'44*
Border Patrol *'43*

David Drake (1963-)
David Searching *'97*
Philadelphia *'93*

Dona Drake (1914-89)
The Road to Morocco *'42*
Louisiana Purchase *'41*

Frances Drake (1908-2000)
I'd Give My Life *'36*
The Invisible Ray *'36*
Forsaking All Others *'35*
Les Miserables *'35*
Mad Love *'35*

Gabrielle Drake (1944-)
Cry Terror *'76*
Au Pair Girls *'72*

Larry Drake (1950-)
Dark Asylum *'01*
Desert Heat *'99*
Paranoia *'98*
The Treat *'98*
Bean *'97*
The Beast *'96*
Overnight Delivery *'96*
Power 98 *'96*
The Journey of August King *'95*
Darkman 2: The Return of Durant *'94*
Dr. Giggles *'92*
Murder in New Hampshire: The Pamela Smart Story *'91*
Darkman *'90*
Tales from the Crypt *'89*
Dark Night of the Scarecrow *'81*
This Stuff'll Kill Ya! *'71*

Tom Drake (1918-82)
Savage Abduction *'73*
The Spectre of Edgar Allen Poe *'73*
Cycle Psycho *'72*
Johnny Reno *'66*
The Singing Nun *'66*
House of the Black Death *'65*
Warkill *'65*
The Bramble Bush *'60*
Cyclops *'56*
FBI Girl *'52*
The Great Rupert *'50*
The Hills of Home *'48*
Words and Music *'48*
Cass Timberlane *'47*
I'll Be Yours *'47*
Courage of Lassie *'46*
Meet Me in St. Louis *'44*
Two Girls and a Sailor *'44*
The White Cliffs of Dover *'44*
The Howards of Virginia *'40*

Polly Draper (1957-)
Second Best *'05*
Shooting Livien *'05*
Dinner Rush *'00*
Hitman's Journal *'99*
The Tic Code *'99*
Gold Diggers: The Secret of Bear Mountain *'95*
Schemes *'95*
A Million to Juan *'94*
Danielle Steel's Heartbeat *'93*
The Pick-Up Artist *'87*
Making Mr. Right *'86*

Thomas Draper
Bikini Med School *'98*
Bikini House Calls *'96*

Rachel Dratch
I Hate Valentine's Day *'09*
My Life in Ruins *'09*
Harold *'08*
Spring Breakdown *'08*
I Now Pronounce You Chuck and Larry *'07*
Click *'06*
The Pleasure Drivers *'05*
Down With Love *'03*

Jamie Draven
Badland *'07*
Butterfly Collectors *'99*

Milena Dravic (1940-)
WR: Mysteries of the Organism *'71*
Man Is Not a Bird *'65*

Alfred Drayton (1881-1949)
Things Happen at Night *'48*
Nicholas Nickleby *'46*
First a Girl *'35*
Jack Ahoy *'34*
Red Ensign *'34*

Dr. Dre (1965-)
Training Day *'01*
The Wash *'01*
The Show *'95*
Gunmen *'93*

Alex Dreier (1916-2000)
Lady Cocoa *'75*
Loners *'72*

Fran Drescher (1957-)
Picking Up the Pieces *'99*
The Beautician and the Beast *'97*
Jack *'96*
Car 54, Where Are You? *'94*
We're Talkin' Serious Money *'92*
Cadillac Man *'90*
UHF *'89*
Wedding Band *'89*
Rosebud Beach Hotel *'85*
This Is Spinal Tap *'84*
Doctor Detroit *'83*
Ragtime *'81*
Gorp *'80*
The Hollywood Knights *'80*
Summer of Fear *'78*
Saturday Night Fever *'77*

Sonia Dresdel (1909-76)
The Clouded Yellow *'51*
The Fallen Idol *'49*
While I Live *'47*

Curley Dresden (1900-53)
Fighting Valley *'43*
Law of the Saddle *'43*
Trigger Men *'41*
Wyoming Outlaw *'39*
Pals of the Saddle *'38*
Santa Fe Stampede *'38*
Rough Ridin' Rhythm *'37*

John Dresden
No Dead Heroes *'87*
Final Mission *'84*
Raw Force *'81*

Louise Dresser (1878-1965)
David Harum *'34*
Scarlet Empress *'34*
The World Moves On *'34*
Doctor Bull *'33*
The Garden of Eden *'28*
The Eagle *'25*

Lieux Dressler (1930-)
Truck Stop Women *'74*
Grave of the Vampire *'72*

Marie Dressler (1868-1934)
Dinner at Eight *'33*
Tugboat Annie *'33*
Emma *'32*
Politics *'31*
Reducing *'31*
Anna Christie *'30*
Let Us Be Gay *'30*
Min & Bill *'30*
The Divine Lady *'29*
Vagabond Lover *'29*
The Patsy *'28*
Tillie Wakes Up *'17*
Tillie's Punctured Romance *'14*

Valerie Dreville
Heartbeat Detector *'07*
La Sentinelle *'92*

Ellen Drew (1913-2003)
Baron of Arizona *'51*
Great Missouri Raid *'51*
Man in the Saddle *'51*
Stars in My Crown *'50*
Man from Colorado *'49*
Isle of the Dead *'45*
China Sky *'44*
Dark Mountain *'44*
That's My Baby! *'44*
The Monster and the Girl *'41*
Night of January 16th *'41*
Buck Benny Rides Again *'40*
Christmas in July *'40*
The Texas Rangers Ride Again *'40*
The Gracie Allen Murder Case *'39*
If I Were King *'38*

Gene Drew (1926-90)
Truck Stop Women *'74*
Steel Arena *'72*
Sweet Georgia *'72*

Griffin (Griffen) Drew (1968-)
The Kid with the X-Ray Eyes *'99*
Dinosaur Valley Girls *'96*
Friend of the Family *'95*
Masseuse *'95*
Sinful Intrigue *'95*
Dinosaur Island *'93*

Roland (Walter Goss) Drew (1900-88)
Across the Pacific *'42*
The Invisible Killer *'40*
Evangeline *'29*

Sarah Drew
Front of the Class *'08*
Radio *'03*

Nancy Drexel (1910-89)
Man from Hell's Edges *'32*
Mason of the Mounted *'32*
Texas Buddies *'32*

James Dreyfus (1968-)
Color Me Kubrick *'05*
Notting Hill *'99*
Boyfriends *'96*

Jean-Claude Dreyfus (1946-)
Two Brothers *'04*
A Very Long Engagement *'04*
The Lady and the Duke *'01*
The City of Lost Children *'95*
Son of Gascogne *'95*
Delicatessen *'92*

Julie Dreyfus (1972-)
Inglourious Basterds *'09*
Kill Bill Vol. 2 *'04*
Kill Bill Vol. 1 *'03*

Lorin Dreyfuss (1944-)
Dutch Treat *'86*
Detective School Dropouts *'85*

Richard Dreyfuss (1947-)
Piranha 3D *'10*
My Life in Ruins *'09*
W. *'08*
Tin Man *'07*
Poseidon *'06*
Coast to Coast *'04*
Silver City *'04*
Who is Cletis Tout? *'02*
The Day Reagan Was Shot *'01*
The Crew *'00*
Fail Safe *'00*
Lansky *'99*
Krippendorf's Tribe *'98*
Jack London's The Call of the Wild *'97 (N)*
Oliver Twist *'97*
James and the Giant Peach *'96 (V)*
Night Falls on Manhattan *'96*
Trigger Happy *'96*
The American President *'95*
The Last Word *'95*
Mr. Holland's Opus *'95*
Silent Fall *'94*
Another Stakeout *'93*
Lost in Yonkers *'93*
Once Around *'91*
Prisoner of Honor *'91*
What about Bob? *'91*
Postcards from the Edge *'90*
Rosencrantz & Guildenstern Are Dead *'90*
Always *'89*
Let It Ride *'89*
Moon over Parador *'88*
Nuts *'87*
Stakeout *'87*
Tin Men *'87*
Down and Out in Beverly Hills *'86*
Stand by Me *'86*
The Buddy System *'83*
Whose Life Is It Anyway? *'81*
The Competition *'80*
Second Coming of Suzanne *'80*
The Big Fix *'78*
Close Encounters of the Third Kind *'77*
The Goodbye Girl *'77*
Inserts *'76*
Victory at Entebbe *'76*
Jaws *'75*
The Apprenticeship of Duddy Kravitz *'74*
American Graffiti *'73*
Dillinger *'73*
Hello Down There *'69*
The Graduate *'67*
Valley of the Dolls *'67*

Moosie Drier (1964-)
Charlie and the Great Balloon Chase *'82*
The Hollywood Knights *'80*
Homeward Bound *'80*
Ants *'77*

Deborah Driggs (1963-)
Night Rhythms *'92*
Total Exposure *'91*

Brian Drillinger (1960-)
How to Go Out on a Date in Queens *'06*
I Shot a Man in Vegas *'96*
Brighton Beach Memoirs *'86*

Carol Drinkwater (1948-)
An Awfully Big Adventure *'94*
Father *'90*

Bobby Driscoll (1937-68)
Peter Pan *'53 (V)*
Treasure Island *'50*
So Dear to My Heart *'49*
The Window *'49*
O.S.S. *'46*
Identity Unknown *'45*
The Fighting Sullivans *'42*

Robert Drivas (1938-86)
God Told Me To *'76*
Road Movie *'72*
The Illustrated Man *'69*
Cool Hand Luke *'67*

Minnie Driver (1971-)
Motherhood *'09*
Ripple Effect *'07*
Ella Enchanted *'04*
The Phantom of the Opera *'04*
Owning Mahowny *'03*
High Heels and Low Lifes *'01*
Beautiful *'00*
Return to Me *'00*
Slow Burn *'00*
An Ideal Husband *'99*
South Park: Bigger, Longer and Uncut *'99 (V)*

The Pentagon Wars '98
Armistead Maupin's More Tales of the City '97
Jerusalem '96
Picture Perfect '96
Jeffrey '95
Mighty Aphrodite '95
Mr. Holland's Opus '95
Dead Badge '94
Digger '94
I Love Trouble '94
Mother '94
Armistead Maupin's Tales of the City '93
The Cemetery Club '93
Look Who's Talking Now '93
Over the Hill '93
Sinatra '92
In the Spirit '90
Look Who's Talking, Too '90
Dad '89
Look Who's Talking '89
Steel Magnolias '89
Working Girl '88
Moonstruck '87
Walls of Glass '85
Idolmaker '80
King of America '80
Rich Kids '79
Wanderers '79
The Seagull '75
Death Wish '74
Lilith '64

Bill Duke (1943-)

The Go-Getter '07
X-Men: The Last Stand '06
Yellow '06
Get Rich or Die Tryin' '05
National Security '03
Red Dragon '02
Exit Wounds '01
Never Again '01
Fever '99
Foolish '99
The Limey '99
Dying to Get Rich '98
Payback '98
Menace II Society '93
Bird on a Wire '90
Predator '87
Commando '85
American Gigolo '79

Patty Duke (1946-)

Love Finds a Home '09
Bigger Than the Sky '05
Murder Without Conviction '04
Little John '02
A Season for Miracles '99
Harvest of Fire '95
Family of Strangers '93
Grave Secrets: The Legacy of Hilltop Drive '92
Prelude to a Kiss '92
Amityville 4: The Evil Escapes '89
Best Kept Secrets '88
George Washington: The Forging of a Nation '86
Something Special '86
George Washington '84
September Gun '83
By Design '82
The Babysitter '80
Mom, the Wolfman and Me '80
The Miracle Worker '79
Family Upside Down '78
The Swarm '78
Curse of the Black Widow '77
Fire '77
Killer on Board '77
You'll Like My Mother '72
She Waits '71
My Sweet Charlie '70
Valley of the Dolls '67
Billie '65
The Miracle Worker '62
The 4D Man '59
The Goddess '58

Robin Duke (1954-)

Hostage for a Day '94
I Love Trouble '94
Motorama '91
Club Paradise '86
The Last Polka '84

David Dukes (1945-2000)

Stephen King's Rose Red '02
Tick Tock '00
Supreme Sanction '99
Gods and Monsters '98
The Love Letter '98
Tinseltown '97
Last Stand at Saber River '96
Norma Jean and Marilyn '95
And the Band Played On '93
Me and the Kid '93
Held Hostage '91
The Josephine Baker Story '90
The Rutanga Tapes '90
Snow Kill '90
Strange Interlude '90
See You in the Morning '89
War & Remembrance: The Final Chapter '89
War & Remembrance '88
Catch the Heat '87
Date with an Angel '87
Rawhead Rex '87
The Men's Club '86
Cat on a Hot Tin Roof '84
George Washington '84
The Winds of War '83
Without a Trace '83
Miss All-American Beauty '82
Portrait of a Rebel: Margaret Sanger '82
Only When I Laugh '81
The First Deadly Sin '80
Mayflower: The Pilgrims' Adventure '79
The Triangle Factory Fire Scandal '79
Wild Party '74
The Strawberry Statement '70

Caitlin Dulany

Class of 1999 2: The Substitute '93
Maniac Cop 3: Badge of Silence '93

Keir Dullea (1936-)

The Accidental Husband '08
The Good Shepherd '06
The Audrey Hepburn Story '00
Oh, What a Night '92
Blind Date '84
Next One '84
2010: The Year We Make Contact '84
Brainwaves '82
No Place to Hide '81
The Hostage Tower '80
Leopard in the Snow '78
Love Under Pressure '78
Full Circle '77
Welcome to Blood City '77
Black Christmas '75
Paul and Michelle '74
Paperback Hero '73
Black Water Gold '69
2001: A Space Odyssey '68
Madame X '66
The Thin Red Line '64
Mail Order Bride '63
David and Lisa '62
The Hoodlum Priest '61

Douglass Dumbrille (1890-1974)

Shake, Rattle and Rock '57
The Ten Commandments '56
Jupiter's Darling '55
Son of Paleface '52
Abbott and Costello in the Foreign Legion '50
Riding High '50
Last of the Wild Horses '49
Spook Busters '48
Blonde Savage '47
The Road to Utopia '46
Under Nevada Skies '46
Jungle Woman '44
Lost in a Harem '44
Uncertain Glory '44
Weird Woman '44
Castle in the Desert '42
A Gentleman After Dark '42
I Married an Angel '42
Ride 'Em Cowboy '42
Big Store '41
Michael Shayne: Private Detective '40
Virginia City '40
Charlie Chan at Treasure Island '39
Charlie Chan in City of Darkness '39
Mr. Moto in Danger Island '39
The Three Musketeers '39
The Mysterious Rider '38
A Day at the Races '37
The Firefly '37
Mr. Deeds Goes to Town '36
The Princess Comes Across '36
Crime and Punishment '35
The Lives of a Bengal Lancer '35
Naughty Marietta '35
Operator 13 '34
Treasure Island '34
Baby Face '33
Heroes for Sale '33
King of the Jungle '33
Rustler's Roundup '33

Denise Dumont (1955-)

Heart of Midnight '89
Kiss of the Spider Woman '85

James DuMont

Fast Girl '07
Combination Platter '93

Jose Dumont (1950-)

Behind the Sun '01
At Play in the Fields of the Lord '91

Margaret Dumont (1889-1965)

Zotz! '62
Shake, Rattle and Rock '57
Three for Bedroom C '52
The Horn Blows at Midnight '45
Up in Arms '44
Rhythm Parade '43
Sing Your Worries Away '42
Tales of Manhattan '42
Big Store '41
Never Give a Sucker an Even Break '41
At the Circus '39
The Women '39
A Day at the Races '37
Youth on Parole '37
A Night at the Opera '35
Duck Soup '33
Animal Crackers '30
The Cocoanuts '29

Ulises Dumont (1937-)

Time for Revenge '82
The Lion's Share '79

Dennis Dun (1954-)

Thousand Pieces of Gold '91
The Last Emperor '87
Prince of Darkness '87
Big Trouble in Little China '86

Steffi Duna (1910-92)

Law of the Pampas '39
Panama Lady '39
Way Down South '39
Dancing Pirate '36
I Conquer the Sea '36

Donnie Dunagan (1934-)

Bambi '42 (V)
Son of Frankenstein '39

Faye Dunaway (1941-)

Midnight Bayou '09
Cougar Club '07
The Gene Generation '07
Pandemic '07
Rain '06
Ghosts Never Sleep '05
Anonymous Rex '04
Blind Horizon '04
Chronicle of the Raven '04
The Rules of Attraction '02
Running Mates '00
The Yards '00
The Messenger: The Story of Joan of Arc '99
The Thomas Crown Affair '99
Gia '98
Rebecca '97
The Twilight of the Golds '97
Albino Alligator '96
The Chamber '96
Drunks '96
Dunston Checks In '95
Arizona Dream '94
Don Juan DeMarco '94
The Temp '93
Double Edge '92
Scorchers '92
Silhouette '91
The Handmaid's Tale '90
Wait until Spring, Bandini '90
Burning Secret '89
Cold Sassy Tree '89
The Gamble '88
Barfly '87
Casanova '87
Midnight Crossing '87
Beverly Hills Madam '86
Agatha Christie's Thirteen at Dinner '85
Christopher Columbus '85
Ordeal by Innocence '84
Supergirl '84
The Wicked Lady '83
Country Girl '82
Mommie Dearest '81
The First Deadly Sin '80
The Champ '79
Eyes of Laura Mars '78
The Disappearance of Aimee '76
Network '76
Voyage of the Damned '76
The Four Musketeers '75
Three Days of the Condor '75
Chinatown '74
The Three Musketeers '74
The Towering Inferno '74
Oklahoma Crude '73
The Deadly Trap '71
Little Big Man '70
The Arrangement '69
The Thomas Crown Affair '68
Bonnie & Clyde '67

Adrian Dunbar (1958-)

Eye of the Dolphin '06
Kidnapped '05
Suspicion '03
Triggermen '02
How Harry Became a Tree '01
Shooters '00
Relative Strangers '99
The General '98
Melissa '97
Innocent Lies '95
Widow's Peak '94
A Woman's Guide to Adultery '93
The Crying Game '92
The Playboys '92
Hear My Song '91
My Left Foot '89

Rockmond Dunbar

Alien Raiders '08
The Family That Preys '08
Jada '08
Dirty Laundry '07
Kiss Kiss Bang Bang '05

Andrew Duncan

Morgan Stewart's Coming Home '87
The Gig '85
Slap Shot '77
Shame of the Jungle '75 (V)
Loving '70
The Rain People '69

Angus Duncan (1936-)

How to Seduce a Woman '74
Hard Frame '70

Archie Duncan

Ring of Bright Water '69
Postman's Knock '62

Arletta Duncan (1914-95)

Roaring Speedboats '37
Fighting Champ '33
The Gallant Fool '33
Frankenstein '31

Bob Duncan (1904-67)

Border Feud '47
Colorado Serenade '46

Bud Duncan (1883-1960)

Hillbilly Blitzkrieg '42
Snuffy Smith, Yard Bird '42

Carmen Duncan (1942-)

Counterstrike '03
Moving Targets '87
Bootleg '85
Dark Forces '83
Now and Forever '82

Julie Duncan

Haunted Ranch '43
Along the Sundown Trail '42
Fugitive Valley '41

Kenne Duncan (1903-72)

Revenge of the Virgins '62 (N)
The Sinister Urge '60
Night of the Ghouls '59
The Astounding She-Monster '58
Flesh and the Spur '57
Cyclotrode "X" '46
Manhunt of Mystery Island '45
Rough Riders of Cheyenne '45
Raiders of Sunset Pass '43
Dynamite Canyon '41
Outlaws of the Rio Grande '41
Riding the Sunset Trail '41
The Spider Returns '41
Pinto Canyon '40
The Spider's Web '38
Make-Up '37

Lindsay Duncan (1950-)

Alice in Wonderland '10
Longford '06
Starter for Ten '06
Under the Tuscan Sun '03
Almost Strangers '01
Oliver Twist '00
An Ideal Husband '99
Mansfield Park '99
Shooting the Past '99
A Midsummer Night's Dream '96
City Hall '95
The Rector's Wife '94
Body Parts '91
The Reflecting Skin '91
Traffik '90
A Year in Provence '89
Loose Connections '87
Prick Up Your Ears '87
Grown Ups '80

Mary Duncan (1895-1993)

Morning Glory '33
State's Attorney '31
City Girl '30

Michael Clarke Duncan (1957-)

Cats & Dogs: The Revenge of Kitty Galore '10 (V)
Street Fighter: The Legend of Chun-Li '09
Delgo '08 (V)
Kung Fu Panda '08 (V)
Welcome Home Roscoe Jenkins '08
American Crude '07
The Last Mimzy '07
Slipstream '07
Air Bud 6: Air Buddies '06 (V)
One Way '06
School for Scoundrels '06
Talladega Nights: The Ballad of Ricky Bobby '06
The Island '05
Racing Stripes '05 (V)
Sin City '05
D.E.B.S. '04
Brother Bear '03 (V)
Daredevil '03
The Scorpion King '02
Cats & Dogs '01 (V)
Planet of the Apes '01
See Spot Run '01
They Call Me Sirr '00
The Whole Nine Yards '00
The Green Mile '99
Armageddon '98

Michaelle Duncan

The Broken '08
Driving Lessons '06

Neil Duncan (1958-)

Sleeping with Strangers '94
Split Second '92
Murder on Line One '90

Peter Duncan (1954-)

The Lifetaker '89
The Old Curiosity Shop '75

Rachel Duncan (1985-)

Amityville Dollhouse '96
Last Stand at Saber River '96
The Crazysitter '94

Sandy Duncan (1946-)

Never Again '01
The Swan Princess '94 (V)
Rock-a-Doodle '92 (V)
The Fox and the Hound '81 (V)
The Cat from Outer Space '78
Roots '77
Million Dollar Duck '71
Star Spangled Girl '71

Jennifer (Jennie) Dundas Lowe (1971-)

Puccini for Beginners '06
Changing Lanes '02
Swimming '00
The First Wives Club '96
Legal Eagles '86
Heaven Help Us '85
The Hotel New Hampshire '84
Mrs. Soffel '84
The Beniker Gang '83

Claude Duneton

Trois Couleurs: Bleu '93
The Double Life of Veronique '91

Christine Dunford

How to Go Out on a Date in Queens '06
Ulee's Gold '97

Katherine Dunham (1909-2006)

Mambo '55
Casbah '48

Robert Dunham (1931-2001)

Godzilla vs. Megalon '76
The Green Slime '68
Face of Another '66

Rosemary Dunham

The Wolves of Kromer '98
Mistress Pamela '74

Stephen Dunham (1964-)

Monster-in-Law '05
The Mummy '99

Dawn Dunlap (1962-)

Barbarian Queen '85
Heartbreaker '83
Forbidden World '82

Lesley Dunlop (1956-)

Tess of the D'Urbervilles '98
The Dying Truth '86
Agatha Christie's Thirteen at Dinner '85

Haunted: The Ferryman '74

Vic Dunlop

Wishful Thinking '92
Martians Go Home! '90
Jud '71

Carolyn Dunn

Hitler's Daughter '90
Breaking All the Rules '85

Conrad Dunn

Animal 2 '07
The Last Don 2 '98
Mask of Death '97
Silent Trigger '97
Inside Edge '92

Eddie Dunn (1896-1951)

Call Northside 777 '48
Mexican Spitfire at Sea '42
Billy the Kid '41
South of Santa Fe '32
Sunrise Trail '31

Emma Dunn (1875-1966)

I Married a Witch '42
Talk of the Town '42
The Great Dictator '40
You Can't Fool Your Wife '40
The Secret of Dr. Kildare '39
Son of Frankenstein '39
The Duke of West Point '38
Madame X '37
Blessed Event '32
Hell's House '32
Morals for Women '31

Geoffrey Dunn

Voyage of the Heart '90
The Leather Boys '63

Harvey B. Dunn (1894-1968)

The Sinister Urge '60
Teenagers from Outer Space '59
Bride of the Monster '55

James Dunn (1905-67)

The Oscar '66
The Bramble Bush '60
Killer McCoy '47
That Brennan Girl '46
A Tree Grows in Brooklyn '45
The Ghost and the Guest '43
Shadows over Shanghai '38
Living on Love '37
Baby, Take a Bow '34
Bright Eyes '34
Stand Up and Cheer '34
365 Nights in Hollywood '34
Bad Girl '31

Josephine Dunn (1906-83)

Between Fighting Men '32
Our Modern Maidens '29
The Singing Fool '28

Kevin Dunn (1956-)

Transformers: Revenge of the Fallen '09
Vicky Cristina Barcelona '08
Lions for Lambs '07
Transformers '07
All the King's Men '06
The Black Dahlia '06
Gridiron Gang '06
A Perfect Day '06
Stir of Echoes '99
Godzilla '98
Small Soldiers '98
Snake Eyes '98
Almost Heroes '97
The Second Civil War '97
The Sixth Man '97
Chain Reaction '96
Picture Perfect '96
JAG '95
Mad Love '95
Nixon '95
Little Big League '94
Dave '93
Chaplin '92
Hot Shots! '91
Only the Lonely '91
Taken Away '89
Mississippi Burning '88

Liam Dunn (1917-76)

Blazing Saddles '74
Young Frankenstein '74
Emperor of the North Pole '73
Catch-22 '70

Michael Dunn

Teen Alien '78
The Abdication '74

Michael Dunn (1934-73)

Dr. Frankenstein's Castle of Freaks '74
The Freakmaker '73
Werewolf of Washington '73
House of the Damned '71
Murders in the Rue Morgue '71
Boom! '68
Madigan '68
You're a Big Boy Now '66
Ship of Fools '65

Nora Dunn (1952-)

The Answer Man '09
It's Complicated '09
Pineapple Express '08
Southland Tales '06
Love for Rent '05
November '05
Laws of Attraction '04
Bruce Almighty '03
Die Mommie Die! '03
Runaway Jury '03
Cherish '02
Heartbreakers '01
Max Keeble's Big Move '01
What's the Worst That Could Happen? '01
What Planet Are You From? '00
Drop Dead Gorgeous '99
Three Kings '99
Air Bud 2: Golden Receiver '98
Bulworth '98
The Last Supper '96
I Love Trouble '94
Shake, Rattle & Rock! '94
Born Yesterday '93
Passion Fish '92
Stepping Out '91
Miami Blues '90
How I Got into College '89
Working Girl '88

Ralph Dunn (1900-68)

Three on a Ticket '47
Too Many Winners '47
Larceny in her Heart '46

Roger Dunn

Owning Mahowny '03
Ignition '01
The Sandy Bottom Orchestra '00

Ryan Dunn (1977-)

Jackass Number Two '06
Jackass: The Movie '02

John Dunn-Hill

Secret Window '04
Varian's War '01
Wilder '00
La Deroute '98
Bleeders '97

Dominick Dunne (1925-)

An Alan Smithee Film: Burn, Hollywood, Burn '97
Addicted to Love '96

Dominique Dunne (1959-82)

Diary of a Teenage Hitchhiker '82
Haunting of Harrington House '82
Poltergeist '82
The Shadow Riders '82
Magic on Love Island '80

Griffin Dunne (1955-)

Last Night '10
The Great Buck Howard '09
Snow Angels '07
Game 6 '05
40 Days and 40 Nights '02
Blonde '01
Lisa Picard Is Famous '01
The Android Affair '95
I Like It Like That '94
Quiz Show '94
Search and Destroy '94
Hotel Room '93
Love Matters '93
The Pickle '93
Big Girls Don't Cry... They Get Even '92
Straight Talk '92
My Girl '91
Once Around '91
Secret Weapon '90
White Palace '90
Me and Him '89
The Big Blue '88
Lip Service '88
Amazon Women on the Moon '87
Who's That Girl? '87
After Hours '85
Almost You '85
From Here to Maternity '85
Cold Feet '84
Johnny Dangerously '84
An American Werewolf in London '81
The Fan '81
Chilly Scenes of Winter '79
The Other Side of the Mountain '75

Irene Dunne (1898-1990)

Never a Dull Moment '50
I Remember Mama '48
Life with Father '47
Anna and the King of Siam '46
A Guy Named Joe '44
The White Cliffs of Dover '44
Together Again '43
Penny Serenade '41
My Favorite Wife '40
Love Affair '39
Joy of Living '38
The Awful Truth '37
Show Boat '36
Theodora Goes Wild '36
Magnificent Obsession '35
Roberta '35
Sweet Adeline '35
Stingaree '34
Ann Vickers '33
No Other Woman '33
Bachelor Apartment '31
Cimarron '31
Consolation Marriage '31

Murphy Dunne (1942-)

Live from Baghdad '03
Blues Brothers 2000 '98
Bad Manners '84
Going Berserk '83
The Blues Brothers '80
The Big Bus '76

Robin Dunne (1976-)

Beyond Sherwood Forest '09
Jack and Jill vs. the World '08
Species 3 '04
The Snow Walker '03
American Psycho 2: All American Girl '02
The Skulls 2 '02
Au Pair 2: The Fairy Tale Continues '01
The Fraternity '01
Cruel Intentions 2 '99

Steve (Stephen) Dunne (1918-77)

I Married a Woman '56
Above and Beyond '53
The Underworld Story '50
The Big Sombrero '49
Son of Rusty '47
Colonel Effingham's Raid '45

Mildred Dunnock (1901-91)

The Pick-Up Artist '87
And Baby Makes Six '79
One Summer Love '76
Spiral Staircase '75
Murder or Mercy '74
Brand New Life '72
Whatever Happened to Aunt Alice? '69
Behold a Pale Horse '64
Sweet Bird of Youth '62
Butterfield 8 '60
The Nun's Story '59
Peyton Place '57
Baby Doll '56
Love Me Tender '56
The Trouble with Harry '55
Viva Zapata! '52
Death of a Salesman '51
I Want You '51
The Corn Is Green '45

Rosemary Dunsmore (1953-)

Orphan '09
Wedding Wars '06
Dreamcatcher '03
Breaking the Surface: The Greg Louganis Story '96
Personals '90
Blades of Courage '88
After the Promise '87
Anne of Avonlea '87
Dancing in the Dark '86

Kirsten Dunst (1982-)

All Good Things '09
How to Lose Friends & Alienate People '08
Spider-Man 3 '07
Marie Antoinette '06
Elizabethtown '05
Eternal Sunshine of the Spotless Mind '04
Spider-Man 2 '04
Wimbledon '04
Kaena: The Prophecy '03 (V)
Levity '03
Mona Lisa Smile '03
Spider-Man '02
The Cat's Meow '01
crazy/beautiful '01
Get Over It! '01
Bring It On '00
The Crow: Salvation '00
Luckytown '00
Deeply '99
The Devil's Arithmetic '99
Dick '99
Drop Dead Gorgeous '99
Lover's Prayer '99
The Virgin Suicides '99
All I Wanna Do '98
Kiki's Delivery Service '98 (V)
Small Soldiers '98
Anastasia '97 (V)
Tower of Terror '97
True Heart '97
Wag the Dog '97
Mother Night '96
Jumanji '95
Interview with the Vampire '94
Little Women '94

Wilson Dunster

Yankee Zulu '95
The Rutanga Tapes '90
Swift Justice '88

Don Duong (1957-)

We Were Soldiers '02
Green Dragon '01
Three Seasons '98

Anny (Annie Legras) Duperey (1947-)

Charlemagne '95
Germinal '93
Les Comperes '83
From Hell to Victory '79
Bobby Deerfield '77
Pardon Mon Affaire '76
No Problem '75
Stavisky '74
The Women '68
Two or Three Things I Know about Her '66

Daphne Lynn Duplaix (1976-)

Survival Island '02
Foolish '99
Lost and Found '99

Mark Duplass

Greenberg '10
Humpday '09
Hannah Takes the Stairs '07

Starletta DuPois

Friday After Next '02
Big Momma's House '00
Three Strikes '00
The Road to Galveston '96
A Raisin in the Sun '89
Hollywood Shuffle '87

Elaine DuPont

The Beach Girls and the Monster '65
The Ghost of Dragstrip Hollow '59

Albert Dupontel (1964-)

Chrysalis '07
Avenue Montaigne '06
A Very Long Engagement '04
Irreversible '02
A Self-Made Hero '95

Monique Dupree

Bachelor Party in the Bungalow of the Damned '08
Skeleton Key 2: 667, the Neighbor of the Beast '08

June Duprez (1918-84)

Calcutta '47
That Brennan Girl '46
And Then There Were None '45
Brighton Strangler '45
None But the Lonely Heart '44
Tiger Fangs '43
The Lion Has Wings '40
The Thief of Bagdad '40
The Four Feathers '39
Spy in Black '39

Paul Dupuis (1913-76)

Against the Wind '48
Johnny Frenchman '46

Roy Dupuis (1963-)

Autumn Hearts: A New Beginning '07
That Beautiful Somewhere '06
The Rocket '05
Bleeders '97
Entangled '93
Being at Home with Claude '92

Erica Durance (1978-)

Beyond Sherwood Forest '09
The Butterfly Effect 2 '06
House of the Dead '03
Sasquatch '02

David Durand (1920-98)

Boy's Reformatory '39
Viva Villa! '34

Kevin Durand (1974-)

Legion '10
Robin Hood '10
X-Men Origins: Wolverine '09
Smokin' Aces '07
3:10 to Yuma '07
Who's Your Monkey '07
Wild Hogs '07

Christopher Durang (1949-)

Simply Irresistible '99
Housesitter '92
The Butcher's Wife '91
In the Spirit '90
Mr. North '88
Heaven Help Us '85

Jack Durant

Four Jacks and a Jill '41
365 Nights in Hollywood '34

Jimmy Durante (1893-1980)

Alice Through the Looking Glass '66
It's a Mad, Mad, Mad, Mad World '63
Billy Rose's Jumbo '62
The Great Rupert '50
On an Island with You '48
It Happened in Brooklyn '47
Ziegfeld Follies '46
Two Girls and a Sailor '44
The Man Who Came to Dinner '41
Melody Ranch '40
Little Miss Broadway '38
Hollywood Party '34
Palooka '34
The Lost Stooges '33
What! No Beer? '33
Speak Easily '32

Deanna Durbin (1921-)

For the Love of Mary '48
Up in Central Park '48
I'll Be Yours '47
Something in the Wind '47
Because of Him '45
Can't Help Singing '45
Lady on a Train '45
His Butler's Sister '44
The Amazing Mrs. Holiday '43
It Started with Eve '41
Nice Girl? '41
It's a Date '40
Spring Parade '40
First Love '39
Three Smart Girls Grow Up '39
Mad About Music '38
That Certain Age '38
100 Men and a Girl '37
Three Smart Girls '36

John Durbin

King of the Hill '93
No Way Back '90
Ain't No Way Back '89
Dr. Caligari '89
Tapeheads '89

Richard Durden

From Paris With Love '10
Pumpkinhead 4: Blood Feud '07
The First 9 1/2 Weeks '98

Minta Durfee (1889-1975)

Savage Intruder '68
Miracle Kid '42
Mickey '17

Anna Marie Duringer (1925-)

Veronika Voss '82
The Lacemaker '77

Romain Duris (1974-)

Afterwards '08
Moliere '07
Inside Paris '06
The Beat My Heart Skipped '05
Russian Dolls '05
Le Divorce '03
L'Auberge Espagnole '02
The Crazy Stranger '98
When the Cat's Away '96

Charles Durning (1933-)

Break '09
Deal '08
The Golden Boys '08
iMurders '08
Forget About It '06
Local Color '06
Miracle Dogs Too '06
River's End '05
A Boyfriend for Christmas '04
One Last Ride '03
Mr. St. Nick '02
L.A.P.D.: To Protect and Serve '01
Hostage Hotel '00
Lakeboat '00
O Brother Where Art Thou? '00

State and Main '00
Backlash '99
Hi-Life '98
Jerry and Tom '98
Shelter '98
The Last Supper '96
Mrs. Santa Claus '96
One Fine Day '96
Spy Hard '96
The Grass Harp '95
Home for the Holidays '95
The Kennedys of Massachusetts '95
A Woman of Independent Means '94
The Hudsucker Proxy '93
The Music of Chance '93
The Story Lady '93
When a Stranger Calls Back '93
The Water Engine '92
The Return of Eliot Ness '91
V.I. Warshawski '91
Cat Chaser '90
Dick Tracy '90
Dinner at Eight '89
Project: Alien '89
Cop '88
Far North '88
Happy New Year '87
Kenny Rogers as the Gambler, Part 3: The Legend Continues '87
The Man Who Broke 1,000 Chains '87
The Rosary Murders '87
A Tiger's Tale '87
Big Trouble '86
Brenda Starr '86
Death of a Salesman '86
The Legend of Sleepy Hollow '86
Solarbabies '86
Tough Guys '86
Where the River Runs Black '86
The Man with One Red Shoe '85
Stand Alone '85
Stick '85
Hadley's Rebellion '84
Mass Appeal '84
To Be or Not to Be '83
Two of a Kind '83
The Best Little Whorehouse in Texas '82
Tootsie '82
The Best Little Girl in the World '81
Dark Night of the Scarecrow '81
Sharky's Machine '81
True Confessions '81
Attica '80
Crisis at Central High '80
Die Laughing '80
The Final Countdown '80
The Muppet Movie '79
North Dallas Forty '79
When a Stranger Calls '79
The Fury '78
Special Olympics '78
Tilt '78
The Choirboys '77
An Enemy of the People '77
Twilight's Last Gleaming '77
Breakheart Pass '76
Harry & Walter Go to New York '76
Dog Day Afternoon '75
The Hindenburg '75
Queen of the Stardust Ballroom '75
The Front Page '74
The Connection '73
Sisters '73
The Sting '73
I Walk the Line '70

Dick Durock (1938-)

The Return of Swamp Thing '89
Swamp Thing '82
The Enforcer '76

Jason Durr (1968-)

Killer Tongue '96
Sharpe's Battle '94
A Dark Adapted Eye '93

Michael Durrell (1943-)

Magma: Volcanic Disaster '06
Illegal in Blue '95
Family Sins '87
V '83

Fred Durst (1970-)

Population 436 '06
Sorry, Haters '05

Ian Dury (1942-2000)

The Crow 2: City of Angels '96
Split Second '92
The Raggedy Rawney '90

Dan Duryea (1907-68)

The Bamboo Saucer '68
Five Golden Dragons '67
The Flight of the Phoenix '65
Platinum High School '60
Battle Hymn '57
Night Passage '57
Ride Clear of Diablo '54
Silver Lode '54
Terror Street '54
Thunder Bay '53
The Underworld Story '50
Winchester '73 '50
Too Late for Tears '49
Criss Cross '48
Black Angel '46
Along Came Jones '45
Great Flamarion '45
Lady on a Train '45
Scarlet Street '45
The Valley of Decision '45
Ministry of Fear '44
None But the Lonely Heart '44
Woman in the Window '44
Sahara '43
The Pride of the Yankees '42
Ball of Fire '41
The Little Foxes '41

George Duryea

See Tom Keene

Marj Dusay (1936-)

Love Walked In '97
Made in Heaven '87
Pendulum '69
Sweet November '68

Vittorio Duse

Queen of Hearts '89
Mad Dog Killer '77

Jaroslav Dusek (1961-)

Up and Down '04
Divided We Fall '00

Ann Dusenberry (1953-)

Basic Training '86
Long Time Gone '86
The Men's Club '86
Lies '83
Cutter's Way '81
Killjoy '81
Heart Beat '80
Desperate Women '78
Little Women '78
The Possessed '77

Eliza Dushku (1980-)

The Alphabet Killer '08
Bottle Shock '08
Nobel Son '08
Sex and Breakfast '07
Wrong Turn '03
City by the Sea '02
The New Guy '02
Jay and Silent Bob Strike Back '01
Soul Survivors '01
Bring It On '00
Race the Sun '96
Journey '95
Bye Bye, Love '94
True Lies '94
That Night '93
This Boy's Life '93

Nancy Dussault (1936-)

The Nurse '97
The In-Laws '79

Marta Dusseldorp (1973-)

After the Deluge '03
Innocence '00

Andre Dussollier (1946-)

Micmacs '09
Private Fears in Public Places '06
Tell No One '06
Lemming '05
A Very Long Engagement '04
Amelie '01 (N)
Same Old Song '97
Colonel Chabert '94
Un Coeur en Hiver '93
Sand and Blood '87
Melo '86
Three Men and a Cradle '85
Love Unto Death '84
Life Is a Bed of Roses '83
Le Beau Mariage '82
Perceval '78
And Now My Love '74

Jacques Dutronc (1943-)

Merci pour le Chocolat '00
Place Vendome '98
Van Gogh '92
Tricheurs '84
Every Man for Himself '79
L'Etat Sauvage '78

Charles S. Dutton (1951-)

Legion '10
Fame '09
The Express '08
The Bronx Is Burning '07
Honeydripper '07
Against the Ropes '04
Secret Window '04
Gothika '03
Conviction '02
Eye See You '01
Deadlocked '00
For Love or Country: The Arturo Sandoval Story '00
Aftershock: Earthquake in New York '99
Cookie's Fortune '99
Random Hearts '99
The '60s '99
Black Dog '98
Blind Faith '98
Mimic '97
True Women '97
Get On the Bus '96
A Time to Kill '96
Cry, the Beloved Country '95
Nick of Time '95
Zooman '95
Foreign Student '94
A Low Down Dirty Shame '94
The Piano Lesson '94
Surviving the Game '94
Menace II Society '93
Rudy '93
Alien 3 '92
The Distinguished Gentleman '92
Mississippi Masala '92
Q & A '90
Jacknife '89
An Unremarkable Life '89
Crocodile Dundee 2 '88
The Murder of Mary Phagan '87
Cat's Eye '85

Tim Dutton (1964-)

The Bourne Identity '02
Oliver Twist '00
Darkness Falls '98
Frenchman's Creek '98
Hard to Forget '98
St. Ives '98
Melissa '97
Rhodes '97
Tom & Viv '94

Daniel Duval (1944-)

District 13: Ultimatum '09
Grocer's Son '07
Time to Leave '05
Time of the Wolf '03

Will It Snow for Christmas? '96

Diane Duval

See Julie Bishop

James Duval (1973-)

The Art of Travel '08
The Pacific and Eddy '07
Mad Cowgirl '06
Roman '06
Chasing Ghosts '05
Window Theory '04
Players '03
Comic Book Villains '02
May '02
The Doe Boy '01
Donnie Darko '01
Gone in 60 Seconds '00
The Weekend '00
Go '99
SLC Punk! '99
A River Made to Drown In '97
Independence Day '96
Nowhere '96
The Doom Generation '95
Totally F***ed Up '94

Josey Duval

New York's Finest '87
Sex, Drugs, and Rock-n-Roll '84

Maria Duval (1939-)

Samson vs. the Vampire Women '61
The Living Coffin '58

Clea DuVall (1977-)

The Killing Room '09
Passengers '08
Anamorph '07
Two Weeks '06
The Grudge '04
Identity '03
21 Grams '03
How to Make a Monster '01
John Carpenter's Ghosts of Mars '01
The Slaughter Rule '01
Thirteen Conversations About One Thing '01
The Astronaut's Wife '99
But I'm a Cheerleader '99
Committed '99
Girl, Interrupted '99
She's All That '99
Wildflowers '99
The Faculty '98
The Defenders: Payback '97

Robert Duvall (1931-)

Crazy Heart '09
Get Low '09
The Road '09
Four Christmases '08
Lucky You '07
We Own the Night '07
Broken Trail '06
Thank You for Smoking '06
Kicking & Screaming '05
Assassination Tango '03
Gods and Generals '03
Open Range '03
Secondhand Lions '03
John Q '02
Gone in 60 Seconds '00
A Shot at Glory '00
The 6th Day '00
A Civil Action '98
Deep Impact '98
The Apostle '97
The Gingerbread Man '97
A Family Thing '96
The Man Who Captured Eichmann '96
Phenomenon '96
Sling Blade '96
The Scarlet Letter '95
Something to Talk About '95
The Paper '94
The Stars Fell on Henrietta '94
Falling Down '93
Geronimo: An American Legend '93
Wrestling Ernest Hemingway '93
Newsies '92
The Plague '92

Stalin '92
Hearts of Darkness: A Filmmaker's Apocalypse '91
Rambling Rose '91
Days of Thunder '90
The Handmaid's Tale '90
A Show of Force '90
Lonesome Dove '89
Colors '88
Hotel Colonial '88
Let's Get Harry '87
Belizaire the Cajun '86
The Lightship '86
The Natural '84
The Stone Boy '84
Tender Mercies '83
The Terry Fox Story '83
The Godfather 1902-1959: The Complete Epic '81
The Pursuit of D.B. Cooper '81
True Confessions '81
The Great Santini '80
Apocalypse Now '79
Ike '79
The Betsy '78
Invasion of the Body Snatchers '78
The Eagle Has Landed '77
The Greatest '77
Network '76
The Seven-Per-Cent Solution '76
Breakout '75
The Killer Elite '75
The Conversation '74
The Godfather, Part 2 '74
Badge 373 '73
Lady Ice '73
The Godfather '72
The Great Northfield Minnesota Raid '72
Joe Kidd '72
Tomorrow '72
Lawman '71
THX 1138 '71
M*A*S*H '70
The Rain People '69
True Grit '69
Bullitt '68
Countdown '68
The Detective '68
The Chase '66
Captain Newman, M.D. '63
To Kill a Mockingbird '62

Shelley Duvall (1949-)

The 4th Floor '99
Russell Mulcahy's Tale of the Mummy '99
Boltneck '98
Home Fries '98
My Teacher Ate My Homework '98
Horton Foote's Alone '97
The Twilight of the Ice Nymphs '97
Changing Habits '96
Portrait of a Lady '96
The Underneath '95
Suburban Commando '91
Mother Goose Rock 'n' Rhyme '90
Roxanne '87
Frankenweenie '84
Rapunzel '82
Rumpelstiltskin '82
Time Bandits '81
Popeye '80
The Shining '80
Annie Hall '77
3 Women '77
Nashville '75
Thieves Like Us '74
McCabe & Mrs. Miller '71
Brewster McCloud '70

Wayne Duvall (1958-)

Duplicity '09
Leatherheads '08
Pride and Glory '08
Killing Emmett Young '02
A Better Way to Die '00
O Brother Where Art Thou? '00
Hard Rain '97
Warlords 3000 '93
Final Approach '91

Janine Duvitsky (1952-)

Grown Ups '80
Dracula '79

Pierre Dux (1908-90)

La Lectrice '88
La Vie Continue '82
The Day and the Hour '63
Les Grandes Manoeuvres '55
Monsieur Vincent '47

Ann Dvorak (1912-79)

I Was an American Spy '51
A Life of Her Own '50
Our Very Own '50
Return of Jesse James '50
The Long Night '47
Out of the Blue '47
The Private Affairs of Bel Ami '47
Abilene Town '46
Flame of the Barbary Coast '45
Manhattan Merry-Go-Round '37
"G" Men '35
Massacre '34
The Strange Love of Molly Louvain '32
Three on a Match '32
The Guardsman '31
Scarface '31

Peter Dvorsky

Mesmer '94
The Kiss '88
Videodrome '83

Dorothy Dwan (1906-81)

The Fighting Legion '30
The Peacock Fan '29
Great K & A Train Robbery '26
The Perfect Clown '25
The Wizard of Oz '25

Earl Dwire (1883-1940)

Purple Vigilantes '38
Lightning Bill Crandall '37
Riding On '37
Trouble in Texas '37
Cavalcade of the West '36
Pinto Rustlers '36
Stormy Trails '36
Assassin of Youth '35
Between Men '35
Big Calibre '35
Lawless Frontier '35
Lawless Range '35
Pecos Kid '35
Rider of the Law '35
Saddle Aces '35
Toll of the Desert '35
Unconquered Bandit '35
Wagon Trail '35
The Star Packer '34
Tombstone Terror '34

Bill Dwyer

Little Shots of Happiness '97
Ski School 2 '94

Hilary Dwyer (1935-)

Cry of the Banshee '70
Wuthering Heights '70
The Oblong Box '69
The Conqueror Worm '68

Leslie Dwyer (1906-86)

Die, Monster, Die! '65
Black Tide '58
Where There's a Will '55
Roadhouse Girl '53
Immortal Battalion '44

Franklin Dyall (1874-1950)

The Private Life of Henry VIII '33
Easy Virtue '27

Valentine Dyall (1908-85)

The Body in the Library '84
The Haunting '63
Horror Hotel '60
Suspended Alibi '56
The Golden Salamander '51

Room to Let *'49*
The Ghost of Rashmon Hall *'47*
Brief Encounter *'46*
Frenzy *'46*
Pink String and Sealing Wax *'45*
Henry V *'44*
Hotel Reserve *'44*

Cameron Dye (1967-)
The Tavern *'00*
The Apocalypse *'96*
Out of the Dark *'88*
Heated Vengeance *'87*
Scenes from the Goldmine *'87*
Stranded *'87*
Fraternity Vacation *'85*
Body Rock *'84*
Joy of Sex *'84*
The Last Starfighter *'84*
Valley Girl *'83*

Dale Dye (1944-)
The Great Raid *'05*
44 Minutes: The North Hollywood Shootout *'03*
Missing Brendan *'03*
Band of Brothers *'01*
Rules of Engagement *'00*
Saving Private Ryan *'98*
Operation Delta Force 2: Mayday *'97*
Rough Riders *'97*
Starship Troopers *'97*
Mission: Impossible *'96*
Trial and Error *'96*
Within the Rock *'96*
Sgt. Bilko *'95*
Under Siege 2: Dark Territory *'95*
Endangered *'94*
Guarding Tess *'94*
Natural Born Killers *'94*
Outbreak *'94*
The Puppet Masters *'94*
Uncivilized *'94*
Heaven and Earth *'93*
Sniper *'92*
Under Siege *'92*
Blue Sky *'91*
JFK *'91*
Relentless 2: Dead On *'91*
Servants of Twilight *'91*
The Court Martial of Jackie Robinson *'90*
Fire Birds *'90*
The Fourth War *'90*
Kid *'90*
Always *'89*
Born on the Fourth of July *'89*
Casualties of War *'89*
Spontaneous Combustion *'89*
Billionaire Boys Club *'87*
Invaders from Mars *'86*
Platoon *'86*

John Dye (1963-)
Heart of the Beholder *'05*
Best of the Best *'89*
Campus Man *'87*

Danny Dyer (1977-)
Closure *'07*
Outlaw *'07*
The Other Half *'06*
Severance *'06*
The Business *'05*
High Heels and Low Lifes *'01*
Mean Machine *'01*
Borstal Boy *'00*
Greenfingers *'00*
Human Traffic *'99*
The Trench *'99*

Karen Dyer
Corrupt *'99*
Urban Menace *'99*

William J. Dyer
Desert of the Lost *'27*
All Night *'18*

Russell Dykstra
Introducing the Dwights *'07*
Romulus, My Father *'07*
Criminal Ways *'03*
Garage Days *'03*
Ned Kelly *'03*
Soft Fruit *'99*

Matthew Dyktynski
Japanese Story *'03*
Heaven's Burning *'97*
Road to Nhill *'97*
Love and Other Catastrophes *'95*

Bob Dylan (1941-)
Masked and Anonymous *'03*
Backtrack *'89*
Hearts of Fire *'87*
Pat Garrett & Billy the Kid *'73*

Louise Dylan
Emma *'09*
Vampire Killers *'09*

Peter Dyneley (1921-77)
Soul Patrol *'80*
The Manster *'59*
Strange Awakening *'58*
Beau Brummel *'54*

Richard Dysart (1929-)
Hard Rain *'97*
Todd McFarlane's Spawn *'97 (V)*
Panther *'95*
Truman *'95*
Marilyn & Bobby: Her Final Affair *'94*
Back to the Future, Part 3 *'90*
Day One *'89*
Wall Street *'87*
L.A. Law *'86*
The Last Days of Patton *'86*
The Rumor Mill *'86*
The Falcon and the Snowman *'85*
Mask *'85*
Pale Rider *'85*
Warning Sign *'85*
The Thing *'82*
Bitter Harvest *'81*
Churchill and the Generals *'81*
The People vs. Jean Harris *'81*
Bogie: The Last Hero *'80*
The Ordeal of Dr. Mudd *'80*
Being There *'79*
Meteor *'79*
Prophecy *'79*
An Enemy of the People *'77*
Riding with Death *'76*
The Day of the Locust *'75*
The Hindenburg *'75*
The Autobiography of Miss Jane Pittman *'74*
The Terminal Man *'74*
The Hospital *'71*
The Lost Man *'69*
Petulia *'68*

Richard Dyszel (1947-)
Night Beast *'83*
The Alien Factor *'78*

Alexis Dziena (1984-)
When in Rome *'09*
Fool's Gold *'08*
Nick & Norah's Infinite Playlist *'08*
Tenderness *'08*
Sex and Breakfast *'07*
Broken Flowers *'05*
Pizza *'05*
Mimic 3: Sentinel *'03*

George Dzundza (1945-)
National Lampoon's Adam & Eve *'05*
City by the Sea *'02*
Above Suspicion *'00*
Instinct *'99*
Species 2 *'98*
Trading Favors *'97*
The Limbic Region *'96*
That Darn Cat *'96*
Crimson Tide *'95*
Dangerous Minds *'95*
The Enemy Within *'94*
Basic Instinct *'92*
The Butcher's Wife *'91*
Impulse *'90*
White Hunter, Black Heart *'90*
The Beast *'88*
Glory Years *'87*
No Way Out *'87*
No Mercy *'86*
Broken Badge *'85*
Brotherly Love *'85*
Best Defense *'84*
Act of Passion: The Lost Honor of Kathryn Beck *'83*
Streamers *'83*
A Long Way Home *'81*
The Deer Hunter *'78*
Loose in New York *'74*

Sheila E (1957-)
The Adventures of Ford Fairlane *'90*
Krush Groove *'85*

Nicholas Eadie (1958-)
Celia: Child of Terror *'89*
Return to Snowy River *'88*

Angela Eads
Things 2 *'97*
Dead Girls *'90*

George Eads (1967-)
Monte Walsh *'03*
The Spring *'00*

James Eagles (1907-59)
Heroes of the Hills *'38*
The Painted Trail *'38*
Racing Blood *'36*
Sunset Range *'35*

Mitch Eakins
Tunnel Rats *'08*
Boxboarders! *'07*

Michael Ealy (1973-)
Takers *'10*
Miracle at St. Anna *'08*
Seven Pounds *'08*
November *'05*
Sleeper Cell *'05*
Barbershop 2: Back in Business *'04*
Never Die Alone *'04*
2 Fast 2 Furious *'03*
Barbershop *'02*

Edward Earle (1882-1972)
Command Decision *'48*
I Accuse My Parents *'45*
Bordertown Gunfighters *'43*
California Joe *'43*
The Duke of West Point *'38*
The Revenge Rider *'35*
Ticket to a Crime *'34*
Spite Marriage *'29*
The Wind *'28*

Harry Earles (1902-85)
Freaks *'32*
The Unholy Three *'30*
The Unholy Three *'25*

Jason Earles (1977-)
Hannah Montana: The Movie *'09*
Space Buddies *'08 (V)*
American Pie Presents Band Camp *'05*

Bo Eason
Tornado! *'96*
Miami Rhapsody *'95*

Carlos East (1942-94)
Fantastic Balloon Voyage *'76*
Fearmaker *'71*
The Fear Chamber *'68*
The Snake People *'68*

Jeff East (1957-)
Another Chance *'88*
Pumpkinhead *'88*
Deadly Blessing *'81*
Mary and Joseph: A Story of Faith *'79*
Summer of Fear *'78*
The Campus Corpse *'77*
Flight of the Grey Wolf *'76*
Huckleberry Finn *'74*
Tom Sawyer *'73*

Leslie Easterbrook (1951-)
Retribution Road *'07*
A Dead Calling *'06*
The Devil's Rejects *'05*
The Biggest Fan *'02*
Police Academy 7: Mission to Moscow *'94*
Police Academy 6: City under Siege *'89*
Police Academy 5: Assignment Miami Beach *'88*
The Taking of Flight 847: The Uli Derickson Story *'88*
Police Academy 3: Back in Training *'86*
Police Academy *'84*
Private Resort *'84*

Steve Eastin
When a Stranger Calls *'06*
A Man Apart *'03*
Matchstick Men *'03*
Catch Me If You Can *'02*
Agent Red *'00*
Peril *'00*
Stealth Fighter *'99*
Little Bigfoot 2: The Journey Home *'97*
Last Man Standing *'95*

Todd Eastland
Mommy 2: Mommy's Day *'96*
Pledge Night *'90*

George Eastman (1854-1932)
Hands of Steel *'86*
After the Fall of New York *'85*
Blastfighter *'85*
Detective School Dropouts *'85*
Ironmaster *'82*
Grim Reaper *'81*
Bloody Avenger *'80*
Belle Starr *'79*
Kiss Me, Kill Me *'73*
Call of the Wild *'72*

Rodney Eastman (1967-)
The Caveman's Valentine *'01*
Sand *'00*
Blue Ridge Fall *'99*
Beverly Hills Bodysnatchers *'89*
Deadly Weapon *'88*
A Nightmare on Elm Street 4: Dream Master *'88*
A Nightmare on Elm Street 3: Dream Warriors *'87*

Michael Easton (1967-)
The '70s *'00*
Murder at Devil's Glen *'99*
Total Recall 2070: Machine Dreams *'99*

Richard Easton (1933-)
Revolutionary Road *'08*
Pizza *'05*
Dead Again *'91*
Henry V *'89*
The Red Badge of Courage *'51*

Robert Easton (1930-)
Just One Night *'00*
Working Girl *'88*
The Giant Spider Invasion *'75*
Heavy Traffic *'73*
Johnny Got His Gun *'71*
When Hell Broke Loose *'58*
Belles on Their Toes *'52*

Sam Easton
Decoys: The Second Seduction *'07*
Final Destination 3 *'06*

Sheena Easton (1959-)
All Dogs Go to Heaven 2 *'95 (V)*
Body Bags *'93*
Indecent Proposal *'93*

Alison Eastwood (1972-)
One Long Night *'07*
How to Go Out on a Date in Queens *'06*
Don't Tell *'05*
The Lost Angel *'04*
Poolhall Junkies *'02*
Power Play *'02*
If You Only Knew *'00*
The Spring *'00*
Black & White *'99*
Friends & Lovers *'99*
Just a Little Harmless Sex *'99*
Breakfast of Champions *'98*
Midnight in the Garden of Good and Evil *'97*
Tightrope *'84*

Clint Eastwood (1930-)
Gran Torino *'08*
Million Dollar Baby *'04*
Blood Work *'02*
Space Cowboys *'00*
True Crime *'99*
Absolute Power *'97*
The Bridges of Madison County *'95*
Casper *'95*
In the Line of Fire *'93*
A Perfect World *'93*
Unforgiven *'92*
The Rookie *'90*
White Hunter, Black Heart *'90*
Pink Cadillac *'89*
The Dead Pool *'88*
Heartbreak Ridge *'86*
Pale Rider *'85*
City Heat *'84*
Tightrope *'84*
Sudden Impact *'83*
Firefox *'82*
Honkytonk Man *'82*
Any Which Way You Can *'80*
Bronco Billy *'80*
Escape from Alcatraz *'79*
Every Which Way But Loose *'78*
The Gauntlet *'77*
The Enforcer *'76*
The Outlaw Josey Wales *'76*
The Eiger Sanction *'75*
Thunderbolt & Lightfoot *'74*
High Plains Drifter *'73*
Magnum Force *'73*
Joe Kidd *'72*
Dirty Harry *'71*
Play Misty for Me *'71*
The Beguiled *'70*
Kelly's Heroes *'70*
Two Mules for Sister Sara *'70*
Paint Your Wagon *'69*
Coogan's Bluff *'68*
Where Eagles Dare *'68*
The Good, the Bad and the Ugly *'67*
Hang 'Em High *'67*
For a Few Dollars More *'65*
A Fistful of Dollars *'64*
Lafayette Escadrille *'58*
Escapade in Japan *'57*
Away All Boats *'56*
Francis in the Navy *'55*
Revenge of the Creature *'55*
Tarantula *'55*

Jayne (Jane) Eastwood (1946-)
Real Time *'08*
You Kill Me *'07*
Wedding Wars *'06*
Dawn of the Dead *'04*
Life with Judy Garland—Me and My Shadows *'01*
That Old Feeling *'96*
Hostile Takeover *'88*
Kidnapping of Baby John Doe *'88*
Night Friend *'87*
My Pleasure Is My Business *'74*

Kyle Eastwood (1968-)
Honkytonk Man *'82*
The Outlaw Josey Wales *'76*

Marjorie Eaton (1901-86)
Street Music *'81*
The Attic *'80*
The Atomic Brain *'64*
Night Tide *'63*

Mary Eaton (1901-48)
Glorifying the American Girl *'30*
The Cocoanuts *'29*

Roberta Eaton
The Crude Oasis *'95*
Split Second *'92*

Shirley Eaton (1936-)
Kiss and Kill *'68*
Eight on the Lam *'67*
Around the World Under the Sea *'65*
Goldfinger *'64*
Girl Hunters *'63*
What a Carve-Up! *'62*
Carry On Constable *'60*
Carry On Nurse *'59*
Carry On Sergeant *'58*
The Naked Truth *'58*
Doctor at Large *'57*
Three Men in a Boat *'56*
Doctor in the House *'53*

Wallace (Wallas) Eaton (1917-95)
Plunge Into Darkness *'77*
Isadora *'68*

John Eaves
Skier's Dream *'88*
Fire and Ice *'87*

Al Eben (1915-2003)
Korea Patrol *'47*
White Pongo *'45*

Luke Eberl (1986-)
A Painted House *'03*
Planet of the Apes *'01*

Christine Ebersole (1953-)
Confessions of a Shopaholic *'09*
Double Platinum *'99*
True Crime *'99*
My Favorite Martian *'98*
An Unexpected Life *'97*
Black Sheep *'96*
Til There Was You *'96*
An Unexpected Family *'96*
Pie in the Sky *'95*
My Girl 2 *'94*
Richie Rich *'94*
Gypsy *'93*
Folks! *'92*
Dead Again *'91*
Ghost Dad *'90*
Mac and Me *'88*
Acceptable Risks *'86*
Amadeus *'84*
Thief of Hearts *'84*
Tootsie *'82*

Eriq Ebouaney
Disgrace *'08*
The Front Line *'06*
The Nativity Story *'06*
Cape of Good Hope *'04*
Femme Fatale *'02*
Lumumba *'01*

Buddy Ebsen (1908-2003)
The Beverly Hillbillies *'93*
Stone Fox *'87*
The Return of the Beverly Hillbillies *'81*
The Bastard *'78*
The Adventures of Tom Sawyer *'73*
The President's Plane Is Missing *'71*
The Andersonville Trial *'70*
The One and Only, Genuine, Original Family Band *'68*
Mail Order Bride *'63*
The Interns *'62*

Breakfast at Tiffany's *'61*
Attack! *'56*
Between Heaven and Hell *'56*
Davy Crockett and the River Pirates *'56*
Davy Crockett, King of the Wild Frontier *'55*
Red Garters *'54*
Rodeo King and the Senorita *'51*
Silver City Bonanza *'51*
Thunder in God's Country *'51*
Sing Your Worries Away *'42*
Girl of the Golden West *'38*
My Lucky Star *'38*
Broadway Melody of 1938 *'37*
Born to Dance *'36*
Captain January *'36*
Broadway Melody of 1936 *'35*

Maude Eburne (1875-1960)
The Boogie Man Will Get You *'42*
The Border Legion *'40*
Courageous Dr. Christian *'40*
Doughnuts & Society *'36*
Ruggles of Red Gap *'35*
Ladies They Talk About *'33*
Panama Flo *'32*
The Vampire Bat *'32*
The Guardsman *'31*

Aimee (Amy) Eccles (1949-)
Humanoid Defender *'85*
Lovelines *'84*
The Concrete Jungle *'82*
Group Marriage *'72*
Little Big Man *'70*

Christopher Eccleston (1964-)
Amelia *'09*
G.I. Joe: The Rise of Cobra *'09*
The Seeker: The Dark Is Rising *'07*
Perfect Parents *'06*
28 Days Later *'02*
Othello *'01*
The Others *'01*
Gone in 60 Seconds *'00*
Invisible Circus *'00*
eXistenZ *'99*
Heart *'99*
Elizabeth *'98*
A Price above Rubies *'97*
Jude *'96*
Cracker: To Be a Somebody *'94*
Shallow Grave *'94*
Let Him Have It *'91*

Alonso Echanove (1954-)
In the Middle of Nowhere *'93*
Vintage Model *'92*

Juan Echanove (1961-)
No News from God *'01*
The Flower of My Secret *'95*

Pablo Echarri
Chronicle of an Escape *'06*
Burnt Money *'00*

Emilio Echeverria
The Alamo *'04*
Die Another Day *'02*
Amores Perros *'00*

Guy Ecker (1959-)
Night Terror *'89*
Devil Wears White *'86*

Aaron Eckhart (1968-)
Love Happens *'09*
The Dark Knight *'08*
Meet Bill *'07*
No Reservations *'07*
Towelhead *'07*
The Black Dahlia *'06*
Thank You for Smoking *'06*
Conversations with Other Women *'05*
Suspect Zero *'04*
The Core *'03*
The Missing *'03*
Paycheck *'03*
Possession *'02*
Erin Brockovich *'00*
Nurse Betty *'00*
The Pledge *'00*
Any Given Sunday *'99*
Molly *'99*
Thursday *'98*
Your Friends & Neighbors *'98*
In the Company of Men *'96*

James Eckhouse (1955-)
Jimmy & Judy *'06*
One True Thing *'98*
Robin Cook's Terminal *'96*
Junior *'94*
Leaving Normal *'92*
The Christmas Wife *'88*
Blue Heaven *'84*

Billy Eckstine (1914-93)
Jo Jo Dancer, Your Life Is Calling *'86*
Skirts Ahoy! *'52*

Jean-Philippe Ecoffey (1959-)
Cold Showers *'05*
Wolves in the Snow *'02*
Ma Vie en Rose *'97*
Portraits Chinois *'96*
Fiesta *'95*
Mina Tannenbaum *'93*
The Possessed *'88*

Paul Eddington (1927-95)
The Camomile Lawn *'92*
The Devil Rides Out *'68*

Helen Jerome Eddy (1897-1990)
Klondike Annie *'36*
A Shot in the Dark *'35*
Frisco Jenny *'32*
The Divine Lady *'29*
The Country Kid *'23*
County Fair *'20*
Pollyanna *'20*
The Tong Man *'19*
Rebecca of Sunnybrook Farm *'17*

Nelson Eddy (1901-67)
Northwest Outpost *'47*
The Phantom of the Opera *'43*
I Married an Angel *'42*
The Chocolate Soldier *'41*
Bitter Sweet *'40*
New Moon *'40*
Balalaika *'39*
Let Freedom Ring *'39*
Girl of the Golden West *'38*
Rosalie *'38*
Sweethearts *'38*
Maytime *'37*
Rose Marie *'36*
Naughty Marietta *'35*
Dancing Lady *'33*

Alfred Edel (1932-93)
Terror 2000 *'92*
My Father Is Coming *'91*

Gregg Edelman (1958-)
Little Children *'06*
Green Card *'90*

Herb Edelman (1930-96)
Cracking Up *'83*
On the Right Track *'81*
Strike Force *'81*
A Cry for Love *'80*
Marathon *'80*
Goin' Coconuts *'78*
Special Olympics *'78*
Charge of the Model T's *'76*
The Yakuza *'75*
A Strange and Deadly Occurrence *'74*
The Way We Were *'73*
I Love You, Alice B. Toklas! *'68*
The Odd Couple *'68*
Barefoot in the Park *'67*

Lisa Edelstein (1966-)
Grilled *'06*
Say Uncle *'05*
Dean Koontz's Black River *'01*
Keeping the Faith *'00*
What Women Want *'00*

Barbara Eden (1934-)
Loco Love *'03*
A Very Brady Sequel *'96*
Lethal Charm *'90*
Chattanooga Choo Choo *'84*
Return of the Rebels *'81*
Harper Valley P.T.A. *'78*
The Amazing Dobermans *'76*
How to Break Up a Happy Divorce *'76*
The Stranger Within *'74*
The Woman Hunter *'72*
Quick, Let's Get Married *'71*
Ride the Wild Surf *'64*
The Brass Bottle *'63*
7 Faces of Dr. Lao *'63*
Five Weeks in a Balloon *'62*
The Wonderful World of the Brothers Grimm *'62*
Voyage to the Bottom of the Sea *'61*
Flaming Star *'60*
From the Terrace *'60*
Back from Eternity *'56*

Harry Eden (1990-)
Flashbacks of a Fool *'08*
Oliver Twist *'05*
Pure *'02*

Jerome (Jerry Stallion) Eden
The Defilers *'65*
Color Me Blood Red *'64*
2000 Maniacs *'64*
Blood Feast *'63*

Mark Eden (1928-)
The Crimson Cult *'68*
Doctor Zhivago *'65*
Seance on a Wet Afternoon *'64*
The L-Shaped Room *'62*

Richard Eden (1956-)
Whitewash: The Clarence Brandley Story *'02*
Undercover Angel *'99*
Public Enemies *'96*
Liberty & Bash *'90*

Robert Edeson (1868-1931)
King of Kings *'27*
Walking Back *'26*
Braveheart *'25*
The Prisoner of Zenda *'22*
On the Night Stage *'15*

George Edgely
Common Law Wife *'63*
Free, White, and 21 *'62*

Joel Edgerton (1974-)
$9.99 *'08 (V)*
Smokin' Aces *'07*
Whisper *'07*
Kinky Boots *'06*
Open Window *'06*
King Arthur *'04*
Ned Kelly *'03*
The Night We Called It a Day *'03*
The Hard Word *'02*
Erskinville Kings *'99*

Gigi Edgley
Newcastle *'08*
Showdown at Area 51 *'07*

Valerie Edmond (1969-)
Saving Grace *'00*
Love and Rage *'99*
One More Kiss *'99*
The Crow Road *'96*

Dartanyan Edmonds (1972-)
Deliver Us from Eva *'03*
Rangers *'00*
Ride *'98*

Elizabeth Edmonds
Experience Preferred... But Not Essential *'83*
Scrubbers *'82*

Louis Edmonds (1923-2001)
Next Year in Jerusalem *'98*
House of Dark Shadows *'70*

Adrian Edmondson
Miss Austen Regrets *'07*
Supergrass *'87*

Bobby Edner (1988-)
Welcome to Paradise *'07*
Spy Kids 3-D: Game Over *'03*
The Day the World Ended *'01*
The Trial of Old Drum *'00*

Beatie Edney (1962-)
In Your Dreams *'07*
Highlander: Endgame *'00*
The Tenant of Wildfell Hall *'96*
The Affair *'95*
In the Name of the Father *'93*
The Dark Angel *'91*
Mister Johnson *'91*
Diary of a Mad Old Man *'88*
Highlander *'86*

Richard Edson (1954-)
Columbus Day *'08*
The Kid and I *'05*
Frankenfish *'04*
Land of Plenty *'04*
Starsky & Hutch *'04*
Sunshine State *'02*
Time Code *'00*
The Million Dollar Hotel *'99*
Thick as Thieves *'99*
Double Tap *'98*
Lulu on the Bridge *'98*
This World, Then the Fireworks *'97*
Intimate Betrayal *'96*
An Occasional Hell *'96*
Scorpion Spring *'96*
Things I Never Told You *'96*
Wedding Bell Blues *'96*
The Winner *'96*
Bad Love *'95*
Destiny Turns on the Radio *'95*
Jury Duty *'95*
Strange Days *'95*
Attack of the 50 Ft. Woman *'93*
Joey Breaker *'93*
Love, Cheat & Steal *'93*
Posse *'93*
Super Mario Bros. *'93*
Jungle Fever *'91*
Do the Right Thing *'89*
Let It Ride *'89*
Eight Men Out *'88*
Tougher Than Leather *'88*
Good Morning, Vietnam *'87*
Ferris Bueller's Day Off *'86*
Howard the Duck *'86*
Platoon *'86*
Desperately Seeking Susan *'85*
Stranger than Paradise *'84*

Allan Edwall (1924-97)
The Sacrifice *'86*
Fanny and Alexander *'83*
Brothers Lionheart *'77*
The New Land *'73*
The Emigrants *'72*

Anthony Edwards (1962-)
Motherhood *'09*
The Forgotten *'04*
Thunderbirds *'04*
Northfork *'03*
Jackpot *'01*
Playing by Heart *'98*
In Cold Blood *'96*
Charlie's Ghost: The Secret of Coronado *'94*
The Client *'94*
Hometown Boy Makes Good *'93*
Delta Heat *'92*
Landslide *'92*
Pet Sematary 2 *'92*
El Diablo *'90*
Downtown *'89*
Hawks *'89*
How I Got into College *'89*
Miracle Mile *'89*
Mr. North *'88*
Revenge of the Nerds 2: Nerds in Paradise *'87*
Summer Heat *'87*
Top Gun *'86*
Going for the Gold: The Bill Johnson Story *'85*
Gotcha! *'85*
The Sure Thing *'85*
Revenge of the Nerds *'84*
Heart Like a Wheel *'83*
Fast Times at Ridgemont High *'82*

Barbara (Lee) Edwards (1960-)
House Party 3 *'94*
Another Chance *'88*
Malibu Express *'85*

Bill Edwards (1918-99)
War Lover *'62*
First Man into Space *'59*
Ladies of the Chorus *'49*

Blake Edwards (1922-)
Panhandle *'48*
Strangler of the Swamp *'46*

Bruce Edwards (1914-2002)
Federal Agents vs. Underworld, Inc. *'49*
The Black Widow *'47*
Queen of the Amazons *'47*
The Fallen Sparrow *'43*
Hitler: Dead or Alive *'43*
The Iron Major *'43*

Cliff Edwards (1895-1971)
Fun & Fancy Free *'47 (V)*
Sagebrush Law *'43*
Lawless Plainsmen *'42*
Dumbo *'41 (V)*
Power Dive *'41*
His Girl Friday *'40*
Pinocchio *'40 (V)*
Gone with the Wind *'39*
Girl of the Golden West *'38*
Saratoga *'37*
Red Salute *'35*
Dance Fools Dance *'31*
Laughing Sinners *'31*
Parlor, Bedroom and Bath *'31*
Sidewalks of New York *'31*
The Sin of Madelon Claudet *'31*
Doughboys *'30*

Cory Edwards
Hoodwinked Too! Hood vs. Evil *'10*
Hoodwinked *'05 (V)*

Dean Edwards
A New Wave *'07*
Tony n' Tina's Wedding *'07*

Edward Edwards
Jesse Stone: Death in Paradise *'06*
Noriega: God's Favorite *'00*

Gail Edwards
A Perfect Little Murder *'90*
Get Crazy *'83*

Glynn Edwards (1931-)
Get Carter *'71*
Zulu *'64*

Henry Edwards (1882-1952)
The Golden Salamander *'51*
Madeleine *'50*

Hilton Edwards (1903-82)
The Quare Fellow *'62*
Victim *'61*
Othello *'52*

James Edwards (1918-70)
Patton *'70*
The Manchurian Candidate *'62*
Pork Chop Hill *'59*
Men in War *'57*
The Killing *'56*
The Member of the Wedding *'52*
The Steel Helmet *'51*
Home of the Brave *'49*
The Set-Up *'49*

Jennifer Edwards (1959-)
Overexposed *'90*
All's Fair *'89*
Peter Gunn *'89*
Perfect Match *'88*
Sunset *'88*
That's Life! *'86*
The Man Who Loved Women *'83*
S.O.B. *'81*
Heidi *'67*

Jimmy Edwards
Three Men in a Boat *'56*
Innocents in Paris *'53*

Lance Edwards
A Woman, Her Men and Her Futon *'92*
Peacemaker *'90*

Luke Edwards (1980-)
Cheaters *'00*
Little Big League *'94*
Mother's Boys *'94*
Newsies *'92*
Guilty by Suspicion *'91*
The Wizard *'89*

Mark Edwards (1942-)
Tower of Evil *'72*
Blood from the Mummy's Tomb *'71*
The Boldest Job in the West *'71*

Megan Edwards
Tattoo, a Love Story *'02*
Poison Ivy 3: The New Seduction *'97*

Meredith Edwards (1917-99)
A Christmas Reunion *'93*
The Electronic Monster *'57*
Race for Life *'55*
The Gambler & the Lady *'52*
The Magnet *'50*

Penny Edwards (1928-98)
Heart of the Rockies *'51*
North of the Great Divide *'50*
Sunset in the West *'50*
Trail of Robin Hood *'50*

Ronnie Clair Edwards (1933-)
8 Seconds *'94*
A Day for Thanks on Walton's Mountain *'82*
Future Cop *'76*

Sam Edwards (1915-2004)
The Beatniks *'60*
Guns Don't Argue *'57*
Gang Busters *'55*
Twelve o'Clock High *'49*
Bambi *'42 (V)*

Snitz Edwards (1862-1937)
The Red Mill *'27*
April Fool *'26*
Battling Butler *'26*
The Cruise of the Jasper B *'26*
The Phantom of the Opera *'25*
Seven Chances *'25*
The Thief of Baghdad *'24*
Souls for Sale *'23*

Stacy Edwards (1965-)
Superbad *'07*
Joshua *'02*

Support Your Local Gunfighter *'71*
Rio Lobo *'70*
Over the Hill Gang *'69*
Support Your Local Sheriff *'69*
Firecreek *'68*
Never a Dull Moment *'68*
Once Upon a Time in the West *'68*
The Way West *'67*
The Rare Breed *'66*
Four for Texas *'63*
Pocketful of Miracles *'61*
The Girl in Lover's Lane *'60*
Gunfight at the O.K. Corral *'57*
Night Passage *'57*
Pardners *'56*
Artists and Models *'55*
Kiss Me Deadly *'55*
The Man from Laramie *'55*
Cattle Queen of Montana *'54*
Ride Clear of Diablo *'54*
The Moonlighter *'53*
Vera Cruz *'53*
The Bushwackers *'52*
Kansas City Confidential *'52*
Rancho Notorious *'52*
The Ring *'52*
High Lonesome *'50*
Rawhide *'50*
Ticket to Tomahawk *'50*
She Shoulda Said No *'49*

Idris Elba (1972-)

The Losers *'10*
Takers *'10*
Obsessed *'09*
The Unborn *'09*
The Human Contract *'08*
Prom Night *'08*
RocknRolla *'08*
American Gangster *'07*
Daddy's Little Girls *'07*
The Reaping *'07*
This Christmas *'07*
28 Weeks Later *'07*
The Gospel *'05*
Sometimes in April *'05*
Ultraviolet *'98*

Vincent Elbaz

The 4 Musketeers *'05*
Almost Peaceful *'02*

Dana Elcar (1927-2005)

Inside Out *'91*
Toughlove *'85*
All of Me *'84*
Code of Honor *'84*
Blue Skies Again *'83*
Forbidden Love *'82*
Help Wanted: Male *'82*
Condorman *'81*
The Nude Bomb *'80*
Missiles of October *'74*
Dying Room Only *'73*
The Sting *'73*
The Bravos *'72*
Fireball Forward *'72*
A Gunfight *'71*
Adam at 6 a.m. *'70*
Soldier Blue *'70*
The Learning Tree *'69*
The Fool Killer *'65*

Ron Eldard (1965-)

The Tenth Circle *'08*
Already Dead *'07*
Diggers *'06*
Freedomland *'06*
House of Sand and Fog *'03*
Ghost Ship *'02*
Just a Kiss *'02*
Black Hawk Down *'01*
Mystery, Alaska *'99*
The Runner *'99*
Deep Impact *'98*
Delivered *'98*
When Trumpets Fade *'98*
Bastard out of Carolina *'96*
The Last Supper *'96*
Sleepers *'96*
Sex and the Other Man *'95*
Scent of a Woman *'92*
Drop Dead Fred *'91*
True Love *'89*

Kevin Eldon (1960-)

Hot Fuzz *'07*
High Heels and Low Lifes *'01*

George Eldredge (1914-92)

An Annapolis Story *'55*
Hi-Jacked *'50*
Mom & Dad *'47*
Sonora Stagecoach *'44*
The Lone Star Trail *'43*
Sherlock Holmes and the Secret Weapon *'42*
Buzzy Rides the Range *'40*
Take Me Back to Oklahoma *'40*

John Eldredge (1904-61)

Loophole *'54*
Horror Island *'41*

Florence Eldridge (1901-88)

Inherit the Wind *'60*
Christopher Columbus *'49*
Mary of Scotland *'36*
Les Miserables *'35*

John Eldridge (1917-60)

I Married a Monster from Outer Space *'58*
Square Dance Jubilee *'51*
Seven Were Saved *'47*
Bad Men of the Border *'45*
Dangerous Passage *'44*
The Black Cat *'41*
Dangerous *'35*

Carmen Electra (1972-)

Disaster Movie *'08*
Meet the Spartans *'08*
Christmas in Wonderland *'07*
Epic Movie *'07*
Full of It *'07*
I Want Candy *'07*
Date Movie *'06*
Hot Tamale *'06*
Scary Movie 4 *'06*
Cheaper by the Dozen 2 *'05*
Dirty Love *'05*
Getting Played *'05*
Searching for Bobby D *'05*
Starsky & Hutch *'04*
My Boss's Daughter *'03*
Whacked! *'02*
Get Over It! *'01*
Perfume *'01*
Sol Goode *'01*
Scary Movie *'00*
The Mating Habits of the Earthbound Human *'99*
The Chosen One: Legend of the Raven *'98*
American Vampire *'97*

Karra Elejalde (1960-)

Timecrimes *'07*
Tierra *'95*
Running Out of Time *'94*

Erika Eleniak (1969-)

Lady Jayne Killer *'03*
Breakaway *'02*
He Sees You When You're Sleeping *'02*
Shakedown *'02*
The Opponent *'01*
Aftershock: Earthquake in New York *'99*
Final Voyage *'99*
Stealth Fighter *'99*
First Degree *'98*
Captive *'97*
Tales from the Crypt Presents Bordello of Blood *'96*
A Pyromaniac's Love Story *'95*
Chasers *'94*
Girl in the Cadillac *'94*
The Beverly Hillbillies *'93*
Under Siege *'92*
Broken Angel *'88*
E.T.: The Extra-Terrestrial *'82*

Sandor Eles (1936-2002)

And Soon the Darkness *'70*
The Evil of Frankenstein *'64*

Bodhi (Pine) Elfman (1969-)

Collateral *'04*
Coyote Waits *'03*
Gone in 60 Seconds *'00*
Keeping the Faith *'00*
Sand *'00*
The Mod Squad *'99*
The Pirates of Silicon Valley *'99*
Enemy of the State *'98*

Danny Elfman (1953-)

Tim Burton's Corpse Bride *'05 (V)*
The Nightmare Before Christmas *'93 (V)*
Forbidden Zone *'80*

Jenna Elfman (1971-)

Touched *'05*
Clifford's Really Big Movie *'04 (V)*
Looney Tunes: Back in Action *'03*
Town and Country *'01*
Keeping the Faith *'00*
EDtv *'99*
Can't Hardly Wait *'98*
Krippendorf's Tribe *'98*

Taina Elg (1930-)

Hercules in New York *'70*
The Bacchantes *'63*
Les Girls *'57*
Diane *'55*
The Prodigal *'55*

Nicholas Elia

The Shortcut *'09*
When a Man Falls in the Forest *'07*
White Noise *'05*

Alix Elias

Munchies *'87*
True Stories *'86*
Rock 'n' Roll High School *'79*
Citizens Band *'77*

Arie Elias (1921-)

Bonjour Monsieur Shlomi *'03*
James' Journey to Jerusalem *'03*

Carmen Elias

A Love to Keep *'07*
To Die (Or Not) *'99*
The Flower of My Secret *'95*

Hector Elias

Envy *'04*
Buddy Boy *'99*
Katherine *'75*

Christine Elise (1965-)

Route 30 *'08*
The Hit *'01*
Nowhere to Land *'00*
Escape from Mars *'99*
Boiling Point *'93*
Child's Play 2 *'90*

Kimberly Elise (1971-)

Gifted Hands: The Ben Carson Story *'09*
The Great Debaters *'07*
Pride *'07*
Diary of a Mad Black Woman *'05*
The Manchurian Candidate *'04*
Woman, Thou Art Loosed *'04*
John Q *'02*
Bojangles *'01*
Bait *'00*
The Loretta Claiborne Story *'00*
Beloved *'98*
Set It Off *'96*

Shannon Elizabeth (1973-)

Night of the Demons *'09*
Deal *'08*
The Kid and I *'05*
Cursed *'04*
Johnson Family Vacation *'04*
Love Actually *'03*
American Pie 2 *'01*
Jay and Silent Bob Strike Back *'01*
13 Ghosts *'01*
Tomcats *'01*
Scary Movie *'00*
Seamless *'00*
American Pie *'99*
Dish Dogs *'98*

Hector Elizondo (1936-)

Valentine's Day *'10*
Georgia Rule *'07*
Love in the Time of Cholera *'07*
Music Within *'07*
The Celestine Prophecy *'06*
I-See-You.Com *'06*
The Princess Diaries 2: Royal Engagement *'04*
Raising Helen *'04*
How High *'01*
The Princess Diaries *'01*
Tortilla Soup *'01*
Entropy *'99*
Runaway Bride *'99*
Safe House *'99*
The Other Sister *'98*
Dear God *'96*
Turbulence *'96*
Being Human *'94*
Beverly Hills Cop 3 *'94*
Exit to Eden *'94*
Getting Even with Dad *'94*
Perfect Alibi *'94*
Backstreet Justice *'93*
Chains of Gold *'92*
Samantha *'92*
Scott Turow's The Burden of Proof *'92*
There Goes the Neighborhood *'92*
Final Approach *'91*
Frankie and Johnny *'91*
Necessary Roughness *'91*
Forgotten Prisoners *'90*
Pretty Woman *'90*
Taking Care of Business *'90*
Leviathan *'89*
Courage *'86*
Nothing in Common *'86*
My Sweet Victim *'85*
Out of the Darkness *'85*
The Flamingo Kid *'84*
Private Resort *'84*
Young Doctors in Love *'82*
The Fan *'81*
American Gigolo *'79*
Cuba *'79*
The Dain Curse *'78*
Diary of the Dead *'76*
Report to the Commissioner *'74*
The Taking of Pelham One Two Three *'74*
Pocket Money *'72*
Born to Win *'71*
Valdez Is Coming *'71*

Ronit Elkabetz (1966-)

The Girl on the Train *'09*
The Band's Visit *'07*
Or (My Treasure) *'04*
Late Marriage *'01*

Jeremie Èlkaim

You'll Get Over It *'02*
Come Undone *'00*

Harry Ellerbe (1901-92)

The Fall of the House of Usher *'60*
Desk Set *'57*

Duke Ellington (1899-1974)

Anatomy of a Murder *'59*
Cabin in the Sky *'43*
Murder at the Vanities *'34*
Check & Double Check *'30*

Biff (Elliott) Elliot (1923-)

The Dark *'79*
The Hard Ride *'71*
Pork Chop Hill *'59*
House of Bamboo *'55*

Jane Elliot (1947-)

Zertigo Diamond Caper *'82*
Change of Habit *'69*

Ramblin' Jack Elliot (1931-)

Roadie *'80*
Honkytonk Nights *'78*

Shawn Elliot

Caught *'96*
Hurricane Streets *'96*

Alison Elliott (1970-)

The Assassination of Jesse James by the Coward Robert Ford *'07*
Griffin & Phoenix *'06*
The Song of the Lark *'01*
The Miracle Worker *'00*
The Eternal *'99*
The External *'99*
The Wings of the Dove *'97*
The Buccaneers *'95*
Indictment: The McMartin Trial *'95*
The Spitfire Grill *'95*
The Underneath *'95*
Wyatt Earp *'94*
Home Before Midnight *'84*

Beverley Elliott

We'll Meet Again *'02*
My Very Best Friend *'96*

Bob Elliott (1923-)

Cabin Boy *'94*
Quick Change *'90*
Vengeance *'80*

Chris Elliott (1960-)

Dance Flick *'09*
I'll Believe You *'07*
Pigs *'07*
Scary Movie 4 *'06*
Osmosis Jones *'01*
Scary Movie 2 *'01*
Nutty Professor 2: The Klumps *'00*
Snow Day *'00*
There's Something about Mary *'98*
Kingpin *'96*
Cabin Boy *'94*
CB4: The Movie *'93*
Groundhog Day *'93*
The Abyss *'89*
New York Stories *'89*
Manhunter *'86*

David Elliott

Ali *'01*
Pearl *'78*
The Possession of Joel Delaney *'72*

David James Elliott (1960-)

Dodson's Journey *'01*
Clockwatchers *'97*
Holiday Affair *'96*
Degree of Guilt *'95*
JAG *'95*
Lethal Charm *'90*

Denholm Elliott (1922-92)

Catherine Cookson's The Black Candle *'92*
Noises Off *'92*
Scorchers *'92*
Codename Kyril *'91*
One Against the Wind *'91*
Toy Soldiers *'91*
A Murder of Quality *'90*
Indiana Jones and the Last Crusade *'89*
The Bourne Identity *'88*
Deep Cover *'88*
Hanna's War *'88*
September *'88*
Stealing Heaven *'88*
Maurice *'87*
Over Indulgence *'87*
Hotel du Lac *'86*
A Room with a View *'86*
The Whoopee Boys *'86*
Bleak House *'85*
Defense of the Realm *'85*
Transmutations *'85*
A Private Function *'84*
The Razor's Edge *'84*
The Hound of the Baskervilles *'83*
Trading Places *'83*
The Wicked Lady *'83*
Brimstone & Treacle *'82*
The Missionary *'82*
The Two Faces of Evil *'82*
Raiders of the Lost Ark *'81*
Rude Awakening *'81*
Cuba *'79*
Saint Jack *'79*
Zulu Dawn *'79*
The Boys from Brazil *'78*
Watership Down *'78 (V)*
A Bridge Too Far *'77*
The Hound of the Baskervilles *'77*
Orde Wingate *'76*
Robin and Marian *'76*
To the Devil, a Daughter *'76*
Voyage of the Damned *'76*
Russian Roulette *'75*
The Apprenticeship of Duddy Kravitz *'74*
It's Not the Size That Counts *'74*
A Doll's House *'73*
Vault of Horror *'73*
The House that Dripped Blood *'71*
Quest for Love *'71*
Too Late the Hero *'70*
The Night They Raided Minsky's *'69*
Dr. Jekyll and Mr. Hyde *'68*
Strange Case of Dr. Jekyll & Mr. Hyde *'68*
Alfie *'66*
Holy Terror *'65*
King Rat *'65*
The Leather Boys *'63*
The Cruel Sea *'53*
The Sound Barrier *'52*

Edythe Elliott (1888-1978)

Homesteaders of Paradise Valley *'47*
Santa Fe Uprising *'46*
The Great Mike *'44*

John Elliott

Rio Grande Ranger *'37*
Single Handed Sanders *'32*

John Elliott (1876-1956)

The Wizard of Gore *'70*
Law of the Saddle *'43*
Two-Fisted Justice *'43*
Rock River Renegades *'42*
Saddle Mountain Roundup *'41*
Death Rides the Range *'40*
Phantom Rancher *'39*
The Phantom of the Range *'38*
Riding On *'37*
A Face in the Fog *'36*
Rogue's Tavern *'36*
Big Calibre *'35*
Bulldog Courage *'35*
Danger Trails *'35*
The Midnight Phantom *'35*
Rider of the Law *'35*
Saddle Aces *'35*
Sunset Range *'35*
Toll of the Desert *'35*
Trails of the Wild *'35*
Unconquered Bandit *'35*
The Gallant Fool *'33*
Riders of the Desert *'32*
Mother and Son *'31*
Two Fisted Justice *'31*

Peter Elliott (1913-75)

Missing Link *'88*
Curse of the Demon *'57*

Peter Anthony Elliott

Vanilla Gorilla *'09*
Maiden Voyage: Ocean Hijack *'04*
Pre-Madonnas: Rebels Without a Clue *'95*

Flower & Snake '04
Azumi '03
The Happiness of the Katakuris '01
Visitor Q '01

Lena Endre (1955-)
Faithless '00
Jerusalem '96
Sunday's Children '94
The Best Intentions '92
The Visitors '89

Georgia Engel (1948-)
Open Season '06 (V)
Signs of Life '89
The Day the Women Got Even '80
The Outside Man '73

Tina Engel (1950-)
The Promise '94
The Boat Is Full '81
The Second Awakening of Christa Klages '78

Constanze Engelbrecht (1955-2000)
The Count of Monte Cristo '99
Fiorile '93

Wera Engels (1909-88)
Hong Kong Nights '35
Fugitive Road '34

Audie England (1971-)
Free Enterprise '98
Legion '98
A Place Called Truth '98
Shame, Shame, Shame '98
Red Shoe Diaries 8: Night of Abandon '97
Delta of Venus '95
Miami Hustle '95
Venus Rising '95

Randall England
Asylum of the Damned '03
Dream Machine '91

Sue England
Teenage Crime Wave '55
Kidnapped '48

Bradford English
Sweet Nothing in My Ear '08
Halloween 6: The Curse of Michael Myers '95
Sex, Love and Cold Hard Cash '93
Capone '89

Marla English (1935-)
Flesh and the Spur '57
Voodoo Woman '57

Zach English (1983-)
The Thorn Birds: The Missing Years '96
The Real McCoy '93

Robert Englund (1947-)
Red '08
Zombie Strippers '08
Black Swarm '07
Freddy vs. Jason '03
Python '00
Wish You Were Dead '00
The Prince and the Surfer '99
Dee Snider's Strangeland '98
Meet the Deedles '98
Perfect Target '98
Urban Legend '98
Wishmaster '97
Killer Tongue '96
The Paper Brigade '96
The Mangler '94
Wes Craven's New Nightmare '94
Dance Macabre '91
Freddy's Dead: The Final Nightmare '91
The Adventures of Ford Fairlane '90
A Nightmare on Elm Street 5: Dream Child '89
The Phantom of the Opera '89
A Nightmare on Elm Street 4: Dream Master '88
A Nightmare on Elm Street 3: Dream Warriors '87
A Nightmare on Elm Street 2: Freddy's Revenge '85
A Nightmare on Elm Street '84
V: The Final Battle '84
V '83
Mysterious Two '82
Dead and Buried '81
Galaxy of Terror '81
Eaten Alive '76
Great Smokey Roadblock '76
A Star Is Born '76
Stay Hungry '76
Buster and Billie '74
Slashed Dreams '74

Bill Engvall
Bait Shop '08
Delta Farce '07

Takaaki Enoki (1956-)
Moon over Tao '97
Heaven & Earth '90

John Enos (1962-)
Everybody Wants to Be Italian '08
Finish Line '08
San Saba '08
Shark Swarm '08
Missionary Man '07
Love Thy Neighbor '02
Phone Booth '02
Brigham City '01
Dead Sexy '01
Red Shoe Diaries: Luscious Lola '00
Stealth Fighter '99
Miami Hustle '95
Ravenhawk '95
Red Shoe Diaries 6: How I Met My Husband '95
Bullet '94
Till the End of the Night '94

Rene Enriquez (1933-90)
Bulletproof '88
The Evil That Men Do '84
Ants '77
Harry and Tonto '74

Michael Ensign (1944-)
Born Yesterday '93
Life Stinks '91
House '86
Jekyll & Hyde... Together Again '82

John Entwhistle (1944-2002)
The Kids Are Alright '79
Tommy '75

Brenda Epperson (1965-)
Storybook '95
Amore! '93

Dieter Eppler (1927-)
The Sprinter '84
The Torture Chamber of Dr. Sadism '69
Strangler of Blackmoor Castle '63
The Slaughter of the Vampires '62

Mike Epps (1970-)
The Hangover '09
Janky Promoters '09
Next Day Air '09
Soul Men '08
Welcome Home Roscoe Jenkins '08
Resident Evil: Extinction '07
Talk to Me '07
Something New '06
Guess Who '05
The Honeymooners '05
Roll Bounce '05
Resident Evil: Apocalypse '04
The Fighting Temptations '03
All About the Benjamins '02
Friday After Next '02
Dr. Dolittle 2 '01 (V)
How High '01
Bait '00
Next Friday '00

Omar Epps (1973-)
A Day in the Life '09
Against the Ropes '04
Alfie '04
Big Trouble '02
Conviction '02
Perfume '01
Brother '00
Dracula 2000 '00
Love and Basketball '00
In Too Deep '99
The Mod Squad '99
The Wood '99
Breakfast of Champions '98
First Time Felon '97
Scream 2 '97
Deadly Voyage '96
Higher Learning '94
Major League 2 '94
Daybreak '93
The Program '93
Juice '92

Shareeka Epps
Mother and Child '09
Half Nelson '06

Kathryn Erbe (1966-)
The Runaway '00
Stir of Echoes '99
Naked City: Justice with a Bullet '98
Dream with the Fishes '97
The Addiction '95
Breathing Lessons '94
D2: The Mighty Ducks '94
Kiss of Death '94
Rich in Love '93
What about Bob? '91

Andoni Erburu (1988-)
Broken Silence '01
Secrets of the Heart '97

Stipe Erceg
The Baader Meinhof Complex '08
The Ring Finger '05
The Edukators '04

Richard Erdman (1925-)
The Learning Curve '01
Tomboy '85
Namu, the Killer Whale '66
Saddle the Wind '58
The Blue Gardenia '53
Stalag 17 '53
Cry Danger '51
The Stooge '51
Objective, Burma! '45

Oris Erhuero
Sometimes in April '05
Black Mask 2: City of Masks '02

Ethan Erickson (1973-)
Fear Runs Silent '99
Jawbreaker '98

Kandis Erickson
Seance '06
Death Valley: The Revenge of Bloody Bill '04

Leif Erickson (1911-86)
D.C. Cab '84
Penitentiary 2 '82
Rocky 3 '82
Twilight's Last Gleaming '77
Winterhawk '76
Abduction '75
Force Five '75
The Carpetbaggers '64
Roustabout '64
Strait-Jacket '64
A Gathering of Eagles '63
Istanbul '57
Fastest Gun Alive '56
Tea and Sympathy '56
On the Waterfront '54
Invaders from Mars '53
Trouble along the Way '53
Abbott and Costello Meet Captain Kidd '52
Never Wave at a WAC '52
Sailor Beware '52
With a Song in My Heart '52
Hill Number One '51
The Showdown '50
Three Secrets '50
Joan of Arc '48
Miss Tatlock's Millions '48
The Snake Pit '48
Blonde Savage '47
Arabian Nights '42
Night Monster '42
Pardon My Sarong '42
H.M. Pulham Esquire '41
One Third of a Nation '39
The Big Broadcast of 1938 '38
Conquest '37
Waikiki Wedding '37
Desert Gold '36

Devon Ericson (1952-)
Can You Hear the Laughter? The Story of Freddie Prinze '79
The Runaway Barge '75

John Ericson (1927-)
Primary Target '89
House of the Dead '78
Zone of the Dead '78
Hustler Squad '76
The Bounty Man '72
The Bamboo Saucer '68
7 Faces of Dr. Lao '63
Forty Guns '57
Green Fire '55
Bad Day at Black Rock '54
Rhapsody '54
The Student Prince '54

Kaj-Erik Eriksen (1979-)
Captains Courageous '95
Kurt Vonnegut's Monkey House '91
Short Time '90

R. Lee Ermey (1944-)
Toy Story 3 '10 (V)
The Texas Chainsaw Massacre: The Beginning '06
Man of the House '05
The Texas Chainsaw Massacre '03
Willard '03
The Salton Sea '02
Jericho '01
On the Borderline '01
Saving Silverman '01
Taking Sides '01
Chaos Factor '00
Skipped Parts '00
Avalanche '99
Life '99
Toy Story 2 '99 (V)
You Know My Name '99
Apartment Complex '98
Gunshy '98
The Sender '98
Dead Men Can't Dance '97
Rough Riders '97
Switchback '97
Weapons of Mass Distraction '97
The Frighteners '96
Prefontaine '96
Soul of the Game '96
Chain of Command '95
Dead Man Walking '95
The Fighter '95
Leaving Las Vegas '95
Murder in the First '95
Seven '95
Toy Story '95 (V)
Under the Hula Moon '95
French Silk '94
Love Is a Gun '94
On Deadly Ground '94
Body Snatchers '93
Hexed '93
Sommersby '93
The Terror Within 2 '91
Endless Descent '90
I'm Dangerous Tonight '90
Kid '90
The Take '90
Demonstone '89
Fletch Lives '89
The Siege of Firebase Gloria '89
Mississippi Burning '88
Full Metal Jacket '87
Apocalypse Now '79
The Boys in Company C '77

George Ernest (1921-)
Racing Luck '35
Justice Rides Again '32

Mario Erpichini
The Best Man '97
Escape from Death Row '73

Krista Errickson (1964-)
Martial Outlaw '93
Killer Image '92
Mortal Passions '90
First Time '82
Jekyll & Hyde... Together Again '82

Melissa Errico (1970-)
Loverboy '05
Life or Something Like It '02
Mockingbird Don't Sing '01
Frequency '00

Leon Errol (1881-1951)
The Noose Hangs High '48
Higher and Higher '44
The Invisible Man's Revenge '44
Slightly Terrific '44
Mexican Spitfire at Sea '42
Hurry, Charlie, Hurry '41
Never Give a Sucker an Even Break '41
Mexican Spitfire '40
Pop Always Pays '40
Make a Wish '37
The Great Ziegfeld '36
We're Not Dressing '34

Patrick Ersgard
Rancid '04
Backlash '99
Living in Peril '97
Dreaming of Rita '94
Mandroid '93
The Visitors '89

Homayon Ershadi
The Kite Runner '07
The Taste of Cherry '96

Eileen Erskine (1914-95)
This Happy Breed '47
Great Expectations '46

Marilyn Erskine (1924-)
Above and Beyond '53
Westward the Women '51

Victor Ertmanis
Holiday Affair '96
Brainscan '94
Paris, France '94

Bill Erwin (1914-)
Chairman of the Board '97
The Color of Evening '95
Fallen Angels 1 '93
Hard Knox '83
Huckleberry Finn '75

Mike Erwin (1978-)
Chaos Theory '08
Freshman Orientation '04
Hulk '03

Stuart Erwin (1902-67)
The Misadventures of Merlin Jones '63
Heading for Heaven '47
Killer Dill '47
The Great Mike '44
Blondie for Victory '42
The Bride Came C.O.D. '41
Cracked Nuts '41
Back Door to Heaven '39
Hollywood Cavalcade '39
It Could Happen to You '39
Mr. Boggs Steps Out '38
Second Honeymoon '37
Small Town Boy '37
Pigskin Parade '36
Ceiling Zero '35
Bachelor Bait '34
Chained '34
Palooka '34
Viva Villa! '34
Going Hollywood '33
Hold Your Man '33
Misleading Lady '32
Strangers in Love '32

Eberhard Esche
Trace of Stones '66
Divided Heaven '64

Jaime Escobedo
The Bad News Bears in Breaking Training '77
The Bad News Bears '76

Carl Esmond (1908-2004)
The World in His Arms '52
Without Love '45
The Master Race '44
Ministry of Fear '44
The Story of Dr. Wassell '44
The Navy Comes Through '42
Panama Hattie '42
Dawn Patrol '38

Jill Esmond (1908-90)
A Man Called Peter '55
Bedelia '46
Casanova Brown '44
The White Cliffs of Dover '44
Journey for Margaret '42
On the Sunny Side '42
F.P. 1 '33
Skin Game '31
State's Attorney '31

Bella Esperance
Lady Dragon 2 '93
Lady Dragon '92

Giancarlo Esposito (1958-)
Gospel Hill '08
The Box '07
Feel the Noise '07
Racing Daylight '07
Last Holiday '06
Rain '06
Sherrybaby '06
Back in the Day '05
Carlito's Way: Rise to Power '05
Chupacabra Terror '05
Derailed '05
Hate Crime '05
Blind Horizon '04
Ali '01
Monkeybone '01
Pinero '01
Homicide: The Movie '00
Big City Blues '99
Naked City: Justice with a Bullet '98
Phoenix '98
Twilight '98
The Keeper '96
Nothing to Lose '96
Blue in the Face '95
Reckless '95
Smoke '95
The Usual Suspects '95
Fresh '94
Amos and Andrew '93
Bob Roberts '92
Malcolm X '92
Night on Earth '91
King of New York '90
Mo' Better Blues '90
Do the Right Thing '89
School Daze '88
Sweet Lorraine '87
Trading Places '83
Taps '81

Gianni Esposito (1930-74)
Paris Belongs to Us '60
Les Miserables '57

Jennifer Esposito (1973-)
Conspiracy '08
American Crude '07
Crash '05
Breakin' All The Rules '04
Taxi '04
Master of Disguise '02

Rip It Off *'02*
Welcome to Collinwood *'02*
Backflash *'01*
Don't Say a Word *'01*
Dracula 2000 *'00*
Just One Time *'00*
The Proposal *'00*
The Bachelor *'99*
Summer of Sam *'99*
I Still Know What You Did Last Summer *'98*
The Sunshine Boys *'95*

Piera Degli Esposti (1939-)
The Unknown Woman *'06*
A Joke of Destiny, Lying in Wait Around the Corner Like a Bandit *'84*

Ato Essandoh (1972-)
Garden State *'04*
Saving Face *'04*

Eileen Essell (1922-)
Charlie and the Chocolate Factory *'05*
The Producers *'05*
Finding Neverland *'04*
Duplex *'03*

Paul Esser (1913-88)
Daughters of Darkness *'71*
The Kaiser's Lackey *'51*
The Merry Wives of Windsor *'50*

David Essex (1947-)
Journey of Honor *'91*
Silver Dream Racer *'83*
That'll Be the Day *'73*
Octaman *'71*

Susie Essman
Loving Leah *'09*
Bolt *'08 (V)*
The Man *'05*

Christine Estabrook (1952-)
Presumed Innocent *'90*
Second Sight *'89*
Almost You *'85*

Gloria Estefan (1957-)
For Love or Country: The Arturo Sandoval Story *'00*
Music of the Heart *'99*

Laura Esterman
Suspended Animation *'02*
Awakenings *'90*

Robert Estes (1963-)
How to Go Out on a Date in Queens *'06*
Counterstrike *'03*
Aces: Iron Eagle 3 *'92*
Phantom of the Mall: Eric's Revenge *'89*
Trapper County War *'89*

Will Estes (1978-)
Mimic 2 *'01*
My Husband's Double Life *'01*
Terror Tract *'00*
U-571 *'00*
Blue Ridge Fall *'99*
The Road Home *'95*

Emilio Estevez (1962-)
Arthur and the Invisibles *'06 (V)*
Bobby *'06*
Rated X *'00*
Sand *'00*
Late Last Night *'99*
D3: The Mighty Ducks *'96*
Mission: Impossible *'96*
The War at Home *'96*
D2: The Mighty Ducks *'94*
Another Stakeout *'93*
Judgment Night *'93*
National Lampoon's Loaded Weapon 1 *'93*
Freejack *'92*
The Mighty Ducks *'92*
Men at Work *'90*
Young Guns 2 *'90*
Nightbreaker *'89*
Never on Tuesday *'88*
Young Guns *'88*
Stakeout *'87*
Wisdom *'87*
Maximum Overdrive *'86*
The Breakfast Club *'85*
St. Elmo's Fire *'85*
That Was Then... This Is Now *'85*
Nightmares *'83*
The Outsiders *'83*
Repo Man *'83*
In the Custody of Strangers *'82*
Tex *'82*

Ines Estevez (1964-)
Life According to Muriel *'97*
Killing Grandpa *'91*

Joe Estevez (1950-)
San Franpsycho *'06*
Autopsy: A Love Story *'02*
No Turning Back *'01*
Acts of Betrayal *'98*
The Catcher *'98*
No Code of Conduct *'98*
Lethal Seduction *'97*
Equal Impact *'96*
Breakaway *'95*
Dillinger and Capone *'95*
The Mosaic Project *'95*
Werewolf *'95*
The Deadly Secret *'94*
Money to Burn *'94*
Beach Babes from Beyond *'93*
Dark Universe *'93*
Expert Weapon *'93*
Eye of the Stranger *'93*
Fatal Justice *'93*
In a Moment of Passion *'93*
Armed for Action *'92*
Eddie Presley *'92*
L.A. Goddess *'92*
Murder-in-Law *'92*
Dark Rider *'91*
Lockdown *'90*
Soultaker *'90*
Terminal Exposure *'89*
Fatal Pulse *'88*
South of Reno *'87*
Zero Boys *'86*
The California Kid *'74*
Gator King *'70*

Ramon Estevez (1963-)
Blood on the Badge *'92*
Cadence *'89*

Renee Estevez (1967-)
Storm Tracker *'99*
Good Girls Don't *'95*
Endangered *'94*
Uncivilized *'94*
Single White Female *'92*
Forbidden Sun *'89*
Heathers *'89*
Marked for Murder *'89*
Bulldance *'88*
Intruder *'88*
Sleepaway Camp 2: Unhappy Campers *'88*

Erik Estrada (1949-)
Kickin' It Old Skool *'07*
Border Blues *'03*
National Lampoon's Van Wilder *'02*
The Modern Adventures of Tom Sawyer *'99*
Panic in the Skies *'96*
The Final Goal *'94*
Gang Justice *'94*
National Lampoon's Loaded Weapon 1 *'93*
The Divine Enforcer *'91*
Do or Die *'91*
Caged Fury *'90*
Guns *'90*
The Last Riders *'90*
Night of the Wilding *'90*
A Show of Force *'90*
Spirits *'90*
Alien Seed *'89*
Andy and the Airwave Rangers *'89*
Twisted Justice *'89*
The Dirty Dozen: The Fatal Mission *'88*
Hour of the Assassin *'86*
Lightblast *'85*
Honeyboy *'82*
The Line *'80*
Midway *'76*
The Cross & the Switchblade *'72*
Jailbreakin' *'72*
The New Centurions *'72*

Alberto Estrella (1962-)
Esmeralda Comes by Night *'98*
Optic Fiber *'97*
On the Air *'95*

Pat Estrin
Dennis the Menace: Dinosaur Hunter *'93*
Act of Vengeance *'74*
America First *'70*

Makiko Esumi
Pistol Opera *'02*
Maborosi *'95*

Pierre Etaix (1928-)
Max, Mon Amour *'86*
Pickpocket *'59*

Alex Etel
Return to Cranford *'09*
Cranford *'08*

Alex(ander Nathan) Etel
The Water Horse: Legend of the Deep *'07*
Millions *'05*

Treva Etienne
Green Street Hooligans 2 *'09*
ESL: English as a Second Language *'05*
Pirates of the Caribbean: The Curse of the Black Pearl *'03*
Black Hawk Down *'01*
Eyes Wide Shut *'99*

Ruth Etting (1896-1978)
Hips, Hips, Hooray *'34*
Roman Scandals *'33*

Cynthia Ettinger
Frailty *'02*
Down, Out and Dangerous *'95*

Shari Eubank (1947-)
Chesty Anderson USN *'76*
Supervixens *'75*

Bob Eubanks (1938-)
Roger & Me *'89*
Johnny Dangerously *'84*

Corey Michael Eubanks
Forced to Kill *'93*
Payback *'90*

Son Eun-seo
Blood Pledge *'09*

Wesley Eure (1950-)
C.H.O.M.P.S. *'79*
Jennifer *'78*
The Toolbox Murders *'78*

Alice Evans (1974-)
The Christmas Card *'06*
Fascination *'04*
102 Dalmatians *'00*

Art Evans (1942-)
Metro *'96*
Tales from the Hood *'95*
CB4: The Movie *'93*
The Finishing Touch *'92*
Trespass *'92*
Die Hard 2: Die Harder *'90*
The Mighty Quinn *'89*
Mom *'89*
School Daze *'88*
White of the Eye *'88*
Jo Jo Dancer, Your Life Is Calling *'86*
Native Son *'86*
Fright Night *'85*
A Soldier's Story *'84*
The In-Laws *'79*
King *'78*

Chris Evans (1981-)
The Losers *'10*
Scott Pilgrim vs. the World *'10*
Battle for Terra *'09 (V)*
Push *'09*
The Loss of a Teardrop Diamond *'08*
Street Kings *'08*
Fantastic Four: Rise of the Silver Surfer *'07*
The Nanny Diaries *'07*
Sunshine *'07*
TMNT (Teenage Mutant Ninja Turtles) *'07 (V)*
Fantastic Four *'05*
Fierce People *'05*
London *'05*
Cellular *'04*
The Perfect Score *'04*
Not Another Teen Movie *'01*

Clifford Evans (1912-85)
One Brief Summer *'70*
Kiss of the Vampire *'62*
The Curse of the Werewolf *'61*
The Gilded Cage *'54*
I'll Get You *'53*
While I Live *'47*
The Foreman Went to France *'42*
The Courageous Mr. Penn *'41*
Love on the Dole *'41*
The Mutiny of the Elsinore *'39*
River of Unrest *'36*

Dale Evans (1912-2001)
Bells of Coronado *'50*
Trigger, Jr. *'50*
Twilight in the Sierras *'50*
Down Dakota Way *'49*
The Golden Stallion *'49*
Susanna Pass *'49*
Apache Rose *'47*
Bells of San Angelo *'47*
Home in Oklahoma *'47*
Lights of Old Santa Fe *'47*
Helldorado *'46*
My Pal Trigger *'46*
Rainbow over Texas *'46*
Roll on Texas Moon *'46*
Song of Arizona *'46*
Under Nevada Skies *'46*
Along the Navaho Trail *'45*
Bells of Rosarita *'45*
Don't Fence Me In *'45*
Sunset in El Dorado *'45*
Utah *'45*
Cowboy & the Senorita *'44*
San Fernando Valley *'44*
Song of Nevada *'44*
The Yellow Rose of Texas *'44*

Daniel Evans (1973-)
Daniel Deronda *'02*
Great Expectations *'99*

Douglas Evans (1904-68)
Actors and Sin *'52*
Leave It to the Marines *'51*
Sky High *'51*
North of the Great Divide *'50*
The Golden Stallion *'49*
My Dog Shep *'46*
The Green Hornet *'39*

Edith Evans (1888-1976)
Nasty Habits *'77*
The Slipper and the Rose *'76*
Craze *'74*
A Doll's House *'73*
David Copperfield *'70*
Scrooge *'70*
Crooks & Coronets *'69*
The Madwoman of Chaillot *'69*
The Chalk Garden *'64*
Tom Jones *'63*
The Nun's Story *'59*
Look Back in Anger *'58*
The Importance of Being Earnest *'52*
The Last Days of Dolwyn *'49*
The Queen of Spades *'49*

Evans Evans (1936-)
Dead Bang *'89*
The Iceman Cometh *'73*
The Story of a Love Story *'73*
Bonnie & Clyde *'67*

Gene Evans (1922-98)
The Shadow Riders *'82*
The Concrete Cowboys *'79*
Devil Times Five *'74*
Gentle Savage *'73*
Walking Tall *'73*
The Bounty Man *'72*
Apache Uprising *'66*
Nevada Smith *'66*
Shock Corridor *'63*
Gold of the Seven Saints *'61*
Operation Petticoat *'59*
The Helen Morgan Story *'57*
The Sad Sack *'57*
Crashout *'55*
Cattle Queen of Montana *'54*
Donovan's Brain *'53*
Mutiny *'52*
Ace in the Hole *'51*
Fixed Bayonets! *'51*
I Was an American Spy *'51*
The Steel Helmet *'51*
Armored Car Robbery *'50*
It Happens Every Spring *'49*

Joan Evans (1934-)
No Name on the Bullet *'59*
Skirts Ahoy! *'52*
Our Very Own *'50*

John Evans (1934-)
UKM: The Ultimate Killing Machine *'06*
Escape Clause *'96*
Long Road Home *'91*
I've Heard the Mermaids Singing *'87*

Josh Evans (1971-)
The Doors *'91*
Ricochet *'91*
Born on the Fourth of July *'89*

Josh Ryan Evans (1982-2002)
Dr. Seuss' How the Grinch Stole Christmas *'00*
P.T. Barnum *'99*

Lee Evans (1965-)
The History of Mr. Polly *'07*
Doogal *'05 (V)*
Freeze Frame *'04*
The Medallion *'03*
Dinotopia *'02 (V)*
The Ladies Man *'00*
There's Something about Mary *'98*
The Fifth Element *'97*
Mouse Hunt *'97*
Funny Bones *'94*

Linda Evans (1942-)
The Stepsister *'97*
The Gambler Returns: The Luck of the Draw *'93*
Kenny Rogers as the Gambler, Part 2: The Adventure Continues *'83*
Tom Horn *'80*
Avalanche Express *'79*
Standing Tall *'78*
Hunter *'76*
Mitchell *'75*
The Klansman *'74*
Confessions of Tom Harris *'72*
Beach Blanket Bingo *'65*
Those Calloways *'65*

Madge Evans (1909-81)
Sinners in Paradise *'38*
Pennies from Heaven *'36*
David Copperfield *'35*
Transatlantic Tunnel *'35*
Stand Up and Cheer *'34*
Dinner at Eight *'33*
Hallelujah, I'm a Bum *'33*
The Mayor of Hell *'33*
Three Broadway Girls *'32*

Maurice Evans (1901-89)
Agatha Christie's A Caribbean Mystery *'83*
The Jerk *'79*
Terror in the Wax Museum *'73*
Beneath the Planet of the Apes *'70*
Invasion of the Body Stealers *'69*
Planet of the Apes *'68*
Rosemary's Baby *'68*
The War Lord *'65*
The Tempest *'63*
Androcles and the Lion *'52*
Scrooge *'35*
Wedding Rehearsal *'32*

Mike Evans (1949-2006)
The House on Skull Mountain *'74*
The Voyage of the Yes *'72*

Mitch Evans
Alien Massacre *'67*
Gallery of Horrors *'67*

Monica Evans (1940-)
Robin Hood *'73 (V)*
The Odd Couple *'68*

Muriel Evans (1910-2000)
Roll, Wagons, Roll *'39*
The House of Secrets *'37*
King of the Pecos *'36*
Law for Tombstone *'35*
The New Frontier *'35*
The Throwback *'35*
Manhattan Melodrama *'34*
The Prizefighter and the Lady *'33*

Peter Evans
Seven Days of Grace *'06*
Impostors *'80*

Rex Evans (1903-69)
The Matchmaker *'58*
The Wrong Road *'37*

Robert Evans (1930-)
The Kid Stays in the Picture *'02 (N)*
An Alan Smithee Film: Burn, Hollywood, Burn *'97*
The Best of Everything *'59*
The Fiend Who Walked the West *'58*
Man of a Thousand Faces *'57*

Robin Evans
Rage of Honor *'87*
One Dark Night *'82*

Rupert Evans
Emma *'09*
Guantanamero *'07*
Hellboy *'04*

Shaun Evans (1980-)
Boy A *'07*
Cashback *'06*
Being Julia *'04*
The Boys and Girl From County Clare *'03*

Terrence Evans
Mr. Fix It *'06*
The Texas Chainsaw Massacre *'03*
Curse 2: The Bite *'88*

Terry Evans
Mongrel *'83*
Cody *'77*

Troy Evans (1948-)
The Black Dahlia *'06*
Alien Fury: Countdown to Invasion *'00*
I'll Remember April *'99*
The Frighteners *'96*
Bodily Harm *'95*

Father and Scout '94
My Summer Story '94
Ace Ventura: Pet Detective '93
Article 99 '92
Kuffs '92
The Lawnmower Man '92

Edith Evanson (1900-80)

The Girl in the Red Velvet Swing '55
Silver Star '55
The Day the Earth Stood Still '51
Caged '50
The Damned Don't Cry '50
The Magnificent Yankee '50
Forever Amber '47
The Jade Mask '45

Eve (1978-)

Whip It '09
Flashbacks of a Fool '08
Barbershop 2: Back in Business '04
The Cookout '04
The Woodsman '04
Barbershop '02

Alice Eve

She's Out of My League '10
Crossing Over '09
Big Nothing '06
Starter for Ten '06

Trevor Eve (1951-)

Troy '04
Possession '02
David Copperfield '99
Heat of the Sun '99
Appetite '98
Dracula '79

Judith Evelyn (1913-67)

The Tingler '59
The Egyptian '54
Rear Window '54

Kimberly Evenson (1932-)

Kandyland '87
The Big Bet '85
Porky's Revenge '85

Barbara Everest (1890-1968)

Tony Draws a Horse '51
Madeleine '50
The Valley of Decision '45
Gaslight '44
Jane Eyre '44
Phantom Fiend '35

Chad Everett (1936-)

Break '09
The Pink Conspiracy '07
Anchorman: The Legend of Ron Burgundy '04
Mulholland Drive '01
Hard to Forget '98
Psycho '98
When Time Expires '97
Official Denial '93
The Rousters '90
Heroes Stand Alone '89
Jigsaw Murders '89
Fever Pitch '85
Airplane 2: The Sequel '82
Intruder Within '81
Centennial '78
The Impossible Years '68
Johnny Tiger '66
The Singing Nun '66
Made in Paris '65
Rome Adventure '62

Francine Everett (1920-99)

Dirty Gertie from Harlem U.S.A. '46
Tall, Tan and Terrific '46

Rupert Everett (1959-)

St. Trinian's '07
Shrek the Third '07 (V)
Stardust '07
The Chronicles of Narnia: The Lion, the Witch and the Wardrobe '05 (V)
A Different Loyalty '04
People '04
Shrek 2 '04 (V)
Stage Beauty '04
Dangerous Liaisons '03
To Kill a King '03
Unconditional Love '03
The Importance of Being Earnest '02
The Wild Thornberrys Movie '02 (V)
The Next Best Thing '00
An Ideal Husband '99
Inspector Gadget '99
William Shakespeare's A Midsummer Night's Dream '99
Shakespeare in Love '98
B. Monkey '97
My Best Friend's Wedding '97
Cemetery Man '95
Dunston Checks In '95
The Madness of King George '94
Ready to Wear '94
Inside Monkey Zetterland '93
The Comfort of Strangers '91
Hearts of Fire '87
The Right Hand Man '87
Dance with a Stranger '85
Another Country '84
The Far Pavilions '84

Todd Everett

Blood on the Badge '92
The Capture of Grizzly Adams '82

Tom Everett (1948-)

The Alamo '04
XXX '02
Air Force One '97
My Fellow Americans '96
Eddie Presley '92
Best of the Best '89
Leatherface: The Texas Chainsaw Massacre 3 '89
Prison '88
Friday the 13th, Part 4: The Final Chapter '84

Nancy Everhard (1959-)

The China Lake Murders '90
This Gun for Hire '90
Deepstar Six '89
Demonstone '89
Double Revenge '89
The Trial of the Incredible Hulk '89

Angie Everhart (1969-)

Bugs '03
Heart of Stone '01
The Stray '00
The Substitute 4: Failure is Not an Option '00
Welcome to Hollywood '00
D.R.E.A.M. Team '99
Running Red '99
Bitter Sweet '98
Something About Sex '98
Executive Target '97
Another 9 1/2 Weeks '96
Tales from the Crypt Presents Bordello of Blood '96
Trigger Happy '96
Jade '95

Rex Everhart (1920-2000)

Beauty and the Beast '91 (V)
Family Business '89

Jason Evers (1922-2005)

Basket Case 2 '90
Barracuda '78
Claws '77
Fer-De-Lance '74
Escape from the Planet of the Apes '71
The Green Berets '68

Cory (Corinna) Everson (1959-)

Felony '95
Double Impact '91

Briana Evigan

S. Darko: A Donnie Darko Tale '09
Sorority Row '09
Step Up 2 the Streets '08
Spectre '96

Greg Evigan (1953-)

Mail Order Bride '08
Poison Ivy 4: The Secret Society '08
Cerberus '05
River's End '05
Arizona Summer '03
He Sees You When You're Sleeping '02
One of Her Own '97
Spectre '96
TekWar '94
Lies Before Kisses '92
Deepstar Six '89
Private Road: No Trespassing '87
Stripped to Kill '87

Pat Evison (1924-)

What the Moon Saw '90
Starstruck '82
Tim '79

John Ewart (1928-94)

Which Way Home '90
The Quest '86
Prince and the Great Race '83
Blue Fire Lady '78
Newsfront '78
Island Trader '71

Dwight Ewell

Jay and Silent Bob Strike Back '01
Intern '00
Man of the Century '99
Chasing Amy '97
Flirt '95

Tom Ewell (1909-94)

Easy Money '83
They Only Kill Their Masters '72
State Fair '62
The Girl Can't Help It '56
The Seven Year Itch '55
Lost in Alaska '52
Adam's Rib '50
A Life of Her Own '50
Mr. Music '50

Barbara Ewing (1944-)

Brothers of the Head '06
Guardian of the Abyss '82
Dracula Has Risen from the Grave '68

Richard Eyer (1945-)

The Seventh Voyage of Sinbad '58
The Invisible Boy '57
Canyon River '56
The Kettles in the Ozarks '56
Desperate Hours '55

Peter Eyre (1942-)

The Affair of the Necklace '01
Don Quixote '00
The Golden Bowl '00
Dangerous Beauty '98
The Tango Lesson '97
Surviving Picasso '96
Joseph '95
Princess Caraboo '94
Scarlett '94
Sharpe's Gold '94
Orlando '92
Diamond's Edge '88
Hedda '75

William Eythe (1918-57)

Colonel Effingham's Raid '45
House on 92nd Street '45
Wilson '44
A Wing and a Prayer '44
The Ox-Bow Incident '43

Bessie Eyton (1890-1965)

Heart of Texas Ryan '17
The Spoilers '14

Maynard Eziashi (1965-)

Ace Ventura: When Nature Calls '95
Bopha! '93
Mister Johnson '91
Twenty-One '91

Shelley Fabares (1944-)

The Canterville Ghost '91
For Love or Money '88
Hot Pursuit '87
Memorial Day '83
Great American Traffic Jam '80
Sky Hei$t '75
Brian's Song '71
Clambake '67
Spinout '66
Girl Happy '65
Ride the Wild Surf '64

Matthew Faber

Palindromes '04
Hard Luck '01
Ride with the Devil '99
Welcome to the Dollhouse '95
Bob Roberts '92

Fabian (1942-)

Mr. Rock 'n' Roll: The Alan Freed Story '99
Runaway Daughters '94
Get Crazy '83
Kiss Daddy Goodbye '81
Soul Hustler '76
Little Laura & Big John '73
Thunder Alley '67
Fireball 500 '66
Dear Brigitte '65
Ride the Wild Surf '64
Five Weeks in a Balloon '62
The Longest Day '62
Mr. Hobbs Takes a Vacation '62
North to Alaska '60

Ava Fabian (1962-)

Capital Punishment '96
Last Man Standing '95
Auntie Lee's Meat Pies '92
Ski School '91
Welcome Home, Roxy Carmichael '90
To Die For '89

Francoise Fabian (1935-)

5x2 '04
La Buche '00
Reunion '88
The French Woman '79
Love by Appointment '76
Salut l'Artiste '74
Happy New Year '73
My Night at Maud's '69
Belle de Jour '67
The Thief of Paris '67
Mam'zelle Pigalle '58
That Naughty Girl '58
Fernandel the Dressmaker '57
Dressmaker '56

Patrick Fabian

Snow 2: Brain Freeze '08
Twitches Too '07
Twitches '05
Snow '04

Joel Fabiani (1936-)

Snake Eyes '98
Reuben, Reuben '83
President's Mistress '78

Fabio (1961-)

Bubble Boy '01
Death Becomes Her '92
Scenes from a Mall '91
Exorcist 3: Legion '90

Nanette Fabray (1920-)

Teresa's Tattoo '94
Personal Exemptions '88
Amy '81
The Man in the Santa Claus Suit '79
Harper Valley P.T.A. '78
The Happy Ending '69
Alice Through the Looking Glass '66
The Band Wagon '53
The Private Lives of Elizabeth & Essex '39

Pierre Fabre (1933-2006)

Bed and Board '70
The 317th Platoon '65

Aldo Fabrizi (1905-90)

The Flowers of St. Francis '50
Open City '45

Franco Fabrizi (1916-95)

Ginger & Fred '86
Aurora '84
Act of Aggression '73
Hit Men '73
A Woman of Rome '56
Il Bidone '55
I Vitelloni '53

Valeria Fabrizi (1938-)

Women in Cell Block 7 '77
Beauty on the Beach '61

Peter Facinelli (1973-)

The Twilight Saga: Eclipse '10
The Twilight Saga: New Moon '09
Finding Amanda '08
Twilight '08
All the Good Ones Are Married '07
Arc '06
Hollow Man 2 '06
The Lather Effect '06
Touch the Top of the World '06
The Scorpion King '02
Riding in Cars with Boys '01
Tempted '01
The Big Kahuna '00
Blue Ridge Fall '99
Supernova '99
Can't Hardly Wait '98
Dancer, Texas—Pop. 81 '98
Telling You '98
Calm at Sunset '96
Foxfire '96

Robert Factor

Bad Channels '92
Ninja Academy '90
Fear '88

Bill Fagerbakke (1957-)

Space Buddies '08 (V)
The SpongeBob SquarePants Movie '04 (V)
Quigley '03
Gargoyles, The Movie: The Heroes Awaken '94 (V)
Stephen King's The Stand '94
The Reluctant Agent '89

Jeff Fahey (1954-)

Planet Terror '07
The Hunt for Eagle One: Crash Point '06
Frederick Forsyth's Icon '05
Locusts: The 8th Plague '05
Manticore '05
No Witness '04
Inferno '01
Blind Heat '00
Revelation '00
Detour '99
Johnny 2.0 '99
No Tomorrow '99
Time Served '99
Beneath the Bermuda Triangle '98
Catherine's Grove '98
Extramarital '98
When Justice Fails '98
Operation: Delta Force '97
The Underground '97
Lethal Tender '96
Smalltime '96
Virtual Seduction '96
Darkman 3: Die Darkman Die '95
Eye of the Wolf '95
Northern Passage '95
Serpent's Lair '95
The Sweeper '95
Firefall '94
Sketch Artist 2: Hands That See '94
Temptation '94
Wyatt Earp '94
Blindsided '93
The Hit List '93
Quick '93
Woman of Desire '93
The Lawnmower Man '92
Sketch Artist '92
Body Parts '91
Iran: Days of Crisis '91
Iron Maze '91
Curiosity Kills '90
Impulse '90
The Last of the Finest '90
White Hunter, Black Heart '90
True Blood '89
Backfire '88
Split Decisions '88
Wrangler '88
Psycho 3 '86
Execution of Raymond Graham '85
Silverado '85

Mary-Anne Fahey (1956-)

Celia: Child of Terror '89
Mutant Hunt '87
The Dunera Boys '85

Matty Fain (1905-71)

The Thirteenth Man '37
Social Error '35

Elinor Fair (1903-57)

Night Rider '32
Let 'er Go Gallegher '28
Yankee Clipper '27
Big Stakes '22
Kismet '20

Jody Fair

The Ghost of Dragstrip Hollow '59
The Brain Eaters '58
High School Confidential '58

Bruce Fairbairn (1947-99)

Cyclone '87
Nightstick '87
The Vampire Hookers '78

Christopher Fairbank

Tess of the D'Urbervilles '08
Below '02
The Scarlet Pimpernel '99
The Scarlet Pimpernel 2: Mademoiselle Guillotine '99
The Scarlet Pimpernel 3: The Kidnapped King '99
How Many Miles to Babylon? '82

Douglas Fairbanks, Sr. (1883-1939)

Private Life of Don Juan '34
Mr. Robinson Crusoe '32
Reaching for the Moon '31
The Iron Mask '29
The Taming of the Shrew '29
The Gaucho '27
A Kiss for Mary Pickford '27
The Black Pirate '26
Don Q., Son of Zorro '25
The Thief of Baghdad '24
Robin Hood '22
The Nut '21
The Three Musketeers '21
Mark of Zorro '20
The Mollycoddle '20
His Majesty, the American '19
When the Clouds Roll By '19
American Aristocracy '17
The Americano '17
Down to Earth '17

The Man from Painted Post *'17*
Reaching for the Moon *'17*
Flirting with Fate *'16*
His Picture in the Papers *'16*
Matrimaniac *'16*
Reggie Mixes In *'16*
The Lamb *'15*

Douglas Fairbanks, Jr. (1909-2000)

Ghost Story *'81*
The Hostage Tower *'80*
Mister Drake's Duck *'50*
Sinbad, the Sailor *'47*
The Corsican Brothers *'42*
Angels Over Broadway *'40*
Gunga Din *'39*
Having a Wonderful Time *'38*
Having Wonderful Time *'38*
Joy of Living *'38*
The Rage of Paris *'38*
The Young in Heart *'38*
Prisoner of Zenda *'37*
When Thief Meets Thief *'37*
Accused *'36*
Mimi *'35*
Catherine the Great *'34*
Morning Glory *'33*
Scarlet Dawn *'32*
Union Depot *'32*
Little Caesar *'30*
Our Modern Maidens *'29*
Party Girls *'29*
A Woman of Affairs *'28*

Craig Fairbrass (1964-)

Rise of the Footsoldier *'07*
White Noise 2: The Light *'07*
The Long Weekend *'05*
Killing Time *'97*
Galaxis *'95*
Proteus *'95*
Cliffhanger *'93*
Nightscare *'93*

Morgan Fairchild (1950-)

The Initiation of Sarah *'06*
Shock to the System *'06*
Arizona Summer *'03*
Peril *'00*
Unshackled *'00*
Nice Guys Sleep Alone *'99*
Holy Man *'98*
Criminal Hearts *'95*
Venus Rising *'95*
Gospa *'94*
Based on an Untrue Story *'93*
Body Chemistry 3: Point of Seduction *'93*
Freaked *'93*
Test Tube Teens from the Year 2000 *'93*
Writer's Block *'91*
Even Angels Fall *'90*
Mob Boss *'90*
Haunting of Sarah Hardy *'89*
Phantom of the Mall: Eric's Revenge *'89*
Sleeping Beauty *'89*
Midnight Cop *'88*
Campus Man *'87*
Deadly Illusion *'87*
Red Headed Stranger *'87*
North and South Book 2 *'86*
Pee-wee's Big Adventure *'85*
The Zany Adventures of Robin Hood *'84*
Honeyboy *'82*
The Seduction *'82*
The Concrete Cowboys *'79*
Initiation of Sarah *'78*

Virginia Brown Faire (1904-80)

Peter Pan *'24*
Cricket on the Hearth *'23*
Monte Cristo *'22*

Heather Fairfield

No Secrets *'91*
A Girl of the Limberlost *'90*
The War of the Roses *'89*

Michael Fairman (1934-)

Dark Streets *'08*
Dead Silence *'07*
Thirteen Days *'00*
Forces of Nature *'99*
The Nurse *'97*
The Banker *'89*

Donald Adeosun Faison (1974-)

Next Day Air *'09*
Something New *'06*
Bachelor Party Vegas *'05*
King's Ransom *'05*
Good Boy! *'03 (V)*
Uptown Girls *'03*
Big Fat Liar *'02*
Double Whammy *'01*
Josie and the Pussycats *'01*
Remember the Titans *'00*
Supreme Sanction *'99*
Trippin' *'99*
Never 2 Big *'98*
Clueless *'95*
New Jersey Drive *'95*
Waiting to Exhale *'95*
Sugar Hill *'94*

Frankie Faison (1949-)

Adam *'09*
Breaking Point *'09*
Cirque du Freak: The Vampire's Assistant *'09*
For Sale by Owner *'09*
Tyler Perry's Meet the Browns *'08*
The Cookout *'04*
In Good Company *'04*
White Chicks *'04*
Gods and Generals *'03*
Highwaymen *'03*
Red Dragon *'02*
Showtime *'02*
Down to Earth *'01*
Hannibal *'01*
A Little Inside *'01*
The Sleepy Time Gal *'01*
Thirteen Conversations About One Thing *'01*
The Thomas Crown Affair *'99*
Julian Po *'97*
Mother Night *'96*
The Rich Man's Wife *'96*
Stephen King's The Langoliers *'95*
The Stupids *'95*
I Love Trouble *'94*
The Spider and the Fly *'94*
Sommersby *'93*
Freejack *'92*
City of Hope *'91*
The Silence of the Lambs *'91*
Betsy's Wedding *'90*
Do the Right Thing *'89*
Coming to America *'88*
Mississippi Burning *'88*
Manhunter *'86*
The Money Pit *'86*
Exterminator 2 *'84*
Ragtime *'81*

Matthew Faison

Lily in Winter *'94*
Taken Away *'89*

Adam Faith (1940-2003)

McVicar *'80*
Yesterday's Hero *'79*
Beat Girl *'60*

Dolores Faith (1942-)

The Human Duplicators *'64*
The Phantom Planet *'61*

Marianne Faithfull (1946-)

Irina Palm *'07*
Marie Antoinette *'06*
Paris, je t'aime *'06*
Intimacy *'00*
Absolutely Fabulous: The Last Shout *'96*
Crimetime *'96*
Moondance *'95*
Shopping *'93*
When Pigs Fly *'93*
The Turn of the Screw *'92*
Assault on Agathon *'75*
Madhouse Mansion *'74*
Hamlet *'69*
The Girl on a Motorcycle *'68*
I'll Never Forget What's 'Isname *'67*

Eduardo Fajardo (1918-)

The Killer Must Kill Again *'75*
Lisa and the Devil *'75*
Mean Machine *'73*
Sting of the West *'72*
Django *'68*
Stranger in Paso Bravo *'68*

Lola Falana (1942-)

Lady Cocoa *'75*
The Klansman *'74*
The Liberation of L.B. Jones *'70*
A Man Called Adam *'66*

Edie Falco (1963-)

Freedomland *'06*
The Great New Wonderful *'06*
The Quiet *'05*
Sunshine State *'02*
Judy Berlin *'99*
Random Hearts *'99*
Cop Land *'97*
A Price above Rubies *'97*
Hurricane Streets *'96*
The Addiction *'95*
The Sunshine Boys *'95*
Laws of Gravity *'92*
Trust *'91*
Sweet Lorraine *'87*

Andre Falcon (1924-)

A Slightly Pregnant Man *'79*
Happy New Year *'73*
The Mad Adventures of Rabbi Jacob *'73*

Lisanne Falk

Shattered Image *'98*
The First to Go *'97*
Suicide Kings *'97*
Night on Earth *'91*
Heathers *'89*

Peter Falk (1927-)

Next *'07*
Three Days to Vegas *'07*
The Thing About My Folks *'05*
Shark Tale *'04 (V)*
The Lost World *'02*
Three Days of Rain *'02*
Undisputed *'02*
Corky Romano *'01*
Made *'01*
Enemies of Laughter *'00*
Lakeboat *'00*
Money Kings *'98*
Pronto *'97*
Roommates *'95*
The Sunshine Boys *'95*
Faraway, So Close! *'93*
The Player *'92*
In the Spirit *'90*
Tune in Tomorrow *'90*
Cookie *'89*
Vibes *'88*
Wings of Desire *'88*
Happy New Year *'87*
The Princess Bride *'87*
Big Trouble *'86*
...All the Marbles *'81*
The Great Muppet Caper *'81*
The In-Laws *'79*
Brink's Job *'78*
The Cheap Detective *'78*
Griffin and Phoenix: A Love Story *'76*
Mikey & Nicky *'76*
Murder by Death *'76*
A Woman under the Influence *'74*
Columbo: Murder by the Book *'71*
Husbands *'70*
Castle Keep *'69*
Anzio *'68*
Columbo: Prescription Murder *'67*
Luv *'67*
The Great Race *'65*
Robin and the 7 Hoods *'64*
The Balcony *'63*
Beach Party *'63*
It's a Mad, Mad, Mad, Mad World *'63*
Pressure Point *'62*
Pocketful of Miracles *'61*
Murder, Inc. *'60*
The Bloody Brood *'59*

Rossella Falk (1926-)

The Black Belly of the Tarantula *'71*
Modesty Blaise *'66*
8 1/2 *'63*

Deborah Fallender

S.O.S. Titanic *'79*
Jabberwocky *'77*

Jimmy Fallon (1974-)

Whip It *'09*
Arthur and the Invisibles *'06 (V)*
Factory Girl *'06*
Fever Pitch *'05*
Taxi *'04*
Anything Else *'03*
Band of Brothers *'01*
Almost Famous *'00*

Bingbing Fan

Flash Point *'07*
Lost in Beijing *'07*

Roger Fan

Annapolis *'06*
Better Luck Tomorrow *'02*
Corky Romano *'01*

Mary Fanaro

Truth or Dare? *'86*
Demon Queen *'80*

Richard Fancy

Adventures of Power *'08*
Midnight Clear *'06*

Al Fann (1925-)

Frankie and Johnny *'91*
Parasite *'82*
Sophisticated Gents *'81*

Dakota Fanning (1994-)

The Runaways *'10*
The Twilight Saga: Eclipse *'10*
Coraline *'09 (V)*
Push *'09*
The Twilight Saga: New Moon *'09*
Fragments *'08*
Hounddog *'08*
The Secret Life of Bees *'08*
Charlotte's Web *'06*
Dreamer: Inspired by a True Story *'05*
Hide and Seek *'05*
Lilo & Stitch 2: Stitch Has a Glitch *'05 (V)*
Nine Lives *'05*
War of the Worlds *'05*
Man on Fire *'04*
Dr. Seuss' The Cat in the Hat *'03*
Uptown Girls *'03*
Sweet Home Alabama *'02*
Taken *'02 (N)*
Trapped *'02*
I Am Sam *'01*

Elle Fanning (1998-)

The Curious Case of Benjamin Button *'08*
Phoebe in Wonderland *'08*
Reservation Road *'07*
Babel *'06*
Because of Winn-Dixie *'05*
The Door in the Floor *'04*

Franco Fantasia (1928-)

Emerald Jungle *'80*
Mountain of the Cannibal God *'79*
Adios, Sabata *'71*
Revenge of the Musketeers *'63*

Ennio Fantastichini (1955-)

Saturn in Opposition *'07*
Napoleon *'03*
The Blonde *'92*
The Station *'92*
Open Doors *'89*

Sergio Fantoni (1930-)

The Belly of an Architect *'91*
Hornet's Nest *'70*
What Did You Do in the War, Daddy? *'66*
Do Not Disturb *'65*
Von Ryan's Express *'65*
The Prize *'63*
Atom Age Vampire *'61*
Esther and the King *'60*
The Giant of Marathon *'60*
The Hit Man *'60*

Stephanie Faracy (1952-)

Flightplan *'05*
Safety Patrol *'98*
Hocus Pocus *'93*
The Great Outdoors *'88*
Blind Date *'87*

Golshifteh Farahani

Body of Lies *'08*
Boutique *'04*

Daniel Faraldo

Full Fathom Five *'90*
Above the Law *'88*

Debrah Farentino (1961-)

Stephen King's The Storm of the Century *'99*
Dead Air *'94*
Son of the Pink Panther *'93*
Bugsy *'91*
Mortal Sins *'90*
Capone *'89*

James Farentino (1938-)

Termination Man *'97*
Bulletproof *'96*
Honor Thy Father and Mother: The True Story of the Menendez Brothers *'94*
In the Line of Duty: A Cop for the Killing *'90*
Naked Lie *'89*
Her Alibi *'88*
Family Sins *'87*
Sins *'85*
License to Kill *'84*
A Summer to Remember *'84*
The Cradle Will Fall *'83*
Dead and Buried *'81*
The Final Countdown *'80*
Silent Victory: The Kitty O'Neil Story *'79*
The Possessed *'77*
The War Lord *'65*
Ensign Pulver *'64*
Psychomania *'63*

Debra Fares

Killer Tomatoes Eat France *'91*
Killer Tomatoes Strike Back *'90*

Antonio Fargas (1946-)

Extreme Honor *'01*
Three Strikes *'00*
The Suburbans *'99*
Milo *'98*
Howling 6: The Freaks *'90*
The Borrower *'89*
I'm Gonna Git You Sucka *'88*
Shakedown *'88*
Florida Straits *'87*
Night of the Sharks *'87*
Crimewave *'85*
Streetwalkin' *'85*
Firestarter *'84*
The Ambush Murders *'82*
Nurse *'80*
Milo Milo *'79*
Pretty Baby *'78*
Car Wash *'76*
Cornbread, Earl & Me *'75*
Huckleberry Finn *'75*
Busting *'74*
Foxy Brown *'74*
Across 110th Street *'72*
Shaft *'71*
Gator King *'70*

Betty Faria (1941-)

The Story of Fausta *'88*
Bye Bye Brazil *'79*

Carolyn Farina

Metropolitan *'90*
The Mayor of Hell *'33*

Dennis Farina (1944-)

Bottle Shock *'08*
What Happens in Vegas *'08*
Purple Violets *'07*
You Kill Me *'07*
Empire Falls *'05*
Paparazzi *'04*
Big Trouble *'02*
Stealing Harvard *'02*
Sidewalks of New York *'01*
Bad Seed *'00*
Reindeer Games *'00*
Snatch *'00*
The Mod Squad *'99*
Out of Sight *'98*
Saving Private Ryan *'98*
Bella Mafia *'97*
Eddie *'96*
That Old Feeling *'96*
Get Shorty *'95*
Little Big League *'94*
Out of Annie's Past *'94*
Another Stakeout *'93*
High Stakes *'93*
Mac *'93*
Striking Distance *'93*
Drug Wars 2: The Cocaine Cartel *'92*
Street Crimes *'92*
We're Talkin' Serious Money *'92*
Men of Respect *'91*
The Hillside Strangler *'89*
Midnight Run *'88*
Jo Jo Dancer, Your Life Is Calling *'86*
Manhunter *'86*
Code of Silence *'85*
Thief *'81*

Daniela Farinacci

Look Both Ways *'05*
Lantana *'01*

Gabriella Farinon (1941-)

Assignment Outer Space *'61*
Blood and Roses *'61*

Anna Faris (1976-)

Alvin and the Chipmunks: The Squeakuel *'09 (V)*
Cloudy with a Chance of Meatballs *'09 (V)*
Observe and Report *'09*
The House Bunny *'08*
Mama's Boy *'07*
Smiley Face *'07*
My Super Ex-Girlfriend *'06*
Scary Movie 4 *'06*
Brokeback Mountain *'05*
Just Friends *'05*
Southern Belles *'05*
Waiting *'05*
Lost in Translation *'03*
Scary Movie 3 *'03*
The Hot Chick *'02*
May *'02*
Scary Movie 2 *'01*
Scary Movie *'00*

Sean Faris (1982-)

Forever Strong *'08*
Never Back Down *'08*
Yours, Mine & Ours *'05*
Sleepover *'04*
Brotherhood 2: The Young Warlocks *'01*

Albert Farley

See Alberto (Albert Farley) Farnese

Chris Farley (1964-97)

Almost Heroes *'97*
Dirty Work *'97*
Beverly Hills Ninja *'96*
Black Sheep *'96*
Tommy Boy *'95*
Airheads *'94*
Billy Madison *'94*
Coneheads *'93*
Wayne's World 2 *'93*

Jim Farley (1882-1947)
The Midnight Phantom *'35*
The General *'26*

John Farley
Believers *'07*
Blonde and Blonder *'07*

Kevin Farley
An American Carol *'08*
Dog Gone *'08*
Blonde and Blonder *'07*
Danny Roane: First Time Director *'06*
Frank McKlusky, C.I. *'02*

Morgan Farley (1898-1988)
Goodbye My Fancy *'51*
Abbott and Costello Meet the Killer, Boris Karloff *'49*
Barricade *'49*
Open Secret *'48*

Sean Farley (1976-)
Tainted *'98*
Crimewave *'85*

Teresa Farley
Breeders *'86*
Bad Girls Dormitory *'84*

Frances Farmer (1913-70)
Son of Fury *'42*
South of Pago Pago *'40*
Toast of New York *'37*
Come and Get It *'36*
Rhythm on the Range *'36*

Gary Farmer (1953-)
All Hat *'07*
Disappearances *'06*
The Big Empty *'04*
Evergreen *'04*
A Thief of Time *'04*
The Republic of Love *'03*
Twist *'03*
Adaptation *'02*
Skins *'02*
The Score *'01*
Angels Don't Sleep Here *'00*
Heater *'99*
Smoke Signals *'98*
Moonshine Highway *'96*
Dead Man *'95*
Henry & Verlin *'94*
Sioux City *'94*
Tales from the Crypt Presents Demon Knight *'94*
Blown Away *'93*
Powwow Highway *'89*
Big Town *'87*

Mimsy Farmer (1945-)
Codename: Wildgeese *'84*
The Black Cat *'81*
Autopsy *'74*
Allonsanfan *'73*
Four Flies on Grey Velvet *'72*
More *'69*
Road to Salina *'68*
Devil's Angels *'67*
Spencer's Mountain *'63*

Suzan Farmer (1943-)
Death in Deep Water *'74*
The Graveyard *'74*
Dracula, Prince of Darkness *'66*
Rasputin the Mad Monk *'66*
Die, Monster, Die! *'65*
The Devil-Ship Pirates *'64*

Vera Farmiga (1973-)
Orphan *'09*
Up in the Air *'09*
The Boy in the Striped Pajamas *'08*
Nothing But the Truth *'08*
Quid Pro Quo *'08*
In Tranzit *'07*
Joshua *'07*
Never Forever *'07*
Breaking and Entering *'06*
The Departed *'06*
Running Scared *'06*
Down to the Bone *'04*
The Manchurian Candidate *'04*
Dummy *'02*
Love in the Time of Money *'02*
Snow White: The Fairest of Them All *'02*
15 Minutes *'01*
Autumn in New York *'00*
Return to Paradise *'98*

Alberto (Albert Farley) Farnese (1926-96)
Scalps *'83*
The Conqueror & the Empress *'64*
Two Gladiators *'64*
Gladiator of Rome *'63*
The Giants of Thessaly *'60*

Matt Farnsworth
Iowa *'05*
The Stepdaughter *'00*

Richard Farnsworth (1920-2000)
The Straight Story *'99*
Lassie *'94*
The Fire Next Time *'93*
Highway to Hell *'92*
Havana *'90*
Misery *'90*
The Two Jakes *'90*
The River Pirates *'88*
Witchery *'88*
Space Rage *'86*
Anne of Green Gables *'85*
Chase *'85*
Into the Night *'85*
Sylvester *'85*
The Natural *'84*
Rhinestone *'84*
The Grey Fox *'83*
Independence Day *'83*
Waltz across Texas *'83*
Legend of the Lone Ranger *'81*
Ruckus *'81*
Resurrection *'80*
Tom Horn *'80*
Comes a Horseman *'78*
Strange New World *'75*
Texas Across the River *'66*

Franklyn Farnum (1878-1961)
Prison Train *'38*
Ghost Rider *'35*
Hopalong Cassidy *'35*
Powdersmoke Range *'35*
The Silver Bullet *'34*
Mark of the Spur *'32*
Battling with Buffalo Bill *'31*
The Scarlet Car *'17*

William Farnum (1876-1953)
Jack & the Beanstalk *'52*
Lone Star *'52*
Trail of Robin Hood *'50*
Gun Cargo *'49*
God's Country *'46*
My Dog Shep *'46*
Wildfire *'45*
The Silver Bullet *'42*
Today I Hang *'42*
Gangs of Sonora *'41*
Adventures of Red Ryder *'40*
South of the Border *'39*
Santa Fe Stampede *'38*
Git Along Little Dogies *'37*
Public Cowboy No. 1 *'37*
The Clutching Hand *'36*
Custer's Last Stand *'36*
Kid Ranger *'36*
Undersea Kingdom *'36*
The Vigilantes Are Coming *'36*
Between Men *'35*
The Crusades *'35*
Powdersmoke Range *'35*
The Silver Streak *'34*
Supernatural *'33*
The Drifter *'32*
Law of the Sea *'32*
Mr. Robinson Crusoe *'32*
A Connecticut Yankee *'31*
Painted Desert *'31*
Ten Nights in a Bar-Room *'31*
Dubarry *'30*
The Spoilers *'14*

Derek Farr (1912-86)
Truth about Women *'58*
Man on the Run *'49*
Spellbound *'41*

Felicia Farr (1932-)
Charley Varrick *'73*
Kotch *'71*
Kiss Me, Stupid! *'64*
3:10 to Yuma *'57*
The First Texan *'56*
Jubal *'56*

Jamie Farr (1936-)
A Grandpa for Christmas *'07*
Fearless Tiger *'94*
Curse 2: The Bite *'88*
Scrooged *'88*
Speed Zone *'88*
Happy Hour *'87*
Combat Academy *'86*
Cannonball Run 2 *'84*
For Love or Money *'84*
M*A*S*H: Goodbye, Farewell & Amen *'83*
Cannonball Run *'81*
Return of the Rebels *'81*
Arnold *'73*
Heavy Traffic *'73*
With Six You Get Eggroll *'68*
Who's Minding the Mint? *'67*
The Loved One *'65*
No Time for Sergeants *'58*
Blackboard Jungle *'55*

Judi Farr
Walking on Water *'02*
The Year My Voice Broke *'87*

Patricia Farr (1915-48)
Mistaken Identity *'36*
Tailspin Tommy *'34*

David Farrar (1908-95)
The 300 Spartans *'62*
Beat Girl *'60*
John Paul Jones *'59*
Let's Make Up *'55*
Pearl of the South Pacific *'55*
Sea Chase *'55*
The Black Shield of Falworth *'54*
The Obsessed *'51*
The Small Back Room *'49*
Black Narcissus *'47*
Frieda *'47*
The World Owes Me a Living *'47*
Murder in the Footlights *'46*
Echo Murders *'45*
Meet Sexton Blake *'44*
The Hooded Terror *'38*

Charles Farrell (1901-88)
The Abominable Dr. Phibes *'71*
The Vampire Lovers *'70*
Girl Hunters *'63*
The Sheriff of Fractured Jaw *'59*
Crimson Pirate *'52*
Night and the City *'50*
They Made Me a Fugitive *'47*
Meet Sexton Blake *'44*
After Tomorrow *'32*
Lucky Star *'29*
Street Angel *'28*
7th Heaven *'27*

Charles Farrell (1901-90)
Just Around the Corner *'38*
Moonlight Sonata *'38*
Aggie Appleby, Maker of Men *'33*
City Girl *'30*
Old Ironsides *'26*

Colin Farrell (1938-)
The Imaginarium of Doctor Parnassus *'09*
A Bridge Too Far *'77*
The Land That Time Forgot *'75*
Oh! What a Lovely War *'69*

Colin Farrell (1976-)
Crazy Heart *'09*
In Bruges *'08*
Pride and Glory *'08*
Cassandra's Dream *'07*
Ask the Dust *'06*
Miami Vice *'06*
The New World *'05*
Alexander *'04*
A Home at the End of the World *'04*
Daredevil *'03*
The Recruit *'03*
S.W.A.T. *'03*
Veronica Guerin *'03*
Hart's War *'02*
Minority Report *'02*
Phone Booth *'02*
American Outlaws *'01*
Tigerland *'00*
Ordinary Decent Criminal *'99*
Falling for a Dancer *'98*
The War Zone *'98*

Glenda Farrell (1904-71)
Disorderly Orderly *'64*
Kissin' Cousins *'64*
The Girl in the Red Velvet Swing *'55*
Heading for Heaven *'47*
City Without Men *'43*
Johnny Eager *'42*
A Night for Crime *'42*
Talk of the Town *'42*
Twin Beds *'42*
Prison Break *'38*
Breakfast for Two *'37*
Hollywood Hotel *'37*
Gold Diggers of 1937 *'36*
Go Into Your Dance *'35*
Gold Diggers of 1935 *'35*
Bureau of Missing Persons *'33*
Gambling Ship *'33*
Havana Widows *'33*
Lady for a Day *'33*
Mystery of the Wax Museum *'33*
I Am a Fugitive from a Chain Gang *'32*
Little Caesar *'30*

Mike Farrell (1939-)
Out at the Wedding *'07*
Sins of the Mind *'97*
Silent Motive *'91*
Dark River: A Father's Revenge *'90*
Lockdown *'90*
Vanishing Act *'88*
M*A*S*H: Goodbye, Farewell & Amen *'83*
Memorial Day *'83*
Prime Suspect *'82*
Sex and the Single Parent *'82*
Damien: The Leper Priest *'80*
Targets *'68*
Escape from Planet Earth *'67*
The Graduate *'67*

Nicholas Farrell (1955-)
The Diary of Anne Frank *'08*
Amazing Grace *'06*
Driving Lessons *'06*
Bait *'02*
Bloody Sunday *'01*
Charlotte Gray *'01*
Beautiful People *'99*
Legionnaire *'98*
Hamlet *'96*
Sharpe's Regiment *'96*
Twelfth Night *'96*
The Choir *'95*
A Midwinter's Tale *'95*
Othello *'95*
To Play the King *'93*
Hold the Dream *'86*

Sharon Farrell (1946-)
Beyond Desire *'94*
Arcade *'93*
One Man Force *'89*
Can't Buy Me Love *'87*
Night of the Comet *'84*
Baby Broker *'81*
Rage *'80*
The Stunt Man *'80*
The Premonition *'75*
It's Alive *'74*
The Love Machine *'71*
Marlowe *'69*
The Reivers *'69*
40 Pounds of Trouble *'62*

Terry Farrell (1963-)
Deep Core *'00*
Legion *'98*
Red Sun Rising *'94*
Danielle Steel's Star *'93*
Hellraiser 3: Hell on Earth *'92*
Off the Mark *'87*
Back to School *'86*
Beverly Hills Madam *'86*

Timothy Farrell (1923-89)
Gun Girls *'56*
Jail Bait *'54*
Glen or Glenda? *'53*
The Devil's Sleep *'51*
Pin Down Girls *'51*
Test Tube Babies *'48*

Tommy Farrell (1921-2004)
Kissin' Cousins *'64*
Meet Danny Wilson *'52*
Pirates of the High Seas *'50*

Mia Farrow (1945-)
Be Kind Rewind *'08*
The Ex *'07*
Arthur and the Invisibles *'06*
The Omen *'06*
Purpose *'02*
A Girl Thing *'01*
Coming Soon *'99*
Miracle at Midnight *'98*
Miami Rhapsody *'95*
Reckless *'95*
Widow's Peak *'94*
Husbands and Wives *'92*
Shadows and Fog *'92*
Alice *'90*
Crimes & Misdemeanors *'89*
New York Stories *'89*
Another Woman *'88*
September *'88*
Radio Days *'87*
Hannah and Her Sisters *'86*
The Purple Rose of Cairo *'85*
Broadway Danny Rose *'84*
Supergirl *'84*
Zelig *'83*
The Last Unicorn *'82 (V)*
A Midsummer Night's Sex Comedy *'82*
Hurricane *'79*
Avalanche *'78*
Death on the Nile *'78*
A Wedding *'78*
Full Circle *'77*
The Great Gatsby *'74*
High Heels *'72*
See No Evil *'71*
Secret Ceremony *'69*
Dandy in Aspic *'68*
Rosemary's Baby *'68*
Guns at Batasi *'64*

Tisa Farrow (1951-)
Grim Reaper *'81*
Search and Destroy *'81*
The Last Hunter *'80*
Zombie *'80*
Manhattan *'79*
Winter Kills *'79*
Fingers *'78*
Initiation of Sarah *'78*
Strange Shadows in an Empty Room *'76*
Some Call It Loving *'73*
And Hope to Die *'72*

Michael Fassbender (1977-)
Jonah Hex *'10*
Blood Creek *'09*
Fish Tank *'09*
Inglourious Basterds *'09*
300 *'07*

Rainer Werner Fassbinder (1946-82)
Kamikaze '89 *'83*
Shadow of Angels *'76*
Fox and His Friends *'75*
Tenderness of the Wolves *'73*
The American Soldier *'70*
Beware of a Holy Whore *'70*
Whity *'70*

Ron Fassler (1957-)
Alien Nation: The Enemy Within *'96*
Alien Nation: Dark Horizon *'94*

Fat Joe (1970-)
Empire *'02*
Thicker than Water *'99*
Urban Menace *'99*

Joey Fatone (1977-)
Beethoven's Big Break *'08*
The Cooler *'03*
My Big Fat Greek Wedding *'02*
On the Line *'01*

Andrew Faulds (1922-2000)
Lisztomania *'75*
The Devils *'71*

James Faulkner (1948-)
The Bank Job *'08*
Day of Wrath *'06*
Agent Cody Banks 2: Destination London *'04*
I Capture the Castle *'02*
The Target *'02*
All the Little Animals *'98*
A Kid in Aladdin's Palace *'97*
Crimetime *'96*
Wavelength *'96*
The Blackheath Poisonings *'92*
Devices and Desires *'91*
The Maid *'90*
Flashpoint Africa *'84*
Albino *'76*
Conduct Unbecoming *'75*

Sally Faulkner (1944-)
Alien Prey *'78*
Vampyres *'74*

Stephanie Faulkner
Virus *'82*
Death Journey *'76*
Ghetto Revenge *'71*

Renee Faure (1918-2005)
The Judge and the Assassin *'75*
La Chartreuse de Parme *'48*

Chad Faust (1980-)
Descent *'07*
Nearing Grace *'05*
Saved! *'04*

David Faustino (1974-)
The Boston Strangler: The Untold Story *'08*
National Lampoon Presents RoboDoc *'08*
MacArthur Park *'01*
Killer Bud *'00*
Alien Nation: Millennium *'96*
Perfect Harmony *'91*

Pierfrancesco Favino (1969-)
The Chronicles of Narnia: Prince Caspian *'08*
Miracle at St. Anna *'08*
Saturn in Opposition *'07*
The Unknown Woman *'06*
Our Italian Husband *'04*
The Last Kiss *'01*

Jon Favreau (1966-)
Iron Man 2 *'10*
Couples Retreat *'09*
G-Force *'09 (V)*
I Love You, Man *'09*
Four Christmases *'08*
Iron Man *'08*

The Break-Up '06
Open Season '06 (V)
The Big Empty '04
Wimbledon '04
Daredevil '03
Elf '03
Something's Gotta Give '03
Made '01
Love & Sex '00
The Replacements '00
Rocky Marciano '99
Deep Impact '98
Very Bad Things '98
Dogtown '97
Just Your Luck '96
Persons Unknown '96
Swingers '96
Batman Forever '95
Notes from Underground '95
P.C.U. '94
Rudy '93

Alan Fawcett
Blindside '88
A Conspiracy of Love '87

Farrah Fawcett (1946-2009)
The Cookout '04
Baby '00
Dr. T & the Women '00
The Apostle '97
Dalva '95
A Good Day to Die '95
Man of the House '95
The Substitute Wife '94
Double Exposure: The Story of Margaret Bourke-White '89
See You in the Morning '89
Small Sacrifices '89
Poor Little Rich Girl: The Barbara Hutton Story '87
Between Two Women '86
Extremities '86
The Burning Bed '85
The Red Light Sting '84
Cannonball Run '81
Murder in Texas '81
Saturn 3 '80
Sunburn '79
Logan's Run '76
Murder on Flight 502 '75
Myra Breckinridge '70

George Fawcett (1860-1939)
Drums of Jeopardy '31
Personal Maid '31
Tempest '28
The Wedding March '28
The Flesh and the Devil '27
Spring Fever '27
Son of the Sheik '26
The Mad Whirl '25
Up the Ladder '25
The Greatest Question '19
Heart of Texas Ryan '17

William "Bill" Fawcett (1894-1974)
Jesse James Meets Frankenstein's Daughter '65
King Rat '65
Gun Glory '57
Storm Rider '57
Seminole Uprising '55
Black Hills '48
Check Your Guns '48
The Tioga Kid '48
Wild Country '47
Driftin' River '46

Dorothy Fay (1915-2003)
Trigger Pals '39
Law of the Texan '38
The Stranger from Arizona '38

Frank Fay (1897-1961)
Love Nest '51
Spotlight Scandals '43

Meagen Fay
The Country Bears '02
Armistead Maupin's Tales of the City '93

Alice Faye (1915-98)
Every Girl Should Have One '78
Magic of Lassie '78
State Fair '62
The Gang's All Here '43
Hello, Frisco, Hello '43
The Great American Broadcast '41
That Night in Rio '41
Week-End in Havana '41
Lillian Russell '40
Tin Pan Alley '40
Hollywood Cavalcade '39
Rose of Washington Square '39
Alexander's Ragtime Band '38
In Old Chicago '37
On the Avenue '37
The Poor Little Rich Girl '36
Stowaway '36
365 Nights in Hollywood '34

Denise Faye
American Pie 2 '01
The Next Step '95

Frank Faylen (1905-85)
Gunfight at the O.K. Corral '57
Seventh Cavalry '56
The McConnell Story '55
Red Garters '54
Riot in Cell Block 11 '54
Hangman's Knot '52
The Sniper '52
Detective Story '51
Copper Canyon '50
The Nevadan '50
Francis the Talking Mule '49
The Road to Rio '47
Welcome Stranger '47
Blue Skies '46
It's a Wonderful Life '46
The Lost Weekend '45
Across the Pacific '42
Wake Island '42
Sergeant York '41
Tanks a Million '41
Gone with the Wind '39
Waterfront '39

Louise Fazenda (1895-1962)
The Old Maid '39
Colleen '36
Doughnuts & Society '36
Wonder Bar '34
Gun Smoke '31
On with the Show '29
The Bat '26
The Night Club '25

Ron Fazio
Basket Case 2 '90
The Toxic Avenger, Part 2 '89
The Toxic Avenger, Part 3: The Last Temptation of Toxie '89

Michael Feast (1946-)
The Deaths of Ian Stone '07
Penelope '06
Velvet Goldmine '98
Touching Evil '97

Angela Featherstone (1965-)
What Doesn't Kill You '08
Federal Protection '02
One Way Out '02
Pressure '02
Skipped Parts '00
The Guilty '99
Palmetto '98
200 Cigarettes '98
Con Air '97
Family of Cops 2: Breach of Faith '97
The Wedding Singer '97
Zero Effect '97
Illtown '96
Family of Cops '95
Dark Angel: The Ascent '94

Jan Fedder
Soul Kitchen '09
Das Boot '81

Birgitte Federspiel (1925-2005)
Babette's Feast '87
Ordet '55

Melinda Fee (1942-)
Doin' Time '85
Aliens Are Coming '80
Fade to Black '80

Caroleen Feeney
Happy Hour '03
Avalanche '99
Bad Manners '98
Cadillac Ranch '96
Denise Calls Up '95

Bekim Fehmiu (1936-)
Battle of the Eagles '79
Ride to Glory '71
The Adventurers '70

Brendan Fehr (1977-)
The Long Weekend '05
Biker Boyz '03
Nemesis Game '03
Edge of Madness '02
The Forsaken '01
Kill Me Later '01
Christina's House '99

Oded Fehr (1970-)
Resident Evil: Extinction '07
Deuce Bigalow: European Gigolo '05
Dreamer: Inspired by a True Story '05
Sleeper Cell '05
Resident Evil: Apocalypse '04
The Mummy Returns '01
Texas Rangers '01
Deuce Bigalow: Male Gigolo '99
The Mummy '99

Trevor Fehrman (1981-)
Clerks 2 '06
Now You Know '02

Martin Feifel (1964-)
Rosenstrasse '03
What to Do in Case of Fire '02

Halley Feiffer
Gentlemen Broncos '09
Margot at the Wedding '07
Stephanie Daley '06
The Squid and the Whale '05

J.J. Feild (1978-)
Northanger Abbey '07
O Jerusalem '07
The Shadow in the North '07
Ruby in the Smoke '06
The Secret Life of Mrs. Beeton '06
The Intended '02
Last Orders '01

Alan Feinstein (1941-)
The Hunt for the Night Stalker '91
The Two Worlds of Jenny Logan '79
Bunco '77
The Hunted Lady '77
Joe Panther '76

Fritz Feld (1900-93)
Get Smart, Again! '89
Barfly '87
History of the World: Part 1 '81
Herbie Goes Bananas '80
World's Greatest Lover '77
The Strongest Man in the World '75
Promises! Promises! '63
The Errand Boy '61
Kentucky Jubilee '51
Sky High '51
The Lovable Cheat '49
Mexican Hayride '48
The Noose Hangs High '48
Iceland '42
Four Jacks and a Jill '41
At the Circus '39

Everything Happens at Night '39
The Affairs of Annabel '38
Bringing Up Baby '38
Campus Confessions '38
Gold Diggers in Paris '38
Last Command '28

Clarence Felder (1938-)
The Hidden '87
Killing Floor '85

Andrea Feldman (1948-72)
Heat '72
Trash '70

Ben Feldman (1980-)
The Perfect Man '05
When Do We Eat? '05

Corey Feldman (1971-)
Lost Boys: The Tribe '08
No Witness '04
The Million Dollar Kid '99
Legion '98
Storm Trooper '98
Born Bad '97
Evil Obsession '96
Red Line '96
South Beach Academy '96
Tales from the Crypt Presents Bordello of Blood '96
Voodoo '95
A Dangerous Place '94
Dream a Little Dream 2 '94
National Lampoon's Last Resort '94
Blown Away '93
Lipstick Camera '93
The Magic Voyage '93 (V)
National Lampoon's Loaded Weapon 1 '93
Meatballs 4 '92
Round Trip to Heaven '92
Stepmonster '92
Edge of Honor '91
Rock 'n' Roll High School Forever '91
Teenage Mutant Ninja Turtles: The Movie '90 (V)
The 'Burbs '89
Dream a Little Dream '89
License to Drive '88
The Lost Boys '87
Stand by Me '86
Friday the 13th, Part 5: A New Beginning '85
The Goonies '85
Friday the 13th, Part 4: The Final Chapter '84
Gremlins '84
The Fox and the Hound '81 (V)

Marty Feldman (1933-82)
Slapstick of Another Kind '84
Yellowbeard '83
In God We Trust '80
The Adventures of Sherlock Holmes' Smarter Brother '78
The Last Remake of Beau Geste '77
Sex with a Smile '76
Silent Movie '76
Young Frankenstein '74
Think Dirty '70

Tibor Feldman (1947-)
Fat Guy Goes Nutzoid '86
The River is Red '48

Barbara Feldon (1941-)
The Last Request '06
Get Smart, Again! '89
Children of Divorce '80
A Guide for the Married Woman '78
No Deposit, No Return '76
Smile '75
Playmates '72

Tovah Feldshuh (1952-)
Love Comes Lately '07
O Jerusalem '07
Just My Luck '06
Lady in the Water '06

The Tollbooth '04
Kissing Jessica Stein '02
Friends and Family '01
Happy Accidents '00
The Corruptor '99
A Walk on the Moon '99
A Day in October '92
Blue Iguana '88
Brewster's Millions '85
Cheaper to Keep Her '80
Idolmaker '80
The Triangle Factory Fire Scandal '79
Holocaust '78
Terror Out of the Sky '78
The Amazing Howard Hughes '77

Mario Feliciani (1918-)
Assassination in Rome '65
Revolt of the Barbarians '64

Jose Feliciano (1945-)
Fargo '96
Aaron Loves Angela '75

Norman Fell (1924-98)
The Destiny of Marty Fine '96
Hexed '93
For the Boys '91
The Bone Yard '90
Stripped to Kill '87
Transylvania 6-5000 '85
On the Right Track '81
Paternity '81
For the Love of It '80
The End '78
Cleopatra Jones & the Casino of Gold '75
Death Stalk '74
Charley Varrick '73
The Stone Killer '73
The Boatniks '70
Catch-22 '70
If It's Tuesday, This Must Be Belgium '69
Bullitt '68
The Graduate '67
The Killers '64
It's a Mad, Mad, Mad, Mad World '63
Inherit the Wind '60
Ocean's 11 '60
Pork Chop Hill '59

Tom Felleghi
Hornet's Nest '70
Revenge of the Barbarians '60

Federico Fellini (1920-93)
Fellini: I'm a Born Liar '03
Intervista '87
We All Loved Each Other So Much '77
Fellini's Roma '72 (V)
Alex in Wonderland '70
Ciao Federico! Fellini Directs Satyricon '69
The Miracle '48

Julian Fellowes (1950-)
The Young Victoria '09
The Aristocrats '99
Behind the Lines '97
The Final Cut '95
Sharpe's Rifles '93
Damage '92
Goldeneye: The Secret Life of Ian Fleming '89
Baby... Secret of the Lost Legend '85

Rockliffe Fellowes (1885-1950)
Monkey Business '31
The Charlatan '29
Regeneration '15

Edith Fellows (1923-)
In the Mood '87
The Grace Kelly Story '83
Heart of the Rio Grande '42
Her First Romance '40
Music in My Heart '40
Pennies from Heaven '36
The Rider of Death Valley '32

Hansjorg Felmy (1931-2007)
The Mad Executioners '65
The Monster of London City '64
Brainwashed '60

Tom Felton (1987-)
Harry Potter and the Half-Blood Prince '09
The Disappeared '08
Harry Potter and the Order of the Phoenix '07
Harry Potter and the Goblet of Fire '05
Harry Potter and the Prisoner of Azkaban '04
Harry Potter and the Chamber of Secrets '02
Harry Potter and the Sorcerer's Stone '01
Anna and the King '99
The Borrowers '97

Verna Felton (1890-1966)
The Jungle Book '67 (V)
Sleeping Beauty '59 (V)
The Oklahoman '56
Lady and the Tramp '55 (V)
Picnic '55
Belles on Their Toes '52
Cinderella '50 (V)
Dumbo '41 (V)

Freddy Fender (1937-2006)
The Milagro Beanfield War '88
She Came to the Valley '77

Edwige Fenech (1948-)
Hostel: Part 2 '07
Phantom of Death '87
You've Got to Have Heart '77
Sex with a Smile '76
Escape from Death Row '73
The Case of the Bloody Iris '72
Your Vice is a Closed Room and Only I Have the Key '72
The Next Victim '71
Blade of the Ripper '70
Five Dolls for an August Moon '70
The Seducers '70

Mei Feng
Spring Fever '09
A Time to Live and a Time to Die '85

Tanya Fenmore
Lisa '90
My Stepmother Is an Alien '88

Sherilyn Fenn (1965-)
Novel Romance '06
Nightwaves '03
United States of Leland '03
Swindle '02
Off Season '01
Cement '99
Darkness Falls '98
Outside Ozona '98
Just Write '97
Lovelife '97
National Lampoon's The Don's Analyst '97
The Assassination File '96
Boxing Helena '93
Fatal Instinct '93
Three of Hearts '93
Desire and Hell at Sunset Motel '92
Of Mice and Men '92
Ruby '92
Diary of a Hitman '91
Dillinger '91
Backstreet Dreams '90
Meridian: Kiss of the Beast '90
Wild at Heart '90
True Blood '89
Crime Zone '88
Two Moon Junction '88
The Wraith '87

Zombie High *'87*
Just One of the Guys *'85*
Silence of the Heart *'84*
The Wild Life *'84*

Tod Fennell (1984-)

The Kid *'97*
Stalked *'94*

Parker Fennelly (1891-1988)

How to Frame a Figg *'71*
The Kettles on Old MacDonald's Farm *'57*

George Fenneman (1919-97)

The Marx Brothers in a Nutshell *'90*
How to Succeed in Business without Really Trying *'67*
The Thing *'51*

Shelby Fenner (1978-)

The Guardian *'06*
Local Boys *'02*

Frank Fenton (1906-57)

Naked Hills *'56*
Island in the Sky *'53*
The Clay Pigeon *'49*
The Golden Stallion *'49*
Mexican Hayride *'48*
Isle of Forgotten Sins *'43*

Lance Fenton (1966-)

Heathers *'89*
Night of the Demons *'88*

Leslie Fenton (1902-78)

The House of Secrets *'37*
Fugitive Road *'34*
Marie Galante *'34*
F.P. 1 *'33*
Lady Killer *'33*
The Strange Love of Molly Louvain *'32*
Murder at Midnight *'31*
Public Enemy *'31*
Lazybones *'25*

Simon Fenton (1976-)

A Knight in Camelot *'98*
The Rector's Wife *'94*
Matinee *'92*

Perry Fenwick (1962-)

The Winslow Boy *'98*
The Raggedy Rawney *'90*
Party! Party! *'83*

Colm Feore (1958-)

Changeling *'08*
Guns *'08*
24 : Redemption *'08*
WarGames 2: The Dead Code *'08*
Bury My Heart at Wounded Knee *'07*
Hearts of War *'07*
Bon Cop Bad Cop *'06*
The Deal *'05*
The Exorcism of Emily Rose *'05*
Slings & Arrows: Season 2 *'05*
The Chronicles of Riddick *'04*
And Starring Pancho Villa as Himself *'03*
Highwaymen *'03*
National Security *'03*
Paycheck *'03*
Chicago *'02*
Point of Origin *'02*
The Sum of All Fears *'02*
Widows *'02*
The Caveman's Valentine *'01*
The Day Reagan Was Shot *'01*
Ignition *'01*
Pearl Harbor *'01*
Sins of the Father *'01*
The Perfect Son *'00*
The Insider *'99*
Stephen King's The Storm of the Century *'99*
Titus *'99*
Airborne *'98*
City of Angels *'98*
The Red Violin *'98*
Critical Care *'97*
Face/Off *'97*
Hostile Waters *'97*
The Lesser Evil *'97*
Night Falls on Manhattan *'96*
The Wrong Guy *'96*
The Escape *'95*
Truman *'95*
Where's the Money, Noreen? *'95*
The Spider and the Fly *'94*
32 Short Films about Glenn Gould *'93*
Beautiful Dreamers *'92*
Dr. Bethune *'90*
Personals *'90*
Blades of Courage *'88*

Heino Ferch (1963-)

The Trojan Horse *'08*
The 4 Musketeers *'05*
Downfall *'04*
Napoleon *'03*
Extreme Ops *'02*
The Tunnel *'01*
The Harmonists *'99*
Straight Shooter *'99*
Lucie Aubrac *'98*
Tower of the Firstborn *'98*
Winter Sleepers *'97*

Pamelyn Ferdin (1959-)

The Toolbox Murders *'78*
Charlotte's Web *'73 (V)*
Smoke *'70*

Tawny (Ellis) Fere

Rockula *'90*
Night Children *'89*
Angel 3: The Final Chapter *'88*

Adam Ferency (1951-)

The Interrogation *'82*
Mother of Kings *'82*
Fever *'81*

Dylan Fergus

Hellbent *'04*
6ixtynin9 *'99*

Al Ferguson (1888-1971)

Rose Marie *'54*
Lightning Raiders *'45*
Law of the Saddle *'43*
Laramie Kid *'35*
The Three Musketeers *'33*
Mystery Trooper *'32*
Near the Rainbow's End *'30*
Tarzan the Tiger *'29*
Tentacles of the North *'26*

Chloe Ferguson (1989-)

The Quiet Room *'96*
Alien Visitor *'95*

Colin Ferguson (1972-)

Because I Said So *'07*
Confessions of a Sociopathic Social Climber *'05*
The Opposite of Sex *'98*
Armistead Maupin's More Tales of the City *'97*
A Prayer in the Dark *'97*
Rowing Through *'96*

Craig Ferguson (1962-)

How to Train Your Dragon *'10 (V)*
Niagara Motel *'06*
I'll Be There *'03*
Life Without Dick *'01*
Born Romantic *'00*
Chain of Fools *'00*
Saving Grace *'00*
The Big Tease *'99*

Frank Ferguson (1899-1978)

Battle Cry *'55*
Johnny Guitar *'53*
Abbott and Costello Meet Frankenstein *'48*

J. Don Ferguson

The Second Chance *'06*
Running Mates *'86*
Loveless *'83*

Jay R. Ferguson (1989-)

The Killer Inside Me *'10*
Blue Ridge Fall *'99*
Campfire Tales *'98*

Mark Ferguson (1961-)

Hercules the Legendary Journeys, Vol. 3: The Circle of Fire *'94*
Hercules the Legendary Journeys, Vol. 4: In the Underworld *'94*

Matthew Ferguson (1973-)

Cube 2: Hypercube *'02*
The Wall *'99*
Lilies *'96*
The Club *'94*
Eclipse *'94*
Love and Human Remains *'93*
On My Own *'92*

Phoebe Ferguson (1993-)

The Quiet Room *'96*
Alien Visitor *'95*

Stacy "Fergie" Ferguson (1975-)

Marmaduke *'10 (V)*
Nine *'09*
Planet Terror *'07*
Poseidon *'06*

Tom Ferguson (1946-)

Biohazard: The Alien Force *'95*
Dark Universe *'93*

Anouk Ferjac (1932-)

Peppermint Soda *'77*
This Man Must Die *'70*

Jodelle Ferland (1994-)

Case 39 *'10*
The Twilight Saga: Eclipse *'10*
Wonderful World *'09*
Celine *'08*
Seed *'08*
Pictures of Hollis Woods *'07*
Silent Hill *'06*
Masters of Horror: The V Word *'05*
Tideland *'05*
Too Cool for Christmas *'04*
Mermaid *'00*

Vanessa Ferlito (1970-)

Wall Street 2: Money Never Sleeps *'10*
Julie & Julia *'09*
Madea Goes to Jail *'09*
Nothing Like the Holidays *'08*
Death Proof *'07*
Shadowboxer *'06*
Man of the House *'05*
Spider-Man 2 *'04*
Undefeated *'03*
On_Line *'01*

Fernando Fernan-Gomez (1921-2007)

Butterfly *'98*
The Grandfather *'98*
Belle Epoque *'92*
The Stilts *'84*
Mama Turns a Hundred *'79*
Spirit of the Beehive *'73*

Fernandel (1903-71)

Fernandel the Dressmaker *'57*
The Man in the Raincoat *'57*
Pantaloons *'57*
Paris Holiday *'57*
Around the World in 80 Days *'56*
Dressmaker *'56*
The French Touch *'54*
The Sheep Has Five Legs *'54*
Forbidden Fruit *'52*
Little World of Don Camillo *'51*
The Red Inn *'51*
Topaze *'51*
Well-Digger's Daughter *'46*
Nais *'45*
Le Schpountz *'38*
Harvest *'37*
Angele *'34*

Miguel Fernandes

Sorry, Wrong Number *'89*
True Believer *'89*
Spasms *'82*
The Kidnapping of the President *'80*

Abel Fernandez (1930-)

Pork Chop Hill *'59*
Rose Marie *'54*

Eduardo Fernandez

Before the Fall *'08*
The Method *'05*

Emilio Fernandez (1904-86)

Bring Me the Head of Alfredo Garcia *'74*
The Wild Bunch *'69*
Return of the Magnificent Seven *'66*
The Night of the Iguana *'64*

Esther Fernandez (1917-99)

Pancho Villa Returns *'50*
Two Years before the Mast *'46*

Evelina Fernandez

Gabriela *'01*
Luminarias *'99*
American Me *'92*

Jaime Fernandez

Samson vs. the Vampire Women *'61*
Massacre *'56*

Jesus Fernandez

Tristana *'70*
Nazarin *'58*

Juan Fernandez (1956-)

The Collector *'09*
A Love to Keep *'07*
The Lost City *'05*
Bad Education *'04*
A Man Apart *'03*
Dead Tides *'97*
Fire on the Amazon *'93*
Liquid Dreams *'92*
Cat Chaser *'90*
Kinjite: Forbidden Subjects *'89*
Crocodile Dundee 2 *'88*
Salvador *'86*
The Amazing Transplant *'70*

Shiloh Fernandez

Red *'08*
Interstate *'07*

Rudolf Fernau (1898-1985)

Strangler of Blackmoor Castle *'63*
The Invisible Dr. Mabuse *'62*

Abel Ferrara (1952-)

Ms. 45 *'81*
Driller Killer *'79*

Adam Ferrara

Paul Blart: Mall Cop *'09*
Definitely, Maybe *'08*
The Town That Banned Christmas *'06*

Ashley Ferrare

Cyclone *'87*
Revenge of the Ninja *'83*

Christina Ferrare (1950-)

Mary, Mary, Bloody Mary *'76*
The Impossible Years *'68*

Isabella Ferrari

Quiet Chaos *'08*
Saturn in Opposition *'07*

Nick Ferrari

Baby It's You *'82*
Sweet Sweetback's Baadasssss Song *'71*

Rebecca Ferratti (1964-)

To the Limit *'95*
Hard Vice *'94*
Vegas Vice *'94*
Small Kill *'93*
Cheerleader Camp *'88*
Gor *'88*
Outlaw of Gor *'87*

Conchata Ferrell (1943-)

Mr. Deeds *'02*
Crime and Punishment in Suburbia *'00*
Erin Brockovich *'00*
My Fellow Americans *'96*
Touch *'96*
The Buccaneers *'95*
Freeway *'95*
Heaven and Earth *'93*
Samurai Cowboy *'93*
True Romance *'93*
Backfield in Motion *'91*
Eye on the Sparrow *'91*
Family Prayers *'91*
Edward Scissorhands *'90*
Goodbye, Miss 4th of July *'88*
Mystic Pizza *'88*
Portrait of a White Marriage *'88*
Where the River Runs Black *'86*
Who'll Save Our Children? *'82*
Heartland *'81*
Rape and Marriage: The Rideout Case *'80*
To Love Again *'80*
Lost Legacy: A Girl Called Hatter Fox *'77*
Network *'76*
Deadly Hero *'75*

Tyra Ferrell (1962-)

The Perfect Score *'04*
The Corner *'00*
Better Off Dead *'94*
Equinox *'93*
Poetic Justice *'93*
Ulterior Motives *'92*
White Men Can't Jump *'92*
Boyz N the Hood *'91*
Jungle Fever *'91*
School Daze *'88*
Lady Beware *'87*

Will Ferrell (1968-)

The Other Guys *'10*
Land of the Lost *'09*
Semi-Pro *'08*
Step Brothers *'08*
Blades of Glory *'07*
Curious George *'06 (V)*
Stranger Than Fiction *'06*
Talladega Nights: The Ballad of Ricky Bobby *'06*
Bewitched *'05*
Kicking & Screaming *'05*
Melinda and Melinda *'05*
The Producers *'05*
Wedding Crashers *'05*
The Wendell Baker Story *'05*
Winter Passing *'05*
Anchorman: The Legend of Ron Burgundy *'04*
Starsky & Hutch *'04*
Boat Trip *'03*
Elf *'03*
Old School *'03*
Jay and Silent Bob Strike Back *'01*
Zoolander *'01*
The Ladies Man *'00*
Austin Powers 2: The Spy Who Shagged Me *'99*
Dick *'99*
The Suburbans *'99*
Superstar *'99*
A Night at the Roxbury *'98*
Austin Powers: International Man of Mystery *'97*

Andrea Ferreol (1947-)

Iris Blond *'98*
Francesco *'93*
Sweet Killing *'93*
The Phantom of the Opera *'90*
Stroke of Midnight *'90*
The Sleazy Uncle *'89*
A Zed & Two Noughts *'88*
Control *'87*
The Last Metro *'80*
Three Brothers *'80*
Milo Milo *'79*
The Tin Drum *'79*
Despair *'78*
La Grande Bouffe *'73*

Jose Ferrer (1909-92)

A Life of Sin *'92*
Hired to Kill *'91*
Old Explorers *'90*
Strange Interlude *'90*
Christopher Columbus *'85*
Seduced *'85*
Dune *'84*
The Evil That Men Do *'84*
George Washington *'84*
Samson and Delilah *'84*
The Being *'83*
To Be or Not to Be *'83*
Blood Tide *'82*
A Midsummer Night's Sex Comedy *'82*
Berlin Tunnel 21 *'81*
Peter and Paul *'81*
The Big Brawl *'80*
Bloody Birthday *'80*
Gideon's Trumpet *'80*
Pleasure Palace *'80*
The Fifth Musketeer *'79*
Natural Enemies *'79*
The Swarm *'78*
Zoltan... Hound of Dracula *'78*
The Private Files of J. Edgar Hoover *'77*
Who Has Seen the Wind? *'77*
The Big Bus *'76*
The Sentinel *'76*
Voyage of the Damned *'76*
The Art of Crime *'75*
Paco *'75*
Order to Kill *'73*
Enter Laughing *'67*
The Greatest Story Ever Told *'65*
Ship of Fools *'65*
Lawrence of Arabia *'62*
The Caine Mutiny *'54*
Deep in My Heart *'54*
Miss Sadie Thompson *'53*
Moulin Rouge *'52*
Crisis *'50*
Cyrano de Bergerac *'50*
Whirlpool *'49*
Joan of Arc *'48*

Leilani Sarelle Ferrer (1966-)

Breach of Trust *'95*
Sketch Artist 2: Hands That See *'94*
Barbarians at the Gate *'93*
Basic Instinct *'92*
The Harvest *'92*
Shag: The Movie *'89*
Neon Maniacs *'86*

Lupita Ferrer (1947-)

Balboa *'82*
Children of Sanchez *'79*

Mel Ferrer (1917-2008)

Catherine the Great *'95*
Outrage! *'86*
Deadly Game *'83*
One Shoe Makes It Murder *'82*
The Great Alligator *'81*
City of the Walking Dead *'80*
Emerald Jungle *'80*
The Fifth Floor *'80*
The Visitor *'80*
Norseman *'78*
Hi-Riders *'77*
Eaten Alive *'76*
Brannigan *'75*
The Tempter *'74*
The Fall of the Roman Empire *'64*
Paris When It Sizzles *'64*
Sex and the Single Girl *'64*

The Longest Day '62
Blood and Roses '61
The Hands of Orlac '60
Elena and Her Men '56
War and Peace '56
Knights of the Round Table '53
Lili '53
Rancho Notorious '52
Scaramouche '52
Born to Be Bad '50
Lost Boundaries '49

Miguel Ferrer (1954-)
The Man '05
The Manchurian Candidate '04
Silver City '04
Sunshine State '02
Traffic '00
Mulan '98 (V)
Where's Marlowe? '98
Mr. Magoo '97
The Disappearance of Garcia Lorca '96
Stephen King's The Night Flier '96
Incident at Deception Ridge '94
Stephen King's The Stand '94
Another Stakeout '93
Blank Check '93
Hot Shots! Part Deux '93
It's All True '93 (N)
Point of No Return '93
Royce '93
Scam '93
The Harvest '92
Twin Peaks: Fire Walk with Me '92
Drug Wars: The Camarena Story '90
The Guardian '90
Revenge '90
Deepstar Six '89
Python Wolf '88
RoboCop '87
Flashpoint '84
Lovelines '84
Star Trek 3: The Search for Spock '84

Tony Ferrer
Blind Rage '78
The Vengeance of Fu Manchu '67

America Ferrera (1984-)
How to Train Your Dragon '10 (V)
Our Family Wedding '10
The Sisterhood of the Traveling Pants 2 '08
Towards Darkness '07
Steel City '06
How the Garcia Girls Spent Their Summer '05
Sisterhood of the Traveling Pants '05
Real Women Have Curves '02

Martin Ferrero (1947-)
Air Bud 3: World Pup '00
The Tailor of Panama '00
Gods and Monsters '98
Jurassic Park '93
Stop! or My Mom Will Shoot '92
High Spirits '88
Planes, Trains & Automobiles '87

Eve Ferret
Foreign Body '86
Haunted Honeymoon '86

Claudia Ferri
The Christmas Choir '08
Mambo Italiano '03
Bonanno: A Godfather's Story '99
The Assignment '97

Noel Ferrier (1930-97)
Great Expectations: The Untold Story '87
Return of Captain Invincible '83

The Year of Living Dangerously '82
Adventures of Eliza Fraser '76

Carla Ferrigno
Black Roses '88
Seven Magnificent Gladiators '84

Lou Ferrigno (1952-)
Hulk '03
Ping! '99
The Godson '98
...And God Spoke '94
Cage 2: The Arena of Death '94
Return to Frogtown '92
Hangfire '91
Death of the Incredible Hulk '90
Liberty & Bash '90
All's Fair '89
The Cage '89
Sinbad of the Seven Seas '89
The Trial of the Incredible Hulk '89
Desert Warrior '88
The Incredible Hulk Returns '88
Hercules 2 '85
Seven Magnificent Gladiators '84
Hercules '83
The Incredible Hulk '77

Barbara Ferris (1943-)
The Krays '90
A Chorus of Disapproval '89
Nice Girl Like Me '69
Children of the Damned '63

John Ferris
Monique '76
Torpedo Attack '72

Pam Ferris (1948-)
Children of Men '06
Jane Eyre '06
Death to Smoochy '02
The Turn of the Screw '99
Our Mutual Friend '98
Matilda '96
Meantime '81

Samantha Ferris
Grace '09
Shattered '07

Dan Ferro (1960-)
Blow '01
Sgt. Bilko '95

Turi Ferro (1921-2001)
Malicious '74
Seduction of Mimi '72

David Ferry (1951-)
Thin Air '00
Boondock Saints '99
The Passion of Ayn Rand '99
Project: Genesis '93
The Last Winter '89
Tales of the Klondike: Race for Number One '87
Men of Steel '77

Gabriele Ferzetti (1925-)
Othello '95
Voyage of Terror: The Achille Lauro Affair '90
Julia and Julia '87
Quo Vadis '85
Basileus Quartet '82
Vatican Conspiracy '81
The Psychic '78
The Night Porter '74
Hitler: The Last Ten Days '73
Counter Punch '71
French Intrigue '70
On Her Majesty's Secret Service '69
L'Avventura '60
That Long Night in '43 '60
Angel in a Taxi '59
The Wayward Wife '52

Larry Fessenden (1963-)
Wendy and Lucy '08
Broken Flowers '05
Headspace '02
Margarita Happy Hour '01
You Are Here * '00
Habit '97
River of Grass '94

Stepin Fetchit (1902-85)
Amazing Grace '74
The Sun Shines Bright '53
Miracle in Harlem '48
Love Is News '37
On the Avenue '37
Charlie Chan in Egypt '35
Steamboat Round the Bend '35
David Harum '34
Judge Priest '34
Stand Up and Cheer '34
The World Moves On '34
Wild Horse '31

Darrell Fetty
Blood Beach '81
Stunts '77

Debra Feuer
Night Angel '90
Homeboy '88
To Live & Die in L.A. '85
Red Flag: The Ultimate Game '81
The Hollywood Knights '80

Mark Feuerstein (1971-)
Defiance '08
In Her Shoes '05
Masters of Horror: Pro-Life '05
Abandon '02
Rules of Engagement '00
Trial by Media '00
What Women Want '00
Woman on Top '00
Giving It Up '99
The Muse '99

Edwige Feuillere (1907-98)
Woman Hater '49
The Eagle Has Two Heads '48
L'Idiot '46
De Mayerling a Sarajevo '40
Topaze '33

Peggy (Margaret) Feury (1924-85)
All of Me '84
The Orphan '79
Witch Who Came from the Sea '76
Red, White & Busted '75

Norman Feusier (1886-1945)
Border Vengeance '35
Diamond Trail '33

Laurence Fevrier
Time Regained '99
Tatie Danielle '91

Tina Fey (1970-)
Date Night '10
The Invention of Lying '09
Baby Mama '08
Ponyo '08 (V)
Mean Girls '04

Kveta Fialova (1929-)
Murder Czech Style '66
Lemonade Joe '64

William Fichtner (1956-)
Prison Break: The Final Break '09
The Dark Knight '08
Blades of Glory '07
First Snow '07
Ultraviolet '06
The Chumscrubber '05
Crash '05
Empire Falls '05

The Longest Yard '05
Mr. & Mrs. Smith '05 (V)
The Moguls '05
Nine Lives '05
Equilibrium '02
The Healer '02
Black Hawk Down '01
Pearl Harbor '01
What's the Worst That Could Happen? '01
Drowning Mona '00
Passion of Mind '00
The Perfect Storm '00
Go '99
The Settlement '99
Armageddon '98
Contact '97
Switchback '97
Albino Alligator '96
Heat '95
Strange Days '95
The Underneath '95
Virtuosity '95

Colin Fickes
The New Twenty '08
Roger Dodger '02

Shelby Fiddis
Cheech and Chong's The Corsican Brothers '84
Cheech and Chong: Things Are Tough All Over '82

Adam Fidusiewicz (1985-)
In Desert and Wilderness '01
Lansdown '01

John Fiedler (1925-2005)
Pooh's Heffalump Movie '05 (V)
Piglet's Big Movie '03 (V)
The Emperor's New Groove '00 (V)
I Am the Cheese '83
The Fox and the Hound '81 (V)
Sharky's Machine '81
Harper Valley P.T.A. '78
The Many Adventures of Winnie the Pooh '77 (V)
Bad Ronald '74
True Grit '69
The Odd Couple '68
A Fine Madness '66
Kiss Me, Stupid! '64
A Raisin in the Sun '61
Twelve Angry Men '57

Arabella Field (1970-)
Blowin' Smoke '99
Godzilla '98
Dante's Peak '97
The Pompatus of Love '95
Laws of Gravity '92

Betty Field (1913-73)
Coogan's Bluff '68
Birdman of Alcatraz '62
Butterfield 8 '60
Peyton Place '57
Bus Stop '56
Picnic '55
The Great Gatsby '49
The Southerner '45
The Great Moment '44
Tomorrow the World '44
Blues in the Night '41
Kings Row '41
The Shepherd of the Hills '41
Of Mice and Men '39
What a Life '39

Chelsea Field (1957-)
The Unsaid '01
Tom Clancy's Netforce '98
Wicked '98
Flipper '96
Indictment: The McMartin Trial '95
The Wrong Woman '95
Andre '94
The Birds 2: Land's End '94
A Passion to Kill '94
Texas '94
Dust Devil '93
Extreme Justice '93

Hotel Room '93
Royce '93
Snapdragon '93
The Dark Half '91
Harley Davidson and the Marlboro Man '91
The Last Boy Scout '91
Skin Deep '89
Prison '88
Commando '85

David Field
The Night We Called It a Day '03
Blood Crime '02
Chopper '00
Mr. Accident '99
Two Hands '98
Blackrock '97

Karin (Karen) Field
The Demons '74
The Mad Butcher '72
Web of the Spider '70
The Alley Cats '65
Cave of the Living Dead '65

Mary Field (1896-1968)
To Hell and Back '55
I Married a Witch '42
Mrs. Miniver '42
Wake Island '42

Sally Field (1946-)
Two Weeks '06
Legally Blonde 2: Red White & Blonde '03
Say It Isn't So '01
Where the Heart Is '00
A Cooler Climate '99
Homeward Bound 2: Lost in San Francisco '96 (V)
An Eye for an Eye '95
Forrest Gump '94
A Woman of Independent Means '94
Homeward Bound: The Incredible Journey '93 (V)
Mrs. Doubtfire '93
Soapdish '91
Not Without My Daughter '90
Steel Magnolias '89
Punchline '88
Surrender '87
Murphy's Romance '85
Places in the Heart '84
Kiss Me Goodbye '82
Absence of Malice '81
Back Roads '81
Smokey and the Bandit 2 '80
Beyond the Poseidon Adventure '79
Norma Rae '79
The End '78
Hooper '78
Heroes '77
Smokey and the Bandit '77
Stay Hungry '76
Sybil '76
Home for the Holidays '72
Maybe I'll Come Home in the Spring '71
Maybe I'll Be Home in the Spring '70
The Way West '67

Shirley Anne Field (1936-)
Lady Chatterley '92
Hear My Song '91
Getting It Right '89
Shag: The Movie '89
Two by Forsyth '86
My Beautiful Laundrette '85
House of the Living Dead '73
Alfie '66
Doctor in Clover '66
Kings of the Sun '63
War Lover '62
Beat Girl '60
The Entertainer '60
Peeping Tom '60
Saturday Night and Sunday Morning '60

Todd Field (1964-)
Rip It Off '02
Eyes Wide Shut '99

The Haunting '99
Stranger than Fiction '99
Broken Vessels '98
Farmer & Chase '96
Walking and Talking '96
Sleep with Me '94
Ruby in Paradise '93
Back to Back '90
Full Fathom Five '90
Eye of the Eagle 2 '89
Gross Anatomy '89

Virginia Field (1917-92)
A Connecticut Yankee in King Arthur's Court '49
John Loves Mary '48
Christmas Eve '47
Dance, Girl, Dance '40
Waterloo Bridge '40
Mr. Moto Takes a Vacation '39
Mr. Moto's Last Warning '39
Mr. Takes a Vacation '39
Charlie Chan at Monte Carlo '37
Think Fast, Mr. Moto '37
Lloyds of London '36

Dorothy Fielding
The Preppie Murder '89
The Abduction of Kari Swenson '87
Fright Night '85

Emma Fielding (1966-)
Return to Cranford '09
Cranford '08
Inspector Lynley Mysteries: A Great Deliverance '01
Pandaemonium '00
Speedy Death '99
A Respectable Trade '98
The Scarlet Tunic '97

Fenella Fielding (1930-)
Arrivederci, Baby! '66
Carry On Screaming '66
Doctor in Clover '66

Margaret Fielding (1895-1974)
The Moon's Our Home '36
A Woman in Grey '20

Marjorie Fielding (1892-1956)
The Franchise Affair '52
The Lavender Hill Mob '51
Conspirator '49
The Demi-Paradise '43

Charlie (Charles) Fields (1971-)
The Beniker Gang '83
Fish Hawk '79

Christopher John Fields
Alien 3 '92
The Gun in Betty Lou's Handbag '92
Indecency '92

Holly Fields
Interceptor Force '99
Wishmaster 2: Evil Never Dies '98
Runaway Daughters '94
Seedpeople '92

Kim Fields (1969-)
Uninvited Guest '99
The Kid with the Broken Halo '82

Norman Fields
Dirty Mind of Young Sally '72
Octaman '71

Robert Fields (1938-)
Anna '87
The Sporting Club '72
The Incident '67

Stanley Fields (1884-1941)
The Great Plane Robbery '40
Wide Open Faces '38

Three Legionnaires '37
The Gay Desperado '36
Island of Lost Souls '32
Justice Rides Again '32
Cimarron '31

Tony Fields (1958-95)

Across the Moon '94
Backstreet Dreams '90
Body Beat '88
Trick or Treat '86

W.C. Fields (1879-1946)

Sensations of 1945 '44
Tales of Manhattan '42
Never Give a Sucker an Even Break '41
The Bank Dick '40
My Little Chickadee '40
You Can't Cheat an Honest Man '39
The Big Broadcast of 1938 '38
David Copperfield '35
Mississippi '35
It's a Gift '34
Mrs. Wiggs of the Cabbage Patch '34
Six of a Kind '34
The Barber Shop '33
International House '33
The Dentist '32
Pharmacist '32
Running Wild '27
It's the Old Army Game '26
Sally of the Sawdust '25
Pool Sharks '15

Joseph Fiennes (1970-)

The Color of Freedom '07
The Darwin Awards '06
Running with Scissors '06
The Great Raid '05
The Merchant of Venice '04
Luther '03
Sinbad: Legend of the Seven Seas '03 (V)
Leo '02
Dust '01
Killing Me Softly '01
Enemy at the Gates '00
Rancid Aluminium '00
Forever Mine '99
Elizabeth '98
Shakespeare in Love '98
The Very Thought of You '98
Stealing Beauty '96
The Vacillations of Poppy Carew '94

Ralph Fiennes (1962-)

Clash of the Titans '10
Nanny McPhee 2 '10
The Wildest Dream: Conquest of Everest '10 (V)
Bernard and Doris '08
The Duchess '08
The Hurt Locker '08
In Bruges '08
The Reader '08
Harry Potter and the Order of the Phoenix '07
Land of the Blind '06
The Chumscrubber '05
The Constant Gardener '05
Harry Potter and the Goblet of Fire '05
Wallace & Gromit in The Curse of the Were-Rabbit '05 (V)
The White Countess '05
The Good Thief '03
Maid in Manhattan '02
Red Dragon '02
Spider '02
The Miracle Maker: The Story of Jesus '00 (V)
The End of the Affair '99
Onegin '99
Sunshine '99
The Avengers '98
Prince of Egypt '98 (V)
Oscar and Lucinda '97
The English Patient '96
Strange Days '95
Quiz Show '94
Schindler's List '93
Emily Bronte's Wuthering Heights '92
Prime Suspect '92
A Dangerous Man: Lawrence after Arabia '91

Harvey Fierstein (1954-)

Duplex '03
Death to Smoochy '02
Common Ground '00
Playing Mona Lisa '00
Double Platinum '99
Mulan '98 (V)
Safe Men '98
Kull the Conqueror '97
Independence Day '96
Dr. Jekyll and Ms. Hyde '95
Bullets over Broadway '94
Mrs. Doubtfire '93
The Harvest '92
Tidy Endings '88
Torch Song Trilogy '88
Apology '86
Garbo Talks '84

Mike Figgis (1948-)

One Night Stand '97
Internal Affairs '90

George Figgs (1947-)

Polyester '81
Female Trouble '74
Pink Flamingos '72
Multiple Maniacs '70

Efrain Figueroa

ESL: English as a Second Language '05
The Visit '00
Eastside '99
The Apostate '98
Desperate Measures '98
Star Maps '97

Kasia (Katarzyna) Figura (1962-)

Dead Man's Bounty '06
Zemsta '02
Too Fast, Too Young '96
Fatal Past '94
Ready to Wear '94
Near Misses '91
Train to Hollywood '86

Michael Filipowich

Kill Switch '08
Mean Streak '99

Nathan Fillion (1971-)

Trucker '08
Waitress '07
White Noise 2: The Light '07
Slither '06
Serenity '05
Outing Riley '04
Water's Edge '03

Clyde Fillmore (1875-1946)

Laura '44
Watch on the Rhine '43
My Sister Eileen '42
Nurse Marjorie '20

Dennis Fimple (1940-2002)

House of 1000 Corpses '03
My Heroes Have Always Been Cowboys '91
Of Mice and Men '81
The $5.20 an Hour Dream '80
The Evictors '79
Creature from Black Lake '76
King Kong '76
Winterhawk '76
Truck Stop Women '74

Jon Finch (1941-)

Kingdom of Heaven '05
Lurking Fear '94
Unexplained Laughter '89
Witching Time '84
And Nothing But the Truth '82
Doktor Faustus '82
Peter and Paul '81
Breaking Glass '80
Death on the Nile '78
Game of Seduction '76
The Final Programme '73
Lady Caroline Lamb '73
Frenzy '72
Macbeth '71

Peter Finch (1916-77)

Raid on Entebbe '77
Network '76
The Abdication '74
Shattered '72
Sunday, Bloody Sunday '71
Red Tent '69
Far from the Madding Crowd '67
The Flight of the Phoenix '65
First Men in the Moon '64
Girl with Green Eyes '64
The Pumpkin Eater '64
The Sins of Rachel Cade '61
Kidnapped '60
No Love for Johnnie '60
Operation Amsterdam '60
The Trials of Oscar Wilde '60
The Nun's Story '59
Pursuit of the Graf Spee '57
Robbery under Arms '57
Windom's Way '57
Make Me an Offer '55
The Warriors '55
The Detective '54
Elephant Walk '54
The Story of Robin Hood & His Merrie Men '52
Wooden Horse '50
Eureka Stockade '49
Train of Events '49
The Fighting Rats of Tobruk '44

Deborah Findlay

Me Without You '01
Wives and Daughters '01
Heat of the Sun '99

Larry Fine (1902-75)

The Outlaws Is Coming! '65
Around the World in a Daze '63
Four for Texas '63
It's a Mad, Mad, Mad, Mad World '63
Three Stooges in Orbit '62
Snow White and the Three Stooges '61
The Three Stooges Meet Hercules '61
Have Rocket Will Travel '59
Gold Raiders '51
Hollywood Party '34
Dancing Lady '33
The Lost Stooges '33
Myrt and Marge '33

Travis Fine (1968-)

Tomcats '01
My Antonia '94
Child's Play 3 '91

Anthony Finetti

Prime Time Murder '92
The Expendables '89

Sticky Fingaz

See Kirk "Sticky Fingaz" Jones

Fyvush Finkel (1923-)

A Serious Man '09
The Crew '00
Q & A '90

Carrie Finklea

Simon Says '07
Elephant '03

Frank Finlay (1926-)

Lighthouse Hill '04
The Statement '03
The Pianist '02
Station Jim '01
Longitude '00
Dreaming of Joseph Lees '99
The Magical Legend of the Leprechauns '99
A Mind to Murder '96
Romance and Rejection '96
Stiff Upper Lips '96
Gospa '94
Stalin '92
Cthulhu Mansion '91
The Return of the Musketeers '89
Casanova '87
Arch of Triumph '85
In the Secret State '85
Lifeforce '85
A Christmas Carol '84
The Death of Adolf Hitler '84
The Ploughman's Lunch '83
Enigma '82
Return of the Soldier '82
Murder by Decree '79
The Thief of Baghdad '78
Wild Geese '78
Bouquet of Barbed Wire '76
The Four Musketeers '75
The Three Musketeers '74
Neither the Sea Nor the Sand '73
Shaft in Africa '73
Gumshoe '72
Assault '70
Cromwell '70
Molly Maguires '70
Inspector Clouseau '68
I'll Never Forget What's 'Is-name '67
Robbery '67
A Study in Terror '66
Othello '65
The Loneliness of the Long Distance Runner '62

James Finlayson (1887-1953)

To Be or Not to Be '42
A Chump at Oxford '40
Saps at Sea '40
The Flying Deuces '39
Block-heads '38
All Over Town '37
Pick a Star '37
Way Out West '37
Bohemian Girl '36
Our Relations '36
Bonnie Scotland '35
The Devil's Brother '33
Pack Up Your Troubles '32
Laurel & Hardy: Chickens Come Home '31
Pardon Us '31
No Man's Law '27

Jon Finlayson

A Kink in the Picasso '90
Lonely Hearts '82

Cameron Finley (1987-)

Perfect Game '00
Hope Floats '98
Leave It to Beaver '97

Evelyn Finley (1916-89)

Trail Riders '42
Dynamite Canyon '41

Margot Finley (1980-)

Tourist Trap '98
Ronnie and Julie '97
In Cold Blood '96

William Finley (1944-)

The Black Dahlia '06
The Funhouse '81
The Fury '78
Eaten Alive '76
Phantom of the Paradise '74
Sisters '73
The Wedding Party '69

John Finn (1952-)

The Hunted '03
Analyze That '02
Catch Me If You Can '02
Deadlocked '00
Atomic Train '99
True Crime '99
Crazy Horse '96
Turbulence '96
Cover-Up '91
Quicksand: No Escape '91
Glory '89

John Finnegan

Finish Line '89
An American Tail '86 (V)

Kate Finneran

Baby on Board '08
Night of the Living Dead '90

Warren Finnerty (1925-74)

Cockfighter '74
Panic in Needle Park '71
Easy Rider '69
Free Grass '69
Cool Hand Luke '67
The Brig '64
The Connection '61

Albert Finney (1936-)

Before the Devil Knows You're Dead '07
The Bourne Ultimatum '07
Amazing Grace '06
A Good Year '06
Tim Burton's Corpse Bride '05 (V)
Big Fish '03
The Gathering Storm '02
My Uncle Silas '01
Erin Brockovich '00
Traffic '00
Simpatico '99
Breakfast of Champions '98
A Rather English Marriage '98
Washington Square '97
Nostromo '96
The Run of the Country '95
The Browning Version '94
A Man of No Importance '94
Rich in Love '93
The Playboys '92
The Green Man '91
Miller's Crossing '90
The Endless Game '89
The Image '89
Orphans '87
Pope John Paul II '84
Under the Volcano '84
The Dresser '83
Loophole '83
Annie '82
Shoot the Moon '82
Looker '81
Wolfen '81
The Duellists '77
Murder on the Orient Express '74
Alpha Beta '73
Gumshoe '72
Scrooge '70
Two for the Road '67
Tom Jones '63
The Victors '63
The Entertainer '60
Saturday Night and Sunday Morning '60

Shirley Jo Finney

Echo Park '86
Wilma '77

Angela Finocchiaro (1955-)

My Brother Is an Only Child '07
Don't Tell '05
Volere Volare '92

Elena Fiore

Seven Beauties '76
Seduction of Mimi '72

John Fiore

Tony n' Tina's Wedding '07
Hit and Runway '01

Maria Fiore

Thor and the Amazon Women '60
Neapolitan Carousel '54

Linda Fiorentino (1960-)

Liberty Stands Still '02
What Planet Are You From? '00
Where the Money Is '00
Dogma '99
Ordinary Decent Criminal '99
Body Count '97
Kicked in the Head '97
Men in Black '97
Larger Than Life '96
Unforgettable '96
Bodily Harm '95
Jade '95
Charlie's Ghost: The Secret of Coronado '94
The Desperate Trail '94
The Last Seduction '94
Acting on Impulse '93
Chain of Desire '93
Beyond the Law '92
Queens Logic '91
Shout '91
Strangers '91
The Neon Empire '89
The Moderns '88
Wildfire '88
After Hours '85
Gotcha! '85
Vision Quest '85

Ann(e) Firbank (1933-)

Flame to the Phoenix '85
Lillie '79
Asylum '72
Persuasion '71

Eddie Firestone (1920-2007)

Duel '71
Two for the Seesaw '62
The Law and Jake Wade '58

MacKenzie Firgens (1975-)

The Pink Conspiracy '07
Sweet Insanity '06
Against the Wall '04
Groove '00

Colin Firth (1960-)

A Christmas Carol '09 (V)
A Single Man '09
The Accidental Husband '08
Easy Virtue '08
Mamma Mia! '08
The Last Legion '07
St. Trinian's '07
Then She Found Me '07
When Did You Last See Your Father? '07
Nanny McPhee '06
Where the Truth Lies '05
Bridget Jones: The Edge of Reason '04
Trauma '04
Girl with a Pearl Earring '03
Love Actually '03
What a Girl Wants '03
The Importance of Being Earnest '02
Bridget Jones's Diary '01
Conspiracy '01
Relative Values '99
The Turn of the Screw '99
My Life So Far '98
Shakespeare in Love '98
A Thousand Acres '97
The English Patient '96
Fever Pitch '96
Nostromo '96
Pride and Prejudice '95
The Widowing of Mrs. Holroyd '95
Circle of Friends '94
Playmaker '94
The Advocate '93
Hostages '93
Wings of Fame '93
Femme Fatale '90
Valmont '89
Apartment Zero '88
Dutch Girls '87
A Month in the Country '87
The Secret Garden '87
Another Country '84

Jonathan Firth (1967-)

The Prince & Me 3: A Royal Honeymoon '08
The Prince & Me 2: Royal Wedding '06
Luther '03
Bait '02
Victoria & Albert '01
Far from the Madding Crowd '97
Middlemarch '93
Emily Bronte's Wuthering Heights '92

Peter Firth (1953-)
The Greatest Game Ever Played '05
Me & Mrs. Jones '02
Pearl Harbor '01
Chill Factor '99
Mighty Joe Young '98
The Garden of Redemption '97
An Awfully Big Adventure '94
Shadowlands '93
The Perfect Husband '92
Prisoner of Honor '91
The Hunt for Red October '90
Innocent Victim '90
Burndown '89
The Incident '89
Born of Fire '87
Northanger Abbey '87
Letter to Brezhnev '86
Lifeforce '85
Fire and Sword '82
Tess '79
Equus '77
Joseph Andrews '77
King Arthur, the Young Warlord '75

Jenna Fischer (1974-)
Solitary Man '10
The Promotion '08
Blades of Glory '07
The Brothers Solomon '07
Walk Hard: The Dewey Cox Story '07
Slither '06

Kai (Kay) Fischer (1934-)
The Goalie's Anxiety at the Penalty Kick '71
The Hellfire Club '61
Uncle Was a Vampire '59

Kate Fischer (1973-)
Blood Surf '00
Sirens '94

Vera Fischer (1950-)
Quilombo '84
Love Strange Love '82
I Love You '81

Patrick Fischler (1969-)
The Great Buck Howard '09
Garden Party '08
The Black Dahlia '06

Nancy Fish (1938-)
Reflections in the Dark '94
Ghost in the Machine '93
Death Becomes Her '92
Exorcist 3: Legion '90

Laurence Fishburne (1963-)
Predators '10
Armored '09
Tortured '08
21 '08
Bobby Z '07
Fantastic Four: Rise of the Silver Surfer '07 (V)
Akeelah and the Bee '06
Bobby '06
Five Fingers '06
Mission: Impossible 3 '06
Assault on Precinct 13 '05
Biker Boyz '03
The Matrix Reloaded '03
The Matrix Revolutions '03
Mystic River '03
Osmosis Jones '01 (V)
Once in the Life '00
The Matrix '99
Always Outgunned Always Outgunned '98
Event Horizon '97
Miss Evers' Boys '97
Fled '96
Hoodlum '96
Othello '95
The Tuskegee Airmen '95
Bad Company '94
Higher Learning '94
Just Cause '94
Searching for Bobby Fischer '93
What's Love Got to Do with It? '93
Deep Cover '92
Boyz N the Hood '91
Class Action '91
Hearts of Darkness: A Filmmaker's Apocalypse '91
Decoration Day '90
King of New York '90
Cadence '89
For Us, the Living '88
Red Heat '88
School Daze '88
Gardens of Stone '87
A Nightmare on Elm Street 3: Dream Warriors '87
Quicksilver '86
Death Wish 2 '82
A Rumor of War '80
Willie & Phil '80
Apocalypse Now '79
Cornbread, Earl & Me '75

Carrie Fisher (1956-)
Sorority Row '09
The Women '08
Cougar Club '07
Undiscovered '05
Stateside '04
Charlie's Angels: Full Throttle '03
Wonderland '03
Jay and Silent Bob Strike Back '01
Scream 3 '00
Austin Powers: International Man of Mystery '97
This Is My Life '92
Drop Dead Fred '91
Soapdish '91
Sibling Rivalry '90
Sweet Revenge '90
The 'Burbs '89
Loverboy '89
When Harry Met Sally... '89
Appointment with Death '88
She's Back '88
Amazon Women on the Moon '87
The Time Guardian '87
Hannah and Her Sisters '86
Hollywood Vice Sqaud '86
From Here to Maternity '85
The Man with One Red Shoe '85
Garbo Talks '84
Return of the Jedi '83
Frankenstein '82
Thumbelina '82
Under the Rainbow '81
The Blues Brothers '80
The Empire Strikes Back '80
Mr. Mike's Mondo Video '79
Star Wars '77
Shampoo '75

Cindy Fisher
Liar's Moon '82
Hometown U.S.A. '79

Eddie Fisher (1928-)
Butterfield 8 '60
Bundle of Joy '56
All About Eve '50

Frances Fisher (1952-)
In the Valley of Elah '07
Sex and Death 101 '07
The Night of the White Pants '06
Mrs. Harris '05
Laws of Attraction '04
Blue Car '03
House of Sand and Fog '03
The Rising Place '02
The Audrey Hepburn Story '00
Gone in 60 Seconds '00
The Big Tease '99
True Crime '99
Titanic '97
Trading Favors '97
Wild America '97
Female Perversions '96
Babyfever '94
Molly and Gina '94
The Stars Fell on Henrietta '94
Attack of the 50 Ft. Woman '93
Praying Mantis '93
Devlin '92
Unforgiven '92
Deadly Conspiracy '91
Frame Up '91
Lucy and Desi: Before the Laughter '91
Sudie & Simpson '90
Cold Sassy Tree '89
Patty Hearst '88
Heart '87
Tough Guys Don't Dance '87
Can She Bake a Cherry Pie? '83

Gregor Fisher (1953-)
Oliver Twist '07
Kidnapped '05
The Merchant of Venice '04
Love Actually '03
The Railway Children '00
The Girl in the Picture '86
1984 '84

Isla Fisher (1976-)
Confessions of a Shopaholic '09
Definitely, Maybe '08
Dr. Seuss' Horton Hears a Who! '08 (V)
Hot Rod '07
The Lookout '07
Wedding Daze '06
London '05
Wedding Crashers '05
Criminal Ways '03
Dallas 362 '03
Scooby-Doo '02

Jaishon Fisher (1996-)
Gifted Hands: The Ben Carson Story '09
Lakeview Terrace '08

Joely Fisher (1967-)
Inspector Gadget '99
Kidnapped in Paradise '98
The Companion '94

Kay Fisher
See Kai (Kay) Fischer

Noel Fisher (1984-)
A Dog Named Christmas '09
Red '08
Pope Dreams '06
National Lampoon's Holiday Reunion '03
Max Keeble's Big Move '01

Rashiya Fisher
See Rah Digga

Shug Fisher (1907-84)
Huckleberry Finn '75
Smoke '70
The Giant Gila Monster '59

Stephen H. Fisher
Hellboy '04
Van Helsing '04

Thomas (Tom) Fisher (1968-)
Van Helsing '04
Shanghai Knights '03

Tricia Leigh Fisher (1969-)
Arizona Dream '94
Hostile Intentions '94
Book of Love '91
C.H.U.D. 2: Bud the Chud '89
Hollywood Chaos '89
Pretty Smart '87

Schuyler Fisk (1982-)
I'm Reed Fish '06
Orange County '02
Skeletons in the Closet '00
Snow Day '00
The Baby-Sitters' Club '95

Robert (Fisk) Fiske (1899-1944)
Before I Hang '40
Green Archer '40
Law and Order '40
Mystic Circle Murder '39
Adventure in Sahara '38
Purple Vigilantes '38
Devil Diamond '37
Roaring Six Guns '37
Sky Parade '36

Alan Fisler
Student Affairs '88
New York's Finest '87
If Looks Could Kill '86

Mark Fite
Off the Lip '04
Stuart Bliss '98

Rick Fitts
Hanoi Hilton '87
Platoon Leader '87

Peter Fitz (1931-)
Club Extinction '89
Au Revoir les Enfants '87
The Wannsee Conference '84
The Oppermann Family '82

Lewis Fitz-Gerald (1958-)
Border Patrol '01
Pitch Black '00
Dead Heart '96
A Cry in the Dark '88
The Four Minute Mile '88
Rikky and Pete '88
Winner Takes All '84
Breaker Morant '80

Barry Fitzgerald (1888-1961)
Broth of a Boy '59
The Catered Affair '56
The Quiet Man '52
Union Station '50
The Story of Seabiscuit '49
Miss Tatlock's Millions '48
The Naked City '48
Welcome Stranger '47
The Saint Strikes Back: Criminal Court '46
Two Years before the Mast '46
And Then There Were None '45
The Stork Club '45
Going My Way '44
None But the Lonely Heart '44
The Amazing Mrs. Holiday '43
How Green Was My Valley '41
The Sea Wolf '41
Tarzan's Secret Treasure '41
The Long Voyage Home '40
The Saint Strikes Back '39
Bringing Up Baby '38
Dawn Patrol '38
Four Men and a Prayer '38
Marie Antoinette '38
Juno and the Paycock '30 (N)

Ciaran Fitzgerald (1983-)
The General '98
The Boxer '97
The Canterville Ghost '96
The Last of the High Kings '96
Into the West '92

Ella Fitzgerald (1917-96)
Uncle Tom's Cabin '69 (V)
Let No Man Write My Epitaph '60
Pete Kelly's Blues '55
Ride 'Em Cowboy '42

Geraldine Fitzgerald (1913-2005)
Arthur 2: On the Rocks '88
Bloodlink '86
Poltergeist 2: The Other Side '86
Dixie: Changing Habits '85
Easy Money '83
Kennedy '83
Arthur '81
Lovespell '79
The Mango Tree '77
Diary of the Dead '76
Harry and Tonto '74
The Last American Hero '73
Rachel, Rachel '68
The Pawnbroker '65
Ten North Frederick '58
The Obsessed '51
O.S.S. '46
The Strange Affair of Uncle Harry '45
Wilson '44
Watch on the Rhine '43
Dark Victory '39
Wuthering Heights '39
The Mill on the Floss '37
Department Store '35

Gerry Fitzgerald
Superbabies: Baby Geniuses 2 '04
Baby Geniuses '98

Glenn Fitzgerald (1971-)
Confess '05
40 Days and 40 Nights '02
The Believer '01
Buffalo Soldiers '01
Series 7: The Contenders '01
101 Ways (The Things a Girl Will Do to Keep Her Volvo) '00
Tully '00
The Sixth Sense '99
A Price above Rubies '97
Manny & Lo '96
Flirting with Disaster '95

Leo Fitzgerald
Superbabies: Baby Geniuses 2 '04
Baby Geniuses '98

Myles Fitzgerald
Superbabies: Baby Geniuses 2 '04
Baby Geniuses '98

Patrick Fitzgerald (1962-)
Day at the Beach '98
Poltergeist: The Legacy '96

Sean Fitzgerald
The Power Within '95
Storybook '95

Tac Fitzgerald (1981-)
Black Hawk Down '01
Here on Earth '00

Tara Fitzgerald (1968-)
Jane Eyre '06
Like Father Like Son '05
I Capture the Castle '02
Dark Blue World '01
Rancid Aluminium '00
New World Disorder '99
Conquest '98
Frenchman's Creek '98
The Woman in White '97
Brassed Off '96
The Tenant of Wildfell Hall '96
The Englishman Who Went up a Hill But Came down a Mountain '95
A Man of No Importance '94
Sirens '94
The Vacillations of Poppy Carew '94
The Camomile Lawn '92
Catherine Cookson's The Black Candle '92
Hear My Song '91

Walter Fitzgerald (1896-1976)
The Adventures of Sadie '55
Treasure Island '50
The Fallen Idol '49
Blanche Fury '48
San Demetrio, London '47
Great Day '46

Colleen (Ann) Fitzpatrick (1972-)
Get Over It! '01
Rock Star '01
Scary Movie 2 '01 (V)
Da Hip Hop Witch '00
Dracula 2000 '00
St. Patrick's Day '99
Higher Learning '94
Hairspray '88

Gabrielle Fitzpatrick (1967-)
Desert Heat '99
Mr. Nice Guy '98

Jim (James) Fitzpatrick (1959-)
Operation Delta Force 3: Clear Target '98
U.S. Seals '98

Kate Fitzpatrick (1948-)
Fantasy Man '84
Return of Captain Invincible '83
Night Nurse '77

Leo Fitzpatrick (1978-)
El Camino '08
Winter of Frozen Dreams '08
How to Rob a Bank '07
Fay Grim '06
Personal Velocity: Three Portraits '02
Bully '01
Storytelling '01
Take It to the Limit '00
Kids '95

Michael Fitzpatrick
Pay Off '89
Blood Tracks '86

Neil Fitzpatrick (1934-2005)
Mr. Reliable: A True Story '95
A Cry in the Dark '88
Ground Zero '88

Richard Fitzpatrick
Survival of the Dead '09
Bridal Fever '08
Sticks and Stones '08
Coast to Coast '04
Confessions of a Teenage Drama Queen '04
Verdict in Blood '02
New Blood '99
Fatal Combat '96
Trilogy of Terror 2 '96
When the Bullet Hits the Bone '96

Emily Fitzroy (1860-1954)
The Frontiersmen '38
Don Quixote '35
The Trail of '98 '28
The Cheerful Fraud '27
Mockery '27
Bardelys the Magnificent '26
The Bat '26
Are Parents People? '25

Paul Fix (1901-83)
Wanda Nevada '79
Grayeagle '77
Night of the Lepus '72
Shoot Out '71
Zabriskie Point '70
El Dorado '67
Nevada Smith '66
Shenandoah '65
Sons of Katie Elder '65
The Outrage '64
Mail Order Bride '63
To Kill a Mockingbird '62
Lafayette Escadrille '58
Jet Pilot '57
Man in the Shadow '57
Night Passage '57
The Bad Seed '56
Man in the Vault '56
Blood Alley '55
The High and the Mighty '54
Hondo '53
Island in the Sky '53
Johnny Guitar '53
She Wore a Yellow Ribbon '49
Red River '48
Tycoon '47
Fighting Seabees '44
Captive Wild Woman '43
Hitler: Dead or Alive '43
Sherlock Holmes and the Secret Weapon '42

South of Santa Fe '42
Black Friday '40
Dr. Cyclops '40
The Great Plane Robbery '40
Mutiny on the Blackhawk '39
Star Reporter '39
Hard to Hold '37
Mannequin '37
Phantom Patrol '36
The Prisoner of Shark Island '36
Desert Trail '35
His Fighting Blood '35
The Throwback '35
Valley of Wanted Men '35
Gun Law '33
Somewhere in Sonora '33
Fargo Express '32
The Fighting Sheriff '31
Lucky Star '29

Cash Flagg

See Ray Dennis Steckler

Fannie Flagg (1944-)

Crazy in Alabama '99
My Best Friend Is a Vampire '88
Grease '78
Five Easy Pieces '70

Joe Flaherty (1941-)

Home on the Range '04 (V)
National Security '03
Slackers '02
Happy Gilmore '96
Snowboard Academy '96
The Wrong Guy '96
A Pig's Tale '94
Runaway Daughters '94
Stuart Saves His Family '94
Looking for Miracles '90
Back to the Future, Part 2 '89
Wedding Band '89
Who's Harry Crumb? '89
Speed Zone '88
Blue Monkey '87
One Crazy Summer '86
Really Weird Tales '86
Sesame Street Presents: Follow That Bird '85
Going Berserk '83
Heavy Metal '81 (V)
Stripes '81
Used Cars '80
1941 '79
Tunnelvision '76

Lanny Flaherty (1935-)

Home Fries '98
Tom and Huck '95
Sommersby '93
The Ballad of the Sad Cafe '91

Pat Flaherty (1903-70)

The Red House '47
Sergeant York '41
Midnight Limited '40
My Son, My Son '40

Didier Flamand (1947-)

Factotum '06
Love '05
The Chorus '04
The Chateau '01
The Crimson Rivers '01
Women '97

Georges Flament (1903-90)

The 400 Blows '59
La Chienne '31

Fionnula Flanagan (1941-)

The Invention of Lying '09
Yes Man '08
Slipstream '07
Four Brothers '05
Transamerica '05
Tears of the Sun '03
Divine Secrets of the Ya-Ya Sisterhood '02
The Others '01
For Love or Country: The Arturo Sandoval Story '00
Waking Ned Devine '98
Kings in Grass Castles '97
Some Mother's Son '96
White Mile '94
Money for Nothing '93
Death Dreams '92
Mad at the Moon '92
A Winner Never Quits '86
Youngblood '86
James Joyce's Women '85
The Ewok Adventure '84
Young Love, First Love '79
Mary White '77
In the Region of Ice '76
Picture of Dorian Gray '74
Cold Comfort Farm '71

Tommy Flanagan (1965-)

Smokin' Aces 2: Assassins' Ball '10
Hero Wanted '08
Smokin' Aces '07
When a Stranger Calls '06
The Last Drop '05
Alien vs. Predator '04
Trauma '04
All About the Benjamins '02
Attila '01
Strictly Sinatra '01
Gladiator '00
Ratcatcher '99
Sunset Strip '99
Braveheart '95

Ed Flanders (1934-95)

Bye Bye, Love '94
Citizen Cohn '92
Exorcist 3: Legion '90
The Final Days '89
Special Bulletin '83
Tomorrow's Child '82
The Pursuit of D.B. Cooper '81
True Confessions '81
Sophia Loren: Her Own Story '80
Backstairs at the White House '79
Blind Ambition '79
The Ninth Configuration '79
Salem's Lot '79
The Amazing Howard Hughes '77
Mary White '77
Eleanor & Franklin '76
Things in Their Season '74
Trial of the Catonsville Nine '72
The Passing of Evil '70
The Grasshopper '69

Sean Patrick Flanery (1965-)

The Boondock Saints II: All Saints Day '09
Crystal River '08
The Insatiable '06
Into the Fire '05
The Gunman '03
Borderline '02
Lone Hero '02
Acceptable Risk '01
Eye See You '01
Ride the Wild Fields '00
Body Shots '99
Boondock Saints '99
Simply Irresistible '99
Best Men '98
Eden '98
Girl '98
Zack & Reba '98
Pale Saints '97
Suicide Kings '97
Just Your Luck '96
The Grass Harp '95
Powder '95
Raging Angels '95

Susan Flannery (1943-)

Anatomy of a Seduction '79
Gumball Rally '76

Maureen Flannigan (1973-)

A Day Without a Mexican '04
At Any Cost '00
Teenage Bonnie & Klepto Clyde '93

Barry Flatman

Daniel's Daughter '08
Saw 3 '06
The Witness Files '00
Random Encounter '98
Open Season '95

John Flaus (1934-)

Lilian's Story '95
In Too Deep '90
Bootleg '85
Blood Money '80

James Flavin (1906-76)

In Cold Blood '67
Night Passage '57
Francis in the Haunted House '56
Abbott and Costello Go to Mars '53
Armored Car Robbery '50
Abbott and Costello Meet the Killer, Boris Karloff '49
Blondie Hits the Jackpot '49
Cloak and Dagger '46
Easy to Wed '46
The Shanghai Cobra '45
Abroad with Two Yanks '44
Hollywood Canteen '44
Laura '44
Uncertain Glory '44
Air Force '43
So Proudly We Hail '43
Brand of Hate '34
King Kong '33

Flea (1962-)

Rugrats Go Wild! '03 (V)
The Wild Thornberrys Movie '02 (V)
Liar's Poker '99
Fear and Loathing in Las Vegas '98
The Big Lebowski '97
The Chase '93
Motorama '91
My Own Private Idaho '91
Back to the Future, Part 2 '89
Dudes '87

John Fleck (1951-)

On_Line '01
Gunshy '98
The Comrades of Summer '92
Mutant on the Bounty '89
Tapeheads '89

Erick Fleeks (1948-)

Campfire Tales '98
Phat Beach '96

James Fleet (1954-)

Little Dorrit '08
Tristram Shandy: A Cock and Bull Story '05
The Phantom of the Opera '04
Two Men Went to War '02
Charlotte Gray '01
Kevin & Perry Go Large '00
Frenchman's Creek '98
Grave Indiscretions '96
Moll Flanders '96
Sense and Sensibility '95
Cracker: The Big Crunch '94
Four Weddings and a Funeral '94

Mick Fleetwood (1942-)

Burning Down the House '01
Zero Tolerance '93
The Running Man '87

Susan Fleetwood (1944-95)

Persuasion '95
The Buddha of Suburbia '92
The Krays '90
White Mischief '88
The Sacrifice '86
Heat and Dust '82

Charles Fleischer (1950-)

Zodiac '07
The Polar Express '04
The 4th Tenor '02
Boltneck '98
Ground Control '98
Permanent Midnight '98
Gridlock'd '96
Tales from the Crypt Presents Demon Knight '94
We're Back! A Dinosaur's Story '93 (V)
Carry On Columbus '92
Straight Talk '92
Back to the Future, Part 2 '89
Honey, I Shrunk the Kids '89 (V)
Bad Dreams '88
Who Framed Roger Rabbit '88 (V)
A Nightmare on Elm Street '84

Larry Fleishman

Mulberry Street '06
Gang Wars '75

Noah Fleiss (1984-)

Brick '06
Evergreen '04
Storytelling '01
Double Parked '00
Things You Can Tell Just by Looking at Her '00
The Truth About Jane '00
Joe the King '99
An Unexpected Life '97
An Unexpected Family '96
A Mother's Prayer '95
Josh and S.A.M. '93

Eric Fleming (1925-66)

The Glass Bottom Boat '66
Curse of the Undead '59
Queen of Outer Space '58
Fright '56
Conquest of Space '55

Ian Fleming (1888-1969)

The Trials of Oscar Wilde '60
Land of Fury '55
Norman Conquest '53
Recoil '53
Butler's Dilemma '43
Murder at the Baskervilles '37
When Thief Meets Thief '37
The Triumph of Sherlock Holmes '35

Lone Fleming (1949-)

Return of the Evil Dead '75
Tombs of the Blind Dead '72
It Happened at Nightmare Inn '70

Rhonda Fleming (1923-)

The Nude Bomb '80
The Crowded Sky '60
Alias Jesse James '59
The Big Circus '59
Bullwhip '58
Gun Glory '57
Gunfight at the O.K. Corral '57
Slightly Scarlet '56
While the City Sleeps '56
Tennessee's Partner '55
Pony Express '53
Cavalry Charge '51
Cry Danger '51
A Connecticut Yankee in King Arthur's Court '49
The Great Lover '49
Adventure Island '47
Out of the Past '47
Abilene Town '46
The Spiral Staircase '46
Spellbound '45
Since You Went Away '44

Jason Flemyng (1966-)

Clash of the Titans '10
The Curious Case of Benjamin Button '08
Bobby Z '07
The Riddle '07
Stardust '07
PU-239 '06
Telling Lies '06
Layer Cake '05
Transporter 2 '05
Lighthouse Hill '04
Seed of Chucky '04
The League of Extraordinary Gentlemen '03
Below '02
The Body '01
From Hell '01
Mean Machine '01
Rock Star '01
Bruiser '00
Snatch '00
Deep Rising '98
Lock, Stock and 2 Smoking Barrels '98
The Red Violin '98
Tess of the D'Urbervilles '98
Spice World: The Movie '97
Alive and Kicking '96
Stealing Beauty '96
Hollow Reed '95
Rob Roy '95
A Question of Attribution '91

Robert Flemyng (1912-95)

The Choir '95
Kafka '91
Oh! What a Lovely War '69
Blood Beast Terror '67
Vanity Fair '67
The Horrible Dr. Hichcock '62
Cast a Dark Shadow '55
The Man Who Never Was '55
The Blue Lamp '49
Conspirator '49
The Guinea Pig '48

Flesh N Bone

Thicker than Water '99
Winner Takes All '98

Alan Fletcher (1957-)

Gross Misconduct '93
Fran '85

Bramwell Fletcher (1904-88)

Random Harvest '42
The Undying Monster '42
White Cargo '42
The Scarlet Pimpernel '34
The Mummy '32
Daughter of the Dragon '31
Raffles '30

Brendan Fletcher (1981-)

BloodRayne 2: Deliverance '07
RV '06
Tideland '05
Death Valley '04
Eighteen '04
The Final Cut '04
Ginger Snaps Back: The Beginning '04
Freddy vs. Jason '03
Heart of America '03
The Unsaid '01
Jimmy Zip '00
The Five Senses '99
Summer's End '99
Air Bud '97
Trucks '97
Contagious '96
Dead Ahead '96

Dexter Fletcher (1966-)

In Your Dreams '07
Doom '05
Layer Cake '05
Stander '03
Below '02
Lock, Stock and 2 Smoking Barrels '98
The Raggedy Rawney '90
Twisted Obsession '90
The Rachel Papers '89
Lionheart '87
The Long Good Friday '80

Diane Fletcher (1944-)

The Aristocrats '99
The Final Cut '95
To Play the King '93
House of Cards '90

Dusty Fletcher (1897-1954)

Boardinghouse Blues '48
Killer Diller '48

Louise Fletcher (1934-)

A Dennis the Menace Christmas '07
Aurora Borealis '06
Dancing in Twilight '05
Finding Home '03
A Time to Remember '03
Big Eden '00
More Dogs Than Bones '00
The Devil's Arithmetic '99
A Map of the World '99
Time Served '99
Cruel Intentions '98
Love Kills '98
Breast Men '97
Love to Kill '97
Sins of the Mind '97
Frankenstein and Me '96
High School High '96
Two Days in the Valley '96
Edie & Pen '95
Virtuosity '95
The Haunting of Seacliff Inn '94
Tollbooth '94
Tryst '94
Return to Two Moon Junction '93
The Player '92
Blind Vision '91
Blue Steel '90
Nightmare on the 13th Floor '90
Best of the Best '89
Final Notice '89
Shadowzone '89
Two Moon Junction '88
Flowers in the Attic '87
Islands '87
J. Edgar Hoover '87
The Boy Who Could Fly '86
Invaders from Mars '86
Nobody's Fool '86
Firestarter '84
A Summer to Remember '84
Talk to Me '84
Brainstorm '83
Strange Invaders '83
Strange Behavior '81
Mama Dracula '80
Lady in Red '79
The Magician of Lublin '79
Natural Enemies '79
The Cheap Detective '78
The Exorcist 2: The Heretic '77
One Flew Over the Cuckoo's Nest '75
Russian Roulette '75
Thieves Like Us '74

Neil Fletcher

Creature of Destruction '67
Zontar, the Thing from Venus '66

Page Fletcher

Ordeal in the Arctic '93
Friends, Lovers & Lunatics '89
Humongous '82

Suzanne Fletcher

Bloodsucking Pharoahs of Pittsburgh '90
Sleepwalk '88

Sam Flint (1882-1980)

Leave It to the Marines '51
Sky High '51
Command Decision '48
Lights of Old Santa Fe '47
Boss of Boomtown '44
The Chinese Cat '44
Spy Smasher '42
Spy Smasher Returns '42
Roaring Six Guns '37
A Face in the Fog '36
The Lawless Nineties '36
Red Lights Ahead '36
Red River Valley '36
Evelyn Prentice '34

Jay C. Flippen (1900-71)
Firecreek '68
Hellfighters '68
The Plunderers '60
Studs Lonigan '60
The Restless Breed '58
Jet Pilot '57
Night Passage '57
The Killing '56
The King and Four Queens '56
Run of the Arrow '56
Seventh Cavalry '56
Far Country '55
Oklahoma! '55
The Wild One '54
Devil's Canyon '53
Flying Leathernecks '51
The Lemon Drop Kid '51
Buccaneer's Girl '50
Winchester '73 '50
The Yellow Cab Man '50
They Live by Night '49
A Woman's Secret '49
Marie Galante '34

Josh Flitter (1994-)
Santa Buddies '09 (V)
Ace Ventura Jr.: Pet Detective '08
Dr. Seuss' Horton Hears a Who! '08 (V)
Snow Buddies '08 (V)
License to Wed '07
Nancy Drew '07
Air Bud 6: Air Buddies '06 (V)
Big Momma's House 2 '06
The Greatest Game Ever Played '05

Bjorn Floberg (1947-)
Uno '04
Kitchen Stories '03
Insomnia '97

Calista Flockhart (1964-)
The Last Shot '04
Things You Can Tell Just by Looking at Her '00
William Shakespeare's A Midsummer Night's Dream '99
Drunks '96
Jane Doe '96
Telling Lies in America '96
The Birdcage '95

Suzanne Flon (1918-2005)
Avenue Montaigne '06
Joyeux Noel '05
One Deadly Summer '83
Mr. Klein '76
Zita '68
Action Man '67
The Train '65
Un Singe en Hiver '62
Moulin Rouge '52

Michael Flood
Death Nurse '87
Crazy Fat Ethel II '85
Criminally Insane '75

Sheila Florance (1916-91)
A Woman's Tale '92
Cactus '86

Dann Florek (1950-)
Beautiful Joe '00
From the Earth to the Moon '98
Hard Rain '97
The Flintstones '94
Getting Even with Dad '94
Angel Heart '87

Florelle (1901-74)
The Crime of Monsieur Lange '36
Liliom '35

Stefano Satta Flores
The Sniper '78
We All Loved Each Other So Much '77

Von Flores (1960-)
The Confessor '04
Tracked '98
The Assignment '97
Frame by Frame '95
Eclipse '94

Holly Floria (1966-)
Private Wars '93
Bikini Island '91
Presumed Guilty '91
Netherworld '90

George "Buck" Flower (1936-)
Sundown: The Vampire in Retreat '08
Relentless '89
Cheerleader Camp '88
Pumpkinhead '88
They Live '88
Sorority Babes in the Slime-ball Bowl-A-Rama '87
In Search of a Golden Sky '84
Escape from New York '81
The Capture of Bigfoot '79
Mountain Family Robinson '79
Further Adventures of the Wilderness Family, Part 2 '77
Across the Great Divide '76
Candy Tangerine Man '75
Devil & Leroy Basset '73
Dirty Mind of Young Sally '72

Kim Flowers
Alien: Resurrection '97
Nobody's Perfect '90

Robert Floyd
Soul's Midnight '06
The Song of the Lark '01
Cold Hearts '99
The Darwin Conspiracy '99

Roger Floyd
Big City Blues '99
The Walking Dead '94

Susan Floyd (1968-)
Domestic Disturbance '01
Random Hearts '99
Breathing Room '96

Darlanne Fluegel (1956-)
Darkman 3: Die Darkman Die '95
Relative Fear '95
Breaking Point '94
Scanner Cop '94
Slaughter of the Innocents '93
Pet Sematary 2 '92
Lock Up '89
Project: Alien '89
Bulletproof '88
Deadly Stranger '88
Freeway '88
Running Scared '86
Tough Guys '86
To Live & Die in L.A. '85
Concrete Beat '84
Once Upon a Time in America '84
The Last Fight '82
Battle Beyond the Stars '80
Eyes of Laura Mars '78

Patrick Flueger
Brothers '09
Last Resort '09

Joel Fluellen (1907-90)
Man Friday '75
A Dream for Christmas '73
The Great White Hope '70
Run Silent, Run Deep '58
Sitting Bull '54
The Jackie Robinson Story '50
No Time for Romance '48

Barbara Flynn (1948-)
Return to Cranford '09
Cranford '08
Miss Potter '06
Elizabeth I '05
Lorna Doone '01
Wives and Daughters '01
King Lear '98
Cracker: Best Boys '95
Cracker: Brotherly Love '95
Cracker: True Romance '95
Cracker: To Be a Somebody '94

Colleen Flynn (1962-)
Serving in Silence: The Margarethe Cammermeyer Story '95
Incident at Deception Ridge '94
The Temp '93

Errol Flynn (1909-59)
Assault of the Rebel Girls '59
Istanbul '57
The King's Rhapsody '55
Let's Make Up '55
The Warriors '55
The Master of Ballantrae '53
Against All Flags '52
Adventures of Captain Fabian '51
Kim '50
Montana '50
Rocky Mountain '50
That Forsyte Woman '50
Adventures of Don Juan '49
It's a Great Feeling '49
Silver River '48
Cry Wolf '47
Escape Me Never '47
Never Say Goodbye '46
Objective, Burma! '45
San Antonio '45
Uncertain Glory '44
Edge of Darkness '43
Northern Pursuit '43
Thank Your Lucky Stars '43
Desperate Journey '42
Gentleman Jim '42
Dive Bomber '41
Footsteps in the Dark '41
They Died with Their Boots On '41
Santa Fe Trail '40
The Sea Hawk '40
Virginia City '40
Dodge City '39
The Private Lives of Elizabeth & Essex '39
The Adventures of Robin Hood '38
Dawn Patrol '38
Four's a Crowd '38
The Sisters '38
The Prince and the Pauper '37
The Charge of the Light Brigade '36
Captain Blood '35

Jerome Flynn (1963-)
A Mind to Murder '96
Edward II '92
A Summer Story '88

Joe Flynn (1924-74)
Crusade: A March through Time '06
The Rescuers '77 (V)
The Strongest Man in the World '75
Gentle Savage '73
Superdad '73
Now You See Him, Now You Don't '72
The Barefoot Executive '71
How to Frame a Figg '71
Million Dollar Duck '71
The Computer Wore Tennis Shoes '69
My Dog, the Thief '69
Divorce American Style '67
McHale's Navy Joins the Air Force '65
McHale's Navy '64
Lover Come Back '61

Kimberly Flynn
Boys Life '94
Rhythm Thief '94
Revolution! A Red Comedy '91

Michael Flynn (1944-)
Partners in Crime '99
Address Unknown '96
Out of Annie's Past '94

Miriam Flynn (1952-)
National Lampoon's Christmas Vacation 2: Cousin Eddie's Big Island Adventure '03
The Land Before Time 6: The Secret of Saurus Rock '98 (V)
The Land Before Time 5: The Mysterious Island '97 (V)
Vegas Vacation '96
National Lampoon's Christmas Vacation '89
18 Again! '88
National Lampoon's Vacation '83

Neil Flynn (1960-)
Indiana Jones and the Kingdom of the Crystal Skull '08
Hoot '06
Mean Girls '04

Sean Flynn (1943-70)
Mission to Venice '63
Son of Captain Blood '62

Steve Flynn
Jesse Stone: Death in Paradise '06
Scarred City '98
Ulee's Gold '97
Without Warning: The James Brady Story '91

Brandon Fobbs
Tunnel Rats '08
Pride '07

Spiros Focas (1937-)
White Palace '90
Rambo 3 '88
The Jewel of the Nile '85
Rocco and His Brothers '60

Nina Foch (1924-)
How to Deal '03
Pumpkin '02
Hush '98
Til There Was You '96
Armistead Maupin's Tales of the City '93
Morning Glory '93
Sliver '93
Skin Deep '89
Dixie Lanes '88
Child of Glass '78
Jennifer '78
Mahogany '75
Salty '73
Columbo: Prescription Murder '67
Cash McCall '60
Spartacus '60
The Ten Commandments '56
Illegal '55
Executive Suite '54
Scaramouche '52
An American in Paris '51
St. Benny the Dip '51
The Dark Past '49
A Song to Remember '45
Cry of the Werewolf '44
Return of the Vampire '43

Brenda Fogarty
Fairy Tales '76
Deadly Fieldtrip '74

Vladimar Fogel (1902-29)
Bed and Sofa '27
The Girl with the Hat Box '27

Adam Fogerty
Legend of the Bog '08
Greenfingers '00

Dan Fogler
Fanboys '09
Taking Woodstock '09
Dr. Seuss' Horton Hears a Who! '08 (V)
Kung Fu Panda '08 (V)
The Wedding Bros. '08
Balls of Fury '07
Good Luck Chuck '07

Freda Foh Shen
Red Doors '05
Mulan '98 (V)
The Tiger Woods Story '98

Joe Folau
The Legend of Johnny Lingo '03
The Other Side of Heaven '02

Dennis Folbigge
Howling 4: The Original Nightmare '88
Zulu '64

Dave Foley (1963-)
Suck '09
California Dreaming '07
Netherbeast Incorporated '07
Postal '07
Sky High '05
Prom Queen '04
White Coats '04
Stark Raving Mad '02
Swindle '02
Monkeybone '01
On the Line '01
Dick '99
Blast from the Past '98
A Bug's Life '98 (V)
From the Earth to the Moon '98
Sink or Swim '97
Kids in the Hall: Brain Candy '96
The Wrong Guy '96
It's Pat: The Movie '94

Ellen Foley (1951-)
Married to the Mob '88
Fatal Attraction '87

Jeremy Foley (1983-)
Soccer Dog: The Movie '98
Dante's Peak '97

Macka Foley
WarCat '88
Las Vegas Weekend '85

Michael Foley (1954-)
Prison Planet '92
The Divine Enforcer '91
Karate Cop '91

Scott Foley (1973-)
The Last Templar '09
Below '02
Scream 3 '00
Forever Love '98

Abel Folk (1959-)
The Cheetah Girls 2 '06
Art Heist '05
The Dancer Upstairs '02
Sharpe's Gold '94

Alison Folland (1978-)
Milwaukee, Minnesota '03
Things Behind the Sun '01
Boys Don't Cry '99
All Over Me '96
Before and After '95
To Die For '95

Megan Follows (1968-)
Christmas Child '03
2 Brothers & a Bride '03
Anne of Green Gables: The Continuing Story '99
Under the Piano '95
The Chase '91
The Nutcracker Prince '91 (V)
Back to Hannibal: The Return of Tom Sawyer and Huckleberry Finn '90
Termini Station '89
A Time of Destiny '88
Anne of Avonlea '87
Stacking '87
Anne of Green Gables '85
Silver Bullet '85
Hockey Night '84

Bridget Fonda (1964-)
The Snow Queen '02
Kiss of the Dragon '01
Monkeybone '01
The Whole Shebang '01
South of Heaven, West of Hell '00
Lake Placid '99
The Break Up '98
Finding Graceland '98
Mr. Jealousy '98
A Simple Plan '98
In the Gloaming '97
Jackie Brown '97
Grace of My Heart '96
Touch '96
Balto '95 (V)
City Hall '95
Rough Magic '95
Camilla '94
It Could Happen to You '94
The Road to Wellville '94
Bodies, Rest & Motion '93
Little Buddha '93
Point of No Return '93
Army of Darkness '92
Single White Female '92
Singles '92
Doc Hollywood '91
Iron Maze '91
Frankenstein Unbound '90
The Godfather, Part 3 '90
Leather Jackets '90
Out of the Rain '90
Strapless '90
Scandal '89
Shag: The Movie '89
Aria '88
Jacob Have I Loved '88
Light Years '88 (V)
You Can't Hurry Love '88

Henry Fonda (1905-82)
On Golden Pond '81
Summer Solstice '81
Gideon's Trumpet '80
Oldest Living Graduate '80
Home to Stay '79
Meteor '79
Roots: The Next Generation '79
Wanda Nevada '79
Battleforce '78
City on Fire '78
The Swarm '78
Last Four Days '77
Rollercoaster '77
Tentacles '77
Great Smokey Roadblock '76
Midway '76
The Red Pony '76
My Name Is Nobody '74
Ash Wednesday '73
Night Flight from Moscow '73
Sometimes a Great Notion '71
The Cheyenne Social Club '70
There Was a Crooked Man '70
Too Late the Hero '70
The Boston Strangler '68
Firecreek '68
Madigan '68
Once Upon a Time in the West '68
Yours, Mine & Ours '68
A Big Hand for the Little Lady '66
Battle of the Bulge '65
In Harm's Way '65
The Rounders '65
The Best Man '64
Fail-Safe '64
Sex and the Single Girl '64
How the West Was Won '63
Spencer's Mountain '63
Advise and Consent '62
The Longest Day '62
Warlock '59
Stage Struck '57
The Tin Star '57
Twelve Angry Men '57
War and Peace '56
The Wrong Man '56
Mister Roberts '55
Jigsaw '49

Fort Apache '48
The Fugitive '48
On Our Merry Way '48
Daisy Kenyon '47
The Long Night '47
My Darling Clementine '46
Immortal Sergeant '43
The Ox-Bow Incident '43
Big Street '42
The Magnificent Dope '42
The Male Animal '42
Tales of Manhattan '42
The Lady Eve '41
The Grapes of Wrath '40
Lillian Russell '40
Return of Frank James '40
Drums Along the Mohawk '39
Jesse James '39
The Story of Alexander Graham Bell '39
Young Mr. Lincoln '39
Jezebel '38
Mad Miss Manton '38
Spawn of the North '38
That Certain Woman '37
Wings of the Morning '37
You Only Live Once '37
The Moon's Our Home '36
The Trail of the Lonesome Pine '36
The Farmer Takes a Wife '35
I Dream Too Much '35

Jane Fonda (1937-)

Georgia Rule '07
Monster-in-Law '05
Stanley and Iris '90
Old Gringo '89
The Morning After '86
Agnes of God '85
The Dollmaker '84
On Golden Pond '81
Rollover '81
9 to 5 '80
The China Syndrome '79
The Electric Horseman '79
California Suite '78
Comes a Horseman '78
Coming Home '78
Fun with Dick and Jane '77
Julia '77
A Doll's House '73
Steelyard Blues '73
Klute '71
They Shoot Horses, Don't They? '69
Barbarella '68
Spirits of the Dead '68
Barefoot in the Park '67
Any Wednesday '66
The Chase '66
The Game Is Over '66
Cat Ballou '65
Circle of Love '64
Joy House '64
Sunday in New York '63
Period of Adjustment '62
Walk on the Wild Side '62
Tall Story '60

Peter Fonda (1939-)

The Boondock Saints II: All Saints Day '09
Journey to the Center of the Earth '08
Ghost Rider '07
3:10 to Yuma '07
The Heart Is Deceitful Above All Things '04
A Thief of Time '04
The Maldonado Miracle '03
The Laramie Project '02
Second Skin '00
South of Heaven, West of Hell '00
Thomas and the Magic Railroad '00
The Limey '99
The Passion of Ayn Rand '99
The Tempest '99
Ulee's Gold '97
Escape from L.A. '96
Grace of My Heart '96 (V)
Nadja '95
Love and a .45 '94
Molly and Gina '94
Bodies, Rest & Motion '93
Deadfall '93
South Beach '92
Fatal Mission '89
The Rose Garden '89
Mercenary Fighters '88
Hawken's Breed '87
Certain Fury '85
Jungle Heat '84
Spasms '82
Split Image '82
Cannonball Run '81
The Hostage Tower '80
Wanda Nevada '79
High Ballin' '78
Outlaw Blues '77
Fighting Mad '76
Futureworld '76
92 in the Shade '76
Killer Force '75
Race with the Devil '75
Dirty Mary Crazy Larry '74
Hired Hand '71
The Last Movie '71
Easy Rider '69
Spirits of the Dead '68
The Trip '67
The Wild Angels '66
Lilith '64
Tammy and the Doctor '63
The Victors '63

Phil Fondacaro (1958-)

George A. Romero's Land of the Dead '05
The Creeps '97
Dollman vs Demonic Toys '93
Meridian: Kiss of the Beast '90
Ghoulies 2 '87
Troll '86

Benson Fong (1916-87)

Kung Fu: The Movie '86
The Strongest Man in the World '75
Our Man Flint '66
Girls! Girls! Girls! '62
Conquest of Space '55
His Majesty O'Keefe '53
Korea Patrol '47
Deception '46
The Scarlet Clue '45
The Shanghai Cobra '45
Charlie Chan in the Secret Service '44
The Chinese Cat '44
The Purple Heart '44

Leo Fong (1928-)

Showdown '93
Killpoint '84
The Last Reunion '80
Blind Rage '78
Enforcer from Death Row '78

Lyndsy Fonseca

Hot Tub Time Machine '10
Kick-Ass '10
Remember the Daze '07

Frank Fontaine (1920-)

Nightwaves '03
Random Encounter '98

Joan Fontaine (1917-)

The Witches '66
Voyage to the Bottom of the Sea '61
Island in the Sun '57
Until They Sail '57
Beyond a Reasonable Doubt '56
Casanova's Big Night '54
The Bigamist '53
Decameron Nights '53
Ivanhoe '52
Othello '52
Born to Be Bad '50
September Affair '50
Emperor Waltz '48
Letter from an Unknown Woman '48
You Gotta Stay Happy '48
Frenchman's Creek '44
Jane Eyre '44
This Above All '42
Suspicion '41
Rebecca '40
Gunga Din '39
The Women '39
The Duke of West Point '38
Maid's Night Out '38
A Damsel in Distress '37
A Million to One '37

Genevieve Fontanel (1936-)

Grain of Sand '84
The Man Who Loved Women '77

Shawn Fonteno

The Wash '01
Three Strikes '00

Dolores Fonzi (1978-)

The Aura '05
The Bottom of the Sea '03
Burnt Money '00

Hallie Foote (1953-)

Horton Foote's Alone '97
The Habitation of Dragons '91
Courtship '87
The Little Match Girl '87
On Valentine's Day '86
1918 '85

Horton Foote, Jr. (1954-)

Blood Red '88
On Valentine's Day '86
1918 '85

Dick Foran (1910-79)

Brighty of the Grand Canyon '67
Studs Lonigan '60
Atomic Submarine '59
Deputy Marshal '50
El Paso '49
Guest Wife '45
The Mummy's Tomb '42
Private Buckaroo '42
Ride 'Em Cowboy '42
Horror Island '41
Riders of Death Valley '41
The Fighting 69th '40
The House of the Seven Gables '40
The Mummy's Hand '40
My Little Chickadee '40
Winners of the West '40
Boy Meets Girl '38
Four Daughters '38
The Sisters '38
The Black Legion '37
Earthworm Tractors '36
Petrified Forest '36
Dangerous '35
Shipmates Forever '35

June Foray (1917-)

The Adventures of Rocky & Bullwinkle '00 (V)
Mulan '98 (V)
Thumbelina '94 (V)
DuckTales the Movie: Treasure of the Lost Lamp '90 (V)
Who Framed Roger Rabbit '88 (V)
Looney Looney Looney Bugs Bunny Movie '81 (V)
Sabaka '55

Brenda Forbes (1909-96)

The Man Upstairs '93
The White Cliffs of Dover '44
Mrs. Miniver '42

Bryan Forbes (1926-)

December Flower '84
The Slipper and the Rose '76
A Shot in the Dark '64
The Guns of Navarone '61
The League of Gentlemen '60
Quatermass 2 '57
The Baby and the Battleship '56
The Colditz Story '55
Wooden Horse '50

Mary Forbes (1883-1974)

You Gotta Stay Happy '48
Tender Comrade '43
You Can't Cheat an Honest Man '39
You Can't Take It with You '38
The Awful Truth '37
Vanity Fair '32

Michelle Forbes (1967-)

Johnson County War '02
Perfume '01
Homicide: The Movie '00
Escape from L.A. '96
Black Day Blue Night '95
Swimming with Sharks '94
Kalifornia '93

Ralph Forbes (1896-1951)

Frenchman's Creek '44
Convicts at Large '38
Legion of Missing Men '37
Make a Wish '37
I'll Name the Murderer '36
Bombay Mail '34
Riptide '34
Twentieth Century '34
The Phantom Broadcast '33
Smilin' Through '33
Inside the Lines '30
The Trail of '98 '28

Scott Forbes

Charade '53
Rocky Mountain '50

Anitra Ford (1942-)

The Longest Yard '74
Invasion of the Bee Girls '73
Stacey '73
The Big Bird Cage '72

Ann Ford

Logan's Run '76
The Love Machine '71

Bette Ford

The Landlady '98
Sudden Impact '83

Constance Ford (1923-93)

All Fall Down '62
Rome Adventure '62
Home from the Hill '60
A Summer Place '59
The Last Hunt '56

Courtney Ford

Alien Raiders '08
Fling '08

Dorothy Ford (1923-)

Jack & the Beanstalk '52
On Our Merry Way '48

Faith Ford (1960-)

The Pacifier '05
Beethoven's 5th '03
Sometimes They Come Back... For More '99
A Weekend in the Country '96
North '94
Murder So Sweet '93
You Talkin' to Me? '87

Francis Ford (1881-1953)

The Quiet Man '52
She Wore a Yellow Ribbon '49
Far Frontier '48
Accomplice '46
Girls in Chains '43
Lucky Cisco Kid '40
Stagecoach '39
The Texans '38
Charlie Chan at the Circus '36
Steamboat Round the Bend '35
Man from Monterey '33
Justice Rides Again '32
Battling with Buffalo Bill '31

Glenn Ford (1916-2006)

Final Verdict '91
Raw Nerve '91
Border Shootout '90
Casablanca Express '89
Virus '82
Day of the Assassin '81
Happy Birthday to Me '81
The Visitor '80
The Sacketts '79
Superman: The Movie '78
Midway '76
Santee '73
Smith! '69
Is Paris Burning? '66
The Money Trap '65
The Rounders '65
The Courtship of Eddie's Father '62
Experiment in Terror '62
The Four Horsemen of the Apocalypse '62
Pocketful of Miracles '61
Cimarron '60
The Gazebo '59
It Started with a Kiss '59
Cowboy '58
The Sheepman '58
Torpedo Run '58
Don't Go Near the Water '57
3:10 to Yuma '57
Fastest Gun Alive '56
Jubal '56
The Teahouse of the August Moon '56
Americano '55
Blackboard Jungle '55
Interrupted Melody '55
The Violent Men '55
Human Desire '54
Appointment in Honduras '53
The Big Heat '53
Man from the Alamo '53
Affair in Trinidad '52
The Green Glove '52
Follow the Sun '51
The White Tower '50
Lust for Gold '49
Man from Colorado '49
The Loves of Carmen '48
Gilda '46
A Stolen Life '46
The Desperadoes '43
Destroyer '43
So Ends Our Night '41
Texas '41
Blondie Plays Cupid '40
The Lady in Question '40

Harrison Ford (1884-1957)

The Nervous Wreck '26
The Average Woman '24
Little Old New York '23
Foolish Wives '22
Shadows '22
Hawthorne of the USA '19
The Primitive Lover '16

Harrison Ford (1942-)

Extraordinary Measures '10
Morning Glory '10
Crossing Over '09
Indiana Jones and the Kingdom of the Crystal Skull '08
Firewall '06
Hollywood Homicide '03
K-19: The Widowmaker '02
What Lies Beneath '00
Random Hearts '99
Six Days, Seven Nights '98
Air Force One '97
The Devil's Own '96
Sabrina '95
Clear and Present Danger '94
The Fugitive '93
Patriot Games '92
Regarding Henry '91
Presumed Innocent '90
Indiana Jones and the Last Crusade '89
Frantic '88
Working Girl '88
The Mosquito Coast '86
Witness '85
Indiana Jones and the Temple of Doom '84
Return of the Jedi '83
Blade Runner '82
Raiders of the Lost Ark '81
The Empire Strikes Back '80
Apocalypse Now '79
The Frisco Kid '79
Hanover Street '79
More American Graffiti '79
Force 10 from Navarone '78
Heroes '77
Star Wars '77
Dynasty '76
The Conversation '74
American Graffiti '73
Getting Straight '70
Zabriskie Point '70
Dead Heat on a Merry-Go-Round '66

Luke Ford (1981-)

The Black Balloon '09
The Mummy: Tomb of the Dragon Emperor '08

Maria Ford (1966-)

Dark Planet '97
Future Fear '97
The Glass Cage '96
The Wasp Woman '96
Alien Terminator '95
Burial of the Rats '95
Machine Gun Blues '95
Night Hunter '95
The Showgirl Murders '95
Stripteaser '95
Angel of Destruction '94
H.P. Lovecraft's Necronomicon: Book of the Dead '93
Deathstalker 4: Match of Titans '92
Final Judgment '92
Ring of Fire 2: Blood and Steel '92
Saturday Night Special '92
The Unnamable 2: The Statement of Randolph Carter '92
Futurekick '91
The Haunting of Morella '91
Naked Obsession '91
Ring of Fire '91
The Rain Killer '90
Slumber Party Massacre 3 '90
Masque of the Red Death '89
Stripped to Kill II: Live Girls '89
Dance of the Damned '88

Mick Ford (1957-)

How to Get Ahead in Advertising '89
Scum '79

Paul Ford (1901-76)

Lola '69
The Comedians '67
The Russians Are Coming, the Russians Are Coming '66
Never Too Late '65
Who's Got the Action? '63
Advise and Consent '62
The Music Man '62
The Matchmaker '58
Missouri Traveler '58
The Teahouse of the August Moon '56
Perfect Strangers '50
Lust for Gold '49

Peter Ford

The Thorn Birds: The Missing Years '96
Fair Game '85

Ross Ford (1923-88)

Reform School Girl '57
Project Moon Base '53
Blue Canadian Rockies '52
Jungle Patrol '48

Ruth Ford (1915-)

The Eyes of the Amaryllis '82
Strange Impersonation '46
The Woman Who Came Back '45

The Lady Is Willing *'42*

Steven Ford (1956-)
Black Hawk Down *'01*
Against the Law *'98*
When Harry Met Sally... *'89*
Body Count *'87*

Trent Ford
September Dawn *'07*
How to Deal *'03*
Slap Her, She's French *'02*

Wallace Ford (1898-1966)
A Patch of Blue *'65*
Warlock *'59*
Last Hurrah *'58*
The Matchmaker *'58*
The First Texan *'56*
The Rainmaker *'56*
A Lawless Street *'55*
The Man from Laramie *'55*
The Maverick Queen *'55*
She Couldn't Say No *'52*
Painting the Clouds With Sunshine *'51*
The Furies *'50*
Harvey *'50*
Great Jesse James Raid *'49*
The Set-Up *'49*
Coroner Creek *'48*
Dead Reckoning *'47*
T-Men *'47*
Black Angel *'46*
Crack-Up *'46*
Blood on the Sun *'45*
Spellbound *'45*
The Ape Man *'43*
Shadow of a Doubt *'43*
All Through the Night *'42*
Inside the Law *'42*
The Mummy's Tomb *'42*
Seven Days' Leave *'42*
Blues in the Night *'41*
Wheel of Fortune *'41*
The Mummy's Hand *'40*
Back Door to Heaven *'39*
Jericho *'38*
Exiled to Shanghai *'37*
Mad About Money *'37*
O.H.M.S. *'37*
Swing It, Sailor! *'37*
Rogue's Tavern *'36*
Get That Man *'35*
The Informer *'35*
Mysterious Mr. Wong *'35*
One Frightened Night *'35*
The Whole Town's Talking *'35*
The Lost Patrol *'34*
Employees' Entrance *'33*
Night of Terror *'33*
The Beast of the City *'32*
Freaks *'32*
Skyscraper Souls *'32*
Possessed *'31*

Willa Ford (1981-)
Friday the 13th *'09*
Impulse *'08*

Ken Foree (1948-)
Brotherhood of Blood *'08*
Brutal Massacre: A Comedy *'07*
Devil's Den *'06*
The Devil's Rejects *'05*
The Dentist *'96*
Leatherface: The Texas Chainsaw Massacre 3 *'89*
Glitz *'88*
From Beyond *'86*
Dawn of the Dead *'78*

Amanda Foreman
All I Want for Christmas *'07*
Jam *'06*

Deborah Foreman (1962-)
Sundown: The Vampire in Retreat *'08*
Lunatics: A Love Story *'92*
Sundown *'91*
The Experts *'89*
Friends, Lovers & Lunatics *'89*
Lobster Man from Mars *'89*
Destroyer *'88*
Waxwork *'88*
April Fool's Day *'86*
My Chauffeur *'86*
3:15—The Moment of Truth *'86*
Real Genius *'85*
Valley Girl *'83*

Jamie Foreman (1958-)
Botched *'07*
Layer Cake *'05*
Oliver Twist *'05*
I'll Sleep When I'm Dead *'03*
Breathtaking *'00*
Gangster No. 1 *'00*
Saving Grace *'00*
Nil by Mouth *'96*

Michelle Foreman
Sunset Strip *'91*
Stripped to Kill *'87*

Mark Forest (1933-)
Goliath and the Sins of Babylon *'64*
Hercules vs. the Sons of the Sun *'64*
The Lion of Thebes *'64*
Terror of Rome Against the Son of Hercules *'64*
Colossus of the Arena *'62*
Son of Samson *'62*
Goliath and the Dragon *'61*
Mole Men Against the Son of Hercules *'61*

Michael Forest (1929-)
Cast Away *'00*
Body of Evidence *'92*
Lensman *'84 (V)*
The Message *'77*
Dirt Gang *'71*
Atlas *'60*
The Beast from Haunted Cave *'60*
Ski Troop Attack *'60*

Sara Forestier
A Few Days in September *'06*
Games of Love and Chance *'03*

Maud Forget (1982-)
La Vie Promise *'02*
Bad Company *'99*

Farrah Forke (1967-)
Kate's Addiction *'99*
Ground Control *'98*
National Lampoon's Favorite Deadly Sins *'95*

Claire Forlani (1972-)
Beer for My Horses *'08*
Flashbacks of a Fool *'08*
In the Name of the King: A Dungeon Siege Tale *'08*
Carolina Moon *'07*
Mister Foe *'07*
Green Street Hooligans *'05*
Bobby Jones: Stroke of Genius *'04*
Memron *'04*
Gone Dark *'03*
The Medallion *'03*
Northfork *'03*
Triggermen *'02*
Antitrust *'00*
Boys and Girls *'00*
Mystery Men *'99*
Basil *'98*
Meet Joe Black *'98*
Basquiat *'96*
The Last Time I Committed Suicide *'96*
The Rock *'96*
Mallrats *'95*
JFK: Reckless Youth *'93*

Carol Forman (1919-97)
Federal Agents vs. Underworld, Inc. *'49*
The Black Widow *'47*

Milos Forman (1932-)
Keeping the Faith *'00*
New Year's Day *'89*
Heartburn *'86*

Richard Foronjy (1937-)
Man of the House *'95*
DaVinci's War *'92*
The Public Eye *'92*
Midnight Run *'88*
The Morning After *'86*
Prince of the City *'81*

Veronica Forque (1955-)
I Love You Baby *'01*
Kika *'94*
Why Do They Call It Love When They Mean Sex? *'92*

Alan Forrest
The Phantom Bullet *'26*
Eyes of Julia Deep *'18*

Christine Forrest
Monkey Shines *'88*
Martin *'77*

Frederic Forrest (1938-)
All the King's Men *'06*
Path to War *'02*
The House Next Door *'01*
Militia *'99*
Sweetwater: A True Rock Story *'99*
Black Thunder *'98*
Boogie Boy *'98*
The First 9 1/2 Weeks *'98*
Implicated *'98*
Point Blank *'98*
Whatever *'98*
The End of Violence *'97*
Horton Foote's Alone *'97*
Crash Dive *'96*
Andersonville *'95*
One Night Stand *'95*
Against the Wall *'94*
Chasers *'94*
Lassie *'94*
Dario Argento's Trauma *'93*
Double Obsession *'93*
Falling Down *'93*
Hidden Fears *'93*
Rain Without Thunder *'93*
Citizen Cohn *'92*
The Habitation of Dragons *'91*
Hearts of Darkness: A Filmmaker's Apocalypse *'91*
Twin Sisters *'91*
Cat Chaser *'90*
The Two Jakes *'90*
Double Exposure: The Story of Margaret Bourke-White *'89*
Lonesome Dove *'89*
Music Box *'89*
Best Kept Secrets *'88*
Gotham *'88*
Return *'88*
Shadow on the Sun *'88*
Tucker: The Man and His Dream *'88*
Valentino Returns *'88*
Saigon: Year of the Cat *'87*
Stacking *'87*
The Deliberate Stranger *'86*
The Adventures of Huckleberry Finn *'85*
Quo Vadis *'85*
Where Are the Children? *'85*
The Stone Boy *'84*
Valley Girl *'83*
Calamity Jane *'82*
Hammett *'82*
One from the Heart *'82*
Apocalypse Now *'79*
The Rose *'79*
It's Alive 2: It Lives Again *'78*
Missouri Breaks *'76*
Permission To Kill *'75*
The Conversation *'74*
Larry *'74*
The Don Is Dead *'73*
When the Legends Die *'72*

Irene Forrest
Bride of Re-Animator *'89*
Sitting Ducks *'80*

Sally Forrest (1928-)
Son of Sinbad *'55*
Hard, Fast and Beautiful *'51*
The Strange Door *'51*
Vengeance Valley *'51*
Mystery Street *'50*
Streets of Sin *'49*

Steve Forrest (1924-)
S.W.A.T. *'03*
Killer: A Journal of Murder *'95*
Amazon Women on the Moon *'87*
Gunsmoke: Return to Dodge *'87*
The Last of the Mohicans *'85*
Spies Like Us *'85*
Sahara *'83*
Hotline *'82*
Mommie Dearest *'81*
Roughnecks *'80*
A Rumor of War *'80*
Captain America *'79*
North Dallas Forty *'79*
The Deerslayer *'78*
The Hatfields & the McCoys *'75*
The Hanged Man *'74*
The Wild Country *'71*
Flaming Star *'60*
Heller in Pink Tights *'60*
Battle Circus *'53*
Clown *'53*
The Ghost Ship *'43*

William Forrest (1902-89)
Billy the Kid Versus Dracula *'66*
Good Neighbor Sam *'64*
The Horse Soldiers *'59*
Jailhouse Rock *'57*
I'll See You in My Dreams *'51*
Dead Reckoning *'47*
Fighting Seabees *'44*
Air Force *'43*
The Masked Marvel *'43*
Wake Island *'42*
Dive Bomber *'41*
International Lady *'41*

Cay Forrester (1921-2005)
Door to Door Maniac *'61*
D.O.A. *'49*

Constance Forslund (1950-)
Village of the Damned *'95*
River's Edge *'87*
A Shining Season *'79*
Dear Detective *'78*

Kathrine (Kate) Forster (1969-)
Mulholland Drive *'01*
Hollywood Harry *'86*

Robert Forster (1941-)
The Code *'09*
Ghosts of Girlfriends Past *'09*
Jack and Jill vs. the World *'08*
Cleaner *'07*
Dragon Wars *'07*
Rise: Blood Hunter *'07*
Firewall *'06*
Lucky Number Slevin *'06*
Charlie's Angels: Full Throttle *'03*
Confidence *'03*
Grand Theft Parsons *'03*
Undefeated *'03*
Due East *'02*
Human Nature *'02*
Like Mike *'02*
Lone Hero *'02*
Murder in Greenwich *'02*
Diamond Men *'01*
Finder's Fee *'01*
Mulholland Drive *'01*
Road to Riches *'01*
Family Tree *'00*
Kiss Toledo Goodbye *'00*
Lakeboat *'00*
Me, Myself, and Irene *'00*
It's the Rage *'99*
Supernova *'99*
Outside Ozona *'98*
Psycho *'98*
Rear Window *'98*
Hindsight *'97*
Jackie Brown *'97*
Night Vision *'97*
Uncle Sam *'96*
Scanner Cop 2: Volkin's Revenge *'94*
Scanners: The Showdown *'94*
Cover Story *'93*
Maniac Cop 3: Badge of Silence *'93*
Sex, Love and Cold Hard Cash *'93*
In Between *'92*
Committed *'91*
Diplomatic Immunity *'91*
29th Street *'91*
Peacemaker *'90*
Satan's Princess *'90*
The Banker *'89*
Once a Hero *'88*
Counterforce *'87*
Delta Force *'86*
Hollywood Harry *'86*
Vigilante *'83*
Walking the Edge *'83*
Goliath Awaits *'81*
Alligator *'80*
The Black Hole *'79*
Avalanche *'78*
Standing Tall *'78*
Stunts *'77*
The City *'76*
The Death Squad *'73*
The Don Is Dead *'73*
Journey Through Rosebud *'72*
Medium Cool *'69*
The Stalking Moon *'69*

Rudolph Forster (1884-1968)
The Mad Executioners *'65*
The Return of Dr. Mabuse *'61*
The Threepenny Opera *'31*

Bruce Forsyth (1928-)
Bedknobs and Broomsticks *'71*
Star! *'68*

Rosemary Forsyth (1945-)
Sweet Nothing in My Ear *'08*
A Time to Remember *'03*
John Carpenter's Ghosts of Mars *'01*
Girl *'98*
Daylight *'96*
Disclosure *'94*
A Friendship in Vienna *'88*
The Gladiator *'86*
Gray Lady Down *'77*
My Father's House *'75*
City Beneath the Sea *'71*
Columbo: Murder by the Book *'71*
Whatever Happened to Aunt Alice? *'69*
Texas Across the River *'66*
Shenandoah *'65*
The War Lord *'65*

Drew Forsythe (1950-)
Billy's Holiday *'95*
Wrangler *'88*
Burke & Wills *'85*
A Test of Love *'84*
Doctors and Nurses *'82*

Henderson Forsythe (1917-2006)
Carolina Skeletons *'92*
Teamster Boss: The Jackie Presser Story *'92*
Midnight Murders *'91*
Sessions *'83*
Crisis at Central High *'80*

John Forsythe (1918-)
Charlie's Angels: Full Throttle *'03 (V)*
Charlie's Angels *'00 (V)*
Scrooged *'88*
Mysterious Two *'82*
Sizzle *'81*
A Time for Miracles *'80*
And Justice for All *'79*
Cruise into Terror *'78*
Users *'78*
Sniper *'75*
Cry Panic *'74*
Terror on the 40th Floor *'74*
Murder Once Removed *'71*
The Happy Ending *'69*
Topaz *'69*
In Cold Blood *'67*
Madame X *'66*
Kitten with a Whip *'64*
The Ambassador's Daughter *'56*
The Trouble with Harry *'55*
Escape from Fort Bravo *'53*
Destination Tokyo *'43*

William Forsythe
Final Approach *'08*
Blue Hill Avenue *'01*

William Forsythe (1955-)
88 Minutes *'08*
iMurders *'08*
Stiletto *'08*
Hack! *'07*
Halloween *'07*
Masters of Horror: We All Scream for Ice Cream *'07*
Freedomland *'06*
Jam *'06*
The Devil's Rejects *'05*
The Last Letter *'04*
City by the Sea *'02*
Hard Cash *'01*
Camouflage *'00*
Luck of the Draw *'00*
Big City Blues *'99*
Blue Streak *'99*
Deuce Bigalow: Male Gigolo *'99*
Four Days *'99*
Hitman's Journal *'99*
The Last Marshal *'99*
Malicious Intent *'99*
Soundman *'99*
For Which He Stands *'98*
Highway Hitcher *'98*
Row Your Boat *'98*
Firestorm *'97*
First Time Felon *'97*
Hell's Kitchen NYC *'97*
Gotti *'96*
The Rock *'96*
The Substitute *'96*
The Immortals *'95*
Palookaville *'95*
Things to Do in Denver When You're Dead *'95*
Virtuosity *'95*
Beyond Desire *'94*
Direct Hit *'93*
Relentless 3 *'93*
American Me *'92*
The Gun in Betty Lou's Handbag *'92*
Career Opportunities *'91*
Out for Justice *'91*
Stone Cold *'91*
The Waterdance *'91*
Dick Tracy *'90*
Torrents of Spring *'90*
Dead Bang *'89*
Sons *'89*
Patty Hearst *'88*
Extreme Prejudice *'87*
Raising Arizona *'87*
Weeds *'87*
The Lightship *'86*
The Long, Hot Summer *'86*
Once Upon a Time in America *'84*
Savage Dawn *'84*

Josef Forte (1896-1967)
Pals of the Saddle *'38*
Reefer Madness *'38*

Marlene Forte
Our Song *'01*
Mob Queen *'98*
The Bronx War *'90*

Will Forte (1970-)
MacGruber '10
The Brothers Solomon '07
Beerfest '06
Around the World in 80 Days '04

Albert Fortell (1952-)
Time Troopers '89
Scandalous '88
Nuclear Conspiracy '85

Robert Fortier (1926-2005)
3 Women '77
Incubus '65

John Fortune (1939-)
Calendar Girls '03
The Tailor of Panama '00
Bloodbath at the House of Death '85

Bob Fosse (1927-87)
The Little Prince '74
My Sister Eileen '55
The Affairs of Dobie Gillis '53
Give a Girl a Break '53
Kiss Me Kate '53

Nicole Fosse (1963-)
A Chorus Line '85
All That Jazz '79

Brigitte Fossey (1946-)
The Last Butterfly '92
The Future of Emily '85
Enigma '82
Chanel Solitaire '81
La Boum '81
Quintet '79
Blue Country '77
The Man Who Loved Women '77
Going Places '74
Honor Among Thieves '68
The Wanderer '67
Forbidden Games '52

Anthony Foster
See Anthony (Jose, J. Antonio, J.A.) Mayans

Barry Foster (1931-2002)
After Pilkington '88
Beyond the Next Mountain '87
Maurice '87
The Whistle Blower '87
Heat and Dust '82
Smiley's People '82
Orde Wingate '76
Quiet Day in Belfast '74
Frenzy '72
Inspector Clouseau '68
Robbery '67
King and Country '64

Ben Foster (1980-)
The Messenger '09
Pandorum '09
Birds of America '08
30 Days of Night '07
3:10 to Yuma '07
Alpha Dog '06
X-Men: The Last Stand '06
Hostage '05
The Heart Is Deceitful Above All Things '04
The Punisher '04
11:14 '03
Northfork '03
Big Trouble '02
Get Over It! '01
Liberty Heights '99

Dianne Foster (1928-)
Iowa '05
The King of the Roaring '20s: The Story of Arnold Rothstein '61
Last Hurrah '58
The Brothers Rico '57
Night Passage '57
The Kentuckian '55
The Violent Men '55

Edward Foster (1906-89)
The Ghost and the Guest '43
Held for Ransom '38

Frances Foster (1924-97)
Crooklyn '94
Enemy Territory '87

George Foster
Centipede '05
Killer Me '01

Gloria Foster (1936-2001)
The Matrix Reloaded '03
The Matrix '99
Percy & Thunder '93
City of Hope '91
The House of Dies Drear '88
Leonard Part 6 '87
Man & Boy '71
To All My Friends on Shore '71
The Angel Levine '70
Nothing but a Man '64
The Cool World '63

Helen Foster (1906-82)
Young Blood '33
Boiling Point '32
Ghost City '32
The Saddle Buster '32
Linda '29
The Road to Ruin '28

Jodie Foster (1963-)
Motherhood '09
Nim's Island '08
The Brave One '07
Inside Man '06
Flightplan '05
A Very Long Engagement '04
The Dangerous Lives of Altar Boys '02
Panic Room '02
Anna and the King '99
Contact '97
Maverick '94
Nell '94
Sommersby '93
Shadows and Fog '92
Little Man Tate '91
The Silence of the Lambs '91
Backtrack '89
The Accused '88
Five Corners '88
Stealing Home '88
Siesta '87
The Blood of Others '84
The Hotel New Hampshire '84
Mesmerized '84
Svengali '83
O'Hara's Wife '82
Carny '80
Foxes '80
Candleshoe '78
Bugsy Malone '76
Freaky Friday '76
The Little Girl Who Lives down the Lane '76
Taxi Driver '76
Alice Doesn't Live Here Anymore '74
Smile, Jenny, You're Dead '74
One Little Indian '73
Tom Sawyer '73
Napoleon and Samantha '72

Jon Foster (1984-)
The Informers '09
The Mysteries of Pittsburgh '08
Tenderness '08
Stay Alive '06
The Door in the Floor '04
Murder in Greenwich '02

Julia Foster (1942-)
Thirteenth Reunion '81
F. Scott Fitzgerald in Hollywood '76
Great McGonagall '75
Half a Sixpence '67

Alfie '66
The Loneliness of the Long Distance Runner '62

Kimberly Foster (1961-)
Broken Trust '93
It Takes Two '88

Meg Foster (1948-)
Spoiler '98
The Man in the Iron Mask '97
Space Marines '96
Backlash: Oblivion 2 '95
Immortal Combat '94
Lady in Waiting '94
Oblivion '94
Shrunken Heads '94
Undercover '94
Best of the Best 2 '93
Hidden Fears '93
Project: Shadowchaser '92
To Catch a Killer '92
Diplomatic Immunity '91
Futurekick '91
Relentless 2: Dead On '91
Backstab '90
Blind Fury '90
Jezebel's Kiss '90
Leviathan '89
Relentless '89
Stepfather 2: Make Room for Daddy '89
Tripwire '89
They Live '88
Masters of the Universe '87
The Wind '87
The Emerald Forest '85
The Osterman Weekend '83
Ticket to Heaven '81
Carny '80
The Legend of Sleepy Hollow '79
The Scarlet Letter '79
Different Story '78
James Dean '76
Things in Their Season '74
Thumb Tripping '72
Adam at 6 a.m. '70

Norman Foster (1900-76)
Journey into Fear '42
Suicide Squad '35
Rafter Romance '34
Pilgrimage '33
Skyscraper Souls '32

Phil Foster (1914-85)
Bang the Drum Slowly '73
Hail '73
Conquest of Space '55

Preston Foster (1902-70)
The Time Travelers '64
Man From Galveston '63
Law and Order '53
The Marshal's Daughter '53
Kansas City Confidential '52
Tomahawk '51
Three Desperate Men '50
The Big Cat '49
I Shot Jesse James '49
Ramrod '47
The Harvey Girls '46
The Valley of Decision '45
Guadalcanal Diary '43
My Friend Flicka '43
American Empire '42
A Gentleman After Dark '42
Thunder Birds '42
The Roundup '41
Sea Devils '37
Annie Oakley '35
The Informer '35
Last Days of Pompeii '35
Hoopla '33
Ladies They Talk About '33
Doctor X '32
I Am a Fugitive from a Chain Gang '32
The Last Mile '32
Two Seconds '32

Sara Foster (1981-)
Bachelor Party 2: The Last Temptation '08
The Big Bounce '04

D.E.B.S. '04

Stacie Foster
Cyber-Tracker 2 '95
Steel Frontier '94

Susanna Foster (1924-)
Detour '92
The Climax '44
The Phantom of the Opera '43

Robert Fotrer
See Anthony (Jose, J. Antonio, J.A.) Mayans

Byron Foulger (1899-1968)
The Devil's Partner '58
Red Desert '50
Outlaw Gang '49
Bells of San Fernando '47
Hoppy Serves a Writ '43
The Panther's Claw '42
Sullivan's Travels '41
Heroes of the Saddle '40
Prisoner of Zenda '37

Robert Foulk (1908-89)
Emperor of the North Pole '73
Robin and the 7 Hoods '64

Derek Fowlds (1937-)
Over the Hill '93
Frankenstein Created Woman '66
Hotel Paradiso '66

Harry Fowler (1926-)
Flight from Singapore '62
Lucky Jim '58
Fire Maidens from Outer Space '56

Douglas Fowley (1911-98)
The White Buffalo '77
From Noon Till Three '76
The Good Guys and the Bad Guys '69
Poor White Trash '57
Lonesome Trail '55
The High and the Mighty '54
Cat Women of the Moon '53
Singin' in the Rain '52
Tarzan's Peril '51
Armored Car Robbery '50
Rider from Tucson '50
Battleground '49
Susanna Pass '49
Behind Locked Doors '48
Desperate '47
Fall Guy '47
Wild Country '47
Larceny in her Heart '46
Scared to Death '46
Along the Navaho Trail '45
One Body Too Many '44
Shake Hands with Murder '44
Colt Comrades '43
Lost Canyon '43
Meet the Mob '42
Mr. Wise Guy '42
Sunset on the Desert '42
Tanks a Million '41
Charlie Chan at Treasure Island '39
It Could Happen to You '39
Mr. Moto's Gamble '38
Charlie Chan on Broadway '37
On the Avenue '37
Big Brown Eyes '36

Bernard Fox (1927-)
The Mummy '99
Titanic '97
The Private Eyes '80
House of the Dead '78
Zone of the Dead '78
Arnold '73
Munster, Go Home! '66
Strange Bedfellows '65

Colin Fox (1938-)
Deathlands: Homeward Bound '03
Webs '03
The Doorbell Rang: A Nero Wolfe Mystery '01

Angels in the Infield '00
A House Divided '00
Left Behind: The Movie '00
Daylight '96
Beautiful Dreamers '92
Canada's Sweetheart: The Saga of Hal C. Banks '85
War Between the Tates '76
My Pleasure Is My Business '74

David Fox (1941-)
Population 436 '06
That Beautiful Somewhere '06
The Saddest Music in the World '03
Grey Owl '99
Conquest '98
When Night Is Falling '95
Black Fox: Good Men and Bad '94
Ordinary Magic '93

Edward Fox (1937-)
Oliver Twist '07
Lassie '05
Stage Beauty '04
The Republic of Love '03
All the Queen's Men '02
Daniel Deronda '02
The Importance of Being Earnest '02
Nicholas Nickleby '02
Lost in Space '98
A Dance to the Music of Time '97
Prince Valiant '97
Gulliver's Travels '95
A Month by the Lake '95
The Crucifer of Blood '91
Robin Hood '91
Anastasia: The Mystery of Anna '86
The Shooting Party '85
Wild Geese 2 '85
The Bounty '84
The Dresser '83
Never Say Never Again '83
Shaka Zulu '83
Gandhi '82
Edward and Mrs. Simpson '80
The Mirror Crack'd '80
The Cat and the Canary '79
The Big Sleep '78
Force 10 from Navarone '78
Soldier of Orange '78
A Bridge Too Far '77
The Duellists '77
The Squeeze '77
The Day of the Jackal '73
A Doll's House '73
The Go-Between '71
Skullduggery '70
Battle of Britain '69
Oh! What a Lovely War '69
Portrait of a Lady '67
Morgan: A Suitable Case for Treatment '66
The Mind Benders '63

Emilia Fox (1974-)
Ballet Shoes '07
Cashback '06
Keeping Mum '05
The Tiger and the Snow '05
Helen of Troy '03
The Republic of Love '03
The Pianist '02
Three Blind Mice '02
David Copperfield '99
The Scarlet Pimpernel '99
Shooting the Past '99
Catherine Cookson's The Round Tower '98
Rebecca '97

Huckleberry Fox (1975-)
Pharoah's Army '95
The Blue Yonder '86
A Winner Never Quits '86
Konrad '85
Misunderstood '84

James Fox (1939-)
Sherlock Holmes '09
Mister Lonely '07
Charlie and the Chocolate Factory '05

The Prince & Me '04
Cambridge Spies '03
The Lost World '02
The Mystic Masseur '01
The Golden Bowl '00
Sexy Beast '00
Up at the Villa '00
Lover's Prayer '99
Mickey Blue Eyes '99
Circle of Passion '97
Kings in Grass Castles '97
Leo Tolstoy's Anna Karenina '96
The Choir '95
Catherine Cookson's The Dwelling Place '94
Doomsday Gun '94
Fall from Grace '94
The Old Curiosity Shop '94
Heart of Darkness '93
The Remains of the Day '93
Afraid of the Dark '92
Hostage '92
Patriot Games '92
A Question of Attribution '91
The Russia House '90
Farewell to the King '89
The Mighty Quinn '89
High Season '88
Shadow on the Sun '88
The Whistle Blower '87
Absolute Beginners '86
Greystoke: The Legend of Tarzan, Lord of the Apes '84
A Passage to India '84
Performance '70
Isadora '68
Thoroughly Modern Millie '67
The Chase '66
King Rat '65
Those Magnificent Men in Their Flying Machines '65
The Servant '63
The Magnet '50

Jerry Fox
Hollywood Chainsaw Hookers '88
Evil Spawn '87

Jorja Fox (1968-)
Memento '00
Happy Hell Night '92
The Kill-Off '90

Kerry Fox (1966-)
Bright Star '09
P.D. James: The Murder Room '04
The Gathering '02
Intimacy '00
To Walk with Lions '99
Immortality '98
The Hanging Garden '97
Welcome to Sarajevo '97
The Affair '95
Country Life '95
Friends '95
A Village Affair '95
Rainbow Warrior '94
Shallow Grave '94
The Last Days of Chez Nous '92
An Angel at My Table '89

Lauren Fox (1977-)
Standing on Fishes '99
I Love You, I Love You Not '97

Laurence Fox (1978-)
A Room With a View '08
Becoming Jane '07
The Last Drop '05
Deathwatch '02
The Hole '01

Matthew Fox (1966-)
Speed Racer '08
Vantage Point '08
Smokin' Aces '07
We Are Marshall '06
Behind the Mask '99
My Boyfriend's Back '93

Megan Fox (1986-)
Jonah Hex '10
Jennifer's Body '09
Transformers: Revenge of the Fallen '09

How to Lose Friends & Alienate People '08
Transformers '07
Confessions of a Teenage Drama Queen '04

Michael Fox (1921-96)
The Longest Yard '74
Bloody Mama '70
The Dunwich Horror '70

Michael J. Fox (1961-)
Interstate 60 '02
Stuart Little 2 '02 (V)
Atlantis: The Lost Empire '01 (V)
Stuart Little '99 (V)
The Frighteners '96
Homeward Bound 2: Lost in San Francisco '96 (V)
Mars Attacks! '96
The American President '95
Blue in the Face '95
Coldblooded '94
Greedy '94
Where the Rivers Flow North '94
For Love or Money '93
Homeward Bound: The Incredible Journey '93 (V)
Life with Mikey '93
Doc Hollywood '91
The Hard Way '91
Back to the Future, Part 3 '90
Back to the Future, Part 2 '89
Casualties of War '89
Bright Lights, Big City '88
Light of Day '87
The Secret of My Success '87
Back to the Future '85
Poison Ivy '85
Teen Wolf '85
High School USA '84
Class of 1984 '82
Midnight Madness '80

Peter Fox
Diamond Run '90
A Minor Miracle '83

Rick Fox (1969-)
Tyler Perry's Meet the Browns '08
Holes '03
The Collectors '99
Resurrection '99

Samantha Fox (1951-)
Warrior Queen '87
Delivery Boys '84
Violated '84

Sidney (Sydney) Fox (1910-42)
Don Quixote '35
Midnight '34
Murders in the Rue Morgue '32

Spencer Fox (1993-)
Air Bud 6: Air Buddies '06 (V)
The Groomsmen '06
The Incredibles '04 (V)

Vivica A. Fox (1964-)
Cover '08
Private Valentine: Blonde & Dangerous '08
San Saba '08
Father of Lies '07
Kickin' It Old Skool '07
Three Can Play That Game '07
Getting Played '05
The Salon '05
Blast '04
Ella Enchanted '04
Kill Bill Vol. 2 '04
Boat Trip '03
Kill Bill Vol. 1 '03
Motives '03
Juwanna Mann '02
Little Secrets '02
Kingdom Come '01
Two Can Play That Game '01
Hendrix '00
Idle Hands '99
A Saintly Switch '99
Teaching Mrs. Tingle '99
Solomon '98
Why Do Fools Fall in Love? '98
Batman and Robin '97
Soul Food '97
Booty Call '96
Independence Day '96
Set It Off '96
The Tuskegee Airmen '95
Born on the Fourth of July '89

Earle Foxe (1891-1973)
Justice Rides Again '32
They Never Come Back '32
Union Depot '32
Four Sons '28
Hangman's House '28

Robert Foxworth (1941-)
Kiss the Bride '07
Transformers '07 (V)
The Librarian: Return to King Solomon's Mines '06
Syriana '05
Beyond the Stars '89
Double Standard '88
Peter and Paul '81
The Black Marble '79
Prophecy '79
Damien: Omen 2 '78
Deathmoon '78
Ants '77
The Invisible Strangler '76
The Treasure of Matecumbe '76
Frankenstein '73

Jeff Foxworthy (1958-)
The Fox and the Hound 2 '06 (V)
Racing Stripes '05 (V)

Jamie Foxx (1967-)
Valentine's Day '10
Law Abiding Citizen '09
The Soloist '09
The Kingdom '07
Dreamgirls '06
Miami Vice '06
Jarhead '05
Stealth '05
Breakin' All The Rules '04
Collateral '04
Ray '04
Shade '03
Ali '01
Bait '00
Held Up '00
Any Given Sunday '99
The Players Club '98
Booty Call '96
The Great White Hype '96
The Truth about Cats and Dogs '96

Redd Foxx (1922-91)
Harlem Nights '89
Norman, Is That You? '76
Cotton Comes to Harlem '70

Charles Foy (1898-1984)
The Wagons Roll at Night '41
Mutiny in the Big House '39

Claire Foy (1984-)
Season of the Witch '10
Little Dorrit '08

Eddie Foy, Jr. (1905-83)
Deadly Game '77
30 Is a Dangerous Age, Cynthia '68
Gidget Goes Hawaiian '61
Bells Are Ringing '60
The Pajama Game '57
Lucky Me '54
The Farmer Takes a Wife '53
Wilson '44
Yankee Doodle Dandy '42
Four Jacks and a Jill '41
Myrt and Marge '33

Victoria Foyt
Going Shopping '05
Deja Vu '98
Last Summer In the Hamptons '96
Babyfever '94

Carla Fracci (1936-)
Life of Verdi '82
Nijinsky '80

Tracy Fraim
Best Men '98
Fear '96
Dream Machine '91

James Frain (1969-)
Everybody's Fine '09
The Front Line '06
Into the Blue '05
The Count of Monte Cristo '02
Path to War '02
Arabian Nights '00
The Miracle Maker: The Story of Jesus '00 (V)
Reindeer Games '00
Where the Heart Is '00
Sunshine '99
Titus '99
Elizabeth '98
Hilary and Jackie '98
Red Meat '98
The Mill on the Floss '97
Rasputin: Dark Servant of Destiny '96
The Buccaneers '95
Loch Ness '95
Nothing Personal '95

Jonathan Frakes (1952-)
Star Trek: Nemesis '02
Star Trek: Insurrection '98
Star Trek: First Contact '96
Gargoyles, The Movie: The Heroes Awaken '94 (V)
Star Trek: Generations '94
North and South Book 1 '85

David "Shark" Fralick (1962-)
When I Find the Ocean '06
Clawed: The Legend of Sasquatch '05
Uncle Sam '96
Femme Fontaine: Killer Babe for the C.I.A. '95
The Legend of Wolf Mountain '92
Dark Rider '91
Invasion Force '90
Soultaker '90

Peter Frampton (1950-)
Almost Famous '00
Sgt. Pepper's Lonely Hearts Club Band '78

C.V. France (1868-1949)
Night Train to Munich '40
If I Were King '38
Skin Game '31

Richard France (1930-)
Vortex '81
Dawn of the Dead '78
The Crazies '73

Guillermo Francella
Rudo y Cursi '09
The Secret in Their Eyes '09

Victor Francen (1888-1977)
The Beast with Five Fingers '46
San Antonio '45
The Mask of Dimitrios '44
Madame Curie '43
The Tuttles of Tahiti '42
J'Accuse '37

Anthony (Tony) Franciosa (1928-2006)
City Hall '95
Double Threat '92
Backstreet Dreams '90
Ghost Writer '89
Death House '88
Blood Vows: The Story of a Mafia Wife '87
Stagecoach '86
Side Show '84
La Cicada '83
Daughter of Death '82
Death Wish 2 '82
Kiss My Grits '82
Unsane '82
The World Is Full of Married Men '80
Curse of the Black Widow '77
The Drowning Pool '75
Ghost in the Noonday Sun '74
Across 110th Street '72
Earth II '71
Web of the Spider '70
Fathom '67
Assault on a Queen '66
Rio Conchos '64
Period of Adjustment '62
Career '59
The Naked Maja '59
The Long, Hot Summer '58
A Face in the Crowd '57
This Could Be the Night '57

Alec B. Francis (1867-1934)
His Private Secretary '33
Mata Hari '32
Evangeline '29
Tramp, Tramp, Tramp '26
Charley's Aunt '25
The Mad Whirl '25
Beau Brummel '24
Little Church Around the Corner '23
Beyond the Rocks '22
The Wishing Ring '14

Anne Francis (1930-)
Lover's Knot '96
The Double O Kid '92
Little Vegas '90
Return '88
Laguna Heat '87
Poor Little Rich Girl: The Barbara Hutton Story '87
Mazes and Monsters '82
The Rebels '79
Born Again '78
Banjo Hackett '76
Cry Panic '74
Fireball Forward '72
Haunts of the Very Rich '72
Pancho Villa '72
The Love God? '70
Wild Women '70
Funny Girl '68
More Dead Than Alive '68
The Crowded Sky '60
Don't Go Near the Water '57
Forbidden Planet '56
Battle Cry '55
Blackboard Jungle '55
Bad Day at Black Rock '54
Susan Slept Here '54
A Lion in the Streets '53
A Lion Is in the Streets '53
Portrait of Jennie '48
Summer Holiday '48

Arlene Francis (1908-2001)
The Thrill of It All! '63
One, Two, Three '61
All My Sons '48
Murders in the Rue Morgue '32

Clive Francis (1946-)
Longitude '00
Sharpe's Company '94
The Bretts '88
Poldark '75
Man Who Had Power Over Women '70

Derek Francis (1923-84)
Murder Motel '74
What's Good for the Goose '69
Rasputin the Mad Monk '66
Tomb of Ligeia '64

Genie Francis (1960-)
The Note 2: Taking a Chance on Love '09
The Note '07
Disney's Teacher's Pet '04 (V)
Thunderbirds '04
North and South Book 2 '86
North and South Book 1 '85

Ivor Francis (1918-86)
House of the Dead '78
Zone of the Dead '78
Wackiest Wagon Train in the West '77
Hard Frame '70

Jan Francis (1951-)
Bloodlines '05
Champions '84

Jon Francis
See Jon(athan) Gries

Kay Francis (1899-1968)
Four Jills in a Jeep '44
Charley's Aunt '41
It's a Date '40
Little Men '40
In Name Only '39
Wonder Bar '34
One Way Passage '32
Strangers in Love '32
Trouble in Paradise '32
Vice Squad '31
Raffles '30
The Cocoanuts '29

Noel Francis (1906-59)
Stone of Silver Creek '35
Fire Alarm '32
My Pal, the King '32
Bachelor Apartment '31
Smart Money '31
Smart Woman '31

Paul Francis
Tears of the Sun '03
Warlock 3: The End of Innocence '98

Robert Francis (1930-55)
The Long Gray Line '55
The Caine Mutiny '54

Ryan Francis (1977-)
Straight into Darkness '04
Social Misfits '00
The River Pirates '88

James Franciscus (1934-91)
Secret Weapons '85
Butterfly '82
Jacqueline Bouvier Kennedy '81
Nightkill '80
Killer Fish '79
Good Guys Wear Black '78
The Greek Tycoon '78
Puzzle '78
Secrets of Three Hungry Wives '78
The Amazing Dobermans '76
Hunter '76
The Man Inside '76
One of My Wives Is Missing '76
Jonathan Livingston Seagull '73
The Cat o' Nine Tails '71
Beneath the Planet of the Apes '70
Marooned '69
The Valley of Gwangi '69
Snow Treasure '67

Don Francks (1932-)
Summer of the Monkeys '98
Bogus '96
Conspiracy of Fear '96
Degree of Guilt '95
Madonna: Innocence Lost '95
The Christmas Wife '88
Big Town '87
Rock & Rule '83 (V)
Heavy Metal '81 (V)
My Bloody Valentine '81
Summer's Children '79
Fast Company '78
Drying Up the Streets '76
Finian's Rainbow '68

Rainbow Sun Francks (1979-)
Love Come Down '00
Love Song '00

Dave Franco
Greenberg '10
The Shortcut '09

James Franco (1978-)
Date Night '10
Eat, Pray, Love '10
Milk '08
Nights in Rodanthe '08
Pineapple Express '08
An American Crime '07
In the Valley of Elah '07
Spider-Man 3 '07
Annapolis '06
The Dead Girl '06
Flyboys '06
Tristan & Isolde '06
The Ape '05
The Great Raid '05
Spider-Man 2 '04
The Company '03
City by the Sea '02
Deuces Wild '02
Sonny '02
Spider-Man '02
James Dean '01
At Any Cost '00
Whatever It Takes '00

Jess (Jesus) Franco (1930-)
Ilsa, the Wicked Warden '78
Rites of Frankenstein '72
Venus in Furs '70
The Diabolical Dr. Z '65

Margarita Franco
3 Ninjas: High Noon at Mega Mountain '97
3 Ninjas '92

Ramon Franco (1963-)
Shattered Image '93
Kiss Me a Killer '91
Tour of Duty '87
Heartbreak Ridge '86

Diana Franco-Galindo
Behind the Wall '08
Goodbye Solo '08

Deborah Francois
The Page Turner '06
The Child '05

Jacques Francois (1920-2003)
The Gift '82
Too Shy to Try '78
The Barkleys of Broadway '49

Billy Franey (1885-1940)
Somewhere in Sonora '33
Ghost Valley '32

Astrid Frank (1945-)
Au Pair Girls '72
Her and She and Him '69

Ben Frank (1934-90)
Hollywood Vice Sqaud '86
Hollywood Zap '86
Don't Answer the Phone '80

Billy Frank
Track 16 '02
Nudity Required '90
Grotesque '87

Charles Frank (1947-)
CSA: The Confederate States of America '04
Danielle Steel's Changes '91
LBJ: The Early Years '88
Lucky Stiff '88
The Right Stuff '83
The Chisholms '79
A Guide for the Married Woman '78

Snowblind '78
Tarantulas: The Deadly Cargo '77

Dan Frank (1959-)
Intimate Deception '96
Great Bikini Off-Road Adventure '94

Diana Frank (1965-)
Club Vampire '98
Pale Blood '91
Monster High '89
The Glass Jungle '88

Gary Frank (1950-)
Prison of Secrets '97
The Distinguished Gentleman '92
Getting Up and Going Home '92
Take Down '92
Deadly Weapon '88
Enemy Territory '87
Enola Gay: The Men, the Mission, the Atomic Bomb '80
The Night the City Screamed '80

Horst Frank (1929-99)
Albino '76
Cold Blood '75
The Grand Duel '73
Dead Are Alive '72
Code Name Alpha '67
Desert Commandos '67
The Vengeance of Fu Manchu '67
The Head '59

Jason David Frank (1973-)
Turbo: A Power Rangers Movie '96
Mighty Morphin Power Rangers: The Movie '95

Jerry Frank
The Big Doll House '71
The Flaming Teen-Age '56

Joanna Frank (1941-)
Say Anything '89
Always '85
The Savage Seven '68

Marilyn Dodds Frank
The Game of Their Lives '05
The Company '03
Sweet Lies '88

Tony Frank (1943-2000)
Rush '91
Riverbend '89

Mark Frankel (1962-96)
For Roseanna '96
Solitaire for 2 '94
Leon the Pig Farmer '93
Young Catherine '91

Al Franken (1951-)
Harvard Man '01
From the Earth to the Moon '98
Stuart Saves His Family '94
One More Saturday Night '86
Trading Places '83
All You Need Is Cash '78
Tunnelvision '76

Steve Franken (1932-)
Freeway '88
The Fiendish Plot of Dr. Fu Manchu '80
Terror Out of the Sky '78
Ants '77
Which Way to the Front? '70

Paul Frankeur (1905-75)
Phantom of Liberty '74
The Milky Way '68
Le Deuxieme Souffle '66
License to Kill '64
Le Gentleman D'Epsom '62
Un Singe en Hiver '62
Nana '55

William Frankfather (1944-98)
Trading Favors '97
Born Yesterday '93
Cool World '92
Defense Play '88

Aretha Franklin (1942-)
Blues Brothers 2000 '98
The Blues Brothers '80

Bonnie Franklin (1944-)
Your Place or Mine '83
Portrait of a Rebel: Margaret Sanger '82
Breaking Up Is Hard to Do '79

David Franklin (1962-)
Rock & Roll Cowboys '92
Early Frost '84

Diane Franklin (1963-)
Terrorvision '86
Better Off Dead '85
Second Time Lucky '84
Amityville 2: The Possession '82
Last American Virgin '82

Don Franklin (1960-)
American Girl: Chrissa Stands Strong '09
Black Dawn '05
Asteroid '97
Fast Forward '84

Gloria Franklin (1923-84)
Without Warning '52
Drums of Fu Manchu '40

Joe Franklin (1926-)
29th Street '91
Ghoul School '90

John Franklin (1967-)
Children of the Corn 666: Isaac's Return '99
Tammy and the T-Rex '94
The Addams Family '91
Children of the Corn '84

Pamela Franklin (1950-)
Eleanor & Franklin '76
Food of the Gods '76
Screamer '74
The Legend of Hell House '73
Satan's School for Girls '73
The Witching '72
And Soon the Darkness '70
David Copperfield '70
The Night of the Following Day '69
The Prime of Miss Jean Brodie '69
The Nanny '65
Flipper's New Adventure '64
A Tiger Walks '64
The Horse Without a Head '63
The Innocents '61

Richard Franklin (1948-)
Cyborg Soldier '08
Into the Night '85

William Franklyn (1925-2006)
Splitting Heirs '93
The Satanic Rites of Dracula '73
Quatermass 2 '57

Chloe Franks (1963-)
Ivanhoe '82
The Littlest Horse Thieves '76
The House that Dripped Blood '71

Mary Frann (1943-98)
Fatal Charm '92
I'm Dangerous Tonight '90

Adrienne Frantz
Hack! '07
Jimmy Zip '00

Arthur Franz (1920-2006)
Bogie: The Last Hero '80
Sisters of Death '76
The Human Factor '75
Missiles of October '74
Dream No Evil '70
Atomic Submarine '59
Monster on the Campus '59
The Young Lions '58
Hellcats of the Navy '57
Beyond a Reasonable Doubt '56
The Caine Mutiny '54
Invaders from Mars '53
Flight to Mars '52
The Member of the Wedding '52
The Sniper '52
Abbott and Costello Meet the Invisible Man '51
Sands of Iwo Jima '49
Jungle Patrol '48

Dennis Franz (1944-)
City of Angels '98
American Buffalo '95
Children of Fury '94
The Player '92
Die Hard 2: Die Harder '90
Kiss Shot '89
The Package '89
Body Double '84
Psycho 2 '83
Blow Out '81
Dressed to Kill '80
The Fury '78
A Wedding '78

Eduard Franz (1902-83)
Johnny Got His Gun '71
The Story of Ruth '60
The Burning Hills '56
The Indian Fighter '55
Lady Godiva '55
Sins of Jezebel '54
Dream Wife '53
Latin Lovers '53
Everything I Have is Yours '52
One Minute to Zero '52
The Great Caruso '51
The Thing '51
The Magnificent Yankee '50
Francis the Talking Mule '49
Outpost in Morocco '49
Whirlpool '49
The Scar '48

Elizabeth Franz (1941-)
Christmas With the Kranks '04
Stephen King's Thinner '96
The Substance of Fire '96
Sabrina '95

Daniel Franzee
Last Resort '09
Whirlygirl '04

Daniel Franzese (1978-)
Killer Pad '06
Cruel World '05
Mean Girls '04
Stateside '04
Bully '01

Francis Frappat
The Butterfly '02
Noir et Blanc '86

Bill Fraser (1908-87)
Little Dorrit, Film 1: Nobody's Fault '88
Little Dorrit, Film 2: Little Dorrit's Story '88
Pirates '86
Eye of the Needle '81
The Corn Is Green '79
Naughty Knights '71
Captain Nemo and the Underwater City '69
Alias John Preston '56

Brendan Fraser (1968-)
Extraordinary Measures '10
Furry Vengeance '10
G.I. Joe: The Rise of Cobra '09
Inkheart '09
Journey to the Center of the Earth '08
The Mummy: Tomb of the Dragon Emperor '08
The Air I Breathe '07
Journey to the End of the Night '06
The Last Time '06
Crash '05
Dickie Roberts: Former Child Star '03
Looney Tunes: Back in Action '03
The Quiet American '02
Monkeybone '01
The Mummy Returns '01
Bedazzled '00
Dudley Do-Right '99
The Mummy '99
Blast from the Past '98
Gods and Monsters '98
George of the Jungle '97
Still Breathing '97
The Twilight of the Golds '97
Glory Daze '96
Mrs. Winterbourne '96
Now and Then '95
The Passion of Darkly Noon '95
Airheads '94
Dark Side of Genius '94
The Scout '94
With Honors '94
Younger & Younger '94
Twenty Bucks '93
Encino Man '92
School Ties '92
Dogfight '91

Brent Fraser (1967-)
The Little Death '95
Wild Orchid 2: Two Shades of Blue '92

Duncan Fraser
The Lost Treasure of the Grand Canyon '08
Masters of Horror: The Washingtonians '07
Merlin's Apprentice '06
The Exorcism of Emily Rose '05
Octopus 2: River of Fear '02
When Danger Follows You Home '97
Unforgettable '96
Captains Courageous '95
Timecop '94
Call of the Wild '93
The Reflecting Skin '91
Watchers '88

Elisabeth Fraser (1920-2005)
A Patch of Blue '65
Two for the Seesaw '62
Ask Any Girl '59
The Tunnel of Love '58
Young at Heart '54
Hills of Oklahoma '50
The Man Who Came to Dinner '41

Helen Fraser (1942-)
Start the Revolution without Me '70
Repulsion '65

Hugh Fraser
Sharpe's Challenge '06
Chaos & Cadavers '03
P.D. James: Death in Holy Orders '03
Sharpe's Waterloo '97
Sharpe's Mission '96
Sharpe's Siege '96
Sharpe's Battle '94
Sharpe's Company '94
Sharpe's Enemy '94
Sharpe's Gold '94
Sharpe's Honour '94
The Bretts '88
The Draughtsman's Contract '82

John Fraser (1931-)
Schizo '77
Isadora '68
Doctor in Clover '66
Repulsion '65
Horsemasters '61
The Trials of Oscar Wilde '60

Laura Fraser (1976-)
The Boys Are Back '09
Florence Nightingale '08
The Flying Scotsman '06
Nina's Heavenly Delights '06
Casanova '05
16 Years of Alcohol '03
A Knight's Tale '01
Station Jim '01
Kevin & Perry Go Large '00
A Christmas Carol '99
Forgive and Forget '99
The Match '99
Titus '99
Virtual Sexuality '99
Left Luggage '98
Neil Gaiman's NeverWhere '96
Small Faces '95

Liz Fraser (1933-)
Chicago Joe & the Showgirl '90
Adventures of a Taxi Driver '76
The Americanization of Emily '64
Carry On Cruising '62
Carry On Regardless '61
Doctor in Love '60
Two-Way Stretch '60

Phyllis Fraser (1911-2006)
The Little Valentino '79
Tough to Handle '37
Winds of the Wasteland '36

Richard Fraser (1913-72)
The Cobra Strikes '48
The Private Affairs of Bel Ami '47
Blonde for a Day '46
The Undercover Woman '46
Bedlam '45
The Tiger Woman '45
White Pongo '45

Ronald Fraser (1930-97)
The Mystery of Edwin Drood '93
The Blackheath Poisonings '92
Let Him Have It '91
Rentadick '72
Too Late the Hero '70
The Killing of Sister George '69
Fathom '67

Sally Fraser
Dangerous Charter '62
Giant from the Unknown '58
The War of the Colossal Beast '58
It Conquered the World '56

Stuart Fratkin (1963-)
Prehysteria '93
Remote '93
Ski School '91
Dr. Alien '88

William Frawley (1887-1966)
Rancho Notorious '52
Abbott and Costello Meet the Invisible Man '51
The Lemon Drop Kid '51
Rhubarb '51
Kill the Umpire '50
Pretty Baby '50
East Side, West Side '49
Babe Ruth Story '48
Down to Earth '47
Miracle on 34th Street '47
Monsieur Verdoux '47
Mother Wore Tights '47
The Inner Circle '46
The Virginian '46
Flame of the Barbary Coast '45
Lady on a Train '45
Fighting Seabees '44
Whistling in Brooklyn '43
Gentleman Jim '42
Roxie Hart '42
Wildcat '42
Blondie in Society '41
The Bride Came C.O.D. '41
Cracked Nuts '41
Footsteps in the Dark '41
Golden Gloves '40
One Night in the Tropics '40
Rhythm on the River '40
The Adventures of Huckleberry Finn '39
Rose of Washington Square '39
Mad About Music '38
Blossoms on Broadway '37
Double or Nothing '37
Desire '36
The General Died at Dawn '36
The Princess Comes Across '36
Something to Sing About '36
Strike Me Pink '36
Alibi Ike '35
Harmony Lane '35
Here is My Heart '34

Jane Frazee (1918-85)
Last of the Wild Horses '49
Grand Canyon Trail '48
Under California Stars '48
On the Old Spanish Trail '47
Springtime in the Sierras '47
The Gay Ranchero '42

Dan Frazer (1921-)
Lord Love a Duck '66
Lilies of the Field '63

Liz Frazer
See Liz Fraser

Robert Frazer (1891-1944)
Lawmen '44
Partners of the Trail '44
Dawn Express '42
Gangs of Sonora '41
Renfrew on the Great White Trail '38
We're in the Legion Now '37
The Clutching Hand '36
Death from a Distance '36
Fighting Parson '35
Fighting Pilot '35
The Miracle Rider '35
Trails of the Wild '35
The Fighting Trooper '34
Found Alive '34
Monte Carlo Nights '34
Mystery Trooper '32
The Saddle Buster '32
The White Zombie '32
Ten Nights in a Bar-Room '31
The Drake Case '29

Rupert Frazer (1947-)
Back Home '90
The Girl in a Swing '89
Empire of the Sun '87
Testament of Youth '79

Joe Frazier (1944-)
Just the Ticket '98
Home of Angels '94

Ron Frazier
Presumed Innocent '90
Fat Man and Little Boy '89

Sheila Frazier (1948-)
The Hitter '79
The Lazarus Syndrome '79
Three the Hard Way '74
Superfly T.N.T. '73
Firehouse '72
Superfly '72

Stan Freberg (1926-)
It's a Mad, Mad, Mad, Mad World '63
Lady and the Tramp '55 (V)

Peter Frechette (1956-)
Paint It Black '89
The Kindred '87
The Hills Have Eyes, Part 2 '84
No Small Affair '84

Judah Friedlander (1969-)
I Hate Valentine's Day *'09*
Meet Dave *'08*
Chapter 27 *'07*
Date Movie *'06*
Feast *'06*
Duane Hopwood *'05*
Pizza *'05*
The Unseen *'05*
Along Came Polly *'04*
American Splendor *'03*
Showtime *'02*

Will Friedle (1976-)
Everything You Want *'05*
National Lampoon's Gold Diggers *'04*
My Date with the President's Daughter *'98*
Trojan War *'97*

David Friedman (1923-)
Sex and Buttered Popcorn *'91*
Blood Feast *'63*

Peter Friedman (1949-)
The Savages *'07*
King of the Corner *'04*
Power and Beauty *'02*
Someone Like You *'01*
I Shot Andy Warhol *'96*
The Heidi Chronicles *'95*
Safe *'95*
Blink *'93*
Single White Female *'92*
The Seventh Sign *'88*
Christmas Evil *'80*

Georg Friedrich
Eight Miles High *'08*
North Face *'08*

John Friedrich
The Final Terror *'83*
A Rumor of War *'80*
Wanderers *'79*
Forever *'78*
The Boy in the Plastic Bubble *'76*

Anna Friel (1976-)
Land of the Lost *'09*
Goal 2: Living the Dream *'07*
Goal! The Dream Begins *'06*
Niagara Motel *'06*
Irish Jam *'05*
Timeline *'03*
Me Without You *'01*
The War Bride *'01*
An Everlasting Piece *'00*
Sunset Strip *'99*
William Shakespeare's A Midsummer Night's Dream *'99*
The Land Girls *'98*
Our Mutual Friend *'98*
Rogue Trader *'98*
St. Ives *'98*

Colin Friels (1952-)
Solo *'06*
Child Star: The Shirley Temple Story *'01*
Dark City *'97*
Angel Baby *'95*
Back of Beyond *'95*
Cosi *'95*
Mr. Reliable: A True Story *'95*
A Good Man in Africa *'94*
Class Action *'91*
Darkman *'90*
Dingo *'90*
Grievous Bodily Harm *'89*
The Gold & Glory *'88*
Ground Zero *'88*
High Tide *'87*
Warm Nights on a Slow-Moving Train *'87*
Kangaroo *'86*
Malcolm *'86*
Monkey Grip *'82*

Philip Friend (1915-87)
Vulture *'67*
Buccaneer's Girl *'50*
Great Day *'46*

Rupert Friend (1981-)
Cheri *'09*
The Young Victoria *'09*
The Boy in the Striped Pajamas *'08*
The Last Legion *'07*
The Moon & the Stars *'07*
Outlaw *'07*
The Libertine *'05*
Mrs. Palfrey at the Claremont *'05*
Pride and Prejudice *'05*

Trixie Friganza (1870-1955)
Myrt and Marge *'33*
Free and Easy *'30*

Arno Frisch (1975-)
Funny Games *'97*
Benny's Video *'92*

Willy Fritsch (1901-73)
The Bellboy and the Playgirls *'62*
Congress Dances *'31*
Woman in the Moon *'29*
Spies *'28*

Lou Frizzell (1920-79)
Devil Dog: The Hound of Hell *'78*
Steel Cowboy *'78*
The Other *'72*
Duel *'71*

Gert Frobe (1912-88)
Sidney Sheldon's Bloodline *'79*
The Serpent's Egg *'78*
Shadow Man *'75*
Ten Little Indians *'75*
Ludwig *'72*
Dollars *'71*
Those Daring Young Men in Their Jaunty Jalopies *'69*
Chitty Chitty Bang Bang *'68*
I Killed Rasputin *'67*
Those Fantastic Flying Fools *'67*
Triple Cross *'67*
Is Paris Burning? *'66*
Those Magnificent Men in Their Flying Machines *'65*
Tonio Kroger *'65*
Goldfinger *'64*
The Longest Day *'62*
Testament of Dr. Mabuse *'62*
The Three Penny Opera *'62*
The Return of Dr. Mabuse *'61*
The Thousand Eyes of Dr. Mabuse *'60*
The Eternal Waltz *'54*
Party Girls for Sale *'54*

Gustav Froehlich (1902-87)
Homecoming *'28*
Metropolis *'26*

Samuel Froler (1957-)
Pulse *'03*
Private Confessions *'98*
The Best Intentions *'92*

Ewa Froling (1952-)
The Girl With the Dragon Tattoo *'09*
The Last Dance *'93*
The Ox *'91*
Fanny and Alexander *'83*

Milton Frome (1908-89)
The St. Valentine's Day Massacre *'67*
Batman *'66*
The Nutty Professor *'63*
Pardners *'56*
Ride 'Em Cowgirl *'41*

Alex Frost
The Vicious Kind *'09*
Drillbit Taylor *'08*
Elephant *'03*

Lee Frost (1935-2007)
Black Gestapo *'75*
The Thing with Two Heads *'72*
Tomb of the Undead *'72*

Lindsay Frost (1962-)
Collateral Damage *'02*
The Ring *'02*
Monolith *'93*
Danielle Steel's Palomino *'91*
Dead Heat *'88*

Nick Frost (1972-)
Pirate Radio *'09*
Wild Child *'08*
Hot Fuzz *'07*
Kinky Boots *'06*
Shaun of the Dead *'04*

Sadie Frost (1967-)
Uprising *'01*
Love, Honour & Obey *'00*
Rancid Aluminium *'00*
Captain Jack *'98*
Final Cut *'98*
Flypaper *'97*
Crimetime *'96*
Magic Hunter *'96*
A Pyromaniac's Love Story *'95*
The Cisco Kid *'94*
Paper Marriage *'93*
Shopping *'93*
Splitting Heirs *'93*
Bram Stoker's Dracula *'92*
Dark Obsession *'90*
The Krays *'90*

Terry Frost (1906-93)
Black Hills *'48*
The Hawk of Powder River *'48*
Trail of the Mounties *'47*
The Monster Maker *'44*
Waterfront *'44*
California Joe *'43*

Catherine Frot (1956-)
The Page Turner *'06*
Chaos *'01*
The Dinner Game *'98*
The New Eve *'98*
Un Air de Famille *'96*
Sorceress *'88*
Elsa, Elsa *'85*

Jordan Fry (1993-)
Meet the Robinsons *'07 (V)*
Charlie and the Chocolate Factory *'05*

Stephen Fry (1957-)
Alice in Wonderland *'10*
St. Trinian's *'07*
V for Vendetta *'06*
The Hitchhiker's Guide to the Galaxy *'05 (V)*
MirrorMask *'05*
Tristram Shandy: A Cock and Bull Story *'05*
Le Divorce *'03*
Gosford Park *'01*
Longitude *'00*
Relative Values *'99*
Spice World: The Movie *'97*
Wilde *'97*
Lone Justice 3: Showdown at Plum Creek *'96*
Mr. Toad's Wild Ride *'96*
Cold Comfort Farm *'94*
I.Q. *'94*
Stalag Luft *'93*
Peter's Friends *'92*

Taylor Fry (1981-)
A Little Princess *'95*
Lone Justice *'93*
Necessary Parties *'88*

Brittain Frye
Slumber Party Massacre 3 *'90*
Hide and Go Shriek *'87*

Dwight Frye (1899-1943)
Dead Men Walk *'43*
Frankenstein Meets the Wolfman *'42*
The Ghost of Frankenstein *'42*
Drums of Fu Manchu *'40*
Sinners in Paradise *'38*
The Bride of Frankenstein *'35*
The Crime of Dr. Crespi *'35*
The Invisible Man *'33*
The Vampire Bat *'32*
The Black Camel *'31*
Dracula *'31*
Frankenstein *'31*
The Maltese Falcon *'31*

Sean Frye (1966-)
Deadline Assault *'90*
E.T.: The Extra-Terrestrial *'82*

Soleil Moon Frye (1976-)
The Proud Family Movie *'05 (V)*
I've Been Waiting for You *'98*
Motel Blue *'98*
Piranha *'95*
Twisted Love *'95*
Pumpkinhead 2: Blood Wings *'94*
The St. Tammany Miracle *'94*
The Liar's Club *'93*
Invitation to Hell *'84*

Virgil Frye
Born in America *'90*
Secret of the Ice Cave *'89*
Body Beat *'88*
Colors *'88*
Hot Moves *'84*
Revenge of the Ninja *'83*
Running Hot *'83*
Dr. Heckyl and Mr. Hype *'80*
Up from the Depths *'79*

Sheng Fu
Life Gamble *'04*
Heaven & Hell *'78*

Jun Fubuki
Pulse *'01*
Seance *'00*
Charisma *'99*

Gaby Fuchs
The Werewolf vs. the Vampire Woman *'70*
Mark of the Devil *'69*

Leo Fuchs (1910-94)
Avalon *'90*
American Matchmaker *'40*

Joachim Fuchsberger (1927-)
The Last Tomahawk *'65*
The Mysterious Magician *'65*
Carpet of Horror *'64*
The Black Abbot *'63*
Curse of the Yellow Snake *'63*
Inn on the River *'62*
Dead Eyes of London *'61*
The Strange Countess *'61*

Alan Fudge (1944-)
Nightmare on the 13th Floor *'90*
Too Young to Die *'90*
The Children of An Lac *'80*
Bug *'75*

Carlos Fuentes
Boystown *'07*
Km. 0 *'00*

Miguel Angel Fuentes
Fitzcarraldo *'82*
The Puma Man *'80*

Athol Fugard (1932-)
The Killing Fields *'84*
Gandhi *'82*

Patrick Fugit (1982-)
Cirque du Freak: The Vampire's Assistant *'09*
Horsemen *'09*
The Good Life *'07*
Bickford Shmeckler's Cool Ideas *'06*
Wristcutters: A Love Story *'06*
The Moguls *'05*
Dead Birds *'04*
Saved! *'04*
Spun *'02*
White Oleander *'02*
Almost Famous *'00*

Takako Fuji (1972-)
The Grudge 2 *'06*
The Grudge *'04*
Ju-On: The Grudge *'03*
Ju-On 2 *'00*

Tatsuya Fuji (1941-)
Bright Future *'03*
The Empire of Passion *'76*
In the Realm of the Senses *'76*
Gappa the Trifibian Monster *'67*

Kahori Fujii (1965-)
Linda Linda Linda *'05*
Ju-On 2 *'00*

Yoshikazu Fujiki
Talking Head *'92*
Stray Dog *'91*

Yu Fujiki (1931-2005)
Yog, Monster from Space *'71*
Godzilla vs. Mothra *'64*
King Kong vs. Godzilla *'63*

Jun Fujimaki (1936-)
100 Monsters *'68*
Daimajin *'66*

Shiho Fujimura
Wrath of Daimajin *'66*
Shinobi no Mono 2: Vengeance *'63*
Shinobi no Mono *'62*

Shunji Fujimura (1934-)
Death Note 3: L, Change the World *'08*
Death Note *'06*

Hiroshi Fujioka (1946-)
K2: The Ultimate High *'92*
Ghostwarrior *'86*
Tidal Wave *'75*

John Fujioka (1925-)
Pearl Harbor *'01*
American Samurai *'92*
The Last Samurai *'90*
A Conspiracy of Love *'87*
Midway *'76*

Susumu Fujita (1912-91)
The Battle of the Japan Sea *'70*
Yojimbo *'61*
The Human Condition: Road to Eternity *'59*
The Hidden Fortress *'58*
No Regrets for Our Youth *'46*
The Men Who Tread on the Tiger's Tail *'45*

Toyo Fujita
The Dragon Painter *'19*
The Tong Man *'19*

Kamatari (Keita) Fujiwara (1905-85)
Yojimbo *'61*
The Hidden Fortress *'58*
Seven Samurai *'54*

Tatsuya Fujiwara
Death Note 3: L, Change the World *'08*
Death Note 2: The Last Name *'07*
Death Note *'06*

Kyoko Fukada
Kamikaze Girls *'04*
Onmyoji 2 *'03*
Dolls *'02*
Ringu 2 *'99*

Mitsuru Fukikoshi
The Twilight Samurai *'02*
Samurai Fiction *'99*

Lucio Fulci (1927-96)
Demonia *'90*
Manhattan Baby *'82*
Gates of Hell *'80*
Zombie *'80*

Christopher Fulford (1955-)
Millions *'05*
Goodbye, Mr. Chips *'02*
Eye See You *'01*
Bedrooms and Hallways *'98*
The Sculptress *'97*
Moll Flanders *'96*
Immortal Beloved *'94*
Prayer for the Dying *'87*

Dale Fuller (1885-1948)
The Unchastened Woman *'25*
Greed *'24*
The Marriage Circle *'24*

Dolores Fuller (1923-)
Bride of the Monster *'55*
Jail Bait *'54*
Glen or Glenda? *'53*
Mesa of Lost Women *'52*

Drew Fuller
The Circuit *'08*
Blonde Ambition *'07*
The Ultimate Gift *'07*

Frances Fuller (1907-80)
Homebodies *'74*
The Girl in the Red Velvet Swing *'55*
One Sunday Afternoon *'33*

Jonathan Fuller
Castle Freak *'95*
Last Man Standing *'95*
Suspect Device *'95*
Arcade *'93*
The Pit & the Pendulum *'91*

Kurt Fuller (1952-)
Van Wilder: Freshman Year *'08*
The Pursuit of Happyness *'06*
Don't Come Knocking *'05*
Ray *'04*
Anger Management *'03*
Auto Focus *'02*
Joshua *'02*
The New Guy *'02*
Angels in the Infield *'00*
Scary Movie *'00*
Diamonds *'99*
Pushing Tin *'99*
French Exit *'97*
Moonbase *'97*
Reflections in the Dark *'94*
Calendar Girl *'93*
Wayne's World *'92*
Bingo *'91*
Eve of Destruction *'90*
Miracle Mile *'89*
No Holds Barred *'89*
Elvira, Mistress of the Dark *'88*
The Running Man *'87*

Lance Fuller (1928-2001)
The Bride & the Beast *'58*
Voodoo Woman *'57*
Girls in Prison *'56*
Apache Woman *'55*
Kentucky Rifle *'55*
Cattle Queen of Montana *'54*

Nancy Belle Fuller
Sky Hei$t *'75*
Hard Part Begins *'73*

Olive Fuller
See Olive Carey

Penny Fuller (1940-)
The Beverly Hillbillies *'93*
Danielle Steel's Star *'93*
Lies Before Kisses *'92*
Miss Rose White *'92*
Fire and Rain *'89*
As Summers Die *'86*
George Washington: The Forging of a Nation *'86*
Cat on a Hot Tin Roof *'84*
License to Kill *'84*
Your Place or Mine *'83*

Lois Gibbs and the Love Canal '82
A Piano for Mrs. Cimino '82
All the President's Men '76

Robert Fuller (1934-)
Maverick '94
Donner Pass: The Road to Survival '84
The Gatling Gun '72
The Hard Ride '71
Whatever Happened to Aunt Alice? '69
Sinai Commandos '68
Return of the Magnificent Seven '66
The Brain from Planet Arous '57

Samuel Fuller (1911-97)
The End of Violence '97
La Vie de Boheme '93
Sons '89
Return to Salem's Lot '87
Slapstick of Another Kind '84
State of Things '82
White Dog '82
1941 '79
The American Friend '77
The Young Nurses '73
Pierrot le Fou '65

Fiona Fullerton (1956-)
Spymaker: The Secret Life of Ian Fleming '90
The Charmer '87
Shaka Zulu '83

Christina (Kristina) Fulton (1967-)
Red Shoe Diaries: Luscious Lola '00
The Girl with the Hungry Eyes '94
Hard Drive '94
Red Shoe Diaries 3: Another Woman's Lipstick '93
Bram Stoker's Dracula '92

Julie Fulton
My Brother's Keeper '95
Lethal Charm '90

Rad Fulton
See James Westmoreland

Soren Fulton
Fragments '08
Saving Sarah Cain '07
South of Pico '07
Thunderbirds '04

Eiji Funakoshi (1933-2007)
Gamera vs. Guiron '69
Gamera, the Invincible '66
Being Two Isn't Easy '62
Fires on the Plain '59

Stephen Fung
House of Fury '05
Special Unit 2002 '01
Gen-X Cops '99

Willie Fung (1896-1945)
Burma Convoy '41
Saddle Mountain Roundup '41
Come on, Cowboys '37

Annette Funicello (1942-)
Back to the Beach '87
Lots of Luck '85
Head '68
Thunder Alley '67
Dr. Goldfoot and the Bikini Machine '66
Fireball 500 '66
Beach Blanket Bingo '65
How to Stuff a Wild Bikini '65
Monkey's Uncle '65
Bikini Beach '64
Muscle Beach Party '64
Pajama Party '64
Beach Party '63
The Misadventures of Merlin Jones '63

Babes in Toyland '61
Horsemasters '61
The Shaggy Dog '59

Joseph Fuqua (1963-)
David Searching '97
Gettysburg '93

John Furey
A Killing Spring '02
The Wolves '95
Mutant on the Bounty '89
Friday the 13th, Part 2 '81

Edward Furlong (1977-)
Night of the Demons '09
Living & Dying '07
Jimmy & Judy '06
The Crow: Wicked Prayer '05
Cruel World '05
Three Blind Mice '02
Animal Factory '00
Detroit Rock City '99
American History X '98
Pecker '98
Before and After '95
The Grass Harp '95
Brainscan '94
Little Odessa '94
A Home of Our Own '93
Last Action Hero '93
American Heart '92
Pet Sematary 2 '92
Terminator 2: Judgment Day '91

Benno Furmann (1972-)
Mutant Chronicles '08
North Face '08
Speed Racer '08
Crusade: A March through Time '06
Joyeux Noel '05
My House in Umbria '03
The Order '03
Anatomy '00
The Princess and the Warrior '00

Yvonne Furneaux (1928-)
Frankenstein's Great Aunt Tillie '83
Repulsion '65
The Lion of Thebes '64
La Dolce Vita '60
The Mummy '59
The Warriors '55
The House of the Arrow '53
The Master of Ballantrae '53

Betty Furness (1916-94)
The President's Mystery '36
Swing Time '36
Here Comes Cookie '35
Magnificent Obsession '35
Beggars in Ermine '34
Aggie Appleby, Maker of Men '33

Deborra-Lee Furness (1960-)
Sleepwalking '08
Jindabyne '06
The Real Macaw '98
Angel Baby '95
Voyager '91
The Last of the Finest '90
Shame '87

Judith Furse
Carry On Spying '64
Black Narcissus '47

Joseph Furst (1916-2005)
The Dunera Boys '85
Diamonds Are Forever '71
Brides of Fu Manchu '66

Stephen Furst (1955-)
National Lampoon's Christmas Vacation 2: Cousin Eddie's Big Island Adventure '03
Little Bigfoot 2: The Journey Home '97

Magic Kid 2 '94
Magic Kid '92
The Dream Team '89
Up the Creek '84
Silent Rage '82
Getting Wasted '80
Midnight Madness '80
The Unseen '80
Swim Team '79
Take Down '79
The Bastard '78
National Lampoon's Animal House '78
Prime Time '77

George Furth (1932-)
Goodbye, Lover '99
Doctor Detroit '83
The Man with Two Brains '83
Prime Time '77
Norman, Is That You? '76
Butch Cassidy and the Sundance Kid '69

Toru Furuya
Paprika '06 (V)
Toward the Terra '80 (V)

Ed Fury (1934-)
Dinosaur Valley Girls '96
Colossus and the Amazon Queen '64
Samson Against the Sheik '62
Ursus in the Valley of the Lions '62
Wild Women of Wongo '59

Dan Futterman (1967-)
A Mighty Heart '07
Enough '02
Urbania '00
1999 '98
Shooting Fish '98
When Trumpets Fade '98
Breathing Room '96
Far Harbor '96
The Birdcage '95
Class of '61 '92

Herbert (Fuchs) Fux (1927-2007)
The Uranium Conspiracy '78
Jack the Ripper '76
Lady Frankenstein '72
Mark of the Devil '69
Island of Lost Girls '68

Jim Fyfe
Tanner on Tanner '04
The Frighteners '96

Mak Fyfe
UKM: The Ultimate Killing Machine '06
Prom Queen '04

Robert Fyfe
Around the World in 80 Days '04
Xtro '83

Franky G. (1965-)
The Devil's Tomb '09
Saw 2 '05
Confidence '03
The Italian Job '03
Manito '03
Wonderland '03

Marianne Gaba (1939-)
How to Stuff a Wild Bikini '65
The Choppers '61

Richard Gabai (1964-)
Black Horizon '01
Virtual Girl '00
Sexual Roulette '96
Vice Girls '96
Assault of the Party Nerds 2: Heavy Petting Detective '95
Bikini Drive-In '94
Dinosaur Island '93
Hot Under the Collar '91
Virgin High '90
Assault of the Party Nerds '89

Sasson Gabai
The Band's Visit '07
Escape: Human Cargo '98

Blink of an Eye '92

Martin Gabel (1912-86)
Smile, Jenny, You're Dead '74
Lady in Cement '68
Divorce American Style '67
Goodbye Charlie '64
Marnie '64
The Thief '52

Scilla Gabel (1937-)
Colossus of the Arena '62
Mill of the Stone Women '60
Tarzan's Greatest Adventure '59

Jean Gabin (1904-78)
L'Annee Sainte '76
Le Chat '75
Action Man '67
Any Number Can Win '63
Duke of the Derby '62
Le Gentleman D'Epsom '62
Un Singe en Hiver '62
Le Cas du Dr. Laurent '57
Les Miserables '57
Four Bags Full '56
French Can-Can '55
Napoleon '55
Grisbi '53
Le Plaisir '52
The Walls of Malapaga '49
Moontide '42
Stormy Waters '41
Le Jour Se Leve '39
La Bete Humaine '38
Grand Illusion '37
Pepe Le Moko '37
The Lower Depths '36
Maria Chapdelaine '34
Zou Zou '34

Christopher Gable (1940-98)
The Rainbow '89
The Lair of the White Worm '88
A Woman of Substance '84
The Slipper and the Rose '76
The Boy Friend '71
The Music Lovers '71

Clark Gable (1901-60)
The Misfits '61
It Started in Naples '60
But Not for Me '59
Run Silent, Run Deep '58
Teacher's Pet '58
Band of Angels '57
The King and Four Queens '56
Soldier of Fortune '55
The Tall Men '55
Betrayed '54
Mogambo '53
Never Let Me Go '53
Lone Star '52
Across the Wide Missouri '51
Key to the City '50
To Please a Lady '50
Any Number Can Play '49
Command Decision '48
Homecoming '48
The Hucksters '47
Adventure '45
Somewhere I'll Find You '42
Honky Tonk '41
They Met in Bombay '41
Boom Town '40
Comrade X '40
Strange Cargo '40
Gone with the Wind '39
Idiot's Delight '39
Test Pilot '38
Too Hot to Handle '38
Saratoga '37
Cain and Mabel '36
Love on the Run '36
San Francisco '36
Wife Versus Secretary '36
China Seas '35
Forsaking All Others '35
Mutiny on the Bounty '35
Chained '34
It Happened One Night '34
Manhattan Melodrama '34
Men in White '34

Dancing Lady '33
Hold Your Man '33
The Lost Stooges '33
Night Flight '33
No Man of Her Own '32
Red Dust '32
Strange Interlude '32
Dance Fools Dance '31
The Easiest Way '31
A Free Soul '31
Laughing Sinners '31
Night Nurse '31
Painted Desert '31
Possessed '31
Susan Lenox: Her Fall and Rise '31

Eva Gabor (1924-95)
Naked Gun 2 1/2: The Smell of Fear '91
The Rescuers Down Under '90 (V)
Princess Academy '87
Tales of the Klondike: The Scorn of Women '87
The Rescuers '77 (V)
The Aristocats '70 (V)
A New Kind of Love '63
It Started with a Kiss '59
Gigi '58
Truth about Women '58
Don't Go Near the Water '57
My Man Godfrey '57
Artists and Models '55
The Last Time I Saw Paris '54

Zsa Zsa Gabor (1919-)
A Very Brady Sequel '96
The Beverly Hillbillies '93
Happily Ever After '93 (V)
A Nightmare on Elm Street 3: Dream Warriors '87
Movie Maker '86
Frankenstein's Great Aunt Tillie '83
Every Girl Should Have One '78
Arrivederci, Baby! '66
Picture Mommy Dead '66
Boys' Night Out '62
For the First Time '59
Queen of Outer Space '58
Touch of Evil '58
Death of a Scoundrel '56
Lili '53
Lovely to Look At '52
Moulin Rouge '52
We're Not Married '52

John Gabriel
Hell's Bloody Devils '70
The Hunters '58

Ruth Gabriel (1975-)
Nostromo '96
Running Out of Time '94

Monique Gabrielle (1963-)
Evil Toons '90
Silk 2 '89
Not of This Earth '88
Amazon Women on the Moon '87
Deathstalker 2: Duel of the Titans '87
Emmanuelle 5 '87
Screen Test '85
Bachelor Party '84
Hard to Hold '84
Hot Moves '84
Black Venus '83

Gabriel Gabrio (1887-1946)
Harvest '37
Pepe Le Moko '37

Josh Gad
The Rocker '08
21 '08

James Gaddas (1960-)
Girls' Night '97
Catherine Cookson's The Black Candle '92

Analia Gade
Murder Mansion '70
Madame Sans-Gene '62

Ariel Gade (1997-)
Aliens vs. Predator: Requiem '07
Envy '04
Dark Water '02

John Gaden (1941-)
A Little Bit of Soul '97
The Wedding Party '97

Antonio Gades (1936-2004)
El Amor Brujo '86
Carmen '83
Blood Wedding '81

Anna Gael (1943-)
Zeta One '69
Therese & Isabelle '67

Jim Gaffigan (1966-)
Going the Distance '10
Away We Go '09
The Love Guru '08
The Great New Wonderful '06
Stephanie Daley '06
13 Going on 30 '04
No Sleep 'Til Madison '02
Final '01
Super Troopers '01
30 Years to Life '01

Mo Gaffney (1958-)
Jailbait! '00
Drop Dead Gorgeous '99
The Shot '96

Kevin Gage (1959-)
Last Resort '09
Big Stan '07
Chaos '05
Paparazzi '04
May '02
Blow '01
Dee Snider's Strangeland '98
Double Tap '98
Gunshy '98
Point Blank '98
Heat '95

Patricia Gage
The Little Kidnappers '90
Rabid '77

Holly Gagnier (1962-)
The Undertaker's Wedding '97
Alligator 2: The Mutation '90
Girls Just Want to Have Fun '85

Trevor Gagnon (1995-)
Shorts: The Adventures of the Wishing Rock '09
Fly Me to the Moon '08 (V)

Jenny Gago (1953-)
Alien Nation: Millennium '96
Grand Avenue '96
My Family '94
Sweet 15 '90
Old Gringo '89

Max Gail (1943-)
Facing the Enemy '00
Mind Lies '00
Not in This Town '97
Good Luck '96
Forest Warrior '95
Deadly Target '94
Pontiac Moon '94
Sodbusters '94
Street Crimes '92
Judgment in Berlin '88
The Game of Love '87
Where Are the Children? '85
D.C. Cab '84
Heartbreakers '84
Aliens Are Coming '80
Pearl '78
Night Moves '75
Cardiac Arrest '74
Dirty Harry '71

Boyd Gaines (1953-)
Second Best '05
The Confession '98
I'm Not Rappaport '96
The Discovery Program '89

Call Me '88
Piece of Cake '88
Heartbreak Ridge '86
The Sure Thing '85
Porky's '82

Jim Gaines (1955-)
Fist of Steel '93
Codename: Terminate '90
Commando Invasion '87
Blood Debts '83

Richard Gaines (1904-75)
Ace in the Hole '51
Humoresque '46
The Enchanted Cottage '45
Mr. Winkle Goes to War '44
The More the Merrier '43

M.C. Gainey (1948-)
Unearthed '07
Wild Hogs '07
Beerfest '06
Are We There Yet? '05
The Dukes of Hazzard '05
Club Dread '04
Sideways '04
The Cooler '03
Wonderland '03
The Country Bears '02
The New Guy '02
Happy, Texas '99
Con Air '97
Breakdown '96
Citizen Ruth '96
The Fan '96
One Man's Justice '95
Leap of Faith '92
El Diablo '90
Starman '84

Courtney Gains (1965-)
Sweet Home Alabama '02
King Cobra '98
No Code of Conduct '98
The Killing Grounds '97
Behind Enemy Lines '96
Memphis Belle '90
The 'Burbs '89
Colors '88
Can't Buy Me Love '87
The Children of Times Square '86
Back to the Future '85
Lust in the Dust '85
Children of the Corn '84
Hardbodies '84

Charlotte Gainsbourg (1972-)
Antichrist '09
I'm Not There '07
I Do '06
The Science of Sleep '06
Lemming '05
Happily Ever After '04
21 Grams '03
My Wife is an Actress '01
La Buche '00
Jane Eyre '96
Love, etc. '96
Grosse Fatigue '94
The Cement Garden '93
Night Sun '90
The Little Thief '89
Le Petit Amour '87
Love Songs '84

Serge Gainsbourg (1928-91)
I Love You All '80
Too Pretty to Be Honest '72
French Intrigue '70
Slogan '69
The Fury of Hercules '61
Samson '61
Voulez-Vous Danser avec Moi? '59

Paulina Gaitan
Sin Nombre '09
Trade '07

Cristina Gajoni
Andy Warhol's Frankenstein '74
Ursus in the Valley of the Lions '62

Janusz Gajos (1939-)
Zemsta '02
Trois Couleurs: Blanc '94
The Decalogue '88
The Interrogation '82

Michel Galabru (1924-)
Belle Epoque '92
Uranus '91
La Cage aux Folles 3: The Wedding '86
Subway '85
La Cage aux Folles 2 '81
La Cage aux Folles '78
L'Amour en Herbe '77
The Judge and the Assassin '75
Soldat Duroc... Ca Va Etre Ta Fete! '75
The Gendarme of Saint-Tropez '64

David Gale (1936-91)
The Guyver '91
Syngenor '90
Bride of Re-Animator '89
The Brain '88
Re-Animator '84
Savage Weekend '80

Ed Gale (1963-)
O Brother Where Art Thou? '00
Chopper Chicks in Zombietown '91

Eddra Gale (1921-2001)
Revenge of the Cheerleaders '76
8 1/2 '63

Joan Gale (1915-82)
Devil Diamond '37
The Miracle Rider '35

June Gale (1918-96)
Charlie Chan at Treasure Island '39
It Could Happen to You '39
Rainbow's End '35
Swifty '35

Vincent Gale
Mail Order Bride '08
Firewall '06
Meltdown '06
The Final Cut '04
The Twelve Days of Christmas Eve '04
Brotherhood of Murder '99
Every Mother's Worst Fear '98
Baby Monitor: Sound of Fear '97
The Escape '95
Bye Bye Blues '89

Johnny Galecki (1975-)
Table for Three '09
Hancock '08
Happy Endings '05
Bookies '03
Vanilla Sky '01
Bounce '00
Playing Mona Lisa '00
Morgan's Ferry '99
The Opposite of Sex '98
Bean '97
I Know What You Did Last Summer '97
Suicide Kings '97
Backfield in Motion '91
National Lampoon's Christmas Vacation '89

Michael Galeota (1984-)
Clubhouse Detectives '96
Rattled '96

Juan Luis Galiardo (1940-)
The Girl of Your Dreams '99
Tango '98
Don Juan, My Love '90

Anna Galiena (1954-)
Excellent Cadavers '99
The Leading Man '96
Moses '96
Three Lives and Only One Death '96

Being Human '94
Jamon, Jamon '93
The Hairdresser's Husband '92
Rorret '87

Zach Galifianakis (1969-)
Dinner for Schmucks '10
Youth in Revolt '10
G-Force '09
The Hangover '09
Up in the Air '09
Gigantic '08
What Happens in Vegas '08
Below '02
Out Cold '01

Kelly Galindo
The Malibu Beach Vampires '91
Angels of the City '89

Nacho Galindo (1908-73)
Born Reckless '59
Wetbacks '56
Green Fire '55
Borderline '50
Border River '47

Annie Galipeau (1979-)
Grey Owl '99
Map of the Human Heart '93

Frank Gallacher (1948-)
December Boys '07
Till Human Voices Wake Us '02
Dark City '97
Mr. Reliable: A True Story '95
Proof '91
Waterfront '83

Bronagh Gallagher (1972-)
Botched '07
Tristan & Isolde '06
The Wicked, Wicked West '97
Mary Reilly '95
Pulp Fiction '94
The Commitments '91

David Gallagher (1985-)
Little Secrets '02
Angels in the Endzone '98

Megan Gallagher (1960-)
A Time to Remember '03
Breaking Free '95
Crosscut '95
Trade Off '95
The Birds 2: Land's End '94
In a Stranger's Hand '92
The Ambulance '90

Patrick Gallagher (1968-)
Night at the Museum '06
Silent Partner '05
In Enemy Hands '04

Peter Gallagher (1955-)
Adam '09
Center Stage: Turn It Up '08
How to Deal '03
Mr. Deeds '02
Anne Rice's The Feast of All Saints '01
Perfume '01
Protection '01
Center Stage '00
Cupid & Cate '00
The Last Debate '00
American Beauty '99
Brotherhood of Murder '99
House on Haunted Hill '99
Cafe Society '97
Johnny Skidmarks '97
The Man Who Knew Too Little '97
Path to Paradise '97
Last Dance '96
Titanic '96
To Gillian on Her 37th Birthday '96

The Underneath '95
While You Were Sleeping '95
Mrs. Parker and the Vicious Circle '94
Mother's Boys '94
White Mile '94
Fallen Angels 1 '93
Fallen Angels 2 '93
The Hudsucker Proxy '93
Malice '93
Short Cuts '93
Watch It '93
Bob Roberts '92
The Player '92
An Inconvenient Woman '91
Late for Dinner '91
Tune in Tomorrow '90
sex, lies and videotape '89
The Caine Mutiny Court Martial '88
High Spirits '88
Long Day's Journey into Night '88
The Murder of Mary Phagan '87
My Little Girl '87
Dreamchild '85
Private Contentment '83
Summer Lovers '82
Idolmaker '80
Skag '79

Richard "Skeets" Gallagher (1891-1955)
Zis Boom Bah '41
Danger on the Air '38
Hats Off '37
Bachelor Bait '34
Riptide '34
Merrily We Go to Hell '32
Possessed '31

James Gallanders (1970-)
Charlie & Me '08
The Third Miracle '99

Camillo Gallardo
Of Love and Shadows '94
Singles '92

Carlos Gallardo
Planet Terror '07
Eastside '99
Desperado '95
El Mariachi '93

Lucy Gallardo
How the Garcia Girls Spent Their Summer '05
The Exterminating Angel '62

Rosa Maria Gallardo
The Brainiac '61
Creature of the Walking Dead '60

Silvania Gallardo (1953-)
Prison Stories: Women on the Inside '91
Out of the Dark '88
Silence of the Heart '84

John Gallaudet (1903-83)
In Cold Blood '67
Outcasts of the Trail '49
I Promise to Pay '37
Alibi for Murder '36
Pennies from Heaven '36

Ely Galleani
Redneck '73
Five Dolls for an August Moon '70

Gina Gallego (1959-)
Personals '90
My Demon Lover '87
Lust in the Dust '85

Georges Galley (1926-)
Gorilla '56
Femmes de Paris '53

Ida Galli (1942-)
The Case of the Scorpion's Tail '71
Eagles Over London '69

Rosina Galli (1906-69)
Gauchos of El Dorado '41
Escape to Paradise '39
Fisherman's Wharf '39

Ketti Gallian (1912-72)
Under the Pampas Moon '35
Marie Galante '34

Zach Galligan (1963-)
Infested: Invasion of the Killer Bugs '02
Gabriela '01
The Tomorrow Man '01
Arthur's Quest '99
Raw Nerve '99
Storm Trooper '98
The First to Go '97
Prince Valiant '97
Cupid '96
Cyborg 3: The Recycler '95
Caroline at Midnight '93
Ice '93
Warlock: The Armageddon '93
All Tied Up '92
Round Trip to Heaven '92
Psychic '91
Waxwork 2: Lost in Time '91
Zandalee '91
Gremlins 2: The New Batch '90
Mortal Passions '90
Rebel Storm '90
The Lawrenceville Stories '88
Waxwork '88
Gremlins '84

Joseph (Joe) Gallison
Critic's Choice '63
All the Young Men '60

Kyle Gallner
A Nightmare on Elm Street '10
The Haunting in Connecticut '09
Jennifer's Body '09
Gardens of the Night '08
Red '08
Sublime '07
Red Eye '05

Carla Gallo (1975-)
Insanitarium '08
Mission: Impossible 3 '06
Spanking the Monkey '94

Michaela Gallo (1990-)
Beethoven's 4th '01
Beethoven's 3rd '00

Robert Gallo (1945-)
Sinners '89
Mayhem '87

Vincent Gallo (1961-)
Tetro '09
Moscow Zero '06
The Brown Bunny '03
Get Well Soon '01
Hide and Seek '00
Freeway 2: Confessions of a Trickbaby '99
Buffalo 66 '97
Truth or Consequences, N.M. '97
The Funeral '96
Nenette and Boni '96
Palookaville '95
Angela '94
Arizona Dream '94
The House of the Spirits '93

Tom Gallop
The Bourne Ultimatum '07
The Bourne Supremacy '04

Don Galloway (1937-2009)
Two Moon Junction '88
Demon Rage '82
Snowblind '78
Rough Night in Jericho '67

Jack Galloway
A Different Loyalty '04
Codename: Icarus '85

Anna Galvin
Masters of Horror: Right to Die '07

Tin Man '07

Rita Gam (1928-)
Midnight '89
Distortions '87
Seeds of Evil '76
Klute '71
Shoot Out '71
The King of Kings '61
Mohawk '56
The Thief '52

Brian Gamble
The Keeper '09
The Perfect Daughter '96

Mason Gamble (1986-)
A Gentleman's Game '01
Arlington Road '99
Rushmore '98
Bad Moon '96
Dennis the Menace '93

Nathan Gamble
The Dark Knight '08
Marley & Me '08
The Mist '07
Babel '06

Jacques Gamblin (1957-)
Carnage '02
Dr. Akagi '98
Pedale Douce '96

Michael Gambon (1940-)
The Book of Eli '10
Emma '09
Fantastic Mr. Fox '09 (V)
Harry Potter and the Half-Blood Prince '09
Brideshead Revisited '08
Cranford '08
Harry Potter and the Order of the Phoenix '07
Amazing Grace '06
The Good Shepherd '06
The Omen '06
Harry Potter and the Goblet of Fire '05
Layer Cake '05
Being Julia '04
Harry Potter and the Prisoner of Azkaban '04
The Life Aquatic with Steve Zissou '04
Sky Captain and the World of Tomorrow '04
Angels in America '03
Deep Blue '03 (N)
Open Range '03
Sylvia '03
Path to War '02
Almost Strangers '01
Charlotte Gray '01
Gosford Park '01
High Heels and Low Lifes '01
Wives and Daughters '01
Longitude '00
The Insider '99
The Last September '99
Sleepy Hollow '99
Dancing at Lughnasa '98
Plunkett & Macleane '98
The Gambler '97
Midnight in Saint Petersburg '97
The Wings of the Dove '97
Samson and Delilah '96
Bullet to Beijing '95
The Innocent Sleep '95
Mary Reilly '95
Nothing Personal '95
The Browning Version '94
Clean Slate '94
Faith '94
A Man of No Importance '94
Squanto: A Warrior's Tale '94
Two Deaths '94
Toys '92
The Heat of the Day '91
Mobsters '91
The Cook, the Thief, His Wife & Her Lover '90
The Rachel Papers '89
Missing Link '88
The Singing Detective '86

Turtle Diary '86
Forbidden Passion: The Oscar Wilde Movie '85
The Beast Must Die '75

The Game (1979-)
Street Kings '08
Waist Deep '06

Robin Gammell
The Girl Next Door '98
His Bodyguard '98
Last Night '98
Bone Daddy '97
If These Walls Could Talk '96
Inhumanoid '96
Sinatra '92
Guilty by Suspicion '91
Gore Vidal's Lincoln '88
Project X '87
Missing Pieces '83
Full Circle '77
Panic in Echo Park '77

James Gammon (1940-)
Appaloosa '08
In the Electric Mist '08
The Final Season '07
The Far Side of Jericho '06
Outlaw Trail '06
Don't Come Knocking '05
Silver City '04
Cold Mountain '03
Monte Walsh '03
The Country Bears '02 (V)
Life or Something Like It '02
The Cell '00
The Iron Giant '99 (V)
You Know My Name '99
The Hi-Lo Country '98
One Man's Hero '98
Point Blank '98
The Man in the Iron Mask '97
Traveller '96
Larry McMurtry's Streets of Laredo '95
Truman '95
Wild Bill '95
Cabin Boy '94
Hard Vice '94
Major League 2 '94
Natural Born Killers '94
Vegas Vice '94
Wyatt Earp '94
The Adventures of Huck Finn '93
Running Cool '93
Crisscross '92
Leaving Normal '92
Coupe de Ville '90
I Love You to Death '90
Revenge '90
Major League '89
Roe vs. Wade '89
Gore Vidal's Lincoln '88
The Milagro Beanfield War '88
Ironweed '87
Hard Traveling '85
Vision Quest '85
Ballad of Gregorio Cortez '83
The McCullochs '75
Deadly Encounter '72
Cool Hand Luke '67

Ken Gampu (1929-2003)
American Ninja 4: The Annihilation '91
Enemy Unseen '91
Act of Piracy '89
Scavengers '87
Flashpoint Africa '84
Kill and Kill Again '81
Chain Gang Killings '80
Soul Patrol '80
African Rage '78
The Naked Prey '66
Dingaka '65

Yvonne Gamy
Manon of the Spring '87
Letters from My Windmill '54

Chester Gan (1908-59)
Crash Dive '43
Across the Pacific '42
Carson City Kid '40

Nitin Ganatra (1967-)
The Mistress of Spices '05
Pure '02

Marguerite Gance
La Chute de la Maison Usher '28
Napoleon '27

Michel Gand
See Jean-Pierre Bouvier

James Gandolfini (1961-)
In the Loop '09
The Taking of Pelham 123 '09
Where the Wild Things Are '09
Miracle at St. Anna '08
All the King's Men '06
Lonely Hearts '06
Romance & Cigarettes '05
Surviving Christmas '04
The Last Castle '01
The Man Who Wasn't There '01
The Mexican '01
Wildflowers '99
A Civil Action '98
8mm '98
The Mighty '98
Dance with the Devil '97
Fallen '97
She's So Lovely '97
Twelve Angry Men '97
The Juror '96
Night Falls on Manhattan '96
Crimson Tide '95
Get Shorty '95
New World '95
Angie '94
Terminal Velocity '94
Italian Movie '93
Mr. Wonderful '93
Money for Nothing '93
True Romance '93
A Stranger Among Us '92

Tony Ganios (1959-)
Die Hard 2: Die Harder '90
Porky's Revenge '85
Porky's 2: The Next Day '83
Porky's '82
Continental Divide '81
Wanderers '79

Richard Ganoung
Billy's Hollywood Screen Kiss '98
Parting Glances '86

Richard Gant (1940-)
Daddy Day Camp '07
Kingdom Come '01
Johnny B. '00
Nutty Professor 2: The Klumps '00
Sour Grapes '98
Bean '97
Raven '97
The Glimmer Man '96
Jason Goes to Hell: The Final Friday '93
The Freshman '90
Krush Groove '85

Robert Gant
Kiss Me Deadly '08
Save Me '07

Peter Gantzler
The Boss of It All '06
Italian for Beginners '01

Paul Ganus (1961-)
The Silencer '92
Crash and Burn '90

Bruno Ganz (1941-)
The Baader Meinhof Complex '08
The Reader '08
Youth Without Youth '07
Have No Fear: The Life of Pope John Paul II '05
Downfall '04
The Manchurian Candidate '04
Luther '03
Bread and Tulips '01
Eternity and a Day '97
Saint-Ex: The Story of the Storyteller '95
Faraway, So Close! '93
The Last Days of Chez Nous '92
Children of Nature '91
Strapless '90
Wings of Desire '88
In the White City '83
Nosferatu the Vampyre '79
Black and White As Day and Night '78
Knife in the Head '78
The American Friend '77
Lumiere '76
The Marquise of O '76

Teresa Ganzel (1957-)
Clifford's Really Big Movie '04 (V)
C.O.D. '83

Yehoram Gaon (1939-)
Dead End Street '83
Operation Thunderbolt '77
Eagles Attack at Dawn '70

Siqin Gaowa (1949-)
The Day the Sun Turned Cold '94
Women from the Lake of Scented Souls '94

Romola Garai (1982-)
Emma '09
The Other Man '08
Atonement '07
Amazing Grace '06
Renaissance '06
Scoop '06
The Incredible Journey of Mary Bryant '05
Dirty Dancing: Havana Nights '04
Rory O'Shea Was Here '04
Vanity Fair '04
Daniel Deronda '02
I Capture the Castle '02
Nicholas Nickleby '02

Kaz Garas (1940-)
Humanoids from the Deep '96
Puppet Master 5: The Final Chapter '94
Fast Gun '93
Naked Vengeance '85
Final Mission '84
Ben '72
The Last Safari '67

Matthew Garber (1956-77)
The Gnome-Mobile '67
Mary Poppins '64
The Three Lives of Thomasina '63

Terri Garber (1960-)
North and South Book 2 '86
North and South Book 1 '85

Victor Garber (1949-)
The Last Templar '09
Milk '08
Home Room '02
Tuck Everlasting '02
Call Me Claus '01
Legally Blonde '01
Life with Judy Garland—Me and My Shadows '01
Torso '01
Annie '99
Invisible Child '99
Cinderella '97
Titanic '97
The First Wives Club '96
Jeffrey '95
Exotica '94
Kleptomania '94
Life with Mikey '93
Queen '93
Sleepless in Seattle '93
Godspell '73

Greta Garbo (1905-90)
The Love Goddesses '65
Two-Faced Woman '41
Ninotchka '39
Conquest '37
Camille '36
Anna Karenina '35
The Painted Veil '34
Queen Christina '33
As You Desire Me '32
Grand Hotel '32
Mata Hari '32
Susan Lenox: Her Fall and Rise '31
Anna Christie '30
Romance '30
The Kiss '29
The Single Standard '29
The Mysterious Lady '28
Wild Orchids '28
A Woman of Affairs '28
The Flesh and the Devil '27
The Temptress '26
Joyless Street '25
The Atonement of Gosta Berling '24

Ingrid Garbo
Touch Me Not '74
Dracula's Great Love '72

John Garces
Kid and the Killers '74
Robby '68

Mauricio Garces (1926-89)
The Brainiac '61
The Living Head '59

Paula Garces (1974-)
Harold & Kumar Escape from Guantanamo Bay '08
Man of the House '05
Harold and Kumar Go to White Castle '04
Spin '04
Marci X '03
Clockstoppers '02
Cash Crop '01

Adam Garcia (1973-)
Standing Still '05
Confessions of a Teenage Drama Queen '04
Fascination '04
The First $20 Million is Always the Hardest '02
Riding in Cars with Boys '01
Bootmen '00
Coyote Ugly '00

Aimee Garcia (1978-)
Dragon Wars '07
A Lot Like Love '05
Dirty '05

Allan Garcia (1887-1938)
South of Santa Fe '32
The Circus '19

Andy Garcia (1956-)
New York, I Love You '09
The Pink Panther 2 '09
Beverly Hills Chihuahua '08 (V)
The Line '08
The Air I Breathe '07
Ocean's Thirteen '07
Smokin' Aces '07
The Lost City '05
Modigliani '04
Ocean's Twelve '04
Twisted '04
Confidence '03
The Man from Elysian Fields '01
Ocean's Eleven '01
The Unsaid '01
For Love or Country: The Arturo Sandoval Story '00
Lakeboat '00
Desperate Measures '98
Just the Ticket '98
The Disappearance of Garcia Lorca '96
Hoodlum '96
Night Falls on Manhattan '96
Steal Big, Steal Little '95
Things to Do in Denver When You're Dead '95
When a Man Loves a Woman '94
Hero '92
Jennifer 8 '92
Dead Again '91
The Godfather, Part 3 '90
Internal Affairs '90
A Show of Force '90
Black Rain '89
American Roulette '88
Blood Money: The Story of Clinton and Nadine '88
Stand and Deliver '88
The Untouchables '87
8 Million Ways to Die '85
Mean Season '85
Blue Skies Again '83
A Night in Heaven '83

Carolina Garcia
Car Babes '06
Supercross: The Movie '05

Darnell Garcia
Blind Rage '78
Enforcer from Death Row '78

Eddie Garcia (1921-)
Relax... It's Just Sex! '98
Twilight People '72
Woman Hunt '72
Beast of the Yellow Night '70

Jeff Garcia
Barnyard '06 (V)
Jimmy Neutron: Boy Genius '01 (V)

Jerry Garcia (1942-95)
Hell's Angels Forever '83
Gimme Shelter '70

Jesse Garcia
The Comebacks '07
Quinceanera '06

Joanna Garcia (1979-)
The Initiation of Sarah '06
Not Another Teen Movie '01

Jorge Garcia (1973-)
Deck the Halls '06
The Good Humor Man '05
Little Athens '05

Jose Garcia
People '04
Apres-Vous '03

Jsu Garcia (1963-)
The Go-Getter '07
The Lost City '05
Sueno '05
Along Came Polly '04
Klepto '03
Collateral Damage '02
We Were Soldiers '02
The Quickie '01
Devil in the Flesh 2 '00
Traffic '00
Candyman 3: Day of the Dead '98
Woo '97
Red Shoe Diaries: Four on the Floor '96
Vampire in Brooklyn '95
In the Heat of Passion '91
Predator 2 '90
Slaves of New York '89
The Lawless Land '88
Tropical Snow '88
Wildcats '86
Gotcha! '85
A Nightmare on Elm Street '84

Juan Garcia
Feast 2: Sloppy Seconds '08
Bounce '00
The Banker '89

Nicole Garcia (1946-)
La Petite Lili '03
Alias Betty '01
Overseas: Three Women with Man Trouble '90
Peril '85
Corrupt '84
Bolero '82
Mon Oncle d'Amerique '80
Le Cavaleur '78

Stenio Garcia (1933-)
Me You Them '00
At Play in the Fields of the Lord '91

Luce Garcia-Ville
Nathalie Granger '72
Last Year at Marienbad '61

Ginette Garcin (1928-)
Charles et Lucie '79
Blue Country '77
Cousin, Cousine '76

Henri Garcin (1929-)
The Dress '96
The Eighth Day '95
One Hundred and One Nights '95
Someone Behind the Door '71

Betty Garde
Caged '50
Call Northside 777 '48

Micah Gardener
Atomic Dog '98
Carpool '96

Vincent Gardenia (1922-92)
The Super '91
Tragedy of Flight 103: The Inside Story '91
Age Old Friends '89
Skin Deep '89
Moonstruck '87
Little Shop of Horrors '86
The Odd Squad '86
Brass '85
Movers and Shakers '85
Kennedy '83
Death Wish 2 '82
The Last Flight of Noah's Ark '80
Home Movies '79
Marciano '79
Greased Lightning '77
Death Wish '74
The Front Page '74
Lucky Luciano '74
Bang the Drum Slowly '73
Cold Turkey '71
Little Murders '71
Jenny '70
Where's Poppa? '70
The Hustler '61
Parrish '61

Reginald Gardiner (1903-80)
Do Not Disturb '65
Mr. Hobbs Takes a Vacation '62
Rock-A-Bye Baby '57
Birds & the Bees '56
Black Widow '54
The Halls of Montezuma '50
The Dolly Sisters '46
Christmas in Connecticut '45
The Horn Blows at Midnight '45
Immortal Sergeant '43
Sweet Rosie O'Grady '43
Captains of the Clouds '42
The Man Who Came to Dinner '41
Sundown '41
A Yank in the R.A.F. '41
Doctor Takes a Wife '40
The Great Dictator '40
The Flying Deuces '39
Everybody Sing '38
Marie Antoinette '38
A Damsel in Distress '37
Born to Dance '36

Arthur Gardner (1910-)
Mystic Circle Murder '39
Assassin of Youth '35

Ava Gardner (1922-90)
Harem '86
The Long, Hot Summer '86
A.D. '85
Regina '83
The Kidnapping of the President '80
City on Fire '78
The Cassandra Crossing '76
The Sentinel '76
Permission To Kill '75

Earthquake '74
Life & Times of Judge Roy Bean '72
Mayerling '68
The Bible '66
The Night of the Iguana '64
Seven Days in May '64
55 Days at Peking '63
The Naked Maja '59
On the Beach '59
Around the World in 80 Days '56
Bhowani Junction '56
The Barefoot Contessa '54
Knights of the Round Table '53
Mogambo '53
Lone Star '52
The Snows of Kilimanjaro '52
My Forbidden Past '51
Pandora and the Flying Dutchman '51
Show Boat '51
East Side, West Side '49
The Bribe '48
One Touch of Venus '48
The Hucksters '47
Singapore '47
The Killers '46
Whistle Stop '46
Reunion in France '42

David Gardner

When Angels Fly '82
Bethune '77

Joan Gardner (1915-99)

The Challenge '38
Dark Journey '37
The Man Who Could Work Miracles '37
Private Life of Don Juan '34
The Scarlet Pimpernel '34
Wedding Rehearsal '32

Katya Gardner

Stir of Echoes 2: The Homecoming '07
Careful '92

Jennifer Gareis (1970-)

Boat Trip '03
Gangland '00
Luckytown '00
Miss Congeniality '00
The 6th Day '00

Allen (Goorwitz) Garfield (1939-)

The Majestic '01
Absence of the Good '99
Obsession '97
Crime of the Century '96
Diabolique '96
Destiny Turns on the Radio '95
Jack and His Friends '92
Family Prayers '91
Club Fed '90
Let It Ride '89
Night Visitor '89
Beverly Hills Cop 2 '87
Desert Bloom '86
The Cotton Club '84
Irreconcilable Differences '84
Get Crazy '83
State of Things '82
Continental Divide '81
Leave 'Em Laughing '81
One Trick Pony '80
The Stunt Man '80
Brink's Job '78
Fyre '78
Sketches of a Strangler '78
Skateboard '77
Mother, Jugs and Speed '76
The Virginia Hill Story '76
Nashville '75
Paco '75
Busting '74
The Conversation '74
Slither '73
The Candidate '72
Get to Know Your Rabbit '72
Bananas '71
Cry Uncle '71
Hi, Mom! '70
The Owl and the Pussycat '70
Greetings '68

Andrew Garfield

The Imaginarium of Doctor Parnassus '09
Boy A '07
Lions for Lambs '07

John Garfield (1913-52)

Force of Evil '49
Jigsaw '49
Body and Soul '47
Gentleman's Agreement '47
Humoresque '46
The Postman Always Rings Twice '46
Pride of the Marines '45
Hollywood Canteen '44
Air Force '43
Destination Tokyo '43
The Fallen Sparrow '43
Thank Your Lucky Stars '43
Tortilla Flat '42
Out of the Fog '41
The Sea Wolf '41
Castle on the Hudson '40
Juarez '39
They Made Me a Criminal '39
Four Daughters '38

John David Garfield (1943-94)

The Other Side of the Mountain '75
White Line Fever '75
Golden Voyage of Sinbad '73
The Stepmother '71
MacKenna's Gold '69
That Cold Day in the Park '69
Savage Intruder '68
The Swimmer '68

Art Garfunkel (1941-)

Boxing Helena '93
Mother Goose Rock 'n' Rhyme '90
Short Fuse '88
Carnal Knowledge '71
Catch-22 '70

Edward (Ed) Gargan (1902-64)

San Fernando Valley '44
The Falcon Takes Over '42
Spring Parade '40
The Saint Strikes Back '39
Hands Across the Table '35
Belle of the Nineties '34

William Gargan (1905-79)

Dynamite '49
Strange Impersonation '46
Till the End of Time '46
The Canterville Ghost '44
Miss Annie Rooney '42
Who Done It? '42
Cheers for Miss Bishop '41
I Wake Up Screaming '41
They Knew What They Wanted '40
Broadway Serenade '39
Devil's Party '38
You Only Live Once '37
Alibi for Murder '36
Milky Way '36
Sky Parade '36
Aggie Appleby, Maker of Men '33
Lucky Devils '33
Night Flight '33
The Animal Kingdom '32
Rain '32

Troy Garity (1973-)

My One and Only '09
Fragments '08
Lake City '08
Sunshine '07
After the Sunset '04
Barbershop 2: Back in Business '04
Milwaukee, Minnesota '03
Soldier's Girl '03
Barbershop '02
Bandits '01
Steal This Movie! '00

Gabriel Garko (1974-)

Callas Forever '02
His Secret Life '01

Gianni "John" Garko (1935-)

Metallica '85
Devilfish '84
The Psychic '78
Waterloo '71
Gunslinger '70
Five for Hell '67
Saul and David '64
The Avenger '62
The Mongols '60
Kapo '59

Beverly Garland (1926-2008)

National Lampoon's Christmas Vacation 2: Cousin Eddie's Big Island Adventure '03
Haunted Symphony '94
The World's Oldest Living Bridesmaid '92
Gamble on Love '86
It's My Turn '80
Roller Boogie '79
Where the Red Fern Grows '74
The Voyage of the Yes '72
Pretty Poison '68
Twice-Told Tales '63
The Gunslinger '56
It Conquered the World '56
Desperate Hours '55
Swamp Women '55
The Go-Getter '54
D.O.A. '49

Judy Garland (1922-69)

That's Entertainment '74
A Child Is Waiting '63
I Could Go on Singing '63
Gay Purr-ee '62 (V)
Judgment at Nuremberg '61
A Star Is Born '54
Summer Stock '50
In the Good Old Summertime '49
Easter Parade '48
The Pirate '48
Words and Music '48
The Harvey Girls '46
Till the Clouds Roll By '46
Ziegfeld Follies '46
The Clock '45
Meet Me in St. Louis '44
Strictly G.I. '44
Girl Crazy '43
Presenting Lily Mars '43
Thousands Cheer '43
For Me and My Gal '42
Babes on Broadway '41
Life Begins for Andy Hardy '41
Ziegfeld Girl '41
Andy Hardy Meets Debutante '40
Little Nellie Kelly '40
Strike Up the Band '40
Babes in Arms '39
The Wizard of Oz '39
Everybody Sing '38
Listen, Darling '38
Love Finds Andy Hardy '38
Broadway Melody of 1938 '37
Thoroughbreds Don't Cry '37
Pigskin Parade '36

Richard Garland (1927-69)

Panic in the Year Zero! '62
The Undead '57

Jeff Garlin (1962-)

Toy Story 3 '10 (V)
The Rocker '08
Strange Wilderness '08
WALL-E '08 (V)
I Want Someone to Eat Cheese With '06
Sleepover '04
Daddy Day Care '03

Lee Garlington (1953-)

A Lot Like Love '05
Guarding Eddy '04
Johnson Family Vacation '04
The Hot Chick '02
The Sum of All Fears '02
Along for the Ride '00
Can of Worms '00
The Babysitter '95
Reflections in the Dark '94
My Life '93
A Killing in a Small Town '90
Cold Sassy Tree '89
Three Fugitives '89
The Seventh Sign '88
Psycho 3 '86

Alice Garner (1969-)

Jindabyne '06
Strange Planet '99
Love and Other Catastrophes '95
Monkey Grip '82

James Garner (1928-)

Battle for Terra '09 (V)
The Ultimate Gift '07
The Notebook '04
Divine Secrets of the Ya-Ya Sisterhood '02
Atlantis: The Lost Empire '01 (V)
The Last Debate '00
Space Cowboys '00
One Special Night '99
Legalese '98
Twilight '98
Dead Silence '96
My Fellow Americans '96
Larry McMurtry's Streets of Laredo '95
Breathing Lessons '94
Maverick '94
Barbarians at the Gate '93
Fire in the Sky '93
The Distinguished Gentleman '92
Decoration Day '90
My Name Is Bill W. '89
Sunset '88
Murphy's Romance '85
The Glitter Dome '84
Tank '83
Victor/Victoria '82
The Fan '81
The Castaway Cowboy '74
One Little Indian '73
They Only Kill Their Masters '72
A Man Called Sledge '71
Skin Game '71
Support Your Local Gunfighter '71
Marlowe '69
Support Your Local Sheriff '69
How Sweet It Is! '68
The Pink Jungle '68
Hour of the Gun '67
Duel at Diablo '66
Grand Prix '66
The Americanization of Emily '64
36 Hours '64
The Great Escape '63
Move Over, Darling '63
The Thrill of It All! '63
The Wheeler Dealers '63
Boys' Night Out '62
The Children's Hour '61
Cash McCall '60
Alias Jesse James '59
Up Periscope '59
Darby's Rangers '58
Sayonara '57

Jennifer Garner (1972-)

Valentine's Day '10
Ghosts of Girlfriends Past '09
The Invention of Lying '09
Catch and Release '07
Juno '07
The Kingdom '07
Elektra '05
13 Going on 30 '04
Daredevil '03
Catch Me If You Can '02
Pearl Harbor '01
Dude, Where's My Car? '00
Aftershock: Earthquake in New York '99
1999 '98
Mr. Magoo '97
Rose Hill '97
Washington Square '97
Larry McMurtry's Dead Man's Walk '96

Katrina Garner

Halloween Night '90
Hack O'Lantern '87

Kelli Garner (1984-)

Going the Distance '10
G-Force '09
Taking Woodstock '09
Havoc 2: Normal Adolescent Behavior '07
Lars and the Real Girl '07
Dreamland '06
Born Killers '05
London '05
Man of the House '05
Thumbsucker '05
The Aviator '04
Bully '01

Peggy Ann Garner (1931-84)

Betrayal '78
A Wedding '78
The Cat '66
Black Widow '54
Eight Witnesses '54
The Big Cat '49
The Lovable Cheat '49
Daisy Kenyon '47
A Tree Grows in Brooklyn '45
Jane Eyre '44
The Keys of the Kingdom '44
Blondie Brings Up Baby '39

Gale Garnett (1942-)

32 Short Films about Glenn Gould '93
Mr. & Mrs. Bridge '90
The Children '80

Tay Garnett (1898-1977)

Challenge To Be Free '76
Strong Man '26

Janeane Garofalo (1964-)

Labor Pains '09
Ratatouille '07 (V)
The Wild '06 (V)
Duane Hopwood '05
Jiminy Glick in LaLa Wood '05
Stay '05
Wonderland '03
Big Trouble '02
The Laramie Project '02
The Search for John Gissing '01
Wet Hot American Summer '01
The Adventures of Rocky & Bullwinkle '00
The Independent '00
Steal This Movie! '00
Titan A.E. '00 (V)
What Planet Are You From? '00
Dogma '99
The Minus Man '99
Mystery Men '99
Thick as Thieves '99
The Bumblebee Flies Anyway '98
Clay Pigeons '98
Dog Park '98
Kiki's Delivery Service '98 (V)
Permanent Midnight '98
200 Cigarettes '98
Cop Land '97
Half-Baked '97
The Matchmaker '97
Romy and Michele's High School Reunion '97
Sweethearts '97
The Cable Guy '96
I Shot a Man in Vegas '96
Kids in the Hall: Brain Candy '96
Larger Than Life '96
Touch '96
The Truth about Cats and Dogs '96
Bye Bye, Love '94
Coldblooded '94
Reality Bites '94
Armistead Maupin's Tales of the City '93

Teri Garr (1949-)

Unaccompanied Minors '06
Ghost World '01
Life Without Dick '01
Dick '99
NightScreams '97
Ronnie and Julie '97
A Simple Wish '97
Changing Habits '96
Michael '96
Dumb & Dumber '94
Perfect Alibi '94
Ready to Wear '94
Mom and Dad Save the World '92
The Player '92
Take Down '92
Mother Goose Rock 'n' Rhyme '90
A Perfect Little Murder '90
Short Time '90
Waiting for the Light '90
Let It Ride '89
Out Cold '89
Full Moon in Blue Water '88
Pack of Lies '87
Miracles '86
After Hours '85
First Born '84
To Catch a King '84
The Black Stallion Returns '83
Mr. Mom '83
The Sting 2 '83
The Tale of the Frog Prince '83
The Escape Artist '82
One from the Heart '82
Prime Suspect '82
Tootsie '82
Honky Tonk Freeway '81
The Black Stallion '79
Mr. Mike's Mondo Video '79
Witches' Brew '79
Close Encounters of the Third Kind '77
Oh, God! '77
Once Upon a Brothers Grimm '77
The Conversation '74
Young Frankenstein '74
Head '68
Speedway '68
Pajama Party '64

Martin Garralaga (1894-1981)

Bela Lugosi Meets a Brooklyn Gorilla '52
The Fighter '52
Shep Comes Home '49
Susanna Pass '49
Riding the California Trail '47
South of Monterey '47
In Old New Mexico '45
For Whom the Bell Tolls '43
Casablanca '42
Boots of Destiny '37

Ivo Garrani (1924-)

Street People '76
Waterloo '71
Atom Age Vampire '61
Black Sunday '60
The Giant of Marathon '60
The Day the Sky Exploded '57
Roland the Mighty '56

Jean-Francoise Garreaud (1947-)

Betty '92
Violette '78

Louis Garrel (1983-)
Frontier of Dawn '08
Love Songs '07
Inside Paris '06

Maurice Garrel (1923-)
Kings and Queen '04
Artemisia '97
Un Coeur en Hiver '93
La Discrete '90

Beau Garrett
Made of Honor '08
Unearthed '07
Turistas '06

Betty Garrett (1919-)
My Sister Eileen '55
Neptune's Daughter '49
On the Town '49
Take Me Out to the Ball Game '49
Words and Music '48

Brad Garrett (1960-)
Hoodwinked Too! Hood vs. Evil '10 (V)
Music & Lyrics '07
Ratatouille '07 (V)
Underdog '07
The Pacifier '05
Tarzan 2 '05 (V)
Garfield: The Movie '04 (V)
Finding Nemo '03 (V)
The Country Bears '02 (V)
Stuart Little 2 '02
Club Land '01
A Bug's Life '98 (V)
Going Postal '98
Suicide Kings '97
Casper '95 (V)

Eliza (Simons) Garrett
Love Is a Gun '94
Terraces '77
Schlock '73

Hank Garrett (1931-)
Blood Frenzy '87
The Boys Next Door '85
Rosebud Beach Hotel '85

Jordan Garrett (1992-)
Death Sentence '07
Saving Shiloh '06
Final Approach '04

Leif Garrett (1961-)
Dickie Roberts: Former Child Star '03
The Whispering '94
Spirit of '76 '91
The Banker '89
Cheerleader Camp '88
Party Line '88
Shaker Run '85
Thunder Alley '85
The Outsiders '83
Long Shot Kids '81
Peter Lundy and the Medicine Hat Stallion '77
Skateboard '77
Walking Tall: The Final Chapter '77
Kid Vengeance '75

Patsy Garrett (1921-)
Dennis the Menace: Dinosaur Hunter '93
For the Love of Benji '77
Benji '74

Roger Garrett
Night of the Cobra Woman '72
The Passing of Evil '70

Spencer Garrett (1963-)
21 '08
I Know Who Killed Me '07
Air Force One '97

Barbara Garrick (1965-)
Brooklyn Lobster '05
Armistead Maupin's More Tales of the City '97
Ellen Foster '97
A Couch in New York '95
Miami Rhapsody '95
Armistead Maupin's Tales of the City '93
The Firm '93
Sleepless in Seattle '93
Eight Men Out '88

John Garrick (1902-66)
Broken Melody '34
Lily of Killarney '34
Lottery Bride '30
Song o' My Heart '30
Song o' My Heart '29

Joaquin Garrido
The Kids Are All Right '10
Solo '96

David Garrison
Homeboys '92
On the Town '91

Robert Garrison
The Karate Kid '84
The Worm Eaters '77

Julia Garro
Gracie '07
Havoc 2: Normal Adolescent Behavior '07

Riccardo Garrone (1926-)
How to Kill 400 Duponts '68
Terror Creatures from the Grave '66
Eva '62
Two Nights with Cleopatra '54

Greer Garson (1908-96)
Little Women '78
The Happiest Millionaire '67
The Singing Nun '66
Invincible Mr. Disraeli '63
Sunrise at Campobello '60
Julius Caesar '53
The Miniver Story '50
That Forsyte Woman '50
Julia Misbehaves '48
Adventure '45
The Valley of Decision '45
Mrs. Parkington '44
Madame Curie '43
Mrs. Miniver '42
Random Harvest '42
Blossoms in the Dust '41
When Ladies Meet '41
Pride and Prejudice '40
Goodbye, Mr. Chips '39

Willie Garson (1964-)
Sex and the City 2 '10
Sex and the City: The Movie '08
Zoom '06
Fever Pitch '05
Little Manhattan '05
Freaky Friday '03
Luster '02
Taken '02
Out Cold '01
What Planet Are You From? '00
Play It to the Bone '99
The Rock '96
Untamed Heart '93

Jennie Garth (1972-)
Telling You '98
My Brother's War '97
Power 98 '96
Danielle Steel's Star '93

Christopher Gartin (1968-)
Friends and Family '01
Tremors 3: Back to Perfection '01
johns '96
Tremors 2: Aftershocks '96
Danielle Steel's Changes '91
Matters of the Heart '90
No Big Deal '83

Steve Garvey (1948-)
BASEketball '98
Ice Cream Man '95
Bloodfist 6: Ground Zero '94
The Scout '94

Elizabeth Garvie (1957-)
Diana: Her True Story '93
Pride and Prejudice '85

John Garwood
A Taste of Hell '73
The Losers '70
Hell's Angels on Wheels '67

Linda Gary
The Land Before Time 4: Journey Through the Mists '96 (V)
The Land Before Time 3: The Time of the Great Giving '95 (V)
The Land Before Time 2: The Great Valley Adventure '94 (V)

Lorraine Gary (1937-)
Jaws: The Revenge '87
1941 '79
The Crash of Flight 401 '78
Jaws 2 '78
Jaws '75
Pray for the Wildcats '74

Tatsuya Gashuin
The Taste of Tea '04
Party 7 '00
Shark Skin Man and Peach Hip Girl '98

Vincent Gaskins
The Dark Dealer '95
The Underneath '95

Kyle Gass (1960-)
Tenacious D in the Pick of Destiny '06
The Cradle Will Rock '99
Bio-Dome '96

Alessandro Gassman (1965-)
Quiet Chaos '08
Transporter 2 '05
Samson and Delilah '96
Steam: A Turkish Bath '96
A Month by the Lake '95
Sacrilege '86

Vittorio Gassman (1922-2000)
Sleepers '96
Abraham '94
The Palermo Connection '91
The Sleazy Uncle '89
The Family '87
Life Is a Bed of Roses '83
The Tempest '82
Sharky's Machine '81
Immortal Bachelor '80
Quintet '79
A Wedding '78
We All Loved Each Other So Much '77
The Desert of the Tartars '76
The Scent of a Woman '75
12 Plus 1 '70
Catch as Catch Can '68
Tiger and the Pussycat '67
Woman Times Seven '67
The Easy Life '63
Il Sorpasso '63
Barabbas '62
The Great War '59
Big Deal on Madonna Street '58
War and Peace '56
Mambo '55
Rhapsody '54
Anna '51
Bitter Rice '49
Lure of the Sila '49

Ana Gasteyer (1967-)
Dare '09
The Women '08
Mean Girls '04
What's the Worst That Could Happen? '01
Gepetto '00
What Women Want '00
Dick '99
Meet the Deedles '98

Michael Gaston
Sugar '09
Body of Lies '08
Home '08
Hurricane Season '08
W. '08
The Notorious Bettie Page '06
Runaway '05
Stay '05
High Crimes '02
Bless the Child '00
Cora Unashamed '00
Ransom '96
The Wedding Banquet '93

Lisa Gastoni (1935-)
Submission '77
Wild, Wild Planet '65
The Great Armored Car Swindle '64
Messalina vs. the Son of Hercules '64
RoGoPaG '62
Tharus Son of Attila '62
The Baby and the Battleship '56
Three Men in a Boat '56
The Runaway Bus '54

Larry Gates (1915-96)
The Henderson Monster '80
Backstairs at the White House '79
Funny Lady '75
Missiles of October '74
Death of a Gunfighter '69
The Sand Pebbles '66
Toys in the Attic '63
The Hoodlum Priest '61
Underworld USA '61
The Young Savages '61
Underworld, U.S.A. '60
The Brothers Rico '57
The Strange One '57
Invasion of the Body Snatchers '56
Above and Beyond '53
Francis Covers the Big Town '53

Nancy Gates (1926-)
Comanche Station '60
The Gunfight at Dodge City '59
Some Came Running '58
The Search for Bridey Murphy '56
Wetbacks '56
Stranger on Horseback '55
Suddenly '54
Torch Song '53
The Atomic City '52
The Member of the Wedding '52
At Sword's Point '51
Check Your Guns '48
The Master Race '44
Nevada '44
The Great Gildersleeve '43

Marjorie Gateson (1891-1977)
International Lady '41
The Duke of West Point '38
Arizona Mahoney '36
Big Brown Eyes '36
Goin' to Town '35
Happiness Ahead '34

Edi Gathegi (1979-)
My Bloody Valentine 3D '09
The Twilight Saga: New Moon '09
Twilight '08
Gone Baby Gone '07

John Gatins
Leprechaun 3 '95
Witchboard 2: The Devil's Doorway '93

Mark Gatiss
Sense & Sensibility '07
Starter for Ten '06

Andy Gatjen (1973-)
In Enemy Hands '04

Jill Gatsby
The Ambulance '90
Return to Salem's Lot '87

Jennifer Gatti (1968-)
Blood Money '99
Double Exposure '93
Street Knight '93

Stephane Gauger
The Rebel '08
Six-String Samurai '98

Valerie Gaunt (1933-)
The Horror of Dracula '58
The Curse of Frankenstein '57

Mikkel Gaup (1968-)
Breaking the Waves '95
Pathfinder '87

Chris Gauthier
The Foursome '06
40 Days and 40 Nights '02

Dan Gauthier (1963-)
Groom Lake '02
Excessive Force 2: Force on Force '95
Illegal in Blue '95
Son-in-Law '93
Shame '92
Teen Witch '89

Dick Gautier (1937-)
Get Smart, Again! '89
Glitch! '88
Marathon '80
Divorce American Style '67

Jean-Yves Gautier
A Chef in Love '96
Three Lives and Only One Death '96
Voyage to the Beginning of the World '96
The Promise '94

Jean Gaven (1922-)
The Story of O '75
The Crucible '57

Erica Gavin (1947-)
Caged Heat '74
Beyond the Valley of the Dolls '70

John Gavin (1928-)
History of the World: Part 1 '81
Sophia Loren: Her Own Story '80
Jennifer '78
House of Shadows '76
The Madwoman of Chaillot '69
Murder for Sale '68
Thoroughly Modern Millie '67
Back Street '61
Breath of Scandal '60
Midnight Lace '60
Psycho '60
Spartacus '60
Imitation of Life '59
A Time to Love & a Time to Die '58

Cassandra Gaviola (1959-)
The Black Room '82
Conan the Barbarian '82

Uri Gavriel
House of Saddam '08
Blink of an Eye '92

Rafi Gavron
Inkheart '09
Nick & Norah's Infinite Playlist '08
Breaking and Entering '06

Peter Gawthorne (1884-1962)
Paid to Kill '54
Ticket of Leave Man '37
Phantom Fiend '35

William Gaxton (1890-1963)
Best Foot Forward '43
The Heat's On '43
It's the Old Army Game '26

Gregory Gay (1900-93)
Seven Doors to Death '44
The Secret Code '42

Ramon Gay (1917-60)
The Curse of the Aztec Mummy '59
The Robot vs. the Aztec Mummy '59

Howard Gaye (1878-1955)
Dante's Inferno '24
Flirting with Fate '16
The Birth of a Nation '15

Lisa Gaye
Class of Nuke 'Em High 3: The Good, the Bad and the Subhumanoid '94
Class of Nuke 'Em High 2: Subhumanoid Meltdown '91
The Toxic Avenger, Part 2 '89
The Toxic Avenger, Part 3: The Last Temptation of Toxie '89

Lisa Gaye (1935-)
Castle of Evil '66
Night of Evil '62
The Sign of Zorro '60
Shake, Rattle and Rock '57
Ten Thousand Bedrooms '57

Marvin Gaye (1939-84)
Chrome and Hot Leather '71
The Ballad of Andy Crocker '69

Nona Gaye (1974-)
Crash '05
The Gospel '05
XXX: State of the Union '05
The Polar Express '04
The Matrix Reloaded '03
The Matrix Revolutions '03
Ali '01

Julie Gayet (1972-)
Shall We Kiss '09
Shall We Kiss? '07
My Best Friend '06
Confusion of Genders '00
One Hundred and One Nights '95

Rebecca Gayheart (1972-)
Bunny Whipped '06
The Christmas Blessing '05
Pipe Dream '02
Harvard Man '01
From Dusk Till Dawn 3: The Hangman's Daughter '99
Jawbreaker '98
Too Smooth '98
Urban Legend '98
Robin Cook's Invasion '97
Scream 2 '97
Nothing to Lose '96
Somebody Is Waiting '96

Jackie Gayle (1926-2002)
Bulworth '98
Mr. Saturday Night '92
Bert Rigby, You're a Fool '89
Plain Clothes '88
Tin Men '87
Pepper and His Wacky Taxi '72

Monica Gayle
Nashville Girl '76
Switchblade Sisters '75

Anna Gaylor (1932-)
The Killing Game '67
Life Upside Down '64

Mitch Gaylord (1961-)
Animal Instincts '92
American Tiger '89
American Anthem '86

George Gaynes (1917-)
The Crucible '96
Police Academy 7: Mission to Moscow '94
Vanya on 42nd Street '94
Stepmonster '92
Police Academy 6: City under Siege '89

Police Academy 5: Assignment Miami Beach '88
Police Academy 4: Citizens on Patrol '87
Police Academy 3: Back in Training '86
Police Academy 2: Their First Assignment '85
It Came Upon a Midnight Clear '84
Micki & Maude '84
Police Academy '84
Dead Men Don't Wear Plaid '82
Tootsie '82
Breaking Up Is Hard to Do '79
Trilogy of Terror '75
The Way We Were '73

Janet Gaynor (1906-84)
The Young in Heart '38
A Star Is Born '37
The Farmer Takes a Wife '35
Lucky Star '29
Street Angel '28
7th Heaven '27
Sunrise '27

Mitzi Gaynor (1930-)
For Love or Money '63
South Pacific '58
Les Girls '57
Birds & the Bees '56
There's No Business Like Show Business '54
Bloodhounds of Broadway '52
We're Not Married '52
My Blue Heaven '50

Eunice Gayson (1931-)
From Russia with Love '63
Dr. No '62
The Revenge of Frankenstein '58
Carry On Admiral '57

Gwen Gaze (1909-)
Two-Fisted Justice '43
West of Pinto Basin '40

Wendy Gazelle
The Net '95
Crooked Hearts '91
Triumph of the Spirit '89
Understudy: The Graveyard Shift 2 '88
Hot Pursuit '87
Sammy & Rosie Get Laid '87

Ben Gazzara (1930-)
Paris, je t'aime '06
Dogville '03
Hysterical Blindness '02
Brian's Song '01
Blue Moon '00
Believe '99
The List '99
Summer of Sam '99
The Thomas Crown Affair '99
Happiness '98
Illuminata '98
The Big Lebowski '97
Buffalo 66 '97
Lady Killer '97
Protector '97
The Spanish Prisoner '97
Stag '97
Vicious Circles '97
Farmer & Chase '96
The Shadow Conspiracy '96
Convict Cowboy '95
The Dogfighters '95
Parallel Lives '94
Blindsided '93
Lies Before Kisses '92
Road House '89
Quicker Than the Eye '88
Secret Obsession '88
Control '87
An Early Frost '85
Tales of Ordinary Madness '83
They All Laughed '81
Question of Honor '80
Saint Jack '79
Sidney Sheldon's Bloodline '79
Opening Night '77
The Trial of Lee Harvey Oswald '77
The Death of Richie '76
High Velocity '76
The Killing of a Chinese Bookie '76
Voyage of the Damned '76
QB VII '74
Neptune Factor '73
Fireball Forward '72
Pursuit '72
Sicilian Connection '72
Shattered Silence '71
Husbands '70
The Bridge at Remagen '69
Joyful Laughter '60
Passionate Thief '60
Anatomy of a Murder '59
The Strange One '57

Michael V. Gazzo (1923-95)
Cookie '89
Sudden Impact '83
The Godfather 1902-1959: The Complete Epic '81
Alligator '80
Kill Castro '80
The Mercenaries '80
Gangsters '79
Love and Bullets '79
Fingers '78
King of the Gypsies '78
Black Sunday '77
The Godfather, Part 2 '74

Devon Gearhart (1995-)
Shorts: The Adventures of the Wishing Rock '09
Funny Games '07
Canvas '06
Bobby Jones: Stroke of Genius '04

Valerie Gearon (1937-2003)
Persuasion '71
Invasion '65

Anthony Geary (1947-)
Carpool Guy '05
Disney's Teacher's Pet '04 (V)
Scorchers '92
Night of the Warrior '91
High Desert Kill '90
Crack House '89
UHF '89
It Takes Two '88
Pass the Ammo '88
You Can't Hurry Love '88
Dangerous Love '87
Penitentiary 3 '87
Kicks '85
The Impostor '84
Johnny Got His Gun '71

Bud Geary (1898-1946)
D-Day on Mars '45
The Topeka Terror '45
Bataan '43
Bordertown Gunfighters '43
Immortal Sergeant '43

Cynthia Geary (1965-)
The Business of Fancydancing '02
Smoke Signals '98
The Killing Grounds '97
When Time Expires '97
The Heist '96
The Awakening '95
8 Seconds '94
To Grandmother's House We Go '94

Karl Geary (1972-)
Mimic 3: Sentinel '03
Hamlet '00
The Book of Stars '99
The Eternal '99
The External '99
Nadja '95

Gordon Gebert (1941-)
To Hell and Back '55
The Narrow Margin '52
Flying Leathernecks '51

Nicholas Gecks (1952-)
Sherlock: Case of Evil '02
Seeing Red '99
Parting Shots '98
The Mill on the Floss '97
Forever Young '85

Martina Gedeck (1961-)
The Baader Meinhof Complex '08
The Good Shepherd '06
The Lives of Others '06
Summer of '04 '06
Mostly Martha '01
Jew-Boy Levi '99

Jason Gedrick (1965-)
Sand Serpents '09
The Christmas Choir '08
Depth Charge '08
Wisegal '08
Kings of South Beach '07
Hidden Places '06
Strange Frequency 2 '01
Summer Catch '01
The Last Don 2 '98
The Last Don '97
Power 98 '96
The Force '94
Crossing the Bridge '92
Still Life '92
Backdraft '91
Rooftops '89
Promised Land '88
Stacking '87
Iron Eagle '86
The Heavenly Kid '85
Massive Retaliation '85
The Zoo Gang '85

Prunella Gee (1950-)
Witching Time '84
Never Say Never Again '83
The Wilby Conspiracy '75

Robbie Gee (1970-)
Underworld '03
Mean Machine '01
Snatch '00

Ellen Geer (1941-)
Neil Simon's The Odd Couple 2 '98
Satan's Princess '90
Hard Traveling '85
Bloody Birthday '80
Over the Edge '79
A Shining Season '79
Babe! '75
Memory of Us '74
Silence '73
Harold and Maude '71
Petulia '68

Kevin Geer
100 Feet '08
The Tavern '00
Sweet Bird of Youth '89

Will Geer (1902-78)
Unknown Powers '80
The Billion Dollar Hobo '78
My Sister, My Love '78
A Woman Called Moses '78
Bunco '77
Moving Violation '76
The Hanged Man '74
Hurricane '74
Memory of Us '74
Executive Action '73
Silence '73
Dear Dead Delilah '72
Jeremiah Johnson '72
Napoleon and Samantha '72
Brother John '70
The Reivers '69
Bandolero! '68
In Cold Blood '67
The President's Analyst '67
Seconds '66
Black Like Me '64
Salt of the Earth '54
Double Crossbones '51
Broken Arrow '50
Comanche Territory '50
To Please a Lady '50
Winchester '73 '50
Lust for Gold '49
Spitfire '34

Judy Geeson (1948-)
The Duke '99
Houdini '99
The Plague Dogs '82 (V)
Danger UXB '81
Inseminoid '80
Adventures of a Taxi Driver '76
Carry On England '76
Poldark '75
Poldark 2 '75
It's Not the Size That Counts '74
Murder on the Midnight Express '74
Doomwatch '72
Dynasty of Fear '72
10 Rillington Place '71
The Executioner '70
It Happened at Nightmare Inn '70
Twinsanity '70
Berserk! '67
To Sir, with Love '67

Sally Geeson (1950-)
Cry of the Banshee '70
The Oblong Box '69
What's Good for the Goose '69

Deborah Geffner (1952-)
Infestation '09
Exterminator 2 '84
All That Jazz '79

Martha Gehman
Going Shopping '05
Threesome '94
Unveiled '94
Father of the Bride '91
A Kiss Before Dying '91
F/X '86
The Flamingo Kid '84

Anna Geislerova (1976-)
Something Like Happiness '05
Zelary '03

Clarence Geldart (1867-1935)
Go-Get-'Em-Haines '35
Jungle Bride '33
Leap Year '21

Bob Geldof (1954-)
Spice World: The Movie '97
The Return of Spinal Tap '92
Pink Floyd: The Wall '82
The Secret Policeman's Other Ball '82
Secret Policeman's Private Parts '81

Alan Gelfant (1956-)
Apartment 12 '06
Next Stop, Wonderland '98
The Destiny of Marty Fine '96
Forced to Kill '93

Daniel Gelin (1921-2002)
Obsession '97
Iran: Days of Crisis '91
Life Is a Long Quiet River '88
Murmur of the Heart '71
Slogan '69
Is Paris Burning? '66
The Testament of Orpheus '59
The Man Who Knew Too Much '56
Plucking the Daisy '56
A Woman of Rome '56
Le Plaisir '52
La Ronde '51
Rendez-vous de Juillet '49

Sarah Michelle Gellar (1977-)
Possession '09
The Air I Breathe '07
Happily N'Ever After '07 (V)
Suburban Girl '07
TMNT (Teenage Mutant Ninja Turtles) '07 (V)
The Grudge 2 '06
The Return '06
Southland Tales '06
The Grudge '04
Scooby-Doo 2: Monsters Unleashed '04
Scooby-Doo '02
Harvard Man '01
She's All That '99
Simply Irresistible '99
Cruel Intentions '98
Small Soldiers '98 (V)
Beverly Hills Family Robinson '97
I Know What You Did Last Summer '97
Scream 2 '97
High Stakes '89

Larry Gelman (1930-)
Prime Time '77
Chatterbox '76
Slumber Party '57 '76

Grant Gelt (1980-)
Mutant Species '95
Avalon '90

Rhoda Gemignani (1940-)
Rocky Marciano '99
Concrete Beat '84

Giuliano Gemma (1938-)
Mad Love '01
Blood at Sundown '88
Unsane '82
The Warning '80
Corleone '79
Battleforce '78
The Desert of the Tartars '76
Smugglers '75
Master Touch '74
Sundance and the Kid '69
Fort Yuma Gold '66
Angelique: The Road to Versailles '65
Erik, the Viking '65
Angelique '64
Goliath and the Sins of Babylon '64
Hercules vs. the Sons of the Sun '64

Ruth Gemmell (1967-)
The Alchemists '99
Fever Pitch '96
Band of Gold '95

Laura Gemser (1950-)
Endgame '85
Women's Prison Massacre '85
Caged Women '84
Ator the Fighting Eagle '83
Black Cobra '83
Love Camp '81
Emmanuelle, the Queen '79
Emmanuelle's Daughter '79
Crime Busters '78
Emmanuelle in the Country '78
Fury '78
Naked Paradise '78
Trap Them & Kill Them '77
Emmanuelle on Taboo Island '76
Emmanuelle, the Joys of a Woman '76

Francois-Eric Gendron (1954-)
Boyfriends & Girlfriends '88
Cloud Waltzing '87

Sophie Gendron
Demons from Her Past '07
Framed for Murder '07

Bryan Genesse (1967-)
We'll Meet Again '02
Agent of Death '99
Cold Harvest '98
Operation Delta Force 3: Clear Target '98
Spoiler '98
Terminal Virus '96
Live Wire: Human Timebomb '95
Terminal Impact '95
Night Siege Project: Shadowchaser 2 '94
California Casanova '89
Loose Screws '85

Leo Genn (1905-78)
Die Screaming, Marianne '73
Mackintosh Man '73
A Lizard in a Woman's Skin '71
Strange Case of Dr. Jekyll & Mr. Hyde '68
Circus of Fear '67
The Longest Day '62
Era Notte a Roma '60
Moby Dick '56
Lady Chatterley's Lover '55
The Miniver Story '50
Wooden Horse '50
The Snake Pit '48
Velvet Touch '48
Green for Danger '47
Henry V '44
Immortal Battalion '44
When Thief Meets Thief '37

Troy Gentile
Hotel for Dogs '09
Drillbit Taylor '08
Tenacious D in the Pick of Destiny '06
The Bad News Bears '05

Minnie Gentry (1916-93)
Def by Temptation '90
Georgia, Georgia '72

Roger Gentry
Alien Massacre '67
Gallery of Horrors '67
Horrors of the Red Planet '64

Carrie Genzel (1971-)
Loch Ness Terror '07
Virtual Seduction '96
Caged Hearts '95

Paul Geoffrey
Emily Bronte's Wuthering Heights '92
Flame to the Phoenix '85
Excalibur '81

Stephen Geoffreys (1964-)
Moon 44 '90
976-EVIL '88
The Chair '87
Fraternity Vacation '85
Fright Night '85

Bill George
See Jay Kirby

Brian George (1952-)
Employee of the Month '06
Touch of Pink '04
Bubble Boy '01
Ghost World '01
Pom Poko '94 (V)
Smokescreen '90

Christopher George (1929-83)
Pieces '83
AngKor: Cambodia Express '81
Enter the Ninja '81
Graduation Day '81
Mortuary '81
Exterminator '80
Gates of Hell '80
Cruise into Terror '78
Day of the Animals '77
Whiskey Mountain '77
Dixie Dynamite '76
Grizzly '76
Mayday at 40,000 Feet '76
Midway '76
Train Robbers '73
Man on a String '71
Chisum '70
El Dorado '67

Chief Dan George (1899-1981)
Americathon '79
The Outlaw Josey Wales '76

Dana Ghia
Burn! '70
Four Dollars of Revenge '66

Massimo Ghini (1954-)
CQ '01
Up at the Villa '00
Tea with Mussolini '99
The Truce '96
Men Men Men '95

Alice Ghostley (1926-2007)
Whispers: An Elephant's Tale '00 (V)
Neil Simon's The Odd Couple 2 '98
Not for Publication '84
Blue Sunshine '78
Grease '78
Gator '76
With Six You Get Eggroll '68
The Graduate '67
To Kill a Mockingbird '62
New Faces of 1952 '54

Ju-Bong Gi
Chain Gang Girls '08
R-Point '04
Save the Green Planet '03

Marcus Giamatti
On the Doll '07
The Business of Strangers '01

Paul Giamatti (1967-)
Cold Souls '09
Duplicity '09
The Last Station '09
John Adams '08
Fred Claus '07
The Nanny Diaries '07
Shoot 'Em Up '07
The Ant Bully '06 (V)
The Hawk Is Dying '06
The Illusionist '06
Lady in the Water '06
Cinderella Man '05
Robots '05 (V)
Sideways '04
American Splendor '03
Confidence '03
Paycheck '03
Big Fat Liar '02
Planet of the Apes '01
Storytelling '01
Big Momma's House '00
Duets '00
If These Walls Could Talk 2 '00
The Cradle Will Rock '99
Man on the Moon '99
The Negotiator '98
Safe Men '98
Saving Private Ryan '98
Tourist Trap '98
The Truman Show '98
Winchell '98
The Break '97
My Best Friend's Wedding '97
Private Parts '96

Louis Giambalvo (1945-)
Gun Shy '00
Gia '98
Illegal in Blue '95
Dead to Rights '93
Fade to Black '93
Question of Faith '93
Mastergate '92
Weekend at Bernie's '89
The Dead Pool '88
The Jagged Edge '85
Ratings Game '84
The Ambush Murders '82

Joseph Gian (1962-)
Mad About You '90
Blackout '88
Night Stalker '87

Rick Gianasi
Sgt. Kabukiman N.Y.P.D. '94
The Occultist '89
Posed for Murder '89
Escape from Safehaven '88
Maximum Thrust '88
Mutant Hunt '87
Robot Holocaust '87

Adriano Giannini (1971-)
Sinbad: Legend of the Seven Seas '03 (V)
Swept Away '02

Giancarlo Giannini (1942-)
Quantum of Solace '08
Casino Royale '06
Man on Fire '04
Incantato '03
My House in Umbria '03
Darkness '02
Joshua '02
CQ '01
Hannibal '01
The Whole Shebang '01
Dune '00
Mimic '97
The Disappearance of Garcia Lorca '96
Heaven Before I Die '96
A Walk in the Clouds '95
Jacob '94
Once Upon a Crime '92
Goodnight, Michelangelo '89
New York Stories '89
The Sleazy Uncle '89
Time to Kill '89
Blood Red '88
Saving Grace '86
Fever Pitch '85
American Dreamer '84
Where's Piccone '84
Lovers and Liars '81
Immortal Bachelor '80
Blood Feud '79
Life Is Beautiful '79
A Night Full of Rain '78
How Funny Can Sex Be? '76
The Innocent '76
Seven Beauties '76
Swept Away... '75
La Grande Bourgeoise '74
The Sensual Man '74
Love and Anarchy '73
Seduction of Mimi '72
The Black Belly of the Tarantula '71
The Secret of Santa Vittoria '69
Anzio '68

Cynthia Gibb (1963-)
Christie's Revenge '07
Demons from Her Past '07
Life with Judy Garland—Me and My Shadows '01 (N)
Volcano: Fire on the Mountain '97
Holiday Affair '96
Sin and Redemption '94
Gypsy '93
The Woman Who Loved Elvis '93
Death Warrant '90
Short Circuit 2 '88
Jack's Back '87
Malone '87
Modern Girls '86
Salvador '86
Youngblood '86
Stardust Memories '80

Donald Gibb
Magic Kid 2 '94
Revenge of the Nerds 4: Nerds in Love '94
Bloodsport '88

Robyn Gibbes (1957-)
What the Moon Saw '90
Wild Horses '82
Gone to Ground '76

Leeza Gibbons (1957-)
The Player '92
Soapdish '91

Marla Gibbs (1946-)
The Brothers '01
The Visit '00
Foolish '99
Lost and Found '99
Lily in Winter '94
The Meteor Man '93
Up Against the Wall '91

Timothy Gibbs (1967-)
Witchboard 2: The Devil's Doorway '93
The Kindred '87
Huckleberry Finn '81 (V)

Josianne Gibert
Sensual Partners '87
The Screaming Dead '72

Rebecca Gibney (1965-)
Introducing the Dwights '07
Joey '98
Paperback Romance '96
Jigsaw '90
Among the Cinders '83

Susan Gibney
Derailed '02
Cabin by the Lake '00
And You Thought Your Parents Were Weird! '91

Deborah Gibson (1970-)
Mega Shark Vs. Giant Octopus '09
Coffee Date '06
Heat Street '87

Henry Gibson (1935-2009)
Big Stan '07
Wedding Crashers '05
A Stranger in the Kingdom '98
Asylum '97
Bio-Dome '96
Mother Night '96
Color of a Brisk and Leaping Day '95
Tom and Jerry: The Movie '93 (V)
Gremlins 2: The New Batch '90
Tune in Tomorrow '90
Around the World in 80 Days '89
Night Visitor '89
Switching Channels '88
Innerspace '87
Long Gone '87
Brenda Starr '86
Monster in the Closet '86
The Incredible Shrinking Woman '81
Tulips '81
The Blues Brothers '80
For the Love of It '80
Kentucky Fried Movie '77
Nashville '75
Charlotte's Web '73 (V)
The Long Goodbye '73
Evil Roy Slade '71
The Outlaws Is Coming! '65
Kiss Me, Stupid! '64
The Nutty Professor '63

Hoot Gibson (1892-1962)
The Horse Soldiers '59
The Marshal's Daughter '53
Arizona Whirlwind '44
Death Valley Rangers '44
Marked Trails '44
Outlaw Trail '44
Sonora Stagecoach '44
Westward Bound '44
The Law Rides Again '43
The Painted Stallion '37
Cavalcade of the West '36
Last Outlaw '36
Lucky Terror '36
The Riding Avenger '36
Feud of the West '35
Fighting Parson '35
Frontier Justice '35
Powdersmoke Range '35
Rainbow's End '35
Sunset Range '35
Swifty '35
Cowboy Counselor '33
The Dude Bandit '33
Boiling Point '32
The Gay Buckaroo '32
Local Badman '32
Man's Land '32
Spirit of the West '32
Clearing the Range '31
Hard Hombre '31
Wild Horse '31
The Concentratin' Kid '30
Roaring Ranch '30
Spurs '30
Trailing Trouble '30
Trigger Tricks '30
Courtin' Wildcats '29
King of the Rodeo '28
The Prairie King '27
The Phantom Bullet '26
Straight Shootin' '17

Martha Gibson
Family of Strangers '93
Outrageous! '77

Mel Gibson (1956-)
Edge of Darkness '10
Paparazzi '04
The Singing Detective '03
Signs '02
We Were Soldiers '02
Chicken Run '00 (V)
The Patriot '00
What Women Want '00
The Million Dollar Hotel '99
Lethal Weapon 4 '98
Payback '98
Conspiracy Theory '97
FairyTale: A True Story '97
Ransom '96
Braveheart '95
Casper '95
Pocahontas '95 (V)
Maverick '94
The Man Without a Face '93
Forever Young '92
Lethal Weapon 3 '92
Air America '90
Bird on a Wire '90
Hamlet '90
Lethal Weapon 2 '89
Tequila Sunrise '88
Lethal Weapon '87
Mad Max: Beyond Thunderdome '85
Attack Force Z '84
The Bounty '84
Mrs. Soffel '84
The River '84
The Road Warrior '82
The Year of Living Dangerously '82
Gallipoli '81
Mad Max '80
Tim '79
Summer City '77

Mimi Gibson (1948-)
Courage of Black Beauty '57
The Monster That Challenged the World '57

Thomas Gibson (1962-)
I'll Believe You '07
Just Buried '07
Category 6 : Day of Destruction '04
Brush with Fate '03
The Lost Empire '01
The Flintstones in Viva Rock Vegas '00
Psycho Beach Party '00
Stardom '00
Eyes Wide Shut '99
Armistead Maupin's More Tales of the City '97
Barcelona '94
Secrets '94
Sleep with Me '94
Armistead Maupin's Tales of the City '93
Love and Human Remains '93
Far and Away '92

Tyrese Gibson (1978-)
Legion '10
Transformers: Revenge of the Fallen '09
Death Race '08
The Take '07
Transformers '07
Annapolis '06
Waist Deep '06
Four Brothers '05
Flight of the Phoenix '04
2 Fast 2 Furious '03
Baby Boy '01
Love Song '00

Virginia Gibson (1928-)
Athena '54
Seven Brides for Seven Brothers '54
Painting the Clouds With Sunshine '51
Tea for Two '50

Wynne Gibson (1899-1987)
Motorcycle Squad '41
Aggie Appleby, Maker of Men '33
Night After Night '32
Man of the World '31

Bond Gideon
Gold of the Amazon Women '79
Stepsisters '74
Storyville '74

Pamela Gidley (1966-)
Luster '02
The Little Vampire '00
Kiss & Tell '99
Liar's Poker '99
Mafia! '98
The Treat '98
Aberration '97
Bombshell '97
Bad Love '95
The Crew '95
The Little Death '95
Firefall '94
S.F.W. '94
Cheatin' Hearts '93
Highway to Hell '92
Liebestraum '91
Disturbed '90
Blue Iguana '88
Cherry 2000 '88
Permanent Record '88
Thrashin' '86

John Gielgud (1904-2000)
Elizabeth '98
Merlin '98
Quest for Camelot '98 (V)
A Dance to the Music of Time '97
Dragonheart '96 (V)
Hamlet '96
The Leopard Son '96 (N)
Looking for Richard '96
Portrait of a Lady '96
First Knight '95
Gulliver's Travels '95
Haunted '95
Shine '95
Scarlett '94
The Power of One '92
Shining Through '92
Prospero's Books '91
Strike It Rich '90
Getting It Right '89
Romance on the Orient Express '89
War & Remembrance: The Final Chapter '89
Appointment with Death '88
Arthur 2: On the Rocks '88
A Man for All Seasons '88
War & Remembrance '88
The Whistle Blower '87
Plenty '85
The Shooting Party '85
Wagner: The Complete Epic '85
Wagner: The Movie '85
The Far Pavilions '84
Scandalous '84
The Scarlet & the Black '83
The Wicked Lady '83
Frankenstein '82
Gandhi '82
The Hunchback of Notre Dame '82
Inside the Third Reich '82
Arthur '81
Brideshead Revisited '81
Chariots of Fire '81
Lion of the Desert '81
Priest of Love '81
Sphinx '81
Caligula '80
The Conductor '80
The Elephant Man '80
The Formula '80
The Human Factor '79
Murder by Decree '79
Les Miserables '78
James Joyce: A Portrait of the Artist as a Young Man '77
Providence '77
Edward the King '75
11 Harrowhouse '74
Murder on the Orient Express '74
QB VII '74
Invitation to the Wedding '73
Probe '72
Julius Caesar '70
Oh! What a Lovely War '69
The Charge of the Light Brigade '68
Sebastian '68
The Shoes of the Fisherman '68
Chimes at Midnight '67
The Loved One '65
Becket '64
Saint Joan '57
Around the World in 80 Days '56
Richard III '55
Romeo and Juliet '54
Julius Caesar '53
Hamlet '48 (V)
The Secret Agent '36

Stefan Gierasch (1926-)
Murder in the First '95
Dave '93
Blood Beach '81
Blue Sunshine '78
Carrie '76
Victory at Entebbe '76
High Plains Drifter '73
Jeremiah Johnson '72

Alan Gifford (1905-89)
Isadora '68
Town without Pity '61
Brainwashed '60
Time Lock '57

Frances Gifford (1919-94)
Riding High '50
Luxury Liner '48
Our Vines Have Tender Grapes '45
Thrill of a Romance '45
American Empire '42
Border Vigilantes '41

Frank Gifford (1930-)
Viva Knievel '77
Up Periscope '59

Gloria Gifford
Vice Versa '88
D.C. Cab '84

Kathie Lee Gifford (1953-)
Model Behavior '00
Dudley Do-Right '99

Roland Gift (1963-)
The Painted Lady '97
Scandal '89
Sammy & Rosie Get Laid '87

Elaine Giftos (1945-)
Angel '84
Tut & Tuttle '81
The Wrestler '73
Gas-s-s-s! '70
The Student Nurses '70

Fabrizio Gifuni
The Girl by the Lake '07
Best of Youth '03

Cam Gigandet
Pandorum '09
The Unborn '09
Never Back Down '08
Twilight '08

Sandro Giglio (1900-79)
For the First Time '59
The War of the Worlds '53

Marie Gignac
No '98
The Confessional '95

Ariadna Gil (1969-)
Appaloosa '08
Pan's Labyrinth '06
Second Skin '99
Talk of Angels '96
Celestial Clockwork '94
Belle Epoque '92

Vincent (Vince Gill) Gil (1939-)
Body Melt '93
Mad Max '80
Solo '77

Andrew S. Gilbert
Look Both Ways '05
Dirty Deeds '02
Paperback Hero '99
Idiot Box '97
Kiss or Kill '97

Billy Gilbert (1894-1971)
The Kissing Bandit '48
Fun & Fancy Free '47 (V)
Trouble Chasers '45
Cooking Up Trouble '44
Ghost Crazy '44
Spotlight Scandals '43
Mr. Wise Guy '42
Song of the Islands '42
Valley of the Sun '42
Melody Master '41
Week-End in Havana '41
The Great Dictator '40
His Girl Friday '40
No, No Nanette '40
Seven Sinners '40
Tin Pan Alley '40
Destry Rides Again '39
Block-heads '38
Breaking the Ice '38
Happy Landing '38
Joy of Living '38
Maid's Night Out '38
Peck's Bad Boy with the Circus '38
The Firefly '37
100 Men and a Girl '37
Snow White and the Seven Dwarfs '37 (V)
Toast of New York '37
Kelly the Second '36

Bob Gilbert
Silver Bandit '50
Red Rock Outlaw '47

Edmund Gilbert (1932-99)
Tom and Jerry: The Movie '93 (V)
Johnny Got His Gun '71
36 Hours '64

Eugenia Gilbert (1902-78)
Courtin' Wildcats '29
Test of Donald Norton '26

Helen Gilbert (1915-95)
Girls in Prison '56
Death Valley '46
God's Country '46
The Falcon Takes Over '42
Andy Hardy Gets Spring Fever '39
The Secret of Dr. Kildare '39

Jody Gilbert (1916-79)
Willard '71
Actors and Sin '52

John Gilbert
Eclipse '94
Desert Nights '29
Bardelys the Magnificent '26
Monte Cristo '22

John Gilbert (1897-1936)
Queen Christina '33
The Phantom of Paris '31
A Woman of Affairs '28
The Flesh and the Devil '27
The Big Parade '25
He Who Gets Slapped '24
The Busher '19

Lou Gilbert
The Great White Hope '70
Goldstein '64

Marcus Gilbert (1958-)
Army of Darkness '92
Riders '88

Melissa Gilbert (1964-)
Safe Harbour '07
Dying to Remember '93
Family of Strangers '93
Undesirable '92
The Lookalike '90
Ice House '89
Blood Vows: The Story of a Mafia Wife '87
Choices '86
Penalty Phase '86
Sylvester '85
Family Secrets '84
The Snow Queen '83
The Miracle Worker '79
The Christmas Coal Mine Miracle '77
Little House on the Prairie '74

Pamela Gilbert
Demonwarp '87
Evil Spawn '87

Sara Gilbert (1975-)
Riding in Cars with Boys '01
High Fidelity '00
Light It Up '99
Desert Blue '98
Dead Beat '94
Poison Ivy '92
Sudie & Simpson '90

Taylor Gilbert
Alone in the T-Shirt Zone '86
Torment '85

Connie Gilchrist (1901-85)
The Misadventures of Merlin Jones '63
Long John Silver '54
Houdini '53
The Half-Breed '51
Here Comes the Groom '51
Stars in My Crown '50
Ticket to Tomahawk '50
A Letter to Three Wives '49
Nothing But Trouble '44
Tortilla Flat '42

Richard Gilden
The Black Klansman '66
Lost, Lonely, and Vicious '59

Nancy Giles (1960-)
Superheroes '07
Loverboy '05
States of Control '98

Rhett Giles
Contract Killers '08
Lost Colony: The Legend of Roanoke '07
Bram Stoker's Way of the Vampire '05

Sandra Giles (1932-)
Daddy-O '59
Lost, Lonely, and Vicious '59

Gwynne Gilford (1946-)
Fade to Black '80
Satan's School for Girls '73
Beware! The Blob '72

Jack Gilford (1907-90)
Arthur 2: On the Rocks '88
Cocoon: The Return '88
Cocoon '85
Caveman '81
Cheaper to Keep Her '80
Wholly Moses! '80
Harry & Walter Go to New York '76
Save the Tiger '73
They Might Be Giants '71
Catch-22 '70
Enter Laughing '67
The Incident '67
A Funny Thing Happened on the Way to the Forum '66

Zach Gilford
Dare '09
Post Grad '09

Dana Gilhooley
Grace Is Gone '07
Outing Riley '04

Thea Gill
Mulligans '08
Seed '08
Masters of Horror: Homecoming '05
Eighteen '04

Marie Gillain (1975-)
Coco Before Chanel '09
On Guard! '03
Harem '99
Elective Affinities '96
L'Appat '94

Aidan Gillen (1968-)
12 Rounds '09
Blackout '07
Shanghai Knights '03
Lorna Doone '01
The Low Down '00
Buddy Boy '99
Some Mother's Son '96
Circle of Friends '94

Walter Giller
Action Man '67
Fanny Hill: Memoirs of a Woman of Pleasure '64

Dana Gillespie (1949-)
Scrubbers '82
The People That Time Forgot '77

Aden (John) Gillett (1958-)
Shadow of the Vampire '00
The 10th Kingdom '00
The Winslow Boy '98
The Borrowers '97
Ivanhoe '97
Under the Lighthouse Dancing '97
The House of Eliott '92

Anita Gillette (1936-)
Shall We Dance? '04
Larger Than Life '96
She's the One '96
Boys on the Side '94
Bob Roberts '92
Moonstruck '87
Brass '85
Marathon '80
Ants '77

David Gilliam (1948-)
Gunpowder '87
Sharks' Treasure '75
Frogs '72

Seth Gilliam
Did You Hear About the Morgans? '09
The Great New Wonderful '06
Personal Velocity: Three Portraits '02
Starship Troopers '97
Tar '97
Courage Under Fire '96
Assault at West Point: The Court-Martial of Johnson Whittaker '94
Jefferson in Paris '94

Terry Gilliam (1940-)
Spies Like Us '85
Monty Python's The Meaning of Life '83
Secret Policeman's Private Parts '81
Monty Python's Life of Brian '79
Monty Python and the Holy Grail '75
And Now for Something Completely Different '72

Larry (Lawrence) Gilliard, Jr.
Kill the Poor '06
Brother to Brother '04
The Machinist '04
Gangs of New York '02
Cecil B. Demented '00
Simply Irresistible '99
Next Stop, Wonderland '98
A Soldier's Sweetheart '98
The Waterboy '98
The Substitute 2: School's Out '97
Lotto Land '95
Money Train '95
Fly by Night '93
Straight out of Brooklyn '91

Andrew Gillies
DC 9/11: Time of Crisis '04
Big Meat Eater '85

Daniel Gillies (1976-)
Captivity '07
Masters of Horror: Dream Cruise '07
Spider-Man 3 '07
The Sensation of Sight '06
Bride & Prejudice '04
Spider-Man 2 '04

Fiona Gillies
Frankenstein '93
A Woman's Guide to Adultery '93

Isabel Gillies (1970-)
Four and a Half Women '05
On_Line '01
I Shot Andy Warhol '96
One Way Out '95
Metropolitan '90

Richard Gilliland (1950-)
Audrey's Rain '03
Home Room '02
Dogwatch '97
Star Kid '97
A Killing in a Small Town '90
Happy Hour '87
Acceptable Risks '86
Challenge of a Lifetime '85
Embassy '85
A Day for Thanks on Walton's Mountain '82
Bug '75

Linda Gillin (1948-)
Windows '80
Terror at Red Wolf Inn '72

Rebecca Gilling (1953-)
Heaven Tonight '93
The Blue Lightning '86
The Naked Country '85

Claude Gillingwater (1870-1939)
The Prisoner of Shark Island '36
Mississippi '35
Green Eyes '34
Illicit '31
My Boy '21

Ann Gillis (1927-)
Big Town After Dark '47
In Society '44
Texas Legionnaires '43
Bambi '42 (V)
'Neath Brooklyn Bridge '42
Nice Girl? '41
The Adventures of Tom Sawyer '38
Peck's Bad Boy with the Circus '38

James Gillis (1943-)
Alien Space Avenger '91
Deranged '87
Night of the Zombies '81
Dracula Sucks '79

Caroline Gillmer
The Monkey's Mask '00
Sorrento Beach '95

Margalo Gillmore (1897-1986)
A Woman's World '54
Cause for Alarm '51
The Happy Years '50
Perfect Strangers '50

Kenneth Gilman
Nights in White Satin '87
Scavengers '87
Bedroom Eyes '86

Alexie Gilmore
World's Greatest Dad '09
Surfer, Dude '08

Art Gilmore (1912-)
The Gallant Hours '60
The Narcotics Story '58 (N)

Danny Gilmore (1973-)
Winter Lily '98
Lilies '96

Denis Gilmore (1949-)
Tomb of Ligeia '64
The Unstoppable Man '59

Lillian Gilmore
Unconquered Bandit '35
The Phantom Flyer '28

Lowell Gilmore (1906-60)
Ma and Pa Kettle at Waikiki '55
Lone Star '52
King Solomon's Mines '50
Calcutta '47
Johnny Angel '45
Picture of Dorian Gray '45
Days of Glory '43

Peter Gilmore
The Abominable Dr. Phibes '71
Oh! What a Lovely War '69
Don't Lose Your Head '66

Virginia Gilmore (1919-86)
The Loves of Edgar Allen Poe '42
Orchestra Wives '42
Western Union '41

Ian Gilmour
Winner Takes All '84
Dangerous Summer '82
The Odd Angry Shot '79
The Chant of Jimmie Blacksmith '78

Jack Gilpin (1951-)
21 '08
The Life Before Her Eyes '07
101 Ways (The Things a Girl Will Do to Keep Her Volvo) '00
From the Earth to the Moon '98
Commandments '96
Last Breath '96
Barcelona '94
White Mile '94
Unnatural Pursuits '91
Quick Change '90
Reversal of Fortune '90
Funny Farm '88
Something Wild '86

Marc Gilpin (1966-)
Computer Wizard '77
Where's Willie? '77

Peri Gilpin (1961-)
Final Fantasy: The Spirits Within '01 (V)
Spring Forward '99

Tom Gilroy
The Blue Tooth Virgin '09
Wild Tigers I Have Known '06
Harry and Max '04
Land and Freedom '95

Jessalyn Gilsig (1971-)
XIII '08
Flood '07
A Cooler Climate '99
Quest for Camelot '98 (V)

Clarence Gilyard, Jr. (1955-)
Left Behind: The Movie '00
Walker: Texas Ranger: One Riot, One Ranger '93
Die Hard '88
Off the Mark '87

Daniel Gimenez Cacho (1961-)
Bad Education '04
Nicotina '03
Jealousy '99
Deep Crimson '96
Midaq Alley '95
On the Air '95
Cabeza de Vaca '90

Erica Gimpel (1964-)
Impostor '02
Santa and Pete '99
Smoke '95
The Fence '94

Teresa Gimpera (1936-)
Crypt of the Living Dead '73
Spirit of the Beehive '73
Feast for the Devil '71
Macabre '69
Black Box Affair '66

Jack Ging (1931-)
Dear Detective '78
Die Sister, Die! '74
Where the Red Fern Grows '74
High Plains Drifter '73
Ssssss '73
That Man Bolt '73
Play Misty for Me '71
Mosby's Marauders '66

Hermione Gingold (1897-1987)
Garbo Talks '84
A Little Night Music '77
Those Fantastic Flying Fools '67
Munster, Go Home! '66
Promise Her Anything '66
Gay Purr-ee '62 (V)
The Music Man '62
The Naked Edge '61
Bell, Book and Candle '58
Gigi '58
Around the World in 80 Days '56
The Adventures of Sadie '55
The Pickwick Papers '54
Tough Guy '53
Butler's Dilemma '43

Bob Ginnaven
The Day It Came to Earth '77
Hootch Country Boys '75

Robert Ginnaven
One False Move '91
Visions of Evil '75

Allen Ginsberg (1926-97)
Superstar: The Life and Times of Andy Warhol '90
Heavy Petting '89

Robert Ginty (1948-)
The Prophet's Game '99
Vampire Time Travelers '98
Taken Alive '95
Lady Dragon '92
Harley Davidson and the Marlboro Man '91
Madhouse '90
Vietnam, Texas '90
Bounty Hunters '89
Loverboy '89
Out on Bail '89
Codename: Vengeance '87
Three Kinds of Heat '87
Programmed to Kill '86
Mission... Kill '85
Exterminator 2 '84
Warrior of the Lost World '84
White Fire '84
Gold Raiders '83
The Act '82
The Alchemist '81
Exterminator '80
Coming Home '78

Frank Gio
Assassination Tango '03
Analyze That '02

Backtrack '89
Once Upon a Time in America '84

Vahina Giocante (1981-)
Lila Says '04
Marie Baie des Anges '97

Rocky Giordani
Cop and a Half '93
After Dark, My Sweet '90
Tapeheads '89

Daniela Giordano (1948-)
The Girl in Room 2A '76
Inquisition '76
Gunslinger '70
Four Times That Night '69

Domiziana Giordano (1960-)
Interview with the Vampire '94
Nouvelle Vague '90
Nostalghia '83

Maria Angela Giordano
The Devil's Daughter '91
Mad Dog Killer '77

Ty(rone) Giordano (1976-)
Untraceable '08
A Lot Like Love '05
The Family Stone '05

Florence Giorgetti (1944-)
The Lacemaker '77
Monique '76

Elenora Giorgi (1953-)
Creepers '85
Nudo di Donna '83
Beyond Obsession '82
Inferno '80
To Forget Venice '79
The Sex Machine '75

Tony Giorgio
American Me '92
The Lonely Guy '84
The Sting 2 '83
Escape to Witch Mountain '75
Foxy Brown '74
Magnum Force '73
The Godfather '72
Changes '69
The Wrecking Crew '68

Carmine D. Giovinazzo (1973-)
In Enemy Hands '04
Players '03
Big Shot: Confessions of a Campus Bookie '02
Black Hawk Down '01
The Learning Curve '01
Terror Tract '00
For Love of the Game '99

Hippolyte Giradot
One Day You'll Understand '08
The Perfume of Yvonne '94

Chaim Girafi
More Dogs Than Bones '00
The Impossible Spy '87

Joseph Girard (1871-1949)
Sergeant York '41
The Spider Returns '41
Mystery of the Hooded Horseman '37
Aces and Eights '36
His Fighting Blood '35
The Ivory Handled Gun '35
Kentucky Blue Streak '35
Social Error '35
The Tonto Kid '35
The Fighting Trooper '34
Hurricane Express '32
Defenders of the Law '31
King of the Rodeo '28
Tentacles of the North '26
Laughing at Danger '24

Remy Girard (1950-)
Human Trafficking '05
The Barbarian Invasions '03
Varian's War '01
The Boys '97
Jesus of Montreal '89

Simone-Elise Girard
Shattered Glass '03
After the Storm '01

Michele Girardon (1938-75)
Devil of the Desert Against the Son of Hercules '62
Death in the Garden '56

Annie Girardot (1931-)
Hidden '05
The Piano Teacher '01
Les Miserables '95
Mussolini & I '85
Jacko & Lise '82
La Vie Continue '82
Jupiter's Thigh '81
Le Cavaleur '78
Dear Detective '77
Gypsy '75
Le Gitan '75
Dillinger Is Dead '69
The Organizer '64
Love and the Frenchwoman '60
Rocco and His Brothers '60

Etienne Girardot
Breakfast for Two '37
The Great Garrick '37
Twentieth Century '34

Hippolyte Girardot (1955-)
A Christmas Tale '08
Flight of the Red Balloon '08
Quiet Chaos '08
Lady Chatterley '06
Paris, je t'aime '06
House of 9 '05
La Moustache '05
Kings and Queen '04
Modigliani '04
Love After Love '94
Barjo '93
Love Without Pity '91
Manon of the Spring '87

Claude Giraud (1936-)
The Mad Adventures of Rabbi Jacob '73
Phedre '68
Angelique: The Road to Versailles '65
Angelique '64
Circle of Love '64

Joyce Giraud (1975-)
Miss Cast Away '04
Latin Dragon '03

Roland Giraud (1942-)
Mr. Frost '89
Three Men and a Cradle '85

Bernard Giraudeau (1947-)
La Petite Lili '03
Water Drops on Burning Rocks '99
Ridicule '96
The Favorite Son '94
Passion of Love '82
La Boum '81
Bilitis '77
Le Gitan '75

Cindy Girling
Devotion '95
Daughter of Death '82

Ennio Girolami (1934-)
Beauty on the Beach '61
Nights of Cabiria '57

Massimo Girotti (1918-2003)
Facing Windows '03
The Monster '96
Quo Vadis '85
The Innocent '76
Mr. Klein '76
Last Tango in Paris '73
Torture Chamber of Baron Blood '72
Red Tent '69
Teorema '68
The Giants of Thessaly '60
Senso '54
Sins of Rome '54
Story of a Love Affair '50
Ossessione '42
The Iron Crown '41

Jackie Giroux
Trick or Treats '82
The Cross & the Switchblade '72

Annabeth Gish (1972-)
American Girl: Chrissa Stands Strong '09
The Celestine Prophecy '06
Knots '05
Buying the Cow '02
A Death in the Family '02
Pursuit of Happiness '01
Race to Space '01
Double Jeopardy '99
SLC Punk! '99
Steel '97
True Women '97
Beautiful Girls '96
Don't Look Back '96
The Last Supper '96
Nixon '95
Scarlett '94
Wyatt Earp '94
Coupe de Ville '90
Shag: The Movie '89
When He's Not a Stranger '89
Mystic Pizza '88
Hiding Out '87
Desert Bloom '86

Dorothy Gish (1898-1968)
The Cardinal '63
Romola '25
Orphans of the Storm '21
Hearts of the World '18
Home Sweet Home '14
Judith of Bethulia '14

Lillian Gish (1896-1993)
The Whales of August '87
Sweet Liberty '86
The Adventures of Huckleberry Finn '85
Hambone & Hillie '84
Hobson's Choice '83
A Wedding '78
The Comedians '67
Follow Me, Boys! '66
The Love Goddesses '65
The Unforgiven '60
The Cobweb '55
The Night of the Hunter '55
Portrait of Jennie '48
Duel in the Sun '46
Commandos Strike at Dawn '43
His Double Life '33
The Wind '28
Romola '25
The White Sister '23
Orphans of the Storm '21
Way Down East '20
Broken Blossoms '19
The Greatest Question '19
True Heart Susie '19
Hearts of the World '18
Intolerance '16
Sold for Marriage '16
The Birth of a Nation '15
Home Sweet Home '14
Judith of Bethulia '14
Battle of Elderbush Gulch '13

Sheila Gish (1942-2005)
Highlander: Endgame '00
Mansfield Park '99
Jewels '92
Highlander '86
A Day in the Death of Joe Egg '71

Heinrich Giskes
Ancient Relic '02
Under the Pavement Lies the Strand '75

Robert Gist (1924-98)
Jack the Giant Killer '62
One Minute to Zero '52
Jigsaw '49

Neil Giuntoli
Henry: Portrait of a Serial Killer 2: Mask of Sanity '96
Memphis Belle '90
Capone '89

Paul(o) Giusti
Emmanuelle on Taboo Island '76
Innocents with Dirty Hands '76
L'Annee Sainte '76

Adele Givens
Beauty Shop '05
Queens of Comedy '01
The Players Club '98

Robin Givens (1964-)
The Family That Preys '08
Head of State '03
Antibody '02
Blankman '94
Foreign Student '94
Boomerang '92
The Penthouse '92
A Rage in Harlem '91
The Women of Brewster Place '89
Beverly Hills Madam '86

George Givot (1903-84)
China Gate '57
Lady and the Tramp '55 *(V)*
Three Sailors and a Girl '53
April in Paris '52
Du Barry Was a Lady '43
Leather Burners '43
Thin Ice '37
Hollywood Party '34

Liliana Glabczynska
See Liliana Komorowska

Frances Gladwin
Frontier Outlaws '44
Thundering Gunslingers '44

Etienne Glaser (1937-)
Speak Up! It's So Dark '93
The Mozart Brothers '86

Paul Michael Glaser (1943-)
Starsky & Hutch '04
Something's Gotta Give '03
Jealousy '84
Single Bars, Single Women '84
Wait Till Your Mother Gets Home '83
Phobia '80
Fiddler on the Roof '71

Ned Glass (1906-84)
Street Music '81
Papa's Delicate Condition '63
Kid Galahad '62
West Side Story '61
The Rebel Set '59
Fright '56
Requiem for a Heavyweight '56

Ron Glass (1945-)
Death at a Funeral '10
Lakeview Terrace '08
Serenity '05
Incognito '99
Back in Business '96
It's My Party '95
Houseguest '94
Deep Space '87
The Crash of Flight 401 '78

Seamon Glass (1925-)
Winterhawk '76
This Is Not a Test '62

Isabel Glasser (1958-)
Tactical Assault '99
Second Chances '98
Mother '96
Circumstances Unknown '95
The Surgeon '94
Death Ring '93
Forever Young '92
Pure Country '92

Phillip Glasser (1978-)
Voodoo Dawn '99
A Troll in Central Park '94 *(V)*
An American Tail: Fievel Goes West '91 *(V)*
Satan's Princess '90
An American Tail '86 *(V)*

Summer Glau (1981-)
The Initiation of Sarah '06
Mammoth '06
Serenity '05

Bob Glaudini
Coastlines '02
Parasite '82
The Alchemist '81

Lola Glaudini (1971-)
Invincible '06
Groove '00

Louise Glaum (1900-70)
The Leopard Woman '20
Sex '20
Return of Draw Egan '16
The Three Musketeers '16

Karen Glave
Blind Faith '98
Last Night '98

Matthew Glave
Corky Romano '01
Rock Star '01
Mutiny '99
Ricochet River '98
Plump Fiction '97
True Women '97
The Wedding Singer '97
Baby's Day Out '94

Eugene Robert Glazer (1942-)
New Blood '99
Loving Evangeline '98
It's My Party '95
Bounty Tracker '93
The Substitute '93
The Five Heartbeats '91
Stepping Out '91
Dollman '90
Eve of Destruction '90
Harlem Nights '89
I'm Gonna Git You Sucka '88
Stand and Deliver '88
Hollywood Shuffle '87
Hunter's Blood '87
No Way Out '87
Vendetta '85

Jackie Gleason (1916-87)
Nothing in Common '86
Izzy & Moe '85
Smokey and the Bandit, Part 3 '83
The Sting 2 '83
The Toy '82
Smokey and the Bandit 2 '80
Mr. Billion '77
Smokey and the Bandit '77
Don't Drink the Water '69
How to Commit Marriage '69
Papa's Delicate Condition '63
Soldier in the Rain '63
Requiem for a Heavyweight '62
The Hustler '61
All Through the Night '42
Orchestra Wives '42
Springtime in the Rockies '42

James Gleason (1886-1959)
Last Hurrah '58
Man or Gun '58
Loving You '57
Man in the Shadow '57
Rock-A-Bye Baby '57
The Night of the Hunter '55
Suddenly '54
Forever Female '53
Movie Stuntmen '53
We're Not Married '52
What Price Glory? '52
I'll See You in My Dreams '51
The Jackpot '50
Key to the City '50
Riding High '50
The Yellow Cab Man '50
Miss Grant Takes Richmond '49
The Dude Goes West '48
Smart Woman '48
The Bishop's Wife '47
Down to Earth '47
Tycoon '47
The Clock '45
A Tree Grows in Brooklyn '45
Arsenic and Old Lace '44
A Guy Named Joe '44
The Keys of the Kingdom '44
Crash Dive '43
The Falcon Takes Over '42
Footlight Serenade '42
Tales of Manhattan '42
Here Comes Mr. Jordan '41
Meet John Doe '41
Tanks a Million '41
Ex-Mrs. Bradford '36
Hot Tip '35
Search for Beauty '34
Hoopla '33
The Crooked Circle '32
A Free Soul '31
Suicide Fleet '31

Joanna Gleason (1950-)
My Sassy Girl '08
The Women '08
Wedding Daze '06
The Wedding Planner '01
Road Ends '98
Boogie Nights '97
If These Walls Could Talk '96
Edie & Pen '95
For Richer, for Poorer '92
F/X 2: The Deadly Art of Illusion '91
Crimes & Misdemeanors '89
Heartburn '86

Mary Pat Gleason
I Now Pronounce You Chuck and Larry '07
Marilyn Hotchkiss' Ballroom Dancing & Charm School '06
Wristcutters: A Love Story '06
Underclassman '05
A Cinderella Story '04
Memron '04

Pat Gleason
Battling Marshal '48
Criminal Court '46
Detour '46
Rogue's Gallery '44
I Killed That Man '42
Swing It, Professor '37

Paul Gleason (1939-2006)
National Lampoon's Van Wilder '02
Not Another Teen Movie '01
Social Misfits '00
The Brutal Truth '99
No Code of Conduct '98
The Thin Red Line '98
Money Talks '97
The Shadow Conspiracy '96
Digital Man '94
I Love Trouble '94
Boiling Point '93
Maniac Cop 3: Badge of Silence '93
Running Cool '93
Wishman '93
There Goes My Baby '92
Wild Cactus '92

Rich Girl '91
Fourth Story '90
Miami Blues '90
Night Game '89
Die Hard '88
Ghost Chase '88
Johnny Be Good '88
She's Having a Baby '88
Forever, Lulu '87
Morgan Stewart's Coming Home '87
The Breakfast Club '85
Challenge of a Lifetime '85
The Ewoks: Battle for Endor '85
Trading Places '83
He Knows You're Alone '80
Doc Savage '75
Private Duty Nurses '71

Russell Gleason (1908-45)

Condemned to Live '35
Hot Tip '35
I Can't Escape '34
All Quiet on the Western Front '30
The Flying Fool '29

Nicholas Gleaves

Half Light '05
Poldark '96

Robert Gleckler (1887-1939)

Whipsaw '35
Defenders of the Law '31
The Sea God '30

Brendan Gleeson (1954-)

Green Zone '10
The Secret of Kells '09 (V)
In Bruges '08
Black Irish '07
Harry Potter and the Order of the Phoenix '07
The Tiger's Tale '06
Harry Potter and the Goblet of Fire '05
Kingdom of Heaven '05
In My Country '04
Troy '04
The Village '04
Cold Mountain '03
Dark Blue '03
Gangs of New York '02
Harrison's Flowers '02
28 Days Later '02
A. I.: Artificial Intelligence '01
Mission: Impossible 2 '00
The Tailor of Panama '00
Lake Placid '99
This Is My Father '99
The General '98
The Break '97
The Butcher Boy '97
I Went Down '97
Michael Collins '96
Trojan Eddie '96
Turbulence '96
Braveheart '95

Paul Gleeson

Komodo '99
Idiot Box '97

Redmond M. Gleeson

2 Brothers & a Bride '03
St. Patrick's Day '99

Iain Glen (1961-)

The Diary of Anne Frank '08
The Last Legion '07
Resident Evil: Extinction '07
Kidnapped '05
Kingdom of Heaven '05
Tara Road '05
Resident Evil: Apocalypse '04
Darkness '02
Gabriel & Me '01
Lara Croft: Tomb Raider '01
Wives and Daughters '01
Beautiful Creatures '00
The Wyvern Mystery '00
Mararia '98
The Painted Lady '97
The Young Americans '93
Fools of Fortune '90
Mountains of the Moon '90
Rosencrantz & Guildenstern Are Dead '90

J. Frank Glendon (1886-1937)

Lion's Den '36
Sucker Money '34
Border Romance '30
Mid-Channel '20

Philip Glenister (1963-)

Cranford '08
Byron '03
Calendar Girls '03
The Other Boleyn Girl '03
State of Play '03
Horatio Hornblower: The Adventure Continues '01
Vanity Fair '99
Sharpe's Justice '97

Robert Glenister (1960-)

Sirens '02
Just Visiting '01

Montgomery Glenn

See Silvano Tranquilli

Roy Glenn (1905-71)

Guess Who's Coming to Dinner '67
Carmen Jones '54
Jungle Drums of Africa '53

Scott Glenn (1942-)

Nights in Rodanthe '08
W. '08
The Bourne Ultimatum '07
Freedom Writers '07
Journey to the End of the Night '06
Puerto Vallarta Squeeze '04
A Painted House '03
Buffalo Soldiers '01
The Seventh Stream '01
The Shipping News '01
Training Day '01
Vertical Limit '00
The Last Marshal '99
The Virgin Suicides '99
Naked City: A Killer Christmas '98
Naked City: Justice with a Bullet '98
Absolute Power '97
Carla's Song '97
Firestorm '97
Courage Under Fire '96
Edie & Pen '95
Reckless '95
Tall Tale: The Unbelievable Adventures of Pecos Bill '95
Night of the Running Man '94
Past Tense '94
The Spy Within '94
Extreme Justice '93
Shadowhunter '93
Slaughter of the Innocents '93
The Player '92
Backdraft '91
My Heroes Have Always Been Cowboys '91
The Silence of the Lambs '91
Women & Men: In Love There Are No Rules '91
The Hunt for Red October '90
Intrigue '90
Miss Firecracker '89
Verne Miller '88
Man on Fire '87
Off Limits '87
As Summers Die '86
Silverado '85
Wild Geese 2 '85
The River '84
The Keep '83
The Right Stuff '83
The Challenge '82
Personal Best '82
Urban Cowboy '80
Apocalypse Now '79
More American Graffiti '79
She Came to the Valley '77
Fighting Mad '76
Nashville '75
The Shrieking '73
Angels Hard As They Come '71
The Baby Maker '70

Sharon Gless (1943-)

The State Within '06
Tales of the Unexpected '91
Letting Go '85
Hobson's Choice '83
The Star Chamber '83
Hardhat & Legs '80
Revenge of the Stepford Wives '80
Centennial '78
The Crash of Flight 401 '78

Stacey Glick (1971-)

Three o'Clock High '87
Brighton Beach Memoirs '86

Brian Glover (1934-97)

Stiff Upper Lips '96
Royal Deceit '94
Leon the Pig Farmer '93
Alien 3 '92
Kafka '91
The Company of Wolves '85
The McGuffin '85
An American Werewolf in London '81

Bruce Glover (1932-)

Simon Says '07
Night of the Scarecrow '95
Warlock: The Armageddon '93
Hider in the House '90
Killcrazy '89
Ghost Town '88
Big Bad Mama 2 '87
Stunts '77
Black Gunn '72
Diamonds Are Forever '71
C.C. & Company '70

Crispin Glover (1964-)

Alice in Wonderland '10
Hot Tub Time Machine '10
9 '09 (V)
Freezer Burn: The Invasion of Laxdale '08
Beowulf '07 (V)
Epic Movie '07
Simon Says '07
The Wizard of Gore '07
Drop Dead Sexy '05
Charlie's Angels: Full Throttle '03
Willard '03
Like Mike '02
Bartleby '01
Fast Sofa '01
Charlie's Angels '00
Nurse Betty '00
The People vs. Larry Flynt '96
Dead Man '95
Chasers '94
Even Cowgirls Get the Blues '94
Hotel Room '93
What's Eating Gilbert Grape '93
Rubin & Ed '92
The Doors '91
Little Noises '91
Where the Heart Is '90
Wild at Heart '90
Back to the Future, Part 2 '89
Twister '89
River's Edge '87
At Close Range '86
Back to the Future '85
Friday the 13th, Part 4: The Final Chapter '84
Racing with the Moon '84
Teachers '84
My Tutor '82

Danny Glover (1947-)

Death at a Funeral '10
Night Train '09
2012 '09
Be Kind Rewind '08
Blindness '08
Gospel Hill '08
Honeydripper '07
Shooter '07
Barnyard '06 (V)
Dreamgirls '06
Poor Man's Game '06
The Shaggy Dog '06
Manderlay '05
The Cookout '04
Saw '04
Good Fences '03
The Royal Tenenbaums '01
3 A.M. '01
Boesman & Lena '00
Freedom Song '00
Antz '98 (V)
Beloved '98
Lethal Weapon 4 '98
Prince of Egypt '98 (V)
Buffalo Soldiers '97
Gone Fishin' '97
John Grisham's The Rainmaker '97
Switchback '97
America's Dream '95
Operation Dumbo Drop '95
Angels in the Outfield '94
Maverick '94
Bopha! '93
Queen '93
The Saint of Fort Washington '93
Lethal Weapon 3 '92
Grand Canyon '91
Pure Luck '91
A Rage in Harlem '91
Flight of the Intruder '90
Predator 2 '90
To Sleep with Anger '90
Dead Man Out '89
Lethal Weapon 2 '89
Lonesome Dove '89
A Raisin in the Sun '89
Bat 21 '88
Lethal Weapon '87
Mandela '87
The Color Purple '85
Silverado '85
Stand-In '85
Witness '85
Iceman '84
Places in the Heart '84
Memorial Day '83
Out '82
Chu Chu & the Philly Flash '81
Keeping On '81
Escape from Alcatraz '79

Jamie Glover (1969-)

In His Life: The John Lennon Story '00
Joseph '95

John Glover (1944-)

On Edge '03
Dead Broke '99
The Tempest '99
Payback '98
Batman and Robin '97
Love! Valour! Compassion! '96
In the Mouth of Madness '95
Schemes '95
Assault at West Point: The Court-Martial of Johnson Whittaker '94
Automatic '94
Night of the Running Man '94
Ed and His Dead Mother '93
What Ever Happened To... '93
Drug Wars 2: The Cocaine Cartel '92
Dead on the Money '91
El Diablo '90
Gremlins 2: The New Batch '90
Meet the Hollowheads '89
Traveling Man '89
The Chocolate War '88
Masquerade '88
Rocket Gibraltar '88
Scrooged '88
Nutcracker: Money, Madness & Murder '87
Apology '86
52 Pick-Up '86
Something Special '86
An Early Frost '85
A Killing Affair '85
Ernie Kovacs: Between the Laughter '84
The Evil That Men Do '84
Kennedy '83
A Little Sex '82
The Mountain Men '80
Last Embrace '79
Annie Hall '77
Julia '77

Julian Glover (1935-)

The Young Victoria '09
Mirrors '08
Scoop '06
Troy '04
Harry Potter and the Chamber of Secrets '02
Two Men Went to War '02
Vatel '00
The Infiltrator '95
Indiana Jones and the Last Crusade '89
Treasure Island '89
Tusks '89
The Fourth Protocol '87
Hearts of Fire '87
Mandela '87
The Secret Garden '87
Kim '84
Heat and Dust '82
Ivanhoe '82
For Your Eyes Only '81
The Empire Strikes Back '80
Luther '74
The Story of Jacob & Joseph '74
Antony and Cleopatra '73
Hitler: The Last Ten Days '73
Theatre of Death '67
The Alphabet Murders '65
Girl with Green Eyes '64
Tom Jones '63

Kara Glover

The Beat '88
Caribe '87

Savion Glover (1973-)

Bojangles '01
Bamboozled '00
The Wall '99
Tap '89

Susan Glover

WarGames 2: The Dead Code '08
Jericho Mansions '03
Random Encounter '98
Eye '96

Vadim Glowna (1941-)

Agnes and His Brothers '04
Advertising Rules! '01
Cross of Iron '76

Carlin Glynn (1940-)

Judy Berlin '99
Blessing '94
Night Game '89
Blood Red '88
Gardens of Stone '87
The Trip to Bountiful '85
Sixteen Candles '84
Continental Divide '81

Mathias Gnaedinger (1941-)

Journey of Hope '90
The Boat Is Full '81

Hiromi Go (1955-)

Samurai Cowboy '93
MacArthur's Children '85

George Gobel (1919-91)

Ellie '84
The Fantastic World of D.C. Collins '84
Better Late Than Never '79
Rabbit Test '78
Birds & the Bees '56
I Married a Woman '56

Justin Gocke (1978-)

The Witching of Ben Wagner '95
My Grandpa Is a Vampire '92

Jean-Luc Godard (1930-)

King Lear '87
First Name: Carmen '83
Contempt '64
Cleo from 5 to 7 '61
Le Petit Soldat '60

Alf Goddard (1897-1981)

Butler's Dilemma '43
Non-Stop New York '37

Beth Goddard (1969-)

Take Me '01
The Last Seduction 2 '98

John Goddard

Naked Youth '59
Storm Rider '57

Mark Goddard (1936-)

Lost in Space '98
Strange Invaders '83
Roller Boogie '79
Blue Sunshine '78
The Death Squad '73

Paul Goddard

Holy Smoke '99
The Matrix '99

Paulette Goddard (1911-90)

Time of Indifference '64
Sins of Jezebel '54
Unholy Four '54
The Torch '50
On Our Merry Way '48
An Ideal Husband '47
Unconquered '47
Diary of a Chambermaid '46
So Proudly We Hail '43
Reap the Wild Wind '42
Star Spangled Rhythm '42
Pot o' Gold '41
The Ghost Breakers '40
The Great Dictator '40
Second Chorus '40
The Women '39
The Young in Heart '38
Modern Times '36

Trevor Goddard (1965-2003)

Flexing with Monty '10
Pirates of the Caribbean: The Curse of the Black Pearl '03
Dead Tides '97
First Encounter '97
Shadow Warriors '97
Fast Money '96
Prey of the Jaguar '96
Yesterday's Target '96
Men of War '94

Godfrey (1969-)

What Up? '08
Phat Girlz '06
Soul Plane '04

Arthur Godfrey (1903-83)

Angel's Brigade '79
Flatbed Annie and Sweetiepie: Lady Truckers '79
Great Bank Hoax '78
Where Angels Go, Trouble Follows '68
The Glass Bottom Boat '66
Four for Texas '63

Derek Godfrey (1924-83)

Hands of the Ripper '71
A Midsummer Night's Dream '68
The Vengeance of She '68

Patrick Godfrey (1933-)

The Importance of Being Earnest '02
Ever After: A Cinderella Story '98
Heat and Dust '82

Jacques Godin (1930-)

Being at Home with Claude '92
Double Identity '89

The Victory '81
The Man Inside '76

Maurice Godin

Boat Trip '03
Double Take '97
The Awakening '95
Vanished '95

Adam Godley

The X Files: I Want to Believe '08
The Old Curiosity Shop '07
Charlie and the Chocolate Factory '05

Judith Godreche (1972-)

L'Auberge Espagnole '02
Quicksand '01
Entropy '99
The Man in the Iron Mask '98
Ridicule '96
The Disenchanted '90
Sons '89

Vanda Godsell (1919-90)

This Sporting Life '63
The Victors '63

Alexander Godunov (1949-95)

The Dogfighters '95
North '94
The Runestone '91
Waxwork 2: Lost in Time '91
Die Hard '88
The Money Pit '86
Witness '85

Angela Goethals (1977-)

V.I. Warshawski '91
Home Alone '90
Heartbreak Hotel '88

Dave Goetz

Muppets from Space '99 (V)
Muppet Treasure Island '96 (V)
The Muppet Christmas Carol '92 (V)
Labyrinth '86
The Dark Crystal '82 (V)
The Muppet Movie '79 (V)

Peter Michael Goetz (1941-)

The Empty Mirror '99
Infinity '96
The Buccaneers '95
Father of the Bride Part 2 '95
The Water Engine '92
Father of the Bride '91
My Girl '91
Tagget '90
Glory '89
Jumpin' Jack Flash '86
King Kong Lives '86
Beer '85
Wolfen '81

Bernhard Goetzke (1884-1964)

Dr. Mabuse, The Gambler '22
Destiny '21
The Indian Tomb '21

John Goff

Party Plane '90
Night Stalker '87
Getting Over '81
The Capture of Bigfoot '79
The Alpha Incident '76
Devil & Leroy Basset '73

Norris Goff (1906-78)

Goin' to Town '44
So This Is Washington '43
Two Weeks to Live '43
The Bashful Bachelor '42
Dreaming Out Loud '40

Walton Goggins (1971-)

Predators '10
That Evening Sun '09
Fragments '08
Miracle at St. Anna '08
The Architect '06
House of 1000 Corpses '03
The Bourne Identity '02
Shanghai Noon '00
Daddy & Them '99
Red Dirt '99
Major League 3: Back to the Minors '98
The Apostle '97

Juliette Goglia

Fired Up! '09
A Grandpa for Christmas '07

Siena Goines

Jada '08
Rancid '04

Joanna Going (1963-)

Runaway Jury '03
Cupid & Cate '00
Heaven '99
Eden '98
Tom Clancy's Netforce '98
Inventing the Abbotts '97
Little City '97
Phantoms '97
Still Breathing '97
Commandments '96
Keys to Tulsa '96
A Good Day to Die '95
How to Make an American Quilt '95
Wyatt Earp '94

Gila Golan (1940-)

The Valley of Gwangi '69
Catch as Catch Can '68
Our Man Flint '66

Ari Gold

Adventures of Power '08
Groove '00

Tracey Gold (1969-)

Final Approach '08
Dirty Little Secret '98
Wanted '98
The Perfect Daughter '96
Shoot the Moon '82

Adam Goldberg (1970-)

(Untitled) '09
2 Days in Paris '07
Zodiac '07
Deja Vu '06
Keeping Up with the Steins '06
Stay Alive '06
How to Lose a Guy in 10 Days '03
The Salton Sea '02
All Over the Guy '01
A Beautiful Mind '01
Fast Sofa '01
Waking Life '01
EDtv '99
Sunset Strip '99
Babe: Pig in the City '98 (V)
Saving Private Ryan '98
Homeward Bound 2: Lost in San Francisco '96 (V)
Dazed and Confused '93

Whoopi Goldberg (1949-)

Toy Story 3 '10 (V)
Everyone's Hero '06 (V)
Jiminy Glick in LaLa Wood '05
Racing Stripes '05 (V)
The Lion King 1 1/2 '04 (V)
Good Fences '03
Call Me Claus '01
Kingdom Come '01
Monkeybone '01
Rat Race '01
The Adventures of Rocky & Bullwinkle '00
More Dogs Than Bones '00
Alice in Wonderland '99
Girl, Interrupted '99
Jackie's Back '99
The Magical Legend of the Leprechauns '99
The Deep End of the Ocean '98
How Stella Got Her Groove Back '98
A Knight in Camelot '98
The Rugrats Movie '98 (V)
An Alan Smithee Film: Burn, Hollywood, Burn '97
Cinderella '97
In the Gloaming '97
The Associate '96
Bogus '96
Eddie '96
Ghosts of Mississippi '96
Moonlight and Valentino '95
The Sunshine Boys '95
Theodore Rex '95
Boys on the Side '94
Corrina, Corrina '94
The Lion King '94 (V)
The Little Rascals '94
The Pagemaster '94 (V)
Star Trek: Generations '94
Made in America '93
Naked in New York '93
Sister Act 2: Back in the Habit '93
The Player '92
Sarafina! '92
Sister Act '92
Soapdish '91
Ghost '90
Homer and Eddie '89
Kiss Shot '89
The Long Walk Home '89
Clara's Heart '88
Burglar '87
Fatal Beauty '87
The Telephone '87
Jumpin' Jack Flash '86
The Color Purple '85

Harold Goldblatt

Children of the Damned '63
The Mind Benders '63

Jeff Goldblum (1952-)

Morning Glory '10
The Switch '10
Adam Resurrected '08
Fay Grim '06
Man of the Year '06
Pittsburgh '06
The Life Aquatic with Steve Zissou '04
Dallas 362 '03
Igby Goes Down '02
Cats & Dogs '01
Perfume '01
Beyond Suspicion '00
Chain of Fools '00
Holy Man '98
Prince of Egypt '98 (V)
The Lost World: Jurassic Park 2 '97
The Great White Hype '96
Independence Day '96
Trigger Happy '96
Nine Months '95
Powder '95
Hideaway '94
Lush Life '94
Jurassic Park '93
Deep Cover '92
Fathers and Sons '92
The Favor, the Watch, & the Very Big Fish '92
The Player '92
Shooting Elizabeth '92
Framed '90
Twisted Obsession '90
Earth Girls Are Easy '89
Mr. Frost '89
The Tall Guy '89
Vibes '88
Beyond Therapy '86
The Fly '86
Into the Night '85
Silverado '85
Transylvania 6-5000 '85
The Adventures of Buckaroo Banzai Across the Eighth Dimension '84
Ernie Kovacs: Between the Laughter '84
The Three Little Pigs '84
The Big Chill '83
The Right Stuff '83
Threshold '83
Rehearsal for Murder '82
The Legend of Sleepy Hollow '79
Invasion of the Body Snatchers '78
Thank God It's Friday '78
Annie Hall '77
Between the Lines '77
The Sentinel '76
Special Delivery '76
Nashville '75
Death Wish '74

Annie Golden (1951-)

Tom and Francie '05
It Runs in the Family '03
One Way Out '95
The Pebble and the Penguin '94 (V)
Baby Boom '87
Forever, Lulu '87
Love at Stake '87
National Lampoon's Class of '86 '86
Desperately Seeking Susan '85
Key Exchange '85
Streetwalkin' '85
Hair '79

Norman D. Golden, II (1984-)

Moby Dick '98
America's Dream '95
Cop and a Half '93

Olive Golden

See Olive Carey

Devin Goldenberg

Fanatic '82
Cry Uncle '71
Guess What We Learned in School Today? '70

Heather Goldenhersch (1973-)

Wedding Daze '06
Southern Belles '05
Kinsey '04
The Merchant of Venice '04
Spin the Bottle '97

Goldie (1965-)

B.U.S.T.E.D. '99
The World Is Not Enough '99

Ricky Paull Goldin (1968-)

Pastime '91
Mirror, Mirror '90
Lambada '89
The Blob '88
Hyper-Sapien: People from Another Star '86

Danny Goldman

Where the Buffalo Roam '80
Swap Meet '79

Diane Goldner (1956-)

Feast 2: Sloppy Seconds '08
Pulse 2: Afterlife '08
Feast '06

Lelia Goldoni (1937-)

Chain Link '08
Choices '81
Bloodbrothers '78
Fatal Chase '77
The Spell '77
The Disappearance of Aimee '76
Theatre of Death '67
Shadows '60

Renee Goldsberry

Pistol Whipped '08
All About You '01

Clio Goldsmith (1957-)

Heat of Desire '84
La Cicada '83
The Gift '82
Honey '81

Jonathan Goldsmith

Phantom of the Mall: Eric's Revenge '89
Go Tell the Spartans '78

Jenette Goldstein (1960-)

Home Room '02
Fair Game '95
Dead to Rights '93
Lethal Weapon 2 '89
The Presidio '88
Near Dark '87
Aliens '86

Bob(cat) Goldthwait (1962-)

Blow '01
Hercules '97 (V)
Sweethearts '97
Back to Back '96
Destiny Turns on the Radio '95
Out There '95
Radioland Murders '94
Freaked '93 (V)
Shakes the Clown '92
Little Vegas '90
Tapeheads '89
Hot to Trot! '88
Scrooged '88
Burglar '87
Police Academy 4: Citizens on Patrol '87
One Crazy Summer '86
Police Academy 3: Back in Training '86

Tony Goldwyn (1960-)

The Last House on the Left '09
American Gun '05
Ghosts Never Sleep '05
The Sisters '05
The Last Samurai '03
Abandon '02
Joshua '02
An American Rhapsody '01
The Song of the Lark '01
Bounce '00
The 6th Day '00
Tarzan '99 (V)
From the Earth to the Moon '98
Kiss the Girls '97
The Lesser Evil '97
The Boys Next Door '96
The Substance of Fire '96
The Last Word '95
Nixon '95
Pocahontas: The Legend '95
Reckless '95
Truman '95
Doomsday Gun '94
A Woman of Independent Means '94
Love Matters '93
The Pelican Brief '93
Taking the Heat '93
Kuffs '92
Traces of Red '92
Iran: Days of Crisis '91
Ghost '90
Gaby: A True Story '87

Valeria Golino (1966-)

Quiet Chaos '08
The Girl by the Lake '07
Frida '02
Respiro '02
Things You Can Tell Just by Looking at Her '00
Harem '99
Spanish Judges '99
Escape from L.A. '96
An Occasional Hell '96
Four Rooms '95
Leaving Las Vegas '95
Clean Slate '94
Immortal Beloved '94
Hot Shots! Part Deux '93
Hot Shots! '91
The Indian Runner '91
Year of the Gun '91
The King's Whore '90
Torrents of Spring '90
Rain Man '88
A Joke of Destiny, Lying in Wait Around the Corner Like a Bandit '84

Lisa Golm (1891-1964)

Come Back, Little Sheba '52
The Hoodlum '51

Arlene Golonka (1939-)

A Family Affair '01
The Gumshoe Kid '89
Dr. Alien '88
Trained to Kill '88
Foxtrap '85
My Tutor '82
Long Shot Kids '81
The In-Laws '79

Marina Golovine

Olivier, Olivier '92
The Stolen Children '92

Yekaterina (Katia) Golubeva

The Intruder '04
Twentynine Palms '03
Pola X '99
I Can't Sleep '93

Sam Golzari

21 '08
American Dreamz '06

Minna Gombell (1892-1973)

I'll See You in My Dreams '51
Pagan Love Song '50
The Best Years of Our Lives '46
Doomed Caravan '41
High Sierra '41
Second Fiddle '39
The Great Waltz '38
Make Way for Tomorrow '37
The Merry Widow '34
No More Women '34
The Thin Man '34
Hoopla '33
Wild Boys of the Road '33
After Tomorrow '32
Bad Girl '31

Carlos Gomez (1962-)

House of Sand and Fog '03
The Negotiator '98
The Replacement Killers '98
Asteroid '97
Fools Rush In '97
The Peacemaker '97
Desperado '95
Bitter Vengeance '94
Hostile Intentions '94
Silhouette '91

Carmelo Gomez

The Method '05
Between Your Legs '99
Mararia '98
Secrets of the Heart '97
Tierra '95
Running Out of Time '94
The Red Squirrel '93
Vacas '91

Ian Gomez (1964-)

Underclassman '05
Connie and Carla '04
The Last Shot '04
Chasing Papi '03
Get a Clue '02
My Big Fat Greek Wedding '02

Jaime Gomez (1965-)

Devil's Knight '03
Gabriela '01
Training Day '01
Solo '96

Jose Luis Gomez (1940-)

Broken Embraces '09
Goya's Ghosts '06
Rowing with the Wind '88
Roads to the South '78
In Memoriam '76

Michelle Gomez

Oliver Twist '07
The Acid House '98

Panchito Gomez (1963-)

Saints and Sinners '95
Mi Vida Loca '94
Sweet 15 '90
Paco '75

Rick Gomez (1972-)

Transformers '07
Sin City '05
Ray '04

Colin Gordon (1911-72)
The Body Beneath *'70*
Burn Witch, Burn! *'62*
Very Important Person *'61*
The Key Man *'57*
One That Got Away *'57*
John and Julie *'55*

Del Gordon
Last of the Clintons *'35*
Wild Mustang *'35*

Dexter Gordon (1923-90)
Awakenings *'90*
Round Midnight *'86*

Don Gordon (1926-)
The Borrower *'89*
The Beast Within *'82*
The Final Conflict *'81*
The Education of Sonny Carson *'74*
The Mack *'73*
Slaughter *'72*
Zero Population Growth *'72*
Bullitt *'68*

Dorothy Gordon (1924-)
Where the Money Is *'00*
The Haunted Strangler *'58*

Eve Gordon (1960-)
I'll Be Home for Christmas *'98*
Honey, We Shrunk Ourselves *'97*
The Heidi Chronicles *'95*
Leaving Normal *'92*
The Secret Passion of Robert Clayton *'92*
Paradise *'91*
Switched at Birth *'91*
Avalon *'90*

Gale Gordon (1906-95)
The 'Burbs *'89*
Speedway *'68*
Dondi *'61*
The 30-Foot Bride of Candy Rock *'59*
Rally 'Round the Flag, Boys! *'58*
Our Miss Brooks *'56*
Francis Covers the Big Town *'53*
Here We Go Again! *'42*

Gavin Gordon (1901-83)
The Bat *'59*
The Matchmaker *'58*
I Killed That Man *'42*
Turf Boy *'42*
Gangs, Inc. *'41*
Bordertown *'35*
The Bride of Frankenstein *'35*
The Bitter Tea of General Yen *'33*
Female *'33*
American Madness *'32*
Romance *'30*
The Silver Horde *'30*
His First Command *'29*

Gerald Gordon (1934-2001)
Ants *'77*
Force Five *'75*
Hell Up in Harlem *'73*

Hannah Taylor Gordon
Anne Frank: The Whole Story *'01*
Jakob the Liar *'99*

James Gordon (1881-1941)
Trailin' *'21*
The Last of the Mohicans *'20*

Julia Swayne Gordon (1879-1933)
The Smart Set *'28*
It *'27*
Wings *'27*
Scaramouche *'23*

Keith Gordon (1961-)
I Love Trouble *'94*
Static *'87*
Back to School *'86*
Combat Academy *'86*
Legend of Billie Jean *'85*
Christine *'84*
Single Bars, Single Women *'84*
Silent Rebellion *'82*
Kent State *'81*
Dressed to Kill *'80*
All That Jazz *'79*
Home Movies *'79*
Jaws 2 *'78*

Kim Gordon
Boarding Gate *'07*
Last Days *'05*

Leo Gordon (1922-2000)
Alienator *'89*
Bog *'84*
Devil's Angels *'67*
Kitten with a Whip *'64*
The Haunted Palace *'63*
Kings of the Sun *'63*
Shame *'61*
The Jayhawkers *'59*
Black Patch *'57*
Seventh Cavalry *'56*
Soldier of Fortune *'55*
Riot in Cell Block 11 *'54*
Ten Wanted Men *'54*
Hondo *'53*

Lucy Gordon (1980-)
Spider-Man 3 *'07*
Russian Dolls *'05*

Mary Gordon (1882-1963)
The Woman in Green *'49*
Little Giant *'46*
Follow the Leader *'44*
Million Dollar Kid *'44*
Boss of Big Town *'43*
Sherlock Holmes and the Secret Weapon *'42*
Motorcycle Squad *'41*
Riot Squad *'41*
The Adventures of Sherlock Holmes *'39*
Double Wedding *'37*
Texas Cyclone *'32*

Pamela Gordon (1937-2003)
Baadasssss! *'03*
Bloodlust: Subspecies 3 *'93*
Bloodstone: Subspecies 2 *'92*

Philip Gordon
Boogeyman *'05*
The Bridge to Nowhere *'86*
Came a Hot Friday *'85*

Roy Gordon (1896-1978)
The Wasp Woman *'59*
Attack of the 50 Foot Woman *'58*
The Real Glory *'39*
Campus Confessions *'38*
The Great Man Votes *'38*

Ruth Gordon (1896-1985)
The Trouble with Spies *'87*
Voyage of the Rock Aliens *'87*
Maxie *'85*
Mugsy's Girls *'85*
Don't Go to Sleep *'82*
Jimmy the Kid *'82*
Any Which Way You Can *'80*
My Bodyguard *'80*
Every Which Way But Loose *'78*
The Prince of Central Park *'77*
The Big Bus *'76*
Harold and Maude *'71*
Where's Poppa? *'70*
Whatever Happened to Aunt Alice? *'69*
Rosemary's Baby *'68*
Lord Love a Duck *'66*
Inside Daisy Clover *'65*
Action in the North Atlantic *'43*
Edge of Darkness *'43*
Two-Faced Woman *'41*
Abe Lincoln in Illinois *'40*
Dr. Ehrlich's Magic Bullet *'40*

Serena Gordon (1963-)
The Aristocrats *'99*
Goldeneye *'95*
A Tale of Two Cities *'89*
Riders *'88*

Susan Gordon (1949-)
Picture Mommy Dead *'66*
Tormented *'60*
Attack of the Puppet People *'58*

Zachary Gordon
Diary of a Wimpy Kid *'10*
Santa Buddies *'09 (V)*

Joseph Gordon-Levitt (1981-)
Hesher *'10*
Inception *'10*
(500) Days of Summer *'09*
G.I. Joe: The Rise of Cobra *'09*
Killshot *'09*
Women in Trouble *'09*
Miracle at St. Anna *'08*
Stop-Loss *'08*
The Lookout *'07*
Brick *'06*
Shadowboxer *'06*
Latter Days *'04*
Mysterious Skin *'04*
Treasure Planet *'02 (V)*
Manic *'01*
Along for the Ride *'00*
Picking Up the Pieces *'99*
Ten Things I Hate about You *'99*
Halloween: H20 *'98*
Sweet Jane *'98*
The Juror *'96*
The Great Elephant Escape *'95*
Angels in the Outfield *'94*
Holy Matrimony *'94*

Charles Gordone (1925-95)
Angel Heart *'87*
Streetfight *'75*

Sandy Gore (1950-)
Brides of Christ *'91*
Wrangler *'88*
Street Hero *'84*

Galyn Gorg (1964-)
RoboCop 2 *'90*
Body Beat *'88*
Malibu Bikini Shop *'86*

Mel Gorham (1959-)
The Center of the World *'01*
Wishful Thinking *'96*
Blue in the Face *'95*
Curdled *'95*
Smoke *'95*

Marius Goring (1912-98)
Charlie Boy *'81*
Holocaust *'78*
Zeppelin *'71*
Exodus *'60*
The Unstoppable Man *'59*
The Moonraker *'58*
Night Ambush *'57*
Quentin Durward *'55*
The Barefoot Contessa *'54*
Paris Express *'53*
The Red Shoes *'48*
Stairway to Heaven *'46*
The Case of the Frightened Lady *'39*
Spy in Black *'39*

Esther Gorintin (1913-)
Since Otar Left.. *'03*
Carnage *'02*

Buddy Gorman (1921-)
Ghost Chasers *'51*
Mr. Muggs Rides Again *'45*

Burn Gorman
Wuthering Heights *'09*
Layer Cake *'05*

Cliff Gorman (1936-2002)
King of the Jungle *'01*
Ghost Dog: The Way of the Samurai *'99*
The '60s *'99*
Down Came a Blackbird *'94*
Hoffa *'92*
Night and the City *'92*
Angel *'84*
Night of the Juggler *'80*
All That Jazz *'79*
An Unmarried Woman *'78*
Rosebud *'75*
Strike Force *'75*
Class of '63 *'73*
Cops and Robbers *'73*
The Boys in the Band *'70*

Jonathan Gorman
Gang Justice *'94*
Street Soldiers *'91*

Patrick Gorman
The Land That Time Forgot *'09*
Gods and Generals *'03*
Gettysburg *'93*

Robert Gorman (1980-)
Leprechaun *'93*
Mr. Nanny *'93*

Eydie Gorme (1931-)
Ocean's Eleven *'01*
Alice in Wonderland *'85*

Peggy Gormley
The Sleepy Time Gal *'01*
Bad Lieutenant *'92*

Karen (Lynn) Gorney (1945-)
Ripe *'97*
The Hard Way *'91*
Saturday Night Fever *'77*

Walt Gorney (1912-2004)
Friday the 13th, Part 2 *'81*
Friday the 13th *'80*

Lisa Gornick
Tick Tock Lullaby *'07*
Do I Love You? *'02*

Frederic Gorny (1973-)
Jeanne and the Perfect Guy *'98*
Wild Reeds *'94*

Irene Gorovaia (1989-)
The Butterfly Effect *'04*
It Runs in the Family *'03*

Ashley Gorrell
Mail to the Chief *'00*
Thunder in Paradise 3 *'94*

Frank Gorshin (1934-2005)
Beethoven's 3rd *'00*
Luck of the Draw *'00*
Man of the Century *'99*
Bloodmoon *'97*
The Twilight of the Ice Nymphs *'97*
12 Monkeys *'95*
Hail Caesar *'94*
Amore! *'93*
The Meteor Man *'93*
Body Trouble *'92*
Sweet Justice *'92*
Beverly Hills Bodysnatchers *'89*
Midnight *'89*
Hollywood Vice Sqaud *'86*
Hot Resort *'85*
The Uppercrust *'81*
Underground Aces *'80*
Sky Hei$t *'75*
Batman *'66*
That Darn Cat *'65*
The George Raft Story *'61*
The Great Impostor *'61*
Studs Lonigan *'60*
Where the Boys Are *'60*
Dragstrip Girl *'57*
Invasion of the Saucer Men *'57*
Portland Expose *'57*
Between Heaven and Hell *'56*

Marjoe Gortner (1944-)
Wild Bill *'95*
Fire, Ice and Dynamite *'91*
American Ninja 3: Blood Hunt *'89*
The Survivalist *'87*
Hellhole *'85*
Jungle Warriors *'84*
Mausoleum *'83*
Acapulco Gold *'78*
Star Crash *'78*
Sidewinder One *'77*
Viva Knievel *'77*
Bobbie Jo and the Outlaw *'76*
Food of the Gods *'76*
Mayday at 40,000 Feet *'76*
Earthquake *'74*
Pray for the Wildcats *'74*
Marjoe *'72*

Ryan Gosling (1980-)
Blue Valentine *'10*
All Good Things *'09*
Fracture *'07*
Lars and the Real Girl *'07*
Half Nelson *'06*
Stay *'05*
The Notebook *'04*
United States of Leland *'03*
Murder by Numbers *'02*
The Believer *'01*
The Slaughter Rule *'01*
Remember the Titans *'00*

David Goss
Hollywood Cop *'87*
She *'83*

Luke Goss (1968-)
Deep Winter *'08*
Hellboy II: The Golden Army *'08*
Unearthed *'07*
Cold and Dark *'05*
The Man *'05*
Charlie *'04*
Silver Hawk *'04*
Blade 2 *'02*
ZigZag *'02*

Jean-Rene Gossart
Emmanuelle 6 *'88*
Panther Squad *'84*

Mark Paul Gosselaar (1974-)
Dead Man on Campus *'97*
Specimen *'97*
Kounterfeit *'96*
Twisted Love *'95*
The St. Tammany Miracle *'94*
Necessary Parties *'88*

Louis Gossett, Jr. (1936-)
Tyler Perry's Why Did I Get Married Too? *'10*
Cover *'08*
Delgo *'08 (V)*
Daddy's Little Girls *'07*
All In *'06*
Jasper, Texas *'03*
Momentum *'03*
What About Your Friends: Weekend Getaway *'02*
The Inspectors 2: A Shred of Evidence *'00*
The Highway Man *'99*
Love Songs *'99*
Strange Justice: The Clarence Thomas and Anita Hill Story *'99*
Y2K *'99*
The Inspectors *'98*
Bram Stoker's The Mummy *'97*
In His Father's Shoes *'97*
Managua *'97*
Inside *'96*
Run for the Dream: The Gail Devers Story *'96*
Iron Eagle 4 *'95*
Zooman *'95*
Curse of the Starving Class *'94*
Flashfire *'94*
A Good Man in Africa *'94*
Dangerous Relations *'93*
Monolith *'93*
Return to Lonesome Dove *'93*
Aces: Iron Eagle 3 *'92*
Carolina Skeletons *'92*
Diggstown *'92*
Keeper of the City *'92*
Cover-Up *'91*
Murder on the Bayou *'91*
Toy Soldiers *'91*
El Diablo *'90*
The Josephine Baker Story *'90*
The Punisher *'90*
Straight Up *'90*
Sudie & Simpson *'90*
Zora Is My Name! *'90*
Goodbye, Miss 4th of July *'88*
Iron Eagle 2 *'88*
Roots: The Gift *'88*
The Father Clements Story *'87*
The Principal *'87*
Firewalker *'86*
Iron Eagle *'86*
Enemy Mine *'85*
Finders Keepers *'84*
The Guardian *'84*
Jaws 3 *'83*
Sadat *'83*
An Officer and a Gentleman *'82*
Don't Look Back: The Story of Leroy "Satchel" Paige *'81*
Backstairs at the White House *'79*
The Lazarus Syndrome *'79*
He Who Walks Alone *'78*
It Rained All Night the Day I Left *'78*
The Choirboys *'77*
The Deep *'77*
Little Ladies of the Night *'77*
J.D.'s Revenge *'76*
The River Niger *'76*
The White Dawn *'75*
It's Good to Be Alive *'74*
The Laughing Policeman *'74*
Travels with My Aunt *'72*
Skin Game *'71*
The Bushbaby *'70*
A Raisin in the Sun *'61*

Robert Gossett (1954-)
Jimmy Zip *'00*
Arlington Road *'99*

Roland Got (1916-48)
G-Men vs. the Black Dragon *'43*
Across the Pacific *'42*

Walter Gotell (1925-97)
Prince Valiant *'97*
Puppet Master 3: Toulon's Revenge *'90*
Sleepaway Camp 2: Unhappy Campers *'88*
The Living Daylights *'87*
Basic Training *'86*
For Your Eyes Only *'81*
Moonraker *'79*
The Spy Who Loved Me *'77*
Lord Jim *'65*
From Russia with Love *'63*
The Guns of Navarone *'61*
The African Queen *'51*

Michael Gothard (1939-93)
Lifeforce *'85*
For Your Eyes Only *'81*
King Arthur, the Young Warlord *'75*
Young Warlord *'75*
The Devils *'71*
The Valley Obscured by the Clouds *'70*

Gilbert Gottfried (1955-)
Dr. Dolittle *'98 (V)*

Chopping Mall '86
Last Resort '86
Terrorvision '86
The Annihilators '85
The Man with One Red Shoe '85
Ratings Game '84
National Lampoon's Class Reunion '82
Soup for One '82
The Creature Wasn't Nice '81
Spaceship '81
Used Cars '80
Home Movies '79
Pretty Baby '78
Demon Seed '77
Cannonball '76
Dynasty '76
Special Delivery '76
Tunnelvision '76
Phantom of the Paradise '74
Beware! The Blob '72
Hi, Mom! '70
Greetings '68

Heather Graham (1970-)
The Hangover '09
Baby on Board '08
Miss Conception '08
Adrift in Manhattan '07
Bobby '06
Gray Matters '06
Cake '05
Anger Management '03
The Guru '02
From Hell '01
Killing Me Softly '01
Say It Isn't So '01
Sidewalks of New York '01
Austin Powers 2: The Spy Who Shagged Me '99
Bowfinger '99
Committed '99
Kiss & Tell '99
Lost in Space '98
Two Girls and a Guy '98
Boogie Nights '97
Scream 2 '97
Entertaining Angels: The Dorothy Day Story '96
Nowhere '96
Swingers '96
Desert Winds '95
Don't Do It '94
Terrified '94
The Ballad of Little Jo '93
Six Degrees of Separation '93
Diggstown '92
Guilty as Charged '92
Twin Peaks: Fire Walk with Me '92
O Pioneers! '91
Shout '91
I Love You to Death '90
Drugstore Cowboy '89

Jessica Graham
And Then Came Lola '09
2 Minutes Later '07

Julie Graham (1965-)
The History of Mr. Polly '07
Bedrooms and Hallways '98
Preaching to the Perverted '97

Lauren Graham (1967-)
The Answer Man '09
Birds of America '08
Flash of Genius '08
Because I Said So '07
Evan Almighty '07
The Moguls '05
The Pacifier '05
Seeing Other People '04
Bad Santa '03
The Third Wheel '02
Sweet November '01
Chasing Destiny '00
One True Thing '98
Nightwatch '96

Marcus Graham (1963-)
Mulholland Drive '01
Animal Instincts 3: The Seductress '95

Morland Graham (1891-1949)
Bonnie Prince Charlie '48
The Upturned Glass '47
Tower of Terror '42
The Ghost Train '41
Night Train to Munich '40
The Scarlet Pimpernel '34

Ronny Graham (1919-99)
The Substance of Fire '96
Ratings Game '84
Gallipoli '81
World's Greatest Lover '77
New Faces of 1952 '54

Sasha Graham
Rage of the Werewolf '99
Addicted to Murder 2: Tainted Blood '97
The Alien Agenda: Out of the Darkness '96
Addicted to Murder '95

Stephen Graham (1973-)
Season of the Witch '10
The Damned United '09
Public Enemies '09
The Crew '08
Filth and Wisdom '08
This Is England '06
Pit Fighter '05
Satan's Little Helper '04
Gangs of New York '02
Snatch '00

Stuart Graham (1967-)
One Man's Hero '98
The Informant '97
Michael Collins '96

Gloria Grahame (1925-81)
The Nesting '80
The Big Scam '79
Chilly Scenes of Winter '79
Autopsy '74
Mama's Dirty Girls '74
Loners '72
The Todd Killings '71
Odds Against Tomorrow '59
The Cobweb '55
The Man Who Never Was '55
Not as a Stranger '55
Oklahoma! '55
Human Desire '54
The Big Heat '53
The Bad and the Beautiful '52
The Greatest Show on Earth '52
Macao '52
Sudden Fear '52
In a Lonely Place '50
A Woman's Secret '49
Crossfire '47
It Happened in Brooklyn '47
Merton of the Movies '47
Song of the Thin Man '47
It's a Wonderful Life '46

Margot Grahame (1911-82)
Fabulous Joe '47
The Informer '35
The Three Musketeers '35
Broken Melody '34

Gawn Grainger (1940-)
Love and Death on Long Island '97
August '95

Kelsey Grammer (1954-)
Crazy on the Outside '10
Fame '09
An American Carol '08
Swing Vote '08
Even Money '06
X-Men: The Last Stand '06
The Good Humor Man '05
The Big Empty '04
Disney's Teacher's Pet '04 (V)
Benedict Arnold: A Question of Honor '03
Mr. St. Nick '02
15 Minutes '01
Animal Farm '99 (V)
Standing on Fishes '99
Toy Story 2 '99 (V)
The Pentagon Wars '98
The Real Howard Spitz '98
Anastasia '97 (V)
Down Periscope '96
Galaxies Are Colliding '92
Kennedy '83

Sam Grana
The Boys of St. Vincent '93
90 Days '86

Alexander Granach (1893-1945)
The Seventh Cross '44
For Whom the Bell Tolls '43
Hangmen Also Die '42
Joan of Paris '42
Kameradschaft '31
Warning Shadows '23
Nosferatu '22

Daisy Granados (1942-)
A Paradise Under the Stars '99
A Very Old Man with Enormous Wings '88
Portrait of Teresa '79
Memories of Underdevelopment '68

Rosario Granados (1925-97)
A Woman Without Love '51
The Great Madcap '49

Bjorn Granath (1946-)
The Ox '91
Pelle the Conqueror '88

Omari (Omarion) Grandberry (1984-)
Feel the Noise '07
The Proud Family Movie '05 (V)
Fat Albert '04
You Got Served '04

Dario Grandinetti (1959-)
Talk to Her '02
The Day Silence Died '98
The Dark Side of the Heart '92

Pippa Grandison (1970-)
Hotel de Love '96
Dating the Enemy '95
Over the Hill '93

Dorothy Granger (1912-95)
Killer Dill '47
One Body Too Many '44
The Dentist '32
Fighting Fool '32

Farley Granger (1925-)
The Next Big Thing '02
Imagemaker '86
Very Close Quarters '84
The Prowler '81
The Widow '76
Arnold '73
Night Flight from Moscow '73
The Slasher '72
They Call Me Trinity '72
Amuck! '71
Sweet Spirits '71
Deathmask '69
The Girl in the Red Velvet Swing '55
Senso '54
Small Town Girl '53
The Story of Three Loves '53
Behave Yourself! '52
Hans Christian Andersen '52
I Want You '51
Strangers on a Train '51
Our Very Own '50
Side Street '50
They Live by Night '49
Rope '48
The Purple Heart '44
The North Star '43

Michael Granger
Murder by Contract '58
Tarzan and the She-Devil '53

Philip Granger
The Deal '05
Possessed '05
Sasquatch '02
The Amy Fisher Story '93

Stewart Granger (1913-93)
Fine Gold '88
Hell Hunters '87
Wild Geese '78
Code Name Alpha '67
The Last Safari '67
Target for Killing '66
The Trygon Factor '66
The Secret Invasion '64
Sodom and Gomorrah '62
North to Alaska '60
Harry Black and the Tiger '58
Gun Glory '57
Bhowani Junction '56
The Last Hunt '56
Green Fire '55
Moonfleet '55
Beau Brummel '54
All the Brothers Were Valiant '53
Salome '53
Young Bess '53
Prisoner of Zenda '52
Scaramouche '52
King Solomon's Mines '50
Woman Hater '49
Blanche Fury '48
Man of Evil '48
Captain Boycott '47
The Magic Bow '47
Caesar and Cleopatra '46
The Man in Grey '45
Waterloo Road '44
Thursday's Child '43
Secret Mission '42
Convoy '40

Nils T. Granlund (1882-1957)
Take It Big '44
Rhythm Parade '43

William Grannel (1929-86)
Girls Are for Loving '73
The Abductors '72
Ginger '72

Greta Granstedt (1907-87)
Return of Dracula '58
They Never Come Back '32

Beth Grant (1949-)
Fragments '08
Henry Poole Is Here '08
Hide '08
The Perfect Witness '07
Welcome to Paradise '07
Factory Girl '06
Hot Tamale '06
The House of Usher '06
Little Miss Sunshine '06
Matchstick Men '03
Evil Alien Conquerors '02
The Rookie '02
Rock Star '01
Sordid Lives '00
Dance with Me '98
Under Oath '97
Lawn Dogs '96
Speed '94
White Sands '92
The Dark Half '91
Love Field '91
Rain Man '88

Cary Grant (1904-86)
Walk, Don't Run '66
Father Goose '64
Charade '63
That Touch of Mink '62
The Grass Is Greener '61
North by Northwest '59
Operation Petticoat '59
Houseboat '58
Indiscreet '58
An Affair to Remember '57
The Pride and the Passion '57
To Catch a Thief '55
Dream Wife '53
Monkey Business '52
People Will Talk '51
Crisis '50
I Was a Male War Bride '49
Every Girl Should Be Married '48
Mr. Blandings Builds His Dream House '48
The Bachelor and the Bobby-Soxer '47
The Bishop's Wife '47
Night and Day '46
Notorious '46
Without Reservations '46
Arsenic and Old Lace '44
None But the Lonely Heart '44
Destination Tokyo '43
Mr. Lucky '43
Once Upon a Honeymoon '42
Talk of the Town '42
Penny Serenade '41
Suspicion '41
His Girl Friday '40
The Howards of Virginia '40
My Favorite Wife '40
The Philadelphia Story '40
Gunga Din '39
In Name Only '39
Only Angels Have Wings '39
Bringing Up Baby '38
Holiday '38
Amazing Adventure '37
The Awful Truth '37
Toast of New York '37
Topper '37
Big Brown Eyes '36
Suzy '36
Wedding Present '36
The Last Outpost '35
Sylvia Scarlett '35
Wings in the Dark '35
Kiss and Make Up '34
Thirty Day Princess '34
The Eagle and the Hawk '33
Gambling Ship '33
I'm No Angel '33
She Done Him Wrong '33
Blonde Venus '32
The Devil and the Deep '32
Hot Saturday '32
Merrily We Go to Hell '32
Sinners in the Sun '32

Charles Grant (1957-)
Playback '95
Lady in Waiting '94

Crystal Grant (1980-)
Kids in America '05
Teenage Caveman '01

Cy Grant
At the Earth's Core '76
Sea Wife '57

David Marshall Grant (1955-)
The Devil Wears Prada '06
The Stepford Wives '04
Noriega: God's Favorite '00
The Chamber '96
The Lazarus Man '96
The Rock '96
Three Wishes '95
And the Band Played On '93
Forever Young '92
Through the Eyes of a Killer '92
Air America '90
Bat 21 '88
Big Town '87
American Flyers '85
Sessions '83
End of August '82
Happy Birthday, Gemini '80

Faye Grant (1957-)
My Best Friend's Girl '08
Manna from Heaven '02
Drive Me Crazy '99
Vibrations '94
Omen 4: The Awakening '91
Internal Affairs '90
V '83
Senior Trip '81

Frances Grant (1909-82)
Oh Susannah '38
Cavalry '36
Red River Valley '36
The Traitor '36
Thunder Mountain '35

Hugh Grant (1960-)
Did You Hear About the Morgans? '09
Music & Lyrics '07
American Dreamz '06
Bridget Jones: The Edge of Reason '04
Love Actually '03
About a Boy '02
Two Weeks Notice '02
Bridget Jones's Diary '01
Small Time Crooks '00
Mickey Blue Eyes '99
Notting Hill '99
Extreme Measures '96
The Englishman Who Went up a Hill But Came down a Mountain '95
Nine Months '95
Sense and Sensibility '95
An Awfully Big Adventure '94
Four Weddings and a Funeral '94
Restoration '94
Sirens '94
Night Train to Venice '93
The Remains of the Day '93
Bitter Moon '92
The Big Man: Crossing the Line '91
Our Sons '91
Impromptu '90
The Lady and the Highwayman '89
The Bengali Night '88
The Dawning '88
The Lair of the White Worm '88
Rowing with the Wind '88
White Mischief '88
Maurice '87

James Grant (1936-)
The Innocent '93
Prick Up Your Ears '87

Jennifer Grant (1966-)
Blood Relic '05
Savage '96

Kathryn Grant (1933-)
Anatomy of a Murder '59
The Big Circus '59
1001 Arabian Nights '59 (V)
Gunman's Walk '58
The Seventh Voyage of Sinbad '58
The Brothers Rico '57
Operation Mad Ball '57

Kirby Grant (1914-85)
Comin' Round the Mountain '51
Bad Men of the Border '45
The Stranger from Pecos '45
Hi, Good Lookin'! '44
In Society '44
Lawmen '44

Lawrence Grant (1870-1952)
Son of Frankenstein '39
S.O.S. Coast Guard '37
Werewolf of London '35
The Mask of Fu Manchu '32
Shanghai Express '32
Speak Easily '32
Bulldog Drummond '29
Doomsday '28
The Grand Duchess and the Waiter '26

Lee Grant (1927-)
Going Shopping '05
Mulholland Drive '01
Dr. T & the Women '00
It's My Party '95

Citizen Cohn '92
Defending Your Life '91
A Billion for Boris '90
Big Town '87
Teachers '84
Visiting Hours '82
Charlie Chan and the Curse of the Dragon Queen '81
For Ladies Only '81
Little Miss Marker '80
Backstairs at the White House '79
Damien: Omen 2 '78
My Sister, My Love '78
The Swarm '78
Airport '77 '77
The Spell '77
Voyage of the Damned '76
The Seagull '75
Shampoo '75
Internecine Project '73
Portnoy's Complaint '72
Plaza Suite '71
There Was a Crooked Man '70
The Big Bounce '69
Marooned '69
Buona Sera, Mrs. Campbell '68
Divorce American Style '67
In the Heat of the Night '67
Valley of the Dolls '67
The Balcony '63
Detective Story '51

Leon Grant
Playing for Keeps '86
Beat Street '84

Micah Grant
Terminal Bliss '91
High Desert Kill '90

Rachel Grant
Brotherhood of Blood '08
The Purifiers '04

Richard E. Grant (1957-)
Filth and Wisdom '08
Garfield: A Tail of Two Kitties '06 (V)
Penelope '06
Color Me Kubrick '05
Tim Burton's Corpse Bride '05 (V)
The Story of an African Farm '04
Bright Young Things '03
Monsieur N. '03
The Hound of the Baskervilles '02
Sherlock: Case of Evil '02
Gosford Park '01
Strictly Sinatra '01
The Little Vampire '00
The Miracle Maker: The Story of Jesus '00 (V)
A Christmas Carol '99
The Match '99
The Scarlet Pimpernel '99
The Scarlet Pimpernel 2: Mademoiselle Guillotine '99
The Scarlet Pimpernel 3: The Kidnapped King '99
St. Ives '98
A Merry War '97
The Serpent's Kiss '97
Spice World: The Movie '97
Portrait of a Lady '96
A Royal Scandal '96
Twelfth Night '96
Cold Light of Day '95
Jack and Sarah '95
Ready to Wear '94
The Age of Innocence '93
Bram Stoker's Dracula '92
The Player '92
Codename Kyril '91
Hudson Hawk '91
L.A. Story '91
Warlock '91
Henry & June '90
Mountains of the Moon '90
How to Get Ahead in Advertising '89
Withnail and I '87

Rodney A. Grant (1959-)
Don't Come Knocking '05
The Jack Bull '99
Wild Wild West '99
White Wolves 3: Cry of the White Wolf '98
The Killing Grounds '97
Two for Texas '97
The Substitute '96
The Last Ride '94
Wagons East '94
Geronimo: An American Legend '93
Son of the Morning Star '91
Dances with Wolves '90

Salim Grant (1977-)
What About Your Friends: Weekend Getaway '02
The Hitman '91

Schuyler Grant (1971-)
Anne of Green Gables: The Continuing Story '99
Wrestling with Alligators '98
Anne of Avonlea '87
Anne of Green Gables '85

Shelby Grant (1940-)
The Witchmaker '69
Fantastic Voyage '66
Our Man Flint '66

Stacy Grant
The Fear: Halloween Night '99
One Special Night '99

Allan Granville
Prey for the Hunter '92
Black Terrorist '85

Bonita Granville (1923-88)
Lone Ranger '56
Guilty of Treason '50
Breakfast in Hollywood '46
Love Laughs at Andy Hardy '46
Hitler's Children '43
The Glass Key '42
Now, Voyager '42
H.M. Pulham Esquire '41
The Mortal Storm '40
Nancy Drew and the Hidden Staircase '39
Nancy Drew, Reporter '39
Nancy Drew—Trouble Shooter '39
Hard to Get '38
Nancy Drew—Detective '38
Call It a Day '37
Quality Street '37
These Three '36

Charley Grapewin (1869-1956)
Follow the Boys '44
They Died with Their Boots On '41
The Grapes of Wrath '40
Johnny Apollo '40
Rhythm on the River '40
The Texas Rangers Ride Again '40
The Wizard of Oz '39
Of Human Hearts '38
Shopworn Angel '38
Three Comrades '38
Captains Courageous '37
The Good Earth '37
Libeled Lady '36
Petrified Forest '36
Without Orders '36
Ah, Wilderness! '35
Alice Adams '35
One Frightened Night '35
Anne of Green Gables '34
Two Alone '34
Heroes for Sale '33
Pilgrimage '33
Torch Singer '33
Hell's House '32

Bertram Grassby (1880-1953)
When a Man Loves '27
Mid-Channel '20

Karen Grassle (1944-)
Wyatt Earp '94
Harry's War '84
Cocaine: One Man's Seduction '83
President's Mistress '78
Little House on the Prairie '74

Bill Gratton
Devil in the Flesh 2 '00
Syngenor '90

Ernest Graves (1919-83)
Hercules in New York '70
One Plus One '61

Karron Graves
The Crucible '96
The Fig Tree '87

Peter Graves (1911-94)
The Adventurers '70
Krakatoa East of Java '69
The Magic Christian '69
The Admirable Crichton '57
Canyon River '56
Encore '52
Maytime in Mayfair '49
Bees in Paradise '44

Peter Graves (1925-2010)
Men in Black 2 '02
These Old Broads '01
Number One with a Bullet '87
Mad Mission 3 '84
The Guns and the Fury '83
The Winds of War '83
Airplane 2: The Sequel '82
Savannah Smiles '82
Airplane! '80
Survival Run '80
The Clonus Horror '79
The Rebels '79
Cruise Missile '78
The Slipper and the Rose '76
Scream of the Wolf '74
Where Have All the People Gone? '74
The President's Plane Is Missing '71
Sergeant Ryker '68
Texas Across the River '66
The Legend of the Sea Wolf '58
Beginning of the End '57
Poor White Trash '57
It Conquered the World '56
The Court Martial of Billy Mitchell '55
Let's Make Up '55
The Night of the Hunter '55
Killers from Space '54
Beneath the 12-Mile Reef '53
Stalag 17 '53
Red Planet Mars '52

Ralph Graves (1900-77)
Three Texas Steers '39
Ticket to a Crime '34
That Certain Thing '28
Extra Girl '23
Dream Street '21
The Greatest Question '19

Rupert Graves (1963-)
God on Trial '08
Death at a Funeral '07
V for Vendetta '06
Extreme Ops '02
All My Loved Ones '00
Cleopatra '99
Dreaming of Joseph Lees '99
Sweet Revenge '98
Bent '97
Mrs. Dalloway '97
Different for Girls '96
The Tenant of Wildfell Hall '96
The Innocent Sleep '95
Intimate Relations '95
The Madness of King George '94

Damage '92
Where Angels Fear to Tread '91
The Children '90
A Handful of Dust '88
Fortunes of War '87
Maurice '87
A Room with a View '86

Teresa Graves (1949-2002)
Get Christie Love! '74
That Man Bolt '73

Fernand Gravey (1905-70)
The Madwoman of Chaillot '69
How to Steal a Million '66
La Ronde '51
The Fantastic Night '42
The Great Waltz '38
Bitter Sweet '33

Carla Gravina (1941-)
Boomerang '76
And Now My Love '74
Salut l'Artiste '74
The Tempter '74
Alfredo, Alfredo '72

Cesare Gravina (1858-1954)
The Wedding March '28
Merry-Go-Round '23
Foolish Wives '22

Billy Gray (1938-)
Werewolves on Wheels '71
Two for the Seesaw '62
By the Light of the Silvery Moon '53
The Girl Next Door '53
The Day the Earth Stood Still '51
On Moonlight Bay '51

Bruce Gray (1939-)
Chasing Freedom '04
A Killing Spring '02
My Big Fat Greek Wedding '02
The Last Debate '00
Dangerous Evidence: The Lori Jackson Story '99
The Happy Face Murders '99
Odd Birds '85

Charles Gray (1928-2000)
Mr. & Mrs. Loving '96
Dreams Lost, Dreams Found '87
The Jigsaw Man '84
An Englishman Abroad '83
Shock Treatment '81
The Mirror Crack'd '80
The House on Garibaldi Street '79
Silver Bears '78
The Seven-Per-Cent Solution '76
The Beast Must Die '75
The Rocky Horror Picture Show '75
Murder on the Midnight Express '74
Diamonds Are Forever '71
The Executioner '70
Nine Ages of Nakedness '69 (N)
The Devil Rides Out '68
The Man Outside '68
Night of the Generals '67
You Only Live Twice '67

Coleen Gray (1922-)
A Cry from the Mountain '85
The Phantom Planet '61
The Leech Woman '59
The Killing '56
Kansas City Confidential '52
Riding High '50
Red River '48
Kiss of Death '47
Nightmare Alley '47

David Barry Gray
Lawn Dogs '96
Soldier Boyz '95

Cops and Robbersons '94
S.F.W. '94

Dolores Gray (1924-2002)
Designing Woman '57
The Opposite Sex '56
Kismet '55

Donald Gray (1914-78)
Flight from Vienna '56
Island of Desire '52
Murder on the Campus '52
The Four Feathers '39

Dorian Gray (1934-)
Colossus and the Amazon Queen '64
Il Grido '57
Nights of Cabiria '57

Dulcie Gray (1919-)
Angels One Five '54
The Franchise Affair '52
A Man About the House '47
Mine Own Executioner '47

Elspet Gray (1929-)
Catherine Cookson's The Wingless Bird '97
The Girl in a Swing '89

Erin Gray (1950-)
Loaded '08
Ghouls '07
A Dangerous Place '94
Honor Thy Father and Mother: The True Story of the Menendez Brothers '94
T-Force '94
Jason Goes to Hell: The Final Friday '93
Official Denial '93
Breaking Home Ties '87
Born Beautiful '82
Six Pack '82
Buck Rogers in the 25th Century '79
The Ultimate Imposter '79

Eve Gray (1900-83)
Death on the Set '35
Department Store '35
Night Birds '31

Gary Gray (1936-2006)
The Painted Hills '51
The Next Voice You Hear '50
Two Weeks with Love '50
Rachel and the Stranger '48

Gary LeRoi Gray
Noah's Arc: Jumping the Broom '08
Slappy and the Stinkers '97

Lawrence Gray (1898-1970)
A Face in the Fog '36
Man of the World '31
It's a Great Life '29
The Patsy '28
Love 'Em and Leave 'Em '26
Are Parents People? '25

Linda Gray (1940-)
Accidental Meeting '93
Bonanza: The Return '93
Kenny Rogers as the Gambler, Part 3: The Legend Continues '87
Haywire '80
The Wild and the Free '80
The Two Worlds of Jenny Logan '79
The Grass Is Always Greener Over the Septic Tank '78

Lorna Gray
See Adrian Booth
Spoilers of the North '47

MacKenzie Gray (1957-)
My Teacher Ate My Homework '98
Strip Search '97

Macy Gray (1967-)
Idlewild '06
Shadowboxer '06
The Crow: Wicked Prayer '05
Domino '05
Around the World in 80 Days '04
Scary Movie 3 '03
Training Day '01

Marc Gray
Which Way Home '90
Flirting '89

Nadia Gray (1923-94)
Two for the Road '67
Maniac '63
The Captain's Table '60
La Dolce Vita '60
Une Parisienne '58
Valley of the Eagles '51
The Spider and the Fly '49

Pamela Gray
Corn '02
The Devil's Advocate '97
Commandments '96

Rebecca Gray
The Coroner '98
Tinseltown '97
A Matter of Honor '95

Sally Gray (1916-2006)
Keeper '76
I'll Get You '53
The Hidden Room '49
Obsession '49
They Made Me a Fugitive '47
Dangerous Moonlight '41
Lady in Distress '39
The Saint in London '39
Mr. Reeder in Room 13 '38

Sam Gray (1923-)
Burnzy's Last Call '95
Heart '87
Wolfen '81
Christmas Evil '80

Spalding Gray (1941-2004)
How High '01
Kate & Leopold '01
Revolution #9 '01
Coming Soon '99
Bliss '96
Diabolique '96
Drunks '96
Glory Daze '96
Gray's Anatomy '96
Beyond Rangoon '95
Bad Company '94
The Paper '94
King of the Hill '93
The Pickle '93
Twenty Bucks '93
Monster in a Box '92
Straight Talk '92
Heavy Petting '89
The Image '89
Our Town '89
Beaches '88
Clara's Heart '88
Spalding Gray: Terrors of Pleasure '88
Stars and Bars '88
Swimming to Cambodia '87
True Stories '86
Almost You '85
Hard Choices '84
The Killing Fields '84

Vivean Gray (1924-)
The Last Wave '77
Picnic at Hanging Rock '75

Willoughby Gray (1916-93)
Absolution '81
Waterloo '71

Ari Graynor (1983-)
Youth in Revolt '10
Whip It '09
Nick & Norah's Infinite Playlist '08
The Great New Wonderful '06

Game 6 *'05*
Book of Love *'04*

Denise Grayson

Though None Go With Me *'06*
Corn *'02*

Jerry Grayson

Pushing Tin *'99*
Mob Queen *'98*

Kathryn Grayson (1922-)

The Desert Song *'53*
Kiss Me Kate *'53*
So This Is Love *'53*
Lovely to Look At *'52*
Show Boat *'51*
The Toast of New Orleans *'50*
That Midnight Kiss *'49*
The Kissing Bandit *'48*
It Happened in Brooklyn *'47*
Till the Clouds Roll By *'46*
Anchors Aweigh *'45*
Thousands Cheer *'43*
Rio Rita *'42*
Andy Hardy's Private Secretary *'41*

Irene Grazioli

The Red Violin *'98*
Mediterraneo *'91*

Jose Greco (1918-2000)

Ship of Fools *'65*
Goliath and the Sins of Babylon *'64*

Juliette Greco (1927-)

Uncle Tom's Cabin *'69*
Elena and Her Men *'56*
The Green Glove *'52*
Orpheus *'49*

Alice Greczyn (1986-)

Sex Drive *'08*
Shrooms *'07*
The Dukes of Hazzard *'05*

Adolph Green (1915-2002)

I Want to Go Home *'89*
Follies in Concert *'85*
Lily in Love *'85*
My Favorite Year *'82*
Simon *'80*

Al Green (1946-)

On the Line *'01*
Beverly Hills Cop 3 *'94*

Anthony Green (1970-)

Anaconda 3: The Offspring *'08*
The Scarlet Pimpernel *'99*
The Scarlet Pimpernel 2: Mademoiselle Guillotine *'99*
The Scarlet Pimpernel 3: The Kidnapped King *'99*

Brian Austin Green (1973-)

Impact Point *'08*
Domino *'05*
Cock & Bull Story *'03*
Fish Without a Bicycle *'03*
Laws of Deception *'97*
An American Summer *'90*
Kid *'90*

Brian Lane Green (1962-)

Circuit *'02*
Friends and Family *'01*

Calvin Green

Zombie Strippers *'08*
Exotica *'94*

Danny Green (1903-73)

The Seventh Voyage of Sinbad *'58*
The Ladykillers *'55*
Non-Stop New York *'37*

Eva Green (1980-)

The Golden Compass *'07*
Casino Royale *'06*
Kingdom of Heaven *'05*

Harry Green (1892-1958)

A King in New York *'57*
Be Yourself *'30*
The Light of Western Stars *'30*

Janet-Laine Green

Anne of Green Gables: The Continuing Story *'99*
When the Dark Man Calls *'95*
Medicine River *'94*
Cowboys Don't Cry *'88*
Kidnapping of Baby John Doe *'88*
Bullies *'86*

Jordan-Claire Green (1991-)

The Twelve Dogs of Christmas *'05*
School of Rock *'03*

Kerri Green (1967-)

Blue Flame *'93*
Tainted Blood *'93*
Three for the Road *'87*
Lucas *'86*
The Goonies *'85*
Summer Rental *'85*

Marika Green

Emmanuelle *'74*
Pickpocket *'59*

Mitzie Green (1920-69)

Bloodhounds of Broadway *'52*
Lost in Alaska *'52*
Little Orphan Annie *'32*
Tom Sawyer *'30*

Nigel Green (1924-72)

The Ruling Class *'72*
The Pink Jungle *'68*
The Wrecking Crew *'68*
Africa Texas Style *'67*
Deadlier Than the Male *'67*
Khartoum *'66*
Tobruk *'66*
The Ipcress File *'65*
Masque of the Red Death *'65*
The Skull *'65*
Zulu *'64*
Jason and the Argonauts *'63*
Mysterious Island *'61*
Beat Girl *'60*
Sword of Sherwood Forest *'60*
Corridors of Blood *'58*
Reach for the Sky *'56*

Robson Green (1964-)

Little Devil *'07*
Like Father Like Son *'05*
Me & Mrs. Jones *'02*
Take Me *'01*
The Last Musketeer *'00*
Catherine Cookson's The Gambling Man *'98*
Reckless: The Sequel *'98*
Reckless *'97*
Touching Evil *'97*

Scott Green

Paranoid Park *'07*
Last Days *'05*

Seth Green (1974-)

Old Dogs *'09*
Sex Drive *'08*
Scooby-Doo 2: Monsters Unleashed *'04*
Without a Paddle *'04*
The Italian Job *'03*
Party Monster *'03*
Austin Powers In Goldmember *'02*
America's Sweethearts *'01*
Josie and the Pussycats *'01*
Knockaround Guys *'01*
Rat Race *'01*
The Trumpet of the Swan *'01 (V)*
Austin Powers 2: The Spy Who Shagged Me *'99*
Idle Hands *'99*
Can't Hardly Wait *'98*
Enemy of the State *'98*
Stonebrook *'98*
Austin Powers: International Man of Mystery *'97*
Airborne *'93*
Arcade *'93*
My Stepmother Is an Alien *'88*
Can't Buy Me Love *'87*
Radio Days *'87*
Something Special *'86*
The Hotel New Hampshire *'84*

Tom Green (1971-)

Freezer Burn: The Invasion of Laxdale *'08*
Bob the Butler *'05*
Stealing Harvard *'02*
Freddy Got Fingered *'01*
Charlie's Angels *'00*
Road Trip *'00*

Bryan Greenberg (1950-)

Bride Wars *'09*
Nobel Son *'08*
Love and Debate *'06*
Prime *'05*

Esther Greenberg

Lupo *'70*
Sallah *'63*

Shon Greenblatt

There Goes My Baby *'92*
Freddy's Dead: The Final Nightmare *'91*

William Greenblatt (1987-)

Ms. Scrooge *'97*
The Abduction *'96*
Homecoming *'96*

Angela Greene (1923-78)

The Cosmic Man *'59*
Night of the Blood Beast *'58*

Ashley Greene (1987-)

The Twilight Saga: Eclipse *'10*
The Twilight Saga: New Moon *'09*
Twilight *'08*

Billoah Greene

Preaching to the Choir *'05*
Levity *'03*

Daniel Greene

Me, Myself, and Irene *'00*
American Tiger *'89*
The Opponent *'89*
Skeleton Coast *'89*
Elvira, Mistress of the Dark *'88*
Hands of Steel *'86*
Weekend Warriors *'86*
Pulsebeat *'85*

Ellen Greene (1952-)

The Cooler *'03*
States of Control *'98*
One Fine Day *'96*
Killer: A Journal of Murder *'95*
Murdered Innocence *'94*
The Professional *'94*
Wagons East *'94*
Fathers and Sons *'92*
Rock-a-Doodle *'92 (V)*
Stepping Out *'91*
Glory! Glory! *'90*
Pump Up the Volume *'90*
Dinner at Eight *'89*
Me and Him *'89*
Talk Radio *'88*
Little Shop of Horrors *'86*
Next Stop, Greenwich Village *'76*

Graham Greene (1952-)

The Twilight Saga: New Moon *'09*
All Hat *'07*
Just Buried *'07*
Luna: Spirit of the Whale *'07*
A Lobster Tale *'06*
When I Find the Ocean *'06*
Transamerica *'05*
A Thief of Time *'04*
Coyote Waits *'03*
Shattered City: The Halifax Explosion *'03*
Skins *'02*
Snow Dogs *'02*
Christmas in the Clouds *'01*
Lost and Delirious *'01*
The Green Mile *'99*
Grey Owl *'99*
Shattered Image *'98*
The Education of Little Tree *'97*
Wounded *'97*
Eye *'96*
Sabotage *'96*
Die Hard: With a Vengeance *'95*
Camilla *'94*
Maverick *'94*
Medicine River *'94*
North *'94*
The Pathfinder *'94*
Savage Land *'94*
Benefit of the Doubt *'93*
The Broken Chain *'93*
Cooperstown *'93*
Huck and the King of Hearts *'93*
Rain Without Thunder *'93*
Spirit Rider *'93*
Clearcut *'92*
The Last of His Tribe *'92*
Thunderheart *'92*
Lost in the Barrens *'91*
Dances with Wolves *'90*
Powwow Highway *'89*

James Greene (1926-)

Philadelphia Experiment 2 *'93*
Pals *'87*
The Moon Stallion *'85*

Joe "Mean Joe" Greene (1946-)

Smokey and the Bandit 2 *'80*
Lady Cocoa *'75*
The Black Six *'74*
Twisted Brain *'74*

Jon Greene

Swift Justice *'88*
Alley Cat *'84*

Kim Morgan Greene (1960-)

Grizzly Mountain *'97*
The Corporation *'96*
The Soft Kill *'94*
Scorned *'93*

Leon Greene (1933-)

A Challenge for Robin Hood *'68*
The Devil Rides Out *'68*

Lorne Greene (1915-87)

The Alamo: Thirteen Days to Glory *'87*
Vasectomy: A Delicate Matter *'86*
A Time for Miracles *'80*
Klondike Fever *'79*
The Bastard *'78*
Battlestar Galactica *'78*
Mission Galactica: The Cylon Attack *'78*
Roots *'77*
The Trial of Lee Harvey Oswald *'77*
Tidal Wave *'75*
Earthquake *'74*
The Errand Boy *'61*
The Trap *'59*
The Buccaneer *'58*
Peyton Place *'57*
Autumn Leaves *'56*
Tight Spot *'55*
The Silver Chalice *'54*

Michael Greene (1934-)

Last Man Standing *'95*
Rubin & Ed *'92*
In the Heat of Passion *'91*
Nightmare on the 13th Floor *'90*
Johnny Be Good *'88*
Moon over Parador *'88*
The Night Before *'88*
White of the Eye *'88*
Lost in America *'85*
Americana *'81*
The Clones *'73*
The Naked Angels *'69*

Michele Greene (1962-)

A Woman Hunted *'03*
Redeemer *'02*
A Family Affair *'01*
Fugitive Mind *'99*
Wild Grizzly *'99*
Stranger in the House *'97*
Daddy's Girl *'96*
How the West Was Fun *'95*
Stranger by Night *'94*
The Unborn 2 *'94*
Silent Victim *'92*
Danielle Steel's Palomino *'91*
I Posed for Playboy *'91*
Double Standard *'88*

Peter Greene (1965-)

Final Engagement *'07*
End Game *'06*
Black Cloud *'04*
Nobody's Baby *'01*
Ticker *'01*
Blue Streak *'99*
Out in Fifty *'99*
Black Cat Run *'98*
Double Tap *'98*
Permanent Midnight *'98*
Trading Favors *'97*
The Rich Man's Wife *'96*
Sworn Enemies *'96*
Bang *'95*
The Usual Suspects *'95*
The Mask *'94*
Pulp Fiction *'94*
Clean, Shaven *'93*
Judgment Night *'93*
Laws of Gravity *'92*

Richard Greene (1918-85)

Special Effects *'85*
Tales from the Crypt *'72*
The Castle of Fu Manchu *'68*
Island of the Lost *'68*
Kiss and Kill *'68*
Sword of Sherwood Forest *'60*
Robin Hood: The Movie *'55*
Captain Scarlett *'53*
The Black Castle *'52*
Forever Amber *'47*
The Hound of the Baskervilles *'39*
The Little Princess *'39*
Stanley and Livingstone *'39*
Four Men and a Prayer *'38*
My Lucky Star *'38*

Shecky Greene (1926-)

Lovelines *'84*
Splash *'84*
The Love Machine *'71*

Kate Greenfield (1987-)

Night Gallery *'69*
Robinson Crusoe of Clipper Island *'36*

Kate Greenhouse

Touch the Top of the World *'06*
Webs *'03*
The Miracle Worker *'00*
The Assistant *'97*

Raymond Greenleaf (1892-1963)

When Gangland Strikes *'56*
Pier 23 *'51*
Storm Warning *'51*
David Harding, Counterspy *'50*
Harriet Craig *'50*

Brad Greenquist (1959-)

The Diary of Ellen Rimbauer *'03*
Crime and Punishment in Suburbia *'00*
Lost Souls *'00*
Inherit the Wind *'99*
Gang Related *'96*
The Yearling *'94*
Pet Sematary *'89*
The Bedroom Window *'87*
Mutants In Paradise *'84*

Sydney Greenstreet (1879-1954)

Flamingo Road *'49*
It's a Great Feeling *'49*
Malaya *'49*
Velvet Touch *'48*
The Hucksters *'47*
The Verdict *'46*
Christmas in Connecticut *'45*
Conflict *'45*
Hollywood Canteen *'44*
The Mask of Dimitrios *'44*
Passage to Marseilles *'44*
Background to Danger *'43*
Across the Pacific *'42*
Casablanca *'42*
The Maltese Falcon *'41*
They Died with Their Boots On *'41*

Bruce Greenwood (1956-)

Dinner for Schmucks *'10*
A Dog Named Christmas *'09*
Star Trek *'09*
Cyborg Soldier *'08*
The Summit *'08*
Firehouse Dog *'07*
I'm Not There *'07*
National Treasure: Book of Secrets *'07*
Deja Vu *'06*
Eight Below *'06*
Capote *'05*
Racing Stripes *'05*
American Meltdown *'04*
Being Julia *'04*
I, Robot *'04*
The Riverman *'04*
The Core *'03*
Hollywood Homicide *'03*
The Republic of Love *'03*
Ararat *'02*
Below *'02*
The Magnificent Ambersons *'02*
Swept Away *'02*
A Girl Thing *'01*
Here on Earth *'00*
Hide and Seek *'00*
Rules of Engagement *'00*
Thirteen Days *'00*
Double Jeopardy *'99*
Thick as Thieves *'99*
The Color of Courage *'98*
Disturbing Behavior *'98*
The Lost Son *'98*
Father's Day *'96*
The Sweet Hereafter *'96*
Bitter Vengeance *'94*
The Companion *'94*
Dream Man *'94*
Exotica *'94*
Treacherous Beauties *'94*
Adrift *'93*
Rio Diablo *'93*
Passenger 57 *'92*
Servants of Twilight *'91*
The Little Kidnappers *'90*
Wild Orchid *'90*
Spy *'89*
Another Chance *'88*
In the Line of Duty: The FBI Murders *'88*
The Climb *'87*
Striker's Mountain *'87*
Malibu Bikini Shop *'86*

Charlotte Greenwood (1890-1978)

Glory *'56*
Oklahoma! *'55*
Dangerous When Wet *'53*
Great Dan Patch *'49*
The Gang's All Here *'43*
Springtime in the Rockies *'42*
Moon over Miami *'41*
Down Argentine Way *'40*
Young People *'40*
Flying High *'31*

Palmy Days *'31*
Parlor, Bedroom and Bath *'31*

Joan Greenwood (1921-87)
Little Dorrit, Film 1: Nobody's Fault *'88*
Little Dorrit, Film 2: Little Dorrit's Story *'88*
The Hound of the Baskervilles *'77*
The Moon-Spinners *'64*
Tom Jones *'63*
Mysterious Island *'61*
Stage Struck *'57*
Moonfleet *'55*
The Detective *'54*
The Importance of Being Earnest *'52*
The Man in the White Suit *'51*
Mr. Peek-A-Boo *'50*
Kind Hearts and Coronets *'49*
The October Man *'48*
Whiskey Galore *'48*
Frenzy *'46*
A Girl in a Million *'46*
He Found a Star *'41*

Dabbs Greer (1917-2007)
Sundown: The Vampire in Retreat *'08*
The Green Mile *'99*
Little Giants *'94*
Pacific Heights *'90*
Two Moon Junction *'88*
The Cheyenne Social Club *'70*
Shenandoah *'65*
Roustabout *'64*
Cash McCall *'60*
The Day of the Outlaw *'59*
It! The Terror from Beyond Space *'58*
Invasion of the Body Snatchers *'56*
An Annapolis Story *'55*
Private Hell 36 *'54*
Rose Marie *'54*
Above and Beyond *'53*
Trouble along the Way *'53*

Jane Greer (1924-2001)
Immediate Family *'89*
Just Between Friends *'86*
Against All Odds *'84*
Billie *'65*
Where Love Has Gone *'64*
Man of a Thousand Faces *'57*
Clown *'53*
Prisoner of Zenda *'52*
Big Steal *'49*
Station West *'48*
Out of the Past *'47*
Sinbad, the Sailor *'47*
They Won't Believe Me *'47*
The Bamboo Blonde *'46*
Dick Tracy, Detective *'45*
George White's Scandals *'45*

Judy Greer (1971-)
Marmaduke *'10*
Love Happens *'09*
Maneater *'09*
27 Dresses *'08*
American Dreamz *'06*
The Great New Wonderful *'06*
The TV Set *'06*
Elizabethtown *'05*
Cursed *'04*
13 Going on 30 *'04*
The Village *'04*
I Love Your Work *'03*
Adaptation *'02*
The Wedding Planner *'01*
The Specials *'00*
What Planet Are You From? *'00*
What Women Want *'00*
Sunset Strip *'99*
Three Kings *'99*
Jawbreaker *'98*
Kissing a Fool *'98*

Michael Greer (1943-2002)
Messiah of Evil *'74*
Fortune and Men's Eyes *'71*

Bradley Gregg (1966-)
Eye of the Storm *'91*
Class of 1999 *'90*
Madhouse *'90*

Clark Gregg (1964-)
Iron Man 2 *'10*
(500) Days of Summer *'09*
Choke *'08*
Iron Man *'08*
Hoot *'06*
In the Land of Women *'06*
When a Stranger Calls *'06*
In Enemy Hands *'04*
In Good Company *'04*
Spartan *'04*
11:14 *'03*
Lovely & Amazing *'02*
We Were Soldiers *'02*
The Adventures of Sebastian Cole *'99*
Tyson *'95*
I Love Trouble *'94*
Lana in Love *'92*

Everley Gregg (1903-59)
A Stolen Face *'52*
The Woman in Question *'50*
Brief Encounter *'46*
Great Expectations *'46*
Pygmalion *'38*
The Ghost Goes West *'36*
The Private Life of Henry VIII *'33*

John Gregg (1940-)
To End All Wars *'01*
Ebbtide *'94*
Trouble in Paradise *'88*
Heatwave *'83*

Julie Gregg (1944-)
The Seekers *'79*
From Hell to Borneo *'64*

Virginia Gregg (1916-86)
No Way Back *'74*
Walk in the Spring Rain *'70*
Columbo: Prescription Murder *'67*
Spencer's Mountain *'63*
Psycho *'60 (V)*
The Hanging Tree *'59*
Operation Petticoat *'59*
D.I. *'57*
Portland Expose *'57*
Love Is a Many-Splendored Thing *'55*
The Amazing Mr. X *'48*

Ezio Greggio (1954-)
2001: A Space Travesty *'00*
Screw Loose *'99*
Silence of the Hams *'93*

Pascal Greggory (1954-)
La Vie en Rose *'07*
The Page Turner *'06*
Gabrielle *'05*
La Vie Promise *'02*
Confusion of Genders *'00*
The Messenger: The Story of Joan of Arc *'99*
Time Regained *'99*
Those Who Love Me Can Take the Train *'98*
Queen Margot *'94*
Pauline at the Beach *'83*
Le Beau Mariage *'82*

Rose Gregorio (1932-)
Maze *'01*
Tarantella *'95*
City of Hope *'91*
Five Corners *'88*
The Last Innocent Man *'87*
Desperate Characters *'71*
The Swimmer *'68*

Andre Gregory (1934-)
Goodbye, Lover *'99*
Celebrity *'98*
Last Summer In the Hamptons *'96*
The Shadow *'94*
Vanya on 42nd Street *'94*
The Linguini Incident *'92*
The Bonfire of the Vanities *'90*
The Last Temptation of Christ *'88*
Some Girls *'88*
Street Smart *'87*
The Mosquito Coast *'86*
Always *'85*
Follies in Concert *'85*
Protocol *'84*
Author! Author! *'82*
My Dinner with Andre *'81*

Celia Gregory (1952-)
Children of the Full Moon *'84*
Agatha *'79*

Dorian Gregory (1971-)
Getting Played *'05*
Deliver Us from Eva *'03*

James Gregory (1911-2002)
Wait Till Your Mother Gets Home *'83*
Great American Traffic Jam *'80*
The Bastard *'78*
The Strongest Man in the World *'75*
Shoot Out *'71*
Beneath the Planet of the Apes *'70*
The Love God? *'70*
The Ambushers *'67*
Clambake *'67*
Murderers' Row *'66*
The Silencers *'66*
Sons of Katie Elder *'65*
A Distant Trumpet *'64*
Captain Newman, M.D. *'63*
PT 109 *'63*
The Manchurian Candidate *'62*
Two Weeks in Another Town *'62*
Gun Glory *'57*
Nightfall *'56*

Leo Gregory (1978-)
Green Street Hooligans *'05*
Stoned *'05*
Pulse *'03*

Mark Gregory (1965-)
War Bus Commando *'89*
Thunder Warrior 3 *'88*
Escape from the Bronx *'85*
Thunder Warrior *'85*
Thunder Warrior 2 *'85*

Mary Gregory
Coming Home *'78*
Sleeper *'73*
Lassie: Well of Love *'70*

Michael Gregory (1944-)
Retribution Road *'07*
Spider's Web *'01*
Zero Tolerance *'93*

Natalie Gregory (1975-)
Oliver & Company *'88 (V)*
Alice in Wonderland *'85*

Nick Gregory
Last Summer In the Hamptons *'96*
Happy Hell Night *'92*

Sebastian Gregory
See Anthony (Tony) Vorno

Thea Gregory (1929-)
Paid to Kill *'54*
Profile *'54*

Joan Gregson
Grindstone Road *'07*
Sea People *'00*

John Gregson (1919-75)
Fright *'71*
Hans Brinker *'69*
Night of the Generals *'67*
The Frightened City *'61*
The Captain's Table *'60*
S.O.S. Pacific *'60*
Sea of Sand *'58*
Above Us the Waves *'56*
Three Cases of Murder *'55*
Angels One Five *'54*
Genevieve *'53*
The Lavender Hill Mob *'51*

Stephen Greif (1944-)
Casanova *'05*
The Dying Truth *'86*
The Great Riviera Bank Robbery *'79*

Robert Greig (1879-1958)
Sullivan's Travels *'41*
Devil Doll *'36*
The Great Ziegfeld *'36*
Trouble in Paradise *'32*
Tonight or Never *'31*
Animal Crackers *'30*

Kim Greist (1958-)
Zoe *'01*
Homeward Bound 2: Lost in San Francisco *'96*
Last Exit to Earth *'96*
Houseguest *'94*
Roswell: The U.F.O. Cover-Up *'94*
Homeward Bound: The Incredible Journey *'93*
Duplicates *'92*
Payoff *'91*
Why Me? *'90*
Punchline *'88*
Throw Momma from the Train *'87*
Manhunter *'86*
Brazil *'85*
C.H.U.D. *'84*

Joyce Grenfell (1910-79)
The Americanization of Emily *'64*
The Pure Hell of St. Trinian's *'61*
Blue Murder at St. Trinian's *'56*
The Belles of St. Trinian's *'53*
Genevieve *'53*
The Happiest Days of Your Life *'50*

Adrian Grenier (1976-)
Adventures of Power *'08*
Tony n' Tina's Wedding *'07*
The Devil Wears Prada *'06*
Anything Else *'03*
Hart's War *'02*
Love in the Time of Money *'02*
A. I.: Artificial Intelligence *'01*
Harvard Man *'01*
Cecil B. Demented *'00*
The Adventures of Sebastian Cole *'99*
Drive Me Crazy *'99*

Zach Grenier (1954-)
Zodiac *'07*
Pulse *'06*
Rescue Dawn *'06*
Swordfish *'01*
Chasing Sleep *'00*
Shaft *'00*
Ride with the Devil *'99*
Donnie Brasco *'96*
Maximum Risk *'96*
Twister *'96*

Macha Grenon (1968-)
The Secret *'07*
Familia *'05*
Cafe Ole *'00*
Jack Higgins' The Windsor Protocol *'97*
Sworn Enemies *'96*
Legends of the North *'95*
The Pianist *'91*

Googy Gress
The Morgue *'07*
Bloodhounds of Broadway *'89*
Promised Land *'88*
Vibes *'88*
Babes in Toyland *'86*
First Turn On *'83*

Joel Gretsch (1963-)
National Treasure: Book of Secrets *'07*
Glass House: The Good Mother *'06*
The Emperor's Club *'02*
Taken *'02*
The Legend of Bagger Vance *'00*

Laurent Grevill (1961-)
I've Loved You So Long *'08*
Look at Me *'04*
I Can't Sleep *'93*
Camille Claudel *'89*

Kevin Grevioux
Underworld: Rise of the Lycans *'09*
Slayer *'06*

Denise Grey (1896-1996)
La Boum *'81*
Sputnik *'61*
Carve Her Name with Pride *'58*
Devil in the Flesh *'46*

Jennifer Grey (1960-)
Keith *'08*
Bounce *'00*
Outrage *'98*
Red Meat *'98*
Since You've Been Gone *'97*
Lover's Knot *'96*
Portraits of a Killer *'95*
Eyes of a Witness *'94*
A Case for Murder *'93*
Wind *'92*
Criminal Justice *'90*
Stroke of Midnight *'90*
Bloodhounds of Broadway *'89*
Light Years *'88 (V)*
Dirty Dancing *'87*
Ferris Bueller's Day Off *'86*
American Flyers *'85*
The Cotton Club *'84*
Reckless *'84*
Red Dawn *'84*

Joel Grey (1932-)
A Christmas Carol *'99*
Dancer in the Dark *'99*
The Empty Mirror *'99*
The Dangerous *'95*
The Fantasticks *'95*
The Music of Chance *'93*
The Player *'92*
Kafka *'91*
Queenie *'87*
Remo Williams: The Adventure Begins *'85*
Buffalo Bill & the Indians *'76*
The Seven-Per-Cent Solution *'76*
Cabaret *'72*
Man on a String *'71*
Come September *'61*

Nan Grey (1918-93)
The House of the Seven Gables *'40*
The Invisible Man Returns *'40*
Three Smart Girls Grow Up *'39*
The Tower of London *'39*
The Black Doll *'38*
Danger on the Air *'38*
The Jury's Secret *'38*
Dracula's Daughter *'36*
Three Smart Girls *'36*

Shirley Grey (1902-81)
Circumstantial Evidence *'35*
The Mystery of the Mary Celeste *'35*
Bombay Mail *'34*
Green Eyes *'34*
His Greatest Gamble *'34*
The Little Giant *'33*
Treason *'33*
Cornered *'32*
Drifting Souls *'32*
Get That Girl *'32*
Hurricane Express *'32*
The Riding Tornado *'32*
Texas Cyclone *'32*
Uptown New York *'32*

Virginia Grey (1917-2004)
Bachelor in Paradise *'69*
Madame X *'66*
Love Has Many Faces *'65*
Naked Kiss *'64*
Portrait in Black *'60*
Crime of Passion *'57*
All That Heaven Allows *'55*
The Last Command *'55*
The Rose Tattoo *'55*
Slaughter Trail *'51*
Bullfighter & the Lady *'50*
Three Desperate Men *'50*
Threat *'49*
Mexican Hayride *'48*
Unknown Island *'48*
Who Killed Doc Robbin? *'48*
Unconquered *'47*
House of Horrors *'46*
Swamp Fire *'46*
Idaho *'43*
Sweet Rosie O'Grady *'43*
Bells of Capistrano *'42*
Grand Central Murder *'42*
Tarzan's New York Adventure *'42*
Big Store *'41*
Whistling in the Dark *'41*
Another Thin Man *'39*
Broadway Serenade *'39*
The Michigan Kid *'28*
Uncle Tom's Cabin *'27*

Zena Grey (1988-)
The Shaggy Dog *'06*
In Good Company *'04*
Max Keeble's Big Move *'01*
Summer Catch *'01*

Michael Greyeyes (1967-)
The New World *'05*
Sunshine State *'02*
ZigZag *'02*
The Lost Child *'00*
Skipped Parts *'00*
The Magnificent Seven *'98*
The Minion *'98*
Smoke Signals *'98*
Firestorm *'97*
True Women *'97*
Crazy Horse *'96*
Dance Me Outside *'95*
Geronimo *'93*

Clinton Greyn (1936-)
The Love Machine *'71*
Raid on Rommel *'71*

Bill Gribble
Dogs of Hell *'83*
The Wild and the Free *'80*

Eddie Gribbon (1890-1965)
The Phantom Rider *'36*
Rio Rattler *'35*
Dames Ahoy *'30*

Harry Gribbon (1885-1961)
Ride Him, Cowboy *'32*
The Cameraman *'28*
The Tomboy *'24*

Richard Grieco (1965-)
Forget About It *'06*
Webs *'03*
Final Payback *'99*
Harold Robbins' Body Parts *'99*
Against the Law *'98*
The Apostate *'98*
Blackheart *'98*
Heaven or Vegas *'98*
A Night at the Roxbury *'98*
Mutual Needs *'97*
When Time Expires *'97*
Inhumanoid *'96*
The Demolitionist *'95*
Rebel Run *'94*
Sin and Redemption *'94*
Suspicious Agenda *'94*
A Vow to Kill *'94*
Born to Run *'93*

Tomcat: Dangerous Desires '93
If Looks Could Kill '91
Mobsters '91

Helmut Griem (1932-2004)

Escape '90
La Passante '83
Malou '83
Les Rendez-vous D'Anna '78
The Desert of the Tartars '76
Voyage of the Damned '76
Children of Rage '75
Cabaret '72
Ludwig '72
McKenzie Break '70
The Damned '69

David Alan Grier (1955-)

Dance Flick '09
The Poker House '09
Gym Teacher: The Movie '08
Bewitched '05
The Muppets' Wizard of Oz '05
The Woodsman '04
Baadasssss! '03
King of Texas '02
15 Minutes '01
The Adventures of Rocky & Bullwinkle '00
Angels in the Infield '00
Return to Me '00
Three Strikes '00
Freeway 2: Confessions of a Trickbaby '99
A Saintly Switch '99
The '60s '99
Stuart Little '99 (V)
McHale's Navy '97
Top of the World '97
Jumanji '95
Tales from the Hood '95
Blankman '94
In the Army Now '94
Boomerang '92
The Player '92
Almost an Angel '90
Loose Cannons '90
I'm Gonna Git You Sucka '88
Off Limits '87
Beer '85
A Soldier's Story '84

Pam Grier (1949-)

Back in the Day '05
The Adventures of Pluto Nash '02
Anne Rice's The Feast of All Saints '01
Bones '01
John Carpenter's Ghosts of Mars '01
Love the Hard Way '01
3 A.M. '01
Snow Day '00
Wilder '00
Fortress 2: Re-Entry '99
Holy Smoke '99
In Too Deep '99
No Tomorrow '99
Jawbreaker '98
Jackie Brown '97
Strip Search '97
Woo '97
Escape from L.A. '96
Mars Attacks! '96
Original Gangstas '96
Serial Killer '95
Posse '93
Bill & Ted's Bogus Journey '91
Class of 1999 '90
The Package '89
Above the Law '88
On the Edge '86
Badge of the Assassin '85
Stand Alone '85
The Vindicator '85
Something Wicked This Way Comes '83
Tough Enough '83
Fort Apache, the Bronx '81
Greased Lightning '77
Drum '76
Bucktown '75
Friday Foster '75
Sheba, Baby '75
Foxy Brown '74
The Arena '73
Coffy '73
Scream Blacula Scream '73
The Big Bird Cage '72
Twilight People '72
The Big Doll House '71
Beyond the Valley of the Dolls '70

Roosevelt "Rosie" Grier (1932-)

Sophisticated Gents '81
The Seekers '79
The Glove '78
The Big Push '75
The Treasure of Jamaica Reef '74
The Thing with Two Heads '72
Black Brigade '69
The Desperate Mission '60

Jon(athan) Gries (1957-)

Crazy on the Outside '10
Taken '08
The Astronaut Farmer '07
The Comebacks '07
Frank '07
September Dawn '07
Car Babes '06
The Sasquatch Gang '06
Stick It '06
The Big Empty '04
Napoleon Dynamite '04
Northfork '03
The Rundown '03
The Snow Walker '03
Jackpot '01
Twin Falls Idaho '99
Casualties '97
Fever '91
Rainbow Drive '90
Kill Me Again '89
Pucker Up and Bark Like a Dog '89
Fright Night 2 '88
Number One with a Bullet '87
Real Genius '85
Joy Sticks '83
More American Graffiti '79
Swap Meet '79
Will Penny '67

John Griesemer (1947-)

Henry Hill '00
Where the Rivers Flow North '94

Joe Grifasi (1944-)

13 Going on 30 '04
Bought and Sold '03
61* '01
Looking for an Echo '99
The Naked Man '98
One Fine Day '96
Sunday '96
Two Bits '96
Batman Forever '95
Money Train '95
Heavy '94
Natural Born Killers '94
Benny & Joon '93
Household Saints '93
City of Hope '91
The Feud '90
Presumed Innocent '90
Chances Are '89
Perfect Witness '89
Ironweed '87
Matewan '87
F/X '86
Bad Medicine '85
Brewster's Millions '85
The Pope of Greenwich Village '84
Still of the Night '82
Gentleman Bandit '81
On the Yard '79
The Deer Hunter '78

Simone Griffeth (1955-)

The Patriot '86
Hot Target '85
Delusion '80
Death Race 2000 '75
Sixteen '72

Ethel Griffies (1878-1975)

The Birds '63
Castle in the Desert '42
Dead Men Tell '41
The Mystery of Edwin Drood '35

Eddie Griffin (1968-)

Beethoven's Big Break '08
Norbit '07
Redline '07
Urban Justice '07
Date Movie '06
Deuce Bigalow: European Gigolo '05
Irish Jam '05
The Wendell Baker Story '05
Who Made the Potatoe Salad? '05
Blast '04
My Baby's Daddy '04
Scary Movie 3 '03
John Q '02
The New Guy '02
Pinocchio '02 (V)
Undercover Brother '02
Double Take '01
Deuce Bigalow: Male Gigolo '99
Foolish '99
The Mod Squad '99
Picking Up the Pieces '99
The Walking Dead '94
The Last Boy Scout '91

Josephine Griffin (1928-)

The Spanish Gardener '57
Postmark for Danger '56
The Man Who Never Was '55

Kathy Griffin (1960-)

Shrek Forever After '10 (V)
Bachelor Party Vegas '05
Dirty Love '05
Beethoven's 5th '03
On Edge '03
Enemies of Laughter '00
Intern '00
Muppets from Space '99
The Cable Guy '96
It's Pat: The Movie '94
Pulp Fiction '94

Lorie Griffin

Aloha Summer '88
Cheerleader Camp '88

Luke Griffin

Speed Dating '07
St. Patrick: The Irish Legend '00

Lynne Griffin (1952-)

Santa Baby '06
Obsessed '88
Strange Brew '83

Merv Griffin (1925-2007)

Alice in Wonderland '85
The Lonely Guy '84
The Man with Two Brains '83
So This Is Love '53

Nikki Griffin (1978-)

The Fast and the Furious: Tokyo Drift '06
The Dukes of Hazzard '05

Renee Griffin (1968-)

Death Match '94
Number One Fan '94

Rhonda Griffin

The Creeps '97
Hideous '97

Robert E. (Bob) Griffin (1902-60)

Monster from Green Hell '58
Crime of Passion '57
I Was a Teenage Werewolf '57

Tim Griffin (1969-)

The Bourne Supremacy '04
Lover Girl '97

Tony Griffin (1959-)

Robin Hood: Men in Tights '93
Evil Laugh '86

Andy Griffith (1926-)

Waitress '07
Daddy & Them '99
Spy Hard '96
Return to Mayberry '85
Rustler's Rhapsody '85
Fatal Vision '84
Murder in Coweta County '83
Murder in Texas '81
From Here to Eternity '79
Centennial '78
Deadly Game '77
Hearts of the West '75
Savages '75
Pray for the Wildcats '74
Winter Kill '74
No Time for Sergeants '58
A Face in the Crowd '57

Anthony Griffith

Masters of Horror: Deer Woman '05
Panther '95
Tales from the Hood '95

Charles B. Griffith (1930-2007)

Hollywood Boulevard '76
Atlas '60
It Conquered the World '56

Corinne Griffith (1894-1979)

The Divine Lady '29
The Garden of Eden '28

Eva Griffith (1962-)

Ride a Wild Pony '75
The Turn of the Screw '74

Gordon Griffith (1907-58)

Outlaws of the Range '36
Little Annie Rooney '25

Hugh Griffith (1912-80)

The Big Scam '79
Legend of the Werewolf '75
The Passover Plot '75
Craze '74
Luther '74
Diary of Forbidden Dreams '73
The Final Programme '73
Doctor Phibes Rises Again '72
The Abominable Dr. Phibes '71
The Canterbury Tales '71
Who Slew Auntie Roo? '71
Cry of the Banshee '70
Start the Revolution without Me '70
Wuthering Heights '70
The Fixer '68
Oliver! '68
Oh Dad, Poor Dad (Momma's Hung You in the Closet & I'm Feeling So Sad) '67
How to Steal a Million '66
Term of Trial '63
Tom Jones '63
The Counterfeit Traitor '62
Mutiny on the Bounty '62
Exodus '60
Ben-Hur '59
Lucky Jim '58
Beggar's Opera '54
The Sleeping Tiger '54
Kind Hearts and Coronets '49
The Last Days of Dolwyn '49

James J. Griffith (1916-93)

The Legend of Sleepy Hollow '79
The Amazing Transparent Man '60
Bullwhip '58
Man From God's Country '58
Tribute to a Bad Man '56

Jeff Griffith

The 13th Mission '91
Nam Angels '88

Katherine Griffith

Mid-Channel '20
Pollyanna '20
Discontent '16

Kenneth Griffith (1921-2006)

The Englishman Who Went up a Hill But Came down a Mountain '95
Four Weddings and a Funeral '94
The Final Option '82
Night of the Laughing Dead '75
Revenge '71
The Assassination Bureau '69
Koroshi '67
The Frightened City '61
Circus of Horrors '60
Tiger Bay '59
Lucky Jim '58
A Night to Remember '58
1984 '56

Melanie Griffith (1957-)

The Night We Called It a Day '03
Shade '03
Stuart Little 2 '02 (V)
Tart '01
Along for the Ride '00
Cecil B. Demented '00
Crazy in Alabama '99
RKO 281 '99
Another Day in Paradise '98
Celebrity '98
Shadow of Doubt '98
Lolita '97
Two Much '96
Buffalo Girls '95
Mulholland Falls '95
Now and Then '95
Milk Money '94
Nobody's Fool '94
Born Yesterday '93
Shining Through '92
A Stranger Among Us '92
Paradise '91
The Bonfire of the Vanities '90
In the Spirit '90
Pacific Heights '90
Women & Men: Stories of Seduction '90
Cherry 2000 '88
The Milagro Beanfield War '88
Stormy Monday '88
Working Girl '88
Something Wild '86
Fear City '85
Body Double '84
She's in the Army Now '81
Underground Aces '80
Steel Cowboy '78
Joyride '77
One on One '77
The Drowning Pool '75
Night Moves '75
Smile '75
Harrad Experiment '73

Raymond Griffith (1894-1937)

All Quiet on the Western Front '30
Hands Up '26
The Night Club '25
Paths to Paradise '25
White Tiger '23

Thomas Ian Griffith (1962-)

Timecop 2: The Berlin Decision '03
Black Point '01
Final Encounter '00
Avalanche '99
John Carpenter's Vampires '97
Kull the Conqueror '97
Behind Enemy Lines '96
Hollow Point '95
Beyond Forgiveness '94
Crackerjack '94
Excessive Force '93
Ulterior Motives '92
The Karate Kid: Part 3 '89

Tom Griffith (1945-)

Night Beast '83
The Alien Factor '78

Tracy Griffith (1965-)

Skeeter '93
All Tied Up '92
The Finest Hour '91
Fast Food '89
The First Power '89
Sleepaway Camp 3: Teenage Wasteland '89
The Good Mother '88

Linda Griffiths (1956-)

Reno and the Doc '84
Lianna '83
Overdrawn at the Memory Bank '83

Michael Griffiths

Timeless '96
Living in Oblivion '94

Rachel Griffiths (1968-)

Comanche Moon '08
Step Up '06
Angel Rodriguez '05
After the Deluge '03
Ned Kelly '03
The Hard Word '02
The Rookie '02
Blow '01
Blow Dry '00
Very Annie Mary '00
Me Myself I '99
Among Giants '98
Amy '98
Hilary and Jackie '98
My Best Friend's Wedding '97
My Son the Fanatic '97
Welcome to Woop Woop '97
Jude '96
Children of the Revolution '95
Cosi '95
Muriel's Wedding '94

Richard Griffiths (1947-)

Harry Potter and the Half-Blood Prince '09
Bedtime Stories '08
Ballet Shoes '07
Harry Potter and the Order of the Phoenix '07
The History Boys '06
Venus '06
The Hitchhiker's Guide to the Galaxy '05 (V)
Harry Potter and the Chamber of Secrets '02
Harry Potter and the Sorcerer's Stone '01
Vatel '00
Sleepy Hollow '99
Guarding Tess '94
Blame It on the Bellboy '92
Naked Gun 2 1/2: The Smell of Fear '91
Withnail and I '87
Shanghai Surprise '86
A Private Function '84
Whoops Apocalypse '83

Jeff Griggs (1963-)

Forbidden Games '95
Breaking Point '94
Eden '93
Eden 2 '93
Eden 3 '93
Eden 4 '93

Johanna Grika

Vice Academy 3 '91
Visitants '87

Frank Grillo

The Express '08
iMurders '08
Pride and Glory '08
April's Shower '03

Dan Grimaldi
Chasing the Green *'09*
Joey *'85*
Don't Go in the House *'80*

Eva Grimaldi
Quiet Days in Clichy *'90*
The Black Cobra *'87*

Frank Grimes (1947-)
Catherine Cookson's The Wingless Bird *'97*
The Dive *'89*
Crystalstone *'88*

Gary Grimes (1955-)
Cahill: United States Marshal *'73*
Class of '44 *'73*
Culpepper Cattle Co. *'72*
Summer of '42 *'71*

Scott Grimes (1971-)
Robin Hood *'10*
Who's Your Monkey *'07*
Band of Brothers *'01*
Mystery, Alaska *'99*
Night Life *'90*
Critters 2: The Main Course *'88*
Critters *'86*
It Came Upon a Midnight Clear *'84*

Shenae Grimes
Picture This! *'08*
True Confessions of a Hollywood Starlet *'08*

Tammy Grimes (1934-)
High Art *'98*
A Modern Affair *'94*
Backstreet Justice *'93*
Mr. North *'88*
America *'86*
The Stuff *'85*
No Big Deal *'83*
The Last Unicorn *'82 (V)*
The Runner Stumbles *'79*

Jim Grimshaw
Chill Factor *'99*
Basket Case 3: The Progeny *'92*

Herbert Grimwood (1875-1929)
Romola *'25*
When the Clouds Roll By *'19*

Anouk Grinberg (1963-)
Mon Homme *'96*
A Self-Made Hero *'95*

Nikolai Grinko (1920-89)
Stalker *'79*
Solaris *'72*
Andrei Rublev *'66*

Rupert Grint (1988-)
Harry Potter and the Half-Blood Prince *'09*
Harry Potter and the Order of the Phoenix *'07*
Driving Lessons *'06*
Harry Potter and the Goblet of Fire *'05*
Harry Potter and the Prisoner of Azkaban *'04*
Harry Potter and the Chamber of Secrets *'02*
Harry Potter and the Sorcerer's Stone *'01*

Stephen Grives (1951-)
Scooby-Doo *'02*
Inseminoid *'80*
Flambards *'78*

George Grizzard (1928-2007)
Flags of Our Fathers *'06*
Small Time Crooks *'00*
Scarlett *'94*
Iran: Days of Crisis *'91*
Caroline? *'90*
False Witness *'89*
The Deliberate Stranger *'86*
Embassy *'85*
Bachelor Party *'84*
Wrong Is Right *'82*
Attica *'80*
Oldest Living Graduate *'80*
Seems Like Old Times *'80*
Comes a Horseman *'78*
The Stranger Within *'74*
Pueblo Affair *'73*
Advise and Consent *'62*
From the Terrace *'60*

Charles Grodin (1935-)
The Ex *'07*
My Summer Story *'94*
Beethoven's 2nd *'93*
Dave *'93*
Heart and Souls *'93*
So I Married an Axe Murderer *'93*
Beethoven *'92*
Clifford *'92*
Taking Care of Business *'90*
Midnight Run *'88*
You Can't Hurry Love *'88*
The Couch Trip *'87*
Ishtar *'87*
Grown Ups *'86*
Last Resort *'86*
Movers and Shakers *'85*
The Lonely Guy *'84*
The Woman in Red *'84*
The Great Muppet Caper *'81*
The Incredible Shrinking Woman *'81*
It's My Turn *'80*
Seems Like Old Times *'80*
Real Life *'79*
Sunburn *'79*
The Grass Is Always Greener Over the Septic Tank *'78*
Heaven Can Wait *'78*
Just Me & You *'78*
King Kong *'76*
11 Harrowhouse *'74*
The Heartbreak Kid *'72*
Catch-22 *'70*
Rosemary's Baby *'68*
The Meanest Men in the West *'67*
Sex and the College Girl *'64*

Kathryn Grody (1946-)
Limbo *'99*
Hombres Armados *'97*
The Lemon Sisters *'90*
Quick Change *'90*
Parents *'89*

Harry Groener (1951-)
Manna from Heaven *'02*
Buddy Boy *'99*

Clare Grogan (1962-)
Comfort and Joy *'84*
Gregory's Girl *'80*

David Groh (1941-)
Blowback *'99*
Acts of Betrayal *'98*
Spoiler *'98*
Last Exit to Earth *'96*
White Cargo *'96*
Illegal in Blue *'95*
Broken Vows *'87*
Hot Shot *'86*
Zertigo Diamond Caper *'82*
A Hero Ain't Nothin' but a Sandwich *'78*
Victory at Entebbe *'76*

Ake Gronberg (1914-69)
Sawdust & Tinsel *'53*
Monika *'52*

Herbert Gronemeyer (1956-)
Spring Symphony *'86*
Das Boot *'81*

Sam Groom (1939-)
Deadly Eyes *'82*
Deadly Games *'80*
Run for the Roses *'78*
Beyond the Bermuda Triangle *'75*
Betrayal *'74*
The Baby Maker *'70*

Arye Gross (1960-)
Grey Gardens *'09*
Minority Report *'02*
Burning Down the House *'01*
Big Eden *'00*
Gone in 60 Seconds *'00*
Seven Girlfriends *'00*
Arthur's Quest *'99*
Big City Blues *'99*
In the Company of Spies *'99*
The Prince and the Surfer *'99*
Timelock *'99*
Spoiler *'98*
Tinseltown *'97*
Mother Night *'96*
Hexed *'93*
The Opposite Sex and How to Live With Them *'93*
Boris and Natasha: The Movie *'92*
A Midnight Clear *'92*
Shaking the Tree *'92*
For the Boys *'91*
Coupe de Ville *'90*
A Matter of Degrees *'90*
The Experts *'89*
Tequila Sunrise *'88*
The Couch Trip *'87*
House 2: The Second Story *'87*
Soul Man *'86*

Edan Gross (1978-)
Best of the Best 2 *'93*
And You Thought Your Parents Were Weird! *'91*

Lance Gross
Our Family Wedding *'10*
Tyler Perry's Meet the Browns *'08*

Mary Gross (1953-)
40 Days and 40 Nights *'02*
Jailbait! *'00*
The Santa Clause *'94*
There Goes the Neighborhood *'92*
Troop Beverly Hills *'89*
Big Business *'88*
Casual Sex? *'88*
Feds *'88*
Baby Boom *'87*
The Couch Trip *'87*
Club Paradise *'86*

Michael Gross (1947-)
Mrs. Harris *'05*
Tremors 3: Back to Perfection *'01*
Ground Control *'98*
True Heart *'97*
Kounterfeit *'96*
Sometimes They Come Back... Again *'96*
Tremors 2: Aftershocks *'96*
In the Heat of Passion 2: Unfaithful *'94*
Snowbound: The Jim and Jennifer Stolpa Story *'94*
Firestorm: 72 Hours in Oakland *'93*
Alan & Naomi *'92*
Undesirable *'92*
Cool As Ice *'91*
Midnight Murders *'91*
A Connecticut Yankee in King Arthur's Court *'89*
Tremors *'89*
Big Business *'88*
In the Line of Duty: The FBI Murders *'88*
Summer Fantasy *'84*

Paul Gross (1959-)
The Trojan Horse *'08*
Slings & Arrows: Season 2 *'05*
Men with Brooms *'02*
20,000 Leagues Under the Sea *'97*
Whale Music *'94*
Armistead Maupin's Tales of the City *'93*
Aspen Extreme *'93*
Northern Extremes *'93*
Buffalo Jump *'90*
Cold Comfort *'90*

Sylvester Groth (1958-)
Inglourious Basterds *'09*
My Fuhrer *'07*

Brigitte Grothum (1933-)
Inn on the River *'62*
The Strange Countess *'61*

Logan Grove
Arc *'06*
Christmas Do-Over *'06*

Deborah Grover
Where the Truth Lies *'05*
The Christmas Wife *'88*

Gulshan Grover (1955-)
My Faraway Bride *'06*
Eastside *'99*
Tales of the Kama Sutra 2: Monsoon *'98*
Monsoon *'97*
Rudyard Kipling's the Second Jungle Book: Mowgli and Baloo *'97*

Robin Groves
Silver Bullet *'85*
The Nesting *'80*

Robert Grubb (1950-)
Salem's Lot *'04*
Mad Max: Beyond Thunderdome *'85*
Remember Me *'85*
Gallipoli *'81*
My Brilliant Career *'79*

Gary Grubbs
Deal *'08*
Double Take *'01*
Gone Fishin' *'97*
The Ernest Green Story *'93*
Without Warning: The James Brady Story *'91*
Foxfire *'87*
Fatal Vision *'84*

Franz Gruber
X from Outer Space *'67*
Terror Beneath the Sea *'66*
Deutschland im Jahre Null *'47*

Ioan Gruffudd (1974-)
W. *'08*
Fantastic Four: Rise of the Silver Surfer *'07*
Amazing Grace *'06*
The TV Set *'06*
Fantastic Four *'05*
King Arthur *'04*
This Girl's Life *'03*
The Gathering *'02*
Another Life *'01*
Black Hawk Down *'01*
Horatio Hornblower: The Adventure Continues *'01*
102 Dalmatians *'00*
Shooters *'00*
Very Annie Mary *'00*
Great Expectations *'99*
Horatio Hornblower *'99*
Solomon and Gaenor *'98*
Poldark *'96*

Greg Grunberg (1966-)
Star Trek *'09 (V)*
Mission: Impossible 3 *'06*
The Ladykillers *'04*
The Medicine Show *'01*
Hollow Man *'00*
Dinner and Driving *'97*

Gustav Grundgens (1899-1963)
Liebelei *'32*
M *'31*

Olivier Gruner (1960-)
Interceptor Force 2 *'02*
Extreme Honor *'01*
Crackerjack 3 *'00*
Interceptor Force *'99*
Velocity Trap *'99*
T.N.T. *'98*
Mercenary 2: Thick and Thin *'97*
Mars *'96*
Mercenary *'96*
Savage *'96*
The Fighter *'95*
Automatic *'94*
Nemesis *'93*
Angel Town *'89*

Ilka Gruning (1876-1964)
Desperate *'47*
Casablanca *'42*
Underground *'41*
Joyless Street *'25*

Stefan Gryff (1939-)
One Against the Wind *'91*
Legend of the Werewolf *'75*

Dorka Gryllus
Soul Kitchen *'09*
Irina Palm *'07*

Ah-Leh Gua (1944-)
Fleeing by Night *'00*
Eat Drink Man Woman *'94*
The Wedding Banquet *'93*

Nicky Guadagni
The Golden Spiders: A Nero Wolfe Mystery *'00*
Cube *'98*

Christopher Guard (1953-)
A Woman of Substance *'84*
The Lord of the Rings *'78 (V)*

Dominic Guard (1956-)
Absolution *'81*
Picnic at Hanging Rock *'75*
The Go-Between *'71*

Kit Guard (1894-1961)
El Diablo Rides *'39*
Six Gun Rhythm *'39*
Carnival Lady *'33*
Fighting Champ *'33*

Pippa Guard (1952-)
Scarlett *'94*
All or Nothing at All *'93*
Unsuitable Job for a Woman *'82*

Harry Guardino (1925-95)
Fist of Honor *'92*
The Neon Empire *'89*
Sophisticated Gents *'81*
Any Which Way You Can *'80*
Goldengirl *'79*
Matilda *'78*
Rollercoaster *'77*
The Enforcer *'76*
St. Ives *'76*
Whiffs *'75*
Get Christie Love! *'74*
They Only Kill Their Masters *'72*
Dirty Harry *'71*
Octaman *'71*
Lovers and Other Strangers *'70*
Madigan *'68*
The Adventures of Bullwhip Griffin *'66*
Hell Is for Heroes *'62*
The Five Pennies *'59*
Pork Chop Hill *'59*
Houseboat *'58*

Justin Guarini (1978-)
Fast Girl *'07*
From Justin to Kelly *'03*

Vincent Guastaferro
Liberty Heights *'99*
Sweet and Lowdown *'99*
Nitti: The Enforcer *'88*

Irina Gubanova (1940-)
Private Life *'82*
War and Peace *'68*

Matthew Grey Gubler
Alvin and the Chipmunks: The Squeakuel *'09 (V)*
(500) Days of Summer *'09*
Alvin and the Chipmunks *'07 (V)*

Florence Guerin (1965-)
Bizarre *'87*
Black Venus *'83*

Blanca Guerra (1953-)
In the Middle of Nowhere *'93*
Danzon *'91*
Santa Sangre *'90*
Erendira *'83*

Alvaro Guerrero
Amores Perros *'00*
In the Country Where Nothing Happens *'99*

Evelyn Guerrero (1949-)
Cheech and Chong: Things Are Tough All Over *'82*
Cheech and Chong's Nice Dreams *'81*
Cheech and Chong's Next Movie *'80*
The Toolbox Murders *'78*

Franco Guerrero
Deathfight *'93*
The Kick Fighter *'91*
Warriors of the Apocalypse *'85*
American Commandos *'84*
One Armed Executioner *'80*

Monica Guerritore (1958-)
The Endless Game *'89*
Together? *'79*

Fausto Guerzoni (1904-)
Black Orpheus *'58*
The Bicycle Thief *'48*

Christopher Guest (1948-)
The Invention of Lying *'09*
Night at the Museum: Battle of the Smithsonian *'09*
For Your Consideration *'06*
Mrs. Henderson Presents *'05*
A Mighty Wind *'03*
Best in Show *'00*
Small Soldiers *'98 (V)*
Waiting for Guffman *'96*
A Few Good Men *'92*
The Return of Spinal Tap *'92*
Sticky Fingers *'88*
The Princess Bride *'87*
Beyond Therapy *'86*
Little Shop of Horrors *'86*
This Is Spinal Tap *'84*
A Piano for Mrs. Cimino *'82*
Heartbeeps *'81*
The Last Word *'80*
The Long Riders *'80*
Blind Ambition *'79*
Girlfriends *'78*
Shame of the Jungle *'75 (V)*

Cornelia Guest
Gardens of the Night *'08*
Second Sight *'89*

Lance Guest (1960-)
Flu Birds *'08*
Mach 2 *'00*
Plan B *'97*
The Wizard of Loneliness *'88*
Jaws: The Revenge *'87*
My Father, My Rival *'85*
Just the Way You Are *'84*
The Last Starfighter *'84*
Roommate *'84*
I Ought to Be in Pictures *'82*
Halloween 2: The Nightmare Isn't Over! *'81*

Nicholas Guest (1955-)
Nemesis 4: Cry of Angels *'97*
Night Hunter *'95*
Kickboxer 4: The Aggressor *'94*
Puppet Master 5: The Final Chapter *'94*
Brain Smasher... A Love Story *'93*

My Daughter's Keeper '93
Nemesis '93
Chrome Soldiers '92
Forever: A Ghost of a Love Story '92
Grand Tour: Disaster in Time '92
Dollman '90
Assassin '89
National Lampoon's Christmas Vacation '89
Strange Case of Dr. Jekyll & Mr. Hyde '89
Criminal Act '88
Trading Places '83
The Long Riders '80

Makhouredia Gueye

Xala '75
Mandabi '68

Carla Gugino (1971-)

Race to Witch Mountain '09
The Unborn '09
Watchmen '09
Women in Trouble '09
Righteous Kill '08
American Gangster '07
The Lookout '07
Rise: Blood Hunter '07
Even Money '06
Night at the Museum '06
Sin City '05
The Singing Detective '03
Spy Kids 3-D: Game Over '03
Spy Kids 2: The Island of Lost Dreams '02
The Center of the World '01
The Jimmy Show '01
The One '01
She Creature '01
Spy Kids '01
A Season for Miracles '99
Judas Kiss '98
Snake Eyes '98
Lovelife '97
Homeward Bound 2: Lost in San Francisco '96 (V)
Jaded '96
The War at Home '96
Wedding Bell Blues '96
The Buccaneers '95
Miami Rhapsody '95
Red Hot '95
Son-in-Law '93
This Boy's Life '93
Murder Without Motive '92

Noel Guglielmi

Red Sands '09
Splinter '06
Harsh Times '05

Wandisa Guida (1937-)

Gladiator of Rome '63
I, Vampiri '56

Giovanni Guidelli (1966-)

Fiorile '93
Where Angels Fear to Tread '91

Anthony Guidera

L.A. Dicks '05
Red Shoe Diaries 7: Burning Up '96
Undercover '94

Darrel Guilbeau (1962-)

Murder-in-Law '92
Lauderdale '89

Ann Guilbert (1928-)

Sour Grapes '98
Grumpier Old Men '95

Nancy Guild (1925-99)

Francis Covers the Big Town '53
Abbott and Costello Meet the Invisible Man '51
Black Magic '49
Somewhere in the Night '46

Paul Guilfoyle (1902-61)

Apache '54
Actors and Sin '52
Follow Me Quietly '49
The Judge '49
The Millerson Case '47
The Missing Corpse '45
It Happened Tomorrow '44
The Seventh Cross '44
The Saint Takes Over '40
Law of the Underworld '38
The Crime of Dr. Crespi '35

Paul Guilfoyle (1955-)

Live from Baghdad '03
Session 9 '01
Anywhere But Here '99
Entropy '99
Random Hearts '99
In Dreams '98
The Negotiator '98
One Tough Cop '98
Primary Colors '98
Air Force One '97
Amistad '97
Cafe Society '97
L.A. Confidential '97
Path to Paradise '97
Celtic Pride '96
Extreme Measures '96
Looking for Richard '96
Manny & Lo '96
Night Falls on Manhattan '96
Ransom '96
Striptease '96
A Couch in New York '95
Heaven's Prisoners '95
Amelia Earhart: The Final Flight '94
Gospa '94
Little Odessa '94
Mother's Boys '94
Fallen Angels 2 '93
Mrs. Doubtfire '93
The Night We Never Met '93
Class of '61 '92
Dead Ahead: The Exxon Valdez Disaster '92
Final Analysis '92
Hoffa '92
True Colors '91
Cadillac Man '90
Curiosity Kills '90
Dealers '89
Beverly Hills Cop 2 '87
The Serpent and the Rainbow '87
Three Men and a Baby '87
Wall Street '87
Billy Galvin '86
Howard the Duck '86

Robert Guillaume (1937-)

The Lion King 1 1/2 '04 (V)
Big Fish '03
Silicon Towers '99
His Bodyguard '98
The Lion King: Simba's Pride '98 (V)
First Kid '96
Pandora's Clock '96
Panic in the Skies '96
Run for the Dream: The Gail Devers Story '96
A Good Day to Die '95
Cosmic Slop '94
The Lion King '94 (V)
The Meteor Man '93
Mastergate '92
The Penthouse '92
You Must Remember This '92
Death Warrant '90
Fire and Rain '89
Lean on Me '89
They Still Call Me Bruce '86
Wanted Dead or Alive '86
North and South Book 1 '85
The Kid with the 200 I.Q. '83
Prince Jack '83
The Kid with the Broken Halo '82
Seems Like Old Times '80
The Kid from Left Field '79
Superfly T.N.T. '73

Sophie Guillemin (1977-)

He Loves Me ... He Loves Me Not '02
With a Friend Like Harry '00
L'Ennui '98

Fernando Guillen (1932-)

Mouth to Mouth '95
Why Do They Call It Love When They Mean Sex? '92
Women on the Verge of a Nervous Breakdown '88

Sienna Guillory (1975-)

Inkheart '09
Eragon '06
Resident Evil: Apocalypse '04
Sorted '04
Helen of Troy '03
Love Actually '03
The Time Machine '02

Francis Guinan

Hannibal '01
Guinevere '99
Lansky '99
Shining Through '92

Tim Guinee (1962-)

Cyrus '10
Iron Man 2 '10
The Private Lives of Pippa Lee '09
Fragments '08
Iron Man '08
Stargate: The Ark of Truth '08
Broken English '07
Sweet Land '05
A Hole in One '04
Ladder 49 '04
Impostor '02
Personal Velocity: Three Portraits '02
The Road from Coorain '02
The Young Girl and the Monsoon '99
Blade '98
John Carpenter's Vampires '97
The Three Lives of Karen '97
Beavis and Butt-Head Do America '96 (V)
Courage Under Fire '96
Lily Dale '96
Sudden Manhattan '96
Black Day Blue Night '95
Follow the River '95
How to Make an American Quilt '95
The Pompatus of Love '95
Breathing Lessons '94
Men of War '94
Chain of Desire '93
The Night We Never Met '93
Once Around '91
American Blue Note '89
Tai-Pan '86

Rick Guinn

Mountain Charlie '80
Buffalo Rider '78

Alec Guinness (1914-2000)

Mute Witness '95
A Foreign Field '93
Kafka '91
Monsignor Quixote '91
A Handful of Dust '88
Little Dorrit, Film 1: Nobody's Fault '88
Little Dorrit, Film 2: Little Dorrit's Story '88
Edwin '84
A Passage to India '84
Lovesick '83
Return of the Jedi '83 (V)
Smiley's People '82
The Empire Strikes Back '80
Little Lord Fauntleroy '80
Raise the Titanic '80
Tinker, Tailor, Soldier, Spy '80
Star Wars '77
Murder by Death '76
Brother Sun, Sister Moon '73
Hitler: The Last Ten Days '73
Cromwell '70
Scrooge '70
The Comedians '67
Hotel Paradiso '66
The Quiller Memorandum '66
Doctor Zhivago '65
The Fall of the Roman Empire '64
Damn the Defiant '62
Lawrence of Arabia '62
Tunes of Glory '60
Our Man in Havana '59
The Horse's Mouth '58
The Bridge on the River Kwai '57
A Majority of One '56
The Swan '56
The Ladykillers '55
The Prisoner '55
To Paris with Love '55
The Detective '54
Captain's Paradise '53
Malta Story '53
The Promoter '52
The Lavender Hill Mob '51
The Man in the White Suit '51
Last Holiday '50
Kind Hearts and Coronets '49
Oliver Twist '48
Great Expectations '46

Julien Guiomar (1928-)

Leolo '92
My New Partner '84
Swashbuckler '84
A Very Curious Girl '69
The Thief of Paris '67
The King of Hearts '66

Tom Guiry (1981-)

Yonkers Joe '08
Black Irish '07
Prisoner '07
Steel City '06
The Mudge Boy '03
Mystic River '03
Scotland, PA '02
Black Hawk Down '01
Tigerland '00
U-571 '00
Ride with the Devil '99
All I Wanna Do '98
Wrestling with Alligators '98
Lassie '94
The Sandlot '93

Henri Guisol (1904-94)

Murder at 45 R.P.M. '65
The Twilight Girls '57
Bizarre Bizarre '39
The Crime of Monsieur Lange '36

Tito Guizar (1908-99)

On the Old Spanish Trail '47
Blondie Goes Latin '42
The Gay Ranchero '42

Clu Gulager (1928-)

Feast 2: Sloppy Seconds '08
Feast '06
Gunfighter '98
Eddie Presley '92
The Killing Device '92
My Heroes Have Always Been Cowboys '91
Tapeheads '89
I'm Gonna Git You Sucka '88
Teen Vamp '88
The Uninvited '88
The Hidden '87
Hunter's Blood '87
The Offspring '87
Into the Night '85
A Nightmare on Elm Street 2: Freddy's Revenge '85
Return of the Living Dead '85
Chattanooga Choo Choo '84
The Initiation '84
Kenny Rogers as the Gambler, Part 2: The Adventure Continues '83
Lies '83
Living Proof: The Hank Williams Jr. Story '83
Kenny Rogers as the Gambler '80
Touched by Love '80
Force of One '79
Willa '79
He Who Walks Alone '78
A Question of Love '78
Snowblind '78
The Other Side of Midnight '77
Wonderland Cove '75
Hit Lady '74
McQ '74
Smile, Jenny, You're Dead '74
The Glass House '72
The Last Picture Show '71
Winning '69
And Now Miguel '66
The Killers '64

Sean Gullette (1968-)

Happy Accidents '00
Requiem for a Dream '00
Pi '98

Dorothy Gulliver (1908-97)

Faces '68
Fighting Caballero '35
The Fighting Marshal '32
Outlaw Justice '32
Shadow of the Eagle '32
The Galloping Ghost '31
Under Montana Skies '30

Leo Gullotta (1946-)

Men Men Men '95
La Scorta '94
Sinbad of the Seven Seas '89

David Gulpilil (1954-)

Australia '08
The Proposition '05
Rabbit-Proof Fence '02
Until the End of the World '91
Dark Age '88
Crocodile Dundee '86
The Last Wave '77
Mad Dog Morgan '76
Walkabout '71

Mamie Gummer

Taking Woodstock '09
The Loss of a Teardrop Diamond '08
Stop-Loss '08
Evening '07

Devon Gummersall (1978-)

Earth vs. the Spider '01
Dick '99
When Trumpets Fade '98
Lured Innocence '97
Trading Favors '97
Independence Day '96
It's My Party '95

Anna Gunn (1968-)

Nobody's Baby '01
Enemy of the State '98
Without Evidence '96

David Gunn (1972-)

The Convent '00
Vampire Journals '96

Janet Gunn (1961-)

Inferno '01
Lost Voyage '01
The Nurse '97
Carnosaur 3: Primal Species '96
Marquis de Sade '96
The Quest '96

Moses Gunn (1929-93)

Memphis '91
Perfect Harmony '91
The Women of Brewster Place '89
The House of Dies Drear '88
Heartbreak Ridge '86
Certain Fury '85
Charlotte Forten's Mission: Experiment in Freedom '85
Killing Floor '85
Firestarter '84
The NeverEnding Story '84
Amityville 2: The Possession '82
Ragtime '81
Aaron Loves Angela '75
Cornbread, Earl & Me '75
Rollerball '75
Amazing Grace '74
The Iceman Cometh '73
Haunts of the Very Rich '72
Shaft's Big Score '72
Shaft '71
Wild Rovers '71
The Great White Hope '70
The Hot Rock '70
Black Brigade '69

Sean Gunn (1974-)

The Specials '00
Stricken '98
Tromeo & Juliet '95

Dan Gunther

Devil's Pond '03
Lewis and Clark and George '97
Denise Calls Up '95

Bob Gunton (1945-)

The Lazarus Project '08
Player 5150 '08
24 : Redemption '08
Dead Silence '07
Fracture '07
Numb '07
Pandemic '07
Believe in Me '06
Boat Trip '03
Dallas 362 '03
61* '01
The Perfect Storm '00
Running Mates '00
Bats '99
Elvis Meets Nixon '98
Patch Adams '98
Buffalo Soldiers '97
Changing Habits '96
The Glimmer Man '96
Ace Ventura: When Nature Calls '95
Broken Arrow '95
In Pursuit of Honor '95
Kingfish: A Story of Huey P. Long '95
Roswell: The U.F.O. Cover-Up '94
The Shawshank Redemption '94
Demolition Man '93
Father Hood '93
Lone Justice '93
Wild Palms '93
Dead Ahead: The Exxon Valdez Disaster '92
Sinatra '92
Mission of the Shark '91
Judgment '90
Cookie '89
Glory '89
Matewan '87
The Pick-Up Artist '87
Static '87
Lois Gibbs and the Love Canal '82
Rollover '81

Neena Gupta

Cotton Mary '99
In Custody '94

Alizia Gur (1942-)

Beast of Morocco '66
From Russia with Love '63

Sigrid Gurie (1911-69)

Enemy of Women '44
Three Faces West '40
The Adventures of Marco Polo '38
Algiers '38

Sharon Gurney (1950-)

Raw Meat '72
Cold Comfort Farm '71
Crucible of Horror '69

Eric Gurry (1966-)

Something Special '86
The Zoo Gang '85
Bad Boys '83

Kick (Christopher) Gurry

Speed Racer '08
Daltry Calhoun '05

Phantom Ranger '38
The Rangers' Roundup '38
Rollin' Plains '38
Songs and Bullets '38
Border Phantom '37
Gun Lords of Stirrup Basin '37
Paroled to Die '37
The Red Rope '37
Sing, Cowboy, Sing '37
Tex Rides with the Boy Scouts '37
Cavalry '36
Lightnin' Bill Carson '36
Stormy Trails '36
The Traitor '36

Sandy Hackett

Ex-Cop '93
Hamburger... The Motion Picture '86

Penne Hackforth-Jones (1943-)

Paradise Road '97
Image of Death '77
Alvin Purple '73

Gene Hackman (1930-)

Welcome to Mooseport '04
Runaway Jury '03
Behind Enemy Lines '01
Heartbreakers '01
Heist '01
The Mexican '01
The Royal Tenenbaums '01
The Replacements '00
Under Suspicion '00
Antz '98 (V)
Enemy of the State '98
Twilight '98
Absolute Power '97
The Chamber '96
Extreme Measures '96
The Birdcage '95
Crimson Tide '95
Get Shorty '95
The Quick and the Dead '95
Wyatt Earp '94
The Firm '93
Geronimo: An American Legend '93
Unforgiven '92
Class Action '91
Company Business '91
Loose Cannons '90
Narrow Margin '90
Postcards from the Edge '90
The Package '89
Another Woman '88
Bat 21 '88
Full Moon in Blue Water '88
Mississippi Burning '88
Split Decisions '88
No Way Out '87
Superman 4: The Quest for Peace '87
Hoosiers '86
Power '86
Target '85
Twice in a Lifetime '85
Misunderstood '84
Uncommon Valor '83
Under Fire '83
All Night Long '81
Eureka! '81
Reds '81
Superman 2 '80
Superman: The Movie '78
A Bridge Too Far '77
The Domino Principle '77
March or Die '77
America at the Movies '76
Bite the Bullet '75
French Connection 2 '75
Night Moves '75
The Conversation '74
Young Frankenstein '74
Zandy's Bride '74
Scarecrow '73
The Poseidon Adventure '72
Prime Cut '72
The French Connection '71
Doctors' Wives '70
I Never Sang for My Father '70
Downhill Racer '69
The Gypsy Moths '69
Marooned '69
Riot '69
Bonnie & Clyde '67
Hawaii '66
Lilith '64

Michiko Hada (1968-)

Flowers of Shanghai '98
Rowing Through '96
The Mystery of Rampo '94

Jonathan Hadary (1948-)

Intolerable Cruelty '03
A Simple Wish '97
Private Parts '96
The New Age '94
As Is '85

Suheil Haddad

The Milky Way '97
Cup Final '92

Ellie Haddington

Lawless Heart '01
The Wyvern Mystery '00

Dayle Haddon (1949-)

Fiesta '95
Cyborg '89
Bedroom Eyes '86
North Dallas Forty '79
The Cheaters '76
Paperback Hero '73
The World's Greatest Athlete '73

Peter Haddon (1898-1962)

Secret of Stamboul '36
The Silent Passenger '35

Ron Haddrick (1929-)

Quigley Down Under '90
Great Expectations: The Untold Story '87
Camel Boy '84 (V)
Dawn! '83

Sara Haden (1897-1981)

The Great Rupert '50
A Life of Her Own '50
Love Laughs at Andy Hardy '46
Mr. Ace '46
She Wolf of London '46
Our Vines Have Tender Grapes '45
She Wouldn't Say Yes '45
Andy Hardy's Double Life '42
Somewhere I'll Find You '42
Andy Hardy Meets Debutante '40
The Shop Around the Corner '40
Andy Hardy Gets Spring Fever '39
The Poor Little Rich Girl '36
Mad Love '35
Magnificent Obsession '35
Anne of Green Gables '34
Spitfire '34
Finishing School '33

Bill Hader (1978-)

Hoodwinked Too! Hood vs. Evil '10 (V)
Adventureland '09
Cloudy with a Chance of Meatballs '09 (V)
Ice Age: Dawn of the Dinosaurs '09 (V)
Night at the Museum: Battle of the Smithsonian '09
Forgetting Sarah Marshall '08
Pineapple Express '08
Tropic Thunder '08
Hot Rod '07
Superbad '07

Reed Hadley (1911-74)

Brain of Blood '71
Kansas Pacific '53
Baron of Arizona '51
The Half-Breed '51
Little Big Horn '51
Motor Patrol '50
Return of Jesse James '50
Riders of the Range '50
I Shot Jesse James '49
Last of the Wild Horses '49
Rimfire '49
Panhandle '48
Return of Wildfire '48
A Southern Yankee '48
Dark Corner '46
Doll Face '46
If I'm Lucky '46
Guadalcanal Diary '43
Whistling in the Dark '41
Ziegfeld Girl '41
The Bank Dick '40
Zorro's Fighting Legion '39
Hollywood Stadium Mystery '38
The Sunset Murder Case '38

Linal Haft

Solo '06
Soft Fruit '99

Marianne Hagan

Rick '03
I Think I Do '97
Halloween 6: The Curse of Michael Myers '95

Molly Hagan (1962-)

The Lucky Ones '08
Miracle in Lane Two '00
Playing Mona Lisa '00
Election '99
Ringmaster '98
French Exit '97
Some Kind of Wonderful '87
Code of Silence '85

Richard Hageman (1882-1966)

The Great Caruso '51
New Orleans '47

Jean Hagen (1923-77)

Alexander: The Other Side of Dawn '77
Dead Ringer '64
Panic in the Year Zero! '62
Sunrise at Campobello '60
The Shaggy Dog '59
The Big Knife '55
Latin Lovers '53
Singin' in the Rain '52
Adam's Rib '50
The Asphalt Jungle '50
A Life of Her Own '50
Side Street '50

Ross Hagen (1938-)

Midnight Tease 2 '95
Bikini Drive-In '94
Dinosaur Island '93
Blood Games '90
Alienator '89
Marked for Murder '89
B.O.R.N. '88
Warlords '88
Commando Squad '87
Phantom Empire '87
Star Slammer '87
Armed Response '86
Avenging Angel '85
Angel '84
Night Creature '79
Fowl Play '75
Bad Charleston Charlie '73
The Deadly and the Beautiful '73
Angels' Wild Women '72
Hellcats '68
Speedway '68

Uta Hagen (1919-2004)

Reversal of Fortune '90
The Boys from Brazil '78
The Other '72

Kristi Hager

Wanted '08
Sure Fire '90

Julie Hagerty (1955-)

Confessions of a Shopaholic '09
She's the Man '06
Just Friends '05
Pizza '05
A Guy Thing '03
The Badge '02
Freddy Got Fingered '01
Storytelling '01
Held Up '00
Jackie's Back '99
The Story of Us '99
Tourist Trap '98
Boys Will Be Boys '97
U-Turn '97
The Wife '95
Noises Off '92
What about Bob? '91
Reversal of Fortune '90
Bloodhounds of Broadway '89
Rude Awakening '89
Necessary Parties '88
Beyond Therapy '86
Bad Medicine '85
Goodbye, New York '85
Lost in America '85
Airplane 2: The Sequel '82
A Midsummer Night's Sex Comedy '82
Airplane! '80
The Day the Women Got Even '80

Michael G. (Mike) Hagerty (1953-)

Rampage: The Hillside Strangler Murders '04
Best Laid Plans '99
Inspector Gadget '99
Speed 2: Cruise Control '97

Merle Haggard (1937-)

Huckleberry Finn '75
Hillbillies in a Haunted House '67

Dan Haggerty (1941-)

Big Stan '07
Grizzly Mountain '97
Abducted 2: The Reunion '94
Cheyenne Warrior '94
The Magic Voyage '93 (V)
Ice Pawn '92
Deadly Diamonds '91
Mind Trap '91
Soldier's Fortune '91
The Inheritor '90
Repo Jake '90
Spirit of the Eagle '90
Chance '89
The Channeler '89
The Chilling '89
Elves '89
Night Wars '88
Abducted '86
The Capture of Grizzly Adams '82
California Gold Rush '81
King of the Mountain '81
Desperate Women '78
Terror Out of the Sky '78
The Adventures of Frontier Fremont '75
Life & Times of Grizzly Adams '74
When the North Wind Blows '74
The Shrieking '73
Starbird and Sweet William '73
Bury Me an Angel '71
The Tender Warrior '71
Angels Die Hard '70

Don Haggerty (1914-88)

The Killers '64
Hell Is for Heroes '62
The Gunfight at Dodge City '59
Loophole '54
Command Decision '48

Dylan Haggerty (1984-)

Interview with the Assassin '02
Grizzly Mountain '97

Sean Haggerty

Rhythm Thief '94
Spare Me '92

Kenichi Hagiwara (1950-)

Traffic Jam '91
Kagemusha '80

Masato Hagiwara

Onmyoji '01
Cure '97

Michael Hagiwara

Josh Kirby... Time Warrior: Chapter 5, Journey to the Magic Cavern '96
Prehysteria 2 '94

Marvin Hagler (1954-)

Indio 2: The Revolt '92
Indio '90

Larry Hagman (1939-)

Primary Colors '98
Nixon '95
S.O.B. '81
President's Mistress '78
The Eagle Has Landed '77
Intimate Strangers '77
The Big Bus '76
Mother, Jugs and Speed '76
Harry and Tonto '74
Hurricane '74
Antonio '73
Beware! The Blob '72
Deadly Encounter '72
No Place to Run '72
Hired Hand '71
Three in the Cellar '70
The Group '66
In Harm's Way '65
Ensign Pulver '64
Fail-Safe '64

Archie Hahn

Amazon Women on the Moon '87
Glory Years '87
Meatballs 2 '84
Protocol '84
This Is Spinal Tap '84
Pray TV '80
Cannonball '76
Phantom of the Paradise '74

Eric Hahn

Fist of Glory '95
Crossfire '89
Nam Angels '88

Gisela Hahn (1943-)

Devil Hunter '08
Alien Contamination '81
Big Boss '77
Mr. Scarface '77
Rulers of the City '76
Jungle Inferno '72

Jess Hahn (1922-98)

White Fire '84
Mama Dracula '80
Mean Frank and Crazy Tony '75
Escape from Death Row '73
The Grand Duel '73
Sicilian Connection '72
The Night of the Following Day '69
Triple Cross '67
Secret Agent Super Dragon '66
Topkapi '64

Jessica Hahn (1959-)

Bikini Summer 2 '92
Thunder & Mud '89

Kathryn Hahn (1974-)

The Goods: Live Hard, Sell Hard '09
Revolutionary Road '08
Step Brothers '08
The Last Mimzy '07
The Holiday '06
A Lot Like Love '05
Win a Date with Tad Hamilton! '04
How to Lose a Guy in 10 Days '03

Charles Haid (1943-)

Home on the Range '04 (V)
The Third Miracle '99
Broken Trust '95
Cooperstown '93
The Fire Next Time '93
Freeze Frame '92
Storyville '92
In the Line of Duty: A Cop for the Killing '90
Nightbreed '90
Capone '89
The Chinatown Murders: Man against the Mob '89
Fire and Rain '89
Cop '88
The Great Escape 2: The Untold Story '88
The Rescue '88
Weekend War '88
Children in the Crossfire '84
Twirl '81
Altered States '80
The Bastard '78
Deathmoon '78
Oliver's Story '78
Who'll Stop the Rain? '78
The Choirboys '77

Ion Haiduc

Ghouls '07
Bloodlust: Subspecies 3 '93
Bloodstone: Subspecies 2 '92

Stacy Haiduk (1968-)

The Sitter '07
Attack of the Sabretooth '05
Gabriela '01
The Darwin Conspiracy '99
Desert Thunder '99
The Beneficiary '97
Yesterday's Target '96
Luther the Geek '90
Steel and Lace '90

David Haig (1955-)

My Boy Jack '07
Two Weeks Notice '02
Station Jim '01
Four Weddings and a Funeral '94
The Moon Stallion '85

Sid Haig (1939-)

Brotherhood of Blood '08
A Dead Calling '06
The Devil's Rejects '05
House of the Dead 2: Dead Aim '05
House of 1000 Corpses '03
Jackie Brown '97
The Forbidden Dance '90
Wizards of the Lost Kingdom 2 '89
Warlords '88
Commando Squad '87
Aftermath '85
Galaxy of Terror '81
Busting '74
Foxy Brown '74
Coffy '73
The Deadly and the Beautiful '73
Emperor of the North Pole '73
The Big Bird Cage '72
The Big Doll House '71
C.C. & Company '70
Pit Stop '67
Track of the Vampire '66
Spider Baby '64

Kenneth Haigh (1929-)

The Bitch '78
Cleopatra '63
Teenage Bad Girl '59

Louisa Haigh

Shipwrecked '90
Murderers Among Us: The Simon Wiesenthal Story '89

Marian Hailey (1941-)

Jenny '70
Lovers and Other Strangers '70

Corey Haim (1972-2010)

Crank: High Voltage '09
Snowboard Academy '96
Demolition High '95
Life 101 '95
Dream a Little Dream 2 '94
Fast Getaway 2 '94
National Lampoon's Last Resort '94
Anything for Love '93
Blown Away '93

Just One of the Girls *'93*
The Double O Kid *'92*
Oh, What a Night *'92*
Dream Machine *'91*
Fast Getaway *'91*
Prayer of the Rollerboys *'91*
Dream a Little Dream *'89*
License to Drive *'88*
Watchers *'88*
The Lost Boys *'87*
Lucas *'86*
Murphy's Romance *'85*
Secret Admirer *'85*
Silver Bullet *'85*
A Time to Live *'85*
First Born *'84*

Jeanette Hain (1969-)
The Journey to Kafiristan *'01*
The Trio *'97*

Patricia Haines (1936-)
The Virgin Witch *'70*
Night Caller from Outer Space *'66*

Richard Haines (1990-)
An African Dream *'90*
Alien from L.A. *'87*

William Haines (1900-73)
The Girl Said No *'37*
Way Out West *'37*
Free and Easy *'30*
Speedway *'29*
Show People *'28*
The Smart Set *'28*
Spring Fever *'27*
West Point *'27*
Little Annie Rooney *'25*
Souls for Sale *'23*

Jester Hairston (1901-2000)
I'm Gonna Git You Sucka *'88*
The Alamo *'60*

Alison Haislip
The Indian *'07*
Into the Arms of Strangers *'07*

Khrystyne Haje (1968-)
Cyborg 3: The Recycler *'95*
Scanner Cop 2: Volkin's Revenge *'94*
Scanners: The Showdown *'94*

Haji (1946-)
Ilsa, Harem Keeper of the Oil Sheiks *'76*
Supervixens *'75*
Beyond the Valley of the Dolls *'70*
Faster, Pussycat! Kill! Kill! *'65*
Motor Psycho *'65*

Alan Hale (1892-1950)
Many Rivers to Cross *'55*
Stars in My Crown *'50*
Adventures of Don Juan *'49*
The Inspector General *'49*
My Girl Tisa *'48*
South of St. Louis *'48*
Pursued *'47*
The Man I Love *'46*
Night and Day *'46*
God is My Co-Pilot *'45*
Roughly Speaking *'45*
The Adventures of Mark Twain *'44*
Action in the North Atlantic *'43*
Destination Tokyo *'43*
Thank Your Lucky Stars *'43*
This Is the Army *'43*
Captains of the Clouds *'42*
Desperate Journey *'42*
Gentleman Jim *'42*
Juke Girl *'42*
Footsteps in the Dark *'41*
Manpower *'41*
Strawberry Blonde *'41*
The Fighting 69th *'40*
Santa Fe Trail *'40*
The Sea Hawk *'40*
They Drive by Night *'40*
Virginia City *'40*
Dodge City *'39*
The Man in the Iron Mask *'39*
The Private Lives of Elizabeth & Essex *'39*
The Adventures of Marco Polo *'38*
The Adventures of Robin Hood *'38*
Algiers *'38*
Listen, Darling *'38*
The Prince and the Pauper *'37*
Stella Dallas *'37*
Thin Ice *'37*
When Thief Meets Thief *'37*
Our Relations *'36*
The Crusades *'35*
The Good Fairy *'35*
Last Days of Pompeii *'35*
Great Expectations *'34*
Imitation of Life *'34*
It Happened One Night *'34*
Little Minister *'34*
The Lost Patrol *'34*
Of Human Bondage *'34*
The Scarlet Letter *'34*
Union Depot *'32*
The Sin of Madelon Claudet *'31*
Susan Lenox: Her Fall and Rise *'31*
The Leatherneck *'28*
Power *'28*
Dick Turpin *'25*
The Covered Wagon *'23*
Robin Hood *'22*
The Trap *'22*
The Four Horsemen of the Apocalypse *'21*

Alan Hale, Jr. (1918-90)
Back to the Beach *'87*
Hambone & Hillie *'84*
Johnny Dangerously *'84*
The Fifth Musketeer *'79*
The North Avenue Irregulars *'79*
Rescue from Gilligan's Island *'78*
The Giant Spider Invasion *'75*
There Was a Crooked Man *'70*
The Crawling Hand *'63*
Hard Drivin' *'60*
Up Periscope *'59*
Battle Hymn *'57*
All Mine to Give *'56*
Canyon River *'56*
The Indian Fighter *'55*
Young at Heart *'54*
Big Trees *'52*
Mr. Walkie Talkie *'52*
At Sword's Point *'51*
Home Town Story *'51*
The Underworld Story *'50*
The West Point Story *'50*
It Happens Every Spring *'49*
Rim of the Canyon *'49*
It Happened on 5th Avenue *'47*
The Spirit of West Point *'47*
Watch on the Rhine *'43*
To the Shores of Tripoli *'42*
Wake Island *'42*
Dive Bomber *'41*
Four Men and a Prayer *'38*

Barbara Hale (1921-)
Perry Mason: The Case of the Lost Love *'87*
Perry Mason Returns *'85*
Flight of the Grey Wolf *'76*
The Giant Spider Invasion *'75*
Airport *'70*
Buckskin *'68*
The Oklahoman *'56*
Seventh Cavalry *'56*
The Far Horizons *'55*
A Lion in the Streets *'53*
A Lion Is in the Streets *'53*
Last of the Comanches *'52*
The Jackpot *'50*
The Clay Pigeon *'49*
Jolson Sings Again *'49*
The Window *'49*
The Boy with the Green Hair *'48*
First Yank into Tokyo *'45*
West of the Pecos *'45*
The Falcon in Hollywood *'44*
Goin' to Town *'44*

Binnie Hale (1899-1984)
Love from a Stranger *'37*
The Phantom Light *'35*

Creighton Hale (1882-1965)
Action in the North Atlantic *'43*
Watch on the Rhine *'43*
Dive Bomber *'41*
Sergeant York *'41*
Shop Angel *'32*
The Cat and the Canary *'27*
The Marriage Circle *'24*
Broken Hearts of Broadway *'23*
The Idol Dancer *'20*
Way Down East *'20*

Doug Hale
Manhunter *'83*
The Night They Robbed Big Bertha's *'75*

Georgina Hale (1943-)
Preaching to the Perverted *'97*
Castaway *'87*
Mahler *'74*
The Boy Friend *'71*
The Devils *'71*

Jean Hale (1938-)
In Like Flint *'67*
The St. Valentine's Day Massacre *'67*
Psychomania *'63*

Jonathan Hale (1891-1966)
Shadow Puppets *'07*
Men of the Fighting Lady *'54*
Scandal Sheet *'52*
The Judge *'49*
Call Northside 777 *'48*
Silver River *'48*
Blondie Knows Best *'46*
Easy to Wed *'46*
End of the Road *'44*
Hollywood Canteen *'44*
Footlight Glamour *'43*
It's a Great Life *'43*
Blondie for Victory *'42*
Blondie Goes Latin *'42*
Blondie Goes to College *'42*
Blondie's Blessed Event *'42*
Hangmen Also Die *'42*
Blondie in Society *'41*
Blondie Has Trouble *'40*
Blondie Plays Cupid *'40*
Johnny Apollo *'40*
The Saint Takes Over *'40*
The Saint's Double Trouble *'40*
Blondie Brings Up Baby *'39*
Blondie Meets the Boss *'39*
The Saint Strikes Back *'39*
The Story of Alexander Graham Bell *'39*
Blondie *'38*
Breaking the Ice *'38*
Bringing Up Baby *'38*
The Duke of West Point *'38*
Exiled to Shanghai *'37*
Saratoga *'37*
You Only Live Once *'37*
The Devil Is a Sissy *'36*

Louise Closser Hale (1872-1933)
The Barbarian *'33*
Today We Live *'33*
Shanghai Express *'32*
Devotion *'31*
Platinum Blonde *'31*
Big Boy *'30*

Monte Hale (1921-2009)
Missourians *'50*
Trail of Robin Hood *'50*
The Vanishing Westerner *'50*
Outcasts of the Trail *'49*
Pioneer Marshal *'49*
Son of God's Country *'48*
Under Colorado Skies *'47*
Rough Riders of Cheyenne *'45*

Sonnie Hale (1902-59)
It's Love Again *'36*
First a Girl *'35*
Evergreen *'34*

Tony Hale (1970-)
The Answer Man *'09*
The Goods: Live Hard, Sell Hard *'09*
The Tale of Despereaux *'08 (V)*
Because I Said So *'07*
Larry the Cable Guy: Health Inspector *'06*
RV *'06*
Stranger Than Fiction *'06*
Fortunes *'05*

Brian Haley (1963-)
Gran Torino *'08*
Pearl Harbor *'01*
McHale's Navy *'97*
That Darn Cat *'96*
Baby's Day Out *'94*
Little Giants *'94*

Jack Haley (1899-1979)
People Are Funny *'46*
George White's Scandals *'45*
Treasure of Fear *'45*
Higher and Higher *'44*
One Body Too Many *'44*
Take It Big *'44*
Moon over Miami *'41*
The Wizard of Oz *'39*
Alexander's Ragtime Band *'38*
Rebecca of Sunnybrook Farm *'38*
Thanks for Everything *'38*
Pick a Star *'37*
Pigskin Parade *'36*
The Poor Little Rich Girl *'36*

Jackie Earle Haley (1961-)
A Nightmare on Elm Street *'10*
Shutter Island *'09*
Watchmen *'09*
Fragments *'08*
Semi-Pro *'08*
All the King's Men *'06*
Little Children *'06*
Maniac Cop 3: Badge of Silence *'93*
Dollman *'90*
The Zoo Gang *'85*
Losin' It *'82*
Breaking Away *'79*
The Bad News Bears Go to Japan *'78*
The Bad News Bears in Breaking Training *'77*
Damnation Alley *'77*
The Bad News Bears *'76*

H.B. Halicki (1941-89)
Deadline Auto Theft *'83*
The Junkman *'82*
Gone in 60 Seconds *'74*

Albert Hall (1937-)
Not Easily Broken *'09*
Ali *'01*
Beloved *'98*
Get On the Bus *'96*
Devil in a Blue Dress *'95*
Major Payne *'95*
Malcolm X *'92*
Hearts of Darkness: A Filmmaker's Apocalypse *'91*
Separate but Equal *'91*
Betrayed *'88*
Uncle Tom's Cabin *'87*
The Long, Hot Summer *'86*
Sophisticated Gents *'81*
Apocalypse Now *'79*

Anthony Michael Hall (1968-)
The Dark Knight *'08*
Final Approach *'08*
Funny Valentine *'05*
All About the Benjamins *'02*
The Dead Zone *'02*
The Caveman's Valentine *'01*
Freddy Got Fingered *'01*
Hitched *'01*
61* *'01*
Happy Accidents *'00*
Fallen Angel *'99*
The Pirates of Silicon Valley *'99*
Bomb Squad *'97*
Exit in Red *'97*
The Killing Grounds *'97*
Trojan War *'97*
The Death Artist *'95*
The Grave *'95*
Hail Caesar *'94*
Me and the Mob *'94*
Texas *'94*
The Adventures of a Gnome Named Gnorm *'93*
Six Degrees of Separation *'93*
Into the Sun *'92*
Edward Scissorhands *'90*
Johnny Be Good *'88*
Out of Bounds *'86*
The Breakfast Club *'85*
Weird Science *'85*
Sixteen Candles *'84*
National Lampoon's Vacation *'83*
Six Pack *'82*

Arch Hall, Jr. (1945-)
Deadwood *'65*
Nasty Rabbit *'64*
The Sadist *'63*
Eegah! *'62*
Wild Guitar *'62*
The Choppers *'61*

Arch (Archie) Hall, Sr. (1908-78)
The Thrill Killers *'65*
Wild Guitar *'62*
Border Badmen *'45*
His Brother's Ghost *'45*
The Lone Rider in Frontier Fury *'41*

Arsenio Hall (1956-)
Black Dynamite *'09*
Igor *'08 (V)*
The Proud Family Movie *'05 (V)*
Harlem Nights *'89*
Coming to America *'88*
Amazon Women on the Moon *'87*

Brad Hall (1958-)
Must Love Dogs *'05*
Bye Bye, Love *'94*
The Guardian *'90*
Limit Up *'89*
Worth Winning *'89*
Troll *'86*

Bug Hall (1985-)
Mortuary *'05*
Arizona Summer *'03*
Footsteps *'03*
Get a Clue *'02*
Skipped Parts *'00*
Safety Patrol *'98*
Honey, We Shrunk Ourselves *'97*
The Big Green *'95*
The Stupids *'95*
The Little Rascals *'94*

Craig Hall
Eagle vs. Shark *'07*
Ike: Countdown to D-Day *'04*
The Vector File *'03*

Delores Hall
Leap of Faith *'92*
Lethal Weapon 3 *'92*

Ellen Hall (1922-99)
Raiders of the Border *'44*
Range Law *'44*

Evelyn Hall
Hell's Angels *'30*
The Return of Dr. Fu Manchu *'30*

Gabriella Hall (1966-)
The Seductress *'00*
The Portrait *'99*
Lolida 2000 *'97*
Sexual Roulette *'96*
Shadow Dancer *'96*

Grayson Hall (1922-85)
Night of Dark Shadows *'71*
Adam at 6 a.m. *'70*
House of Dark Shadows *'70*
The Night of the Iguana *'64*
Satan in High Heels *'61*

Hanna Hall (1987-)
Halloween *'07*
The Virgin Suicides *'99*
Homecoming *'96*
Forrest Gump *'94*

Harriet Hall (1948-2007)
The Witching of Ben Wagner *'95*
Foxfire *'87*

Henry Hall (1898-1989)
Command Decision *'48*
Lightning Raiders *'45*
The Ape Man *'43*
Stagecoach Buckaroo *'42*
The Ape *'40*
Circle of Death *'36*
Inside Information *'34*
Rainbow Ranch *'33*
Midnight Warning *'32*

Huntz Hall (1920-99)
Auntie Lee's Meat Pies *'92*
Cyclone *'87*
Ratings Game *'84*
The Escape Artist *'82*
Gas Pump Girls *'79*
Valentino *'77*
Gentle Giant *'67*
Bowery Boys Meet the Monsters *'54*
Clipped Wings *'53*
Here Come the Marines *'52*
Ghost Chasers *'51*
Blues Busters *'50*
Master Minds *'49*
Smugglers' Cove *'48*
Spook Busters *'48*
Bowery Buckaroos *'47*
Hard-Boiled Mahoney *'47*
A Walk in the Sun *'46*
Mr. Muggs Rides Again *'45*
Follow the Leader *'44*
Million Dollar Kid *'44*
Clancy Street Boys *'43*
Ghost on the Loose *'43*
Kid Dynamite *'43*
Junior Army *'42*
Junior G-Men of the Air *'42*
Let's Get Tough *'42*
Mr. Wise Guy *'42*
'Neath Brooklyn Bridge *'42*
Smart Alecks *'42*
Bowery Blitzkrieg *'41*
Pride of the Bowery *'41*
Spooks Run Wild *'41*
Zis Boom Bah *'41*
Junior G-Men *'40*
They Made Me a Criminal *'39*
Angels with Dirty Faces *'38*
Crime School *'38*
Little Tough Guys *'38*
Dead End *'37*

Irma P. Hall (1937-)
Bad Lieutenant: Port of Call New Orleans *'09*
Hurricane Season *'08*
Tyler Perry's Meet the Browns *'08*
Collateral *'04*
The Ladykillers *'04*
Our America *'02*
A Lesson Before Dying *'99*
A Slipping Down Life *'99*
Beloved *'98*
The Love Letter *'98*
Patch Adams *'98*
Buddy *'97*
Midnight in the Garden of Good and Evil *'97*
Soul Food *'97*
Steel *'97*

A Family Thing '96
Nothing to Lose '96

James Hall (1900-40)
Millie '31
Hell's Angels '30
Four Sons '28
Hotel Imperial '27

Jerry Hall (1956-)
Merci Docteur Rey '04
R.P.M. '97
Savage Hearts '95
Batman '89
Running out of Luck '86

Jon Hall (1913-79)
The Beach Girls and the Monster '65
Hell Ship Mutiny '57
Deputy Marshal '50
Pirate Ship '49
The Prince of Thieves '48
The Last of the Redmen '47
Cobra Woman '44
The Invisible Man's Revenge '44
Ali Baba and the Forty Thieves '43
Arabian Nights '42
Invisible Agent '42
The Tuttles of Tahiti '42
Kit Carson '40
South of Pago Pago '40
The Hurricane '37
The Lion Man '36
Charlie Chan in Shanghai '35

Juanita Hall (1901-68)
Flower Drum Song '61
South Pacific '58
Paradise in Harlem '40

Kevin Peter Hall (1955-91)
Highway to Hell '92
Predator 2 '90
Harry and the Hendersons '87
Predator '87
Misfits of Science '85

Landon Hall
The Escort '97
Witchcraft 9: Bitter Flesh '96
Over the Wire '95
Stolen Hearts '95

Lois Hall (1926-2006)
Kalifornia '93
Dead Again '91
Pirates of the High Seas '50

Michael C. Hall (1971-)
Gamer '09
Paycheck '03

Michael Keys Hall
Flight of Black Angel '91
Blackout '88

Philip Baker Hall (1931-)
All Good Things '09
Fired Up! '09
The Lodger '09
Wonderful World '09
You Kill Me '07
Zodiac '07
Islander '06
The Matador '06
The Shaggy Dog '06
The Amityville Horror '05
Duck '05
The Zodiac '05
In Good Company '04
Bruce Almighty '03
Die Mommie Die! '03
Dogville '03
Path to War '02
The Sum of All Fears '02
A Gentleman's Game '01
The Contender '00
Lost Souls '00
Rules of Engagement '00
The Cradle Will Rock '99
The Insider '99
Let the Devil Wear Black '99
Magnolia '99
The Talented Mr. Ripley '99
Enemy of the State '98
Psycho '98
Rush Hour '98
Sour Grapes '98
The Truman Show '98
Witness to the Mob '98
Air Force One '97
Boogie Nights '97
Hard Eight '96
Hit Me '96
The Rock '96
Kiss of Death '94
A Thousand Heroes '92
Blue Desert '91
Dark River: A Father's Revenge '90
Three o'Clock High '87
Secret Honor '85
The Last Reunion '80
The Bastard '78
Terror Out of the Sky '78

Pooch Hall
Christmas at Water's Edge '04
Blue Hill Avenue '01

Porter Hall (1888-1953)
Ace in the Hole '51
The Half-Breed '51
The Beautiful Blonde from Bashful Bend '49
Intruder in the Dust '49
Miracle on 34th Street '47
Singapore '47
Unconquered '47
Murder, He Says '45
Weekend at the Waldorf '45
Double Indemnity '44
Going My Way '44
The Great Moment '44
Miracle of Morgan's Creek '44
The Woman of the Town '44
The Desperadoes '43
Sullivan's Travels '41
Arizona '40
His Girl Friday '40
Mr. Smith Goes to Washington '39
They Shall Have Music '39
Bulldog Drummond's Peril '38
Bulldog Drummond Escapes '37
Make Way for Tomorrow '37
The Plainsman '37
Souls at Sea '37
The General Died at Dawn '36
Petrified Forest '36
The Princess Comes Across '36
Satan Met a Lady '36
The Story of Louis Pasteur '36
The Case of the Lucky Legs '35
The Thin Man '34

Rebecca Hall (1982-)
Frost/Nixon '08
Vicky Cristina Barcelona '08
The Prestige '06
Starter for Ten '06
Wide Sargasso Sea '06
Like a Brother '05
The Camomile Lawn '92

Regina Hall (1970-)
Death at a Funeral '10
Law Abiding Citizen '09
First Sunday '08
The Elder Son '06
Scary Movie 4 '06
The Honeymooners '05
King's Ransom '05
Malibu's Most Wanted '03
Scary Movie 3 '03
The Other Brother '02
Paid in Full '02
Scary Movie 2 '01
Disappearing Acts '00
Scary Movie '00

Ron Hall
Vampire Assassin '05
Raw Target '95
Triple Impact '92

Ruth Hall (1910-2003)
The Return of Casey Jones '34
Man from Monterey '33
Strawberry Roan '33
The Three Musketeers '33
Between Fighting Men '32
Dynamite Ranch '32
Kid from Spain '32
Ride Him, Cowboy '32
Monkey Business '31

Sam Hall
Extraordinary Measures '10
South of Hell Mountain '70

Scott H. Hall
Color Me Blood Red '64
Blood Feast '63

Shannah Hall
The Princess & the Call Girl '84
Boogey Man 2 '83

Thurston Hall (1883-1958)
The Go-Getter '54
Night Stage to Galveston '52
Rim of the Canyon '49
Up in Central Park '48
Son of Rusty '47
Colonel Effingham's Raid '45
West of the Pecos '45
In Society '44
Something for the Boys '44
Song of Nevada '44
Crash Dive '43
Footlight Glamour '43
The Great Gildersleeve '43
I Dood It '43
Call of the Canyon '42
Twin Beds '42
The Invisible Woman '40
Each Dawn I Die '39
Jeepers Creepers '39
Mutiny on the Blackhawk '39
You Can't Cheat an Honest Man '39
Amazing Dr. Clitterhouse '38
Campus Confessions '38
Hard to Get '38
I Promise to Pay '37
Murder in Greenwich Village '37
Lady from Nowhere '36
Theodora Goes Wild '36
The Black Room '35

William Hall (1903-86)
Harmon of Michigan '41
The Spy Ring '38

Zooey Hall (1947-)
I Dismember Mama '74
Fortune and Men's Eyes '71

Lillian Hall-Davis (1896-1933)
The Farmer's Wife '28
The Ring '27
The Last of the Mohicans '20

Charles Hallahan (1943-97)
Mind Lies '00
Dante's Peak '97
The Fan '96
The Pest '96
The Rich Man's Wife '96
Warlock: The Armageddon '93
Wild Palms '93
Body of Evidence '92
True Believer '89
A Winner Never Quits '86
Pale Rider '85
Vision Quest '85
The Thing '82
Margin for Murder '81
Nightwing '79

John Hallam (1941-)
Lifeforce '85
Under Capricorn '82
Dragonslayer '81
The Offence '73

Jane Hallaren
A Night in the Life of Jimmy Reardon '88
Lianna '83
Body Heat '81

May Hallatt (1876-1969)
Separate Tables '58
Black Narcissus '47

Gisli Halldorsson (1927-98)
Devil's Island '96
Cold Fever '95
Children of Nature '91

Tom Hallick (1941-)
A Rare Breed '81
Hangar 18 '80

John Halliday (1880-1947)
The Philadelphia Story '40
That Certain Age '38
Desire '36
The Dark Angel '35
Happiness Ahead '34
Finishing School '33
Consolation Marriage '31
Millie '31
Smart Woman '31

Lori Hallier (1959-)
Running Wild '99
Blacklight '98
Recipe for Revenge '98
Night of the Twisters '95
Blindside '88
Higher Education '88
The Gunfighters '87
My Bloody Valentine '81

William (Bill) Halligan (1883-1957)
Jive Junction '43
Turf Boy '42
Blonde Comet '41
Robot Pilot '41

Johnny Hallyday (1943-)
The Pink Panther 2 '09
Crimson Rivers 2: Angels of the Apocalypse '05
Crime Spree '03
The Man on the Train '02
Conseil de Famille '86
Detective '85

Billy Halop (1920-76)
Too Late for Tears '49
Junior Army '42
Junior G-Men of the Air '42
Blues in the Night '41
Pride of the Bowery '41
Junior G-Men '40
They Made Me a Criminal '39
Angels with Dirty Faces '38
Crime School '38
Little Tough Guys '38
Dead End '37

Luke Halpin (1948-)
Flipper '96
Matinee '92
Shock Waves '77
If It's Tuesday, This Must Be Belgium '69
Island of the Lost '68
Flipper's Odyssey '66
Flipper's New Adventure '64
Flipper '63
Peter Pan '60

Brett Halsey (1933-)
First Degree '95
Beyond Justice '92
Black Cat '90
Demonia '90
Dangerous Obsession '88
The Crash of Flight 401 '78
Four Times That Night '69
Magnificent Adventurer '63
Twice-Told Tales '63
Return to Peyton Place '61
The Girl in Lover's Lane '60
Atomic Submarine '59
Four Fast Guns '59
Jet Over the Atlantic '59
Return of the Fly '59
Submarine Seahawk '59
To Hell and Back '55
Ma and Pa Kettle at Home '54

Michael Halsey
Postmortem '98
Mean Guns '97
Dollman '90
Treasure Island '89
Under the Gun '88

Julie Halston (1954-)
A Very Serious Person '06
Joe Gould's Secret '00
David Searching '97

Rodger Halston
Carnosaur 3: Primal Species '96
Alien Terminator '95

Charles Halton (1876-1959)
Friendly Persuasion '56
A Star Is Born '54
Carrie '52
Here Comes the Groom '51
Guns of Fury '49
My Dear Secretary '49
If You Knew Susie '48
The Best Years of Our Lives '46
It's a Wonderful Life '46
Sister Kenny '46
Rhapsody in Blue '45
A Tree Grows in Brooklyn '45
Enemy of Women '44
The Thin Man Goes Home '44
Up in Arms '44
Wilson '44
Heaven Can Wait '43
Across the Pacific '42
Captains of the Clouds '42
In Old California '42
The Lady Is Willing '42
Saboteur '42
The Spoilers '42
To Be or Not to Be '42
Dance Hall '41
Lady Scarface '41
Look Who's Laughing '41
Mr. & Mrs. Smith '41
Dr. Cyclops '40
Doctor Takes a Wife '40
Foreign Correspondent '40
The Shop Around the Corner '40
Stranger on the Third Floor '40
They Drive by Night '40
Virginia City '40
The Westerner '40
Dodge City '39
Golden Boy '39
Jesse James '39
Juarez '39
Nancy Drew, Reporter '39
Young Mr. Lincoln '39
I Am the Law '38
Mad Miss Manton '38
Room Service '38
The Saint in New York '38
The Young in Heart '38
Dead End '37
Pick a Star '37
Prisoner of Zenda '37
Come and Get It '36
Dodsworth '36
The Adventurer '17

Mie Hama (1943-)
King Kong Escapes '67
You Only Live Twice '67
What's Up, Tiger Lily? '66
King Kong vs. Godzilla '63

Yuko Hamada
Shogun Assassin 2: Lightning Swords of Death '73
Gamera vs. Guiron '69

Jun Hamamura
Shogun Assassin 2: Lightning Swords of Death '73
100 Monsters '68

Veronica Hamel (1945-)
Bone Eater '07
Secrets '94
High Stakes '93
Taking Care of Business '90
A New Life '88
Sessions '83
The Gathering: Part 2 '79
Snowblind '78
The Gathering '77
Cannonball '76

Jayne Hamil
Vice Academy 2 '90
Vice Academy '88

Mark Hamill (1952-)
Comic Book: The Movie '04
Jay and Silent Bob Strike Back '01
Laserhawk '99
Watchers Reborn '98
When Time Expires '97
Phantom 2040 Movie: The Ghost Who Walks '95 (V)
Village of the Damned '95
The Raffle '94
Silk Degrees '94
Batman: Mask of the Phantasm '93 (V)
Body Bags '93
Midnight Ride '92
Sleepwalkers '92
Time Runner '92
Black Magic Woman '91
The Guyver '91
Slipstream '89
Return of the Jedi '83
Britannia Hospital '82
The Night the Lights Went Out in Georgia '81
The Big Red One '80
The Empire Strikes Back '80
Corvette Summer '78
Star Wars '77
The City '76
Eric '75

Pete Hamill (1935-)
The Insider '99
One Fine Day '96

Antony (Tony) Hamilton (1953-95)
Fatal Instinct '92
Howling 4: The Original Nightmare '88
Mirrors '85
Samson and Delilah '84
Nocturna '79

Bernie Hamilton (1929-2008)
Bucktown '75
Scream Blacula Scream '73
The Losers '70
The Lost Man '69
Captain Sinbad '63
The Young One '61

Carrie Hamilton (1963-2002)
Cool World '92
Shag: The Movie '89
Tokyo Pop '88

Derek Hamilton
Angels Fall '07
Nightstalker '02
Taboo '02
Extremedays '01
Out Cold '01
Ripper: Letter from Hell '01

George Hamilton (1939-)
Too Cool for Christmas '04
Hollywood Ending '02
P.T. Barnum '99
Rough Riders '97
8 Heads in a Duffel Bag '96
Playback '95
Vanished '95
Amore! '93
Once Upon a Crime '92
Doc Hollywood '91
The Godfather, Part 3 '90
Poker Alice '87
Monte Carlo '86
Two Fathers' Justice '85
Zorro, the Gay Blade '81
Express to Terror '79
From Hell to Victory '79
Love at First Bite '79
The Seekers '79
Sextette '78
Users '78

The Happy Hooker Goes to Washington '77
Killer on Board '77
The Dead Don't Die '75
Once Is Not Enough '75
Medusa '74
Evel Knievel '72
Togetherness '70
Viva Maria! '65
The Victors '63
Two Weeks in Another Town '62
Angel Baby '61
By Love Possessed '61
Home from the Hill '60
Where the Boys Are '60
Crime and Punishment, USA '59

Hale Hamilton (1883-1942)

One Man's Journey '33
The Champ '32
Murder at Midnight '31
Susan Lenox: Her Fall and Rise '31

Jane (Veronica Hart) Hamilton (1962-)

Beauty School '93
Bloodsucking Pharoahs of Pittsburgh '90
Wildest Dreams '90
Bedroom Eyes 2 '89
Cleo/Leo '89
Deranged '87
New York's Finest '87
Slammer Girls '87

John Hamilton (1887-1958)

Outcasts of the City '58
On the Waterfront '54
Bandit King of Texas '49
Too Many Winners '47
Swingtime Johnny '43
I Killed That Man '42
Phantom Killer '42
The Fatal Hour '40
Flash Gordon Conquers the Universe '40
The Saint's Double Trouble '40

Josh Hamilton (1968-)

Away We Go '09
Broken English '07
Diggers '06
Outsourced '06
Four and a Half Women '05
The Bourne Identity '02
West of Here '02
On_Line '01
Urbania '00
Blowin' Smoke '99
The '60s '99
The House of Yes '97
Don't Look Back '96
The Proprietor '96
Kicking and Screaming '95
With Honors '94
Alive '93
O Pioneers! '91
Sitting Bull '54

Judd Hamilton

Fanatic '82
Star Crash '78
Gun Crazy '69

Linda Hamilton (1956-)

In Your Dreams '07
The Kid and I '05
Smile '05
A Girl Thing '01
Sex & Mrs. X '00
Skeletons in the Closet '00
The Secret Life of Girls '99
The Color of Courage '98
Rescuers: Stories of Courage—Two Couples '98
Dante's Peak '97
The Shadow Conspiracy '96
A Mother's Prayer '95
Separate Lives '94
Silent Fall '94
Terminator 2: Judgment Day '91
Mr. Destiny '90
Black Moon Rising '86
King Kong Lives '86
Secret Weapons '85
Children of the Corn '84
The Stone Boy '84
The Terminator '84
Tag: The Assassination Game '82
Rape and Marriage: The Rideout Case '80

Lisa Gay Hamilton (1964-)

Beastly '10
Mother and Child '09
The Soloist '09
Deception '08
Honeydripper '07
Nine Lives '05
The Sum of All Fears '02
The Truth About Charlie '02
Hamlet '01
A House Divided '00
True Crime '99
Beloved '98
Jackie Brown '97
Drunks '96
Last Breath '96
Nick and Jane '96
Palookaville '95
Extreme Vengeance '90
Krush Groove '85

Mahlon Hamilton (1880-1960)

Little Old New York '23
Peg o' My Heart '22
Daddy Long Legs '19

Margaret Hamilton (1902-85)

The Night Strangler '72
The Anderson Tapes '71
Journey Back to Oz '71 (V)
Brewster McCloud '70
13 Ghosts '60
Comin' Round the Mountain '51
People Will Talk '51
Riding High '50
The Red Pony '49
The Sin of Harold Diddlebock '47
George White's Scandals '45
Guest in the House '44
City Without Men '43
Twin Beds '42
The Invisible Woman '40
My Little Chickadee '40
The Wizard of Oz '39
The Adventures of Tom Sawyer '38
Breaking the Ice '38
Four's a Crowd '38
A Slight Case of Murder '38
Nothing Sacred '37
You Only Live Once '37
The Moon's Our Home '36
These Three '36
Broadway Bill '34

Murray Hamilton (1923-86)

The Last Days of Patton '86
Too Scared to Scream '85
Mazes and Monsters '82
Brubaker '80
The Amityville Horror '79
Last Cry for Help '79
1941 '79
Casey's Shadow '78
Jaws 2 '78
The Drowning Pool '75
Jaws '75
The Way We Were '73
The Tattered Web '71
If It's Tuesday, This Must Be Belgium '69
The Boston Strangler '68
The Brotherhood '68
No Way to Treat a Lady '68
Sergeant Ryker '68
The Graduate '67
Seconds '66
Papa's Delicate Condition '63
The Hustler '61
Anatomy of a Murder '59
The FBI Story '59
Darby's Rangers '58
Houseboat '58
No Time for Sergeants '58
Spirit of St. Louis '57

Neil Hamilton (1899-1984)

Batman '66
Good Neighbor Sam '64
The Patsy '64
The Devil's Hand '61
X Marks the Spot '42
King of the Texas Rangers '41
The Saint Strikes Back '39
Hollywood Stadium Mystery '38
Tarzan and His Mate '34
One Sunday Afternoon '33
The Animal Kingdom '32
Tarzan, the Ape Man '32
What Price Hollywood? '32
Laughing Sinners '31
The Sin of Madelon Claudet '31
The Return of Dr. Fu Manchu '30
The Love Trap '29
America '24
Isn't Life Wonderful '24
The White Rose '23

Patricia Hamilton

Anne of Green Gables: The Continuing Story '99
Holiday Affair '96
The Christmas Wife '88
Anne of Avonlea '87
Anne of Green Gables '85
Who Has Seen the Wind? '77
A House Without a Christmas Tree '72 (V)

Richard Hamilton (1920-2004)

Message in a Bottle '98
Reach the Rock '98
Sommersby '93
In Country '89
Greetings '68

Suzanna Hamilton (1960-)

Duel of Hearts '92
Tale of a Vampire '92
Out of Africa '85
Wetherby '85
1984 '84
Brimstone & Treacle '82

Victoria Hamilton (1971-)

Scoop '06
Wide Sargasso Sea '06
Goodbye, Mr. Chips '02
Victoria & Albert '01
Mansfield Park '99
King Lear '98
Persuasion '95

Wendy Hamilton

The Dallas Connection '94
Ski School 2 '94
The Scars of Dracula '70

Harry Hamlin (1951-)

Strange Wilderness '08
Disappearance '02
Shoot or Be Shot '02
Perfume '01
Road to Riches '01
Silent Predators '99
Frogs for Snakes '98
The Hunted '98
Allie & Me '97
Ebbtide '94
Murder So Sweet '93
Save Me '93
Under Investigation '93
Take Down '92
Deceptions '90
Dinner at Eight '89
Laguna Heat '87
Target: Favorite Son '87
L.A. Law '86
Maxie '85
Blue Skies Again '83
Making Love '82
Clash of the Titans '81
King of the Mountain '81
Movie, Movie '78

Jon Hamm

Shrek Forever After '10 (V)
A Single Man '09 (V)
The Day the Earth Stood Still '08
We Were Soldiers '02

Warren Hammack

Mars Needs Women '66
Zontar, the Thing from Venus '66
The Eye Creatures '65

Hammer (1962-)

One Man's Justice '95
Last Action Hero '93

Alvin Hammer (1915-93)

Command Decision '48
A Walk in the Sun '46

Ben Hammer (1925-)

(Untitled) '09
Subterfuge '98
Crazy People '90
Survival Quest '89
Beastmaster '82
The Execution of Private Slovik '74
Invasion of the Bee Girls '73
Johnny Got His Gun '71

John Hammil (1948-)

Phantoms '97
Young Guns 2 '90
Crossover Dreams '85

Brandon Hammond (1984-)

Our America '02
Soul Food '97
The Fan '96
Tales from the Hood '95

Darrell Hammond (1955-)

Wieners '08
Epic Movie '07
Netherbeast Incorporated '07
Ira & Abby '06
New York Minute '04
Agent Cody Banks '03
The King and I '99 (V)
Blues Brothers 2000 '98
Celtic Pride '96

John Hammond

The Prodigal '83
The Blue and the Gray '82
Enforcer from Death Row '78

Kay Hammond (1909-80)

The Girl in the Red Velvet Swing '55
Blithe Spirit '45
Abraham Lincoln '30

Nicholas Hammond (1950-)

Stealth '05
Salem's Lot '04
Black Cobra 2 '89
Trouble in Paradise '88
The Martian Chronicles: Part 1 '79
The Martian Chronicles: Part 3 '79
Chinese Web '78
Spiderman: The Deadly Dust '78
The Amazing Spider-Man '77
The Sound of Music '65

Roger Hammond (1936-)

Around the World in 80 Days '04
A Good Woman '04
Lady Chatterley '92
A Dangerous Man: Lawrence after Arabia '91

Olivia Hamnett

The Ripper '97
Deadly Possession '88
Earthling '80
The Last Wave '77
Plunge Into Darkness '77

Walter Hampden (1879-1955)

The Prodigal '55
Sabrina '54
Five Fingers '52
The Adventures of Mark Twain '44
Reap the Wild Wind '42
They Died with Their Boots On '41
The Hunchback of Notre Dame '39

Emily Hampshire (1981-)

The Cradle '06
It's a Boy Girl Thing '06
Snow Cake '06
Posers '02
The Happy Face Murders '99
Love Letters '99
Eye '96

Susan Hampshire (1938-)

Coming Home '98
Cry Terror '76
The Story of David '76
Neither the Sea Nor the Sand '73
Baffled '72
Living Free '72
David Copperfield '70
Those Daring Young Men in Their Jaunty Jalopies '69
Vanity Fair '67
The Fighting Prince of Donegal '66
The Trygon Factor '66
The Three Lives of Thomasina '63

Danielle Hampton (1978-)

Detention '03
Ginger Snaps '01

James Hampton (1936-)

Sling Blade '96
World War III '86
Teen Wolf '85
Condorman '81
Tut & Tuttle '81
Hangar 18 '80
The China Syndrome '79
The Amazing Howard Hughes '77
Bunco '77
Hawmps! '76
Force Five '75
The Longest Yard '74

Lionel Hampton (1908-2002)

Force of Impulse '60
The Benny Goodman Story '55

Paul Hampton (1945-)

Deadly Exposure '93
They Came from Within '75
Hit! '73
Lady Sings the Blues '72
Private Duty Nurses '71
More Dead Than Alive '68

Maggie Han (1959-)

Open Season '95
The Last Emperor '87

Master Bong Soo Han (1933-2007)

Force: Five '81
Kill the Golden Goose '79

Suk-kyu Han

Shiri '99
No. 3 '97

Herbie Hancock (1940-)

Indecent Proposal '93
Round Midnight '86

John Hancock (1939-)

Sundown: The Vampire in Retreat '08
Why Me? '90
Traxx '87
In the Custody of Strangers '82
Archer: The Fugitive from the Empire '81
The Black Marble '79

Lou Hancock

Miracle Mile '89
Evil Dead 2: Dead by Dawn '87

Sheila Hancock (1933-)

The Boy in the Striped Pajamas '08
Yes '04
Bait '02
Love or Money '01
Love and Death on Long Island '97
The Buccaneers '95
A Business Affair '93
Three Men and a Little Lady '90
Hawks '89
Buster '88
The Anniversary '68
The Moon-Spinners '64

Irene Handl (1901-87)

Riding High '78
Adventures of a Private Eye '77
The Private Life of Sherlock Holmes '70
Wonderwall: The Movie '69
Smashing Time '67
Morgan: A Suitable Case for Treatment '66
Doctor in Love '60
No Kidding '60
School for Scoundrels '60
Small Hotel '57
A Kid for Two Farthings '55
The Belles of St. Trinian's '53
Brief Encounter '46
Mr. Emmanuel '44
The Girl in the News '41
Night Train to Munich '40

Evan Handler (1961-)

Sex and the City 2 '10
Sex and the City: The Movie '08
Cash Crop '01
Harvest '98
Ransom '96
Natural Born Killers '94
Sweet Lorraine '87
Ruby's Dream '82
Taps '81

Taylor Handley

September Dawn '07
The Texas Chainsaw Massacre: The Beginning '06

Marina Hands

Lady Chatterley '06
Tell No One '06
The Barbarian Invasions '03

James Handy

Ash Wednesday '02
15 Minutes '01
Unbreakable '00
K-911 '99
Time Served '99
Gang Related '96
Rave Review '95
The O.J. Simpson Story '94
False Arrest '92
The Rocketeer '91
Arachnophobia '90
K-9 '89
The Preppie Murder '89
Bird '88
Burglar '87
The Verdict '82

Scott Handy

The Haunted Airman '06
The Gospel of John '03

Anne Haney (1934-2001)

Psycho '98
The Lesser Evil '97
Liar Liar '97

Midnight in the Garden of Good and Evil '97
Changing Habits '96
The American President '95
The Bad Seed '85

Daryl Haney (1963-)
Concealed Weapon '94
Lords of the Deep '89
Daddy's Boys '87

Perla Haney-Jardine
Untraceable '08
Spider-Man 3 '07
Kill Bill Vol. 2 '04
Dark Water '02

Helen Hanft (1934-)
Used People '92
Stardust Memories '80

Roger Hanin (1925-)
Day of Atonement '93
My Other Husband '85
Rocco and His Brothers '60
Sois Belle et Tais-Toi '58

Larry Hankin (1940-)
The Independent '00
Money Talks '97
Billy Madison '94
Prehysteria 2 '94
Out on a Limb '92
T Bone N Weasel '92
Black Magic Woman '91
Armed and Dangerous '86
Escape from Alcatraz '79

Colin Hanks (1977-)
The Great Buck Howard '09
The House Bunny '08
My Mom's New Boyfriend '08
Untraceable '08
Alone With Her '07
Careless '07
Rx '06
Tenacious D in the Pick of Destiny '06
King Kong '05
Standing Still '05
11:14 '03
Orange County '02
Band of Brothers '01
Get Over It! '01
Whatever It Takes '00
That Thing You Do! '96

Jim Hanks (1961-)
Black Ops '07
Purgatory House '04
Xtro 3: Watch the Skies '95
Buford's Beach Bunnies '92

Tom Hanks (1956-)
Toy Story 3 '10 (V)
Angels & Demons '09
The Great Buck Howard '09
Charlie Wilson's War '07
The Simpsons Movie '07 (V)
The Da Vinci Code '06
Elvis Has Left the Building '04
The Ladykillers '04
The Polar Express '04
The Terminal '04
Catch Me If You Can '02
Road to Perdition '02
Cast Away '00
The Green Mile '99
Toy Story 2 '99 (V)
Saving Private Ryan '98
You've Got Mail '98
That Thing You Do! '96
Apollo 13 '95
Toy Story '95 (V)
Forrest Gump '94
Fallen Angels 2 '93
Philadelphia '93
Sleepless in Seattle '93
A League of Their Own '92
Radio Flyer '92 (N)
The Bonfire of the Vanities '90
Joe Versus the Volcano '90
The 'Burbs '89
Turner and Hooch '89
Big '88
Punchline '88
Dragnet '87
Every Time We Say Goodbye '86
The Money Pit '86
Nothing in Common '86
The Man with One Red Shoe '85
Volunteers '85
Bachelor Party '84
Splash '84
Mazes and Monsters '82
He Knows You're Alone '80

Jenny Hanley (1947-)
Flesh and Blood Show '73
The Scars of Dracula '70
On Her Majesty's Secret Service '69

Jimmy Hanley (1918-70)
Radio Cab Murder '54
The Blue Lamp '49
Room to Let '49
Captive Heart '47
It Always Rains on Sunday '47
Immortal Battalion '44
Salute John Citizen '42
Gaslight '40
Housemaster '38

Bert Hanlon (1890-1972)
A Slight Case of Murder '38
Park Avenue Logger '37
Wings in the Dark '35
Too Busy to Work '32

Adam Hann-Byrd (1982-)
Halloween: H20 '98
The Ice Storm '97
Diabolique '96
Jumanji '95
Digger '94
Little Man Tate '91

Daryl Hannah (1960-)
Dark Honeymoon '08
Shark Swarm '08
Vice '08
All the Good Ones Are Married '07
Hearts of War '07
Keeping Up with the Steins '06
The Big Empty '04
Kill Bill Vol. 2 '04
Silver City '04
Casa de los Babys '03
The Job '03
Kill Bill Vol. 1 '03
Northfork '03
A Walk to Remember '02
Hard Cash '01
Jack and the Beanstalk: The Real Story '01
Jackpot '01
Cowboy Up '00
Dancing at the Blue Iguana '00
Hide and Seek '00
Diplomatic Siege '99
Speedway Junky '99
Wildflowers '99
Hi-Life '98
My Favorite Martian '98
Rear Window '98
The Gingerbread Man '97
The Last Don '97
The Real Blonde '97
The Last Days of Frankie the Fly '96
Two Much '96
Grumpier Old Men '95
The Tie That Binds '95
The Little Rascals '94
Attack of the 50 Ft. Woman '93
Grumpy Old Men '93
Memoirs of an Invisible Man '92
At Play in the Fields of the Lord '91
Crazy People '90
Crimes & Misdemeanors '89
Steel Magnolias '89
High Spirits '88
Roxanne '87
Wall Street '87
The Clan of the Cave Bear '86
Legal Eagles '86
The Pope of Greenwich Village '84
Reckless '84
Splash '84
The Final Terror '83
Blade Runner '82
Summer Lovers '82
Hard Country '81
The Fury '78

John Hannah (1962-)
The Mummy: Tomb of the Dragon Emperor '08
The Last Legion '07
Ghost Son '06
I'm with Lucy '02
The Mummy Returns '01
Circus '00
Pandaemonium '00
The Hurricane '99
The Mummy '99
The Love Bug '97
Resurrection Man '97
Sliding Doors '97
The Final Cut '96
Romance and Rejection '96
The Innocent Sleep '95
Madagascar Skin '95
Faith '94
Four Weddings and a Funeral '94

Page Hannah (1964-)
Shag: The Movie '89
Creepshow 2 '87
My Man Adam '86
Racing with the Moon '84

Alyson Hannigan (1974-)
Date Movie '06
American Wedding '03
Rip It Off '02
American Pie 2 '01
Boys and Girls '00
American Pie '99
Dead Man on Campus '97
My Stepmother Is an Alien '88

Donna Hanover (1950-)
Series 7: The Contenders '01
Just the Ticket '98
The People vs. Larry Flynt '96

Lawrence Hanray (1874-1947)
On Approval '44
Mimi '35
The Private Life of Henry VIII '33

Glen Hansard
Once '06
The Commitments '91

Gale Hansen (1969-)
Double Vision '92
Shaking the Tree '92
The Finest Hour '91
Dead Poets Society '89
The Deadly and the Beautiful '73

Gunnar Hansen (1947-)
Brutal Massacre: A Comedy '07
Hellblock 13 '97
Freakshow '95
Mosquito '95
Hollywood Chainsaw Hookers '88
The Demon Lover '77
The Texas Chainsaw Massacre '74

Heidi Hansen
Superbug Super Agent '76
Fanny Hill: Memoirs of a Woman of Pleasure '64

Holger Juul Hansen (1924-)
The Kingdom 2 '97
The Kingdom '95

Joachim Hansen (1930-2007)
Anne of Green Gables '85
Frozen Alive '64
Secret of the Black Trunk '62

Patti Hansen (1956-)
Hard to Hold '84
They All Laughed '81

Paul Hansen
The Return of Count Yorga '71
Count Yorga, Vampire '70

Peter Hansen (1921-)
Cavalry Charge '51
When Worlds Collide '51

Valda Hansen (1932-93)
Wham-Bam, Thank You Spaceman '75
Cain's Cutthroats '71
Night of the Ghouls '59

William Hansen (1911-75)
Homebodies '74
Willard '71
The Member of the Wedding '52

Dave Hanson
Gamers '06
Slap Shot 2: Breaking the Ice '02
Slap Shot '77

Lars Hanson (1886-1965)
Walpurgis Night '41
The Informer '29
Homecoming '28
The Wind '28
The Flesh and the Devil '27
The Atonement of Gosta Berling '24

Katy Hansz
Fresh Cut Grass '04
Coffee and Cigarettes '03

Thomas Hanzon (1962-)
Faithless '00
Private Confessions '98

Setsuko Hara (1920-)
Tokyo Story '53
Early Summer '51
The Idiot '51
Late Spring '49
No Regrets for Our Youth '46

Kiwako Harada (1965-)
Godzilla vs. King Ghidora '91
Days of Hell '84

Meiko Harada (1958-)
Akira Kurosawa's Dreams '90
Ran '85
Nomugi Pass '79

Ryuuji Harada
Kibakichi '04
Kibakichi 2 '04

Yoshio Harada
Azumi '03
9 Souls '03
Party 7 '00
The Hunted '94
Ronin Gai '90
Shogun's Samurai—The Yagyu Clan Conspiracy '78

Haya Harareet (1931-)
The Interns '62
Journey Beneath the Desert '61
Ben-Hur '59
Hill 24 Doesn't Answer '55

Clement Harari (1919-)
Train of Life '98
Flight of the Eagle '82
The Fiendish Plot of Dr. Fu Manchu '80
Monkeys, Go Home! '66
Double Agents '59

David Harbour
Quantum of Solace '08
Revolutionary Road '08
Brokeback Mountain '05

Matthew Harbour (1990-)
Equilibrium '02
The Witness Files '00
Time at the Top '99

James Harcourt (1873-1951)
The Hidden Room '49
Obsession '49
Johnny Frenchman '46
Night Train to Munich '40
I Met a Murderer '39
The Avenging Hand '36

Diana Hardcastle
A Good Woman '04
If Only '04
Catherine Cookson's The Tide of Life '96
Fortunes of War '87

Ernest Harden, Jr. (1952-)
The Hit '06
Gang Boys '97
White Men Can't Jump '92
The Final Terror '83
White Mama '80

Marcia Gay Harden (1959-)
The Courageous Heart of Irena Sendler '09
Whip It '09
The Christmas Cottage '08
Home '08
The Maiden Heist '08
Sex & Lies in Sin City: The Ted Binion Scandal '08
Into the Wild '07
The Invisible '07
The Mist '07
Rails & Ties '07
American Dreamz '06
Canvas '06
The Dead Girl '06
The Hoax '06
American Gun '05
The Bad News Bears '05
P.S. '04
Welcome to Mooseport '04
Casa de los Babys '03
Mona Lisa Smile '03
Mystic River '03
King of Texas '02
Gaudi Afternoon '01
Pollock '00
Space Cowboys '00
Thin Air '00
Small Vices: A Spenser Mystery '99
Desperate Measures '98
Meet Joe Black '98
Curtain Call '97
Flubber '97
Path to Paradise '97
The Daytrippers '96
Far Harbor '96
The First Wives Club '96
Spy Hard '96
Convict Cowboy '95
The Spitfire Grill '95
Safe Passage '94
Crush '93
Sinatra '92
Used People '92
Fever '91
Late for Dinner '91
Miller's Crossing '90

Crofton Hardester
Devastator '85
Android '82

Kate Hardie (1969-)
Heart '99
Croupier '97
The Krays '90
Conspiracy '89
Mona Lisa '86

Jerry Hardin (1929-)
Hidalgo '04
The Firm '93
The Hot Spot '90
Blaze '89
Wanted Dead or Alive '86
Cujo '83
Wolf Lake '79

Melora Hardin (1967-)
27 Dresses '08
Boxboarders! '07
The Comebacks '07
The Hot Chick '02
Seven Girlfriends '00
Absolute Power '97
Chameleon '95
The Undercover Kid '95
Reckless Kelly '93
The Rocketeer '91
Big Man on Campus '89
Dead Poets Society '89
Lambada '89
Iron Eagle '86
The North Avenue Irregulars '79

Ty Hardin (1930-)
Bad Jim '89
Rooster: Spurs of Death! '83
You're Jinxed, Friend, You've Met Sacramento '70
Berserk! '67
One Step to Hell '67
Battle of the Bulge '65
Palm Springs Weekend '63
PT 109 '63
Merrill's Marauders '62
I Married a Monster from Outer Space '58

Ann Harding (1901-81)
The Man in the Gray Flannel Suit '56
Promise to Murder '56
The Magnificent Yankee '50
Two Weeks with Love '50
It Happened on 5th Avenue '47
Mission to Moscow '43
Love from a Stranger '37
Double Harness '33
The Animal Kingdom '32
Devotion '31
Condemned '29

John Harding
The Impossible Years '68
This Property Is Condemned '66
Crime and Punishment, USA '59

Kay Harding (1924-84)
The Mummy's Curse '44
Scarlet Claw '44

Lyn Harding (1876-1952)
The Mutiny of the Elsinore '39
Murder at the Baskervilles '37
The Man Who Lived Again '36
Old Spanish Custom '36
Spy of Napoleon '36
The Speckled Band '31

Kadeem Hardison (1965-)
Made of Honor '08
What Up? '08
Biker Boyz '03
Showtime '02
Instinct to Kill '01
30 Years to Life '01
Dancing in September '00
Blind Faith '98
The Sixth Man '97
Drive '96
Panther '95
Vampire in Brooklyn '95
Renaissance Man '94
Dream Date '93
Gunmen '93
White Men Can't Jump '92
Def by Temptation '90
I'm Gonna Git You Sucka '88
School Daze '88
Beat Street '84

24-7 '97
In the Name of the Father '93

Gerald Harper (1929-)
If It's a Man, Hang Up '75
The Admirable Crichton '57

Hill Harper (1973-)
The Breed '06
The Badge '02
The Skulls '00
The Visit '00
In Too Deep '99
Loving Jezebel '99
Slaves of Hollywood '99
He Got Game '98
Mama Flora's Family '98
Hav Plenty '97
The Nephew '97
Steel '97
Get On the Bus '96
Zooman '95

Jessica Harper (1954-)
Minority Report '02
Safe '95
Mr. Wonderful '93
Big Man on Campus '89
Eat a Bowl of Tea '89
Blue Iguana '88
Imagemaker '86
My Favorite Year '82
Pennies from Heaven '81
Shock Treatment '81
Stardust Memories '80
The Evictors '79
Suspiria '77
Inserts '76
Phantom of the Paradise '74

Kyra Harper
Swann '96
Buffalo Jump '90

Robert Harper (1951-)
Molly '99
The Wrong Man '93
Final Analysis '92
Running Mates '92
Held Hostage '91
Not Quite Human '87
Once Upon a Time in America '84

Tess Harper (1950-)
Kiss the Bride '07
No Country for Old Men '07
Saving Sarah Cain '07
Broken Bridges '06
Jam '06
Karla '06
Loggerheads '05
The Rising Place '02
The In Crowd '00
The Jackal '97
The Road to Galveston '96
Children of Fury '94
Christy '94
My New Gun '92
The Turning '92
The Man in the Moon '91
My Heroes Have Always Been Cowboys '91
Daddy's Dyin'... Who's Got the Will? '90
Dark River: A Father's Revenge '90
Criminal Law '89
Far North '88
Her Alibi '88
Ishtar '87
Crimes of the Heart '86
Flashpoint '84
Reckless Disregard '84
A Summer to Remember '84
Amityville 3: The Demon '83
Chiefs '83
Tender Mercies '83

Valerie Harper (1940-)
Drop-Out Mother '88
The Execution '85
Blame It on Rio '84
Don't Go to Sleep '82
The Last Married Couple in America '80
The Shadow Box '80
Chapter Two '79
Night Terror '76
Freebie & the Bean '74
Thursday's Game '74

Cindy Harrel
The Final Terror '83
Model Behavior '82

Jim Harrell (1918-2000)
A Family Thing '96
Don't Open the Door! '74

Rebecca Harrell (1980-)
Suspended Animation '02
Prancer '89

Brett Harrelson
Dee Snider's Strangeland '98
From Dusk Till Dawn 2: Texas Blood Money '98
The People vs. Larry Flynt '96

Woody Harrelson (1962-)
Defendor '09
Management '09
The Messenger '09
2012 '09
Zombieland '09
Semi-Pro '08
Seven Pounds '08
Sleepwalking '08
Surfer, Dude '08
Transsiberian '08
Battle in Seattle '07
No Country for Old Men '07
The Walker '07
A Prairie Home Companion '06
A Scanner Darkly '06
The Big White '05
North Country '05
The Prize Winner of Defiance, Ohio '05
After the Sunset '04
She Hate Me '04
Anger Management '03
Go Further '03
Scorched '02
Austin Powers 2: The Spy Who Shagged Me '99
EDtv '99
Play It to the Bone '99
The Hi-Lo Country '98
Palmetto '98
The Thin Red Line '98
Wag the Dog '97
Welcome to Sarajevo '97
Kingpin '96
The People vs. Larry Flynt '96
Sunchaser '96
Money Train '95
The Cowboy Way '94
Natural Born Killers '94
Indecent Proposal '93
Ted & Venus '93
White Men Can't Jump '92
Doc Hollywood '91
Mother Goose Rock 'n' Rhyme '90
Cool Blue '88
Eye of the Demon '87
Wildcats '86

William Harrigan (1894-1966)
Flying Leathernecks '51
Exiled to Shanghai '37
"G" Men '35
Whipsaw '35
The Invisible Man '33

Laura Elena Harring (1964-)
The Caller '08
Love in the Time of Cholera '07
Nancy Drew '07
Ghost Son '06
Inland Empire '06
All Souls Day '05
The King '05
The Punisher '04
Loco Love '03
Willard '03
Derailed '02
John Q '02
Mulholland Drive '01
Black Scorpion 2: Ground Zero '96
Exit to Eden '94
Rio Diablo '93
Dead Women in Lingerie '90
The Forbidden Dance '90
Silent Night, Deadly Night 3: Better Watch Out! '89
The Alamo: Thirteen Days to Glory '87

Cheryl Francis Harrington
Legal Deceit '95
Perfume '91

Desmond Harrington (1976-)
Exit Speed '08
Life is Hot in Cracktown '08
3-Way '04
Wrong Turn '03
Ghost Ship '02
We Were Soldiers '02
The Hole '01
My First Mister '01
Riding in Cars with Boys '01
The Messenger: The Story of Joan of Arc '99

Jay Harrington (1971-)
A Little Inside '01
Octopus '00

Laura Harrington (1958-)
Paulie '98
The Devil's Advocate '97
Dead Air '94
Linda '93
The Secret '93
What's Eating Gilbert Grape '93
Perfect Witness '89
Maximum Overdrive '86

Pat Harrington (1929-)
These Old Broads '01
Ablaze '00
The Affair '73
Easy Come, Easy Go '67
The President's Analyst '67
Move Over, Darling '63

Peter Harrington
Diamond Run '00
Time Chasers '95

Richard Harrington
Cravings '06
The Proposition '96

Barbara Harris (1937-)
The Midnight Meat Train '08
Grosse Pointe Blank '97
Dirty Rotten Scoundrels '88
Nice Girls Don't Explode '87
Peggy Sue Got Married '86
The North Avenue Irregulars '79
The Seduction of Joe Tynan '79
Movie, Movie '78
Family Plot '76
Freaky Friday '76
Nashville '75
Plaza Suite '71
Who Is Harry Kellerman and Why Is He Saying Those Terrible Things About Me? '71
Oh Dad, Poor Dad (Momma's Hung You in the Closet & I'm Feeling So Sad) '67
A Thousand Clowns '65

Baxter Harris (1940-)
Species 2 '98
Home Alone 3 '97
Stephen King's The Langoliers '95

Brad Harris (1933-)
Seven Magnificent Gladiators '84
Hercules '83
King of Kong Island '78
The Freakmaker '73
Jungle Inferno '72
The Mad Butcher '72
Island of Lost Girls '68
Rattler Kid '68
Goliath Against the Giants '63
The Fury of Hercules '61
Samson '61

Cynthia Harris (1934-)
Pancho Barnes '88
Three Men and a Baby '87
Izzy & Moe '85
Reuben, Reuben '83
Edward and Mrs. Simpson '80
Isadora '68

Danielle Harris (1977-)
Halloween II '09
Super Capers '09
Halloween '07
Rugrats Go Wild! '03 (V)
The Wild Thornberrys Movie '02 (V)
Killer Bud '00
Urban Legend '98
Back to Back '96
Daylight '96
Wish upon a Star '96
Roseanne: An Unauthorized Biography '94
The Woman Who Loved Elvis '93
The Last Boy Scout '91
Nightmare '91
Marked for Death '90
Halloween 5: The Revenge of Michael Myers '89
Halloween 4: The Return of Michael Myers '88

Danneel Harris (1979-)
The Back-Up Plan '10
Fired Up! '09
Harold & Kumar Escape from Guantanamo Bay '08
Still Waiting '08

David Harris (1959-)
Undercover '87
Badge of the Assassin '85
The Warriors '79
She-Devils on Wheels '68

Ed Harris (1949-)
Appaloosa '08
Cleaner '07
Gone Baby Gone '07
National Treasure: Book of Secrets '07
Two Tickets to Paradise '06
Empire Falls '05
A History of Violence '05
Winter Passing '05
The Human Stain '03
Masked and Anonymous '03
Radio '03
The Hours '02
A Beautiful Mind '01
Buffalo Soldiers '01
Enemy at the Gates '00
Pollock '00
The Prime Gig '00
The Third Miracle '99
Stepmom '98
The Truman Show '98
Absolute Power '97
Riders of the Purple Sage '96
The Rock '96
Apollo 13 '95
An Eye for an Eye '95
Nixon '95
Just Cause '94
Milk Money '94
Stephen King's The Stand '94
The Firm '93
Needful Things '93
Glengarry Glen Ross '92
Running Mates '92
China Moon '91
Paris Trout '91
State of Grace '90
The Abyss '89
Jacknife '89
To Kill a Priest '89
The Last Innocent Man '87
Walker '87
Alamo Bay '85
Code Name: Emerald '85
A Flash of Green '85
Sweet Dreams '85
Places in the Heart '84
Swing Shift '84
The Right Stuff '83
Under Fire '83
Creepshow '82
Knightriders '81
Borderline '80
The Seekers '79
Coma '78

Edna Mae Harris (1910-97)
Paradise in Harlem '40
Lying Lips '39
The Spirit of Youth '37

Estelle Harris (1926-)
Toy Story 3 '10 (V)
Tarzan 2 '05 (V)
Disney's Teacher's Pet '04 (V)
Home on the Range '04 (V)
Brother Bear '03 (V)
Good Advice '01
Playing Mona Lisa '00
What's Cooking? '00
Lost and Found '99
Toy Story 2 '99 (V)
Chairman of the Board '97
Downhill Willie '96
Once Upon a Time in America '84

Fox Harris (1936-88)
Alienator '89
Dr. Caligari '89
Warlords '88
Repo Man '83

Gail Harris (1964-)
Cellblock Sisters: Banished Behind Bars '95
Forbidden Games '95
Virtual Desire '95

George Harris (1949-)
Eye of the Dolphin '06
The Interpreter '05
Layer Cake '05
Black Hawk Down '01
Soul Survivor '95

Hank Harris
Hellbent '04
Milwaukee, Minnesota '03
Pumpkin '02

Harriet Sansom Harris (1955-)
Moonlight Serenade '09
Memento '00
Nurse Betty '00

Jamie Harris (1963-)
The New World '05
Rick '03
The Next Big Thing '02
Lost Battalion '01

Jared Harris (1961-)
Extraordinary Measures '10
The Curious Case of Benjamin Button '08
The Shadow in the North '07
Lady in the Water '06
The Notorious Bettie Page '06
Ocean's Twelve '04
Resident Evil: Apocalypse '04
I Love Your Work '03
The Other Boleyn Girl '03
Sylvia '03
Dummy '02
Igby Goes Down '02
Mr. Deeds '02
How to Kill Your Neighbor's Dog '01
Lush '01
Perfume '01
Shadow Magic '00
Two of Us '00
The Weekend '00
The Eternal '99
The External '99
Happiness '98
Lost in Space '98
B. Monkey '97
Father's Day '96
I Shot Andy Warhol '96
Sunday '96
Blue in the Face '95
Dead Man '95
Nadja '95
Smoke '95
Tall Tale: The Unbelievable Adventures of Pecos Bill '95
Natural Born Killers '94
The Public Eye '92

Jim Harris
Waitress '81
Squeeze Play '79

Jo Ann Harris (1949-)
Deadly Games '80
Act of Vengeance '74
The Beguiled '70

Jonathan Harris (1914-2002)
Toy Story 2 '99 (V)
A Bug's Life '98 (V)

Julie Harris (1925-)
The Golden Boys '08
Bad Manners '98
Ellen Foster '97
Carried Away '95
One Christmas '95
Scarlett '94
Secrets '94
Housesitter '92
The Dark Half '91
The Christmas Wife '88
Gorillas in the Mist '88
The Woman He Loved '88
Backstairs at the White House '79
The Bell Jar '79
America at the Movies '76
The Last of Mrs. Lincoln '76
Voyage of the Damned '76
The Hiding Place '75
Home for the Holidays '72
The People Next Door '70
Reflections in a Golden Eye '67
Harper '66
You're a Big Boy Now '66
Holy Terror '65
The Haunting '63
Requiem for a Heavyweight '62
Victoria Regina '61
A Doll's House '59
Truth about Women '58
I Am a Camera '55
East of Eden '54
The Member of the Wedding '52

Julius W. Harris (1923-2004)
Shrunken Heads '94
Murder on the Bayou '91
Prayer of the Rollerboys '91
Crimewave '85
Missing Pieces '83
Victory at Entebbe '76
The Taking of Pelham One Two Three '74
Black Caesar '73
Hell Up in Harlem '73
Live and Let Die '73
Shaft's Big Score '72
Superfly '72
Nothing but a Man '64

Kirk Harris
Hard Luck '01
Loser '97

Lara Harris (1967-)
April's Shower '03
I'll Take You There '99
Habitat '97
Inhumanoid '96
The Dogfighters '95
All Tied Up '92
The Fourth War '90
Blood Red '88
No Man's Land '87

Laura Harris (1976-)
Merlin and the Book of Beasts '09
Corporate Affairs '07
Severance '06
Going Greek '01

The Highway Man *'99*
The Faculty *'98*
Just the Ticket *'98*
Suicide Kings *'97*

Leigh Anne Harris (1954-)
I, the Jury *'82*
Sorceress *'82*

Lynette Harris (1954-)
I, the Jury *'82*
Sorceress *'82*

Mel Harris (1957-)
Arc *'06*
Purple Heart *'05*
Hangman's Curse *'03*
Firetrap *'01*
Out of Time *'00*
Sonic Impact *'99*
Sharon's Secret *'95*
Broken Lullaby *'94*
The Pagemaster *'94*
The Secretary *'94*
The Spider and the Fly *'94*
Suture *'93*
Desperate Motives *'92*
Raising Cain *'92*
Scott Turow's The Burden of Proof *'92*
Cameron's Closet *'89*
K-9 *'89*
My Brother's Wife *'89*
Wanted Dead or Alive *'86*

Michael (M.K.) Harris
I Love You, Don't Touch Me! *'97*
Mr. Stitch *'95*
Dead Air *'94*
Sleepstalker: The Sandman's Last Rites *'94*
The Soft Kill *'94*
Shattered Image *'93*
Suture *'93*
The Horseplayer *'91*
Satan's Princess *'90*
Slumber Party Massacre 3 *'90*
Genuine Risk *'89*
Shriek of the Mutilated *'74*

Michelle Harris
Tennessee *'08*
A Matter of Love *'78*

Naomie Harris (1976-)
Sex & Drugs & Rock & Roll *'10*
Ninja Assassin *'09*
August *'08*
Explicit Ills *'08*
Street Kings *'08*
Pirates of the Caribbean: At World's End *'07*
Miami Vice *'06*
Pirates of the Caribbean: Dead Man's Chest *'06*
Tristram Shandy: A Cock and Bull Story *'05*
After the Sunset *'04*
Trauma *'04*
28 Days Later *'02*

Neil Patrick Harris (1973-)
Beastly *'10*
Harold & Kumar Escape from Guantanamo Bay *'08*
The Christmas Blessing *'05*
Harold and Kumar Go to White Castle *'04*
Undercover Brother *'02*
The Next Best Thing *'00*
Joan of Arc *'99*
The Proposition *'97*
Starship Troopers *'97*
Animal Room *'95*
The Man in the Attic *'94*
My Antonia *'94*
Snowbound: The Jim and Jennifer Stolpa Story *'94*
Cold Sassy Tree *'89*
Clara's Heart *'88*
Purple People Eater *'88*

Phil Harris (1906-95)
Rock-a-Doodle *'92 (V)*
Robin Hood *'73 (V)*
The Gatling Gun *'72*
The Aristocats *'70 (V)*
The Jungle Book *'67 (V)*
The Patsy *'64*
The Wheeler Dealers *'63*
Goodbye, My Lady *'56*
The High and the Mighty *'54*
Here Comes the Groom *'51*
I Love a Bandleader *'45*
Buck Benny Rides Again *'40*
Dreaming Out Loud *'40*
Man About Town *'39*
Melody Cruise *'32*

Rachael Harris (1968-)
Diary of a Wimpy Kid *'10*
The Hangover *'09*
Evan Almighty *'07*
License to Wed *'07*
For Your Consideration *'06*
Kicking & Screaming *'05*

Richard Harris (1932-2002)
Kaena: The Prophecy *'03 (V)*
The Count of Monte Cristo *'02*
Harry Potter and the Chamber of Secrets *'02*
Harry Potter and the Sorcerer's Stone *'01*
Gladiator *'00*
Grizzly Falls *'99*
To Walk with Lions *'99*
The Hunchback *'97*
Smilla's Sense of Snow *'96*
This Is the Sea *'96*
Trojan Eddie *'96*
Cry, the Beloved Country *'95*
Savage Hearts *'95*
Abraham *'94*
King of the Wind *'93*
Wrestling Ernest Hemingway *'93*
Patriot Games *'92*
Silent Tongue *'92*
Unforgiven *'92*
The Field *'90*
Mack the Knife *'89*
Game for Vultures *'86*
Martin's Day *'85*
Your Ticket Is No Longer Valid *'84*
Triumphs of a Man Called Horse *'83*
Tarzan, the Ape Man *'81*
Highpoint *'80*
The Last Word *'80*
Wild Geese *'78*
Golden Rendezvous *'77*
Gulliver's Travels *'77*
Orca *'77*
The Cassandra Crossing *'76*
The Return of a Man Called Horse *'76*
Robin and Marian *'76*
Juggernaut *'74*
99 & 44/100 Dead *'74*
The Deadly Trackers *'73*
The Hero *'71*
Man in the Wilderness *'71*
Cromwell *'70*
A Man Called Horse *'70*
Molly Maguires *'70*
Camelot *'67*
Caprice *'67*
The Bible *'66*
Hawaii *'66*
The Heroes of Telemark *'65*
Major Dundee *'65*
The Red Desert *'64*
This Sporting Life *'63*
Mutiny on the Bounty *'62*
The Guns of Navarone *'61*
The Wreck of the Mary Deare *'59*

Ricky Harris (1962-)
Woman, Thou Art Loosed *'04*
Bones *'01*
Simon Sez *'99*
Thick as Thieves *'99*

Robert H. Harris (1909-81)
Valley of the Dolls *'67*
Apache Uprising *'66*
How to Make a Monster *'58*
The Invisible Boy *'57*

Robin Harris (1953-90)
Sorority House Massacre 2: Nighty Nightmare *'92*
Hard to Die *'90*
House Party *'90*
Mo' Better Blues *'90*
I'm Gonna Git You Sucka *'88*

Rosalind Harris
Mrs. Santa Claus *'96*
Fiddler on the Roof *'71*

Rosemary Harris (1930-)
Is Anybody There? *'08*
Before the Devil Knows You're Dead *'07*
Spider-Man 3 *'07*
Being Julia *'04*
Spider-Man 2 *'04*
Spider-Man *'02*
Blow Dry *'00*
The Gift *'00*
Sunshine *'99*
My Life So Far *'98*
Hamlet *'96*
Tom & Viv *'94*
The Camomile Lawn *'92*
Crossing Delancey *'88*
Heartbreak House *'86*
The Ploughman's Lunch *'83*
To the Lighthouse *'83*
The Chisholms *'79*
Beau Brummel *'54*

Rossie (Ross) Harris (1969-)
Zapped Again *'89*
Two Kinds of Love *'85*
Testament *'83*
Amber Waves *'82*
Airplane! *'80*

Sean Harris
Outlaw *'07*
Brothers of the Head *'06*
See No Evil: The Moors Murders *'06*
Asylum *'05*
Trauma *'04*
24 Hour Party People *'01*

Shawntae Harris
See Da Brat

Stacy Harris (1918-73)
Bloody Mama *'70*
The Hunters *'58*
New Orleans After Dark *'58*
The Redhead from Wyoming *'53*

Steve Harris (1965-)
12 Rounds *'09*
Quarantine *'08*
Diary of a Mad Black Woman *'05*
The Unseen *'05*
Bringing Down the House *'03*
Minority Report *'02*
Rip It Off *'02*
The Skulls *'00*
The Mod Squad *'99*
The Rock *'96*
Sugar Hill *'94*

Ted Harris (1938-91)
Uforia *'81*
Blacula *'72*

Tip "T.I." Harris (1980-)
Takers *'10*
ATL *'06*

Wood Harris (1969-)
Next Day Air *'09*
Not Easily Broken *'09*
Southland Tales *'06*
Dirty *'05*
Paid in Full *'02*
Hendrix *'00*
Remember the Titans *'00*
Small Vices: A Spenser Mystery *'99*

Zelda Harris (1985-)
He Got Game *'98*
The Baby-Sitters' Club *'95*
Crooklyn *'94*
The Piano Lesson *'94*

Anthony Harrison (1961-)
House of the Dead *'03*
Blackwoods *'02*

Cathryn Harrison (1960-)
Heat of the Sun *'99*
The Choir *'95*
Clarissa *'91*
A Handful of Dust *'88*
Empire State *'87*
The Dresser *'83*
Blue Fire Lady *'78*
Images *'72*
Pied Piper *'72*

Emily Harrison
Valley of the Heart's Delight *'07*
Curse of the Puppet Master: The Human Experiment *'98*

George Harrison (1943-2001)
Shanghai Surprise *'86*
Water *'85*
Monty Python's Life of Brian *'79*
All You Need Is Cash *'78*
Let It Be *'70*
Yellow Submarine *'68 (V)*
Magical Mystery Tour *'67*
Help! *'65*
A Hard Day's Night *'64*

Gregory Harrison (1952-)
Au Pair 3: Adventure in Paradise *'09*
Maneater *'09*
Au Pair 2: The Fairy Tale Continues *'01*
Au Pair *'99*
First Daughter *'99*
Running Wild *'99*
Air Bud 2: Golden Receiver *'98*
It's My Party *'95*
Hard Evidence *'94*
Cadillac Girls *'93*
Caught in the Act *'93*
Duplicates *'92*
Bare Essentials *'91*
Body Chemistry 2: Voice of a Stranger *'91*
Dangerous Pursuit *'89*
North Shore *'87*
The Hasty Heart *'86*
Oceans of Fire *'86*
Seduced *'85*
Razorback *'84*
For Ladies Only *'81*
Enola Gay: The Men, the Mission, the Atomic Bomb *'80*
Centennial *'78*
The Gathering *'77*
Trilogy of Terror *'75*

Jenilee Harrison (1959-)
Fists of Iron *'94*
Prime Target *'91*
Curse 3: Blood Sacrifice *'90*
Tank *'83*

Jenna Harrison
Against the Dark *'08*
Telling Lies *'06*

Kathleen Harrison (1892-1995)
A Cry from the Streets *'57*
Cast a Dark Shadow *'55*
Let's Make Up *'55*
Where There's a Will *'55*
The Pickwick Papers *'54*
A Christmas Carol *'51*
Trio *'50*
The Winslow Boy *'48*
The Ghost Train *'41*
Night Must Fall *'37*
The Ghoul *'34*

Linda Harrison (1945-)
Cocoon *'85*
Beneath the Planet of the Apes *'70*
Planet of the Apes *'68*

Lottie Harrison
Driftin' River *'46*
Lost in a Harem *'44*

Matthew Harrison (1968-)
Ace of Hearts *'08*
The House Next Door *'01*

Michelle Harrison
The Invisible *'07*
Luna: Spirit of the Whale *'07*
Come as You Are *'05*
Pressure *'02*

Mya Harrison
See Mya

Noel Harrison (1936-)
Deja Vu *'98*
Tagget *'90*

Rex Harrison (1908-90)
Anastasia: The Mystery of Anna *'86*
Heartbreak House *'86*
Time to Die *'83*
Ashanti, Land of No Mercy *'79*
The Fifth Musketeer *'79*
Deadly Thief *'78*
The Prince and the Pauper *'78*
Doctor Dolittle *'67*
The Honey Pot *'67*
The Agony and the Ecstasy *'65*
My Fair Lady *'64*
Cleopatra *'63*
Midnight Lace *'60*
The Reluctant Debutante *'58*
King Richard and the Crusaders *'54*
Main Street to Broadway *'53*
The Long Dark Hall *'51*
Unfaithfully Yours *'48*
The Ghost and Mrs. Muir *'47*
Anna and the King of Siam *'46*
I Live in Grosvenor Square *'46*
Blithe Spirit *'45*
Major Barbara *'41*
Night Train to Munich *'40*
The Citadel *'38*
Sidewalks of London *'38*
Men Are Not Gods *'37*
Storm in a Teacup *'37*

Richard Harrison (1935-)
Ninja Powerforce *'90*
Ninja Showdown *'90*
The Channeler *'89*
Ninja Strike Force *'88*
Terminal Force *'88*
Ninja Commandments *'87*
Ninja Operation: Licensed to Terminate *'87*
Blood Debts *'83*
Ninja Champion *'80*
Fireback *'78*
Mad Dog Killer *'77*
Thirty-Six Hours of Hell *'77*
Between God, the Devil & a Winchester *'72*
His Name Was King *'71*
Messalina vs. the Son of Hercules *'64*
Two Gladiators *'64*
Giants of Rome *'63*
Gunfight at Red Sands *'63*
The Invincible Gladiator *'63*
Gladiators 7 *'62*
The Invincible Gladiator *'62*
Medusa Against the Son of Hercules *'62*

Schae Harrison (1962-)
Interlocked *'98*
Magic Island *'95*

David Harrod
The Thin Red Line *'98*
The House on Todville Road *'95*
The Tuskegee Airmen *'95*
Armed for Action *'92*
Blood on the Badge *'92*

Jamie Harrold
Flannel Pajamas *'06*
The Last Winter *'06*
Corn *'02*
The Sum of All Fears *'02*
A Glimpse of Hell *'01*
The Score *'01*
Henry Hill *'00*
101 Ways (The Things a Girl Will Do to Keep Her Volvo) *'00*
Swimming *'00*
I Think I Do *'97*
I Shot Andy Warhol *'96*
Chain of Desire *'93*
Family Pictures *'93*

Kathryn Harrold (1950-)
A Woman's a Helluva Thing *'01*
The '70s *'00*
Outrage *'98*
The Companion *'94*
Deadly Desire *'91*
Rainbow Drive *'90*
Dead Solid Perfect *'88*
Someone to Love *'87*
Raw Deal *'86*
Into the Night *'85*
Heartbreakers *'84*
The Sender *'82*
Yes, Giorgio *'82*
Modern Romance *'81*
The Pursuit of D.B. Cooper *'81*
Bogie: The Last Hero *'80*
The Hunter *'80*
Nightwing *'79*

John Harron (1903-39)
Midnight Warning *'32*
The White Zombie *'32*
The Night Cry *'26*
West-Bound Limited *'23*

Robert "Bobbie" Harron (1893-1920)
The Greatest Question *'19*
True Heart Susie *'19*
Hearts of the World *'18*
Hoodoo Ann *'16*
The Birth of a Nation *'15*
Home Sweet Home *'14*
Judith of Bethulia *'14*
Battle of Elderbush Gulch *'13*

Lisa Harrow (1943-)
Sunday *'96*
That Eye, the Sky *'94*
The Last Days of Chez Nous *'92*
Shaker Run *'85*
Under Capricorn *'82*
The Final Conflict *'81*
From a Far Country: Pope John Paul II *'81*
All Creatures Great and Small *'74*

Deborah Harry (1945-)
Elegy *'08*
My Life Without Me *'03*
All I Want *'02*
Deuces Wild *'02*
The Fluffer *'01*
Six Ways to Sunday *'99*
Cop Land *'97*
Dead Beat *'94*
Heavy *'94*
Body Bags *'93*
Intimate Stranger *'91*
Mother Goose Rock 'n' Rhyme *'90*
Tales from the Darkside: The Movie *'90*
New York Stories *'89*
Hairspray *'88*
Satisfaction *'88*
Forever, Lulu *'87*
Videodrome *'83*
Union City *'81*
Mr. Mike's Mondo Video *'79*
The Foreigner *'78*

Jackee Harry
See Jackee
The Last Days of Summer *'07*

Ray Harryhausen (1920-)
Comic Book: The Movie *'04*
Mighty Joe Young *'98*
Spies Like Us *'85*

Margo Harshman (1986-)
Sorority Row *'09*
College Road Trip *'08*
Recipe for Disaster *'03*

Christina Hart
Helter Skelter *'76*
Games Girls Play *'75*
Johnny Firecloud *'75*
The Runaway Barge *'75*

Christopher Hart
Idle Hands *'99*
Addams Family Values *'93*
The Addams Family *'91*

Dianne Lee Hart
Pom Pom Girls *'76*
The Giant Spider Invasion *'75*

Dolores Hart (1938-)
The Plunderers *'60*
Where the Boys Are *'60*
King Creole *'58*
Lonelyhearts *'58*
Loving You *'57*

Dorothy Hart (1923-2004)
Loan Shark *'52*
Tarzan's Savage Fury *'52*
I Was a Communist for the FBI *'51*
The Naked City *'48*

Ian Hart (1964-)
Tristram Shandy: A Cock and Bull Story *'05*
Finding Neverland *'04*
The Hound of the Baskervilles *'02*
Harry Potter and the Sorcerer's Stone *'01*
Killing Me Softly *'01*
Strictly Sinatra *'01*
Aberdeen *'00*
American Women *'00*
Born Romantic *'00*
Liam *'00*
Longitude *'00*
The End of the Affair *'99*
Spring Forward *'99*
Wonderland *'99*
Frogs for Snakes *'98*
Monument Ave. *'98*
B. Monkey *'97*
The Butcher Boy *'97*
Michael Collins *'96*
Robinson Crusoe *'96*
The Englishman Who Went up a Hill But Came down a Mountain *'95*
Hollow Reed *'95*
Land and Freedom *'95*
Nothing Personal *'95*
Backbeat *'94*
The Hours and Times *'92*

John Hart (1917-)
Blackenstein *'73*
The Fighting Redhead *'50*

Kevin Hart
Death at a Funeral *'10*
Not Easily Broken *'09*
Lone Wolf *'88*
Mindkiller *'87*

Kevin Hart (1980-)
Fool's Gold *'08*
Meet Dave *'08*
Scary Movie 4 *'06*
In the Mix *'05*
Along Came Polly *'04*
Soul Plane *'04*
Scary Movie 3 *'03*

Linda Hart
The First $20 Million is Always the Hardest *'02*
Crazy in Alabama *'99*
Tin Cup *'96*
Gypsy *'93*
A Perfect World *'93*

Melissa Joan Hart (1976-)
Holiday in Handcuffs *'07*
Backflash *'01*
Drive Me Crazy *'99*
Sabrina the Teenage Witch *'96*

Neal Hart (1870-1949)
The Dude Bandit *'33*
Trigger Tricks *'30*
Sands of Sacrifice *'21*

Pamela Hart
Changing Lanes *'02*
Next Stop, Wonderland *'98*
Pi *'98*
The Proposition *'97*

Roxanne Hart (1952-)
The Good Girl *'02*
Home Room *'02*
Moonlight Mile *'02*
Follow the Stars Home *'01*
The Runaway *'00*
Horton Foote's Alone *'97*
Our Mother's Murder *'97*
Once Around *'91*
Tagget *'90*
Vengeance *'89*
Pulse *'88*
The Last Innocent Man *'87*
Highlander *'86*
Samaritan: The Mitch Snyder Story *'86*
Oh, God! You Devil *'84*
Old Enough *'84*
The Tender Age *'84*
Special Bulletin *'83*
The Verdict *'82*

Shad Hart
The Reagans *'04*
Big Brother Trouble *'00*

Susan Hart (1941-)
Dr. Goldfoot and the Bikini Machine *'66*
Ghost in the Invisible Bikini *'66*
Pajama Party *'64*
Ride the Wild Surf *'64*
The Slime People *'63*

Teddy Hart (1897-1971)
Mickey One *'65*
Ma and Pa Kettle at Waikiki *'55*

William S. Hart (1864-1946)
Show People *'28*
Tumbleweeds *'25*
Three Word Brand *'21*
The Cradle of Courage *'20*
The Toll Gate *'20*
Wagon Tracks *'19*
Blue Blazes Rawden *'18*
Narrow Trail *'17*
Hell's Hinges *'16*
Return of Draw Egan *'16*
The Bargain *'15*
The Disciple *'15*
The Fugitive: Taking of Luke McVane *'15*
On the Night Stage *'15*

Douglas Harter
Invasion Force *'90*
White Fury *'90*

Pat Hartigan (1881-1951)
Ranson's Folly *'26*
King of the Wild Horses *'24*

Clabe Hartley
Trancers 5: Sudden Deth *'94*
Trancers 4: Jack of Swords *'93*

Mariette Hartley (1940-)
Novel Romance *'06*
Encino Man *'92*
1969 *'89*
Passion in Paradise *'89*
Silence of the Heart *'84*
M.A.D.D.: Mothers Against Drunk Driving *'83*
Improper Channels *'82*
O'Hara's Wife *'82*
No Place to Hide *'81*
Nightmare at 43 Hillcrest *'74*
Genesis II *'73*
The Return of Count Yorga *'71*
Marnie *'64*
Drums of Africa *'63*
Ride the High Country *'62*

Pat Hartley
Edie in Ciao! Manhattan *'72*
Rainbow Bridge *'71*

Steven Hartley
The Walker *'07*
A Dog of Flanders *'99*

Elizabeth Hartman (1941-87)
The Secret of NIMH *'82 (V)*
Walking Tall *'73*
The Beguiled *'70*
The Fixer *'68*
The Group *'66*
You're a Big Boy Now *'66*
A Patch of Blue *'65*

Margot Hartman
Voyage to the Planet of Prehistoric Women *'68*
Curse of the Living Corpse *'64*

Phil Hartman (1948-98)
Kiki's Delivery Service *'98 (V)*
Small Soldiers *'98*
The Second Civil War *'97*
Jingle All the Way *'96*
Sgt. Bilko *'95*
The Crazysitter *'94*
Greedy *'94*
Houseguest *'94*
CB4: The Movie *'93*
Coneheads *'93*
Daybreak *'93*
National Lampoon's Loaded Weapon 1 *'93*
So I Married an Axe Murderer *'93*
Quick Change *'90*
Fletch Lives *'89*
How I Got into College *'89*
Amazon Women on the Moon *'87*
Blind Date *'87*
Jumpin' Jack Flash *'86*
Last Resort *'86*
Three Amigos *'86*
Pee-wee's Big Adventure *'85*
Weekend Pass *'84*
The Pee-wee Herman Show *'82*
Cheech and Chong's Next Movie *'80*

Lisa Hartman Black (1956-)
Bare Essentials *'91*
Red Wind *'91*
The Return of Eliot Ness *'91*
The Take *'90*
Full Exposure: The Sex Tape Scandals *'89*
The Seventeenth Bride *'84*
Where the Boys Are '84 *'84*
Deadly Blessing *'81*
Just Tell Me You Love Me *'80*
Magic on Love Island *'80*

William Hartnell (1908-75)
This Sporting Life *'63*
The Mouse That Roared *'59*
Carry On Sergeant *'58*
Brighton Rock *'47*
Appointment with Crime *'45*
Immortal Battalion *'44*

Rona Hartner (1973-)
Le Divorce *'03*
Time of the Wolf *'03*
Dad On the Run *'00*
The Crazy Stranger *'98*

Josh Hartnett (1978-)
August *'08*
Resurrecting the Champ *'07*
30 Days of Night *'07*
The Black Dahlia *'06*
Lucky Number Slevin *'06*
Mozart and the Whale *'05*
Sin City *'05*
Wicker Park *'04*
Hollywood Homicide *'03*
40 Days and 40 Nights *'02*
Black Hawk Down *'01*
O *'01*
Pearl Harbor *'01*
Town and Country *'01*
Blow Dry *'00*
Here on Earth *'00*
The Virgin Suicides *'99*
The Faculty *'98*
Halloween: H20 *'98*

Joshua Harto (1979-)
The Dark Knight *'08*
Iron Man *'08*

Rainbow Harvest
Fever *'91*
Mirror, Mirror *'90*
Old Enough *'84*

Alex Harvey
Fire Down Below *'97*
Gettysburg *'93*

Don Harvey
Corn *'02*
Sparkler *'99*
The Con *'98*
The Thin Red Line *'98*
Crime of the Century *'96*
Last Dance *'96*
Sawbones *'95*
Better Off Dead *'94*
Men of War *'94*
Tank Girl *'94*
American Heart *'92*
Mission of the Shark *'91*
Prey of the Chameleon *'91*
Die Hard 2: Die Harder *'90*
Casualties of War *'89*
The Beast *'88*
Eight Men Out *'88*

Forrester Harvey (1890-1945)
Mrs. Miniver *'42*
The Wolf Man *'41*
Thoroughbreds Don't Cry *'37*
The Eagle and the Hawk *'33*

Harry Harvey (1901-85)
The Narrow Margin *'52*
Ace in the Hole *'51*
Tea for Two *'50*
I'm from Arkansas *'44*
The Spider Returns *'41*
Ridin' the Trail *'40*
Code of the Fearless *'39*
In Old Montana *'39*
Phantom Rancher *'39*
Here's Flash Casey *'38*
King of the Sierras *'38*
The Reckless Way *'36*

Harry Harvey, Jr. (1929-78)
King of the Sierras *'38*
Reefer Madness *'38*

John Harvey
The Stranglers of Bombay *'60*
X The Unknown *'56*
Four Jills in a Jeep *'44*

Laurence Harvey (1928-73)
Escape to the Sun *'72*
Night Watch *'72*
The Magic Christian *'69*
Dandy in Aspic *'68*
Spy with a Cold Nose *'66*
Darling *'65*
Of Human Bondage *'64*
The Outrage *'64*
The Manchurian Candidate *'62*
Walk on the Wild Side *'62*
The Wonderful World of the Brothers Grimm *'62*
Summer and Smoke *'61*
The Alamo *'60*
Butterfield 8 *'60*
Expresso Bongo *'59*
Room at the Top *'59*
The Silent Enemy *'58*
Truth about Women *'58*
Three Men in a Boat *'56*
I Am a Camera *'55*
King Richard and the Crusaders *'54*
Romeo and Juliet *'54*
Innocents in Paris *'53*
Man on the Run *'49*
House of Darkness *'48*

Paul Harvey (1882-1955)
Three for the Show *'55*
April in Paris *'52*
Thunder in God's Country *'51*
Riding High *'50*
Side Street *'50*
The Yellow Cab Man *'50*
Call Northside 777 *'48*
John Loves Mary *'48*
A Southern Yankee *'48*
The Bamboo Blonde *'46*
Easy to Wed *'46*
Helldorado *'46*
A Night in Casablanca *'46*
Blondie's Blessed Event *'42*
High Sierra *'41*
Out of the Fog *'41*
Arizona *'40*
Meet Dr. Christian *'39*
A Slight Case of Murder *'38*
23 1/2 Hours Leave *'37*
Alibi Ike *'35*
The Whole Town's Talking *'35*

Rodney Harvey (1967-98)
Guncrazy *'92*
My Own Private Idaho *'91*
Five Corners *'88*
Salsa *'88*

Steve Harvey (1956-)
Racing Stripes *'05 (V)*
Johnson Family Vacation *'04*
You Got Served *'04*
The Fighting Temptations *'03*
Love Don't Cost a Thing *'03*

Terence Harvey
From Hell *'01*
The Phantom of the Opera *'89*

Tom Harvey
Moving Target *'96*
And Then You Die *'88*
Second Wind *'76*

Verna Harvey (1952-)
That'll Be the Day *'73*
The Nightcomers *'72*

Kazuo Hasegawa (1908-84)
An Actor's Revenge *'63*
The Crucified Lovers *'54*
Gate of Hell *'54*

Riki Hashimoto
Daimajin *'66*
Return of Daimajin *'66*
Wrath of Daimajin *'66*

David Haskell (1948-2000)
Body Double *'84*
Godspell *'73*

Peter Haskell (1934-)
Robot Wars *'93*
Child's Play 3 *'91*
The Cracker Factory *'79*
Fantastic Seven *'79*
Christina *'74*
Legend of Earl Durand *'74*
The Ballad of Andy Crocker *'69*
Finnegan's Wake *'65*

Susan Haskell (1968-)
Black Point *'01*
No Turning Back *'01*
Smart House *'00*
Mrs. Winterbourne *'96*

Imogen Hassall (1942-80)
The Bloodsuckers *'70*
When Dinosaurs Ruled the Earth *'70*

Tamer Hassan
Wrong Turn 3: Left for Dead *'09*
The Business *'05*
Layer Cake *'05*

O.E. Hasse (1903-78)
State of Siege *'73*
The Elusive Corporal *'62*
Above Us the Waves *'56*
Betrayed *'54*
I Confess *'53*
The Big Lift *'50*

Danny Hassel (1967-)
A Nightmare on Elm Street 5: Dream Child *'89*
A Nightmare on Elm Street 4: Dream Master *'88*

David Hasselhoff (1952-)
Anaconda 3: The Offspring *'08*
Kickin' It Old Skool *'07*
Click *'06*
A Dirty Shame *'04*
Dodgeball: A True Underdog Story *'04*
The SpongeBob SquarePants Movie *'04*
The Big Tease *'99*
Baywatch the Movie: Forbidden Paradise *'95*
Ring of the Musketeers *'93*
Bail Out *'90*
The Final Alliance *'89*
Fire and Rain *'89*
Witchery *'88*
Terror at London Bridge *'85*
Cartier Affair *'84*
Star Crash *'78*
Revenge of the Cheerleaders *'76*

Marilyn Hassett (1947-)
Twenty Dollar Star *'91*
Messenger of Death *'88*
Body Count *'87*
The Bell Jar *'79*
The Other Side of the Mountain, Part 2 *'78*
Two Minute Warning *'76*
The Other Side of the Mountain *'75*

Signe Hasso (1910-2002)
The True and the False *'55*
Crisis *'50*
A Double Life *'47*
Where There's Life *'47*
A Scandal in Paris *'46*
House on 92nd Street *'45*
Johnny Angel *'45*
The Seventh Cross *'44*
The Story of Dr. Wassell *'44*
Heaven Can Wait *'43*
Journey for Margaret *'42*

Bob Hastings (1925-)
Shadow Force *'92*
Snowballing *'85*
The Munsters' Revenge *'81*
Harper Valley P.T.A. *'78*
McHale's Navy Joins the Air Force *'65*
McHale's Navy *'64*

Richard Hatch (1945-)
InAlienable *'08*
Unseen Evil *'99*
Delta Force Commando 2 *'90*
Ghetto Blaster *'89*
Party Line *'88*
Heated Vengeance *'87*
Prisoners of the Lost Universe *'84*
Charlie Chan and the Curse of the Dragon Queen *'81*
Battlestar Galactica *'78*
Deadman's Curve *'78*
Mission Galactica: The Cylon Attack *'78*
The Hatfields & the McCoys *'75*

Riley Hatch
America '24
Little Old New York '23

Mary Hatcher (1929-)
Tales of Robin Hood '52
The Big Wheel '49
Holiday in Havana '49
Variety Girl '47

Teri Hatcher (1964-)
Coraline '09 (V)
Resurrecting the Champ '07
Momentum '03
Spy Kids '01
Running Mates '00
Fever '99
Since You've Been Gone '97
Tomorrow Never Dies '97
Two Days in the Valley '96
Heaven's Prisoners '95
Brain Smasher... A Love Story '93
All Tied Up '92
The Cool Surface '92
Straight Talk '92
Dead in the Water '91
Soapdish '91
The Big Picture '89
Tango and Cash '89

Hurd Hatfield (1918-98)
Her Alibi '88
Crimes of the Heart '86
King David '85
The Word '78
Thief '71
The Boston Strangler '68
Lamp at Midnight '66
Mickey One '65
Invincible Mr. Disraeli '63
El Cid '61
The King of Kings '61
Tarzan and the Slave Girl '50
The Unsuspected '47
Diary of a Chambermaid '46
Picture of Dorian Gray '45
Dragon Seed '44

Amy Hathaway
Smiling Fish & Goat on Fire '99
Joyride '97

Anne Hathaway (1982-)
Alice in Wonderland '10
Valentine's Day '10
Bride Wars '09
Get Smart '08
Passengers '08
Rachel Getting Married '08
Becoming Jane '07
The Devil Wears Prada '06
Brokeback Mountain '05
Hoodwinked '05 (V)
Ella Enchanted '04
The Princess Diaries 2: Royal Engagement '04
Nicholas Nickleby '02
The Other Side of Heaven '02
The Princess Diaries '01

Noah Hathaway (1971-)
Mortal Danger '94
Troll '86
The NeverEnding Story '84

Shawn Hatosy (1975-)
Bad Lieutenant: Port of Call New Orleans '09
Public Enemies '09
Familiar Strangers '08
The Lazarus Project '08
Nobel Son '08
Alpha Dog '06
Factory Girl '06
The Cooler '03
Dallas 362 '03
11:14 '03
A Guy Thing '03
Soldier's Girl '03
John Q '02
Tangled '01
Borstal Boy '00
Down to You '00
Anywhere But Here '99
Outside Providence '99
Simpatico '99
Witness Protection '99
The Thin Red Line '98
In and Out '97
The Postman '97

Eriko Hatsune
Apartment 1303 '07
Uzumaki '00

D.R.O. Hatswell (1898-1976)
The Quiet Man '52
Peg o' My Heart '22

Raymond Hatton (1887-1971)
Flesh and the Spur '57
Invasion of the Saucer Men '57
Motorcycle Gang '57
Shake, Rattle and Rock '57
Girls in Prison '56
Day the World Ended '55
Kentucky Jubilee '51
Blazing Guns '50
Guns of Justice '50
Last Bullet '50
Marshal of Heldorado '50
Operation Haylift '50
Outlaw Fury '50
Rangeland Empire '50
Sudden Death '50
Rolling Home '48
Land of the Lawless '47
Border Bandits '46
Gentleman from Texas '46
Northwest Trail '46
The Stranger from Pecos '45
Lawmen '44
Partners of the Trail '44
Raiders of the Border '44
Range Law '44
Ghost Rider '43
Six Gun Gospel '43
Texas Kid '43
Below the Border '42
Dawn on the Great Divide '42
Down Texas Way '42
Ghost Town Law '42
Reap the Wild Wind '42
Riders of the West '42
West of the Law '42
Arizona Bound '41
Forbidden Trails '41
Gunman from Bodie '41
Covered Wagon Days '40
Heroes of the Saddle '40
Oklahoma Renegades '40
Pioneers of the West '40
Rocky Mountain Rangers '40
Cowboys from Texas '39
Frontier Horizon '39
The Kansas Terrors '39
Rough Riders' Roundup '39
Wall Street Cowboy '39
Wyoming Outlaw '39
Come on Rangers '38
The Texans '38
Desert Gold '36
The Vigilantes Are Coming '36
Rustlers of Red Dog '35
Buffalo Stampede '33
Hidden Gold '33
Lady Killer '33
Terror Trail '33
The Three Musketeers '33
Cornered '32
The Crooked Circle '32
Drifting Souls '32
Uptown New York '32
Rogue of the Rio Grande '30
The Silver Horde '30
We're in the Navy Now '27
Behind the Front '26
The Fighting American '24
The Virginian '23
Peck's Bad Boy '21
Male and Female '19
The Little American '17

Rondo Hatton (1894-1946)
The Brute Man '46
House of Horrors '46
Jungle Captive '45
The Pearl of Death '44

Sabine Haudepin
Hotel America '81
The Last Metro '80

Aysha Hauer (1966-)
Welcome Says the Angel '01
Witchcraft 5: Dance with the Devil '92

Rutger Hauer (1944-)
Goal 2: Living the Dream '07
Moving McAllister '07
The Hunt for Eagle One: Crash Point '06
Batman Begins '05
Dracula 3: Legacy '05
Mirror Wars: Reflection One '05
Sin City '05
Salem's Lot '04
Dracula 2: Ascension '03
Confessions of a Dangerous Mind '02
Scorcher '02
The 10th Kingdom '00
Turbulence 3: Heavy Metal '00
Wilder '00
New World Disorder '99
Partners in Crime '99
Tactical Assault '99
Merlin '98
Bleeders '97
Bone Daddy '97
Hostile Waters '97
Jack London's The Call of the Wild '97
Redline '97
Tales from a Parallel Universe: Eating Pattern '97
Blast '96
Crossworlds '96
Omega Doom '96
Precious Find '96
Mr. Stitch '95
Amelia Earhart: The Final Flight '94
Beyond Forgiveness '94
Fatherland '94
Forbidden Choices '94
Surviving the Game '94
Arctic Blue '93
Blind Side '93
Nostradamus '93
Voyage '93
Beyond Justice '92
Buffy the Vampire Slayer '92
Past Midnight '92
Split Second '92
Deadlock '91
Blind Fury '90
The Blood of Heroes '89
Bloodhounds of Broadway '89
Escape from Sobibor '87
The Hitcher '86
Wanted Dead or Alive '86
Flesh and Blood '85
Ladyhawke '85
A Breed Apart '84
Mysteries '84
Fatal Error '83
The Osterman Weekend '83
Blade Runner '82
Inside the Third Reich '82
Chanel Solitaire '81
Eureka! '81
Nighthawks '81
Spetters '80
Soldier of Orange '78
Cold Blood '75
Katie Tippel '75
The Wilby Conspiracy '75
Dandelions '74
Turkish Delight '73

Angelika Hauff (1923-83)
The Life and Loves of Mozart '59
Tromba, the Tiger Man '52
The Marriage of Figaro '49

Thomas Hauff
DC 9/11: Time of Crisis '04
My Father, My Rival '85

Vicky Haughton
Whale Rider '02
Her Majesty '01

Darla Haun (1964-)
Dracula: Dead and Loving It '95
Married People, Single Sex '93
Red Snow '91

Lindsey Haun
Shrooms '07
Broken Bridges '06
Brave New Girl '04

Ullrich Haupt (1887-1931)
Morocco '30
The Iron Mask '29
Tempest '28
Captain Swagger '25

Cole Hauser (1975-)
The Family That Preys '08
Tortured '08
The Stone Angel '07
The Break-Up '06
The Cave '05
Dirty '05
Paparazzi '04
Tears of the Sun '03
2 Fast 2 Furious '03
Hart's War '02
White Oleander '02
Pitch Black '00
A Shot at Glory '00
Tigerland '00
The Hi-Lo Country '98
Gang Boys '97
Good Will Hunting '97
All Over Me '96
Higher Learning '94
Dazed and Confused '93
School Ties '92

Fay Hauser
The Hot Chick '02
Candyman 2: Farewell to the Flesh '94
Jo Jo Dancer, Your Life Is Calling '86
Christmas Lilies of the Field '84
Marvin & Tige '84
Jimmy the Kid '82

Wings Hauser (1948-)
Avenging Angel '07
The Stone Angel '07
The Insider '99
Gang Boys '97
Tales from the Hood '95
Victim of Desire '94
Watchers 3 '94
In Between '92
Mind, Body & Soul '92
Beastmaster 2: Through the Portal of Time '91
Deadly Conspiracy '91
Frame Up '91
Living to Die '91
Pale Blood '91
The Art of Dying '90
Coldfire '90
Exiled in America '90
The Killer's Edge '90
Reason to Die '90
Street Asylum '90
Wilding '90
Bedroom Eyes 2 '89
The Carpenter '89
L.A. Bounty '89
Marked for Murder '89
Out of Sight, Out of Her Mind '89
The Siege of Firebase Gloria '89
Dead Man Walking '88
Hostage '87
Nightmare at Noon '87
No Safe Haven '87
Tough Guys Don't Dance '87
The Wind '87
Jo Jo Dancer, Your Life Is Calling '86
The Long, Hot Summer '86
Code of Honor '84
A Soldier's Story '84
Deadly Force '83
Mutant '83
Homework '82
Vice Squad '82

Richie Havens (1941-)
Perfect Harmony '91
Street Hunter '90
Boss' Son '78

June Haver (1926-2005)
The Girl Next Door '53
Love Nest '51
Look for the Silver Lining '49
The Dolly Sisters '46

Phyllis Haver (1899-1960)
Battle of the Sexes '28
The Fighting Eagle '27
The Nervous Wreck '26

Nigel Havers (1949-)
Penelope '06
Element of Doubt '96
Catherine Cookson's The Glass Virgin '95
The Burning Season '94
Lie Down with Lions '94
Quiet Days in Clichy '90
Farewell to the King '89
The Charmer '87
Empire of the Sun '87
The Little Princess '87
The Whistle Blower '87
Hold the Dream '86
Burke & Wills '85
A Passage to India '84
Chariots of Fire '81
Who Is Killing the Great Chefs of Europe? '78

Thom Haverstock
Fall from Innocence '88
Skullduggery '79

Alex Havier (1911-45)
They Were Expendable '45
Bataan '43

June Havoc (1916-)
Return to Salem's Lot '87
Follow the Sun '51
Gentleman's Agreement '47
Brewster's Millions '45
Timber Queen '44
Hello, Frisco, Hello '43
My Sister Eileen '42
Sing Your Worries Away '42
Four Jacks and a Jill '41

Robin Hawdon (1939-)
When Dinosaurs Ruled the Earth '70
Zeta One '69
Bedazzled '68

Keeley Hawes (1977-)
Flashbacks of a Fool '08
Death at a Funeral '07
Tristram Shandy: A Cock and Bull Story '05
Under the Greenwood Tree '05
Chaos & Cadavers '03
Me & Mrs. Jones '02
Tipping the Velvet '02
Othello '01
Wives and Daughters '01
The Last September '99
The Avengers '98
Our Mutual Friend '98
Retribution '98
The Moonstone '97

Jeremy Hawk (1918-2002)
Lucky Jim '58
Who Done It? '56
Race for Life '55

Ethan Hawke (1971-)
Brooklyn's Finest '09
Daybreakers '09
New York, I Love You '09
What Doesn't Kill You '08
Before the Devil Knows You're Dead '07
Fast Food Nation '06
The Hottest State '06
Assault on Precinct 13 '05
Lord of War '05
Before Sunset '04
Taking Lives '04
The Jimmy Show '01
Tape '01
Training Day '01
Waking Life '01
Hamlet '00
Joe the King '99
Snow Falling on Cedars '99
Gattaca '97
Great Expectations '97
The Newton Boys '97
Before Sunrise '94
Floundering '94
Reality Bites '94
Search and Destroy '94
White Fang 2: The Myth of the White Wolf '94
Alive '93
Rich in Love '93
A Midnight Clear '92
Waterland '92
Mystery Date '91
White Fang '91
Dad '89
Dead Poets Society '89
Explorers '85

John Hawkes (1959-)
Winter's Bone '10
S. Darko: A Donnie Darko Tale '09
Zombie Strippers '08
Miami Vice '06
Wristcutters: A Love Story '06
Me and You and Everyone We Know '05
Identity '03
Hardball '01
The Perfect Storm '00
Sand '00
A Slipping Down Life '99
I Still Know What You Did Last Summer '98
Playing God '96
Night of the Scarecrow '95
Roadracers '94
Murder Rap '87

Terri Hawkes
The Killing Man '94
Watch It '93

Jack Hawkins (1910-73)
Tales That Witness Madness '73
Theatre of Blood '73
Escape to the Sun '72
Restless '72
Young Winston '72
Nicholas and Alexandra '71
Waterloo '71
When Eight Bells Toll '71
Lola '69
Oh! What a Lovely War '69
Those Daring Young Men in Their Jaunty Jalopies '69
Lord Jim '65
Guns at Batasi '64
Zulu '64
Lawrence of Arabia '62
The League of Gentlemen '60
Ben-Hur '59
The Bridge on the River Kwai '57
The Third Key '57
Land of Fury '55
Land of the Pharaohs '55
The Prisoner '55
Angels One Five '54
The Cruel Sea '53
Malta Story '53
Mandy '53
The Adventurers '51
No Highway in the Sky '51
The Black Rose '50
The Elusive Pimpernel '50
The Fallen Idol '49
The Small Back Room '49
Bonnie Prince Charlie '48
Phantom Fiend '35
A Shot in the Dark '33

Jimmy Hawkins (1941-)
Zotz! '62
Private Hell 36 '54

Sally Hawkins (1976-)
An Education '09
Happy-Go-Lucky '08

Cassandra's Dream *'07*
Persuasion *'07*
Layer Cake *'05*
Vera Drake *'04*
Byron *'03*
All or Nothing *'02*
Tipping the Velvet *'02*

Screamin' Jay Hawkins (1929-2000)

Dance with the Devil *'97*
A Rage in Harlem *'91*
Mystery Train *'89*
Two Moon Junction *'88*

Monte Hawley (1901-50)

Look Out Sister *'48*
Miracle in Harlem *'48*
Tall, Tan and Terrific *'46*
Gang War *'40*
Mystery in Swing *'40*
Double Deal *'39*
The Duke Is Tops *'38*

Richard Hawley

Jane Eyre *'97*
Captives *'94*
Paper Marriage *'93*

Wanda (Petit) Hawley (1895-1963)

American Pluck *'25*
Smouldering Fires *'25*
Affairs of Anatol *'21*

Goldie Hawn (1945-)

The Banger Sisters *'02*
Town and Country *'01*
The Out-of-Towners *'99*
Everyone Says I Love You *'96*
The First Wives Club *'96*
Crisscross *'92*
Death Becomes Her *'92*
Housesitter *'92*
Deceived *'91*
Bird on a Wire *'90*
Overboard *'87*
Wildcats *'86*
Protocol *'84*
Swing Shift *'84*
Best Friends *'82*
Lovers and Liars *'81*
Private Benjamin *'80*
Seems Like Old Times *'80*
Foul Play *'78*
The Duchess and the Dirt-water Fox *'76*
Shampoo *'75*
The Girl from Petrovka *'74*
The Sugarland Express *'74*
Butterflies Are Free *'72*
Dollars *'71*
There's a Girl in My Soup *'70*
Cactus Flower *'69*
The One and Only, Genuine, Original Family Band *'68*

Jill Haworth (1945-)

The Freakmaker *'73*
Tower of Evil *'72*
The Ballad of Andy Crocker *'69*
In Harm's Way *'65*
Exodus *'60*

Vinton (Hayworth) Haworth (1906-70)

Spartacus *'60*
Junior G-Men of the Air *'42*
The Pride of the Yankees *'42*
Blind Fools *'40*
Law of the Underworld *'38*
Without Orders *'36*

Elizabeth Hawthorne

Underworld: Rise of the Lycans *'09*
The Chronicles of Narnia: The Lion, the Witch and the Wardrobe *'05*
Alex *'92*

Nigel Hawthorne (1929-2001)

Call Me Claus *'01*
Victoria & Albert *'01*
The Big Brass Ring *'99*
Tarzan *'99 (V)*
Madeline *'98*
The Object of My Affection *'98*
Uncorked *'98*
The Winslow Boy *'98*
Amistad *'97*
Murder in Mind *'97*
Inside *'96*
Twelfth Night *'96*
Richard III *'95*
The Madness of King George *'94*
Demolition Man *'93*
Freddie the Frog *'92 (V)*
Tartuffe *'90*
The Black Cauldron *'85 (V)*
Jenny's War *'85*
Mapp & Lucia *'85*
Pope John Paul II *'84*
Firefox *'82*
Gandhi *'82*
S*P*Y*S *'74*

Charles Hawtrey (1914-88)

Carry On Abroad *'72*
Carry On Matron *'72*
Carry On at Your Convenience *'71*
Carry On Camping *'71*
Carry On Henry VIII *'71*
Carry On Loving *'70*
Carry On Up the Jungle *'70*
Carry On Again Doctor *'69*
Zeta One *'69*
Carry On Up the Khyber *'68*
The Terrornauts *'67*
Carry On Cowboy *'66*
Carry On Screaming *'66*
Don't Lose Your Head *'66*
Carry On Cleo *'65*
Carry On Spying *'64*
Carry On Cabby *'63*
Carry On Jack *'63*
Carry On Regardless *'61*
Carry On Constable *'60*
Carry On Sergeant *'58*
Room to Let *'49*
A Canterbury Tale *'44*
Sabotage *'36*

Kay Hawtrey (1926-)

Focus *'01*
At the Midnight Hour *'95*
Funeral Home *'82*

Alexandra Hay (1944-93)

How Come Nobody's On Our Side? *'73*
The Love Machine *'71*
Model Shop *'69*

Christian Hay (1944-)

Autopsy *'74*
You're Jinxed, Friend, You've Met Sacramento *'70*

Colin Hay (1953-)

The Wild *'06 (V)*
Heaven's Burning *'97*
Cosi *'95*

Will Hay (1888-1949)

Hey! Hey! USA! *'38*
Oh, Mr. Porter *'37*

Sessue Hayakawa (1889-1973)

Hell to Eternity *'60*
The Swiss Family Robinson *'60*
Green Mansions *'59*
The Geisha Boy *'58*
The Bridge on the River Kwai *'57*
House of Bamboo *'55*
Three Came Home *'50*
Tokyo Joe *'49*
Daughter of the Dragon *'31*
The Dragon Painter *'19*
The Tong Man *'19*
The Cheat *'15*
The Wrath of the Gods *'14*

Marc Hayashi

The Laserman *'90*
White of the Eye *'88*
Chan Is Missing *'82*

Harry Hayden (1884-1955)

Double Dynamite *'51*
Pier 23 *'51*
Gun Crazy *'49*
Merton of the Movies *'47*
The Rains Came *'39*

James Hayden (1954-83)

Once Upon a Time in America *'84*
Don't Go in the Woods *'81*

Linda Hayden (1953-)

Therese: The Story of Saint Therese of Lisieux *'04*
The Barcelona Kill *'77*
The House on Straw Hill *'76*
Madhouse *'74*
The Blood on Satan's Claw *'71*
Taste the Blood of Dracula *'70*
Baby Love *'69*

Russell Hayden (1912-81)

Apache Chief *'50*
Blazing Guns *'50*
Guns of Justice *'50*
Last Bullet *'50*
Marshal of Heldorado *'50*
Outlaw Fury *'50*
Rangeland Empire *'50*
Sudden Death *'50*
Rolling Home *'48*
Seven Were Saved *'47*
Trail of the Mounties *'47*
Where the North Begins *'47*
'Neath Canadian Skies *'46*
Lost City of the Jungle *'45*
Gambler's Choice *'44*
Frontier Law *'43*
Lawless Plainsmen *'42*
Border Vigilantes *'41*
Doomed Caravan *'41*
In Old Colorado *'41*
Knights of the Range *'40*
The Light of Western Stars *'40*
Santa Fe Marshal *'40*
The Showdown *'40*
Hopalong Cassidy: Renegade Trail *'39*
Law of the Pampas *'39*
Renegade Trail *'39*
The Frontiersmen *'38*
The Mysterious Rider *'38*

Sterling Hayden (1916-86)

The Blue and the Gray *'82*
Deadly Strangers *'82*
Venom *'82*
Gas *'81*
The Godfather 1902-1959: The Complete Epic *'81*
9 to 5 *'80*
Winter Kills *'79*
King of the Gypsies *'78*
1900 *'76*
Spaghetti Western *'75*
The Final Programme *'73*
The Long Goodbye *'73*
The Godfather *'72*
Cobra *'71*
Loving *'70*
Dr. Strangelove, or: How I Learned to Stop Worrying and Love the Bomb *'64*
Terror in a Texas Town *'58*
Crime of Passion *'57*
Zero Hour! *'57*
The Killing *'56*
The Last Command *'55*
Shotgun *'55*
Crime Wave *'54*
Prince Valiant *'54*
Suddenly *'54*
Fighter Attack *'53*
Johnny Guitar *'53*
Kansas Pacific *'53*
Flat Top *'52*
Hellgate *'52*
The Star *'52*
The Denver & Rio Grande *'51*
The Asphalt Jungle *'50*
El Paso *'49*
Bahama Passage *'42*

Richard Haydn (1905-85)

Young Frankenstein *'74*
Clarence, the Cross-eyed Lion *'65*
The Sound of Music *'65*
Mutiny on the Bounty *'62*
Please Don't Eat the Daisies *'60*
Jupiter's Darling *'55*
Money from Home *'53*
Never Let Me Go *'53*
The Merry Widow *'52*
Pride of St. Louis *'52*
Emperor Waltz *'48*
Sitting Pretty *'48*
Forever Amber *'47*
Singapore *'47*
Adventure *'45*
Thunder Birds *'42*
Charley's Aunt *'41*

Julie Haydon (1910-94)

It's Pat: The Movie *'94*
Come on Danger! *'32*

Helen Haye (1874-1957)

Man of Evil *'48*
The Case of the Frightened Lady *'39*
Spy in Black *'39*
Sidewalks of London *'38*
The 39 Steps *'35*
Skin Game *'31*

Salma Hayek (1966-)

Grown Ups *'10*
Cirque du Freak: The Vampire's Assistant *'09*
Beverly Hills Chihuahua *'08 (V)*
Ask the Dust *'06*
Lonely Hearts *'06*
After the Sunset *'04*
Once Upon a Time in Mexico *'03*
Spy Kids 3-D: Game Over *'03*
Frida *'02*
Hotel *'01*
In the Time of the Butterflies *'01*
Chain of Fools *'00*
Time Code *'00*
Traffic *'00*
Dogma *'99*
Wild Wild West *'99*
The Faculty *'98*
54 *'98*
The Velocity of Gary *'98*
Breaking Up *'97*
Fools Rush In *'97*
The Hunchback *'97*
Fled *'96*
Desperado *'95*
Fair Game *'95*
Four Rooms *'95*
From Dusk Till Dawn *'95*
Midaq Alley *'95*
Mi Vida Loca *'94*
Roadracers *'94*

Jeff Hayenga

The Unborn *'91*
Prince of Pennsylvania *'88*

Allan Hayes

Neon Maniacs *'86*
Sam's Son *'84*

Allison Hayes (1930-77)

The Crawling Hand *'63*
Attack of the 50 Foot Woman *'58*
The Undead *'57*
The Unearthly *'57*
Zombies of Moratau *'57*
The Gunslinger *'56*
Francis Joins the WACs *'54*

Anthony Hayes (1977-)

Newcastle *'08*
Look Both Ways *'05*
The Boys *'98*

Bernadene Hayes (1903-87)

Santa Fe Marshal *'40*
Heroes in Blue *'39*
Panama Lady *'39*
Sweetheart of the Navy *'37*

Billie Hayes (1924-)

Pufnstuf *'70*
Li'l Abner *'59*

George "Gabby" Hayes (1885-1969)

The Cariboo Trail *'50*
El Paso *'49*
Return of the Bad Men *'48*
Home in Oklahoma *'47*
Lights of Old Santa Fe *'47*
Trail Street *'47*
Badman's Territory *'46*
Great Expectations *'46*
Helldorado *'46*
My Pal Trigger *'46*
Rainbow over Texas *'46*
Roll on Texas Moon *'46*
Song of Arizona *'46*
Under Nevada Skies *'46*
Along the Navaho Trail *'45*
Bells of Rosarita *'45*
Don't Fence Me In *'45*
Sunset in El Dorado *'45*
Utah *'45*
Tall in the Saddle *'44*
Bordertown Gunfighters *'43*
Calling Wild Bill Elliott *'43*
Death Valley Manhunt *'43*
Man from Thunder River *'43*
War of the Wildcats *'43*
Heart of the Golden West *'42*
Man from Cheyenne *'42*
Ridin' Down the Canyon *'42*
Romance on the Range *'42*
Sons of the Pioneers *'42*
South of Santa Fe *'42*
Sunset on the Desert *'42*
Sunset Serenade *'42*
Bad Man of Deadwood *'41*
In Old Cheyenne *'41*
Jesse James at Bay *'41*
Nevada City *'41*
Red River Valley *'41*
Robin Hood of the Pecos *'41*
Sheriff of Tombstone *'41*
The Border Legion *'40*
Carson City Kid *'40*
Colorado *'40*
Dark Command *'40*
Melody Ranch *'40*
Ranger and the Lady *'40*
Wagons Westward *'40*
Young Bill Hickok *'40*
Young Buffalo Bill *'40*
Arizona Kid *'39*
Days of Jesse James *'39*
Hopalong Cassidy: Renegade Trail *'39*
In Old Caliente *'39*
Renegade Trail *'39*
Saga of Death Valley *'39*
Southward Ho! *'39*
Wall Street Cowboy *'39*
Billy the Kid Returns *'38*
Come on Rangers *'38*
The Frontiersmen *'38*
Borderland *'37*
The Plainsman *'37*
Rustler's Valley *'37*
Hopalong Cassidy Returns *'36*
The Lawless Nineties *'36*
Smokey Smith *'36*
Song of the Trail *'36*
The Texas Rangers *'36*
Three on the Trail *'36*
Hopalong Cassidy *'35*
Justice of the Range *'35*
Lawless Frontier *'35*
Swifty *'35*
Texas Terror *'35*
The Throwback *'35*
Thunder Mountain *'35*
Beggars in Ermine *'34*
Blue Steel *'34*
Brand of Hate *'34*
House of Mystery *'34*
In Old Santa Fe *'34*
The Lost City *'34*
Lucky Texan *'34*
The Man from Hell *'34*
Man from Utah *'34*
Monte Carlo Nights *'34*
Mystery Liner *'34*
'Neath the Arizona Skies *'34*
Randy Rides Alone *'34*
The Return of Casey Jones *'34*
The Star Packer *'34*
Tombstone Terror *'34*
Breed of the Border *'33*
Fighting Champ *'33*
The Gallant Fool *'33*
Galloping Romeo *'33*
The Outlaw Tamer *'33*
The Phantom Broadcast *'33*
Riders of Destiny *'33*
The Sphinx *'33*
West of the Divide *'33*
Boiling Point *'32*
Border Devils *'32*
Broadway to Cheyenne *'32*
Man from Hell's Edges *'32*
Night Rider *'32*
Riders of the Desert *'32*
Texas Buddies *'32*
Without Honors *'32*
Cavalier of the West *'31*
The Nevada Buckaroo *'31*
Pleasure *'31*

Gloria Hayes

Judgment Day *'88*
Witchboard *'87*

Grace Hayes (1895-1989)

Zis Boom Bah *'41*
Rainbow over Broadway *'33*

Helen Hayes (1900-93)

Agatha Christie's Murder with Mirrors *'85*
Agatha Christie's A Caribbean Mystery *'83*
Agatha Christie's Murder is Easy *'82*
Candleshoe *'78*
Family Upside Down *'78*
Victory at Entebbe *'76*
One of Our Dinosaurs Is Missing *'75*
Herbie Rides Again *'74*
Airport *'70*
Third Man on the Mountain *'59*
Anastasia *'56*
Main Street to Broadway *'53*
Stage Door Canteen *'43*
Night Flight *'33*
Arrowsmith *'32*
A Farewell to Arms *'32*
The Sin of Madelon Claudet *'31*

Isaac Hayes (1942-2008)

Kill Switch *'08*
Soul Men *'08*
Hustle & Flow *'05*
Anonymous Rex *'04*
Dr. Dolittle 2 *'01 (V)*
Reindeer Games *'00*
Shaft *'00*
Six Ways to Sunday *'99*
South Park: Bigger, Longer and Uncut *'99 (V)*
Woo *'97*
Flipper *'96*
Illtown *'96*
Uncle Sam *'96*
Backlash: Oblivion 2 *'95*
It Could Happen to You *'94*
Oblivion *'94*
Acting on Impulse *'93*
Deadly Exposure *'93*
Posse *'93*
Robin Hood: Men in Tights *'93*
Final Judgment *'92*
Guilty as Charged *'92*
Prime Target *'91*
I'm Gonna Git You Sucka *'88*
Counterforce *'87*
Dead Aim *'87*
Nightstick *'87*
Jailbait: Betrayed By Innocence *'86*

Escape from New York '81
It Seemed Like a Good Idea at the Time '75
Truck Turner '74

Linda Hayes (1922-95)
Ridin' Down the Canyon '42
Romance on the Range '42
South of Santa Fe '42
Mexican Spitfire '40
Danger on the Air '38

Margaret (Maggie) Hayes (1916-77)
Girls' Town '59
Good Day for a Hanging '58
Omar Khayyam '57
Blackboard Jungle '55
In Old Colorado '41
Sullivan's Travels '41

Patricia Hayes (1909-98)
A Fish Called Wanda '88
Little Dorrit, Film 1: Nobody's Fault '88
Little Dorrit, Film 2: Little Dorrit's Story '88
Willow '88
The NeverEnding Story '84
The Corn Is Green '79
Super Bitch '73

Peter Lind Hayes (1915-98)
The 5000 Fingers of Dr. T '53
Seven Days' Leave '42
Playmates '41
Zis Boom Bah '41

Sean P. Hayes (1970-)
Igor '08 (V)
Soul Men '08
The Bucket List '07
Win a Date with Tad Hamilton! '04
Dr. Seuss' The Cat in the Hat '03 (V)
Pieces of April '03
Cats & Dogs '01 (V)
Billy's Hollywood Screen Kiss '98

Tony Haygarth (1945-)
Ghostboat '06
Under the Greenwood Tree '05
Fakers '04
Chicken Run '00 (V)
Don Quixote '00
Swept from the Sea '97
The Return of the Borrowers '96
The Infiltrator '95
Royal Deceit '94
The Borrowers '93
Devices and Desires '91
A Month in the Country '87
A Private Function '84
Dracula '79

Lisa Hayland
Fatal Passion '94
Novel Desires '92

Grace Hayle (1888-1963)
Loving You '57
The Great Dictator '40
The Moon's Our Home '36

Cyd Hayman (1944-)
The Godsend '79
After Julius '78
Rogue Male '76

David Hayman (1950-)
The Boy in the Striped Pajamas '08
Speed Dating '07
Where the Truth Lies '05
The Tailor of Panama '00
Vertical Limit '00
The Match '99
My Name Is Joe '98
Behind the Lines '97
The Jackal '97
Rob Roy '95
Hope and Glory '87
Sid & Nancy '86

A Sense of Freedom '78

Dick Haymes (1916-80)
Betrayal '74
St. Benny the Dip '51
One Touch of Venus '48
Up in Central Park '48
State Fair '45
Four Jills in a Jeep '44
Du Barry Was a Lady '43

Cal Haynes
Fyre '78
Kemek '70

Linda Haynes (1947-)
Human Experiments '79
Rolling Thunder '77
Latitude Zero '69

Loren Haynes
Eve of Destruction '90
The Expendables '89

Roberta Haynes (1929-)
The Adventurers '70
Hell Ship Mutiny '57
Return to Paradise '53
The Fighter '52

Jim Haynie (1940-)
Avenging Angel '07
United States of Leland '03
The Peacemaker '97
The Bridges of Madison County '95
Danielle Steel's Star '93
Grand Tour: Disaster in Time '92
Sleepwalkers '92
Too Much Sun '90
From Hollywood to Deadwood '89
Men Don't Leave '89
Jack's Back '87
On the Edge '86
Hard Traveling '85
Out '82
Bitter Harvest '81

Robert Hays (1947-)
The Santa Trap '02
Dr. T & the Women '00
The Abduction '96
Homeward Bound 2: Lost in San Francisco '96
Vanished '95
Cyber Bandits '94
No Dessert Dad, 'Til You Mow the Lawn '94
Homeward Bound: The Incredible Journey '93
Raw Justice '93
Hot Chocolate '92
Honeymoon Academy '90
Running Against Time '90
Murder by the Book '87
Cat's Eye '85
Scandalous '84
Trenchcoat '83
Utilities '83
Airplane 2: The Sequel '82
Touched '82
California Gold Rush '81
Take This Job & Shove It '81
Airplane! '80
The Fall of the House of Usher '80
Initiation of Sarah '78
The Young Pioneers '76

Dennis Haysbert (1955-)
Vanilla Gorilla '09
Breach '07
The Color of Freedom '07
Jarhead '05
Sinbad: Legend of the Seven Seas '03 (V)
Far from Heaven '02
Love and Basketball '00
What's Cooking? '00
The Minus Man '99
Random Hearts '99
The Thirteenth Floor '99
Major League 3: Back to the Minors '98
Absolute Power '97
Standoff '97
Heat '95

Waiting to Exhale '95
Major League 2 '94
Widow's Kiss '94
Return to Lonesome Dove '93
Suture '93
Mr. Baseball '92
Love Field '91
Navy SEALS '90
Major League '89

David Hayter (1969-)
Guyver 2: Dark Hero '94
The Castle of Cagliostro '80 (V)

James Hayter (1907-83)
Not Tonight Darling '72
The Blood on Satan's Claw '71
A Challenge for Robin Hood '68
Cop-Out '67
Abandon Ship '57
Beau Brummel '54
The Pickwick Papers '54
Four Sided Triangle '53
Tom Brown's School Days '51
Morning Departure '50
Trio '50
The Fallen Idol '49

Chard Hayward (1949-)
Violent Zone '89
The Killing Game '87

David Hayward
Accidental Meeting '93
Thousand Pieces of Gold '91
Who'll Save Our Children? '82
Delusion '80

Louis Hayward (1909-85)
Terror in the Wax Museum '73
The Christmas Kid '68
Chuka '67
Promise to Murder '56
The Search for Bridey Murphy '56
Black Arrow '48
The Strange Woman '46
And Then There Were None '45
Dance, Girl, Dance '40
My Son, My Son '40
The Son of Monte Cristo '40
The Man in the Iron Mask '39
The Duke of West Point '38
The Saint in New York '38
Anthony Adverse '36

Rachel Hayward
Call of the Wild '04
Cruel and Unusual '01
The Fear: Halloween Night '99
Anything for Love '93
Breaking All the Rules '85

Susan Hayward (1918-75)
Say Goodbye, Maggie Cole '72
The Honey Pot '67
Valley of the Dolls '67
Where Love Has Gone '64
Stolen Hours '63
Back Street '61
I Want to Live! '58
Top Secret Affair '57
The Conqueror '56
I'll Cry Tomorrow '55
Soldier of Fortune '55
Demetrius and the Gladiators '54
Garden of Evil '54
The Lusty Men '52
The Snows of Kilimanjaro '52
With a Song in My Heart '52
David and Bathsheba '51
I'd Climb the Highest Mountain '51
Rawhide '50

House of Strangers '49
My Foolish Heart '49
Tulsa '49
Lost Moment '47
Smash-Up: The Story of a Woman '47
They Won't Believe Me '47
Canyon Passage '46
Deadline at Dawn '46
Fighting Seabees '44
The Hairy Ape '44
Jack London '44
I Married a Witch '42
Reap the Wild Wind '42
Star Spangled Rhythm '42
Young and Willing '42
Adam Had Four Sons '41
Beau Geste '39

Chris Haywood (1949-)
Jindabyne '06
Innocence '00
Blackrock '97
Kiss or Kill '97
Lust and Revenge '95
Shine '95
Alex '92
A Woman's Tale '92
Sweet Talker '91
Quigley Down Under '90
The Navigator '88
The Tale of Ruby Rose '87
Malcolm '86
Burke & Wills '85
Attack Force Z '84
The Coca-Cola Kid '84
Man of Flowers '84
Razorback '84
Heatwave '83
Waterfront '83
Freedom '82
Breaker Morant '80
Newsfront '78

Rita Hayworth (1918-87)
Road to Salina '68
The Rover '67
The Poppy Is Also a Flower '66
The Love Goddesses '65
The Money Trap '65
Circus World '64
They Came to Cordura '59
Separate Tables '58
Fire Down Below '57
Pal Joey '57
Miss Sadie Thompson '53
Salome '53
Affair in Trinidad '52
The Lady from Shanghai '48
The Loves of Carmen '48
Down to Earth '47
Gilda '46
Tonight and Every Night '45
Cover Girl '44
Tales of Manhattan '42
You Were Never Lovelier '42
Blood and Sand '41
Strawberry Blonde '41
You'll Never Get Rich '41
Angels Over Broadway '40
Blondie On a Budget '40
The Lady in Question '40
Music in My Heart '40
Susan and God '40
Only Angels Have Wings '39
Hard to Hold '37
Hit the Saddle '37
Trouble in Texas '37
Charlie Chan in Egypt '35

Jonathan Haze (1929-)
The St. Valentine's Day Massacre '67
Track of the Vampire '66
The Terror '63
X: The Man with X-Ray Eyes '63
Little Shop of Horrors '60
Teenage Caveman '58
Carnival Rock '57
Poor White Trash '57
Rock All Night '57
The Gunslinger '56
It Conquered the World '56
Apache Woman '55
Day the World Ended '55
Swamp Women '55

Monster from the Ocean Floor '54

James Hazeldine (1948-2002)
Emma '97
My Friend Walter '93

Noni Hazlehurst (1954-)
Candy '06
Little Fish '05
True Colors '87
Fran '85
Waterfront '83
Monkey Grip '82

Saifei He (1963-)
Temptress Moon '96
Blush '95

Anthony Head (1954-)
Repo! The Genetic Opera '08
Persuasion '07
Imagine Me & You '06
Scoop '06
And Starring Pancho Villa as Himself '03
I'll Be There '03

Murray Head (1946-)
Beaumarchais the Scoundrel '96
White Mischief '88
Sunday, Bloody Sunday '71
A Coeur Joie '67

Lena Headey (1976-)
The Broken '08
The Contractor '07
St. Trinian's '07
300 '07
Imagine Me & You '06
The Brothers Grimm '05
The Cave '05
The Gathering Storm '02
Possession '02
Ripley's Game '02
Aberdeen '00
Gossip '99
Onegin '99
Merlin '98
Twice upon a Yesterday '98
Face '97
Mrs. Dalloway '97
Grave Indiscretions '96
Century '94
Rudyard Kipling's The Jungle Book '94
The Summer House '94
Waterland '92

Glenne Headley
The Joneses '10
Kit Kittredge: An American Girl '08

Shari Headley (1964-)
Towelhead '07
Johnson Family Vacation '04
The Preacher's Wife '96
Coming to America '88

Glenne Headly (1955-)
Raising Flagg '06
The Moguls '05
Around the Bend '04
Confessions of a Teenage Drama Queen '04
Eulogy '04
Women vs. Men '02
Bartleby '01
A Girl Thing '01
What's the Worst That Could Happen? '01
The Sandy Bottom Orchestra '00
Time Code '00
Babe: Pig in the City '98 (V)
Breakfast of Champions '98
My Own Country '98
Winchell '98
The X-Files '98
Pronto '97
Bastard out of Carolina '96
Two Days in the Valley '96
Mr. Holland's Opus '95
Sgt. Bilko '95
Getting Even with Dad '94
And the Band Played On '93

Hotel Room '93
Ordinary Magic '93
Grand Isle '92
Mortal Thoughts '91
Dick Tracy '90
Paperhouse '89
Dirty Rotten Scoundrels '88
Stars and Bars '88
Nadine '87
Making Mr. Right '86
Seize the Day '86
Fandango '85
The Purple Rose of Cairo '85
Doctor Detroit '83

Anthony Heald (1944-)
Accepted '06
X-Men: The Last Stand '06
Red Dragon '02
Proof of Life '00
Deep Rising '98
8mm '98
A Time to Kill '96
Bushwhacked '95
The Client '94
Kiss of Death '94
The Ballad of Little Jo '93
Whispers in the Dark '92
The Silence of the Lambs '91
Postcards from the Edge '90

Elizabeth Healey
The Hive '08
Croc '07

Myron Healey (1922-2005)
Pulse '88
Claws '77
Smoke in the Wind '75
Cavalry Command '63
Varan the Unbelievable '61
Guns Don't Argue '57
The Unearthly '57
Gang Busters '55
Bonanza Town '51
Down to Earth '47

David Healy (1932-95)
Unnatural Pursuits '91
Supergirl '84
The Sign of Four '83
Lust for a Vampire '71

Mary Healy (1918-)
The 5000 Fingers of Dr. T '53
Zis Boom Bah '41
Second Fiddle '39

Pat Healy (1971-)
Great World of Sound '07
Rescue Dawn '06

Patricia Healy
Mr. Fix It '06
Undertow '04
Sweet Poison '91
Ultraviolet '91

Ted Healy (1896-1937)
Hollywood Hotel '37
Varsity Show '37
San Francisco '36
Mad Love '35
Reckless '35
Hollywood Party '34
Dancing Lady '33
Myrt and Marge '33

Darin Heames
Cock & Bull Story '03
The Fear '94
Night of the Demons 2 '94

Amber Heard (1986-)
The Joneses '10
The Informers '09
The Stepfather '09
Zombieland '09
Never Back Down '08
Pineapple Express '08
Remember the Daze '07
North Country '05

Daphne Heard (1904-83)
Jude the Obscure '71
Macbeth '70

John Heard (1946-)
The Lucky Ones *'08*
Brothers Three *'07*
The Great Debaters *'07*
Dead Lenny *'06*
Gamers *'06*
The Guardian *'06*
Steel City *'06*
The Chumscrubber *'05*
The Deal *'05*
Sweet Land *'05*
Tracks *'05*
Mind the Gap *'04*
White Chicks *'04*
Monday Night Mayhem *'02*
O *'01*
The Pilot's Wife *'01*
Animal Factory *'00*
Perfect Murder, Perfect Town *'00*
Pollock *'00*
The Pact *'99*
The Witness *'99*
Desert Blue *'98*
Executive Power *'98*
Snake Eyes *'98*
Men *'97*
187 *'97*
My Fellow Americans *'96*
Before and After *'95*
In the Line of Fire *'93*
Me & Veronica *'93*
The Pelican Brief *'93*
Dead Ahead: The Exxon Valdez Disaster *'92*
Gladiator *'92*
Home Alone 2: Lost in New York *'92*
Radio Flyer *'92*
Waterland *'92*
Deceived *'91*
Mindwalk: A Film for Passionate Thinkers *'91*
Rambling Rose *'91*
Awakenings *'90*
Blown Away *'90*
The End of Innocence *'90*
Home Alone *'90*
The Package *'89*
Beaches *'88*
Betrayed *'88*
Big *'88*
The Milagro Beanfield War *'88*
The Seventh Sign *'88*
Out on a Limb *'87*
The Telephone *'87*
After Hours *'85*
Heaven Help Us *'85*
Too Scared to Scream *'85*
The Trip to Bountiful *'85*
C.H.U.D. *'84*
Violated *'84*
Best Revenge *'83*
Legs *'83*
Cat People *'82*
Cutter's Way *'81*
Heart Beat *'80*
Chilly Scenes of Winter *'79*
On the Yard *'79*
The Scarlet Letter *'79*
Between the Lines *'77*
First Love *'77*
Rush It *'77*

Ann Hearn (1953-)
The War at Home *'96*
A Woman of Independent Means *'94*
Lorenzo's Oil *'92*
Mirror, Mirror *'90*
The Accused *'88*

Edward Hearn
Fighting Hero *'34*
Local Badman *'32*

George Hearn (1934-)
Durango *'99*
Barney's Great Adventure *'98*
The Devil's Own *'96*
All Dogs Go to Heaven 2 *'95* (V)
Annie: A Royal Adventure *'95*
The Vanishing *'93*
Sneakers *'92*
See You in the Morning *'89*
Sweeney Todd: The Demon Barber of Fleet Street *'84*
A Piano for Mrs. Cimino *'82*
Sanctuary of Fear *'79*

Richard Hearne (1908-79)
The Time of His Life *'55*
Butler's Dilemma *'43*

Patty (Patricia Campbell) Hearst (1954-)
A Dirty Shame *'04*
Cecil B. Demented *'00*
Pecker *'98*
Serial Mom *'94*
Cry-Baby *'90*

Rick Hearst (1965-)
Carpool Guy *'05*
Warlock 3: The End of Innocence *'98*
Crossing the Line *'90*

Darrell Heath
Woo *'97*
Don't Be a Menace to South Central While Drinking Your Juice in the Hood *'95*

Thomas Heathcote (1917-86)
Luther *'74*
Demons of the Mind *'72*
Village of the Damned *'60*
Above Us the Waves *'56*

Jean Heather (1921-95)
Murder, He Says *'45*
Double Indemnity *'44*

Clifford Heatherley (1888-1937)
The Church Mouse *'34*
Bitter Sweet *'33*
If I Were Rich *'33*
Champagne *'28*

Joey Heatherton (1944-)
Cry-Baby *'90*
The Happy Hooker Goes to Washington *'77*
Bluebeard *'72*
The Ballad of Andy Crocker *'69*
My Blood Runs Cold *'65*
Where Love Has Gone *'64*

Patricia Heaton (1959-)
Front of the Class *'08*
The New Age *'94*
Beethoven *'92*
Memoirs of an Invisible Man *'92*

Tom Heaton
Mail Order Bride *'08*
Mermaid *'00*
Call of the Wild *'93*
April Fool's Day *'86*

David Heavener (1958-)
The Catcher *'98*
Fugitive X *'96*
Eye of the Stranger *'93*
Kill or Be Killed *'93*
L.A. Goddess *'92*
Prime Target *'91*
Ragin' Cajun *'90*
Deadly Reactor *'89*
Killcrazy *'89*
Twisted Justice *'89*
Outlaw Force *'87*

Heavy D
See Dwight "Heavy D" Myers
Black Listed *'03*

Anne Heche (1969-)
The Other Guys *'10*
Spread *'09*
What Love Is *'07*
Birth *'04*
Gracie's Choice *'04*
John Q *'02*
Prozac Nation *'01*
Beyond Suspicion *'00*
One Kill *'00*
The Third Miracle *'99*
Psycho *'98*
Return to Paradise *'98*
Six Days, Seven Nights *'98*
I Know What You Did Last Summer *'97*
Subway Stories *'97*
Volcano *'97*
Wag the Dog *'97*
Donnie Brasco *'96*
If These Walls Could Talk *'96*
The Juror *'96*
Walking and Talking *'96*
Kingfish: A Story of Huey P. Long *'95*
Pie in the Sky *'95*
Wild Side *'95*
Against the Wall *'94*
Girls in Prison *'94*
Milk Money *'94*
A Simple Twist of Fate *'94*
The Adventures of Huck Finn *'93*
O Pioneers! *'91*

Gina Hecht
The Last Word *'08*
Seven Pounds *'08*
A Stranger's Heart *'07*

Jessica Hecht (1965-)
Jesse Stone: Thin Ice *'09*
Starting Out in the Evening *'07*
The Forgotten *'04*
Saving Face *'04*
Sideways *'04*
Intimate Betrayal *'96*

Paul Hecht (1941-)
Last Call: The Final Chapter of F. Scott Fitzgerald *'02*
Private Parts *'96*
Mary and Joseph: A Story of Faith *'79*
The Savage Bees *'76*
The Reincarnation of Peter Proud *'75*

Ted Hecht (1908-69)
Riding the California Trail *'47*
So Proudly We Hail *'43*

Eileen Heckart (1919-2001)
The First Wives Club *'96*
Breathing Lessons *'94*
Heartbreak Ridge *'86*
Table Settings *'84*
White Mama *'80*
Backstairs at the White House *'79*
Sorrows of Gin *'79*
The Hiding Place *'75*
Zandy's Bride *'74*
Butterflies Are Free *'72*
No Way to Treat a Lady *'68*
Up the Down Staircase *'67*
Heller in Pink Tights *'60*
A Doll's House *'59*
Hot Spell *'58*
The Bad Seed *'56*
Bus Stop *'56*
Somebody Up There Likes Me *'56*

Andrew Heckler
Time Code *'00*
Stir *'98*

Dan Hedaya (1940-)
Strangers with Candy *'06*
Robots *'05* (V)
American Cousins *'02*
Swimfan *'02*
Mulholland Drive *'01*
Quicksand *'01*
The Shaft *'01*
The Crew *'00*
Shaft *'00*
Dick *'99*
The Hurricane *'99*
Locked in Silence *'99*
The Extreme Adventures of Super Dave *'98*
A Night at the Roxbury *'98*
Alien: Resurrection *'97*
The Garden of Redemption *'97*
A Life Less Ordinary *'97*
The Second Civil War *'97*
Daylight *'96*
The First Wives Club *'96*
Marvin's Room *'96*
Ransom *'96*
Clueless *'95*
Freeway *'95*
To Die For *'95*
The Usual Suspects *'95*
Maverick *'94*
Based on an Untrue Story *'93*
Benny & Joon *'93*
Boiling Point *'93*
Fallen Angels 2 *'93*
For Love or Money *'93*
Four Eyes and Six Guns *'93*
Mr. Wonderful *'93*
Rookie of the Year *'93*
The Addams Family *'91*
Joe Versus the Volcano *'90*
Pacific Heights *'90*
Tune in Tomorrow *'90*
The Reluctant Agent *'89*
Courage *'86*
Running Scared *'86*
Slow Burn *'86*
A Smoky Mountain Christmas *'86*
Wise Guys *'86*
Blood Simple *'85*
Commando *'85*
The Adventures of Buckaroo Banzai Across the Eighth Dimension *'84*
Reckless *'84*
Tightrope *'84*
The Hunger *'83*
Endangered Species *'82*
The Prince of Central Park *'77*

Jon Heder (1977-)
When in Rome *'09*
Blades of Glory *'07*
Mama's Boy *'07*
Moving McAllister *'07*
Surf's Up *'07* (V)
The Benchwarmers *'06*
Monster House *'06* (V)
School for Scoundrels *'06*
Just like Heaven *'05*
Napoleon Dynamite *'04*

Amel Hedhili
Honey & Ashes *'96*
The Silences of the Palace *'94*

Serene Hedin
Hawken's Breed *'87*
Boggy Creek II *'83*

David Hedison (1928-)
Fugitive Mind *'99*
Undeclared War *'91*
License to Kill *'89*
A.D. *'85*
The Naked Face *'84*
Kenny Rogers as the Gambler, Part 2: The Adventure Continues *'83*
ffolkes *'80*
The Power Within *'79*
The Art of Crime *'75*
Live and Let Die *'73*
Kemek *'70*
The Fly *'58*
Enemy Below *'57*

Jack Hedley (1930-)
New York Ripper *'82*
For Your Eyes Only *'81*
Goodbye, Mr. Chips *'69*
The Anniversary *'68*
The Very Edge *'63*

Garrett Hedlund (1984-)
Death Sentence *'07*
Georgia Rule *'07*
Eragon *'06*
Four Brothers *'05*
Friday Night Lights *'04*
Troy *'04*

Tippi Hedren (1935-)
Tribute *'09*
The Last Confederate: The Story of Robert Adams *'05*
Raising Genius *'04*
Darkwolf *'03*
Mind Lies *'00*
The Break Up *'98*
Footsteps *'98*
Citizen Ruth *'96*
The Birds 2: Land's End *'94*
Inevitable Grace *'94*
Teresa's Tattoo *'94*
Treacherous Beauties *'94*
Through the Eyes of a Killer *'92*
Pacific Heights *'90*
Deadly Spygames *'89*
In the Cold of the Night *'89*
Foxfire Light *'82*
Harrad Experiment *'73*
Mr. Kingstreet's War *'71*
A Countess from Hong Kong *'67*
Satan's Harvest *'65*
Marnie *'64*
The Birds *'63*

Deborah Hedwall
Shadrach *'98*
Sessions *'83*

Astrid Heeren
Silent Night, Bloody Night *'73*
Castle Keep *'69*

Richard Heffer
Mad Death *'83*
Waterloo *'71*

Meghan Heffern
American Pie Presents: Beta House *'07*
Insecticidal *'05*

Kevin Heffernan (1968-)
Strange Wilderness *'08*
Beerfest *'06*
The Lather Effect *'06*
The Dukes of Hazzard *'05*
Sky High *'05*
Club Dread *'04*
Super Troopers *'01*

Wayne Heffley (1927-)
Johnny Got His Gun *'71*
Submarine Seahawk *'59*

Kyle T. Heffner
Asylum of the Damned *'03*
Mutant on the Bounty *'89*
Flashdance *'83*

Marta Heflin (1945-)
Come Back to the Five & Dime Jimmy Dean, Jimmy Dean *'82*
A Star Is Born *'76*

Nora Heflin (1950-)
Chilly Scenes of Winter *'79*
Our Time *'74*

Van Heflin (1910-71)
Airport *'70*
The Ruthless Four *'70*
The Big Bounce *'69*
The Man Outside *'68*
The Greatest Story Ever Told *'65*
Cry of Battle *'63*
They Came to Cordura *'59*
Gunman's Walk *'58*
3:10 to Yuma *'57*
Patterns *'56*
Battle Cry *'55*
Black Widow *'54*
A Woman's World *'54*
Shane *'53*
Prowler *'51*
Tomahawk *'51*
East Side, West Side *'49*
Madame Bovary *'49*
Act of Violence *'48*
The Three Musketeers *'48*
Green Dolphin Street *'47*
The Possessed *'47*
The Strange Love of Martha Ivers *'46*
Till the Clouds Roll By *'46*
Presenting Lily Mars *'43*
Grand Central Murder *'42*
Johnny Eager *'42*
H.M. Pulham Esquire *'41*
Santa Fe Trail *'40*
Back Door to Heaven *'39*
Flight from Glory *'37*
A Woman Rebels *'36*

Hugh Hefner (1926-)
Miss March *'09*
The House Bunny *'08*
Comic Book: The Movie *'04*
Hugh Hefner: Once Upon a Time *'92*
Beverly Hills Cop 2 *'87*
History of the World: Part 1 *'81*

Rene Heger (1978-)
In Enemy Hands *'04*

O.P. Heggie (1879-1936)
The Bride of Frankenstein *'35*
Anne of Green Gables *'34*
The Count of Monte Cristo *'34*
Midnight *'34*
Peck's Bad Boy *'34*
Smilin' Through *'33*
Devotion *'31*
The Return of Dr. Fu Manchu *'30*
The Mysterious Dr. Fu Manchu *'29*

Robert Hegyes (1951-)
Bob Roberts *'92*
Just Tell Me You Love Me *'80*
Underground Aces *'80*

Peter Hehir (1949-)
Sweet Talker *'91*
Fast Talking *'86*
I Live with Me Dad *'86*
Two Friends *'86*

Sasha Hehn
Melody in Love *'78*
Secrets of Sweet Sixteen *'74*

Katherine Heigl (1978-)
Killers *'10*
The Ugly Truth *'09*
27 Dresses *'08*
Knocked Up *'07*
Caffeine *'06*
The Ringer *'05*
Side Effects *'05*
Love's Enduring Promise *'04*
Love Comes Softly *'03*
MTV's Wuthering Heights *'03*
Valentine *'01*
100 Girls *'00*
Bug Buster *'99*
The Tempest *'99*
Bride of Chucky *'98*
Prince Valiant *'97*
Stand-Ins *'97*
Wish upon a Star *'96*
Under Siege 2: Dark Territory *'95*
King of the Hill *'93*
My Father the Hero *'93*

Elayne Heilveil
The Adventures of Nellie Bly *'81*
Birds of Prey *'72*

Laurie Heineman
Lady in Red *'79*
Save the Tiger *'73*

Amelia Heinle (1973-)
Earth vs. the Spider *'01*
Liar's Poker *'99*
The Limey *'99*
Black Cat Run *'98*
Quicksilver Highway *'98*
Uncorked *'98*

Maria Heiskanen
Everlasting Moments *'08*
Lights in the Dusk *'06*

Jayne Heitmeyer (1960-)
Black Swarm *'07*
Snakeman *'05*

Voodoo Moon '05
An American Affair '99
Believe '99
Beyond Redemption '99
Requiem for Murder '99
Dead End '98
Sir Arthur Conan Doyle's The Lost World '98
Face the Evil '97
Hawk's Vengeance '96
Sci-Fighters '96
Suspicious Minds '96

Simon Helberg (1980-)
Mama's Boy '07
Walk Hard: The Dewey Cox Story '07
A Cinderella Story '04

Brit Helfer (1959-)
Body Trouble '92
Alley Cat '84

Tricia Helfer
Battlestar Galactica: The Plan '09
Spiral '07
Memory '06

Marg Helgenberger (1958-)
Columbus Day '08
Mr. Brooks '07
In Good Company '04
Erin Brockovich '00
Perfect Murder, Perfect Town '00
The Happy Face Murders '99
Species 2 '98
Elmore Leonard's Gold Coast '97
Fire Down Below '97
The Last Time I Committed Suicide '96
Bad Boys '95
Frame by Frame '95
Species '95
The Cowboy Way '94
Lie Down with Lions '94
Fallen Angels 2 '93
Stephen King's The Tommy-knockers '93
Death Dreams '92
Desperate Motives '92
Through the Eyes of a Killer '92
Crooked Hearts '91
Blind Vengeance '90
After Midnight '89
Always '89
China Beach '88

Erik Hell (1911-73)
The Passion of Anna '70
The Rite '69
Port of Call '48

Richard Hell (1949-)
Desperately Seeking Susan '85
Geek Maggot Bingo '83
Smithereens '82

Thomas Hellberg
Man from Mallorca '84
The Assignment '78

Randee Heller
Matter of Trust '98
Danielle Steel's Changes '91
The Karate Kid '84
Can You Hear the Laughter? The Story of Freddie Prinze '79
Fast Break '79

Anne Helm (1938-)
Nightmare in Wax '69
The Unkissed Bride '66
Follow That Dream '61

Brigitte Helm (1906-96)
The Love of Jeanne Ney '27
Metropolis '26

Fay Helm (1913-2003)
One Body Too Many '44
Phantom Lady '44
Calling Dr. Death '43
The Wolf Man '41
Blondie On a Budget '40
Blondie Brings Up Baby '39

Levon Helm (1943-)
In the Electric Mist '08
Shooter '07
The Three Burials of Melquiades Estrada '05
Fire Down Below '97
Feeling Minnesota '96
End of the Line '88
Man Outside '88
Smooth Talk '85
The Dollmaker '84
Best Revenge '83
The Right Stuff '83
Coal Miner's Daughter '80

Charlotte J. Helmkamp (1961-)
Frankenhooker '90
Posed for Murder '89

Katherine Helmond (1934-)
A Grandpa for Christmas '07
Cars '06 (V)
Beethoven's 5th '03
Mr. St. Nick '02
The Perfect Nanny '00
Fear and Loathing in Las Vegas '98
Ms. Scrooge '97
The Spy Within '94
Amore! '93
Inside Monkey Zetterland '93
The Lady in White '88
Overboard '87
Shadey '87
World War III '86
Brazil '85
Jack & the Beanstalk '83
Diary of a Teenage Hitch-hiker '82
Rosie: The Rosemary Clooney Story '82
Time Bandits '81
Scout's Honor '80
Pearl '78
Family Plot '76
The Autobiography of Miss Jane Pittman '74
Larry '74
The Hospital '71

Tom Helmore (1904-95)
Flipper's New Adventure '64
Vertigo '58
Designing Woman '57
This Could Be the Night '57
The Tender Trap '55
Trouble along the Way '53

Ed Helms
The Goods: Live Hard, Sell Hard '09
The Hangover '09
Monsters vs. Aliens '09 (V)
Harold & Kumar Escape from Guantanamo Bay '08
Meet Dave '08
Evan Almighty '07

Frits Helmuth (1931-2004)
Flickering Lights '01
Memories of a Marriage '90

Robert Helpmann (1909-86)
Patrick '78
Puzzle '78
The Mango Tree '77
The Tales of Hoffmann '51
The Red Shoes '48
Henry V '44

Sheila Helpmann (1916-94)
The Getting of Wisdom '77
Image of Death '77

Percy Helton (1894-1971)
Crashout '55
Kiss Me Deadly '55

David Hemblen
Rollerball '02
Family of Cops 2: Breach of Faith '97
Booty Call '96
The Sweet Hereafter '96
Hollow Point '95
Brainscan '94
Exotica '94
Mesmer '94
A Man in Uniform '93
The Adjuster '91
Speaking Parts '89
Short Circuit 2 '88
Family Viewing '87
The Room '87

Mark Hembrow (1955-)
Swimming Upstream '03
Desperate Prey '94
Out of the Body '88
Return to Snowy River '88
High Tide '87

Margaux Hemingway (1955-96)
Bad Love '95
Inner Sanctum 2 '94
Double Obsession '93
Deadly Rivals '92
Deadly Conspiracy '91
Inner Sanctum '91
Over the Brooklyn Bridge '83
They Call Me Bruce? '82
Killer Fish '79
Lipstick '76

Mariel Hemingway (1961-)
The Golden Boys '08
In Her Line of Fire '06
Perfume '01
First Daughter '99
The Sex Monster '99
Little Men '98
Road Ends '98
Deconstructing Harry '97
Bad Moon '96
The Crying Child '96
Deceptions 2: Edge of Deception '94
Falling from Grace '92
Into the Badlands '92
Delirious '91
Steal the Sky '88
Sunset '88
Superman 4: The Quest for Peace '87
Creator '85
Mean Season '85
Star 80 '83
Personal Best '82
Manhattan '79
Lipstick '76

Toby Hemingway
Feast of Love '07
The Covenant '06

David Hemmings (1941-2003)
The League of Extraordinary Gentlemen '03
The Night We Called It a Day '03
Gangs of New York '02
Last Orders '01
Mean Machine '01
Spy Game '01
Gladiator '00
A Mind to Murder '96
The Rainbow '89
The Turn of the Screw '89
The Key to Rebecca '85
Dark Forces '83
Man, Woman & Child '83
The Snow Queen '83
Calamity Jane '82
Disappearance '81
Beyond Reasonable Doubt '80
Beyond Erotica '79
Charlie Muffin '79
Just a Gigolo '79
Murder by Decree '79
Thirst '79
Power Play '78
Blood Relatives '77
Islands in the Stream '77
The Squeeze '77
Deep Red: Hatchet Murders '75
The Old Curiosity Shop '75
Juggernaut '74
The Love Machine '71
Barbarella '68
The Charge of the Light Brigade '68
Camelot '67
Blow-Up '66
The Girl Getters '66

Nolan Hemmings
In a Day '06
Last Orders '01

Anouska (Anoushka) Hempel (1941-)
Tiffany Jones '75
Blacksnake! '73
The Scars of Dracula '70
On Her Majesty's Secret Service '69

John Hemphill
Hostage for a Day '94
Sodbusters '94

Sherman Hemsley (1938-)
Screwed '00
Home of Angels '94
Mr. Nanny '93
Camp Cucamonga: How I Spent My Summer Vacation '90
Club Fed '90
Ghost Fever '87
Combat Academy '86
Alice in Wonderland '85
Ghost Dance '83
Love at First Bite '79

Chris Hemsworth (1983-)
A Perfect Getaway '09
Star Trek '09

Zulay Henao
Fighting '09
Feel the Noise '07

George Henare (1945-)
The Legend of Johnny Lingo '03
The Vector File '03
The Silent One '86

Richard Hench (1955-)
Endangered '94
Uncivilized '94
Tomb '86
Bio Hazard '85

Bill Henderson (1925-)
Smiling Fish & Goat on Fire '99
Trippin' '99
City Slickers '91
Movie Maker '86
Murphy's Law '86
Clue '85
The Adventures of Buckaroo Banzai Across the Eighth Dimension '84
Get Crazy '83

Dell Henderson (1883-1956)
Love Affair '39
Rainbow over Broadway '33
The Crowd '28
The Patsy '28
Show People '28

Don Henderson (1931-97)
Preaching to the Perverted '97
The Adventures of Baron Munchausen '89
The Island '80
The Ghoul '75

Doug(las) Henderson (1918-78)
The Manchurian Candidate '62
King Dinosaur '55
From Here to Eternity '53

Florence Henderson (1934-)
The Brady Bunch Movie '95
Shakes the Clown '92
A Very Brady Christmas '88
Song of Norway '70

Jo Henderson (1934-88)
Matewan '87
Rachel River '87
Lianna '83

Josh Henderson
April Fool's Day '08
Step Up '06

Marcia Henderson (1930-87)
Canyon River '56
Naked Hills '56
Thunder Bay '53

Martin Henderson (1974-)
Battle in Seattle '07
Smokin' Aces '07
Flyboys '06
Little Fish '05
Bride & Prejudice '04
Torque '04
The Ring '02
Windtalkers '02

Sarah Henderson
The Reckoning '03
Kids '95

Shirley Henderson (1966-)
Life During Wartime '09
Miss Pettigrew Lives for a Day '08
Wild Child '08
I Really Hate My Job '07
Marie Antoinette '06
Harry Potter and the Goblet of Fire '05
Tristram Shandy: A Cock and Bull Story '05
Bridget Jones: The Edge of Reason '04
Yes '04
American Cousins '02
Close Your Eyes '02
Harry Potter and the Chamber of Secrets '02
Once Upon a Time in the Midlands '02
The Way We Live Now '02
Wilbur Wants to Kill Himself '02
Bridget Jones's Diary '01
24 Hour Party People '01
Topsy Turvy '99
Wonderland '99
Rob Roy '95
Trainspotting '95
Clarissa '91

Ty Henderson
Happy Hour '87
The Competition '80

Daniel Hendler (1976-)
Lost Embrace '04
The Bottom of the Sea '03

Tony Hendra (1941-)
Life with Mikey '93
This Is Spinal Tap '84

Benjamin Hendrickson (1950-2006)
Spanking the Monkey '94
Manhunter '86

Elaine Hendrix (1971-)
Coffee Date '06
Bam Bam & Celeste '05
What the #$*! Do We Know? '04
Inspector Gadget 2 '02
Mr. St. Nick '02
Wish You Were Dead '00
Molly '99
Superstar '99
The Parent Trap '98
Romy and Michele's High School Reunion '97
Last Dance '91

Wanda Hendrix (1928-81)
My Outlaw Brother '51
The Admiral Was a Lady '50
Prince of Foxes '49
Miss Tatlock's Millions '48
Saddle Tramp '47
Welcome Stranger '47

Gloria Hendry (1949-)
Pumpkinhead 2: Blood Wings '94
Bare Knuckles '77
Black Belt Jones '74
Black Caesar '73
Hell Up in Harlem '73
Live and Let Die '73
Slaughter's Big Ripoff '73

Ian Hendry (1931-84)
The Bitch '78
The Passenger '75
Captain Kronos: Vampire Hunter '74
Killer with Two Faces '74
Theatre of Blood '73
Tales from the Crypt '72
Get Carter '71
McKenzie Break '70
Journey to the Far Side of the Sun '69
The Saint '68
Vendetta for the Saint '68
The Hill '65
Repulsion '65
Children of the Damned '63
Room at the Top '59

Sonja Henie (1912-69)
It's a Pleasure '45
Wintertime '43
Iceland '42
Sun Valley Serenade '41
Everything Happens at Night '39
Second Fiddle '39
Happy Landing '38
My Lucky Star '38
Thin Ice '37
One in a Million '36

Brad William Henke (1971-)
Choke '08
Hollywoodland '06
Sherrybaby '06
The Assassination of Richard Nixon '05
Must Love Dogs '05
The Zodiac '05
Mr. Wrong '95

Barry (Shabaka) Henley (1954-)
Miami Vice '06
Four Brothers '05
Collateral '04
The Terminal '04
Ali '01
Life '99
How Stella Got Her Groove Back '98
Patch Adams '98
Fear of a Black Hat '94

Georgie Henley
The Chronicles of Narnia: Prince Caspian '08
The Chronicles of Narnia: The Lion, the Witch and the Wardrobe '05

Marilu Henner (1952-)
Enemies of Laughter '00
Man on the Moon '99
Titanic '96
Chasers '94
Chains of Gold '92
Grand Larceny '92
Noises Off '92
L.A. Story '91
Ladykillers '88
Grown Ups '86
Love with a Perfect Stranger '86
Perfect '85
Rustler's Rhapsody '85
Stark '85
Cannonball Run 2 '84
Johnny Dangerously '84
The Man Who Loved Women '83
Hammett '82
Bloodbrothers '78
Between the Lines '77

Jill(ian) Hennessey (1969-)
Wild Hogs *'07*
Love in the Time of Money *'02*
Exit Wounds *'01*
Jackie, Ethel, Joan: The Kennedy Women *'01*
Autumn in New York *'00*
Nuremberg *'00*
Two Ninas *'00*
Chutney Popcorn *'99*
Dead Broke *'99*
Komodo *'99*
Molly *'99*
Row Your Boat *'98*
Most Wanted *'97*
I Shot Andy Warhol *'96*
A Smile Like Yours *'96*

Andre Hennicke
Youth Without Youth *'07*
Antibodies *'05*
Sophie Scholl: The Final Days *'05*

Eva Henning (1920-)
Devil's Wanton *'49*
Three Strange Loves *'49*

Sam Hennings
Indecent Behavior 3 *'95*
Drop Zone *'94*
Seedpeople *'92*
Night Angel *'90*
Mission Manila *'87*

Monika Henreid
The California Kid *'74*
Omega Man *'71*
Dead Ringer *'64*

Paul Henreid (1908-92)
The Exorcist 2: The Heretic *'77*
The Madwoman of Chaillot *'69*
The Four Horsemen of the Apocalypse *'62*
Never So Few *'59*
Ten Thousand Bedrooms *'57*
Battle Shock *'56*
Deep in My Heart *'54*
Tall Lie *'53*
A Stolen Face *'52*
The Scar *'48*
Song of Love *'47*
Deception *'46*
The Spanish Main *'45*
Casablanca *'42*
Joan of Paris *'42*
Now, Voyager *'42*
Night Train to Munich *'40*
Goodbye, Mr. Chips *'39*

David Henrie (1989-)
The Wizards of Waverly Place: The Movie *'09*
Arizona Summer *'03*

Lance Henriksen (1940-)
Screamers: The Hunting *'09*
Appaloosa *'08*
Pistol Whipped *'08*
Prairie Fever *'08*
Black Ops *'07*
Bone Dry *'07*
In the Spider's Web *'07*
Pumpkinhead 4: Blood Feud *'07*
Pumpkinhead 3: Ashes to Ashes *'06*
When a Stranger Calls *'06 (V)*
Hellraiser: Hellworld *'05*
Tarzan 2 *'05 (V)*
Alien vs. Predator *'04*
Madhouse *'04*
Modigliani *'04*
Paranoia 1.0 *'04*
Starkweather *'04*
The Invitation *'03*
Mimic 3: Sentinel *'03*
Antibody *'02*
Sasquatch *'02*
Unspeakable *'02*
Lost Voyage *'01*
Scream 3 *'00*
Tarzan *'99 (V)*
Face the Evil *'97*
Gunfighter's Moon *'96*
The Last Assassins *'96*
Profile for Murder *'96*
Baja *'95*
Dead Man *'95*
Felony *'95*
Operation Intercept *'95*
Powder *'95*
The Quick and the Dead *'95*
Wes Craven Presents Mind Ripper *'95*
Boulevard *'94*
Color of Night *'94*
Nature of the Beast *'94*
No Escape *'94*
Spitfire *'94*
The Criminal Mind *'93*
Excessive Force *'93*
Hard Target *'93*
Knights *'93*
Man's Best Friend *'93*
The Outfit *'93*
Super Mario Bros. *'93*
Alien 3 *'92*
Delta Heat *'92*
Jennifer 8 *'92*
Comrades in Arms *'91*
The Pit & the Pendulum *'91*
Stone Cold *'91*
The Last Samurai *'90*
The Horror Show *'89*
Johnny Handsome *'89*
Survival Quest *'89*
Deadly Intent *'88*
The Hit List *'88*
Pumpkinhead *'88*
Near Dark *'87*
Aliens *'86*
Choke Canyon *'86*
The Jagged Edge *'85*
Savage Dawn *'84*
The Terminator *'84*
Nightmares *'83*
The Right Stuff *'83*
Piranha 2: The Spawning *'82*
Prince of the City *'81*
The Visitor *'80*
Damien: Omen 2 *'78*
Network *'76*
Dog Day Afternoon *'75*

Anders Henrikson (1896-1965)
Miss Julie *'50*
A Woman's Face *'38*
Intermezzo *'36*

Krister Henriksson (1946-)
Reconstruction *'03*
Faithless *'00*

Buck Henry (1930-)
The Last Shot *'04*
Town and Country *'01*
Breakfast of Champions *'98*
I'm Losing You *'98*
1999 *'98*
Curtain Call *'97*
The Real Blonde *'97*
Kurt Vonnegut's Harrison Bergeron *'95*
To Die For *'95*
Grumpy Old Men *'93*
Short Cuts *'93*
Keep the Change *'92*
The Linguini Incident *'92*
Mastergate *'92*
The Player *'92*
Defending Your Life *'91*
Tune in Tomorrow *'90*
Dark Before Dawn *'89*
Rude Awakening *'89*
Aria *'88*
Eating Raoul *'82*
Gloria *'80*
Old Boyfriends *'79*
Heaven Can Wait *'78*
The Man Who Fell to Earth *'76*
The Day of the Dolphin *'73 (V)*
Is There Sex After Death? *'71*
Catch-22 *'70*
The Graduate *'67*

Charlotte Henry (1913-80)
Bowery Blitzkrieg *'41*
God's Country and the Man *'37*
The Mandarin Mystery *'37*
Charlie Chan at the Opera *'36*
March of the Wooden Soldiers *'34*

Gloria Henry (1923-)
Kill the Umpire *'50*
Miss Grant Takes Richmond *'49*

Gloria Lynne Henry
The Devil's Advocate *'97*
Phantasm 3: Lord of the Dead *'94*

Gregg Henry (1952-)
The Black Dahlia *'06*
In the Land of Women *'06*
Slither *'06*
United 93 *'06*
Silent Partner *'05*
Ballistic: Ecks vs. Sever *'02*
Femme Fatale *'02*
Sin *'02*
Sleep Easy, Hutch Rimes *'00*
The Big Brass Ring *'99*
Payback *'98*
Star Trek: Insurrection *'98*
Robin Cook's Terminal *'96*
Bodily Harm *'95*
Sharon's Secret *'95*
Kiss of a Killer *'93*
The Positively True Adventures of the Alleged Texas Cheerleader-Murdering Mom *'93*
Fever *'91*
Fair Game *'89*
The Last of Philip Banter *'87*
The Patriot *'86*
Body Double *'84*
Scarface *'83*
Funny Money *'82*
Just Before Dawn *'80*
Hot Rod *'79*
Mean Dog Blues *'78*
Pearl *'78*

Hank Henry (1906-81)
Robin and the 7 Hoods *'64*
Pal Joey *'57*

Judith Henry
Germinal *'93*
La Discrete *'90*

Justin Henry (1971-)
Lost *'05*
Finding Home *'03*
Chasing Destiny *'00*
Andersonville *'95*
Sweet Hearts Dance *'88*
Martin's Day *'85*
Sixteen Candles *'84*
Tiger Town *'83*
Kramer vs. Kramer *'79*

Lenny Henry (1958-)
Penelope *'06*
Bernard and the Genie *'91*
True Identity *'91*

Linda Henry
The Business *'05*
Beautiful Thing *'95*

Louise Henry
Charlie Chan on Broadway *'37*
In Old Kentucky *'35*

Martha Henry (1938-)
Clean *'04*
The Republic of Love *'03*
Anne of Green Gables: The Continuing Story *'99*
Long Day's Journey Into Night *'96*
Glory Enough for All: The Discovery of Insulin *'92*
White Light *'90*
Dancing in the Dark *'86*

Mike Henry (1939-)
Smokey and the Bandit, Part 3 *'83*
Smokey and the Bandit 2 *'80*
Smokey and the Bandit *'77*
Adios Amigo *'75*
The Longest Yard *'74*
The Green Berets *'68*
More Dead Than Alive *'68*

Pat Henry (1924-82)
The Detective *'68*
Lady in Cement *'68*

Robert "Buzzy" Henry (1931-71)
Danny Boy *'46*
Wild West *'46*
The Great Mike *'44*
Turf Boy *'42*
The Phantom Pinto *'41*
Buzzy Rides the Range *'40*
Rio Grande Ranger *'37*
The Unknown Ranger *'36*
Western Frontier *'35*

Thomas B(rowne). Henry (1907-80)
Showdown at Boot Hill *'58*
Beginning of the End *'57*
Blood of Dracula *'57*
The Brain from Planet Arous *'57*
20 Million Miles to Earth *'57*

Tim Henry
Masters of Horror: We All Scream for Ice Cream *'07*
125 Rooms of Comfort *'83*
The Dawson Patrol *'78*
Vengeance Is Mine *'74*

William Henry (1918-82)
The Alamo *'60*
Mister Roberts *'55*
Marshal of Cedar Rock *'53*
Movie Stuntmen *'53*
Motor Patrol *'50*
Trail to San Antone *'47*
G.I. War Brides *'46*
The Adventures of Mark Twain *'44*
Navy Way *'44*
Dance Hall *'41*
A Man to Remember *'39*
Campus Confessions *'38*
Four Men and a Prayer *'38*
Double or Nothing *'37*
Madame X *'37*
Tarzan Escapes *'36*
China Seas *'35*

Douglas Henshall (1965-)
It's All About Love *'03*
Gentlemen's Relish *'01*
Lawless Heart *'01*
Anna Karenina *'00*
Twice upon a Yesterday *'98*
Kull the Conqueror *'97*
Orphans *'97*
Sharpe's Justice *'97*
Angels and Insects *'95*

John Henshaw
See No Evil: The Moors Murders *'06*
This Is Not a Love Song *'02*

John Hensley
Shutter *'08*
Teeth *'07*

Lisa Hensley
15 Amore *'98*
Paradise Road *'97*
Dating the Enemy *'95*
Mr. Reliable: A True Story *'95*
Brides of Christ *'91*
The 13th Floor *'88*

Pamela Hensley (1950-)
Double Exposure *'82*
The Nude Bomb *'80*
Buck Rogers in the 25th Century *'79*
The Rebels *'79*
Doc Savage *'75*

Shuler Hensley (1967-)
The Legend of Zorro *'05*
Van Helsing *'04*
The Bread, My Sweet *'01*

Darrin Dewitt Henson (1972-)
Life Support *'07*
The Salon *'05*

Elden (Ratliff) Henson (1977-)
Deja Vu *'06*
Marilyn Hotchkiss' Ballroom Dancing & Charm School *'06*
The Butterfly Effect *'04*
The Battle of Shaker Heights *'03*
Dumb and Dumberer: When Harry Met Lloyd *'03*
Evil Alien Conquerors *'02*
Manic *'01*
O *'01*
Idle Hands *'99*
She's All That *'99*
The Mighty *'98*
D3: The Mighty Ducks *'96*
The Mighty Ducks *'92*

Gladys Henson (1897-1983)
The Leather Boys *'63*
Those People Next Door *'52*
The Magnet *'50*
Train of Events *'49*

Jim Henson (1936-90)
Into the Night *'85*
Sesame Street Presents: Follow That Bird *'85 (V)*
The Muppets Take Manhattan *'84 (V)*
The Dark Crystal *'82 (V)*
The Muppet Movie *'79 (V)*

John Henson (1967-)
Bar Hopping *'00*
Stag *'97*

Nicky Henson (1945-)
Love or Money *'01*
Me Without You *'01*
Parting Shots *'98*
Number 1 of the Secret Service *'77*
Psychomania *'73*
The Conqueror Worm *'68*

Taraji P. Henson (1970-)
Date Night *'10*
The Karate Kid *'10*
I Can Do Bad All By Myself *'09*
Not Easily Broken *'09*
The Curious Case of Benjamin Button *'08*
The Family That Preys *'08*
Hurricane Season *'08*
Smokin' Aces *'07*
Talk to Me *'07*
Something New *'06*
Four Brothers *'05*
Hustle & Flow *'05*
Hair Show *'04*
Baby Boy *'01*

Natasha Henstridge (1974-)
Deception *'08*
Species 3 *'04*
The Whole Ten Yards *'04*
Power and Beauty *'02*
Chilly Dogs *'01*
John Carpenter's Ghosts of Mars *'01*
A Better Way to Die *'00*
Bounce *'00*
Caracara *'00*
It Had to Be You *'00*
Jason and the Argonauts *'00*
Second Skin *'00*
The Whole Nine Yards *'00*
Dog Park *'98*
Species 2 *'98*
Standoff *'97*
Adrenalin: Fear the Rush *'96*
Maximum Risk *'96*
Species *'95*

Audrey Hepburn (1929-93)
Always *'89*
Love Among Thieves *'86*
They All Laughed *'81*
Sidney Sheldon's Bloodline *'79*
Robin and Marian *'76*
Two for the Road *'67*
Wait until Dark *'67*
How to Steal a Million *'66*
My Fair Lady *'64*
Paris When It Sizzles *'64*
Charade *'63*
Breakfast at Tiffany's *'61*
The Children's Hour *'61*
The Unforgiven *'60*
Green Mansions *'59*
The Nun's Story *'59*
Funny Face *'57*
Love in the Afternoon *'57*
War and Peace *'56*
Sabrina *'54*
Roman Holiday *'53*
The Lavender Hill Mob *'51*

Katharine Hepburn (1907-2003)
One Christmas *'95*
Love Affair *'94*
The Man Upstairs *'93*
Grace Quigley *'84*
On Golden Pond *'81*
The Corn Is Green *'79*
Olly Olly Oxen Free *'78*
Love Among the Ruins *'75*
Rooster Cogburn *'75*
Trojan Women *'71*
The Madwoman of Chaillot *'69*
The Lion in Winter *'68*
Guess Who's Coming to Dinner *'67*
Long Day's Journey into Night *'62*
Suddenly, Last Summer *'59*
Desk Set *'57*
The Rainmaker *'56*
Summertime *'55*
Pat and Mike *'52*
The African Queen *'51*
Adam's Rib *'50*
State of the Union *'48*
Song of Love *'47*
Undercurrent *'46*
Without Love *'45*
Dragon Seed *'44*
Stage Door Canteen *'43*
Keeper of the Flame *'42*
Woman of the Year *'42*
The Philadelphia Story *'40*
Bringing Up Baby *'38*
Holiday *'38*
Quality Street *'37*
Stage Door *'37*
Mary of Scotland *'36*
A Woman Rebels *'36*
Alice Adams *'35*
Break of Hearts *'35*
Sylvia Scarlett *'35*
Little Minister *'34*
Spitfire *'34*
Christopher Strong *'33*
Little Women *'33*
Morning Glory *'33*
A Bill of Divorcement *'32*

Bernard Hepton (1925-)
Emma *'97*
Eminent Domain *'91*
Woman in Black *'89*
Stealing Heaven *'88*
The Charmer *'87*
The Lady's Not for Burning *'87*
Shadey *'87*
Mansfield Park *'85*
Smiley's People *'82*
Tinker, Tailor, Soldier, Spy *'80*
Orde Wingate *'76*
Get Carter *'71*

Charles Herbert (1948-)
13 Ghosts *'60*
The Fly *'58*
Gun Glory *'57*

Holmes Herbert (1882-1956)
Command Decision *'48*
Calling Dr. Death *'43*
Invisible Agent *'42*

Sherlock Holmes and the Secret Weapon *'42*
British Intelligence *'40*
Bad Boy *'39*
Stanley and Livingstone *'39*
Here's Flash Casey *'38*
The House of Secrets *'37*
Sons of Steel *'35*
Dangerous Appointment *'34*
The Invisible Man *'33*
Mystery of the Wax Museum *'33*
Dr. Jekyll and Mr. Hyde *'32*
Shop Angel *'32*
Daughter of the Dragon *'31*
The Charlatan *'29*
The Kiss *'29*
Say It With Songs *'29*
Through the Breakers *'28*
When a Man Loves *'27*
Up the Ladder *'25*
A Woman of the World *'25*

Hugh Herbert (1887-1952)
The Beautiful Blonde from Bashful Bend *'49*
On Our Merry Way *'48*
A Song Is Born *'48*
It's a Great Life *'43*
Sherlock Holmes and the Secret Weapon *'42*
The Black Cat *'41*
The Villain Still Pursued Her *'41*
Eternally Yours *'39*
Four's a Crowd *'38*
Gold Diggers in Paris *'38*
The Great Waltz *'38*
Hollywood Hotel *'37*
Sing Me a Love Song *'37*
Colleen *'36*
One Rainy Afternoon *'36*
Gold Diggers of 1935 *'35*
A Midsummer Night's Dream *'35*
Sweet Adeline *'35*
Fashions of 1934 *'34*
Bureau of Missing Persons *'33*
Diplomaniacs *'33*
Lost Squadron *'32*
Hook, Line and Sinker *'30*

Percy Herbert (1920-92)
Blacksnake! *'73*
The Fiend *'71*
Man in the Wilderness *'71*
Too Late the Hero *'70*
Carry On Cowboy *'66*
One Million Years B.C. *'66*
Call Me Bwana *'63*
Carry On Jack *'63*
Mutiny on the Bounty *'62*
The Guns of Navarone *'61*
Mysterious Island *'61*
Serious Charge *'59*
The Bridge on the River Kwai *'57*

Becky Herbst (1977-)
Donor Unknown *'95*
Shrunken Heads *'94*

Carla Herd
Deathstalker 3 *'89*
Wild Zone *'89*

Richard Herd (1932-)
I Married a Monster *'98*
The Survivor *'98*
Cosmic Slop *'94*
The Judas Project: The Ultimate Encounter *'94*
V *'83*
Lovely... But Deadly *'82*
Wolf Lake *'79*
Terror Out of the Sky *'78*

Dolores Heredia (1966-)
Rudo y Cursi *'09*
Santitos *'99*
On the Air *'95*

Wilson Jermaine Heredia (1971-)
iMurders *'08*
Rent *'05*

Eileen Herlie (1920-2008)
Angel with the Trumpet *'50*
Hamlet *'48*

Jacques Herlin (1932-)
Torrents of Spring *'90*
Ironmaster *'82*

Roberto Herlitzka (1937-)
The Favorite Son *'94*
Summer Night with Greek Profile, Almond Eyes & Scent of Basil *'87*

David Herman (1967-)
Idiocracy *'06*
The Lather Effect *'06*
Dude, Where's My Car? *'00*
Table One *'00*
Office Space *'98*

Jack Herman
The Naked Witch *'64*
The Yesterday Machine *'63*

Jimmy Herman
Coyote Waits *'03*
Crazy Horse *'96*
Medicine River *'94*
Warrior Spirit *'94*
Geronimo *'93*
Dances with Wolves *'90*

Paul Herman (1946-)
Somebody to Love *'94*
New York Stories *'89*
The Last Temptation of Christ *'88*
The Squeeze *'87*

Pee-wee Herman
See Paul (Pee-wee Herman) Reubens

Woody Herman (1913-87)
New Orleans *'47*
Sensations of 1945 *'44*
Wintertime *'43*

Irm Hermann (1942-)
A Woman in Berlin *'08*
The Last Five Days *'82*
Mother Kusters Goes to Heaven *'76*
Fear of Fear *'75*
Ali: Fear Eats the Soul *'74*
The Bitter Tears of Petra von Kant *'72*
The Merchant of Four Seasons *'71*

Jay Hernandez (1978-)
Takers *'10*
American Son *'08*
Lakeview Terrace *'08*
Nothing Like the Holidays *'08*
Quarantine *'08*
Hostel: Part 2 *'07*
Hostel *'06*
World Trade Center *'06*
Carlito's Way: Rise to Power *'05*
Friday Night Lights *'04*
Torque *'04*
The Rookie *'02*
crazy/beautiful *'01*

Jonathan Hernandez (1983-)
The Hammer *'07*
A Million to Juan *'94*
My Family *'94*

Juan Carlos Hernandez
Carlito's Way: Rise to Power *'05*
High Crimes *'02*

Juano Hernandez (1901-70)
They Call Me Mr. Tibbs! *'70*
The Sins of Rachel Cade *'61*
Sergeant Rutledge *'60*
The Mark of the Hawk *'57*
Something of Value *'57*
Stars in My Crown *'50*
Intruder in the Dust *'49*

Sergio Hernandez
The Sacred Family *'04*
Johnny 100 Pesos *'93*

Vicky Hernandez
Proof of Life *'00*
Details of a Duel: A Question of Honor *'89*

Blake Heron (1982-)
11:14 *'03*
We Were Soldiers *'02*
Cheaters *'00*
Wind River *'98*
Shiloh *'97*
Trilogy of Terror 2 *'96*

Marcel Herrand (1897-1953)
Fanfan la Tulipe *'51*
Children of Paradise *'44*
Les Visiteurs du Soir *'42*

Mark Herrier (1954-)
Porky's Revenge *'85*
Spraggue *'84*
Porky's 2: The Next Day *'83*
Tank *'83*
Porky's *'82*

Aggie Herring (1876-1939)
Suicide Squad *'35*
That Certain Thing *'28*
Oliver Twist *'22*

Laura (Martinez) Herring
See Laura Elena Harring

Edward Herrmann (1943-)
The Skeptic *'09*
I Think I Love My Wife *'07*
Relative Strangers *'06*
Wedding Daze *'06*
The Aviator *'04*
Intolerable Cruelty *'03*
The Emperor's Club *'02*
The Cat's Meow *'01*
Double Take *'01*
James Dean *'01*
The Shaft *'01*
Atomic Train *'99*
Vendetta *'99*
Saint Maybe *'98*
Critical Care *'97*
Pandora's Clock *'96*
Soul of the Game *'96*
Nixon *'95*
Foreign Student *'94*
Richie Rich *'94*
Born Yesterday *'93*
A Foreign Field *'93*
My Boyfriend's Back *'93*
Sweet Poison *'91*
Big Business *'88*
The Lawrenceville Stories *'88*
The Lost Boys *'87*
Overboard *'87*
Murrow *'86*
Compromising Positions *'85*
The Man with One Red Shoe *'85*
The Purple Rose of Cairo *'85*
Harry's War *'84*
Mrs. Soffel *'84*
Memorial Day *'83*
A Little Sex *'82*
Death Valley *'81*
The Private History of a Campaign That Failed *'81*
Reds *'81*
Freedom Road *'79*
The North Avenue Irregulars *'79*
Portrait of a Stripper *'79*
Sorrows of Gin *'79*
Take Down *'79*
The Betsy *'78*
Brass Target *'78*
Love Affair: The Eleanor & Lou Gehrig Story *'77*
Eleanor & Franklin *'76*
The Great Waldo Pepper *'75*
The Great Gatsby *'74*
The Day of the Dolphin *'73*
The Paper Chase *'73*

Mark Herron
Girl in Gold Boots *'69*
8 1/2 *'63*

Adam Herschman
Soul Men *'08*
Accepted *'06*

Gary Hershberger (1964-)
The Siege of Firebase Gloria *'89*
Free Ride *'86*
Paradise Motel *'84*

Barbara Hershey (1948-)
Love Comes Lately *'07*
Riding the Bullet *'04*
11:14 *'03*
Daniel Deronda *'02*
Lantana *'01*
Drowning on Dry Land *'00*
Passion *'99*
Breakfast of Champions *'98*
Frogs for Snakes *'98*
A Soldier's Daughter Never Cries *'98*
Portrait of a Lady *'96*
The Last of the Dogmen *'95*
The Pallbearer *'95*
Abraham *'94*
A Dangerous Woman *'93*
Falling Down *'93*
Return to Lonesome Dove *'93*
Splitting Heirs *'93*
Swing Kids *'93*
The Public Eye *'92*
Defenseless *'91*
Paris Trout *'91*
A Killing in a Small Town *'90*
Tune in Tomorrow *'90*
Beaches *'88*
The Last Temptation of Christ *'88*
A World Apart *'88*
Shy People *'87*
Tin Men *'87*
Hannah and Her Sisters *'86*
Hoosiers *'86*
Passion Flower *'86*
My Wicked, Wicked Ways *'84*
The Natural *'84*
The Entity *'83*
The Nightingale *'83*
The Right Stuff *'83*
Americana *'81*
Take This Job & Shove It *'81*
Angel on My Shoulder *'80*
The Stunt Man *'80*
From Here to Eternity *'79*
Choice of Weapons *'76*
Flood! *'76*
The Last Hard Men *'76*
Boxcar Bertha *'72*
Diamonds *'72*
The Baby Maker *'70*
The Liberation of L.B. Jones *'70*
The Pursuit of Happiness *'70*
Last Summer *'69*
With Six You Get Eggroll *'68*

Jean Hersholt (1886-1956)
Melody for Three *'41*
They Meet Again *'41*
Courageous Dr. Christian *'40*
Dr. Christian Meets the Women *'40*
Remedy for Riches *'40*
Meet Dr. Christian *'39*
Mr. Moto in Danger Island *'39*
Alexander's Ragtime Band *'38*
Happy Landing *'38*
Heidi *'37*
One in a Million *'36*
Reunion *'36*
Break of Hearts *'35*
Mark of the Vampire *'35*
The Cat and the Fiddle *'34*
Men in White *'34*
The Painted Veil *'34*
Dinner at Eight *'33*
The Beast of the City *'32*
Emma *'32*
Grand Hotel *'32*
Hearts of Humanity *'32*
The Mask of Fu Manchu *'32*
Skyscraper Souls *'32*
The Phantom of Paris *'31*
Private Lives *'31*
The Sin of Madelon Claudet *'31*
Susan Lenox: Her Fall and Rise *'31*
Hell Harbor *'30*
Battle of the Sexes *'28*
Greed *'24*
Heart's Haven *'22*
Tess of the Storm Country *'22*
The Disciple *'15*

Gerard Herter
Adios, Sabata *'71*
Hornet's Nest *'70*
Last Day of the War *'69*
Any Gun Can Play *'67*

Brighton Hertford (1986-)
Can of Worms *'00*
Mystery Kids *'99*
Evil Has a Face *'96*

Irene Hervey (1910-98)
Play Misty for Me *'71*
Mickey *'48*
Mr. Peabody & the Mermaid *'48*
Gang Busters *'42*
Night Monster *'42*
Destry Rides Again *'39*
East Side of Heaven *'39*
The Girl Said No *'37*
Charlie Chan in Shanghai *'35*
Motive for Revenge *'35*
The Count of Monte Cristo *'34*
Dude Ranger *'34*

Jason Hervey (1972-)
Trading Favors *'97*
Back to School *'86*
Back to the Future *'85*
Pee-wee's Big Adventure *'85*
Frankenweenie *'84*
Ratings Game *'84*

Werner Herzog (1942-)
Encounters at the End of the World *'07 (N)*
Mister Lonely *'07*
Julien Donkey-boy *'99*
Man of Flowers *'84*
Burden of Dreams *'82*

Kam Heskin (1973-)
The Prince & Me 3: A Royal Honeymoon *'08*
The Prince & Me 2: Royal Wedding *'06*
Dirty Love *'05*
This Girl's Life *'03*
Vlad *'03*

Grant Heslov (1963-)
Good Night, and Good Luck *'05*
Sleeper Cell *'05*
The Scorpion King *'02*
Dante's Peak *'97*
Black Sheep *'96*
Congo *'95*
True Lies *'94*

Annelise Hesme (1976-)
Avenue Montaigne *'06*
Priceless *'06*
Alexander *'04*

David A(lexander) Hess (1942-)
Let It Rock *'86*
House on the Edge of the Park *'84*
Avalanche Express *'79*
Last House on the Left *'72*

Joe Hess
Bloodmoon *'97*
Master Blaster *'85*

Sandra Hess (1968-)
Mortal Kombat 2: Annihilation *'97*
Beastmaster 3: The Eye of Braxus *'95*
Endangered *'94*
Uncivilized *'94*

Howard Hesseman (1940-)
Halloween II *'09*
The Rocker *'08*
Nanny Insanity *'06*
About Schmidt *'02*
Gridlock'd *'96*
Out of Sync *'95*
Home for Christmas *'93*
Hot Chocolate *'92*
Rubin & Ed *'92*
The Diamond Trap *'91*
Inside Out *'91*
Murder in New Hampshire: The Pamela Smart Story *'91*
Amazon Women on the Moon *'87*
Heat *'87*
Flight of the Navigator *'86*
My Chauffeur *'86*
Clue *'85*
Police Academy 2: Their First Assignment *'85*
The Princess Who Never Laughed *'84*
Silence of the Heart *'84*
This Is Spinal Tap *'84*
Doctor Detroit *'83*
One Shoe Makes It Murder *'82*
Honky Tonk Freeway *'81*
Great American Traffic Jam *'80*
Americathon *'79*
Tarantulas: The Deadly Cargo *'77*
The Big Bus *'76*
Jackson County Jail *'76*
Tunnelvision *'76*
Private Lessons *'75*
Shampoo *'75*
The Sunshine Boys *'75*
Steelyard Blues *'73*
Billy Jack *'71*
A Session with The Committee *'68*

Catherine Hessling (1900-79)
Renoir Shorts *'27*
Charleston *'26*

Charlton Heston (1924-2008)
Cats & Dogs *'01 (V)*
Planet of the Apes *'01*
Town and Country *'01*
Any Given Sunday *'99*
Gideon *'99*
Hercules *'97 (N)*
Alaska *'96*
Hamlet *'96*
The Avenging Angel *'95*
In the Mouth of Madness *'95*
True Lies *'94*
Tombstone *'93*
Wayne's World 2 *'93*
Solar Crisis *'92*
A Thousand Heroes *'92*
The Crucifer of Blood *'91*
Almost an Angel *'90*
The Little Kidnappers *'90*
Treasure Island *'89*
A Man for All Seasons *'88*
Nairobi Affair *'88*
Proud Men *'87*
Chiefs *'83*
Mother Lode *'82*
The Awakening *'80*
The Mountain Men *'80*
The Prince and the Pauper *'78*
Gray Lady Down *'77*
America at the Movies *'76 (N)*
The Last Hard Men *'76*

Midway '76
Two Minute Warning '76
Airport '75 '75
The Four Musketeers '75
Earthquake '74
The Three Musketeers '74
Antony and Cleopatra '73
Soylent Green '73
Call of the Wild '72
Omega Man '71
Beneath the Planet of the Apes '70
Julius Caesar '70
Elizabeth, the Queen '68
Planet of the Apes '68
Will Penny '67
Khartoum '66
The Agony and the Ecstasy '65
The Greatest Story Ever Told '65
Major Dundee '65
The War Lord '65
55 Days at Peking '63
Diamond Head '62
El Cid '61
Ben-Hur '59
The Wreck of the Mary Deare '59
The Big Country '58
The Buccaneer '58
Touch of Evil '58
Three Violent People '57
The Ten Commandments '56
The Far Horizons '55
The Private War of Major Benson '55
Naked Jungle '54
Arrowhead '53
Pony Express '53
The Greatest Show on Earth '52
Ruby Gentry '52

Lori Heuring (1973-)
The Poker Club '08
False Prophets '06
The Locket '02
Taboo '02
Seduced: Pretty When You Cry '01
True Blue '01
The In Crowd '00

Jennifer Love Hewitt (1979-)
Delgo '08 (V)
Tropic Thunder '08
Garfield: A Tail of Two Kitties '06
Confessions of a Sociopathic Social Climber '05
Garfield: The Movie '04
If Only '04
The Truth About Love '04
The Tuxedo '02
Heartbreakers '01
The Audrey Hepburn Story '00
The Suburbans '99
Can't Hardly Wait '98
I Still Know What You Did Last Summer '98
Telling You '98
I Know What You Did Last Summer '97
Trojan War '97
House Arrest '96
Home for Christmas '93
Sister Act 2: Back in the Habit '93

Martin Hewitt (1958-)
Bombshell '97
Night Fire '94
Secret Games 2: The Escort '93
Night Rhythms '92
Secret Games '92
Carnal Crimes '91
Crime Lords '91
Private War '90
White Ghost '88
Killer Party '86
Out of Control '85
Yellowbeard '83
Endless Love '81
Alien Predators '80

Paul Hewitt
Tom Clancy's Netforce '98
Hijacking Hollywood '97
A Perfect World '93

Sean Hewitt
Battlefield Earth '00
My Own Country '98
Swann '96
The Sender '82
Big Zapper '73

David Hewlett (1968-)
Splice '09
A Dog's Breakfast '07
Darklight '04
Ice Men '04
Cypher '02
The Triangle '01
The Life Before This '99
Cube '98
The Boys of St. Vincent '93
Desire and Hell at Sunset Motel '92
The Penthouse '92
Scanners 2: The New Order '91
Where the Heart Is '90
Pin... '88

Siobhan Hewlett
Irina Palm '07
Monsieur N. '03

Virginia Hey (1952-)
Bullet Down Under '94
Obsession: A Taste for Fear '89
The Road Warrior '82

Kirby Heyborne (1977-)
Together Again for the First Time '08
Saints and Soldiers '03

Weldon Heyburn (1910-51)
The Chinese Cat '44
Westward Bound '44
Code of the Outlaw '42
Rock River Renegades '42
Criminals Within '41
Panama Patrol '39
Sea Racketeers '37
The Thirteenth Man '37
Convention Girl '35

Louis Jean Heydt (1905-60)
Island in the Sky '53
The Kid From Cleveland '49
The Big Sleep '46
Our Vines Have Tender Grapes '45
They Were Expendable '45
Thirty Seconds Over Tokyo '44
Zombies on Broadway '44
Dive Bomber '41
Power Dive '41
Sleepers West '41
The Great McGinty '40
Charlie Chan at Treasure Island '39
Before Morning '33

Chris Heyerdahl
The Twilight Saga: New Moon '09
Blade: Trinity '04
Catwoman '04
Varian's War '01
Requiem for Murder '99
The Witness '99

Herbert (Hayes) Heyes (1889-1958)
The Far Horizons '55
Bedtime for Bonzo '51
A Place in the Sun '51
Behind Locked Doors '48
The Cobra Strikes '48
Teenage '44
Calling Wild Bill Elliott '43

Barton Heyman (1937-96)
Dead Man Walking '95
Raising Cain '92
Roadside Prophets '92
Awakenings '90

Static '87
Billy Galvin '86
Cruising '80
He Who Walks Alone '78
The Exorcist '73
Let's Scare Jessica to Death '71
Valdez Is Coming '71
The Naked Flame '68

Anne Heywood (1932-)
Sadat '83
The Shaming '79
I Want What I Want '72
Scenes from a Murder '72
The Chairman '69
The Very Edge '63
The Brain '62
Carthage in Flames '60
Doctor at Large '57

Herbert Heywood (1881-1964)
Swingtime Johnny '43
Legion of the Lawless '40

Pat Heywood (1927-)
Wish You Were Here '87
Rude Awakening '81
10 Rillington Place '71
Girly '70

Sung Hi Lee (1970-)
The Art of War 3: Retribution '08
National Lampoon's Christmas Vacation 2: Cousin Eddie's Big Island Adventure '03

Ruth Hiatt
Ridin' Thru '35
Sunset Trail '32

Edward Hibbert (1955-)
A Different Loyalty '04
The Lion King 1 1/2 '04 (V)
Friends and Family '01
The First Wives Club '96

John Benjamin Hickey (1963-)
Living Proof '08
Freedom Writers '07
The Seeker: The Dark Is Rising '07
Flags of Our Fathers '06
Infamous '06
Changing Lanes '02
The Anniversary Party '01
Hamlet '01
Life with Judy Garland—Me and My Shadows '01
The Bone Collector '99
The General's Daughter '99
The Lady in Question '99
Finding North '97
The Ice Storm '97
Eddie '96
Love! Valour! Compassion! '96

Marguerite Hickey (1963-)
Grizzly Mountain '97
Mirrors '85

Tom Hickey (1944-)
Rory O'Shea Was Here '04
Possession '02
Raining Stones '93
Unnatural Pursuits '91
Nuns on the Run '90

William Hickey (1928-97)
Mouse Hunt '97
Love Is All There Is '96
Twisted '96
Forget Paris '95
The Jerky Boys '95
The Maddening '95
Major Payne '95
The Nightmare Before Christmas '93 (V)
The Runestone '91
Any Man's Death '90
Mob Boss '90
My Blue Heaven '90
Tales from the Darkside: The Movie '90

National Lampoon's Christmas Vacation '89
Pink Cadillac '89
Puppet Master '89
Sea of Love '89
Sons '89
Bright Lights, Big City '88
Da '88
Hobo's Christmas '87
The Name of the Rose '86
One Crazy Summer '86
Prizzi's Honor '85
Remo Williams: The Adventure Begins '85
Walls of Glass '85
Mikey & Nicky '76
The Boston Strangler '68
Invitation to a Gunfighter '64

Catherine Hickland (1956-)
Millions '90
Ghost Town '88
Witchery '88

Darryl Hickman (1931-)
Johnny Shiloh '63
Geronimo's Revenge '60
Texas John Slaughter: Geronimo's Revenge '60
The Tingler '59
Tea and Sympathy '56
Island in the Sky '53
The Happy Years '50
Fighting Father Dunne '48
The Devil on Wheels '47
Underworld Scandal '47
Two Years before the Mast '46
Leave Her to Heaven '45
Keeper of the Flame '42
Men of Boys Town '41

Dwayne Hickman (1934-)
A Night at the Roxbury '98
High School USA '84
My Dog, the Thief '69
Dr. Goldfoot and the Bikini Machine '66
Cat Ballou '65
How to Stuff a Wild Bikini '65
Ski Party '65
Rally 'Round the Flag, Boys! '58
The Sun Comes Up '49

Howard Hickman (1880-1949)
Watch on the Rhine '43
Dive Bomber '41
Bullet Code '40
Gone with the Wind '39
Western Gold '37
Hell-Ship Morgan '36
Civilization '16

Anthony Hickox (1959-)
Blast '04
Prince Valiant '97
Lobster Man from Mars '89

Catherine Hicks (1951-)
Poison Ivy 4: The Secret Society '08
Eight Days a Week '97
Turbulence '96
Animal Room '95
Dillinger and Capone '95
Redwood Curtain '95
Secret Ingredient '92
Running Against Time '90
She's Out of Control '89
Spy '89
Child's Play '88
Souvenir '88
Laguna Heat '87
Like Father, Like Son '87
Peggy Sue Got Married '86
Star Trek 4: The Voyage Home '86
Fever Pitch '85
Garbo Talks '84
The Razor's Edge '84
Better Late Than Never '83
Death Valley '81

Marilyn: The Untold Story '80

Dan Hicks
Class Action '91
Evil Dead 2: Dead by Dawn '87
My Blue Heaven '50

James Hicks
Miss Monday '98
Swing '98

Kevin Hicks
Final Notice '89
Higher Education '88
Blood Relations '87

Michele Hicks (1973-)
Northfork '03
Everything Put Together '00
Twin Falls Idaho '99

Russell Hicks (1895-1957)
Seventh Cavalry '56
Mr. Walkie Talkie '52
As You Were '51
Kentucky Jubilee '51
Air Raid Wardens '43
Hitler: Dead or Alive '43
King of the Cowboys '43
Tarzan's New York Adventure '42
Dive Bomber '41
Sergeant York '41
The Bank Dick '40
Blind Fools '40
Johnny Apollo '40
Hollywood Cavalcade '39
The Real Glory '39
Stanley and Livingstone '39
The Big Broadcast of 1938 '38
Pick a Star '37
Charlie Chan in Shanghai '35
Devil Dogs of the Air '35
Before Morning '33

Sir Seymour Hicks (1891-1949)
Fame Is the Spur '47
Scrooge '35
The Secret of the Loch '34

Taral Hicks (1975-)
The Salon '05
Belly '98
Subway Stories '97
A Bronx Tale '93

Tommy Redmond Hicks (1962-)
Daughters of the Dust '91
She's Gotta Have It '86
Joe's Bed-Stuy Barbershop: We Cut Heads '83

William T. Hicks
Order of the Black Eagle '87
Unmasking the Idol '86
Death Screams '83
House of Death '82
Day of Judgment '81
Challenge '74

Joan Hickson (1906-98)
Century '94
A Murder Is Announced '87
A Pocketful of Rye '87
The Body in the Library '84
Great Expectations '81
A Day in the Death of Joe Egg '71
Carry On Loving '70
Carry On Regardless '61
Carry On Constable '60
No Kidding '60
Sea Wife '57
Doctor in the House '53
Seven Days to Noon '50
The Guinea Pig '48

Bokuzen Hidari (1894-1971)
Along with Ghosts '69
The Lower Depths '57
Seven Samurai '54

Sachiko Hidari (1930-2001)
Under the Flag of the Rising Sun '72
The Insect Woman '63
She and He '63

Tom Hiddleston
Return to Cranford '09
Wallander: Firewall '08
Wallander: One Step Behind '08
Wallander: Sidetracked '08
Miss Austen Regrets '07

Martha Higareda
Street Kings '08
Borderland '07

Chieko Higashiyama (1890-1980)
Tokyo Story '53
Early Summer '51

Wilbur Higby (1867-1934)
Until They Get Me '18
Hoodoo Ann '16
Matrimaniac '16
Reggie Mixes In '16

Robert Higden (1958-)
Swamp Devil '08
Black Swarm '07

David Anthony Higgens (1961-)
The Wrong Guy '96
Coldblooded '94

Anthony (Corlan) Higgins (1947-)
The Last Minute '01
Alive and Kicking '96
Moses '96
For Love or Money '93
Nostradamus '93
Sweet Killing '93
One Against the Wind '91
Darlings of the Gods '90
Max, Mon Amour '86
The Bride '85
Cold Room '84
She'll Be Wearing Pink Pajamas '84
The Draughtsman's Contract '82
Quartet '81
Raiders of the Lost Ark '81
Vampire Circus '71
Something for Everyone '70
Taste the Blood of Dracula '70

Clare Higgins (1955-)
Cassandra's Dream '07
Bigger Than the Sky '05
The Libertine '05
Catherine Cookson's The Secret '00
Small Faces '95
Circle of Deceit '94
Fatherland '94
Bad Behavior '92
Hellbound: Hellraiser 2 '88
Wonderland '88
Hellraiser '87

Colin Higgins (1941-88)
Hope and Glory '87
Into the Night '85

Joe Higgins (1925-98)
Milo Milo '79
Namu, the Killer Whale '66
Flipper's New Adventure '64

John Michael Higgins (1963-)
Couples Retreat '09
Fired Up! '09
The Ugly Truth '09
Still Waiting '08
Yes Man '08
Evan Almighty '07
Fred Claus '07
Walk Hard: The Dewey Cox Story '07
The Break-Up '06

The Mayor of Casterbridge '03
The Statement '03
Veronica Guerin '03
Road to Perdition '02
The Sum of All Fears '02
Jason and the Argonauts '00
The Weight of Water '00
The Lost Son '98
Ivanhoe '97
Jane Eyre '97
Oscar and Lucinda '97
Some Mother's Son '96
The Affair '95
Mary Reilly '95
Persuasion '95
Catherine Cookson's The Man Who Cried '93
A Dark Adapted Eye '93
Hostages '93
December Bride '91

Cindy Hinds

Deadline '82
The Brood '79

Samuel S. Hinds (1875-1948)

The Bribe '48
It's a Wonderful Life '46
Scarlet Street '45
The Strange Affair of Uncle Harry '45
Weekend at the Waldorf '45
Cobra Woman '44
Jungle Woman '44
Son of Dracula '43
Grand Central Murder '42
Pardon My Sarong '42
Ride 'Em Cowboy '42
The Strange Case of Dr. Rx '42
Back Street '41
Blossoms in the Dust '41
Man Made Monster '41
It's a Date '40
Charlie McCarthy, Detective '39
Destry Rides Again '39
The Secret of Dr. Kildare '39
Devil's Party '38
Forbidden Valley '38
The Jury's Secret '38
Test Pilot '38
You Can't Take It with You '38
The Black Legion '37
Double or Nothing '37
Navy Blue and Gold '37
Rhythm on the Range '36
The Raven '35
Deluge '33
Gabriel Over the White House '33

Brendan P. Hines

Heavy Petting '07
Ordinary Sinner '02

Cheryl Hines (1965-)

Labor Pains '09
The Ugly Truth '09
Bart Got a Room '08
Henry Poole Is Here '08
Space Chimps '08 (V)
Waitress '07
Bickford Shmeckler's Cool Ideas '06
Keeping Up with the Steins '06
RV '06
Cake '05
Herbie: Fully Loaded '05

Damon Hines

Lethal Weapon 4 '98
Once Upon a Time ... When We Were Colored '95
What's Love Got to Do with It? '93
Lethal Weapon 3 '92
Lethal Weapon 2 '89
Scrooged '88
Barfly '87
Lethal Weapon '87
The Adventures of Buckaroo Banzai Across the Eighth Dimension '84
Ratings Game '84

Gregory Hines (1946-2003)

Bojangles '01
The Red Sneakers '01
Echo of Murder '00
Once in the Life '00
Things You Can Tell Just by Looking at Her '00
The Tic Code '99
Color of Justice '97
Subway Stories '97
The Cherokee Kid '96
Good Luck '96
The Preacher's Wife '96
Trigger Happy '96
A Stranger in Town '95
Waiting to Exhale '95
Bleeding Hearts '94
Dead Air '94
Renaissance Man '94
T Bone N Weasel '92
A Rage in Harlem '91
White Lie '91
Eve of Destruction '90
Tap '89
Off Limits '87
Running Scared '86
White Nights '85
The Cotton Club '84
The Muppets Take Manhattan '84
Puss 'n Boots '84
Deal of the Century '83
Eubie! '82
History of the World: Part 1 '81
Wolfen '81

Johnny Hines (1895-1970)

The Speed Spook '24
A Girl's Folly '17
Tillie Wakes Up '17

Robert Hines (1929-)

Devices and Desires '91
Echoes '88
Hellraiser '87

Ronald Hines (1929-)

Pack of Lies '87
We'll Meet Again '82
Elizabeth R '72

Pat Hingle (1923-2009)

The List '07
Two Tickets to Paradise '06
Waltzing Anna '06
The Runaway '00
Shaft '00
Muppets from Space '99
Batman and Robin '97
Hunter's Moon '97
A Thousand Acres '97
Larger Than Life '96
Batman Forever '95
One Christmas '95
The Quick and the Dead '95
Truman '95
Lightning Jack '94
Batman Returns '92
Citizen Cohn '92
The Habitation of Dragons '91
The Grifters '90
Batman '89
The Land Before Time '88 (V)
LBJ: The Early Years '88
Baby Boom '87
In 'n Out '86
Manhunt for Claude Dallas '86
Maximum Overdrive '86
Brewster's Millions '85
Broken Badge '85
The Falcon and the Snowman '85
Lady from Yesterday '85
Going Berserk '83
Running Brave '83
Sudden Impact '83
The Act '82
When Hell Was in Session '82
Of Mice and Men '81
The Private History of a Campaign That Failed '81
Elvis: The Movie '79
Norma Rae '79
Running Scared '79
Wild Times '79
The Gauntlet '77
Tarantulas: The Deadly Cargo '77
Hazel's People '73
Running Wild '73
Bloody Mama '70
The Ballad of Andy Crocker '69
Hang 'Em High '67
Nevada Smith '66
Invitation to a Gunfighter '64
The Ugly American '63
The Strange One '57

Marin Hinkle (1966-)

Weather Girl '09
The Haunting of Molly Hartley '08
Quarantine '08
Rails & Ties '07
Turn the River '07
Four and a Half Women '05
The Next Big Thing '02
Winds of Terror '01

Brent Hinkley (1962-)

Say It Isn't So '01
The Silence of the Lambs '91

Tommy Hinkley (1960-)

The Little Vampire '00
The Human Shield '92
Back to the Beach '87

Skip Hinnant (1940-)

Nine Lives of Fritz the Cat '74 (V)
Fritz the Cat '72 (V)

Darby Hinton (1957-)

Malibu Express '85
Firecracker '81
The Treasure of Jamaica Reef '74

Michael Hinz (1939-)

Touch Me Not '74
The Bridge '59

Bill (William Heinzman) Hinzman (1936-)

Revenge of the Living Zombies '88
The Majorettes '87
Night of the Living Dead '68

Paul Hipp (1963-)

South of Pico '07
Two Tickets to Paradise '06
Teenage Caveman '01
Cleopatra's Second Husband '00
More Dogs Than Bones '00
Waking the Dead '00
Another Day in Paradise '98
Midnight in the Garden of Good and Evil '97
Vicious Circles '97
The Funeral '96
Bad Channels '92

Mikijiro Hira

Azumi 2 '05
Pistol Opera '02
The Mystery of Rampo '94

Akihiko Hirata (1927-84)

Godzilla vs. the Cosmic Monster '74
Son of Godzilla '66
King Kong vs. Godzilla '63
Mothra '62
The Secret of the Telegian '61
H-Man '59
Godzilla, King of the Monsters '56
Samurai 2: Duel at Ichijoji Temple '55

Thora Hird (1911-2003)

Lost for Words '99
The Wedding Gift '93
Consuming Passions '88
The Nightcomers '72
Rattle of a Simple Man '64
Term of Trial '63
A Kind of Loving '62
The Entertainer '60
Dangerous Youth '58
The Frightened Man '52
Conspirator '49

Ingvar Hirdwall (1934-)

The Girl With the Dragon Tattoo '09
The Man on the Roof '76

Ryoko Hirosue

Departures '08
Wasabi '01

Daniel Hirsch

Lady Avenger '89
Zero Boys '86
Sky High '84

Emile Hirsch (1985-)

Taking Woodstock '09
Milk '08
Speed Racer '08
The Air I Breathe '07
Into the Wild '07
Alpha Dog '06
Imaginary Heroes '05
Lords of Dogtown '05
The Girl Next Door '04
The Mudge Boy '03
The Dangerous Lives of Altar Boys '02
The Emperor's Club '02
Wild Iris '01
Gargantua '98

Judd Hirsch (1935-)

A Beautiful Mind '01
Man on the Moon '99
Out of the Cold '99
Rocky Marciano '99
Color of Justice '97
Independence Day '96
The Great Escape 2: The Untold Story '88
Running on Empty '88
Brotherly Love '85
Teachers '84
The Goodbye People '83
Without a Trace '83
Marriage Is Alive and Well '80
Ordinary People '80
King of the Gypsies '78
Sooner or Later '78
Legend of Valentino '75
Fury on Wheels '71

Lou Hirsch

Thunderbirds '04
Honey, I Shrunk the Kids '89 (V)

Robert Hirsch (1929-)

Mortal Transfer '01
The Hunchback of Notre Dame '57
Plucking the Daisy '56

David Julian Hirsh

Coast to Coast '04
Blue Hill Avenue '01

Hallee Hirsh (1987-)

Make the Yuletide Gay '09
Happy Endings '05
Speak '04
My Sister's Keeper '02
Joe Gould's Secret '00
Spring Forward '99
You've Got Mail '98

Alice Hirson (1929-)

Blind Date '87
Miss All-American Beauty '82

Christianne Hirt

Firestorm '97
For the Moment '94
Tokyo Cowboy '94
Blades of Courage '88

Alfred Hitchcock (1899-1980)

Family Plot '76
The Birds '63
Psycho '60
The Lady Vanishes '38
Blackmail '29
The Lodger '26

Michael Hitchcock (1958-)

Danny Roane: First Time Director '06
Pretty Persuasion '05
A Mighty Wind '03
Best in Show '00
Happy, Texas '99

Patricia Hitchcock (1928-)

Psycho '60
Strangers on a Train '51

Robyn Hitchcock

Women in Trouble '09
The Manchurian Candidate '04

Iben Hjejle (1971-)

Cheri '09
Defiance '08
The Boss of It All '06
Cuban Blood '03
The Emperor's New Clothes '01
Flickering Lights '01
High Fidelity '00
Mifune '99

Jesse Hlubik

Masters of Horror: Sick Girl '06
Roman '06

Josie Ho

Street Fighter: The Legend of Chun-Li '09
Exiled '06
Vampire Effect '03
So Close '02
The Cave of the Silken Web '67

Judith Hoag (1968-)

Return to Halloweentown '06
Halloweentown High '04
Halloweentown 2: Kalabar's Revenge '01
Halloweentown '98
Acting on Impulse '93
Switched at Birth '91
Danielle Steel's Fine Things '90
A Matter of Degrees '90
Teenage Mutant Ninja Turtles: The Movie '90

Florence Hoath (1984-)

Back to the Secret Garden '01
The Governess '98
FairyTale: A True Story '97

Doug Hobart

The Death Curse of Tartu '66
The Professor '58

Rose Hobart (1906-2000)

Cass Timberlane '47
The Farmer's Daughter '47
Conflict '45
Susan and God '40
Convention Girl '35
Dr. Jekyll and Mr. Hyde '32
East of Borneo '31

Halliwell Hobbes (1877-1962)

You Gotta Stay Happy '48
Casanova Brown '44
Gaslight '44
Sherlock Holmes Faces Death '43
Journey for Margaret '42
Son of Fury '42
To Be or Not to Be '42
The Undying Monster '42
You Can't Take It with You '38
Charlie Chan in Shanghai '35
Dr. Jekyll and Mr. Hyde '32
The Lady Refuses '31

Chelsea Hobbs (1984-)

Clawed: The Legend of Sasquatch '05
The Snow Queen '02

Katrina Hobbs (1971-)

SuperFire '02
Absent Without Leave '95

Peter Hobbs (1918-)

In the Mood '87
Next One '84
Good Neighbor Sam '64

Rebecca Hobbs

Siam Sunset '99
The Ugly '96

William Hobbs (1939-)

Captain Kronos: Vampire Hunter '74
The Three Musketeers '74

Mara Hobel (1971-)

Personal Velocity: Three Portraits '02
Broadway Damage '98
Mommie Dearest '81
Sorrows of Gin '79

Valerie Hobson (1917-98)

The Promoter '52
The Voice of Merrill '52
Interrupted Journey '49
Kind Hearts and Coronets '49
The Rocking Horse Winner '49
Train of Events '49
Blanche Fury '48
Great Expectations '46
The Adventures of Tartu '43
Contraband '40
Clouds over Europe '39
Spy in Black '39
Drums '38
When Thief Meets Thief '37
Secret of Stamboul '36
The Bride of Frankenstein '35
The Mystery of Edwin Drood '35
Werewolf of London '35

Danny Hoch (1970-)

We Own the Night '07
Washington Heights '02
Black Hawk Down '01
White Boyz '99
Subway Stories '97

Kristen Hocking

See Kristen Dalton

Kane Hodder (1951-)

Bundy: A Legacy of Evil '08
Hack! '07
Darkwolf '03
Jason X '01
Watchers Reborn '98
Wishmaster '97
Pumpkinhead 2: Blood Wings '94
Jason Goes to Hell: The Final Friday '93
Friday the 13th, Part 8: Jason Takes Manhattan '89
Friday the 13th, Part 7: The New Blood '88

Douglas Hodge (1960-)

Mansfield Park '07
Scenes of a Sexual Nature '06
Vanity Fair '04
The Way We Live Now '02
Hollow Reed '95
Middlemarch '93
A Fatal Inversion '92
Buddy's Song '91
Dark Obsession '90
Salome's Last Dance '88

Edwin Hodge (1985-)

Hangman's Curse '03
Coastlines '02
My Teacher Ate My Homework '98

Kate Hodge (1966-)

Desire '95
The Hidden 2 '94
Rapid Fire '92
Love Kills '91
Leatherface: The Texas Chainsaw Massacre 3 '89

Mike Hodge (1947-)
Boycott *'02*
Fiona *'98*
Office Killer *'97*

Patricia Hodge (1946-)
Lies and Whispers *'98*
The Moonstone *'97*
The Leading Man *'96*
The Heat of the Day *'91*
Spymaker: The Secret Life of Ian Fleming *'90*
The Shell Seekers *'89*
Diamond's Edge *'88*
Sunset *'88*
Betrayal *'83*

Eddie Hodges (1947-)
Live a Little, Love a Little *'68*
Summer Magic *'63*
The Adventures of Huckleberry Finn *'60*
A Hole in the Head *'59*

Tom (Thomas E.) Hodges (1965-)
Since You've Been Gone *'97*
The Baby Doll Murders *'92*
Lucas *'86*

Earle Hodgins (1893-1964)
The Man Who Shot Liberty Valance *'62*
The Topeka Terror *'45*
Colt Comrades *'43*
Hoppy Serves a Writ *'43*
The Lone Star Trail *'43*
The Bashful Bachelor *'42*
Inside the Law *'42*
Boss of Bullion City *'41*
Law and Order *'40*
Range Busters *'40*
Santa Fe Marshal *'40*
Call the Mesquiteers *'38*
Purple Vigilantes *'38*
The Rangers' Roundup *'38*
Heroes of the Alamo *'37*
A Lawman Is Born *'37*
Aces and Eights *'36*
Law for Tombstone *'35*

Leyland Hodgson (1894-1949)
Bedlam *'45*
International Lady *'41*
My Son, My Son *'40*
The Eagle and the Hawk *'33*

John Hodiak (1914-55)
Dragonfly Squadron *'54*
Ambush at Tomahawk Gap *'53*
Conquest of Cochise *'53*
Across the Wide Missouri *'51*
The Miniver Story *'50*
Battleground *'49*
Malaya *'49*
The Bribe *'48*
Command Decision *'48*
Homecoming *'48*
Love from a Stranger *'47*
The Harvey Girls *'46*
Somewhere in the Night *'46*
Lifeboat *'44*

Biddy Hodson
Hellboy *'04*
Loaded *'94*

Tyler Hoechlin (1987-)
Grizzly Rage *'07*
Road to Perdition *'02*

Heinz Hoenig
Antibodies *'05*
Judgment in Berlin *'88*

Paul Hoerbiger (1894-1981)
The Third Man *'49*
The Mozart Story *'48*

Tobias Hoesl (1961-)
The Polar Bear King *'94*
Mines of Kilimanjaro *'87*

Dennis Hoey (1893-1960)
David and Bathsheba *'51*
Golden Earrings *'47*
Where There's Life *'47*
Anna and the King of Siam *'46*
Roll on Texas Moon *'46*
She Wolf of London *'46*
Terror by Night *'46*
House of Fear *'45*
A Thousand and One Nights *'45*
The Pearl of Death *'44*
Spider Woman *'44*
Uncertain Glory *'44*
Sherlock Holmes and the Secret Weapon *'42*
Son of Fury *'42*
The Mystery of the Mary Celeste *'35*
Power *'34*

Abbie Hoffman (1936-89)
Born on the Fourth of July *'89*
Heavy Petting *'89*

Basil Hoffman (1941-)
The Ice Runner *'93*
The Double O Kid *'92*
Communion *'89*
Lambada *'89*
Ratings Game *'84*
Love at First Bite *'79*

Bridget Hoffman
Time Trackers *'88*
The Castle of Cagliostro *'80 (V)*

David Hoffman (1904-61)
Children in the Crossfire *'84*
Wolf Lake *'79*
A Woman's World *'54*

Dustin Hoffman (1937-)
Kung Fu Panda *'08 (V)*
Last Chance Harvey *'08*
The Tale of Despereaux *'08 (V)*
Mr. Magorium's Wonder Emporium *'07*
Perfume: The Story of a Murderer *'06*
Stranger Than Fiction *'06*
The Lost City *'05*
Racing Stripes *'05 (V)*
Finding Neverland *'04*
I Heart Huckabees *'04*
Meet the Fockers *'04*
Confidence *'03*
Runaway Jury *'03*
Moonlight Mile *'02*
The Messenger: The Story of Joan of Arc *'99*
Mad City *'97*
Sphere *'97*
Wag the Dog *'97*
Sleepers *'96*
American Buffalo *'95*
Outbreak *'94*
Hero *'92*
Billy Bathgate *'91*
Hook *'91*
Dick Tracy *'90*
Common Threads: Stories from the Quilt *'89 (N)*
Family Business *'89*
Rain Man *'88*
Ishtar *'87*
Death of a Salesman *'86*
Tootsie *'82*
Agatha *'79*
Kramer vs. Kramer *'79*
Straight Time *'78*
All the President's Men *'76*
Marathon Man *'76*
Lenny *'74*
Papillon *'73*
Alfredo, Alfredo *'72*
Straw Dogs *'72*
Who Is Harry Kellerman and Why Is He Saying Those Terrible Things About Me? *'71*
Little Big Man *'70*
Midnight Cowboy *'69*
The Graduate *'67*
Madigan's Millions *'67*

Elizabeth Hoffman (1927-)
Dante's Peak *'97*
Fear No Evil *'80*

Erika Hoffman
The Final Cut *'95*
To Play the King *'93*

Gaby Hoffman (1982-)
Life During Wartime *'09*
Perfume *'01*
Black and White *'99*
Coming Soon *'99*
All I Wanna Do *'98*
200 Cigarettes *'98*
Volcano *'97*
Everyone Says I Love You *'96*
Now and Then *'95*
The Man Without a Face *'93*
Sleepless in Seattle *'93*
This Is My Life *'92*
Field of Dreams *'89*
Uncle Buck *'89*

Gertrude Hoffman
Caged *'50*
The Ape *'40*

Gus Hoffman
Gifted Hands: The Ben Carson Story *'09*
Rebound *'05*

Jackie Hoffman (1960-)
Queer Duck: The Movie *'06 (V)*
Robots *'05 (V)*
A Dirty Shame *'04*
Garden State *'04*
Kissing Jessica Stein *'02*

Jake Hoffman (1981-)
Jiminy Glick in LaLa Wood *'05*
National Lampoon's Adam & Eve *'05*

Jane Hoffman (1911-2004)
Static *'87*
Senior Trip *'81*
Sybil *'76*
Up the Sandbox *'72*

Jenna Hoffman
See Jenna Byrne

Linda Hoffman
Captured *'99*
Beneath the Bermuda Triangle *'98*
The Dentist 2: Brace Yourself *'98*
Mission of Death *'97*
The Dentist *'96*

Philip Seymour Hoffman (1967-)
The Invention of Lying *'09*
Mary and Max *'09*
Pirate Radio *'09*
Doubt *'08*
Synecdoche, New York *'08*
Before the Devil Knows You're Dead *'07*
Charlie Wilson's War *'07*
The Savages *'07*
Mission: Impossible 3 *'06*
Strangers with Candy *'06*
Capote *'05*
Empire Falls *'05*
Along Came Polly *'04*
Cold Mountain *'03*
Owning Mahowny *'03*
Love Liza *'02*
Punch-Drunk Love *'02*
Red Dragon *'02*
25th Hour *'02*
Almost Famous *'00*
State and Main *'00*
Flawless *'99*
Magnolia *'99*
The Talented Mr. Ripley *'99*
Happiness *'98*
Patch Adams *'98*
The Big Lebowski *'97*
Boogie Nights *'97*
Montana *'97*
Hard Eight *'96*
Twister *'96*
Nobody's Fool *'94*
When a Man Loves a Woman *'94*
The Yearling *'94*
Joey Breaker *'93*
Leap of Faith *'92*
Scent of a Woman *'92*

Rick Hoffman (1970-)
The Condemned *'07*
Hostel *'06*
Cellular *'04*
Blood Work *'02*

Robert Hoffman
Step Up 2 the Streets *'08*
Joe Panther *'76*
Eyes Behind the Stars *'72*
A Black Veil for Lisa *'68*
How I Learned to Love Women *'66*

Robert Hoffman, III (1980-)
Aliens in the Attic *'09*
She's the Man *'06*

Shawn Hoffman
Karla *'06*
Adventures in Dinosaur City *'92*

Susan Lee Hoffman
Acts of Betrayal *'98*
Wizards of the Lost Kingdom 2 *'89*

Thom Hoffman (1957-)
Black Book *'06*
Dogville *'03*
Soul Assassin *'01*
Orlando *'92*
Lily Was Here *'89*
The 4th Man *'79*

Jutta Hoffmann (1941-)
Bandits *'99*
The Third *'72*

Pato Hoffmann
The Last Winter *'06*
Cheyenne Warrior *'94*

Susanna Hoffs (1959-)
Austin Powers In Goldmember *'02*
The Allnighter *'87*

Charlie Hofheimer (1981-)
Black Hawk Down *'01*
Music of the Heart *'99*
Father's Day *'96*

Isabella Hofmann (1958-)
Midnight Bayou *'09*
Homicide: The Movie *'00*
Atomic Dog *'98*
The Colony *'98*
Tripwire *'89*

Marco Hofschneider (1969-)
Urban Legends 2: Final Cut *'00*
The Island of Dr. Moreau *'96*
Foreign Student *'94*
Immortal Beloved *'94*
Europa, Europa *'91*

Bosco Hogan (1949-)
In the Name of the Father *'93*
Count Dracula *'77*
James Joyce: A Portrait of the Artist as a Young Man *'77*
Zardoz *'73*

Chris Hogan
On Edge *'03*
Dancing at the Blue Iguana *'00*

Dick Hogan (1917-95)
Action in the North Atlantic *'43*
So Proudly We Hail *'43*

Gabriel Hogan (1973-)
Bridal Fever *'08*
Head in the Clouds *'04*
Show Me *'04*
The Halfback of Notre Dame *'96*

Heather Hogan
The Land Before Time 4: Journey Through the Mists *'96 (V)*
The Land Before Time 3: The Time of the Great Giving *'95 (V)*
The Land Before Time 2: The Great Valley Adventure *'94 (V)*

Hulk Hogan (1953-)
Shadow Warriors *'97*
Shadow Warriors 2: Hunt for the Death Merchant *'97*
3 Ninjas: High Noon at Mega Mountain *'97*
The Ultimate Weapon *'97*
Santa with Muscles *'96*
The Secret Agent Club *'96*
Thunder in Paradise 2 *'94*
Thunder in Paradise 3 *'94*
Mr. Nanny *'93*
Thunder in Paradise *'93*
Suburban Commando *'91*
Gremlins 2: The New Batch *'90*
No Holds Barred *'89*

Michael Hogan
A Simple Curve *'05*
End of Summer *'97*
Clearcut *'92*
Smokescreen *'90*
Lost *'86*
The Peanut Butter Solution *'85*

Michael Hogan
Battlestar Galactica: The Plan *'09*
Coffee and Cigarettes *'03*

Pat Hogan (1920-66)
Indian Paint *'64*
Seventh Cavalry *'56*
Davy Crockett, King of the Wild Frontier *'55*
Savage Wilderness *'55*

Paul Hogan (1939-)
Strange Bedfellows *'04*
Crocodile Dundee in Los Angeles *'01*
Flipper *'96*
Lightning Jack *'94*
Almost an Angel *'90*
Crocodile Dundee 2 *'88*
Crocodile Dundee *'86*
Anzacs: The War Down Under *'85*

Robert Hogan (1936-)
Maze *'01*
Gone Are the Days *'84*
Lady in Red *'79*
Memory of Us *'74*

Siobhan Fallon Hogan (1972-)
New in Town *'09*
Baby Mama *'08*
Charlotte's Web *'06*
Fever Pitch *'05*
Dogville *'03*
Holes *'03*
What's the Worst That Could Happen? *'01*
Krippendorf's Tribe *'98*
The Negotiator *'98*
Men in Black *'97*
Forrest Gump *'94*

Susan Hogan
Everything's Gone Green *'06*
A Father's Choice *'00*
Take Me Home: The John Denver Story *'00*
Rupert's Land *'98*
When Danger Follows You Home *'97*
Impolite *'92*
White Fang *'91*
Title Shot *'81*
Phobia *'80*
The Brood *'79*
One Night Stand *'78*

B.J. Hogg (1955-)
Resurrection Man *'97*
Rudyard Kipling's the Second Jungle Book: Mowgli and Baloo *'97*

Brian Hogg
Eden Valley *'94*
Catherine Cookson's The Black Candle *'92*

Ian Hogg (1937-)
Rasputin: Dark Servant of Destiny *'96*
The Legacy *'79*

Arthur Hohl (1889-1964)
Mystery of the Riverboat *'44*
Son of Fury *'42*
Blondie Has Trouble *'40*
Village Tale *'35*
The Whole Town's Talking *'35*
Massacre *'34*
The Sign of the Cross *'33*
Island of Lost Souls *'32*

Solbjorg Hojfeldt (1947-)
The Kingdom 2 *'97*
The Kingdom *'95*

Allen Holbrook
Lightning Bill *'35*
Circle Canyon *'33*
Fighting Cowboy *'33*

David Holbrook
Creepshow 2 *'87*
Return to Salem's Lot *'87*

Hal Holbrook (1925-)
Killshot *'09*
That Evening Sun *'09*
Into the Wild *'07*
Shade *'03*
Purpose *'02*
The Majestic *'01*
Men of Honor *'00*
Waking the Dead *'00*
The Bachelor *'99*
Hush *'98*
Judas Kiss *'98*
My Own Country *'98*
Cats Don't Dance *'97 (V)*
Eye of God *'97*
Hercules *'97 (V)*
Operation: Delta Force *'97*
Carried Away *'95*
The Firm *'93*
A Killing in a Small Town *'90*
Day One *'89*
Fletch Lives *'89*
Sorry, Wrong Number *'89*
The Unholy *'88*
Wall Street *'87*
Dress Gray *'86*
North and South Book 2 *'86*
Behind Enemy Lines *'85*
North and South Book 1 *'85*
George Washington *'84*
Girls Night Out *'83*
The Star Chamber *'83*
Creepshow *'82*
When Hell Was in Session *'82*
Killing of Randy Webster *'81*
The Kidnapping of the President *'80*
Murder by Natural Causes *'79*
Natural Enemies *'79*
Rituals *'79*
Capricorn One *'78*
The Fog *'78*
Julia *'77*
Our Town *'77*
All the President's Men *'76*
Midway *'76*
The Girl from Petrovka *'74*
Magnum Force *'73*
Pueblo Affair *'73*
They Only Kill Their Masters *'72*
The Great White Hope *'70*
The People Next Door *'70*
Wild in the Streets *'68*
The Group *'66*

Kristin Holby
Manhunter *'86*
Trading Places *'83*

Kathryn Holcomb
Skag *'79*
Our Time *'74*

Sarah Holcomb (1960-)
Caddyshack *'80*
Happy Birthday, Gemini *'80*
National Lampoon's Animal House *'78*

Alexandra Holden (1977-)
A Dead Calling *'06*
Special *'06*
Wasted *'06*
Everything You Want *'05*
Window Theory *'04*
How to Deal *'03*
American Gun *'02*
The Hot Chick *'02*
Sugar & Spice *'01*
Uprising *'01*
Dancer, Texas—Pop. 81 *'98*
In and Out *'97*

Diane Holden
Black Starlet *'74*
Grave of the Vampire *'72*

Fay Holden (1895-1973)
The Big Hangover *'50*
Samson and Delilah *'50*
Love Laughs at Andy Hardy *'46*
Andy Hardy's Double Life *'42*
Andy Hardy's Private Secretary *'41*
Blossoms in the Dust *'41*
H.M. Pulham Esquire *'41*
Life Begins for Andy Hardy *'41*
Ziegfeld Girl *'41*
Andy Hardy Meets Debutante *'40*
Bitter Sweet *'40*
Andy Hardy Gets Spring Fever *'39*
Love Finds Andy Hardy *'38*
Double or Nothing *'37*

Frankie J. Holden (1952-)
Introducing the Dwights *'07*
Ebbtide *'94*
High Tide *'87*

Gina Holden (1975-)
Love Happens *'09*
Screamers: The Hunting *'09*
The Christmas Cottage *'08*
The Butterfly Effect 2 *'06*
Final Destination 3 *'06*

Gloria Holden (1908-91)
The Adventures of Rusty *'45*
Having Wonderful Crime *'45*
Behind the Rising Sun *'43*
A Gentleman After Dark *'42*
Hawaii Calls *'38*
The Life of Emile Zola *'37*
Dracula's Daughter *'36*
Wife Versus Secretary *'36*

Jan Holden (1931-2005)
One Brief Summer *'70*
The Stranglers of Bombay *'60*
Fire Maidens from Outer Space *'56*

Laurie Holden (1972-)
Meet Market *'08*
The Mist *'07*
Silent Hill *'06*
Bailey's Billion$ *'05*
Fantastic Four *'05*
The Majestic *'01*
The Magnificent Seven *'98*
Past Perfect *'98*
Expect No Mercy *'95*
The Pathfinder *'94*

Marjean Holden
Hostage *'05*
Mortal Kombat 2: Annihilation *'97*
Ballistic *'94*
Philadelphia Experiment 2 *'93*
Secret Agent 00-Soul *'89*
Stripped to Kill II: Live Girls *'89*

Peter Holden (1930-)
Pandemic *'09*
The Great Man Votes *'38*

Rebecca Holden (1953-)
Twenty Dollar Star *'91*
The Sisterhood *'88*

William Holden (1918-81)
S.O.B. *'81*
Earthling *'80*
When Time Ran Out *'80*
Ashanti, Land of No Mercy *'79*
Escape to Athena *'79*
Damien: Omen 2 *'78*
Network *'76*
21 Hours at Munich *'76*
The Towering Inferno *'74*
Wild Rovers *'71*
When Wolves Cry *'69*
The Wild Bunch *'69*
The Devil's Brigade *'68*
Casino Royale *'67*
Alvarez Kelly *'66*
Paris When It Sizzles *'64*
The Seventh Dawn *'64*
The Counterfeit Traitor *'62*
The World of Suzie Wong *'60*
The Horse Soldiers *'59*
The Key *'58*
The Bridge on the River Kwai *'57*
The Bridges at Toko-Ri *'55*
Love Is a Many-Splendored Thing *'55*
Picnic *'55*
Country Girl *'54*
Executive Suite *'54*
Sabrina *'54*
Escape from Fort Bravo *'53*
Forever Female *'53*
The Moon Is Blue *'53*
Stalag 17 *'53*
Boots Malone *'52*
Born Yesterday *'50*
Sunset Boulevard *'50*
Union Station *'50*
The Dark Past *'49*
Dear Wife *'49*
Man from Colorado *'49*
Miss Grant Takes Richmond *'49*
Rachel and the Stranger *'48*
Young and Willing *'42*
Texas *'41*
Arizona *'40*
Our Town *'40*
Golden Boy *'39*
Invisible Stripes *'39*

Kris Holden-Ried
Never Forget *'08*
Autumn Hearts: A New Beginning *'07*
A Broken Life *'07*
Niagara Motel *'06*
Waking Up Wally *'05*
Touch of Pink *'04*
Hendrix *'00*
Night of the Demons 3 *'97*
Young Ivanhoe *'95*

Geoffrey Holder (1930-)
Charlie and the Chocolate Factory *'05 (N)*
Boomerang *'92*
Swashbuckler *'76*
The Noah *'75 (V)*
Live and Let Die *'73*
The Man Without a Country *'73*
Everything You Always Wanted to Know about Sex (But Were Afraid to Ask) *'72*
Krakatoa East of Java *'69*
Doctor Dolittle *'67*

Philip Holder
Under the Lighthouse Dancing *'97*
Iris *'89*

Roy Holder (1946-)
The Land That Time Forgot *'75*
Loot... Give Me Money, Honey! *'70*
Othello *'65*
Whistle down the Wind *'61*

Ticky Holgado (1944-2004)
A Very Long Engagement *'04*
And Now Ladies and Gentlemen *'02*
French Twist *'95*
Delicatessen *'92*

Hope Holiday (1938-)
The Rounders *'65*
The Apartment *'60*

Anthony Holland (1928-88)
The Lonely Lady *'83*
Oh, God! Book 2 *'80*
All That Jazz *'79*
King of the Gypsies *'78*

Edna Holland (1895-1982)
Blood of Dracula *'57*
Shep Comes Home *'49*

Eric Holland (1933-)
Masquerade *'88*
Gardens of Stone *'87*

John Holland (1908-93)
They Saved Hitler's Brain *'64*
Girl in Black Stockings *'57*
House of Errors *'42*
Gentleman from Dixie *'41*
Up in the Air *'40*
Defenders of the Law *'31*
Morals for Women *'31*
Hell Harbor *'30*

Tom Holland (1943-)
The Soloist *'09*
Stephen King's The Langoliers *'95*
Model Shop *'69*

Tom Hollander (1969-)
In the Loop *'09*
Valkyrie *'08*
The Company *'07*
Elizabeth: The Golden Age *'07*
Pirates of the Caribbean: At World's End *'07*
The Darwin Awards *'06*
A Good Year *'06*
Land of the Blind *'06*
Pirates of the Caribbean: Dead Man's Chest *'06*
The Libertine *'05*
Pride and Prejudice *'05*
Paparazzi *'04*
Cambridge Spies *'03*
Possession *'02*
Enigma *'01*
Gosford Park *'01*
Lawless Heart *'01*
Wives and Daughters *'01*
Maybe Baby *'99*
Bedrooms and Hallways *'98*
The Very Thought of You *'98*

Judy Holliday (1922-65)
Bells Are Ringing *'60*
Full of Life *'56*
Solid Gold Cadillac *'56*
It Should Happen to You *'54*
Phffft! *'54*
The Marrying Kind *'52*
Adam's Rib *'50*
Born Yesterday *'50*

Kene Holliday
Great World of Sound *'07*
The Josephine Baker Story *'90*

Polly Holliday (1937-)
Stick It *'06*
The Parent Trap *'98*
Mr. Wrong *'95*
Mrs. Doubtfire *'93*
Moon over Parador *'88*
Konrad *'85*
Lots of Luck *'85*
Gremlins *'84*
All the President's Men *'76*

Earl Holliman (1928-)
Perfect Tenant *'99*
Gunsmoke: Return to Dodge *'87*
The Solitary Man *'82*
Sharky's Machine *'81*
Alexander: The Other Side of Dawn *'77*
Cry Panic *'74*
I Love You, Goodbye *'74*
Smoke *'70*
Tribes *'70*
Anzio *'68*
Sons of Katie Elder *'65*
Armored Command *'61*
Summer and Smoke *'61*
The Desperate Mission *'60*
Last Train from Gun Hill *'59*
The Trap *'59*
Hot Spell *'58*
Don't Go Near the Water *'57*
Gunfight at the O.K. Corral *'57*
Forbidden Planet *'56*
Giant *'56*
The Rainmaker *'56*
Big Combo *'55*
The Bridges at Toko-Ri *'55*
I Died a Thousand Times *'55*
Broken Lance *'54*

Tommy Hollis (1954-2001)
Primary Colors *'98*
The Piano Lesson *'94*
Malcolm X *'92*

Ellen Hollman
Fling *'08*
Road House 2: Last Call *'06*

Bridget Holloman (1958-2006)
Evils of the Night *'85*
Slumber Party '57 *'76*

Laurel Holloman (1971-)
The Rising Place *'02*
Lush *'01*
Loving Jezebel *'99*
Tumbleweeds *'98*
Boogie Nights *'97*
The First to Go *'97*
The Myth of Fingerprints *'97*
Prefontaine *'96*
The Incredibly True Adventure of Two Girls in Love *'95*

Carol Holloway (1892-1979)
The Saphead *'21*
The Sea Lion *'21*

Julian Holloway (1944-)
Porridge *'91*
Carry On Henry VIII *'71*

Stanley Holloway (1890-1982)
The Private Life of Sherlock Holmes *'70*
Mrs. Brown, You've Got a Lovely Daughter *'68*
In Harm's Way *'65*
My Fair Lady *'64*
On the Fiddle *'61*
No Love for Johnnie *'60*
Beggar's Opera *'54*
The Lavender Hill Mob *'51*
Passport to Pimlico *'49*
Hamlet *'48*
This Happy Breed *'47*
Brief Encounter *'46*
Nicholas Nickleby *'46*
Immortal Battalion *'44*
Salute John Citizen *'42*
Cotton Queen *'37*
Lily of Killarney *'34*

Sterling Holloway (1905-92)
The Many Adventures of Winnie the Pooh *'77 (V)*
Super Seal *'77*
Thunder and Lightning *'77*
The Aristocats *'70 (V)*
Live a Little, Love a Little *'68*
The Jungle Book *'67 (V)*
The Adventures of Huckleberry Finn *'60*
Shake, Rattle and Rock *'57*
Kentucky Rifle *'55*
Alice in Wonderland *'51 (V)*
The Beautiful Blonde from Bashful Bend *'49*
Robin Hood of Texas *'47*
Trail to San Antone *'47*
Death Valley *'46*
Sioux City Sue *'46*
A Walk in the Sun *'46*
The Three Caballeros *'45 (V)*
Wildfire *'45*
Bambi *'42 (V)*
The Lady Is Willing *'42*
Cheers for Miss Bishop *'41*
Dumbo *'41 (V)*
Melody Master *'41*
Twilight on the Rio Grande *'41*
Remember the Night *'40*
Varsity Show *'37*
Doubting Thomas *'35*
I Live My Life *'35*
Life Begins at Forty *'35*
The Merry Widow *'34*
Tomorrow's Children *'34*
International House *'33*
Wild Boys of the Road *'33*

Ellen Holly (1931-)
School Daze *'88*
Cops and Robbers *'73*

Lauren Holly (1963-)
Fatwa *'06*
Raising Flagg *'06*
The Chumscrubber *'05*
The Pleasure Drivers *'05*
In Enemy Hands *'04*
The Final Hit *'02*
King of Texas *'02*
Jackie, Ethel, Joan: The Kennedy Women *'01*
Spirited Away *'01 (V)*
What Women Want *'00*
Any Given Sunday *'99*
Entropy *'99*
Money Kings *'98*
No Looking Back *'98*
Beautiful Girls *'96*
Down Periscope *'96*
A Smile Like Yours *'96*
Turbulence *'96*
Sabrina *'95*
Dumb & Dumber *'94*
Dangerous Heart *'93*
Dragon: The Bruce Lee Story *'93*
Fugitive Among Us *'92*
The Adventures of Ford Fairlane *'90*
Archie: Return to Riverdale *'90*
Band of the Hand *'86*
Seven Minutes in Heaven *'86*

Ryan Hollyman
The Audrey Hepburn Story *'00*
Seducing Maarya *'99*

Astrid Holm
Master of the House *'25*
Haxan: Witchcraft through the Ages *'22*
The Phantom Chariot *'20*

Celeste Holm (1919-)
Alchemy *'05*
Still Breathing *'97*
Murder by the Book *'87*
Three Men and a Baby *'87*
Backstairs at the White House *'79*
Bittersweet Love *'76*
Death Cruise *'74*
Tom Sawyer *'73*
Cinderella *'64*
High Society *'56*
The Tender Trap *'55*
All About Eve *'50*
Champagne for Caesar *'50*
Come to the Stable *'49*
A Letter to Three Wives *'49 (V)*
Road House *'48*
The Snake Pit *'48*
Gentleman's Agreement *'47*

Claus Holm
Tiger of Eschnapur *'59*
Journey to the Lost City *'58*

Ian Holm (1931-)
O Jerusalem *'07*
Ratatouille *'07 (V)*
Renaissance *'06*
Strangers with Candy *'06*
Lord of War *'05*
The Aviator *'04*
The Day After Tomorrow *'04*
Garden State *'04*
Lord of the Rings: The Return of the King *'03*
The Emperor's New Clothes *'01*
From Hell *'01*
Lord of the Rings: The Fellowship of the Ring *'01*
Beautiful Joe *'00*
Bless the Child *'00*
Esther Kahn *'00*
Joe Gould's Secret *'00*
The Last of the Blonde Bombshells *'00*
The Miracle Maker: The Story of Jesus *'00 (V)*
Animal Farm *'99 (V)*
eXistenZ *'99*
The Match *'99*
King Lear *'98*
The Fifth Element *'97*
A Life Less Ordinary *'97*
Night Falls on Manhattan *'96*
The Return of the Borrowers *'96*
The Sweet Hereafter *'96*
Big Night *'95*
Loch Ness *'95*
The Madness of King George *'94*
Mary Shelley's Frankenstein *'94*
The Advocate *'93*
The Borrowers *'93*
Kafka *'91*
Naked Lunch *'91*
Hamlet *'90*
The Endless Game *'89*
Henry V *'89*
Another Woman *'88*
Brazil *'85*
Dance with a Stranger *'85*
Dreamchild *'85*
Wetherby *'85*
Greystoke: The Legend of Tarzan, Lord of the Apes *'84*
Singleton's Pluck *'84*
Inside the Third Reich *'82*
Return of the Soldier *'82*
Chariots of Fire *'81*
Time Bandits *'81*
Alien *'79*
S.O.S. Titanic *'79*
Holocaust *'78*
The Lost Boys *'78*
The Thief of Baghdad *'78*
The Man in the Iron Mask *'77*
March or Die *'77*
Robin and Marian *'76*
Shout at the Devil *'76*
Juggernaut *'74*
Young Winston *'72*
Mary, Queen of Scots *'71*
Oh! What a Lovely War *'69*
The Fixer *'68*
A Midsummer Night's Dream *'68*

Clare Holman (1964-)
Dot.Kill *'05*
Tom & Viv *'94*
Afraid of the Dark *'92*

Let Him Have It '91
Catherine Cookson's The Fifteen Streets '90

Harry Holman (1874-1947)
Inside the Law '42
Mexican Spitfire at Sea '42
Shadows on the Sage '42
Fugitive Road '34
Night Alarm '34

Rex Holman (1928-)
Panic in the Year Zero! '62
The Choppers '61

Ashton Holmes (1978-)
Smart People '08
Havoc 2: Normal Adolescent Behavior '07
What We Do Is Secret '07
Wind Chill '07
Peaceful Warrior '06
A History of Violence '05

Katie Holmes (1978-)
Mad Money '08
Thank You for Smoking '06
Batman Begins '05
First Daughter '04
Pieces of April '03
The Singing Detective '03
Abandon '02
Phone Booth '02
The Gift '00
Wonder Boys '00
Go '99
Teaching Mrs. Tingle '99
Disturbing Behavior '98
The Ice Storm '97

Luree Holmes (1942-)
How to Stuff a Wild Bikini '65
Pajama Party '64

Phillips Holmes (1909-42)
Housemaster '38
General Spanky '36
Great Expectations '34
Dinner at Eight '33
Penthouse '33
An American Tragedy '31
Criminal Code '31

Prudence Wright Holmes
In Dreams '98
Kingpin '96

Stuart Holmes (1884-1971)
People Will Talk '51
My Pal, the King '32
When a Man Loves '27
Beyond the Trail '26
The Prisoner of Zenda '22
The Four Horsemen of the Apocalypse '21

Taylor Holmes (1872-1959)
Sleeping Beauty '59 (V)
Tobor the Great '54
Beware, My Lovely '52
Hoodlum Empire '52
Rhubarb '51
Copper Canyon '50
Double Deal '50
Act of Violence '48
Boomerang '47
Nightmare Alley '47
Before Morning '33

Teck Holmes (1976-)
National Lampoon's Van Wilder '02
Love Song '00

Tina Holmes (1973-)
Shelter '07
Half Nelson '06
Taken '02
Prince of Central Park '00
Edge of Seventeen '99

Wendell Holmes (1915-62)
The Absent-Minded Professor '61
Elmer Gantry '60
Compulsion '59
Never Steal Anything Small '59
Good Day for a Hanging '58
Lost Boundaries '49

Karen Holness
Twitches Too '07
Twitches '05

Rosie Holotik
Encounter with the Unknown '75
Twisted Brain '74
Don't Look in the Basement '73

Charlene Holt (1939-96)
El Dorado '67
Red Line 7000 '65
Man's Favorite Sport? '63

David Holt (1927-2003)
The Adventures of Tom Sawyer '38
Last Days of Pompeii '35

Hans Holt (1909-2002)
Almost Angels '62
The Embezzled Heaven '58
The Mozart Story '48

Jack Holt (1888-1951)
Across the Wide Missouri '51
King of the Bullwhip '51
Red Desert '50
Trail of Robin Hood '50
Task Force '49
Loaded Pistols '48
Wild Frontier '47
The Chase '46
Flight to Nowhere '46
My Pal Trigger '46
Renegade Girl '46
They Were Expendable '45
Cat People '42
Holt of the Secret Service '42
Thunder Birds '42
The Great Plane Robbery '40
San Francisco '36
The Littlest Rebel '35
Maker of Men '31
The Smart Set '28
The Little American '17

Jennifer Holt (1920-97)
The Hawk of Powder River '48
Range Renegades '48
Stage to Mesa City '48
The Tioga Kid '48
Buffalo Bill Rides Again '47
Fighting Vigilantes '47
Ghost Town Renegades '47
Trail of the Mounties '47
Where the North Begins '47
Song of Old Wyoming '45
Outlaw Trail '44
Frontier Law '43
The Lone Star Trail '43
Raiders of Sunset Pass '43
The Silver Bullet '42

Jim Holt (1956-)
The Prince & Me 2: Royal Wedding '06
The Monkey's Mask '00
Fever '88

Patrick Holt (1912-93)
Psychomania '73
When Dinosaurs Ruled the Earth '70
Vulture '67
Flight from Singapore '62
It Takes a Thief '59
Men of Sherwood Forest '57
Alias John Preston '56
Suspended Alibi '56
Unholy Four '54

Sandrine Holt (1971-)
Fire Serpent '07
Resident Evil: Apocalypse '04
Happy Hour '03
Ballistic: Ecks vs. Sever '02
Mission '00
Loving Jezebel '99
Gunslinger's Revenge '98
1999 '98
Once a Thief '96
Legends of the North '95
Pocahontas: The Legend '95
Rapa Nui '93
Black Robe '91

Tim Holt (1918-73)
This Stuff'll Kill Ya! '71
The Yesterday Machine '63
The Monster That Challenged the World '57
Gunplay '51
His Kind of Woman '51
Hot Lead '51
Dynamite Pass '50
Rider from Tucson '50
Riders of the Range '50
Storm over Wyoming '50
Mysterious Desperado '49
Treasure of the Sierra Madre '48
My Darling Clementine '46
Hitler's Children '43
Sagebrush Law '43
The Magnificent Ambersons '42
Back Street '41
Fifth Avenue Girl '39
Stagecoach '39
Law West of Tombstone '38
Stella Dallas '37

Ula Holt
Tarzan and the Green Goddess '38
The New Adventures of Tarzan '35

Mark Holton (1958-)
Convicted '04
Leprechaun '93
A League of Their Own '92
Easy Wheels '89
Pee-wee's Big Adventure '85
Stoogemania '85

Sean Holton
Presumed Guilty '91
White Fury '90
Operation Warzone '89

Tenen Holtz
The Trail of '98 '28
Exit Smiling '26

Maria Holvoe
The Last Warrior '89
Worth Winning '89

Arabella Holzbog (1966-)
Red Shoe Diaries: Swimming Naked '00
Carnosaur 2 '94
Evil Lives '92
Stone Cold '91
The Last Samurai '90

Robert E. Homans (1874-1947)
The Scarlet Clue '45
Rogue's Gallery '44
X Marks the Spot '42
I Take This Oath '40
Suicide Squad '35
Man from Hell's Edges '32
Young America '32
The Concentratin' Kid '30
Spurs '30
Trigger Tricks '30

Lluis Homar (1957-)
Broken Embraces '09
Body Armour '07
Fermat's Room '07
The Backwoods '06
Bad Education '04
Valentin '03
What It's All About '95
Celestial Clockwork '94
If They Tell You I Fell '89

David Homb
Street Soldiers '91
The Channeler '89

Skip Homeier (1930-)
Starbird and Sweet William '73
The Voyage of the Yes '72
The Ghost and Mr. Chicken '66
Johnny Shiloh '63
Comanche Station '60
The Tall T '57
The Burning Hills '56
Black Widow '54
Cry Vengeance '54
Ten Wanted Men '54
Fixed Bayonets! '51
The Gunfighter '50
The Halls of Montezuma '50
Tomorrow the World '44

Oscar Homolka (1898-1978)
The Executioner '70
Song of Norway '70
The Madwoman of Chaillot '69
Dr. Jekyll and Mr. Hyde '68
Strange Case of Dr. Jekyll & Mr. Hyde '68
Billion Dollar Brain '67
Funeral in Berlin '66
The Long Ships '64
Boys' Night Out '62
Mooncussers '62
The Wonderful World of the Brothers Grimm '62
Mr. Sardonicus '61
The Key '58
A Farewell to Arms '57
War and Peace '56
The Seven Year Itch '55
The House of the Arrow '53
The White Tower '50
I Remember Mama '48
Mission to Moscow '43
Ball of Fire '41
Comrade X '40
The Invisible Woman '40
Seven Sinners '40
Rhodes '36
Sabotage '36

James Hong (1929-)
The Day the Earth Stood Still '08
Kung Fu Panda '08 (V)
Balls of Fury '07
Shanghai Kiss '07
American Fusion '05
Latin Dragon '03
The Art of War '00
Epoch '00
G2: Mortal Conquest '99
Breakout '98
Broken Vessels '98
Mulan '98 (V)
Bloodsport 3 '97
Red Corner '97
The Secret Agent Club '96
South Beach Academy '96
Bloodsport 2: The Next Kumite '95
Femme Fontaine: Killer Babe for the C.I.A. '95
Gladiator Cop: The Swordsman 2 '95
Bad Company '94
Operation Golden Phoenix '94
The Shadow '94
Question of Faith '93
Wayne's World 2 '93
Body Trouble '92
L.A. Goddess '92
Merlin '92
Talons of the Eagle '92
Crime Lords '91
Caged Fury '90
Dragonfight '90
Tax Season '90
The Brotherhood of the Rose '89
Shadowzone '89
Tango and Cash '89
The Vineyard '89
The Jitters '88
Black Widow '87
Revenge of the Nerds 2: Nerds in Paradise '87
Big Trouble in Little China '86
The Golden Child '86
When Hell Was in Session '82
Yes, Giorgio '82
Airplane! '80
Go Tell the Spartans '78
Bethune '77
The Dynamite Brothers '74
Missiles of October '74
The Sand Pebbles '66
China Gate '57

Kojiro Hongo (1938-)
Along with Ghosts '69
Destroy All Planets '68
Gamera vs. Gaos '67
Gamera vs. Barugon '66
Wrath of Daimajin '66

Shiriohona Hongsopon
The Iron Ladies 2 '03
The Iron Ladies '00

Darla Hood (1931-79)
The Bat '59
Bohemian Girl '36

Don Hood (1940-2003)
Dean Koontz's Mr. Murder '98
Blind Vengeance '90
Marie '85
Absence of Malice '81

Morag Hood (1942-2002)
A Shot at Glory '00
War and Peace '73

Shaun Hood
Blind Eye '06
Visitor Q '01

Joel Hookey
Blind Eye '06
Visitor Q '01

Brian Hooks (1973-)
Fool's Gold '08
Soul Plane '04
Nothin' 2 Lose '00
Three Strikes '00
Phat Beach '96

Jan Hooks (1957-)
Jiminy Glick in LaLa Wood '05
Simon Birch '98
Coneheads '93
A Dangerous Woman '93
Batman Returns '92
Pee-wee's Big Adventure '85

Kevin Hooks (1958-)
Innerspace '87
Backstairs at the White House '79
Can You Hear the Laughter? The Story of Freddie Prinze '79
Take Down '79
Aaron Loves Angela '75
Sounder '72

Robert Hooks (1937-)
Seventeen Again '00
Free of Eden '98
Posse '93
Passenger 57 '92
Heat Wave '90
The Execution '85
Words by Heart '84
Fast Walking '82
Sophisticated Gents '81
Backstairs at the White House '79
A Woman Called Moses '78
Aaron Loves Angela '75
Black Brigade '69
Sweet Love, Bitter '67

Ewan Hooper (1935-)
Kinky Boots '06
Dracula Has Risen from the Grave '68

Tobe Hooper (1946-)
Body Bags '93
Sleepwalkers '92

Peter Hooten (1950-)
2020 Texas Gladiators '85
Deadly Mission '78
Dr. Strange '78
The Inglorious Bastards '78
Slashed Dreams '74
Fantasies '73

William Hootkins (1948-2005)
Color Me Kubrick '05
The Magnificent Ambersons '02
The Omega Code '99
This World, Then the Fireworks '97
Death Machine '95
Dust Devil '93
Hear My Song '91
American Gothic '88
Valentino '77

Joseph Hoover
The Astro-Zombies '67
Hell Is for Heroes '62
The Man Who Shot Liberty Valance '62

Phil Hoover
Acapulco Gold '78
Black Gestapo '75
Policewomen '73
Chain Gang Women '72

Barclay Hope
Charlie & Me '08
Too Cool for Christmas '04
Range of Motion '00

Bob Hope (1903-2003)
The Muppet Movie '79
Cancel My Reservation '72
Bachelor in Paradise '69
How to Commit Marriage '69
Private Navy of Sgt. O'Farrell '68
Eight on the Lam '67
Boy, Did I Get a Wrong Number! '66
The Oscar '66
I'll Take Sweden '65
Call Me Bwana '63
Critic's Choice '63
A Global Affair '63
The Road to Hong Kong '62
The Facts of Life '60
Alias Jesse James '59
Paris Holiday '57
The Seven Little Foys '55
Casanova's Big Night '54
Here Come the Girls '53
Off Limits '53
The Road to Bali '53
Scared Stiff '53
Son of Paleface '52
The Lemon Drop Kid '51
Fancy Pants '50
The Great Lover '49
Sorrowful Jones '49
The Paleface '48
My Favorite Brunette '47
The Road to Rio '47
Where There's Life '47
Monsieur Beaucaire '46
The Road to Utopia '46
The Princess and the Pirate '44
Strictly G.I. '44
They Got Me Covered '43
My Favorite Blonde '42
The Road to Morocco '42
Star Spangled Rhythm '42
Caught in the Draft '41
Louisiana Purchase '41
The Road to Zanzibar '41
The Ghost Breakers '40
The Road to Singapore '40
Never Say Die '39
Rhythm Romance '39
The Big Broadcast of 1938 '38
College Swing '38
Give Me a Sailor '38
Thanks for the Memory '38

Leslie Hope (1965-)
Jesse Stone: Thin Ice '09
Never Back Down '08
American Meltdown '04
The Incredible Mrs. Ritchie '03
Bruiser '00
The Life Before This '99
Restless Spirits '99

Bram Stoker's Shadowbuilder '98
Summer of the Monkeys '98
This Matter of Marriage '98
Conspiracy of Fear '96
Rowing Through '96
First Degree '95
Schemes '95
Fun '94
Paris, France '94
Caught in the Act '93
Sweet Killing '93
The Abduction of Allison Tate '92
The Big Slice '90
Doppelganger: The Evil Within '90
Men at Work '90
It Takes Two '88
Kansas '88
Talk Radio '88
Sword of Gideon '86
Prep School '81

Nicholas Hope (1958-)
The Night We Called It a Day '03
Lust and Revenge '95
Bad Boy Bubby '93

Richard Hope
Antonia and Jane '91
A Casualty of War '90
Bellman and True '88
Piece of Cake '88
Singleton's Pluck '84

Tamara Hope (1984-)
Sand Serpents '09
September Dawn '07
The Nickel Children '05
A Different Loyalty '04
Prom Queen '04
Saint Ralph '04
Shall We Dance? '04
Shattered City: The Halifax Explosion '03
The Deep End '01
The Sandy Bottom Orchestra '00

Vida Hope (1918-63)
Angels One Five '54
Roadhouse Girl '53
The Woman in Question '50
They Made Me a Fugitive '47

William Hope (1955-)
Finding Rin Tin Tin '07
The Detonator '06
Submerged '05
Hellbound: Hellraiser 2 '88
Aliens '86

Alan Hopgood (1934-)
Hotel de Love '96
Road Games '81
My Brilliant Career '79

Anthony Hopkins (1937-)
The Wolfman '09
Beowulf '07 (V)
Fracture '07
Slipstream '07
All the King's Men '06
Bobby '06
Proof '05
The World's Fastest Indian '05
Alexander '04
The Human Stain '03
Bad Company '02
Red Dragon '02
Hannibal '01
Hearts in Atlantis '01
Dr. Seuss' How the Grinch Stole Christmas '00 (N)
Mission: Impossible 2 '00
Instinct '99
Titus '99
The Mask of Zorro '98
Meet Joe Black '98
Amistad '97
The Edge '97
Surviving Picasso '96
August '95
Nixon '95
Legends of the Fall '94
The Road to Wellville '94
The Innocent '93
The Remains of the Day '93
Shadowlands '93
The Trial '93
Bram Stoker's Dracula '92
Chaplin '92
The Efficiency Expert '92
Freejack '92
Howard's End '92
The Silence of the Lambs '91
Desperate Hours '90
One Man's War '90
A Chorus of Disapproval '89
Great Expectations '89
The Dawning '88
The Tenth Man '88
The Good Father '87
84 Charing Cross Road '86
Arch of Triumph '85
Guilty Conscience '85
Mussolini & I '85
The Bounty '84
A Married Man '84
The Hunchback of Notre Dame '82
Peter and Paul '81
A Change of Seasons '80
The Elephant Man '80
Mayflower: The Pilgrims' Adventure '79
International Velvet '78
Magic '78
Audrey Rose '77
A Bridge Too Far '77
The Lindbergh Kidnapping Case '76
Victory at Entebbe '76
All Creatures Great and Small '74
The Girl from Petrovka '74
Juggernaut '74
QB VII '74
A Doll's House '73
War and Peace '73
Young Winston '72
When Eight Bells Toll '71
Hamlet '69
The Looking Glass War '69
The Lion in Winter '68

Bo Hopkins (1942-)
Shade '03
Big Brother Trouble '00
Cowboy Up '00
A Crack in the Floor '00
Time Served '99
From Dusk Till Dawn 2: Texas Blood Money '98
U-Turn '97
November Conspiracy '96
Uncle Sam '96
The Feminine Touch '95
Painted Hero '95
Texas Payback '95
Cheyenne Warrior '94
Wyatt Earp: Return to Tombstone '94
The Ballad of Little Jo '93
Inside Monkey Zetterland '93
President's Target '93
Blood Ties '92
Center of the Web '92
The Legend of Wolf Mountain '92
Big Bad John '90
Bounty Hunters '89
The Final Alliance '89
Trapper County War '89
Nightmare at Noon '87
A Smoky Mountain Christmas '86
What Comes Around '85
Mutant '83
Plutonium Incident '82
Sweet 16 '81
Casino '80
The Fifth Floor '80
Rodeo Girl '80
More American Graffiti '79
Midnight Express '78
Tentacles '77
The Invasion of Johnson County '76
A Small Town in Texas '76
The Day of the Locust '75
The Killer Elite '75
Posse '75
The Runaway Barge '75
American Graffiti '73
Man Who Loved Cat Dancing '73
White Lightning '73
Culpepper Cattle Co. '72
The Getaway '72
The Only Way Home '72
The Wild Bunch '69

Bruce Hopkins (1955-)
You Move You Die '07
Beyond Justice '01
Dead Evidence '00

Harold Hopkins (1944-)
Joey '98
Resistance '92
Fantasy Man '84
Monkey Grip '82
Gallipoli '81
Sara Dane '81
Demonstrator '71

Jermaine "Huggy" Hopkins (1973-)
Def Jam's How to Be a Player '97
Phat Beach '96
Juice '92

Joan Hopkins (1915-2002)
Man on the Run '49
The Weaker Sex '49

Josh Hopkins (1970-)
The Hades Factor '06
The Insatiable '06
Love & Sex '00
The Perfect Storm '00
The Pirates of Silicon Valley '99

Miriam Hopkins (1902-72)
Savage Intruder '68
The Chase '66
Fanny Hill: Memoirs of a Woman of Pleasure '64
The Children's Hour '61
Carrie '52
The Heiress '49
A Gentleman After Dark '42
Virginia City '40
The Old Maid '39
Men Are Not Gods '37
These Three '36
Barbary Coast '35
Becky Sharp '35
Splendor '35
Dr. Jekyll and Mr. Hyde '32
Trouble in Paradise '32
The Smiling Lieutenant '31

Nikita Hopkins
Pooh's Heffalump Movie '05 (V)
Piglet's Big Movie '03 (V)

Paul Hopkins (1968-)
My First Wedding '04
Armistead Maupin's More Tales of the City '97
Snowboard Academy '96
A Young Connecticut Yankee in King Arthur's Court '95

Rhonda Leigh Hopkins
Cover Girl Models '75
Summer School Teachers '75
Tidal Wave '75

Telma Hopkins (1948-)
The Love Guru '08
Trancers 3: Deth Lives '92
Vital Signs '90
Trancers '84
The Kid with the Broken Halo '82

Rolf Hoppe (1930-)
Go for Zucker '05
Palmetto '98
Schtonk '92
Spring Symphony '86
Mephisto '81

Dennis Hopper (1936-)
Elegy '08
Hell Ride '08
Sleepwalking '08
Swing Vote '08
Memory '06
10th & Wolf '06
Americano '05
The Crow: Wicked Prayer '05
George A. Romero's Land of the Dead '05
House of 9 '05
The Night We Called It a Day '03
Firestarter 2: Rekindled '02
Leo '02
The Target '02
Unspeakable '02
Knockaround Guys '01
L.A.P.D.: To Protect and Serve '01
Ticker '01
Choke '00
Jason and the Argonauts '00
Luck of the Draw '00
EDtv '99
Jesus' Son '99
The Prophet's Game '99
Straight Shooter '99
The Apostate '98
Meet the Deedles '98
Road Ends '98
Tycus '98
The Blackout '97
Lured Innocence '97
Space Truckers '97
Top of the World '97
Basquiat '96
The Last Days of Frankie the Fly '96
Samson and Delilah '96
Carried Away '95
Waterworld '95
Chasers '94
Search and Destroy '94
Speed '94
Witch Hunt '94
Boiling Point '93
Red Rock West '93
Super Mario Bros. '93
True Romance '93
Nails '92
Sunset Heat '92
Double-Crossed '91
Eye of the Storm '91
Hearts of Darkness: A Filmmaker's Apocalypse '91
The Indian Runner '91
Paris Trout '91
Superstar: The Life and Times of Andy Warhol '90
Backtrack '89
Chattahoochee '89
Flashback '89
Blood Red '88
Riders of the Storm '88
Black Widow '87
O.C. and Stiggs '87
The Pick-Up Artist '87
River's Edge '87
Straight to Hell '87
Blue Velvet '86
Hoosiers '86
Let It Rock '86
Running out of Luck '86
The Texas Chainsaw Massacre 2 '86
My Science Project '85
Stark '85
The Inside Man '84
The Osterman Weekend '83
Rumble Fish '83
King of the Mountain '81
Reborn '81
Out of the Blue '80
Apocalypse Now '79
Wild Times '79
The American Friend '77
Bloodbath '76
Mad Dog Morgan '76
Tracks '76
The Last Movie '71
Easy Rider '69
True Grit '69
Head '68
Cool Hand Luke '67
The Glory Stompers '67
The Trip '67
Planet of Blood '66
Sons of Katie Elder '65
Night Tide '63
The Young Land '59
Gunfight at the O.K. Corral '57
Giant '56
Rebel without a Cause '55

Hedda Hopper (1885-1966)
Breakfast in Hollywood '46
Reap the Wild Wind '42
Midnight '39
Maid's Night Out '38
Tarzan's Revenge '38
Thanks for the Memory '38
Dangerous Holiday '37
Vogues of 1938 '37
The Dark Hour '36
Doughnuts & Society '36
Dracula's Daughter '36
Alice Adams '35
I Live My Life '35
One Frightened Night '35
Pilgrimage '33
As You Desire Me '32
Speak Easily '32
Flying High '31
Let Us Be Gay '30
The Racketeer '29
The Dropkick '27
Don Juan '26
Skinner's Dress Suit '26
Sherlock Holmes '22
Seven Keys to Baldpate '17

Tim Hopper
School of Rock '03
Pipe Dream '02

Victoria Hopper (1909-2007)
The Mill on the Floss '37
Lorna Doone '34

William Hopper (1915-70)
The Deadly Mantis '57
20 Million Miles to Earth '57
The Bad Seed '56
The First Texan '56
Conquest of Space '55
Rebel without a Cause '55
The High and the Mighty '54
Sitting Bull '54
The Fighting 69th '40

Russell Hopton (1900-45)
West of the Pecos '45
Zombies on Broadway '44
Hopalong Cassidy: Renegade Trail '39
Renegade Trail '39
Death from a Distance '36
Last Outlaw '36
Valley of Wanted Men '35
The World Accuses '35
The Girl from Missouri '34
Curtain at Eight '33
I'm No Angel '33
The Little Giant '33
The Miracle Woman '31

Barbara Horan
Bayou Romance '86
Malibu Bikini Shop '86

Gerard Horan
Nicholas Nickleby '02
A Midwinter's Tale '95
Much Ado about Nothing '93
Look Back in Anger '89

James Horan (1954-)
Counter Measures '99
The Haunting of Seacliff Inn '94
Image of Passion '86

Michael Hordern (1911-95)
Middlemarch '93
Freddie the Frog '92 (V)
The Green Man '91
Dark Obsession '90
The Secret Garden '87
Suspicion '87
The Trouble with Spies '87
Lady Jane '85
Young Sherlock Holmes '85
Yellowbeard '83
Ivanhoe '82
The Missionary '82
Oliver Twist '82
The Medusa Touch '78
Watership Down '78 (V)
Joseph Andrews '77
The Slipper and the Rose '76
The Old Curiosity Shop '75
Royal Flash '75
Mackintosh Man '73
Theatre of Blood '73
Demons of the Mind '72
Pied Piper '72
The Possession of Joel Delaney '72
Anne of the Thousand Days '69
Where Eagles Dare '68
How I Won the War '67
I'll Never Forget What's 'Isname '67
The Taming of the Shrew '67
A Funny Thing Happened on the Way to the Forum '66
Khartoum '66
Lamp at Midnight '66
The Spy Who Came in from the Cold '65
Dr. Syn, Alias the Scarecrow '64
Cleopatra '63
Sink the Bismarck '60
The Spaniard's Curse '58
The Spanish Gardener '57
The Baby and the Battleship '56
The Man Who Never Was '55
The Warriors '55
Grand National Night '53
The Promoter '52
A Christmas Carol '51
Train of Events '49

Sharon Horgan (1970-)
Imagine Me & You '06
Valiant '05 (V)

Keisuke Horibe
Party 7 '00
Shark Skin Man and Peach Hip Girl '98

Tad Horino (1921-2002)
Kung Pow! Enter the Fist '02
Galaxina '80

Sacha Horler
Look Both Ways '05
Soft Fruit '99
Praise '98

Camilla Horn (1906-96)
Matinee Idol '33
Tempest '28
Faust '26

Michelle Horn (1987-)
Loving Annabelle '06
Hostage '05
Little Athens '05

David Horne (1898-1970)
Men of Two Worlds '46
Spitfire '42
Night Train to Munich '40
Crimes at the Dark House '39
Late Extra '35

Geoffrey Horne (1933-)
Bonjour Tristesse '57
The Bridge on the River Kwai '57

Lena Horne (1917-)
The Wiz '78
Death of a Gunfighter '69
The Duchess of Idaho '50
Words and Music '48
Till the Clouds Roll By '46
Ziegfeld Follies '46
Broadway Rhythm '44
Two Girls and a Sailor '44
Cabin in the Sky '43
I Dood It '43
Stormy Weather '43
Thousands Cheer '43
Panama Hattie '42
The Duke Is Tops '38

Victoria Horne (1911-2003)
Harvey '50
Abbott and Costello Meet the Killer, Boris Karloff '49

Wil Horneff (1979-)
Cash Crop '01
Harvest '98
Born to Be Wild '95
Oldest Confederate Widow Tells All '95
The Yearling '94
Ghost in the Machine '93

Craig Horner
See No Evil '06
Swimming Upstream '03

Penelope Horner
Dracula '73
Man Who Had Power Over Women '70
Half a Sixpence '67

Russell Hornsby
Stuck '07
Edmond '05
Get Rich or Die Tryin' '05
After the Sunset '04
Big Fat Liar '02

David Horovitch (1945-)
Goodbye, Mr. Chips '02
Max '02
102 Dalmatians '00
Solomon and Gaenor '98
Ivanhoe '97
The Sculptress '97
Paper Marriage '93
Piece of Cake '88

Adam Horovitz (1966-)
Roadside Prophets '92
A Kiss Before Dying '91
Long Road Home '91
Lost Angels '89

Sam Horrigan (1981-)
Brink '98
Little Giants '94

Jane Horrocks (1964-)
Brothers of the Head '06
Garfield: A Tail of Two Kitties '06 (V)
Tim Burton's Corpse Bride '05 (V)
Born Romantic '00
Chicken Run '00 (V)
Little Voice '98
Second Best '94
Deadly Advice '93
Catherine Cookson's The Fifteen Streets '90
Life Is Sweet '90
Memphis Belle '90
The Witches '90
The Dressmaker '89
Getting It Right '89

Chelah Horsdal (1973-)
Elegy '08
Gym Teacher: The Movie '08
Passengers '08
Masters of Horror: Dreams in the Witch House '05

Michael Horse (1951-)
Bone Eater '07
Navajo Blues '97
Lakota Woman: Siege at Wounded Knee '94
Wagons East '94
The Avenging '92
House of Cards '92
Passenger 57 '92
Border Shootout '90
Deadly Weapon '88
Buckeye and Blue '87
Legend of the Lone Ranger '81

Anna Maria Horsford (1948-)
Our Family Wedding '10
Broken Bridges '06
Friday After Next '02
How High '01
Dancing in September '00
Lockdown '00
Nutty Professor 2: The Klumps '00
Dear God '96
One Fine Day '96
Set It Off '96
Friday '95
Widow's Kiss '94
Murder Without Motive '92
Presumed Innocent '90
Taken Away '89
Street Smart '87
Heartburn '86
Charlotte Forten's Mission: Experiment in Freedom '85
St. Elmo's Fire '85
Times Square '80

John Horsley (1915-)
Sink the Bismarck '60
Black Tide '58
The Runaway Bus '54
Recoil '53
The Frightened Man '52

John David Horsley
The Girl from Missouri '34
Finishing School '33
Flaming Signal '33

Lee Horsley (1955-)
Showdown at Area 51 '07
French Silk '94
Unlawful Passage '94
Danielle Steel's Palomino '91
Agatha Christie's Thirteen at Dinner '85
Sword & the Sorcerer '82

Jochen Horst (1961-)
Luther '03
The Cement Garden '93

Edward Everett Horton (1886-1970)
Cold Turkey '71
Sex and the Single Girl '64
It's a Mad, Mad, Mad, Mad World '63
Pocketful of Miracles '61
Down to Earth '47
Her Husband's Affairs '47
Lady on a Train '45
Arsenic and Old Lace '44
Summer Storm '44
Forever and a Day '43
The Gang's All Here '43
Thank Your Lucky Stars '43
I Married an Angel '42
The Magnificent Dope '42
Springtime in the Rockies '42
Here Comes Mr. Jordan '41
Sunny '41
Ziegfeld Girl '41
Bluebeard's Eighth Wife '38
College Swing '38
Holiday '38
Angel '37
The Great Garrick '37
Lost Horizon '37
Shall We Dance '37
The Singing Kid '36
The Devil Is a Woman '35
The Private Secretary '35
Top Hat '35
The Gay Divorcee '34
Kiss and Make Up '34
The Merry Widow '34
Sing and Like It '34
Trouble in Paradise '32
The Front Page '31
Lonely Wives '31
Reaching for the Moon '31
Smart Woman '31

Helen Horton
Alien '79 (V)
The Chairman '69

Peter Horton (1953-)
From the Earth to the Moon '98
The End of Violence '97
Into Thin Air: Death on Everest '97
Crazy Horse '96
Death Benefit '96
Two Days in the Valley '96
The Baby-Sitters' Club '95
Singles '92
Side Out '90
Amazon Women on the Moon '87
Where the River Runs Black '86
Children of the Corn '84

Robert Horton (1924-)
The Green Slime '68
Men of the Fighting Lady '54

Dominique Horwitz
Shooting Dogs '05
Stalingrad '94

Bobby Hosea
The Veteran '06
All About You '01
61* '01
Under Heavy Fire '01
Gargantua '98
Independence Day '96
French Silk '94
The O.J. Simpson Story '94

Marjorie Hoshelle (1918-89)
Dangerous Crossing '53
Blonde for a Day '46

Shizuko Hoshi
Memoirs of a Geisha '05
Charlotte Sometimes '02
M. Butterfly '93
Come See the Paradise '90

Yuriko Hoshi (1943-)
Last War '68
Ghidrah the Three Headed Monster '65
Godzilla vs. Mothra '64

Bob Hoskins (1942-)
A Christmas Carol '09 (V)
Doomsday '08
Outlaw '07
Ruby Blue '07
Garfield: A Tail of Two Kitties '06 (V)
Hollywoodland '06
Paris, je t'aime '06
Mrs. Henderson Presents '05
Son of the Mask '05
Stay '05
Unleashed '05
Beyond the Sea '04
Vanity Fair '04
The Lost World '02
Maid in Manhattan '02
The Sleeping Dictionary '02
Last Orders '01
Don Quixote '00
Enemy at the Gates '00
Noriega: God's Favorite '00
David Copperfield '99
Felicia's Journey '99
White River '99
American Virgin '98
Captain Jack '98
Parting Shots '98
Cousin Bette '97
Spice World: The Movie '97
24-7 '97
Michael '96
The Secret Agent '96
Balto '95 (V)
Nixon '95
World War II: When Lions Roared '94
Super Mario Bros. '93
Blue Ice '92
The Favor, the Watch, & the Very Big Fish '92
Passed Away '92
Hook '91
The Inner Circle '91
Shattered '91
Heart Condition '90
Mermaids '90
The Raggedy Rawney '90
Who Framed Roger Rabbit '88
The Lonely Passion of Judith Hearne '87
Prayer for the Dying '87
Mona Lisa '86
Sweet Liberty '86
Brazil '85
The Dunera Boys '85
Mussolini & I '85
The Cotton Club '84
Lassiter '84
Beyond the Limit '83
Pink Floyd: The Wall '82
Flickers '80
The Long Good Friday '80
Zulu Dawn '79
Cry Terror '76
Inserts '76
Royal Flash '75

Shigeki Hosokawa
Death Note 3: L, Change tne World '08
Death Note 2: The Last Name '07
Death Note '06

Allison Hossack (1965-)
The Gambler, the Girl and the Gunslinger '09
Escape from Mars '99
White Light '90

Robert Hossein (1927-)
Venus Beauty Institute '98
Wax Mask '97
Bolero '82
Le Professionnel '81
Don Juan (Or If Don Juan Were a Woman) '73
Carbon Copy '69
Angelique and the Sultan '68
The Battle of El Alamein '68
Murder for Sale '68
Untamable Angelique '67
Angelique and the King '66
Angelique: The Road to Versailles '65
Angelique '64
Le Repos du Guerrier '62
Love on a Pillow '62
Madame Sans-Gene '62
Double Agents '59

Barry Hostetler
Mystery Mansion '83
The Worm Eaters '77

Emil Hostina
Catacombs '07
Vlad '03

Yukihiro Hotaru
Boogiepop and Others '00
Cure '97
Zeram 2 '94
Zeram '91

Donald Hotton
The Freeway Maniac '88
The Hearse '80

Germain Houde (1952-)
Night Zoo '87
Les Bons Debarras '81

Serge Houde (1953-)
The Invisible '07
Eighteen '04
The Lathe of Heaven '02
Hidden Agenda '01
Wilder '00
Legends of the North '95

Harry Houdini (1874-1926)
The Man from Beyond '22
The Houdini Serial '20

James Houghton (1948-)
Superstition '82
More American Graffiti '79

Katharine Houghton (1945-)
The Night We Never Met '93
Ethan Frome '92
Billy Bathgate '91
Mr. North '88
The Eyes of the Amaryllis '82
Seeds of Evil '76
Guess Who's Coming to Dinner '67

Nicholas Hoult (1989-)
A Single Man '09
Wah-Wah '05
The Weather Man '05
About a Boy '02

Djimon Hounsou (1964-)
Push '09
Never Back Down '08
Blood Diamond '06
Eragon '06
Beauty Shop '05
Constantine '05
The Island '05
Biker Boyz '03
Lara Croft Tomb Raider: The Cradle of Life '03
The Four Feathers '02
In America '02
Gladiator '00
Deep Rising '98
Amistad '97

Ned Hourani
Fist of Steel '93
Raiders of the Sun '92
Triple Impact '92

Billy House (1890-1961)
People Will Talk '51
Santa Fe '51
Where Danger Lives '50
Egg and I '47
Bedlam '45

Ron House
Stoogemania '85
Bullshot '83

Arthur Houseman (1889-1942)
The Bat '26
Manhandled '24

John Houseman (1902-88)
Another Woman '88
Bright Lights, Big City '88
Gore Vidal's Lincoln '88
The Naked Gun: From the Files of Police Squad '88
Scrooged '88
A.D. '85
The Winds of War '83
Murder by Phone '82
Ghost Story '81
The Babysitter '80
A Christmas Without Snow '80
Gideon's Trumpet '80
My Bodyguard '80
Wholly Moses! '80
Old Boyfriends '79
The Cheap Detective '78
The Fog '78
Our Town '77
St. Ives '76
Rollerball '75
Three Days of the Condor '75
The Paper Chase '73
Seven Days in May '64

Jerry Houser (1952-)
A Very Brady Christmas '88
Forbidden Love '82
Magic '78
Slap Shot '77
Class of '44 '73
Summer of '42 '71

Arthur Housman
Racing Blood '36
The Singing Fool '28
Braveheart '25

Allan Houston (1971-)
Laws of Attraction '04
Black and White '99

Donald Houston (1923-91)
Tales That Witness Madness '73
The Bushbaby '70
Where Eagles Dare '68
The Viking Queen '67
A Study in Terror '66
Maniac '63
The Prince and the Pauper '62
The 300 Spartans '62
The Mark '61
Room at the Top '59
Doctor in the House '53
Crow Hollow '52

George Houston (1898-1944)
The Lone Rider in Cheyenne '42
Texas Justice '42
Border Roundup '41
The Lone Rider Crosses the Rio '41
The Lone Rider in Frontier Fury '41
The Lone Rider in Ghost Town '41
Frontier Scout '38
The Great Waltz '38
Wallaby Jim of the Islands '37
Captain Calamity '36
Let's Sing Again '36

Glyn Houston (1926-)
Conspiracy '89
River Beat '54

Joff Houston
Ninja: American Warrior '90
Ninja Death Squad '87

Marques Houston (1981-)
Fat Albert '04
You Got Served '04
Bebe's Kids '92 (V)

Renee Houston (1902-)
Legend of the Werewolf '75
Repulsion '65
The Flesh and the Fiends '60
The Horse's Mouth '58
Time Without Pity '57
The Belles of St. Trinian's '53

Whitney Houston (1963-)
Cinderella '97
The Preacher's Wife '96
Waiting to Exhale '95
The Bodyguard '92

Anders (Tofting) Hove (1956-)
Mifune '99
Bloodstorm: Subspecies 4 '98
Bloodlust: Subspecies 3 '93
Bloodstone: Subspecies 2 '92
Subspecies '90

Adrian Hoven (1922-81)
Fear of Fear '75
Fox and His Friends '75
Mark of the Devil '69
Castle of the Creeping Flesh '68
Cave of the Living Dead '65
Tromba, the Tiger Man '52

Natasha Hovey (1967-)
Demons '86
Acqua e Sapone '83

Adam Coleman Howard
No Secrets '91
Slaves of New York '89
Quiet Cool '86

Alan Howard (1937-)
P.D. James: Death in Holy Orders '03
The Secret Rapture '94
A Casualty of War '90
The Cook, the Thief, His Wife & Her Lover '90
Strapless '90
The Heroes of Telemark '65

Andrew Howard
Revolver '05
The Lion in Winter '03
Below '02
Shooters '00

Anne Howard (1925-91)
The Ghost of Rashmon Hall '47
All This and Heaven Too '40
Little Men '40
The Prince and the Pauper '37
Anthony Adverse '36
Lloyds of London '36
Great Expectations '34
Jane Eyre '34

Anne Marie Howard (1960-)
Shopgirl '05
The Weather Man '05
Blue Streak '99
Prince of Darkness '87
Model Behavior '82

Arliss Howard (1955-)
The Time Traveler's Wife '09
Awake '07
Birth '04
Big Bad Love '02
The Song of the Lark '01
A Map of the World '99
You Know My Name '99
The Lesser Evil '97
The Lost World: Jurassic Park 2 '97
William Faulkner's Old Man '97
Beyond the Call '96
johns '96
The Man Who Captured Eichmann '96
The Infiltrator '95
To Wong Foo, Thanks for Everything, Julie Newmar '95
Natural Born Killers '94
The Sandlot '93 (V)
Tales of Erotica '93
Wilder Napalm '93
Crisscross '92
Ruby '92
Till Death Do Us Part '92
For the Boys '91
Iran: Days of Crisis '91
Somebody Has to Shoot the Picture '90
Men Don't Leave '89
Plain Clothes '88
Tequila Sunrise '88
Full Metal Jacket '87
Hands of a Stranger '87
The Lightship '86
Door to Door '84
The Prodigal '83

Arthur Howard (1910-95)
Another Country '84
Paradisio '61
The Belles of St. Trinian's '53
The Happiest Days of Your Life '50
The Reckless Way '36

Barbara Howard
Where's Marlowe? '98
Lucky Stiff '88
Running Mates '86

Ben Howard
The Land That Time Forgot '75
Oh! What a Lovely War '69

Bob Howard (1906-86)
Junction 88 '47
Murder with Music '45

Boothe Howard (1887-1936)
Oh Susannah '38
Red River Valley '36
Mystery Liner '34

Brie Howard
The Runnin' Kind '89
Android '82

Bryce Dallas Howard (1981-)
The Twilight Saga: Eclipse '10
Terminator Salvation '09
The Loss of a Teardrop Diamond '08
Spider-Man 3 '07
As You Like It '06
Lady in the Water '06
Manderlay '05
Book of Love '04
The Village '04

Clint Howard (1959-)
Foreign Exchange '08
Senior Skip Day '08
Curious George '06 (V)
River's End '05
Beethoven's 5th '03
Heart of America '03
House of the Dead '03
The Missing '03
Austin Powers In Goldmember '02
Blackwoods '02
Dr. Seuss' How the Grinch Stole Christmas '00
Little Nicky '00
Arthur's Quest '99
Austin Powers 2: The Spy Who Shagged Me '99
EDtv '99
The Million Dollar Kid '99
Ping! '99
From the Earth to the Moon '98
The Waterboy '98
Under Oath '97
Barb Wire '96
Body Armor '96
Humanoids from the Deep '96
Rattled '96
Santa with Muscles '96
That Thing You Do! '96
Apollo 13 '95
Dillinger and Capone '95
Ice Cream Man '95
Bigfoot: The Unforgettable Encounter '94
Cheyenne Warrior '94
Leprechaun 2 '94
Carnosaur '93
Forced to Kill '93
Far and Away '92
Backdraft '91
Disturbed '90
Silent Night, Deadly Night 4: Initiation '90
Tango and Cash '89
B.O.R.N. '88
End of the Line '88
Freeway '88
The Wraith '87
Cocoon '85
Gung Ho '85
Get Crazy '83
Cotton Candy '82
Evilspeak '82
Night Shift '82
Rock 'n' Roll High School '79
Grand Theft Auto '77
The Death of Richie '76
Eat My Dust '76
The Red Pony '76
Huckleberry Finn '75
Salty '73
The Wild Country '71
Gentle Giant '67

Curly Howard (1903-52)
Hollywood Party '34
Dancing Lady '33
The Lost Stooges '33
Myrt and Marge '33

Esther Howard (1892-1965)
Detour '46
Murder, My Sweet '44
Klondike Annie '36
Vice Squad '31

Frank Howard (1970-)
That Was Then.. This Is Now '85
Hard Knox '83

Jeffrey Howard
The Wedding Banquet '93
Simple Men '92

John Howard (1913-95)
The High and the Mighty '54
Make Haste to Live '54
Radar Secret Service '50
The Fighting Kentuckian '49
Love from a Stranger '47
The Undying Monster '42
The Invisible Woman '40
The Philadelphia Story '40
The Texas Rangers Ride Again '40
Bulldog Drummond's Bride '39
Bulldog Drummond's Secret Police '39
What a Life '39
Arrest Bulldog Drummond '38
Bulldog Drummond's Peril '38
Bulldog Drummond Comes Back '37
Bulldog Drummond's Revenge '37
Lost Horizon '37

John Howard (1952-)
Jindabyne '06
Japanese Story '03
The Road from Coorain '02
Dating the Enemy '95
Young Einstein '89
The Highest Honor '84
Prince and the Great Race '83
The Club '81

Joyce Howard (1922-)
Appointment with Crime '45
The Night Has Eyes '42

Kathleen Howard (1879-1956)
Crash Dive '43
Blossoms in the Dust '41
Young People '40
First Love '39
It's a Gift '34

Ken Howard (1944-)
Grey Gardens '09
Rambo '08
Smother '08
Michael Clayton '07
Arc '06
Dreamer: Inspired by a True Story '05
In Her Shoes '05
Perfect Murder, Perfect Town '00
Tactical Assault '99
At First Sight '98
The Net '95
Mastergate '92
Ulterior Motives '92
Murder in New Hampshire: The Pamela Smart Story '91
Oscar '91
Strange Interlude '90
Rage of Angels: The Story Continues '86
Pudd'nhead Wilson '84
Rage of Angels '83
Second Thoughts '83
The Thorn Birds '83
Country Girl '82
Damien: The Leper Priest '80
Manhunter '74
1776 '72

Kevyn Major Howard
Alien Nation '88
Full Metal Jacket '87
Sudden Impact '83

Kyle Howard (1978-)
Holiday in Handcuffs '07
Orange County '02
Baby Geniuses '98
Address Unknown '96
House Arrest '96
The Paper Brigade '96
Robo Warriors '96
Skeletons '96

Leo Howard (1997-)
Aussie and Ted's Great Adventure '09
Shorts: The Adventures of the Wishing Rock '09

Leslie Howard (1893-1943)
Pimpernel Smith '42
Spitfire '42
The Forty-Ninth Parallel '41
Gone with the Wind '39
Intermezzo '39
Pygmalion '38
Stand-In '37
Petrified Forest '36
Romeo and Juliet '36
Of Human Bondage '34
The Scarlet Pimpernel '34
Smilin' Through '33
The Animal Kingdom '32
Devotion '31
A Free Soul '31

Lisa Howard (1963-)
Bounty Hunters 2: Hardball '97
Bounty Hunters '96
Rolling Vengeance '87
Sabaka '55

Mary Howard (1912-89)
The Loves of Edgar Allen Poe '42
Billy the Kid '41
Abe Lincoln in Illinois '40
All Over Town '37

Moe Howard (1897-1975)
Dr. Death, Seeker of Souls '73
The Outlaws Is Coming! '65
Around the World in a Daze '63
Four for Texas '63
It's a Mad, Mad, Mad, Mad World '63
Three Stooges in Orbit '62
Snow White and the Three Stooges '61
The Three Stooges Meet Hercules '61
Have Rocket Will Travel '59
Gold Raiders '51
Swing Parade of 1946 '46
Hollywood Party '34
Dancing Lady '33
The Lost Stooges '33

Rance Howard (1929-)
Walk Hard: The Dewey Cox Story '07
Sister Aimee: The Aimee Semple McPherson Story '06
The Alamo '04
Eye See You '01
A Crack in the Floor '00
Psycho '98
The Student Affair '97
Ghosts of Mississippi '96
Bigfoot: The Unforgettable Encounter '94
Ed Wood '94
Forced to Kill '93
Far and Away '92
Dark Before Dawn '89
B.O.R.N. '88
Grand Theft Auto '77
Eat My Dust '76
Huckleberry Finn '75
Where the Lilies Bloom '74
Bloody Trail '72
The Wild Country '71
Cool Hand Luke '67

Ron Howard (1954-)
Osmosis Jones '01 (V)
The Independent '00
Return to Mayberry '85
Bitter Harvest '81
More American Graffiti '79
Grand Theft Auto '77
Eat My Dust '76
The Shootist '76
The First Nudie Musical '75
Huckleberry Finn '75
The Migrants '74
American Graffiti '73
Run, Stranger, Run '73
The Wild Country '71
Smoke '70
Village of the Giants '65
The Courtship of Eddie's Father '62
The Music Man '62
Door to Door Maniac '61

Ronald Howard (1918-96)
Pattern for Plunder '62
The Naked Edge '61
The Queen of Spades '49
Night Beat '48

Shawn Michael Howard (1969-)
Boycott '02
The Rats '01
Sunset Park '96

Shemp Howard (1895-1955)
Gold Raiders '51
Africa Screams '49
Blondie Knows Best '46
Trouble Chasers '45
Cooking Up Trouble '44
Ghost Crazy '44
It Ain't Hay '43
Pittsburgh '42
Private Buckaroo '42
The Strange Case of Dr. Rx '42
Buck Privates '41
Cracked Nuts '41
Hold That Ghost '41
The Bank Dick '40
The Invisible Woman '40
Convention Girl '35

Susan Howard (1944-)
The Power Within '79
Moonshine County Express '77
Sidewinder One '77

Terrence Howard (1969-)
Fighting '09
The Princess and the Frog '09 (V)
Iron Man '08
August Rush '07
Awake '07
The Brave One '07
The Hunting Party '07
The Perfect Holiday '07
Pride '07
Idlewild '06
Animal '05
Crash '05
Four Brothers '05
Get Rich or Die Tryin' '05
Hustle & Flow '05
The Salon '05
Ray '04
Biker Boyz '03
Boycott '02
Hart's War '02
Angel Eyes '01
Glitter '01
Intimate Affairs '01
Big Momma's House '00
Love Beat the Hell Outta Me '00
The Best Man '99
Never 2 Big '98
Spark '98
johns '96
Sunset Park '96
The Jacksons: An American Dream '92

Traylor Howard (1966-)
Son of the Mask '05
Me, Myself, and Irene '00
Dirty Work '97

Trevor Howard (1916-88)
The Dawning '88
The Unholy '88
White Mischief '88
Foreign Body '86
Dust '85
This Lightning Always Strikes Twice '85
Flashpoint Africa '84
George Washington '84
Shaka Zulu '83
Sword of the Valiant '83
Deadly Game '82
Gandhi '82
Inside the Third Reich '82
The Missionary '82
Sea Wolves '81
Windwalker '81
Staying On '80
Hurricane '79
Meteor '79
Stevie '78
Superman: The Movie '78
Slavers '77
Adventures of Eliza Fraser '76
Albino '76
The Bawdy Adventures of Tom Jones '76
Conduct Unbecoming '75
Hennessy '75
Roboman '75
The Count of Monte Cristo '74
Craze '74
11 Harrowhouse '74
The Graveyard '74
Catholics '73
A Doll's House '73
The Offence '73
Ludwig '72
Catch Me a Spy '71
Mary, Queen of Scots '71
The Night Visitor '70
Ryan's Daughter '70
Battle of Britain '69
Lola '69
The Charge of the Light Brigade '68
Triple Cross '67
The Poppy Is Also a Flower '66
Morituri '65
Operation Crossbow '65
Von Ryan's Express '65
Father Goose '64
Invincible Mr. Disraeli '63
Mutiny on the Bounty '62
The Key '58
Around the World in 80 Days '56
The Gift Horse '52
The Clouded Yellow '51
The Golden Salamander '51
The Third Man '49
Green for Danger '47
They Made Me a Fugitive '47
Brief Encounter '46
I See a Dark Stranger '46

Vanessa Howard (1948-)
Picture of Dorian Gray '74
Girly '70
Blood Beast Terror '67

Kevin Howarth
Cold and Dark '05
Razor Blade Smile '98

Clark Howat (1917-)
Billy Jack '71
The Giant Claw '57

Brian Howe
Gran Torino '08
Dark Heart '06
The Pursuit of Happyness '06
RV '06
Catch Me If You Can '02

Anthony Howell
The Other Boleyn Girl '03
Wives and Daughters '01

C. Thomas Howell (1966-)
The Land That Time Forgot '09
The Pledge '08
The Haunting of Marsten Manor '07
The Far Side of Jericho '06
Crimson Force '05
The Keeper: The Legend of Omar Khayyam '05
The Glass Trap '04
Hidalgo '04
The Hillside Strangler '04
The Lost Angel '04

Gods and Generals '03
The Hitcher 2: I've Been Waiting '03
Net Games '03
Burning Down the House '01
Dead Evidence '00
Avalanche '99
The Crimson Code '99
Cybercity '99
The Million Dollar Kid '99
The Prince and the Surfer '99
Shepherd '99
Dead Fire '98
First Degree '98
Last Lives '98
Matter of Trust '98
Stalker '98
Baby Face Nelson '97
Dilemma '97
Laws of Deception '97
The Big Fall '96
Pure Danger '96
Hourglass '95
Suspect Device '95
The Sweeper '95
Dangerous Indiscretion '94
Payback '94
Shameless '94
Teresa's Tattoo '94
Acting on Impulse '93
Gettysburg '93
Jailbait '93
That Night '93
Breaking the Rules '92
Nickel & Dime '92
Tattle Tale '92
To Protect and Serve '92
Curiosity Kills '90
Eyes of the Panther '90
Kid '90
Side Out '90
Far Out Man '89
The Return of the Musketeers '89
Into the Homeland '87
A Tiger's Tale '87
The Hitcher '86
Soul Man '86
Secret Admirer '85
Grandview U.S.A. '84
Red Dawn '84
The Outsiders '83
Tank '83
E.T.: The Extra-Terrestrial '82

Hoke Howell (1930-97)
Vice Girls '96
Alienator '89
B.O.R.N. '88
Humanoids from the Deep '80
Bad Charleston Charlie '73

Jean Howell (1927-96)
Crime of Passion '57
The Fast and the Furious '54

Kenneth Howell (1913-66)
Hurry, Charlie, Hurry '41
Junior G-Men '40
Little Red Schoolhouse '36
The Eagle and the Hawk '33

Peter Howell
Almost Strangers '01
Shadowlands '93

Virginia Howell
Star Reporter '39
Spitfire '34

Ursula Howells (1922-2005)
Jewels '92
Girly '70
The Gilded Cage '54

Frankie Howerd (1922-92)
Night of the Laughing Dead '75
Naughty Knights '71
Carry On Up the Jungle '70
Carry On Doctor '68
The Great St. Trinian's Train Robbery '66
Cool Mikado '63

The Runaway Bus '54

Glenn Howerton (1976-)
The Strangers '08
Two Weeks '06

Bobby Howes (1895-1972)
Happy Go Lovely '51
Murder in the Footlights '46

Reed Howes (1900-64)
The Sinister Urge '60
My Dog Shep '46
Dead or Alive '44
Law of the Saddle '43
Fugitive Valley '41
Covered Wagon Days '40
Lightning Strikes West '40
Phantom Rancher '39
Roll, Wagons, Roll '39
Six Gun Rhythm '39
A Million to One '37
The Clutching Hand '36
Custer's Last Stand '36
Confidential '35
Feud of the West '35
Queen of the Jungle '35
The Singing Fool '28
Cyclone Cavalier '25

Sally Ann Howes (1930-)
Death Ship '80
Chitty Chitty Bang Bang '68
The Admirable Crichton '57
Anna Karenina '48
Nicholas Nickleby '46
Dead of Night '45
Pink String and Sealing Wax '45
Thursday's Child '43

Steve Howey (1977-)
Bride Wars '09
Stan Helsing '09
Still Waiting '08
DOA: Dead or Alive '06
Supercross: The Movie '05

Peter Howitt (1957-)
Kiss and Tell '96
The Magician '93

Chris Howland (1928-)
The Mad Executioners '65
Fanny Hill: Memoirs of a Woman of Pleasure '64

Jobyna Howland (1880-1936)
Topaze '33
Hook, Line and Sinker '30

Noel Howlett (1901-84)
Woman of Straw '64
Victim '61
Serious Charge '59

Olin Howlin (1886-1959)
The Blob '58
Storm Rider '57
Last of the Wild Horses '49
Apache Rose '47
The Wistful Widow of Wagon Gap '47
Nancy Drew, Reporter '39
Girl of the Golden West '38
Earthworm Tractors '36
Satan Met a Lady '36

Karl Howman
Party! Party! '83
The House on Straw Hill '76

Leonard Earl Howze
The Ringer '05
Barbershop 2: Back in Business '04
Barbershop '02

Jack Hoxie (1885-1965)
Gun Law '33
Law and Lawless '33
Trouble Busters '33
Outlaw Justice '32
Backfire '22
Blue Blazes Rawden '18

Cristina Hoyos (1946-)
El Amor Brujo '86
Carmen '83

Blood Wedding '81

Arthur Hoyt (1874-1953)
The Great McGinty '40
In the Money '34
His Private Secretary '33
American Madness '32
The Devil and the Deep '32
Dynamite Ranch '32

Carol Hoyt
Midnight Confessions '95
Illegal Entry: Formula for Fear '93

John Hoyt (1905-91)
Flesh Gordon '72
The Time Travelers '64
X: The Man with X-Ray Eyes '63
Merrill's Marauders '62
Curse of the Undead '59
Attack of the Puppet People '58
The Conqueror '56
Forever Darling '56
Wetbacks '56
Blackboard Jungle '55
The Girl in the Red Velvet Swing '55
Sins of Jezebel '54
Julius Caesar '53
The Black Castle '52
Loan Shark '52
The Lost Continent '51
Great Dan Patch '49
Trapped '49
Winter Meeting '48
O.S.S. '46

Vera Hruba Ralston
See Vera Hruba Ralston

Rudolf Hrusinsky (1921-94)
The Elementary School '91
My Sweet Little Village '86
Larks on a String '68
Murder Czech Style '66

Brigitte Lin Ching Hsia
See Brigitte Lin

Jun Hu
Red Cliff '08
Infernal Affairs 2 '03

Kelly Hu (1967-)
The Tournament '09
Dim Sum Funeral '08
Farmhouse '08
Stiletto '08
Shanghai Kiss '07
Devil's Den '06
Underclassman '05
The Librarian: Quest for the Spear '04
Cradle 2 the Grave '03
X2: X-Men United '03
The Scorpion King '02
No Way Back '96
Strange Days '95
Surf Ninjas '93
The Doors '91
Harley Davidson and the Marlboro Man '91
Friday the 13th, Part 8: Jason Takes Manhattan '89

Sibelle Hu
China Heat '90
Lethal Panther '90

Ying Huang
Madame Butterfly '95
Opium and Kung-Fu Master '84

Patrick Huard
Bon Cop Bad Cop '06
The Boys '97

Marin Huba
I Served the King of England '07
Divided We Fall '00

David Huband (1958-)
Cinderella Man '05
Cube: Zero '04
Wrong Turn '03

Dirty Pictures '00

Elizabeth Hubbard (1933-)
Center Stage '00
Cold River '81

John Hubbard (1914-88)
Gunfight at Comanche Creek '64
Mexican Hayride '48
Cowboy & the Senorita '44
The Mummy's Tomb '42
Road Show '41

Cork Hubbert (1952-2003)
The Ballad of the Sad Cafe '91
Caveman '81

Henry Hubchen (1947-)
Go for Zucker '05
Jacob the Liar '74

Grischa Huber
Malou '83
Under the Pavement Lies the Strand '75

Harold Huber (1904-59)
A Gentleman After Dark '42
Charlie Chan in Rio '41
Dance, Girl, Dance '40
Beau Geste '39
Charlie Chan in City of Darkness '39
Mr. Moto's Gamble '38
Mysterious Mr. Moto '38
A Slight Case of Murder '38
Charlie Chan at Monte Carlo '37
Charlie Chan on Broadway '37
The Gay Desperado '36
Kelly the Second '36
Klondike Annie '36
San Francisco '36
Ladies They Talk About '33
Frisco Jenny '32

Janet Hubert-Whitten (1956-)
30 Years to Life '01
New Eden '94

Season Hubley (1951-)
Kiss the Sky '98
Stepfather 3: Father's Day '92
Total Exposure '91
Child in the Night '90
Prettykill '87
The Key to Rebecca '85
Agatha Christie's A Caribbean Mystery '83
Vice Squad '82
Escape from New York '81
Elvis: The Movie '79
Hardcore '79
Mrs. R's Daughter '79

Whip Hubley (1957-)
A Cinderella Story '04
Armistead Maupin's More Tales of the City '97
Black Scorpion 2: Ground Zero '96
Daddy's Girl '96
Executive Decision '96
A Very Brady Sequel '96
Unveiled '94
Desire and Hell at Sunset Motel '92
Devlin '92
A Connecticut Yankee in King Arthur's Court '89
Russkies '87
Top Gun '86

Paul (Christian) Hubschmid (1917-2001)
Manon '68
Funeral in Berlin '66
The Indian Tomb '59
Tiger of Eschnapur '59
Journey to the Lost City '58
The Day the Sky Exploded '57

The Beast from 20,000 Fathoms '53
Bagdad '49

Cooper Huckabee (1951-)
Gettysburg '93
Love Field '91
Night Eyes '90
Cohen and Tate '88
The Curse '87
The Funhouse '81
Getting Wasted '80
Joni '79

Steffany Huckaby
Death Tunnel '05
The Pleasure Drivers '05

Walter Hudd (1897-1963)
Sink the Bismarck '60
Cast a Dark Shadow '55
I Know Where I'm Going '45
Black Limelight '38
Housemaster '38
Elephant Boy '37
Rembrandt '36

David Huddleston (1930-)
The Producers '05
The Big Lebowski '97
Life with Mikey '93
Double Exposure: The Story of Margaret Bourke-White '89
Frantic '88
The Tracker '88
When the Bough Breaks '86
Santa Claus: The Movie '85
Finnegan Begin Again '84
Go for It '83
Smokey and the Bandit 2 '80
Crime Busters '78
Billy Two Hats '74
Blazing Saddles '74
McQ '74
On the Run '73
Rio Lobo '70

Michael Huddleston
Wyatt Earp '94
Bad Channels '92
Bombs Away! '86
Four Friends '81
World's Greatest Lover '77

Vanessa Anne Hudgens (1988-)
Beastly '10
Bandslam '09
High School Musical 3: Senior Year '08
High School Musical 2 '07
High School Musical '06
Thunderbirds '04
Thirteen '03

Reginald (Reggie) Hudlin (1961-)
Joe's Apartment '96 (V)
Posse '93
She's Gotta Have It '86

Bill Hudson (1949-)
Hysterical '83
KISS Meets the Phantom of the Park '78

Ernie Hudson (1945-)
Smokin' Aces 2: Assassins' Ball '10
Dragonball: Evolution '09
Meteor '09
Final Approach '08
All Hat '07
Marilyn Hotchkiss' Ballroom Dancing & Charm School '06
Miss Congeniality 2: Armed and Fabulous '05
Clifford's Really Big Movie '04 (V)
Miss Congeniality '00
Nowhere to Land '00
Red Letters '00
The Watcher '00
Corrupt '99
Interceptor Force '99

Paper Bullets '99
Shark Attack '99
Stealth Fighter '99
Urban Menace '99
Best of the Best: Without Warning '98
For Which He Stands '98
Never 2 Big '98
A Stranger in the Kingdom '98
Levitation '97
Mr. Magoo '97
Operation: Delta Force '97
The Cherokee Kid '96
Just Your Luck '96
The Substitute '96
Tornado! '96
The Basketball Diaries '95
Congo '95
Airheads '94
The Cowboy Way '94
In the Army Now '94
No Escape '94
Speechless '94
Sugar Hill '94
The Crow '93
Wild Palms '93
The Hand that Rocks the Cradle '92
Ghostbusters 2 '89
Leviathan '89
Trapper County War '89
The Wrong Guys '88
Weeds '87
Ghostbusters '84
Joy of Sex '84
Going Berserk '83
Spacehunter: Adventures in the Forbidden Zone '83
Penitentiary 2 '82
The $5.20 an Hour Dream '80
The Jazz Singer '80
Dolemite 2: Human Tornado '76

Gary Hudson (1956-)
Sea Beast '08
Angels Fall '07
Termination Point '07
Snakeman '05
I Downloaded a Ghost '04
Extreme Limits '01
My Husband's Double Life '01
The Stepdaughter '00
Bridge of Dragons '99
Eye of the Killer '99
Black Thunder '98
Serial Killer '95
Texas Payback '95
The Wrong Woman '95
The Force '94
Scanner Cop '94
Sexual Intent '94
Indecent Behavior '93
Martial Outlaw '93
Mind Twister '93
Wild Cactus '92
Night Angel '90

Jennifer Hudson (1981-)
Fragments '08
The Secret Life of Bees '08
Sex and the City: The Movie '08
Dreamgirls '06

John Hudson (1922-96)
When Gangland Strikes '56
Return to Paradise '53

Kate Hudson (1979-)
The Killer Inside Me '10
Bride Wars '09
Nine '09
Fool's Gold '08
My Best Friend's Girl '08
You, Me and Dupree '06
The Skeleton Key '05
Raising Helen '04
Alex & Emma '03
How to Lose a Guy in 10 Days '03
Le Divorce '03
The Four Feathers '02
About Adam '00
Almost Famous '00
Dr. T & the Women '00

Gossip '99
Desert Blue '98
Ricochet River '98
200 Cigarettes '98

Larry Hudson (1921-61)
Tank Commando '59
The Creature Walks among Us '56

Oliver Hudson (1976-)
Carolina Moon '07
Black Christmas '06
The Breed '06
New Best Friend '02
Going Greek '01
The Smokers '00
The Out-of-Towners '99

Rochelle Hudson (1914-72)
Alien Massacre '67
The Night Walker '64
Strait-Jacket '64
Rebel without a Cause '55
Sky Liner '49
The Devil's Cargo '48
Bush Pilot '47
Mr. Moto Takes a Chance '38
Reunion '36
Curly Top '35
Les Miserables '35
Life Begins at Forty '35
Show Them No Mercy '35
Bachelor Bait '34
Imitation of Life '34
Mr. Skitch '33
Wild Boys of the Road '33
Beyond the Rockies '32
The Savage Girl '32

Rock Hudson (1925-85)
World War III '86
The Ambassador '84
The Vegas Strip Wars '84
The Mirror Crack'd '80
The Martian Chronicles: Part 1 '79
The Martian Chronicles: Part 2 '79
The Martian Chronicles: Part 3 '79
Avalanche '78
Embryo '76
Showdown '73
Darling Lili '70
Hornet's Nest '70
The Undefeated '69
Ice Station Zebra '68
Seconds '66
Tobruk '66
Strange Bedfellows '65
Send Me No Flowers '64
A Gathering of Eagles '63
Man's Favorite Sport? '63
Come September '61
Lover Come Back '61
Pillow Talk '59
Battle Hymn '57
A Farewell to Arms '57
Something of Value '57
Tarnished Angels '57
Giant '56
Written on the Wind '56
All That Heaven Allows '55
Magnificent Obsession '54
Gun Fury '53
Sea Devils '53
Bend of the River '52
Here Come the Nelsons '52
Horizons West '52
The Lawless Breed '52
Tomahawk '51
Winchester '73 '50

Toni Hudson
The Uninvited '88
Just One of the Guys '85
Prime Risk '84

William (Bill) Hudson (1925-74)
Attack of the 50 Foot Woman '58
The Screaming Skull '58
The Amazing Colossal Man '57

Objective, Burma! '45

Jon Huertas
Generation Kill '08
The Objective '08
Believers '07
The Insatiable '06

Matthias Hues (1959-)
Suicide Ride '97
Alone in the Woods '95
Cyberzone '95
Death Match '94
Digital Man '94
Fists of Iron '94
Bounty Tracker '93
TC 2000 '93
Black Belt '92
Mission of Justice '92
Talons of the Eagle '92
Fist Fighter '88

Brent Huff (1961-)
The Glass Trap '04
Submerged '00
The Bad Pack '98
Final Justice '94
Falling from Grace '92
Stormquest '87
Armed Response '86
Deadly Passion '85
Nine Deaths of the Ninja '85
The Perils of Gwendoline '84

Cady Huffman
Dare '09
Space Marines '96

David Huffman (1945-85)
Agatha Christie's Sparkling Cyanide '83
Last Plane Out '83
Firefox '82
St. Helen's, Killer Volcano '82
Blood Beach '81
Ice Castles '79
The Onion Field '79
F.I.S.T. '78
The Winds of Kitty Hawk '78

Felicity Huffman (1962-)
Phoebe in Wonderland '08
Georgia Rule '07
Transamerica '05
Christmas With the Kranks '04
Raising Helen '04
Out of Order '03
Path to War '02
Snap Decision '01
A Slight Case of Murder '99
The Spanish Prisoner '97
Hackers '95
Quicksand: No Escape '91
Stephen King's Golden Years '91

Kymberley Huffman
K-9 3: P.I. '01
Sleeping with Strangers '94

Billy Hufsey (1958-)
Magic Kid '92
Off the Wall '82

Daniel Hugh-Kelly (1954-)
Jackie, Ethel, Joan: The Kennedy Women '01
Chill Factor '99
Passing Glory '99
Atomic Dog '98
From the Earth to the Moon '98
Star Trek: Insurrection '98
The Tuskegee Airmen '95
Bad Company '94
The Good Son '93
Cujo '83
Nowhere to Hide '83

Andrew Hughes (1908-85)
Destroy All Monsters '68
Terror Beneath the Sea '66

Barnard Hughes (1915-2006)
The Cradle Will Rock '99
Neil Simon's The Odd Couple 2 '98
The Fantasticks '95
Past the Bleachers '95
Primal Secrets '94
Sister Act 2: Back in the Habit '93
Doc Hollywood '91
Day One '89
The Incident '89
Da '88
Hobo's Christmas '87
The Lost Boys '87
The Adventures of Huckleberry Finn '85
Maxie '85
Under the Biltmore Clock '85
Where Are the Children? '85
Little Gloria... Happy at Last '84
Agatha Christie's A Caribbean Mystery '83
Best Friends '82
Tron '82
First Monday in October '81
Homeward Bound '80
Sanctuary of Fear '79
Oh, God! '77
Sisters '73
Rage '72
Cold Turkey '71
The Hospital '71
Where's Poppa? '70
Midnight Cowboy '69

Brendan Hughes
Sundown: The Vampire in Retreat '08
Howling 6: The Freaks '90
To Die For '89
Return to Horror High '87

Carol Hughes (1915-85)
Home in Oklahoma '47
Miracle Kid '42
Desperate Cargo '41
Robot Pilot '41
Silver Stallion '41
The Border Legion '40
Flash Gordon Conquers the Universe '40
Space Soldiers Conquer the Universe '40
Love Affair '39
The Man from Music Mountain '38
Renfrew of the Royal Mounted '37
Earthworm Tractors '36
Three Men on a Horse '36

Charles Hughes
Call of the Forest '49
The Frontiersmen '38

Finola Hughes (1960-)
Tycus '98
Prison of Secrets '97
The Crying Child '96
Dark Side of Genius '94
Aspen Extreme '93
Soapdish '91
Nutcracker Sweet '84
Staying Alive '83

Frank John Hughes (1967-)
Kings of South Beach '07
Catch Me If You Can '02
Band of Brothers '01
Deranged '01
Angel's Dance '99
Happy Hell Night '92

Geraldine Hughes
Gran Torino '08
Rocky Balboa '06

Heather Hughes
Blood Freak '72
Flesh Feast '69

Helen Hughes (1929-)
Night of the Twisters '95
The Amityville Curse '90
Kidnapping of Baby John Doe '88
My Father, My Rival '85
The Peanut Butter Solution '85

Incubus '82
Off Your Rocker '80
Outrageous! '77

Jason Hughes (1971-)
Killing Me Softly '01
Plain Jane '01
Shooters '00

Kathleen Hughes (1928-)
Cult of the Cobra '55
It Came from Outer Space '53

Kay Hughes (1914-98)
Dick Tracy: The Spider Strikes '37
The Mandarin Mystery '37
Ride, Ranger, Ride '36
The Three Mesquiteers '36
The Vigilantes Are Coming '36

Lloyd Hughes (1897-1958)
Blake of Scotland Yard '36
A Face in the Fog '36
Kelly of the Secret Service '36
Little Red Schoolhouse '36
The Midnight Phantom '35
Social Error '35
Drums of Jeopardy '31
Big Boy '30
Where East Is East '29
Ella Cinders '26
The Lost World '25
The Sea Hawk '24
Tess of the Storm Country '22
Beau Revel '21
Dangerous Hours '19

Mary Beth Hughes (1919-95)
Loophole '54
Close to My Heart '51
Square Dance Jubilee '51
Holiday Rhythm '50
Last of the Wild Horses '49
Rimfire '49
Inner Sanctum '48
Return of Wildfire '48
Great Flamarion '45
I Accuse My Parents '45
The Lady Confesses '45
Take It Big '44
Timber Queen '44
The Ox-Bow Incident '43
Blue, White and Perfect '42
Orchestra Wives '42
Charlie Chan in Rio '41
The Great American Broadcast '41
Sleepers West '41
Lucky Cisco Kid '40

Miko Hughes (1986-)
Fly Boy '99
Mercury Rising '98
Spawn '97
Zeus and Roxanne '96
Apollo 13 '95
Cops and Robbersons '94
Wes Craven's New Nightmare '94
Jack the Bear '93
Pet Sematary '89

Roddy Hughes (1891-1970)
Old Mother Riley's Jungle Treasure '51
The Last Days of Dolwyn '49

Sharon Hughes
Grotesque '87
Chained Heat '83

Tresa Hughes
Sarah, Plain and Tall: Skylark '93
Coming Home '78

Wendy Hughes (1952-)
Paradise Road '97
Lust and Revenge '95
Princess Caraboo '94
Wild Orchid 2: Two Shades of Blue '92

A Woman Named Jackie '91
The Heist '89
Happy New Year '87
Warm Nights on a Slow-Moving Train '87
Echoes of Paradise '86
An Indecent Obsession '85
Remember Me '85
Careful, He Might Hear You '84
My First Wife '84
Dangerous Summer '82
Lonely Hearts '82
Touch & Go '80
Kostas '79
My Brilliant Career '79
Newsfront '78
Puzzle '78
High Rolling in a Hot Corvette '77
Alternative '76
Jock Petersen '74

D.L. Hughley (1964-)
Spy School '08
Soul Plane '04
Chasing Papi '03
Scary Movie 3 '03
The Brothers '01
Inspector Gadget '99 (V)

Michael Hui
Robin-B-Hood '06
Chinese Box '97

Steve Huison (1963-)
Chaos & Cadavers '03
The Navigators '01
The Full Monty '96

Claude Hulbert (1900-64)
The Dummy Talks '43
Bulldog Jack '35

Jack Hulbert (1892-1978)
Bulldog Jack '35
Jack Ahoy '34

Tom Hulce (1953-)
Stranger Than Fiction '06
The Hunchback of Notre Dame '96 (V)
The Heidi Chronicles '95
Mary Shelley's Frankenstein '94
Fearless '93
Black Rainbow '91
The Inner Circle '91
Parenthood '89
Dominick & Eugene '88
Slamdance '87
Echo Park '86
The Rise & Rise of Daniel Rocket '86
Amadeus '84
Those Lips, Those Eyes '80
National Lampoon's Animal House '78
September 30, 1955 '77

Dianne Hull (1948-)
The New Adventures of Pippi Longstocking '88
Christmas Evil '80
The Fifth Floor '80
Haywire '80
The Onion Field '79
Aloha, Bobby and Rose '74
Girls on the Road '73

Henry Hull (1890-1977)
The Fool Killer '65
Master of the World '61
The Sheriff of Fractured Jaw '59
The Buccaneer '58
Return of Jesse James '50
Colorado Territory '49
El Paso '49
The Fountainhead '49
Great Dan Patch '49
The Great Gatsby '49
Rimfire '49
Portrait of Jennie '48
Objective, Burma! '45
Lifeboat '44
The Woman of the Town '44
High Sierra '41
My Son, My Son '40

Return of Frank James '40
Jesse James '39
Stanley and Livingstone '39
Boys Town '38
Three Comrades '38
Werewolf of London '35
Great Expectations '34
Midnight '34

Josephine Hull (1884-1957)
Harvey '50
Arsenic and Old Lace '44
After Tomorrow '32

Warren Hull (1903-74)
Bowery Blitzkrieg '41
The Spider Returns '41
Hidden Enemy '40
Yukon Flight '40
Star Reporter '39
Hawaii Calls '38
The Spider's Web '38

Anthony Hulme
Mysterious Mr. Nicholson '47
The Body Vanished '39

Lachy Hulme (1971-)
Macbeth '06
The Matrix Revolutions '03
The Crocodile Hunter: Collision Course '02

George Humbert (1880-1963)
Music in My Heart '40
The California Trail '33
Hearts of Humanity '32

Benita Hume (1906-67)
It Happened in New Orleans '36
Suzy '36
Tarzan Escapes '36
Power '34
Private Life of Don Juan '34
Gambling Ship '33
Lady of the Lake '28

Mark Humphrey
Vipers '08
Treacherous Beauties '94
Iron Eagle 2 '88

Renee Humphrey (1975-)
Hard Luck '01
Jay and Silent Bob Strike Back '01
Chicks, Man '99
The Sex Monster '99
Lover Girl '97
Cadillac Ranch '96
The Cure '95
Devil in a Blue Dress '95
French Kiss '95
Mallrats '95
Fun '94
Jailbait '93

Alf Humphreys
X2: X-Men United '03
The Stickup '01
My Bloody Valentine '81

Cecil Humphreys (1883-1947)
The Razor's Edge '46
Accused '36

William Humphreys (1874-1942)
The Unholy Three '25
Beau Brummel '24

Barry Humphries (1934-)
Mary and Max '09 (N)
Finding Nemo '03 (V)
Nicholas Nickleby '02
Spice World: The Movie '97
Welcome to Woop Woop '97
The Leading Man '96
Immortal Beloved '94
Les Patterson Saves the World '90
Shock Treatment '81
The Getting of Wisdom '77
Barry McKenzie Holds His Own '74

Bedazzled *'68*

Tessa Humphries

Paradise Road *'97*
Out of the Body *'88*
Cassandra *'87*

Robert Hundar

See Claudio Undari

Hui Siu Hung

Breaking News *'04*
Running out of Time *'99*

Sammo Hung (1952-)

Around the World in 80 Days *'04*
Zu Warriors *'01*
Mr. Nice Guy *'98*
Painted Skin *'93*
The Prisoner *'90*
Dragons Forever *'88*
Paper Marriage *'88*
Eastern Condors *'87*
The Millionaire's Express *'86*
Heart of Dragon *'85*
Project A *'83*
Zu: Warriors from the Magic Mountain *'83*
The Prodigal Son *'82*
Spooky Encounters *'80*

Charlie Hunnam (1980-)

Children of Men *'06*
Green Street Hooligans *'05*
Cold Mountain *'03*
Abandon *'02*
Nicholas Nickleby *'02*

Arthur Hunnicutt (1911-79)

Winterhawk *'76*
Harry and Tonto *'74*
The Bounty Man *'72*
Shoot Out *'71*
El Dorado *'67*
Apache Uprising *'66*
Born Reckless *'59*
The Tall T *'57*
The Kettles in the Ozarks *'56*
The French Line *'54*
Devil's Canyon *'53*
The Big Sky *'52*
The Lusty Men *'52*
She Couldn't Say No *'52*
Distant Drums *'51*
The Red Badge of Courage *'51*
Broken Arrow *'50*
Stars in My Crown *'50*
Ticket to Tomahawk *'50*
Border Incident *'49*
Great Dan Patch *'49*
Abroad with Two Yanks *'44*
Wildcat *'42*

Gayle Hunnicutt (1943-)

Turnaround *'87*
Dream Lover *'85*
Target *'85*
Flashpoint Africa *'84*
A Woman of Substance *'84*
Return of the Man from U.N.C.L.E. *'83*
The Martian Chronicles: Part 2 *'79*
The Martian Chronicles: Part 3 *'79*
Once in Paris... *'79*
Sell Out *'76*
Strange Shadows in an Empty Room *'76*
Shadow Man *'75*
Spiral Staircase *'75*
The Legend of Hell House *'73*
Scorpio *'73*
The Golden Bowl *'72*
Freelance *'71*
The Love Machine *'71*
Marlowe *'69*
The Wild Angels *'66*

Bonnie Hunt (1964-)

Toy Story 3 *'10 (V)*
Cars *'06 (V)*
I Want Someone to Eat Cheese With *'06*
Cheaper by the Dozen 2 *'05*
Loggerheads *'05*
Cheaper by the Dozen *'03*
Stolen Summer *'02*
Monsters, Inc. *'01 (V)*
Return to Me *'00*
The Green Mile *'99*
Random Hearts *'99*
A Bug's Life *'98 (V)*
Kissing a Fool *'98*
Subway Stories *'97*
Getting Away With Murder *'96*
Jerry Maguire *'96*
Jumanji *'95*
Now and Then *'95*
Only You *'94*
Beethoven's 2nd *'93*
Dave *'93*
Beethoven *'92*
Rain Man *'88*

Brad Hunt

Just Add Water *'07*
Cherish *'02*
Dream with the Fishes *'97*
Fire Down Below *'97*

Crystal Hunt

Sydney White *'07*
The Derby Stallion *'05*

David Hunt

The Dead Pool *'88*
Date with an Angel *'87*

Eleanor Hunt (-1981)

We're in the Legion Now *'37*
Yellow Cargo *'36*
Go-Get-'Em-Haines *'35*
Whoopee! *'30*

Gareth Hunt (1943-2007)

Parting Shots *'98*
A Chorus of Disapproval *'89*
It Couldn't Happen Here *'88*
Bloodbath at the House of Death *'85*
Funny Money *'82*
The World Is Full of Married Men *'80*

Helen Hunt (1963-)

Then She Found Me *'07*
Bobby *'06*
Empire Falls *'05*
A Good Woman *'04*
The Curse of the Jade Scorpion *'01*
Cast Away *'00*
Dr. T & the Women *'00*
Pay It Forward *'00*
What Women Want *'00*
As Good As It Gets *'97*
Twister *'96*
Kiss of Death *'94*
Bob Roberts *'92*
Into the Badlands *'92*
Mr. Saturday Night *'92*
Only You *'92*
Trancers 3: Deth Lives *'92*
Murder in New Hampshire: The Pamela Smart Story *'91*
The Waterdance *'91*
Dark River: A Father's Revenge *'90*
Trancers 2: The Return of Jack Deth *'90*
Next of Kin *'89*
Miles from Home *'88*
Stealing Home *'88*
Project X *'87*
Peggy Sue Got Married *'86*
Girls Just Want to Have Fun *'85*
Quarterback Princess *'85*
Code of Honor *'84*
Trancers *'84*
Bill: On His Own *'83*
Desperate Lives *'82*
The Best Little Girl in the World *'81*
Child Bride of Short Creek *'81*
Rollercoaster *'77*
The Spell *'77*
Death Scream *'75*
Pioneer Woman *'73*

Jimmy Hunt (1939-)

Invaders from Mars *'53*
Belles on Their Toes *'52*
The Capture *'50*
Rusty's Birthday *'49*
Pitfall *'48*
Song of Love *'47*

Linda Hunt (1945-)

Stranger Than Fiction *'06*
A Lot Like Love *'05*
Yours, Mine & Ours *'05*
Dragonfly *'02*
Eat Your Heart Out *'96*
The Relic *'96*
Pocahontas *'95 (V)*
Ready to Wear *'94*
Younger & Younger *'94*
Rain Without Thunder *'93*
Twenty Bucks *'93*
If Looks Could Kill *'91*
Kindergarten Cop *'90*
She-Devil *'89*
The Room *'87*
Waiting for the Moon *'87*
Eleni *'85*
Silverado *'85*
The Bostonians *'84*
Dune *'84*
The Year of Living Dangerously *'82*
Popeye *'80*

Marsha Hunt (1917-)

Johnny Got His Gun *'71*
The Plunderers *'60*
Bombers B-52 *'57*
Actors and Sin *'52*
Raw Deal *'48*
Carnegie Hall *'47*
Smash-Up: The Story of a Woman *'47*
The Valley of Decision *'45*
Blossoms in the Dust *'41*
Star Reporter *'39*
Helltown *'38*
Thunder Pass *'37*
Thunder Trail *'37*
Desert Gold *'36*

Marsha A. Hunt (1947-)

Howling 2: Your Sister Is a Werewolf *'85*
Britannia Hospital *'82*
The Sender *'82*
Dracula A.D. 1972 *'72*

Martita Hunt (1900-69)

The Unsinkable Molly Brown *'64*
The Wonderful World of the Brothers Grimm *'62*
The Brides of Dracula *'60*
Song Without End *'60*
Me and the Colonel *'58*
The Admirable Crichton *'57*
Anastasia *'56*
Three Men in a Boat *'56*
The King's Rhapsody *'55*
The Story of Robin Hood & His Merrie Men *'52*
Anna Karenina *'48*
Little Ballerina *'47*
Great Expectations *'46*
Nine Days a Queen *'36*
Sabotage *'36*
When Knights Were Bold *'36*
First a Girl *'35*

William Dennis Hunt

Peephole *'93*
Flesh Gordon 2: Flesh Gordon Meets the Cosmic Cheerleaders *'90*

Bill Hunter (1940-)

Finding Nemo *'03 (V)*
Kangaroo Jack *'02*
The Echo of Thunder *'98*
Moby Dick *'98*
Road to Nhill *'97*
Race the Sun *'96*
River Street *'95*
The Adventures of Priscilla, Queen of the Desert *'94*
The Custodian *'94*
Muriel's Wedding *'94*
The Last Days of Chez Nous *'92*
Strictly Ballroom *'92*
Fever *'88*
Rikky and Pete *'88*
The Hit *'85*
An Indecent Obsession *'85*
Rebel *'85*
Heatwave *'83*
Return of Captain Invincible *'83*
1915 *'82*
Hard Knocks *'80*
In Search of Anna *'79*
Newsfront *'78*

Dirk Hunter

Undead *'05*

Holly Hunter (1958-)

The Big White *'05*
Nine Lives *'05*
The Incredibles *'04 (V)*
Little Black Book *'04*
Levity *'03*
Thirteen *'03*
Moonlight Mile *'02*
Harlan County War *'00*
O Brother Where Art Thou? *'00*
Things You Can Tell Just by Looking at Her *'00*
Time Code *'00*
Jesus' Son *'99*
Living Out Loud *'98*
Woman Wanted *'98*
A Life Less Ordinary *'97*
Copycat *'95*
Crash *'95*
Home for the Holidays *'95*
The Firm *'93*
The Piano *'93*
The Positively True Adventures of the Alleged Texas Cheerleader-Murdering Mom *'93*
Crazy in Love *'92*
Murder on the Bayou *'91*
Once Around *'91*
Always *'89*
Animal Behavior *'89*
Miss Firecracker *'89*
Roe vs. Wade *'89*
End of the Line *'88*
Broadcast News *'87*
Raising Arizona *'87*
Blood Simple *'85*
Swing Shift *'84*
Urge to Kill *'84*
Svengali *'83*
The Burning *'82*

Ian Hunter

Order of the Black Eagle *'87*
Unmasking the Idol *'86*
Call It a Day *'37*
The Devil Is a Sissy *'36*

Ian Hunter (1900-75)

Doctor Blood's Coffin *'62*
Flame Over India *'60*
Pursuit of the Graf Spee *'57*
Bedelia *'46*
Andy Hardy's Private Secretary *'41*
Billy the Kid *'41*
Dr. Jekyll and Mr. Hyde *'41*
Smilin' Through *'41*
Ziegfeld Girl *'41*
Bitter Sweet *'40*
Broadway Melody of 1940 *'40*
The Long Voyage Home *'40*
Strange Cargo *'40*
Broadway Serenade *'39*
The Little Princess *'39*
Tarzan Finds a Son *'39*
The Tower of London *'39*
The Adventures of Robin Hood *'38*
The Sisters *'38*
That Certain Woman *'37*
A Midsummer Night's Dream *'35*
The Phantom Light *'35*
The Church Mouse *'34*
Easy Virtue *'27*
The Ring *'27*

Jeffrey Hunter (1925-69)

The Christmas Kid *'68*
Private Navy of Sgt. O'Farrell *'68*
A Witch Without a Broom *'68*
A Guide for the Married Man *'67*
Man From Galveston *'63*
The Longest Day *'62*
No Man Is an Island *'62*
The King of Kings *'61*
Hell to Eternity *'60*
Sergeant Rutledge *'60*
Last Hurrah *'58*
The Great Locomotive Chase *'56*
The Searchers *'56*
Seven Cities of Gold *'55*
Sailor of the King *'53*
Belles on Their Toes *'52*

Kaki Hunter (1955-)

Porky's Revenge *'85*
Just the Way You Are *'84*
Porky's 2: The Next Day *'83*
Porky's *'82*
Whose Life Is It Anyway? *'81*
Roadie *'80*
Willie & Phil *'80*

Kim Hunter (1922-2002)

Out of the Cold *'99*
Midnight in the Garden of Good and Evil *'97*
A Price above Rubies *'97*
Two Evil Eyes *'90*
Drop-Out Mother *'88*
The Kindred *'87*
Backstairs at the White House *'79*
Dark August *'76*
Bad Ronald *'74*
Born Innocent *'74*
Escape from the Planet of the Apes *'71*
Beneath the Planet of the Apes *'70*
Planet of the Apes *'68*
The Swimmer *'68*
Lamp at Midnight *'66*
Lilith *'64*
Requiem for a Heavyweight *'56*
A Streetcar Named Desire *'51*
Stairway to Heaven *'46*
The Seventh Victim *'43*
Tender Comrade *'43*

Rachel Hunter (1969-)

Strike *'07*
MacArthur Park *'01*
Rock Star *'01*
TripFall *'00*
Just a Little Harmless Sex *'99*
Two Shades of Blue *'98*

Ronald Hunter

Jakarta *'88*
Adventure of the Action Hunters *'87*
Rage of Angels *'83*
The Lazarus Syndrome *'79*

Ross Hunter (1916-96)

Reform School Girl *'57*
Louisiana Hayride *'44*

Tab Hunter (1931-)

Cameron's Closet *'89*
Out of the Dark *'88*
Grotesque *'87*
Lust in the Dust *'85*
Grease 2 *'82*
Pandemonium *'82*
Polyester *'81*
The Kid from Left Field *'79*
The Big Push *'75*
The Arousers *'70*
Hostile Guns *'67*
The Loved One *'65*
Ride the Wild Surf *'64*
Operation Bikini *'63*
They Came to Cordura *'59*
Damn Yankees *'58*
Gunman's Walk *'58*
Lafayette Escadrille *'58*
The Burning Hills *'56*
Battle Cry *'55*
Sea Chase *'55*
Island of Desire *'52*

Thomas Hunter (1932-)

Escape from the KGB *'87*
Battle of the Commandos *'71*
The Vampire Happening *'71*
Web of Deception *'71*

Sam Huntington (1982-)

Fanboys *'09*
Superman Returns *'06*
River's End *'05*
Freshman Orientation *'04*
In Enemy Hands *'04*
Sleepover *'04*
Not Another Teen Movie *'01*
Detroit Rock City *'99*
Jungle 2 Jungle *'96*

G.P. (Tim) Huntley, Jr. (1904-71)

Journey for Margaret *'42*
They Died with Their Boots On *'41*
Beau Geste *'39*
Mr. Takes a Vacation *'39*
The Charge of the Light Brigade *'36*

Raymond Huntley (1904-90)

Hot Millions *'68*
The Mummy *'59*
Our Man in Havana *'59*
Room at the Top *'59*
The Prisoner *'55*
I'll Never Forget You *'51*
The Long Dark Hall *'51*
I See a Dark Stranger *'46*
Immortal Battalion *'44*
Night Train to Munich *'40*

Isabelle Huppert (1955-)

Comedy of Power *'06*
Private Property *'06*
Gabrielle *'05*
I Heart Huckabees *'04*
Time of the Wolf *'03*
8 Women *'02*
La Vie Promise *'02*
The Piano Teacher *'01*
Comedy of Innocence *'00*
Les Destinees *'00*
Merci pour le Chocolat *'00*
La Separation *'98*
The Swindle *'97*
Elective Affinities *'96*
La Ceremonie *'95*
Amateur *'94*
Love After Love *'94*
The Separation *'94*
Madame Bovary *'91*
La Vengeance d'une Femme *'89*
The Possessed *'88*
The Story of Women *'88*
The Bedroom Window *'87*
Cactus *'86*
Sincerely Charlotte *'86*
My Best Friend's Girl *'84*
Entre-Nous *'83*
La Truite *'83*
Passion *'82*
Coup de Torchon *'81*
Heaven's Gate *'81*
Loulou *'80*
Every Man for Himself *'79*
Violette *'78*
The Lacemaker *'77*
The Judge and the Assassin *'75*
Rosebud *'75*
Going Places *'74*

Paige Hurd (1992-)

Beauty Shop *'05*
Cradle 2 the Grave *'03*

Rachel Hurd-Wood (1990-)

Perfume: The Story of a Murderer *'06*
An American Haunting *'05*
Peter Pan *'03*

Elizabeth Hurley (1965-)

Dawg *'02*
Serving Sara *'02*

Double Whammy '01
Bedazzled '00
The Weight of Water '00
Austin Powers 2: The Spy Who Shagged Me '99
EDtv '99
My Favorite Martian '98
Permanent Midnight '98
Austin Powers: International Man of Mystery '97
Dangerous Ground '96
Samson and Delilah '96
Shameless '94
Sharpe's Enemy '94
Nightscare '93
Passenger 57 '92
Kill Cruise '90
Christabel '89
Rowing with the Wind '88

Richard Hurndall

Running Blind '78
I, Monster '71

Brandon Hurst (1866-1947)

Stanley and Livingstone '39
House of Mystery '34
The Lost Patrol '34
The Midnight Lady '32
Murders in the Rue Morgue '32
The White Zombie '32
Murder at Midnight '31
The Man Who Laughs '27
Made for Love '26
The Thief of Baghdad '24
The Hunchback of Notre Dame '23
Dr. Jekyll and Mr. Hyde '20

David Hurst (1926-)

Kelly's Heroes '70
Tony Draws a Horse '51

Michael Hurst (1957-)

The Tattooist '07
Hercules the Legendary Journeys, Vol. 1: And the Amazon Women '94
Hercules the Legendary Journeys, Vol. 2: The Lost Kingdom '94
Hercules the Legendary Journeys, Vol. 3: The Circle of Fire '94
Hercules the Legendary Journeys, Vol. 4: In the Underworld '94
Desperate Remedies '93
Death Warmed Up '85

Paul Hurst (1888-1953)

Missourians '50
The Vanishing Westerner '50
Outcasts of the Trail '49
Pioneer Marshal '49
Who Killed Doc Robbin? '48
Under Colorado Skies '47
Treasure of Fear '45
Girl Rush '44
Caught in the Draft '41
Bad Lands '39
Gone with the Wind '39
It Could Happen to You '39
Alexander's Ragtime Band '38
Prison Break '38
Legion of Missing Men '37
Hold Your Man '33
The Sphinx '33
The Big Stampede '32
My Pal, the King '32
Panama Flo '32
13th Guest '32
Mountain Justice '30
Paradise Island '30
The Red Raiders '27
Battling Bunyon '24

Ryan Hurst (1976-)

Chasing the Green '09
The Ladykillers '04
Lone Star State of Mind '02
Taken '02
We Were Soldiers '02
Remember the Titans '00

Veronica Hurst (1931-)

Second Best Secret Agent in the Whole Wide World '65
Peeping Tom '60
Angels One Five '54
The Gilded Cage '54

John Hurt (1940-)

An Englishman in New York '09
The Limits of Control '09
New York, I Love You '09
Hellboy II: The Golden Army '08
Indiana Jones and the Kingdom of the Crystal Skull '08
Outlander '08
Recount '08
Perfume: The Story of a Murderer '06 (N)
V for Vendetta '06
Manderlay '05
The Proposition '05
Shooting Dogs '05
The Skeleton Key '05
Valiant '05 (V)
Hellboy '04
Dogville '03 (N)
Owning Mahowny '03
Bait '02
Captain Corelli's Mandolin '01
Harry Potter and the Sorcerer's Stone '01
Miranda '01
Lost Souls '00
New Blood '99
All the Little Animals '98
Brute '97
The Climb '97
Contact '97
Love and Death on Long Island '97
Dead Man '95
Rob Roy '95
Wild Bill '95
Even Cowgirls Get the Blues '94
Second Best '94
Thumbelina '94 (V)
Monolith '93
Shades of Fear '93
King Ralph '91
The Field '90
Frankenstein Unbound '90
Little Sweetheart '90
Scandal '89
Aria '88
The Bengali Night '88
White Mischief '88
Spaceballs '87
Vincent: The Life and Death of Vincent van Gogh '87 (V)
From the Hip '86
Jake Speed '86
After Darkness '85
The Black Cauldron '85 (V)
The Hit '85
Champions '84
1984 '84
Success Is the Best Revenge '84
The Osterman Weekend '83
Partners '82
The Plague Dogs '82 (V)
Disappearance '81
Heaven's Gate '81
History of the World: Part 1 '81
Night Crossing '81
The Elephant Man '80
Alien '79
The Lord of the Rings '78 (V)
Midnight Express '78
The Shout '78
Watership Down '78 (V)
East of Elephant Rock '76
The Ghoul '75
The Naked Civil Servant '75
Pied Piper '72
Cry of the Penguins '71
10 Rillington Place '71
A Man for All Seasons '66

Mary Beth Hurt (1948-)

Untraceable '08
The Walker '07
The Dead Girl '06
Lady in the Water '06
Perception '06
The Exorcism of Emily Rose '05
Red Dragon '02
Family Man '00
Bringing Out the Dead '99
Affliction '97
From the Journals of Jean Seberg '95
The Age of Innocence '93
My Boyfriend's Back '93
Six Degrees of Separation '93
Light Sleeper '92
Defenseless '91
Parents '89
Slaves of New York '89
Baby Girl Scott '87
Compromising Positions '85
D.A.R.Y.L. '85
The World According to Garp '82
A Change of Seasons '80
Chilly Scenes of Winter '79
Interiors '78

William Hurt (1950-)

Robin Hood '10
Endgame '09
The Incredible Hulk '08
Vantage Point '08
The Yellow Handkerchief '08
Into the Wild '07
Mr. Brooks '07
Noise '07
Beautiful Ohio '06
The Good Shepherd '06
A History of Violence '05
The King '05
Syriana '05
The Blue Butterfly '04
The Village '04
Changing Lanes '02
Master Spy: The Robert Hanssen Story '02
Tuck Everlasting '02
A. I.: Artificial Intelligence '01
The Contaminated Man '01
The Flamingo Rising '01
Rare Birds '01
Varian's War '01
Dune '00
The Miracle Maker: The Story of Jesus '00 (V)
The Big Brass Ring '99
The 4th Floor '99
Silent Witness '99
The Simian Line '99
Sunshine '99
Lost in Space '98
One True Thing '98
Dark City '97
Loved '97
The Proposition '97
Jane Eyre '96
Michael '96
A Couch in New York '95
Smoke '95
Second Best '94
Trial by Jury '94
Mr. Wonderful '93
The Plague '92
The Doctor '91
Until the End of the World '91
Alice '90
I Love You to Death '90
The Accidental Tourist '88
A Time of Destiny '88
Broadcast News '87
Children of a Lesser God '86
Kiss of the Spider Woman '85
The Big Chill '83
Gorky Park '83
Body Heat '81
Eyewitness '81
Altered States '80

Ferlin Husky (1927-)

Hillbillies in a Haunted House '67
Las Vegas Hillbillys '66

Toby Huss (1966-)

World's Greatest Dad '09
Rescue Dawn '06
The Country Bears '02 (V)
Human Nature '02
Beavis and Butt-Head Do America '96 (V)
Dear God '96
Dogs: The Rise and Fall of an All-Girl Bookie Joint '96
Down Periscope '96

Olivia Hussey (1951-)

Three Priests '08
Tortilla Heaven '07
Seven Days of Grace '06
Headspace '02
Bloody Proof '99
Shame, Shame, Shame '98
Ice Cream Man '95
Quest of the Delta Knights '93
Save Me '93
Undeclared War '91
The Jeweller's Shop '90
Psycho 4: The Beginning '90
Stephen King's It '90
Distortions '87
Ivanhoe '82
Virus '82
Escape 2000 '81
The Man with Bogart's Face '80
The Cat and the Canary '79
The Bastard '78
Death on the Nile '78
Black Christmas '75
Ricco '74
H-Bomb '71
Romeo and Juliet '68

Ruth Hussey (1911-2005)

The Facts of Life '60
Stars and Stripes Forever '52
Hill Number One '51
Mr. Music '50
The Great Gatsby '49
The Uninvited '44
Marine Raiders '43
Tender Comrade '43
H.M. Pulham Esquire '41
Northwest Passage '40
The Philadelphia Story '40
Susan and God '40
Another Thin Man '39
The Women '39
Madame X '37

Francis Huster (1947-)

The Dinner Game '98
I Married a Dead Man '82
Another Man, Another Chance '77
Lumiere '76

Anjelica Huston (1951-)

When in Rome '09
Choke '08
The Kreutzer Sonata '08
The Darjeeling Limited '07
Martian Child '07
Art School Confidential '06
The Hades Factor '06
Material Girls '06
Seraphim Falls '06
These Foolish Things '06
The Life Aquatic with Steve Zissou '04
Daddy Day Care '03
Kaena: The Prophecy '03 (V)
Blood Work '02
The Man from Elysian Fields '01
Mists of Avalon '01
The Royal Tenenbaums '01
The Golden Bowl '00
Agnes Browne '99
Ever After: A Cinderella Story '98
Phoenix '98
Buffalo 66 '97
Buffalo Girls '95
The Crossing Guard '94
The Perez Family '94
Addams Family Values '93
And the Band Played On '93
Family Pictures '93
Manhattan Murder Mystery '93
The Player '92
The Addams Family '91
The Grifters '90
The Witches '90
Crimes & Misdemeanors '89
Enemies, a Love Story '89
Lonesome Dove '89
A Handful of Dust '88
Mr. North '88
The Dead '87
Gardens of Stone '87
Prizzi's Honor '85
The Cowboy & the Ballerina '84
Ice Pirates '84
This Is Spinal Tap '84
Beauty and the Beast '83.
Comic Book Kids '82
The Postman Always Rings Twice '81
The Last Tycoon '76
Hamlet '69

Danny Huston (1962-)

Clash of the Titans '10
Edge of Darkness '10
Robin Hood '10
X-Men Origins: Wolverine '09
How to Lose Friends & Alienate People '08
John Adams '08
The Kreutzer Sonata '08
I Really Hate My Job '07
The Number 23 '07
30 Days of Night '07
Alpha Male '06
Children of Men '06
The Hades Factor '06
Marie Antoinette '06
The Constant Gardener '05
The Proposition '05
The Aviator '04
Birth '04
Silver City '04
21 Grams '03
Time Code '00
Leo Tolstoy's Anna Karenina '96

Jack Huston (1982-)

Shrink '09
Outlander '08
Miss Austen Regrets '07
Shrooms '07

John Huston (1906-87)

Mr. Corbett's Ghost '90
The Black Cauldron '85 (N)
Lovesick '83
A Minor Miracle '83
Cannery Row '82 (N)
Fatal Attraction '80
The Return of the King '80 (V)
The Visitor '80
Jaguar Lives '79
Winter Kills '79
Wise Blood '79
Battleforce '78
The Hobbit '78 (V)
The Word '78
Angela '77
Tentacles '77
Breakout '75
The Wind and the Lion '75
Chinatown '74
Battle for the Planet of the Apes '73
Man in the Wilderness '71
Ride to Glory '71
Myra Breckinridge '70
Candy '68
Casino Royale '67
The Bible '66 (N)
The Cardinal '63

Virginia Huston (1925-81)

Flight to Mars '52
Night Stage to Galveston '52
Sudden Fear '52
Tarzan's Peril '51
The Doolins of Oklahoma '49
Flamingo Road '49
Out of the Past '47
Nocturne '46

Walter Huston (1884-1950)

December 7th: The Movie '91
The Furies '50
Summer Holiday '48
Treasure of the Sierra Madre '48
Dragonwyck '46
Duel in the Sun '46
And Then There Were None '45
Dragon Seed '44
Edge of Darkness '43
Mission to Moscow '43
The North Star '43
The Outlaw '43
In This Our Life '42
The Shanghai Gesture '42
Yankee Doodle Dandy '42
The Devil & Daniel Webster '41
The Maltese Falcon '41
Of Human Hearts '38
Dodsworth '36
Rhodes '36
Transatlantic Tunnel '35
Ann Vickers '33
Gabriel Over the White House '33
The Prizefighter and the Lady '33
American Madness '32
The Beast of the City '32
Rain '32
Criminal Code '31
Abraham Lincoln '30
The Virginian '29

Michael Hutchence (1960-97)

Frankenstein Unbound '90
Dogs in Space '87

Josh Hutcherson (1992-)

The Kids Are All Right '10
Cirque du Freak: The Vampire's Assistant '09
Fragments '08
Journey to the Center of the Earth '08
Bridge to Terabithia '07
Firehouse Dog '07
RV '06
Kicking & Screaming '05
Little Manhattan '05
Zathura '05
Howl's Moving Castle '04 (V)
Miracle Dogs '03

David Hutcheson (1905-76)

The Abominable Dr. Phibes '71
No Highway in the Sky '51
Murder in the Footlights '46

Geoffrey Hutchings (1939-)

It's All About Love '03
Heart of Darkness '93
Wish You Were Here '87

Eleanor Hutchins

Milk and Honey '03
Margarita Happy Hour '01

Will Hutchins (1932-)

Maverick '94
Slumber Party '57 '76
Magnum Force '73
Clambake '67
The Shooting '66
Spinout '66
Merrill's Marauders '62
Lafayette Escadrille '58
No Time for Sergeants '58

Fiona Hutchinson

Rage '95
American Gothic '88

Josephine Hutchinson (1904-98)

The Adventures of Huckleberry Finn '60
North by Northwest '59
Love Is Better Than Ever '52

Cass Timberlane '47
The Tender Years '47
Somewhere in the Night '46
My Son, My Son '40
Son of Frankenstein '39
The Story of Louis Pasteur '36
Happiness Ahead '34

Doug Hutchison (1960-)
Punisher: War Zone '08
Moola '07
No Good Deed '02
The Salton Sea '02
I Am Sam '01
Bait '00
The Green Mile '99

Ken Hutchison (1948-)
Ladyhawke '85
Deadly Strangers '82

Candy Hutson
The Land Before Time 4: Journey Through the Mists '96 (V)
The Land Before Time 3: The Time of the Great Giving '95 (V)
The Land Before Time 2: The Great Valley Adventure '94 (V)
Hider in the House '90

William Hutt (1920-2007)
The Trojan Horse '08
The Statement '03
Long Day's Journey Into Night '96
The Fixer '68

Betty Hutton (1921-2007)
The Greatest Show on Earth '52
Sailor Beware '52
Annie Get Your Gun '50
Let's Dance '50
The Perils of Pauline '47
Here Come the Waves '45
The Stork Club '45
Miracle of Morgan's Creek '44
Star Spangled Rhythm '42

Brian Hutton
Last Train from Gun Hill '59
Carnival Rock '57

Jim Hutton (1933-79)
Psychic Killer '75
Nightmare at 43 Hillcrest '74
Don't Be Afraid of the Dark '73
They Call It Murder '71
Bachelor in Paradise '69
The Green Berets '68
Hellfighters '68
Who's Minding the Mint? '67
Walk, Don't Run '66
The Hallelujah Trail '65
Major Dundee '65
Never Too Late '65
Sunday in New York '63
The Horizontal Lieutenant '62
Period of Adjustment '62
The Honeymoon Machine '61
Where the Boys Are '60

Lauren Hutton (1943-)
The Joneses '10
Caracara '00
Just a Little Harmless Sex '99
54 '98
A Rat's Tale '98
My Father the Hero '93
Guilty as Charged '92
Missing Pieces '91
Fear '90
Millions '90
Forbidden Sun '89
Bulldance '88
Scandalous '88
Malone '87
Timestalkers '87
Monte Carlo '86
Trade Secrets '86
From Here to Maternity '85
Once Bitten '85
Scandal Sheet '85
Lassiter '84
The Cradle Will Fall '83
The Snow Queen '83
Starflight One '83
Paternity '81
Zorro, the Gay Blade '81
American Gigolo '79
A Wedding '78
Viva Knievel '77
Welcome to L.A. '77
Gator '76
Nashville '75
The Gambler '74
Paper Lion '68

Marion Hutton (1919-87)
Love Happy '50
In Society '44

Pascale Hutton
A Simple Curve '05
Ginger Snaps: Unleashed '04

Robert Hutton (1920-94)
Cry of the Banshee '70
They Came from Beyond Space '67
Vulture '67
The Slime People '63
Cinderfella '60
Invisible Invaders '59
Naked Youth '59
Outcasts of the City '58
Showdown at Boot Hill '58
Big Bluff '55
Slaughter Trail '51
The Steel Helmet '51
Hollywood Canteen '44
Destination Tokyo '43

Timothy Hutton (1960-)
The Ghost Writer '10
Brief Interviews With Hideous Men '09
The Killing Room '09
The Alphabet Killer '08
Lymelife '08
The Last Mimzy '07
When a Man Falls in the Forest '07
The Good Shepherd '06
Heavens Fall '06
The Kovak Box '06
Last Holiday '06
Stephanie Daley '06
Kinsey '04
Secret Window '04
Sunshine State '02
Deliberate Intent '01
The Doorbell Rang: A Nero Wolfe Mystery '01
Winds of Terror '01
Deterrence '00
The Golden Spiders: A Nero Wolfe Mystery '00
Just One Night '00
The General's Daughter '99
Aldrich Ames: Traitor Within '98
Money Kings '98
Beautiful Girls '96
City of Industry '96
Mr. & Mrs. Loving '96
Playing God '96
The Substance of Fire '96
French Kiss '95
The Last Word '95
The Temp '93
The Dark Half '91
Strangers '91
Q & A '90
Torrents of Spring '90
Everybody's All American '88
A Time of Destiny '88
Made in Heaven '87
The Falcon and the Snowman '85
Turk 182! '85
Iceman '84
Daniel '83
A Long Way Home '81
Taps '81
Father Figure '80
Oldest Living Graduate '80
Ordinary People '80
And Baby Makes Six '79
Friendly Fire '79
Young Love, First Love '79

Eugene Hutz
Filth and Wisdom '08
Everything is Illuminated '05

Brody Hutzler
Beach Kings '08
Totally Blonde '01

Richard Huw
A Certain Justice '99
The Buccaneers '95
Getting It Right '89
The Four Minute Mile '88

Jeong-min Hwang (1969-)
Chain Gang Girls '08
Black House '07
Save the Green Planet '03

Sin-Hye Hwang
301/302 '95
301, 302 '94

Leila Hyams (1905-77)
Yellow Dust '36
Ruggles of Red Gap '35
Freaks '32
Island of Lost Souls '32
Red Headed Woman '32
The Phantom of Paris '31
The Big House '30
Spite Marriage '29

Pam Hyatt
He Sees You When You're Sleeping '02
Holiday Affair '96

Jacquelyn Hyde (1930-92)
House of Terror '72
Take the Money and Run '69

Jonathan Hyde (1947-)
The Contract '07
Attila '01
The Prince and the Pauper '01
Princess of Thieves '01
Joan of Arc '99
The Mummy '99
Titanic '97
Anaconda '96
Jumanji '95
Richie Rich '94
Fellow Traveler '89
An Indecent Obsession '85

Alex Hyde-White (1958-)
Pursuit of Happiness '01
Mars '96
Unknown Origin '95
Wyatt Earp: Return to Tombstone '94
Silent Victim '92
Ironclads '90
Pretty Woman '90
Indiana Jones and the Last Crusade '89
The Phantom of the Opera '89
Time Trackers '88
Echoes in the Darkness '87
Biggles '85
The First Olympics: Athens 1896 '84
The Seekers '79

Wilfrid Hyde-White (1903-91)
Heartburn '86
Fanny Hill '83
The Toy '82
Tarzan, the Ape Man '81
Damien: The Leper Priest '80
In God We Trust '80
Oh, God! Book 2 '80
Scout's Honor '80
The Cat and the Canary '79
The Rebels '79
King Solomon's Treasure '76
Brand New Life '72
Skullduggery '70
The Magic Christian '69
My Fair Lady '64
In Search of the Castaways '62
On the Fiddle '61
Flame Over India '60
Two-Way Stretch '60
Carry On Nurse '59
Teenage Bad Girl '59
Truth about Women '58
Up the Creek '58
Tarzan and the Lost Safari '57
The Vicious Circle '57
John and Julie '55
Quentin Durward '55
Tarzan's Hidden Jungle '55
Betrayed '54
The Browning Version '51
The Golden Salamander '51
Angel with the Trumpet '50
Last Holiday '50
Mister Drake's Duck '50
The Third Man '49
Ghosts of Berkeley Square '47
The Man Who Knew Too Much '34

Martha Hyer (1924-)
The Day of the Wolves '71
Catch as Catch Can '68
The House of 1000 Dolls '67
The Chase '66
Night of the Grizzly '66
Picture Mommy Dead '66
Sons of Katie Elder '65
Bikini Beach '64
The Carpetbaggers '64
First Men in the Moon '64
Ice Palace '60
The Best of Everything '59
Mistress of the World '59
Houseboat '58
Some Came Running '58
Battle Hymn '57
My Man Godfrey '57
Paris Holiday '57
The Delicate Delinquent '56
Francis in the Navy '55
Cry Vengeance '54
Lucky Me '54
Sabrina '54
Scarlet Spear '54
Abbott and Costello Go to Mars '53
Geisha Girl '52
The Clay Pigeon '49

Diana Hyland (1936-77)
The Boy in the Plastic Bubble '76
Hercules and the Princess of Troy '65
One Man's Way '63

Frances Hyland (1927-2004)
When the Dark Man Calls '95
Broken Lullaby '94
The Lotus Eaters '93
Happy Birthday to Me '81
Home to Stay '79

Scott Hylands (1943-)
Freezer Burn: The Invasion of Laxdale '08
Ignition '01
36 Hours to Die '99
The Halfback of Notre Dame '96
Titanic '96
Decoy '95
Ordeal in the Arctic '93
Tales of the Klondike: In a Far Country '87
Coming Out Alive '84
Savage Hunger '84
The Winds of Kitty Hawk '78
The Boys in Company C '77
Earthquake '74
Slipstream '73
Earth II '71
Fools '70
Daddy's Gone A-Hunting '69

Jane Hylton (1927-79)
Circus of Horrors '60
The Manster '59
Dear Murderer '47
It Always Rains on Sunday '47
The Upturned Glass '47

Richard Hylton (1920-62)
Fixed Bayonets! '51
The Halls of Montezuma '50
Lost Boundaries '49

Phyllis Hyman (1949-95)
The Kill Reflex '89
School Daze '88

Warren Hymer (1906-48)
Hitler: Dead or Alive '43
Baby Face Morgan '42
Lure of the Islands '42
Meet the Mob '42
Mr. Wise Guy '42
Phantom Killer '42
Birth of the Blues '41
Mr. Moto in Danger Island '39
Joy of Living '38
You and Me '38
Sea Racketeers '37
You Only Live Once '37
Rhythm on the Range '36
San Francisco '36
Tango '36
Confidential '35
Hong Kong Nights '35
Show Them No Mercy '35
In the Money '34
Badmen of Nevada '33
Midnight Mary '33
The Mysterious Rider '33
20,000 Years in Sing Sing '33
One Way Passage '32
The Lone Star Ranger '30
Up the River '30

Joyce Hyser (1956-)
Wedding Band '89
Just One of the Guys '85
The Hollywood Knights '80

Steve Hytner
Bachelor Party Vegas '05
Eurotrip '04
Air Rage '01
Forces of Nature '99
Love Stinks '99
The Prophecy 3: The Ascent '99
The Prophecy 2: Ashtown '97
Down, Out and Dangerous '95
The Shadow '94
In the Line of Fire '93

Stanislav Ianevski (1985-)
Hostel: Part 2 '07
Harry Potter and the Goblet of Fire '05

Mirta Ibarra
Mararia '98
Guantanamera '95
Strawberry and Chocolate '93
Up to a Certain Point '83

Masato Ibu
Azumi '03
Empire of the Sun '87

Ice Cube (1969-)
The Lottery Ticket '10
Janky Promoters '09
First Sunday '08
The Longshots '08
Are We Done Yet? '07
Are We There Yet? '05
XXX: State of the Union '05
Barbershop 2: Back in Business '04
Torque '04
All About the Benjamins '02
Barbershop '02
Friday After Next '02
John Carpenter's Ghosts of Mars '01
Next Friday '00
Thicker than Water '99
Three Kings '99
I Got the Hook-Up '98
The Players Club '98
Anaconda '96
Dangerous Ground '96
Friday '95
The Glass Shield '95
Higher Learning '94
Trespass '92
Boyz N the Hood '91

Ice-T (1958-)
Tracks '05
On the Edge '02
Air Rage '01
Black Horizon '01
Guardian '01
Kept '01
'R Xmas '01
Rhapsody '01
3000 Miles to Graceland '01
Ticker '01
Ablaze '00
Gangland '00
The Guardian '00
Luck of the Draw '00
Agent of Death '99
Corrupt '99
Final Voyage '99
Jacob Two Two Meets the Hooded Fang '99
Judgment Day '99
Leprechaun 5: In the Hood '99
Sonic Impact '99
Stealth Fighter '99
Urban Menace '99
The Wrecking Crew '99
Crazy Six '98
Body Count '97
The Deli '97
Mean Guns '97
Johnny Mnemonic '95
Surviving the Game '94
Tank Girl '94
Who's the Man? '93
Trespass '92
New Jack City '91
Ricochet '91

Etsuko Ichihara (1936-)
The Eel '96
Black Rain '88
Snow Country '57

Hayato Ichihara
Onmyoji 2 '03
All About Lily Chou-Chou '01
Ju-On 2 '00

Raizo Ichikawa (1931-69)
Shinobi no Mono 2: Vengeance '63
Sleepy Eyes of Death: The Chinese Jade '63
Shinobi no Mono '62
Enjo '58
Shin Heike Monogatari '55

Utaemon Ichikawa (1904-99)
47 Ronin, Part 1 '42
47 Ronin, Part 2 '42

Eric Idle (1943-)
Shrek Forever After '10 (V)
Delgo '08 (V)
Shrek the Third '07 (V)
Ella Enchanted '04 (N)
Hollywood Homicide '03
National Lampoon's Christmas Vacation 2: Cousin Eddie's Big Island Adventure '03
Pinocchio '02 (V)
102 Dalmatians '00 (V)
Dudley Do-Right '99
South Park: Bigger, Longer and Uncut '99 (V)
Quest for Camelot '98 (V)
The Secret of NIMH 2 '98 (V)
An Alan Smithee Film: Burn, Hollywood, Burn '97

Mr. Toad's Wild Ride *'96*
Casper *'95*
Splitting Heirs *'93*
Mom and Dad Save the World *'92*
Missing Pieces *'91*
Nuns on the Run *'90*
Too Much Sun *'90*
The Adventures of Baron Munchausen *'89*
Around the World in 80 Days *'89*
Transformers: The Movie *'86 (V)*
National Lampoon's European Vacation *'85*
The Pied Piper of Hamelin *'84*
Monty Python's The Meaning of Life *'83*
Yellowbeard *'83*
Secret Policeman's Private Parts *'81*
Monty Python's Life of Brian *'79*
All You Need Is Cash *'78*
Jabberwocky *'77*
Monty Python and the Holy Grail *'75*
And Now for Something Completely Different *'72*

Cinnamon Idles (1975-)
Sixteen Candles *'84*
Kidco *'83*

Billy Idol (1955-)
Heavy Metal 2000 *'00 (V)*
The Wedding Singer *'97*
Trigger Happy *'96*
The Doors *'91*

Rhys Ifans (1968-)
Greenberg *'10*
Nanny McPhee 2 *'10*
The Informers *'09*
Pirate Radio *'09*
Elizabeth: The Golden Age *'07*
Hannibal Rising *'07*
Four Last Songs *'06*
Garfield: A Tail of Two Kitties *'06 (V)*
Enduring Love *'04*
Vanity Fair *'04*
Danny Deckchair *'03*
Human Nature *'02*
Once Upon a Time in the Midlands *'02*
Formula 51 *'01*
Hotel *'01*
The Shipping News *'01*
Kevin & Perry Go Large *'00*
Little Nicky *'00*
Love, Honour & Obey *'00*
Rancid Aluminium *'00*
The Replacements *'00*
Heart *'99*
Janice Beard *'99*
Notting Hill *'99*
Dancing at Lughnasa *'98*
Twin Town *'97*

Hisashi Igawa (1936-)
Hiroshima *'95*
Rhapsody in August *'91*
Akira Kurosawa's Dreams *'90*
Boiling Point *'90*
Ran *'85*
Goyokin *'69*
Harakiri *'62*

Togo Igawa (1946-)
The Last Samurai *'03*
Incognito *'97*

James Iglehart
Death Force *'78*
Fighting Mad *'77*
Savage! *'73*
Angels Hard As They Come *'71*
Beyond the Valley of the Dolls *'70*

Tsuyoski Ihara
Letters from Iwo Jima *'06*
Retribution *'06*

Steve Ihnat (1934-72)
Hunter *'73*
Countdown *'68*
Hour of the Gun *'67*

Choko Iida (1897-1972)
Drunken Angel *'48*
Record of a Tenement Gentleman *'47*

Diasuke Iijima
Flower & Snake *'04*
Merry Christmas, Mr. Lawrence *'83*

Ryo Ikebe (1918-)
Gorath *'62*
Snow Country *'57*

Peter Illing (1899-1966)
The Electronic Monster *'57*
Bhowani Junction *'56*
Eureka Stockade *'49*
Against the Wind *'48*

Igor Ilyinsky (1904-87)
A Kiss for Mary Pickford *'27*
The Cigarette Girl of Mosselprom *'24*

Eriko Imai
Onmyoji 2 *'03*
Onmyoji *'01*
Andromedia *'00*

Kenji Imai
Sympathy for the Underdog *'71*
Legends of the Poisonous Seductress 2: Quick Draw Okatsu *'69*

Iman (1955-)
The Deli *'97*
Exit to Eden *'94*
Heart of Darkness *'93*
The Linguini Incident *'92*
House Party 2: The Pajama Jam *'91*
L.A. Story *'91*
Lies of the Twins *'91*
Star Trek 6: The Undiscovered Country *'91*
No Way Out *'87*
Surrender *'87*
Out of Africa *'85*
The Human Factor *'79*

Roger Imhof (1875-1958)
Sweetheart of the Navy *'37*
Red Lights Ahead *'36*
San Francisco *'36*
Life Begins at Forty *'35*
Riff Raff *'35*
Steamboat Round the Bend *'35*
David Harum *'34*
Hoopla *'33*

Gary Imhoff (1952-)
Thumbelina *'94 (V)*
The Seniors *'78*

Michael Imperioli (1966-)
The Lovely Bones *'09*
For One More Day *'07*
My Baby's Daddy *'04*
Shark Tale *'04 (V)*
Love in the Time of Money *'02*
Hamlet *'01*
Disappearing Acts *'00*
Witness to the Mob *'98*
Office Killer *'97*
A River Made to Drown In *'97*
Girl 6 *'96*
I Shot Andy Warhol *'96*
Last Man Standing *'96*
Sweet Nothing *'96*
The Addiction *'95*
Bad Boys *'95*
The Basketball Diaries *'95*
Postcards from America *'95*
Household Saints *'93*
Jungle Fever *'91*
Goodfellas *'90*

Celia Imrie (1952-)
Imagine Me & You *'06*
Nanny McPhee *'06*
Wah-Wah *'05*
Calendar Girls *'03*
Doctor Zhivago *'03*
Daniel Deronda *'02*
The Gathering Storm *'02*
Lucky Break *'01*
Station Jim *'01*
A Christmas Carol *'99*
Hilary and Jackie *'98*
The Borrowers *'97*
Into the Blue *'97*
A Midwinter's Tale *'95*
Mary Shelley's Frankenstein *'94*
The Return of the Native *'94*
A Dark Adapted Eye *'93*

Yoshio Inaba (1921-98)
Harakiri *'62*
Seven Samurai *'54*

Francesca Inaudi (1977-)
Don't Tell *'05*
After Midnight *'04*

Ada Ince (1913-)
Rainbow's End *'35*
The Fighting Rookie *'34*
Frontier Days *'34*

John Ince (1878-1947)
Code of the Outlaw *'42*

Ralph Ince (1887-1937)
Law of the Sea *'32*
Lost Squadron *'32*
Men of America *'32*
State's Attorney *'31*

Annabella Incontrera (1943-)
The Slasher *'72*
Return of Sabata *'71*
Challenge of McKenna *'70*
Double Face *'70*
The Assassination Bureau *'69*

Luis Induni (1920-79)
Rape *'76*
Night of the Howling Beast *'75*
Dr. Jekyll and the Wolfman *'71*

Frieda Inescort (1901-76)
A Place in the Sun *'51*
The Underworld Story *'50*
The Judge Steps Out *'49*
The Amazing Mrs. Holiday *'43*
Return of the Vampire *'43*
Shadows on the Stairs *'41*
Sunny *'41*
The Letter *'40*
Pride and Prejudice *'40*
Beauty for the Asking *'39*
Tarzan Finds a Son *'39*
Call It a Day *'37*
If You Could Only Cook *'36*
The Dark Angel *'35*

Eddie Infante
Ethan *'71*
Warkill *'65*
Cavalry Command *'63*

Angelo Infanti (1939-)
La Scorta *'94*
The Inquiry *'87*
Blood Tracks *'86*
The Assisi Underground *'84*
The Black Stallion Returns *'83*
The Scarlet & the Black *'83*
The Squeeze *'77*
The Count of Monte Cristo *'74*
The Godfather *'72*
The Valachi Papers *'72*
Le Mans *'71*
A Man Called Sledge *'71*
Four Dollars of Revenge *'66*

Marty Ingels (1936-)
Round Numbers *'91*
Instant Karma *'90*
How to Seduce a Woman *'74*
If It's Tuesday, This Must Be Belgium *'69*
The Busy Body *'67*

Mariah Inger
Lost Junction *'03*
The Courage to Love *'00*

Randi Ingerman (1967-)
Screw Loose *'99*
Let's Talk About Sex *'98*
Desperate Crimes *'93*
Deadly Rivals *'92*

Barrie Ingham (1934-)
Josh Kirby... Time Warrior: Chapter 5, Journey to the Magic Cavern *'96*
Josh Kirby... Time Warrior: Chapter 6, Last Battle for the Universe *'96*
Josh Kirby... Time Warrior: Chapter 3, Trapped on Toyworld *'95*
Josh Kirby... Time Warrior: Chapter 4, Eggs from 70 Million B.C. *'95*
The Great Mouse Detective *'86 (V)*
A Challenge for Robin Hood *'68*
Invasion *'65*

John Ingle
The Land Before Time 5: The Mysterious Island *'97 (V)*
The Land Before Time 4: Journey Through the Mists *'96 (V)*
The Land Before Time 3: The Time of the Great Giving *'95 (V)*
The Land Before Time 2: The Great Valley Adventure *'94 (V)*

Lee Ingleby (1976-)
Place of Execution *'09*
Master and Commander: The Far Side of the World *'03*
Borstal Boy *'00*

Lloyd Ingraham (1885-1956)
The Caravan Trail *'46*
Partners of the Trail *'44*
Range Law *'44*
Park Avenue Logger *'37*
Captain Calamity *'36*
Everyman's Law *'36*
Red River Valley *'36*
Stormy Trails *'36*
Undercover Man *'36*
Between Men *'35*
Ghost Rider *'35*
Go-Get-'Em-Haines *'35*
Rider of the Law *'35*
Sons of Steel *'35*
Trail of Terror *'35*
Peck's Bad Boy *'34*
Texas Gunfighter *'32*
Scaramouche *'23*

Jack Ingram (1902-69)
Lost in Alaska *'52*
Frontier Fugitives *'45*
Boss of Boomtown *'44*
Boss of Rawhide *'44*
Devil Riders *'44*
The Drifter *'44*
Frontier Outlaws *'44*
Guns of the Law *'44*
Oath of Vengeance *'44*
Outlaw Roundup *'44*
Range Law *'44*
Thundering Gunslingers *'44*
Frontier Law *'43*
The Lone Star Trail *'43*
Raiders of Sunset Pass *'43*
Riders of the Rio Grande *'43*
Arizona Roundup *'42*
The Mysterious Rider *'42*
Sheriff of Tombstone *'41*
Ridin' the Trail *'40*
Wyoming Outlaw *'39*
Valley of Terror *'38*
The Rangers Step In *'37*
Wild Horse Rodeo *'37*
Whistling Bullets *'36*

Rex Ingram (1892-1950)
Elmer Gantry *'60*
The Smallest Show on Earth *'48*
A Thousand and One Nights *'45*
Dark Waters *'44*
Cabin in the Sky *'43*
Sahara *'43*
Talk of the Town *'42*
The Thief of Bagdad *'40*
The Adventures of Huckleberry Finn *'39*
Green Pastures *'36*

Frankie Ingrassia
Election *'99*
The Positively True Adventures of the Alleged Texas Cheerleader-Murdering Mom *'93*

Valeri Inkizhinov (1895-1973)
Samson and the 7 Miracles of the World *'62*
Journey to the Lost City *'58*
Storm over Asia *'28*

George Innes (1938-)
Master and Commander: The Far Side of the World *'03*
Agatha Christie's A Caribbean Mystery *'83*
Ivanhoe *'82*
Archer: The Fugitive from the Empire *'81*
Danger UXB *'81*

Laura Innes
Deep Impact *'98*
Just Like Dad *'96*

Neil Innes (1944-)
Erik the Viking *'89*
Monty Python's Life of Brian *'79*
All You Need Is Cash *'78*
Jabberwocky *'77*
Monty Python and the Holy Grail *'75*
Magical Mystery Tour *'67*

Harold Innocent (1933-93)
Fergie & Andrew: Behind Palace Doors *'93*
Robin Hood: Prince of Thieves *'91*
Henry V *'89*

Annie Shizuka Inoh (1969-)
8 1/2 Women *'99*
Flowers of Shanghai *'98*
Goodbye South, Goodbye *'96*

Rie Inou
Ringu 2 *'99*
Ringu *'98*

Tino Insana (1948-)
The Masters of Menace *'90*
Wedding Band *'89*

Antonella Interlenghi (1960-)
New York Ripper *'82*
Gates of Hell *'80*

Franco Interlenghi (1931-)
I Vitelloni *'53*
The Wayward Wife *'52*
Shoeshine *'47*

Steve Inwood (1947-)
The Human Shield *'92*
Hurry Up or I'll Be Thirty *'73*

Aharon Ipale (1941-)
The Mummy *'99*
A Kid in Aladdin's Palace *'97*
Invisible: The Chronicles of Benjamin Knight *'93*
Tragedy of Flight 103: The Inside Story *'91*
One Man Out *'89*
Too Hot to Handle *'76*

Michael Irby
Law Abiding Citizen *'09*
Flightplan *'05*
The Last Castle *'01*
Pinero *'01*

Jill Ireland (1936-90)
Assassination *'87*
Death Wish 2 *'82*
Love and Bullets *'79*
Breakheart Pass *'76*
From Noon Till Three *'76*
Breakout *'75*
Chino *'75*
Hard Times *'75*
The Mechanic *'72*
The Valachi Papers *'72*
Cold Sweat *'71*
Someone Behind the Door *'71*
The Family *'70*
Rider on the Rain *'70*
Villa Rides *'68*
Robbery under Arms *'57*
Three Men in a Boat *'56*

John Ireland (1914-92)
Waxwork 2: Lost in Time *'91*
Messenger of Death *'88*
Miami Horror *'87*
Tales of the Klondike: Race for Number One *'87*
Flying from the Hawk *'86*
Thunder Run *'86*
Martin's Day *'85*
The Treasure of the Amazon *'84*
Incubus *'82*
Kavik the Wolf Dog *'80*
Marilyn: The Untold Story *'80*
Mission to Glory *'80*
Bordello *'79*
Crossbar *'79*
Midnight Auto Supply *'78*
Delta Fox *'77*
Maniac *'77*
Perfect Killer *'77*
Satan's Cheerleaders *'77*
Tomorrow Never Comes *'77*
Farewell, My Lovely *'75*
The House of Seven Corpses *'73*
Escape to the Sun *'72*
Northeast of Seoul *'72*
Dirty Heroes *'71*
The Adventurers *'70*
Challenge of McKenna *'70*
Dead for a Dollar *'70*
Diary of a Rebel *'68*
Taste of Death *'68*
Arizona Bushwackers *'67*
The Fall of the Roman Empire *'64*
55 Days at Peking *'63*
Wild in the Country *'61*
Spartacus *'60*
Black Tide *'58*
Party Girl *'58*
Gunfight at the O.K. Corral *'57*
The Gunslinger *'56*
Glass Tomb *'55*
Queen Bee *'55*
The Fast and the Furious *'54*
The Bushwackers *'52*
Little Big Horn *'51*
Vengeance Valley *'51*
Return of Jesse James *'50*
All the King's Men *'49*
The Doolins of Oklahoma *'49*
I Shot Jesse James *'49*
Joan of Arc *'48*
Open Secret *'48*
Raw Deal *'48*
Red River *'48*
A Southern Yankee *'48*
The Gangster *'47*
Railroaded *'47*
My Darling Clementine *'46*
A Walk in the Sun *'46*

John Ireland, Jr.
Sundown: The Vampire in Retreat *'08*

Wham-Bam, Thank You Spaceman '75

Kathy Ireland (1963-)
Miami Hustle '95
Backfire! '94
Amore! '93
National Lampoon's Loaded Weapon 1 '93
Mom and Dad Save the World '92
The Player '92
Necessary Roughness '91
Mr. Destiny '90
Side Out '90
Alien from L.A. '87

Vincent Irizarry (1959-)
Heartbreak Ridge '86
Marie '85

Jeremy Irons (1948-)
The Pink Panther 2 '09
Appaloosa '08
The Color of Magic '08
Eragon '06
Inland Empire '06
Casanova '05
Elizabeth I '05
Kingdom of Heaven '05
Being Julia '04
The Merchant of Venice '04
And Now Ladies and Gentlemen '02
Callas Forever '02
Last Call: The Final Chapter of F. Scott Fitzgerald '02
The Time Machine '02
The Fourth Angel '01
Dungeons and Dragons '00
Longitude '00
The Man in the Iron Mask '98
Chinese Box '97
Lolita '97
Stealing Beauty '96
Die Hard: With a Vengeance '95
The Lion King '94 (V)
The House of the Spirits '93
M. Butterfly '93
Damage '92
Waterland '92
Kafka '91
Reversal of Fortune '90
A Chorus of Disapproval '89
Dead Ringers '88
The Mission '86
Swann in Love '84
The Wild Duck '84
Betrayal '83
Moonlighting '82
Brideshead Revisited '81
The French Lieutenant's Woman '81
Nijinsky '80
Love for Lydia '79

Michael Ironside (1950-)
Hardwired '09
Terminator Salvation '09
The Alphabet Killer '08
Mutants '08
Storm Cell '08
Surveillance '08
The Terrorist Next Door '08
The Butcher '07
The Veteran '06
Deepwater '05
Masters of Horror: The V Word '05
The Machinist '04
Anti-Terrorist Cell: Manhunt '01
Children of the Corn: Revelation '01
Extreme Honor '01
Ignition '01
Mindstorm '01
The Shaft '01
Cause of Death '00
Crime and Punishment in Suburbia '00
Heavy Metal 2000 '00 (V)
Nuremberg '00
The Perfect Storm '00
Beyond Redemption '99
Johnny 2.0 '99
The Omega Code '99
Blacklight '98
Blood Money '98
Chicago Cab '98
Bomb Squad '97
Captive '97
Ivory Tower '97
Starship Troopers '97
The Destiny of Marty Fine '96
Kids of the Round Table '96
Robin Cook's Terminal '96
Too Fast, Too Young '96
The Glass Shield '95
One Way Out '95
Portraits of a Killer '95
Probable Cause '95
Fortunes of War '94
The Killing Man '94
Rebel Run '94
Red Scorpion 2 '94
Red Sun Rising '94
Tokyo Cowboy '94
Dead Man's Revenge '93
Father Hood '93
Forced to Kill '93
Mardi Gras for the Devil '93
Point of Impact '93
Save Me '93
Sweet Killing '93
Black Ice '92
Guncrazy '92
Killer Image '92
The Vagrant '92
Common Bonds '91
Deadly Surveillance '91
Highlander 2: The Quickening '91
McBain '91
Neon City '91
Victim of Beauty '91
Payback '90
Total Recall '90
Mindfield '89
Murder by Night '89
Hostile Takeover '88
Surrogate '88
Watchers '88
Extreme Prejudice '87
Ford: The Man & the Machine '87
Hello Mary Lou: Prom Night 2 '87
Top Gun '86
The Falcon and the Snowman '85
Murder in Space '85
Coming Out Alive '84
V: The Final Battle '84
Cross Country '83
Nowhere to Hide '83
Spacehunter: Adventures in the Forbidden Zone '83
Visiting Hours '82
American Nightmare '81
Scanners '81
The Family Man '79

Brittney Irvin (1984-)
Spectacular '09
Hot Rod '07
National Lampoon's Holiday Reunion '03
Wilderness Love '02
Angels in the Infield '00

Amy Irving (1953-)
Adam '09
Hide and Seek '05
Tuck Everlasting '02
Thirteen Conversations About One Thing '01
Traffic '00
Blue Ridge Fall '99
Bossa Nova '99
The Rage: Carrie 2 '99
The Confession '98
One Tough Cop '98
Deconstructing Harry '97
I'm Not Rappaport '96
Carried Away '95
Kleptomania '94
Benefit of the Doubt '93
An American Tail: Fievel Goes West '91 (V)
A Show of Force '90
The Turn of the Screw '89
Crossing Delancey '88
Who Framed Roger Rabbit '88 (V)
Anastasia: The Mystery of Anna '86
Heartbreak House '86
Rumpelstiltskin '86
The Far Pavilions '84
Micki & Maude '84
Yentl '83
The Competition '80
Honeysuckle Rose '80
The Fury '78
Carrie '76
Dynasty '76
James Dean '76

George Irving (1874-1961)
Sergeant York '41
The Abe Lincoln of Ninth Avenue '39
Maid's Night Out '38
The Mandarin Mystery '37
Captain January '36
Merrily We Go to Hell '32
Touchdown '31
The Divorcee '30
Coquette '29

Margaret Irving (1898-1988)
In Society '44
San Francisco '36
Animal Crackers '30

Penny Irving (1950-)
House of Whipcord '75
Big Zapper '73

Bill Irwin (1950-)
Rachel Getting Married '08
Lady in the Water '06
Dr. Seuss' How the Grinch Stole Christmas '00
William Shakespeare's A Midsummer Night's Dream '99
Illuminata '98
Just the Ticket '98
Subway Stories '97
Silent Tongue '92
Hot Shots! '91
Scenes from a Mall '91
Stepping Out '91
My Blue Heaven '90
Eight Men Out '88
Popeye '80

Boyd Irwin (1880-1957)
Madam Satan '30
The Three Musketeers '21

Charles Irwin
Montana '50
The Moonstone '34

Steve Irwin (1962-2006)
Happy Feet '06 (V)
The Crocodile Hunter: Collision Course '02

Tom Irwin (1956-)
Exposed '03
Snow White: The Fairest of Them All '02
The Sandy Bottom Orchestra '00
Holiday Affair '96
My Very Best Friend '96
Mr. Jones '93
Ladykiller '92
Deceived '91

January Isaac
Doomsdayer '01
Doomsdayer '99

Oscar Isaac
Robin Hood '10
Body of Lies '08
The Nativity Story '06
PU-239 '06

Jason Isaacs (1963-)
Green Zone '10
Good '08
Harry Potter and the Order of the Phoenix '07
Friends with Money '06
The State Within '06
The Chumscrubber '05
Harry Potter and the Goblet of Fire '05
Nine Lives '05
Peter Pan '03
Harry Potter and the Chamber of Secrets '02
The Tuxedo '02
Windtalkers '02
Black Hawk Down '01
Hotel '01
The Last Minute '01
Sweet November '01
The Patriot '00
The End of the Affair '99
Armageddon '98
The Last Don 2 '98
St. Ives '98
Soldier '98
Event Horizon '97
Dragonheart '96
Solitaire for 2 '94

Chris Isaak (1956-)
The Informers '09
A Dirty Shame '04
Blue Ridge Fall '99
From the Earth to the Moon '98
Grace of My Heart '96
That Thing You Do! '96
Little Buddha '93
Twin Peaks: Fire Walk with Me '92
The Silence of the Lambs '91
Married to the Mob '88

Margarita Isabel
Lucia, Lucia '03
Cronos '94

Katharine Isabelle (1981-)
Another Cinderella Story '08
Mail Order Bride '08
Everything's Gone Green '06
Ginger Snaps Back: The Beginning '04
Ginger Snaps: Unleashed '04
Show Me '04
Falling Angels '03
Freddy vs. Jason '03
Carrie '02
Due East '02
Insomnia '02
Bones '01
Ginger Snaps '01

Tom Isbell (1957-)
A Case of Deadly Force '86
Behind Enemy Lines '85

Yusuke Iseya
Sukiyaki Western Django '08
Black House '07

Renji Ishibashi
The Great Yokai War '05
One Missed Call 2 '05
Shinobi '05
Flower & Snake '04
One Missed Call '03
The Sea is Watching '02
The Watcher in the Attic '76

Ryo Ishibashi (1956-)
Masters of Horror: Dream Cruise '07
War '07
The Grudge '04
Gozu '03
Suicide Club '02
Audition '99
Back to Back '96
Another Lonely Hitman '95
American Yakuza '94
Blue Tiger '94
The Crossing Guard '94

Takaaki Ishibashi (1961-)
Sukiyaki Western Django '08
Major League 3: Back to the Minors '98
Major League 2 '94

Yuma Ishigaki
Azumi 2 '05
Azumi '03

Akira Ishihama (1935-)
Harakiri '62
The Human Condition: No Greater Love '58

Kenjiro Ishimaru
Onmyoji '01
Ringu 2 '99

Dale Ishimoto (1923-2004)
Midway '76
King Rat '65

Kevin Isola (1970-)
24 Nights '99
The Summer of Ben Tyler '96

Ravil Isyanov
The Good German '06
K-19: The Widowmaker '02
Octopus '00
Doomsdayer '99
Back in the USSR '92

Juzo Itami (1933-97)
MacArthur's Children '85
The Family Game '83

Itsuji Itao
Tokyo Gore Police '08
Big Man Japan '07

Ayumi Ito
Tokyo! '09
All About Lily Chou-Chou '01

Emi Ito (1946-)
Ghidrah the Three Headed Monster '65
Godzilla vs. Mothra '64
Mothra '62

Hideaki Ito
Sukiyaki Western Django '08
Onmyoji 2 '03
The Princess Blade '02
Onmyoji '01

Hisaya Ito (1938-)
Destroy All Monsters '68
Ghidrah the Three Headed Monster '65

Robert Ito (1931-)
The Omega Code '99
Once a Thief '96
Pray for Death '85
The Adventures of Buckaroo Banzai Across the Eighth Dimension '84
Midway '76
Women of the Prehistoric Planet '66

Toshiya Ito (1947-)
Ran '85
Space Riders '83

Yumi Ito (1946-)
Ghidrah the Three Headed Monster '65
Godzilla vs. Mothra '64
Mothra '62

Yunosuke Ito (1919-80)
Shinobi no Mono '62
The Burmese Harp '56
Ikiru '52

Jose Iturbi (1895-1980)
That Midnight Kiss '49
Three Daring Daughters '48
Holiday in Mexico '46
Anchors Aweigh '45
Two Girls and a Sailor '44

Gregory Itzin (1948-)
Forfeit '07
I Know Who Killed Me '07
DC 9/11: Time of Crisis '04
Life or Something Like It '02
Evolution '01
Original Sin '01
Fly Boy '99

Marcel Iures (1951-)
Goal! The Dream Begins '06
The Cave '05
Layer Cake '05
Amen '02
Hart's War '02
The Peacemaker '97

Rosalind Ivan (1880-1959)
The Most Wonderful Time of the Year '08
The Corn Is Green '45
Pillow of Death '45
Pursuit to Algiers '45
Dead Man's Eyes '44

Zeljko Ivanek (1957-)
John Adams '08
Manderlay '05
The Manchurian Candidate '04
The Reagans '04
Dogville '03
Unfaithful '02
Black Hawk Down '01
Hannibal '01
Homicide: The Movie '00
Dancer in the Dark '99
Dash and Lilly '99
A Civil Action '98
From the Earth to the Moon '98
The Rat Pack '98
Ellen Foster '97
Julian Po '97
Courage Under Fire '96
Donnie Brasco '96
Infinity '96
White Squall '96
My Brother's Keeper '95
Truman '95
School Ties '92
Our Sons '91
Echoes in the Darkness '87
Rachel River '87
Mass Appeal '84
The Sender '82

Mark Ivanir (1968-)
The Good Shepherd '06
Schindler's List '93

Vlad Ivanov
Police, Adjective '09
4 Months, 3 Weeks and 2 Days '07

Stan Ivar
High Stakes '93
Creature '85

Terri Ivens (1967-)
Trancers 5: Sudden Deth '94
Trancers 4: Jack of Swords '93

Daniel Ivernel (1920-99)
High Heels '72
Diary of a Chambermaid '64
Manon '50

Robert Ivers (1934-2003)
G.I. Blues '60
The Delicate Delinquent '56

Burl Ives (1909-95)
Two Moon Junction '88
Poor Little Rich Girl: The Barbara Hutton Story '87
Uphill All the Way '85
The Ewok Adventure '84 (N)
White Dog '82
The Bermuda Depths '78
Roots '77
Baker's Hawk '76
Hugo the Hippo '76 (V)
The McMasters '70
Those Fantastic Flying Fools '67
Ensign Pulver '64
The Brass Bottle '63
Summer Magic '63
Let No Man Write My Epitaph '60
The Day of the Outlaw '59
Our Man in Havana '59
The Big Country '58
Cat on a Hot Tin Roof '58
Desire Under the Elms '58
East of Eden '54
So Dear to My Heart '49
Station West '48

Dana Ivey (1942-)
Ghost Town '08
Rush Hour 3 '07

A Very Serious Person '06
Legally Blonde 2: Red White & Blonde '03
Orange County '02
Two Weeks Notice '02
Disney's The Kid '00
Mumford '99
The Imposters '98
Simon Birch '98
Sabrina '95
The Scarlet Letter '95
Addams Family Values '93
The Adventures of Huck Finn '93
Guilty as Sin '93
Class of '61 '92
Home Alone 2: Lost in New York '92
The Addams Family '91
Postcards from the Edge '90
Dirty Rotten Scoundrels '88
Explorers '85

Judith Ivey (1951-)
Pictures of Hollis Woods '07
Flags of Our Fathers '06
Stephen King's Rose Red '02
Mystery, Alaska '99
What the Deaf Man Heard '98
The Devil's Advocate '97
A Life Less Ordinary '97
Washington Square '97
Without Limits '97
The Summer of Ben Tyler '96 (N)
There Goes the Neighborhood '92
Love Hurts '91
Decoration Day '90
Everybody Wins '90
In Country '89
Miles from Home '88
Hello Again '87
Sister, Sister '87
We Are the Children '87
Brighton Beach Memoirs '86
The Long, Hot Summer '86
Compromising Positions '85
Dixie: Changing Habits '85
Harry & Son '84
The Lonely Guy '84
The Woman in Red '84
Piaf '81

Moshe Ivgi (1953-)
Munich '05
Cup Final '92

Dana Ivgy
The Secrets '07
Or (My Treasure) '04

Tommy "T.V." Ivo (1936-)
Belles on Their Toes '52
Operation Haylift '50
Outcasts of the Trail '49

Bob Ivy
Bubba Ho-Tep '03
Phantasm 4: Oblivion '98

Ryo Iwamatsu
Zebraman '04
Samurai Fiction '99

Shima Iwashita (1941-)
Gonza the Spearman '86
MacArthur's Children '85
Double Suicide '69
Red Lion '69
An Autumn Afternoon '62
Harakiri '62

Victor Izay (1923-)
Blood Orgy of the She-Devils '74
The Trial of Billy Jack '74
Billy Jack '71
Premonition '71
The Astro-Zombies '67

Eddie Izzard (1962-)
The Chronicles of Narnia: Prince Caspian '08 (V)
Igor '08 (V)
Valkyrie '08
Ocean's Thirteen '07
My Super Ex-Girlfriend '06
The Wild '06 (V)
Romance & Cigarettes '05
Ocean's Twelve '04
All the Queen's Men '02
The Cat's Meow '01
Circus '00
The Criminal '00
Shadow of the Vampire '00
Mystery Men '99
The Avengers '98
Velvet Goldmine '98

Ja Rule (1976-)
Assault on Precinct 13 '05
Back in the Day '05
The Cookout '04
Scary Movie 3 '03
Half Past Dead '02
The Fast and the Furious '01
Turn It Up '00

Tony Jaa
Ong Bak 2 '08
Ong-Bak '03

Jay Jablonski
Conspiracy '08
Everybody Wants to Be Italian '08

Michael Jace (1965-)
Bats: Human Harvest '07
Cradle 2 the Grave '03
Planet of the Apes '01
The Replacements '00
Thick as Thieves '99
Bombshell '97
Boogie Nights '97
The Fan '96
The Great White Hype '96
Strange Days '95
Forrest Gump '94

Jackee (1956-)
You Got Served '04
Ladybugs '92
The Reluctant Agent '89
The Women of Brewster Place '89

Ian Jacklin
American Streetfighter '96
Capital Punishment '96
Warrior of Justice '96
Death Match '94
Expert Weapon '93
Kickboxer 3: The Art of War '92

Hugh Jackman (1968-)
X-Men Origins: Wolverine '09
Australia '08
Deception '08
Flushed Away '06 (V)
The Fountain '06
Happy Feet '06 (V)
The Prestige '06
Scoop '06
X-Men: The Last Stand '06
Van Helsing '04
X2: X-Men United '03
Kate & Leopold '01
Someone Like You '01
Swordfish '01
X-Men '00
Erskinville Kings '99
Paperback Hero '99

Andrew Jackson (1963-)
Seed '08
Merlin's Apprentice '06
Category 6 : Day of Destruction '04
We'll Meet Again '02
Bram Stoker's Shadowbuilder '98
The Last Don 2 '98
Twists of Terror '98
Family of Cops 2: Breach of Faith '97
Specimen '97

Anne Jackson (1926-)
Rescuers: Stories of Courage "Two Women" '97
Folks! '92
Funny About Love '90
Out on a Limb '87
Sam's Son '84
Blood Debts '83
Blinded by the Light '82
A Woman Called Golda '82
Leave 'Em Laughing '81
The Shining '80
The Bell Jar '79
The Family Man '79
Nasty Habits '77
The Angel Levine '70
Lovers and Other Strangers '70
Secret Life of an American Wife '68
Tall Story '60

Bo Jackson (1962-)
Imagine Me & You '06
The Chamber '96

Brandon T. Jackson (1984-)
The Lottery Ticket '10
Tropic Thunder '08
Roll Bounce '05

Curtis "50 Cent" Jackson (1975-)
Twelve '10
Streets of Blood '09
Righteous Kill '08
Home of the Brave '06
Get Rich or Die Tryin' '05

Eugene Jackson (1916-2001)
Shenandoah '65
Red River Valley '36

Freda Jackson (1909-90)
The Valley of Gwangi '69
Die, Monster, Die! '65
The Brides of Dracula '60
Bhowani Junction '56
Beware of Pity '46
Great Expectations '46
Henry V '44

Glenda Jackson (1936-)
King of the Wind '93
A Murder of Quality '90
Strange Interlude '90
The Rainbow '89
Business As Usual '88
Salome's Last Dance '88
Beyond Therapy '86
Turtle Diary '86
Sakharov '84
And Nothing But the Truth '82
Return of the Soldier '82
Hopscotch '80
Lost and Found '79
The Class of Miss MacMichael '78
House Calls '78
Stevie '78
Nasty Habits '77
Triple Echo '77
The Incredible Sarah '76
Hedda '75
Romantic Englishwoman '75
A Touch of Class '73
Elizabeth R '72
Mary, Queen of Scots '71
The Music Lovers '71
Sunday, Bloody Sunday '71
Women in Love '70
Negatives '68

Gordon Jackson (1923-90)
Noble House '88
Gunpowder '87
The Whistle Blower '87
My Brother Tom '86
A Town Like Alice '85
Hamlet '69
The Prime of Miss Jean Brodie '69
The Fighting Prince of Donegal '66
The Ipcress File '65
Those Magnificent Men in Their Flying Machines '65
The Great Escape '63
Abandon Ship '57
The Baby and the Battleship '56
Death Goes to School '53
Against the Wind '48
Whiskey Galore '48
Pink String and Sealing Wax '45
Nine Men '43
The Foreman Went to France '42

Howard Jackson (1900-66)
Full Contact '93
Out for Blood '93
Dolemite 2: Human Tornado '76

Janet Jackson (1966-)
Tyler Perry's Why Did I Get Married Too? '10
Tyler Perry's Why Did I Get Married? '07
Nutty Professor 2: The Klumps '00
Poetic Justice '93

Jenie Jackson (1921-76)
How Sweet It Is! '68
Ride the High Country '62

Jeremy Jackson (1980-)
Ring of Darkness '04
Baywatch the Movie: Forbidden Paradise '95

John M. Jackson (1950-)
The Invasion '07
The Spitfire Grill '95
Roswell: The U.F.O. Cover-Up '94
An American Story '92
A Thousand Heroes '92
Career Opportunities '91
Love, Lies and Murder '91
Switched at Birth '91
Eve of Destruction '90
Sudie & Simpson '90
Cold Sassy Tree '89
Ginger Ale Afternoon '89
The Hitcher '86

Jonathan Jackson (1982-)
Dirty Dancing: Havana Nights '04
Riding the Bullet '04
Insomnia '02
Tuck Everlasting '02
On the Edge '00
Skeletons in the Closet '00
The Deep End of the Ocean '98
Double Play '96
Camp Nowhere '94

Joshua Jackson (1978-)
Shutter '08
Battle in Seattle '07
Aurora Borealis '06
Bobby '06
Americano '05
Racing Stripes '05 (V)
Venom '05
Cursed '04
I Love Your Work '03
Lone Star State of Mind '02
Ocean's Eleven '01
The Safety of Objects '01
The Skulls '00
Gossip '99
Cruel Intentions '98
Urban Legend '98
Apt Pupil '97
Ronnie and Julie '97
D3: The Mighty Ducks '96
Magic in the Water '95
Robin of Locksley '95
Andre '94
Digger '94
The Mighty Ducks '92

Kate Jackson (1949-)
Miracle Dogs '03
Panic in the Skies '96
Adrift '93
Homewrecker '92 (V)
Loverboy '89
Listen to Your Heart '83
Making Love '82
Dirty Tricks '81
Thunder and Lightning '77
Death at Love House '75
Death Scream '75
Death Cruise '74
Satan's School for Girls '73
Night of Dark Shadows '71

Leonard Jackson (1928-)
Basket Case 2 '90
Ganja and Hess '73

Linda Jackson
Black Bikers from Hell '70
The Outlaw Bikers—Gang Wars '70

Mary Jackson (1910-2005)
A Family Thing '96
Skinned Alive '89
Terror at Red Wolf Inn '72
Targets '68

Mel Jackson (1970-)
Deliver Us from Eva '03
Motives '03
Little Richard '00
Uninvited Guest '99
Soul Food '97

Michael Jackson (1958-2009)
Michael Jackson's This Is It '09
Men in Black 2 '02
The Wiz '78

Neil Jackson
Push '09
The Thirst '06
Alexander '04

Peter Jackson (1961-)
Hot Fuzz '07
Dead Alive '93
Bad Taste '88

Philip Jackson (1948-)
Place of Execution '09
Fanny Hill '07
I Want Candy '07
A Little Trip to Heaven '05
The Intended '02
Little Voice '98
Girls' Night '97
Brassed Off '96
Bad Behavior '92
High Hopes '88

Reggie Jackson (1946-)
The Benchwarmers '06
BASEketball '98
Richie Rich '94
The Naked Gun: From the Files of Police Squad '88

Richard Lee Jackson (1979-)
Avenging Angel '07
Love's Long Journey '05
Bring It On Again '03
Hope Ranch '02
Madison '01
Double Play '96

Sammy Jackson (1937-95)
Shame, Shame on the Bixby Boys '82
Fastest Guitar Alive '68
None But the Brave '65

Samuel L. Jackson (1948-)
Iron Man 2 '10
The Other Guys '10
Astro Boy '09 (V)
Inglourious Basterds '09 (N)
Mother and Child '09
Gospel Hill '08
Iron Man '08
Jumper '08
Lakeview Terrace '08
Soul Men '08
The Spirit '08
Star Wars: The Clone Wars '08 (V)
Black Snake Moan '07
Cleaner '07
1408 '07
Resurrecting the Champ '07
Freedomland '06
Home of the Brave '06
Snakes on a Plane '06
Coach Carter '05
The Man '05
Star Wars: Episode 3—Revenge of the Sith '05
XXX: State of the Union '05
In My Country '04
The Incredibles '04 (V)
Kill Bill Vol. 2 '04
Twisted '04
Basic '03
S.W.A.T. '03
Changing Lanes '02
No Good Deed '02
Star Wars: Episode 2—Attack of the Clones '02
XXX '02
The Caveman's Valentine '01
Formula 51 '01
Rules of Engagement '00
Shaft '00
Unbreakable '00
Deep Blue Sea '99
Star Wars: Episode 1—The Phantom Menace '99
The Negotiator '98
Out of Sight '98
The Red Violin '98
Eve's Bayou '97
Jackie Brown '97
187 '97
Sphere '97
The Great White Hype '96
Hard Eight '96
The Long Kiss Goodnight '96
The Search for One-Eye Jimmy '96
A Time to Kill '96
Tree's Lounge '96
Die Hard: With a Vengeance '95
Fluke '95 (V)
Against the Wall '94
Assault at West Point: The Court-Martial of Johnson Whittaker '94
Fresh '94
Hail Caesar '94
Kiss of Death '94
Losing Isaiah '94
The New Age '94
Pulp Fiction '94
Amos and Andrew '93
Jurassic Park '93
Menace II Society '93
National Lampoon's Loaded Weapon 1 '93
True Romance '93
Fathers and Sons '92
Johnny Suede '92
Juice '92
Jumpin' at the Boneyard '92
Patriot Games '92
White Sands '92
Jungle Fever '91
Betsy's Wedding '90
Def by Temptation '90
Goodfellas '90
Mo' Better Blues '90
Return of Superfly '90
Dead Man Out '89
Coming to America '88
School Daze '88
Ragtime '81

Selmer Jackson (1888-1971)
The Gallant Hours '60
We're Not Married '52
Pitfall '48
Guadalcanal Diary '43
The Fighting Sullivans '42
Gangs, Inc. '41
International Lady '41
Sergeant York '41
They Died with Their Boots On '41
Brigham Young: Frontiersman '40

Johnny Apollo *'40*
The Thirteenth Man *'37*
Alibi Ike *'35*

Sherry Jackson (1942-)
Daughters of the Dust *'91*
Stingray *'78*
Bare Knuckles *'77*
Cotter *'72*
The Adventures of Huckleberry Finn *'60*
Trouble along the Way *'53*
Miracle of Our Lady of Fatima *'52*

Stoney Jackson (1960-)
Trippin' *'99*
Black Scorpion 2: Ground Zero *'96*
Carnival of Wolves *'96*
The Disappearance of Kevin Johnson *'95*
Up Against the Wall *'91*
Sweet Perfection *'90*
Knights of the City *'85*
Streets of Fire *'84*
Roller Boogie *'79*

Tom Jackson (1948-)
Skinwalkers *'07*
Grizzly Falls *'99*
Medicine River *'94*
Spirit Rider *'93*

Victoria Jackson (1959-)
Soccer Mom *'08*
Midnight Clear *'06*
Shut Up and Kiss Me *'05*
Wedding Bell Blues *'96*
The Undercover Kid *'95 (V)*
Based on an Untrue Story *'93*
I Love You to Death *'90*
Dream a Little Dream *'89*
Family Business *'89*
UHF *'89*
Casual Sex? *'88*
Baby Boom *'87*
The Pick-Up Artist *'87*
Stoogemania *'85*

Catherine Jacob (1956-)
Who Killed Bambi? *'03*
The Green House *'96*
Tatie Danielle *'91*

Irene Jacob (1966-)
The Big Brass Ring *'99*
Spy Games *'99*
My Life So Far *'98*
U.S. Marshals *'98*
Incognito *'97*
Beyond the Clouds *'95*
Othello *'95*
Victory *'95*
Trois Couleurs: Rouge *'94*
Trusting Beatrice *'92*
The Double Life of Veronique *'91*
Au Revoir les Enfants *'87*

Derek Jacobi (1938-)
Endgame *'09*
Adam Resurrected *'08*
The Golden Compass *'07*
Guantanamero *'07*
The Old Curiosity Shop *'07*
The Riddle *'07*
Nanny McPhee *'06*
Pinochet's Last Stand *'06*
Underworld: Evolution *'05*
The Gathering Storm *'02*
Two Men Went to War *'02*
The Body *'01*
Gladiator *'00*
Jason and the Argonauts *'00*
Up at the Villa *'00*
The Wyvern Mystery *'00*
Molokai: The Story of Father Damien *'99*
Basil *'98*
Love Is the Devil *'98*
Hamlet *'96*
Breaking the Code *'95*
Circle of Deceit *'94*
Dead Again *'91*
Henry V *'89*
Little Dorrit, Film 1: Nobody's Fault *'88*
Little Dorrit, Film 2: Little Dorrit's Story *'88*
The Tenth Man *'88*
The Secret Garden *'87*
Cyrano de Bergerac *'85*
Philby, Burgess and MacLean: Spy Scandal of the Century *'84*
Enigma *'82*
The Hunchback of Notre Dame *'82*
Inside the Third Reich *'82*
The Secret of NIMH *'82 (V)*
The Human Factor *'79*
The Medusa Touch *'78*
The Odessa File *'74*
Blue Blood *'73*
The Day of the Jackal *'73*
The Strauss Family *'73*
Othello *'65*

Ernst Jacobi (1933-)
The White Ribbon *'09 (N)*
Hamsun *'96*
Germany, Pale Mother *'80*

Lou Jacobi (1913-2009)
I.Q. *'94*
I Don't Buy Kisses Anymore *'92*
Avalon *'90*
Amazon Women on the Moon *'87*
The Boss' Wife *'86*
My Favorite Year *'82*
Arthur *'81*
Chu Chu & the Philly Flash *'81*
Off Your Rocker *'80*
Better Late Than Never *'79*
The Magician of Lublin *'79*
Roseland *'77*
Next Stop, Greenwich Village *'76*
Everything You Always Wanted to Know about Sex (But Were Afraid to Ask) *'72*
Little Murders *'71*
Cotton Comes to Harlem *'70*
Song Without End *'60*
The Diary of Anne Frank *'59*
A Kid for Two Farthings *'55*

Andre Jacobs
Curse of the Crystal Eye *'93*
Prey for the Hunter *'92*
Pursuit *'90*
Emissary *'89*

Danny A. Jacobs (1979-)
Bachelor Party 2: The Last Temptation *'08*
The Cavern *'05*

Gillian Jacobs
The Box *'09*
Choke *'08*
Gardens of the Night *'08*

Jon Jacobs (1966-)
Hard Luck *'01*
Welcome Says the Angel *'01*

Lawrence-Hilton Jacobs (1953-)
Sublime *'07*
Indecent Behavior *'93*
The Jacksons: An American Dream *'92*
Quiet Fire *'91*
Angels of the City *'89*
Chance *'89*
East L.A. Warriors *'89*
Killcrazy *'89*
L.A. Vice *'89*
L.A. Heat *'88*
Paramedics *'88*
The Annihilators *'85*
For the Love of It *'80*
Cooley High *'75*

Mark Evan Jacobs
Bleeding Hearts *'94*
Trusting Beatrice *'92*

Steve Jacobs (1967-)
Father *'90*
Alice to Nowhere *'86*
Echoes of Paradise *'86*

Colombe Jacobsen (1979-)
Men in Black 2 *'02*
D3: The Mighty Ducks *'96*

Peter Jacobson (1965-)
The Starter Wife *'07*
Transformers *'07*
Failure to Launch *'06*
Domino *'05*
Good Night, and Good Luck *'05*
Pipe Dream *'02*
Hit and Runway *'01*
61* *'01*
The Cradle Will Rock *'99*
A Civil Action *'98*
It Could Happen to You *'94*

Ulla Jacobsson (1929-82)
Fox and His Friends *'75*
The Heroes of Telemark *'65*
Zulu *'64*
Smiles of a Summer Night *'55*

Billy Jacoby (1969-)
Dr. Alien *'88*
Party Camp *'87*
Just One of the Guys *'85*
Cujo *'83*
Beastmaster *'82*
Bloody Birthday *'80*

Bobby Jacoby (1973-)
Fear Runs Silent *'99*
Night of the Demons 2 *'94*
The Day My Parents Ran Away *'93*
The Applegates *'89*
Tremors *'89*
Wizards of the Lost Kingdom 2 *'89*
Iron Eagle *'86*

Dale Jacoby
Guardian Angel *'94*
Ring of Fire 2: Blood and Steel *'92*
Bloodmatch *'91*
Ring of Fire *'91*

Scott Jacoby (1956-)
To Die For 2: Son of Darkness *'91*
To Die For *'89*
Return to Horror High *'87*
Midnight Auto Supply *'78*
The Little Girl Who Lives down the Lane *'76*
Bad Ronald *'74*
Rivals *'72*

Carlos Jacott
Fun With Dick and Jane *'05*
Jiminy Glick in LaLa Wood *'05*
Bats *'99*
Mr. Jealousy *'98*
Kicking and Screaming *'95*

Hattie Jacques (1924-80)
Carry On Abroad *'72*
Carry On Matron *'72*
Carry On at Your Convenience *'71*
Carry On Loving *'70*
Carry On Again Doctor *'69*
Carry On Cabby *'63*
Carry On Constable *'60*
Make Mine Mink *'60*
Carry On Nurse *'59*
Carry On Sergeant *'58*
The Square Peg *'58*
A Christmas Carol *'51*

Yves Jacques (1956-)
The Barbarian Invasions *'03*
La Petite Lili *'03*
Napoleon *'03*

Claude Jade (1948-2006)
Love on the Run *'78*
Bed and Board *'70*
Stolen Kisses *'68*

Scott Jaeck (1954-)
Killing Mr. Griffin *'97*
Washington Square *'97*
JAG *'95*

Richard Jaeckel (1926-97)
Martial Outlaw *'93*
The King of the Kickboxers *'91*
Delta Force 2: Operation Stranglehold *'90*
Ghetto Blaster *'89*
Black Moon Rising *'86*
The Dirty Dozen: The Next Mission *'85*
Pacific Inferno *'85*
The Fix *'84*
Starman *'84*
Airplane 2: The Sequel *'82*
Blood Song *'82*
...All the Marbles *'81*
Awakening of Candra *'81*
Cold River *'81*
The $5.20 an Hour Dream *'80*
Herbie Goes Bananas *'80*
The Dark *'79*
Speedtrap *'78*
Day of the Animals *'77*
Twilight's Last Gleaming *'77*
Grizzly *'76*
Jaws of Death *'76*
The Drowning Pool *'75*
Surabaya Conspiracy *'75*
Walking Tall: Part 2 *'75*
Born Innocent *'74*
The Kill *'73*
Pat Garrett & Billy the Kid *'73*
Firehouse *'72*
Ulzana's Raid *'72*
Sometimes a Great Notion *'71*
Chisum *'70*
Latitude Zero *'69*
The Devil's Brigade *'68*
The Green Slime *'68*
The Dirty Dozen *'67*
Once Before I Die *'65*
Town without Pity *'61*
Flaming Star *'60*
The Gallant Hours *'60*
Platinum High School *'60*
Cowboy *'58*
The Lineup *'58*
When Hell Broke Loose *'58*
3:10 to Yuma *'57*
Attack! *'56*
Come Back, Little Sheba *'52*
Hoodlum Empire *'52*
Battleground *'49*
Sands of Iwo Jima *'49*
Jungle Patrol *'48*
A Wing and a Prayer *'44*
Guadalcanal Diary *'43*

Frederick Jaeger (1928-2004)
The Body in the Library *'84*
Nijinsky *'80*
Slaughterday *'77*

Sam Jaeger
Catch and Release *'07*
The Riverman *'04*

Hannes Jaenicke (1960-)
Black Horizon *'01*
Extreme Limits *'01*
Mom's Outta Sight *'01*
Venomous *'01*
Active Stealth *'99*
Bandits *'99*
Nautilus *'99*
Restraining Order *'99*
The Hunted *'98*
The Heist *'96*
Jack Higgins' Midnight Man *'96*
Catherine the Great *'95*
Out of Order *'84*

Chapelle Jaffe
Sin and Redemption *'94*
Confidential *'86*
Overdrawn at the Memory Bank *'83*
One Night Stand *'78*
Who Has Seen the Wind? *'77*

Sam Jaffe (1891-1984)
On the Line *'83*
Battle Beyond the Stars *'80*
Gideon's Trumpet *'80*
Bedknobs and Broomsticks *'71*
The Dunwich Horror *'70*
Night Gallery *'69*
A Guide for the Married Man *'67*
Ben-Hur *'59*
Barbarian and the Geisha *'58*
The Day the Earth Stood Still *'51*
The Asphalt Jungle *'50*
The Accused *'48*
13 Rue Madeleine *'46*
Gunga Din *'39*
Lost Horizon *'37*
Scarlet Empress *'34*

Seth Jaffe
Scorned 2 *'96*
Beverly Hills Bodysnatchers *'89*
Stark *'85*

Melissa Jaffer (1936-)
Weekend of Shadows *'77*
The Cars That Ate Paris *'74*

Madhur Jaffrey (1933-)
Partition *'07*
ABCD *'99*
Chutney Popcorn *'99*
Cotton Mary *'99*
Vanya on 42nd Street *'94*
Heat and Dust *'82*
Autobiography of a Princess *'75*
Shakespeare Wallah *'65*

Saeed Jaffrey (1929-)
Chicken Tikka Masala *'05*
Masala *'91*
The Deceivers *'88*
The Courtesans of Bombay *'85*
My Beautiful Laundrette *'85*
The Razor's Edge *'84*
Gandhi *'82*
Hullabaloo over Georgie & Bonnie's Pictures *'78*
The Man Who Would Be King *'75*
The Wilby Conspiracy *'75*

Sakina Jaffrey (1962-)
The Manchurian Candidate *'04*
Raising Helen *'04*
Revolution #9 *'01*
Chutney Popcorn *'99*
Cotton Mary *'99*
Masala *'91*

Bianca Jagger (1945-)
C.H.U.D. 2: Bud the Chud *'89*
All You Need Is Cash *'78*

Dean Jagger (1903-91)
Evil Town *'87*
Alligator *'80*
Gideon's Trumpet *'80*
Game of Death *'79*
End of the World *'76*
The Lindbergh Kidnapping Case *'76*
Hootch Country Boys *'75*
Visions of Evil *'75*
The Hanged Man *'74*
I Heard the Owl Call My Name *'73*
The Stranger *'73*
The Glass House *'72*
Vanishing Point *'71*
Firecreek *'68*
Billy Rose's Jumbo *'62*
The Honeymoon Machine *'61*
Parrish *'61*
Cash McCall *'60*
Elmer Gantry *'60*
The Nun's Story *'59*
King Creole *'58*
Proud Rebel *'58*
Forty Guns *'57*
X The Unknown *'56*
It's a Dog's Life *'55*
Bad Day at Black Rock *'54*
Executive Suite *'54*
Private Hell 36 *'54*
White Christmas *'54*
The Robe *'53*
The Denver & Rio Grande *'51*
Rawhide *'50*
The C-Man *'49*
Twelve o'Clock High *'49*
Pursued *'47*
I Live in Grosvenor Square *'46*
Sister Kenny *'46*
The North Star *'43*
Valley of the Sun *'42*
Western Union *'41*
Brigham Young: Frontiersman *'40*
Exiled to Shanghai *'37*
Revolt of the Zombies *'36*
Wings in the Dark *'35*

Mick Jagger (1943-)
The Man from Elysian Fields *'01*
Bent *'97*
Freejack *'92*
Running out of Luck *'86*
The Nightingale *'83*
Burden of Dreams *'82*
All You Need Is Cash *'78*
Gimme Shelter *'70*
Ned Kelly *'70*
Performance *'70*
Sympathy for the Devil *'70*

Henry Jaglom (1943-)
Last Summer In the Hamptons *'96*
Venice, Venice *'92*
New Year's Day *'89*
Someone to Love *'87*
Always *'85*
Sitting Ducks *'80*
Psych-Out *'68*

Lisa Jakub (1978-)
Dream House *'98*
The Beautician and the Beast *'97*
The Wicked, Wicked West *'97*
Mrs. Doubtfire *'93*
The Story Lady *'93*
Matinee *'92*
Rambling Rose *'91*
The Phone Call *'89*

Adam James
Mother of Tears *'08*
Lost Battalion *'01*

Anthony James (1942-)
Unforgiven *'92*
Slow Burn *'90*
The Teacher *'74*
Sam Whiskey *'69*
Columbo: Prescription Murder *'67*
The Last Days of Dolwyn *'49*

Brenda James
Slither *'06*
Masters of Horror: Jenifer *'05*
The Incredible Mrs. Ritchie *'03*
Dodson's Journey *'01*

Brion James (1945-99)
The Operator *'01*
The King Is Alive *'00*
Arthur's Quest *'99*
Brown's Requiem *'98*
In God's Hands *'98*
A Place Called Truth *'98*
Bombshell *'97*
The Fifth Element *'97*
Hunter's Moon *'97*
Pterodactyl Woman from Beverly Hills *'97*
American Strays *'96*
Back in Business *'96*
Evil Obsession *'96*
The Killing Jar *'96*
The Lazarus Man *'96*

Precious Find '96
Virtual Assassin '95
Cabin Boy '94
The Companion '94
The Dark '94
Dominion '94
Hong Kong '97 '94
The Last Ride '94
Nature of the Beast '94
Radioland Murders '94
Savage Land '94
Scanner Cop '94
Sketch Artist 2: Hands That See '94
The Soft Kill '94
Steel Frontier '94
Brain Smasher... A Love Story '93
Future Shock '93
Rio Diablo '93
Striking Distance '93
Wishman '93
Black Magic '92
The Player '92
Time Runner '92
Ultimate Desires '91
Another 48 Hrs. '90
Beyond the Silhouette '90
Mutator '90
Street Asylum '90
The Horror Show '89
Mom '89
Red Scorpion '89
Tango and Cash '89
Dead Man Walking '88
Nightmare at Noon '87
Steel Dawn '87
Armed and Dangerous '86
Love Among Thieves '86
Crimewave '85
Enemy Mine '85
Flesh and Blood '85
A Breed Apart '84
Ballad of Gregorio Cortez '83
Blade Runner '82
48 Hrs. '82
Southern Comfort '81
Blue Sunshine '78
KISS Meets the Phantom of the Park '78

Clifton James (1921-)
Raising Flagg '06
The Summer of Ben Tyler '96
Lone Star '95
Carolina Skeletons '92
The Bonfire of the Vanities '90
Eight Men Out '88
Where Are the Children? '85
Talk to Me '84
The Bad News Bears in Breaking Training '77
Rancho Deluxe '75
Sniper '75
Bank Shot '74
Buster and Billie '74
The Man with the Golden Gun '74
The Iceman Cometh '73
The Last Detail '73
Live and Let Die '73
Werewolf of Washington '73
Cool Hand Luke '67
Will Penny '67
Black Like Me '64
David and Lisa '62
The Strange One '57

Colton James
The Derby Stallion '05
The Cell '00

Dalton James (1971-)
My Father the Hero '93
The Substitute '93

David James
District 9 '09
Charley's Aunt '25

Etta James (1938-)
Tap '89
Chuck Berry: Hail! Hail! Rock 'n' Roll '87

Gennie James (1977-)
The River Pirates '88
Broadcast News '87

The Secret Garden '87
A Smoky Mountain Christmas '86

Gerald James (1917-2006)
Tess of the D'Urbervilles '98
Hope and Glory '87

Geraldine James (1950-)
Sherlock Holmes '09
The Last Enemy '08
Northanger Abbey '07 (N)
A Harlot's Progress '06
The Fever '04
Calendar Girls '03
The Hound of the Baskervilles '02
The Luzhin Defence '00
Lover's Prayer '99
The Man Who Knew Too Little '97
Rebecca '97
Moll Flanders '96
Band of Gold '95
If Looks Could Kill '91
The Tall Guy '89
Echoes '88
The Jewel in the Crown '84
Gandhi '82

Gladden James (1892-1948)
Paradise Island '30
The Peacock Fan '29
The Social Secretary '16

Godfrey James (1931-)
Magic in the Mirror: Fowl Play '96
Spellbreaker: Secret of the Leprechauns '96
Leapin' Leprechauns '95
At the Earth's Core '76
The Land That Time Forgot '75

Harry James (1916-83)
The Benny Goodman Story '55
If I'm Lucky '46
Strictly G.I. '44
Two Girls and a Sailor '44
Best Foot Forward '43
Private Buckaroo '42

Hawthorne James
Campfire Tales '98
Heaven's Prisoners '95
Speed '94
The Five Heartbeats '91

Ida James
The Devil's Daughter '39
Hi-De-Ho '35

Jesse James (1989-)
The Amityville Horror '05
The Butterfly Effect '04
Fear of the Dark '02
Slap Her, She's French '02
Blow '01
A Dog of Flanders '99
Hanging Up '99
Message in a Bottle '98
The Gingerbread Man '97

Jessica James (1929-90)
Immediate Family '89
Diner '82
I, the Jury '82

John James (1914-60)
Range Renegades '48
Homesteaders of Paradise Valley '47
The Devil Bat's Daughter '46
Man from Thunder River '43

John James (1956-)
Peril '00
Secret Passions '87

Julie James
Night of the Death Cult '75
Terror Beach '75

Ken James (1948-)
Verdict in Blood '02
The Third Miracle '99

Tracked '98
Landslide '92
Switching Channels '88
Summer's Children '79

Kevin James (1965-)
Grown Ups '10
Paul Blart: Mall Cop '09
I Now Pronounce You Chuck and Larry '07
Barnyard '06 (V)
Grilled '06
Monster House '06 (V)
Hitch '05

Lee James
The Taking of Beverly Hills '91
Cassandra '87

Lennie James (1965-)
The Prisoner '09
Outlaw '07
The State Within '06
Sahara '05
Lucky Break '01
24 Hour Party People '01
Snatch '00
Among Giants '98
Lost in Space '98

Michael James (1959-)
Commando Invasion '87
Warriors of the Apocalypse '85

Oliver James (1980-)
Without a Paddle: Nature's Calling '09
Raise Your Voice '04
What a Girl Wants '03

Paul James
The Architect '06
Cry_Wolf '05
The St. Francisville Experiment '00

Pell James (1977-)
Shrink '09
Surveillance '08
Deceit '06
Broken Flowers '05
The King '05
Undiscovered '05

Peter Francis James (1956-)
The Rosa Parks Story '02
Love Song '00

Raji James
Nina's Heavenly Delights '06
East Is East '99

Ron James
Ernest Rides Again '93
The Boogey Man '80

Sidney James (1913-76)
Carry On Behind '75
Carry On Dick '75
Carry On Abroad '72
Carry On Matron '72
Carry On at Your Convenience '71
Carry On Camping '71
Carry On Henry VIII '71
Carry On Loving '70
Carry On Up the Jungle '70
Carry On Again Doctor '69
Carry On Up the Khyber '68
Carry On Cowboy '66
Don't Lose Your Head '66
Carry On Cleo '65
Carry On Cabby '63
Carry On Cruising '62
What a Carve-Up! '62
Carry On Regardless '61
Carry On Constable '60
The Silent Enemy '58
Quatermass 2 '57
The Smallest Show on Earth '57
Glass Tomb '55
John and Julie '55
Heat Wave '54
The Belles of St. Trinian's '53
Norman Conquest '53
The Lavender Hill Mob '51

Sonny James (1929-)
Hillbillies in a Haunted House '67
Las Vegas Hillbillys '66

Steve James (1955-93)
Bloodfist 5: Human Target '93
Weekend at Bernie's 2 '93
The Player '92
McBain '91
Street Hunter '90
American Ninja 3: Blood Hunt '89
Riverbend '89
Hero and the Terror '88
I'm Gonna Git You Sucka '88
Johnny Be Good '88
Python Wolf '88
American Ninja 2: The Confrontation '87
Avenging Force '86
The P.O.W. Escape '86
Stalking Danger '86
American Ninja '85
The Brother from Another Planet '84
Exterminator '80
The Warriors '79
The Land That Time Forgot '75

Tim James
Journey to the Center of the Earth '08
Funnyman '94

Walter James (1882-1946)
Police Court '32
The Kid Brother '27
Battling Butler '26
Little Annie Rooney '25
The Monster '25
The Idol Dancer '20

Joyce Jameson (1932-87)
Hardbodies '84
Pray TV '80
Savage Run '70
The Comedy of Terrors '64
Good Neighbor Sam '64
The Balcony '63
Tales of Terror '62

Malcom Jamieson
Meridian: Kiss of the Beast '90
Pictures '81

Tadeusz Janczar (1926-97)
Landscape After Battle '70
Kanal '56

Krystyna Janda (1955-)
The Decalogue '88
The Interrogation '82
Man of Iron '81
Mephisto '81
The Conductor '80
Without Anesthesia '78
Man of Marble '76

Thomas Jane (1969-)
Dark Country '09
Killshot '09
Mutant Chronicles '08
The Mist '07
The Tripper '06
The Punisher '04
Dreamcatcher '03
Stander '03
The Sweetest Thing '02
Original Sin '01
61* '01
Under Suspicion '00
Deep Blue Sea '99
Molly '99
The Thin Red Line '98
Thursday '98
The Velocity of Gary '98
Boogie Nights '97
Hollywood Confidential '97
The Crow 2: City of Angels '96
The Last Time I Committed Suicide '96

Buffy the Vampire Slayer '92

Dong-Kun Jang (1972-)
Typhoon '06
The Promise '05
Tae Guk Gi: The Brotherhood of War '04

Conrad Janis (1928-)
The Cable Guy '96
November Conspiracy '96
The Feminine Touch '95
Mr. Saturday Night '92
Sonny Boy '87
Brewster's Millions '85
Oh, God! Book 2 '80
The Buddy Holly Story '78
The Duchess and the Dirtwater Fox '76

Petr Janis
Hostel '06
The Ninth Day '04

Oleg (Yankovsky) Jankowsky (1944-)
Mute Witness '95
My Twentieth Century '90
Nostalghia '83
The Shooting Party '77
The Mirror '75

Allison Janney (1960-)
Away We Go '09
Jennifer's Body '09
Life During Wartime '09
Hairspray '07
Juno '07
Over the Hedge '06 (V)
Strangers with Candy '06
The Chumscrubber '05
Winter Solstice '04
Finding Nemo '03 (V)
How to Deal '03
The Hours '02
A Girl Thing '01
Nurse Betty '00
American Beauty '99
Drop Dead Gorgeous '99
Ten Things I Hate about You '99
Celebrity '98
The Imposters '98
The Object of My Affection '98
Primary Colors '98
Six Days, Seven Nights '98
First Do No Harm '97
The Ice Storm '97
Julian Po '97
Private Parts '96
Big Night '95

Leon Janney (1917-80)
Charly '68
Police Court '32

William Janney (1908-92)
Hopalong Cassidy Returns '36
Coquette '29

Emil Jannings (1884-1950)
The Blue Angel '30
Last Command '28
Faust '26
Tartuffe '25
Variety '25
The Last Laugh '24
Waxworks '24
Othello '22
Fortune's Fool '21
Passion '19

Walter Janovitz (1913-97)
The Hollywood Knights '80
Billy the Kid Versus Dracula '66

Josh Janowicz
On the Doll '07
The Chumscrubber '05

Thom Jansen (1945-)
The Gambler '97
Suite 16 '94

Horst Janson (1935-)
To Catch a King '84

Captain Kronos: Vampire Hunter '74
McKenzie Break '70

David Janssen (1930-80)
City in Fear '80
High Ice '80
S.O.S. Titanic '79
Centennial '78
The Word '78
Golden Rendezvous '77
Swiss Conspiracy '77
Stalk the Wild Child '76
Two Minute Warning '76
Once Is Not Enough '75
Fer-De-Lance '74
Prisoner in the Middle '74
Smile, Jenny, You're Dead '74
Pioneer Woman '73
Birds of Prey '72
Moon of the Wolf '72
Macho Callahan '70
Generation '69
Marooned '69
The Green Berets '68
The Shoes of the Fisherman '68
Dondi '61
The King of the Roaring '20s: The Story of Arnold Rothstein '61
Hell to Eternity '60
Darby's Rangers '58
Lafayette Escadrille '58
Francis in the Haunted House '56
Francis in the Navy '55
To Hell and Back '55
Francis Goes to West Point '52
Yankee Buccaneer '52
Swamp Fire '46

Eilene Janssen (1937-)
On Our Merry Way '48
Who Killed Doc Robbin? '48
Curley '47
Song of Love '47

Famke Janssen (1964-)
100 Feet '08
Taken '08
The Wackness '08
The Ten '07
Turn the River '07
The Treatment '06
X-Men: The Last Stand '06
Hide and Seek '05
Eulogy '04
X2: X-Men United '03
I Spy '02
Don't Say a Word '01
Made '01
Circus '00
Love & Sex '00
X-Men '00
House on Haunted Hill '99
Celebrity '98
Deep Rising '98
The Faculty '98
Monument Ave. '98
Rounders '98
The Gingerbread Man '97
R.P.M. '97
City of Industry '96
Goldeneye '95
Lord of Illusions '95
Model by Day '94
Relentless 4 '94
Fathers and Sons '92

Walther Jansson (1887-1976)
The Mozart Story '48
Destiny '21

Lois January (1912-2006)
Lightning Bill Crandall '37
The Red Rope '37
The Roamin' Cowboy '37
Border Caballero '36
Cocaine Fiends '36
Lightnin' Bill Carson '36
Rogue of the Range '36
Bulldog Courage '35
Skull & Crown '35

The Visitor '07
Fun With Dick and Jane '05
North Country '05
Rumor Has It.. '05
Shall We Dance? '04
Cheaper by the Dozen '03
The Core '03
Intolerable Cruelty '03
The Mudge Boy '03
Changing Lanes '02
Stealing Harvard '02
The Man Who Wasn't There '01
One Night at McCool's '01
Say It Isn't So '01
Sins of the Father '01
Me, Myself, and Irene '00
What Planet Are You From? '00
The Mod Squad '99
Outside Providence '99
Random Hearts '99
Snow Falling on Cedars '99
The Imposters '98
There's Something about Mary '98
Eye of God '97
Into Thin Air: Death on Everest '97
The Boys Next Door '96
Eddie '96
A Couch in New York '95
Flirting with Disaster '95
The Indian in the Cupboard '95
Getting Out '94
It Could Happen to You '94
Trapped in Paradise '94
Wolf '94
And the Band Played On '93
Descending Angel '90
Rising Son '90
Blaze '89
Sea of Love '89
Stealing Home '88
The Witches of Eastwick '87
The Manhattan Project '86
On Valentine's Day '86
The Tender Age '84

Sam Jenkins (1966-)
Fortunes of War '94
Ed and His Dead Mother '93
Twenty Bucks '93

Frank Jenks (1902-62)
The Amazing Colossal Man '57
Motor Patrol '50
Shep Comes Home '49
Blonde Savage '47
That Brennan Girl '46
Kid Sister '45
The Missing Corpse '45
The Phantom of 42nd Street '45
The Falcon in Hollywood '44
His Butler's Sister '44
Rogue's Gallery '44
Shake Hands with Murder '44
Zombies on Broadway '44
Corregidor '43
The Navy Comes Through '42
Back Street '41
The Flame of New Orleans '41
His Girl Friday '40
First Love '26
That Girl from Paris '36

Si Jenks (1876-1970)
Kentucky Jubilee '51
Captain January '36
Fighting Shadows '35
The Outlaw Deputy '35
Rider of the Law '35
Rawhide Romance '34

Michael Jenn
Unleashed '05
Dance with a Stranger '85
Another Country '84

Bruce Jenner (1949-)
The Big Tease '99
Grambling's White Tiger '81
Can't Stop the Music '80

Lucinda Jenney (1954-)
S.W.A.T. '03
The Mothman Prophecies '02
crazy/beautiful '01
Crime and Punishment in Suburbia '00
Thirteen Days '00
Sugar Town '99
Desert Blue '98
G.I. Jane '97
Loved '97
Stephen King's Thinner '96
Leaving Las Vegas '95
A Stranger in Town '95
Next Door '94
American Heart '92
Matinee '92
Thelma & Louise '91
Wired '89
Rain Man '88
Verne Miller '88
The Whoopee Boys '86

Alex Jennings (1957-)
Return to Cranford '09
The Disappeared '08
The Queen '06
The State Within '06
The Four Feathers '02
The Hunley '99
The Wings of the Dove '97
A Midsummer Night's Dream '96
The Franchise Affair '88

Brent Jennings
Boycott '02
Blue Ridge Fall '99
A Lesson Before Dying '99
Life '99
Love Songs '99
The Fixer '97
Children of the Corn 4: The Gathering '96
Soul of the Game '96
Nervous Ticks '93
The Serpent and the Rainbow '87

Byron Jennings
Hamlet '01
The Ice Storm '97
A Simple Twist of Fate '94

Claudia Jennings (1949-79)
Death Sport '78
Fast Company '78
Moonshine County Express '77
The Great Texas Dynamite Chase '76
Sisters of Death '76
Truck Stop Women '74
Gator Bait '73
Group Marriage '72
Unholy Rollers '72
Jud '71
The Love Machine '71
The Stepmother '71

DeWitt Jennings (1879-1937)
Kelly the Second '36
The Fighting Rookie '34
Criminal Code '31
The Bat Whispers '30
The Big House '30
Exit Smiling '26
The Little American '17

Juanita Jennings
Runaway Jury '03
Spirit Lost '96
Laurel Avenue '93

Tom Jennings
Stones of Death '88
Night Master '87
My Brother Tom '86

Waylon Jennings (1937-2002)
Outlaw Justice '98
Maverick '94
Stagecoach '86
Sesame Street Presents: Follow That Bird '85

Rita Jenrette (1949-)
End of the Line '88
Malibu Bikini Shop '86
Zombie Island Massacre '84

Salome Jens (1935-)
Cats & Dogs '01 (V)
I'm Losing You '98
The Grace Kelly Story '83
Tomorrow's Child '82
A Matter of Life and Death '81
Diary of the Dead '76
Savages '72
Seconds '66
The Fool Killer '65
Angel Baby '61

David Jensen (1947-98)
Taking Chances '09
Warbirds '08
Schizopolis '97
The Underneath '95
King of the Hill '93
A Midnight Clear '92

Erik Jensen
The Bronx Is Burning '07
Undermind '03
Borough of Kings '98

Maren Jensen (1956-)
Deadly Blessing '81
Battlestar Galactica '78
Mission Galactica: The Cylon Attack '78

Todd Jensen
The Prince & Me 3: A Royal Honeymoon '08
Finding Rin Tin Tin '07
Target of Opportunity '04
Breeders '97
Operation: Delta Force '97
Alien Chaser '96
Armageddon: The Final Challenge '94
Never Say Die '94
Cyborg Cop '93
Prey for the Hunter '92

Roy Jenson (1935-)
The Car '77
The Wind and the Lion '75
The Bandits '67

Sasha Jenson
Dazed and Confused '93
Dream Trap '90
A Girl to Kill For '90
Halloween 4: The Return of Michael Myers '88

Julia Jentsch (1978-)
I Served the King of England '07
Sophie Scholl: The Final Days '05
The Edukators '04

Jun Jeong
Nightmare '00
Attack the Gas Station '99

Jun-ho Jeong
Another Public Enemy '05
Unborn but Forgotten '02

Ken Jeong (1969-)
Despicable Me '10 (V)
Furry Vengeance '10
All About Steve '09
Couples Retreat '09
The Goods: Live Hard, Sell Hard '09
The Hangover '09
Pineapple Express '08
Young Tiger '74

Ron Jeremy (1953-)
Waiting '00
Boondock Saints '99
Orgazmo '98
They Bite '95

Adele Jergens (1917-2002)
Girls in Prison '56
The Cobweb '55
Day the World Ended '55
Lonesome Trail '55
Big Chase '54
Abbott and Costello Meet the Invisible Man '51
Armored Car Robbery '50
Blues Busters '50
Radar Secret Service '50
The Traveling Saleswoman '50
Treasure of Monte Cristo '50
The Dark Past '49
Ladies of the Chorus '49
Pirate Ship '49
The Fuller Brush Man '48
The Prince of Thieves '48
Down to Earth '47
She Wouldn't Say Yes '45
A Thousand and One Nights '45

Diane Jergens (1937-)
The FBI Story '59
High School Confidential '58
Desk Set '57

Jimmy Jerman
Vampire Night '00
Vampire Time Travelers '98
Amazon Warrior '97

Tim Jerome (1943-)
Thirteen Days '00
A Price above Rubies '97
Billy Bathgate '91

Mary Jerrold (1877-1955)
The Queen of Spades '49
Woman Hater '49
Immortal Battalion '44

George Jessel (1898-1981)
Diary of a Young Comic '79
The Busy Body '67
Valley of the Dolls '67

James Jeter (1921-2007)
The Hollywood Knights '80
Cool Hand Luke '67

Michael Jeter (1952-2003)
The Polar Express '04
Open Range '03
Welcome to Collinwood '02
Jurassic Park 3 '01
The Gift '00
South of Heaven, West of Hell '00
The Green Mile '99
Jakob the Liar '99
True Crime '99
Fear and Loathing in Las Vegas '98
The Naked Man '98
Patch Adams '98
Thursday '98
Zack & Reba '98
Air Bud '97
Mouse Hunt '97
The Boys Next Door '96
Mrs. Santa Claus '96
Waterworld '95
Drop Zone '94
Armistead Maupin's Tales of the City '93
Bank Robber '93
Gypsy '93
Sister Act 2: Back in the Habit '93
The Fisher King '91
Dead Bang '89
Tango and Cash '89
The Money Pit '86
Ragtime '81

Joan Jett (1958-)
Boogie Boy '98
Light of Day '87
Dubeat-E-O '84

Jimmy Jewel (1913-95)
The Krays '90
Arthur's Hallowed Ground '84

Geri Jewell
The Night of the White Pants '06
Two of a Kind '82

Isabel Jewell (1909-72)
Edie in Ciao! Manhattan '72
The Arousers '70
Man in the Attic '53
The Leopard Man '43
The Seventh Victim '43
Gone with the Wind '39
Lost Horizon '37
Marked Woman '37
Swing It, Sailor! '37
Big Brown Eyes '36
Go West, Young Man '36
A Tale of Two Cities '36
Ceiling Zero '35
Evelyn Prentice '34
Manhattan Melodrama '34
Counsellor-at-Law '33
Blessed Event '32

Ronny Jhutti
Nina's Heavenly Delights '06
Wild West '93

Penn Jillette (1955-)
Fear and Loathing in Las Vegas '98
Hackers '95
Penn and Teller Get Killed '90
Light Years '88 (V)
Tough Guys Don't Dance '87

Ann Jillian (1950-)
Little White Lies '89
The Ann Jillian Story '88
Convicted: A Mother's Story '87
Alice in Wonderland '85
Girls of the White Orchid '85
Mae West '84
Mr. Mom '83
Gypsy '62

Joyce Jillson (1938-)
Slumber Party '57 '76
Superchick '71

Yolanda Jilot
JFK: Reckless Youth '93
Diving In '90

Hector Jimenez (1973-)
Gentlemen Broncos '09
Epic Movie '07
Killer Pad '06
Nacho Libre '06

Jose Luis Jimenez (1900-78)
Spiritism '61
The Vampire '57

Lucia Jimenez (1978-)
The Kovak Box '06
Broken Silence '01

Soledad Jiminez (1874-1966)
For Whom the Bell Tolls '43
The Real Glory '39
The Phantom of the Range '38

Elaine Jin
Lost in Beijing '07
Yi Yi '00

Courtney Jines (1992-)
Because of Winn-Dixie '05
Spy Kids 3-D: Game Over '03
Gaudi Afternoon '01

Ma Jingwu
The Day the Sun Turned Cold '94
Raise the Red Lantern '91

Kenzaburo Jo
See Tomisaburo Wakayama

Ebony Jo-Ann
The Other Brother '02
Fly by Night '93

Suzy Joachim
White Chicks '04
Beyond Redemption '99
Ultimate Desires '91

William Job
Anatomy of Terror '74
Privilege '67

Marlene Jobert (1943-)
Swashbuckler '84
Ten Days Wonder '72
Catch Me a Spy '71
Rider on the Rain '70
The Thief of Paris '67
Masculine Feminine '66

Maz Jobrani (1972-)
The Interpreter '05
13 Going on 30 '04
The Medicine Show '01

Adan Jodorowsky
2 Days in Paris '07
Santa Sangre '90

Zita Johann (1904-93)
The Mummy '32
Tiger Shark '32
Struggle '31

David Johansen (1950-)
The Tic Code '99
Cats Don't Dance '97 (V)
Nick and Jane '96
Burnzy's Last Call '95
Car 54, Where Are You? '94
Mr. Nanny '93
Naked in New York '93 (V)
Desire and Hell at Sunset Motel '92
Freejack '92
Tales from the Darkside: The Movie '90
Let It Ride '89
Light Years '88 (V)
Married to the Mob '88
Scrooged '88
Candy Mountain '87

Paul Johansson (1964-)
Novel Romance '06
Dark Side '02
Edge of Madness '02
John Q '02
Hooded Angels '00
Carnival of Souls '98
Wishmaster 2: Evil Never Dies '98
Midnight Witness '93
Martial Law 2: Undercover '91
Soapdish '91

Scarlett Johansson (1984-)
Iron Man 2 '10
He's Just Not That Into You '09
The Other Boleyn Girl '08
The Spirit '08
Vicky Cristina Barcelona '08
The Nanny Diaries '07
The Black Dahlia '06
The Prestige '06
Scoop '06
The Island '05
Match Point '05
A Good Woman '04
In Good Company '04
A Love Song for Bobby Long '04
The Perfect Score '04
The SpongeBob SquarePants Movie '04 (V)
Girl with a Pearl Earring '03
Lost in Translation '03
Eight Legged Freaks '02
An American Rhapsody '01
Ghost World '01
The Man Who Wasn't There '01
Home Alone 3 '97
The Horse Whisperer '97
Manny & Lo '96

I.S. Johar (1920-)
Maya '66
Flame Over India '60

Elton John (1947-)
The Road to El Dorado '00 (N)
Spice World: The Movie '97
Tommy '75
Born to Boogie '72

Gottfried John (1942-)
Piano Tuner of Earthquakes '05
Proof of Life '00
The Ogre '96
Goldeneye '95
Institue Benjamenta or This Dream People Call Human Life '95
Abraham '94
The Mistake '91
Mata Hari '85
Berlin Alexanderplatz '80
The Marriage of Maria Braun '79
In a Year of 13 Moons '78
Mother Kusters Goes to Heaven '76

Karl John (1905-77)
The Mysterious Magician '65
The Lost One '51

Rosamund John (1913-98)
Fame Is the Spur '47
The Upturned Glass '47
Spitfire '42

Glynis Johns (1923-)
Superstar '99
While You Were Sleeping '95
Nukie '93
The Ref '93
Zelly & Me '88
Spraggue '84
Under Milk Wood '73
Vault of Horror '73
Dear Brigitte '65
Mary Poppins '64
Papa's Delicate Condition '63
The Sundowners '60
Shake Hands with the Devil '59
Another Time, Another Place '58
All Mine to Give '56
Around the World in 80 Days '56
Court Jester '56
Land of Fury '55
Rob Roy—The Highland Rogue '53
The Sword & the Rose '53
Encore '52
The Promoter '52
No Highway in the Sky '51
Frieda '47
An Ideal Husband '47
The Adventures of Tartu '43
The Forty-Ninth Parallel '41
South Riding '37

Marcus Johns (1993-)
Canvas '06
The Punisher '04

Mervyn Johns (1899-1992)
Day of the Triffids '63
The Victors '63
No Love for Johnnie '60
1984 '56
Romeo and Juliet '54
The Master of Ballantrae '53
A Christmas Carol '51
Tony Draws a Horse '51
Counterblast '48
Captain Boycott '47
Captive Heart '47
San Demetrio, London '47
Dead of Night '45
Pink String and Sealing Wax '45
The Foreman Went to France '42

Stratford Johns (1925-2002)
Neil Gaiman's NeverWhere '96
Splitting Heirs '93
The Strange Case of the End of Civilization As We Know It '93
A Demon in My View '92
The Lair of the White Worm '88
Salome's Last Dance '88
Car Trouble '85
Dance with a Stranger '85
Great Expectations '81
The Fiendish Plot of Dr. Fu Manchu '80
Who Done It? '56

Tracy C. Johns (1963-)
New Jack City '91
Mo' Better Blues '90
She's Gotta Have It '86

Aaron Johnson (1990-)
Kick-Ass '10
Nowhere Boy '09
Angus, Thongs and Perfect Snogging '08
The Illusionist '06
The Thief Lord '06
Dead Cool '04
Shanghai Knights '03

A.J. (Anthony) Johnson (1967-)
O '01
I Got the Hook-Up '98
The Players Club '98
B.A.P.'s '97
Def Jam's How to Be a Player '97
Double Trouble '91
House Party '90

Amy Jo Johnson (1970-)
Islander '06
Magma: Volcanic Disaster '06
Infested: Invasion of the Killer Bugs '02
Pursuit of Happiness '01
Cold Hearts '99
Sweetwater: A True Rock Story '99
Killing Mr. Griffin '97
Turbo: A Power Rangers Movie '96
Mighty Morphin Power Rangers: The Movie '95

Anne-Marie Johnson (1960-)
Pursuit of Happiness '01
Down in the Delta '98
Asteroid '97
Dream Date '93
True Identity '91
Robot Jox '90
I'm Gonna Git You Sucka '88
Hollywood Shuffle '87

Arch Johnson (1922-97)
The Cheyenne Social Club '70
Gun Glory '57

Ariyan Johnson
Bulworth '98
Just Another Girl on the I.R.T. '93

Arnold Johnson (1922-2000)
My Demon Lover '87
Putney Swope '69

Arte Johnson (1934-)
Assault of the Party Nerds 2: Heavy Petting Detective '95
Munchie '92
Evil Spirits '91
Evil Toons '90
The Red Raven Kiss-Off '90
Tax Season '90
Alice in Wonderland '85
What Comes Around '85
If Things Were Different '79
Love at First Bite '79
Bud and Lou '78
Bunco '77
Charge of the Model T's '76
The President's Analyst '67
That Funny Feeling '65

Ashley Johnson (1983-)
Columbus Day '08
Fast Food Nation '06
Nearing Grace '05
Killer Diller '04
King of the Corner '04
Rustin '01
What Women Want '00
Anywhere But Here '99
Dancer, Texas—Pop. 81 '98
Annie: A Royal Adventure '95
Nine Months '95
Lionheart '90

Bart Johnson
The Cell 2 '09
High School Musical 3: Senior Year '08
High School Musical '06

Ben Johnson (1920-96)
The Evening Star '96
Ruby Jean and Joe '96
Angels in the Outfield '94
Bonanza: The Return '93
Radio Flyer '92
The Chase '91
My Heroes Have Always Been Cowboys '91
Back to Back '90
Dark Before Dawn '89
Cherry 2000 '88
Let's Get Harry '87
Trespasses '86
Champions '84
Red Dawn '84
Soggy Bottom U.S.A. '84
Wild Horses '84
The Shadow Riders '82
Tex '82
Ruckus '81
Terror Train '80
The Sacketts '79
Wild Times '79
The Swarm '78
Grayeagle '77
Breakheart Pass '76
The Red Pony '76
The Savage Bees '76
Town That Dreaded Sundown '76
Bite the Bullet '75
The Sugarland Express '74
Dillinger '73
Train Robbers '73
The Getaway '72
Junior Bonner '72
Bull of the West '71
The Last Picture Show '71
Chisum '70
The Undefeated '69
The Wild Bunch '69
Will Penny '67
The Rare Breed '66
Major Dundee '65
One-Eyed Jacks '61
Tomboy & the Champ '58
Shane '53
Rio Grande '50
Wagon Master '50
Mighty Joe Young '49
She Wore a Yellow Ribbon '49
Three Godfathers '48

Beverly Johnson (1952-)
Crossroads '02
Def Jam's How to Be a Player '97
True Vengeance '97
The Cover Girl Murders '93
Ashanti, Land of No Mercy '79

Bill Johnson
The Texas Chainsaw Massacre 2 '86
It's a Pleasure '45

Brad Johnson (1959-)
Safe Harbour '07
Alien Siege '05
Crossfire Trail '01
Across the Line '00
Left Behind: The Movie '00
Rough Riders '97
Soldier of Fortune Inc. '97
Lone Justice 3: Showdown at Plum Creek '96
The Birds 2: Land's End '94
Dominion '94
Siringo '94
Lone Justice 2 '93
Philadelphia Experiment 2 '93
An American Story '92
Flight of the Intruder '90
Always '89
Nam Angels '88

Bryce Johnson
The Blue Tooth Virgin '09
Private Valentine: Blonde & Dangerous '08
Trucker '08
Sleeping Dogs Lie '06
Freshman Orientation '04
Harry and Max '04
Bring It On Again '03

C. David Johnson (1955-)
Terminal Invasion '02
Aldrich Ames: Traitor Within '98
The Legend of Gator Face '96

Candy Johnson (1944-)
Bikini Beach '64
Muscle Beach Party '64
Pajama Party '64
Beach Party '63

Celia Johnson (1908-82)
The Hostage Tower '80
Staying On '80
Les Miserables '78
The Prime of Miss Jean Brodie '69
A Kid for Two Farthings '55
Captain's Paradise '53
This Happy Breed '47
Brief Encounter '46
In Which We Serve '43

Chic Johnson (1891-1962)
Crazy House '43
All Over Town '37
Country Gentlemen '36

Chubby Johnson
Law and Order '53
Night Riders of Montana '50
Rocky Mountain '50

Clark Johnson (1954-)
The Trojan Horse '08
The Sentinel '06
Re-Generation '04
S.W.A.T. '03
Boycott '02
Deliberate Intent '01
Disappearing Acts '00
Homicide: The Movie '00
Love Come Down '00
Blood Brothers '97
Junior's Groove '97
Rude '96
Soul Survivor '95
Final Round '93
The Finishing Touch '92
Personals '90
Colors '88

Corey Johnson (1961-)
The Fourth Kind '09
The Bourne Ultimatum '07
The Contract '07
A Sound of Thunder '05
Hellboy '04
Endgame '01
Last Run '01
The Mummy '99

Don Johnson (1950-)
Moondance Alexander '07
Goodbye, Lover '99
Tin Cup '96
In Pursuit of Honor '95
Born Yesterday '93
Guilty as Sin '93
Harley Davidson and the Marlboro Man '91
Paradise '91
Tales of the Unexpected '91
The Hot Spot '90
Dead Bang '89
Sweet Hearts Dance '88
The Long, Hot Summer '86
Cease Fire '85
Miami Vice '84
Soggy Bottom U.S.A. '84
Melanie '82
Beulah Land '80
Revenge of the Stepford Wives '80
The Rebels '79
Snowblind '78
The City '76
Law of the Land '76
A Boy and His Dog '75
Return to Macon County '75
Harrad Experiment '73
Zachariah '70

Dots Johnson (1913-86)
Paisan '46
Tall, Tan and Terrific '46

Dwayne "The Rock" Johnson (1972-)
The Other Guys '10
Tooth Fairy '10
Planet 51 '09 (V)
Race to Witch Mountain '09
Get Smart '08
The Game Plan '07
Reno 911! Miami '07
Gridiron Gang '06
Southland Tales '06
Be Cool '05
Doom '05
Walking Tall '04
The Rundown '03
The Scorpion King '02
The Mummy Returns '01

Geordie Johnson (1953-)
Charms for the Easy Life '02
Dangerous Evidence: The Lori Jackson Story '99
A Change of Place '94
Spenser: The Judas Goat '94

Georgann Johnson (1926-)
Twilight Man '96
Shattered Dreams '90
Murphy's Romance '85

Helen Johnson (1954-)
Vice Squad '31
The Divorcee '30
Sin Takes a Holiday '30

Jack Johnson (1987-)
Sleep Easy, Hutch Rimes '00
Lost in Space '98

Jerry Johnson
Code of Honor '82
Kill Squad '81

Joey Johnson
Courier of Death '84
Grad Night '81

Julie Johnson
Barney's Great Adventure '98 (V)
The Islander '88

Karl Johnson (1924-93)
Night of the Ghouls '59
The Unearthly '57
Plan 9 from Outer Space '56

Karl Johnson (1948-)
The Chatterley Affair '06
Four Last Songs '06
Pure '02
Love Is the Devil '98
Saint-Ex: The Story of the Storyteller '95
Wittgenstein '93
Close My Eyes '91

Katie Johnson (1878-1957)
John and Julie '55
The Ladykillers '55

Kay Johnson (1904-75)
Son of Fury '42
The Real Glory '39
Village Tale '35
American Madness '32
Madam Satan '30

Kelly Johnson
Utu '83
Carry Me Back '82
Goodbye Pork Pie '81

Kenneth Johnson (1942-)
The Veteran '06
Major League 3: Back to the Minors '98

Kirsten Johnson
Bride Wars '09
Eclipse '94

Kurt Johnson (1952-86)
Sole Survivor '84
Jane Austen in Manhattan '80

Kyle Johnson (1951-)
Man on the Run '74
The Learning Tree '69

Lamont Johnson (1955-)
Waiting to Exhale '95
Fear of a Black Hat '94
The Five Heartbeats '91
The Brothers Rico '57

Laura Johnson (1957-)
Hope Ranch '02
Judge & Jury '96
Cheatin' Hearts '93
Dario Argento's Trauma '93
Deadly Exposure '93
Fatal Instinct '92
Red Shoe Diaries 2: Double Dare '92
Murderous Vision '91
Nick Knight '89
Beyond Reason '77
Opening Night '77

Lynn-Holly Johnson (1958-)
Fugitive X '96
The Criminal Mind '93
Digging Up Business '91
Hyper Space '89
The Sisterhood '88
Where the Boys Are '84 '84
For Your Eyes Only '81
The Watcher in the Woods '81
Alien Predators '80
Ice Castles '79

Mel Johnson, Jr.
Hideous '97
Total Recall '90
Eubie! '82

Melody Johnson (1982-)
Jason X '01
Jailbait! '00

Michael Johnson (1939-2001)
Lust for a Vampire '71
Anne of the Thousand Days '69

Michelle Johnson (1965-)
Fallen Angel '99
Specimen '97
The Glimmer Man '96
Moving Target '96
When the Bullet Hits the Bone '96
The Donor '94
Illicit Dreams '94
Incident at Deception Ridge '94
Body Shot '93
Blood Ties '92
Death Becomes Her '92
Far and Away '92
Till Murder Do Us Part '92
Wishful Thinking '92
Driving Me Crazy '91
Genuine Risk '89
Jigsaw Murders '89
Slipping into Darkness '88
Waxwork '88

Beaks: The Movie *'87*
A Chorus Line *'85*
Gung Ho *'85*
Blame It on Rio *'84*

Noble Johnson (1881-1978)
North of the Great Divide *'50*
She Wore a Yellow Ribbon *'49*
Hurry, Charlie, Hurry *'41*
The Ghost Breakers *'40*
The Lives of a Bengal Lancer *'35*
King Kong *'33*
The Most Dangerous Game *'32*
The Mummy *'32*
Murders in the Rue Morgue *'32*
The Navigator *'24*
The Leopard Woman *'20*

Penny Johnson (1961-)
DC 9/11: Time of Crisis *'04*
Deliberate Intent *'01*
The Road to Galveston *'96*
Fear of a Black Hat *'94*
What's Love Got to Do with It? *'93*

Rebekah Johnson (1976-)
Liberty Heights *'99*
Ruby Jean and Joe *'96*

Reggie Johnson
Seven Hours to Judgment *'88*
Platoon *'86*

Richard Johnson (1927-)
The Boy in the Striped Pajamas *'08*
The Raven *'07 (N)*
Lara Croft: Tomb Raider *'01*
Breaking the Code *'95*
The Camomile Lawn *'92*
Duel of Hearts *'92*
The Crucifer of Blood *'91*
Diving In *'90*
Spymaker: The Secret Life of Ian Fleming *'90*
Treasure Island *'89*
A Man for All Seasons *'88*
Turtle Diary *'86*
Lady Jane *'85*
The Great Alligator *'81*
Screamers *'80*
Zombie *'80*
The Big Scam *'79*
The Four Feathers *'78*
The Comeback *'77*
Beyond the Door *'75*
Hennessy *'75*
Fifth Day of Peace *'72*
Restless *'72*
Deadlier Than the Male *'67*
The Rover *'67*
Khartoum *'66*
The Witch *'66*
The Amorous Adventures of Moll Flanders *'65*
Operation Crossbow *'65*
The Pumpkin Eater *'64*
Tomb of Ligeia *'64*
The Haunting *'63*
Never So Few *'59*

Rick Johnson (1961-)
Rustin *'01*
Foreign Student *'94*

Rita Johnson (1913-65)
All Mine to Give *'56*
The Big Clock *'48*
They Won't Believe Me *'47*
The Perfect Marriage *'46*
The Naughty Nineties *'45*
My Friend Flicka *'43*
The Major and the Minor *'42*
Here Comes Mr. Jordan *'41*
Edison the Man *'40*
Broadway Serenade *'39*
Honolulu *'39*
Smashing the Rackets *'38*

Robin Johnson (1964-)
Splitz *'84*
Times Square *'80*

Ron Johnson (1973-)
Shadow Dancer *'96*
Zebrahead *'92*

Russell Johnson (1924-)
Undesirable *'92*
Blue Movies *'88*
The Great Skycopter Rescue *'82*
The Bastard *'78*
Rescue from Gilligan's Island *'78*
Fatal Chase *'77*
Rock All Night *'57*
Ma and Pa Kettle at Waikiki *'55*
Many Rivers to Cross *'55*
This Island Earth *'55*
Ride Clear of Diablo *'54*
It Came from Outer Space *'53*
Law and Order *'53*
Loan Shark *'52*

Ryan Thomas Johnson
Criminal Ways *'03*
Carnosaur 2 *'94*

Samuel Johnson
$9.99 *'08 (V)*
After the Deluge *'03*
Strange Fits of Passion *'99*

Stacii Jae Johnson
Da Hip Hop Witch *'00*
Parental Guidance *'98*

Steve Johnson
Angel of H.E.A.T. *'82*
Lemora, Lady Dracula *'73*

Sunny Johnson (1953-84)
The Red Light Sting *'84*
Flashdance *'83*
Dr. Heckyl and Mr. Hype *'80*

Tor Johnson (1903-71)
The Beast of Yucca Flats *'61*
Night of the Ghouls *'59*
The Unearthly *'57*
The Black Sleep *'56*
Carousel *'56*
Plan 9 from Outer Space *'56*
Bride of the Monster *'55*
Houdini *'53*
Abbott and Costello in the Foreign Legion *'50*
Behind Locked Doors *'48*
Human Gorilla *'48*

Van Johnson (1916-2008)
Three Days to a Kill *'91*
Delta Force Commando 2 *'90*
The Purple Rose of Cairo *'85*
Scorpion with Two Tails *'82*
The Kidnapping of the President *'80*
Eagles Over London *'69*
Where Angels Go, Trouble Follows *'68*
Yours, Mine & Ours *'68*
Divorce American Style *'67*
The Doomsday Flight *'66*
The Pied Piper of Hamelin *'57*
End of the Affair *'55*
Brigadoon *'54*
The Caine Mutiny *'54*
The Last Time I Saw Paris *'54*
Men of the Fighting Lady *'54*
Easy to Love *'53*
Go for Broke! *'51*
Invitation *'51*
It's a Big Country *'51*
Three Guys Named Mike *'51*
The Big Hangover *'50*
The Duchess of Idaho *'50*
Battleground *'49*
In the Good Old Summertime *'49*
Command Decision *'48*
State of the Union *'48*
Easy to Wed *'46*
Thrill of a Romance *'45*
Weekend at the Waldorf *'45*
A Guy Named Joe *'44*
Thirty Seconds Over Tokyo *'44*
Two Girls and a Sailor *'44*
The White Cliffs of Dover *'44*
The Human Comedy *'43*
Madame Curie *'43*
Too Many Girls *'40*

Victoria (Vicki) Johnson
Starship Invasions *'77*
Grizzly *'76*

Bobby Johnston
DC 9/11: Time of Crisis *'04*
Body Strokes *'95*
Sinful Intrigue *'95*
Hollywood's New Blood *'88*

Grace Johnston
One Good Cop *'91*
God Bless the Child *'88*

James Johnston
Clean *'04*
Never Pick Up a Stranger *'79*

J.J. Johnston (1933-)
Lakeboat *'00*
K-911 *'99*
The Fixer *'97*
Stranger by Night *'94*
Mad Dog and Glory *'93*
Things Change *'88*
Fatal Attraction *'87*

John Dennis Johnston
Firestarter 2: Rekindled *'02*
Mercenary 2: Thick and Thin *'97*
In Pursuit of Honor *'95*
Wyatt Earp *'94*
Fever *'91*
Miracle in the Wilderness *'91*
Big Bad John *'90*
Pink Cadillac *'89*
Into Thin Air *'85*
A Breed Apart *'84*
Streets of Fire *'84*
The Beast Within *'82*
Dear Detective *'78*
KISS Meets the Phantom of the Park *'78*

Kristen Johnston (1967-)
Music & Lyrics *'07*
Strangers with Candy *'06*
The Flintstones in Viva Rock Vegas *'00*
Austin Powers 2: The Spy Who Shagged Me *'99*

Margaret Johnston (1918-2002)
Sebastian *'68*
Burn Witch, Burn! *'62*
A Man About the House *'47*

Oliver Johnston (1888-1966)
A Countess from Hong Kong *'67*
Tomb of Ligeia *'64*
A King in New York *'57*

Shaun Johnston
September Dawn *'07*
The Christmas Blessing *'05*

Shawn Johnston
Bury My Heart at Wounded Knee *'07*
Ms. Bear *'97*

Sue Johnston
Little Dorrit *'08*
Imagine Me & You *'06*

Kim Johnston-Ulrich (1955-)
Rumpelstiltskin *'96*
Blood Ties *'92*

Marilyn Joi
Hospital of Terror *'78*
Black Samurai *'77*
Kentucky Fried Movie *'77*

Mirjana Jokovic (1967-)
Underground *'95*
Vukovar *'94*
Eversmile New Jersey *'89*

Angelina Jolie (1975-)
Salt *'10*
Changeling *'08*
Kung Fu Panda *'08 (V)*
Wanted *'08*
Beowulf *'07 (V)*
A Mighty Heart *'07*
The Good Shepherd *'06*
Mr. & Mrs. Smith *'05*
Alexander *'04*
The Fever *'04*
Shark Tale *'04 (V)*
Sky Captain and the World of Tomorrow *'04*
Taking Lives *'04*
Beyond Borders *'03*
Lara Croft Tomb Raider: The Cradle of Life *'03*
Life or Something Like It *'02*
Lara Croft: Tomb Raider *'01*
Original Sin *'01*
Gone in 60 Seconds *'00*
The Bone Collector *'99*
Girl, Interrupted *'99*
Pushing Tin *'99*
Gia *'98*
Playing by Heart *'98*
George Wallace *'97*
Hell's Kitchen NYC *'97*
True Women *'97*
Foxfire *'96*
Love Is All There Is *'96*
Mojave Moon *'96*
Playing God *'96*
Without Evidence *'96*
Hackers *'95*
Cyborg 2 *'93*

Adrien Jolivet
Apres Lui *'07*
In the Arms of My Enemy *'07*

I. Stanford Jolley (1900-78)
The Rebel Set *'59*
The Violent Years *'56*
Outlaw Fury *'50*
King of the Rocketmen *'49*
Rimfire *'49*
Sands of Iwo Jima *'49*
Check Your Guns *'48*
Wild Country *'47*
Ambush Trail *'46*
Cyclotrode "X" *'46*
Flaming Bullets *'45*
Frontier Fugitives *'45*
Lightning Raiders *'45*
Outlaw Roundup *'44*
The Black Raven *'43*
The Return of the Rangers *'43*
Rangers Take Over *'42*
Trail of the Silver Spurs *'41*
Midnight Limited *'40*

Al Jolson (1886-1950)
Rhapsody in Blue *'45*
Rose of Washington Square *'39*
The Singing Kid *'36*
Go Into Your Dance *'35*
Wonder Bar *'34*
Hallelujah, I'm a Bum *'33*
Big Boy *'30*
Say It With Songs *'29*
The Singing Fool *'28*
The Jazz Singer *'27*

Joe Jonas (1989-)
Jonas Brothers: The 3D Concert Experience *'09*
Camp Rock *'08*

Wesley Jonathan (1978-)
Remember the Daze *'07*
Crossover *'06*
Roll Bounce *'05*
Baadasssss! *'03*

Allan Jones (1908-92)
A Swingin' Summer *'65*
One Night in the Tropics *'40*
Everybody Sing *'38*
A Day at the Races *'37*
The Firefly *'37*
Rose Marie *'36*
Show Boat *'36*
A Night at the Opera *'35*

Allison Jones
Ellen Foster *'97*
Nightjohn *'96*

Andras Jones (1968-)
The Demolitionist *'95*
Far from Home *'89*
A Nightmare on Elm Street 4: Dream Master *'88*
Sorority Babes in the Slimeball Bowl-A-Rama *'87*

Andy Jones
Behind the Wall *'08*
Rare Birds *'01*

Angela Jones
The Debt *'98*
Curdled *'95*
Pulp Fiction *'94*

Angus T. Jones (1993-)
The Christmas Blessing *'05*
Audrey's Rain *'03*
Bringing Down the House *'03*
The Rookie *'02*
See Spot Run *'01*

Ashley Jones (1976-)
The Devil's Prey *'01*
The King's Guard *'01*
The Fire Next Time *'93*

Barry Jones (1893-1981)
War and Peace *'56*
The Glass Slipper *'55*
Brigadoon *'54*
Demetrius and the Gladiators *'54*
Prince Valiant *'54*
Return to Paradise *'53*
The Clouded Yellow *'51*
Madeleine *'50*
Seven Days to Noon *'50*
Uneasy Terms *'48*

Ben Jones (1941-)
Joe Gould's Secret *'00*
Primary Colors *'98*
Deep in the Heart *'83*
Don't Change My World *'83*

Billy "Red" Jones (1913-2000)
Ninja Death Squad *'87*
The Phantom Flyer *'28*

Bruce Jones (1953-)
24-7 *'97*
Raining Stones *'93*

Buck Jones (1891-1942)
Below the Border *'42*
Dawn on the Great Divide *'42*
Down Texas Way *'42*
Ghost Town Law *'42*
Riders of the West *'42*
West of the Law *'42*
Arizona Bound *'41*
Forbidden Trails *'41*
Gunman from Bodie *'41*
Riders of Death Valley *'41*
Wagons Westward *'40*
Law of the Texan *'38*
The Stranger from Arizona *'38*
Sandflow *'37*
The Phantom Rider *'36*
The Crimson Trail *'35*
The Ivory Handled Gun *'35*
Law for Tombstone *'35*
Stone of Silver Creek *'35*
The Throwback *'35*
When a Man Sees Red *'34*
The California Trail *'33*
Treason *'33*
Hello Trouble *'32*
Ridin' for Justice *'32*
White Eagle *'32*
Border Law *'31*
The Fighting Sheriff *'31*
Range Feud *'31*
The Dawn Trail *'30*
Lazybones *'25*

Carolyn Jones (1929-83)
Halloween with the Addams Family *'79*
The Shaming *'79*
Little Ladies of the Night *'77*
Eaten Alive *'76*
Color Me Dead *'69*
How the West Was Won *'63*
Ice Palace *'60*
Career *'59*
A Hole in the Head *'59*
Last Train from Gun Hill *'59*
King Creole *'58*
Marjorie Morningstar *'58*
Invasion of the Body Snatchers *'56*
The Man Who Knew Too Much *'56*
The Seven Year Itch *'55*
The Tender Trap *'55*
The Big Heat *'53*
House of Wax *'53*
The Road to Bali *'53*
The War of the Worlds *'53*

Cherry Jones (1956-)
Amelia *'09*
Mother and Child *'09*
24 : Redemption *'08*
Ocean's Twelve *'04*
The Village *'04*
Divine Secrets of the Ya-Ya Sisterhood *'02*
Signs *'02*
Cora Unashamed *'00*
Erin Brockovich *'00*
The Perfect Storm *'00*
The Cradle Will Rock *'99*
The Lady in Question *'99*
Murder in a Small Town *'99*
The Horse Whisperer *'97*
Julian Po *'97*
Big Town *'87*

Christopher Jones (1941-)
Ryan's Daughter *'70*
The Looking Glass War *'69*
Three in the Attic *'68*
Wild in the Streets *'68*

Claude Earl Jones
Bride of Re-Animator *'89*
Miracle Mile *'89*
Impulse *'84*
Evilspeak *'82*

Clyde Jones
Father of Lies *'07*
Love Beat the Hell Outta Me *'00*
Delta Heat *'92*
Crack House *'89*
The Siege of Firebase Gloria *'89*

Cody Jones (1985-)
Running Wild *'99*
Rent-A-Kid *'95*

Darby Jones (1910-86)
Zombies on Broadway *'44*
I Walked with a Zombie *'43*

Davy Jones (1946-)
The Brady Bunch Movie *'95*
Head *'68*

Dean Jones (1935-)
The Love Bug *'97*
That Darn Cat *'96*
Clear and Present Danger *'94*
Beethoven *'92*
Other People's Money *'91*
Fire and Rain *'89*
The Long Days of Summer *'80*
Born Again *'78*
When Every Day Was the Fourth of July *'78*
Herbie Goes to Monte Carlo *'77*
Once Upon a Brothers Grimm *'77*
The Shaggy D.A. *'76*

O-lan Jones (1950-)
American Virgin *'98*
Natural Born Killers *'94*
Pacific Heights *'90*
Miracle Mile *'89*

Orlando Jones (1968-)
Beyond a Reasonable Doubt *'09*
Cirque du Freak: The Vampire's Assistant *'09*
Primeval *'07*
House of D *'04*
Biker Boyz *'03*
Drumline *'02*
The Time Machine *'02*
Double Take *'01*
Evolution *'01*
Say It Isn't So *'01*
Bedazzled *'00*
Chain of Fools *'00*
The Replacements *'00*
Liberty Heights *'99*
Waterproof *'99*
Office Space *'98*

Paul Jones (1942-)
Demons of the Mind *'72*
Privilege *'67*

Peter Jones (1920-2000)
Whoops Apocalypse *'83*
Hot Millions *'68*
John and Julie *'55*
Man of Evil *'48*

Rashida Jones (1976-)
I Love You, Man *'09*
New in Town *'09*
Little Black Book *'04*
Now You Know *'02*

Richard Jones (1946-)
Where the Heart Is *'00*
The Newton Boys *'97*
Two for Texas *'97*
The Good Old Boys *'95*
Lone Star *'95*
Under Siege *'92*
Another Pair of Aces: Three of a Kind *'91*
Blue Sky *'91*

Richard T. Jones (1972-)
Tyler Perry's Why Did I Get Married Too? *'10*
Vantage Point *'08*
Tyler Perry's Why Did I Get Married? *'07*
Twisted *'04*
G *'02*
Moonlight Mile *'02*
Phone Booth *'02*
Beyond Suspicion *'00*
Lockdown *'00*
Incognito *'99*
The Wood *'99*
Event Horizon *'97*
Hollywood Confidential *'97*
Kiss the Girls *'97*
The Trigger Effect *'96*
Renaissance Man *'94*

Robert Earl Jones (1911-2006)
Rain Without Thunder *'93*
Maniac Cop 2 *'90*
Witness *'85*
The Cotton Club *'84*
Sleepaway Camp *'83*
Trading Places *'83*
Cold River *'81*
Sophisticated Gents *'81*
Cockfighter *'74*
The Sting *'73*

Rosie Jones
Ganjasaurus Rex *'87*
Alice to Nowhere *'86*

Sam Jones (1954-)
Strange Fruit *'04*
Dead Sexy *'01*
T.N.T. *'98*
American Strays *'96*
Where Truth Lies *'96*
Texas Payback *'95*
Ballistic *'94*
Fists of Iron *'94*
Hard Vice *'94*
Vegas Vice *'94*
Expert Weapon *'93*
Lady Dragon 2 *'93*
Thunder in Paradise *'93*
DaVinci's War *'92*
Fist of Honor *'92*
Maximum Force *'92*
Night Rhythms *'92*
The Other Woman *'92*
In Gold We Trust *'91*
One Man Force *'89*
Driving Force *'88*
Silent Assassins *'88*
Under the Gun *'88*
WhiteForce *'88*
Jane & the Lost City *'87*
My Chauffeur *'86*
Flash Gordon *'80*

Sam Jones, III (1983-)
Glory Road *'06*
Home of the Brave *'06*
ZigZag *'02*
Snipes *'01*

Sarah Jones
Love Finds a Home *'09*
Love Takes Wing *'09*
Still Green *'07*
Bamboozled *'00*

Sharon Lee Jones
Josh Kirby... Time Warrior: Chapter 3, Trapped on Toyworld *'95*
Leapin' Leprechauns *'95*

Shirley Jones (1934-)
Grandma's Boy *'06*
Hidden Places *'06*
Raising Genius *'04*
Manna from Heaven *'02*
Shriek If You Know What I Did Last Friday the 13th *'00*
Gideon *'99*
Ping! *'99*
Black Devil Doll from Hell *'84*
Tank *'83*
Who'll Save Our Children? *'82*
The Children of An Lac *'80*
Beyond the Poseidon Adventure *'79*
Last Cry for Help *'79*
The Girls of Huntington House *'73*
The Cheyenne Social Club *'70*
The Happy Ending *'69*
Silent Night, Lonely Night *'69*
Bedtime Story *'63*
The Courtship of Eddie's Father *'62*
The Music Man *'62*
Two Rode Together *'61*
Elmer Gantry *'60*
Never Steal Anything Small *'59*
Carousel *'56*
Oklahoma! *'55*

Simon Jones (1950-)
The Hitchhiker's Guide to the Galaxy *'05*
Operation Delta Force 2: Mayday *'97*
The Devil's Own *'96*
Miracle on 34th Street *'94*
Green Card *'90*
Club Paradise *'86*
Privates on Parade *'84*
Monty Python's The Meaning of Life *'83*
The Hitchhiker's Guide to the Galaxy *'81*

Steve Jones (1955-)
The Big Bounce *'04*
The Filth and the Fury *'99*

Tamala Jones (1974-)
Daddy Day Camp *'07*
What Love Is *'07*
Who's Your Caddy? *'07*
Nora's Hair Salon *'04*
Head of State *'03*
The Brothers *'01*
On the Line *'01*
Two Can Play That Game *'01*
The Ladies Man *'00*
Little Richard *'00*
Next Friday *'00*
Turn It Up *'00*
Blue Streak *'99*
The Wood *'99*
Booty Call *'96*

Terry Jones (1942-)
Mr. Toad's Wild Ride *'96*
Erik the Viking *'89*
Monty Python's The Meaning of Life *'83*
The Secret Policeman's Other Ball *'82*
Secret Policeman's Private Parts *'81*
Monty Python's Life of Brian *'79*
Jabberwocky *'77*
Monty Python and the Holy Grail *'75*
And Now for Something Completely Different *'72*

Toby Jones (1967-)
Sex & Drugs & Rock & Roll *'10*
Creation *'09*
City of Ember *'08*
Frost/Nixon *'08*
W. *'08*
The Mist *'07*
The Old Curiosity Shop *'07*
St. Trinian's *'07*
Amazing Grace *'06*
A Harlot's Progress *'06*
Infamous *'06*
The Painted Veil *'06*
Elizabeth I *'05*
Harry Potter and the Chamber of Secrets *'02 (V)*
In Love and War *'01*
Love or Money *'01*

Tom Jones (1940-)
Agnes Browne *'99*
Mars Attacks! *'96*
The Jerky Boys *'95*
The Last Days of Dolwyn *'49*

Tommy Lee Jones (1946-)
In the Electric Mist *'08*
In the Valley of Elah *'07*
No Country for Old Men *'07*
A Prairie Home Companion *'06*
Man of the House *'05*
The Three Burials of Melquiades Estrada *'05*
The Hunted *'03*
The Missing *'03*
Men in Black 2 *'02*
Rules of Engagement *'00*
Space Cowboys *'00*
Double Jeopardy *'99*
Small Soldiers *'98 (V)*
U.S. Marshals *'98*
Men in Black *'97*
Volcano *'97*
Batman Forever *'95*
The Good Old Boys *'95*
Blown Away *'94*
The Client *'94*
Cobb *'94*
Natural Born Killers *'94*
The Fugitive *'93*
Heaven and Earth *'93*
House of Cards *'92*
Under Siege *'92*
Blue Sky *'91*
JFK *'91*
Fire Birds *'90*
Lonesome Dove *'89*
The Package *'89*
Gotham *'88*
Stormy Monday *'88*
Big Town *'87*
Broken Vows *'87*
Black Moon Rising *'86*
Yuri Nosenko, KGB *'86*
The Park Is Mine *'85*
Cat on a Hot Tin Roof *'84*
The River Rat *'84*
Nate and Hayes *'83*
The Executioner's Song *'82*
Back Roads *'81*
Coal Miner's Daughter *'80*
The Betsy *'78*
Eyes of Laura Mars *'78*
The Amazing Howard Hughes *'77*
Rolling Thunder *'77*
Jackson County Jail *'76*
Eliza's Horoscope *'70*
Love Story *'70*

Tyler Patrick Jones (1994-)
G-Force *'09*
The Bad News Bears *'05*
Yours, Mine & Ours *'05*
Red Dragon *'02*

Vinnie Jones (1965-)
Smokin' Aces 2: Assassins' Ball *'10*
(Untitled) *'09*
Year One *'09*
Hell Ride *'08*
Legend of the Bog *'08*
Loaded *'08*
The Midnight Meat Train *'08*
The Condemned *'07*
The Riddle *'07*
Rush Hour 3 *'07*
Strike *'07*
Tooth and Nail *'07*
Garfield: A Tail of Two Kitties *'06 (V)*
The Other Half *'06*
Played *'06*
She's the Man *'06*
X-Men: The Last Stand *'06*
Johnny Was *'05*
Submerged *'05*
The Big Bounce *'04*
Blast *'04*
Eurotrip *'04*
Night at the Golden Eagle *'02*
Mean Machine *'01*
Swordfish *'01*
Gone in 60 Seconds *'00*
Snatch *'00*
Lock, Stock and 2 Smoking Barrels *'98*

Betsy Jones-Moreland (1930-2006)
The Last Woman on Earth *'61*
Creature from the Haunted Sea *'60*

Samson Jorah
The Snow Walker *'03*
Never Cry Wolf *'83*

Richard Jordahl
To the Shores of Hell *'65*
The Starfighters *'63*

Bobby Jordan (1923-65)
Spook Busters *'48*
Bowery Buckaroos *'47*
Hard-Boiled Mahoney *'47*
Clancy Street Boys *'43*
Kid Dynamite *'43*
Junior Army *'42*
Let's Get Tough *'42*
'Neath Brooklyn Bridge *'42*
Bowery Blitzkrieg *'41*
Flying Wild *'41*
Pride of the Bowery *'41*
Spooks Run Wild *'41*
Boys of the City *'40*
That Gang of Mine *'40*
Young Tom Edison *'40*
They Made Me a Criminal *'39*
Angels with Dirty Faces *'38*
Crime School *'38*
A Slight Case of Murder *'38*
Dead End *'37*

Clint Jordan
Down to the Bone *'04*
Milk and Honey *'03*
Virgil Bliss *'01*

Dorothy Jordan (1906-88)
The Searchers *'56*
One Man's Journey *'33*
The Cabin in the Cotton *'32*
Lost Squadron *'32*
Min & Bill *'30*

James Carroll Jordan (1950-)
Tales of the Unexpected *'91*
Slashdance *'89*
Diary of a Teenage Hitchhiker *'82*

Jeremy Jordan (1973-)
Never Been Kissed *'99*
Nowhere *'96*

Jim Jordan (1896-1988)
The Rescuers *'77 (V)*
Here We Go Again! *'42*
Look Who's Laughing *'41*

Joanne Moore Jordan
I Dismember Mama *'74*
Faces *'68*

Laura Jordan
Joy Ride 2: Dead Ahead *'08*
Thr3e *'07*
The Night of the White Pants *'06*
Berkeley *'05*

Leslie Jordan (1955-)
Eating Out 3: All You Can Eat *'09*
Chasing Christmas *'05*
Madhouse *'04*
Sordid Lives *'00*
Jason Goes to Hell: The Final Friday *'93*
Ski Patrol *'89*
Frankenstein General Hospital *'88*

Louis Jordan (1908-75)
Look Out Sister *'48*
Reet, Petite and Gone *'47*
Beware *'46*

Lydia Grace Jordan
Pistol Whipped *'08*
Into the Fire *'05*
The Thing About My Folks *'05*

Marian Jordan (1897-1961)
Here We Go Again! *'42*
Look Who's Laughing *'41*

Marsha Jordan (1939-)
Class Reunion *'72*
Sweet Georgia *'72*
Count Yorga, Vampire *'70*
Lady Godiva Rides *'68*

Nick Jordan
See Aldo Canti

Patrick Jordan (1923-)
Too Late the Hero *'70*
The Heroes of Telemark *'65*
The Victors *'63*

Richard Jordan (1938-93)
Gettysburg *'93*
Posse *'93*
Primary Motive *'92*
Heaven Is a Playground *'91*
The Hunt for the Night Stalker *'91*
Shout *'91*
Timebomb *'91*
The Hunt for Red October *'90*
Romero *'89*
The Murder of Mary Phagan *'87*
The Secret of My Success *'87*
The Men's Club *'86*
Solarbabies *'86*
A Flash of Green *'85*
Mean Season *'85*
Dune *'84*
Washington Mistress *'81*
Raise the Titanic *'80*
The Big Scam *'79*
Old Boyfriends *'79*
Interiors *'78*
Les Miserables *'78*
Logan's Run *'76*
Rooster Cogburn *'75*
The Yakuza *'75*
Trial of the Catonsville Nine *'72*
Chato's Land *'71*
Lawman *'71*
Valdez Is Coming *'71*

William Jordan
Kingpin *'96*
The Doors *'91*
The Red Fury *'84*
The Buddy Holly Story *'78*
I Wanna Hold Your Hand *'78*
King *'78*

Daniel Jordano
Playing for Keeps *'86*
Alphabet City *'84*

Victor Jory (1902-82)
The Mountain Men *'80*
Devil Dog: The Hound of Hell *'78*
Frasier the Sensuous Lion *'73*
Papillon *'73*
Cheyenne Autumn *'64*
The Miracle Worker *'62*
The Fugitive Kind *'60*
Death of a Scoundrel *'56*
Manfish *'56*
Sabaka *'55*
Valley of the Kings *'54*
Cat Women of the Moon *'53*
Man from the Alamo *'53*
Son of Ali Baba *'52*
The Capture *'50*
The Cariboo Trail *'50*
A Woman's Secret *'49*
The Loves of Carmen *'48*
South of St. Louis *'48*
Buckskin Frontier *'43*
Colt Comrades *'43*
Hoppy Serves a Writ *'43*
The Kansan *'43*
Leather Burners *'43*
Power of the Press *'43*
Border Vigilantes *'41*
Charlie Chan in Rio *'41*
Riders of the Timberline *'41*
Green Archer *'40*
Knights of the Range *'40*
The Light of Western Stars *'40*
Dodge City *'39*
Each Dawn I Die *'39*
Gone with the Wind *'39*
Susannah of the Mounties *'39*
The Adventures of Tom Sawyer *'38*
Bulldog Drummond at Bay *'37*
Hell-Ship Morgan *'36*
A Midsummer Night's Dream *'35*

Jackie Joseph (1933-)
Gremlins 2: The New Batch *'90*
Gremlins *'84*
Get Crazy *'83*
The Cheyenne Social Club *'70*
Little Shop of Horrors *'60*

Paterson Joseph (1964-)
The Beach *'00*
Greenfingers *'00*
Neil Gaiman's NeverWhere *'96*
In the Name of the Father *'93*

Ron Joseph
Mexican Blow *'02*
Navy SEALS *'90*

Erland Josephson (1923-)
Saraband *'03*
Faithless *'00*
Ulysses' Gaze *'95*
Good Evening, Mr. Wallenberg *'93*
Sofie *'92*
Meeting Venus *'91*
The Ox *'91*

Doctor in the House '53
Rob Roy—The Highland Rogue '53
The Sword & the Rose '53
The Voice of Merrill '52
David and Bathsheba '51
The Lady Says No '51
Whiskey Galore '48

Katherine Justice (1942-)
Captain America 2: Death Too Soon '79
Frasier the Sensuous Lion '73
The Stepmother '71
Five Card Stud '68
Columbo: Prescription Murder '67

John Justin (1917-2002)
Lisztomania '75
The Sound Barrier '52
The Thief of Bagdad '40

William Justine
Trauma '62
The Bride & the Beast '58

Jeff Kaake (1959-)
D.R.E.A.M. Team '99
Border Shootout '90

Suzanne Kaaren (1912-2004)
The Devil Bat '41
Phantom Ranger '38
Undercover Man '36

Nikolaj Lie Kaas (1973-)
Just Another Love Story '08
PU-239 '06
Adam's Apples '05
Brothers '04
Reconstruction '03
Flickering Lights '01
The Idiots '99

Jane Kaczmarek (1955-)
Pleasantville '98
All's Fair '89
D.O.A. '88
Vice Versa '88
The Heavenly Kid '85
Door to Door '84
Falling in Love '84

Karen Kadler (1934-84)
The Beatniks '60
It Conquered the World '56

Piotr Kadochnikev
Ivan the Terrible, Part 2 '46
Ivan the Terrible, Part 1 '44

Charlotte Kady
Revenge of the Musketeers '94
L.627 '92

Hakeem Kae-Kazim
The Fourth Kind '09
The Front Line '06
The Librarian: Return to King Solomon's Mines '06

Takeshi Kaga
Death Note 3: L, Change the World '08
Death Note 2: The Last Name '07
Death Note '06

Diane Kagan
Mr. & Mrs. Bridge '90
The Life and Assassination of the Kingfish '76

Elaine Kagan
Sharon's Secret '95
Babyfever '94

Kyoko Kagawa (1931-)
Mothra '62
The Lower Depths '57
The Crucified Lovers '54
Sansho the Bailiff '54
Mother '52

Teruyuki Kagawa
Tokyo Sonata '09
Sukiyaki Western Django '08
The Mystery of Rampo '94

David Kagen (1948-)
Body Chemistry '90
Conspiracy: The Trial of the Chicago Eight '87
Friday the 13th, Part 6: Jason Lives '86

Steve Kahan (1930-)
Lethal Weapon 4 '98
Demolition Man '93
Warlock: The Armageddon '93
Lethal Weapon 3 '92
Predator 2 '90
Lethal Weapon 2 '89
Scrooged '88
Lethal Weapon '87

Wolf Kahler (1946-)
One Against the Wind '91
Raiders of the Lost Ark '81

Madeline Kahn (1942-99)
Judy Berlin '99
A Bug's Life '98 (V)
Nixon '95
Mixed Nuts '94
For Richer, for Poorer '92
Kurt Vonnegut's Monkey House '91
Betsy's Wedding '90
An American Tail '86 (V)
Wanted: The Perfect Guy '86
Clue '85
City Heat '84
Slapstick of Another Kind '84
Yellowbeard '83
History of the World: Part 1 '81
First Family '80
Happy Birthday, Gemini '80
Simon '80
Wholly Moses! '80
The Muppet Movie '79
The Adventures of Sherlock Holmes' Smarter Brother '78
The Cheap Detective '78
High Anxiety '77
Blazing Saddles '74
Young Frankenstein '74
The Hideaways '73
Paper Moon '73
What's Up, Doc? '72

Alexander Kaidanovsky (1946-95)
Magic Hunter '96
Stalker '79

Chen Kaige (1952-)
Together '02
The Emperor and the Assassin '99

Khalil Kain (1965-)
Baadasssss! '03
Bones '01
Execution of Justice '99
Passing Glory '99
The Tiger Woods Story '98
Love Jones '96
Zooman '95
Renaissance Man '94
Juice '92

Joel Kaiser (1956-)
Dead Certain '92
Home for Christmas '90

Oldrich Kaiser
I Served the King of England '07
Dark Blue World '01

Suki Kaiser (1967-)
Bloodhounds 2 '96
Virtual Assassin '95

Elizabeth Kaitan (1960-)
South Beach Academy '96
Virtual Encounters '96
Desperate Crimes '93
Beretta's Island '92
Vice Academy 3 '91
Roller Blade Warriors: Taken By Force '90
Nightwish '89
Aftershock '88
Assault of the Killer Bimbos '88
Friday the 13th, Part 7: The New Blood '88
Necromancer: Satan's Servant '88
Silent Night, Deadly Night 2 '87
Slave Girls from Beyond Infinity '87

Meiko Kaji
Lady Snowblood '73
Blind Woman's Curse '70

Tomohiro Kaku
Hana & Alice '04
Ju-On 2 '00

Bonita Kalem
Escape from Cell Block 3 '74
Women Unchained '72

Toni Kalem (1956-)
American Strays '96
Billy Galvin '86
Silent Rage '82
Wanderers '79

Patricia Kalember (1957-)
Path to War '02
Signs '02
A Time for Dancing '00
Degree of Guilt '95
A Far Off Place '93
Big Girls Don't Cry... They Get Even '92
Jacob's Ladder '90
Fletch Lives '89

Jean-Pierre Kalfon (1938-)
Heartbeat Detector '07
Total Western '00
The Cry of the Owl '87
Condorman '81
The Valley Obscured by the Clouds '70
Weekend '67

Mindy Kaling (1979-)
Despicable Me '10 (V)
License to Wed '07

Helena Kallianiotes
Backtrack '89
Five Easy Pieces '70

Alexander Kalyagin (1942-)
A Slave of Love '78
An Unfinished Piece for a Player Piano '77

Woo-seong Kam (1970-)
R-Point '04
Spider Forest '04

Danny Kamekona (1926-96)
Robot Wars '93
Robot Jox '90
The Karate Kid: Part 2 '86

Stanley Kamel (1943-2008)
Domino '05
Escape under Pressure '00
Running Red '99
Stonebrook '98
Honor Thy Father and Mother: The True Story of the Menendez Brothers '94
Murder by Numbers '89

Antoine Kamerling (1966-)
Dominion: Prequel to the Exorcist '05
Soul Assassin '01
Suite 16 '94

Ryunosuke Kamiki
Big Man Japan '07
The Great Yokai War '05

Dan Kamin (1947-)
The Rookie '02
America's Dream '95
Another Pair of Aces: Three of a Kind '91

Ida Kaminska (1899-1980)
The Angel Levine '70
The Shop on Main Street '65

Kris Kamm (1964-)
Andersonville '95
Wyatt Earp '94
Born to Ride '91
When the Party's Over '91

Fritz Kampers (1891-1950)
Kameradschaft '31
Westfront 1918 '30

Hanae Kan
Nobody Knows '04
Pistol Opera '02

Akiko Kana
The Imperial Japanese Empire '85
Samurai Reincarnation '81

Melina Kanakaredes (1967-)
Percy Jackson & The Olympians: The Lightning Thief '10
Into the Fire '05
15 Minutes '01
Rounders '98
Saint Maybe '98
The Long Kiss Goodnight '96

Anna Kanakis (1962-)
After the Fall of New York '85
Warriors of the Wasteland '83

Steve Kanaly (1946-)
Scorpio One '97
Midnight Blue '96
Pumpkinhead 2: Blood Wings '94
Double Trouble '91
Driving Me Crazy '91
Eye of the Eagle 3 '91
Headhunter '89
Fleshburn '84
Balboa '82
Midway '76
The Wind and the Lion '75

Sean Kanan (1966-)
Hack! '07
Carpool Guy '05
Chasing Holden '01
Chaos Factor '00
Rich Girl '91
The Karate Kid: Part 3 '89

Hiroshi Kanbe
The Twilight Samurai '02
Samurai Fiction '99

Takashi Kanda (1918-86)
100 Monsters '68
Spook Warfare '68

Big Daddy Kane (1968-)
Dead Heist '07
Gunmen '93
Posse '93

Carol Kane (1952-)
The Pacifier '05
Confessions of a Teenage Drama Queen '04
Audrey's Rain '03
Love in the Time of Money '02
My First Mister '01
Noah's Ark '99
The Tic Code '99
Jawbreaker '98
Gone Fishin' '97
Office Killer '97
American Strays '96
Sunset Park '96
Tree's Lounge '96
Big Bully '95
The Pallbearer '95
The Crazysitter '94
Addams Family Values '93
Ted & Venus '93
When a Stranger Calls Back '93
Baby on Board '92
In the Soup '92
The Lemon Sisters '90
My Blue Heaven '90
Flashback '89
Drop-Out Mother '88
License to Drive '88
Scrooged '88
Sticky Fingers '88
Ishtar '87
The Princess Bride '87
Jumpin' Jack Flash '86
Transylvania 6-5000 '85
Burning Rage '84
Racing with the Moon '84
The Secret Diary of Sigmund Freud '84
Strong Medicine '84
Over the Brooklyn Bridge '83
Norman Loves Rose '82
Pandemonium '82
Keeping On '81
The Muppet Movie '79
When a Stranger Calls '79
My Sister, My Love '78
Annie Hall '77
Valentino '77
World's Greatest Lover '77
Harry & Walter Go to New York '76
Dog Day Afternoon '75
Hester Street '75
The Last Detail '73
Wedding in White '72
Carnal Knowledge '71
Desperate Characters '71

Christian Kane (1974-)
Hide '08
Four Sheets to the Wind '07
Taxi '04
Just Married '03
Secondhand Lions '03
Life or Something Like It '02
Crossfire Trail '01
Summer Catch '01
Love Song '00

Ivan Kane
Bound '96
Gettysburg '93
Platoon '86

Marjorie "Babe" Kane (1909-92)
The Dentist '32
Pharmacist '32
Be Yourself '30
Border Romance '30
Sunny Skies '30
The Great Gabbo '29

Michael Kane
The Gunfighters '87
Lonely Are the Brave '62

Sandra Kane
Teenage Gang Debs '66
Mutiny on the Blackhawk '39

Tom Kane (1962-)
Star Wars: The Clone Wars '08 (V)
Rugrats Go Wild! '03 (V)
The Powerpuff Girls Movie '02 (V)
The Wild Thornberrys Movie '02 (V)

Nobuo Kaneko (1923-95)
The Human Condition: A Soldier's Prayer '61
Ikiru '52

Takeshi Kaneshiro (1911-)
Red Cliff '08
Warlords '08
Perhaps Love '05
House of Flying Daggers '04
Returner '02
Chungking Express '95
Fallen Angels '95

Hye-jeong Kang (1982-)
Three ... Extremes '04
Oldboy '03

Shin-il Kang
Black House '07
Another Public Enemy '05
Public Enemy '02

Sung Kang (1972-)
War '07
The Fast and the Furious: Tokyo Drift '06
Better Luck Tomorrow '02

Tim Kang
Rambo '08
Robot Stories '03

John Kani
Endgame '09
The Ghost and the Darkness '96
Sarafina! '92
An African Dream '90
Options '88
Killing Heat '84
Master Harold and the Boys '84

Alexis Kanner (1942-2003)
Nightfall '88
Kings and Desperate Men '83
Twinsanity '70

Miho Kanno
Dolls '02
Tomie '99

China Kantner (1971-)
The Evening Star '96
Airheads '94
The Stoned Age '94

Ivar Kants (1949-)
Gallagher's Travels '87
The Naked Country '85
Silver City '84
Plumber '79

Jack Kao (1958-)
Ghosted '09
Flowers of Shanghai '98
Goodbye South, Goodbye '96

John Kapelos (1956-)
Everybody Wants to Be Italian '08
Stick It '06
Shallow Ground '04
Mimic 3: Sentinel '03
Cold Blooded '00
The Deep End of the Ocean '98
The Late Shift '96
The Shadow '94
Man Trouble '92
Internal Affairs '90
All's Fair '89
Nick Knight '89
The Boost '88
Roxanne '87
Nothing in Common '86
The Breakfast Club '85

Gabe Kaplan (1945-)
Tulips '81
Fast Break '79
Nobody's Perfekt '79

Jonathan Kaplan (1947-)
Cannonball '76
Hollywood Boulevard '76

Mady Kaplan (1956-)
The Falcon and the Snowman '85
The Deer Hunter '78

Marvin Kaplan (1924-)
Witchboard 2: The Devil's Doorway '93
Fangs '75

Masaya Kato (1963-)
Brother '00
Nobody '99
Drive '96
Crime Broker '94
Crimebroker '93
The Seventh Floor '93
Talking Head '92

Takeshi Kato (1929-)
Ran '85
None But the Brave '65

Rosanne Katon (1954-)
Bachelor Party '84
Zapped! '82
Lunch Wagon '81
Motel Hell '80
Chesty Anderson USN '76
The Muthers '76
She Devils in Chains '76
The Swinging Cheerleaders '74

Shintaro Katsu (1932-97)
Ronin Gai '90
The Razor: Sword of Justice '72
Zatoichi vs. Yojimbo '70
Zatoichi: The Blind Swordsman and the Fugitives '68
Zatoichi: The Blind Swordsman's Vengeance '66
Zatoichi: The Blind Swordsman and the Chess Expert '65
Zatoichi: Master Ichi and a Chest of Gold '64
Zatoichi: Zatoichi's Flashing Sword '64
Zatoichi: The Life and Opinion of Masseur Ichi '62

Andreas Katsulas (1947-2006)
Path to Paradise '97
The Fugitive '93
Blame It on the Bellboy '92
Communion '89
Next of Kin '89
Someone to Watch Over Me '87
Milo Milo '79

Nicky Katt (1970-)
The Brave One '07
Death Proof '07
Planet Terror '07
Snow Angels '07
Sin City '05
I Love Your Work '03
School of Rock '03
Secondhand Lions '03
Full Frontal '02
Insomnia '02
Waking Life '01
Boiler Room '00
Way of the Gun '00
The Limey '99
Delivered '98
One True Thing '98
Phantoms '97
johns '96
subUrbia '96
The Babysitter '95

William Katt (1950-)
Bone Eater '07
The Man from Earth '07
River's End '05
Circuit '02
Twin Falls Idaho '99
Deadly Game '98
Jawbreaker '98
Mother Teresa: In the Name of God's Poor '97
Rough Riders '97
Daddy's Girl '96
Rattled '96
Piranha '95
American Cop '94
The Paperboy '94
Stranger by Night '94
Tollbooth '94
Desperate Motives '92
House 4: Home Deadly Home '91
Naked Obsession '91
Last Call '90
Swimsuit '89
Wedding Band '89
White Ghost '88
Perry Mason: The Case of the Lost Love '87
House '86
Baby...Secret of the Lost Legend '85
Perry Mason Returns '85
Thumbelina '82
Pippin '81
Butch and Sundance: The Early Days '79
Big Wednesday '78
First Love '77
Carrie '76

Chris Kattan (1970-)
Bollywood Hero '09
Delgo '08 (V)
Christmas in Wonderland '07
Undead or Alive '07
Adam & Steve '05
Undercover Brother '02
Corky Romano '01
Monkeybone '01
House on Haunted Hill '99
A Night at the Roxbury '98

Jonathan Katz (1946-)
Daddy Day Care '03
The Independent '00

Judah Katz (1960-)
Crown Heights '02
Dirty Pictures '00

Omri Katz (1976-)
Hocus Pocus '93
Adventures in Dinosaur City '92
Matinee '92

Yftach Katzur (1958-)
Young Love—Lemon Popsicle 7 '87
Atalia '85
Baby Love '83
Hot Bubblegum '81

Adam Kaufman
Loving Leah '09
Between '05

Andy Kaufman (1949-84)
Heartbeeps '81
In God We Trust '80
God Told Me To '76

David Kaufman (1969-)
Invisible: The Chronicles of Benjamin Knight '93
The Last Prostitute '91

Gunther Kaufman (1947-)
Kamikaze '89 '83
In a Year of 13 Moons '78
Whity '70

Christine Kaufmann (1944-)
Bagdad Cafe '88
Welcome to 18 '87
Murders in the Rue Morgue '71
Taras Bulba '62
Town without Pity '61
The Last Days of Pompeii '60

Joseph Kaufmann
Heavy Traffic '73
Johnny Got His Gun '71
Jud '71
Private Duty Nurses '71

Maurice Kaufmann (1928-97)
Next Victim '74
The Abominable Dr. Phibes '71
Fright '71
The Hero '71
Die! Die! My Darling! '65

Caroline Kava
Born on the Fourth of July '89
Little Nikita '88

Christine Kavanagh
In His Life: The John Lennon Story '00
Catherine Cookson's The Glass Virgin '95
The Blackheath Poisonings '92
Monkey Boy '90

John Kavanagh
The Black Dahlia '06
Alexander '04
Benedict Arnold: A Question of Honor '03
The Informant '97
Sharpe's Sword '94
Widow's Peak '94
Bellman and True '88
Cal '84

Ingrid Kavelaars (1971-)
Harm's Way '07
White Coats '04

Julie Kavner (1951-)
The Simpsons Movie '07 (V)
Click '06
The Lion King 1 1/2 '04 (V)
Judy Berlin '99
Dr. Dolittle '98 (V)
Deconstructing Harry '97
Forget Paris '95
I'll Do Anything '93
Shadows and Fog '92
This Is My Life '92
Alice '90
Awakenings '90
New York Stories '89
Radio Days '87
Surrender '87
Hannah and Her Sisters '86
Bad Medicine '85
Revenge of the Stepford Wives '80
Katherine '75

Tamio Kawaji (1938-)
Gappa the Trifibian Monster '67
Tokyo Drifter '66
Story of a Prostitute '65

Chojuro Kawarazaki (1903-81)
47 Ronin, Part 1 '42
47 Ronin, Part 2 '42

Kunitaro Kawarazaki
47 Ronin, Part 1 '42
47 Ronin, Part 2 '42

Hiroyuki Kawase (1964-)
Godzilla vs. Megalon '76
Godzilla vs. the Smog Monster '72

Seizaburo Kawazu (1908-83)
Snake Woman's Curse '68
Yojimbo '61
A Geisha '53

Yusuke Kawazu (1935-)
Fighting Elegy '66
The Human Condition: A Soldier's Prayer '61
The Cruel Story of Youth '60
The Human Condition: Road to Eternity '59

Barnaby Kay
Conspiracy '01
Oscar and Lucinda '97

Beatrice Kay
Underworld USA '61
Underworld, U.S.A. '60

Bernard Kay (1928-)
The Conqueror Worm '68
Doctor Zhivago '65

Billy Kay (1984-)
The Battle of Shaker Heights '03
L.I.E. '01

Charles Kay (1930-)
Have No Fear: The Life of Pope John Paul II '05
The Importance of Being Earnest '02
Beautiful People '99
Henry V '89
Fortunes of War '87

Dianne Kay (1955-)
Andy and the Airwave Rangers '89
Portrait of a Showgirl '82
1941 '79

Dominic Scott Kay (1996-)
Front of the Class '08
Charlotte's Web '06 (V)

Jody Kay
Death Screams '83
House of Death '82
One Armed Executioner '80

Mary Ellen Kay (1929-)
Thunder Pass '54
Border Saddlemates '52
Colorado Sundown '52
Government Agents vs. Phantom Legion '51
Rodeo King and the Senorita '51
Silver City Bonanza '51
Thunder in God's Country '51

Melody Kay
Camp Nowhere '94
The NeverEnding Story 3: Escape from Fantasia '94

Yuzo Kayama (1937-)
Zero '84
The Battle of the Japan Sea '70
Red Beard '65
Attack Squadron '63
Sanjuro '62

Caren Kaye (1951-)
Pumpkinhead 2: Blood Wings '94
Satan's Princess '90
Poison Ivy '85
Help Wanted: Male '82
My Tutor '82
Kill Castro '80
The Mercenaries '80

Celia Kaye (1941-)
Final Comedown '72
Island of the Blue Dolphins '64

Danny Kaye (1913-87)
The Madwoman of Chaillot '69
The Five Pennies '59
Me and the Colonel '58
Court Jester '56
White Christmas '54
Hans Christian Andersen '52
The Inspector General '49
It's a Great Feeling '49
A Song Is Born '48
The Secret Life of Walter Mitty '47
Kid from Brooklyn '46
Wonder Man '45
Up in Arms '44

David Kaye (1964-)
3000 Miles to Graceland '01
Mermaid '00

Lila Kaye (1929-)
Dragonworld '94
Mrs. 'Arris Goes to Paris '92
Antonia and Jane '91
Nuns on the Run '90
An American Werewolf in London '81

Norman Kaye (1927-2007)
Innocence '00
Heaven's Burning '97
Lust and Revenge '95
Bad Boy Bubby '93
The Killing Beach '92
A Woman's Tale '92
Frenchman's Farm '87
Warm Nights on a Slow-Moving Train '87
Cactus '86
Man of Flowers '84
Where the Green Ants Dream '84
Lonely Hearts '82

Paul Kaye
The Killing Gene '07
It's All Gone, Pete Tong '04

Stubby Kaye (1918-97)
Who Framed Roger Rabbit '88
The Big Push '75
The Way West '67
Cat Ballou '65
Cool Mikado '63
40 Pounds of Trouble '62
Li'l Abner '59
Guys and Dolls '55

Morio Kazama
Samurai Fiction '99
Fall Guy '82

Elia Kazan (1909-2003)
Blues in the Night '41
City for Conquest '40

Lainie Kazan (1942-)
You Don't Mess with the Zohan '08
Bratz '07
Gigli '03
My Big Fat Greek Wedding '02
The Crew '00
If You Only Knew '00
What's Cooking? '00
The Big Hit '98
Safety Patrol '98
Allie & Me '97
Love Is All There Is '96
Movies Money Murder '96
The Cemetery Club '93
I Don't Buy Kisses Anymore '92
29th Street '91
Eternity '90
Beaches '88
Out of the Dark '88
Harry and the Hendersons '87
Delta Force '86
The Journey of Natty Gann '85
Lust in the Dust '85
Obsessive Love '84
Pinocchio '83
Sunset Limousine '83
My Favorite Year '82
One from the Heart '82
A Cry for Love '80
Love Affair: The Eleanor & Lou Gehrig Story '77
Romance of a Horsethief '71
Dayton's Devils '68
Lady in Cement '68

Zoe Kazan (1983-)
I Hate Valentine's Day '09
It's Complicated '09
Me and Orson Welles '09
The Private Lives of Pippa Lee '09
Revolutionary Road '08
Fracture '07

Tim Kazurinsky (1950-)
Poor White Trash '00
Shakes the Clown '92
A Billion for Boris '90
Dinner at Eight '89
Wedding Band '89
Hot to Trot! '88
Police Academy 4: Citizens on Patrol '87
Police Academy 3: Back in Training '86
The Princess and the Pea '83
Continental Divide '81
My Bodyguard '80

James Keach (1948-)
The Dance Goes On '92
The Experts '89
Options '88
Evil Town '87
Wildcats '86
Moving Violations '85
Stand Alone '85
The Razor's Edge '84
Love Letters '83
National Lampoon's Vacation '83
The Long Riders '80
Hurricane '79
Smokey & the Hotwire Gang '79
Slashed Dreams '74
Till Death Do Us Part '72

Stacy Keach (1941-)
Meteor '09
Lone Rider '08
Ring of Death '08
Honeydripper '07
Come Early Morning '06
Fatal Contact: Bird Flu in America '06
The Hollow '04
Miracle Dogs '03
The Santa Trap '02
Sunstorm '01
The Courage to Love '00
Mercy Streets '00
Unshackled '00
Children of the Corn 666: Isaac's Return '99
Fear Runs Silent '99
Militia '99
American History X '98
Future Fear '97
Legend of the Lost Tomb '97
Escape from L.A. '96
Prey of the Jaguar '96
Amanda and the Alien '95
Young Ivanhoe '95
New Crime City: Los Angeles 2020 '94
The Pathfinder '94
Texas '94
Batman: Mask of the Phantasm '93 (V)
Body Bags '93
Raw Justice '93
Rio Diablo '93
Sunset Grill '92
Mission of the Shark '91
Class of 1999 '90
False Identity '90
The Forgotten '89
Mistral's Daughter '84
Princess Daisy '83
The Blue and the Gray '82
Butterfly '82
That Championship Season '82
Cheech and Chong's Nice Dreams '81
Road Games '81
Saturday the 14th '81
The Long Riders '80
A Rumor of War '80
Cheech and Chong's Up in Smoke '79
Diary of a Young Comic '79
Mountain of the Cannibal God '79
The Ninth Configuration '79
Battleforce '78
Gray Lady Down '77
The Squeeze '77
Dynasty '76
The Killer Inside Me '76
Street People '76
Conduct Unbecoming '75
All the Kind Strangers '74
Luther '74
Man of Destiny '73
Watched '73
Fat City '72
Life & Times of Judge Roy Bean '72
The New Centurions '72
Brewster McCloud '70
End of the Road '70
The Heart Is a Lonely Hunter '68

Stacy Keach, Sr. (1914-2003)
Mission of the Shark '91
Ants '77
Missiles of October '74

Betty Kean (1915-86)
Hi, Good Lookin'! '44
Slightly Terrific '44

Marie Kean (1922-94)
The Dead *'87*
The Lonely Passion of Judith Hearne *'87*
Girl with Green Eyes *'64*

Staci Keanan (1975-)
Downhill Willie *'96*
Nowhere *'96*
Lisa *'90*

Edward (Ed Kean, Keene) Keane (1884-1959)
Rogue's Gallery *'44*
Midnight Limited *'40*
Heroes in Blue *'39*
Slander House *'38*
A Night at the Opera *'35*
The Cheat *'31*

James Keane (1952-)
Crazy Heart *'09*
Assassination Tango *'03*
Cannery Row *'82*
Apocalypse Now *'79*

Kerrie Keane
Steel *'97*
Alien Nation: Millennium *'96*
Alien Nation: The Enemy Within *'96*
Malarek *'89*
Distant Thunder *'88*
Obsessed *'88*
Nightstick *'87*
Kung Fu: The Movie *'86*
Hot Pursuit *'84*
Incubus *'82*
Spasms *'82*

Robert Emmett Keane (1883-1981)
Hills of Oklahoma *'50*
Susanna Pass *'49*
Fear in the Night *'47*
Treasure of Fear *'45*
The Man Who Wouldn't Die *'42*
Blind Fools *'40*
Born to Be Wild *'38*

Gillian Kearney (1972-)
The Other Half *'06*
In His Life: The John Lennon Story *'00*
Catherine Cookson's The Tide of Life *'96*

Stephen Kearney
The Nutt House *'95*
Rikky and Pete *'88*

Billy Kearns (1923-92)
Bed and Board *'70*
The Day and the Hour *'63*
Purple Noon *'60*

Charles Keating (1941-)
Deuce Bigalow: European Gigolo *'05*
The Thomas Crown Affair *'99*
The Bodyguard *'92*
Brideshead Revisited *'81*

Dominic Keating
Species 4: The Awakening *'07*
Hollywood Kills *'06*

Fred Keating (1897-1961)
Tin Pan Alley *'40*
Prison Train *'38*
I Live My Life *'35*

Larry Keating (1896-1963)
The Incredible Mr. Limpet *'64*
Stopover Tokyo *'57*
Daddy Long Legs *'55*
Gypsy Colt *'54*
Above and Beyond *'53*
Give a Girl a Break *'53*
A Lion in the Streets *'53*
A Lion Is in the Streets *'53*
Carson City *'52*
Monkey Business *'52*
Follow the Sun *'51*
Francis Goes to the Races *'51*
When Worlds Collide *'51*

Buster Keaton (1895-1966)
Man in the Silk Hat *'83*
A Funny Thing Happened on the Way to the Forum *'66*
Beach Blanket Bingo *'65*
How to Stuff a Wild Bikini *'65*
Railrodder *'65*
Pajama Party *'64*
It's a Mad, Mad, Mad, Mad World *'63*
Days of Thrills and Laughter *'61*
The Adventures of Huckleberry Finn *'60*
Around the World in 80 Days *'56*
Limelight *'52*
Sunset Boulevard *'50*
In the Good Old Summertime *'49*
Boom in the Moon *'46*
God's Country *'46*
Two Girls and a Sailor *'44*
Forever and a Day *'43*
The Villain Still Pursued Her *'41*
Li'l Abner *'40*
New Moon *'40*
Old Spanish Custom *'36*
What! No Beer? *'33*
Speak Easily *'32*
Parlor, Bedroom and Bath *'31*
Sidewalks of New York *'31*
Doughboys *'30*
Free and Easy *'30*
Spite Marriage *'29*
The Cameraman *'28*
Steamboat Bill, Jr. *'28*
College *'27*
Battling Butler *'26*
The General *'26*
Seven Chances *'25*
The Navigator *'24*
Sherlock, Jr. *'24*
Our Hospitality *'23*
Three Ages *'23*
The Saphead *'21*

Diane Keaton (1946-)
Morning Glory *'10*
Mad Money *'08*
Smother *'08*
Because I Said So *'07*
Mama's Boy *'07*
The Family Stone *'05*
Something's Gotta Give *'03*
Town and Country *'01*
Hanging Up *'99*
The Other Sister *'98*
The Only Thrill *'97*
The First Wives Club *'96*
Marvin's Room *'96*
Father of the Bride Part 2 *'95*
Amelia Earhart: The Final Flight *'94*
Look Who's Talking Now *'93 (V)*
Manhattan Murder Mystery *'93*
Running Mates *'92*
Father of the Bride *'91*
The Godfather, Part 3 *'90*
The Lemon Sisters *'90*
The Good Mother *'88*
Baby Boom *'87*
Radio Days *'87*
Crimes of the Heart *'86*
The Little Drummer Girl *'84*
Mrs. Soffel *'84*
Shoot the Moon *'82*
The Godfather 1902-1959: The Complete Epic *'81*
Reds *'81*
Manhattan *'79*
Interiors *'78*
Annie Hall *'77*
Looking for Mr. Goodbar *'77*
Harry & Walter Go to New York *'76*
I Will, I Will for Now *'76*
Love and Death *'75*
The Godfather, Part 2 *'74*
Sleeper *'73*
The Godfather *'72*
Play It Again, Sam *'72*
Lovers and Other Strangers *'70*

Joe Keaton (1867-1946)
The General *'26*
Sherlock, Jr. *'24*
Our Hospitality *'23*

Michael Keaton (1951-)
The Other Guys *'10*
Toy Story 3 *'10 (V)*
Post Grad *'09*
The Merry Gentleman *'08*
The Company *'07*
Cars *'06 (V)*
The Last Time *'06*
Game 6 *'05*
Herbie: Fully Loaded *'05*
White Noise *'05*
First Daughter *'04*
Live from Baghdad *'03*
Quicksand *'01*
A Shot at Glory *'00*
Desperate Measures *'98*
Jack Frost *'98*
Out of Sight *'98*
Jackie Brown *'97*
Multiplicity *'96*
The Paper *'94*
Speechless *'94*
Much Ado about Nothing *'93*
My Life *'93*
Batman Returns *'92*
One Good Cop *'91*
Pacific Heights *'90*
Batman *'89*
The Dream Team *'89*
Beetlejuice *'88*
Clean and Sober *'88*
The Squeeze *'87*
Touch and Go *'86*
Gung Ho *'85*
Johnny Dangerously *'84*
Mr. Mom *'83*
Night Shift *'82*

Caitlin Keats (1972-)
Women in Trouble *'09*
The Lather Effect *'06*
Kill Bill Vol. 2 *'04*

Ele Keats (1973-)
Eros *'04*
White Dwarf *'95*
Mother *'94*
White Wolves 2: Legend of the Wild *'94*
Lipstick Camera *'93*

Steven Keats (1946-94)
Eternity *'90*
The Spring *'89*
In Dangerous Company *'88*
Badge of the Assassin *'85*
The Executioner's Song *'82*
Silent Rage *'82*
For Ladies Only *'81*
Mysterious Island of Beautiful Women *'79*
Black Sunday *'77*
Hester Street *'75*

Brian L. Keaulana (1961-)
Riding Giants *'04*
In God's Hands *'98*

Hugh Keays-Byrne (1947-)
Journey to the Center of the Earth *'99*
Moby Dick *'98*
Resistance *'92*
Kangaroo *'86*
Mad Max *'80*
Death Train *'79*

Arielle Kebbel (1985-)
The Uninvited *'09*
Forever Strong *'08*
Aquamarine *'06*
The Grudge 2 *'06*
John Tucker Must Die *'06*
Outlaw Trail *'06*
American Pie Presents Band Camp *'05*
The Kid and I *'05*
Soul Plane *'04*

Toby Kebbell
The Sorcerer's Apprentice *'10*
RocknRolla *'08*
Control *'07*
Dead Man's Shoes *'04*

Lila Kedrova (1918-2000)
Some Girls *'88*
Sword of the Valiant *'83*
Tell Me a Riddle *'80*
Le Cavaleur *'78*
Widow's Nest *'77*
The Tenant *'76*
Primal Impulse *'74*
Escape to the Sun *'72*
Torn Curtain *'66*
Zorba the Greek *'64*
Modigliani *'58*

James Kee
Coast to Coast *'04*
Double Standard *'88*
Shadow Dancing *'88*

Cornelius Keefe (1900-72)
The Trigger Trio *'37*
Death from a Distance *'36*
Hong Kong Nights *'35*
Kentucky Blue Streak *'35*
Western Courage *'35*
Mystery Liner *'34*
The Adorable Cheat *'28*
Man from Headquarters *'28*

Don Keefer (1916-)
Candy Stripe Nurses *'74*
Sleeper *'73*
The Young Nurses *'73*

Andrew Keegan (1979-)
Doughboys *'08*
A New Wave *'07*
Cruel World *'05*
Extreme Dating *'04*
O *'01*
Teenage Caveman *'01*
The Broken Hearts Club *'00*
Ten Things I Hate about You *'99*
Camp Nowhere *'94*

Howard Keel (1917-2004)
Arizona Bushwackers *'67*
The War Wagon *'67*
Man from Button Willow *'65 (V)*
Day of the Triffids *'63*
Armored Command *'61*
Jupiter's Darling *'55*
Kismet *'55*
Deep in My Heart *'54*
Rose Marie *'54*
Seven Brides for Seven Brothers *'54*
Calamity Jane *'53*
I Love Melvin *'53*
Kiss Me Kate *'53*
Lovely to Look At *'52*
Across the Wide Missouri *'51 (N)*
Show Boat *'51*
Texas Carnival *'51*
Three Guys Named Mike *'51*
Annie Get Your Gun *'50*
Pagan Love Song *'50*

Ruby Keeler (1909-93)
That's Dancing! *'85*
Colleen *'36*
Go Into Your Dance *'35*
Shipmates Forever *'35*
Dames *'34*
Flirtation Walk *'34*
Footlight Parade *'33*
42nd Street *'33*
Gold Diggers of 1933 *'33*

Diane Keen (1946-)
Jekyll and Hyde *'90*
Agatha Christie's Thirteen at Dinner *'85*
Silver Dream Racer *'83*

Geoffrey Keen (1916-2005)
The Living Daylights *'87*
Amin: The Rise and Fall *'82*
For Your Eyes Only *'81*
Moonraker *'79*
Number 1 of the Secret Service *'77*
The Spy Who Loved Me *'77*
Sacco & Vanzetti *'71*
Taste the Blood of Dracula *'70*
Doctor Zhivago *'65*
Dr. Syn, Alias the Scarecrow *'64*
The Mind Benders *'63*
A Matter of WHO *'62*
Sink the Bismarck *'60*
The Third Key *'57*
Postmark for Danger *'56*
The Man Who Never Was *'55*
Angels One Five *'54*
Black Glove *'54*
Doctor in the House *'53*
Genevieve *'53*
Scotland Yard Inspector *'52*
The Clouded Yellow *'51*
Cry, the Beloved Country *'51*
The Fallen Idol *'49*
The Third Man *'49*

Malcolm Keen (1888-1970)
Mr. Reeder in Room 13 *'38*
The Manxman *'29*
The Lodger *'26*

Pat Keen
Without a Clue *'88*
A Kind of Loving *'62*

Monica Keena (1979-)
Night of the Demons *'09*
Loaded *'08*
Brooklyn Rules *'07*
Corporate Affairs *'07*
The Lather Effect *'06*
Left in Darkness *'06*
Man of the House *'05*
Freddy vs. Jason *'03*
Crime and Punishment in Suburbia *'00*
First Daughter *'99*
The Simian Line *'99*
All I Wanna Do *'98*
Ripe *'97*
Snow White: A Tale of Terror *'97*
While You Were Sleeping *'95*

Caroline Keenan (1970-)
Killer Bud *'00*
Vice Girls *'96*

Will Keenan
Wicked Lake *'08*
Margarita Happy Hour *'01*
Waiting *'00*
Tromeo & Juliet *'95*

Tom Keene (1898-1963)
Plan 9 from Outer Space *'56*
Storm over Wyoming *'50*
Trail of Robin Hood *'50*
Lights of Old Santa Fe *'47*
Navy Way *'44*
Arizona Roundup *'42*
Lone Star Law Men *'42*
Western Mail *'42*
Where Trails End *'42*
The Driftin' Kid *'41*
Dynamite Canyon *'41*
Riding the Sunset Trail *'41*
The Painted Trail *'38*
God's Country and the Man *'37*
Where Trails Divide *'37*
Desert Gold *'36*
Drift Fence *'36*
The Glory Trail *'36*
Hong Kong Nights *'35*
Our Daily Bread *'34*
Cheyenne Kid *'33*
Beyond the Rockies *'32*
Come on Danger! *'32*
Ghost Valley *'32*
The Saddle Buster *'32*
Pardon My Gun *'30*
Marked Money *'28*

Catherine Keener (1961-)
Cyrus *'10*
Percy Jackson & The Olympians: The Lightning Thief *'10*
The Soloist *'09*
Where the Wild Things Are *'09*
Hamlet 2 *'08*
Synecdoche, New York *'08*
What Just Happened *'08*
An American Crime *'07*
Into the Wild *'07*
Friends with Money *'06*
The Ballad of Jack and Rose *'05*
Capote *'05*
The 40 Year Old Virgin *'05*
The Interpreter *'05*
Death to Smoochy *'02*
Full Frontal *'02*
Lovely & Amazing *'02*
Simone *'02*
Being John Malkovich *'99*
Simpatico *'99*
8mm *'98*
Out of Sight *'98*
Your Friends & Neighbors *'98*
The Real Blonde *'97*
Box of Moonlight *'96*
The Destiny of Marty Fine *'96*
If These Walls Could Talk *'96*
Walking and Talking *'96*
Living in Oblivion *'94*
Johnny Suede *'92*
Survival Quest *'89*

Eliott Keener (1949-99)
Running Wild *'94*
Hard Target *'93*
Angel Heart *'87*

Eric Keenleyside
Every Second Counts *'08*
Blue Smoke *'07*
The Interpreter *'05*

Matt Keeslar (1972-)
Snowglobe *'07*
Art School Confidential *'06*
Open Window *'06*
The Thirst *'06*
Masters of Horror: Family *'05*
Live from Baghdad *'03*
Stephen King's Rose Red *'02*
Texas Rangers *'01*
Dune *'00*
Psycho Beach Party *'00*
Scream 3 *'00*
Urbania *'00*
Durango *'99*
Splendor *'99*
The Last Days of Disco *'98*
Sour Grapes *'98*
The Deli *'97*
Mr. Magoo *'97*
Waiting for Guffman *'96*
The Run of the Country *'95*
The Stupids *'95*
Safe Passage *'94*

Jack Kehler
Pineapple Express *'08*
Grilled *'06*
Invincible *'06*
Fever Pitch *'05*
Big Trouble *'02*
Love Liza *'02*
Men in Black 2 *'02*
Beyond Suspicion *'00*
Austin Powers 2: The Spy Who Shagged Me *'99*
Dudley Do-Right *'99*
Forces of Nature *'99*
The Mating Habits of the Earthbound Human *'99*
True Crime *'99*
Lethal Weapon 4 *'98*
Sour Grapes *'98*
The Big Lebowski *'97*

The Lesser Evil '97
187 '97
American Strays '96
Death Benefit '96
Lost Highway '96
My Fellow Americans '96
The Shot '96
Desert Winds '95
The Invaders '95
Serpent's Lair '95
Waterworld '95
Across the Moon '94
Cops and Robbersons '94
Love Is a Gun '94
Wyatt Earp '94
Blindsided '93
Casualties of Love: The "Long Island Lolita" Story '93
The Positively True Adventures of the Alleged Texas Cheerleader-Murdering Mom '93
White Sands '92
Grand Canyon '91
The Last Boy Scout '91
Point Break '91
I Love You to Death '90
Bloodstone '88
Year of the Dragon '85
Strange Invaders '83

Jack Kehoe (1938-)

Special '06
Falling Down '93
Servants of Twilight '91
Young Guns 2 '90
The Untouchables '87
A Winner Never Quits '86
The Pope of Greenwich Village '84
On the Nickel '80
The Fish that Saved Pittsburgh '79
Law and Disorder '74
Serpico '73
The Sting '73

Claire Keim (1975-)

The Girl '01
Ripper: Letter from Hell '01

Andrew Keir (1926-97)

Rob Roy '95
Dragonworld '94
Absolution '81
The Thirty-Nine Steps '79
Blood from the Mummy's Tomb '71
Zeppelin '71
The Night Visitor '70
The Viking Queen '67
Daleks—Invasion Earth 2150 A.D. '66
Dracula, Prince of Darkness '66
The Fighting Prince of Donegal '66
Lord Jim '65
The Devil-Ship Pirates '64
Cleopatra '63
Pirates of Blood River '62
Suspended Alibi '56

Harvey Keitel (1947-)

National Treasure: Book of Secrets '07
Arthur and the Invisibles '06 (V)
The Stone Merchant '06
Be Cool '05
The Bridge of San Luis Rey '05
National Treasure '04
Puerto Vallarta Squeeze '04
Crime Spree '03
Cuban Blood '03
Ginostra '02
Red Dragon '02
The Grey Zone '01
Taking Sides '01
Fail Safe '00
Little Nicky '00
Prince of Central Park '00
U-571 '00
Holy Smoke '99
Finding Graceland '98
Gunslinger's Revenge '98
Lulu on the Bridge '98
Shadrach '98
Three Seasons '98
Cop Land '97
FairyTale: A True Story '97
City of Industry '96
Head Above Water '96
Blue in the Face '95
Clockers '95
From Dusk Till Dawn '95
Get Shorty '95
Smoke '95
Ulysses' Gaze '95
Imaginary Crimes '94
Monkey Trouble '94
Pulp Fiction '94
Somebody to Love '94
Dangerous Game '93
The Piano '93
Point of No Return '93
Rising Sun '93
The Young Americans '93
Bad Lieutenant '92
Reservoir Dogs '92
Sister Act '92
Bugsy '91
Mortal Thoughts '91
Thelma & Louise '91
Two Evil Eyes '90
The Two Jakes '90
The January Man '89
Blindside '88
The Last Temptation of Christ '88
The Inquiry '87
The Pick-Up Artist '87
The Men's Club '86
Off Beat '86
Camorra: The Naples Connection '85
Star Knight '85
Corrupt '84
Falling in Love '84
Exposed '83
The Border '82
La Nuit de Varennes '82
Death Watch '80
Saturn 3 '80
Eagle's Wing '79
Blue Collar '78
Fingers '78
The Duellists '77
Welcome to L.A. '77
Buffalo Bill & the Indians '76
Mother, Jugs and Speed '76
Taxi Driver '76
The Virginia Hill Story '76
Shining Star '75
Alice Doesn't Live Here Anymore '74
Mean Streets '73
Who's That Knocking at My Door? '68

Stella Keitel

The Life of Lucky Cucumber '08
Bad Lieutenant '92

Alexander Keith

The Capitol Conspiracy '99
Counter Measures '99

Brian Keith (1921-97)

Rough Riders '97
Entertaining Angels: The Dorothy Day Story '96
National Lampoon's Favorite Deadly Sins '95
Picture Windows '95
Walking Thunder '94 (N)
The Gambler Returns: The Luck of the Draw '93
Escape '90
Welcome Home '89
Young Guns '88
The Alamo: Thirteen Days to Glory '87
Death Before Dishonor '87
World War III '86
Charlie Chan and the Curse of the Dragon Queen '81
Sharky's Machine '81
The Mountain Men '80
The Chisholms '79
Meteor '79
The Seekers '79
Centennial '78
Hooper '78
Joe Panther '76
The Loneliest Runner '76
The Longest Drive '76
The Wind and the Lion '75
The Yakuza '75
Bull of the West '71
Scandalous John '71
McKenzie Break '70
Suppose They Gave a War and Nobody Came? '70
Krakatoa East of Java '69
With Six You Get Eggroll '68
Reflections in a Golden Eye '67
Nevada Smith '66
The Rare Breed '66
The Russians Are Coming, the Russians Are Coming '66
The Hallelujah Trail '65
Those Calloways '65
A Tiger Walks '64
Johnny Shiloh '63
Savage Sam '63
Moon Pilot '62
Deadly Companions '61
The Parent Trap '61
Ten Who Dared '60
The Young Philadelphians '59
Dino '57
Nightfall '56
Run of the Arrow '56
5 Against the House '55
Tight Spot '55
The Violent Men '55
Arrowhead '53

David Keith (1954-)

Bottoms Up '06
In Her Line of Fire '06
Miracle Dogs Too '06
All Souls Day '05
Locusts: The 8th Plague '05
Raise Your Voice '04
Daredevil '03
Epoch: Evolution '03
Hangman's Curse '03
Carrie '02
Behind Enemy Lines '01
Burning Down the House '01
Sabretooth '01
The Stickup '01
World Traveler '01
Epoch '00
Men of Honor '00
U-571 '00
Hot Blooded '98
Poodle Springs '98
Secre of the Andes '98
Invasion of Privacy '96
Judge & Jury '96
Red Blooded 2 '96
Born Wild '95
Deadly Sins '95
Gold Diggers: The Secret of Bear Mountain '95
The Indian in the Cupboard '95
Major League 2 '94
Temptation '94
Texas '94
Till the End of the Night '94
Raw Justice '93
Caged Fear '92
Desperate Motives '92
Liar's Edge '92
Off and Running '90
The Two Jakes '90
The Further Adventures of Tennessee Buck '88
Heartbreak Hotel '88
White of the Eye '88
The Curse '87
The Whoopee Boys '86
Gulag '85
Firestarter '84
Independence Day '83
The Lords of Discipline '83
An Officer and a Gentleman '82
Back Roads '81
Take This Job & Shove It '81
Brubaker '80
The Great Santini '80
The Rose '79

Donald Keith (1903-69)

Outlaw Justice '32
Branded Men '31
Bare Knees '28
We're in the Navy Now '27
Dancing Mothers '26
Free to Love '25
My Lady of Whims '25
Parisian Love '25
The Plastic Age '25

Ian Keith (1899-1960)

It Came from Beneath the Sea '55
The Black Shield of Falworth '54
Dick Tracy's Dilemma '47
Nightmare Alley '47
Dick Tracy vs. Cueball '46
Song of Old Wyoming '45
The Chinese Cat '44
Bordertown Gunfighters '43
Corregidor '43
Five Graves to Cairo '43
Man from Thunder River '43
The Payoff '43
Sundown Kid '43
Mary of Scotland '36
The White Legion '36
The Crusades '35
The Three Musketeers '35
Queen Christina '33
The Sign of the Cross '33
The Phantom of Paris '31
Abraham Lincoln '30
The Divine Lady '29
Manhandled '24

Penelope Keith (1940-)

Coming Home '98
The Norman Conquests, Part 1: Table Manners '78
The Norman Conquests, Part 2: Living Together '78
The Norman Conquests, Part 3: Round and Round the Garden '78
Madhouse Mansion '74

Robert Keith (1898-1966)

Cimarron '60
The Lineup '58
Men in War '57
My Man Godfrey '57
Between Heaven and Hell '56
Written on the Wind '56
Love Me or Leave Me '55
Drum Beat '54
The Wild One '54
Young at Heart '54
Battle Circus '53
Devil's Canyon '53
Small Town Girl '53
Here Comes the Groom '51
I Want You '51
My Foolish Heart '49
Boomerang '47

Rosalind Keith (1916-2000)

Bad Boy '39
Theodora Goes Wild '36

Sheila Keith (1920-2004)

House of the Long Shadows '82
The Comeback '77
The Confessional '75
Frightmare '74

Toby Keith

Beer for My Horses '08
Broken Bridges '06

Peter Keleghan (1959-)

Niagara Motel '06
Jericho Mansions '03
Ginger Snaps '01
Angels in the Infield '00
Escape from Wildcat Canyon '99
Screwballs '83

Joseph Kell (1960-)

White Lies '98
Bone Daddy '97
Cupid '96

Robert Kellard (1915-81)

The Millerson Case '47
Gentleman from Dixie '41
Drums of Fu Manchu '40

Cecil Kellaway (1893-1973)

Quick, Let's Get Married '71
Getting Straight '70
Guess Who's Coming to Dinner '67
Spinout '66
Hush, Hush, Sweet Charlotte '65
The Cardinal '63
Zotz! '62
Interrupted Melody '55
The Prodigal '55
The Beast from 20,000 Fathoms '53
Young Bess '53
Francis Goes to the Races '51
Harvey '50
Kim '50
The Luck of the Irish '48
Portrait of Jennie '48
Unconquered '47
Easy to Wed '46
Monsieur Beaucaire '46
The Postman Always Rings Twice '46
Love Letters '45
Frenchman's Creek '44
It Ain't Hay '43
Bahama Passage '42
I Married a Witch '42
Birth of the Blues '41
Burma Convoy '41
Night of January 16th '41
Brother Orchid '40
The House of the Seven Gables '40
The Letter '40
Mexican Spitfire '40
The Mummy's Hand '40
Gunga Din '39
Wuthering Heights '39
Maid's Night Out '38

Tina Kellegher (1967-)

Scarlett '94
The Snapper '93

Tim Kelleher

Flash of Genius '08
Seven Pounds '08
Thirteen Days '00
Understudy: The Graveyard Shift 2 '88

Hiram Keller (1944-97)

Countryman '83
Lifespan '75
A Real Young Girl '75
Ciao Federico! Fellini Directs Satyricon '69
Fellini Satyricon '69

Joel S. Keller

Brotherhood of Murder '99
The Life Before This '99
The Hanging Garden '97

Marthe Keller (1945-)

Gigantic '08
Chrysalis '07
Women '97
Mon Amie Max '94
Young Catherine '91
The Nightmare Years '89
Dark Eyes '87
Red Kiss '85
The Amateur '82
The Formula '80
Black Sunday '77
Bobby Deerfield '77
Marathon Man '76
And Now My Love '74

Mary Page Keller (1961-)

Timecop 2: The Berlin Decision '03
Venomous '01
Dirty Little Secret '98
Any Place But Home '97
The Colony '95
Ulterior Motives '92
Scared Stiff '87

Melissa Keller

Impact Point '08
Drop Dead Sexy '05

Barbara Kellerman (1949-)

The Chronicles of Narnia '89
Mad Death '83
Quatermass Conclusion '79

Sally Kellerman (1938-)

Delgo '08 (N)
The Prince and the Pauper '07
I Could Never Be Your Woman '06
The Boynton Beach Club '05
Verdict in Blood '02
Bar Hopping '00
American Virgin '98
The Student Affair '97
Mirror, Mirror 2: Raven Dance '94
Ready to Wear '94
Younger & Younger '94
Happily Ever After '93 (V)
Boris and Natasha: The Movie '92
The Player '92
Victim of Beauty '91
Doppelganger: The Evil Within '90
All's Fair '89
Limit Up '89
Secret of the Ice Cave '89
You Can't Hurry Love '88
Meatballs 3 '87
Someone to Love '87
Three for the Road '87
Back to School '86
The KGB: The Secret War '86
That's Life! '86
Moving Violations '85
Secret Weapons '85
Dempsey '83
Dirkham Detective Agency '83
September Gun '83
Fatal Attraction '80
Foxes '80
Loving Couples '80
Serial '80
A Little Romance '79
Centennial '78
It Rained All Night the Day I Left '78
Magee and the Lady '78
Welcome to L.A. '77
The Big Bus '76
Rafferty & the Gold Dust Twins '75
Slither '73
Last of the Red Hot Lovers '72
A Reflection of Fear '72
Brewster McCloud '70
M*A*S*H '70
April Fools '69
The Boston Strangler '68
Hands of a Stranger '62
Reform School Girl '57

Susan Kellerman

Last Holiday '06
Elvira, Mistress of the Dark '88
Oh, Heavenly Dog! '80
Where the Buffalo Roam '80

Barry Kelley (1908-91)

Jack the Giant Killer '62
The Manchurian Candidate '62
Buchanan Rides Alone '58
Law and Order '53
South Sea Woman '53
Carrie '52
Francis Goes to the Races '51
The Well '51
The Asphalt Jungle '50
Ma and Pa Kettle '49
Too Late for Tears '49
The Killer That Stalked New York '47

DeForest Kelley (1920-99)

Star Trek 6: The Undiscovered Country '91
Star Trek 5: The Final Frontier '89

Four Weddings and a Funeral '94
The Magician '93
Duel of Hearts '92
Prisoner of Honor '91
War & Remembrance: The Final Chapter '89
When the Whales Came '89
War & Remembrance '88
Top Secret! '84
Sadat '83
The Winds of War '83
Prisoner of Zenda '79
The Treasure Seekers '79
East of Elephant Rock '76
The Seven-Per-Cent Solution '76
The Belstone Fox '73
Blockhouse '73
Darling Lili '70
The Blue Max '66
Operation Crossbow '65

Lindsay Kemp (1940-)
Sebastiane '79
The Wicker Man '75
Savage Messiah '72

Martin Kemp (1961-)
Back in Business '06
Sugar Town '99
Desire '95
Embrace of the Vampire '95
Boca '94
Cyber Bandits '94
Fleshtone '94
Aspen Extreme '93
Waxwork 2: Lost in Time '91
The Krays '90

Matty Kemp (1907-99)
Law of the Texan '38
Red Lights Ahead '36
Tango '36

Paul Kemp (1899-1953)
Charm of La Boheme '36
M '31

Will(iam) Kemp (1977-)
Step Up 2 the Streets '08
Mindhunters '05
Van Helsing '04

Will Kempe (1963-)
Hit the Dutchman '92
Metropolitan '90
Pledge Night '90

Charles Kemper (1900-50)
On Dangerous Ground '51
Mr. Music '50
The Nevadan '50
Stars in My Crown '50
Ticket to Tomahawk '50
Where Danger Lives '50
The Doolins of Oklahoma '49
Fighting Father Dunne '48

Gerhard Kempinski (1947-)
Beware of Pity '46
Thursday's Child '43

Rachel Kempson (1910-2003)
Deja Vu '98
Stealing Heaven '88
Out of Africa '85
Little Lord Fauntleroy '80
Love for Lydia '79
The Virgin Soldiers '69
The Charge of the Light Brigade '68
Georgy Girl '66
Captive Heart '47

Friederike Kempter
Eight Miles High '08
Eight Miles High '07

Felicity Kendal (1946-)
Parting Shots '98
We're Back! A Dinosaur's Story '93 (V)
The Camomile Lawn '92
Valentino '77
Shakespeare Wallah '65

Jennifer Kendal (1934-84)
Heat and Dust '82
Bombay Talkie '70

Cy Kendall (1898-1953)
Blonde for a Day '46
Girl Rush '44
Outlaw Trail '44
Johnny Eager '42
Tarzan's New York Adventure '42
Billy the Kid '41
The Saint Takes Over '40
The Green Hornet '39
The Shadow Strikes '37
Bulldog Edition '36
King of the Pecos '36

Henry Kendall (1897-1962)
The Voice of Merrill '52
Butler's Dilemma '43
Amazing Adventure '37
The Shadow '36
Death on the Set '35
The Ghost Camera '33
Rich and Strange '32

Katherine Kendall (1969-)
Devil in the Flesh 2 '00
Eye of the Storm '98
Swingers '96

Kay Kendall (1926-59)
The Reluctant Debutante '58
Les Girls '57
Abdulla the Great '56
Quentin Durward '55
Doctor in the House '53
Genevieve '53
The Shadow Man '53
Wings of Danger '52

Suzy Kendall (1944-)
Adventures of a Private Eye '77
Craze '74
Tales That Witness Madness '73
Torso '73
Assault '70
The Bird with the Crystal Plumage '70
Darker than Amber '70
30 Is a Dangerous Age, Cynthia '68
Circus of Fear '67
To Sir, with Love '67

Tony Kendall (1936-)
Oil '78
People Who Own the Dark '75
Return of the Evil Dead '75
When the Screaming Stops '73
Island of Lost Girls '68
The Whip and the Body '63
Hyena of London '62

Anna Kendrick (1985-)
Scott Pilgrim vs. the World '10
The Twilight Saga: Eclipse '10
The Marc Pease Experience '09
The Twilight Saga: New Moon '09
Up in the Air '09
Twilight '08
Rocket Science '07
Camp '03

Alexa Kenin (1962-85)
Pretty in Pink '86
Honkytonk Man '82
A Piano for Mrs. Cimino '82
A House Without a Christmas Tree '72

Arthur Kennedy (1914-90)
Signs of Life '89
Emmanuelle on Taboo Island '76
The Sentinel '76
Let Sleeping Corpses Lie '74
The Tempter '74
Mean Machine '73
My Old Man's Place '71
The President's Plane Is Missing '71
Hail, Hero! '69
Anzio '68
Shark! '68
A Minute to Pray, a Second to Die '67
Fantastic Voyage '66
Nevada Smith '66
Cheyenne Autumn '64
Barabbas '62
Lawrence of Arabia '62
Murder She Said '62
Elmer Gantry '60
A Summer Place '59
Some Came Running '58
Peyton Place '57
Crashout '55
Desperate Hours '55
Impulse '55
The Man from Laramie '55
Bend of the River '52
The Lusty Men '52
Rancho Notorious '52
Champion '49
Too Late for Tears '49
The Window '49
Boomerang '47
Air Force '43
Desperate Journey '42
High Sierra '41
They Died with Their Boots On '41
City for Conquest '40

Beth Kennedy
The Tomorrow Man '01
Jerome '98

Bill Kennedy (1909-97)
Silver City Bonanza '51
Storm over Wyoming '50
Two Lost Worlds '50
People's Choice '46

David Kennedy
Attack Force '06
Reign of Fire '02
Shiner '00

Deborah Kennedy
Swimming Upstream '03
Idiot Box '97
The Wedding Party '97
The Sum of Us '94

Douglas Kennedy (1915-73)
The Amazing Transparent Man '60
The Land Unknown '57
Big Chase '54
Sitting Bull '54
I Was an American Spy '51
Montana '50
South of St. Louis '48
The Lion Hunters '47

Edgar Kennedy (1890-1948)
My Dream Is Yours '49
Unfaithfully Yours '48
The Sin of Harold Diddlebock '47
It Happened Tomorrow '44
Air Raid Wardens '43
Hillbilly Blitzkrieg '42
Snuffy Smith, Yard Bird '42
Blondie in Society '41
Dr. Christian Meets the Women '40
Remedy for Riches '40
Charlie McCarthy, Detective '39
Frolics on Ice '39
The Black Doll '38
Hey! Hey! USA! '38
Peck's Bad Boy with the Circus '38
Double Wedding '37
When's Your Birthday? '37
San Francisco '36
Cowboy Millionaire '35
King Kelly of the U.S.A. '34
The Silver Streak '34
Twentieth Century '34
Duck Soup '33
Hold 'Em Jail '32
Little Orphan Annie '32
Laurel & Hardy: Night Owls '30
Laurel & Hardy: Perfect Day '29
The Better 'Ole '26

George Kennedy (1925-)
The Man Who Came Back '08
Don't Come Knocking '05
Three Bad Men '05
Dennis the Menace Strikes Again '98
Small Soldiers '98 (V)
Cats Don't Dance '97 (V)
Naked Gun 33 1/3: The Final Insult '94
Distant Justice '92
Final Shot: The Hank Gathers Story '92
Driving Me Crazy '91
Hangfire '91
Hired to Kill '91
Naked Gun 2 1/2: The Smell of Fear '91
Brain Dead '89
Ministry of Vengeance '89
Born to Race '88
The Naked Gun: From the Files of Police Squad '88
The Terror Within '88
The Uninvited '88
Counterforce '87
Creepshow 2 '87
Demonwarp '87
The Gunfighters '87
Kenny Rogers as the Gambler, Part 3: The Legend Continues '87
Nightmare at Noon '87
Private Road: No Trespassing '87
Delta Force '86
Radioactive Dreams '86
Bolero '84
Chattanooga Choo Choo '84
The Jesse Owens Story '84
Savage Dawn '84
Wacko '83
Virus '82
Archer: The Fugitive from the Empire '81
Modern Romance '81
A Rare Breed '81
Search and Destroy '81
Death Ship '80
Hotwire '80
Just Before Dawn '80
Steel '80
Backstairs at the White House '79
The Concorde: Airport '79 '79
The Double McGuffin '79
Brass Target '78
Death on the Nile '78
Mean Dog Blues '78
Airport '77 '77
Proof of the Man '77
Airport '75 '75
The Blue Knight '75
The Eiger Sanction '75
The Human Factor '75
Earthquake '74
Thunderbolt & Lightfoot '74
Cahill: United States Marshal '73
Bull of the West '71
Airport '70
The Good Guys and the Bad Guys '69
Guns of the Magnificent Seven '69
Bandolero! '68
The Boston Strangler '68
The Pink Jungle '68
Cool Hand Luke '67
The Dirty Dozen '67
Mirage '66
The Flight of the Phoenix '65
In Harm's Way '65
Shenandoah '65
Sons of Katie Elder '65
Island of the Blue Dolphins '64
McHale's Navy '64
Strait-Jacket '64
Charade '63
Lonely Are the Brave '62

Gerald Kennedy
Puzzle '78
The Mango Tree '77

Gerard Kennedy (1932-)
Body Melt '93
The Lighthorsemen '87
Panic Station '82
Newsfront '78

Graham Kennedy (1934-)
Return of Captain Invincible '83
The Club '81
The Odd Angry Shot '79
Don's Party '76

Jamie Kennedy (1970-)
Extreme Movie '08
Heckler '08
Kickin' It Old Skool '07
Son of the Mask '05
Malibu's Most Wanted '03
Max Keeble's Big Move '01
Seduced: Pretty When You Cry '01
Sol Goode '01
Bait '00
Boiler Room '00
Scream 3 '00
The Specials '00
Bowfinger '99
Sparkler '99
Three Kings '99
Bongwater '98
Enemy of the State '98
Highway Hitcher '98
Stricken '98
Clockwatchers '97
Scream 2 '97
Scream '96

Jayne Kennedy (1951-)
Body & Soul '81
Mysterious Island of Beautiful Women '79
Death Force '78
Fighting Mad '77
The Muthers '76
Group Marriage '72

Joey Kennedy
Innocence '00
Dance Me to My Song '98

Leon Isaac Kennedy (1949-)
Skeleton Coast '89
Penitentiary 3 '87
Hollywood Vice Sqaud '86
Too Scared to Scream '85
Lone Wolf McQuade '83
Penitentiary 2 '82
Body & Soul '81
Penitentiary '79
Death Force '78
Fighting Mad '77

Marklen Kennedy (1967-)
Magenta '96
Witchcraft 5: Dance with the Devil '92

Merle Kennedy (1967-)
May '02
Three Days of Rain '02
Switchback '97
Night of the Demons 2 '94
Nemesis '93

Merna Kennedy (1908-44)
Come on Tarzan '32
The Gay Buckaroo '32
Ghost Valley '32
The Circus '19

Mimi Kennedy (1949-)
In the Loop '09
Death Becomes Her '92
Pump Up the Volume '90
Immediate Family '89

Patricia Kennedy (1917-)
Road to Nhill '97
Country Life '95
My Brilliant Career '79
The Getting of Wisdom '77

Patrick Kennedy (1977-)
The Last Station '09
Me and Orson Welles '09
Atonement '07
Bleak House '05
Cambridge Spies '03

Rigg Kennedy
Hostile Intentions '94
Perfect Alibi '94
Dangerous Relations '93
Maid to Order '87
Slumber Party Massacre '82
Jessi's Girls '75
Girls on the Road '73
R.P.M.* (*Revolutions Per Minute) '70
Dayton's Devils '68

Ryan Kennedy (1982-)
Poison Ivy 4: The Secret Society '08
Storm Cell '08
The Invisible '07

Sheila Kennedy
Dead Boyz Can't Fly '93
Ellie '84
First Turn On '83

Tom Kennedy (1885-1965)
Invasion U.S.A. '52
Pirate Ship '49
The Devil's Cargo '48
Day the Bookies Wept '39
Living on Love '37
Hollywood Party '34
Monkey Business '31
Big News '29
Marked Money '28
We're in the Navy Now '27
Mantrap '26

Kari Kennell
See Kari Whitman

Donald Kenney
Clayton County Line '78
The Bellboy and the Playgirls '62

Doug Kenney
Heavy Metal '81 (V)
National Lampoon's Animal House '78

James Kenney (1930-82)
Above Us the Waves '56
Tough Guy '53

June Kenney
Bloodlust '59
Attack of the Puppet People '58
Earth vs. the Spider '58
Sorority Girl '57
Teenage Doll '57

Kerri Kenney
The Comebacks '07
Waiting '00

Sean Kenney (1942-)
Savage Abduction '73
The Corpse Grinders '71

Tom Kenny (1962-)
World's Greatest Dad '09
Comic Book: The Movie '04
The SpongeBob SquarePants Movie '04 (V)
The Powerpuff Girls Movie '02 (V)
Dead Weekend '95
Shakes the Clown '92

Patsy Kensit (1968-)
Played '06
Shelter Island '03
Dark Side '02
Hell's Gate '01

Strange Frequency 2 *'01*
Things Behind the Sun *'01*
Janice Beard *'99*
Speedway Junky *'99*
The Last Don 2 *'98*
Human Bomb *'97*
Grace of My Heart *'96*
Angels and Insects *'95*
At the Midnight Hour *'95*
Tunnel Vision *'95*
Dream Man *'94*
Fall from Grace *'94*
Kleptomania *'94*
Bitter Harvest *'93*
Full Eclipse *'93*
Blame It on the Bellboy *'92*
The Turn of the Screw *'92*
Timebomb *'91*
Twenty-One *'91*
Blue Tornado *'90*
Bullseye! *'90*
Chicago Joe & the Showgirl *'90*
Does This Mean We're Married? *'90*
Kill Cruise *'90*
A Chorus of Disapproval *'89*
Lethal Weapon 2 *'89*
Absolute Beginners *'86*
Silas Marner *'85*
Monty Python and the Holy Grail *'75*
The Great Gatsby *'74*

Anne Kent
Catherine Cookson's The Gambling Man *'98*
Widow's Peak *'94*

Barbara Kent (1906-)
Oliver Twist *'33*
Vanity Fair *'32*
Chinatown After Dark *'31*
Indiscreet *'31*
Feet First *'30*
The Dropkick *'27*
The Flesh and the Devil *'27*
No Man's Law *'27*

Crauford Kent (1881-1953)
Tea for Two *'50*
The Charlatan *'29*
Seven Keys to Baldpate *'29*
Virtue's Revolt *'24*

Dorothea Kent (1916-90)
It Happened on 5th Avenue *'47*
Behind the Mask *'46*
King of the Cowboys *'43*
Danger Ahead *'40*

Elizabeth Kent
Trapped Alive *'93*
Mindwarp *'91*

Gary Kent (1933-)
Satan's Sadists *'69*
The Thrill Killers *'65*

Jean Kent (1921-)
The Haunted Strangler *'58*
Bonjour Tristesse *'57*
The Browning Version *'51*
The Woman in Question *'50*
The Gay Lady *'49*
Man of Evil *'48*
The Magic Bow *'47*
Sleeping Car to Trieste *'45*
Bees in Paradise *'44*

Julie Kent
Center Stage *'00*
Dancers *'87*

Kenneth Kent (1892-1963)
Dangerous Moonlight *'41*
House of Mystery *'41*
Night Train to Munich *'40*

Larry Kent (1900-67)
Viva Las Vegas *'63*
Seas Beneath *'31*
Hangman's House *'28*
Eyes Right! *'26*

Marjorie Kent
See Marjorie Ann Mutchie

Robert Kent (1908-55)
Big Town After Dark *'47*
Shoot to Kill *'47*
The Phantom Rider *'46*
Blonde Comet *'41*
East Side of Heaven *'39*
The Phantom Creeps *'39*
Gang Bullets *'38*
The Gladiator *'38*
Mr. Moto Takes a Chance *'38*
Charlie Chan at Monte Carlo *'37*
Dimples *'36*

Dambisa Kente (1958-2002)
Cry, the Beloved Country *'95*
Friends *'95*

Michael Kenworthy
Return of the Living Dead 2 *'88*
Lensman *'84 (V)*

Doris Kenyon (1897-1979)
Counsellor-at-Law *'33*
No Marriage Ties *'33*
Young America *'32*
Burning Daylight *'28*
Monsieur Beaucaire *'24*
A Girl's Folly *'17*

Gwen Kenyon (1916-99)
In Old New Mexico *'45*
Charlie Chan in the Secret Service *'44*
The Great Mike *'44*
Lawless Plainsmen *'42*
Meet the Mob *'42*

Sandy Kenyon (1924-)
The Loch Ness Horror *'82*
The Arousers *'70*

Leila Kenzle (1960-)
Identity *'03*
Enemies of Laughter *'00*

Danny Keogh (1948-)
Operation Delta Force 3: Clear Target *'98*
Kill Slade *'89*

Jimmy Keogh
Bloom *'03*
The Matchmaker *'97*

Evelyne Ker (1935-2005)
A Nos Amours *'84*
Love Play *'60*

Ken Kercheval (1935-)
Beretta's Island *'92*
Corporate Affairs *'90*
California Casanova *'89*
Calamity Jane *'82*
Too Far to Go *'79*
Devil Dog: The Hound of Hell *'78*
Judge Horton and the Scottsboro Boys *'76*
Pretty Poison *'68*

Robert Kerman
Cannibal Holocaust *'80*
Emerald Jungle *'80*

Joey Kern (1976-)
The Sasquatch Gang *'06*
Pizza *'05*
Cabin Fever *'03*
Grind *'03*

Roger Kern (1948-)
Delos Adventure *'86*
The Young Pioneers *'76*

Joanna Kerns (1954-)
All Over the Guy *'01*
Emma's Wish *'98*
No Dessert Dad, 'Til You Mow the Lawn *'94*
The Nightman *'93*
The Great Los Angeles Earthquake *'91*
An American Summer *'90*
The Preppie Murder *'89*
Street Justice *'89*

Cross My Heart *'88*
Broken Badge *'85*
A Bunny's Tale *'85*
A*P*E* *'76*

Bill Kerr (1924-)
Sweet Talker *'91*
The Lighthorsemen *'87*
Miracle Down Under *'87*
Dusty *'85*
The Coca-Cola Kid *'84*
Razorback *'84*
Vigil *'84*
1915 *'82*
Pirate Movie *'82*
The Year of Living Dangerously *'82*
Deadline *'81*
Gallipoli *'81*

Deborah Kerr (1921-2007)
Hold the Dream *'86*
A Woman of Substance *'84*
America at the Movies *'76*
The Arrangement *'69*
The Gypsy Moths *'69*
Casino Royale *'67*
Marriage on the Rocks *'65*
The Chalk Garden *'64*
The Night of the Iguana *'64*
The Grass Is Greener *'61*
The Innocents *'61*
The Naked Edge *'61*
The Sundowners *'60*
Beloved Infidel *'59*
Separate Tables *'58*
An Affair to Remember *'57*
Bonjour Tristesse *'57*
Heaven Knows, Mr. Allison *'57*
The King and I *'56*
Tea and Sympathy *'56*
End of the Affair *'55*
Dream Wife *'53*
From Here to Eternity *'53*
Julius Caesar *'53*
Young Bess *'53*
Prisoner of Zenda *'52*
Quo Vadis *'51*
King Solomon's Mines *'50*
Black Narcissus *'47*
The Hucksters *'47*
I See a Dark Stranger *'46*
The Life and Death of Colonel Blimp *'43*
The Day Will Dawn *'42*
The Courageous Mr. Penn *'41*
Love on the Dole *'41*
Major Barbara *'41*

E. Katherine Kerr (1937-)
Songcatcher *'99*
The Siege *'98*
The Buccaneers *'95*
Suspect *'87*
Children of a Lesser God *'86*
Power *'86*
Reuben, Reuben *'83*

Edward Kerr (1966-)
Legalese *'98*
Above Suspicion *'95*
Magic Island *'95*

John Kerr (1931-)
The Pit and the Pendulum *'61*
The Crowded Sky *'60*
South Pacific *'58*
Tea and Sympathy *'56*
The Cobweb *'55*

Kristen Kerr
Strictly Sexual *'08*
Flight of the Living Dead: Outbreak on a Plane *'07*

Linda Kerridge (1959-)
Down Twisted *'89*
Alien from L.A. *'87*
Mixed Blood *'84*
Surf 2 *'84*
Strangers Kiss *'83*
Fade to Black *'80*

J.M. Kerrigan (1884-1964)
Fastest Gun Alive *'56*
Mrs. Mike *'49*
Fighting Seabees *'44*
Action in the North Atlantic *'43*
The Flying Irishman *'39*
The Great Man Votes *'38*
Hot Tip *'35*
The Informer *'35*
The Lost Patrol *'34*
The Black Camel *'31*
Song o' My Heart *'30*
Song o' My Heart *'29*
Little Old New York *'23*

John Kerry
Memorial Valley Massacre *'88*
Bad Georgia Road *'77*

Norman Kerry (1889-1956)
Tanks a Million *'41*
Bachelor Apartment *'31*
The Claw *'27*
The Unknown *'27*
The Phantom of the Opera *'25*
The Hunchback of Notre Dame *'23*
Is Money Everything? *'23*
Merry-Go-Round *'23*
Amarilly of Clothesline Alley *'18*

Paul Kersey (1970-)
Hulk *'03*
Missing Pieces *'00*

Brian Kerwin (1949-)
27 Dresses *'08*
Common Ground *'00*
Flash *'98*
Mr. Jealousy *'98*
Critical Choices *'97*
The Myth of Fingerprints *'97*
Unlikely Angel *'97*
Volcano: Fire on the Mountain *'97*
Getting Away With Murder *'96*
Jack *'96*
Gold Diggers: The Secret of Bear Mountain *'95*
It Came from Outer Space 2 *'95*
Hard Promises *'92*
Love Field *'91*
Switched at Birth *'91*
Code Name: Chaos *'90*
Torch Song Trilogy *'88*
King Kong Lives *'86*
Murphy's Romance *'85*
Nickel Mountain *'85*
Wet Gold *'84*
Miss All-American Beauty *'82*
Getting Wasted *'80*
Hometown U.S.A. *'79*
A Real American Hero *'78*

Lance Kerwin (1960-)
Enemy Mine *'85*
Fourth Wise Man *'85*
Side Show *'84*
The Snow Queen *'83*
The Mysterious Stranger *'82*
Shooting *'82*
Children of Divorce *'80*
Salem's Lot *'79*
The Loneliest Runner *'76*
Reflections of Murder *'74*

Maureen Kerwin (1949-)
Reunion *'88*
The Destructors *'74*

William Kerwin (1927-89)
A Taste of Blood *'67*
Playgirl Killer *'66*
2000 Maniacs *'64*
Blood Feast *'63*

Ian Reed Kesler
Finish Line *'08*
Poster Boy *'04*

Jillian Kesner (1950-2007)
Roots of Evil *'91*
Beverly Hills Vamp *'88*
Trick or Treats *'82*
Firecracker *'81*
Starhops *'78*

Quin Kessler
Wishman *'93*
She *'83*

Sara Kestelman (1944-)
Lady Jane *'85*
Lisztomania *'75*
Zardoz *'73*

Boyd Kestner (1964-)
The Insatiable *'06*
Black Hawk Down *'01*
Cleopatra's Second Husband *'00*
The Art of Murder *'99*
The General's Daughter *'99*
Entertaining Angels: The Dorothy Day Story *'96*
Lethal Lolita—Amy Fisher: My Story *'92*

Bryan Kestner (1964-)
In Dark Places *'97*
Fire Birds *'90*

Janet Key (1945-92)
And Now the Screaming Starts *'73*
Dracula A.D. 1972 *'72*

Evelyn Keyes (1919-2008)
Wicked Stepmother *'89*
Return to Salem's Lot *'87*
Around the World in 80 Days *'56*
The Seven Year Itch *'55*
Prowler *'51*
Mrs. Mike *'49*
The Killer That Stalked New York *'47*
The Jolson Story *'46*
A Thousand and One Nights *'45*
The Desperadoes *'43*
Here Comes Mr. Jordan *'41*
Before I Hang *'40*
The Lady in Question *'40*
Slightly Honorable *'40*
Gone with the Wind *'39*
Union Pacific *'39*

Irwin Keyes (1952-)
Intolerable Cruelty *'03*
Backlash: Oblivion 2 *'95*
The Flintstones *'94*
Frankenstein General Hospital *'88*

Mark Keyloun (1960-)
Separate Vacations *'86*
Gimme an F *'85*
Mike's Murder *'84*

Skander Keynes
The Chronicles of Narnia: Prince Caspian *'08*
The Chronicles of Narnia: The Lion, the Witch and the Wardrobe *'05*

Alicia Keys
The Nanny Diaries *'07*
Smokin' Aces *'07*

Konstantin Khabensky
Wanted *'08*
Day Watch *'06*
Night Watch *'04*

Malika Khadijah
ATL *'06*
Sky High *'05*

Simbi Khali (1971-)
We Were Soldiers *'02*
A Thin Line Between Love and Hate *'96*

Chulpan Khamatova (1975-)
Good Bye, Lenin! *'03*
Advertising Rules! *'01*

Persis Khambatta (1950-98)
Deadly Intent *'88*
Phoenix the Warrior *'88*
First Strike *'85*
Warrior of the Lost World *'84*
Megaforce *'82*
Nighthawks *'81*
Star Trek: The Motion Picture *'79*
Conduct Unbecoming *'75*
The Wilby Conspiracy *'75*

Aamir Khan (1965-)
St. Trinian's *'07*
Lagaan: Once upon a Time in India *'01*
Earth *'98*

Irfan Khan
Slumdog Millionaire *'08*
A Mighty Heart *'07*
Partition *'07*
The Namesake *'06*
The Warrior *'81*

Sajid Khan (1952-)
Heat and Dust *'82*
Maya *'66*

Shaheen Khan
Bend It Like Beckham *'02*
Bhaji on the Beach *'94*

Arsinee Khanjian (1958-)
Adoration *'08*
Ararat *'02*
Felicia's Journey *'99*
Late August, Early September *'98*
Ms. Scrooge *'97*
Irma Vep *'96*
The Sweet Hereafter *'96*
Exotica *'94*
Calendar *'93*
The Adjuster *'91*
Speaking Parts *'89*
Family Viewing *'87*

Rahul Khanna (1972-)
The Emperor's Club *'02*
Earth *'98*

Kulbashan Kharbanda
Water *'05*
Lagaan: Once upon a Time in India *'01*
Fire *'96*

Anupam Kher (1955-)
The Other End of the Line *'08*
The Mistress of Spices *'05*
Bride & Prejudice *'04*
Bend It Like Beckham *'02*

Kiron Kher
Silent Waters *'03*
Devdas *'02*

Nozha Khouadra
The New Eve *'98*
Bye-Bye *'96*
Honey & Ashes *'96*

Makram Khoury (1945-)
House of Saddam *'08*
Free Zone *'05*
Munich *'05*
The Body *'01*
The Milky Way *'97*
Double Edge *'92*

Leleti Khumalo (1970-)
Cry, the Beloved Country *'95*
Sarafina! *'92*

Guy Kibbee (1882-1956)
Fort Apache *'48*
Three Godfathers *'48*
The Horn Blows at Midnight *'45*
Dixie Jamboree *'44*
Power of the Press *'43*
Miss Annie Rooney *'42*
Whistling in Dixie *'42*
It Started with Eve *'41*
Our Town *'40*

Babes in Arms '39
Let Freedom Ring '39
Mr. Smith Goes to Washington '39
Joy of Living '38
Of Human Hearts '38
Three Comrades '38
Captain January '36
Earthworm Tractors '36
Little Lord Fauntleroy '36
Three Men on a Horse '36
Captain Blood '35
Dames '34
Wonder Bar '34
Footlight Parade '33
42nd Street '33
Gold Diggers of 1933 '33
Havana Widows '33
Lady for a Day '33
Rain '32
Scarlet Dawn '32
The Strange Love of Molly Louvain '32
Two Seconds '32
Union Depot '32
Flying High '31
Laughing Sinners '31
Man of the World '31

Milton Kibbee (1896-1970)
Homesteaders of Paradise Valley '47
Jungle Siren '42

Sandrine Kiberlain (1968-)
Apres-Vous '03
Alias Betty '01
For Sale '98
Seventh Heaven '98
Beaumarchais the Scoundrel '96
A Self-Made Hero '95

Kid Rock (1971-)
Larry the Cable Guy: Health Inspector '06
Biker Boyz '03
Joe Dirt '01

Jonathan Kidd
The 7th Commandment '61
Seven Thieves '60

Michael Kidd (1915-2007)
Smile '75
It's Always Fair Weather '55

Janet Kidder
Ginger Snaps: Unleashed '04
Dark Side '02

Margot Kidder (1948-)
Halloween II '09
On the Other Hand, Death '08
Common Ground '00
Tribulation '00
My Teacher Ate My Homework '98
Junior's Groove '97
Never Met Picasso '96
Bloodknot '95
Phantom 2040 Movie: The Ghost Who Walks '95 (V)
Young Ivanhoe '95
Beanstalk '94
Henry & Verlin '94
Windrunner '94
To Catch a Killer '92
Mob Story '90
Vanishing Act '88
Louisiana '87
Superman 4: The Quest for Peace '87
Keeping Track '86
Little Treasure '85
The Glitter Dome '84
Superman 3 '83
Trenchcoat '83
Heartaches '82
Some Kind of Hero '82
Miss Right '81
Shoot the Sun Down '81
Superman 2 '80
Willie & Phil '80
The Amityville Horror '79
Mr. Mike's Mondo Video '79
Superman: The Movie '78
92 in the Shade '76
Black Christmas '75
The Great Waldo Pepper '75
The Reincarnation of Peter Proud '75
Quiet Day in Belfast '74
Sisters '73
The Bounty Man '72
Quackser Fortune Has a Cousin in the Bronx '70

Nicole Kidman (1966-)
Nine '09
Australia '08
The Golden Compass '07
The Invasion '07
Margot at the Wedding '07
Fur: An Imaginary Portrait of Diane Arbus '06
Happy Feet '06 (V)
Bewitched '05
The Interpreter '05
Birth '04
The Stepford Wives '04
Cold Mountain '03
Dogville '03
The Human Stain '03
Birthday Girl '02
The Hours '02
Moulin Rouge '01
The Others '01
Eyes Wide Shut '99
Practical Magic '98
The Peacemaker '97
The Leading Man '96
Portrait of a Lady '96
Batman Forever '95
To Die For '95
Malice '93
My Life '93
Far and Away '92
Billy Bathgate '91
Days of Thunder '90
Dead Calm '89
Flirting '89
Night Master '87
Windrider '86
Archer's Adventure '85
BMX Bandits '83
Prince and the Great Race '83

James Kidnie
Swamp Devil '08
Resurrection '99
Rescuers: Stories of Courage—Two Couples '98
Hostile Intent '97
Gate 2 '92
Body Parts '91

Richard Kiel (1939-)
Happy Gilmore '96
Think Big '90
Pale Rider '85
Mad Mission 3 '84
Hysterical '83
War of the Wizards '83
So Fine '81
Moonraker '79
Force 10 from Navarone '78
They Went That-a-Way & That-a-Way '78
The Spy Who Loved Me '77
Silver Streak '76
Flash & Firecat '75
The Longest Yard '74
The Human Duplicators '64
Roustabout '64
Eegah! '62
The Phantom Planet '61

Sue Kiel
Survivor '87
Red Heat '85

Wolfgang Kieling (1924-85)
Out of Order '84
The Oppermann Family '82
The Vengeance of Fu Manchu '67

Udo Kier (1944-)
Mother of Tears '08
Holly '07
BloodRayne '06
Manderlay '05
Masters of Horror: Cigarette Burns '05
Evil Eyes '04
Modigliani '04
Paranoia 1.0 '04
Dogville '03
All the Queen's Men '02
Feardotcom '02
He Sees You When You're Sleeping '02
Headspace '02
Doomsdayer '01
Invincible '01
The Last Minute '01
Critical Mass '00
Just One Night '00
Life in the Fast Lane '00
Red Letters '00
Shadow of the Vampire '00
Dancer in the Dark '99
Doomsdayer '99
End of Days '99
Spy Games '99
Blade '98
Modern Vampires '98
Betty '97
The End of Violence '97
The Kingdom 2 '97
Prince Valiant '97
The Adventures of Pinocchio '96
Barb Wire '96
Red Shoe Diaries 7: Burning Up '96
Breaking the Waves '95
Johnny Mnemonic '95
The Kingdom '95
Ace Ventura: Pet Detective '93
For Love or Money '93
Terror 2000 '92
Zentropa '92
My Own Private Idaho '91
Seduction: The Cruel Woman '89
Medea '88
The Stationmaster's Wife '77
Suspiria '77
The House on Straw Hill '76
The Story of O '75
Andy Warhol's Dracula '74
Andy Warhol's Frankenstein '74
Mark of the Devil '69

Robbie Kiger (1973-)
Welcome Home, Roxy Carmichael '90
Children of the Corn '84
Table for Five '83

Susan Kiger (1953-)
Death Screams '83
House of Death '82
The Return '80
H.O.T.S. '79
Seven '79

Laura Kightlinger (1969-)
Mama's Boy '07
The Shaggy Dog '06
Kicking & Screaming '05
Must Love Dogs '05
Anchorman: The Legend of Ron Burgundy '04
Down With Love '03

Rya Kihlstedt (1970-)
Women in Trouble '09
She Creature '01
Deep Impact '98
Home Alone 3 '97
Jaded '96
The Buccaneers '95

Jorgen Kiil (1931-2003)
Webmaster '98
Parallel Corpse '83

Kirin Kiki
Pistol Opera '02
Returner '02

Rinko Kikuchi (1981-)
The Brothers Bloom '09
The Sky Crawlers '08
Babel '06
Funky Forest: The First Contact '06

Nicholas Kilbertus
Rescuers: Stories of Courage—Two Couples '98
The Defenders: Payback '97
The Kiss '88

Craig Kilborn (1962-)
Full of It '07
The Benchwarmers '06
The Shaggy Dog '06
Old School '03

Percy Kilbride (1888-1964)
Ma and Pa Kettle at Waikiki '55
Ma and Pa Kettle at Home '54
Ma and Pa Kettle on Vacation '53
Ma and Pa Kettle at the Fair '52
Ma and Pa Kettle Back On the Farm '51
Ma and Pa Kettle Go to Town '50
Riding High '50
Ma and Pa Kettle '49
You Gotta Stay Happy '48
Egg and I '47
Riff-Raff '47
Welcome Stranger '47
She Wouldn't Say Yes '45
The Southerner '45
State Fair '45
The Adventures of Mark Twain '44
Guest in the House '44
The Woman of the Town '44
George Washington Slept Here '42
Keeper of the Flame '42

Terence (Terry) Kilburn (1926-)
Lolita '62
Fiend without a Face '58
National Velvet '44
Goodbye, Mr. Chips '39
They Shall Have Music '39
A Christmas Carol '38

Richard Kiley (1922-99)
Patch Adams '98
Phenomenon '96
Secrets '94
Jurassic Park '93 (V)
Mastergate '92
The Canterville Ghost '91
Separate but Equal '91
The Final Days '89
Howard the Duck '86 (V)
A.D. '85
The Adventures of Huckleberry Finn '85
The Bad Seed '85
George Washington '84
The Thorn Birds '83
Pray TV '82
Endless Love '81
Angel on My Shoulder '80
Looking for Mr. Goodbar '77
The Little Prince '74
Jigsaw '71
Murder Once Removed '71
Night Gallery '69
Pendulum '69
Blackboard Jungle '55
Pickup on South Street '53
The Sniper '52

Victor Kilian (1891-1979)
One Too Many '51
Unknown World '51
Rimfire '49
Dangerous Passage '44
Dr. Cyclops '40
Young Tom Edison '40
The Adventures of Tom Sawyer '38
Prison Break '38
It Happened in Hollywood '37
Lady from Nowhere '36
Riff Raff '35

Taram Killam (1982-)
My Best Friend's Girl '08
Just Married '03

Val Kilmer (1959-)
MacGruber '10
Bad Lieutenant: Port of Call New Orleans '09
The Chaos Experiment '09
Hardwired '09
Streets of Blood '09
The Thaw '09
Columbus Day '08
Comanche Moon '08
Conspiracy '08
Delgo '08 (V)
Felon '08
XIII '08
Dead Man's Bounty '06
Deja Vu '06
Moscow Zero '06
Played '06
10th & Wolf '06
Kiss Kiss Bang Bang '05
Mindhunters '05
Alexander '04
Spartan '04
Stateside '04
The Missing '03
Wonderland '03
The Salton Sea '02
Hard Cash '01
Pollock '00
Red Planet '00
Joe the King '99
At First Sight '98
Prince of Egypt '98 (V)
The Saint '97
The Ghost and the Darkness '96
The Island of Dr. Moreau '96
Batman Forever '95
Heat '95
The Real McCoy '93
Tombstone '93
True Romance '93
Thunderheart '92
The Doors '91
Gore Vidal's Billy the Kid '89
Kill Me Again '89
Willow '88
The Man Who Broke 1,000 Chains '87
The Murders in the Rue Morgue '86
Top Gun '86
Real Genius '85
Top Secret! '84

Kevin Kilner (1958-)
Julia '08
A Stranger's Heart '07
Inside '06
A Cinderella Story '04
Raising Helen '04
Smart House '00
Home Alone 3 '97
Music from Another Room '97
Danielle Steel's Heartbeat '93

Lincoln Kilpatrick (1932-2004)
Piranha '95
Fortress '93
Prison '88
Deadly Force '83
Omega Man '71

Patrick Kilpatrick (1949-)
Already Dead '07
Gamebox 1.0 '04
Minority Report '02
The Substitute 4: Failure is Not an Option '00
Free Willy 3: The Rescue '97
Last Stand at Saber River '96
Riot '96
Beastmaster 3: The Eye of Braxus '95
3 Ninjas Knuckle Up '95
Open Fire '94
Scanner Cop 2: Volkin's Revenge '94
Scanners: The Showdown '94
Showdown '93
The Cellar '90
Class of 1999 '90
Death Warrant '90
Roanoak '86
Remo Williams: The Adventure Begins '85

Bobby Kim
Kill Line '91
Manchurian Avenger '84

Daniel Dae Kim (1968-)
The Adjustment Bureau '10
The Cave '05
Momentum '03
American Shaolin: King of the Kickboxers 2 '92

Evan C. Kim
The Dead Pool '88
Go Tell the Spartans '78

Gyu-ri Kim
Nightmare '00
Whispering Corridors '98

Hye-su Kim
The Red Shoes '05
3 Extremes 2 '02

Jacqueline Kim (1965-)
Red Doors '05
Charlotte Sometimes '02
The Hollywood Sign '01
The Operator '01
Brokedown Palace '99
Volcano '97

Joon Kim
Gang Justice '94
Street Soldiers '91

Joy Kim
Blood Alley '55
The High and the Mighty '54

Randall Duk Kim (1943-)
The Last Airbender '10
Dragonball: Evolution '09
Kung Fu Panda '08 (V)
Memoirs of a Geisha '05
The Matrix Reloaded '03

Seo-hyeong Kim
Black House '07
Hidden Floor '06

Bruce (Kemp) Kimball
Cain's Cutthroats '71
Rebel Vixens '69

Billy Kimbley
Silver City Bonanza '51
Shep Comes Home '49

Charles Kimbrough (1936-)
The Wedding Planner '01
The Hunchback of Notre Dame '96 (V)
The Good Mother '88
Switching Channels '88
Sunday in the Park with George '86

Clinton Kimbrough (1933-96)
Night Call Nurses '72
Bloody Mama '70

Bruce Kimmel (1947-)
The Creature Wasn't Nice '81
Spaceship '81
The First Nudie Musical '75

Dana Kimmell (1959-)
Friday the 13th, Part 3 '82
Sweet 16 '81

Kenneth Kimmins (1941-)
My Best Friend Is a Vampire '88
Eleanor: First Lady of the World '82

Isao Kimura (1923-81)
Black Lizard '68
Stray Dog '49

Yoshino Kimura
Sukiyaki Western Django '08

Masters of Horror: Dream Cruise '07

Aron Kincaid (1943-)

The Proud and the Damned '72
Creature of Destruction '67
Ghost in the Invisible Bikini '66
Ski Party '65

Danielle Kind

Christie's Revenge '07
Posers '02

Richard Kind (1956-)

A Serious Man '09
Big Stan '07
The Neighbor '07
Raising Flagg '06
The Wild '06 (V)
Bewitched '05
Elvis Has Left the Building '04
Dog Gone Love '03
Quicksand '01
A Bug's Life '98 (V)
Sink or Swim '97
Tom and Jerry: The Movie '93 (V)
All-American Murder '91

Helmo Kinderman

The Secret Invasion '64
The Magic Fountain '61

Kevin Kindlin

Heartstopper '92
Revenge of the Living Zombies '88
The Majorettes '87

Adrienne King (1960-)

Friday the 13th, Part 2 '81
Friday the 13th '80

Alan King (1927-2004)

Mind the Gap '04
Sunshine State '02
Rush Hour 2 '01
Casino '95
The Infiltrator '95
Night and the City '92
The Bonfire of the Vanities '90
Enemies, a Love Story '89
Memories of Me '88
Cat's Eye '85
Author! Author! '82
I, the Jury '82
Just Tell Me What You Want '80
Pleasure Palace '80
How to Pick Up Girls '78
The Anderson Tapes '71
The Helen Morgan Story '57

Andrea King (1919-2003)

Inevitable Grace '94
The Linguini Incident '92
Blackenstein '73
House of the Black Death '65
Band of Angels '57
Red Planet Mars '52
The World in His Arms '52
The Lemon Drop Kid '51
Buccaneer's Girl '50
Mr. Peabody & the Mermaid '48
The Beast with Five Fingers '46
The Man I Love '46
God is My Co-Pilot '45

Atlas King

The Thrill Killers '65
Incredibly Strange Creatures Who Stopped Living and Became Mixed-Up Zombies '63

B.B. King (1925-)

Soul Power '08
Blues Brothers 2000 '98
Amazon Women on the Moon '87

Benjamin King

A Little Inside '01
Spider's Web '01

Brad King (1917-91)

Outlaws of the Desert '41
Riders of the Timberline '41
Twilight on the Trail '41

Brett King (1920-99)

Flying Leathernecks '51
Battleground '49

Cammie King (1934-)

Bambi '42 (V)
Gone with the Wind '39

Charles King

The Unnamable '88
Law and Order '42
Mystery Trooper '32

Charles King (1889-1944)

Riders of the Rio Grande '43
The Lone Rider Crosses the Rio '41
Outlaws of the Rio Grande '41
Oklahoma Frontier '39
The Silver Bullet '34
The Gay Buckaroo '32
The Dawn Trail '30
Behind That Curtain '29
Broadway Melody '29

Charles "Blackie" King (1895-1957)

Law of the Lash '47
Ambush Trail '46
The Caravan Trail '46
Colorado Serenade '46
Outlaw of the Plains '46
Border Badmen '45
Flaming Bullets '45
Gangster's Den '45
His Brother's Ghost '45
Shadows of Death '45
Three in the Saddle '45
Boss of Rawhide '44
Dead or Alive '44
Devil Riders '44
Frontier Outlaws '44
Oath of Vengeance '44
Rustler's Hideout '44
Thundering Gunslingers '44
Wild Horse Phantom '44
California Joe '43
Land of Hunted Men '43
Raiders of Red Gap '43
Texas Kid '43
Two-Fisted Justice '43
Along the Sundown Trail '42
Arizona Stagecoach '42
Below the Border '42
Prairie Pals '42
Rangers Take Over '42
Trail Riders '42
Where Trails End '42
Trigger Men '41
Battling Outlaw '40
Death Rides the Range '40
Lightning Strikes West '40
Down the Wyoming Trail '39
Mesquite Buckaroo '39
Trigger Pals '39
Wild Horse Canyon '39
Gun Packer '38
The Phantom of the Range '38
Songs and Bullets '38
Thunder in the Desert '38
The Gambling Terror '37
God's Country and the Man '37
Hittin' the Trail '37
A Lawman Is Born '37
Lightning Bill Crandall '37
Mystery of the Hooded Horseman '37
The Red Rope '37
Riders of the Rockies '37
Ridin' the Lone Trail '37
Santa Fe Bound '37
Sing, Cowboy, Sing '37
Tex Rides with the Boy Scouts '37
Desert Phantom '36
Headin' for the Rio Grande '36
Last of the Warrens '36
The Law Rides '36
The Lawless Nineties '36
Lucky Terror '36
Red River Valley '36
Rip Roarin' Buckaroo '36
Fighting Parson '35
His Fighting Blood '35
Silent Valley '35
Trail of Terror '35
Inside Information '34
Fighting Champ '33
The Lone Avenger '33
Young Blood '33
Outlaw Justice '32
Branded Men '31
The Pocatello Kid '31
Range Law '31
Two Gun Man '31
Oklahoma Cyclone '30

Charmion King (1925-2007)

Jackie, Ethel, Joan: The Kennedy Women '01
Broken Lullaby '94
Anne of Green Gables '85

Chris Thomas King (1962-)

Kill Switch '08
Ray '04
O Brother Where Art Thou? '00

Claude King (1875-1941)

Three on the Trail '36
The Moonstone '34
The Mysterious Dr. Fu Manchu '29

Damu King (1917-91)

Blackjack '78
Black Godfather '74
Black Starlet '74

Dave King (1929-2002)

Revolution '85
The Long Good Friday '80
Naughty Knights '71

Erik King

Atomic Train '99
True Crime '99
Joey Breaker '93
Casualties of War '89

Georgia King

The Duchess '08
Little Dorrit '08
Wild Child '08

Jaime (James) King (1979-)

My Bloody Valentine 3D '09
The Spirit '08
Lies & Alibis '06
The Tripper '06
Cheaper by the Dozen 2 '05
Pretty Persuasion '05
The River King '05
Sin City '05
Two for the Money '05
White Chicks '04
Bulletproof Monk '03
Lone Star State of Mind '02
Slackers '02
Blow '01
Happy Campers '01
Pearl Harbor '01

Joe King (1883-1951)

Dark Town '04
Alexander's Ragtime Band '38
San Quentin '37
Woman in the Shadows '34
Shifting Sands '18
Until They Get Me '18

Joey King (1999-)

Ramona and Beezus '10
Dr. Seuss' Horton Hears a Who! '08 (V)

John King, III (1909-87)

Psycho from Texas '75
Black Bikers from Hell '70
The Outlaw Bikers—Gang Wars '70

John "Dusty" King (1909-87)

Renegade Girl '46
Haunted Ranch '43
Two-Fisted Justice '43
Arizona Stagecoach '42
Boot Hill Bandits '42
Law of the Jungle '42
Rock River Renegades '42
Texas to Bataan '42
Thunder River Feud '42
Trail Riders '42
Fugitive Valley '41
Kid's Last Ride '41
Saddle Mountain Roundup '41
Tonto Basin Outlaws '41
Trail of the Silver Spurs '41
Tumbledown Ranch in Arizona '41
Underground Rustlers '41
Half a Soldier '40
Midnight Limited '40
Range Busters '40
Trailing Double Trouble '40
West of Pinto Basin '40
Mr. Takes a Vacation '39
Charlie Chan in Honolulu '38
Ace Drummond '36

Kenneth King

Jade '95
Polyester '81

Kent Masters King (1974-)

Johnny B. '00
Her Name Is Cat '99

Larry King (1933-)

Shrek Forever After '10 (V)
Bee Movie '07 (V)
Shrek the Third '07 (V)
Shrek 2 '04 (V)
America's Sweethearts '01
An Alan Smithee Film: Burn, Hollywood, Burn '97
Dave '93
Eddie and the Cruisers 2: Eddie Lives! '89
Pink Nights '87

Leslie King

Cotton Candy '82
Gas Pump Girls '79

Mabel King (1932-99)

Dead Men Don't Die '91
Scrooged '88
The Jerk '79
The Wiz '78
Ganja and Hess '73

Meegan King

Money to Burn '83
Humanoids from the Deep '80
Sweater Girls '78

Morgana King (1930-)

A Brooklyn State of Mind '97
A Time to Remember '87
The Godfather, Part 2 '74
The Godfather '72

Perry King (1948-)

Framed for Murder '07
The Day After Tomorrow '04
The Perfect Wife '00
A Cry in the Night '93
Jericho Fever '93
Switch '91
Danielle Steel's Kaleidoscope '90
The Prize Pulitzer '89
Disaster at Silo 7 '88
The Hasty Heart '86
Killing Hour '84
Class of 1984 '82
Search and Destroy '81
City in Fear '80
The Cracker Factory '79
Love's Savage Fury '79
Different Story '78
Andy Warhol's Bad '77
The Choirboys '77
Lipstick '76
Mandingo '75
The Lords of Flatbush '74
Wild Party '74
The Possession of Joel Delaney '72
Slaughterhouse Five '72

Regina King (1971-)

Our Family Wedding '10
Living Proof '08
Grindin' '07
Year of the Dog '07
The Ant Bully '06 (V)
Miss Congeniality 2: Armed and Fabulous '05
A Cinderella Story '04
Ray '04
Daddy Day Care '03
Legally Blonde 2: Red White & Blonde '03
Down to Earth '01
If These Walls Could Talk 2 '00
Love and Action in Chicago '99
Where the Truth Lies '99
Enemy of the State '98
How Stella Got Her Groove Back '98
Mighty Joe Young '98
Jerry Maguire '96
A Thin Line Between Love and Hate '96
Friday '95
Higher Learning '94
Poetic Justice '93

Rowena King

The Bucket List '07
A Perfect Day '06
Romance and Rejection '96
Framed '93
To Play the King '93
Wide Sargasso Sea '92

Stephen King (1947-)

Stephen King's Thinner '96
Stephen King's The Langoliers '95
Stephen King's The Stand '94
Sleepwalkers '92
Stephen King's Golden Years '91
Pet Sematary '89
Creepshow 2 '87
Maximum Overdrive '86
Creepshow '82

Tony King

Cannibal Apocalypse '80
The Last Hunter '80
Sparkle '76
Report to the Commissioner '74
Gordon's War '73
Hell Up in Harlem '73

Walter Woolf King (1899-1984)

The Helen Morgan Story '57
Smart Alecks '42
Today I Hang '42
Yank in Libya '42
Go West '40
Swiss Miss '38
Call It a Day '37
A Night at the Opera '35
Golden Dawn '30

Wright King (1923-)

Missiles of October '74
Invasion of the Bee Girls '73
King Rat '65
Dangerous Charter '62

Yolanda King (1955-)

Selma, Lord, Selma '99
Ghosts of Mississippi '96
America's Dream '95

Zalman King (1941-)

Galaxy of Terror '81
Blue Sunshine '78
The Passover Plot '75
Ski Bum '75
Deadly Fieldtrip '74
Smile, Jenny, You're Dead '74
Some Call It Loving '73

Guy Kingsford (1911-86)

Sahara '43
House of Errors '42

Walter Kingsford (1881-1958)

Velvet Touch '48
My Favorite Blonde '42
The Man in the Iron Mask '39
It Could Happen to You '37
The Invisible Ray '36
The Story of Louis Pasteur '36

Ben Kingsley (1943-)

Prince of Persia: The Sands of Time '10
Shutter Island '09
Elegy '08
Fifty Dead Men Walking '08
The Love Guru '08
Transsiberian '08
The Wackness '08
War, Inc. '08
The Last Legion '07
You Kill Me '07
BloodRayne '06
Lucky Number Slevin '06
Mrs. Harris '05
Oliver Twist '05
A Sound of Thunder '05
Suspect Zero '04
Thunderbirds '04
House of Sand and Fog '03
Tuck Everlasting '02
A. I.: Artificial Intelligence '01 (N)
Anne Frank: The Whole Story '01
The Triumph of Love '01
Rules of Engagement '00
Sexy Beast '00
What Planet Are You From? '00
Alice in Wonderland '99
Dostoevsky's Crime and Punishment '99
The Confession '98
Parting Shots '98
The Assignment '97
Photographing Fairies '97
Weapons of Mass Distraction '97
Moses '96
Twelfth Night '96
Joseph '95
Species '95
Death and the Maiden '94
Dave '93
Schindler's List '93
Searching for Bobby Fischer '93
Freddie the Frog '92 (V)
Sneakers '92
Bugsy '91
The Children '90
The Fifth Monkey '90
Murderers Among Us: The Simon Wiesenthal Story '89
Slipstream '89
Pascali's Island '88
Without a Clue '88
Maurice '87
Turtle Diary '86
Harem '85
Silas Marner '85
Betrayal '83
Gandhi '82
Hard Labour '73

Danitza Kingsley

Jack's Back '87
South of Reno '87
Amazons '86

Susan Kingsley (1946-84)

The Dollmaker '84
Old Enough '84

Alex Kingston (1963-)

Lost in Austen '08
Crashing '07
Alpha Dog '06
Sweet Land '05
Warrior Queen '03
Essex Boys '99
Croupier '97
Moll Flanders '96
Carrington '95
The Infiltrator '95

Mark Kingston (1934-)
Intimate Contact *'87*
Hitler: The Last Ten Days *'73*

Natalie Kingston (1905-91)
His Private Secretary *'33*
Tarzan the Tiger *'29*
His First Flame *'26*

Amelia Kinkade (1963-)
Night of the Demons 3 *'97*
Night of the Demons 2 *'94*

Laurence Kinlan (1983-)
Ned Kelly *'03*
An Everlasting Piece *'00*

Kathleen Kinmont (1965-)
Gangland *'00*
The Corporate Ladder *'97*
That Thing You Do! *'96*
Stormswept *'95*
Texas Payback *'95*
C.I.A. 2: Target Alexa *'94*
Final Round *'93*
C.I.A.: Code Name Alexa *'92*
Sweet Justice *'92*
Final Impact *'91*
Night of the Warrior *'91*
The Art of Dying *'90*
Roller Blade Warriors: Taken By Force *'90*
Bride of Re-Animator *'89*
SnakeEater 2: The Drug Buster *'89*
Halloween 4: The Return of Michael Myers *'88*
Phoenix the Warrior *'88*
Rush Week *'88*
Fraternity Vacation *'85*
Hardbodies *'84*

Greg Kinnear (1963-)
Green Zone *'10*
The Last Song *'10*
Baby Mama *'08*
Flash of Genius *'08*
Ghost Town *'08*
Feast of Love *'07*
Fast Food Nation *'06*
Invincible *'06*
Little Miss Sunshine *'06*
The Matador *'06*
The Bad News Bears *'05*
Robots *'05 (V)*
Godsend *'04*
Stuck On You *'03*
Auto Focus *'02*
We Were Soldiers *'02*
Dinner with Friends *'01*
Someone Like You *'01*
The Gift *'00*
Loser *'00*
Nurse Betty *'00*
What Planet Are You From? *'00*
Mystery Men *'99*
You've Got Mail *'98*
As Good As It Gets *'97*
Dear God *'96*
A Smile Like Yours *'96*
Sabrina *'95*

Rory Kinnear
Five Days *'07*
Mansfield Park *'07*
Secret Smile *'05*

Roy Kinnear (1934-88)
The Return of the Musketeers *'89*
A Man for All Seasons *'88*
Pirates *'86*
The Zany Adventures of Robin Hood *'84*
Hawk the Slayer *'81*
The Adventures of Sherlock Holmes' Smarter Brother *'78*
Herbie Goes to Monte Carlo *'77*
The Hound of the Baskervilles *'77*
The Four Musketeers *'75*
Juggernaut *'74*
Pied Piper *'72*
Melody *'71*
Willy Wonka & the Chocolate Factory *'71*
Taste the Blood of Dracula *'70*
How I Won the War *'67*
Help! *'65*
The Hill *'65*

Kathy Kinney (1954-)
This Boy's Life *'93*
Three Fugitives *'89*
Parting Glances *'86*

Terry Kinney (1954-)
Turn the River *'07*
The Game of Their Lives *'05*
Runaway *'05*
The Laramie Project *'02*
Save the Last Dance *'01*
House of Mirth *'00*
Luminous Motion *'00*
Oxygen *'99*
That Championship Season *'99*
The Young Girl and the Monsoon *'99*
Don't Look Down *'98*
Critical Choices *'97*
George Wallace *'97*
Fly Away Home *'96*
Sleepers *'96*
Devil in a Blue Dress *'95*
The Good Old Boys *'95*
Body Snatchers *'93*
The Firm *'93*
JFK: Reckless Youth *'93*
The Last of the Mohicans *'92*
Talent for the Game *'91*
Murder Ordained *'87*

Houka Kinoshita
Shinobi *'05*
Ichi the Killer *'01*
Onmyoji *'01*

Leonid Kinskey (1903-98)
Can't Help Singing *'45*
Fighting Seabees *'44*
That's My Baby! *'44*
Casablanca *'42*
I Married an Angel *'42*
Lady for a Night *'42*
Somewhere I'll Find You *'42*
Broadway Limited *'41*
That Night in Rio *'41*
Down Argentine Way *'40*
Day-Time Wife *'39*
Everything Happens at Night *'39*
The Great Waltz *'38*
Les Miserables *'35*
The Lives of a Bengal Lancer *'35*
Duck Soup *'33*

Klaus Kinski (1926-91)
Cobra Verde *'88*
Timestalkers *'87*
Crawlspace *'86*
Gangster's Law *'86*
Creature *'85*
Star Knight *'85*
Codename: Wildgeese *'84*
The Little Drummer Girl *'84*
The Secret Diary of Sigmund Freud *'84*
Beauty and the Beast *'83*
Android *'82*
Burden of Dreams *'82*
Fitzcarraldo *'82*
The Soldier *'82*
Venom *'82*
Buddy Buddy *'81*
Schizoid *'80*
The French Woman *'79*
Nosferatu the Vampyre *'79*
Woyzeck *'78*
Night of the Assassin *'77*
Operation Thunderbolt *'77*
Jack the Ripper *'76*
Lifespan *'75*
Primal Impulse *'74*
Heroes in Hell *'73*
Aguirre, the Wrath of God *'72*
Count Dracula *'71*
Fistful of Death *'71*
His Name Was King *'71*
Slaughter Hotel *'71*
Creature with the Blue Hand *'70*
Double Face *'70*
Rough Justice *'70*
The Ruthless Four *'70*
Shoot the Living, Pray for the Dead *'70*
Venus in Furs *'70*
Web of the Spider *'70*
And God Said to Cain *'69*
Liberators *'69*
Twice a Judas *'69*
A Bullet for the General *'68*
Deadly Sanctuary *'68*
Psychopath *'68*
Circus of Fear *'67*
Five for Hell *'67*
Five Golden Dragons *'67*
Target for Killing *'66*
Doctor Zhivago *'65*
Fighting Fists of Shanghai Joe *'65*
For a Few Dollars More *'65*
The Squeaker *'65*
The Indian Scarf *'63*
Door with the Seven Locks *'62*
Inn on the River *'62*
Dead Eyes of London *'61*
The Avenger *'60*
A Time to Love & a Time to Die *'58*

Nastassja Kinski (1959-)
Dangerous Liaisons *'03*
Rip It Off *'02*
An American Rhapsody *'01*
The Day the World Ended *'01*
Say Nothing *'01*
Town and Country *'01*
The Claim *'00*
Red Letters *'00*
Dying to Get Rich *'98*
The Lost Son *'98*
Playing by Heart *'98*
Savior *'98*
Your Friends & Neighbors *'98*
Bella Mafia *'97*
Little Boy Blue *'97*
One Night Stand *'97*
Father's Day *'96*
Somebody Is Waiting *'96*
Crackerjack *'94*
Terminal Velocity *'94*
Faraway, So Close! *'93*
The Blonde *'92*
Torrents of Spring *'90*
Magdalene *'88*
Spring Symphony *'86*
Harem *'85*
Revolution *'85*
The Hotel New Hampshire *'84*
Maria's Lovers *'84*
Unfaithfully Yours *'84*
Boarding School *'83*
Exposed *'83*
Moon in the Gutter *'83*
Paris, Texas *'83*
Cat People *'82*
One from the Heart *'82*
For Your Love Only *'79*
Tess *'79*
Stay As You Are *'78*
The Wrong Move *'78*
To the Devil, a Daughter *'76*

Nikolai Kinski (1976-)
Klimt *'06*
Aeon Flux *'05*
Tortilla Soup *'01*

Bruce Kirby (1928-)
Blood Money *'99*
Interlocked *'98*
Rave Review *'95*
Mr. Wonderful *'93*
Getting Up and Going Home *'92*
Throw Momma from the Train *'87*
Armed and Dangerous *'86*
Fyre *'78*
The Young Graduates *'71*
Catch-22 *'70*

Bruno Kirby (1949-2006)
Played *'06*
American Tragedy *'00*
A Slipping Down Life *'99*
Spy Games *'99*
Stuart Little *'99 (V)*
Donnie Brasco *'96*
Sleepers *'96*
The Basketball Diaries *'95*
Fallen Angels 2 *'93*
Golden Gate *'93*
Mastergate *'92*
City Slickers *'91*
The Freshman *'90*
Bert Rigby, You're a Fool *'89*
We're No Angels *'89*
When Harry Met Sally... *'89*
Nitti: The Enforcer *'88*
Good Morning, Vietnam *'87*
Tin Men *'87*
Flesh and Blood *'85*
Birdy *'84*
This Is Spinal Tap *'84*
Kiss My Grits *'82*
The Godfather 1902-1959: The Complete Epic *'81*
Modern Romance *'81*
Borderline *'80*
Where the Buffalo Roam *'80*
Between the Lines *'77*
The Godfather, Part 2 *'74*
Cinderella Liberty *'73*
Harrad Experiment *'73*

George Kirby (1924-95)
Trouble in Mind *'86*
Oh Dad, Poor Dad (Momma's Hung You in the Closet & I'm Feeling So Sad) *'67*

Jay Kirby (1920-64)
Sundown Riders *'48*
Border Patrol *'43*
Colt Comrades *'43*
Hoppy Serves a Writ *'43*
Leather Burners *'43*
Lost Canyon *'43*

Luke Kirby (1978-)
Labor Pains *'09*
All Hat *'07*
The Stone Angel *'07*
Window Theory *'04*
Mambo Italiano *'03*
Shattered Glass *'03*
Halloween: Resurrection *'02*
Lost and Delirious *'01*

Michael Kirby (1925-97)
Shadows and Fog *'92*
Swoon *'91*
Another Woman *'88*
Find the Lady *'76*
The Girl in Blue *'74*

James Kirk (1986-)
Dr. Dolittle 3 *'06*
She's the Man *'06*
Category 7 : The End of the World *'05*
Confessions of a Sociopathic Social Climber *'05*
Two for the Money *'05*
Final Destination 2 *'03*
X2: X-Men United *'03*
Due East *'02*
A Season on the Brink *'02*
Mindstorm *'01*
National Lampoon's Golf Punks *'99*

Joe (Joseph) Kirk (1903-75)
Abbott and Costello Go to Mars *'53*
Impact *'49*
The Noose Hangs High *'48*
The Naughty Nineties *'45*
Smart Alecks *'42*

Justin Kirk (1969-)
Ask the Dust *'06*
Flannel Pajamas *'06*
Puccini for Beginners *'06*
Angels in America *'03*
Love! Valour! Compassion! *'96*

Pamela Kirk
See Pam(ela) Austin

Phyllis Kirk (1926-2006)
The Sad Sack *'57*
Back from Eternity *'56*
Crime Wave *'54*
River Beat *'54*
House of Wax *'53*
The Iron Mistress *'52*
Three Guys Named Mike *'51*
A Life of Her Own *'50*
Our Very Own *'50*
Two Weeks with Love *'50*

Tommy Kirk (1941-)
Attack of the 60-Foot Centerfold *'95*
Blood of Ghastly Horror *'72*
It's Alive! *'68*
Ghost in the Invisible Bikini *'66*
Mars Needs Women *'66*
The Unkissed Bride *'66*
Monkey's Uncle *'65*
Village of the Giants *'65*
Pajama Party *'64*
The Misadventures of Merlin Jones *'63*
Savage Sam *'63*
Son of Flubber *'63*
Bon Voyage! *'62*
Escapade in Florence *'62*
Moon Pilot *'62*
The Absent-Minded Professor *'61*
Babes in Toyland *'61*
Horsemasters *'61*
The Swiss Family Robinson *'60*
The Shaggy Dog *'59*
Old Yeller *'57*

Donald Kirke (1901-71)
A Night for Crime *'42*
Oh Susannah *'38*
Country Gentlemen *'36*

Sally Kirkland (1944-)
Flexing with Monty *'10*
Big Stan *'07*
Coffee Date *'06*
Adam & Steve *'05*
What's Up, Scarlet? *'05*
Out of the Black *'01*
Another Woman's Husband *'00*
Wish You Were Dead *'00*
EDtv *'99*
Starry Night *'99*
Dead Silence *'98*
Get a Clue! *'98*
Paranoia *'98*
Amnesia *'96*
Excess Baggage *'96*
Cheatin' Hearts *'93*
Eye of the Stranger *'93*
Gunmen *'93*
The Woman Who Loved Elvis *'93*
Double Jeopardy *'92*
Double Threat *'92*
Forever: A Ghost of a Love Story *'92*
Hit the Dutchman *'92*
The Player *'92*
Primary Motive *'92*
Prime Time Murder *'92*
In the Heat of Passion *'91*
JFK *'91*
Bullseye! *'90*
Heat Wave *'90*
Revenge *'90*
Superstar: The Life and Times of Andy Warhol *'90*
Two Evil Eyes *'90*
Best of the Best *'89*
Cold Feet *'89*
High Stakes *'89*
Paint It Black *'89*
White Hot *'88*
Anna *'87*
Talking Walls *'85*
Fatal Games *'84*
Love Letters *'83*
Private Benjamin *'80*
Hometown U.S.A. *'79*
Breakheart Pass *'76*
Pipe Dreams *'76*
A Star Is Born *'76*
Bite the Bullet *'75*
Crazy Mama *'75*
Death Scream *'75*
The Noah *'75 (V)*
Big Bad Mama *'74*
Candy Stripe Nurses *'74*
Cinderella Liberty *'73*
The Sting *'73*
The Way We Were *'73*
The Young Nurses *'73*
Fury on Wheels *'71*
Coming Apart *'69*
Futz *'69*
Blue *'68*

Bryan Kirkwood
Hellbent *'04*
The Devil's Prey *'01*

Gene Kirkwood (1945-)
The Crossing Guard *'94*
Night and the City *'92*

Jack Kirkwood (1895-1964)
Fancy Pants *'50*
Never a Dull Moment *'50*

Langley Kirkwood
Invictus *'09*
In My Country *'04*

Stan Kirsch (1968-)
Shallow Ground *'04*
Highlander: The Gathering *'92*

Rudiger Kirschstein (1941-)
Coup de Grace *'78*
An Occurrence at Owl Creek Bridge/Coup de Grace *'62*

Mia Kirshner (1975-)
Miss Conception *'08*
The Black Dahlia *'06*
The Iris Effect *'04*
New Best Friend *'02*
Now & Forever *'02*
Not Another Teen Movie *'01*
Cowboys and Angels *'00*
Innocents *'00*
Out of the Cold *'99*
Speed of Life *'99*
Mad City *'97*
The Crow 2: City of Angels *'96*
Leo Tolstoy's Anna Karenina *'96*
The Grass Harp *'95*
Johnny's Girl *'95*
Murder in the First *'95*
Exotica *'94*
Cadillac Girls *'93*
Love and Human Remains *'93*

Terry Kiser (1939-)
Forest Warrior *'95*
Pet Shop *'94*
Tammy and the T-Rex *'94*
Weekend at Bernie's 2 *'93*
Into the Sun *'92*
Mannequin 2: On the Move *'91*
Weekend at Bernie's *'89*
Friday the 13th, Part 7: The New Blood *'88*
The Offspring *'87*
Surf 2 *'84*
Starflight One *'83*
Making Love *'82*
Steel *'80*

Keiko Kishi (1932-)
The Makioka Sisters *'83*
Master Mind *'73*
Kwaidan *'64*
Qui Etes Vous, Mr. Sorge? *'61*
Snow Country *'57*

Ittoku Kishibe
Hula Girls *'06*
Zatoichi *'03*
Onmyoji *'01*
Shark Skin Man and Peach Hip Girl *'98*

Kyoko Kishida (1930-2006)
Face of Another '66
Woman in the Dunes '64
Shinobi no Mono '62
The Human Condition: A Soldier's Prayer '61

Shin Kishida (1939-82)
Shogun Assassin '80
Murders in the Doll House '79

Goro Kishitani
One Missed Call '03
Graveyard of Honor '02
Returner '02

Charles Kissinger (1925-91)
Grizzly '76
Sheba, Baby '75
Asylum of Satan '72
Three on a Meathook '72

Jeremy James Kissner
Brotherhood of Blood '08
A Dog of Flanders '99

Tawny Kitaen (1961-)
Dead Tides '97
Playback '95
Hercules the Legendary Journeys, Vol. 3: The Circle of Fire '94
Hercules the Legendary Journeys, Vol. 4: In the Underworld '94
White Hot '88
Crystal Heart '87
Glory Years '87
Happy Hour '87
Witchboard '87
Instant Justice '86
Bachelor Party '84
The Perils of Gwendoline '84

Kazuki Kitamura
Azumi 2 '05
Azumi '03
The Way To Fight '96

Kazuo Kitamura (1927-2007)
Shinobi '05
Black Rain '88
Tora! Tora! Tora! '70

Takeshi "Beat" Kitano (1948-)
Zatoichi '03
Brother '00
Kikujiro '99
Taboo '99
Fireworks '97
Sonatine '96
Johnny Mnemonic '95
Boiling Point '90
Violent Cop '89
Merry Christmas, Mr. Lawrence '83

Michael Kitchen (1948-)
Lorna Doone '01
Oliver Twist '00
Proof of Life '00
The Railway Children '00
The World Is Not Enough '99
Reckless: The Sequel '98
Mrs. Dalloway '97
Reckless '97
A Royal Scandal '96
Wilderness '96
The Buccaneers '95
Goldeneye '95
Kidnapped '95
Doomsday Gun '94
Fatherland '94
To Play the King '93
Enchanted April '92
Fools of Fortune '90
The Russia House '90
The Dive '89
Out of Africa '85
The Brontes of Haworth '73

Taylor Kitsch (1981-)
X-Men Origins: Wolverine '09
Gospel Hill '08
The Covenant '06
Snakes on a Plane '06

Supakorn Kitsuwon
The Legend of Suriyothai '02
Tears of the Black Tiger '00

Eartha Kitt (1928-2008)
And Then Came Love '07
Preaching to the Choir '05
Holes '03
Anything But Love '02
Anne Rice's The Feast of All Saints '01
The Emperor's New Groove '00 (V)
Harriet the Spy '96
Boomerang '92
Ernest Scared Stupid '91
Living Doll '90
Erik the Viking '89
Master of Dragonard Hill '89
Dragonard '88
The Pink Chiquitas '86
Naughty Knights '71
The Mark of the Hawk '57
New Faces of 1952 '54

Tory Kittles
Next '07
Get Rich or Die Tryin' '05
Frankenfish '04
Big Shot: Confessions of a Campus Bookie '02

John Kitzmiller (1913-65)
Uncle Tom's Cabin '69
Cave of the Living Dead '65
Dr. No '62

Barry Kivel
Bound '96
One Fine Day '96

Alf Kjellin (1920-88)
The Victors '63
The Iron Mistress '52
Summer Interlude '50
Torment '44

Bjorn Kjellman (1963-)
All Things Fair '95
The Best Intentions '92

Gary Klar (1947-)
Devlin '92
Chattahoochee '89

Burghart Klaussner
The White Ribbon '09
The Edukators '04

Uri Klauzner
Free Zone '05
Year Zero '04
Kippur '00
Kadosh '99

Martin Klebba (1969-)
Feast 2: Sloppy Seconds '08
Pirates of the Caribbean: At World's End '07
Pirates of the Caribbean: Dead Man's Chest '06
El Matador '03

Chris Klein (1979-)
Street Fighter: The Legend of Chun-Li '09
Hank and Mike '08
Day Zero '07
The Good Life '07
American Dreamz '06
Full Count '06
Just Friends '05
The Long Weekend '05
United States of Leland '03
Rollerball '02
We Were Soldiers '02
American Pie 2 '01
Say It Isn't So '01
Here on Earth '00
American Pie '99
Election '99

Erik S. Klein (1926-2002)
Anton, the Magician '78
Under the Pear Tree '73
The Second Track '62

Gerard Klein
Frantic '88
La Passante '83

Nita Klein
Dr. Petiot '90
Muriel '63

Robert Klein (1942-)
Reign Over Me '07
Ira & Abby '06
How to Lose a Guy in 10 Days '03
People I Know '02
Two Weeks Notice '02
The Safety of Objects '01
Labor Pains '99
Next Stop, Wonderland '98
Primary Colors '98
One Fine Day '96
Mixed Nuts '94
Radioland Murders '94
The Marx Brothers in a Nutshell '90
Tales from the Darkside: The Movie '90
Dangerous Curves '88
A Secret Space '88
Poison Ivy '85
Table Settings '84
Pajama Tops '83
Your Place or Mine '83
The Last Unicorn '82 (V)
The Bell Jar '79
Nobody's Perfekt '79
Hooper '78
Rivals '72
The Owl and the Pussycat '70
The Pursuit of Happiness '70

Silke Klein (1974-)
Felicidades '00
Tierra '95

Rudolf Klein-Rogge (1888-1955)
Crimes of Dr. Mabuse '32
Spies '28
Metropolis '26
Kriemhilde's Revenge '24
Warning Shadows '23
Dr. Mabuse, The Gambler '22
Destiny '21
The Cabinet of Dr. Caligari '19

Werner Klemperer (1920-2000)
Judgment at Nuremberg '61
Istanbul '57

Kevin Kline (1947-)
Definitely, Maybe '08
The Tale of Despereaux '08 (V)
Trade '07
As You Like It '06
The Pink Panther '06
A Prairie Home Companion '06
Jiminy Glick in LaLa Wood '05
De-Lovely '04
The Emperor's Club '02
Orange County '02
The Anniversary Party '01
Life as a House '01
The Road to El Dorado '00 (V)
Wild Wild West '99
William Shakespeare's A Midsummer Night's Dream '99
The Ice Storm '97
In and Out '97
Fierce Creatures '96
The Hunchback of Notre Dame '96 (V)
Looking for Richard '96
French Kiss '95
Princess Caraboo '94
Dave '93
George Balanchine's The Nutcracker '93 (N)
Chaplin '92
Consenting Adults '92
Grand Canyon '91
Soapdish '91
I Love You to Death '90
The January Man '89
A Fish Called Wanda '88
Cry Freedom '87
Violets Are Blue '86
Silverado '85
The Big Chill '83
The Pirates of Penzance '83
Sophie's Choice '82

Richard Kline (1944-)
I Now Pronounce You Chuck and Larry '07
Liberty Heights '99
Treehouse Hostage '99
The Feminine Touch '95

Heidi Kling (1962-)
D3: The Mighty Ducks '96
The Mighty Ducks '92
Out on a Limb '92

Evan J. Klisser
Prey for the Hunter '92
Hellgate '89

Brian Klugman
Vacancy 2: The First Cut '08
Dreamland '06

Jack Klugman (1922-)
When Do We Eat? '05
The Twilight of the Golds '97
Dear God '96
Parallel Lives '94
Around the World in 80 Days '89
One of My Wives Is Missing '76
Two Minute Warning '76
Goodbye Columbus '69
The Detective '68
Hail Mafia '65
I Could Go on Singing '63
Days of Wine and Roses '62
Twelve Angry Men '57

Heidi Klum (1973-)
Ella Enchanted '04
Blow Dry '00

Vincent Klyn
Mexican Blow '02
Gangland '00
Urban Menace '99
Nemesis '93
Bloodmatch '91
Point Break '91
Dollman '90
Cyborg '89

Skelton Knaggs (1911-55)
Dick Tracy Meets Gruesome '47
Forever Amber '47
Dick Tracy vs. Cueball '46
Bedlam '45
Isle of the Dead '45

Evalyn Knapp (1908-81)
Hawaiian Buckaroo '38
Rawhide '38
Bulldog Edition '36
Mistaken Identity '36
Confidential '35
In Old Santa Fe '34
The Perils of Pauline '34
His Private Secretary '33
The Strange Love of Molly Louvain '32
Smart Money '31

Katrin Knappe
The Woman and the Stranger '84
Jadup and Boel '81

Herbert Knaup (1956-)
Agnes and His Brothers '04
Nuremberg '00
Run Lola Run '98

Hildegarde Knef (1925-2002)
Witchery '88
The Future of Emily '85
Bluebeard '63
The Three Penny Opera '62
Svengali '55
Diplomatic Courier '52
The Snows of Kilimanjaro '52
Unnatural '52
The Murderers Are Among Us '46

David Knell (1961-)
Chopper Chicks in Zombietown '91
Spring Break '83
Bitter Harvest '81

Robert Knepper (1959-)
Prison Break: The Final Break '09
The Day the Earth Stood Still '08
Transporter 3 '08
Hitman '07
Good Night, and Good Luck '05
Hostage '05
Species 3 '04
Jackie, Ethel, Joan: The Kennedy Women '01
Love & Sex '00
Absence of the Good '99
Kidnapped in Paradise '98
The Undercover Kid '95 (V)
Getting Out '94
Gas Food Lodging '92
Where the Day Takes You '92
Young Guns 2 '90
Renegades '89
Wild Thing '87
That's Life! '86

Bobby Knight (1940-)
Anger Management '03
Blue Chips '94

Christopher Knight (1957-)
Madagascar: Escape 2 Africa '08 (V)
Nowhere '96
The Brady Bunch Movie '95
The Doom Generation '95
Good Girls Don't '95
A Very Brady Christmas '88
Diary of a Teenage Hitchhiker '82
Cotter '72

David Knight (1927-)
Nightmare '63
Missiles from Hell '58
Across the Bridge '57

David Edwin Knight (1972-)
Who Shot Pat? '92
Demons 2 '87

Esmond Knight (1906-87)
The Element of Crime '84
Peeping Tom '60
Sink the Bismarck '60
Missiles from Hell '58
The River '51
Hamlet '48
The Red Shoes '48
Black Narcissus '47
A Canterbury Tale '44
Henry V '44
Contraband '40
The Arsenal Stadium Mystery '39

Fuzzy Knight (1901-76)
Hostile Guns '67
Naked Hills '56
Oklahoma Annie '51
Apache Chief '50
Blazing Guns '50
Hills of Oklahoma '50
Last Bullet '50
Marshal of Heldorado '50
Rangeland Empire '50
Sudden Death '50
Rimfire '49
The Adventures of Gallant Bess '48
Bad Men of the Border '45
Boss of Boomtown '44
Hi, Good Lookin'! '44
Take It Big '44
Frontier Law '43
The Lone Star Trail '43
The Silver Bullet '42
Stagecoach Buckaroo '42
Arizona Cyclone '41
Boss of Bullion City '41
Bury Me Not on the Lone Prairie '41
Horror Island '41
Man from Montana '41
The Masked Rider '41
The Shepherd of the Hills '41
Law and Order '40
My Little Chickadee '40
Pony Post '40
Riders of Pasco Basin '40
Chip of the Flying U '39
Oklahoma Frontier '39
The Cowboy and the Lady '38
Spawn of the North '38
Kelly of the Secret Service '36
Song of the Gringo '36
Song of the Trail '36
The Trail of the Lonesome Pine '36
Trails of the Wild '35
To the Last Man '33

Gladys Knight (1944-)
I Can Do Bad All By Myself '09
Hollywood Homicide '03
Twenty Bucks '93
Pipe Dreams '76

Harlan E. Knight
Whistlin' Dan '32
The Fighting Sheriff '31

Jack Knight
A Lobster Tale '06
Class of 1999 2: The Substitute '93

Lily Knight (1956-)
The Assassination of Richard Nixon '05
An Unremarkable Life '89
Static '87

Matthew Knight
The Grudge 3 '09
All the Good Ones Are Married '07
Christmas in Wonderland '07
Skinwalkers '07
The Greatest Game Ever Played '05

Michael E. Knight (1959-)
Hexed '93
Date with an Angel '87

Sandra Knight (1940-)
Track of the Vampire '66
The Terror '63
Tower of London '62
Frankenstein's Daughter '58
Thunder Road '58

Shirley Knight (1937-)
Paul Blart: Mall Cop '09
The Private Lives of Pippa Lee '09
Grandma's Boy '06
Love and Debate '06
Open Window '06
Divine Secrets of the Ya-Ya Sisterhood '02
My Louisiana Sky '02
P.S. Your Cat is Dead! '02
The Salton Sea '02
Angel Eyes '01
75 Degrees '00
As Good As It Gets '97
Little Boy Blue '97
Diabolique '96
If These Walls Could Talk '96
Somebody Is Waiting '96
A Good Day to Die '95
Indictment: The McMartin Trial '95
Color of Night '94
Stuart Saves His Family '94
The Sender '82

Endless Love '81
Beyond the Poseidon Adventure '79
Return to Earth '76
21 Hours at Munich '76
Juggernaut '74
Secrets '71
The Rain People '69
Petulia '68
Dutchman '67
The Group '66
Sweet Bird of Youth '62
Ice Palace '60

Ted (Edward) Knight (1923-86)
Caddyshack '80
Countdown '68
Psycho '60

Trenton Knight (1982-)
Invisible Mom '96
The Tin Soldier '95
Charlie's Ghost: The Secret of Coronado '94
The Skateboard Kid 2 '94

Tuesday Knight (1969-)
The Theory of the Leisure Class '01
Cool and the Crazy '94
Cover Story '93
A Nightmare on Elm Street 4: Dream Master '88

Wayne Knight (1955-)
Punisher: War Zone '08
Forfeit '07
Who's Your Monkey '07
Black Cloud '04
Master Spy: The Robert Hanssen Story '02
Rat Race '01
Tarzan '99 (V)
Toy Story 2 '99 (V)
For Richer or Poorer '97
Space Jam '96
Chameleon '95
To Die For '95
Fallen Angels 2 '93
Jurassic Park '93
Basic Instinct '92
Dead Again '91
JFK '91

William Knight (1934-)
Action U.S.A. '89
The Lost Platoon '89

Wyatt Knight (1955-)
Porky's Revenge '85
Porky's 2: The Next Day '83
Porky's '82

Keira Knightley (1985-)
Last Night '10
The Duchess '08
The Edge of Love '08
Atonement '07
Pirates of the Caribbean: At World's End '07
Silk '07
Pirates of the Caribbean: Dead Man's Chest '06
Domino '05
The Jacket '05
Pride and Prejudice '05
King Arthur '04
Doctor Zhivago '03
Love Actually '03
Pirates of the Caribbean: The Curse of the Black Pearl '03
Bend It Like Beckham '02
Pure '02
The Hole '01
Princess of Thieves '01
Oliver Twist '00

Zachery Knighton (1978-)
The Hitcher '07
The Mudge Boy '03

Ohad Knoller (1976-)
Beaufort '07
The Bubble '06
Yossi & Jagger '02
Under the Domim Tree '95

Sascha Knopf (1971-)
He Was a Quiet Man '07
What's the Worst That Could Happen? '01
Blackmale '99

Andrew Knott (1979-)
The History Boys '06
Black Beauty '94
The Secret Garden '93

Don Knotts (1924-2006)
Air Bud 6: Air Buddies '06 (V)
Chicken Little '05 (V)
Pleasantville '98
Cats Don't Dance '97 (V)
Big Bully '95
Return to Mayberry '85
Cannonball Run 2 '84
The Private Eyes '80
The Apple Dumpling Gang Rides Again '79
Prize Fighter '79
Hot Lead & Cold Feet '78
Herbie Goes to Monte Carlo '77
No Deposit, No Return '76
The Apple Dumpling Gang '75
How to Frame a Figg '71
The Love God? '70
The Shakiest Gun in the West '68
The Reluctant Astronaut '67
The Ghost and Mr. Chicken '66
The Incredible Mr. Limpet '64
It's a Mad, Mad, Mad, Mad World '63
Move Over, Darling '63
No Time for Sergeants '58

Beyonce Knowles (1981-)
Obsessed '09
Cadillac Records '08
Dreamgirls '06
The Pink Panther '06
The Fighting Temptations '03
Austin Powers In Goldmember '02
Carmen: A Hip Hopera '01

Elizabeth Knowles
Wild Riders '71
Lady Godiva Rides '68

Patric Knowles (1911-95)
Arnold '73
Chisum '70
The Devil's Brigade '68
Auntie Mame '58
Band of Angels '57
Mutiny '52
Tarzan's Savage Fury '52
Three Came Home '50
Big Steal '49
Monsieur Beaucaire '46
O.S.S. '46
Hit the Ice '43
Frankenstein Meets the Wolfman '42
The Strange Case of Dr. Rx '42
Who Done It? '42
How Green Was My Valley '41
The Wolf Man '41
Beauty for the Asking '39
Five Came Back '39
The Adventures of Robin Hood '38
Four's a Crowd '38
The Sisters '38
The Charge of the Light Brigade '36

Alexander Knox (1907-95)
Joshua Then and Now '85
Cry of the Innocent '80
The Chosen '77
Puppet on a Chain '72
Nicholas and Alexandra '71
Shalako '68
Villa Rides '68
Accident '67
Khartoum '66
Modesty Blaise '66
Woman of Straw '64
The Longest Day '62
Operation Amsterdam '60
The Wreck of the Mary Deare '59
The Vikings '58
Alias John Preston '56
Reach for the Sky '56
The Sleeping Tiger '54
Europa '51 '52
I'd Climb the Highest Mountain '51
Man in the Saddle '51
The Judge Steps Out '49
Tokyo Joe '49
Sister Kenny '46
Wilson '44
Commandos Strike at Dawn '43
The Sea Wolf '41
The Four Feathers '39

Elyse Knox (1917-)
I Wouldn't Be in Your Shoes '48
Don Winslow of the Coast Guard '43
Hit the Ice '43
The Mummy's Tomb '42
Sheriff of Tombstone '41
Tanks a Million '41

Mickey Knox (1922-)
Cemetery Man '95
Frankenstein Unbound '90
Western Pacific Agent '51
Killer McCoy '47

Patricia Knox
Flaming Bullets '45
I Accuse My Parents '45

Terence Knox (1946-)
The Invaders '95
The Spy Within '94
Murder So Sweet '93
Children of the Corn 2: The Final Sacrifice '92
Forever: A Ghost of a Love Story '92
Snow Kill '90
Tripwire '89
City Killer '87
Distortions '87
The Mighty Pawns '87
Murder Ordained '87
Tour of Duty '87
Humanoid Defender '85
Rebel Love '85
Circle of Power '83

Johnny Knoxville (1971-)
Jackass Number Two '06
Daltry Calhoun '05
The Dukes of Hazzard '05
Lords of Dogtown '05
The Ringer '05
A Dirty Shame '04
Walking Tall '04
Grand Theft Parsons '03
Big Trouble '02
Deuces Wild '02
Jackass: The Movie '02
Men in Black 2 '02
Life Without Dick '01

Erik Knudsen
Youth in Revolt '10
Saw 2 '05

Peggy Knudsen (1923-80)
Istanbul '57
Copper Canyon '50
The Big Sleep '46
Humoresque '46
Never Say Goodbye '46
A Stolen Life '46

Gustav Knuth (1901-87)
Heidi '65
Tromba, the Tiger Man '52

Philip Ko
Interpol Connection '92
Opium and Kung-Fu Master '84

Mpho Koaho
It's a Boy Girl Thing '06
Saw 3 '06
Get Rich or Die Tryin' '05
Detention '03
Crown Heights '02
Snipes '01
Down in the Delta '98

Hirohoshi Kobayashi
Death Note 3: L, Change the World '08
Ichi the Killer '01

Keiju Kobayashi (1923-)
Godzilla 1985 '85
Tidal Wave '75
Sanjuro '62

Megumi Kobayashi (1977-)
Rebirth of Mothra 2 '97
Rebirth of Mothra '96

Nenji Kobayashi (1943-)
The Hidden Blade '04
The Twilight Samurai '02

Shoji Kobayashi (-1996)
Godzilla vs. King Ghidora '91
Youth of the Beast '63

Yukiko Kobayashi (1946-)
Yog, Monster from Space '71
Destroy All Monsters '68

Jeff Kober (1953-)
Aces 'n Eights '08
A Man Apart '03
Lost Voyage '01
American Tragedy '00
Militia '99
The Colony '98
The Maker '98
Elmore Leonard's Gold Coast '97
The Big Fall '96
Demolition High '95
One Man's Justice '95
Automatic '94
Tank Girl '94
Lone Justice '93
The Baby Doll Murders '92
Keep the Change '92
The First Power '89
Alien Nation '88
China Beach '88
Lucky Stiff '88
Out of Bounds '86

Bogumil Kobiela
Hands Up '81
Ashes and Diamonds '58

Edward I. Koch (1924-)
Somewhere in the City '97
New York Stories '89

Marianne Koch (1931-)
A Place Called Glory '66
A Fistful of Dollars '64
Frozen Alive '64
The Monster of London City '64
Coast of Skeletons '63

Pete Koch
Adventures in Dinosaur City '92
Heartbreak Ridge '86

Sebastian Koch (1962-)
Black Book '06
Operation Valkyrie '04
Napoleon '03
Gloomy Sunday '02
The Tunnel '01

Rebekah Kochan
Eating Out 3: All You Can Eat '09
Eating Out 2: Sloppy Seconds '06

Barbara Kodetova (1970-)
Children of Dune '03
Dune '00

Boris Kodjoe (1973-)
Surrogates '09
Starship Troopers 3: Marauder '08
Madea's Family Reunion '06
The Gospel '05
Brown Sugar '02

David Koechner (1962-)
Extract '09
The Goods: Live Hard, Sell Hard '09
My One and Only '09
Get Smart '08
Semi-Pro '08
The Brothers Solomon '07
The Comebacks '07
Barnyard '06 (V)
Larry the Cable Guy: Health Inspector '06
Let's Go to Prison '06
Snakes on a Plane '06
Thank You for Smoking '06
Unaccompanied Minors '06
Daltry Calhoun '05
The Dukes of Hazzard '05
The 40 Year Old Virgin '05
Waiting '05
Yours, Mine & Ours '05
Anchorman: The Legend of Ron Burgundy '04
A Guy Thing '03
My Boss's Daughter '03

Frederick Koehler (1975-)
Death Race '08
Little Chenier: A Cajun Story '06
Touched '05
Divine Secrets of the Ya-Ya Sisterhood '02

Walter Koenig (1936-)
InAlienable '08
Bone Eater '07
Mad Cowgirl '06
Star Trek: Generations '94
Star Trek 6: The Undiscovered Country '91
Moontrap '89
Star Trek 5: The Final Frontier '89
Star Trek 4: The Voyage Home '86
Star Trek 3: The Search for Spock '84
Star Trek 2: The Wrath of Khan '82
Star Trek: The Motion Picture '79

Michiyo Kogure (1918-90)
Street of Shame '56
Shin Heike Monogatari '55
A Geisha '53

Kenji Kohashi
The World Sinks Except Japan '06
Azumi '03

Fumiyo Kohinata
Black House '07
Dark Water '02
Ringu 2 '99

Fred Kohler, Sr. (1889-1938)
Forbidden Valley '38
The Texas Rangers '36
Mississippi '35
Honor of the Range '34
Deluge '33
The Fiddlin' Buckaroo '33
Texas Bad Man '32
Fighting Caravans '31
Other Men's Women '31
Underworld '27
Riders of the Purple Sage '25
Anna Christie '23

Fred Kohler, Jr. (1912-93)
Daniel Boone: Trail Blazer '56
Tough Assignment '49
Calling Wild Bill Elliott '43
Bahama Passage '42
Western Mail '42
Nevada City '41
Pigskin Parade '36
The Prisoner of Shark Island '36
Pecos Kid '35
Toll of the Desert '35
The Man from Hell '34
The Rider of Death Valley '32
The Iron Horse '24

Juliane Kohler (1965-)
Nowhere in Africa '02
Aimee & Jaguar '98

Lee Kohlmar (1873-1946)
Death from a Distance '36
Love in Bloom '35

Susan Kohner (1936-)
The Gene Krupa Story '59
Imitation of Life '59
Dino '57
To Hell and Back '55

Hiroshi Koizumi (1926-)
Dagora, the Space Monster '65
Ghidrah the Three Headed Monster '65
Godzilla vs. Mothra '64
Attack of the Mushroom People '63
Matango '63
Mothra '62

Kyoko Koizumi
Tokyo Sonata '09
Onmyoji '01

Clarence (C. William) Kolb (1874-1964)
Impact '49
Something for the Boys '44
Caught in the Draft '41
Night of January 16th '41
His Girl Friday '40
Michael Shayne: Private Detective '40
Honolulu '39
Give Me a Sailor '38

Scott Kolk (1905-93)
Murder in Greenwich Village '37
All Quiet on the Western Front '30

Henry Kolker (1870-1947)
The Real Glory '39
Union Pacific '39
The Cowboy and the Lady '38
Charlie Chan in Paris '35
Mad Love '35
The Mystery Man '35
The Ghost Walks '34
Baby Face '33
Rasputin and the Empress '33
The Devil and the Deep '32
Coquette '29

Amos Kollek (1947-)
Whore 2 '94
Double Edge '92
Goodbye, New York '85

Tetsu Komai (1893-1970)
The Real Glory '39
The Princess Comes Across '36
Hong Kong Nights '35
Bulldog Drummond '29

Hosei Komatsu (1924-2003)
A Taxing Woman's Return '88

Double Suicide '69

Rich Komenich

The Amityville Horror '05
Henry: Portrait of a Serial Killer 2: Mask of Sanity '96
Two Wrongs Make a Right '89

Liliana Komorowska (1956-)

Extreme Ops '02
The Art of War '00
The Assignment '97
Martial Outlaw '93
Scanners 3: The Takeover '92

Maja Komorowska (1937-)

The Decalogue '88
Year of the Quiet Sun '84
Contract '80
Maids of Wilko '79
Family Life '71

Manami Konishi (1978-)

Retribution '06
Steamboy '05 (V)

Magda Konopka (1943-)

When Dinosaurs Ruled the Earth '70
Satanik '69

Karin Konoval

The Tooth Fairy '06
Alone in the Dark '05
We'll Meet Again '02

Phyllis Konstam (1907-76)

Skin Game '31
Murder '30

Louis Koo

Flash Point '07
Robin-B-Hood '06
Zu Warriors '01

Guich Koock (1944-)

Picasso Trigger '89
Square Dance '87
American Ninja '85
Seven '79

Kool Moe Dee (1962-)

Crossroads '02
Storm Trooper '98

Thomas Kopache

Love Finds a Home '09
A Stranger's Heart '07
Ten 'Til Noon '06
Stigmata '99

Milos Kopecky (1922-96)

Lemonade Joe '64
Fabulous Adventures of Baron Munchausen '61
The Original Fabulous Adventures of Baron Munchausen '61

Bernie Kopell (1933-)

Get Smart '08
Bug Buster '99
Get Smart, Again! '89
Combat Academy '86
The Loved One '65
Good Neighbor Sam '64

Kim Kopf

Stormswept '95
Witchcraft 8: Salem's Ghost '95

Karen Kopins

Lady in Waiting '94
Archie: Return to Riverdale '90
Jake Speed '86
Creator '85
Once Bitten '85

Aya Koren (1979-)

Bonjour Monsieur Shlomi '03
Yossi & Jagger '02

Mia Korf

Blood Brothers '97
Color of Justice '97

Arnold Korff (1870-1944)

Doughboys '30
The Haunted Castle '21

Jon Korkes

Syngenor '90
Jaws of Satan '81
The Day of the Dolphin '73
Little Murders '71
Catch-22 '70

Baltasar Kormakur (1966-)

No Such Thing '01
101 Reykjavik '00
Devil's Island '96

Harvey Korman (1927-2008)

The Flintstones in Viva Rock Vegas '00
Gideon '99
The Secret of NIMH 2 '98 (V)
Jingle All the Way '96
Dracula: Dead and Loving It '95
The Flintstones '94 (V)
Radioland Murders '94
Based on an Untrue Story '93
Betrayal of the Dove '92
Munchies '87
The Longshot '86
Alice in Wonderland '85
Gone Are the Days '84
Curse of the Pink Panther '83
History of the World: Part 1 '81
Herbie Goes Bananas '80
Americathon '79
Bud and Lou '78
High Anxiety '77
Blazing Saddles '74
Huckleberry Finn '74
April Fools '69
Lord Love a Duck '66

Mary Kornman (1915-73)

Swing It, Professor '37
The Adventurous Knights '35
Desert Trail '35
Queen of the Jungle '35
Roaring Roads '35
College Humor '33

Alix Koromzay (1971-)

Blood Work '02
Mimic 2 '01
Children of the Corn 666: Isaac's Return '99
The Haunting '99
Nightwatch '96

Charlie Korsmo (1978-)

Can't Hardly Wait '98
The Doctor '91
Hook '91
What about Bob? '91
Dick Tracy '90
Heat Wave '90
Men Don't Leave '89

Robert F. (Bob) Kortman (1887-1967)

Guns of the Law '44
Fugitive Valley '41
Hopalong Cassidy: Renegade Trail '39
Oklahoma Frontier '39
Law of the Texan '38
The Rangers Step In '37
Sandflow '37
Robinson Crusoe of Clipper Island '36
The Crimson Trail '35
Feud of the West '35
Swifty '35
Wild Mustang '35
When a Man Sees Red '34
The Fiddlin' Buckaroo '33
Phantom Thunderbolt '33
Rainbow Ranch '33
Terror Trail '33
Trail Drive '33
Come on Tarzan '32
Island of Lost Souls '32
The Lone Defender '32

Fritz Kortner (1892-1970)

Woman in Brown '48
Somewhere in the Night '46
Pandora's Box '28
The Hands of Orlac '25
Warning Shadows '23
Backstairs '21

Charles Korvin (1907-98)

Ship of Fools '65
Tarzan's Savage Fury '52
Berlin Express '48
The Killer That Stalked New York '47

Dina Korzun

Cold Souls '09
Forty Shades of Blue '05

Sylva Koscina (1933-94)

Lisa and the Devil '75
Hit Men '73
The Slasher '72
Hornet's Nest '70
Deadly Sanctuary '68
The Secret War of Harry Frigg '68
Deadlier Than the Male '67
Juliet of the Spirits '65
The Hit Man '60
Hercules Unchained '59
Uncle Was a Vampire '59
Hercules '58

Martin Kosleck (1907-94)

The Flesh Eaters '64
36 Hours '64
House of Horrors '46
She Wolf of London '46
Pursuit to Algiers '45
The Mummy's Curse '44
Weird Woman '44
All Through the Night '42
International Lady '41
Underground '41
Foreign Correspondent '40

Paul Koslo (1944-)

Downdraft '96
Judge & Jury '96
Chained Heat 2 '92
Project: Shadowchaser '92
Xtro 2: The Second Encounter '91
Robot Jox '90
A Night in the Life of Jimmy Reardon '88
The Annihilators '85
Roots: The Next Generation '79
Maniac '77
Rooster Cogburn '75
Joe Kidd '72
Omega Man '71
Vanishing Point '71
The Losers '70

David Kossoff (1919-2005)

The Mouse on the Moon '62
The Two Faces of Dr. Jekyll '60
The Mouse That Roared '59
1984 '56
Who Done It? '56
A Kid for Two Farthings '55
Svengali '55

Maria Kosti (1951-)

Night of the Death Cult '75
Exorcism '74

Nick Kostopoulos

Addicted to Murder 3: Bloodlust '99
The Alien Agenda: Under the Skin '97

Kane (Takeshi) Kosugi (1973-)

DOA: Dead or Alive '06
Journey of Honor '91
Nine Deaths of the Ninja '85
Pray for Death '85
Revenge of the Ninja '83

Sho Kosugi (1948-)

Ninja Assassin '09
Journey of Honor '91
Blind Fury '90
Aloha Summer '88
Black Eagle '88
Rage of Honor '87
Nine Deaths of the Ninja '85
Pray for Death '85
Ninja 3: The Domination '84
Revenge of the Ninja '83
Enter the Ninja '81
Kingfisher the Killer '81

Yoshio Kosugi (1903-68)

The Human Condition: No Greater Love '58
Seven Samurai '54
The Men Who Tread on the Tiger's Tail '45

Eva Kotamanidou (1936-)

Weeping Meadow '04
Landscape in the Mist '88
The Travelling Players '75

Elias Koteas (1961-)

The Killer Inside Me '10
Defendor '09
The Fourth Kind '09
The Haunting in Connecticut '09
Shutter Island '09
Two Lovers '09
The Curious Case of Benjamin Button '08
Dark Streets '08
Prisoner '07
Shooter '07
Skinwalkers '07
Zodiac '07
The Greatest Game Ever Played '05
Ararat '02
Collateral Damage '02
Harrison's Flowers '02
Simone '02
Novocaine '01
Shot in the Heart '01
Dancing at the Blue Iguana '00
Lost Souls '00
Living Out Loud '98
The Thin Red Line '98
Apt Pupil '97
Fallen '97
Gattaca '97
Hit Me '96
Crash '95
The Prophecy '95
Sugartime '95
Camilla '94
Exotica '94
Power of Attorney '94
Chain of Desire '93
Cyborg 2 '93
Teenage Mutant Ninja Turtles 3 '93
The Adjuster '91
Almost an Angel '90
Desperate Hours '90
Look Who's Talking, Too '90
Teenage Mutant Ninja Turtles: The Movie '90
Friends, Lovers & Lunatics '89
Malarek '89
Blood Red '88
Full Moon in Blue Water '88
Tucker: The Man and His Dream '88
Gardens of Stone '87
Some Kind of Wonderful '87

Oded Kotler (1937-)

Hanna K. '83
My Michael '75

Yaphet Kotto (1937-)

Witless Protection '08
Stiletto Dance '01
Homicide: The Movie '00
The Defenders: Payback '97
Out of Sync '95
Two If by Sea '95
Dead Badge '94
The Puppet Masters '94
Almost Blue '93
Extreme Justice '93
In Self Defense '93
Chrome Soldiers '92
Freddy's Dead: The Final Nightmare '91
Hangfire '91
After the Shock '90
Jigsaw Murders '89
Ministry of Vengeance '89
Tripwire '89
Midnight Run '88
A Whisper to a Scream '88
Prettykill '87
The Running Man '87
Terminal Entry '87
Eye of the Tiger '86
Harem '86
Badge of the Assassin '85
The Park Is Mine '85
Warning Sign '85
The Star Chamber '83
Fighting Back '82
Brubaker '80
Rage '80
Alien '79
Blue Collar '78
Monkey Hustle '77
Raid on Entebbe '77
Drum '76
Friday Foster '75
Sharks' Treasure '75
Report to the Commissioner '74
Truck Turner '74
Live and Let Die '73
Across 110th Street '72
Housewife '72
Man & Boy '71
Five Card Stud '68
The Thomas Crown Affair '68
Nothing but a Man '64

Adam Kotz (1962-)

Suspicion '03
All the King's Men '99
Shot Through the Heart '98
Touching Evil '97
Max and Helen '90

Hubert Kounde (1970-)

The Constant Gardener '05
How I Killed My Father '03
Simon the Magician '99
Hate '95
Cafe au Lait '94

Nancy Kovack (1935-)

The Silencers '66
Frankie and Johnny '65
The Outlaws Is Coming! '65
Diary of a Madman '63
Jason and the Argonauts '63

Ernie Kovacs (1919-62)

North to Alaska '60
Strangers When We Meet '60
Our Man in Havana '59
Bell, Book and Candle '58
Operation Mad Ball '57

Geza Kovacs

Return to the Lost World '93
Baby on Board '92

Lajos Kovacs (1944-)

Kontroll '03
Woyzeck '94
Maria's Day '84

Martin Kove (1946-)

Devil's Knight '03
Con Games '02
Crocodile 2: Death Swamp '01
Extreme Honor '01
Under Heavy Fire '01
Final Payback '99
Timelock '99
Nowhere Land '98
Baby Face Nelson '97
Grizzly Mountain '97
Shadow Warriors '97
Shadow Warriors 2: Hunt for the Death Merchant '97
Top of the World '97
Judge & Jury '96
Mercenary '96
Final Equinox '95
Without Mercy '95
Death Match '94
Endangered '94
Uncivilized '94
Wyatt Earp '94
Wyatt Earp: Return to Tombstone '94
Future Shock '93
The Outfit '93
President's Target '93
Shootfighter: Fight to the Death '93
To Be the Best '93
Firehawk '92
Project: Shadowchaser '92
White Light '90
The Karate Kid: Part 3 '89
Higher Ground '88
Steele Justice '87
The Karate Kid: Part 2 '86
Rambo: First Blood, Part 2 '85
The Karate Kid '84
Laboratory '80
Seven '79
Death Race 2000 '75
Last House on the Left '72

Jeff Kovski

Zone 39 '96
Life '95

Shigeru Koyama

Azumi 2 '05
Black Rain '89

Yukimi Koyanagi

Tokyo Sonata '09
Ringu 0 '01

Koyuki (1976-)

Blood: The Last Vampire '09
The Last Samurai '03
Pulse '01

Andras Kozak (1943-2005)

The Red and the White '68
The Round Up '66

Harley Jane Kozak (1957-)

Emma's Wish '98
Dark Planet '97
Titanic '96
The Android Affair '95
Magic in the Water '95
The Amy Fisher Story '93
The Favor '92
All I Want for Christmas '91
Necessary Roughness '91
The Taking of Beverly Hills '91
Arachnophobia '90
Side Out '90
Parenthood '89
When Harry Met Sally... '89

Linda Kozlowski (1958-)

Crocodile Dundee in Los Angeles '01
Village of the Damned '95
Backstreet Justice '93
The Neighbor '93
Almost an Angel '90
Crocodile Dundee 2 '88
Pass the Ammo '88
Target: Favorite Son '87
Crocodile Dundee '86

Jeroen Krabbe (1944-)

Transporter 3 '08
Deuce Bigalow: European Gigolo '05
Ocean's Twelve '04
Jesus '00
The Sky Is Falling '00
An Ideal Husband '99
Dangerous Beauty '98
Ever After: A Cinderella Story '98
Left Luggage '98
Only Love '98
The Odyssey '97
Business for Pleasure '96
The Disappearance of Garcia Lorca '96

Farinelli '94
Immortal Beloved '94
For a Lost Soldier '93
The Fugitive '93
King of the Hill '93
Stalin '92
Kafka '91
The Prince of Tides '91
Robin Hood '91
Till There Was You '91
The Punisher '90
Secret Weapon '90
Scandal '89
Crossing Delancey '88
A World Apart '88
Code Name: Dancer '87
The Living Daylights '87
Jumpin' Jack Flash '86
No Mercy '86
Turtle Diary '86
A Flight of Rainbirds '81
The 4th Man '79
Soldier of Orange '78

Jane Krakowski (1966-)
Cirque du Freak: The Vampire's Assistant '09
Kit Kittredge: An American Girl '08
The Rocker '08
Surf's Up '07 (V)
Open Season '06 (V)
Pretty Persuasion '05
Alfie '04
Marci X '03
Ice Age '02 (V)
The Flintstones in Viva Rock Vegas '00
Go '99
Dance with Me '98
Stepping Out '91
National Lampoon's Vacation '83
No Big Deal '83

Clare Kramer
The Thirst '06
Bring It On '00

Eric Allen Kramer (1962-)
Grilled '06
American Wedding '03
The Colony '98
Robin Hood: Men in Tights '93
The Comrades of Summer '92
Quest for the Mighty Sword '90

Grant Kramer
See Grant Cramer

Jeffrey Kramer (1952-)
Halloween 2: The Nightmare Isn't Over! '81
Jaws 2 '78
Hollywood Boulevard '76

Stephanie Kramer (1956-)
The Cutting Edge: Going for the Gold '05
Twin Sisters '91
Terror at London Bridge '85
The Man with Two Brains '83

Robert Krantz
Winners Take All '87
Paradise Motel '84

Fran Kranz
Wieners '08
Careless '07
The Night of the White Pants '06
The TV Set '06
The Village '04
Whirlygirl '04

John Krasinski (1979-)
Away We Go '09
Brief Interviews With Hideous Men '09
It's Complicated '09
Monsters vs. Aliens '09 (V)
Leatherheads '08
License to Wed '07
A New Wave '07
Shrek the Third '07 (V)
Smiley Face '07
The Holiday '06
Duane Hopwood '05
Jarhead '05
Kinsey '04

Brian Krause (1972-)
Supernova '09
Loch Ness Terror '07
Protecting the King '07
Return to Cabin by the Lake '01
Within the Rock '96
Breaking Free '95
Naked Souls '95
The Liar's Club '93
Sleepwalkers '92
December '91
Return to the Blue Lagoon '91
An American Summer '90

Peter Krause (1965-)
Beastly '10
Civic Duty '06
We Don't Live Here Anymore '04
Lovelife '97

Werner Krauss (1884-1959)
Jud Suess '40
Joyless Street '25
Secrets of a Soul '25
Tartuffe '25
Variety '25
Waxworks '24
Othello '22
Shattered '21
The Cabinet of Dr. Caligari '19

Lenny Kravitz (1964-)
Precious: Based on the Novel by Sapphire '09
The Brave One '07

Nicolette Krebitz (1971-)
All the Queen's Men '02
The Tunnel '01
Bandits '99

Hans Kremer (1954-)
Mendel '98
The Promise '94

Connie Kreski (1946-95)
Black Bird '75
The Trackers '71

Nathan Kress
Gym Teacher: The Movie '08
Babe: Pig in the City '98 (V)

Thomas Kretschmann (1962-)
The Young Victoria '09
Hellboy II: The Golden Army '08 (V)
Transsiberian '08
Valkyrie '08
Wanted '08
In Tranzit '07
Next '07
The Celestine Prophecy '06
Have No Fear: The Life of Pope John Paul II '05
King Kong '05
Downfall '04
Head in the Clouds '04
In Enemy Hands '04
Karate Dog '04
Resident Evil: Apocalypse '04
Blade 2 '02
The Pianist '02
U-571 '00
Esther '98
Prince Valiant '97
Total Reality '97
The Stendahl Syndrome '95
Stalingrad '94

Kurt Kreuger (1916-2006)
Unfaithfully Yours '48
Dark Corner '46
Mademoiselle Fifi '44
Manhunt in the African Jungles '43
Sahara '43

Kristin Kreuk (1982-)
Street Fighter: The Legend of Chun-Li '09
Partition '07
Eurotrip '04
Snow White: The Fairest of Them All '02

Elisabeth (Lisa) Kreuzer (1945-)
Birgitt Haas Must Be Killed '83
A Man Like Eva '83
Basileus Quartet '82
The American Friend '77
Kings of the Road—In the Course of Time '76
Alice in the Cities '74

David Kriegel
Speed '94
Alive '93
Quest of the Delta Knights '93

Anneline Kriel
Reason to Die '90
Kill and Kill Again '81

Alice Krige (1955-)
The Contract '07
The Line of Beauty '06
Lonely Hearts '06
Silent Hill '06
Children of Dune '03
Dinotopia '02
Reign of Fire '02
Attila '01
The Little Vampire '00
In the Company of Spies '99
Molokai: The Story of Father Damien '99
Habitat '97
The Twilight of the Ice Nymphs '97
Hidden in America '96
Star Trek: First Contact '96
Donor Unknown '95
Institue Benjamenta or This Dream People Call Human Life '95
Joseph '95
Sharpe's Honour '94
Ladykiller '92
Sleepwalkers '92
Iran: Days of Crisis '91
Code Name: Chaos '90
Max and Helen '90
See You in the Morning '89
Haunted Summer '88
Barfly '87
King David '85
Chariots of Fire '81
Ghost Story '81
A Tale of Two Cities '80

Harry Krimer (1896-1991)
Heart of a Nation '43
Napoleon '27

Sylvia Kristel (1952-)
Beauty School '93
Hot Blood '89
Dracula's Widow '88
Casanova '87
The Big Bet '85
Mata Hari '85
Red Heat '85
Emmanuelle 4 '84
Mysteries '84
Private School '83
Lady Chatterley's Lover '81
The Nude Bomb '80
Tigers in Lipstick '80
The Concorde: Airport '79 '79
The Fifth Musketeer '79
Good-bye, Emmanuelle '77
Emmanuelle, the Joys of a Woman '76
Game of Seduction '76
Private Lessons '75
Because of the Cats '74
Emmanuelle '74

Marta Kristen (1945-)
Lost in Space '98
Body Count '97
Battle Beyond the Stars '80
Gemini Affair '74
Terminal Island '73
Beach Blanket Bingo '65
Savage Sam '63

Jason Kristofer (1972-)
The Crossing Guard '94
Spy Trap '88

Romano Kristoff
Slash '87
Warbus '85

Kris Kristofferson (1936-)
For Sale by Owner '09
He's Just Not That Into You '09
Powder Blue '09
Lords of the Street '08
Snow Buddies '08 (V)
Disappearances '06
Fast Food Nation '06
Dreamer: Inspired by a True Story '05
The Jacket '05
The Wendell Baker Story '05
Blade: Trinity '04
Silver City '04
Blade 2 '02
Chelsea Walls '01
Eye See You '01
Planet of the Apes '01
Perfect Murder, Perfect Town '00
Limbo '99
Molokai: The Story of Father Damien '99
Blade '98
Dance with Me '98
The Land Before Time 6: The Secret of Saurus Rock '98 (V)
Outlaw Justice '98
Payback '98
A Soldier's Daughter Never Cries '98
Tom Clancy's Netforce '98
Fire Down Below '97
Girls' Night '97
Two for Texas '97
Lone Star '95
Pharoah's Army '95
The Road Home '95
Sodbusters '94
Cheatin' Hearts '93
Knights '93
No Place to Hide '93
Christmas in Connecticut '92
Another Pair of Aces: Three of a Kind '91
Miracle in the Wilderness '91
Original Intent '91
Night of the Cyclone '90
Pair of Aces '90
Millennium '89
Welcome Home '89
Big Top Pee-wee '88
The Tracker '88
Last Days of Frank & Jesse James '86
Stagecoach '86
Trouble in Mind '86
Flashpoint '84
Songwriter '84
Act of Passion: The Lost Honor of Kathryn Beck '83
Heaven's Gate '81
Rollover '81
Freedom Road '79
Convoy '78
Semi-Tough '77
The Sailor Who Fell from Grace with the Sea '76
A Star Is Born '76
Alice Doesn't Live Here Anymore '74
Bring Me the Head of Alfredo Garcia '74
Blume in Love '73
Pat Garrett & Billy the Kid '73
The Last Movie '71

Berry Kroeger (1912-91)
Demon Seed '77
The Incredible Two-Headed Transplant '71
Seven Thieves '60
Man in the Vault '56
Blood Alley '55
Yellowneck '55
Guilty of Treason '50
Gun Crazy '49
Act of Violence '48

Gary Kroeger (1957-)
Secret Ingredient '92
Archie: Return to Riverdale '90
A Man Called Sarge '90

Joachim Krol (1957-)
Gloomy Sunday '02
Anne Frank: The Whole Story '01
The Princess and the Warrior '00
Run Lola Run '98
Maybe... Maybe Not '94

Josef Kroner (1924-98)
Another Way '82
The Shop on Main Street '65

Margareta Krook (1925-2001)
Pay Off '89
The Adventures of Picasso '80
Persona '66

Chad Krowchuk
Poltergeist: The Legacy '96
Heck's Way Home '95

Frank Krueger
Break '09
The Pink Conspiracy '07

Manfred Krug (1937-)
Trace of Stones '66
The Boxer and Death '63
Minna von Barnhelm or The Soldier's Fortune '62
On the Sunny Side '62
Five Cartridges '60

Alma Kruger (1868-1960)
Forever Amber '47
A Scandal in Paris '46
The Great Waltz '38
100 Men and a Girl '37
Craig's Wife '36
These Three '36

Christiane Kruger (1945-)
Anne of Green Gables '85
Le Dernier Combat '84
Little Mother '71
Double Face '70

Diane Kruger (1976-)
Inglourious Basterds '09
The Color of Freedom '07
The Hunting Party '07
National Treasure: Book of Secrets '07
Joyeux Noel '05
National Treasure '04
Troy '04
Wicker Park '04
The Target '02
Whatever You Say '02

Hardy Kruger (1928-)
Operation Valkyrie '04
The Inside Man '84
Wrong Is Right '82
Blue Fin '78
Wild Geese '78
A Bridge Too Far '77
Barry Lyndon '75
Paper Tiger '74
What the Peeper Saw '72
Battle of Neretva '69
Red Tent '69
The Secret of Santa Vittoria '69
The Defector '66
The Flight of the Phoenix '65
Hatari! '62
Sundays & Cybele '62
Bachelor of Hearts '58
One That Got Away '57
Liane, Jungle Goddess '56

Otto Kruger (1885-1974)
The Wonderful World of the Brothers Grimm '62
Cash McCall '60
The Young Philadelphians '59
Black Widow '54
High Noon '52
Payment on Demand '51
Smart Woman '48
Jungle Captive '45
The Woman Who Came Back '45
Wonder Man '45
Cover Girl '44
Murder, My Sweet '44
Corregidor '43
Hitler's Children '43
Power of the Press '43
Saboteur '42
Dr. Ehrlich's Magic Bullet '40
Another Thin Man '39
Black Eyes '39
Housemaster '38
I Am the Law '38
Thanks for the Memory '38
They Won't Forget '37
Dracula's Daughter '36
Chained '34
Men in White '34
Treasure Island '34
The Prizefighter and the Lady '33

Ulrike Krumbiegel
A Woman in Berlin '08
Antibodies '05

David Krumholtz (1978-)
Harold & Kumar Escape from Guantanamo Bay '08
Walk Hard: The Dewey Cox Story '07
Bobby '06
Kill the Poor '06
Tenacious D in the Pick of Destiny '06
Guess Who '05
Harold and Kumar Go to White Castle '04
Looking for Kitty '04
Ray '04
Big Shot: Confessions of a Campus Bookie '02
The Santa Clause 2 '02
Scorched '02
You Stupid Man '02
The Mexican '01
Sidewalks of New York '01
Liberty Heights '99
Ten Things I Hate about You '99
Slums of Beverly Hills '98
The Ice Storm '97
The Santa Clause '94
Addams Family Values '93
Life with Mikey '93

Gene Krupa (1909-73)
The Benny Goodman Story '55
The Glenn Miller Story '54
Ball of Fire '41
Rhythm Romance '39

Olek Krupa (1955-)
Burn After Reading '08
The Italian Job '03
Behind Enemy Lines '01
Thirteen Days '00
Blue Streak '99
No Vacancy '99
Home Alone 3 '97
Kicked in the Head '97
Mac '93
Ivory Hunters '90

Jack Kruschen (1922-2002)
Cheaters '84
Money to Burn '83
Mountain Man '77

Ride the Man Down '53
The Road to Utopia '46
Santa Fe Uprising '46
Dangerous Passage '44
Follow the Leader '44
The Law Rides Again '43
The Payoff '43
X Marks the Spot '42
Footsteps in the Dark '41
Gentleman from Dixie '41
In Old Caliente '39
Captains Courageous '37
Dangerous Holiday '37
Dancing Pirate '36
Strike Me Pink '36
Yellow Cargo '36
Headline Woman '35
The Fighting Rookie '34
The Kennel Murder Case '33
To the Last Man '33
A Farewell to Arms '32

Eriq La Salle (1962-)

Inside Out '05
Johnny Was '05
Biker Boyz '03
Crazy as Hell '02
One Hour Photo '02
Rebound: The Legend of Earl "The Goat" Manigault '96
Color of Night '94
DROP Squad '94
Jacob's Ladder '90
Coming to America '88
Cut and Run '85

Lucille La Verne

See Lucille LaVerne
Pilgrimage '33

John La Zar

See John Lazar

Barbara Laage (1920-88)

Bed and Board '70
Therese & Isabelle '67
The Respectful Prostitute '52

Samuel Labarthe

Le Divorce '03
Strayed '03
The Green House '96
The Accompanist '93

Patti LaBelle (1944-)

Cover '08
Preaching to the Choir '05
Fire and Rain '89
Sing '89
Unnatural Causes '86
A Soldier's Story '84

Shia LaBeouf (1986-)

Wall Street 2: Money Never Sleeps '10
New York, I Love You '09
Transformers: Revenge of the Fallen '09
Eagle Eye '08
Indiana Jones and the Kingdom of the Crystal Skull '08
Disturbia '07
Surf's Up '07 (V)
Transformers '07
Bobby '06
A Guide to Recognizing Your Saints '06
Constantine '05
The Greatest Game Ever Played '05
I, Robot '04
The Battle of Shaker Heights '03
Charlie's Angels: Full Throttle '03
Dumb and Dumberer: When Harry Met Lloyd '03
Holes '03

Halina Labonarska (1947-)

A Woman and a Woman '80
Provincial Actors '79

Matthew Laborteaux (1966-)

Deadly Friend '86
Shattered Spirits '86
Aliens Are Coming '80
King of the Gypsies '78
Tarantulas: The Deadly Cargo '77
A Woman under the Influence '74

Patrick Laborteaux (1965-)

JAG '95
3 Ninjas '92
Heathers '89
Prince of Bel Air '87

Elina Labourdette (1919-)

Lola '61
The Ladies of the Bois de Bologne '44

Dominique Labourier (1943-)

Jonah Who Will Be 25 in the Year 2000 '76
Celine and Julie Go Boating '74

Catherine Lacey (1904-79)

The Private Life of Sherlock Holmes '70
The Servant '63
Pink String and Sealing Wax '45
Cottage to Let '41
The Lady Vanishes '38

Ingrid Lacey

In Love and War '96
Funnyman '94
A Woman's Guide to Adultery '93

Margaret Lacey (1910-88)

Our Town '03
Diamonds Are Forever '71
Seance on a Wet Afternoon '64

Ronald Lacey (1935-91)

Landslide '92
Jailbird Rock '88
The Lone Runner '88
Into the Darkness '86
Flesh and Blood '85
The Adventures of Buckaroo Banzai Across the Eighth Dimension '84
Making the Grade '84
The Hound of the Baskervilles '83
Sahara '83
Firefox '82
Raiders of the Lost Ark '81
Nijinsky '80
Next Victim '74
Crucible of Terror '72
Disciple of Death '72
The Fearless Vampire Killers '67

Stephen Lack (1946-)

All the Vermeers in New York '91
Dead Ringers '88
Perfect Strangers '84
Scanners '81
Fatal Attraction '80

Elizabeth Lackey (1971-)

Blood Crime '02
Boa '02

Frank Lackteen (1894-1968)

The Sea Wolf '41
Red Barry '38
Rustler's Roundup '33
Treason '33
Texas Pioneers '32
The Pony Express '25

Andre Lacombe

Dr. Petiot '90
The Bear '89

Ghalia Lacroix

For Ever Mozart '96
The Silences of the Palace '94

John Lacy (1965-)

Zodiac '07
Wildcard '92

Preston Lacy

The Life of Lucky Cucumber '08
Jackass Number Two '06

Alan Ladd (1913-64)

The Carpetbaggers '64
Duel of Champions '61
All the Young Men '60
The Badlanders '58
Deep Six '58
Proud Rebel '58
Hell on Frisco Bay '55
The McConnell Story '55
Drum Beat '54
Botany Bay '53
Shane '53
The Iron Mistress '52
Branded '50
The Great Gatsby '49
Calcutta '47
My Favorite Brunette '47
Saigon '47
The Blue Dahlia '46
O.S.S. '46
Two Years before the Mast '46
Salty O'Rourke '45
China '43
The Glass Key '42
Joan of Paris '42
Star Spangled Rhythm '42
This Gun for Hire '42
The Black Cat '41
Citizen Kane '41
Gangs, Inc. '41
They Met in Bombay '41
Captain Caution '40
Her First Romance '40
The Howards of Virginia '40
Island of Lost Souls '32

Cheryl Ladd (1951-)

Though None Go With Me '06
A Dog of Flanders '99
Every Mother's Worst Fear '98
Permanent Midnight '98
Dancing with Danger '93
Poison Ivy '92
Danielle Steel's Changes '91
Jekyll and Hyde '90
Lisa '90
Fulfillment '89
Millennium '89
Romance on the Orient Express '89
The Hasty Heart '86
Purple Hearts '84
The Grace Kelly Story '83
Now and Forever '82
The Treasure of Jamaica Reef '74
Satan's School for Girls '73

David Ladd (1947-)

The Treasure of Jamaica Reef '74
Raw Meat '72
Catlow '71
Misty '61
A Dog of Flanders '59

Diane Ladd (1939-)

Montana Sky '07
Come Early Morning '06
Inland Empire '06
When I Find the Ocean '06
The World's Fastest Indian '05
Gracie's Choice '04
Forever Together '00
28 Days '00
Daddy & Them '99
Get a Clue! '98
Primary Colors '98
Family of Cops 2: Breach of Faith '97
James Dean: Live Fast, Die Young '97

Citizen Ruth '96
Ghosts of Mississippi '96
Mrs. Munck '95
Raging Angels '95
Mother '94
Carnosaur '93
The Cemetery Club '93
Father Hood '93
Hold Me, Thrill Me, Kiss Me '93
Hush Little Baby '93
Forever: A Ghost of a Love Story '92
A Kiss Before Dying '91
Rambling Rose '91
Code Name: Chaos '90
The Lookalike '90
Wild at Heart '90
National Lampoon's Christmas Vacation '89
Plain Clothes '88
Black Widow '87
I Married a Centerfold '84
The Grace Kelly Story '83
Something Wicked This Way Comes '83
Desperate Lives '82
All Night Long '81
Willa '79
Embryo '76
Alice Doesn't Live Here Anymore '74
Chinatown '74
Rebel Rousers '69
The Wild Angels '66

Jordan Ladd (1975-)

Grace '09
Death Proof '07
Hostel: Part 2 '07
Waiting '05
Club Dread '04
Madhouse '04
Cabin Fever '03
Dog Gone Love '03
The Specials '00
Never Been Kissed '99
Every Mother's Worst Fear '98
Stand-Ins '97
Nowhere '96
Embrace of the Vampire '95

Walter Ladengast (1899-1980)

Nosferatu the Vampyre '79
Every Man for Himself & God Against All '75

John Lafayette

Loverboy '05
White Sands '92
Full Fathom Five '90

Pat Laffan

How Harry Became a Tree '01
American Women '00
The Snapper '93

Patricia Laffan (1919-)

Devil Girl from Mars '54
Quo Vadis '51

James Lafferty

S. Darko: A Donnie Darko Tale '09
A Season on the Brink '02

Art LaFleur (1944-)

Ace Ventura Jr.: Pet Detective '08
The Santa Clause 2 '02
Beethoven's 4th '01
The Replacements '00
The Garbage-Picking, Field Goal-Kicking Philadelphia Phenomenon '98
Hijacking Hollywood '97
Lewis and Clark and George '97
First Kid '96
Man of the House '95
Jack the Bear '93
The Sandlot '93
Forever Young '92
Live! From Death Row '92
Oscar '91
Rampage '87
Trancers '84
Zone Troopers '84

Jekyll & Hyde.. Together Again '82
The Hollywood Knights '80

Sarah Lafleur

Lake Placid 2 '07
Terminal Invasion '02

Bernadette LaFont (1938-)

I Do '06
Genealogies of a Crime '97
Son of Gascogne '95
Dingo '90
Waiting for the Moon '87
The Perils of Gwendoline '84
Violette '78
The Mother and the Whore '73
Too Pretty to Be Honest '72
Catch Me a Spy '71
A Very Curious Girl '69
The Thief of Paris '67
It Means That to Me '60
Les Bonnes Femmes '60
Le Beau Serge '58
Les Mistons '57

Roc Lafortune (1956-)

The List '99
The Minion '98
The Boys '97

Alicia Lagano

Believe in Me '06
The Truth About Jane '00

Marika Lagercrantz (1954-)

The Girl With the Dragon Tattoo '09
All Things Fair '95
Dreaming of Rita '94

Caroline Lagerfelt (1947-)

August '08
Glam '97
Home at Last '88
Iron Eagle '86

Valerie Lagrange (1942-)

Cat and Mouse '78
Weekend '67
A Man and a Woman '66
Morgan the Pirate '60

Ernesto Laguardia

Esmeralda Comes by Night '98
Like A Bride '94

Bert Lahr (1895-1967)

The Night They Raided Minsky's '69
Rose Marie '54
Meet the People '44
Ship Ahoy '42
Sing Your Worries Away '42
The Wizard of Oz '39
Just Around the Corner '38
Flying High '31

Christine Lahti (1950-)

Obsessed '09
Yonkers Joe '08
Out of the Ashes '03
Women vs. Men '02
The Pilot's Wife '01
Trial by Media '00
Hope '97
Subway Stories '97
A Weekend in the Country '96
Pie in the Sky '95
Hideaway '94
The Fear Inside '92
The Good Fight '92
Leaving Normal '92
Crazy from the Heart '91
The Doctor '91
Funny About Love '90
Gross Anatomy '89
Miss Firecracker '89
Running on Empty '88
Housekeeping '87
Stacking '87
Just Between Friends '86
Single Bars, Single Women '84

Swing Shift '84
The Executioner's Song '82
Whose Life Is It Anyway? '81
The Henderson Monster '80
And Justice for All '79

Leon Lai (1966-)

Infernal Affairs 3 '03
3 Extremes 2 '02
Fallen Angels '95
Wicked City '92

Me Me Lai (1952-)

The Element of Crime '84
Emerald Jungle '80
Au Pair Girls '72
Crucible of Terror '72

Leah Lail (1966-)

Late Last Night '99
Something About Sex '98
Body Waves '92

Cleo Laine (1927-)

The Last of the Blonde Bombshells '00
On the Town '91

Robin Laing

Joyeux Noel '05
Borstal Boy '00
Dr. Bell and Mr. Doyle: The Dark Beginnings of Sherlock Holmes '00
Relative Strangers '99

Stuart Laing (1969-)

Cambridge Spies '03
Lawless Heart '01

Jenny Laird (1917-2001)

Village of the Damned '60
Black Narcissus '47
Beware of Pity '46

Alan Lake (1941-84)

Don't Open Till Christmas '84
Freelance '71

Alice Lake (1889-1967)

Broken Hearts of Broadway '23
Playing Dead '15

Arthur Lake (1905-87)

Blondie Hits the Jackpot '49
Blondie Knows Best '46
Footlight Glamour '43
It's a Great Life '43
Blondie for Victory '42
Blondie Goes Latin '42
Blondie Goes to College '42
Blondie's Blessed Event '42
Blondie in Society '41
Blondie Has Trouble '40
Blondie On a Budget '40
Blondie Plays Cupid '40
Blondie Brings Up Baby '39
Blondie Meets the Boss '39
Blondie Takes a Vacation '39
Blondie '38
Exiled to Shanghai '37
23 1/2 Hours Leave '37
The Silver Streak '34
On with the Show '29
Skinner's Dress Suit '26

Don Lake (1956-)

Best in Show '00
Hostage for a Day '94
Sodbusters '94
Big Town '87

Florence Lake (1904-80)

Savage Intruder '68
Goin' to Town '44
Crash Dive '43
Next Time I Marry '38
Quality Street '37
Romance '30

Ricki Lake (1968-)

Loving Leah '09
A Dirty Shame '04
Cecil B. Demented '00
Murder She Purred: A Mrs. Murphy Mystery '98
Mrs. Winterbourne '96

Cabin Boy *'94*
Serial Mom *'94*
Based on an Untrue Story *'93*
Inside Monkey Zetterland *'93*
Skinner *'93*
Buffy the Vampire Slayer *'92*
Where the Day Takes You *'92*
The Chase *'91*
Cry-Baby *'90*
Last Exit to Brooklyn *'90*
Babycakes *'89*
Cookie *'89*
Hairspray *'88*
Working Girl *'88*

Sanoe Lake
Cruel World *'05*
Blue Crush *'02*

Veronica Lake (1919-73)
Flesh Feast *'69*
Ramrod *'47*
Saigon *'47*
The Blue Dahlia *'46*
So Proudly We Hail *'43*
The Glass Key *'42*
I Married a Witch *'42*
Star Spangled Rhythm *'42*
This Gun for Hire *'42*
Sullivan's Travels *'41*

Christine Lakin (1979-)
Super Capers *'09*
The Hottie and the Nottie *'08*
Dark Mirror *'07*
Mystery Kids *'99*
Boltneck *'98*

Padma Lakshmi (1970-)
Sharpe's Challenge *'06*
The Mistress of Spices *'05*
Glitter *'01*

Lorena Lalazquez (1937-)
Doctor of Doom *'62*
Samson vs. the Vampire Women *'61*
Wrestling Women vs. the Aztec Mummy *'59*

James Lally (1956-)
Critical Care *'97*
Working Girl *'88*

Michael David Lally (1942-)
Cool World *'92*
The Nesting *'80*

Mick (Michael) Lally (1945-)
The Secret of Kells *'09 (V)*
Circle of Friends *'94*
A Man of No Importance *'94*
The Secret of Roan Inish *'94*
Fools of Fortune *'90*

Ben Lam
Flash Point *'07*
So Close *'02*

Ching-Ying Lam
Exorcist Master *'93*
Heroes Shed No Tears *'86*

Ching-Ying Lam (1952-97)
Mr. Vampire *'86*
The Prodigal Son *'82*

Ka-tung Lam
Exiled *'06*
Infernal Affairs 3 *'03*

Suet Lam
Dog Bite Dog *'06*
Exiled *'06*
Running Out of Time 2 *'06*
Full Time Killer *'01*

Maurice LaMarche (1958-)
Barnyard *'06 (V)*
Queer Duck: The Movie *'06 (V)*
Inspector Gadget's Biggest Caper Ever *'05 (V)*
Team America: World Police *'04 (V)*
Hey Arnold! The Movie *'02 (V)*
Pom Poko *'94 (V)*

Hedy Lamarr (1913-2000)
The Love of Three Queens *'54*
Copper Canyon *'50*
Samson and Delilah *'50*
Dishonored Lady *'47*
The Strange Woman *'46*
Experiment Perilous *'45*
The Heavenly Body *'44*
Crossroads *'42*
Tortilla Flat *'42*
White Cargo *'42*
H.M. Pulham Esquire *'41*
Ziegfeld Girl *'41*
Boom Town *'40*
Comrade X *'40*
I Take This Woman *'40*
Algiers *'38*
Ecstasy *'33*

Phil LaMarr (1967-)
Shark Tale *'04 (V)*
Free Enterprise *'98*
Bio-Dome *'96*
Pulp Fiction *'94*

Jean LaMarre
Deadly Voyage *'96*
Fresh *'94*
Malcolm X *'92*

Fernando Lamas (1915-82)
The Cheap Detective *'78*
Murder on Flight 502 *'75*
Powder Keg *'70*
100 Rifles *'69*
Violent Ones *'68*
Revenge of the Musketeers *'63*
Rose Marie *'54*
Dangerous When Wet *'53*
The Girl Who Had Everything *'53*
The Merry Widow *'52*
Rich, Young and Pretty *'51*

Lorenzo Lamas (1958-)
Mega Shark Vs. Giant Octopus *'09*
Blood Angels *'05*
18 Fingers of Death *'05*
Alien 3000 *'04*
Lethal *'04*
Sci-Fighter *'04*
Latin Dragon *'03*
Hope Ranch *'02*
The Immortal *'01*
The Muse *'99*
Undercurrent *'99*
The Debt *'98*
Mask of Death *'97*
The Rage *'96*
Blood for Blood *'95*
Gladiator Cop: The Swordsman 2 *'95*
Terminal Justice: Cybertech P.D. *'95*
Bad Blood *'94*
C.I.A. 2: Target Alexa *'94*
Bounty Tracker *'93*
Final Round *'93*
C.I.A.: Code Name Alexa *'92*
SnakeEater 3: His Law *'92*
The Swordsman *'92*
Final Impact *'91*
Killing Streets *'91*
Night of the Warrior *'91*
SnakeEater *'89*
SnakeEater 2: The Drug Buster *'89*
Body Rock *'84*
Take Down *'79*
Grease *'78*

Debra Lamb (1963-)
Evil Spirits *'91*
The Invisible Maniac *'90*
Rock & the Money-Hungry Party Girls *'89*
Stripped to Kill II: Live Girls *'89*
Beverly Hills Vamp *'88*
B.O.R.N. *'88*

Larry Lamb
Blood: The Last Vampire *'09*
Essex Boys *'99*
Fool's Gold: The Story of the Brink's-Mat Robbery *'92*
Buster *'88*
Shadey *'87*
Transmutations *'85*

Adam Lamberg (1984-)
When Do We Eat? *'05*
The Lizzie McGuire Movie *'03*

Anne Louise Lambert (1956-)
Napoleon *'96 (V)*
Lilian's Story *'95*
Great Expectations: The Untold Story *'87*
The Draughtsman's Contract *'82*
Picnic at Hanging Rock *'75*

Christopher Lambert (1959-)
Day of Wrath *'06*
The Target *'02*
Druids *'01*
Highlander: Endgame *'00*
Fortress 2: Re-Entry *'99*
Gideon *'99*
Resurrection *'99*
Beowulf *'98*
Mean Guns *'97*
Nirvana *'97*
Adrenalin: Fear the Rush *'96*
North Star *'96*
Mortal Kombat 1: The Movie *'95*
The Road Killers *'95*
Highlander: The Final Dimension *'94*
The Hunted *'94*
Fortress *'93*
Gunmen *'93*
Knight Moves *'93*
Highlander: The Gathering *'92*
Highlander 2: The Quickening *'91*
Priceless Beauty *'90*
Why Me? *'90*
To Kill a Priest *'89*
The Sicilian *'87*
Highlander *'86*
Love Songs *'85*
Subway *'85*
Greystoke: The Legend of Tarzan, Lord of the Apes *'84*
Love Songs *'84*

Jack Lambert (1899-1976)
Three Cases of Murder *'55*
Hue and Cry *'47*
Nine Men *'43*
The Ghost Goes West *'36*

Jack Lambert (1920-2002)
Neither the Sea Nor the Sand *'73*
The Day of the Outlaw *'59*
Machine Gun Kelly *'58*
Kiss Me Deadly *'55*
Montana Belle *'52*
North of the Great Divide *'50*
Stars in My Crown *'50*
Dick Tracy's Dilemma *'47*
The Unsuspected *'47*

Mark Lambert
Durango *'99*
Cracker: Brotherly Love *'95*

Paul Lambert (1922-97)
Soldier's Revenge *'84*
Mama's Dirty Girls *'74*
Missiles of October *'74*

Heath Lamberts (1941-2005)
Tom and Huck *'95*
Ordinary Magic *'93*
To Kill a Clown *'72*

Ellie Lambetti (1926-83)
A Matter of Dignity *'57*
Girl in Black *'56*

Lloyd Lamble
Sea Wife *'57*
The Belles of St. Trinian's *'53*

Vassili Lambrinos
Last Rites *'88*
That Man Bolt *'73*

Anne Lambton (1954-)
A Different Loyalty *'04*
American History X *'98*
Love Is the Devil *'98*

Karen Lamm (1952-2001)
Ants *'77*
The Hatfields & the McCoys *'75*

Duncan Lamont (1918-78)
The Creeping Flesh *'72*
Frankenstein Created Woman *'66*
The Devil-Ship Pirates *'64*
The Evil of Frankenstein *'64*
Murder at the Gallop *'63*
Quentin Durward *'55*
The Golden Coach *'52*
The Woman in Question *'50*

Marten Lamont (1911-)
Redwood Forest Trail *'50*
Federal Operator 99 *'45*
Son of Fury *'42*
International Lady *'41*

Molly Lamont (1910-2001)
The Devil Bat's Daughter *'46*
Somewhere I'll Find You *'42*
The Awful Truth *'37*

Pascal Lamorisse (1950-)
Voyage en Balloon *'59*
The Red Balloon *'56*

Jake LaMotta (1921-)
Mob War *'88*
Hangmen *'87*
The Hustler *'61*

John Lamotta
Showdown *'94*
We're Talkin' Serious Money *'92*
One More Chance *'90*
Revenge of the Ninja *'83*

Dorothy Lamour (1914-96)
Creepshow 2 *'87*
The Love Goddesses *'65*
Pajama Party *'64*
Donovan's Reef *'63*
The Road to Hong Kong *'62*
The Road to Bali *'53*
The Greatest Show on Earth *'52*
Here Comes the Groom *'51*
On Our Merry Way *'48*
My Favorite Brunette *'47*
The Road to Rio *'47*
The Road to Utopia *'46*
They Got Me Covered *'43*
The Road to Morocco *'42*
Star Spangled Rhythm *'42*
Caught in the Draft *'41*
The Road to Zanzibar *'41*
Johnny Apollo *'40*
The Road to Singapore *'40*
Man About Town *'39*
The Big Broadcast of 1938 *'38*
Spawn of the North *'38*
The Hurricane *'37*
Swing High, Swing Low *'37*
Dixiana *'30*

Lisa Lampanelli
Delta Farce *'07*
Larry the Cable Guy: Health Inspector *'06*

Jutta Lampe (1937-)
Rosenstrasse *'03*
The Possessed *'88*
Marianne and Juliane *'82*
Sisters, Or the Balance of Happiness *'79*

Zohra Lampert (1937-)
Alan & Naomi *'92*
Stanley and Iris *'90*
American Blue Note *'89*
Izzy & Moe *'85*
Alphabet City *'84*
Teachers *'84*
Isle of Secret Passion *'82*
Opening Night *'77*
The Connection *'73*
Let's Scare Jessica to Death *'71*
Bye Bye Braverman *'67*
A Fine Madness *'66*
Splendor in the Grass *'61*

Chus (Maria Jesus) Lampreave (1930-)
Chef's Special *'08*
Volver *'06*
The Flower of My Secret *'95*
I'm the One You're Looking For *'88*
Matador *'86*
What Have I Done to Deserve This? *'85*

Gunter Lamprecht (1930-)
Red Kiss *'85*
Berlin Alexanderplatz *'80*

Sarah Lancashire (1964-)
Wuthering Heights *'09*
Oliver Twist *'07*
When Did You Last See Your Father? *'07*
Gentlemen's Relish *'01*
Seeing Red *'99*

Ann Lancaster (1920-70)
The Railway Children *'70*
Hot Millions *'68*

Burt Lancaster (1913-94)
Separate but Equal *'91*
The Jeweller's Shop *'90*
The Phantom of the Opera *'90*
Voyage of Terror: The Achille Lauro Affair *'90*
Field of Dreams *'89*
Rocket Gibraltar *'88*
Control *'87*
Barnum *'86*
On Wings of Eagles *'86*
Tough Guys *'86*
Little Treasure *'85*
Scandal Sheet *'85*
Local Hero *'83*
The Osterman Weekend *'83*
Atlantic City *'81*
Zulu Dawn *'79*
Go Tell the Spartans *'78*
The Island of Dr. Moreau *'77*
Twilight's Last Gleaming *'77*
America at the Movies *'76*
Buffalo Bill & the Indians *'76*
The Cassandra Crossing *'76*
Moses *'76*
1900 *'76*
Victory at Entebbe *'76*
Conversation Piece *'75*
Executive Action *'73*
Scorpio *'73*
Ulzana's Raid *'72*
Lawman *'71*
Valdez Is Coming *'71*
Airport *'70*
Castle Keep *'69*
The Gypsy Moths *'69*
The Scalphunters *'68*
The Swimmer *'68*
The Professionals *'66*
The Hallelujah Trail *'65*
The Train *'65*
Seven Days in May *'64*
A Child Is Waiting *'63*
The Leopard *'63*
The List of Adrian Messenger *'63*
Birdman of Alcatraz *'62*
Judgment at Nuremberg *'61*
The Young Savages *'61*
Elmer Gantry *'60*
The Unforgiven *'60*
The Devil's Disciple *'59*
Run Silent, Run Deep *'58*
Separate Tables *'58*
Gunfight at the O.K. Corral *'57*
Sweet Smell of Success *'57*
The Rainmaker *'56*
Trapeze *'56*
The Kentuckian *'55*
The Rose Tattoo *'55*
Apache *'54*
From Here to Eternity *'53*
His Majesty O'Keefe *'53*
South Sea Woman *'53*
Three Sailors and a Girl *'53*
Vera Cruz *'53*
Come Back, Little Sheba *'52*
Crimson Pirate *'52*
Jim Thorpe: All American *'51*
Vengeance Valley *'51*
The Flame & the Arrow *'50*
All My Sons *'48*
Criss Cross *'48*
Sorry, Wrong Number *'48*
Brute Force *'47*
The Killers *'46*

James Lancaster
Leprechaun 2 *'94*
Gettysburg *'93*

Stuart Lancaster (1920-2000)
Beneath the Valley of the Ultra-Vixens *'79*
Mistress of the Apes *'79*
Mantis in Lace *'68*
Born Losers *'67*
Faster, Pussycat! Kill! Kill! *'65*

James Lance
Bronson *'09*
Mr. Right *'06*
The Search for John Gissing *'01*

Karl Lanchbury (1944-)
Vampyres *'74*
The House that Vanished *'73*

Elsa Lanchester (1902-86)
Die Laughing *'80*
Murder by Death *'76*
Arnold *'73*
Terror in the Wax Museum *'73*
Willard *'71*
My Dog, the Thief *'69*
Blackbeard's Ghost *'67*
Easy Come, Easy Go *'67*
That Darn Cat *'65*
Pajama Party *'64*
Bell, Book and Candle *'58*
Witness for the Prosecution *'57*
The Glass Slipper *'55*
Androcles and the Lion *'52*
Buccaneer's Girl *'50*
Mystery Street *'50*
Come to the Stable *'49*
The Inspector General *'49*
The Secret Garden *'49*
The Big Clock *'48*
The Bishop's Wife *'47*
Northwest Outpost *'47*
The Razor's Edge *'46*
The Spiral Staircase *'46*
Forever and a Day *'43*
Lassie, Come Home *'43*
Son of Fury *'42*
Tales of Manhattan *'42*
Beachcomber *'38*
The Ghost Goes West *'36*
Rembrandt *'36*
The Bride of Frankenstein *'35*
David Copperfield *'35*
Naughty Marietta *'35*
The Private Life of Henry VIII *'33*

Micheline Lanctot (1947-)
Blood Relatives *'77*
The Apprenticeship of Duddy Kravitz *'74*
Addie Land
The Sasquatch Gang *'06*
Evergreen *'04*
Geoffrey Land
Hospital of Terror *'78*
Black Heat *'76*
Against a Crooked Sky *'75*
The Female Bunch *'69*
Paul Land (1956-)
Spring Break *'83*
Idolmaker *'80*
Rodolfo Landa
Neutron vs. the Maniac *'62*
Neutron vs. the Amazing Dr. Caronte *'61*
The Criminal Life of Archibaldo de la Cruz *'55*
David Landau (1878-1935)
The Man with Two Faces *'34*
Gabriel Over the White House *'33*
No Marriage Ties *'33*
One Man's Journey *'33*
False Faces *'32*
Horse Feathers *'32*
The Purchase Price *'32*
Union Depot *'32*
Street Scene *'31*
Juliet Landau (1965-)
Hack! *'07*
Going Shopping *'05*
Ravager *'97*
Theodore Rex *'95*
Ed Wood *'94*
Direct Hit *'93*
Neon City *'91*
Martin Landau (1931-)
9 *'09 (V)*
City of Ember *'08*
Hollywood Homicide *'03*
The Majestic *'01*
Ready to Rumble *'00*
Shiner *'00*
Bonanno: A Godfather's Story *'99*
EDtv *'99*
Sleepy Hollow *'99*
Rounders *'98*
The X-Files *'98*
B.A.P.'s *'97*
The Adventures of Pinocchio *'96*
City Hall *'95*
The Color of Evening *'95*
Joseph *'95*
Ed Wood *'94*
Eye of the Stranger *'93*
Intersection *'93*
No Place to Hide *'93*
Sliver *'93*
12:01 *'93*
Legacy of Lies *'92*
Mistress *'91*
Firehead *'90*
Max and Helen *'90*
Real Bullets *'90*
By Dawn's Early Light *'89*
Crimes & Misdemeanors *'89*
The Neon Empire *'89*
Paint It Black *'89*
Tucker: The Man and His Dream *'88*
Cyclone *'87*
Death Blow *'87*
Empire State *'87*
Run If You Can *'87*
Sweet Revenge *'87*
Kung Fu: The Movie *'86*
Access Code *'84*
The Being *'83*
Alone in the Dark *'82*
The Fall of the House of Usher *'80*
The Last Word *'80*
The Return *'80*
Meteor *'79*
Space: 1999—Alien Attack *'79*
Strange Shadows in an Empty Room *'76*
Destination Moonbase Alpha *'75*
Black Gunn *'72*
A Town Called Hell *'72*
They Call Me Mr. Tibbs! *'70*
The Hallelujah Trail *'65*
Cleopatra *'63*
The Gazebo *'59*
North by Northwest *'59*
Pork Chop Hill *'59*
Dinsdale Landen (1931-2003)
Catherine Cookson's The Wingless Bird *'97*
Morons from Outer Space *'85*
Anatomy of Terror *'74*
Digby, the Biggest Dog in the World *'73*
David Lander (1947-)
Scary Movie *'00*
The Modern Adventures of Tom Sawyer *'99*
Ava's Magical Adventure *'94*
Tom and Jerry: The Movie *'93 (V)*
Betrayal of the Dove *'92*
A League of Their Own *'92*
Steel and Lace *'90*
Funland *'89*
The Man with One Red Shoe *'85*
Used Cars *'80*
1941 *'79*
The Tell-Tale Heart *'60*
Audrey Landers (1959-)
Bachelor Party 2: The Last Temptation *'08*
California Casanova *'89*
Ghost Writer *'89*
Getting Even *'86*
A Chorus Line *'85*
Deadly Twins *'85*
Underground Aces *'80*
1941 *'79*
Tennessee Stallion *'78*
Harry Landers (1921-)
The Gallant Hours *'60*
The Indian Fighter *'55*
Phantom from Space *'53*
The C-Man *'49*
Judy Landers (1961-)
Expert Weapon *'93*
The Divine Enforcer *'91*
Club Fed *'90*
Ghost Writer *'89*
Dr. Alien *'88*
Armed and Dangerous *'86*
Stewardess School *'86*
Deadly Twins *'85*
Doin' Time *'85*
Hellhole *'85*
The Black Marble *'79*
Tennessee Stallion *'78*
The Yum-Yum Girls *'78*
Michael Landes (1972-)
Homecoming *'09*
Possession *'09*
Last Chance Harvey *'08*
Final Destination 2 *'03*
Rescuers: Stories of Courage "Two Women" *'97*
Dream for an Insomniac *'96*
An American Summer *'90*
Steve Landesberg (1945-)
Forgetting Sarah Marshall *'08*
The Souler Opposite *'97*
The Crazysitter *'94*
Sodbusters *'94*
Home for Christmas *'93*
Mission of the Shark *'91*
Final Notice *'89*
Leader of the Band *'87*
Blade *'72*
Clayton Landey
Assault of the Killer Bimbos *'88*
First & Ten: The Team Scores Again *'85*
Janet Landgard
Land Raiders *'69*
The Swimmer *'68*
Gudrun Landgrebe (1950-)
Advertising Rules! *'01*
The Berlin Affair *'85*
Colonel Redl *'84*
A Woman in Flames *'84*
Sonny Landham (1941-)
Best of the Best 2 *'93*
Taxi Dancers *'93*
Three Days to a Kill *'91*
Lock Up *'89*
Predator *'87*
The Dirty Dozen: The Next Mission *'85*
Fleshburn *'84*
48 Hrs. *'82*
Southern Comfort *'81*
Elissa Landi (1904-48)
Corregidor *'43*
After the Thin Man *'36*
The Count of Monte Cristo *'34*
The Sign of the Cross *'33*
Marla Landi (1937-)
Pirates of Blood River *'62*
First Man into Space *'59*
Across the Bridge *'57*
Sal Landi
The Indian *'07*
Xtro 3: Watch the Skies *'95*
Back to Back *'90*
Savage Streets *'83*
D.W. Landingham
Karate Cop *'91*
Omega Cop *'90*
Carole Landis (1919-48)
Out of the Blue *'47*
A Scandal in Paris *'46*
Having Wonderful Crime *'45*
Four Jills in a Jeep *'44*
Wintertime *'43*
Orchestra Wives *'42*
Dance Hall *'41*
I Wake Up Screaming *'41*
Moon over Miami *'41*
Road Show *'41*
Topper Returns *'41*
One Million B.C. *'40*
Cowboys from Texas *'39*
Three Texas Steers *'39*
Daredevils of the Red Circle *'38*
Cullen Landis (1895-1975)
The Broken Mask *'28*
Soul of the Beast *'23*
Forrest Landis (1994-)
Spy School *'08*
Cheaper by the Dozen 2 *'05*
Benji: Off the Leash! *'04*
Cheaper by the Dozen *'03*
Jessie Royce Landis (1904-72)
Airport *'70*
Critic's Choice *'63*
Gidget Goes to Rome *'63*
Bon Voyage! *'62*
Boys' Night Out *'62*
Goodbye Again *'61*
North by Northwest *'59*
My Man Godfrey *'57*
I Married a Woman *'56*
The Swan *'56*
To Catch a Thief *'55*
It Happens Every Spring *'49*
My Foolish Heart *'49*
John Landis (1950-)
Diamonds *'99*
Freeway 2: Confessions of a Trickbaby *'99*
Laws of Deception *'97*
Silence of the Hams *'93*
Sleepwalkers *'92*
Venice, Venice *'92*
Body Chemistry 2: Voice of a Stranger *'91*
Darkman *'90*
Spontaneous Combustion *'89*
The Muppets Take Manhattan *'84*
The Blues Brothers *'80*
1941 *'79*
Death Race 2000 *'75*
Battle for the Planet of the Apes *'73*
Schlock *'73*
Margaret Landis (1890-1981)
The Confession *'20*
Amarilly of Clothesline Alley *'18*
Monte Landis (1936-)
Yellowbeard *'83*
Candy Stripe Nurses *'74*
Young Frankenstein *'74*
Targets *'68*
The Mouse That Roared *'59*
Nina Landis
Komodo *'99*
Rikky and Pete *'88*
Joe Lando (1961-)
Counterstrike *'03*
No Code of Conduct *'98*
Any Place But Home *'97*
Alien Nation: The Enemy Within *'96*
Seeds of Doubt *'96*
Avice Landon (1910-76)
The Blood on Satan's Claw *'71*
The Leather Boys *'63*
Hal Landon, Jr. (1941-)
Bill & Ted's Bogus Journey *'91*
Eraserhead *'78*
Laurene Landon (1958-)
The Ambulance *'90*
Maniac Cop 2 *'90*
Wicked Stepmother *'89*
Maniac Cop *'88*
It's Alive 3: Island of the Alive *'87*
America 3000 *'86*
Hundra *'85*
Yellow Hair & the Fortress of Gold *'84*
I, the Jury *'82*
Michael Landon (1936-91)
Sam's Son *'84*
The Loneliest Runner *'76*
Little House on the Prairie *'74*
The Errand Boy *'61*
Legend of Tom Dooley *'59*
God's Little Acre *'58*
High School Confidential *'58*
Fight for the Title *'57*
I Was a Teenage Werewolf *'57*
Rosalyn Landor (1958-)
Disney's Teacher's Pet *'04 (V)*
Guardian of the Abyss *'82*
Pavel Landovsky (1936-)
The Unbearable Lightness of Being *'88*
The Uppercrust *'81*
Ali Landry (1973-)
Bella *'06*
Outta Time *'01*
Repli-Kate *'01*
Karen Landry
Roadracers *'94*
Heartbreak Hotel *'88*
Patti Rocks *'88*
The Personals *'83*
Margaret Landry (1922-2005)
Gildersleeve on Broadway *'43*
The Leopard Man *'43*
Tamara Landry (1962-)
Bikini Med School *'98*
Bikini House Calls *'96*
Beach Babes from Beyond *'93*
David Landsberg
Dutch Treat *'86*
Detective School Dropouts *'85*
Valerie Landsburg (1958-)
The Triangle Factory Fire Scandal *'79*
Thank God It's Friday *'78*
Abbe Lane (1932-)
Twilight Zone: The Movie *'83*
Americano *'55*
Ride Clear of Diablo *'54*
Allan "Rocky" Lane (1904-73)
El Paso Stampede *'53*
Marshal of Cedar Rock *'53*
Night Riders of Montana *'50*
Trail of Robin Hood *'50*
Bandit King of Texas *'49*
Oklahoma Badlands *'48*
Homesteaders of Paradise Valley *'47*
Wild Frontier *'47*
Santa Fe Uprising *'46*
Stagecoach to Denver *'46*
Vigilantes of Boom Town *'46*
Silver City Kid *'45*
The Topeka Terror *'45*
Perils of the Darkest Jungle *'44*
Panama Lady *'39*
Maid's Night Out *'38*
Charlie Chan at the Olympics *'37*
Night Nurse *'31*
Charles Lane (1869-1945)
Sadie Thompson *'28*
The Winning of Barbara Worth *'26*
Romola *'25*
The White Sister *'23*
Dr. Jekyll and Mr. Hyde *'20*
Charles Lane (1905-2007)
Acting on Impulse *'93*
War & Remembrance *'88*
Date with an Angel *'87*
Murphy's Romance *'85*
Strange Invaders *'83*
Sunset Limousine *'83*
The Winds of War *'83*
Strange Behavior *'81*
Little Dragons *'80*
Billie *'65*
Good Neighbor Sam *'64*
Papa's Delicate Condition *'63*
But Not for Me *'59*
The Mating Game *'59*
Teacher's Pet *'58*
The Affairs of Dobie Gillis *'53*
Borderline *'50*
Riding High *'50*
Call Northside 777 *'48*
I Wake Up Screaming *'41*
The Invisible Woman *'40*
It's a Date *'40*
Rhythm on the River *'40*
Mr. Smith Goes to Washington *'39*
Twentieth Century *'34*
Charles Lane (1953-)
Posse *'93*
True Identity *'91*
Colin Lane
The Blood Oranges *'97*
Broken Harvest *'94*
Diane Lane (1965-)
Killshot *'09*
Jumper *'08*
Nights in Rodanthe *'08*
Untraceable *'08*
Hollywoodland *'06*
Fierce People *'05*
Must Love Dogs *'05*
Under the Tuscan Sun *'03*
Unfaithful *'02*
The Glass House *'01*
Hardball *'01*
The Perfect Storm *'00*
My Dog Skip *'99*
The Virginian *'99*
A Walk on the Moon *'99*
Grace & Glorie *'98*
Gunshy *'98*
Murder at 1600 *'97*
The Only Thrill *'97*
Jack *'96*
Trigger Happy *'96*
Judge Dredd *'95*
Oldest Confederate Widow Tells All *'95*
A Streetcar Named Desire *'95*
Wild Bill *'95*
Fallen Angels 1 *'93*
Indian Summer *'93*
Knight Moves *'93*
Chaplin *'92*
My New Gun *'92*
Descending Angel *'90*
Priceless Beauty *'90*
Vital Signs *'90*
Lonesome Dove *'89*
Big Town *'87*
Lady Beware *'87*
The Cotton Club *'84*
Streets of Fire *'84*
The Outsiders *'83*
Rumble Fish *'83*
Ladies and Gentlemen, the Fabulous Stains *'82*
Miss All-American Beauty *'82*
Six Pack *'82*
Child Bride of Short Creek *'81*
National Lampoon Goes to the Movies *'81*
Touched by Love *'80*
A Little Romance *'79*
Frederic Lane
See Frederic Lehne
Jackie Lane (1947-)
Venus Against the Son of Hercules *'62*
Dangerous Youth *'58*
Kent Lane
Defiant *'70*
Changes *'69*
Krista Lane (1959-)
Thrilled to Death *'88*
Sensations *'87*
Lenita Lane (1901-95)
The Bat *'59*
Castle in the Desert *'42*
Lola Lane (1909-81)
Deadline at Dawn *'46*
Buckskin Frontier *'43*
Lost Canyon *'43*
Four Daughters *'38*
Hollywood Hotel *'37*
Marked Woman *'37*
Death from a Distance *'36*
Ticket to a Crime *'34*
Woman Condemned *'33*
Lupino Lane (1892-1959)
The Deputy Drummer *'35*
Golden Dawn *'30*
The Love Parade *'29*
Isn't Life Wonderful *'24*
Mike Lane (1931-)
Curse of the Crystal Eye *'93*
Cold War Killers *'86*
Code Name: Zebra *'84*
Zebra Force *'76*
A Name for Evil *'70*
The Harder They Fall *'56*
Nathan Lane (1956-)
Astro Boy *'09 (V)*
Swing Vote *'08*
The Producers *'05*
Disney's Teacher's Pet *'04 (V)*

The Lion King 1 1/2 *'04 (V)*
Win a Date with Tad Hamilton! *'04*
Austin Powers In Goldmember *'02*
Nicholas Nickleby *'02*
Stuart Little 2 *'02 (V)*
Isn't She Great *'00*
Love's Labour's Lost *'00*
Titan A.E. *'00 (V)*
Trixie *'00*
Stuart Little *'99 (V)*
At First Sight *'98*
The Lion King: Simba's Pride *'98 (V)*
Mouse Hunt *'97*
The Boys Next Door *'96*
The Birdcage *'95*
Jeffrey *'95*
The Lion King *'94 (V)*
Life with Mikey *'93*
Frankie and Johnny *'91*
He Said, She Said *'91*
Ironweed *'87*

Nora Lane (1905-48)
Six Gun Trail *'38*
Borderland *'37*
The Outlaw Deputy *'35*
Western Frontier *'35*
Sally *'29*

Priscilla Lane (1917-95)
Arsenic and Old Lace *'44*
Saboteur *'42*
Silver Queen *'42*
Blues in the Night *'41*
The Roaring Twenties *'39*
Four Daughters *'38*
Varsity Show *'37*

Richard Lane (1899-1982)
The Jackie Robinson Story *'50*
Take Me Out to the Ball Game *'49*
Sioux City Sue *'46*
Bullfighters *'45*
Louisiana Hayride *'44*
Mr. Winkle Goes to War *'44*
Slightly Terrific *'44*
Air Force *'43*
Arabian Nights *'42*
Junior G-Men of the Air *'42*
Ride 'Em Cowboy *'42*
Time to Kill *'42*
Sunny *'41*
Day the Bookies Wept *'39*
It Could Happen to You *'39*
Mr. Moto in Danger Island *'39*
Mutiny on the Blackhawk *'39*

Rosemary Lane (1914-74)
Harvest Melody *'43*
Oklahoma Kid *'39*
Four Daughters *'38*
Gold Diggers in Paris *'38*
Hollywood Hotel *'37*
Varsity Show *'37*

Eric Laneuville (1952-)
Fear of a Black Hat *'94*
Love at First Bite *'79*
Shoot It Black, Shoot It Blue *'74*
Omega Man *'71*

Doreen Lang (1918-99)
Almost an Angel *'90*
Missiles of October *'74*

Judith Lang
Count Yorga, Vampire *'70*
The Trip *'67*

June Lang (1915-)
Wee Willie Winkie *'37*
Captain January *'36*
Bonnie Scotland *'35*

Katherine Kelly Lang (1961-)
The Corporation *'96*
Subliminal Seduction *'96*
Till the End of the Night *'94*

k.d. lang (1961-)
Eye of the Beholder *'99*
The Last Don *'97*
Teresa's Tattoo *'94*
Salmonberries *'91*

Matthew Lang
The Rules of Attraction *'02*
We Were Soldiers *'02*

Perry Lang (1959-)
Sunshine State *'02*
Mortuary Academy *'91*
Little Vegas *'90*
Eight Men Out *'88*
Jailbird Rock *'88*
Jocks *'87*
Sahara *'83*
Spring Break *'83*
O'Hara's Wife *'82*
Tag: The Assassination Game *'82*
Body & Soul *'81*
Alligator *'80*
The Big Red One *'80*
A Rumor of War *'80*
Girls Next Door *'79*
1941 *'79*
Great Ride *'78*
Greedy Terror *'78*

Robert Lang (1934-2004)
Mrs. Palfrey at the Claremont *'05*
Cider with Rosie *'99*
I'm the Girl He Wants to Kill *'74*

Stephen Lang (1952-)
Avatar *'09*
The Men Who Stare at Goats *'09*
Public Enemies *'09*
Save Me *'07*
The Treatment *'06*
Gods and Generals *'03*
After the Storm *'01*
Eye See You *'01*
The Proposal *'00*
Trixie *'00*
Escape: Human Cargo *'98*
A Town Has Turned to Dust *'98*
Fire Down Below *'97*
Niagara, Niagara *'97*
Gang in Blue *'96*
An Occasional Hell *'96*
The Shadow Conspiracy *'96*
The Amazing Panda Adventure *'95*
Tall Tale: The Unbelievable Adventures of Pecos Bill *'95*
Gettysburg *'93*
Guilty as Sin *'93*
Tombstone *'93*
Another You *'91*
The Hard Way *'91*
Last Exit to Brooklyn *'90*
Finish Line *'89*
Project X *'87*
Band of the Hand *'86*
Death of a Salesman *'86*
Manhunter *'86*
King of America *'80*

Glenn Langan (1917-91)
The Amazing Colossal Man *'57*
Big Chase *'54*
Hangman's Knot *'52*
Treasure of Monte Cristo *'50*
The Snake Pit *'48*
Dragonwyck *'46*
Hangover Square *'45*
Something for the Boys *'44*

Harry Langdon (1884-1944)
House of Errors *'42*
Double Trouble *'41*
Misbehaving Husbands *'41*
Mad About Money *'37*
Long Pants *'27*
Ella Cinders *'26*
His First Flame *'26*
Strong Man *'26*
Tramp, Tramp, Tramp *'26*

Libby Langdon
Corn *'02*
A Shot at Glory *'00*
Federal Hill *'94*

Lillian Langdon (1884-1944)
Daddy Long Legs *'19*
His Majesty, the American *'19*
Shifting Sands *'18*
The Americano *'17*
Flirting with Fate *'16*
The Lamb *'15*

Sue Ane Langdon (1936-)
Zapped! *'82*
The Evictors *'79*
The Cheyenne Social Club *'70*
A Guide for the Married Man *'67*
A Fine Madness *'66*
Frankie and Johnny *'65*
The Rounders *'65*
Roustabout *'64*

Allison Lange (1978-)
Single White Female 2: The Psycho *'05*
The Hillside Strangler *'04*
Out of the Black *'01*
Christina's House *'99*

Artie Lange (1967-)
Beer League *'06*
Waltzing Anna *'06*
Boat Trip *'03*
Old School *'03*
The Bachelor *'99*
The 4th Floor *'99*
Lost and Found *'99*
Mystery Men *'99*
Dirty Work *'97*

Carl Lange (1909-99)
Creature with the Blue Hand *'70*
The Torture Chamber of Dr. Sadism *'69*
Carpet of Horror *'64*

Hope Lange (1931-2003)
Cooperstown *'93*
Tune in Tomorrow *'90*
Ford: The Man & the Machine *'87*
Blue Velvet *'86*
A Nightmare on Elm Street 2: Freddy's Revenge *'85*
I Am the Cheese *'83*
The Prodigal *'83*
Beulah Land *'80*
Pleasure Palace *'80*
Death Wish *'74*
Fer-De-Lance *'74*
I Love You, Goodbye *'74*
The Love Bug *'68*
Pocketful of Miracles *'61*
Wild in the Country *'61*
The Best of Everything *'59*
The Young Lions *'58*
Peyton Place *'57*
Bus Stop *'56*

Jessica Lange (1949-)
Grey Gardens *'09*
Bonneville *'06*
Broken Flowers *'05*
Don't Come Knocking *'05*
Big Fish *'03*
Masked and Anonymous *'03*
Normal *'03*
Prozac Nation *'01*
Titus *'99*
Hush *'98*
Cousin Bette *'97*
A Thousand Acres *'97*
Rob Roy *'95*
A Streetcar Named Desire *'95*
Losing Isaiah *'94*
Night and the City *'92*
Blue Sky *'91*
Cape Fear *'91*
O Pioneers! *'91*
Men Don't Leave *'89*
Music Box *'89*
Everybody's All American *'88*
Far North *'88*
Crimes of the Heart *'86*
Sweet Dreams *'85*
Cat on a Hot Tin Roof *'84*
Country *'84*
Frances *'82*
Tootsie *'82*
The Postman Always Rings Twice *'81*
How to Beat the High Cost of Living *'80*
All That Jazz *'79*
King Kong *'76*

Ted Lange (1947-)
Perfume *'91*
Terminal Exposure *'89*
Glitch! *'88*

Jack Langedijk
One Way Out *'02*
Codename: Jaguar *'00*
Left Behind: The Movie *'00*
The Pact *'99*
Dead End *'98*
A Young Connecticut Yankee in King Arthur's Court *'95*
Blind Fear *'89*
Evil Judgment *'85*

Frank Langella (1940-)
Wall Street 2: Money Never Sleeps *'10*
All Good Things *'09*
The Box *'09*
The Caller *'08*
Frost/Nixon *'08*
The Tale of Despereaux *'08 (V)*
Starting Out in the Evening *'07*
Superman Returns *'06*
Back in the Day *'05*
Good Night, and Good Luck *'05*
How You Look to Me *'05*
House of D *'04*
Sweet November *'01*
Innocents *'00*
Jason and the Argonauts *'00*
Stardom *'00*
The Ninth Gate *'99*
I'm Losing You *'98*
Small Soldiers *'98 (V)*
Lolita *'97*
Eddie *'96*
Moses *'96*
Cutthroat Island *'95*
Bad Company *'94*
Brainscan *'94*
Doomsday Gun *'94*
Junior *'94*
Dave *'93*
Body of Evidence *'92*
1492: Conquest of Paradise *'92*
Kurt Vonnegut's Monkey House *'91*
True Identity *'91*
And God Created Woman *'88*
Masters of the Universe *'87*
The Men's Club *'86*
Sphinx *'81*
Those Lips, Those Eyes *'80*
Dracula *'79*
The Seagull *'75*
The Deadly Trap *'71*
Diary of a Mad Housewife *'70*
The Twelve Chairs *'70*

Sarah Langenfeld
Bloodlink *'86*
Gold Raiders *'83*
The Act *'82*

Heather Langenkamp (1964-)
Fugitive Mind *'99*
The Demolitionist *'95*
Wes Craven's New Nightmare *'94*
Shocker *'89*
A Nightmare on Elm Street 3: Dream Warriors *'87*
Nickel Mountain *'85*
A Nightmare on Elm Street *'84*

A.J. (Allison Joy) Langer (1974-)
On Edge *'03*
Meet the Deedles *'98*
Escape from L.A. *'96*
The Ghost Brigade *'93*
The People under the Stairs *'91*

Frances Langford (1913-2005)
Deputy Marshal *'50*
Melody Time *'48 (V)*
The Bamboo Blonde *'46*
Dixie Jamboree *'44*
Girl Rush *'44*
Yankee Doodle Dandy *'42*
Dreaming Out Loud *'40*
Too Many Girls *'40*
Born to Dance *'36*

Wallace (Wally) Langham (1965-)
The Great Buck Howard *'09*
I Want Someone to Eat Cheese With *'06*
Little Miss Sunshine *'06*
On Edge *'03*
God's Lonely Man *'96*
The Chocolate War *'88*
The Invisible Kid *'88*
Thunder Run *'86*

Amanda Langlet
Triple Agent *'04*
A Summer's Tale *'96*
Pauline at the Beach *'83*

Lisa Langlois (1959-)
Mindfield *'89*
The Nest *'88*
Transformations *'88*
Truth or Die *'86*
Joy of Sex *'84*
The Man Who Wasn't There *'83*
Class of 1984 *'82*
Deadly Eyes *'82*
Blood Relatives *'77*

Margaret Langrick (1971-)
Boxcar Blues *'90*
Cold Comfort *'90*
American Boyfriends *'89*
Thunderground *'89*
Harry and the Hendersons *'87*
My American Cousin *'85*

Caroline Langrishe (1958-)
Cleopatra *'99*
Mosley *'98*
Parting Shots *'98*
Rogue Trader *'98*
Sharpe's Justice *'97*
Sharpe's Regiment *'96*
Eagle's Wing *'79*

Murray Langston
Wishful Thinking *'92*
Digging Up Business *'91*
Up Your Alley *'89*
Night Patrol *'85*

Brooke Langton (1970-)
Primeval *'07*
The Benchwarmers *'06*
Playing Mona Lisa *'00*
The Replacements *'00*
Reach the Rock *'98*
Listen *'96*
Swingers *'96*

David Langton (1912-94)
The Whistle Blower *'87*
Quintet *'79*
Abandon Ship *'57*

Jeff Langton
Maximum Force *'92*
Final Impact *'91*

Paul Langton (1913-80)
The Cosmic Man *'59*
It! The Terror from Beyond Space *'58*
The Incredible Shrinking Man *'57*
The Big Knife *'55*
To Hell and Back *'55*
The Snow Creature *'54*
They Were Expendable *'45*
Thirty Seconds Over Tokyo *'44*

Guy Lankester
Pandaemonium *'00*
Tower of the Firstborn *'98*

Kim Lankford (1962-)
Street Corner Justice *'96*
Cameron's Closet *'89*
Octagon *'80*
Malibu Beach *'78*

Frank Lanning (1872-1945)
The Lone Defender *'32*
Stand and Deliver *'28*
The Unknown *'27*

Les Lannom
Southern Comfort *'81*
Centennial *'78*
Stingray *'78*

Jenya Lano
Ten 'Til Noon *'06*
Stealing Candy *'04*
Deathlands: Homeward Bound *'03*

Victor Lanoux (1936-)
Louisiana *'87*
Scene of the Crime *'87*
National Lampoon's European Vacation *'85*
Dog Day *'83*
Make Room for Tomorrow *'81*
Investigation *'79*
One Wild Moment *'78*
A Woman at Her Window *'77*
Cousin, Cousine *'76*
Pardon Mon Affaire *'76*
The French Detective *'75*

Angela Lansbury (1925-)
Nanny McPhee *'06*
Anastasia *'97 (V)*
Mrs. Santa Claus *'96*
Mrs. 'Arris Goes to Paris *'92*
Beauty and the Beast *'91 (V)*
The Shell Seekers *'89*
Rage of Angels: The Story Continues *'86*
The Company of Wolves *'85*
The First Olympics: Athens 1896 *'84*
Little Gloria... Happy at Last *'84*
Sweeney Todd: The Demon Barber of Fleet Street *'84*
The Pirates of Penzance *'83*
The Last Unicorn *'82 (V)*
The Mirror Crack'd *'80*
The Lady Vanishes *'79*
Death on the Nile *'78*
Bedknobs and Broomsticks *'71*
Something for Everyone *'70*
The Amorous Adventures of Moll Flanders *'65*
The Greatest Story Ever Told *'65*
Harlow *'65*
The World of Henry Orient *'64*
All Fall Down *'62*
Blue Hawaii *'62*
The Manchurian Candidate *'62*
Breath of Scandal *'60*
The Long, Hot Summer *'58*
The Reluctant Debutante *'58*
Court Jester *'56*
A Lawless Street *'55*
Mutiny *'52*
Samson and Delilah *'50*
State of the Union *'48*
The Three Musketeers *'48*
The Private Affairs of Bel Ami *'47*
The Harvey Girls *'46*

Picture of Dorian Gray *'45*
Gaslight *'44*
National Velvet *'44*

David Lansbury (1961-)
From Other Worlds *'04*
Cupid & Cate *'00*
A Stranger in the Kingdom *'98*
Truman *'95*
Parallel Lives *'94*
Gas Food Lodging *'92*

John Lansing
More American Graffiti *'79*
Sunnyside *'79*

Joi Lansing (1928-72)
Big Foot *'72*
Hillbillies in a Haunted House *'67*
Atomic Submarine *'59*
A Hole in the Head *'59*
Touch of Evil *'58*
The Brave One *'56*
The Finger Man *'55*
Son of Sinbad *'55*
The French Line *'54*
The Merry Widow *'52*
Singin' in the Rain *'52*
Pier 23 *'51*
Two Tickets to Broadway *'51*
Neptune's Daughter *'49*
Easter Parade *'48*
Julia Misbehaves *'48*

Robert Lansing (1929-94)
The Nest *'88*
Island Claw *'80*
S*H*E *'79*
Acapulco Gold *'78*
Empire of the Ants *'77*
Bittersweet Love *'76*
Scalpel *'76*
The Widow *'76*
The Grissom Gang *'71*
Namu, the Killer Whale *'66*
Talion *'66*
Under the Yum-Yum Tree *'63*
The 4D Man *'59*

Matt Lanter
The Cutting Edge 3: Chasing the Dream *'08*
Disaster Movie *'08*
Star Wars: The Clone Wars *'08 (V)*
WarGames 2: The Dead Code *'08*

Virginia Lantry
No Way Back *'90*
Ain't No Way Back *'89*

Gerard Lanvin (1950-)
The Taste of Others *'00*
Mon Homme *'96*
The Favorite Son *'94*

Mario Lanza (1921-59)
For the First Time *'59*
The Seven Hills of Rome *'58*
Because You're Mine *'52*
The Great Caruso *'51*
The Toast of New Orleans *'50*
That Midnight Kiss *'49*

Fabio Lanzoni
See Fabio

Anthony LaPaglia (1959-)
$9.99 *'08 (V)*
The Architect *'06*
Happy Feet *'06 (V)*
Played *'06*
Winter Solstice *'04*
Happy Hour *'03*
The Guys *'02*
I'm with Lucy *'02*
The Salton Sea *'02*
The Bank *'01*
Dead Heat *'01*
Lantana *'01*
Autumn in New York *'00*
Company Man *'00*
House of Mirth *'00*
Lansky *'99*
Summer of Sam *'99*
Sweet and Lowdown *'99*
Phoenix *'98*
The Garden of Redemption *'97*
Brilliant Lies *'96*
Commandments *'96*
Paperback Romance *'96*
Tree's Lounge *'96*
Bulletproof Heart *'95*
Chameleon *'95*
Empire Records *'95*
The Client *'94*
The Custodian *'94*
Mixed Nuts *'94*
Past Tense *'94*
So I Married an Axe Murderer *'93*
Black Magic *'92*
Innocent Blood *'92*
Keeper of the City *'92*
Whispers in the Dark *'92*
He Said, She Said *'91*
One Good Cop *'91*
29th Street *'91*
Betsy's Wedding *'90*
Criminal Justice *'90*
Mortal Sins *'90*
Slaves of New York *'89*
Nitti: The Enforcer *'88*

Jonathan LaPaglia (1967-)
Plain Truth *'04*
Under Hellgate Bridge *'99*
Inferno *'98*

Daniel Lapaine (1971-)
Shanghai *'09*
The 10th Kingdom *'00*
Brokedown Palace *'99*
Dangerous Beauty *'98*
1999 *'98*
Polish Wedding *'97*
Muriel's Wedding *'94*

Francine Lapensee
Bounty Hunter 2002 *'94*
Demon Wind *'90*
Born Killer *'89*
Hollywood's New Blood *'88*

Andrzej Lapicki (1924-)
The Deluge *'73*
Everything for Sale *'68*

Peter Lapis
Undeclared War *'91*
Death Blow *'87*

Victor Laplace (1943-)
Letters from the Park *'88*
Under the Earth *'86*

Jane Lapotaire (1944-)
Shooting Fish *'98*
Surviving Picasso *'96*
The Dark Angel *'91*
Murder by Moonlight *'91*
Eureka! *'81*
Piaf *'81*
The Asphyx *'72*
Crescendo *'69*

Alexandra Maria Lara (1978-)
The Reader *'08*
The Company *'07*
Control *'07*
I Really Hate My Job *'07*
Youth Without Youth *'07*
Doctor Zhivago *'03*
The Tunnel *'01*

Joe Lara (1962-)
Doomsdayer *'01*
Doomsdayer *'99*
Operation: Delta Force *'97*
Warhead *'96*
Final Equinox *'95*
Hologram Man *'95*
Live Wire: Human Timebomb *'95*
American Cyborg: Steel Warrior *'94*
Steel Frontier *'94*

John Larch (1922-94)
The Amityville Horror *'79*
Future Cop *'76*
Bad Ronald *'74*
Winter Kill *'74*
Santee *'73*
Dirty Harry *'71*
Play Misty for Me *'71*
Hail, Hero! *'69*
The Wrecking Crew *'68*
Man in the Shadow *'57*

Vincent Laresca (1974-)
El Cantante *'06*
The Fast and the Furious: Tokyo Drift *'06*
.45 *'06*
The Aviator *'04*
Empire *'02*
Hard Cash *'01*
Just One Time *'00*
Forever Mine *'99*
Music from Another Room *'97*
Ripe *'97*
Money Train *'95*
Juice *'92*

Corey Large (1975-)
Loaded *'08*
Chasing Ghosts *'05*
Window Theory *'04*

Veronica Lario (1956-)
Sotto, Sotto *'85*
Unsane *'82*

Bryan Larkin
Born on the Fourth of July *'89*
She-Devil *'89*

Chris Larkin (1967-)
Friends & Crocodiles *'05*
Hitler: The Rise of Evil *'03*
Master and Commander: The Far Side of the World *'03*
Shackleton *'02*
The Flamingo Rising *'01*
Angels and Insects *'95*

Linda Larkin (1970-)
Aladdin and the King of Thieves *'96 (V)*
The Return of Jafar *'94 (V)*
Aladdin *'92 (V)*

Mary Laroche (1920-99)
Psychomania *'73*
Gidget *'59*
The Lineup *'58*
Run Silent, Run Deep *'58*

Michele Laroque (1960-)
The Neighbor *'07*
The Closet *'00*
Ma Vie en Rose *'97*
Pedale Douce *'96*
Nelly et Monsieur Arnaud *'95*

Scott LaRose
Comic Book: The Movie *'04*
Booty Call *'96*

Pierre Larquey (1884-1962)
Topaze *'51*
Le Corbeau *'43*

Tito Larriva
Just a Little Harmless Sex *'99*
True Stories *'86*
The Pee-wee Herman Show *'82*

John Larroquette (1947-)
Kill Your Darlings *'06*
Southland Tales *'06*
Beethoven's 5th *'03*
Recipe for Disaster *'03*
The Texas Chainsaw Massacre *'03 (N)*
Walter and Henry *'01*
Isn't She Great *'00*
The 10th Kingdom *'00*
The Defenders: Payback *'97*
Richie Rich *'94*
Madhouse *'90*
Tune in Tomorrow *'90*
Second Sight *'89*
Blind Date *'87*
Convicted *'86*
Summer Rental *'85*
Choose Me *'84*
Meatballs 2 *'84*
Star Trek 3: The Search for Spock *'84*
Twilight Zone: The Movie *'83*
Cat People *'82*
Green Ice *'81*
Stripes *'81*
Altered States *'80*
Heart Beat *'80*
The Texas Chainsaw Massacre *'74 (N)*

Larry the Cable Guy (1963-)
Witless Protection *'08*
Delta Farce *'07*
Cars *'06*
Larry the Cable Guy: Health Inspector *'06*

Eric Larsen (1961-)
Young & Free *'78*
Trap on Cougar Mountain *'72*

Ham Larsen
Mountain Family Robinson *'79*
Further Adventures of the Wilderness Family, Part 2 *'77*

Keith Larsen (1924-2006)
Whitewater Sam *'78*
Trap on Cougar Mountain *'72*
Mission Batangas *'69*
Dial Red O *'55*
Flat Top *'52*

Bobby Larson (1930-2002)
Leather Burners *'43*
The Underdog *'43*

Brie Larson (1989-)
Greenberg *'10*
Scott Pilgrim vs. the World *'10*
Hoot *'06*

Darrell Larson (1951-)
Shadrach *'98*
Stepmom *'98*
Stuart Saves His Family *'94*
Hero *'92*
The Last Innocent Man *'87*
Murder Ordained *'87*
City Limits *'85*
Mike's Murder *'84*
Red, White & Busted *'75*
The Girls of Huntington House *'73*
The Student Nurses *'70*

Eric Larson (1905-88)
Demon Wind *'90*
The Uninvited *'88*
'68 *'87*

Wolf Larson (1959-)
Shakedown *'02*
Crash & Byrnes *'99*
Storm Chasers: Revenge of the Twister *'98*
The Heist *'96*
Expect No Mercy *'95*
Tracks of a Killer *'95*

Ali Larter (1976-)
Obsessed *'09*
Marigold *'07*
National Lampoon's The Stoned Aged *'07*
Resident Evil: Extinction *'07*
A Lot Like Love *'05*
Confess *'05*
3-Way *'04*
Final Destination 2 *'03*
American Outlaws *'01*
Jay and Silent Bob Strike Back *'01*
Legally Blonde *'01*
Final Destination *'00*
Drive Me Crazy *'99*
Giving It Up *'99*
House on Haunted Hill *'99*
Varsity Blues *'98*

Eva LaRue (1966-)
Lakeview Terrace *'08*
Crash and Burn *'90*
The Barbarians *'87*
Lawless Plainsmen *'42*

Frank LaRue (1878-1960)
Range Renegades *'48*
Border Bandits *'46*
Devil Riders *'44*
Battling Outlaw *'40*
Range Busters *'40*
Riders of Pasco Basin *'40*
Mesquite Buckaroo *'39*
Trigger Pals *'39*
Overland Stage Raiders *'38*
Songs and Bullets *'38*
Boothill Brigade *'37*
Gun Lords of Stirrup Basin *'37*
A Lawman Is Born *'37*
Lightning Bill Crandall *'37*
The Phantom Rider *'36*
Red River Valley *'36*
His Fighting Blood *'35*
The Throwback *'35*
Law of the Sea *'32*
Sidewalks of New York *'31*

Jack LaRue (1902-84)
Gangs, Inc. *'41*
Under the Pampas Moon *'35*
Gambling Ship *'33*

Lash LaRue (1917-96)
Pair of Aces *'90*
The Dark Power *'85*
The Black Lash *'52*
King of the Bullwhip *'51*
Thundering Trail *'51*
Outlaw Country *'49*
Stage to Mesa City *'48*
Border Feud *'47*
Cheyenne Takes Over *'47*
Fighting Vigilantes *'47*
Ghost Town Renegades *'47*
Heartaches *'47*
Law of the Lash *'47*
Return of the Lash *'47*
The Caravan Trail *'46*
Wild West *'46*
Song of Old Wyoming *'45*
Master Key *'44*

Robert LaSardo (1963-)
Death Race *'08*
Never Down *'06*
Dirty *'05*
Latin Dragon *'03*
Mercy Streets *'00*
Double Tap *'98*
Running Woman *'98*
The Real Thing *'97*
Under Oath *'97*
Gang Related *'96*
Tiger Heart *'96*
Waterworld *'95*

David Lascher (1972-)
A Call to Remember *'97*
White Squall *'96*

Dieter Laser (1942-)
The Man Inside *'90*
The Lost Honor of Katharina Blum *'75*

Michael Laskin (1951-)
Bounce *'00*
Limbo *'99*
The Disappearance of Kevin Johnson *'95*
Passion Fish *'92*
Eight Men Out *'88*
The Personals *'83*

Kathleen Lasky
Getting Gotti *'94*
Lethal Lolita—Amy Fisher: My Story *'92*
Love & Murder *'91*

Hanna Laslo
Adam Resurrected *'08*
Free Zone *'05*

Tommy Lasorda (1927-)
Homeward Bound 2: Lost in San Francisco *'96 (V)*
Ladybugs *'92*
Americathon *'79*

Dagmar Lassander (1943-)
S.A.S. San Salvador *'84*
The Black Cat *'81*
Flatfoot *'78*
Dandelions *'74*
The Frightened Woman *'71*
Hatchet for the Honeymoon *'70*

Louise Lasser (1939-)
National Lampoon's Gold Diggers *'04*
Club Land *'01*
Requiem for a Dream *'00*
Mystery Men *'99*
Happiness *'98*
Sudden Manhattan *'96*
The Night We Never Met *'93*
Frankenhooker *'90*
Modern Love *'90*
Rude Awakening *'89*
Sing *'89*
Blood Rage *'87*
Surrender *'87*
Crimewave *'85*
For Ladies Only *'81*
In God We Trust *'80*
Just Me & You *'78*
Slither *'73*
Everything You Always Wanted to Know about Sex (But Were Afraid to Ask) *'72*
Bananas *'71*
Take the Money and Run *'69*

Sarah Lassez
Mad Cowgirl *'06*
In Pursuit *'00*
The Blackout *'97*
Nowhere *'96*
Malicious *'95*
Roosters *'95*

Rolf Lassgard (1955-)
After the Wedding *'06*
Under the Sun *'98*
The White Lioness *'96*

Sydney Lassick (1922-2003)
American Vampire *'97*
Sisters *'97*
Freeway *'95*
Money to Burn *'94*
Deep Cover *'92*
Shakes the Clown *'92*
Committed *'91*
Cool As Ice *'91*
The Art of Dying *'90*
Smooth Talker *'90*
Out on Bail *'89*
Tale of Two Sisters *'89*
Curse 2: The Bite *'88*
Sonny Boy *'87*
Night Patrol *'85*
Silent Madness *'84*
Monaco Forever *'83*
Alligator *'80*
The Unseen *'80*
The Billion Dollar Hobo *'78*
Carrie *'76*

Lyle Latell (1904-67)
Dick Tracy Meets Gruesome *'47*
Dick Tracy's Dilemma *'47*
Dick Tracy vs. Cueball *'46*
Dick Tracy, Detective *'45*

Dick Latessa (1930-)
The Great New Wonderful *'06*
Alfie *'04*
The Event *'03*
Stigmata *'99*
Rockabye *'86*
Izzy & Moe *'85*
Pudd'nhead Wilson *'84*

Anne Latham
Thieves Like Us '74
Mind Warp '72

Louise Latham (1922-)
In Cold Blood '96
Crazy from the Heart '91
Love Field '91
Paradise '91
Toughlove '85
Mass Appeal '84
Lois Gibbs and the Love Canal '82
Pray TV '82
Backstairs at the White House '79
Dying Room Only '73
White Lightning '73
Adam at 6 a.m. '70
Marnie '64

Philip Latham (1927-)
The Two Faces of Evil '82
Dracula, Prince of Darkness '66
The Devil-Ship Pirates '64

Sanaa Lathan (1971-)
Powder Blue '09
Wonderful World '09
The Family That Preys '08
A Raisin in the Sun '08
Something New '06
Alien vs. Predator '04
Out of Time '03
Brown Sugar '02
Catfish in Black Bean Sauce '00
Disappearing Acts '00
Love and Basketball '00
The Best Man '99
The Wood '99
Blade '98

Hugh Latimer (1913-2006)
The Cosmic Monsters '58
Rogue's Yarn '56
Someone at the Door '50

Michael Latimer (1941-)
Man of Violence '71
Prehistoric Women '67

Frank Latimore (1925-98)
Patton '70
The Sergeant '68
The Dolly Sisters '46
The Razor's Edge '46
Shock! '46
13 Rue Madeleine '46

Zoltan Latonovits
Sinbad '71
Cold Days '66

Ney Latorraca (1944-)
The Fable of the Beautiful Pigeon Fancier '88
The Dolphin '87
Opera do Malandro '87

Matt Lattanzi (1959-)
Diving In '90
Catch Me... If You Can '89
Roxanne '87
My Tutor '82
Rich and Famous '81

Andy Lau (1961-)
Warlords '08
House of Flying Daggers '04
Infernal Affairs 3 '03
Running on Karma '03
Infernal Affairs '02
Full Time Killer '01
Running out of Time '99
The Legend of Drunken Master '94
Days of Being Wild '91
As Tears Go By '88

Carina Lau (1964-)
Ashes of Time Redux '08
2046 '04
Infernal Affairs 2 '03
Infernal Affairs 3 '03
Ashes of Time '94
Days of Being Wild '91
Project A: Part 2 '87

Damian Lau (1949-)
Jet Li's The Enforcer '95
The Heroic Trio '93
Duel to the Death '82
Last Hurrah for Chivalry '78

Tak-Wah Lau
See Andy Lau

Chantal Lauby
Mr. Average '06
You and Me '06

Chester Lauck (1901-80)
Goin' to Town '44
So This Is Washington '43
Two Weeks to Live '43
The Bashful Bachelor '42
Dreaming Out Loud '40

Philippe Laudenbach (1936-)
Four Adventures of Reinette and Mirabelle '89
Confidentially Yours '83

Andrew Lauer (1965-)
Gun Shy '00
I'll Be Home for Christmas '98
Screamers '96
Never on Tuesday '88

Jack Laufer
The Learning Curve '01
The Man Who Captured Eichmann '96
And the Band Played On '93
Lost in Yonkers '93

John Laughlin
Love's Abiding Joy '06
Storm Trooper '98
Back to Back '96
Improper Conduct '94
Night Fire '94
Sexual Malice '93
The Lawnmower Man '92
Memphis '91
Motorama '91
Midnight Crossing '87
Space Rage '86
Agatha Christie's Murder with Mirrors '85
Crimes of Passion '84
Footloose '84
The Hills Have Eyes, Part 2 '84

Tom Laughlin (1939-)
The Trial of Billy Jack '74
Billy Jack '71
Born Losers '67
Tall Story '60
South Pacific '58

Charles Laughton (1899-1962)
Advise and Consent '62
Spartacus '60
Witness for the Prosecution '57
Hobson's Choice '53
Salome '53
Young Bess '53
Abbott and Costello Meet Captain Kidd '52
The Strange Door '51
Arch of Triumph '48
The Big Clock '48
The Bribe '48
Man on the Eiffel Tower '48
The Paradine Case '47
Because of Him '45
Captain Kidd '45
The Canterville Ghost '44
Forever and a Day '43
This Land Is Mine '43
Tales of Manhattan '42
The Tuttles of Tahiti '42
It Started with Eve '41
They Knew What They Wanted '40
The Hunchback of Notre Dame '39
Jamaica Inn '39
Beachcomber '38
Sidewalks of London '38
Rembrandt '36
Les Miserables '35
Mutiny on the Bounty '35
Ruggles of Red Gap '35
The Barretts of Wimpole Street '34
The Private Life of Henry VIII '33
The Sign of the Cross '33
The Devil and the Deep '32
Island of Lost Souls '32
The Old Dark House '32

S. John Launer (1919-2006)
Crime of Passion '57
I Was a Teenage Werewolf '57

Rik Launspach (1958-)
Manderlay '05
The Delivery '99

Cyndi Lauper (1953-)
Life with Mikey '93
Mother Goose Rock 'n' Rhyme '90
Off and Running '90
Vibes '88

Matthew Laurance (1950-)
Perfect Assassins '98
Eddie and the Cruisers 2: Eddie Lives! '89
Eddie and the Cruisers '83

Mitchell Laurance (1950-)
The Portrait '93
The Hand that Rocks the Cradle '92
Syngenor '90
Stepfather 2: Make Room for Daddy '89
A Conspiracy of Love '87

Carole Laure (1951-)
Surrogate '88
Sweet Country '87
Heartbreakers '84
Maria Chapdelaine '84
Victory '81
Dirty Dishes '78
Get Out Your Handkerchiefs '78
Born for Hell '76
Strange Shadows in an Empty Room '76
Sweet Movie '75
The Apprentice '71

Stan Laurel (1890-1965)
Days of Thrills and Laughter '61
Utopia '51
Bullfighters '45
Nothing But Trouble '44
Air Raid Wardens '43
Great Guns '41
A Chump at Oxford '40
Saps at Sea '40
The Flying Deuces '39
Block-heads '38
Swiss Miss '38
Pick a Star '37
Way Out West '37
Bohemian Girl '36
Our Relations '36
Bonnie Scotland '35
Hollywood Party '34
Laurel & Hardy Spooktacular '34
March of the Wooden Soldiers '34
The Devil's Brother '33
Laurel & Hardy and the Family '33
Laurel & Hardy: Stan "Helps" Ollie '33
Sons of the Desert '33
Laurel & Hardy: At Work '32
Pack Up Your Troubles '32
Laurel & Hardy: Be Big '31
Laurel & Hardy: Chickens Come Home '31
Laurel & Hardy: Laughing Gravy '31
Pardon Us '31
Laurel & Hardy: Another Fine Mess '30
Laurel & Hardy: Below Zero '30
Laurel & Hardy: Blotto '30
Laurel & Hardy: Brats '30
Laurel & Hardy: Hog Wild '30
Laurel & Hardy: Night Owls '30
Laurel & Hardy On the Lam '30
Laurel & Hardy: Berth Marks '29
Laurel & Hardy: Men O'War '29
Laurel & Hardy: Perfect Day '29
Laurel & Hardy: The Hoose-Gow '29

Andrew Lauren (1969-)
G '02
Far Harbor '96

Ashley Lauren
See Ashley Laurence

Greg Lauren (1970-)
Friends and Family '01
The Prophet's Game '99
Boys Life '94

Rod Lauren (1940-)
Once Before I Die '65
The Crawling Hand '63

Tammy Lauren (1969-)
Wishmaster '97
The Last Flight of Noah's Ark '80

Veronica Lauren (1980-)
Homeward Bound 2: Lost in San Francisco '96
Homeward Bound: The Incredible Journey '93

Andy Laurence
Family Tree '00
Mysterious Mr. Nicholson '47

Ashley Laurence (1971-)
Chill '06
Hellraiser: Hellseeker '02
Cypress Edge '99
Warlock 3: The End of Innocence '98
The Real Thing '97
Cupid '96
Felony '95
The Fighter '95
Outside the Law '95
Triplecross '95
American Cop '94
Lurking Fear '94
Hellraiser 3: Hell on Earth '92
Mikey '92
One Last Run '89
Hellbound: Hellraiser 2 '88
Hellraiser '87

Michael Laurence
Room 314 '07
The Operator '01

Phil Laurensen
The Gore-Gore Girls '72
The Wizard of Gore '70

James Laurenson (1935-)
Ghostboat '06
Three Blind Mice '02
The Cat's Meow '01
Sharpe's Mission '96
Sharpe's Regiment '96
Sharpe's Siege '96
Cold Light of Day '95
A House in the Hills '93
Codename Kyril '91
Rainbow Drive '90
Heartbreakers '84
Pink Floyd: The Wall '82
Rude Awakening '81
Assault '70

Agnes Laurent
Girl in His Pocket '57
The Twilight Girls '57

Melanie Laurent
Inglourious Basterds '09
Paris '08
The Beat My Heart Skipped '05

Remy Laurent (1957-89)
The Gift '82
La Cage aux Folles '78

Joanie Laurer (1970-)
Cougar Club '07
Frank McKlusky, C.I. '02
Alien Fury: Countdown to Invasion '00

Dan Lauria (1947-)
Alien Trespass '09
Dear Me: A Blogger's Tale '08
Finish Line '08
The Spirit '08
The Bronx Is Burning '07
Big Momma's House 2 '06
Common Ground '00
Full Disclosure '00
Hangman '00
Fear Runs Silent '99
Dean Koontz's Mr. Murder '98
From the Earth to the Moon '98
Ricochet River '98
True Friends '98
Dogwatch '97
Prison of Secrets '97
Wide Awake '97
Independence Day '96
In the Line of Duty: Ambush in Waco '93
In the Line of Duty: A Cop for the Killing '90
Skin '89
Stakeout '87

Hugh Laurie (1959-)
Monsters vs. Aliens '09 (V)
Street Kings '08
Valiant '05 (V)
Flight of the Phoenix '04
Stuart Little 2 '02
Life with Judy Garland—Me and My Shadows '01
Maybe Baby '99
Stuart Little '99
The Man in the Iron Mask '98
The Borrowers '97
Cousin Bette '97
Spice World: The Movie '97
101 Dalmatians '96
Sense and Sensibility '95
All or Nothing at All '93
Peter's Friends '92
Strapless '90

John Laurie (1897-1980)
The Reptile '66
Devil Girl from Mars '54
Love in Pawn '53
Encore '52
Madeleine '50
No Trace '50
Trio '50
Bonnie Prince Charlie '48
Hamlet '48
Man of Evil '48
Mine Own Executioner '47
The World Owes Me a Living '47
Henry V '44
Immortal Battalion '44
Dangerous Moonlight '41
Clouds over Europe '39
The Four Feathers '39
Edge of the World '37
Nine Days a Queen '36
The 39 Steps '35
Juno and the Paycock '30

Piper Laurie (1932-)
Hesher '10
Hounddog '08
The Dead Girl '06
Eulogy '04
Possessed '00
Inherit the Wind '99
St. Patrick's Day '99
The Faculty '98
Horton Foote's Alone '97
The Road to Galveston '96
The Grass Harp '95
The Crossing Guard '94
Dario Argento's Trauma '93
Rich in Love '93
Wrestling Ernest Hemingway '93
Storyville '92
Other People's Money '91
Rising Son '90
Dream a Little Dream '89
Appointment with Death '88
Distortions '87
Tiger Warsaw '87
Children of a Lesser God '86
Return to Oz '85
Toughlove '85
Mae West '84
The Thorn Birds '83
Skag '79
Tim '79
Boss' Son '78
Ruby '77
Carrie '76
The Hustler '61
Days of Wine and Roses '58
Until They Sail '57
Dangerous Mission '54
Son of Ali Baba '52
Francis Goes to the Races '51

Charlotte Laurier (1966-)
2 Seconds '98
Les Bons Debarras '81

Lucie Laurier (1975-)
Bon Cop Bad Cop '06
Seducing Doctor Lewis '03
Stiletto Dance '01
Strip Search '97

Ed Lauter (1940-)
The Number 23 '07
The Prince and the Pauper '07
Seraphim Falls '06
Art Heist '05
Into the Fire '05
The Longest Yard '05
Starship Troopers 2: Hero of the Federation '04
Seabiscuit '03
Not Another Teen Movie '01
Thirteen Days '00
Malicious Intent '99
A Bright Shining Lie '98
For Which He Stands '98
Allie & Me '97
Coyote Summer '96
Mercenary '96
Rattled '96
Breach of Trust '95
Leaving Las Vegas '95
Mulholland Falls '95
Ravenhawk '95
The Sweeper '95
Black Water '94
Digital Man '94
Girl in the Cadillac '94
Trial by Jury '94
Extreme Justice '93
Murder So Sweet '93
True Romance '93
Under Investigation '93
School Ties '92
The Rocketeer '91
Stephen King's Golden Years '91
Goodbye, Miss 4th of July '88
Revenge of the Nerds 2: Nerds in Paradise '87
The Last Days of Patton '86
Youngblood '86
Yuri Nosenko, KGB '86
Death Wish 3 '85
Girls Just Want to Have Fun '85
Nickel Mountain '85
Real Genius '85
Cartier Affair '84
Finders Keepers '84
Lassiter '84
Big Score '83
Cujo '83

Timerider '83
The Amateur '82
In the Custody of Strangers '82
Death Hunt '81
Eureka! '81
Love's Savage Fury '79
Magic '78
The Chicken Chronicles '77
Breakheart Pass '76
Family Plot '76
King Kong '76
The Longest Yard '74
The Migrants '74
Class of '63 '73
The Last American Hero '73

Harry Lauter (1914-90)
Escape from the Planet of the Apes '71
Tarzan's Fight for Life '58
Trader Tom of the China Seas '54
Thunder in God's Country '51
Bandit King of Texas '49

Heiner Lauterbach
Dresden '06
Men... '85

Kathrin Lautner
Two Bits & Pepper '95
Final Impact '91
The Last Riders '90
Night of the Wilding '90
Spirits '90

Taylor Lautner (1992-)
The Twilight Saga: Eclipse '10
The Twilight Saga: New Moon '09
Twilight '08
The Adventures of Sharkboy and Lavagirl in 3-D '05
Cheaper by the Dozen 2 '05

Rene Lavan (1968-)
Christmas With the Kranks '04
Dirty Dancing: Havana Nights '04
Bitter Sugar '96

Dominque Lavanant (1944-)
The Monster '96
Three Men and a Cradle '85
Hotel America '81
French Fried Vacation '79

Denis Lavant (1961-)
Mister Lonely '07
A Very Long Engagement '04
Beau Travail '98
The Lovers on the Bridge '91
Mauvais Sang '86
Boy Meets Girl '84

Lucille LaVerne (1872-1945)
Snow White and the Seven Dwarfs '37 (V)
Kentucky Kernels '34
Hearts of Humanity '32
Wayne Murder Case '32
An American Tragedy '31
The White Rose '23

Amos Lavi
Lemon Tree '08
Blink of an Eye '92

Daliah Lavi (1942-)
Those Fantastic Flying Fools '67
The Silencers '66
Spy with a Cold Nose '66
Lord Jim '65
Apache's Last Battle '64
The Whip and the Body '63
Two Weeks in Another Town '62
The Return of Dr. Mabuse '61

Gabriele Lavia (1942-)
Revenge of the Dead '84
Zeder '83
Deep Red: Hatchet Murders '75

Avril Lavigne (1984-)
The Flock '07
Fast Food Nation '06
Over the Hedge '06 (V)

Linda Lavin (1937-)
Collected Stories '02
I Want to Go Home '89
See You in the Morning '89
Maricela '88
The Muppets Take Manhattan '84
A Matter of Life and Death '81
The $5.20 an Hour Dream '80

Marc Lavoine (1962-)
The Good Thief '03
Fiesta '95
L'Enfer '93

Adam LaVorgna (1981-)
Outside Providence '99
I'll Be Home for Christmas '98

John Phillip Law (1937-)
CQ '01
Hindsight '97
My Magic Dog '97
Cold Heat '90
Alienator '89
Space Mutiny '88
Thunder Warrior 3 '88
Moon in Scorpio '86
L.A. Bad '85
American Commandos '84
Attack Force Z '84
Night Train to Terror '84
No Time to Die '84
Overthrow '82
Tarzan, the Ape Man '81
African Rage '78
The Cassandra Crossing '76
Spiral Staircase '75
Golden Voyage of Sinbad '73
The Last Movie '71
The Love Machine '71
Barbarella '68
Danger: Diabolik '68
The Sergeant '68
The Russians Are Coming, the Russians Are Coming '66

Jude Law (1972-)
Repo Men '10
The Imaginarium of Doctor Parnassus '09
Sherlock Holmes '09
My Blueberry Nights '07
Sleuth '07
All the King's Men '06
Breaking and Entering '06
The Holiday '06
Alfie '04
The Aviator '04
Closer '04
I Heart Huckabees '04
Lemony Snicket's A Series of Unfortunate Events '04
Sky Captain and the World of Tomorrow '04
Cold Mountain '03
Road to Perdition '02
A. I.: Artificial Intelligence '01
Enemy at the Gates '00
Love, Honour & Obey '00
eXistenZ '99
The Talented Mr. Ripley '99
Final Cut '98
Immortality '98
Bent '97
Gattaca '97
I Love You, I Love You Not '97
Midnight in the Garden of Good and Evil '97
Music from Another Room '97
Wilde '97
Shopping '93

Phyllida Law (1932-)
Miss Austen Regrets '07
Day of Wrath '06
Miss Potter '06
Pinochet's Last Stand '06
A Little Trip to Heaven '05
Brush with Fate '03
The Time Machine '02
Two Men Went to War '02
The Magical Legend of the Leprechauns '99
I Want You '98
The Winter Guest '97
Emma '96
Leo Tolstoy's Anna Karenina '96
Before the Rain '94
All or Nothing at All '93
Much Ado about Nothing '93
Peter's Friends '92
Hitler: The Last Ten Days '73

Christopher Lawford (1955-)
The World's Fastest Indian '05
Counterstrike '03
The 6th Day '00
Thirteen Days '00
Mary, Mother of Jesus '99
The Confession '98
Kiss Me, Guido '97
The Abduction '96
The Russia House '90
Mr. North '88

Peter Lawford (1923-84)
Body & Soul '81
Angel's Brigade '79
Mysterious Island of Beautiful Women '79
Fantasy Island '76
Rosebud '75
They Only Kill Their Masters '72
One More Time '70
Togetherness '70
April Fools '69
Buona Sera, Mrs. Campbell '68
Salt & Pepper '68
A Man Called Adam '66
The Oscar '66
Harlow '65
Dead Ringer '64
Advise and Consent '62
The Longest Day '62
Sergeants 3 '62
Exodus '60
Ocean's 11 '60
Never So Few '59
It Should Happen to You '54
Royal Wedding '51
Little Women '49
Easter Parade '48
Julia Misbehaves '48
On an Island with You '48
Good News '47
It Happened in Brooklyn '47
Picture of Dorian Gray '45
Son of Lassie '45
The Canterville Ghost '44
The White Cliffs of Dover '44
Immortal Sergeant '43
Sahara '43
Junior Army '42
Mrs. Miniver '42
Thunder Birds '42

Lucy Lawless (1968-)
Angel of Death '09
Bedtime Stories '08
Boogeyman '05
Eurotrip '04
Spider-Man '02
Hercules the Legendary Journeys, Vol. 1: And the Amazon Women '94

Yvonne Lawley (1914-99)
Death in Brunswick '90
Among the Cinders '83

Sean Lawlor
Mega Shark Vs. Giant Octopus '09
Red Roses and Petrol '03

Stephanie Lawlor
Hot T-Shirts '79
Cherry Hill High '76

Barbara Lawrence (1928-)
Kronos '57
Man in the Shadow '57
Oklahoma! '55
Here Come the Nelsons '52
The Star '52
A Letter to Three Wives '49
The Street with No Name '48

Bruno Lawrence (1941-95)
Jack Be Nimble '94
Rainbow Warrior '94
The Efficiency Expert '92
Grievous Bodily Harm '89
Rikky and Pete '88
The Bridge to Nowhere '86
An Indecent Obsession '85
The Quiet Earth '85
Heart of the Stag '84
Treasure of the Yankee Zephyr '83
Utu '83
Smash Palace '82

Carol Lawrence (1934-)
Shattered Image '93
Summer of Fear '78
New Faces of 1952 '54

Carolyn Lawrence (1964-)
The SpongeBob SquarePants Movie '04 (V)
Jimmy Neutron: Boy Genius '01 (V)

Cary Lawrence
Canvas: The Fine Art of Crime '92
The Dance Goes On '92

Delphi Lawrence (1926-2002)
Frozen Alive '64
Murder on Approval '56
Three Stops to Murder '53

Elizabeth Lawrence (1922-2000)
Unbreakable '00
The Crucible '96
Sleeping with the Enemy '91

Gertrude Lawrence (1898-1952)
Stage Door Canteen '43
Men Are Not Gods '37
Rembrandt '36
Mimi '35

Jennifer Lawrence
Winter's Bone '10
The Poker House '09
The Burning Plain '08

Joey Lawrence (1976-)
Together Again for the First Time '08
Killer Pad '06
Tequila Body Shots '99
Radioland Murders '94
Mrs. Doubtfire '93
Chains of Gold '92
Oliver & Company '88 (V)
Pulse '88
Wait Till Your Mother Gets Home '83

John Lawrence (1931-92)
They Live '88
The Asphyx '72
The Manchurian Candidate '62

Joseph Lawrence
Rest Stop '06
Confessions of a Sociopathic Social Climber '05
Urban Legends 2: Final Cut '00

Marc Lawrence (1910-2005)
Gotti '96
Ruby '92
The Big Easy '87
Night Train to Terror '84
Cataclysm '81
Foul Play '78
Goin' Coconuts '78
King of Kong Island '78
Marathon Man '76
The Man with the Golden Gun '74
Frasier the Sensuous Lion '73
Pigs '73
Dream No Evil '70
Krakatoa East of Java '69
Abbott and Costello in the Foreign Legion '50
The Asphalt Jungle '50
The Black Hand '50
Jigsaw '49
Tough Assignment '49
Cloak and Dagger '46
'Neath Brooklyn Bridge '42
This Gun for Hire '42
The Monster and the Girl '41
Brigham Young: Frontiersman '40
Charlie Chan at the Wax Museum '40
Johnny Apollo '40
Invisible Stripes '39
Adventure in Sahara '38
I Am the Law '38
The Spider's Web '38
Murder in Greenwich Village '37
San Quentin '37
Vengeance '37

Mark Christopher Lawrence (1964-)
That Darn Cat '96
Fear of a Black Hat '94

Martin Lawrence (1965-)
Death at a Funeral '10
College Road Trip '08
Welcome Home Roscoe Jenkins '08
Wild Hogs '07
Big Momma's House 2 '06
Open Season '06 (V)
Rebound '05
Bad Boys 2 '03
National Security '03
Black Knight '01
What's the Worst That Could Happen? '01
Big Momma's House '00
Blue Streak '99
Life '99
Nothing to Lose '96
A Thin Line Between Love and Hate '96
Bad Boys '95
You So Crazy '94
Boomerang '92
House Party 2: The Pajama Jam '91
Talkin' Dirty after Dark '91
House Party '90

Matthew Lawrence (1980-)
The Comebacks '07
The Hot Chick '02
Family Tree '00
All I Wanna Do '98
Angels in the Endzone '98
Boltneck '98
Kiki's Delivery Service '98 (V)
Undesirable '92
Tales from the Darkside: The Movie '90

Michael Lawrence
The Price of Milk '00
Othello '52
Elizabeth of Ladymead '48

Peter Lee Lawrence (1943-73)
Garringo '69
They Paid with Bullets: Chicago 1929 '69
Special Forces '68

Rosina Lawrence (1913-97)
Pick a Star '37
Way Out West '37
General Spanky '36
Charlie Chan's Secret '35

Scott Lawrence
Timecop '94
Laurel Avenue '93
God's Bloody Acre '75

Sharon Lawrence (1963-)
Lies & Alibis '06
Aftershock: Earthquake in New York '99
Gossip '99
The Only Thrill '97
Degree of Guilt '95
The Heidi Chronicles '95

Sheldon Lawrence
Sweet Beat '59
Black Tide '58

Stephanie Lawrence (1949-2000)
The Phantom of the Opera '89
Buster '88

Steve Lawrence (1935-)
Ocean's Eleven '01
The Yards '00
Blues Brothers 2000 '98
Alice in Wonderland '85
The Lonely Guy '84
The Blues Brothers '80
Express to Terror '79

Steven Anthony Lawrence (1995-)
Kicking & Screaming '05
Rebound '05
Cheaper by the Dozen '03

Vicki Lawrence
Hannah Montana: The Movie '09
National Lampoon's Attack of the 5 Ft. 2 Women '94

Robert Lawrenson
Beyond Sherwood Forest '09

Bianca Lawson (1979-)
Breakin' All The Rules '04
Anne Rice's The Feast of All Saints '01
Bones '01
Save the Last Dance '01
Boltneck '98

Denis Lawson (1947-)
Jekyll '07
Bleak House '05
Horatio Hornblower '99
Catherine Cookson's The Round Tower '98
A Royal Scandal '96
Local Hero '83
Return of the Jedi '83

Leigh Lawson (1945-)
The Courageous Heart of Irena Sendler '09
Casanova '05
Being Julia '04
Back to the Secret Garden '01
Battling for Baby '92
O Pioneers! '91
Madame Sousatzka '88
Tears in the Rain '88
Sword of the Valiant '83
Agatha Christie's Murder is Easy '82
Fire and Sword '82
Charlie Boy '81
Disraeli '79
Tess '79
Love Among the Ruins '75
It's Not the Size That Counts '74
Madhouse Mansion '74
Brother Sun, Sister Moon '73

Louise Lawson
Creeping Terror *'64*
The Bellboy and the Playgirls *'62*

Maggie Lawson (1980-)
Cleaner *'07*
Winter Break *'02*
Model Behavior *'00*

Priscilla Lawson (1914-58)
Flash Gordon: Rocketship *'40*
Girl of the Golden West *'38*
Heroes of the Hills *'38*

Richard Lawson (1947-)
Christmas at Water's Edge *'04*
Black Listed *'03*
Blue Hill Avenue *'01*
How Stella Got Her Groove Back *'98*
Pandora's Clock *'96*
The Forgotten *'89*
The Reluctant Agent *'89*
Johnnie Gibson F.B.I. *'87*
Streets of Fire *'84*
Poltergeist *'82*
Coming Home *'78*
Fist *'76*
Homeboy *'75*
Foxstyle *'73*
Scream Blacula Scream *'73*

Sarah Lawson (1928-)
The Devil Rides Out *'68*
Island of the Burning Doomed *'67*

Shannon Lawson
Last Call: The Final Chapter of F. Scott Fitzgerald *'02*
Possessed *'00*
Anne of Green Gables: The Continuing Story *'99*
Heck's Way Home *'95*

Wilfred Lawson (1900-66)
Room at the Top *'59*
War and Peace *'56*
The Prisoner *'55*
Man of Evil *'48*
Thursday's Child *'43*
The Night Has Eyes *'42*
Tower of Terror *'42*
Pygmalion *'38*
The Terror *'38*

Marlene Lawston
Dan in Real Life *'07*
Flightplan *'05*

Chas Lawther
Urban Legends 2: Final Cut *'00*
Love Letters *'99*

Frank Lawton (1904-69)
A Night to Remember *'58*
The Winslow Boy *'48*
The Secret Four *'40*
The Mill on the Floss *'37*
Devil Doll *'36*
The Invisible Ray *'36*
David Copperfield *'35*
Cavalcade *'33*
Skin Game *'31*

Evelyn Laye (1900-96)
Say Hello to Yesterday *'71*
Theatre of Death *'67*

John Lazar (1934-)
Attack of the 60-Foot Centerfold *'95*
Night of the Scarecrow *'95*
Over the Wire *'95*
Eddie Presley *'92*
Deathstalker 2: Duel of the Titans *'87*
Every Girl Should Have One *'78*
Beyond the Valley of the Dolls *'70*

Justin Lazard (1967-)
The Brutal Truth *'99*
Universal Soldier: The Return *'99*
Species 2 *'98*
The Big Fall *'96*
Dead Center *'94*

Eugene (Yevgeny) Lazarev
Lord of War *'05*
Pearl Diver *'04*
The Sum of All Fears *'02*
The Saint *'97*
The Ice Runner *'93*

Eusebio Lazaro (1942-)
Twice upon a Yesterday *'98*
The Return of the Musketeers *'89*

George Lazenby (1939-)
Winter Break *'02*
Spider's Web *'01*
Four Dogs Playing Poker *'00*
Fatally Yours *'95*
Twinsitters *'95*
Gettysburg *'93*
Eyes of the Beholder *'92*
Hell Hunters *'87*
Never Too Young to Die *'86*
Saint Jack *'79*
Black Eliminator *'78*
Kill Factor *'78*
Kentucky Fried Movie *'77*
Who Saw Her Die? *'72*
On Her Majesty's Secret Service *'69*

Bruce Le
Clones of Bruce Lee *'80*
The Young Bruce Lee *'80*
Bruce Lee Fights Back from the Grave *'76*
Super Inframan *'76*

Hiep Thi Le (1970-)
Green Dragon *'01*
Heaven and Earth *'93*

Becky Le Beau
See Becky LeBeau

Islid Le Besco (1982-)
A Song of Innocence *'05*
Sade *'00*
Girls Can't Swim *'99*

Maiwenn Le Besco (1976-)
High Tension *'03*
The Fifth Element *'97*
The Elegant Criminal *'92*

Samuel Le Bihan (1965-)
He Loves Me ... He Loves Me Not *'02*
Brotherhood of the Wolf *'01*
Total Western *'00*
For Sale *'98*
Venus Beauty Institute *'98*
Capitaine Conan *'96*
Trois Couleurs: Rouge *'94*

Gene Le Brock (1961-)
Beyond Darkness *'92*
Metamorphosis *'90*
Fortress of Amerikka *'89*

Kelly Le Brock (1960-)
Wrongfully Accused *'98*
Tracks of a Killer *'95*
Hard Bounty *'94*
Betrayal of the Dove *'92*
Hard to Kill *'89*
Weird Science *'85*
The Woman in Red *'84*

Bernard Le Coq (1950-)
Times Have Been Better *'06*
Hidden *'05*
Joyeux Noel *'05*
The Bridesmaid *'04*
Capitaine Conan *'96*
Van Gogh *'92*

Jake Le Doux
See Jake LeDoux

Steve Le Marquand (1967-)
Rodgers & Hammerstein's South Pacific *'01*
Vertical Limit *'00*

John Le Mesurier (1912-83)
A Married Man *'84*
Brideshead Revisited *'81*
The Fiendish Plot of Dr. Fu Manchu *'80*
The Adventures of Sherlock Holmes' Smarter Brother *'78*
Jabberwocky *'77*
Salt & Pepper *'68*
Dead Lucky *'60*
Jack the Ripper *'60*
Brothers in Law *'57*
The Baby and the Battleship *'56*

Paul Le Person
Phantom of Liberty *'74*
The Thief of Paris *'67*

Nicholas Le Prevost (1947-)
Miss Conception *'08*
Half Broken Things *'07*
P.D. James: The Murder Room *'04*
The Camomile Lawn *'92*
A Fatal Inversion *'92*
The Girl in a Swing *'89*

Sylvestria Le Touzel
Happy-Go-Lucky *'08*
Northanger Abbey *'07*
Amazing Grace *'06*
Catherine Cookson's The Gambling Man *'98*
Mansfield Park *'85*

Nicholas Lea (1962-)
Vice *'08*
American Venus *'07*
Shattered *'07*
Category 7 : The End of the World *'05*
Moving Malcolm *'03*
Threshold *'03*
Ignition *'01*
Kiss Tomorrow Goodbye *'00*
Vertical Limit *'00*
Once a Thief *'96*
The Raffle *'94*
Xtro 2: The Second Encounter *'91*

Ron Lea
A Different Loyalty *'04*
Sea People *'00*
A Map of the World *'99*
The Neighbor *'93*
Clearcut *'92*
The Phone Call *'89*

Britt Leach
Baby Boom *'87*
The California Kid *'74*

Rosemary Leach (1925-)
Catherine Cookson's Tilly Trotter *'99*
Berkeley Square *'98*
The Buccaneers *'95*
The Hawk *'93*
The Mystery of Edwin Drood *'93*
The Children *'90*
The Charmer *'87*
A Room with a View *'86*
Turtle Diary *'86*
D.P. *'85*
The Seventeenth Bride *'84*
Disraeli *'79*
Ghost in the Noonday Sun *'74*
That'll Be the Day *'73*

Cloris Leachman (1930-)
Inglourious Basterds *'09*
Love Takes Wing *'09*
New York, I Love You *'09*
Ponyo *'08 (V)*
The Women *'08*
Lake Placid 2 *'07*
Beerfest *'06*
Scary Movie 4 *'06*
The Longest Yard *'05*
Mrs. Harris *'05*
Sky High *'05*
Spanglish *'04*
Alex & Emma *'03*
Bad Santa *'03*
Manna from Heaven *'02*
Hanging Up *'99*
The Iron Giant *'99 (V)*
Music of the Heart *'99*
Beavis and Butt-Head Do America *'96 (V)*
Now and Then *'95*
Double Double Toil and Trouble *'94*
A Troll in Central Park *'94 (V)*
The Beverly Hillbillies *'93*
Fade to Black *'93*
My Boyfriend's Back *'93*
Danielle Steel's Fine Things *'90*
Texasville *'90*
Prancer *'89*
Walk Like a Man *'87*
Shadow Play *'86*
Dixie: Changing Habits *'85*
Ernie Kovacs: Between the Laughter *'84*
The Woman Who Willed a Miracle *'83*
Acorn People *'82*
Miss All-American Beauty *'82*
History of the World: Part 1 *'81*
The Victory *'81*
Foolin' Around *'80*
Herbie Goes Bananas *'80*
Oldest Living Graduate *'80*
Backstairs at the White House *'79*
Mrs. R's Daughter *'79*
The Muppet Movie *'79*
The North Avenue Irregulars *'79*
Scavenger Hunt *'79*
S.O.S. Titanic *'79*
Willa *'79*
Long Journey Back *'78*
High Anxiety *'77*
Mouse and His Child *'77 (V)*
Crazy Mama *'75*
Death Scream *'75*
Someone I Touched *'75*
Daisy Miller *'74*
Death Sentence *'74*
The Migrants *'74*
Thursday's Game *'74*
Young Frankenstein *'74*
Charley and the Angel *'73*
Dillinger *'73*
Dying Room Only *'73*
Run, Stranger, Run *'73*
Brand New Life *'72*
Haunts of the Very Rich *'72*
The Last Picture Show *'71*
The Steagle *'71*
Lovers and Other Strangers *'70*
The People Next Door *'70*
Butch Cassidy and the Sundance Kid *'69*
Silent Night, Lonely Night *'69*
Kiss Me Deadly *'55*

Richard Leacock
That Russell Girl *'08*
The Note *'07*

Viv Leacock (1974-)
White Coats *'04*
I Spy *'02*

Damien Leake
Killing Floor *'85*
Apocalypse Now *'79*

Sharon Leal (1972-)
Tyler Perry's Why Did I Get Married Too? *'10*
Linewatch *'08*
Soul Men *'08*
This Christmas *'07*
Tyler Perry's Why Did I Get Married? *'07*
Dreamgirls *'06*
Face the Music *'00*

Michael Learned (1939-)
American Girl: Chrissa Stands Strong *'09*
Loggerheads *'05*
Dragon: The Bruce Lee Story *'93*
Murder in New Hampshire: The Pamela Smart Story *'91*
Roots: The Gift *'88*
All My Sons *'86*
Deadly Business *'86*
Power *'86*
A Christmas Without Snow *'80*
Nurse *'80*
The Widow *'76*

Denis Leary (1957-)
Ice Age: Dawn of the Dinosaurs *'09 (V)*
Recount *'08*
Ice Age: The Meltdown *'06 (V)*
Dawg *'02*
Ice Age *'02 (V)*
The Secret Lives of Dentists *'02*
Double Whammy *'01*
Final *'01*
Company Man *'00*
Lakeboat *'00*
Sand *'00*
Jesus' Son *'99*
Silent Witness *'99*
The Thomas Crown Affair *'99*
True Crime *'99*
A Bug's Life *'98 (V)*
Monument Ave. *'98*
Small Soldiers *'98*
Love Walked In *'97*
The Matchmaker *'97*
The Real Blonde *'97*
The Second Civil War *'97*
Subway Stories *'97*
Suicide Kings *'97*
Wag the Dog *'97*
Wide Awake *'97*
Underworld *'96*
National Lampoon's Favorite Deadly Sins *'95*
The Neon Bible *'95*
Operation Dumbo Drop *'95*
Two If by Sea *'95*
Natural Born Killers *'94*
Demolition Man *'93*
Gunmen *'93*
Judgment Night *'93*
National Lampoon's Loaded Weapon 1 *'93*
The Ref *'93*
The Sandlot *'93*
Who's the Man? *'93*

Timothy Leary (1920-96)
Conceiving Ada *'97*
Hold Me, Thrill Me, Kiss Me *'93*
Ted & Venus *'93*
Roadside Prophets *'92*
Fatal Skies *'90*
Shocker *'89*
Cheech and Chong's Nice Dreams *'81*

Rex Lease (1901-66)
Lost in Alaska *'52*
Gun Cargo *'49*
People's Choice *'46*
Haunted Ranch *'43*
The Silver Bullet *'42*
Billy the Kid in Santa Fe *'41*
Outlaws of the Rio Grande *'41*
Texas Trouble *'41*
Heroes of the Alamo *'37*
Riding On *'37*
Aces and Eights *'36*
Cavalcade of the West *'36*
The Clutching Hand *'36*
Custer's Last Stand *'36*
Fast Bullets *'36*
Lightnin' Bill Carson *'36*
The Man from Gun Town *'36*
Roaring Guns *'36*
Cowboy & the Bandit *'35*
Cyclone of the Saddle *'35*
Fighting Caballero *'35*
Ghost Rider *'35*
Pals of the Range *'35*
Rough Riding Ranger *'35*
Inside Information *'34*
The Monster Walks *'32*
Chinatown After Dark *'31*
Sunny Skies *'30*

Jean-Pierre Leaud (1944-)
What Time Is It There? *'01*
Irma Vep *'96*
Mon Homme *'96*
Diary of a Seducer *'95*
La Vie de Boheme *'93*
36 Fillete *'88*
Detective *'85*
Love on the Run *'78*
Day for Night *'73*
Last Tango in Paris *'73*
The Mother and the Whore *'73*
Two English Girls *'72*
Bed and Board *'70*
Porcile *'69*
Stolen Kisses *'68*
La Chinoise *'67*
Weekend *'67*
Masculine Feminine *'66*
Alphaville *'65*
The Joy of Knowledge *'65*
Pierrot le Fou *'65*
The 400 Blows *'59*
The Testament of Orpheus *'59*

Becky LeBeau (1962-)
The Malibu Beach Vampires *'91*
Not of This Earth *'88*

Madeleine LeBeau (1921-)
8 1/2 *'63*
Une Parisienne *'58*
Casablanca *'42*

Pierre Lebeau
Bon Cop Bad Cop *'06*
The Boys *'97*

Ivan Lebedeff (1894-1953)
Love on the Run *'36*
Goin' to Town *'35*
Bachelor Apartment *'31*
The Lady Refuses *'31*
They Had to See Paris *'29*
Walking Back *'26*

Matt LeBlanc (1967-)
Charlie's Angels: Full Throttle *'03*
All the Queen's Men *'02*
Charlie's Angels *'00*
Lost in Space *'98*
Ed *'96*
Showdown *'94*
The Ghost Brigade *'93*
Red Shoe Diaries 3: Another Woman's Lipstick *'93*

Geno Lechner (1965-)
Love *'05*
Flirt *'95*

Brian Leckner (1967-)
Joy Ride *'01*
Sgt. Bilko *'95*
Bonanza: The Return *'93*

Michael LeClair
Leave 'Em Laughing *'81*
Anatomy of a Seduction *'79*

Ginette LeClerc (1912-92)
Le Plaisir *'52*
Le Corbeau *'43*
Man from Nowhere *'37*
The Baker's Wife *'33*

Jean LeClerc (1948-)
Blown Away *'93*
Whispers *'89*

Cyril Lecomte
Chrysalis *'07*
The Girl *'01*

Friedrich Ledebur (1900-86)
The 27th Day '57
Moby Dick '56

Erwin Leder (1951-)
Underworld '03
Das Boot '81

Paul Leder (1926-96)
How to Succeed with Girls '64
Five Minutes to Love '63

Francis Lederer (1899-2000)
Terror Is a Man '59
Return of Dracula '58
The Ambassador's Daughter '56
Lisbon '56
Stolen Identity '53
A Woman of Distinction '50
Diary of a Chambermaid '46
The Bridge of San Luis Rey '44
Confessions of a Nazi Spy '39
Midnight '39
One Rainy Afternoon '36
Romance in Manhattan '34
Pandora's Box '28

Otto Lederer
The Cruise of the Jasper B '26
Behind Two Guns '24

Suzanne Lederer (1948-)
Women of Valor '86
Judge Horton and the Scottsboro Boys '76

Brandy Ledford (1969-)
Ice Men '04
We'll Meet Again '02
Zebra Lounge '01

Heath Ledger (1979-2008)
The Imaginarium of Doctor Parnassus '09
The Dark Knight '08
I'm Not There '07
Candy '06
Brokeback Mountain '05
The Brothers Grimm '05
Casanova '05
Lords of Dogtown '05
Ned Kelly '03
The Order '03
The Four Feathers '02
A Knight's Tale '01
Monster's Ball '01
The Patriot '00
Ten Things I Hate about You '99
Two Hands '98

Fernand Ledoux (1897-1993)
Pattes Blanches '49
Les Visiteurs du Soir '42
Volpone '39
La Bete Humaine '38

Jake LeDoux (1985-)
Love Come Down '00
Summer's End '99

Virginie Ledoyen (1976-)
Shall We Kiss '09
Holly '07
Shall We Kiss? '07
The Backwoods '06
The Valet '06
Bon Voyage '03
8 Women '02
The Beach '00
Jeanne and the Perfect Guy '98
Late August, Early September '98
A Soldier's Daughter Never Cries '98
A Single Girl '96
La Ceremonie '95

Richard Leduc
We Will Not Enter the Forest '79
Nous N'Irons Plus au Bois '69

Anna Lee (1913-2004)
Eleanor & Franklin '76
In Like Flint '67
The Sound of Music '65
Jack the Giant Killer '62
What Ever Happened to Baby Jane? '62
The Crimson Kimono '59
The Horse Soldiers '59
Fort Apache '48
The Ghost and Mrs. Muir '47
G.I. War Brides '46
Bedlam '45
Summer Storm '44
Commandos Strike at Dawn '43
Flying Tigers '42
Hangmen Also Die '42
How Green Was My Valley '41
The Secret Four '40
King Solomon's Mines '37
Non-Stop New York '37
O.H.M.S. '37
The Man Who Lived Again '36
The Passing of the Third Floor Back '36
First a Girl '35

Belinda Lee (1935-61)
The Hit Man '60
That Long Night in '43 '60
Who Done It? '56
No Smoking '55
Blackout '54
The Runaway Bus '54
The Belles of St. Trinian's '53

Bernard Lee (1908-81)
Moonraker '79
The Spy Who Loved Me '77
Frankenstein and the Monster from Hell '74
It's Not the Size That Counts '74
The Man with the Golden Gun '74
Live and Let Die '73
Diamonds Are Forever '71
Long Ago Tomorrow '71
10 Rillington Place '71
On Her Majesty's Secret Service '69
You Only Live Twice '67
Thunderball '65
Goldfinger '64
From Russia with Love '63
The Brain '62
Dr. No '62
The L-Shaped Room '62
Whistle down the Wind '61
Across the Bridge '57
The Spanish Gardener '57
The Detective '54
Beat the Devil '53
Sailor of the King '53
The Gift Horse '52
The Adventurers '51
Last Holiday '50
Morning Departure '50
The Blue Lamp '49
The Fallen Idol '49
The Third Man '49
Elizabeth of Ladymead '48
The Courtney Affair '47
The Terror '38
Rhodes '36

Billy Lee (1929-89)
Nevada City '41
Reg'lar Fellers '41
Wagon Wheels '34

Bobby Lee (1972-)
Pineapple Express '08
Kickin' It Old Skool '07

Brandon Lee (1965-93)
The Crow '93
Rapid Fire '92
Showdown in Little Tokyo '91
Laser Mission '90
Kung Fu: The Movie '86
Legacy of Rage '86

Britton Lee
Ironheart '92
The Power of the Ninjitsu '88

Bruce Lee (1940-73)
The Three Avengers '80
Game of Death '79
Chinese Connection 2 '77
Chinese Connection '73
Enter the Dragon '73
Fists of Fury '73
Return of the Dragon '73
Marlowe '69

Byung-hun Lee
G.I. Joe: The Rise of Cobra '09
Three ... Extremes '04
Addicted '02
JSA: Joint Security Area '00

Canada Lee (1907-52)
Cry, the Beloved Country '51
Lost Boundaries '49
Body and Soul '47
Lifeboat '44
Keep Punching '39

Carl Lee (1926-86)
Keeping On '81
Gordon's War '73
Superfly '72
The Cool World '63
The Connection '61

Casey Lee
White Chicks '04
Parental Guidance '98

China Lee (1942-)
Good Times '67
What's Up, Tiger Lily? '66

Christopher Lee (1922-)
Alice in Wonderland '10
The Color of Magic '08 (V)
Star Wars: The Clone Wars '08 (V)
The Golden Compass '07
Charlie and the Chocolate Factory '05
Crimson Rivers 2: Angels of the Apocalypse '05
Star Wars: Episode 3—Revenge of the Sith '05
Tim Burton's Corpse Bride '05 (V)
Lord of the Rings: The Two Towers '02
Star Wars: Episode 2—Attack of the Clones '02
Lord of the Rings: The Fellowship of the Ring '01
Russell Mulcahy's Tale of the Mummy '99
Sleepy Hollow '99
Ivanhoe '97
The Odyssey '97
Moses '96
The Stupids '95
Funnyman '94
Police Academy 7: Mission to Moscow '94
Detonator '93
Double Vision '92
Journey of Honor '91
Sherlock Holmes and the Incident at Victoria Falls '91
Curse 3: Blood Sacrifice '90
Gremlins 2: The New Batch '90
Around the World in 80 Days '89
Murder Story '89
The Return of the Musketeers '89
Treasure Island '89
Jocks '87
The Land of Faraway '87
Desperate Moves '86
The Girl '86
Many Faces of Sherlock Holmes '86
Howling 2: Your Sister Is a Werewolf '85
Rosebud Beach Hotel '85
The Far Pavilions '84
Return of Captain Invincible '83
Shaka Zulu '83
House of the Long Shadows '82
The Last Unicorn '82 (V)
Safari 3000 '82
The Salamander '82
The Boy Who Left Home to Find Out About the Shivers '81
An Eye for an Eye '81
Goliath Awaits '81
Bear Island '80
Serial '80
Captain America 2: Death Too Soon '79
Jaguar Lives '79
1941 '79
Circle of Iron '78
Return from Witch Mountain '78
Airport '77 '77
Starship Invasions '77
Albino '76
Dracula and Son '76
End of the World '76
Keeper '76
To the Devil, a Daughter '76
The Devil's Undead '75
The Four Musketeers '75
The Wicker Man '75
The Man with the Golden Gun '74
The Three Musketeers '74
Dark Places '73
The Satanic Rites of Dracula '73
The Creeping Flesh '72
Dracula A.D. 1972 '72
Hannie Caulder '72
Horror Express '72
Nothing But the Night '72
Raw Meat '72
Count Dracula '71
The House that Dripped Blood '71
I, Monster '71
One More Time '70
The Private Life of Sherlock Holmes '70
The Scars of Dracula '70
Scream and Scream Again '70
Taste the Blood of Dracula '70
The Magic Christian '69
The Oblong Box '69
The Torture Chamber of Dr. Sadism '69
The Castle of Fu Manchu '68
The Crimson Cult '68
The Devil Rides Out '68
Dracula Has Risen from the Grave '68
Kiss and Kill '68
Circus of Fear '67
Five Golden Dragons '67
Island of the Burning Doomed '67
Theatre of Death '67
The Vengeance of Fu Manchu '67
Brides of Fu Manchu '66
Dracula, Prince of Darkness '66
Rasputin the Mad Monk '66
Dr. Terror's House of Horrors '65
She '65
The Skull '65
The Virgin of Nuremberg '65
Castle of the Living Dead '64
The Devil-Ship Pirates '64
The Gorgon '64
Hercules in the Haunted World '64
The Whip and the Body '63
The Longest Day '62
Pirates of Blood River '62
Sherlock Holmes and the Deadly Necklace '62
Scream of Fear '61
The Terror of the Tongs '61
Beat Girl '60
The Hands of Orlac '60
Horror Hotel '60
The Two Faces of Dr. Jekyll '60
The Hound of the Baskervilles '59
The Mummy '59
Uncle Was a Vampire '59
Corridors of Blood '58
The Horror of Dracula '58
Missiles from Hell '58
A Tale of Two Cities '58
The Curse of Frankenstein '57
Night Ambush '57
Alias John Preston '56
Crimson Pirate '52
Moulin Rouge '52
Captain Horatio Hornblower '51
Valley of the Eagles '51
Hamlet '48
Scott of the Antarctic '48

Cinque Lee (1966-)
Rapturious '07
Coffee and Cigarettes '03
Mystery Train '89

Conan Lee
The Eliminators '86
Gymkata '85

Cosette Lee (1910-76)
The Fly '86
Deranged '74

Dae-yeon Lee
Three ... Extremes '04
Sympathy for Mr. Vengeance '02

Danny Lee (1952-)
Organized Crime & Triad Bureau '93
The Untold Story '93
The Killer '90
City on Fire '87
The Mighty Peking Man '77
Sword Masters: The Battle Wizard '77
Super Inframan '76

Davey Lee
Say It With Songs '29
The Singing Fool '28

DeWitt Lee
The Legend of Jedediah Carver '76
Apache Blood '75

Dixie Lee (1911-52)
Love in Bloom '35
Night Life in Reno '31

Dorothy Lee (1911-99)
Cockeyed Cavaliers '34
Hips, Hips, Hooray '34
Half-Shot at Sunrise '30
Hook, Line and Sinker '30
Rio Rita '29

Dragon Lee
Clones of Bruce Lee '80
The Three Avengers '80

Elizabeth Lee
Organized Crime & Triad Bureau '93
Something Weird '68

Eol Lee
Samaritan Girl '04
Addicted '02

Eric Lee (1948-)
Out for Blood '93
Ring of Fire '91

Etta Lee (1906-56)
The Thief of Baghdad '24
The Untamable '23

Florence Lee
City Lights '31
Road Agent '26
Virtue's Revolt '24

Gwen Lee
A Lady of Chance '28

Gypsy Rose Lee (1914-70)
Over the Hill Gang '69
The Trouble with Angels '66
The Stripper '63
My Lucky Star '38

Jae-yong Lee
Chain Gang Girls '08
Save the Green Planet '03

James Kyson Lee
Shutter '08
Asian Stories '06

Jason Lee (1971-)
Alvin and the Chipmunks: The Squeakuel '09
Alvin and the Chipmunks '07
Underdog '07 (V)
Clerks 2 '06
Monster House '06 (V)
The Ballad of Jack and Rose '05
Drop Dead Sexy '05
The Incredibles '04 (V)
Jersey Girl '04
Dreamcatcher '03
A Guy Thing '03
I Love Your Work '03
Big Trouble '02
Stealing Harvard '02
Heartbreakers '01
Jay and Silent Bob Strike Back '01
Vanilla Sky '01
Almost Famous '00
Dogma '99
Mumford '99
Enemy of the State '98
Kissing a Fool '98
Chasing Amy '97
Weapons of Mass Distraction '97
Mallrats '95

Jason Scott Lee (1966-)
Only the Brave '06
Dracula 3: Legacy '05
Lilo & Stitch 2: Stitch Has a Glitch '05 (V)
Dracula 2: Ascension '03
Timecop 2: The Berlin Decision '03
Lilo & Stitch '02 (V)
Arabian Nights '00
Russell Mulcahy's Tale of the Mummy '99
Soldier '98
Murder in Mind '97
Rudyard Kipling's The Jungle Book '94
Dragon: The Bruce Lee Story '93
Map of the Human Heart '93
Rapa Nui '93
The Lookalike '90
Back to the Future, Part 2 '89

Jeong-jin Lee
Seoul Raiders '05
Bloody Beach '00

Jesse Lee (1984-)
A Very Brady Sequel '96
The Brady Bunch Movie '95
From the Mixed-Up Files of Mrs. Basil E. Frankweiler '95
Matinee '92

Joanna Lee (1931-2003)
Making the Grade '84
Sam's Son '84
The Brain Eaters '58
Plan 9 from Outer Space '56

Joie Lee (1962-)
Coffee and Cigarettes '03
Crooklyn '94
Fathers and Sons '92
Mo' Better Blues '90
Bail Jumper '89
School Daze '88
She's Gotta Have It '86

Jon Kit Lee (1967-)
Romeo Must Die '00
The Corruptor '99

Ju-hyeon Lee
Chain Gang Girls *'08*
Save the Green Planet *'03*

Julia Lee
The Hillside Strangler *'04*
Asylum of the Damned *'03*

Kaiulani Lee
Hush *'98*
Before and After *'95*
Zelly & Me *'88*
Cujo *'83*

Kang-sheng Lee
Goodbye, Dragon Inn *'03*
What Time Is It There? *'01*
The Hole *'98*
Rebels of the Neon God *'92*

Karen Lee
Eye on the Sparrow *'91*
Roadhouse 66 *'84*

Kyung-Young Lee
White Badge *'97*
White Badge *'92*

Lila Lee (1901-73)
A Nation Aflame *'37*
Country Gentlemen *'36*
Champagne for Breakfast *'35*
I Can't Escape *'34*
Stand Up and Cheer *'34*
False Faces *'32*
The Unholy Three *'30*
The Adorable Cheat *'28*
Midnight Girl *'25*
Blood and Sand *'22*
Hawthorne of the USA *'19*
Male and Female *'19*

Margaret Lee (1943-)
Rogue *'76*
Slaughter Hotel *'71*
Dorian Gray *'70*
Venus in Furs *'70*
How to Kill 400 Duponts *'68*
Murder for Sale *'68*
Action Man *'67*
Circus of Fear *'67*
Five for Hell *'67*
Five Golden Dragons *'67*
Secret Agent Super Dragon *'66*
Casanova '70 *'65*
Fire Monsters Against the Son of Hercules *'62*

Mark Lee (1958-)
The Junction Boys *'02*
Nowhere to Land *'00*
Chameleon 2: Death Match *'99*
Blackwater Trail *'95*
The Everlasting Secret Family *'88*
The City's Edge *'83*
Gallipoli *'81*

Mary Lee (1925-96)
Back in the Saddle *'41*
Ridin' on a Rainbow *'41*
Gaucho Serenade *'40*
Nancy Drew, Reporter *'39*
South of the Border *'39*

Mi-yeon Lee
Addicted *'02*
Whispering Corridors *'98*
No. 3 *'97*

Michele Lee (1942-)
Along Came Polly *'04*
Broadway Bound *'92*
The Fatal Image *'90*
Bud and Lou *'78*
The Comic *'69*
The Love Bug *'68*
How to Succeed in Business without Really Trying *'67*

Moon Lee (1965-)
Mr. Vampire *'86*
Zu: Warriors from the Magic Mountain *'83*

Peggy Lee (1920-2002)
Lady and the Tramp *'55 (V)*
Pete Kelly's Blues *'55*
Mr. Music *'50*
Stage Door Canteen *'43*

Reggie Lee
Drag Me to Hell *'09*
Frankenfish *'04*

Robbie Lee (1955-)
Switchblade Sisters *'75*
Big Bad Mama *'74*

Robine Lee (1974-)
Hotel for Dogs *'09*
Seven Pounds *'08*
13 Going on 30 *'04*
Deliver Us from Eva *'03*
National Security *'03*
Hav Plenty *'97*

RonReaco Lee (1977-)
Madea Goes to Jail *'09*
Guess Who *'05*
Killer Diller *'04*
How I Spent My Summer Vacation *'97*
Glory *'89*

Ruta Lee (1936-)
Christmas Do-Over *'06*
Funny Bones *'94*
Sweet Bird of Youth *'89*
First & Ten: The Team Scores Again *'85*
Rooster: Spurs of Death! *'83*
Escape from Planet Earth *'67*
Sergeants 3 *'62*
Witness for the Prosecution *'57*

Sam Lee (1975-)
Dog Bite Dog *'06*
Ping Pong *'02*
Special Unit 2002 *'01*
Gen-X Cops *'99*
Biozombie *'98*

Shannon Lee (1969-)
The Gay Bed and Breakfast of Terror *'07*
Epoch *'00*
High Voltage *'98*

Sheryl Lee (1967-)
Winter's Bone *'10*
Paradise, Texas *'05*
Children On Their Birthdays *'02*
Hitched *'01*
Angel's Dance *'99*
Kiss the Sky *'98*
The Blood Oranges *'97*
David *'97*
John Carpenter's Vampires *'97*
This World, Then the Fireworks *'97*
Bliss *'96*
Mother Night *'96*
Follow the River *'95*
Homage *'95*
Notes from Underground *'95*
Backbeat *'94*
Don't Do It *'94*
Fall Time *'94*
Red Shoe Diaries 4: Auto Erotica *'93*
Jersey Girl *'92*
Twin Peaks: Fire Walk with Me *'92*
Love, Lies and Murder *'91*
Wild at Heart *'90*

Sophie Lee (1968-)
He Died With a Felafel in His Hand *'01*
Bootmen *'00*
Holy Smoke *'99*
The Castle *'97*
Muriel's Wedding *'94*

Spike Lee (1957-)
Lisa Picard Is Famous *'01*
Summer of Sam *'99*
Girl 6 *'96*
Crooklyn *'94*
DROP Squad *'94*
Malcolm X *'92*
Jungle Fever *'91*
Mo' Better Blues *'90*
Do the Right Thing *'89*
School Daze *'88*
She's Gotta Have It *'86*

Stan Lee (1922-)
Fantastic Four *'05*
Comic Book: The Movie *'04*
Daredevil *'03*
Hulk *'03*
Mallrats *'95*
The Ambulance *'90*

Stephen Lee (1951-)
Me and the Mob *'94*
Prehysteria *'93*
The Pit & the Pendulum *'91*
Dolls *'87*
Purple Hearts *'84*

Sung-jae Lee
Public Enemy *'02*
Attack the Gas Station *'99*

Tommy Lee (1901-76)
Rooster Cogburn *'75*
The Sand Pebbles *'66*

Tommy Lee (1962-)
10th & Wolf *'06*
The New Guy *'02*

Waise Lee (1959-)
Infernal Affairs 3 *'03*
Running out of Time *'99*
Wing Chun *'94*
Fatal Chase *'92*
Blood Stained Tradewind *'90*
A Bullet in the Head *'90*
A Better Tomorrow, Part 1 *'86*

Will Yun Lee (1971-)
Elektra *'05*
Torque *'04*
Die Another Day *'02*

Yeong-ae Lee
Lady Vengeance *'05*
JSA: Joint Security Area *'00*

Yu-won Lee
Take Care of My Cat *'01*
Attack the Gas Station *'99*

Pete Lee-Wilson
Seven Seconds *'05*
The Garden *'90*

Richard Leech (1922-2004)
The Terror of the Tongs *'61*
The Moonraker *'58*
The Third Key *'57*

Stephen Leeder
Resistance *'92*
Fatal Bond *'91*

Andrea Leeds (1914-74)
The Real Glory *'39*
They Shall Have Music *'39*
The Goldwyn Follies *'38*
Letter of Introduction *'38*
It Could Happen to You *'37*
Stage Door *'37*
Come and Get It *'36*
Song of the Trail *'36*

Lila Leeds (1928-99)
She Shoulda Said No *'49*
The Show-Off *'46*

Phil Leeds (1916-98)
Lost and Found *'99*
Frankie and Johnny *'91*
He Said, She Said *'91*
Ghost *'90*
Enemies, a Love Story *'89*
Saturday the 14th Strikes Back *'88*
Haunting of Harrington House *'82*

Erica Leerhsen (1976-)
Organizm *'08*
Wrong Turn 2: Dead End *'07*
Little Athens *'05*
Anything Else *'03*
The Texas Chainsaw Massacre *'03*
Book of Shadows: Blair Witch 2 *'00*

Jane Leeves (1962-)
Garfield: A Tail of Two Kitties *'06 (V)*
The Event *'03*
James and the Giant Peach *'96 (V)*
Pandora's Clock *'96*
Miracle on 34th Street *'94*
Mr. Write *'92*

Jean (Lefevre) Lefebvre (1919-2004)
No Problem *'75*
The Gendarme of Saint-Tropez *'64*
Duke of the Derby *'62*

Philippe Lefebvre
OSS 117: Cairo, Nest of Spies *'06*
Whatever You Say *'02*

Adam LeFevre (1950-)
Arthur and the Invisibles *'06*
Tadpole *'02*
Hearts in Atlantis *'01*
L.I.E. *'01*
The Ref *'93*
Return of the Secaucus 7 *'80*

Rachelle Lefevre (1979-)
The Twilight Saga: New Moon *'09*
The Summit *'08*
Twilight *'08*
The River King *'05*
The Legend of Butch & Sundance *'04*

Rene Lefevre (1898-1991)
The Crime of Monsieur Lange *'36*
Le Million *'31*

Christian Leffler
Madhouse *'04*
A Girl, 3 Guys and a Gun *'01*

Eva LeGallienne (1899-1991)
Resurrection *'80*
The Devil's Disciple *'59*

Lance LeGault (1935-)
Home on the Range *'04 (V)*
Roadracers *'94*
Shadow Force *'92*
Welcome to Spring Break *'88*
Kidnapped *'87*
Stripes *'81*
Kenny Rogers as the Gambler *'80*
French Quarter *'78*

Sheila LeGay
See Sheila (Manors) Mannors

Phoebe Legere
The Toxic Avenger, Part 2 *'89*
The Toxic Avenger, Part 3: The Last Temptation of Toxie *'89*

Alison Leggatt (1904-90)
Day of the Triffids *'63*
This Happy Breed *'47*
Waterloo Road *'44*

Michael Legge (1978-)
Cowboys & Angels *'04*
Angela's Ashes *'99*

Annie Legras
See Anny (Annie Legras) Duperey

James LeGros (1962-)
Sherman's Way *'08*
Vantage Point *'08*
The Last Winter *'06*
Trust the Man *'06*
November *'05*
Sleeper Cell *'05*
Catch That Kid *'04*
Straight into Darkness *'04*
Big Shot: Confessions of a Campus Bookie *'02*
Lovely & Amazing *'02*
Scotland, PA *'02*
World Traveler *'01*
Common Ground *'00*
If You Only Knew *'00*
Enemy of the State *'98*
Highway Hitcher *'98*
Psycho *'98*
Thursday *'98*
The Myth of Fingerprints *'97*
Pronto *'97*
The Destiny of Marty Fine *'96*
Infinity *'96*
Marshal Law *'96*
Serial Bomber *'96*
Wishful Thinking *'96*
Destiny Turns on the Radio *'95*
The Low Life *'95*
Safe *'95*
Bad Girls *'94*
Don't Do It *'94*
Floundering *'94*
Living in Oblivion *'94*
Nervous Ticks *'93*
Guncrazy *'92*
My New Gun *'92*
Singles *'92*
Where the Day Takes You *'92*
Point Break *'91*
Blood & Concrete: A Love Story *'90*
Leather Jackets *'90*
Drugstore Cowboy *'89*
Hollywood Heartbreak *'89*
Phantasm 2 *'88*
*batteries not included *'87*
Ratings Game *'84*

John Leguizamo (1964-)
Gamer *'09*
Ice Age: Dawn of the Dinosaurs *'09*
The Happening *'08*
Miracle at St. Anna *'08*
Nothing Like the Holidays *'08*
Righteous Kill *'08*
The Babysitters *'07*
Love in the Time of Cholera *'07*
The Take *'07*
Where God Left His Shoes *'07*
The Groomsmen *'06*
Ice Age: The Meltdown *'06 (V)*
Lies & Alibis *'06*
Assault on Precinct 13 *'05*
George A. Romero's Land of the Dead *'05*
The Honeymooners *'05*
Sueno *'05*
Cronicas *'04*
Undefeated *'03*
Collateral Damage *'02*
Empire *'02*
Ice Age *'02 (V)*
Point of Origin *'02*
Spun *'02*
ZigZag *'02*
King of the Jungle *'01*
Moulin Rouge *'01*
What's the Worst That Could Happen? *'01*
Arabian Nights *'00*
Titan A.E. *'00 (V)*
Joe the King *'99*
Summer of Sam *'99*
Dr. Dolittle *'98 (V)*
Frogs for Snakes *'98*
Body Count *'97*
A Brother's Kiss *'97*
Spawn *'97*
Executive Decision *'96*
The Fan *'96*
The Pest *'96*
William Shakespeare's Romeo and Juliet *'96*
A Pyromaniac's Love Story *'95*
To Wong Foo, Thanks for Everything, Julie Newmar *'95*
Carlito's Way *'93*
Super Mario Bros. *'93*
Whispers in the Dark *'92*
Hangin' with the Homeboys *'91*
Out for Justice *'91*
Regarding Henry *'91*
Die Hard 2: Die Harder *'90*
Street Hunter *'90*
Casualties of War *'89*

Kristen Lehman (1970-)
The Sentinel *'06*
Verdict in Blood *'02*
Way of the Gun *'00*
Dog Park *'98*
Bleeders *'97*

Beatrix Lehmann (1903-79)
The Cat and the Canary *'79*
Love for Lydia *'79*

Carla Lehmann (1917-90)
Fame Is the Spur *'47*
Secret Mission *'42*
Cottage to Let *'41*

Frederic Lehne
Octopus 2: River of Fear *'02*
Terror Tract *'00*
Inferno *'98*
Balloon Farm *'97*
Dream Lover *'93*
Man's Best Friend *'93*
This Gun for Hire *'90*
Amityville 4: The Evil Escapes *'89*
Billionaire Boys Club *'87*
Coward of the County *'81*
Ordinary People *'80*

John Lehne
Ladies and Gentlemen, the Fabulous Stains *'82*
A Long Way Home *'81*
The Disappearance of Aimee *'76*
Griffin and Phoenix: A Love Story *'76*
Roboman *'75*

Meme Lei
See Me Me Lai

Fritz Leiber (1882-1949)
Bagdad *'49*
Cry of the Werewolf *'44*
The Story of Louis Pasteur *'36*

Ron Leibman (1937-)
Garden State *'04*
Auto Focus *'02*
Dummy *'02*
Personal Velocity: Three Portraits *'02*
Just the Ticket *'98*
Don King: Only in America *'97*
Night Falls on Manhattan *'96*
Seven Hours to Judgment *'88*
Door to Door *'84*
Phar Lap *'84*
Rhinestone *'84*
Romantic Comedy *'83*
Zorro, the Gay Blade *'81*
Up the Academy *'80*
Norma Rae *'79*
A Question of Guilt *'78*
The Art of Crime *'75*
Slaughterhouse Five *'72*
The Hot Rock *'70*
Where's Poppa? *'70*

Hudson (Heidi) Leick (1969-)
Chill Factor *'99*
Something About Sex *'98*

Don Leifert
Deadly Neighbor *'91*
Galaxy Invader *'85*
Fiend *'83*
The Alien Factor *'78*

Barbara Leigh (1946-)
Mistress of the Apes *'79*
Seven *'79*

Boss '74
Smile, Jenny, You're Dead '74
Junior Bonner '72
The Student Nurses '70

Cassandra Leigh (1968-)
Alien Terminator '95
Caged Heat 3000 '95
Midnight Tease '94

Frank Leigh (1876-1948)
Below the Deadline '29
American Pluck '25
Nurse Marjorie '20

Janet Leigh (1926-2004)
Halloween: H20 '98
The Fog '78
Night of the Lepus '72
Hello Down There '69
Harper '66
Bye, Bye, Birdie '63
The Manchurian Candidate '62
Psycho '60
The Perfect Furlough '59
Touch of Evil '58
The Vikings '58
Jet Pilot '57
My Sister Eileen '55
Pete Kelly's Blues '55
The Black Shield of Falworth '54
Prince Valiant '54
Houdini '53
The Naked Spur '53
Scaramouche '52
Angels in the Outfield '51
It's a Big Country '51
Two Tickets to Broadway '51
That Forsyte Woman '50
Holiday Affair '49
Little Women '49
Act of Violence '48
The Hills of Home '48
Words and Music '48

Jennifer Jason Leigh (1963-)
Greenberg '10
Synecdoche, New York '08
Margot at the Wedding '07
The Jacket '05
The Machinist '04
Palindromes '04
In the Cut '03
Hey Arnold! The Movie '02 (V)
Road to Perdition '02
The Anniversary Party '01
The Quickie '01
The King Is Alive '00
Skipped Parts '00
eXistenZ '99
The Love Letter '98
A Thousand Acres '97
Washington Square '97
Bastard out of Carolina '96
Georgia '95
Kansas City '95
Dolores Claiborne '94
Mrs. Parker and the Vicious Circle '94
The Hudsucker Proxy '93
Short Cuts '93
Single White Female '92
Backdraft '91
Crooked Hearts '91
Rush '91
Buried Alive '90
Last Exit to Brooklyn '90
Miami Blues '90
The Big Picture '89
Heart of Midnight '89
Sister, Sister '87
Undercover '87
The Hitcher '86
The Men's Club '86
Flesh and Blood '85
Girls of the White Orchid '85
Grandview U.S.A. '84
Easy Money '83
Fast Times at Ridgemont High '82
Wrong Is Right '82
The Best Little Girl in the World '81
Eyes of a Stranger '81
Killing of Randy Webster '81
Angel City '80

John Leigh (1965-)
Kidnapped '05
Stickmen '01

Nelson Leigh (1905-85)
The Gallant Hours '60
Ma Barker's Killer Brood '60
Bombers B-52 '57
Texas Masquerade '44

Spencer Leigh
Smart Money '88
The Last of England '87
Caravaggio '86

Steven Leigh
Sword of Honor '94
To Be the Best '93
China White '91
Deadly Bet '91

Suzanna Leigh (1945-)
The Fiend '71
Lust for a Vampire '71
Deadlier Than the Male '67
Paradise, Hawaiian Style '66
Boeing Boeing '65

Vivien Leigh (1913-67)
Ship of Fools '65
Roman Spring of Mrs. Stone '61
A Streetcar Named Desire '51
Anna Karenina '48
Caesar and Cleopatra '46
That Hamilton Woman '41
Waterloo Bridge '40
Gone with the Wind '39
Sidewalks of London '38
Dark Journey '37
Fire Over England '37
Storm in a Teacup '37
21 Days '37

Barbara Leigh-Hunt (1935-)
Wives and Daughters '01
Longitude '00
A Merry War '97
Pride and Prejudice '95
Paper Mask '91
The Plague Dogs '82 (V)
Frenzy '72

Laura Leighton (1968-)
Daniel's Daughter '08
We'll Meet Again '02
Seven Girlfriends '00
Naked City: A Killer Christmas '98

Lillian (Lillianne, Lyllian) Leighton (1874-1956)
Man from Monterey '33
$50,000 Reward '25
Parisian Love '25
Peck's Bad Boy '21
The Jack Knife Man '20

Linda Leighton (1917-2005)
Sundown Kid '43
Code of the Outlaw '42

Margaret Leighton (1922-76)
Choice of Weapons '76
From Beyond the Grave '73
X, Y & Zee '72
The Go-Between '71
The Madwoman of Chaillot '69
The Loved One '65
The Best Man '64
Waltz of the Toreadors '62
Carrington, V.C. '54
The Elusive Pimpernel '50
Under Capricorn '49
Bonnie Prince Charlie '48
The Winslow Boy '48

Roberta Leighton (1953-)
Covergirl '83
Barracuda '78

Harald Leipnitz (1926-2000)
Fight for Gold '86
Hell Hounds of Alaska '73
River of Evil '64

Frederick Leister (1885-1970)
The Time of His Life '55
Green Grow the Rushes '51
Spellbound '41
O.H.M.S. '37

David Leisure (1950-)
Elvis Has Left the Building '04
Three Strikes '00
Ten Things I Hate about You '99
Gangster World '98
Hollywood Safari '96
Nowhere '96
You Can't Hurry Love '88

Donovan Leitch (1968-)
Big City Blues '99
The '60s '99
Love Kills '98
One Night Stand '97
I Shot Andy Warhol '96
Dark Horse '92
Gas Food Lodging '92
Cutting Class '89
Glory '89
And God Created Woman '88
The Blob '88
The In Crowd '88

Matthew Leitch (1975-)
The Detonator '06
AKA '02

Virginia Leith
The Brain that Wouldn't Die '63
Black Widow '54

Tyron Leitso (1976-)
Seed '08
Masters of Horror: Valerie on the Stairs '06
House of the Dead '03
Dinotopia '02
Snow White: The Fairest of Them All '02

Jeremy Lelliott (1982-)
Lady Jayne Killer '03
Disappearance '02

Paul LeMat (1952-)
Big Bad Love '02
American History X '98
Children of Fury '94
Sensation '94
Wishman '93
Woman with a Past '92
Blind Witness '89
Easy Wheels '89
Grave Secrets '89
Puppet Master '89
Hanoi Hilton '87
Into the Homeland '87
The Night They Saved Christmas '87
P.I. Private Investigations '87
Private Investigations '87
Long Time Gone '86
On Wings of Eagles '86
The Burning Bed '85
P.K. and the Kid '85
Rock & Rule '83 (V)
Strange Invaders '83
Jimmy the Kid '82
Death Valley '81
Melvin and Howard '80
More American Graffiti '79
Citizens Band '77
Aloha, Bobby and Rose '74
American Graffiti '73
Firehouse '72

Harvey Lembeck (1923-82)
Fireball 500 '66
Ghost in the Invisible Bikini '66
Beach Blanket Bingo '65
How to Stuff a Wild Bikini '65
Bikini Beach '64
Pajama Party '64
Beach Party '63
Love with the Proper Stranger '63
Between Heaven and Hell '56
The Command '54
Stalag 17 '53

Michael Lembeck (1948-)
Danielle Steel's Heartbeat '93
Conspiracy: The Trial of the Chicago Eight '87
On the Right Track '81
Gorp '80
The In-Laws '79
The Boys in Company C '77

Kris Lemche (1978-)
Final Destination 3 '06
A Simple Curve '05
Ginger Snaps '01

Stephanie Lemelin
Raising Flagg '06
Anonymous Rex '04

Valerie Lemercier (1964-)
Avenue Montaigne '06
Friday Night '02
The Visitors '95

Rachel Lemieux
Mommy 2: Mommy's Day '96
Mommy '95

Tutte Lemkow (1924-91)
Inspector Clouseau '68
The Guns of Navarone '61
The Siege of Sidney Street '60
Moulin Rouge '52

Steve Lemme (1973-)
Beerfest '06
The Dukes of Hazzard '05
Club Dread '04
Super Troopers '01

Chris Lemmon (1954-)
Best of the Best: Without Warning '98
Just the Ticket '98
Land of the Free '98
Wishmaster '97
Thunder in Paradise 2 '94
Thunder in Paradise 3 '94
Thunder in Paradise '93
Corporate Affairs '90
Firehead '90
Lena's Holiday '90
Dad '89
Going Undercover '88
That's Life! '86
Weekend Warriors '86
Swing Shift '84
C.O.D. '83
The Happy Hooker Goes Hollywood '80
Just Before Dawn '80

Jack Lemmon (1925-2001)
The Legend of Bagger Vance '00
Inherit the Wind '99
Tuesdays with Morrie '99
Neil Simon's The Odd Couple 2 '98
Out to Sea '97
Twelve Angry Men '97
Getting Away With Murder '96
Hamlet '96
My Fellow Americans '96
A Weekend in the Country '96
The Grass Harp '95
Grumpier Old Men '95
Grumpy Old Men '93
A Life in the Theater '93
Short Cuts '93
For Richer, for Poorer '92
Glengarry Glen Ross '92
The Player '92
JFK '91
Dad '89
Long Day's Journey into Night '88
The Murder of Mary Phagan '87
That's Life! '86
Macaroni '85
Mass Appeal '84
Missing '82
Buddy Buddy '81
Tribute '80
The China Syndrome '79
Airport '77 '77
The Front Page '74
Prisoner of Second Avenue '74
Save the Tiger '73
Avanti! '72
The Out-of-Towners '70
April Fools '69
The Odd Couple '68
Luv '67
The Fortune Cookie '66
The Great Race '65
Good Neighbor Sam '64
How to Murder Your Wife '64
Irma La Douce '63
Under the Yum-Yum Tree '63
Days of Wine and Roses '62
The Notorious Landlady '62
Wackiest Ship in the Army '61
The Apartment '60
Some Like It Hot '59
Voyage en Balloon '59 (N)
Bell, Book and Candle '58
Cowboy '58
Fire Down Below '57
Operation Mad Ball '57
Mister Roberts '55
My Sister Eileen '55
Three for the Show '55
It Should Happen to You '54
Phffft! '54

Kasi Lemmons (1961-)
Til There Was You '96
DROP Squad '94
Fear of a Black Hat '94
Hard Target '93
Candyman '92
The Silence of the Lambs '91
School Daze '88
Vampire's Kiss '88

Michel Lemoine (1929-)
The Sensuous Teenager '70
Conquest of Mycene '63
Planets Against Us '61

Genevieve Lemon
Soft Fruit '99
Billy's Holiday '95
The Piano '93
Sweetie '89

Ute Lemper (1963-)
Appetite '98
A River Made to Drown In '97
Bogus '96
Moscow Parade '92

Mark Lenard (1928-96)
Star Trek 6: The Undiscovered Country '91
Star Trek 4: The Voyage Home '86
Star Trek 3: The Search for Spock '84
Star Trek: The Motion Picture '79
Noon Sunday '75

Vanessa Lengies (1985-)
Foreign Exchange '08
Still Waiting '08
Stick It '06
The Perfect Man '05
Waiting '05
Ratz '99

Harry J. Lennix (1964-)
Resurrecting the Champ '07
Stomp the Yard '07
Barbershop 2: Back in Business '04
Ray '04
Suspect Zero '04
Black Listed '03
The Human Stain '03
The Matrix Reloaded '03
The Matrix Revolutions '03
Collateral Damage '02
Pumpkin '02
Love and Basketball '00
Titus '99
Get On the Bus '96
Bob Roberts '92
Mo' Money '92
The Five Heartbeats '91

Jarrett Lennon (1982-)
Amityville Dollhouse '96
Short Cuts '93
Servants of Twilight '91

John Lennon (1940-80)
Chuck Berry: Hail! Hail! Rock 'n' Roll '87
Let It Be '70
The Magic Christian '69
Yellow Submarine '68 (V)
How I Won the War '67
Magical Mystery Tour '67
Help! '65
A Hard Day's Night '64

Julian Lennon (1963-)
Leaving Las Vegas '95
The Linguini Incident '92
Chuck Berry: Hail! Hail! Rock 'n' Roll '87

Maria Lennon
Bloom '03
Oktober '98
The Informant '97

Thomas Lennon (1969-)
17 Again '09
Hancock '08
Balls of Fury '07
Reno 911! Miami '07
Conversations with Other Women '05
Herbie: Fully Loaded '05
The Hitchhiker's Guide to the Galaxy '05 (V)
Heights '04
A Guy Thing '03
How to Lose a Guy in 10 Days '03
Le Divorce '03

Annie Lennox (1954-)
Edward II '92
The Room '87
Revolution '85

Jay Leno (1950-)
Igor '08 (V)
Ice Age: The Meltdown '06 (V)
Robots '05 (V)
Calendar Girls '03
Stuck On You '03
The Flintstones '94
Dave '93
We're Back! A Dinosaur's Story '93 (V)
Collision Course '89
Americathon '79
Silver Bears '78

Jack Lenoir (1926-81)
Breakfast in Paris '81
Once in Paris... '79

Rosetta LeNoire (1911-2002)
The Father Clements Story '87
Fritz the Cat '72 (V)

Lotte Lenya (1899-1981)
Semi-Tough '77
From Russia with Love '63
Roman Spring of Mrs. Stone '61
The Threepenny Opera '31

Kay Lenz (1953-)
A Gun, a Car, a Blonde '97
Gunfighter's Moon '96

Trapped in Space '94
Falling from Grace '92
Hitler's Daughter '90
Headhunter '89
Murder by Night '89
Physical Evidence '89
Fear '88
Death Wish 4: The Crackdown '87
Stripped to Kill '87
House '86
Prisoners of the Lost Universe '84
Fast Walking '82
Sanctuary of Fear '79
Initiation of Sarah '78
Mean Dog Blues '78
Great Scout & Cathouse Thursday '76
Moving Violation '76
Rich Man, Poor Man '76
White Line Fever '75

Rick Lenz (1939-)
Little Dragons '80
Scandalous John '71
Cactus Flower '69

Melissa Leo (1960-)
According to Greta '08
The Alphabet Killer '08
Frozen River '08
Lullaby '08
Righteous Kill '08
Black Irish '07
The Cake Eaters '07
Mr. Woodcock '07
Racing Daylight '07
Stephanie Daley '06
American Gun '05
Confess '05
Hide and Seek '05
Runaway '05
The Three Burials of Melquiades Estrada '05
From Other Worlds '04
21 Grams '03
Homicide: The Movie '00
The 24 Hour Woman '99
Last Summer In the Hamptons '96
Scarlett '94
Carolina Skeletons '92
Venice, Venice '92
A Time of Destiny '88
Deadtime Stories '86
Always '85
Silent Witness '85
Streetwalkin' '85

Leon (1962-)
The Brooklyn Heist '08
Cover '08
Little Richard '00
Bats '99
Friends & Lovers '99
Mean Streak '99
Mr. Rock 'n' Roll: The Alan Freed Story '99
The Temptations '98
Pure Danger '96
Spirit Lost '96
Once Upon a Time ... When We Were Colored '95
Waiting to Exhale '95
Above the Rim '94
Bad Attitude '93
Cliffhanger '93
Cool Runnings '93
The Five Heartbeats '91
Colors '88

Carlos Leon
The Cry: La Llorona '07
The Woodsman '04

David Leon
These Foolish Things '06
Beatlemania! The Movie '81

Loles Leon (1950-)
The Girl of Your Dreams '99
Amor de Hombre '97
Don Juan, My Love '90
Tie Me Up! Tie Me Down! '90

Valerie Leon (1945-)
Never Say Never Again '83
The Spy Who Loved Me '77
Blood from the Mummy's Tomb '71

Zeta One '69

Jack E. Leonard
The Fat Spy '66
Three Sailors and a Girl '53

Joshua Leonard (1975-)
Humpday '09
20 Years After '08
The Shaggy Dog '06
Shooting Livien '05
Madhouse '04
Live from Baghdad '03
Two Days '03
Scorched '02
In the Weeds '00
Men of Honor '00
Mission '00
Sacrifice '00
The Blair Witch Project '99

Lu Leonard (1927-2004)
A Climate for Killing '91
Circuitry Man '90
Shadowzone '89
Princess Academy '87

Robert Sean Leonard (1969-)
A Painted House '03
Chelsea Walls '01
Driven '01
A Glimpse of Hell '01
Tape '01
Ground Control '98
The Last Days of Disco '98
I Love You, I Love You Not '97
In the Gloaming '97
Standoff '97
The Boys Next Door '96
Killer: A Journal of Murder '95
Safe Passage '94
The Age of Innocence '93
Married to It '93
Much Ado about Nothing '93
Swing Kids '93
Mr. & Mrs. Bridge '90
Dead Poets Society '89
My Best Friend Is a Vampire '88
Bluffing It '87
The Manhattan Project '86

Sheldon Leonard (1907-97)
Brink's Job '78
Guys and Dolls '55
Breakdown '53
Money from Home '53
Here Come the Nelsons '52
Abbott and Costello Meet the Invisible Man '51
Chained for Life '51
Force of Evil '49
Shep Comes Home '49
Open Secret '48
Sinbad, the Sailor '47
Violence '47
Decoy '46
It's a Wonderful Life '46
Rainbow over Texas '46
Somewhere in the Night '46
Captain Kidd '45
The Falcon in Hollywood '44
Gambler's Choice '44
Timber Queen '44
To Have & Have Not '44
Uncertain Glory '44
Zombies on Broadway '44
City Without Men '43
Harvest Melody '43
Tortilla Flat '42
Week-End in Havana '41

Marco Leonardi (1971-)
Once Upon a Time in Mexico '03
Texas Rangers '01
The Five Senses '99
From Dusk Till Dawn 3: The Hangman's Daughter '99
David '97
Manhattan Merenque! '95
The Stendahl Syndrome '95
Like Water for Chocolate '93
Cinema Paradiso '88

Al Leong
The Shadow '94
Hard Hunted '92
Bill & Ted's Excellent Adventure '89
Die Hard '88
Lethal Weapon '87

Isabella Leong (1978-)
The Mummy: Tomb of the Dragon Emperor '08
Diary '06
Spider Lilies '06
The Eye 3 '05

Tea Leoni (1966-)
Ghost Town '08
You Kill Me '07
Fun With Dick and Jane '05
House of D '04
Spanglish '04
Hollywood Ending '02
People I Know '02
Jurassic Park 3 '01
Family Man '00
Life in the Fast Lane '00
Deep Impact '98
Bad Boys '95
Flirting with Disaster '95
Wyatt Earp '94
A League of Their Own '92

Stephanie Leonidas (1984-)
Crusade: A March through Time '06
Dracula '06
MirrorMask '05
Yes '04

Chauncey Leopardi (1981-)
The Sandlot 3: Heading Home '07
ShadowZone: The Undead Express '96
Sticks and Stones '96
The Big Green '95
Houseguest '94
Huck and the King of Hearts '93
The Sandlot '93

Philippe Leotard (1940-2001)
Les Miserables '95
La Balance '82
Le Choc '82
La Petite Sirene '80
Cat and Mouse '78
Two English Girls '72

Robert Lepage (1957-)
Far Side of the Moon '03
Stardom '00
Jesus of Montreal '89

Ted Leplat
American Kickboxer 1 '91
Emissary '89
Swift Justice '88
The Kirlian Witness '78

Gregoire Leprince-Ringuet
In the Arms of My Enemy '07
Love Songs '07
Strayed '03

Logan Lerman (1992-)
Percy Jackson & The Olympians: The Lightning Thief '10
Gamer '09
My One and Only '09
Meet Bill '07
The Number 23 '07
3:10 to Yuma '07
Hoot '06
The Butterfly Effect '04
A Painted House '03
Riding in Cars with Boys '01
The Patriot '00
What Women Want '00

Ken Lerner
Senseless '98
Mother's Boys '94
Relentless 4 '94
Fallen Angels 1 '93

Unlawful Entry '92
Fast Getaway '91
Relentless '89

Michael Lerner (1941-)
Life During Wartime '09
Yonkers Joe '08
The Last Time '06
Love and Other Disasters '06
When Do We Eat? '05
Poster Boy '04
Elf '03
Mockingbird Don't Sing '01
Attention Shoppers '99
The Mod Squad '99
Russell Mulcahy's Tale of the Mummy '99
Celebrity '98
Godzilla '98
My Favorite Martian '98
Safe Men '98
The Beautician and the Beast '97
For Richer or Poorer '97
No Way Back '96
A Pyromaniac's Love Story '95
Girl in the Cadillac '94
No Escape '94
Radioland Murders '94
The Road to Wellville '94
Amos and Andrew '93
Blank Check '93
The Comrades of Summer '92
Newsies '92
Barton Fink '91
The Closer '91
Omen 4: The Awakening '91
Any Man's Death '90
Maniac Cop 2 '90
Harlem Nights '89
Anguish '88
Eight Men Out '88
Hands of a Stranger '87
The Execution '85
Rita Hayworth: The Love Goddess '83
Strange Invaders '83
National Lampoon's Class Reunion '82
The Postman Always Rings Twice '81
Coast to Coast '80
Outlaw Blues '77
F. Scott Fitzgerald in Hollywood '76
Busting '74
Missiles of October '74
Reflections of Murder '74
The Candidate '72
Firehouse '72

Sam Lerner (1992-)
Monster House '06 (V)
Envy '04

Adelaide Leroux
Seraphine '08
Flanders '06

Maxime LeRoux (1951-)
The Son of the Shark '93
Mama, There's a Man in Your Bed '89

Phillippe LeRoy (1930-)
Mother of Tears '08
Vatel '00
Quo Vadis '85
Three Men and a Cradle '85
The Night Porter '74
The Frightened Woman '71
A Married Woman '65
Castle of the Living Dead '64
Une Femme Mariee '64
Alone Against Rome '62
Le Trou '59

Ed LeSaint (1870-1940)
Justice of the Range '35
Riding Wild '35
Thunder Mountain '35
Treason '33
Texas Bad Man '32
Range Feud '31
The Dawn Trail '30

Carole Lesley
Doctor in Love '60
Dangerous Youth '58

Bethel Leslie (1929-99)
Message in a Bottle '98
Saint Maybe '98
In Cold Blood '96
Long Day's Journey into Night '88
Ironweed '87

Joan Leslie (1925-)
Jubilee Trail '54
Hellgate '52
Man in the Saddle '51
Born to Be Bad '50
Rhapsody in Blue '45
Hollywood Canteen '44
The Sky's the Limit '43
Thank Your Lucky Stars '43
This Is the Army '43
The Male Animal '42
Yankee Doodle Dandy '42
High Sierra '41
Sergeant York '41
The Wagons Roll at Night '41
Love Affair '39

John Leslie
It's Called Murder, Baby '82
Dracula Sucks '79

Nan Leslie (1926-2000)
The Bamboo Saucer '68
Iron Mountain Trail '53
Pioneer Marshal '49
Rim of the Canyon '49
Desperate '47
The Devil Thumbs a Ride '47

Jalil Lespert
Le Petit Lieutenant '05
Sade '00

Mimi Lesseos
Beyond Fear '93
Pushed to the Limit '92
Final Impact '91
The American Angels: Baptism of Blood '89

Anton Lesser (1952-)
Miss Potter '06
River Queen '05
Almost Strangers '01
Charlotte Gray '01
Lorna Doone '01
Vanity Fair '99
Moses '96

Len Lesser (1922-)
Baadasssss! '03
Ain't No Way Back '89
Grandma's House '88
Dubeat-E-O '84
Joy Ride to Nowhere '78
Kelly's Heroes '70
How to Stuff a Wild Bikini '65
Shack Out on 101 '55

Ben Lessy (1902-92)
That Funny Feeling '65
Pajama Party '64
The Jackie Robinson Story '50

Adrian Lester (1970-)
Doomsday '08
Starting Out in the Evening '07
As You Like It '06
Scenes of a Sexual Nature '06
The Day After Tomorrow '04
Dust '01
Born Romantic '00
Jason and the Argonauts '00
Love's Labour's Lost '00
Maybe Baby '99
Primary Colors '98

Bruce Lester (1912-)
Charade '53
Tales of Robin Hood '52
Golden Earrings '47
Shadows on the Stairs '41
British Intelligence '40

The Letter '40
Boy Meets Girl '38

Buddy Lester (1917-2002)
Cracking Up '83
Big Mouth '67
The Patsy '64
The Nutty Professor '63
Sergeants 3 '62
Ocean's 11 '60

Jeff Lester (1955-)
In the Cold of the Night '89
Once a Hero '88

Kate Lester (1857-1924)
The Hunchback of Notre Dame '23
The Social Secretary '16

Mark Lester (1958-)
The Prince and the Pauper '78
Redneck '73
What the Peeper Saw '72
Black Beauty '71
Melody '71
Who Slew Auntie Roo? '71
Eye Witness '70
Oliver! '68
Fahrenheit 451 '66

Ron Lester (1975-)
Not Another Teen Movie '01
Varsity Blues '98
Good Burger '97

James Lesure
Loveless in Los Angeles '07
The Ring 2 '05

David Letch
Dark of the Night '85
Death Warmed Up '85

Shelli Lether
The Sender '98
Born to Run '93

Lori Lethin (1955-)
Return to Horror High '87
Brotherly Love '85
Bloody Birthday '80
The Prey '80

Ken Letner (1932-93)
The Big Sweat '90
Strangers in Paradise '84

Jared Leto (1971-)
Chapter 27 '07
Lonely Hearts '06
Lord of War '05
Alexander '04
Panic Room '02
Highway '01
Requiem for a Dream '00
American Psycho '99
Black and White '99
Fight Club '99
Girl, Interrupted '99
Sunset Strip '99
Basil '98
The Thin Red Line '98
Urban Legend '98
Switchback '97
The Last of the High Kings '96
Prefontaine '96
How to Make an American Quilt '95
Cool and the Crazy '94

Matt Letscher (1970-)
Towelhead '07
Gods and Generals '03
Identity '03
Super Sucker '03
King of Texas '02
Jackie, Ethel, Joan: The Kennedy Women '01
Madison '01
John John in the Sky '00
The Mask of Zorro '98
Lovelife '97

Dan Lett
Get a Clue '02
The Life Before This '99
Blind Faith '98

Frame by Frame *'95*
Under the Piano *'95*
Paris, France *'94*

David Letterman (1947-)
Beavis and Butt-Head Do America *'96 (V)*
Cabin Boy *'94*

Al Lettieri (1928-75)
The Godfather 1902-1959: The Complete Epic *'81*
McQ *'74*
Mr. Majestyk *'74*
The Deadly Trackers *'73*
The Don Is Dead *'73*
The Getaway *'72*
The Godfather *'72*
Pulp *'72*

Katie Leung (1987-)
Harry Potter and the Order of the Phoenix *'07*
Harry Potter and the Goblet of Fire *'05*

Ken Leung (1970-)
Shanghai Kiss *'07*
X-Men: The Last Stand *'06*
Sucker Free City *'05*
Saw *'04*
Red Dragon *'02*

Tony Leung Chiu-Wai (1962-)
Ashes of Time Redux *'08*
Red Cliff *'08*
Lust, Caution *'07*
2046 *'04*
Hero *'03*
Infernal Affairs 3 *'03*
In the Mood for Love *'00*
Tokyo Raiders *'00*
Gorgeous *'99*
Flowers of Shanghai *'98*
Happy Together *'96*
Chungking Express *'95*
Cyclo *'95*
Ashes of Time *'94*
Hard-Boiled *'92*
A Bullet in the Head *'90*

Tony Leung Ka-Fai (1958-)
Ashes of Time Redux *'08*
Three … Extremes *'04*
Double Vision *'02*
Ashes of Time *'94*
The Lover *'92*
The Laserman *'90*
The Prisoner *'90*
A Better Tomorrow, Part 3 *'89*
Prison on Fire *'87*

Clinton Leupp
Trick *'99*
Nick and Jane *'96*

Lynn Levand
Kill or Be Killed *'93*
Hellbent *'88*

Oscar Levant (1906-72)
The Cobweb *'55*
The Band Wagon *'53*
An American in Paris *'51*
The Barkleys of Broadway *'49*
Romance on the High Seas *'48*
Humoresque *'46*
Rhythm on the River *'40*
Dance of Life *'29*

Francois Levantal
Dante 01 *'08*
A Very Long Engagement *'04*
Hate *'95*

Calvin Levels (1954-)
Black Listed *'03*
Within the Rock *'96*
Hellbound *'94*
Point of No Return *'93*
Johnny Suede *'92*
Live! From Death Row *'92*
Adventures in Babysitting *'87*

A Christmas Without Snow *'80*

Sam Levene (1905-80)
God Told Me To *'76*
A Dream of Kings *'69*
Designing Woman *'57*
Sweet Smell of Success *'57*
Three Sailors and a Girl *'53*
Babe Ruth Story *'48*
Boomerang *'47*
The Killers *'46*
The Purple Heart *'44*
Action in the North Atlantic *'43*
I Dood It *'43*
Whistling in Brooklyn *'43*
Shadow of the Thin Man *'41*
Golden Boy *'39*
Mad Miss Manton *'38*
Shopworn Angel *'38*
Three Men on a Horse *'36*

Joanna "JoJo" Levesque (1990-)
True Confessions of a Hollywood Starlet *'08*
Aquamarine *'06*
RV *'06*

Marcel Levesque (1877-1962)
The Fantastic Night *'42*
Judex *'16*
Les Vampires *'15*

Mariette Levesque
Tanya's Island *'81*
Snowballin' *'71*

Zachary Levi (1980-)
Alvin and the Chipmunks: The Squeakuel *'09*
Stuntmen *'09*
Wieners *'08*
Spiral *'07*
Big Momma's House 2 *'06*

Margarita Levieva (1985-)
Spread *'09*
The Invisible *'07*
Noise *'07*

John Levin
Bounce *'00*
Zoltan… Hound of Dracula *'78*

Rachel Levin (1952-)
White Palace *'90*
Gaby: A True Story *'87*

Floyd Levine
Watchers Reborn *'98*
Ice *'93*

Ilana Levine (1963-)
Tanner on Tanner *'04*
Anything But Love *'02*
Just Looking *'99*

Jean Levine
Hollywood in Trouble *'87*
The Newlydeads *'87*

Jerry Levine (1957-)
Ghosts of Mississippi *'96*
Born on the Fourth of July *'89*
Casual Sex? *'88*
Iron Eagle *'86*

Samm Levine (1982-)
Inglourious Basterds *'09*
Pulse *'06*
Club Dread *'04*
Home on the Range *'04 (V)*
Not Another Teen Movie *'01*
Killer McCoy *'47*

Ted Levine (1958-)
American Gangster *'07*
The Assassination of Jesse James by the Coward Robert Ford *'07*
The Hills Have Eyes *'06*
Birth *'04*
The Manchurian Candidate *'04*
Wonderland *'03*
The Truth About Charlie *'02*

Ali *'01*
Evolution *'01*
The Fast and the Furious *'01*
Joy Ride *'01 (V)*
Harlan County War *'00*
Wild Wild West *'99*
From the Earth to the Moon *'98*
Moby Dick *'98*
Ellen Foster *'97*
Flubber *'97*
Mad City *'97*
Switchback *'97*
Georgia *'95*
Heat *'95*
Bullet *'94*
The Mangler *'94*
Detonator *'93*
The Last Outlaw *'93*
Nowhere to Run *'93*
The Silence of the Lambs *'91*
Fulfillment *'89*
Love at Large *'89*
Ironweed *'87*

Connor Christopher Levins (1999-)
The Betrayed *'08*
The Most Wonderful Time of the Year *'08*
Eight Below *'06*

Barry Levinson (1942-)
Bee Movie *'07 (V)*
Jimmy Hollywood *'94*
Quiz Show *'94*
History of the World: Part 1 *'81*

Patrick Levis
Love's Unfolding Dream *'07*
Brink *'98*

Emile Levisetti
Alien Terminator *'95*
Sexual Response *'92*
Bix *'90*

Steve Levitt
Blue Movies *'88*
The Incredible Hulk Returns *'88*
Hunk *'87*
Last Resort *'86*

Uta Levka (1942-)
Scream and Scream Again *'70*
Carmen, Baby *'66*
The Alley Cats *'65*

Eugene Levy (1946-)
Astro Boy *'09 (V)*
Night at the Museum: Battle of the Smithsonian *'09*
Taking Woodstock *'09*
American Pie Presents: Beta House *'07*
American Pie Presents: The Naked Mile *'06*
Curious George *'06 (V)*
For Your Consideration *'06*
Over the Hedge *'06 (V)*
American Pie Presents Band Camp *'05*
Cheaper by the Dozen 2 *'05*
The Man *'05*
New York Minute *'04*
American Wedding *'03*
Bringing Down the House *'03*
Dumb and Dumberer: When Harry Met Lloyd *'03*
A Mighty Wind *'03*
Like Mike *'02*
American Pie 2 *'01*
Club Land *'01*
Down to Earth *'01*
Repli-Kate *'01*
Serendipity *'01*
Best in Show *'00*
The Ladies Man *'00*
American Pie *'99*
The Secret Life of Girls *'99*
Almost Heroes *'97*
Multiplicity *'96*
Waiting for Guffman *'96*
Father of the Bride Part 2 *'95*

Kurt Vonnegut's Harrison Bergeron *'95*
I Love Trouble *'94*
Stay Tuned *'92*
Father of the Bride *'91*
Speed Zone *'88*
Armed and Dangerous *'86*
Club Paradise *'86*
The Last Polka *'84*
Splash *'84*
Going Berserk *'83*
National Lampoon's Vacation *'83*
Heavy Metal *'81 (V)*

Micky Levy
Rails & Ties *'07*
Vampire Time Travelers *'98*

Ori Levy
Operation Thunderbolt *'77*
The Chairman *'69*

James Lew (1952-)
18 Fingers of Death *'05*
Deep Core *'00*
Boogie Boy *'98*
High Voltage *'98*
Balance of Power *'96*
Robo Warriors *'96*
Blood for Blood *'95*
Red Sun Rising *'94*
Private Wars *'93*

Jose Lewgoy (1920-2003)
Cobra Verde *'88*
Kiss of the Spider Woman *'85*
Fitzcarraldo *'82*
Earth Entranced *'66*

Al Lewis (1923-2006)
South Beach Academy *'96*
Car 54, Where Are You? *'94*
My Grandpa Is a Vampire *'92*
Fright House *'89*
Married to the Mob *'88*
The Munsters' Revenge *'81*
Used Cars *'80*
Way He Was *'76*
The Night Strangler *'72*
They Shoot Horses, Don't They? *'69*
Munster, Go Home! *'66*

Ben Lewis
That Russell Girl *'08*
Stir of Echoes 2: The Homecoming *'07*

Brittney Lewis
Rubin & Ed *'92*
Dream Machine *'91*

Charlotte Lewis (1968-)
Mutual Needs *'97*
Navajo Blues *'97*
The Glass Cage *'96*
Decoy *'95*
Embrace of the Vampire *'95*
Red Shoe Diaries 6: How I Met My Husband *'95*
Men of War *'94*
Excessive Force *'93*
Sketch Artist *'92*
Storyville *'92*
Bare Essentials *'91*
Tripwire *'89*
Dial Help *'88*
The Golden Child *'86*
Pirates *'86*

Clea Lewis (1965-)
Confessions of a Shopaholic *'09*
Ice Age: The Meltdown *'06 (V)*
The Rich Man's Wife *'96*

Damian Lewis (1971-)
Alex Rider: Operation Stormbreaker *'06*
The Situation *'06*
Friends & Crocodiles *'05*
An Unfinished Life *'05*
Keane *'04*
Dreamcatcher *'03*
Band of Brothers *'01*
Robinson Crusoe *'96*

David Lewis (1916-2000)
Personal Effects *'09*
Lake Placid *'99*
The Apartment *'60*

Dawnn Lewis (1961-)
The 10th Kingdom *'00*
Race to Freedom: The Story of the Underground Railroad *'94*
I'm Gonna Git You Sucka *'88*

Diana Lewis (1919-97)
Somewhere I'll Find You *'42*
Whistling in Dixie *'42*
Andy Hardy Meets Debutante *'40*
Go West *'40*

Fiona Lewis (1946-)
Innerspace *'87*
Strange Invaders *'83*
Strange Behavior *'81*
Wanda Nevada *'79*
Tintorera… Tiger Shark *'78*
Stunts *'77*
Drum *'76*
Lisztomania *'75*
Blue Blood *'73*
Dracula *'73*
Doctor Phibes Rises Again *'72*
The Fearless Vampire Killers *'67*

Forrest Lewis (1899-1977)
The Monster of Piedras Blancas *'57*
Escape from Fort Bravo *'53*

Gary Lewis (1958-)
Valhalla Rising *'09*
Eragon *'06*
Goal! The Dream Begins *'06*
Joyeux Noel *'05*
Yes *'04*
Warrior Queen *'03*
Gangs of New York *'02*
Pure *'02*
Billy Elliot *'00*
My Name Is Joe *'98*
Postmortem *'98*
Carla's Song *'97*
Orphans *'97*
Hardly Working *'81*

Geoffrey Lewis (1935-)
The Butcher *'07*
The Devil's Rejects *'05*
Down in the Valley *'05*
A Painted House *'03*
A Light in the Darkness *'02*
The New Guy *'02*
Sunstorm *'01*
Way of the Gun *'00*
The Prophet's Game *'99*
Midnight in the Garden of Good and Evil *'97*
Rough Riders *'97*
An Occasional Hell *'96*
Trilogy of Terror 2 *'96*
When the Dark Man Calls *'95*
Army of One *'94*
Maverick *'94*
National Lampoon's Last Resort *'94*
White Fang 2: The Myth of the White Wolf *'94*
The Man Without a Face *'93*
Only the Strong *'93*
Point of No Return *'93*
Wishman *'93*
The Lawnmower Man *'92*
Double Impact *'91*
Disturbed *'90*
Matters of the Heart *'90*
Catch Me… If You Can *'89*
Fletch Lives *'89*
Pink Cadillac *'89*
Tango and Cash *'89*
Out of the Dark *'88*
Pancho Barnes *'88*
Maximum Security *'87*
Lust in the Dust *'85*
Stitches *'85*
Night of the Comet *'84*

Return of the Man from U.N.C.L.E. *'83*
September Gun *'83*
I, the Jury *'82*
Heaven's Gate *'81*
Shoot the Sun Down *'81*
Any Which Way You Can *'80*
Bronco Billy *'80*
Every Which Way But Loose *'78*
Tilt *'78*
When Every Day Was the Fourth of July *'78*
The Return of a Man Called Horse *'76*
The Great Waldo Pepper *'75*
Smile *'75*
The Wind and the Lion *'75*
Macon County Line *'74*
Thunderbolt & Lightfoot *'74*
Culpepper Cattle Co. *'72*
Moon of the Wolf *'72*

George Lewis (1903-95)
Indian Paint *'64*
The Sign of Zorro *'60*
King of the Bullwhip *'51*
Outlaw Fury *'50*
Rangeland Empire *'50*
The Big Sombrero *'49*
Outlaw Gang *'49*
Radar Patrol vs. Spy King *'49*
Border River *'47*
Federal Operator 99 *'45*
Perils of the Darkest Jungle *'44*
Zorro's Black Whip *'44*
Outlaws of the Desert *'41*
Captain Calamity *'36*

Gilbert Lewis (1941-)
Candyman *'92*
The Kid Who Loved Christmas *'90*
Touched *'82*

Greg Lewis
Prehysteria 2 *'94*
Frankie and Johnny *'91*

Gus Lewis (1993-)
Asylum *'05*
Batman Begins *'05*

Huey Lewis (1950-)
Duets *'00*
Shadow of Doubt *'98*
Short Cuts *'93*
Back to the Future *'85*

Jason Lewis
Sex and the City 2 *'10*
Tribute *'09*
Sex and the City: The Movie *'08*
Bobby Z *'07*
Mr. Brooks *'07*
The Attic *'06*
My Faraway Bride *'06*

Jazsmin Lewis (1976-)
Three Can Play That Game *'07*
Barbershop 2: Back in Business *'04*
Barbershop *'02*

Jean Ann Lewis
See Eve Brent

Jenifer Lewis (1957-)
Not Easily Broken *'09*
The Princess and the Frog *'09 (V)*
Tyler Perry's Meet the Browns *'08*
Dirty Laundry *'07*
Who's Your Caddy? *'07*
Cars *'06 (V)*
Madea's Family Reunion *'06*
The Cookout *'04*
Nora's Hair Salon *'04*
Shark Tale *'04 (V)*
Juwanna Mann *'02*
The Brothers *'01*
Cast Away *'00*
Dancing in September *'00*
Little Richard *'00*
Jackie's Back *'99*

Mystery Men '99
Partners '99
The Mighty '98
Girl 6 '96
The Preacher's Wife '96
Corrina, Corrina '94
Deconstructing Sarah '94
Renaissance Man '94
What's Love Got to Do with It? '93

Jenny Lewis (1977-)
Little Boy Blue '97
Foxfire '96
Runaway Daughters '94
Runaway Father '91
Troop Beverly Hills '89
The Wizard '89
A Friendship in Vienna '88
Trading Hearts '87

Jerry Lewis (1926-)
Arizona Dream '94
Funny Bones '94
Mr. Saturday Night '92
Cookie '89
Slapstick of Another Kind '84
Cracking Up '83
King of Comedy '82
Hardly Working '81
Which Way to the Front? '70
Don't Raise the Bridge, Lower the River '68
Big Mouth '67
Boeing Boeing '65
Family Jewels '65
Disorderly Orderly '64
The Patsy '64
It's a Mad, Mad, Mad, Mad World '63
The Nutty Professor '63
Who's Minding the Store? '63
The Errand Boy '61
The Ladies' Man '61
The Bellboy '60
Cinderfella '60
The Geisha Boy '58
Rock-A-Bye Baby '57
The Sad Sack '57
The Delicate Delinquent '56
Hollywood or Bust '56
Pardners '56
Artists and Models '55
The Caddy '53
Money from Home '53
The Road to Bali '53
Scared Stiff '53
Jumping Jacks '52
Sailor Beware '52
The Stooge '51
At War with the Army '50
My Friend Irma '49

Jerry Lee Lewis (1935-)
Chuck Berry: Hail! Hail! Rock 'n' Roll '87
High School Confidential '58

Joe Lewis (1943-)
Force: Five '81
Jaguar Lives '79

Joe E. Lewis (1902-71)
Lady in Cement '68
Private Buckaroo '42
The Holy Terror '37

Johnny Lewis
Felon '08
Aliens vs. Predator: Requiem '07
Palo Alto '07
Raise Your Voice '04

Juliette Lewis (1973-)
The Switch '10
Whip It '09
Catch and Release '07
Aurora Borealis '06
Grilled '06
Daltry Calhoun '05
Chasing Freedom '04
Starsky & Hutch '04
Cold Creek Manor '03
Old School '03
Enough '02
Hysterical Blindness '02
My Louisiana Sky '02
Gaudi Afternoon '01
Picture Claire '01
Way of the Gun '00
The 4th Floor '99
The Other Sister '98
The Evening Star '96
The Basketball Diaries '95
From Dusk Till Dawn '95
Strange Days '95
Mixed Nuts '94
Natural Born Killers '94
Kalifornia '93
Romeo Is Bleeding '93
That Night '93
What's Eating Gilbert Grape '93
Husbands and Wives '92
Cape Fear '91
Crooked Hearts '91
Too Young to Die '90
Meet the Hollowheads '89
National Lampoon's Christmas Vacation '89
My Stepmother Is an Alien '88

Leigh Lewis
Revelation '00
Tribulation '00

Louise Lewis (1914-96)
Blood of Dracula '57
I Was a Teenage Werewolf '57

Matthew Lewis (1989-)
Harry Potter and the Goblet of Fire '05
Harry Potter and the Sorcerer's Stone '01
The Legend of Wolf Mountain '92

Michael Lewis (1939-)
Signs of Life '89
Gruesome Twosome '67

Mitchell Lewis (1880-1956)
Cairo '42
Billy the Kid '41
The Wizard of Oz '39
Linda '29
The Red Lily '24
Salome '22

Monica Lewis
The Concorde: Airport '79 '79
Everything I Have is Yours '52

Phill Lewis (1968-)
Elvis Has Left the Building '04
I Spy '02
Spent '00
Once Upon a Time ... When We Were Colored '95 (N)
Brother Future '91
City Slickers '91

Ralph Lewis (1872-1937)
Sunset Range '35
Swifty '35
Fighting Hero '34
Sucker Money '34
Somewhere in Sonora '33
Dante's Inferno '24
Outside the Law '21
When the Clouds Roll By '19
The Birth of a Nation '15

Richard Lewis (1947-)
Hugo Pool '97
Drunks '96
A Weekend in the Country '96
Danger of Love '95
Leaving Las Vegas '95
Wagons East '94
Robin Hood: Men in Tights '93
Once Upon a Crime '92
The Return of Spinal Tap '92
That's Adequate '90
The Wrong Guys '88
Diary of a Young Comic '79

Robert Lewis (1909-97)
Misbegotten '98
My Very Best Friend '96
Hello Again '87
Monsieur Verdoux '47
Son of Lassie '45

Robert Q. Lewis (1921-91)
Ski Party '65
Good Neighbor Sam '64
An Affair to Remember '57

Ronald Lewis (1928-82)
Paul and Michelle '74
Friends '71
Billy Budd '62
Mr. Sardonicus '61
Scream of Fear '61
Conspiracy of Hearts '60
Bachelor of Hearts '58
Robbery under Arms '57
Helen of Troy '56

Russell Scott Lewis
Green Plaid Shirt '96
Boys Life '94

Sheldon Lewis (1869-1958)
Tombstone Canyon '32
The Phantom '31
Beyond the Trail '26
Lightning Hutch '26
With Kit Carson over the Great Divide '25

Tommy (Tom E.) Lewis (1957-)
The Proposition '05
The Chant of Jimmie Blacksmith '78

Vera Lewis (1873-1956)
Ella Cinders '26
Nurse Marjorie '20

Vicki Lewis (1960-)
California Dreaming '07
Finding Nemo '03 (V)
Pushing Tin '99
Breakfast of Champions '98
Godzilla '98
Mouse Hunt '97

John Ley (1951-)
Out of the Body '88
BMX Bandits '83

Leo Leyden (1929-2007)
Quiet Day in Belfast '74
The Mask '61

Jacob Leygraf
Sunday's Children '94
The Slingshot '93

Johan Leysen (1950-)
Brotherhood of the Wolf '01
The Gambler '97
Trahir '93
Daens '92
Egg '88
The Music Teacher '88
Hail Mary '85

Drue Leyton
Charlie Chan at the Circus '36
Charlie Chan in London '34

John Leyton (1939-)
Schizo '77
Krakatoa East of Java '69
Seaside Swingers '65
Von Ryan's Express '65
Guns at Batasi '64
The Great Escape '63

Thierry Lhermitte (1957-)
Mr. Average '06
Le Divorce '03
And Now Ladies and Gentlemen '02
The Closet '00
The Dinner Game '98
An American Werewolf in Paris '97
Augustin '95
Little Indian, Big City '95
Grosse Fatigue '94
My Best Friend's Girl '84
My New Partner '84
Until September '84
Next Year If All Goes Well '83
French Fried Vacation '79

Baotian Li (1946-)
Shanghai Triad '95
Ju Dou '90

Bin Li (1982-)
Beijing Bicycle '01
The Road Home '01

Bingbing Li
The Forbidden Kingdom '08
Silver Hawk '04

Bruce Li (1950-)
Counter Attack '84
The Three Avengers '80
The Young Bruce Lee '80
Return of the Tiger '78
Chinese Connection 2 '77

Gong Li (1965-)
Shanghai '09
Hannibal Rising '07
Curse of the Golden Flower '06
Miami Vice '06
Memoirs of a Geisha '05
Eros '04
2046 '04
Zhou Yu's Train '02
The Emperor and the Assassin '99
Chinese Box '97
Temptress Moon '96
Shanghai Triad '95
To Live '94
Farewell My Concubine '93
Raise the Red Lantern '91
The Story of Qiu Ju '91
Ju Dou '90
Red Sorghum '87

Jet Li (1963-)
The Expendables '10
The Forbidden Kingdom '08
The Mummy: Tomb of the Dragon Emperor '08
Warlords '08
War '07
Jet Li's Fearless '06
Unleashed '05
Cradle 2 the Grave '03
Hero '03
Kiss of the Dragon '01
The One '01
Romeo Must Die '00
Lethal Weapon 4 '98
Black Mask '96
Jet Li's The Enforcer '95
Meltdown '95
The Bodyguard from Beijing '94
Fist of Legend '94
Once Upon a Time in China III '93
Twin Warriors '93
Once Upon a Time in China II '92
Once Upon a Time in China '91

Xuejian Li (1954-)
Happy Times '00
The Emperor and the Assassin '99
Shanghai Triad '95

Peter Paul Liapis
Fast Getaway 2 '94
Ghoulies 4 '93
For the Love of Angela '82
Starhops '78

Brian Libby
Platoon Leader '87
Silent Rage '82

Liberace (1919-87)
The Loved One '65
Sincerely Yours '56

Johan Libereau
The Witnesses '07
Cold Showers '05

Anne Libert (1946-)
The Demons '74
Erotic Escape '72
Rites of Frankenstein '72
Virgin among the Living Dead '71

Richard Libertini (1933-)
Everybody Wants to Be Italian '08
A Grandpa for Christmas '07
Grilled '06
The 4th Tenor '02
Lethal Weapon 4 '98
Telling You '98
Nell '94
And You Thought Your Parents Were Weird! '91 (V)
Awakenings '90
The Bonfire of the Vanities '90
DuckTales the Movie: Treasure of the Lost Lamp '90 (V)
Animal Behavior '89
Fletch Lives '89
Big Trouble '86
Fletch '85
Fourth Wise Man '85
All of Me '84
Unfaithfully Yours '84
Deal of the Century '83
Going Berserk '83
Soup for One '82
Sharky's Machine '81
Popeye '80
The In-Laws '79
I Wonder Who's Killing Her Now? '76
Catch-22 '70

Richard Liberty (1932-)
Day of the Dead '85
The Crazies '73

Alain Libolt (1943-)
The Lady and the Duke '01
Autumn Tale '98
Army of Shadows '69

Jeremy Licht (1971-)
Next One '84
Twilight Zone: The Movie '83
Lois Gibbs and the Love Canal '82
Father Figure '80
The Seekers '79

Mitchell Lichtenstein (1956-)
The Wedding Banquet '93
Streamers '83

Jeff(rey) Licon (1985-)
Alien Raiders '08
Mysterious Skin '04

Gabriella Licudi (1943-)
The Last Safari '67
The Unearthly Stranger '64

G. Gordon Liddy (1930-)
Adventures in Spying '92
Camp Cucamonga: How I Spent My Summer Vacation '90
Street Asylum '90
Super Force '90
When Nature Calls '85

Anki Liden (1947-)
Expectations '97
My Life As a Dog '85

Mimi Lieber
The Thing About My Folks '05
Wilder Napalm '93
Last Resort '86

Leon Liebgold (1910-93)
The Dybbuk '37
Yidl Mitn Fidl '36

Michael Liebman
2 by 4 '98
The Painted Lady '97

Harry Liedtke
The Finances of the Grand Duke '24
Passion '19

Lo Lieh (1939-2002)
Sex and Zen '93
The Stranger and the Gunfighter '76

Jennifer Lien (1974-)
SLC Punk! '99
American History X '98

Albert Lieven (1906-71)
The Victors '63
Brainwashed '60
Frieda '47
Beware of Pity '46
The Seventh Veil '46
Sleeping Car to Trieste '45
The Life and Death of Colonel Blimp '43
Night Train to Munich '40

Tina Lifford
Hostage '05
Urban Legends: Bloody Mary '05
Amy's O '02
Blood Work '02
The Loretta Claiborne Story '00
The '70s '00
Letters from a Killer '98
The Temptations '98
Mandela and de Klerk '97
America's Dream '95
The Ernest Green Story '93
Grand Canyon '91
Paris Trout '91
Colors '88

John Light (1972-)
Partition '07
Heights '04
Benedict Arnold: A Question of Honor '03
Cambridge Spies '03
The Lion in Winter '03
Purpose '02
Intimate Affairs '01

Judith Light (1949-)
Save Me '07
Ira & Abby '06
Stamp of a Killer '87

Cody Lightning (1986-)
Four Sheets to the Wind '07
Manic '01
Smoke Signals '98
Grand Avenue '96

Crystle Lightning (1981-)
American Pie Presents Band Camp '05
3 Ninjas Knuckle Up '95

Marilyn Lightstone (1941-)
Grand Tour: Disaster in Time '92
Abraxas: Guardian of the Universe '90
Surrogate '88
Anne of Green Gables '85
Wild Pony '83
Spasms '82
Lies My Father Told Me '75

Tom Ligon (1945-)
Judge Horton and the Scottsboro Boys '76
Fury on Wheels '71

Lil' Kim
See Kimberly (Lil' Kim) Jones

Lil' Romeo (1989-)
Internet Dating '08
Honey '03

Dennis (Denis) Lill (1942-)
Element of Doubt '96
Bad Blood '81
Lillie '79

Matthew Lillard (1970-)
What Love Is '07
Bickford Shmeckler's Cool Ideas '06
The Groomsmen '06

The Perfect Score '04
Scooby-Doo 2: Monsters Unleashed '04
Wicker Park '04
Without a Paddle '04
Scooby-Doo '02
Finder's Fee '01
Summer Catch '01
13 Ghosts '01
Love's Labour's Lost '00
She's All That '99
SLC Punk! '99
Spanish Judges '99
Wing Commander '99
Dish Dogs '98
Senseless '98
Telling You '98
The Curve '97
Without Limits '97
Scream '96
Animal Room '95
Hackers '95
Tarantella '95
Serial Mom '94

Beatrice Lillie (1898-1989)
Thoroughly Modern Millie '67
Around the World in 80 Days '56
On Approval '44
Exit Smiling '26

Rachael Lillis
Pokemon 3: The Movie '01 (V)
Pokemon: The First Movie '99 (V)

Evangeline Lilly (1979-)
Afterwards '08
The Hurt Locker '08

Jennifer Lim
Hostel '06
When Evil Calls '06

Brigitte Lin (1954-)
Ashes of Time Redux '08
Chungking Express '95
Ashes of Time '94
The Bride with White Hair '93
The Bride with White Hair 2 '93
Dream Lovers '86
Police Story '85
Fantasy Mission Force '84
Zu: Warriors from the Magic Mountain '83

Chen Chi Lin (1955-)
Heaven & Hell '78
Sword Masters: The Battle Wizard '77

Ching-hsai Lin
See Brigitte Lin

Kelly Lin
Boarding Gate '07
Running Out of Time 2 '06
Full Time Killer '01
Zu Warriors '01

Kay Linaker (1914-2008)
Two Weeks to Live '43
Charlie Chan's Murder Cruise '40
Hidden Enemy '40
Charlie Chan at Monte Carlo '37

Aida Linares
U-Turn '97
Clueless '95

Peter Linari
The Curse of the Jade Scorpion '01
Fat Guy Goes Nutzoid '86

Abbey Lincoln (1930-)
Mo' Better Blues '90
For Love of Ivy '68
Nothing but a Man '64
The Girl Can't Help It '56

Andrew Lincoln (1973-)
Wuthering Heights '09
Scenes of a Sexual Nature '06
These Foolish Things '06
Enduring Love '04
Love Actually '03
Gangster No. 1 '00
The Woman in White '97
Boston Kickout '95

Elmo Lincoln (1889-1952)
Tarzan's New York Adventure '42
Wyoming Outlaw '39
The Adventures of Tarzan '21
Tarzan of the Apes '17
Hoodoo Ann '16

Pamela Lincoln (1937-)
Anatomy of a Psycho '61
The Tingler '59

Gillian Lind (1904-83)
And Now the Screaming Starts '73
Dynasty of Fear '72

Traci Lind (1966-)
No Strings Attached '98
Red Meat '98
The End of Violence '97
Wolverine '96
The Road to Wellville '94
My Boyfriend's Back '93
No Secrets '91
Voyager '91
Class of 1999 '90
The Handmaid's Tale '90
Survival Quest '89
Fright Night 2 '88
A Tiger's Tale '87

Boguslaw Linda (1952-)
The Decalogue '88
Danton '82
Mother of Kings '82

Boguslaw Linda (1952-)
Dead Man's Bounty '06
Flowers of Reverie '84
Fever '81

Chad Lindberg (1976-)
Punk Love '06
Push '06
National Lampoon's Adam & Eve '05
The Rookie '02
The Fast and the Furious '01
October Sky '99
Black Circle Boys '97

Gunnel Lindblom (1931-)
Hunger '66
The Virgin Spring '59
The Seventh Seal '56

Doris Linden
Hillbilly Blitzkrieg '42
Snuffy Smith, Yard Bird '42

Eric Linden (1909-94)
Criminals Within '41
Frolics on Ice '39
Gone with the Wind '39
Here's Flash Casey '38
Sweetheart of the Navy '37
Ah, Wilderness! '35
Let 'Em Have It '35
No Other Woman '33

Hal Linden (1931-)
Out to Sea '97
The Colony '95
A New Life '88
My Wicked, Wicked Ways '84
Starflight One '83
Father Figure '80
How to Break Up a Happy Divorce '76
Mr. Inside, Mr. Outside '74

Jennie Linden (1939-)
Charlie Muffin '79
Hedda '75
Women in Love '70
Nightmare '63

Cec Linder (1921-92)
Heavenly Bodies '84
Deadly Eyes '82
The Devil's Web '74
Vengeance Is Mine '74
A Touch of Class '73
Goldfinger '64
Lolita '62
Quatermass and the Pit '58

Max Linder (1883-1925)
Man in the Silk Hat '83
Seven Years Bad Luck '21
Man in the Silk Hat '15

Viveca Lindfors (1920-95)
Last Summer In the Hamptons '96
Stargate '94
Backstreet Justice '93
The Linguini Incident '92
Child of Darkness, Child of Light '91
Zandalee '91
Exiled in America '90
Exorcist 3: Legion '90
The Ann Jillian Story '88
Lady Beware '87
Rachel River '87
Secret Weapons '85
The Sure Thing '85
Silent Madness '84
Creepshow '82
Inside the Third Reich '82
The Best Little Girl in the World '81
For Ladies Only '81
The Hand '81
Marilyn: The Untold Story '80
Mom, the Wolfman and Me '80
Natural Enemies '79
Girlfriends '78
A Question of Guilt '78
A Wedding '78
Welcome to L.A. '77
Bell from Hell '74
The Way We Were '73
Coming Apart '69
Cauldron of Blood '67
The King of Kings '61
The Story of Ruth '60
Moonfleet '55
Four in a Jeep '51
Adventures of Don Juan '49

Peter Lindgren (1915-81)
The New Land '73
I Am Curious (Yellow) '67

Riki Lindhome (1981-)
The Last House on the Left '09
My Best Friend's Girl '08
Million Dollar Baby '04

Audra Lindley (1918-97)
Sudden Death '95
The New Age '94
Troop Beverly Hills '89
The Spellbinder '88
Stamp of a Killer '87
Desert Hearts '86
Best Friends '82
Cannery Row '82
Revenge of the Stepford Wives '80
The Heartbreak Kid '72

Carl Michael Lindner (1988-)
The Extreme Adventures of Super Dave '98
Krippendorf's Tribe '98
Slappy and the Stinkers '97

Delroy Lindo (1952-)
Up '09 (V)
This Christmas '07
Wondrous Oblivion '06
Domino '05
Sahara '05
The Core '03
Heist '01
The Last Castle '01
The One '01
Gone in 60 Seconds '00
Romeo Must Die '00
The Book of Stars '99
The Cider House Rules '99
Pros & Cons '99
Strange Justice: The Clarence Thomas and Anita Hill Story '99
Glory & Honor '98
The Devil's Advocate '97
First Time Felon '97
A Life Less Ordinary '97
Feeling Minnesota '96
Ransom '96
Soul of the Game '96
The Winner '96
Broken Arrow '95
Clockers '95
Get Shorty '95
Crooklyn '94
Blood In ... Blood Out: Bound by Honor '93
Mr. Jones '93
Malcolm X '92
Bright Angel '91
Mountains of the Moon '90
More American Graffiti '79
Find the Lady '76

Olga Lindo (1899-1968)
The Hidden Room '49
Things Happen at Night '48

Vincent Lindon (1959-)
La Moustache '05
Friday Night '02
Chaos '01
Seventh Heaven '98
A Man in Love '87
Betty Blue '86

Matt Lindquist
In Enemy Hands '04

Margaret Lindsay (1910-81)
Please Don't Eat the Daisies '60
Cass Timberlane '47
Club Havana '46
The Adventures of Rusty '45
The Spoilers '42
British Intelligence '40
The House of the Seven Gables '40
Jezebel '38
Bordertown '35
Dangerous '35
Devil Dogs of the Air '35
"G" Men '35
Baby Face '33
Cavalcade '33
Lady Killer '33

Robert Lindsay (1949-)
Friends & Crocodiles '05
Gideon's Daughter '05
Wimbledon '04
Horatio Hornblower: The Adventure Continues '01
Oliver Twist '00
Horatio Hornblower '99
Fierce Creatures '96
Genghis Cohn '93
Strike It Rich '90
Bert Rigby, You're a Fool '89
That'll Be the Day '73

Stuart Lindsell
Profile '54
Man of Evil '48

George Lindsey (1933-)
Return to Mayberry '85
Robin Hood '73 (V)

Joseph Lindsey
Caught Up '98
Public Enemies '96
Amongst Friends '93

Blake Lindsley (1973-)
Plain Dirty '04
Coastlines '02
Trial by Media '00
Starship Troopers '97
Swingers '96

Pierre Lindstedt (1943-)
The New Land '73
The Emigrants '72

Angela Lindvall (1979-)
Kiss Kiss Bang Bang '05
CQ '01

Helga Line (1932-)
Pulsebeat '85
Black Venus '83
The Mummy's Revenge '73
When the Screaming Stops '73
Horror Express '72
Horror Rises from the Tomb '72
The Saga of the Draculas '72
One Step to Hell '67
Nightmare Castle '65

Richard Lineback
Ready to Rumble '00
Dangerous Evidence: The Lori Jackson Story '99
The Baby Dance '98
Meet the Deedles '98
Varsity Blues '98
The Jackal '97
Tin Cup '96
Twister '96
Natural Born Killers '94
Speed '94
Woman with a Past '92
Beyond the Next Mountain '87

Stephi Lineburg (1982-)
Zoe '01
Breathing Lessons '94
Richie Rich '94

Rosaleen Linehan (1937-)
About Adam '00
Mad About Mambo '00
The Hi-Lo Country '98
The Matchmaker '97
Sharpe's Gold '94

Bai Ling (1972-)
Crank: High Voltage '09
Dim Sum Funeral '08
The Gene Generation '07
Living & Dying '07
Edmond '05
The Beautiful Country '04
My Baby's Daddy '04
She Hate Me '04
Three ... Extremes '04
Point of Origin '02
The Breed '01
The Lost Empire '01
Anna and the King '99
Wild Wild West '99
Row Your Boat '98
Red Corner '97
Somewhere in the City '97
Dead Weekend '95
The Crow '93

Wendy Lingham
Demonstrator '71
Zeta One '69

Paul (Link) Linke (1948-)
The Fear Inside '92
Parenthood '89
Motel Hell '80

Richard Linklater (1961-)
Waking Life '01
Beavis and Butt-Head Do America '96 (V)
The Underneath '95
Slacker '91

Art Linkletter (1912-)
Champagne for Caesar '50
People Are Funny '46

Cody Linley (1989-)
Hoot '06
My Dog Skip '99

Rex Linn (1956-)
Appaloosa '08
The Zodiac '05
After the Sunset '04
Cheaper by the Dozen '03
The Hunted '03
Crossfire Trail '01
Neil Simon's The Odd Couple 2 '98
Rush Hour '98
The Postman '97
Breakdown '96
Ghosts of Mississippi '96
Tin Cup '96
Children of Fury '94
Drop Zone '94
Wyatt Earp '94
Cliffhanger '93

Mark Linn-Baker (1954-)
Adam '09
Noises Off '92
Bare Essentials '91
Me and Him '89 (V)
Ghostwriter '84
My Favorite Year '82
Manhattan '79

Laura Linney (1964-)
John Adams '08
The Other Man '08
Breach '07
The Nanny Diaries '07
The Savages '07
Driving Lessons '06
The Hottest State '06
Jindabyne '06
Man of the Year '06
The Exorcism of Emily Rose '05
The Squid and the Whale '05
Kinsey '04
P.S. '04
The Life of David Gale '03
Love Actually '03
Mystic River '03
The Laramie Project '02
The Mothman Prophecies '02
Lush '01
Maze '01
Wild Iris '01
House of Mirth '00
Running Mates '00
Love Letters '99
You Can Count On Me '99
The Truman Show '98
Absolute Power '97
Armistead Maupin's More Tales of the City '97
Primal Fear '96
Congo '95
A Simple Twist of Fate '94
Armistead Maupin's Tales of the City '93
Blind Spot '93
Dave '93
Class of '61 '92

Richard Lintern
The Bank Job '08
The House of Eliott '92

Joanne Linville (1928-)
James Dean '01
From the Dead of Night '89
Secrets '77
Scorpio '73

Larry Linville (1939-2000)
No Dessert Dad, 'Til You Mow the Lawn '94
Body Waves '92
Rock 'n' Roll High School Forever '91
Earth Girls Are Easy '89
Blue Movies '88
School Spirit '85
Night Partners '83
The Night Stalker '71
The Stepmother '71

Alex D. Linz (1989-)
Choose Connor '07
Red Dragon '02 (V)
Max Keeble's Big Move '01
Race to Space '01
Bounce '00
Titan A.E. '00 (V)
The Dress Code '99

Tarzan '99 (V)
Home Alone 3 '97
The Cable Guy '96
One Fine Day '96
Vanished '95

Lio (1962-)
Carnage '02
Love After Love '94
Window Shopping '86
Elsa, Elsa '85
The Eighties '83

Leon M. Lion (1879-1947)
Amazing Adventure '37
No. 17 '32

Alberto Lionello (1930-94)
Till Marriage Do Us Part '74
Porcile '69

Therese Liotard (1949-)
My Father's Glory '91
My Mother's Castle '91
The Disenchanted '90
Cloud Waltzing '87
One Sings, the Other Doesn't '77

Ray Liotta (1955-)
Crazy on the Outside '10
Date Night '10
Youth in Revolt '10
Crossing Over '09
Observe and Report '09
Powder Blue '09
Hero Wanted '08
In the Name of the King: A Dungeon Siege Tale '08
The Line '08
Battle in Seattle '07
Bee Movie '07 (V)
Smokin' Aces '07
Wild Hogs '07
Even Money '06
Local Color '06
Revolver '05
Slow Burn '05
The Last Shot '04
Identity '03
John Q '02
Narc '02
Point of Origin '02
Blow '01
Hannibal '01
Heartbreakers '01
A Rumor of Angels '00
Forever Mine '99
Inferno '99
Muppets from Space '99
Phoenix '98
The Rat Pack '98
Cop Land '97
Turbulence '96
Unforgettable '96
Operation Dumbo Drop '95
Corrina, Corrina '94
No Escape '94
Article 99 '92
Unlawful Entry '92
Women & Men: In Love There Are No Rules '91
Goodfellas '90
Field of Dreams '89
Dominick & Eugene '88
Something Wild '86
The Lonely Lady '83

Daniele Liotti (1971-)
Doctor Zhivago '03
Mad Love '01

Eugene Lipinski (1956-)
Alice '09
The Lost Angel '04
The Recruit '03
Bless the Child '00
Restless Spirits '99
Small Vices: A Spenser Mystery '99
Aldrich Ames: Traitor Within '98
Perfectly Normal '91
Riders of the Storm '88
Going Home '86
Moonlighting '82

Maureen Lipman (1946-)
Lighthouse Hill '04
The Pianist '02
Captain Jack '98
Solomon and Gaenor '98
Carry On Columbus '92
The Little Princess '87
Educating Rita '83

Jonathan Lipnicki (1990-)
Like Mike '02
Stuart Little 2 '02
The Little Vampire '00
Stuart Little '99
Jerry Maguire '96

Jonathon Lippe
Blood Voyage '77
Green Eyes '76

David Lipper
Threshold '03
Federal Protection '02
Last Run '01
Bug Buster '99

Sarah K. Lippmann
Addicted to Murder 3: Bloodlust '99
Addicted to Murder 2: Tainted Blood '97

Dennis Lipscomb (1941-)
Automatic '94
Retribution '88
Guilty of Innocence '87
Sister, Sister '87
Slow Burn '86
Eyes of Fire '84
Union City '81

James Lipton
Bolt '08
Igor '08 (V)

Peggy Lipton (1947-)
Jackpot '01
Intern '00
The '70s '00
Skipped Parts '00
The Postman '97
The Spider and the Fly '94
Fatal Charm '92
Twin Peaks: Fire Walk with Me '92
Kinjite: Forbidden Subjects '89
I'm Gonna Git You Sucka '88
Purple People Eater '88
Mosby's Marauders '66

Robert Lipton
A Woman, Her Men and Her Futon '92
Lethal Woman '88

LisaRaye (1967-)
Beauty Shop '05
Gang of Roses '03
Civil Brand '02
All About You '01
The Wood '99
The Players Club '98

Joe Lisi (1950-)
Kiss of Death '94
Traces of Red '92
Come See the Paradise '90

Virna Lisi (1937-)
Balzac: A Life of Passion '99
Queen Margot '94
I Love N.Y. '87
Christopher Columbus '85
La Cicada '83
Miss Right '81
Night Flight from Moscow '73
Bluebeard '72
The Statue '71
Carbon Copy '69
The Secret of Santa Vittoria '69
When Wolves Cry '69
Assault on a Queen '66
Casanova '70 '65
How to Murder Your Wife '64

Eva '62

Pavel Liska (1971-)
The Country Teacher '08
Something Like Happiness '05
Up and Down '04

Leon Lissek (1927-)
Bloodmoon '90
The Unbearable Lightness of Being '88
Adventures of Eliza Fraser '76
Blockhouse '73

Peyton List
Shuttle '09
Deep Winter '08
The Greatest Game Ever Played '05

Moira Lister (1923-2007)
The 10th Kingdom '00
Cop-Out '67
Abandon Ship '57
John and Julie '55
Grand National Night '53
The Limping Man '53
Trouble in Store '53
Uneasy Terms '48

Tommy (Tiny) Lister (1958-)
The Dark Knight '08
Bone Dry '07
Who Made the Potatoe Salad? '05
Blast '04
My Baby's Daddy '04
Never Die Alone '04
Asylum of the Damned '03
Confidence '03
Austin Powers In Goldmember '02
The Wash '01
Circus '00
Little Nicky '00
Next Friday '00
Judgment Day '99
Supreme Sanction '99
I Got the Hook-Up '98
Never 2 Big '98
The Players Club '98
Wishmaster 2: Evil Never Dies '98
Body Count '97
The Fifth Element '97
Jackie Brown '97
Phat Beach '96
White Cargo '96
Friday '95
Hologram Man '95
Things to Do in Denver When You're Dead '95
Immortal Combat '94
Men of War '94
Posse '93
9 1/2 Ninjas '90
No Holds Barred '89
Secret Agent 00-Soul '89
Prison '88
Beverly Hills Cop 2 '87
Extreme Prejudice '87

Zoe Lister-Jones
Salt '10
The Wedding Bros. '08

Giorgio Listuzzi (1934-)
White Nights '57
The Roof '56

Litefoot (1969-)
Adaptation '02
Kull the Conqueror '97
Mortal Kombat 2: Annihilation '97
The Indian in the Cupboard '95

John Litel (1892-1972)
Sitting Bull '54
Montana Belle '52
The Fuller Brush Girl '50
Outpost in Morocco '49
Rusty's Birthday '49
Pitfall '48
Cass Timberlane '47
Northwest Trail '46

San Antonio '45
Boss of Big Town '43
So Proudly We Hail '43
Invisible Agent '42
They Died with Their Boots On '41
Castle on the Hudson '40
The Fighting 69th '40
Nancy Drew and the Hidden Staircase '39
Nancy Drew, Reporter '39
Nancy Drew—Trouble Shooter '39
Amazing Dr. Clitterhouse '38
Nancy Drew—Detective '38
A Slight Case of Murder '38
The Black Legion '37

John Lithgow (1945-)
Leap Year '10
Confessions of a Shopaholic '09
Kinsey '04
Orange County '02
Shrek '01 (V)
Don Quixote '00
Rugrats in Paris: The Movie '00 (V)
A Civil Action '98
Homegrown '97
Johnny Skidmarks '97
Hollow Point '95
My Brother's Keeper '95
Redwood Curtain '95
The Tuskegee Airmen '95
A Good Man in Africa '94
Princess Caraboo '94
Silent Fall '94
World War II: When Lions Roared '94
Cliffhanger '93
Love, Cheat & Steal '93
The Pelican Brief '93
The Wrong Man '93
Raising Cain '92
At Play in the Fields of the Lord '91
Ricochet '91
Ivory Hunters '90
Memphis Belle '90
Out Cold '89
Traveling Man '89
Distant Thunder '88
Baby Girl Scott '87
Harry and the Hendersons '87
The Manhattan Project '86
Santa Claus: The Movie '85
The Adventures of Buckaroo Banzai Across the Eighth Dimension '84
Footloose '84
The Glitter Dome '84
Mesmerized '84
2010: The Year We Make Contact '84
The Day After '83
Goldilocks & the Three Bears '83
Terms of Endearment '83
Twilight Zone: The Movie '83
I'm Dancing as Fast as I Can '82
The World According to Garp '82
Blow Out '81
Mom, the Wolfman and Me '80
Oldest Living Graduate '80
All That Jazz '79
Rich Kids '79
The Big Fix '78
Obsession '76
Dealing: Or the Berkeley-to-Boston Forty-Brick Lost-Bag Blues '72

Paulie (Litowsky) Litt
Speed Racer '08
Eternal Sunshine of the Spotless Mind '04
Jersey Girl '04

Ann Little
The Cradle of Courage '20
The Roaring Road '19

Cleavon Little (1939-92)
Perfect Harmony '91
Separate but Equal '91
Fletch Lives '89
Murder by Numbers '89
Gore Vidal's Lincoln '88
The Gig '85
Once Bitten '85
E. Nick: A Legend in His Own Mind '84
Surf 2 '84
Toy Soldiers '84
Double Exposure '82
Jimmy the Kid '82
The Salamander '82
Don't Look Back: The Story of Leroy "Satchel" Paige '81
High Risk '81
Scavenger Hunt '79
FM '78
Greased Lightning '77
Once Upon a Brothers Grimm '77
Blazing Saddles '74
Homecoming: A Christmas Story '71
Vanishing Point '71
Cotton Comes to Harlem '70

Kim Little
Social Intercourse '01
Sorority House Party '92

Mark Little (1959-)
The Wacky World of Wills & Burke '85
Waterfront '83

Michelle Little
Apollo 13 '95
Heartstrings '93
Blood Clan '91
Bluffing It '87
My Demon Lover '87
Radioactive Dreams '86
Appointment with Fear '85

Mickey Little (1941-)
Gun Crazy '49
Guns of Fury '49

Natasha Little (1969-)
Vanity Fair '04
Byron '03
Another Life '01
The Criminal '00
Greenfingers '00
Vanity Fair '99

Rich Little (1938-)
The Late Shift '96
Happy Hour '87
Dirty Tricks '81

Sacheen Little Feather (1947-)
Shoot the Sun Down '81
Johnny Firecloud '75
The Trial of Billy Jack '74

Little JJ (1990-)
Beauty Shop '05
Yours, Mine & Ours '05

Little Nell
See Nell Campbell

Little Richard (1935-)
Mystery, Alaska '99
Why Do Fools Fall in Love? '98
Last Action Hero '93
The Pickle '93
Mother Goose Rock 'n' Rhyme '90
Scenes from the Class Struggle in Beverly Hills '89
Purple People Eater '88
Down and Out in Beverly Hills '86
The Girl Can't Help It '56

Eddie Little Sky (1932-67)
Journey Through Rosebud '72
Savage Run '70

Lucien Littlefield (1895-1960)
Susanna Pass '49
Lights of Old Santa Fe '47
Treasure of Fear '45
One Body Too Many '44
Zorro's Black Whip '44
Bells of Capistrano '42
Hillbilly Blitzkrieg '42
Jeepers Creepers '39
The Gladiator '38
Hollywood Stadium Mystery '38
Wide Open Faces '38
Bulldog Drummond's Revenge '37
Let's Sing Again '36
The Moon's Our Home '36
Kiss and Make Up '34
The Bitter Tea of General Yen '33
Rainbow over Broadway '33
Strangers of the Evening '32
Reducing '31
Tom Sawyer '30
Seven Keys to Baldpate '29
The Cat and the Canary '27
My Best Girl '27
Twinkletoes '26
Charley's Aunt '25
Tumbleweeds '25
Leap Year '21
The Sheik '21

Gary Littlejohn
Badlands '74
Angels Hard As They Come '71
Bury Me an Angel '71

Chia Hui Liu
Drunken Monkey '02
Shaolin & Wu Tang '81
The 36th Chamber of Shaolin '78

Chia Yung Liu
The 36th Chamber of Shaolin '78
Master of the Flying Guillotine '75

Ernest Liu
Get a Clue! '98
From Dusk Till Dawn '95

Gordon (Chia Hui) Liu (1955-)
Chandni Chowk to China '09
Kill Bill Vol. 2 '04
Kill Bill Vol. 1 '03

Harrison Liu
Warriors of Heaven and Earth '03
Black Robe '91
Dr. Bethune '90

Lucy Liu (1968-)
Kung Fu Panda '08 (V)
Code Name: The Cleaner '07
Rise: Blood Hunter '07
Watching the Detectives '07
Lucky Number Slevin '06
Domino '05
Kill Bill Vol. 2 '04
Charlie's Angels: Full Throttle '03
Kill Bill Vol. 1 '03
Ballistic: Ecks vs. Sever '02
Chicago '02
Cypher '02
Hotel '01
Charlie's Angels '00
Shanghai Noon '00
The Mating Habits of the Earthbound Human '99
Molly '99
Play It to the Bone '99
Payback '98
Flypaper '97
City of Industry '96

Matty Liu
Off the Lip '04
In God's Hands '98

Peiqi Liu
Together '02
Shadow Magic '00

Ermo *'94*

Rene Liu (1970-)

Double Vision *'02*
Fleeing by Night *'00*
The Personals *'98*

Terry Liu

Infra-Man *'76*
Super Inframan *'76*

Tony Liu

Human Lanterns *'82*
Enter the Dragon *'73*

Ye Liu

Blood Brothers *'07*
Dark Matter *'07*
Purple Butterfly *'03*

Boris Livanov

Baltic Deputy *'37*
Ten Days That Shook the World *'27*

Blake Lively (1987-)

New York, I Love You *'09*
The Private Lives of Pippa Lee *'09*
The Sisterhood of the Traveling Pants 2 *'08*
Simon Says *'07*
Accepted *'06*
Sisterhood of the Traveling Pants *'05*

Eric Lively (1981-)

Deep Winter *'08*
24 : Redemption *'08*
Sex and Breakfast *'07*
The Breed *'06*
The Butterfly Effect 2 *'06*
Speak *'04*
Uprising *'01*
Crash Course *'00*
American Pie *'99*

Ernie Lively (1947-)

The Sisterhood of the Traveling Pants 2 *'08*
The Legend of Cryin' Ryan *'98*
Senseless *'98*
Accidental Meeting *'93*

Jason Lively (1968-)

Maximum Force *'92*
Rock 'n' Roll High School Forever *'91*
Ghost Chase *'88*
Night of the Creeps *'86*
National Lampoon's European Vacation *'85*

Robin (Robyn) Lively (1972-)

Strike *'07*
Crazy from the Heart *'91*
The Karate Kid: Part 3 *'89*
Not Quite Human 2 *'89*
Teen Witch *'89*
Buckeye and Blue *'87*
Not Quite Human *'87*

Jack Livesey (1901-61)

The World Owes Me a Living *'47*
Never Too Late to Mend *'37*

Roger Livesey (1906-76)

Of Human Bondage *'64*
The Entertainer *'60*
The League of Gentlemen *'60*
The Master of Ballantrae *'53*
Green Grow the Rushes *'51*
Stairway to Heaven *'46*
I Know Where I'm Going *'45*
The Life and Death of Colonel Blimp *'43*
The Girl in the News *'41*
Drums *'38*
Lorna Doone *'34*

Barry Livingston (1953-)

Final Approach *'08*
You Don't Mess with the Zohan *'08*
Invisible Mom 2 *'99*
Steel Sharks *'97*
Invisible Mom *'96*
Easy Wheels *'89*

John Livingston (1961-)

Dopamine *'03*
The Stickup *'01*
Where's Marlowe? *'98*
Dogtown *'97*
Mr. Wrong *'95*

Margaret Livingston (1895-1984)

The Lady Refuses *'31*
The Charlatan *'29*
Seven Keys to Baldpate *'29*
Through the Breakers *'28*
Sunrise *'27*
Up the Ladder *'25*
The Busher *'19*

Robert "Bob" Livingston (1904-88)

Blazing Stewardesses *'75*
I Spit on Your Corpse *'74*
Mysterious Desperado *'49*
Grand Canyon Trail *'48*
The Undercover Woman *'46*
The Cheaters *'45*
Don't Fence Me In *'45*
Death Rides the Plains *'44*
Law of the Saddle *'43*
Raiders of Red Gap *'43*
Gangs of Sonora *'41*
Covered Wagon Days *'40*
Oklahoma Renegades *'40*
Pioneers of the West *'40*
Rocky Mountain Rangers *'40*
Cowboys from Texas *'39*
The Kansas Terrors *'39*
Call the Mesquiteers *'38*
Heroes of the Hills *'38*
Outlaws of Sonora *'38*
Purple Vigilantes *'38*
Circus Girl *'37*
Come on, Cowboys *'37*
Heart of the Rockies *'37*
Hit the Saddle *'37*
Larceny On the Air *'37*
Riders of the Whistling Skull *'37*
Roarin' Lead *'37*
Wild Horse Rodeo *'37*
The Bold Caballero *'36*
Ghost Town Gold *'36*
The Three Mesquiteers *'36*
The Vigilantes Are Coming *'36*

Ron Livingston (1968-)

Dinner for Schmucks *'10*
Going the Distance *'10*
The Time Traveler's Wife *'09*
American Crude *'07*
Holly *'07*
Music Within *'07*
Relative Strangers *'06*
Pretty Persuasion *'05*
Little Black Book *'04*
Winter Solstice *'04*
The Cooler *'03*
44 Minutes: The North Hollywood Shootout *'03*
King of the Ants *'03*
Adaptation *'02*
Buying the Cow *'02*
Band of Brothers *'01*
Beat *'00*
A Rumor of Angels *'00*
Two Ninas *'00*
The Big Brass Ring *'99*
Body Shots *'99*
Campfire Tales *'98*
Office Space *'98*
Swingers *'96*

Shelby Livingston

2000 Maniacs *'64*
Nude on the Moon *'61*

Stanley Livingston (1950-)

Attack of the 60-Foot Centerfold *'95*
Smokey & the Hotwire Gang *'79*
Private Parts *'72*

Kari Lizer (1961-)

Private School *'83*
Smokey Bites the Dust *'81*

LL Cool J (1968-)

The Deal *'08*
Last Holiday *'06*
Edison Force *'05*
Mindhunters *'05*
Slow Burn *'05*
Deliver Us from Eva *'03*
Rugrats Go Wild! *'03 (V)*
S.W.A.T. *'03*
Rollerball *'02*
Kingdom Come *'01*
Charlie's Angels *'00*
Any Given Sunday *'99*
Deep Blue Sea *'99*
In Too Deep *'99*
Caught Up *'98*
Halloween: H20 *'98*
Woo *'97*
Out of Sync *'95*
The Right to Remain Silent *'95*
Toys *'92*
The Hard Way *'91*
Krush Groove *'85*

Suzette Llewellyn

Manderlay *'05*
Welcome II the Terrordome *'95*

Desmond Llewelyn (1914-99)

The World Is Not Enough *'99*
Tomorrow Never Dies *'97*
Goldeneye *'95*
Merlin *'92*
License to Kill *'89*
The Living Daylights *'87*
A View to a Kill *'85*
For Your Eyes Only *'81*
Moonraker *'79*
The Spy Who Loved Me *'77*
The Man with the Golden Gun *'74*
Diamonds Are Forever *'71*
On Her Majesty's Secret Service *'69*
You Only Live Twice *'67*
Thunderball *'65*
Goldfinger *'64*
From Russia with Love *'63*

Christopher Lloyd (1938-)

Piranha 3D *'10*
Meteor *'09*
Santa Buddies *'09*
Fly Me to the Moon *'08*
The Tale of Despereaux *'08 (V)*
Flakes *'07*
Masters of Horror: Valerie on the Stairs *'06*
A Perfect Day *'06*
Hey Arnold! The Movie *'02 (V)*
Interstate 60 *'02*
When Good Ghouls Go Bad *'01*
Wit *'01*
Chasing Destiny *'00*
Wish You Were Dead *'00*
Alice in Wonderland *'99*
Angels in the Endzone *'98*
Baby Geniuses *'98*
It Came from the Sky *'98*
My Favorite Martian *'98*
Premonition *'98*
Quicksilver Highway *'98*
Anastasia *'97 (V)*
The Real Blonde *'97*
Cadillac Ranch *'96*
Changing Habits *'96*
Rent-A-Kid *'95*
The Right to Remain Silent *'95*
Things to Do in Denver When You're Dead *'95*
Angels in the Outfield *'94*
Camp Nowhere *'94*
The Pagemaster *'94 (V)*
Radioland Murders *'94*
Addams Family Values *'93*
Dennis the Menace *'93*
Twenty Bucks *'93*
Dead Ahead: The Exxon Valdez Disaster *'92*
T Bone N Weasel *'92*
The Addams Family *'91*
Suburban Commando *'91*
Back to the Future, Part 3 *'90*
DuckTales the Movie: Treasure of the Lost Lamp *'90 (V)*
Why Me? *'90*
Back to the Future, Part 2 *'89*
The Dream Team *'89*
Eight Men Out *'88*
Track 29 *'88*
Who Framed Roger Rabbit *'88*
Walk Like a Man *'87*
Miracles *'86*
Back to the Future *'85*
Clue *'85*
The Adventures of Buckaroo Banzai Across the Eighth Dimension *'84*
The Cowboy & the Ballerina *'84*
Joy of Sex *'84*
Star Trek 3: The Search for Spock *'84*
Mr. Mom *'83*
September Gun *'83*
To Be or Not to Be *'83*
Pilgrim, Farewell *'82*
Legend of the Lone Ranger *'81*
National Lampoon Goes to the Movies *'81*
The Postman Always Rings Twice *'81*
The Black Marble *'79*
Fantastic Seven *'79*
Lady in Red *'79*
The Onion Field *'79*
Goin' South *'78*
Three Warriors *'77*
One Flew Over the Cuckoo's Nest *'75*

Danny Lloyd (1972-)

Will: G. Gordon Liddy *'82*
The Shining *'80*

Doris Lloyd (1896-1968)

The Time Machine *'60*
G.I. War Brides *'46*
The Invisible Man's Revenge *'44*
Journey for Margaret *'42*
The Black Doll *'38*
Motive for Revenge *'35*
A Shot in the Dark *'35*
Disraeli *'30*
The Drake Case *'29*
Exit Smiling *'26*

Emily Lloyd (1971-)

Boogie Boy *'98*
The Real Thing *'97*
Welcome to Sarajevo *'97*
Under the Hula Moon *'95*
When Saturday Comes *'95*
A River Runs Through It *'92*
Scorchers *'92*
Chicago Joe & the Showgirl *'90*
Cookie *'89*
In Country *'89*
Wish You Were Here *'87*

Emily Ann Lloyd (1984-)

Annie: A Royal Adventure *'95*
Apollo 13 *'95*

Eric Lloyd (1986-)

The Santa Clause 3: The Escape Clause *'06*
The Santa Clause 2 *'02*
Luminous Motion *'00*
Chameleon *'98*
Deconstructing Harry *'97*
Dunston Checks In *'95*
The Santa Clause *'94*

George Lloyd (1897-1967)

I Accuse My Parents *'45*
White Pongo *'45*
San Quentin *'37*

Harold Lloyd (1893-1971)

Days of Thrills and Laughter *'61*
The Sin of Harold Diddlebock *'47*
Milky Way *'36*
Feet First *'30*
Speedy *'28*
The Kid Brother *'27*
For Heaven's Sake *'26*
The Freshman *'25*
Girl Shy *'24*
Safety Last *'23*

Harold Lloyd, Jr. (1931-71)

Married Too Young *'62*
Platinum High School *'60*
Girls' Town *'59*
The Flaming Urge *'53*

Hugh Lloyd (1923-)

Cider with Rosie *'99*
August *'95*

Jake Lloyd (1989-)

Madison *'01*
Race to Space *'01*
Star Wars: Episode 1—The Phantom Menace *'99*
Jingle All the Way *'96*
Unhook the Stars *'96*

Jeremy Lloyd

Murder on the Orient Express *'74*
Doctor in Clover *'66*

Jimmy Lloyd (1918-88)

G.I. Jane *'51*
Miss Grant Takes Richmond *'49*
Riders of the Whistling Pines *'49*
Sea Hound *'47*
The Jolson Story *'46*
The Story of G.I. Joe *'45*

John Bedford Lloyd (1956-)

The Killing Floor *'06*
The Bourne Supremacy *'04*
The Manchurian Candidate *'04*
Super Troopers *'01*
Fair Game *'95*
Killer: A Journal of Murder *'95*
Philadelphia *'93*
Waiting for the Light *'90*
The Abyss *'89*
Crossing Delancey *'88*
Sweet Lorraine *'87*
Tough Guys Don't Dance *'87*

Kathleen Lloyd (1949-)

Fly Boy *'99*
Call to Glory *'84*
Gangster Wars *'81*
The Jayne Mansfield Story *'80*
Take Down *'79*
It's Alive 2: It Lives Again *'78*
The Car *'77*
Skateboard *'77*
Missouri Breaks *'76*

Norman Lloyd (1914-)

In Her Shoes *'05*
The Song of the Lark *'01*
The Adventures of Rocky & Bullwinkle *'00*
Fail Safe *'00*
Journey of Honor *'91*
Amityville 4: The Evil Escapes *'89*
Jaws of Satan *'81*
The Nude Bomb *'80*
Audrey Rose *'77*
Buccaneer's Girl *'50*
A Walk in the Sun *'46*
The Southerner *'45*
Saboteur *'42*

Rollo Lloyd (1883-1938)

The Lives of a Bengal Lancer *'35*

Carnival Lady *'33*

Sabrina Lloyd (1970-)

Racing Daylight *'07*
The Last Request *'06*
The Breakup Artist *'04*
Dopamine *'03*
On Edge *'03*
Father Hood *'93*

Sue Lloyd (1939-)

Bullet to Beijing *'95*
The Bitch *'78*
Number 1 of the Secret Service *'77*
Ned Kelly *'70*
The Ipcress File *'65*
Hysteria *'64*

Charles Lloyd-Pack (1905-83)

If... *'69*
Bedazzled *'68*
The Reptile *'66*
The Terror of the Tongs *'61*
Victim *'61*
The Horror of Dracula *'58*
Stranger in Town *'57*
River Beat *'54*

Roger Lloyd-Pack (1944-)

The History of Mr. Polly *'07*
Harry Potter and the Goblet of Fire *'05*
The Young Poisoner's Handbook *'94*
Fright *'71*

Carmen (Lee) Llywelyn

Cowboys and Angels *'00*
The Mod Squad *'99*
Never Been Kissed *'99*
Chasing Amy *'97*

Candy Lo (1974-)

The Eye *'02*
Time and Tide *'00*
The Cave of the Silken Web *'67*

Chi Muoi Lo

Catfish in Black Bean Sauce *'00*
The Relic *'96*

Lieh Lo (1939-2002)

Human Lanterns *'82*
The 36th Chamber of Shaolin *'78*
Chinese Connection 2 *'77*
King Boxer *'72*
Sword Masters: Brothers Five *'70*

Meng Lo

Life Gamble *'04*
Five Element Ninjas *'82*
Human Lanterns *'82*
Heaven & Hell *'78*

Luigi Lo Cascio (1967-)

Don't Tell *'05*
Best of Youth *'03*
Light of My Eyes *'01*

Enrico Lo Verso (1964-)

Baaria *'09*
Hannibal *'01*
Moses *'96*
Lamerica *'95*
Farinelli *'94*
La Scorta *'94*
The Stolen Children *'92*

Tony LoBianco (1935-)

Endangered Species *'02*
Friends and Family *'01*
Rocky Marciano *'99*
Mafia! *'98*
Bomb Squad *'97*
Sworn to Justice *'97*
The Juror *'96*
Nixon *'95*
Tyson *'95*
The Ascent *'94*
Boiling Point *'93*
Teamster Boss: The Jackie Presser Story *'92*
City of Hope *'91*
The Ten Million Dollar Getaway *'91*

The Ann Jillian Story '88
Blood Ties '87
City Heat '84
Separate Ways '82
Last Cry for Help '79
Marciano '79
Bloodbrothers '78
F.I.S.T. '78
Magee and the Lady '78
Goldenrod '77
God Told Me To '76
Mean Frank and Crazy Tony '75
Mr. Inside, Mr. Outside '74
The Story of Jacob & Joseph '74
Escape from Death Row '73
The Seven-Ups '73
The French Connection '71
Honeymoon Killers '70

Jane Lobre
The Green Room '78
A Gentle Woman '69

Amy Locane (1972-)
Secretary '02
Hell's Gate '01
Bongwater '98
Implicated '98
Route 9 '98
Bram Stoker's The Mummy '97
Ebenezer '97
End of Summer '97
Going All the Way '97
Love to Kill '97
Prefontaine '96
Carried Away '95
Criminal Hearts '95
Airheads '94
School Ties '92
Blue Sky '91
No Secrets '91
Cry-Baby '90
Lost Angels '89

David Lochary (1944-77)
Female Trouble '74
Pink Flamingos '72
Multiple Maniacs '70
Mondo Trasho '69

Hannah Lochner
Jack and Jill vs. the World '08
The Devil's Mercy '07
Harm's Way '07
Encrypt '03

Bruce Locke
Ripper Man '96
RoboCop 3 '91

Katherine Locke (1910-95)
People Will Talk '51
Try and Get Me '50
The Seventh Cross '44

Philip Locke (1928-2004)
Othello '95
Tom & Viv '94
And the Ship Sails On '83
Fiction Makers '67

Ryan Locke
The New Twenty '08
Supercross: The Movie '05

Sondra Locke (1947-)
The Prophet's Game '99
Tales of the Unexpected '91
Ratboy '86
Sudden Impact '83
Rosie: The Rosemary Clooney Story '82
Any Which Way You Can '80
Bronco Billy '80
Second Coming of Suzanne '80
Every Which Way But Loose '78
The Gauntlet '77
Seducers '77
Shadow of Chikara '77
The Outlaw Josey Wales '76
A Reflection of Fear '72
Willard '71
The Heart Is a Lonely Hunter '68

Spencer Locke (1991-)
Resident Evil: Extinction '07
Monster House '06 (V)

Anne Lockhart (1953-)
Bug Buster '99
Big Bad John '90
Dark Tower '87
Troll '86
Hambone & Hillie '84
Savage Hunger '84
Mission Galactica: The Cylon Attack '78
Joyride '77
Slashed Dreams '74

Calvin Lockhart (1934-2007)
Predator 2 '90
The Baron '88
Coming to America '88
The Beast Must Die '75
Let's Do It Again '75
Honeybaby '74
Uptown Saturday Night '74
Cotton Comes to Harlem '70
Dark of the Sun '68

Emma Lockhart
Ace Ventura Jr.: Pet Detective '08
Looking for Comedy in the Muslim World '06

Gene Lockhart (1891-1957)
Carousel '56
The Man in the Gray Flannel Suit '56
Francis Covers the Big Town '53
Face to Face '52
A Girl in Every Port '52
Hoodlum Empire '52
I'd Climb the Highest Mountain '51
Rhubarb '51
The Big Hangover '50
Riding High '50
The Inspector General '49
Madame Bovary '49
That Wonderful Urge '48
Cynthia '47
Her Husband's Affairs '47
Miracle on 34th Street '47
A Scandal in Paris '46
The Strange Woman '46
House on 92nd Street '45
Leave Her to Heaven '45
Action in Arabia '44
Going My Way '44
Mission to Moscow '43
Northern Pursuit '43
Hangmen Also Die '42
Juke Girl '42
Billy the Kid '41
The Devil & Daniel Webster '41
International Lady '41
Meet John Doe '41
The Sea Wolf '41
They Died with Their Boots On '41
Abe Lincoln in Illinois '40
Edison the Man '40
His Girl Friday '40
South of Pago Pago '40
The Story of Alexander Graham Bell '39
Algiers '38
Blondie '38
A Christmas Carol '38
Of Human Hearts '38
Sinners in Paradise '38
The Devil Is a Sissy '36
Earthworm Tractors '36
Something to Sing About '36
Wedding Present '36
Crime and Punishment '35

June Lockhart (1925-)
Holiday in Handcuffs '07
Au Pair 2: The Fairy Tale Continues '01
Lost in Space '98
The Colony '95
Out There '95
Sleep with Me '94
Dead Women in Lingerie '90
The Gift of Love '90
The Big Picture '89
Rented Lips '88
Troll '86
Strange Invaders '83
Butterfly '82
The Capture of Grizzly Adams '82
Deadly Games '80
Just Tell Me You Love Me '80
Walking Through the Fire '80
Curse of the Black Widow '77
Lassie's Great Adventure '62
T-Men '47
Easy to Wed '46
She Wolf of London '46
The Yearling '46
Son of Lassie '45
Meet Me in St. Louis '44
The White Cliffs of Dover '44
Miss Annie Rooney '42
Adam Had Four Sons '41
Sergeant York '41
All This and Heaven Too '40

Heather Locklear (1962-)
Flirting with Forty '09
Flying By '09
Hannah Montana: The Movie '09
Angels Fall '07
The Perfect Man '05
Looney Tunes: Back in Action '03
Uptown Girls '03
Double Tap '98
Money Talks '97
The First Wives Club '96
The Great American Sex Scandal '94
Fade to Black '93
Body Language '92
Illusions '91
The Big Slice '90
Lethal Charm '90
The Return of Swamp Thing '89
City Killer '87
Firestarter '84
Twirl '81

Loryn Locklin
Fortress '93
Taking Care of Business '90
Catch Me... If You Can '89

Gary Lockwood (1937-)
Night of the Scarecrow '95
Terror in Paradise '90
The Wild Pair '87
Survival Zone '84
The Incredible Journey of Dr. Meg Laurel '79
Bad Georgia Road '77
Project: Kill! '77
Manhunter '74
Earth II '71
R.P.M.* (*Revolutions Per Minute) '70
Model Shop '69
Firecreek '68
2001: A Space Odyssey '68
It Happened at the World's Fair '63
The Magic Sword '62
Wild in the Country '61
Tall Story '60

Julia Lockwood
No Kidding '60
Teenage Bad Girl '59

Margaret Lockwood (1911-90)
The Slipper and the Rose '76
Cast a Dark Shadow '55
Trouble in the Glen '54
Bedelia '46
The Man in Grey '45
The Wicked Lady '45
The Girl in the News '41
Night Train to Munich '40
The Stars Look Down '39
Susannah of the Mounties '39
The Lady Vanishes '38
Dr. Syn '37
Lorna Doone '34

Thomas Lockyer
Dog Soldiers '01
Jesus '00
Ultraviolet '98
Incognito '97
The Scarlet Tunic '97
Teenagers from Outer Space '59

Barbara Loden (1932-80)
Iron Cowboy '68
Splendor in the Grass '61

Anne Marie Loder (1969-)
Life-Size '00
Blacklight '98

John Loder (1898-1988)
Small Hotel '57
The Story of Esther Costello '57
Dishonored Lady '47
Brighton Strangler '45
The Woman Who Came Back '45
Abroad with Two Yanks '44
The Hairy Ape '44
Passage to Marseilles '44
How Green Was My Valley '41
Tin Pan Alley '40
Dr. Syn '37
King Solomon's Mines '37
Non-Stop New York '37
The Man Who Lived Again '36
River of Unrest '36
Sabotage '36
Java Head '35
The Silent Passenger '35
Lorna Doone '34
My Song Goes Round the World '34
The Private Life of Henry VIII '33
Wedding Rehearsal '32

Kathryn Loder (1940-)
Foxy Brown '74
The Big Doll House '71

David Lodge (1921-2003)
Edge of Sanity '89
Killer with Two Faces '74
The Railway Children '70
Oh! What a Lovely War '69
What's Good for the Goose '69
Trial & Error '62
The Hellfire Club '61
Two-Way Stretch '60

Jean Lodge (1927-)
Terror Ship '54
Dick Barton Strikes Back '48

John Lodge (1903-85)
The Witchmaker '69
De Mayerling a Sarajevo '40
Bulldog Drummond at Bay '37
River of Unrest '36
The Little Colonel '35
Scarlet Empress '34
Murders in the Zoo '33
Seas Beneath '31

Fiona Loewi (1975-)
Invasion! '99
Blackheart '98
Love and Death on Long Island '97

Jeanette Loff (1906-42)
Fightin' Ranch '30
Fighting Thru '30
King of Jazz '30
Party Girls '29
Annapolis '28

Marianne Lofgren (1910-57)
Only One Night '42
June Night '40

Arthur Loft (1897-1947)
Lights of Old Santa Fe '47
It's a Pleasure '45
Charlie Chan in the Secret Service '44
Woman in the Window '44
Blue, White and Perfect '42
Carson City Kid '40
Riders of Pasco Basin '40
Southward Ho! '39
Gang Bullets '38
I Am the Law '38
Hard to Hold '37
Public Cowboy No. 1 '37
Kid Courageous '35
Western Justice '35

Lenny Y. Loftin
From Dusk Till Dawn 3: The Hangman's Daughter '99
Underground Terror '88

Cecilia Loftus (1876-1943)
The Black Cat '41
Lucky Partners '40

Jacqueline Logan (1901-83)
King of the Kongo '29
Ships in the Night '28
King of Kings '27

Janice Logan (1915-65)
Dr. Cyclops '40
What a Life '39

Phyllis Logan (1956-)
All the King's Men '99
Invasion: Earth '98
Secrets and Lies '95
Freddie the Frog '92 (V)
And a Nightingale Sang '91
Goldeneye: The Secret Life of Ian Fleming '89
The Inquiry '87
The Kitchen Toto '87
The Doctor and the Devils '85
The McGuffin '85
Another Time, Another Place '83

Ricky Dean Logan
Freddy's Dead: The Final Nightmare '91
Back to the Future, Part 3 '90
Back to the Future, Part 2 '89

Robert F. Logan (1941-)
Man Outside '88
Death Ray 2000 '81
Mountain Family Robinson '79
Sea Gypsies '78
Further Adventures of the Wilderness Family, Part 2 '77
Snowbeast '77
Across the Great Divide '76
The Adventures of the Wilderness Family '76

Stanley Logan (1885-1953)
Double Crossbones '51
That Forsyte Woman '50
My Son, My Son '40

Robert Loggia (1930-)
Shrink '09
Forget About It '06
Rain '06
The Deal '05
Return to Me '00
Bonanno: A Godfather's Story '99
Joan of Arc '99
The Suburbans '99
American Virgin '98
Holy Man '98
Flypaper '97
Joe Torre: Curveballs Along the Way '97
National Lampoon's The Don's Analyst '97
The Proposition '97
Wide Awake '97
Independence Day '96
Lost Highway '96
Mistrial '96
Pandora's Clock '96
Smilla's Sense of Snow '96
Man with a Gun '95
Picture Windows '95
The Right to Remain Silent '95
Bad Girls '94
Coldblooded '94
I Love Trouble '94
White Mile '94
Lifepod '93
Mercy Mission '93
Wild Palms '93
Afterburn '92
Gladiator '92
Innocent Blood '92
The Marrying Man '91
Necessary Roughness '91
Code Name: Chaos '90
Intrigue '90
Opportunity Knocks '90
Relentless '89
Running Away '89
Triumph of the Spirit '89
Big '88
Oliver & Company '88 (V)
The Believers '87
Conspiracy: The Trial of the Chicago Eight '87
Echoes in the Darkness '87
Gaby: A True Story '87
Hot Pursuit '87
Target: Favorite Son '87
Armed and Dangerous '86
Over the Top '86
That's Life! '86
The Jagged Edge '85
Prizzi's Honor '85
Curse of the Pink Panther '83
Psycho 2 '83
Scarface '83
An Officer and a Gentleman '82
Trail of the Pink Panther '82
A Woman Called Golda '82
S.O.B. '81
The Ninth Configuration '79
Revenge of the Pink Panther '78
Speedtrap '78
First Love '77
The Greatest Story Ever Told '65
The Three Sisters '65
The Lost Missile '58
The Nine Lives of Elfego Baca '58
The Garment Jungle '57
Somebody Up There Likes Me '56

Donal Logue (1966-)
The Lodger '09
Max Payne '08
The Ex '07
Ghost Rider '07
The Good Life '07
Purple Violets '07
Zodiac '07
Almost Heaven '06
The Groomsmen '06
Just like Heaven '05
American Splendor '03
Confidence '03
Two Days '03
Comic Book Villains '02
The Chateau '01
The Patriot '00
Reindeer Games '00
Steal This Movie! '00
The Tao of Steve '00
The Big Tease '99
The Million Dollar Hotel '99
Runaway Bride '99
Blade '98
A Bright Shining Lie '98
The Thin Red Line '98
Glam '97
Dear God '96

Metro '96
Baja '95
The Crew '95
The Grave '95
And the Band Played On '93
Gettysburg '93
Sneakers '92

Lindsay Lohan (1986-)
Labor Pains '09
Chapter 27 '07
Georgia Rule '07
I Know Who Killed Me '07
Bobby '06
Just My Luck '06
A Prairie Home Companion '06
Herbie: Fully Loaded '05
Confessions of a Teenage Drama Queen '04
Mean Girls '04
Freaky Friday '03
Get a Clue '02
Life-Size '00
The Parent Trap '98

Svea Lohde
Summer of '04 '06
Rosenstrasse '03

Alison Lohman (1979-)
Drag Me to Hell '09
Gamer '09
Beowulf '07 (V)
Things We Lost in the Fire '07
Flicka '06
The Big White '05
Where the Truth Lies '05
Big Fish '03
Matchstick Men '03
White Oleander '02
The Thirteenth Floor '99

Marie Lohr (1890-1975)
Abandon Ship '57
Small Hotel '57
Escapade '55
Counterblast '48
The Magic Bow '47
Pygmalion '38
South Riding '37

Florence Loiret-Caille
The Intruder '04
Time of the Wolf '03

Kristanna Loken (1979-)
In the Name of the King: A Dungeon Siege Tale '08
BloodRayne '06
Lime Salted Love '06
Terminator 3: Rise of the Machines '03
Gangland '00

Gina Lollobrigida (1927-)
Bad Man's River '72
King, Queen, Knave '72
Buona Sera, Mrs. Campbell '68
Private Navy of Sgt. O'Farrell '68
Hotel Paradiso '66
Strange Bedfellows '65
Woman of Straw '64
Imperial Venus '63
Come September '61
The Unfaithfuls '60
Never So Few '59
Solomon and Sheba '59
Where the Hot Wind Blows '59
Four Ways Out '57
The Hunchback of Notre Dame '57
Trapeze '56
A Woman of Rome '56
Beat the Devil '53
Bread, Love and Dreams '53
Beauties of the Night '52
The Wayward Wife '52
Fanfan la Tulipe '51
Young Caruso '51

Herbert Lom (1917-)
Son of the Pink Panther '93
The Devil's Daughter '91
The Pope Must Diet '91
Masque of the Red Death '90
River of Death '90
Skeleton Coast '89
Ten Little Indians '89
Going Bananas '88
King Solomon's Mines '85
Curse of the Pink Panther '83
Dead Zone '83
Whoops Apocalypse '83
Trail of the Pink Panther '82
Peter and Paul '81
Hopscotch '80
The Man with Bogart's Face '80
The Lady Vanishes '79
Revenge of the Pink Panther '78
The Pink Panther Strikes Again '76
Ten Little Indians '75
Return of the Pink Panther '74
And Now the Screaming Starts '73
Asylum '72
Count Dracula '71
Murders in the Rue Morgue '71
Dorian Gray '70
Journey to the Far Side of the Sun '69
Mark of the Devil '69
99 Women '69
Uncle Tom's Cabin '69
Villa Rides '68
Gambit '66
A Shot in the Dark '64
The Horse Without a Head '63
The Phantom of the Opera '62
Tiara Tahiti '62
The Frightened City '61
Mysterious Island '61
Flame Over India '60
Spartacus '60
Third Man on the Mountain '59
Room 43 '58
Fire Down Below '57
War and Peace '56
The Ladykillers '55
Paris Express '53
The Golden Salamander '51
The Black Rose '50
Night and the City '50
Dual Alibi '47
The Seventh Veil '46
Appointment with Crime '45
Hotel Reserve '44
Secret Mission '42

Herbert Lomas
The Ghost Train '41
The Ghost Goes West '36

Carole Lombard (1908-42)
To Be or Not to Be '42
Mr. & Mrs. Smith '41
They Knew What They Wanted '40
In Name Only '39
Made for Each Other '39
Nothing Sacred '37
Swing High, Swing Low '37
My Man Godfrey '36
The Princess Comes Across '36
Hands Across the Table '35
Lady by Choice '34
Now and Forever '34
Twentieth Century '34
We're Not Dressing '34
The Eagle and the Hawk '33
Supernatural '33
No Man of Her Own '32
No One Man '32
Sinners in the Sun '32
Man of the World '31
Big News '29
High Voltage '29
The Racketeer '29
Mack & Carole '28
Power '28

Karina Lombard (1969-)
Footsteps '98
Kull the Conqueror '97
Last Man Standing '96
Legends of the Fall '94
The Firm '93
Wide Sargasso Sea '92

Louise Lombard (1971-)
Hidalgo '04
After the Rain '99
Russell Mulcahy's Tale of the Mummy '99
Esther '98
The House of Eliott '92

Louis Lombardi (1968-)
Doughboys '08
Confidence '03
Deuces Wild '02
The Animal '01
3000 Miles to Graceland '01
The Crew '00
Suicide Kings '97
Father's Day '96
The Immortals '95
The Usual Suspects '95
Beverly Hills Cop 3 '94
Natural Born Killers '94
Amongst Friends '93

Domenick Lombardozzi (1976-)
Find Me Guilty '06
Carlito's Way: Rise to Power '05
S.W.A.T. '03
Love in the Time of Money '02
Just One Time '00
The Young Girl and the Monsoon '99

Ulli Lommel (1944-)
Chinese Roulette '86
Strangers in Paradise '84
Boogey Man 2 '83
Effi Briest '74
The American Soldier '70
Beware of a Holy Whore '70
Whity '70
Love Is Colder Than Death '69
Fanny Hill: Memoirs of a Woman of Pleasure '64

Tadeusz Lomnicki (1927-92)
Hands Up '81
Contract '80
Man of Marble '76
Colonel Wolodyjowski '69
Innocent Sorcerers '60
A Generation '54

Beba Loncar (1943-)
Don't Look in the Attic '81
The Long Ships '64

Alexandra London
Les Destinees '00
Le Bonheur Est Dans le Pre '95
Van Gogh '92

Daniel London
Old Joy '06
Minority Report '02
Four Dogs Playing Poker '00
Patch Adams '98
A Soldier's Sweetheart '98

Jason London (1972-)
The Devil's Tomb '09
All Roads Lead Home '08
Killer Movie '08
Showdown at Area 51 '07
Who's Your Monkey '07
Axe '06
Glass House: The Good Mother '06
Dracula 3: Legacy '05
Dracula 2: Ascension '03
Grind '03
Out Cold '01
The Hound of the Baskervilles '00
Jason and the Argonauts '00
Poor White Trash '00
Spent '00
Alien Cargo '99
The Rage: Carrie 2 '99
Broken Vessels '98
If These Walls Could Talk '96
Serial Bomber '96
My Teacher's Wife '95
To Wong Foo, Thanks for Everything, Julie Newmar '95
Fall Time '94
Safe Passage '94
Dazed and Confused '93
Blood Ties '92
December '91
The Man in the Moon '91

Jeremy London (1972-)
Chasing the Green '09
Ba'al: The Storm God '08
Gods and Generals '03
Journey to the Center of the Earth '99
The Defenders: Taking the First '98
Levitation '97
The Babysitter '95
Breaking Free '95
Mallrats '95
White Wolves 2: Legend of the Wild '94

Julie London (1926-2000)
The George Raft Story '61
Man of the West '58
Saddle the Wind '58
The Girl Can't Help It '56
Task Force '49
The Red House '47
Nabonga '44

Lauren London (1984-)
I Love You, Beth Cooper '09
This Christmas '07
ATL '06

Lisa London (1957-)
Savage Beach '89
H.O.T.S. '79

Tom London (1889-1963)
Tribute to a Bad Man '56
Blue Canadian Rockies '52
Red Desert '50
Brand of Fear '49
Homesteaders of Paradise Valley '47
Under Colorado Skies '47
Alias Billy the Kid '46
Santa Fe Uprising '46
Rough Riders of Cheyenne '45
Sunset in El Dorado '45
Fighting Seabees '44
Zorro's Black Whip '44
Shadows on the Sage '42
Fugitive Valley '41
The Lone Rider in Frontier Fury '41
Flaming Lead '39
Phantom Rancher '39
Roll, Wagons, Roll '39
Southward Ho! '39
Prairie Moon '38
Rio Grande Ranger '37
Western Gold '37
Courage of the North '35
The Miracle Rider '35
Rio Rattler '35
Toll of the Desert '35
Fighting Hero '34
Beyond the Rockies '32
Outlaw Justice '32
Arizona Terror '31
Two Gun Man '31
Westward Bound '30

Tony London
24 Hours in London '00
Sid & Nancy '86

John Lone (1952-)
War '07
Rush Hour 2 '01
The Hunted '94
The Shadow '94
M. Butterfly '93
Shadow of China '91
The Moderns '88
The Last Emperor '87
Echoes of Paradise '86
Year of the Dragon '85
Iceman '84
Americathon '79

Keith Loneker
Lakeview Terrace '08
Leatherheads '08
Out of Sight '98

Audrey Long (1924-)
Indian Uprising '51
David Harding, Counterspy '50
The Adventures of Gallant Bess '48
Desperate '47

Derek Long
Make the Yuletide Gay '09
The Gay Bed and Breakfast of Terror '07

Howie Long (1960-)
3000 Miles to Graceland '01
Firestorm '97
Broken Arrow '95

Jackie Long
The Comebacks '07
ATL '06

Jodi Long (1954-)
Amos and Andrew '93
Patty Hearst '88

Justin Long (1978-)
Going the Distance '10
Youth in Revolt '10
Alvin and the Chipmunks: The Squeakuel '09 (V)
Drag Me to Hell '09
He's Just Not That Into You '09
Planet 51 '09 (V)
Taking Chances '09
Still Waiting '08
Strange Wilderness '08
Zack and Miri Make a Porno '08
Alvin and the Chipmunks '07 (V)
Just Add Water '07
Live Free or Die Hard '07
Walk Hard: The Dewey Cox Story '07
Accepted '06
The Break-Up '06
Dreamland '06
Idiocracy '06
The Sasquatch Gang '06
Herbie: Fully Loaded '05
Waiting '05
Dodgeball: A True Underdog Story '04
Raising Genius '04
Crossroads '02
Happy Campers '01
Jeepers Creepers '01

Kathy Long (1965-)
The Stranger '95
Under the Gun '95
Knights '93

Lotus Long (1909-90)
Phantom of Chinatown '40
Mr. Wong in Chinatown '39
Mystery of Mr. Wong '39
Mysterious Mr. Wong '35

Matt Long
Homecoming '09
Ghost Rider '07
Sydney White '07
Deceit '06

Nia Long (1970-)
Are We Done Yet? '07
Premonition '07
Big Momma's House 2 '06
Are We There Yet? '05
Alfie '04
Baadasssss! '03
Big Momma's House '00
Boiler Room '00
The Broken Hearts Club '00
Held Up '00
If These Walls Could Talk 2 '00
The Best Man '99
In Too Deep '99
Stigmata '99
Never 2 Big '98
Soul Food '97
Love Jones '96
Friday '95
Made in America '93
Boyz N the Hood '91

Richard Long (1927-74)
Death Cruise '74
House on Haunted Hill '58
Cult of the Cobra '55
Ma and Pa Kettle Back On the Farm '51
Ma and Pa Kettle Go to Town '50
Ma and Pa Kettle '49
Criss Cross '48
Egg and I '47
The Stranger '46
Tomorrow Is Forever '46

Shelley Long (1949-)
The Santa Trap '02
Dr. T & the Women '00
A Very Brady Sequel '96
The Brady Bunch Movie '95
Frozen Assets '92
Don't Tell Her It's Me '90
Troop Beverly Hills '89
Hello Again '87
Outrageous Fortune '87
The Money Pit '86
Irreconcilable Differences '84
Losin' It '82
Night Shift '82
Caveman '81
A Small Circle of Friends '80
The Cracker Factory '79

Tom Long
Do or Die '01
The Dish '00
Risk '00
Strange Planet '99
Two Hands '98

Walter Long (1879-1952)
Silver Stallion '41
Flaming Lead '39
Man's Country '38
The Painted Trail '38
Six Shootin' Sheriff '38
The Glory Trail '36
Cornered '32
Sea Devils '31
Yankee Clipper '27
Soul-Fire '25
Little Church Around the Corner '23
Blood and Sand '22
Moran of the Lady Letty '22
The Sheik '21
The Little American '17
Sold for Marriage '16
The Birth of a Nation '15

John Longden (1900-71)
Quatermass 2 '57
Alias John Preston '56
Tower of Terror '42
Clouds over Europe '39
Young and Innocent '37
Juno and the Paycock '30
Blackmail '29

Terence Longdon (1922-)
Another Time, Another Place '58
Carry On Sergeant '58
Murder on the Campus '52

Sue Longhurst
Auntie '73
A Man with a Maid '73

Victoria Longley
Talk '94
Celia: Child of Terror '89

Cody Longo (1988-)
Piranha 3D '10
Bring It On: Fight to the Finish '09

Malisa Longo
Urban Warriors '87
Metallica '85

Tony Longo (1962-)
The Cooler '03
Hard Luck '01
Houseguest '94
Prehysteria '93
Remote '93
Rapid Fire '92
The Last Boy Scout '91
Suburban Commando '91
Bloodhounds of Broadway '89
Worth Winning '89
Fletch '85

Eva Longoria (1975-)
Lower Learning '08
Over Her Dead Body '08
The Sentinel '06
Harsh Times '05

Emily Longstreth
Confessions of a Hit Man '94
Rising Son '90
Too Young to Die '90
The Big Picture '89
Wired to Kill '86
Private Resort '84

Ray Lonnen (1940-)
Belfast Assassin '84
Guardian of the Abyss '82

Michael (Michel) Lonsdale (1931-)
Heartbeat Detector '07
Goya's Ghosts '06
Munich '05
5x2 '04
Ronin '98
Nelly et Monsieur Arnaud '95
The Remains of the Day '93
Souvenir '88
The Name of the Rose '86
The Holcroft Covenant '85
Erendira '83
Enigma '82
Moonraker '79
Mr. Klein '76
Phantom of Liberty '74
The Day of the Jackal '73
Les Assassins de L'Ordre '71
Murmur of the Heart '71
The Bride Wore Black '68
Stolen Kisses '68
Is Paris Burning? '66

Leon Lontoc (1908-74)
The Gallant Hours '60
The Hunters '58

Richard Loo (1903-83)
The Man with the Golden Gun '74
The Sand Pebbles '66
Battle Hymn '57
Love Is a Many-Splendored Thing '55
Five Fingers '52
I Was an American Spy '51
The Steel Helmet '51
The Clay Pigeon '49
Malaya '49
Seven Were Saved '47
Back to Bataan '45
First Yank into Tokyo '45
God is My Co-Pilot '45
Betrayal from the East '44
China Sky '44
The Purple Heart '44
China '43
Across the Pacific '42
Mr. Wong in Chinatown '39
The Bitter Tea of General Yen '33

Michael (Mike) Lookinland (1960-)
The Brady Bunch Movie '95
Stephen King's The Stand '94
A Very Brady Christmas '88

Nancy Loomis (1949-)
Halloween '78
Assault on Precinct 13 '76

Rod Loomis (1942-)
Bill & Ted's Excellent Adventure '89
Jack's Back '87

Theodore Loos (1883-1954)
M '31
Metropolis '26
Kriemhilde's Revenge '24

Tanya Lopert (1942-)
Changing Times '04
Tales of Ordinary Madness '83
Navajo Joe '67

Carmen Lopez
Our Song '01
Curdled '95

George Lopez (1961-)
Marmaduke '10 (V)
The Spy Next Door '10
Valentine's Day '10
Mr. Troop Mom '09
Beverly Hills Chihuahua '08 (V)
Henry Poole Is Here '08
Swing Vote '08
Balls of Fury '07
Tortilla Heaven '07
The Adventures of Sharkboy and Lavagirl in 3-D '05
Real Women Have Curves '02
Bread and Roses '00

Jennifer Lopez (1970-)
The Back-Up Plan '10
Bordertown '06
El Cantante '06
Monster-in-Law '05
An Unfinished Life '05
Jersey Girl '04
Shall We Dance? '04
Gigli '03
Enough '02
Maid in Manhattan '02
Angel Eyes '01
The Wedding Planner '01
The Cell '00
Antz '98 (V)
Out of Sight '98
U-Turn '97
Anaconda '96
Blood & Wine '96
Jack '96
Selena '96
Money Train '95
My Family '94

Kamala Lopez
Erotique '94
Crazy from the Heart '91
Dollman '90
Exiled in America '90
Born in East L.A. '87

Mario Lopez (1973-)
The Dog Who Saved Christmas '09 (V)
Holiday in Handcuffs '07
The Street King '02
Outta Time '01
Big Brother Trouble '00
A Crack in the Floor '00
Eastside '99
Depraved '98
Killing Mr. Griffin '97
Breaking the Surface: The Greg Louganis Story '96

Perry Lopez (1931-)
Chinatown '74
Kelly's Heroes '70
McLintock! '63
Taras Bulba '62
Battle Cry '55
Mister Roberts '55

Priscilla Lopez (1948-)
Tony n' Tina's Wedding '07
Maid in Manhattan '02
Center Stage '00
Chutney Popcorn '99
Jesse '88

Sal Lopez (1954-)
Comanche Moon '08
ESL: English as a Second Language '05

Silver City '04
Price of Glory '00
Luminarias '99
Selena '96
The Fire Next Time '93
American Me '92
Full Metal Jacket '87

Seidy Lopez
Gabriela '01
The Stray '00
Depraved '98
Solo '96
Mi Vida Loca '94

Sergi Lopez (1965-)
Pan's Labyrinth '06
Dirty Pretty Things '03
Jet Lag '02
With a Friend Like Harry '00
An Affair of Love '99
Between Your Legs '99
Lisboa '99
The New Eve '98
Caresses '97
Western '96

Trini Lopez (1937-)
Antonio '73
The Dirty Dozen '67
The Poppy Is Also a Flower '66

Sophie Lorain (1957-)
Mambo Italiano '03
The Sign of Four '01
Home Team '98

Isabel Lorca
She's Having a Baby '88
Lightning: The White Stallion '86

Theodore Lorch (1880-1947)
The Better 'Ole '26
The Man on the Box '25
The Last of the Mohicans '20

Jack Lord (1920-98)
The Doomsday Flight '66
Dr. No '62
God's Little Acre '58
Man of the West '58
The Court Martial of Billy Mitchell '55

Justine Lord (1937-)
Skeezer '82
He Kills Night After Night After Night '69
Night Slasher '69
Fiction Makers '67

Marjorie Lord (1922-)
Boy, Did I Get a Wrong Number! '66
Stop That Cab '51
Riding High '50
The Strange Mrs. Crane '48
Johnny Come Lately '43
Sherlock Holmes in Washington '43
Timber! '42

Stephen Lord (1972-)
The Shepherd: Border Patrol '08
Lethal Dose '03
Pulse '03

Traci Lords (1968-)
Zack and Miri Make a Porno '08
Crazy Eights '06
Novel Romance '06
Deathlands: Homeward Bound '03
Black Mask 2: City of Masks '02
The Killing Club '01
D.R.E.A.M. Team '99
Me & Will '99
Blade '98
Boogie Boy '98
Extramarital '98
Stir '98
Nowhere '96
As Good as Dead '95
The Nutt House '95
Dragstrip Girl '94

Plughead Rewired: Circuitry Man 2 '94
Serial Mom '94
Desperate Crimes '93
Ice '93
Skinner '93
Stephen King's The Tommyknockers '93
Laser Moon '92
Raw Nerve '91
A Time to Die '91
Cry-Baby '90
Shock 'Em Dead '90
Fast Food '89
Not of This Earth '88

Tony Lorea
Smokey & the Hotwire Gang '79
The Deadly and the Beautiful '73

Donna Loren (1947-)
Bikini Beach '64
Muscle Beach Party '64
Pajama Party '64

Sophia Loren (1934-)
Nine '09
Between Strangers '02
Grumpier Old Men '95
Ready to Wear '94
Running Away '89
Courage '86
Aurora '84
Sophia Loren: Her Own Story '80
Blood Feud '79
Firepower '79
Brass Target '78
Angela '77
A Special Day '77
The Cassandra Crossing '76
Get Rita '75
Lady of the Evening '75
Man of La Mancha '72
A Countess from Hong Kong '67
Arabesque '66
Lady L '65
The Love Goddesses '65
Operation Crossbow '65
The Fall of the Roman Empire '64
Marriage Italian Style '64
Yesterday, Today and Tomorrow '64
Boccaccio '70 '62
Madame Sans-Gene '62
El Cid '61
Two Women '61
Breath of Scandal '60
Heller in Pink Tights '60
It Started in Naples '60
The Millionairess '60
Black Orchid '59
Desire Under the Elms '58
Houseboat '58
The Key '58
Legend of the Lost '57
The Pride and the Passion '57
What a Woman! '56
Attila '54
The Gold of Naples '54
Neapolitan Carousel '54
Too Bad She's Bad '54
Two Nights with Cleopatra '54
Quo Vadis '51

Tray Loren
The American Angels: Baptism of Blood '89
Gator Bait 2: Cajun Justice '88
Rocktober Blood '85

Livio Lorenzon (1923-71)
Cjamango '67
The Good, the Bad and the Ugly '67
Challenge of the Gladiator '65
Last Gun '64
The Invincible Gladiator '63
Gladiators 7 '62
The Invincible Gladiator '62
Pirates of the Coast '61

Susanne Loret
Atom Age Vampire '61
Uncle Was a Vampire '59

Teala Loring (1922-)
Fall Guy '47
Hard-Boiled Mahoney '47
Riding the California Trail '47
Delinquent Daughters '44

James Lorinz (1964-)
The Jerky Boys '95
Me and the Mob '94
Frankenhooker '90
Punch the Clock '90
Street Trash '87

Jean-Pierre Lorit
The White Countess '05
Jeanne la Pucelle '94
Trois Couleurs: Rouge '94

Marion Lorne (1883-1968)
The Graduate '67
Strangers on a Train '51

George Loros (1944-)
Shakedown '88
Apology '86

Louise Lorraine (1901-81)
Near the Rainbow's End '30
Exit Smiling '26
The Adventures of Tarzan '21

Peter Lorre (1904-64)
The Comedy of Terrors '64
Muscle Beach Party '64
The Patsy '64
The Raven '63
Five Weeks in a Balloon '62
Tales of Terror '62
Voyage to the Bottom of the Sea '61
The Big Circus '59
Hell Ship Mutiny '57
The Sad Sack '57
Silk Stockings '57
Around the World in 80 Days '56
Meet Me in Las Vegas '56
Promise to Murder '56
20,000 Leagues under the Sea '54
Beat the Devil '53
The Lost One '51
Quicksand '50
Casbah '48
My Favorite Brunette '47
The Beast with Five Fingers '46
Black Angel '46
The Chase '46
The Verdict '46
Arsenic and Old Lace '44
Hollywood Canteen '44
The Mask of Dimitrios '44
Passage to Marseilles '44
Background to Danger '43
All Through the Night '42
The Boogie Man Will Get You '42
Casablanca '42
Invisible Agent '42
The Maltese Falcon '41
Mr. District Attorney '41
They Met in Bombay '41
Strange Cargo '40
Stranger on the Third Floor '40
You'll Find Out '40
Mr. Moto in Danger Island '39
Mr. Moto Takes a Vacation '39
Mr. Moto's Last Warning '39
Mr. Takes a Vacation '39
Mr. Moto Takes a Chance '38
Mr. Moto's Gamble '38
Mysterious Mr. Moto '38
Thank you, Mr. Moto '37
Think Fast, Mr. Moto '37
The Secret Agent '36
Crime and Punishment '35
Mad Love '35

The Man Who Knew Too Much '34
F.P. 1 Doesn't Answer '33
M '31

Joan Lorring (1926-)
Good Sam '48
The Gangster '47
The Verdict '46
The Corn Is Green '45

Diana Lorys (1940-)
House of Psychotic Women '73
Fangs of the Living Dead '68
Villa Rides '68
Lightning Bolt '67
The Texican '66
The Awful Dr. Orloff '62

Susanne Lothar (1960-)
The Reader '08
The Piano Teacher '01
Funny Games '97

Eb Lottimer (1950-)
Diamondbacks '99
Termination Man '97
Bloodfist 7: Manhunt '95
Dead Center '94
Beyond the Call of Duty '92
Quake '92
The Finest Hour '91
Futurekick '91
Streets '90
Lords of the Deep '89
Stripped to Kill II: Live Girls '89
Quicker Than the Eye '88

Alexander Lou
Ninja the Battalion '90
Ninja in the U.S.A. '88
Ninja Condors '87
Mafia vs. Ninja '84

Louanne (1970-)
A Night in the Life of Jimmy Reardon '88
Missing Pieces '83
The Long Days of Summer '80
Oh, God! Book 2 '80

Lance Loud (1950-2001)
Armistead Maupin's Tales of the City '93
Inside Monkey Zetterland '93

Dorothy Loudon (1933-2003)
Midnight in the Garden of Good and Evil '97
Garbo Talks '84

Jackie Loughery (1930-)
D.I. '57
Pardners '56
Abbott and Costello Go to Mars '53

Lori Loughlin (1965-)
Old Dogs '09
Moondance Alexander '07
Critical Mass '00
One of Her Own '97
To Grandmother's House We Go '94
Doing Time on Maple Drive '92
The Night Before '88
Back to the Beach '87
Rad '86
The New Kids '85
Secret Admirer '85
Amityville 3: The Demon '83

Jonathan Loughran (1966-)
The House Bunny '08
Death Proof '07
I Now Pronounce You Chuck and Larry '07
Grandma's Boy '06
Anger Management '03

Bill Louie
Fist of Fear, Touch of Death *'80*
The Bodyguard *'76*

Joe Louis (1914-81)
This Is the Army *'43*
The Spirit of Youth *'37*

Justin Louis (1967-)
Grey Gardens *'09*
The Andromeda Strain *'08*
True Confessions of a Hollywood Starlet *'08*
Shooter *'07*
Dawn of the Dead *'04*
Stiletto Dance *'01*
Everything Put Together *'00*
National Lampoon's Dad's Week Off *'97*
Blood & Donuts *'95*
The Big Slice *'90*
Hello Mary Lou: Prom Night 2 *'87*

Patrick Louis
Cinderella Man *'05*
Lansdown *'01*

Willard Louis (1882-1926)
Don Juan *'26*
Beau Brummel *'24*
Robin Hood *'22*

Julia Louis-Dreyfus (1961-)
Gepetto *'00*
Animal Farm *'99 (V)*
A Bug's Life *'98 (V)*
Deconstructing Harry *'97*
Father's Day *'96*
North *'94*
Jack the Bear *'93*
National Lampoon's Christmas Vacation *'89*
Troll *'86*

Anita Louise (1915-70)
Retreat, Hell! *'52*
Love Letters *'45*
Casanova Brown *'44*
Harmon of Michigan *'41*
The Villain Still Pursued Her *'41*
Wagons Westward *'40*
The Gorilla *'39*
The Little Princess *'39*
Marie Antoinette *'38*
The Sisters *'38*
Call It a Day *'37*
That Certain Woman *'37*
Anthony Adverse *'36*
The Story of Louis Pasteur *'36*
Judge Priest *'34*
Millie *'31*
Square Shoulders *'29*

Tina Louise (1934-)
Johnny Suede *'92*
Dixie Lanes *'88*
O.C. and Stiggs *'87*
Evils of the Night *'85*
Hellriders *'84*
The Day the Women Got Even *'80*
Mean Dog Blues *'78*
Nightmare in Badham County *'76*
Death Scream *'75*
The Stepford Wives *'75*
The Good Guys and the Bad Guys *'69*
The Happy Ending *'69*
How to Commit Marriage *'69*
The Wrecking Crew *'68*
Armored Command *'61*
The Day of the Outlaw *'59*
The Trap *'59*
God's Little Acre *'58*

Todd Louiso (1970-)
The Switch *'10*
School for Scoundrels *'06*
Snakes on a Plane *'06*
Thank You for Smoking *'06*
High Fidelity *'00*
8 Heads in a Duffel Bag *'96*
Jerry Maguire *'96*
The Rock *'96*
Apollo 13 *'95*

Tim Lounibos
Life Tastes Good *'99*
Steel Sharks *'97*
Erotique *'94*

Demi Lovato (1992-)
Princess Protection Program *'09*
Camp Rock *'08*

Alan Love
The Apple *'80*
That Sinking Feeling *'79*

Bessie Love (1898-1986)
Vampyres *'74*
Catlow *'71*
Sunday, Bloody Sunday *'71*
Isadora *'68*
The Poppy Is Also a Flower *'66*
Roman Spring of Mrs. Stone *'61*
Morals for Women *'31*
Broadway Melody *'29*
Dress Parade *'27*
The King on Main Street *'25*
The Lost World *'25*
Soul-Fire *'25*
The Sea Lion *'21*
Intolerance *'16*
Reggie Mixes In *'16*

Courtney Love (1964-)
Trapped *'02*
Beat *'00*
Man on the Moon *'99*
200 Cigarettes *'98*
Basquiat *'96*
Feeling Minnesota *'96*
The People vs. Larry Flynt *'96*
Tapeheads *'89*
Straight to Hell *'87*
Sid & Nancy *'86*

Darlene Love (1938-)
Lethal Weapon 4 *'98*
Lethal Weapon 3 *'92*
Lethal Weapon 2 *'89*
Lethal Weapon *'87*

Darris Love
Janky Promoters *'09*
Sucker Free City *'05*
Shrunken Heads *'94*

Faizon Love (1968-)
Couples Retreat *'09*
A Day in the Life *'09*
The Perfect Holiday *'07*
Who's Your Caddy? *'07*
Idlewild *'06*
Just My Luck *'06*
Animal *'05*
Torque *'04*
Elf *'03*
Wonderland *'03*
Blue Crush *'02*
Made *'01*
Inhumanity *'00*
The Replacements *'00*
Three Strikes *'00*
The Players Club *'98*
Fear of a Black Hat *'94*
Bebe's Kids *'92 (V)*

Lucretia Love
Dr. Heckyl and Mr. Hype *'80*
The Arena *'73*
The She-Beast *'65*

Montagu Love (1877-1943)
Wings over the Pacific *'43*
Lady for a Night *'42*
Sherlock Holmes: The Voice of Terror *'42*
All This and Heaven Too *'40*
Dr. Ehrlich's Magic Bullet *'40*
The Mark of Zorro *'40*
The Son of Monte Cristo *'40*
Gunga Din *'39*
The Adventures of Robin Hood *'38*
A Damsel in Distress *'37*
The Prince and the Pauper *'37*
Prisoner of Zenda *'37*
Lloyds of London *'36*
One in a Million *'36*
The Crusades *'35*
His Double Life *'33*
The Midnight Lady *'32*
Murder on the High Seas *'32*
The Riding Tornado *'32*
Vanity Fair *'32*
Inside the Lines *'30*
Bulldog Drummond *'29*
The Divine Lady *'29*
The Wind *'28*
King of Kings *'27*
Don Juan *'26*
Hands Up *'26*
Son of the Sheik *'26*

Mother Love (1953-)
Twinsitters *'95*
The Surgeon *'94*
Armistead Maupin's Tales of the City *'93*
Mr. Nanny *'93*

Suzanna Love
Boogey Man 2 *'83*
Devonsville Terror *'83*
Olivia *'83*
Brainwaves *'82*
The Boogey Man *'80*
Cocaine Cowboys *'79*

Victor Love (1957-)
A Gun, a Car, a Blonde *'97*
The Assassination File *'96*
Gang Related *'96*
Final Shot: The Hank Gathers Story *'92*
Heaven Is a Playground *'91*
Guilty of Innocence *'87*
Native Son *'86*

Alec Lovejoy (1893-)
Murder on Lenox Avenue *'41*
Moon over Harlem *'39*

Frank Lovejoy (1914-62)
Americano *'55*
The Finger Man *'55*
Shack Out on 101 *'55*
Strategic Air Command *'55*
Men of the Fighting Lady *'54*
The Hitch-Hiker *'53*
House of Wax *'53*
Retreat, Hell! *'52*
The Winning Team *'52*
Goodbye My Fancy *'51*
I Was a Communist for the FBI *'51*
I'll See You in My Dreams *'51*
In a Lonely Place *'50*
South Sea Sinner *'50*
Three Secrets *'50*
Try and Get Me *'50*
Home of the Brave *'49*

Jacqueline Lovell (1974-)
A Place Called Truth *'98*
Erotic House of Wax *'97*
Hideous *'97*
Lolida 2000 *'97*
Femalien *'96*
Head of the Family *'96*

Pedro Lovell (1945-)
Rocky Balboa *'06*
Rocky *'76*

Raymond Lovell (1900-53)
Appointment with Crime *'45*
Hotel Reserve *'44*
Immortal Battalion *'44*
Contraband *'40*
King of the Damned *'36*

Ray Lovelock (1950-)
From Hell to Victory *'79*
You've Got to Have Heart *'77*
Autopsy *'74*
Let Sleeping Corpses Lie *'74*
One Russian Summer *'73*
Fiddler on the Roof *'71*

Ed Lover (1963-)
Gunmen *'93*
Who's the Man? *'93*

Dorothy Lovett (1915-98)
Call Out the Marines *'42*
They Meet Again *'41*
Courageous Dr. Christian *'40*
Dr. Christian Meets the Women *'40*
Remedy for Riches *'40*

Lyle Lovett (1959-)
The Open Road *'09*
The New Guy *'02*
Cookie's Fortune *'99*
Fear and Loathing in Las Vegas *'98*
The Opposite of Sex *'98*
Bastard out of Carolina *'96*
Ready to Wear *'94*
Short Cuts *'93*
The Player *'92*

David Lovgren (1969-)
Something More *'99*
Live Bait *'95*

Jon Lovitz (1957-)
The Benchwarmers *'06*
I Could Never Be Your Woman *'06*
Bailey's Billion$ *'05 (V)*
The Producers *'05*
The Stepford Wives *'04*
Dickie Roberts: Former Child Star *'03*
Adam Sandler's 8 Crazy Nights *'02 (V)*
Cats & Dogs *'01 (V)*
Good Advice *'01*
Rat Race *'01*
3000 Miles to Graceland *'01*
Little Nicky *'00*
Sand *'00*
Small Time Crooks *'00*
Lost and Found *'99*
Happiness *'98*
The Wedding Singer *'97*
The Great White Hype *'96*
High School High *'96*
City Slickers 2: The Legend of Curly's Gold *'94*
North *'94*
Trapped in Paradise *'94*
National Lampoon's Loaded Weapon 1 *'93*
A League of Their Own *'92*
Mom and Dad Save the World *'92*
An American Tail: Fievel Goes West *'91 (V)*
Mr. Destiny *'90*
Big *'88*
My Stepmother Is an Alien *'88*
Jumpin' Jack Flash *'86*
Last Resort *'86*
Three Amigos *'86*

Celia Lovsky (1897-1979)
36 Hours *'64*
I, Mobster *'58*
Rhapsody *'54*

Victor Low (1962-)
Everybody's Famous! *'00*
Character *'97*

Alex Lowe (1968-)
Haunted *'95*
Peter's Friends *'92*

Arthur Lowe (1915-82)
The Strange Case of the End of Civilization As We Know It *'93*
Sweet William *'79*
The Bawdy Adventures of Tom Jones *'76*
No Sex Please—We're British *'73*
O Lucky Man! *'73*
Theatre of Blood *'73*
The Ruling Class *'72*
If... *'69*
This Sporting Life *'63*
Black Tide *'58*
Kind Hearts and Coronets *'49*

Chad Lowe (1968-)
Unfaithful *'02*
Acceptable Risk *'01*
Take Me Home: The John Denver Story *'00*
Apartment Complex *'98*
Floating *'97*
In the Presence of Mine Enemies *'97*
Quiet Days in Hollywood *'97*
Trading Favors *'97*
Siringo *'94*
Highway to Hell *'92*
An Inconvenient Woman *'91*
Nobody's Perfect *'90*
True Blood *'89*
Apprentice to Murder *'88*
Silence of the Heart *'84*

Crystal Lowe (1981-)
Wrong Turn 2: Dead End *'07*
Black Christmas *'06*
Final Destination 3 *'06*
Blood Angels *'05*
Insomnia *'02*
Children of the Corn: Revelation *'01*

Edmund Lowe (1890-1971)
Heller in Pink Tights *'60*
Wings of Eagles *'57*
Good Sam *'48*
Dillinger *'45*
The Enchanted Forest *'45*
Call Out the Marines *'42*
I Love You Again *'40*
Every Day's a Holiday *'38*
The Squeaker *'37*
Bombay Mail *'34*
No More Women *'34*
Dinner at Eight *'33*
Chandu the Magician *'32*
Misleading Lady *'32*
Women of All Nations *'31*
The Eyes of Youth *'19*

Harrison Lowe
Buffalo Soldiers *'97*
Geronimo *'93*

Patrick Lowe
Primal Rage *'90*
Slumber Party Massacre 2 *'87*

Rob Lowe (1964-)
The Invention of Lying *'09*
Stir of Echoes 2: The Homecoming *'07*
A Perfect Day *'06*
Thank You for Smoking *'06*
The Christmas Blessing *'05*
Jiminy Glick in LaLa Wood *'05*
Secret Smile *'05*
Salem's Lot *'04*
View from the Top *'03*
The Christmas Shoes *'02*
Escape under Pressure *'00*
Proximity *'00*
The Specials *'00*
Atomic Train *'99*
Austin Powers 2: The Spy Who Shagged Me *'99*
Dead Silent *'99*
Crazy Six *'98*
For Hire *'98*
Outrage *'98*
Contact *'97*
Hostile Intent *'97*
Living in Peril *'97*
Jack Higgins' Midnight Man *'96*
First Degree *'95*
Jack Higgins' On Dangerous Ground *'95*
Mulholland Falls *'95*
Tommy Boy *'95*
Frank and Jesse *'94*
Stephen King's The Stand *'94*
Wayne's World *'92*
The Dark Backward *'91*
The Finest Hour *'91*
Bad Influence *'90*
Stroke of Midnight *'90*
Masquerade *'88*
Illegally Yours *'87*
Square Dance *'87*
About Last Night... *'86*
Youngblood *'86*
St. Elmo's Fire *'85*
The Hotel New Hampshire *'84*
Oxford Blues *'84*
Class *'83*
The Outsiders *'83*

Susan Lowe
Serial Mom *'94*
Hairspray *'88*
Polyester *'81*
Desperate Living *'77*
Female Trouble *'74*
Multiple Maniacs *'70*

Carey Lowell (1961-)
Fierce Creatures *'96*
Leaving Las Vegas *'95*
Sleepless in Seattle *'93*
Road to Ruin *'91*
The Guardian *'90*
Down Twisted *'89*
License to Kill *'89*
Me and Him *'89*
Club Paradise *'86*
Dangerously Close *'86*

Chris Lowell
Up in the Air *'09*
Graduation *'07*

Tom Lowell (1941-)
The Carpetbaggers *'64*
The Manchurian Candidate *'62*

Curt Lowens (1925-)
Operation Intercept *'95*
Invisible: The Chronicles of Benjamin Knight *'93*
Mandroid *'93*
A Midnight Clear *'92*
Werewolf in a Girl's Dormitory *'61*

Elina Lowensohn (1967-)
Fay Grim *'06*
Dark Water *'02*
Get Well Soon *'01*
Quicksand *'01*
Six Ways to Sunday *'99*
Immortality *'98*
In the Presence of Mine Enemies *'97*
Basquiat *'96*
I'm Not Rappaport *'96*
Jane Doe *'96*
Nadja *'95*
Amateur *'94*
My Antonia *'94*
Simple Men *'92*

Andrew Lowery (1970-)
Conspiracy of Fear *'96*
Color of Night *'94*
JFK: Reckless Youth *'93*
My Boyfriend's Back *'93*
School Ties *'92*

Carolyn Lowery
Octopus *'00*
Vicious Circles *'97*

Robert Lowery (1914-71)
The Undertaker and His Pals *'67*
Johnny Reno *'66*
The Rise and Fall of Legs Diamond *'60*
Western Pacific Agent *'51*
Border Rangers *'50*
Gunfire *'50*
I Shot Billy the Kid *'50*
Train to Tombstone *'50*
Call of the Forest *'49*
Outlaw Gang *'49*
Shep Comes Home *'49*
Highway 13 *'48*
Big Town *'47*
Queen of the Amazons *'47*
Death Valley *'46*
God's Country *'46*
House of Horrors *'46*
Dangerous Passage *'44*

Joanna Lumley (1946-)
Doogal *'05 (V)*
Tim Burton's Corpse Bride *'05 (V)*
Ella Enchanted *'04*
Eurotrip *'04*
The Cat's Meow *'01*
Whispers: An Elephant's Tale *'00 (V)*
Maybe Baby *'99*
Coming Home *'98*
Parting Shots *'98*
A Rather English Marriage *'98*
Prince Valiant *'97*
Absolutely Fabulous: The Last Shout *'96*
James and the Giant Peach *'96 (V)*
Innocent Lies *'95*
Cold Comfort Farm *'94*
Shirley Valentine *'89*
Weather in the Streets *'84*
Curse of the Pink Panther *'83*
The Satanic Rites of Dracula *'73*
On Her Majesty's Secret Service *'69*

Dayton Lummis (1903-88)
The First Texan *'56*
Loophole *'54*

Barbara Luna (1939-)
The Concrete Jungle *'82*
The Hanged Man *'74*
Gentle Savage *'73*
The Gatling Gun *'72*
Firecreek *'68*
Mail Order Bride *'63*

Diego Luna (1979-)
Rudo y Cursi *'09*
Milk *'08*
Mister Lonely *'07*
Criminal *'04*
Dirty Dancing: Havana Nights *'04*
The Terminal *'04*
Nicotina *'03*
Open Range *'03*
Frida *'02*
John Carpenter Presents Vampires: Los Muertos *'02*
Y Tu Mama Tambien *'01*

Art Lund (1915-90)
Bucktown *'75*
Black Caesar *'73*
The Last American Hero *'73*

Deanna Lund (1937-)
Red Wind *'91*
Elves *'89*
Hardly Working *'81*
Dr. Goldfoot and the Bikini Machine *'66*

Jana Lund (1933-91)
Married Too Young *'62*
Frankenstein 1970 *'58*
Loving You *'57*

John Lund (1913-92)
Wackiest Ship in the Army *'61*
Dakota Incident *'56*
Latin Lovers *'53*
The Duchess of Idaho *'50*
My Friend Irma *'49*
A Foreign Affair *'48*
Miss Tatlock's Millions *'48*
The Perils of Pauline *'47*
To Each His Own *'46*

Lucille Lund (1913-2002)
Prison Shadows *'36*
The Black Cat *'34*

Nicole Lund
Grizzly Mountain *'97*
The Legend of Wolf Mountain *'92*

Zoe Lund
See Zoe Tamerlis

Christine Lunde
Masque of the Red Death *'90*
Hardcase and Fist *'89*
Dead End City *'88*

Dolph Lundgren (1959-)
The Expendables *'10*
Command Performance *'09*
Direct Contact *'09*
Universal Soldier: Regeneration *'09*
Diamond Dogs *'07*
Missionary Man *'07*
Detention *'03*
Hidden Agenda *'01*
Agent Red *'00*
Jill the Ripper *'00*
Bridge of Dragons *'99*
The Last Warrior *'99*
Storm Catcher *'99*
Sweepers *'99*
The Minion *'98*
The Peacekeeper *'98*
Blackjack *'97*
Silent Trigger *'97*
Johnny Mnemonic *'95*
Army of One *'94*
Hidden Assassin *'94*
Men of War *'94*
Pentathlon *'94*
Universal Soldier *'92*
Cover-Up *'91*
Showdown in Little Tokyo *'91*
I Come in Peace *'90*
The Punisher *'90*
Red Scorpion *'89*
Masters of the Universe *'87*
Rocky 4 *'85*
A View to a Kill *'85*

William Lundigan (1914-75)
Terror Ship *'54*
The White Orchid *'54*
I'd Climb the Highest Mountain *'51*
Love Nest *'51*
Follow Me Quietly *'49*
Pinky *'49*
State Department File 649 *'49*
Dishonored Lady *'47*
Andy Hardy's Double Life *'42*
The Fighting 69th *'40*
Three Smart Girls Grow Up *'39*
Danger on the Air *'38*
Wives under Suspicion *'38*

Vic Lundin
Robinson Crusoe on Mars *'64*
Promises! Promises! *'63*
Two for the Seesaw *'62*
Ma Barker's Killer Brood *'60*

Steve Lundquist
Killer Tomatoes Eat France *'91*
Killer Tomatoes Strike Back *'90*
Return of the Killer Tomatoes! *'88*

Jessica Lundy (1966-)
Just a Little Harmless Sex *'99*
Something About Sex *'98*
RocketMan *'97*
The Stupids *'95*
I Love Trouble *'94*
Single White Female *'92*
Madhouse *'90*
Bright Lights, Big City *'88*
Caddyshack 2 *'88*
Vampire's Kiss *'88*

Kenneth Lundy
Sioux City Sue *'46*
Junior G-Men *'40*

Jamie Luner (1971-)
Threshold *'03*
Sacrifice *'00*
Confessions of Sorority Girls *'94*
The St. Tammany Miracle *'94*

Sihung Lung (1930-2002)
Crouching Tiger, Hidden Dragon *'00*
Eat Drink Man Woman *'94*
The Wedding Banquet *'93*
Pushing Hands *'92*

Ti Lung (1946-)
The Legend of Drunken Master *'94*
A Better Tomorrow, Part 1 *'86*
Duel of Fists *'71*

Tien Hsiang Lung
Five Element Ninjas *'82*
House of Traps *'81*

Cherie Lunghi (1953-)
Back to the Secret Garden *'01*
Horatio Hornblower *'99*
An Alan Smithee Film: Burn, Hollywood, Burn *'97*
The Canterville Ghost *'96*
The Buccaneers *'95*
Jack and Sarah *'95*
Mary Shelley's Frankenstein *'94*
Intrigue *'90*
To Kill a Priest *'89*
The Lady's Not for Burning *'87*
Tales of the Klondike: The Unexpected *'87*
Harem *'86*
The Mission *'86*
King David *'85*
Letters to an Unknown Lover *'84*
Parker *'84*
Praying Mantis *'83*
The Sign of Four *'83*
Oliver Twist *'82*
Excalibur *'81*

Kathleen Luong (1976-)
Missing Brendan *'03*
Two Days in the Valley *'96*

Roldano Lupi (1909-89)
The Giant of Metropolis *'61*
The Mongols *'60*

Ida Lupino (1914-95)
My Boys Are Good Boys *'78*
Food of the Gods *'76*
Devil's Rain *'75*
Junior Bonner *'72*
While the City Sleeps *'56*
The Big Knife *'55*
Private Hell 36 *'54*
The Bigamist *'53*
Beware, My Lovely *'52*
On Dangerous Ground *'51*
Lust for Gold *'49*
Road House *'48*
Escape Me Never *'47*
The Man I Love *'46*
Hollywood Canteen *'44*
Forever and a Day *'43*
Thank Your Lucky Stars *'43*
Moontide *'42*
High Sierra *'41*
Out of the Fog *'41*
The Sea Wolf *'41*
They Drive by Night *'40*
The Adventures of Sherlock Holmes *'39*
Sea Devils *'37*
The Gay Desperado *'36*
One Rainy Afternoon *'36*
Paris in Spring *'35*
Search for Beauty *'34*
The Ghost Camera *'33*

Alberto Lupo (1924-84)
Django Shoots First *'74*
The Agony and the Ecstasy *'65*
Coriolanus, Man without a Country *'64*
The Lion of Thebes *'64*
The Bacchantes *'63*
Atom Age Vampire *'61*
The Giant of Marathon *'60*
Herod the Great *'60*
The Hit Man *'60*

Patti LuPone (1949-)
City by the Sea *'02*
Monday Night Mayhem *'02*
Heist *'01*
Cold Blooded *'00*
State and Main *'00*
Bonanno: A Godfather's Story *'99*
Just Looking *'99*
Summer of Sam *'99*
The 24 Hour Woman *'99*
Song Spinner *'95*
The Water Engine *'92*
Family Prayers *'91*
Driving Miss Daisy *'89*
LBJ: The Early Years *'88*
Wise Guys *'86*
Witness *'85*
Fighting Back *'82*
Piaf *'81 (N)*
1941 *'79*
King of the Gypsies *'78*

Robert LuPone (1946-)
American Tragedy *'00*
Palookaville *'95*
High Stakes *'89*

Federico Luppi (1934-)
Fermat's Room *'07*
Swindled *'04*
The Devil's Backbone *'01*
Lisboa *'99*
Autumn Sun *'98*
Hombres Armados *'97*
Martin (Hache) *'97*
Extasis *'96*
Cronos *'94*
A Place in the World *'92*
Killing Grandpa *'91*
Mayalunta *'86*
Funny, Dirty Little War *'83*
Time for Revenge *'82*

John Lupton (1926-93)
Private Parts *'72*
Jesse James Meets Frankenstein's Daughter *'65*
The Rebel Set *'59*
Battle Cry *'55*
Diane *'55*
All the Brothers Were Valiant *'53*
Escape from Fort Bravo *'53*

Peter Lupus (1932-)
Acting on Impulse *'93*
Think Big *'90*
Pulsebeat *'85*
Escapist *'83*
Challenge of the Gladiator *'65*
Muscle Beach Party *'64*

Luis Luque (1956-)
Manhunt *'01*
What Your Eyes Don't See *'99*

Evan Lurie (1954-)
Mortal Challenge *'97*
Hologram Man *'95*
Shadow Warriors *'95*
T-Force *'94*
American Kickboxer 2: To the Death *'93*
Ring of Fire 2: Blood and Steel *'92*
Martial Law 2: Undercover *'91*

John Lurie (1952-)
New Rose Hotel *'98*
Blue in the Face *'95*
The Last Temptation of Christ *'88*
Down by Law *'86*
Permanent Vacation *'84*
Stranger than Paradise *'84*

Jaques Lussier (1960-)
Norman's Awesome Experience *'88*
Pouvoir Intime *'87*

Aaron Lustig (1956-)
Tuesdays with Morrie *'99*
Pinocchio's Revenge *'96*
The Shadow *'94*
Stuart Saves His Family *'94*
Bad Channels *'92*

William Lustig (1955-)
Army of Darkness *'92*
Darkman *'90*
Maniac *'80*

Eric Lutes (1962-)
The Twelve Dogs of Christmas *'05*
Bram Stoker's The Mummy *'97*
Distant Justice *'92*

Alfred Lutter (1962-)
The Bad News Bears in Breaking Training *'77*
The Bad News Bears *'76*

Kellan Lutz (1985-)
A Nightmare on Elm Street *'10*
The Twilight Saga: Eclipse *'10*
The Twilight Saga: New Moon *'09*
Deep Winter *'08*
Twilight *'08*
Stick It *'06*

Franc Luz (1950-)
Ghost Town *'88*
The Nest *'88*
Ecstasy *'84*

Maria Pia Luzi
Planets Against Us *'61*
La Notte *'60*

Aleksei Lyarsky
My Apprenticeship *'39*
My Childhood *'38*

Desi Lydic
Stan Helsing *'09*
Out at the Wedding *'07*

Christine Lydon (1966-)
Merchants of Death *'99*
Vampires of Sorority Row: Kickboxers From Hell *'99*
Amazon Warrior *'97*

Gary Lydon (1954-)
The Last September *'99*
Nothing Personal *'95*

James Lydon
Corky of Gasoline Alley *'51*
Gasoline Alley *'51*
When Willie Comes Marching Home *'50*
Cynthia *'47*

Jimmy Lydon (1923-)
Island in the Sky *'53*
The Magnificent Yankee *'50*
Life with Father *'47*
Strange Illusion *'45*
Little Men *'40*
Tom Brown's School Days *'40*
Back Door to Heaven *'39*

John (Johnny Rotten) Lydon (1956-)
The Independent *'00*
The Filth and the Fury *'99*
Corrupt *'84*

Reg Lye (1912-88)
Freedom *'82*
King Rat *'65*
Walk into Hell *'57*

Leslie Lyles
Slippery Slope *'06*
Coming Soon *'99*
My Teacher's Wife *'95*

Dorothy Lyman (1947-)
I Love Trouble *'94*
Ruby in Paradise *'93*
Camp Cucamonga: How I Spent My Summer Vacation *'90*
Ollie Hopnoodle's Haven of Bliss *'88*
Summer Fantasy *'84*
The 300 Year Weekend *'71*

Will Lyman
What Doesn't Kill You *'08*
Little Children *'06 (N)*
American Meltdown *'04*
The Siege *'98*
Floating *'97*

Alfred Lynch (1931-2003)
The Krays *'90*
Blockhouse *'73*
The Hill *'65*
On the Fiddle *'61*

David Lynch (1946-)
Nadja *'95*
Twin Peaks: Fire Walk with Me *'92*
Zelly & Me *'88*

Finbar Lynch
To Kill a King *'03*
King Lear *'98*

Helen Lynch (1900-65)
Smouldering Fires *'25*
The Return of Grey Wolf *'22*

Jane Lynch (1960-)
Shrek Forever After *'10 (V)*
Julie & Julia *'09*
Mr. Troop Mom *'09*
Post Grad *'09*
Weather Girl *'09*
Adventures of Power *'08*
Another Cinderella Story *'08*
The Rocker *'08*
Role Models *'08*
Space Chimps *'08 (V)*
Spring Breakdown *'08*
Alvin and the Chipmunks *'07*
Walk Hard: The Dewey Cox Story *'07*
Eye of the Dolphin *'06*
For Your Consideration *'06*
Talladega Nights: The Ballad of Ricky Bobby *'06*
Bam Bam & Celeste *'05*
The 40 Year Old Virgin *'05*
Sleepover *'04*
Exposed *'03*
A Mighty Wind *'03*

Jimmy Lynch
Avenging Disco Godfather *'76*
Dolemite 2: Human Tornado *'76*

John Lynch (1961-)
The Bridge of San Luis Rey *'05*
Lassie *'05*
Conspiracy of Silence *'03*
Evelyn *'02*
The Seventh Stream *'01*
The Quarry *'98*
Sliding Doors *'97*
Moll Flanders *'96*
Some Mother's Son *'96*
This Is the Sea *'96*
Angel Baby *'95*
Nothing Personal *'95*
Princess Caraboo *'94*
The Secret of Roan Inish *'94*
In the Name of the Father *'93*
The Secret Garden *'93*
Edward II *'92*
The Railway Station Man *'92*
Hardware *'90*
Monkey Boy *'90*
Cal *'84*

John Carroll Lynch (1963-)
Hesher *'10*
Love Happens *'09*
Gran Torino *'08*
Full of It *'07*
Things We Lost in the Fire *'07*
Zodiac *'07*
Looking for Comedy in the Muslim World *'06*
Mozart and the Whale *'05*
Catch That Kid *'04*
Confidence *'03*
Gothika *'03*
Live from Baghdad *'03*
The Good Girl *'02*
Bubble Boy *'01*
Tuesdays with Morrie *'99*
From the Earth to the Moon *'98*

Restaurant *'98*
Face/Off *'97*
A Thousand Acres *'97*
Volcano *'97*
Fargo *'96*

Kate Lynch

Coast to Coast *'04*
Lethal Lolita—Amy Fisher: My Story *'92*
Def-Con 4 *'85*
Reckless Disregard *'84*
Meatballs *'79*
Summer's Children *'79*

Kelly Lynch (1959-)

Havoc 2: Normal Adolescent Behavior *'07*
The Jacket *'05*
Dallas 362 *'03*
Joe Somebody *'01*
The Slaughter Rule *'01*
Charlie's Angels *'00*
Brotherhood of Murder *'99*
Cold Around the Heart *'97*
Homegrown *'97*
Mr. Magoo *'97*
Persons Unknown *'96*
Heaven's Prisoners *'95*
Virtuosity *'95*
White Man's Burden *'95*
Forbidden Choices *'94*
Imaginary Crimes *'94*
Three of Hearts *'93*
For Better and for Worse *'92*
Curly Sue *'91*
Desperate Hours *'90*
Drugstore Cowboy *'89*
Road House *'89*
Warm Summer Rain *'89*
Bright Lights, Big City *'88*
Cocktail *'88*
Osa *'85*

Ken Lynch (1910-90)

My Pleasure Is My Business *'74*
Legend of Tom Dooley *'59*
Pork Chop Hill *'59*
I Married a Monster from Outer Space *'58*
Run Silent, Run Deep *'58*

Mark Lynch

Dance of the Dead *'08*
The Other Half *'06*

Pauline Lynch

Attila *'01*
Trainspotting *'95*

Richard Lynch (1940-)

Diamond Run *'00*
Eastside *'99*
Total Force *'98*
Under Oath *'97*
Terminal Virus *'96*
Warrior of Justice *'96*
Cyborg 3: The Recycler *'95*
Destination Vegas *'95*
Dragon Fury *'95*
Midnight Confessions *'95*
Werewolf *'95*
Scanner Cop *'94*
Terrified *'94*
H.P. Lovecraft's Necronomicon: Book of the Dead *'93*
Showdown *'93*
Double Threat *'92*
Inside Edge *'92*
Maximum Force *'92*
Merlin *'92*
Alligator 2: The Mutation *'90*
The Forbidden Dance *'90*
Invasion Force *'90*
Lockdown *'90*
Puppet Master 3: Toulon's Revenge *'90*
Trancers 2: The Return of Jack Deth *'90*
High Stakes *'89*
One Man Force *'89*
Aftershock *'88*
Bad Dreams *'88*
The Baron *'88*
Little Nikita *'88*
The Barbarians *'87*
Nightforce *'86*
Cut and Run *'85*
Invasion U.S.A. *'85*
Savage Dawn *'84*
Sword & the Sorcerer *'82*
Sizzle *'81*
The Formula *'80*
Steel *'80*
Death Sport *'78*
Delta Fox *'77*
God Told Me To *'76*
The Premonition *'75*
Scarecrow *'73*

Susan Lynch (1971-)

Duane Hopwood *'05*
Enduring Love *'04*
Casa de los Babys *'03*
Red Roses and Petrol *'03*
16 Years of Alcohol *'03*
From Hell *'01*
The Mapmaker *'01*
Beautiful Creatures *'00*
Nora *'00*
Amongst Women *'98*
Waking Ned Devine *'98*
Ivanhoe *'97*
Kings in Grass Castles *'97*
A Royal Scandal *'96*
The Secret of Roan Inish *'94*
Northern Lights *'79*

Helen Lynd (1902-92)

So Proudly We Hail *'43*
Hats Off *'37*

Paul Lynde (1926-82)

The Villain *'79*
Rabbit Test *'78*
Hugo the Hippo *'76 (V)*
Charlotte's Web *'73 (V)*
Journey Back to Oz *'71 (V)*
How Sweet It Is! *'68*
The Glass Bottom Boat *'66*
Beach Blanket Bingo *'65*
Send Me No Flowers *'64*
Bye, Bye, Birdie *'63*
Son of Flubber *'63*
Under the Yum-Yum Tree *'63*
New Faces of 1952 *'54*

Nicholas Lyndhurst (1961-)

David Copperfield *'99*
Gulliver's Travels *'95*
Stalag Luft *'93*

Amy Lyndon

Big City Blues *'99*
Slaves of Hollywood *'99*

Simon Lyndon (1971-)

Chopper *'00*
Blackrock *'97*

Carol Lynley (1942-)

Drowning on Dry Land *'00*
Howling 6: The Freaks *'90*
Spirits *'90*
Blackout *'88*
Dark Tower *'87*
Vigilante *'83*
Balboa *'82*
The Cat and the Canary *'79*
Bad Georgia Road *'77*
Washington Affair *'77*
Fantasy Island *'76*
Flood! *'76*
Four Deuces *'75*
If It's a Man, Hang Up *'75*
Death Stalk *'74*
Beware! The Blob *'72*
Cotter *'72*
The Poseidon Adventure *'72*
The Night Stalker *'71*
Blood Island *'68*
The Cardinal *'63*
The Stripper *'63*
Under the Yum-Yum Tree *'63*
Return to Peyton Place *'61*
The Light in the Forest *'58*

Ann Lynn (1939-)

Baby Love *'69*
Estate of Insanity *'64*

Betty Lynn (1926-)

Return to Mayberry *'85*
Texas John Slaughter: Geronimo's Revenge *'60*
Meet Me in Las Vegas *'56*
Payment on Demand *'51*
Cheaper by the Dozen *'50*
Father Was a Fullback *'49*
June Bride *'48*

Cheryl Lynn

Fate *'90*
Emanon *'86*
Thunder Run *'86*

Diana Lynn (1924-71)

An Annapolis Story *'55*
The Kentuckian *'55*
Bedtime for Bonzo *'51*
My Friend Irma *'49*
Every Girl Should Be Married *'48*
Miracle of Morgan's Creek *'44*
The Major and the Minor *'42*

Emmett Lynn (1897-1958)

The Fighting Redhead *'50*
Trail of the Mounties *'47*
The Caravan Trail *'46*
Song of Old Wyoming *'45*
Frontier Outlaws *'44*
The Return of the Rangers *'43*
Sundown Kid *'43*

Fonda Lynn

Ninja Brothers of Blood *'89*
Deadly Darling *'85*

George Lynn (1906-64)

Teenage Frankenstein *'58*
To Be or Not to Be *'42*

Jeffrey Lynn (1909-95)

Tony Rome *'67*
Home Town Story *'51*
A Letter to Three Wives *'49*
For the Love of Mary *'48*
Underground *'41*
All This and Heaven Too *'40*
The Fighting 69th *'40*
The Roaring Twenties *'39*
Four Daughters *'38*

Jenny Lynn

The Greed of William Hart *'48*
Ticket of Leave Man *'37*

Jonathan Lynn (1943-)

Greedy *'94*
Three Men and a Little Lady *'90*

Mara Lynn (1927-88)

G.I. Jane *'51*
Leave It to the Marines *'51*
Sky High *'51*
Prehistoric Women *'50*

Meredith Scott Lynn

How to Go Out on a Date in Queens *'06*
When Do We Eat? *'05*
Hollywood Homicide *'03*
Legally Blonde *'01*
Forces of Nature *'99*
Standing on Fishes *'99*
Billy's Hollywood Screen Kiss *'98*
I Love You, Don't Touch Me! *'97*

Peter George Lynn (1906-67)

Mr. Wong in Chinatown *'39*
Mystery Plane *'39*
Wolf Call *'39*

Theresa Lynn (1964-)

Psycho Sisters *'98*
Private Parts *'96*
Vampire Vixens from Venus *'94*

Melanie Lynskey (1977-)

Away We Go *'09*
The Informant! *'09*
Up in the Air *'09*
Comanche Moon *'08*
Flags of Our Fathers *'06*
Say Uncle *'05*
Serial Slayer *'03*
Shattered Glass *'03*
Abandon *'02*
Stephen King's Rose Red *'02*
Sweet Home Alabama *'02*
Coyote Ugly *'00*
Shooters *'00*
Ever After: A Cinderella Story *'98*
Heavenly Creatures *'94*

Ben Lyon (1901-79)

Mad About Money *'37*
Crimson Romance *'34*
I Cover the Waterfront *'33*
The Crooked Circle *'32*
Indiscreet *'31*
Night Nurse *'31*
Hell's Angels *'30*

Earle Lyon (1926-)

Lonesome Trail *'55*
Silver Star *'55*
Silent Raiders *'54*

Richard Lyon (1934-)

The Tender Years *'47*
Anna and the King of Siam *'46*

Sue Lyon (1946-)

Alligator *'80*
End of the World *'76*
The Invisible Strangler *'76*
Autopsy *'74*
Evel Knievel *'72*
Four Rode Out *'69*
Flim-Flam Man *'67*
Tony Rome *'67*
The Night of the Iguana *'64*
Lolita *'62*

Wendy Lyon

Hello Mary Lou: Prom Night 2 *'87*
Anne of Green Gables *'85*

Natasha Lyonne (1979-)

Loving Leah *'09*
Robots *'05 (V)*
Blade: Trinity *'04*
Madhouse *'04*
Die Mommie Die! *'03*
Party Monster *'03*
Comic Book Villains *'02*
Night at the Golden Eagle *'02*
ZigZag *'02*
American Pie 2 *'01*
Fast Sofa *'01*
The Grey Zone *'01*
Kate & Leopold *'01*
Scary Movie 2 *'01*
If These Walls Could Talk 2 *'00*
American Pie *'99*
But I'm a Cheerleader *'99*
Detroit Rock City *'99*
Freeway 2: Confessions of a Trickbaby *'99*
Krippendorf's Tribe *'98*
Modern Vampires *'98*
Slums of Beverly Hills *'98*
Everyone Says I Love You *'96*

Bruce Lyons

The Navigator *'88*
Model Behavior *'82*

Cliff Lyons (1901-74)

The Horse Soldiers *'59*
She Wore a Yellow Ribbon *'49*

Elena Lyons (1973-)

Club Dread *'04*
Face the Music *'00*

James Lyons (1960-2007)

I Shot Andy Warhol *'96*
Frisk *'95*
Postcards from America *'95*
Poison *'91*

Jennifer Lyons (1977-)

Transylmania *'09*
Killer Pad *'06*
Tequila Body Shots *'99*
Tiger Heart *'96*

Phyllis Lyons (1960-)

The Rat Pack *'98*
Casualties of Love: The "Long Island Lolita" Story *'93*

Robert F. Lyons (1940-)

Counter Measures *'99*
The Omega Code *'99*
Ripper Man *'96*
American Eagle *'90*
Platoon Leader *'87*
Murphy's Law *'86*
Cease Fire *'85*
Black Oak Conspiracy *'77*
Shoot Out *'71*
The Todd Killings *'71*
Getting Straight *'70*

Susan Lyons (1957-)

Napoleon *'96 (V)*
Ebbtide *'94*
The Winds of Jarrah *'83*

Tom Lyons

Factotum *'06*
Burn! *'70*

Lya Lys

Confessions of a Nazi Spy *'39*
L'Age D'Or *'30*

Stanislav Lyubshin (1933-)

To See Paris and Die *'93*
The Theme *'79*

Monika M.

Nekromantik 2 *'91*
Nekromantik *'87*

Tzi Ma

Rush Hour 3 *'07*
Akeelah and the Bee *'06*
Red Doors *'05*
The Ladykillers *'04*
The Quiet American *'02*
Catfish in Black Bean Sauce *'00*
Rush Hour *'98*
Dante's Peak *'97*
Red Corner *'97*
Chain Reaction *'96*
Golden Gate *'93*
Rapid Fire *'92*

Hidde Maas (1944-)

The Delivery *'99*
Amsterdamned *'88*

Byron Mabe (1932-2001)

The Doberman Gang *'72*
The Defilers *'65*

Ricky Mabe (1983-)

Zack and Miri Make a Porno *'08*
Believe *'99*
Little Men *'98*

Kate Maberly (1982-)

Boogeyman 3 *'08*
Murderous Intent *'06*
Gulliver's Travels *'95*
Stephen King's The Langoliers *'95*
The Secret Garden *'93*

Eric Mabius (1971-)

Nature of the Beast *'07*
Voodoo Moon *'05*
The Job *'03*
Resident Evil *'02*
On the Borderline *'01*
Tempted *'01*
The Crow: Salvation *'00*
The Minus Man *'99*
Splendor *'99*
Wirey Spindell *'99*
Around the Fire *'98*
Cruel Intentions *'98*
Black Circle Boys *'97*
I Shot Andy Warhol *'96*
Lawn Dogs *'96*
Welcome to the Dollhouse *'95*

Moms (Jackie) Mabley (1894-1975)

Amazing Grace *'74*
Boardinghouse Blues *'48*
Killer Diller *'48*

Luke Mably (1976-)

Deceit *'06*
The Prince & Me 2: Royal Wedding *'06*
Color Me Kubrick *'05*
The Prince & Me *'04*

Sunny Mabrey (1975-)

Final Approach *'08*
San Saba *'08*
Snakes on a Plane *'06*
One Last Thing *'05*
XXX: State of the Union *'05*
Species 3 *'04*
The New Guy *'02*

Bernie Mac (1958-2008)

Old Dogs *'09*
Madagascar: Escape 2 Africa *'08 (V)*
Soul Men *'08*
Ocean's Thirteen *'07*
Pride *'07*
Transformers *'07*
Guess Who *'05*
Inspector Gadget's Biggest Caper Ever *'05 (V)*
Mr. 3000 *'04*
Ocean's Twelve *'04*
Bad Santa *'03*
Charlie's Angels: Full Throttle *'03*
Head of State *'03*
Ocean's Eleven *'01*
What's the Worst That Could Happen? *'01*
Life *'99*
The Players Club *'98*
Def Jam's How to Be a Player *'97*
Don King: Only in America *'97*
Booty Call *'96*
Get On the Bus *'96*
Friday *'95*
Above the Rim *'94*
House Party 3 *'94*

Anne MacAdams (1925-2003)

Don't Look in the Basement *'73*
Common Law Wife *'63*

Cal Macaninch (1969-)

Dear Frankie *'04*
A Mind to Murder *'96*

Hayes Macarthur

The Game Plan *'07*
National Lampoon's The Stoned Aged *'07*

James MacArthur (1937-)

Storm Chasers: Revenge of the Twister *'98*
Hang 'Em High *'67*
Mosby's Marauders *'66*
Battle of the Bulge *'65*
Bedford Incident *'65*
Cry of Battle *'63*
Spencer's Mountain *'63*
The Interns *'62*
Kidnapped *'60*
The Swiss Family Robinson *'60*
Third Man on the Mountain *'59*
The Light in the Forest *'58*

Charles Macaulay (1927-99)

The Big Red One *'80*
Blacula *'72*

Marc Macaulay (1948-)

Cleaner *'07*
The Punisher *'04*
Holy Man *'98*
Wild Things *'98*
Cop and a Half *'93*
Hidden Fears *'93*

Donald MacBride (1889-1957)

Meet Danny Wilson *'52*
Holiday Rhythm *'50*
Buck Privates Come Home *'47*

Egg and I '47
A Night to Remember '42
High Sierra '41
The Invisible Woman '40
Michael Shayne: Private Detective '40
Murder over New York '40
The Saint's Double Trouble '40
Blondie Takes a Vacation '39
Charlie Chan at Treasure Island '39
The Flying Irishman '39
The Great Man Votes '38
Room Service '38

Catriona MacCall

See Katherine (Katriona) MacColl

Ralph Macchio (1961-)

Beer League '06
Forever Together '00
The Secret of NIMH 2 '98 (V)
Naked in New York '93
My Cousin Vinny '92
Too Much Sun '90
The Karate Kid: Part 3 '89
Distant Thunder '88
Crossroads '86
The Karate Kid: Part 2 '86
The Karate Kid '84
Teachers '84
The Outsiders '83
Up the Academy '80

Aldo Maccione (1935-)

The Chambermaid on the Titanic '97
Too Shy to Try '78
Loves & Times of Scaramouche '76
Lady of the Evening '75
Loose in New York '74

Katherine (Katriona) MacColl (1954-)

The House by the Cemetery '83
The Beyond '82
Gates of Hell '80

Simon MacCorkindale (1952-)

The Girl Next Door '98
At the Midnight Hour '95
Family of Cops '95
Obsessive Love '84
Jaws 3 '83
Robbers of the Sacred Mountain '83
Sword & the Sorcerer '82
Cabo Blanco '81
The Manions of America '81
Visitor from the Grave '81
Quatermass Conclusion '79
The Riddle of the Sands '79
Death on the Nile '78

Aimi MacDonald

Number 1 of the Secret Service '77
Vendetta for the Saint '68

Ann-Marie MacDonald (1958-)

Better Than Chocolate '99
I've Heard the Mermaids Singing '87

Bill MacDonald

Mercy '00
One Kill '00
The Corruptor '99

Edmund MacDonald (1908-51)

Shoot to Kill '47
Detour '46
The Lady Confesses '45
Castle in the Desert '42
The Strange Case of Dr. Rx '42
Timber! '42
Prison Break '38

Ian MacDonald (1914-78)

This Woman Is Dangerous '52
Thunder in God's Country '51
Montana '50

J. Farrell MacDonald (1875-1952)

Outlaw Gang '49
Shep Comes Home '49
Panhandle '48
Texas Masquerade '44
The Ape Man '43
Phantom Killer '42
Snuffy Smith, Yard Bird '42
In Old Cheyenne '41
Riders of the Timberline '41
I Take This Oath '40
Knights of the Range '40
Susannah of the Mounties '39
Come on Rangers '38
Gang Bullets '38
Shadows of the Orient '37
Riff Raff '35
Square Shooter '35
Romance in Manhattan '34
Hearts of Humanity '32
No Man of Her Own '32
Phantom Express '32
Probation '32
13th Guest '32
The Easiest Way '31
Other Men's Women '31
Touchdown '31
Song o' My Heart '30
Sunrise '27
Sky High '22

James MacDonald

Hollywood Homicide '03
Phone Booth '02
Sour Grapes '98
Cinderella '50 (V)

Jeanette MacDonald (1901-65)

The Sun Comes Up '49
Three Daring Daughters '48
Cairo '42
I Married an Angel '42
Smilin' Through '41
Bitter Sweet '40
New Moon '40
Broadway Serenade '39
Girl of the Golden West '38
Sweethearts '38
The Firefly '37
Maytime '37
Rose Marie '36
San Francisco '36
Naughty Marietta '35
The Cat and the Fiddle '34
The Merry Widow '34
One Hour with You '32
Lottery Bride '30
Monte Carlo '30
The Love Parade '29

Jennifer MacDonald

Campfire Tales '98
Alien Chaser '96
Headless Body in Topless Bar '96
Dead Weekend '95
Clean, Shaven '93

Kelly Macdonald (1977-)

Choke '08
In the Electric Mist '08
The Merry Gentleman '08
No Country for Old Men '07
Nanny McPhee '06
The Girl in the Cafe '05
Lassie '05
Tristram Shandy: A Cock and Bull Story '05
Finding Neverland '04
Brush with Fate '03
State of Play '03
Gosford Park '01
Strictly Sinatra '01
Entropy '99
Splendor '99
Two Family House '99
The Loss of Sexual Innocence '98
My Life So Far '98
Cousin Bette '97
Stella Does Tricks '96
Trainspotting '95

Kenneth MacDonald (1950-2001)

Touching Evil '97
Storm over Wyoming '50
U-Boat Prisoner '44
Six Gun Gospel '43
The Durango Kid '40
Border Vengeance '35

Norm MacDonald (1963-)

Grown Ups '10
Senior Skip Day '08
Deuce Bigalow: European Gigolo '05
Dr. Dolittle 2 '01 (V)
Screwed '00
Dr. Dolittle '98 (V)
Dirty Work '97
The People vs. Larry Flynt '96
Billy Madison '94

Ray Macdonald

The Eye 3 '05
Babes on Broadway '41

Scott MacDonald

Jarhead '05
Straight into Darkness '04
A Rat's Tale '98 (V)

Shauna Macdonald

The Descent '05
Saint Ralph '04
Shattered City: The Halifax Explosion '03

Wallace MacDonald (1891-1978)

Between Fighting Men '32
Daring Danger '32
Hello Trouble '32
The Riding Tornado '32
Texas Cyclone '32
Two-Fisted Law '32
Range Feud '31
Fightin' Ranch '30
Red Signals '27
The Sea Hawk '24

Wendy MacDonald

Broken Trust '93
Dark Side of the Moon '90
Blood Frenzy '87
Heat Street '87
Mayhem '87

William Macdonald

Mail Order Bride '08
White Noise 2: The Light '07
Hollow Man 2 '06

Andie MacDowell (1958-)

Barnyard '06 (V)
Beauty Shop '05
Tara Road '05
Crush '02
Ginostra '02
Harrison's Flowers '02
Dinner with Friends '01
Town and Country '01
Muppets from Space '99
The Muse '99
Just the Ticket '98
Shadrach '98
The End of Violence '97
Michael '96
Multiplicity '96
Unstrung Heroes '95
Bad Girls '94
Four Weddings and a Funeral '94
Groundhog Day '93
Short Cuts '93
Deception '92
The Player '92
Hudson Hawk '91
The Object of Beauty '91
Women & Men: In Love There Are No Rules '91
Green Card '90
sex, lies and videotape '89
St. Elmo's Fire '85
Greystoke: The Legend of Tarzan, Lord of the Apes '84

Rita Macedo (1928-93)

The Curse of the Crying Woman '61
Nazarin '58
The Criminal Life of Archibaldo de la Cruz '55

Sterling Macer (1963-)

Double Take '01
The Beast '96
Dragon: The Bruce Lee Story '93

Angus MacFadyen (1964-)

Shadowheart '09
Impulse '08
San Saba '08
Killer Wave '07
Redline '07
Fatwa '06
.45 '06
Saw 3 '06
The Pleasure Drivers '05
Divine Secrets of the Ya-Ya Sisterhood '02
Equilibrium '02
A Woman's a Helluva Thing '01
Jason and the Argonauts '00
Second Skin '00
Styx '00
The Cradle Will Rock '99
Titus '99
Facade '98
The Rat Pack '98
Nevada '97
Still Breathing '97
Warriors of Virtue '97
The Brylcreem Boys '96
Braveheart '95
The Lost Language of Cranes '92

Matthew MacFadyen (1974-)

Robin Hood '10
Incendiary '08
Pride and Prejudice '05
The Way We Live Now '02
Almost Strangers '01
Enigma '01

Seth MacFarlane (1973-)

Tooth Fairy '10
Hellboy II: The Golden Army '08 (V)

Matthew Macfayden

Frost/Nixon '08
Little Dorrit '08
Death at a Funeral '07
Middletown '06

Moyna MacGill (1895-1975)

Three Daring Daughters '48
The Strange Affair of Uncle Harry '45
Frenchman's Creek '44
Gaslight '40

Niall MacGinnis (1913-78)

Krakatoa East of Java '69
The Viking Queen '67
Island of Terror '66
The War Lord '65
A Face in the Rain '63
Jason and the Argonauts '63
Sword of Sherwood Forest '60
Tarzan's Greatest Adventure '59
Curse of the Demon '57
Helen of Troy '56
Lust for Life '56
Betrayed '54
Martin Luther '53
No Highway in the Sky '51
Anna Karenina '48
Captain Boycott '47
Henry V '44
The Day Will Dawn '42
Edge of the World '37

Jack MacGowran (1918-73)

The Exorcist '73
King Lear '71
Start the Revolution without Me '70
Age of Consent '69
Wonderwall: The Movie '69
The Fearless Vampire Killers '67
Cul de Sac '66
Doctor Zhivago '65
Lord Jim '65
The Brain '62
The Quiet Man '52

Tara MacGowran (1964-)

The Dawning '88
Las Vegas Serial Killer '86
Secret Places '85

Ali MacGraw (1938-)

Glam '97
Natural Causes '94
Murder Elite '86
The Winds of War '83
Just Tell Me What You Want '80
Players '79
Convoy '78
The Getaway '72
Love Story '70
Goodbye Columbus '69

Justina Machado (1972-)

The Accidental Husband '08
In the Electric Mist '08
Fatal Contact: Bird Flu in America '06
Little Fugitive '06
Torque '04
Final Destination 2 '03
Sticks '98

Ignacy Machowski (1920-2001)

Contract '80
First Spaceship on Venus '60
Shadow '56

Gabriel Macht (1972-)

Whiteout '09
The Spirit '08
Because I Said So '07
The Good Shepherd '06
Archangel '05
A Love Song for Bobby Long '04
Grand Theft Parsons '03
The Recruit '03
Bad Company '02
American Outlaws '01
Behind Enemy Lines '01
The Audrey Hepburn Story '00
101 Ways (The Things a Girl Will Do to Keep Her Volvo) '00

Stephen Macht (1942-)

DC 9/11: Time of Crisis '04
Watchers Reborn '98
Galgameth '96
Siringo '94
Trancers 5: Sudden Deth '94
Trancers 4: Jack of Swords '93
Amityville 1992: It's About Time '92
Trancers 3: Deth Lives '92
Graveyard Shift '90
Blind Witness '89
A Friendship in Vienna '88
The Monster Squad '87
Agatha Christie's A Caribbean Mystery '83
American Dream '81
Killjoy '81
Enola Gay: The Men, the Mission, the Atomic Bomb '80
Galaxina '80
Nightwing '79
The Choirboys '77

Angus MacInnes (1947-)

Strange Brew '83
The Sender '82
Outland '81

Keegan Macintosh (1984-)

At the Midnight Hour '95
The Road Home '95
Henry & Verlin '94

Martha MacIsaac (1984-)

The Last House on the Left '09
The Thaw '09
Superbad '07

Daniel MacIvor (1962-)

Beefcake '99
The Five Senses '99
Eclipse '94

Betty Mack (1901-80)

Rough Ridin' Rhythm '37
Outlaw Rule '36
Last of the Clintons '35
Toll of the Desert '35
Fighting Texans '33
The Forty-Niners '32

Charles Emmet Mack (1900-27)

The First Auto '27
Old San Francisco '27
A Woman of the World '25
America '24
Dream Street '21

Helen Mack (1913-86)

Power Dive '41
His Girl Friday '40
Fit for a King '37
I Promise to Pay '37
The Wrong Road '37
Milky Way '36
The Return of Peter Grimm '35
She '35
Kiss and Make Up '34
The California Trail '33
Son of Kong '33
Fargo Express '32
Melody Cruise '32
Struggle '31

Kerry Mack (1957-)

Fantasy Man '84
Savage Attraction '83
Fair Game '82

Wayne Mack (1924-93)

Mardi Gras Massacre '78
Crypt of Dark Secrets '76
Storyville '74

Dorothy Mackaill (1903-90)

Bulldog Drummond at Bay '37
Curtain at Eight '33
No Man of Her Own '32
Kept Husbands '31
Ranson's Folly '26
Shore Leave '25

Barry Mackay (1906-85)

Sailing Along '38
Gangway '37
The Private Secretary '35
Evergreen '34

Fulton Mackay (1922-87)

Porridge '91
Defense of the Realm '85
Local Hero '83
A Sense of Freedom '78
Nothing But the Night '72

George MacKay

The Boys Are Back '09
The Old Curiosity Shop '07

John MacKay

The Rook '99
Niagara, Niagara '97
Simple Men '92
Trust '91
Alligator Eyes '90
The Rejuvenator '88
I Was a Teenage TV Terrorist '87
Fat Guy Goes Nutzoid '86
Krush Groove '85

Dear Detective '78
Great Ride '78
Greedy Terror '78

Carol MacReady

Wondrous Oblivion '06
102 Dalmatians '00
Agatha Christie's Murder is Easy '82

George Macready (1908-73)

The Return of Count Yorga '71
Tora! Tora! Tora! '70
Night Gallery '69
The Great Race '65
Dead Ringer '64
The Human Duplicators '64
Seven Days in May '64
Where Love Has Gone '64
Taras Bulba '62
Two Weeks in Another Town '62
Paths of Glory '57
I Beheld His Glory '53
Julius Caesar '53
The Stranger Wore a Gun '53
Vera Cruz '53
The Green Glove '52
Detective Story '51
Tarzan's Peril '51
The Nevadan '50
The Doolins of Oklahoma '49
Knock on Any Door '49
The Big Clock '48
Black Arrow '48
Coroner Creek '48
Down to Earth '47
Gilda '46
The Seventh Cross '44

Tim Maculan

Inside Out '05

Bruce MacVittie

Just Like the Son '06
2B Perfectly Honest '04
Where the Money Is '00
Hi-Life '98
Stonewall '95
Devlin '92

Bill Macy (1922-)

Mr. Woodcock '07
The Holiday '06
Surviving Christmas '04
Analyze This '98
Me, Myself & I '92
The Doctor '91
Sibling Rivalry '90
Bad Medicine '85
Movers and Shakers '85
My Favorite Year '82
Serial '80
Diary of a Young Comic '79
Fantastic Seven '79
The Jerk '79
The Late Show '77
Oh! Calcutta! '72

William H. Macy (1950-)

Marmaduke '10
Shorts: The Adventures of the Wishing Rock '09
Bart Got a Room '08
The Deal '08
The Maiden Heist '08
The Tale of Despereaux '08 (V)
He Was a Quiet Man '07
Wild Hogs '07
Bobby '06
Everyone's Hero '06 (V)
Thank You for Smoking '06
Edmond '05
Sahara '05
Cellular '04
In Enemy Hands '04
Spartan '04
Stealing Sinatra '04
The Cooler '03
Out of Order '03
Seabiscuit '03
Welcome to Collinwood '02
Focus '01
Jurassic Park 3 '01
Panic '00
State and Main '00
Happy, Texas '99
Magnolia '99
Mystery Men '99
A Slight Case of Murder '99
A Civil Action '98
The Con '98
Jerry and Tom '98
Pleasantville '98
Psycho '98
The Secret of NIMH 2 '98 (V)
Air Force One '97
Boogie Nights '97
Wag the Dog '97
Down Periscope '96
Fargo '96
Ghosts of Mississippi '96
Hit Me '96
Andersonville '95
Mr. Holland's Opus '95
Murder in the First '95
Being Human '94
Children of Fury '94
The Client '94
Dead on Sight '94
Evolver '94 (V)
Oleanna '94
Benny & Joon '93
Searching for Bobby Fischer '93
Twenty Bucks '93
A Private Matter '92
The Water Engine '92
Homicide '91
Things Change '88
Foolin' Around '80

Ciaran Madden (1945-)

Ivanhoe '97
Fortunes of War '87
A Married Man '84
The Beast Must Die '75

John Madden (1949-)

The Replacements '00
Little Giants '94
P.K. and the Kid '85

Peter Madden (1910-76)

Frankenstein Created Woman '66
Doctor Zhivago '65
Woman of Straw '64
Kiss of the Vampire '62
The Loneliness of the Long Distance Runner '62
Missiles from Hell '58

Victor Maddern (1926-93)

Carry On Spying '64
I'm All Right Jack '59
Blood of the Vampire '58
Abandon Ship '57
Sailor of the King '53
The Shadow Man '53

Anna Madeley

Affinity '08
The Old Curiosity Shop '07
The Secret Life of Mrs. Beeton '06

Rebecca Mader (1979-)

The Men Who Stare at Goats '09
Great World of Sound '07
The Devil Wears Prada '06
Mimic 3: Sentinel '03

Amy Madigan (1957-)

Living Proof '08
Gone Baby Gone '07
Winter Passing '05
The Laramie Project '02
Shot in the Heart '01
The Sleepy Time Gal '01
Pollock '00
A Time for Dancing '00
A Bright Shining Lie '98
With Friends Like These '98
Loved '97
Female Perversions '96
Riders of the Purple Sage '96
The Dark Half '91
Field of Dreams '89
Roe vs. Wade '89
Uncle Buck '89
Prince of Pennsylvania '88
Alamo Bay '85
Twice in a Lifetime '85
Places in the Heart '84
Streets of Fire '84
Love Letters '83
Nowhere to Hide '83
The Ambush Murders '82
Love Child '82

James Madio (1975-)

Doughboys '08
The Box '07
Searching for Bobby D '05
Band of Brothers '01
The Basketball Diaries '95
Hero '92

Guy Madison (1922-96)

Computer Wizard '77
Where's Willie? '77
Hell Commandos '69
Place in Hell '69
Special Forces '68
Bang Bang Kid '67
Superargo '67
Five Giants from Texas '66
The Snake Hunter Strangler '66
Cold Steel for Tortuga '65
Apache's Last Battle '64
The Conqueror & the Empress '64
Executioner of Venice '63
Jet Over the Atlantic '59
Bullwhip '58
5 Against the House '55
Savage Wilderness '55
The Command '54
Drums in the Deep South '51
Till the End of Time '46
Since You Went Away '44

Noel Madison (1897-1975)

Footsteps in the Dark '41
The Great Plane Robbery '40
Charlie Chan in City of Darkness '39
Sailing Along '38
Gangway '37
The House of Secrets '37
A Nation Aflame '37
Cocaine Fiends '36

Philip Madoc (1934-)

A Mind to Kill '95
A Very British Coup '88
Space: 1999—Alien Attack '79

Ruth Madoc (1943-)

Very Annie Mary '00
Agatha Christie's The Pale Horse '96

Madonna (1959-)

Arthur and the Invisibles '06 (V)
Swept Away '02
The Next Best Thing '00
Evita '96
Girl 6 '96
Blue in the Face '95
Four Rooms '95
Dangerous Game '93
Body of Evidence '92
A League of Their Own '92
Shadows and Fog '92
Truth or Dare '91
Dick Tracy '90
Bloodhounds of Broadway '89
Who's That Girl? '87
Shanghai Surprise '86
Desperately Seeking Susan '85
Certain Sacrifice '80

Teresa Madruga (1953-)

Two Drifters '05
In the White City '83

Michael Madsen (1959-)

Break '09
Deep Winter '08
Hell Ride '08
Last Hour '08
Lost Treasure of the Maya '08
Vice '08
Afghan Knights '07
Boarding Gate '07
Crash and Burn '07
Croc '07
Living & Dying '07
Tooth and Nail '07
All In '06
BloodRayne '06
Scary Movie 4 '06
UKM: The Ultimate Killing Machine '06
Chasing Ghosts '05
L.A. Dicks '05
The Last Drop '05
Sin City '05
Kill Bill Vol. 2 '04
44 Minutes: The North Hollywood Shootout '03
Kill Bill Vol. 1 '03
My Boss's Daughter '03
Die Another Day '02
Extreme Honor '01
L.A.P.D.: To Protect and Serve '01
Choke '00
High Noon '00
The Inspectors 2: A Shred of Evidence '00
Luck of the Draw '00
Sacrifice '00
The Stray '00
Agent of Death '99
Detour '99
Supreme Sanction '99
Voodoo Dawn '99
Catherine's Grove '98
The Florentine '98
The Maker '98
The Sender '98
Species 2 '98
Surface to Air '98
Trail of a Serial Killer '98
Diary of a Serial Killer '97
Executive Target '97
Love to Kill '97
Donnie Brasco '96
The Last Days of Frankie the Fly '96
Red Line '96
The Winner '96
Free Willy 2: The Adventure Home '95
Man with a Gun '95
Mulholland Falls '95
Species '95
Dead Connection '94
Season of Change '94
Wyatt Earp '94
Almost Blue '93
Final Combination '93
Free Willy '93
The Getaway '93
A House in the Hills '93
Money for Nothing '93
Beyond the Law '92
Fatal Instinct '92
Inside Edge '92
Reservoir Dogs '92
Straight Talk '92
Trouble Bound '92
The Doors '91
Thelma & Louise '91
The End of Innocence '90
Iguana '89
Kill Me Again '89
Shadows in the Storm '88
The Natural '84
Racing with the Moon '84
One for the Road '82

Virginia Madsen (1963-)

The Haunting in Connecticut '09
Diminished Capacity '08
The Astronaut Farmer '07
The Number 23 '07
Ripple Effect '07
Firewall '06
A Prairie Home Companion '06
Brave New Girl '04
Sideways '04
American Gun '02
Crossfire Trail '01
Full Disclosure '00
The Haunting '99
The Florentine '98
The Apocalypse Watch '97
John Grisham's The Rainmaker '97
Ghosts of Mississippi '96
Just Your Luck '96
The Prophecy '95
Bitter Vengeance '94
Blue Tiger '94
Caroline at Midnight '93
Linda '93
Becoming Colette '92
Candyman '92
Highlander 2: The Quickening '91
Love Kills '91
Victim of Love '91
The Hot Spot '90
Ironclads '90
The Heart of Dixie '89
Third Degree Burn '89
Gotham '88
Hot to Trot! '88
Mr. North '88
Long Gone '87
Slamdance '87
Zombie High '87
Fire with Fire '86
Modern Girls '86
Creator '85
The Hearst and Davies Affair '85
Dune '84
Electric Dreams '84

Aki Maeda

Azumi 2 '05
Linda Linda Linda '05

Beverly (Bibari) Maeda (1948-)

Face of Another '66
Son of Godzilla '66

Christian Maelen

Remedy '05
This Thing of Ours '03
Wisegirls '02
I Think I Do '97

Mia Maestro (1978-)

The Summit '08
The Box '07
Poseidon '06
Deepwater '05
The Motorcycle Diaries '04
Frida '02
In the Time of the Butterflies '01
For Love or Country: The Arturo Sandoval Story '00
Time Code '00
Tango '98

Stella Maeve

The Runaways '10
Harold '08

Roma Maffia (1958-)

The Blue Tooth Virgin '09
Yonkers Joe '08
Holes '03
Things You Can Tell Just by Looking at Her '00
Double Jeopardy '99
Route 9 '98
The Defenders: Payback '97
Kiss the Girls '97
Mistrial '96
The Heidi Chronicles '95
Nick of Time '95
Disclosure '94

Dominic Mafham (1968-)

The Scarlet Pimpernel '99
Our Mutual Friend '98
Shooting Fish '98

Robbie Magasiva

The Tattooist '07
Stickmen '01

Cass Magda

Blade Boxer '97
Hawk's Vengeance '96

Patrick Magee (1922-82)

The Monster Club '85
The Black Cat '81
Chariots of Fire '81
Rough Cut '80
Sleep of Death '79
Telefon '77
Barry Lyndon '75
A Killer in Every Corner '74
Luther '74
And Now the Screaming Starts '73
The Final Programme '73
Asylum '72
Demons of the Mind '72
Young Winston '72
A Clockwork Orange '71
The Fiend '71
King Lear '71
Trojan Women '71
Cromwell '70
Anzio '68
Portrait in Terror '66
Die, Monster, Die! '65
Masque of the Red Death '65
The Skull '65
Seance on a Wet Afternoon '64
Zulu '64
Dementia 13 '63
The Very Edge '63

Jad Mager (1969-)

Big City Blues '99
Blue Flame '93

Brandon Maggart (1933-)

Running Mates '92
The World According to Garp '82
Christmas Evil '80
Dressed to Kill '80

Maggie Q

Balls of Fury '07
Naked Weapon '03

Pupella Maggio (1910-99)

Amarcord '74
The Valachi Papers '72

Santiago Magill (1977-)

City of M '01
I Love You Baby '01

Benoit Magimel (1974-)

A Girl Cut in Two '07
Crimson Rivers 2: Angels of the Apocalypse '05
The Bridesmaid '04
The Piano Teacher '01
Children of the Century '99
Les Voleurs '96
A Single Girl '96
Life Is a Long Quiet River '88

Licia Maglietta (1954-)

Agata and the Storm '04
Bread and Tulips '01

Anna Magnani (1907-73)

Fellini's Roma '72
The Secret of Santa Vittoria '69
Mamma Roma '62
The Fugitive Kind '60
Joyful Laughter '60
Passionate Thief '60
And the Wild, Wild Women '59
The Rose Tattoo '55
The Golden Coach '52
Bellissima '51
Amore '48
The Miracle '48
Peddlin' in Society '47
Open City '45
Teresa Venerdi '41

Donna Magnani

Epoch '00
29th Street '91

Pierre Magnier

Cyrano de Bergerac '25
La Roue '23

Ann Magnuson (1956-)
United States of Leland *'03*
Night at the Golden Eagle *'02*
Panic Room *'02*
The Caveman's Valentine *'01*
Glitter *'01*
Kitchen Privileges *'00*
Love & Sex *'00*
From the Earth to the Moon *'98*
Small Soldiers *'98*
Levitation *'97*
Still Breathing *'97*
Before and After *'95*
Cabin Boy *'94*
Tank Girl *'94*
Checking Out *'89*
Heavy Petting *'89*
Love at Large *'89*
A Night in the Life of Jimmy Reardon *'88*
Sleepwalk *'88*
Tequila Sunrise *'88*
Making Mr. Right *'86*
Desperately Seeking Susan *'85*
Perfect Strangers *'84*
The Hunger *'83*
Vortex *'81*

Billy Magnussen
Twelve *'10*
Happy Tears *'09*

Kate Magowan
Stardust *'07*
It's All Gone, Pete Tong *'04*

Pierre Maguelon (1933-)
Alice et Martin *'98*
Cyrano de Bergerac *'90*
Bed and Board *'70*

Kathleen Maguire
Flipper *'63*
Edge of the City *'57*

Mary Maguire
Black Eyes *'39*
Mysterious Mr. Moto *'38*

Tobey Maguire (1975-)
Brothers *'09*
Tropic Thunder *'08*
Spider-Man 3 *'07*
The Good German *'06*
Spider-Man 2 *'04*
Seabiscuit *'03*
Spider-Man *'02*
Cats & Dogs *'01 (V)*
Wonder Boys *'00*
The Cider House Rules *'99*
Ride with the Devil *'99*
Fear and Loathing in Las Vegas *'98*
Pleasantville *'98*
Deconstructing Harry *'97*
The Ice Storm *'97*
Joyride *'97*
Revenge of the Red Baron *'93*

Valerie Mahaffey (1953-)
My First Wedding *'04*
Seabiscuit *'03*
Jungle 2 Jungle *'96*
National Lampoon's Senior Trip *'95*
Witch Hunt *'94*
They Watch *'93*
Code Name: Dancer *'87*
The Rise & Rise of Daniel Rocket *'86*
Women of Valor *'86*

George Maharis (1928-)
Sword & the Sorcerer *'82*
The Crash of Flight 401 *'78*
Return to Fantasy Island *'77*
Murder on Flight 502 *'75*
Desperados *'69*
Land Raiders *'69*
Last Day of the War *'69*
Exodus *'60*

Bill Maher (1956-)
Religulous *'08*
Pizza Man *'91*
Cannibal Women in the Avocado Jungle of Death *'89*
House 2: The Second Story *'87*

Joseph Maher (1934-98)
Surviving Picasso *'96*
Bulletproof Heart *'95*
I.Q. *'94*
The Shadow *'94*
Sister Act *'92*
Funny Farm *'88*
My Stepmother Is an Alien *'88*
The Evil That Men Do *'84*
Frankenweenie *'84*
Under the Rainbow *'81*

Sean Maher (1975-)
Wedding Wars *'06*
Serenity *'05*
Brian's Song *'01*

Grace Mahlaba
Being Human *'94*
Bopha! *'93*

Bruce Mahler (1950-)
Funland *'89*
Police Academy 6: City under Siege *'89*

Shiek Mahmud-Bey
Leprechaun 6: Back 2 Tha Hood *'03*
Buffalo Soldiers *'01*
Mercy Streets *'00*
Small Vices: A Spenser Mystery *'99*
Path to Paradise *'97*
Joe's Apartment *'96*
Night Falls on Manhattan *'96*

Michael Mahonen (1964-)
Captured *'99*
By Way of the Stars *'92*
Giant Steps *'92*

Brian Mahoney
Boondock Saints *'99*
Red Snow *'91*

Jock Mahoney (1919-89)
Bad Bunch *'76*
The Glory Stompers *'67*
The Walls of Hell *'64*
Three Blondes in His Life *'61*
Tarzan the Magnificent *'60*
A Time to Love & a Time to Die *'58*
Battle Hymn *'57*
The Land Unknown *'57*
Cow Town *'50*
The Nevadan *'50*
Rim of the Canyon *'49*

John Mahoney (1940-)
Dan in Real Life *'07*
Atlantis: The Lost Empire *'01 (V)*
The Broken Hearts Club *'00*
The Iron Giant *'99 (V)*
Antz *'98 (V)*
Primal Fear *'96*
She's the One *'96*
The American President *'95*
Reality Bites *'94*
The Hudsucker Proxy *'93*
In the Line of Fire *'93*
Striking Distance *'93*
Article 99 *'92*
The Secret Passion of Robert Clayton *'92*
The Water Engine *'92*
Barton Fink *'91*
Love Hurts *'91*
The Ten Million Dollar Getaway *'91*
Unnatural Pursuits *'91*
The Russia House *'90*
Dinner at Eight *'89*
The Image *'89*
Say Anything *'89*
Betrayed *'88*
Eight Men Out *'88*
Frantic *'88*
Moonstruck *'87*
Suspect *'87*
Tin Men *'87*
The Manhattan Project *'86*
Trapped in Silence *'86*

Tim Maier
Turnaround *'87*
Raw Courage *'84*

Aissa Maiga (1975-)
Bamako *'06*
Paris, je t'aime *'06*
Russian Dolls *'05*

Steven Mailer (1966-)
Ride with the Devil *'99*
24 Nights *'99*
Red Meat *'98*
Quiet Days in Hollywood *'97*
Getting In *'94*

Robert Mailhouse
All I Want for Christmas *'07*
Just a Little Harmless Sex *'99*

Caludette Maille
Like A Bride *'94*
Like Water for Chocolate *'93*

Deborah Mailman (1972-)
Rabbit-Proof Fence *'02*
Radiance *'98*

Laurie Main (1922-)
Tarzan, the Ape Man *'81*
Private Parts *'72*

Marjorie Main (1890-1975)
The Kettles on Old MacDonald's Farm *'57*
Friendly Persuasion *'56*
The Kettles in the Ozarks *'56*
Ma and Pa Kettle at Waikiki *'55*
The Long, Long Trailer *'54*
Ma and Pa Kettle at Home *'54*
Rose Marie *'54*
Ma and Pa Kettle on Vacation *'53*
The Belle of New York *'52*
Ma and Pa Kettle at the Fair *'52*
It's a Big Country *'51*
Ma and Pa Kettle Back On the Farm *'51*
Mr. Imperium *'51*
Ma and Pa Kettle Go to Town *'50*
Summer Stock *'50*
Ma and Pa Kettle *'49*
Egg and I *'47*
The Wistful Widow of Wagon Gap *'47*
The Harvey Girls *'46*
The Show-Off *'46*
Undercurrent *'46*
Murder, He Says *'45*
Heaven Can Wait *'43*
Johnny Come Lately *'43*
We Were Dancing *'42*
Honky Tonk *'41*
The Shepherd of the Hills *'41*
A Woman's Face *'41*
Dark Command *'40*
I Take This Woman *'40*
Susan and God *'40*
They Shall Have Music *'39*
The Women *'39*
Little Tough Guys *'38*
Dead End *'37*
Stella Dallas *'37*
The Wrong Road *'37*

Giorgio Maiocchi
The Iron Ladies 2 *'03*
The Iron Ladies *'00*

Guy Mairesse (1924-)
A Reason to Live, a Reason to Die *'73*
The Diabolical Dr. Z *'65*

Valerie Mairesse (1955-)
One to Another *'06*
The Sacrifice *'86*
Investigation *'79*
One Sings, the Other Doesn't *'77*

Marne Maitland (1920-92)
Fellini's Roma *'72*
The Bushbaby *'70*
The Reptile *'66*
The Terror of the Tongs *'61*
The Stranglers of Bombay *'60*
Bhowani Junction *'56*

Tina Majorino (1985-)
What We Do Is Secret *'07*
Think Tank *'06*
Napoleon Dynamite *'04*
Alice in Wonderland *'99*
Santa Fe *'97*
True Women *'97*
Waterworld *'95*
Andre *'94*
Corrina, Corrina *'94*
When a Man Loves a Woman *'94*

Austin Majors (1995-)
The Ant Bully *'06 (V)*
Treasure Planet *'02 (V)*

Lee Majors (1940-)
The Brothers Solomon *'07*
When I Find the Ocean *'06*
Arizona Summer *'03*
Big Fat Liar *'02*
Out Cold *'01*
Trojan War *'97*
The Cover Girl Murders *'93*
Chinatown Connection *'90*
Keaton's Cop *'90*
Scrooged *'88*
A Smoky Mountain Christmas *'86*
The Cowboy & the Ballerina *'84*
Starflight One *'83*
The Agency *'81*
Last Chase *'81*
High Noon: Part 2 *'80*
Steel *'80*
Killer Fish *'79*
Norseman *'78*
Francis Gary Powers: The True Story of the U-2 Spy *'76*
The Bionic Woman *'75*
The Ballad of Andy Crocker *'69*
Will Penny *'67*
Strait-Jacket *'64*

Heike Makatsch (1971-)
Love Actually *'03*
Aimee & Jaguar *'98*
Obsession *'97*

Miriam Makeba
Soul Power *'08*
Sarafina! *'92*

Chris Makepeace (1964-)
Synapse *'95*
Aloha Summer *'88*
Captive Hearts *'87*
Vamp *'86*
Undergrads *'85*
Savage Hunger *'84*
The Terry Fox Story *'83*
Mazes and Monsters *'82*
The Mysterious Stranger *'82*
Last Chase *'81*
My Bodyguard *'80*

Yoko Maki
The Grudge *'04*
The Princess Blade *'02*

Wendy Makkena (1963-)
Air Bud *'97*
Finding North *'96*
Death Benefit *'96*
Serving in Silence: The Margarethe Cammermeyer Story *'95*
Camp Nowhere *'94*
Sister Act 2: Back in the Habit *'93*
Sister Act *'92*
Eight Men Out *'88*

Mako (1933-2006)
Rise: Blood Hunter *'07*
TMNT (Teenage Mutant Ninja Turtles) *'07 (V)*
Memoirs of a Geisha *'05*
Bulletproof Monk *'03*
Pearl Harbor *'01*
Rugrats in Paris: The Movie *'00 (V)*
Seven Years in Tibet *'97*
Sworn to Justice *'97*
Balance of Power *'96*
Riot in the Streets *'96*
Blood for Blood *'95*
A Dangerous Place *'94*
Highlander: The Final Dimension *'94*
Red Sun Rising *'94*
Rising Sun *'93*
Sidekicks *'93*
My Samurai *'92*
Hiroshima: Out of the Ashes *'90*
Pacific Heights *'90*
Taking Care of Business *'90*
Fatal Mission *'89*
An Unremarkable Life *'89*
Tucker: The Man and His Dream *'88*
The Wash *'88*
Armed Response *'86*
Kung Fu: The Movie *'86*
The P.O.W. Escape *'86*
Girls of the White Orchid *'85*
Conan the Destroyer *'84*
The Nightingale *'83*
Testament *'83*
Conan the Barbarian *'82*
When Hell Was in Session *'82*
An Eye for an Eye *'81*
Under the Rainbow *'81*
The Big Brawl *'80*
The Killer Elite *'75*
The Island at the Top of the World *'74*
The Streets of San Francisco *'72*
Private Navy of Sgt. O'Farrell *'68*
The Sand Pebbles *'66*
The Ugly Dachshund *'65*

Lawrence Makoare (1968-)
Lord of the Rings: The Return of the King *'03*
Die Another Day *'02*

Sergei Makovetsky
12 *'07*
Of Freaks and Men *'98*

Khoury J. Makram
See Makram Khoury

Dragan Maksimovic (1949-2001)
Pretty Village, Pretty Flame *'96*
Meetings with Remarkable Men *'79*

Mala (1906-52)
The Tuttles of Tahiti *'42*
Call of the Yukon *'38*
Hawk of the Wilderness *'38*
Robinson Crusoe of Clipper Island *'36*
Robinson Crusoe of Mystery Island *'36*

Patrick Malahide (1945-)
Brideshead Revisited *'08*
Five Days *'07*
Murderous Intent *'06*
Elizabeth I *'05*
Friends & Crocodiles *'05*
Sahara *'05*
Eurotrip *'04*
Goodbye, Mr. Chips *'02*
Captain Corelli's Mandolin *'01*
Victoria & Albert *'01*
All the King's Men *'99*
Fortress 2: Re-Entry *'99*
Heaven *'99*
Ordinary Decent Criminal *'99*
Deacon Brodie *'98*
Miracle at Midnight *'98*
The Beautician and the Beast *'97*
The Long Kiss Goodnight *'96*
Til There Was You *'96*
Cutthroat Island *'95*
Kidnapped *'95*
A Man of No Importance *'94*
Two Deaths *'94*
Middlemarch *'93*
December Bride *'91*
The Franchise Affair *'88*
A Month in the Country *'87*
The Singing Detective *'86*
Comfort and Joy *'84*

Christophe MaLavoy (1952-)
Madame Bovary *'91*
The Cry of the Owl *'87*
Peril *'85*

Paolo Malco
The House by the Cemetery *'83*
New York Ripper *'82*
Scorpion with Two Tails *'82*
Watch Me When I Kill *'77*

Romany Malco (1968-)
Saint John of Las Vegas *'09*
Baby Mama *'08*
The Love Guru *'08*
The Ex *'07*
The 40 Year Old Virgin *'05*
The Tuxedo *'02*
The Chateau *'01*
Urban Menace *'99*

Christopher Malcolm (1946-)
Daphne *'07*
We'll Meet Again *'82*
The Great Riviera Bank Robbery *'79*

Robyn Malcolm (1965-)
Boogeyman *'05*
Perfect Strangers *'03*

Paula Malcomson
Caprica *'09*
Hamlet *'00*

Karl Malden (1914-2009)
Nuts *'87*
Billy Galvin *'86*
Alice in Wonderland *'85*
Fatal Vision *'84*
Urge to Kill *'84*
The Sting 2 *'83*
Miracle on Ice *'81*
Beyond the Poseidon Adventure *'79*
Meteor *'79*
Skag *'79*
Ricco *'74*
The Streets of San Francisco *'72*
The Cat o' Nine Tails *'71*
Wild Rovers *'71*
Patton *'70*
Blue *'68*
Hot Millions *'68*
Billion Dollar Brain *'67*
Hotel *'67*
The Adventures of Bullwhip Griffin *'66*
Murderers' Row *'66*
Nevada Smith *'66*
The Cincinnati Kid *'65*
Cheyenne Autumn *'64*
Dead Ringer *'64*
How the West Was Won *'63*
All Fall Down *'62*
Birdman of Alcatraz *'62*
Gypsy *'62*
The Great Impostor *'61*
One-Eyed Jacks *'61*
Parrish *'61*
Pollyanna *'60*
The Hanging Tree *'59*
Bombers B-52 *'57*

Fear Strikes Out *'57*
Baby Doll *'56*
On the Waterfront *'54*
I Confess *'53*
Diplomatic Courier *'52*
Ruby Gentry *'52*
A Streetcar Named Desire *'51*
The Gunfighter *'50*
The Halls of Montezuma *'50*
Where the Sidewalk Ends *'50*
Boomerang *'47*
Kiss of Death *'47*
13 Rue Madeleine *'46*
They Knew What They Wanted *'40*

Ruth Maleczech

The Ballad of Little Jo *'93*
In the Soup *'92*
Anna *'87*

Jonathan Malen (1987-)

Charlie Bartlett *'07*
Possessed *'00*

Arthur Malet (1927-)

A Little Princess *'95*
Beastmaster 2: Through the Portal of Time *'91*
Hook *'91*
The Black Cauldron *'85 (V)*
Halloween *'78*
Munster, Go Home! *'66*
King Rat *'65*

Laurent Malet (1955-)

The Possessed *'88*
Sword of Gideon *'86*
Querelle *'83*
Invitation au Voyage *'82*
Jacko & Lise *'82*
Roads to the South *'78*
Blood Relatives *'77*

Ryan Malgarini (1992-)

Freaky Friday *'03*
United States of Leland *'03*

Wendie Malick (1950-)

Alvin and the Chipmunks: The Squeakuel *'09*
Confessions of a Shopaholic *'09*
Racing Stripes *'05*
Waiting *'05*
Raising Genius *'04*
On Edge *'03*
Manna from Heaven *'02*
Strange Frequency 2 *'01*
The Emperor's New Groove *'00 (V)*
Dead Husbands *'98*
Jerome *'98*
North Shore Fish *'97*
Trojan War *'97*
The American President *'95*
Madonna: Innocence Lost *'95*
Scrooged *'88*

Keram Malicki-Sanchez (1974-)

Happy Campers *'01*
Cherry Falls *'00*
Skin Deep *'94*

Art Malik (1952-)

The Wolfman *'09*
Nina's Heavenly Delights *'06*
Fakers *'04*
Cleopatra *'99*
Catherine Cookson's Colour Blind *'98*
Path to Paradise *'97*
Booty Call *'96*
A Kid in King Arthur's Court *'95*
True Lies *'94*
Uncovered *'94*
City of Joy *'92*
The Killing Beach *'92*
Year of the Comet *'92*
The Living Daylights *'87*
Harem *'86*
Transmutations *'85*
The Jewel in the Crown *'84*

Joshua Malina (1966-)

View from the Top *'03*
Bulworth *'98*
From the Earth to the Moon *'98*
The American President *'95*
In the Line of Fire *'93*

Judith Malina (1926-)

Let It Snow *'99*
The Deli *'97*
Music from Another Room *'97*
Household Saints *'93*
The Addams Family *'91*
Awakenings *'90*
Enemies, a Love Story *'89*

Ross Malinger (1984-)

Club Vampire *'98*
Frog and Wombat *'98*
Toothless *'97*
Little Bigfoot *'96*
Sudden Death *'95*
Bye Bye, Love *'94*
Sleepless in Seattle *'93*
Late for Dinner *'91*
Eve of Destruction *'90*

Cylia Malki (1976-)

La Moustache *'05*
Daughter of Keltoum *'01*

Sam Malkin

Blood Relations *'87*
Caribe *'87*

John Malkovich (1953-)

Jonah Hex *'10*
The Great Buck Howard *'09*
Afterwards *'08*
Burn After Reading *'08*
Changeling *'08*
Disgrace *'08*
Gardens of the Night *'08*
Mutant Chronicles *'08*
Beowulf *'07 (V)*
In Tranzit *'07*
Art School Confidential *'06*
Eragon *'06*
Klimt *'06*
Color Me Kubrick *'05*
The Hitchhiker's Guide to the Galaxy *'05*
The Libertine *'05*
Johnny English *'03*
Napoleon *'03*
Ripley's Game *'02*
Hotel *'01*
Knockaround Guys *'01*
I'm Going Home *'00*
Shadow of the Vampire *'00*
Being John Malkovich *'99*
The Messenger: The Story of Joan of Arc *'99*
RKO 281 *'99*
Time Regained *'99*
The Man in the Iron Mask *'98*
Rounders *'98*
Con Air *'97*
The Ogre *'96*
Portrait of a Lady *'96*
Beyond the Clouds *'95*
The Convent *'95*
Mary Reilly *'95*
Mulholland Falls *'95*
Alive *'93 (N)*
Heart of Darkness *'93*
In the Line of Fire *'93*
Jennifer 8 *'92*
Of Mice and Men *'92*
Shadows and Fog *'92*
The Object of Beauty *'91*
Queens Logic *'91*
The Sheltering Sky *'90*
Dangerous Liaisons *'88*
Miles from Home *'88*
Empire of the Sun *'87*
The Glass Menagerie *'87*
Death of a Salesman *'86*
Making Mr. Right *'86*
Rocket to the Moon *'86*
True West *'86*
Eleni *'85*
The Killing Fields *'84*
Places in the Heart *'84*
American Dream *'81*

Miles Malleson (1888-1969)

The Brides of Dracula *'60*
Peeping Tom *'60*
The Horror of Dracula *'58*
Brothers in Law *'57*
The King's Rhapsody *'55*
Captain's Paradise *'53*
A Christmas Carol *'51*
The Golden Salamander *'51*
Kind Hearts and Coronets *'49*
Train of Events *'49*
Dead of Night *'45*
The Thief of Bagdad *'40*
Nine Days a Queen *'36*

Perry Mallette

Thou Shalt Not Kill...Except *'87*
Going Back *'83*

Brian Mallon

Gods and Generals *'03*
Gettysburg *'93*

Patricia "Boots" Mallory (1913-58)

Here's Flash Casey *'38*
Powdersmoke Range *'35*
Sing Sing Nights *'35*
Carnival Lady *'33*
Wolf Dog *'33*

Matt Malloy

Wedding Daze *'06*
Spartan *'04*
Tanner on Tanner *'04*
Elephant *'03*
United States of Leland *'03*
Changing Lanes *'02*
The Great Gatsby *'01*
Dr. T & the Women *'00*
Everything Put Together *'00*
Running Mates *'00*
Cookie's Fortune *'99*
Drop Dead Gorgeous *'99*
Election *'99*
In the Company of Men *'96*
Surviving Desire *'91*

Tom Malloy

The Alphabet Killer *'08*
The Attic *'06*
Gravesend *'97*

Jan Malmsjo (1932-)

Fanny and Alexander *'83*
Scenes from a Marriage *'73*

Birger Malmsten (1920-91)

The Silence *'63*
Summer Interlude *'50*
To Joy *'50*
Three Strange Loves *'49*
Night Is My Future *'47*

Bonz Malone

Bomb the System *'05*
White Boyz *'99*
Slam *'98*

Dorothy Malone (1925-)

Basic Instinct *'92*
Rest in Pieces *'87*
Day Time Ended *'80*
Off Your Rocker *'80*
Winter Kills *'79*
Abduction *'75*
The Man Who Would Not Die *'75*
Beach Party *'63*
The Last Voyage *'60*
Warlock *'59*
Man of a Thousand Faces *'57*
Tarnished Angels *'57*
Sincerely Yours *'56*
Tension at Table Rock *'56*
Written on the Wind *'56*
Artists and Models *'55*
At Gunpoint *'55*
Battle Cry *'55*
The Fast and the Furious *'54*
Loophole *'54*
Private Hell 36 *'54*
Pushover *'54*
Young at Heart *'54*
Law and Order *'53*
Scared Stiff *'53*
Torpedo Alley *'53*
The Bushwackers *'52*
The Nevadan *'50*
Colorado Territory *'49*
South of St. Louis *'48*
The Killer That Stalked New York *'47*
The Big Sleep *'46*
Night and Day *'46*

Jena Malone (1984-)

The Messenger *'09*
The Ruins *'08*
The Go-Getter *'07*
Into the Wild *'07*
Four Last Songs *'06*
The Ballad of Jack and Rose *'05*
Pride and Prejudice *'05*
Howl's Moving Castle *'04 (V)*
Saved! *'04*
Cold Mountain *'03*
Hitler: The Rise of Evil *'03*
United States of Leland *'03*
The Badge *'02*
Corn *'02*
The Dangerous Lives of Altar Boys *'02*
Donnie Darko *'01*
Life as a House *'01*
Cheaters *'00*
The Book of Stars *'99*
For Love of the Game *'99*
Stepmom *'98*
Contact *'97*
Ellen Foster *'97*
Hope *'97*
Bastard out of Carolina *'96*
Hidden in America *'96*

Mollie Malone (1888-1952)

Battling Bunyon *'24*
Straight Shootin' *'17*

Nancy Malone (1935-)

Man Who Loved Cat Dancing *'73*
Fright *'56*

Patrick Malone (1969-)

Face the Music *'00*
Hostage High *'97*
Grand Canyon *'91*
Rock 'n' Roll High School Forever *'91*

Michael Maloney (1957-)

The Young Victoria *'09*
Pinochet's Last Stand *'06*
P.D. James: The Murder Room *'04*
Me & Mrs. Jones *'02*
The Painted Lady *'97*
Hamlet *'96*
A Midwinter's Tale *'95*
Othello *'95*
Truly, Madly, Deeply *'91*
Henry V *'89*
Sharma & Beyond *'84*

Peter Maloney

Washington Square *'97*
Robot in the Family *'94*

H.F. Maltby (1880-1963)

Pygmalion *'38*
Young and Innocent *'37*

Natassia Malthe (1974-)

BloodRayne 2: Deliverance *'07*
DOA: Dead or Alive *'06*
Bound by Lies *'05*
Confessions of a Sociopathic Social Climber *'05*
Call Me: The Rise and Fall of Heidi Fleiss *'04*

Leonard Maltin (1950-)

Forgotten Silver *'96*
Gremlins 2: The New Batch *'90*
The Lost Stooges *'33 (N)*

Eily Malyon (1879-1961)

She Wolf of London *'46*
Treasure of Fear *'45*
The Seventh Cross *'44*
I Married a Witch *'42*

Barbara Mamabolo (1986-)

Brave New Girl *'04*
Dangerous Evidence: The Lori Jackson Story *'99*

Peter Mamakos (1918-)

The Conqueror *'56*
Pier 23 *'51*

David Mamet (1947-)

The Water Engine *'92*
Black Widow *'87*

Tony Mamet

Spartan *'04*
Lakeboat *'00*

Robert Mammone

The Condemned *'07*
The Great Raid *'05*
Salem's Lot *'04*
Heaven's Burning *'97*
The Crossing *'92*

Method Man

The Wackness *'08*
Garden State *'04*

Biff Manard (1939-)

Trancers 2: The Return of Jack Deth *'90*
Zone Troopers *'84*

Michael Manasseri (1974-)

Sunstorm *'01*
When Danger Follows You Home *'97*
License to Drive *'88*

Melissa Manchester (1951-)

For the Boys *'91*
The Great Mouse Detective *'86 (V)*

Al Mancini (1932-2007)

The Ticket *'97*
My Summer Story *'94*
Mission Manila *'87*
The Dirty Dozen *'67*

Ray "Boom Boom" Mancini (1961-)

Redbelt *'08*
Body and Soul *'98*
The Search for One-Eye Jimmy *'96*
Wishful Thinking *'92*
Timebomb *'91*
Backstreet Dreams *'90*
The Dirty Dozen: The Fatal Mission *'88*
Oceans of Fire *'86*

Nick Mancuso (1948-)

Contract Killers *'08*
Vanessa *'07*
Blind Eye *'06*
Call of the Wild *'04*
Firefight *'03*
Revelation *'00*
Tribulation *'00*
Captured *'99*
The Pact *'99*
Total Recall 2070: Machine Dreams *'99*
Against the Law *'98*
Loving Evangeline *'98*
Matter of Trust *'98*
Misbegotten *'98*
Past Perfect *'98*
Perfect Assassins *'98*
Twists of Terror *'98*
Laws of Deception *'97*
The Ex *'96*
The Invader *'96*
Marquis de Sade *'96*
Provocateur *'96*
Under Siege 2: Dark Territory *'95*
A Young Connecticut Yankee in King Arthur's Court *'95*
Young Ivanhoe *'95*
Flinch *'94*
Suspicious Agenda *'94*
The Takeover *'94*
Wild Palms *'93*
Lies Before Kisses *'92*
Rapid Fire *'92*
Fatal Exposure *'91*
Lena's Holiday *'90*
Double Identity *'89*
Death of an Angel *'86*
Half a Lifetime *'86*
Embassy *'85*
Blame It on the Night *'84*
Heartbreakers *'84*
Love Songs *'84*
Maria Chapdelaine *'84*
Tell Me That You Love Me *'84*
Legend of Walks Far Woman *'82*
Mother Lode *'82*
Ticket to Heaven *'81*
Death Ship *'80*
The House on Garibaldi Street *'79*
Nightwing *'79*

Elena Mandalis

Head On *'98*
Only the Brave *'94*

Robert Mandan (1932-)

The Nutt House *'95*
National Lampoon's Last Resort *'94*
Perry Mason: The Case of the Lost Love *'87*
In Love with an Older Woman *'82*
Zapped! *'82*
Return of the Rebels *'81*

Howie Mandel (1955-)

Tribulation *'00*
Kurt Vonnegut's Harrison Bergeron *'95*
Shake, Rattle & Rock! *'94*
Gremlins 2: The New Batch *'90 (V)*
Mother Goose Rock 'n' Rhyme *'90*
Little Monsters *'89*
Walk Like a Man *'87*
A Fine Mess *'86*
Gremlins *'84 (V)*
The Princess Who Never Laughed *'84*
Gas *'81*

Miles Mander (1888-1946)

Brighton Strangler *'45*
Picture of Dorian Gray *'45*
Murder, My Sweet *'44*
The Pearl of Death *'44*
Scarlet Claw *'44*
The White Cliffs of Dover *'44*
Five Graves to Cairo *'43*
Guadalcanal Diary *'43*
Return of the Vampire *'43*
To Be or Not to Be *'42*
Shadows on the Stairs *'41*
Primrose Path *'40*
The Little Princess *'39*
Stanley and Livingstone *'39*
The Three Musketeers *'39*
The Tower of London *'39*
Wuthering Heights *'39*
Mad Miss Manton *'38*
Youth on Parole *'37*
Don Quixote *'35*
The Three Musketeers *'35*
Matinee Idol *'33*
The Private Life of Henry VIII *'33*
Murder *'30*

Barbara Mandrell (1948-)

Burning Rage *'84*
The Concrete Cowboys *'79*

Neil Mandt (1969-)

Last Stop for Paul *'08*
Arthur's Quest *'99*
Hijacking Hollywood *'97*

Aasif Mandvi

The Last Airbender *'10*
The Proposal *'09*

Music & Lyrics *'07*
Sorry, Haters *'05*
The War Within *'05*
Spider-Man 2 *'04*
The Mystic Masseur *'01*
ABCD *'99*

Costas Mandylor (1962-)
Saw 6 *'09*
Saw 5 *'08*
Nobody *'07*
Saw 4 *'07*
Saw 3 *'06*
The Game of Their Lives *'05*
Gangland *'00*
The Pledge *'00*
Bonanno: A Godfather's Story *'99*
Stealth Fighter *'99*
The Fury Within *'98*
Shame, Shame, Shame *'98*
Shelter *'98*
Double Take *'97*
Just Write *'97*
Stand-Ins *'97*
Last Exit to Earth *'96*
Crosscut *'95*
Delta of Venus *'95*
Fist of the North Star *'95*
Portraits of a Killer *'95*
Venus Rising *'95*
Virtuosity *'95*
Almost Dead *'94*
Fatal Past *'94*
The Doors *'91*
Mobsters *'91*
Soapdish *'91*
Triumph of the Spirit *'89*

Louis Mandylor (1966-)
Silent Venom *'08*
Redline *'07*
The Game of Their Lives *'05*
Gang of Roses *'03*
Lady Jayne Killer *'03*
My Big Fat Greek Wedding *'02*
Price of Glory *'00*
Rogue Force *'99*
Mafia! *'98*
The Quest *'96*

Tyler Mane (1966-)
Halloween II *'09*
Halloween *'07*
The Devil's Rejects *'05*
Troy *'04*
Black Mask 2: City of Masks *'02*
How to Make a Monster *'01*
X-Men *'00*

Marshall Manesh (1950-)
Pirates of the Caribbean: At World's End *'07*
Car Babes *'06*
Kazaam *'96*

Larry Manetti (1947-)
The Corporation *'96*
Subliminal Seduction *'96*
Body Chemistry 4: Full Exposure *'95*
Exit *'95*
C.I.A. 2: Target Alexa *'94*
The Take *'90*
Magnum P.I.: Don't Eat the Snow in Hawaii *'80*

Nino Manfredi (1921-2004)
Alberto Express *'92*
In the Name of the Pope-King *'85*
Cafe Express *'83*
Nudo di Donna *'83*
Spaghetti House *'82*
We All Loved Each Other So Much *'77*
Down & Dirty *'76*
Bread and Chocolate *'73*
Head of the Family *'71*

Joe Manganiello (1976-)
Behind Enemy Lines 3: Colombia *'08*
Impact Point *'08*
Spider-Man 3 *'07*
Spider-Man *'02*

Anthony Mangano
All Saint's Day *'98*
8 Heads in a Duffel Bag *'96*
Point Break *'91*

Silvana Mangano (1930-89)
Dark Eyes *'87*
Dune *'84*
Conversation Piece *'75*
Ludwig *'72*
Death in Venice *'71*
The Decameron *'70*
Teorema *'68*
Oedipus Rex *'67*
Barabbas *'62*
The Great War *'59*
Mambo *'55*
Ulysses *'55*
The Gold of Naples *'54*
Anna *'51*
Bitter Rice *'49*
Lure of the Sila *'49*

Alec Mango (1911-89)
The Cosmic Monsters *'58*
The Seventh Voyage of Sinbad *'58*
Race for Life *'55*

Camryn Manheim (1961-)
Jesse Stone: Thin Ice *'09*
Slipstream *'07*
Marilyn Hotchkiss' Ballroom Dancing & Charm School *'06*
An Unfinished Life *'05*
Twisted *'04*
Scary Movie 3 *'03*
Dark Water *'02*
A Girl Thing *'01*
The Loretta Claiborne Story *'00*
The 10th Kingdom *'00*
What Planet Are You From? *'00*
The Tic Code *'99*
Happiness *'98*
David Searching *'97*
Romy and Michele's High School Reunion *'97*
Wide Awake *'97*
Sudden Impact *'83*

Karin Mani
Avenging Angel *'85*
Alley Cat *'84*

Jim Maniaci
The Rock *'96*
Timebomb *'91*

Cindy Manion
The Toxic Avenger *'86*
Preppies *'82*

Paulus Manker (1958-)
King of Thieves *'04*
My Twentieth Century *'90*

Blu Mankuma
Tin Man *'07*
Connor's War *'06*
Fierce People *'05*
Jasper, Texas *'03*
Johnson County War *'02*
Halloweentown 2: Kalabar's Revenge *'01*
Mermaid *'00*
Atomic Train *'99*
Premonition *'98*
A Call to Remember *'97*
Bliss *'96*
Dead Silence *'96*
Watchers *'88*

Dudley Manlove (1914-96)
The Creation of the Humanoids *'62*
Plan 9 from Outer Space *'56*

Alakina Mann (1990-)
Girl with a Pearl Earring *'03*
The Others *'01*

Byron Mann
Blonde and Blonder *'07*
Catwoman *'04*
Sniper 3 *'04*
The Corruptor *'99*
Double Edge *'97*
Red Corner *'97*
Street Fighter *'94*

Danny Mann
Babe: Pig in the City *'98 (V)*
Babe *'95 (V)*
Balto *'95 (V)*
Pocahontas *'95 (V)*

David Mann
Madea Goes to Jail *'09*
Tyler Perry's Meet the Browns *'08*

Gabriel Mann (1972-)
Dark Streets *'08*
80 Minutes *'08*
Love and Mary *'07*
Valley of the Heart's Delight *'07*
A Lot Like Love *'05*
Born Killers *'05*
Dominion: Prequel to the Exorcist *'05*
Don't Come Knocking *'05*
The Bourne Supremacy *'04*
The Life of David Gale *'03*
Abandon *'02*
The Bourne Identity *'02*
Buffalo Soldiers *'01*
Josie and the Pussycats *'01*
Summer Catch *'01*
Things Behind the Sun *'01*
Cherry Falls *'00*
Sleep Easy, Hutch Rimes *'00*
No Vacancy *'99*
Outside Providence *'99*
American Virgin *'98*
High Art *'98*
Kiss of Fire *'98*

Hank Mann (1887-1971)
The Stranger from Arizona *'38*
City Lights *'31*
The Dawn Trail *'30*
Spite Marriage *'29*

John Mann (1962-)
Personal Effects *'09*
Underworld: Evolution *'05*
Turbulence 3: Heavy Metal *'00*

Leonard Mann (1947-)
Cut and Run *'85*
Corrupt *'84*
Night School *'81*
Perfect Crime *'79*

Leslie Mann (1972-)
I Love You Phillip Morris *'10*
Funny People *'09*
17 Again *'09*
Shorts: The Adventures of the Wishing Rock *'09*
Drillbit Taylor *'08*
Knocked Up *'07*
The 40 Year Old Virgin *'05*
Orange County *'02*
Stealing Harvard *'02*
Perfume *'01*
Time Code *'00*
Big Daddy *'99*
George of the Jungle *'97*
The Cable Guy *'96*
Last Man Standing *'96*
She's the One *'96*
Things I Never Told You *'96*

Margaret Mann (1868-1941)
The Law Rides *'36*
Kentucky Blue Streak *'35*
Four Sons *'28*

Robert Mann
Black Christmas *'06*
Assault of the Party Nerds *'89*

Tamela Mann
Madea Goes to Jail *'09*
Tyler Perry's Meet the Browns *'08*

Terrence Mann (1951-)
True Women *'97*
Mrs. Santa Claus *'96*
Critters 4 *'91*
The Ten Million Dollar Getaway *'91*
Critters 2: The Main Course *'88*
Light Years *'88 (V)*
Critters *'86*
A Chorus Line *'85*

Tracy Mann (1957-)
Fast Talking *'86*
Hard Knocks *'80*

Yanka (Doris Keating) Mann
Flesh Feast *'69*
Pagan Island *'60*

Guido Mannari
Cop in Blue Jeans *'78*
Driver's Seat *'73*

David Manners (1901-98)
The Mystery of Edwin Drood *'35*
The Black Cat *'34*
The Moonstone *'34*
The Death Kiss *'33*
Torch Singer *'33*
A Bill of Divorcement *'32*
The Mummy *'32*
They Call It Sin *'32*
Three Broadway Girls *'32*
Dracula *'31*
The Miracle Woman *'31*

Sheila Manners
See Sheila (Manors) Mannors

Lucie Mannheim (1895-1976)
Hotel Reserve *'44*
High Command *'37*
The 39 Steps *'35*

Ettore Manni (1927-79)
City of Women *'81*
Street People *'76*
Heroes in Hell *'73*
Jungle Master *'72*
Angelique and the Sultan *'68*
The Battle of El Alamein *'68*
Untamable Angelique *'67*
Mademoiselle *'66*
Giants of Rome *'63*
Hercules and the Captive Women *'63*
The Battle of Austerlitz *'60*
Angel in a Taxi *'59*
Attila *'54*
Two Nights with Cleopatra *'54*

Vic Manni
Trapped in Paradise *'94*
29th Street *'91*

Sarah Manninen
Never Forget *'08*
Touch the Top of the World *'06*
Eternal *'04*

Marilyn Manning
The Sadist *'63*
What's Up Front *'63*
Eegah! *'62*

Taryn Manning (1978-)
The Devil's Tomb *'09*
Last Resort *'09*
Jack and Jill vs. the World *'08*
Cult *'07*
Weirdsville *'07*
Banshee *'06*
The Breed *'06*
A Lot Like Love *'05*
Hustle & Flow *'05*
Cold Mountain *'03*
Crossroads *'02*
8 Mile *'02*
crazy/beautiful *'01*

Sheila (Manors) Mannors (1911-2003)
Nancy Drew, Reporter *'39*
Torture Ship *'39*
Waterfront *'39*
Cocaine Fiends *'36*
Desert Phantom *'36*
Kelly of the Secret Service *'36*
Prescott Kid *'36*
Lawless Range *'35*
Westward Ho *'35*
Cowboy Counselor *'33*
Texas Pioneers *'32*

Dinah Manoff (1958-)
The Lost Child *'00*
Welcome Home, Roxy Carmichael *'90*
Bloodhounds of Broadway *'89*
Backfire *'88*
Child's Play *'88*
Table Settings *'84*
I Ought to Be in Pictures *'82*
For Ladies Only *'81*
Ordinary People *'80*
Grease *'78*
The Possessed *'77*

Miki (Predrag) Manojlovic (1950-)
Irina Palm *'07*
Mortal Transfer *'01*
Criminal Lovers *'99*
Set Me Free *'99*
Black Cat, White Cat *'98*
Cabaret Balkan *'98*
Artemisia *'97*
Portraits Chinois *'96*
Someone Else's America *'96*
Underground *'95*
Tito and Me *'92*
Every Other Weekend *'91*
When Father Was Away on Business *'85*

J.P. Manoux (1969-)
Minutemen *'08*
Knocked Up *'07*
Eurotrip *'04*

Jayne Mansfield (1932-67)
Single Room Furnished *'68*
A Guide for the Married Man *'67*
The Fat Spy *'66*
Las Vegas Hillbillys *'66*
Dog Eat Dog *'64*
Promises! Promises! *'63*
Panic Button *'62*
The George Raft Story *'61*
The Loves of Hercules *'60*
It Takes a Thief *'59*
The Sheriff of Fractured Jaw *'59*
Will Success Spoil Rock Hunter? *'57*
The Female Jungle *'56*
The Girl Can't Help It *'56*
Hell on Frisco Bay *'55*
Illegal *'55*
Pete Kelly's Blues *'55*
Underwater! *'55*

Martha Mansfield (1899-1927)
Is Money Everything? *'23*
Dr. Jekyll and Mr. Hyde *'20*

Leonor Manso (1948-)
Made in Argentina *'86*
House of Shadows *'76*
Far Away and Long Ago *'74*

Alan Manson (1920-2002)
Whiffs *'75*
Let's Scare Jessica to Death *'71*
The Rain People *'69*

Amy Manson
Blood Monkey *'07*
Pumpkinhead 4: Blood Feud *'07*

Ted Manson
Crystal River *'08*
Gordy *'95*

Paul Mantee (1936-)
Memorial Day *'98*
Lurking Fear *'94*
When Hell Was in Session *'82*
The Manitou *'78*
Robinson Crusoe on Mars *'64*

Gina Mantegna (1990-)
The Neighbor *'07*
In the Land of Women *'06*
Unaccompanied Minors *'06*
Uncle Nino *'03*

Joe Mantegna (1947-)
Hank and Mike *'08*
The Last Hit Man *'08*
Redbelt *'08*
Witless Protection *'08*
Cougar Club *'07*
The Simpsons Movie *'07 (V)*
Edmond *'05*
The Kid and I *'05*
Nine Lives *'05*
Stateside *'04*
Uncle Nino *'03*
Women vs. Men *'02*
The Trumpet of the Swan *'01 (V)*
Lakeboat *'00*
More Dogs Than Bones *'00*
Thin Air *'00*
Turbulence 3: Heavy Metal *'00*
Liberty Heights *'99*
My Little Assassin *'99*
The Runner *'99*
Small Vices: A Spenser Mystery *'99*
Body and Soul *'98*
Celebrity *'98*
For Hire *'98*
Hoods *'98*
Jerry and Tom *'98*
The Last Don 2 *'98*
The Rat Pack *'98*
The Wonderful Ice Cream Suit *'98*
A Call to Remember *'97*
Face Down *'97*
The Last Don *'97*
Albino Alligator *'96*
Persons Unknown *'96*
Stephen King's Thinner *'96*
Underworld *'96*
Up Close and Personal *'96*
Above Suspicion *'95*
Captain Nuke and the Bomber Boys *'95*
An Eye for an Eye *'95*
For Better or Worse *'95*
Forget Paris *'95*
National Lampoon's Favorite Deadly Sins *'95*
Airheads *'94*
Baby's Day Out *'94*
State of Emergency *'94*
Fallen Angels 2 *'93*
Searching for Bobby Fischer *'93*
Body of Evidence *'92*
The Comrades of Summer *'92*
The Water Engine *'92*
Bugsy *'91*
Family Prayers *'91*
Homicide *'91*
Queens Logic *'91*
Alice *'90*
The Godfather, Part 3 *'90*
Wait until Spring, Bandini *'90*
Things Change *'88*
House of Games *'87*
Suspect *'87*
Weeds *'87*
Critical Condition *'86*
The Money Pit *'86*
Off Beat *'86*
Three Amigos *'86*
Compromising Positions *'85*
Second Thoughts *'83*
Elvis: The Movie *'79*

Bronwen Mantel
Gothika *'03*
Pin... *'88*

Henriette Mantel

A Very Brady Sequel *'96*
The Brady Bunch Movie *'95*

Joe Mantell (1920-)

Chinatown *'74*
The Birds *'63*
Marty *'55*

Michael Mantell

Ocean's Thirteen *'07*
Secretary *'02*
Chain of Command *'00*
Gun Shy *'00*
Sins of the Mind *'97*
Dead Funny *'94*
The Night We Never Met *'93*
City of Hope *'91*
Eight Men Out *'88*

Fernando Soto Mantequilla (1911-80)

Invasion of the Vampires *'61*
The Illusion Travels by Streetcar *'53*
Boom in the Moon *'46*

Randolph Mantooth (1945-)

Fire Serpent *'07*
Agent Red *'00*
Terror at London Bridge *'85*
The Seekers *'79*

Robert Manuel

Life Is a Bed of Roses *'83*
Rififi *'54*

Lesley Manville (1956-)

A Christmas Carol *'09 (V)*
Perfect Parents *'06*
All or Nothing *'02*
Plain Jane *'01*
Topsy Turvy *'99*
The Painted Lady *'97*
Secrets and Lies *'95*
High Hopes *'88*
High Season *'88*
Dance with a Stranger *'85*
Grown Ups *'80*

Linda Manz (1961-)

Gummo *'97*
The Snow Queen *'83*
Long Shot Kids *'81*
Out of the Blue *'80*
Orphan Train *'79*
Wanderers *'79*
Days of Heaven *'78*

Dagmar Manzel

The Mistake *'91*
Coming Out *'89*

Angela (Mao Ying) Mao (1952-)

When Taekwondo Strikes *'83*
Return of the Tiger *'78*
Enter the Dragon *'73*

Marla Maples (1963-)

Loving Annabelle *'06*
Black and White *'99*
Happiness *'98*

William Mapother (1965-)

Hurt *'09*
Moola *'07*
The Lather Effect *'06*
The Zodiac *'05*
The Grudge *'04*
Suspect Zero *'04*
In the Bedroom *'01*

Adele Mara (1923-)

Sands of Iwo Jima *'49*
Night Time in Nevada *'48*
Robin Hood of Texas *'47*
The Inner Circle *'46*
Bells of Rosarita *'45*
The Tiger Woman *'45*
Twilight on the Rio Grande *'41*

Kate Mara (1983-)

Iron Man 2 *'10*
The Open Road *'09*
Transsiberian *'08*
Full of It *'07*
Shooter *'07*
We Are Marshall *'06*
Zoom *'06*
Brokeback Mountain *'05*
Urban Legends: Bloody Mary *'05*
Random Hearts *'99*

Mary Mara (1960-)

K-PAX *'01*
Lloyd *'00*
Bound *'96*
Love Potion #9 *'92*
Mr. Saturday Night *'92*

Rooney Mara

A Nightmare on Elm Street *'10*
Dare *'09*

Steve Marachuk

Hot Target *'85*
Piranha 2: The Spawning *'82*
Waikiki *'80*

Jean Marais (1913-98)

Stealing Beauty *'96*
Peau D'Ane *'71*
Donkey Skin *'70*
The Rape of the Sabines *'61*
The Battle of Austerlitz *'60*
The Testament of Orpheus *'59*
Girl in His Pocket *'57*
White Nights *'57*
Elena and Her Men *'56*
Orpheus *'49*
The Eagle Has Two Heads *'48*
Ruyblas *'48*
The Storm Within *'48*
Beauty and the Beast *'46*
Eternal Return *'43*

Josie Maran (1978-)

The Aviator *'04*
Little Black Book *'04*
Van Helsing *'04*

Cindy Maranne

Provoked *'89*
Slashdance *'89*

Dominique Marcas (1920-)

The Butterfly *'02*
La Vie de Boheme *'93*
Dr. Petiot *'90*

Marcel Marceau (1923-2007)

Silent Movie *'76*
Barbarella *'68*

Sophie Marceau (1966-)

Alex & Emma *'03*
Belphegar: Phantom of the Louvre *'01*
Lost and Found *'99*
William Shakespeare's A Midsummer Night's Dream *'99*
The World Is Not Enough *'99*
Firelight *'97*
Leo Tolstoy's Anna Karenina *'96*
Beyond the Clouds *'95*
Braveheart *'95*
Revenge of the Musketeers *'94*
Police *'85*
Fort Saganne *'84*
La Boum *'81*

Elspeth March (1911-99)

The Magician of Lublin *'79*
Goodbye, Mr. Chips *'69*
Woman Times Seven *'67*
The Three Lives of Thomasina *'63 (V)*
Roman Spring of Mrs. Stone *'61*
Midnight Lace *'60*
Quo Vadis *'51*
Mr. Emmanuel *'44*

Fredric March (1897-1975)

The Iceman Cometh *'73*
Hombre *'67*
Seven Days in May *'64*
Inherit the Wind *'60*
The Man in the Gray Flannel Suit *'56*
Alexander the Great *'55*
The Bridges at Toko-Ri *'55*
Desperate Hours *'55*
A Christmas Carol *'54*
Executive Suite *'54*
Death of a Salesman *'51*
It's a Big Country *'51*
Christopher Columbus *'49*
The Best Years of Our Lives *'46*
The Adventures of Mark Twain *'44*
Tomorrow the World *'44*
I Married a Witch *'42*
So Ends Our Night *'41*
Susan and God *'40*
Nothing Sacred *'37*
A Star Is Born *'37*
Anthony Adverse *'36*
Mary of Scotland *'36*
Anna Karenina *'35*
The Dark Angel *'35*
Les Miserables *'35*
The Barretts of Wimpole Street *'34*
Death Takes a Holiday *'34*
The Eagle and the Hawk *'33*
The Sign of the Cross *'33*
Smilin' Through *'33*
Dr. Jekyll and Mr. Hyde *'32*
Merrily We Go to Hell *'32*
Strangers in Love *'32*

Jane March (1973-)

The Stone Merchant *'06*
Dracula: The Dark Prince *'01*
Tarzan and the Lost City *'98*
Circle of Passion *'97*
Provocateur *'96*
Color of Night *'94*
The Lover *'92*

Stephanie March (1974-)

The Invention of Lying *'09*
Flannel Pajamas *'06*
Jesse Stone: Night Passage *'06*
The Treatment *'06*
Mr. & Mrs. Smith *'05*
Head of State *'03*

Georges Marchal (1920-97)

Belle de Jour *'67*
Death in the Garden *'56*
The French Way *'40*

Corinne Marchand (1937-)

Bandits *'86*
Borsalino *'70*
Cleo from 5 to 7 *'61*

Guy Marchand (1937-)

Apres Lui *'07*
Inside Paris *'06*
Paid *'06*
New World *'95*
May Wine *'90*
Conseil de Famille *'86*
Heat of Desire *'84*
Petit Con *'84*
Entre-Nous *'83*
Coup de Torchon *'81*
Loulou *'80*
Dear Detective *'77*
Cousin, Cousine *'76*

Nancy Marchand (1928-2000)

Dear God *'96*
Sabrina *'95*
Brain Donors *'92*
Regarding Henry *'91*
The Naked Gun: From the Files of Police Squad *'88*
North and South Book 2 *'86*
The Bostonians *'84*
Agatha Christie's Sparkling Cyanide *'83*
Killjoy *'81*
The Hospital *'71*

Josh Marchette (1973-)

Tequila Body Shots *'99*
Floating *'97*

Ron Marchini

Karate Cop *'91*
Omega Cop *'90*
Return Fire *'88*
Forgotten Warrior *'86*
Wolf *'86*
Death Machines *'76*

David Marciano (1960-)

The Last Don 2 *'98*
The Last Don *'97*
Kiss Shot *'89*
Hellbent *'88*

Vanessa Marcil (1968-)

Nice Guys Sleep Alone *'99*
The Rock *'96*

Joseph Marco

Gladiators 7 *'62*
The Invincible Gladiator *'62*

Paul Marco (1927-2006)

Night of the Ghouls *'59*
Plan 9 from Outer Space *'56*
Bride of the Monster *'55*

Andre Marcon (1948-)

La Vie Promise *'02*
Les Destinees *'00*
Up/Down/Fragile *'95*
Jeanne la Pucelle *'94*

Lisa Marcos

Diary of a Mad Black Woman *'05*
King's Ransom *'05*

Ted Marcoux

Andersonville *'95*
Ghost in the Machine *'93*
The Nightman *'93*

Andrea Marcovicci (1948-)

Jack the Bear *'93*
The Water Engine *'92*
Someone to Love *'87*
The Stuff *'85*
Spraggue *'84*
Kings and Desperate Men *'83*
Packin' It In *'83*
Spacehunter: Adventures in the Forbidden Zone *'83*
The Hand *'81*
The Concorde: Airport '79 *'79*
The Front *'76*
The Devil's Web *'74*

James A. Marcus (1867-1937)

The Lone Avenger *'33*
The Broken Mask *'28*
Sadie Thompson *'28*
The Eagle *'25*
Oliver Twist *'22*

Jeff Marcus (1960-)

Alien Nation: Millennium *'96*
Legal Deceit *'95*
Alien Nation: Dark Horizon *'94*

Richard Marcus

Cannibal Campout *'88*
Deadly Friend *'86*
Enemy Mine *'85*

Stephen Marcus (1962-)

The Greatest Game Ever Played *'05*
Sorted *'04*
Lock, Stock and 2 Smoking Barrels *'98*
My Beautiful Laundrette *'85*

Jordan Marder (1973-)

American History X *'98*
Lord of Illusions *'95*
Walking on Air *'87*

Tom Mardirosian (1947-)

The Dark Half *'91*
Presumed Innocent *'90*

Ivano Marescotti (1946-)

The Moon & the Stars *'07*
King Arthur *'04*
The Monster *'96*

Bam Margera (1979-)

Jackass Number Two *'06*
Jackass: The Movie *'02*

Arthur Margetson (1887-1951)

Sherlock Holmes Faces Death *'43*
Juggernaut *'37*
The Mystery of the Mary Celeste *'35*

Margo (1917-85)

Who's Got the Action? *'63*
I'll Cry Tomorrow *'55*
Viva Zapata! *'52*
Behind the Rising Sun *'43*
The Leopard Man *'43*
Lost Horizon *'37*
Winterset *'36*

Janet Margolin (1943-93)

Ghostbusters 2 *'89*
Distant Thunder *'88*
The Game of Love *'87*
Plutonium Incident *'82*
Last Embrace *'79*
The Triangle Factory Fire Scandal *'79*
Annie Hall *'77*
Planet Earth *'74*
Pray for the Wildcats *'74*
Take the Money and Run *'69*
Buona Sera, Mrs. Campbell *'68*
Enter Laughing *'67*
Nevada Smith *'66*
Morituri *'65*
David and Lisa *'62*

Stuart Margolin (1940-)

The Student Affair *'97*
To Grandmother's House We Go *'94*
Impolite *'92*
Guilty by Suspicion *'91*
Bye Bye Blues *'89*
Iron Eagle 2 *'88*
A Fine Mess *'86*
The Glitter Dome *'84*
Class *'83*
Running Hot *'83*
S.O.B. *'81*
Days of Heaven *'78*
The Big Bus *'76*
Futureworld *'76*
Death Wish *'74*
Kelly's Heroes *'70*
Women of the Prehistoric Planet *'66*

Laura Margolis

The Strangers *'08*
Masters of Horror: Sounds Like *'06*

Mark Margolis (1939-)

The Fountain *'06*
Stay *'05*
2B Perfectly Honest *'04*
Headspace *'02*
Infested: Invasion of the Killer Bugs *'02*
Hardball *'01*
Dinner Rush *'00*
The Tailor of Panama *'00*
Jakob the Liar *'99*
The Thomas Crown Affair *'99*
Pi *'98*
Where the Rivers Flow North *'94*
Descending Angel *'90*
Scarface *'83*

Miriam Margolyes (1941-)

How to Lose Friends & Alienate People *'08*
Flushed Away *'06 (V)*
Happy Feet *'06 (V)*
Being Julia *'04*
Chasing Liberty *'04*
Ladies in Lavender *'04*
Modigliani *'04*
Harry Potter and the Chamber of Secrets *'02*
Cats & Dogs *'01*
Dreaming of Joseph Lees *'99*
End of Days *'99*
Sunshine *'99*
Vanity Fair *'99*
Mulan *'98 (V)*
Different for Girls *'96*
James and the Giant Peach *'96 (V)*
William Shakespeare's Romeo and Juliet *'96*
Babe *'95 (V)*
Balto *'95 (V)*
Cold Comfort Farm *'94*
Immortal Beloved *'94*
The Age of Innocence *'93*
Ed and His Dead Mother *'93*
Stalin *'92*
The Butcher's Wife *'91*
Orpheus Descending *'91*
I Love You to Death *'90*
Pacific Heights *'90*
Little Dorrit, Film 1: Nobody's Fault *'88*
Little Dorrit, Film 2: Little Dorrit's Story *'88*

Michael Margotta (1946-)

Can She Bake a Cherry Pie? *'83*
The Blue Knight *'75*

David Margulies (1937-)

Bought and Sold *'03*
Looking for an Echo *'99*
Last Breath *'96*
Out on a Limb *'92*
Family Prayers *'91*
Funny About Love *'90*
Ghostbusters 2 *'89*
Running on Empty *'88*
9 1/2 Weeks *'86*
Ghostbusters *'84*
Dressed to Kill *'80*
All That Jazz *'79*

Julianna Margulies (1966-)

Beautiful Ohio *'06*
The Darwin Awards *'06*
Snakes on a Plane *'06*
Hitler: The Rise of Evil *'03*
Evelyn *'02*
Ghost Ship *'02*
The Man from Elysian Fields *'01*
Mists of Avalon *'01*
Dinosaur *'00 (V)*
What's Cooking? *'00*
The Big Day *'99*
The Newton Boys *'97*
Paradise Road *'97*
A Price above Rubies *'97*
Traveller *'96*
Out for Justice *'91*

A. L. Mariaux

See Jess (Jesus) Franco

Constance Marie (1965-)

Tortilla Soup *'01*
The Last Marshal *'99*
Selena *'96*
My Family *'94*

Jeanne Marie

Young Nurses in Love *'89*
If Looks Could Kill *'86*

Lisa Marie (1968-)

Sleepy Hollow *'99*
Tail Lights Fade *'99*
Frogs for Snakes *'98*
Breast Men *'97*

Mars Attacks! *'96*
Ed Wood *'94*
Roller Blade *'85*
Dead and Buried *'81*

Jean-Pierre Marielle (1932-)
Micmacs *'09*
The Da Vinci Code *'06*
La Petite Lili *'03*
L'Eleve *'95*
Tous les Matins du Monde *'92*
Uranus *'91*
Menage *'86*
Coup de Torchon *'81*
One Wild Moment *'78*
Four Flies on Grey Velvet *'72*
The Women *'68*

Eli Marienthal (1986-)
Confessions of a Teenage Drama Queen *'04*
The Country Bears *'02*
American Pie 2 *'01*
Jay and Silent Bob Strike Back *'01*
American Pie *'99*
The Iron Giant *'99 (V)*
First Love, Last Rites *'98*
Jack Frost *'98*
Slums of Beverly Hills *'98*

Marietto (1951-)
It Started in Naples *'60*
Angel in a Taxi *'59*

Jacques Marin (1919-2001)
The Island at the Top of the World *'74*
Shaft in Africa *'73*
Darling Lili *'70*
The Night of the Following Day *'69*
How to Steal a Million *'66*
The Train *'65*
Duke of the Derby *'62*
Forbidden Games *'52*

Richard "Cheech" Marin (1946-)
Toy Story 3 *'10 (V)*
Race to Witch Mountain *'09*
Beverly Hills Chihuahua *'08 (V)*
Cars *'06 (V)*
Underclassman *'05*
Christmas With the Kranks *'04*
The Lion King 1 1/2 *'04 (V)*
Good Boy! *'03 (V)*
Once Upon a Time in Mexico *'03*
Spy Kids 3-D: Game Over *'03*
Pinocchio *'02 (V)*
Spy Kids 2: The Island of Lost Dreams *'02*
Spy Kids *'01*
Luminarias *'99*
Picking Up the Pieces *'99*
Paulie *'98*
The Great White Hype *'96*
Tin Cup *'96*
The Courtyard *'95*
Desperado *'95*
From Dusk Till Dawn *'95*
Charlie's Ghost: The Secret of Coronado *'94*
The Cisco Kid *'94*
The Lion King *'94 (V)*
A Million to Juan *'94*
Ring of the Musketeers *'93*
Ferngully: The Last Rain Forest *'92 (V)*
Mother Goose Rock 'n' Rhyme *'90*
The Shrimp on the Barbie *'90*
Far Out Man *'89*
Ghostbusters 2 *'89*
Rude Awakening *'89*
Oliver & Company *'88 (V)*
Born in East L.A. *'87*
Fatal Beauty *'87*
Echo Park *'86*
After Hours *'85*
Cheech and Chong's The Corsican Brothers *'84*
Cheech and Chong: Still Smokin' *'83*
Yellowbeard *'83*
Cheech and Chong: Things Are Tough All Over *'82*
Cheech and Chong's Nice Dreams *'81*
Cheech and Chong's Next Movie *'80*
Cheech and Chong's Up in Smoke *'79*

Rikki Marin
Cheech and Chong's The Corsican Brothers *'84*
Cheech and Chong: Things Are Tough All Over *'82*

Ed Marinaro (1950-)
Urban Legends: Bloody Mary *'05*
Deadly Game *'98*
Panic in the Skies *'96*
Dancing with Danger *'93*
Lethal Lolita—Amy Fisher: My Story *'92*
The Diamond Trap *'91*
Queens Logic *'91*
Dead Aim *'87*
The Game of Love *'87*
Policewoman Centerfold *'83*
Born Beautiful *'82*

Anamaria Marinca
Five Minutes of Heaven *'09*
The Last Enemy *'08*
4 Months, 3 Weeks and 2 Days *'07*

Sonny Marinelli
Dot.Kill *'05*
Boss of Bosses *'99*

Ethier Crispin Marini
See Chris-Pin (Ethier Crispin Martini) Martin

Dan Marino (1961-)
Little Nicky *'00*
Ace Ventura: Pet Detective *'93*

Ken Marino (1968-)
Role Models *'08*
The Ten *'07*
Diggers *'06*
Love for Rent *'05*
Joe Somebody *'01*
Alphabet City *'84*
Prince of the City *'81*

Beth Marion (1912-2003)
Phantom Gold *'38*
The Phantom of the Range *'38*
Everyman's Law *'36*
Rip Roarin' Buckaroo *'36*
Between Men *'35*
Trail of Terror *'35*

George F. Marion, Sr. (1860-1945)
Death from a Distance *'36*
Anna Christie *'30*
The Big House *'30*
Hook, Line and Sinker *'30*
Evangeline *'29*
Anna Christie *'23*

Howard Marion-Crawford (1914-69)
The Castle of Fu Manchu *'68*
The Charge of the Light Brigade *'68*
Kiss and Kill *'68*
Paid to Kill *'54*
Mister Drake's Duck *'50*
Man on the Run *'49*
The Singing Princess *'49*

Mona Maris (1903-91)
Heartbeat *'46*
The Falcon in Mexico *'44*
I Married an Angel *'42*
Underground *'41*
Love on the Run *'36*
Kiss and Make Up *'34*
Seas Beneath *'31*

Sari Maritza (1910-87)
Crimson Romance *'34*
International House *'33*
Greek Street *'30*

Robert Marius
Fist of Glory *'95*
Triple Impact *'92*
The 13th Mission *'91*

Heidi Mark (1971-)
Rock Star *'01*
Red Shoe Diaries: Luscious Lola *'00*

Jane (Jeanne) Marken (1895-1976)
Crazy for Love *'52*
Dedee d'Anvers *'49*
A Day in the Country *'46*
Children of Paradise *'44*
Eternal Return *'43*

Tony Markes
Welcome to Hollywood *'00*
In the Aftermath: Angels Never Sleep *'87*

Enid Markey (1896-1981)
Tarzan of the Apes *'17*
Civilization *'16*
The Fugitive: Taking of Luke McVane *'15*

Kika Markham (1942-)
Longford *'06*
Wonderland *'99*
Deep Cover *'88*
Miss A & Miss M *'86*
Outland *'81*
Two English Girls *'72*

Monte Markham (1935-)
At First Sight *'95*
Piranha *'95*
Defense Play *'88*
Judgment Day *'88*
Hot Pursuit *'87*
Counter Measures *'85*
Hotline *'82*
Off the Wall *'82*
Shame, Shame on the Bixby Boys *'82*
Airport '77 *'77*
Midway *'76*
Hustling *'75*
Ginger in the Morning *'73*
Guns of the Magnificent Seven *'69*

Brian Markinson
High Noon *'09*
Charlie Wilson's War *'07*
RV *'06*
Category 6 : Day of Destruction *'04*
Chasing Freedom *'04*
Angels in America *'03*
The Curse of the Jade Scorpion *'01*
Take Me Home: The John Denver Story *'00*
Sweet and Lowdown *'99*

Ted Markland
American Kickboxer 2: To the Death *'93*
Merlin *'92*
Fatal Mission *'89*
Wanda Nevada *'79*
Angels from Hell *'68*

Margaret Markov (1951-)
The Arena *'73*
Hot Box *'72*
Run, Angel, Run! *'69*

Olivera Markovic (1925-)
Tito and Me *'92*
Siberian Lady Macbeth *'61*

Karl Markovics (1963-)
The Counterfeiters *'07*
All the Queen's Men *'02*

Alfred Marks (1921-96)
Antonia and Jane *'91*
Fanny Hill *'83*
Valentino *'77*
Scream and Scream Again *'70*
The Frightened City *'61*

Hannah Marks (1993-)
The Runaways *'10*
Accepted *'06*

Jennifer Marks
Naked Wishes *'00*
The Strangers *'98*

Winnie Markus (1922-2002)
The Devil in Silk *'56*
The Mozart Story *'48*

Arnold Marle (1888-1970)
The Snake Woman *'61*
Men of Two Worlds *'46*

Ben Marley
From the Earth to the Moon *'98*
The Mosaic Project *'95*

John Marley (1907-84)
On the Edge *'86*
The Glitter Dome *'84*
Robbers of the Sacred Mountain *'83*
Threshold *'83*
Utilities *'83*
The Godfather 1902-1959: The Complete Epic *'81*
Hooper *'78*
It's Alive 2: It Lives Again *'78*
The Car *'77*
The Greatest *'77*
Framed *'75*
Kid Vengeance *'75*
Dead Are Alive *'72*
Deathdream *'72*
The Godfather *'72*
Jory *'72*
A Man Called Sledge *'71*
Love Story *'70*
Faces *'68*

Carla Marlier
Spirits of the Dead *'68*
Any Number Can Win *'63*
The Avenger *'62*
Zazie dans le Metro *'61*

Lucy Marlow (1932-)
My Sister Eileen *'55*
Queen Bee *'55*

Hugh Marlowe (1911-82)
Castle of Evil *'66*
Seven Days in May *'64*
Birdman of Alcatraz *'62*
Elmer Gantry *'60*
Earth vs. the Flying Saucers *'56*
Illegal *'55*
Casanova's Big Night *'54*
Garden of Evil *'54*
Bugles in the Afternoon *'52*
Monkey Business *'52*
The Day the Earth Stood Still *'51*
All About Eve *'50*
Night and the City *'50*
Rawhide *'50*
Come to the Stable *'49*
Twelve o'Clock High *'49*

June Marlowe (1903-84)
The Lone Defender *'32*
Pardon Us *'31*
Don Juan *'26*
The Night Cry *'26*

Linda Marlowe (1944-)
The Green Man *'91*
Mr. Love *'86*
Big Zapper *'73*
He Kills Night After Night After Night *'69*
Night Slasher *'69*

Scott Marlowe (1933-2001)
Counter Measures *'99*
Men in War *'57*

Florence Marly (1919-78)
Dr. Death, Seeker of Souls *'73*
Games *'67*
Planet of Blood *'66*
Tokyo Joe *'49*

Percy Marmont (1883-1977)
Lisbon *'56*
Four Sided Triangle *'53*
Young and Innocent *'37*
The Secret Agent *'36*
Rich and Strange *'32*
Lady of the Lake *'28*
Mantrap *'26*

Richard Marner (1921-2004)
The Sum of All Fears *'02*
Race for Life *'55*
The African Queen *'51*

Mozhan Marno
The Stoning of Soraya M. *'08*
Traitor *'08*

Kelli Maroney (1964-)
Face Down *'97*
Servants of Twilight *'91*
Chopping Mall *'86*
Zero Boys *'86*
Night of the Comet *'84*
Slayground *'84*
Fast Times at Ridgemont High *'82*

Michael Maronna (1977-)
40 Days and 40 Nights *'02*
Slackers *'02*

Adoni Maropis (1963-)
Bone Eater *'07*
Hidalgo *'04*
Bad Company *'02*

Carl Marotte (1959-)
One Kill *'00*
Prisoner of Love *'99*
This Matter of Marriage *'98*
Twists of Terror *'98*
When Justice Fails *'98*
The Ultimate Weapon *'97*
Breaking All the Rules *'85*
Pick-Up Summer *'79*

Erika Marozsan (1972-)
Gloomy Sunday *'02*
Sniper 2 *'02*

Christian Marquand (1927-2000)
Victory at Entebbe *'76*
The Corrupt Ones *'67*
End of Desire *'62*
Love Play *'60*
And God Created Woman *'57*
Attila *'54*

Serge Marquand (1930-2004)
The Big Red One *'80*
Barbarella *'68*
Blood and Roses *'61*
Please Not Now! *'61*

Maria Elena Marques (1926-)
Ambush at Tomahawk Gap *'53*
Across the Wide Missouri *'51*
The Pearl *'48*

Christopher Marquette (1984-)
Fanboys *'09*
Infestation *'09*
Life During Wartime *'09*
Choose Connor *'07*
Graduation *'07*
The Invisible *'07*
Remember the Daze *'07*
American Gun *'05*
Just Friends *'05*
The Girl Next Door *'04*
The Tic Code *'99*

Ron Marquette (-1995)
Red Shoe Diaries 7: Burning Up *'96*
Deadly Past *'95*
Red Shoe Diaries 5: Weekend Pass *'95*
Public Access *'93*

Sean Marquette
Remember the Daze *'07*
13 Going on 30 *'04*
Black Mask 2: City of Masks *'02*

William Marquez
Crazy Heart *'09*
The Lost City *'05*

Andre Marquis
Paco *'75*
The Day of the Wolves *'71*

Juliette Marquis
The Insurgents *'06*
This Girl's Life *'03*

Margaret Marquis (1917-)
Brand of the Outlaws *'36*
Last of the Warrens *'36*

Eddie Marr (1900-87)
I Was a Teenage Werewolf *'57*
The Damned Don't Cry *'50*
Hollywood Canteen *'44*

David Marriott
Monster High *'89*
Operation Warzone *'89*

Moore Marriott (1885-1949)
Oh, Mr. Porter *'37*
The Flying Scotsman *'29*

Sylvia Marriott (1917-)
The Story of Adele H. *'75*
Two English Girls *'72*
Beast of Morocco *'66*
Crimes at the Dark House *'39*

Marlo Marron
Funny Valentine *'05*
Mi Vida Loca *'94*

Kenneth Mars (1936-)
The Land Before Time 6: The Secret of Saurus Rock *'98 (V)*
The Land Before Time 5: The Mysterious Island *'97 (V)*
Citizen Ruth *'96*
The Land Before Time 4: Journey Through the Mists *'96 (V)*
The Land Before Time 3: The Time of the Great Giving *'95 (V)*
The Land Before Time 2: The Great Valley Adventure *'94 (V)*
Thumbelina *'94 (V)*
We're Back! A Dinosaur's Story *'93 (V)*
Shadows and Fog *'92*
Get Smart, Again! *'89*
The Little Mermaid *'89 (V)*
For Keeps *'88*
Rented Lips *'88*
Illegally Yours *'87*
Radio Days *'87*
Beer *'85*
Fletch *'85*
Misfits of Science *'85*
Protocol *'84*
Yellowbeard *'83*
The Apple Dumpling Gang Rides Again *'79*
Goin' Coconuts *'78*
Bunco *'77*
Night Moves *'75*
The Parallax View *'74*
Young Frankenstein *'74*
What's Up, Doc? *'72*
Desperate Characters *'71*
April Fools *'69*
Butch Cassidy and the Sundance Kid *'69*

The Producers '68

Marjorie Mars (1903-91)

Brief Encounter '46
Spy of Napoleon '36

Severin Mars

La Roue '23
J'accuse! '19

Maurice Marsac (1915-2007)

The Big Red One '80
Clarence, the Cross-eyed Lion '65
Werewolf in a Girl's Dormitory '61
Tarzan and the Trappers '58
China Gate '57

Branford Marsalis (1960-)

School Daze '88
Throw Momma from the Train '87

Eddie Marsan (1968-)

Me and Orson Welles '09
Sherlock Holmes '09
God on Trial '08
Hancock '08
Happy-Go-Lucky '08
Little Dorrit '08
I Want Candy '07
Beowulf & Grendel '06
The Illusionist '06
Mission: Impossible 3 '06
V for Vendetta '06
Friends & Crocodiles '05
Vera Drake '04
Gangs of New York '02
The Emperor's New Clothes '01
Gangster No. 1 '00
Dostoevsky's Crime and Punishment '99
Second Sight '99

Heather Marie Marsden

Crash and Burn '07
Lethal '04

James Marsden (1973-)

Death at a Funeral '10
The Box '09
Sex Drive '08
27 Dresses '08
Enchanted '07
Hairspray '07
Lies & Alibis '06
Superman Returns '06
10th & Wolf '06
X-Men: The Last Stand '06
Heights '04
The Notebook '04
The 24th Day '04
X2: X-Men United '03
Interstate 60 '02
Sugar & Spice '01
X-Men '00
Gossip '99
Campfire Tales '98
Disturbing Behavior '98
Bella Mafia '97
Public Enemies '96

Jason Marsden (1975-)

How to Make a Monster '01
Spirited Away '01 (V)
The Lion King: Simba's Pride '98 (V)
White Squall '96
A Goofy Movie '94 (V)

Matthew Marsden (1972-)

DOA: Dead or Alive '06
Anacondas: The Hunt for the Blood Orchid '04
Helen of Troy '03
Black Hawk Down '01
Shiner '00

Roy Marsden (1941-)

A Certain Justice '99
A Mind to Murder '96
Devices and Desires '91
Vanity Fair '67

Carol Marsh (1926-)

The Horror of Dracula '58
A Christmas Carol '51
Alice in Wonderland '50
Brighton Rock '47

Garry Marsh (1902-81)

Who Done It? '56
Those People Next Door '52
The Voice of Merrill '52
Old Mother Riley's Jungle Treasure '51
Someone at the Door '50
Just William's Luck '47
A Girl in a Million '46
Dead of Night '45
Pink String and Sealing Wax '45
Death on the Set '35
Department Store '35

Jamie Marsh

Beethoven's 3rd '00
Best Laid Plans '99
Brainscan '94

Jean Marsh (1934-)

Sense & Sensibility '07
Agatha Christie's The Pale Horse '96
Fatherland '94
A Connecticut Yankee in King Arthur's Court '89
Willow '88
Return to Oz '85
Goliath Awaits '81
The Changeling '80
Frenzy '72
The Unearthly Stranger '64
Horsemasters '61

Joan Marsh (1914-2000)

Follow the Leader '44
Manhunt in the African Jungles '43
Charlie Chan on Broadway '37
Champagne for Breakfast '35
Daring Daughters '33
High Gear '33
Rainbow over Broadway '33
Maker of Men '31
Politics '31

Mae Marsh (1895-1968)

From the Terrace '60
Sergeant Rutledge '60
While the City Sleeps '56
The Tall Men '55
The Quiet Man '52
The Gunfighter '50
My Blue Heaven '50
Impact '49
Fort Apache '48
Three Godfathers '48
Blue, White and Perfect '42
The Fighting Sullivans '42
How Green Was My Valley '41
The White Rose '23
Hoodoo Ann '16
Intolerance '16
The Birth of a Nation '15
Home Sweet Home '14
Judith of Bethulia '14
Battle of Elderbush Gulch '13

Marian Marsh (1913-2006)

House of Errors '42
Gentleman from Dixie '41
When's Your Birthday? '37
Youth on Parole '37
The Black Room '35
Crime and Punishment '35
Daring Daughters '33
Svengali '31

Matthew Marsh (1954-)

An American Haunting '05
Bad Company '02
Miranda '01
Spy Game '01
A Certain Justice '99
An Affair in Mind '89
In the Secret State '85

Michele Marsh

Evil Town '87
Deadly Alliance '78
Fiddler on the Roof '71

Alan Marshal (1909-61)

The Day of the Outlaw '59
House on Haunted Hill '58
The White Cliffs of Dover '44
Lydia '41
Tom, Dick, and Harry '41
The Howards of Virginia '40
The Hunchback of Notre Dame '39
Conquest '37
Night Must Fall '37
After the Thin Man '36
The Garden of Allah '36

Brenda Marshall (1915-92)

Strange Impersonation '46
Background to Danger '43
Captains of the Clouds '42
Footsteps in the Dark '41
The Sea Hawk '40

Bryan Marshall (1938-)

Return to Snowy River '88
The Long Good Friday '80
Because of the Cats '74
Vanity Fair '67

Connie Marshall (1938-)

Kill the Umpire '50
The Green Promise '49
Daisy Kenyon '47
Mother Wore Tights '47

David Anthony Marshall

The Demolitionist '95
Another 48 Hrs. '90

Dodie Marshall

Easy Come, Easy Go '67
Spinout '66

Don Marshall (1936-)

Terminal Island '73
The Thing with Two Heads '72

E.G. Marshall (1910-98)

Absolute Power '97
The Defenders: Payback '97
Miss Evers' Boys '97
Nixon '95
Oldest Confederate Widow Tells All '95
Russian Roulette '93
Stephen King's The Tommyknockers '93
Consenting Adults '92
Ironclads '90
Two Evil Eyes '90
National Lampoon's Christmas Vacation '89
Saigon: Year of the Cat '87
My Chauffeur '86
Power '86
Kennedy '83
Creepshow '82
Eleanor: First Lady of the World '82
Superman 2 '80
The Lazarus Syndrome '79
Interiors '78
Abduction of St. Anne '75
Pursuit '72
The Pursuit of Happiness '70
Tora! Tora! Tora! '70
The Bridge at Remagen '69
The Littlest Angel '69
The Chase '66
Is Paris Burning? '66
The Poppy Is Also a Flower '66
Town without Pity '61
Cash McCall '60
Compulsion '59
The Buccaneer '58
Twelve Angry Men '57
The Mountain '56
The Left Hand of God '55
Broken Lance '54
The Caine Mutiny '54
Pushover '54
The Silver Chalice '54
Call Northside 777 '48
13 Rue Madeleine '46

Garry Marshall (1934-)

Race to Witch Mountain '09
Keeping Up with the Steins '06
Chicken Little '05 (V)
Devil's Knight '03
Orange County '02
The Hollywood Sign '01
Forever Together '00
Never Been Kissed '99
With Friends Like These '98
The Twilight of the Golds '97
Dear God '96
Hocus Pocus '93
A League of Their Own '92
Soapdish '91
Jumpin' Jack Flash '86
Lost in America '85

Herbert Marshall (1890-1966)

The Fly '58
Stage Struck '57
The Virgin Queen '55
The Black Shield of Falworth '54
Angel Face '52
Captain Blackjack '51
The Underworld Story '50
The Secret Garden '49
Crack-Up '46
Duel in the Sun '46
The Razor's Edge '46
The Enchanted Cottage '45
Forever and a Day '43
The Moon and Sixpence '43
The Little Foxes '41
When Ladies Meet '41
Foreign Correspondent '40
The Letter '40
Mad About Music '38
Angel '37
Breakfast for Two '37
Girl's Dormitory '36
If You Could Only Cook '36
A Woman Rebels '36
The Dark Angel '35
The Good Fairy '35
The Painted Veil '34
Riptide '34
Blonde Venus '32
Trouble in Paradise '32
Murder '30

James Marshall (1967-)

Come as You Are '05
The Shaft '01
Luck of the Draw '00
Soccer Dog: The Movie '98
The Ticket '97
Don't Do It '94
Vibrations '94
A Few Good Men '92
Gladiator '92
Twin Peaks: Fire Walk with Me '92

Ken Marshall (1951-)

Double Exposure: The Story of Margaret Bourke-White '89
Feds '88
Krull '83
Tilt '78

Kris Marshall (1973-)

Easy Virtue '08
Death at a Funeral '07
The Merchant of Venice '04
Doctor Zhivago '03
Love Actually '03
Deathwatch '02
The Four Feathers '02

Marion Marshall (1930-)

Sailor Beware '52
The Stooge '51
I Was a Male War Bride '49

Paula Marshall (1964-)

I Know Who Killed Me '07
Cheaper by the Dozen '03
Thursday '98
A Gun, a Car, a Blonde '97
A Family Thing '96
That Old Feeling '96
The New Age '94
Warlock: The Armageddon '93
Hellraiser 3: Hell on Earth '92

Penny Marshall (1947-)

Everybody Wants to Be Italian '08
Alice Upside Down '07
Looking for Comedy in the Muslim World '06
Stateside '04
Get Shorty '95
Hocus Pocus '93
The Hard Way '91
Challenge of a Lifetime '85
Movers and Shakers '85
1941 '79
How Come Nobody's On Our Side? '73
Evil Roy Slade '71

Peter Marshall (1930-)

Americathon '79
A Guide for the Married Woman '78
Return of Jesse James '50

Sarah Marshall (1933-)

French Silk '94
The People vs. Jean Harris '81
Lord Love a Duck '66

Sean Marshall (1965-)

Pete's Dragon '77
Wonderland Cove '75

Trudy Marshall (1920-2004)

Married Too Young '62
Too Many Winners '47
Crash Dive '43
The Fighting Sullivans '42

Tully Marshall (1864-1943)

Behind Prison Walls '43
This Gun for Hire '42
Mr. Boggs Steps Out '38
California Straight Ahead! '37
Night of Terror '33
The Beast of the City '32
The Cabin in the Cotton '32
Red Dust '32
Strangers of the Evening '32
Two-Fisted Law '32
Fighting Caravans '31
Big Trail '30
Tom Sawyer '30
Queen Kelly '29
The Trail of '98 '28
The Cat and the Canary '27
Twinkletoes '26
Smouldering Fires '25
He Who Gets Slapped '24
Broken Hearts of Broadway '23
Let's Go! '23
What Happened to Rosa? '21
Hawthorne of the USA '19

William Marshall (1917-94)

That Brennan Girl '46
State Fair '45

William Marshall (1924-2003)

Vasectomy: A Delicate Matter '86
The Great Skycopter Rescue '82
Twilight's Last Gleaming '77
Scream Blacula Scream '73
Blacula '72
The Boston Strangler '68
Demetrius and the Gladiators '54

Zena Marshall (1926-)

The Terrornauts '67
Dr. No '62

Christina Marsillach (1963-)

Opera '88
Every Time We Say Goodbye '86

Tony Marsina

Last Mercenary '84
Tornado '83

James Marsters (1962-)

Dragonball: Evolution '09
P.S. I Love You '07
Shadow Puppets '07
Strange Frequency 2 '01

Nathaniel Marston (1975-)

Ordinary Sinner '02
Love Is All There Is '96

Lynn(e) Marta (1946-)

Blood Beach '81
Genesis II '73
Joe Kidd '72
Richard Petty Story '72

Judy Marte (1983-)

On the Outs '05
Raising Victor Vargas '03

Henri Marteau (1933-2005)

Indochine '92
La Femme Infidele '69

Arlene Martel (1936-)

Angels from Hell '68
Demon with a Glass Hand '64

June Martel (1909-78)

Santa Fe Stampede '38
Forlorn River '37
Wild Horse Rodeo '37
Arizona Mahoney '36

K.C. Martel (1970-)

White Water Summer '87
E.T.: The Extra-Terrestrial '82
The Munsters' Revenge '81
The Amityville Horror '79

Chris Martell

Flesh Feast '69
Scream, Baby, Scream '69
Gruesome Twosome '67

Donna (Dona Martel) Martell (1927-)

Ten Wanted Men '54
Give a Girl a Break '53
Project Moon Base '53
Abbott and Costello Meet the Killer, Boris Karloff '49

Gillian Martell

Cause Celebre '87
Oliver Twist '85

Peter Martell

See Peter Martellanza

Peter Martellanza (1938-)

Mission Phantom '79
Planet on the Prowl '65

Cynthia Martells

Paid in Full '02
The Wood '99
Broken Trust '95
Zooman '95
A Modern Affair '94
Blind Spot '93

Barbara Marten

Florence Nightingale '08
The Debt '03

Frank Marth (1922-)

Showdown '93
Fright '56

Francois Marthouret (1943-)

La Petite Jerusalem '05
The Lady and the Duke '01
Sitcom '97
Hot Chocolate '92
Marquis '90 (V)

Andrea Martin (1947-)

Black Christmas '06
Brother Bear 2 '06 (V)
The Producers '05
New York Minute '04
My Big Fat Greek Wedding '02
All Over the Guy '01

Jimmy Neutron: Boy Genius '01 (V)
Hedwig and the Angry Inch '00
Loser '00
Believe '99
The Secret of NIMH 2 '98 (V)
Wag the Dog '97
Bogus '96
Guitarman '95
Kurt Vonnegut's Harrison Bergeron '95
Gypsy '93
Ted & Venus '93
Boris and Natasha: The Movie '92
All I Want for Christmas '91
Stepping Out '91
Too Much Sun '90
Rude Awakening '89
Worth Winning '89
Club Paradise '86
Soup for One '82
Black Christmas '75

Anna Maxwell Martin
Becoming Jane '07
Bleak House '05

Barney Martin (1923-2005)
Arthur 2: On the Rocks '88
Arthur '81

Charles Martin (1910-83)
Fighting Black Kings '76
You've Ruined Me, Eddie '58

Chris-Pin (Ethier Crispin Martini) Martin (1894-1953)
Rimfire '49
Return of Wildfire '48
Down Argentine Way '40
Lucky Cisco Kid '40
Stagecoach '39
The Texans '38
The California Trail '33
South of Santa Fe '32

Chris William Martin (1975-)
The Terrorist Next Door '08
Emile '03

Christopher Martin (1963-)
House Party 3 '94
Class Act '91
House Party 2: The Pajama Jam '91
House Party '90

Damon Martin
Amityville 1992: It's About Time '92
Ghoulies 2 '87

Dan Martin (1951-)
Groom Lake '02
Sleepwalkers '92

Dan (Daniel, Danny) Martin (1935-)
Devil's Kiss '75
Surprise Attack '70
The Last Tomahawk '65
Gunfight at Red Sands '63

Dean Martin (1917-95)
That's Dancing! '85
Cannonball Run 2 '84
Cannonball Run '81
Showdown '73
Airport '70
Bandolero! '68
Five Card Stud '68
The Wrecking Crew '68
The Ambushers '67
Rough Night in Jericho '67
Murderers' Row '66
The Silencers '66
Texas Across the River '66
Marriage on the Rocks '65
Sons of Katie Elder '65
Kiss Me, Stupid! '64
Robin and the 7 Hoods '64
Four for Texas '63
Toys in the Attic '63
Who's Got the Action? '63
Sergeants 3 '62
All in a Night's Work '61
Bells Are Ringing '60
Ocean's 11 '60
Career '59
Rio Bravo '59
Some Came Running '58
The Young Lions '58
Ten Thousand Bedrooms '57
Hollywood or Bust '56
Pardners '56
Artists and Models '55
The Caddy '53
Money from Home '53
The Road to Bali '53
Scared Stiff '53
Jumping Jacks '52
Sailor Beware '52
The Stooge '51
At War with the Army '50
My Friend Irma '49

Dean Paul (Dino Martin Jr.) Martin (1951-87)
Backfire '88
Misfits of Science '85
Players '79

Dewey Martin (1923-)
Seven Alone '75
Flight to Fury '66
Savage Sam '63
Ten Thousand Bedrooms '57
Desperate Hours '55
Land of the Pharaohs '55
Men of the Fighting Lady '54
The Big Sky '52
The Thing '51

Dick Martin (1928-)
Bartleby '01
The Trial of Old Drum '00
Air Bud 2: Golden Receiver '98
Carbon Copy '81
The Glass Bottom Boat '66

Duane Martin (1970-)
Deliver Us from Eva '03
Mutiny '99
Scream 2 '97
Woo '97
Down Periscope '96
Above the Rim '94

Duke Martin
Lost Zeppelin '29
Across to Singapore '28

D'Urville Martin (1938-84)
Big Score '83
Blind Rage '78
Death Journey '76
Dolemite '75
Sheba, Baby '75
Boss '74
Hell Up in Harlem '73
Final Comedown '72
Watermelon Man '70

Eddy Martin (1990-)
Rebound '05
The Maldonado Miracle '03

Edie Martin (1880-1964)
The Ladykillers '55
Genevieve '53

George Martin (1926-)
Drunks '96
One Fine Day '96
Blood at Sundown '88
Crossing Delancey '88
Falling in Love '84
Psychopath '68

Gilbert Martin
Beautiful People '99
Rob Roy '95

Gregory Mars Martin
See Mars Callahan
Kalifornia '93

Helen Martin (1909-2000)
I Got the Hook-Up '98
Don't Be a Menace to South Central While Drinking Your Juice in the Hood '95
Doc Hollywood '91
House Party 2: The Pajama Jam '91
Night Angel '90
Hollywood Shuffle '87
A Hero Ain't Nothin' but a Sandwich '78

Ivan Martin
Funny Valentine '05
Prey for Rock and Roll '03

Jared Martin (1943-)
Twinsitters '95
Karate Warrior '88
Quiet Cool '86
The Sea Serpent '85
The Lonely Lady '83
The New Gladiators '83
Second Coming of Suzanne '80

Jean Martin (1922-)
Lucie Aubrac '98
The Messiah '75
The Battle of Algiers '66

Jesse L. Martin (1969-)
Peter and Vandy '09
The Cake Eaters '07
Rent '05

John Martin
Dr. Terror's House of Horrors '65
The Tell-Tale Heart '60
Mesa of Lost Women '52

John Martin (1951-)
The Underneath '95
Dark Before Dawn '89
Black Roses '88
Fire in the Night '85

Jose Martin
The Castle of Fu Manchu '68
Four Dollars of Revenge '66

Justin Martin
A Raisin in the Sun '08
Bloody Murder '99

Kellie Martin (1975-)
Mystery Woman: Mystery Weekend '05
Christy '94
A Goofy Movie '94 (V)
Matinee '92
Troop Beverly Hills '89

Kiel Martin (1944-90)
Convicted: A Mother's Story '87
Child Bride of Short Creek '81
Panic in Needle Park '71

Lewis Martin (1894-1969)
Men of the Fighting Lady '54
The War of the Worlds '53
Ace in the Hole '51

Lock Martin (1916-59)
Invaders from Mars '53
The Day the Earth Stood Still '51

Marion Martin (1918-85)
The Great Mike '44
Mexican Spitfire at Sea '42
Big Store '41
The Man in the Iron Mask '39
Sinners in Paradise '38

Mary Martin (1913-90)
Peter Pan '60
Main Street to Broadway '53
Night and Day '46
Star Spangled Rhythm '42
Birth of the Blues '41
Rhythm on the River '40

Mel Martin (1947-)
Poldark '96
Darlings of the Gods '90
White Hunter, Black Heart '90
Love for Lydia '79

Millicent Martin (1934-)
Return to Halloweentown '06
Mrs. Palfrey at the Claremont '05
Alfie '66
Those Magnificent Men in Their Flying Machines '65
Horsemasters '61

Nan Martin (1927-)
Shallow Hal '01
The Song of the Lark '01
Big Eden '00
Cast Away '00
Matters of the Heart '90
A Nightmare on Elm Street 3: Dream Warriors '87
Proud Men '87
The Young Nurses '73
Goodbye Columbus '69
For Love of Ivy '68
Toys in the Attic '63

Pamela Sue Martin (1953-)
A Cry in the Wild '90
Eye of the Demon '87
Flicks '85
Torchlight '85
Lady in Red '79
Buster and Billie '74
Our Time '74
The Girls of Huntington House '73

Pepper Martin (1936-)
Evil Altar '89
Scream '83
The Longest Yard '74
Angels from Hell '68

Remi Martin (1965-)
Clean '04
The Possessed '88
Conseil de Famille '86

Richard Martin (1919-94)
Four Fast Guns '59
Gunplay '51
Dynamite Pass '50
Rider from Tucson '50
Riders of the Range '50
Storm over Wyoming '50
Mysterious Desperado '49
The Bamboo Blonde '46
Having Wonderful Crime '45
West of the Pecos '45
Nevada '44
Tender Comrade '43

Ross Martin (1920-81)
More Wild, Wild West '80
The Seekers '79
Wild, Wild West Revisited '79
Wild & Wooly '78
Dying Room Only '73
Experiment in Terror '62
Geronimo '62
Conquest of Space '55

Rudolf Martin (1967-)
River's End '05
The Home Front '02
Dracula: The Dark Prince '01
Swordfish '01
Bedazzled '00
Fall '97

Sandy Martin (1950-)
Sparkler '99
Barfly '87
Vendetta '85
Scalpel '76

Sharlene Martin
Possession: Until Death Do You Part '90
Friday the 13th, Part 8: Jason Takes Manhattan '89

Skip Martin (1928-84)
Horror Hospital '73
Masque of the Red Death '65

Steve Martin (1945-)
It's Complicated '09
The Pink Panther 2 '09
Baby Mama '08
The Pink Panther '06
Cheaper by the Dozen 2 '05
Jiminy Glick in LaLa Wood '05
Shopgirl '05
Bringing Down the House '03
Cheaper by the Dozen '03
Looney Tunes: Back in Action '03
Novocaine '01
Joe Gould's Secret '00
Bowfinger '99
The Out-of-Towners '99
Prince of Egypt '98 (V)
The Spanish Prisoner '97
Father of the Bride Part 2 '95
Sgt. Bilko '95
Mixed Nuts '94
A Simple Twist of Fate '94
And the Band Played On '93
Housesitter '92
Leap of Faith '92
Father of the Bride '91
Grand Canyon '91
L.A. Story '91
My Blue Heaven '90
Parenthood '89
Dirty Rotten Scoundrels '88
Planes, Trains & Automobiles '87
Roxanne '87
Little Shop of Horrors '86
Three Amigos '86
Movers and Shakers '85
All of Me '84
The Lonely Guy '84
The Man with Two Brains '83
Dead Men Don't Wear Plaid '82
Pennies from Heaven '81
The Jerk '79
The Kids Are Alright '79
The Muppet Movie '79
Sgt. Pepper's Lonely Hearts Club Band '78

Strother Martin (1919-80)
Hotwire '80
Better Late Than Never '79
The Champ '79
Cheech and Chong's Up in Smoke '79
Love and Bullets '79
Nightwing '79
The Villain '79
Steel Cowboy '78
Slap Shot '77
Hard Times '75
Rooster Cogburn '75
Sssssss '73
Hannie Caulder '72
Pocket Money '72
The Brotherhood of Satan '71
Ballad of Cable Hogue '70
Butch Cassidy and the Sundance Kid '69
True Grit '69
The Wild Bunch '69
Cool Hand Luke '67
Shenandoah '65
Invitation to a Gunfighter '64
McLintock! '63
The Man Who Shot Liberty Valance '62
The Horse Soldiers '59
Black Patch '57
Attack! '56
Kiss Me Deadly '55
Rhubarb '51

Tina Martin
Spellbreaker: Secret of the Leprechauns '96
Leapin' Leprechauns '95

Tony Martin (1912-)
Meet Me in Las Vegas '56
Hit the Deck '55
Easy to Love '53
Here Come the Girls '53
Two Tickets to Broadway '51
Casbah '48
Till the Clouds Roll By '46
Big Store '41
Ziegfeld Girl '41
Music in My Heart '40
Thanks for Everything '38
The Holy Terror '37
Pigskin Parade '36

Tony (Anthony) Martin (1953-)
Candy '06
The Incredible Journey of Mary Bryant '05
Inspector Gadget 2 '02
The Interview '98
A Cry in the Dark '88

Vera Martin
Loyalties '86
The Noose Hangs High '48

Vince Martin
Breaking Loose '90
Night Master '87

Vivian Martin (1893-1987)
The Belles of St. Trinian's '53
The Wishing Ring '14

W.T. Martin
High Stakes '89
Hardhat & Legs '80

Margo Martindale (1951-)
Management '09
Orphan '09
Rails & Ties '07
Rocket Science '07
Superheroes '07
Walk Hard: The Dewey Cox Story '07
Paris, je t'aime '06
Wedding Daze '06
Million Dollar Baby '04
The Human Stain '03
It's All About Love '03
The Hours '02
Proof of Life '00
28 Days '00
Earthly Possessions '99
Ride with the Devil '99
In Dreams '98
Twilight '98
Critical Care '97
Eye of God '97
Ghosts of Mississippi '96
Marvin's Room '96
Dead Man Walking '95
Nobody's Fool '94
Lorenzo's Oil '92

Edward Martindel
Golden Dawn '30
The Singing Fool '28
The Duchess of Buffalo '26

Elsa Martinelli (1932-)
Once Upon a Crime '92
Belle Starr '79
Candy '68
Manon '68
Madigan's Millions '67
Maroc 7 '67
Oldest Profession '67
Woman Times Seven '67
Hail Mafia '65
10th Victim '65
The Trial '63
The V.I.P.'s '63
Hatari! '62
Blood and Roses '61
The Indian Fighter '55

Alessandra Martines (1963-)
And Now Ladies and Gentlemen '02
Les Miserables '95

A. Martinez (1948-)
Once Upon a Wedding '05
Ordinary Sinner '02
What's Cooking? '00
Double Tap '98
Last Rites '98
Wind River '98

The Cherokee Kid '96
Grand Avenue '96
One Night Stand '95
Where's the Money, Noreen? '95
Deconstructing Sarah '94
The Hunt for the Night Stalker '91
Powwow Highway '89
She-Devil '89
Born in East L.A. '87
Centennial '78
Joe Panther '76
Once Upon a Scoundrel '73
Starbird and Sweet William '73
The Cowboys '72
Hard Frame '70

Adrian Martinez

Just Like the Son '06
Mail Order Wife '04
Corn '02

Fele Martinez (1976-)

Bad Education '04
Darkness '02
Lovers of the Arctic Circle '98
Open Your Eyes '97
Thesis '96

Joaquin Martinez (1932-)

The Cowboy Way '94
Jeremiah Johnson '72

Nacho Martinez (1952-96)

Law of Desire '86
Matador '86

Nathalia Martinez

Death Race '08
Terranova '91

Olivier Martinez (1966-)

Blood & Chocolate '07
Taking Lives '04
The Roman Spring of Mrs. Stone '03
S.W.A.T. '03
Angel of Death '02
Unfaithful '02
Before Night Falls '00
The Chambermaid on the Titanic '97
Mon Homme '96
The Horseman on the Roof '95

Vanessa Martinez

Casa de los Babys '03
Limbo '99

Maximillian Martini (1969-)

Redbelt '08
The Great Raid '05
Saving Private Ryan '98

Steven Martini (1978-)

Smiling Fish & Goat on Fire '99
Major Payne '95

Susanna Martinkova

Ring of Death '69
Diary of a Rebel '68

Al Martino (1927-2009)

The Godfather, Part 3 '90
The Godfather '72

Orlando Martins (1899-1985)

Call Me Bwana '63
Simba '55
Men of Two Worlds '46

Laia Marull (1973-)

Take My Eyes '03
Cafe Ole '00

Lee Marvin (1924-87)

Delta Force '86
The Dirty Dozen: The Next Mission '85
Dog Day '83
Gorky Park '83
Death Hunt '81
The Big Red One '80
Avalanche Express '79
Great Scout & Cathouse Thursday '76
Shout at the Devil '76
The Klansman '74
Emperor of the North Pole '73
The Iceman Cometh '73
Pocket Money '72
Prime Cut '72
Monte Walsh '70
Hell in the Pacific '69
Paint Your Wagon '69
Sergeant Ryker '68
The Dirty Dozen '67
The Meanest Men in the West '67
Point Blank '67
The Professionals '66
Cat Ballou '65
Ship of Fools '65
The Killers '64
Donovan's Reef '63
The Man Who Shot Liberty Valance '62
The Comancheros '61
Missouri Traveler '58
Raintree County '57
Attack! '56
I Died a Thousand Times '55
Pete Kelly's Blues '55
Shack Out on 101 '55
Bad Day at Black Rock '54
The Caine Mutiny '54
The Wild One '54
The Big Heat '53
Gun Fury '53
The Stranger Wore a Gun '53
Duel at Silver Creek '52
Hangman's Knot '52
We're Not Married '52
Union Station '50

Brett Marx (1964-)

The Bad News Bears Go to Japan '78
The Bad News Bears in Breaking Training '77
The Bad News Bears '76

Chico Marx (1886-1961)

The Marx Brothers in a Nutshell '90
Love Happy '50
A Night in Casablanca '46
Big Store '41
Go West '40
At the Circus '39
Room Service '38
A Day at the Races '37
A Night at the Opera '35
Duck Soup '33
Horse Feathers '32
Monkey Business '31
Animal Crackers '30
The Cocoanuts '29

Groucho Marx (1890-1977)

The Marx Brothers in a Nutshell '90
Will Success Spoil Rock Hunter? '57
A Girl in Every Port '52
Double Dynamite '51
Love Happy '50
Mr. Music '50
Copacabana '47
A Night in Casablanca '46
Big Store '41
Go West '40
At the Circus '39
Room Service '38
A Day at the Races '37
A Night at the Opera '35
Duck Soup '33
Horse Feathers '32
Monkey Business '31
Animal Crackers '30
The Cocoanuts '29

Harpo Marx (1888-1964)

The Marx Brothers in a Nutshell '90
Love Happy '50
A Night in Casablanca '46
Strictly G.I. '44
Stage Door Canteen '43
Big Store '41
Go West '40
At the Circus '39
Room Service '38
A Day at the Races '37
A Night at the Opera '35
Duck Soup '33
Horse Feathers '32
Monkey Business '31
Animal Crackers '30
The Cocoanuts '29

Zeppo Marx (1901-79)

The Marx Brothers in a Nutshell '90
Duck Soup '33
Horse Feathers '32
Monkey Business '31
Animal Crackers '30
The Cocoanuts '29

Franca Marzi (1926-89)

Nights of Cabiria '57
Island Monster '53

Ron Masak (1936-)

Harper Valley P.T.A. '78
Tora! Tora! Tora! '70

Masako

Ringu 0 '01
Ringu 2 '99
Ringu '98

Masasa

Team America: World Police '04 (V)
Kingdom Come '01

Pierrino Mascarino

Uncle Nino '03
Summer Rental '85

Joseph Mascolo (1935-)

Jaws 2 '78
Love Desperados '68

Marino (Martin) Mase (1939-)

The Belly of an Architect '91
Zorro '74
Les Carabiniers '63

Vladimir Mashkov (1963-)

Behind Enemy Lines '01
The Quickie '01
Dancing at the Blue Iguana '00
The Thief '97

Giulietta Masina (1921-94)

Ginger & Fred '86
The Madwoman of Chaillot '69
Juliet of the Spirits '65
And the Wild, Wild Women '59
Nights of Cabiria '57
Il Bidone '55
La Strada '54
Europa '51 '52
The White Sheik '52
Variety Lights '51

Ace Mask (1948-)

Transylvania Twist '89
Not of This Earth '88

Virginia Maskell

Only Two Can Play '62
Doctor in Love '60

Tatiana Maslany (1985-)

Hardwired '09
An Old-Fashioned Thanksgiving '08
Trapped '06
Ginger Snaps: Unleashed '04

Connie Mason (1937-)

2000 Maniacs '64
Blood Feast '63

Elliot Mason (1897-1949)

On Approval '44
The Ghost Goes West '36

Eric Mason (1934-)

Kiss of the Tarantula '75
Black Starlet '74

Hilary Mason (1917-2006)

Meridian: Kiss of the Beast '90
Robot Jox '90
Dolls '87
Don't Look Now '73
Macbeth '70

Ingrid Mason (1952-)

The Thorn Birds: The Missing Years '96
Death Train '79

Jackie Mason (1934-)

Caddyshack 2 '88
History of the World: Part 1 '81
The Jerk '79

James Mason (1890-1954)

The Upturned Glass '47
The Plainsman '37
Hopalong Cassidy '35
Border Law '31
The Concentratin' Kid '30
For Heaven's Sake '26

James Mason (1909-84)

A.D. '85
The Shooting Party '85
The Assisi Underground '84
George Washington '84
Yellowbeard '83
Dangerous Summer '82
Evil under the Sun '82
Ivanhoe '82
The Verdict '82
ffolkes '80
Murder by Decree '79
Salem's Lot '79
Sidney Sheldon's Bloodline '79
Water Babies '79
The Boys from Brazil '78
Heaven Can Wait '78
Jesus of Nazareth '77
Cross of Iron '76
Kidnap Syndicate '76
Street War '76
Voyage of the Damned '76
Autobiography of a Princess '75
Inside Out '75
Mandingo '75
The Destructors '74
11 Harrowhouse '74
The Last of Sheila '73
Mackintosh Man '73
Bad Man's River '72
Cold Sweat '71
Yin & Yang of Mr. Go '71
Age of Consent '69
Mayerling '68
Cop-Out '67
The Blue Max '66
Georgy Girl '66
Lord Jim '65
The Fall of the Roman Empire '64
The Pumpkin Eater '64
Lolita '62
Tiara Tahiti '62
The Trials of Oscar Wilde '60
Journey to the Center of the Earth '59
North by Northwest '59
Island in the Sun '57
Forever Darling '56
Prince Valiant '54
A Star Is Born '54
20,000 Leagues under the Sea '54
Botany Bay '53
Charade '53
The Desert Rats '53
Julius Caesar '53
The Story of Three Loves '53
Face to Face '52
Five Fingers '52
Prisoner of Zenda '52
The Desert Fox '51
Pandora and the Flying Dutchman '51
Caught '49
East Side, West Side '49
Madame Bovary '49
Reckless Moment '49
Man of Evil '48
Odd Man Out '47
The Seventh Veil '46
The Man in Grey '45
The Wicked Lady '45
Hotel Reserve '44
The Night Has Eyes '42
Secret Mission '42
I Met a Murderer '39
Fire Over England '37
High Command '37
The Mill on the Floss '37
Secret of Stamboul '36
Late Extra '35

Jim Mason

Texas Gunfighter '32
Across to Singapore '28

Laurence Mason

Ali '01
Hackers '95
Parallel Sons '95
The Crow '93

Leroy Mason (1903-47)

Daughter of Don Q '46
The Phantom Rider '46
Vigilantes of Boom Town '46 (N)
California Joe '43
The Man Who Wouldn't Die '42
The Silver Bullet '42
Western Mail '42
Silver Stallion '41
Range Busters '40
Rocky Mountain Rangers '40
Wyoming Outlaw '39
Heroes of the Hills '38
Outlaw Express '38
The Painted Trail '38
Santa Fe Stampede '38
California Straight Ahead! '37
Children of the Wild '37
The Painted Stallion '37
Western Gold '37
Black Gold '36
Go-Get-'Em-Haines '35
The Mystery Man '35
Texas Terror '35
Valley of Wanted Men '35
Dude Ranger '34
The Fighting Trooper '34
When a Man Sees Red '34
Phantom of the Air '33
The Viking '28
Lightning Hutch '26

Madison Mason

Thirteen Days '00
Glitz '88

Marsha Mason (1942-)

Bride & Prejudice '04
Life with Judy Garland—Me and My Shadows '01
Restless Spirits '99
Two Days in the Valley '96
Broken Trust '95
Nick of Time '95
I Love Trouble '94
Drop Dead Fred '91
Dinner at Eight '89
The Image '89
Stella '89
Heartbreak Ridge '86
Trapped in Silence '86
Max Dugan Returns '83
Lois Gibbs and the Love Canal '82
Only When I Laugh '81
Chapter Two '79
Promises in the Dark '79
The Cheap Detective '78
Audrey Rose '77
The Goodbye Girl '77
Blume in Love '73
Cinderella Liberty '73

Pamela Mason (1922-96)

Navy vs. the Night Monsters '66
Door to Door Maniac '61
Charade '53

Tom Mason

Brooklyn Lobster '05
Looking for an Echo '99
Runaway Bride '99
Maternal Instincts '96
My Very Best Friend '96
The Amy Fisher Story '93
Final Appeal '93
Men Don't Leave '89
Mississippi Burning '88
Kicks '85
Aliens Are Coming '80
Walking Through the Fire '80
Apocalypse Now '79

Varvara O. Massalitinova

My Apprenticeship '39
Alexander Nevsky '38
My Childhood '38

Lea Massari (1930-)

Vengeance '86
Christ Stopped at Eboli '79
Les Rendez-vous D'Anna '78
Allonsanfan '73
The Story of a Love Story '73
And Hope to Die '72
Murmur of the Heart '71
The Things of Life '70
L'Avventura '60

Michael Massee

Catwoman '04
Momentum '03
The Theory of the Leisure Class '01
The Last Don '97
Lost Highway '96
One Fine Day '96
Playing God '96
Tales from the Hood '95
The Crow '93
My Father Is Coming '91

Osa Massen (1914-2006)

Outcasts of the City '58
Rocketship X-M '50
Cry of the Werewolf '44
The Master Race '44
Background to Danger '43
Iceland '42
A Woman's Face '41

Andrew Masset (1949-)

From the Earth to the Moon '98
Perfect Crime '97

Anna Massey (1937-)

Affinity '08
Tess of the D'Urbervilles '08
Olivor Twist '07
Pinochet's Last Stand '06
Mrs. Palfrey at the Claremont '05
Agatha Christie: A Life in Pictures '04
The Machinist '04
The Importance of Being Earnest '02
Possession '02
Dark Blue World '01
Captain Jack '98
Deja Vu '98
A Respectable Trade '98
Grave Indiscretions '96
Angels and Insects '95
Haunted '95
Impromptu '90
Mountains of the Moon '90
The Man from the Pru '89
A Tale of Two Cities '89
The Tall Guy '89
Foreign Body '86
Hotel du Lac '86
Anna Karenina '85
Mansfield Park '85
The McGuffin '85

Another Country '84
The Little Drummer Girl '84
The Corn Is Green '79
Sweet William '79
A Doll's House '73
Vault of Horror '73
Frenzy '72
Peeping Tom '60

Athena Massey (1971-)
Harold Robbins' Body Parts '99
Shadow of a Scream '97
Star Portal '97
Termination Man '97
Red Shoe Diaries: Strip Poker '96
Virtual Combat '95
Undercover '94

Daniel Massey (1933-98)
The Miracle Maker: The Story of Jesus '00 (V)
Samson and Delilah '96
The Vacillations of Poppy Carew '94
Catherine Cookson's The Man Who Cried '93
In the Name of the Father '93
Stalin '92
Scandal '89
Intimate Contact '87
Love with a Perfect Stranger '86
Dance with a Stranger '85
Victory '81
The Cat and the Canary '79
The Incredible Sarah '76
Vault of Horror '73
The Golden Bowl '72
Mary, Queen of Scots '71
Star! '68
The Entertainer '60

Edith Massey (1918-84)
Polyester '81
Desperate Living '77
Female Trouble '74
Pink Flamingos '72
Multiple Maniacs '70

Ilona Massey (1910-74)
Love Happy '50
Northwest Outpost '47
Holiday in Mexico '46
Frankenstein Meets the Wolfman '42
Invisible Agent '42
International Lady '41
Melody Master '41
Balalaika '39
Rosalie '38

Raymond Massey (1896-1983)
The President's Plane Is Missing '71
MacKenna's Gold '69
How the West Was Won '63
The Great Impostor '61
The Naked and the Dead '58
Omar Khayyam '57
Battle Cry '55
East of Eden '54
The Desert Song '53
Carson City '52
David and Bathsheba '51
Chain Lightning '50
Barricade '49
The Fountainhead '49
The Possessed '47
Stairway to Heaven '46
God is My Co-Pilot '45
Arsenic and Old Lace '44
Woman in the Window '44
Action in the North Atlantic '43
Desperate Journey '42
Reap the Wild Wind '42
The Forty-Ninth Parallel '41
Abe Lincoln in Illinois '40
Santa Fe Trail '40
Black Limelight '38
Drums '38
Dreaming Lips '37
Fire Over England '37
The Hurricane '37
Prisoner of Zenda '37
Things to Come '36
Under the Red Robe '36
The Scarlet Pimpernel '34
The Old Dark House '32
The Speckled Band '31

Paul Massie (1932-)
The Two Faces of Dr. Jekyll '60
Sapphire '59

Leonide Massine
Neapolitan Carousel '54
The Red Shoes '48

Marina Massironi (1963-)
Agata and the Storm '04
Bread and Tulips '01

Chris Massoglia (1992-)
Cirque du Freak: The Vampire's Assistant '09
A Plumm Summer '08

Master P (1967-)
Internet Dating '08
Soccer Mom '08
Dark Blue '03
Hollywood Homicide '03
Scary Movie 3 '03
Gone in 60 Seconds '00
Lockdown '00
Foolish '99
No Tomorrow '99

Ben Masters (1947-)
Running Mates '92
Noble House '88
The Deliberate Stranger '86
Making Mr. Right '86
Celebrity '85
Dream Lover '85
Key Exchange '85
The Shadow Box '80
Mandingo '75

Chase Masterson (1963-)
Manticore '05
Comic Book: The Movie '04
Terminal Invasion '02
Sometimes They Come Back... For More '99
In a Moment of Passion '93
Married People, Single Sex '93

Christopher K. Masterson (1980-)
The Art of Travel '08
MTV's Wuthering Heights '03
Scary Movie 2 '01
Dragonheart: A New Beginning '00
Campfire Tales '98
Girl '98

Danny Masterson (1976-)
The Brooklyn Heist '08
Yes Man '08
Smiley Face '07
Puff, Puff, Pass '06
Comic Book Villains '02
Dracula 2000 '00
Star Kid '97
Bye Bye, Love '94

Fay Masterson (1974-)
Rancid '04
Sorted '04
Johnson County War '02
Eyes Wide Shut '99
Apartment Complex '98
Cops and Robbersons '94
The Man Without a Face '93
The Power of One '92

Mary Stuart Masterson (1966-)
The Insurgents '06
The Sisters '05
Leo '02
West of Here '02
The Book of Stars '99
Digging to China '98
The Florentine '98
Dogtown '97
Lily Dale '96
Bed of Roses '95
Heaven's Prisoners '95
Bad Girls '94
Radioland Murders '94
Benny & Joon '93
Married to It '93
Mad at the Moon '92
Fried Green Tomatoes '91
Funny About Love '90
Chances Are '89
Immediate Family '89
Mr. North '88
Gardens of Stone '87
My Little Girl '87
Some Kind of Wonderful '87
At Close Range '86
Heaven Help Us '85
The Stepford Wives '75

Peter Masterson (1934-)
Gardens of Stone '87
A Question of Guilt '78
The Stepford Wives '75
The Exorcist '73

Sean Masterson
Deranged '01
Fatal Games '84

Mary Elizabeth Mastrantonio (1958-)
That Russell Girl '08
The Perfect Storm '00
Limbo '99
Witness Protection '99
My Life So Far '98
Two Bits '96
Three Wishes '95
Consenting Adults '92
White Sands '92
Class Action '91
Robin Hood: Prince of Thieves '91
Fools of Fortune '90
The Abyss '89
The January Man '89
Slamdance '87
The Color of Money '86
Scarface '83

Gina Mastrogiacomo (1962-2001)
Bloodhounds '96
Tall, Dark and Deadly '95
Alien Space Avenger '91
Jungle Fever '91

Chiara Mastroianni (1972-)
A Christmas Tale '08
Love Songs '07
Persepolis '07 (V)
Carnage '02
Time Regained '99
For Sale '98
Nowhere '96
Three Lives and Only One Death '96
Diary of a Seducer '95
Ma Saison Preferee '93

Marcello Mastroianni (1923-96)
Three Lives and Only One Death '96
Voyage to the Beginning of the World '96
Beyond the Clouds '95
One Hundred and One Nights '95
I Don't Want to Talk About It '94
Ready to Wear '94
A Fine Romance '92
Used People '92
Everybody's Fine '90
Dark Eyes '87
Intervista '87
Ginger & Fred '86
Henry IV '85
Macaroni '85
Gabriela '84
Beyond Obsession '82
La Nuit de Varennes '82
City of Women '81
Blood Feud '79
A Slightly Pregnant Man '79
Wifemistress '79
Stay As You Are '78
A Special Day '77
We All Loved Each Other So Much '77
Lunatics & Lovers '76
Get Rita '75
Lady of the Evening '75
Salut l'Artiste '74
Allonsanfan '73
Diary of Forbidden Dreams '73
La Grande Bouffe '73
Massacre in Rome '73
Fellini's Roma '72
Divine Nymph '71
The Poppy Is Also a Flower '66
Shoot Loud, Louder, I Don't Understand! '66
Casanova '70 '65
10th Victim '65
Marriage Italian Style '64
The Organizer '64
Yesterday, Today and Tomorrow '64
8 1/2 '63
Divorce—Italian Style '62
A Very Private Affair '62
Il Bell'Antonio '60
La Dolce Vita '60
La Notte '60
Where the Hot Wind Blows '59
Big Deal on Madonna Street '58
White Nights '57
What a Woman! '56
Too Bad She's Bad '54

Shoichiro Masumoto
Azumi 2 '05
Azumi '03

Richard Masur (1948-)
Lovely by Surprise '07
Palindromes '04
61* '01
Noriega: God's Favorite '00
Play It to the Bone '99
Fire Down Below '97
Multiplicity '96
Forget Paris '95
Hiroshima '95
My Brother's Keeper '95
My Girl 2 '94
And the Band Played On '93
The Man Without a Face '93
Six Degrees of Separation '93
Encino Man '92
My Girl '91
Stephen King's It '90
Cast the First Stone '89
Far from Home '89
Flashback '89
Third Degree Burn '89
Higher Ground '88
Hiroshima Maiden '88
License to Drive '88
Rent-A-Cop '88
Shoot to Kill '88
The Believers '87
Walker '87
Hard Lessons '86
Heartburn '86
When the Bough Breaks '86
The Burning Bed '85
Embassy '85
Mean Season '85
My Science Project '85
Wild Horses '84
Adam '83
Nightmares '83
Risky Business '83
Timerider '83
Under Fire '83
The Thing '82
Fallen Angel '81
Heaven's Gate '81
East of Eden '80
Walking Through the Fire '80
Betrayal '78
Who'll Stop the Rain? '78
Semi-Tough '77

Clelia Matania (1918-81)
Don't Look Now '73
The Seven Hills of Rome '58
Neapolitan Carousel '54

Heather Matarazzo (1982-)
Hostel: Part 2 '07
Believe in Me '06
Freshman Orientation '04
The Princess Diaries 2: Royal Engagement '04
Saved! '04
Sorority Boys '02
The Princess Diaries '01
Blue Moon '00
Company Man '00
Scream 3 '00
All I Wanna Do '98
54 '98
The Deli '97
The Devil's Advocate '97
Hurricane Streets '96
Welcome to the Dollhouse '95

Kari Matchett (1970-)
The National Tree '09
Civic Duty '06
Cube 2: Hypercube '02
Cypher '02
Men with Brooms '02

Julian Mateos (1938-96)
Four Rode Out '69
Kashmiri Run '69
Hellbenders '67
Return of the Magnificent Seven '66

Edouard Mathe
Judex '16
Les Vampires '15

Aubrey Mather (1885-1958)
That Forsyte Woman '50
Adventures of Don Juan '49
House of Fear '45
Jane Eyre '44
Hello, Frisco, Hello '43
Mrs. Miniver '42
The Undying Monster '42
Sabotage '36
The Silent Passenger '35

Marie Matheron
Come Undone '00
Western '96

Jerry Mathers (1948-)
Larry the Cable Guy: Health Inspector '06
Down the Drain '89
Back to the Beach '87
The Trouble with Harry '55
Men of the Fighting Lady '54

Marshall Mathers, III
See Eminem

Marissa Mathes (1940-)
Track of the Vampire '66
How to Succeed with Girls '64

Hans Matheson (1975-)
Sherlock Holmes '09
Tess of the D'Urbervilles '08
Doctor Zhivago '03
Deathwatch '02
Mists of Avalon '01
Bodywork '99
Still Crazy '98
Les Miserables '97
Poldark '96
Stella Does Tricks '96

Judy Matheson
Flesh and Blood Show '73
The House that Vanished '73
Crucible of Terror '72
Twins of Evil '71

Michelle Matheson (1971-)
Threesome '94
Test Tube Teens from the Year 2000 '93
Howling 6: The Freaks '90

Tim Matheson (1947-)
Behind Enemy Lines 3: Colombia '08
Redline '07
Don't Come Knocking '05
National Lampoon's Van Wilder '02
She's All That '99
The Story of Us '99
Deadly Game '98
Forever Love '98
Buried Alive 2 '97
Black Sheep '96
Twilight Man '96
A Very Brady Sequel '96
Midnight Heat '95
Tails You Live, Heads You're Dead '95
Fallen Angels 1 '93
Solar Crisis '92
Trial and Error '92
Drop Dead Fred '91
Quicksand: No Escape '91
Sometimes They Come Back '91
Buried Alive '90
Little White Lies '89
Speed Zone '88
Eye of the Demon '87
Blind Justice '86
Fletch '85
Impulse '84
Up the Creek '84
Listen to Your Heart '83
To Be or Not to Be '83
A Little Sex '82
The Apple Dumpling Gang Rides Again '79
Dreamer '79
1941 '79
National Lampoon's Animal House '78
Mary White '77
The Captive: The Longest Drive 2 '76
The Longest Drive '76
The Runaway Barge '75
Magnum Force '73
How to Commit Marriage '69
Yours, Mine & Ours '68

Carole Mathews (1920-)
Showdown at Boot Hill '58
Strange Awakening '58
Swamp Women '55
Shark River '53

George Mathews (-1984)
The Man with the Golden Arm '55
Last of the Comanches '52
Yankee Buccaneer '52

Kerwin Mathews (1926-2007)
Killer Likes Candy '78
Nightmare in Blood '75
Octaman '71
Battle Beneath the Earth '68
Maniac '63
Waltz King '63
Jack the Giant Killer '62
Pirates of Blood River '62
The Devil at 4 O'Clock '61
The Three Worlds of Gulliver '59
The Seventh Voyage of Sinbad '58
The Garment Jungle '57
5 Against the House '55

Thom Mathews (1965-)
Heatseeker '95
Bloodmatch '91
Midnight Cabaret '90
Down Twisted '89
Return of the Living Dead 2 '88
Alien from L.A. '87
Friday the 13th, Part 6: Jason Lives '86

Marion Mathie
Dracula Has Risen from the Grave '68
Lolita '62

Samantha Mathis (1970-)
Buried '10
For One More Day '07
A Stranger's Heart '07
Believe in Me '06
Local Color '06
Kids in America '05
Touched '05
The Punisher '04
Salem's Lot '04
Collected Stories '02
Mists of Avalon '01
Mermaid '00
American Psycho '99
The Simian Line '99
Sweet Jane '98
The American President '95
Broken Arrow '95
How to Make an American Quilt '95
Jack and Sarah '95
Little Women '94
The Music of Chance '93
Super Mario Bros. '93
The Thing Called Love '93
Ferngully: The Last Rain Forest '92 (V)
This Is My Life '92
Pump Up the Volume '90

Jacques Mathou
Ridicule '96
The Hairdresser's Husband '92
Year of the Comet '92
Betty Blue '86

Marie Matiko
Date Movie '06
Counterstrike '03
Gang of Roses '03
The Art of War '00

Elisa Matilla
Valentin '03
Km. 0 '00
Why Do They Call It Love When They Mean Sex? '92

Marlee Matlin (1965-)
Sweet Nothing in My Ear '08
What the #$*! Do We Know? '04
Where the Truth Lies '99
Two Shades of Blue '98
When Justice Fails '98
Dead Silence '96
It's My Party '95
Hear No Evil '93
The Linguini Incident '92
The Player '92
Bridge to Silence '89
Walker '87
Children of a Lesser God '86

Norman Matlock
Crooklyn '94
Wilma '77

John Matshikiza (1954-)
Yankee Zulu '95
Dust Devil '93
Mandela '87
Dust '85

Chieko Matsubara (1945-)
Dolls '02
Black Tight Killers '66
Tokyo Drifter '66

Eiko Matsuda (1947-)
Sweet Evil '95
In the Realm of the Senses '76

Ryuhei Matsuda
Nightmare Detective '06
9 Souls '03
Taboo '99

Yusaku Matsuda (1950-89)
Black Rain '89
The Family Game '83
Murders in the Doll House '79

Hiroki Matsukata
Shogun's Samurai—The Yagyu Clan Conspiracy '78
Magic Serpent '66

Kayo Matsuo
Shogun Assassin '80
Gate of Flesh '64

Masatoshi Matsuo
The World Sinks Except Japan '06
Pulse '01

Yutaka Matsushige
Shinobi '05
Last Life in the Universe '03
One Missed Call '03
The Princess Blade '02
Charisma '99
Rasen '98
Ringu '98

Nanako Matsushima (1973-)
Ringu 2 '99
Rasen '98
Ringu '98

Ken'ichi Matsuyama
Death Note 3: L, Change the World '08
Death Note 2: The Last Name '07
Death Note '06
Linda Linda Linda '05

Takashi Matsuyama
Ju-On 2 '00
Talking Head '92
Stray Dog '91

Keiko Matsuzaka (1952-)
The Happiness of the Katakuris '01
Dr. Akagi '98
Fall Guy '82
The Go-Masters '82

Danilo Mattei
In the Name of the Pope-King '85
Ironmaster '82

Niall Matter
Dr. Dolittle 4: Tail to the Chief '08
Loch Ness Terror '07

Eva Mattes (1954-)
Enemy at the Gates '00
Jew-Boy Levi '99
The Promise '94
A Man Like Eva '83
Celeste '81
Germany, Pale Mother '80
David '79
In a Year of 13 Moons '78
Woyzeck '78
Stroszek '77
The Bitter Tears of Petra von Kant '72

Pam Matteson (1962-)
Prehysteria 3 '95
Punchline '88

Walter Matthau (1920-2000)
Hanging Up '99
Neil Simon's The Odd Couple 2 '98
Out to Sea '97
I'm Not Rappaport '96
The Grass Harp '95
Grumpier Old Men '95
I.Q. '94
Dennis the Menace '93
Grumpy Old Men '93
JFK '91
The Incident '89
The Couch Trip '87
Pirates '86
Movers and Shakers '85
Survivors '83
I Ought to Be in Pictures '82
Buddy Buddy '81
First Monday in October '81
Hopscotch '80
Little Miss Marker '80
California Suite '78
Casey's Shadow '78
House Calls '78
The Bad News Bears '76
The Sunshine Boys '75
Earthquake '74
The Front Page '74
The Laughing Policeman '74
The Taking of Pelham One Two Three '74
Charley Varrick '73
Pete 'n' Tillie '72
Kotch '71
A New Leaf '71
Plaza Suite '71
Cactus Flower '69
Hello, Dolly! '69
Candy '68
The Odd Couple '68
Secret Life of an American Wife '68
A Guide for the Married Man '67
The Fortune Cookie '66
Mirage '66
Ensign Pulver '64
Fail-Safe '64
Goodbye Charlie '64
Charade '63
Who's Got the Action? '63
Lonely Are the Brave '62
Strangers When We Meet '60
King Creole '58
A Face in the Crowd '57
The Indian Fighter '55
The Kentuckian '55

Ulrich Matthes (1959-)
Downfall '04
The Ninth Day '04
Winter Sleepers '97

A.E. Matthews (1869-1960)
Carry On Admiral '57
Made in Heaven '52
Mister Drake's Duck '50
Immortal Battalion '44
The Iron Duke '34

Al Matthews (1942-)
American Roulette '88
Aliens '86
The Sender '82

Brian Matthews (1953-)
Red Nights '87
The Burning '82

Dakin Matthews (1933-)
Thirteen Days '00
The Muse '99
From the Earth to the Moon '98
The Siege '98
Bean '97
Rough Riders '97
The Swan Princess '94 (V)
White Mile '94
And the Band Played On '93
The Temp '93
In a Stranger's Hand '92
Revolver '92
Child's Play 3 '91
My Brother's Wife '89
Naked Lie '89
Permanent Record '88
Nuts '87

Dave Matthews
Lake City '08
You Don't Mess with the Zohan '08
Because of Winn-Dixie '05

DeLane Matthews (1961-)
Running Red '99
From the Earth to the Moon '98
The Invaders '95

Francis Matthews (1927-)
The McGuffin '85
Dracula, Prince of Darkness '66
Rasputin the Mad Monk '66
Murder Ahoy '64
The Hellfire Club '61
Corridors of Blood '58
The Revenge of Frankenstein '58
Small Hotel '57
Bhowani Junction '56

Fritz Matthews
Born Killer '89
Hell on the Battleground '88
Deadly Prey '87

Jessie Matthews (1907-81)
The Hound of the Baskervilles '77
Candles at Nine '44
Forever and a Day '43
Sailing Along '38
Gangway '37
It's Love Again '36
First a Girl '35
Evergreen '34

John Matthews
A Secret Space '88
Sleuth '72

Junius Matthews
The Many Adventures of Winnie the Pooh '77 (V)
The Sword in the Stone '63 (V)

Lester Matthews (1900-75)
The Far Horizons '55
King Richard and the Crusaders '54
Man in the Attic '53
Tales of Robin Hood '52
Objective, Burma! '45
The Invisible Man's Revenge '44
Across the Pacific '42
The Raven '35
Werewolf of London '35

Liesl Matthews (1984-)
Air Force One '97
A Little Princess '95

Sinead Matthews
Happy-Go-Lucky '08
Half Broken Things '07

Terumi Matthews
The Waiting Game '99
The Sticky Fingers of Time '97
Madonna: Innocence Lost '95

Robin Mattson (1956-)
In Between '92
Take Two '87
Captain America '79
Hot Rod '79
Wolf Lake '79
Return to Macon County '75
Candy Stripe Nurses '74
Bonnie's Kids '73
Island of the Lost '68
Namu, the Killer Whale '66

Helena Mattsson
Iron Man 2 '10
Surrogates '09
Species 4: The Awakening '07

Victor Mature (1915-99)
Samson and Delilah '84
Head '68
After the Fox '66
The Big Circus '59
The Long Haul '57
Savage Wilderness '55
Betrayed '54
Dangerous Mission '54
Demetrius and the Gladiators '54
The Egyptian '54
The Robe '53
Androcles and the Lion '52
The Las Vegas Story '52
Million Dollar Mermaid '52
Samson and Delilah '50
Easy Living '49
Kiss of Death '47
My Darling Clementine '46
Footlight Serenade '42
Seven Days' Leave '42
The Shanghai Gesture '42
Song of the Islands '42
I Wake Up Screaming '41
Captain Caution '40
No, No Nanette '40
One Million B.C. '40

John Matuszak (1950-89)
Down the Drain '89
Ghost Writer '89
One Man Force '89
The Goonies '85
Ice Pirates '84
Caveman '81
North Dallas Forty '79
Semi-Tough '77

Johanna (Hannerl) Matz (1932-)
The Life and Loves of Mozart '59
They Were So Young '55
Party Girls for Sale '54

Joan Maude (1908-98)
The Temptress '49
Power '34

Tony Maudsley (1968-)
Place of Execution '09
Vanity Fair '04
The Intended '02
Strange Relations '02

Monica Maughan (1938-)
Road to Nhill '97
A Woman's Tale '92
Cactus '86

Wayne Maunder (1938-)
Crazy Horse and Custer: "The Untold Story" '90
Porky's '82

Sarah Maur-Thorp
River of Death '90
Edge of Sanity '89
Ten Little Indians '89

Carmen Maura (1945-)
Tetro '09
Volver '06
Free Zone '05
800 Bullets '02
Valentin '02
Lisboa '99
Alice et Martin '98
Women '97
Le Bonheur Est Dans le Pre '95
Between Heaven and Earth '93
How to Be a Woman and Not Die in the Attempt '91
Ay, Carmela! '90
Baton Rouge '88
Women on the Verge of a Nervous Breakdown '88
Law of Desire '86
Matador '86
Extramuros '85
What Have I Done to Deserve This? '85
Dark Habits '84
Pepi, Luci, Bom and Other Girls on the Heap '80

Howard Maurer
Ilsa, the Tigress of Siberia '79
Ilsa, the Wicked Warden '78

Joshua Maurer
Taken Away '89
Tour of Duty '87

Nicole Maurey (1925-)
Day of the Triffids '63
The Jayhawkers '59
Me and the Colonel '58
Rogue's Yarn '56
Diary of a Country Priest '50

Claire Maurier (1929-)
Amelie '01
Un Air de Famille '96
La Cage aux Folles '78
A Very Curious Girl '69
Angelique: The Road to Versailles '65
Sweet Ecstasy '62
The 400 Blows '59
Back to the Wall '56

Eve Mauro
The Chaos Experiment '09
Wicked Lake '08

Gerda Maurus (1909-68)
Woman in the Moon '29
Spies '28

Gary Mavers (1964-)
The Unknown Soldier '98
Body & Soul '93

Dawn Maxey
Raising Flagg '06
The Killing Club '01
Ringmaster '98
Normal Life '96
That Thing You Do! '96

Chenoa Maxwell (1969-)
G '02
Hav Plenty '97

Edwin Maxwell (1886-1948)
Woman in Brown '48
Swamp Fire '46
Waterfront '44
Behind Prison Walls '43
Way Down South '39
Motive for Revenge '35
Mystery Liner '34
Night of Terror '33
The Taming of the Shrew '29

Frank Maxwell (1916-2004)
The Haunted Palace '63
Shame '61
Lonelyhearts '58

John Maxwell
Prowler '51
Boss of Big Town '43
The Payoff '43
Honky Tonk '41

Larry Maxwell (1953-96)
Public Access '93
Poison '91

Lois Maxwell (1927-2007)
The Fourth Angel '01
Hard to Forget '98
Eternal Evil '87
A View to a Kill '85
For Your Eyes Only '81
Moonraker '79
The Spy Who Loved Me '77
The Man with the Golden Gun '74
Live and Let Die '73
Diamonds Are Forever '71
On Her Majesty's Secret Service '69
You Only Live Twice '67
Thunderball '65
Goldfinger '64
From Russia with Love '63
The Haunting '63
Dr. No '62
Lolita '62
The Unstoppable Man '59
Kill Me Tomorrow '57
Time Without Pity '57
Submarine Attack '54
Scotland Yard Inspector '52

Marilyn Maxwell (1922-72)
Wild Women '70
Arizona Bushwackers '67
Critic's Choice '63
Rock-A-Bye Baby '57
Off Limits '53
The Lemon Drop Kid '51
Key to the City '50
Champion '49
Summer Holiday '48

The Show-Off '46
Lost in a Harem '44

Paul Maxwell (1920-91)
Cloud Waltzing '87
Going Home '86

Roberta Maxwell (1944-)
Brokeback Mountain '05
Gracie's Choice '04
Full Disclosure '00
Last Night '98
The Postman '97
Mistrial '96
Dead Man Walking '95
Philadelphia '93
Psycho 3 '86
Lois Gibbs and the Love Canal '82
The Changeling '80

Deborah May
Caged Fear '92
Johnny Be Good '88
Rage of Angels '83

Donald May (1927-)
Bogie: The Last Hero '80
Kisses for My President '64

Elaine May (1932-)
Small Time Crooks '00
In the Spirit '90
California Suite '78
A New Leaf '71
Enter Laughing '67
Luv '67

Jack May (1922-97)
He Kills Night After Night After Night '69
Night Slasher '69

Jodhi May (1975-)
Emma '09
Defiance '08
Flashbacks of a Fool '08
Land of the Blind '06
Friends & Crocodiles '05
On a Clear Day '05
The Mayor of Casterbridge '03
The Other Boleyn Girl '03
Daniel Deronda '02
Tipping the Velvet '02
House of Mirth '00
The Aristocrats '99
The Turn of the Screw '99
The Gambler '97
Sister My Sister '94
The Last of the Mohicans '92
Eminent Domain '91
Max and Helen '90
A World Apart '88

Mathilda May (1965-)
A Girl Cut in Two '07
Only Love '98
The Jackal '97
Prince Brat and the Whipping Boy '95
Grosse Fatigue '94
Becoming Colette '92
Naked Tango '91
The Cry of the Owl '87
Lifeforce '85
Letters to an Unknown Lover '84

Herschel Mayall (1863-1941)
Kismet '20
The Bargain '15

Rik Mayall (1958-)
Valiant '05 (V)
Chilly Dogs '01
Jesus Christ Superstar '00
Carry On Columbus '92
Drop Dead Fred '91
Little Noises '91
Whoops Apocalypse '83
An American Werewolf in London '81
Eye of the Needle '81
Shock Treatment '81

Anthony (Jose, J. Antonio, J.A.) Mayans (1939-)
Revenge in the House of Usher '82
Zombie Lake '80
Sex Is Crazy '79
Heat of the Flame '76

Eddie Mayehoff (1911-92)
How to Murder Your Wife '64
Artists and Models '55
The Stooge '51

Jose Mayens
See Anthony (Jose, J. Antonio, J.A.) Mayans

Chip (Christopher) Mayer (1955-)
Fugitive Champion '99
Liar Liar '97
Survivor '87
Our Family Business '81

Ray Mayer (1901-48)
Swing It, Sailor! '37
Special Investigator '36

Peter Mayhew (1944-)
Star Wars: Episode 3—Revenge of the Sith '05
Comic Book: The Movie '04
Return of the Jedi '83
The Empire Strikes Back '80
Star Wars '77

John Maynard (1959-)
Biohazard: The Alien Force '95
Dark Universe '93

Ken Maynard (1895-1973)
Arizona Whirlwind '44
Death Valley Rangers '44
Westward Bound '44
The Law Rides Again '43
Death Rides the Range '40
Lightning Strikes West '40
Flaming Lead '39
Phantom Rancher '39
Six Shootin' Sheriff '38
Whirlwind Horseman '38
Boots of Destiny '37
Trailing Trouble '37
Trails of the Wild '35
Western Courage '35
Western Frontier '35
Honor of the Range '34
In Old Santa Fe '34
Mystery Mountain '34
Drum Taps '33
The Fiddlin' Buckaroo '33
The Lone Avenger '33
Phantom Thunderbolt '33
Strawberry Roan '33
Trail Drive '33
Between Fighting Men '32
Come on Tarzan '32
Dynamite Ranch '32
False Faces '32
Fargo Express '32
Hell Fire Austin '32
Sunset Trail '32
Texas Gunfighter '32
Tombstone Canyon '32
Whistlin' Dan '32
Arizona Terror '31
Branded Men '31
The Pocatello Kid '31
Range Law '31
Two Gun Man '31
Fightin' Ranch '30
The Fighting Legion '30
Fighting Thru '30
Mountain Justice '30
The Red Raiders '27
$50,000 Reward '25

Kermit Maynard (1897-1971)
The Black Lash '52
Trail of Robin Hood '50
Ambush Trail '46
'Neath Canadian Skies '46
Gangster's Den '45
The Stranger from Pecos '45
Devil Riders '44
The Drifter '44
Frontier Outlaws '44
Thundering Gunslingers '44
Raiders of Red Gap '43
Texas Kid '43
Along the Sundown Trail '42
Arizona Stagecoach '42
The Mysterious Rider '42
Prairie Pals '42
Rock River Renegades '42
Trail Riders '42
Billy the Kid '41
Bury Me Not on the Lone Prairie '41
Man from Montana '41
Heroes of the Saddle '40
Pony Post '40
Range Busters '40
Riders of Pasco Basin '40
The Showdown '40
Valley of Terror '38
Galloping Dynamite '37
Roaring Six Guns '37
Rough Ridin' Rhythm '37
Phantom Patrol '36
Song of the Trail '36
Whistling Bullets '36
His Fighting Blood '35
The Fighting Trooper '34
Drum Taps '33
Outlaw Justice '32

Mimi Maynard
Adventures in Dinosaur City '92
False Identity '90

Terence Maynard
Revolver '05
Reign of Fire '02

Belinda Mayne (1958-)
Don't Open Till Christmas '84
White Fire '84

Ferdinand "Ferdy" Mayne (1916-98)
Benefit of the Doubt '93
River of Diamonds '90
A Friendship in Vienna '88
Magdalene '88
Howling 2: Your Sister Is a Werewolf '85
Night Train to Terror '84
The Secret Diary of Sigmund Freud '84
Yellowbeard '83
Frightmare '81
Hawk the Slayer '81
Au Pair Girls '72
The Vampire Happening '71
When Eight Bells Toll '71
The Adventurers '70
The Vampire Lovers '70
The Magic Christian '69
Where Eagles Dare '68
The Fearless Vampire Killers '67
Masters of Venus '62
Our Man in Havana '59
Abandon Ship '57
Captain's Paradise '53
Roadhouse Girl '53
White Fire '53
Made in Heaven '52
The Temptress '49
Echo Murders '45

Juliette Mayniel (1935-)
The Bloodstained Shadow '78
Assassination in Rome '65
The Trojan Horse '62
The Cousins '59
The Horror Chamber of Dr. Faustus '59

Alfredo Mayo (1911-85)
Bell from Hell '74
The Hunt '65
Mission in Morocco '59

Frank Mayo (1886-1963)
Across the Pacific '42
The Fighting 69th '40
Tim Tyler's Luck '37
Hell's Headquarters '32
Doughboys '30
Souls for Sale '23

Virginia Mayo (1920-2005)
Midnight Witness '93
Evil Spirits '91
The Haunted '79
French Quarter '78
Runaways '75
Castle of Evil '66
Jet Over the Atlantic '59
Westbound '58
Great Day in the Morning '56
Pearl of the South Pacific '55
King Richard and the Crusaders '54
The Silver Chalice '54
Devil's Canyon '53
South Sea Woman '53
The Iron Mistress '52
Along the Great Divide '51
Captain Horatio Hornblower '51
Painting the Clouds With Sunshine '51
The Flame & the Arrow '50
The West Point Story '50
Colorado Territory '49
White Heat '49
A Song Is Born '48
Out of the Blue '47
The Secret Life of Walter Mitty '47
The Best Years of Our Lives '46
Kid from Brooklyn '46
Wonder Man '45
Jack London '44
The Princess and the Pirate '44
Seven Days Ashore '44

Whitman Mayo (1930-2001)
Boycott '02
Waterproof '99
Boyz N the Hood '91
Of Mice and Men '81

Karen Mayo-Chandler (1958-2006)
Death Feud '89
Stripped to Kill II: Live Girls '89

Gale Mayron
Almost Blue '93
The Feud '90
Heart of Midnight '89

Melanie Mayron (1952-)
Range of Motion '00
Toothless '97
Ordeal in the Arctic '93
My Blue Heaven '90
Checking Out '89
Sticky Fingers '88
The Boss' Wife '86
Wanted: The Perfect Guy '86
Missing '82
The Best Little Girl in the World '81
Heartbeeps '81
Playing for Time '80
Girlfriends '78
You Light Up My Life '77
Car Wash '76
Great Smokey Roadblock '76
Harry and Tonto '74

Daniel Mays (1978-)
The Bank Job '08
Half Broken Things '07
Middletown '06
Vera Drake '04
All or Nothing '02

Jayma Mays (1979-)
Paul Blart: Mall Cop '09
Epic Movie '07

Jefferson Mays (1965-)
The Notorious Bettie Page '06
Alfie '04

The Big Brass Ring '99
Some Folks Call It a Sling Blade '94

Joshua Gibran Mayweather (1981-)
Nowhere '96
Camp Nowhere '94
Candyman 2: Farewell to the Flesh '94

Bob Maza (1939-2000)
Back of Beyond '95
Reckless Kelly '93
Ground Zero '88
The Fringe Dwellers '86

Debi Mazar (1964-)
The Women '08
Lies & Alibis '06
Be Cool '05
Edmond '05
Collateral '04
The Tuxedo '02
Life in the Fast Lane '00
More Dogs Than Bones '00
The Insider '99
Frogs for Snakes '98
Hush '98
Witness to the Mob '98
Meet Wally Sparks '97
She's So Lovely '97
Space Truckers '97
Girl 6 '96
Nowhere '96
Things I Never Told You '96
Tree's Lounge '96
Bad Love '95
Batman Forever '95
Empire Records '95
Witch Hunt '94
Beethoven's 2nd '93
Inside Monkey Zetterland '93
Money for Nothing '93
In the Soup '92
Jungle Fever '91
Little Man Tate '91
Goodfellas '90

Monet Mazur (1976-)
The House Bunny '08
Monster-in-Law '05
Stoned '05
Torque '04
Whirlygirl '04
Just Married '03
Comic Book Villains '02
40 Days and 40 Nights '02
Stark Raving Mad '02
Angel Eyes '01
The Learning Curve '01
Raging Angels '95

Mike Mazurki (1907-90)
Doin' Time '85
The Adventures of Huckleberry Finn '78
The Incredible Rocky Mountain Race '77
Challenge To Be Free '76
The McCullochs '75
Cheyenne Autumn '64
Donovan's Reef '63
The Errand Boy '61
Some Like It Hot '59
Hell Ship Mutiny '57
Man in the Vault '56
Blood Alley '55
Pier 23 '51
Night and the City '50
Come to the Stable '49
Neptune's Daughter '49
The Noose Hangs High '48
Killer Dill '47
Nightmare Alley '47
Sinbad, the Sailor '47
Unconquered '47
Abbott and Costello in Hollywood '45
Dick Tracy, Detective '45
The Canterville Ghost '44
Murder, My Sweet '44
Behind the Rising Sun '43
The Shanghai Gesture '42

Paul Mazursky (1930-)
National Lampoon Presents Cattle Call '06
Coast to Coast '04
Big Shot's Funeral '01
Crazy in Alabama '99
A Slight Case of Murder '99
Antz '98 (V)
Why Do Fools Fall in Love? '98
Weapons of Mass Distraction '97
Touch '96
Two Days in the Valley '96
Faithful '95
Miami Rhapsody '95
Love Affair '94
Man Trouble '92
Enemies, a Love Story '89
Scenes from the Class Struggle in Beverly Hills '89
Moon over Parador '88
Punchline '88
Into the Night '85
History of the World: Part 1 '81
A Man, a Woman, and a Bank '79
A Star Is Born '76
Harry and Tonto '74
Alex in Wonderland '70
Blackboard Jungle '55

Marcello Mazzarello (1965-)
Felicidades '00
Time Regained '99

Joseph Mazzello (1983-)
The Sensation of Sight '06
Simon Birch '98
The Lost World: Jurassic Park 2 '97
Star Kid '97
The Cure '95
Three Wishes '95
The River Wild '94
Jurassic Park '93
Shadowlands '93
Jersey Girl '92
Radio Flyer '92
Presumed Innocent '90

M.C. Lyte (1971-)
Civil Brand '02
An Alan Smithee Film: Burn, Hollywood, Burn '97
Fly by Night '93

Rachel McAdams (1976-)
Morning Glory '10
Sherlock Holmes '09
State of Play '09
The Time Traveler's Wife '09
The Lucky Ones '08
Married Life '07
The Family Stone '05
Red Eye '05
Wedding Crashers '05
Mean Girls '04
The Notebook '04
The Hot Chick '02

Anndi McAfee (1979-)
Land Before Time 7: The Stone of Cold Fire '00 (V)
The Land Before Time 6: The Secret of Saurus Rock '98 (V)
The Land Before Time 5: The Mysterious Island '97 (V)
Conagher '91

Scott McAfee
The Land Before Time 4: Journey Through the Mists '96 (V)
The Land Before Time 3: The Time of the Great Giving '95 (V)
The Land Before Time 2: The Great Valley Adventure '94 (V)

Des McAleer
When the Sky Falls '99
I Want You '98
Kings in Grass Castles '97
This Is the Sea '96
Butterfly Kiss '94
Hidden Agenda '90
Four Days in July '85

Ray McAnally (1926-89)
My Left Foot *'89*
We're No Angels *'89*
A Perfect Spy *'88*
Taffin *'88*
A Very British Coup *'88*
Empire State *'87*
The Fourth Protocol *'87*
The Mission *'86*
No Surrender *'86*
Cal *'84*
Danny Boy *'82*
Sea of Sand *'58*

Marianne McAndrew (1938-)
The Bat People *'74*
Hello, Dolly! *'69*

Andrea McArdle (1963-)
Annie *'99*
Rainbow *'78*

Alex McArthur (1957-)
Hydra *'09*
Lost Colony: The Legend of Roanoke *'07*
Stealing Candy *'04*
Suspended Animation *'02*
Route 666 *'01*
Devil in the Flesh *'98*
Kiss the Girls *'97*
Lady Killer *'97*
Sharon's Secret *'95*
Drug Wars 2: The Cocaine Cartel *'92*
Race for Glory *'89*
Rampage *'87*
Silent Witness *'85*
Urge to Kill *'84*

Hugh McArthur
Panama Patrol *'39*
Marihuana *'36*

Alphonso McAuley
Pride *'07*
Glory Road *'06*
Fat Albert *'04*

James McAvoy (1979-)
The Last Station *'09*
Wanted *'08*
Atonement *'07*
Becoming Jane *'07*
The Last King of Scotland *'06*
Penelope *'06*
Starter for Ten *'06*
The Chronicles of Narnia: The Lion, the Witch and the Wardrobe *'05*
Rory O'Shea Was Here *'04*
Wimbledon *'04*
Bright Young Things *'03*
Children of Dune *'03*
State of Play *'03*

May McAvoy (1901-84)
Gun Glory *'57*
The Jazz Singer *'27*
Ben-Hur *'26*
Lady Windermere's Fan *'25*

Diane McBain (1941-)
Puppet Master 5: The Final Chapter *'94*
Flying from the Hawk *'86*
Donner Pass: The Road to Survival *'84*
Monster *'78*
Deathhead Virgin *'74*
Thunder Alley *'67*
Spinout *'66*
A Distant Trumpet *'64*
Mary, Mary *'63*
Parrish *'61*

Tom McBeath
Off Season *'01*
Firestorm *'97*

Daron McBee (1961-)
Mortal Kombat 2: Annihilation *'97*
T-Force *'94*
The Killing Zone *'90*

Jack McBrayer
Cats & Dogs: The Revenge of Kitty Galore *'10*
Despicable Me *'10 (V)*
Forgetting Sarah Marshall *'08*
Walk Hard: The Dewey Cox Story *'07*

Chi McBride (1961-)
American Son *'08*
First Sunday *'08*
The Brothers Solomon *'07*
Annapolis *'06*
Let's Go to Prison *'06*
Roll Bounce *'05*
Waiting *'05*
I, Robot *'04*
The Terminal *'04*
Cradle 2 the Grave *'03*
Narc *'02*
Paid in Full *'02*
Undercover Brother *'02*
Dancing in September *'00*
Disney's The Kid *'00*
Gone in 60 Seconds *'00*
Mercury Rising *'98*
The Frighteners *'96*
Hoodlum *'96*
Cosmic Slop *'94*
What's Love Got to Do with It? *'93*

Danny McBride
Despicable Me *'10 (V)*
Land of the Lost *'09*
Up in the Air *'09*
The Foot Fist Way *'08*
Pineapple Express *'08*
Tropic Thunder *'08*
The Heartbreak Kid *'07*
Hot Rod *'07*
All the Real Girls *'03*

Jon McBride
Terror House *'97*
Feeders *'96*
Blades *'89*
Woodchipper Massacre *'89*
Cannibal Campout *'88*

Michelle McBride
Masque of the Red Death *'90*
Subspecies *'90*

Simon McBurney (1957-)
Body of Lies *'08*
The Duchess *'08*
Friends with Money *'06*
The Last King of Scotland *'06*
The Manchurian Candidate *'04*
Mesmer *'94*
Kafka *'91*

Debra McCabe
Sticks and Stones *'08*
Saw 3 *'06*

Richard McCabe (1960-)
Wallander: Firewall *'08*
Wallander: One Step Behind *'08*
Wallander: Sidetracked *'08*
The Constant Gardener *'05*
Master and Commander: The Far Side of the World *'03*
Heat of the Sun *'99*
Notting Hill *'99*

Ruth McCabe
Rory O'Shea Was Here *'04*
American Women *'00*
An Everlasting Piece *'00*
Talk of Angels *'96*
The Snapper *'93*
My Left Foot *'89*

Tony McCabe (-1968)
Something Weird *'68*
Suburban Roulette *'67*

Frankie McCafferty (1967-)
The Informant *'97*
Fools of Fortune *'90*

John McCafferty
The Perfect Gift *'95*
Deathrow Gameshow *'88*

James McCaffrey (1960-)
Feel the Noise *'07*
Fresh Cut Grass *'04*
American Splendor *'03*
The Tic Code *'99*
Nick and Jane *'96*
Burnzy's Last Call *'95*
Schemes *'95*

Frances Lee McCain (1944-)
Patch Adams *'98*
Question of Faith *'93*
The Lookalike *'90*
Broken Badge *'85*
Gremlins *'84*
Tex *'82*
Two of a Kind *'82*
Real Life *'79*

Catriona McCall
See Katherine (Katriona) MacColl

Mitzi McCall
World's Greatest Dad *'09*
The Opposite Sex and How to Live With Them *'93*

Ross McCall (1976-)
Green Street Hooligans 2 *'09*
Green Street Hooligans *'05*
Lethal Dose *'03*
The Return of the Borrowers *'96*

William (Bill, Billy) McCall (1870-1938)
Outlaws of the Range *'36*
Lightning Bill *'35*
Trailing Trouble *'30*
Rounding Up the Law *'22*

Irish McCalla (1929-2002)
Hands of a Stranger *'62*
She Demons *'58*

Holt McCallany (1964-)
The Losers *'10*
Vantage Point *'08*
The Upside of Anger *'05*
Below *'02*
Kiss Tomorrow Goodbye *'00*
Men of Honor *'00*
Three Kings *'99*
The Peacemaker *'97*
Rough Riders *'97*
The Search for One-Eye Jimmy *'96*
Tecumseh: The Last Warrior *'95*
Tyson *'95*
Alien 3 *'92*
Creepshow 2 *'87*

Lon (Bud) McCallister (1923-2005)
The Big Cat *'49*
The Story of Seabiscuit *'49*
The Red House *'47*
Stage Door Canteen *'43*

David McCallum (1933-)
Coming Home *'98*
Mortal Challenge *'97*
Shattered Image *'93*
The Haunting of Morella *'91*
Hear My Song *'91*
The Wind *'87*
Behind Enemy Lines *'85*
Terminal Choice *'85*
Return of the Man from U.N.C.L.E. *'83*
The Watcher in the Woods *'81*
King Solomon's Treasure *'76*
Kingfisher Caper *'76*
She Waits *'71*
Around the World Under the Sea *'65*
The Great Escape *'63*
Billy Budd *'62*

A Night to Remember *'58*
Robbery under Arms *'57*

Joanna McCallum
Tom & Viv *'94*
The Franchise Affair *'88*
Testament of Youth *'79*

John McCallum (1918-)
Devil on Horseback *'54*
Valley of the Eagles *'51*
The Woman in Question *'50*
It Always Rains on Sunday *'47*

Macon McCalman (1932-2005)
Doc Hollywood *'91*
Fleshburn *'84*
The Ultimate Imposter *'79*

Mercedes McCambridge (1918-2004)
Echoes *'83*
The Concorde: Airport '79 *'79*
The Sacketts *'79*
The Exorcist *'73 (V)*
The Girls of Huntington House *'73*
Sixteen *'72*
The President's Plane Is Missing *'71*
99 Women *'69*
Deadly Sanctuary *'68*
Angel Baby *'61*
Cimarron *'60*
Suddenly, Last Summer *'59*
Touch of Evil *'58*
A Farewell to Arms *'57*
Giant *'56*
Tender Is the Night *'55*
Johnny Guitar *'53*
All the King's Men *'49*

Tom McCamus (1955-)
Cairo Time *'09*
Waking Up Wally *'05*
Confessions of a Teenage Drama Queen *'04*
Ginger Snaps Back: The Beginning *'04*
Siblings *'04*
The Passion of Ayn Rand *'99*
Long Day's Journey Into Night *'96*
The Sweet Hereafter *'96*
First Degree *'95*
A Man in Uniform *'93*
Norman's Awesome Experience *'88*

Chuck McCann (1936-)
Storyville *'92*
DuckTales the Movie: Treasure of the Lost Lamp *'90 (V)*
That's Adequate *'90*
Cameron's Closet *'89*
Thrashin' *'86*
Rosebud Beach Hotel *'85*
C.H.O.M.P.S. *'79*
If Things Were Different *'79*
Foul Play *'78*
They Went That-a-Way & That-a-Way *'78*
The Projectionist *'71*
The Heart Is a Lonely Hunter *'68*

Donal McCann (1943-99)
Illuminata *'98*
The Nephew *'97*
The Serpent's Kiss *'97*
Stealing Beauty *'96*
December Bride *'91*
The Miracle *'91*
The Dead *'87*
Rawhead Rex *'87*
Out of Africa *'85*
Cal *'84*
Hard Way *'80*
Screamer *'74*

Henry McCann
The Ghost of Dragstrip Hollow *'59*
Submarine Seahawk *'59*

Martin McCann
Closing the Ring *'07*
My Boy Jack *'07*

Rory McCann (1969-)
The Crew *'08*
Beowulf & Grendel *'06*
Alexander *'04*

Sean McCann (1935-)
Wedding Wars *'06*
The River King *'05*
Miracle *'04*
The Reagans *'04*
A Separate Peace *'04*
A House Divided *'00*
Tracked *'98*
Affliction *'97*
Gang in Blue *'96*
Swann *'96*
Iron Eagle 4 *'95*
The Air Up There *'94*
Trapped in Paradise *'94*
Guilty as Sin *'93*
Trial and Error *'92*
Run *'91*
Mindfield *'89*
Unnatural Causes *'86*
Canada's Sweetheart: The Saga of Hal C. Banks *'85*
Quiet Day in Belfast *'74*

Brian McCardie (1965-)
The Damned United *'09*
Rip It Off *'02*
200 Cigarettes *'98*
Speed 2: Cruise Control *'97*
The Ghost and the Darkness *'96*
Kidnapped *'95*
Rob Roy *'95*

Fred McCarren (1952-)
Red Flag: The Ultimate Game *'81*
Marriage Is Alive and Well *'80*
How to Pick Up Girls *'78*

Andrew McCarthy (1963-)
The Good Guy *'10*
The National Tree *'09*
The Spiderwick Chronicles *'08*
2B Perfectly Honest *'04*
Anything But Love *'02*
Nowhere in Sight *'01*
Beyond Redemption *'99*
New Waterford Girl *'99*
New World Disorder *'99*
I'm Losing You *'98*
Perfect Assassins *'98*
Stag *'97*
Escape Clause *'96*
The Heist *'96*
Things I Never Told You *'96*
The Courtyard *'95*
Mulholland Falls *'95*
Dead Funny *'94*
Dream Man *'94*
Getting In *'94*
Mrs. Parker and the Vicious Circle *'94*
Night of the Running Man *'94*
The Joy Luck Club *'93*
Weekend at Bernie's 2 *'93*
Only You *'92*
Year of the Gun *'91*
Quiet Days in Clichy *'90*
Club Extinction *'89*
Weekend at Bernie's *'89*
Fresh Horses *'88*
Kansas *'88*
Less Than Zero *'87*
Mannequin *'87*
Waiting for the Moon *'87*
Pretty in Pink *'86*
Heaven Help Us *'85*
St. Elmo's Fire *'85*
The Beniker Gang *'83*
Class *'83*

Francis X. (Frank) McCarthy
Nightwaves *'03*
A Case of Deadly Force *'86*
The Man with Two Brains *'83*

Dead Men Don't Wear Plaid *'82*

James McCarthy
To End All Wars *'01*
Oktober *'98*

Jenny McCarthy (1972-)
Wieners *'08*
Witless Protection *'08*
John Tucker Must Die *'06*
Santa Baby *'06*
Dirty Love *'05*
Scary Movie 3 *'03*
Crazy Little Thing *'02*
Python *'00*
Scream 3 *'00*
Diamonds *'99*
BASEketball *'98*
Things to Do in Denver When You're Dead *'95*

Kevin McCarthy (1914-)
Loving Annabelle *'06*
The Sister-in-Law *'95*
Just Cause *'94*
The Distinguished Gentleman *'92*
Duplicates *'92*
Matinee *'92*
Dead on the Money *'91*
Final Approach *'91*
Ghoulies 3: Ghoulies Go to College *'91*
The Rose and the Jackal *'90*
The Sleeping Car *'90*
Texas Guns *'90*
Fast Food *'89*
UHF *'89*
For Love or Money *'88*
LBJ: The Early Years *'88*
Dark Tower *'87*
Hostage *'87*
Innerspace *'87*
Poor Little Rich Girl: The Barbara Hutton Story *'87*
The Midnight Hour *'86*
Invitation to Hell *'84*
Ratings Game *'84*
Twilight Zone: The Movie *'83*
My Tutor *'82*
Rosie: The Rosemary Clooney Story *'82*
The Howling *'81*
Hero at Large *'80*
Those Lips, Those Eyes *'80*
Invasion of the Body Snatchers *'78*
Piranha *'78*
Buffalo Bill & the Indians *'76*
The Seagull *'75*
Dan Candy's Law *'73*
Order to Kill *'73*
Ace High *'68*
Dead Right *'68*
Hotel *'67*
A Big Hand for the Little Lady *'66*
Mirage *'66*
The Three Sisters *'65*
The Best Man *'64*
A Gathering of Eagles *'63*
40 Pounds of Trouble *'62*
Invasion of the Body Snatchers *'56*
An Annapolis Story *'55*
Stranger on Horseback *'55*
Death of a Salesman *'51*

Lin McCarthy (1918-2002)
D.I. *'57*
Yellowneck *'55*

Melissa McCarthy
The Back-Up Plan *'10*
The Nines *'07*

Molly McCarthy
The Flamingo Kid *'84*
Blast of Silence *'61*
The Great St. Louis Bank Robbery *'59*

Neil McCarthy (1933-85)
Where Eagles Dare *'68*
The Hill *'65*

Emer McCourt
Boston Kickout '95
Riff Raff '92
London Kills Me '91

Malachy McCourt (1931-)
Ash Wednesday '02
The Guru '02
JFK: Reckless Youth '93
Q (The Winged Serpent) '82
Manny's Orphans '78

Alec McCowen (1925-)
Gangs of New York '02
Longitude '00
The Age of Innocence '93
Maria's Child '93
Henry V '89
Cry Freedom '87
Personal Services '87
A Dedicated Man '86
Forever Young '85
Hanover Street '79
Stevie '78
Frenzy '72
Travels with My Aunt '72
The Witches '66
A Night to Remember '58
The Silent Enemy '58
Time Without Pity '57

Larry McCoy
The Players Club '98
Bulletproof '96

Lisa Ray McCoy
See LisaRaye

Matt McCoy (1958-)
The Town That Banned Christmas '06
National Security '03
Beethoven's 4th '01
Forever Together '00
Rangers '00
Tales of the Kama Sutra 2: Monsoon '98
Buck and the Magic Bracelet '97
L.A. Confidential '97
Monsoon '97
The Apocalypse '96
Fast Money '96
Little Bigfoot '96
Rent-A-Kid '95
Synapse '95
Bigfoot: The Unforgettable Encounter '94
Hard Bounty '94
Hard Drive '94
The Soft Kill '94
Dead On '93
Samurai Cowboy '93
The Cool Surface '92
Eyes of the Beholder '92
The Hand that Rocks the Cradle '92
Archie: Return to Riverdale '90
Deepstar Six '89
Police Academy 6: City under Siege '89
Police Academy 5: Assignment Miami Beach '88
Fraternity Vacation '85

Sylvester McCoy (1943-)
Doctor Who '96
Spellbreaker: Secret of the Leprechauns '96
Leapin' Leprechauns '95

Tim McCoy (1891-1978)
Run of the Arrow '56
Below the Border '42
Dawn on the Great Divide '42
Down Texas Way '42
Ghost Town Law '42
Riders of the West '42
West of the Law '42
Arizona Bound '41
Forbidden Trails '41
Gunman from Bodie '41
Outlaws of the Rio Grande '41
Arizona Gangbusters '40
Gun Code '40
Fighting Renegade '39
Outlaw's Paradise '39
Texas Wildcats '39
Lightnin' Carson Rides Again '38
Phantom Ranger '38
Six Gun Trail '38
Aces and Eights '36
Border Caballero '36
Ghost Patrol '36
Lightnin' Bill Carson '36
Lion's Den '36
The Man from Gun Town '36
Prescott Kid '36
Roaring Guns '36
The Traitor '36
Bulldog Courage '35
Fighting Shadows '35
Justice of the Range '35
The Outlaw Deputy '35
The Revenge Rider '35
Riding Wild '35
Square Shooter '35
Man of Action '33
Cornered '32
Daring Danger '32
Fighting Fool '32
The Fighting Marshal '32
The Riding Tornado '32
Texas Cyclone '32
Two-Fisted Law '32

Mark McCracken (1960-)
We Were Soldiers '02
Pumpkinhead 2: Blood Wings '94
Matinee '92

Paul McCrane (1961-)
From the Earth to the Moon '98
The Portrait '93
RoboCop '87
Purple Hearts '84
Fame '80

Darius McCrary (1976-)
Next Day Air '09
Transformers '07 (V)
John Carpenter Presents Vampires: Los Muertos '02
15 Minutes '01
Kingdom Come '01
Don King: Only in America '97
Big Shots '87

Jody McCrea (1934-)
Cry Blood, Apache '70
Free Grass '69
The Glory Stompers '67
Beach Blanket Bingo '65
How to Stuff a Wild Bikini '65
Bikini Beach '64
Muscle Beach Party '64
Pajama Party '64
Beach Party '63
Operation Bikini '63
Force of Impulse '60

Joel McCrea (1905-90)
Cry Blood, Apache '70
Ride the High Country '62
The Gunfight at Dodge City '59
Lafayette Escadrille '58
The First Texan '56
The Oklahoman '56
Stranger on Horseback '55
Stars in My Crown '50
Colorado Territory '49
Four Faces West '48
South of St. Louis '48
Border River '47
Ramrod '47
Saddle Tramp '47
The Virginian '46
Buffalo Bill '44
The Great Moment '44
The More the Merrier '43
The Great Man's Lady '42
The Palm Beach Story '42
Sullivan's Travels '41
Foreign Correspondent '40
Primrose Path '40
They Shall Have Music '39
Union Pacific '39
Dead End '37
Internes Can't Take Money '37
Come and Get It '36
These Three '36
Barbary Coast '35
Our Little Girl '35
Splendor '35
One Man's Journey '33
Bird of Paradise '32
Lost Squadron '32
The Most Dangerous Game '32
Kept Husbands '31
The Silver Horde '30

Helen McCrory (1968-)
Fantastic Mr. Fox '09 (V)
Harry Potter and the Half-Blood Prince '09
Flashbacks of a Fool '08
Becoming Jane '07
The Queen '06
Casanova '05
Enduring Love '04
Dead Gorgeous '02
Charlotte Gray '01
Anna Karenina '00
Split Second '99
Dad Savage '97
Uncovered '94

Bruce McCulloch (1961-)
Stealing Harvard '02
Dick '99
Dog Park '98
Kids in the Hall: Brain Candy '96

Ian McCulloch (1940-)
Witching Time '84
Alien Contamination '81
Doctor Butcher M.D. '80
Zombie '80
Running Blind '78

Kyle McCulloch
Careful '92
Tales from the Gimli Hospital '88

Julie McCullough (1965-)
The St. Tammany Miracle '94
Round Trip to Heaven '92
Big Bad Mama 2 '87

Philo (Philip, P.H., P.M.) McCullough (1890-1981)
Captured in Chinatown '35
Ridin' Thru '35
Inside Information '34
Tarzan the Fearless '33
Sunset Trail '32
The Charlatan '29

Mathew McCurley (1982-)
The Secret Agent Club '96
Little Giants '94

Natalie McCurry
Glass '90
Stones of Death '88
Dead End Drive-In '86

Bill McCutcheon (1924-2002)
Mr. Destiny '90
Tune in Tomorrow '90
Family Business '89
Steel Magnolias '89
Santa Claus Conquers the Martians '64

Hattie McDaniel (1895-1952)
Mickey '48
Never Say Goodbye '46
Since You Went Away '44
Johnny Come Lately '43
George Washington Slept Here '42
In This Our Life '42
The Male Animal '42
The Great Lie '41
They Died with Their Boots On '41
Gone with the Wind '39
Carefree '38
Mad Miss Manton '38
Shopworn Angel '38
Saratoga '37
The Bride Walks Out '36
Libeled Lady '36
Show Boat '36
Alice Adams '35
China Seas '35
Harmony Lane '35
The Little Colonel '35
I'm No Angel '33
Blonde Venus '32

James McDaniel (1958-)
Organizm '08
Steel City '06
Sunshine State '02
Taken '02
Deliberate Intent '01
Livin' for Love: The Natalie Cole Story '00
Out of Time '00
The Road to Galveston '96
Malcolm X '92

Charlie McDermott
Frozen River '08
Disappearances '06

Dean McDermott (1966-)
Saving God '08
Open Range '03
Brian's Song '01
The Wall '99

Dylan McDermott (1962-)
The Messengers '07
The Tenants '06
Edison Force '05
The Mistress of Spices '05
Party Monster '03
Wonderland '03
Texas Rangers '01
Three to Tango '99
Til There Was You '96
Destiny Turns on the Radio '95
Home for the Holidays '95
The Cowboy Way '94
Miracle on 34th Street '94
In the Line of Fire '93
The Fear Inside '92
Into the Badlands '92
Jersey Girl '92
Where Sleeping Dogs Lie '91
Hardware '90
The Neon Empire '89
Steel Magnolias '89
Twister '89
Blue Iguana '88
Hamburger Hill '87

Hugh McDermott (1908-72)
Devil Girl from Mars '54
The Seventh Veil '46

Marc McDermott
The Temptress '26
He Who Gets Slapped '24

Ruth McDevitt (1895-1976)
Homebodies '74
Change of Habit '69
The Shakiest Gun in the West '68
The Birds '63
The Parent Trap '61

Ian McDiarmid (1947-)
Elizabeth I '05
Star Wars: Episode 3—Revenge of the Sith '05
Star Wars: Episode 2—Attack of the Clones '02
All the King's Men '99
Sleepy Hollow '99
Star Wars: Episode 1—The Phantom Menace '99
Touching Evil '97
Rasputin: Dark Servant of Destiny '96
Annie: A Royal Adventure '95
The Awakening '80

Amber McDonald
Without a Paddle: Nature's Calling '09
You Tell Me '06

Audra McDonald (1970-)
A Raisin in the Sun '08
It Runs in the Family '03
Wit '01
The Last Debate '00
Annie '99
Having Our Say: The Delany Sisters' First 100 Years '99

Christopher McDonald (1955-)
The House Bunny '08
Mad Money '08
Player 5150 '08
Superhero Movie '08
American Pie Presents: Beta House '07
Awake '07
Kickin' It Old Skool '07
American Pie Presents: The Naked Mile '06
Broken Flowers '05
Rumor Has It... '05
Grind '03
Children On Their Birthdays '02
61* '01
The Theory of the Leisure Class '01
The Perfect Storm '00
Requiem for a Dream '00
The Skulls '00
Gideon '99
The Iron Giant '99 (V)
SLC Punk! '99
The Faculty '98
Dirty Work '97
The Eighteenth Angel '97
Flubber '97
Into Thin Air: Death on Everest '97
Leave It to Beaver '97
Celtic Pride '96
Happy Gilmore '96
House Arrest '96
Jaded '96
Lawn Dogs '96
The Rich Man's Wife '96
A Smile Like Yours '96
Unforgettable '96
Best of the Best 3: No Turning Back '95
Fair Game '95
My Teacher's Wife '95
The Tuskegee Airmen '95
Monkey Trouble '94
Quiz Show '94
Terminal Velocity '94
Benefit of the Doubt '93
Bums '93
Cover Story '93
Fatal Instinct '93
Grumpy Old Men '93
Conflict of Interest '92
Wild Orchid 2: Two Shades of Blue '92
Fatal Exposure '91
Red Wind '91
Thelma & Louise '91
Playroom '90
Chances Are '89
Paramedics '88
The Boys Next Door '85
Breakin' '84
Chattanooga Choo Choo '84
Where the Boys Are '84 '84
Grease 2 '82

Country Joe McDonald (1942-)
Armistead Maupin's Tales of the City '93
Zachariah '70

Francis McDonald (1891-1968)
Spoilers of the North '47
Bad Men of the Border '45
Mystery Man '44
Mystery of the Riverboat '44
Texas Masquerade '44
Zorro's Black Whip '44
The Kansan '43
The Sea Wolf '41
Carson City Kid '40
The Prisoner of Shark Island '36
Terror Trail '33
Hidden Valley '32
Texas Buddies '32
Morocco '30
The Notorious Lady '27
Battling Butler '26
The Confession '20

Garry McDonald (1948-)
The Shepherd: Border Patrol '08
Rabbit-Proof Fence '02
Moulin Rouge '01
Ghosts Can Do It '87
The Wacky World of Wills & Burke '85
Pirate Movie '82

Grace McDonald (1918-99)
Follow the Boys '44
Gung Ho! '43
It Ain't Hay '43

Jeff (Jeffrey) McDonald (1963-)
Sugar Town '99
Spirit of '76 '91

Kenneth McDonald
The Coast Patrol '25
Dynamite Dan '24

Kevin McDonald (1961-)
Lilo & Stitch 2: Stitch Has a Glitch '05 (V)
Sky High '05
Lilo & Stitch '02 (V)
The Godson '98
Kids in the Hall: Brain Candy '96
National Lampoon's Senior Trip '95

Marie McDonald (1923-65)
Promises! Promises! '63
The Geisha Boy '58
Tell It to the Judge '49
Getting Gertie's Garter '45
It's a Pleasure '45
Guest in the House '44

Mary Ann McDonald
Far Cry from Home '81
Love at First Sight '76

Michael McDonald
Outing Riley '04
The Nutcracker Prince '91 (V)

Miriam McDonald
Poison Ivy 4: The Secret Society '08
Sea Beast '08

Peter McDonald (1972-)
Blow Dry '00
Nora '00
When Brendan Met Trudy '00
Felicia's Journey '99
Captain Jack '98
I Went Down '97

Ryan McDonald (1984-)
The Private Lives of Pippa Lee '09
Art of War 2: The Betrayal '08
Resurrecting the Champ '07
The Ballad of Jack and Rose '05

William McDonald
Subhuman '04
Don't Look Down '98

Ryan McDonell
Meltdown '06
Snakehead Terror '04

Mary McDonnell (1952-)
Crazy Like a Fox *'04*
Donnie Darko *'01*
A Father's Choice *'00*
Behind the Mask *'99*
Mumford *'99*
Evidence of Blood *'97*
Twelve Angry Men *'97*
Independence Day *'96*
Woman Undone *'95*
Blue Chips *'94*
Passion Fish *'92*
Sneakers *'92*
Grand Canyon *'91*
Dances with Wolves *'90*
Matewan *'87*
Tiger Warsaw *'87*

Mary (Elizabeth) McDonough (1961-)
The Locket *'02*
Mom *'89*
Snowballing *'85*
A Day for Thanks on Walton's Mountain *'82*
The Waltons: The Christmas Carol *'80*

Neal McDonough (1966-)
Street Fighter: The Legend of Chun-Li *'09*
88 Minutes *'08*
Forever Strong *'08*
Traitor *'08*
Brothers Three *'07*
The Hitcher *'07*
I Know Who Killed Me *'07*
Tin Man *'07*
Flags of Our Fathers *'06*
The Guardian *'06*
The Last Time *'06*
Walking Tall *'04*
Timeline *'03*
Minority Report *'02*
Band of Brothers *'01*
The Killing Club *'01*
Ravenous *'99*
Grace & Glorie *'98*
Balloon Farm *'97*
Robin Cook's Invasion *'97*
Star Trek: First Contact *'96*
Blue River *'95*
White Dwarf *'95*

Jake McDorman (1986-)
Aquamarine *'06*
Bring It On: All or Nothing *'06*

Frances McDormand (1958-)
Burn After Reading *'08*
Miss Pettigrew Lives for a Day *'08*
Friends with Money *'06*
Aeon Flux *'05*
North Country *'05*
Something's Gotta Give *'03*
City by the Sea *'02*
Laurel Canyon *'02*
The Man Who Wasn't There *'01*
Almost Famous *'00*
Wonder Boys *'00*
Madeline *'98*
Johnny Skidmarks *'97*
Paradise Road *'97*
Fargo *'96*
Hidden in America *'96*
Primal Fear *'96*
Talk of Angels *'96*
Beyond Rangoon *'95*
The Good Old Boys *'95*
Lone Star *'95*
Palookaville *'95*
Short Cuts *'93*
Crazy in Love *'92*
Passed Away *'92*
The Butcher's Wife *'91*
Darkman *'90*
Hidden Agenda *'90*
Chattahoochee *'89*
Mississippi Burning *'88*
Raising Arizona *'87*
Blood Simple *'85*
Crimewave *'85*

Betty McDowall (1933-)
Ballad in Blue *'66*
Dead Lucky *'60*
Jack the Ripper *'60*
Time Lock *'57*

Roddy McDowall (1928-98)
A Bug's Life *'98 (V)*
Rudyard Kipling's the Second Jungle Book: Mowgli and Baloo *'97*
Unlikely Angel *'97*
Last Summer In the Hamptons *'96*
The Color of Evening *'95*
Fatally Yours *'95*
The Grass Harp *'95*
It's My Party *'95*
Star Hunter *'95*
Unknown Origin *'95*
Mirror, Mirror 2: Raven Dance *'94*
Heads *'93*
Deadly Game *'91*
Double Trouble *'91*
An Inconvenient Woman *'91*
Around the World in 80 Days *'89*
The Big Picture *'89*
Cutting Class *'89*
Shakma *'89*
Doin' Time on Planet Earth *'88*
Fright Night 2 *'88*
Dead of Winter *'87*
Overboard *'87*
Alice in Wonderland *'85*
Fright Night *'85*
Mae West *'84*
The Zany Adventures of Robin Hood *'84*
Class of 1984 *'82*
Evil under the Sun *'82*
Charlie Chan and the Curse of the Dragon Queen *'81*
The Return of the King *'80 (V)*
The Martian Chronicles: Part 2 *'79*
The Martian Chronicles: Part 3 *'79*
Scavenger Hunt *'79*
The Cat from Outer Space *'78*
Circle of Iron *'78*
Laserblast *'78*
Rabbit Test *'78*
The Thief of Baghdad *'78*
Embryo *'76*
Flood! *'76*
Funny Lady *'75*
Mean Johnny Barrows *'75*
Dirty Mary Crazy Larry *'74*
Arnold *'73*
Battle for the Planet of the Apes *'73*
The Legend of Hell House *'73*
Conquest of the Planet of the Apes *'72*
Life & Times of Judge Roy Bean *'72*
The Poseidon Adventure *'72*
Bedknobs and Broomsticks *'71*
Escape from the Planet of the Apes *'71*
Night Gallery *'69*
Five Card Stud *'68*
Planet of the Apes *'68*
The Adventures of Bullwhip Griffin *'66*
The Defector *'66*
Lord Love a Duck *'66*
The Greatest Story Ever Told *'65*
Inside Daisy Clover *'65*
The Loved One *'65*
That Darn Cat *'65*
Cleopatra *'63*
The Tempest *'63*
The Longest Day *'62*
Midnight Lace *'60*
Hill Number One *'51*
Everybody's Dancin' *'50*
Kidnapped *'48*
Macbeth *'48*
Holiday in Mexico *'46*
The Keys of the Kingdom *'44*
The White Cliffs of Dover *'44*
Lassie, Come Home *'43*
My Friend Flicka *'43*
On the Sunny Side *'42*
Son of Fury *'42*
How Green Was My Valley *'41*
Man Hunt *'41*

Claire McDowell (1877-1966)
Ben-Hur *'26*
The Show Off *'26*
The Big Parade *'25*
West-Bound Limited *'23*

Malcolm McDowell (1943-)
The Book of Eli *'10*
Halloween II *'09*
Suck *'09*
Bolt *'08*
Coco Chanel *'08*
Delgo *'08 (V)*
Doomsday *'08*
Halloween *'07*
The List *'07*
Mirror Wars: Reflection One *'05*
Bobby Jones: Stroke of Genius *'04*
Hidalgo *'04*
The Company *'03*
I'll Sleep When I'm Dead *'03*
Red Roses and Petrol *'03*
Between Strangers *'02*
Firestarter 2: Rekindled *'02*
I Spy *'02*
Just Visiting *'01*
Princess of Thieves *'01*
The Void *'01*
Can of Worms *'00*
Gangster No. 1 *'00*
Island of the Dead *'00*
St. Patrick: The Irish Legend *'00*
Y2K *'99*
The First 9 1/2 Weeks *'98*
My Life So Far *'98*
Asylum *'97*
Hugo Pool *'97*
Mr. Magoo *'97*
Tales from a Parallel Universe: Giga Shadow *'97*
2103: Deadly Wake *'97*
Kids of the Round Table *'96*
Where Truth Lies *'96*
Yesterday's Target *'96*
Cyborg 3: The Recycler *'95*
Fist of the North Star *'95*
Dangerous Indiscretion *'94*
Milk Money *'94*
Star Trek: Generations *'94*
The Surgeon *'94*
Tank Girl *'94*
Bopha! *'93*
Chain of Desire *'93*
Night Train to Venice *'93*
The Player *'92*
The Light in the Jungle *'91*
Class of 1999 *'90*
Disturbed *'90*
Jezebel's Kiss *'90*
Moon 44 *'90*
Buy & Cell *'89*
Sunset *'88*
The Caller *'87*
Monte Carlo *'86*
Gulag *'85*
Merlin and the Sword *'85*
Blue Thunder *'83*
Cross Creek *'83*
Get Crazy *'83*
Little Red Riding Hood *'83*
Britannia Hospital *'82*
Cat People *'82*
Caligula *'80*
Look Back in Anger *'80*
Time After Time *'79*
Voyage of the Damned *'76*
Royal Flash *'75*
O Lucky Man! *'73*
A Clockwork Orange *'71*
Long Ago Tomorrow *'71*
If... *'69*

Nelson McDowell (1870-1947)
Roll, Wagons, Roll *'39*
Desert Phantom *'36*
Feud of the West *'35*
Lightning Bill *'35*
Texas Jack *'35*
Rustler's Roundup *'33*
Come on Tarzan *'32*
Mason of the Mounted *'32*
The Phantom Bullet *'26*
Oliver Twist *'22*
The Last of the Mohicans *'20*

Randy McDowell
Paranormal Activity *'09*
Dance of the Dead *'08*

Trevyn McDowell (1967-)
Mary Shelley's Frankenstein *'94*
Middlemarch *'93*

James McEachin (1930-)
Double Exposure *'93*
Honeyboy *'82*
He Who Walks Alone *'78*
The Dead Don't Die *'75*
The Groundstar Conspiracy *'72*

Ellen McElduff
Working Girls *'87*
Impostors *'80*

Rob McElhenney (1977-)
Latter Days *'04*
The Tollbooth *'04*

Ian McElhinney (1948-)
The Front Line *'06*
The Mapmaker *'01*
Hamlet *'96*
Small Faces *'95*
A Woman's Guide to Adultery *'93*
The Playboys *'92*

Jack McElhone (1994-)
Dear Frankie *'04*
Young Adam *'03*

Natascha (Natasha) McElhone (1971-)
The Company *'07*
Big Nothing *'06*
Ladies in Lavender *'04*
City of Ghosts *'03*
The Other Boleyn Girl *'03*
Feardotcom *'02*
Laurel Canyon *'02*
Solaris *'02*
The Contaminated Man *'01*
Killing Me Softly *'01*
Love's Labour's Lost *'00*
Ronin *'98*
The Truman Show *'98*
Mrs. Dalloway *'97*
The Devil's Own *'96*
Surviving Picasso *'96*

John McEnery (1945-)
Merlin *'98*
Tess of the D'Urbervilles *'98*
When Saturday Comes *'95*
Black Beauty *'94*
The Buddha of Suburbia *'92*
Codename Kyril *'91*
The Krays *'90*
A.D. *'85*
Gulag *'85*
Pope John Paul II *'84*
Schizo *'77*
The Land That Time Forgot *'75*
One Russian Summer *'73*
Bartleby *'70*

Peter McEnery (1940-)
Florence Nightingale *'85*
Pictures *'81*
The Cat and the Canary *'79*
Primal Impulse *'74*
Tales That Witness Madness *'73*
Entertaining Mr. Sloane *'70*
Negatives *'68*
I Killed Rasputin *'67*
The Fighting Prince of Donegal *'66*
The Game Is Over *'66*
The Moon-Spinners *'64*
Victim *'61*

Annie McEnroe (1955-)
Cop *'88*
True Stories *'86*
Howling 2: Your Sister Is a Werewolf *'85*
Purple Hearts *'84*
Warlords of the 21st Century *'82*
The Hand *'81*
Running Scared *'79*

John McEnroe (1959-)
Anger Management *'03*
Mr. Deeds *'02*

Reba McEntire (1955-)
Charlotte's Web *'06 (V)*
The Fox and the Hound 2 *'06 (V)*
One Night at McCool's *'01*
Forever Love *'98*
Buffalo Girls *'95*
Is There Life Out There? *'94*
North *'94*
The Gambler Returns: The Luck of the Draw *'93*
The Man from Left Field *'93*
Tremors *'89*

Barry McEvoy
An Everlasting Piece *'00*
Gloria *'98*

Geraldine McEwan (1932-)
Carrie's War *'04*
Vanity Fair *'04*
Food of Love *'02*
The Magdalene Sisters *'02*
Pure *'02*
Love's Labour's Lost *'00*
The Love Letter *'99*
Titus *'99*
Moses *'96*
Robin Hood: Prince of Thieves *'91*
Henry V *'89*
Oranges Are Not the Only Fruit *'89*
Foreign Body *'86*
Mapp & Lucia *'85*
No Kidding *'60*

Davenia McFadden (1961-)
Smokin' Aces *'07*
Double Jeopardy *'99*

Gates (Cheryl) McFadden (1949-)
Make the Yuletide Gay *'09*
Star Trek: Nemesis *'02*
Star Trek: Insurrection *'98*
Star Trek: First Contact *'96*
Star Trek: Generations *'94*
Taking Care of Business *'90*

Joseph McFadden (1975-)
Cranford *'08*
Dad Savage *'97*
The Crow Road *'96*
Small Faces *'95*

George "Spanky" McFarland (1928-93)
The Aurora Encounter *'85*
Peck's Bad Boy with the Circus *'38*
General Spanky *'36*
The Trail of the Lonesome Pine *'36*
Kentucky Kernels *'34*

Hayley McFarland
Fragments *'08*
An American Crime *'07*

Douglas McFerran
Johnny English *'03*
Antitrust *'00*
Sliding Doors *'97*

William F. McGaha
Iron Horsemen *'71*
The Speed Lovers *'68*

Mark McGann (1961-)
Shackleton *'02*
Endgame *'01*
Samson and Delilah *'96*
Catherine the Great *'95*
Let Him Have It *'91*
John & Yoko: A Love Story *'85*

Paul McGann (1959-)
Vampire Killers *'09*
Kidnapped *'05*
Queen of the Damned *'02*
Horatio Hornblower: The Adventure Continues *'01*
Our Mutual Friend *'98*
FairyTale: A True Story *'97*
Doctor Who *'96*
The One That Got Away *'96*
Catherine the Great *'95*
Afraid of the Dark *'92*
Alien 3 *'92*
Paper Mask *'91*
Innocent Victim *'90*
Dealers *'89*
The Rainbow *'89*
Withnail and I *'87*

Darren McGavin (1922-2006)
Smalltime *'96*
Billy Madison *'94*
Happy Hell Night *'92*
Mastergate *'92*
Perfect Harmony *'91*
Blood & Concrete: A Love Story *'90*
Child in the Night *'90*
Around the World in 80 Days *'89*
By Dawn's Early Light *'89*
Captain America *'89*
Dead Heat *'88*
Sunset *'88*
Raw Deal *'86*
Turk 182! *'85*
The Baron and the Kid *'84*
My Wicked, Wicked Ways *'84*
The Natural *'84*
A Christmas Story *'83*
Power, Passion & Murder *'83*
Firebird 2015 A.D. *'81*
Hangar 18 *'80*
Waikiki *'80*
Ike *'79*
The Martian Chronicles: Part 1 *'79*
The Martian Chronicles: Part 2 *'79*
The Martian Chronicles: Part 3 *'79*
Zero to Sixty *'78*
Airport '77 *'77*
No Deposit, No Return *'76*
The Night Strangler *'72*
Richard Petty Story *'72*
Say Goodbye, Maggie Cole *'72*
The Night Stalker *'71*
Tribes *'70*
Mission Mars *'67*
The Delicate Delinquent *'56*
The Court Martial of Billy Mitchell *'55*
The Man with the Golden Arm *'55*
Summertime *'55*
Queen for a Day *'51*

Patrick McGaw
Dream with the Fishes *'97*
Scorpion Spring *'96*
The Basketball Diaries *'95*
Malicious *'95*
Forbidden Choices *'94*
Amongst Friends *'93*

Jack McGee (1928-2003)
Bread and Roses *'00*
Treehouse Hostage *'99*
Chairman of the Board *'97*
The Last Days of Frankie the Fly *'96*

The Quest '96
Crash and Burn '90

Jack McGee (1948-)
The International '09
21 '08

Vic McGee
Alien Massacre '67
Gallery of Horrors '67
Monsters Crash the Pajama Party '65
Horrors of the Red Planet '64

Vonetta McGee (1948-)
Johnny B. '00
You Must Remember This '92
Brother Future '91
To Sleep with Anger '90
Repo Man '83
The Eiger Sanction '75
The Big Bust Out '73
The Norliss Tapes '73
Shaft in Africa '73
Blacula '72

Johnny Rae McGhee
Love Field '91
Project X '87

William (Bill) McGhee (1930-2007)
1918 '85
Don't Look in the Basement '73

Bruce McGill (1950-)
Law Abiding Citizen '09
Obsessed '09
Recount '08
Vantage Point '08
The Good Life '07
Humble Pie '07
The Lookout '07
Valley of the Heart's Delight '07
Behind Enemy Lines 2: Axis of Evil '06
Outlaw Trail '06
Cinderella Man '05
Elizabethtown '05
Slow Burn '05
Collateral '04
Legally Blonde 2: Red White & Blonde '03
Live from Baghdad '03
Matchstick Men '03
Runaway Jury '03
Path to War '02
The Sum of All Fears '02
Ali '01
Exit Wounds '01
Shallow Hal '01
61* '01
Deep Core '00
The Legend of Bagger Vance '00
Running Mates '00
A Dog of Flanders '99
The Insider '99
Everything That Rises '98
Ground Control '98
Letters from a Killer '98
Murder She Purred: A Mrs. Murphy Mystery '98
Black Sheep '96
Lawn Dogs '96
Rosewood '96
The Good Old Boys '95
Timecop '94
My Cousin Vinny '92
Play Nice '92
The Last Boy Scout '91
Little Vegas '90
Out Cold '89
Three Fugitives '89
End of the Line '88
The Last Innocent Man '87
Waiting for the Moon '87
No Mercy '86
Wildcats '86
Charlotte Forten's Mission: Experiment in Freedom '85
Into the Night '85
Ballad of Gregorio Cortez '83
Silkwood '83
Tough Enough '83
The Hand '81
Whale for the Killing '81
National Lampoon's Animal House '78
Citizens Band '77

Everett McGill (1945-)
My Fellow Americans '96
Under Siege 2: Dark Territory '95
The People under the Stairs '91
Drug Wars: The Camarena Story '90
Jezebel's Kiss '90
Iguana '89
License to Kill '89
Field of Honor '86
Heartbreak Ridge '86
Silver Bullet '85
Dune '84
Quest for Fire '82
Union City '81
Brubaker '80

Paul McGillion
A Dog's Breakfast '07
Loch Ness Terror '07

Kelly McGillis (1957-)
The Monkey's Mask '00
Morgan's Ferry '99
The Settlement '99
At First Sight '98
Ground Control '98
Storm Chasers: Revenge of the Twister '98
The Wicked, Wicked West '97
North '94
The Babe '92
Grand Isle '92
Cat Chaser '90
Winter People '89
The Accused '88
The House on Carroll Street '88
Unsettled Land '88
Made in Heaven '87
Top Gun '86
Witness '85
Code of Honor '84
Reuben, Reuben '83

John C. McGinley (1959-)
Are We Done Yet? '07
Wild Hogs '07
Two Tickets to Paradise '06
Identity '03
Crazy as Hell '02
Stealing Harvard '02
The Animal '01
Highway '01
Get Carter '00
Any Given Sunday '99
The Jack Bull '99
Three to Tango '99
Office Space '98
The Pentagon Wars '98
Flypaper '97
Truth or Consequences, N.M. '97
Mother '96
Nothing to Lose '96
The Rock '96
Set It Off '96
Born to Be Wild '95
Seven '95
Car 54, Where Are You? '94
Mother's Boys '94
On Deadly Ground '94
Surviving the Game '94
Wagons East '94
Hear No Evil '93
The Last Outlaw '93
Watch It '93
Article 99 '92
A Midnight Clear '92
Highlander 2: The Quickening '91
Little Noises '91
Point Break '91
Suffering Bastards '90
Fat Man and Little Boy '89
Lost Angels '89
Prisoners of Inertia '89
Talk Radio '88
Wall Street '87
Platoon '86

Sean McGinley (1956-)
The Tiger's Tale '06
On a Clear Day '05
Freeze Frame '04
Conspiracy of Silence '03
Dead Bodies '03
American Women '00
The Claim '00
Dr. Bell and Mr. Doyle: The Dark Beginnings of Sherlock Holmes '00
The General '98
The Break '97
The Butcher Boy '97
The Informant '97
Resurrection Man '97
Michael Collins '96
Trojan Eddie '96
Braveheart '95
Family '94
The Field '90

Ted McGinley (1958-)
The Note 2: Taking a Chance on Love '09
The Note '07
Daybreak '01
Pearl Harbor '01
Face the Music '00
Dick '99
Every Mother's Worst Fear '98
Major League 3: Back to the Minors '98
Tails You Live, Heads You're Dead '95
Covert Assassin '94
Revenge of the Nerds 4: Nerds in Love '94
Linda '93
Revenge of the Nerds 3: The Next Generation '92
Blue Tornado '90
Physical Evidence '89
Revenge of the Nerds '84

Scott McGinnis (1958-)
You Can't Hurry Love '88
Odd Jobs '85
Thunder Alley '85
Making the Grade '84
Joy Sticks '83

Boris McGiver (1962-)
Connie and Carla '04
Little Odessa '94

John McGiver (1912-75)
Mame '74
The Adventures of Tom Sawyer '73
Arnold '73
Lawman '71
Bachelor in Paradise '69
Midnight Cowboy '69
The Glass Bottom Boat '66
Made in Paris '65
Marriage on the Rocks '65
A Global Affair '63
Man's Favorite Sport? '63
Who's Got the Action? '63
Who's Minding the Store? '63
The Manchurian Candidate '62
Mr. Hobbs Takes a Vacation '62
Period of Adjustment '62
Breakfast at Tiffany's '61
The Gazebo '59
Love in the Afternoon '57
The Man in the Raincoat '57
I Married a Woman '56

Mike McGlone (1972-)
Bad City '06
Fortunes '05
The War Within '05
Hardball '01
Dinner Rush '00
The Bone Collector '99
One Tough Cop '98
Subway Stories '97
Ed '96
She's the One '96
The Brothers McMullen '94

Frank McGlynn (1866-1951)
Rogue's Gallery '44
Western Gold '37
Custer's Last Stand '36
The Prisoner of Shark Island '36
These Three '36
Hopalong Cassidy '35
America '24

Patrick McGoohan (1928-2009)
Treasure Planet '02 (V)
The Phantom '96
A Time to Kill '96
Braveheart '95
Baby... Secret of the Lost Legend '85
Three Sovereigns for Sarah '85
Kings and Desperate Men '83
Jamaica Inn '82
Scanners '81
Hard Way '80
Escape from Alcatraz '79
Brass Target '78
The Man in the Iron Mask '77
Silver Streak '76
Mary, Queen of Scots '71
Ice Station Zebra '68
Koroshi '67
Dr. Syn, Alias the Scarecrow '64
The Three Lives of Thomasina '63
The Quare Fellow '62
I Am a Camera '55

Barry McGovern (1948-)
Miracle at Midnight '98
Braveheart '95
Joe Versus the Volcano '90
Riders to the Sea '88

Elizabeth McGovern (1961-)
A Room With a View '08
Daphne '07
Buffalo Soldiers '01
The Flamingo Rising '01
House of Mirth '00
The Scarlet Pimpernel '99
The Scarlet Pimpernel 2: Mademoiselle Guillotine '99
The Scarlet Pimpernel 3: The Kidnapped King '99
Twice upon a Yesterday '98
The Wings of the Dove '97
Broken Glass '96
The Summer of Ben Tyler '96
Broken Trust '95
King of the Hill '93
Me & Veronica '93
The Favor '92
The Handmaid's Tale '90
A Shock to the System '90
Tune in Tomorrow '90
Women & Men: Stories of Seduction '90
Johnny Handsome '89
She's Having a Baby '88
The Bedroom Window '87
Native Son '86
Once Upon a Time in America '84
Racing with the Moon '84
Lovesick '83
Snow White and the Seven Dwarfs '83
Ragtime '81
Ordinary People '80

Terence McGovern (1942-)
DuckTales the Movie: Treasure of the Lost Lamp '90 (V)
Americathon '79

James McGowan (1960-)
All the Good Ones Are Married '07
Christie's Revenge '07

J(ohn) P(aterson) McGowan (1880-1952)
Heart of the Rockies '37
Hit the Saddle '37
The Three Mesquiteers '36
When Lightning Strikes '34
The Outlaw Tamer '33
Somewhere in Sonora '33
The Red Raiders '27
Red Signals '27

Rose McGowan (1975-)
Fifty Dead Men Walking '08
Death Proof '07
Planet Terror '07
The Black Dahlia '06
The Killing Yard '01
Monkeybone '01
Road to Riches '01
Ready to Rumble '00
The Last Stop '99
Devil in the Flesh '98
Jawbreaker '98
Southie '98
Going All the Way '97
Lewis and Clark and George '97
Phantoms '97
Bio-Dome '96
Nowhere '96
Scream '96
The Doom Generation '95
Encino Man '92

Tom McGowan (1921-)
Dog Gone Love '03
As Good As It Gets '97
Bean '97
The Birdcage '95
Mrs. Parker and the Vicious Circle '94

Zach McGowan
Seal Team '08
The Hunt for Eagle One: Crash Point '06

Michael McGrady
The Deep End of the Ocean '98
Operation Delta Force 2: Mayday '97
Malevolence '95
White Dwarf '95
The Babe '92

Walter McGrail (1888-1970)
Code of the Fearless '39
The Green Hornet '39
The Shadow Strikes '37
Sunset Range '35
Night Nurse '31
The Lone Star Ranger '30

Alethea McGrath
Alien Visitor '95
That Eye, the Sky '94

Brian McGrath
A Love Divided '01
Falling for a Dancer '98

Debra McGrath (1954-)
DC 9/11: Time of Crisis '04
Termini Station '89

Derek McGrath (1951-)
Daniel's Daughter '08
Full of It '07
Stuart Bliss '98
Chameleon '95
Freaked '93
She's Out of Control '89

Douglas McGrath (1958-)
Company Man '00
Pale Rider '85
Porky's '82

Matt McGrath (1969-)
The Notorious Bettie Page '06
The Broken Hearts Club '00
Boys Don't Cry '99
The Imposters '98
1999 '98
The Member of the Wedding '97
Last Breath '96
Bob Roberts '92
Desperate Hours '90

Charles McGraw (1914-80)
Twilight's Last Gleaming '77
The Killer Inside Me '76
A Boy and His Dog '75
Johnny Got His Gun '71
Pendulum '69
Tell Them Willie Boy Is Here '69
The Busy Body '67
In Cold Blood '67
The Birds '63
The Horizontal Lieutenant '62
Cimarron '60
Spartacus '60
The Defiant Ones '58
Saddle the Wind '58
The Bridges at Toko-Ri '55
Loophole '54
The Narrow Margin '52
One Minute to Zero '52
His Kind of Woman '51
Armored Car Robbery '50
Ma and Pa Kettle Go to Town '50
Side Street '50
Border Incident '49
Threat '49
T-Men '47
The Killers '46

Melinda McGraw (1963-)
The Dark Knight '08
Nutty Professor 2: The Klumps '00
Wrongfully Accused '98

Tim McGraw (1967-)
The Blind Side '09
Four Christmases '08
Flicka '06
Black Cloud '04
Friday Night Lights '04

Michael McGreevey (1948-)
The Strongest Man in the World '75
Death of a Gunfighter '69
Sammy, the Way-Out Seal '62

Angela Punch McGregor (1953-)
The Efficiency Expert '92
Double Deal '84
A Test of Love '84
We of the Never Never '82
The Island '80
Survivor '80
The Chant of Jimmie Blacksmith '78
Newsfront '78

Charles McGregor (1922-96)
The Baron '88
Superfly '72

Ewan McGregor (1971-)
The Ghost Writer '10
I Love You Phillip Morris '10
Amelia '09
Angels & Demons '09
The Men Who Stare at Goats '09
Deception '08
Incendiary '08
Cassandra's Dream '07
Alex Rider: Operation Stormbreaker '06
Miss Potter '06
Scenes of a Sexual Nature '06
The Island '05
Robots '05 (V)
Star Wars: Episode 3—Revenge of the Sith '05
Stay '05
Valiant '05 (V)
Big Fish '03
Down With Love '03

Todd McKee (1963-)
Devil in the Flesh 2 *'00*
Blade Boxer *'97*

Michael McKeever
Around the Fire *'98*
Junior *'86*
The Three Stooges Meet Hercules *'61*

Danica McKellar (1976-)
Hack! *'07*
Raising Genius *'04*
Sidekicks *'93*
Camp Cucamonga: How I Spent My Summer Vacation *'90*

Don McKellar (1963-)
Blindness *'08*
Slings & Arrows: Season 2 *'05*
Clean *'04*
The Event *'03*
Sea People *'00*
eXistenZ *'99*
The Passion of Ayn Rand *'99*
Last Night *'98*
The Red Violin *'98*
In the Presence of Mine Enemies *'97*
Never Met Picasso *'96*
When Night Is Falling *'95*
Exotica *'94*
The Adjuster *'91*
Highway 61 *'91*
Roadkill *'89*

Ian McKellen (1939-)
The Prisoner *'09*
The Golden Compass *'07 (V)*
Stardust *'07 (N)*
The Da Vinci Code *'06*
Flushed Away *'06 (V)*
X-Men: The Last Stand *'06*
Asylum *'05*
Doogal *'05 (V)*
Emile *'03*
Lord of the Rings: The Return of the King *'03*
X2: X-Men United *'03*
Lord of the Rings: The Two Towers *'02*
Lord of the Rings: The Fellowship of the Ring *'01*
X-Men *'00*
David Copperfield *'99*
Gods and Monsters *'98*
Apt Pupil *'97*
Bent *'97*
Swept from the Sea *'97*
Rasputin: Dark Servant of Destiny *'96*
Jack and Sarah *'95*
Richard III *'95*
Cold Comfort Farm *'94*
Heaven's a Drag *'94 (N)*
Restoration *'94*
The Shadow *'94*
And the Band Played On *'93*
Armistead Maupin's Tales of the City *'93*
The Ballad of Little Jo *'93*
Six Degrees of Separation *'93*
Scandal *'89*
Windmills of the Gods *'88*
Plenty *'85*
The Keep *'83*
The Scarlet Pimpernel *'82*
Priest of Love *'81*

Alex McKenna (1984-)
Campfire Tales *'98*
Joey *'98*
Safety Patrol *'98*
The Stupids *'95*

Chris(topher) McKenna (1977-)
Prairie Fever *'08*
King of the Ants *'03*

Siobhan McKenna (1923-86)
Doctor Zhivago *'65*
Of Human Bondage *'64*
Playboy of the Western World *'62*
The King of Kings *'61*
The Adventurers *'51*

T.P. McKenna (1929-)
Red Scorpion *'89*
Valmont *'89*
Bleak House *'85*
The Doctor and the Devils *'85*
To the Lighthouse *'83*
James Joyce: A Portrait of the Artist as a Young Man *'77*
All Creatures Great and Small *'74*
Next Victim *'74*
Straw Dogs *'72*
Beast in the Cellar *'70*
The Charge of the Light Brigade *'68*
Ulysses *'67*
Girl with Green Eyes *'64*
The Siege of Sidney Street *'60*

Virginia McKenna (1931-)
Sliding Doors *'97*
The Camomile Lawn *'92*
Duel of Hearts *'92*
The First Olympics: Athens 1896 *'84*
Disappearance *'81*
The Chosen *'77*
Christian the Lion *'76*
The Gathering Storm *'74*
Waterloo *'71*
An Elephant Called Slowly *'69*
Ring of Bright Water *'69*
Born Free *'66*
The Wreck of the Mary Deare *'59*
Carve Her Name with Pride *'58*
The Smallest Show on Earth *'57*
Simba *'55*
The Cruel Sea *'53*

Dallas McKennon (1919-)
Mystery Mansion *'83*
Lady and the Tramp *'55 (V)*

Ben(jamin) McKenzie (1978-)
88 Minutes *'08*
Junebug *'05*

Fay McKenzie (1918-)
Heart of the Rio Grande *'42*
Down Mexico Way *'41*
Death Rides the Range *'40*
Ghost Town Riders *'38*
Boss Cowboy *'35*

Jacqueline McKenzie (1967-)
Divine Secrets of the Ya-Ya Sisterhood *'02*
On the Beach *'00*
Deep Blue Sea *'99*
Under the Lighthouse Dancing *'97*
Angel Baby *'95*
Mr. Reliable: A True Story *'95*
Talk *'94*
Traps *'93*
Romper Stomper *'92*

Julia McKenzie (1941-)
Return to Cranford *'09*
Cranford *'08*
These Foolish Things *'06*
Bright Young Things *'03*
The Old Curiosity Shop *'94*
Shirley Valentine *'89*

Richard McKenzie (1930-)
In Love and War *'91*
Corvette Summer *'78*

Tim McKenzie
The 13th Floor *'88*
The Lighthorsemen *'87*
Gallipoli *'81*

Doug McKeon (1966-)
The Empty Mirror *'99*
From the Earth to the Moon *'98*
Sub Down *'97*
Where the Red Fern Grows: Part 2 *'92*
Breaking Home Ties *'87*
Turnaround *'87*
Heart of a Champion: The Ray Mancini Story *'85*
Mischief *'85*
Desperate Lives *'82*
Night Crossing *'81*
On Golden Pond *'81*
Centennial *'78*

Nancy McKeon (1966-)
Category 6 : Day of Destruction *'04*
Just Write *'97*
The Wrong Woman *'95*
Teresa's Tattoo *'94*
Where the Day Takes You *'92*
The Lightning Incident *'91*
Poison Ivy *'85*
High School USA *'84*

Philip McKeon (1964-)
Red Surf *'90*
Return to Horror High *'87*

Charles McKeown
The Adventures of Baron Munchausen *'89*
Erik the Viking *'89*

Fintan McKeown
Conspiracy of Silence *'03*
Waking Ned Devine *'98*

Leo McKern (1920-2002)
Molokai: The Story of Father Damien *'99*
A Foreign Field *'93*
Monsignor Quixote *'91*
Travelling North *'87*
Agatha Christie's Murder with Mirrors *'85*
Ladyhawke *'85*
The French Lieutenant's Woman *'81*
The Blue Lagoon *'80*
The House on Garibaldi Street *'79*
The Adventures of Sherlock Holmes' Smarter Brother *'78*
Candleshoe *'78*
The Omen *'76*
Massacre in Rome *'73*
Ryan's Daughter *'70*
The Shoes of the Fisherman *'68*
The Amorous Adventures of Moll Flanders *'65*
Help! *'65*
King and Country *'64*
Doctor in Distress *'63*
The Horse Without a Head *'63*
The Day the Earth Caught Fire *'61*
The Mouse That Roared *'59*
Time Without Pity *'57*
X The Unknown *'56*

Kevin McKidd (1973-)
Percy Jackson & The Olympians: The Lightning Thief *'10*
Made of Honor *'08*
Hannibal Rising *'07*
The Last Legion *'07*
Kingdom of Heaven *'05*
De-Lovely *'04*
The Purifiers *'04*
16 Years of Alcohol *'03*
Max *'02*
Dog Soldiers *'01*
Anna Karenina *'00*
Topsy Turvy *'99*
The Acid House *'98*
Bedrooms and Hallways *'98*
Behind the Lines *'97*
Dad Savage *'97*
Small Faces *'95*
Trainspotting *'95*

Robert McKim (1886-1927)
The Bat *'26*
Heart's Haven *'22*
Monte Cristo *'22*
Wagon Tracks *'19*
Blue Blazes Rawden *'18*
Hell's Hinges *'16*
The Disciple *'15*

Bill McKinney (1931-)
Undertow *'04*
Asylum of the Damned *'03*
It Came from Outer Space 2 *'95*
City Slickers 2: The Legend of Curly's Gold *'94*
Lone Justice 2 *'93*
The China Lake Murders *'90*
Against All Odds *'84*
Heart Like a Wheel *'83*
St. Helen's, Killer Volcano *'82*
Tex *'82*
Bronco Billy *'80*
The Gauntlet *'77*
Cannonball *'76*
The Outlaw Josey Wales *'76*
The Shootist *'76*
The Parallax View *'74*
Deliverance *'72*
Angel Unchained *'70*
She-Freak *'67*

Gregory McKinney (1957-98)
Recoil *'97*
Star Quest *'94*
A Brilliant Disguise *'93*

Kurt McKinney (1962-)
Cupid & Cate *'00*
Sworn to Justice *'97*
No Retreat, No Surrender *'86*

Mark McKinney (1959-)
Slings & Arrows: Season 2 *'05*
Falling Angels *'03*
The Saddest Music in the World *'03*
Jacob Two Two Meets the Hooded Fang *'99*
The Out-of-Towners *'99*
Superstar *'99*
Dog Park *'98*
A Night at the Roxbury *'98*
Spice World: The Movie *'97*
Kids in the Hall: Brain Candy *'96*

Mira McKinney (1892-1978)
Heart of the Rockies *'51*
Rough Riders of Cheyenne *'45*
Double Trouble *'41*

Nina Mae McKinney (1912-67)
Pinky *'49*
The Devil's Daughter *'39*
Hallelujah! *'29*

Mona McKinnon (1929-90)
Plan 9 from Outer Space *'56*
Jail Bait *'54*

Ray McKinnon (1957-)
The Blind Side *'09*
That Evening Sun *'09*
The Missing *'03*
The Badge *'02*
O Brother Where Art Thou? *'00*
Goodbye, Lover *'99*
Larry McMurtry's Dead Man's Walk *'96*
The Net *'95*
A Perfect World *'93*
Indecency *'92*
Paris Trout *'91*

Craig McLachlan (1965-)
The Great Raid *'05*
Absent Without Leave *'95*

Clifford McLaglen (1892-1978)
Late Extra *'35*
The Mystery of the Mary Celeste *'35*

Victor McLaglen (1886-1959)
Around the World in 80 Days *'56*
Lady Godiva *'55*
Many Rivers to Cross *'55*
Prince Valiant *'54*
Trouble in the Glen *'54*
The Quiet Man *'52*
Rio Grande *'50*
She Wore a Yellow Ribbon *'49*
Fort Apache *'48*
Whistle Stop *'46*
The Princess and the Pirate *'44*
Forever and a Day *'43*
Call Out the Marines *'42*
Broadway Limited *'41*
South of Pago Pago *'40*
Gunga Din *'39*
Let Freedom Ring *'39*
Devil's Party *'38*
Sea Devils *'37*
Wee Willie Winkie *'37*
Klondike Annie *'36*
The Informer *'35*
The Lost Patrol *'34*
Murder at the Vanities *'34*
No More Women *'34*
Laughing at Life *'33*
Dishonored *'31*
Women of All Nations *'31*
A Girl in Every Port *'28*
Hangman's House *'28*
The Unholy Three *'25*

Brandon Jay McLaren
Dr. Dolittle: Million Dollar Mutts *'09*
She's the Man *'06*

Hollis McLaren
Atlantic City *'81*
Lost and Found *'79*
Outrageous! *'77*
Vengeance Is Mine *'74*

Ron McLarty (1947-)
Into the Fire *'05*
Mean Streak *'99*
The Postman *'97*
Two Bits *'96*
The Feud *'90*
Enormous Changes *'83*
Tiger Town *'83*
Trumps *'83*

Bill McLaughlin
Silk *'86*
Naked Vengeance *'85*

Duane McLaughlin
Finding Buck McHenry *'00*
The Runaway *'00*

Dylan McLaughlin
Alice Upside Down *'07*
Kicking & Screaming *'05*

Ellen McLaughlin (1957-)
Everything Relative *'96*
The Bed You Sleep In *'93*

Gibb McLaughlin (1884-1960)
Inspector Hornleigh *'39*
Mr. Reeder in Room 13 *'38*
Bulldog Jack *'35*
The Old Curiosity Shop *'35*
Power *'34*
The Scarlet Pimpernel *'34*
The Private Life of Henry VIII *'33*

Maya McLaughlin
Milo *'98*
Children of the Night *'92*

David McLean (1922-95)
Death Sport *'78*
Hughes & Harlow: Angels in Hell *'77*

The Strangler *'64*

B.J. McLellan
Little Men *'98*
Summer of the Monkeys *'98*

Zoe McLellan (1974-)
Dungeons and Dragons *'00*
Stonebrook *'98*

Catherine McLeod (1921-97)
A Blueprint for Murder *'53*
Sword of Venus *'53*
I've Always Loved You *'46*

Duncan McLeod (1918-)
Tomb of the Undead *'72*
Beyond the Valley of the Dolls *'70*

Gordon McLeod (1890-1961)
Meet Sexton Blake *'44*
Clouds over Europe *'39*

Kenneth McLeod
Virtual Combat *'95*
Deadly Target *'94*
Guardian Angel *'94*
Out for Blood *'93*
Showdown *'93*
Judgment Day *'88*

Samantha McLeod
Snakes on a Plane *'06*
Insecticidal *'05*

Allyn Ann McLerie (1926-)
Living Proof: The Hank Williams Jr. Story *'83*
And Baby Makes Six *'79*
A Shining Season *'79*
Death Scream *'75*
Someone I Touched *'75*
Cinderella Liberty *'73*
The Way We Were *'73*
Jeremiah Johnson *'72*
They Shoot Horses, Don't They? *'69*
Calamity Jane *'53*
The Desert Song *'53*

John McLiam (1918-94)
Split Decisions *'88*
The Ambush Murders *'82*
The Five of Me *'81*
Freedom Road *'79*
The Iceman Cometh *'73*
Showdown *'73*
Sleeper *'73*
Cool Hand Luke *'67*
In Cold Blood *'67*

Rachel McLish (1955-)
Ravenhawk *'95*
Aces: Iron Eagle 3 *'92*

Marshall McLuhan (1911-80)
Third Walker *'79*
Annie Hall *'77*

Pauline McLynn (1962-)
An Everlasting Piece *'00*
When Brendan Met Trudy *'00*
Angela's Ashes *'99*

Ed McMahon (1923-2009)
For Which He Stands *'98*
Safety Patrol *'98*
Just Write *'97*
Butterfly *'82*
Great American Traffic Jam *'80*
The Kid from Left Field *'79*
Fun with Dick and Jane *'77*
Slaughter's Big Ripoff *'73*
The Incident *'67*
Daughter of Horror *'55 (N)*

Horace McMahon (1906-71)
The Detective *'68*
Never Steal Anything Small *'59*

The Delicate Delinquent '56
My Sister Eileen '55
Abbott and Costello Go to Mars '53
Detective Story '51
Birth of the Blues '41
Melody Ranch '40
The Wrong Road '37

Julian McMahon (1968-)
Meet Market '08
Fantastic Four: Rise of the Silver Surfer '07
Premonition '07
Prisoner '07
Fantastic Four '05
Chasing Sleep '00
Magenta '96
Wet and Wild Summer '92

Cody McMains (1985-)
Madison '01
Not Another Teen Movie '01
Bring It On '00

Don McManus
The 6th Day '00
True Colors '91

James McManus
Black Dynamite '09
La Cucaracha '99
The Big Empty '98

Michael McManus (1961-)
Hard to Forget '98
Tales from a Parallel Universe: Eating Pattern '97
Tales from a Parallel Universe: Giga Shadow '97
Tales from a Parallel Universe: I Worship His Shadow '97
Tales from a Parallel Universe: Super Nova '97
Funland '89
Speaking Parts '89
Poltergeist '82
Captain America '79

John McMartin (1929-)
No Reservations '07
Kinsey '04
The Dish '00
Separate but Equal '91
Little Sweetheart '90
A Shock to the System '90
Day One '89
Gore Vidal's Lincoln '88
Roots: The Gift '88
Legal Eagles '86
Murrow '86
Native Son '86
Dream Lover '85
Private Contentment '83
Sweet Charity '69

Niles McMaster
Alice Sweet Alice '76
Bloodsucking Freaks '75

Ciaran McMenamin (1975-)
The Last Minute '01
To End All Wars '01
David Copperfield '99
The Trench '99

Kenneth McMillan (1932-89)
Three Fugitives '89
Malone '87
Acceptable Risks '86
Armed and Dangerous '86
Cat's Eye '85
Dixie: Changing Habits '85
Runaway Train '85
Concrete Beat '84
Dune '84
Killing Hour '84
The Pope of Greenwich Village '84
Protocol '84
Reckless '84
Blue Skies Again '83
In the Custody of Strangers '82
Partners '82
Eyewitness '81
Heartbeeps '81
Ragtime '81
True Confessions '81
Whose Life Is It Anyway? '81
Borderline '80
Carny '80
Hide in Plain Sight '80
Chilly Scenes of Winter '79
Salem's Lot '79
Bloodbrothers '78
Girlfriends '78
Johnny We Hardly Knew Ye '77
The Taking of Pelham One Two Three '74

Richard McMillan
Cube: Zero '04
A Different Loyalty '04
The Sandy Bottom Orchestra '00
Bram Stoker's Shadowbuilder '98
Naked City: A Killer Christmas '98
M. Butterfly '93
Ordeal in the Arctic '93

Roddy McMillan (1923-79)
Killer with Two Faces '74
The Battle of the Sexes '60

Ross McMillan
The Saddest Music in the World '03
The Twilight of the Ice Nymphs '97

W.G. McMillan
See Will MacMillan

James McMullan (1929-)
Sex Through a Window '72
Shenandoah '65

Sam McMurray (1952-)
Lake Placid 2 '07
Stealing Sinatra '04
Lone Star State of Mind '02
Lucky Numbers '00
Drop Dead Gorgeous '99
The Mod Squad '99
Slappy and the Stinkers '97
Savage '96
Getting Even with Dad '94
National Lampoon's Attack of the 5 Ft. 2 Women '94
L.A. Story '91
Stone Cold '91
Raising Arizona '87
C.H.U.D. '84
Union City '81

Pamela McMyler
Blood Beach '81
The $5.20 an Hour Dream '80
The Stick-Up '77

Mercedes McNab (1981-)
The Pink Conspiracy '07
White Wolves 3: Cry of the White Wolf '98
Escape from Atlantis '97
Savage Land '94
Addams Family Values '93

Barbara McNair (1934-2007)
The Organization '71
They Call Me Mr. Tibbs! '70
Venus in Furs '70
Change of Habit '69
Stiletto '69
Dead Right '68

Kevin McNally (1956-)
Valkyrie '08
Pirates of the Caribbean: At World's End '07
Pirates of the Caribbean: Dead Man's Chest '06
Bloodlines '05
Irish Jam '05
De-Lovely '04
The Phantom of the Opera '04
Johnny English '03
Pirates of the Caribbean: The Curse of the Black Pearl '03
Shackleton '02
Conspiracy '01
High Heels and Low Lifes '01
When the Sky Falls '99
Abraham '94
Jekyll and Hyde '90
Cry Freedom '87
The Berlin Affair '85
Poldark 2 '75

Stephen McNally (1913-94)
Dear Detective '78
Hi-Riders '77
Black Gunn '72
The Fiend Who Walked the West '58
Tribute to a Bad Man '56
A Bullet Is Waiting '54
Make Haste to Live '54
Devil's Canyon '53
Split Second '53
The Black Castle '52
Diplomatic Courier '52
Duel at Silver Creek '52
No Way Out '50
Winchester '73 '50
Criss Cross '48
Magnificent Doll '46
Thirty Seconds Over Tokyo '44
Air Raid Wardens '43
For Me and My Gal '42
Keeper of the Flame '42

Terrance McNally (1939-)
Earth Girls Are Easy '89
Tap '89

Brian McNamara (1960-)
The Gunman '03
The Ghost of Spoon River '00
Where the Truth Lies '99
Mystery Date '91
When the Party's Over '91
Arachnophobia '90
The Betty Ford Story '87
Billionaire Boys Club '87
Short Circuit '86
Detective Sadie & Son '84

Julianne McNamara (1965-)
Class of Fear '91
Saturday the 14th Strikes Back '88

Maggie McNamara (1928-78)
The Cardinal '63
Three Coins in the Fountain '54
The Moon Is Blue '53

Pat McNamara
Ash Wednesday '02
Commandments '96
The Daytrippers '96
Trusting Beatrice '92

William McNamara (1965-)
Time Lapse '01
Paper Bullets '99
Implicated '98
Ringmaster '98
Sweet Jane '98
Glam '97
Stag '97
The Brylcreem Boys '96
Natural Enemy '96
Copycat '95
Storybook '95
Black Water '94
Chasers '94
Girl in the Cadillac '94
Radio Inside '94
Surviving the Game '94
Doing Time on Maple Drive '92
Wildflower '91
Texasville '90
Dream a Little Dream '89
The Beat '88
Opera '88
Stealing Home '88

Penny McNamee
See No Evil '06
Salem's Lot '04

Gus McNaughton (1881-1969)
Clouds over Europe '39
Sidewalks of London '38
The 39 Steps '35

Julia McNeal (1961-)
The Refrigerator '91
The Unbelievable Truth '90

Howard McNear (1905-69)
Kiss Me, Stupid! '64
Fun in Acapulco '63
The Errand Boy '61
Follow That Dream '61
Escape from Fort Bravo '53

Ian McNeice (1950-)
The Black Dahlia '06
The Hitchhiker's Guide to the Galaxy '05 (V)
Oliver Twist '05
White Noise '05
Around the World in 80 Days '04
Freeze Frame '04
Children of Dune '03
I'll Be There '03
The Body '01
Conspiracy '01
The Fourth Angel '01
Dune '00
A Certain Justice '99
David Copperfield '99
The Beautician and the Beast '97
A Life Less Ordinary '97
Ace Ventura: When Nature Calls '95
The Englishman Who Went up a Hill But Came down a Mountain '95
Funny Bones '94
No Escape '94
The Blackheath Poisonings '92
Year of the Comet '92
The Russia House '90
Valmont '89
The Lonely Passion of Judith Hearne '87

Claudia McNeil (1916-93)
Roll of Thunder, Hear My Cry '78
Cry Panic '74
The Migrants '74
A Raisin in the Sun '61

Kate McNeil (1959-)
One Kill '00
Escape Clause '96
Shadow Dancer '96
Sudden Death '95
Monkey Shines '88
The House on Sorority Row '83

Scott McNeil (1962-)
Bionicle 3: Web of Shadows '05 (V)
Sleeping with Strangers '94

Jimmy (James Vincent) McNichol (1967-)
Escape from El Diablo '83
Blinded by the Light '82
Night Warning '82
Smokey Bites the Dust '81

Kristy McNichol (1962-)
Baby of the Bride '91
The Forgotten One '89
Two Moon Junction '88
You Can't Hurry Love '88
Women of Valor '86
Dream Lover '85
Just the Way You Are '84
Blinded by the Light '82
Pirate Movie '82
White Dog '82
The Night the Lights Went Out in Georgia '81
Only When I Laugh '81
Little Darlings '80
My Old Man '79
The End '78
The Summer of My German Soldier '78

Kevin McNulty (1955-)
A Call to Remember '97
Tricks '97
Maternal Instincts '96
Titanic '96
Live Bait '95
The NeverEnding Story 3: Escape from Fantasia '94
Timecop '94
Anything for Love '93
Impolite '92

Matthew McNulty (1982-)
Messengers 2: The Scarecrow '09
Return to Cranford '09
See No Evil: The Moors Murders '06

Sandy McPeak (1935-97)
Eye on the Sparrow '91
Inside Out '91
The Flight '89
The Taking of Flight 847: The Uli Derickson Story '88
My Mother's Secret Life '84
Tarantulas: The Deadly Cargo '77
Ode to Billy Joe '76

Marnie McPhail (1966-)
Stir of Echoes 2: The Homecoming '07
The Greatest Game Ever Played '05
RFK '02

Kris McQuade (1952-)
December Boys '07
Ned Kelly '03
Better Than Sex '00
Billy's Holiday '95
Resistance '92
Strictly Ballroom '92
Two Friends '86
The Coca-Cola Kid '84

Murdock McQuarrie
See Murdock MacQuarrie

Butterfly McQueen (1911-95)
The Mosquito Coast '86
The Adventures of Huckleberry Finn '85
Amazing Grace '74
Killer Diller '48
Duel in the Sun '46
I Dood It '43
Gone with the Wind '39

Chad McQueen (1960-)
Surface to Air '98
Trail of a Serial Killer '98
Red Line '96
Indecent Behavior 2 '94
Money to Burn '94
New York Cop '94
Number One Fan '94
Death Ring '93
Firepower '93
Possessed by the Night '93
Sexual Malice '93
Where the Red Fern Grows: Part 2 '92
Martial Law '90
Nightforce '86
Fever Pitch '85
The Karate Kid '84
Skateboard '77

Justus E. McQueen
See L.Q. Jones

Steve McQueen (1930-80)
Minutemen '08
The Hunter '80
Tom Horn '80
An Enemy of the People '77
The Towering Inferno '74
Papillon '73
The Getaway '72
Junior Bonner '72
Le Mans '71
The Reivers '69
Bullitt '68
The Thomas Crown Affair '68
Nevada Smith '66
The Sand Pebbles '66
The Cincinnati Kid '65
Baby, the Rain Must Fall '64
The Great Escape '63
Love with the Proper Stranger '63
Soldier in the Rain '63
Hell Is for Heroes '62
War Lover '62
The Honeymoon Machine '61
The Magnificent Seven '60
The Great St. Louis Bank Robbery '59
Never So Few '59
The Blob '58
Never Love a Stranger '58
Somebody Up There Likes Me '56

Alan McRae
3 Ninjas: High Noon at Mega Mountain '97
3 Ninjas '92
The Slayer '82

Elizabeth McRae
The Conversation '74
The Incredible Mr. Limpet '64

Frank McRae (1952-)
Asteroid '97
Lightning Jack '94
Last Action Hero '93
Sketch Artist '92
Farewell to the King '89
License to Kill '89
Lock Up '89
*batteries not included '87
National Lampoon's Vacation '83
Cannery Row '82
1941 '79

Hilton McRae (1949-)
Voices from a Locked Room '95
The Secret Rapture '94

Leslie McRae
Blood Orgy of the She-Devils '74
Girl in Gold Boots '69

Gerald McRaney (1948-)
The A-Team '10
Get Low '09
Saving Shiloh '06
Ike: Countdown to D-Day '04
Danger Beneath the Sea '02
Take Me Home: The John Denver Story '00
Murder by Moonlight '91
Blind Vengeance '90
Dynamite and Gold '88
City Killer '87
Hobo's Christmas '87
American Justice '86
The NeverEnding Story '84
The Haunting Passion '83
Mind Warp '72
Night of Bloody Horror '69

Peter McRobbie (1943-)
The Notorious Bettie Page '06
Brokeback Mountain '05
Corn '02
Kill by Inches '99
The Neon Bible '95

And the Band Played On '93
Johnny Suede '92

Ian McShane (1942-)
Case 39 '10
Coraline '09 (V)
Death Race '08
Kung Fu Panda '08 (V)
The Golden Compass '07 (V)
Hot Rod '07
The Seeker: The Dark Is Rising '07
Shrek the Third '07 (V)
Scoop '06
We Are Marshall '06
Nine Lives '05
Agent Cody Banks '03
Nemesis Game '03
Sexy Beast '00
D.R.E.A.M. Team '99
Grand Larceny '92
War & Remembrance: The Final Chapter '89
The Great Escape 2: The Untold Story '88
War & Remembrance '88
Young Charlie Chaplin '88
The Murders in the Rue Morgue '86
A.D. '85
Too Scared to Scream '85
Torchlight '85
Ordeal by Innocence '84
Exposed '83
The Grace Kelly Story '83
Disraeli '79
The Fifth Musketeer '79
The Great Riviera Bank Robbery '79
Yesterday's Hero '79
Code Name: Diamond Head '77
Journey into Fear '74
The Terrorists '74
The Last of Sheila '73
Freelance '71
Battle of Britain '69
If It's Tuesday, This Must Be Belgium '69

Jenny (Jennifer) McShane
Shark Attack 3: Megalodon '02
The Watcher '00
Shark Attack '99
Tales of the Kama Sutra 2: Monsoon '98
Monsoon '97
Stag '97
The Rage '96
Terminal Impact '95
Never Say Die '94
Hit the Dutchman '92

Kitty McShane (1898-1964)
Old Mother Riley's Jungle Treasure '51
Old Mother Riley, Headmistress '50
Old Mother Riley's New Venture '49
Old Mother Riley's Ghosts '41

Michael McShane (1957-)
Happily N'Ever After '07 (V)
Memron '04
Kaena: The Prophecy '03 (V)
Treasure Planet '02 (V)
Drop Dead Gorgeous '99
A Bug's Life '98 (V)
Office Space '98
Tom and Huck '95
Richie Rich '94
Robin Hood: Prince of Thieves '91

Gerard McSorley (1950-)
The Front Line '06
Middletown '06
The Constant Gardener '05
Rory O'Shea Was Here '04
Dead Bodies '03
Veronica Guerin '03
Bloody Sunday '01
Felicia's Journey '99
Ordinary Decent Criminal '99
The Boxer '97
Michael Collins '96
Some Mother's Son '96
Moondance '95
Nothing Personal '95
An Awfully Big Adventure '94
Widow's Peak '94
In the Name of the Father '93

Monica McSwain
What About Your Friends: Weekend Getaway '02
The Little Match Girl '84

Virginia McSweeney
See Virginia Valli

Malcolm "Bud" McTaggart (1910-49)
Billy the Kid Trapped '42
Meet the Mob '42
Gangs of Sonora '41
Six Gun Rhythm '39

Graham McTavish
Green Street Hooligans 2 '09
Pandemic '09
Rambo '08

Janet McTeer (1962-)
Daphne '07
Five Days '07
Sense & Sensibility '07
As You Like It '06
Tideland '05
The Intended '02
The King Is Alive '00
Waking the Dead '00
Songcatcher '99
Tumbleweeds '98
Carrington '95
Saint-Ex: The Story of the Storyteller '95
Catherine Cookson's The Black Velvet Gown '92
Emily Bronte's Wuthering Heights '92
Hawks '89

Patrick McVey (1910-73)
Top of the Heap '72
Desperate Characters '71
The Detective '68

Paul McVey (1898-1973)
Phantom of Chinatown '40
Buried Alive '39

Tyler McVey (1912-2003)
The Gallant Hours '60
Attack of the Giant Leeches '59
Night of the Blood Beast '58
From Here to Eternity '53

Daniel McVicar (1958-)
Alone in the Woods '95
Guardian Angel '94
Scorned '93

Margaret McWade (1872-1956)
Mr. Deeds Goes to Town '36
Theodora Goes Wild '36
The Confession '20

Robert McWade (1872-1938)
California Straight Ahead! '37
Healer '36
Next Time We Love '36
Kept Husbands '31
Feet First '30

Jillian McWhirter
The Dentist 2: Brace Yourself '98
Progeny '98
Bloodfist 7: Manhunt '95
Last Man Standing '95
Rage '95
Stranglehold '94
Beyond the Call of Duty '92
Dune Warriors '91
After Midnight '89

Caroline McWilliams (1945-)
Switched at Birth '91
Mermaids '90
Into Thin Air '85
Shattered Vows '84
Rage '80

Anne Meacham (1925-)
Seizure '74
Lilith '64

Courtland Mead (1988-)
Emma's Wish '98
Tom and Huck '95
Dragonworld '94
The Little Rascals '94

Taylor Mead (1924-)
Coffee and Cigarettes '03
Frogs for Snakes '98
Superstar: The Life and Times of Andy Warhol '90

Jayne Meadows (1920-)
The Story of Us '99
Casino '95
The Player '92
City Slickers '91
Murder by Numbers '89
Ratings Game '84
Miss All-American Beauty '82
James Dean '76
Norman, Is That You? '76
David and Bathsheba '51
The Luck of the Irish '48
Song of the Thin Man '47
Lady in the Lake '46

Joyce Meadows
Zebra in the Kitchen '65
The Girl in Lover's Lane '60
The Brain from Planet Arous '57
Flesh and the Spur '57

Stanley Meadows (1931-)
Performance '70
The Terrornauts '67

Stephen Meadows
Sunstroke '92
Ultraviolet '91
A Cry in the Wild '90
The End of Innocence '90

Tim Meadows (1961-)
Grown Ups '10
Aliens in the Attic '09
Shredderman Rules '07
Walk Hard: The Dewey Cox Story '07
The Benchwarmers '06
The Cookout '04
Mean Girls '04
The Ladies Man '00
It's Pat: The Movie '94

Karen Meagher
Wide Sargasso Sea '06
Threads '85
Experience Preferred.. But Not Essential '83

Ray Meagher (1944-)
Dark Age '88
Bootleg '85
Nowhere to Hide '83
Breaker Morant '80
The Odd Angry Shot '79
The Chant of Jimmie Blacksmith '78

Colm Meaney (1953-)
Alice '09
The Damned United '09
Law Abiding Citizen '09
Kings '07
Five Fingers '06
The Hades Factor '06
A Lobster Tale '06
Layer Cake '05
The Boys and Girl From County Clare '03
King of Texas '02
How Harry Became a Tree '01
Four Days '99
The Magical Legend of the Leprechauns '99
Mystery, Alaska '99
This Is My Father '99
Monument Ave. '98
Claire Dolan '97
Con Air '97
The Last of the High Kings '96
The Englishman Who Went up a Hill But Came down a Mountain '95
The Van '95
War of the Buttons '95
The Road to Wellville '94
Scarlett '94
The Snapper '93
Far and Away '92
Into the West '92
The Last of the Mohicans '92
The Commitments '91
Die Hard 2: Die Harder '90

Kevin Meaney
Shut Up and Kiss Me '05
Plump Fiction '97

Russell Means (1939-)
Pathfinder '07
Unearthed '07
Black Cloud '04
Cowboy Up '00
Black Cat Run '98
Wind River '98
Buffalo Girls '95
Natural Born Killers '94
The Pathfinder '94
Wagons East '94
Windrunner '94
The Last of the Mohicans '92

Anne Meara (1929-)
Night at the Museum '06
Like Mike '02
Get Well Soon '01
The Independent '00
Judy Berlin '99
Southie '98
The Daytrippers '96
The Search for One-Eye Jimmy '96
Heavyweights '94
Kiss of Death '94
Reality Bites '94
Awakenings '90
That's Adequate '90
My Little Girl '87
The Longshot '86
Fame '80
Nasty Habits '77
Lovers and Other Strangers '70
The Out-of-Towners '70

Michael Mears (1957-)
Sylvia '03
Sharpe's Legend '97
The Old Curiosity Shop '94
Sharpe's Rifles '93

Scott Mechlowicz (1981-)
Peaceful Warrior '06
Eurotrip '04
Mean Creek '04

Julio Oscar Mechoso (1955-)
Janky Promoters '09
The Go-Getter '07
Planet Terror '07
The Legend of Zorro '05
The Lost City '05
Assassination Tango '03
Pumpkin '02
Heartbreakers '01
Jurassic Park 3 '01
All the Pretty Horses '00
Missing Pieces '00
Krippendorf's Tribe '98
Virus '98
Switchback '97
White Squall '96
Bad Boys '95

Karen Medak
Galaxies Are Colliding '92
Treacherous Crossing '92
A Girl to Kill For '90

Kay Medford (1920-80)
Windows '80
Lola '69
Funny Girl '68
The Busy Body '67
A Fine Madness '66
Butterfield 8 '60
The Rat Race '60

Harriet Medin (1914-2005)
Blood Beach '81
Blood and Black Lace '64
The Ghost '63
The Whip and the Body '63
The Horrible Dr. Hichcock '62

Ofelia Medina (1950-)
Innocent Voices '04
Frida '84

Patricia Medina (1920-)
The Big Push '75
The Killing of Sister George '69
Latitude Zero '69
Snow White and the Three Stooges '61
Missiles from Hell '58
Mr. Arkadin '55
Botany Bay '53
Abbott and Costello in the Foreign Legion '50
The Jackpot '50
Francis the Talking Mule '49
The Three Musketeers '48
Hotel Reserve '44
The Day Will Dawn '42
Spitfire '42
Dinner at the Ritz '37

Frank Medrano (1954-)
Shade '03
The Apostate '98
Kissing a Fool '98
The Replacement Killers '98
Telling You '98
Winchell '98
Suicide Kings '97
The Fan '96
Sleepers '96

Heather Medway
Serpent's Lair '95
The Fear '94

Michael Medwin (1923-)
The Jigsaw Man '84
A Countess from Hong Kong '67
Rattle of a Simple Man '64
Above Us the Waves '56
Genevieve '53
Four in a Jeep '51
Someone at the Door '50
The Gay Lady '49
The Courtney Affair '47

Lew Meehan (1890-1951)
Feud Maker '38
Thunder in the Desert '38
Melody of the Plains '37
Ridin' the Lone Trail '37
Feud of the West '35
Range Riders '35
Ridin' Thru '35
Texas Jack '35
The Silver Bullet '34
Whistlin' Dan '32
The Man From Oklahoma '26
Road Agent '26
Backfire '22

Donald Meek (1880-1946)
Fabulous Joe '47
Magic Town '47
Because of Him '45
Colonel Effingham's Raid '45
State Fair '45
Bathing Beauty '44
The Thin Man Goes Home '44
Two Girls and a Sailor '44
Air Raid Wardens '43
Du Barry Was a Lady '43
They Got Me Covered '43
Keeper of the Flame '42
Tortilla Flat '42
A Woman's Face '41
Dr. Ehrlich's Magic Bullet '40
My Little Chickadee '40
Return of Frank James '40
Blondie Takes a Vacation '39
Hollywood Cavalcade '39
Jesse James '39
Stagecoach '39
Young Mr. Lincoln '39
The Adventures of Tom Sawyer '38
Having a Wonderful Time '38
Little Miss Broadway '38
You Can't Take It with You '38
Breakfast for Two '37
Three Legionnaires '37
Toast of New York '37
One Rainy Afternoon '36
Pennies from Heaven '36
Barbary Coast '35
The Informer '35
Mark of the Vampire '35
The Return of Peter Grimm '35
Village Tale '35
The Whole Town's Talking '35
The Merry Widow '34
Mrs. Wiggs of the Cabbage Patch '34
Murder at the Vanities '34
Personal Maid '31

Jeffrey Meek (1959-)
Timelock '99
Breaking the Surface: The Greg Louganis Story '96
The St. Tammany Miracle '94
Heart Condition '90
Night of the Cyclone '90
Winter People '89

George Meeker (1904-84)
The Invisible Monster '50
Twilight in the Sierras '50
Omoo Omoo, the Shark God '49
Apache Rose '47
Murder Is My Business '46
People's Choice '46
I Accuse My Parents '45
Dead Man's Eyes '44
Seven Doors to Death '44
Dive Bomber '41
High Sierra '41
Michael Shayne: Private Detective '40
Frolics on Ice '39
Danger on the Air '38
Slander House '38
Tango '36
Murder by Television '35
Double Harness '33
Night of Terror '33
Emma '32
Four Sons '28

Ralph Meeker (1920-88)
Winter Kills '79
My Boys Are Good Boys '78
Hi-Riders '77
The Alpha Incident '76
Food of the Gods '76
Brannigan '75
The Dead Don't Die '75
Johnny Firecloud '75
Cry Panic '74
Birds of Prey '72
Mind Snatchers '72
The Anderson Tapes '71
The Night Stalker '71
I Walk the Line '70
The Detective '68
The Dirty Dozen '67
Gentle Giant '67

The St. Valentine's Day Massacre *'67*
Paths of Glory *'57*
Battle Shock *'56*
Run of the Arrow *'56*
Kiss Me Deadly *'55*
Jeopardy *'53*
The Naked Spur *'53*
Four in a Jeep *'51*

Leighton Meester (1986-)
Date Night *'10*
Killer Movie *'08*
Remember the Daze *'07*
Flourish *'06*
Inside *'06*
Hangman's Curse *'03*

Armand Meffre
Jean de Florette *'87*
Manon of the Spring *'87*
Here Comes Santa Claus *'84*
Blue Country *'77*

John Megna (1953-95)
Go Tell the Spartans *'78*
To Kill a Mockingbird *'62*

Don Megowan (1922-81)
The Devil's Brigade *'68*
The Creation of the Humanoids *'62*
The Jayhawkers *'59*
The Creature Walks among Us *'56*
A Lawless Street *'55*

Blanche Mehaffey (1907-68)
Devil Monster *'46*
Held for Ransom *'38*
Silent Code *'35*
Mystery Trooper *'32*
Sunrise Trail *'31*
A Woman of the World *'25*
Battling Orioles *'24*

Tobias Mehler (1976-)
Carrie *'02*
Wishmaster 3: Beyond the Gates of Hell *'01*
Sabrina the Teenage Witch *'96*

Yan-Fang Mei
See Anita (Yim-Fong) Mui

Armin Meier (1943-78)
Mother Kusters Goes to Heaven *'76*
Fear of Fear *'75*

Christian Meier (1970-)
La Mujer de Mi Hermano *'06*
City of M *'01*

Shane Meier (1977-)
Call of the Wild *'04*
Outrage *'98*
Silver Wolf *'98*
Andre *'94*

Thomas Meighan (1879-1936)
Peck's Bad Boy *'34*
Peck's Bad Boy *'21*
Why Change Your Wife? *'20*
Male and Female *'19*
The Forbidden City *'18*

John Meillon (1934-89)
Crocodile Dundee 2 *'88*
Frenchman's Farm *'87*
The Blue Lightning *'86*
Crocodile Dundee *'86*
The Dunera Boys *'85*
Camel Boy *'84 (V)*
Fourth Wish *'75*
Ride a Wild Pony *'75*
The Cars That Ate Paris *'74*
Inn of the Damned *'74*
Walkabout *'71*
Billy Budd *'62*

Tarcisio Meira (1935-)
Boca *'94*
Love Strange Love *'82*
I Love You *'81*

Kurt Meisel (1912-94)
The Odessa File *'74*
A Time to Love & a Time to Die *'58*
Party Girls for Sale *'54*
Wozzeck *'47*

Kathryn Meisle (1960-)
Rosewood *'96*
Basket Case 2 *'90*

Gunter Meisner (1928-94)
Magdalene *'88*
In a Glass Cage *'86*
Between Wars *'74*
Willy Wonka & the Chocolate Factory *'71*

Bent Mejding
Just Another Love Story *'08*
Reptilicus *'62*

Gerardo Mejia (1965-)
Sundown: The Vampire in Retreat *'08*
Loco Love *'03*
A Million to Juan *'94*
Somebody to Love *'94*
Colors *'88*
Can't Buy Me Love *'87*
Winners Take All *'87*

Isabelle Mejias
Scanners 2: The New Order *'91*
Unfinished Business *'89*
Fall from Innocence *'88*
Higher Education *'88*
Meatballs 3 *'87*
The Bay Boy *'85*
Daughter of Death *'82*

Mariangela Melato (1941-)
Dancers *'87*
Summer Night with Greek Profile, Almond Eyes & Scent of Basil *'87*
So Fine *'81*
To Forget Venice *'79*
Swept Away... *'75*
By the Blood of Others *'73*
Love and Anarchy *'73*
Seduction of Mimi *'72*

Lauritz Melchior
Luxury Liner *'48*
Thrill of a Romance *'45*

Wendel Meldrum (1958-)
Melanie Darrow *'97*
National Lampoon's Dad's Week Off *'97*
Sodbusters *'94*
City Boy *'93*
Hush Little Baby *'93*
Beautiful Dreamers *'92*

Nicholas Mele
Impulse *'90*
Capone *'89*
A Nightmare on Elm Street 5: Dream Child *'89*

George Melford (1877-1961)
A Woman's World *'54*
Call Northside 777 *'48*

Jack Melford (1899-1972)
The Ladykillers *'55*
When Thief Meets Thief *'37*
Department Store *'35*

Jill Melford (1934-)
Edge of Sanity *'89*
Abandon Ship *'57*
Blackout *'54*

Claude Melki (1939-94)
A Slightly Pregnant Man *'79*
Six in Paris *'68*

Gilbert Melki (1958-)
Mr. Average *'06*
Angel-A *'05*
Cote d'Azur *'05*
Changing Times *'04*
Intimate Strangers *'04*
Monsieur Ibrahim *'03*

Joseph Mell (1915-77)
Lord Love a Duck *'66*
36 Hours *'64*
I Was a Teenage Werewolf *'57*

Marisa Mell (1939-92)
Mad Dog *'84*
Hostages *'80*
Mad Dog Killer *'77*
Danger: Diabolik *'68*
Secret Agent Super Dragon *'66*

Randle Mell (1951-)
Cookie's Fortune *'99*
Wyatt Earp *'94*
Grand Canyon *'91*

John Cougar Mellencamp (1951-)
Lone Star State of Mind *'02*
Falling from Grace *'92*

Otto Mellies
Minna von Barnhelm or The Soldier's Fortune *'62*
Intrigue and Love *'59*

Tamara Mello
Tortilla Soup *'01*
She's All That *'99*

Andree Melly (1932-)
The Brides of Dracula *'60*
The Belles of St. Trinian's *'53*

Christopher Meloni (1961-)
Carriers *'09*
Gym Teacher: The Movie *'08*
Harold & Kumar Escape from Guantanamo Bay *'08*
Nights in Rodanthe *'08*
Harold and Kumar Go to White Castle *'04*
Murder in Greenwich *'02*
Wet Hot American Summer *'01*
Runaway Bride *'99*
The Souler Opposite *'97*
Bound *'96*

Frank Melton (1907-51)
Tanks a Million *'41*
The Glory Trail *'36*
The Traitor *'36*
David Harum *'34*
Stand Up and Cheer *'34*
365 Nights in Hollywood *'34*

Sid Melton (1920-)
Hit! *'73*
Lady Sings the Blues *'72*
Leave It to the Marines *'51*
The Lost Continent *'51*
Mask of the Dragon *'51*
Savage Drums *'51*
Sky High *'51*
The Steel Helmet *'51*
Stop That Cab *'51*
Hi-Jacked *'50*
Motor Patrol *'50*
Tough Assignment *'49*
Girls in Chains *'43*

Sam Melville (1936-89)
Twice Dead *'88*
Roughnecks *'80*

Murray Melvin (1932-)
The Phantom of the Opera *'04*
The Emperor's New Clothes *'01*
Let Him Have It *'91*
The Krays *'90*
The Bawdy Adventures of Tom Jones *'76*
Lisztomania *'75*
Madhouse Mansion *'74*
The Devils *'71*
Start the Revolution without Me *'70*
The Fixer *'68*
Alfie *'66*
Kaleidoscope *'66*
A Taste of Honey *'61*

Nasser Memarzia
The Situation *'06*
Millions *'05*

George Memmoli (1938-85)
Hot Potato *'76*
Phantom of the Paradise *'74*
Mean Streets *'73*

Carlos Mencia (1967-)
Our Family Wedding *'10*
The Heartbreak Kid *'07*

Stephen Mendel
The Terminal *'04*
Midnight Heat *'95*
Scanner Cop 2: Volkin's Revenge *'94*
Scanners: The Showdown *'94*

Ben Mendelsohn (1969-)
Knowing *'09*
Australia *'08*
$9.99 *'08 (V)*
The New World *'05*
Vertical Limit *'00*
Amy *'98*
Idiot Box *'97*
Cosi *'95*
Metal Skin *'94*
Sirens *'94*
The Efficiency Expert *'92*
Quigley Down Under *'90*
The Year My Voice Broke *'87*

David Mendenhall (1971-)
Streets *'90*
Secret of the Ice Cave *'89*
Going Bananas *'88*
Over the Top *'86*
Witchfire *'86*
Space Raiders *'83*

Eva Mendes (1974-)
Last Night *'10*
The Other Guys *'10*
Bad Lieutenant: Port of Call New Orleans *'09*
The Spirit *'08*
The Women *'08*
Cleaner *'07*
Ghost Rider *'07*
We Own the Night *'07*
Trust the Man *'06*
Hitch *'05*
The Wendell Baker Story *'05*
Once Upon a Time in Mexico *'03*
Out of Time *'03*
Stuck On You *'03*
2 Fast 2 Furious *'03*
All About the Benjamins *'02*
Exit Wounds *'01*
Training Day *'01*
Urban Legends 2: Final Cut *'00*
Children of the Corn 5: Fields of Terror *'98*

Joey Mendicino
Rest Stop: Don't Look Back *'08*
Rest Stop *'06*

Stephen Mendillo (1942-)
The First Wives Club *'96*
Ethan Frome *'92*
King of the Gypsies *'78*
Slap Shot *'77*

Bridgit Mendler
Alvin and the Chipmunks: The Squeakuel *'09*
Labor Pains *'09*
The Clique *'08*

Maria Luisa Mendonca (1970-)
Carandiru *'03*
The 3 Marias *'03*

Mauro Mendonca (1932-)
Love Strange Love *'82*
Dona Flor and Her Two Husbands *'78*

Natalie Mendoza (1978-)
The Descent *'05*
The Great Raid *'05*
Moulin Rouge *'01*
Rodgers & Hammerstein's South Pacific *'01*

Victor Manuel Mendoza (1913-95)
Cowboy *'58*
Garden of Evil *'54*
The Proud Ones *'53*
Susana *'51*

Gonzalo Menendez (1971-)
Fantastic Four: Rise of the Silver Surfer *'07*
The Lost City *'05*

Alex Meneses (1965-)
44 Minutes: The North Hollywood Shootout *'03*
The Flintstones in Viva Rock Vegas *'00*
Living in Peril *'97*
Amanda and the Alien *'95*
Payback *'89*

Bernard Menez (1944-)
Dracula and Son *'76*
No Problem *'75*

John Mengatti (1954-)
Knights of the City *'85*
Meatballs 2 *'84*

Alex Menglet (1956-)
Zone 39 *'96*
A Woman's Tale *'92*

Adolphe Menjou (1890-1963)
Pollyanna *'60*
Paths of Glory *'57*
The Ambassador's Daughter *'56*
Bundle of Joy *'56*
I Married a Woman *'56*
The Sniper *'52*
Across the Wide Missouri *'51*
To Please a Lady *'50*
My Dream Is Yours *'49*
State of the Union *'48*
The Hucksters *'47*
I'll Be Yours *'47*
Heartbeat *'46*
Step Lively *'44*
Hi Diddle Diddle *'43*
Sweet Rosie O'Grady *'43*
Roxie Hart *'42*
You Were Never Lovelier *'42*
Road Show *'41*
Golden Boy *'39*
The Goldwyn Follies *'38*
Letter of Introduction *'38*
Thanks for Everything *'38*
Cafe Metropole *'37*
100 Men and a Girl *'37*
Stage Door *'37*
A Star Is Born *'37*
Milky Way *'36*
One in a Million *'36*
Gold Diggers of 1935 *'35*
Little Miss Marker *'34*
Morning Glory *'33*
A Farewell to Arms *'32*
The Easiest Way *'31*
The Front Page *'31*
Morocco *'30*
The Grand Duchess and the Waiter *'26*
The Sorrows of Satan *'26*
Are Parents People? *'25*
The King on Main Street *'25*
The Swan *'25*
The Marriage Circle *'24*
The Sheik *'21*

Shepard Menken (1921-99)
The Great Caruso *'51*
The Red Menace *'49*

Laura Mennell
Ruslan *'09*
Montana Sky *'07*

Peter Mensah
The Incredible Hulk *'08*
Hidalgo *'04*
Tears of the Sun *'03*
Jason X *'01*

Oleg Menshikov (1960-)
East-West *'99*
Prisoner of the Mountains *'96*
Burnt by the Sun *'94*

Vladimir Menshov
Day Watch *'06*
Night Watch *'04*

Vladimir Mensik (1924-88)
All My Good Countrymen *'68*
Murder Czech Style *'66*

Idina Menzel (1971-)
Enchanted *'07*
Ask the Dust *'06*
Rent *'05*
The Tollbooth *'04*

Heather Menzies (1949-)
Captain America *'79*
Piranha *'78*
Red, White & Busted *'75*
Ssssss *'73*
The Sound of Music *'65*

Robert Menzies (1955-)
Innocence *'00*
Cactus *'86*

Tobias Menzies (1974-)
Casino Royale *'06*
The Low Down *'00*

Christian Meoli
The Song of the Lark *'01*
The Low Life *'95*
Alive *'93*

Julino Mer
The Last Warrior *'99*
Under the Domim Tree *'95*

Kad Merad
Paris 36 *'08*
The Chorus *'04*

Doro Merande (1898-1975)
The Russians Are Coming, the Russians Are Coming *'66*
Kiss Me, Stupid! *'64*
The Gazebo *'59*
The Man with the Golden Arm *'55*
The Seven Year Itch *'55*

Hector Mercado (1949-)
Leather Jacket Love Story *'98*
Nomads *'86*

Beryl Mercer (1862-1939)
Jane Eyre *'34*
Cavalcade *'33*
Smilin' Through *'33*
Supernatural *'33*
Young America *'32*
The Miracle Woman *'31*
Public Enemy *'31*
All Quiet on the Western Front *'30*

Frances Mercer (1915-2000)
Beauty for the Asking *'39*
Smashing the Rackets *'38*

Freddie Mercer (1929-)
Gildersleeve on Broadway *'43*
On the Sunny Side *'42*
Shadows on the Sage *'42*

Mae Mercer (1932-)
Pretty Baby *'78*
The Swinging Cheerleaders *'74*

Frogs *'72*
Dirty Harry *'71*

Marian Mercer (1935-)
Out on a Limb *'92*
The Seagull *'75*

Vivien Merchant (1929-83)
The Offence *'73*
Under Milk Wood *'73*
Frenzy *'72*
Accident *'67*
Alfie *'66*

Denis Mercier
Bogus *'96*
Le Sexe des Etoiles *'93*

Michele Mercier (1939-)
Call of the Wild *'72*
Web of the Spider *'70*
Angelique and the Sultan *'68*
Oldest Profession *'67*
Untamable Angelique *'67*
Angelique and the King *'66*
How I Learned to Love Women *'66*
Angelique: The Road to Versailles *'65*
Casanova '70 *'65*
Angelique *'64*
Black Sabbath *'64*
A Global Affair *'63*
Shoot the Piano Player *'62*

Melina Mercouri (1925-94)
A Dream of Passion *'78*
Nasty Habits *'77*
Once Is Not Enough *'75*
Topkapi *'64*
The Victors *'63*
Phaedra *'61*
Never on Sunday *'60*
Where the Hot Wind Blows *'59*
Stella *'55*

Monique Mercure (1930-)
Set Me Free *'99*
Conquest *'98*
The Red Violin *'98*
When Justice Fails *'98*
Naked Lunch *'91*
Tramp at the Door *'87*
The Odyssey of the Pacific *'82*
Third Walker *'79*

Micole Mercurio (1938-)
Bandits *'01*
While You Were Sleeping *'95*
Colors *'88*

Paul Mercurio (1963-)
The First 9 1/2 Weeks *'98*
Dark Planet *'97*
Back of Beyond *'95*
Cosi *'95*
Joseph *'95*
Exit to Eden *'94*
Strictly Ballroom *'92*

Burgess Meredith (1908-97)
Grumpier Old Men *'95*
Across the Moon *'94*
Camp Nowhere *'94*
Grumpy Old Men *'93*
Mastergate *'92*
Oddball Hall *'91*
Mr. Corbett's Ghost *'90*
Rocky 5 *'90*
State of Grace *'90*
Full Moon in Blue Water *'88*
King Lear *'87*
Outrage! *'86*
Santa Claus: The Movie *'85*
Wet Gold *'84*
Twilight Zone: The Movie *'83*
Rocky 3 *'82*
Thumbelina *'82*
Clash of the Titans *'81*
Last Chase *'81*
True Confessions *'81*
Final Assignment *'80*
When Time Ran Out *'80*
Rocky 2 *'79*
Foul Play *'78*
Great Bank Hoax *'78*
Magic *'78*
The Manitou *'78*
Golden Rendezvous *'77*
Johnny We Hardly Knew Ye *'77*
Burnt Offerings *'76*
92 in the Shade *'76*
Rocky *'76*
The Sentinel *'76*
The Day of the Locust *'75*
The Hindenburg *'75*
Beware! The Blob *'72*
Probe *'72*
Yin & Yang of Mr. Go *'71*
There Was a Crooked Man *'70*
MacKenna's Gold *'69*
Stay Away, Joe *'68*
Torture Garden *'67*
Batman *'66*
A Big Hand for the Little Lady *'66*
Madame X *'66*
In Harm's Way *'65*
The Cardinal *'63*
Advise and Consent *'62*
Jigsaw *'49*
Man on the Eiffel Tower *'48*
On Our Merry Way *'48*
Mine Own Executioner *'47*
Diary of a Chambermaid *'46*
Magnificent Doll *'46*
The Story of G.I. Joe *'45*
That Uncertain Feeling *'41*
Tom, Dick, and Harry *'41*
Castle on the Hudson *'40*
Second Chorus *'40*
Idiot's Delight *'39*
Of Mice and Men *'39*
Winterset *'36*

Don Meredith (1938-)
Three Days of Rain *'02*
Wyatt Earp: Return to Tombstone *'94*
The Night the City Screamed *'80*
Express to Terror *'79*
Banjo Hackett *'76*
Mayday at 40,000 Feet *'76*
Sky Hei$t *'75*
Terror on the 40th Floor *'74*

Ifan Meredith
Metroland *'97*
The Mill on the Floss *'97*

Iris Meredith (1915-80)
Rangers Take Over *'42*
Green Archer *'40*
The Spider's Web *'38*
A Lawman Is Born *'37*
Mystery of the Hooded Horseman *'37*
Rio Grande Ranger *'37*

Judi Meredith (1936-)
Planet of Blood *'66*
Jack the Giant Killer *'62*

Lee Meredith (1947-)
The Sunshine Boys *'75*
The Producers *'68*

Luc Merenda (1942-)
Could It Happen Here? *'77*
The Cheaters *'76*
Violent Professionals *'73*
Le Mans *'71*

Stanislas Merhar (1971-)
Merci Docteur Rey *'04*
Almost Peaceful *'02*
The Count of Monte Cristo *'99*
Dry Cleaning *'97*

Jalal Merhi
Expect No Mercy *'95*
Fearless Tiger *'94*
Operation Golden Phoenix *'94*
TC 2000 *'93*
Talons of the Eagle *'92*
Tiger Claws *'91*

Auriele Meriel
The Butterfly *'02*
The Delivery *'99*

Macha Meril (1940-)
Meeting Venus *'91*
Chinese Roulette *'86*
Vagabond *'85*
Beau Pere *'81*
Robert et Robert *'78*
Deep Red: Hatchet Murders *'75*
Night Train Murders *'75*
Torture Train *'75*
The Defector *'66*
A Married Woman *'65*
Une Femme Mariee *'64*

Eda Reiss Merin (1913-98)
For Better or Worse *'95*
Don't Tell Mom the Babysitter's Dead *'91*
The Reluctant Agent *'89*

Michele Meritz
Classe Tous Risque *'60*
Le Beau Serge *'58*

Philip Merivale (1886-1946)
Sister Kenny *'46*
Nothing But Trouble *'44*
Lady for a Night *'42*
This Above All *'42*

Lee Meriwether (1935-)
The Ultimate Gift *'07*
Brothers O'Toole *'73*
The Undefeated *'69*
Batman *'66*
Namu, the Killer Whale *'66*
The 4D Man *'59*

Una Merkel (1903-86)
Spinout *'66*
A Tiger Walks *'64*
Summer Magic *'63*
The Parent Trap *'61*
Summer and Smoke *'61*
The Mating Game *'59*
The Girl Most Likely *'57*
The Kettles in the Ozarks *'56*
The Kentuckian *'55*
I Love Melvin *'53*
The Merry Widow *'52*
With a Song in My Heart *'52*
Rich, Young and Pretty *'51*
Kill the Umpire *'50*
My Blue Heaven *'50*
It's a Joke, Son! *'47*
Twin Beds *'42*
Cracked Nuts *'41*
The Road to Zanzibar *'41*
The Bank Dick *'40*
Destry Rides Again *'39*
On Borrowed Time *'39*
Rhythm Romance *'39*
Saratoga *'37*
Born to Dance *'36*
Broadway Melody of 1936 *'35*
Riff Raff *'35*
Evelyn Prentice *'34*
The Merry Widow *'34*
Bombshell *'33*
42nd Street *'33*
Midnight Mary *'33*
Red Headed Woman *'32*
They Call It Sin *'32*
The Maltese Falcon *'31*
Private Lives *'31*
Abraham Lincoln *'30*
The Bat Whispers *'30*

S. Epatha Merkerson (1952-)
Mother and Child *'09*
Black Snake Moan *'07*
Slipstream *'07*
Jersey Girl *'04*
Radio *'03*
A Mother's Prayer *'95*
A Place for Annie *'94*
She's Gotta Have It *'86*

Maurizio Merli
Fearless *'77*
Street War *'76*

Jan Merlin (1925-)
Silk 2 *'89*
Twilight People *'72*
Take the Money and Run *'69*
Gunfight at Comanche Creek *'64*

Joanna Merlin (1931-)
City of Angels *'98*
Two Bits *'96*
Class Action *'91*
Mystic Pizza *'88*
Baby It's You *'82*
Fame *'80*

Ethel Merman (1909-84)
Airplane! *'80*
Journey Back to Oz *'71 (V)*
It's a Mad, Mad, Mad, Mad World *'63*
There's No Business Like Show Business *'54*
Stage Door Canteen *'43*
Alexander's Ragtime Band *'38*
Happy Landing *'38*
Strike Me Pink *'36*
Kid Millions *'34*
We're Not Dressing *'34*

Mary Merrall (1890-1973)
The Belles of St. Trinian's *'53*
The Obsessed *'51*
They Made Me a Fugitive *'47*
Nicholas Nickleby *'46*
Dead of Night *'45*
Pink String and Sealing Wax *'45*

Charlotte Merriam (1906-72)
Night Nurse *'31*
One-Punch O'Day *'26*

Lynn Merrick (1919-2007)
Down to Earth *'47*
California Joe *'43*
The Sombrero Kid *'42*
Sundown Fury *'42*

Dina Merrill (1925-)
Shade *'03*
The Other Sister *'98*
Open Season *'95*
Suture *'93*
The Player *'92*
True Colors *'91*
Fear *'90*
Caddyshack 2 *'88*
Twisted *'86*
Anna to the Infinite Power *'84*
Hot Pursuit *'84*
Tenth Month *'79*
A Wedding *'78*
The Greatest *'77*
The Meal *'75*
Running Wild *'73*
I'll Take Sweden *'65*
The Courtship of Eddie's Father *'62*
The Young Savages *'61*
Butterfield 8 *'60*
The Sundowners *'60*
Operation Petticoat *'59*
Desk Set *'57*

Frank Merrill (1893-1966)
Tarzan the Tiger *'29*
The Adventures of Tarzan *'21*

Gary Merrill (1915-90)
The Seekers *'79*
Huckleberry Finn *'74*
Pueblo Affair *'73*
Then Came Bronson *'68*
Clambake *'67*
The Incident *'67*
Around the World Under the Sea *'65*
The Great Impostor *'61*
Mysterious Island *'61*
Missouri Traveler *'58*
A Blueprint for Murder *'53*
Another Man's Poison *'52*
Phone Call from a Stranger *'52*
All About Eve *'50*
Where the Sidewalk Ends *'50*
Twelve o'Clock High *'49*

Ryan Merriman (1983-)
Backwoods *'08*
Comanche Moon *'08*
Final Destination 3 *'06*
The Ring 2 *'05*
Spin *'04*
Halloween: Resurrection *'02*
Dangerous Child *'01*
Smart House *'00*
Just Looking *'99*
Lansky *'99*
The Deep End of the Ocean *'98*
Everything That Rises *'98*

Clive Merrison (1945-)
The History Boys *'06*
Photographing Fairies *'97*
The English Patient *'96*
An Awfully Big Adventure *'94*
Heavenly Creatures *'94*

Lindsay Merrithew
At the Midnight Hour *'95*
Hitler's Daughter *'90*

George Merritt (1890-1977)
I, Monster *'71*
Clouds over Europe *'39*
Young and Innocent *'37*

Theresa Merritt (1922-98)
Billy Madison *'94*
Voodoo Dawn *'89*
The Serpent and the Rainbow *'87*

Jane Merrow (1941-)
The Appointment *'82*
Hands of the Ripper *'71*
The Lion in Winter *'68*
Island of the Burning Doomed *'67*
The Girl Getters *'66*

Susan Merson
American Meltdown *'04*
Lost in Yonkers *'93*

John Merton (1901-59)
Radar Patrol vs. Spy King *'49*
Border Bandits *'46*
Devil Riders *'44*
Rustler's Hideout *'44*
Wild Horse Phantom *'44*
Cowboy Commandos *'43*
Fighting Valley *'43*
Land of Hunted Men *'43*
Boot Hill Bandits *'42*
The Mysterious Rider *'42*
Prairie Pals *'42*
Battling Outlaw *'40*
Billy the Kid in Texas *'40*
Covered Wagon Days *'40*
Code of the Fearless *'39*
Hopalong Cassidy: Renegade Trail *'39*
In Old Montana *'39*
Zorro's Fighting Legion *'39*
Gang Bullets *'38*
Gunsmoke Trail *'38*
Phantom Ranger *'38*
Valley of Terror *'38*
The Rangers Step In *'37*
Roaring Six Guns *'37*
Slaves in Bondage *'37*
Two-Gun Troubador *'37*
Aces and Eights *'36*
Crooked Trail *'36*
Lightnin' Bill Carson *'36*
Lion's Den *'36*
The Gun Ranger *'34*

William Mervyn (1912-76)
The Ruling Class *'72*
The Railway Children *'70*
Murder Ahoy *'64*
The Battle of the Sexes *'60*

John Mese (1963-)
Red Dirt *'99*
Excessive Force 2: Force on Force *'95*
Night of the Scarecrow *'95*

Daniel Mesguich (1952-)
Le Divorce *'03*
The Musketeer *'01*

Hannes Messemer (1924-91)
The Odessa File *'74*
The Defector *'66*
The Great Escape *'63*

Donald E. Messick (1926-97)
Tiny Toon Adventures: How I Spent My Vacation *'91 (V)*
Jetsons: The Movie *'90 (V)*
Flight of Dragons *'82 (V)*
The Hobbit *'78 (V)*

Marc Messier (1947-)
The Boys *'97*
A Wind from Wyoming *'94*

Chris Messina (1974-)
Greenberg *'10*
Away We Go *'09*
Brief Interviews With Hideous Men *'09*
Julie & Julia *'09*
Humboldt County *'08*
Made of Honor *'08*
Vicky Cristina Barcelona *'08*
Towelhead *'07*
Ira & Abby *'06*

Francesco Messina
13 Moons *'02*
In the Soup *'92*

Debra Messing (1968-)
Nothing Like the Holidays *'08*
The Women *'08*
Lucky You *'07*
Purple Violets *'07*
The Starter Wife *'07*
Open Season *'06 (V)*
The Wedding Date *'05*
Along Came Polly *'04*
Garfield: The Movie *'04 (V)*
Hollywood Ending *'02*
The Mothman Prophecies *'02*
Jesus *'00*
McHale's Navy *'97*
A Walk in the Clouds *'95*

Gertrude Messinger (1911-95)
Miracle Kid *'42*
Aces Wild *'37*
The Adventurous Knights *'35*
Fighting Pilot *'35*
Rider of the Law *'35*
Roaring Roads *'35*
Rustler's Paradise *'35*
Social Error *'35*
Wagon Trail *'35*
Hidden Valley *'32*
Riders of the Desert *'32*

Johnny Messner (1970-)
The Art of Travel *'08*
Loaded *'08*
The Poker Club *'08*
Ring of Death *'08*
Believers *'07*
Running Scared *'06*
Hostage *'05*
Anacondas: The Hunt for the Blood Orchid *'04*
Spartan *'04*
The Whole Ten Yards *'04*
Finding Home *'03*
Tears of the Sun *'03*

Sombat Metanee
The Legend of Suriyothai *'02*
Tears of the Black Tiger *'00*

George Metaxa (1899-1950)

The Mask of Dimitrios *'44*
Doctor Takes a Wife *'40*

Laurie Metcalf (1955-)

Toy Story 3 *'10 (V)*
Georgia Rule *'07*
Meet the Robinsons *'07 (V)*
Beer League *'06*
Steel City *'06*
Treasure Planet *'02 (V)*
Runaway Bride *'99*
Toy Story 2 *'99 (V)*
Always Outnumbered Always Outgunned *'98*
Bulworth *'98*
Chicago Cab *'98*
Balloon Farm *'97*
Scream 2 *'97*
U-Turn *'97*
Dear God *'96*
Leaving Las Vegas *'95*
Toy Story *'95 (V)*
Blink *'93*
A Dangerous Woman *'93*
JFK *'91*
Mistress *'91*
Internal Affairs *'90*
Pacific Heights *'90*
Uncle Buck *'89*
Miles from Home *'88*
Stars and Bars *'88*
Candy Mountain *'87*
Making Mr. Right *'86*
Desperately Seeking Susan *'85*
Execution of Raymond Graham *'85*

Mark Metcalf (1946-)

Drive Me Crazy *'99*
Hijacking Hollywood *'97*
Rage *'95*
The Stupids *'95*
Dead Ahead: The Exxon Valdez Disaster *'92*
Mr. North *'88*
One Crazy Summer *'86*
The Final Terror *'83*
National Lampoon's Animal House *'78*
Julia *'77*

Earl Metcalfe (1889-1928)

The Notorious Lady *'27*
With Kit Carson over the Great Divide *'25*

Jesse Metcalfe (1978-)

Beyond a Reasonable Doubt *'09*
Insanitarium *'08*
Loaded *'08*
The Other End of the Line *'08*
John Tucker Must Die *'06*

Ken Metcalfe

Nam Angels *'88*
Savage Justice *'88*
Warriors of the Apocalypse *'85*
TNT Jackson *'75*

Aaron Michael Metchik (1980-)

The Baby-Sitters' Club *'95*
Trading Mom *'94*

Asher Metchik (1986-)

Milo *'98*
Trading Mom *'94*

Saul Meth

Double Agent 73 *'80*
Deadly Weapons *'70*

Method Man (1971-)

Meet the Spartans *'08*
Venom *'05*
My Baby's Daddy *'04*
Soul Plane *'04*
How High *'01*
Belly *'98*

Mayo Methot (1904-51)

Marked Woman *'37*
Goodbye Love *'34*
Counsellor-at-Law *'33*
Corsair *'31*

Svetlana Metkina

Bobby *'06*
The Second Front *'05*

Art Metrano (1937-)

Beverly Hills Bodysnatchers *'89*
Police Academy 3: Back in Training *'86*
Malibu Express *'85*
Police Academy 2: Their First Assignment *'85*
Breathless *'83*
Going Ape! *'81*
How to Beat the High Cost of Living *'80*
Seven *'79*
Prisoner in the Middle *'74*
Slaughter's Big Ripoff *'73*
The Heartbreak Kid *'72*
They Only Kill Their Masters *'72*
Rocket Attack U.S.A. *'58*

Nancy Mette

Meet the Hollowheads *'89*
Matewan *'87*
Key Exchange *'85*

Omar Metwally

Rendition *'07*
Munich *'05*

Jim Metzler (1955-)

Sundown: The Vampire in Retreat *'08*
The Doe Boy *'01*
St. Patrick's Day *'99*
A Gun, a Car, a Blonde *'97*
Cadillac Ranch *'96*
Children of the Corn 3: Urban Harvest *'95*
French Silk *'94*
Plughead Rewired: Circuitry Man 2 *'94*
Delusion *'91*
Love Kills *'91*
One False Move *'91*
Circuitry Man *'90*
Murder by Night *'89*
Old Gringo *'89*
Hot to Trot! *'88*
976-EVIL *'88*
The Little Match Girl *'87*
River's Edge *'87*
On Wings of Eagles *'86*
Tex *'82*
Four Friends *'81*
Squeeze Play *'79*

Paul Meurisse (1912-79)

Gypsy *'75*
Le Gitan *'75*
Army of Shadows *'69*
Le Deuxieme Souffle *'66*
The Monocle *'64*
Picnic on the Grass *'59*
Diabolique *'55*

Anne-Laure Meury

Boyfriends & Girlfriends *'88*
The Aviator's Wife *'80*

Jason Mewes (1974-)

Zack and Miri Make a Porno *'08*
Netherbeast Incorporated *'07*
Bottoms Up *'06*
Clerks 2 *'06*
The Tripper *'06*
The Pleasure Drivers *'05*
R.S.V.P. *'02*
Jay and Silent Bob Strike Back *'01*
Scream 3 *'00*
Dogma *'99*
Chasing Amy *'97*
Mallrats *'95*
Clerks *'94*

Bess Meyer

All I Want for Christmas *'07*
H.P. Lovecraft's Necronomicon: Book of the Dead *'93*
The Inner Circle *'91*

Breckin Meyer (1974-)

Ghosts of Girlfriends Past *'09*
Blue State *'07*
Corporate Affairs *'07*
Caffeine *'06*
Garfield: A Tail of Two Kitties *'06*
Herbie: Fully Loaded *'05*
Rebound *'05*
Blast *'04*
Garfield: The Movie *'04*
Pinocchio *'02 (V)*
Josie and the Pussycats *'01*
Kate & Leopold *'01*
Rat Race *'01*
Road Trip *'00*
Go *'99*
Tail Lights Fade *'99*
Dancer, Texas—Pop. 81 *'98*
54 *'98*
Prefontaine *'96*
Touch *'96*
Clueless *'95*

Dina Meyer (1969-)

Piranha 3D *'10*
Decoys: The Second Seduction *'07*
Crazy Eights *'06*
Saw 3 *'06*
Saw 2 *'05*
Saw *'04*
Federal Protection *'02*
Star Trek: Nemesis *'02*
Unspeakable *'02*
Eye See You *'01*
Time Lapse *'01*
Bats *'99*
Stranger than Fiction *'99*
Nowhere Land *'98*
Poodle Springs *'98*
Starship Troopers *'97*
Dragonheart *'96*
Johnny Mnemonic *'95*

Emile Meyer (1910-87)

King of the Wild Stallions *'59*
The Fiend Who Walked the West *'58*
Good Day for a Hanging *'58*
The Lineup *'58*
Blackboard Jungle *'55*
The Girl in the Red Velvet Swing *'55*
Stranger on Horseback *'55*
Riot in Cell Block 11 *'54*
Shane *'53*

Hans Meyer (1925-)

Brotherhood of the Wolf *'01*
Mauvais Sang *'86*
Le Magnifique *'76*

Michael Meyer (1957-)

The Biggest Fan *'02*
Virtual Desire *'95*
Crossfire *'89*

Russ Meyer (1922-2004)

Amazon Women on the Moon *'87*
Motor Psycho *'65*

Torben Meyer (1884-1975)

Judgment at Nuremberg *'61*
The Matchmaker *'58*
Sullivan's Travels *'41*
Thin Ice *'37*

Ari Meyers (1969-)

Dark Horse *'92*
Think Big *'90*
Shakma *'89*
License to Kill *'84*

Harry Meyers

See Harry C. (Henry) Myers

Seth Meyers

Spring Breakdown *'08*
American Dreamz *'06*
Perception *'06*

Gerard Meylan

The Town Is Quiet *'00*
Marius and Jeannette *'97*
Nenette and Boni *'96*

Michelle Meyrink (1962-)

Permanent Record *'88*
Nice Girls Don't Explode *'87*
One Magic Christmas *'85*
Real Genius *'85*
Joy of Sex *'84*
Revenge of the Nerds *'84*
Valley Girl *'83*

Myriam Meziere (1949-)

Mouth to Mouth *'95*
Jonah Who Will Be 25 in the Year 2000 *'76*

Giovanna Mezzogiorno (1974-)

Love in the Time of Cholera *'07*
Don't Tell *'05*
Facing Windows *'03*
The Last Kiss *'01*

Vittorio Mezzogiorno (1942-94)

Cafe Express *'83*
L'Homme Blesse *'83*
Moon in the Gutter *'83*
Car Crash *'80*
Three Brothers *'80*

Robert Miano (1942-)

The Indian *'07*
The Still Life *'07*
The Stickup *'01*
Dungeons and Dragons *'00*
Loser *'00*
Luckytown *'00*
Detour *'99*
Thick as Thieves *'99*
Matter of Trust *'98*
Smoke Signals *'98*
Laws of Deception *'97*
Donnie Brasco *'96*
Opposite Corners *'96*
Taxi Dancers *'93*
Chained Heat *'83*

Cora Miao (1958-)

Eat a Bowl of Tea *'89*
Dim Sum: A Little Bit of Heart *'85*

Tien Miao

Goodbye, Dragon Inn *'03*
What Time Is It There? *'01*
The Hole *'98*
Rebels of the Neon God *'92*

Gertrude Michael (1911-64)

Bugles in the Afternoon *'52*
Caged *'50*
Flamingo Road *'49*
Behind Prison Walls *'43*
The Last Outpost *'35*
Cleopatra *'34*
Murder at the Vanities *'34*
Search for Beauty *'34*
I'm No Angel *'33*

Ralph Michael (1907-94)

Diary of a Mad Old Man *'88*
The Heroes of Telemark *'65*
Murder Most Foul *'65*
Children of the Damned *'63*
A Night to Remember *'58*
Abandon Ship *'57*
San Demetrio, London *'47*
Johnny Frenchman *'46*
Dead of Night *'45*

Sean Michael

See Sean Michael Afable

Genia Michaela

Is There Life Out There? *'94*
Fallen Angels 2 *'93*

Dario Michaelis (1927-)

The Day the Sky Exploded *'57*
I, Vampiri *'56*

Al Michaels (1944-)

BASEketball *'98*
Homeward Bound 2: Lost in San Francisco *'96 (V)*

Bret Michaels (1963-)

In God's Hands *'98*
No Code of Conduct *'98*

Julie Michaels

Jason Goes to Hell: The Final Friday *'93*
Witchboard 2: The Devil's Doorway *'93*
Road House *'89*

Mimi Michaels

Meteor *'09*
Boogeyman 3 *'08*
Sister Aimee: The Aimee Semple McPherson Story *'06*

Pat Michaels

The Cut Throats *'69*
Santa Fe Uprising *'46*

Joel Michaely

Cult *'07*
Cruel World *'05*

Alyson Michalka (1989-)

Bandslam *'09*
Cow Belles *'06*

Jeff Michalski

Star Maps *'97*
Pet Shop *'94*

Francoise Michaud

The Butterfly *'02*
Eminent Domain *'91*

Dominique Michel (1932-)

The Barbarian Invasions *'03*
King of the Airwaves *'94*
The Decline of the American Empire *'86*

Marc Michel

Umbrellas of Cherbourg *'64*
Lola *'61*
Le Trou *'59*

Marcella Michelangeli

Could It Happen Here? *'77*
Padre Padrone *'77*
And God Said to Cain *'69*

Michael Michele (1966-)

Dark Blue *'03*
How to Lose a Guy in 10 Days *'03*
Ali *'01*
Homicide: The Movie *'00*
The Sixth Man *'97*
The Substitute 2: School's Out *'97*
New Jack City *'91*

Helena Michell (1963-)

Devices and Desires *'91*
Piece of Cake *'88*

Keith Michell (1928-)

The Deceivers *'88*
My Brother Tom *'86*
Memorial Day *'83*
Grendel, Grendel, Grendel *'82 (V)*
Ruddigore *'82*
Tenth Month *'79*
The Story of David *'76*
The Story of Jacob & Joseph *'74*
Six Wives of Henry VIII *'71*
The Executioner *'70*
Soldier in Love *'67*
The Hellfire Club *'61*

Anne Michelle (1952-)

The Haunted *'79*
French Quarter *'78*
House of Whipcord *'75*
Mistress Pamela *'74*
The Virgin Witch *'70*

Janee Michelle

The House on Skull Mountain *'74*
Scream Blacula Scream *'73*

Shelley Michelle

Married People, Single Sex *'93*
Bikini Summer *'91*
Sunset Strip *'91*

Maria Michi (1921-80)

Last Tango in Paris *'73*
Redneck *'73*
Paisan *'46*
Open City *'45*

Terry Michos

The Great Skycopter Rescue *'82*
The Warriors *'79*

Eric Micklewood (1911-2003)

Nine Men *'43*
Salute John Citizen *'42*

Tracy Middendorf (1970-)

Just Add Water *'07*
The Assassination of Richard Nixon *'05*
Wes Craven's New Nightmare *'94*

Frank Middlemass (1919-2006)

One Against the Wind *'91*
The Bretts *'88*
Oliver Twist *'85*
The Island *'80*

Charles Middleton (1879-1949)

Spook Busters *'48*
Northwest Trail *'46*
Strangler of the Swamp *'46*
Western Union *'41*
Flash Gordon Conquers the Universe *'40*
Flash Gordon: Rocketship *'40*
Space Soldiers Conquer the Universe *'40*
Flash Gordon: Mars Attacks the World *'39*
Oklahoma Kid *'39*
Way Down South *'39*
Wyoming Outlaw *'39*
Dick Tracy Returns *'38*
Hollywood Cowboy *'37*
Yodelin' Kid from Pine Ridge *'37*
Rocketship *'36*
Hopalong Cassidy *'35*
The Miracle Rider *'35*
Square Shooter *'35*
David Harum *'34*
Mrs. Wiggs of the Cabbage Patch *'34*
Murder at the Vanities *'34*
Mystery Ranch *'34*
Duck Soup *'33*
The Strange Love of Molly Louvain *'32*
Too Busy to Work *'32*
An American Tragedy *'31*
The Miracle Woman *'31*
Palmy Days *'31*

Fran Middleton

Martin *'77*
Love Thrill Murders *'71*

Guy Middleton (1906-73)

Oh! What a Lovely War *'69*
The Belles of St. Trinian's *'53*
The Happiest Days of Your Life *'50*
A Man About the House *'47*
The Demi-Paradise *'43*
Dangerous Moonlight *'41*

Noelle Middleton (1926-)

The Vicious Circle *'57*
John and Julie *'55*
Carrington, V.C. *'54*

Ray Middleton (1908-84)

A Christmas Carol *'54*
Jubilee Trail *'54*
I Dream of Jeannie *'52*
Lady for a Night *'42*
Lady from Louisiana *'42*

Robert Middleton (1911-77)

Harrad Experiment *'73*
Gold of the Seven Saints *'61*
Career *'59*
The Law and Jake Wade *'58*

Tarnished Angels '57
Court Jester '56
Love Me Tender '56
Desperate Hours '55

Dale Midkiff (1959-)

Boxboarders! '07
Flight of the Living Dead: Outbreak on a Plane '07
Love's Unending Legacy '07
Love's Unfolding Dream '07
Love's Abiding Joy '06
Love's Enduring Promise '04
Love Comes Softly '03
Video Voyeur: The Susan Wilson Story '02
Route 666 '01
Air Bud 3: World Pup '00
Alien Fury: Countdown to Invasion '00
Another Woman's Husband '00
The Crow: Salvation '00
The Magnificent Seven '98
Any Place But Home '97
Toothless '97
Love Potion #9 '92
Blackmail '91
Pet Sematary '89
Elvis and Me '88
Nightmare Weekend '86
Streetwalkin' '85

Bette Midler (1945-)

Cats & Dogs: The Revenge of Kitty Galore '10 (V)
The Women '08
Then She Found Me '07
The Stepford Wives '04
Drowning Mona '00
Isn't She Great '00
What Women Want '00
The First Wives Club '96
That Old Feeling '96
Get Shorty '95
Gypsy '93
Hocus Pocus '93
For the Boys '91
Scenes from a Mall '91
Stella '89
Beaches '88
Big Business '88
Oliver & Company '88 (V)
Outrageous Fortune '87
Down and Out in Beverly Hills '86
Ruthless People '86
Jinxed '82
The Rose '79
The Thorn '74
Hawaii '66

Anne-Marie Mieville (1945-)

Comment Ca Va? '76
Here and Elsewhere '76

Toshiro Mifune (1920-97)

Picture Bride '94
Shadow of the Wolf '92
Journey of Honor '91
The Challenge '82
Shogun '80
1941 '79
Winter Kills '79
Love and Faith '78
Shogun's Samurai—The Yagyu Clan Conspiracy '78
Proof of the Man '77
Midway '76
Paper Tiger '74
Red Sun '71
The Battle of the Japan Sea '70
Zatoichi vs. Yojimbo '70
Hell in the Pacific '69
Red Lion '69
Samurai Banners '69
Samurai Rebellion '67
Sword of Doom '67
Grand Prix '66
Red Beard '65
Attack Squadron '63
High & Low '62
Sanjuro '62
Yojimbo '61
The Bad Sleep Well '60
The Gambling Samurai '60
I Bombed Pearl Harbor '60
Saga of the Vagabond '59
The Hidden Fortress '58
Rikisha-Man '58
The Lower Depths '57
Throne of Blood '57
Samurai 3: Duel at Ganryu Island '56
I Live in Fear '55
Samurai 1: Musashi Miyamoto '55
Samurai 2: Duel at Ichijoji Temple '55
Seven Samurai '54
Life of Oharu '52
The Idiot '51
Rashomon '51
Scandal '50
A Quiet Duel '49
Stray Dog '49
Drunken Angel '48

Julia Migenes (1949-)

The Krays '90
Berlin Blues '89
Mack the Knife '89

R.A. Mihailoff

Pumpkinhead 2: Blood Wings '94
Leatherface: The Texas Chainsaw Massacre 3 '89

Tatsuya Mihashi (1923-2004)

Black House '07
Dolls '02
Tora! Tora! Tora! '70
What's Up, Tiger Lily? '66
None But the Brave '65
High & Low '62
The Burmese Harp '56

Dash Mihok (1974-)

The Longshots '08
Punisher: War Zone '08
Firehouse Dog '07
I Am Legend '07
Loveless in Los Angeles '07
Superheroes '07
Hollywoodland '06
10th & Wolf '06
Kiss Kiss Bang Bang '05
Connie and Carla '04
The Day After Tomorrow '04
Death Valley '04
Hustle '04
Basic '03
Dark Blue '03
The Guru '02
Finder's Fee '01
The Perfect Storm '00
White Boyz '99
Telling You '98
The Thin Red Line '98

Takashi Miike (1960-)

The Neighbor No. Thirteen '05
Last Life in the Universe '03

Hiroshi Mikami

Premonition '04
Parasite Eve '97

Nadia Mikhalkov

Burnt by the Sun '94
Anna '93

Nikita Mikhalkov (1945-)

12 '07
Burnt by the Sun '94
Anna '93
Close to Eden '90
Siberiade '79
An Unfinished Piece for a Player Piano '77

Norihei Miki (1923-99)

Black Rain '88
Himatsuri '85

Mads Mikkelsen (1965-)

Clash of the Titans '10
Coco Chanel & Igor Stravinksy '09
Valhalla Rising '09
After the Wedding '06
Casino Royale '06
Adam's Apples '05
King Arthur '04
The Green Butchers '03
Wilbur Wants to Kill Himself '02
Flickering Lights '01
Pusher '96

Izabella Miko (1981-)

Clash of the Titans '10
Dark Streets '08
Crashing '07
The House of Usher '06
The Forsaken '01
Coyote Ugly '00

Rentaro Mikuni (1923-)

Rikyu '90
A Taxing Woman's Return '88
The Go-Masters '82
Nomugi Pass '79
Vengeance Is Mine '79
Swords of Death '71
Kwaidan '64
Harakiri '62
The Burmese Harp '56
Samurai 1: Musashi Miyamoto '55

Frank Milan

Joy of Living '38
Hollywood Cowboy '37

Lita Milan (1933-)

I, Mobster '58
The Left-Handed Gun '58
Never Love a Stranger '58
Naked in the Sun '57
Poor White Trash '57
The Ride Back '57

Alyssa Milano (1972-)

Pathology '08
Wisegal '08
Dickie Roberts: Former Child Star '03
Goldrush: A Real Life Alaskan Adventure '98
Body Count '97
Hugo Pool '97
Fear '96
Glory Daze '96
Public Enemies '96
Deadly Sins '95
Embrace of the Vampire '95
Poison Ivy 2: Lily '95
Confessions of Sorority Girls '94
Double Dragon '94
Casualties of Love: The "Long Island Lolita" Story '93
Conflict of Interest '92
Little Sister '92
Where the Day Takes You '92
Commando '85
Old Enough '84

Adolph Milar (1886-1950)

The Savage Girl '32
Bulldog Drummond '29
The Michigan Kid '28

David Milbern

See David Millbern

Oliver Milburn (1973-)

The Descent '05
Me Without You '01
Tess of the D'Urbervilles '98
The Choir '95
Loaded '94

Ben Miles (1967-)

Ninja Assassin '09
V for Vendetta '06
Under the Greenwood Tree '05
Three Blind Mice '02
Catherine Cookson's The Round Tower '98

Bernard Miles (1907-91)

Sapphire '59
The Smallest Show on Earth '57
The Man Who Knew Too Much '56
Never Let Me Go '53
The Guinea Pig '48
Fame Is the Spur '47
Great Expectations '46
Nicholas Nickleby '46
In Which We Serve '43

Betty Miles (1910-92)

Sonora Stagecoach '44
Westward Bound '44
Law of the Saddle '43
The Law Rides Again '43
Lone Star Law Men '42
The Driftin' Kid '41
Riding the Sunset Trail '41

Elaine Miles (1960-)

Wyvern '09
The Business of Fancydancing '02
Smoke Signals '98

Joanna Miles (1940-)

Jesse Stone: Thin Ice '09
Sex and Breakfast '07
Monte Walsh '03
Crossfire Trail '01
Horton Foote's Alone '97
The Avenging Angel '95
Cooperstown '93
The Water Engine '92
Rosencrantz & Guildenstern Are Dead '90
Blackout '88
Sound of Murder '82
Sophisticated Gents '81
The Orphan '79
The Dark Secret of Harvest Home '78
Bug '75
The Ultimate Warrior '75
Born Innocent '74

Kate Miles

Longford '06
The Truth About Love '04

Kevin Miles

The Chant of Jimmie Blacksmith '78
Endplay '75
The Cars That Ate Paris '74

Lillian Miles (1907-72)

Reefer Madness '38
Get That Man '35

Maria Miles

Catherine Cookson's The Cinder Path '94
Cold Comfort Farm '94

Peter Miles (1938-2002)

Trigger, Jr. '50
The Red Pony '49
Who Killed Doc Robbin? '48

Rosalind Miles

The Black Six '74
I Spit on Your Corpse '74
The Manhandlers '73
Shaft's Big Score '72

Sarah Miles (1941-)

The Silent Touch '94
White Mischief '88
Hope and Glory '87
Queenie '87
Harem '86
Steaming '86
Ordeal by Innocence '84
Venom '82
The Big Sleep '78
Dynasty '76
The Sailor Who Fell from Grace with the Sea '76
Lady Caroline Lamb '73
Man Who Loved Cat Dancing '73
Ryan's Daughter '70
Blow-Up '66
Those Magnificent Men in Their Flying Machines '65
The Servant '63
Term of Trial '63

Sherry Miles (1952-)

Jailbreakin' '72
The Todd Killings '71
The Velvet Vampire '71

Sylvia Miles (1932-)

Denise Calls Up '95
Superstar: The Life and Times of Andy Warhol '90
She-Devil '89
Sleeping Beauty '89
Crossing Delancey '88
Spike of Bensonhurst '88
No Big Deal '83
Evil under the Sun '82
The Funhouse '81
Deadly Thief '78
Zero to Sixty '78
The Sentinel '76
Farewell, My Lovely '75
Heat '72
The Last Movie '71
Who Killed Mary What's 'Er Name? '71
Midnight Cowboy '69
Psychomania '63
Parrish '61

Vera Miles (1929-)

Separate Lives '94
Into the Night '85
The Initiation '84
Psycho 2 '83
Brainwaves '82
Mazes and Monsters '82
Our Family Business '81
Roughnecks '80
And I Alone Survived '78
Run for the Roses '78
Fire '77
Twilight's Last Gleaming '77
Judge Horton and the Scottsboro Boys '76
The Castaway Cowboy '74
A Strange and Deadly Occurrence '74
One Little Indian '73
Baffled '72
Molly & Lawless John '72
Jigsaw '71
Mission Batangas '69
Hellfighters '68
Sergeant Ryker '68
Gentle Giant '67
Follow Me, Boys! '66
Those Calloways '65
A Tiger Walks '64
The Man Who Shot Liberty Valance '62
Back Street '61
Psycho '60
The FBI Story '59
Autumn Leaves '56
The Searchers '56
The Wrong Man '56

Vicki (Allison Louise Downe) Miles

Scum of the Earth '63
Nature's Playmates '62

Kim Milford (1950-88)

Corvette Summer '78
Laserblast '78

Penelope Milford (1948-)

Henry: Portrait of a Serial Killer 2: Mask of Sanity '96
Normal Life '96
Cold Justice '89
Heathers '89
Bloodlink '86
The Burning Bed '85
The Golden Seal '83
Rosie: The Rosemary Clooney Story '82
Take This Job & Shove It '81
The Last Word '80
Oldest Living Graduate '80
Seizure: The Story of Kathy Morris '80
Coming Home '78

Christina Milian (1981-)

Bring It On: Fight to the Finish '09
Snowglobe '07
Pulse '06
Be Cool '05
Man of the House '05
Love Don't Cost a Thing '03
American Pie '99

Tomas Milian (1937-)

The Lost City '05
Washington Heights '02
For Love or Country: The Arturo Sandoval Story '00
Traffic '00
The Yards '00
Amistad '97
Fools Rush In '97
The Burning Season '94
The Cowboy Way '94
Nails '92
JFK '91
Cat Chaser '90
Drug Wars: The Camarena Story '90
Havana '90
Revenge '90
Salome '85
Identification of a Woman '82
Almost Human '79
Blood and Guns '79
Cop in Blue Jeans '78
Sonny and Jed '73
Don't Torture a Duckling '72
Counter Punch '71
Companeros '70
Time of Indifference '64
Boccaccio '70 '62
Il Bell'Antonio '60

Ivana Milicevic (1974-)

Witless Protection '08
Casino Royale '06
Running Scared '06
Just like Heaven '05
Head Over Heels '01

Frank Military

The Last Castle '01
Everybody Wins '90
Dead Bang '89
Nutcracker: Money, Madness & Murder '87

John Miljan (1892-1960)

Mrs. Mike '49
Queen of the Amazons '47
I Accuse My Parents '45
Wildfire '45
Boss of Big Town '43
The Fallen Sparrow '43
Motorcycle Squad '41
Riot Squad '41
Young Bill Hickok '40
Arizona Mahoney '36
Charlie Chan in Paris '35
Mississippi '35
Under the Pampas Moon '35
Belle of the Nineties '34
The Ghost Walks '34
What! No Beer? '33
Emma '32
Kid from Spain '32
Politics '31
Possessed '31
Susan Lenox: Her Fall and Rise '31
Show Girl in Hollywood '30
The Unholy Three '30
Speedway '29
Yankee Clipper '27
The Unchastened Woman '25

Hugh Millais

The Dogs of War '81
Images '72
McCabe & Mrs. Miller '71

Robyn Millan

Murph the Surf '75
Murder Motel '74
The Witchmaker '69

Victor Millan (1920-)

Boulevard Nights '79
The FBI Story '59
Terror in a Texas Town '58
Touch of Evil '58

Gloria Milland

Goliath Against the Giants '63
Revenge of the Musketeers '63
Beauty on the Beach '61

Ray Milland (1905-86)

Game for Vultures '86
Masks of Death '86
The Sea Serpent '85

Starflight One *'83*
Our Family Business *'81*
The Attic *'80*
Survival Run *'80*
Blackout *'78*
Cruise into Terror *'78*
Oil *'78*
Oliver's Story *'78*
The Uncanny *'78*
Slavers *'77*
Swiss Conspiracy *'77*
The Last Tycoon *'76*
Mayday at 40,000 Feet *'76*
Rich Man, Poor Man *'76*
The Dead Don't Die *'75*
Escape to Witch Mountain *'75*
Night of the Laughing Dead *'75*
Terror in the Wax Museum *'73*
The Big Game *'72*
Embassy *'72*
Frogs *'72*
The Thing with Two Heads *'72*
Quick, Let's Get Married *'71*
Love Story *'70*
X: The Man with X-Ray Eyes *'63*
Panic in the Year Zero! *'62*
Premature Burial *'62*
Lisbon *'56*
The Girl in the Red Velvet Swing *'55*
A Man Alone *'55*
Dial "M" for Murder *'54*
Bugles in the Afternoon *'52*
The Thief *'52*
Close to My Heart *'51*
Rhubarb *'51*
Copper Canyon *'50*
A Life of Her Own *'50*
A Woman of Distinction *'50*
It Happens Every Spring *'49*
The Big Clock *'48*
Golden Earrings *'47*
The Lost Weekend *'45*
Ministry of Fear *'44*
The Uninvited *'44*
Forever and a Day *'43*
The Major and the Minor *'42*
Reap the Wild Wind *'42*
Star Spangled Rhythm *'42*
Doctor Takes a Wife *'40*
Beau Geste *'39*
Everything Happens at Night *'39*
Bulldog Drummond Escapes *'37*
Easy Living *'37*
Next Time We Love *'36*
Three Smart Girls *'36*
Charlie Chan in London *'34*
We're Not Dressing *'34*
Ambassador Bill *'31*
Blonde Crazy *'31*
The Flying Scotsman *'29*

Gregory Millar

Lethal Weapon 3 *'92*
Uncaged *'91*

Marjie Millar

When Gangland Strikes *'56*
Money from Home *'53*

David Millbern (1957-)

Ice Spiders *'07*
Christmas Do-Over *'06*
In Her Line of Fire *'06*
Chupacabra Terror *'05*
Gods and Monsters *'98*
Amanda and the Alien *'95*
Bikini Summer *'91*
Sorceress *'82*

David Millburn

See David Millbern

Allan Miller (1929-)

Warlock *'91*
Obsessive Love *'84*
Pearl *'78*

Andrew Miller

Cube *'98*
The Last of the Dogmen *'95*

Ann Miller (1919-2004)

Mulholland Drive *'01*
The Opposite Sex *'56*
Hit the Deck *'55*
Deep in My Heart *'54*
Kiss Me Kate *'53*
Small Town Girl *'53*
Lovely to Look At *'52*
Texas Carnival *'51*
Watch the Birdie *'50*
On the Town *'49*
Easter Parade *'48*
Melody Ranch *'40*
Too Many Girls *'40*
Room Service *'38*
You Can't Take It with You *'38*

Annette Miller

Lift *'01*
The Imported Bridegroom *'89*

Aubree Miller (1979-)

The Ewoks: Battle for Endor *'85*
The Ewok Adventure *'84*

Barry Miller (1958-)

Flawless *'99*
Love Affair *'94*
The Pickle *'93*
Love at Large *'89*
The Last Temptation of Christ *'88*
Peggy Sue Got Married *'86*
Roommate *'84*
The Chosen *'81*
Fame *'80*
Saturday Night Fever *'77*

Ben Miller (1966-)

The Prince & Me *'04*
Johnny English *'03*

Bodil Miller (1928-)

Reptilicus *'62*
Ma and Pa Kettle on Vacation *'53*

Brendan Miller

Red Sands *'09*
The Last Days of Summer *'07*

Charles F. Miller (1891-1955)

Call Northside 777 *'48*
The Spider Returns *'41*
Phantom of Chinatown *'40*

Cheryl Miller (1943-)

Mountain Man *'77*
Dr. Death, Seeker of Souls *'73*
Clarence, the Cross-eyed Lion *'65*

Christa Miller (1964-)

The Andromeda Strain *'08*
The Operator *'01*
Smiling Fish & Goat on Fire *'99*

Colleen Miller (1932-)

Gunfight at Comanche Creek *'64*
Man in the Shadow *'57*

C.T. Miller

Friend of the Family *'95*
Lap Dancing *'95*

David Keith Miller

Turn of the Blade *'97*
Playing Dangerous *'95*

Dax Miller

Blood Surf *'00*
The Convent *'00*

Dean Miller (1924-2004)

Because You're Mine *'52*
Everything I Have is Yours *'52*

Dennis Miller (1953-)

What Happens in Vegas *'08*
Joe Dirt *'01*
Murder at 1600 *'97*
Tales from the Crypt Presents Bordello of Blood *'96*
The Net *'95*
Never Talk to Strangers *'95*
Disclosure *'94*
Madhouse *'90*
The Everlasting Secret Family *'88*
The Quest *'86*

Denny Miller (1934-)

Buck and the Preacher *'72*
The Party *'68*

Dick Miller (1928-)

Small Soldiers *'98*
National Lampoon's Attack of the 5 Ft. 2 Women *'94*
Pulp Fiction *'94*
Runaway Daughters *'94*
Shake, Rattle & Rock! *'94*
Tales from the Crypt Presents Demon Knight *'94*
Batman: Mask of the Phantasm *'93 (V)*
Fallen Angels 1 *'93*
Fallen Angels 2 *'93*
Amityville 1992: It's About Time *'92*
Body Waves *'92*
Matinee *'92*
Quake *'92*
Unlawful Entry *'92*
Motorama *'91*
Evil Toons *'90*
Gremlins 2: The New Batch *'90*
Far from Home *'89*
Under the Boardwalk *'89*
Amazon Women on the Moon *'87*
Innerspace *'87*
Project X *'87*
Chopping Mall *'86*
Night of the Creeps *'86*
After Hours *'85*
Explorers *'85*
Gremlins *'84*
The Terminator *'84*
All the Right Moves *'83*
Get Crazy *'83*
Heart Like a Wheel *'83*
Lies *'83*
Twilight Zone: The Movie *'83*
Heartbeeps *'81*
The Howling *'81*
Dr. Heckyl and Mr. Hype *'80*
Used Cars *'80*
Lady in Red *'79*
Rock 'n' Roll High School *'79*
Piranha *'78*
Starhops *'78*
New York, New York *'77*
Cannonball *'76*
Hollywood Boulevard *'76*
Crazy Mama *'75*
Big Bad Mama *'74*
Candy Stripe Nurses *'74*
Truck Turner *'74*
The Young Nurses *'73*
Night Call Nurses *'72*
The St. Valentine's Day Massacre *'67*
The Trip *'67*
The Wild Angels *'66*
The Terror *'63*
X: The Man with X-Ray Eyes *'63*
Premature Burial *'62*
Atlas *'60*
Little Shop of Horrors *'60*
A Bucket of Blood *'59*
Carnival Rock *'57*
Rock All Night *'57*
Sorority Girl *'57*
The Undead *'57*
The Gunslinger *'56*
It Conquered the World *'56*

Eve Miller (1933-77)

Kansas Pacific *'53*
April in Paris *'52*
Big Trees *'52*
The Winning Team *'52*

F.E. (Flourney) Miller (1887-1971)

Yes, Sir, Mr. Bones *'51*
Mystery in Swing *'40*
Bronze Buckaroo *'39*
Harlem Rides the Range *'39*
Harlem on the Prairie *'38*

Gabrielle Miller (1973-)

The Silencer *'99*
Rupert's Land *'98*

Geri Miller

Trash *'70*
Flesh *'68*

Glenn Miller (1904-44)

Orchestra Wives *'42*
Sun Valley Serenade *'41*

Ivan Miller (1888-1967)

Frontier Vengeance *'40*
Call of the Yukon *'38*

J. Matthew Miller

2 Minutes Later *'07*
Open Cam *'05*

Jason Miller (1939-2001)

Finding Home *'03*
Mommy *'95*
Murdered Innocence *'94*
Rudy *'93*
Small Kill *'93*
Exorcist 3: Legion *'90*
Light of Day *'87*
Vengeance *'86*
Toy Soldiers *'84*
Monsignor *'82*
That Championship Season *'82*
The Best Little Girl in the World *'81*
The Henderson Monster *'80*
Marilyn: The Untold Story *'80*
The Ninth Configuration *'79*
The Dain Curse *'78*
F. Scott Fitzgerald in Hollywood *'76*
A Home of Our Own *'75*
The Exorcist *'73*

Jean Miller

Speak of the Devil *'90*
Silent Night, Deadly Night 2 *'87*

Jeremy Miller (1976-)

The Willies *'90*
Emanon *'86*

Joel McKinnon Miller

Friday After Next *'02*
The Swan Princess *'94 (V)*

Johnny Miller

The Flying Scotsman *'06*
Byron *'03*

Jonny Lee Miller (1972-)

Emma *'09*
Endgame *'09*
Aeon Flux *'05*
Melinda and Melinda *'05*
Mindhunters *'05*
Dracula 2000 *'00*
Love, Honour & Obey *'00*
Mansfield Park *'99*
Plunkett & Macleane *'98*
Retribution *'98*
Afterglow *'97*
Behind the Lines *'97*
Larry McMurtry's Dead Man's Walk *'96*
Hackers *'95*
Trainspotting *'95*

Joshua John Miller (1974-)

The Wizard of Gore *'07*
And You Thought Your Parents Were Weird! *'91*
Class of 1999 *'90*
Teen Witch *'89*
Near Dark *'87*
River's Edge *'87*
Stoogemania *'85*

Kathleen Miller (1945-)

Coming Home *'78*
Fighting Mad *'76*
Strange New World *'75*

Kelly Miller

Newsbreak *'00*
George of the Jungle *'97*

Kenny (Ken) Miller (1931-)

Bloodstalkers *'76*
Surf Party *'64*

Kristen Miller (1977-)

All In *'06*
Single White Female 2: The Psycho *'05*
Team America: World Police *'04 (V)*

Kristine Miller (1929-)

High Lonesome *'50*
Too Late for Tears *'49*
Jungle Patrol *'48*

Larry Miller (1953-)

The Other End of the Line *'08*
Senior Skip Day *'08*
Bee Movie *'07 (V)*
Blonde Ambition *'07*
The Final Season *'07*
The Ant Bully *'06 (V)*
Keeping Up with the Steins *'06*
Kiss Kiss Bang Bang *'05*
Life of the Party *'05*
Final Approach *'04*
The Princess Diaries 2: Royal Engagement *'04*
A Mighty Wind *'03*
Max Keeble's Big Move *'01*
The Princess Diaries *'01*
What's the Worst That Could Happen? *'01*
Best in Show *'00*
Nutty Professor 2: The Klumps *'00*
The Big Tease *'99*
The Minus Man *'99*
Pros & Cons *'99*
Ten Things I Hate about You *'99*
Carnival of Souls *'98*
Chairman of the Board *'97*
For Richer or Poorer *'97*
Dear God *'96*
Waiting for Guffman *'96*
Corrina, Corrina *'94*
Radioland Murders *'94*
Dream Lover *'93*
Undercover Blues *'93*
Carry On Columbus *'92*
The Favor *'92*
Frozen Assets *'92*
Suburban Commando *'91*
Almost an Angel *'90*
Pretty Woman *'90*
Three Fugitives *'89*

Linda Miller (1942-)

Elvis and Me *'88*
Alice Sweet Alice *'76*
One Summer Love *'76*
King Kong Escapes *'67*

Lorraine Miller (1922-78)

Ambush Trail *'46*
Border Badmen *'45*
Frontier Fugitives *'45*
Riders of the Rio Grande *'43*

Mark Miller (1953-)

Love Field *'91*
Savannah Smiles *'82*
Ginger in the Morning *'73*

Mark Thomas Miller (1960-)

Mom *'89*
Blue De Ville *'86*
Misfits of Science *'85*

Martin Miller (1899-1969)

Children of the Damned *'63*
The Phantom of the Opera *'62*
Peeping Tom *'60*
Man on the Run *'49*
Frenzy *'46*
Hotel Reserve *'44*

Marvin Miller (1913-85)

Kiss Daddy Goodbye *'81*
The Day the Earth Froze *'59 (N)*
Sleeping Beauty *'59 (V)*
Forbidden Planet *'56 (V)*
Off Limits *'53*
Red Planet Mars *'52*
Dead Reckoning *'47*

Mary Louise Miller (1924-)

The Night Cry *'26*
Sparrows *'26*

Mindi Miller (1950-)

Caged Fury *'90*
Nudity Required *'90*
Hollywood Boulevard 2 *'89*
The Big Turnaround *'88*
Deadly Embrace *'88*
Return Fire *'88*
Penitentiary 3 *'87*
Amazons *'86*
Body Double *'84*
Hercules *'83*
Sacred Ground *'83*
Hell Up in Harlem *'73*

Mirta Miller (1948-)

Icebox Murders *'82*
Cria Cuervos *'76*
Dracula's Great Love *'72*
Dr. Jekyll and the Wolfman *'71*

Omar Benson Miller (1978-)

The Express *'08*
Miracle at St. Anna *'08*
Grindin' *'07*
Things We Lost in the Fire *'07*
Get Rich or Die Tryin' *'05*
Shall We Dance? *'04*
Undefeated *'03*
8 Mile *'02*

Patsy Ruth Miller (1905-95)

Lonely Wives *'31*
The First Auto *'27*
So This Is Paris *'26*
Head Winds *'25*
The Hunchback of Notre Dame *'23*
The Sheik *'21*

Penelope Ann Miller (1964-)

Free Style *'09*
Blonde Ambition *'07*
The Messengers *'07*
Carry Me Home *'04*
National Lampoon's Holiday Reunion *'03*
Rudy: The Rudy Giulani Story *'03*
Dead in a Heartbeat *'02*
Along Came a Spider *'01*
A Woman's a Helluva Thing *'01*
Along for the Ride *'00*
Full Disclosure *'00*
Killing Moon *'00*
Rocky Marciano *'99*
The Break Up *'98*
Outside Ozona *'98*
Ruby Bridges *'98*
The Last Don *'97*
Little City *'97*
The Relic *'96*
The Shadow *'94*
Witch Hunt *'94*
Carlito's Way *'93*
Chaplin *'92*
The Gun in Betty Lou's Handbag *'92*
Year of the Comet *'92*
Other People's Money *'91*
Awakenings *'90*
The Freshman *'90*
Kindergarten Cop *'90*
Dead Bang *'89*
Downtown *'89*
Our Town *'89*
Big Top Pee-wee *'88*
Biloxi Blues *'88*
Miles from Home *'88*
Adventures in Babysitting *'87*

Percy Miller

See Master P

Rebecca Miller (1962-)
Mrs. Parker and the Vicious Circle *'94*
The Pickle *'93*
Consenting Adults *'92*
Wind *'92*
The Murder of Mary Phagan *'87*

Roger Miller (1936-92)
Lucky Luke *'94 (V)*
Robin Hood *'73 (V)*

Sarah Jane Miller
Mommy 2: Mommy's Day *'96*
Mommy *'95*

Sherry Miller
It's a Boy Girl Thing *'06*
A Killing Spring *'02*
Tribulation *'00*
This Matter of Marriage *'98*
Sabrina the Teenage Witch *'96*
Rent-A-Kid *'95*

Sidney Miller (1916-2004)
There Goes Kelly *'45*
Men of Boys Town *'41*
Boys Town *'38*
Little Red Schoolhouse *'36*
Rafter Romance *'34*

Sienna Miller (1981-)
G.I. Joe: The Rise of Cobra *'09*
The September Issue *'09*
The Edge of Love *'08*
The Mysteries of Pittsburgh *'08*
Interview *'07*
Stardust *'07*
Factory Girl *'06*
Casanova *'05*
Layer Cake *'05*
Alfie *'04*

Stephen E. Miller
Air Bud *'97*
Home Is Where the Hart Is *'88*
The Stepfather *'87*
Jane Doe *'83*

Tangi Miller (1974-)
Love and Other Four Letter Words *'07*
Leprechaun 6: Back 2 Tha Hood *'03*
The Other Brother *'02*

T.J. Miller
She's Out of My League *'10*
Cloverfield *'08*
The Alien Agenda: Out of the Darkness *'96*

Ty Miller (1964-)
Trancers 5: Sudden Deth *'94*
Trancers 4: Jack of Swords *'93*

Walter Miller (1892-1940)
Wild Horse Rodeo *'37*
Ghost Patrol *'36*
The Ivory Handled Gun *'35*
Law for Tombstone *'35*
Rustlers of Red Dog *'35*
Stone of Silver Creek *'35*
The Fighting Trooper *'34*
Tailspin Tommy *'34*
Blessed Event *'32*
The Lone Defender *'32*
Ridin' for Justice *'32*
Shadow of the Eagle *'32*
The Galloping Ghost *'31*
Rogue of the Rio Grande *'30*

Wentworth Miller (1972-)
Stealth *'05 (V)*
The Human Stain *'03*
Underworld *'03*
Dinotopia *'02*

Christiane Millet
The Taste of Others *'00*
November Moon *'85*

Arthur Millett (1874-1952)
The Nevada Buckaroo *'31*
The Wildcat *'26*

Andra Millian
Nightfall *'88*
Stacy's Knights *'83*

James Millican (1910-55)
A Lion in the Streets *'53*
Bugles in the Afternoon *'52*
Carson City *'52*
Scandal Sheet *'52*
The Winning Team *'52*
I Was a Communist for the FBI *'51*
Last of the Wild Horses *'49*
Man from Colorado *'49*
Outlaw Gang *'49*
Rimfire *'49*
The Adventures of Gallant Bess *'48*
Return of Wildfire *'48*
Spoilers of the North *'47*

Deanna Milligan (1972-)
Suspicious River *'00*
Must Be Santa *'99*

Dustin Milligan
Extract *'09*
The Messengers *'07*
The Butterfly Effect 2 *'06*
In the Land of Women *'06*

Spike Milligan (1918-2002)
Monty Python's Life of Brian *'79*
The Hound of the Baskervilles *'77*
Great McGonagall *'75*
Ghost in the Noonday Sun *'74*
Digby, the Biggest Dog in the World *'73*
Rentadick *'72*
The Magic Christian *'69*
Postman's Knock *'62*
Down Among the Z Men *'52*
Goon Movie *'52*

Angie Milliken
The Condemned *'07*
Solo *'06*
Paperback Hero *'99*
Dead Heart *'96*
Talk *'94*

Alley Mills (1951-)
Tainted Blood *'93*
Going Berserk *'83*
Rape and Marriage: The Rideout Case *'80*

Barbara Mills
Chain Gang Women *'72*
Sweet Georgia *'72*

Brooke Mills (1985-)
The Student Teachers *'73*
The Big Doll House *'71*
Dream No Evil *'70*

Donna Mills (1942-)
Too Cool for Christmas *'04*
False Arrest *'92*
The World's Oldest Living Bridesmaid *'92*
Runaway Father *'91*
Alice in Wonderland *'85*
Waikiki *'80*
Bunco *'77*
Curse of the Black Widow *'77*
Fire *'77*
The Hunted Lady *'77*
Beyond the Bermuda Triangle *'75*
Murph the Surf *'75*
Killer with Two Faces *'74*
One Deadly Owner *'74*
Haunts of the Very Rich *'72*
Play Misty for Me *'71*
The Incident *'67*

Eddie Mills (1972-)
Winter Break *'02*
At Any Cost *'00*

The Tempest *'99*
Dancer, Texas—Pop. 81 *'98*
Heartwood *'98*

Grace Mills
Night of the Howling Beast *'75*
Exorcism *'74*

Hayley Mills (1946-)
2B Perfectly Honest *'04*
A Troll in Central Park *'94 (V)*
Back Home *'90*
Appointment with Death *'88*
Deadly Strangers *'82*
The Flame Trees of Thika *'81*
Bananas Boat *'78*
Kingfisher Caper *'76*
Cry of the Penguins *'71*
Endless Night *'71*
Africa Texas Style *'67*
The Trouble with Angels *'66*
That Darn Cat *'65*
The Chalk Garden *'64*
The Moon-Spinners *'64*
Summer Magic *'63*
In Search of the Castaways *'62*
The Parent Trap *'61*
Whistle down the Wind *'61*
Pollyanna *'60*
Tiger Bay *'59*

John Mills (1908-)
Hamlet *'96*
Martin Chuzzlewit *'94*
Frankenstein *'93*
Around the World in 80 Days *'89*
The Lady and the Highwayman *'89*
A Tale of Two Cities *'89*
Who's That Girl? *'87*
Hold the Dream *'86*
Masks of Death *'86*
When the Wind Blows *'86 (V)*
Agatha Christie's Murder with Mirrors *'85*
A Woman of Substance *'84*
Sahara *'83*
Gandhi *'82*
Quatermass Conclusion *'79*
The Thirty-Nine Steps *'79*
Zulu Dawn *'79*
The Big Sleep *'78*
Dr. Strange *'78*
Choice of Weapons *'76*
The Human Factor *'75*
Lady Caroline Lamb *'73*
Oklahoma Crude *'73*
Young Winston *'72*
Ryan's Daughter *'70*
Oh! What a Lovely War *'69*
A Black Veil for Lisa *'68*
Africa Texas Style *'67*
Chuka *'67*
The Wrong Box *'66*
King Rat *'65*
Operation Crossbow *'65*
The Chalk Garden *'64*
Tiara Tahiti *'62*
The Swiss Family Robinson *'60*
Tunes of Glory *'60*
Tiger Bay *'59*
The Vicious Circle *'57*
Above Us the Waves *'56*
Around the World in 80 Days *'56*
The Baby and the Battleship *'56*
War and Peace *'56*
The Colditz Story *'55*
End of the Affair *'55*
Escapade *'55*
Hobson's Choice *'53*
The October Man *'48*
Scott of the Antarctic *'48*
This Happy Breed *'47*
Great Expectations *'46*
Waterloo Road *'44*
In Which We Serve *'43*
We Dive at Dawn *'43*
Cottage to Let *'41*
Goodbye, Mr. Chips *'39*
The Green Cockatoo *'37*
O.H.M.S. *'37*

Nine Days a Queen *'36*
The Ghost Camera *'33*

Judson Mills (1969-)
Chill Factor *'99*
Major League 3: Back to the Minors *'98*
Joyride *'97*

Juliet Mills (1941-)
The Other Sister *'98*
Waxwork 2: Lost in Time *'91*
The Cracker Factory *'79*
Alexander: The Other Side of Dawn *'77*
Barnaby and Me *'77*
Beyond the Door *'75*
QB VII *'74*
Jonathan Livingston Seagull *'73*
Avanti! *'72*
Oh! What a Lovely War *'69*
The Rare Breed *'66*
Carry On Jack *'63*
The October Man *'48*

Zach Mills
Kit Kittredge: An American Girl *'08*
Mr. Magorium's Wonder Emporium *'07*

Bill Milner
Sex & Drugs & Rock & Roll *'10*
Is Anybody There? *'08*
Son of Rambow *'07*

Martin Milner (1927-)
Nashville Beat *'89*
The Seekers *'79*
Flood! *'76*
Hurricane *'74*
Columbo: Murder by the Book *'71*
Valley of the Dolls *'67*
Zebra in the Kitchen *'65*
13 Ghosts *'60*
Compulsion *'59*
Gunfight at the O.K. Corral *'57*
Sweet Smell of Success *'57*
Francis in the Navy *'55*
Mister Roberts *'55*
Pete Kelly's Blues *'55*
Belles on Their Toes *'52*
I Want You *'51*
The Halls of Montezuma *'50*
Our Very Own *'50*
Sands of Iwo Jima *'49*
Life with Father *'47*

Jean-Roger Milo (1957-)
Lucie Aubrac *'98*
L.627 *'92*

Sandra Milo (1935-)
Incantato *'03*
Dead for a Dollar *'70*
Bang Bang Kid *'67*
Juliet of the Spirits *'65*
8 1/2 *'63*
Vanina Vanini *'61*
Classe Tous Risque *'60*
Generale Della Rovere *'60*
Herod the Great *'60*

Andy Milonakis (1976-)
Still Waiting *'08*
Wieners *'08*
Who's Your Caddy? *'07*
Killer Pad *'06*
Waiting *'05*

Ernest Milton (1890-1974)
Cat Girl *'57*
Alice in Wonderland *'50*
The Foreman Went to France *'42*
The Scarlet Pimpernel *'34*

Gerald Milton
Underworld USA *'61*
China Gate *'57*

Mantoyo Mimasu
47 Ronin, Part 1 *'42*
47 Ronin, Part 2 *'42*

Yvette Mimieux (1939-)
Obsessive Love *'84*
Circle of Power *'83*
Night Partners *'83*
Forbidden Love *'82*
The Black Hole *'79*
Devil Dog: The Hound of Hell *'78*
Outside Chance *'78*
Snowbeast *'77*
Jackson County Jail *'76*
Legend of Valentino *'75*
Hit Lady *'74*
Journey into Fear *'74*
Neptune Factor *'73*
Dark of the Sun *'68*
Three in the Attic *'68*
Caper of the Golden Bulls *'67*
Monkeys, Go Home! *'66*
Toys in the Attic *'63*
Diamond Head *'62*
The Four Horsemen of the Apocalypse *'62*
The Wonderful World of the Brothers Grimm *'62*
Platinum High School *'60*
The Time Machine *'60*
Where the Boys Are *'60*

Kaho Minami
The Great Yokai War *'05*
Angel Dust *'96*

Leo Minaya
How the Garcia Girls Spent Their Summer *'05*
Manito *'03*

Christiane Minazzoli (1931-)
Betty *'92*
The Story of O *'75*

Esther Minciotti (1883-1962)
Full of Life *'56*
Marty *'55*

Sal Mineo (1939-76)
Escape from the Planet of the Apes *'71*
Krakatoa East of Java *'69*
Cheyenne Autumn *'64*
The Longest Day *'62*
Exodus *'60*
The Gene Krupa Story *'59*
Tonka *'58*
Dino *'57*
Giant *'56*
Rock, Pretty Baby *'56*
Somebody Up There Likes Me *'56*
The Private War of Major Benson *'55*
Rebel without a Cause *'55*

Jan Miner (1917-2004)
Mermaids *'90*
Willie & Phil *'80*
Lenny *'74*

Rachel Miner (1980-)
The Butterfly Effect 3: Revelation *'09*
Hide *'08*
Cult *'07*
The Still Life *'07*
Tooth and Nail *'07*
The Black Dahlia *'06*
Fatwa *'06*
Love and Debate *'06*
Circadian Rhythm *'05*
Little Athens *'05*
Bully *'01*

Ming Na (1968-)
Push *'09*
Final Fantasy: The Spirits Within *'01 (V)*
Mulan *'98 (V)*
One Night Stand *'97*
Hong Kong '97 *'94*
Star Quest *'94*
Street Fighter *'94*
The Joy Luck Club *'93*

Max Minghella (1985-)
Brief Interviews With Hideous Men *'09*
How to Lose Friends & Alienate People *'08*

Art School Confidential *'06*
Bee Season *'05*
Syriana *'05*

Elvira Minguez (1965-)
Che *'08*
The Reckoning *'03*
The Dancer Upstairs *'02*

Birgit Minichmayr
Cherry Blossoms *'08*
The Crown Prince *'06*
Falling *'06*
Taking Sides *'01*

Claudette Mink (1975-)
Shattered *'07*
Children of the Corn: Revelation *'01*
Deadly Heroes *'96*

Liza Minnelli (1946-)
Sex and the City 2 *'10*
The Oh in Ohio *'06*
Jackie's Back *'99*
Parallel Lives *'94*
Stepping Out *'91*
Arthur 2: On the Rocks *'88*
Rent-A-Cop *'88*
That's Dancing! *'85*
A Time to Live *'85*
The Muppets Take Manhattan *'84*
The Princess and the Pea *'83*
King of Comedy *'82*
Arthur *'81*
New York, New York *'77*
A Matter of Time *'76*
Silent Movie *'76*
Cabaret *'72*
Journey Back to Oz *'71 (V)*
The Sterile Cuckoo *'69*
In the Good Old Summertime *'49*

Byron Keith Minns
Black Dynamite *'09*
South Central *'92*

Kylie Minogue (1968-)
Doogal *'05 (V)*
Moulin Rouge *'01*
Cut *'00*
Bio-Dome *'96*
Street Fighter *'94*

Bob Minor (1942-)
Black Eliminator *'78*
The Swinging Cheerleaders *'74*

Kelly Jo Minter (1966-)
The People under the Stairs *'91*
Miracle Mile *'89*
A Nightmare on Elm Street 5: Dream Child *'89*
Popcorn *'89*
Summer School *'87*

Kristin Minter (1965-)
The Bread, My Sweet *'01*
Tick Tock *'00*
The Apostate *'98*
Savage *'96*
Flashfire *'94*
There Goes My Baby *'92*
Cool As Ice *'91*

Mary Miles Minter (1902-84)
Nurse Marjorie *'20*
Eyes of Julia Deep *'18*

Christopher Mintz-Plasse (1989-)
How to Train Your Dragon *'10 (V)*
Kick-Ass *'10*
Marmaduke *'10 (V)*
Year One *'09*
Role Models *'08*
Superbad *'07*

Frank Minucci
Friends and Family *'01*
A Brother's Kiss *'97*
Tar *'97*

Fabrizio Mioni (1930-)
Hercules *'58*
Roland the Mighty *'56*

Miou-Miou (1950-)
The Science of Sleep *'06*
Dry Cleaning *'97*
Women *'97*
The Eighth Day *'95*
Little Indian, Big City *'95*
Germinal *'93*
May Fools *'90*
La Lectrice *'88*
Menage *'86*
My Other Husband *'85*
Dog Day *'83*
Entre-Nous *'83*
Josepha *'82*
Roads to the South *'78*
This Sweet Sickness *'77*
Jonah Who Will Be 25 in the Year 2000 *'76*
No Problem *'75*
Going Places *'74*
The Mad Adventures of Rabbi Jacob *'73*

Brigitte Mira (1910-2005)
Chinese Roulette *'86*
Berlin Alexanderplatz *'80*
Mother Kusters Goes to Heaven *'76*
Every Man for Himself & God Against All *'75*
Fear of Fear *'75*
Ali: Fear Eats the Soul *'74*
Tenderness of the Wolves *'73*

Irene Miracle (1954-)
Puppet Master *'89*
The Last of Philip Banter *'87*
In the Shadow of Kilimanjaro *'86*
Inferno *'80*
Night Train Murders *'75*
Torture Train *'75*

Evan Mirand
Megalodon *'03*
My Best Friend Is a Vampire *'88*
Weekend War *'88*
Brotherhood of Justice *'86*

Aurora Miranda (1915-2005)
The Three Caballeros *'45 (V)*
Phantom Lady *'44*

Carmen Miranda (1909-55)
Scared Stiff *'53*
Nancy Goes to Rio *'50*
A Date with Judy *'48*
Copacabana *'47*
Doll Face *'46*
If I'm Lucky *'46*
Greenwich Village *'44*
Something for the Boys *'44*
The Gang's All Here *'43*
Springtime in the Rockies *'42*
That Night in Rio *'41*
Week-End in Havana *'41*
Down Argentine Way *'40*

Isa Miranda (1909-82)
The Night Porter *'74*
Twitch of the Death Nerve *'71*
Dorian Gray *'70*
Dog Eat Dog *'64*
Just Another Pretty Face *'58*
Summertime *'55*
Seven Deadly Sins *'53*
La Ronde *'51*
The Walls of Malapaga *'49*
La Signora di Tutti *'34*

Robert Miranda
Blue Streak *'99*
Black Thunder *'98*
For Which He Stands *'98*
The Rat Pack *'98*
Steel Sharks *'97*
Gotti *'96*
Desire *'95*
Lost in Yonkers *'93*
What's Love Got to Do with It? *'93*
Sister Act *'92*
Chips, the War Dog *'90*
Sons *'89*

Soledad Miranda (1943-72)
Count Dracula *'71*
Sound of Horror *'64*

Helen Mirren (1946-)
Inkheart *'09*
The Last Station *'09*
State of Play *'09*
National Treasure: Book of Secrets *'07*
The Queen *'06*
Shadowboxer *'06*
Elizabeth I *'05*
The Hitchhiker's Guide to the Galaxy *'05 (V)*
The Clearing *'04*
Raising Helen *'04*
Calendar Girls *'03*
The Roman Spring of Mrs. Stone *'03*
Gosford Park *'01*
Last Orders *'01*
No Such Thing *'01*
Greenfingers *'00*
The Pledge *'00*
The Passion of Ayn Rand *'99*
Teaching Mrs. Tingle *'99*
Prince of Egypt *'98 (V)*
Critical Care *'97*
The Painted Lady *'97*
Losing Chase *'96*
Some Mother's Son *'96*
The Madness of King George *'94*
Royal Deceit *'94*
The Hawk *'93*
Prime Suspect *'92*
The Comfort of Strangers *'91*
Where Angels Fear to Tread *'91*
The Cook, the Thief, His Wife & Her Lover *'90*
Dr. Bethune *'90*
Red King, White Knight *'89*
When the Whales Came *'89*
Pascali's Island *'88*
Cause Celebre *'87*
The Gospel According to Vic *'87*
The Mosquito Coast *'86*
Coming Through *'85*
White Nights *'85*
Cal *'84*
2010: The Year We Make Contact *'84*
Excalibur *'81*
Priest of Love *'81*
Caligula *'80*
The Fiendish Plot of Dr. Fu Manchu *'80*
Hussy *'80*
The Long Good Friday *'80*
S.O.S. Titanic *'79*
O Lucky Man! *'73*
Savage Messiah *'72*
Age of Consent *'69*
A Midsummer Night's Dream *'68*

Masao Mishima (1906-73)
Harakiri *'62*
The Human Condition: No Greater Love *'58*

Dorian Missick (1976-)
Mama's Boy *'07*
Lucky Number Slevin *'06*
Two Weeks Notice *'02*

Karen Mistal
Cannibal Women in the Avocado Jungle of Death *'89*
Return of the Killer Tomatoes! *'88*

Mr. T (1952-)
Cloudy with a Chance of Meatballs *'09 (V)*
Not Another Teen Movie *'01*
Freaked *'93*
Straight Line *'88*
D.C. Cab *'84*
Penitentiary 2 *'82*
Rocky 3 *'82*

Mr. Wiggles
See Ludacris

Jorge Mistral (1920-72)
The Sword and the Cross *'58*
Wuthering Heights *'53*

Jimi Mistry (1973-)
RocknRolla *'08*
Partition *'07*
Blood Diamond *'06*
Dead Fish *'04*
Ella Enchanted *'04*
Touch of Pink *'04*
The Truth About Love *'04*
The Guru *'02*
The Mystic Masseur *'01*
Born Romantic *'00*
East Is East *'99*

Brian Stokes Mitchell (1957-)
One Last Thing *'05*
Call Me Claus *'01*
Ruby's Bucket of Blood *'01*
Double Platinum *'99*

Cameron Mitchell (1918-94)
Jack-O *'95*
Trapped Alive *'93*
Crossing the Line *'90*
Terror in Beverly Hills *'90*
Action U.S.A. *'89*
Easy Kill *'89*
Killers *'88*
Memorial Valley Massacre *'88*
Rage to Kill *'88*
Space Mutiny *'88*
Swift Justice *'88*
Codename: Vengeance *'87*
Deadly Prey *'87*
Hollywood Cop *'87*
The Messenger *'87*
The Offspring *'87*
Bloodlink *'86*
Nightforce *'86*
Tomb *'86*
Mission... Kill *'85*
Go for the Gold *'84*
Killpoint *'84*
Night Train to Terror *'84*
The Guns and the Fury *'83*
Prince Jack *'83*
Code of Honor *'82*
It's Called Murder, Baby *'82*
My Favorite Year *'82*
Cataclysm *'81*
The Demon *'81*
Frankenstein Island *'81*
Kill Squad *'81*
Raw Force *'81*
Texas Lightning *'81*
The Last Reunion *'80*
Silent Scream *'80*
The Bastard *'78*
Enforcer from Death Row *'78*
Supersonic Man *'78*
The Swarm *'78*
The Toolbox Murders *'78*
Haunts *'77*
Return to Fantasy Island *'77*
Scalp Merchant *'77*
Slavers *'77*
Texas Detour *'77*
Viva Knievel *'77*
Flood! *'76*
The Longest Drive *'76*
The Hanged Man *'74*
The Klansman *'74*
Medusa *'74*
The Stranger *'73*
The Big Game *'72*
Buck and the Preacher *'72*
Slaughter *'72*
Thief *'71*
The Andersonville Trial *'70*
Nightmare in Wax *'69*
Rebel Rousers *'69*
Autopsy of a Ghost *'67*
Hombre *'67*
Ride in the Whirlwind *'66*
Knives of the Avenger *'65*
Minnesota Clay *'65*
Blood and Black Lace *'64*
Dog Eat Dog *'64*
Last Gun *'64*
Caesar the Conqueror *'63*
The Invaders *'63*
Conquest of the Normans *'62*
The Unstoppable Man *'59*
Escapade in Japan *'57*
All Mine to Give *'56*
Carousel *'56*
Tension at Table Rock *'56*
House of Bamboo *'55*
Love Me or Leave Me *'55*
The Tall Men *'55*
Desiree *'54*
Garden of Evil *'54*
How to Marry a Millionaire *'53*
Flight to Mars *'52*
Death of a Salesman *'51*
The Adventures of Gallant Bess *'48*
Homecoming *'48*
They Were Expendable *'45*

Charlotte Mitchell (1926-)
Persuasion *'71*
Village of the Damned *'60*

Chuck "Porky" Mitchell (1928-92)
Ghost Chase *'88*
Swift Justice *'88*
Hollywood Zap *'86*
Porky's Revenge *'85*
Goodbye Cruel World *'82*
Porky's *'82*
Penitentiary *'79*

Daryl (Chill) Mitchell (1965-)
Inside Man *'06*
The Country Bears *'02*
13 Moons *'02*
Black Knight *'01*
Lucky Numbers *'00*
Galaxy Quest *'99*
The Pooch and the Pauper *'99 (V)*
Ten Things I Hate about You *'99*
Home Fries *'98*
Quiet Days in Hollywood *'97*
Toothless *'97*
A Thin Line Between Love and Hate *'96*
Sgt. Bilko *'95*
Fly by Night *'93*

Donna Mitchell
Bomb the System *'05*
Mona Lisa Smile *'03*
Two Bits *'96*
The Portrait *'93*
Psycho 4: The Beginning *'90*

Duke Mitchell (1926-81)
The Executioner *'78*
Bela Lugosi Meets a Brooklyn Gorilla *'52*

E. Roger Mitchell (1971-)
Boycott *'02*
How I Spent My Summer Vacation *'97*

Eddy Mitchell (1942-)
Le Bonheur Est Dans le Pre *'95*
Coup de Torchon *'81*

Elizabeth Mitchell (1970-)
Running Scared *'06*
The Santa Clause 3: The Escape Clause *'06*
The Santa Clause 2 *'02*
Double Bang *'01*
Frequency *'00*
Molly *'99*
Gia *'98*

Eric Mitchell
Underground U.S.A. *'84*
The Foreigner *'78*
Rome '78 *'78*

Ewing Mitchell (1910-88)
Above and Beyond *'53*
Cavalry Charge *'51*

Gene Mitchell
Flipping *'96*
The Takeover *'94*

Geneva Mitchell
Fighting Shadows *'35*
Western Courage *'35*

Gordon Mitchell (1923-2003)
Commando Invasion *'87*
Mines of Kilimanjaro *'87*
Rush *'84*
Frankenstein '80 *'79*
Operation Orient *'78*
Slaughterday *'77*
The Big Bust Out *'73*
Fistful of Death *'71*
Beyond the Law *'68*
Erik, the Viking *'65*
Fighting Fists of Shanghai Joe *'65*
Ali Baba and the Seven Saracens *'64*
Battle of Valiant *'63*
Vulcan God of Fire *'62*
The Giant of Metropolis *'61*

Grant Mitchell (1874-1957)
It Happened on 5th Avenue *'47*
Easy to Wed *'46*
Conflict *'45*
Laura *'44*
The Amazing Mrs. Holiday *'43*
Cairo *'42*
My Sister Eileen *'42*
Footsteps in the Dark *'41*
The Great Lie *'41*
The Man Who Came to Dinner *'41*
The Grapes of Wrath *'40*
The Last Gangster *'37*
Next Time We Love *'36*
Gold Diggers of 1935 *'35*
In Person *'35*
365 Nights in Hollywood *'34*
Heroes for Sale *'33*
20,000 Years in Sing Sing *'33*
No Man of Her Own *'32*
Three on a Match *'32*

Gwen Mitchell
Black Force 2 *'78*
Shaft *'71*

Heather Mitchell
Rogue *'07*
A Little Bit of Soul *'97*
Proof *'91*
The Everlasting Secret Family *'88*

James Mitchell (1920-)
Border Incident *'49*
Colorado Territory *'49*

John Cameron Mitchell (1963-)
Hedwig and the Angry Inch *'00*
David Searching *'97*
Book of Love *'91*

Julien Mitchell (1888-1954)
Bedelia *'46*
Echo Murders *'45*
Hotel Reserve *'44*

Kel Mitchell (1978-)
Ganked *'05*
Clifford's Really Big Movie *'04 (V)*
The Adventures of Rocky & Bullwinkle *'00*
Mystery Men *'99*
Good Burger *'97*

Kenneth Mitchell (1974-)
Miracle *'04*
Charms for the Easy Life *'02*

Kirsty Mitchell (1974-)
Almost Heaven *'06*
I Downloaded a Ghost *'04*
Lighthouse Hill *'04*
A Shot at Glory *'00*

Laurie Mitchell (1922-)
Missile to the Moon *'59*
Queen of Outer Space *'58*

Mark Mitchell (1955-)
Inspector Gadget 2 *'02*
The Outing *'87*

Mary Mitchell (1940-)
A Swingin' Summer *'65*
Spider Baby *'64*
Dementia 13 *'63*
Panic in the Year Zero! *'62*

Millard Mitchell (1900-53)
Here Come the Girls *'53*
The Naked Spur *'53*
Singin' in the Rain *'52*
The Gunfighter *'50*
Winchester '73 *'50*
Twelve o'Clock High *'49*
A Foreign Affair *'48*
A Double Life *'47*

Radha Mitchell (1973-)
The Code *'09*
The Crazies *'09*
Surrogates *'09*
The Children of Huang Shi *'08*
Henry Poole Is Here *'08*
Feast of Love *'07*
Rogue *'07*
PU-239 *'06*
Silent Hill *'06*
Melinda and Melinda *'05*
Mozart and the Whale *'05*
Finding Neverland *'04*
Man on Fire *'04*
Visitors *'03*
Phone Booth *'02*
Dead Heat *'01*
Nobody's Baby *'01*
Uprising *'01*
Cleopatra's Second Husband *'00*
Cowboys and Angels *'00*
Everything Put Together *'00*
Pitch Black *'00*
High Art *'98*
Love and Other Catastrophes *'95*

Red Mitchell (1964-94)
8 Seconds *'94*
Forever Evil *'87*

Sasha Mitchell (1967-)
Gangland *'00*
Luck of the Draw *'00*
Kickboxer 4: The Aggressor *'94*
Class of 1999 2: The Substitute *'93*
Kickboxer 3: The Art of War *'92*
Kickboxer 2: The Road Back *'90*
Spike of Bensonhurst *'88*

Scoey Mitchell (1930-)
Jo Jo Dancer, Your Life Is Calling *'86*
The Voyage of the Yes *'72*

Sharon Mitchell (1956-)
Kamikaze Hearts *'91*
Maniac *'80*

Silas Weir Mitchell
Prairie Fever *'08*
The Whole Ten Yards *'04*
Johnson County War *'02*

Steve Mitchell
Incident at Channel Q *'86*
The Sibling *'72*
Submarine Seahawk *'59*

Thomas Mitchell (1892-1962)
By Love Possessed *'61*
Pocketful of Miracles *'61*
While the City Sleeps *'56*

High Noon '52
The Big Wheel '49
Silver River '48
Dark Mirror '46
It's a Wonderful Life '46
Adventure '45
Buffalo Bill '44
Dark Waters '44
The Keys of the Kingdom '44
Wilson '44
Bataan '43
Immortal Sergeant '43
The Outlaw '43
The Black Swan '42
The Fighting Sullivans '42
Joan of Paris '42
Moontide '42
Song of the Islands '42
Tales of Manhattan '42
This Above All '42
Out of the Fog '41
Angels Over Broadway '40
The Long Voyage Home '40
Our Town '40
Gone with the Wind '39
The Hunchback of Notre Dame '39
Mr. Smith Goes to Washington '39
Only Angels Have Wings '39
Stagecoach '39
The Hurricane '37
I Promise to Pay '37
Lost Horizon '37
Make Way for Tomorrow '37
Theodora Goes Wild '36

Warren Mitchell (1926-)

Knights & Emeralds '87
Foreign Body '86
The Dunera Boys '85
The Last Bastion '84
Waterfront '83
Norman Loves Rose '82
Bananas Boat '78
Jabberwocky '77
The Assassination Bureau '69
Arrivederci, Baby! '66
Help! '65
The Unearthly Stranger '64
Postman's Knock '62
The Crawling Eye '58

Yvonne Mitchell (1925-79)

The Incredible Sarah '76
Demons of the Mind '72
Crucible of Horror '69
Johnny Nobody '61
Conspiracy of Hearts '60
The Trials of Oscar Wilde '60
Sapphire '59
Tiger Bay '59
Escapade '55
The Queen of Spades '49

Ilan Mitchell-Smith (1969-)

Identity Crisis '90
The Chocolate War '88
Journey to the Center of the Earth '88
Weird Science '85

Bentley Mitchum (1970-)

Conviction '02
U.S. Navy SEALS: Dead or Alive '02
U.S. SEALs: Dead or Alive '02
Shark Attack '99
Chained Heat 3: Hell Mountain '98
On the Border '98
Deadly Exposure '93
Ruby in Paradise '93
Teenage Bonnie & Klepto Clyde '93
Demonic Toys '90

Chris Mitchum (1943-)

Diamondbacks '99
Lethal Seduction '97
Fugitive X '96
Biohazard: The Alien Force '95
Striking Point '94
Tombstone '93
Death Feud '89
Aftershock '88
Faceless '88
Angel of Death '86
American Commandos '84
The Executioner, Part 2: Frozen Scream '84
No Time to Die '84
My Champion '81
Day Time Ended '80
Desperate Target '80
A Rumor of War '80
One Man Jury '78
Stingray '78
The Last Hard Men '76
Ricco '74
Mean Machine '73
Big Foot '72
Big Jake '71
H-Bomb '71
Rio Lobo '70

Jim Mitchum (1941-)

Fatal Mission '89
Marked for Murder '89
Mercenary Fighters '88
Hollywood Cop '87
Code Name: Zebra '84
Blackout '78
Monster '78
Maniac '77
The Invincible Six '68
In Harm's Way '65
Ride the Wild Surf '64
The Victors '63
Girls' Town '59
Thunder Road '58

John Mitchum (1919-2001)

Escapes '86
The Enforcer '76
The Outlaw Josey Wales '76
The Hanged Man '74
Magnum Force '73
Big Foot '72
Bloody Trail '72
Dirty Harry '71
The Devil's Sleep '51

Julie Mitchum (1914-2003)

House on Haunted Hill '58
The High and the Mighty '54

Robert Mitchum (1917-97)

James Dean: Live Fast, Die Young '97
Dead Man '95
Backfire! '94
Tombstone '93 (N)
Woman of Desire '93
Midnight Ride '92
Cape Fear '91
Thompson's Last Run '90
The Brotherhood of the Rose '89
War & Remembrance: The Final Chapter '89
Mr. North '88
Scrooged '88
War & Remembrance '88
The Hearst and Davies Affair '85
North and South Book 1 '85
The Ambassador '84
Maria's Lovers '84
The Winds of War '83
One Shoe Makes It Murder '82
That Championship Season '82
The Agency '81
Nightkill '80
The Amsterdam Kill '78
The Big Sleep '78
Breakthrough '78
Matilda '78
The Last Tycoon '76
Midway '76
Farewell, My Lovely '75
The Yakuza '75
Ryan's Daughter '70
The Good Guys and the Bad Guys '69
Secret Ceremony '69
Anzio '68
Five Card Stud '68
Villa Rides '68
El Dorado '67
The Way West '67
The List of Adrian Messenger '63
The Longest Day '62
Two for the Seesaw '62
Cape Fear '61
The Grass Is Greener '61
Home from the Hill '60
The Sundowners '60
The Hunters '58
Thunder Road '58
Enemy Below '57
Fire Down Below '57
Heaven Knows, Mr. Allison '57
The Night of the Hunter '55
Not as a Stranger '55
River of No Return '54
Second Chance '53
Angel Face '52
The Lusty Men '52
Macao '52
One Minute to Zero '52
She Couldn't Say No '52
His Kind of Woman '51
My Forbidden Past '51
The Racket '51
Where Danger Lives '50
Big Steal '49
Holiday Affair '49
The Red Pony '49
Blood on the Moon '48
Rachel and the Stranger '48
Crossfire '47
Out of the Past '47
Pursued '47
Till the End of Time '46
Undercurrent '46
The Story of G.I. Joe '45
West of the Pecos '45
Girl Rush '44
Nevada '44
Thirty Seconds Over Tokyo '44
Colt Comrades '43
False Colors '43
Gung Ho! '43
Hopalong Cassidy: Riders of the Deadline '43
Hoppy Serves a Writ '43
The Human Comedy '43
Leather Burners '43
The Lone Star Trail '43

Labina Mitevska (1975-)

I Want You '98
Before the Rain '94

Rhona Mitra (1976-)

Underworld: Rise of the Lycans '09
Doomsday '08
The Number 23 '07
Shooter '07
Skinwalkers '07
Highwaymen '03
The Life of David Gale '03
Sweet Home Alabama '02
Get Carter '00
Beowulf '98
A Kid in Aladdin's Palace '97

Koji Mitsui

Woman in the Dunes '64
The Hidden Fortress '58

Tomokazu Miura

The Taste of Tea '04
The Imperial Japanese Empire '85

Asumi Miwa (1982-)

The Great Yokai War '05
Boogiepop and Others '00
Uzumaki '00

Art Mix (1895-1972)

Yodelin' Kid from Pine Ridge '37
Powdersmoke Range '35
Rustlers of Red Dog '35
Way of the West '35
Border Devils '32
Mason of the Mounted '32

Ruth Mix (1907-77)

Custer's Last Stand '36
The Riding Avenger '36
Saddle Aces '35
The Tonto Kid '35

Tom Mix (1880-1940)

The Miracle Rider '35
Hidden Gold '33
Rustler's Roundup '33
Terror Trail '33
Justice Rides Again '32
My Pal, the King '32
The Rider of Death Valley '32
Texas Bad Man '32
Great K & A Train Robbery '26
Dick Turpin '25
Riders of the Purple Sage '25
Sky High '22
Trailin' '21
Child of the Prairie '18
Heart of Texas Ryan '17
In the Days of the Thundering Herd & the Law & the Outlaw '14

Jerod Mixon (1981-)

The New Guy '02
Me, Myself, and Irene '00

Katy Mixon

All About Steve '09
State of Play '09
Four Christmases '08
The Quiet '05

Seiji Miyaguchi (1913-85)

The Human Condition: No Greater Love '58
Seven Samurai '54
Early Summer '51

Kuniko Miyake (1916-92)

Good Morning '59
Early Summer '51

Nobuko Miyamoto (1945-)

Minbo—Or the Gentle Art of Japanese Extortion '92
A Taxing Woman's Return '88
A Taxing Woman '87
Tampopo '86
The Funeral '84

Hiroyuki Miyasako

Black House '07
The Great Yokai War '05

Junko Miyazono

Legends of the Poisonous Seductress 2: Quick Draw Okatsu '69
Legends of the Poisonous Seductress 3: Okatsu the Fugitive '69
Legends of the Poisonous Seductress 1: Female Demon Ohyaku '68

Eric Miyeni

Dangerous Ground '96
Cry, the Beloved Country '95

Kim Miyori (1951-)

The Grudge 2 '06
Metro '96
Body Shot '93
Hiroshima: Out of the Ashes '90
The Punisher '90
The Big Picture '89
When the Bough Breaks '86
John & Yoko: A Love Story '85

Eiko Miyoshi

The Hidden Fortress '58
Snow Country '57
I Live in Fear '55
Samurai 1: Musashi Miyamoto '55
No Regrets for Our Youth '46

Isaac Mizrahi (1961-)

Hollywood Ending '02
Celebrity '98
For Love or Money '93

Kenji Mizuhashi

Funky Forest: The First Contact '06
Pulse '01
Moonlight Whispers '99

Asami Mizukawa

Pray '05
Dark Water '02

Kumi Mizuno (1937-)

War of the Gargantuas '70
Godzilla vs. Monster Zero '68
Godzilla vs. the Sea Monster '66
What's Up, Tiger Lily? '66
Frankenstein Conquers the World '64
Attack of the Mushroom People '63
Matango '63

Genevieve Mnich (1942-)

Seraphine '08
Beau Pere '81
The Mother and the Whore '73

Henry Moan

O'Horten '09
Kristin Lavransdatter '95

Mary Ann Mobley (1939-)

Crazy Horse and Custer: "The Untold Story" '90
My Dog, the Thief '69
Girl Happy '65
Harum Scarum '65

Roger Mobley (1949-)

Emil and the Detectives '64
Jack the Giant Killer '62

Tony Mockus, Sr.

Charming Billy '98
Backdraft '91

Matthew Modine (1959-)

Sex & Lies in Sin City: The Ted Binion Scandal '08
The Neighbor '07
Kettle of Fish '06
Transporter 2 '05
Hitler: The Rise of Evil '03
Hollywood North '03
Le Divorce '03
Redeemer '02
The American '01
In the Shadows '01
Jack and the Beanstalk: The Real Story '01
Nobody's Baby '01
Flowers for Algernon '00
Any Given Sunday '99
The Maker '98
What the Deaf Man Heard '98
The Blackout '97
The Real Blonde '97
Cutthroat Island '95
Fluke '95
The Browning Version '94
Bye Bye, Love '94
Jacob '94
And the Band Played On '93
Equinox '93
Short Cuts '93
Wind '92
Memphis Belle '90
Pacific Heights '90
Gross Anatomy '89
The Gamble '88
Married to the Mob '88
Full Metal Jacket '87
Orphans '87
Vision Quest '85
Birdy '84
The Hotel New Hampshire '84
Mrs. Soffel '84
Private School '83
Streamers '83
Baby It's You '82

Gaston Modot (1887-1970)

Casque d'Or '52
Beauty and the Devil '50
Children of Paradise '44
The Rules of the Game '39
Grand Illusion '37
L'Age D'Or '30
Under the Roofs of Paris '29

Enrica Maria Modugno (1958-)

The Story of Boys & Girls '91
Kaos '85

Ralph (Ralf) Moeller (1959-)

Seed '08
Pathfinder '07
Beerfest '06
The Scorpion King '02
Gladiator '00
The Bad Pack '98
The Viking Sagas '95
Best of the Best 2 '93

Donald Moffat (1930-)

61* '01
Cookie's Fortune '99
The Evening Star '96
A Smile Like Yours '96
Clear and Present Danger '94
Is There Life Out There? '94
Trapped in Paradise '94
Armistead Maupin's Tales of the City '93
Love, Cheat & Steal '93
Housesitter '92
Teamster Boss: The Jackie Presser Story '92
Class Action '91
Regarding Henry '91
When the Time Comes '91
The Bonfire of the Vanities '90
Danielle Steel's Kaleidoscope '90
Music Box '89
The Bourne Identity '88
Far North '88
Necessary Parties '88
The Unbearable Lightness of Being '88
The Best of Times '86
Alamo Bay '85
License to Kill '84
The Right Stuff '83
The Thing '82
Jacqueline Bouvier Kennedy '81
The Long Days of Summer '80
On the Nickel '80
Mrs. R's Daughter '79
Promises in the Dark '79
Strangers: The Story of a Mother and Daughter '79
Winter Kills '79
Mary White '77
Showdown '73
The Great Northfield Minnesota Raid '72
Rachel, Rachel '68

D.W. Moffett (1954-)

Twisted '04
Thirteen '03
Kill Me Later '01
Traffic '00
Molly '99
Stealing Beauty '96
The Little Death '95
Rough Magic '95
Falling Down '93
In the Deep Woods '91
Danielle Steel's Fine Things '90
Lisa '90
Pacific Heights '90
Black Widow '87
The Misfit Brigade '87
An Early Frost '85

Gregory Moffett

Robot Monster '53
Let's Dance '50

Michelle Moffett
Indecent Behavior '93
Deathstalker 4: Match of Titans '92
Wild Cactus '92
Hired to Kill '91

Sharyn Moffett (1936-)
The Judge Steps Out '49
The Body Snatcher '45

Jerry Mofokeng
Tsotsi '05
Mandela and de Klerk '97

Carl Mohner (1916-2005)
A Woman at Her Window '77
Wanted: Babysitter '75
Cave of the Living Dead '65
Last Gun '64
Sink the Bismarck '60
It Takes a Thief '59
The Last Bridge '54
Rififi '54

Gerald Mohr (1914-68)
The Angry Red Planet '59
Terror in the Haunted House '58
Money from Home '53
Duel at Silver Creek '52
Invasion U.S.A. '52
The Ring '52
The Sniper '52
Son of Ali Baba '52
Detective Story '51
Sirocco '51
Hunt the Man Down '50
King of the Cowboys '43
The Monster and the Girl '41
Charlie Chan at Treasure Island '39
Love Affair '39

Jay Mohr (1970-)
Street Kings '08
Christmas Do-Over '06
Even Money '06
The Groomsmen '06
Are We There Yet? '05
King's Ransom '05
Seeing Other People '04
The Adventures of Pluto Nash '02
Simone '02
Dean Koontz's Black River '01
Cherry Falls '00
Pay It Forward '00
Go '99
From the Earth to the Moon '98
Mafia! '98
Paulie '98 (V)
Playing by Heart '98
Small Soldiers '98
200 Cigarettes '98
Suicide Kings '97
Jerry Maguire '96
Picture Perfect '96
For Better or Worse '95

Wotan Wilke Mohring
Antibodies '05
The Experiment '01

Zia Mohyeddin (1933-)
We Are the Children '87
Bombay Talkie '70

Richard Moir (1950-)
Welcome to Woop Woop '97
Wrangler '88
An Indecent Obsession '85
Remember Me '85
Heatwave '83
Panic Station '82
In Search of Anna '79
The Odd Angry Shot '79

Marisa Moitzi
See Marisa Mell

Jose Mojica Marins (1929-)
Hallucinations of a Deranged Mind '78
Awakenings of the Beast '68
Strange World of Coffin Joe '68
At Midnight, I'll Take Your Soul '63

Karen Mok (1970-)
Vampire Effect '03
So Close '02
Black Mask '96
Fallen Angels '95

Zakes Mokae (1935-)
Krippendorf's Tribe '98
Vampire in Brooklyn '95
Waterworld '95
Dust Devil '93
Percy & Thunder '93
Body Parts '91
A Rage in Harlem '91
Dad '89
A Dry White Season '89
Gross Anatomy '89
Cry Freedom '87
The Serpent and the Rainbow '87
Master Harold and the Boys '84
Agatha Christie's A Caribbean Mystery '83
The Comedians '67
A World of Strangers '62

Albert Mol (1917-2004)
Dear Boys '80
Business is Business '71

Gretchen Mol (1973-)
An American Affair '09
The Memory Keeper's Daughter '08
The Ten '07
3:10 to Yuma '07
The Notorious Bettie Page '06
Puccini for Beginners '06
The Shape of Things '03
The Magnificent Ambersons '02
Get Carter '00
The Cradle Will Rock '99
Forever Mine '99
Just Looking '99
Sweet and Lowdown '99
The Thirteenth Floor '99
Celebrity '98
Finding Graceland '98
New Rose Hotel '98
Rounders '98
Music from Another Room '97
Calm at Sunset '96
The Funeral '96
The Last Time I Committed Suicide '96

Karin Molander (1889-1978)
Thomas Graal's First Child '18
Thomas Graal's Best Film '17

Jeff Moldovan
Trancers 5: Sudden Deth '94
Master Blaster '85

Alfred Molina (1953-)
Prince of Persia: The Sands of Time '10
The Sorcerer's Apprentice '10
An Education '09
The Lodger '09
The Pink Panther 2 '09
Nothing Like the Holidays '08
The Company '07
The Moon & the Stars '07
Silk '07
As You Like It '06
The Da Vinci Code '06
The Hoax '06
Steamboy '05 (V)
Cronicas '04
Spider-Man 2 '04
Coffee and Cigarettes '03
Identity '03
Luther '03
My Life Without Me '03
Frida '02
Texas Rangers '01
Chocolat '00
The Miracle Maker: The Story of Jesus '00 (V)
Dudley Do-Right '99
The Imposters '98
Pete's Meteor '98
Rescuers: Stories of Courage—Two Couples '98
The Treat '98
Boogie Nights '97
The Man Who Knew Too Little '97
Leo Tolstoy's Anna Karenina '96
Mojave Moon '96
Scorpion Spring '96
Before and After '95
Dead Man '95
Species '95
Maverick '94
The Perez Family '94
White Fang 2: The Myth of the White Wolf '94
The Trial '93
When Pigs Fly '93
Enchanted April '92
American Friends '91
Not Without My Daughter '90
A Night of Love '87
Prick Up Your Ears '87
Letter to Brezhnev '86
Ladyhawke '85
Meantime '81
Raiders of the Lost Ark '81
The Big Scam '79

Angela Molina (1955-)
Baaria '09
Carnage '02
Live Flesh '97
1492: Conquest of Paradise '92
Half of Heaven '86
Camorra: The Naples Connection '85
The Eyes, the Mouth '83
Demons in the Garden '82
That Obscure Object of Desire '77

Enrique Molina
A Paradise Under the Stars '99
Hello, Hemingway '90

Jacinto (Jack) Molina
See Paul Naschy

Rolando Molina (1971-)
crazy/beautiful '01
Next Friday '00

Charles Moll (1943-)
Combat Academy '86
Night Train to Terror '84
Cataclysm '81

Georgia Moll (1938-)
What a Way to Die '70
Contempt '64
Thief of Baghdad '61

Richard Moll (1943-)
The Christmas Cottage '08
The Biggest Fan '02
Evolution '01
Scary Movie 2 '01
Spiders 2: Breeding Ground '01
Boltneck '98
Dish Dogs '98
The Survivor '98
Living in Peril '97
The Glass Cage '96
The Secret Agent Club '96
Galaxis '95
Storybook '95
Beanstalk '94
The Flintstones '94
No Dessert Dad, 'Til You Mow the Lawn '94
Dream Date '93
National Lampoon's Loaded Weapon 1 '93
Sidekicks '93
Highlander: The Gathering '92
Driving Me Crazy '91
Think Big '90
Wicked Stepmother '89
Survivor '87
House '86
Dungeonmaster '83
Metalstorm: The Destruction of Jared Syn '83
Savage Journey '83
Sword & the Sorcerer '82
Hard Country '81

Jordi Molla (1968-)
Knight and Day '10
Che '08
Elizabeth: The Golden Age '07
The Stone Merchant '06
The Alamo '04
Bad Boys 2 '03
Blow '01
Second Skin '99
Jamon, Jamon '93

Jenny Mollen (1979-)
My Best Friend's Girl '08
National Lampoon Presents Cattle Call '06
Return of the Living Dead: Rave to the Grave '05

Clothilde Mollet
The Page Turner '06
Amelie '01

Dearbhla Molloy (1946-)
Frankie Starlight '95
Paddy '70

Patrick Molloy
Phantom Brother '88
Plutonium Baby '87

Tibor Molnar (1921-82)
The Red and the White '68
The Round Up '66

Robert Moloney
Storm Cell '08
Touch the Top of the World '06
Sweetwater: A True Rock Story '99

Alessandro Momo
The Scent of a Woman '75
Malicious '74

Kaori Momoi
Sukiyaki Western Django '08
Memoirs of a Geisha '05

Sloane Momsen (1997-)
Daddy Day Care '03
We Were Soldiers '02
Dr. Seuss' How the Grinch Stole Christmas '00

Taylor Momsen (1993-)
Paranoid Park '07
Underdog '07
We Were Soldiers '02
Dr. Seuss' How the Grinch Stole Christmas '00

Dominic Monaghan (1976-)
X-Men Origins: Wolverine '09
Shooting Livien '05
The Purifiers '04
Lord of the Rings: The Return of the King '03
Lord of the Rings: The Two Towers '02
Lord of the Rings: The Fellowship of the Ring '01

Michelle Monaghan (1976-)
Eagle Eye '08
Made of Honor '08
Trucker '08
Gone Baby Gone '07
The Heartbreak Kid '07
Mission: Impossible 3 '06
Kiss Kiss Bang Bang '05
Mr. & Mrs. Smith '05
North Country '05
The Bourne Supremacy '04
Winter Solstice '04
It Runs in the Family '03

Dan Monahan (1955-)
Stephen King's The Night Flier '96
Porky's Revenge '85
Porky's 2: The Next Day '83
Porky's '82

Jeff Monahan
Bruiser '00
One Way Out '95

Richard Monahan
Fixed Bayonets! '51
Pier 23 '51
The Steel Helmet '51

Karen Moncrieff (1963-)
Xtro 3: Watch the Skies '95
Deathfight '93
Midnight Witness '93

Julie Mond
Exit Speed '08
Rest Stop: Don't Look Back '08

Merwin Mondesir
Godsend '04
Bones '01

Jorge Mondragon (1903-97)
Spiritism '61
The New Invisible Man '58

Daniella Monet (1989-)
Nancy Drew '07

Richard Monette (1944-)
Murder by Night '89
Higher Education '88
Hello Mary Lou: Prom Night 2 '87
Dancing in the Dark '86
Far Cry from Home '81
Big Zapper '73

Corbett Monica (1930-98)
The Passing of Evil '70
The Grasshopper '69

Mo'Nique (1968-)
Precious: Based on the Novel by Sapphire '09
Welcome Home Roscoe Jenkins '08
Beerfest '06
Phat Girlz '06
Shadowboxer '06
Domino '05
Hair Show '04
Soul Plane '04
Good Fences '03
Half Past Dead '02
Queens of Comedy '01
Two Can Play That Game '01
Three Strikes '00

Debra Monk (1949-)
The Producers '05
Palindromes '04
Plain Dirty '04
Eloise at the Plaza '03
Milwaukee, Minnesota '03
Dark Water '02
The Doorbell Rang: A Nero Wolfe Mystery '01
Center Stage '00
The Devil's Advocate '97
Ellen Foster '97
Extreme Measures '96
The First Wives Club '96
Bed of Roses '95
Redwood Curtain '95

Sophie Monk
Spring Breakdown '08
Date Movie '06

Bob Monkhouse
All or Nothing at All '93
Dentist In the Chair '60
Carry On Sergeant '58

Yvonne Monlaur (1940-)
License to Kill '64
Ladies' Man '62
The Terror of the Tongs '61
The Brides of Dracula '60
Circus of Horrors '60

Carlo Monni (1943-)
The Tesseract '03
Dial Help '88
Berlinguer I Love You '77

Valentine Monnier
After the Fall of New York '85
Devilfish '84

Lawrence Monoson (1965-)
Machine Gun Blues '95
And the Band Played On '93
Dangerous Love '87
Gaby: A True Story '87
Mask '85
Last American Virgin '82

Marilyn Monroe (1926-62)
The Love Goddesses '65
The Misfits '61
Let's Make Love '60
Some Like It Hot '59
The Prince and the Showgirl '57
Bus Stop '56
The Seven Year Itch '55
River of No Return '54
There's No Business Like Show Business '54
Gentlemen Prefer Blondes '53
How to Marry a Millionaire '53
Clash by Night '52
Don't Bother to Knock '52
Monkey Business '52
Niagara '52
We're Not Married '52
As Young As You Feel '51
Home Town Story '51
Let's Make It Legal '51
Love Nest '51
All About Eve '50
The Asphalt Jungle '50
Love Happy '50
Ticket to Tomahawk '50
Ladies of the Chorus '49

Meredith Monroe
Masters of Horror: Family '05
Full Ride '02
New Best Friend '02

Mircea Monroe
Into the Blue 2: The Reef '09
Fast Girl '07
One Long Night '07
All Souls Day '05

Steve Monroe
School for Scoundrels '06
House of the Dead 2: Dead Aim '05
The Santa Trap '02
Going Greek '01
Cast Away '00
Miss Congeniality '00
Inherit the Wind '99
Can't Hardly Wait '98

Renzo Montagnani (1930-77)
Voyage of Terror: The Achille Lauro Affair '90
A Joke of Destiny, Lying in Wait Around the Corner Like a Bandit '84
You've Got to Have Heart '77
The Mad Adventures of Rabbi Jacob '73
The Libertine '69

Lee Montague (1927-)
Jekyll and Hyde '90
Madame Sousatzka '88
Mahler '74
Brother Sun, Sister Moon '73
Moulin Rouge '52

Monte Montague (1891-1959)
Radio Patrol '37
Quick Trigger Lee '31
Trigger Tricks '30
Courtin' Wildcats '29
King of the Rodeo '28

Paolo Montalban (1973-)
The Great Raid '05
American Adobo '02
Cinderella '97

Ricardo Montalban (1920-2009)
The Ant Bully '06 *(V)*
Spy Kids 3-D: Game Over '03
Spy Kids 2: The Island of Lost Dreams '02
The Naked Gun: From the Files of Police Squad '88
Cannonball Run 2 '84
Star Trek 2: The Wrath of Khan '82
Mission to Glory '80
Return to Fantasy Island '77
Fantasy Island '76
Joe Panther '76
Train Robbers '73
Conquest of the Planet of the Apes '72
Fireball Forward '72
Escape from the Planet of the Apes '71
Ride to Glory '71
Black Water Gold '69
Sweet Charity '69
Blue '68
Iron Cowboy '68
Alice Through the Looking Glass '66
Madame X '66
The Singing Nun '66
The Money Trap '65
Cheyenne Autumn '64
Pirate Warrior '64
The Desperate Mission '60
Let No Man Write My Epitaph '60
Sayonara '57
Latin Lovers '53
Across the Wide Missouri '51
Mystery Street '50
Two Weeks with Love '50
Battleground '49
Border Incident '49
Neptune's Daughter '49
On an Island with You '48

Lenny Montana (1926-92)
Blood Song '82
Evilspeak '82
Pandemonium '82
...All the Marbles '81
Below the Belt '80
The Big Brawl '80
Defiance '79
The Jerk '79
Seven '79
Fingers '78
They Went That-a-Way & That-a-Way '78
The Godfather '72

Monte Montana (1910-98)
Down Dakota Way '49
Circle of Death '36

Yves Montand (1921-91)
Jean de Florette '87
Manon of the Spring '87
Choice of Arms '83
Roads to the South '78
Delusions of Grandeur '76
Vincent, Francois, Paul and the Others '76
Lovers Like Us '75
The Savage '75
State of Siege '73
Cesar & Rosalie '72
Le Cercle Rouge '70
On a Clear Day You Can See Forever '70
Z '69
Grand Prix '66
Is Paris Burning? '66
La Guerre Est Finie '66
Le Joli Mai '62 *(N)*
My Geisha '62
Goodbye Again '61
Let's Make Love '60
Where the Hot Wind Blows '59
The Crucible '57
The Wide Blue Road '57
Napoleon '55
Wages of Fear '55

Cory Monteith (1982-)
Hybrid '07
Kraken: Tentacles of the Deep '06

Lisa Montell (1933-)
The Nine Lives of Elfego Baca '58
Ten Thousand Bedrooms '57
She Gods of Shark Reef '56

Fernanda Montenegro (1929-)
House of Sand '05
Central Station '98

Rosenda Monteros (1935-)
Cauldron of Blood '67
She '65
Mighty Jungle '64
Tiara Tahiti '62
Battle Shock '56
The White Orchid '54

Elisa Montes (1936-)
Return of the Magnificent Seven '66
Texas, Adios '66
As If It Were Raining '63

Enrico Montesano (1945-)
Sotto, Sotto '85
Lobster for Breakfast '82

Liliane Montevecchi (1932-)
King Creole '58
Me and the Colonel '58
The Young Lions '58
Meet Me in Las Vegas '56

Maria Montez (1918-51)
Portrait of an Assassin '49
Cobra Woman '44
Ali Baba and the Forty Thieves '43
Arabian Nights '42
Boss of Bullion City '41

Belinda J. Montgomery (1950-)
Stone Fox '87
Silent Madness '84
Tell Me That You Love Me '84
Stone Cold Dead '80
Blackout '78
The Man from Atlantis '77
The Bravos '72
The Todd Killings '71

Chuck Montgomery
Fay Grim '06
Amateur '94

Dan Montgomery, Jr. (1969-)
Club Dread '04
You Stupid Man '02
On the Line '01
The Last Man '00
Red Dirt '99

Douglass Montgomery (1907-66)
Harmony Lane '35
The Mystery of Edwin Drood '35
Little Women '33

Elizabeth Montgomery (1933-95)
Deadline Assault '90
Amos '85
Missing Pieces '83
The Court Martial of Billy Mitchell '55

Flora Montgomery (1974-)
Basic Instinct 2 '06
Benedict Arnold: A Question of Honor '03
When Brendan Met Trudy '00
A Certain Justice '99

George Montgomery (1916-2000)
Bomb at 10:10 '67
Hallucination '67
Hostile Guns '67
Battle of the Bulge '65
Satan's Harvest '65
Warkill '65
From Hell to Borneo '64
Samar '62
The Steel Claw '61
King of the Wild Stallions '59
Man From God's Country '58
Black Patch '57
Canyon River '56
Seminole Uprising '55
Indian Uprising '51
Sword of Monte Cristo '51
The Texas Rangers '51
Orchestra Wives '42
Roxie Hart '42
Young People '40
Rough Riders' Roundup '39

Julia Montgomery (1960-)
Revenge of the Nerds 4: Nerds in Love '94
Revenge of the Nerds 3: The Next Generation '92
Black Snow '89
Savage Justice '88
The Kindred '87
South of Reno '87
Stewardess School '86
Revenge of the Nerds '84
Up the Creek '84
Girls Night Out '83

Lee Montgomery (1961-)
Into the Fire '88
The Midnight Hour '86
Girls Just Want to Have Fun '85
Prime Risk '84
Mutant '83
Baker's Hawk '76
Savage Is Loose '74
Ben '72
Pete 'n' Tillie '72

Matthew Montgomery
Redwoods '09
Long-Term Relationship '06

Poppy Montgomery (1972-)
Between '05
How to Lose Your Lover '04
Blonde '01
Life '99
The Other Sister '98
Dead Man on Campus '97

Robert Montgomery (1904-81)
Eye Witness '49
June Bride '48
Lady in the Lake '46
They Were Expendable '45
Here Comes Mr. Jordan '41
Mr. & Mrs. Smith '41
The Last of Mrs. Cheyney '37
Night Must Fall '37
Forsaking All Others '35
Hide-Out '34
Riptide '34
The Lost Stooges '33
Night Flight '33
The Easiest Way '31
Private Lives '31
The Big House '30
The Divorcee '30
Free and Easy '30

Silvia Monti (1946-)
Sicilian Connection '72
A Lizard in a Woman's Skin '71
The Brain '69

Anna Maria Monticelli (1952-)
Nomads '86
The Empty Beach '85
My First Wife '84
Heatwave '83
Smash Palace '82

Luigi Montini (1934-)
Mediterraneo '91
Satanik '69

Alex Montoya (1907-70)
Escape from Fort Bravo '53
West to Glory '47

Pascale Montpetit (1961-)
Savage Messiah '02
Street Heart '98
Eclipse '94
H '90

Michael Monty (1936-2006)
The Firing Line '91
The 13th Mission '91
Slash '87

Jim Moody (1949-)
Who's the Man? '93
Bad Boys '83

King Moody (1929-2001)
The Dark Backward '91
Get Smart, Again! '89
Sweet November '68
Five Minutes to Love '63
Teenagers from Outer Space '59

Lynne Moody (1948-)
The Reading Room '05
Ellen Foster '97
Last Light '93
A Fight for Jenny '90
Agatha Christie's A Caribbean Mystery '83
Wait Till Your Mother Gets Home '83
Some Kind of Hero '82
White Dog '82
Roots: The Next Generation '79
The Evil '78
Las Vegas Lady '76
Nightmare in Badham County '76
Scream Blacula Scream '73

Ralph Moody (1886-1971)
The Last Hunt '56
The Road to Bali '53

Ron Moody (1924-)
A Kid in King Arthur's Court '95
The Strange Case of the End of Civilization As We Know It '93
Wrong Is Right '82
Dominique Is Dead '79
Unidentified Flying Oddball '79
Dog Pound Shuffle '75
Legend of the Werewolf '75
David Copperfield '70
The Twelve Chairs '70
Oliver! '68
Murder Most Foul '65
The Mouse on the Moon '62

Jung-Hee Moon
The Wishing Stairs '03
3 Extremes 2 '02

Keith Moon (1946-78)
The Kids Are Alright '79
Sextette '78
Tommy '75
That'll Be the Day '73
200 Motels '71

Sheri Moon Zombie (1970-)
Halloween II '09
Halloween '07
The Devil's Rejects '05
House of 1000 Corpses '03

Dennis Mooney
Death Row Diner '88
Hollywood Chainsaw Hookers '88

Laura Mooney (1976-)
Little Nemo: Adventures in Slumberland '92 *(V)*
She's Out of Control '89

Paul Mooney
Bamboozled '00
Dance with a Stranger '85

Alvy Moore (1921-97)
Intruder '88
They're Playing with Fire '84
Scream '83
Smokey & the Hotwire Gang '79
A Boy and His Dog '75
The Specialist '75
The Brotherhood of Satan '71
The Witchmaker '69
Three Nuts in Search of a Bolt '64
Move Over, Darling '63
Designing Woman '57
An Annapolis Story '55
5 Against the House '55
The Wild One '54
The War of the Worlds '53

Archie Moore (1913-98)
Breakheart Pass '76
My Sweet Charlie '70
The Carpetbaggers '64
The Adventures of Huckleberry Finn '60

Ben Moore
She-Freak '67
Suburban Roulette '67
Moonshine Mountain '64
2000 Maniacs '64

Candy Moore (1947-)
Lunch Wagon '81
Tomboy & the Champ '58

Christina Moore
Delta Farce '07
Without a Paddle '04

Christine Moore
Lurkers '88
Prime Evil '88
Thrilled to Death '88

Clayton Moore (1914-99)
Justice of the West '61
Lone Ranger '56
Jungle Drums of Africa '53
Radar Men from the Moon '52
The Adventures of Frank and Jesse James '48
Far Frontier '48
G-Men Never Forget '48
Jesse James Rides Again '47
Cyclotrode "X" '46
The Black Dragons '42
Nyoka and the Tigermen '42
International Lady '41
The Son of Monte Cristo '40

Colleen Moore (1902-88)
The Scarlet Letter '34
Ella Cinders '26
Twinkletoes '26
Broken Hearts of Broadway '23
The Sky Pilot '21
The Busher '19
Little Orphan Annie '18

Constance Moore (1920-2005)
Delightfully Dangerous '45
Argentine Nights '40
Buck Rogers Conquers the Universe '39
Charlie McCarthy, Detective '39
Destination Saturn '39
Mutiny on the Blackhawk '39
You Can't Cheat an Honest Man '39
Prison Break '38
Wives under Suspicion '38

Deborah Maria Moore (1963-)
Jack Higgins' Midnight Man '96
Jack Higgins' On Dangerous Ground '95
Chaplin '92
Into the Sun '92
Bullseye! '90
Lionheart '87

Del Moore (1917-70)
The Patsy '64
The Nutty Professor '63

Demi Moore (1962-)
The Joneses '10
Happy Tears '09
Flawless '07
Mr. Brooks '07
Bobby '06
Half Light '05
Charlie's Angels: Full Throttle '03
Passion of Mind '00
Deconstructing Harry '97
G.I. Jane '97
Beavis and Butt-Head Do America '96 *(V)*
The Hunchback of Notre Dame '96 *(V)*
If These Walls Could Talk '96
The Juror '96
Striptease '96
Now and Then '95
The Scarlet Letter '95
Disclosure '94
Indecent Proposal '93
A Few Good Men '92
The Butcher's Wife '91
Mortal Thoughts '91
Nothing But Trouble '91
Ghost '90
We're No Angels '89
The Seventh Sign '88
Wisdom '87
About Last Night... '86
One Crazy Summer '86
St. Elmo's Fire '85
Blame It on Rio '84
No Small Affair '84
Parasite '82
Young Doctors in Love '82
Choices '81

Dennie Moore (1907-78)
Dive Bomber '41
Sylvia Scarlett '35

Dennis Moore (1908-64)
Tribute to a Bad Man '56
King of the Bullwhip '51
Range Renegades '48
The Tioga Kid '48
Colorado Serenade '46
Driftin' River '46
D-Day on Mars '45
The Purple Monster Strikes '45
Master Key '44
The Mummy's Curse '44
Raiders of Ghost City '44
Black Market Rustlers '43
Cowboy Commandos '43
Frontier Law '43
Land of Hunted Men '43
Texas Justice '42
Arizona Bound '41
Billy the Kid in Santa Fe '41
Border Roundup '41
Spooks Run Wild '41
East Side Kids '40
Rocky Mountain Rangers '40
Across the Plains '39
Mutiny in the Big House '39

Wild Horse Canyon '39
The Sunset Murder Case '38

Dickie Moore (1925-)
Out of the Past '47
Heaven Can Wait '43
Jive Junction '43
Miss Annie Rooney '42
Sergeant York '41
The Gladiator '38
Little Red Schoolhouse '36
The World Accuses '35
Gabriel Over the White House '33
Oliver Twist '33
Blonde Venus '32

Dorothy Moore (1919-2005)
Blondie Meets the Boss '39
Blondie '38
Vivacious Lady '38

Dudley Moore (1935-2002)
A Weekend in the Country '96
The Disappearance of Kevin Johnson '95
Parallel Lives '94
The Pickle '93
Blame It on the Bellboy '92
Crazy People '90
The Adventures of Milo & Otis '89 (N)
Milo & Otis '89 (N)
Arthur 2: On the Rocks '88
Like Father, Like Son '87
Santa Claus: The Movie '85
Best Defense '84
Micki & Maude '84
Unfaithfully Yours '84
Lovesick '83
Romantic Comedy '83
Six Weeks '82
Arthur '81
Wholly Moses! '80
10 '79
Foul Play '78
The Hound of the Baskervilles '77
Those Daring Young Men in Their Jaunty Jalopies '69
Bedazzled '68
30 Is a Dangerous Age, Cynthia '68
The Wrong Box '66

Duke Moore (1913-76)
The Sinister Urge '60
Night of the Ghouls '59
Plan 9 from Outer Space '56

Frank Moore
Blood & Donuts '95
Hostage for a Day '94
Kings and Desperate Men '83
Rabid '77
Patchwork Girl of Oz '14

Gar Moore (1920-85)
The Underworld Story '50
Abbott and Costello Meet the Killer, Boris Karloff '49
Paisan '46

Ida Moore (1882-1964)
Rock-A-Bye Baby '57
Leave It to the Marines '51
Money Madness '47

Jeanie Moore
Dream Trap '90
The Final Alliance '89
Vampire at Midnight '88

Joanna Moore (1934-97)
Scout's Honor '80
Iron Horsemen '71
The Dunwich Horror '70
Countdown '68
Never a Dull Moment '68
Man From Galveston '63
Son of Flubber '63
Follow That Dream '61
Monster on the Campus '59
Touch of Evil '58

Joel David Moore (1977-)
Avatar '09
Beyond a Reasonable Doubt '09
The Hottie and the Nottie '08
The Dead One '07
Shanghai Kiss '07
Spiral '07
Art School Confidential '06
Grandma's Boy '06

John Moore (1970-)
Military Intelligence and You! '06
Pitch Black '00

Juanita Moore (1922-)
Runaways '75
A Dream for Christmas '73
Foxstyle '73
The Singing Nun '66
Papa's Delicate Condition '63
Imitation of Life '59
The Girl Can't Help It '56

Julianne Moore (1961-)
The Kids Are All Right '10
Chloe '09
The Private Lives of Pippa Lee '09
A Single Man '09
Blindness '08
I'm Not There '07
Next '07
Savage Grace '07
Children of Men '06
Freedomland '06
Trust the Man '06
The Prize Winner of Defiance, Ohio '05
The Forgotten '04
Laws of Attraction '04
Marie and Bruce '04
Far from Heaven '02
The Hours '02
Evolution '01
Hannibal '01
The Shipping News '01
World Traveler '01
The Ladies Man '00
Cookie's Fortune '99
The End of the Affair '99
An Ideal Husband '99
Magnolia '99
A Map of the World '99
Chicago Cab '98
Psycho '98
The Big Lebowski '97
Boogie Nights '97
The Lost World: Jurassic Park 2 '97
The Myth of Fingerprints '97
Surviving Picasso '96
Assassins '95
Nine Months '95
Roommates '95
Safe '95
Vanya on 42nd Street '94
Benny & Joon '93
The Fugitive '93
Short Cuts '93
Body of Evidence '92
The Gun in Betty Lou's Handbag '92
The Hand that Rocks the Cradle '92
Cast a Deadly Spell '91
Tales from the Darkside: The Movie '90

Kaycee Moore
Daughters of the Dust '91
Killer of Sheep '77

Kenya Moore (1971-)
I Know Who Killed Me '07
No Turning Back '01
Senseless '98

Kieron Moore (1924-2007)
Arabesque '66
The Thin Red Line '64
Day of the Triffids '63
Doctor Blood's Coffin '62
The 300 Spartans '62
The Siege of Sidney Street '60
Darby O'Gill & the Little People '59
The Key '58
Recoil '53
David and Bathsheba '51
Anna Karenina '48
A Man About the House '47
Mine Own Executioner '47

Lisa Bronwyn Moore
I'm Not There '07
The Aviator '04
Head in the Clouds '04
The Reagans '04
Mambo Italiano '03
The Sum of All Fears '02
The Courage to Love '00
Isn't She Great '00
A Walk on the Moon '99
Bleeders '97
The Education of Little Tree '97

Mandy Moore (1984-)
Because I Said So '07
Dedication '07
License to Wed '07
American Dreamz '06
Brother Bear 2 '06 (V)
Southland Tales '06
Racing Stripes '05 (V)
Romance & Cigarettes '05
Chasing Liberty '04
Saved! '04
How to Deal '03
All I Want '02
A Walk to Remember '02
The Princess Diaries '01

Mary Moore
Murder at 1600 '97
D-Day on Mars '45

Mary Tyler Moore (1937-)
Labor Pains '99
Keys to Tulsa '96
Flirting with Disaster '95
The Last Best Year '90
Gore Vidal's Lincoln '88
Just Between Friends '86
Finnegan Begin Again '84
Six Weeks '82
Ordinary People '80
Change of Habit '69
Thoroughly Modern Millie '67

Matt Moore (1888-1960)
Devon's Ghost: Legend of the Bloody Boy '05
I Bury the Living '58
An Affair to Remember '57
That Forsyte Woman '50
Deluge '33
Consolation Marriage '31
Coquette '29
The Unholy Three '25
White Tiger '23
Pride of the Clan '18
20,000 Leagues under the Sea '16
Traffic in Souls '13

Melba Moore (1945-)
The Fighting Temptations '03
All Dogs Go to Heaven '89 (V)
Charlotte Forten's Mission: Experiment in Freedom '85

Melissa Moore (1963-)
Stormswept '95
Evil Lives '92
Sorority House Massacre 2: Nighty Nightmare '92
Hard to Die '90
The Invisible Maniac '90
The Killing Zone '90
Vampire Cop '90
Scream Dream '89

Michael Moore (1954-)
Capitalism: A Love Story '09
The Fever '04
Lucky Numbers '00
The Insider '99
The Big One '98 (N)
Canadian Bacon '94
Roger & Me '89

Norma Moore (1935-)
Poor White Trash 2 '75
Fear Strikes Out '57

Owen Moore (1887-1939)
She Done Him Wrong '33
As You Desire Me '32
The Red Mill '27
Married? '26

Pauline Moore (1914-2001)
Motorcycle Squad '41
Carson City Kid '40
Young Buffalo Bill '40
Charlie Chan at Treasure Island '39
Days of Jesse James '39
The Three Musketeers '39
Charlie Chan at the Olympics '37
Love Is News '37

Richard Moore (1925-)
Human Bomb '97
Band of Gold '95

R.J. (Geoffrey) Moore (1966-)
Fit to Kill '93
Hard Hunted '92

Roger Moore (1928-)
Cats & Dogs: The Revenge of Kitty Galore '10
Boat Trip '03
The Enemy '01
D.R.E.A.M. Team '99
Spice World: The Movie '97
The Quest '96
Bed & Breakfast '92
Fire, Ice and Dynamite '91
Bullseye! '90
A View to a Kill '85
The Naked Face '84
Octopussy '83
Cannonball Run '81
For Your Eyes Only '81
Sea Wolves '81
ffolkes '80
Escape to Athena '79
Moonraker '79
Wild Geese '78
The Spy Who Loved Me '77
Shout at the Devil '76
Street People '76
That Lucky Touch '75
The Man with the Golden Gun '74
Live and Let Die '73
The Man Who Haunted Himself '70
The Saint '68
Vendetta for the Saint '68
Fiction Makers '67
Gold of the Seven Saints '61
The Rape of the Sabines '61
The Sins of Rachel Cade '61
Diane '55
Interrupted Melody '55
The King's Thief '55
The Last Time I Saw Paris '54

Rudy Ray Moore (1937-2008)
Vampire Assassin '05
Devil's Son-in-Law '77
Monkey Hustle '77
Avenging Disco Godfather '76
Dolemite 2: Human Tornado '76
Dolemite '75

Sam Moore (1935-)
Night at the Golden Eagle '02
Tapeheads '89

Shemar Moore (1970-)
Diary of a Mad Black Woman '05
Motives '03
The Brothers '01
Mama Flora's Family '98
Never 2 Big '98

Shiela Moore (1938-)
The Reflecting Skin '91
Bye Bye Blues '89
Overdrawn at the Memory Bank '83

Stephan Campbell Moore (1979-)
Season of the Witch '10
Amazing Grace '06
The History Boys '06
A Good Woman '04
Bright Young Things '03

Stephen Moore (1937-)
Prince of Poisoners: The Life and Crimes of William Palmer '98
Under Suspicion '92
Clockwise '86

Tedde Moore
A Christmas Story '83
Second Wind '76

Terry Moore (1929-)
The Still Life '07
Kill Your Darlings '06
Second Chances '98
Beverly Hills Brats '89
Death Blow '87
Hellhole '85
Kill Factor '78
Platinum High School '60
Why Must I Die? '60
Peyton Place '57
Between Heaven and Hell '56
Postmark for Danger '56
Daddy Long Legs '55
Shack Out on 101 '55
Beneath the 12-Mile Reef '53
Come Back, Little Sheba '52
The Great Rupert '50
Mighty Joe Young '49
Gaslight '44
Since You Went Away '44

Toby Moore
A Separate Peace '04
Murder in Greenwich '02

Victor Moore (1876-1962)
The Seven Year Itch '55
We're Not Married '52
On Our Merry Way '48
It Happened on 5th Avenue '47
Ziegfeld Follies '46
The Heat's On '43
Star Spangled Rhythm '42
Louisiana Purchase '41
Make Way for Tomorrow '37
Gold Diggers of 1937 '36
Swing Time '36

Vivienne Moore
Miss Conception '08
Emma '72

Agnes Moorehead (1906-74)
Charlotte's Web '73 (V)
Dear Dead Delilah '72
What's the Matter with Helen? '71
Bachelor in Paradise '69
The Ballad of Andy Crocker '69
Alice Through the Looking Glass '66
The Singing Nun '66
Hush, Hush, Sweet Charlotte '65
How the West Was Won '63
Who's Minding the Store? '63
Pollyanna '60
The Bat '59
Raintree County '57
The Conqueror '56
Meet Me in Las Vegas '56
The Opposite Sex '56
Pardners '56
All That Heaven Allows '55
The Left Hand of God '55
Magnificent Obsession '54
Main Street to Broadway '53
The Story of Three Loves '53
Adventures of Captain Fabian '51
Captain Blackjack '51
Show Boat '51
Caged '50
The Stratton Story '49
Johnny Belinda '48
Station West '48
Summer Holiday '48
Dark Passage '47
Lost Moment '47
Our Vines Have Tender Grapes '45
Dragon Seed '44
Jane Eyre '44
Mrs. Parkington '44
The Seventh Cross '44
Since You Went Away '44
Tomorrow the World '44
Big Street '42
Journey into Fear '42
The Magnificent Ambersons '42
Citizen Kane '41

Natalie Moorhead (1901-92)
The Thin Man '34
Dancing Man '33
The King Murder '32
Murder on the High Seas '32
Illicit '31
Morals for Women '31
Hook, Line and Sinker '30

Tiriel Mora (1958-)
Garage Days '03
The Castle '97

Esai Morales (1962-)
Caprica '09
The Line '08
Fast Food Nation '06
How to Go Out on a Date in Queens '06
American Fusion '05
Once Upon a Wedding '05
Paid in Full '02
Atomic Train '99
The Wonderful Ice Cream Suit '98
Dogwatch '97
The Real Thing '97
The Disappearance of Garcia Lorca '96
Scorpion Spring '96
The Burning Season '94
Deadlock 2 '94
Don't Do It '94
In the Army Now '94
My Family '94
Rapa Nui '93
Freejack '92
Naked Tango '91
Ultraviolet '91
Bloodhounds of Broadway '89
La Bamba '87
The Principal '87
On Wings of Eagles '86
L.A. Bad '85
Bad Boys '83

Ines Morales
Curse of the Devil '73
House of Psychotic Women '73

Santos Morales
Hot to Trot! '88
The Boys in Company C '77

Dan Moran
Winter of Frozen Dreams '08
Rick '03
Mob Queen '98

Dolores Moran (1924-82)
The Man I Love '46
The Horn Blows at Midnight '45
To Have & Have Not '44

Dylan Moran (1971-)
Run, Fatboy, Run '07

Tristram Shandy: A Cock and Bull Story *'05*
Shaun of the Dead *'04*

Erin Moran (1961-)
Galaxy of Terror *'81*
Twirl *'81*
Watermelon Man *'70*
How Sweet It Is! *'68*

Frank Moran (1887-1967)
Return of the Ape Man *'44*
Motorcycle Squad *'41*
Ships in the Night *'28*

Jackie Moran (1923-90)
There Goes Kelly *'45*
Since You Went Away *'44*
Let's Go Collegiate *'41*
The Gang's All Here *'40*
Old Swimmin' Hole *'40*
Tomboy *'40*
Buck Rogers Conquers the Universe *'39*
The Adventures of Tom Sawyer *'38*
Mad About Music *'38*

Lee Moran (1890-1961)
High Gear *'33*
Pardon My Gun *'30*
On with the Show *'29*
My Lady of Whims *'25*
The Tomboy *'24*

Lois Moran
Behind That Curtain *'29*
Just Suppose *'26*

Nick Moran (1969-)
Silent Partner *'05*
Chaos & Cadavers *'03*
Another Life *'01*
The Musketeer *'01*
The Proposal *'00*
Rancid Aluminium *'00*
New Blood *'99*
Lock, Stock and 2 Smoking Barrels *'98*
Miss Monday *'98*

Pat Moran
Desperate Living *'77*
Female Trouble *'74*
Pink Flamingos *'72*
Multiple Maniacs *'70*

Patrick Moran (1960-)
Biohazard: The Alien Force *'95*
Dark Universe *'93*

Peggy Moran (1918-2002)
King of the Cowboys *'43*
Horror Island *'41*
Argentine Nights *'40*
The Mummy's Hand *'40*
One Night in the Tropics *'40*
Spring Parade *'40*

Polly Moran (1883-1952)
Adam's Rib *'50*
Hollywood Party *'34*
Politics *'31*
Reducing *'31*

Rob Moran (1963-)
Shallow Hal *'01*
Me, Myself, and Irene *'00*
There's Something about Mary *'98*
Kingpin *'96*
Dumb & Dumber *'94*

Rick Moranis (1954-)
Brother Bear 2 *'06 (V)*
Brother Bear *'03 (V)*
Honey, We Shrunk Ourselves *'97*
Big Bully *'95*
The Flintstones *'94*
Little Giants *'94*
Splitting Heirs *'93*
Honey, I Blew Up the Kid *'92*
My Blue Heaven *'90*
Ghostbusters 2 *'89*
Honey, I Shrunk the Kids *'89*
Parenthood *'89*
Spaceballs *'87*
Club Paradise *'86*
Head Office *'86*
Little Shop of Horrors *'86*
Brewster's Millions *'85*
Ghostbusters *'84*
Hockey Night *'84*
The Last Polka *'84*
Streets of Fire *'84*
The Wild Life *'84*
Strange Brew *'83*

Richard Morant (1945-)
Scandal *'89*
John & Yoko: A Love Story *'85*
Mad Death *'83*
Poldark *'75*
Mahler *'74*

Laura Morante (1956-)
Moliere *'07*
Avenue Montaigne *'06*
Private Fears in Public Places *'06*
Empire of the Wolves *'05*
The Dancer Upstairs *'02*
The Son's Room *'00*
The Tragedy of a Ridiculous Man *'81*

Milburn (Milt) Morante (1887-1964)
Ghost Rider *'43*
Between Men *'35*
Wolf Blood *'25*

Kestie Morassi
Wolf Creek *'05*
Strange Bedfellows *'04*
Dirty Deeds *'02*

Kenneth More (1914-82)
A Tale of Two Cities *'80*
Unidentified Flying Oddball *'79*
Leopard in the Snow *'78*
Where Time Began *'77*
The Slipper and the Rose *'76*
Scrooge *'70*
Battle of Britain *'69*
Oh! What a Lovely War *'69*
Dark of the Sun *'68*
The Longest Day *'62*
Flame Over India *'60*
Sink the Bismarck *'60*
The Sheriff of Fractured Jaw *'59*
A Night to Remember *'58*
The Admirable Crichton *'57*
Reach for the Sky *'56*
The Adventures of Sadie *'55*
Doctor in the House *'53*
Genevieve *'53*
Never Let Me Go *'53*
The Clouded Yellow *'51*
No Highway in the Sky *'51*
Morning Departure *'50*
Man on the Run *'49*
Scott of the Antarctic *'48*

Jeanne Moreau (1928-)
One Day You'll Understand *'08*
Go West *'05*
Time to Leave *'05*
Balzac: A Life of Passion *'99*
Ever After: A Cinderella Story *'98*
I Love You, I Love You Not *'97*
The Proprietor *'96*
Beyond the Clouds *'95*
Catherine the Great *'95*
The Summer House *'94*
A Foreign Field *'93*
Map of the Human Heart *'93*
Alberto Express *'92*
The Lover *'92 (N)*
La Femme Nikita *'91*
The Old Lady Who Walked in the Sea *'91*
Until the End of the World *'91*
Heat of Desire *'84*
Your Ticket Is No Longer Valid *'84*
La Truite *'83*
Querelle *'83*
The Last Tycoon *'76*
Lumiere *'76*
Mr. Klein *'76*
Going Places *'74*
Nathalie Granger *'72*
The Little Theatre of Jean Renoir *'71*
Alex in Wonderland *'70*
Monte Walsh *'70*
The Bride Wore Black *'68*
Chimes at Midnight *'67*
Oldest Profession *'67*
Mademoiselle *'66*
The Train *'65*
Viva Maria! *'65*
Diary of a Chambermaid *'64*
The Fire Within *'64*
The Trial *'63*
The Victors *'63*
Eva *'62*
Jules and Jim *'62*
Dangerous Liaisons *'60*
La Notte *'60*
The 400 Blows *'59*
The Lovers *'59*
Frantic *'58*
Back to the Wall *'56*
Grisbi *'53*

Marguerite Moreau (1977-)
Beverly Hills Chihuahua *'08 (V)*
Off the Lip *'04*
Runaway Jury *'03*
Two Days *'03*
Firestarter 2: Rekindled *'02*
The Locket *'02*
Queen of the Damned *'02*
Wet Hot American Summer *'01*

Marsha Moreau (1977-)
The Last Winter *'89*
Miracle at Moreaux *'86*

Nathaniel Moreau (1978-)
George's Island *'91*
The Last Winter *'89*

Sylvie Moreau (1964-)
Familia *'05*
The Widow of Saint-Pierre *'00*
Post Mortem *'99*

Yolande Moreau (1953-)
Micmacs *'09*
Seraphine *'08*
Paris, je t'aime *'06*
Amelie *'01*
Vagabond *'85*

Elizabeth Morehead
Sand Trap *'97*
Interceptor *'92*

Mantan Moreland (1902-73)
The Young Nurses *'73*
Spider Baby *'64*
Juke Joint *'47*
Tall, Tan and Terrific *'46*
The Jade Mask *'45*
The Scarlet Clue *'45*
The Shanghai Cobra *'45*
Charlie Chan in the Secret Service *'44*
The Chinese Cat *'44*
Meeting at Midnight *'44*
Pin-Up Girl *'44*
Revenge of the Zombies *'43*
Footlight Serenade *'42*
Law of the Jungle *'42*
Phantom Killer *'42*
The Strange Case of Dr. Rx *'42*
Cracked Nuts *'41*
King of the Zombies *'41*
Let's Go Collegiate *'41*
The Gang's All Here *'40*
Up in the Air *'40*
Frontier Scout *'38*
Harlem on the Prairie *'38*
Next Time I Marry *'38*
Two-Gun Man from Harlem *'38*
The Spirit of Youth *'37*

Andre Morell (1909-78)
10 Rillington Place *'71*
Dark of the Sun *'68*
Plague of the Zombies *'66*
Woman of Straw *'64*
The Hound of the Baskervilles *'59*
Quatermass and the Pit *'58*
The Bridge on the River Kwai *'57*
The Baby and the Battleship *'56*
The Man Who Never Was *'55*
A Stolen Face *'52*
The Clouded Yellow *'51*
Madeleine *'50*
Seven Days to Noon *'50*

Rina Morelli (1908-)
The Innocent *'76*
The Leopard *'63*
Il Bell'Antonio *'60*
The Inveterate Bachelor *'58*
The Iron Crown *'41*

Antonio Moreno (1887-1967)
The Searchers *'56*
Creature from the Black Lagoon *'54*
Captain from Castile *'47*
Valley of the Sun *'42*
Rose of Rio Grande *'38*
It *'27*
The Temptress *'26*

Catalina Sandino Moreno (1981-)
The Twilight Saga: Eclipse *'10*
Che *'08*
Love in the Time of Cholera *'07*
Fast Food Nation *'06*
The Hottest State *'06*
Journey to the End of the Night *'06*
Paris, je t'aime *'06*
Maria Full of Grace *'04*

Jose Elias Moreno (1910-69)
Night of the Bloody Apes *'68*
Santa Claus *'59*

Lea Moreno (1977-)
Doom Runners *'97*
Jungle Boy *'96*

Rene L. Moreno (1969-)
Band of Brothers *'01*
Tequila Body Shots *'99*

Rita Moreno (1931-)
King of the Corner *'04*
Casa de los Babys *'03*
Pinero *'01*
Blue Moon *'00*
Slums of Beverly Hills *'98*
The Spree *'96*
Angus *'95*
The Wharf Rat *'95*
I Like It Like That *'94*
Italian Movie *'93*
Age Isn't Everything *'91*
Portrait of a Showgirl *'82*
The Four Seasons *'81*
Happy Birthday, Gemini *'80*
Anatomy of a Seduction *'79*
Boss' Son *'78*
The Ritz *'76*
Carnal Knowledge *'71*
Marlowe *'69*
The Night of the Following Day *'69*
Popi *'69*
Cry of Battle *'63*
Summer and Smoke *'61*
West Side Story *'61*
The King and I *'56*
Seven Cities of Gold *'55*
Garden of Evil *'54*
Cattle Town *'52*
The Ring *'52*
Singin' in the Rain *'52*
Pagan Love Song *'50*
The Toast of New Orleans *'50*

Michele Moretti (1977-)
Apres-Vous *'03*
Wild Reeds *'94*

Nanni Moretti (1953-)
Quiet Chaos *'08*
The Son's Room *'00*
Caro Diario *'93*
Palombella Rossa *'89*

Chloe Grace Moretz (1997-)
Diary of a Wimpy Kid *'10*
Kick-Ass *'10*
(500) Days of Summer *'09*
The Eye *'08*
Big Momma's House 2 *'06*
The Amityville Horror *'05*

George Morfogen (1933-)
Twenty Bucks *'93*
Deadly Business *'86*
Yuri Nosenko, KGB *'86*

Boyd 'Red' Morgan (1915-88)
The Adventures of Buckaroo Banzai Across the Eighth Dimension *'84*
The Amazing Transparent Man *'60*

Chad Morgan
Taken *'02*
Whatever *'98*

Chesty Morgan (1928-)
Double Agent 73 *'80*
Deadly Weapons *'70*

Cindy Morgan (1954-)
Tron *'82*
Caddyshack *'80*

Clive Morgan (1896-1984)
Gunga Din *'39*
The Lives of a Bengal Lancer *'35*

Debbi (Deborah) Morgan (1956-)
Back in the Day *'05*
Coach Carter *'05*
Woman, Thou Art Loosed *'04*
Love and Basketball *'00*
The Runaway *'00*
Asunder *'99*
The Hurricane *'99*
She's All That *'99*
Eve's Bayou *'97*
Guilty of Innocence *'87*
The Jesse Owens Story *'84*
Monkey Hustle *'77*
Mandingo *'75*

Dennis Morgan (1910-94)
Pearl of the South Pacific *'55*
Cattle Town *'52*
This Woman Is Dangerous *'52*
Painting the Clouds With Sunshine *'51*
Perfect Strangers *'50*
Pretty Baby *'50*
It's a Great Feeling *'49*
Christmas in Connecticut *'45*
God is My Co-Pilot *'45*
Thank Your Lucky Stars *'43*
Captains of the Clouds *'42*
In This Our Life *'42*
The Fighting 69th *'40*
Kitty Foyle *'40*
Waterfront *'39*
The Great Ziegfeld *'36*
I Conquer the Sea *'36*

Frank Morgan (1890-1949)
Key to the City *'50*
Any Number Can Play *'49*
The Stratton Story *'49*
Summer Holiday *'48*
The Three Musketeers *'48*
Courage of Lassie *'46*
Casanova Brown *'44*
The White Cliffs of Dover *'44*
The Human Comedy *'43*
Thousands Cheer *'43*
Tortilla Flat *'42*
White Cargo *'42*
Honky Tonk *'41*
Boom Town *'40*
Broadway Melody of 1940 *'40*
The Mortal Storm *'40*
The Shop Around the Corner *'40*
Balalaika *'39*
Broadway Serenade *'39*
The Wizard of Oz *'39*
Rosalie *'38*
Sweethearts *'38*
The Last of Mrs. Cheyney *'37*
Saratoga *'37*
Dancing Pirate *'36*
Dimples *'36*
The Great Ziegfeld *'36*
The Good Fairy *'35*
I Live My Life *'35*
Naughty Marietta *'35*
The Cat and the Fiddle *'34*
Hallelujah, I'm a Bum *'33*
The Half Naked Truth *'32*
Manhandled *'24*

Gary Morgan (1950-)
The Power Within *'95*
Storybook *'95*
The California Kid *'74*

Gene Morgan (1893-1940)
Alibi for Murder *'36*
Rogue of the Rio Grande *'30*

Harry (Henry) Morgan (1915-)
The Incident *'89*
Dragnet *'87*
Agatha Christie's Sparkling Cyanide *'83*
M*A*S*H: Goodbye, Farewell & Amen *'83*
Roughnecks *'80*
Scout's Honor *'80*
The Apple Dumpling Gang Rides Again *'79*
Backstairs at the White House *'79*
Better Late Than Never *'79*
Roots: The Next Generation *'79*
Wild, Wild West Revisited *'79*
The Bastard *'78*
The Cat from Outer Space *'78*
The Shootist *'76*
The Apple Dumpling Gang *'75*
Charley and the Angel *'73*
Snowball Express *'72*
The Barefoot Executive *'71*
Scandalous John *'71*
Support Your Local Gunfighter *'71*
Support Your Local Sheriff *'69*
Flim-Flam Man *'67*
What Did You Do in the War, Daddy? *'66*
Frankie and Johnny *'65*
How the West Was Won *'63*
Inherit the Wind *'60*
The Mountain Road *'60*
Murder, Inc. *'60*
It Started with a Kiss *'59*
The Teahouse of the August Moon *'56*
Far Country *'55*
The Glenn Miller Story *'54*
Torch Song *'53*
Bend of the River *'52*
Boots Malone *'52*
High Noon *'52*
Scandal Sheet *'52*
The Well *'51*
The Showdown *'50*
Holiday Affair *'49*
All My Sons *'48*
The Big Clock *'48*
The Smallest Show on Earth *'48*

The Gangster '47
Dragonwyck '46
State Fair '45
A Wing and a Prayer '44
Crash Dive '43
The Ox-Bow Incident '43
Orchestra Wives '42
To the Shores of Tripoli '42

Helen Morgan (1900-41)
Frankie and Johnny '36
Show Boat '36
Go Into Your Dance '35
Marie Galante '34
Applause '29

Jaye P. Morgan (1931-)
Confessions of a Dangerous Mind '02
Night Patrol '85

Jeffrey Dean Morgan (1966-)
The Losers '10
All Good Things '09
Shanghai '09
Taking Woodstock '09
Watchmen '09
The Accidental Husband '08
P.S. I Love You '07
Jam '06
Six: The Mark Unleashed '04
Legal Deceit '95
Undercover '94
Uncaged '91

Melissa Morgan
See Liz Renay

Michele Morgan (1920-)
The Other Brother '02
Bulworth '98
Everybody's Fine '90
Cat and Mouse '78
The Lost Command '66
Bluebeard '63
Les Grandes Manoeuvres '55
The Proud Ones '53
The Fallen Idol '49
Fabiola '48
The Chase '46
La Symphonie Pastorale '46
Higher and Higher '44
Passage to Marseilles '44
Heart of a Nation '43
Joan of Paris '42
Stormy Waters '41

Nancy Morgan (1949-)
Lucky Luke '94
Danielle Steel's Heartbeat '93
The Nest '88
Pray TV '80
Americathon '79
Backstairs at the White House '79
Grand Theft Auto '77

Ralph Morgan (1882-1956)
Heart of the Rockies '51
The Creeper '48
Song of the Thin Man '47
Enemy of Women '44
The Monster Maker '44
Weird Woman '44
Gang Busters '42
Night Monster '42
Dick Tracy vs. Crime Inc. '41
Way Down South '39
Shadows over Shanghai '38
Mannequin '37
General Spanky '36
Yellowstone '36
Condemned to Live '35
Magnificent Obsession '35
Transatlantic Merry-Go-Round '34
The Kennel Murder Case '33
Rasputin and the Empress '33
Strange Interlude '32

Richard Morgan (1958-2006)
The Wicked '89
Innocent Prey '88

Shelley Taylor Morgan
Malibu Express '85
My Tutor '82

Stafford Morgan
The Capture of Bigfoot '79
The Alpha Incident '76

Terence Morgan (1921-2005)
The Lifetaker '89
Tread Softly Stranger '58
The Scamp '57
Svengali '55
The Love of Three Queens '54

Tracy Morgan (1968-)
Death at a Funeral '10
Cloudy with a Chance of Meatballs '09 (V)
G-Force '09 (V)
First Sunday '08
Little Man '06
Are We There Yet? '05
The Longest Yard '05
Head of State '03
Frank McKlusky, C.I. '02
30 Years to Life '01
Half-Baked '97
A Thin Line Between Love and Hate '96

Trevor Morgan (1986-)
Local Color '06
The Prize Winner of Defiance, Ohio '05
Mean Creek '04
Uncle Nino '03
The Rookie '02
The Glass House '01
Jurassic Park 3 '01
The Patriot '00
A Rumor of Angels '00
I'll Remember April '99
The Sixth Sense '99
Barney's Great Adventure '98
In the Doghouse '98

Wendy Morgan
Pictures '81
The Mirror Crack'd '80

Maia Morgenstern (1962-)
The Passion of the Christ '04
Ulysses' Gaze '95
The Oak '93
Trahir '93

Stephanie Morgenstern (1965-)
Cafe Ole '00
Maelstrom '00
P.T. Barnum '99
The Sweet Hereafter '96

Masayuki Mori (1911-73)
The Bad Sleep Well '60
When a Woman Ascends the Stairs '60
Princess Yang Kwei Fei '55
Ugetsu '53
The Idiot '51
Rashomon '51
The Men Who Tread on the Tiger's Tail '45

Naoki Mori
Living Hell: A Japanese Chainsaw Massacre '00
Spice World: The Movie '97

Toshia Mori (1912-95)
The Bitter Tea of General Yen '33
The Secrets of Wu Sin '32

Pat Moriarity (1896-1962)
Kings Row '41
Mutiny in the Big House '39

Cathy Moriarty (1961-)
The Bounty Hunter '10
Analyze That '02
Prince of Central Park '00
But I'm a Cheerleader '99
Crazy in Alabama '99
The Crimson Code '99
New Waterford Girl '99
Digging to China '98
Gloria '98
P.U.N.K.S. '98
A Brother's Kiss '97
Cop Land '97
Dream with the Fishes '97
Hugo Pool '97
Foxfire '96
Opposite Corners '96
Casper '95
Forget Paris '95
Pontiac Moon '94
Runaway Daughters '94
Another Stakeout '93
Me and the Kid '93
The Gun in Betty Lou's Handbag '92
The Mambo Kings '92
Matinee '92
Soapdish '91
Kindergarten Cop '90
Burndown '89
White of the Eye '88
Neighbors '81
Raging Bull '80

James Moriarty
Ten Benny '98
Someone to Watch Over Me '87

Michael Moriarty (1941-)
Taken '02
Along Came a Spider '01
James Dean '01
Mindstorm '01
Cold Blooded '00
The Art of Murder '99
Shiloh 2: Shiloh Season '99
Woman Wanted '98
Managua '97
Shiloh '97
Calm at Sunset '96
Courage Under Fire '96
Crime of the Century '96
A Good Day to Die '95
Full Fathom Five '90
Secret of the Ice Cave '89
Tailspin: Behind the Korean Airline Tragedy '89
Nitti: The Enforcer '88
Windmills of the Gods '88
Dark Tower '87
Hanoi Hilton '87
It's Alive 3: Island of the Alive '87
Return to Salem's Lot '87
Bloodlink '86
Troll '86
Odd Birds '85
Pale Rider '85
The Stuff '85
Q (The Winged Serpent) '82
Sound of Murder '82
Reborn '81
Too Far to Go '79
Holocaust '78
Who'll Stop the Rain? '78
The Winds of Kitty Hawk '78
Report to the Commissioner '74
Shoot It Black, Shoot It Blue '74
Bang the Drum Slowly '73
The Last Detail '73
My Old Man's Place '71

P. H. Moriarty (1939-)
The Riddle '07
Children of Dune '03
Dune '00
Lock, Stock and 2 Smoking Barrels '98
The Long Good Friday '80

Tara Morice (1964-)
Salem's Lot '04
Sorrento Beach '95
Metal Skin '94
Strictly Ballroom '92

Philippe Morier-Genoud
Time Regained '99
Trois Couleurs: Blanc '94
Cyrano de Bergerac '90
Au Revoir les Enfants '87
Confidentially Yours '83

Johnny Morina
Home Team '98
Kids of the Round Table '96
The Other Side of the Law '95
The Boys of St. Vincent '93

Yoshiyuki Morishita
Funky Forest: The First Contact '06
The Happiness of the Katakuris '01
Ringu 0 '01
Wild Zero '00
Shark Skin Man and Peach Hip Girl '98

Patricia Morison (1914-)
Song Without End '60
The Prince of Thieves '48
Return of Wildfire '48
Queen of the Amazons '47
Song of the Thin Man '47
Dressed to Kill '46
Without Love '45
Calling Dr. Death '43
The Fallen Sparrow '43
The Roundup '41

Alanis Morissette (1974-)
Jay and Silent Bob Strike Back '01
Dogma '99

Noriyuki "Pat" Morita (1932-2005)
American Fusion '05
18 Fingers of Death '05
Elvis Has Left the Building '04
Karate Dog '04
The Biggest Fan '02
Desert Heat '99
I'll Remember April '99
King Cobra '98
Mulan '98 (V)
Bloodsport 3 '97
Bloodsport 2: The Next Kumite '95
Timemaster '95
Even Cowgirls Get the Blues '94
The Next Karate Kid '94
North '94
Auntie Lee's Meat Pies '92
Honeymoon in Vegas '92
Mastergate '92
Miracle Beach '92
Do or Die '91
Hiroshima: Out of the Ashes '90
Lena's Holiday '90
Collision Course '89
The Karate Kid: Part 3 '89
Captive Hearts '87
Babes in Toyland '86
The Karate Kid: Part 2 '86
Alice in Wonderland '85
Amos '85
Night Patrol '85
The Karate Kid '84
Slapstick of Another Kind '84
The Vegas Strip Wars '84
For the Love of It '80
When Time Ran Out '80
I Wonder Who's Killing Her Now? '76
Midway '76
Cancel My Reservation '72
Evil Roy Slade '71
The Shakiest Gun in the West '68
Thoroughly Modern Millie '67

Louisa Moritz (1946-)
Chained Heat '83
Last American Virgin '82
True Confessions '81
New Year's Evil '78
Death Race 2000 '75
One Flew Over the Cuckoo's Nest '75

Henning Moritzen (1928-)
Allegro '05
The Celebration '98
Sofie '92
Memories of a Marriage '90
Cries and Whispers '72

Yuko Moriyama (1968-)
Zeram 2 '94
Zeram '91

Karen Morley (1909-2003)
Beloved Enemy '36
Healer '36
The Littlest Rebel '35
Our Daily Bread '34
Dinner at Eight '33
Gabriel Over the White House '33
The Mask of Fu Manchu '32
Mata Hari '32
Politics '31
Scarface '31
The Sin of Madelon Claudet '31

Robert Morley (1908-92)
A Troll in Central Park '94 (V)
Istanbul '90
Around the World in 80 Days '89
The Lady and the Highwayman '89
War & Remembrance: The Final Chapter '89
Little Dorrit, Film 1: Nobody's Fault '88
Little Dorrit, Film 2: Little Dorrit's Story '88
War & Remembrance '88
The Trouble with Spies '87
The Wind '87
Alice in Wonderland '85
Second Time Lucky '84
High Road to China '83
Loophole '83
Deadly Game '82
The Great Muppet Caper '81
Oh, Heavenly Dog! '80
The Human Factor '79
Scavenger Hunt '79
Who Is Killing the Great Chefs of Europe? '78
Hugo the Hippo '76 (V)
Theatre of Blood '73
When Eight Bells Toll '71
Cromwell '70
Song of Norway '70
Lola '69
Hot Millions '68
Woman Times Seven '67
A Study in Terror '66
The Trygon Factor '66
The Alphabet Murders '65
The Loved One '65
Those Magnificent Men in Their Flying Machines '65
Of Human Bondage '64
Topkapi '64
Ladies Who Do '63
Murder at the Gallop '63
The Battle of the Sexes '60
Around the World in 80 Days '56
Quentin Durward '55
Beau Brummel '54
Beat the Devil '53
Curtain Up '53
The African Queen '51
The Small Back Room '49
Ghosts of Berkeley Square '47
I Live in Grosvenor Square '46
The Foreman Went to France '42
Major Barbara '41
Marie Antoinette '38

Stanley Morner
See Dennis Morgan

Alicia Moro
Hot Blood '89
Slugs '87
Exterminators in the Year 3000 '83

Mike Moroff
Three Bad Men '05
The Crew '00
My Little Assassin '99
The Wonderful Ice Cream Suit '98
Angel Town '89
The Cage '89

Michael Morra
See Rockets Redglare

Geoff Morrell
Rogue '07
Marking Time '03

George Morrell (1871-1955)
The Phantom Pinto '41
Buzzy Rides the Range '40

Priscilla Morrill (1927-94)
Right of Way '84
The People vs. Jean Harris '81

Adrian Morris (1903-41)
Angels with Dirty Faces '38
Radio Patrol '37

Anita Morris (1944-94)
Radioland Murders '94
Home for Christmas '93
Me and the Kid '93
Martians Go Home! '90
Off and Running '90
Bloodhounds of Broadway '89
A Sinful Life '89
Aria '88
18 Again! '88
Absolute Beginners '86
Blue City '86
Ruthless People '86
A Smoky Mountain Christmas '86
The Hotel New Hampshire '84
Maria's Lovers '84

Aubrey Morris (1930-)
She Creature '01
Lifeforce '85
Lisztomania '75
A Clockwork Orange '71
Night Caller from Outer Space '66

Barboura Morris (1932-75)
The Dunwich Horror '70
The St. Valentine's Day Massacre '67
The Trip '67
The Haunted Palace '63
X: The Man with X-Ray Eyes '63
Atlas '60
A Bucket of Blood '59
The Wasp Woman '59
Machine Gun Kelly '58
Sorority Girl '57
Teenage Doll '57

Beth Morris (1949-)
That'll Be the Day '73
Crucible of Terror '72

Chester Morris (1901-70)
The Great White Hope '70
Gambler's Choice '44
Wagons Westward '40
Five Came Back '39
Law of the Underworld '38
Smashing the Rackets '38
Flight from Glory '37
I Promise to Pay '37
Frankie and Johnny '36
They Met in a Taxi '36
Tomorrow at Seven '33
Red Headed Woman '32
Sinners in the Sun '32

Corsair *'31*
The Bat Whispers *'30*
The Big House *'30*
The Divorcee *'30*
Playing Around *'30*
Alibi *'29*

Colleen Morris
Prehysteria *'93*
Crossing the Line *'90*

David Morris (1924-)
Mr. Right *'06*
Charlie and the Chocolate Factory *'05*

Dorothy Morris (1922-)
Club Havana *'46*
Thirty Seconds Over Tokyo *'44*
Bataan *'43*

Frances Morris
Boss Cowboy *'35*
Pals of the Range *'35*
The Ridin' Fool *'31*

Garrett Morris (1944-)
Dog Gone *'08*
The Salon *'05*
Jackpot *'01*
Little Richard *'00*
Twin Falls Idaho *'99*
Black Scorpion 2: Ground Zero *'96*
Santa with Muscles *'96*
Black Scorpion *'95*
Machine Gun Blues *'95*
Almost Blue *'93*
Children of the Night *'92*
Severed Ties *'92*
Motorama *'91*
The Underachievers *'88*
Husbands, Wives, Money, and Murder *'86*
The Stuff *'85*
Cooley High *'75*
The Anderson Tapes *'71*
Where's Poppa? *'70*

Greg Morris (1934-96)
Vegas *'78*
The Doomsday Flight *'66*

Haviland (Haylie) Morris (1959-)
Cherry Crush *'07*
Rick *'03*
Home Alone 3 *'97*
Larry McMurtry's Dead Man's Walk *'96*
Gremlins 2: The New Batch *'90*
For Love or Money *'88*
Who's That Girl? *'87*
Sixteen Candles *'84*

Howard Morris (1919-2005)
The Wonderful Ice Cream Suit *'98*
It Came from Outer Space 2 *'95*
Tom and Jerry: The Movie *'93 (V)*
Life Stinks *'91*
End of the Line *'88*
Splash *'84*
Portrait of a Showgirl *'82*
History of the World: Part 1 *'81*
The Munsters' Revenge *'81*
High Anxiety *'77*
The Many Adventures of Winnie the Pooh *'77 (V)*
The Nutty Professor *'63*
40 Pounds of Trouble *'62*

Iona Morris (1957-)
Next Time *'99*
Rain Without Thunder *'93*

Jane Morris
Pet Shop *'94*
Frankie and Johnny *'91*
Pretty Woman *'90*
Nothing in Common *'86*

Jeff Morris (1934-2004)
The Crossing Guard *'94*
Payday *'73*
Kelly's Heroes *'70*

John Morris
Toy Story 3 *'10 (V)*
Toy Story 2 *'99 (V)*
Toy Story *'95 (V)*

Jonathan Morris (1960-)
Bloodstorm: Subspecies 4 *'98*
Vampire Journals *'96*
The Fantasticks *'95*

Judy Morris (1947-)
Best Enemies *'86*
Phar Lap *'84*
Razorback *'84*
In Search of Anna *'79*
Plumber *'79*
Cass *'78*
Between Wars *'74*

Julian Morris (1983-)
Sorority Row *'09*
Donkey Punch *'08*
Cry_Wolf *'05*
Whirlygirl *'04*

Kathryn Morris (1969-)
Resurrecting the Champ *'07*
Mindhunters *'05*
Minority Report *'02*
Inherit the Wind *'99*
Inferno *'98*
Sleepstalker: The Sandman's Last Rites *'94*

Kirk Morris (1938-)
Terror of the Steppes *'64*
Devil of the Desert Against the Son of Hercules *'62*
Maciste in Hell *'60*

Lana Morris (1930-98)
Radio Cab Murder *'54*
The Woman in Question *'50*
The Gay Lady *'49*
The Weaker Sex *'49*

Mary Morris (1915-88)
Train of Events *'49*
Pimpernel Smith *'42*
The Thief of Bagdad *'40*

Phil Morris (1959-)
Meet the Spartans *'08*
Bottoms Up *'06*
Comic Book: The Movie *'04*
Atlantis: The Lost Empire *'01 (V)*
Incognito *'99*
Clay Pigeons *'98*
Devil in the Flesh *'98*
Legal Deceit *'95*
P.I. Private Investigations *'87*

Robert Morris (1940-)
One Deadly Owner *'74*
Frankenstein Created Woman *'66*

Wayne Morris (1914-59)
Paths of Glory *'57*
Plunder Road *'57*
Lonesome Trail *'55*
The Bushwackers *'52*
Task Force *'49*
John Loves Mary *'48*
Kid Galahad *'37*

Ann Morrison
Battle Circus *'53*
Close to My Heart *'51*

Jenny (Jennifer) Morrison (1979-)
Star Trek *'09*
Table for Three *'09*
Big Stan *'07*
Flourish *'06*
Mr. & Mrs. Smith *'05*
Surviving Christmas *'04*
Grind *'03*
Big Shot: Confessions of a Campus Bookie *'02*
Urban Legends 2: Final Cut *'00*
Stir of Echoes *'99*
Intersection *'93*

Kenny Morrison (1974-)
Little Athens *'05*
NeverEnding Story 2: The Next Chapter *'91*
The Quick and the Dead *'87*

Pete Morrison (1890-1973)
Trailing Trouble *'30*
Trigger Tricks *'30*

Sammy (Earnest) Morrison (1912-89)
Follow the Leader *'44*
Let's Get Tough *'42*
'Neath Brooklyn Bridge *'42*
Flying Wild *'41*
Spooks Run Wild *'41*

Shelley Morrison (1936-)
Devil Times Five *'74*
Castle of Evil *'66*

Temuera Morrison (1961-)
Couples Retreat *'09*
The Marine 2 *'09*
River Queen *'05*
Star Wars: Episode 3—Revenge of the Sith *'05*
The Beautiful Country *'04*
Star Wars: Episode 2—Attack of the Clones *'02*
Vertical Limit *'00*
From Dusk Till Dawn 3: The Hangman's Daughter *'99*
Six Days, Seven Nights *'98*
Speed 2: Cruise Control *'97*
Barb Wire *'96*
The Island of Dr. Moreau *'96*
Once Were Warriors *'94*

Billy Morrissette
Get a Clue! *'98*
Severed Ties *'92*

David Morrissey (1963-)
Nowhere Boy *'09*
Is Anybody There? *'08*
The Other Boleyn Girl *'08*
The Reaping *'07*
Sense & Sensibility *'07*
The Water Horse: Legend of the Deep *'07*
Basic Instinct 2 *'06*
Derailed *'05*
Stoned *'05*
State of Play *'03*
Captain Corelli's Mandolin *'01*
Born Romantic *'00*
Robert Louis Stevenson's The Game of Death *'99*
Hilary and Jackie *'98*
Our Mutual Friend *'98*
The One That Got Away *'96*
Being Human *'94*
Framed *'93*
Robin Hood *'91*
Cause Celebre *'87*

Eamon Morrissey (1943-)
The Seventh Stream *'01*
Eat the Peach *'86*

Neil Morrissey (1962-)
Triggermen *'02*
The Match *'99*
A Woman's Guide to Adultery *'93*

Byron Morrow (1911-2006)
Missiles of October *'74*
Johnny Got His Gun *'71*

Edwin Morrow (1980-)
We Were Soldiers *'02*
What About Your Friends: Weekend Getaway *'02*
Soul of the Game *'96*

Jeff Morrow (1913-93)
Blood Legacy *'73*
Octaman *'71*
The Story of Ruth *'60*
The Giant Claw *'57*
Hour of Decision *'57*
Kronos *'57*
The Creature Walks among Us *'56*
The First Texan *'56*
Pardners *'56*
This Island Earth *'55*
The Robe *'53*

Jo Morrow (1940-)
Dr. Death, Seeker of Souls *'73*
Sunday in New York *'63*
13 Ghosts *'60*
Legend of Tom Dooley *'59*
Our Man in Havana *'59*
The Three Worlds of Gulliver *'59*

Mari Morrow
Uninvited Guest *'99*
Dead Man on Campus *'97*
Def Jam's How to Be a Player *'97*
Children of the Corn 3: Urban Harvest *'95*

Max Morrow (1991-)
That Russell Girl *'08*
The Christmas Shoes *'02*
Jacob Two Two Meets the Hooded Fang *'99*

Neyle Morrow
The Crimson Kimono *'59*
China Gate *'57*
Run of the Arrow *'56*
The Steel Helmet *'51*

Patricia Morrow (1944-)
Surf Party *'64*
The Kettles on Old MacDonald's Farm *'57*

Rob Morrow (1962-)
The Bucket List *'07*
Going Shopping *'05*
The Emperor's Club *'02*
The Guru *'02*
Maze *'01*
The Thin Blue Lie *'00*
Labor Pains *'99*
Only Love *'98*
Last Dance *'96*
Mother *'96*
Quiz Show *'94*
Private Resort *'84*

Susan Morrow (1931-85)
Battle Cry *'55*
Cat Women of the Moon *'53*
Corky of Gasoline Alley *'51*
Gasoline Alley *'51*

Vic Morrow (1932-82)
1990: The Bronx Warriors *'83*
Twilight Zone: The Movie *'83*
B.A.D. Cats *'80*
Humanoids from the Deep *'80*
The Evictors *'79*
Express to Terror *'79*
The Seekers *'79*
Wild & Wooly *'78*
Curse of the Black Widow *'77*
Funeral for an Assassin *'77*
The Bad News Bears *'76*
The Treasure of Matecumbe *'76*
Wanted: Babysitter *'75*
The California Kid *'74*
Death Stalk *'74*
Dirty Mary Crazy Larry *'74*
The Adventures of Tom Sawyer *'73*
The Glass House *'72*
Cimarron *'60*
God's Little Acre *'58*
King Creole *'58*
Men in War *'57*
Tribute to a Bad Man *'56*
Blackboard Jungle *'55*

Barry Morse (1918-)
I Really Hate My Job *'07*
Anne of Green Gables: The Continuing Story *'99*
JFK: Reckless Youth *'93*
Glory! Glory! *'90*
Sadat *'83*
Whoops Apocalypse *'83*
The Changeling *'80*
A Tale of Two Cities *'80*
The Martian Chronicles: Part 2 *'79*
The Martian Chronicles: Part 3 *'79*
Space: 1999—Alien Attack *'79*
Power Play *'78*
Welcome to Blood City *'77*
Love at First Sight *'76*
Destination Moonbase Alpha *'75*
Asylum *'72*
The Golden Bowl *'72*
Kings of the Sun *'63*
No Trace *'50*

David Morse (1953-)
Mother and Child *'09*
Hounddog *'08*
The Hurt Locker *'08*
John Adams *'08*
Passengers *'08*
Disturbia *'07*
16 Blocks *'06*
Down in the Valley *'05*
Dreamer: Inspired by a True Story *'05*
Nearing Grace *'05*
Double Vision *'02*
Hearts in Atlantis *'01*
The Slaughter Rule *'01*
Bait *'00*
Proof of Life *'00*
Crazy in Alabama *'99*
Dancer in the Dark *'99*
The Green Mile *'99*
The Negotiator *'98*
Contact *'97*
The Long Kiss Goodnight *'96*
The Rock *'96*
Stephen King's The Langoliers *'95*
Tecumseh: The Last Warrior *'95*
12 Monkeys *'95*
The Crossing Guard *'94*
The Getaway *'93*
The Good Son *'93*
Dead Ahead: The Exxon Valdez Disaster *'92*
The Indian Runner *'91*
Desperate Hours *'90*
The Brotherhood of the Rose *'89*
Shattered Vows *'84*
Prototype *'83*
Inside Moves *'80*

Helen Morse (1946-)
Iris *'89*
Far East *'85*
A Town Like Alice *'85*
Agatha *'79*
Caddie *'76*
Picnic at Hanging Rock *'75*

Laila Morse (1945-)
Love, Honour & Obey *'00*
Great Expectations *'99*
Nil by Mouth *'96*

Robert Morse (1931-)
Wild Palms *'93*
The Boatniks *'70*
Where Were You When the Lights Went Out? *'68*
A Guide for the Married Man *'67*
How to Succeed in Business without Really Trying *'67*
Oh Dad, Poor Dad (Momma's Hung You in the Closet & I'm Feeling So Sad) *'67*
The Loved One *'65*
The Matchmaker *'58*

Robin Morse (1915-58)
Rock All Night *'57*
Marty *'55*

Glenn Morshower (1959-)
The Men Who Stare at Goats *'09*
Delta Farce *'07*
Transformers *'07*
All the King's Men *'06*
Behind Enemy Lines 2: Axis of Evil *'06*
Good Night, and Good Luck *'05*
Hostage *'05*
The Last Shot *'04*
Black Hawk Down *'01*
Pearl Harbor *'01*
The Jack Bull *'99*
My Little Assassin *'99*
Dominion *'94*
84 Charlie MoPic *'89*
Tango and Cash *'89*
Drive-In *'76*

Viggo Mortensen (1958-)
The Road *'09*
Appaloosa *'08*
Good *'08*
Eastern Promises *'07*
A History of Violence *'05*
Hidalgo *'04*
Lord of the Rings: The Return of the King *'03*
Lord of the Rings: The Two Towers *'02*
Lord of the Rings: The Fellowship of the Ring *'01*
28 Days *'00*
A Walk on the Moon *'99*
A Perfect Murder *'98*
Psycho *'98*
G.I. Jane *'97*
Albino Alligator *'96*
Daylight *'96*
Portrait of a Lady *'96*
The Crew *'95*
Crimson Tide *'95*
The Passion of Darkly Noon *'95*
The Prophecy *'95*
American Yakuza *'94*
Boiling Point *'93*
Carlito's Way *'93*
The Young Americans *'93*
Deception *'92*
The Indian Runner *'91*
The Reflecting Skin *'91*
Young Guns 2 *'90*
Leatherface: The Texas Chainsaw Massacre 3 *'89*
Fresh Horses *'88*
Prison *'88*
Salvation! *'87*
Witness *'85*

Janne Mortil
Johnny's Girl *'95*
Tokyo Cowboy *'94*
Nightmare at Bittercreek *'91*

Emily Mortimer (1971-)
The Pink Panther 2 *'09*
Shutter Island *'09*
Chaos Theory *'08*
Redbelt *'08*
Transsiberian *'08*
Lars and the Real Girl *'07*
Paris, je t'aime *'06*
The Pink Panther *'06*
Match Point *'05*
Dear Frankie *'04*
Howl's Moving Castle *'04 (V)*
Bright Young Things *'03*
2 Brothers & a Bride *'03*
Young Adam *'03*
Lovely & Amazing *'02*
The Sleeping Dictionary *'02*
Formula 51 *'01*
Disney's The Kid *'00*
Love's Labour's Lost *'00*
Scream 3 *'00*
Cider with Rosie *'99*
Noah's Ark *'99*
Coming Home *'98*
Elizabeth *'98*
The Saint *'97*
The Ghost and the Darkness *'96*
The Last of the High Kings *'96*
Catherine Cookson's The Glass Virgin *'95*
Sharpe's Sword *'94*

Cookie Mueller (1949-89)
Polyester '81
Desperate Living '77
Female Trouble '74
Pink Flamingos '72
Multiple Maniacs '70

Maureen Mueller
Larger Than Life '96
Oldest Confederate Widow Tells All '95
The New Age '94
In a Shallow Grave '88

Armin Mueller-Stahl (1930-)
Angels & Demons '09
The International '09
Eastern Promises '07
Local Color '06
The Story of an African Farm '04
Jesus '00
Inferno '99
Jakob the Liar '99
The Third Miracle '99
The Thirteenth Floor '99
The X-Files '98
The Assistant '97
The Game '97
In the Presence of Mine Enemies '97
The Peacemaker '97
Twelve Angry Men '97
The Ogre '96
A Pyromaniac's Love Story '95
Red Hot '95
Shine '95
Theodore Rex '95
Holy Matrimony '94
The Last Good Time '94
The House of the Spirits '93
Utz '93
The Power of One '92
Kafka '91
Night on Earth '91
Avalon '90
Music Box '89
Midnight Cop '88
Lethal Obsession '87
Angry Harvest '85
Forget Mozart '85
Colonel Redl '84
A Love in Germany '84
Jacob the Liar '74
The Third '72
Five Cartridges '60

Marianne Muellerleile (1948-)
Return to Me '00
A Smile Like Yours '96
Curse 2: The Bite '88
The Trouble with Dick '88

Amanda Muggleton
Idiot Box '97
Queen of the Road '84

Ulrich Muhe (1953-2007)
Amen '02
Straight Shooter '99
Funny Games '97
Benny's Video '92
The Woman and the Stranger '84

Anita (Yim-Fong) Mui (1963-2003)
Rumble in the Bronx '96
Jet Li's The Enforcer '95
The Legend of Drunken Master '94
The Executioners '93
The Heroic Trio '93
A Better Tomorrow, Part 3 '89
Miracles '89

Esther Muir (1903-95)
Misbehaving Husbands '41
A Day at the Races '37
Racing Luck '35
So This Is Africa '33

Gavin Muir (1900-72)
Night Tide '63
Abbott and Costello Meet the Invisible Man '51
O.S.S. '46
House of Fear '45
Sherlock Holmes Faces Death '43
Charlie Chan at the Race Track '36
Mary of Scotland '36

Oliver Muirhead
MVP (Most Valuable Primate) '00
The Duke '99

Madhabi Mukherjee (1943-)
Charulata '64
The Big City '63

Diana Muldaur (1938-)
Return of Frank Cannon '80
Beyond Reason '77
McQ '74
Planet Earth '74
The Other '72

Patrick Muldoon (1969-)
The Chaos Experiment '09
Christmas Town '08
Ice Spiders '07
Military Intelligence and You! '06
Miracle Dogs Too '06
A Boyfriend for Christmas '04
Heart of America '03
Blackwoods '02
Whacked! '02
Hell's Gate '01
Chain of Command '00
The Crimson Code '99
Stigmata '99
The Arrival 2 '98
Black Cat Run '98
Wicked '98
Starship Troopers '97
Rage and Honor 2: Hostile Takeover '93

Nancy Mulford
Act of Piracy '89
Skeleton Coast '89

Kate Mulgrew (1955-)
Perception '06
Star Trek: Nemesis '02
Captain Nuke and the Bomber Boys '95
Camp Nowhere '94
Danielle Steel's Daddy '91
Round Numbers '91
Roots: The Gift '88
Throw Momma from the Train '87
Remo Williams: The Adventure Begins '85
A Stranger Is Watching '82
The Manions of America '81
A Time for Miracles '80
Lovespell '79
The Word '78

Jack Mulhall (1887-1979)
'Neath Canadian Skies '46
Dawn Express '42
I Killed That Man '42
Mr. Wise Guy '42
Desperate Cargo '41
International Lady '41
Saddle Mountain Roundup '41
Held for Ransom '38
Outlaws of Sonora '38
100 Men and a Girl '37
Radio Patrol '37
Tim Tyler's Luck '37
The Clutching Hand '36
Custer's Last Stand '36
A Face in the Fog '36
Kelly of the Secret Service '36
Rogue's Tavern '36
Roaring Roads '35
Skull & Crown '35
Mystery Squadron '33
The Three Musketeers '33
Hell's Headquarters '32
Murder on the High Seas '32
Show Girl in Hollywood '30

Edward Mulhare (1923-97)
Out to Sea '97
Megaforce '82
Caprice '67
Our Man Flint '66
Von Ryan's Express '65
Hill 24 Doesn't Answer '55

Michael Mulheren
Ash Wednesday '02
The Curse of the Jade Scorpion '01
Johnny Suede '92

Matt Mulhern (1960-)
Sunchaser '96
Biloxi Blues '88
Extreme Prejudice '87

Chris Mulkey (1948-)
Dragon Wars '07
Broken Trail '06
The Curiosity of Chance '06
Dreamland '06
Little Chenier: A Cajun Story '06
Love and Debate '06
Mysterious Skin '04
Radio '03
Jimmy Zip '00
Requiem for Murder '99
Sugar Town '99
Psychopath '97
Sub Down '97
Weapons of Mass Distraction '97
Behind Enemy Lines '96
Dead Cold '96
The Fan '96
Bound and Gagged: A Love Story '93
Ghost in the Machine '93
Deadbolt '92
Gas Food Lodging '92
The Silencer '92
Runaway Father '91
Write to Kill '91
Rainbow Drive '90
K-9000 '89
Roe vs. Wade '89
Heartbreak Hotel '88
In Dangerous Company '88
Patti Rocks '88
Tricks of the Trade '88
The Hidden '87
Jack's Back '87

Martin Mull (1943-)
Killers '10
A Boyfriend for Christmas '04
Attention Shoppers '99
Zack & Reba '98
Beverly Hills Family Robinson '97
Jingle All the Way '96
Movies Money Murder '96
Edie & Pen '95
How the West Was Fun '95
The Day My Parents Ran Away '93
Mrs. Doubtfire '93
Ted & Venus '93
Miracle Beach '92
Mr. Write '92
The Player '92
Dance with Death '91
Think Big '90
Cutting Class '89
Far Out Man '89
Ski Patrol '89
Home Is Where the Hart Is '88
Portrait of a White Marriage '88
Rented Lips '88
O.C. and Stiggs '87
The Boss' Wife '86
Pecos Bill '86
Clue '85
Flicks '85
Lots of Luck '85
Bad Manners '84
Mr. Mom '83
Take This Job & Shove It '81
My Bodyguard '80
Serial '80
FM '78

Megan Mullally (1958-)
Fame '09
Bee Movie '07 (V)
Rebound '05
Disney's Teacher's Pet '04 (V)
Stealing Harvard '02
Monkeybone '01
Everything Put Together '00
Winchell '98
Rainbow Drive '90
Last Resort '86

Peter Mullan (1954-)
Boy A '07
The Last Legion '07
Children of Men '06
On a Clear Day '05
Criminal '04
Young Adam '03
Session 9 '01
The Claim '00
Miss Julie '99
Ordinary Decent Criminal '99
My Name Is Joe '98

Jack Mullaney (1932-82)
George! '70
Spinout '66
Tickle Me '65
The Honeymoon Machine '61

Arthur Mullard
Morgan: A Suitable Case for Treatment '66
Postman's Knock '62

Greg Mullavey (1939-)
Cock & Bull Story '03
Deadly Conspiracy '91
Not Quite Human 2 '89
Body Count '87
Husbands, Wives, Money, and Murder '86
I Dismember Mama '74
The Love Machine '71
C.C. & Company '70

Barbara Mullen (1914-79)
The Very Edge '63
It Takes a Thief '59
Murder in the Footlights '46

Conor Mullen
The Honeymooners '03
Reckless '97

Marie Mullen (1963-)
When Brendan Met Trudy '00
Dancing at Lughnasa '98

Patty Mullen
Frankenhooker '90
Doom Asylum '88

David Muller
Spiral '07
Ernest in the Army '97

Harrison Muller
Miami Cops '89
2020 Texas Gladiators '85
The Final Executioner '83
She '83
Violent Breed '83

Michel Muller (1966-)
Wasabi '01
Like a Fish Out of Water '99
Train of Life '98

Paul Muller (1923-)
The Arena '73
Lady Frankenstein '72
Count Dracula '71
Virgin among the Living Dead '71
Fangs of the Living Dead '68
Nightmare Castle '65
Goliath and the Sins of Babylon '64
Four Ways Out '57
The Black Devils of Kali '55
Two Nights with Cleopatra '54

Carey Mulligan (1985-)
Wall Street 2: Money Never Sleeps '10
Brothers '09
An Education '09
My Boy Jack '07
Northanger Abbey '07
Bleak House '05
Pride and Prejudice '05

Richard Mulligan (1932-2000)
Gore Vidal's Lincoln '88
Oliver & Company '88 (V)
Poker Alice '87
Babes in Toyland '86
A Fine Mess '86
Doin' Time '85
The Heavenly Kid '85
Meatballs 2 '84
Micki & Maude '84
Teachers '84
S.O.B. '81
Scavenger Hunt '79
The Big Bus '76
The Hideaways '73
Pueblo Affair '73
Little Big Man '70
The Group '66

Terry David Mulligan (1942-)
Masters of Horror: Homecoming '05
Can of Worms '00
Sweetwater: A True Rock Story '99
Deadly Sins '95

Rod Mullinar (1942-)
Dead Calm '89
Echoes of Paradise '86
Breakfast in Paris '81
Breaker Morant '80
Patrick '78

Dermot Mulroney (1963-)
Flash of Genius '08
The Memory Keeper's Daughter '08
Georgia Rule '07
Gracie '07
Zodiac '07
Griffin & Phoenix '06
The Family Stone '05
Must Love Dogs '05
The Wedding Date '05
Undertow '04
About Schmidt '02
Lovely & Amazing '02
Intimate Affairs '01
The Safety of Objects '01
Trixie '00
Where the Money Is '00
Goodbye, Lover '99
My Best Friend's Wedding '97
Bastard out of Carolina '96
Box of Moonlight '96
The Trigger Effect '96
Copycat '95
How to Make an American Quilt '95
Kansas City '95
Angels in the Outfield '94
Bad Girls '94
Living in Oblivion '94
Family Pictures '93
The Last Outlaw '93
Point of No Return '93
The Thing Called Love '93
Samantha '92
Silent Tongue '92
There Goes My Baby '92
Where the Day Takes You '92
Bright Angel '91
Career Opportunities '91
Longtime Companion '90
Staying Together '89
Survival Quest '89
Sunset '88
Young Guns '88
Long Gone '87

Kieran Mulroney (1965-)
Quigley '03
Pursuit of Happiness '01
From the Earth to the Moon '98
God's Lonely Man '96
The Immortals '95
The Spitfire Grill '95
Sensation '94
Gettysburg '93
Career Opportunities '91
Nowhere to Run '88

Kelsey Mulrooney (1987-)
Second Chances '98
She's So Lovely '97
The Christmas Box '95

Samantha Mumba (1983-)
Johnny Was '05
The Time Machine '02

Danny Mummert (1934-)
Blondie Hits the Jackpot '49
Blondie Knows Best '46
Footlight Glamour '43
It's a Great Life '43
Blondie for Victory '42
Blondie Goes Latin '42
Blondie Goes to College '42
Blondie's Blessed Event '42
Blondie in Society '41
Blondie Has Trouble '40
Blondie On a Budget '40
Blondie Plays Cupid '40
Blondie Brings Up Baby '39
Blondie Meets the Boss '39
Blondie Takes a Vacation '39

Billy Mumy (1954-)
Comic Book: The Movie '04
Twilight Zone: The Movie '83
Bless the Beasts and Children '71
Dear Brigitte '65
Sammy, the Way-Out Seal '62

Liliana Mumy (1995-)
Snow Buddies '08 (V)
The Santa Clause 3: The Escape Clause '06
Cheaper by the Dozen 2 '05
Lilo & Stitch 2: Stitch Has a Glitch '05 (V)
Howl's Moving Castle '04 (V)
Cheaper by the Dozen '03
The Santa Clause 2 '02

Misty Mundae (1979-)
The Rage '07
Masters of Horror: Sick Girl '06
Lust for Dracula '04
Screaming Dead '03

Mary Munday (1926-97)
Pressure Point '62
Serpent Island '54

Herbert Mundin (1898-1939)
The Adventures of Robin Hood '38
Mutiny on the Bounty '35
Cavalcade '33
Hoopla '33

Kevin Mundy (1977-)
Jailbait! '00
Better Than Chocolate '99

Ian Mune (1941-)
Ike: Countdown to D-Day '04
Dangerous Orphans '86
Sleeping Dogs '77

Paul Muni (1895-1967)
The Last Angry Man '59
Angel on My Shoulder '46
A Song to Remember '45
Commandos Strike at Dawn '43
Stage Door Canteen '43
Juarez '39

The Good Earth '37
The Life of Emile Zola '37
The Story of Louis Pasteur '36
Black Fury '35
Bordertown '35
I Am a Fugitive from a Chain Gang '32
Scarface '31

Frankie Muniz (1985-)
Extreme Movie '08
Walk Hard: The Dewey Cox Story '07
Stay Alive '06
Racing Stripes '05 (V)
Agent Cody Banks 2: Destination London '04
Agent Cody Banks '03
Big Fat Liar '02
Deuces Wild '02
It Had to Be You '00
Miracle in Lane Two '00
My Dog Skip '99
What the Deaf Man Heard '98

Pep Munne (1953-)
Barcelona '94
Where Time Began '77

Amparo Munoz (1954-)
A Paradise Under the Stars '99
Mama Turns a Hundred '79

Caroline Munro (1950-)
Black Cat '90
Faceless '88
Slaughter High '86
Don't Open Till Christmas '84
Fanatic '82
Maniac '80
Star Crash '78
The Spy Who Loved Me '77
At the Earth's Core '76
I Don't Want to Be Born '75
Captain Kronos: Vampire Hunter '74
Golden Voyage of Sinbad '73
Doctor Phibes Rises Again '72
Dracula A.D. 1972 '72
The Abominable Dr. Phibes '71
Gun Crazy '69
Casino Royale '67

Janet Munro (1934-72)
The Day the Earth Caught Fire '61
Horsemasters '61
The Swiss Family Robinson '60
Darby O'Gill & the Little People '59
Third Man on the Mountain '59
The Crawling Eye '58
The Young and the Guilty '58
Small Hotel '57

Lochlyn Munro (1966-)
Art of War 2: The Betrayal '08
Space Buddies '08 (V)
Daddy Day Camp '07
Hack! '07
The Benchwarmers '06
Final Move '06
Little Man '06
The Tooth Fairy '06
Chasing Ghosts '05
Dirty Love '05
White Chicks '04
Freddy vs. Jason '03
A Guy Thing '03
Heart of America '03
Net Games '03
Pressure '02
Rock My World '02
Chilly Dogs '01
Kill Me Later '01
Camouflage '00
Dracula 2000 '00
Scary Movie '00
High Voltage '98
A Night at the Roxbury '98
Dead Man on Campus '97
Downhill Willie '96
Trancers 5: Sudden Deth '94
Wagons East '94
Anything for Love '93

Neil Munro
Beethoven Lives Upstairs '92
Gate 2 '92
Confidential '86
Dancing in the Dark '86

Jules Munshin (1915-70)
Ten Thousand Bedrooms '57
On the Town '49
Take Me Out to the Ball Game '49
That Midnight Kiss '49
Easter Parade '48

Ona Munson (1906-56)
The Red House '47
Dakota '45
Idaho '43
Lady from Louisiana '42
The Shanghai Gesture '42
Wagons Westward '40
Gone with the Wind '39

Silvia Munt
Secrets of the Heart '97
Extasis '96
Butterfly Wings '91

John Mylong Munz
See John (Jack) Mylong

Kunio Murai
Legends of the Poisonous Seductress 1: Female Demon Ohyaku '68
Snake Woman's Curse '68

Fuyuki Murakami (1911-2007)
Godzilla vs. Monster Zero '68
Godzilla, King of the Monsters '56

Katsumi Muramatsu
Ringu 2 '99
Ringu '98

Jean Murat (1888-1968)
Dishonorable Discharge '57
Rich, Young and Pretty '51
Eternal Return '43
Carnival in Flanders '35

Takehiro Murata (1960-)
When the Last Sword is Drawn '02
Godzilla 2000 '99
Okoge '93
Minbo—Or the Gentle Art of Japanese Extortion '92

George Murcell (1925-98)
Cutthroat Island '95
Year of the Gun '91

Enrique Murciano (1973-)
How to Go Out on a Date in Queens '06
The Lost City '05
Miss Congeniality 2: Armed and Fabulous '05
Black Hawk Down '01
Traffic '00
Speed 2: Cruise Control '97

Vince Murdocco
L.A. Wars '94
Ring of Fire 2: Blood and Steel '92
Ring of Fire '91
Flesh Gordon 2: Flesh Gordon Meets the Cosmic Cheerleaders '90

George Murdock (1930-)
Serial Killing 101 '04
Orange County '02
Spider's Web '01
Scorpio One '97
Crosscut '95
Firepower '93
Grand Tour: Disaster in Time '92
Strange Case of Dr. Jekyll & Mr. Hyde '89
In Love with an Older Woman '82
Mission Galactica: The Cylon Attack '78
Breaker! Breaker! '77
The Bravos '72

Jack Murdock (1922-2001)
Rain Man '88
Altered States '80

Tim Murdock
They Were Expendable '45
Thirty Seconds Over Tokyo '44

Caterina Murino
XIII '08
Casino Royale '06

Christopher Murney (1943-)
Winning Girls Through Psychic Mind Control '02
Barton Fink '91
The Ten Million Dollar Getaway '91
Murder by the Book '87
Maximum Overdrive '86
The Last Dragon '85

Peter Murnik (1965-)
Hard Rain '97
Rowing Through '96
Andersonville '95
Golden Gate '93
Body Parts '91

Hideo Murota
A Taxing Woman '87
Shogun's Samurai—The Yagyu Clan Conspiracy '78
Snake Woman's Curse '68

Aaron Murphy (1992-)
Boogeyman '05
The World's Fastest Indian '05
Rain '01

Annette Murphy (1967-)
Race '99
Star Maps '97

Audie Murphy (1924-71)
The Texican '66
Arizona Raiders '65
Gunfight at Comanche Creek '64
The Unforgiven '60
No Name on the Bullet '59
Night Passage '57
Walk the Proud Land '56
To Hell and Back '55
Ride Clear of Diablo '54
Gunsmoke '53
Duel at Silver Creek '52
The Red Badge of Courage '51

Barri Murphy
Armed for Action '92
Action U.S.A. '89

Ben Murphy (1942-)
The Cradle Will Fall '83
The Winds of War '83
Time Walker '82
The Chisholms '79
Riding with Death '76

Brittany Murphy (1977-2009)
The Expendables '10
Deadline '09
Tribute '09
The Ramen Girl '08
The Dead Girl '06
The Groomsmen '06
Happy Feet '06 (V)
Love and Other Disasters '06
Sin City '05
Little Black Book '04
Good Boy! '03 (V)
Just Married '03
Uptown Girls '03
8 Mile '02
Spun '02
Don't Say a Word '01
Riding in Cars with Boys '01
Sidewalks of New York '01
Summer Catch '01
Cherry Falls '00
Common Ground '00
Trixie '00
The Devil's Arithmetic '99
Drop Dead Gorgeous '99
Girl, Interrupted '99
Bongwater '98
Phoenix '98
Zack & Reba '98
The Prophecy 2: Ashtown '97
Drive '96
Clueless '95
Freeway '95

Charlie (Charles Q.) Murphy (1959-)
The Perfect Holiday '07
Unearthed '07
King's Ransom '05
Roll Bounce '05
CB4: The Movie '93

Cillian Murphy (1976-)
Inception '10
The Dark Knight '08
The Edge of Love '08
Sunshine '07
Watching the Detectives '07
The Wind That Shakes the Barley '06
Batman Begins '05
Red Eye '05
Girl with a Pearl Earring '03
28 Days Later '02
The Way We Live Now '02
Disco Pigs '01
How Harry Became a Tree '01
On the Edge '00

Donald Murphy (1910-95)
Lord Love a Duck '66
Frankenstein's Daughter '58
Shack Out on 101 '55

Donna Murphy (1958-)
Sherman's Way '08
The Nanny Diaries '07
Spider-Man 2 '04
Center Stage '00
The Last Debate '00
The Astronaut's Wife '99
Star Trek: Insurrection '98

Dwain Murphy
How She Move '08
Saving God '08

Eddie Murphy (1961-)
Shrek Forever After '10 (V)
Imagine That '09
Meet Dave '08
Norbit '07
Shrek the Third '07 (V)
Dreamgirls '06
Shrek 2 '04 (V)
Daddy Day Care '03
The Haunted Mansion '03
The Adventures of Pluto Nash '02
I Spy '02
Showtime '02
Dr. Dolittle 2 '01
Shrek '01 (V)
Nutty Professor 2: The Klumps '00
Bowfinger '99
Life '99
Dr. Dolittle '98
Holy Man '98
Mulan '98 (V)
Metro '96
The Nutty Professor '96
Vampire in Brooklyn '95
Beverly Hills Cop 3 '94
Boomerang '92
The Distinguished Gentleman '92
Another 48 Hrs. '90
Harlem Nights '89
Coming to America '88
Beverly Hills Cop 2 '87
The Golden Child '86
Best Defense '84
Beverly Hills Cop '84
Trading Places '83
48 Hrs. '82

Gary Murphy
U.S. Navy SEALS: Dead or Alive '02
U.S. SEALs: Dead or Alive '02

George Murphy (1902-92)
It's a Big Country '51
Battleground '49
Border Incident '49
Cynthia '47
Having Wonderful Crime '45
Broadway Rhythm '44
Show Business '44
Step Lively '44
Bataan '43
This Is the Army '43
For Me and My Gal '42
The Navy Comes Through '42
A Girl, a Guy and a Gob '41
Tom, Dick, and Harry '41
Broadway Melody of 1940 '40
Little Nellie Kelly '40
Letter of Introduction '38
Little Miss Broadway '38
Broadway Melody of 1938 '37
Kid Millions '34

Horace Murphy (1880-1975)
Bad Man of Deadwood '41
Down the Wyoming Trail '39
Rollin' Plains '38
The Stranger from Arizona '38
Wide Open Faces '38
Boothill Brigade '37
Border Phantom '37
Come on, Cowboys '37
Paroled to Die '37
Sing, Cowboy, Sing '37
Tex Rides with the Boy Scouts '37
Last of the Warrens '36
Undercover Man '36

Jimmy Murphy (1931-)
Platinum High School '60
Curse of the Undead '59

Johnny Murphy
War of the Buttons '95
The Commitments '91

Kim Murphy (1974-)
The In Crowd '00
Campfire Tales '98
Houseguest '94

Mary Murphy
The Wind That Shakes the Barley '06
Crime and Punishment, USA '59

Mary Murphy (1931-)
I Love You, Goodbye '74
40 Pounds of Trouble '62
The Electronic Monster '57
Desperate Hours '55
A Man Alone '55
The Maverick Queen '55
Sitting Bull '54
The Wild One '54
Houdini '53
Main Street to Broadway '53
Carrie '52

Maurice Murphy (1913-78)
Abe Lincoln in Illinois '40
Delinquent Parents '38
Found Alive '34
Tailspin Tommy '34
Pilgrimage '33

Megan Murphy
Money Buys Happiness '99
Shredder Orpheus '89

Michael Murphy (1938-)
According to Greta '08
Away From Her '06
X-Men: The Last Stand '06
Heights '04
Silver City '04
Tanner on Tanner '04
Footsteps '03
Live from Baghdad '03
The Day Reagan Was Shot '01
Breaking the Surface: The Greg Louganis Story '96
Private Parts '96
Kansas City '95
Clean Slate '94
Batman Returns '92
Dead Ahead: The Exxon Valdez Disaster '92
Folks! '92
Shocker '89
Tailspin: Behind the Korean Airline Tragedy '89
The Caine Mutiny Court Martial '88
Tanner '88 '88
Salvador '86
Cloak & Dagger '84
Mesmerized '84
Talk to Me '84
The Year of Living Dangerously '82
Strange Behavior '81
Hot Money '79
Manhattan '79
The Class of Miss MacMichael '78
Great Bank Hoax '78
An Unmarried Woman '78
The Front '76
Nashville '75
The Autobiography of Miss Jane Pittman '74
I Love You, Goodbye '74
Phase 4 '74
The Thief Who Came to Dinner '73
McCabe & Mrs. Miller '71
Brewster McCloud '70
Count Yorga, Vampire '70
M*A*S*H '70
That Cold Day in the Park '69
Countdown '68
Double Trouble '67

Rosemary Murphy (1927-)
Dust '01
Message in a Bottle '98
The Tuskegee Airmen '95
For the Boys '91
A Woman Named Jackie '91
The Attic '80
Julia '77
Eleanor & Franklin '76
Walking Tall '73
Ben '72
You'll Like My Mother '72
Any Wednesday '66
To Kill a Mockingbird '62

Timothy Murphy
National Treasure: Book of Secrets '07
Shallow Ground '04

Timothy Patrick Murphy (1959-88)
Doin' Time on Planet Earth '88
Sam's Son '84
The Seekers '79

William Murphy
Sands of Iwo Jima '49
The Story of G.I. Joe '45

Barbara Murray (1929-)
The Bretts '88
A Cry from the Streets '57
Death Goes to School '53
Another Man's Poison '52
The Frightened Man '52
Tony Draws a Horse '51

Beverly Murray

The Carpenter '89
Cathy's Curse '77

Bill Murray (1950-)

Fantastic Mr. Fox '09 (V)
Get Low '09
The Limits of Control '09
Zombieland '09
City of Ember '08
Get Smart '08
Garfield: A Tail of Two Kitties '06 (V)
Broken Flowers '05
The Lost City '05
Garfield: The Movie '04 (V)
The Life Aquatic with Steve Zissou '04
Coffee and Cigarettes '03
Lost in Translation '03
Osmosis Jones '01
The Royal Tenenbaums '01
Charlie's Angels '00
Hamlet '00
The Cradle Will Rock '99
Rushmore '98
Wild Things '98
With Friends Like These '98
The Man Who Knew Too Little '97
Kingpin '96
Larger Than Life '96
Space Jam '96
Ed Wood '94
Groundhog Day '93
Mad Dog and Glory '93
What about Bob? '91
Quick Change '90
Ghostbusters 2 '89
Scrooged '88
Little Shop of Horrors '86
Ghostbusters '84
The Razor's Edge '84
Tootsie '82
Stripes '81
Caddyshack '80
Where the Buffalo Roam '80
Meatballs '79
Mr. Mike's Mondo Video '79
All You Need Is Cash '78
Shame of the Jungle '75 (V)

Brian Murray (1937-)

Nearing Grace '05
Treasure Planet '02 (V)
Bob Roberts '92

Chad Michael Murray (1981-)

Home of the Brave '06
House of Wax '05
A Cinderella Story '04
Freaky Friday '03

Charles Murray

The Boob '26
The Wizard of Oz '25

David Murray

Cowboys & Angels '04
Veronica Guerin '03

Don Murray (1929-)

Kickboxer the Champion '91
Ghosts Can't Do It '90
Made in Heaven '87
Mistress '87
Peggy Sue Got Married '86
Radioactive Dreams '86
Scorpion '86
Something in Common '86
Quarterback Princess '85
License to Kill '84
I Am the Cheese '83
Endless Love '81
Justin Morgan Had a Horse '81
Return of the Rebels '81
If Things Were Different '79
Rainbow '78
Deadly Hero '75
Confessions of Tom Harris '72
Conquest of the Planet of the Apes '72
Cotter '72
Sweet Love, Bitter '67
The Viking Queen '67
Baby, the Rain Must Fall '64
One Man's Way '63
Advise and Consent '62
The Hoodlum Priest '61
Shake Hands with the Devil '59
Bus Stop '56

Forbes Murray (1844-1982)

Leather Burners '43
The Spider's Web '38

Jaime Murray (1977-)

Botched '07
The Deaths of Ian Stone '07

James Murray (1901-36)

All the King's Men '99
Skull & Crown '35
Baby Face '33
High Gear '33
Frisco Jenny '32
The Crowd '28

Jan Murray (1916-2006)

Banjo Hackett '76
The Day of the Wolves '71
Which Way to the Front? '70
The Busy Body '67
Thunder Alley '67

Joel Murray (1963-)

The Cable Guy '96
Scrooged '88
One Crazy Summer '86

Ken Murray (1903-88)

Follow Me, Boys! '66
The Man Who Shot Liberty Valance '62
The Marshal's Daughter '53

Mae Murray (1889-1965)

Bachelor Apartment '31
A Mormon Maid '17

Stephen Murray (1912-83)

Elizabeth R '72
Four Sided Triangle '53
Alice in Wonderland '50
The Magnet '50
Pygmalion '38

Peter Murray-Hill (1908-57)

The Ghost Train '41
Mr. Reeder in Room 13 '38

Kate Murtagh (1920-)

Doctor Detroit '83
Switchblade Sisters '75

James Murtaugh

Two Weeks '06
Private Parts '96
The Rosary Murders '87
The River is Red '48

Lionel Murton (1915-2006)

Carry On Admiral '57
Meet the Navy '46

Tony Musante (1936-)

We Own the Night '07
The Yards '00
The Deep End of the Ocean '98
Collector's Item '89
The Pope of Greenwich Village '84
High Ice '80
Breaking Up Is Hard to Do '79
Fatal Chase '77
The Grissom Gang '71
The Bird with the Crystal Plumage '70
The Detective '68
The Incident '67

Clarence Muse (1889-1979)

The Black Stallion '79
A Dream for Christmas '73
Great Dan Patch '49
Watch on the Rhine '43
Gentleman from Dixie '41
The Invisible Ghost '41
Broken Strings '40
That Gang of Mine '40
Way Down South '39
Prison Train '38
The Spirit of Youth '37
The White Zombie '32

Musidora

Judex '16
Les Vampires '15

Victoria (Tory) Mussett (1978-)

The Condemned '07
Boogeyman '05

Louis Mustillo (1947-)

Dudley Do-Right '99
Just the Ticket '98

Marjorie Ann Mutchie (1939-)

Blondie Hits the Jackpot '49
Blondie Knows Best '46
Footlight Glamour '43
It's a Great Life '43

Ellen Muth (1981-)

SuperFire '02
A Gentleman's Game '01
Cora Unashamed '00
The Truth About Jane '00
The Young Girl and the Monsoon '99

Ornella Muti (1955-)

The Heart Is Deceitful Above All Things '04
People '04
Last Run '01
The Count of Monte Cristo '99
Esther '98
Somewhere in the City '97
Once Upon a Crime '92
Oscar '91
Wait until Spring, Bandini '90
Casanova '87
Swann in Love '84
Tales of Ordinary Madness '83
Flash Gordon '80
Life Is Beautiful '79
Leonor '75
Summer Affair '71

Roger Mutton

The Charge of the Light Brigade '68
The Girl on a Motorcycle '68

Jake Muxworthy (1978-)

The Art of Travel '08
Borderland '07
The Take '07
Born Killers '05

Mya (1979-)

Cover '08
Cursed '04
Dirty Dancing: Havana Nights '04
Shall We Dance? '04

Bruce Myers

The Mahabharata '89
The Unbearable Lightness of Being '88
The Awakening '80

Carmel Myers (1900-80)

Chinatown After Dark '31
Pleasure '31
Ben-Hur '26
Beau Brummel '24
All Night '18

Dwight "Heavy D" Myers (1967-)

Step Up '06
Dallas 362 '03
Big Trouble '02
The Cider House Rules '99

Harry C. (Henry) Myers (1886-1938)

Rainbow over Broadway '33
Convicted '32
The Savage Girl '32
City Lights '31
Getting Gertie's Garter '27
Exit Smiling '26
The Marriage Circle '24

Johann Myers

The Medallion '03
24-7 '97

Kim Myers (1966-)

Letters from a Killer '98
Hellraiser 4: Bloodline '95
White Palace '90
A Nightmare on Elm Street 2: Freddy's Revenge '85

Lou Myers (1945-)

All About You '01
Tin Cup '96
The Piano Lesson '94

Mike Myers (1963-)

Shrek Forever After '10 (V)
Inglourious Basterds '09
The Love Guru '08
Shrek the Third '07 (V)
Shrek 2 '04 (V)
Dr. Seuss' The Cat in the Hat '03
View from the Top '03
Austin Powers In Goldmember '02
Shrek '01 (V)
Austin Powers 2: The Spy Who Shagged Me '99
Mystery, Alaska '99
54 '98
Pete's Meteor '98
Austin Powers: International Man of Mystery '97
So I Married an Axe Murderer '93
Wayne's World 2 '93
Wayne's World '92

Susan Myers

Desperate Women '78
The Spell '77

Peter Mygind (1963-)

The Kingdom 2 '97
The Kingdom '95

Bruce Myles (1940-)

A Woman's Tale '92
Sweet Talker '91
A Cry in the Dark '88

Sophia Myles (1980-)

Outlander '08
Mister Foe '07
Art School Confidential '06
Dracula '06
The Hades Factor '06
Tristan & Isolde '06
Underworld: Evolution '05
Thunderbirds '04
Underworld '03
Oliver Twist '00

John (Jack) Mylong (1892-1975)

The Mermaids of Tiburon '62
Robot Monster '53
For Whom the Bell Tolls '43

Arden Myrin

Heart of the Beholder '05
Christmas With the Kranks '04

Jim Nabors (1932-)

Return to Mayberry '85
Cannonball Run 2 '84
Stroker Ace '83
The Best Little Whorehouse in Texas '82

Matheus Nachtergaele (1969-)

City of God '02
Mango Yellow '02

Nikolai Nademsky (1892-1937)

Earth '30
Zvenigora '28

George Nader (1921-2002)

Beyond Atlantis '73
The House of 1000 Dolls '67
The Human Duplicators '64
Away All Boats '56
Lady Godiva '55
Carnival Story '54
Sins of Jezebel '54
Robot Monster '53

Michael Nader (1945-)

The Finishing Touch '92
The Flash '90
Nick Knight '89
The Great Escape 2: The Untold Story '88
Lady Mobster '88
The Trip '67

Lycia Naff (1962-)

Chopper Chicks in Zombietown '91
Lethal Weapon '87

Kazu Nagahama

Ringu 2 '99
Ringu '98

Toshiya Nagasawa

Azumi 2 '05
The Great Yokai War '05
Shinobi '05

Masatoshi Nagase (1966-)

The Hidden Blade '04
The Sea is Watching '02
Electric Dragon 80,000V '01
Party 7 '00
Cold Fever '95
Autumn Moon '92
Mystery Train '89

Anne Nagel (1912-66)

The Spirit of West Point '47
Don Winslow of the Navy '43
Dawn Express '42
The Mad Monster '42
The Secret Code '42
Stagecoach Buckaroo '42
Man Made Monster '41
Argentine Nights '40
Black Friday '40
Winners of the West '40
The Green Hornet '39
Gang Bullets '38
Hoosier Schoolboy '37
Three Legionnaires '37

Conrad Nagel (1897-1970)

All That Heaven Allows '55
Woman in Brown '48
The Adventures of Rusty '45
Wedding Present '36
Yellow Cargo '36
Dangerous Corner '34
Ann Vickers '33
The Divorcee '30
Dubarry '30
The Kiss '29
The Michigan Kid '28
The Mysterious Lady '28

Alan Naggar

Cleo/Leo '89
New York's Finest '87

Parminder K. Nagra (1975-)

In Your Dreams '07
Ella Enchanted '04
Bend It Like Beckham '02

Philippe Nahon (1938-)

High Tension '03
Irreversible '02
Brotherhood of the Wolf '01
The Chateau '01
I Stand Alone '98

Ajay Naidu (1972-)

The Accidental Husband '08
Righteous Kill '08
Perception '06
The Honeymooners '05
The War Within '05
K-PAX '01
More Dogs Than Bones '00
You Are Here * '00
Chutney Popcorn '99
Office Space '98
Pi '98
subUrbia '96
Touch and Go '86
Where the River Runs Black '86

Jimmy Nail (1954-)

The 10th Kingdom '00
Still Crazy '98
Evita '96
Crusoe '89
Dream Demon '88
Howling 2: Your Sister Is a Werewolf '85
Morons from Outer Space '85

Joanne Nail (1947-)

The Visitor '80
Switchblade Sisters '75

J. Carrol Naish (1900-73)

Dracula vs. Frankenstein '71
Force of Impulse '60
This Could Be the Night '57
Hit the Deck '55
The Last Command '55
Rage at Dawn '55
Sitting Bull '54
Beneath the 12-Mile Reef '53
Fighter Attack '53
Clash by Night '52
Across the Wide Missouri '51
The Denver & Rio Grande '51
Annie Get Your Gun '50
The Black Hand '50
Rio Grande '50
The Toast of New Orleans '50
That Midnight Kiss '49
The Fugitive '48
The Kissing Bandit '48
The Beast with Five Fingers '46
Humoresque '46
Getting Gertie's Garter '45
The Southerner '45
Strange Confession '45
Dragon Seed '44
House of Frankenstein '44
Jungle Woman '44
The Monster Maker '44
Waterfront '44
Behind the Rising Sun '43
Calling Dr. Death '43
Sahara '43
The Corsican Brothers '42
Dr. Renault's Secret '42
Tales of Manhattan '42
Birth of the Blues '41
Blood and Sand '41
That Night in Rio '41
Down Argentine Way '40
Golden Gloves '40
Beau Geste '39
King of Alcatraz '38
Sea Racketeers '37
Thunder Trail '37
The Charge of the Light Brigade '36
Charlie Chan at the Circus '36
Special Investigator '36
Black Fury '35
Captain Blood '35
Confidential '35
The Lives of a Bengal Lancer '35
Under the Pampas Moon '35
Mystery Squadron '33
No Other Woman '33
The World Gone Mad '33
Kid from Spain '32
Tiger Shark '32
Two Seconds '32
The Royal Bed '31

Laurence Naismith (1908-92)

Amazing Mr. Blunden '72
Diamonds Are Forever '71
Quest for Love '71
The Bushbaby '70
The Valley of Gwangi '69
Jason and the Argonauts '63
The Prince and the Pauper '62

Greyfriars Bobby '61
Sink the Bismarck '60
The Trials of Oscar Wilde '60
Village of the Damned '60
The World of Suzie Wong '60
Third Man on the Mountain '59
A Night to Remember '58
Abandon Ship '57
Robbery under Arms '57
The Man Who Never Was '55
Carrington, V.C. '54
Love in Pawn '53
Room to Let '49
Train of Events '49

Takashi Naito (1955-)
After Life '98
Maborosi '95
Merry Christmas, Mr. Lawrence '83

Taketoshi Naito (1926-)
Samurai Fiction '99
After Life '98
The Human Condition: A Soldier's Prayer '61

Rick Najera
How the Garcia Girls Spent Their Summer '05
A Day Without a Mexican '04
Red Surf '90

Kathy Najimy (1957-)
WALL-E '08 (V)
Bam Bam & Celeste '05
Getting Played '05
Say Uncle '05
Rat Race '01
The Wedding Planner '01
If These Walls Could Talk 2 '00
Attention Shoppers '99
Bride of Chucky '98
Hope Floats '98
Zack & Reba '98
Cats Don't Dance '97 (V)
Nevada '97
Jeffrey '95
It's Pat: The Movie '94
Hocus Pocus '93
Sister Act 2: Back in the Habit '93
Sister Act '92
The Fisher King '91
Soapdish '91

Tatsuya Nakadai (1932-)
Wicked City '92
Ran '85
The Wolves '82
Hunter in the Dark '80
Kagemusha '80
Phoenix '78
Today We Kill, Tomorrow We Die '71
The Battle of the Japan Sea '70
Goyokin '69
Kojiro '67
Samurai Rebellion '67
Sword of Doom '67
Face of Another '66
Kwaidan '64
Harakiri '62
High & Low '62
Sanjuro '62
The Human Condition: A Soldier's Prayer '61
Yojimbo '61
When a Woman Ascends the Stairs '60
The Human Condition: Road to Eternity '59
Enjo '58
The Human Condition: No Greater Love '58

Anna Nakagawa
Cure '97
The Silk Road '92

Sanae Nakahara (1935-)
Shogun's Samurai—The Yagyu Clan Conspiracy '78
Lady Snowblood '73
Under the Flag of the Rising Sun '72

Kiichi Nakai (1961-)
Riding Alone for Thousands of Miles '05
Onmyoji 2 '03
Warriors of Heaven and Earth '03
When the Last Sword is Drawn '02

Haruo Nakajima (1929-)
War of the Gargantuas '70
Latitude Zero '69
Frankenstein Conquers the World '64
King Kong vs. Godzilla '63
Matango '63

Tomoko Nakajima
The Taste of Tea '04
Parasite Eve '97

Ganjiro Nakamura (1902-83)
An Actor's Revenge '63
Odd Obsession '60
Drifting Weeds '59
Enjo '58
The Lower Depths '57

Katsuo Nakamura (1938-)
Steamboy '05 (V)
Samurai Banners '69
Kwaidan '64

Kinnosuke Nakamura (1932-97)
Shogun's Samurai—The Yagyu Clan Conspiracy '78
Swords of Death '71
Goyokin '69
Samurai Banners '69

Satoshi Nakamura (1908-92)
That Man Bolt '73
The Manster '59

Shido Nakamura (1972-)
Red Cliff '08
Jet Li's Fearless '06
Letters from Iwo Jima '06
The Neighbor No. Thirteen '05
Ping Pong '02

Shiro Nakamura
Death Note 3: L, Change the World '08 (V)
Death Note 2: The Last Name '07 (V)
Death Note '06 (V)

Suzy Nakamura
Stark Raving Mad '02
Strawberry Fields '97

Tadao Nakamura (1933-)
What's Up, Tiger Lily? '66
The Secret of the Telegian '61

Tamao Nakamura (1939-)
Sleepy Eyes of Death: The Chinese Jade '63
The Human Condition: A Soldier's Prayer '61

Tetsu Nakamura
Latitude Zero '69
The Manster '59

Toru Nakamura (1965-)
Purple Butterfly '03
Tokyo Raiders '00
Gen-X Cops '99
Blue Tiger '94
New York Cop '94

Hideo Nakano
The Rug Cop '06
Nobody '99

Miki Nakatani
Train Man: Densha Otoko '05
When the Last Sword is Drawn '02
Ringu 2 '99
Ringu '98

Rodion Nakhapetov
Border Blues '03
A Slave of Love '78

Reggie Nalder (1911-91)
Dracula Sucks '79
Salem's Lot '79
Zoltan... Hound of Dracula '78
Mark of the Devil 2 '72
The Bird with the Crystal Plumage '70
Mark of the Devil '69
The Day and the Hour '63

Nita Naldi (1897-1961)
You Can't Fool Your Wife '40
Cobra '25
The Ten Commandments '23
Blood and Sand '22
The Man from Beyond '22
Dr. Jekyll and Mr. Hyde '20

Leonardo Nam (1979-)
He's Just Not That Into You '09
Vantage Point '08
The Fast and the Furious: Tokyo Drift '06
The Perfect Score '04

Joe Namath (1943-)
Chattanooga Choo Choo '84
Marriage Is Alive and Well '80
Avalanche Express '79
C.C. & Company '70

Shiro Namiki
Wild Zero '00
Ringu 2 '99

Jack Nance (1943-96)
Little Witches '96
Lost Highway '96
The Secret Agent Club '96
The Demolitionist '95
Voodoo '95
Across the Moon '94
Meatballs 4 '92
Motorama '91
The Hot Spot '90
Wild at Heart '90
Colors '88
Barfly '87
Blue Velvet '86
Dune '84
Ghoulies '84
Eraserhead '78
Breaker! Breaker! '77
Fury on Wheels '71

Chieko Naniwa (1908-73)
Snow Country '57
A Geisha '53

Erica Nann (1962-)
Mind Twister '93
Legion of Iron '90

Isabelle Nanty (1962-)
Amelie '01
Tatie Danielle '91

Igal Naor
House of Saddam '08
Rendition '07
Munich '05

Neriah Napaul (1972-)
The Bikini Car Wash Company 2 '92
The Bikini Car Wash Company '90

Alan Napier (1903-88)
The Bastard '78
Batman '66
The Loved One '65
Marnie '64
36 Hours '64
The Sword in the Stone '63 (V)
Premature Burial '62
Wild in the Country '61
Journey to the Center of the Earth '59
Until They Sail '57
The Mole People '56
Across the Wide Missouri '51
The Great Caruso '51
The Strange Door '51
Tarzan's Peril '51
Challenge to Lassie '49
Master Minds '49
Criss Cross '48
Tarzan's Magic Fountain '48
Adventure Island '47
Forever Amber '47
Lured '47
House of Horrors '46
A Scandal in Paris '46
Hangover Square '45
Isle of the Dead '45
Action in Arabia '44
The Hairy Ape '44
Mademoiselle Fifi '44
Ministry of Fear '44
Thirty Seconds Over Tokyo '44
The Uninvited '44
Cat People '42
The House of the Seven Gables '40
The Secret Four '40

Charles Napier (1936-)
The Goods: Live Hard, Sell Hard '09
Annapolis '06
The Manchurian Candidate '04
Extreme Honor '01
Nutty Professor 2: The Klumps '00
Austin Powers 2: The Spy Who Shagged Me '99
The Big Tease '99
Cypress Edge '99
Austin Powers: International Man of Mystery '97
Hunter's Moon '97
Steel '97
The Cable Guy '96
Riot '96
Ripper Man '96
Felony '95
Hard Justice '95
Jury Duty '95
Max Is Missing '95
3 Ninjas Knuckle Up '95
Tyson '95
Ballistic '94
Mortal Danger '94
Silk Degrees '94
Body Shot '93
Raw Justice '93
Skeeter '93
Center of the Web '92
Eyes of the Beholder '92
Indio 2: The Revolt '92
Return to Frogtown '92
Treacherous Crossing '92
The Silence of the Lambs '91
Soldier's Fortune '91
Dragonfight '90
Ernest Goes to Jail '90
Future Zone '90
The Grifters '90
Miami Blues '90
One Man Force '89
The Hit List '88
The Incredible Hulk Returns '88
Married to the Mob '88
Deep Space '87
Kidnapped '87
Night Stalker '87
Instant Justice '86
Something Wild '86
Rambo: First Blood, Part 2 '85
In Search of a Golden Sky '84
The Blues Brothers '80
Last Embrace '79
Citizens Band '77
Supervixens '75
Beyond the Valley of the Dolls '70

Jessica Napier (1979-)
The Alice '04
Cut '00
Love Serenade '96

Marshall Napier
Strange Planet '99
Starlight Hotel '90
The Navigator '88

Russell Napier (1910-75)
The Mark '61
Unholy Four '54

Toni Naples (1952-)
Dinosaur Island '93
Deathstalker 2: Duel of the Titans '87

Tony Nappo
Hank and Mike '08
Better Than Chocolate '99

Tony Nardi (1958-)
Bonanno: A Godfather's Story '99
La Deroute '98
Speaking Parts '89

Daniela Nardini (1968-)
Sirens '02
Reckless '97

Tom Nardini (1945-)
Self-Defense '83
Africa Texas Style '67

Kathrine Narducci (1965-)
Two Family House '99
A Bronx Tale '93

Darling Narita
Pups '99
Bang '95

Mikio Narita
Shogun's Samurai—The Yagyu Clan Conspiracy '78
Zatoichi: The Blind Swordsman and the Chess Expert '65

Nas (1973-)
Murda Muzik '03
Ticker '01
Belly '98

Arthur J. Nascarelli
The Groomsmen '06
Running Scared '06
Remedy '05
The Cooler '03
Wisegirls '02
Bringing Out the Dead '99
Cop Land '97

Paul Naschy (1934-)
The Craving '80
Human Beasts '80
Inquisition '76
Night of the Howling Beast '75
People Who Own the Dark '75
The Devil's Possessed '74
Exorcism '74
Curse of the Devil '73
House of Psychotic Women '73
The Mummy's Revenge '73
The Rue Morgue Massacres '73
Dracula's Great Love '72
The Hanging Woman '72
Horror Rises from the Tomb '72
Vengeance of the Zombies '72
Dr. Jekyll and the Wolfman '71
The Fury of the Wolfman '70
The Werewolf vs. the Vampire Woman '70
Dracula vs. Frankenstein '69

Chris Nash
Mischief '85
Silent Witness '85

Graham Nash (1942-)
Elvis Meets Nixon '98
Gimme Shelter '70

Marilyn Nash (1924-)
Unknown World '51
Monsieur Verdoux '47
The Rains Came '39

Mary Nash (1885-1976)
Cobra Woman '44
The Philadelphia Story '40
Easy Living '37
Heidi '37

Niecy Nash (1970-)
Not Easily Broken '09
Code Name: The Cleaner '07
Reno 911! Miami '07
Guess Who '05
Cookie's Fortune '99

Noreen Nash (1924-)
Phantom from Space '53
Storm over Wyoming '50
The Devil on Wheels '47
The Red Stallion '47
The Tender Years '47

Kais Nashef
American East '07
Paradise Now '05

Deborah Ann Nassar
Dance of the Damned '88
Stripped to Kill '87

Joseph Nasser
Voyage of Terror: The Achille Lauro Affair '90
The Taking of Flight 847: The Uli Derickson Story '88

Frank Nasso
Dot.Kill '05
Prince of Central Park '00

Marie-Jose Nat (1940-)
Les Violons du Bal '74
Embassy '72
Love and the Frenchwoman '60

Anthony Natale
His Bodyguard '98
Mr. Holland's Opus '95

Adam Nathan
I Was a Teenage TV Terrorist '87
Parting Glances '86

Stephen Nathan (1948-)
You Light Up My Life '77
The First Nudie Musical '75
1776 '72

Louis Natheaux
Captain Calamity '36
Go-Get-'Em-Haines '35
Dress Parade '27

Zoe Nathenson
One Night Stand '97
The Raggedy Rawney '90
Mona Lisa '86
Those Glory, Glory Days '83

Francesca "Kitten" Natividad (1948-)
Night at the Golden Eagle '02
Eddie Presley '92
Tomb '86
Doin' Time '85
The Wild Life '84
My Tutor '82
Beneath the Valley of the Ultra-Vixens '79

Yui Natsukawa
When the Last Sword is Drawn '02
Onmyoji '01

Gonin 2 '96

Mari Natsuki (1952-)

Ping Pong '02
Remembering the Cosmos Flower '99
Samurai Fiction '99
The Hunted '94

Yosuke Natsuki (1936-)

Dagora, the Space Monster '65
Ghidrah the Three Headed Monster '65
Attack Squadron '63
I Bombed Pearl Harbor '60

Masako Natsume (1958-85)

The Imperial Japanese Empire '85
MacArthur's Children '85
Antarctica '84

Isao Natsuyagi

The Wolves '82
Shogun's Samurai—The Yagyu Clan Conspiracy '78
Goyokin '69

Mildred Natwick (1905-94)

Dangerous Liaisons '88
Kiss Me Goodbye '82
Daisy Miller '74
A House Without a Christmas Tree '72
If It's Tuesday, This Must Be Belgium '69
Barefoot in the Park '67
Tammy and the Bachelor '57
Court Jester '56
The Trouble with Harry '55
Against All Flags '52
The Quiet Man '52
Cheaper by the Dozen '50
She Wore a Yellow Ribbon '49
The Kissing Bandit '48
Three Godfathers '48
The Enchanted Cottage '45
Yolanda and the Thief '45
The Long Voyage Home '40

Myron Natwick

Masters of Horror: The Washingtonians '07
DC 9/11: Time of Crisis '04
Shallow Ground '04
Project Vampire '93

David Naughton (1951-)

Brutal Massacre: A Comedy '07
Sky Blue '03 (V)
A Crack in the Floor '00
Mirror, Mirror 3: The Voyeur '96
Ice Cream Man '95
Beanstalk '94
Desert Steel '94
Amityville: A New Generation '93
Body Bags '93
Wild Cactus '92
Overexposed '90
The Sleeping Car '90
Steel and Lace '90
Private Affairs '89
Kidnapped '87
Boy in Blue '86
Separate Vacations '86
Getting Physical '84
Not for Publication '84
Hot Dog... The Movie! '83
Separate Ways '82
An American Werewolf in London '81
Midnight Madness '80

James Naughton (1945-)

Suburban Girl '07
The Devil Wears Prada '06
Factory Girl '06
Fascination '04
The Truth About Jane '00
Oxygen '99
First Kid '96
The First Wives Club '96
The Birds 2: Land's End '94
Blown Away '90
The Good Mother '88
The Glass Menagerie '87
Cat's Eye '85
A Stranger Is Watching '82
Second Wind '76
The Paper Chase '73

Naturi Naughton

The Lottery Ticket '10
Notorious '09

Demetrius Navarro

Purple Heart '05
The Wash '01
187 '97
Soldier Boyz '95

Nieves Navarro (1938-)

Blood at Sundown '88
Day of the Maniac '77
Trap Them & Kill Them '77
The Slasher '72

John P. Navin, Jr. (1968-)

Losin' It '82
Taps '81

Cliff Nazarro (1904-61)

'Neath Canadian Skies '46
Rhythm Parade '43
Hillbilly Blitzkrieg '42
Dive Bomber '41
In Old Colorado '41
Singing Buckaroo '37

Alla Nazimova (1879-1945)

The Bridge of San Luis Rey '44
Since You Went Away '44
Blood and Sand '41
Salome '22
Camille '21

Amedeo Nazzari (1907-79)

The Valachi Papers '72
Nefertiti, Queen of the Nile '64
Journey Beneath the Desert '61
The Naked Maja '59
Nights of Cabiria '57
Lure of the Sila '49

Anna Neagle (1904-86)

Teenage Bad Girl '59
The King's Rhapsody '55
Let's Make Up '55
Maytime in Mayfair '49
Elizabeth of Ladymead '48
The Courtney Affair '47
I Live in Grosvenor Square '46
Forever and a Day '43
Sunny '41
No, No Nanette '40
Nurse Edith Cavell '39
London Melody '37
Bitter Sweet '33

Billie Neal (1955-99)

Sweet Nothing '96
Consenting Adults '92
Mortal Thoughts '91
Down by Law '86

Diane Neal (1975-)

Dracula 3: Legacy '05
Dracula 2: Ascension '03

Dylan Neal (1969-)

Chupacabra Terror '05
40 Days and 40 Nights '02
Prom Night 3: The Last Kiss '89

Edwin Neal (1945-)

Neurotic Cabaret '90
Future Kill '85
The Texas Chainsaw Massacre '74

Elise Neal (1970-)

Hustle & Flow '05
Paid in Full '02
The Rising Place '02
Brian's Song '01
Mission to Mars '00
Restaurant '98
Def Jam's How to Be a Player '97
Money Talks '97
Scream 2 '97
Rosewood '96

Ella Neal

Doctor Satan's Robot '40
Mysterious Doctor Satan '40

Patricia Neal (1926-)

Flying By '09
Cookie's Fortune '99
Heidi '93
Caroline? '90
An Unremarkable Life '89
Love Leads the Way '84
Shattered Vows '84
Ghost Story '81
All Quiet on the Western Front '79
The Bastard '78
Love Affair: The Eleanor & Lou Gehrig Story '77
Widow's Nest '77
Eric '75
Things in Their Season '74
Run, Stranger, Run '73
Homecoming: A Christmas Story '71
The Subject Was Roses '68
In Harm's Way '65
Hud '63
Breakfast at Tiffany's '61
A Face in the Crowd '57
The Stranger from Venus '54
Diplomatic Courier '52
The Day the Earth Stood Still '51
Bright Leaf '50
Three Secrets '50
The Fountainhead '49
John Loves Mary '48

Peggy Neal (1947-)

X from Outer Space '67
Terror Beneath the Sea '66

Rome Neal

Pinero '01
Hamlet '00

Siri Neal (1972-)

Urban Ghost Story '98
The Children '90

Tom Neal (1914-72)

Danger Zone '51
Fingerprints Don't Lie '51
G.I. Jane '51
King of the Bullwhip '51
Stop That Cab '51
Apache Chief '50
I Shot Billy the Kid '50
Radar Secret Service '50
Red Desert '50
Train to Tombstone '50
Great Jesse James Raid '49
Hat Box Mystery '47
The Brute Man '46
Club Havana '46
Detour '46
My Dog Shep '46
First Yank into Tokyo '45
Behind the Rising Sun '43
Bowery at Midnight '42
Miracle Kid '42
Andy Hardy Meets Debutante '40
Courageous Dr. Christian '40

Kevin Nealon (1953-)

Aliens in the Attic '09
Grandma's Boy '06
Anger Management '03
Daddy Day Care '03
Good Boy! '03
Adam Sandler's 8 Crazy Nights '02 (V)
Bar Hopping '00
Little Nicky '00
The Principal Takes a Holiday '98
The Wedding Singer '97
Happy Gilmore '96
All I Want for Christmas '91
Roxanne '87

Christopher Neame (1947-)

Species 3 '04
The Apocalypse Watch '97
Project Shadowchaser 3000 '95
Hellbound '94
Street Knight '93
Boris and Natasha: The Movie '92
Still Not Quite Human '92
Edge of Honor '91
Suburban Commando '91
Bloodstone '88
D.O.A. '88
Transformations '88
Steel Dawn '87
Love Among Thieves '86
Dracula A.D. 1972 '72

Holly Near (1949-)

Dogfight '91
Minnie and Moskowitz '71

Jesus Nebot

No Turning Back '01
Dementia '98

Claire Nebout (1964-)

On Guard! '03
Venus Beauty Institute '98
Beaumarchais the Scoundrel '96
Ponette '95
Scene of the Crime '87

Vaclav Neckar (1943-)

Larks on a String '68
Closely Watched Trains '66

Raisa Nedashkovskaya (1943-)

Commissar '68
The Tsar's Bride '66

Tracey Needham (1967-)

Backlash '99
Buried Alive 2 '97
Last Stand at Saber River '96
Sensation '94

Nique Needles (1964-)

Beverly Hills Family Robinson '97
The Four Minute Mile '88
Dogs in Space '87

Ted Neeley (1943-)

Hard Country '81
Of Mice and Men '81
Shadow of Chikara '77
Jesus Christ, Superstar '73

Cam Neely (1965-)

Me, Myself, and Irene '00
Dumb & Dumber '94

Mark Neely

The Siege of Firebase Gloria '89
Off the Mark '87
The Bastard '78

Liam Neeson (1952-)

The A-Team '10
Clash of the Titans '10
The Wildest Dream: Conquest of Everest '10 (N)
Chloe '09
Five Minutes of Heaven '09
The Chronicles of Narnia: Prince Caspian '08 (V)
The Other Man '08
Ponyo '08 (V)
Taken '08
Seraphim Falls '06
Batman Begins '05
The Chronicles of Narnia: The Lion, the Witch and the Wardrobe '05 (V)
Kingdom of Heaven '05
Kinsey '04
Love Actually '03
Gangs of New York '02
K-19: The Widowmaker '02
Gun Shy '00
The Haunting '99
Star Wars: Episode 1—The Phantom Menace '99
Les Miserables '97
Michael Collins '96
Before and After '95
Rob Roy '95
Nell '94
Schindler's List '93
Deception '92
Ethan Frome '92
Husbands and Wives '92
Leap of Faith '92
Shining Through '92
Under Suspicion '92
The Big Man: Crossing the Line '91
Darkman '90
Next of Kin '89
The Dead Pool '88
The Good Mother '88
High Spirits '88
Satisfaction '88
Prayer for the Dying '87
Suspect '87
Duet for One '86
Hold the Dream '86
The Mission '86
Lamb '85
The Bounty '84
A Woman of Substance '84
Krull '83
Excalibur '81

Baelyn Neff

The Pacific and Eddy '07
I-See-You.Com '06

Hildegarde Neff

See Hildegarde Knef

Akemi Negisha

Lady Snowblood '73
Sex and Fury '73
Snake Woman's Curse '68

Toshie Negishi (1954-)

Azumi 2 '05
The Great Yokai War '05
Masters of Horror: Imprint '05
Okoge '93
Akira Kurosawa's Dreams '90

Natalia (Natalya) Negoda (1964-)

Back in the USSR '92
The Comrades of Summer '92
Little Vera '88

Francois Negret (1966-)

Night and Day '91
Au Revoir les Enfants '87

Pola Negri (1894-1987)

The Moon-Spinners '64
Hi Diddle Diddle '43
Hotel Imperial '27
A Woman of the World '25
One Arabian Night '21
Passion '19
Gypsy Blood '18

Mary Joan Negro

No Big Deal '83
The Family Man '79

Taylor Negron (1958-)

Entry Level '07
Three Days to Vegas '07
Call Me Claus '01
The Fluffer '01
Lloyd '00
Loser '00
A Kid in Aladdin's Palace '97
Bio-Dome '96
Mr. Stitch '95
Inevitable Grace '94
The Last Boy Scout '91
Nothing But Trouble '91
Punchline '88
The Whoopee Boys '86
Bad Medicine '85
Better Off Dead '85
Easy Money '83

Regine Nehy

Lakeview Terrace '08
Pride '07

David Neidorf

Rainbow Drive '90
Empire of the Sun '87
Undercover '87
Hoosiers '86
Platoon '86

Hildegard(e) Neil (1939-)

Antony and Cleopatra '73
A Touch of Class '73
The Man Who Haunted Himself '70

Richard Neil

Blondes Have More Guns '95
The Disappearance of Kevin Johnson '95

James Neill (1860-1931)

King of Kings '27
The Cheat '15

Noel Neill (1920-)

Superman Returns '06
Invasion U.S.A. '52
Atom Man vs. Superman '50
The Adventures of Frank and Jesse James '48
Here Come the Waves '45
The Stork Club '45

Sam Neill (1948-)

Daybreakers '09
Irresistible '06
Merlin's Apprentice '06
The Incredible Journey of Mary Bryant '05
Little Fish '05
Wimbledon '04
Yes '04
Doctor Zhivago '03
Perfect Strangers '03
Dirty Deeds '02
Jurassic Park 3 '01
The Dish '00
Sally Hemings: An American Scandal '00
Bicentennial Man '99
Molokai: The Story of Father Damien '99
Merlin '98
Sweet Revenge '98
Event Horizon '97
The Horse Whisperer '97
Snow White: A Tale of Terror '97
Forgotten Silver '96
In Cold Blood '96
Children of the Revolution '95
Country Life '95
In the Mouth of Madness '95
Victory '95
Rainbow Warrior '94
Restoration '94
Rudyard Kipling's The Jungle Book '94
Sirens '94
Family Pictures '93
Jurassic Park '93
The Piano '93
Question of Faith '93
Hostage '92
Memoirs of an Invisible Man '92
Fever '91
One Against the Wind '91
Until the End of the World '91
Death in Brunswick '90
The Hunt for Red October '90
Dead Calm '89
A Cry in the Dark '88
Reilly: Ace of Spies '87
For Love Alone '86
The Good Wife '86
Plenty '85
Attack Force Z '84
The Blood of Others '84
Enigma '82
Ivanhoe '82
The Final Conflict '81
From a Far Country: Pope John Paul II '81
Possession '81
My Brilliant Career '79
Sleeping Dogs '77

Don Nakaya Neilsen
Blood Ring '93
Fist of Steel '93

John Neilson (1944-2000)
Terror at Red Wolf Inn '72
Honky '71

George Neise (1916-96)
The Three Stooges Meet Hercules '61
Outcasts of the City '58

Stacey Nelkin (1959-)
Everything Relative '96
Halloween 3: Season of the Witch '82
Children of Divorce '80
Up the Academy '80
The Triangle Factory Fire Scandal '79

David Nell
See David Knell

Nathalie Nell (1950-)
Echoes '83
Rape of Love '79

Kate Nelligan (1951-)
Premonition '07
Walter and Henry '01
The Cider House Rules '99
U.S. Marshals '98
Calm at Sunset '96
Up Close and Personal '96
How to Make an American Quilt '95
Margaret's Museum '95
A Mother's Prayer '95
Wolf '94
Fatal Instinct '93
Terror Stalks the Class Reunion '93
Diamond Fleece '92
Shadows and Fog '92
Frankie and Johnny '91
The Prince of Tides '91
Love and Hate: A Marriage Made in Hell '90
Control '87
Eleni '85
Without a Trace '83
Crossover '82
Eye of the Needle '81
Therese Raquin '80
Dracula '79
Bethune '77
Romantic Englishwoman '75
The Count of Monte Cristo '74

Nelly (1978-)
The Longest Yard '05
Snipes '01

Adam Nelson
Mystic River '03
Phantoms '97
The Abyss '89

Ann Nelson (1916-92)
My Girl '91
Ghosts That Still Walk '77

Barry Nelson (1920-2007)
Island Claw '80
The Shining '80
Pete 'n' Tillie '72
Airport '70
Mary, Mary '63
Bataan '43
The Human Comedy '43
Johnny Eager '42
Shadow of the Thin Man '41

Bob Nelson (1956-)
Brain Donors '92
Miracles '86
Ryder P.I. '86
Sorceress '82

Bobby Nelson (1923-93)
Boothill Brigade '37
The Red Rope '37
Cowboy & the Bandit '35
Cyclone of the Saddle '35
Ghost Rider '35
Rough Riding Ranger '35
Way of the West '35
Cowboy Counselor '33
Two Fisted Justice '31
Roaring Ranch '30

Craig Richard Nelson (1947-)
My Bodyguard '80
The Grass Is Always Greener Over the Septic Tank '78
3 Women '77
The Paper Chase '73

Craig T. Nelson (1946-)
The Proposal '09
Blades of Glory '07
The Family Stone '05
The Incredibles '04 (V)
Dirty Pictures '00
The Skulls '00
The Devil's Advocate '97
Ghosts of Mississippi '96
If These Walls Could Talk '96
I'm Not Rappaport '96
Probable Cause '95
The Fire Next Time '93
Drug Wars: The Camarena Story '90
The Josephine Baker Story '90
Me and Him '89
Murderers Among Us: The Simon Wiesenthal Story '89
Troop Beverly Hills '89
Turner and Hooch '89
Action Jackson '88
Red Riding Hood '88
Rachel River '87
Poltergeist 2: The Other Side '86
Call to Glory '84
The Killing Fields '84
All the Right Moves '83
Man, Woman & Child '83
The Osterman Weekend '83
Silkwood '83
Diary of a Teenage Hitchhiker '82
Poltergeist '82
Murder in Texas '81
Private Benjamin '80
Rage '80
Stir Crazy '80
Where the Buffalo Roam '80
And Justice for All '79
Flesh Gordon '72 (V)
The Return of Count Yorga '71

Danny Nelson
A Good Baby '99
Blood Salvage '90

David Nelson (1936-)
Cry-Baby '90
High School USA '84
The Big Circus '59
The Day of the Outlaw '59
Peyton Place '57
Here Come the Nelsons '52

Ed Nelson (1928-)
Jackie Chan's Who Am I '98
Cries of Silence '97
The Bone Yard '90
Deadly Weapon '88
Brenda Starr '86
Baby Broker '81
Enola Gay: The Men, the Mission, the Atomic Bomb '80
Return of Frank Cannon '80
Anatomy of a Seduction '79
Acapulco Gold '78
For the Love of Benji '77
Midway '76
Airport '75 '75
Shining Star '75
Man From Galveston '63
Soldier in the Rain '63
A Bucket of Blood '59
T-Bird Gang '59
The Devil's Partner '58
Night of the Blood Beast '58
Carnival Rock '57
Invasion of the Saucer Men '57
Teenage Doll '57
Swamp Women '55

Gene Nelson (1920-96)
The Atomic Man '56
The Way Out '56
Oklahoma! '55
Crime Wave '54
Three Sailors and a Girl '53
Lullaby of Broadway '51
Painting the Clouds With Sunshine '51
Tea for Two '50
The West Point Story '50

Harriet Hilliard Nelson (1909-94)
The Kid with the 200 I.Q. '83
Here Come the Nelsons '52
Hi, Good Lookin'! '44
Take It Big '44
Honeymoon Lodge '43
Swingtime Johnny '43
Follow the Fleet '36

Herbert Nelson (1913-90)
Future Cop '76
When the North Wind Blows '74

Ian Nelson
True Confessions of a Hollywood Starlet '08
Bratz '07

Jerry Nelson (1934-)
The Muppet Christmas Carol '92 (V)
The Muppet Movie '79 (V)

John Allen Nelson (1959-)
Shelter '98
Deathstalker 3 '89
Killer Klowns from Outer Space '88
Saigon Commandos '88
Hunk '87

Judd Nelson (1959-)
The Boondock Saints II: All Saints Day '09
Infected '08
Netherbeast Incorporated '07
Nevermore '07
The Lost Angel '04
Cybermutt '02
Dark Asylum '01
Jay and Silent Bob Strike Back '01
Lost Voyage '01
Return to Cabin by the Lake '01
Cabin by the Lake '00
Light It Up '99
Mr. Rock 'n' Roll: The Alan Freed Story '99
Steel '97
Blackwater Trail '95
Circumstances Unknown '95
Airheads '94
Blindfold: Acts of Obsession '94
Flinch '94
Hail Caesar '94
Caroline at Midnight '93
Entangled '93
Every Breath '93
Conflict of Interest '92
Primary Motive '92
The Dark Backward '91
New Jack City '91
Hiroshima: Out of the Ashes '90
Far Out Man '89
Relentless '89
Billionaire Boys Club '87
Blue City '86
From the Hip '86
Transformers: The Movie '86 (V)
The Breakfast Club '85
Fandango '85
St. Elmo's Fire '85
Making the Grade '84

Lloyd Nelson (1927-2007)
The Wild World of Batwoman '66
Curse of the Stone Hand '64
The Incredible Petrified World '58
Man Beast '55

Lori Nelson (1933-)
The Pied Piper of Hamelin '57
Untamed Youth '57
Hot Rod Girl '56
Mohawk '56
Pardners '56
Day the World Ended '55
I Died a Thousand Times '55
Ma and Pa Kettle at Waikiki '55
Revenge of the Creature '55
Francis Goes to West Point '52
Ma and Pa Kettle at the Fair '52

Margaret Nelson
Scalp Merchant '77
Picnic at Hanging Rock '75

Novella Nelson (1939-)
Dear Wendy '05
Preaching to the Choir '05
Antwone Fisher '02
A Perfect Murder '98
Manny & Lo '96
Mercy '96

Ozzie Nelson (1906-75)
The Impossible Years '68
Here Come the Nelsons '52
People Are Funny '46
Take It Big '44
Big Street '42

Peter Nelson
Eye of the Eagle 3 '91
Sounds of Silence '91
The Expendables '89
Silk 2 '89
Crime Zone '88
V '83

Portia Nelson (1921-2001)
The Other '72
The Sound of Music '65

Ricky Nelson (1940-85)
Over the Hill Gang '69
Wackiest Ship in the Army '61
Rio Bravo '59
The Story of Three Loves '53
Here Come the Nelsons '52

Ruth Nelson (1905-92)
The Haunting Passion '83
A Christmas Without Snow '80
3 Women '77
Humoresque '46
Wilson '44

Sandra Nelson (1962-)
De-Lovely '04
Life as a House '01
The Halfback of Notre Dame '96
Maternal Instincts '96

Sean Nelson (1980-)
The Freebie '10
My Effortless Brilliance '08
The Corner '00
The Wood '99
A Stranger in the Kingdom '98
American Buffalo '95
Fresh '94

Steven Nelson
Men Cry Bullets '00
Little Ninjas '92

Tim Blake Nelson (1965-)
American Violet '09
Saint John of Las Vegas '09
The Incredible Hulk '08
The Astronaut Farmer '07
Come Early Morning '06
The Darwin Awards '06
Fido '06
Hoot '06
The Big White '05
The Moguls '05
Syriana '05
The Last Shot '04
Meet the Fockers '04
Scooby-Doo 2: Monsters Unleashed '04
Holes '03
2 Brothers & a Bride '03
Wonderland '03
Cherish '02
The Good Girl '02
Minority Report '02
O Brother Where Art Thou? '00
The Thin Red Line '98

Tracy Nelson (1963-)
A Grandpa for Christmas '07
Perfect Game '00
The Perfect Nanny '00
Perfect Tenant '99
The Night Caller '97
The Game of Love '87
Down and Out in Beverly Hills '86
Maria's Lovers '84
Yours, Mine & Ours '68

Willie Nelson (1933-)
Beer for My Horses '08
Surfer, Dude '08
Blonde Ambition '07
Fighting with Anger '07
The Dukes of Hazzard '05
The Big Bounce '04
Austin Powers 2: The Spy Who Shagged Me '99
Outlaw Justice '98
Gone Fishin' '97
Half-Baked '97
Starlight '97
Wag the Dog '97
Another Pair of Aces: Three of a Kind '91
Pair of Aces '90
Texas Guns '90
Dynamite and Gold '88
Baja Oklahoma '87
Red Headed Stranger '87
Amazons '86
Last Days of Frank & Jesse James '86
Stagecoach '86
Songwriter '84
Hell's Angels Forever '83
Barbarosa '82
Coming Out of the Ice '82
Thief '81
Honeysuckle Rose '80
The Electric Horseman '79

Corin "Corky" Nemec (1971-)
The Boston Strangler: The Untold Story '08
Bundy: A Legacy of Evil '08
National Lampoon Presents RoboDoc '08
Sea Beast '08
Mosquitoman '05
Brother's Keeper '02
Killer Bud '00
The First to Go '97
The War at Home '96
Operation Dumbo Drop '95
Drop Zone '94
Stephen King's The Stand '94
White Wolves 2: Legend of the Wild '94
Solar Crisis '92
Tucker: The Man and His Dream '88

Neil Nephew
Panic in the Year Zero! '62
The Young Savages '61

Francesca Neri (1964-)
Collateral Damage '02
Hannibal '01
Live Flesh '97
Flight of the Innocent '93
Outrage '93

Rosalba Neri (1940-)
The Arena '73
Devil's Wedding Night '73
Lady Frankenstein '72
Amuck! '71
Slaughter Hotel '71
The Seducers '70
The Castle of Fu Manchu '68
Murder for Sale '68
The Lion of Thebes '64
Conquest of Mycene '63

David Nerman
Nightwaves '03
The Witness Files '00
The Minion '98
Sir Arthur Conan Doyle's The Lost World '98
Witchboard 3: The Possession '95
The Scorpio Factor '90

Franco Nero (1942-)
Letters to Juliet '10
David '97
The Painted Lady '97
Talk of Angels '96
The Innocent Sleep '95
Young Catherine '91
Die Hard 2: Die Harder '90
Magdalene '88
Windmills of the Gods '88
Django Strikes Again '87
Sweet Country '87
Challenge to White Fang '86
The Girl '86
Wagner: The Complete Epic '85
Wagner: The Movie '85
Day of the Cobra '84
Querelle '83
The Salamander '82
Enter the Ninja '81
The Man with Bogart's Face '80
Shark Hunter '79
Force 10 from Navarone '78
Last Four Days '77
Submission '77
21 Hours at Munich '76
Legend of Valentino '75
Sardinia Kidnapped '75
Spaghetti Western '75
Blood Brothers '74
Street Law '74
High Crime '73
Redneck '73
Confessions of a Police Captain '72
Fifth Day of Peace '72
Devil's Crude '71
Companeros '70
Tristana '70
The Virgin and the Gypsy '70
Battle of Neretva '69
Ring of Death '69
Django '68
Camelot '67
The Bible '66
Texas, Adios '66
Wild, Wild Planet '65

Toni Nero
No Dead Heroes '87
Silent Night, Deadly Night '84

Caroline Neron (1973-)
Eternal '04
Strip Search '97

Cathleen Nesbitt (1888-1982)
Family Plot '76
Promise Her Anything '66
The Trygon Factor '66
The Parent Trap '61
Separate Tables '58
An Affair to Remember '57
Black Widow '54
Desiree '54
Man of Evil '48
Men of Two Worlds '46
Nicholas Nickleby '46
Pygmalion '38
The Passing of the Third Floor Back '36

Derren Nesbitt (1932-)
Funny Money '82
Horrors of Burke & Hare '71
Where Eagles Dare '68
The Blue Max '66
Victim '61

James Nesbitt (1966-)
Five Minutes of Heaven '09
Jekyll '07
Match Point '05
Millions '05
Bloody Sunday '01
Lucky Break '01
Waking Ned Devine '98
Resurrection Man '97
Welcome to Sarajevo '97
Go Now '96

Michael Nesmith (1942-)
Tapeheads '89
Head '68

Ottola Nesmith
Witness for the Prosecution '57
Return of the Vampire '43

Loni Nest (1915-)
Joyless Street '25
The Golem '20

Lois Nettleton (1927-2008)
The Christmas Card '06
The Feminine Touch '95
Mirror, Mirror 2: Raven Dance '94
Manhunt for Claude Dallas '86
Brass '85
Soggy Bottom U.S.A. '84
The Best Little Whorehouse in Texas '82
Butterfly '82
Deadly Blessing '81
Centennial '78
The Man in the Glass Booth '75
Bull of the West '71
The Good Guys and the Bad Guys '69
The Bamboo Saucer '68
Mail Order Bride '63
Period of Adjustment '62

Alex Neuberger (1992-)
Underdog '07
Running Scared '06

Martin Neufeld
Relative Fear '95
H '90

Dorothy Neumann (1912-94)
Private Parts '72
The Terror '63
The Ghost of Dragstrip Hollow '59
The Undead '57

Jenny Neumann
Delos Adventure '86
Stage Fright '83
Hell Night '81
Mistress of the Apes '79
Swim Team '79

Bebe Neuwirth (1958-)
Fame '09
Game 6 '05
The Big Bounce '04
How to Lose a Guy in 10 Days '03
Le Divorce '03
Tadpole '02
Cupid & Cate '00
Dash and Lilly '99
Liberty Heights '99
Summer of Sam '99
Celebrity '98
The Faculty '98
The Adventures of Pinocchio '96
The Associate '96
All Dogs Go to Heaven 2 '95 (V)
Jumanji '95
Malice '93
The Paint Job '93
Wild Palms '93
Bugsy '91
Green Card '90
Say Anything '89

Chantal Neuwirth
Gabrielle '05
A Very Long Engagement '04
Rendez-Moi Ma Peau '81

Suzanne Neve
Portrait of a Lady '67
Naked Evil '66

Aaron Neville (1941-)
The Last Ride '94
Posse '93
Zandalee '91

John Neville (1925-)
Hollywood North '03
Moving Malcolm '03
The Statement '03
Spider '02
The Duke '99
Goodbye, Lover '99
Sunshine '99
My Teacher Ate My Homework '98
Urban Legend '98
The X-Files '98
Behind the Lines '97
The Fifth Element '97
Sabotage '96
Swann '96
Dangerous Minds '95
Song Spinner '95
Baby's Day Out '94
Little Women '94
The Road to Wellville '94
The Adventures of Baron Munchausen '89
A Study in Terror '66
The Unearthly Stranger '64
Billy Budd '62

Brooke Nevin (1982-)
Infestation '09
Sherman's Way '08
The Comebacks '07
Too Cool for Christmas '04
Running Wild '99

Robyn Nevin (1942-)
The Matrix Reloaded '03
The Matrix Revolutions '03
Angel Baby '95
Resistance '92
Careful, He Might Hear You '84
The Chant of Jimmie Blacksmith '78
The Irishman '78
Fourth Wish '75

Claudette Nevins
Star Trek: Insurrection '98
Sweet Evil '95
Widow's Kiss '94
Child of Darkness, Child of Light '91
Sleeping with the Enemy '91
Tuff Turf '85
Don't Go to Sleep '82
Take Your Best Shot '82
...All the Marbles '81
Jacqueline Bouvier Kennedy '81
The Possessed '77
The Mask '61

Anzhelika Nevolina (1962-)
Of Freaks and Men '98
Creation of Adam '93

Derek Newark (1933-98)
Bellman and True '88
The Offence '73
The Blue Max '66

George Newbern (1964-)
Saw 6 '09
A Dennis the Menace Christmas '07
Crazy Eights '06
If These Walls Could Talk 2 '00
Friends & Lovers '99
The Simple Life of Noah Dearborn '99
The Evening Star '96
Far Harbor '96
Father of the Bride Part 2 '95
Witness to the Execution '94
Father of the Bride '91
Doppelganger: The Evil Within '90
It Takes Two '88
Paramedics '88
Switching Channels '88
Adventures in Babysitting '87
My Little Girl '87

William "Billy" Newell (1894-1967)
Escape from Fort Bravo '53
Doctor Satan's Robot '40
The Invisible Killer '40
Mysterious Doctor Satan '40
Slander House '38
The Mandarin Mystery '37
Bulldog Edition '36

Bob Newhart (1929-)
The Librarian: Curse of the Judas Chalice '08
The Librarian: Return to King Solomon's Mines '06
The Librarian: Quest for the Spear '04
Elf '03
Legally Blonde 2: Red White & Blonde '03
In and Out '97
The Rescuers Down Under '90 (V)
First Family '80
Little Miss Marker '80
Marathon '80
The Rescuers '77 (V)
Thursday's Game '74
Cold Turkey '71
Catch-22 '70
On a Clear Day You Can See Forever '70
Hot Millions '68
Hell Is for Heroes '62

James Newill (1911-75)
Boss of Rawhide '44
Guns of the Law '44
Outlaw Roundup '44
Fighting Valley '43
The Return of the Rangers '43
Rangers Take Over '42
The Great American Broadcast '41
Danger Ahead '40
Murder on the Yukon '40
Sky Bandits '40
Yukon Flight '40
Fighting Mad '39
Renfrew on the Great White Trail '38
Renfrew of the Royal Mounted '37

Anthony Newlands (1926-95)
Scream and Scream Again '70
Circus of Fear '67

Anthony Newley (1931-99)
Boris and Natasha: The Movie '92
The Garbage Pail Kids Movie '87
Outrage! '86
Stagecoach '86
Alice in Wonderland '85
Blade in Hong Kong '85
It Seemed Like a Good Idea at the Time '75
The Old Curiosity Shop '75
Sweet November '68
Doctor Dolittle '67
Let's Get Married '60
Fire Down Below '57
Above Us the Waves '56
X The Unknown '56
Those People Next Door '52
Oliver Twist '48
Little Ballerina '47

Alec Newman (1974-)
Moonlight Serenade '09
The Gene Generation '07
Children of Dune '03
Dr. Bell and Mr. Doyle: The Dark Beginnings of Sherlock Holmes '00
Dune '00
Catherine Cookson's The Rag Nymph '96

Barry Newman (1938-)
Grilled '06
What the #$*! Do We Know? '04
40 Days and 40 Nights '02
Good Advice '01
True Blue '01
Bowfinger '99
Goodbye, Lover '99
The Limey '99
Brown's Requiem '98
Daylight '96
Fatal Vision '84
Having It All '82
Amy '81
Deadline '81
City on Fire '78
The Salzburg Connection '72
Vanishing Point '71

Daniel Newman (1976-)
Road Trip: Beer Pong '09
Endgame '01
The Return of the Borrowers '96
Shopping '93

Laraine Newman (1952-)
Dr. Seuss' Horton Hears a Who! '08 (V)
Barnyard '06 (V)
The Modern Adventures of Tom Sawyer '99
Jingle All the Way '96
Alone in the Woods '95
The Flintstones '94
Coneheads '93
Revenge of the Red Baron '93
Witchboard 2: The Devil's Doorway '93
Problem Child 2 '91
Invaders from Mars '86
Perfect '85
Her Life as a Man '83
Wholly Moses! '80
Mr. Mike's Mondo Video '79
Tunnelvision '76

Nanette Newman (1934-)
The Mystery of Edwin Drood '93
The Stepford Wives '75
Long Ago Tomorrow '71
Captain Nemo and the Underwater City '69
The Madwoman of Chaillot '69
Oh! What a Lovely War '69
The Wrong Arm of the Law '63

Paul Newman (1925-2008)
Cars '06 (V)
Empire Falls '05
Our Town '03
Road to Perdition '02
Where the Money Is '00
Message in a Bottle '98
Twilight '98
Nobody's Fool '94
The Hudsucker Proxy '93
Mr. & Mrs. Bridge '90
Blaze '89
Fat Man and Little Boy '89
The Color of Money '86
Harry & Son '84
The Verdict '82
Absence of Malice '81
Fort Apache, the Bronx '81
When Time Ran Out '80
Quintet '79
Slap Shot '77
Buffalo Bill & the Indians '76
Silent Movie '76
The Drowning Pool '75
The Towering Inferno '74
Mackintosh Man '73
The Sting '73
Life & Times of Judge Roy Bean '72
Pocket Money '72
Sometimes a Great Notion '71
Butch Cassidy and the Sundance Kid '69
Winning '69
The Secret War of Harry Frigg '68
Cool Hand Luke '67
Hombre '67
Harper '66
Torn Curtain '66
Lady L '65
The Outrage '64
Hud '63
A New Kind of Love '63
The Prize '63
Sweet Bird of Youth '62
The Hustler '61
Paris Blues '61
Exodus '60
From the Terrace '60
The Young Philadelphians '59
Cat on a Hot Tin Roof '58
The Left-Handed Gun '58
The Long, Hot Summer '58
Rally 'Round the Flag, Boys! '58
The Helen Morgan Story '57
Until They Sail '57
Bang the Drum Slowly '56
Somebody Up There Likes Me '56
The Silver Chalice '54

Phyllis Newman (1933-)
The Human Stain '03
It Had to Be You '00
The Beautician and the Beast '97
A Price above Rubies '97
A Secret Space '88
Follies in Concert '85
Bye Bye Braverman '67
Picnic '55

Ryan Newman (1998-)
Lower Learning '08
Zoom '06

Stephen D. Newman (1943-)
Yuri Nosenko, KGB '86
Sophie's Choice '82

Julie Newmar (1935-)
Backlash: Oblivion 2 '95
To Wong Foo, Thanks for Everything, Julie Newmar '95
Oblivion '94
Nudity Required '90
Body Beat '88
Deep Space '87
Evils of the Night '85
Streetwalkin' '85
Ecstasy '84
Hysterical '83
Terraces '77
MacKenna's Gold '69
For Love or Money '63
Li'l Abner '59
Seven Brides for Seven Brothers '54

Lisa Marie Newmyer
A Scanner Darkly '06
Sin City '05
The House on Todville Road '95
The Texas Chainsaw Massacre 4: The Next Generation '95

John Haymes Newton (1965-)
Operation Sandman: Warriors in Hell '00
Alive '93
Desert Kickboxer '92

Margit Evelyn Newton
Hell of the Living Dead '83
The Last Hunter '80

Mary Newton
Zero Hour! '57
Tomorrow the World '44

Matt Newton (1977-)
Poster Boy '04
Dahmer '02

Robert Newton (1905-56)
Around the World in 80 Days '56
The High and the Mighty '54
Long John Silver '54
The Desert Rats '53
Androcles and the Lion '52
Blackbeard the Pirate '52
Tom Brown's School Days '51
Treasure Island '50
The Hidden Room '49
Obsession '49
Oliver Twist '48
Odd Man Out '47
This Happy Breed '47
Henry V '44
Gaslight '40
Jamaica Inn '39
Beachcomber '38
The Green Cockatoo '37
21 Days '37

Thandie Newton (1972-)
2012 '09
RocknRolla '08
W. '08
Norbit '07
Run, Fatboy, Run '07
The Pursuit of Happyness '06
Crash '05
The Chronicles of Riddick '04
Shade '03
The Truth About Charlie '02
Mission: Impossible 2 '00
Beloved '98
Besieged '98
Gridlock'd '96
The Leading Man '96
The Journey of August King '95
Jefferson in Paris '94
Loaded '94
The Young Americans '93
Flirting '89

Theodore Newton (1942-)
Ace of Aces '33
The Sphinx '33

Wayne Newton (1942-)
Ocean's Eleven '01
Elvis Meets Nixon '98
Vegas Vacation '96
Best of the Best 2 '93
The Dark Backward '91
The Adventures of Ford Fairlane '90
License to Kill '89

Olivia Newton-John (1948-)
Sordid Lives '00
It's My Party '95
Two of a Kind '83
Xanadu '80
Grease '78

Richard Ney (1916-2004)
Premature Burial '62
The Lovable Cheat '49
Mrs. Miniver '42

Anne Neyland
Jailhouse Rock '57
Motorcycle Gang '57

Marina Neyolova (1947-)
Autumn Marathon '79
The Errors of Youth '78

Hot Fuzz *'07*
Pirates of the Caribbean: At World's End *'07*
Alex Rider: Operation Stormbreaker *'06*
Flushed Away *'06 (V)*
Notes on a Scandal *'06*
Pirates of the Caribbean: Dead Man's Chest *'06*
The Constant Gardener *'05*
Doogal *'05 (V)*
Gideon's Daughter *'05*
The Girl in the Cafe *'05*
The Hitchhiker's Guide to the Galaxy *'05*
Underworld: Evolution *'05*
Shaun of the Dead *'04*
Love Actually *'03*
State of Play *'03*
Underworld *'03*
AKA *'02*
I Capture the Castle *'02*
Lawless Heart *'01*
Lucky Break *'01*
Blow Dry *'00*
Longitude *'00*
Still Crazy *'98*
FairyTale: A True Story *'97*
Alive and Kicking *'96*
Being Human *'94*
Antonia and Jane *'91*
The Phantom of the Opera *'89*
Agatha Christie's Thirteen at Dinner *'85*

Miho Nikaido (1966-)
Flirt *'95*
Tokyo Decadence *'91*

Esko Nikkari (1938-2006)
The Match Factory Girl *'90*
The Winter War *'89*

Jan Niklas (1947-)
Plain Truth *'04*
The House of the Spirits *'93*
Club Extinction *'89*
The Rose Garden *'89*
Anastasia: The Mystery of Anna *'86*
Colonel Redl *'84*

Valery (Valeri Nikolayev) Nikolaev (1963-)
The Terminal *'04*
Aberration *'97*
The Saint *'97*
U-Turn *'97*

Tony Nikolakopoulos
Criminal Ways *'03*
Head On *'98*

Anna Q. Nilsson (1888-1974)
Fighting Father Dunne *'48*
Riders of the Timberline *'41*
The Toll Gate *'20*
Seven Keys to Baldpate *'17*
Regeneration *'15*

Inger Nilsson (1959-)
Pippi in the South Seas *'70*
Pippi on the Run *'70*
Pippi Goes on Board *'69*
Pippi Longstocking *'69*

Maj-Britt Nilsson (1924-2006)
Secrets of Women *'52*
Summer Interlude *'50*
To Joy *'50*

Rob Nilsson (1940-)
Rainbow Drive *'90*
Heat and Sunlight *'87*
Northern Lights *'79*

Derek Nimmo (1930-99)
One of Our Dinosaurs Is Missing *'75*
Coast of Skeletons *'63*

Leonard Nimoy (1931-)
Star Trek *'09*
Atlantis: The Lost Empire *'01 (V)*
David *'97*
The Pagemaster *'94 (V)*
Never Forget *'91*
Star Trek 6: The Undiscovered Country *'91*
Star Trek 5: The Final Frontier *'89*
Star Trek 4: The Voyage Home *'86*
Transformers: The Movie *'86 (V)*
Aladdin and His Wonderful Lamp *'84*
Star Trek 3: The Search for Spock *'84*
Star Trek 2: The Wrath of Khan *'82*
A Woman Called Golda *'82*
Seizure: The Story of Kathy Morris *'80*
Star Trek: The Motion Picture *'79*
Invasion of the Body Snatchers *'78*
Baffled *'72*
Catlow *'71*
The Balcony *'63*
The Brain Eaters *'58*
Them! *'54*
Kid Monk Baroni *'52*
Zombies of the Stratosphere *'52*
Rhubarb *'51*

Chaicham Nimpulsawasdi
The Iron Ladies 2 *'03*
The Iron Ladies *'00*

Najwa Nimri (1972-)
The Method *'05*
Sex and Lucia *'01*
Before Night Falls *'00*
Lovers of the Arctic Circle *'98*
Open Your Eyes *'97*

Annibale Ninchi (1887-1967)
Time Out for Love *'61*
La Dolce Vita *'60*

Yvette Nipar (1964-)
Black Horizon *'01*
Kept *'01*
Submerged *'00*
Twilight Man *'96*
Doctor Mordrid: Master of the Unknown *'90*
Ski Patrol *'89*
Run If You Can *'87*

Joe Nipote
Soul's Midnight *'06*
Casper *'95 (V)*

Naomi Nishida
The Happiness of the Katakuris *'01*
Godzilla 2000 *'99*

Toshiyuki Nishida
The Ramen Girl *'08*
The Silk Road *'92*

Hidetoshi Nishijima
Black House *'07*
Dolls *'02*

Ko Nishimura
Lady Snowblood *'73*
Legends of the Poisonous Seductress 2: Quick Draw Okatsu *'69*
Snake Woman's Curse *'68*
Yojimbo *'61*

John Nishio
Overkill *'86*
Dim Sum: A Little Bit of Heart *'85*

Greta Nissen (1906-88)
Melody Cruise *'32*
Ambassador Bill *'31*
Women of All Nations *'31*
The King on Main Street *'25*

Ronald Nitschke (1950-)
Sons of Trinity *'95*
The Innocent *'93*

Barbara Niven (1953-)
Redline *'07*
Serial Killing 101 *'04*
Alone with a Stranger *'99*
Depraved *'98*
I Married a Monster *'98*
Taken Alive *'95*
Psycho Cop *'88*

David Niven (1909-83)
Better Late Than Never *'83*
Curse of the Pink Panther *'83*
Trail of the Pink Panther *'82*
Sea Wolves *'81*
Rough Cut *'80*
The Big Scam *'79*
Escape to Athena *'79*
Candleshoe *'78*
Death on the Nile *'78*
Murder by Death *'76*
No Deposit, No Return *'76*
Paper Tiger *'74*
King, Queen, Knave *'72*
The Statue *'71*
The Brain *'69*
The Impossible Years *'68*
Casino Royale *'67*
Lady L *'65*
The Pink Panther *'64*
Bedtime Story *'63*
55 Days at Peking *'63*
The Guns of Navarone *'61*
Please Don't Eat the Daisies *'60*
Ask Any Girl *'59*
Separate Tables *'58*
Bonjour Tristesse *'57*
My Man Godfrey *'57*
Around the World in 80 Days *'56*
Birds & the Bees *'56*
The King's Thief *'55*
Carrington, V.C. *'54*
The Moon Is Blue *'53*
Happy Go Lovely *'51*
The Lady Says No *'51*
The Elusive Pimpernel *'50*
The Toast of New Orleans *'50*
Bonnie Prince Charlie *'48*
The Bishop's Wife *'47*
Magnificent Doll *'46*
The Perfect Marriage *'46*
Stairway to Heaven *'46*
Immortal Battalion *'44*
Spitfire *'42*
Bachelor Mother *'39*
Eternally Yours *'39*
The Real Glory *'39*
Wuthering Heights *'39*
Bluebeard's Eighth Wife *'38*
Dawn Patrol *'38*
Four Men and a Prayer *'38*
Dinner at the Ritz *'37*
Prisoner of Zenda *'37*
Beloved Enemy *'36*
The Charge of the Light Brigade *'36*
Dodsworth *'36*
Rose Marie *'36*
Barbary Coast *'35*
Splendor *'35*

Kip Niven (1945-)
Blind Ambition *'79*
New Year's Evil *'78*
Midway *'76*
Magnum Force *'73*

Alessandro Nivola (1972-)
Coco Before Chanel *'09*
The Eye *'08*
$5 a Day *'08*
The Company *'07*
Goal 2: Living the Dream *'07*
Grace Is Gone *'07*
The Darwin Awards *'06*
Goal! The Dream Begins *'06*
Junebug *'05*
The Sisters *'05*
The Clearing *'04*
Carolina *'03*
Laurel Canyon *'02*
Jurassic Park 3 *'01*
Love's Labour's Lost *'00*
Time Code *'00*
Best Laid Plans *'99*
Mansfield Park *'99*
I Want You *'98*
Reach the Rock *'98*
Face/Off *'97*

Tommy Nix
Sin City *'05*
Roadracers *'94*

Allan Nixon (1920-95)
Mesa of Lost Women *'52*
Prehistoric Women *'50*

Cynthia Nixon (1966-)
Sex and the City 2 *'10*
An Englishman in New York *'09*
Lymelife *'08*
Sex and the City: The Movie *'08*
The Babysitters *'07*
Little Manhattan *'05*
One Last Thing *'05*
Tanner on Tanner *'04*
Igby Goes Down *'02*
Papa's Angels *'00*
Marvin's Room *'96*
Let It Ride *'89*
Tanner '88 *'88*
The Manhattan Project *'86*
Amadeus *'84*
I Am the Cheese *'83*

Kimberly Nixon
Angus, Thongs and Perfect Snogging *'08*
Cranford *'08*
Easy Virtue *'08*
Wild Child *'08*

Marion (Marian) Nixon (1904-83)
Captain Calamity *'36*
The Reckless Way *'36*
Tango *'36*
Doctor Bull *'33*
Pilgrimage *'33*
After Tomorrow *'32*
Too Busy to Work *'32*
Say It With Songs *'29*
Hands Up *'26*
Spangles *'26*

Marni Nixon (1930-)
Mulan *'98 (V)*
I Think I Do *'97*
The Sound of Music *'65*
Daughter of Horror *'55 (V)*

Mojo Nixon (1956-)
Super Mario Bros. *'93*
Rock 'n' Roll High School Forever *'91*

Stephanie Niznik (1967-)
Spiders 2: Breeding Ground *'01*
Epoch *'00*
Inferno *'98*
Memorial Day *'98*

Chelsea Noble (1964-)
Left Behind: The Movie *'00*
Instant Karma *'90*

Christian Noble (1961-)
Human Desires *'97*
Illegal Affairs *'96*

James Noble (1922-)
Chances Are *'89*
When the Bough Breaks *'86*
Dempsey *'83*
The Woman Who Willed a Miracle *'83*
One Summer Love *'76*
Roboman *'75*

John Noble (1948-)
Running Scared *'06*
Lord of the Rings: The Return of the King *'03*
The Monkey's Mask *'00*

Nancy Lee Noble
Just for the Hell of It *'68*
She-Devils on Wheels *'68*
The Girl, the Body and the Pill *'67*

Ray Noble (1907-78)
Here We Go Again! *'42*
A Damsel in Distress *'37*

Trisha Noble (1943-)
Deadline *'81*
The Private Eyes *'80*

Bernard Noel (1926-70)
A Married Woman *'65*
The Fire Within *'64*
Une Femme Mariee *'64*

Chris Noel (1941-)
The Tormentors *'71*
The Glory Stompers *'67*

Magali Noel (1932-)
The Eighties *'83*
Les Rendez-vous D'Anna *'78*
Amarcord *'74*
Season for Assassins *'71*
La Dolce Vita *'60*
Elena and Her Men *'56*

Noelia Noel (1933-)
Night of the Bloody Apes *'68*
Sputnik *'61*

Ulrich Noethen (1959-)
My Fuhrer *'07*
Downfall *'04*
The Harmonists *'99*

Yumiko Nogawa
The Sea is Watching *'02*
Zatoichi: The Blind Swordsman and the Fugitives *'68*
Story of a Prostitute *'65*
Gate of Flesh *'64*

Natalija Nogulich (1950-)
Confessions of Sorority Girls *'94*
Hoffa *'92*
Homicide *'91*
The Guardian *'90*
Sister, Sister *'87*

Philippe Noiret (1930-2006)
On Guard! *'03*
Grosse Fatigue *'94*
The Postman *'94*
Revenge of the Musketeers *'94*
I Don't Kiss *'91*
The Palermo Connection *'91*
Uranus *'91*
Life and Nothing But *'89*
The Return of the Musketeers *'89*
Cinema Paradiso *'88*
The Family *'87*
Aurora *'84*
Fort Saganne *'84*
My New Partner *'84*
Next Summer *'84*
Birgitt Haas Must Be Killed *'83*
Coup de Torchon *'81*
Jupiter's Thigh *'81*
Three Brothers *'80*
Who Is Killing the Great Chefs of Europe? *'78*
Dear Detective *'77*
The Purple Taxi *'77*
A Woman at Her Window *'77*
The Desert of the Tartars *'76*
Old Gun *'76*
The Judge and the Assassin *'75*
Le Secret *'74*
The Clockmaker *'73*
La Grande Bouffe *'73*
Night Flight from Moscow *'73*
The Holes *'72*
Murphy's War *'71*
The Assassination Bureau *'69*
Justine *'69*
Topaz *'69*
Night of the Generals *'67*
Woman Times Seven *'67*
Lady L *'65*
Zazie dans le Metro *'61*

Bob Nolan (1908-80)
Melody Time *'48 (V)*
Lights of Old Santa Fe *'47*
Song of Arizona *'46*
King of the Cowboys *'43*
Heart of the Golden West *'42*
Sunset on the Desert *'42*

Doris Nolan (1916-98)
Follies Girl *'43*
Holiday *'38*

Jeannette Nolan (1911-98)
The Horse Whisperer *'97*
Street Justice *'89*
Cloak & Dagger *'84*
The Fox and the Hound *'81 (V)*
The Manitou *'78*
The Rescuers *'77 (V)*
Babe! *'75*
The Reluctant Astronaut *'67*
My Blood Runs Cold *'65*
The Man Who Shot Liberty Valance *'62*
Psycho *'60 (V)*
Seventh Cavalry *'56*
Tribute to a Bad Man *'56*
A Lawless Street *'55*
Hangman's Knot *'52*
Macbeth *'48*
Abandoned *'47*
Saddle Tramp *'47*

John Nolan (1933-2000)
Following *'99*
The Terror *'79*
In the Steps of a Dead Man *'74*

Lloyd Nolan (1902-85)
Hannah and Her Sisters *'86*
It Came Upon a Midnight Clear *'84*
Prince Jack *'83*
My Boys Are Good Boys *'78*
Galyon *'77*
Abduction of St. Anne *'75*
Earthquake *'74*
Airport *'70*
Ice Station Zebra *'68*
Sergeant Ryker *'68*
Never Too Late *'65*
Circus World *'64*
Girl Hunters *'63*
Susan Slade *'61*
Portrait in Black *'60*
Abandon Ship *'57*
Peyton Place *'57*
The Last Hunt *'56*
Island in the Sky *'53*
The Lemon Drop Kid *'51*
Easy Living *'49*
The Sun Comes Up *'49*
The Street with No Name *'48*
Lady in the Lake *'46*
Somewhere in the Night *'46*
House on 92nd Street *'45*
A Tree Grows in Brooklyn *'45*
Bataan *'43*
Guadalcanal Diary *'43*
Blue, White and Perfect *'42*
Just Off Broadway *'42*
The Man Who Wouldn't Die *'42*
Time to Kill *'42*
Blues in the Night *'41*
Sleepers West *'41*
House Across the Bay *'40*
Johnny Apollo *'40*
Michael Shayne: Private Detective *'40*
Every Day's a Holiday *'38*
King of Alcatraz *'38*
Internes Can't Take Money *'37*
Big Brown Eyes *'36*
The Texas Rangers *'36*
"G" Men *'35*

Mary Nolan (1905-48)
Undertow *'30*
Desert Nights *'29*
West of Zanzibar *'28*

Tom Nolan (1948-)
Voyage of the Rock Aliens *'87*
School Spirit *'85*

Amaury Nolasco (1970-)
Armored '09
Prison Break: The Final Break '09
Max Payne '08
Street Kings '08
Transformers '07
The Benchwarmers '06
Mr. 3000 '04

Michelle Nolden
The Time Traveler's Wife '09
All Hat '07
Show Me '04
Rudy: The Rudy Giulani Story '03
Cybermutt '02
Men with Brooms '02

Claude Nollier (1919-)
Forbidden Fruit '52
Moulin Rouge '52

Jacques Nolot (1943-)
Before I Forget '07
Under the Sand '00
Artemisia '97
Nenette and Boni '96
I Don't Kiss '91

Nick Nolte (1941-)
The Mysteries of Pittsburgh '08
The Spiderwick Chronicles '08 (V)
Tropic Thunder '08
Chicago 10 '07 (V)
A Few Days in September '06
Over the Hedge '06 (V)
Paris, je t'aime '06
Peaceful Warrior '06
The Beautiful Country '04
Clean '04
Hotel Rwanda '04
The Good Thief '03
Hulk '03
Northfork '03
Intimate Affairs '01
The Golden Bowl '00
Trixie '00
Simpatico '99
Breakfast of Champions '98
The Thin Red Line '98
Affliction '97
Afterglow '97
U-Turn '97
Mother Night '96
Nightwatch '96
Mulholland Falls '95
Blue Chips '94
I Love Trouble '94
Jefferson in Paris '94
I'll Do Anything '93
Lorenzo's Oil '92
The Player '92
Cape Fear '91
The Prince of Tides '91
Another 48 Hrs. '90
Everybody Wins '90
Q & A '90
Farewell to the King '89
New York Stories '89
Three Fugitives '89
Extreme Prejudice '87
Weeds '87
Down and Out in Beverly Hills '86
Grace Quigley '84
Teachers '84
Under Fire '83
Cannery Row '82
48 Hrs. '82
Heart Beat '80
North Dallas Forty '79
Who'll Stop the Rain? '78
The Deep '77
Rich Man, Poor Man '76
Return to Macon County '75
The Runaway Barge '75
The California Kid '74
Death Sentence '74
Winter Kill '74

Hironobu Nomura (1965-)
Executive Koala '06
Retribution '06
Flower & Snake '04

Mansai Nomura
Onmyoji 2 '03
Onmyoji '01

Takashi Nomura
Suicide Club '02
Ran '85

Tom NonDorf
Rage of the Werewolf '99
Addicted to Murder 2: Tainted Blood '97

John Ford Noonan (1943-)
Flirting with Disaster '95
Adventures in Babysitting '87

Tom Noonan (1951-)
The House of the Devil '09
Where the Wild Things Are '09 (V)
The Alphabet Killer '08
Synecdoche, New York '08
Snow Angels '07
Seraphim Falls '06
Eight Legged Freaks '02
Knockaround Guys '01
The Pledge '00
The Astronaut's Wife '99
Phoenix '98
Heat '95
The Wife '95
What Happened Was... '94
Last Action Hero '93
RoboCop 2 '90
Mystery Train '89
The Monster Squad '87
Manhunter '86
The Man with One Red Shoe '85
Wolfen '81

Tommy Noonan (1921-68)
Three Nuts in Search of a Bolt '64
Promises! Promises! '63
The Girl Most Likely '57
The Ambassador's Daughter '56
A Star Is Born '54
Gentlemen Prefer Blondes '53
Adam's Rib '50
Return of Jesse James '50
Jungle Patrol '48

Kathleen Noone (1945-)
Citizen Ruth '96
Serpent's Lair '95

Nora-Jane Noone (1984-)
Legend of the Bog '08
The Descent '05
The Magdalene Sisters '02

Ghita Norby (1935-)
O'Horten '09
Everlasting Moments '08
The Kingdom 2 '97
Hamsun '96
The Kingdom '95
Like It Never Was Before '95
The Best Intentions '92
Sofie '92
Freud Leaving Home '91
Memories of a Marriage '90
Babette's Feast '87 (N)
The Wolf at the Door '87
The Inheritance '76

Christine Norden (1924-88)
Night Beat '48
Mine Own Executioner '47

Jeffrey Nordling (1962-)
Surfer, Dude '08
Flicka '06
Wilderness Love '02
Turbulence 2: Fear of Flying '99
Saint Maybe '98
True Women '97
D3: The Mighty Ducks '96
A Stranger in Town '95
Holy Matrimony '94
And the Band Played On '93
Dangerous Heart '93

Carsten Norgaard (1963-)
Alien vs. Predator '04
Red Shoe Diaries 6: How I Met My Husband '95
Out of Annie's Past '94

Eduardo Noriega (1916-2007)
Transsiberian '08
The Devil's Backbone '01
Burnt Money '00
The Yellow Fountain '99
Open Your Eyes '97
Thesis '96

Eduardo Noriega (1918-)
Vantage Point '08
The Method '05
The Far Horizons '55
Seven Cities of Gold '55

Felix Noriego (1930-)
Battle Cry '55
To Hell and Back '55

Lucille Norman (1921-98)
Carson City '52
Painting the Clouds With Sunshine '51

Maidie Norman (1913-98)
Sixteen '72
What Ever Happened to Baby Jane? '62

Susan Norman
Safe '95
Poison '91

Zack Norman
Festival at Cannes '02
Crosscut '95
Babyfever '94
Venice, Venice '92
Cadillac Man '90
America '86
Romancing the Stone '84
Sitting Ducks '80
Tracks '76

Mabel Normand (1894-1930)
Extra Girl '23
What Happened to Rosa? '21
Mickey '17
Mabel & Fatty '16
Charlie Chaplin ... Our Hero! '15
Tillie's Punctured Romance '14

David Norona (1972-)
Mrs. Santa Claus '96
Twisted '96

Bruce Norris (1960-)
The Sixth Sense '99
A Civil Action '98
Reach the Rock '98

Chuck Norris (1939-)
Dodgeball: A True Underdog Story '04
Forest Warrior '95
Top Dog '95
Hellbound '94
Sidekicks '93
Walker: Texas Ranger: One Riot, One Ranger '93
The Hitman '91
Delta Force 2: Operation Stranglehold '90
Braddock: Missing in Action 3 '88
Hero and the Terror '88
Delta Force '86
Firewalker '86
Code of Silence '85
Invasion U.S.A. '85
Missing in Action 2: The Beginning '85
Missing in Action '84
Lone Wolf McQuade '83
Forced Vengeance '82
Silent Rage '82
An Eye for an Eye '81
Slaughter in San Francisco '81
Octagon '80
Force of One '79
Game of Death '79
Good Guys Wear Black '78
Breaker! Breaker! '77
Enter the Dragon '73
Return of the Dragon '73
The Student Teachers '73

Dean Norris
Linewatch '08
The Cell '00
Three Strikes '00
My Little Assassin '99
Starship Troopers '97
Without Limits '97
The Lawnmower Man '92
Hard to Kill '89
Lethal Weapon 2 '89

Edward Norris (1911-2002)
Mysterious Desperado '49
Heartaches '47
Decoy '46
End of the Road '44
Wings over the Pacific '43
The Man with Two Lives '42
Back in the Saddle '41
Road Show '41
The Lady in Question '40
They Won't Forget '37
Show Them No Mercy '35
Wagon Trail '35

Mike Norris (1963-)
Carnival of Wolves '96
Dragon Fury 2 '96
Ripper Man '96
Death Ring '93
Delta Force 3: The Killing Game '91
Survival Game '87
Born American '86

Terry Norris (1930-)
Innocence '00
Road to Nhill '97

Simon Norrthon (1967-)
Like It Never Was Before '95
Speak Up! It's So Dark '93

Alan North (1920-2000)
I'll Take You There '99
The Jerky Boys '95
Crazy People '90
Glory '89
Lean on Me '89
Rachel River '87
Billy Galvin '86
Highlander '86

Heather North (1950-)
The Barefoot Executive '71
Git! '65

Jay North (1952-)
Scout's Honor '80
The Teacher '74
Maya '66
Zebra in the Kitchen '65

J.J. North
Psycho Sisters '98
Hellblock 13 '97
Attack of the 60-Foot Centerfold '95
Vampire Vixens from Venus '94

Noelle North
Diary of a Teenage Hitchhiker '82
Sweater Girls '78
Slumber Party '57 '76

Sheree North (1933-2005)
Dying to Get Rich '98
Defenseless '91
Maniac Cop '88
Legs '83
Marilyn: The Untold Story '80
Only Once in a Lifetime '79
Portrait of a Stripper '79
Telefon '77
Most Wanted '76
The Shootist '76
Breakout '75
Winter Kill '74
Charley Varrick '73
Snatched '72
Lawman '71
The Organization '71
The Gypsy Moths '69
The Trouble with Girls (and How to Get into It) '69
Then Came Bronson '68

Ted North (1916-)
The Devil Thumbs a Ride '47
The Unsuspected '47
Thunder Birds '42
Charlie Chan in Rio '41

Jeremy Northam (1961-)
Creation '09
The Invasion '07
Tristram Shandy: A Cock and Bull Story '05
Bobby Jones: Stroke of Genius '04
The Singing Detective '03
The Statement '03
Cypher '02
Possession '02
Enigma '01
Gosford Park '01
The Golden Bowl '00
Happy, Texas '99
An Ideal Husband '99
Gloria '98
The Winslow Boy '98
Mimic '97
Emma '96
Carrington '95
The Net '95
A Village Affair '95
Voices from a Locked Room '95
Emily Bronte's Wuthering Heights '92
A Fatal Inversion '92
Suspicion '87

Ryan Northcott (1980-)
Ripper: Letter from Hell '01
Mystery, Alaska '99

Alex Norton (1950-)
Pirates of the Caribbean: Dead Man's Chest '06
The Count of Monte Cristo '02
Beautiful Creatures '00
Orphans '97
Squanto: A Warrior's Tale '94
Hidden City '87
Comfort and Joy '84
Gregory's Girl '80
A Sense of Freedom '78

Barry Norton (1909-56)
Devil Monster '46
Captain Calamity '36
Dishonored '31
Dracula (Spanish Version) '31

Edgar Norton (1868-1953)
Son of Frankenstein '39
Thirty Day Princess '34
Dr. Jekyll and Mr. Hyde '32
The Lady Refuses '31
The Love Parade '29
The King on Main Street '25

Edward Norton (1969-)
The Invention of Lying '09
The Incredible Hulk '08
Pride and Glory '08
The Illusionist '06
The Painted Veil '06
Down in the Valley '05
Kingdom of Heaven '05
The Italian Job '03
Death to Smoochy '02
Frida '02
Red Dragon '02
25th Hour '02
The Score '01
Keeping the Faith '00
Fight Club '99
American History X '98
Rounders '98
Everyone Says I Love You '96
The People vs. Larry Flynt '96
Primal Fear '96

Jack Norton (1889-1958)
The Bank Dick '40
Finishing School '33

Jim Norton (1938-)
The Boy in the Striped Pajamas '08
Driving Lessons '06
Conspiracy of Silence '03
Midnight's Child '93
Memoirs of an Invisible Man '92
Hidden Agenda '90

Ken Norton (1945-)
The Man Who Came Back '08
Dirty Work '97
Kiss and Be Killed '91
Oceans of Fire '86
Drum '76
Mandingo '75

Richard Norton (1950-)
Amazons and Gladiators '01
Nautilus '99
Black Thunder '98
Mr. Nice Guy '98
Fugitive X '96
Under the Gun '95
Tough and Deadly '94
Cyber-Tracker '93
Deathfight '93
Direct Hit '93
Rage and Honor 2: Hostile Takeover '93
Ironheart '92
Lady Dragon '92
Rage and Honor '92
Raiders of the Sun '92
The Kick Fighter '91
China O'Brien 2 '89
Crossfire '89
Hyper Space '89
China O'Brien '88
Equalizer 2000 '86
The Millionaire's Express '86
Gymkata '85

Terry Norton
American Kickboxer 1 '91
Emissary '89

Judy Norton-Taylor (1958-)
A Day for Thanks on Walton's Mountain '82
The Waltons: The Christmas Carol '80

Brandy Norwood (1979-)
Osmosis Jones '01 (V)
Double Platinum '99
I Still Know What You Did Last Summer '98
Cinderella '97

Jack Noseworthy (1969-)
Surrogates '09
Aces 'n Eights '08
A Dennis the Menace Christmas '07
Phat Girlz '06
Poster Boy '04
Unconditional Love '03
Undercover Brother '02
Cecil B. Demented '00
U-571 '00
Idle Hands '99
Murder at Devil's Glen '99
Event Horizon '97
Barb Wire '96
Breakdown '96
The Brady Bunch Movie '95
A Place for Annie '94

S.F.W. '94
Alive '93
Encino Man '92

Ralph Nossek

My Life in Ruins '09
Citizen X '95
Chicago Joe & the Showgirl '90

Christopher Noth (1956-)

Sex and the City 2 '10
My One and Only '09
Sex and the City: The Movie '08
The Perfect Man '05
Mr. 3000 '04
Searching for Paradise '02
Double Whammy '01
The Glass House '01
Cast Away '00
A Texas Funeral '99
The Confession '98
Cold Around the Heart '97
Rough Riders '97
Burnzy's Last Call '95
Jakarta '88
Baby Boom '87
Apology '86
Off Beat '86
Smithereens '82

Michael Nouri (1945-)

The Proposal '09
Invincible '06
Last Holiday '06
The Boynton Beach Club '05
The Terminal '04
Klepto '03
Lovely & Amazing '02
Terminal Error '02
61* '01
Finding Forrester '00
This Matter of Marriage '98
Overkill '96
Hologram Man '95
To the Limit '95
American Yakuza '94
Fortunes of War '94
The Hidden 2 '94
Inner Sanctum 2 '94
Lady in Waiting '94
No Escape, No Return '93
Black Ice '92
DaVinci's War '92
Danielle Steel's Changes '91
Psychic '91
Total Exposure '91
Little Vegas '90
Shattered Dreams '90
Project: Alien '89
Thieves of Fortune '89
The Hidden '87
Between Two Women '86
Imagemaker '86
Rage of Angels: The Story Continues '86
Spraggue '84
Flashdance '83
Gangster Wars '81

B.J. Novak (1979-)

Inglourious Basterds '09
Knocked Up '07

Eva Novak (1898-1988)

Red Signals '27
Laughing at Danger '24
Sky High '22
Trailin' '21

Frank Novak (1945-)

Virtual Seduction '96
Watchers 3 '94

Jane Novak (1896-1990)

Three Word Brand '21
Wagon Tracks '19

John Novak (1955-)

Wishmaster 4: The Prophecy Fulfilled '02
Wishmaster 3: Beyond the Gates of Hell '01

Kim Novak (1933-)

Liebestraum '91
The Children '90
The Mirror Crack'd '80
Just a Gigolo '79
The White Buffalo '77
Tales That Witness Madness '73
The Amorous Adventures of Moll Flanders '65
Kiss Me, Stupid! '64
Of Human Bondage '64
Boys' Night Out '62
The Notorious Landlady '62
Strangers When We Meet '60
Bell, Book and Candle '58
Vertigo '58
Pal Joey '57
The Eddy Duchin Story '56
5 Against the House '55
The Man with the Golden Arm '55
Picnic '55
The French Line '54
Phffft! '54
Pushover '54

Mel Novak

Vampire Assassin '05
Capital Punishment '96
Expert Weapon '93
Lovely... But Deadly '82
Family Reunion '79
Cat in the Cage '68

Bojana Novakovic

Edge of Darkness '10
Solo '06
Marking Time '03

Ramon Novarro (1899-1968)

Heller in Pink Tights '60
Crisis '50
Big Steal '49
The Cat and the Fiddle '34
The Barbarian '33
Mata Hari '32
Across to Singapore '28
The Student Prince in Old Heidelberg '27
Ben-Hur '26
The Red Lily '24
Scaramouche '23
The Prisoner of Zenda '22

Tamar Novas

Broken Embraces '09
The Sea Inside '04

Don Novello (1943-)

Atlantis: The Lost Empire '01 (V)
The Adventures of Rocky & Bullwinkle '00
Just One Night '00
Just the Ticket '98
Jack '96
Casper '95
One Night Stand '95
Armistead Maupin's Tales of the City '93
Teenage Bonnie & Klepto Clyde '93
Spirit of '76 '91
The Godfather, Part 3 '90
New York Stories '89
Tucker: The Man and His Dream '88

Ivor Novello (1893-1951)

Phantom Fiend '35
The Lodger '26
The White Rose '23

Jay Novello (1904-82)

What Did You Do in the War, Daddy? '66
Harum Scarum '65
The Pride and the Passion '57
Jaguar '56
The Prodigal '55
Sabaka '55
Crime Wave '54
Ma and Pa Kettle on Vacation '53
Cattle Town '52
Miracle of Our Lady of Fatima '52
Bad Man of Deadwood '41
Robin Hood of the Pecos '41
Sheriff of Tombstone '41
The Border Legion '40

Tom Novembre (1959-)

The Ice Rink '99
An American Werewolf in Paris '97
Elsa, Elsa '85

Nancho Novo (1958-)

Lovers of the Arctic Circle '98
Tierra '95
The Red Squirrel '93

Jarmila Novotna (1908-94)

The Great Caruso '51
The Search '48

Jerzy Nowak (1923-)

The Healer '02
Trois Couleurs: Blanc '94

Tom Nowicki

Conjurer '08
Flash '98
Kiss of Fire '98
Nightjohn '96

Zachi Noy (1953-)

Young Love—Lemon Popsicle 7 '87
Baby Love '83
Private Manoeuvres '83
Hot Bubblegum '81

Joanna Noyes

Nightwaves '03
Bleeders '97
The Reaper '97

Bruce Nozick

Gale Force '01
Tuesdays with Morrie '99
Hit the Dutchman '92
Killer Instinct '92

Winston Ntshona (1941-)

Tarzan and the Lost City '98
Night of the Cyclone '90
A Dry White Season '89

Danny Nucci (1968-)

Backwoods '08
The Sandlot 3: Heading Home '07
Break a Leg '03
American Cousins '02
Firestarter 2: Rekindled '02
Codename: Jaguar '00
Friends & Lovers '99
Love Walked In '97
Titanic '97
The Big Squeeze '96
Eraser '96
The Rock '96
That Old Feeling '96
Crimson Tide '95
Homage '95
Roosters '95
Book of Love '91
The Children of Times Square '86

Carole Nugent

Lost, Lonely, and Vicious '59
Belles on Their Toes '52

Eddie Nugent (1904-95)

Doughnuts & Society '36
Prison Shadows '36
Kentucky Blue Streak '35
Night Nurse '31
Vagabond Lover '29

Elliott Nugent (1900-80)

Welcome Stranger '47
Romance '30
The Unholy Three '30

Ted Nugent

Beer for My Horses '08
Tapeheads '89

Yoichi Numata

The Princess Blade '02
Ringu 2 '99
Ringu '98

Miguel A. Nunez, Jr. (1964-)

Kickin' It Old Skool '07
The Adventures of Pluto Nash '02
Juwanna Mann '02
Scooby-Doo '02
MacArthur Park '01
If You Only Knew '00
Life '99
For Richer or Poorer '97
Lethal Weapon 3 '92
Return of the Living Dead '85

Osmar Nunez

The Proposal '09
Beethoven's Big Break '08
A Year Without Love '05

Bill Nunn (1953-)

A Raisin in the Sun '08
Firehouse Dog '07
Spider-Man 3 '07
Spider-Man 2 '04
Runaway Jury '03
People I Know '02
Spider-Man '02
Lockdown '00
The Substitute 4: Failure is Not an Option '00
Foolish '99
Passing Glory '99
The Tic Code '99
Always Outnumbered Always Outgunned '98
He Got Game '98
The Legend of 1900 '98
Quicksilver Highway '98
Blood Brothers '97
Ellen Foster '97
Kiss the Girls '97
Mad City '97
Bulletproof '96
Extreme Measures '96
Mr. & Mrs. Loving '96
The Affair '95
Money Train '95
Things to Do in Denver When You're Dead '95
True Crime '95
Canadian Bacon '94
Candyman 2: Farewell to the Flesh '94
The Last Seduction '94
Save Me '93
Sister Act '92
New Jack City '91
Regarding Henry '91
White Lie '91
Def by Temptation '90
Mo' Better Blues '90
Do the Right Thing '89
School Daze '88

Teri Nunn (1961-)

Follow That Car '80
Thank God It's Friday '78

Rudolf Nureyev (1938-93)

Exposed '83
Valentino '77

Maila Nurmi

See Vampira

Loredana Nusciak (1942-)

Django '68
Gladiators 7 '62

Danny Nussbaum

Beautiful People '99
24-7 '97

Mike Nussbaum (1923-)

The Water Engine '92
Things Change '88
House of Games '87

Jeff Nuttal (1933-2004)

Beaumarchais the Scoundrel '96
Captives '94
Robin Hood '91

Mayf Nutter (1941-)

Hunter's Blood '87
The $5.20 an Hour Dream '80

France Nuyen (1939-)

A Smile Like Yours '96
A Passion to Kill '94
The Joy Luck Club '93
China Cry '91
Code Name: Diamond Head '77
Return to Fantasy Island '77
The Big Game '72
Black Water Gold '69
Diamond Head '62
South Pacific '58

N!xau (1944-2003)

The Gods Must Be Crazy 2 '89
The Gods Must Be Crazy '84

Carrie Nye (1937-2006)

Hello Again '87
Creepshow '82
The Group '66

Carroll Nye (1901-74)

Gone with the Wind '39
Lottery Bride '30

Louis Nye (1933-2005)

O.C. and Stiggs '87
Alice in Wonderland '85
Harper Valley P.T.A. '78
Charge of the Model T's '76
A Guide for the Married Man '67
Good Neighbor Sam '64
The Wheeler Dealers '63
The Facts of Life '60

Andy Nyman

Death at a Funeral '07
Severance '06

Lena Nyman (1944-)

The Adventures of Picasso '80
Autumn Sonata '78
I Am Curious (Yellow) '67

Michael Nyquist

Downloading Nancy '08
Mother of Mine '05
London Voodoo '04

Pascal Nzonzi

Lumumba '01
Night on Earth '91

Henry O

A Thousand Years of Good Prayers '07
The Lost Empire '01
Dragonheart: A New Beginning '00
Romeo Must Die '00
Shanghai Noon '00

Jack Oakie (1903-78)

Lover Come Back '61
The Rat Race '60
Around the World in 80 Days '56
Tomahawk '51
It Happened Tomorrow '44
Hello, Frisco, Hello '43
Wintertime '43
Iceland '42
Song of the Islands '42
The Great American Broadcast '41
The Great Dictator '40
Little Men '40
Tin Pan Alley '40
Young People '40
The Affairs of Annabel '38
Thanks for Everything '38
Toast of New York '37
Colleen '36
The Texas Rangers '36
That Girl from Paris '36
Murder at the Vanities '34
College Humor '33
The Eagle and the Hawk '33
Uptown New York '32
Touchdown '31

Simon Oakland (1922-83)

Emperor of the North Pole '73
The Night Strangler '72
Chato's Land '71
The Night Stalker '71
On a Clear Day You Can See Forever '70
Bullitt '68
Tony Rome '67
The Sand Pebbles '66
Follow That Dream '61
West Side Story '61
Murder, Inc. '60
Psycho '60
The Rise and Fall of Legs Diamond '60
I Want to Live! '58

Wheeler Oakman (1890-1949)

Teenage '44
The Ape Man '43
Meet the Mob '42
Double Trouble '41
Wolf Call '39
Slaves in Bondage '37
Aces and Eights '36
Death from a Distance '36
Ghost Patrol '36
The Man from Gun Town '36
Roaring Guns '36
Song of the Trail '36
Trails of the Wild '35
Frontier Days '34
In Old Santa Fe '34
The Lost Jungle '34
Man of Action '33
Boiling Point '32
The Riding Tornado '32
Texas Cyclone '32
Two-Fisted Law '32
Roaring Ranch '30
On with the Show '29
The Broken Mask '28
Outside the Law '21
Peck's Bad Boy '21
The Spoilers '14

Simon Oates

Jewels '92
Doomwatch '72
The Terrornauts '67

Warren Oates (1928-82)

Blue Thunder '83
Tough Enough '83
The Blue and the Gray '82
The Border '82
Stripes '81
East of Eden '80
And Baby Makes Six '79
My Old Man '79
1941 '79
Brink's Job '78
Gunfire '78
Prime Time '77
Sleeping Dogs '77
Dixie Dynamite '76
Drum '76
92 in the Shade '76
Race with the Devil '75
The White Dawn '75
Badlands '74
Bring Me the Head of Alfredo Garcia '74
Cockfighter '74
Dillinger '73
The Thief Who Came to Dinner '73
Tom Sawyer '73
Hired Hand '71
Two Lane Blacktop '71
There Was a Crooked Man '70
Crooks & Coronets '69
The Wild Bunch '69
In the Heat of the Night '67
Return of the Magnificent Seven '66
The Shooting '66
Shenandoah '65
Mail Order Bride '63
Ride the High Country '62

Devin Oatway (1978-)

Galgameth '96
Camp Nowhere '94

Philip Ober (1902-82)

The Ghost and Mr. Chicken '66
The Facts of Life '60

Beloved Infidel '59
The Mating Game '59
North by Northwest '59
Escapade in Japan '57
From Here to Eternity '53
Come Back, Little Sheba '52
The Magnificent Yankee '50
Never a Dull Moment '50

Merle Oberon (1911-79)

Interval '73
Hotel '67
The Oscar '66
Deep in My Heart '54
Desiree '54
Berlin Express '48
A Song to Remember '45
Dark Waters '44
Forever and a Day '43
Stage Door Canteen '43
Lydia '41
That Uncertain Feeling '41
The Lion Has Wings '40
Wuthering Heights '39
The Cowboy and the Lady '38
The Divorce of Lady X '38
Beloved Enemy '36
These Three '36
The Dark Angel '35
Broken Melody '34
Private Life of Don Juan '34
The Scarlet Pimpernel '34
The Private Life of Henry VIII '33
Wedding Rehearsal '32

Jacqueline Obradors (1967-)

A Man Apart '03
Atlantis: The Lost Empire '01 (V)
Tortilla Soup '01
Deuce Bigalow: Male Gigolo '99
Six Days, Seven Nights '98
Soldier Boyz '95

Anna (Ana Garcia) Obregon (1955-)

Bolero '84
Treasure of the Four Crowns '82
Car Crash '80

Claudio Obregon (1955-)

Esmeralda Comes by Night '98
Midaq Alley '95
Reed: Insurgent Mexico '73

Rodrigo Obregon

L.A. Wars '94
Enemy Gold '93
Fit to Kill '93
Hard Hunted '92
Tides of War '90
Picasso Trigger '89
Savage Beach '89
Django Strikes Again '87
Hard Ticket to Hawaii '87

Hugh O'Brian (1925-)

Wyatt Earp: Return to Tombstone '94
The Gambler Returns: The Luck of the Draw '93
Doin' Time on Planet Earth '88
Twins '88
The Seekers '79
Cruise into Terror '78
Fantasy Island '76
The Shootist '76
Killer Force '75
Murder on Flight 502 '75
Probe '72
Wild Women '70
Africa Texas Style '67
Assassination in Rome '65
In Harm's Way '65
Love Has Many Faces '65
Alias Jesse James '59
The Fiend Who Walked the West '58
Broken Lance '54
There's No Business Like Show Business '54
Man from the Alamo '53
The Lawless Breed '52
Red Ball Express '52
Son of Ali Baba '52
Little Big Horn '51
Vengeance Valley '51
Return of Jesse James '50
Rocketship X-M '50

Austin O'Brien (1981-)

The Baby-Sitters' Club '95
Lawnmower Man 2: Beyond Cyberspace '95
My Girl 2 '94
Last Action Hero '93
Prehysteria '93

Clay O'Brien (1961-)

Cahill: United States Marshal '73
One Little Indian '73
The Cowboys '72

Conan O'Brien (1963-)

The Great Buck Howard '09
Queer Duck: The Movie '06 (V)

Dave O'Brien (1912-69)

Enemy of the Law '45
Flaming Bullets '45
Frontier Fugitives '45
Marked for Murder '45
The Phantom of 42nd Street '45
Three in the Saddle '45
Boss of Rawhide '44
Dead or Alive '44
Gangsters of the Frontier '44
Guns of the Law '44
Fighting Valley '43
The Return of the Rangers '43
Bowery at Midnight '42
King of the Stallions '42
Law and Order '42
Rangers Take Over '42
Billy the Kid in Santa Fe '41
The Devil Bat '41
Double Trouble '41
The Phantom Pinto '41
The Spider Returns '41
Spooks Run Wild '41
Buzzy Rides the Range '40
Danger Ahead '40
Murder on the Yukon '40
Sky Bandits '40
That Gang of Mine '40
Yukon Flight '40
Daughter of the Tong '39
Phantom Rancher '39
The Singing Cowgirl '39
Water Rustlers '39
Law of the Texan '38
Reefer Madness '38
Brothers of the West '37
Lightning Bill Crandall '37
Lion's Den '36

Donald O'Brien (1930-2003)

Quest for the Mighty Sword '90
Doctor Butcher M.D. '80
Trap Them & Kill Them '77
The Train '65

Edmond O'Brien (1915-85)

Lucky Luciano '74
99 & 44/100 Dead '74
They Only Kill Their Masters '72
Jigsaw '71
Dream No Evil '70
The Love God? '70
The Wild Bunch '69
The Doomsday Flight '66
Fantastic Voyage '66
Rio Conchos '64
Seven Days in May '64
Birdman of Alcatraz '62
The Longest Day '62
The Man Who Shot Liberty Valance '62
Moon Pilot '62
The Great Impostor '61
The Last Voyage '60
Up Periscope '59
Stopover Tokyo '57
D-Day, the Sixth of June '56
The Girl Can't Help It '56
1984 '56
Pete Kelly's Blues '55
The Barefoot Contessa '54
The Bigamist '53
The Hitch-Hiker '53
Julius Caesar '53
The Denver & Rio Grande '51
The Admiral Was a Lady '50
D.O.A. '49
White Heat '49
For the Love of Mary '48
A Double Life '47
The Killers '46
The Amazing Mrs. Holiday '43
A Girl, a Guy and a Gob '41
The Hunchback of Notre Dame '39

George O'Brien (1900-85)

Cheyenne Autumn '64
Gold Raiders '51
She Wore a Yellow Ribbon '49
Bullet Code '40
Legion of the Lawless '40
Racketeers of the Range '39
Hollywood Cowboy '37
Park Avenue Logger '37
Windjammer '37
Cowboy Millionaire '35
Thunder Mountain '35
When a Man's a Man '35
Daniel Boone '34
Dude Ranger '34
Mystery Ranch '34
Painted Desert '31
Seas Beneath '31
The Lone Star Ranger '30
Sunrise '27
The Iron Horse '24

Gerry O'Brien

Speed Dating '07
Veronica Guerin '03

Joan O'Brien (1936-)

It Happened at the World's Fair '63
Samar '62
The Alamo '60
Operation Petticoat '59

Kieran O'Brien (1973-)

Goal! The Dream Begins '06
Bloodlines '05
Tristram Shandy: A Cock and Bull Story '05
Jason and the Argonauts '00
Virtual Sexuality '99
Cracker: Brotherly Love '95
Cracker: True Romance '95
Bellman and True '88

Margaret O'Brien (1937-)

Amy '81
Heller in Pink Tights '60
Glory '56
Little Women '49
The Secret Garden '49
Our Vines Have Tender Grapes '45
The Canterville Ghost '44
Jane Eyre '44
Meet Me in St. Louis '44
Thousands Cheer '43
Journey for Margaret '42

Maria O'Brien (1950-)

In a Stranger's Hand '92
Promised a Miracle '88

Maureen O'Brien (1944-)

American Women '00
Falling for a Dancer '98
The Land Girls '98
The Lost Boys '78

Myles O'Brien

Scorned 2 '96
Sexual Roulette '96

Niall O'Brien

Secret of the Cave '06
Broken Harvest '94
Class of '61 '92
Rawhead Rex '87
Excalibur '81
Lovespell '79

Pat O'Brien (1899-1983)

Ragtime '81
Scout's Honor '80
The End '78
Some Like It Hot '59
Last Hurrah '58
Kill Me Tomorrow '57
Jubilee Trail '54
The Boy with the Green Hair '48
Fighting Father Dunne '48
Riff-Raff '47
Crack-Up '46
Having Wonderful Crime '45
His Butler's Sister '44
Bombardier '43
The Iron Major '43
Marine Raiders '43
Broadway '42
The Navy Comes Through '42
Castle on the Hudson '40
The Fighting 69th '40
Knute Rockne: All American '40
Slightly Honorable '40
Torrid Zone '40
The Night of Nights '39
Angels with Dirty Faces '38
Boy Meets Girl '38
San Quentin '37
Ceiling Zero '35
Devil Dogs of the Air '35
Flirtation Walk '34
Bombshell '33
Bureau of Missing Persons '33
The World Gone Mad '33
American Madness '32
Hell's House '32
Consolation Marriage '31
Flying High '31
The Front Page '31
Personal Maid '31

Pat J. O'Brien

Doomed Caravan '41
Hawaiian Buckaroo '38
Tim Tyler's Luck '37

Peter O'Brien (1960-)

The Return '06
Hotel de Love '96
Angel of Fury '93
A Kink in the Picasso '90
The Grand Duel '73

Richard O'Brien (1942-)

Night Train '09
Elvira's Haunted Hills '02
Dungeons and Dragons '00
Dark City '97
Spice World: The Movie '97
Robin Hood... The Legend: The Time of the Wolf '85
Shock Treatment '81
The Rocky Horror Picture Show '75

Shauna O'Brien (1970-)

The Seductress '00
The Escort '97
Body Armor '96
Friend of the Family 2 '96
Fugitive Rage '96
Friend of the Family '95
Over the Wire '95

Tom O'Brien (1965-)

A Thousand Heroes '92
The Accused '88
The Big Easy '87

Virginia O'Brien (1921-2001)

Merton of the Movies '47
The Harvey Girls '46
The Show-Off '46
Till the Clouds Roll By '46
Meet the People '44
Two Girls and a Sailor '44
Du Barry Was a Lady '43
Thousands Cheer '43
Panama Hattie '42
Ship Ahoy '42
Big Store '41
Lady Be Good '41

Erin O'Brien-Moore (1902-79)

Destination Moon '50
The Black Legion '37
Our Little Girl '35
His Greatest Gamble '34

Jeffrey Obrow

The Kindred '87
The Power '80

Pat O'Bryan

976-EVIL 2: The Astral Factor '91
Relentless '89
976-EVIL '88

Sean O'Bryan

The Princess Diaries 2: Royal Engagement '04
Raising Helen '04
Big Fat Liar '02
The Princess Diaries '01
Nice Guys Sleep Alone '99
I'll Be Home for Christmas '98
The Twilight of the Golds '97

Brian F. O'Byrne (1967-)

Brooklyn's Finest '09
The International '09
Before the Devil Knows You're Dead '07
No Reservations '07
Bug '06
The New World '05
Million Dollar Baby '04
Bandits '01
Disco Pigs '01
The Mapmaker '01
An Everlasting Piece '00
Amongst Women '98

Ric Ocasek (1949-)

Hairspray '88
Made in Heaven '87

Andrea Occhipinti (1957-)

Amor de Hombre '97
Running Away '89
Control '87
The Family '87
Bolero '84
El Barbaro '84
A Blade in the Dark '83
Conquest '83
New York Ripper '82

P.J. Ochlan

Quigley '03
Little Man Tate '91

Jesus Ochoa (1959-)

Innocent Voices '04
Man on Fire '04
Nicotina '03

Juan Manuel Ochoa

Alias, La Gringa '91
The City and the Dogs '85

Uwe Ochsenknecht (1956-)

Luther '03
Kaspar Hauser '93
Schtonk '92
Fire, Ice and Dynamite '91
Men... '85
Das Boot '81

Arthur O'Connell (1908-81)

The Hiding Place '75
Huckleberry Finn '74
Ben '72
They Only Kill Their Masters '72
The Last Valley '71
There Was a Crooked Man '70
The Reluctant Astronaut '67
Fantastic Voyage '66
The Silencers '66
Monkey's Uncle '65
Kissin' Cousins '64
7 Faces of Dr. Lao '63
Follow That Dream '61
The Great Impostor '61
Misty '61
Pocketful of Miracles '61
Cimarron '60
Anatomy of a Murder '59
Gidget '59
Operation Petticoat '59
Man of the West '58
Operation Mad Ball '57
Bus Stop '56
The Man in the Gray Flannel Suit '56
Solid Gold Cadillac '56
Picnic '55
Open Secret '48
Blondie's Blessed Event '42
Law of the Jungle '42
Citizen Kane '41

Charlie O'Connell (1975-)

Kraken: Tentacles of the Deep '06
The Devil's Prey '01
Dude, Where's My Car? '00
Derby '71

Deirdre O'Connell

What Happens in Vegas '08
Stephanie Daley '06
Imaginary Heroes '05
Winter Passing '05
Hearts in Atlantis '01
Murder in a Small Town '99
Lifeform '96
Fearless '93
Cool World '92
Falling from Grace '92
Straight Talk '92
Pastime '91

Hugh O'Connell

Personal Maid '31
The Smiling Lieutenant '31

Jerry O'Connell (1974-)

Piranha 3D '10
Midnight Bayou '09
Obsessed '09
Baby on Board '08
Yours, Mine & Ours '05
Buying the Cow '02
Kangaroo Jack '02
Tomcats '01
Mission to Mars '00
Body Shots '99
The '60s '99
Can't Hardly Wait '98
What the Deaf Man Heard '98
Scream 2 '97
Jerry Maguire '96
Joe's Apartment '96
Blue River '95
Hole in the Sky '95
Calendar Girl '93
Ollie Hopnoodle's Haven of Bliss '88
Stand by Me '86

Patrick O'Connell (1934-)

We'll Meet Again '82
McKenzie Break '70

Raoul O'Connell

Lifeform '96
Frisk '95
Boys Life '94

Taaffe O'Connell

Galaxy of Terror '81
Caged Fury '80

Carroll O'Connor (1925-2001)

Return to Me '00
Gideon '99
36 Hours to Die '99
The Father Clements Story '87
Convicted '86
Brass '85
Law and Disorder '74
Doctors' Wives '70
Kelly's Heroes '70
Death of a Gunfighter '69
Marlowe '69
The Devil's Brigade '68
For Love of Ivy '68

Point Blank '67
Waterhole Number 3 '67
Hawaii '66
What Did You Do in the War, Daddy? '66
In Harm's Way '65
Cleopatra '63
Lonely Are the Brave '62
Parrish '61
Johnny Frenchman '46

Derrick O'Connor (1941-)
Daredevil '03
End of Days '99
Deep Rising '98
How to Make an American Quilt '95
Dealers '89
Lethal Weapon 2 '89
Hope and Glory '87

Donald O'Connor (1925-2003)
Out to Sea '97
Toys '92
A Time to Remember '87
Alice in Wonderland '85
Pandemonium '82
Ragtime '81
That Funny Feeling '65
The Wonders of Aladdin '61
Francis in the Navy '55
Francis Joins the WACs '54
There's No Business Like Show Business '54
Francis Covers the Big Town '53
I Love Melvin '53
Francis Goes to West Point '52
Singin' in the Rain '52
Double Crossbones '51
Francis Goes to the Races '51
Francis the Talking Mule '49
Something in the Wind '47
Private Buckaroo '42
Beau Geste '39

Frances O'Connor (1967-)
Darwin's Darkest Hour '09
Book of Love '04
Timeline '03
The Importance of Being Earnest '02
Windtalkers '02
A. I.: Artificial Intelligence '01
About Adam '00
Bedazzled '00
Madame Bovary '00
Mansfield Park '99
Kiss or Kill '97
A Little Bit of Soul '97
The Wedding Party '97
Love and Other Catastrophes '95

Frank O'Connor (1882-1959)
Bury Me Not on the Lone Prairie '41
The Sunset Murder Case '38

Glynnis O'Connor (1956-)
Graduation '07
New Best Friend '02
Saint Maybe '98
Ellen Foster '97
Past the Bleachers '95
To Heal a Nation '88
A Conspiracy of Love '87
The Deliberate Stranger '86
Johnny Dangerously '84
Melanie '82
Night Crossing '81
Those Lips, Those Eyes '80
California Dreaming '79
The Dark Side of Love '79
Our Town '77
The Boy in the Plastic Bubble '76
Ode to Billy Joe '76
Kid Vengeance '75
Someone I Touched '75

Hazel O'Connor
Car Trouble '85
Breaking Glass '80

Kevin J. O'Connor (1964-)
Flight of the Living Dead: Outbreak on a Plane '07
There Will Be Blood '07
Kettle of Fish '06
Seraphim Falls '06
Van Helsing '04
Chill Factor '99
The Mummy '99
Black Cat Run '98
Deep Rising '98
Gods and Monsters '98
The Love Bug '97
Hit Me '96
Lord of Illusions '95
Virtuosity '95
Canadian Bacon '94
Color of Night '94
No Escape '94
Equinox '93
Hero '92
Love at Large '89
Signs of Life '89
Steel Magnolias '89
The Caine Mutiny Court Martial '88
The Moderns '88
Candy Mountain '87
Peggy Sue Got Married '86
Special Effects '85
Bogie: The Last Hero '80
Let's Scare Jessica to Death '71

Renee O'Connor (1971-)
Boogeyman 2 '07
Follow the River '95
Darkman 2: The Return of Durant '94
Hercules the Legendary Journeys, Vol. 2: The Lost Kingdom '94

Robert Emmett O'Connor
Picture Snatcher '33
Up the River '30

Robert Emmett O'Connor (1885-1962)
A Night at the Opera '35
Kid from Spain '32

Sinead O'Connor (1966-)
The Butcher Boy '97
Emily Bronte's Wuthering Heights '92

Tim O'Connor (1927-)
Naked Gun 2 1/2: The Smell of Fear '91
Manhunter '74
Winter Kill '74
Sssssss '73
Across 110th Street '72
The Groundstar Conspiracy '72

Una O'Connor (1880-1959)
Witness for the Prosecution '57
Fighting Father Dunne '48
Hopalong Cassidy: Unexpected Guest '47
Christmas in Connecticut '45
The Canterville Ghost '44
This Land Is Mine '43
Strawberry Blonde '41
The Sea Hawk '40
The Adventures of Robin Hood '38
Personal Property '37
Lloyds of London '36
The Bride of Frankenstein '35
David Copperfield '35
The Informer '35
The Barretts of Wimpole Street '34
Chained '34
Stingaree '34
Cavalcade '33
The Invisible Man '33

Hugh O'Conor (1975-)
Speed Dating '07
Bloom '03
Deathwatch '02
Chocolat '00
The Young Poisoner's Handbook '94
My Left Foot '89
Da '88
Lamb '85

Joe Odagiri
Retribution '06
Shinobi '05
Azumi '03
Bright Future '03

Nell O'Day (1909-89)
Boss of Rawhide '44
The Return of the Rangers '43
Stagecoach Buckaroo '42
Arizona Cyclone '41
Bury Me Not on the Lone Prairie '41
Man from Montana '41
The Masked Rider '41
Law and Order '40
Pony Post '40

Denis O'Dea (1905-78)
Esther and the King '60
The Story of Esther Costello '57
Mogambo '53
Niagara '52
Captain Horatio Hornblower '51
The Long Dark Hall '51
Treasure Island '50
The Fallen Idol '49
Under Capricorn '49

Judith O'Dea (1945-)
Serial Slayer '03
Night of the Living Dead '68

Deborah Odell
Time Bomb '08
All the Good Ones Are Married '07
Godsend '04
Protection '01

Georgia O'Dell (1892-1950)
West of Nevada '36
Big Calibre '35

Jennifer O'Dell (1974-)
Nevermore '07
Slayer '06
Window Theory '04

Tony O'Dell
Chopping Mall '86
The Karate Kid '84

Bob Odenkirk (1962-)
Danny Roane: First Time Director '06
Sink or Swim '97
The Cable Guy '96
The Truth about Cats and Dogs '96
Waiting for Guffman '96
Clean Slate '94
Wayne's World 2 '93

Christophe Odent
Nouvelle Vague '90
First Name: Carmen '83

Devon Odessa
Mad Cowgirl '06
The Omega Code '99

Odetta (1930-)
The Fire Next Time '93
The Autobiography of Miss Jane Pittman '74

Anthony O'Donnell
Agatha Christie: A Life in Pictures '04
Nuts in May '76

Cathy O'Donnell (1925-70)
Ben-Hur '59
Terror in the Haunted House '58
The Man from Laramie '55
The Love of Three Queens '54
Detective Story '51
The Miniver Story '50
Side Street '50
They Live by Night '49
The Amazing Mr. X '48
The Best Years of Our Lives '46

Chris O'Donnell (1970-)
Cats & Dogs: The Revenge of Kitty Galore '10
Kit Kittredge: An American Girl '08
Max Payne '08
The Company '07
The Sisters '05
Kinsey '04
Vertical Limit '00
The Bachelor '99
Cookie's Fortune '99
Batman and Robin '97
The Chamber '96
In Love and War '96
Batman Forever '95
Mad Love '95
Circle of Friends '94
The Three Musketeers '93
Scent of a Woman '92
School Ties '92
Blue Sky '91
Fried Green Tomatoes '91
Men Don't Leave '89

David O'Donnell
A Christmas Proposal '08
Dear Me: A Blogger's Tale '08
Lime Salted Love '06
Magma: Volcanic Disaster '06

Keir O'Donnell
Paul Blart: Mall Cop '09
Taking Chances '09
Pathology '08
Flakes '07
Wedding Crashers '05

Rosie O'Donnell (1962-)
America '09
Tarzan '99 (V)
The Twilight of the Golds '97
Wide Awake '97
Beautiful Girls '96
Harriet the Spy '96
A Very Brady Sequel '96
Now and Then '95
Car 54, Where Are You? '94
Exit to Eden '94
The Flintstones '94
Another Stakeout '93
Sleepless in Seattle '93
A League of Their Own '92

"Spec" (Walter) O'Donnell (1911-86)
Hello Trouble '32
Sparrows '26
The Country Kid '23

Martha O'Driscoll (1922-98)
Carnegie Hall '47
Criminal Court '46
Here Come the Co-Eds '45
House of Dracula '45
Follow the Boys '44
Crazy House '43
The Fallen Sparrow '43
Reap the Wild Wind '42
Young and Willing '42

Steve Oedekerk (1961-)
Barnyard '06 (V)
Kung Pow! Enter the Fist '02
High Strung '91

Gregoire Oestermann
I Do '06
Look at Me '04
Lucie Aubrac '98

Bernadette O'Farrell (1924-99)
Robin Hood: The Movie '55
Scotland Yard Inspector '52
The Happiest Days of Your Life '50

Conor O'Farrell
Stir of Echoes '99
From the Earth to the Moon '98
Baby of the Bride '91

George Offerman, Jr. (1917-63)
A Walk in the Sun '46
The Fighting Sullivans '42
Frontier Vengeance '40
The Outlaw Deputy '35

Nick Offerman (1970-)
Taking Chances '09
The Go-Getter '07
Wristcutters: A Love Story '06
Miss Congeniality 2: Armed and Fabulous '05
November '05
Sin City '05
Groove '00
Treasure Island '99

Damian O'Flynn (1907-82)
Daniel Boone: Trail Blazer '56
The Devil on Wheels '47
Crack-Up '46
Wake Island '42
X Marks the Spot '42

Ken Ogata (1937-)
The Hidden Blade '04
Gonin 2 '96
The Pillow Book '95
Mishima: A Life in Four Chapters '85
The Ballad of Narayama '83
Virus '82
Eijanaika '81
Samurai Reincarnation '81
Vengeance Is Mine '79

Mayumi Ogawa (1939-)
The Go-Masters '82
Vengeance Is Mine '79
Zatoichi: The Blind Swordsman's Vengeance '66

Bulle Ogier (1939-)
The Duchess of Langeais '07
Belle Toujours '06
Merci Docteur Rey '04
Shattered Image '98
Venus Beauty Institute '98
Somewhere in the City '97
Irma Vep '96
Son of Gascogne '95
Candy Mountain '87
Tricheurs '84
Maitresse '76
Celine and Julie Go Boating '74
The Discreet Charm of the Bourgeoisie '72
La Salamandre '71
The Valley Obscured by the Clouds '70

Ian Ogilvy (1943-)
Fugitive Mind '99
The Disappearance of Kevin Johnson '95
Puppet Master 5: The Final Chapter '94
Death Becomes Her '92
Eddie Presley '92
Invasion of Privacy '92
Anna Karenina '85
And Now the Screaming Starts '73
From Beyond the Grave '73
No Sex Please—We're British '73
Waterloo '71
Wuthering Heights '70
The Conqueror Worm '68
The Invincible Six '68
Cop-Out '67
The She-Beast '65

Jorgo Ognenovski
Stalked '99
Warrior of Justice '96

Dean O'Gorman (1976-)
The Legend of Bloody Mary '08
Beyond Justice '01
When Love Comes '98
Young Hercules '97

Gail O'Grady (1963-)
An American Carol '08
All I Want for Christmas '07
The Sitter '07
Lucky Seven '03
Hope Ranch '02
Another Woman's Husband '00
Lip Service '00
Sleep Easy, Hutch Rimes '00
Deuce Bigalow: Male Gigolo '99
The Three Lives of Karen '97
Celtic Pride '96
That Old Feeling '96
Spellcaster '91
Nobody's Perfect '90
Blackout '88

Olivia Oguma
Robot Stories '03
The Flamingo Rising '01

Shun Oguri
Azumi 2 '05
The Neighbor No. Thirteen '05
Reincarnation '05
Azumi '03

Sandra Oh (1971-)
Ramona and Beezus '10
Defendor '09
Hard Candy '06
The Night Listener '06
Cake '05
Sorry, Haters '05
Sideways '04
Break a Leg '03
Rick '03
Under the Tuscan Sun '03
Big Fat Liar '02
Long Life, Happiness and Prosperity '02
The Princess Diaries '01
Dancing at the Blue Iguana '00
Waking the Dead '00
Guinevere '99
Last Night '98
Bean '97
Double Happiness '94

Soon-Teck Oh (1943-)
True Blue '01
Mulan '98 (V)
Yellow '98
Beverly Hills Ninja '96
Red Sun Rising '94
A Home of Our Own '93
Missing in Action 2: The Beginning '85
East of Eden '80
Fantastic Seven '79
The Man with the Golden Gun '74

Michael O'Hagan (1941-)
Quicksand '01
For Love or Country: The Arturo Sandoval Story '00

Brian O'Halloran (1969-)
Brutal Massacre: A Comedy '07
Clerks 2 '06
Jay and Silent Bob Strike Back '01
Chasing Amy '97
Mallrats '95
Clerks '94

Lost in Space *'98*
Quest for Camelot *'98 (V)*
Air Force One *'97*
The Fifth Element *'97*
Basquiat *'96*
Murder in the First *'95*
The Scarlet Letter *'95*
Immortal Beloved *'94*
The Professional *'94*
Fallen Angels 2 *'93*
Romeo Is Bleeding *'93*
True Romance *'93*
Bram Stoker's Dracula *'92*
JFK *'91*
Rosencrantz & Guildenstern Are Dead *'90*
State of Grace *'90*
Chattahoochee *'89*
Criminal Law *'89*
Track 29 *'88*
We Think the World of You *'88*
Prick Up Your Ears *'87*
Sid & Nancy *'86*
Meantime *'81*

Gabriel Olds (1972-)
Life of the Party *'05*
Now & Forever *'02*
Urbania *'00*
A Town Has Turned to Dust *'98*
Without Limits *'97*
Andersonville *'95*
Animal Room *'95*
Calendar Girl *'93*

Matt O'Leary (1987-)
American Son *'08*
Death Sentence *'07*
Brick *'06*
Spy Kids 3-D: Game Over *'03*
Frailty *'02*
Spy Kids 2: The Island of Lost Dreams *'02*
Domestic Disturbance *'01*

William O'Leary
Candyman 2: Farewell to the Flesh *'94*
In the Line of Duty: Ambush in Waco *'93*
Flight of Black Angel *'91*
Hot Shots! *'91*
Nice Girls Don't Explode *'87*

Larisa Oleynik (1981-)
Together Again for the First Time *'08*
Pope Dreams *'06*
100 Girls *'00*
A Time for Dancing *'00*
Ten Things I Hate about You *'99*
The Baby-Sitters' Club *'95*

Ken Olin (1954-)
Til There Was You *'96*
Queens Logic *'91*
The Game of Love *'87*

Lena Olin (1955-)
Remember Me *'10*
The Reader *'08*
Awake *'07*
Casanova *'05*
Hollywood Homicide *'03*
United States of Leland *'03*
Darkness *'02*
Queen of the Damned *'02*
Ignition *'01*
Chocolat *'00*
Mystery Men *'99*
The Ninth Gate *'99*
Polish Wedding *'97*
Night Falls on Manhattan *'96*
The Night and the Moment *'94*
Mr. Jones *'93*
Romeo Is Bleeding *'93*
Havana *'90*
Enemies, a Love Story *'89*
The Unbearable Lightness of Being *'88*
After the Rehearsal *'84*

Ingrid Oliu
Real Women Have Curves *'02*
Stand and Deliver *'88*

Luis Oliva
The Christmas Choir *'08*
The Cutting Edge 3: Chasing the Dream *'08*

Barret Oliver (1973-)
Cocoon: The Return *'88*
The Secret Garden *'87*
Cocoon *'85*
D.A.R.Y.L. *'85*
Frankenweenie *'84*
Invitation to Hell *'84*
The NeverEnding Story *'84*

Charles Oliver
The Hooded Terror *'38*
The Green Cockatoo *'37*
The Avenging Hand *'36*
Midnight at the Wax Museum *'36*

Christian Oliver (1972-)
Tribute *'09*
Speed Racer *'08*
The Good German *'06*
Subject Two *'06*
Kept *'01*
Eat Your Heart Out *'96*

David Oliver (1900-78)
The Invisible Killer *'40*
Postal Inspector *'36*

David Oliver (1962-92)
Miracle in the Wilderness *'91*
The Horror Show *'89*
Defense Play *'88*
Night of the Creeps *'86*

Edna May Oliver (1883-1942)
Pride and Prejudice *'40*
Drums Along the Mohawk *'39*
Nurse Edith Cavell *'39*
Second Fiddle *'39*
The Story of Vernon and Irene Castle *'39*
Little Miss Broadway *'38*
Rosalie *'38*
Romeo and Juliet *'36*
A Tale of Two Cities *'36*
David Copperfield *'35*
Ann Vickers *'33*
Little Women *'33*
Hold 'Em Jail *'32*
Cimarron *'31*
Half-Shot at Sunrise *'30*
Lucky Devil *'25*

Gordon Oliver (1911-95)
The Spiral Staircase *'46*
Seven Days Ashore *'44*
Follies Girl *'43*
Blondie *'38*
San Quentin *'37*
Youth on Parole *'37*

Guy Oliver
Nevada *'27*
A Woman of the World *'25*

Michael Oliver (1981-)
Problem Child 2 *'91*
Problem Child *'90*

Rochelle Oliver (1937-)
Scent of a Woman *'92*
An Unremarkable Life *'89*
Courtship *'87*
On Valentine's Day *'86*
1918 *'85*

Stephen Oliver (1942-)
Savage Abduction *'73*
Cycle Psycho *'72*
Werewolves on Wheels *'71*
Angels from Hell *'68*
Motor Psycho *'65*

Susan Oliver (1937-90)
Tomorrow's Child *'82*
Hardly Working *'81*
Widow's Nest *'77*
Ginger in the Morning *'73*
Black Brigade *'69*
Disorderly Orderly *'64*
Guns of Diablo *'64*
Butterfield 8 *'60*

The Gene Krupa Story *'59*

Robert Oliveri (1978-)
Honey, I Blew Up the Kid *'92*
Edward Scissorhands *'90*
Honey, I Shrunk the Kids *'89*

Ramiro Oliveros
Hundra *'85*
Rape *'76*

Laurence Olivier (1907-89)
Sky Captain and the World of Tomorrow *'04*
A Voyage 'Round My Father *'89*
Ebony Tower *'86*
Peter the Great *'86*
Wagner: The Complete Epic *'85*
Wagner: The Movie *'85*
Wild Geese 2 *'85*
The Bounty *'84*
The Jigsaw Man *'84*
Brideshead Revisited *'81*
Clash of the Titans *'81*
The Jazz Singer *'80*
Dracula *'79*
A Little Romance *'79*
The Betsy *'78*
The Boys from Brazil *'78*
A Bridge Too Far *'77*
Jesus of Nazareth *'77*
Marathon Man *'76*
The Seven-Per-Cent Solution *'76*
Love Among the Ruins *'75*
Lady Caroline Lamb *'73*
The Merchant of Venice *'73*
Sleuth *'72*
Nicholas and Alexandra *'71*
David Copperfield *'70*
Battle of Britain *'69*
Oh! What a Lovely War *'69*
Romeo and Juliet *'68 (N)*
The Shoes of the Fisherman *'68*
Khartoum *'66*
Othello *'65*
Term of Trial *'63*
The Entertainer *'60*
Spartacus *'60*
The Devil's Disciple *'59*
The Prince and the Showgirl *'57*
Richard III *'55*
Beggar's Opera *'54*
Carrie *'52*
Hamlet *'48*
This Happy Breed *'47 (N)*
Henry V *'44*
The Demi-Paradise *'43*
The Forty-Ninth Parallel *'41*
That Hamilton Woman *'41*
Pride and Prejudice *'40*
Rebecca *'40*
Clouds over Europe *'39*
Wuthering Heights *'39*
The Divorce of Lady X *'38*
Fire Over England *'37*
21 Days *'37*
As You Like It *'36*
I Stand Condemned *'36*

Paul Olivier (1876-1948)
A Nous la Liberte *'31*
Le Million *'31*

Dawn Olivieri
Hydra *'09*
Devil's Den *'06*

Silvio Oliviero
Gotti *'96*
Understudy: The Graveyard Shift 2 *'88*
A Whisper to a Scream *'88*
Graveyard Shift *'87*
Psycho Girls *'86*

Walter Olkewicz (1948-)
Meeting Daddy *'98*
Milo *'98*
Pronto *'97*
The Good Old Boys *'95*
The Client *'94*
1941 *'79*

Can I Do It... Till I Need Glasses? *'77*

Edward James Olmos (1949-)
Battlestar Galactica: The Plan *'09*
Beverly Hills Chihuahua *'08 (V)*
Splinter *'06*
In the Time of the Butterflies *'01*
The Road to El Dorado *'00 (V)*
Bonanno: A Godfather's Story *'99*
Gossip *'99*
The Wall *'99*
The Wonderful Ice Cream Suit *'98*
Hollywood Confidential *'97*
Twelve Angry Men *'97*
Caught *'96*
The Disappearance of Garcia Lorca *'96*
Larry McMurtry's Dead Man's Walk *'96*
The Limbic Region *'96*
Selena *'96*
Roosters *'95*
The Burning Season *'94*
A Million to Juan *'94*
Mirage *'94*
My Family *'94 (N)*
American Me *'92*
Talent for the Game *'91*
Triumph of the Spirit *'89*
Stand and Deliver *'88*
Saving Grace *'86*
Ballad of Gregorio Cortez *'83*
Blade Runner *'82*
Virus *'82*
Wolfen *'81*
Zoot Suit *'81*

Dan Olmstead
The Manchurian Candidate *'04*
Philadelphia *'93*

Gertrude (Olmstead) Olmsted (1904-75)
The Cheerful Fraud *'27*
The Boob *'26*
Sweet Adeline *'26*
California Straight Ahead *'25*
Cobra *'25*
The Monster *'25*

Alex O'Loughlin (1977-)
Whiteout *'09*
The Invisible *'07*
Feed *'05*
The Incredible Journey of Mary Bryant *'05*

Gerald S. O'Loughlin (1921-)
Three Strikes *'00*
Crime of the Century *'96*
Quicksilver *'86*
Crimes of Passion *'84*
Frances *'82*
A Matter of Life and Death *'81*
Pleasure Palace *'80*
Blind Ambition *'79*
The Crash of Flight 401 *'78*
The Valachi Papers *'72*
Desperate Characters *'71*
In Cold Blood *'67*
A Fine Madness *'66*
Ensign Pulver *'64*

Ashley (Fuller) Olsen (1986-)
New York Minute *'04*
Charlie's Angels: Full Throttle *'03*
Billboard Dad *'98*
How the West Was Fun *'95*
It Takes Two *'95*
Double Double Toil and Trouble *'94*
To Grandmother's House We Go *'94*

Eric Christian Olsen (1977-)
The Back-Up Plan *'10*
Fired Up! *'09*
Sunshine Cleaning *'09*
The Comebacks *'07*
License to Wed *'07*
Beerfest *'06*
Cellular *'04*
Death Valley *'04*
Dumb and Dumberer: When Harry Met Lloyd *'03*
The Hot Chick *'02*
Local Boys *'02*
Not Another Teen Movie *'01*

Gary Olsen (1957-2000)
24 Hours in London *'00*
Winter Flight *'84*

Larry Olsen (1938-)
Who Killed Doc Robbin? *'48*
Curley *'47*

Mary-Kate Olsen (1986-)
Beastly *'10*
The Wackness *'08*
New York Minute *'04*
Charlie's Angels: Full Throttle *'03*
Billboard Dad *'98*
How the West Was Fun *'95*
It Takes Two *'95*
Double Double Toil and Trouble *'94*
To Grandmother's House We Go *'94*

Merlin Olsen (1940-2010)
Mitchell *'75*
The Undefeated *'69*

Moroni Olsen (1899-1954)
The Long, Long Trailer *'54*
Father's Little Dividend *'51*
Father of the Bride *'50*
The Fountainhead *'49*
Task Force *'49*
Call Northside 777 *'48*
The Long Night *'47*
The Possessed *'47*
Notorious *'46*
Buffalo Bill *'44*
Cobra Woman *'44*
Air Force *'43*
Ali Baba and the Forty Thieves *'43*
The Glass Key *'42*
Reunion in France *'42*
Dive Bomber *'41*
Brigham Young: Frontiersman *'40*
Allegheny Uprising *'39*
Rose of Washington Square *'39*
Susannah of the Mounties *'39*
Snow White and the Seven Dwarfs *'37 (V)*
Mary of Scotland *'36*
Yellow Dust *'36*
Annie Oakley *'35*
The Three Musketeers *'35*

Ole Olsen (1892-1963)
Crazy House *'43*
All Over Town *'37*
Country Gentlemen *'36*

Richard Olsen
Stephen King's The Night Flier *'96*
Wildflower *'91*

James Olson (1943-)
Rachel River *'87*
Commando *'85*
Amityville 2: The Possession *'82*
Ragtime *'81*
My Sister, My Love *'78*
The Spell *'77*
Someone I Touched *'75*
Strange New World *'75*
Missiles of October *'74*
The Groundstar Conspiracy *'72*

The Andromeda Strain *'71*
Paper Man *'71*
Crescendo *'69*
Rachel, Rachel *'68*
The Three Sisters *'65*
The Strange One *'57*

Kaitlin Olson (1975-)
Leap Year *'10*
Weather Girl *'09*

Nancy Olson (1928-)
Making Love *'82*
Airport '75 *'75*
Snowball Express *'72*
Son of Flubber *'63*
The Absent-Minded Professor *'61*
Pollyanna *'60*
Battle Cry *'55*
Big Jim McLain *'52*
Mr. Music *'50*
Sunset Boulevard *'50*
Union Station *'50*

Ty Olsson
High Noon *'09*
Christmas Caper *'07*

Niclas Olund (1977-)
Expectations *'97*
The Slingshot *'93*

Timothy Olyphant (1968-)
The Crazies *'09*
A Perfect Getaway *'09*
Stop-Loss *'08*
Catch and Release *'07*
Hitman *'07*
Live Free or Die Hard *'07*
Meet Bill *'07*
The Girl Next Door *'04*
Dreamcatcher *'03*
A Man Apart *'03*
Coastlines *'02*
Rock Star *'01*
The Safety of Objects *'01*
Beyond Suspicion *'00*
The Broken Hearts Club *'00*
Gone in 60 Seconds *'00*
Go *'99*
No Vacancy *'99*
When Trumpets Fade *'98*
Ellen Foster *'97*
Scream 2 *'97*
The First Wives Club *'96*

Bingo O'Malley
Bob Roberts *'92*
Two Evil Eyes *'90*

Daragh O'Malley (1954-)
Sharpe's Challenge *'06*
Longitude *'00*
Cleopatra *'99*
The Magnificent Seven *'98*
Sharpe's Justice *'97*
Sharpe's Revenge *'97*
Sharpe's Waterloo *'97*
Sharpe's Mission *'96*
Sharpe's Regiment *'96*
Sharpe's Siege *'96*
Sharpe's Battle *'94*
Sharpe's Company *'94*
Sharpe's Enemy *'94*
Sharpe's Gold *'94*
Sharpe's Honour *'94*
Sharpe's Sword *'94*
Sharpe's Eagle *'93*
Sharpe's Rifles *'93*

J. Pat O'Malley (1901-85)
A Small Killing *'81*
Willard *'71*
Star! *'68*
The Jungle Book *'67 (V)*
Hey There, It's Yogi Bear *'64 (V)*
101 Dalmatians *'61 (V)*
Courage of Black Beauty *'57*
Witness for the Prosecution *'57*
Lassie, Come Home *'43*

Michael O'Malley (1966-)
Meet Dave *'08*
The Perfect Man *'05*

28 Days '00

Pat O'Malley (1891-1966)
Invasion of the Body Snatchers '56
The Adventures of Ichabod and Mr. Toad '49 (V)
Stunt Pilot '39
Fighting Marines '36
The Miracle Rider '35
Evelyn Prentice '34
The Perils of Pauline '34
The Fighting Marshal '32
Night Life in Reno '31
Spangles '26
The Fighting American '24
The Virginian '23

Rex O'Malley (1901-76)
Midnight '39
Camille '36

Kate O'Mara (1939-)
Nativity '78
Whose Child Am I? '75
The Horror of Frankenstein '70
The Vampire Lovers '70

Mollie O'Mara
Escape from Safehaven '88
Girls School Screamers '86

Omarion
See Omari (Omarion) Grandberry

Judd Omen
Bounty Tracker '93
Dollman '90
Howling 2: Your Sister Is a Werewolf '85
Pee-wee's Big Adventure '85

Afemo Omilami (1950-)
Hounddog '08
Drumline '02
Bringing Out the Dead '99
DROP Squad '94

Pat O'Moore (1909-83)
The Two Mrs. Carrolls '47
Sahara '43

Andy On
The Kumite '03
Black Mask 2: City of Masks '02

Anny Ondra (1903-87)
Blackmail '29
The Manxman '29

Anne O'Neal (1893-1971)
Gun Crazy '49
Open Secret '48

Frederick O'Neal (1905-92)
Free, White, and 21 '62
The Sins of Rachel Cade '61
Tarzan's Peril '51

Griffin O'Neal (1964-)
Evil Lives '92
Ghoulies 3: Ghoulies Go to College '91
Night Children '89
Assault of the Killer Bimbos '88
The Wraith '87
April Fool's Day '86
The Children of Times Square '86
Hadley's Rebellion '84
The Escape Artist '82

Patrick O'Neal (1927-94)
Under Siege '92
For the Boys '91
Alice '90
Q & A '90
New York Stories '89
Perry Mason Returns '85
The Stuff '85
Spraggue '84
Make Me an Offer '80
The Stepford Wives '75
Silent Night, Bloody Night '73
The Way We Were '73
El Condor '70
Castle Keep '69
Stiletto '69
Secret Life of an American Wife '68
Where Were You When the Lights Went Out? '68
Alvarez Kelly '66
A Fine Madness '66
In Harm's Way '65
King Rat '65
From the Terrace '60
The Black Shield of Falworth '54

Ron O'Neal (1937-2004)
On the Edge '02
Original Gangstas '96
Up Against the Wall '91
Hyper Space '89
Hero and the Terror '88
Mercenary Fighters '88
Trained to Kill '88
As Summers Die '86
Red Dawn '84
St. Helen's, Killer Volcano '82
Sophisticated Gents '81
Freedom Road '79
The Hitter '79
When a Stranger Calls '79
Superfly T.N.T. '73
Superfly '72

Ryan O'Neal (1941-)
Malibu's Most Wanted '03
People I Know '02
Epoch '00
Coming Soon '99
The List '99
An Alan Smithee Film: Burn, Hollywood, Burn '97
Sink or Swim '97
Zero Effect '97
Faithful '95
The Man Upstairs '93
Chances Are '89
Small Sacrifices '89
Tough Guys Don't Dance '87
Fever Pitch '85
Irreconcilable Differences '84
Partners '82
Green Ice '81
So Fine '81
The Main Event '79
The Driver '78
Oliver's Story '78
A Bridge Too Far '77
Barry Lyndon '75
Paper Moon '73
The Thief Who Came to Dinner '73
What's Up, Doc? '72
Wild Rovers '71
Love Story '70
The Big Bounce '69

Shaquille O'Neal (1972-)
Scary Movie 4 '06
Good Burger '97
Steel '97
Kazaam '96
Blue Chips '94

Tatum O'Neal (1963-)
The Runaways '10
My Brother '06
The Home Front '02
Basquiat '96
Little Noises '91
Certain Fury '85
Goldilocks & the Three Bears '83
Circle of Two '80
Little Darlings '80
International Velvet '78
The Bad News Bears '76
Paper Moon '73

Ty O'Neal (1978-)
American Outlaws '01
Bug Buster '99
D2: The Mighty Ducks '94

Barbara O'Neil (1910-80)
Flame of the Islands '55
Angel Face '52
Whirlpool '49
I Remember Mama '48
Secret Beyond the Door '48
All This and Heaven Too '40
Gone with the Wind '39
The Tower of London '39
I Am the Law '38
Stella Dallas '37

Nance O'Neil (1875-1965)
Cimarron '31
The Royal Bed '31

Nancy O'Neil (1908-95)
Jack Ahoy '34
The Secret of the Loch '34

Sally O'Neil (1908-68)
Convention Girl '35
Sixteen Fathoms Deep '34
On with the Show '29
Battle of the Sexes '28
Battling Butler '26

Angela O'Neill
Enemy Unseen '91
River of Diamonds '90
Sorority House Massacre '86

Chris O'Neill (1945-97)
2 by 4 '98
Backbeat '94
James Joyce's Women '85

Dick O'Neill (1928-98)
My Summer Story '94
Dark Justice '91
She's Out of Control '89
The Mosquito Coast '86
Wolfen '81
The Jerk '79
Prime Time '77
The Taking of Pelham One Two Three '74
Hail '73
Pretty Poison '68
Gamera, the Invincible '66

Ed O'Neill (1946-)
Spartan '04
Nobody's Baby '01
Lucky Numbers '00
The 10th Kingdom '00
The Bone Collector '99
The Spanish Prisoner '97
Prefontaine '96
Blue Chips '94
Little Giants '94
Wayne's World 2 '93
Wayne's World '92
Dutch '91
The Adventures of Ford Fairlane '90
Sibling Rivalry '90
Disorganized Crime '89
K-9 '89
When Your Lover Leaves '83
Cruising '80
The Day the Women Got Even '80
Deliverance '72

Henry O'Neill (1891-1961)
Scandal Sheet '52
Holiday Affair '49
The Virginian '46
The Heavenly Body '44
Nothing But Trouble '44
Air Raid Wardens '43
Whistling in Brooklyn '43
Johnny Eager '42
White Cargo '42
Billy the Kid '41
Honky Tonk '41
Men of Boys Town '41
Shadow of the Thin Man '41
Castle on the Hudson '40
The Fighting 69th '40
Confessions of a Nazi Spy '39
Amazing Dr. Clitterhouse '38
It Happened in New Orleans '36
Black Fury '35
Massacre '34
Lady Killer '33
America '24

Jennifer O'Neill (1948-)
The Corporate Ladder '97
Bad Love '95
The Cover Girl Murders '93
Discretion Assured '93
Invasion of Privacy '92
Perfect Family '92
Committed '91
Personals '90
Full Exposure: The Sex Tape Scandals '89
I Love N.Y. '87
A.D. '85
Chase '85
Scanners '81
Cloud Dancer '80
Steel '80
Force of One '79
Love's Savage Fury '79
The Psychic '78
The Innocent '76
The Reincarnation of Peter Proud '75
Whiffs '75
Lady Ice '73
Summer of '42 '71
Rio Lobo '70

Kel O'Neill
Redacted '07
Stephanie Daley '06
Domino '05
XX/XY '02

Kevin O'Neill
Five Minutes of Heaven '09
Cycle Vixens '79

Maggie O'Neill (1967-)
Little Devil '07
Mansfield Park '07
Invasion: Earth '98
Under Suspicion '92

Maire O'Neill (1887-1952)
Great Day '46
Sidewalks of London '38
Juno and the Paycock '30

Michael O'Neill
Transformers '07
Dreamcatcher '03
Seabiscuit '03
The Legend of Bagger Vance '00
Dancer, Texas—Pop. 81 '98
Sunchaser '96
The Gun in Betty Lou's Handbag '92
Gore-Met Zombie Chef from Hell '87

Remy O'Neill
To Die For 2: Son of Darkness '91
Hollywood Hot Tubs 2: Educating Crystal '89

Terry O'Neill (1948-)
The League of Extraordinary Gentlemen '03
Kull the Conqueror '97
Dragonheart '96

Alannah Ong
New York Minute '04
Double Happiness '94

Yoko Ono (1933-)
Let It Be '70
The Magic Christian '69

Peter Onorati (1954-)
Ordinary Sinner '02
Dancing in September '00
The Art of Murder '99
Just Looking '99
Shelter '98
True Friends '98
Tycus '98
RocketMan '97
Dead Ahead '96
Not Like Us '96
Donor Unknown '95
Camp Nowhere '94
Fire Birds '90
Goodfellas '90

Lupe Ontiveros (1942-)
Our Family Wedding '10
Dark Mirror '07
Tortilla Heaven '07
Mr. St. Nick '02
Real Women Have Curves '02
Gabriela '01
Storytelling '01
Chuck & Buck '00
Picking Up the Pieces '99
Candyman 3: Day of the Dead '98
As Good As It Gets '97
Selena '96
My Family '94
El Norte '83

Michael Ontkean (1950-)
A Killing Spring '02
Just a Little Harmless Sex '99
Summer of the Monkeys '98
Swann '96
Legacy of Lies '92
Postcards from the Edge '90
Bye Bye Blues '89
Cold Front '89
Street Justice '89
Clara's Heart '88
The Allnighter '87
Maid to Order '87
The Blood of Others '84
Just the Way You Are '84
Making Love '82
Willie & Phil '80
Slap Shot '77
Girls on the Road '73
Where the Eagle Flies '72
The Witching '72
Peacekillers '71

Amanda Ooms (1964-)
Everlasting Moments '08
Wilderness '96
The Women on the Roof '89

Marian Opania (1943-)
Hero of the Year '85
Man of Iron '81

Dhobi Oparei
Seven Seconds '05
Thunderbirds '04

David Opatoshu (1918-96)
Forty Days of Musa Dagh '85
Americathon '79
Who'll Stop the Rain? '78
Conspiracy of Terror '75
Romance of a Horsethief '71
Death of a Gunfighter '69
The Fixer '68
The Defector '66
Torn Curtain '66
Exodus '60
The Light Ahead '39

Anne Openshaw
Narc '02
We'll Meet Again '02

Alan Oppenheimer (1930-)
Trancers 5: Sudden Deth '94
Invisible: The Chronicles of Benjamin Knight '93
Trancers 4: Jack of Swords '93
Child of Darkness, Child of Light '91
Blind Ambition '79
A Pleasure Doing Business '79
Helter Skelter '76
The Bionic Woman '75
The Groundstar Conspiracy '72
Star! '68

Don Opper (1949-)
Critters 3 '91
Critters 4 '91
The Forgotten '89
Critters 2: The Main Course '88
Critters '86
Android '82

Terry O'Quinn (1952-)
Old School '03
Hometown Legend '02
The Locket '02
American Outlaws '01
Winds of Terror '01
Rated X '00
Murder in a Small Town '99
The X-Files '98
Breast Men '97
Ghosts of Mississippi '96
Primal Fear '96
The Shadow Conspiracy '96
JAG '95
Shadow Warriors '95
Don't Talk to Strangers '94
Amityville: A New Generation '93
Lipstick Camera '93
Tombstone '93
The Cutting Edge '92
The Good Fight '92
My Samurai '92
Take Down '92
Wildcard '92
Company Business '91
Prisoners of the Sun '91
The Rocketeer '91
Son of the Morning Star '91
When the Time Comes '91
Blind Fury '90
The Forgotten One '89
Roe vs. Wade '89
Stepfather 2: Make Room for Daddy '89
Pin... '88
Young Guns '88
Black Widow '87
The Stepfather '87
SpaceCamp '86
Women of Valor '86
Mischief '85
Silver Bullet '85
Mrs. Soffel '84
Places in the Heart '84
Heaven's Gate '81
Mahler '74

Alessio Orano
Lisa and the Devil '75
The Count of Monte Cristo '74
Summer Affair '71

Geraldine O'Rawe
Disco Pigs '01
Amongst Women '98
I Want You '98
Resurrection Man '97
Some Mother's Son '96
Circle of Friends '94

Jerry Orbach (1935-2004)
Prince of Central Park '00
Aladdin and the King of Thieves '96 (V)
The Adventures of a Gnome Named Gnorm '93
Broadway Bound '92
Mastergate '92
Mr. Saturday Night '92
Straight Talk '92
Universal Soldier '92
Beauty and the Beast '91 (V)
Delirious '91
Delusion '91
Out for Justice '91
Toy Soldiers '91
Dead Women in Lingerie '90
Last Exit to Brooklyn '90
California Casanova '89
Crimes & Misdemeanors '89
Dirty Dancing '87
I Love N.Y. '87
Out on a Limb '87
Someone to Watch Over Me '87
F/X '86
Imagemaker '86
Love Among Thieves '86
Brewster's Millions '85
Prince of the City '81
Underground Aces '80
Foreplay '75

24 Hours in a Woman's Life *'61*

Roy Orbison (1936-88)

Chuck Berry: Hail! Hail! Rock 'n' Roll *'87*
Roadie *'80*
Fastest Guitar Alive *'68*

Cyril O'Reilly (1958-)

Air Rage *'01*
Shadow of a Scream *'97*
Bloodfist 7: Manhunt *'95*
Philadelphia Experiment 2 *'93*
The Cool Surface *'92*
Navy SEALS *'90*
Dance of the Damned *'88*
On Wings of Eagles *'86*
Purple Hearts *'84*
Porky's 2: The Next Day *'83*
Porky's *'82*

Joan Orenstein

The Hanging Garden *'97*
Charlie Grant's War *'80*

Fereshteh Sadr Orfani

The Circle *'00*
The White Balloon *'95*

Liana Orfei (1937-)

Casanova '70 *'65*
Nefertiti, Queen of the Nile *'64*
Pirate Warrior *'64*
The Avenger *'62*
The Giant of Metropolis *'61*
Pirates of the Coast *'61*
Mill of the Stone Women *'60*

Moira Orfei (1931-)

The Scent of a Woman *'75*
The Triumph of Hercules *'66*
Terror of the Steppes *'64*
Two Gladiators *'64*
The Beast of Babylon Against the Son of Hercules *'63*
Ursus in the Valley of the Lions *'62*
Mole Men Against the Son of Hercules *'61*

Silvio Orlando (1957-)

After Midnight *'04*
Light of My Eyes *'01*
The Son's Room *'00*
Not of This World *'99*
Children of Hannibal *'98*
Palombella Rossa *'89*

Tony Orlando (1944-)

Waking Up in Reno *'02*
Rosie: The Rosemary Clooney Story *'82*

Julia Ormond (1965-)

Che *'08*
The Curious Case of Benjamin Button *'08*
Kit Kittredge: An American Girl *'08*
Surveillance *'08*
I Know Who Killed Me *'07*
Inland Empire *'06*
Resistance *'03*
Varian's War *'01*
The Prime Gig *'00*
Animal Farm *'99 (V)*
Smilla's Sense of Snow *'96*
First Knight *'95*
Sabrina *'95*
Captives *'94*
Legends of the Fall *'94*
Nostradamus *'93*
Stalin *'92*
Young Catherine *'91*
Traffik *'90*

Alan Ormsby (1944-)

Children Shouldn't Play with Dead Things *'72*
Deathdream *'72*

Anya Ormsby

Thunder County *'74*
Children Shouldn't Play with Dead Things *'72*

Ed O'Ross (1949-)

Delta Farce *'07*
Nobody *'07*
Curious George *'06 (V)*
Mindstorm *'01*
Y2K *'99*
Dark Planet *'97*
Navajo Blues *'97*
Hoodlum *'96*
Play Nice *'92*
Universal Soldier *'92*
Another 48 Hrs. *'90*
Tailspin: Behind the Korean Airline Tragedy *'89*
Red Heat *'88*
Full Metal Jacket *'87*
The Hidden *'87*
Lethal Weapon *'87*
Ruby's Dream *'82*

Heather O'Rourke (1975-88)

Poltergeist 3 *'88*
Poltergeist 2: The Other Side *'86*
Poltergeist *'82*

Ashley Rose Orr (1990-)

Carry Me Home *'04*
Child Star: The Shirley Temple Story *'01*

Christopher Orr

Robin Cook's Invasion *'97*
D3: The Mighty Ducks *'96*

Leland Orser (1960-)

Taken *'08*
The Good German *'06*
Twisted *'04*
Confidence *'03*
Daredevil *'03*
Runaway Jury *'03*
Brother's Keeper *'02*
Pearl Harbor *'01*
The Bone Collector *'99*
Resurrection *'99*
Saving Private Ryan *'98*
Very Bad Things *'98*
Alien: Resurrection *'97*
Excess Baggage *'96*
Independence Day *'96*
Lifeform *'96*

Marina Orsini (1967-)

Steel Toes *'06*
Eddie and the Cruisers 2: Eddie Lives! *'89*
Battle of the Worlds *'61*

Umberto Orsini (1934-)

Good-bye, Emmanuelle *'77*
A Woman at Her Window *'77*
Emmanuelle, the Joys of a Woman *'76*
The Outside Man *'73*
Cesar & Rosalie *'72*
The Family *'70*
Mademoiselle *'66*

Dyana Ortelli

Luminarias *'99*
Alienator *'89*

Frank Orth (1880-1962)

The Great Rupert *'50*
Heartaches *'47*
I Wake Up Screaming *'41*
Nancy Drew and the Hidden Staircase *'39*
Nancy Drew—Detective *'38*

Zak Orth (1970-)

Peter and Vandy *'09*
(Untitled) *'09*
Kill the Poor *'06*
The Baxter *'05*
Prime *'05*
Wet Hot American Summer *'01*
Down to You *'00*
Loser *'00*
When Trumpets Fade *'98*
In and Out *'97*
Rose Hill *'97*
My Teacher's Wife *'95*

Ana Ortiz (1971-)

Tortilla Heaven *'07*
Mr. St. Nick *'02*

Antonio Ortiz

Illegal Tender *'07*
Just Like the Son *'06*
Knights of the South Bronx *'05*

Humberto Ortiz (1979-)

Arcade *'93*
Dollman *'90*

John Ortiz

Pride and Glory *'08*
Aliens vs. Predator: Requiem *'07*
American Gangster *'07*
El Cantante *'06*
Miami Vice *'06*
Take the Lead *'06*
Narc *'02*
The Last Marshal *'99*
Riot in the Streets *'96*

Meaghan Ory

Blonde and Blonder *'07*
Merlin's Apprentice *'06*
Decoys *'04*

Romano Orzari (1964-)

The Last Hit Man *'08*
Bugs *'03*
Wolves in the Snow *'02*
Stiletto Dance *'01*
Wilder *'00*

Andrew Osborn (1912-85)

Angels One Five *'54*
Blackout *'54*
Spaceways *'53*
Three Stops to Murder *'53*

Lyn Osborn (1926-58)

The Amazing Colossal Man *'57*
Invasion of the Saucer Men *'57*

Ted Osborn (1905-87)

Charlie Chan at the Wax Museum *'40*
Buried Alive *'39*

Bud Osborne (1884-1964)

Night of the Ghouls *'59*
Gun Glory *'57*
Tribute to a Bad Man *'56*
Bride of the Monster *'55*
Border Bandits *'46*
The Caravan Trail *'46*
Outlaw of the Plains *'46*
Wild West *'46*
Border Badmen *'45*
His Brother's Ghost *'45*
Dead or Alive *'44*
Range Law *'44*
Rustler's Hideout *'44*
Wild Horse Phantom *'44*
Six Gun Gospel *'43*
Death Rides the Range *'40*
West of Pinto Basin *'40*
Wild Horse Valley *'40*
Across the Plains *'39*
Western Gold *'37*
Where Trails Divide *'37*
The Crimson Trail *'35*
Lightning Bill *'35*
The Outlaw Deputy *'35*
Ridin' Thru *'35*
Riding Speed *'35*
Rustlers of Red Dog *'35*
Deadwood Pass *'33*
Diamond Trail *'33*
Rustler's Roundup *'33*
When a Man Rides Alone *'33*
Mark of the Spur *'32*
The Riding Tornado *'32*
Battling with Buffalo Bill *'31*
Apache Kid's Escape *'30*
The Fighting Stallion *'26*

Holmes Osborne (1952-)

The Box *'09*
Meet Bill *'07*
Southland Tales *'06*
A Lot Like Love *'05*
Dreamer: Inspired by a True Story *'05*
Cheaper by the Dozen *'03*
Identity *'03*
The Quiet American *'02*
Waking Up in Reno *'02*
Donnie Darko *'01*
Crazy in Alabama *'99*
Election *'99*
The Mod Squad *'99*
From the Earth to the Moon *'98*
Affliction *'97*
That Thing You Do! *'96*

John Osborne (1929-94)

The Power of One *'92*
Get Carter *'71*

Vivienne Osborne (1896-1961)

Captain Caution *'40*
Primrose Path *'40*
Let's Sing Again *'36*
The Phantom Broadcast *'33*
Supernatural *'33*
Tomorrow at Seven *'33*
Two Seconds *'32*

Ozzy Osbourne (1948-)

Austin Powers In Goldmember *'02*
Little Nicky *'00*
The Jerky Boys *'95*
Decline of Western Civilization 2: The Metal Years *'88*
Trick or Treat *'86*

Sharon Osbourne

Garfield: A Tail of Two Kitties *'06 (V)*
It's a Boy Girl Thing *'06*

Henry Oscar (1891-1969)

The Brides of Dracula *'60*
The Spaniard's Curse *'58*
Postmark for Danger *'56*
The Greed of William Hart *'48*
The Courageous Mr. Penn *'41*
The Four Feathers *'39*
Black Limelight *'38*
The Terror *'38*
Spy of Napoleon *'36*
The Man Who Knew Too Much *'34*

Per Oscarsson (1927-)

Dreaming of Rita *'94*
House of Angels *'92*
Sleep of Death *'79*
Blockhouse *'73*
The New Land *'73*
Endless Night *'71*
The Last Valley *'71*
Secrets *'71*
The Night Visitor *'70*
Dandy in Aspic *'68*
Hunger *'66*
The Doll *'62*

Brian O'Shaughnessy (1931-2001)

Alien Chaser *'96*
Claws *'85*
Mr. Kingstreet's War *'71*

Kevin O'Shea (1915-)

The Purple Heart *'44*
A Wing and a Prayer *'44*

Marc O'Shea

I'll Sleep When I'm Dead *'03*
This Is the Sea *'96*

Michael O'Shea (1906-73)

Bloodhounds of Broadway *'52*
Fixed Bayonets! *'51*
The Underworld Story *'50*
The Big Wheel *'49*
Parole, Inc. *'49*
Threat *'49*
Smart Woman *'48*
The Last of the Redmen *'47*
Violence *'47*
It's a Pleasure *'45*
Jack London *'44*
Something for the Boys *'44*
Lady of Burlesque *'43*

Milo O'Shea (1925-)

The Butcher Boy *'97*
The Matchmaker *'97*
The Playboys *'92*
Only the Lonely *'91*
Opportunity Knocks *'90*
The Dream Team *'89*
Once a Hero *'88*
Broken Vows *'87*
Two by Forsyth *'86*
The Purple Rose of Cairo *'85*
Portrait of a Rebel: Margaret Sanger *'82*
The Verdict *'82*
A Time for Miracles *'80*
Danger in the Skies *'79*
Peter Lundy and the Medicine Hat Stallion *'77*
It's Not the Size That Counts *'74*
Theatre of Blood *'73*
Sacco & Vanzetti *'71*
The Angel Levine *'70*
Loot... Give Me Money, Honey! *'70*
Paddy *'70*
Barbarella *'68*
Romeo and Juliet *'68*
Ulysses *'67*
Carry On Cabby *'63*

Tessie O'Shea (1913-95)

Dr. Jekyll and Mr. Hyde *'68*
The Russians Are Coming, the Russians Are Coming *'66*
Immortal Battalion *'44*

Karen Oshima

One Missed Call 2 *'05*
One Missed Call *'03*

Yukari Oshima (1963-)

Supercop 2 *'93*
Fatal Chase *'92*
Interpol Connection *'92*
The Millionaire's Express *'86*

K.T. Oslin (1941-)

Murder So Sweet *'93*
The Thing Called Love *'93*

Emily Osment (1992-)

Hannah Montana: The Movie *'09*
Soccer Mom *'08*
Spy Kids 3-D: Game Over *'03*
Spy Kids 2: The Island of Lost Dreams *'02*
Sarah, Plain and Tall: Winter's End *'99*

Haley Joel Osment (1988-)

The Jungle Book 2 *'03 (V)*
Secondhand Lions *'03*
The Country Bears *'02 (V)*
A. I.: Artificial Intelligence *'01*
Pay It Forward *'00*
I'll Remember April *'99*
The Sixth Sense *'99*
Bogus *'96*
Last Stand at Saber River *'96*
Forrest Gump *'94*

Cliff Osmond (1937-)

In Search of a Golden Sky *'84*
The Adventures of Nellie Bly *'81*
Hangar 18 *'80*
Mountain Man *'77*
Joe Panther *'76*
Sharks' Treasure *'75*
Invasion of the Bee Girls *'73*
Sweet Sugar *'72*
The Fortune Cookie *'66*
Kiss Me, Stupid! *'64*

Donny Osmond (1957-)

College Road Trip *'08*
Joseph and the Amazing Technicolor Dreamcoat *'00*
Mulan *'98 (V)*
Goin' Coconuts *'78*

Lesley Osmond

House of Darkness *'48*
Mysterious Mr. Nicholson *'47*

Marie Osmond (1959-)

The Gift of Love *'90*
Goin' Coconuts *'78*
Hugo the Hippo *'76 (V)*

Yelba Osorio

Valentina's Tango *'07*
Shut Up and Kiss Me *'05*
Riot in the Streets *'96*

Jeffery Osterhage (1953-)

Sex Crimes *'92*
Big Bad John *'90*
Dark Before Dawn *'89*
Masque of the Red Death *'89*
Buckeye and Blue *'87*
South of Reno *'87*
The Shadow Riders *'82*
The Sacketts *'79*

Robert Osterloh (1918-2001)

I Bury the Living *'58*
An Annapolis Story *'55*
One Minute to Zero *'52*
Prowler *'51*
Gun Crazy *'49*

Bibi Osterwald (1918-2002)

As Good As It Gets *'97*
Great Smokey Roadblock *'76*
Bank Shot *'74*
A Fine Madness *'66*
The World of Henry Orient *'64*
Parrish *'61*

William Ostrander (1959-)

Red Heat *'85*
Christine *'84*
Mike's Murder *'84*
Fire and Ice *'83 (V)*

Ren Osugi (1951-)

Zebraman *'04*
The Twilight Samurai *'02*
Uzumaki *'00*
Charisma *'99*
Cure *'97*
Fireworks *'97*
Sonatine *'96*

Aisling O'Sullivan (1968-)

Me & Mrs. Jones *'02*
The American *'01*
The Wyvern Mystery *'00*
The War Zone *'98*
The Butcher Boy *'97*

Maureen O'Sullivan (1911-98)

The Habitation of Dragons *'91*
The River Pirates *'88*
Stranded *'87*
Hannah and Her Sisters *'86*
Peggy Sue Got Married *'86*
Too Scared to Scream *'85*
The Tall T *'57*
All I Desire *'53*
Where Danger Lives *'50*
The Big Clock *'48*
Tarzan's New York Adventure *'42*
Tarzan's Secret Treasure *'41*
Pride and Prejudice *'40*
Tarzan Finds a Son *'39*
A Day at the Races *'37*
Devil Doll *'36*
Tarzan Escapes *'36*
Anna Karenina *'35*
David Copperfield *'35*
The Barretts of Wimpole Street *'34*
Hide-Out *'34*
Tarzan and His Mate *'34*
The Thin Man *'34*
Tugboat Annie *'33*
Skyscraper Souls *'32*
Strange Interlude *'32*
Tarzan, the Ape Man *'32*
A Connecticut Yankee *'31*
Song o' My Heart *'30*
Song o' My Heart *'29*

Patton Oswalt (1969-)
Big Fan '09
The Informant! '09
Observe and Report '09
All Roads Lead Home '08
Ratatouille '07 (V)
Sex and Death 101 '07
Failure to Launch '06
Blade: Trinity '04
Starsky & Hutch '04

Akira Otaka
Charisma '99
Cure '97

Rikiya Otaka
Ringu 2 '99
Ringu '98

Hideji Otaki (1925-)
Black House '07
Minbo—Or the Gentle Art of Japanese Extortion '92
Tampopo '86
The Funeral '84
Kagemusha '80

Cheri Oteri (1962-)
Private Valentine: Blonde & Dangerous '08
Surveillance '08
Shrek the Third '07 (V)
The Ant Bully '06 (V)
Dumb and Dumberer: When Harry Met Lloyd '03
Sol Goode '01
Love & Sex '00
Scary Movie '00
Liar Liar '97

Carre Otis (1968-)
Under Heavy Fire '01
Exit in Red '97
Wild Orchid '90

Annette O'Toole (1953-)
Here on Earth '00
Final Justice '98
The Christmas Box '95
The Kennedys of Massachusetts '95
My Brother's Keeper '95
Imaginary Crimes '94
Kiss of a Killer '93
Love Matters '93
Jewels '92
White Lie '91
A Girl of the Limberlost '90
Stephen King's It '90
Love at Large '89
Cross My Heart '88
Broken Vows '87
Superman 3 '83
Cat People '82
48 Hrs. '82
Foolin' Around '80
King of the Gypsies '78
One on One '77
War Between the Tates '76
Smile '75

Peter O'Toole (1932-)
The Christmas Cottage '08
Ratatouille '07 (V)
Stardust '07
Venus '06
Casanova '05
Lassie '05
Troy '04
Bright Young Things '03
Hitler: The Rise of Evil '03
Rock My World '02
Joan of Arc '99
Molokai: The Story of Father Damien '99
Coming Home '98
FairyTale: A True Story '97
Phantoms '97
Gulliver's Travels '95
Wings of Fame '93
The Seventh Coin '92
The Dark Angel '91
King Ralph '91
The Nutcracker Prince '91 (V)
High Spirits '88
The Last Emperor '87
Club Paradise '86
Creator '85
Kim '84
Supergirl '84
Svengali '83
My Favorite Year '82
Masada '81
Caligula '80
The Stunt Man '80
Zulu Dawn '79
Power Play '78
Foxtrot '76
Rogue Male '76
Man Friday '75
Rosebud '75
Under Milk Wood '73
Man of La Mancha '72
The Ruling Class '72
Murphy's War '71
Goodbye, Mr. Chips '69
The Lion in Winter '68
Casino Royale '67
Night of the Generals '67
The Bible '66
How to Steal a Million '66
Lord Jim '65
What's New Pussycat? '65
Becket '64
Lawrence of Arabia '62
Kidnapped '60

Nobuko Otowa (1925-95)
Last War '68
Onibaba '64
The Island '61

Angelica Ott
Fight for Gold '86
Hell Hounds of Alaska '73

John Ottavino
Bob Roberts '92
Malcolm X '92

James Ottaway (1908-99)
Absolution '81
That'll Be the Day '73

Rafaela (Rafael, Raphaella) Ottiano (1888-1942)
Devil Doll '36
Curly Top '35
She Done Him Wrong '33

Barry Otto (1941-)
Australia '08
Newcastle '08
$9.99 '08 (V)
Dead Letter Office '98
Mr. Nice Guy '98
Kiss or Kill '97
Oscar and Lucinda '97
Cosi '95
Lilian's Story '95
Mr. Reliable: A True Story '95
The Custodian '94
Strictly Ballroom '92
Howling 3: The Marsupials '87
Bliss '85

Goetz Otto (1967-)
Downfall '04
The Girl of Your Dreams '99
Beowulf '98

Kevin Otto
Diamond Girl '98
Who Shot Pat? '92

Miranda Otto (1967-)
The Starter Wife '07
War of the Worlds '05
Flight of the Phoenix '04
Danny Deckchair '03
Lord of the Rings: The Return of the King '03
Close Your Eyes '02
The Healer '02
Human Nature '02
Lord of the Rings: The Two Towers '02
The Way We Live Now '02
What Lies Beneath '00
The Jack Bull '99
Dead Letter Office '98
In the Winter Dark '98
The Thin Red Line '98
Doing Time for Patsy Cline '97
The Well '97
Love Serenade '96
The Last Days of Chez Nous '92
The Nostradamus Kid '92
The 13th Floor '88

Assita Ouedraogo
La Promesse '96
Yaaba '89

Rasmane Ouedraogo
La Promesse '96
Tilai '90
Yaaba '89

Stephen Ouimette
Slings & Arrows: Season 2 '05
Heater '99

Andre Oumansky (1933-)
Spy Games '99
Othello '95
Burnt by the Sun '94
Joy House '64

Gerard Oury (1919-2006)
The Prize '63
Back to the Wall '56
The Love of Three Queens '54

Sverre Anker Ousdal (1944-)
Insomnia '97
Hamsun '96
Kristin Lavransdatter '95
The Last Place on Earth '85

Maria Ouspenskaya (1876-1949)
Frankenstein Meets the Wolfman '42
The Shanghai Gesture '42
Kings Row '41
The Wolf Man '41
Beyond Tomorrow '40
Dance, Girl, Dance '40
Dr. Ehrlich's Magic Bullet '40
Waterloo Bridge '40
Love Affair '39
The Rains Came '39
Conquest '37
Dodsworth '36

Levani Outchanechvili (1958-)
25th Hour '02
The Legend of Suram Fortress '85

Peter Outerbridge (1966-)
Saw 6 '09
Lucky Number Slevin '06
Population 436 '06
Men with Brooms '02
The Rendering '02
Lip Service '00
Mission to Mars '00
Better Than Chocolate '99
Escape from Mars '99
Escape Velocity '99
Thrill Seekers '99
Closer and Closer '96
Kissed '96
The Android Affair '95
Another Woman '94
For the Moment '94
Paris, France '94
Cool Runnings '93
Victim of Beauty '91

Kati Outinen (1961-)
The Man Without a Past '02
The Match Factory Girl '90

Park Overall (1957-)
Sparkler '99
The Good Old Boys '95
The Gambler Returns: The Luck of the Draw '93
Undercover Blues '93
The Vanishing '93
House of Cards '92
Kindergarten Cop '90
Lost Angels '89
Biloxi Blues '88
Mississippi Burning '88
Tainted '88

Kellie Overbey (1964-)
Love Thy Neighbor '02
Sweet and Lowdown '99

Lynne Overman (1887-1943)
Reap the Wild Wind '42
Roxie Hart '42
Caught in the Draft '41
Edison the Man '40
Union Pacific '39
Paris in Spring '35
Little Miss Marker '34
Midnight '34

Frank Overton (1918-67)
To Kill a Mockingbird '62
Desire Under the Elms '58

Rick Overton (1954-)
Dinner for Schmucks '10
A Plumm Summer '08
Off the Lip '04
Serial Killing 101 '04
Eight Legged Freaks '02
EDtv '99
National Lampoon's Attack of the 5 Ft. 2 Women '94
The High Crusade '92
Blind Fury '90
Earth Girls Are Easy '89
A Sinful Life '89
Million Dollar Mystery '87
Traxx '87
Odd Jobs '85
Beverly Hills Cop '84

Baard Owe (1936-)
O'Horten '09
The Kingdom 2 '97
The Kingdom '95
Medea '88
Gertrud '64

Bill Owen (1914-99)
Singleton's Pluck '84
The Comeback '77
In Celebration '75
Georgy Girl '66
Carry On Cabby '63
Carry On Regardless '61
The Hellfire Club '61
The Gay Lady '49

Chris Owen (1980-)
Dear Wendy '05
National Lampoon's Gold Diggers '04
National Lampoon's Van Wilder '02
American Pie 2 '01
Ready to Rumble '00
American Pie '99
October Sky '99
Angus '95

Clive Owen (1965-)
The Boys Are Back '09
Duplicity '09
The International '09
Elizabeth: The Golden Age '07
Shoot 'Em Up '07
Children of Men '06
Inside Man '06
The Pink Panther '06
Derailed '05
Sin City '05
Closer '04
King Arthur '04
Beyond Borders '03
I'll Sleep When I'm Dead '03
The Bourne Identity '02
Gosford Park '01
Greenfingers '00
Second Sight '99
Split Second '99
Bent '97
Croupier '97
The Rich Man's Wife '96
Century '94
The Return of the Native '94
The Magician '93
Class of '61 '92
Close My Eyes '91
Lorna Doone '90

Garry Owen (1897-1951)
Dark Mirror '46
Call of the Yukon '38
San Quentin '37
Hold Your Man '33

Harriet Owen
Return to Never Land '02 (V)
Relative Strangers '99

Lloyd Owen (1966-)
Miss Potter '06
The Republic of Love '03
Dead Gorgeous '02
Catherine Cookson's The Cinder Path '94

Michael Owen
Youth Aflame '44
Dick Tracy vs. Crime Inc. '41

Reginald Owen (1887-1972)
The Thrill of It All! '63
Red Garters '54
The Miniver Story '50
Challenge to Lassie '49
Julia Misbehaves '48
The Pirate '48
The Three Musketeers '48
Diary of a Chambermaid '46
Monsieur Beaucaire '46
Captain Kidd '45
The Valley of Decision '45
The Canterville Ghost '44
National Velvet '44
Above Suspicion '43
Madame Curie '43
Cairo '42
I Married an Angel '42
Mrs. Miniver '42
Random Harvest '42
Reunion in France '42
Somewhere I'll Find You '42
We Were Dancing '42
White Cargo '42
Woman of the Year '42
Charley's Aunt '41
Tarzan's Secret Treasure '41
They Met in Bombay '41
A Woman's Face '41
The Real Glory '39
A Christmas Carol '38
Everybody Sing '38
Rosalie '38
The Bride Wore Red '37
Conquest '37
Madame X '37
Personal Property '37
The Great Ziegfeld '36
Love on the Run '36
Rose Marie '36
A Tale of Two Cities '36
Anna Karenina '35
The Good Fairy '35
Fashions of 1934 '34
Here is My Heart '34
Of Human Bondage '34
Double Harness '33
Queen Christina '33
A Study in Scarlet '33
Ghost City '32

Rena Owen (1962-)
Nemesis Game '03
Players '03
Soul Assassin '01
Dance Me to My Song '98
When Love Comes '98
Once Were Warriors '94

Seena Owen (1894-1966)
Queen Kelly '29
Intolerance '16
The Lamb '15

Ciaran Owens
Agnes Browne '99
Angela's Ashes '99

Eamon Owens (1983-)
The Boys and Girl From County Clare '03
St. Patrick: The Irish Legend '00
The General '98
The Butcher Boy '97

Gary Owens (1936-)
Digging Up Business '91
Killcrazy '89
I'm Gonna Git You Sucka '88

Patricia Owens (1925-2000)
Hell to Eternity '60
The Fly '58
The Law and Jake Wade '58
Sayonara '57
The Happiest Days of Your Life '50

Earl Owensby (1936-)
The Rutherford County Line '87
Dogs of Hell '83
Manhunter '83
The Wolfman '82
Death Driver '78
Challenge '74

Monroe Owsley (1900-37)
Goin' to Town '35
Ex-Lady '33

Catherine Oxenberg (1961-)
The Vector File '03
Road Rage '01
Sanctimony '01
Frozen in Fear '00
The Collectors '99
The Omega Code '99
Time Served '99
Deadly Game '98
Boys Will Be Boys '97
Heaven Before I Die '96
Treacherous Beauties '94
Charles & Diana: A Palace Divided '93
Rubdown '93
Sexual Response '92
Overexposed '90
K-9000 '89
Swimsuit '89
The Lair of the White Worm '88

Ben Oxenbould
Black Water '07
Fatty Finn '84

David Oxley (1920-85)
House of the Living Dead '73
Night Ambush '57

David Oyelowo
A Raisin in the Sun '08
Sweet Nothing in My Ear '08
Five Days '07
As You Like It '06
A Sound of Thunder '05

Moishe Oysher (1907-58)
The Singing Blacksmith '38
The Cantor's Son '37

Frank Oz (1944-)
Star Wars: Episode 3—Revenge of the Sith '05 (V)
Zathura '05 (V)
Star Wars: Episode 2—Attack of the Clones '02 (V)
Monsters, Inc. '01 (V)
Muppets from Space '99 (V)
Star Wars: Episode 1—The Phantom Menace '99 (V)
Blues Brothers 2000 '98
Muppet Treasure Island '96 (V)
Innocent Blood '92
The Muppet Christmas Carol '92 (V)
Sesame Street Presents: Follow That Bird '85 (V)
Spies Like Us '85
The Muppets Take Manhattan '84 (V)
Return of the Jedi '83 (V)
The Dark Crystal '82 (V)
An American Werewolf in London '81

The Great Muppet Caper '81 (V)
The Blues Brothers '80
The Empire Strikes Back '80
The Muppet Movie '79 (V)

Eitaro (Sakae, Saka Ozawa) Ozawa (1909-88)
Sandakan No. 8 '74
The Human Condition: No Greater Love '58
Princess Yang Kwei Fei '55
Ugetsu '53
Record of a Tenement Gentleman '47

Sakae (Saka) Ozawa
See Eitaro (Sakae, Saka Ozawa) Ozawa

Shoichi Ozawa (1929-)
Black Rain '88
The Ballad of Narayama '83
The Pornographers '66

Yuya Ozeki (1996-)
The Grudge '04
Ju-On: The Grudge '03

Madeleine Ozeray (1908-89)
Crime and Punishment '35
Liliom '35

Jack Paar (1918-2004)
Love Nest '51
Walk Softly, Stranger '50
Easy Living '49

Judy Pace (1946-)
Frogs '72
Brian's Song '71
Cotton Comes to Harlem '70
Three in the Cellar '70

Lee Pace (1979-)
Marmaduke '10
Possession '09
A Single Man '09
Miss Pettigrew Lives for a Day '08
The Fall '06
The Good Shepherd '06
Infamous '06
The White Countess '05
Soldier's Girl '03

Tom Pace
Blood Orgy of the She-Devils '74
Girl in Gold Boots '69
The Astro-Zombies '67

Frederico Pacifici (1955-)
Fluke '95
Flight of the Innocent '93

Al Pacino (1940-)
88 Minutes '08
Righteous Kill '08
Ocean's Thirteen '07
Two for the Money '05
The Merchant of Venice '04
Gigli '03
The Recruit '03
Insomnia '02
People I Know '02
Simone '02
Any Given Sunday '99
The Insider '99
The Devil's Advocate '97
Donnie Brasco '96
Looking for Richard '96
Two Bits '96
City Hall '95
Heat '95
Carlito's Way '93
Glengarry Glen Ross '92
Scent of a Woman '92
Frankie and Johnny '91
Dick Tracy '90
The Godfather, Part 3 '90
Sea of Love '89
Revolution '85
Scarface '83
Author! Author! '82
The Godfather 1902-1959: The Complete Epic '81
Cruising '80
And Justice for All '79
Bobby Deerfield '77
America at the Movies '76
Dog Day Afternoon '75
The Godfather, Part 2 '74
Scarecrow '73
Serpico '73
The Godfather '72
Panic in Needle Park '71

David Packer (1962-)
The Killing Club '01
No Strings Attached '98
Silent Motive '91
The Runnin' Kind '89
Trust Me '89
You Can't Hurry Love '88

Joanna Pacula (1957-)
Forget About It '06
The Hit '01
The Art of Murder '99
Crash & Byrnes '99
My Giant '98
Virus '98
The White Raven '98
The Haunted Sea '97
Business for Pleasure '96
Heaven Before I Die '96
Not Like Us '96
Captain Nuke and the Bomber Boys '95
Timemaster '95
Deep Red '94
The Last Gasp '94
Every Breath '93
Silence of the Hams '93
Tombstone '93
Under Investigation '93
Warlock: The Armageddon '93
Black Ice '92
Eyes of the Beholder '92
Husbands and Lovers '91
Marked for Death '90
The Kiss '88
Options '88
Sweet Lies '88
Death Before Dishonor '87
Escape from Sobibor '87
Not Quite Paradise '86
Gorky Park '83

Jared Padalecki (1982-)
Friday the 13th '09
The Christmas Cottage '08
Cry_Wolf '05
House of Wax '05
New York Minute '04
A Little Inside '01

Sarah Padden (1881-1967)
My Dog Shep '46
Wild West '46
Song of Old Wyoming '45
Wildfire '45
Girl Rush '44
Range Law '44
Law and Order '42
The Mad Monster '42
Riders of the West '42
Snuffy Smith, Yard Bird '42
In Old Colorado '41
Reg'lar Fellers '41
Three Comrades '38
Exiled to Shanghai '37
Tomorrow's Children '34
Cross Examination '32
The Midnight Lady '32

Hugh Paddick (1915-2000)
Naughty Knights '71
The Killing of Sister George '69

Pilar Padilla
In the Time of the Butterflies '01
Bread and Roses '00

Robert Padilla
Twisted Nightmare '87
The Great Gundown '75

Lea Padovani (1920-91)
The Naked Maja '59
Modigliani '58

Dira Paes (1969-)
Mango Yellow '02
Chronically Unfeasible '00
The Emerald Forest '85

David Paetkau (1978-)
Final Destination 2 '03
National Lampoon's Holiday Reunion '03

Michael J. Pagan
See No Evil '06
The Gospel '05
How Stella Got Her Groove Back '98

Anita Page (1910-2008)
After Midnight '33
Jungle Bride '33
Skyscraper Souls '32
The Easiest Way '31
Reducing '31
Sidewalks of New York '31
Free and Easy '30
Broadway Melody '29
Our Modern Maidens '29
Speedway '29
Our Dancing Daughters '28

Bradley Page (1901-85)
The Affairs of Annabel '38
Mistaken Identity '36
Champagne for Breakfast '35

Diamond Dallas Page (1956-)
The Devil's Rejects '05
Ready to Rumble '00

Dorothy Page (1904-61)
Ride 'Em Cowgirl '41
The Singing Cowgirl '39
Water Rustlers '39

Ellen Page (1987-)
Inception '10
Whip It '09
Smart People '08
An American Crime '07
Juno '07
The Stone Angel '07
The Tracey Fragments '07
Hard Candy '06
X-Men: The Last Stand '06
I Downloaded a Ghost '04

Gale Page (1911-83)
Knute Rockne: All American '40
They Drive by Night '40
Amazing Dr. Clitterhouse '38
Crime School '38
Four Daughters '38

Genevieve Page (1930-)
Buffet Froid '79
The Private Life of Sherlock Holmes '70
Gun Crazy '69
Mayerling '68
Belle de Jour '67
The Day and the Hour '63
El Cid '61
Song Without End '60
Girl in His Pocket '57
Fanfan la Tulipe '51

Geraldine Page (1924-87)
Riders to the Sea '88
My Little Girl '87
Native Son '86
The Adventures of Huckleberry Finn '85
The Bride '85
The Trip to Bountiful '85
Walls of Glass '85
White Nights '85
The Dollmaker '84
Harry's War '84
Loving '84
The Pope of Greenwich Village '84
I'm Dancing as Fast as I Can '82
Honky Tonk Freeway '81
Interiors '78
Nasty Habits '77
The Rescuers '77 (V)
The Day of the Locust '75
Hazel's People '73
Pete 'n' Tillie '72
The Beguiled '70
Whatever Happened to Aunt Alice? '69
The Happiest Millionaire '67
ABC Stage 67: Truman Capote's A Christmas Memory '66
Barefoot in Athens '66
You're a Big Boy Now '66
The Three Sisters '65
Toys in the Attic '63
Sweet Bird of Youth '62
Summer and Smoke '61
Hondo '53

Grant Page (1939-)
Road Games '81
Deathcheaters '76

Harrison Page (1941-)
Carnosaur '93
Lionheart '90
Backstairs at the White House '79
Beyond the Valley of the Dolls '70

Joanna Page (1978-)
Love Actually '03
Very Annie Mary '00
David Copperfield '99

Joy Page (1924-2008)
Conquest of Cochise '53
Fighter Attack '53
Casablanca '42

Ken Page (1954-)
The Alamo '04
The Nightmare Before Christmas '93 (V)
The Kid Who Loved Christmas '90

LaWanda Page (1920-2002)
Friday '95
The Meteor Man '93
Shakes the Clown '92
Mausoleum '83
Zapped! '82
B.A.D. Cats '80

Michelle Page (1987-)
Together Again for the First Time '08
I Know Who Killed Me '07

Patti Page (1927-)
Boys' Night Out '62
Dondi '61
Elmer Gantry '60

Paul Page (1903-74)
Palmy Days '31
Pleasure '31

Tony Page (1939-84)
Q (The Winged Serpent) '82
Gangsters '79

Melinda Page Hamilton
Corporate Affairs '07
Sleeping Dogs Lie '06

Alfred Paget (1880-1925)
Intolerance '16
The Lamb '15
Battle of Elderbush Gulch '13

Debra Paget (1933-)
The Haunted Palace '63
The Mercenaries '62
Tales of Terror '62
Why Must I Die? '60
The Indian Tomb '59
Tiger of Eschnapur '59
From the Earth to the Moon '58
Journey to the Lost City '58
Omar Khayyam '57
The Last Hunt '56
Love Me Tender '56
The Ten Commandments '56
Demetrius and the Gladiators '54
Prince Valiant '54
Belles on Their Toes '52
Stars and Stripes Forever '52
Broken Arrow '50
House of Strangers '49

Nicola Pagett (1945-)
An Awfully Big Adventure '94
Privates on Parade '84
A Woman of Substance '84
Oliver's Story '78
The Seducer '69
The Viking Queen '67

Marcel Pagliero (1907-80)
Dedee d'Anvers '49
Open City '45

Stratos Pahis
The Enchantress '85
The Travelling Players '75

Liana Pai
Happy Accidents '00
The Siege '98

Janis Paige (1922-)
Natural Causes '94
Love at the Top '86
Angel on My Shoulder '80
Magic on Love Island '80
Bachelor in Paradise '69
Please Don't Eat the Daisies '60
Silk Stockings '57
Romance on the High Seas '48
Winter Meeting '48
Hollywood Canteen '44

Mabel Paige (1880-1954)
The Scar '48
Nocturne '46
Murder, He Says '45

Peter Paige
Say Uncle '05
Our America '02

Robert Paige (1910-87)
Abbott and Costello Go to Mars '53
The Green Promise '49
The Red Stallion '47
Can't Help Singing '45
Son of Dracula '43
Pardon My Sarong '42
The Monster and the Girl '41
Golden Gloves '40
Cain and Mabel '36

Yasmin Paige
Ballet Shoes '07
Wondrous Oblivion '06

Geraldine Pailhas (1971-)
5x2 '04
They Came Back '04
Don Juan DeMarco '94
Suite 16 '94

Didier Pain
On Guard! '03
My Father's Glory '91
My Mother's Castle '91

Cathy Paine
Image of Death '77
Helter Skelter '76

Heidi Paine
Wizards of the Demon Sword '94
Lethal Games '90
Wildest Dreams '90
Alien Seed '89
New York's Finest '87

Josh Pais (1964-)
Gentlemen Broncos '09
Teeth '07
Year of the Dog '07
Phone Booth '02
Scotland, PA '02
Swimming '00
Music of the Heart '99

Nestor Paiva (1905-66)
Jesse James Meets Frankenstein's Daughter '65
Ballad of a Gunfighter '64
They Saved Hitler's Brain '64
Girls! Girls! Girls! '62
Frontier Uprising '61
The Nine Lives of Elfego Baca '58
Outcasts of the City '58
The Mole People '56
Revenge of the Creature '55
Tarantula '55
Creature from the Black Lagoon '54
Five Fingers '52
Double Dynamite '51
The Great Caruso '51
Follow Me Quietly '49
Shoot to Kill '47
Fear '46
The Road to Utopia '46
The Falcon in Mexico '44
The Purple Heart '44
Hold That Ghost '41
Beau Geste '39
Prison Train '38

Maria Pakulnis (1956-)
The Decalogue '88
No End '84

Holly Palance (1950-)
The Strange Case of the End of Civilization As We Know It '93
Cast the First Stone '89
The Best of Times '86
Tuxedo Warrior '82
The Omen '76

Jack Palance (1919-2006)
Prancer Returns '01
Sarah, Plain and Tall: Winter's End '99
Treasure Island '99
Ebenezer '97
Buffalo Girls '95
City Slickers 2: The Legend of Curly's Gold '94
Cops and Robbersons '94
The Swan Princess '94 (V)
Cyborg 2 '93
Keep the Change '92
Solar Crisis '92
City Slickers '91
Batman '89
Tango and Cash '89
Bagdad Cafe '88
Gor '88
Young Guns '88
Outlaw of Gor '87
Black Cobra '83
Alone in the Dark '82
Hawk the Slayer '81
Bloody Avenger '80
Hell's Brigade: The Final Assault '80
Unknown Powers '80
Angel's Brigade '79
Cocaine Cowboys '79
The Last Ride of the Dalton Gang '79
Cop in Blue Jeans '78
One Man Jury '78
Big Boss '77
The Last Contract '77
Mr. Scarface '77
Portrait of a Hitman '77
Welcome to Blood City '77
Rulers of the City '76
The Sensuous Nurse '76
Four Deuces '75
God's Gun '75
Great Adventure '75
The Hatfields & the McCoys '75
Craze '74
Dracula '73
Oklahoma Crude '73
Sting of the West '72
Battle of the Commandos '71
Chato's Land '71
Companeros '70
The Horsemen '70
The McMasters '70
Monte Walsh '70
Desperados '69
Deadly Sanctuary '68
Dr. Jekyll and Mr. Hyde '68

Strange Case of Dr. Jekyll & Mr. Hyde *'68*
Torture Garden *'67*
Alice Through the Looking Glass *'66*
The Professionals *'66*
Contempt *'64*
Barabbas *'62*
The Battle of Austerlitz *'60*
The Mongols *'60*
Revak the Rebel *'60*
Lonely Man *'57*
Attack! *'56*
Requiem for a Heavyweight *'56*
The Big Knife *'55*
I Died a Thousand Times *'55*
The Silver Chalice *'54*
Arrowhead *'53*
Man in the Attic *'53*
Second Chance *'53*
Shane *'53*
Sudden Fear *'52*
The Halls of Montezuma *'50*
Panic in the Streets *'50*

Joe Palese
The Box *'03*
Sinners *'89*

David Palffy (1969-)
House of the Dead *'03*
He Sees You When You're Sleeping *'02*
Storm *'87*

Adrianne Palicki (1983-)
Legion *'10*
Women in Trouble *'09*

Ron Palillo (1954-)
Committed *'91*
Hellgate *'89*
SnakeEater *'89*
Doin' Time *'85*

Michael Palin (1943-)
Fierce Creatures *'96*
Mr. Toad's Wild Ride *'96*
American Friends *'91*
A Fish Called Wanda *'88*
Brazil *'85*
A Private Function *'84*
Monty Python's The Meaning of Life *'83*
The Missionary *'82*
The Secret Policeman's Other Ball *'82*
Secret Policeman's Private Parts *'81*
Time Bandits *'81*
Monty Python's Life of Brian *'79*
All You Need Is Cash *'78*
Jabberwocky *'77*
Monty Python and the Holy Grail *'75*
And Now for Something Completely Different *'72*
John Cleese on How to Irritate People *'68*

Anna Palk (1943-90)
The Nightcomers *'72*
Fahrenheit 451 *'66*

Aleksa Palladino (1980-)
Before the Devil Knows You're Dead *'07*
Wrong Turn 2: Dead End *'07*
Storytelling *'01*
The Adventures of Sebastian Cole *'99*
Red Dirt *'99*
Wrestling with Alligators *'98*
Manny & Lo *'96*

Erik Palladino (1968-)
Buried *'10*
Crash and Burn *'07*
Return to House on Haunted Hill *'07*
The Thirst *'06*
Alchemy *'05*
L.A. Dicks *'05*
Latter Days *'04*
Finder's Fee *'01*
Life Without Dick *'01*
U-571 *'00*

Can't Hardly Wait *'98*

Kumar Pallana (1919-)
Bomb the System *'05*
The Terminal *'04*
The Royal Tenenbaums *'01*

Anita Pallenberg (1944-)
Cheri *'09*
Mister Lonely *'07*
Performance *'70*
Dillinger Is Dead *'69*
Barbarella *'68*
Candy *'68*

Eugene Pallette (1889-1954)
The Cheaters *'45*
Pin-Up Girl *'44*
Sensations of 1945 *'44*
Step Lively *'44*
The Gang's All Here *'43*
Heaven Can Wait *'43*
It Ain't Hay *'43*
The Kansan *'43*
Big Street *'42*
The Male Animal *'42*
Silver Queen *'42*
The Bride Came C.O.D. *'41*
The Lady Eve *'41*
The Mark of Zorro *'40*
Young Tom Edison *'40*
First Love *'39*
Mr. Smith Goes to Washington *'39*
The Adventures of Robin Hood *'38*
100 Men and a Girl *'37*
Topper *'37*
The Ghost Goes West *'36*
My Man Godfrey *'36*
Stowaway *'36*
Bordertown *'35*
Steamboat Round the Bend *'35*
The Kennel Murder Case *'33*
The Half Naked Truth *'32*
Shanghai Express *'32*
Strangers of the Evening *'32*
Gun Smoke *'31*
The Sea God *'30*
The Love Parade *'29*
The Virginian *'29*
Mantrap *'26*
The Three Musketeers *'21*
Intolerance *'16*
The Birth of a Nation *'15*

Joseph Pallister
Broadcast Bombshells *'95*
Bikini Bistro *'94*

Gabriella Pallotta (1938-)
Hero of Rome *'63*
The Mongols *'60*
Il Grido *'57*
The Roof *'56*

Mimmo Palmara (1928-81)
A Long Ride From Hell *'68*
Two Gladiators *'64*
The Trojan Horse *'62*
The Last Days of Pompeii *'60*

Ulf Palme (1920-93)
Dreams *'55*
Miss Julie *'50*

Betsy Palmer (1929-)
Waltzing Anna *'06*
The Fear: Halloween Night *'99*
Still Not Quite Human *'92*
Friday the 13th, Part 2 *'81*
Friday the 13th *'80*
The Last Angry Man *'59*
The Tin Star *'57*
The Long Gray Line *'55*
Mister Roberts *'55*
Queen Bee *'55*

Byron Palmer (1925-)
Ma and Pa Kettle at Waikiki *'55*
Man in the Attic *'53*

Geoffrey Palmer (1927-)
The Pink Panther 2 *'09*
Peter Pan *'03*
Mrs. Brown *'97*
Tomorrow Never Dies *'97*
Stalag Luft *'93*
A Question of Attribution *'91*
Christabel *'89*
A Fish Called Wanda *'88*

Gregg (Hunter) Palmer (1927-)
The Rebel Set *'59*
From Hell It Came *'57*
Zombies of Moratau *'57*
The Creature Walks among Us *'56*
To Hell and Back *'55*
Francis Goes to West Point *'52*

Gretchen Palmer (1961-)
I Got the Hook-Up *'98*
Chopper Chicks in Zombietown *'91*

Hubbel Palmer
Humble Pie *'07*
The Sasquatch Gang *'06*

Keke Palmer (1993-)
Shrink *'09*
The Longshots *'08*
Cleaner *'07*
Jump In! *'07*
Akeelah and the Bee *'06*
Madea's Family Reunion *'06*
Knights of the South Bronx *'05*

Lewis Lemperuer Palmer
The Disappeared *'08*
Don't Tell *'05*

Lilli Palmer (1914-86)
The Holcroft Covenant *'85*
The Boys from Brazil *'78*
What the Peeper Saw *'72*
Murders in the Rue Morgue *'71*
Sebastian *'68*
The Amorous Adventures of Moll Flanders *'65*
The Miracle of the White Stallions *'63*
Adorable Julia *'62*
The Counterfeit Traitor *'62*
Conspiracy of Hearts *'60*
But Not for Me *'59*
Modigliani *'58*
The Devil in Silk *'56*
The Long Dark Hall *'51*
My Girl Tisa *'48*
Body and Soul *'47*
Beware of Pity *'46*
Cloak and Dagger *'46*
Chamber of Horrors *'40*
The Secret Agent *'36*

Maria Palmer (1924-81)
Outcasts of the City *'58*
By the Light of the Silvery Moon *'53*
Days of Glory *'43*

Rebecca Palmer
Blood Trails *'06*
Intimacy *'00*

Renzo Palmer (1929-88)
Street Law *'74*
Sting of the West *'72*
Eagles Over London *'69*

Shirley Palmer (1908-2000)
Somewhere in Sonora *'33*
Campus Knights *'29*

Teresa Palmer (1986-)
Bedtime Stories *'08*
Restraint *'08*
December Boys *'07*
The Grudge 2 *'06*

Zoie Palmer
Godsend *'04*
The Reagans *'04*

Chazz Palminteri (1952-)
Yonkers Joe *'08*
Body Armour *'07*
Arthur and the Invisibles *'06 (V)*
A Guide to Recognizing Your Saints *'06*
Little Man *'06*
Push *'06*
Running Scared *'06*
Animal *'05*
Hoodwinked *'05 (V)*
In the Mix *'05*
Noel *'04*
One Last Ride *'03*
Poolhall Junkies *'02*
Down to Earth *'01*
Boss of Bosses *'99*
Excellent Cadavers *'99*
Stuart Little *'99 (V)*
Analyze This *'98*
Hurlyburly *'98*
Scarred City *'98*
Diabolique *'96*
Faithful *'95*
Jade *'95*
The Last Word *'95*
Mulholland Falls *'95*
The Usual Suspects *'95*
Bullets over Broadway *'94*
The Perez Family *'94*
A Bronx Tale *'93*
Innocent Blood *'92*
There Goes the Neighborhood *'92*
Oscar *'91*

Carlos Palomino (1949-)
Die Watching *'93*
Geronimo: An American Legend *'93*
My Samurai *'92*
Nasty Hero *'89*
Strangers Kiss *'83*

Gwyneth Paltrow (1973-)
Iron Man 2 *'10*
Two Lovers *'09*
Iron Man *'08*
The Good Night *'07*
Infamous *'06*
Running with Scissors *'06*
Proof *'05*
Sky Captain and the World of Tomorrow *'04*
Sylvia *'03*
View from the Top *'03*
Austin Powers In Goldmember *'02*
Possession *'02*
The Anniversary Party *'01*
The Royal Tenenbaums *'01*
Shallow Hal *'01*
Bounce *'00*
Duets *'00*
The Talented Mr. Ripley *'99*
Hush *'98*
A Perfect Murder *'98*
Shakespeare in Love *'98*
Great Expectations *'97*
Sliding Doors *'97*
Emma *'96*
Hard Eight *'96*
Moonlight and Valentino *'95*
The Pallbearer *'95*
Seven *'95*
Jefferson in Paris *'94*
Mrs. Parker and the Vicious Circle *'94*
Flesh and Bone *'93*
Malice *'93*
Hook *'91*

Luciana Paluzzi (1931-)
The Klansman *'74*
Medusa *'74*
Hit Men *'73*
Manhunt *'73*
Black Gunn *'72*
Captain Nemo and the Underwater City *'69*
99 Women *'69*
A Black Veil for Lisa *'68*
The Green Slime *'68*
Murder for Sale *'68*
Chuka *'67*

One-Eyed Soldiers *'67*
Thunderball *'65*
Muscle Beach Party *'64*
Return to Peyton Place *'61*
Carlton Browne of the F.O. *'59*
Tiger of Eschnapur *'59*
Journey to the Lost City *'58*

Rebecca Pan
In the Mood for Love *'00*
Days of Being Wild *'91*

Danielle Panabaker (1987-)
Friday the 13th *'09*
Mr. Brooks *'07*
Empire Falls *'05*
Sky High *'05*
Yours, Mine & Ours *'05*

Kay Panabaker (1990-)
Fame *'09*
Moondance Alexander *'07*
Nancy Drew *'07*
The Prince and the Pauper *'07*

Alessandra Panaro (1939-)
The Bacchantes *'63*
Conquest of Mycene *'63*
Executioner of Venice *'63*
Rocco and His Brothers *'60*

Richard Panebianco (1971-)
Dogfight *'91*
China Girl *'87*

Michael Panes (1963-)
(Untitled) *'09*
Broken English *'07*
Watching the Detectives *'07*
Fabled *'02*
The Anniversary Party *'01*

Hayden Panettiere (1989-)
Hoodwinked Too! Hood vs. Evil *'10 (V)*
The Cove *'09*
I Love You, Beth Cooper *'09*
The Good Student *'08*
Shanghai Kiss *'07*
The Architect *'06*
Bring It On: All or Nothing *'06*
Ice Princess *'05*
Racing Stripes *'05*
Raising Helen *'04*
Normal *'03*
The Affair of the Necklace *'01*
Joe Somebody *'01*
Dinosaur *'00 (V)*
Remember the Titans *'00*
A Bug's Life *'98 (V)*

Andrew Pang
Petty Crimes *'02*
The Corruptor *'99*

Franklin Pangborn (1889-1958)
Romance on the High Seas *'48*
I'll Be Yours *'47*
The Sin of Harold Diddlebock *'47*
The Great Moment *'44*
Hail the Conquering Hero *'44*
His Butler's Sister *'44*
Honeymoon Lodge *'43*
Two Weeks to Live *'43*
Call Out the Marines *'42*
The Palm Beach Story *'42*
The Flame of New Orleans *'41*
A Girl, a Guy and a Gob *'41*
Never Give a Sucker an Even Break *'41*
Sullivan's Travels *'41*
The Bank Dick *'40*
Christmas in July *'40*
Spring Parade *'40*
Fifth Avenue Girl *'39*
Topper Takes a Trip *'39*
Bluebeard's Eighth Wife *'38*
Carefree *'38*

Four's a Crowd *'38*
Just Around the Corner *'38*
Vivacious Lady *'38*
All Over Town *'37*
Dangerous Holiday *'37*
Easy Living *'37*
Hats Off *'37*
It Happened in Hollywood *'37*
Living on Love *'37*
The Mandarin Mystery *'37*
A Star Is Born *'37*
Doughnuts & Society *'36*
My Man Godfrey *'36*
Tango *'36*
King Kelly of the U.S.A. *'34*
Flying Down to Rio *'33*
The Half Naked Truth *'32*
Getting Gertie's Garter *'27*
Exit Smiling *'26*

Corrado Pani (1936-2005)
Watch Me When I Kill *'77*
The Girl with a Suitcase *'60*

Ty Panitz (1999-)
Santa Buddies *'09 (V)*
Because I Said So *'07*
Yours, Mine & Ours *'05*

Archie Panjabi (1972-)
Traitor *'08*
A Mighty Heart *'07*
A Good Year *'06*
The Constant Gardener *'05*
Bend It Like Beckham *'02*
East Is East *'99*

Stuart Pankin (1946-)
Miss Cast Away *'04*
Chasing Destiny *'00*
Honey, We Shrunk Ourselves *'97*
Down, Out and Dangerous *'95*
Beanstalk *'94*
Father and Scout *'94*
I Love Trouble *'94*
Squanto: A Warrior's Tale *'94*
Silence of the Hams *'93*
Betrayal of the Dove *'92*
The Vagrant *'92*
Life Stinks *'91*
Mannequin 2: On the Move *'91*
Arachnophobia *'90*
That's Adequate *'90*
Second Sight *'89*
Fatal Attraction *'87*
Love at Stake *'87*
Dirt Bike Kid *'86*
The Hollywood Knights *'80*

John Pankow (1954-)
Bride Wars *'09*
The Object of My Affection *'98*
A Stranger Among Us *'92*
Mortal Thoughts *'91*
Year of the Gun *'91*
Johnny Be Good *'88*
Monkey Shines *'88*
Talk Radio *'88*
To Live & Die in L.A. *'85*

Joe Pantoliano (1951-)
Cats & Dogs: The Revenge of Kitty Galore *'10 (V)*
Canvas *'06*
Deceit *'06*
Larry the Cable Guy: Health Inspector *'06*
Wedding Daze *'06*
The Moguls *'05*
Racing Stripes *'05 (V)*
Second Best *'05*
Bad Boys 2 *'03*
Daredevil *'03*
The Adventures of Pluto Nash *'02*
Cats & Dogs *'01 (V)*
A Better Way to Die *'00*
Memento *'00*
Ready to Rumble *'00*
Black and White *'99*
The Life Before This *'99*
The Matrix *'99*
New Blood *'99*
Hoods *'98*

The Taxman '98
U.S. Marshals '98
Tinseltown '97
Top of the World '97
Bound '96
Natural Enemy '96
Bad Boys '95
The Immortals '95
The Last Word '95
Steal Big, Steal Little '95
Baby's Day Out '94
Robot in the Family '94
The Spy Within '94
Teresa's Tattoo '94
Calendar Girl '93
Dangerous Heart '93
The Fugitive '93
Me and the Kid '93
Three of Hearts '93
Through the Eyes of a Killer '92
Used People '92
Zandalee '91
El Diablo '90
The Last of the Finest '90
Short Time '90
Downtown '89
Nightbreaker '89
Tales from the Crypt '89
The In Crowd '88
Midnight Run '88
Empire of the Sun '87
La Bamba '87
Scenes from the Goldmine '87
The Squeeze '87
Running Scared '86
The Goonies '85
Mean Season '85
Eddie and the Cruisers '83
The Final Terror '83
Risky Business '83
Idolmaker '80

Cecile Paoli

Sharpe's Revenge '97
Sharpe's Waterloo '97
Riders '88

Connor Paolo

Snow Angels '07
Alexander '04

Michael (Mike) Papajohn (1964-)

I Know Who Killed Me '07
Spider-Man 3 '07
The Last Shot '04
Spider-Man '02
Whacked! '02
The Animal '01
Rustin '01
Charlie's Angels '00
For Love of the Game '99
My Giant '98
Spawn '97
Eraser '96
The Indian in the Cupboard '95
Naked Souls '95
Dominion '94
Little Big League '94
The Babe '92
The Last Boy Scout '91
Predator 2 '90

Irene Papas (1926-)

Captain Corelli's Mandolin '01
Yerma '99
The Odyssey '97
Party '96
Jacob '94
High Season '88
Sweet Country '87
Into the Night '85
The Assisi Underground '84
Erendira '83
Lion of the Desert '81
Christ Stopped at Eboli '79
Sidney Sheldon's Bloodline '79
Iphigenia '77
The Message '77
Moses '76
Don't Torture a Duckling '72
1931: Once Upon a Time in New York '72
Trojan Women '71
Anne of the Thousand Days '69
A Dream of Kings '69
Z '69
The Brotherhood '68
The Moon-Spinners '64
Zorba the Greek '64
The Guns of Navarone '61
The Unfaithfuls '60
Tribute to a Bad Man '56
Attila '54

Ike Pappas (1933-)

The Package '89
Moon over Parador '88

Anna Paquin (1982-)

The Courageous Heart of Irena Sendler '09
Trick 'r Treat '08
Blue State '07
Bury My Heart at Wounded Knee '07
X-Men: The Last Stand '06
The Squid and the Whale '05
Steamboy '05 (V)
X2: X-Men United '03
Darkness '02
25th Hour '02
Buffalo Soldiers '01
Almost Famous '00
Finding Forrester '00
X-Men '00
It's the Rage '99
She's All That '99
A Walk on the Moon '99
Hurlyburly '98
Amistad '97
The Member of the Wedding '97
Fly Away Home '96
Jane Eyre '96
The Piano '93

Vanessa Paradis (1972-)

The Girl on the Bridge '98
Elisa '94

John Paragon (1954-)

UHF '89
Elvira, Mistress of the Dark '88
Pee-wee's Big Adventure '85
Eating Raoul '82
The Pee-wee Herman Show '82

Kiri Paramore

Ned Kelly '03
Doing Time for Patsy Cline '97
The Last Days of Chez Nous '92
Flirting '89

Rawiri Paratene

The Legend of Johnny Lingo '03
Whale Rider '02

J.D. Pardo

The Burning Plain '08
Supercross: The Movie '05
A Cinderella Story '04
Hope Ranch '02

Michael Parducci

Hit and Runway '01
Gravesend '97

Kip Pardue (1976-)

Princess: A Modern Fairytale '08
Ripple Effect '07
South of Pico '07
The Wizard of Gore '07
Wasted '06
Imaginary Heroes '05
Loggerheads '05
Undiscovered '05
The Heart Is Deceitful Above All Things '04
The Iris Effect '04
Devil's Pond '03
Thirteen '03
This Girl's Life '03
The Rules of Attraction '02
Driven '01
Road to Riches '01
Remember the Titans '00

Jessica Pare (1982-)

Suck '09
Wicker Park '04
Posers '02
Lost and Delirious '01
Stardom '00

Michael Pare (1958-)

Direct Contact '09
Dark World '08
100 Feet '08
The Perfect Sleep '08
Seed '08
Tunnel Rats '08
BloodRayne 2: Deliverance '07
BloodRayne '06
Heart of America '03
Blackwoods '02
Sanctimony '01
Peril '00
In the Dead of Space '99
Men of Means '99
The Debt '98
Hope Floats '98
Falling Fire '97
Mission of Death '97
Strip Search '97
2103: Deadly Wake '97
Bad Moon '96
Carver's Gate '96
Deadly Heroes '96
Sworn Enemies '96
The Dangerous '95
Raging Angels '95
Triplecross '95
Village of the Damned '95
Solar Force '94
Warriors '94
Point of Impact '93
Blink of an Eye '92
Into the Sun '92
Sunset Heat '92
The Closer '91
Killing Streets '91
The Last Hour '91
Dragonfight '90
Moon 44 '90
Eddie and the Cruisers 2: Eddie Lives! '89
World Gone Wild '88
Women's Club '87
Instant Justice '86
Space Rage '86
The Philadelphia Experiment '84
Streets of Fire '84
Eddie and the Cruisers '83

Marisa Paredes (1946-)

Four Last Songs '06
The Devil's Backbone '01
All About My Mother '99
Life Is Beautiful '98
Doctor Chance '97
Deep Crimson '96
Talk of Angels '96
Three Lives and Only One Death '96
The Flower of My Secret '95
High Heels '91
In a Glass Cage '86
Dark Habits '84

Mila Parely (1917-)

Three Stops to Murder '53
Le Plaisir '52
Beauty and the Beast '46
The Rules of the Game '39

Monique Parent (1965-)

The Pornographer '00
The Catcher '98
James Dean: Live Fast, Die Young '97
Tender Flesh '97
Illegal Affairs '96
Mirror, Mirror 3: The Voyeur '96
Dark Secrets '95
Masseuse '95
Midnight Confessions '95
The Perfect Gift '95
Stripshow '95
Married People, Single Sex 2: For Better or Worse '94
Play Time '94
Buford's Beach Bunnies '92

Judy Parfitt (1935-)

Little Dorrit '08
Asylum '05
Girl with a Pearl Earring '03
Berkeley Square '98
Ever After: A Cinderella Story '98
Wilde '97
Element of Doubt '96
The Return of the Borrowers '96
Dolores Claiborne '94
Midnight's Child '93
The Blackheath Poisonings '92
Dark Obsession '90
Getting It Right '89
The Charmer '87
Maurice '87
Office Romances '86
The Jewel in the Crown '84
Hamlet '69

Woodrow Parfrey (1922-84)

Backstairs at the White House '79
The Outlaw Josey Wales '76
Oklahoma Crude '73
Dirty Harry '71
Sam Whiskey '69

Anne Parillaud (1960-)

Sex is Comedy '02
The Man in the Iron Mask '98
Shattered Image '98
Frankie Starlight '95
Six Days, Six Nights '94
Map of the Human Heart '93
Innocent Blood '92
La Femme Nikita '91

Jerry Paris (1925-86)

Evil Roy Slade '71
Zero Hour! '57
D-Day, the Sixth of June '56
Marty '55
The Caine Mutiny '54
The Wild One '54

Sarah Parish (1968-)

The Wedding Date '05
Sirens '02

Annie Parisse (1975-)

Definitely, Maybe '08
Monster-in-Law '05
Prime '05
How to Lose a Guy in 10 Days '03

Ji-yeon Park

Time '06
The Wishing Stairs '03
Memento Mori '00

Joong-Hoon Park (1964-)

The Truth About Charlie '02
Double Edge '97

Kris Park

Ordinary Sinner '02
Drive Me Crazy '99
I Love You, I Love You Not '97

Ray Park (1974-)

G.I. Joe: The Rise of Cobra '09
What We Do Is Secret '07
Slayer '06
Ballistic: Ecks vs. Sever '02
X-Men '00
Star Wars: Episode 1—The Phantom Menace '99

Reg Park (1928-2007)

Hercules in the Haunted World '64
Hercules, Prisoner of Evil '64
Hercules and the Captive Women '63

Yong-woo Park

Blood Rain '05
The Warrior '01

Lar Park-Lincoln (1961-)

Friday the 13th, Part 7: The New Blood '88
House 2: The Second Story '87
Princess Academy '87

Evan Dexter Parke (1968-)

All Roads Lead Home '08
King Kong '05
Brother's Keeper '02
Nightstalker '02
Planet of the Apes '01
The Replacements '00
The Cider House Rules '99

MacDonald Parke (1891-1960)

The Mouse That Roared '59
Summertime '55

Anthony Ray Parker

The Marine '06
The Matrix '99

Cecil Parker (1897-1971)

Oh! What a Lovely War '69
A Study in Terror '66
Lady L '65
Carry On Jack '63
Heavens Above '63
The Brain '62
On the Fiddle '61
The Pure Hell of St. Trinian's '61
The Wreck of the Mary Deare '59
A Tale of Two Cities '58
The Admirable Crichton '57
Court Jester '56
The Ladykillers '55
The Detective '54
Tony Draws a Horse '51
Under Capricorn '49
The Weaker Sex '49
Captain Boycott '47
The Magic Bow '47
Caesar and Cleopatra '46
Dangerous Moonlight '41
The Stars Look Down '39
Housemaster '38
The Lady Vanishes '38
Storm in a Teacup '37
The Man Who Lived Again '36

Cecilia Parker (1914-93)

Andy Hardy's Double Life '42
Grand Central Murder '42
Andy Hardy Meets Debutante '40
Andy Hardy Gets Spring Fever '39
Love Finds Andy Hardy '38
Hollywood Cowboy '37
Roll Along Cowboy '37
Sweetheart of the Navy '37
Ah, Wilderness! '35
Naughty Marietta '35
Honor of the Range '34
The Lost Jungle '34
Mystery Ranch '34
Rainbow Ranch '33
Riders of Destiny '33
Trail Drive '33
Tombstone Canyon '32

Chris Parker

Red Nights '87
Permanent Vacation '84

Corey Parker (1965-)

Mr. & Mrs. Loving '96
A Mother's Prayer '95
Broadway Bound '92
The Lost Language of Cranes '92
I'm Dangerous Tonight '90
White Palace '90
Big Man on Campus '89
How I Got into College '89
Biloxi Blues '88

Ed Parker (1931-90)

Curse of the Pink Panther '83
Kill the Golden Goose '79

Eddie (Ed, Eddy, Edwin) Parker (1900-60)

The Secret Code '42
God's Country and the Man '37
Ghost Rider '35
Lucky Texan '34

Eleanor Parker (1922-)

Dead on the Money '91
She's Dressed to Kill '79
The Bastard '78
Fantasy Island '76
Home for the Holidays '72
Maybe I'll Come Home in the Spring '71
Maybe I'll Be Home in the Spring '70
Hans Brinker '69
Tiger and the Pussycat '67
The Oscar '66
The Sound of Music '65
Panic Button '62
Return to Peyton Place '61
Home from the Hill '60
A Hole in the Head '59
The King and Four Queens '56
Interrupted Melody '55
The Man with the Golden Arm '55
Many Rivers to Cross '55
Naked Jungle '54
Valley of the Kings '54
Above and Beyond '53
Escape from Fort Bravo '53
Scaramouche '52
Detective Story '51
Caged '50
Chain Lightning '50
Three Secrets '50
It's a Great Feeling '49
Escape Me Never '47
Never Say Goodbye '46
Pride of the Marines '45
Hollywood Canteen '44
Mission to Moscow '43

Erica Parker

See Erica Durance

F. William Parker

Warm Blooded Killers '01
Jack Frost '97
Hard Eight '96

Fess Parker (1926-)

Hell Is for Heroes '62
Alias Jesse James '59
The Jayhawkers '59
The Light in the Forest '58
Old Yeller '57
Davy Crockett and the River Pirates '56
The Great Locomotive Chase '56
Westward Ho, the Wagons! '56
Battle Cry '55
Davy Crockett, King of the Wild Frontier '55
Them! '54
Island in the Sky '53

Jameson Parker (1947-)

Curse of the Crystal Eye '93
Spy '89
Prince of Darkness '87
American Justice '86
Agatha Christie's A Caribbean Mystery '83
White Dog '82
Callie and Son '81
A Small Circle of Friends '80
Anatomy of a Seduction '79
The Gathering: Part 2 '79

Jean Parker (1915-2005)

Apache Uprising '66
A Lawless Street '55
The Gunfighter '50
Rolling Home '48
Bluebeard '44
Dead Man's Eyes '44
Lady in the Death House '44

Navy Way '44
One Body Too Many '44
Flying Blind '41
Power Dive '41
Beyond Tomorrow '40
Knights of the Range '40
The Flying Deuces '39
The Ghost Goes West '36
The Texas Rangers '36
Operator 13 '34
Two Alone '34
Gabriel Over the White House '33
Lady for a Day '33
Little Women '33
Rasputin and the Empress '33

Kim Parker

Fiend without a Face '58
Fire Maidens from Outer Space '56

Lara Parker (1942-)

Foxfire Light '82
The Solitary Man '82
The Lazarus Syndrome '79
Race with the Devil '75
Night of Dark Shadows '71
Hi, Mom! '70

Lloyd "Sunshine" Parker (1928-99)

Spittin' Image '83
Cannery Row '82

Mary-Louise Parker (1964-)

Solitary Man '10
The Spiderwick Chronicles '08
The Assassination of Jesse James by the Coward Robert Ford '07
Romance & Cigarettes '05
Saved! '04
Angels in America '03
Master Spy: The Robert Hanssen Story '02
Pipe Dream '02
Red Dragon '02
Cupid & Cate '00
The Five Senses '99
Goodbye, Lover '99
Let the Devil Wear Black '99
The Simple Life of Noah Dearborn '99
Legalese '98
The Maker '98
Saint Maybe '98
Murder in Mind '97
Portrait of a Lady '96
Reckless '95
Sugartime '95
Boys on the Side '94
Bullets over Broadway '94
The Client '94
A Place for Annie '94
Mr. Wonderful '93
Naked in New York '93
Fried Green Tomatoes '91
Grand Canyon '91
Longtime Companion '90
Signs of Life '89

Michael Parker (1969-)

Kill Line '91
My Own Private Idaho '91

Molly Parker (1972-)

Hollywoodland '06
The Wicker Man '06
Nine Lives '05
The Confessor '04
Break a Leg '03
Marion Bridge '02
Max '02
Men with Brooms '02
Pure '02
The Center of the World '01
Rare Birds '01
The War Bride '01
Suspicious River '00
Waking the Dead '00
The Five Senses '99
Sunshine '99
Wonderland '99
In the Shadows '98
Kissed '96
Hole in the Sky '95

Anything for Love '93

Monica Parker

Coming Out Alive '84
Improper Channels '82

Nathaniel Parker (1962-)

The Secret Life of Bees '08
The Great Debaters '07
Pride '07
Stardust '07
Bleak House '05
The Haunted Mansion '03
Inspector Lynley Mysteries: A Great Deliverance '01
Lover's Prayer '99
Vanity Fair '99
David '97
Far from the Madding Crowd '97
Into Thin Air: Death on Everest '97
Beverly Hills Ninja '96
Othello '95
A Village Affair '95
Squanto: A Warrior's Tale '94
Catherine Cookson's The Black Candle '92
Wide Sargasso Sea '92
Hamlet '90
Piece of Cake '88

Nicole Ari Parker (1970-)

Imagine That '09
Welcome Home Roscoe Jenkins '08
King's Ransom '05
Brown Sugar '02
Dancing in September '00
The Loretta Claiborne Story '00
Remember the Titans '00
Blue Streak '99
Loving Jezebel '99
Spark '98
200 Cigarettes '98
Boogie Nights '97
The End of Violence '97
The Incredibly True Adventure of Two Girls in Love '95

Noelle Parker (1969-)

Newsbreak '00
L.A. Rules: The Pros and Cons of Breathing '94
Lethal Lolita—Amy Fisher: My Story '92
Ernest Saves Christmas '88
Twisted '86
The Whoopee Boys '86

Norman Parker

Question of Faith '93
Killing Hour '84

Paula Jai Parker (1969-)

Cover '08
Animal '05
Hustle & Flow '05
The Proud Family Movie '05 (V)
My Baby's Daddy '04
She Hate Me '04
Phone Booth '02
30 Years to Life '01
The Breaks '99
Woo '97
Sprung '96
Tales from the Hood '95
Cosmic Slop '94

Sachi (MacLaine) Parker (1956-)

Welcome Home, Roxy Carmichael '90
Riders to the Sea '88
Peggy Sue Got Married '86
The Dancing Princesses '84

Sarah Jessica Parker (1965-)

Sex and the City 2 '10
Did You Hear About the Morgans? '09
Sex and the City: The Movie '08

Smart People '08
Failure to Launch '06
Strangers with Candy '06
The Family Stone '05
Life Without Dick '01
State and Main '00
Dudley Do-Right '99
Extreme Measures '96
The First Wives Club '96
Mars Attacks! '96
The Substance of Fire '96
Til There Was You '96
If Lucy Fell '95
Miami Rhapsody '95
The Sunshine Boys '95
Ed Wood '94
Hocus Pocus '93
Striking Distance '93
Honeymoon in Vegas '92
L.A. Story '91
Flight of the Navigator '86
Girls Just Want to Have Fun '85
Going for the Gold: The Bill Johnson Story '85
Somewhere Tomorrow '85
First Born '84
Footloose '84

Suzy Parker (1932-2003)

The Interns '62
The Best of Everything '59
Ten North Frederick '58
Funny Face '57

Trey Parker (1969-)

Team America: World Police '04 (V)
South Park: Bigger, Longer and Uncut '99 (V)
BASEketball '98
Orgazmo '98
Cannibal! The Musical '96

Willard Parker (1912-96)

Bandit Queen '51
David Harding, Counterspy '50
Great Jesse James Raid '49
You Gotta Stay Happy '48
A Slight Case of Murder '38

Gerard Parkes

A House Divided '00
Rescuers: Stories of Courage "Two Women" '97
It Takes Two '95
The Last Winter '89
Speaking Parts '89
Spasms '82
The Apprentice '71

Shaun Parkes (1972-)

The Mummy Returns '01
Human Traffic '99

Barbara Parkins (1942-)

Calendar Girl Murders '84
To Catch a King '84
Breakfast in Paris '81
Bear Island '80
Law of the Land '76
Shout at the Devil '76
Christina '74
Asylum '72
Puppet on a Chain '72
Snatched '72
The Deadly Trap '71
The Mephisto Waltz '71
Valley of the Dolls '67

Katharine Parkinson

Pirate Radio '09
Easy Virtue '08

Bert Parks (1914-92)

The Freshman '90
Shining Star '75

Catherine Parks (1956-)

Body of Influence '93
Friday the 13th, Part 3 '82

James Parks (1968-)

Death Proof '07
The Listening '06
Spent '00

You Know My Name '99

Larry Parks (1914-75)

Love Is Better Than Ever '52
Jolson Sings Again '49
Down to Earth '47
Her Husband's Affairs '47
The Jolson Story '46
Destroyer '43
Power of the Press '43
Blondie Goes to College '42
The Boogie Man Will Get You '42
You Were Never Lovelier '42
Harmon of Michigan '41

Michael Parks (1938-)

Smokin' Aces 2: Assassins' Ball '10
Three Priests '08
The Assassination of Jesse James by the Coward Robert Ford '07
The Dead One '07
Death Proof '07
Planet Terror '07
The Listening '06
Kill Bill Vol. 2 '04
Kill Bill Vol. 1 '03
Big Bad Love '02
From Dusk Till Dawn 3: The Hangman's Daughter '99
Wicked '98
Julian Po '97
Niagara, Niagara '97
From Dusk Till Dawn '95
Death Wish 5: The Face of Death '94
Stranger by Night '94
Storyville '92
The Hitman '91
The China Lake Murders '90
Gore Vidal's Billy the Kid '89
Welcome to Spring Break '88
Arizona Heat '87
Stamp of a Killer '87
Club Life '86
The Return of Josey Wales '86
Chase '85
French Quarter Undercover '85
Savannah Smiles '82
Hard Country '81
ffolkes '80
The Evictors '79
Breakthrough '78
Midnight Auto Supply '78
Night Cries '78
The Private Files of J. Edgar Hoover '77
Sidewinder One '77
The Last Hard Men '76
The Savage Bees '76
Then Came Bronson '68
The Bible '66

Tammy Parks (1965-)

Attack of the 60-Foot Centerfold '95
Play Time '94

Trina Parks

The Muthers '76
Darktown Strutters '74
Diamonds Are Forever '71

Parkyakarkus (Harry Einstein) (1904-58)

Yank in Libya '42
Strike Me Pink '36

Steve Parlavecchio (1970-)

The First to Go '97
Bandwagon '95
Amongst Friends '93

Dita Parlo (1906-71)

Grand Illusion '37
L'Atalante '34
Homecoming '28

Chris Parnell (1967-)

Labor Pains '09
Harold '08
Hot Rod '07
Walk Hard: The Dewey Cox Story '07
I'm Reed Fish '06

Ira & Abby '06
Anchorman: The Legend of Ron Burgundy '04
Evil Alien Conquerors '02

Emory Parnell (1892-1979)

Man of the West '58
Pardners '56
Ma and Pa Kettle at Home '54
Shadows of Tombstone '53
Lost in Alaska '52
Ma and Pa Kettle at the Fair '52
Ma and Pa Kettle Back On the Farm '51
Trail of Robin Hood '50
The Show-Off '46
Colonel Effingham's Raid '45
Casanova Brown '44
Miracle of Morgan's Creek '44
I Married a Witch '42
They All Kissed the Bride '42

Marriam Parris

Maryam '00
Club Vampire '98

Helen Parrish (1924-59)

Overland Mail '42
Sunset Serenade '42
They All Kissed the Bride '42
X Marks the Spot '42
You'll Find Out '40
First Love '39
Three Smart Girls Grow Up '39
Little Tough Guys '38
Mad About Music '38
Big Trail '30

Hunter Parrish (1987-)

It's Complicated '09
RV '06
Down in the Valley '05

Julie Parrish (1940-2003)

The Doberman Gang '72
Fireball 500 '66
Paradise, Hawaiian Style '66

Leslie Parrish (1935-)

The Invisible Strangler '76
The Giant Spider Invasion '75
Sex and the Single Girl '64
For Love or Money '63
The Manchurian Candidate '62
Li'l Abner '59

Steve Parrish

Scanners 3: The Takeover '92
Midnight '89

David Parry (1954-)

Auntie Lee's Meat Pies '92
Dr. Caligari '89
The Lost Platoon '89

Natasha Parry (1930-)

Haunted: The Ferryman '74
Oh! What a Lovely War '69
The Rough and the Smooth '59
Crow Hollow '52

Tom Parsekian

Club Life '86
Hot Resort '85

Frederick Parslow

Wrangler '88
The Last Wave '77

Estelle Parsons (1927-)

Empire Falls '05
The Love Letter '98
Looking for Richard '96
That Darn Cat '96
A Private Matter '92
Dick Tracy '90
Come Along with Me '84
Gentleman Bandit '81
Backstairs at the White House '79

Foreplay '75
For Pete's Sake '74
I Never Sang for My Father '70
I Walk the Line '70
Watermelon Man '70
Don't Drink the Water '69
Rachel, Rachel '68
Bonnie & Clyde '67

Jim Parsons (1973-)

The Great New Wonderful '06
Garden State '04

Karyn Parsons (1968-)

13 Moons '02
The Ladies Man '00
Mixing Nia '98
Gulliver's Travels '95
Major Payne '95
Class Act '91

Mike Parsons

The Ravagers '65
The Walls of Hell '64

Milton Parsons

Castle in the Desert '42
Dead Men Tell '41

Nancy Parsons (1942-2001)

Lakota Woman: Siege at Wounded Knee '94
Wishman '93
Ladybugs '92
Porky's Revenge '85
Porky's 2: The Next Day '83
Sudden Impact '83
Porky's '82
Motel Hell '80

Percy Parsons (1878-1944)

Dangerous Moonlight '41
Rhodes '36
Power '34
Blackmail '29

Dolly Parton (1946-)

Hannah Montana: The Movie '09
Frank McKlusky, C.I. '02
Jackie's Back '99
Unlikely Angel '97
The Beverly Hillbillies '93
Straight Talk '92
Steel Magnolias '89
A Smoky Mountain Christmas '86
Rhinestone '84
The Best Little Whorehouse in Texas '82
9 to 5 '80

Julia Parton (1964-)

Good Girls Don't '95
Vice Academy 3 '91

Ross Partridge

Baghead '08
Amityville: A New Generation '93

Adam Pascal (1970-)

Rent '05
School of Rock '03
SLC Punk! '99

Christine Pascal (1953-96)

Le Grand Chemin '87
Sincerely Charlotte '86
Maids of Wilko '79
Spoiled Children '77
The Best Way '76
The Clockmaker '73

Mary Ann Pascal (1958-)

Lethal Lolita—Amy Fisher: My Story '92
Writer's Block '91

Olivia Pascal (1957-)

Bloody Moon '83
C.O.D. '83

Isabelle Pasco (1966-)

Invisible Circus '00
Sous Sol '96

Prospero's Books '91
High Frequency '88

Nicholas Pasco

The Undertaker's Wedding '97
Red Blooded 2 '96

Richard Pasco (1926-)

Mrs. Brown '97
The Watcher in the Woods '81
Rasputin the Mad Monk '66
The Gorgon '64
Sword of Sherwood Forest '60
Room at the Top '59

Adrian Pasdar (1965-)

Home Movie '08
Secondhand Lions '03
The Big Day '99
Mutiny '99
A Brother's Kiss '97
Wounded '97
Just Like a Woman '95
The Pompatus of Love '95
The Last Good Time '94
Carlito's Way '93
The Ghost Brigade '93
Grand Isle '92
The Lost Capone '90
Vital Signs '90
Cookie '89
Torn Apart '89
Made in USA '88
Near Dark '87
Streets of Gold '86
Top Gun '86

Pier Paolo Pasolini (1922-75)

The Canterbury Tales '71
The Decameron '70
Oedipus Rex '67

Giorgio Pasotti (1973-)

After Midnight '04
The Last Kiss '01

David Pasquesi

I Want Someone to Eat Cheese With '06
Strangers with Candy '06

Cyndi Pass

Hindsight '97
The Night Caller '97
Serial Killer '95
The Force '94
Scanner Cop '94
Bounty Tracker '93
Deadbolt '92
Desperate Motives '92
Mission of Justice '92
Bikini Island '91

George Pastell (1976-)

Vendetta for the Saint '68
The Stranglers of Bombay '60
The Mummy '59
The Gambler & the Lady '52

Reagan Pasternak (1977-)

Just Buried '07
Cake '05
Verdict in Blood '02
Jailbait! '00

Earl Pastko

Just Business '08
Subhuman '04
Masterminds '96
The Sweet Hereafter '96
Eclipse '94
Highway 61 '91

Rosana Pastor (1960-)

Mad Love '01
The Break '97
Land and Freedom '95

Vincent Pastore (1946-)

College Road Trip '08
Doughboys '08
The Devil's Dominoes '07
The Last Request '06
Bachelor Party Vegas '05
Remedy '05
Revolver '05
Shark Tale '04 (V)
A Tale of Two Pizzas '03
This Thing of Ours '03
American Cousins '02
Deuces Wild '02
Serving Sara '02
Made '01
Blue Moon '00
Hitman's Journal '99
The Hurricane '99
Mickey Blue Eyes '99
A Slight Case of Murder '99
Under Hellgate Bridge '99
Mafia! '98
Witness to the Mob '98
Gotti '96
Walking and Talking '96
West New York '96
The Jerky Boys '95
Money Train '95
It Could Happen to You '94
Carlito's Way '93
The Ref '93
Awakenings '90
Goodfellas '90
True Love '89

Robert Pastorelli (1954-2004)

Be Cool '05
Women vs. Men '02
Rodgers & Hammerstein's South Pacific '01
Bait '00
Modern Vampires '98
A Simple Wish '97
Eraser '96
Michael '96
The Yarn Princess '94
The Paint Job '93
Sister Act 2: Back in the Habit '93
Striking Distance '93
Folks! '92
Dances with Wolves '90
Beverly Hills Cop 2 '87

Willie Pastrano (1935-97)

Alligator Alley '72
Wild Rebels '71

Patachou (1918-)

Belphegar: Phantom of the Louvre '01
The Adventures of Felix '99
French Can-Can '55

Michael Pataki (1938-)

One More Chance '90
Death House '88
Halloween 4: The Return of Michael Myers '88
The Underachievers '88
American Anthem '86
Remo Williams: The Adventure Begins '85
Rocky 4 '85
Delinquent School Girls '84
Dead and Buried '81
The Last Word '80
Love at First Bite '79
On the Edge: The Survival of Dana '79
The Onion Field '79
When Every Day Was the Fourth of July '78
Zoltan... Hound of Dracula '78
The Amazing Spider-Man '77
The Bat People '74
The Last Porno Flick '74
The Baby '72
Grave of the Vampire '72
Dirt Gang '71

Elsa Pataky (1976-)

Snakes on a Plane '06
Beyond Re-Animator '03

Wally Patch (1888-1970)

Calling Paul Temple '48
Butler's Dilemma '43
Cottage to Let '41
Night Train to Munich '40
Inspector Hornleigh '39
Pygmalion '38
Don Quixote '35
The Private Life of Henry VIII '33

Michael Pate (1920-2008)

Howling 3: The Marsupials '87
Camel Boy '84 (V)
Return of Captain Invincible '83
The Singing Nun '66
McLintock! '63
Tower of London '62
Curse of the Undead '59
Green Mansions '59
Westbound '58
The Oklahoman '56
Seventh Cavalry '56
A Lawless Street '55
King Richard and the Crusaders '54
Hondo '53
Houdini '53
Julius Caesar '53
Face to Face '52
Five Fingers '52
The Strange Door '51

Dev Patel

The Last Airbender '10
Slumdog Millionaire '08

Bill Paterson (1945-)

Little Dorrit '08
Miss Potter '06
Doctor Zhivago '03
Crush '02
Wives and Daughters '01
Heart '99
The Match '99
Hilary and Jackie '98
Retribution '98
Spice World: The Movie '97
The Crow Road '96
Chaplin '92
The Object of Beauty '91
Truly, Madly, Deeply '91
Traffik '90
The Witches '90
The Adventures of Baron Munchausen '89
The Rachel Papers '89
Coming Up Roses '87
Dutch Girls '87
Hidden City '87
Defense of the Realm '85
Comfort and Joy '84
The Killing Fields '84
A Private Function '84
The Ploughman's Lunch '83

Mandy Patinkin (1952-)

Pinero '01
Strange Justice: The Clarence Thomas and Anita Hill Story '99
Lulu on the Bridge '98
Hombres Armados '97
The Hunchback '97
Broken Glass '96
Squanto: A Warrior's Tale '94
The Music of Chance '93
The Doctor '91
True Colors '91
Dick Tracy '90
Impromptu '90
Alien Nation '88
The House on Carroll Street '88
The Princess Bride '87
Sunday in the Park with George '86
Follies in Concert '85
Maxie '85
Daniel '83
Yentl '83
Ragtime '81
Night of the Juggler '80
French Postcards '79
Last Embrace '79
The Big Fix '78

Tatjana Patitz (1966-)

Restraining Order '99
Rising Sun '93

Angela Paton

The Final Season '07
American Wedding '03
United States of Leland '03
The Con '98
Trapped in Paradise '94
Groundhog Day '93
Dirty Harry '71

Laurie Paton

The Amy Fisher Story '93
Norman's Awesome Experience '88

Jason Patric (1966-)

The Losers '10
Downloading Nancy '08
Walker Payne '06
The Alamo '04
Narc '02
Your Friends & Neighbors '98
Incognito '97
Speed 2: Cruise Control '97
Sleepers '96
The Journey of August King '95
Geronimo: An American Legend '93
Denial: The Dark Side of Passion '91
Rush '91
After Dark, My Sweet '90
Frankenstein Unbound '90
The Beast '88
The Lost Boys '87
Solarbabies '86
Toughlove '85

Dennis Patrick (1918-2002)

The Air Up There '94
Heated Vengeance '87
Choices '81
Missiles of October '74
Dear Dead Delilah '72
Joe '70
The Time Travelers '64

Dorothy Patrick (1922-87)

Men of the Fighting Lady '54
Thunder Pass '54
Torch Song '53
Follow Me Quietly '49
New Orleans '47

Gail Patrick (1911-80)

Brewster's Millions '45
We Were Dancing '42
Love Crazy '41
Doctor Takes a Wife '40
My Favorite Wife '40
King of Alcatraz '38
Mad About Music '38
Wives under Suspicion '38
Stage Door '37
Murder With Pictures '36
My Man Godfrey '36
Mississippi '35
Death Takes a Holiday '34
Murder at the Vanities '34
Wagon Wheels '34
Badmen of Nevada '33
Murders in the Zoo '33
The Mysterious Rider '33
The Phantom Broadcast '33
To the Last Man '33

Gregory Patrick

A Woman Obsessed '93
Sexpot '88

Jason Patrick

My Sister's Keeper '09
In the Valley of Elah '07

Lee Patrick (1911-82)

Black Bird '75
7 Faces of Dr. Lao '63
Summer and Smoke '61
Pillow Talk '59
Vertigo '58
Caged '50
The Fuller Brush Girl '50
Inner Sanctum '48
Gambler's Choice '44
Mrs. Parkington '44
In This Our Life '42
Somewhere I'll Find You '42
Footsteps in the Dark '41
The Maltese Falcon '41
Fisherman's Wharf '39
Invisible Stripes '39
Law of the Underworld '38

Marcus Patrick

Descent '07
Love and Other Four Letter Words '07

Nigel Patrick (1913-81)

Mackintosh Man '73
The Executioner '70
Battle of Britain '69
The Virgin Soldiers '69
Johnny Nobody '61
The League of Gentlemen '60
The Trials of Oscar Wilde '60
Sapphire '59
Raintree County '57
The Pickwick Papers '54
Grand National Night '53
Encore '52
The Sound Barrier '52
The Browning Version '51
Pandora and the Flying Dutchman '51
Morning Departure '50
Trio '50
Uneasy Terms '48

Robert Patrick (1958-)

Alien Trespass '09
The Men Who Stare at Goats '09
Strange Wilderness '08
Balls of Fury '07
Bridge to Terabithia '07
Firewall '06
Flags of Our Fathers '06
The Marine '06
Walk the Line '05
Ladder 49 '04
Charlie's Angels: Full Throttle '03
Backflash '01
Eye See You '01
Spy Kids '01
Texas Rangers '01
All the Pretty Horses '00
Angels Don't Sleep Here '00
Mexico City '00
Rogue Force '99
Tactical Assault '99
A Texas Funeral '99
The Faculty '98
Forgotten City '98
From Dusk Till Dawn 2: Texas Blood Money '98
Perfect Assassins '98
Asylum '97
Cop Land '97
The Only Thrill '97
Striptease '96
Decoy '95
Double Dragon '94
Hong Kong '97 '94
The Last Gasp '94
Body Shot '93
Fire in the Sky '93
Last Action Hero '93
Zero Tolerance '93
The Cool Surface '92
Terminator 2: Judgment Day '91
Die Hard 2: Die Harder '90
Future Hunters '88
Eye of the Eagle '87
Behind Enemy Lines '85

Luana Patten (1938-96)

Follow Me, Boys! '66
Johnny Tremain & the Sons of Liberty '58
Rock, Pretty Baby '56
So Dear to My Heart '49

Elizabeth Patterson (1875-1966)

Tall Story '60
Pal Joey '57
Intruder in the Dust '49
Welcome Stranger '47
Colonel Effingham's Raid '45
Lady on a Train '45
Follow the Boys '44
The Sky's the Limit '43
I Married a Witch '42
My Sister Eileen '42
Remember the Night '40
Bulldog Drummond's Bride '39
Bluebeard's Eighth Wife '38
Go West, Young Man '36
Hide-Out '34
Hold Your Man '33
A Bill of Divorcement '32
No Man of Her Own '32

James Patterson (1932-72)

Castle Keep '69
Lilith '64

Jay Patterson (1954-)

Excessive Force 2: Force on Force '95
Nobody's Fool '94
McBain '91
Double Exposure: The Story of Margaret Bourke-White '89
D.O.A. '88
Nadine '87
Street Smart '87
Heaven Help Us '85

John D. Patterson (1940-2005)

Helltown '38
Forlorn River '37

Kenneth Patterson

Private Hell 36 '54
Hard, Fast and Beautiful '51

Lee Patterson (1929-)

Bullseye! '90
Chato's Land '71
He Lives: The Search for the Evil One '67
Jack the Ripper '60
The Spaniard's Curse '58
The Key Man '57
The Story of Esther Costello '57
Time Lock '57
Above Us the Waves '56

Lorna Patterson (1956-)

The Impostor '84
Airplane! '80

Marne Patterson (1980-)

Remember the Daze '07
Pope Dreams '06
Camp Nowhere '94

Neva Patterson (1922-)

Women of Valor '86
V '83
The Runaways '75
David and Lisa '62
An Affair to Remember '57
Desk Set '57
Solid Gold Cadillac '56

Pat Patterson

The Body Shop '72
Gas-s-s-s! '70
Moonshine Mountain '64

Rocky Patterson (1945-)

Time Tracers '97
The Dark Dealer '95
Armed for Action '92
Blood on the Badge '92
Nail Gun Massacre '86

Ross Patterson (1977-)

Stuntmen '09
Garden Party '08
Strike '07
The New Guy '02

Sarah Patterson (1972-)

Tick Tock Lullaby '07
Do I Love You? '02
Snow White '89
The Company of Wolves '85

Scott Patterson (1958-)

Saw 5 '08
Her Best Move '07
Saw 4 '07
Alien Nation: Dark Horizon '94
Little Big League '94

Cold Room '84
Oxford Blues '84

Barbara Payton (1927-67)

Four Sided Triangle '53
Bride of the Gorilla '51
Drums in the Deep South '51
Kiss Tomorrow Goodbye '50
Only the Valiant '50
Great Jesse James Raid '49
Trapped '49

Pamela Payton-Wright (1941-)

In Dreams '98
Resurrection '80

Nello Pazzafini

A Long Ride From Hell '68
Death Ray '67
Fort Yuma Gold '66

Rock Peace

Killer Tomatoes Strike Back '90
Return of the Killer Tomatoes! '88
Attack of the Killer Tomatoes '77

Mary Peach (1934-)

Disraeli '79
Ballad in Blue '66
A Gathering of Eagles '63
No Love for Johnnie '60
Room at the Top '59

Trevor Peacock (1931-)

Fred Claus '07
Madame Bovary '00
A Christmas Carol '99
For Roseanna '96
Neil Gaiman's NeverWhere '96

E.J. Peaker (1942-)

The Banker '89
Hello, Dolly! '69

Adele Pearce

See Pamela Blake

Alice Pearce (1913-66)

The Glass Bottom Boat '66
Dear Brigitte '65
The Belle of New York '52

Craig Pearce

The Seventh Floor '93
Vicious '88

Guy Pearce (1967-)

The Road '09
Bedtime Stories '08
Fragments '08
The Hurt Locker '08
Traitor '08
Death Defying Acts '07
First Snow '07
Factory Girl '06
The Proposition '05
Two Brothers '04
The Count of Monte Cristo '02
The Hard Word '02
Till Human Voices Wake Us '02
The Time Machine '02
Memento '00
Rules of Engagement '00
Ravenous '99
A Slipping Down Life '99
L.A. Confidential '97
Flynn '96
Dating the Enemy '95
The Adventures of Priscilla, Queen of the Desert '94
Heaven Tonight '93
The Hunting '92

Jacqueline Pearce (1943-)

Princess Caraboo '94
White Mischief '88
Don't Raise the Bridge, Lower the River '68
Plague of the Zombies '66
The Reptile '66

Joanne Pearce

Morons from Outer Space '85

Whoops Apocalypse '83

Mary Vivian Pearce

Pecker '98
Serial Mom '94
Cry-Baby '90
Hairspray '88
Polyester '81
Desperate Living '77
Female Trouble '74
Pink Flamingos '72
Multiple Maniacs '70
Mondo Trasho '69

Slade Pearce (1995-)

Air Bud 6: Air Buddies '06
Yours, Mine & Ours '05

Patricia Pearcy

Delusion '80
Squirm '76

Aaron Pearl (1972-)

Montana Sky '07
All I Want '02
The Spring '00

Barry Pearl (1950-)

Avenging Angel '85
Grease '78

Randy Pearlstein (1971-)

Dead Man on Campus '97
Revenge of the Radioactive Reporter '91

Corey Pearson (1974-)

Jiminy Glick in LaLa Wood '05
Going Greek '01
Summer Catch '01

David Pearson

Masters of Horror: Sounds Like '06
Tomb '86

Drew Pearson (1897-1969)

The Day the Earth Stood Still '51
Betrayal from the East '44

James Anthony Pearson

Control '07
Kidnapped '05

Neil Pearson (1959-)

The State Within '06
Bridget Jones: The Edge of Reason '04
Rhodes '97
Fever Pitch '96
The Secret Rapture '94

Richard Pearson (1918-)

Pirates '86
Thirteenth Reunion '81
Therese Raquin '80
The Woman in Question '50

Virginia Pearson (1886-1958)

Lightning Hutch '26
The Taxi Mystery '26
The Phantom of the Opera '25
The Wizard of Oz '25

Harold (Hal) Peary (1908-85)

Clambake '67
Wetbacks '56
Gildersleeve on Broadway '43
The Great Gildersleeve '43
Here We Go Again! '42
Seven Days' Leave '42
Look Who's Laughing '41

Patsy Pease (1956-)

Improper Conduct '94
He Knows You're Alone '80

Sierra Pecheur

Kalifornia '93
Bronco Billy '80
3 Women '77

Bob Peck (1945-99)

The Miracle Maker: The Story of Jesus '00 (V)

FairyTale: A True Story '97
Smilla's Sense of Snow '96
Surviving Picasso '96
Jurassic Park '93
Catherine Cookson's The Black Velvet Gown '92
Slipstream '89
After Pilkington '88
The Kitchen Toto '87
Edge of Darkness '86
Parker '84

Cecilia Peck (1958-)

Blue Flame '93
The Portrait '93
Ambition '91
Torn Apart '89
My Best Friend Is a Vampire '88
Wall Street '87

George Peck

Curse of the Puppet Master: The Human Experiment '98
Dawn of the Mummy '82

Gregory Peck (1916-2003)

Moby Dick '98
The Portrait '93
Cape Fear '91
Other People's Money '91
Old Gringo '89
Amazing Grace & Chuck '87
The Scarlet & the Black '83
The Blue and the Gray '82
Sea Wolves '81
The Boys from Brazil '78
MacArthur '77
The Omen '76
Billy Two Hats '74
Shoot Out '71
I Walk the Line '70
The Chairman '69
MacKenna's Gold '69
Marooned '69
The Stalking Moon '69
Arabesque '66
Mirage '66
Behold a Pale Horse '64
Captain Newman, M.D. '63
How the West Was Won '63
To Kill a Mockingbird '62
Cape Fear '61
The Guns of Navarone '61
Beloved Infidel '59
On the Beach '59
Pork Chop Hill '59
The Big Country '58
The Bravados '58
Designing Woman '57
The Man in the Gray Flannel Suit '56
Moby Dick '56
Roman Holiday '53
The Snows of Kilimanjaro '52
The World in His Arms '52
Captain Horatio Hornblower '51
David and Bathsheba '51
The Gunfighter '50
Only the Valiant '50
Twelve o'Clock High '49
Gentleman's Agreement '47
The Paradine Case '47
Duel in the Sun '46
The Yearling '46
Spellbound '45
The Valley of Decision '45
The Keys of the Kingdom '44
Days of Glory '43

J. Eddie Peck (1958-)

Blind Heat '00
To Grandmother's House We Go '94
Lambada '89
Curse 2: The Bite '88
Dangerously Close '86

Josh Peck (1986-)

Aliens in the Attic '09 (V)
Ice Age: Dawn of the Dinosaurs '09 (V)
What Goes Up '09
Drillbit Taylor '08
The Wackness '08

Ice Age: The Meltdown '06 (V)
Special '06
Mean Creek '04
Max Keeble's Big Move '01

Tony Peck (1956-)

Carnosaur 3: Primal Species '96
Die Hard: With a Vengeance '95
Fit to Kill '93
The Magic Bubble '93
Hard Hunted '92
Inside Edge '92
Poor Little Rich Girl: The Barbara Hutton Story '87
Brenda Starr '86

Sam Peckinpah (1925-84)

The Visitor '80
Gunfire '78
Invasion of the Body Snatchers '56
An Annapolis Story '55

Chris Pederson

Point Break '91
Platoon '86
Suburbia '83

Tom Pedi

The Iceman Cometh '73
The Iceman Cometh '60

David Peel (1920-82)

The Brides of Dracula '60
The Hands of Orlac '60

Nia Peeples (1961-)

Connor's War '06
Inside Out '05
Half Past Dead '02
Alone with a Stranger '99
Blues Brothers 2000 '98
Poodle Springs '98
Tower of Terror '97
Bloodhounds 2 '96
Robin Cook's Terminal '96
Mr. Stitch '95
Deadlock 2 '94
Improper Conduct '94
Return to Lonesome Dove '93
I Don't Buy Kisses Anymore '92
Deepstar Six '89
Swimsuit '89
North Shore '87

Joan Peers (1911-75)

The Tip-Off '31
Applause '29

Lisa Peers (1956-)

Glass '90
Solo '77

Amanda Peet (1972-)

2012 '09
$5 a Day '08
What Doesn't Kill You '08
The X Files: I Want to Believe '08
The Ex '07
Martian Child '07
Griffin & Phoenix '06
A Lot Like Love '05
Melinda and Melinda '05
Syriana '05
The Whole Ten Yards '04
Identity '03
Something's Gotta Give '03
Changing Lanes '02
High Crimes '02
Igby Goes Down '02
Saving Silverman '01
Isn't She Great '00
Two Ninas '00
Whipped '00
The Whole Nine Yards '00
Body Shots '99
1999 '98
Southie '98
Ellen Foster '97
Grind '96
One Fine Day '96
She's the One '96

Simon Pegg (1970-)

Ice Age: Dawn of the Dinosaurs '09 (V)

Star Trek '09
How to Lose Friends & Alienate People '08
The Good Night '07
Hot Fuzz '07
Run, Fatboy, Run '07
Big Nothing '06
Mission: Impossible 3 '06
George A. Romero's Land of the Dead '05
Shaun of the Dead '04

Luke Pegler

The Condemned '07
See No Evil '06

Edward Peil, Sr. (1883-1959)

The Lone Rider in Frontier Fury '41
Trigger Men '41
The Gay Buckaroo '32
Justice Rides Again '32
Local Badman '32
$50,000 Reward '25
The Dragon Painter '19

Mary Beth Peil

Mirrors '08
The List '07
The Reagans '04
Neil Simon's The Odd Couple 2 '98

Ashley Peldon (1984-)

Aliens in the Attic '09 (V)
Night Skies '07
Get a Clue! '98
With Friends Like These '98
Cats Don't Dance '97 (V)
Deceived '91

Courtney Peldon (1981-)

InAlienable '08
Mortuary '05
National Lampoon's Adam & Eve '05
Wild Grizzly '99

Pele (1940-)

Hot Shot '86
A Minor Miracle '83
Victory '81

Lisa Pelikan (1954-)

Color of Justice '97
Into the Badlands '92
Return to the Blue Lagoon '91
Lionheart '90
Ghoulies '84
Swing Shift '84
The Best Little Girl in the World '81
Jennifer '78
Julia '77

Valentine Pelka (1956-)

Under the Tuscan Sun '03
The Last of the Blonde Bombshells '00
Ivanhoe '97
First Knight '95
Monsignor Quixote '91
Rowing with the Wind '88
Hold the Dream '86

Oana Pellea

I Really Hate My Job '07
High Tension '03

Raymond Pellegrin (1925-2007)

Street War '76
Taste of Death '68
Scandal Man '67
Le Deuxieme Souffle '66
Imperial Venus '63
A Woman of Rome '56
Napoleon '55

Frank Pellegrino (1957-)

Friends and Family '01
Execution of Justice '99
Mickey Blue Eyes '99
Tarantella '95

Mark Pellegrino (1965-)

An American Affair '09
The Number 23 '07

Caffeine '06
Capote '05
Twisted '04
The Hunted '03
Mulholland Drive '01
Say It Isn't So '01
Drowning Mona '00
Midnight Witness '93
Prayer of the Rollerboys '91
Blood & Concrete: A Love Story '90

Clara Peller (1903-87)

Moving Violations '85
The Stuff '85

Andree Pelletier (1950-)

Third Walker '79
Outrageous! '77

Michelle-Barbara Pelletier

Twist '03
P.T. Barnum '99
La Deroute '98
The Lotus Eaters '93

Yves Pelletier (1961-)

2 Seconds '98
Karmina '96

Mark Pellington (1965-)

Almost Famous '00
Jerry Maguire '96

Matti Pellonpaa (1951-95)

La Vie de Boheme '93
Night on Earth '91
Zombie and the Ghost Train '91
Ariel '89
Leningrad Cowboys Go America '89

Meeno Peluce (1970-)

Nightstalker '81
Scout's Honor '80
The Amityville Horror '79

Ana Luisa Peluffo (1929-)

The Living Head '59
The New Invisible Man '58

Ron Pember (1934-)

Suspicion '87
Bullshot '83
The Land That Time Forgot '75

Steve Pemberton

Mr. Bean's Holiday '07
Lassie '05
Under the Greenwood Tree '05

George Pembroke (1900-72)

The Black Dragons '42
Dawn Express '42
I Killed That Man '42
Gangs, Inc. '41
Buried Alive '39

Candela Pena (1973-)

Take My Eyes '03
Torremolinos 73 '03
All About My Mother '99
Running Out of Time '94

Elizabeth Pena (1959-)

Nothing Like the Holidays '08
Adrift in Manhattan '07
Dragon Wars '07
Goal 2: Living the Dream '07
Love Comes Lately '07
How the Garcia Girls Spent Their Summer '05
The Lost City '05
Sueno '05
Transamerica '05
The Incredibles '04 (V)
Impostor '02
ZigZag '02
On the Borderline '01
Things Behind the Sun '01
Tortilla Soup '01
Seven Girlfriends '00
Aldrich Ames: Traitor Within '98

Dee Snider's Strangeland '98
Highway Hitcher '98
Rush Hour '98
The Second Civil War '97
Contagious '96
Free Willy 2: The Adventure Home '95
The Invaders '95
It Came from Outer Space 2 '95
Lone Star '95
Across the Moon '94
Dead Funny '94
Fugitive Among Us '92
The Waterdance '91
Blue Steel '90
Drug Wars: The Camarena Story '90
Jacob's Ladder '90
Vibes '88
*batteries not included '87
La Bamba '87
Down and Out in Beverly Hills '86
Crossover Dreams '85
They All Laughed '81
Thief '81
Times Square '80
El Super '79

Julio Pena (1912-72)
Horror Express '72
The Werewolf vs. the Vampire Woman '70
Satanik '69

Michael Pena (1976-)
Observe and Report '09
The Lucky Ones '08
Lions for Lambs '07
Shooter '07
World Trade Center '06
Crash '05
Little Athens '05
United States of Leland '03
Buffalo Soldiers '01
Bellyfruit '99
Running Free '94

Beverly Penberthy (1949-)
Judas Kiss '98
Bloodsucking Pharoahs of Pittsburgh '90

Austin Pendleton (1940-)
Lovely by Surprise '07
Bad City '06
The Notorious Bettie Page '06
Raising Flagg '06
Christmas With the Kranks '04
Finding Nemo '03 (V)
Uptown Girls '03
A Beautiful Mind '01
The 4th Floor '99
Joe the King '99
Men of Means '99
Amistad '97
A River Made to Drown In '97
The Mirror Has Two Faces '96
The Proprietor '96
Trial and Error '96
Two Days in the Valley '96
Home for the Holidays '95
Guarding Tess '94
Four Eyes and Six Guns '93
Mr. Nanny '93
My Boyfriend's Back '93
Rain Without Thunder '93
My Cousin Vinny '92
The Ballad of the Sad Cafe '91
Mr. & Mrs. Bridge '90
Hello Again '87
Short Circuit '86
Talk to Me '84
Simon '80
Starting Over '79
Great Smokey Roadblock '76
The Front Page '74
The Thief Who Came to Dinner '73
What's Up, Doc? '72
Catch-22 '70
Petulia '68

Cedric Pendleton (1973-)
Summer Catch '01
Nothin' 2 Lose '00

Nat Pendleton (1895-1967)
Buck Privates Come Home '47
Scared to Death '46
Northwest Passage '40
At the Circus '39
The Secret of Dr. Kildare '39
Shopworn Angel '38
Gangway '37
Sing Me a Love Song '37
The Great Ziegfeld '36
Reckless '35
Manhattan Melodrama '34
Sing and Like It '34
The Thin Man '34
Penthouse '33
The Sign of the Cross '33
Hell Fire Austin '32
Horse Feathers '32
Blonde Crazy '31

Steve Pendleton (1908-84)
I Married a Woman '56
Sky Liner '49
Seas Beneath '31

Peng Peng
Vengeance is a Golden Blade '69
The Cave of the Silken Web '67

Thaao Penghlis (1945-)
Les Patterson Saves the World '90
The Lookalike '90
Altered States '80

Susan Penhaligon (1949-)
Leopard in the Snow '78
Patrick '78
Soldier of Orange '78
Count Dracula '77
Nasty Habits '77
Bouquet of Barbed Wire '76
The Confessional '75
The Land That Time Forgot '75
No Sex Please—We're British '73

Bruce Penhall (1960-)
Enemy Gold '93
Fit to Kill '93
Hard Hunted '92
Do or Die '91
Picasso Trigger '89
Savage Beach '89

Lea Penman (1895-1962)
We're No Angels '55
Fancy Pants '50

Christopher Penn (1965-2006)
Holly '07
The Darwin Awards '06
After the Sunset '04
Starsky & Hutch '04
Shelter Island '03
Murder by Numbers '02
Stealing Harvard '02
American Pie 2 '01
Corky Romano '01
Cement '99
The Florentine '98
One Tough Cop '98
Trail of a Serial Killer '98
Deceiver '97
The Boys Club '96
The Funeral '96
Fist of the North Star '95
Mulholland Falls '95
To Wong Foo, Thanks for Everything, Julie Newmar '95
Under the Hula Moon '95
Imaginary Crimes '94
Beethoven's 2nd '93
Best of the Best 2 '93
Josh and S.A.M. '93
The Music of Chance '93
The Pickle '93
Short Cuts '93
True Romance '93
Reservoir Dogs '92
Futurekick '91
Mobsters '91
Leather Jackets '90
Best of the Best '89
Made in USA '88
At Close Range '86
Pale Rider '85
Footloose '84
The Wild Life '84
All the Right Moves '83
Rumble Fish '83

Kal Penn (1977-)
Harold & Kumar Escape from Guantanamo Bay '08
Epic Movie '07
The Namesake '06
National Lampoon's Van Wilder 2: The Rise of Taj '06
Superman Returns '06
A Lot Like Love '05
Bachelor Party Vegas '05
Dancing in Twilight '05
Son of the Mask '05
Ball & Chain '04
Harold and Kumar Go to White Castle '04
Love Don't Cost a Thing '03
Malibu's Most Wanted '03
National Lampoon's Van Wilder '02

Leonard Penn (1907-75)
Streets of Sin '49
Girl of the Golden West '38

Matthew Penn
Delta Force 3: The Killing Game '91
Playing for Keeps '86

Robin Wright Penn (1966-)
A Christmas Carol '09 (V)
The Private Lives of Pippa Lee '09
State of Play '09
What Just Happened '08

Sean Penn (1960-)
Crossing Over '09
Milk '08
What Just Happened '08
All the King's Men '06
The Assassination of Richard Nixon '05
The Interpreter '05
It's All About Love '03
Mystic River '03
21 Grams '03
I Am Sam '01
Before Night Falls '00
Up at the Villa '00
The Weight of Water '00
Sweet and Lowdown '99
Hurlyburly '98
The Thin Red Line '98
The Game '97
Hugo Pool '97
Loved '97
She's So Lovely '97
U-Turn '97
Dead Man Walking '95
Carlito's Way '93
State of Grace '90
Casualties of War '89
We're No Angels '89
Colors '88
Cool Blue '88
Judgment in Berlin '88
At Close Range '86
Shanghai Surprise '86
The Falcon and the Snowman '85
Crackers '84
Racing with the Moon '84
Bad Boys '83
Fast Times at Ridgemont High '82
Killing of Randy Webster '81
Taps '81

Larry Pennell (1928-)
Bubba Ho-Tep '03
The Fear: Halloween Night '99
The FBI Story '59
The Far Horizons '55

Nicholas Pennell (1939-95)
Cry of the Penguins '71
Isadora '68
Rasputin the Mad Monk '66

Jonathan Penner (1962-)
Cleopatra's Second Husband '00
Let the Devil Wear Black '99
Down Periscope '96
The Last Supper '96
Wedding Bell Blues '96
Bloodfist 7: Manhunt '95
A Fool and His Money '88

Alan Penney
Around the World in 80 Ways '86
Gone to Ground '76

Jack Pennick (1895-1964)
The Man Who Shot Liberty Valance '62
The Alamo '60
The Horse Soldiers '59
Mister Roberts '55
The Beast from 20,000 Fathoms '53
She Wore a Yellow Ribbon '49
They Were Expendable '45
Lady from Louisiana '42
Sergeant York '41
Stagecoach '39

Chris Pennock (1944-)
Running Woman '98
Frances '82
The Great Texas Dynamite Chase '76

Joe Penny (1956-)
Anti-Terrorist Cell: Manhunt '01
The Prophet's Game '99
Family of Cops 3 '98
Family of Cops 2: Breach of Faith '97
Danger of Love '95
Blood Vows: The Story of a Mafia Wife '87
Gangster Wars '81
Bloody Birthday '80
Lifepod '80
Deathmoon '78

Sydney Penny (1971-)
Hidden Places '06
Child of Darkness, Child of Light '91
Bernadette '90
Running Away '89
Hyper-Sapien: People from Another Star '86
News at Eleven '86
Pale Rider '85
The Capture of Grizzly Adams '82
Tut & Tuttle '81

John Penrose (1914-83)
The Shadow Man '53
Kind Hearts and Coronets '49

Rupert Penry-Jones (1970-)
Persuasion '07
Casanova '05
Match Point '05
Cambridge Spies '03
The Four Feathers '02
Charlotte Gray '01
Virtual Sexuality '99
Hilary and Jackie '98

Del Pentacost
Coyote Ugly '00
O Brother Where Art Thou? '00

George Peppard (1928-94)
The Tigress '93
Night of the Fox '90
Silence Like Glass '90
The Chinatown Murders: Man against the Mob '89
Target Eagle '84
Your Ticket Is No Longer Valid '84
Treasure of the Yankee Zephyr '83
Battle Beyond the Stars '80
From Hell to Victory '79
Torn Between Two Lovers '79
Damnation Alley '77
Newman's Law '74
The Bravos '72
The Groundstar Conspiracy '72
The Executioner '70
Pendulum '69
Rough Night in Jericho '67
The Blue Max '66
Tobruk '66
Operation Crossbow '65
The Carpetbaggers '64
How the West Was Won '63
The Victors '63
Breakfast at Tiffany's '61
Home from the Hill '60
Pork Chop Hill '59
The Strange One '57
Bang the Drum Slowly '56

Barbara Pepper (1915-69)
Kiss Me, Stupid! '64
Murder, He Says '45
Girls in Chains '43
Hollywood Stadium Mystery '38
Wide Open Faces '38
Last Outlaw '36
Rogue's Tavern '36
Our Daily Bread '34

Barry Pepper (1970-)
Seven Pounds '08
Flags of Our Fathers '06
The Three Burials of Melquiades Estrada '05
The Snow Walker '03
25th Hour '02
We Were Soldiers '02
Knockaround Guys '01
61* '01
Battlefield Earth '00
We All Fall Down '00
The Green Mile '99
Enemy of the State '98
Saving Private Ryan '98
Firestorm '97
Dead Silence '96

Marilia Pera (1943-)
Central Station '98
Tieta of Agreste '96
Mixed Blood '84
Pixote '81

Piper Perabo (1977-)
Carriers '09
Beverly Hills Chihuahua '08
The Lazarus Project '08
Because I Said So '07
First Snow '07
Imagine Me & You '06
Perception '06
The Prestige '06
10th & Wolf '06
The Cave '05
Cheaper by the Dozen 2 '05
Edison Force '05
George and the Dragon '04
Cheaper by the Dozen '03
Slap Her, She's French '02
Lost and Delirious '01
The Adventures of Rocky & Bullwinkle '00
Coyote Ugly '00
White Boyz '99

Ed Peranio
Desperate Living '77
Female Trouble '74
Multiple Maniacs '70

Daniel Percival
Lost in Austen '08
National Lampoon's Van Wilder 2: The Rise of Taj '06

Lance Percival
Yellow Submarine '68 (V)
Postman's Knock '62

Eileen (Elaine Persey) Percy (1901-73)
Spring Fever '27
The Phantom Bullet '26
Let's Go! '23
Down to Earth '17
The Man from Painted Post '17
Reaching for the Moon '17

Esme Percy (1887-1957)
Dead of Night '45
Pygmalion '38
21 Days '37
Accused '36
Old Spanish Custom '36
Bitter Sweet '33

Wayne Pere
Soundman '99
An American Summer '90

Missy Peregrym (1982-)
Stick It '06
Call Me: The Rise and Fall of Heidi Fleiss '04

Tony Perenski
Varsity Blues '98
The Texas Chainsaw Massacre 4: The Next Generation '95
The Underneath '95

George Perez (1972-)
Valentina's Tango '07
Manhattan Merenque! '95
Bounty Tracker '93

Jose Perez (1940-)
Miami Blues '90
Courage '86
One Shoe Makes It Murder '82
Short Eyes '79

Manny Perez
Illegal Tender '07
Bella '06
El Cantante '06
Yellow '06
Washington Heights '02

Marco Perez
Trade '07
Amores Perros '00

Rosie Perez (1964-)
Pineapple Express '08
The Take '07
Just Like the Son '06
Human Nature '02
Widows '02
King of the Jungle '01
The Road to El Dorado '00 (V)
The 24 Hour Woman '99
A Brother's Kiss '97
Dance with the Devil '97
Subway Stories '97
It Could Happen to You '94
Somebody to Love '94
Fearless '93
Untamed Heart '93
White Men Can't Jump '92
Night on Earth '91
Criminal Justice '90
Do the Right Thing '89

Timothy Paul Perez
The Street King '02
Relax... It's Just Sex! '98

Vincent Perez (1964-)
On Guard! '03
Queen of the Damned '02
Bride of the Wind '01
I Dreamed of Africa '00
Time Regained '99

Shot Through the Heart '98
Those Who Love Me Can Take the Train '98
The Treat '98
Swept from the Sea '97
The Crow 2: City of Angels '96
Talk of Angels '96
Beyond the Clouds '95
Queen Margot '94
Indochine '92
Cyrano de Bergerac '90

Francois Perier (1919-2002)

Tartuffe '84
Stavisky '74
Just Before Nightfall '71
Le Cercle Rouge '70
Z '69
Le Samourai '67
The Organizer '64
The Testament of Orpheus '59
Nights of Cabiria '57
Gervaise '56
Orpheus '49
Sylvia and the Phantom '45

George Periolat (1876-1940)

Nurse Marjorie '20
Eyes of Julia Deep '18

Anthony Perkins (1932-92)

A Demon in My View '92
In the Deep Woods '91
I'm Dangerous Tonight '90
Psycho 4: The Beginning '90
Daughter of Darkness '89
Edge of Sanity '89
Destroyer '88
Psycho 3 '86
Crimes of Passion '84
The Glory Boys '84
Psycho 2 '83
The Sins of Dorian Gray '82
The Double Negative '80
ffolkes '80
The Black Hole '79
Twice a Woman '79
Winter Kills '79
Les Miserables '78
Mahogany '75
Murder on the Orient Express '74
Life & Times of Judge Roy Bean '72
Ten Days Wonder '72
Someone Behind the Door '71
Catch-22 '70
Pretty Poison '68
Is Paris Burning? '66
The Fool Killer '65
Ravishing Idiot '64
The Trial '63
Goodbye Again '61
Phaedra '61
Psycho '60
Tall Story '60
Green Mansions '59
On the Beach '59
Desire Under the Elms '58
The Matchmaker '58
Fear Strikes Out '57
Lonely Man '57
The Tin Star '57
Friendly Persuasion '56
The Actress '53

Elizabeth Perkins (1960-)

Fierce People '05
Jiminy Glick in LaLa Wood '05
Kids in America '05
Must Love Dogs '05
The Ring 2 '05
The Thing About My Folks '05
Speak '04
Finding Nemo '03 (V)
All I Want '02
My Sister's Keeper '02
Cats & Dogs '01
If These Walls Could Talk 2 '00
28 Days '00
Crazy in Alabama '99
From the Earth to the Moon '98
I'm Losing You '98
Rescuers: Stories of Courage "Two Women" '97
Moonlight and Valentino '95
The Flintstones '94
Miracle on 34th Street '94
Indian Summer '93
The Doctor '91
He Said, She Said '91
Avalon '90
Enid Is Sleeping '90
Love at Large '89
Big '88
Sweet Hearts Dance '88
About Last Night... '86
From the Hip '86

Emily Perkins (1977-)

Another Cinderella Story '08
She's the Man '06
Ginger Snaps Back: The Beginning '04
Ginger Snaps: Unleashed '04
Ginger Snaps '01
Prozac Nation '01
Small Sacrifices '89

Millie Perkins (1938-)

The Lost City '05
The Chamber '96
Bodily Harm '95
Pistol: The Birth of a Legend '90
Two Moon Junction '88
Wall Street '87
At Close Range '86
A.D. '85
License to Kill '84
Shattered Vows '84
The Haunting Passion '83
Table for Five '83
Witch Who Came from the Sea '76
Cockfighter '74
Wild in the Streets '68
Ride in the Whirlwind '66
The Shooting '66
Ensign Pulver '64
Wild in the Country '61
The Diary of Anne Frank '59

Osgood Perkins (1892-1937)

Gold Diggers of 1937 '36
Scarface '31
Love 'Em and Leave 'Em '26

Oz (Osgood) Perkins, II (1974-)

Quigley '03
Secretary '02
Legally Blonde '01
Wolf '94
Six Degrees of Separation '93
Psycho 2 '83

Orli Perl (1972-)

Pick a Card '97
Under the Domim Tree '95

Max Perlich (1968-)

Protecting the King '07
Punk Love '06
The Missing '03
Deuces Wild '02
Blow '01
Sol Goode '01
Homicide: The Movie '00
The Independent '00
Freeway 2: Confessions of a Trickbaby '99
Goodbye, Lover '99
House on Haunted Hill '99
Sometimes They Come Back... For More '99
Gummo '97
Truth or Consequences, N.M. '97
Beautiful Girls '96
The Curse of Inferno '96
Homeward Bound 2: Lost in San Francisco '96
Georgia '95
Dead Beat '94
Maverick '94
Shake, Rattle & Rock! '94
Terrified '94
Born Yesterday '93
Cliffhanger '93
The Butcher's Wife '91
Rush '91
Drugstore Cowboy '89
Plain Clothes '88
Can't Buy Me Love '87
Ferris Bueller's Day Off '86

Rhea Perlman (1948-)

Beethoven's Big Break '08
The Christmas Choir '08
Love Comes Lately '07
10 Items or Less '06
Houdini '99
In the Doghouse '98
Carpool '96
Matilda '96
Sunset Park '96
Canadian Bacon '94
To Grandmother's House We Go '94
Ted & Venus '93
We're Back! A Dinosaur's Story '93 (V)
There Goes the Neighborhood '92
Class Act '91
Enid Is Sleeping '90
Stamp of a Killer '87
Amazing Stories '85
Ratings Game '84
Intimate Strangers '77

Ron Perlman (1950-)

Marmaduke '10 (V)
Season of the Witch '10
Dark Country '09
The Devil's Tomb '09
Hellboy II: The Golden Army '08
In the Name of the King: A Dungeon Siege Tale '08
Mutant Chronicles '08
Outlander '08
How to Go Out on a Date in Queens '06
The Last Winter '06
Local Color '06
Masters of Horror: Pro-Life '05
The Second Front '05
Tarzan 2 '05 (V)
Comic Book: The Movie '04
Hellboy '04
Hoodlum & Son '03
Blade 2 '02
Shakedown '02
Star Trek: Nemesis '02
The King's Guard '01
The Shaft '01
Enemy at the Gates '00
Operation Sandman: Warriors in Hell '00
Price of Glory '00
Titan A.E. '00 (V)
The Trial of Old Drum '00
Happy, Texas '99
Houdini '99
Supreme Sanction '99
Frogs for Snakes '98
The Magnificent Seven '98
A Town Has Turned to Dust '98
Alien: Resurrection '97
Betty '97
Prince Valiant '97
The Second Civil War '97
Tinseltown '97
Body Armor '96
The Island of Dr. Moreau '96
The Last Supper '96
The City of Lost Children '95
Fluke '95
Mr. Stitch '95
Phantom 2040 Movie: The Ghost Who Walks '95 (V)
Cronos '94
Police Academy 7: Mission to Moscow '94
Sensation '94
The Adventures of Huck Finn '93
Double Exposure '93
Romeo Is Bleeding '93
When the Bough Breaks '93
Sleepwalkers '92
Blind Man's Bluff '91
The Name of the Rose '86
Ice Pirates '84
Quest for Fire '82

Florence Pernel (1966-)

Trois Couleurs: Blanc '94
Trois Couleurs: Bleu '93

Gigi Perreau (1941-)

Hell on Wheels '67
Journey to the Center of Time '67
Girls' Town '59
Dance with Me, Henry '56
The Man in the Gray Flannel Suit '56
Never a Dull Moment '50
My Foolish Heart '49
Song of Love '47

Paul Perri (1953-)

Without Evidence '96
Hellraiser 4: Bloodline '95
Delta Force 2: Operation Stranglehold '90
Manhunter '86
Hit & Run '82

Mireille Perrier (1959-)

The Ice Rink '99
Trahir '93
Love Without Pity '91
Toto le Heros '91
Chocolat '88
Mauvais Sang '86
Boy Meets Girl '84

Olivier Perrier (1940-)

Blame It on Fidel '06
Read My Lips '01
Les Destinees '00

Pierre Perrier

One to Another '06
Cold Showers '05

Jack Perrin (1896-1967)

Sunrise at Campobello '60
When Gangland Strikes '56
The Court Martial of Billy Mitchell '55
Ten Wanted Men '54
Them! '54
Bandit Queen '51
I Shot Billy the Kid '50
The North Star '43
New Moon '40
West of Pinto Basin '40
The Story of Vernon and Irene Castle '39
Gun Grit '36
Texas Jack '35
Hell Fire Austin '32
Apache Kid's Escape '30
The Man From Oklahoma '26
Midnight Faces '26

Jacques Perrin (1941-)

Oceans '09 (N)
Le Petit Lieutenant '05
The Chorus '04
Brotherhood of the Wolf '01
Winged Migration '01 (N)
Flight of the Innocent '93
Cinema Paradiso '88
Love Songs '84
Le Crabe Tambour '77
Black and White in Color '76
The Desert of the Tartars '76
State of Siege '73
Peau D'Ane '71
Donkey Skin '70
Z '69
The Young Girls of Rochefort '68
The 317th Platoon '65
The Girl with a Suitcase '60

Maxence Perrin

Paris 36 '08
The Chorus '04

Valerie Perrine (1944-)

The Moguls '05
What Women Want '00
Brown's Requiem '98
A Place Called Truth '98
Shame, Shame, Shame '98
Curtain Call '97
The Break '95
Girl in the Cadillac '94
Boiling Point '93
Bright Angel '91
Sweet Bird of Youth '89
Maid to Order '87
Water '85
The Three Little Pigs '84
When Your Lover Leaves '83
The Border '82
The Agency '81
Can't Stop the Music '80
Superman 2 '80
The Electric Horseman '79
The Magician of Lublin '79
Superman: The Movie '78
Mr. Billion '77
Lenny '74
The Last American Hero '73
Slaughterhouse Five '72

Harold Perrineau, Jr. (1963-)

Felon '08
Gardens of the Night '08
28 Weeks Later '07
The Matrix Reloaded '03
The Matrix Revolutions '03
On_Line '01
Woman on Top '00
The Best Man '99
The Tempest '99
The Edge '97
Blood & Wine '96
William Shakespeare's Romeo and Juliet '96
Smoke '95

Joe Perrino (1982-)

The Bumblebee Flies Anyway '98
The Mighty '98
Sleepers '96

Leslie Perrins (1902-62)

Man on the Run '49
Mr. Reeder in Room 13 '38
Nine Days a Queen '36
The Silent Passenger '35
The Living Dead '33

Michel Perron

Lost Junction '03
The Sign of Four '01
Battlefield Earth '00

Francois Perrot (1924-)

Life and Nothing But '89
Women's Prison Massacre '85
My Best Friend's Girl '84
Le Choc '82

Felton Perry (1942-)

Buck and the Magic Bracelet '97
Dumb & Dumber '94
RoboCop 3 '91
RoboCop 2 '90
Checking Out '89
RoboCop '87
Sudden Death '77
Magnum Force '73
Walking Tall '73
Night Call Nurses '72

Jeff(rey) Perry (1955-)

Diminished Capacity '08
Wild Things '98
Kingfish: A Story of Huey P. Long '95
Playmaker '94

Jeffrey S. (Jeff) Perry

The Chronicles of Narnia '89
Oxford Blues '84

John Bennett Perry (1941-)

Loaded '08
Protecting the King '07
Fools Rush In '97
George of the Jungle '97
The Last Fling '86
A Matter of Life and Death '81
Only When I Laugh '81

Lou Perry

The Texas Chainsaw Massacre 2 '86
Last Night at the Alamo '83

Luke Perry (1966-)

Angel and the Badman '09
The Pledge '08
Silent Venom '08
Alice Upside Down '07
The Sandlot 3: Heading Home '07
Dishdogz '05
Johnson County War '02
The Enemy '01
The Triangle '01
Attention Shoppers '99
Storm Tracker '99
The Florentine '98
Indiscreet '98
The Fifth Element '97
Robin Cook's Invasion '97
American Strays '96
Last Breath '96
Normal Life '96
Riot in the Streets '96
8 Seconds '94
Buffy the Vampire Slayer '92
Terminal Bliss '91
Sweet Trash '70

Matthew Perry (1969-)

17 Again '09
Birds of America '08
Numb '07
The Whole Ten Yards '04
Serving Sara '02
The Whole Nine Yards '00
Three to Tango '99
Almost Heroes '97
Fools Rush In '97
She's Out of Control '89
A Night in the Life of Jimmy Reardon '88
The Whole Shootin' Match '79

Rod Perry (1941-)

Black Gestapo '75
Black Godfather '74

Roger Perry (1933-)

Roller Boogie '79
Conspiracy of Terror '75
The Thing with Two Heads '72
The Return of Count Yorga '71
Count Yorga, Vampire '70
The Cat '66

Tyler Perry (1969-)

Tyler Perry's Why Did I Get Married Too? '10
I Can Do Bad All By Myself '09
Madea Goes to Jail '09
Star Trek '09
The Family That Preys '08
Tyler Perry's Meet the Browns '08
Tyler Perry's Why Did I Get Married? '07
Madea's Family Reunion '06
Diary of a Mad Black Woman '05

Maria Perschy (1938-)

People Who Own the Dark '75
Exorcism '74
Horror of the Zombies '74
House of Psychotic Women '73
The Rue Morgue Massacres '73
Last Day of the War '69
The Castle of Fu Manchu '68
A Witch Without a Broom '68
The Mad Executioners '65
633 Squadron '64
Man's Favorite Sport? '63
No Survivors, Please '63

Lisa Jane Persky (1955-)

Grilled '06
An American Rhapsody '01

My First Mister *'01*
Meat Loaf: To Hell and Back *'00*
Perfect Assassins *'98*
Female Perversions *'96*
Dead Funny *'94*
Pontiac Moon *'94*
Coneheads *'93*
The Last of the Finest *'90*
Vital Signs *'90*
Great Balls of Fire *'89*
When Harry Met Sally... *'89*
The Big Easy *'87*
Peggy Sue Got Married *'86*
The Sure Thing *'85*
The Cotton Club *'84*
Shattered Vows *'84*
Breathless *'83*
American Pop *'81 (V)*
The Great Santini *'80*
KISS Meets the Phantom of the Park *'78*

Nehemiah Persoff (1920-)
An American Tail: Fievel Goes West *'91 (V)*
The Last Temptation of Christ *'88*
Twins *'88*
An American Tail *'86 (V)*
Sadat *'83*
Yentl *'83*
The Henderson Monster *'80*
The Rebels *'79*
Killing Stone *'78*
Francis Gary Powers: The True Story of the U-2 Spy *'76*
Voyage of the Damned *'76*
Eric *'75*
Missiles of October *'74*
The Stranger Within *'74*
Deadly Harvest *'72*
The People Next Door *'70*
A Global Affair *'63*
The Comancheros *'61*
Al Capone *'59*
The Day of the Outlaw *'59*
Green Mansions *'59*
Never Steal Anything Small *'59*
Some Like It Hot *'59*
The Badlanders *'58*
Men in War *'57*
The Wrong Man *'56*
On the Waterfront *'54*

Essy Persson (1941-)
Cry of the Banshee *'70*
Mission Stardust *'68*
Vibration *'68*
Therese & Isabelle *'67*
I, a Woman *'66*

Maria Persson (1959-)
Pippi in the South Seas *'70*
Pippi on the Run *'70*
Pippi Goes on Board *'69*
Pippi Longstocking *'69*

Jon Pertwee (1919-96)
The House that Dripped Blood *'71*
Carry On Screaming *'66*
Ladies Who Do *'63*
Mister Drake's Duck *'50*

Sean Pertwee (1964-)
Mutant Chronicles *'08*
Botched *'07*
Goal 2: Living the Dream *'07*
Goal! The Dream Begins *'06*
When Evil Calls *'06*
The Last Drop *'05*
Dog Soldiers *'01*
Formula 51 *'01*
Seven Days to Live *'01*
Love, Honour & Obey *'00*
Cleopatra *'99*
Russell Mulcahy's Tale of the Mummy *'99*
Soldier *'98*
Event Horizon *'97*
Deadly Voyage *'96*
Stiff Upper Lips *'96*
Blue Juice *'95*
Shopping *'93*
Clarissa *'91*

Jorge Perugorria (1965-)
Che *'08*
Life According to Muriel *'97*
Guantanamera *'95*
Strawberry and Chocolate *'93*

Frank Pesce
Night Vision *'97*
Trapped in Paradise *'94*
The Pamela Principle *'91*
29th Street *'91*
Vigilante *'83*

Joe Pesci (1943-)
The Good Shepherd *'06*
Lethal Weapon 4 *'98*
Gone Fishin' *'97*
8 Heads in a Duffel Bag *'96*
Casino *'95*
Jimmy Hollywood *'94*
With Honors *'94*
A Bronx Tale *'93*
Home Alone 2: Lost in New York *'92*
Lethal Weapon 3 *'92*
My Cousin Vinny *'92*
The Public Eye *'92*
JFK *'91*
The Super *'91*
Betsy's Wedding *'90*
Goodfellas *'90*
Home Alone *'90*
Backtrack *'89*
Lethal Weapon 2 *'89*
Man on Fire *'87*
Once Upon a Time in America *'84*
Easy Money *'83*
I'm Dancing as Fast as I Can *'82*
Ruby's Dream *'82*
Eureka! *'81*
Raging Bull *'80*
Family Enforcer *'76*

Lisa Pescia
The Dark Dancer *'95*
Body Chemistry 2: Voice of a Stranger *'91*
Body Chemistry *'90*

Donna Pescow (1954-)
Partners *'99*
Dead Husbands *'98*
Ivory Tower *'97*
Glory Years *'87*
Policewoman Centerfold *'83*
Saturday Night Fever *'77*

Bernadette Peters (1948-)
Living Proof *'08*
It Runs in the Family *'03*
Bobbie's Girl *'02*
Let It Snow *'99*
What the Deaf Man Heard *'98*
Anastasia *'97 (V)*
Cinderella *'97*
The Odyssey *'97*
Alice *'90*
Impromptu *'90*
The Last Best Year *'90*
Pink Cadillac *'89*
Slaves of New York *'89*
Sunday in the Park with George *'86*
Sleeping Beauty *'83*
Annie *'82*
Heartbeeps *'81*
Pennies from Heaven *'81*
Tulips *'81*
The Jerk *'79*
The Martian Chronicles: Part 2 *'79*
The Martian Chronicles: Part 3 *'79*
Silent Movie *'76*
The Longest Yard *'74*

Brock Peters (1927-2005)
The Locket *'02*
The Wild Thornberrys Movie *'02 (V)*
The Secret *'93*
Star Trek 6: The Undiscovered Country *'91*
Alligator 2: The Mutation *'90*
To Heal a Nation *'88*
Star Trek 4: The Voyage Home *'86*
Agatha Christie's A Caribbean Mystery *'83*
The Adventures of Huckleberry Finn *'78*
Framed *'75*
Slaughter's Big Ripoff *'73*
Soylent Green *'73*
The McMasters *'70*
Ace High *'68*
Daring Game *'68*
The Incident *'67*
The Pawnbroker *'65*
The L-Shaped Room *'62*
To Kill a Mockingbird *'62*
Carmen Jones *'54*

Clarke Peters (1952-)
Endgame *'09*
Freedomland *'06*
The Corner *'00*
A Casualty of War *'90*
Mona Lisa *'86*
Outland *'81*

House Peters, Sr. (1880-1967)
Head Winds *'25*
Human Hearts *'22*
The Leopard Woman *'20*

House Peters, Jr. (1916-2008)
Man From God's Country *'58*
Black Patch *'57*
Red Planet Mars *'52*
Outlaw Country *'49*
Public Cowboy No. 1 *'37*

Jean Peters (1926-2000)
Peter and Paul *'81*
A Man Called Peter *'55*
Apache *'54*
Broken Lance *'54*
Three Coins in the Fountain *'54*
A Blueprint for Murder *'53*
Pickup on South Street *'53*
Niagara *'52*
Viva Zapata! *'52*
As Young As You Feel *'51*
It Happens Every Spring *'49*
Captain from Castile *'47*

Luan Peters (1948-)
Land of the Minotaur *'77*
Flesh and Blood Show *'73*
Not Tonight Darling *'72*
Freelance *'71*
Man of Violence *'71*
Twins of Evil *'71*

Molly Peters (1942-)
Target for Killing *'66*
Thunderball *'65*

Ralph Peters (1903-59)
Sky Liner *'49*
Meeting at Midnight *'44*
I Married a Witch *'42*
Outlaws of the Rio Grande *'41*
Death Rides the Range *'40*
Six Gun Rhythm *'39*
Man's Country *'38*
Rough Ridin' Rhythm *'37*

Rick Peters (1967-)
The Happy Face Murders *'99*
American Virgin *'98*
Elvis Meets Nixon *'98*
This Matter of Marriage *'98*
The Disappearance of Kevin Johnson *'95*
Night of the Demons 2 *'94*

Robert Peters
From Other Worlds *'04*
Baadasssss! *'03*

Scott Peters (1930-94)
They Saved Hitler's Brain *'64*
Girl Hunters *'63*

Susan Peters (1921-52)
Andy Hardy's Double Life *'42*
Random Harvest *'42*

Werner Peters (1918-71)
The Bird with the Crystal Plumage *'70*
The Corrupt Ones *'67*
A Fine Madness *'66*
The Phantom of Soho *'64*
36 Hours *'64*
Curse of the Yellow Snake *'63*
The Counterfeit Traitor *'62*
The Kaiser's Lackey *'51*

Chris Petersen
Vampire Raiders—Ninja Queen *'89*
Ninja Masters of Death *'85*
Little Dragons *'80*
When Every Day Was the Fourth of July *'78*

Colin Petersen
A Cry from the Streets *'57*
The Scamp *'57*

Oscar Petersen
Mama Africa *'02*
The Quarry *'98*

Pat Petersen (1966-)
Cold River *'81*
Little Dragons *'80*

Stewart Petersen (1960-)
Pony Express Rider *'76*
Against a Crooked Sky *'75*
Seven Alone *'75*
Where the Red Fern Grows *'74*

William L. Petersen (1953-)
The Contender *'00*
The Skulls *'00*
Gunshy *'98*
Kiss the Sky *'98*
The Rat Pack *'98*
Twelve Angry Men *'97*
The Beast *'96*
Fear *'96*
The Kennedys of Massachusetts *'95*
Mulholland Falls *'95*
In the Kingdom of the Blind the Man with One Eye Is King *'94*
Deadly Currents *'93*
Return to Lonesome Dove *'93*
Hard Promises *'92*
Keep the Change *'92*
Passed Away *'92*
Young Guns 2 *'90*
Cousins *'89*
Amazing Grace & Chuck *'87*
Long Gone *'87*
Manhunter *'86*
To Live & Die in L.A. *'85*

Alan C. Peterson
Deathlands: Homeward Bound *'03*
Run *'91*

Amanda Peterson (1971-)
Windrunner *'94*
Fatal Charm *'92*
I Posed for Playboy *'91*
Listen to Me *'89*
The Lawless Land *'88*
Can't Buy Me Love *'87*
Explorers *'85*

Annika Peterson
The Man from Earth *'07*
Frederick Forsyth's Icon *'05*

Bob Peterson
Up *'09 (V)*
Finding Nemo *'03 (V)*
Monsters, Inc. *'01 (V)*

Cassandra Peterson (1951-)
Elvira's Haunted Hills *'02*
Acting on Impulse *'93*
Ted & Venus *'93*
Elvira, Mistress of the Dark *'88*
Echo Park *'86*
Pee-wee's Big Adventure *'85*
Balboa *'82*
Jekyll & Hyde... Together Again *'82*
Working Girls *'75*

Dorothy Peterson (1900-79)
Woman in the Window *'44*
Air Force *'43*
Too Many Husbands *'40*
Peck's Bad Boy *'34*
I'm No Angel *'33*
The Beast of the City *'32*

Eric Peterson (1980-)
Henry & Verlin *'94*
Tramp at the Door *'87*

Kimberlee Peterson (1980-)
Legend of the Lost Tomb *'97*
Homecoming *'96*

Vidal Peterson
Wizards of the Lost Kingdom *'85*
Something Wicked This Way Comes *'83*

Edward Petherbridge (1936-)
Gulliver's Travels *'95*
An Awfully Big Adventure *'94*
Strange Interlude *'90*
Lovers of Their Time *'85*

Pascale Petit (1938-)
Four Times That Night *'69*
End of Desire *'62*

Victor Petit
Street Warriors *'77*
Night of the Death Cult *'75*
Terror Beach *'75*

Isabelle Petit-Jacques
The Man on the Train *'02*
The Girl on the Bridge *'98*

Steven Petrarca
Sparkler *'99*
The Lesser Evil *'97*

Gio Petre (1937-)
The Doll *'62*
Gorilla *'56*

Ian Petrella (1974-)
Crimes of Passion *'84*
A Christmas Story *'83*

Alexei Petrenko
12 *'07*
Rasputin *'85*

Mario Petri
The Conqueror & the Empress *'64*
The Beast of Babylon Against the Son of Hercules *'63*

Hay Petrie (1895-1948)
Great Expectations *'46*
A Canterbury Tale *'44*
On Approval *'44*
Spellbound *'41*
Contraband *'40*
Clouds over Europe *'39*
Crimes at the Dark House *'39*
The Four Feathers *'39*
Spy in Black *'39*
21 Days *'37*
The Ghost Goes West *'36*
The Old Curiosity Shop *'35*
The Private Life of Henry VIII *'33*

Howard Petrie (1906-68)
Rocky Mountain *'50*
Border River *'47*

Susan Petrie
Snapshot *'77*
They Came from Within *'75*
Vengeance Is Mine *'74*

Ciro Petrone
Gomorrah *'08*

Marisa Petroro
Everybody Wants to Be Italian *'08*
No Witness *'04*

Joanna Pettet (1944-)
Terror in Paradise *'90*
Sweet Country *'87*
Double Exposure *'82*
Cry of the Innocent *'80*
Return of Frank Cannon *'80*
The Evil *'78*
A Killer in Every Corner *'74*
Pioneer Woman *'73*
Blue *'68*
Casino Royale *'67*
Night of the Generals *'67*
Robbery *'67*
The Group *'66*

Christopher Pettiet (1976-2000)
Carried Away *'95*
The Goodbye Bird *'93*
Fatal Exposure *'91*
Point Break *'91*

Brian Pettifer
Conspiracy *'01*
If... *'69*

Valarie Pettiford (1960-)
Stomp the Yard *'07*
Glitter *'01*
Street Hunter *'90*

Frank Pettingell (1891-1966)
Trial & Error *'62*
Butler's Dilemma *'43*
Gaslight *'40*

Madison Pettis
Free Style *'09*
The Game Plan *'07*

Lori Petty (1964-)
Masters of Horror: Fair Haired Child *'06*
Karate Dog *'04 (V)*
Prey for Rock and Roll *'03*
Firetrap *'01*
MacArthur Park *'01*
Route 666 *'01*
Blood Money *'98*
Relax... It's Just Sex! *'98*
Serial Bomber *'96*
The Glass Shield *'95*
In the Army Now *'94*
Tank Girl *'94*
Free Willy *'93*
A League of Their Own *'92*
Point Break *'91*
Cadillac Man *'90*

Richard Petty (1937-)
Cars *'06 (V)*
Richard Petty Story *'72*
Speedway *'68*

Ross Petty
Spenser: A Savage Place *'94*
The Housekeeper *'86*

Tom Petty (1950-)
The Postman *'97*
Made in Heaven *'87*

Alex Pettyfer
Beastly *'10*
Wild Child *'08*
Alex Rider: Operation Stormbreaker *'06*

Angelique Pettyjohn (1943-92)
The Wizard of Speed and Time *'88*
Bio Hazard *'85*
The Lost Empire *'83*
Repo Man *'83*
Confessions of Tom Harris *'72*
G.I. Executioner *'71*
Hell's Belles *'69*
Mad Doctor of Blood Island *'68*

Clambake '67

Katija Pevec (1988-)

Yours, Mine & Ours '05
Air Bud 5: Buddy Spikes Back '03

Joseph Pevney (1920-)

The Plunderers '60
The Street with No Name '48
Body and Soul '47
Nocturne '46

Penny Peyser (1951-)

Indecent Behavior '93
Messenger of Death '88
The Frisco Kid '79
The In-Laws '79

Dedee Pfeiffer (1965-)

The Prince and the Pauper '07
Meat Loaf: To Hell and Back '00
Up Close and Personal '96
Deadly Past '95
Double Exposure '93
Falling Down '93
Running Cool '93
Shoot '92
A Climate for Killing '91
King's Ransom '91
Red Surf '90
The Horror Show '89
Brothers in Arms '88
The Midnight Hour '86
Vamp '86
Toughlove '85

Michelle Pfeiffer (1957-)

Cheri '09
Personal Effects '09
Hairspray '07
Stardust '07
I Could Never Be Your Woman '06
Sinbad: Legend of the Seven Seas '03 (V)
White Oleander '02
I Am Sam '01
What Lies Beneath '00
The Story of Us '99
William Shakespeare's A Midsummer Night's Dream '99
The Deep End of the Ocean '98
Prince of Egypt '98 (V)
A Thousand Acres '97
One Fine Day '96
To Gillian on Her 37th Birthday '96
Up Close and Personal '96
Dangerous Minds '95
Wolf '94
The Age of Innocence '93
Batman Returns '92
Frankie and Johnny '91
Love Field '91
The Russia House '90
The Fabulous Baker Boys '89
Dangerous Liaisons '88
Married to the Mob '88
Tequila Sunrise '88
Amazon Women on the Moon '87
The Witches of Eastwick '87
Sweet Liberty '86
Into the Night '85
Ladyhawke '85
Power, Passion & Murder '83
Scarface '83
Grease 2 '82
The Solitary Man '82
Callie and Son '81
Charlie Chan and the Curse of the Dragon Queen '81
B.A.D. Cats '80
Falling in Love Again '80
The Hollywood Knights '80

JoAnn Pflug (1940-)

The Day the Women Got Even '80
Scream of the Wolf '74
Catlow '71
They Call It Murder '71
M*A*S*H '70

Liz Phair (1967-)

Seeing Other People '04
Cherish '02

Linh Dan Pham (1973-)

Dante 01 '08
The Beat My Heart Skipped '05
Indochine '92

Joe Phelan

See Joe Estevez

Shawn (Michael) Phelan (1975-98)

Breaking the Rules '92
Toy Soldiers '91
Caroline? '90

Peter Phelps (1960-)

Ned Kelly '03
Lantana '01
Zone 39 '96
Blackwater Trail '95
Merlin '92
Rock & Roll Cowboys '92
Breaking Loose '90
Starlight Hotel '90
The Lighthorsemen '87

Mekhi Phifer (1975-)

A Day in the Life '09
Nora's Hair Salon 2: A Cut Above '08
This Christmas '07
Puff, Puff, Pass '06
Slow Burn '05
Dawn of the Dead '04
Honey '03
8 Mile '02
Impostor '02
The Other Brother '02
Paid in Full '02
Brian's Song '01
Carmen: A Hip Hopera '01
O '01
Shaft '00
A Lesson Before Dying '99
Uninvited Guest '99
I Still Know What You Did Last Summer '98
Hell's Kitchen NYC '97
Soul Food '97
High School High '96
Clockers '95

John Philbin (1965-)

The Crew '95
Point Break '91
Martians Go Home! '90
The Four Minute Mile '88
North Shore '87
Shy People '87

Mary Philbin (1903-93)

The Man Who Laughs '27
The Phantom of the Opera '25
Merry-Go-Round '23
Human Hearts '22

Regis Philbin (1934-)

Shrek Forever After '10 (V)
Shrek the Third '07 (V)
The Breakup Artist '04
Cheaper by the Dozen '03
Little Nicky '00
Dudley Do-Right '99
Night and the City '92
The Bad News Bears Go to Japan '78
Sextette '78

James Philbrook (1924-82)

Last Day of the War '69
Finger on the Trigger '65
Sound of Horror '64
The Thin Red Line '64

Dominic Philie

For Hire '98
The Boys '97

Gerard Philipe (1922-59)

Dangerous Liaisons '60
Fever Mounts at El Pao '59
Modigliani '58
The Red and the Black '57
Les Grandes Manoeuvres '55
The Proud Ones '53
Beauties of the Night '52
Fanfan la Tulipe '51
La Ronde '51
Beauty and the Devil '50
La Chartreuse de Parme '48
Devil in the Flesh '46
L'Idiot '46

Busy Philipps (1979-)

Made of Honor '08
White Chicks '04
Home Room '02
The Smokers '00

Emo Philips (1956-)

Meet the Parents '91
UHF '89

Gina Philips (1970-)

Love and Debate '06
Chronicle of the Raven '04
Jeepers Creepers '01

Gina Philips (1970-)

Bella Mafia '97
Breaking Free '95

Lee Philips (1927-99)

Psychomania '63
The Hunters '58
Peyton Place '57

Mary (Phillips) Philips (1900-75)

Prince Valiant '54
Leave Her to Heaven '45
A Farewell to Arms '32

Ryan Phillippe (1974-)

MacGruber '10
Stop-Loss '08
Breach '07
Five Fingers '06
Flags of Our Fathers '06
Crash '05
Igby Goes Down '02
Gosford Park '01
Antitrust '00
Company Man '00
Way of the Gun '00
Cruel Intentions '98
54 '98
Playing by Heart '98
Homegrown '97
I Know What You Did Last Summer '97
Little Boy Blue '97
Lifeform '96
Nowhere '96
White Squall '96

Angie Phillips

Duets '00
Manny & Lo '96

Barney (Bernard) Phillips (1913-82)

Savage Run '70
The Sand Pebbles '66
I Was a Teenage Werewolf '57
A Blueprint for Murder '53

Bijou Phillips (1980-)

Choke '08
Dark Streets '08
Hostel: Part 2 '07
What We Do Is Secret '07
The Wizard of Gore '07
Venom '05
Pulse '03
Bully '01
Fast Sofa '01
Tart '01
Almost Famous '00
Black and White '99

Bill Phillips (1908-57)

The Last Hunt '56
Thirty Seconds Over Tokyo '44

Bobbie Phillips (1972-)

Chameleon 3: Dark Angel '00
Red Shoe Diaries: Luscious Lola '00
Chameleon 2: Death Match '99
American Virgin '98
Carnival of Souls '98
Chameleon '98
Back in Action '94
Hail Caesar '94
Ring of Fire 3: Lion Strike '94
TC 2000 '93

Chris Phillips

Doug's 1st Movie '99 (V)
Felix the Cat: The Movie '91 (V)

Chynna Phillips (1968-)

Bye Bye Birdie '95
The Prize Pulitzer '89
Say Anything '89
Caddyshack 2 '88
Goodbye, Miss 4th of July '88
The Invisible Kid '88

Dorothy Phillips

The Corn Is Green '79
Heart of Humanity '18

Eddie (Edward) Phillips (1899-1965)

Phantom Patrol '36
The Throwback '35
Probation '32
Big Boy '30
Lightning Hutch '26
Virtue's Revolt '24
The Love Light '21

Ethan Phillips (1955-)

The Babysitters '07
California Dreaming '07
The Island '05
From the Earth to the Moon '98
The Shadow '94
Green Card '90
Bloodhounds of Broadway '89
Glory '89
Lean on Me '89

Frank Phillips (1912-94)

The Quatermass Experiment '56
Dam Busters '55
The Runaway Bus '54

Gary Phillips

Island of Blood '82
Whodunit '82

Grace Phillips

Alien Fury: Countdown to Invasion '00
The New Yorker '98
Truth or Consequences, N.M. '97
All the Vermeers in New York '91

John Phillips (1915-95)

Max and Helen '90
The Mummy's Shroud '67
Village of the Damned '60
Black Angel '46

Jonathan Phillips (1963-)

Bronson '09
Dead Gorgeous '02
The Mystery of Edwin Drood '93
Clarissa '91

Joseph C. Phillips (1962-)

Let's Talk About Sex '98
Strictly Business '91

Julianne Phillips (1960-)

Allie & Me '97
Big Bully '95
Where's the Money, Noreen? '95
A Vow to Kill '94
Getting Up and Going Home '92
Fletch Lives '89
Skin Deep '89
Seven Hours to Judgment '88
Sweet Lies '88
Summer Fantasy '84

Kate Phillips

See Kay Linaker

Kevin Phillips

Pride '07
Rock the Paint '05

Leslie Phillips (1924-)

Venus '06
Color Me Kubrick '05
Millions '05
Lara Croft: Tomb Raider '01
Agatha Christie's The Pale Horse '96
The Canterville Ghost '96
August '95
Carry On Columbus '92
Mountains of the Moon '90
Scandal '89
Empire of the Sun '87
Maroc 7 '67
Doctor in Clover '66
Very Important Person '61
Carry On Constable '60
Doctor in Love '60
No Kidding '60
The Smallest Show on Earth '57
The Limping Man '53
Train of Events '49

Lou Diamond Phillips (1962-)

Angel and the Badman '09
Love Takes Wing '09
Che '08
Lone Rider '08
Never Forget '08
Termination Point '07
Hollywood Homicide '03
Lone Hero '02
Stark Raving Mad '02
Red Water '01
Route 666 '01
A Better Way to Die '00
Hangman '00
Bats '99
Brokedown Palace '99
In a Class of His Own '99
Picking Up the Pieces '99
Supernova '99
Another Day in Paradise '98
The Big Hit '98
Courage Under Fire '96
Undertow '95
The Wharf Rat '95
Boulevard '94
Dangerous Touch '94
Sioux City '94
Teresa's Tattoo '94
Extreme Justice '93
Shadow of the Wolf '92
Ambition '91
The Dark Wind '91
Harley '90
A Show of Force '90
Young Guns 2 '90
Disorganized Crime '89
The First Power '89
Renegades '89
Dakota '88
Stand and Deliver '88
Young Guns '88
La Bamba '87
Trespasses '86

MacKenzie Phillips (1959-)

The Jacket '05
True Friends '98
Love Child '82
More American Graffiti '79
Eleanor & Franklin '76
Rafferty & the Gold Dust Twins '75
Miles to Go Before I Sleep '74
American Graffiti '73

Margaret "Peg" Phillips (1918-2002)

How the West Was Fun '95
Dogfight '91

Michelle Phillips (1944-)

Kids in America '05
Harry and Max '04
Sweetwater: A True Rock Story '99
Army of One '94
Rubdown '93
Scissors '91
Let It Ride '89
Assault and Matrimony '87
American Anthem '86
Secrets of a Married Man '84
Sidney Sheldon's Bloodline '79
Valentino '77
The California Kid '74
The Death Squad '73
Dillinger '73

Nathan Phillips (1980-)

Redline '07
Snakes on a Plane '06
Wolf Creek '05

Robert Phillips (1925-)

The Car '77
The Killing of a Chinese Bookie '76
Adios Amigo '75
Mitchell '75
Detroit 9000 '73
Slaughter '72
MacKenna's Gold '69
The Dirty Dozen '67
Hour of the Gun '67
Cat Ballou '65
The Killers '64

Sally Phillips (1970-)

Bridget Jones: The Edge of Reason '04
Bridget Jones's Diary '01

Samantha (Sam) Phillips (1966-)

The Dallas Connection '94
Sexual Malice '93
Deceit '89
Phantasm 2 '88

Sian Phillips (1934-)

P.D. James: The Murder Room '04
Attila '01
The Aristocrats '99
Ivanhoe '97
The Return of the Borrowers '96
The Vacillations of Poppy Carew '94
The Borrowers '93
Heidi '93
Valmont '89
The Doctor and the Devils '85
The Ewoks: Battle for Endor '85
Dune '84
Smiley's People '82
The Carpathian Eagle '81
Clash of the Titans '81
Nijinsky '80
Tinker, Tailor, Soldier, Spy '80
Murphy's War '71
Goodbye, Mr. Chips '69

Sydney Coale Phillips

Maximum Breakout '91
Cause of Death '90

Wendy Phillips (1953-)

Bugsy '91
Midnight Run '88
Death Be Not Proud '75

Max Phipps (1939-2000)

What the Moon Saw '90
Dark Age '88
Sky Pirates '87
The Blue Lightning '86
Nate and Hayes '83
Return of Captain Invincible '83
The Road Warrior '82

Nicholas Phipps (1913-80)

Doctor in Love '60
Captain's Paradise '53
Maytime in Mayfair '49
Elizabeth of Ladymead '48

William Phipps (1923-)
Cavalry Command *'63*
The War of the Worlds *'53*
Loan Shark *'52*
Five *'51*
Cinderella *'50 (V)*
The Vanishing Westerner *'50*

Joaquin Rafael (Leaf) Phoenix (1974-)
Two Lovers *'09*
Reservation Road *'07*
We Own the Night *'07*
Walk the Line *'05*
Hotel Rwanda *'04*
Ladder 49 *'04*
The Village *'04*
Brother Bear *'03 (V)*
It's All About Love *'03*
Signs *'02*
Buffalo Soldiers *'01*
Gladiator *'00*
Quills *'00*
The Yards *'00*
Clay Pigeons *'98*
8mm *'98*
Return to Paradise *'98*
Inventing the Abbotts *'97*
U-Turn *'97*
To Die For *'95*
Parenthood *'89*
Russkies *'87*
SpaceCamp *'86*

Rain Phoenix (1973-)
Kids in America *'05*
Harry and Max *'04*
O *'01*
Spent *'00*
Even Cowgirls Get the Blues *'94*

River Phoenix (1970-93)
The Thing Called Love *'93*
Silent Tongue *'92*
Sneakers *'92*
Dogfight *'91*
My Own Private Idaho *'91*
I Love You to Death *'90*
Indiana Jones and the Last Crusade *'89*
Little Nikita *'88*
A Night in the Life of Jimmy Reardon *'88*
Running on Empty *'88*
The Mosquito Coast *'86*
Stand by Me *'86*
Explorers *'85*

Summer Phoenix (1978-)
The Believer *'01*
Dinner Rush *'00*
Esther Kahn *'00*
SLC Punk! *'99*
Girl *'98*

Jesdaporn Pholdee (1977-)
The Eye 2 *'04*
The Iron Ladies 2 *'03*
The Iron Ladies *'00*

Maurice Pialat (1925-2003)
Under Satan's Sun *'87*
A Nos Amours *'84*
This Man Must Die *'70*

Jean Piat
Tower of Screaming Virgins *'68*
The Would-Be Gentleman *'58*

Ben Piazza (1934-91)
Guilty by Suspicion *'91*
Clean and Sober *'88*
Consenting Adult *'85*
Scene of the Crime *'85*
The Five of Me *'81*
The Children of An Lac *'80*
Nightwing *'79*
The Hanging Tree *'59*
A Dangerous Age *'57*

Tony Pica (1933-)
House of Psychotic Women *'73*
Yesterday, Today and Tomorrow *'64*

Robert Picardo (1953-)
Chasing the Green *'09*
Masters of Horror: Homecoming *'05*
Small Soldiers *'98*
Menno's Mind *'96*
Star Trek: First Contact *'96*
Revenge of the Nerds 4: Nerds in Love *'94*
Runaway Daughters *'94*
Wagons East *'94*
White Mile *'94*
Matinee *'92*
Frame Up *'91*
Motorama *'91*
Gremlins 2: The New Batch *'90*
China Beach *'88*
976-EVIL *'88*
Innerspace *'87*
Jack's Back *'87*
Munchies *'87*
Back to School *'86*
Explorers *'85*
The Howling *'81*

Michel Piccoli (1925-)
The Duchess of Langeais *'07*
Belle Toujours *'06*
I'm Going Home *'00*
Genealogies of a Crime *'97*
Passion in the Desert *'97*
Beaumarchais the Scoundrel *'96*
Party *'96*
Traveling Companion *'96*
One Hundred and One Nights *'95*
Martha and I *'91*
La Belle Noiseuse *'90*
May Fools *'90*
La Puritaine *'86*
Mauvais Sang *'86*
Peril *'85*
Dangerous Moves *'84*
Prize of Peril *'84*
La Passante *'83*
Beyond Obsession *'82*
La Nuit de Varennes *'82*
Passion *'82*
Atlantic City *'81*
L'Etat Sauvage *'78*
Spoiled Children *'77*
Mado *'76*
Vincent, Francois, Paul and the Others *'76*
Leonor *'75*
The Infernal Trio *'74*
Phantom of Liberty *'74*
Wedding in Blood *'74*
La Grande Bouffe *'73*
The Discreet Charm of the Bourgeoisie *'72*
Ten Days Wonder *'72*
The Things of Life *'70*
Dillinger Is Dead *'69*
Topaz *'69*
Danger: Diabolik *'68*
The Milky Way *'68*
The Young Girls of Rochefort *'68*
Belle de Jour *'67*
The Game Is Over *'66*
La Guerre Est Finie *'66*
Lady L *'65*
Contempt *'64*
Diary of a Chambermaid *'64*
The Day and the Hour *'63*
Le Doulos *'61*
Death in the Garden *'56*

Paul Picerni (1922-)
Fearmaker *'71*
The Scalphunters *'68*
The Brothers Rico *'57*
Dial Red O *'55*
To Hell and Back *'55*
House of Wax *'53*
Cattle Town *'52*
I Was a Communist for the FBI *'51*

Irving Pichel (1891-1954)
How Green Was My Valley *'41 (N)*
Torture Ship *'39*
Dick Tracy *'37*
Dracula's Daughter *'36*
General Spanky *'36*
Badmen of Nevada *'33*
Oliver Twist *'33*
An American Tragedy *'31*
The Cheat *'31*

Jean-Francois Pichette
Mouvements du Desir *'94*
Being at Home with Claude *'92*

Joe Pichler (1987-)
Children On Their Birthdays *'02*
Beethoven's 4th *'01*
When Good Ghouls Go Bad *'01*
Beethoven's 3rd *'00*
Shiloh 2: Shiloh Season *'99*
Varsity Blues *'98*

John Pickard (1913-93)
Seminole Uprising *'55*
Above and Beyond *'53*
Hellgate *'52*
Government Agents vs. Phantom Legion *'51*

Raymond Pickard (1982-)
The Borrowers *'97*
The Canterville Ghost *'96*

Sorrels Pickard (1940-2003)
Hardbodies *'84*
Running Hot *'83*

James Pickens, Jr. (1954-)
Venom *'05*
Home Room *'02*
Liberty Heights *'99*
A Slight Case of Murder *'99*
RocketMan *'97*
Bloodhounds *'96*
Ghosts of Mississippi *'96*
Gridlock'd *'96*
Sharon's Secret *'95*
Lily in Winter *'94*
Sodbusters *'94*

Slim Pickens (1919-83)
Crazy Horse and Custer: "The Untold Story" *'90*
Charlie and the Great Balloon Chase *'82*
Pink Motel *'82*
The Howling *'81*
Story of a Cowboy Angel *'81*
Honeysuckle Rose *'80*
Tom Horn *'80*
Beyond the Poseidon Adventure *'79*
1941 *'79*
Sweet Creek County War *'79*
The Swarm *'78*
Mr. Billion *'77*
Shadow of Chikara *'77*
The White Buffalo *'77*
Banjo Hackett *'76*
Hawmps! *'76*
Pony Express Rider *'76*
The Apple Dumpling Gang *'75*
Babe! *'75*
Rancho Deluxe *'75*
White Line Fever *'75*
Blazing Saddles *'74*
Legend of Earl Durand *'74*
Ginger in the Morning *'73*
Pat Garrett & Billy the Kid *'73*
Poor Pretty Eddie *'73*
The Cowboys *'72*
The Getaway *'72*
Iron Horsemen *'71*
Ride to Glory *'71*
Ballad of Cable Hogue *'70*
Never a Dull Moment *'68*
Flim-Flam Man *'67*
Rough Night in Jericho *'67*
Talion *'66*
In Harm's Way *'65*
Major Dundee *'65*
Dr. Strangelove, or: How I Learned to Stop Worrying and Love the Bomb *'64*
One-Eyed Jacks *'61*
The Desperate Mission *'60*
The Sheepman *'58*
Phantom Stallion *'54*
Iron Mountain Trail *'53*
Shadows of Tombstone *'53*
Border Saddlemates *'52*
Colorado Sundown *'52*
Rocky Mountain *'50*

Josh Picker
Beverly Hills Family Robinson *'97*
Alex *'92*
Flirting *'89*

Marc Pickering
Cashback *'06*
Sleepy Hollow *'99*

Sarah Pickering
Little Dorrit, Film 1: Nobody's Fault *'88*
Little Dorrit, Film 2: Little Dorrit's Story *'88*

Blake Pickett
Dark Universe *'93*
HauntedWeen *'91*

Bobby "Boris" Pickett (1940-)
Lobster Man from Mars *'89*
Frankenstein General Hospital *'88*
Hot Money *'79*

Cindy Pickett (1947-)
The Village Barbershop *'08*
Hate Crime *'05*
The Stepdaughter *'00*
Atomic Dog *'98*
Coyote Summer *'96*
Painted Hero *'95*
Evolver *'94*
The Goodbye Bird *'93*
Son-in-Law *'93*
Sleepwalkers *'92*
Wildcard *'92*
Crooked Hearts *'91*
Original Intent *'91*
Deepstar Six *'89*
Hot to Trot! *'88*
Echoes in the Darkness *'87*
Ferris Bueller's Day Off *'86*
The Men's Club *'86*
Call to Glory *'84*
Circle of Power *'83*
Hysterical *'83*
Margin for Murder *'81*
Night Games *'80*

Jack Pickford
The Bat *'26*
Exit Smiling *'26*

Mary Pickford (1893-1979)
Coquette *'29*
The Taming of the Shrew *'29*
A Kiss for Mary Pickford *'27*
My Best Girl *'27*
Sparrows *'26*
Little Annie Rooney *'25*
Tess of the Storm Country *'22*
The Love Light *'21*
Pollyanna *'20*
Suds *'20*
Daddy Long Legs *'19*
Amarilly of Clothesline Alley *'18*
Pride of the Clan *'18*
Stella Maris *'18*
The Little American *'17*
A Poor Little Rich Girl *'17*
Rebecca of Sunnybrook Farm *'17*

Christina Pickles (1938-)
The Family Holiday *'07*
Sol Goode *'01*
Angels Don't Sleep Here *'00*
Murder She Purred: A Mrs. Murphy Mystery *'98*
Weapons of Mass Distraction *'97*
The Wedding Singer *'97*
William Shakespeare's Romeo and Juliet *'96*
Revenge of the Nerds 4: Nerds in Love *'94*
Rush It *'77*
Seizure *'74*

Vivian Pickles (1933-)
Suspicion *'87*
Candleshoe *'78*
Elizabeth R *'72*
Harold and Maude *'71*
Sunday, Bloody Sunday *'71*

Ronald Pickup (1941-)
The Christmas Miracle of Jonathan Toomey *'07*
Horatio Hornblower *'99*
Ivanhoe *'97*
The Rector's Wife *'94*
Scarlett *'94*
My Friend Walter *'93*
Journey of Honor *'91*
Dr. Bethune *'90*
Jekyll and Hyde *'90*
A Murder of Quality *'90*
The Attic: The Hiding of Anne Frank *'88*
Fortunes of War *'87*
The Mission *'86*
Eleni *'85*
Ivanhoe *'82*
Life of Verdi *'82*
Nijinsky *'80*

Molly Picon (1898-1992)
Cannonball Run 2 *'84*
Cannonball Run *'81*
Murder on Flight 502 *'75*
For Pete's Sake *'74*
Fiddler on the Roof *'71*
Come Blow Your Horn *'63*
Mamele *'38*
Yidl Mitn Fidl *'36*
East and West *'24*

Jim Piddock (1956-)
The Seeker: The Dark Is Rising *'07*
For Your Consideration *'06*
Love for Rent *'05*
A Different Loyalty *'04*
She Creature *'01*
Traces of Red *'92*

Rebecca Pidgeon (1963-)
How to Be *'08*
Redbelt *'08*
Jesse Stone: Sea Change *'07*
Edmond *'05*
Shopgirl *'05*
Heist *'01*
State and Main *'00*
The Winslow Boy *'98*
The Spanish Prisoner *'97*
Homicide *'91*
The Dawning *'88*

Walter Pidgeon (1897-1984)
Sextette *'78*
The Lindbergh Kidnapping Case *'76*
Two Minute Warning *'76*
Murder on Flight 502 *'75*
Neptune Factor *'73*
Funny Girl *'68*
Cinderella *'64*
Advise and Consent *'62*
Big Red *'62*
Voyage to the Bottom of the Sea *'61*
Forbidden Planet *'56*
The Glass Slipper *'55 (N)*
Hit the Deck *'55*
Deep in My Heart *'54*
Executive Suite *'54*
The Last Time I Saw Paris *'54*
Men of the Fighting Lady *'54*
Dream Wife *'53*
The Bad and the Beautiful *'52*
Million Dollar Mermaid *'52*
Quo Vadis *'51 (N)*
The Miniver Story *'50*
That Forsyte Woman *'50*
Command Decision *'48*
Julia Misbehaves *'48*
Cass Timberlane *'47*
Holiday in Mexico *'46*
Weekend at the Waldorf *'45*
Mrs. Parkington *'44*
Madame Curie *'43*
Mrs. Miniver *'42*
White Cargo *'42*
Blossoms in the Dust *'41*
How Green Was My Valley *'41*
Man Hunt *'41*
Dark Command *'40*
House Across the Bay *'40*
It's a Date *'40*
Girl of the Golden West *'38*
Listen, Darling *'38*
Shopworn Angel *'38*
Too Hot to Handle *'38*
Saratoga *'37*
Big Brown Eyes *'36*

Franciszek Pieczka
Mother of Kings *'82*
Jadup and Boel *'81*

Jacques Pieller
The Town Is Quiet *'00*
Time Regained *'99*
Three Lives and Only One Death *'96*

Claude Pieplu (1956-)
This Sweet Sickness *'77*
The Best Way *'76*
Phantom of Liberty *'74*
Wedding in Blood *'74*

Adrienne Pierce
Styx *'00*
Warriors from Hell *'90*

Bradley Michael Pierce (1982-)
The Borrowers *'97*
Doom Runners *'97*
Jumanji *'95*
The Undercover Kid *'95*
Beauty and the Beast *'91 (V)*

Brock Pierce (1938-)
Legend of the Lost Tomb *'97*
First Kid *'96*

Charles B. Pierce (1938-)
Boggy Creek II *'83*
Grayeagle *'77*
Town That Dreaded Sundown *'76*
Winterhawk *'76*

David Hyde Pierce (1959-)
Hellboy *'04 (V)*
Down With Love *'03*
Full Frontal *'02*
Treasure Planet *'02 (V)*
Osmosis Jones *'01 (V)*
Wet Hot American Summer *'01*
Chain of Fools *'00*
Isn't She Great *'00*
Jackie's Back *'99*
The Mating Habits of the Earthbound Human *'99 (N)*
A Bug's Life *'98 (V)*
Nixon *'95*
Wolf *'94*
The Fisher King *'91*
Little Man Tate *'91*
Bright Lights, Big City *'88*
Crossing Delancey *'88*
Vampire's Kiss *'88*

Jill Pierce
Omega Doom *'96*
Cyborg Soldier *'94*
Darkroom *'90*

Justin Pierce (1975-2000)
Next Friday *'00*
Blackmale *'99*
A Brother's Kiss *'97*
Kids *'95*

Norman Pierce
The Four Feathers *'39*
Ticket of Leave Man *'37*

Preston Pierce (1940-)
Whiskey Mountain *'77*
I Spit on Your Corpse *'74*

Stack Pierce
24 Hours to Midnight *'92*
Enemy Unseen *'91*
A Rage in Harlem *'91*
Murphy's Fault *'88*
Night Call Nurses *'72*

Tony Pierce
Big Bully *'95*
Trancers 3: Deth Lives *'92*

Wendell Pierce (1962-)
I Think I Love My Wife *'07*
Life Support *'07*
Stay Alive *'06*
A Hole in One *'04*
Land of Plenty *'04*
Ray *'04*
Brown Sugar *'02*
The 24 Hour Woman *'99*
Bulworth *'98*
Get On the Bus *'96*
Hackers *'95*
Waiting to Exhale *'95*
Bye Bye, Love *'94*
It Could Happen to You *'94*
Family Business *'89*
The Money Pit *'86*

Eric Pierpoint (1950-)
Liar Liar *'97*
Alien Nation: Millennium *'96*
Alien Nation: The Enemy Within *'96*
Little Witches *'96*
Where Truth Lies *'96*
Alien Nation: Body and Soul *'95*
Blood for Blood *'95*
The Stranger *'95*
Alien Nation: Dark Horizon *'94*
Sex, Love and Cold Hard Cash *'93*

Olivier Pierre (1953-)
The Lonely Lady *'83*
The Sender *'82*

Frederic Pierrot (1960-)
I've Loved You So Long *'08*
A Song of Innocence *'05*
They Came Back *'04*
Monsieur N. *'03*
The Girl from Paris *'02*
Artemisia *'97*
For Ever Mozart *'96*
Land and Freedom *'95*

Sarah Pierse
Heavenly Creatures *'94*
The Navigator *'88*

Emma Pierson
Little Dorrit *'08*
Bloodlines *'05*

Geoffrey Pierson (1949-)
Sleeping Dogs Lie *'06*
Spartan *'04*
Venomous *'01*
Necessary Parties *'88*

Angela Pietropinto
A Tale of Two Pizzas *'03*
Shaft *'00*
Finding North *'97*
Welcome to the Dollhouse *'95*
It Could Happen to You *'94*
Honeymoon in Vegas *'92*
Goodfellas *'90*

Roger Pigaut
Angelique and the Sultan *'68*
Untamable Angelique *'67*
Antoine et Antoinette *'47*

Alexandra Pigg (1962-)
Bullseye! *'90*
Chicago Joe & the Showgirl *'90*
Strapless *'90*
Smart Money *'88*
Letter to Brezhnev *'86*

Tim Pigott-Smith (1946-)
V for Vendetta *'06*
Alexander *'04*
Johnny English *'03*
The Four Feathers *'02*
Bloody Sunday *'01*
The Remains of the Day *'93*
The Jewel in the Crown *'84*
The Hunchback of Notre Dame *'82*
The Lost Boys *'78*

Luciano Pigozzi
See Alan Collins

Rosamund Pike (1979-)
An Education *'09*
Surrogates *'09*
Fracture *'07*
Doom *'05*
The Libertine *'05*
Pride and Prejudice *'05*
Die Another Day *'02*

Joe Pilato (1949-)
Fatal Passion *'94*
Married People, Single Sex *'93*
Day of the Dead *'85*

Nova Pilbeam (1919-)
Counterblast *'48*
Young and Innocent *'37*
Nine Days a Queen *'36*
The Man Who Knew Too Much *'34*

Mitch Pileggi (1952-)
Recount *'08*
The X Files: I Want to Believe *'08*
Gun Shy *'00*
The X-Files *'98*
Ravenhawk *'95*
Shocker *'89*
Brothers in Arms *'88*

Lorraine Pilkington (1975-)
In a Day *'06*
Human Traffic *'99*
The Nephew *'97*
The Last of the High Kings *'96*
The Miracle *'91*

Alison Pill (1985-)
Scott Pilgrim vs. the World *'10*
Milk *'08*
Dan in Real Life *'07*
Dear Wendy *'05*
Confessions of a Teenage Drama Queen *'04*
Plain Truth *'04*
A Separate Peace *'04*
Pieces of April *'03*
The Pilot's Wife *'01*
Baby *'00*
Skipped Parts *'00*

Jeffrey Pillars
Bloodmoon *'97*
Ernest Rides Again *'93*

Soren Pilmark (1955-)
Flickering Lights *'01*
The Kingdom 2 *'97*
The Kingdom *'95*

Daniel Pilon (1940-)
Shoot 'Em Up *'07*
Left Behind: The Movie *'00*
Sex & Mrs. X *'00*
The Collectors *'99*
The Ultimate Weapon *'97*
Poltergeist: The Legacy *'96*
Suspicious Minds *'96*
Obsessed *'88*
Starship Invasions *'77*
Brannigan *'75*
Snowballin' *'71*
The Red Half-Breed *'70*
In Trouble *'67*

Donald Pilon (1941-)
It's My Turn, Laura Cadieux *'98*
A Wind from Wyoming *'94*
Keeping Track *'86*

Left for Dead *'78*
The Pyx *'73*

Silvia Pinal (1931-)
Vintage Model *'92*
Simon of the Desert *'66*
The Exterminating Angel *'62*
Viridiana *'61*

Bronson Pinchot (1959-)
Second Best *'05*
Winning Girls Through Psychic Mind Control *'02*
Out of the Cold *'99*
All New Adventures of Laurel and Hardy: For Love or Mummy *'98*
Quest for Camelot *'98 (V)*
Slappy and the Stinkers *'97*
Courage Under Fire *'96*
The First Wives Club *'96*
It's My Party *'95*
Stephen King's The Langoliers *'95*
Beverly Hills Cop 3 *'94*
The Great American Sex Scandal *'94*
True Romance *'93*
Blame It on the Bellboy *'92*
Second Sight *'89*
After Hours *'85*
Hot Resort *'85*
Beverly Hills Cop *'84*
The Flamingo Kid *'84*
Risky Business *'83*

Chris Pine (1980-)
Carriers *'09*
Star Trek *'09*
Bottle Shock *'08*
Smokin' Aces *'07*
Blind Dating *'06*
Just My Luck *'06*
The Princess Diaries 2: Royal Engagement *'04*

Larry Pine
Chasing the Green *'09*
Islander *'06*
Outsourced *'06*
The Clearing *'04*
2 Brothers & a Bride *'03*
The Shipping News *'01*
Let It Snow *'99*
A Stranger in the Kingdom *'98*
Sunday *'96*
Dead Man Walking *'95*
Vanya on 42nd Street *'94*
Plain Clothes *'88*
Anna *'87*
Hullabaloo over Georgie & Bonnie's Pictures *'78*

Phillip Pine (1920-)
Money to Burn *'83*
Pot, Parents, and Police *'71*
The Lost Missile *'58*
Murder by Contract *'58*
Men in War *'57*
The Phantom from 10,000 Leagues *'56*

Robert Pine (1941-)
All I Want for Christmas *'07*
Love's Unfolding Dream *'07*
Lost Voyage *'01*
Body Count *'97*
Sins of the Mind *'97*
Independence Day *'96*
Are You Lonesome Tonight *'92*
Mysterious Two *'82*
Enola Gay: The Men, the Mission, the Atomic Bomb *'80*
Empire of the Ants *'77*
Munster, Go Home! *'66*

Miguel Pinero (1946-88)
Almost You *'85*
Alphabet City *'84*
Short Eyes *'79*

John Pinette (1962-)
The Punisher *'04*
My 5 Wives *'00*
Simon Sez *'99*

Jada Pinkett Smith (1971-)
The Human Contract *'08*
Madagascar: Escape 2 Africa *'08 (V)*
The Women *'08*
Reign Over Me *'07*
Madagascar *'05 (V)*
Collateral *'04*
The Matrix Reloaded *'03*
The Matrix Revolutions *'03*
Ali *'01*
Kingdom Come *'01*
Bamboozled *'00*
Princess Mononoke *'98 (V)*
Return to Paradise *'98*
Scream 2 *'97*
Woo *'97*
If These Walls Could Talk *'96*
The Nutty Professor *'96*
Set It Off *'96*
The Inkwell *'94*
Jason's Lyric *'94*
A Low Down Dirty Shame *'94*
Tales from the Crypt Presents Demon Knight *'94*
Menace II Society *'93*

Rob Pinkston
Extreme Movie *'08*
The Sasquatch Gang *'06*
The Derby Stallion *'05*

Ryan Pinkston
College *'08*
Extreme Movie *'08*
Foreign Exchange *'08*
Full of It *'07*

Arnold Pinnock
Twitches Too *'07*
Twitches *'05*
Must Be Santa *'99*

Danny Pino
The Burning Plain *'08*
Flicka *'06*
Rx *'06*
Between *'05*

Dominique Pinon (1955-)
Micmacs *'09*
Dante 01 *'08*
Roman de Gare *'07*
When Evil Calls *'06*
A Very Long Engagement *'04*
Amelie *'01*
Like a Fish Out of Water *'99*
Alien: Resurrection *'97*
The City of Lost Children *'95*
Alberto Express *'92*
Delicatessen *'92*
Moon in the Gutter *'83*
Diva *'82*

Gordon Pinsent (1930-)
Away From Her *'06*
The Confessor *'04*
Saint Ralph *'04*
Fallen Angel *'03*
The Shipping News *'01*
Pale Saints *'97*
A Vow to Kill *'94*
Blood Clan *'91*
Babar: The Movie *'88 (V)*
John and the Missus *'87*
Who Has Seen the Wind? *'77*
Newman's Law *'74*
Blacula *'72*
Colossus: The Forbin Project *'70*
The Thomas Crown Affair *'68*

Leah K. Pinsent (1968-)
Virus *'96*
The Little Kidnappers *'90*
Brutal Glory *'89*
Double Identity *'89*
April Fool's Day *'86*
The Bay Boy *'85*

Danny Pintauro (1976-)
The Great American Sex Scandal *'94*

The Beniker Gang *'83*
Cujo *'83*

Harold Pinter (1930-2008)
Wit *'01*
The Tailor of Panama *'00*
Mansfield Park *'99*
Breaking the Code *'95*
Accident *'67*

Billie Piper
Mansfield Park *'07*
The Shadow in the North *'07*
Ruby in the Smoke *'06*

Frederick Piper (1902-79)
The Frightened City *'61*
The Blue Lamp *'49*
Hue and Cry *'47*
San Demetrio, London *'47*
Johnny Frenchman *'46*
Pink String and Sealing Wax *'45*
Nine Men *'43*
Oh, Mr. Porter *'37*
Sabotage *'36*

Kelly Piper
Rawhead Rex *'87*
Maniac *'80*

Roddy Piper (1951-)
Kickin' It Old Skool *'07*
Blind Eye *'06*
Honor *'06*
Cybercity *'99*
Shepherd *'99*
The Bad Pack *'98*
Dead Tides *'97*
First Encounter *'97*
Marked Man *'96*
Sci-Fighters *'96*
Terminal Rush *'96*
Jungleground *'95*
Back in Action *'94*
Immortal Combat *'94*
No Contest *'94*
Tough and Deadly *'94*
Buy & Cell *'89*
Hell Comes to Frogtown *'88*
They Live *'88*
Body Slam *'87*

Grant Piro
Darkness Falls *'03*
The Outsider *'02*
Mr. Accident *'99*

Mark Pirro (1956-)
Curse of the Queerwolf *'87*
A Polish Vampire in Burbank *'80*

Carlo Pisacane (1891-)
Joyful Laughter *'60*
Paisan *'46*

Joe Piscopo (1951-)
Dead Lenny *'06*
The Last Request *'06*
Bartleby *'01*
Captain Nuke and the Bomber Boys *'95*
Open Season *'95*
Two Bits & Pepper *'95*
Huck and the King of Hearts *'93*
Sidekicks *'93*
Dead Heat *'88*
Wise Guys *'86*
Johnny Dangerously *'84*
American Tickler *'76*
King Kong *'76*

Marie-France Pisier (1944-)
Paid *'06*
The Ice Rink *'99*
Time Regained *'99*
Son of Gascogne *'95*
Prize of Peril *'84*
Hot Touch *'82*
Chanel Solitaire *'81*
Miss Right *'81*
French Postcards *'79*
We Will Not Enter the Forest *'79*
Love on the Run *'78*
The Other Side of Midnight *'77*

Barocco *'76*
Cousin, Cousine *'76*
Celine and Julie Go Boating *'74*
Diary of a Suicide *'73*
Nous N'Irons Plus au Bois *'69*

Luigi Pistilli (1929-96)
Your Vice is a Closed Room and Only I Have the Key *'72*
The Case of the Scorpion's Tail *'71*
The Scorpion's Tail *'71*
Twitch of the Death Nerve *'71*
Eagles Over London *'69*
The Libertine *'69*
The Good, the Bad and the Ugly *'67*

Kimberly Pistone
WhiteForce *'88*
Blue De Ville *'86*

Mario Pisu (1910-76)
The Sensuous Nurse *'76*
Juliet of the Spirits *'65*

Maria Pitillo (1965-)
Godzilla *'98*
Dear God *'96*
Bye Bye, Love *'94*
Natural Born Killers *'94*
Cooperstown *'93*
True Romance *'93*
The Lost Capone *'90*
Bright Lights, Big City *'88*
Spike of Bensonhurst *'88*

Noam Pitlik (1932-99)
The Big Bounce *'69*
Iron Cowboy *'68*

John Paul (J.P.) Pitoc
Species 3 *'04*
In the Weeds *'00*
Trick *'99*

Sacha (Sascha) Pitoeff (1920-90)
Inferno *'80*
Diary of a Suicide *'73*
Last Year at Marienbad *'61*
Anastasia *'56*

Anne Pitoniak (1922-2007)
Where the Money Is *'00*
A Thousand Acres *'97*
House of Cards *'92*
The Ballad of the Sad Cafe *'91*
Old Gringo *'89*
The Wizard of Loneliness *'88*
Best Seller *'87*
Sister, Sister *'87*
Agnes of God *'85*
Old Enough *'84*

Brad Pitt (1963-)
Inglourious Basterds *'09*
Burn After Reading *'08*
The Curious Case of Benjamin Button *'08*
The Assassination of Jesse James by the Coward Robert Ford *'07*
Ocean's Thirteen *'07*
Babel *'06*
Mr. & Mrs. Smith *'05*
Ocean's Twelve *'04*
Troy *'04*
Sinbad: Legend of the Seven Seas *'03 (V)*
Confessions of a Dangerous Mind *'02*
The Mexican *'01*
Ocean's Eleven *'01*
Spy Game *'01*
Snatch *'00*
Fight Club *'99*
Meet Joe Black *'98*
Seven Years in Tibet *'97*
The Devil's Own *'96*
Sleepers *'96*
Seven *'95*
12 Monkeys *'95*
Interview with the Vampire *'94*

Legends of the Fall '94
Kalifornia '93
True Romance '93
Cool World '92
The Favor '92
Johnny Suede '92
A River Runs Through It '92
Thelma & Louise '91
Too Young to Die '90
Across the Tracks '89
Cutting Class '89
Happy Together '89
The Dark Side of the Sun '88

Charles Pitt

Moving Target '89
Monaco Forever '83

Ingrid Pitt (1937-)

Hanna's War '88
Transmutations '85
The Final Option '82
The Wicker Man '75
The House that Dripped Blood '71
The Vampire Lovers '70
Where Eagles Dare '68
Sound of Horror '64

Michael Pitt (1981-)

Funny Games '07
Silk '07
Delirious '06
The Hawk Is Dying '06
Last Days '05
The Heart Is Deceitful Above All Things '04
The Village '04
The Dreamers '03
Murder by Numbers '02
Bully '01
Hedwig and the Angry Inch '00

Carl Pitti (1917-2003)

Gun Glory '57
Tribute to a Bad Man '56
Billy the Kid '41

Tom Pittman

Invasion of the Bee Girls '73
The Zodiac Killer '71
Black Patch '57

Jacob Pitts

21 '08
Eurotrip '04
A Separate Peace '04

Zasu Pitts (1898-1963)

It's a Mad, Mad, Mad, Mad World '63
The Thrill of It All! '63
This Could Be the Night '57
Francis Joins the WACs '54
The Denver & Rio Grande '51
Francis the Talking Mule '49
Life with Father '47
Breakfast in Hollywood '46
The Perfect Marriage '46
The Bashful Bachelor '42
Meet the Mob '42
Mexican Spitfire at Sea '42
Broadway Limited '41
No, No Nanette '40
Eternally Yours '39
Nurse Edith Cavell '39
Sing Me a Love Song '37
Way Out West '37
Hot Tip '35
Ruggles of Red Gap '35
Dames '34
Mrs. Wiggs of the Cabbage Patch '34
Sing and Like It '34
Two Alone '34
Aggie Appleby, Maker of Men '33
Mr. Skitch '33
The Crooked Circle '32
Justice Rides Again '32
Strangers of the Evening '32
The Guardsman '31
Lottery Bride '30
Monte Carlo '30
Sin Takes a Holiday '30
Risky Business '28
Sunny Side Up '28
The Wedding March '28
Lazybones '25
Greed '24

Byrne Piven (1929-2002)

Madison '01
Wavelength '96

Jeremy Piven (1965-)

Marmaduke '10 (V)
The Goods: Live Hard, Sell Hard '09
RocknRolla '08
The Kingdom '07
Smokin' Aces '07
Keeping Up with the Steins '06
Two for the Money '05
Chasing Liberty '04
Old School '03
Runaway Jury '03
Scary Movie 3 '03
Black Hawk Down '01
Highway '01
Rush Hour 2 '01
Serendipity '01
The Crew '00
Family Man '00
Red Letters '00
Phoenix '98
Very Bad Things '98
Don King: Only in America '97
Grosse Pointe Blank '97
Just Write '97
Kiss the Girls '97
Music from Another Room '97
The Real Thing '97
Larger Than Life '96
Wavelength '96
Heat '95
Miami Rhapsody '95
Car 54, Where Are You? '94
Floundering '94
P.C.U. '94
Twogether '94
Judgment Night '93
12:01 '93
Bob Roberts '92
Singles '92
Body Chemistry 2: Voice of a Stranger '91
The Grifters '90
Say Anything '89

Conrad Pla (1966-)

Eternal '04
The Rendering '02
Swindle '02

Lou Place (1912-)

Apache Woman '55
Swamp Women '55

Mary Kay Place (1947-)

Youth in Revolt '10
It's Complicated '09
City of Ember '08
Mama's Boy '07
Lonesome Jim '06
Nine Lives '05
Evergreen '04
Killer Diller '04
Latter Days '04
Silver City '04
Human Nature '02
Sweet Home Alabama '02
My First Mister '01
The Safety of Objects '01
A Woman's a Helluva Thing '01
Being John Malkovich '99
Girl, Interrupted '99
Pecker '98
Eye of God '97
John Grisham's The Rainmaker '97
Citizen Ruth '96
Manny & Lo '96
My Very Best Friend '96
Teresa's Tattoo '94
Armistead Maupin's Tales of the City '93
Captain Ron '92
Samantha '92
Bright Angel '91
Crazy from the Heart '91
A New Life '88
Portrait of a White Marriage '88
The Girl Who Spelled Freedom '86
Explorers '85
Smooth Talk '85
For Love or Money '84
The Big Chill '83
Waltz across Texas '83
Modern Problems '81
Private Benjamin '80
More American Graffiti '79
Starting Over '79
New York, New York '77

Michele Placido (1946-)

The Unknown Woman '06
Searching for Paradise '02
Lamerica '95
Drug Wars 2: The Cocaine Cartel '92
Forever Mary '89
Private Affairs '89
Big Business '88
Summer Night with Greek Profile, Almond Eyes & Scent of Basil '87
The Sicilian Connection '85
Three Brothers '80
Ernesto '79
Till Marriage Do Us Part '74
Black Hand '73

Tony Plana (1952-)

The Dead One '07
Towards Darkness '07
Goal! The Dream Begins '06
The Lost City '05
Cuban Blood '03 (V)
Fidel '02
Half Past Dead '02
Noriega: God's Favorite '00
Backlash '99
My Little Assassin '99
187 '97
Santa Fe '97
Sub Down '97
Primal Fear '96
The Burning Season '94
A Million to Juan '94
JFK '91
One Good Cop '91
Drug Wars: The Camarena Story '90
Havana '90
In the Line of Duty: A Cop for the Killing '90
Sweet 15 '90
Why Me? '90
The Hillside Strangler '89
Romero '89
Break of Dawn '88
Born in East L.A. '87
Salvador '86
Latino '85

Roger Planchon (1931-)

The Return of Martin Guerre '83
Roads to the South '78

Nigel Planer (1955-)

Flood '07
Mr. Toad's Wild Ride '96
Supergrass '87

Scott Plank (1958-2002)

Holes '03
Frozen in Fear '00
Moonbase '97
Marshal Law '96
Without Evidence '96
Saints and Sinners '95
Dying to Remember '93
Red Shoe Diaries 4: Auto Erotica '93
Pastime '91
The In Crowd '88

Dana Plato (1964-99)

Blade Boxer '97
High School USA '84
Return to Boggy Creek '77
Beyond the Bermuda Triangle '75

Edward Platt (1916-74)

Atlantis, the Lost Continent '61
North by Northwest '59
The Rebel Set '59
Gunman's Walk '58
Designing Woman '57
Rock, Pretty Baby '56
Written on the Wind '56
Rebel without a Cause '55

Louise Platt (1915-2003)

Captain Caution '40
Stagecoach '39
Spawn of the North '38

Marc Platt (1913-)

Down to Earth '47
Tonight and Every Night '45

Oliver Platt (1960-)

2012 '09
Year One '09
Frost/Nixon '08
The Bronx Is Burning '07
Martian Child '07
The Ten '07
Casanova '05
The Ice Harvest '05
Loverboy '05
Kinsey '04
Pieces of April '03
Ash Wednesday '02
Liberty Stands Still '02
ZigZag '02
Don't Say a Word '01
Gun Shy '00
Ready to Rumble '00
Bicentennial Man '99
Lake Placid '99
Three to Tango '99
Bulworth '98
Dangerous Beauty '98
Dr. Dolittle '98
The Imposters '98
Simon Birch '98
Executive Decision '96
A Time to Kill '96
The Infiltrator '95
Tall Tale: The Unbelievable Adventures of Pecos Bill '95
Funny Bones '94
Benny & Joon '93
Indecent Proposal '93
The Temp '93
The Three Musketeers '93
Beethoven '92
Diggstown '92
Flatliners '90
Postcards from the Edge '90
Working Girl '88

Alice Playten (1947-)

Doug's 1st Movie '99 (V)
Felix the Cat: The Movie '91 (V)
Legend '86

Aubrey Plaza

Scott Pilgrim vs. the World '10
Funny People '09

Angela Pleasence (1941-)

The Favor, the Watch, & the Very Big Fish '92
Stealing Heaven '88
A Christmas Carol '84
The Godsend '79
Six Wives of Henry VIII '71

Donald Pleasence (1919-95)

Halloween 6: The Curse of Michael Myers '95
The Advocate '93
Shadows and Fog '92
Millions '90
River of Death '90
American Tiger '89
Buried Alive '89
Casablanca Express '89
Halloween 5: The Revenge of Michael Myers '89
Ten Little Indians '89
Deep Cover '88
The Great Escape 2: The Untold Story '88
Ground Zero '88
Halloween 4: The Return of Michael Myers '88
Hanna's War '88
The House of Usher '88
Django Strikes Again '87
Phantom of Death '87
Prince of Darkness '87
The Room '87
Specters '87
Warrior Queen '87
Into the Darkness '86
Arch of Triumph '85
Creepers '85
Mansfield Park '85
The Monster Club '85
Nothing Underneath '85
Operation 'Nam '85
The Ambassador '84
The Black Arrow '84
A Breed Apart '84
To Kill a Stranger '84
The Treasure of the Amazon '84
Warrior of the Lost World '84
Devonsville Terror '83
Frankenstein's Great Aunt Tillie '83
Treasure of the Yankee Zephyr '83
Alone in the Dark '82
Escape from New York '81
Halloween 2: The Nightmare Isn't Over! '81
The Puma Man '80
All Quiet on the Western Front '79
Better Late Than Never '79
Dracula '79
Gold of the Amazon Women '79
Jaguar Lives '79
Night Creature '79
The Shaming '79
The Bastard '78
The Dark Secret of Harvest Home '78 (N)
Halloween '78
Power Play '78
Sgt. Pepper's Lonely Hearts Club Band '78
The Uncanny '78
Blood Relatives '77
The Eagle Has Landed '77
Goldenrod '77
Land of the Minotaur '77
Oh, God! '77
Telefon '77
Tomorrow Never Comes '77
Choice of Weapons '76
The Last Tycoon '76
Escape to Witch Mountain '75
Hearts of the West '75
I Don't Want to Be Born '75
The Passover Plot '75
Barry McKenzie Holds His Own '74
The Black Windmill '74
The Count of Monte Cristo '74
Journey into Fear '74
Dr. Jekyll and Mr. Hyde '73
The Freakmaker '73
From Beyond the Grave '73
The Rainbow Gang '73
Tales That Witness Madness '73
Pied Piper '72
Raw Meat '72
Wedding in White '72
House of the Damned '71
THX 1138 '71
Soldier Blue '70
The Madwoman of Chaillot '69
Night of the Generals '67
Will Penny '67
You Only Live Twice '67
Cul de Sac '66
Fantastic Voyage '66
The Greatest Story Ever Told '65
The Hallelujah Trail '65
The Great Escape '63
What a Carve-Up! '62
Horsemasters '61
The Battle of the Sexes '60
Circus of Horrors '60
The Flesh and the Fiends '60
The Hands of Orlac '60
No Love for Johnnie '60
Look Back in Anger '58
A Tale of Two Cities '58
1984 '56

Jesse Plemons (1988-)

Observe and Report '09
Children On Their Birthdays '02
Like Mike '02

John Pleshette (1942-)

James Dean '01
The Curse of Inferno '96
Eye of the Stranger '93
Lies of the Twins '91
Burning Rage '84
The Kid with the Broken Halo '82
The Trial of Lee Harvey Oswald '77

Suzanne Pleshette (1937-2008)

Spirited Away '01 (V)
The Lion King: Simba's Pride '98 (V)
Battling for Baby '92
The Queen of Mean '90
Alone in the Neon Jungle '87
Dixie: Changing Habits '85
Kojak: The Belarus File '85
For Love or Money '84
One Cooks, the Other Doesn't '83
Help Wanted: Male '82
Hot Stuff '80
Oh, God! Book 2 '80
If Things Were Different '79
The Shaggy D.A. '76
Legend of Valentino '75
Support Your Local Gunfighter '71
Hard Frame '70
Suppose They Gave a War and Nobody Came? '70
If It's Tuesday, This Must Be Belgium '69
Blackbeard's Ghost '67
The Adventures of Bullwhip Griffin '66
Nevada Smith '66
The Ugly Dachshund '65
A Distant Trumpet '64
The Birds '63
40 Pounds of Trouble '62
Rome Adventure '62
The Geisha Boy '58

George Plimpton (1927-2003)

Soul Power '08
Just Visiting '01
Just Cause '94
Little Man Tate '91
Easy Wheels '89
A Fool and His Money '88
Volunteers '85
Reds '81
Rio Lobo '70
The Detective '68

Martha Plimpton (1970-)

Remember Me '10
The Sleepy Time Gal '01
The Defenders: Taking the First '98
Pecker '98
200 Cigarettes '98
The Defenders: Payback '97
Eye of God '97
Music from Another Room '97
Beautiful Girls '96
I Shot Andy Warhol '96
I'm Not Rappaport '96
Last Summer In the Hamptons '96
Forbidden Choices '94
Mrs. Parker and the Vicious Circle '94
My Life's in Turnaround '94
A Woman at War '94
Chantilly Lace '93
Daybreak '93
Inside Monkey Zetterland '93
Josh and S.A.M. '93
Samantha '92
Silence Like Glass '90

Stanley and Iris *'90*
Parenthood *'89*
Another Woman *'88*
Running on Empty *'88*
Stars and Bars *'88*
Shy People *'87*
The Mosquito Coast *'86*
The Goonies *'85*
The River Rat *'84*
Rollover *'81*

Jack Plotnick (1968-)
Sleeping Dogs Lie *'06*
Down With Love *'03*
Say It Isn't So *'01*
Gods and Monsters *'98*
Chairman of the Board *'97*

Anna-Louise Plowman (1975-)
Cambridge Spies *'03*
The Foreigner *'03*

Melinda Plowman
Billy the Kid Versus Dracula *'66*
Home Town Story *'51*

Hilda Plowright (1890-1973)
36 Hours *'64*
Separate Tables *'58*

Joan Plowright (1929-)
The Spiderwick Chronicles *'08*
Curious George *'06 (V)*
Mrs. Palfrey at the Claremont *'05*
I Am David *'04*
Bringing Down the House *'03*
Callas Forever *'02*
Rock My World *'02*
Back to the Secret Garden *'01*
Dinosaur *'00 (V)*
Tea with Mussolini *'99*
Aldrich Ames: Traitor Within *'98*
Dance with Me *'98*
The Assistant *'97*
Jane Eyre *'96*
101 Dalmatians *'96*
Surviving Picasso *'96*
Mr. Wrong *'95*
A Pyromaniac's Love Story *'95*
The Scarlet Letter *'95*
Sorrento Beach *'95*
A Place for Annie *'94*
The Return of the Native *'94*
The Summer House *'94*
Widow's Peak *'94*
Dennis the Menace *'93*
Last Action Hero *'93*
Enchanted April *'92*
Stalin *'92*
And a Nightingale Sang *'91*
Avalon *'90*
I Love You to Death *'90*
The Dressmaker *'89*
Drowning by Numbers *'87*
A Dedicated Man *'86*
Revolution *'85*
Brimstone & Treacle *'82*
Britannia Hospital *'82*
Equus *'77*
The Merchant of Venice *'73*
The Entertainer *'60*
Time Without Pity *'57*

Eve Plumb (1958-)
Nowhere *'96*
...And God Spoke *'94*
I'm Gonna Git You Sucka *'88*
A Very Brady Christmas *'88*
Little Women *'78*
Secrets of Three Hungry Wives *'78*
Alexander: The Other Side of Dawn *'77*
Force of Evil *'77*

Amanda Plummer (1957-)
Affinity *'08*
Red *'08*
Satan's Little Helper *'04*
Mimic 3: Sentinel *'03*
My Life Without Me *'03*
Get a Clue *'02*
Triggermen *'02*
Seven Days to Live *'01*
8 1/2 Women *'99*
The Million Dollar Hotel *'99*
Apartment Complex *'98*
Hercules *'97 (V)*
A Simple Wish *'97*
Don't Look Back *'96*
Drunks *'96*
The Final Cut *'96*
Freeway *'95*
The Prophecy *'95*
The Right to Remain Silent *'95*
Under the Piano *'95*
Butterfly Kiss *'94*
Pulp Fiction *'94*
Last Light *'93*
Needful Things *'93*
Nostradamus *'93*
So I Married an Axe Murderer *'93*
Freejack *'92*
Miss Rose White *'92*
The Fisher King *'91*
Joe Versus the Volcano *'90*
Prisoners of Inertia *'89*
Gryphon *'88*
Riders to the Sea *'88*
Courtship *'87*
Made in Heaven *'87*
Static *'87*
The Dollmaker *'84*
The Hotel New Hampshire *'84*
Daniel *'83*
The World According to Garp *'82*

Christopher Plummer (1927-)
The Imaginarium of Doctor Parnassus *'09*
The Last Station *'09*
9 *'09 (V)*
Up *'09 (V)*
The Summit *'08*
Already Dead *'07*
Autumn Hearts: A New Beginning *'07*
Closing the Ring *'07*
Inside Man *'06*
The Lake House *'06*
Must Love Dogs *'05*
The New World *'05*
Syriana *'05*
Alexander *'04*
National Treasure *'04*
Cold Creek Manor *'03*
The Gospel of John *'03 (N)*
Ararat *'02*
Nicholas Nickleby *'02*
A Beautiful Mind *'01*
Lucky Break *'01*
American Tragedy *'00*
Dracula 2000 *'00*
Full Disclosure *'00*
Nuremberg *'00*
Possessed *'00*
Hidden Agenda *'99*
The Insider *'99*
Blackheart *'98*
Winchell *'98*
Conspiracy of Fear *'96*
Skeletons *'96*
Kurt Vonnegut's Harrison Bergeron *'95*
12 Monkeys *'95*
Crackerjack *'94*
Dolores Claiborne *'94*
Wolf *'94*
Impolite *'92*
Liar's Edge *'92*
Malcolm X *'92*
Rock-a-Doodle *'92 (V)*
Star Trek 6: The Undiscovered Country *'91*
Young Catherine *'91*
Firehead *'90*
Red Blooded American Girl *'90*
Where the Heart Is *'90*
Mindfield *'89*
Light Years *'88 (V)*
Shadow Dancing *'88*
Souvenir *'88*
Dragnet *'87*
I Love N.Y. *'87*
An American Tail *'86 (V)*
The Boss' Wife *'86*
Boy in Blue *'86*
Many Faces of Sherlock Holmes *'86*
Lily in Love *'85*
Dreamscape *'84*
Little Gloria... Happy at Last *'84*
Ordeal by Innocence *'84*
Prototype *'83*
The Scarlet & the Black *'83*
The Thorn Birds *'83*
The Amateur *'82*
Disappearance *'81*
Eyewitness *'81*
Highpoint *'80*
The Shadow Box *'80*
Somewhere in Time *'80*
Hanover Street *'79*
Murder by Decree *'79*
Riel *'79*
The Assignment *'78*
The Day That Shook the World *'78*
International Velvet *'78*
The Silent Partner *'78*
Star Crash *'78*
Conduct Unbecoming *'75*
The Man Who Would Be King *'75*
Spiral Staircase *'75*
Return of the Pink Panther *'74*
The Pyx *'73*
Waterloo *'71*
Battle of Britain *'69*
Night of the Generals *'67*
Triple Cross *'67*
Inside Daisy Clover *'65*
The Sound of Music *'65*
The Fall of the Roman Empire *'64*
A Doll's House *'59*
Stage Struck *'57*

Glenn Plummer (1966-)
Janky Promoters *'09*
The Longshots *'08*
Saw 2 *'05*
The Day After Tomorrow *'04*
Baadasssss! *'03*
Shade *'03*
Poolhall Junkies *'02*
The Salton Sea *'02*
MacArthur Park *'01*
Rhapsody *'01*
Ruby's Bucket of Blood *'01*
The Corner *'00*
Love Beat the Hell Outta Me *'00*
Rangers *'00*
Interceptor Force *'99*
Spy Games *'99*
Thursday *'98*
One Night Stand *'97*
Pronto *'97*
Speed 2: Cruise Control *'97*
The Destiny of Marty Fine *'96*
Smalltime *'96*
The Substitute *'96*
Up Close and Personal *'96*
Convict Cowboy *'95*
Showgirls *'95*
Strange Days *'95*
Things to Do in Denver When You're Dead *'95*
Speed *'94*
Menace II Society *'93*
South Central *'92*
Pastime *'91*
Colors *'88*

Gerard Plunkett
Eight Below *'06*
Two for the Money *'05*
A Cooler Climate *'99*
My Husband's Secret Life *'98*
Baby Monitor: Sound of Fear *'97*

Werner Pochath (1939-93)
Devil Hunter *'08*
Laser Mission *'90*
Thunder Warrior 3 *'88*
Shark Hunter *'79*
Flatfoot *'78*

Denis Podalydes (1963-)
Almost Peaceful *'02*
Mortal Transfer *'01*
Comedy of Innocence *'00*
Children of the Century *'99*
Pas Tres Catholique *'93*

Rick Podell (1946-)
World Gone Wild *'88*
Lunch Wagon *'81*

Rossana Podesta (1934-)
The Sensual Man *'74*
The Virgin of Nuremberg *'65*
Alone Against Rome *'62*
Sodom and Gomorrah *'62*
Helen of Troy *'56*
Ulysses *'55*

Fernando Poe, Jr. (1939-2004)
The Ravagers *'65*
The Walls of Hell *'64*

Amy Poehler (1971-)
Hoodwinked Too! Hood vs. Evil *'10 (V)*
Alvin and the Chipmunks: The Squeakuel *'09 (V)*
Monsters vs. Aliens *'09 (V)*
Baby Mama *'08*
Dr. Seuss' Horton Hears a Who! *'08 (V)*
Hamlet 2 *'08*
Spring Breakdown *'08*
Blades of Glory *'07*
The Ex *'07*
Mr. Woodcock *'07*
Shrek the Third *'07 (V)*
Tenacious D in the Pick of Destiny *'06*
Envy *'04*
Mean Girls *'04*
Wet Hot American Summer *'01*

Benoit Poelvoorde
Coco Before Chanel *'09*
Man Bites Dog *'91*

Clarence Poesy
In Bruges *'08*
Harry Potter and the Goblet of Fire *'05*

Judith Pogany
The Midas Touch *'89*
A Hungarian Fairy Tale *'87*

Kathryn Pogson
Millions *'05*
Over Indulgence *'87*
The Company of Wolves *'85*

Ken Pogue
A Dog Named Christmas *'09*
Johnson County War *'02*
Crossfire Trail *'01*
Out of Time *'00*
The 6th Day *'00*
The Jack Bull *'99*
National Lampoon's Dad's Week Off *'97*
Bad Moon *'96*
In the Lake of the Woods *'96*
The Amy Fisher Story *'93*
Still Not Quite Human *'92*
Blind Man's Bluff *'91*
The Hitman *'91*
Run *'91*
Where the Heart Is *'90*
Crazy Moon *'87*
Dead of Winter *'87*
Keeping Track *'86*
Miracle at Moreaux *'86*
The Grey Fox *'83*
July Group *'81*
Suzanne *'80*
Second Wind *'76*

Eric Pohlmann (1913-79)
Tiffany Jones *'75*
Carry On Spying *'64*
Glass Tomb *'55*
Terror Street *'54*
The Belles of St. Trinian's *'53*
Mogambo *'53*
Three Stops to Murder *'53*
The Gambler & the Lady *'52*
Moulin Rouge *'52*
Blackout *'50*

Larry Poindexter (1959-)
S.W.A.T. *'03*
Black Horizon *'01*
Poison *'01*
Steel Sharks *'97*
Body Chemistry 4: Full Exposure *'95*
Sorceress *'94*
Blue Movies *'88*
American Ninja 2: The Confrontation *'87*

Priscilla Pointer (1924-)
Carried Away *'95*
The Magic Bubble *'93*
Disturbed *'90*
A Nightmare on Elm Street 3: Dream Warriors *'87*
Blue Velvet *'86*
Rumpelstiltskin *'86*
The Falcon and the Snowman *'85*
Mysterious Two *'82*
Archer: The Fugitive from the Empire *'81*
The Competition *'80*
Honeysuckle Rose *'80*
The Onion Field *'79*

Jean Poiret (1926-92)
The Elegant Criminal *'92*
Cop Au Vin *'85*
The Last Metro *'80*

Kim Poirier
Decoys: The Second Seduction *'07*
Dawn of the Dead *'04*
Decoys *'04*

Earl C. Poitier (1974-)
Drumline *'02*
Remember the Titans *'00*

Sidney Poitier (1924-)
The Simple Life of Noah Dearborn *'99*
Free of Eden *'98*
The Jackal *'97*
Mandela and de Klerk *'97*
A Good Day to Die *'95*
Sneakers *'92*
Separate but Equal *'91*
Little Nikita *'88*
Shoot to Kill *'88*
Piece of the Action *'77*
Let's Do It Again *'75*
The Wilby Conspiracy *'75*
Uptown Saturday Night *'74*
Buck and the Preacher *'72*
The Organization *'71*
Brother John *'70*
They Call Me Mr. Tibbs! *'70*
The Lost Man *'69*
For Love of Ivy *'68*
Guess Who's Coming to Dinner *'67*
In the Heat of the Night *'67*
To Sir, with Love *'67*
Duel at Diablo *'66*
Bedford Incident *'65*
The Greatest Story Ever Told *'65*
A Patch of Blue *'65*
The Slender Thread *'65*
The Long Ships *'64*
Lilies of the Field *'63*
Pressure Point *'62*
Paris Blues *'61*
A Raisin in the Sun *'61*
All the Young Men *'60*
The Defiant Ones *'58*
Band of Angels *'57*
Edge of the City *'57*
The Mark of the Hawk *'57*
Something of Value *'57*
Goodbye, My Lady *'56*
Blackboard Jungle *'55*
Red Ball Express *'52*
Cry, the Beloved Country *'51*
No Way Out *'50*

Sydney Tamiia Poitier (1973-)
Death Proof *'07*
Nine Lives *'05*
MacArthur Park *'01*
Noah's Ark *'99*
True Crime *'99*
Free of Eden *'98*

Simon Poland
Nemesis 4: Cry of Angels *'97*
Alien from L.A. *'87*

Roman Polanski (1933-)
Rush Hour 3 *'07*
Zemsta *'02*
Grosse Fatigue *'94*
A Pure Formality *'94*
Back in the USSR *'92*
The Tenant *'76*
Andy Warhol's Dracula *'74*
Chinatown *'74*
Diary of Forbidden Dreams *'73*
Ciao Federico! Fellini Directs Satyricon *'69*
The Magic Christian *'69*
The Fearless Vampire Killers *'67*
Innocent Sorcerers *'60*
A Generation *'54*

Victor Poletti
Meeting Venus *'91*
And the Ship Sails On *'83*

Maurice Poli
Urban Warriors *'87*
Gangster's Law *'86*
Five Dolls for an August Moon *'70*

Mark Polish (1972-)
The Astronaut Farmer *'07*
The Bridge of San Luis Rey *'05*
The Good Thief *'03*
Northfork *'03*
Twin Falls Idaho *'99*

Michael Polish (1972-)
The Bridge of San Luis Rey *'05*
The Good Thief *'03*
Twin Falls Idaho *'99*

Jon Polito (1950-)
The Wedding Bros. *'08*
American Gangster *'07*
Cougar Club *'07*
Big Nothing *'06*
Grilled *'06*
The Family Plan *'05*
The Honeymooners *'05*
The Last Shot *'04*
The Box *'03*
The Singing Detective *'03*
Women vs. Men *'02*
The Man Who Wasn't There *'01*
Mimic 2 *'01*
The Adventures of Rocky & Bullwinkle *'00*
Homicide: The Movie *'00*
Angel's Dance *'99*
Russell Mulcahy's Tale of the Mummy *'99*
Apartment Complex *'98*
Nowhere Land *'98*
With Friends Like These *'98*
Music from Another Room *'97*
Robin Cook's Invasion *'97*
Homeward Bound 2: Lost in San Francisco *'96 (V)*
Just Your Luck *'96*
Bushwhacked *'95*
Fluke *'95*
The Invaders *'95*
Blankman *'94*
Girls in Prison *'94*
The Crow *'93*
Fallen Angels 2 *'93*
Barton Fink *'91*
The Freshman *'90*
Leather Jackets *'90*
Miller's Crossing *'90*

Deadly Business '86
Fire with Fire '86
Highlander '86

Lina Polito (1954-)
All Screwed Up '74
Blood Brothers '74

Haydee Politoff (1946-)
Dracula's Great Love '72
La Collectionneuse '67

Vic Polizos
Light It Up '99
Winchell '98
Kiss of a Killer '93
C.H.U.D. '84

Oscar Polk (1899-1949)
Gone with the Wind '39
Green Pastures '36

Stephen Polk
Cherish '02
Drowning on Dry Land '00
Destination Vegas '95

Ben Pollack (1903-71)
The Benny Goodman Story '55
The Glenn Miller Story '54

Sydney Pollack (1934-2008)
Made of Honor '08
Michael Clayton '07
Avenue Montaigne '06
The Interpreter '05
Changing Lanes '02
Eyes Wide Shut '99
Random Hearts '99
A Civil Action '98
Death Becomes Her '92
Husbands and Wives '92
The Player '92
Tootsie '82

Cheryl Pollak (1967-)
Art House '98
No Strings Attached '98
Betty '97
Sin and Redemption '94
Crossing the Bridge '92
Night Life '90
Pump Up the Volume '90
Swimsuit '89
The Dark Side of the Sun '88
My Best Friend Is a Vampire '88

Kevin Pollak (1958-)
Numb '07
Niagara Motel '06
The Santa Clause 3: The Escape Clause '06
Hostage '05
The Whole Ten Yards '04
Frank McKlusky, C.I. '02
Juwanna Mann '02
The Santa Clause 2 '02
Stolen Summer '02
Dr. Dolittle 2 '01
3000 Miles to Graceland '01
The Wedding Planner '01
Deterrence '00
Steal This Movie! '00
The Whole Nine Yards '00
Deal of a Lifetime '99
End of Days '99
She's All That '99
From the Earth to the Moon '98
Hoods '98
Outside Ozona '98
Ruby Bridges '98
National Lampoon's The Don's Analyst '97
Truth or Consequences, N.M. '97
House Arrest '96
That Thing You Do! '96
Casino '95
Chameleon '95
Grumpier Old Men '95
Miami Rhapsody '95
The Usual Suspects '95
Canadian Bacon '94
Clean Slate '94
Grumpy Old Men '93
Indian Summer '93
The Opposite Sex and How to Live With Them '93
Wayne's World 2 '93
A Few Good Men '92
Another You '91
L.A. Story '91
Ricochet '91
Avalon '90
Willow '88

Tracy Pollan (1960-)
The Natalee Holloway Story '09
The Kennedys of Massachusetts '95
A Stranger Among Us '92
Danielle Steel's Fine Things '90
Bright Lights, Big City '88
Promised Land '88
The Abduction of Kari Swenson '87
The Tender Age '84
Baby It's You '82

Daphne Pollard (1890-1978)
Our Relations '36
Bonnie Scotland '35
The Lady Refuses '31

Michael J. Pollard (1939-)
House of 1000 Corpses '03
Out of the Black '01
Along for the Ride '00
Stir '98
Tumbleweeds '98
The Odyssey '97
Trigger Happy '96
Skeeter '93
Split Second '92
Motorama '91
The Arrival '90
The Art of Dying '90
Dick Tracy '90
I Come in Peace '90
Why Me? '90
Fast Food '89
Next of Kin '89
Night Visitor '89
Season of Fear '89
Sleepaway Camp 3: Teenage Wasteland '89
Tango and Cash '89
American Gothic '88
Riders of the Storm '88
Scrooged '88
Heated Vengeance '87
Roxanne '87
America '86
The Patriot '86
Melvin and Howard '80
Between the Lines '77
Vengeance Is Mine '74
Legend of Frenchie King '71
Bonnie & Clyde '67
Caprice '67
Enter Laughing '67
The Wild Angels '66

Snub Pollard (1886-1962)
The Errand Boy '61
Rollin' Plains '38
Arizona Days '37
A Nation Aflame '37
Riders of the Rockies '37
Tex Rides with the Boy Scouts '37
The White Legion '36

Sarah Polley (1979-)
Splice '09
John Adams '08
Beowulf & Grendel '06
Don't Come Knocking '05
Dawn of the Dead '04
Siblings '04
The Event '03
My Life Without Me '03
No Such Thing '01
The Claim '00
Love Come Down '00
The Weight of Water '00
eXistenZ '99
Go '99
Guinevere '99
The Life Before This '99
Last Night '98
White Lies '98
The Hanging Garden '97
Junior's Groove '97
The Sweet Hereafter '96
Exotica '94
Lantern Hill '90
The Adventures of Baron Munchausen '89
Babar: The Movie '88 (V)
Big Town '87

David Pollock (1961-)
The Bad News Bears Go to Japan '78
The Bad News Bears in Breaking Training '77
The Bad News Bears '76

Dee Pollock (1937-2005)
The Plunderers '60
Legend of Tom Dooley '59
Beware, My Lovely '52

Eileen Pollock (1947-)
Far and Away '92
Four Days in July '85

Ellen Pollock (1903-97)
Horror Hospital '73
The Time of His Life '55
Non-Stop New York '37

Teri Polo (1969-)
Full of It '07
Meet the Fockers '04
Beyond Borders '03
Domestic Disturbance '01
The Unsaid '01
Meet the Parents '00
A Prayer in the Dark '97
The Arrival '96
Aspen Extreme '93
Golden Gate '93
The House of the Spirits '93
Quick '93
Passed Away '92
Born to Ride '91
Mystery Date '91
The Phantom of the Opera '90

John Polson (1965-)
Mission: Impossible 2 '00
The Boys '98
Idiot Box '97
Back of Beyond '95
Sirens '94
The Sum of Us '94
Dangerous Game '90

Max Pomeranc (1984-)
Fluke '95
Journey '95
Searching for Bobby Fischer '93

Ellen Pompeo (1969-)
Art Heist '05
Life of the Party '05
Eternal Sunshine of the Spotless Mind '04
Old School '03
Undermind '03
Moonlight Mile '02

Carlos Ponce (1972-)
Couples Retreat '09
Just My Luck '06
Deuce Bigalow: European Gigolo '05

Eusebio Poncela (1947-)
800 Bullets '02
Intacto '01
Martin (Hache) '97
A Shadow You Soon Will Be '94
Law of Desire '86
Matador '86
Cannibal Man '71

Lily Pons (1904-76)
That Girl from Paris '36
I Dream Too Much '35

Merce Pons (1966-)
Km. 0 '00
Caresses '97

Chris Pontius (1974-)
Jackass Number Two '06
Jackass: The Movie '02

Yvan Ponton (1945-)
The Boys '97
Scanners 2: The New Order '91
Pouvoir Intime '87
Men of Steel '77

Olaf Pooley
Crucible of Horror '69
Naked Evil '66

Bray Poor
Two Ninas '00
Anima '98

Iggy Pop (1947-)
Suck '09
Coffee and Cigarettes '03
Snow Day '00
The Crow 2: City of Angels '96
Dead Man '95
Tank Girl '94
Cry-Baby '90
Hardware '90
Sid & Nancy '86

Carly Pope (1980-)
Stuntmen '09
Beneath '07
Itty Bitty Titty Committee '07
Two for the Money '05
Eighteen '04
White Coats '04
Window Theory '04
Nemesis Game '03
Finder's Fee '01
A Cooler Climate '99

Marc Poppel
Separate Lives '94
Damned River '89

Anna Popplewell (1988-)
The Chronicles of Narnia: Prince Caspian '08
The Chronicles of Narnia: The Lion, the Witch and the Wardrobe '05
The Little Vampire '00

Albert "Poppy" Popwell (1926-99)
Scissors '91
Wild at Heart '90
The Siege of Firebase Gloria '89
Who's That Girl? '87
Sudden Impact '83
The Buddy Holly Story '78
The Enforcer '76
Cleopatra Jones & the Casino of Gold '75
Charley Varrick '73
Cleopatra Jones '73
Magnum Force '73
Fuzz '72
Dirty Harry '71
Coogan's Bluff '68
The Harder They Fall '56
The Joe Louis Story '53

Johnny Popwell
Manhunter '83
Challenge '74

Paul Porcasi
The Devil and the Deep '32
Morocco '30

Jorge Porcel (1936-)
Carlito's Way '93
Naked Is Better '73

Colleen Porch
S.I.S. '08
All In '06
Starship Troopers 2: Hero of the Federation '04

Marc Porel (1949-83)
The Psychic '78
The Innocent '76
Don't Torture a Duckling '72

Paulina Porizkova (1965-)
Second Best '05
Dark Asylum '01
Intern '00
Partners in Crime '99
Thursday '98
Long Time Since '97
Female Perversions '96
Wedding Bell Blues '96
Arizona Dream '94
Her Alibi '88
Portfolio '88
Anna '87

Maria Poroshina
Day Watch '06
Night Watch '04

Louise Portal (1951-)
Heading South '05
The Barbarian Invasions '03
Sous Sol '96
The Decline of the American Empire '86
The Klutz '73

Robert Portal
In Your Dreams '07
Mrs. Dalloway '97
Stiff Upper Lips '96

Andrew Porter
Juncture '07
Road Kill USA '93

Billy Porter
The Broken Hearts Club '00
Intern '00
Twisted '96

Brett Porter (1956-)
Stiletto Dance '01
Firehead '90

Don Porter (1912-96)
The Christmas Coal Mine Miracle '77
Mame '74
The Norliss Tapes '73
The Candidate '72
Bachelor in Paradise '69
Live a Little, Love a Little '68
Our Miss Brooks '56
The Racket '51
Buck Privates Come Home '47
She Wolf of London '46
Night Monster '42
Who Done It? '42

Eric Porter (1928-95)
Oliver Twist '85
Churchill and the Generals '81
Little Lord Fauntleroy '80
The Thirty-Nine Steps '79
Hennessy '75
Antony and Cleopatra '73
The Belstone Fox '73
Hitler: The Last Ten Days '73
Hands of the Ripper '71
Macbeth '70
Kaleidoscope '66
The Heroes of Telemark '65
The Fall of the Roman Empire '64
The Pumpkin Eater '64

Jean Porter (1925-)
G.I. Jane '51
Kentucky Jubilee '51
Abbott and Costello in Hollywood '45
Bathing Beauty '44
San Fernando Valley '44
Inside Information '34

Robert Porter
Deadly Fieldtrip '74
The Jesus Trip '71

Scott Porter
The Good Guy '10
Bandslam '09
Prom Night '08
Speed Racer '08

Susie Porter
Better Than Sex '00
Bootmen '00
The Monkey's Mask '00
Two Hands '98
Idiot Box '97
Paradise Road '97
Welcome to Woop Woop '97

Blanca Portillo
Broken Embraces '09
Goya's Ghosts '06
Volver '06

Eric Portman (1903-69)
Bedford Incident '65
The Naked Edge '61
The Colditz Story '55
The Spider and the Fly '49
Dear Murderer '47
Great Day '46
Men of Two Worlds '46
A Canterbury Tale '44
We Dive at Dawn '43
The Forty-Ninth Parallel '41
One of Our Aircraft Is Missing '41
Moonlight Sonata '38
The Crimes of Stephen Hawke '36
Murder in the Old Red Barn '36

Natalie Portman (1981-)
Hesher '10
Brothers '09
New York, I Love You '09
The Other Boleyn Girl '08
Mr. Magorium's Wonder Emporium '07
My Blueberry Nights '07
Goya's Ghosts '06
Paris, je t'aime '06
V for Vendetta '06
Free Zone '05
Star Wars: Episode 3—Revenge of the Sith '05
Closer '04
Garden State '04
Cold Mountain '03
Star Wars: Episode 2—Attack of the Clones '02
Where the Heart Is '00
Anywhere But Here '99
Star Wars: Episode 1—The Phantom Menace '99
Beautiful Girls '96
Everyone Says I Love You '96
Mars Attacks! '96
Heat '95
The Professional '94

Richard Portnow (1950-)
The Indian '07
Perfect Stranger '07
Tony n' Tina's Wedding '07
Find Me Guilty '06
Double Bang '01
Double Down '01
The Ghost of Spoon River '00
Happy Accidents '00
Desert Thunder '99
Ghost Dog: The Way of the Samurai '99
The Substitute 3: Winner Takes All '99
Witness Protection '99
Going Postal '98
Private Parts '96
Donor Unknown '95
Man of the House '95
S.F.W. '94
Trial by Jury '94
Sister Act '92
Barton Fink '91
Kindergarten Cop '90
Meet the Hollowheads '89
Say Anything '89
In Dangerous Company '88
Good Morning, Vietnam '87

Brian Posehn (1966-)
The Devil's Rejects '05
Pom Poko '94 (V)

Parker Posey (1968-)
Happy Tears '09
The Eye '08
Spring Breakdown '08
Broken English '07
Fay Grim '06
For Your Consideration '06
The Oh in Ohio '06

Superman Returns '06
Adam & Steve '05
Blade: Trinity '04
Laws of Attraction '04
The Event '03
A Mighty Wind '03
Personal Velocity: Three Portraits '02
The Sweetest Thing '02
The Anniversary Party '01
Josie and the Pussycats '01
Best in Show '00
Scream 3 '00
Henry Fool '98
You've Got Mail '98
Armistead Maupin's More Tales of the City '97
Clockwatchers '97
The House of Yes '97
Basquiat '96
The Daytrippers '96
Drunks '96
subUrbia '96
Waiting for Guffman '96
The Doom Generation '95
Flirt '95
Frisk '95
Kicking and Screaming '95
Party Girl '94
Sleep with Me '94
Armistead Maupin's Tales of the City '93
Dazed and Confused '93

Markie Post (1950-)
Holiday in Handcuffs '07
I've Been Waiting for You '98
There's Something about Mary '98
Glitz '88
Tricks of the Trade '88
Scene of the Crime '85
TripleCross '85

Mikey Post
Rest Stop: Don't Look Back '08
Rest Stop '06

Saskia Post (1961-)
Dogs in Space '87
One Night Stand '84

William Post, Jr. (1901-89)
Call Northside 777 '48
House on 92nd Street '45
Sherlock Holmes and the Secret Weapon '42
Ship Ahoy '42

Pete Postlethwaite (1945-)
Closing the Ring '07
Valley of the Heart's Delight '07
Ghost Son '06
The Omen '06
Aeon Flux '05
The Constant Gardener '05
Red Mercury '05
Strange Bedfellows '04
Gone Dark '03
Shattered City: The Halifax Explosion '03
Between Strangers '02
Dark Water '02
Triggermen '02
The Shipping News '01
Cowboy Up '00
Alice in Wonderland '99
Animal Farm '99
Butterfly Collectors '99
Lost for Words '99
When the Sky Falls '99
Among Giants '98
Amistad '97
Brute '97
The Lost World: Jurassic Park 2 '97
The Serpent's Kiss '97
Brassed Off '96
Crimetime '96
Dragonheart '96
James and the Giant Peach '96 (V)
William Shakespeare's Romeo and Juliet '96
The Usual Suspects '95
When Saturday Comes '95
Martin Chuzzlewit '94
Sharpe's Company '94
Sharpe's Enemy '94
Suite 16 '94
In the Name of the Father '93
The Last of the Mohicans '92
Split Second '92
Waterland '92
Hamlet '90
The Dressmaker '89
To Kill a Priest '89
Distant Voices, Still Lives '88
A Private Function '84

Laurens C. Postma
To Live and Die in Hong Kong '89
Heroes Three '84

Tom Poston (1921-2007)
The Princess Diaries 2: Royal Engagement '04
Beethoven's 5th '03
The Story of Us '99
Krippendorf's Tribe '98
A Perfect Little Murder '90
Carbon Copy '81
Up the Academy '80
Cold Turkey '71
Soldier in the Rain '63
The Tempest '63
Zotz! '62

Victor Potel (1889-1947)
Miracle of Morgan's Creek '44
Last of the Clintons '35
Inside Information '34
Thunder Over Texas '34
Border Romance '30
Doughboys '30
Paradise Island '30
Captain Swagger '25
Anna Christie '23

Franka Potente (1974-)
Che '08
Romulus, My Father '07
The Bourne Supremacy '04
I Love Your Work '03
All I Want '02
The Bourne Identity '02
Blow '01
Storytelling '01
Anatomy '00
The Princess and the Warrior '00
Run Lola Run '98

Brian Poth (1975-)
Angel of Death '09
Dog Gone Love '03
Venomous '01

Chris Potter (1960-)
The Good Witch '08
The Pacifier '05
Arachnid '01
The Waiting Game '98

Madeleine Potter (1963-)
The White Countess '05
The Golden Bowl '00
Spellbreaker: Secret of the Leprechauns '96
Two Evil Eyes '90
Bloodhounds of Broadway '89
Slaves of New York '89
Hello Again '87
The Bostonians '84

Martin Potter (1944-)
Gunpowder '87
The Only Way '70
Twinsanity '70
Ciao Federico! Fellini Directs Satyricon '69
Fellini Satyricon '69

Monica Potter (1971-)
The Last House on the Left '09
Lower Learning '08
Saw '04
I'm with Lucy '02
Along Came a Spider '01
Head Over Heels '01
A Cool, Dry Place '98
Patch Adams '98
The Very Thought of You '98
Con Air '97
Without Limits '97

Andrew Lee Potts (1979-)
Alice '09
Return to House on Haunted Hill '07
Dead Fish '04

Annie Potts (1952-)
Queen Sized '08
Elvis Has Left the Building '04
Toy Story 2 '99 (V)
Toy Story '95 (V)
Breaking the Rules '92
Texasville '90
Ghostbusters 2 '89
Who's Harry Crumb? '89
Pass the Ammo '88
Bayou Romance '86
Jumpin' Jack Flash '86
Pretty in Pink '86
Crimes of Passion '84
Ghostbusters '84
It Came Upon a Midnight Clear '84
Heartaches '82
Flatbed Annie and Sweetiepie: Lady Truckers '79
Corvette Summer '78
King of the Gypsies '78

Cliff (Potter) Potts (1947-)
Counter Measures '99
Sahara '83
The Last Ride of the Dalton Gang '79
Little Women '78
The Groundstar Conspiracy '72
Silent Running '71

Jonathan Potts
Jason X '01
Torso '01

Jose Maria Pou (1944-)
The Sea Inside '04
Beloved/Friend '99

Ely Pouget (1961-)
Total Reality '97
Death Machine '95
Lawnmower Man 2: Beyond Cyberspace '95
Red Shoe Diaries 5: Weekend Pass '95
Tall, Dark and Deadly '95
Silent Victim '92
Endless Descent '90
Cool Blue '88

Georges Poujouly (1940-2000)
Frantic '58
Forbidden Games '52

CCH Pounder (1952-)
Avatar '09
Orphan '09
Boycott '02
Things Behind the Sun '01
Cora Unashamed '00
Disappearing Acts '00
End of Days '99
Race '99
Final Justice '98
Tom Clancy's Netforce '98
Face/Off '97
Aladdin and the King of Thieves '96 (V)
If These Walls Could Talk '96
White Dwarf '95
Zooman '95
Tales from the Crypt Presents Demon Knight '94
Benny & Joon '93
The Disappearance of Christina '93
The Ernest Green Story '93
Lifepod '93
Question of Faith '93
Return to Lonesome Dove '93
Sliver '93
RoboCop 3 '91
Postcards from the Edge '90
Psycho 4: The Beginning '90
Bagdad Cafe '88
Prizzi's Honor '85
Union City '81

Melvil Poupaud (1973-)
The Broken '08
A Christmas Tale '08
Broken English '07
Time to Leave '05
Le Divorce '03
Time Regained '99
Genealogies of a Crime '97
A Summer's Tale '96
Three Lives and Only One Death '96
Diary of a Seducer '95
The Lover '92

Henri Poupon (1882-1953)
Harvest '37
Angele '34

Andre Pousse
Deadly Sting '73
Killer '73

Addison Powell (1921-)
The Rosary Murders '87
The Man Without a Country '73

Brittney Powell (1972-)
Dragonworld '94
Airborne '93
To Be the Best '93

Charles Powell (1963-)
Lost Junction '03
Fear of the Dark '02
Grey Owl '99
Screamers '96
Cheyenne Warrior '94

Clifton Powell (1956-)
Internet Dating '08
Jada '08
Father of Lies '07
Norbit '07
The Gospel '05
Who Made the Potatoe Salad? '05
Never Die Alone '04
Ray '04
Woman, Thou Art Loosed '04
Civil Brand '02
Friday After Next '02
Bones '01
The Brothers '01
Lockdown '00
The Breaks '99
Selma, Lord, Selma '99
Caught Up '98
The Pentagon Wars '98
Phantoms '97
Dead Presidents '95

Dick Powell (1904-63)
Susan Slept Here '54
The Bad and the Beautiful '52
Cry Danger '51
Mrs. Mike '49
Pitfall '48
Station West '48
Cornered '45
It Happened Tomorrow '44
Meet the People '44
Murder, My Sweet '44
Star Spangled Rhythm '42
In the Navy '41
Christmas in July '40
Hard to Get '38
Hollywood Hotel '37
On the Avenue '37
Varsity Show '37
Colleen '36
Gold Diggers of 1937 '36
Stage Struck '36
Gold Diggers of 1935 '35
A Midsummer Night's Dream '35
Shipmates Forever '35
Dames '34
Flirtation Walk '34
Happiness Ahead '34
Wonder Bar '34
Footlight Parade '33
42nd Street '33
Gold Diggers of 1933 '33
Blessed Event '32
Too Busy to Work '32

Eleanor Powell (1912-82)
The Duchess of Idaho '50
Sensations of 1945 '44
I Dood It '43
Thousands Cheer '43
Ship Ahoy '42
Lady Be Good '41
Broadway Melody of 1940 '40
Honolulu '39
Rosalie '38
Broadway Melody of 1938 '37
Born to Dance '36
Broadway Melody of 1936 '35

Esteban Louis Powell (1977-)
Bunny Whipped '06
Hitman's Run '99
Powder '95

Jane Powell (1929-)
The Sandy Bottom Orchestra '00
Mayday at 40,000 Feet '76
Enchanted Island '58
The Girl Most Likely '57
Hit the Deck '55
Athena '54
Deep in My Heart '54
Seven Brides for Seven Brothers '54
Small Town Girl '53
Three Sailors and a Girl '53
Rich, Young and Pretty '51
Royal Wedding '51
Nancy Goes to Rio '50
Two Weeks with Love '50
A Date with Judy '48
Luxury Liner '48
Three Daring Daughters '48
Holiday in Mexico '46
Delightfully Dangerous '45

Lee Powell (1908-44)
Fighting Devil Dogs '43
Along the Sundown Trail '42
Prairie Pals '42
Tumbleweed Trail '42
Trigger Pals '39
The Lone Ranger '38

Marcus Powell (1932-2000)
Kill by Inches '99
The Rejuvenator '88

Michael Powell (1905-90)
Peeping Tom '60
Edge of the World '37

Robert Powell (1944-)
The Mystery of Edwin Drood '93
The Jigsaw Man '84
Dark Forces '83
Shaka Zulu '83
What Waits Below '83
Frankenstein '82
The Hunchback of Notre Dame '82
Jane Austen in Manhattan '80
Survivor '80
The Thirty-Nine Steps '79
The Four Feathers '78
Jesus of Nazareth '77
Tommy '75
Mahler '74
The Asphyx '72
Asylum '72
Jude the Obscure '71
Secrets '71

William Powell (1892-1984)
Mister Roberts '55
The Girl Who Had Everything '53
How to Marry a Millionaire '53
It's a Big Country '51
Mr. Peabody & the Mermaid '48
Life with Father '47
The Senator Was Indiscreet '47
Song of the Thin Man '47
Ziegfeld Follies '46
The Heavenly Body '44
The Thin Man Goes Home '44
Crossroads '42
Love Crazy '41
Shadow of the Thin Man '41
I Love You Again '40
Another Thin Man '39
Double Wedding '37
The Last of Mrs. Cheyney '37
After the Thin Man '36
Ex-Mrs. Bradford '36
The Great Ziegfeld '36
Libeled Lady '36
My Man Godfrey '36
Reckless '35
Star of Midnight '35
Evelyn Prentice '34
Fashions of 1934 '34
Manhattan Melodrama '34
The Thin Man '34
Double Harness '33
The Kennel Murder Case '33
One Way Passage '32
Man of the World '31
Feel My Pulse '28
Last Command '28
Nevada '27
Romola '25
Sherlock Holmes '22

Power
Black and White '99
Belly '98

Chad Power (1984-)
3 Ninjas Knuckle Up '95
3 Ninjas '92

Dave Power (1978-)
Shuttle '09
U-571 '00

Hartley Power (1894-1966)
Dead of Night '45
Evergreen '34

Romina Power
Deadly Sanctuary '68
How I Learned to Love Women '66

Taryn Power (1953-)
Sinbad and the Eye of the Tiger '77
Tracks '76
The Count of Monte Cristo '74

Tyrone Power (1913-58)
Abandon Ship '57
Witness for the Prosecution '57
The Eddy Duchin Story '56
The Long Gray Line '55
Diplomatic Courier '52
I'll Never Forget You '51
The Black Rose '50
Rawhide '50
Prince of Foxes '49
The Luck of the Irish '48
That Wonderful Urge '48
Captain from Castile '47
Nightmare Alley '47
The Razor's Edge '46
Crash Dive '43
The Black Swan '42
Son of Fury '42
This Above All '42
Blood and Sand '41
A Yank in the R.A.F. '41
Brigham Young: Frontiersman '40
Johnny Apollo '40
The Mark of Zorro '40

Day-Time Wife '39
Jesse James '39
The Rains Came '39
Rose of Washington Square '39
Second Fiddle '39
Alexander's Ragtime Band '38
Marie Antoinette '38
Cafe Metropole '37
In Old Chicago '37
Love Is News '37
Second Honeymoon '37
Thin Ice '37
Girl's Dormitory '36
Lloyds of London '36
Braveheart '25

Tyrone Power, Jr. (1959-)
Evil Lives '92
California Casanova '89
Shag: The Movie '89
Cocoon '85

Tyrone Power, Sr. (1869-1931)
Big Trail '30
Test of Donald Norton '26
Red Kimono '25
Dream Street '21

Alexandra Powers (1967-)
Double Down '01
Storm Tracker '99
Last Man Standing '96
Rising Sun '93
The Seventh Coin '92
Cast a Deadly Spell '91
Dangerous Pursuit '89
Dead Poets Society '89
Plain Clothes '88
Sonny Boy '87
Mask '85
Silence of the Heart '84

Beverly (Hills) Powers
Knights & Emeralds '87
Sixteen '72
Brides of the Beast '68
The Comedy of Terrors '64
Kissin' Cousins '64

Lucille Powers (1911-81)
Texas Bad Man '32
Two Gun Man '31

Mala Powers (1931-2007)
Daddy's Gone A-Hunting '69
Escape from Planet Earth '67
Storm Rider '57
Rage at Dawn '55
City That Never Sleeps '53
Cyrano de Bergerac '50

Stefanie Powers (1942-)
Scott Turow's The Burden of Proof '92
Shadow on the Sun '88
Family Secrets '84
Mistral's Daughter '84
Escape to Athena '79
Little Moon & Jud McGraw '78
The Invisible Strangler '76
The Man Inside '76
Return to Earth '76
It Seemed Like a Good Idea at the Time '75
Sky Hei$t '75
Herbie Rides Again '74
Manhunter '74
Gone with the West '72
No Place to Run '72
Paper Man '71
The Boatniks '70
Crescendo '69
Die! Die! My Darling! '65
Love Has Many Faces '65
McLintock! '63
Palm Springs Weekend '63
Experiment in Terror '62
The Interns '62

Tom Powers (1890-1955)
Lucky Me '54
Destination Moon '50
The Nevadan '50
Mexican Hayride '48
Station West '48
Up in Central Park '48
Son of Rusty '47
The Blue Dahlia '46
Double Indemnity '44

Leon Pownall (1943-2006)
Shattered City: The Halifax Explosion '03
The Day Reagan Was Shot '01
Dirty Pictures '00
Hiroshima '95
How the West Was Fun '95
Spenser: The Judas Goat '94
Love and Hate: A Marriage Made in Hell '90
Bye Bye Blues '89
Termini Station '89

Clare Powney (1963-)
The Girl '86
Operation Julie '85

Beata Pozniak
Cyxork 7 '06
JFK '91

Jose Maria Prada (1925-78)
The Diabolical Dr. Z '65
The Hunt '65

Bruno Pradal (1949-92)
November Moon '85
Charlie Bravo '80

Lilia Prado (1928-2006)
The Illusion Travels by Streetcar '53
Wuthering Heights '53
Mexican Bus Ride '51

Jerome Pradon (1964-)
Jesus Christ Superstar '00
Simon Sez '99

Michael Praed (1960-)
Darkness Falls '98
To Die For 2: Son of Darkness '91
Writer's Block '91
Riders '88
Nightflyers '87
Robin Hood... The Legend: Robin Hood and the Sorcerer '83
Robin Hood... The Legend: The Swords of Wayland '83

Stanley Prager (1917-72)
Gun Crazy '49
A Foreign Affair '48
You Gotta Stay Happy '48

Pras (1972-)
Nora's Hair Salon '04
Da Hip Hop Witch '00
Turn It Up '00
Mystery Men '99

Eric Prat
Brotherhood of the Wolf '01
Tatie Danielle '91

Joan Prather (1951-)
The Deerslayer '78
Devil's Rain '75
Smile '75
Big Bad Mama '74

Chris Pratt
Bride Wars '09
Jennifer's Body '09
Strangers with Candy '06

Judson Pratt (1916-2002)
The Horse Soldiers '59
Monster on the Campus '59

Keri Lynn Pratt (1978-)
I Hope They Serve Beer in Hell '09

The Smokers '00
Cruel Intentions 2 '99

Kyla Pratt (1986-)
Dr. Dolittle: Million Dollar Mutts '09
Hotel for Dogs '09
Dr. Dolittle 4: Tail to the Chief '08
Dr. Dolittle 3 '06
The Proud Family Movie '05 (V)
Fat Albert '04
Dr. Dolittle 2 '01
Love and Basketball '00
Barney's Great Adventure '98
Dr. Dolittle '98

Purnell Pratt (1885-1941)
Come on Rangers '38
Emma '32
Bachelor Apartment '31
The Silver Horde '30
On with the Show '29

Susan May Pratt (1974-)
Who's Your Monkey '07
Undermind '03
Charms for the Easy Life '02
Searching for Paradise '02
Center Stage '00
Drive Me Crazy '99
Ten Things I Hate about You '99

Victoria Pratt
Brotherhood of Blood '08
Journey to the Center of the Earth '08
What Love Is '07
Kraken: Tentacles of the Deep '06
House of the Dead 2: Dead Aim '05

George Pravda (1918-85)
The Duchess of Duke Street '78
Frankenstein Must Be Destroyed '69

Joana Preiss
Boarding Gate '07
Inside Paris '06

Wolfgang Preiss (1910-2002)
Club Extinction '89
A Bridge Too Far '77
Raid on Rommel '71
Cave of the Living Dead '65
The Mad Executioners '65
The Train '65
Von Ryan's Express '65
The Invisible Dr. Mabuse '62
Testament of Dr. Mabuse '62
The Return of Dr. Mabuse '61
Mill of the Stone Women '60
The Thousand Eyes of Dr. Mabuse '60
Mistress of the World '59

June Preisser (1920-84)
Strike Up the Band '40
Babes in Arms '39

Albert Prejean (1893-1979)
Princess Tam Tam '35
Under the Roofs of Paris '29
Italian Straw Hat '27
The Crazy Ray '22

Otto Preminger (1906-86)
The Hobbit '78 (V)
Stalag 17 '53
They Got Me Covered '43

Luis Prendes (1913-98)
Alien Predators '80
The Christmas Kid '68
Ursus in the Valley of the Lions '62

Jordan Prentice
In Bruges '08
Weirdsville '07

Paula Prentiss (1939-)
Mrs. Winterbourne '96
M.A.D.D.: Mothers Against Drunk Driving '83
Packin' It In '83
Buddy Buddy '81
Saturday the 14th '81
The Black Marble '79
No Room to Run '78
The Stepford Wives '75
The Parallax View '74
Last of the Red Hot Lovers '72
Born to Win '71
Catch-22 '70
Bachelor in Paradise '69
In Harm's Way '65
What's New Pussycat? '65
The World of Henry Orient '64
Man's Favorite Sport? '63
The Horizontal Lieutenant '62
The Honeymoon Machine '61
Where the Boys Are '60

Robert Prentiss
The Alamo '04
Total Exposure '91

Laura Prepon (1980-)
Come Early Morning '06
Karla '06
Slackers '02

Judy Prescott
Islander '06
Hit and Runway '01

Robert Prescott
Michael Clayton '07
Blue De Ville '86
Real Genius '85
Bachelor Party '84

Micheline Presle (1922-)
Transfixed '01
Bad Company '99
A Chef in Love '96
Diary of a Seducer '95
Pas Tres Catholique '93
I Want to Go Home '89
A Slightly Pregnant Man '79
Legend of Frenchie King '71
The King of Hearts '66
The Nun '66
Hail Mafia '65
The Prize '63
Time Out for Love '61
Mistress of the World '59
The Bride Is Much Too Beautiful '58
Adventures of Captain Fabian '51
Devil in the Flesh '46
The Fantastic Night '42
The French Way '40

Brian Presley
Borderland '07
Home of the Brave '06
Guarding Eddy '04

Elvis Presley (1935-77)
This Is Elvis '81
Change of Habit '69
Charro! '69
The Trouble with Girls (and How to Get into It) '69
Live a Little, Love a Little '68
Speedway '68
Stay Away, Joe '68
Clambake '67
Double Trouble '67
Easy Come, Easy Go '67
Paradise, Hawaiian Style '66
Spinout '66
Frankie and Johnny '65
Girl Happy '65
Harum Scarum '65
Tickle Me '65
Kissin' Cousins '64
Roustabout '64
Fun in Acapulco '63

It Happened at the World's Fair '63
Viva Las Vegas '63
Blue Hawaii '62
Girls! Girls! Girls! '62
Kid Galahad '62
Follow That Dream '61
Wild in the Country '61
Flaming Star '60
G.I. Blues '60
King Creole '58
Jailhouse Rock '57
Loving You '57
Love Me Tender '56

Priscilla Presley (1946-)
Naked Gun 33 1/3: The Final Insult '94
Naked Gun 2 1/2: The Smell of Fear '91
The Adventures of Ford Fairlane '90
The Naked Gun: From the Files of Police Squad '88

Harve Presnell (1933-)
Bait Shop '08
Flags of Our Fathers '06
Old School '03
Super Sucker '03
Mr. Deeds '02
Escanaba in da Moonlight '01
Jackie, Ethel, Joan: The Kennedy Women '01
Family Man '00
The Legend of Bagger Vance '00
A Bright Shining Lie '98
Everything That Rises '98
Patch Adams '98
Saving Private Ryan '98
Face/Off '97
Julian Po '97
Fargo '96
Larger Than Life '96
The Whole Wide World '96
Paint Your Wagon '69
The Unsinkable Molly Brown '64

Nathalie Press
Fifty Dead Men Walking '08
In Tranzit '07
Red Road '06
My Summer of Love '05

Jaime Pressly (1977-)
I Love You, Man '09
Dr. Seuss' Horton Hears a Who! '08 (V)
DOA: Dead or Alive '06
Bachelor Party Vegas '05
Cruel World '05
Karate Dog '04
Torque '04
Survival Island '02
Joe Dirt '01
Not Another Teen Movie '01
Ticker '01
Tomcats '01
100 Girls '00
Poor White Trash '00
Ringmaster '98
Poison Ivy 3: The New Seduction '97

Lawrence Pressman (1939-)
American Dreamz '06
The Far Side of Jericho '06
DC 9/11: Time of Crisis '04
American Wedding '03
American Pie '99
The Maker '98
Mighty Joe Young '98
The Late Shift '96
Sunchaser '96
Trial and Error '96
Angus '95
White Hot: The Mysterious Murder of Thelma Todd '91
Fire and Rain '89
Hanoi Hilton '87
The Deliberate Stranger '86
On Wings of Eagles '86
For Love or Money '84
The Winds of War '83

Rehearsal for Murder '82
Blind Ambition '79
The Gathering: Part 2 '79
The Gathering '77
The Trial of Lee Harvey Oswald '77
Rich Man, Poor Man '76
The Man in the Glass Booth '75
Winter Kill '74
The Hellstrom Chronicle '71
Shaft '71

Jason Presson (1971-)
The Lady in White '88
Saturday the 14th Strikes Back '88
Explorers '85
The Stone Boy '84

Jo Prestia (1960-)
Irreversible '02
The Dreamlife of Angels '98

Billy Preston (1946-)
Wired '89
Blame It on the Night '84
Let It Be '70

Carrie Preston (1967-)
Duplicity '09
That Evening Sun '09
Doubt '08
Ready? OK! '08
Lovely by Surprise '07
Towelhead '07
Transamerica '05

Cynthia (Cyndy, Cindy) Preston (1968-)
Lone Rider '08
Nanny Insanity '06
The Event '03
Facing the Enemy '00
The Thin Blue Lie '00
Total Recall 2070: Machine Dreams '99
Premonition '98
The Ultimate Weapon '97
Black Fox: The Price of Peace '94
Whale Music '94
Prom Night 3: The Last Kiss '89
The Brain '88
Pin... '88
The Darkside '87

J.A. Preston
Harvest of Fire '95
A Few Good Men '92
Fire Birds '90
Remo Williams: The Adventure Begins '85
Body Heat '81
The Spook Who Sat by the Door '73

John Preston
Ready? OK! '08
Courage of the North '35

Kelly Preston (1962-)
The Last Song '10
Old Dogs '09
The Tenth Circle '08
Death Sentence '07
Broken Bridges '06
Sky High '05
Convicted '04
Eulogy '04
Dr. Seuss' The Cat in the Hat '03
View from the Top '03
What a Girl Wants '03
Bar Hopping '00
Battlefield Earth '00
Daddy & Them '99
For Love of the Game '99
Holy Man '98
Jack Frost '98
Addicted to Love '96
Citizen Ruth '96
Jerry Maguire '96
Nothing to Lose '96
From Dusk Till Dawn '95
Mrs. Munck '95
Cheyenne Warrior '94
Double Cross '94
Love Is a Gun '94
Only You '92

The Perfect Bride *'91*
Run *'91*
The Experts *'89*
The Spellbinder *'88*
Twins *'88*
Amazon Women on the Moon *'87*
Love at Stake *'87*
A Tiger's Tale *'87*
52 Pick-Up *'86*
SpaceCamp *'86*
Mischief *'85*
Secret Admirer *'85*
Christine *'84*
Metalstorm: The Destruction of Jared Syn *'83*

Mike (Michael) Preston (1938-)
Blade in Hong Kong *'85*
Hot Pursuit *'84*
Metalstorm: The Destruction of Jared Syn *'83*
The Road Warrior *'82*
Surabaya Conspiracy *'75*

Robert Preston (1918-87)
Outrage! *'86*
Finnegan Begin Again *'84*
The Last Starfighter *'84*
September Gun *'83*
Rehearsal for Murder *'82*
Victor/Victoria *'82*
S.O.B. *'81*
The Chisholms *'79*
Semi-Tough *'77*
My Father's House *'75*
Mame *'74*
Junior Bonner *'72*
How the West Was Won *'63*
The Music Man *'62*
Savage Wilderness *'55*
Face to Face *'52*
My Outlaw Brother *'51*
Best of the Badmen *'50*
Tulsa *'49*
Blood on the Moon *'48*
Reap the Wild Wind *'42*
This Gun for Hire *'42*
Wake Island *'42*
Night of January 16th *'41*
Beau Geste *'39*
Union Pacific *'39*
King of Alcatraz *'38*

Wayde Preston (1929-92)
Smokey & the Judge *'80*
Today We Kill, Tomorrow We Die *'71*
A Long Ride From Hell *'68*

Giancarlo Prete (1942-2001)
Escape from the Bronx *'85*
Tornado *'83*
Warriors of the Wasteland *'83*
Street Law *'74*
Sting of the West *'72*
Fistful of Death *'71*

Daniel Prevost (1939-)
Whatever You Say *'02*
The Dinner Game *'98*
Uranus *'91*

Francoise Prevost (1930-97)
L'Amour en Herbe *'77*
Spirits of the Dead *'68*
Time Out for Love *'61*
Love Play *'60*
Paris Belongs to Us *'60*

Marie Prevost (1898-1937)
Tango *'36*
Hands Across the Table *'35*
The Sin of Madelon Claudet *'31*
The Flying Fool *'29*
Party Girls *'29*
Getting Gertie's Garter *'27*
The Marriage Circle *'24*
Yankee Doodle in Berlin *'19*

Alan Price (1941-)
Oh, Alfie *'75*
O Lucky Man! *'73*

Dennis Price (1915-73)
Horror Hospital *'73*
Theatre of Blood *'73*
Pulp *'72*
Rites of Frankenstein *'72*
The Screaming Dead *'72*
Twins of Evil *'71*
The Horror of Frankenstein *'70*
Venus in Furs *'70*
Murder Most Foul *'65*
Cool Mikado *'63*
The V.I.P.'s *'63*
The Wrong Arm of the Law *'63*
What a Carve-Up! *'62*
Victim *'61*
The Millionairess *'60*
No Love for Johnnie *'60*
School for Scoundrels *'60*
Tunes of Glory *'60*
The Naked Truth *'58*
Eight Witnesses *'54*
The Adventurers *'51*
I'll Never Forget You *'51*
Kind Hearts and Coronets *'49*
Dear Murderer *'47*
The Magic Bow *'47*
Echo Murders *'45*
A Canterbury Tale *'44*

Hal Price (1886-1964)
Lawmen *'44*
Rustler's Hideout *'44*
Trigger Men *'41*
Across the Plains *'39*
Man from Texas *'39*
Melody of the Plains *'37*
Where Trails Divide *'37*
Cavalry *'36*
Desert Phantom *'36*

Kate Price (1872-1943)
Linda *'29*
The Perfect Clown *'25*
Amarilly of Clothesline Alley *'18*

Lindsay Price (1976-)
Club Dread *'04*
No Turning Back *'01*

Marc Price (1968-)
Killer Tomatoes Eat France *'91*
The Rescue *'88*
Trick or Treat *'86*

Molly Price (1966-)
What Goes Up *'09*
Chasing Sleep *'00*
Kiss Me, Guido *'97*
Risk *'94*
Jersey Girl *'92*

Nancy Price (1880-1970)
The Three Weird Sisters *'48*
Secret Mission *'42*
The Speckled Band *'31*

Oliver Price
Dark Corners *'06*
Parasite *'03*

Richard Price (1949-)
Ransom *'96*
Night and the City *'92*
Shocker *'89*
Wanderers *'79*

Stanley Price (1892-1955)
Roaring City *'51*
The Invisible Monster *'50*
Outlaw Fury *'50*
Rangeland Empire *'50*
Sudden Death *'50*
Outlaw Gang *'49*
Rimfire *'49*
Tough Assignment *'49*
Son of Zorro *'47*
The Driftin' Kid *'41*
Dynamite Canyon *'41*
The Singing Cowgirl *'39*

Sue Price (1965-)
Nemesis 4: Cry of Angels *'97*
Nemesis 3: Time Lapse *'96*
Nemesis 2: Nebula *'94*

Vincent Price (1911-93)
The Thief and the Cobbler *'96 (V)*
Edward Scissorhands *'90*
Once Upon a Midnight Scary *'90 (N)*
Backtrack *'89*
Dead Heat *'88*
The Offspring *'87*
The Whales of August *'87*
Escapes *'86*
The Great Mouse Detective *'86 (V)*
Bloodbath at the House of Death *'85*
The Monster Club *'85*
Snow White and the Seven Dwarfs *'83*
House of the Long Shadows *'82*
Ruddigore *'82*
The Boy Who Left Home to Find Out About the Shivers *'81 (V)*
Scavenger Hunt *'79*
Butterfly Ball *'76 (N)*
It's Not the Size That Counts *'74*
Journey into Fear *'74*
Madhouse *'74*
Theatre of Blood *'73*
Doctor Phibes Rises Again *'72*
The Abominable Dr. Phibes *'71*
Cry of the Banshee *'70*
Scream and Scream Again *'70*
The Oblong Box *'69*
The Trouble with Girls (and How to Get into It) *'69*
The Conqueror Worm *'68*
More Dead Than Alive *'68*
Spirits of the Dead *'68 (N)*
The House of 1000 Dolls *'67*
The Jackals *'67*
Dr. Goldfoot and the Bikini Machine *'66*
Masque of the Red Death *'65*
The Comedy of Terrors *'64*
The Last Man on Earth *'64*
Nefertiti, Queen of the Nile *'64*
Pirate Warrior *'64*
Tomb of Ligeia *'64*
Beach Party *'63*
Diary of a Madman *'63*
The Haunted Palace *'63*
The Raven *'63*
Twice-Told Tales *'63*
Tales of Terror *'62*
Tower of London *'62*
Master of the World *'61*
The Pit and the Pendulum *'61*
The Fall of the House of Usher *'60*
The Bat *'59*
The Big Circus *'59*
Return of the Fly *'59*
The Tingler *'59*
The Fly *'58*
House on Haunted Hill *'58*
The Ten Commandments *'56*
While the City Sleeps *'56*
Son of Sinbad *'55*
Casanova's Big Night *'54*
Dangerous Mission *'54*
House of Wax *'53*
The Las Vegas Story *'52*
Adventures of Captain Fabian *'51*
Baron of Arizona *'51*
His Kind of Woman *'51*
Champagne for Caesar *'50*
Bagdad *'49*
Abbott and Costello Meet Frankenstein *'48 (V)*
The Bribe *'48*
The Three Musketeers *'48*
Up in Central Park *'48*
The Long Night *'47*
Dragonwyck *'46*
Shock! *'46*
Leave Her to Heaven *'45*
The Keys of the Kingdom *'44*
Laura *'44*
Wilson *'44*
The Song of Bernadette *'43*
Brigham Young: Frontiersman *'40*
The House of the Seven Gables *'40*
The Invisible Man Returns *'40*
The Private Lives of Elizabeth & Essex *'39*
The Tower of London *'39*
Service De Luxe *'38*

Robert Prichard
Alien Space Avenger *'91*
Class of Nuke 'Em High *'86*
The Toxic Avenger *'86*

Dan Priest (1924-2004)
Rattlers *'76*
Black Like Me *'64*

Martin Priest
Zebrahead *'92*
The Plot Against Harry *'69*
Nothing but a Man *'64*

Pat Priest (1936-)
Some Call It Loving *'73*
The Incredible Two-Headed Transplant *'71*
Easy Come, Easy Go *'67*

Jason Priestley (1969-)
Luna: Spirit of the Whale *'07*
Termination Point *'07*
Hot Tamale *'06*
Masters of Horror: The Screwfly Solution *'06*
Die Mommie Die! *'03*
Cherish *'02*
Dark Side *'02*
Double Down *'01*
The Fourth Angel *'01*
Common Ground *'00*
Homicide: The Movie *'00*
Kiss Tomorrow Goodbye *'00*
Eye of the Beholder *'99*
The Highway Man *'99*
Standing on Fishes *'99*
Love and Death on Long Island *'97*
Sink or Swim *'97*
Coldblooded *'94*
Calendar Girl *'93*
Tombstone *'93*
Nowhere to Run *'88*
The Boy Who Could Fly *'86*

Aurore Prieto
Dr. Petiot *'90*
Therese *'86*

Paco Christian Prieto (1955-)
Street Law *'95*
Only the Strong *'93*

Suzy Prim (1896-1991)
Heart of a Nation *'43*
The Lower Depths *'36*

Louis Prima (1910-78)
The Jungle Book *'67 (V)*
Manhattan Merry-Go-Round *'37*

Barry Primus (1938-)
Righteous Kill *'08*
When Will I Be Loved *'04*
James Dean *'01*
Elmore Leonard's Gold Coast *'97*
Crime of the Century *'96*
Flipping *'96*
Trade Off *'95*
Night and the City *'92*
Denial: The Dark Side of Passion *'91*
Guilty by Suspicion *'91*
Cannibal Women in the Avocado Jungle of Death *'89*
Torn Apart *'89*
Big Business *'88*
The Stranger *'87*
Down and Out in Beverly Hills *'86*
Brotherly Love *'85*
Talking Walls *'85*
Shooting *'82*
Absence of Malice *'81*
Heartland *'81*
Night Games *'80*
New York, New York *'77*
Autopsy *'74*
Boxcar Bertha *'72*

Prince (1958-)
Graffiti Bridge *'90*
Under the Cherry Moon *'86*
Purple Rain *'84*

Clayton Prince (1965-)
Dark Justice *'91*
Hairspray *'88*

Faith Prince (1957-)
It Had to Be You *'00*
A Season for Miracles *'99*
Picture Perfect *'96*
Big Bully *'95*
Dave *'93*
My Father the Hero *'93*
The Last Dragon *'85*

Jonathan Prince (1958-)
Private School *'83*
Pray TV *'82*

Steven Prince
The Alamo *'04*
Allie & Me *'97*

William Prince (1913-96)
The Portrait *'93*
The Taking of Beverly Hills *'91*
Second Sight *'89*
Spontaneous Combustion *'89*
Vice Versa *'88*
Nuts *'87*
Spies Like Us *'85*
The Soldier *'82*
City in Fear *'80*
The Promise *'79*
Johnny We Hardly Knew Ye *'77*
Family Plot *'76*
Network *'76*
The Stepford Wives *'75*
Missiles of October *'74*
Cyrano de Bergerac *'50*
Lust for Gold *'49*
Carnegie Hall *'47*
Dead Reckoning *'47*
Objective, Burma! *'45*
Destination Tokyo *'43*

Victoria Principal (1950-)
The Abduction *'96*
Scott Turow's The Burden of Proof *'92*
Nightmare *'91*
Blind Witness *'89*
Naked Lie *'89*
Mistress *'87*
Pleasure Palace *'80*
Fantasy Island *'76*
I Will, I Will for Now *'76*
Earthquake *'74*
Life & Times of Judge Roy Bean *'72*

Andrew Prine (1936-)
Daltry Calhoun *'05*
Critical Mass *'00*
Witchouse 2: Blood Coven *'00*
Possums *'99*
Without Evidence *'96*
Serial Killer *'95*
Deadly Exposure *'93*
Gettysburg *'93*
Mission of the Shark *'91*
Chill Factor *'90*
The Eliminators *'86*
The Last of the Mohicans *'85*
Donner Pass: The Road to Survival *'84*
They're Playing with Fire *'84*
V *'83*
Amityville 2: The Possession *'82*
Callie and Son *'81*
A Small Killing *'81*
The Evil *'78*
The Christmas Coal Mine Miracle *'77*
Grizzly *'76*
Riding with Death *'76*
Town That Dreaded Sundown *'76*
The Centerfold Girls *'74*
Barn of the Naked Dead *'73*
Crypt of the Living Dead *'73*
One Little Indian *'73*
Simon, King of the Witches *'71*
Generation *'69*
Bandolero! *'68*
The Devil's Brigade *'68*
Texas Across the River *'66*
The Miracle Worker *'62*

Aileen Pringle (1895-1989)
Sons of Steel *'35*
Jane Eyre *'34*
Convicted *'32*
Police Court *'32*
Murder at Midnight *'31*

Bryan Pringle (1935-2002)
Getting It Right *'89*
Haunted Honeymoon *'86*
Saturday Night and Sunday Morning *'60*

Joan Pringle
Original Sin *'01*
Incognito *'99*
J.D.'s Revenge *'76*

Sandra Prinsloo
Claws *'85*
The Gods Must Be Crazy *'84*
The Outcast *'84*
African Rage *'78*

Freddie Prinze, Jr. (1976-)
Delgo *'08 (V)*
Jack and Jill vs. the World *'08*
Brooklyn Rules *'07*
Happily N'Ever After *'07 (V)*
Scooby-Doo 2: Monsters Unleashed *'04*
Scooby-Doo *'02*
Head Over Heels *'01*
Summer Catch *'01*
Boys and Girls *'00*
Down to You *'00*
She's All That *'99*
Sparkler *'99*
Wing Commander *'99*
I Still Know What You Did Last Summer *'98*
Money Kings *'98*
Hostage High *'97*
The House of Yes *'97*
I Know What You Did Last Summer *'97*
To Gillian on Her 37th Birthday *'96*

Ted Prior (1959-)
The P.A.C.K. *'96*
Mutant Species *'95*
Possessed by the Night *'93*
Center of the Web *'92*
Raw Nerve *'91*
Future Zone *'90*
Born Killer *'89*
Final Sanction *'89*
Hardcase and Fist *'89*
Jungle Assault *'89*
Hell on the Battleground *'88*
Deadly Prey *'87*
Killer Workout *'86*
Killzone *'85*
Sledgehammer *'83*

Albert Priscoe
The Prairie King *'27*
The Love Light *'21*

David Pritchard
Slashed Dreams *'74*
The Devil's Brigade *'68*

Michael Pritchard
Lightblast *'85*
Massive Retaliation *'85*

Lucien Prival (1900-94)
Panama Menace *'41*
Hell's Angels *'30*
Party Girls *'29*

Jurgen Prochnow (1941-)
Primeval *'07*
Beerfest *'06*
The Celestine Prophecy *'06*
The Da Vinci Code *'06*
Heart of America *'03*
House of the Dead *'03*
Dark Asylum *'01*
Last Run *'01*
Ripper: Letter from Hell *'01*
Heaven's Fire *'99*
The Last Stop *'99*
Wing Commander *'99*
Esther *'98*
The Fall *'98*
The Replacement Killers *'98*
Air Force One *'97*
DNA *'97*
Human Bomb *'97*
The English Patient *'96*
In the Mouth of Madness *'95*
Jack Higgins' On Dangerous Ground *'95*
Judge Dredd *'95*
The Other Side of the Law *'95*
Lie Down with Lions *'94*
The Fire Next Time *'93*
Body of Evidence *'92*
Hurricane Smith *'92*
Interceptor *'92*
Jewels *'92*
Twin Peaks: Fire Walk with Me *'92*
Robin Hood *'91*
The Fourth War *'90*
Kill Cruise *'90*
The Man Inside *'90*
A Dry White Season *'89*
The Seventh Sign *'88*
Beverly Hills Cop 2 *'87*
The Cop & the Girl *'86*
Blitz *'85*
Forbidden *'85*
My Sweet Victim *'85*
Dune *'84*
The Keep *'83*
Das Boot *'81*
The Lost Honor of Katharina Blum *'75*
Tenderness of the Wolves *'73*

Emily Procter (1968-)
Big Momma's House 2 *'06*
Body Shots *'99*
Guinevere *'99*
Breast Men *'97*

Marland Proctor (1941-88)
Terrorists *'88*
All the Lovin' Kinfolk *'70*

Phil(ip) Proctor (1940-)
The Rugrats Movie *'98 (V)*
Lobster Man from Mars *'89*
J-Men Forever! *'79*
A Safe Place *'71*

Tome Proculi
See Anthony (Jose, J. Antonio, J.A.) Mayans

Tim Progosh
I Downloaded a Ghost *'04*
My Teacher Ate My Homework *'98*

Luigi Proietti
Revenge of the Musketeers *'94*
The Libertine *'69*

Greg Proops
Cyxork 7 *'06*
Kaena: The Prophecy *'03 (V)*
The Nightmare Before Christmas *'93 (V)*

Melissa Prophet (1957-)
Invasion U.S.A. *'85*
Better Late Than Never *'83*
Van Nuys Blvd. *'79*

John Prosky
Heart of the Beholder *'05*
Groom Lake *'02*

Robert Prosky (1930-2008)
The Skeptic *'09*
Eye See You *'01*
Dudley Do-Right *'99*
Mad City *'97*
The Chamber *'96*
Dead Man Walking *'95*
The Scarlet Letter *'95*
Miracle on 34th Street *'94*
Hit Woman: The Double Edge *'93*
Last Action Hero *'93*
Mrs. Doubtfire *'93*
Rudy *'93*
Far and Away *'92*
Hoffa *'92*
Teamster Boss: The Jackie Presser Story *'92*
Age Isn't Everything *'91*
Funny About Love *'90*
Green Card *'90*
Gremlins 2: The New Batch *'90*
From the Dead of Night *'89*
The Heist *'89*
Things Change *'88*
Big Shots *'87*
Broadcast News *'87*
The Murder of Mary Phagan *'87*
World War III *'86*
Into Thin Air *'85*
Christine *'84*
The Natural *'84*
The Keep *'83*
The Lords of Discipline *'83*
Thief *'81*

Joe Prospero (1988-)
Finding Neverland *'04*
My Uncle Silas *'01*

Protasio
Border Lost *'08*
Lost Treasure of the Maya *'08*

Kirsten Prout
The Twilight Saga: Eclipse *'10*
Elektra *'05*

Jed Prouty (1879-1956)
Remedy for Riches *'40*
The Gracie Allen Murder Case *'39*
Hollywood Cavalcade *'39*
Danger on the Air *'38*
100 Men and a Girl *'37*
Small Town Boy *'37*
Broadway Melody *'29*
It's a Great Life *'29*
Ella Cinders *'26*

David Proval (1942-)
Smokin' Aces *'07*
Murder Without Conviction *'04*
Bookies *'03*
13 Moons *'02*
Double Down *'01*
The Hollywood Sign *'01*
Mob Queen *'98*
The Siege *'98*
Flipping *'96*
The Phantom *'96*
Four Rooms *'95*
To the Limit *'95*
Being Human *'94*
Romeo Is Bleeding *'93*
Innocent Blood *'92*
Vice Versa *'88*
Wizards *'77 (V)*
Cinderella Liberty *'73*
Mean Streets *'73*

Dorothy Provine (1937-)
Never a Dull Moment *'68*
Who's Minding the Mint? *'67*
That Darn Cat *'65*
Good Neighbor Sam *'64*
It's a Mad, Mad, Mad, Mad World *'63*
The 30-Foot Bride of Candy Rock *'59*

Jon(athan) Provost (1950-)
This Property Is Condemned *'66*
Lassie's Great Adventure *'62*
Escapade in Japan *'57*
All Mine to Give *'56*
Back from Eternity *'56*

David Prowse (1935-)
Comic Book: The Movie *'04*
Return of the Jedi *'83*
The Empire Strikes Back *'80*
Jabberwocky *'77*
Star Wars *'77*
Frankenstein and the Monster from Hell *'74*
Blacksnake! *'73*
A Clockwork Orange *'71*
Vampire Circus *'71*
The Horror of Frankenstein *'70*
Casino Royale *'67*

Juliet Prowse (1937-96)
Dingaka *'65*
Can-Can *'60*
G.I. Blues *'60*

Anna Prucnal (1940-)
City of Women *'81*
Sweet Movie *'75*

Harold P. Pruett (1969-2002)
The Perfect Daughter *'96*
Precious Find *'96*
Spellcaster *'91*
Summer Camp Nightmare *'86*

Karl Pruner
Welcome to Mooseport *'04*
Bugs *'03*
The Recruit *'03*
Threshold *'03*
Finding Buck McHenry *'00*
Total Recall 2070: Machine Dreams *'99*
This Matter of Marriage *'98*
The Fixer *'97*

Alex Prusmack
In Enemy Hands *'04*

Jonathan Pryce (1947-)
G.I. Joe: The Rise of Cobra *'09*
Return to Cranford *'09*
Bedtime Stories *'08*
Leatherheads *'08*
My Zinc Bed *'08*
The Moon & the Stars *'07*
Pirates of the Caribbean: At World's End *'07*
Brothers of the Head *'06*
Pirates of the Caribbean: Dead Man's Chest *'06*
Renaissance *'06*
The Brothers Grimm *'05*
The New World *'05*
De-Lovely *'04*
Pirates of the Caribbean: The Curse of the Black Pearl *'03*
Unconditional Love *'03*
What a Girl Wants *'03*
The Affair of the Necklace *'01*
Bride of the Wind *'01*
Very Annie Mary *'00*
Robert Louis Stevenson's The Game of Death *'99*
Stigmata *'99*
Ronin *'98*
Behind the Lines *'97*
David *'97*
Tomorrow Never Dies *'97*
Evita *'96*
Carrington *'95*
A Troll in Central Park *'94 (V)*
The Age of Innocence *'93*
Barbarians at the Gate *'93*
A Business Affair *'93*
Deadly Advice *'93*
Shades of Fear *'93*
Shopping *'93*
Thicker Than Water *'93*
Freddie the Frog *'92 (V)*
Glengarry Glen Ross *'92*
The Adventures of Baron Munchausen *'89*
The Man from the Pru *'89*
The Rachel Papers *'89*
Consuming Passions *'88*
Man on Fire *'87*
Haunted Honeymoon *'86*
Jumpin' Jack Flash *'86*
Brazil *'85*
The Doctor and the Devils *'85*
Loophole *'83*
The Ploughman's Lunch *'83*
Praying Mantis *'83*
Something Wicked This Way Comes *'83*
Agatha Christie's Murder is Easy *'82*
Breaking Glass *'80*
Voyage of the Damned *'76*

Ainslie Pryor (1921-58)
The Last Hunt *'56*
The Girl in the Red Velvet Swing *'55*

Nicholas Pryor (1935-)
American Tragedy *'00*
Hail Caesar *'94*
Hoffa *'92*
Pacific Heights *'90*
Brain Dead *'89*
Nightbreaker *'89*
Morgan Stewart's Coming Home *'87*
The Falcon and the Snowman *'85*
Into Thin Air *'85*
Risky Business *'83*
East of Eden *'80*
The $5.20 an Hour Dream *'80*
Last Song *'80*
The Fish that Saved Pittsburgh *'79*
Damien: Omen 2 *'78*
Gumball Rally *'76*
The Life and Assassination of the Kingfish *'76*
Night Terror *'76*
Force Five *'75*
The Happy Hooker *'75*
Smile *'75*

Richard Pryor (1940-2005)
Lost Highway *'96*
Trigger Happy *'96*
Another You *'91*
Harlem Nights *'89*
See No Evil, Hear No Evil *'89*
Moving *'88*
Critical Condition *'86*
Jo Jo Dancer, Your Life Is Calling *'86*
Brewster's Millions *'85*
Superman 3 *'83*
Some Kind of Hero *'82*
The Toy *'82*
Bustin' Loose *'81*
In God We Trust *'80*
Stir Crazy *'80*
Wholly Moses! *'80*
Blue Collar *'78*
California Suite *'78*
The Wiz *'78*
Greased Lightning *'77*
Which Way Is Up? *'77*
Bingo Long Traveling All-Stars & Motor Kings *'76*
Car Wash *'76*
Silver Streak *'76*
Adios Amigo *'75*
Uptown Saturday Night *'74*
Hit! *'73*
The Mack *'73*
Some Call It Loving *'73*
Lady Sings the Blues *'72*
Dynamite Chicken *'70*
Black Brigade *'69*
Wild in the Streets *'68*
The Busy Body *'67*

Roger Pryor (1901-74)
Identity Unknown *'45*
Kid Sister *'45*
Meet the Mob *'42*
Flying Blind *'41*
Panama Menace *'41*
Power Dive *'41*
The Man They Could Not Hang *'39*
Headline Woman *'35*
Belle of the Nineties *'34*
Lady by Choice *'34*

Wojtek Psoniak
See Wojciech Pszoniak

Wojciech Pszoniak (1942-)
Chaos *'01*
Korczak *'90*
Angry Harvest *'85*
Danton *'82*
Land of Promise *'74*

Wojtek Pszoniak
See Wojciech Pszoniak

Lou Taylor Pucci (1985-)
The Answer Man *'09*
Brief Interviews With Hideous Men *'09*
Carriers *'09*
Horsemen *'09*
The Informers *'09*
Explicit Ills *'08*
The Go-Getter *'07*
The Chumscrubber *'05*
Empire Falls *'05*
Thumbsucker *'05*
Personal Velocity: Three Portraits *'02*

Vladimir Pucholt (1942-)
Loves of a Blonde *'65*
Black Peter *'63*

Jesus Puente
Hatchet for the Honeymoon *'70*
Rattler Kid *'68*

Tito Puente (1925-2000)
The Mambo Kings *'92*
Radio Days *'87*

Robert Pugh (1950-)
The Last Legion *'07*
Kinky Boots *'06*
Longford *'06*
Bloodlines *'05*
Master and Commander: The Far Side of the World *'03*
The Intended *'02*
Enigma *'01*
Sword of Honour *'01*
A Mind to Murder *'96*
Priest *'94*
Thicker Than Water *'93*
Danger UXB *'81*
Nighthawks *'81*

Willard Pugh
Puppet Master 5: The Final Chapter *'94*
CB4: The Movie *'93*
Eddie Presley *'92*
Ambition *'91*
A Rage in Harlem *'91*
Traxx *'87*
Native Son *'86*
The Color Purple *'85*

Frank Puglia (1892-1975)
Girls! Girls! Girls! *'62*
20 Million Miles to Earth *'57*
The Black Hand *'50*
Bagdad *'49*
Without Reservations *'46*
Ali Baba and the Forty Thieves *'43*
For Whom the Bell Tolls *'43*
Casablanca *'42*
Billy the Kid *'41*
The Fatal Hour *'40*
In Old Caliente *'39*
Bulldog Drummond's Revenge *'37*
Viva Villa! *'34*
Romola *'25*

Aldo Puglisi (1935-)
Marriage Italian Style *'64*
Seduced and Abandoned *'64*

Ian Puleston-Davies
Tess of the D'Urbervilles *'08*
Ghostboat *'06*
Strange Relations *'02*

Benjamin Pullen (1972-)
Intern *'00*
An Ideal Husband *'99*
Prince Valiant *'97*

Keisha Knight Pulliam (1979-)
Madea Goes to Jail *'09*
Beauty Shop *'05*
The Gospel *'05*
Christmas at Water's Edge *'04*
Motives *'03*
What About Your Friends: Weekend Getaway *'02*
A Connecticut Yankee in King Arthur's Court *'89*
The Little Match Girl *'87*

Bill Pullman (1953-)
The Killer Inside Me *'10*
Bottle Shock *'08*
Nobel Son *'08*
Phoebe in Wonderland *'08*
Surveillance *'08*
You Kill Me *'07*
Scary Movie 4 *'06*
Dear Wendy *'05*
The Grudge *'04*
Rick *'03*
Igby Goes Down *'02*
Ignition *'01*
Lucky Numbers *'00*
Titan A.E. *'00 (V)*
Brokedown Palace *'99*
The Guilty *'99*
Lake Placid *'99*
Spy Games *'99*
The Virginian *'99*
The End of Violence *'97*
Zero Effect *'97*
Independence Day *'96*
Lost Highway *'96*
Mistrial *'96*
Casper *'95*
Mr. Wrong *'95*
While You Were Sleeping *'95*
The Last Seduction *'94*
Wyatt Earp *'94*
Malice *'93*
Nervous Ticks *'93*
Sleepless in Seattle *'93*
Sommersby *'93*
Crazy in Love *'92*
The Favor *'92*
A League of Their Own *'92*
Newsies *'92*
Singles *'92*
Bright Angel *'91*
Going Under *'91*
Liebestraum *'91*
Sibling Rivalry *'90*
Brain Dead *'89*
Cold Feet *'89*
The Accidental Tourist *'88*
Rocket Gibraltar *'88*
The Serpent and the Rainbow *'87*
Spaceballs *'87*
Ruthless People *'86*

Lilo (Liselotte) Pulver (1929-)
The Nun *'66*
A Global Affair *'63*
A Time to Love & a Time to Die *'58*

Lucy Punch
Dinner for Schmucks *'10*
(Untitled) *'09*
St. Trinian's *'07*
Being Julia *'04*

Bernard Punsley (1923-2004)
Junior G-Men of the Air '42
Junior G-Men '40
Angels with Dirty Faces '38
Crime School '38
Dead End '37

Romano Puppo
The Great Alligator '81
Spaghetti Western '75

Dick Purcell (1908-44)
Captain America '44
Timber Queen '44
Phantom Killer '42
X Marks the Spot '42
Flying Blind '41
King of the Zombies '41
The Abe Lincoln of Ninth Avenue '39
Heroes in Blue '39
Irish Luck '39
Tough Kid '39
Wine, Women and Horses '37

Dominic Purcell (1970-)
Blood Creek '09
Prison Break: The Final Break '09
Primeval '07
Blade: Trinity '04
3-Way '04

James Purcell
Sabotage '96
Another Woman '94
Playroom '90
White Light '90

Leah Purcell (1970-)
Jindabyne '06
The Proposition '05
Somersault '04
Lantana '01

Lee Purcell (1957-)
Movies Money Murder '96
Long Road Home '91
The Incredible Hulk Returns '88
To Heal a Nation '88
Jailbait: Betrayed By Innocence '86
Space Rage '86
Eddie Macon's Run '83
Valley Girl '83
Homework '82
Killing at Hell's Gate '81
Kenny Rogers as the Gambler '80
Stir Crazy '80
Big Wednesday '78
Summer of Fear '78
The Amazing Howard Hughes '77
Mr. Majestyk '74
The Witching '72
Adam at 6 a.m. '70

Noel Purcell (1900-85)
Mutiny on the Bounty '62
No Kidding '60
Lust for Life '56
Land of Fury '55
Grand National Night '53
Encore '52
Captain Boycott '47

Reginald Purdell (1896-1953)
Brighton Rock '47
Candles at Nine '44
Clouds over Europe '39
The Old Curiosity Shop '35

Edmund Purdom (1924-)
After the Fall of New York '85
Don't Open Till Christmas '84
Ator the Fighting Eagle '83
Big Boss '77
Mr. Scarface '77
Rulers of the City '76
Dr. Frankenstein's Castle of Freaks '74
Nefertiti, Queen of the Nile '64
Herod the Great '60
The King's Thief '55
The Prodigal '55
Athena '54
The Egyptian '54
The Student Prince '54

Carolyn Purdy-Gordon
Dolls '87
From Beyond '86
Re-Animator '84

James Purefoy (1964-)
The Summit '08
Beau Brummell: This Charming Man '06
George and the Dragon '04
Vanity Fair '04
The Mayor of Casterbridge '03
Resident Evil '02
A Knight's Tale '01
Don Quixote '00
Dead of Night '99
Mansfield Park '99
Maybe Baby '99
Bedrooms and Hallways '98
A Dance to the Music of Time '97
Catherine Cookson's The Tide of Life '96
The Tenant of Wildfell Hall '96
Feast of July '95

Om Puri (1950-)
Charlie Wilson's War '07
Code 46 '03
The Mystic Masseur '01
East Is East '99
Such a Long Journey '98
My Son the Fanatic '97
The Ghost and the Darkness '96
Brothers in Trouble '95
In Custody '94
Wolf '94
City of Joy '92
Spices '86
Gandhi '82

Linda Purl (1953-)
Fear of the Dark '02
Perfect Tenant '99
Mighty Joe Young '98
Incident at Deception Ridge '94
Natural Causes '94
Accidental Meeting '93
In Self Defense '93
Body Language '92
Spies, Lies and Naked Thighs '91
Web of Deceit '90
Viper '88
Outrage! '86
Visiting Hours '82
The Adventures of Nellie Bly '81
High Country '81
The Manions of America '81
The Night the City Screamed '80
The Flame Is Love '79
Last Cry for Help '79
Little Ladies of the Night '77
Eleanor & Franklin '76
The Young Pioneers '76
Crazy Mama '75

Alycia Purrott
The Cutting Edge 3: Chasing the Dream '08
Jailbait! '00

Edna Purviance (1894-1958)
The Chaplin Revue '58
The Kid '21
Three Charlies and One Phoney! '18
The Cure '17
The Immigrant '17
Burlesque on Carmen '16
The Fireman '16
Pawnshop '16
The Vagabond '16
Charlie Chaplin: Night at the Show '15
Charlie Chaplin ... Our Hero! '15

Alexandra Purvis (1988-)
Now & Forever '02
Ronnie and Julie '97
Contagious '96
Poltergeist: The Legacy '96

Roberto Purvis
The Moon & the Stars '07
Red Riding Hood '03

Jeff Pustil
Real Time '08
The Killing Man '94

John Putch (1961-)
Same River Twice '97
The Souler Opposite '97
Camp Nowhere '94
Fallen Angels 2 '93
Curfew '88
Impure Thoughts '86
Jaws 3 '83

Hanna Putnam
Feast 2: Sloppy Seconds '08
Nightmare Man '06

Bruno Putzulu
Monsieur N. '03
In Praise of Love '01
L'Appat '94

Hy Pyke (1935-)
Halloween Night '90
Hack O'Lantern '87
Lemora, Lady Dracula '73

Denver Pyle (1920-97)
Maverick '94
Mountain Man '77
Hawmps! '76
Winterhawk '76
The Adventures of Frontier Fremont '75
Escape to Witch Mountain '75
Life & Times of Grizzly Adams '74
Murder or Mercy '74
The Legend of Hillbilly John '73
Bonnie & Clyde '67
The Rounders '65
Shenandoah '65
Mail Order Bride '63
Geronimo '62
The Man Who Shot Liberty Valance '62
The Alamo '60
The Horse Soldiers '59
King of the Wild Stallions '59
Naked Hills '56
Seventh Cavalry '56
To Hell and Back '55
Ride Clear of Diablo '54
Johnny Guitar '53
Hills of Utah '51
Oklahoma Annie '51
Dynamite Pass '50
Rim of the Canyon '49
Too Late for Tears '49
Where the North Begins '47

Missi Pyle (1973-)
Taking Chances '09
Harold & Kumar Escape from Guantanamo Bay '08
Meet Market '08
Soccer Mom '08
Spring Breakdown '08
American Crude '07
Entry Level '07
Alex Rider: Operation Stormbreaker '06
Just My Luck '06
Charlie and the Chocolate Factory '05
Along Came Polly '04
Anchorman: The Legend of Ron Burgundy '04
Dodgeball: A True Underdog Story '04
50 First Dates '04
Soul Plane '04
BachelorMan '03
Big Fish '03
Bringing Down the House '03
Exposed '03
Josie and the Pussycats '01
Galaxy Quest '99
Trick '99
As Good As It Gets '97

Natasha Pyne
Madhouse '74
The Devil-Ship Pirates '64

John Pyper-Ferguson (1964-)
Black Dawn '05
I'll Take You There '99
The Tempest '99
The Waiting Game '98
For Richer or Poorer '97
Drive '96
Hard Core Logo '96
Space Marines '96
Killer Image '92
Showdown at Williams Creek '91
Bird on a Wire '90

Maggie Q (1979-)
New York, I Love You '09
Deception '08
Live Free or Die Hard '07
Mission: Impossible 3 '06

Q-Tip
She Hate Me '04
Love Goggles '99

Gregory Qaiyum
See GQ

Shu Qi (1976-)
Three Times '05
The Transporter '02

Shaobo Qin (1982-)
Ocean's Thirteen '07
Ocean's Twelve '04
Ocean's Eleven '01

Xu Qing (1969-)
The Emperor's Shadow '96
Life on a String '90

Yun Qu
Stomp the Yard '07
Jet Li's Fearless '06

John Quade (1938-)
And You Thought Your Parents Were Weird! '91
The Tracker '88
Tigershark '87
Fury to Freedom: The Life Story of Raul Ries '85
Dirkham Detective Agency '83
Peter Lundy and the Medicine Hat Stallion '77
The Last Hard Men '76
Night Terror '76
The Outlaw Josey Wales '76

Stephen Quadros
Auntie Lee's Meat Pies '92
C.I.A.: Code Name Alexa '92
Shock 'Em Dead '90

Buddy Quaid (1974-)
Psycho Beach Party '00
Ice House '89

Dennis Quaid (1954-)
Legion '10
Battle for Terra '09 (V)
G.I. Joe: The Rise of Cobra '09
Horsemen '09
Pandorum '09
The Express '08
Smart People '08
Vantage Point '08
American Dreamz '06
Yours, Mine & Ours '05
The Alamo '04
The Day After Tomorrow '04
Flight of the Phoenix '04
In Good Company '04
Cold Creek Manor '03
Far from Heaven '02
The Rookie '02
Dinner with Friends '01
Frequency '00
Traffic '00
Any Given Sunday '99
Everything That Rises '98
The Parent Trap '98
Playing by Heart '98
Savior '98
Switchback '97
Dragonheart '96
Gang Related '96
Something to Talk About '95
Wyatt Earp '94
Flesh and Bone '93
Undercover Blues '93
Wilder Napalm '93
Come See the Paradise '90
Postcards from the Edge '90
Great Balls of Fire '89
D.O.A. '88
Everybody's All American '88
The Big Easy '87
Innerspace '87
Suspect '87
Enemy Mine '85
Dreamscape '84
Bill: On His Own '83
Jaws 3 '83
The Right Stuff '83
Tough Enough '83
Johnny Belinda '82
All Night Long '81
Bill '81
Caveman '81
The Night the Lights Went Out in Georgia '81
Gorp '80
The Long Riders '80
Breaking Away '79
The Seniors '78
I Never Promised You a Rose Garden '77
September 30, 1955 '77

Randy Quaid (1953-)
Balls Out: Gary the Tennis Coach '09
Real Time '08
Goya's Ghosts '06
Brokeback Mountain '05
Category 7 : The End of the World '05
The Ice Harvest '05
Category 6 : Day of Destruction '04
Home on the Range '04 (V)
Black Cadillac '03
Carolina '03
Grind '03
Milwaukee, Minnesota '03
National Lampoon's Christmas Vacation 2: Cousin Eddie's Big Island Adventure '03
The Adventures of Pluto Nash '02
Frank McKlusky, C.I. '02
The Day the World Ended '01
Not Another Teen Movie '01
The Adventures of Rocky & Bullwinkle '00
Mail to the Chief '00
Sand '00
The Thin Blue Lie '00
Bug Buster '99
The Magical Legend of the Leprechauns '99
Purgatory '99
Last Rites '98
P.U.N.K.S. '98
Hard Rain '97
Protector '97
Get On the Bus '96
Independence Day '96
Kingpin '96
Last Dance '96
Moonshine Highway '96
Vegas Vacation '96
Larry McMurtry's Streets of Laredo '95
Legends of the North '95
Woman Undone '95
Bye Bye, Love '94
Curse of the Starving Class '94
Major League 2 '94
Next Door '94
The Paper '94
Frankenstein '93
Freaked '93
Days of Thunder '90
Martians Go Home! '90
Quick Change '90
Texasville '90
Bloodhounds of Broadway '89
National Lampoon's Christmas Vacation '89
Out Cold '89
Parents '89
Caddyshack 2 '88
Dead Solid Perfect '88
LBJ: The Early Years '88
Moving '88
No Man's Land '87
Sweet Country '87
The Wraith '87
Fool for Love '86
The Slugger's Wife '85
A Streetcar Named Desire '84
The Wild Life '84
National Lampoon's Vacation '83
Inside the Third Reich '82
Heartbeeps '81
Of Mice and Men '81
Foxes '80
The Guyana Tragedy: The Story of Jim Jones '80
The Long Riders '80
To Race the Wind '80
The Last Ride of the Dalton Gang '79
Midnight Express '78
The Choirboys '77
Three Warriors '77
Bound for Glory '76
Missouri Breaks '76
Breakout '75
The Apprenticeship of Duddy Kravitz '74
The Last Detail '73
Paper Moon '73
What's Up, Doc? '72
The Last Picture Show '71
Targets '68

John Qualen (1899-1987)
I'll Take Sweden '65
A Patch of Blue '65
Those Calloways '65
Cheyenne Autumn '64
7 Faces of Dr. Lao '63
The Man Who Shot Liberty Valance '62
Terror in the Haunted House '58
The Searchers '56
At Gunpoint '55
Sea Chase '55
The High and the Mighty '54
Passion '54
Big Steal '49
The Fugitive '48
The Scar '48
Song of Scheherazade '47
Adventure '45
Captain Kidd '45
Dark Waters '44
Casablanca '42
The Jungle Book '42
Larceny, Inc. '42
Tortilla Flat '42
The Devil & Daniel Webster '41
Out of the Fog '41
Angels Over Broadway '40
Blondie On a Budget '40
The Grapes of Wrath '40
His Girl Friday '40
Knute Rockne: All American '40
The Long Voyage Home '40
Black Fury '35
Charlie Chan in Paris '35
Our Daily Bread '34
365 Nights in Hollywood '34

DJ Qualls (1978-)
All About Steve '09
Road Trip: Beer Pong '09
Familiar Strangers '08
Delta Farce '07
I'm Reed Fish '06
Hustle & Flow '05
Little Athens '05
The Core '03
Comic Book Villains '02

Kevin Quinn
Wild Country *'05*
GhostWatcher *'02*

Louis Quinn (1915-88)
Unholy Rollers *'72*
Superchick *'71*

Martha Quinn (1961-)
Bad Channels *'92*
The Return of Spinal Tap *'92*
Chopper Chicks in Zombietown *'91*
Motorama *'91*
Eddie and the Cruisers 2: Eddie Lives! *'89*
Tapeheads *'89*

Pat Quinn (1937-)
Clean and Sober *'88*
Zachariah *'70*
Alice's Restaurant *'69*

Patricia Quinn (1944-)
Witching Time *'84*
Monty Python's The Meaning of Life *'83*
Shock Treatment *'81*
The Rocky Horror Picture Show *'75*

Terry Quinn
The Witching *'72*
The Two Faces of Dr. Jekyll *'60*

Adolfo "Shabba Doo" Quinones
Deadly Dancer *'90*
Lambada *'89*
Breakin' *'84*
Breakin' 2: Electric Boogaloo *'84*

Jonathan Quint
Silicon Towers *'99*
Floating *'97*

Pauline Quirke (1959-)
Carrie's War *'04*
David Copperfield *'99*
The Sculptress *'97*

Oscar Quitak
Tangiers *'83*
The Revenge of Frankenstein *'58*

Jocelyn Quivrin
The Romance of Astrea and Celadon *'07*
Empire of the Wolves *'05*

Beulah Quo (1923-2002)
The Children of An Lac *'80*
The Seventh Dawn *'64*
Girls! Girls! Girls! *'62*

Marianne Quon (1923-91)
Charlie Chan in the Secret Service *'44*
China *'43*

Ellie Raab (1977-)
The Ref *'93*
Eyes of an Angel *'91*
The Fabulous Baker Boys *'89*

Kurt Raab (1946-88)
Angry Harvest *'85*
Mussolini & I *'85*
Parker *'84*
Tricheurs *'84*
The Stationmaster's Wife *'77*
Satan's Brew *'76*
Fox and His Friends *'75*
Tenderness of the Wolves *'73*
The American Soldier *'70*
Beware of a Holy Whore *'70*
Why Does Herr R. Run Amok? *'69*

Birgitte Raaberg (1954-)
The Kingdom 2 *'97*
The Kingdom *'95*

Francisco Rabal (1926-2001)
Goya in Bordeaux *'99*
Talk of Angels *'96*
Tie Me Up! Tie Me Down! *'90*
A Time of Destiny *'88*
Camorra: The Naples Connection *'85*
Padre Nuestro *'85*
The Holy Innocents *'84*
The Stilts *'84*
Reborn *'81*
City of the Walking Dead *'80*
Hostages *'80*
Stay As You Are *'78*
Sorcerer *'77*
El Muerto *'75*
Exorcism's Daughter *'74*
Devil's Crude *'71*
Eagles Over London *'69*
Diary of a Rebel *'68*
Belle de Jour *'67*
The Eclipse *'66*
The Nun *'66*
Viridiana *'61*
Nazarin *'58*
The Wide Blue Road *'57*

Lily Rabe (1982-)
All Good Things *'09*
What Just Happened *'08*
No Reservations *'07*

Pamela Rabe (1959-)
Paradise Road *'97*
The Well *'97*
Cosi *'95*
Sirens *'94*

Olivier Rabourdin
Taken *'08*
Kings and Queen *'04*

Francine Racette (1947-)
Au Revoir les Enfants *'87*
Lumiere *'76*
Mr. Klein *'76*
Four Flies on Grey Velvet *'72*

Alan Rachins (1947-)
Leave It to Beaver *'97*
Meet Wally Sparks *'97*
The Stepsister *'97*
Showgirls *'95*
Star Quest *'94*
Heart Condition *'90*
Mistress *'87*
L.A. Law *'86*
Always *'85*

Victoria Racimo (1945-)
White Fang 2: The Myth of the White Wolf *'94*
Ernest Goes to Camp *'87*
Roanoak *'86*
Prophecy *'79*
Green Eyes *'76*
Search for the Gods *'75*
Journey Through Rosebud *'72*
G.I. Executioner *'71*

Kurt Rackelmann (1910-73)
Carbide and Sorrel *'63*
First Spaceship on Venus *'60*

Damaine Radcliff
Glory Road *'06*
Step Up *'06*

Daniel Radcliffe (1989-)
Harry Potter and the Half-Blood Prince *'09*
December Boys *'07*
Harry Potter and the Order of the Phoenix *'07*
My Boy Jack *'07*
Harry Potter and the Goblet of Fire *'05*
Harry Potter and the Prisoner of Azkaban *'04*
Harry Potter and the Chamber of Secrets *'02*
Harry Potter and the Sorcerer's Stone *'01*
The Tailor of Panama *'00*
David Copperfield *'99*

Rosemary Radcliffe
Anne of Green Gables: The Continuing Story *'99*
Anne of Green Gables *'85*

Sascha Radetsky (1977-)
Center Stage *'00*
Home at Last *'88*

Basil Radford (1897-1952)
Passport to Pimlico *'49*
Whiskey Galore *'48*
The Winslow Boy *'48*
Captive Heart *'47*
Dead of Night *'45*
The Girl in the News *'41*
Night Train to Munich *'40*
The Lady Vanishes *'38*
Young and Innocent *'37*

Natalie Radford (1959-)
Last Call: The Final Chapter of F. Scott Fitzgerald *'02*
Agent Red *'00*
Killing Moon *'00*
P.T. Barnum *'99*
The Android Affair *'95*
Spenser: The Judas Goat *'94*
JFK: Reckless Youth *'93*
Tomcat: Dangerous Desires *'93*

Giovanni Lambardo Radice (1954-)
Deadly Impact *'84*
Cannibal Apocalypse *'80*

Ken Radley
Mr. Reliable: A True Story *'95*
Sniper *'92*

Gilda Radner (1946-89)
Haunted Honeymoon *'86*
Movers and Shakers *'85*
The Woman in Red *'84*
Hanky Panky *'82*
First Family *'80*
Mr. Mike's Mondo Video *'79*
All You Need Is Cash *'78*
The Last Detail *'73*

Jerzy Radziwilowicz (1950-)
The Story of Marie and Julien *'03*
No End *'84*
Passion *'82*
Man of Iron *'81*
Man of Marble *'76*

Cassidy Rae (1976-)
Extremedays *'01*
National Lampoon's Favorite Deadly Sins *'95*
Evolver *'94*

Charlotte Rae (1926-)
Another Woman's Husband *'00*
Nowhere *'96*
Thunder in Paradise *'93*
Tom and Jerry: The Movie *'93 (V)*
The Worst Witch *'86*
Words by Heart *'84*
The Triangle Factory Fire Scandal *'79*
Sidewinder One *'77*
Queen of the Stardust Ballroom *'75*
Bananas *'71*
The Hot Rock *'70*
Jenny *'70*
Hello Down There *'69*

John Rae
Oh! What a Lovely War *'69*
Morgan: A Suitable Case for Treatment *'66*

Paul Rae
The Circuit *'08*
Daddy Day Camp *'07*

Raekwon (1970-)
Scary Movie 3 *'03*
Black and White *'99*

Bob Rafelson (1933-)
Always *'85*
Head *'68*

Cyril Raffaelli (1974-)
District 13: Ultimatum *'09*
Live Free or Die Hard *'07*
District B13 *'04*

Giuliano Raffaelli
And God Said to Cain *'69*
Blood and Black Lace *'64*

Chips Rafferty (1909-71)
Skullduggery *'70*
Double Trouble *'67*
Wackiest Ship in the Army *'61*
The Sundowners *'60*
Walk into Hell *'57*
The Desert Rats *'53*
Eureka Stockade *'49*
Overlanders *'46*
The Fighting Rats of Tobruk *'44*
Forty Thousand Horsemen *'41*

Frances Rafferty (1922-2004)
Curley *'47*
Money Madness *'47*
Abbott and Costello in Hollywood *'45*
Mrs. Parkington *'44*

Deborah Raffin (1953-)
Morning Glory *'93*
Scanners 2: The New Order *'91*
Night of the Fox *'90*
Noble House *'88*
Claudia *'85*
Death Wish 3 *'85*
Jungle Heat *'84*
Agatha Christie's Sparkling Cyanide *'83*
Killing at Hell's Gate *'81*
For the Love of It *'80*
Haywire *'80*
Touched by Love *'80*
Willa *'79*
Hanging on a Star *'78*
How to Pick Up Girls *'78*
Snowblind *'78*
Maniac *'77*
God Told Me To *'76*
Nightmare in Badham County *'76*
The Sentinel *'76*
Once Is Not Enough *'75*
The Dove *'74*
Forty Carats *'73*

George Raft (1895-1980)
Sextette *'78*
Casino Royale *'67*
Five Golden Dragons *'67*
Ocean's 11 *'60*
Jet Over the Atlantic *'59*
Some Like It Hot *'59*
Around the World in 80 Days *'56*
A Bullet for Joey *'55*
Black Widow *'54*
Man from Cairo *'54*
I'll Get You *'53*
Loan Shark *'52*
Outpost in Morocco *'49*
Christmas Eve *'47*
Mr. Ace *'46*
Nocturne *'46*
Whistle Stop *'46*
Johnny Angel *'45*
Follow the Boys *'44*
Background to Danger *'43*
Stage Door Canteen *'43*
Broadway *'42*
Manpower *'41*
House Across the Bay *'40*
They Drive by Night *'40*
Each Dawn I Die *'39*
Invisible Stripes *'39*
Spawn of the North *'38*
You and Me *'38*
Souls at Sea *'37*
The Bowery *'33*
Night After Night *'32*
Palmy Days *'31*
Scarface *'31*

Rags Ragland (1905-46)
The Canterville Ghost *'44*
Meet the People *'44*
Du Barry Was a Lady *'43*
Whistling in Brooklyn *'43*
Panama Hattie *'42*
Whistling in Dixie *'42*
Whistling in the Dark *'41*

Joe Ragno
Day at the Beach *'98*
Jane Doe *'96*
No Way Home *'96*
The Babe *'92*

William Ragsdale (1961-)
The Reaping *'07*
Road House 2: Last Call *'06*
Just a Little Harmless Sex *'99*
National Lampoon's Favorite Deadly Sins *'95*
Mannequin 2: On the Move *'91*
Fright Night 2 *'88*
Fright Night *'85*
Smooth Talk *'85*

Rah Digga (1972-)
Carmen: A Hip Hopera *'01*
13 Ghosts *'01*

Bashar Rahal
Direct Contact *'09*
Target of Opportunity *'04*

Umberto Raho (1922-)
The Blonde *'92*
Aladdin *'86*
Amuck! *'71*
The Night Evelyn Came Out of the Grave *'71*
The Bird with the Crystal Plumage *'70*
Satanik *'69*
The Ghost *'63*

Aishwarya Rai (1973-)
The Pink Panther 2 *'09*
The Last Legion *'07*
The Mistress of Spices *'05*
Bride & Prejudice *'04*
Devdas *'02*

Victor Raider-Wexler (1943-)
Die Mommie Die! *'03*
Tom Clancy's Netforce *'98*

Steve Railsback (1948-)
The Devil's Rejects *'05*
The Box *'03*
Ed Gein *'01*
Made Men *'99*
Me & Will *'99*
Disturbing Behavior *'98*
Stranger in the House *'97*
Termination Man *'97*
Barb Wire *'96*
Street Corner Justice *'96*
Calendar Girl *'93*
Final Mission *'93*
In the Line of Fire *'93*
Nukie *'93*
Private Wars *'93*
Save Me *'93*
Forever: A Ghost of a Love Story *'92*
Quake *'92*
Sunstroke *'92*
Scissors *'91*
Alligator 2: The Mutation *'90*
Assassin *'89*
The Forgotten *'89*
Deadly Intent *'88*
Blue Monkey *'87*
Distortions *'87*
Scenes from the Goldmine *'87*
The Survivalist *'87*
The Wind *'87*
Armed and Dangerous *'86*
Lifeforce *'85*
Torchlight *'85*
The Golden Seal *'83*
Trick or Treats *'82*
Escape 2000 *'81*
Deadly Games *'80*
The Stunt Man *'80*
From Here to Eternity *'79*
Angela *'77*
Helter Skelter *'76*

Sam Raimi (1959-)
Stephen King's The Stand *'94*
Body Bags *'93*
Indian Summer *'93*
Innocent Blood *'92*
Maniac Cop *'88*
Evil Dead 2: Dead by Dawn *'87*
Thou Shalt Not Kill...Except *'87*
Evil Dead *'83*

Theodore (Ted) Raimi (1965-)
Angel of Death *'09*
The Midnight Meat Train *'08*
My Name Is Bruce *'08*
Spider-Man 3 *'07*
The Grudge *'04*
Spider-Man 2 *'04*
Players *'03*
Spider-Man *'02*
The Shot *'96*
Clear and Present Danger *'94*
Stuart Saves His Family *'94*
Hard Target *'93*
Skinner *'93*
Army of Darkness *'92*
Eddie Presley *'92*
The Finishing Touch *'92*
Lunatics: A Love Story *'92*
Patriot Games *'92*
Darkman *'90*
Shocker *'89*
Evil Dead 2: Dead by Dawn *'87*
Thou Shalt Not Kill...Except *'87*
Crimewave *'85*
Evil Dead *'83*

Ruggero Raimondi
La Truite *'83*
Life Is a Bed of Roses *'83*

Raimu (1883-1946)
The Hammer *'07*
Well-Digger's Daughter *'46*
Heart of a Nation *'43*
Cesar *'36*
The Baker's Wife *'33*
Fanny *'32*
Marius *'31*

Rain (1982-)
Ninja Assassin *'09*
Speed Racer *'08*

Douglas Rain (1928-)
2010: The Year We Make Contact *'84 (V)*
2001: A Space Odyssey *'68 (V)*

Jeramie Rain (1948-)
The Abductors *'72*
Last House on the Left *'72*

Jack Raine (1897-1979)
The Killing of Sister George *'69*
The Girl in the Red Velvet Swing *'55*
Above and Beyond *'53*
The Ghoul *'34*
Night Birds *'31*

Luise Rainer (1910-)
The Gambler *'97*
Tiefland *'44*
The Great Waltz *'38*
The Good Earth *'37*
The Great Ziegfeld *'36*

Christina Raines (1952-)
North Shore *'87*
Quo Vadis *'85*
Nightmares *'83*
Silver Dream Racer *'83*
Touched by Love *'80*

Centennial *'78*
The Duellists *'77*
The Sentinel *'76*
Nashville *'75*
Russian Roulette *'75*
The Shrieking *'73*
Stacey *'73*

Ella Raines (1921-88)
Ride the Man Down *'53*
Impact *'49*
Brute Force *'47*
The Senator Was Indiscreet *'47*
The Strange Affair of Uncle Harry *'45*
Hail the Conquering Hero *'44*
Phantom Lady *'44*
Tall in the Saddle *'44*

Frances Raines (1962-)
Disconnected *'87*
Breeders *'86*
The Mutilator *'85*

Ford Rainey (1908-2005)
Bed & Breakfast *'92*
The Cellar *'90*
Backstairs at the White House *'79*
Strangers: The Story of a Mother and Daughter *'79*
Mountain Man *'77*
Babel *'75*
Strange New World *'75*
Sixteen *'72*
My Sweet Charlie *'70*
The Gypsy Moths *'69*
The Sand Pebbles *'66*
Flaming Star *'60*
3:10 to Yuma *'57*

Claude Rains (1889-1967)
The Greatest Story Ever Told *'65*
Lawrence of Arabia *'62*
Battle of the Worlds *'61*
The Pied Piper of Hamelin *'57*
Lisbon *'56*
Paris Express *'53*
Where Danger Lives *'50*
The White Tower *'50*
The Unsuspected *'47*
Angel on My Shoulder *'46*
Caesar and Cleopatra *'46*
Deception *'46*
Notorious *'46*
Mr. Skeffington *'44*
Passage to Marseilles *'44*
Forever and a Day *'43*
The Phantom of the Opera *'43*
Casablanca *'42*
Moontide *'42*
Now, Voyager *'42*
Here Comes Mr. Jordan *'41*
Kings Row *'41*
The Wolf Man *'41*
The Sea Hawk *'40*
Juarez *'39*
Mr. Smith Goes to Washington *'39*
They Made Me a Criminal *'39*
The Adventures of Robin Hood *'38*
Four Daughters *'38*
The Prince and the Pauper *'37*
They Won't Forget *'37*
Anthony Adverse *'36*
The Last Outpost *'35*
The Mystery of Edwin Drood *'35*
The Evil Mind *'34*
The Invisible Man *'33*

Francia Raisa
The Cutting Edge 3: Chasing the Dream *'08*
Shredderman Rules *'07*

Pierre-Loup Rajot (1958-)
The Adventures of Felix *'99*
The New Eve *'98*

Mary Lynn Rajskub (1971-)
Julie & Julia *'09*
Sunshine Cleaning *'09*
Humble Pie *'07*
Firewall *'06*
Grilled *'06*
Little Miss Sunshine *'06*
Mysterious Skin *'04*
Legally Blonde 2: Red White & Blonde *'03*
Serial Slayer *'03*
Punch-Drunk Love *'02*
Sweet Home Alabama *'02*
Sunset Strip *'99*

Tommy (Thomas) Rall (1929-)
Dancers *'87*
My Sister Eileen *'55*
Seven Brides for Seven Brothers *'54*
Kiss Me Kate *'53*

Giovanna Ralli (1935-)
Sex with a Smile *'76*
Caper of the Golden Bulls *'67*
What Did You Do in the War, Daddy? *'66*
Era Notte a Roma *'60*

Christopher Ralph (1977-)
The Skulls 2 *'02*
Hendrix *'00*

Jessie Ralph (1864-1944)
They Met in Bombay *'41*
The Bank Dick *'40*
The Blue Bird *'40*
Drums Along the Mohawk *'39*
Double Wedding *'37*
The Last of Mrs. Cheyney *'37*
After the Thin Man *'36*
Little Lord Fauntleroy *'36*
San Francisco *'36*
Yellow Dust *'36*
I Live My Life *'35*
Les Miserables *'35*
Paris in Spring *'35*
Evelyn Prentice *'34*
Murder at the Vanities *'34*
One Night of Love *'34*

Sheryl Lee Ralph (1956-)
Deterrence *'00*
Personals *'00*
Bogus *'96*
White Man's Burden *'95*
Witch Hunt *'94*
Sister Act 2: Back in the Habit *'93*
The Distinguished Gentleman *'92*
Mistress *'91*
To Sleep with Anger *'90*
The Mighty Quinn *'89*
Oliver & Company *'88 (V)*
Codename: Foxfire *'85*

Esther Ralston (1902-94)
Tin Pan Alley *'40*
Slander House *'38*
The Spy Ring *'38*
Shadows of the Orient *'37*
We're in the Legion Now *'37*
To the Last Man *'33*
Lonely Wives *'31*
Old Ironsides *'26*
$50,000 Reward *'25*
Lucky Devil *'25*
Peter Pan *'24*
Oliver Twist *'22*

Jobyna Ralston (1900-67)
The Kid Brother *'27*
Wings *'27*
For Heaven's Sake *'26*
The Freshman *'25*
Girl Shy *'24*

John Ralston
Demons from Her Past *'07*
Earthstorm *'06*
Power and Beauty *'02*

Vera Hruba Ralston (1923-2003)
Jubilee Trail *'54*
Hoodlum Empire *'52*
The Fighting Kentuckian *'49*
Dakota *'45*

Cecil Ramage (1895-1988)
Kind Hearts and Coronets *'49*
King of the Damned *'36*
Secret of Stamboul *'36*

Enrique Rambal (1924-71)
The Man and the Monster *'65*
The Exterminating Angel *'62*

Marjorie Rambeau (1889-1970)
Man of a Thousand Faces *'57*
A Man Called Peter *'55*
Forever Female *'53*
Torch Song *'53*
Abandoned *'47*
Broadway *'42*
Primrose Path *'40*
Santa Fe Marshal *'40*
The Rains Came *'39*
The Easiest Way *'31*
Laughing Sinners *'31*
Min & Bill *'30*

Dack Rambo (1942-94)
Ultra Warrior *'92*
River of Diamonds *'90*
The Spring *'89*
Waikiki *'80*
Hit Lady *'74*

Henry Ramer
The Big Slice *'90*
Hockey Night *'84*
Reno and the Doc *'84*
Starship Invasions *'77*
It Seemed Like a Good Idea at the Time *'75*
My Pleasure Is My Business *'74*

Carlos Ramirez (1914-86)
Wassup Rockers *'06*
Anchors Aweigh *'45*
Bathing Beauty *'44*
Two Girls and a Sailor *'44*

Dania Ramirez (1979-)
Quarantine *'08*
Illegal Tender *'07*
X-Men: The Last Stand *'06*
Fat Albert *'04*
She Hate Me *'04*
South Seas Massacre *'74*

Edgar Ramirez (1977-)
Che *'08*
Vantage Point *'08*
The Bourne Ultimatum *'07*
Domino *'05*

Efren Ramirez (1973-)
Crank: High Voltage *'09*
Moola *'07*
Crank *'06*
Employee of the Month *'06*
Napoleon Dynamite *'04*

Frank Ramirez
Details of a Duel: A Question of Honor *'89*
Miracle in Rome *'88*
Code of Honor *'82*
Smith! *'69*

Harold Ramis (1944-)
Year One *'09*
Knocked Up *'07*
Walk Hard: The Dewey Cox Story *'07*
The Last Kiss *'06*
I'm with Lucy *'02*
Orange County *'02*
As Good As It Gets *'97*
Airheads *'94*
Love Affair *'94*
Ghostbusters 2 *'89*
Stealing Home *'88*
Baby Boom *'87*
Ghostbusters *'84*
Heavy Metal *'81 (V)*
Stripes *'81*

Haley Ramm (1992-)
Walking Tall: Lone Justice *'07*
X-Men: The Last Stand *'06*
Flightplan *'05*
Yours, Mine & Ours *'05*

Eulalia Ramon (1959-)
Goya in Bordeaux *'99*
Outrage *'93*
Letters from Alou *'90*

Rudy Ramos (1950-)
The Spy Within *'94*
Blindsided *'93*
Colors *'88*
Open House *'86*
Quicksilver *'86*

Charlotte Rampling (1945-)
Life During Wartime *'09*
Babylon A.D. *'08*
Deception *'08*
The Duchess *'08*
Basic Instinct 2 *'06*
Heading South *'05*
Lemming *'05*
I'll Sleep When I'm Dead *'03*
The Statement *'03*
Swimming Pool *'03*
The Fourth Angel *'01*
My Uncle Silas *'01*
Spy Game *'01*
Aberdeen *'00*
Signs & Wonders *'00*
Under the Sand *'00*
Great Expectations *'99*
The Wings of the Dove *'97*
Invasion of Privacy *'96*
Hammers over the Anvil *'91*
D.O.A. *'88*
Angel Heart *'87*
Mascara *'87*
Max, Mon Amour *'86*
The Verdict *'82*
Stardust Memories *'80*
Orca *'77*
The Purple Taxi *'77*
Foxtrot *'76*
Farewell, My Lovely *'75*
Sardinia Kidnapped *'75*
Ski Bum *'75*
Caravan to Vaccares *'74*
The Night Porter *'74*
'Tis a Pity She's a Whore *'73*
Zardoz *'73*
Asylum *'72*
The Damned *'69*
Georgy Girl *'66*

Anne Elizabeth Ramsay (1960-)
The Final Cut *'96*
A League of Their Own *'92*

Bruce Ramsay (1968-)
Jericho Mansions *'03*
Island of the Dead *'00*
Bonanno: A Godfather's Story *'99*
Hit Me *'96*
Curdled *'95*
Hellraiser 4: Bloodline *'95*
Dead Beat *'94*
Killing Zoe *'94*
The New Age *'94*
Alive *'93*

Remak Ramsay (1937-)
Addicted to Love *'96*
Mr. & Mrs. Bridge *'90*
The Dining Room *'86*

Bobby Ramsen
It's Alive 2: It Lives Again *'78*
Hell Up in Harlem *'73*

Anne Ramsey (1929-88)
Perfect Alibi *'94*
Meet the Hollowheads *'89*
Another Chance *'88*
Dr. Hackenstein *'88*
The River Pirates *'88*
Throw Momma from the Train *'87*
Weeds *'87*
Deadly Friend *'86*
The Goonies *'85*
A Small Killing *'81*
Marilyn: The Untold Story *'80*
White Mama *'80*
The Black Marble *'79*
Goin' South *'78*
The Boy in the Plastic Bubble *'76*

David Ramsey
Mother and Child *'09*
Fatal Contact: Bird Flu in America *'06*
Hair Show *'04*
Pay It Forward *'00*
Mutiny *'99*

Laura Ramsey (1982-)
Shrink *'09*
The Ruins *'08*
The Covenant *'06*
She's the Man *'06*
Cruel World *'05*
Venom *'05*

Logan Ramsey (1921-2000)
Dr. Hackenstein *'88*
Say Yes! *'86*
The Beast Within *'82*
Conspiracy of Terror *'75*
Red, White & Busted *'75*
Confessions of Tom Harris *'72*
Fury on Wheels *'71*
Head *'68*
The Hoodlum Priest *'61*

Lois Ramsey
Road to Nhill *'97*
River Street *'95*

Marion Ramsey (1947-)
Police Academy 6: City under Siege *'89*
Police Academy 5: Assignment Miami Beach *'88*
Police Academy 3: Back in Training *'86*

Natalie Ramsey (1975-)
Cruel Intentions 3 *'04*
Children of the Corn 666: Isaac's Return *'99*

Wes Ramsey
Brotherhood of Blood *'08*
Dark Honeymoon *'08*
Slippery Slope *'06*
Latter Days *'04*

Stacey Linn Ramsower
The Baby-Sitters' Club *'95*
The Quick and the Dead *'95*
Tank Girl *'94*

Nick Ramus (1952-2007)
3 Ninjas Knuckle Up *'95*
Geronimo *'93*
Journey to Spirit Island *'92*

Frederica Ranchi (1939-)
Son of Samson *'62*
The Wide Blue Road *'57*

Sally Rand
The Sunset Murder Case *'38*
Sunny Side Up *'28*
The Fighting Eagle *'27*
Getting Gertie's Garter *'27*
Braveheart *'25*

Cestmir Randa (1923-86)
A Prayer for Katarina Horovitzova *'69*
Transport from Paradise *'65*

Monica Randal
See Monica Randall

Addison Randall (1949-)
Chance *'89*
Deadly Breed *'89*
Hollow Gate *'88*

Addison "Jack" Randall (1906-45)
Covered Wagon Trails *'40*
Across the Plains *'39*
Wild Horse Canyon *'39*
Gun Packer *'38*
Gunsmoke Trail *'38*
Man's Country *'38*
Red Lights Ahead *'36*

Anne Randall
Stacey *'73*
Hell's Bloody Devils *'70*

Jack Randall
See Addison "Jack" Randall

Lexi (Faith) Randall (1980-)
Sarah, Plain and Tall: Winter's End *'99*
The Stars Fell on Henrietta *'94*
The War *'94*
Heidi *'93*
Sarah, Plain and Tall: Skylark *'93*
Sarah, Plain and Tall *'91*

Meg Randall (1926-)
Ma and Pa Kettle Back On the Farm *'51*
Ma and Pa Kettle Go to Town *'50*
Ma and Pa Kettle *'49*
Abandoned *'47*

Monica Randall (1942-)
Cria Cuervos *'76*
Inquisition *'76*
Witches' Mountain *'71*
Commando Attack *'67*
Five Giants from Texas *'66*

Stacie Randall
Detour *'99*
Evil Obsession *'96*
Excessive Force 2: Force on Force *'95*
Dream a Little Dream 2 *'94*
Trancers 5: Sudden Deth *'94*
Trancers 4: Jack of Swords *'93*
Eddie Presley *'92*

Tony Randall (1920-2004)
Down With Love *'03*
Fatal Instinct *'93*
Gremlins 2: The New Batch *'90 (V)*
That's Adequate *'90*
King of Comedy *'82*
Foolin' Around *'80*
Scavenger Hunt *'79*
Everything You Always Wanted to Know about Sex (But Were Afraid to Ask) *'72*
Hello Down There *'69*
The Littlest Angel *'69*
The Alphabet Murders *'65*
Robin and the 7 Hoods *'64*
Send Me No Flowers *'64*
The Brass Bottle *'63*
7 Faces of Dr. Lao *'63*
Boys' Night Out *'62*
Lover Come Back *'61*
The Adventures of Huckleberry Finn *'60*
Let's Make Love *'60*
The Mating Game *'59*
Pillow Talk *'59*
Will Success Spoil Rock Hunter? *'57*

Steven Randazzo
The Wedding Bros. *'08*
Mac *'93*
In the Soup *'92*
Jungle Fever *'91*

Monica Randel
See Monica Randall

Ron Randell (1918-2005)

Girl in Black Stockings *'57*
The Story of Esther Costello *'57*
Counterspy Meets Scotland Yard *'50*
Omoo Omoo, the Shark God *'49*
The Loves of Carmen *'48*

Theresa Randle (1967-)

The Hunt for Eagle One: Crash Point *'06*
Bad Boys 2 *'03*
Livin' for Love: The Natalie Cole Story *'00*
Spawn *'97*
Girl 6 *'96*
Space Jam *'96*
Bad Boys *'95*
Beverly Hills Cop 3 *'94*
Sugar Hill *'94*
CB4: The Movie *'93*
Malcolm X *'92*
Jungle Fever *'91*

Anders Randolf (1870-1930)

The Kiss *'29*
The Viking *'28*
Old San Francisco *'27*
Ranson's Folly *'26*
The Idol Dancer *'20*
The Love Flower *'20*

Donald Randolph (1906-93)

The Deadly Mantis *'57*
Gunsmoke *'53*

Jane Randolph (1919-)

Abbott and Costello Meet Frankenstein *'48*
Open Secret *'48*
Railroaded *'47*
Curse of the Cat People *'44*
Cat People *'42*
The Falcon's Brother *'42*

John Randolph (1915-2004)

Sunset Strip *'99*
You've Got Mail *'98*
A Price above Rubies *'97*
A Foreign Field *'93*
Iron Maze *'91*
National Lampoon's Christmas Vacation *'89*
The Wizard of Loneliness *'88*
As Summers Die *'86*
Prizzi's Honor *'85*
Frances *'82*
Lovely... But Deadly *'82*
The Adventures of Nellie Bly *'81*
Backstairs at the White House *'79*
Blind Ambition *'79*
The Winds of Kitty Hawk *'78*
Secrets *'77*
F. Scott Fitzgerald in Hollywood *'76*
King Kong *'76*
The Runaways *'75*
Missiles of October *'74*
Serpico *'73*
Conquest of the Planet of the Apes *'72*
Escape from the Planet of the Apes *'71*
There Was a Crooked Man *'70*
Pretty Poison *'68*
Seconds *'66*

Katherine Randolph

Black Ops *'07*
Girl Play *'04*

Lillian Randolph (1898-1980)

Magic *'78*
How to Seduce a Woman *'74*

Ty Randolph

See Mindi Miller

Windsor Taylor Randolph

See Mindi Miller

Robert Random (1943-)

Danger Zone 3: Steel Horse War *'90*
Danger Zone 2 *'89*

Salvo Randone (1906-91)

Fellini Satyricon *'69*
Spirits of the Dead *'68*
10th Victim *'65*
The Mercenaries *'62*

Joe Ranft (1960-2005)

Cars *'06 (V)*
Finding Nemo *'03 (V)*
Toy Story 2 *'99 (V)*
A Bug's Life *'98 (V)*

Dan Ranger

Cop-Out *'91*
The Last Ride *'91*

Arthur (L.) Rankin (1900-47)

Terror Trail *'33*
Fighting Fool *'32*
Below the Deadline *'29*
Walking Back *'26*

Kenny Ransom

The Crocodile Hunter: Collision Course *'02*
Border Patrol *'01*
Prison for Children *'93*
There Goes My Baby *'92*

Tim Ransom (1963-)

Courage Under Fire *'96*
Vital Signs *'90*
The Dressmaker *'89*

Prunella Ransome (1943-)

Man in the Wilderness *'71*
Far from the Madding Crowd *'67*

James Ransone

Generation Kill *'08*
The Good Humor Man *'05*

Michael Rapaport (1970-)

Big Fan *'09*
A Day in the Life *'09*
Grilled *'06*
Special *'06*
Hitch *'05*
This Girl's Life *'03*
Comic Book Villains *'02*
Triggermen *'02*
Dr. Dolittle 2 *'01 (V)*
King of the Jungle *'01*
Bamboozled *'00*
Chain of Fools *'00*
Kiss Toledo Goodbye *'00*
Lucky Numbers *'00*
Men of Honor *'00*
The 6th Day *'00*
Small Time Crooks *'00*
Deep Blue Sea *'99*
The Naked Man *'98*
Palmetto *'98*
A Brother's Kiss *'97*
Cop Land *'97*
Kicked in the Head *'97*
Subway Stories *'97*
Beautiful Girls *'96*
Illtown *'96*
Metro *'96*
The Basketball Diaries *'95*
Mighty Aphrodite *'95*
The Pallbearer *'95*
Higher Learning *'94*
Kiss of Death *'94*
The Scout *'94*
Hand Gun *'93*
Money for Nothing *'93*
True Romance *'93*
Zebrahead *'92*

Anthony Rapp (1971-)

Danny Roane: First Time Director *'06*
Rent *'05*
A Beautiful Mind *'01*
Road Trip *'00*
Man of the Century *'99*
David Searching *'97*
Dazed and Confused *'93*
Six Degrees of Separation *'93*
School Ties *'92*
Far from Home *'89*
Adventures in Babysitting *'87*

David Rappaport (1952-90)

Peter Gunn *'89*
The Bride *'85*
Mysteries *'84*

Sheeri Rappaport (1977-)

Seeing Other People *'04*
Serial Slayer *'03*
United States of Leland *'03*
Little Witches *'96*

Kseniya Rappoport (1974-)

The Double Hour *'09*
The Unknown Woman *'06*

Eva Ras (1941-)

The Love Affair, or The Case of the Missing Switchboard Operator *'67*
Man Is Not a Bird *'65*

Renato Rascel (1912-91)

The Secret of Santa Vittoria *'69*
Uncle Was a Vampire *'59*
The Seven Hills of Rome *'58*

David Rasche (1944-)

In the Loop *'09*
Burn After Reading *'08*
Perception *'06*
The Sentinel *'06*
Final Approach *'04*
Off the Lip *'04*
Exposed *'03*
Just Married *'03*
Divine Secrets of the Ya-Ya Sisterhood *'02*
Hostage Hotel *'00*
The Big Tease *'99*
Friends & Lovers *'99*
The Settlement *'99*
Tourist Trap *'98*
That Old Feeling *'96*
Dead Weekend *'95*
Out There *'95*
Bigfoot: The Unforgettable Encounter *'94*
A Million to Juan *'94*
Twenty Bucks *'93*
Bingo *'91*
Delirious *'91*
Silhouette *'91*
The Masters of Menace *'90*
An Innocent Man *'89*
Wedding Band *'89*
Wicked Stepmother *'89*
Made in Heaven *'87*
Native Son *'86*
Manhattan *'79*
Sanctuary of Fear *'79*

Phylicia Rashad (1949-)

A Raisin in the Sun *'08*
The Old Settler *'01*
The Visit *'00*
Loving Jezebel *'99*
Free of Eden *'98*
Once Upon a Time ... When We Were Colored *'95*
False Witness *'89*
Uncle Tom's Cabin *'87*

Sharif Rashed

Hell's Kitchen NYC *'97*
Blue in the Face *'95*
Crooklyn *'94*

Rie Rasmussen

Angel-A *'05*
Femme Fatale *'02*

Fritz Rasp (1891-1976)

The Threepenny Opera *'31*
Diary of a Lost Girl *'29*
Spies *'28*
The Love of Jeanne Ney *'27*
Metropolis *'26*

Julien Rassam (1968-)

Queen Margot *'94*
The Accompanist *'93*

Ivan Rassimov (1938-2003)

Emerald Jungle *'80*
Shock *'79*
Man from Deep River *'77*
Your Vice is a Closed Room and Only I Have the Key *'72*
The Next Victim *'71*
Blade of the Ripper *'70*
Cjamango *'67*
Planet of the Vampires *'65*

Rada Rassimov (1938-)

Torture Chamber of Baron Blood *'72*
The Good, the Bad and the Ugly *'67*

Victor Rasuk (1984-)

Che *'08*
Stop-Loss *'08*
Adrift in Manhattan *'07*
Feel the Noise *'07*
Bonneville *'06*
I'm Reed Fish *'06*
Lords of Dogtown *'05*
Haven *'04*
Raising Victor Vargas *'03*

Thalmus Rasulala (1939-91)

Mom and Dad Save the World *'92*
New Jack City *'91*
Blind Vengeance *'90*
The Package *'89*
Above the Law *'88*
Bulletproof *'88*
Born American *'86*
Sophisticated Gents *'81*
The Last Hard Men *'76*
Adios Amigo *'75*
Bucktown *'75*
Friday Foster *'75*
Blacula *'72*

Mikhail Rasumny (1890-1956)

The Kissing Bandit *'48*
Anna and the King of Siam *'46*
For Whom the Bell Tolls *'43*
Wake Island *'42*

Jeremy Ratchford (1965-)

Angel Eyes *'01*
The Crew *'00*
Fly Away Home *'96*
Moonshine Highway *'96*
Prom Night 3: The Last Kiss *'89*

Sandy Ratcliff (1950-)

Yesterday's Hero *'79*
Family Life *'71*

Basil Rathbone (1892-1967)

Many Faces of Sherlock Holmes *'86*
Autopsy of a Ghost *'67*
Hillbillies in a Haunted House *'67*
Ghost in the Invisible Bikini *'66*
Planet of Blood *'66*
Voyage to the Prehistoric Planet *'65*
The Comedy of Terrors *'64*
The Magic Sword *'62*
Tales of Terror *'62*
Victoria Regina *'61*
Last Hurrah *'58*
The Black Sleep *'56*
Court Jester *'56*
We're No Angels *'55*
Casanova's Big Night *'54*
A Christmas Carol *'54*
The Adventures of Ichabod and Mr. Toad *'49 (N)*
The Woman in Green *'49*
Dressed to Kill *'46*
Heartbeat *'46*
Terror by Night *'46*
House of Fear *'45*
Pursuit to Algiers *'45*
Bathing Beauty *'44*
Frenchman's Creek *'44*
The Pearl of Death *'44*
Scarlet Claw *'44*
Spider Woman *'44*
Above Suspicion *'43*
Sherlock Holmes Faces Death *'43*
Sherlock Holmes in Washington *'43*
Crossroads *'42*
Sherlock Holmes and the Secret Weapon *'42*
Sherlock Holmes: The Voice of Terror *'42*
The Black Cat *'41*
International Lady *'41*
The Mark of Zorro *'40*
Rhythm on the River *'40*
The Adventures of Sherlock Holmes *'39*
The Hound of the Baskervilles *'39*
Son of Frankenstein *'39*
The Tower of London *'39*
The Adventures of Marco Polo *'38*
The Adventures of Robin Hood *'38*
Dawn Patrol *'38*
If I Were King *'38*
Love from a Stranger *'37*
Make a Wish *'37*
The Garden of Allah *'36*
Romeo and Juliet *'36*
A Tale of Two Cities *'36*
Anna Karenina *'35*
Captain Blood *'35*
David Copperfield *'35*
Last Days of Pompeii *'35*
Sin Takes a Holiday *'30*

Jackson Rathbone (1984-)

The Last Airbender *'10*
The Twilight Saga: Eclipse *'10*
Hurt *'09*
S. Darko: A Donnie Darko Tale *'09*
The Twilight Saga: New Moon *'09*
Twilight *'08*

Benjamin Ratner

Moving Malcolm *'03*
Ignition *'01*
Firestorm *'97*
Bounty Hunters *'96*

Gregory Ratoff (1897-1960)

Exodus *'60*
Abdulla the Great *'56*
All About Eve *'50*
Cafe Metropole *'37*
I'm No Angel *'33*
Skyscraper Souls *'32*

Devin Ratray (1977-)

Surrogates *'09*
Home Alone 2: Lost in New York *'92*
Home Alone *'90*
Spy Trap *'88*

Peter Ratray (1941-)

Stonewall *'95*
Will: G. Gordon Liddy *'82*

Heather Rattray (1966-)

Basket Case 2 *'90*
Mountain Family Robinson *'79*
Sea Gypsies *'78*
Further Adventures of the Wilderness Family, Part 2 *'77*
Across the Great Divide *'76*

John Ratzenberger (1947-)

Toy Story 3 *'10 (V)*
Up *'09 (V)*
The Village Barbershop *'08*
WALL-E *'08 (V)*
Ratatouille *'07 (V)*
Cars *'06 (V)*
Finding Nemo *'03 (V)*
Monsters, Inc. *'01 (V)*
Spirited Away *'01 (V)*
Tick Tock *'00*
Toy Story 2 *'99 (V)*
A Bug's Life *'98 (V)*
Under Pressure *'98*
One Night Stand *'97*
That Darn Cat *'96*
Toy Story *'95 (V)*
Camp Cucamonga: How I Spent My Summer Vacation *'90*
House 2: The Second Story *'87*
Timestalkers *'87*
Combat Academy *'86*
Gandhi *'82*
Outland *'81*
Ragtime *'81*
The Empire Strikes Back *'80*
Motel Hell *'80*
The Bitch *'78*
A Bridge Too Far *'77*
Twilight's Last Gleaming *'77*

Andrea Rau (1949-)

Beyond Erotica *'79*
Daughters of Darkness *'71*

Siegfried Rauch (1932-)

Sons of Trinity *'95*
Alien Contamination *'81*
The Big Red One *'80*
We Will Not Enter the Forest *'79*
The Uranium Conspiracy *'78*
Patton *'70*
Nous N'Irons Plus au Bois *'69*

Rick Ravanello

Smoke Jumpers *'08*
The Cave *'05*

Gina Ravarra

See Gina Ravera

Raven (1985-)

The Cheetah Girls 2 *'06*
Everyone's Hero *'06 (V)*
The Princess Diaries 2: Royal Engagement *'04*
The Cheetah Girls *'03*
Dr. Dolittle 2 *'01*
Dr. Dolittle *'98*
Queen *'93*

Mike Raven (1924-97)

Crucible of Terror *'72*
Disciple of Death *'72*
I, Monster *'71*
Lust for a Vampire *'71*

Raven-Symone

See Raven
College Road Trip *'08*

Christopher Ravenscroft (1946-)

A Mind to Murder *'96*
Henry V *'89*

Kim Raver (1969-)

Night at the Museum *'06*
Mind the Gap *'04*

Gina Ravera (1968-)

The Great Debaters *'07*
The Temptations *'98*
Kiss the Girls *'97*
Soul Food *'97*
Soul of the Game *'96*
Showgirls *'95*

emile de ravin (1981-)

High Noon *'09*

Navi Rawat (1977-)

Loveless in Los Angeles *'07*
Undead or Alive *'07*
Feast *'06*
House of Sand and Fog *'03*

Adrian Rawlins (1958-)

The Old Curiosity Shop *'07*
Wilbur Wants to Kill Himself *'02*
Breaking the Waves *'95*
Woman in Black *'89*

The Candidate '72
Jeremiah Johnson '72
The Hot Rock '70
Butch Cassidy and the Sundance Kid '69
Downhill Racer '69
Tell Them Willie Boy Is Here '69
Barefoot in the Park '67
The Chase '66
This Property Is Condemned '66
Inside Daisy Clover '65
The Iceman Cometh '60

Rockets Redglare (1948-2001)
In the Soup '92
Cookie '89
Mystery Train '89
Shakedown '88
Salvation! '87
Down by Law '86
After Hours '85

Corin Redgrave (1939-2010)
Enduring Love '04
To Kill a King '03
Close Your Eyes '02
Enigma '01
Ultraviolet '98
The Ice House '97
The Woman in White '97
Persuasion '95
Four Weddings and a Funeral '94
In the Name of the Father '93
Excalibur '81
Between Wars '74
When Eight Bells Toll '71
Oh! What a Lovely War '69
The Charge of the Light Brigade '68

Jemma Redgrave (1965-)
Mansfield Park '07
Lassie '05
Like Father Like Son '05
I'll Be There '03
The Acid House '98
Mosley '98
Diana: Her True Story '93
The Buddha of Suburbia '92
Howard's End '92
Dream Demon '88

Lynn Redgrave (1943-)
Confessions of a Shopaholic '09
The Jane Austen Book Club '07
The White Countess '05
Kinsey '04
Peter Pan '03
Unconditional Love '03
My Sister's Keeper '02
Spider '02
The Wild Thornberrys Movie '02 (V)
How to Kill Your Neighbor's Dog '01
Varian's War '01
The Next Best Thing '00
Deeply '99
A Season for Miracles '99
The Simian Line '99
All I Wanna Do '98
Gods and Monsters '98
White Lies '98
Toothless '97
Shine '95
The Great American Sex Scandal '94
What Ever Happened To... '93
Getting It Right '89
Midnight '89
Morgan Stewart's Coming Home '87
Walking on Air '87
The Bad Seed '85
Rehearsal for Murder '82
Shooting '82
To Love Again '80
Centennial '78
Sooner or Later '78
The Big Bus '76
The Happy Hooker '75
The Turn of the Screw '74
Everything You Always Wanted to Know about Sex (But Were Afraid to Ask) '72
The Virgin Soldiers '69
Smashing Time '67
Georgy Girl '66
Girl with Green Eyes '64
Tom Jones '63

Michael Redgrave (1908-85)
Dr. Jekyll and Mr. Hyde '73
The Go-Between '71
Nicholas and Alexandra '71
Twinsanity '70
Battle of Britain '69
Goodbye, Mr. Chips '69
Oh! What a Lovely War '69
Heidi '67
The Heroes of Telemark '65
The Hill '65
The Loneliness of the Long Distance Runner '62
The Innocents '61
Shake Hands with the Devil '59
The Wreck of the Mary Deare '59
Time Without Pity '57
1984 '56
Dam Busters '55
Mr. Arkadin '55
The Sea Shall Not Have Them '55
The Importance of Being Earnest '52
The Browning Version '51
Secret Beyond the Door '48
Captive Heart '47
Fame Is the Spur '47
Dead of Night '45
Kipps '41
Lady in Distress '39
The Stars Look Down '39
The Lady Vanishes '38

Vanessa Redgrave (1937-)
Letters to Juliet '10
Atonement '07
Evening '07
How About You '07
The Riddle '07
Venus '06
The Keeper: The Legend of Omar Khayyam '05
The White Countess '05
The Fever '04
Merci Docteur Rey '04
Byron '03
Good Boy! '03 (V)
The Gathering Storm '02
The Locket '02
Jack and the Beanstalk: The Real Story '01
If These Walls Could Talk 2 '00
The Pledge '00
A Rumor of Angels '00
The Cradle Will Rock '99
Girl, Interrupted '99
Deep Impact '98
Deja Vu '98
Lulu on the Bridge '98
Bella Mafia '97
Mrs. Dalloway '97
Wilde '97
Looking for Richard '96
Mission: Impossible '96
Smilla's Sense of Snow '96
A Month by the Lake '95
Down Came a Blackbird '94
Little Odessa '94
Mother's Boys '94
The House of the Spirits '93
Shades of Fear '93
They Watch '93
What Ever Happened To... '93
Howard's End '92
The Ballad of the Sad Cafe '91
Orpheus Descending '91
Young Catherine '91
Consuming Passions '88
A Man for All Seasons '88
Prick Up Your Ears '87
Peter the Great '86
Steaming '86
Three Sovereigns for Sarah '85
Wagner: The Complete Epic '85
Wagner: The Movie '85
Wetherby '85
The Bostonians '84
Snow White and the Seven Dwarfs '83
Bear Island '80
Playing for Time '80
Agatha '79
Yanks '79
Julia '77
The Seven-Per-Cent Solution '76
Out of Season '75
Murder on the Orient Express '74
The Devils '71
Mary, Queen of Scots '71
Trojan Women '71
Oh! What a Lovely War '69
The Charge of the Light Brigade '68
Isadora '68
Camelot '67
Blow-Up '66
A Man for All Seasons '66
Morgan: A Suitable Case for Treatment '66

Juli Reding (1935-)
Tormented '60
Why Must I Die? '60
Mission in Morocco '59

Nick Reding (1962-)
In Love and War '01
Croupier '97
Mister Johnson '91

Christian Redl (1948-)
Yella '07
The Trio '97
Lea '96

Redman (1970-)
Seed of Chucky '04
Scary Movie 3 '03
How High '01

Amanda Redman (1959-)
Suspicion '03
Sexy Beast '00
King Lear '98
Body & Soul '93
Richard's Things '80

Joyce Redman (1918-)
The Rector's Wife '94
Othello '65
Tom Jones '63

Teal Redmann (1982-)
Dumb and Dumberer: When Harry Met Lloyd '03
Chameleon 3: Dark Angel '00

Eddie Redmayne
Powder Blue '09
The Other Boleyn Girl '08
Tess of the D'Urbervilles '08
The Yellow Handkerchief '08
Elizabeth: The Golden Age '07
Savage Grace '07
The Good Shepherd '06
Murderous Intent '06

Liam Redmond (1913-89)
The Last Safari '67
The Ghost and Mr. Chicken '66
Curse of the Demon '57
Devil on Horseback '54

Moira Redmond (1928-2006)
Catherine Cookson's The Wingless Bird '97
Nightmare '63
Doctor in Love '60

Sarah Jane Redmond
The Invitation '03
Dead in a Heartbeat '02
Suspicious River '00

Siobhan Redmond (1959-)
Beautiful People '99
Every Woman Knows a Secret '99
Captives '94
Look Back in Anger '89

Yekaterina Rednikova (1973-)
Archangel '05
Border Blues '03
The Thief '97

Manning Redwood (1929-2006)
Outland '81
Shock Treatment '81

Alan Reed (1936-)
Shinbone Alley '70 (V)
Tarnished Angels '57
The Far Horizons '55
Lady and the Tramp '55 (V)
A Woman's World '54
Actors and Sin '52
The Postman Always Rings Twice '46
Days of Glory '43

Alan Reed, Jr.
Peyton Place '57
Rock, Pretty Baby '56

Alyson Reed (1958-)
High School Musical '06
Manhattan Merenque! '95
Skin Deep '89
A Chorus Line '85

Bobby Reed
A Simple Promise '07

Donald Reed (1901-73)
Slaves in Bondage '37
Evangeline '29

Donna Reed (1921-86)
The Benny Goodman Story '55
The Far Horizons '55
The Last Time I Saw Paris '54
The Caddy '53
From Here to Eternity '53
Gun Fury '53
Trouble along the Way '53
Hangman's Knot '52
Scandal Sheet '52
Green Dolphin Street '47
It's a Wonderful Life '46
Picture of Dorian Gray '45
They Were Expendable '45
The Human Comedy '43
Thousands Cheer '43
Shadow of the Thin Man '41

George Reed (1866-1952)
Strange Illusion '45
Green Pastures '36

Hal Reed
The Doberman Gang '72
The Zodiac Killer '71

Jerry Reed (1937-2008)
The Waterboy '98
Bat 21 '88
What Comes Around '85
Smokey and the Bandit, Part 3 '83
Survivors '83
Hot Stuff '80
Smokey and the Bandit 2 '80
The Concrete Cowboys '79
High Ballin' '78
Smokey and the Bandit '77
Gator '76

Lou Reed (1942-)
Blue in the Face '95
Faraway, So Close! '93
Superstar: The Life and Times of Andy Warhol '90
Get Crazy '83
One Trick Pony '80

Marshall Reed (1917-80)
The Hard Ride '71
They Saved Hitler's Brain '64
The Lineup '58
Lawmen '44

Maxwell Reed (1919-74)
The Notorious Landlady '62
Roadhouse Girl '53
Sea Devils '53
The Clouded Yellow '51
Flame of Araby '51
Blackout '50
Night Beat '48
Dear Murderer '47

Nikki Reed (1988-)
The Twilight Saga: Eclipse '10
The Twilight Saga: New Moon '09
Familiar Strangers '08
Twilight '08
Cherry Crush '07
American Gun '05
Lords of Dogtown '05
Thirteen '03

Oliver Reed (1938-99)
Gladiator '00
Jeremiah '98
Parting Shots '98
The Bruce '96
Funny Bones '94
Return to Lonesome Dove '93
Severed Ties '92
Hired to Kill '91
The Pit & the Pendulum '91
Prisoner of Honor '91
The Revenger '90
The Adventures of Baron Munchausen '89
The Lady and the Highwayman '89
Master of Dragonard Hill '89
The Return of the Musketeers '89
Skeleton Coast '89
Treasure Island '89
Captive Rage '88
Dragonard '88
Gor '88
The House of Usher '88
Rage to Kill '88
Captive '87
Castaway '87
The Misfit Brigade '87
Christopher Columbus '85
The Black Arrow '84
Fanny Hill '83
The Sting 2 '83
Two of a Kind '83
Spasms '82
Venom '82
Condorman '81
Lion of the Desert '81
Dr. Heckyl and Mr. Hype '80
The Brood '79
The Big Sleep '78
The Class of Miss MacMichael '78
The Prince and the Pauper '78
Maniac '77
Tomorrow Never Comes '77
Triple Echo '77
Burnt Offerings '76
Great Scout & Cathouse Thursday '76
Sell Out '76
The Four Musketeers '75
Lisztomania '75
Royal Flash '75
Ten Little Indians '75
Tommy '75
The Three Musketeers '74
Blue Blood '73
One Russian Summer '73
Zero Population Growth '72
The Devils '71
Women in Love '70
The Assassination Bureau '69
Dante's Inferno: Life of Dante Gabriel Rossetti '69
Blood Island '68
Oliver! '68
I'll Never Forget What's 'Isname '67
The Girl Getters '66
Trap '66
Paranoiac '62
Pirates of Blood River '62
The Curse of the Werewolf '61
Beat Girl '60
No Love for Johnnie '60
Sword of Sherwood Forest '60
The Two Faces of Dr. Jekyll '60

Pamela Reed (1949-)
Life of the Party '05
Tanner on Tanner '04
Proof of Life '00
Standing on Fishes '99
Why Do Fools Fall in Love? '98
Bean '97
Critical Choices '97
Santa Fe '97
Junior '94
Bob Roberts '92
Passed Away '92
Woman with a Past '92
Cadillac Man '90
Caroline? '90
Kindergarten Cop '90
Chattahoochee '89
Tanner '88 '88
Rachel River '87
The Best of Times '86
The Clan of the Cave Bear '86
Scandal Sheet '85
The Goodbye People '83
The Right Stuff '83
Young Doctors in Love '82
Eyewitness '81
The Long Riders '80
Melvin and Howard '80

Penelope Reed
Hired to Kill '91
Amazons '86

Philip Reed (1908-96)
The Girl in the Red Velvet Swing '55
Bandit Queen '51
Unknown Island '48
Big Town '47
Big Town After Dark '47
Song of Scheherazade '47
Song of the Thin Man '47
Underworld Scandal '47
A Gentleman After Dark '42
Madame X '37
Klondike Annie '36
Female '33

Robert Reed (1932-92)
Prime Target '91
A Very Brady Christmas '88
Death of a Centerfold '81
Casino '80
Nurse '80
Love's Savage Fury '79
The Seekers '79
Bud and Lou '78
No Prince for My Cinderella '78
The Hunted Lady '77
The Boy in the Plastic Bubble '76
Nightmare in Badham County '76
Rich Man, Poor Man '76
Haunts of the Very Rich '72
Snatched '72
The Love Bug '68
Star! '68
Bloodlust '59
The Hunters '58

Shanna Reed (1956-)
The Night Caller '97
Alien Avengers '96
Rattled '96
The Sister-in-Law '95
Don't Talk to Strangers '94
The Banker '89
Legs '83

Suzanne Reed
Up from the Depths '79
Beyond the Bermuda Triangle '75

Execution of Raymond Graham '85
Heaven Help Us '85
The Blood of Others '84
Atlantic City '81
Circle of Two '80
Death Ship '80
The Double Negative '80
Highpoint '80
Crossbar '79
The Rainbow Gang '73
The Andromeda Strain '71
This Property Is Condemned '66
Holy Terror '65
Invincible Mr. Disraeli '63
One Plus One '61

Michael Earl Reid

Asylum of the Damned '03
Army of Darkness '92

R.D. Reid

Dawn of the Dead '04
Dirty Pictures '00

Sheila Reid (1937-)

The Winter Guest '97
Zero Population Growth '72
Othello '65

Tara Reid (1975-)

Senior Skip Day '08
Vipers '08
Strike '07
Alone in the Dark '05
The Crow: Wicked Prayer '05
Incubus '05
Knots '05
Silent Partner '05
Devil's Pond '03
My Boss's Daughter '03
National Lampoon's Van Wilder '02
American Pie 2 '01
Josie and the Pussycats '01
Just Visiting '01
Dr. T & the Women '00
American Pie '99
Body Shots '99
Murder at Devil's Glen '99
Around the Fire '98
Girl '98
Urban Legend '98
The Big Lebowski '97

Tim Reid (1944-)

The Reading Room '05
For Real '02
Race to Freedom: The Story of the Underground Railroad '94
Mastergate '92
You Must Remember This '92
The Fourth War '90
Stephen King's It '90
Dead Bang '89

Wallace Reid (1891-1923)

Affairs of Anatol '21
Hawthorne of the USA '19
The Roaring Road '19
The Birth of a Nation '15

Timothy Reifsnyder (1986-)

Hearts in Atlantis '01
Wide Awake '97

Halina Reijn (1975-)

Black Book '06
Zus & Zo '01

Charles Nelson Reilly (1931-2007)

Boys Will Be Boys '97
A Troll in Central Park '94 (V)
Rock-a-Doodle '92 (V)
All Dogs Go to Heaven '89 (V)
Body Slam '87
Cannonball Run 2 '84

Hugh Reilly (1916-98)

Chuka '67
Lassie's Great Adventure '62

John C. Reilly (1965-)

Cyrus '10
Cirque du Freak: The Vampire's Assistant '09
9 '09 (V)
The Promotion '08
Step Brothers '08
Walk Hard: The Dewey Cox Story '07
Year of the Dog '07
A Prairie Home Companion '06
Talladega Nights: The Ballad of Ricky Bobby '06
Tenacious D in the Pick of Destiny '06
The Aviator '04
Criminal '04
Anger Management '03
Chicago '02
Dark Water '02
Gangs of New York '02
The Good Girl '02
The Hours '02
The Anniversary Party '01
The Perfect Storm '00
For Love of the Game '99
Magnolia '99
Never Been Kissed '99
The Settlement '99
Chicago Cab '98
The Thin Red Line '98
Boogie Nights '97
Hard Eight '96
Nightwatch '96
Boys '95
Georgia '95
Dolores Claiborne '94
The River Wild '94
Fallen Angels 1 '93
What's Eating Gilbert Grape '93
Hoffa '92
Out on a Limb '92
Days of Thunder '90
State of Grace '90
Casualties of War '89
We're No Angels '89
Touch and Go '86
Missing Pieces '83

Kelly Reilly (1977-)

Me and Orson Welles '09
Sherlock Holmes '09
The Libertine '05
Mrs. Henderson Presents '05
Pride and Prejudice '05
Russian Dolls '05
Dead Bodies '03
L'Auberge Espagnole '02
Last Orders '01
Poldark '96

Luke Reilly

Zebrahead '92
Bye Bye Blues '89

Robert Reilly

Frankenstein Meets the Space Monster '65
Lilith '64

Tom Reilly (1959-)

Mirror Images 2 '93
Kiss and Be Killed '91

Gary Reineke

Spider '02
The Golden Spiders: A Nero Wolfe Mystery '00
George's Island '91

Carl Reiner (1922-)

Ocean's Thirteen '07
Ocean's Twelve '04
Good Boy! '03 (V)
Ocean's Eleven '01
The Adventures of Rocky & Bullwinkle '00
Slums of Beverly Hills '98
The Right to Remain Silent '95
Spirit of '76 '91
Summer School '87
Pinocchio '83
Dead Men Don't Wear Plaid '82
The Jerk '79
The End '78
Generation '69
A Guide for the Married Man '67
The Russians Are Coming, the Russians Are Coming '66
It's a Mad, Mad, Mad, Mad World '63
The Thrill of It All! '63
Gidget Goes Hawaiian '61
The Gazebo '59

Rob Reiner (1945-)

Everyone's Hero '06 (V)
Alex & Emma '03
Dickie Roberts: Former Child Star '03
EDtv '99
The Muse '99
The Story of Us '99
Primary Colors '98
The First Wives Club '96
Trigger Happy '96
For Better or Worse '95
Bullets over Broadway '94
Bye Bye, Love '94
Mixed Nuts '94
Sleepless in Seattle '93
The Return of Spinal Tap '92
Spirit of '76 '91
Postcards from the Edge '90
Throw Momma from the Train '87
Johnny Appleseed '86
This Is Spinal Tap '84
The Jerk '79
Thursday's Game '74
How Come Nobody's On Our Side? '73
Where's Poppa? '70
Enter Laughing '67

Tracy Reiner (1964-)

Apollo 13 '95
A League of Their Own '92
Frankie and Johnny '91
Masque of the Red Death '89
New Year's Day '89
When Harry Met Sally... '89
Jumpin' Jack Flash '86
Nothing in Common '86

Judge Reinhold (1958-)

Swing Vote '08
The Santa Clause 3: The Escape Clause '06
Clifford's Really Big Movie '04 (V)
The Hollow '04
National Lampoon's Holiday Reunion '03
Dead in a Heartbeat '02
The Santa Clause 2 '02
Whacked! '02
Beethoven's 4th '01
Beethoven's 3rd '00
Enemies of Laughter '00
Newsbreak '00
Ping! '99
Boltneck '98
Last Lives '98
Tom Clancy's Netforce '98
Crackerjack 2 '97
Homegrown '97
As Good as Dead '95
The Right to Remain Silent '95
The Wharf Rat '95
Beverly Hills Cop 3 '94
The Santa Clause '94
Bank Robber '93
Four Eyes and Six Guns '93
Baby on Board '92
Black Magic '92
Near Misses '91
A Soldier's Tale '91
Zandalee '91
Daddy's Dyin'... Who's Got the Will? '90
Enid Is Sleeping '90
Rosalie Goes Shopping '89
Promised a Miracle '88
Vice Versa '88
Beverly Hills Cop 2 '87
Head Office '86
Off Beat '86
Ruthless People '86
Beverly Hills Cop '84
Gremlins '84
Roadhouse 66 '84
The Lords of Discipline '83
Fast Times at Ridgemont High '82
Pandemonium '82
Stripes '81
On the Edge: The Survival of Dana '79
Running Scared '79

Ann Reinking (1949-)

Micki & Maude '84
Annie '82
All That Jazz '79

Michelle Reis (1970-)

Flowers of Shanghai '98
Fallen Angels '95

Vivian Reis

Broken Lullaby '94
Stalked '94

Geri Reischl (1959-)

I Dismember Mama '74
The Brotherhood of Satan '71

Hans Reiser (1919-92)

The Great Escape '63
Secret of the Black Trunk '62

Paul Reiser (1956-)

The Thing About My Folks '05
Purpose '02
Strange Relations '02
Women vs. Men '02
One Night at McCool's '01
The Story of Us '99
Bye Bye, Love '94
Mr. Write '92
Family Prayers '91
The Marrying Man '91
Crazy People '90
Cross My Heart '88
Beverly Hills Cop 2 '87
Aliens '86
From Here to Maternity '85
Odd Jobs '85
Beverly Hills Cop '84
Sunset Limousine '83
Diner '82

Robbie Reist

See Robbie (Reist) Rist

Jack Reitzen (1924-98)

Kentucky Jubilee '51
Mask of the Dragon '51

David Reivers

Free Style '09
Jump In! '07

Winston Rekert (1949-)

Art of War 2: The Betrayal '08
Smoke Jumpers '08
Savage Island '03
A Cooler Climate '99
The Last Stop '99
Loving Evangeline '98
The World's Oldest Living Bridesmaid '92
Glory! Glory! '90
Eternal Evil '87
Toby McTeague '87
Agnes of God '85
Dead Wrong '83
Heartaches '82
Suzanne '80

Maria Therese Relin (1966-)

Quo Vadis '85
Secret Places '85

James Remar (1953-)

The Unborn '09
Pineapple Express '08
Ratatouille '07 (V)
Sharpshooter '07
American Meltdown '04
Blade: Trinity '04
The Girl Next Door '04
Ike: Countdown to D-Day '04
Duplex '03
Fear X '03
Lady Jayne Killer '03
2 Fast 2 Furious '03
Guardian '01
The Guardian '00
Hellraiser 5: Inferno '00
What Lies Beneath '00
Blowback '99
D.R.E.A.M. Team '99
Rites of Passage '99
Inferno '98
Psycho '98
Born Bad '97
Mortal Kombat 2: Annihilation '97
The Phantom '96
The Quest '96
Robo Warriors '96
One Good Turn '95
Across the Moon '94
Boys on the Side '94
Confessions of a Hit Man '94
Miracle on 34th Street '94
Renaissance Man '94
The Surgeon '94
Blink '93
Fatal Instinct '93
The Tigress '93
Fatal Charm '92
Indecency '92
Deadlock '91
White Fang '91
Silence Like Glass '90
Tales from the Darkside: The Movie '90
The Dream Team '89
Drugstore Cowboy '89
Rent-A-Cop '88
The Clan of the Cave Bear '86
Quiet Cool '86
The Cotton Club '84
48 Hrs. '82
Windwalker '81
Cruising '80
The Warriors '79

Erika Remberg (1932-)

The Lickerish Quartet '70
Cave of the Living Dead '65
Circus of Horrors '60

Lee Remick (1935-91)

Around the World in 80 Days '89
Bridge to Silence '89
Jesse '88
Nutcracker: Money, Madness & Murder '87
The Vision '87
Follies in Concert '85
Toughlove '85
Mistral's Daughter '84
The Snow Queen '83
The Competition '80
Haywire '80
Tribute '80
The Europeans '79
Ike '79
Torn Between Two Lovers '79
Breaking Up '78
The Medusa Touch '78
Telefon '77
The Omen '76
Hennessy '75
Hustling '75
QB VII '74
Touch Me Not '74
Sometimes a Great Notion '71
Loot... Give Me Money, Honey! '70
The Detective '68
No Way to Treat a Lady '68
The Hallelujah Trail '65
Baby, the Rain Must Fall '64
The Tempest '63
The Wheeler Dealers '63
Days of Wine and Roses '62
Experiment in Terror '62
Anatomy of a Murder '59
The Long, Hot Summer '58
A Face in the Crowd '57

Bert Remsen (1925-99)

Sundown: The Vampire in Retreat '08
Crime of the Century '96
Humanoids from the Deep '96
Maverick '94
Evil Spirits '91
Only the Lonely '91
Daddy's Dyin'... Who's Got the Will? '90
Payback '90
Peacemaker '90
Miss Firecracker '89
Curfew '88
South of Reno '87
Eye of the Tiger '86
Tai-Pan '86
Terrorvision '86
Code of Silence '85
Burning Rage '84
I Married a Centerfold '84
Lies '83
M.A.D.D.: Mothers Against Drunk Driving '83
Policewoman Centerfold '83
Joni '79
A Wedding '78
Tarantulas: The Deadly Cargo '77
Nashville '75
Sweet Hostage '75
Thieves Like Us '74
The Death Squad '73
McCabe & Mrs. Miller '71
Dead Ringer '64
Pork Chop Hill '59

Kerry Remsen

Pumpkinhead '88
Ghoulies 2 '87
Appointment with Fear '85

Albert Remy (1912-67)

The Train '65
Shoot the Piano Player '62
The 400 Blows '59
Children of Paradise '44

Ronald Remy

Mad Doctor of Blood Island '68
The Vampire People '66
No Man Is an Island '62

Richie Ren

Seoul Raiders '05
Silver Hawk '04

Duncan Renaldo (1904-80)

The Capture '50
Guns of Fury '49
In Old New Mexico '45
South of the Rio Grande '45
Fighting Seabees '44
Perils of the Darkest Jungle '44
Border Patrol '43
For Whom the Bell Tolls '43
Manhunt in the African Jungles '43
Tiger Fangs '43
Down Mexico Way '41
Gauchos of El Dorado '41
Outlaws of the Desert '41
Panama Menace '41
Covered Wagon Days '40
Gaucho Serenade '40
Heroes of the Saddle '40
Oklahoma Renegades '40
Pioneers of the West '40
Rocky Mountain Rangers '40
Cowboys from Texas '39
The Kansas Terrors '39
Rough Riders' Roundup '39
South of the Border '39
Rose of Rio Grande '38
Spawn of the North '38
The Painted Stallion '37
Roaring Speedboats '37
Zorro Rides Again '37
Trader Horn '31

Tito Renaldo

The Story of G.I. Joe '45
For Whom the Bell Tolls '43

Simone Renant (1911-2004)

Dear Detective '77
That Man from Rio '64
Dangerous Liaisons '60
Jenny Lamour '47

Renaud (1952-)

Crime Spree '03
Germinal '93

Francis Renaud (1967-)
Chrysalis *'07*
Perfect Love *'96*
Pigalle *'95*

Madeleine Renaud (1900-94)
Le Plaisir *'52*
Stormy Waters *'41*
Maria Chapdelaine *'34*

Isabelle Renauld (1966-)
Monsieur Ibrahim *'03*
Eternity and a Day *'97*
Perfect Love *'96*

Georges Renavent (1894-1969)
Manhunt in the African Jungles *'43*
Whistlin' Dan *'32*
East of Borneo *'31*
Rio Rita *'29*

Liz Renay (1926-2007)
Desperate Living *'77*
Blackenstein *'73*
Lady Godiva Rides *'68*
Deadwood *'65*
The Thrill Killers *'65*
Nasty Rabbit *'64*

Mark Rendall (1988-)
My One and Only *'09*
Charlie Bartlett *'07*
30 Days of Night *'07*
A Different Loyalty *'04*

Victor Rendina (1916-85)
Racing with the Moon *'84*
The Man Who Wasn't There *'83*
The Godfather *'72*

Liz Rene
See Liz Renay

Brad Renfro (1982-2008)
10th & Wolf *'06*
The Jacket *'05*
The Job *'03*
Deuces Wild *'02*
Bully *'01*
Ghost World *'01*
Happy Campers *'01*
Tart *'01*
The Theory of the Leisure Class *'01*
Skipped Parts *'00*
Apt Pupil *'97*
Sleepers *'96*
Telling Lies in America *'96*
The Cure *'95*
Tom and Huck *'95*
The Client *'94*

Jeremie Renier (1981-)
In Bruges *'08*
Lorna's Silence *'08*
Summer Hours *'08*
Private Property *'06*
The Child *'05*
Brotherhood of the Wolf *'01*
Criminal Lovers *'99*
La Promesse *'96*

Yannick Renier (1975-)
Born in 68 *'08*
Love Songs *'07*
Private Property *'06*

Serge Renko
The Romance of Astrea and Celadon *'07*
Triple Agent *'04*
Rendezvous in Paris *'95*

Patrick Renna (1979-)
P.U.N.K.S. *'98*
Address Unknown *'96*
The Big Green *'95*
Blue River *'95*
Beanstalk *'94*
The Sandlot *'93*
Son-in-Law *'93*

Deborah Rennard (1959-)
Lionheart *'90*
Land of Doom *'84*

Jeremy Renner (1971-)
The Hurt Locker *'08*
The Assassination of Jesse James by the Coward Robert Ford *'07*
28 Weeks Later *'07*
A Little Trip to Heaven *'05*
North Country *'05*
12 and Holding *'05*
S.W.A.T. *'03*
Dahmer *'02*
Fish in a Barrel *'01*

Callum Keith Rennie (1960-)
Case 39 *'10*
Battlestar Galactica: The Plan *'09*
The X Files: I Want to Believe *'08*
Code Name: The Cleaner *'07*
The Invisible *'07*
Normal *'07*
Shattered *'07*
Tin Man *'07*
Whole New Thing *'05*
Blade: Trinity *'04*
Falling Angels *'03*
Now & Forever *'02*
Slap Shot 2: Breaking the Ice *'02*
Picture Claire *'01*
Torso *'01*
Memento *'00*
Suspicious River *'00*
eXistenZ *'99*
The Highway Man *'99*
The Last Stop *'99*
The Life Before This *'99*
Last Night *'98*
Tricks *'97*
Curtis's Charm *'96*
Hard Core Logo *'96*
Masterminds *'96*
Double Happiness *'94*

Michael Rennie (1909-71)
Surabaya Conspiracy *'75*
Die Screaming, Marianne *'73*
Dracula vs. Frankenstein *'69*
The Battle of El Alamein *'68*
The Devil's Brigade *'68*
Commando Attack *'67*
Hotel *'67*
Mary, Mary *'63*
Third Man on the Mountain *'59*
Missiles from Hell *'58*
Omar Khayyam *'57*
Mambo *'55*
Seven Cities of Gold *'55*
Soldier of Fortune *'55*
Demetrius and the Gladiators *'54*
Desiree *'54*
Dangerous Crossing *'53*
The Robe *'53*
Sailor of the King *'53*
Five Fingers *'52*
Phone Call from a Stranger *'52*
The Day the Earth Stood Still *'51*
I'll Never Forget You *'51*
The Black Rose *'50*
Trio *'50*
Uneasy Terms *'48*
The Wicked Lady *'45*
Tower of Terror *'42*

Ginette Reno (1946-)
Mambo Italiano *'03*
It's My Turn, Laura Cadieux *'98*
Leolo *'92*

Jean Reno (1948-)
Armored *'09*
Couples Retreat *'09*
The Pink Panther 2 *'09*
The Da Vinci Code *'06*
Flushed Away *'06 (V)*
Flyboys *'06*
The Pink Panther *'06*
Crimson Rivers 2: Angels of the Apocalypse *'05*
Empire of the Wolves *'05*
The Tiger and the Snow *'05*
Hotel Rwanda *'04*
Jet Lag *'02*
Rollerball *'02*
The Crimson Rivers *'01*
Just Visiting *'01*
Wasabi *'01*
Godzilla *'98*
Ronin *'98*
For Roseanna *'96*
Mission: Impossible *'96*
Beyond the Clouds *'95*
French Kiss *'95*
The Visitors *'95*
The Professional *'94*
La Femme Nikita *'91*
The Big Blue *'88*
Subway *'85*
Le Dernier Combat *'84*

John Reno
Bloodspell *'87*
Mirror of Death *'87*

Kelly Reno (1966-)
Brady's Escape *'84*
The Black Stallion Returns *'83*
The Black Stallion *'79*

Jean Renoir (1894-1979)
The Little Theatre of Jean Renoir *'71*
The Rules of the Game *'39*

Pierre Renoir (1885-1952)
Children of Paradise *'44*
La Marseillaise *'37*
Madame Bovary *'34*

Sophie Renoir
Boyfriends & Girlfriends *'88*
Le Beau Mariage *'82*

Robin Renucci (1956-)
Comedy of Power *'06*
The Dreamers *'03*
Taking Sides *'01*
Children of the Century *'99*

Andrea Renzi (1963-)
The Spectator *'04*
His Secret Life *'01*

Eva Renzi (1944-)
Night of the Assassin *'77*
The Bird with the Crystal Plumage *'70*
The Pink Jungle *'68*
Funeral in Berlin *'66*

Maggie Renzi
Passion Fish *'92*
City of Hope *'91*
Eight Men Out *'88*
Matewan *'87*
The Brother from Another Planet *'84*
Return of the Secaucus 7 *'80*

Lisa Repo Martell (1971-)
Touch of Pink *'04*
American Boyfriends *'89*

Stafford Repp (1918-74)
Batman *'66*
Plunder Road *'57*

Dan Resin
Caddyshack *'80*
Hail *'73*

Antonio Resines (1954-)
Two Tough Guys *'03*
The Girl of Your Dreams *'99*
How to Be a Woman and Not Die in the Attempt *'91*
Skyline *'84*

Frank Ressel (1925-85)
Sabata *'69*
Tarzana, the Wild Girl *'69*
Blood and Black Lace *'64*

Dale Resteghini (1968-)
Da Hip Hop Witch *'00*
Colorz of Rage *'97*

Tommy Rettig (1941-96)
The Cobweb *'55*
River of No Return *'54*
The 5000 Fingers of Dr. T *'53*

Raoul Retzer (1919-74)
2069: A Sex Odyssey *'78*
The Vampire Happening *'71*

Gloria Reuben (1964-)
Life Support *'07*
Little John *'02*
Anne Rice's The Feast of All Saints *'01*
Cold Blooded *'00*
Shaft *'00*
Inferno *'99*
Indiscreet *'98*
Johnny's Girl *'95*
Nick of Time *'95*
Dead Air *'94*
Timecop *'94*
Percy & Thunder *'93*

Paul (Pee-wee Herman) Reubens (1952-)
Life During Wartime *'09*
The Tripper *'06*
Disney's Teacher's Pet *'04 (V)*
Blow *'01*
South of Heaven, West of Hell *'00*
Mystery Men *'99*
Dr. Dolittle *'98 (V)*
Buddy *'97*
Matilda *'96*
Dunston Checks In *'95*
The Nightmare Before Christmas *'93 (V)*
Batman Returns *'92*
Buffy the Vampire Slayer *'92*
Big Top Pee-wee *'88*
Back to the Beach *'87*
Flight of the Navigator *'86 (V)*
Pee-wee's Big Adventure *'85*
Meatballs 2 *'84*
Pinocchio *'83*
Pandemonium *'82*
The Pee-wee Herman Show *'82*
Cheech and Chong's Nice Dreams *'81*
The Blues Brothers *'80*
Cheech and Chong's Next Movie *'80*

Thekla Reuten (1975-)
In Bruges *'08*
Highlander: The Source *'07*
Rosenstrasse *'03*
Everybody's Famous! *'00*

Anne Revere (1903-90)
A Place in the Sun *'51*
Secret Beyond the Door *'48*
Body and Soul *'47*
Forever Amber *'47*
Gentleman's Agreement *'47*
Dragonwyck *'46*
The Keys of the Kingdom *'44*
National Velvet *'44*
The Thin Man Goes Home *'44*
The Song of Bernadette *'43*
The Falcon Takes Over *'42*
The Howards of Virginia *'40*

Dorothy Revier (1904-93)
Circumstantial Evidence *'35*
Green Eyes *'34*
When a Man Sees Red *'34*
The King Murder *'32*
The Secrets of Wu Sin *'32*
The Black Camel *'31*
Dance of Life *'29*
The Dropkick *'27*

Clive Revill (1930-)
Possums *'99*
The Thief and the Cobbler *'96 (V)*
Dracula: Dead and Loving It *'95*
The Sea Wolf *'93*
Let Him Have It *'91*
Mack the Knife *'89*
Rumpelstiltskin *'86*
George Washington *'84*
Zorro, the Gay Blade *'81*
The Empire Strikes Back *'80*
Charlie Muffin *'79*
Matilda *'78*
One of Our Dinosaurs Is Missing *'75*
The Black Windmill *'74*
Ghost in the Noonday Sun *'74*
The Little Prince *'74*
The Legend of Hell House *'73*
Avanti! *'72*
Escape to the Sun *'72*
The Buttercup Chain *'70*
The Private Life of Sherlock Holmes *'70*
The Assassination Bureau *'69*
Fathom *'67*
A Fine Madness *'66*
Kaleidoscope *'66*
Modesty Blaise *'66*

Rex
Robinson Crusoe of Clipper Island *'36*
Robinson Crusoe of Mystery Island *'36*
King of the Wild Horses *'24*

Simon Rex (1974-)
Scary Movie 4 *'06*
Karate Dog *'04*
Scary Movie 3 *'03*
The Forsaken *'01*
Going Greek *'01*
Shriek If You Know What I Did Last Friday the 13th *'00*

Alejandro Rey (1930-87)
Stickfighter *'89*
Terrorvision *'86*
Moscow on the Hudson *'84*
The Grace Kelly Story *'83*
Rita Hayworth: The Love Goddess *'83*
The Ninth Configuration *'79*
The Stepmother *'71*
Fun in Acapulco *'63*
Solomon and Sheba *'59*

Antonia Rey (1927-)
Tarantella *'95*
Spike of Bensonhurst *'88*
King of the Gypsies *'78*

Fernando Rey (1917-94)
1492: Conquest of Paradise *'92*
Naked Tango *'91*
The Tunnel *'89*
Moon over Parador *'88*
Angel of Death *'86*
Saving Grace *'86*
A.D. *'85*
The Hit *'85*
Padre Nuestro *'85*
Star Knight *'85*
Monsignor *'82*
Cabo Blanco *'81*
Honey *'81*
Quintet *'79*
The Assignment *'78*
Elisa, Vida Mia *'77*
That Obscure Object of Desire *'77*
The Desert of the Tartars *'76*
Insanity *'76*
Seven Beauties *'76*
French Connection 2 *'75*
Autopsy *'74*
La Grande Bourgeoise *'74*
Antony and Cleopatra *'73*
High Crime *'73*
The Discreet Charm of the Bourgeoisie *'72*
A Town Called Hell *'72*
The French Connection *'71*
The Adventurers *'70*
Cold Eyes of Fear *'70*
Companeros *'70*
Tristana *'70*
Guns of the Magnificent Seven *'69*
Villa Rides *'68*
Chimes at Midnight *'67*
Navajo Joe *'67*
Attack of the Robots *'66*
The Castilian *'63*
Goliath Against the Giants *'63*
Viridiana *'61*
Mission in Morocco *'59*
Pantaloons *'57*
The Miracle of Marcelino *'55*

Mony Rey
Not Without My Daughter *'90*
Mademoiselle *'66*

Walter Reyer (1922-99)
The Indian Tomb *'59*
Tiger of Eschnapur *'59*
Journey to the Lost City *'58*

Ernie Reyes, Jr. (1972-)
Indiana Jones and the Kingdom of the Crystal Skull *'08*
The Rundown *'03*
Poolhall Junkies *'02*
Rush Hour 2 *'01*
White Wolves 2: Legend of the Wild *'94*
Surf Ninjas *'93*
Teenage Mutant Ninja Turtles 2: The Secret of the Ooze *'91*

Judy Reyes (1967-)
The Poker Club *'08*
Washington Heights *'02*
Jack and His Friends *'92*

Julian Reyes (1961-)
Mi Vida Loca *'94*
Point Break *'91*

Kamar Reyes
See Kamar De Los Reyes

Dominique Reymond
Summer Hours *'08*
Demonlover *'02*
Come Undone *'00*
Les Destinees *'00*
Will It Snow for Christmas? *'96*

Janine Reynaud (1930-)
The Case of the Scorpion's Tail *'71*
The Scorpion's Tail *'71*
The Sensuous Teenager *'70*
Castle of the Creeping Flesh *'68*

Burt Reynolds (1936-)
Deal *'08*
Delgo *'08 (V)*
In the Name of the King: A Dungeon Siege Tale *'08*
Broken Bridges *'06*
End Game *'06*
Forget About It *'06*
Grilled *'06*
The Dukes of Hazzard *'05*
The Longest Yard *'05*
Without a Paddle *'04*
The Final Hit *'02*
Johnson County War *'02*
Snapshots *'02*
Driven *'01*
The Hollywood Sign *'01*
Tempted *'01*
The Crew *'00*
Hostage Hotel *'00*
Big City Blues *'99*
Mystery, Alaska *'99*
Pups *'99*
Waterproof *'99*
Crazy Six *'98*
Universal Soldier 3: Unfinished Business *'98*
Bean *'97*
Boogie Nights *'97*
Hunter's Moon *'97*
Meet Wally Sparks *'97*
Raven *'97*
The Cherokee Kid *'96*

Citizen Ruth '96
Frankenstein and Me '96
Striptease '96
Trigger Happy '96
The Maddening '95
Cop and a Half '93
The Man from Left Field '93
The Player '92
Modern Love '90
All Dogs Go to Heaven '89 (V)
Breaking In '89
Physical Evidence '89
Rent-A-Cop '88
Switching Channels '88
Heat '87
Malone '87
Sherman's March '86
Stick '85
Uphill All the Way '85
Cannonball Run 2 '84
City Heat '84
The Man Who Loved Women '83
Smokey and the Bandit, Part 3 '83
Stroker Ace '83
Best Friends '82
The Best Little Whorehouse in Texas '82
Cannonball Run '81
Paternity '81
Sharky's Machine '81
Rough Cut '80
Smokey and the Bandit 2 '80
Starting Over '79
The End '78
Hooper '78
Semi-Tough '77
Smokey and the Bandit '77
Gator '76
Silent Movie '76
The Hustle '75
The Longest Yard '74
Man Who Loved Cat Dancing '73
Shamus '73
White Lightning '73
Deliverance '72
Everything You Always Wanted to Know about Sex (But Were Afraid to Ask) '72
Fuzz '72
Hard Frame '70
Savage Run '70
Skullduggery '70
100 Rifles '69
Sam Whiskey '69
Iron Cowboy '68
Shark! '68
Navajo Joe '67
Operation C.I.A. '65
Angel Baby '61
Armored Command '61

Craig Reynolds (1907-49)

Nevada '44
I Take This Oath '40
Slander House '38

Debbie Reynolds (1932-)

Return to Halloweentown '06
Connie and Carla '04
Halloweentown High '04
Halloweentown 2: Kalabar's Revenge '01
These Old Broads '01
Rugrats in Paris: The Movie '00 (V)
Halloweentown '98
Kiki's Delivery Service '98 (V)
Zack & Reba '98
In and Out '97
Mother '96
Wedding Bell Blues '96
Heaven and Earth '93
Battling for Baby '92
The Bodyguard '92
Detective Sadie & Son '84
Charlotte's Web '73 (V)
What's the Matter with Helen? '71
How Sweet It Is! '68
Divorce American Style '67
The Singing Nun '66
Goodbye Charlie '64
The Unsinkable Molly Brown '64
How the West Was Won '63
Mary, Mary '63
The Rat Race '60
The Gazebo '59
It Started with a Kiss '59
The Mating Game '59
This Happy Feeling '58
Tammy and the Bachelor '57
Bundle of Joy '56
The Catered Affair '56
Meet Me in Las Vegas '56
Hit the Deck '55
The Tender Trap '55
Athena '54
Susan Slept Here '54
The Affairs of Dobie Gillis '53
Give a Girl a Break '53
I Love Melvin '53
Singin' in the Rain '52
Skirts Ahoy! '52
Mr. Imperium '51
Three Little Words '50
Two Weeks with Love '50

Gene Reynolds (1925-)

Country Girl '54
Jungle Patrol '48
Junior G-Men of the Air '42
The Tuttles of Tahiti '42
Andy Hardy's Private Secretary '41
Life Begins for Andy Hardy '41
The Flying Irishman '39
They Shall Have Music '39
Boys Town '38
Love Finds Andy Hardy '38
In Old Chicago '37

Marjorie Reynolds (1916-97)

His Kind of Woman '51
Home Town Story '51
Monsieur Beaucaire '46
The Time of Their Lives '46
Ministry of Fear '44
Holiday Inn '42
Robin Hood of the Pecos '41
Doomed to Die '40
The Fatal Hour '40
Midnight Limited '40
Up in the Air '40
The Abe Lincoln of Ninth Avenue '39
Gone with the Wind '39
Mr. Wong in Chinatown '39
Mystery Plane '39
Racketeers of the Range '39
Stunt Pilot '39
Man's Country '38
Six Shootin' Sheriff '38
Western Trails '38
Murder in Greenwich Village '37
Tex Rides with the Boy Scouts '37

Michael J. Reynolds (1939-)

Ms. Scrooge '97
Wicked City '89 (V)
The Big Turnaround '88
War Between the Tates '76

Peter Reynolds (1926-75)

The Great Armored Car Swindle '64
The Hands of Orlac '60
It Takes a Thief '59
Devil Girl from Mars '54

Robert Reynolds

Element of Doubt '96
Tunnel Vision '95
Traps '93
Daughter of Darkness '89

Ryan Reynolds (1976-)

Buried '10
Adventureland '09
The Proposal '09
X-Men Origins: Wolverine '09
Chaos Theory '08
Definitely, Maybe '08
The Nines '07
Smokin' Aces '07
School of Life '06
The Amityville Horror '05
Just Friends '05
Waiting '05
Blade: Trinity '04
Harold and Kumar Go to White Castle '04
The In-Laws '03
Buying the Cow '02
National Lampoon's Van Wilder '02
Finder's Fee '01
We All Fall Down '00
Coming Soon '99
Dick '99
The Alarmist '98
Boltneck '98
Sabrina the Teenage Witch '96
Ordinary Magic '93

Simon Reynolds (1969-)

The Prize Winner of Defiance, Ohio '05
Gate 2 '92

Vera Reynolds (1900-62)

The Monster Walks '32
Tangled Destinies '32
Risky Business '28
Sunny Side Up '28
The Night Club '25
The Road to Yesterday '25

William Reynolds (1931-)

A Distant Trumpet '64
The Land Unknown '57
All That Heaven Allows '55
Cult of the Cobra '55
Gunsmoke '53
Carrie '52
Francis Goes to West Point '52
Son of Ali Baba '52

Ving Rhames (1961-)

Piranha 3D '10
Echelon Conspiracy '09
The Goods: Live Hard, Sell Hard '09
Surrogates '09
The Tournament '09
Saving God '08
Animal 2 '07
A Broken Life '07
I Now Pronounce You Chuck and Larry '07
Idlewild '06
Mission: Impossible 3 '06
Animal '05
Back in the Day '05
Dawn of the Dead '04
Dark Blue '03
Lilo & Stitch '02 (V)
Little John '02
RFK '02
Sin '02
Undisputed '02
Baby Boy '01
Final Fantasy: The Spirits Within '01 (V)
Sins of the Father '01
American Tragedy '00
Holiday Heart '00
Mission: Impossible 2 '00
Bringing Out the Dead '99
Entrapment '99
Out of Sight '98
Body Count '97
Con Air '97
Don King: Only in America '97
Dangerous Ground '96
Mission: Impossible '96
Rosewood '96
Striptease '96
DROP Squad '94
Kiss of Death '94
Pulp Fiction '94
Dave '93
The Saint of Fort Washington '93
Homicide '91
The People under the Stairs '91
Flight of the Intruder '90
Jacob's Ladder '90
Rising Son '90
The Long Walk Home '89
Patty Hearst '88

Caroline Rhea (1964-)

Fast Girl '07
The Perfect Man '05
Christmas With the Kranks '04

Phillip Rhee (1960-)

Best of the Best: Without Warning '98
Best of the Best 3: No Turning Back '95
Best of the Best 2 '93
Best of the Best '89
Silent Assassins '88

Simon Rhee (1957-)

Kung Pow! Enter the Fist '02
The Substitute 4: Failure is Not an Option '00
Best of the Best 2 '93
Best of the Best '89

Ashlie Rhey (1961-)

Bikini Drive-In '94
Midnight Tease '94
Play Time '94

Julian Rhind-Tutt (1968-)

Oliver Twist '07
The Shadow in the North '07
The River King '05
To Kill a King '03
Lara Croft: Tomb Raider '01
Miranda '01
Heat of the Sun '99
The Trench '99
Reckless '97
The Madness of King George '94

Barbara Rhoades (1947-)

Sex and the Single Parent '82
The Day the Women Got Even '80
Serial '80
The Choirboys '77
The Goodbye Girl '77
Conspiracy of Terror '75
Hunter '73
Scream Blacula Scream '73
Up the Sandbox '72
The Shakiest Gun in the West '68

Bobby Rhodes (1947-)

Demons 2 '87
The Last Hunter '80

Brian Rhodes (1947-)

DC 9/11: Time of Crisis '04
Nemesis Game '03

Cynthia Rhodes (1957-)

Curse of the Crystal Eye '93
Dirty Dancing '87
Runaway '84
Flashdance '83
Staying Alive '83

Donnelly Rhodes (1937-)

Loch Ness Terror '07
Pressure '02
Wilderness Love '02
Big and Hairy '98
Guitarman '95
Dirty Work '92
The Penthouse '92
Kurt Vonnegut's Monkey House '91
Showdown at Williams Creek '91
After the Promise '87
Goldenrod '77
Hard Part Begins '73

Dusty Rhodes (1945-)

Heroes of the Heart '94
Gold Raiders '83

Erik Rhodes (1906-90)

Mysterious Mr. Moto '38
Special Investigator '36
Charlie Chan in Paris '35
Top Hat '35
The Gay Divorcee '34

Grandon Rhodes (1904-87)

Revenge of the Creature '55
Too Many Winners '47
Magnificent Doll '46

Hari Rhodes (1932-92)

Backstairs at the White House '79
Coma '78
A Woman Called Moses '78
Mayday at 40,000 Feet '76
Detroit 9000 '73
A Dream for Christmas '73
Conquest of the Planet of the Apes '72
Earth II '71
Drums of Africa '63
Shock Corridor '63

Marjorie Rhodes (1903-79)

Hands of the Ripper '71
Decameron Nights '53
Those People Next Door '52
Great Day '46
Butler's Dilemma '43

Busta Rhymes (1972-)

Breaking Point '09
Halloween: Resurrection '02
Narc '02
Finding Forrester '00
Shaft '00
The Rugrats Movie '98 (V)

Matthew Rhys (1974-)

The Edge of Love '08
Virgin Territory '07
Beau Brummell: This Charming Man '06
Love and Other Disasters '06
Fakers '04
Sorted '04
Deathwatch '02
The Lost World '02
Shooters '00
Very Annie Mary '00
Heart '99
Titus '99

Paul Rhys (1963-)

Hellraiser: Deader '05
Food of Love '02
King Lear '98
A Dance to the Music of Time '97
Gallowglass '95
Nina Takes a Lover '94
Becoming Colette '92
Chaplin '92
Vincent & Theo '90

John Rhys-Davies (1944-)

Anacondas: Trail of Blood '09
Anaconda 3: The Offspring '08
In the Name of the King: A Dungeon Siege Tale '08
Kiss Me Deadly '08
Chupacabra Terror '05
The Game of Their Lives '05
Dragon Storm '04
The Lost Angel '04
The Princess Diaries 2: Royal Engagement '04
Helen of Troy '03
The Jungle Book 2 '03 (V)
Lord of the Rings: The Return of the King '03
The Medallion '03
Vlad '03
Endangered Species '02
Lord of the Rings: The Two Towers '02 (V)
Scorcher '02
Lord of the Rings: The Fellowship of the Ring '01
Sabretooth '01
Brittanic '00
Au Pair '99
Britannic '99
Secre of the Andes '98
Bloodsport 3 '97
Cats Don't Dance '97 (V)
Aladdin and the King of Thieves '96 (V)
Glory Daze '96
The Great White Hype '96
Marquis de Sade '96
Catherine the Great '95
Beyond Forgiveness '94
Robot in the Family '94
Cyborg Cop '93
Return to the Lost World '93
Ring of the Musketeers '93
Canvas: The Fine Art of Crime '92
The Double O Kid '92
The High Crusade '92
The Lost World '92
The Seventh Coin '92
Sunset Grill '92
The Unnamable 2: The Statement of Randolph Carter '92
Journey of Honor '91
Rebel Storm '90
Secret Weapon '90
Great Expectations '89
Indiana Jones and the Last Crusade '89
The Trial of the Incredible Hulk '89
Tusks '89
War & Remembrance: The Final Chapter '89
Higher Ground '88
Nairobi Affair '88
Noble House '88
War & Remembrance '88
Waxwork '88
The Little Match Girl '87
The Living Daylights '87
In the Shadow of Kilimanjaro '86
King Solomon's Mines '85
Kim '84
Best Revenge '83
Sadat '83
Sahara '83
Sword of the Valiant '83
Ivanhoe '82
Victor/Victoria '82
Raiders of the Lost Ark '81
Sphinx '81
Shogun '80
Nativity '78

Griff Rhys Jones (1953-)

The Misadventures of Mr. Wilt '90
Morons from Outer Space '85

Jonathan Rhys Meyers (1977-)

From Paris With Love '10
The Children of Huang Shi '08
August Rush '07
Mission: Impossible 3 '06
Match Point '05
Alexander '04
Vanity Fair '04
The Lion in Winter '03
Pulse '03
The Tesseract '03
Bend It Like Beckham '02
The Magnificent Ambersons '02
Prozac Nation '01
Tangled '01
Ride with the Devil '99
Titus '99
The Governess '98
The Loss of Sexual Innocence '98
The Maker '98
Velvet Goldmine '98
B. Monkey '97
Killer Tongue '96
Michael Collins '96
Samson and Delilah '96
Telling Lies in America '96

Candice Rialson (1952-)
Moonshine County Express '77
Chatterbox '76
Hollywood Boulevard '76
Summer School Teachers '75
Candy Stripe Nurses '74
Mama's Dirty Girls '74

Renie Riano (1899-1971)
Nancy Drew and the Hidden Staircase '39
Nancy Drew—Trouble Shooter '39
Nancy Drew—Detective '38

Alfonso Ribeiro (1971-)
Ticks '93
The Mighty Pawns '87

Jacques Riberolles (1929-82)
The Young Girls of Rochefort '68
Please Not Now! '61

Giovanni Ribisi (1974-)
Avatar '09
Public Enemies '09
Perfect Stranger '07
The Dead Girl '06
The Dog Problem '06
10th & Wolf '06
The Big White '05
Flight of the Phoenix '04
Sky Captain and the World of Tomorrow '04
Basic '03
Cold Mountain '03
I Love Your Work '03
Lost in Translation '03
Heaven '01
Shot in the Heart '01
Boiler Room '00
The Gift '00
Gone in 60 Seconds '00
It's the Rage '99
The Mod Squad '99
The Virgin Suicides '99 (N)
First Love, Last Rites '98
The Other Sister '98
Saving Private Ryan '98
The Postman '97
subUrbia '96
That Thing You Do! '96
Promised a Miracle '88

Marissa Ribisi (1974-)
True Crime '99
Changing Habits '96
Armistead Maupin's Tales of the City '93
Dazed and Confused '93

Christina Ricci (1980-)
New York, I Love You '09
Speed Racer '08
Black Snake Moan '07
Home of the Brave '06
Penelope '06
Cursed '04
Anything Else '03
I Love Your Work '03
Monster '03
The Gathering '02
The Laramie Project '02
Pumpkin '02
All Over the Guy '01
Miranda '01
Prozac Nation '01
Bless the Child '00
The Man Who Cried '00
No Vacancy '99
Sleepy Hollow '99
Desert Blue '98
Fear and Loathing in Las Vegas '98
The Opposite of Sex '98
Pecker '98
Small Soldiers '98 (V)
200 Cigarettes '98
Buffalo 66 '97
The Ice Storm '97
Bastard out of Carolina '96
The Last of the High Kings '96
That Darn Cat '96
Casper '95
Gold Diggers: The Secret of Bear Mountain '95
Now and Then '95
Addams Family Values '93
The Cemetery Club '93
The Addams Family '91
The Hard Way '91
Mermaids '90

Alex Rice
The New World '05
Coyote Waits '03
Skinwalker '02

Bill Rice (1931-2006)
Coffee and Cigarettes '03
Landlord Blues '87
Doomed Love '83
Vortex '81

Brett Rice (1954-)
Conjurer '08
Bobby Jones: Stroke of Genius '04
Final Cut '88

Florence Rice (1911-74)
Boss of Big Town '43
The Ghost and the Guest '43
Mr. District Attorney '41
At the Circus '39
Sweethearts '38
Double Wedding '37
Navy Blue and Gold '37

Frank Rice (1892-1936)
The Gore-Gore Girls '72
The Ivory Handled Gun '35
The Fiddlin' Buckaroo '33
Phantom Thunderbolt '33
Somewhere in Sonora '33
Trail Drive '33
Hello Trouble '32
Sunset Trail '32
Border Law '31
The Fighting Legion '30
Red Signals '27
Dynamite Dan '24

Joan Rice (1930-97)
The Horror of Frankenstein '70
His Majesty O'Keefe '53
The Story of Robin Hood & His Merrie Men '52

Mandy Rice-Davies (1944-)
Absolute Beginners '86
Black Venus '83
Kuni Lemel in Tel Aviv '77

Adam Rich (1968-)
Zertigo Diamond Caper '82
The Devil & Max Devlin '81

Allan Rich (1926-)
The Last Word '08
Matters of the Heart '90
Archer: The Fugitive from the Empire '81
The Seekers '79

Charlie Rich (1932-95)
Weeds '87
Take This Job & Shove It '81

Christopher Rich (1953-)
The Joy Luck Club '93
Midnight Murders '91
Archie: Return to Riverdale '90
Prisoners of Inertia '89

Claude Rich (1929-)
La Buche '00
Balzac: A Life of Passion '99
Capitaine Conan '96
The Green House '96
Revenge of the Musketeers '94
Maria Chapdelaine '84
Le Crabe Tambour '77
The Bride Wore Black '68
Is Paris Burning? '66
The Burning Court '62
The Elusive Corporal '62

Delphine Rich
Mr. Average '06
Bad Company '99

Eli Rich
Deadly Diamonds '91
Nudity Required '90
Murderlust '86

Irene Rich (1891-1988)
Angel and the Badman '47
The Lady in Question '40
The Mortal Storm '40
That Certain Age '38
The Champ '32
Held for Murder '32
They Had to See Paris '29
Beau Brummel '24
The Trap '22

Lillian Rich
Mark of the Spur '32
Braveheart '25

Cliff Richard (1940-)
Expresso Bongo '59
Serious Charge '59

Emily Richard (1948-)
Empire of the Sun '87
The Life and Adventures of Nicholas Nickleby '81

Firmine Richard (1947-)
8 Women '02
Mama, There's a Man in Your Bed '89

Jean Richard (1921-2001)
Elena and Her Men '56
Seven Deadly Sins '53

Jean-Louis Richard (1921-)
After Sex '97
Jeanne la Pucelle '94
La Sentinelle '92
Le Choc '82
Le Professionnel '81
The Last Metro '80
It Means That to Me '60

Nathalie Richard (1962-)
Le Divorce '03
Confusion of Genders '00
Irma Vep '96
Up/Down/Fragile '95

Pierre Richard (1934-)
A Chef in Love '96
Les Comperes '83
La Chevre '81
Too Shy to Try '78
The Daydreamer '75
Return of the Tall Blond Man with One Black Shoe '74
The Tall Blond Man with One Black Shoe '72

Robert Ri'chard (1983-)
The Comebacks '07
Coach Carter '05
House of Wax '05
Anne Rice's The Feast of All Saints '01
Alley Cats Strike '00
Light It Up '99
In His Father's Shoes '97

Addison Richards (1887-1964)
Call Northside 777 '48
A Southern Yankee '48
The Millerson Case '47
Criminal Court '46
Bells of Rosarita '45
Betrayal from the East '44
Fighting Seabees '44
Since You Went Away '44
Air Force '43
The Fighting Sullivans '42
The Man with Two Lives '42
Ridin' Down the Canyon '42
Underground Agent '42
Dive Bomber '41
Sheriff of Tombstone '41
Bad Lands '39
The Black Legion '37
Our Daily Bread '34

Ann Richards (1917-2006)
Breakdown '53
Sorry, Wrong Number '48
Lost Honeymoon '47
Love from a Stranger '47
Badman's Territory '46
Love Letters '45

Ariana Richards (1979-)
Tremors 3: Back to Perfection '01
The Lost World: Jurassic Park 2 '97
Angus '95
Jurassic Park '93
Grand Tour: Disaster in Time '92
Switched at Birth '91
Spaced Invaders '90
Prancer '89
Tremors '89

Beah Richards (1926-2000)
Beloved '98
Inside Out '91
Drugstore Cowboy '89
Acceptable Risks '86
As Summers Die '86
Sophisticated Gents '81
A Christmas Without Snow '80
Roots: The Next Generation '79
A Dream for Christmas '73
Guess Who's Coming to Dinner '67
Gone Are the Days '63
Purlie Victorious '63
The Miracle Worker '62

Cordelia Richards
Original Sin '01
North Shore Fish '97

Denise Richards (1972-)
Blonde and Blonder '07
Edmond '05
Elvis Has Left the Building '04
Love Actually '03
Scary Movie 3 '03
Empire '02
The Third Wheel '02
Undercover Brother '02
You Stupid Man '02
Good Advice '01
Valentine '01
Drop Dead Gorgeous '99
Tail Lights Fade '99
The World Is Not Enough '99
Wild Things '98
Starship Troopers '97
Nowhere '96
Tammy and the T-Rex '94

Evan Richards (1970-)
Mute Witness '95
Society '92
Dream Machine '91
Rock 'n' Roll High School Forever '91
Down and Out in Beverly Hills '86

Jeff Richards (1922-89)
Born Reckless '59
It's a Dog's Life '55
Seven Brides for Seven Brothers '54
Above and Beyond '53
Battle Circus '53
Angels in the Outfield '51
Kill the Umpire '50

Keith Richards (1915-87)
Chuck Berry: Hail! Hail! Rock 'n' Roll '87
The Kids Are Alright '79
Gimme Shelter '70
Queen of the Amazons '47

Kim Richards (1964-)
Black Snake Moan '07
Escape '90
Tuff Turf '85
Meatballs 2 '84
Devil Dog: The Hound of Hell '78
Return from Witch Mountain '78
Assault on Precinct 13 '76
Escape to Witch Mountain '75

Kyle Richards (1969-)
Curfew '88
The Watcher in the Woods '81
Halloween '78
Eaten Alive '76

Lisa Richards
Eating '90
Return '88
The Prince of Central Park '77

Michael Richards (1948-)
Bee Movie '07 (V)
Trial and Error '96
Unstrung Heroes '95
Airheads '94
Coneheads '93
So I Married an Axe Murderer '93
Problem Child '90
UHF '89
Transylvania 6-5000 '85
Ratings Game '84

Michele Lamar Richards (1954-)
Top Dog '95
The Bodyguard '92

Paul Richards (1934-)
Kiss Daddy Goodnight '87
Beach Girls '82
Four Fast Guns '59
Pushover '54

Paul (E.) Richards (1924-74)
Beneath the Planet of the Apes '70
All the Young Men '60

Tom Richards (1922-)
The Cursed Mountain Mystery '93
Dawn! '83
Plunge Into Darkness '77

Cameron Richardson
Women in Trouble '09
Familiar Strangers '08
Alvin and the Chipmunks '07
The Good Humor Man '05
Supercross: The Movie '05

Derek Richardson (1976-)
Hostel '06
Dumb and Dumberer: When Harry Met Lloyd '03

Ian Richardson (1934-2007)
Becoming Jane '07
Hogfather '06 (V)
Joyeux Noel '05
From Hell '01
Dr. Bell and Mr. Doyle: The Dark Beginnings of Sherlock Holmes '00
102 Dalmatians '00
The King and I '99 (V)
A Knight in Camelot '98
B.A.P.'s '97
Dark City '97
Incognito '97
The Woman in White '97
A Royal Scandal '96 (N)
Catherine the Great '95
The Final Cut '95
A Change of Place '94
Foreign Affairs '93
M. Butterfly '93
To Play the King '93
Year of the Comet '92
Monsignor Quixote '91
House of Cards '90
The Phantom of the Opera '90
Rosencrantz & Guildenstern Are Dead '90
Burning Secret '89
Troubles '88
Cry Freedom '87
The Fourth Protocol '87
Mountbatten: The Last Viceroy '86
Brazil '85
The Hound of the Baskervilles '83
The Sign of Four '83
Whoops Apocalypse '83
Tinker, Tailor, Soldier, Spy '80
Charlie Muffin '79
A Midsummer Night's Dream '68

Jack (H.) Richardson (1883-1957)
They Never Come Back '32
Trigger Tricks '30
Marked Money '28
Dynamite Dan '24
The Toll Gate '20

Jackie Richardson
Under the Piano '95
Another Woman '94

Jay Richardson
Fugitive Rage '96
Illegal Affairs '96
Attack of the 60-Foot Centerfold '95
Killing for Love '95
Victim of Desire '94
Wizards of the Demon Sword '94
Teenage Exorcist '93
Mind, Body & Soul '92
Sins of Desire '92
Original Intent '91
Vice Academy 3 '91
Bad Girls from Mars '90
Vice Academy 2 '90
Alienator '89
The Channeler '89
Slashdance '89
Death Row Diner '88
Hollywood Chainsaw Hookers '88
The Newlydeads '87
Gator King '70

Joely Richardson (1965-)
The Christmas Miracle of Jonathan Toomey '07
The Last Mimzy '07
Fatal Contact: Bird Flu in America '06
The Fever '04
Fallen Angel '03
The Affair of the Necklace '01
The Patriot '00
Return to Me '00
Maybe Baby '99
In the Shadows '98
Wrestling with Alligators '98
Event Horizon '97
101 Dalmatians '96
Hollow Reed '95
Loch Ness '95
Sister My Sister '94
I'll Do Anything '93
Lady Chatterley '92
Shining Through '92
King Ralph '91
Drowning by Numbers '87
Wetherby '85
The Charge of the Light Brigade '68

John Richardson (1936-)
Broadcast Bombshells '95
Cosmos: War of the Planets '80
Frankenstein '80 '79
Eyeball '78
War in Space '77
Torso '73
The Vengeance of She '68
One Million Years B.C. '66
She '65
Black Sunday '60

Kevin M. Richardson (1964-)
Star Wars: The Clone Wars *'08 (V)*
Queer Duck: The Movie *'06 (V)*
The Wild *'06 (V)*
The Matrix Revolutions *'03*
The Country Bears *'02 (V)*
Lilo & Stitch *'02 (V)*
The Wild Thornberrys Movie *'02 (V)*
Whispers: An Elephant's Tale *'00 (V)*
Bound *'96*
Pom Poko *'94 (V)*

Lee Richardson (1926-99)
Sarah, Plain and Tall: Skylark *'93*
A Stranger Among Us *'92*
Q & A *'90*
The Fly 2 *'89*
The Believers *'87*
Sweet Lorraine *'87*
Tiger Warsaw *'87*
Prizzi's Honor *'85*

Marie Richardson (1959-)
Evil *'03*
Faithless *'00*
Eyes Wide Shut *'99*

Miranda Richardson (1958-)
The Young Victoria *'09*
Fred Claus *'07*
Merlin's Apprentice *'06*
Paris, je t'aime *'06*
Southland Tales *'06*
Gideon's Daughter *'05*
Harry Potter and the Goblet of Fire *'05*
Wah-Wah *'05*
The Phantom of the Opera *'04*
The Prince & Me *'04*
Falling Angels *'03*
The Hours *'02*
Snow White: The Fairest of Them All *'02*
Spider *'02*
Chicken Run *'00 (V)*
Get Carter *'00*
The Miracle Maker: The Story of Jesus *'00 (V)*
Alice in Wonderland *'99*
The Big Brass Ring *'99*
Jacob Two Two Meets the Hooded Fang *'99*
The King and I *'99 (V)*
Sleepy Hollow *'99*
Merlin *'98*
St. Ives *'98*
The Apostle *'97*
A Dance to the Music of Time *'97*
The Designated Mourner *'97*
The Evening Star *'96*
Swann *'96*
Kansas City *'95*
Saint-Ex: The Story of the Storyteller *'95*
Century *'94*
Fatherland *'94*
The Night and the Moment *'94*
Tom & Viv *'94*
The Bachelor *'93*
The Crying Game *'92*
Damage *'92*
Enchanted April *'92*
Twisted Obsession *'90*
After Pilkington *'88*
Eat the Rich *'87*
Empire of the Sun *'87*
Dance with a Stranger *'85*
Transmutations *'85*
A Woman of Substance *'84*

Natasha Richardson (1963-2009)
The Wildest Dream: Conquest of Everest *'10 (V)*
Wild Child *'08*
Evening *'07*
Asylum *'05*
The White Countess *'05*
Maid in Manhattan *'02*
Waking Up in Reno *'02*
Chelsea Walls *'01*
Blow Dry *'00*
The Parent Trap *'98*
Nell *'94*
Widow's Peak *'94*
Hostages *'93*
The Favor, the Watch, & the Very Big Fish *'92*
Past Midnight *'92*
The Comfort of Strangers *'91*
The Handmaid's Tale *'90*
Fat Man and Little Boy *'89*
Patty Hearst *'88*
Gothic *'87*
A Month in the Country *'87*

Patricia Richardson (1951-)
California Dreaming *'07*
Blonde *'01*
Dead Simple *'01*
Ulee's Gold *'97*
In Country *'89*
Christmas Evil *'80*

Peter Richardson (1951-)
Carry On Columbus *'92*
Supergrass *'87*

Ralph Richardson (1902-83)
Wagner: The Complete Epic *'85*
Give My Regards to Broad Street *'84*
Greystoke: The Legend of Tarzan, Lord of the Apes *'84*
Dragonslayer *'81*
Early Days *'81*
Time Bandits *'81*
Charlie Muffin *'79*
Watership Down *'78 (V)*
The Man in the Iron Mask *'77*
A Doll's House *'73*
Invitation to the Wedding *'73*
Lady Caroline Lamb *'73*
O Lucky Man! *'73*
Tales from the Crypt *'72*
Who Slew Auntie Roo? *'71*
Battle of Britain *'69*
The Looking Glass War *'69*
Oh! What a Lovely War *'69*
Chimes at Midnight *'67 (N)*
Khartoum *'66*
The Wrong Box *'66*
Doctor Zhivago *'65*
Woman of Straw *'64*
Long Day's Journey into Night *'62*
The 300 Spartans *'62*
Exodus *'60*
Our Man in Havana *'59*
Richard III *'55*
The Sound Barrier *'52*
The Fallen Idol *'49*
The Heiress *'49*
Anna Karenina *'48*
The Day Will Dawn *'42*
The Lion Has Wings *'40*
Clouds over Europe *'39*
The Four Feathers *'39*
The Citadel *'38*
The Divorce of Lady X *'38*
Amazing Adventure *'37*
The Man Who Could Work Miracles *'37*
South Riding *'37*
Thunder in the City *'37*
Things to Come *'36*
Bulldog Jack *'35*
Java Head *'35*
The Ghoul *'34*

Regina Richardson
Nine Deaths of the Ninja *'85*
Tightrope *'84*

Russell Richardson
The Rookie *'02*
Ancient Evil: Scream of the Mummy *'00*
Tigerland *'00*

Salli Richardson (1967-)
I Am Legend *'07*
Anacondas: The Hunt for the Blood Orchid *'04*
Biker Boyz *'03*
Antwone Fisher *'02*
Never 2 Big *'98*
True Women *'97*
The Great White Hype *'96*
Soul of the Game *'96*
Gargoyles, The Movie: The Heroes Awaken *'94 (V)*
Lily in Winter *'94*
A Low Down Dirty Shame *'94*
Sioux City *'94*
Posse *'93*
How U Like Me Now? *'92*
Up Against the Wall *'91*

Sy Richardson
Floundering *'94*
Ring of Fire 2: Blood and Steel *'92*
Street Asylum *'90*
Backtrack *'89*
Tapeheads *'89*
Three Fugitives *'89*
Bad Dreams *'88*
Colors *'88*
Dead Man Walking *'88*
They Live *'88*
Straight to Hell *'87*
Repo Man *'83*
Fairy Tales *'76*

LaTanya Richardson Jackson
Freedomland *'06*
Kill Bill Vol. 2 *'04*
The Fighting Temptations *'03*
Introducing Dorothy Dandridge *'99*
U.S. Marshals *'98*
Julian Po *'97*
Losing Isaiah *'94*
When a Man Loves a Woman *'94*

Carole Richert
The Night and the Moment *'94*
Tous les Matins du Monde *'92*

William Richert (1944-)
Manic *'01*
The Man in the Iron Mask *'97*
My Own Private Idaho *'91*

Julian Richings (1955-)
Shoot 'Em Up *'07*
The Tracey Fragments *'07*
My Life Without Me *'03*
Wrong Turn *'03*
The Claim *'00*
Cube *'98*

Charles Richman (-1940)
In Old Kentucky *'35*
Struggle *'31*

Peter Mark Richman (1927-)
Poolhall Junkies *'02*
Naked Gun 2 1/2: The Smell of Fear *'91*
Friday the 13th, Part 8: Jason Takes Manhattan *'89*
Judgment Day *'88*
City Killer *'87*
Dempsey *'83*
PSI Factor *'80*
Blind Ambition *'79*
Black Orchid *'59*
The Strange One *'57*

Anthony Richmond (1942-)
One Wish Too Many *'55*
Devil Girl from Mars *'54*

B.L. Richmond
See Branscombe Richmond

Branscombe Richmond (1955-)
Black Cloud *'04*
The Scorpion King *'02*
To the Limit *'95*
Vegas Vice *'94*
Jericho Fever *'93*
Christopher Columbus: The Discovery *'92*
DaVinci's War *'92*
Inside Edge *'92*
The Taking of Beverly Hills *'91*

Deon Richmond (1978-)
National Lampoon's Van Wilder *'02*
Not Another Teen Movie *'01*
Scream 3 *'00*
Trippin' *'99*

Fiona Richmond (1945-)
Eat the Rich *'87*
The House on Straw Hill *'76*

Kane Richmond (1906-73)
Behind the Mask *'46*
The Tiger Woman *'45*
Haunted Harbor *'44*
Action in the North Atlantic *'43*
Spy Smasher *'42*
Spy Smasher Returns *'42*
Motorcycle Squad *'41*
Anything for a Thrill *'37*
Devil Diamond *'37*
Tough to Handle *'37*
Racing Blood *'36*
The Reckless Way *'36*
Confidential *'35*
Silent Code *'35*
The Lost City *'34*
Cavalier of the West *'31*
Politics *'31*

Warner Richmond (1886-1948)
Colorado Serenade *'46*
Wild West *'46*
Wild Horse Canyon *'39*
Doomed at Sundown *'37*
A Lawman Is Born *'37*
Where Trails Divide *'37*
Headin' for the Rio Grande *'36*
Song of the Gringo *'36*
The New Frontier *'35*
Rainbow's End *'35*
The Lost Jungle *'34*
Big News *'29*
The Speed Spook *'24*

Andy Richter (1966-)
Aliens in the Attic *'09*
Madagascar: Escape 2 Africa *'08 (V)*
Semi-Pro *'08*
Talladega Nights: The Ballad of Ricky Bobby *'06*
Madagascar *'05 (V)*
New York Minute *'04*
Seeing Other People *'04*
Elf *'03*
My Boss's Daughter *'03*
Big Trouble *'02*
Frank McKlusky, C.I. *'02*
Dr. Dolittle 2 *'01*
Pootie Tang *'01*
Scary Movie 2 *'01*
Dr. T & the Women *'00*
Cabin Boy *'94*
The Positively True Adventures of the Alleged Texas Cheerleader-Murdering Mom *'93*

Deborah Richter (1961-)
The Banker *'89*
Cyborg *'89*
Promised Land *'88*
Square Dance *'87*
Hot Moves *'84*
Twirl *'81*
The Rebels *'79*
Swap Meet *'79*

Jason James Richter (1980-)
Laserhawk *'99*
Ricochet River *'98*
Free Willy 3: The Rescue *'97*
Free Willy 2: The Adventure Home *'95*
Cops and Robbersons *'94*
The NeverEnding Story 3: Escape from Fantasia *'94*
Free Willy *'93*

Paul Richter (1896-1961)
Kriemhilde's Revenge *'24*
Siegfried *'24*
Dr. Mabuse, The Gambler *'22*
The Indian Tomb *'21*

Tony Rickards
Castaway *'87*
Robbery *'85*
Great Gold Swindle *'84*
Waterfront *'83*

Don Rickles (1926-)
Toy Story 3 *'10 (V)*
Toy Story 2 *'99 (V)*
Dennis the Menace Strikes Again *'98*
Quest for Camelot *'98 (V)*
Dirty Work *'97*
Casino *'95*
Toy Story *'95 (V)*
Innocent Blood *'92*
Keaton's Cop *'90*
For the Love of It *'80*
Kelly's Heroes *'70*
Enter Laughing *'67*
Beach Blanket Bingo *'65*
Bikini Beach *'64*
Muscle Beach Party *'64*
Pajama Party *'64*
X: The Man with X-Ray Eyes *'63*
The Rat Race *'60*
Run Silent, Run Deep *'58*

Alan Rickman (1946-)
Alice in Wonderland *'10*
The Wildest Dream: Conquest of Everest *'10 (V)*
Harry Potter and the Half-Blood Prince *'09*
Bottle Shock *'08*
Nobel Son *'08*
Harry Potter and the Order of the Phoenix *'07*
Sweeney Todd: The Demon Barber of Fleet Street *'07*
Perfume: The Story of a Murderer *'06*
Snow Cake *'06*
Harry Potter and the Goblet of Fire *'05*
The Hitchhiker's Guide to the Galaxy *'05 (V)*
Harry Potter and the Prisoner of Azkaban *'04*
Love Actually *'03*
Harry Potter and the Chamber of Secrets *'02*
Harry Potter and the Sorcerer's Stone *'01*
The Search for John Gissing *'01*
Blow Dry *'00*
Dogma *'99*
Galaxy Quest *'99*
Dark Harbor *'98*
Judas Kiss *'98*
Michael Collins *'96*
Rasputin: Dark Servant of Destiny *'96*
Sense and Sensibility *'95*
An Awfully Big Adventure *'94*
Mesmer *'94*
Fallen Angels 1 *'93*
Bob Roberts *'92*
Close My Eyes *'91*
Robin Hood: Prince of Thieves *'91*
Truly, Madly, Deeply *'91*
Closet Land *'90*
Quigley Down Under *'90*
The January Man *'89*
Die Hard *'88*
Therese Raquin *'80*

Allen Rickman
I Was a Teenage Zombie *'87*
Shock! Shock! Shock! *'87*

Maria Ricossa
The Note 2: Taking a Chance on Love *'09*
The Note *'07*
The In-Laws *'03*
Bojangles *'01*
Dead Man Out *'89*

Stephane Rideau (1976-)
Come Undone *'00*
Sitcom *'97*
Full Speed *'96*
Wild Reeds *'94*

John Ridgely (1909-68)
As You Were *'51*
Cavalry Charge *'51*
Room for One More *'51*
Border Incident *'49*
Task Force *'49*
Cry Wolf *'47*
Nora Prentiss *'47*
The Possessed *'47*
The Big Sleep *'46*
The Man I Love *'46*
My Reputation *'46*
God is My Co-Pilot *'45*
Pride of the Marines *'45*
Arsenic and Old Lace *'44*
Air Force *'43*
Destination Tokyo *'43*

Robert Ridgely (1931-96)
Boogie Nights *'97*
Hard Eight *'96*
Philadelphia *'93*
The Ref *'93*
Beverly Hills Cop 2 *'87*
Rosie: The Rosemary Clooney Story *'82*
Who Am I This Time? *'82*
Prime Time *'77*

Stanley Ridges (1891-1951)
No Way Out *'50*
Task Force *'49*
The Possessed *'47*
Mr. Ace *'46*
Because of Him *'45*
God is My Co-Pilot *'45*
The Master Race *'44*
The Story of Dr. Wassell *'44*
Wilson *'44*
Air Force *'43*
The Lady Is Willing *'42*
To Be or Not to Be *'42*
Mr. District Attorney *'41*
The Sea Wolf *'41*
Sergeant York *'41*
They Died with Their Boots On *'41*
Black Friday *'40*
Each Dawn I Die *'39*
Union Pacific *'39*
If I Were King *'38*
Internes Can't Take Money *'37*

Freddy Ridgeway
Fangs of the Wild *'54*
A Blueprint for Murder *'53*

Harry Riebauer (1921-99)
The Great Escape *'63*
Strangler of Blackmoor Castle *'63*

Leni Riefenstahl (1902-2003)
Tiefland *'44*
The Blue Light *'32*

Eden Riegel (1981-)
Henry Hill *'00*
Prince of Egypt *'98 (V)*

Peter Riegert (1947-)
King of the Corner *'04*
Bojangles *'01*
How to Kill Your Neighbor's Dog *'01*
In the Weeds *'00*
Passion of Mind *'00*
Traffic *'00*
The Baby Dance *'98*
Hi-Life *'98*

Jerry and Tom '98
Face Down '97
North Shore Fish '97
Infinity '96
The Infiltrator '95
Pie in the Sky '95
Bleeding Hearts '94
Coldblooded '94
The Mask '94
Barbarians at the Gate '93
Gypsy '93
Utz '93
Passed Away '92
The Object of Beauty '91
Oscar '91
The Runestone '91
A Shock to the System '90
That's Adequate '90
Crossing Delancey '88
A Man in Love '87
The Stranger '87
News at Eleven '86
Local Hero '83
National Lampoon Goes to the Movies '81
Americathon '79
Chilly Scenes of Winter '79
National Lampoon's Animal House '78

Richard Riehle (1948-)
Messengers 2: The Scarecrow '09
Red '08
The Man from Earth '07
Midnight Clear '06
The Twelve Dogs of Christmas '05
Home on the Range '04 (V)
Mysterious Skin '04
Palindromes '04
Bandits '01
The Fluffer '01
Say It Isn't So '01
Au Pair '99
Deuce Bigalow: Male Gigolo '99
Desperate Measures '98
Lethal Weapon 4 '98
Office Space '98
The Lesser Evil '97
Trading Favors '97
Ghosts of Mississippi '96
Soul of the Game '96
A Stranger in Town '95
Dominion '94
Holy Matrimony '94
Lightning Jack '94
A Dangerous Woman '93
Lone Justice 2 '93
Body of Evidence '92
Hero '92
Of Mice and Men '92
The Public Eye '92
Glory '89

Katja Riemann (1963-)
Blood & Chocolate '07
My Fuhrer '07
Agnes and His Brothers '04
Rosenstrasse '03
Balzac: A Life of Passion '99
Bandits '99
The Harmonists '99
Maybe... Maybe Not '94

Adam Rifkin (1966-)
National Lampoon's The Stoned Aged '07
Welcome to Hollywood '00
Something About Sex '98
The Dark Backward '91

Richard Rifkin
Eragon '06
Assault of the Party Nerds '89

Ron Rifkin (1939-)
Pulse '06
Dragonfly '02
The Sum of All Fears '02
Deliberate Intent '01
The Majestic '01
Boiler Room '00
Flowers for Algernon '00
Keeping the Faith '00
The Negotiator '98
L.A. Confidential '97
I'm Not Rappaport '96
Last Summer In the Hamptons '96
The Substance of Fire '96
Norma Jean and Marilyn '95
Wolf '94
Manhattan Murder Mystery '93
Courage '86
Ratings Game '84
The Chosen '81
Mrs. R's Daughter '79
Silent Running '71

Jorge (George) Rigaud (1905-84)
The Case of the Bloody Iris '72
Horror Express '72
One Step to Hell '67
Black Box Affair '66
The Castilian '63
Quatorze Juliet '32

Cathy Rigby (1952-)
Challenge of a Lifetime '85
The Great Wallendas '78

Edward Rigby (1879-1951)
The Happiest Days of Your Life '50
Salute John Citizen '42
Convoy '40
Young and Innocent '37
Lorna Doone '34

Terence Rigby (1937-2008)
Color Me Kubrick '05
Mona Lisa Smile '03
Essex Boys '99
Plunkett & Macleane '98
The Young Americans '93
Tinker, Tailor, Soldier, Spy '80
Get Carter '71

Diana Rigg (1938-)
The Painted Veil '06
The American '01
Victoria & Albert '01
Speedy Death '99
Parting Shots '98
Rebecca '97
Moll Flanders '96
Samson and Delilah '96
A Good Man in Africa '94
Genghis Cohn '93
Running Delilah '93
Mrs. 'Arris Goes to Paris '92
Snow White '89
Unexplained Laughter '89
The Worst Witch '86
Bleak House '85
Evil under the Sun '82
The Great Muppet Caper '81
A Little Night Music '77
In This House of Brede '75
Theatre of Blood '73
The Hospital '71
Julius Caesar '70
The Assassination Bureau '69
On Her Majesty's Secret Service '69
A Midsummer Night's Dream '68

Rebecca Rigg (1967-)
Ellie Parker '05
Tunnel Vision '95
The Efficiency Expert '92
The Hunting '92
Fortress '85
Doctors and Nurses '82

Rob Riggle
Killers '10
The Other Guys '10
The Goods: Live Hard, Sell Hard '09

Mitchell Riggs
Kaaterskill Falls '01
Spin the Bottle '97

Amanda Righetti
Friday the 13th '09
Return to House on Haunted Hill '07

Massimo Righi
Death Ray '67
Black Sabbath '64
Blood and Black Lace '64

Alex(andre) Rignault (1901-85)
Numero Deux '75
The Horror Chamber of Dr. Faustus '59
Eternal Return '43

Lucia Rijker (1967-)
Million Dollar Baby '04
The Dreamers '03

Brad Rijn
Special Effects '85
Perfect Strangers '84
Smithereens '82

Robin Riker (1952-)
Stepmonster '92
Body Chemistry 2: Voice of a Stranger '91
Alligator '80

Charlotte Riley
Wuthering Heights '09
Easy Virtue '08

Elaine Riley (1923-)
Dial Red O '55
Clipped Wings '53
Rider from Tucson '50
Hopalong Cassidy: Borrowed Trouble '48
Hopalong Cassidy: The Devil's Playground '46

Jack Riley (1935-)
Rugrats Go Wild! '03 (V)
Rugrats in Paris: The Movie '00 (V)
The Rugrats Movie '98 (V)
Portrait of a White Marriage '88
Night Patrol '85
Attack of the Killer Tomatoes '77
McCabe & Mrs. Miller '71

Jeannine Riley (1939-)
Wackiest Wagon Train in the West '77
Electra Glide in Blue '73
The Comic '69
Big Mouth '67

Larry Riley (1953-92)
Dead Solid Perfect '88
Long Gone '87
Crackers '84
A Soldier's Story '84

Michael Riley (1962-)
The Tenth Circle '08
Cube: Zero '04
The Way We Live Now '02
Pale Saints '97
French Kiss '95
Heck's Way Home '95
The Prince '95
...And God Spoke '94
Race to Freedom: The Story of the Underground Railroad '94
Because Why? '93
To Catch a Killer '92
Perfectly Normal '91

Talulah Riley
St. Trinian's '07
Pride and Prejudice '05

Tom Riley
I Want Candy '07
Return to House on Haunted Hill '07
A Few Days in September '06

Walter Rilla (1894-1980)
Frozen Alive '64
The Gamma People '56
The Golden Salamander '51
Mr. Emmanuel '44
House of Mystery '41
Black Eyes '39
The Scarlet Pimpernel '34
The Finances of the Grand Duke '24

Shane Rimmer (1932-)
Space Truckers '97
Crusoe '89
Dreamchild '85
Out of Africa '85
Charlie Muffin '79
The People That Time Forgot '77
S*P*Y*S '74
Dr. Strangelove, or: How I Learned to Stop Worrying and Love the Bomb '64

Blanche Ring (1877-1961)
Having Wonderful Crime '45
It's the Old Army Game '26

Cyril Ring (1892-1967)
I Wake Up Screaming '41
The Cocoanuts '29

Molly Ringwald (1968-)
Not Another Teen Movie '01
Cowboy Up '00
Cut '00
In the Weeds '00
The Brutal Truth '99
Requiem for Murder '99
Teaching Mrs. Tingle '99
Office Killer '97
Since You've Been Gone '97
Baja '95
Malicious '95
Some Folks Call It a Sling Blade '94
Stephen King's The Stand '94
Face the Music '92
Betsy's Wedding '90
Strike It Rich '90
Women & Men: Stories of Seduction '90
For Keeps '88
Fresh Horses '88
King Lear '87
The Pick-Up Artist '87
Johnny Appleseed '86
Pretty in Pink '86
The Breakfast Club '85
P.K. and the Kid '85
Sixteen Candles '84
Packin' It In '83
Spacehunter: Adventures in the Forbidden Zone '83
The Tempest '82

Scott Rinker
Gamers '06
Shoot or Be Shot '02

Lisa Rinna (1963-)
Another Woman's Husband '00
Vanished '95
Robot Wars '93

David Rintoul (1948-)
Horatio Hornblower: The Adventure Continues '01
Pride and Prejudice '85
Legend of the Werewolf '75

Nicole Rio
Visitants '87
Sorority House Massacre '86
Zero Boys '86

Marjorie (Reardon) Riordan (1921-84)
The Hoodlum '51
South of Monterey '47
Pursuit to Algiers '45
Stage Door Canteen '43

Vincent Riotta
Under the Tuscan Sun '03
Car Trouble '85

Kelly Ripa (1970-)
Delgo '08 (V)
Fly Me to the Moon '08 (V)
Cheaper by the Dozen '03

Maurice Ripke
Living & Dying '07
Mad Bad '07

Fay Ripley (1966-)
Dead Gorgeous '02
For Roseanna '96
Mute Witness '95

Michael Ripper (1913-2000)
No Surrender '86
The Creeping Flesh '72
Girly '70
The Scars of Dracula '70
Taste the Blood of Dracula '70
Dracula Has Risen from the Grave '68
Plague of the Zombies '66
The Reptile '66
Where the Bullets Fly '66
The Devil-Ship Pirates '64
Pirates of Blood River '62
The Curse of the Werewolf '61
The Brides of Dracula '60
Dead Lucky '60
The Mummy '59
Quatermass 2 '57
Eye Witness '49

Leon Rippy
Gridiron Gang '06
The Alamo '04
The Life of David Gale '03
Eight Legged Freaks '02
The Patriot '00
Stargate '94
Beyond the Law '92
Kuffs '92
Eye of the Storm '91
The Hot Spot '90
Moon 44 '90
Young Guns 2 '90
Jesse '88
Track 29 '88

Maurice Risch (1943-)
Beau Pere '81
The Last Metro '80

Elisabeth Risdon (1887-1958)
Scaramouche '52
Guilty of Treason '50
Hills of Oklahoma '50
Down Dakota Way '49
The Amazing Mrs. Holiday '43
The Lady Is Willing '42
Mexican Spitfire at Sea '42
Reap the Wild Wind '42
High Sierra '41
Mexican Spitfire '40
The Great Man Votes '38
Make Way for Tomorrow '37
Mannequin '37
Theodora Goes Wild '36
Crime and Punishment '35

Miriam Riselle
Tevye '39
The Singing Blacksmith '38

Jeff Risk
Code of Honor '82
Kill Squad '81

Michael Risley
The Poker Club '08
Revolution #9 '01

Jacques Rispal (1923-86)
Le Chat '75
Act of Aggression '73
Bed and Board '70

Michael Rispoli (1960-)
The Taking of Pelham 123 '09
Yonkers Joe '08
Black Irish '07
The Bronx Is Burning '07
Invincible '06
One Last Thing '05
The Weather Man '05
Mr. 3000 '04
Death to Smoochy '02
Summer of Sam '99
The Third Miracle '99
Two Family House '99
Rounders '98
Scarred City '98
Snake Eyes '98
Volcano '97
Homeward Bound 2: Lost in San Francisco '96
While You Were Sleeping '95
Household Saints '93
Night and the City '92

Roberto Risso
Gladiator of Rome '63
Revenge of the Musketeers '63
Bread, Love and Dreams '53

Robbie (Reist) Rist (1964-)
Unseen Evil '99
Teenage Mutant Ninja Turtles: The Movie '90 (V)
She's Out of Control '89
Iron Eagle '86
He Is My Brother '75

Lazar Ristovski (1952-)
King of Thieves '04
Underground '95
Tito and Me '92

Steven Ritch
City of Fear '59
Plunder Road '57
Seminole Uprising '55

Cyril Ritchard (1897-1977)
The Hobbit '78 (V)
Hans Brinker '69
Half a Sixpence '67
Peter Pan '60
Blackmail '29

Bob Ritchie
See Kid Rock

Clint Ritchie (1938-)
Peacekillers '71
The St. Valentine's Day Massacre '67

Jill Ritchie (1974-)
Herbie: Fully Loaded '05
Little Athens '05
Breakin' All The Rules '04
D.E.B.S. '04
Seeing Other People '04
Face the Music '00

June Ritchie (1939-)
A Kind of Loving '62
The Mouse on the Moon '62
The Three Penny Opera '62

Blake Ritson
Emma '09
God on Trial '08
Mansfield Park '07
AKA '02

Martin Ritt (1914-90)
The Slugger's Wife '85
Conrack '74

Huntley Ritter
September Dawn '07
Dark Heart '06

Jason Ritter (1980-)
Peter and Vandy '09
The Deal '08
W. '08
Full Count '06
Happy Endings '05
Raise Your Voice '04
Freddy vs. Jason '03
Swimfan '02
Mumford '99

John Ritter (1948-2003)
Clifford's Really Big Movie '04 (V)
Bad Santa '03
Tadpole '02
Panic '00
Terror Tract '00
TripFall '00
The Million Dollar Kid '99
Bride of Chucky '98
Dead Husbands '98
It Came from the Sky '98
Shadow of Doubt '98
A Gun, a Car, a Blonde '97
Montana '97
Sink or Swim '97
Mercenary '96
Nowhere '96

Sling Blade '96
The Colony '95
North '94
Danielle Steel's Heartbeat '93
Prison for Children '93
Noises Off '92
Stay Tuned '92
Problem Child 2 '91
Problem Child '90
Stephen King's It '90
My Brother's Wife '89
Skin Deep '89
Tricks of the Trade '88
Real Men '87
The Last Fling '86
A Smoky Mountain Christmas '86
Unnatural Causes '86
Letting Go '85
Sunset Limousine '83
Flight of Dragons '82 (V)
In Love with an Older Woman '82
Pray TV '82
They All Laughed '81
Comeback Kid '80
Hero at Large '80
Wholly Moses! '80
Americathon '79
The Stone Killer '73
The Other '72
The Barefoot Executive '71
Evil Roy Slade '71
Scandalous John '71

Krysten Ritter

She's Out of My League '10
Confessions of a Shopaholic '09
What Happens in Vegas '08

Tex Ritter (1905-74)

The Girl from Tobacco Row '66
The Marshal's Daughter '53
Holiday Rhythm '50
Enemy of the Law '45
Flaming Bullets '45
Frontier Fugitives '45
Marked for Murder '45
Three in the Saddle '45
Dead or Alive '44
Gangsters of the Frontier '44
The Lone Star Trail '43
The Pioneers '41
Take Me Back to Oklahoma '40
Down the Wyoming Trail '39
Man from Texas '39
Roll, Wagons, Roll '39
Rollin' Plains '38
Utah Trail '38
Arizona Days '37
Hittin' the Trail '37
Mystery of the Hooded Horseman '37
Riders of the Rockies '37
Sing, Cowboy, Sing '37
Tex Rides with the Boy Scouts '37
Trouble in Texas '37
Headin' for the Rio Grande '36
Song of the Gringo '36

Thelma Ritter (1905-69)

The Incident '67
Boeing Boeing '65
For Love or Money '63
How the West Was Won '63
Move Over, Darling '63
A New Kind of Love '63
Birdman of Alcatraz '62
The Misfits '61
A Hole in the Head '59
Pillow Talk '59
Daddy Long Legs '55
Rear Window '54
The Farmer Takes a Wife '53
Pickup on South Street '53
Titanic '53
With a Song in My Heart '52
As Young As You Feel '51
All About Eve '50
Perfect Strangers '50
Father Was a Fullback '49
A Letter to Three Wives '49
Miracle on 34th Street '47

Al Ritz (1901-65)

Argentine Nights '40
The Gorilla '39
The Three Musketeers '39
The Goldwyn Follies '38
On the Avenue '37
One in a Million '36

Harry Ritz (1906-86)

Silent Movie '76
Blazing Stewardesses '75
Argentine Nights '40
The Gorilla '39
The Three Musketeers '39
The Goldwyn Follies '38
On the Avenue '37
One in a Million '36

Jimmy Ritz (1903-85)

Blazing Stewardesses '75
Argentine Nights '40
The Gorilla '39
The Three Musketeers '39
The Goldwyn Follies '38
On the Avenue '37
One in a Million '36

Emmanuelle Riva (1927-)

Trois Couleurs: Bleu '93
Leon Morin, Priest '61
Hiroshima, Mon Amour '59
Kapo '59

Carlos Rivas (1928-2003)

True Grit '69
They Saved Hitler's Brain '64
The Black Scorpion '57
The King and I '56

Geoffrey Rivas

Luminarias '99
Running Red '99

Naike Rivelli (1974-)

Ancient Relic '02
The Count of Monte Cristo '99

Chita Rivera (1933-)

Mayflower Madam '87
Pippin '81
Once Upon a Brothers Grimm '77
Sweet Charity '69

Elilio Rivera

Next Day Air '09
El Matador '03

Mabel Rivera

The Orphanage '07
The Sea Inside '04

Rene Rivera

Break a Leg '03
Rangers '00

Enrique Rivero

The Blood of a Poet '30
Tournament '29

George Rivero

See Jorge (George) Rivero

Jorge (George) Rivero (1938-)

Warrior of Justice '96
Werewolf '95
Ice '93
Fist Fighter '88
Counterforce '87
Target Eagle '84
Conquest '83
Day of the Assassin '81
Priest of Love '81
Bordello '79
The Last Hard Men '76
Rio Lobo '70
Soldier Blue '70
Sin of Adam & Eve '67

Julian Rivero (1890-1976)

Underground Agent '42
The Lone Rider Crosses the Rio '41
Arizona Gangbusters '40
Death Rides the Range '40
Heroes of the Alamo '37
Ridin' the Lone Trail '37
Phantom Patrol '36
Western Justice '35
Law and Lawless '33
Beyond the Rockies '32
Man from Hell's Edges '32
Night Rider '32

Joan Rivers (1933-)

Joan Rivers: A Piece of Work '10
Intern '00
Whispers: An Elephant's Tale '00 (V)
Napoleon '96 (V)
Serial Mom '94
Les Patterson Saves the World '90
Spaceballs '87
The Muppets Take Manhattan '84

Victor Rivers

What's Cooking? '00
Two for Texas '97
A Million to Juan '94
Blood In ... Blood Out: Bound by Honor '93
Black Magic Woman '91

Jorge Rivier

See Jorge (George) Rivero

George Riviere (1924-)

The Virgin of Nuremberg '65
Castle of Blood '64
Journey Beneath the Desert '61

George(s) Riviere

See Jorge (George) Rivero

Julien Riviere

Ma Vie en Rose '97
Les Voleurs '96

Marie Riviere (1956-)

Time to Leave '05
The Lady and the Duke '01
Girls Can't Swim '99
Autumn Tale '98
A Tale of Winter '92
Four Adventures of Reinette and Mirabelle '89
Summer '86
The Aviator's Wife '80

George Riviya

See Jorge (George) Rivero

Gianni Rizzo (1925-92)

Sabata '69
Mission Stardust '68
Desert Commandos '67

Bert Roach (1891-1971)

The Great Waltz '38
San Francisco '36
Daring Daughters '33
The Crowd '28
Smouldering Fires '25

Daryl Roach

Gang Boys '97
Watchers 3 '94

Martin Roach

Cube: Zero '04
Blue Hill Avenue '01
The Wall '99

Linus Roache (1964-)

Yonkers Joe '08
Before the Rains '07
Find Me Guilty '06
Batman Begins '05
12 and Holding '05
The Chronicles of Riddick '04
The Forgotten '04
Beyond Borders '03
The Gathering Storm '02
Hart's War '02
RFK '02
Pandaemonium '00
Siam Sunset '99
Shot Through the Heart '98
The Wings of the Dove '97
Priest '94

Adam Roarke (1938-96)

Sioux City '94
Trespasses '86
Beach Girls '82
The Stunt Man '80
Hughes & Harlow: Angels in Hell '77
Four Deuces '75
Dirty Mary Crazy Larry '74
How Come Nobody's On Our Side? '73
This Is a Hijack '73
Frogs '72
The Losers '70
Hell's Belles '69
The Savage Seven '68
Hell's Angels on Wheels '67
Women of the Prehistoric Planet '66

Jason Robards, Sr. (1892-1963)

Western Pacific Agent '51 (N)
Rimfire '49
Mr. Blandings Builds His Dream House '48
Return of the Bad Men '48
Desperate '47
Riff-Raff '47
Trail Street '47
Bedlam '45
Isle of the Dead '45
Mademoiselle Fifi '44
The Fatal Hour '40
Stunt Pilot '39
Sweetheart of the Navy '37
Fighting Marines '36
The Miracle Rider '35
Crimson Romance '34
Carnival Lady '33
Woman Condemned '33
Wayne Murder Case '32
White Eagle '32

Jason Robards, Jr. (1922-2000)

Magnolia '99
Beloved '98
Enemy of the State '98
Heartwood '98
The Real Macaw '98
A Thousand Acres '97
Crimson Tide '95
Journey '95
The Enemy Within '94
Little Big League '94
My Antonia '94
The Paper '94
The Adventures of Huck Finn '93
Heidi '93
Philadelphia '93
The Trial '93
Storyville '92
Black Rainbow '91
An Inconvenient Woman '91
Mark Twain and Me '91
Final Warning '90
Quick Change '90
Dream a Little Dream '89
Parenthood '89
Bright Lights, Big City '88
The Christmas Wife '88
The Good Mother '88
Reunion '88
Breaking Home Ties '87
Laguna Heat '87
Square Dance '87
The Long, Hot Summer '86
Sakharov '84
You Can't Take It with You '84
The Day After '83
Max Dugan Returns '83
Something Wicked This Way Comes '83
Burden of Dreams '82
Cabo Blanco '81
Legend of the Lone Ranger '81
Haywire '80
Melvin and Howard '80
Raise the Titanic '80
Hurricane '79
A Christmas to Remember '78
Comes a Horseman '78
Julia '77
All the President's Men '76
A Boy and His Dog '75
Mr. Sycamore '74
A House Without a Christmas Tree '72
Johnny Got His Gun '71
Murders in the Rue Morgue '71
Ballad of Cable Hogue '70
Fools '70
Julius Caesar '70
Tora! Tora! Tora! '70
The Night They Raided Minsky's '69
Isadora '68
Once Upon a Time in the West '68
Divorce American Style '67
Hour of the Gun '67
The St. Valentine's Day Massacre '67
Any Wednesday '66
A Big Hand for the Little Lady '66
A Thousand Clowns '65
Long Day's Journey into Night '62
By Love Possessed '61
The Iceman Cometh '60
A Doll's House '59

Sam Robards (1961-)

Perestroika '09
Awake '07
Catch That Kid '04
A. I.: Artificial Intelligence '01
Hamlet '01
Life as a House '01
Bounce '00
American Beauty '99
Dinner and Driving '97
Beautiful Girls '96
The Man Who Captured Eichmann '96
Donor Unknown '95
Mrs. Parker and the Vicious Circle '94
Ready to Wear '94
The Ballad of Little Jo '93
Casualties of War '89
Bright Lights, Big City '88
Pancho Barnes '88
Not Quite Paradise '86
Fandango '85
Into Thin Air '85
The Tempest '82

Andrew Robb

School of Life '06
Dreamcatcher '03

AnnaSophia Robb (1993-)

Race to Witch Mountain '09
Jumper '08
Sleepwalking '08
Spy School '08
Bridge to Terabithia '07
The Reaping '07
Because of Winn-Dixie '05
Charlie and the Chocolate Factory '05

David Robb (1947-)

Behind the Lines '97
The Crow Road '96
The Flame Trees of Thika '81

R.D. Robb (1972-)

Eight Days a Week '97
A Christmas Story '83

Amy Robbins (1971-)

Strange Relations '02
All the Little Animals '98
Rudyard Kipling's the Second Jungle Book: Mowgli and Baloo '97

Brian Robbins (1964-)

DaVinci's War '92
C.H.U.D. 2: Bud the Chud '89
Cellar Dweller '87

Gale Robbins (1921-80)

Parasite '82
The Girl in the Red Velvet Swing '55
The Belle of New York '52
The Fuller Brush Girl '50
Three Little Words '50
The Barkleys of Broadway '49
My Girl Tisa '48

Marty Robbins (1925-82)

Hell on Wheels '67
Road to Nashville '67
Ballad of a Gunfighter '64

Ryan Robbins

Passengers '08
Horsey '99

Skeeter Bill Robbins (1887-1933)

Fighting Parson '35
Cowboy Counselor '33
The Dude Bandit '33
Boiling Point '32
Man's Land '32
Hard Hombre '31

Tim Robbins (1958-)

City of Ember '08
The Lucky Ones '08
Noise '07
Catch a Fire '06
Tenacious D in the Pick of Destiny '06
War of the Worlds '05
Zathura '05
Anchorman: The Legend of Ron Burgundy '04
Code 46 '03
Mystic River '03
Human Nature '02
The Truth About Charlie '02
Antitrust '00
High Fidelity '00
Mission to Mars '00
Arlington Road '99
Austin Powers 2: The Spy Who Shagged Me '99
Nothing to Lose '96
I.Q. '94
Ready to Wear '94
The Shawshank Redemption '94
The Hudsucker Proxy '93
Short Cuts '93
Bob Roberts '92
The Player '92
Jungle Fever '91
Cadillac Man '90
Jacob's Ladder '90
Erik the Viking '89
Miss Firecracker '89
Tapeheads '89
Twister '89
Bull Durham '88
Five Corners '88
Howard the Duck '86
Top Gun '86
Fraternity Vacation '85
Quarterback Princess '85
The Sure Thing '85
No Small Affair '84
Toy Soldiers '84

Richard Rober (1910-52)

Jet Pilot '57
Kid Monk Baroni '52
Man in the Saddle '51
The Well '51
The Woman on Pier 13 '50
Task Force '49
Call Northside 777 '48

David Roberson

Steel Sharks '97
The O.J. Simpson Story '94

Yves Robert (1920-2002)

The Judge and the Assassin '75
Les Grandes Manoeuvres '55

Lyda Roberti

Torch Singer '33
Kid from Spain '32

Allene Roberts (1928-)

The Hoodlum '51
Union Station '50

The Red House '47

Arthur Roberts (1938-)

The Capitol Conspiracy '99
Illegal Entry: Formula for Fear '93
Not of This Earth '88
Revenge of the Ninja '83
Deadly Vengeance '81

Bart Roberts

See Rex Reason

Beatrice Roberts

Pioneers of the West '40
Park Avenue Logger '37

Beverly Roberts (1914-2009)

Buried Alive '39
Call of the Yukon '38
The Singing Kid '36

Bret Roberts

S. Darko: A Donnie Darko Tale '09
Beach Kings '08
Rampage: The Hillside Strangler Murders '04
Cock & Bull Story '03
Nightstalker '02

Christian Roberts (1944-)

The Adventurers '70
Desperados '69
The Anniversary '68
To Sir, with Love '67

Conrad Roberts

The Scorpion King '02
The Million Dollar Hotel '99
The Serpent and the Rainbow '87
The Mosquito Coast '86

Dallas Roberts (1970-)

Shrink '09
Joshua '07
Lovely by Surprise '07
3:10 to Yuma '07
Flicka '06
The Notorious Bettie Page '06
Walk the Line '05
Winter Passing '05
A Home at the End of the World '04

Daniel Roberts

Valiant '05 (V)
Walking on Water '02

David Roberts

Fool's Gold '08
Me Myself I '99

Des Roberts

Black Bikers from Hell '70
The Outlaw Bikers—Gang Wars '70

Doris Roberts (1930-)

Aliens in the Attic '09
Grandma's Boy '06
I-See-You.Com '06
Keeping Up with the Steins '06
Dickie Roberts: Former Child Star '03
A Time to Remember '03
All Over the Guy '01
My Giant '98
The Night We Never Met '93
Used People '92
Honeymoon Academy '90
National Lampoon's Christmas Vacation '89
Simple Justice '89
The Fig Tree '87
Number One with a Bullet '87
Ordinary Heroes '85
Hester Street '75
The Taking of Pelham One Two Three '74
Honeymoon Killers '70

Edith Roberts (1899-1935)

Man from Headquarters '28
The Taxi Mystery '26

Emma Roberts

Lymelife '08
Persuasion '95

Emma Roberts (1991-)

Twelve '10
Valentine's Day '10
Hotel for Dogs '09
Wild Child '08
Nancy Drew '07
Aquamarine '06
Blow '01

Eric Roberts (1956-)

The Expendables '10
The Chaos Experiment '09
Cyclops '08
Dark Honeymoon '08
The Dark Knight '08
Depth Charge '08
Witless Protection '08
The Butcher '07
Pandemic '07
DOA: Dead or Alive '06
A Guide to Recognizing Your Saints '06
One Way '06
Phat Girlz '06
Final Approach '04
Miss Cast Away '04
Six: The Mark Unleashed '04
Border Blues '03
Break a Leg '03
National Security '03
Breakaway '02
Con Games '02
Endangered Species '02
Spun '02
Fast Sofa '01
The King's Guard '01
The Long Ride Home '01
Mindstorm '01
Sanctimony '01
Stiletto Dance '01
Cecil B. Demented '00
Frozen in Fear '00
Luck of the Draw '00
Mercy Streets '00
No Alibi '00
Race Against Time '00
TripFall '00
Agent of Death '99
Heaven's Fire '99
Hitman's Run '99
La Cucaracha '99
Lansky '99
Purgatory '99
Restraining Order '99
Wildflowers '99
Bitter Sweet '98
Dead End '98
Facade '98
Past Perfect '98
T.N.T. '98
Two Shades of Blue '98
Most Wanted '97
The Odyssey '97
The Prophecy 2: Ashtown '97
American Strays '96
Doctor Who '96
The Glass Cage '96
In Cold Blood '96
Power 98 '96
Public Enemies '96
The Grave '95
Heaven's Prisoners '95
The Immortals '95
It's My Party '95
Saved by the Light '95
Babyfever '94
Firefall '94
The Hard Truth '94
Love Is a Gun '94
Nature of the Beast '94
Sensation '94
The Specialist '94
Best of the Best 2 '93
By the Sword '93
Love, Cheat & Steal '93
Voyage '93
Final Analysis '92
Fugitive Among Us '92
A Family Matter '91
Lonely Hearts '91
The Ambulance '90
Descending Angel '90
The Lost Capone '90
Best of the Best '89
Rude Awakening '89
Blood Red '88
Options '88
To Heal a Nation '88
Nobody's Fool '86
Slow Burn '86
Runaway Train '85
The Coca-Cola Kid '84
The Pope of Greenwich Village '84
Star 80 '83
Raggedy Man '81
King of the Gypsies '78

Ewan Roberts (1914-83)

Day of the Triffids '63
Curse of the Demon '57

Florence Roberts (1860-1940)

Harmony Lane '35
Sons of Steel '35
Hoopla '33
Torch Singer '33
Kept Husbands '31

Francesca Roberts

Prison Stories: Women on the Inside '91
The Heart of Dixie '89

Ian Roberts

Tsotsi '05
Wah-Wah '05
Tarzan and the Lost City '98
Mandela and de Klerk '97
Terminal Impact '95
The Power of One '92
Violated '53

Jay Roberts, Jr.

Warlords 3000 '93
Aftershock '88
White Phantom: Enemy of Darkness '87

Jeremy Roberts (1954-)

Herbie: Fully Loaded '05
The Thirteenth Floor '99
Jungle Boy '96

J.H. Roberts (1884-1961)

Uneasy Terms '48
Spitfire '42
The Courageous Mr. Penn '41
Young and Innocent '37
Nine Days a Queen '36

Joe Roberts

Cider with Rosie '99
Shakespeare in Love '98

Judith Anna Roberts

The Nanny Diaries '07
Eraserhead '78

Julia Roberts (1967-)

Eat, Pray, Love '10
Valentine's Day '10
Duplicity '09
Charlie Wilson's War '07
The Ant Bully '06 (V)
Charlotte's Web '06 (V)
Closer '04
Ocean's Twelve '04
Mona Lisa Smile '03
Confessions of a Dangerous Mind '02
Full Frontal '02
America's Sweethearts '01
The Mexican '01
Ocean's Eleven '01
Erin Brockovich '00
Notting Hill '99
Runaway Bride '99
Stepmom '98
Conspiracy Theory '97
My Best Friend's Wedding '97
Everyone Says I Love You '96
Michael Collins '96
Mary Reilly '95
Something to Talk About '95
I Love Trouble '94
Ready to Wear '94
The Pelican Brief '93
The Player '92
Dying Young '91
Hook '91
Sleeping with the Enemy '91
Flatliners '90
Pretty Woman '90
Steel Magnolias '89
Blood Red '88
Mystic Pizza '88
Satisfaction '88
Baja Oklahoma '87
Firehouse '87

Ken Roberts (1910-)

Fatal Pulse '88
The Great Land of Small '86

Kimberly Roberts

Get a Clue '02
Range of Motion '00
Vice Girls '96

Lee Roberts

Battling Marshal '48
Law of the Lash '47

Leonard Roberts (1972-)

Red Sands '09
Drumline '02
Joe and Max '02
The '60s '99
Love Jones '96

Lynne Roberts (1922-78)

Because of You '52
Dynamite Pass '50
Hunt the Man Down '50
Eyes of Texas '48
Robin Hood of Texas '47
Sioux City Sue '46
Dr. Renault's Secret '42
Frolics on Ice '39
In Old Caliente '39
Rough Riders' Roundup '39
Southward Ho! '39
Billy the Kid Returns '38
Call the Mesquiteers '38
Come on Rangers '38
Hollywood Stadium Mystery '38
Shine on, Harvest Moon '38
Heart of the Rockies '37

Mark Roberts (1921-2006)

Bulletproof '96
Posse '75

Michael D. Roberts (1947-)

Live! From Death Row '92
Rain Man '88
Ice Pirates '84
Heartbreaker '83

Pascale Roberts (1933-)

The Town Is Quiet '00
Marius and Jeannette '97
Le Grand Chemin '87
Friends '71
The Peking Blond '68
Dishonorable Discharge '57

Pernell Roberts (1928-2010)

Around the World in 80 Days '89
The Night Train to Kathmandu '88
High Noon: Part 2 '80
Hot Rod '79
Magic of Lassie '78
Paco '75
Sniper '75
The Bravos '72
Four Rode Out '69
Kashmiri Run '69
The Errand Boy '61
Ride Lonesome '59
The Sheepman '58

Rachel Roberts (1927-80)

Charlie Chan and the Curse of the Dragon Queen '81
The Hostage Tower '80
Sorrows of Gin '79
When a Stranger Calls '79
Yanks '79
Foul Play '78
Picnic at Hanging Rock '75
Murder on the Orient Express '74
Alpha Beta '73
The Belstone Fox '73
O Lucky Man! '73
Baffled '72
Wild Rovers '71
Doctors' Wives '70
This Sporting Life '63
Saturday Night and Sunday Morning '60
Our Man in Havana '59

Rick Roberts (1965-)

Pontypool '09
The Note '07
Man of the Year '06
Love and Human Remains '93

Roy Roberts (1900-75)

The Strongest Man in the World '75
I'll Take Sweden '65
The King and Four Queens '56
Second Chance '53
The Enforcer '51
Santa Fe '51
Borderline '50
Force of Evil '49
He Walked by Night '48
Colonel Effingham's Raid '45
Guadalcanal Diary '43
The Fighting Sullivans '42

Sebastien Roberts (1972-)

Black Swarm '07
One Way '06

Shawn Roberts (1984-)

Edge of Darkness '10
I Love You, Beth Cooper '09
Diary of the Dead '07

Tanya Roberts (1954-)

Deep Down '94
Sins of Desire '92
Almost Pregnant '91
Inner Sanctum '91
Legal Tender '90
Night Eyes '90
Purgatory '89
Body Slam '87
A View to a Kill '85
Sheena '84
Hearts & Armour '83
Beastmaster '82
California Dreaming '79
Racquet '79
Tourist Trap '79
Fingers '78
The Yum-Yum Girls '78
Forced Entry '75

Teal Roberts

Fatal Games '84
Hardbodies '84

Ted Jan Roberts (1979-)

Hollywood Safari '96
Tiger Heart '96
The Power Within '95
A Dangerous Place '94
Magic Kid 2 '94
Magic Kid '92

Theodore Roberts (1861-1928)

The Ten Commandments '23
Affairs of Anatol '21
Suds '20
The Roaring Road '19

Tony Roberts (1939-)

Dead Broke '99
Our Sons '91
Switch '91
Popcorn '89
18 Again! '88
Radio Days '87
Hannah and Her Sisters '86
Seize the Day '86
Key Exchange '85
Amityville 3: The Demon '83
Packin' It In '83
A Midsummer Night's Sex Comedy '82
Just Tell Me What You Want '80
Question of Honor '80
Stardust Memories '80
If Things Were Different '79
Annie Hall '77
The Lindbergh Kidnapping Case '76
Lovers Like Us '75
The Savage '75
The Taking of Pelham One Two Three '74
Serpico '73
Play It Again, Sam '72
Million Dollar Duck '71
Star Spangled Girl '71

Tracey Roberts (1914-2002)

The Naked Flame '68
The Prodigal '55
Actors and Sin '52
Queen for a Day '51

Wink Roberts (1955-)

The Day It Came to Earth '77
The First Time '69

Alex Robertson

Fanny Hill '07
Wide Sargasso Sea '06

Brittany Robertson

The Tenth Circle '08
Dan in Real Life '07
Frank '07

Cliff Robertson (1925-)

Spider-Man 3 '07
Riding the Bullet '04
Spider-Man 2 '04
Spider-Man '02
Family Tree '00
Mach 2 '00
Race '99
Escape from L.A. '96
Renaissance Man '94
Wind '92
Wild Hearts Can't Be Broken '91
Dead Reckoning '89
Ford: The Man & the Machine '87
Malone '87
The Key to Rebecca '85
Shaker Run '85
Brainstorm '83
Class '83
Star 80 '83
Two of a Kind '82
Danger in the Skies '79
Dominique Is Dead '79
Midway '76
Obsession '76
Return to Earth '76
Shoot '76
My Father's House '75
Out of Season '75
Three Days of the Condor '75
The Man Without a Country '73
The Great Northfield Minnesota Raid '72
Too Late the Hero '70
Charly '68
The Devil's Brigade '68
The Honey Pot '67
Love Has Many Faces '65
The Best Man '64
633 Squadron '64
PT 109 '63
Sunday in New York '63
The Interns '62
All in a Night's Work '61
Underworld USA '61
Underworld, U.S.A. '60
Gidget '59
Days of Wine and Roses '58
The Naked and the Dead '58
The Girl Most Likely '57
Autumn Leaves '56
Picnic '55

Dale Robertson (1923-)
The Last Ride of the Dalton Gang *'79*
Melvin Purvis: G-Man *'74*
One-Eyed Soldiers *'67*
Man from Button Willow *'65 (V)*
Coast of Skeletons *'63*
Dakota Incident *'56*
Son of Sinbad *'55*
Sitting Bull *'54*
Devil's Canyon *'53*
The Farmer Takes a Wife *'53*

Finlay Robertson
The Disappeared *'08*
In a Day *'06*

Francoise Robertson
We All Fall Down *'00*
The Minion *'98*
Twists of Terror *'98*
Armistead Maupin's More Tales of the City *'97*

Iain Robertson (1981-)
Basic Instinct 2 *'06*
The Match *'99*
Plunkett & Macleane *'98*
Small Faces *'95*

Jenny Robertson (1963-)
Twitches *'05*
The Boys Next Door *'96*
Danger of Love *'95*
The Nightman *'93*
Bull Durham *'88*
Jacob Have I Loved *'88*

Kathleen Robertson (1973-)
The Terrorist Next Door *'08*
Tin Man *'07*
Hollywoodland *'06*
XX/XY *'02*
Scary Movie 2 *'01*
Torso *'01*
Beautiful *'00*
Psycho Beach Party *'00*
Splendor *'99*
Dog Park *'98*
Nowhere *'96*
Blown Away *'93*

Ken Robertson
Yellow Hair & the Fortress of Gold *'84*
Nighthawks *'78*

Kimmy Robertson (1954-)
Speed 2: Cruise Control *'97*
Leprechaun 2 *'94*
Beauty and the Beast *'91 (V)*

Robbie Robertson (1943-)
The Crossing Guard *'94*
Carny *'80*

Steven Robertson (1980-)
Joyeux Noel *'05*
Rory O'Shea Was Here *'04*
Devil's Gift *'84*

Willard Robertson (1886-1948)
Air Force *'43*
Night of January 16th *'41*
Brigham Young: Frontiersman *'40*
Remember the Night *'40*
Larceny On the Air *'37*
Park Avenue Logger *'37*
Two Alone *'34*
Supernatural *'33*
Tugboat Annie *'33*
The Rider of Death Valley *'32*

William Robertson
Dark August *'76*
Operator 13 *'34*

James Robertson-Justice
Doctor in Clover *'66*
The Trygon Factor *'66*
Doctor in Love *'60*

Paul Robeson (1898-1976)
Tales of Manhattan *'42*
Jericho *'38*
Big Fella *'37*
King Solomon's Mines *'37*
Show Boat *'36*
Song of Freedom *'36*
Sanders of the River *'35*
Emperor Jones *'33*
Body and Soul *'24*

George Robey (1869-1954)
Henry V *'44*
Salute John Citizen *'42*
Don Quixote *'35*

Wendy Robie
Were the World Mine *'08*
The People under the Stairs *'91*

Kim Robillard
Ali *'01*
Home Fries *'98*
Breakdown *'96*
The Fan *'96*
Chrome Soldiers *'92*
Rain Man *'88*

Dany Robin (1927-95)
Don't Lose Your Head *'66*
Waltz of the Toreadors *'62*

Michel Robin
Merci pour le Chocolat *'00*
Marquis *'90 (V)*
La Chevre *'81*

Herb Robins
The Worm Eaters *'77*
The Thrill Killers *'65*

Jessie Robins (1905-91)
The Fearless Vampire Killers *'67*
Magical Mystery Tour *'67*

Laila Robins (1959-)
Slippery Slope *'06*
Searching for Paradise *'02*
Oxygen *'99*
True Crime *'99*
The Blood Oranges *'97*
Female Perversions *'96*
Live Nude Girls *'95*
Welcome Home, Roxy Carmichael *'90*
An Innocent Man *'89*
Planes, Trains & Automobiles *'87*

Mikul Robins
Witchcraft 11: Sisters in Blood *'00*
Witchcraft 9: Bitter Flesh *'96*

Oliver Robins (1971-)
Poltergeist 2: The Other Side *'86*
Poltergeist *'82*

Andrew (Andy) Robinson (1942-)
Running Woman *'98*
Pumpkinhead 2: Blood Wings *'94*
Fatal Charm *'92*
Into the Badlands *'92*
There Goes My Baby *'92*
Trancers 3: Deth Lives *'92*
Child's Play 3 *'91*
Prime Target *'91*
Shoot to Kill *'88*
Hellraiser *'87*
Cobra *'86*
Mask *'85*
Not My Kid *'85*
Someone I Touched *'75*
Charley Varrick *'73*
Dirty Harry *'71*

Ann (Robin) Robinson (1935-)
War of the Worlds *'05*
Attack from Mars *'88*
Dragnet *'54*
The War of the Worlds *'53*

Bill Robinson (1878-1949)
Stormy Weather *'43*
Just Around the Corner *'38*
Rebecca of Sunnybrook Farm *'38*
The Little Colonel *'35*
The Littlest Rebel *'35*
Dixiana *'30*

Bruce Robinson (1946-)
Still Crazy *'98*
The Story of Adele H. *'75*

Bumper Robinson
Death Valley *'04*
The Old Settler *'01*

Charles Robinson (1945-)
The House Bunny *'08*
Land of the Free *'98*
Set It Off *'96*
Fatal Chase *'77*
Black Gestapo *'75*
Daring Dobermans *'73*
The Brotherhood of Satan *'71*
Shenandoah *'65*

Chris Robinson (1938-)
Viper *'88*
Ace of Hearts *'85*
Savannah Smiles *'82*
Amy *'81*
Sunshine Run *'79*
Thunder County *'74*
Women's Prison Escape *'74*
Stanley *'72*
Darker than Amber *'70*

Claudia Robinson
Back in the USSR *'92*
Wide Sargasso Sea *'92*

Craig Robinson (1971-)
Hot Tub Time Machine *'10*
Shrek Forever After *'10 (V)*
Fanboys *'09*
Miss March *'09*
Post Grad *'09*
Pineapple Express *'08*
Zack and Miri Make a Porno *'08*
Daddy's Little Girls *'07*
Dragon Wars *'07*
Knocked Up *'07*
Walk Hard: The Dewey Cox Story *'07*

Dar Robinson (1947-86)
Cyclone *'87*
Stick *'85*

Eartha D. Robinson (1960-)
The Old Settler *'01*
Daughters of the Dust *'91*

Edward G. Robinson (1893-1973)
Soylent Green *'73*
Song of Norway *'70*
MacKenna's Gold *'69*
Never a Dull Moment *'68*
The Peking Blond *'68*
The Cincinnati Kid *'65*
Cheyenne Autumn *'64*
Good Neighbor Sam *'64*
The Outrage *'64*
Robin and the 7 Hoods *'64*
The Prize *'63*
My Geisha *'62*
Two Weeks in Another Town *'62*
Seven Thieves *'60*
A Hole in the Head *'59*
A Bullet for Joey *'55*
Hell on Frisco Bay *'55*
Illegal *'55*
Tight Spot *'55*
The Violent Men *'55*
Actors and Sin *'52*
House of Strangers *'49*
It's a Great Feeling *'49*
All My Sons *'48*
Key Largo *'48*
The Red House *'47*
The Stranger *'46*
Our Vines Have Tender Grapes *'45*
Scarlet Street *'45*
Double Indemnity *'44*
Mr. Winkle Goes to War *'44*
Woman in the Window *'44*
Destroyer *'43*
Larceny, Inc. *'42*
Tales of Manhattan *'42*
Manpower *'41*
The Sea Wolf *'41*
Brother Orchid *'40*
Dr. Ehrlich's Magic Bullet *'40*
Confessions of a Nazi Spy *'39*
Amazing Dr. Clitterhouse *'38*
Bullets or Ballots *'38*
I Am the Law *'38*
A Slight Case of Murder *'38*
Kid Galahad *'37*
The Last Gangster *'37*
Thunder in the City *'37*
Barbary Coast *'35*
The Whole Town's Talking *'35*
The Man with Two Faces *'34*
The Little Giant *'33*
Tiger Shark *'32*
Two Seconds *'32*
Smart Money *'31*
Little Caesar *'30*

Frances Robinson (1916-71)
Smilin' Through *'41*
Riders of Pasco Basin *'40*
Forbidden Valley *'38*
Red Barry *'38*
Tim Tyler's Luck *'37*

Holly Robinson (1964-)
The Jacksons: An American Dream *'92*
Howard the Duck *'86*

Jay Robinson (1930-)
Dying to Remember *'93*
Sinatra *'92*
Transylvania Twist *'89*
Malibu Bikini Shop *'86*
Partners *'82*
Three the Hard Way *'74*
This Is a Hijack *'73*
Everything You Always Wanted to Know about Sex (But Were Afraid to Ask) *'72*
My Man Godfrey *'57*
The Virgin Queen *'55*
Demetrius and the Gladiators *'54*
The Robe *'53*

Joe Robinson (1929-)
Diamonds Are Forever *'71*
Tor *'64*
The Invaders *'63*
Thor and the Amazon Women *'60*
A Kid for Two Farthings *'55*

John Robinson
Just Business *'08*
Sticks and Stones *'08*
Killer Wave *'07*
Remember the Daze *'07*
Head in the Clouds *'04*
A Woman's a Helluva Thing *'01*
Simon Birch *'98*
Zero Patience *'94*

John Robinson (1908-79)
Nothing But the Night *'72*
The Longest Day *'62*
Ghost Ship *'53*
Uneasy Terms *'48*
The Lion Has Wings *'40*

John Robinson (1985-)
Wendy and Lucy *'08*
Transformers *'07*
Seraphim Falls *'06*
Lords of Dogtown *'05*
Elephant *'03*

Karen Robinson
Lars and the Real Girl *'07*
Jasper, Texas *'03*
My Louisiana Sky *'02*
My Teacher Ate My Homework *'98*
Stalked *'94*

Keith D. Robinson
Dear John *'10*
This Christmas *'07*
Dreamgirls *'06*
Fat Albert *'04*

Leon Robinson (1962-)
Buffalo Soldiers *'01*
The Father Clements Story *'87*
Band of the Hand *'86*
Streetwalkin' *'85*
Sole Survivor *'84*

Linette Robinson
Blue Hill Avenue *'01*
The Wall *'99*

Madeleine Robinson (1916-2008)
Camille Claudel *'89*
I Married a Dead Man *'82*
Mission to Venice *'63*
Duke of the Derby *'62*

Paul Michael Robinson
Kept *'01*
The Capitol Conspiracy *'99*
Friend of the Family 2 *'96*

Phyllis Robinson
Sunshine Run *'79*
Thunder County *'74*

Roger Robinson (1940-)
Brother to Brother *'04*
Burnzy's Last Call *'95*
Newman's Law *'74*

Sherry Robinson
Hot Summer in Barefoot County *'74*
Gruesome Twosome *'67*

"Sugar Ray" Robinson (1921-89)
Candy *'68*
The Detective *'68*
Paper Lion *'68*

Wendy Raquel Robinson (1967-)
Something New *'06*
Rebound *'05*
Two Can Play That Game *'01*
Miss Congeniality *'00*
Ringmaster *'98*

Zuleikha Robinson (1977-)
The Namesake *'06*
Hidalgo *'04*
The Merchant of Venice *'04*

German Robles (1929-)
Genie of Darkness *'62*
The Brainiac *'61*
Curse of Nostradamus *'60*
The Monster Demolisher *'60*
The Living Head *'59*
The Vampire's Coffin *'58*
The Vampire *'57*

Rudy Robles (1910-70)
Omoo Omoo, the Shark God *'49*
Across the Pacific *'42*
The Real Glory *'39*

Flora Robson (1902-84)
A Tale of Two Cities *'80*
Les Miserables *'78*
Restless *'72*
Beast in the Cellar *'70*
Blood Island *'68*
Those Magnificent Men in Their Flying Machines *'65*
Guns at Batasi *'64*
55 Days at Peking *'63*
Murder at the Gallop *'63*
Romeo and Juliet *'54*
Malta Story *'53*
Black Narcissus *'47*
Frieda *'47*
Caesar and Cleopatra *'46*
Great Day *'46*
Saratoga Trunk *'45*
Bahama Passage *'42*
The Lion Has Wings *'40*
The Sea Hawk *'40*
Invisible Stripes *'39*
Wuthering Heights *'39*
Fire Over England *'37*
Catherine the Great *'34*

Greer Robson (1971-)
Starlight Hotel *'90*
Smash Palace *'82*

May Robson (1858-1942)
Joan of Paris *'42*
Playmates *'41*
The Texas Rangers Ride Again *'40*
Nurse Edith Cavell *'39*
The Adventures of Tom Sawyer *'38*
Bringing Up Baby *'38*
Four Daughters *'38*
The Texans *'38*
A Star Is Born *'37*
It Happened in New Orleans *'36*
Wife Versus Secretary *'36*
Anna Karenina *'35*
Reckless *'35*
Lady by Choice *'34*
Dancing Lady *'33*
Dinner at Eight *'33*
Lady for a Day *'33*
One Man's Journey *'33*
Little Orphan Annie *'32*
Red Headed Woman *'32*
Strange Interlude *'32*

Wayne Robson (1946-)
Welcome to Mooseport *'04*
Wrong Turn *'03*
Harlan County War *'00*
Cube *'98*
Murder She Purred: A Mrs. Murphy Mystery *'98*
Affliction *'97*
Two If by Sea *'95*
Stand Off *'93*
Love & Murder *'91*
Bye Bye Blues *'89*
And Then You Die *'88*
The Grey Fox *'83*

Patricia Roc (1915-2003)
Captain Blackjack *'51*
Man on the Eiffel Tower *'48*
Canyon Passage *'46*
Johnny Frenchman *'46*
The Wicked Lady *'45*

Pascale Rocard (1960-)
Field of Honor *'87*
Police *'85*
The Rascals *'81*

Daniela Rocca (1938-95)
Divorce—Italian Style *'62*
The Mercenaries *'62*
The Giant of Marathon *'60*
Revenge of the Barbarians *'60*

Stefania Rocca (1971-)
Don't Tell *'05*
The 4 Musketeers *'05*
Operation Valkyrie *'04*
Heaven *'01*
Jesus *'00*
Love's Labour's Lost *'00*
The Talented Mr. Ripley *'99*
Solomon *'98*

Alex Rocco (1936-)
Smokin' Aces *'07*
Find Me Guilty *'06*
Jam *'06*
The Job *'03*
Big Shot: Confessions of a Campus Bookie *'02*
The Country Bears *'02*
The Wedding Planner *'01*
Dudley Do-Right *'99*
Goodbye, Lover *'99*
A Bug's Life *'98 (V)*
Just Write *'97*

Forgive and Forget '99
The Acid House '98
David '97
Moses '96
The Last of the Mohicans '92
The Big Man: Crossing the Line '91
Hidden Agenda '90
Danger UXB '81
When Eight Bells Toll '71
Oh! What a Lovely War '69
Ulysses '67

Michael Rogen

Punch the Clock '90
Doom Asylum '88

Seth Rogen (1982-)

Funny People '09
Monsters vs. Aliens '09 (V)
Observe and Report '09
Dr. Seuss' Horton Hears a Who! '08 (V)
Kung Fu Panda '08 (V)
Pineapple Express '08
The Spiderwick Chronicles '08 (V)
Zack and Miri Make a Porno '08
Knocked Up '07
Shrek the Third '07 (V)
Superbad '07
You, Me and Dupree '06
The 40 Year Old Virgin '05

Austin Rogers

Ace Ventura Jr.: Pet Detective '08
How to Eat Fried Worms '06

Bill Rogers (1930-2004)

The Girl, the Body and the Pill '67
Shanty Tramp '67
A Taste of Blood '67

Charles "Buddy" Rogers (1904-99)

Mexican Spitfire at Sea '42
Double Trouble '41
My Best Girl '27
Wings '27

Clyde Rogers

See Rik van Nutter

Ginger Rogers (1911-95)

That's Dancing! '85
Quick, Let's Get Married '71
Cinderella '64
Tight Spot '55
Black Widow '54
Forever Female '53
Monkey Business '52
We're Not Married '52
Storm Warning '51
Perfect Strangers '50
The Barkleys of Broadway '49
Heartbeat '46
Magnificent Doll '46
Weekend at the Waldorf '45
I'll Be Seeing You '44
Tender Comrade '43
The Major and the Minor '42
Once Upon a Honeymoon '42
Roxie Hart '42
Tales of Manhattan '42
Tom, Dick, and Harry '41
Kitty Foyle '40
Lucky Partners '40
Primrose Path '40
Bachelor Mother '39
Fifth Avenue Girl '39
The Story of Vernon and Irene Castle '39
Carefree '38
Having a Wonderful Time '38
Having Wonderful Time '38
Vivacious Lady '38
Shall We Dance '37
Stage Door '37
Follow the Fleet '36
Swing Time '36
In Person '35
Roberta '35
Star of Midnight '35
Top Hat '35
The Gay Divorcee '34
Rafter Romance '34
Romance in Manhattan '34
Finishing School '33
Flying Down to Rio '33
42nd Street '33
Gold Diggers of 1933 '33
Shriek in the Night '33
13th Guest '32
Suicide Fleet '31
The Tip-Off '31

Ivan Rogers (1954-)

Slow Burn '90
Ballbuster '89
Two Wrongs Make a Right '89
Crazed Cop '88

Jean Rogers (1916-91)

Whistling in Brooklyn '43
Brigham Young: Frontiersman '40
Flash Gordon: Rocketship '40
Flash Gordon: Mars Attacks the World '39
Ace Drummond '36
Rocketship '36

Jimmy Rogers (1915-2000)

Mystery Man '44
Texas Masquerade '44
False Colors '43
Hopalong Cassidy: Riders of the Deadline '43

Kenny Rogers (1938-)

The Gambler Returns: The Luck of the Draw '93
Rio Diablo '93
The Return of Spinal Tap '92
Kenny Rogers as the Gambler, Part 3: The Legend Continues '87
Wild Horses '84
Kenny Rogers as the Gambler, Part 2: The Adventure Continues '83
Six Pack '82
Coward of the County '81
Kenny Rogers as the Gambler '80

Michael Rogers

In the Spider's Web '07
Children of the Corn: Revelation '01

Mimi Rogers (1956-)

Storm Cell '08
Big Nothing '06
Dancing in Twilight '05
Jesse Stone: Stone Cold '05
The Door in the Floor '04
Seeing Other People '04
Dumb and Dumberer: When Harry Met Lloyd '03
The Gunman '03
Charms for the Easy Life '02
Ginger Snaps '01
Common Ground '00
Seven Girlfriends '00
Cruel Intentions 2 '99
The Devil's Arithmetic '99
Lost in Space '98
Austin Powers: International Man of Mystery '97
Tricks '97
Weapons of Mass Distraction '97
The Mirror Has Two Faces '96
Tree's Lounge '96
Bulletproof Heart '95
Full Body Massage '95
Far from Home: The Adventures of Yellow Dog '94
Monkey Trouble '94
Reflections in the Dark '94
Dark Horse '92
Ladykiller '92
The Player '92
Shooting Elizabeth '92
White Sands '92
Deadlock '91
The Doors '91
The Palermo Connection '91
The Rapture '91
Desperate Hours '90
Fourth Story '90
Hider in the House '90
The Rousters '90
The Mighty Quinn '89
Someone to Watch Over Me '87
Street Smart '87
Embassy '85
Gung Ho '85
Blue Skies Again '83

Paul Rogers (1917-)

The Return of the Native '94
The Tenth Man '88
Edwin '84
The Looking Glass War '69
A Midsummer Night's Dream '68
Stolen Hours '63
Billy Budd '62
The Mark '61
The Trials of Oscar Wilde '60
Our Man in Havana '59
Svengali '55
Beau Brummel '54

Reg Rogers (1964-)

Lovely by Surprise '07
Analyze That '02
Attila '01
I'll Take You There '99
Runaway Bride '99

Roxanne Rogers

Punk Vacation '90
Slow Moves '84

Roy Rogers (1912-98)

Alias Jesse James '59
Son of Paleface '52
Heart of the Rockies '51
Bells of Coronado '50
North of the Great Divide '50
Sunset in the West '50
Trail of Robin Hood '50
Trigger, Jr. '50
Twilight in the Sierras '50
Down Dakota Way '49
The Golden Stallion '49
Susanna Pass '49
Eyes of Texas '48
Far Frontier '48
Grand Canyon Trail '48
Melody Time '48
Night Time in Nevada '48
Under California Stars '48
Apache Rose '47
Bells of San Angelo '47
Home in Oklahoma '47
Lights of Old Santa Fe '47
On the Old Spanish Trail '47
Springtime in the Sierras '47
Helldorado '46
My Pal Trigger '46
Rainbow over Texas '46
Roll on Texas Moon '46
Song of Arizona '46
Under Nevada Skies '46
Along the Navaho Trail '45
Bells of Rosarita '45
Don't Fence Me In '45
Sunset in El Dorado '45
Utah '45
Cowboy & the Senorita '44
San Fernando Valley '44
Song of Nevada '44
The Yellow Rose of Texas '44
Hands Across the Border '43
Idaho '43
King of the Cowboys '43
Silver Spurs '43
Song of Texas '43
Texas Legionnaires '43
The Gay Ranchero '42
Heart of the Golden West '42
Man from Cheyenne '42
Ridin' Down the Canyon '42
Romance on the Range '42
Sons of the Pioneers '42
South of Santa Fe '42
Sunset on the Desert '42
Sunset Serenade '42
Bad Man of Deadwood '41
In Old Cheyenne '41
Jesse James at Bay '41
Nevada City '41
Red River Valley '41
Robin Hood of the Pecos '41
Sheriff of Tombstone '41
The Border Legion '40
Carson City Kid '40
Colorado '40
Dark Command '40
Ranger and the Lady '40
Young Bill Hickok '40
Young Buffalo Bill '40
Arizona Kid '39
Days of Jesse James '39
Frontier Pony Express '39
In Old Caliente '39
Jeepers Creepers '39
Rough Riders' Roundup '39
Saga of Death Valley '39
Southward Ho! '39
Wall Street Cowboy '39
Billy the Kid Returns '38
Come on Rangers '38
Old Barn Dance '38
Shine on, Harvest Moon '38
Under Western Stars '38
Wild Horse Rodeo '37
Old Corral '36

Steve Rogers

Triple Impact '92
Trident Force '88

Tristan Rogers (1946-)

Night Eyes 3 '93
Evil Lives '92
The Rescuers Down Under '90 (V)
Flesh and Blood Show '73

Wayne Rogers (1933-)

Miracle Dogs '03
Ghosts of Mississippi '96
The Goodbye Bird '93
Passion in Paradise '89
Drop-Out Mother '88
The Killing Time '87
The Girl Who Spelled Freedom '86
The Gig '85
Lady from Yesterday '85
Chiefs '83
Hot Touch '82
Once in Paris... '79
Pocket Money '72
Cool Hand Luke '67

Will Rogers (1879-1935)

Doubting Thomas '35
In Old Kentucky '35
Life Begins at Forty '35
Steamboat Round the Bend '35
David Harum '34
Judge Priest '34
Doctor Bull '33
Mr. Skitch '33
Too Busy to Work '32
Ambassador Bill '31
A Connecticut Yankee '31
They Had to See Paris '29

Elisabeth Rohm (1973-)

The Kreutzer Sonata '08
San Saba '08
Miss Congeniality 2: Armed and Fabulous '05

Maria Rohm (1949-)

Count Dracula '71
Dorian Gray '70
Venus in Furs '70
Kiss and Kill '68
The House of 1000 Dolls '67

Clayton Rohner (1961-)

Border Patrol '01
The Big Day '99
Sometimes They Come Back... For More '99
Where's Marlowe? '98
The Relic '96
Naked Souls '95
Caroline at Midnight '93
I, Madman '89
Nightwish '89
Bat 21 '88
P.I. Private Investigations '87
Private Investigations '87
April Fool's Day '86
Just One of the Guys '85

Alba Rohrwacher (1979-)

Days and Clouds '07
My Brother Is an Only Child '07

Eduardo Lopez Rojas (1937-99)

My Family '94
Reed: Insurgent Mexico '73

Gustavo Rojo (1926-)

The Valley of Gwangi '69
The Christmas Kid '68
A Witch Without a Broom '68
Apache's Last Battle '64
No Survivors, Please '63
It Started with a Kiss '59

Helena Rojo (1944-)

Mary, Mary, Bloody Mary '76
Aguirre, the Wrath of God '72

Maria Rojo (1943-)

Esmeralda Comes by Night '98
Midaq Alley '95
Forbidden Homework '92
Danzon '91
Homework '90
Break of Dawn '88
Mary, My Dearest '83
Candy Stripe Nurses '74

Ruben Rojo (1922-93)

Cauldron of Blood '67
Samson in the Wax Museum '63
The Brainiac '61
The Great Madcap '49

Gilbert Roland (1905-94)

Barbarosa '82
Cabo Blanco '81
The Sacketts '79
Islands in the Stream '77
Running Wild '73
Between God, the Devil & a Winchester '72
The Ruthless Four '70
Go Kill and Come Back '68
Any Gun Can Play '67
The Poppy Is Also a Flower '66
Cheyenne Autumn '64
Samar '62
The Big Circus '59
Three Violent People '57
Around the World in 80 Days '56
The Racers '55
Treasure of Pancho Villa '55
Underwater! '55
The French Line '54
Beneath the 12-Mile Reef '53
Thunder Bay '53
The Bad and the Beautiful '52
Miracle of Our Lady of Fatima '52
Bullfighter & the Lady '50
Crisis '50
The Furies '50
The Torch '50
Malaya '49
The Dude Goes West '48
Riding the California Trail '47
South of Monterey '47
Captain Kidd '45
The Sea Hawk '40
Thunder Pass '37
Thunder Trail '37
She Done Him Wrong '33
The Plastic Age '25

Gylian Roland (1941-)

Deadly Sunday '82
Barn of the Naked Dead '73

Tutta Rolf (1907-94)

Dollar '38
Swedenhielms '35

Guy Rolfe (1911-2003)

Retro Puppet Master '99
Puppet Master 5: The Final Chapter '94
Puppet Master 4 '93
The Dark Angel '91
Puppet Master 3: Toulon's Revenge '90
Dolls '87
And Now the Screaming Starts '73
The Alphabet Murders '65
Mr. Sardonicus '61
The Stranglers of Bombay '60
Young Bess '53
Home to Danger '51
The Spider and the Fly '49

Kirsten Rolffes (1928-2000)

The Kingdom 2 '97
The Kingdom '95
Sofie '92

Esther Rolle (1920-98)

Down in the Delta '98
My Fellow Americans '96
Rosewood '96
How to Make an American Quilt '95
Scarlett '94
To Dance with the White Dog '93
House of Cards '92
The Kid Who Loved Christmas '90
Age Old Friends '89
Driving Miss Daisy '89
The Mighty Quinn '89
A Raisin in the Sun '89
P.K. and the Kid '85
I Know Why the Caged Bird Sings '79
The Summer of My German Soldier '78

Henry Rollins (1961-)

The Devil's Tomb '09
Suck '09
Wrong Turn 2: Dead End '07
Feast '06
Lies & Alibis '06
Bad Boys 2 '03
The New Guy '02
Time Lapse '01
Morgan's Ferry '99
Jack Frost '98
Lost Highway '96
Heat '95
Johnny Mnemonic '95
The Chase '93

Howard E. Rollins, Jr. (1950-96)

Drunks '96
For Us, the Living '88
The House of Dies Drear '88
Johnnie Gibson F.B.I. '87
The Children of Times Square '86
A Soldier's Story '84
The Member of the Wedding '83
Ragtime '81
King '78

Rose Rollins (1978-)

13 Moons '02
Undisputed '02

Mark Rolston (1956-)

Saw 6 '09
Backwoods '08
Protecting the King '07
The Departed '06
Scorcher '02
Wicked Ways '99
From the Earth to the Moon '98
Letters from a Killer '98
Rush Hour '98
George Wallace '97
Hard Rain '97
Daylight '96
Eraser '96
Humanoids from the Deep '96
Best of the Best 3: No Turning Back '95
Scanner Cop '94
The Shawshank Redemption '94

Body of Evidence '92
The Comrades of Summer '92
Lethal Weapon 2 '89
Prancer '89
A Sinful Life '89
Survival Quest '89
Weeds '87
Aliens '86

Yvonne Romain (1938-)
The Last of Sheila '73
Double Trouble '67
Devil Doll '64
The Curse of the Werewolf '61
The Frightened City '61

Candice Roman
The Big Bird Cage '72
Unholy Rollers '72

Freddie Roman (1937-)
Finding North '97
Sweet Lorraine '87

Leticia Roman (1939-)
Fanny Hill: Memoirs of a Woman of Pleasure '64
The Girl Who Knew Too Much '63
Gold of the Seven Saints '61
G.I. Blues '60

Ruth Roman (1924-99)
Echoes '83
The Sacketts '79
Day of the Animals '77
Impulse '74
The Killing Kind '73
The Baby '72
Love Has Many Faces '65
Great Day in the Morning '56
Far Country '55
Blowing Wild '54
Invitation '51
Strangers on a Train '51
Three Secrets '50
Barricade '49
Beyond the Forest '49
Champion '49
The Window '49
Good Sam '48
Since You Went Away '44

Susan (Suzan) Roman (1957-)
Rock & Rule '83 (V)
Rabid '77
Weekend with the Babysitter '70

Viviane Romance (1909-91)
Any Number Can Win '63
Panique '47
Princess Tam Tam '35

Beatrice Romand (1952-)
Autumn Tale '98
Four Adventures of Reinette and Mirabelle '89
Summer '86
House of the Yellow Carpet '84
Le Beau Mariage '82
Claire's Knee '71

Carla Romanelli
The Lonely Lady '83
Steppenwolf '74
Fighting Fists of Shanghai Joe '65

Andy Romano (1936-)
Eraser '96
Fast Money '96
Ghosts of Mississippi '96
Listen '96
Two Bits '96
Chameleon '95
Under Siege 2: Dark Territory '95
Drop Zone '94
Tryst '94
Afterburn '92
Unlawful Entry '92
Pump Up the Volume '90
Over the Edge '79

Get Christie Love! '74

Christy Carlson Romano
The Cutting Edge 3: Chasing the Dream '08
The Cutting Edge: Going for the Gold '05
Looking for an Echo '99

Lou Romano (1972-)
Toy Story 3 '10 (V)
Ratatouille '07 (V)

Ray Romano (1957-)
Ice Age: Dawn of the Dinosaurs '09 (V)
The Last Word '08
Grilled '06
Ice Age: The Meltdown '06 (V)
Eulogy '04
Welcome to Mooseport '04
Ice Age '02 (V)

Renato Romano
Frankenstein '80 '79
The Bird with the Crystal Plumage '70
Dorian Gray '70

Rino Romano (1969-)
Rocky Marciano '99
The Club '94

Stephanie Romanov
Thirteen Days '00
Sunset Strip '99

Anna Romantowska (1950-)
The Interrogation '82
A Woman and a Woman '80

Richard Romanus (1943-)
Cops and Robbersons '94
Point of No Return '93
To Protect and Serve '92
Oscar '91
Hollywood Heartbreak '89
The Couch Trip '87
Murphy's Law '86
Protocol '84
Strangers Kiss '83
Heavy Metal '81 (V)
Sitting Ducks '80
Wizards '77 (V)
Night Terror '76
Mean Streets '73

Robert Romanus (1956-)
Route 30 '08
The Resurrected '91
Pulse '88
Bad Medicine '85
Fast Times at Ridgemont High '82

Lina Romay (1922-)
Love Laughs at Andy Hardy '46
Adventure '45

Lina Romay (1954-)
Tender Flesh '97
Revenge in the House of Usher '82
Sex Is Crazy '79
Ilsa, the Wicked Warden '78
Jack the Ripper '76
Female Vampire '73
The Perverse Countess '73
Rites of Frankenstein '72

Cindy Rome
Knock Outs '92
Swift Justice '88

Sydne Rome (1947-)
The Puma Man '80
Just a Gigolo '79
Twist '76
That Lucky Touch '75
Wanted: Babysitter '75
Diary of Forbidden Dreams '73
Order to Kill '73
Sundance and the Kid '69

Rachel Romen
Ransom Money '70

The Girl from Tobacco Row '66

Cesar Romero (1907-94)
Mortuary Academy '91
Simple Justice '89
Judgment Day '88
Lust in the Dust '85
Mission to Glory '80
The Big Push '75
The Strongest Man in the World '75
The Spectre of Edgar Allen Poe '73
Now You See Him, Now You Don't '72
The Proud and the Damned '72
The Computer Wore Tennis Shoes '69
Crooks & Coronets '69
Gun Crazy '69
Latitude Zero '69
Hot Millions '68
Madigan's Millions '67
Batman '66
Marriage on the Rocks '65
The Castilian '63
Donovan's Reef '63
Ocean's 11 '60
Around the World in 80 Days '56
Americano '55
The Racers '55
The Shadow Man '53
Vera Cruz '53
FBI Girl '52
Jungle '52
Scotland Yard Inspector '52
Happy Go Lovely '51
The Lost Continent '51
The Beautiful Blonde from Bashful Bend '49
Julia Misbehaves '48
Captain from Castile '47
Wintertime '43
Orchestra Wives '42
Springtime in the Rockies '42
Tales of Manhattan '42
Dance Hall '41
The Great American Broadcast '41
Week-End in Havana '41
Lucky Cisco Kid '40
Charlie Chan at Treasure Island '39
The Little Princess '39
Happy Landing '38
My Lucky Star '38
Wee Willie Winkie '37
The Devil Is a Woman '35
The Good Fairy '35
Show Them No Mercy '35
The Thin Man '34

George A. Romero (1940-)
Dawn of the Dead '78
Martin '77
Night of the Living Dead '68

Joanelle Romero
Miracle in the Wilderness '91
Powwow Highway '89
Lost Legacy: A Girl Called Hatter Fox '77

Ned Romero (1925-)
The Lost Child '00
The Magnificent Seven '98
Children of the Corn 2: The Final Sacrifice '92
House 4: Home Deadly Home '91
The Last of the Mohicans '85
The Deerslayer '78
I Will Fight No More Forever '75

Rebecca Romijn (1972-)
Lake City '08
Lies & Alibis '06
X-Men: The Last Stand '06
Godsend '04
The Punisher '04

X2: X-Men United '03
Femme Fatale '02
Rollerball '02
Simone '02
X-Men '00
Austin Powers 2: The Spy Who Shagged Me '99

Tiny Ron
Alien Nation: The Enemy Within '96
Alien Nation: Body and Soul '95
The Rocketeer '91

Paul Ronan (1965-)
Speed Dating '07
Bloom '03
Durango '99
The Devil's Own '96

Saoirse Ronan (1994-)
The Lovely Bones '09
City of Ember '08
Atonement '07
The Christmas Miracle of Jonathan Toomey '07
Death Defying Acts '07
I Could Never Be Your Woman '06

Maurice Ronet (1927-83)
Beau Pere '81
Sphinx '81
Sidney Sheldon's Bloodline '79
Don Juan (Or If Don Juan Were a Woman) '73
The Deadly Trap '71
Swimming Pool '70
La Femme Infidele '69
La Piscine '69
How Sweet It Is! '68
The Women '68
Scandal Man '67
L'Odeur des Fauves '66
The Lost Command '66
The Fire Within '64
The Victors '63
Time Out for Love '61
Purple Noon '60
Carve Her Name with Pride '58
Frantic '58
Without Warning '52
Rendez-vous de Juillet '49

Fabrizio Rongione (1973-)
Lorna's Silence '08
The Child '05
Rosetta '99

Linda Ronstadt (1946-)
Chuck Berry: Hail! Hail! Rock 'n' Roll '87
The Pirates of Penzance '83
FM '78

Michael Roof
The Dukes of Hazzard '05
XXX: State of the Union '05
XXX '02
Black Hawk Down '01

Michael Rooker (1956-)
The Marine 2 '09
Meteor '09
Super Capers '09
Jumper '08
Whisper '07
Full Count '06
Slither '06
Chasing Ghosts '05
The Box '03
Undisputed '02
Replicant '01
Here on Earth '00
Newsbreak '00
The 6th Day '00
Table One '00
The Bone Collector '99
Rogue Force '99
Wicked Ways '99
Bram Stoker's Shadowbuilder '98
Brown's Requiem '98
The Replacement Killers '98
Deceiver '97
Back to Back '96

Bastard out of Carolina '96
Keys to Tulsa '96
Rosewood '96
The Trigger Effect '96
Mallrats '95
The Hard Truth '94
Cliffhanger '93
Tombstone '93
Afterburn '92
The Dark Half '91
JFK '91
Days of Thunder '90
Henry: Portrait of a Serial Killer '90
Music Box '89
Sea of Love '89
Above the Law '88
Eight Men Out '88
Mississippi Burning '88
Light of Day '87

Mickey Rooney (1920-)
Night at the Museum '06
The Last Confederate: The Story of Robert Adams '05
Babe: Pig in the City '98
Boys Will Be Boys '97
The Road Home '95
The Gambler Returns: The Luck of the Draw '93
The Magic Voyage '93 (V)
Revenge of the Red Baron '93
The Legend of Wolf Mountain '92
Little Nemo: Adventures in Slumberland '92 (V)
Maximum Force '92
Sweet Justice '92
My Heroes Have Always Been Cowboys '91
Silent Night, Deadly Night 5: The Toymaker '91
Home for Christmas '90
Erik the Viking '89
Lightning: The White Stallion '86
Ace of Hearts '85
It Came Upon a Midnight Clear '84
Bill: On His Own '83
The Odyssey of the Pacific '82
Bill '81
The Fox and the Hound '81 (V)
Leave 'Em Laughing '81
Senior Trip '81
The Black Stallion '79
The Dark Side of Love '79
Magic of Lassie '78
The Domino Principle '77
Pete's Dragon '77
Find the Lady '76
Rachel's Man '75
Thunder County '74
Women's Prison Escape '74
Pulp '72
Evil Roy Slade '71
Journey Back to Oz '71 (V)
Manipulator '71
The Comic '69
How to Stuff a Wild Bikini '65
The Secret Invasion '64
It's a Mad, Mad, Mad, Mad World '63
Requiem for a Heavyweight '62
Breakfast at Tiffany's '61
The King of the Roaring '20s: The Story of Arnold Rothstein '61
Platinum High School '60
Operation Mad Ball '57
Francis in the Haunted House '56
The Bridges at Toko-Ri '55
The Atomic Kid '54
Off Limits '53
My Outlaw Brother '51
Quicksand '50
The Big Wheel '49
Summer Holiday '48
Words and Music '48
Killer McCoy '47
Love Laughs at Andy Hardy '46
National Velvet '44

Girl Crazy '43
The Human Comedy '43
Thousands Cheer '43
Andy Hardy's Double Life '42
Andy Hardy's Private Secretary '41
Babes on Broadway '41
Life Begins for Andy Hardy '41
Men of Boys Town '41
Andy Hardy Meets Debutante '40
Strike Up the Band '40
Young Tom Edison '40
The Adventures of Huckleberry Finn '39
Andy Hardy Gets Spring Fever '39
Babes in Arms '39
Mickey the Great '39
Boys Town '38
Love Finds Andy Hardy '38
Captains Courageous '37
Hoosier Schoolboy '37
Thoroughbreds Don't Cry '37
The Devil Is a Sissy '36
Healer '36
Little Lord Fauntleroy '36
Ah, Wilderness! '35
A Midsummer Night's Dream '35
Riff Raff '35
Hide-Out '34
Manhattan Melodrama '34
My Pal, the King '32

Tim Rooney (1947-)
Storyville '74
Village of the Giants '65

Jemima Rooper (1981-)
Lost in Austen '08
The Black Dahlia '06
Kinky Boots '06
A Sound of Thunder '05
Snapshots '02
The Railway Children '00

Camilla Overbye Roos (1969-)
The Guilty '99
Facade '98
On the Border '98
Hotel Room '93

Buddy Roosevelt (1898-1973)
Tribute to a Bad Man '56
Boss Cowboy '35
Powdersmoke Range '35
Range Riders '35
Circle Canyon '33
Lightning Range '33
Westward Bound '30

Amanda Root (1963-)
Daniel Deronda '02
Anna Karenina '00
Deep in the Heart (of Texas) '98
Jane Eyre '96
Breaking the Code '95
Persuasion '95
Catherine Cookson's The Man Who Cried '93
This Lightning Always Strikes Twice '85

Bonnie Root (1975-)
Rails & Ties '07
Don't Tell '05
In the Weeds '00
Coming Soon '99

Stephen (Steve) Root (1951-)
Bob Funk '09
The Men Who Stare at Goats '09
The Soloist '09
Leatherheads '08
Mad Money '08
Over Her Dead Body '08
Ice Age: The Meltdown '06 (V)
Idiocracy '06
Just Friends '05
Anchorman: The Legend of Ron Burgundy '04

Dodgeball: A True Underdog Story *'04*
Jersey Girl *'04*
The Ladykillers *'04*
Raising Genius *'04*
Surviving Christmas *'04*
Finding Nemo *'03 (V)*
The Country Bears *'02 (V)*
Ice Age *'02 (V)*
O Brother Where Art Thou? *'00*
Bicentennial Man *'99*
From the Earth to the Moon *'98*
Krippendorf's Tribe *'98*
Office Space *'98*
Pandora's Clock *'96*
The Road to Galveston *'96*
Night of the Scarecrow *'95*
Bye Bye, Love *'94*
Dave *'93*
Extreme Justice *'93*
Bed & Breakfast *'92*
Buffy the Vampire Slayer *'92*
Till Murder Do Us Part *'92*
Guilty by Suspicion *'91*
RoboCop 3 *'91*
Stephen King's Golden Years *'91*
V.I. Warshawski *'91*
Ghost *'90*
Black Rain *'89*
Crocodile Dundee 2 *'88*
Monkey Shines *'88*

Henry Roquemore (1886-1943)
Gunsmoke Trail *'38*
Inside Information *'34*
Apache Kid's Escape *'30*

Noel Roquevert (1892-1973)
Une Parisienne *'58*
Nana *'55*
Fanfan la Tulipe *'51*
Antoine et Antoinette *'47*
Le Corbeau *'43*

Hayden Rorke (1910-87)
The Night Walker *'64*
Spencer's Mountain *'63*
Above and Beyond *'53*
Project Moon Base *'53*
South Sea Woman *'53*
Double Crossbones *'51*
Francis Goes to the Races *'51*

Tom Rosales (1948-)
John Carpenter's Vampires *'97*
Bail Out *'90*

Bert Rosario
A Million to Juan *'94*
Cold Justice *'89*

Tony Rosato (1954-)
Rent-A-Kid *'95*
The Good Fight *'92*
Switching Channels *'88*
Busted Up *'86*
City of Shadows *'86*
Hog Wild *'80*

Francoise Rosay (1891-1974)
The Pedestrian *'73*
Me and the Colonel *'58*
Seven Deadly Sins *'53*
The Red Inn *'51*
September Affair *'50*
Johnny Frenchman *'46*
Bizarre Bizarre *'39*
Carnival in Flanders *'35*

Alan Roscoe
Cheyenne Kid *'33*
Dynamite Ranch *'32*

Anika Noni Rose (1972-)
The Princess and the Frog *'09 (V)*
Just Add Water *'07*
The Starter Wife *'07*
Dreamgirls *'06*
From Justin to Kelly *'03*

Gabrielle Rose (1954-)
Grace *'09*
Lost Boys: The Tribe *'08*
On the Other Hand, Death *'08*
Beneath *'07*
The Five Senses *'99*
The Sweet Hereafter *'96*
Timecop *'94*
Devlin *'92*
The Adjuster *'91*
Speaking Parts *'89*
Family Viewing *'87*

George Rose (1920-88)
Pound Puppies and the Legend of Big Paw *'88 (V)*
You Can't Take It with You *'84*
The Pirates of Penzance *'83*
The Hideaways *'73*
A New Leaf *'71*
The Pink Jungle *'68*
The Flesh and the Fiends *'60*
Jack the Ripper *'60*
The Devil's Disciple *'59*
A Night to Remember *'58*

Jamie Rose (1960-)
Chopper Chicks in Zombietown *'91*
To Die Standing *'91*
Playroom *'90*
Rebel Love *'85*
Heartbreakers *'84*
Tightrope *'84*
In Love with an Older Woman *'82*
Twirl *'81*

Laurie Rose (1948-)
Blood Voyage *'77*
Working Girls *'75*
The Abductors *'72*
Hot Box *'72*
Woman Hunt *'72*

Nectar Rose
Roman *'06*
The Hazing *'04*

Robin Pearson Rose
Lucy and Desi: Before the Laughter *'91*
Last Resort *'86*

Roger Rose
Comic Book: The Movie *'04*
Ski Patrol *'89*

Sherrie Rose (1966-)
Me & Will *'99*
Devil in the Flesh *'98*
The Nurse *'97*
Black Scorpion 2: Ground Zero *'96*
New Crime City: Los Angeles 2020 *'94*
Double Threat *'92*
Maximum Force *'92*
Martial Law 2: Undercover *'91*

Rose Marie (1925-)
Shriek If You Know What I Did Last Friday the 13th *'00*
Ghetto Blaster *'89*
Witchboard *'87*
Cheaper to Keep Her *'80*
Memory of Us *'74*
Dead Heat on a Merry-Go-Round *'66*

Roseanne (1952-)
Home on the Range *'04 (V)*
Blue in the Face *'95*
Even Cowgirls Get the Blues *'94*
The Woman Who Loved Elvis *'93*
Backfield in Motion *'91*
Freddy's Dead: The Final Nightmare *'91*
Look Who's Talking, Too *'90 (V)*
She-Devil *'89*

John Roselius
Con Air *'97*
Devil in a Blue Dress *'95*
JAG *'95*

Ed Roseman (1875-1957)
America *'24*
Sands of Sacrifice *'21*

Sascha Rosemann
In Enemy Hands *'04*

Romy Rosemont
An American Crime *'07*
Shopgirl *'05*
John John in the Sky *'00*

Michael Rosenbaum (1972-)
Kickin' It Old Skool *'07*
Racing Stripes *'05 (V)*
Bringing Down the House *'03*
Poolhall Junkies *'02*
Sorority Boys *'02*
Sweet November *'01*
Urban Legend *'98*

Alan Rosenberg (1950-)
Righteous Kill *'08*
Robots *'05 (V)*
Crash Course *'00*
The Temptations *'98*
Witch Hunt *'94*
In a Stranger's Hand *'92*
Impulse *'90*
After Midnight *'89*
Capone *'89*
Miracle Mile *'89*
White of the Eye *'88*
Happy Birthday, Gemini *'80*
Wanderers *'79*

Michael Rosenberg (1900-72)
Mirele Efros *'38*
The Two Sisters *'37*
His Wife's Lover *'31*

Maxie "Slapsie" Rosenbloom (1903-76)
The Bellboy *'60*
I Married a Monster from Outer Space *'58*
Hollywood or Bust *'56*
Abbott and Costello Meet the Keystone Kops *'54*
Trouble Chasers *'45*
Cooking Up Trouble *'44*
Ghost Crazy *'44*
Here Comes Kelly *'43*
The Boogie Man Will Get You *'42*
To the Shores of Tripoli *'42*
Louisiana Purchase *'41*
Each Dawn I Die *'39*
Amazing Dr. Clitterhouse *'38*
Mr. Moto's Gamble *'38*
Kelly the Second *'36*

George Rosener (1879-1945)
In Old Cheyenne *'41*
Carson City Kid *'40*
Union Depot *'32*

Rick Rosenthal (1949-)
Halloween: Resurrection *'02*
Distant Thunder *'88*

Rosette (1959-)
A Tale of Winter *'92*
Summer *'86*
Pauline at the Beach *'83*

Jose Rosette (1975-)
Machined *'06*
San Franpsycho *'06*
I Got Five on It *'05*

Carolina Rosi (1966-)
Abraham *'94*
The Palermo Connection *'91*

Stelvio Rosi (1938-)
Great Treasure Hunt *'72*
The Hanging Woman *'72*
Hell Commandos *'69*

Annie Ross (1930-)
Short Cuts *'93*
Basket Case 3: The Progeny *'92*
Basket Case 2 *'90*
Pump Up the Volume *'90*
Superman 3 *'83*
Funny Money *'82*
Yanks *'79*
Dressed for Death *'74*

Anthony Ross (1909-55)
Country Girl *'54*
Perfect Strangers *'50*

Betsy King Ross (1921-89)
The Phantom Empire *'35*
Fighting with Kit Carson *'33*

Beverly Ross
Crazed *'82*
S.O.S. Titanic *'79*

Charlotte Ross (1968-)
Ring of Death *'08*
Montana Sky *'07*
Moola *'07*
Kidnapped in Paradise *'98*
Foreign Student *'94*
Love and a .45 *'94*
Savage Land *'94*

Chelcie Ross (1942-)
Drag Me to Hell *'09*
Waking Up in Reno *'02*
Madison *'01*
The Majestic *'01*
Snap Decision *'01*
The Gift *'00*
Charming Billy *'98*
A Simple Plan *'98*
Chain Reaction *'96*
Evil Has a Face *'96*
Amos and Andrew *'93*
Rudy *'93*
Basic Instinct *'92*
Legacy of Lies *'92*
Bill & Ted's Bogus Journey *'91*
The Last Boy Scout *'91*
Rainbow Drive *'90*
Major League *'89*
Above the Law *'88*
Keep My Grave Open *'80*

David Ross (1945-)
Station Jim *'01*
Oliver Twist *'00*
Six Ways to Sunday *'99*
Vanity Fair *'99*
Mary Reilly *'95*
Splitting Heirs *'93*

David W. Ross
Quinceanera *'06*
Love the Hard Way *'01*

Diana Ross (1944-)
Double Platinum *'99*
The Wiz *'78*
Mahogany *'75*
Lady Sings the Blues *'72*

Evan Ross (1988-)
According to Greta *'08*
Gardens of the Night *'08*
Life is Hot in Cracktown *'08*
Linewatch *'08*
Life Support *'07*
Pride *'07*
ATL *'06*

Gene Ross (1930-)
Lost Highway *'96*
Halloween 4: The Return of Michael Myers *'88*
Keep My Grave Open *'80*
Encounter with the Unknown *'75*
Poor White Trash 2 *'75*
Don't Open the Door! *'74*
Don't Look in the Basement *'73*

Herbert Ross (1927-2001)
Play It Again, Sam *'72*
Goodbye, Mr. Chips *'69*

Howard (Red) Ross (1934-96)
The New Gladiators *'83*
New York Ripper *'82*
The Legend of the Wolf Woman *'77*
Five Dolls for an August Moon *'70*
Diary of a Rebel *'68*

Hugh Ross
Bronson *'09*
The Assassination of Jesse James by the Coward Robert Ford *'07 (N)*
For Love of the Game *'99*

Katharine Ross (1942-)
Eye of the Dolphin *'06*
Donnie Darko *'01*
A Climate for Killing *'91*
Conagher *'91*
Red Headed Stranger *'87*
The Shadow Riders *'82*
Wrong Is Right *'82*
Murder in Texas *'81*
The Final Countdown *'80*
Rodeo Girl *'80*
The Legacy *'79*
Murder by Natural Causes *'79*
The Betsy *'78*
The Swarm *'78*
Voyage of the Damned *'76*
The Stepford Wives *'75*
Pigs *'73*
Get to Know Your Rabbit *'72*
They Only Kill Their Masters *'72*
Fools *'70*
Butch Cassidy and the Sundance Kid *'69*
Tell Them Willie Boy Is Here *'69*
Hellfighters *'68*
Games *'67*
The Graduate *'67*
The Singing Nun *'66*
Shenandoah *'65*

Kimberly Ross (1959-2006)
Pumpkinhead *'88*
Nightmare at Noon *'87*
The Last Starfighter *'84*

Lee Ross (1971-)
Goal! The Dream Begins *'06*
Secret Society *'00*
Dreaming of Joseph Lees *'99*
Metroland *'97*
Secrets and Lies *'95*
Buddy's Song *'91*

Lonny Ross
The Rocker *'08*
Good Luck Chuck *'07*

Marion Ross (1928-)
Superhero Movie *'08*
The Last Best Sunday *'98*
The Evening Star *'96*
On the Edge: The Survival of Dana *'79*
Pearl *'78*
Grand Theft Auto *'77*
Teacher's Pet *'58*
Forever Female *'53*

Matt Ross (1970-)
Turn the River *'07*
Last Holiday *'06*
Good Night, and Good Luck *'05*
The Aviator *'04*
Stephen King's Rose Red *'02*
Just Visiting *'01*
American Psycho *'99*
Pushing Tin *'99*
Face/Off *'97*
Ed's Next Move *'96*

Merrie Lynn Ross
Class of 1984 *'82*
The Lucifer Complex *'78*
Way He Was *'76*

Michael Ross (1911-93)
Attack of the 50 Foot Woman *'58*
D.O.A. *'49*

Milton Ross (1876-1941)
False Faces *'18*
Narrow Trail *'17*

Monty Ross
She's Gotta Have It *'86*
Joe's Bed-Stuy Barbershop: We Cut Heads *'83*

Ricco Ross (1960-)
Aliens *'86*
The Dirty Dozen: The Next Mission *'85*

Ron Ross
Battle Beyond the Stars *'80*
Joy Ride to Nowhere *'78*

Shavar Ross (1971-)
The House of Dies Drear *'88*
Friday the 13th, Part 5: A New Beginning *'85*

Shirley Ross
Mindkiller *'87*
Night Vision *'87*

Shirley Ross (1913-75)
Rhythm Romance *'39*
The Big Broadcast of 1938 *'38*
Thanks for the Memory *'38*
Blossoms on Broadway *'37*
Waikiki Wedding *'37*
San Francisco *'36*

Stanley Ralph Ross (1936-2000)
Babe: Pig in the City *'98 (V)*
Candy Stripe Nurses *'74*

Ted Ross (1934-2002)
Arthur 2: On the Rocks *'88*
Stealing Home *'88*
Arthur *'81*
The Wiz *'78*

Tracee Ellis Ross (1972-)
Labor Pains *'09*
Daddy's Little Girls *'07*
Life Support *'07*
I-See-You.Com *'06*
Far Harbor *'96*

Yolonda Ross
United States of Leland *'03*
Antwone Fisher *'02*

Gavin Rossdale (1965-)
How to Rob a Bank *'07*
Constantine *'05*
The Game of Their Lives *'05*

Isabella Rossellini (1952-)
Two Lovers *'09*
Infected *'08*
The Architect *'06*
Brand Upon the Brain! *'06 (N)*
Infamous *'06*
Heights *'04*
King of the Corner *'04*
Monte Walsh *'03*
Napoleon *'03*
The Saddest Music in the World *'03*
Empire *'02*
Roger Dodger *'02*
Don Quixote *'00*
The Sky Is Falling *'00*
The Imposters *'98*
Left Luggage *'98*
Merlin *'98*
The Odyssey *'97*
Crime of the Century *'96*
The Funeral *'96*
Big Night *'95*
Immortal Beloved *'94*
Wyatt Earp *'94*
Fallen Angels 1 *'93*
Fearless *'93*
The Innocent *'93*
The Pickle *'93*
Death Becomes Her *'92*
Lies of the Twins *'91*
Ivory Hunters *'90*
Wild at Heart *'90*
Cousins *'89*

Red Riding Hood *'88*
Zelly & Me *'88*
Siesta *'87*
Tough Guys Don't Dance *'87*
Blue Velvet *'86*
White Nights *'85*
A Matter of Time *'76*

Carol Rossen (1937-)
The Fury *'78*
The Stepford Wives *'75*

Kathryn Rossetter
Whatever *'98*
Shakedown *'88*

Leo Rossi (1959-)
The Last Letter *'04*
The Business of Fancydancing *'02*
One Night at McCool's *'01*
Crackerjack 3 *'00*
Analyze This *'98*
Sticks *'98*
True Friends *'98*
In Cold Blood *'96*
Wedding Bell Blues *'96*
Felony *'95*
Mutant Species *'95*
Rave Review *'95*
Beyond Desire *'94*
Fast Getaway 2 *'94*
Relentless 4 *'94*
Casualties of Love: The "Long Island Lolita" Story *'93*
Raw Justice *'93*
Relentless 3 *'93*
We're Talkin' Serious Money *'92*
Where the Day Takes You *'92*
Fast Getaway *'91*
Relentless 2: Dead On *'91*
Maniac Cop 2 *'90*
Relentless *'89*
The Accused *'88*
The Hit List *'88*
River's Edge *'87*
Heart Like a Wheel *'83*

Theo Rossi
Last Resort *'09*
Red Sands *'09*

Eleanora Rossi-Drago (1925-2007)
Dorian Gray *'70*
Camille 2000 *'69*
Uncle Tom's Cabin *'69*

Giacomo "Jack" Rossi-Stuart (1931-)
Reactor *'78*
Zorro *'74*
The Night Evelyn Came Out of the Grave *'71*
Hornet's Nest *'70*
Macabre *'69*
Diary of a Rebel *'68*
Kill, Baby, Kill *'66*
Knives of the Avenger *'65*
Planet on the Prowl *'65*
The Last Man on Earth *'64*
Gunfight at Red Sands *'63*
The Avenger *'62*

Kim Rossi-Stuart (1969-)
Pinocchio *'02*
Beyond the Clouds *'95*

Paul Rossilli (1948-)
Bayou Romance *'86*
The Haunting Passion *'83*

Norman Rossington (1928-99)
Let Him Have It *'91*
The Krays *'90*
Raw Meat *'72*
Man in the Wilderness *'71*
The Charge of the Light Brigade *'68*
Negatives *'68*
A Hard Day's Night *'64*
Lawrence of Arabia *'62*
Saturday Night and Sunday Morning *'60*
Carry On Sergeant *'58*

Ronato Rossini
See Howard (Red) Ross

Leonard Rossiter (1926-84)
Water *'85*
Britannia Hospital *'82*
The Pink Panther Strikes Again *'76*
Luther *'74*
2001: A Space Odyssey *'68*
King Rat *'65*

Angelo Rossitto (1908-91)
The Offspring *'87*
Mad Max: Beyond Thunderdome *'85*
Brain of Blood *'71*
Dracula vs. Frankenstein *'71*
Invasion of the Saucer Men *'57*
Daughter of Horror *'55*
Mesa of Lost Women *'52*
The Corpse Vanishes *'42*

Rick Rossovich (1957-)
Miracle in Lane Two *'00*
Telling You *'98*
Legend of the Lost Tomb *'97*
Truth or Consequences, N.M. *'97*
Black Scorpion *'95*
Cover Me *'95*
Fatally Yours *'95*
New Crime City: Los Angeles 2020 *'94*
The Gambler Returns: The Luck of the Draw *'93*
Tropical Heat *'93*
Secret Ingredient *'92*
Navy SEALS *'90*
Paint It Black *'89*
The Spellbinder *'88*
Let's Get Harry *'87*
Roxanne *'87*
The Morning After *'86*
Top Gun *'86*
Warning Sign *'85*
Streets of Fire *'84*
The Terminator *'84*
The Lords of Discipline *'83*
Losin' It *'82*

Emmy Rossum (1986-)
Dare *'09*
Dragonball: Evolution *'09*
Poseidon *'06*
The Day After Tomorrow *'04*
The Phantom of the Opera *'04*
Mystic River *'03*
An American Rhapsody *'01*
Songcatcher *'99*

Carlo Rota
Saw 5 *'08*
Boondock Saints *'99*
32 Short Films about Glenn Gould *'93*

Andrea Roth (1967-)
The Collector *'09*
The Skeptic *'09*
Bridal Fever *'08*
Chasing Christmas *'05*
Sasquatch *'02*
Wilderness Love *'02*
The Stepdaughter *'00*
Hidden Agenda *'99*
Executive Power *'98*
Crossworlds *'96*
Divided by Hate *'96*
A Change of Place *'94*
The Club *'94*
The Good Fight *'92*
Seedpeople *'92*

Cecilia (Celia) Roth (1958-)
Lucia, Lucia *'03*
All About My Mother *'99*
Second Skin *'99*
Martin (Hache) *'97*
A Place in the World *'92*
The Stranger *'87*
Labyrinth of Passion *'82*

Eli Roth (1972-)
Inglourious Basterds *'09*
Death Proof *'07*

Cabin Fever *'03*

Gene Roth (1903-76)
Attack of the Giant Leeches *'59*
Earth vs. the Spider *'58*
She Demons *'58*
Pirates of the High Seas *'50*
Homesteaders of Paradise Valley *'47*

Joanna Roth (1965-)
Stalin *'92*
The Real Charlotte *'91*
Rosencrantz & Guildenstern Are Dead *'90*

Lillian Roth (1910-80)
Alice Sweet Alice *'76*
Ladies They Talk About *'33*
Animal Crackers *'30*
Madam Satan *'30*
The Love Parade *'29*

Louis Roth (1947-94)
Ninja Connection *'90*
Clash of the Ninja *'86*

Martha Roth
The Man and the Monster *'65*
Massacre *'56*

Nick Roth
Berkeley *'05*
Brave New Girl *'04*

Tim Roth (1961-)
The Incredible Hulk *'08*
Funny Games *'07*
Virgin Territory *'07*
Youth Without Youth *'07*
Even Money *'06*
Don't Come Knocking *'05*
The Beautiful Country *'04*
Silver City *'04*
To Kill a King *'03*
Dark Water *'02*
Killing Emmett Young *'02*
Invincible *'01*
The Musketeer *'01*
Planet of the Apes *'01*
Lucky Numbers *'00*
Vatel *'00*
The Million Dollar Hotel *'99*
The Legend of 1900 *'98*
Deceiver *'97*
Everyone Says I Love You *'96*
Gridlock'd *'96*
Hoodlum *'96*
No Way Home *'96*
Four Rooms *'95*
Rob Roy *'95*
Captives *'94*
Little Odessa *'94*
Pulp Fiction *'94*
Bodies, Rest & Motion *'93*
Heart of Darkness *'93*
Jumpin' at the Boneyard *'92*
The Perfect Husband *'92*
Reservoir Dogs *'92*
The Cook, the Thief, His Wife & Her Lover *'90*
Rosencrantz & Guildenstern Are Dead *'90*
Vincent & Theo *'90*
To Kill a Priest *'89*
A World Apart *'88*
Agatha Christie's Murder with Mirrors *'85*
The Hit *'85*
Return to Waterloo *'85*
Meantime *'81*

Adam Rothenberg
Mad Money *'08*
Tennessee *'08*

Teryl Rothery (1965-)
Whisper *'07*
White Noise 2: The Light *'07*
The Sandlot 2 *'05*
The Twelve Days of Christmas Eve *'04*
Threshold *'03*
Video Voyeur: The Susan Wilson Story *'02*
Mr. Rice's Secret *'00*

John Rothman (1949-)
Brooklyn Lobster *'05*
Welcome to Mooseport *'04*

Say It Isn't So *'01*
The Siege *'98*
Hostile Waters *'97*
Copycat *'95*
Gettysburg *'93*
The Boost *'88*

Cynthia Rothrock (1957-)
Sci-Fighter *'04*
Night Vision *'97*
Sworn to Justice *'97*
Fast Getaway 2 *'94*
Guardian Angel *'94*
Undefeatable *'94*
Angel of Fury *'93*
Lady Dragon 2 *'93*
Rage and Honor 2: Hostile Takeover *'93*
Honor and Glory *'92*
Lady Dragon *'92*
Rage and Honor *'92*
24 Hours to Midnight *'92*
Fast Getaway *'91*
Martial Law 2: Undercover *'91*
Tiger Claws *'91*
Martial Law *'90*
China O'Brien 2 *'89*
No Retreat, No Surrender 2 *'89*
China O'Brien *'88*
The Millionaire's Express *'86*

Paolo Rotondo
Stickmen *'01*
The Ugly *'96*

Yella Rottlaender
Alice in the Cities *'74*
The Scarlet Letter *'73*

Brigitte Rouan (1965-)
Love Songs *'07*
Time of the Wolf *'03*
After Sex *'97*
Olivier, Olivier *'92*
Overseas: Three Women with Man Trouble *'90*

Alida Rouffe (1874-1949)
Cesar *'36*
Fanny *'32*

Richard Roundtree (1942-)
Final Approach *'08*
Speed Racer *'08*
Brick *'06*
Boat Trip *'03*
Joe and Max *'02*
Corky Romano *'01*
Antitrust *'00*
Shaft *'00*
Having Our Say: The Delany Sisters' First 100 Years *'99*
Any Place But Home *'97*
George of the Jungle *'97*
Steel *'97*
Original Gangstas *'96*
Once Upon a Time ... When We Were Colored *'95*
Seven *'95*
Theodore Rex *'95*
Ballistic *'94*
Gypsy Angels *'94*
Amityville: A New Generation *'93*
Body of Influence *'93*
Bonanza: The Return *'93*
Mind Twister *'93*
Sins of the Night *'93*
Bloodfist 3: Forced to Fight *'92*
Christmas in Connecticut *'92*
Deadly Rivals *'92*
Getting Even *'92*
A Time to Die *'91*
Bad Jim *'89*
The Banker *'89*
Crack House *'89*
Miami Cops *'89*
Night Visitor *'89*
Angel 3: The Final Chapter *'88*
Maniac Cop *'88*
Party Line *'88*
Jocks *'87*

Opposing Force *'87*
Game for Vultures *'86*
A.D. *'85*
The Baron and the Kid *'84*
City Heat *'84*
Killpoint *'84*
Big Score *'83*
Young Warriors *'83*
One Down, Two to Go! *'82*
Q (The Winged Serpent) *'82*
Day of the Assassin *'81*
An Eye for an Eye *'81*
Escape to Athena *'79*
The Last Contract *'77*
Portrait of a Hitman *'77*
Man Friday *'75*
Earthquake *'74*
Shaft in Africa *'73*
Diamonds *'72*
Embassy *'72*
Firehouse *'72*
Shaft's Big Score *'72*
Shaft *'71*

Robert Rounseville (1914-74)
Carousel *'56*
The Tales of Hoffmann *'51*

Mickey Rourke (1955-)
The Expendables *'10*
Iron Man 2 *'10*
The Informers *'09*
Killshot *'09*
The Wrestler *'08*
Alex Rider: Operation Stormbreaker *'06*
Domino *'05*
Sin City *'05*
Man on Fire *'04*
Once Upon a Time in Mexico *'03*
Spun *'02*
Picture Claire *'01*
They Crawl *'01*
Animal Factory *'00*
Get Carter *'00*
The Pledge *'00*
Out in Fifty *'99*
Point Blank *'98*
Thursday *'98*
Buffalo 66 *'97*
Double Team *'97*
Exit in Red *'97*
John Grisham's The Rainmaker *'97*
Another 9 1/2 Weeks *'96*
Bullet *'94*
Fall Time *'94*
The Last Ride *'94*
Francesco *'93*
The Last Outlaw *'93*
White Sands *'92*
Harley Davidson and the Marlboro Man *'91*
Desperate Hours *'90*
Wild Orchid *'90*
Johnny Handsome *'89*
Homeboy *'88*
Angel Heart *'87*
Barfly *'87*
Prayer for the Dying *'87*
9 1/2 Weeks *'86*
Year of the Dragon *'85*
The Pope of Greenwich Village *'84*
Rumble Fish *'83*
Diner *'82*
Body Heat *'81*
Eureka! *'81*
Heaven's Gate *'81*
City in Fear *'80*
Fade to Black *'80*
Rape and Marriage: The Rideout Case *'80*
1941 *'79*

Graham Rouse (1934-)
The Odd Angry Shot *'79*
Weekend of Shadows *'77*
Ride a Wild Pony *'75*

Anne Roussel (1960-)
Wolves in the Snow *'02*
The Music Teacher *'88*
Trade Secrets *'86*

Myriem Roussel (1962-)
Sacrilege *'86*
Hail Mary *'85*
First Name: Carmen *'83*

Nathalie Roussel
My Father's Glory *'91*
My Mother's Castle *'91*

Jean-Paul Roussillon (1931-)
A Christmas Tale *'08*
The Girl from Paris *'02*
Same Old Song *'97*
Baxter *'89*

Brandon Routh (1979-)
Scott Pilgrim vs. the World *'10*
Stuntmen *'09*
Table for Three *'09*
Fling *'08*
Life is Hot in Cracktown *'08*
Zack and Miri Make a Porno *'08*
Superman Returns *'06*

Alison Routledge
The Bridge to Nowhere *'86*
The Quiet Earth *'85*

Jordan Routledge
Gabriel & Me *'01*
East Is East *'99*

Jean-Paul Rouve
La Vie en Rose *'07*
A Very Long Engagement *'04*

Catherine Rouvel (1939-)
Va Savoir *'01*
Sand and Blood *'87*
Black and White in Color *'76*
Les Assassins de L'Ordre *'71*
Borsalino *'70*
La Rupture *'70*
Picnic on the Grass *'59*

Jean-Louis Roux (1923-)
The Courage to Love *'00*
The Third Miracle *'99*

Jack Rovello (1994-)
Lonesome Jim *'06*
The Hours *'02*

Dominic Rowan (1971-)
David *'97*
Emma *'97*

Kelly Rowan (1967-)
Jack and Jill vs. the World *'08*
Greenmail *'01*
Proximity *'00*
The Truth About Jane *'00*
Three to Tango *'99*
Loving Evangeline *'98*
187 *'97*
Black Fox: Good Men and Bad *'94*
Candyman 2: Farewell to the Flesh *'94*
Adrift *'93*
The Gate *'87*

Brad Rowe (1970-)
Shelter *'07*
The Insatiable *'06*
Though None Go With Me *'06*
Love for Rent *'05*
Shut Up and Kiss Me *'05*
Fish Without a Bicycle *'03*
Lucky Seven *'03*
The '70s *'00*
Body Shots *'99*
Christina's House *'99*
Billy's Hollywood Screen Kiss *'98*
Stonebrook *'98*

Douglas Rowe
Writer's Block *'91*
Appointment with Fear *'85*

Kimberly Rowe
Knocking on Death's Door *'99*

Rumble in the Streets '96

Leanne Rowe

Oliver Twist '05
Warrior Queen '03

Misty Rowe (1950-)

Goodnight, Sweet Marilyn '89
Meatballs 2 '84
Double Exposure '82
The Man with Bogart's Face '80
A Pleasure Doing Business '79
Goodbye, Norma Jean '75
Hitchhikers '72

Nevan Rowe

Nutcase '83
Sleeping Dogs '77

Nicholas (Nick) Rowe (1966-)

Shanghai '09
Beau Brummell: This Charming Man '06
A Harlot's Progress '06
Shackleton '02
Longitude '00
Sharpe's Enemy '94
The Lawrenceville Stories '88
Young Sherlock Holmes '85

Rosie Rowell

Gabriel & Me '01
Kiss and Tell '96

Victoria Rowell (1960-)

Home of the Brave '06
Black Listed '03
Motives '03
Anne Rice's The Feast of All Saints '01
Barb Wire '96
Dumb & Dumber '94
The Distinguished Gentleman '92

Henry Rowland (1914-84)

Beneath the Valley of the Ultra-Vixens '79
Supervixens '75
36 Hours '64

Oscar Rowland

Bats '99
Promised Land '88

Paige Rowland (1967-)

Doomsdayer '99
Riot '96

Rodney Rowland (1964-)

I Know Who Killed Me '07
Dancing at the Blue Iguana '00
The 6th Day '00
Marshal Law '96

Steve Rowland (1932-)

Naked Youth '59
Gun Glory '57

David Rowlands

Minnie and Moskowitz '71
Husbands '70

Gena Rowlands (1934-)

Broken English '07
Paris, je t'aime '06
The Skeleton Key '05
The Notebook '04
Taking Lives '04
The Incredible Mrs. Ritchie '03
Charms for the Easy Life '02
Hysterical Blindness '02
Wild Iris '01
The Weekend '00
Grace & Glorie '98
Hope Floats '98
The Mighty '98
Paulie '98
Playing by Heart '98
She's So Lovely '97
Unhook the Stars '96
The Neon Bible '95
Something to Talk About '95
Parallel Lives '94
Ted & Venus '93
Crazy in Love '92
Night on Earth '91
Once Around '91
Montana '90
Another Woman '88
The Betty Ford Story '87
Light of Day '87
An Early Frost '85
Love Streams '84
Rapunzel '82
The Tempest '82
Gloria '80
Strangers: The Story of a Mother and Daughter '79
Brink's Job '78
A Question of Love '78
Opening Night '77
Two Minute Warning '76
A Woman under the Influence '74
Minnie and Moskowitz '71
Faces '68
Tony Rome '67
A Child Is Waiting '63
Lonely Are the Brave '62

Polly Rowles (1914-2001)

Power '86
Springtime in the Rockies '37

Richard Roxburgh (1962-)

Murderous Intent '06
The Silence '06
Stealth '05
Van Helsing '04
The League of Extraordinary Gentlemen '03
The Hound of the Baskervilles '02
The Road from Coorain '02
Blonde '01
Moulin Rouge '01
Mission: Impossible 2 '00
The Last September '99
Passion '99
In the Winter Dark '98
Doing Time for Patsy Cline '97
Oscar and Lucinda '97
The Wedding Party '97
Billy's Holiday '95
Children of the Revolution '95
Talk '94

Deep Roy (1957-)

Star Trek '09
Charlie and the Chocolate Factory '05
Tim Burton's Corpse Bride '05 (V)
Alien from L.A. '87
Starship '87

Lise Roy

The Courage to Love '00
The Boys of St. Vincent '93

Maxim Roy (1972-)

Infected '08
Picture This! '08
WarGames 2: The Dead Code '08
Rudy: The Rudy Giulani Story '03
A Woman Hunted '03
Federal Protection '02
Hidden Agenda '01
Cause of Death '00
Stalker '98

Allan Royal (1944-)

The Good Witch '08
DC 9/11: Time of Crisis '04
The Pirates of Silicon Valley '99
Men of Steel '77

Lionel Royce (1886-1946)

White Pongo '45
Manhunt in the African Jungles '43
My Favorite Blonde '42
Panama Menace '41
The Road to Zanzibar '41

Roselyn Royce

Retrievers '82
Sizzle Beach U.S.A. '74

Virginia Roye

Pace That Kills '28
The Road to Ruin '28

Selena Royle (1904-83)

Robot Monster '53
The Big Hangover '50
The Damned Don't Cry '50
The Heiress '49
My Dream Is Yours '49
A Date with Judy '48
The Smallest Show on Earth '48
Summer Holiday '48
Cass Timberlane '47
Courage of Lassie '46
The Harvey Girls '46
Mrs. Parkington '44
Thirty Seconds Over Tokyo '44
The Fighting Sullivans '42

William Royle (1887-1940)

Heroes of the Saddle '40
Mr. Wong in Chinatown '39
Mutiny in the Big House '39
The Rains Came '39

Andre Royo

August '08
G '02

Gregory Rozakis (1943-89)

Five Corners '88
Abduction '75

Spela Rozin (1945-)

The Secret Invasion '64
Son of Hercules in the Land of Darkness '63

Christian Rub (1887-1956)

Pinocchio '40 (V)
100 Men and a Girl '37
No Other Woman '33

Alma Rubens (1897-1931)

She Goes to War '29
The Americano '17

Jan Rubes (1920-2009)

The Republic of Love '03
Believe '99
Rescuers: Stories of Courage—Two Couples '98
The White Raven '98
Flood: A River's Rampage '97
Music from Another Room '97
Serving in Silence: The Margarethe Cammermeyer Story '95
The Birds 2: Land's End '94
D2: The Mighty Ducks '94
Mesmer '94
By Way of the Stars '92
Devlin '92
Class Action '91
Deceived '91
The Amityville Curse '90
Descending Angel '90
Blind Fear '89
Courage Mountain '89
The Kiss '88
Blood Relations '87
Dead of Winter '87
Charlie Grant's War '80

Andrew Rubin (1946-)

From the Earth to the Moon '98
Sunnyside '79

Benny Rubin (1899-1986)

The Tender Trap '55
Torch Song '53
The Noose Hangs High '48
The Bashful Bachelor '42
Mr. Wise Guy '42
Sunny '41
Zis Boom Bah '41
Sunny Skies '30
It's a Great Life '29

Jennifer Rubin (1964-)

Amazons and Gladiators '01
Beyond Justice '01
Sanctimony '01
Deal of a Lifetime '99
Last Lives '98
Twists of Terror '98
Kisses in the Dark '97
Loved '97
Plump Fiction '97
Little Witches '96
Screamers '96
The Wasp Woman '96
Saints and Sinners '95
Deceptions 2: Edge of Deception '94
Playmaker '94
Red Scorpion 2 '94
Stranger by Night '94
Bitter Harvest '93
The Crush '93
The Fear Inside '92
A Woman, Her Men and Her Futon '92
Delusion '91
Victim of Beauty '91
Bad Dreams '88
Blueberry Hill '88
Permanent Record '88
A Nightmare on Elm Street 3: Dream Warriors '87

Daphne Rubin-Vega (1969-)

Virgin '03
Flawless '99
Wild Things '98

Saul Rubinek (1949-)

Julia '08
The Trojan Horse '08
A Broken Life '07
Jesse Stone: Sea Change '07
War '07
Jesse Stone: Night Passage '06
Call Me: The Rise and Fall of Heidi Fleiss '04
Coast to Coast '04
White Coats '04
And Starring Pancho Villa as Himself '03
Baadasssss! '03
Hollywood North '03
The Singing Detective '03
Triggermen '02
The Doorbell Rang: A Nero Wolfe Mystery '01
Rush Hour 2 '01
The Contender '00
Family Man '00
The Golden Spiders: A Nero Wolfe Mystery '00
Lakeboat '00
Dick '99
36 Hours to Die '99
Bad Manners '98
Past Perfect '98
Blackjack '97
Color of Justice '97
Pale Saints '97
The Android Affair '95
Hiroshima '95
Nixon '95
Open Season '95
Synapse '95
Getting Even with Dad '94
I Love Trouble '94
And the Band Played On '93
The Quarrel '93
True Romance '93
Undercover Blues '93
Man Trouble '92
Unforgiven '92
The Bonfire of the Vanities '90
Obsessed '88
Outside Chance of Maximillian Glick '88
Wall Street '87
Half a Lifetime '86
Against All Odds '84
Soup for One '82
Young Doctors in Love '82
The Agency '81
Ticket to Heaven '81
Death Ship '80
Highpoint '80

Giulia Rubini (1935-)

Adios, Hombre '68
Stranger in Paso Bravo '68
Journey Beneath the Desert '61

Sergio Rubini (1959-)

The Passion of the Christ '04
The Count of Monte Cristo '99
The Talented Mr. Ripley '99
Nirvana '97
A Pure Formality '94
The Blonde '92
Intervista '87

John Rubinstein (1946-)

Choose Connor '07
Perfect Murder, Perfect Town '00
Mercy '96
Norma Jean and Marilyn '95
Another Stakeout '93
Shadow on the Sun '88
Someone to Watch Over Me '87
Happily Ever After '82
Killjoy '81
She's Dressed to Kill '79
The Car '77
Defiant '70
Getting Straight '70
Zachariah '70
The Trouble with Girls (and How to Get into It) '69

Zelda Rubinstein (1936-2010)

The Wild Card '03
Little Witches '96
Acting on Impulse '93
Teen Witch '89
Anguish '88
Poltergeist 3 '88
Poltergeist 2: The Other Side '86
Sixteen Candles '84
Poltergeist '82
Under the Rainbow '81

Jack Rubio

Valentina's Tango '07
Loser '97

Richard Ruccolo (1972-)

All Over the Guy '01
Deranged '01
Luck of the Draw '00

Alan Ruck (1960-)

Extraordinary Measures '10
I Love You, Beth Cooper '09
Ghost Town '08
InAlienable '08
Kickin' It Old Skool '07
Cheaper by the Dozen '03
Everything Put Together '00
From the Earth to the Moon '98
Twister '96
Speed '94
Star Trek: Generations '94
Young Guns 2 '90
Three Fugitives '89
Three for the Road '87
Ferris Bueller's Day Off '86
Hard Knox '83

Lamman Rucker

Tyler Perry's Meet the Browns '08
Tyler Perry's Why Did I Get Married? '07

Paul Rudd (1969-)

Dinner for Schmucks '10
I Love You, Man '09
Monsters vs. Aliens '09 (V)
Year One '09
Forgetting Sarah Marshall '08
Over Her Dead Body '08
Role Models '08
The Ex '07
Knocked Up '07
Reno 911! Miami '07
The Ten '07
Walk Hard: The Dewey Cox Story '07
Diggers '06
I Could Never Be Your Woman '06
Night at the Museum '06
The Oh in Ohio '06
The Baxter '05
The 40 Year Old Virgin '05
Anchorman: The Legend of Ron Burgundy '04
P.S. '04
The Shape of Things '03
Two Days '03
The Chateau '01
The Great Gatsby '01
Wet Hot American Summer '01
The Cider House Rules '99
The Object of My Affection '98
200 Cigarettes '98
The Locusts '97
Overnight Delivery '96
William Shakespeare's Romeo and Juliet '96
Clueless '95
Halloween 6: The Curse of Michael Myers '95
Runaway Daughters '94
Beulah Land '80
Last Song '80
Johnny We Hardly Knew Ye '77

Michael Rudder

Buying Time '89
Blindside '88

John Ruddock (1897-1981)

Lawrence of Arabia '62
Martin Luther '53
The Fallen Idol '49

Herbert Rudley (1911-2006)

Beloved Infidel '59
The Jayhawkers '59
The Young Lions '58
The Black Sleep '56
Artists and Models '55
The Scar '48
Decoy '46
A Walk in the Sun '46
Rhapsody in Blue '45
The Seventh Cross '44
Abe Lincoln in Illinois '40

Rita Rudner (1955-)

A Weekend in the Country '96
Peter's Friends '92

Lars Rudolph (1966-)

The Princess and the Warrior '00
The Inheritors '98

Maya Rudolph (1972-)

Grown Ups '10
Shrek Forever After '10 (V)
Away We Go '09
Bollywood Hero '09
Shrek the Third '07 (V)
Idiocracy '06
A Prairie Home Companion '06
50 First Dates '04
Duplex '03
Chuck & Buck '00

Joshua Rudoy (1975-)

Flatliners '90
Harry and the Hendersons '87

Reed Rudy

Zapped Again '89
Free Ride '86

Sara Rue (1979-)

Danny Roane: First Time Director '06
The Ring '02
Gypsy 83 '01
A Slipping Down Life '99

Kurt Russell (1951-)
Death Proof *'07*
Poseidon *'06*
Dreamer: Inspired by a True Story *'05*
Jiminy Glick in LaLa Wood *'05*
Sky High *'05*
Miracle *'04*
Dark Blue *'03*
Interstate 60 *'02*
3000 Miles to Graceland *'01*
Vanilla Sky *'01*
Soldier *'98*
Breakdown *'96*
Escape from L.A. *'96*
Executive Decision *'96*
Stargate *'94*
Tombstone *'93*
Captain Ron *'92*
Unlawful Entry *'92*
Backdraft *'91*
Tango and Cash *'89*
Winter People *'89*
Tequila Sunrise *'88*
Overboard *'87*
The Best of Times *'86*
Big Trouble in Little China *'86*
Mean Season *'85*
Swing Shift *'84*
Silkwood *'83*
Amber Waves *'82*
The Thing *'82*
Escape from New York *'81*
The Fox and the Hound *'81 (V)*
Used Cars *'80*
Elvis: The Movie *'79*
The Christmas Coal Mine Miracle *'77*
The Captive: The Longest Drive 2 *'76*
The Longest Drive *'76*
Search for the Gods *'75*
Sniper *'75*
The Strongest Man in the World *'75*
Charley and the Angel *'73*
Superdad *'73*
Now You See Him, Now You Don't *'72*
The Barefoot Executive *'71*
The Computer Wore Tennis Shoes *'69*
The Horse in the Gray Flannel Suit *'68*
The One and Only, Genuine, Original Family Band *'68*
Follow Me, Boys! *'66*
Mosby's Marauders *'66*
Guns of Diablo *'64*
It Happened at the World's Fair *'63*

Lucy Russell (1972-)
Tristan & Isolde *'06*
The Lady and the Duke *'01*
Following *'99*

Monte Russell
Lily in Winter *'94*
Laurel Avenue *'93*

Nipsey Russell (1918-2005)
Car 54, Where Are You? *'94*
Posse *'93*
The Wiz *'78*

Reb Russell (1905-78)
Outlaw Rule *'36*
Border Vengeance *'35*
The Man from Hell *'34*

Robert Russell
Dune *'00*
Bedazzled *'68*
The Conqueror Worm *'68*

Rosalind Russell (1908-76)
Where Angels Go, Trouble Follows *'68*
Oh Dad, Poor Dad (Momma's Hung You in the Closet & I'm Feeling So Sad) *'67*
The Trouble with Angels *'66*
Gypsy *'62*
Auntie Mame *'58*
A Majority of One *'56*
Picnic *'55*
Never Wave at a WAC *'52*
A Woman of Distinction *'50*
Tell It to the Judge *'49*
Velvet Touch *'48*
Sister Kenny *'46*
Roughly Speaking *'45*
She Wouldn't Say Yes *'45*
My Sister Eileen *'42*
They Met in Bombay *'41*
His Girl Friday *'40*
The Women *'39*
The Citadel *'38*
Four's a Crowd *'38*
Night Must Fall *'37*
Craig's Wife *'36*
China Seas *'35*
Forsaking All Others *'35*
Reckless *'35*
Evelyn Prentice *'34*

T.E. Russell
30 Years to Life *'01*
Bellyfruit *'99*

Theresa Russell (1957-)
Dark World *'08*
Spider-Man 3 *'07*
Empire Falls *'05*
The Box *'03*
Love Comes Softly *'03*
Now & Forever *'02*
The Believer *'01*
Earth vs. the Spider *'01*
The House Next Door *'01*
Luckytown *'00*
Running Woman *'98*
Wild Things *'98*
Grave Indiscretions *'96*
The Proposition *'96*
Public Enemies *'96*
Trade Off *'95*
A Young Connecticut Yankee in King Arthur's Court *'95*
Being Human *'94*
The Spy Within *'94*
Thicker Than Water *'93*
A Woman's Guide to Adultery *'93*
Cold Heaven *'92*
Kafka *'91*
Whore *'91*
Impulse *'90*
Physical Evidence *'89*
Aria *'88*
Track 29 *'88*
Black Widow *'87*
Insignificance *'85*
The Razor's Edge *'84*
Eureka! *'81*
Blind Ambition *'79*
Straight Time *'78*
The Last Tycoon *'76*

Tony Russell (1925-)
The Hard Ride *'71*
Wild, Wild Planet *'65*

William Russell (1884-1929)
The Gay Dog *'54*
Anna Christie *'23*

Chelsea Russo (1990-)
An Unexpected Life *'97*
An Unexpected Family *'96*

Deanna Russo
Believers *'07*
Rest Stop *'06*

Gianni Russo (1941-)
Harvard Man *'01*
Lepke *'75*
The Godfather, Part 2 *'74*
The Godfather *'72*

James Russo (1953-)
Break *'09*
Public Enemies *'09*
Dark World *'08*
Stiletto *'08*
Black Ops *'07*
The Pink Conspiracy *'07*
All In *'06*
Broken Trail *'06*
Chill *'06*
The Hit *'06*
Come as You Are *'05*
Confessions of a Pit Fighter *'05*
The Box *'03*
Open Range *'03*
The House Next Door *'01*
Deep Core *'00*
Jimmy Zip *'00*
Detour *'99*
The Ninth Gate *'99*
Paper Bullets *'99*
Sonic Impact *'99*
Voodoo Dawn *'99*
Bitter Sweet *'98*
First Degree *'98*
My Husband's Secret Life *'98*
Laws of Deception *'97*
Love to Kill *'97*
The Postman *'97*
The Real Thing *'97*
Under Oath *'97*
American Strays *'96*
Donnie Brasco *'96*
No Way Home *'96*
Condition Red *'95*
Panther *'95*
The Set Up *'95*
Bad Girls *'94*
The Secretary *'94*
Dangerous Game *'93*
Dario Argento's Trauma *'93*
Cold Heaven *'92*
DaVinci's War *'92*
Illicit Behavior *'91*
Intimate Stranger *'91*
A Kiss Before Dying *'91*
My Own Private Idaho *'91*
We're No Angels *'89*
Blue Iguana *'88*
Freeway *'88*
China Girl *'87*
Extremities *'86*
Beverly Hills Cop *'84*
Once Upon a Time in America *'84*
Fast Times at Ridgemont High *'82*
Vortex *'81*

John A. Russo (1939-)
The Groomsmen *'06*
The Majorettes *'87*
Night of the Living Dead *'68*

Michael Russo
Pure Danger *'96*
Demonic Toys *'90*
Nitti: The Enforcer *'88*

Rene Russo (1954-)
Two for the Money *'05*
Yours, Mine & Ours *'05*
Big Trouble *'02*
Showtime *'02*
The Adventures of Rocky & Bullwinkle *'00*
The Thomas Crown Affair *'99*
Lethal Weapon 4 *'98*
Buddy *'97*
Ransom *'96*
Tin Cup *'96*
Get Shorty *'95*
Outbreak *'94*
In the Line of Fire *'93*
Freejack *'92*
Lethal Weapon 3 *'92*
One Good Cop *'91*
Mr. Destiny *'90*
Major League *'89*

Leon Russom (1941-)
Prison Break: The Final Break *'09*
The Big Lebowski *'97*
A Private Matter *'92*
A Thousand Heroes *'92*
Long Road Home *'91*
Silver Bullet *'85*

Richard Rust (1938-)
Double Revenge *'89*
The Great Gundown *'75*
The Student Nurses *'70*
The Naked Angels *'69*
Underworld USA *'61*
Comanche Station *'60*
Legend of Tom Dooley *'59*

Babe Ruth (1895-1948)
The Pride of the Yankees *'42*
Headin' Home *'20*

Mary Ruth
Gentleman from Dixie *'41*
Riot Squad *'41*

Ann Rutherford (1917-)
They Only Kill Their Masters *'72*
Operation Haylift *'50*
Adventures of Don Juan *'49*
The Secret Life of Walter Mitty *'47*
Whistling in Brooklyn *'43*
Andy Hardy's Double Life *'42*
Orchestra Wives *'42*
Whistling in Dixie *'42*
Andy Hardy's Private Secretary *'41*
Life Begins for Andy Hardy *'41*
Whistling in the Dark *'41*
Andy Hardy Meets Debutante *'40*
Pride and Prejudice *'40*
Andy Hardy Gets Spring Fever *'39*
Gone with the Wind *'39*
A Christmas Carol *'38*
Love Finds Andy Hardy *'38*
Of Human Hearts *'38*
Public Cowboy No. 1 *'37*
Doughnuts & Society *'36*
Fighting Marines *'36*
The Lawless Nineties *'36*
Melody Trail *'35*
Ghost City *'32*

Camilla Rutherford (1976-)
Land of the Blind *'06*
Gosford Park *'01*

Kelly Rutherford (1968-)
Acceptable Risk *'01*
Angels Don't Sleep Here *'00*
Chaos Factor *'00*
I Love Trouble *'94*

Margaret Rutherford (1892-1972)
Chimes at Midnight *'67*
A Countess from Hong Kong *'67*
The Alphabet Murders *'65*
Murder Most Foul *'65*
Murder Ahoy *'64*
Murder at the Gallop *'63*
The V.I.P.'s *'63*
The Mouse on the Moon *'62*
Murder She Said *'62*
The Smallest Show on Earth *'57*
The Runaway Bus *'54*
Curtain Up *'53*
Innocents in Paris *'53*
Trouble in Store *'53*
The Importance of Being Earnest *'52*
The Happiest Days of Your Life *'50*
Passport to Pimlico *'49*
Blithe Spirit *'45*
The Demi-Paradise *'43*

Susan Ruttan (1950-)
The Legend of Butch & Sundance *'04*
Love Kills *'98*
Funny About Love *'90*
A Perfect Little Murder *'90*
Sweet 15 *'90*
Chances Are *'89*
Fire and Rain *'89*
Bad Dreams *'88*
Eye of the Demon *'87*
L.A. Law *'86*
Bad Manners *'84*

Barbara Rutting (1927-)
The Squeaker *'65*
The Phantom of Soho *'64*
River of Evil *'64*
Town without Pity *'61*
A Time to Love & a Time to Die *'58*
The Last Bridge *'54*

Sif Ruud (1916-)
Like It Never Was Before *'95*
Face to Face *'76*

Wolf Ruvinskis (1921-99)
Neutron vs. the Death Robots *'62*
Neutron vs. the Maniac *'62*
Neutron and the Black Mask *'61*
Neutron vs. the Amazing Dr. Caronte *'61*

Basil Ruysdael (1888-1960)
Davy Crockett, King of the Wild Frontier *'55*
Carrie *'52*
People Will Talk *'51*
Broken Arrow *'50*
High Lonesome *'50*
Colorado Territory *'49*
The Cocoanuts *'29*

David Ryall (1935-)
Around the World in 80 Days *'04*
The Embalmer *'03*
Two Men Went to War *'02*
One Against the Wind *'91*
Truly, Madly, Deeply *'91*

Amanda Ryan
Inspector Lynley Mysteries: A Great Deliverance *'01*
Brittanic *'00*
Britannic *'99*
David Copperfield *'99*
Metroland *'97*
Poldark *'96*

Amy Ryan (1970-)
Green Zone *'10*
Bob Funk *'09*
Changeling *'08*
Before the Devil Knows You're Dead *'07*
Chicago 10 *'07 (V)*
Dan in Real Life *'07*
Gone Baby Gone *'07*
Looking for Comedy in the Muslim World *'06*
Capote *'05*
Keane *'04*

Anne Ryan
Three o'Clock High *'87*
All the Lovin' Kinfolk *'70*

Blanchard Ryan (1967-)
The Brooklyn Heist *'08*
Pistol Whipped *'08*
Beerfest *'06*
Open Water *'03*

Eddie Ryan (1923-)
It Happened on 5th Avenue *'47*
Breakfast in Hollywood *'46*
The Fighting Sullivans *'42*

Edmon Ryan (1905-84)
Tora! Tora! Tora! *'70*
Two for the Seesaw *'62*
Mystery Street *'50*
Side Street *'50*
Hey! Hey! USA! *'38*

Eileen Ryan (1928-)
The Assassination of Richard Nixon *'05*
Eight Legged Freaks *'02*
Anywhere But Here *'99*
The Crossing Guard *'94*
Benny & Joon *'93*
Winter People *'89*
At Close Range *'86*

Fran Ryan (1926-2000)
Suture *'93*
Archie: Return to Riverdale *'90*
Chances Are *'89*
Gunsmoke: Return to Dodge *'87*
Quiet Cool *'86*
Pale Rider *'85*
Eyes of Fire *'84*
Private School *'83*
Johnny Belinda *'82*
Story of a Cowboy Angel *'81*
Deadly Game *'77*

Ger Ryan
Forgive and Forget *'99*
Amongst Women *'98*
Moll Flanders *'96*
The Van *'95*
Family *'94*

James Ryan
Aussie and Ted's Great Adventure *'09 (V)*
Second Best *'05*
Redemption: Kickboxer 5 *'95*
The Last Samurai *'90*
Pursuit *'90*
Rage to Kill *'88*
Space Mutiny *'88*
Go for the Gold *'84*
Kill and Kill Again *'81*
Kill or Be Killed *'80*

Jeri Ryan (1968-)
Down With Love *'03*
Dracula 2000 *'00*
The Last Man *'00*
Men Cry Bullets *'00*

John P. Ryan (1938-)
Bound *'96*
American Cyborg: Steel Warrior *'94*
C.I.A. 2: Target Alexa *'94*
Hoffa *'92*
Star Time *'92*
White Sands *'92*
Delta Force 3: The Killing Game *'91*
Class of 1999 *'90*
Delta Force 2: Operation Stranglehold *'90*
Eternity *'90*
Best of the Best *'89*
Paramedics *'88*
Rent-A-Cop *'88*
Death Wish 4: The Crackdown *'87*
Three o'Clock High *'87*
Avenging Force *'86*
City of Shadows *'86*
Runaway Train *'85*
Breathless *'83*
The Right Stuff *'83*
The Postman Always Rings Twice *'81*
It's Alive 2: It Lives Again *'78*
Death Scream *'75*
It's Alive *'74*
Cops and Robbers *'73*
Shamus *'73*

Kathleen Ryan (1922-85)
Try and Get Me *'50*
Captain Boycott *'47*
Odd Man Out *'47*

Lisa Dean Ryan (1972-)
The Stepdaughter *'00*
Twisted Love *'95*
Hostile Intentions *'94*

Marisa Ryan (1974-)
Brooklyn Lobster *'05*
Riding in Cars with Boys *'01*
Wet Hot American Summer *'01*
Cold Hearts *'99*
Slaves to the Underground *'96*

Max Ryan (1967-)
Death Race *'08*
Thr3e *'07*
The League of Extraordinary Gentlemen *'03*

Meg Ryan (1961-)
The Deal *'08*
My Mom's New Boyfriend *'08*
The Women *'08*
In the Land of Women *'06*
Against the Ropes *'04*
In the Cut *'03*
Kate & Leopold *'01*

Proof of Life '00
Hanging Up '99
City of Angels '98
Hurlyburly '98
You've Got Mail '98
Anastasia '97 (V)
Addicted to Love '96
Courage Under Fire '96
French Kiss '95
I.Q. '94
Restoration '94
When a Man Loves a Woman '94
Flesh and Bone '93
Sleepless in Seattle '93
Prelude to a Kiss '92
The Doors '91
Joe Versus the Volcano '90
When Harry Met Sally... '89
D.O.A. '88
The Presidio '88
Promised Land '88
Innerspace '87
Armed and Dangerous '86
Top Gun '86
Amityville 3: The Demon '83
Rich and Famous '81

Michelle Ryan

I Want Candy '07
Jekyll '07
Mansfield Park '07
Cashback '06

Mitchell Ryan (1928-)

Aftershock: Earthquake in New York '99
Grosse Pointe Blank '97
Liar Liar '97
The Devil's Own '96
Halloween 6: The Curse of Michael Myers '95
Speechless '94
Danielle Steel's Star '93
Hot Shots! Part Deux '93
The Opposite Sex and How to Live With Them '93
Aces: Iron Eagle 3 '92
Dirty Work '92
Blue Sky '91
Judgment '90
Double Exposure: The Story of Margaret Bourke-White '89
Winter People '89
Lethal Weapon '87
Fatal Vision '84
The Choice '81
Death of a Centerfold '81
The Five of Me '81
Of Mice and Men '81
Angel City '80
Sergeant Matlovich vs. the U.S. Air Force '78
The Christmas Coal Mine Miracle '77
Peter Lundy and the Medicine Hat Stallion '77
Midway '76
Electra Glide in Blue '73
High Plains Drifter '73
Magnum Force '73
My Old Man's Place '71
Monte Walsh '70
Thunder Road '58

Peggy Ryan (1924-2004)

Here Come the Co-Eds '45
Miss Annie Rooney '42

Remi Ryan (1984-)

Ava's Magical Adventure '94
RoboCop 3 '91

R.L. Ryan (1946-91)

Street Trash '87
Class of Nuke 'Em High '86
Eat and Run '86

Robert Ryan (1909-73)

Executive Action '73
The Iceman Cometh '73
The Man Without a Country '73
And Hope to Die '72
Lawman '71
The Love Machine '71
Captain Nemo and the Underwater City '69
The Wild Bunch '69
Anzio '68
The Busy Body '67
The Dirty Dozen '67
Hour of the Gun '67
A Minute to Pray, a Second to Die '67
The Professionals '66
Battle of the Bulge '65
Billy Budd '62
The Longest Day '62
The King of Kings '61
Ice Palace '60
The Day of the Outlaw '59
Odds Against Tomorrow '59
God's Little Acre '58
Lonelyhearts '58
Men in War '57
Back from Eternity '56
Escape to Burma '55
House of Bamboo '55
The Tall Men '55
Bad Day at Black Rock '54
The Naked Spur '53
Beware, My Lovely '52
Clash by Night '52
Horizons West '52
Flying Leathernecks '51
On Dangerous Ground '51
The Racket '51
Best of the Badmen '50
Born to Be Bad '50
The Woman on Pier 13 '50
Caught '49
The Set-Up '49
Act of Violence '48
Berlin Express '48
The Boy with the Green Hair '48
Return of the Bad Men '48
Crossfire '47
Trail Street '47
Behind the Rising Sun '43
Bombardier '43
The Iron Major '43
Marine Raiders '43
The Sky's the Limit '43
Tender Comrade '43

Sheila Ryan (1921-75)

On Top of Old Smoky '53
Fingerprints Don't Lie '51
Gold Raiders '51
Mask of the Dragon '51
Western Pacific Agent '51
Ringside '49
The Cobra Strikes '48
Heartaches '47
Railroaded '47
Getting Gertie's Garter '45
Something for the Boys '44
Dead Men Tell '41
Great Guns '41

Steve Ryan

Entry Level '07
The Rangers' Roundup '38

Thomas Ryan

The Relic '96
Body Count '87

Thomas Jay Ryan (1962-)

Fay Grim '06
Eternal Sunshine of the Spotless Mind '04
The Legend of Bagger Vance '00
Henry Fool '98

Tim Ryan (1899-1956)

From Here to Eternity '53
Here Come the Marines '52
Detour '46
Ghost Crazy '44
Harmon of Michigan '41

Tim Ryan (1958-)

The Lightning Incident '91
The Runestone '91
China Beach '88

Will Ryan (1939-)

Thumbelina '94 (V)
The Land Before Time '88 (V)
An American Tail '86 (V)

Derek Rydall (1968-)

Night Visitor '89
Phantom of the Mall: Eric's Revenge '89
Popcorn '89

Georg Rydeberg (1907-83)

Hour of the Wolf '68
Walpurgis Night '41
Dollar '38
A Woman's Face '38

Bobby Rydell (1942-)

Mr. Rock 'n' Roll: The Alan Freed Story '99
Marco Polo, Jr. '72 (V)
Bye, Bye, Birdie '63

Christopher Rydell (1963-)

By the Sword '93
Dario Argento's Trauma '93
Flesh and Bone '93
For the Boys '91
In the Deep Woods '91
Side Out '90
Blood and Sand '89
How I Got into College '89
Gotcha! '85

Mark Rydell (1934-)

Hollywood Ending '02
James Dean '01
Havana '90
Punchline '88
The Long Goodbye '73

Alfred Ryder (1919-95)

Bogie: The Last Hero '80
Probe '72
True Grit '69
T-Men '47

Winona Ryder (1971-)

The Informers '09
The Private Lives of Pippa Lee '09
Star Trek '09
The Last Word '08
Sex and Death 101 '07
The Ten '07
The Darwin Awards '06
A Scanner Darkly '06
Mr. Deeds '02
Simone '02
Autumn in New York '00
Lost Souls '00
Girl, Interrupted '99
Celebrity '98
Alien: Resurrection '97
The Crucible '96
Looking for Richard '96
Boys '95
How to Make an American Quilt '95
Little Women '94
Reality Bites '94
The Age of Innocence '93
The House of the Spirits '93
Bram Stoker's Dracula '92
Night on Earth '91
Edward Scissorhands '90
Mermaids '90
Welcome Home, Roxy Carmichael '90
Great Balls of Fire '89
Heathers '89
1969 '89
Beetlejuice '88
Square Dance '87
Lucas '86

Joseph Rye

Alien vs. Predator '04
Born to Lose '99

Patrick Ryecart (1952-)

Coming Home '98
Parting Shots '98
Heart of Darkness '93
Twenty-One '91
Goldeneye: The Secret Life of Ian Fleming '89
The Bretts '88
True Colors '87
Jenny's War '85
Silas Marner '85

Georgina Rylance (1979-)

Pulse 2: Afterlife '08
Hellraiser: Deader '05
Seven Seconds '05

Mark Rylance (1960-)

The Other Boleyn Girl '08
Intimacy '00
Angels and Insects '95
Institue Benjamenta or This Dream People Call Human Life '95
Prospero's Books '91

Ryo

Black House '07
Azumi '03

Rex Ryon (1953-)

The Man in the Iron Mask '97
Jack's Back '87

Chishu Ryu (1904-93)

Akira Kurosawa's Dreams '90
The Battle of the Japan Sea '70
An Autumn Afternoon '62
The Human Condition: A Soldier's Prayer '61
Good Morning '59
Equinox Flower '58
Twenty-Four Eyes '54
Tokyo Story '53
Early Summer '51
Late Spring '49
Record of a Tenement Gentleman '47

Daisuke Ryu

Nezulla the Rat Monster '02
Ran '85

RZA (1966-)

Funny People '09
Life is Hot in Cracktown '08
American Gangster '07
Derailed '05
Coffee and Cigarettes '03
Scary Movie 3 '03

Bruno S (1932-)

Stroszek '77
Every Man for Himself & God Against All '75

Daryl Sabara (1992-)

World's Greatest Dad '09
Havoc 2: Normal Adolescent Behavior '07
Her Best Move '07
Keeping Up with the Steins '06
The Polar Express '04 (V)
Spy Kids 3-D: Game Over '03
Spy Kids 2: The Island of Lost Dreams '02
Spy Kids '01

Antonio Sabato, Jr. (1972-)

Bugs '03
Testosterone '03
Mindstorm '01
Chaos Factor '00
Fatal Error '99
The Big Hit '98
High Voltage '98
Wolverine '96
Jailbreakers '94

Antonio (Tony) Sabato (1943-)

High Voltage '98
Thundersquad '85
Crimebusters '79
Reactor '78
This Time I'll Make You Rich '75
New Mafia Boss '72
Black Lemons '70
Twice a Judas '69
Beyond the Law '68

Bo Sabato

L.A. Crackdown 2 '88
Neon Maniacs '86

Ernie Sabella (1949-)

The Lion King 1 1/2 '04 (V)
The Lion King: Simba's Pride '98 (V)
The Lion King '94 (V)

Kyle Sabihy (1983-)

Analyze That '02
Analyze This '98

Patrick Sabongui (1975-)

High Noon '09
Merlin and the Book of Beasts '09

Marcel Sabourin (1935-)

Lilies '96
The Hitman '91

Sabu (1924-63)

A Tiger Walks '64
Mistress of the World '59
Jaguar '56
Jungle Hell '55
The Treasure of Bengal '53
Pardon My Trunk '52
Savage Drums '51
Black Narcissus '47
Cobra Woman '44
Arabian Nights '42
The Jungle Book '42
The Thief of Bagdad '40
Drums '38
Elephant Boy '37

Robert Sacchi (1941-)

Cold Heat '90
The Man with Bogart's Face '80

Orlando Sacha (1929-2001)

Alias, La Gringa '91
To Die Standing '91
Crime Zone '88

Adrienne Sachs

In the Cold of the Night '89
Two to Tango '88

Robin Sachs (1951-)

Megalodon '03
Northfork '03
Galaxy Quest '99
Cold War Killers '86
Deadly Recruits '86

Salli Sachse (1943-)

Devil's Angels '67
The Trip '67

Graham Sack (1981-)

Dunston Checks In '95
A Pig's Tale '94

Katee Sackhoff

The Last Sentinel '07
White Noise 2: The Light '07
Halloween: Resurrection '02

Martin Sacks

Do or Die '01
Slate, Wyn & Me '87

Michael Sacks (1948-)

Bunco '77
The Sugarland Express '74
Slaughterhouse Five '72

Jose Sacristan (1937-)

A Place in the World '92
El Diputado '78

Keiji Sada (1926-64)

An Autumn Afternoon '62
The Human Condition: Road to Eternity '59
The Human Condition: No Greater Love '58

Nicholas Sadler

Idle Hands '99
Sawbones '95
Acting on Impulse '93

William Sadler (1950-)

Jesse Stone: Thin Ice '09
Shadowheart '09
The Good Student '08
August Rush '07
The Mist '07
A New Wave '07
Jimmy & Judy '06
Confess '05
Devour '05
Purple Heart '05
Kinsey '04
The Battle of Shaker Heights '03
The Green Mile '99
Disturbing Behavior '98
Reach the Rock '98
RocketMan '97
Poltergeist: The Legacy '96
Solo '96
Roadracers '94
The Shawshank Redemption '94
Tales from the Crypt Presents Demon Knight '94
Freaked '93
Trespass '92
Bill & Ted's Bogus Journey '91
Rush '91
Die Hard 2: Die Harder '90
The Hot Spot '90
Tagget '90
Hard to Kill '89
Tales from the Crypt '89
Project X '87

Tom Sadoski (1976-)

The New Twenty '08
Happy Hour '03
Loser '00

Jonathan Sadowski

Spring Breakdown '08
She's the Man '06

Isabelle Sadoyan (1928-)

Summer Hours '08
The Eighth Day '95
Trois Couleurs: Bleu '93

Marianne Saegebrecht (1945-)

Left Luggage '98
Dust Devil '93
Martha and I '91
Rosalie Goes Shopping '89
The War of the Roses '89
Bagdad Cafe '88
Moon over Parador '88
Sugarbaby '85

Hinako Saeki

Uzumaki '00
Rasen '98

Libuse Safrankova (1953-)

All My Loved Ones '00
Kolya '96
The Elementary School '91

Elizabeth Sagal (1961-)

Skinheads: The Second Coming of Hate '88
Howard the Duck '86
Flashdance '83

Katey Sagal (1954-)

I'm Reed Fish '06
Smart House '00 (V)
Mr. Headmistress '98
The Good Mother '88

Jonathan Sagalle (1962-)

Deadly Outbreak '96
Schindler's List '93
Young Love—Lemon Popsicle 7 '87
Baby Love '83
Drifting '82
Hot Bubblegum '81

Bill Sage (1962-)

The New Twenty '08
Tennessee '08
Blue Blood '07
Heavens Fall '06
The Maldonado Miracle '03

William Sage

Mysterious Skin '04
Sin '02
Desert Saints '01
Double Parked '00
Urbania '00
American Psycho '99
High Art '98
Rift '96
Boys '95

Flirt '95
Two Plus One '95
Simple Men '92

Melissa Sagemiller (1974-)
Mr. Woodcock '07
The Guardian '06
Sleeper Cell '05
Standing Still '05
The Clearing '04
Sorority Boys '02
Get Over It! '01
Soul Survivors '01

Ray Sager
The Gore-Gore Girls '72
This Stuff'll Kill Ya! '71
The Wizard of Gore '70
Just for the Hell of It '68
Blast-Off Girls '67
The Girl, the Body and the Pill '67
Gruesome Twosome '67

Bob Saget (1956-)
New York Minute '04
Father and Scout '94
To Grandmother's House We Go '94

Ludivine Sagnier (1979-)
A Girl Cut in Two '07
Love Songs '07
Moliere '07
A Secret '07
Paris, je t'aime '06
La Petite Lili '03
Peter Pan '03
Swimming Pool '03
8 Women '02
My Wife is an Actress '01
Water Drops on Burning Rocks '99

Ken Sagoes (1967-)
Death by Dialogue '88
A Nightmare on Elm Street 4: Dream Master '88

Luis Saguar
Against the Wall '04
Silver City '04

Elena Sahagun
Firetrap '01
Teenage Exorcist '93
Uncaged '91

Kenji Sahara (1932-)
Yog, Monster from Space '71
War of the Gargantuas '70
Godzilla's Revenge '69
Destroy All Monsters '68
Son of Godzilla '66
Ghidrah the Three Headed Monster '65
Godzilla vs. Mothra '64
Attack of the Mushroom People '63
King Kong vs. Godzilla '63
Matango '63
Mothra '62
H-Man '59
The Mysterians '58
Rodan '56

Amir Ali Said (1996-)
Inside Man '06
Game 6 '05

Eva Marie Saint (1924-)
Superman Returns '06
Because of Winn-Dixie '05
Don't Come Knocking '05
I Dreamed of Africa '00
Papa's Angels '00
Titanic '96
My Antonia '94
Kiss of a Killer '93
Danielle Steel's Palomino '91
Voyage of Terror: The Achille Lauro Affair '90
Breaking Home Ties '87
The Last Days of Patton '86
Nothing in Common '86
Fatal Vision '84
Love Leads the Way '84
Jane Doe '83
When Hell Was in Session '82
The Best Little Girl in the World '81
The Curse of King Tut's Tomb '80
A Christmas to Remember '78
Cancel My Reservation '72
Loving '70
The Stalking Moon '69
Grand Prix '66
The Russians Are Coming, the Russians Are Coming '66
The Sandpiper '65
36 Hours '64
All Fall Down '62
Exodus '60
North by Northwest '59
Raintree County '57
On the Waterfront '54

Michael St. Clair (1921-2001)
Our Man Flint '66
Von Ryan's Express '65

Julie St. Claire (1970-)
Dark World '08
Stealing Candy '04
Extreme Limits '01

Lili St. Cyr (1918-99)
The Naked and the Dead '58
Son of Sinbad '55

Michael St. Gerard (1961-)
Replikator: Cloned to Kill '94
Star Time '92
Great Balls of Fire '89
Hairspray '88
Senior Week '88

Tabitha St. Germain
Bionicle 3: Web of Shadows '05 (V)
Popeye's Voyage: The Quest for Pappy '04

Soledad St. Hilaire (1950-)
The Maldonado Miracle '03
Real Women Have Curves '02
crazy/beautiful '01

Raymond St. Jacques (1930-90)
Timebomb '91
Glory '89
Voodoo Dawn '89
They Live '88
The Wild Pair '87
The Evil That Men Do '84
Sophisticated Gents '81
Kill Castro '80
The Mercenaries '80
The Private Files of J. Edgar Hoover '77
Search for the Gods '75
Final Comedown '72
Cotton Comes to Harlem '70
Dead Right '68
The Green Berets '68
The Comedians '67

Susan St. James (1946-)
Don't Cry, It's Only Thunder '82
Sex and the Single Parent '82
Carbon Copy '81
How to Beat the High Cost of Living '80
Love at First Bite '79
S.O.S. Titanic '79
Desperate Women '78
Night Cries '78
Outlaw Blues '77
Where Angels Go, Trouble Follows '68

Al "Fuzzy" St. John (1892-1963)
The Black Lash '52
King of the Bullwhip '51
Thundering Trail '51
Outlaw Country '49
Stage to Mesa City '48
Border Feud '47
Cheyenne Takes Over '47
Fighting Vigilantes '47
Ghost Town Renegades '47
Law of the Lash '47
Return of the Lash '47
My Dog Shep '46
Outlaw of the Plains '46
Gangster's Den '45
His Brother's Ghost '45
Lightning Raiders '45
Shadows of Death '45
Death Rides the Plains '44
Devil Riders '44
The Drifter '44
Frontier Outlaws '44
Oath of Vengeance '44
Rustler's Hideout '44
Thundering Gunslingers '44
Wild Horse Phantom '44
Dead Men Walk '43
Law of the Saddle '43
Raiders of Red Gap '43
Billy the Kid Trapped '42
Law and Order '42
The Lone Rider in Cheyenne '42
The Mysterious Rider '42
Prairie Pals '42
Sundown Fury '42
Texas Justice '42
Billy the Kid in Santa Fe '41
Border Roundup '41
The Lone Rider Crosses the Rio '41
The Lone Rider in Frontier Fury '41
The Lone Rider in Ghost Town '41
Texas Trouble '41
Trigger Men '41
Battling Outlaw '40
Billy the Kid in Texas '40
Trigger Pals '39
Call of the Yukon '38
Gunsmoke Trail '38
The Rangers' Roundup '38
Songs and Bullets '38
Melody of the Plains '37
The Roamin' Cowboy '37
Sing, Cowboy, Sing '37
A Face in the Fog '36
Pinto Rustlers '36
West of Nevada '36
His Private Secretary '33
Riders of Destiny '33
Police Court '32
Riders of the Desert '32
Oklahoma Cyclone '30
Dance of Life '29
She Goes to War '29
Mabel & Fatty '16

Betta St. John (1929-)
Horror Hotel '60
Tarzan the Magnificent '60
Corridors of Blood '58
Tarzan and the Lost Safari '57
Alias John Preston '56
Tarzan's Hidden Jungle '55
The Student Prince '54
All the Brothers Were Valiant '53
Dream Wife '53

Christopher St. John
Top of the Heap '72
Shaft '71

Howard St. John (1905-74)
Strange Bedfellows '65
Strait-Jacket '64
Lover Come Back '61
Li'l Abner '59
I Died a Thousand Times '55
Illegal '55
The Tender Trap '55
Close to My Heart '51
Goodbye My Fancy '51
Born Yesterday '50
Counterspy Meets Scotland Yard '50
David Harding, Counterspy '50
The Sun Sets at Dawn '50
Shockproof '49

Jill St. John (1940-)
The Trip '02
Out There '95
The Player '92
Around the World in 80 Days '89
The Act '82
The Concrete Jungle '82
Diamonds Are Forever '71
Eight on the Lam '67
Tony Rome '67
The Oscar '66
Come Blow Your Horn '63
Who's Minding the Store? '63
Roman Spring of Mrs. Stone '61

Kristoff St. John
Carpool Guy '05
Finish Line '89

Michelle St. John
The Business of Fancydancing '02
Smoke Signals '98
Coyote Summer '96
Pocahontas '95 (V)
Geronimo '93
Spirit Rider '93
Where the Spirit Lives '89

Trevor St. John (1971-)
The King's Guard '01
Dogtown '97

Hubert Saint Macary (1949-)
Lucie Aubrac '98
Genealogies of a Crime '97
Diary of a Seducer '95

Matthew St. Patrick (1968-)
Alien Raiders '08
War '07
Steel Sharks '97

Irma St. Paule (1927-2007)
Where the Money Is '00
Fever '99

John St. Polis (1873-1946)
Rocky Mountain Rangers '40
Phantom Ranger '38
The Shadow Strikes '37
Death from a Distance '36
Terror Trail '33
Coquette '29
Party Girls '29
The Unknown '27
The Phantom of the Opera '25
The Untamable '23
The Four Horsemen of the Apocalypse '21

Lucile Saint-Simon (1937-)
The Hands of Orlac '60
Les Bonnes Femmes '60

Marin Sais (1890-1971)
The Fighting Redhead '50
Lightning Raiders '45
Frontier Outlaws '44
Billy the Kid in Santa Fe '41
Rawhide Romance '34

James Saito (1955-)
Robot Stories '03
Henry Fool '98
The Adventures of Buckaroo Banzai Across the Eighth Dimension '84

Tak Sakaguchi
Azumi 2 '05
Death Trance '05
Shinobi '05
Azumi '03
Battlefield Baseball '03
Versus '00

Frankie Sakai (1929-96)
Master Mind '73
Last War '68
Mothra '62

Sachio Sakai (1929-)
Godzilla's Revenge '69
Godzilla, King of the Monsters '56
Samurai 2: Duel at Ichijoji Temple '55

Hideo Sakaki
Azumi '03
Battlefield Baseball '03
Versus '00

S.Z. Sakall (1884-1955)
The Student Prince '54
Small Town Girl '53
It's a Big Country '51
Lullaby of Broadway '51
Painting the Clouds With Sunshine '51
Montana '50
Tea for Two '50
In the Good Old Summertime '49
Look for the Silver Lining '49
My Dream Is Yours '49
Romance on the High Seas '48
Cynthia '47
The Dolly Sisters '46
Never Say Goodbye '46
Christmas in Connecticut '45
San Antonio '45
Wonder Man '45
Hollywood Canteen '44
Wintertime '43
Casablanca '42
Yankee Doodle Dandy '42
Ball of Fire '41
The Devil & Miss Jones '41
That Night in Rio '41
It's a Date '40
Spring Parade '40

Ryuichi Sakamoto (1952-)
New Rose Hotel '98
The Last Emperor '87
Merry Christmas, Mr. Lawrence '83

Sumiko Sakamoto (1936-)
The Ballad of Narayama '83
The Pornographers '66

Amy Sakasitz
House Arrest '96
Mad Love '95
Dennis the Menace '93
A Home of Our Own '93

Harold Sakata (1920-82)
Black Eliminator '78
Goin' Coconuts '78
Kill Factor '78
Jaws of Death '76
Impulse '74
The Wrestler '73
Goldfinger '64

Nancy Sakovich (1961-)
Category 6 : Day of Destruction '04
Coast to Coast '04
The Jesse Ventura Story '99

Gene Saks (1921-)
Deconstructing Harry '97
I.Q. '94
Nobody's Fool '94
A Fine Romance '92
The One and Only '78
Prisoner of Second Avenue '74
A Thousand Clowns '65

Yoshiko Sakuma (1939-)
The Makioka Sisters '83
Samurai Banners '69

Renato Sala
Full Metal Ninja '89
Ninja of the Magnificence '89

Abel Salazar (1917-95)
The Man and the Monster '65
The Brainiac '61
The Curse of the Crying Woman '61
The Living Head '59
The Vampire's Coffin '58
The Vampire '57

Theresa Saldana (1954-)
Thrill Seekers '99
Angel Town '89
Double Revenge '89
The Night Before '88
The Evil That Men Do '84
Raging Bull '80
Defiance '79
I Wanna Hold Your Hand '78

Zoe Saldana (1978-)
Death at a Funeral '10
The Losers '10
Takers '10
Avatar '09
The Skeptic '09
Star Trek '09
Vantage Point '08
Guess Who '05
Haven '04
The Terminal '04
Pirates of the Caribbean: The Curse of the Black Pearl '03
Crossroads '02
Drumline '02
Get Over It! '01
Snipes '01
Center Stage '00

Charles "Chic" Sale (1885-1936)
You Only Live Once '37
The Fighting Westerner '35
Treasure Island '34
Men of America '32

Dahlia Salem
Love Finds a Home '09
Return to Cabin by the Lake '01

Kario Salem
Savage '96
Killing Zoe '94
1492: Conquest of Paradise '92
Triumph of the Spirit '89
Tut & Tuttle '81
Centennial '78

Pamela Salem (1950-)
Quicksand '01
After Darkness '85
Salome '85
Never Say Never Again '83

Meredith Salenger (1970-)
The Third Wheel '02
Bug Buster '99
Lake Placid '99
No Code of Conduct '98
Glory Daze '96
Village of the Damned '95
Dead Beat '94
Edge of Honor '91
Dream a Little Dream '89
The Kiss '88
A Night in the Life of Jimmy Reardon '88
The Journey of Natty Gann '85

Enrico Maria Salerno (1926-94)
The Cheaters '76
Night Train Murders '75
Torture Train '75
The Bird with the Crystal Plumage '70
That Long Night in '43 '60

Soupy Sales (1926-2009)
..And God Spoke '94
Critic's Choice '63

John Salew (1897-1961)
Black Glove '54
Kind Hearts and Coronets '49

Beware of Pity *'46*

Diane Salinger (1951-)
20 Years After *'08*
Rest Stop *'06*
The Kid with the X-Ray Eyes *'99*
Last Summer In the Hamptons *'96*
One Night Stand *'95*
The Scarlet Letter *'95*
The Magic Bubble *'93*
Venice, Venice *'92*
The Butcher's Wife *'91*
The Morning After *'86*
Creature *'85*
Pee-wee's Big Adventure *'85*

Emmanuel Salinger (1964-)
Triple Agent *'04*
Kill by Inches *'99*
My Sex Life... Or How I Got into an Argument *'96*
One Hundred and One Nights *'95*
La Sentinelle *'92*

Matt Salinger (1960-)
Bigger Than the Sky *'05*
Black Dawn *'05*
Babyfever *'94*
Fortunes of War *'94*
Firehawk *'92*
Captain America *'89*
Options *'88*
Manhunt for Claude Dallas *'86*
Power *'86*

Jason Salkey (1962-)
The Turn of the Screw *'99*
Sharpe's Rifles *'93*

Pascale Salkin
Window Shopping *'86*
The Eighties *'83*

John Salley (1964-)
The Comebacks *'07*
Coast to Coast *'04*
Mr. 3000 *'04*
Eddie *'96*
Bad Boys *'95*

Peter Sallis (1921-)
Wallace & Gromit in The Curse of the Were-Rabbit *'05 (V)*
Taste the Blood of Dracula *'70*
The Curse of the Werewolf *'61*

Tomi Salmela (1957-)
Night on Earth *'91*
The Winter War *'89*

Gustavo Salmeron
Body Armour *'07*
Twice upon a Yesterday *'98*

Albert Salmi (1928-90)
Breaking In *'89*
Gore Vidal's Billy the Kid *'89*
Jesse *'88*
Born American *'86*
Fatal Vision *'84*
Hard to Hold *'84*
The Guns and the Fury *'83*
Love Child *'82*
St. Helen's, Killer Volcano *'82*
Superstition *'82*
Dragonslayer *'81*
Kill Castro *'80*
The Mercenaries *'80*
Steel *'80*
Sweet Creek County War *'79*
Black Oak Conspiracy *'77*
Empire of the Ants *'77*
Moonshine County Express *'77*
Viva Knievel *'77*
Lawman *'71*
Menace on the Mountain *'70*
The Ambushers *'67*
Hour of the Gun *'67*
The Meanest Men in the West *'67*
The Outrage *'64*
The Unforgiven *'60*
The Bravados *'58*
Bang the Drum Slowly *'56*

Colin Salmon (1965-)
Punisher: War Zone *'08*
Alien vs. Predator *'04*
Freeze Frame *'04*
The Statement *'03*
Die Another Day *'02*
Dinotopia *'02*
Resident Evil *'02*
Anti-Terrorist Cell: Manhunt *'01*
The World Is Not Enough *'99*
Immortality *'98*
Tomorrow Never Dies *'97*
Captives *'94*

Sonya Salomaa
Christmas Caper *'07*
Blood Angels *'05*
Firefight *'03*
House of the Dead *'03*

Lea Salonga (1971-)
Mulan *'98 (V)*
Redwood Curtain *'95*
Aladdin *'92 (V)*
My Neighbor Totoro *'88 (V)*

Frank S. Salsedo
Magic in the Water *'95*
Creepshow 2 *'87*

Jennifer Salt (1944-)
Out of the Darkness *'85*
Sisters *'73*
Play It Again, Sam *'72*
Hi, Mom! *'70*

Gino Saltamerenda
Young Caruso *'51*
The Bicycle Thief *'48*

Montserrat Salvador
Caresses *'97*
If They Tell You I Fell *'89*

Renato Salvatori (1933-88)
La Cicada *'83*
State of Siege *'73*
Burn! *'70*
The Organizer *'64*
RoGoPaG *'62*
Era Notte a Roma *'60*
Rocco and His Brothers *'60*
And the Wild, Wild Women *'59*
Big Deal on Madonna Street *'58*

Andy Samberg (1978-)
Cloudy with a Chance of Meatballs *'09 (V)*
Space Chimps *'08 (V)*
Hot Rod *'07*

Aldo Sambrel (1937-)
Hot Blood *'89*
Emmanuelle in the Country *'78*
Voodoo Black Exorcist *'73*
Navajo Joe *'67*
The Texican *'66*

Udo Samel (1953-)
Go for Zucker *'05*
The Piano Teacher *'01*
Killer Condom *'95*
Kaspar Hauser *'93*
Knife in the Head *'78*

Sami Samir
God's Sandbox *'02*
Yellow Asphalt *'01*

Emma Samms (1960-)
Humanoids from the Deep *'96*
Star Quest *'94*
Treacherous Beauties *'94*
Delirious *'91*
Illusions *'91*
The Shrimp on the Barbie *'90*
A Connecticut Yankee in King Arthur's Court *'89*
The Lady and the Highwayman *'89*
Goliath Awaits *'81*

Mercedes Sampietro (1947-)
Broken Silence *'01*
Second Skin *'99*

Candy Samples (1940-)
Beneath the Valley of the Ultra-Vixens *'79*
Flesh Gordon *'72*

Cindy Sampson
The Christmas Choir *'08*
Swamp Devil *'08*
Mama Africa *'02*

Paul Sampson
Deuces Wild *'02*
Whacked! *'02*
If You Only Knew *'00*
Detour *'99*

Robert Sampson (1932-)
The Arrival *'90*
Dark Side of the Moon *'90*
Netherworld *'90*
Robot Jox *'90*
Re-Animator *'84*
Gates of Hell *'80*
The Grass Is Always Greener Over the Septic Tank *'78*
Ethan *'71*
Lassie: Well of Love *'70*

Will Sampson (1935-87)
Poltergeist 2: The Other Side *'86*
Roanoak *'86*
Insignificance *'85*
Fish Hawk *'79*
From Here to Eternity *'79*
Standing Tall *'78*
Vegas *'78*
The Hunted Lady *'77*
Orca *'77*
The White Buffalo *'77*
Buffalo Bill & the Indians *'76*
The Outlaw Josey Wales *'76*
One Flew Over the Cuckoo's Nest *'75*

Jeffrey D. Sams (1966-)
Hope *'97*
Just Write *'97*
Rose Hill *'97*
Soul Food *'97*
Waiting to Exhale *'95*
Fly by Night *'93*

Russell Sams (1977-)
The Flock *'07*
The Rules of Attraction *'02*

Joanne Samuel (1959-)
Gallagher's Travels *'87*
Queen of the Road *'84*
Mad Max *'80*
Alison's Birthday *'79*

Laura San Giacomo (1962-)
With Friends Like These *'98*
Suicide Kings *'97*
The Apocalypse *'96*
Eat Your Heart Out *'96*
The Right to Remain Silent *'95*
Nina Takes a Lover *'94*
Stephen King's The Stand *'94*
Stuart Saves His Family *'94*
Under Suspicion *'92*
Where the Day Takes You *'92 (V)*
Once Around *'91*
Pretty Woman *'90*
Quigley Down Under *'90*
Vital Signs *'90*
sex, lies and videotape *'89*
Miles from Home *'88*

Olga San Juan (1927-)
The Beautiful Blonde from Bashful Bend *'49*
One Touch of Venus *'48*
Variety Girl *'47*
Blue Skies *'46*

Hiroyuki (Henry) Sanada (1960-)
Speed Racer *'08*
Rush Hour 3 *'07*
Sunshine *'07*
The Promise *'05*
The White Countess *'05*
The Last Samurai *'03*
The Twilight Samurai *'02*
Onmyoji *'01*
Ringu 2 *'99*
Rasen *'98*
Ringu *'98*
Royal Warriors *'86*
Shogun's Ninja *'83*
Samurai Reincarnation *'81*
Shogun's Samurai—The Yagyu Clan Conspiracy *'78*

Jon Sanborne
Addicted to Murder 3: Bloodlust *'99*
Rage of the Werewolf *'99*

Jaime Sanchez (1938-)
Pinero *'01*
The Wild Bunch *'69*
The Pawnbroker *'65*

Kiele Sanchez
A Perfect Getaway *'09*
Insanitarium *'08*

Lucia Sanchez (1969-)
Carnage *'02*
Sitcom *'97*

Marisol Padilla Sanchez (1973-)
Traffic *'00*
Fever *'99*
Dementia *'98*

Otto Sanchez
Kill the Poor *'06*
Push *'06*
Bad Boys 2 *'03*

Paul Sanchez
Navy SEALS *'90*
Platoon *'86*

Pedro Sanchez (1924-95)
Night and the City *'92*
White Fang and the Hunter *'85*
Any Gun Can Play *'67*

Roselyn Sanchez (1973-)
The Perfect Sleep *'08*
The Game Plan *'07*
Rush Hour 3 *'07*
Yellow *'06*
Edison Force *'05*
Underclassman *'05*
Basic *'03*
Boat Trip *'03*
Chasing Papi *'03*
Nightstalker *'02*
Rush Hour 2 *'01*

Susi Sanchez
The Milk of Sorrow *'09*
A Love to Keep *'07*

Victoria Sanchez (1976-)
Eternal *'04*
Codename: Jaguar *'00*
P.T. Barnum *'99*

Aitana Sanchez-Gijon (1968-)
The Backwoods *'06*
The Machinist *'04*
I'm Not Scared *'03*
Jealousy *'99*
Yerma *'99*
The Chambermaid on the Titanic *'97*
Love Walked In *'97*
Mouth to Mouth *'95*
A Walk in the Clouds *'95*
The Perfect Husband *'92*
Rowing with the Wind *'88*

Fernando (Fernand) Sancho (1916-90)
Blood at Sundown *'88*
Return of the Evil Dead *'75*
Voodoo Black Exorcist *'73*
Dr. Orloff and the Invisible Man *'72*
Orloff and the Invisible Man *'70*

Jose Sancho (1944-)
Arachnid *'01*
Live Flesh *'97*
Ay, Carmela! *'90*

Paul Sand (1935-)
Sweet Land *'05*
Chuck & Buck *'00*
Frozen Assets *'92*
Getting Up and Going Home *'92*
Teen Wolf Too *'87*
The Last Fling *'86*
Can't Stop the Music *'80*
Second Coming of Suzanne *'80*
Wholly Moses! *'80*
The Legend of Sleepy Hollow *'79*
Great Bank Hoax *'78*
Once Upon a Brothers Grimm *'77*

Dominique Sanda (1948-)
The Crimson Rivers *'01*
Joseph *'95*
I, the Worst of All *'90*
Voyage of Terror: The Achille Lauro Affair *'90*
Cabo Blanco *'81*
Voyage en Douce *'81*
Damnation Alley *'77*
The Inheritance *'76*
1900 *'76*
Steppenwolf *'74*
Mackintosh Man *'73*
The Story of a Love Story *'73*
The Conformist *'71*
The Garden of the Finzi-Continis *'71*
First Love *'70*
A Gentle Woman *'69*

Walter Sande (1906-71)
I'll Take Sweden *'65*
The Gallant Hours *'60*
Canyon River *'56*
Rim of the Canyon *'49*
The Red House *'47*
Nocturne *'46*
Don Winslow of the Navy *'43*

Casey Sander (1956-)
16 Blocks *'06*
Mystery Woman: Mystery Weekend *'05*
Crosscut *'95*

Otto Sander (1941-)
The Promise *'94*
Faraway, So Close! *'93*
Wings of Desire *'88*
Rosa Luxemburg *'86*
The Marquise of O *'76*

John Sanderford
Leprechaun *'93*
The Alchemist *'81*

Christopher Sanders (1960-)
Lilo & Stitch 2: Stitch Has a Glitch *'05 (V)*
Lilo & Stitch *'02 (V)*

Dirk Sanders (1934-2002)
Pierrot le Fou *'65*
Black Tights *'60*

George Sanders (1906-72)
Psychomania *'73*
Doomwatch *'72*
Endless Night *'71*
Invasion of the Body Stealers *'69*
Good Times *'67*
The Jungle Book *'67 (V)*
One Step to Hell *'67*
The Quiller Memorandum *'66*
The Amorous Adventures of Moll Flanders *'65*
A Shot in the Dark *'64*
In Search of the Castaways *'62*
The Last Voyage *'60*
Village of the Damned *'60*
Solomon and Sheba *'59*
From the Earth to the Moon *'58*
Outcasts of the City *'58*
Rock-A-Bye Baby *'57*
Death of a Scoundrel *'56*
While the City Sleeps *'56*
Jupiter's Darling *'55*
The King's Thief *'55*
Moonfleet *'55*
King Richard and the Crusaders *'54*
Voyage in Italy *'53*
Ivanhoe *'52*
Captain Blackjack *'51*
All About Eve *'50*
Samson and Delilah *'50*
Forever Amber *'47*
The Ghost and Mrs. Muir *'47*
Lured *'47*
The Private Affairs of Bel Ami *'47*
The Saint Strikes Back: Criminal Court *'46*
A Scandal in Paris *'46*
The Strange Woman *'46*
Hangover Square *'45*
Picture of Dorian Gray *'45*
The Strange Affair of Uncle Harry *'45*
Action in Arabia *'44*
Summer Storm *'44*
The Moon and Sixpence *'43*
This Land Is Mine *'43*
The Black Swan *'42*
The Falcon Takes Over *'42*
The Falcon's Brother *'42*
Son of Fury *'42*
Tales of Manhattan *'42*
Man Hunt *'41*
Sundown *'41*
Bitter Sweet *'40*
Foreign Correspondent *'40*
The House of the Seven Gables *'40*
Rebecca *'40*
The Saint Takes Over *'40*
The Saint's Double Trouble *'40*
The Son of Monte Cristo *'40*
Allegheny Uprising *'39*
Confessions of a Nazi Spy *'39*
Mr. Moto's Last Warning *'39*
Nurse Edith Cavell *'39*
The Saint in London *'39*
The Saint Strikes Back *'39*
Four Men and a Prayer *'38*
Love Is News *'37*
Lloyds of London *'36*

Henry Sanders (1942-)
Rocky Balboa *'06*
Rainbow Drive *'90*
Deadly Sunday *'82*
Boss' Son *'78*
Killer of Sheep *'77*

Hugh Sanders (1911-66)
The Finger Man *'55*
The Fighter *'52*
Pride of St. Louis *'52*
Storm Warning *'51*
The Damned Don't Cry *'50*
The Magnificent Yankee *'50*

Jay O. Sanders (1953-)
Edge of Darkness *'10*
I Hate Valentine's Day *'09*
Revolutionary Road *'08*
Half Nelson *'06*
Wedding Daze *'06*
Shooting Livien *'05*
The Day After Tomorrow *'04*
Widows *'02*
Along Came a Spider *'01*

My Husband's Double Life *'01*
Dead Dog *'00*
Boss of Bosses *'99*
Earthly Possessions *'99*
The Jack Bull *'99*
Music of the Heart *'99*
The Confession *'98*
Neil Simon's The Odd Couple 2 *'98*
Tumbleweeds *'98*
Wrestling with Alligators *'98*
For Richer or Poorer *'97*
Kiss the Girls *'97*
The Matchmaker *'97*
Daylight *'96*
The Big Green *'95*
Three Wishes *'95*
Angels in the Outfield *'94*
Down Came a Blackbird *'94*
Kiss of Death *'94*
Hostages *'93*
My Boyfriend's Back *'93*
JFK *'91*
Meeting Venus *'91*
V.I. Warshawski *'91*
Mr. Destiny *'90*
Glory *'89*
Assault of the Killer Bimbos *'88*

Richard Sanders (1940-)

Forbidden Choices *'94*
Neon City *'91*
Diary of a Teenage Hitchhiker *'82*

Martyn Sanderson (1938-)

An Angel at My Table *'89*
Beyond Reasonable Doubt *'80*
Solo *'77*

Will Sanderson (1980-)

In the Name of the King: A Dungeon Siege Tale *'08*
Seed *'08*
BloodRayne *'06*
Alone in the Dark *'05*
Heart of America *'03*
House of the Dead *'03*
Blackwoods *'02*

William Sanderson (1948-)

Beyond the Wall of Sleep *'06*
Disappearances *'06*
Gods and Generals *'03*
Monte Walsh *'03*
Crossfire Trail *'01*
Nice Guys Sleep Alone *'99*
George Wallace *'97*
Last Man Standing *'96*
Lone Justice 3: Showdown at Plum Creek *'96*
Andersonville *'95*
Forest Warrior *'95*
Hologram Man *'95*
Phoenix *'95*
Mirror, Mirror 2: Raven Dance *'94*
Wagons East *'94*
Return to Lonesome Dove *'93*
Sometimes They Come Back *'91*
Mirror, Mirror *'90*
Circle Man *'87*
Last Man Standing *'87*
Fletch *'85*
City Heat *'84*
Ballad of Gregorio Cortez *'83*
Blade Runner *'82*
Raggedy Man *'81*
Savage Weekend *'80*
The Onion Field *'79*
Fight for Your Life *'77*

Elizabeth Sandifer (1962-)

Animal Instincts 2 *'94*
Indecent Behavior 2 *'94*

Adam Sandler (1966-)

Grown Ups *'10*
Funny People *'09*
Bedtime Stories *'08*
You Don't Mess with the Zohan *'08*
I Now Pronounce You Chuck and Larry *'07*
Reign Over Me *'07*
Click *'06*
Deuce Bigalow: European Gigolo *'05*
The Longest Yard *'05*
50 First Dates *'04*
Spanglish *'04*
Anger Management *'03*
Adam Sandler's 8 Crazy Nights *'02 (V)*
The Hot Chick *'02*
Mr. Deeds *'02*
Punch-Drunk Love *'02*
Little Nicky *'00*
Big Daddy *'99*
The Waterboy *'98*
Dirty Work *'97*
The Wedding Singer *'97*
Bulletproof *'96*
Happy Gilmore *'96*
Airheads *'94*
Billy Madison *'94*
Mixed Nuts *'94*
Coneheads *'93*
Shakes the Clown *'92*
Going Overboard *'89*

Debra Sandlund (1962-)

Victimless Crimes *'90*
Murder by Numbers *'89*
Tough Guys Don't Dance *'87*

Steve Sandor (1937-)

Stryker *'83*
The Only Way Home *'72*
Hell's Angels '69 *'69*

Miguel (Michael) Sandoval (1951-)

Bottle Shock *'08*
Tortilla Heaven *'07*
Marilyn Hotchkiss' Ballroom Dancing & Charm School *'06*
Nine Lives *'05*
Ballistic: Ecks vs. Sever *'02*
Collateral Damage *'02*
Human Nature *'02*
Blow *'01*
Wild Iris *'01*
The Crew *'00*
Thin Air *'00*
Things You Can Tell Just by Looking at Her *'00*
Apartment Complex *'98*
Route 9 *'98*
The Fixer *'97*
Mrs. Winterbourne *'96*
Scorpion Spring *'96*
Up Close and Personal *'96*
Breach of Trust *'95*
Fair Game *'95*
Clear and Present Danger *'94*
Girls in Prison *'94*
Dancing with Danger *'93*
Lone Justice *'93*
White Sands *'92*
Jungle Fever *'91*
El Diablo *'90*
Walker *'87*
Howard the Duck *'86*

Nick Sandow

Connie and Carla *'04*
Swimfan *'02*
Return to Paradise *'98*

Stefania Sandrelli (1946-)

The Last Kiss *'01*
Stealing Beauty *'96*
Of Love and Shadows *'94*
Jamon, Jamon *'93*
The Sleazy Uncle *'89*
The Family *'87*
We All Loved Each Other So Much *'77*
1900 *'76*
Alfredo, Alfredo *'72*
The Black Belly of the Tarantula *'71*
The Conformist *'71*
Partner *'68*
Seduced and Abandoned *'64*
Divorce—Italian Style *'62*

Billy (Billie) Sands (1911-84)

Harrad Experiment *'73*
McHale's Navy Joins the Air Force *'65*
McHale's Navy *'64*

Diana Sands (1934-73)

Honeybaby *'74*
Georgia, Georgia *'72*
Doctors' Wives *'70*
A Raisin in the Sun *'61*

Julian Sands (1958-)

Beyond Sherwood Forest *'09*
Bollywood Hero *'09*
Stargate: The Ark of Truth *'08*
Ocean's Thirteen *'07*
The Haunted Airman *'06*
The Medallion *'03*
Napoleon *'03*
The Home Front *'02*
Stephen King's Rose Red *'02*
Hotel *'01*
Mercy *'00*
Time Code *'00*
Vatel *'00*
The Million Dollar Hotel *'99*
The Loss of Sexual Innocence *'98*
The Phantom of the Opera *'98*
Circle of Passion *'97*
End of Summer *'97*
Long Time Since *'97*
One Night Stand *'97*
The Great Elephant Escape *'95*
Leaving Las Vegas *'95*
Black Water *'94*
The Browning Version *'94*
Witch Hunt *'94*
Boxing Helena *'93*
Warlock: The Armageddon *'93*
Crazy in Love *'92*
Grand Isle *'92*
Tale of a Vampire *'92*
The Turn of the Screw *'92*
Husbands and Lovers *'91*
Murder by Moonlight *'91*
Naked Lunch *'91*
Warlock *'91*
Arachnophobia *'90*
Impromptu *'90*
Night Sun *'90*
Vibes *'88*
Gothic *'87*
The Room *'87*
Siesta *'87*
Harem *'86*
A Room with a View *'86*
After Darkness *'85*
The Doctor and the Devils *'85*
The Killing Fields *'84*
Oxford Blues *'84*
Privates on Parade *'84*

Stark Sands (1978-)

Generation Kill *'08*
Pretty Persuasion *'05*
Catch That Kid *'04*
Chasing Liberty *'04*
Shall We Dance? *'04*
Die Mommie Die! *'03*
11:14 *'03*

Tommy Sands (1937-)

None But the Brave *'65*
Babes in Toyland *'61*

Steve Sandvoss

Fling *'08*
Kiss the Bride *'07*
Rumor Has It... *'05*

Ellen Sandweiss

Brutal Massacre: A Comedy *'07*
Evil Dead *'83*

Gary Sandy (1945-)

Mommy 2: Mommy's Day *'96*
Troll *'86*
Great Smokey Roadblock *'76*
Hail *'73*

Erskine Sanford (1885-1969)

The Lady from Shanghai *'48*
Crack-Up *'46*
Ministry of Fear *'44*
The Magnificent Ambersons *'42*
Citizen Kane *'41*

Garwin Sanford (1955-)

Termination Point *'07*
Merlin's Apprentice *'06*
Get Carter *'00*
Life-Size *'00*
Mr. Rice's Secret *'00*
Firestorm *'97*
Ronnie and Julie *'97*
Maternal Instincts *'96*
My Very Best Friend *'96*
Unforgettable *'96*
Heartstrings *'93*
Quarantine *'89*

Isabel Sanford (1917-2004)

Desperate Moves *'86*
Love at First Bite *'79*
Guess Who's Coming to Dinner *'67*

Ralph Sanford (1899-1963)

Kentucky Jubilee *'51*
Hi-Jacked *'50*
Sioux City Sue *'46*
There Goes Kelly *'45*
A Night for Crime *'42*

Thomas Sangster (1990-)

Bright Star *'09*
Nowhere Boy *'09*
The Last Legion *'07*
Nanny McPhee *'06*
Tristan & Isolde *'06*
Love Actually *'03*
Bobbie's Girl *'02*
Station Jim *'01*

Shiro Sano (1955-)

Oh! My Zombie Mermaid *'04*
The Princess Blade *'02*
Godzilla 2000 *'99*
Evil Dead Trap 2: Hideki *'91*
Violent Cop *'89*

Maya Sansa

The Listening *'06*
Best of Youth *'03*

Ken Sansom

Pooh's Heffalump Movie *'05 (V)*
Piglet's Big Movie *'03 (V)*

Claudio Santamaria (1974-)

Casino Royale *'06*
Agata and the Storm *'04*
The Last Kiss *'01*
Besieged *'98*

Ray Santiago (1984-)

12 Rounds *'09*
Meet the Fockers *'04*
Girlfight *'99*

Renoly Santiago (1974-)

Daylight *'96*
Dangerous Minds *'95*
Hackers *'95*

Saundra Santiago (1957-)

Hi-Life *'98*
Nick and Jane *'96*
Beat Street *'84*
Miami Vice *'84*

Ruben Santiago-Hudson (1956-)

American Gangster *'07*
Mr. Brooks *'07*
Winning Girls Through Psychic Mind Control *'02*
Domestic Disturbance *'01*
The Red Sneakers *'01*
American Tragedy *'00*
Shaft *'00*
Rear Window *'98*
The Devil's Advocate *'97*
Which Way Home *'90*

Santo (1917-84)

Samson in the Wax Museum *'63*
Invasion of the Zombies *'61*
Samson vs. the Vampire Women *'61*

Espartaco (Spartaco) Santoni (1932-98)

Lisa and the Devil *'75*
Exorcism's Daughter *'74*
The Castilian *'63*

Reni Santoni (1939-)

28 Days *'00*
Dr. Dolittle *'98 (V)*
The Late Shift *'96*
Private Parts *'96*
The Package *'89*
The Pick-Up Artist *'87*
Cobra *'86*
Brewster's Millions *'85*
Bad Boys *'83*
Dead Men Don't Wear Plaid *'82*
Dirty Harry *'71*
The Student Nurses *'70*
Guns of the Magnificent Seven *'69*
Anzio *'68*
Enter Laughing *'67*

Rodrigo Santoro (1975-)

I Love You Phillip Morris *'10*
Post Grad *'09*
Che *'08*
Lion's Den *'08*
Redbelt *'08*
300 *'07*
Carandiru *'03*
Charlie's Angels: Full Throttle *'03*
Love Actually *'03*
The Roman Spring of Mrs. Stone *'03*
Behind the Sun *'01*

Gaston Santos

Swamp of the Lost Monster *'65*
The Living Coffin *'58*
Black Pit of Dr. M *'47*

Joe Santos (1931-)

Beyond Suspicion *'00*
The Postman *'97*
Tyson *'95*
Trial by Jury *'94*
Mo' Money *'92*
Sinatra *'92*
Deadly Desire *'91*
The Last Boy Scout *'91*
Revenge *'90*
Fear City *'85*
Ratings Game *'84*
Zandy's Bride *'74*
Shaft's Big Score *'72*

Thomas Santschi (1878-1931)

Phantom of the West *'31*
Ten Nights in a Bar-Room *'31*
Paradise Island *'30*
Paths to Paradise *'25*
The Cradle of Courage *'20*
Little Orphan Annie *'18*
The Spoilers *'14*

Michael Sanville

Dreams Come True *'84*
First Turn On *'83*

Carlos Sanz

Beer for My Horses *'08*
The Take *'07*
Crank *'06*

Horatio Sanz (1969-)

Lucky You *'07*
School for Scoundrels *'06*
The Man *'05*
Rebound *'05*
Boat Trip *'03*
The New Guy *'02*
Tomcats *'01*

Jorge Sanz (1969-)

I Love You Baby *'01*
The Girl of Your Dreams *'99*
The Break *'97*
The Garden of Redemption *'97*
Zafarinas *'94*
Belle Epoque *'92*
Why Do They Call It Love When They Mean Sex? *'92*
Lovers: A True Story *'90*
If They Tell You I Fell *'89*

Margarita Sanz (1954-)

Frida *'02*
Midaq Alley *'95*

Al Sapienza (1962-)

The American Mall *'08*
Guns *'08*
Sharpshooter *'07*
Back in the Day *'05*
Bomb the System *'05*
Megalodon *'03*
Endangered Species *'02*
The Hollywood Sign *'01*
Blind Heat *'00*
Sweet Evil *'98*
Animal Instincts 2 *'94*
The Voyeur *'94*

Bob Sapp

Player 5150 *'08*
Big Stan *'07*
The Longest Yard *'05*

Alice Sapritch (1916-90)

A Slightly Pregnant Man *'79*
Delusions of Grandeur *'76*

Mia Sara (1967-)

Hoodlum & Son *'03*
Jack and the Beanstalk: The Real Story *'01*
Black Day Blue Night *'95*
Bullet to Beijing *'95*
The Maddening *'95*
The Pompatus of Love *'95*
The Set Up *'95*
Undertow *'95*
Timecop *'94*
Blindsided *'93*
By the Sword *'93*
Call of the Wild *'93*
Caroline at Midnight *'93*
A Stranger Among Us *'92*
A Climate for Killing *'91*
Any Man's Death *'90*
Daughter of Darkness *'89*
Apprentice to Murder *'88*
Shadows in the Storm *'88*
Queenie *'87*
Ferris Bueller's Day Off *'86*
Legend *'86*

Barbara Sarafian

Moscow, Belgium *'08*
8 1/2 Women *'99*

Richard Sarafian (1935-)

Dr. Dolittle 2 *'01 (V)*
Bulworth *'98*
Bound *'96*
Gotti *'96*
Miami Hustle *'95*
The Crossing Guard *'94*
Sex, Love and Cold Hard Cash *'93*
Ruby *'92*
Bugsy *'91*

Chris Sarandon (1942-)

Loggerheads *'05*
Perfume *'01*
Race Against Time *'00*
Let the Devil Wear Black *'99*
Little Men *'98*
Road Ends *'98*
The Reaper *'97*
Tales from the Crypt Presents Bordello of Blood *'96*
Edie & Pen *'95*

Nightlife '90

Suzanne Savoy

The Man with the Perfect Swing '95
The Cellar '90

Devon Sawa (1978-)

Devil's Den '06
Extreme Dating '04
Extreme Ops '02
Slackers '02
Final Destination '00
The Guilty '99
Idle Hands '99
SLC Punk! '99
Around the Fire '98
A Cool, Dry Place '98
Wild America '97
The Boys Club '96
Night of the Twisters '95
Robin of Locksley '95
Little Giants '94

Kenji Sawada

The Happiness of the Katakuris '01
Mishima: A Life in Four Chapters '85
Samurai Reincarnation '81

Yasuka Sawaguchi

Orochi, the Eight Headed Dragon '94
Godzilla 1985 '85

Keiko Sawai

Godzilla vs. Monster Zero '68
Frankenstein Conquers the World '64

Tetsu Sawaki

Boogiepop and Others '00
Audition '99

Julia Sawalha (1968-)

Cranford '08
Chicken Run '00 (V)
Mr. Toad's Wild Ride '96
A Midwinter's Tale '95
Pride and Prejudice '95
Martin Chuzzlewit '94

Nadim Sawalha (1935-)

The Nativity Story '06
Cleopatra '99
The Awakening '80
The Wind and the Lion '75

Ikio Sawamura (1905-75)

War of the Gargantuas '70
Godzilla's Revenge '69
Yojimbo '61

Joseph (Joe) Sawyer (1906-82)

The Kettles in the Ozarks '56
The Killing '56
Mr. Walkie Talkie '52
As You Were '51
Comin' Round the Mountain '51
Indian Uprising '51
Operation Haylift '50
The Traveling Saleswoman '50
Coroner Creek '48
Fighting Father Dunne '48
Big Town After Dark '47
G.I. War Brides '46
The Naughty Nineties '45
Raiders of Ghost City '44
The Outlaw '43
Tanks a Million '41
They Died with Their Boots On '41
The Border Legion '40
Lucky Cisco Kid '40
Melody Ranch '40
Confessions of a Nazi Spy '39
The Roaring Twenties '39
The Black Legion '37
San Quentin '37
Murder With Pictures '36
Petrified Forest '36
Special Investigator '36
The Informer '35
College Humor '33

John Saxon (1935-)

Masters of Horror: Pelts '06
Outta Time '01
Final Payback '99
From Dusk Till Dawn '95
Beverly Hills Cop 3 '94
Killing Obsession '94
Wes Craven's New Nightmare '94
No Escape, No Return '93
Animal Instincts '92
The Baby Doll Murders '92
Hellmaster '92
Maximum Force '92
Blackmail '91
Deadly Conspiracy '91
Payoff '91
The Arrival '90
Blood Salvage '90
Crossing the Line '90
The Last Samurai '90
The Final Alliance '89
My Mom's a Werewolf '89
Aftershock '88
Criminal Act '88
Death House '88
Welcome to Spring Break '88
A Nightmare on Elm Street 3: Dream Warriors '87
Hands of Steel '86
Fever Pitch '85
Half Slave, Half Free '85
A Nightmare on Elm Street '84
Prisoners of the Lost Universe '84
Big Score '83
Scorpion with Two Tails '82
Unsane '82
Wrong Is Right '82
Blood Beach '81
Battle Beyond the Stars '80
Beyond Evil '80
Cannibal Apocalypse '80
The Electric Horseman '79
Running Scared '79
The Bees '78
Deadly Thief '78
Fast Company '78
The Glove '78
Moonshine County Express '77
Raid on Entebbe '77
Swiss Conspiracy '77
Strange Shadows in an Empty Room '76
Black Christmas '75
Mitchell '75
Strange New World '75
Planet Earth '74
Enter the Dragon '73
Joe Kidd '72
Snatched '72
Mr. Kingstreet's War '71
Death of a Gunfighter '69
The Appaloosa '66
The Doomsday Flight '66
Night Caller from Outer Space '66
Planet of Blood '66
The Ravagers '65
The Cardinal '63
The Girl Who Knew Too Much '63
Mr. Hobbs Takes a Vacation '62
The Plunderers '60
Portrait in Black '60
The Unforgiven '60
The Reluctant Debutante '58
This Happy Feeling '58
Rock, Pretty Baby '56

Diane Sayer (1938-2001)

Kitten with a Whip '64
The Strangler '64

Philip Sayer (1947-89)

A.D. '85
Slayground '84
Xtro '83
Green Horizon '80

Alexei Sayle (1952-)

The Thief Lord '06
Tipping the Velvet '02
Swing '98
Deadly Currents '93
Reckless Kelly '93
Carry On Columbus '92
Siesta '87
Whoops Apocalypse '83

John Sayles (1950-)

Girlfight '99
Gridlock'd '96
My Life's in Turnaround '94
Matinee '92
Straight Talk '92
City of Hope '91
Little Vegas '90
Eight Men Out '88
Matewan '87
Something Wild '86
Unnatural Causes '86
The Brother from Another Planet '84
Hard Choices '84
Lianna '83
The Howling '81
Return of the Secaucus 7 '80
Piranha '78

Syd Saylor (1895-1962)

Abbott and Costello Meet the Invisible Man '51
Ambush Trail '46
Harvest Melody '43
Helltown '38
Arizona Days '37
Forlorn River '37
Sea Racketeers '37
Headin' for the Rio Grande '36
Kelly of the Secret Service '36
Kelly the Second '36
Prison Shadows '36
Sky Parade '36
The Three Mesquiteers '36
Dude Ranger '34
The Lost Jungle '34
When a Man Sees Red '34
Law of the Sea '32
The Light of Western Stars '30

John Sayre

Crystal's Diary '99
Crack Up '97

Kyu Sazanka (1914-71)

Yojimbo '61
Fires on the Plain '59

Leonardo Sbaraglia (1970-)

Carmen '03
Intacto '01
Burnt Money '00
Wild Horses '95

Raphael Sbarge (1964-)

Home Room '02
Pearl Harbor '01
Message in a Bottle '98
Quicksilver Highway '98
Independence Day '96
The Hidden 2 '94
Carnosaur '93
Prison for Children '93
Murder 101 '91
Back to Hannibal: The Return of Tom Sawyer and Huckleberry Finn '90
Billionaire Boys Club '87
My Man Adam '86
My Science Project '85
Vision Quest '85
Risky Business '83
Abuse '82

Mattia Sbragia (1952-)

The Passion of the Christ '04
Heaven '01
Year of the Gun '91
Dial Help '88

Greta Scacchi (1960-)

Brideshead Revisited '08
The Trojan Horse '08
Miss Austen Regrets '07
Broken Trail '06
Flightplan '05
Beyond the Sea '04
Daniel Deronda '02
Festival at Cannes '02
Cotton Mary '99
Love and Rage '99
The Red Violin '98
The Odyssey '97
The Serpent's Kiss '97
Emma '96
Rasputin: Dark Servant of Destiny '96
Cosi '95
Country Life '95
The Browning Version '94
Jefferson in Paris '94
Desire '93
The Killing Beach '92
The Player '92
Fires Within '91
Shattered '91
Presumed Innocent '90
White Mischief '88
Good Morning, Babylon '87
A Man in Love '87
Ebony Tower '86
Burke & Wills '85
Defense of the Realm '85
The Coca-Cola Kid '84
Waterfront '83
Heat and Dust '82

Gia Scala (1934-72)

The Guns of Navarone '61
The Tunnel of Love '58
Don't Go Near the Water '57
The Garment Jungle '57

Prunella Scales (1932-)

Station Jim '01
Emma '97
Stiff Upper Lips '96
Breaking the Code '95
An Awfully Big Adventure '94
The Rector's Wife '94
Second Best '94
Wolf '94
My Friend Walter '93
Howard's End '92
A Question of Attribution '91
A Chorus of Disapproval '89
Consuming Passions '88
The Lonely Passion of Judith Hearne '87
Mapp & Lucia '85
The Wicked Lady '83
Room at the Top '59

Jack Scalia (1951-)

End Game '06
Kraken: Tentacles of the Deep '06
Red Eye '05
Silent Predators '99
Chained Heat 3: Hell Mountain '98
First Degree '98
Under Oath '97
Act of War '96
Dark Breed '96
The Silencers '95
Storybook '95
Tall, Dark and Deadly '95
T-Force '94
Amore! '93
Casualties of Love: The "Long Island Lolita" Story '93
Shattered Image '93
Undesirable '92
Deadly Desire '91
Illicit Behavior '91
Runaway Father '91
After the Shock '90
Endless Descent '90
Fear City '85
The Amazons '84

Tiare Scanda (1974-)

I Love You Baby '01
A Lost Year '93

Carlo Scandiuzzi

Darkdrive '98
Killing Zoe '94
Red Snow '91
Shredder Orpheus '89

Sean Scanlan

A Mind to Murder '96
A Sense of Freedom '78

Kevin Scannell

Backfield in Motion '91
Shoot to Kill '88

Michelle Scarabelli (1955-)

Alien Nation: Millennium '96
Alien Nation: The Enemy Within '96
Alien Nation: Body and Soul '95
The Colony '95
The Wrong Woman '95
Alien Nation: Dark Horizon '94
Deadbolt '92
Age Old Friends '89
SnakeEater 2: The Drug Buster '89
Perfect Timing '84

Sam Scarber

Dark Heart '06
Shocker '89

Adrian Scarborough (1968-)

The History Boys '06
Vera Drake '04

Margaret Scarborough

Loco Love '03
Sunstorm '01

Don Scardino (1949-)

Cruising '80
He Knows You're Alone '80
Squirm '76

Hal Scardino (1984-)

Marvin's Room '96
The Indian in the Cupboard '95
Searching for Bobby Fischer '93

Alan Scarfe (1946-)

Sanctuary '98
Back in Business '96
Once a Thief '96
The Wrong Guy '96
Heart of Darkness '93
Jericho Fever '93
Iron Eagle 2 '88
Python Wolf '88
Keeping Track '86
The Bay Boy '85
Joshua Then and Now '85
The Deserters '83
Cathy's Curse '77

Jonathan Scarfe (1975-)

Vipers '08
Carolina Moon '07
Hearts of War '07
Liberty Stands Still '02
Blood Money '99
White Lies '98
The Lesser Evil '97
Our Mother's Murder '97
Eye '96

Renato Scarpa (1939-)

For Roseanna '96
The Postman '94
Volere Volare '92
The Icicle Thief '89
St. Michael Had a Rooster '72

Carmen Scarpitta (1933-)

In the Name of the Pope-King '85
La Cage aux Folles '78

Diana Scarwid (1955-)

Tribute '09
Valley of the Heart's Delight '07
Local Color '06
The Clearing '04
A Guy Thing '03
Party Monster '03
Path to War '02
Dirty Pictures '00
What Lies Beneath '00
From the Earth to the Moon '98
Ruby Bridges '98
Critical Choices '97
Bastard out of Carolina '96
If These Walls Could Talk '96
The Cure '95
Gold Diggers: The Secret of Bear Mountain '95
The Neon Bible '95
Truman '95
JFK: Reckless Youth '93
After the Promise '87
Brenda Starr '86
Extremities '86
The Ladies Club '86
Psycho 3 '86
A Bunny's Tale '85
Rumble Fish '83
Silkwood '83
Strange Invaders '83
Desperate Lives '82
Mommie Dearest '81
Inside Moves '80
Forever '78
Pretty Baby '78
Bunco '77
The Possessed '77

Monica Scattini (1957-)

Men Men Men '95
Priceless Beauty '90

Cassie Scerbo

Soccer Mom '08
Bring It On: In It to Win It '07

Kirsten Schaal (1978-)

Shrek Forever After '10 (V)
Toy Story 3 '10 (V)

Wendy Schaal (1954-)

Loving Annabelle '06
Small Soldiers '98
Out There '95
Going Under '91
When the Time Comes '91
Innerspace '87
Munchies '87
Creature '85
Fatal Vision '84
Where the Boys Are '84 '84

Sam Schacht (1936-)

Heart of Midnight '89
A Secret Space '88

Doris Schade (1924-)

Rosenstrasse '03
Marianne and Juliane '82

Johnathon Schaech (1969-)

Takers '10
Organizm '08
The Poker Club '08
Prom Night '08
Quarantine '08
Sex & Lies in Sin City: The Ted Binion Scandal '08
Angels Fall '07
Masters of Horror: The Washingtonians '07
Little Chenier: A Cajun Story '06
Road House 2: Last Call '06
Blood Crime '02
The Forsaken '01
How to Kill Your Neighbor's Dog '01
Sol Goode '01
Caracara '00
If You Only Knew '00
The Brutal Truth '99
Houdini '99
Splendor '99
Finding Graceland '98
Hush '98
Welcome to Woop Woop '97
Invasion of Privacy '96
That Thing You Do! '96
The Doom Generation '95
How to Make an American Quilt '95
Poison Ivy 2: Lily '95

Joshua Schaefer

Eight Days a Week '97
johns '96
No Dessert Dad, 'Til You Mow the Lawn '94

Laura Schaefer
Curse 4: The Ultimate Sacrifice '90
Catacombs '89
Ghost Town '88

Eric Schaeffer (1962-)
Mind the Gap '04
One Night at McCool's '01
Wirey Spindell '99
Gunshy '98
Fall '97
If Lucy Fell '95
My Life's in Turnaround '94

Rebecca Schaeffer (1967-89)
The End of Innocence '90
Voyage of Terror: The Achille Lauro Affair '90
Scenes from the Class Struggle in Beverly Hills '89

Natalie Schafer (1900-91)
I'm Dangerous Tonight '90
Rescue from Gilligan's Island '78
Susan Slade '61
Forever Darling '56
The Girl Next Door '53
Caught '49
The Time of Your Life '48
Wonder Man '45

William Schallert (1922-)
Shake, Rattle & Rock! '94
Matinee '92
Held Hostage '91
House Party 2: The Pajama Jam '91
The Incident '89
War & Remembrance: The Final Chapter '89
War & Remembrance '88
Innerspace '87
The Grace Kelly Story '83
Twilight Zone: The Movie '83
Blind Ambition '79
The Strongest Man in the World '75
Death Sentence '74
Trial of the Catonsville Nine '72
Man on a String '71
Colossus: The Forbin Project '70
The Computer Wore Tennis Shoes '69
Sam Whiskey '69
Speedway '68
Lonely Are the Brave '62
The Gallant Hours '60
The Incredible Shrinking Man '57
Man in the Shadow '57
Tarnished Angels '57
The Gunslinger '56
An Annapolis Story '55
The High and the Mighty '54
Them! '54
Sword of Venus '53
Invasion U.S.A. '52
The Man from Planet X '51

Mike Schank
Storytelling '01
American Movie '99

Tom Schanley (1961-)
Lone Rider '08
Footsteps '98
Nothing Underneath '85

Heidi Schanz
Universal Soldier: The Return '99
Mixing Nia '98
Shame, Shame, Shame '98
Body Language '95

Sabrina Scharf
Hunter '73
Easy Rider '69
Hell's Angels on Wheels '67

Alexander Scheer
Eight Miles High '08
Eight Miles High '07
Advertising Rules! '01

Roy Scheider (1932-2008)
Dark Honeymoon '08
Blue Blood '07
Chicago 10 '07 (V)
Hearts of War '07
Dracula 3: Legacy '05
The Punisher '04
Dracula 2: Ascension '03
King of Texas '02
Love Thy Neighbor '02
Daybreak '01
Time Lapse '01
Angels Don't Sleep Here '00
Chain of Command '00
The Doorway '00
RKO 281 '99
The Peacekeeper '98
Silver Wolf '98
The White Raven '98
Executive Target '97
John Grisham's The Rainmaker '97
The Myth of Fingerprints '97
Plato's Run '96
The Rage '96
Covert Assassin '94
Romeo Is Bleeding '93
Naked Lunch '91
The Fourth War '90
The Russia House '90
Somebody Has to Shoot the Picture '90
Listen to Me '89
Night Game '89
Cohen and Tate '88
52 Pick-Up '86
The Men's Club '86
Mishima: A Life in Four Chapters '85 (N)
2010: The Year We Make Contact '84
Blue Thunder '83
Tiger Town '83
Still of the Night '82
All That Jazz '79
Last Embrace '79
Jaws 2 '78
Sorcerer '77
Marathon Man '76
Jaws '75
The Outside Man '73
The Seven-Ups '73
The French Connection '71
Klute '71
Loving '70
Stiletto '69
Paper Lion '68
Curse of the Living Corpse '64

Raynor Scheine (1942-)
A Stranger's Heart '07
The Sentinel '06
The Rookie '02
The War '94

Clemens Scheitz
Stroszek '77
Heart of Glass '74

Carl Schell (1928-)
Quick, Let's Get Married '71
Werewolf in a Girl's Dormitory '61

Catherine Schell (1946-)
On the Third Day '83
Gulliver's Travels '77
Return of the Pink Panther '74
On Her Majesty's Secret Service '69

Maria Schell (1926-2005)
Christmas Lilies of the Field '84
Samson and Delilah '84
La Passante '83
Inside the Third Reich '82
Just a Gigolo '79
Twist '76
Voyage of the Damned '76
The Odessa File '74
99 Women '69
End of Desire '62
The Mark '61
Cimarron '60
The Hanging Tree '59
The Brothers Karamazov '58
White Nights '57
Gervaise '56
Napoleon '55
The Last Bridge '54
Angel with the Trumpet '50

Maximilian Schell (1930-)
The Brothers Bloom '09
Coast to Coast '04
Festival at Cannes '02
The Song of the Lark '01
Joan of Arc '99
Deep Impact '98
Left Luggage '98
The Eighteenth Angel '97
John Carpenter's Vampires '97
Telling Lies in America '96
The Thorn Birds: The Missing Years '96
Abraham '94
Little Odessa '94
A Far Off Place '93
Miss Rose White '92
Stalin '92
Young Catherine '91
The Freshman '90
The Rose Garden '89
Peter the Great '86
The Assisi Underground '84
The Chosen '81
Avalanche Express '79
The Black Hole '79
Players '79
Together? '79
The Day That Shook the World '78
A Bridge Too Far '77
Julia '77
Cross of Iron '76
St. Ives '76
The Man in the Glass Booth '75
The Odessa File '74
The Pedestrian '73
First Love '70
Krakatoa East of Java '69
Simon Bolivar '69
The Castle '68
Heidi '67
Topkapi '64
Judgment at Nuremberg '61
The Young Lions '58

Ronnie Schell (1931-)
Jetsons: The Movie '90 (V)
Gus '76

August Schellenberg (1936-)
Bury My Heart at Wounded Knee '07
Missionary Man '07
Eight Below '06
The New World '05
The Unsaid '01
High Noon '00
Out of Time '00
Free Willy 3: The Rescue '97
True Heart '97
Crazy Horse '96
Grand Avenue '96
Free Willy 2: The Adventure Home '95
Tecumseh: The Last Warrior '95
Getting Gotti '94
Lakota Woman: Siege at Wounded Knee '94
Free Willy '93
Geronimo '93
Iron Will '93
Black Robe '91
Striker's Mountain '87
Tramp at the Door '87
Confidential '86
Mark of Cain '84

David Scheller
Eight Miles High '08
The Lost Samaritan '08
Eight Miles High '07
Extreme Ops '02

Mary Kate Schellhardt (1978-)
Apollo 13 '95
What's Eating Gilbert Grape '93

Wolfgang Schenck (1934-)
Effi Briest '74
Tenderness of the Wolves '73

Robert Schenkkan (1953-)
Act of Vengeance '86
The Manhattan Project '86
Sanctuary of Fear '79

Jean Schertler
Runaway Bride '99
Pecker '98

Rosanna Schiaffino (1938-)
Simon Bolivar '69
Code Name Alpha '67
The Rover '67
Arrivederci, Baby! '66
The Witch '66
The Long Ships '64
The Victors '63
RoGoPaG '62
Two Weeks in Another Town '62
Roland the Mighty '56

Vincent Schiavelli (1948-2005)
Baadasssss! '03
Death to Smoochy '02
The 4th Tenor '02
Hey Arnold! The Movie '02 (V)
Snow White: The Fairest of Them All '02
Three Strikes '00
Desert Heat '99
Man on the Moon '99
The Pooch and the Pauper '99
The Prince and the Surfer '99
Treehouse Hostage '99
Milo '98
Tomorrow Never Dies '97
Back to Back '96
The People vs. Larry Flynt '96
Two Much '96
The Courtyard '95
Lord of Illusions '95
Prince Brat and the Whipping Boy '95
3 Ninjas Knuckle Up '95
Lurking Fear '94
Batman Returns '92
Miracle Beach '92
Ghost '90
Playroom '90
Waiting for the Light '90
Cold Feet '89
Valmont '89
Better Off Dead '85
Lots of Luck '85
The Adventures of Buckaroo Banzai Across the Eighth Dimension '84
Amadeus '84
Ratings Game '84
Fast Times at Ridgemont High '82
Night Shift '82 (V)
The Return '80
One Flew Over the Cuckoo's Nest '75

Dieter Schidor (1949-87)
Schnelles Geld '84
Cross of Iron '76

Richard Schiff (1959-)
Solitary Man '10
Last Chance Harvey '08
Civic Duty '06
Ray '04
People I Know '02
I Am Sam '01
What's the Worst That Could Happen? '01
Along for the Ride '00
Gun Shy '00
Lucky Numbers '00
Whatever It Takes '00
Crazy in Alabama '99
Forces of Nature '99
Heaven '99
Deep Impact '98
Dr. Dolittle '98
Living Out Loud '98
The Pentagon Wars '98
The Lost World: Jurassic Park 2 '97
The Trigger Effect '96
City Hall '95
Hoffa '92

Claudia Schiffer (1970-)
Love Actually '03
Life Without Dick '01
In Pursuit '00
Black and White '99
Friends & Lovers '99
The Blackout '97
Richie Rich '94

Joseph Schildkraut (1895-1964)
The Diary of Anne Frank '59
Monsieur Beaucaire '46
The Cheaters '45
Flame of the Barbary Coast '45
The Shop Around the Corner '40
Idiot's Delight '39
The Man in the Iron Mask '39
Mr. Moto Takes a Vacation '39
Mr. Takes a Vacation '39
The Rains Came '39
The Three Musketeers '39
Marie Antoinette '38
The Life of Emile Zola '37
Souls at Sea '37
The Garden of Allah '36
The Crusades '35
Cleopatra '34
Viva Villa! '34
King of Kings '27
The Road to Yesterday '25
Orphans of the Storm '21
Wandering Jew '20

Gus Schilling (1908-57)
Gasoline Alley '51
The Lady from Shanghai '48
It's a Pleasure '45
A Thousand and One Nights '45
Citizen Kane '41

Tom Schilling (1982-)
Agnes and His Brothers '04
Before the Fall '04

Vivian Schilling (1968-)
Savage Land '94
Future Shock '93
In a Moment of Passion '93
The Legend of Wolf Mountain '92
Project: Eliminator '91
Soultaker '90
Terror Eyes '87

Tom Schioler (1956-)
Maniac Warriors '88
Storm '87

Steve Schirripa (1958-)
Must Love Dogs '05
Something About Sex '98

Sharon Schlarth
Eat and Run '86
Dead As a Doorman '85

Charlie Schlatter (1966-)
Out at the Wedding '07
Miss Cast Away '04
Ed '96
Police Academy 7: Mission to Moscow '94
Sunset Heat '92
All-American Murder '91
Bright Lights, Big City '88
18 Again! '88
Heartbreak Hotel '88

Ariane Schluter (1966-)
The Dress '96
1-900 '94

Kyle Schmid (1984-)
The Thaw '09
Joy Ride 2: Dead Ahead '08
Sisterhood of the Traveling Pants '05
The Cheetah Girls '03
Alley Cats Strike '00

Walter Schmidinger (1933-)
Hanussen '88
From the Life of the Marionettes '80

Kevin G. Schmidt (1988-)
Cheaper by the Dozen 2 '05
The Butterfly Effect '04
Catch That Kid '04

Marlene Schmidt (1937-)
Scorchy '76
The Stepmother '71

Niels Bruno Schmidt
The Baader Meinhof Complex '08
School's Out '99

Wolfgang Schmidt
See Ray Dennis Steckler

Christiane Schmidtmer (1940-2003)
The Giant Spider Invasion '75
The Big Doll House '71
Boeing Boeing '65

Sybille Schmitz (1909-55)
F.P. 1 Doesn't Answer '33
Vampyr '31
Diary of a Lost Girl '29

August Schmolzer (1958-)
Bride of the Wind '01
Requiem for Dominic '91

Stefan Schnabel (1912-99)
Anna '87
Two Weeks in Another Town '62
The 27th Day '57
Houdini '53

Monica Schnarre (1971-)
Love on the Side '04
Turbulence 3: Heavy Metal '00
Dead Fire '98
The Peacekeeper '98
Bulletproof Heart '95
Fearless Tiger '94
The Death Merchant '91
Waxwork 2: Lost in Time '91

Bonnie Schneider
Murderlust '86
Mama Dracula '80

Dan Schneider (1966-)
Good Burger '97
The Big Picture '89
Happy Together '89
Better Off Dead '85

Helmuth Schneider (1920-72)
Fifth Day of Peace '72
Angelique and the Sultan '68
Captain Sinbad '63

John Schneider (1960-)
Conjurer '08
Shark Swarm '08
Lake Placid 2 '07
Sydney White '07
Collier & Co.: Hot Pursuit '06
Snow Day '00

True Women '97
Night of the Twisters '95
Texas '94
Ministry of Vengeance '89
Speed Zone '88
Christmas Comes to Willow Creek '87
The Curse '87
Cocaine Wars '86
Stagecoach '86
Eddie Macon's Run '83
Smokey and the Bandit '77

Maria Schneider (1952-)
Jane Eyre '96
Les Nuits Fauves '92
Crime of Honor '85
Mama Dracula '80
The Passenger '75
Wanted: Babysitter '75
Last Tango in Paris '73

Michael Schneider (1939-)
Schindler's List '93
Double Edge '92
The Last Winter '84

Paul Schneider (1973-)
Away We Go '09
Bright Star '09
The Assassination of Jesse James by the Coward Robert Ford '07
Lars and the Real Girl '07
Elizabethtown '05
The Family Stone '05
How to Lose Your Lover '04
All the Real Girls '03

Rob Schneider (1963-)
Grown Ups '10
American Virgin '09
You Don't Mess with the Zohan '08
American Crude '07
Big Stan '07
I Now Pronounce You Chuck and Larry '07
The Benchwarmers '06
Click '06
Grandma's Boy '06
Deuce Bigalow: European Gigolo '05
The Longest Yard '05
Around the World in 80 Days '04
50 First Dates '04
Adam Sandler's 8 Crazy Nights '02 (V)
The Hot Chick '02
Mr. Deeds '02
The Animal '01
Little Nicky '00
Big Daddy '99
Deuce Bigalow: Male Gigolo '99
Muppets from Space '99
Dying to Get Rich '98
Knock Off '98
The Waterboy '98
The Adventures of Pinocchio '96
Down Periscope '96
Judge Dredd '95
The Beverly Hillbillies '93
Demolition Man '93
Surf Ninjas '93
Home Alone 2: Lost in New York '92

Romy Schneider (1938-82)
La Passante '83
Death Watch '80
Sidney Sheldon's Bloodline '79
A Simple Story '79
A Woman at Her Window '77
Innocents with Dirty Hands '76
Mado '76
Old Gun '76
The Infernal Trio '74
The Last Train '74
Assassination of Trotsky '72
Cesar & Rosalie '72
Ludwig '72
The Hero '71
Swimming Pool '70
The Things of Life '70
La Piscine '69
Triple Cross '67
What's New Pussycat? '65
Good Neighbor Sam '64
The Trial '63
The Victors '63
Boccaccio '70 '62

Andrea Schober (1964-)
Chinese Roulette '86
The Merchant of Four Seasons '71

Michael Schoeffling (1960-)
Wild Hearts Can't Be Broken '91
Longtime Companion '90
Mermaids '90
Slaves of New York '89
Let's Get Harry '87
Belizaire the Cajun '86
Sylvester '85
Vision Quest '85
Racing with the Moon '84
Sixteen Candles '84

Jill Schoelen (1970-)
When a Stranger Calls Back '93
Adventures in Spying '92
There Goes My Baby '92
Rich Girl '91
Cutting Class '89
The Phantom of the Opera '89
Popcorn '89
Curse 2: The Bite '88
Billionaire Boys Club '87
The Stepfather '87
Babes in Toyland '86
That Was Then... This Is Now '85
Thunder Alley '85
D.C. Cab '84
Hot Moves '84

Ingrid Schoeller
They Paid with Bullets: Chicago 1929 '69
Psychopath '68

Margareta Schoen (1895-1985)
Kriemhilde's Revenge '24
Siegfried '24

Hinnerk Schoenemann
Yella '07
Unveiled '05

Ingeborg (Inge) Schoener (1935-)
Mr. Superinvisible '73
Mark of the Devil '69
Cold Steel for Tortuga '65

Dietmar Schoenherr (1926-)
Journey of Hope '90
The Monster of London City '64

Andrew Schofield
Liam '00
Sid & Nancy '86

Annabel Schofield (1963-)
Exit in Red '97
Body Armor '96
Midnight Blue '96
Solar Crisis '92
Dragonard '88

David Schofield (1951-)
Pirates of the Caribbean: Dead Man's Chest '06
The Musketeer '01
Gladiator '00
Leo Tolstoy's Anna Karenina '96
Band of Gold '95
Jekyll and Hyde '90
An American Werewolf in London '81

Tom Scholte
Goldrush: A Real Life Alaskan Adventure '98
Live Bait '95

Jason Schombing (1963-)
K-9 3: P.I. '01
Asylum '97
Robin Cook's Invasion '97
3 Ninjas Kick Back '94
Timecop '94

Reiner Schone (1942-)
My Little Assassin '99
Mortal Kombat 2: Annihilation '97
Crash Dive '96
The Gunfighters '87
Return of Sabata '71

Frank Schorpion
No Alibi '00
Escape from Wildcat Canyon '99
Dead End '98
Random Encounter '98

Bob Schott (1949-)
Head of the Family '96
In the Line of Fire '93
Out for Blood '93
Future Hunters '88

Maria Schrader (1965-)
Rosenstrasse '03
Advertising Rules! '01
Aimee & Jaguar '98
Burning Life '94

Lisa Schrage
China White '91
Food of the Gods: Part 2 '88
Hello Mary Lou: Prom Night 2 '87

Bitty Schram (1968-)
Cleopatra's Second Husband '00
Kissing a Fool '98
Caught '96
One Fine Day '96
My Family Treasure '93
A League of Their Own '92

Max Schreck (1879-1936)
The Street '23
Nosferatu '22

Avery Schreiber (1935-2002)
The Student Affair '97
Saturday the 14th Strikes Back '88
Hunk '87
Caveman '81
Galaxina '80
Silent Scream '80
Flatbed Annie and Sweetiepie: Lady Truckers '79

Liev Schreiber (1967-)
Repo Men '10
Salt '10
Taking Woodstock '09
X-Men Origins: Wolverine '09
Defiance '08
Chicago 10 '07 (V)
Love in the Time of Cholera '07
The Omen '06
The Painted Veil '06
The Manchurian Candidate '04
Hitler: The Rise of Evil '03
The Sum of All Fears '02
Kate & Leopold '01
Hamlet '00
Scream 3 '00
The Hurricane '99
Jakob the Liar '99
RKO 281 '99
Spring Forward '99
A Walk on the Moon '99
Twilight '98
Phantoms '97
Scream 2 '97
Since You've Been Gone '97
Sphere '97
The Daytrippers '96
Ransom '96
Scream '96
Walking and Talking '96
Buffalo Girls '95
Denise Calls Up '95
The Sunshine Boys '95
Mixed Nuts '94
Party Girl '94

Pablo Schreiber (1978-)
Nights in Rodanthe '08
Into the Fire '05
The Manchurian Candidate '04
The Mudge Boy '03
A Painted House '03

Greta Schroder (1891-1967)
Nosferatu '22
The Golem '20

Rick Schroder (1970-)
The Andromeda Strain '08
Journey to the Center of the Earth '08
Black Cloud '04
Poolhall Junkies '02
Lost Battalion '01
Murder at Devil's Glen '99
Ebenezer '97
Hostage High '97
Crimson Tide '95
Texas '94
Call of the Wild '93
Return to Lonesome Dove '93
There Goes My Baby '92
Across the Tracks '89
Lonesome Dove '89
Two Kinds of Love '85
Hansel and Gretel '82
Earthling '80
The Last Flight of Noah's Ark '80
Little Lord Fauntleroy '80
The Champ '79

Barbet Schroeder (1941-)
The Duchess of Langeais '07
Paris, je t'aime '06
Celine and Julie Go Boating '74
Six in Paris '68

Carly Schroeder (1990-)
Gracie '07
Eye of the Dolphin '06
Firewall '06
Mean Creek '04
The Lizzie McGuire Movie '03

Steven Schub
Devil's Den '06
No Vacancy '99
The Thirteenth Floor '99
Footsteps '98
Caught '96

Karin Schubert (1944-)
Delusions of Grandeur '76
Till Marriage Do Us Part '74
Cold Eyes of Fear '70

John Schuck (1940-)
The Curse of the Jade Scorpion '01
The Trial of Old Drum '00
Holy Matrimony '94
Tales from the Crypt Presents Demon Knight '94
Star Trek 6: The Undiscovered Country '91
My Mom's a Werewolf '89
Second Sight '89
The New Adventures of Pippi Longstocking '88
Star Trek 4: The Voyage Home '86
Finders Keepers '84
Butch and Sundance: The Early Days '79
Thieves Like Us '74
Blade '72
Hammersmith Is Out '72
McCabe & Mrs. Miller '71
Brewster McCloud '70
M*A*S*H '70

Rudolf Schuendler (1906-88)
The American Friend '77
Suspiria '77

Al Schuerman
The Bible and Gun Club '96
Presumed Guilty '91

Rebecca Schull (1929-)
Flannel Pajamas '06
Analyze This '98
Neil Simon's The Odd Couple 2 '98
That Darn Cat '96
My Life '93

Albert Schultz
White Lies '98
Ebenezer '97
Beethoven Lives Upstairs '92

Dwight Schultz (1947-)
The A-Team '10
Star Trek: First Contact '96
The Temp '93
Woman with a Past '92
Fat Man and Little Boy '89
The Long Walk Home '89
When Your Lover Leaves '83
Alone in the Dark '82

Sarah Ann Schultz
Lies and Illusions '09

Matt Schulze (1972-)
The Flock '07
Mr. Brooks '07
Final Move '06
Torque '04
Blade 2 '02
The Transporter '02
The Fast and the Furious '01
Dementia '98

Paul Schulze
Rambo '08
Panic Room '02
Don't Say a Word '01
Alien Fury: Countdown to Invasion '00
Drowning Mona '00
Grind '96
Illtown '96
Hand Gun '93
Laws of Gravity '92

Wendy Schumacher (1971-)
Fugitive Rage '96
Scorned 2 '96
Animal Instincts 3: The Seductress '95
Star Hunter '95

Hans Schumm (1896-1990)
Spy Smasher '42
Spy Smasher Returns '42

Reinhold Schunzel (1886-1954)
Woman in Brown '48
Golden Earrings '47
Notorious '46
The Threepenny Opera '31
Fortune's Fool '21

Maurice Schutz (1866-1955)
Vampyr '31
Passion of Joan of Arc '28
Napoleon '27

Jennifer Schwalbach Smith (1971-)
Clerks 2 '06
Jay and Silent Bob Strike Back '01

Maurice Schwartz (1891-1960)
Salome '53
Tevye '39
Uncle Moses '32

Scott Schwartz (1969-)
Alien 3000 '04
Bridge of Dragons '99
A Time to Live '85
A Christmas Story '83
Kidco '83
The Toy '82

Jason Schwartzman (1980-)
Scott Pilgrim vs. the World '10
Fantastic Mr. Fox '09 (V)
Funny People '09
The Marc Pease Experience '09
The Darjeeling Limited '07
Walk Hard: The Dewey Cox Story '07
Marie Antoinette '06
Bewitched '05
The Hitchhiker's Guide to the Galaxy '05
Shopgirl '05
I Heart Huckabees '04
Simone '02
Slackers '02
Spun '02
CQ '01
Rushmore '98

Jaecki Schwarz
Burning Life '94
I Was Nineteen '68

Simon Schwarz
North Face '08
The Inheritors '98

Arnold Schwarzenegger (1947-)
The Expendables '10
Around the World in 80 Days '04
The Rundown '03
Terminator 3: Rise of the Machines '03
Collateral Damage '02
The 6th Day '00
End of Days '99
Batman and Robin '97
Eraser '96
Jingle All the Way '96
Junior '94
True Lies '94
Dave '93
Last Action Hero '93
Beretta's Island '92
Terminator 2: Judgment Day '91
Kindergarten Cop '90
Total Recall '90
Red Heat '88
Twins '88
Predator '87
The Running Man '87
Raw Deal '86
Commando '85
Red Sonja '85
Conan the Destroyer '84
The Terminator '84
Conan the Barbarian '82
The Jayne Mansfield Story '80
The Villain '79
Stay Hungry '76
The Long Goodbye '73
Hercules in New York '70

Eric Schweig (1967-)
Bury My Heart at Wounded Knee '07
It Waits '05
The Missing '03
Mr. Barrington '03
Skins '02
Big Eden '00
Larry McMurtry's Dead Man's Walk '96
Follow the River '95
Tom and Huck '95
Pontiac Moon '94
Squanto: A Warrior's Tale '94
The Broken Chain '93
The Last of the Mohicans '92

Til Schweiger (1963-)
Inglourious Basterds *'09*
Already Dead *'07*
Body Armour *'07*
One Way *'06*
Deuce Bigalow: European Gigolo *'05*
In Enemy Hands *'04*
King Arthur *'04*
Lara Croft Tomb Raider: The Cradle of Life *'03*
Joe and Max *'02*
What to Do in Case of Fire *'02*
Driven *'01*
Intimate Affairs *'01*
SLC Punk! *'99*
Judas Kiss *'98*
The Replacement Killers *'98*
Brute *'97*
Maybe... Maybe Not *'94*

Jan Schweiterman (1972-)
Warlock 3: The End of Innocence *'98*
Good Burger *'97*

David Schwimmer (1966-)
Madagascar: Escape 2 Africa *'08 (V)*
Nothing But the Truth *'08*
Big Nothing *'06*
Duane Hopwood *'05*
Madagascar *'05 (V)*
Band of Brothers *'01*
Hotel *'01*
Uprising *'01*
It's the Rage *'99*
Picking Up the Pieces *'99*
Kissing a Fool *'98*
Six Days, Seven Nights *'98*
Apt Pupil *'97*
Breast Men *'97*
Since You've Been Gone *'97*
The Pallbearer *'95*
Flight of the Intruder *'90*

Rusty Schwimmer
Broken Trail *'06*
The Hawk Is Dying *'06*
Mozart and the Whale *'05*
North Country *'05*
Runaway Jury *'03*
John John in the Sky *'00*
The Perfect Storm *'00*
Los Locos Posse *'97*
North Shore Fish *'97*
Prison of Secrets *'97*
Lone Justice 3: Showdown at Plum Creek *'96*
Twister *'96*
A Little Princess *'95*
Jason Goes to Hell: The Final Friday *'93*
Lone Justice 2 *'93*
T Bone N Weasel *'92*

Hanna Schygulla (1943-)
The Edge of Heaven *'07*
The Girl of Your Dreams *'99*
Lea *'96*
Dead Again *'91*
The Summer of Miss Forbes *'88*
Casanova *'87*
Forever, Lulu *'87*
Barnum *'86*
Delta Force *'86*
A Love in Germany *'84*
Sheer Madness *'84*
La Nuit de Varennes *'82*
Passion *'82*
Berlin Alexanderplatz *'80*
The Marriage of Maria Braun *'79*
The Wrong Move *'78*
Effi Briest *'74*
The Bitter Tears of Petra von Kant *'72*
The Merchant of Four Seasons *'71*
Beware of a Holy Whore *'70*
Whity *'70*
Gods of the Plague *'69*
Love Is Colder Than Death *'69*

Why Does Herr R. Run Amok? *'69*

Yvonne Scio (1969-)
Sorority Boys *'02*
Redline *'97*

Steve Scionti
Megalodon *'03*
Mom's Outta Sight *'01*

Annabella Sciorra (1960-)
Find Me Guilty *'06*
12 and Holding *'05*
Chasing Liberty *'04*
King of the Jungle *'01*
Above Suspicion *'00*
Once in the Life *'00*
Mr. Jealousy *'98*
New Rose Hotel *'98*
What Dreams May Come *'98*
Asteroid *'97*
Cop Land *'97*
Highball *'97*
Little City *'97*
The Funeral *'96*
Underworld *'96*
The Addiction *'95*
The Cure *'95*
The Innocent Sleep *'95*
National Lampoon's Favorite Deadly Sins *'95*
Mr. Wonderful *'93*
The Night We Never Met *'93*
Romeo Is Bleeding *'93*
The Hand that Rocks the Cradle *'92*
Whispers in the Dark *'92*
The Hard Way *'91*
Jungle Fever *'91*
Prison Stories: Women on the Inside *'91*
Cadillac Man *'90*
Internal Affairs *'90*
Reversal of Fortune *'90*
True Love *'89*

Edith Scob (1937-)
Summer Hours *'08*
Heartbeat Detector *'07*
Bon Voyage *'03*
The Man on the Train *'02*
Brotherhood of the Wolf *'01*
Comedy of Innocence *'00*
Time Regained *'99*
The Milky Way *'68*
The Burning Court *'62*
The Horror Chamber of Dr. Faustus *'59*

Dean Scofield (1957-)
The Last Assassins *'96*
Prehysteria 2 *'94*
Eden 3 *'93*
Eden 4 *'93*

Paul Scofield (1922-2008)
Animal Farm *'99 (V)*
The Crucible *'96*
Martin Chuzzlewit *'94*
Quiz Show *'94*
Utz *'93*
Hamlet *'90*
Mr. Corbett's Ghost *'90*
Henry V *'89*
When the Whales Came *'89*
The Attic: The Hiding of Anne Frank *'88*
Anna Karenina *'85*
The Curse of King Tut's Tomb *'80 (N)*
Scorpio *'73*
King Lear *'71*
Bartleby *'70*
A Man for All Seasons *'66*
The Train *'65*
Carve Her Name with Pride *'58*

Tracy Scoggins (1959-)
The Strange Case of Dr. Jekyll and Mr. Hyde *'06*
Asylum of the Damned *'03*
A Crack in the Floor *'00*
The Great American Sex Scandal *'94*
Alien Intruder *'93*
Dead On *'93*

Dollman vs Demonic Toys *'93*
Play Murder for Me *'91*
Timebomb *'91*
Ultimate Desires *'91*
Beyond the Silhouette *'90*
Demonic Toys *'90*
The Red Raven Kiss-Off *'90*
Watchers 2 *'90*
The Gumshoe Kid *'89*
One Last Run *'89*
In Dangerous Company *'88*
Toy Soldiers *'84*
Twirl *'81*

Peter Scolari (1954-)
A Plumm Summer *'08*
The Polar Express *'04*
From the Earth to the Moon *'98*
That Thing You Do! *'96*
Camp Nowhere *'94*
Fallen Angels 2 *'93*
Ticks *'93*
Perfect Harmony *'91*
Corporate Affairs *'90*
Rosebud Beach Hotel *'85*

Zvee Scooler (1899-1985)
Trumps *'83*
Uncle Moses *'32*

Martin Scorsese (1942-)
Shark Tale *'04 (V)*
Gangs of New York *'02*
The Muse *'99*
With Friends Like These *'98*
Quiz Show *'94*
Search and Destroy *'94*
The Age of Innocence *'93*
Guilty by Suspicion *'91*
Akira Kurosawa's Dreams *'90*
Round Midnight *'86*
After Hours *'85*
Cannonball *'76*
Taxi Driver *'76*
Boxcar Bertha *'72*

Nicolette Scorsese
Aspen Extreme *'93*
Boxing Helena *'93*

Izabela Scorupco (1970-)
Cougar Club *'07*
Exorcist: The Beginning *'04*
Reign of Fire *'02*
Vertical Limit *'00*
Goldeneye *'95*

Adam Scott (1973-)
Leap Year *'10*
Piranha 3D *'10*
The Vicious Kind *'09*
August *'08*
Step Brothers *'08*
Corporate Affairs *'07*
The Matador *'06*
The Return *'06*
Monster-in-Law *'05*
The Aviator *'04*
Off the Lip *'04*
Torque *'04*
Two Days *'03*
High Crimes *'02*
The Lesser Evil *'97*

Alex Scott (1929-)
Romper Stomper *'92*
Next of Kin *'82*
The Asphyx *'72*
The Abominable Dr. Phibes *'71*
Fahrenheit 451 *'66*

Andrew Scott
Dead Bodies *'03*
The American *'01*
Nora *'00*

Ashley Scott (1977-)
12 Rounds *'09*
Strange Wilderness *'08*
Into the Blue *'05*
Lost *'05*
Walking Tall *'04*

Bainbridge Scott
Death Chase *'87*
Hell Squad *'85*

Brenda Scott (1943-)
Simon, King of the Witches *'71*
Johnny Tiger *'66*

Campbell Scott (1962-)
Phoebe in Wonderland *'08*
Crashing *'07*
Music & Lyrics *'07*
Duma *'05*
The Dying Gaul *'05*
The Exorcism of Emily Rose *'05*
Loverboy *'05*
Saint Ralph *'04*
Roger Dodger *'02*
The Secret Lives of Dentists *'02*
Follow the Stars Home *'01*
Hamlet *'01*
Lush *'01*
The Pilot's Wife *'01*
Invasion! *'99*
Spring Forward *'99*
Hi-Life *'98*
The Imposters *'98*
The Love Letter *'98*
The Spanish Prisoner *'97*
The Daytrippers *'96*
Big Night *'95*
The Kennedys of Massachusetts *'95*
Mrs. Parker and the Vicious Circle *'94*
The Innocent *'93*
Singles *'92*
Dead Again *'91*
Dying Young *'91*
Longtime Companion *'90*
No Way Back *'90*
The Sheltering Sky *'90*
Ain't No Way Back *'89*

Carey Scott (1965-)
Diving In *'90*
Making the Grade *'84*

Debralee Scott (1953-)
Police Academy *'84*
Just Tell Me You Love Me *'80*
Deathmoon *'78*
Our Time *'74*
Dirty Harry *'71*

Donovan Scott (1946-)
I Know Who Killed Me *'07*
Sheena *'84*
Goldilocks & the Three Bears *'83*
Savannah Smiles *'82*
Zorro, the Gay Blade *'81*
1941 *'79*

Dougray Scott (1965-)
Dr. Jekyll and Mr. Hyde *'08*
Hitman *'07*
The Truth About Love *'04*
To Kill a King *'03*
Dark Water *'02*
Ripley's Game *'02*
Enigma *'01*
Arabian Nights *'00*
Mission: Impossible 2 *'00*
Deep Impact *'98*
Ever After: A Cinderella Story *'98*
Behind the Lines *'97*
Twin Town *'97*
Another 9 1/2 Weeks *'96*
The Crow Road *'96*

Eric Scott (1958-)
A Day for Thanks on Walton's Mountain *'82*
The Waltons: The Christmas Carol *'80*

Fred Scott (1902-91)
The Black Six *'74*
Rodeo Rhythm *'42*
Ridin' the Trail *'40*
Code of the Fearless *'39*
In Old Montana *'39*
The Rangers' Roundup *'38*
Songs and Bullets *'38*
Melody of the Plains *'37*

The Roamin' Cowboy *'37*
Singing Buckaroo *'37*
Two-Gun Troubador *'37*

Geoffrey Scott (1942-)
The Morning After *'86*
First & Ten: The Team Scores Again *'85*

George C. Scott (1927-99)
Inherit the Wind *'99*
Rocky Marciano *'99*
Gloria *'98*
Twelve Angry Men *'97*
Titanic *'96*
Angus *'95*
Prince Brat and the Whipping Boy *'95*
Tyson *'95*
Deadly Currents *'93*
Malice *'93*
Descending Angel *'90*
Exorcist 3: Legion *'90*
The Rescuers Down Under *'90 (V)*
Pals *'87*
Choices *'86*
The Last Days of Patton *'86*
The Murders in the Rue Morgue *'86*
A Christmas Carol *'84*
Firestarter *'84*
Oliver Twist *'82*
Taps *'81*
The Changeling *'80*
The Formula *'80*
Hardcore *'79*
Movie, Movie *'78*
The Prince and the Pauper *'78*
Islands in the Stream *'77*
The Hindenburg *'75*
Bank Shot *'74*
Savage Is Loose *'74*
The Day of the Dolphin *'73*
Oklahoma Crude *'73*
The New Centurions *'72*
Rage *'72*
The Hospital *'71*
They Might Be Giants *'71*
Patton *'70*
Petulia *'68*
Flim-Flam Man *'67*
The Bible *'66*
Dr. Strangelove, or: How I Learned to Stop Worrying and Love the Bomb *'64*
The List of Adrian Messenger *'63*
The Hustler *'61*
Anatomy of a Murder *'59*
The Hanging Tree *'59*

Gordon Scott (1926-2007)
Death Ray *'67*
Tramplers *'66*
Hercules and the Princess of Troy *'65*
Marauder *'65*
Coriolanus, Man without a Country *'64*
The Beast of Babylon Against the Son of Hercules *'63*
Conquest of Mycene *'63*
Gladiator of Rome *'63*
Hero of Rome *'63*
Samson and the 7 Miracles of the World *'62*
Tarzan the Magnificent *'60*
Tarzan's Greatest Adventure *'59*
Tarzan and the Trappers *'58*
Tarzan's Fight for Life *'58*
Tarzan and the Lost Safari *'57*
Tarzan's Hidden Jungle *'55*

Gregg Scott
Savage Island *'03*
Ghosthouse *'88*

Jacqueline Scott (1935-)
Empire of the Ants *'77*
Charley Varrick *'73*
Duel *'71*
Smoke *'70*

Death of a Gunfighter *'69*

Janette Scott (1938-)
Day of the Triffids *'63*
Paranoiac *'62*
School for Scoundrels *'60*
Helen of Troy *'56*

Jay Scott (1931-)
Grave of the Vampire *'72*
All the Lovin' Kinfolk *'70*
The Cut Throats *'69*

Jill Scott
Hounddog *'08*
Tyler Perry's Why Did I Get Married? *'07*

John Scott (1930-)
Horror of Party Beach *'64*
The Tell-Tale Heart *'60*

Judith Scott
Flightplan *'05*
Guess Who *'05*
Murder She Purred: A Mrs. Murphy Mystery *'98*
Soul Survivor *'95*
Burn Witch, Burn! *'62*

Kathryn Leigh Scott (1933-)
The Last Days of Patton *'86*
Murrow *'86*
Visitor from the Grave *'81*
Witches' Brew *'79*
House of Dark Shadows *'70*

Keith Scott (1954-)
The Adventures of Rocky & Bullwinkle *'00 (V)*
George of the Jungle *'97 (N)*

Ken Scott (1928-86)
Fantastic Voyage *'66*
The Fiend Who Walked the West *'58*
Stopover Tokyo *'57*

Kenn Scott
Sworn to Justice *'97*
Shootfighter: Fight to the Death *'93*
Showdown *'93*

Kente Scott (1977-)
Antwone Fisher *'02*
They Call Me Sirr *'00*

Kimberly Scott (1961-)
Guess Who *'05*
United States of Leland *'03*
K-PAX *'01*
Bellyfruit *'99*
Toothless *'97*
Batman Forever *'95*
Flatliners *'90*
The Abyss *'89*

Larry B. Scott (1961-)
The Bad Pack *'98*
Fear of a Black Hat *'94*
Revenge of the Nerds 4: Nerds in Love *'94*
Super Force *'90*
SnakeEater 2: The Drug Buster *'89*
Extreme Prejudice *'87*
Revenge of the Nerds 2: Nerds in Paradise *'87*
The Children of Times Square *'86*
Iron Eagle *'86*
My Man Adam *'86*
SpaceCamp *'86*
That Was Then... This Is Now *'85*
The Karate Kid *'84*
Revenge of the Nerds *'84*
A Hero Ain't Nothin' but a Sandwich *'78*
Wilma *'77*

Lizabeth Scott (1922-)
Pulp *'72*
Loving You *'57*
Silver Lode *'54*
Scared Stiff *'53*
A Stolen Face *'52*
The Racket *'51*
Easy Living *'49*
Too Late for Tears *'49*

Pitfall *'48*
Dead Reckoning *'47*
The Strange Love of Martha Ivers *'46*

Margaretta Scott (1912-2005)

Crescendo *'69*
Calling Paul Temple *'48*
Counterblast *'48*
Man of Evil *'48*
The Girl in the News *'41*
Action for Slander *'38*
Things to Come *'36*

Martha Scott (1914-2003)

Adam *'83*
Father Figure *'80*
The Turning Point *'77*
Ben-Hur *'59*
Sayonara *'57*
The Ten Commandments *'56*
Desperate Hours *'55*
Hi Diddle Diddle *'43*
War of the Wildcats *'43*
Cheers for Miss Bishop *'41*
The Howards of Virginia *'40*
Our Town *'40*

Pippa Scott (1935-)

Sound of Murder *'82*
Bad Ronald *'74*
Cold Turkey *'71*
Petulia *'68*

Randolph Scott (1898-1987)

Ride the High Country *'62*
Comanche Station *'60*
Ride Lonesome *'59*
Buchanan Rides Alone *'58*
Westbound *'58*
Decision at Sundown *'57*
The Tall T *'57*
Seventh Cavalry *'56*
A Lawless Street *'55*
Rage at Dawn *'55*
Ten Wanted Men *'54*
The Stranger Wore a Gun *'53*
Carson City *'52*
Hangman's Knot *'52*
Man in the Saddle *'51*
Santa Fe *'51*
The Cariboo Trail *'50*
The Nevadan *'50*
The Doolins of Oklahoma *'49*
Coroner Creek *'48*
Return of the Bad Men *'48*
Christmas Eve *'47*
Trail Street *'47*
Abilene Town *'46*
Badman's Territory *'46*
Captain Kidd *'45*
China Sky *'44*
Bombardier *'43*
The Desperadoes *'43*
Gung Ho! *'43*
Pittsburgh *'42*
The Spoilers *'42*
To the Shores of Tripoli *'42*
Western Union *'41*
My Favorite Wife *'40*
Virginia City *'40*
Jesse James *'39*
Susannah of the Mounties *'39*
Rebecca of Sunnybrook Farm *'38*
The Texans *'38*
Follow the Fleet *'36*
Go West, Young Man *'36*
The Last of the Mohicans *'36*
The Fighting Westerner *'35*
Roberta *'35*
She *'35*
Village Tale *'35*
Wagon Wheels *'34*
Buffalo Stampede *'33*
Heritage of the Desert *'33*
Man of the Forest *'33*
Murders in the Zoo *'33*
Supernatural *'33*
To the Last Man *'33*
Hot Saturday *'32*
Island of Lost Souls *'32*
When the West Was Young *'32*

Seann William Scott (1976-)

Balls Out: Gary the Tennis Coach *'09*
Ice Age: Dawn of the Dinosaurs *'09 (V)*
Planet 51 *'09 (V)*
The Promotion *'08*
Role Models *'08*
Mr. Woodcock *'07*
Ice Age: The Meltdown *'06 (V)*
Southland Tales *'06*
The Dukes of Hazzard *'05*
American Wedding *'03*
Bulletproof Monk *'03*
Old School *'03*
The Rundown *'03*
Stark Raving Mad *'02*
American Pie 2 *'01*
Evolution *'01*
Jay and Silent Bob Strike Back *'01*
Dude, Where's My Car? *'00*
Final Destination *'00*
Road Trip *'00*
American Pie *'99*

Susan Scott

See Nieves Navarro

Terry Scott

Carry On Matron *'72*
Carry On Loving *'70*
Carry On Up the Jungle *'70*
Carry On Up the Khyber *'68*
Carry On Sergeant *'58*

Timothy Scott (1938-95)

Lone Justice *'93*
Return to Lonesome Dove *'93*
Fried Green Tomatoes *'91*
Inside Out *'91*
Love Me Deadly *'73*

Tom Everett Scott (1970-)

Race to Witch Mountain *'09*
Because I Said So *'07*
National Lampoon's Van Wilder *'02*
Boiler Room *'00*
Inherit the Wind *'99*
Invasion! *'99*
The Love Letter *'99*
One True Thing *'98*
An American Werewolf in Paris *'97*
Dead Man on Campus *'97*
That Thing You Do! *'96*
The River is Red *'48*

William Lee Scott (1973-)

Farmhouse *'08*
The Go-Getter *'07*
The Butterfly Effect *'04*
Killer Diller *'04*
Dumb and Dumberer: When Harry Met Lloyd *'03*
Identity *'03*
Pearl Harbor *'01*
Gone in 60 Seconds *'00*
Black and White *'99*
October Sky *'99*
The Opposite of Sex *'98*

Zachary Scott (1914-65)

The Young One *'61*
Flame of the Islands *'55*
Shotgun *'55*
Appointment in Honduras *'53*
Wings of Danger *'52*
Let's Make It Legal *'51*
Born to Be Bad *'50*
Pretty Baby *'50*
Flamingo Road *'49*
South of St. Louis *'48*
Cass Timberlane *'47*
Mildred Pierce *'45*
The Southerner *'45*
The Mask of Dimitrios *'44*

Kristin Scott Thomas (1960-)

Confessions of a Shopaholic *'09*
Easy Virtue *'08*
I've Loved You So Long *'08*
The Other Boleyn Girl *'08*
The Golden Compass *'07 (V)*
The Walker *'07*
Tell No One *'06*
The Valet *'06*
Keeping Mum *'05*
Gosford Park *'01*
Life as a House *'01*
Up at the Villa *'00*
Random Hearts *'99*
Sweet Revenge *'98*
The Horse Whisperer *'97*
The English Patient *'96*
Angels and Insects *'95*
The Confessional *'95*
Gulliver's Travels *'95*
The Pompatus of Love *'95*
Richard III *'95*
Four Weddings and a Funeral *'94*
An Unforgettable Summer *'94*
The Bachelor *'93*
Body & Soul *'93*
Weep No More My Lady *'93*
Bitter Moon *'92*
Framed *'90*
Spymaker: The Secret Life of Ian Fleming *'90*
The Endless Game *'89*
A Handful of Dust *'88*
The Tenth Man *'88*
Under the Cherry Moon *'86*

Serena Scott Thomas (1961-)

The Thirst *'06*
Hostage *'05*
The World Is Not Enough *'99*
Relax... It's Just Sex! *'98*
Nostromo *'96*
Diana: Her True Story *'93*
Harnessing Peacocks *'92*

Andrea Scotti (1931-)

The Legend of the Wolf Woman *'77*
Hercules vs. the Sons of the Sun *'64*
The Beast of Babylon Against the Son of Hercules *'63*
Atom Age Vampire *'61*

Nick Scotti

The Last Request *'06*
Perception *'06*
Kiss Me, Guido *'97*

Vito Scotti (1918-96)

I Wonder Who's Killing Her Now? *'76*
The McCullochs *'75*
Caper of the Golden Bulls *'67*
What Did You Do in the War, Daddy? *'66*
Von Ryan's Express *'65*
Two Weeks in Another Town *'62*

Alexander Scourby (1913-85)

The Stuff *'85*
Seven Thieves *'60*
Me and the Colonel *'58*
The Big Heat *'53*
The Redhead from Wyoming *'53*
Affair in Trinidad *'52*
Because of You *'52*

Don Scribner

Rapid Assault *'99*
Wild Man *'89*
Slave Girls from Beyond Infinity *'87*

Angus Scrimm (1926-)

Phantasm 4: Oblivion *'98*
Vampirella *'96*
Phantasm 3: Lord of the Dead *'94*
Mindwarp *'91*
Subspecies *'90*
Transylvania Twist *'89*
Phantasm 2 *'88*
The Lost Empire *'83*
Phantasm *'79*

Linda Scruggs

Las Vegas Lady *'76*
Shoot It Black, Shoot It Blue *'74*

Sean Scully (1947-)

Sara Dane *'81*
The Prince and the Pauper *'62*

Terry Scully (1936-2001)

The Asphyx *'72*
He Kills Night After Night After Night *'69*

Matthew Scurfield (1948-)

A Different Loyalty *'04*
Bait *'02*
A Murder of Quality *'90*

Sandra Seacat

Crazy in Alabama *'99*
The Destiny of Marty Fine *'96*
The New Age *'94*
Promised Land *'88*

Susan Seaforth Hayes (1943-)

Dream Machine *'91*
Billie *'65*

Steven Seagal

Ruslan *'09*
Against the Dark *'08*
Black Dawn *'05*

Steven Seagal (1952-)

The Keeper *'09*
Kill Switch *'08*
Pistol Whipped *'08*
Urban Justice *'07*
Attack Force *'06*
Shadow Man *'06*
Submerged *'05*
The Foreigner *'03*
Half Past Dead *'02*
Exit Wounds *'01*
Ticker *'01*
The Patriot *'99*
My Giant *'98*
Fire Down Below *'97*
Executive Decision *'96*
The Glimmer Man *'96*
Under Siege 2: Dark Territory *'95*
On Deadly Ground *'94*
Under Siege *'92*
Out for Justice *'91*
Marked for Death *'90*
Hard to Kill *'89*
Above the Law *'88*

Jocelyn Seagrave (1968-)

Dark Justice *'00*
Moonbase *'97*

Jenny Seagrove (1958-)

Zoe *'01*
Deadly Game *'91*
Sherlock Holmes and the Incident at Victoria Falls *'91*
Bullseye! *'90*
The Guardian *'90*
A Chorus of Disapproval *'89*
Magic Moments *'89*
Appointment with Death *'88*
Hold the Dream *'86*
A Woman of Substance *'84*
Local Hero *'83*
Nate and Hayes *'83*

Elizabeth Seal

Vampire Circus *'71*
Radio Cab Murder *'54*

Douglas Seale (1913-99)

Aladdin *'92 (V)*
Almost an Angel *'90*
Mr. Destiny *'90*
Ernest Saves Christmas *'88*

Orlando Seale

Miss Conception *'08*
Caffeine *'06*
Everything You Want *'05*

Franklyn Seales (1952-90)

Southern Comfort *'81*
The Onion Field *'79*

Nick Searcy (1959-)

The Expendables *'10*
The Last Song *'10*
The Ugly Truth *'09*
Eagle Eye *'08*
An American Crime *'07*
The Comebacks *'07*
Welcome to Paradise *'07*
The Dead Girl *'06*
Flicka *'06*
The Assassination of Richard Nixon *'05*
Head of State *'03*
Runaway Jury *'03*
Cast Away *'00*
From the Earth to the Moon *'98*
Perfect Crime *'97*
The War *'94*

Jackie Searl (1921-91)

That Certain Age *'38*
Peck's Bad Boy *'34*
The Return of Casey Jones *'34*
High Gear *'33*
Topaze *'33*
Hearts of Humanity *'32*

Fred F. Sears (1913-57)

Bonanza Town *'51*
Counterspy Meets Scotland Yard *'50*
Down to Earth *'47*

Heather Sears (1935-94)

Estate of Insanity *'64*
The Phantom of the Opera *'62*
Room at the Top *'59*
The Story of Esther Costello *'57*

James Seay (1914-92)

The Amazing Colossal Man *'57*
Beginning of the End *'57*
Man in the Vault *'56*
Phantom from Space *'53*
Close to My Heart *'51*
The Strange Mrs. Crane *'48*
Heartaches *'47*
Ridin' Down the Canyon *'42*
Turf Boy *'42*
In Old Colorado *'41*

Heidi Lenhart Seban

Au Pair 3: Adventure in Paradise *'09*
Au Pair 2: The Fairy Tale Continues *'01*
Au Pair *'99*

Dorothy Sebastian (1906-57)

Rough Riders' Roundup *'39*
They Never Come Back *'32*
His First Command *'29*
The Single Standard *'29*
Spite Marriage *'29*
Our Dancing Daughters *'28*
A Woman of Affairs *'28*

Lobo Sebastian

Columbus Day *'08*
Crash and Burn *'07*
Dirty *'05*
The Longest Yard *'05*
Next Friday *'00*
Major League 3: Back to the Minors *'98*
187 *'97*

Tracy Sebastian

Running Cool *'93*
On the Air Live with Captain Midnight *'79*

Jean Seberg (1938-79)

Airport *'70*
Macho Callahan *'70*
Paint Your Wagon *'69*
Pendulum *'69*
A Fine Madness *'66*
Moment to Moment *'66*
Lilith *'64*
Time Out for Love *'61*
Let No Man Write My Epitaph *'60*
Love Play *'60*
Breathless *'59*
The Mouse That Roared *'59*
Bonjour Tristesse *'57*
Saint Joan *'57*

Douta Seck

Sugar Cane Alley *'83*
Xala *'75*

Harry Secombe (1921-2001)

Song of Norway *'70*
Down Among the Z Men *'52*
Goon Movie *'52*

Kyle Secor (1958-)

Beat *'00*
Homicide: The Movie *'00*
Children of Fury *'94*
Drop Zone *'94*
Untamed Heart *'93*
Silent Victim *'92*
City Slickers *'91*
Delusion *'91*
Sleeping with the Enemy *'91*
The Heart of Dixie *'89*

Jon Seda (1970-)

One Long Night *'07*
Bad Boys 2 *'03*
The Street King *'02*
Undisputed *'02*
Double Bang *'01*
Love the Hard Way *'01*
Homicide: The Movie *'00*
Price of Glory *'00*
Thin Air *'00*
Dear God *'96*
Mistrial *'96*
Primal Fear *'96*
Selena *'96*
Sunchaser *'96*
12 Monkeys *'95*
I Like It Like That *'94*
Carlito's Way *'93*
Gladiator *'92*

Amy Sedaris (1961-)

Shrek Forever After *'10 (V)*
Dance Flick *'09*
Jennifer's Body *'09*
Old Dogs *'09*
Gym Teacher: The Movie *'08*
Shrek the Third *'07 (V)*
Snow Angels *'07*
I Want Someone to Eat Cheese With *'06*
Strangers with Candy *'06*
Bewitched *'05*
Chicken Little *'05 (V)*
My Baby's Daddy *'04*
Elf *'03*
Maid in Manhattan *'02*

Margaret Seddon (1872-1968)

Mr. Deeds Goes to Town *'36*
The Return of Casey Jones *'34*
Smilin' Through *'33*
Little Church Around the Corner *'23*
Headin' Home *'20*

Kyra Sedgwick (1965-)

Gamer *'09*
The Game Plan *'07*
Loverboy *'05*
The Woodsman *'04*
Secondhand Lions *'03*
Behind the Red Door *'02*
Just a Kiss *'02*
Personal Velocity: Three Portraits *'02*
What's Cooking? *'00*
Labor Pains *'99*
Critical Care *'97*
Montana *'97*

Losing Chase '96
Phenomenon '96
The Low Life '95
Murder in the First '95
Something to Talk About '95
Family Pictures '93
Heart and Souls '93
Miss Rose White '92
Singles '92
Pyrates '91
Women & Men: In Love There Are No Rules '91
Mr. & Mrs. Bridge '90
Born on the Fourth of July '89
Kansas '88
Tai-Pan '86
War & Love '84

Robert Sedgwick

Tune in Tomorrow '90
Nasty Hero '89
Morgan Stewart's Coming Home '87

Miriam Seegar

Strangers of the Evening '32
The Dawn Trail '30
Seven Keys to Baldpate '29

Andrew Seeley

The Shortcut '09
Another Cinderella Story '08

George Segal (1934-)

Three Days to Vegas '07
Heights '04
Houdini '99
The Cable Guy '96
The Mirror Has Two Faces '96
November Conspiracy '96
The Babysitter '95
The Feminine Touch '95
Flirting with Disaster '95
It's My Party '95
To Die For '95
Army of One '94
Deep Down '94
Direct Hit '93
Look Who's Talking Now '93
Taking the Heat '93
Me, Myself & I '92
For the Boys '91
All's Fair '89
The Endless Game '89
Look Who's Talking '89
Killing 'Em Softly '85
Not My Kid '85
Stick '85
Cold Room '84
The Zany Adventures of Robin Hood '84
Deadly Game '82
Carbon Copy '81
The Last Married Couple in America '80
Lost and Found '79
Who Is Killing the Great Chefs of Europe? '78
Fun with Dick and Jane '77
Rollercoaster '77
The Duchess and the Dirtwater Fox '76
Black Bird '75
Russian Roulette '75
The Terminal Man '74
Blume in Love '73
A Touch of Class '73
Born to Win '71
The Hot Rock '70
Loving '70
The Owl and the Pussycat '70
Where's Poppa? '70
The Bridge at Remagen '69
No Way to Treat a Lady '68
Bye Bye Braverman '67
The St. Valentine's Day Massacre '67
The Lost Command '66
The Quiller Memorandum '66
Who's Afraid of Virginia Woolf? '66
King Rat '65
Ship of Fools '65
Invitation to a Gunfighter '64

Jonathan Segal

See Jonathan Sagalle

Yonathan Segal

See Jonathan Sagalle

Zohra Segal

See Zohra Sehgal

Jonathan Segall

See Jonathan Sagalle

Pamela Segall (1966-)

Disney's Teacher's Pet '04 (V)
Kiki's Delivery Service '98 (V)
Plump Fiction '97
Eat Your Heart Out '96
Bed of Roses '95
Sgt. Bilko '95
Gate 2 '92
After Midnight '89
Say Anything '89
Something Special '86
Bad Manners '84

Noah Segan (1983-)

Still Green '07
What We Do Is Secret '07
Brick '06
Adam & Steve '05

Paolo Seganti (1966-)

Camera: The Walking Mountain '08
Cradle 2 the Grave '03
Sex & Mrs. X '00
Tea with Mussolini '99
L.A. Confidential '97
Still Breathing '97

Jason Segel (1980-)

Despicable Me '10 (V)
I Love You, Man '09
Forgetting Sarah Marshall '08
The Good Humor Man '05
11:14 '03
Slackers '02
SLC Punk! '99
Dead Man on Campus '97

Santiago Segura (1965-)

Agent Cody Banks 2: Destination London '04
Blade 2 '02
The Girl of Your Dreams '99
Dance with the Devil '97
The Day of the Beast '95

Zohra Sehgal (1912-)

Chicken Tikka Masala '05
The Mystic Masseur '01
Bhaji on the Beach '94
Masala '91
The Courtesans of Bombay '85

Emmanuelle Seigner (1966-)

The Diving Bell and the Butterfly '07
La Vie en Rose '07
Four Last Songs '06
Happily Ever After '04
Buddy Boy '99
The Ninth Gate '99
Place Vendome '98
Nirvana '97
R.P.M. '97
Bitter Moon '92
Frantic '88

Louis Seigner (1903-95)

Mr. Klein '76
This Special Friendship '67
The Eclipse '66
The Would-Be Gentleman '58
Seven Deadly Sins '53

Mathilde Seigner (1968-)

The Girl from Paris '02
Alias Betty '01
With a Friend Like Harry '00
Time Regained '99
Venus Beauty Institute '98
Dry Cleaning '97
The Man I Love '97

Jerry Seinfeld (1954-)

Bee Movie '07 (V)
Ratings Game '84

Rapulana Seiphemo

Tsotsi '05
Tarzan and the Lost City '98

John Seitz (1892-1979)

The Bread, My Sweet '01
Forced March '90
Out of the Rain '90
Five Corners '88
Hard Choices '84
The Prowler '81

Johnny Sekka (1934-2006)

The Message '77
The Bloodsuckers '70
The Last Safari '67
Khartoum '66
Woman of Straw '64

David Selby (1941-)

End Game '06
Horton Foote's Alone '97
Soldier of Fortune Inc. '97
D3: The Mighty Ducks '96
Headless Body in Topless Bar '96
White Squall '96
Intersection '93
Grave Secrets: The Legacy of Hilltop Drive '92
Dying Young '91
Rich and Famous '81
Rich Kids '79
The Girl in Blue '74
Up the Sandbox '72
Night of Dark Shadows '71

Nicholas Selby (1925-)

House of Cards '90
Macbeth '71
A Midsummer Night's Dream '68

Sarah Selby (1905-80)

Huckleberry Finn '75
An Affair to Remember '57
Stopover Tokyo '57
Battle Cry '55
Men of the Fighting Lady '54
Battle Circus '53

Viveka Seldahl (1944-2001)

A Song for Martin '01
House of Angels '92

Marian Seldes (1928-)

Home '08
Mona Lisa Smile '03
Hollywood Ending '02
Town and Country '01
Duets '00
If These Walls Could Talk 2 '00
The Haunting '99
Digging to China '98
Affliction '97
Home Alone 3 '97
Tom and Huck '95
Truman '95
Fingers '78
Crime and Punishment, USA '59

William (Bill) Self (1921-)

The Thing '51
Sands of Iwo Jima '49
The Story of G.I. Joe '45

Edgar Selge

Fashion Victims '07
The Experiment '01

Elizabeth Sellars (1923-)

A Voyage 'Round My Father '89
The Mummy's Shroud '67
The Chalk Garden '64
Never Let Go '60
Three Cases of Murder '55
Desiree '54
Recoil '53
Madeleine '50

Connie Sellecca (1955-)

The Brotherhood of the Rose '89
The Last Fling '86
Captain America 2: Death Too Soon '79
She's Dressed to Kill '79
The Bermuda Depths '78

Tom Selleck (1945-)

Killers '10
Jesse Stone: Thin Ice '09
Jesse Stone: Sea Change '07
Meet the Robinsons '07 (V)
Jesse Stone: Death in Paradise '06
Jesse Stone: Night Passage '06
Jesse Stone: Stone Cold '05
Ike: Countdown to D-Day '04
Monte Walsh '03
Crossfire Trail '01
Running Mates '00
The Love Letter '99
In and Out '97
Last Stand at Saber River '96
Ruby Jean and Joe '96
Broken Trust '95
Open Season '95
Christopher Columbus: The Discovery '92
Folks! '92
Mr. Baseball '92
Quigley Down Under '90
Three Men and a Little Lady '90
An Innocent Man '89
Her Alibi '88
Three Men and a Baby '87
Lassiter '84
Runaway '84
High Road to China '83
The Shadow Riders '82
Magnum P.I.: Don't Eat the Snow in Hawaii '80
The Concrete Cowboys '79
The Sacketts '79
Coma '78
The Gypsy Warriors '78
Bunco '77
Washington Affair '77
Midway '76
Most Wanted '76
Terminal Island '73
Daughters of Satan '72
Myra Breckinridge '70

Peter Sellers (1925-80)

Trail of the Pink Panther '82
The Fiendish Plot of Dr. Fu Manchu '80
Being There '79
Prisoner of Zenda '79
Revenge of the Pink Panther '78
America at the Movies '76
Murder by Death '76
The Pink Panther Strikes Again '76
Great McGonagall '75
Ghost in the Noonday Sun '74
Return of the Pink Panther '74
Blockhouse '73
The Optimists '73
Hoffman '70
There's a Girl in My Soup '70
The Magic Christian '69
I Love You, Alice B. Toklas! '68
The Party '68
The Bobo '67
Casino Royale '67
Woman Times Seven '67
After the Fox '66
The Wrong Box '66
What's New Pussycat? '65
Dr. Strangelove, or: How I Learned to Stop Worrying and Love the Bomb '64
The Pink Panther '64
A Shot in the Dark '64
The World of Henry Orient '64
Heavens Above '63
The Wrong Arm of the Law '63
Lolita '62
Only Two Can Play '62
The Road to Hong Kong '62
Trial & Error '62
Waltz of the Toreadors '62
The Battle of the Sexes '60
The Millionairess '60
Never Let Go '60
Two-Way Stretch '60
Carlton Browne of the F.O. '59
I'm All Right Jack '59
The Mouse That Roared '59
The Naked Truth '58
Tom Thumb '58
Up the Creek '58
The Smallest Show on Earth '57
John and Julie '55
The Ladykillers '55
Down Among the Z Men '52
Goon Movie '52

Sabrina Sellers

See Sabrina Siani

Charles Sellon (1870-1937)

In Old Kentucky '35
Life Begins at Forty '35
Bright Eyes '34
Ride Him, Cowboy '32
Behind Office Doors '31
Bulldog Drummond '29
Vagabond Lover '29
The Prairie King '27
The Monster '25

Morton Selten (1860-1939)

The Thief of Bagdad '40
The Ghost Goes West '36

David Selvas (1971-)

Beloved/Friend '99
Caresses '97

Katy Selverstone (1918-2006)

Divine Secrets of the Ya-Ya Sisterhood '02
Seven Girlfriends '00

Clarissa Selwynne (1886-1948)

Jane Eyre '34
My Pal, the King '32
The Love Trap '29

Milton Selzer (1918-)

Miss Rose White '92
Tapeheads '89
The Triangle Factory Fire Scandal '79
The Evil '78

Harry Semels (1887-1946)

Stone of Silver Creek '35
Ghost Valley '32
Texas Buddies '32
America '24

Larry Semon (1889-1928)

Underworld '27
The Perfect Clown '25
The Wizard of Oz '25

Aparna Sen (1945-)

Hullabaloo over Georgie & Bonnie's Pictures '78
Bombay Talkie '70

Nandana Sen (1967-)

Marigold '07
The War Within '05
Seducing Maarya '99

Paola Senatore (1949-)

Emerald Jungle '80
Mean Machine '73

Koreya Senda (1904-94)

Tora! Tora! Tora! '70
Face of Another '66
H-Man '59
Gate of Hell '54

Joe Seneca (1914-96)

The Saint of Fort Washington '93
Mississippi Masala '92
Murder on the Bayou '91
Mo' Better Blues '90
The Blob '88
School Daze '88
Crossroads '86
Samaritan: The Mitch Snyder Story '86
Half Slave, Half Free '85
The Verdict '82
Wilma '77

Noriko Sengoku (1922-)

Okoge '93
Godzilla vs. Monster Zero '68
Snow Country '57

Mack Sennett (1880-1960)

Man in the Silk Hat '83
Abbott and Costello Meet the Keystone Kops '54
Charlie Chaplin ... Our Hero! '15

Heyon-a Seong

Time '06
Cello '05

Silu Seppala

Zombie and the Ghost Train '91
Leningrad Cowboys Go America '89

Greg Serano

Beer for My Horses '08
Conspiracy '08

Massimo Serato (1916-89)

The Bloodstained Shadow '78
Don't Look Now '73
Camille 2000 '69
Challenge of the Gladiator '65
10th Victim '65
Wild, Wild Planet '65
The Lion of Thebes '64
Battle of Valiant '63
Hero of Rome '63
Venus Against the Son of Hercules '62
The Naked Maja '59
The Love of Three Queens '54

Rade Serbedzija (1946-)

The Code '09
The Eye '08
Quarantine '08
Shooter '07
The Elder Son '06
Moscow Zero '06
The Fog '05
Go West '05
The Keeper: The Legend of Omar Khayyam '05
Eurotrip '04
The Fever '04
The Quiet American '02
Quicksand '01
Rodgers & Hammerstein's South Pacific '01
Mission: Impossible 2 '00
Snatch '00
Space Cowboys '00
Eyes Wide Shut '99
Stigmata '99
Lies and Whispers '98
Mighty Joe Young '98
Polish Wedding '97
The Saint '97
Broken English '96
The Truce '96
Before the Rain '94

Ivan Sergei (1972-)

High Noon '09
The Break-Up '06
Santa Baby '06

Playing Mona Lisa '00
The Big Day '99
The Opposite of Sex '98
Gunfighter's Moon '96
Once a Thief '96

Brian Sergent

Eagle vs. Shark '07
Meet the Feebles '89 (V)

Yahoo Serious (1954-)

Mr. Accident '99
Reckless Kelly '93
Young Einstein '89

Reita Serizawa

Ju-On 2 '00
Ringu 2 '99

Andy Serkis (1964-)

Sex & Drugs & Rock & Roll '10
Inkheart '09
Little Dorrit '08
Extraordinary Rendition '07
Sugarhouse '07
Alex Rider: Operation Stormbreaker '06
Flushed Away '06 (V)
Longford '06
The Prestige '06
King Kong '05
13 Going on 30 '04
Lord of the Rings: The Return of the King '03
Deathwatch '02
Lord of the Rings: The Two Towers '02 (V)
Lord of the Rings: The Fellowship of the Ring '01
24 Hour Party People '01
The Jolly Boys' Last Stand '00
Oliver Twist '00
Pandaemonium '00
Shiner '00
Among Giants '98
Career Girls '97
Stella Does Tricks '96

Assumpta Serna (1957-)

Piano Tuner of Earthquakes '05
Managua '97
The Craft '96
Hidden Assassin '94
Sharpe's Company '94
Sharpe's Enemy '94
Chain of Desire '93
Nostradamus '93
Sharpe's Eagle '93
Sharpe's Rifles '93
The Fencing Master '92
Revolver '92
I, the Worst of All '90
Wild Orchid '90
Matador '86

Pepe Serna (1944-)

The Black Dahlia '06
Devil's Knight '03
Latin Dragon '03
A Million to Juan '94
American Me '92
The Rookie '90
Bad Jim '89
The Forgotten '89
Break of Dawn '88
Fandango '85
The Adventures of Buckaroo Banzai Across the Eighth Dimension '84
Ballad of Gregorio Cortez '83
Scarface '83
The Jerk '79
Tarantulas: The Deadly Cargo '77
Sniper '75
Shoot Out '71
The Student Nurses '70

Jacques Sernas (1925-)

Superfly T.N.T. '73
Hornet's Nest '70
Fort Yuma Gold '66
55 Days at Peking '63
La Dolce Vita '60
Helen of Troy '56
The Golden Salamander '51

Raymond Serra (1931-2003)

Wannabes '01
Men of Means '99
Gotti '96
Marilyn & Bobby: Her Final Affair '94
Sugar Hill '94
Nasty Hero '89
A Time to Remember '87
Alphabet City '84
Splitz '84
Hardhat & Legs '80
Hooch '76

Diego Serrano (1973-)

The 24 Hour Woman '99
Mixing Nia '98

Julieta Serrano (1933-)

A Love to Keep '07
Caresses '97
Tie Me Up! Tie Me Down! '90
Women on the Verge of a Nervous Breakdown '88
Matador '86
Dark Habits '84

Nestor Serrano (1957-)

Definitely, Maybe '08
Sueno '05
The Day After Tomorrow '04
Runaway Jury '03
Undefeated '03
City by the Sea '02
Empire '02
Showtime '02
Bait '00
Bringing Out the Dead '99
The Insider '99
The Negotiator '98
Bad Boys '95
City Hall '95
I Love Trouble '94
Hangin' with the Homeboys '91
Lethal Weapon 2 '89
Brenda Starr '86
The Money Pit '86

Christian Serratos (1990-)

The Twilight Saga: Eclipse '10
The Twilight Saga: New Moon '09
Twilight '08

Michel Serrault (1928-2007)

Joyeux Noel '05
The Butterfly '02
The Girl from Paris '02
Belphegar: Phantom of the Louvre '01
Artemisia '97
The Swindle '97
Beaumarchais the Scoundrel '96
Le Bonheur Est Dans le Pre '95
Nelly et Monsieur Arnaud '95
The Old Lady Who Walked in the Sea '91
Dr. Petiot '90
La Cage aux Folles 3: The Wedding '86
La Cage aux Folles 2 '81
The Associate '79
Buffet Froid '79
La Cage aux Folles '78
The Holes '72
The King of Hearts '66
Love on a Pillow '62
Diabolique '55

Henri Serre (1931-)

The Fire Within '64
Jules and Jim '62

Jean Servais (1910-76)

The Devil's Nightmare '71
Black Jesus '68
Super Brother '68
Murder at 45 R.P.M. '65
The Liars '64
That Man from Rio '64
Fever Mounts at El Pao '59
Tamango '59
Rififi '54
Le Plaisir '52 (N)

Toni Servillo

Gomorrah '08
Il Divo '08
The Girl by the Lake '07

Matt Servitto

Big Fan '09
Two Family House '99

Almira Sessions (1888-1974)

Oklahoma Annie '51
Diary of a Chambermaid '46
Miracle of Morgan's Creek '44
The Heat's On '43

John Sessions (1953-)

The Last Station '09
Oliver Twist '07
The Good Shepherd '06
Lighthouse Hill '04
The Merchant of Venice '04
William Shakespeare's A Midsummer Night's Dream '99
Tom Jones '98
Cousin Bette '97
The Scarlet Tunic '97
A Midwinter's Tale '95
Princess Caraboo '94
Freddie the Frog '92 (V)
Sweet Revenge '90
Henry V '89

Greg Sestero

The Room '03
Retro Puppet Master '99

Roshan Seth (1942-)

The Cheetah Girls: One World '08
Proof '05
Vertical Limit '00
Such a Long Journey '98
Solitaire for 2 '94
Street Fighter '94
The Buddha of Suburbia '92
Mississippi Masala '92
Stalin '92
London Kills Me '91
Mountains of the Moon '90
Not Without My Daughter '90
Little Dorrit, Film 1: Nobody's Fault '88
Little Dorrit, Film 2: Little Dorrit's Story '88
My Beautiful Laundrette '85
Gandhi '82

Asako Seto

Death Note 3: L, Change the World '08
Death Note '06
One Missed Call 2 '05

Bruce Seton (1909-69)

Gorgo '61
The Blue Lamp '49
The Green Cockatoo '37
Love from a Stranger '37
Demon Barber of Fleet Street '36

Ed Setrakian (1928-)

The Great New Wonderful '06
Astoria '00
Day at the Beach '98

Matthew Settle (1969-)

Beneath '07
Blue Smoke '07
The Celestine Prophecy '06
Rancid '04
Divine Secrets of the Ya-Ya Sisterhood '02
The In Crowd '00
U-571 '00

Gerard Sety (1922-98)

Van Gogh '92
Modigliani '58

Adam G. Sevani

Step Up 3D '10
Step Up 2 the Streets '08

Joan Severance (1958-)

Cause of Death '00
The Last Seduction 2 '98
Matter of Trust '98
In Dark Places '97
Black Scorpion 2: Ground Zero '96
Profile for Murder '96
Black Scorpion '95
Dangerous Indiscretion '94
Hard Evidence '94
Payback '94
Lake Consequence '92
Red Shoe Diaries 2: Double Dare '92
Almost Pregnant '91
Another Pair of Aces: Three of a Kind '91
Illicit Behavior '91
The Runestone '91
Write to Kill '91
Bird on a Wire '90
No Holds Barred '89
See No Evil, Hear No Evil '89
Lethal Weapon '87

William Severn (1938-83)

Son of Lassie '45
Journey for Margaret '42

Corey Sevier (1984-)

A Broken Life '07
Decoys: The Second Seduction '07
Decoys '04
Detention '03
Edge of Madness '02
Summer of the Monkeys '98

Chloe Sevigny (1975-)

The Killing Room '09
Zodiac '07
Broken Flowers '05
Manderlay '05
Melinda and Melinda '05
Mrs. Harris '05
The Brown Bunny '03
Dogville '03
Party Monster '03
Shattered Glass '03
Demonlover '02
If These Walls Could Talk 2 '00
American Psycho '99
Boys Don't Cry '99
Julien Donkey-boy '99
A Map of the World '99
The Last Days of Disco '98
Palmetto '98
Gummo '97
Tree's Lounge '96
Kids '95

Carmen Sevilla (1930-)

The Boldest Job in the West '71
Pantaloons '57

Billie Seward (1912-82)

The Man from Gun Town '36
Branded a Coward '35
Justice of the Range '35
The Revenge Rider '35
Trails of the Wild '35

George Sewell

Running Blind '78
Get Carter '71
Kaleidoscope '66

Rufus Sewell (1967-)

Downloading Nancy '08
John Adams '08
Amazing Grace '06
The Holiday '06
The Illusionist '06
Paris, je t'aime '06
Tristan & Isolde '06
The Legend of Zorro '05
Helen of Troy '03
Extreme Ops '02
A Knight's Tale '01
She Creature '01
Arabian Nights '00
Bless the Child '00
In a Savage Land '99
Dangerous Beauty '98
Illuminata '98
Uncorked '98
The Very Thought of You '98
Dark City '97
Hamlet '96
Carrington '95
Victory '95
Cold Comfort Farm '94
A Man of No Importance '94
Middlemarch '93
Twenty-One '91

Andrzej Seweryn (1946-)

Zemsta '02
Lucie Aubrac '98
Genealogies of a Crime '97
Schindler's List '93
The Conductor '80
Without Anesthesia '78
Land of Promise '74

Brendan Sexton, III (1980-)

The Wedding Bros. '08
Winter of Frozen Dreams '08
The Secret '07
Just Like the Son '06
Little Fugitive '06
Love, Ludlow '05
This Revolution '05
Black Hawk Down '01
Session 9 '01
Boys Don't Cry '99
Desert Blue '98
Pecker '98
Spark '98
Hurricane Streets '96
Welcome to the Dollhouse '95

Brent Sexton

Flightplan '05
Radio '03

Amanda Seyfried (1985-)

Dear John '10
Letters to Juliet '10
Chloe '09
Jennifer's Body '09
Mamma Mia! '08
Alpha Dog '06
American Gun '05
Nine Lives '05
Mean Girls '04

Athene Seyler (1889-1990)

Curse of the Demon '57
Beggar's Opera '54
The Franchise Affair '52
Sailing Along '38
Non-Stop New York '37
Private Life of Don Juan '34

Anne Seymour (1909-88)

Gemini Affair '74
Good Neighbor Sam '64
Misty '61
All the King's Men '49

Cara Seymour

An Education '09
The Savages '07
The Notorious Bettie Page '06
Birth '04
Evergreen '04
Hotel Rwanda '04
Adaptation '02
Gangs of New York '02
American Psycho '99
Dancer in the Dark '99
A Good Baby '99

Carolyn Seymour (1947-)

Red Shoe Diaries: Swimming Naked '00
The Break '97
Red Shoe Diaries: Strip Poker '96
Midnight Cabaret '90
Girls of the White Orchid '85
The Assignment '78
The Bitch '78
Gumshoe '72
The Ruling Class '72

Dan Seymour (1915-93)

Return of the Fly '59
Abbott and Costello Meet the Mummy '55
Key Largo '48
Hard-Boiled Mahoney '47
A Night in Casablanca '46
To Have & Have Not '44

Jane Seymour (1951-)

Blind Dating '06
Wedding Crashers '05
Quest for Camelot '98 (V)
Heidi '93
Praying Mantis '93
Are You Lonesome Tonight '92
Sunstroke '92
Matters of the Heart '90
The Tunnel '89
War & Remembrance: The Final Chapter '89
Jack the Ripper '88
Onassis '88
War & Remembrance '88
The Woman He Loved '88
Head Office '86
Lassiter '84
The Haunting Passion '83
Jamaica Inn '82
The Scarlet Pimpernel '82
East of Eden '80
Oh, Heavenly Dog! '80
Somewhere in Time '80
Battlestar Galactica '78
The Four Feathers '78
Killer on Board '77
Sinbad and the Eye of the Tiger '77
The Story of David '76
Live and Let Die '73
The Strauss Family '73
Young Winston '72
The Only Way '70
Oh! What a Lovely War '69

Jeff Seymour

Wedding Bell Blues '96
Rave Review '95

Ralph Seymour

Rain Man '88
Empire of the Sun '87
Killer Party '86
Fletch '85
Meatballs 2 '84

Delphine Seyrig (1932-90)

Window Shopping '86
Grain of Sand '84
I Sent a Letter to My Love '81
The Black Windmill '74
Diary of a Suicide '73
A Doll's House '73
The Discreet Charm of the Bourgeoisie '72
Daughters of Darkness '71
Peau D'Ane '71
Donkey Skin '70
The Milky Way '68
Stolen Kisses '68
Accident '67
Muriel '63
Last Year at Marienbad '61

Sabrina Seyvecou

Born in 68 '08
Cote d'Azur '05

Serif Sezer (1943-)

Steam: A Turkish Bath '96
Yol '82

Ted Shackleford (1946-)

Miracle Dogs '03
The Spider and the Fly '94
Dying to Remember '93
Baby of the Bride '91
Sweet Revenge '87
Summer Fantasy '84

Glenn Shadix (1952-)

The Empty Mirror '99
Red Dirt '99
Chairman of the Board '97

Dunston Checks In *'95*
Dark Side of Genius *'94*
Love Affair *'94*
My Summer Story *'94*
Demolition Man *'93*
The Nightmare Before Christmas *'93 (V)*
Sleepwalkers *'92*
Bingo *'91*
Nightlife *'90*
The Applegates *'89*
Heathers *'89*
Beetlejuice *'88*

Robert (Bobby Ray) Shafer (1958-)
Monster Man *'03*
Psycho Cop 2 *'94*
A Brilliant Disguise *'93*
Psycho Cop *'88*

Paul Shaffer (1949-)
Blues Brothers 2000 *'98*
Hercules *'97 (V)*
The Return of Spinal Tap *'92*
Light Years *'88 (V)*
This Is Spinal Tap *'84*
Mr. Mike's Mondo Video *'79*

Jamal Shah
K2: The Ultimate High *'92*
Traffik *'90*

Naseeruddin Shah (1950-)
The Great New Wonderful *'06*
The League of Extraordinary Gentlemen *'03*
Monsoon Wedding *'01*
Such a Long Journey *'98*
Spices *'86*

Darren Shahlavi (1972-)
Alone in the Dark *'05*
Bloodmoon *'97*

Tupac Shakur (1971-96)
Gang Related *'96*
Gridlock'd *'96*
Above the Rim *'94*
Bullet *'94*
Poetic Justice *'93*
Juice *'92*

Victoria Shalet
Haunted *'95*
The Maid *'90*

Tony Shalhoub (1953-)
American East *'07*
Careless *'07*
Cars *'06 (V)*
The Great New Wonderful *'06*
Against the Ropes *'04*
The Last Shot *'04*
Spy Kids 3-D: Game Over *'03*
Impostor *'02*
Life or Something Like It *'02*
Men in Black 2 *'02*
The Man Who Wasn't There *'01*
Spy Kids *'01*
13 Ghosts *'01*
Galaxy Quest *'99*
That Championship Season *'99*
The Tic Code *'99*
A Civil Action *'98*
The Imposters *'98*
Paulie *'98*
Primary Colors *'98*
The Siege *'98*
Gattaca *'97*
A Life Less Ordinary *'97*
Men in Black *'97*
Big Night *'95*
I.Q. *'94*
Honeymoon in Vegas *'92*
Barton Fink *'91*
Quick Change *'90*

Chuck Shamata
WarGames 2: The Dead Code *'08*
The Sentinel *'06*
Whitewash: The Clarence Brandley Story *'02*
Snap Decision *'01*
The Thin Blue Lie *'00*
Family of Strangers *'93*
Princes in Exile *'90*
Unfinished Business *'89*
Night Friend *'87*
Mafia Princess *'86*
Joshua Then and Now *'85*
Death Weekend *'76*

Jeremy Shamos
The Great New Wonderful *'06*
Kid Colter *'85*

Garry Shandling (1949-)
Iron Man 2 *'10*
Over the Hedge *'06 (V)*
Trust the Man *'06*
Town and Country *'01*
What Planet Are You From? *'00*
Dr. Dolittle *'98 (V)*
Hurlyburly *'98*
Love Affair *'94*
Mixed Nuts *'94*
The Night We Never Met *'93*
Mother Goose Rock 'n' Rhyme *'90*

Sara Shane
Tarzan's Greatest Adventure *'59*
The King and Four Queens *'56*

Michael Shaner
Traveller *'96*
The Expert *'95*
Bloodfist *'89*
Crime Zone *'88*

Amelia Shankley (1972-)
The Little Princess *'87*
Dreamchild *'85*

Don Shanks (1950-)
3 Ninjas Knuckle Up *'95*
The Legend of Wolf Mountain *'92*
Spirit of the Eagle *'90*
Halloween 5: The Revenge of Michael Myers *'89*
The Last of the Mohicans *'85*
Mountain Man *'77*
Life & Times of Grizzly Adams *'74*

Michael Shanks (1970-)
The Lost Treasure of the Grand Canyon *'08*
Stargate: Continuum *'08*
Stargate: The Ark of Truth *'08*
Megasnake *'07*
Suspicious River *'00*
Escape from Mars *'99*
Terror Train *'80*

Al Shannon
Out of the Rain *'90*
The Drifter *'88*

Fay Shannon
See Fay McKenzie

Frank Shannon (1874-1959)
Flash Gordon Conquers the Universe *'40*
Flash Gordon: Rocketship *'40*

Harry Shannon (1890-1964)
Summer and Smoke *'61*
Man or Gun *'58*
Written on the Wind *'56*
Phantom Stallion *'54*
Cow Town *'50*
The Jackie Robinson Story *'50*
The Underworld Story *'50*
Fighting Father Dunne *'48*
The Red House *'47*
The Yellow Rose of Texas *'44*
Idaho *'43*
Song of Texas *'43*
The Lady Is Willing *'42*
Citizen Kane *'41*

Michael Shannon (1974-)
Jonah Hex *'10*
The Runaways *'10*
Bad Lieutenant: Port of Call New Orleans *'09*
Revolutionary Road *'08*
Before the Devil Knows You're Dead *'07*
Lucky You *'07*
Shotgun Stories *'07*
Bug *'06*
Let's Go to Prison *'06*
World Trade Center *'06*
Dead Birds *'04*
The Woodsman *'04*
Bad Boys 2 *'03*
Grand Theft Parsons *'03*
8 Mile *'02*
High Crimes *'02*
Kangaroo Jack *'02*
Pearl Harbor *'01*
Vanilla Sky *'01*
Chicago Cab *'98*

Michael J. Shannon (1943-)
Detonator 2: Night Watch *'95*
We'll Meet Again *'82*
Future Cop *'76*

Molly Shannon (1964-)
What Goes Up *'09*
Igor *'08 (V)*
Snow Buddies *'08*
Evan Almighty *'07*
Year of the Dog *'07*
Gray Matters *'06*
Little Man *'06*
Marie Antoinette *'06*
Scary Movie 4 *'06*
Talladega Nights: The Ballad of Ricky Bobby *'06*
The Twelve Days of Christmas Eve *'04*
American Splendor *'03*
Good Boy! *'03*
My Boss's Daughter *'03*
Osmosis Jones *'01*
Serendipity *'01*
Wet Hot American Summer *'01*
Dr. Seuss' How the Grinch Stole Christmas *'00*
My 5 Wives *'00*
Never Been Kissed *'99*
Superstar *'99*
Analyze This *'98*
A Night at the Roxbury *'98*
Dinner and Driving *'97*
The Phantom of the Opera *'89*

Peggy Shannon (1910-41)
The Case of the Lucky Legs *'35*
Deluge *'33*
False Faces *'32*
Touchdown *'31*

Polly Shannon (1973-)
Hydra *'09*
Hide *'08*
Jesse Stone: Night Passage *'06*
Jesse Stone: Stone Cold *'05*
Do or Die *'03*
Men with Brooms *'02*
The Triangle *'01*
The Girl Next Door *'98*
Hard to Forget *'98*
A Young Connecticut Yankee in King Arthur's Court *'95*

Vicellous Shannon (1981-)
Animal 2 *'07*
Annapolis *'06*
Hart's War *'02*
Dancing in September *'00*
Freedom Song *'00*
The Hurricane *'99*

Omar Sharif (1932-)
The Last Templar *'09*
10,000 B.C. *'08 (N)*
The Crown Prince *'06*
Hidalgo *'04*
Monsieur Ibrahim *'03*
The 13th Warrior *'99*
Heaven Before I Die *'96*
Catherine the Great *'95*
Gulliver's Travels *'95*
Lie Down with Lions *'94*
Beyond Justice *'92*
Grand Larceny *'92*
Mrs. 'Arris Goes to Paris *'92*
The Possessed *'88*
Anastasia: The Mystery of Anna *'86*
Harem *'86*
Peter the Great *'86*
The Far Pavilions *'84*
Top Secret! *'84*
Green Ice *'81*
The Baltimore Bullet *'80*
Oh, Heavenly Dog! *'80*
Pleasure Palace *'80*
Ashanti, Land of No Mercy *'79*
S*H*E *'79*
Sidney Sheldon's Bloodline *'79*
Crime & Passion *'75*
Funny Lady *'75*
Juggernaut *'74*
The Tamarind Seed *'74*
The Last Valley *'71*
The Horsemen *'70*
MacKenna's Gold *'69*
Funny Girl *'68*
Mayerling *'68*
Night of the Generals *'67*
Doctor Zhivago *'65*
Behold a Pale Horse *'64*
The Fall of the Roman Empire *'64*
Lawrence of Arabia *'62*

David Shark
See David "Shark" Fralick

Ray Sharkey (1953-93)
Urban Crossfire *'94*
Cop and a Half *'93*
Caged Fear *'92*
Chrome Soldiers *'92*
Round Trip to Heaven *'92*
Zebrahead *'92*
Relentless 2: Dead On *'91*
The Rain Killer *'90*
The Take *'90*
Act of Piracy *'89*
Capone *'89*
The Neon Empire *'89*
Scenes from the Class Struggle in Beverly Hills *'89*
Wired *'89*
P.I. Private Investigations *'87*
Private Investigations *'87*
No Mercy *'86*
Wise Guys *'86*
Behind Enemy Lines *'85*
Hellhole *'85*
Body Rock *'84*
Dubeat-E-O *'84*
Regina *'83*
Some Kind of Hero *'82*
Heart Beat *'80*
Idolmaker *'80*
Willie & Phil *'80*
Who'll Stop the Rain? *'78*

Kunal Sharma
The Kids Are All Right *'10*
The Cheetah Girls: One World *'08*

John Sharp (1920-92)
Misunderstood *'87*
The Fiendish Plot of Dr. Fu Manchu *'80*

Lesley Sharp
The Diary of Anne Frank *'08*
Carrie's War *'04*
The Full Monty *'96*
Priest *'94*
Naked *'93*
The Rachel Papers *'89*
Rita, Sue & Bob Too *'87*

Lesley Sharp (1964-)
Return to Cranford *'09*
From Hell *'01*
Great Expectations *'99*
Close My Eyes *'91*

Thom Sharp
Heartbreak Ridge *'86*
Stoogemania *'85*

Timm Sharp
Americano *'05*
King of the Ants *'03*
Stark Raving Mad *'02*

Albert Sharpe (1885-1970)
Darby O'Gill & the Little People *'59*
Brigadoon *'54*
Up in Central Park *'48*

Cornelia Sharpe (1947-)
Venom *'82*
S*H*E *'79*
The Arab Conspiracy *'76*
The Reincarnation of Peter Proud *'75*
Busting *'74*
Serpico *'73*

David Sharpe (1911-79)
Colorado Serenade *'46*
Haunted Ranch *'43*
Two-Fisted Justice *'43*
Texas to Bataan *'42*
Trail Riders *'42*
Silver Stallion *'41*
Covered Wagon Trails *'40*
Doomed at Sundown *'37*
Melody of the Plains *'37*
Where Trails Divide *'37*
Gun Grit *'36*
The Adventurous Knights *'35*
Roaring Roads *'35*
Social Error *'35*

Melanie Shatner (1964-)
Surface to Air *'98*
Unknown Origin *'95*
Cthulhu Mansion *'91*
Syngenor *'90*
Star Trek 5: The Final Frontier *'89*

William Shatner (1931-)
Over the Hedge *'06 (V)*
The Wild *'06 (V)*
Miss Congeniality 2: Armed and Fabulous *'05*
Dodgeball: A True Underdog Story *'04*
American Psycho 2: All American Girl *'02*
Groom Lake *'02*
Shoot or Be Shot *'02*
Showtime *'02*
Osmosis Jones *'01 (V)*
Miss Congeniality *'00*
Free Enterprise *'98*
Land of the Free *'98*
Double Play *'96*
Star Trek: Generations *'94*
TekWar *'94*
Family of Strangers *'93*
National Lampoon's Loaded Weapon 1 *'93*
Bill & Ted's Bogus Journey *'91*
Star Trek 6: The Undiscovered Country *'91*
Star Trek 5: The Final Frontier *'89*
Broken Angel *'88*
Star Trek 4: The Voyage Home *'86*
Secrets of a Married Man *'84*
Star Trek 3: The Search for Spock *'84*
Airplane 2: The Sequel *'82*
Star Trek 2: The Wrath of Khan *'82*
Visiting Hours *'82*
The Babysitter *'80*
The Kidnapping of the President *'80*
Riel *'79*
Star Trek: The Motion Picture *'79*
Third Walker *'79*
The Bastard *'78*
The Crash of Flight 401 *'78*
Little Women *'78*
Kingdom of the Spiders *'77*
Whale of a Tale *'76*
Devil's Rain *'75*
The Barbary Coast *'74*
Big Bad Mama *'74*
Impulse *'74*
Pray for the Wildcats *'74*
Pioneer Woman *'73*
The People *'71*
The Andersonville Trial *'70*
White Comanche *'67*
Incubus *'65*
The Outrage *'64*
Judgment at Nuremberg *'61*
Shame *'61*
The Brothers Karamazov *'58*

Shari Shattuck (1960-)
Body Chemistry 3: Point of Seduction *'93*
Dead On *'93*
Out for Blood *'93*
Mad About You *'90*
Arena *'89*
The Spring *'89*
Desert Warrior *'88*
Tainted *'88*
The Uninvited *'88*
Hot Child in the City *'87*
Number One with a Bullet *'87*
Naked Cage *'86*

Grant Shaud (1960-)
Waltzing Anna *'06*
The Crow: Salvation *'00*
From the Earth to the Moon *'98*
The Distinguished Gentleman *'92*
Wall Street *'87*

Charles Shaughnessy (1955-)
The Tale of Despereaux *'08 (V)*
Soldiers of Change *'06*
Kids in America *'05*
Get a Clue *'02*
Something About Sex *'98*

Mickey Shaughnessy (1920-85)
Primal Scream *'87*
My Dog, the Thief *'69*
A Global Affair *'63*
Dondi *'61*
The King of the Roaring '20s: The Story of Arnold Rothstein *'61*
Pocketful of Miracles *'61*
The Adventures of Huckleberry Finn *'60*
Gunman's Walk *'58*
The Sheepman *'58*
Designing Woman *'57*
Jailhouse Rock *'57*
Conquest of Space *'55*
From Here to Eternity *'53*
Last of the Comanches *'52*

Billy Joe Shaver
Bait Shop *'08*
The Apostle *'97*

Helen Shaver (1952-)
Numb *'07*
Tremors 3: Back to Perfection *'01*
Common Ground *'00*
We All Fall Down *'00*
The Sweetest Gift *'98*
The Craft *'96*
Poltergeist: The Legacy *'96*
Rowing Through *'96*
Tremors 2: Aftershocks *'96*
Born to Be Wild *'95*
Open Season *'95*
The Outer Limits: Sandkings *'95*
Morning Glory *'93*
Murder So Sweet *'93*
That Night *'93*
Trial and Error *'92*

Zebrahead '92
Dr. Bethune '90
Innocent Victim '90
Pair of Aces '90
The Land Before Time '88 (V)
The Believers '87
The Color of Money '86
Desert Hearts '86
Lost '86
The Park Is Mine '85
The War Boy '85
Best Defense '84
Coming Out Alive '84
Harry Tracy '83
The Osterman Weekend '83
Gas '81
Off Your Rocker '80
The Amityville Horror '79
High Ballin' '78
In Praise of Older Women '78
Outrageous! '77
Starship Invasions '77
Who Has Seen the Wind? '77
Shoot '76

Anabel Shaw (1923-)
To Hell and Back '55
Gun Crazy '49
Shock! '46

Bill Shaw
Total Reality '97
Ghostriders '87

Bobbi Shaw (1942-)
Ghost in the Invisible Bikini '66
Beach Blanket Bingo '65
How to Stuff a Wild Bikini '65
Ski Party '65
Pajama Party '64

C. Montague Shaw (1884-1968)
Holt of the Secret Service '42
Thunder Birds '42
Mysterious Doctor Satan '40
The Rains Came '39
Zorro's Fighting Legion '39
Square Shoulders '29

Crystal Shaw
Laser Moon '92
Hardbodies '84

Fiona Shaw (1958-)
Harry Potter and the Half-Blood Prince '09
Catch and Release '07
Fracture '07
Harry Potter and the Order of the Phoenix '07
The Black Dahlia '06
Close Your Eyes '02
Harry Potter and the Chamber of Secrets '02
Harry Potter and the Sorcerer's Stone '01
The Seventh Stream '01
The Triumph of Love '01
The Last September '99
RKO 281 '99
The Avengers '98
The Butcher Boy '97
Jane Eyre '96
Leo Tolstoy's Anna Karenina '96
Persuasion '95
Maria's Child '93
Super Mario Bros. '93
Undercover Blues '93
London Kills Me '91
Mountains of the Moon '90
Three Men and a Little Lady '90
My Left Foot '89

John Shaw
Wyvern '09
The Foursome '06

Martin Shaw (1945-)
P.D. James: The Murder Room '04
P.D. James: Death in Holy Orders '03
The Scarlet Pimpernel '99
The Scarlet Pimpernel 2: Mademoiselle Guillotine '99
The Scarlet Pimpernel 3: The Kidnapped King '99
Rhodes '97
Intrigue '90
The Last Place on Earth '85
The Hound of the Baskervilles '83
Golden Voyage of Sinbad '73
Macbeth '71

Oscar Shaw (1887-1967)
Rhythm on the River '40
The Cocoanuts '29
The King on Main Street '25

Paula Shaw (1941-)
Chupacabra Terror '05
We'll Meet Again '02

Reta Shaw (1912-82)
Escape to Witch Mountain '75
The Ghost and Mr. Chicken '66
The Pajama Game '57
All Mine to Give '56
Picnic '55

Robert Shaw (1927-78)
Avalanche Express '79
Force 10 from Navarone '78
Black Sunday '77
The Deep '77
Robin and Marian '76
Swashbuckler '76
Jaws '75
The Taking of Pelham One Two Three '74
The Sting '73
Diamonds '72
A Reflection of Fear '72
A Town Called Hell '72
Young Winston '72
Battle of Britain '69
A Man for All Seasons '66
Battle of the Bulge '65
From Russia with Love '63

Sandie Shaw (1947-)
Eat the Rich '87
Absolute Beginners '86

Sebastian Shaw (1905-94)
High Season '88
Reilly: Ace of Spies '87
Return of the Jedi '83
A Midsummer Night's Dream '68
Spy in Black '39
The Squeaker '37
Department Store '35

Stan Shaw (1952-)
Freedom Song '00
Snake Eyes '98
Daylight '96
Cutthroat Island '95
Houseguest '94
Lifepod '93
Rising Sun '93
Body of Evidence '92
Fried Green Tomatoes '91
The Court Martial of Jackie Robinson '90
Fear '90
Billionaire Boys Club '87
Busted Up '86
The Gladiator '86
Samaritan: The Mitch Snyder Story '86
D.P. '85
Runaway '84
Dirkham Detective Agency '83
Tough Enough '83
Roots: The Next Generation '79
The Boys in Company C '77
Bingo Long Traveling All-Stars & Motor Kings '76
TNT Jackson '75

Susan Shaw (1929-78)
Blonde Blackmailer '58
Fire Maidens from Outer Space '56
The Woman in Question '50
Train of Events '49
It Always Rains on Sunday '47

Vanessa Shaw
Garden Party '08
Horror Hospital '73

Victoria Shaw (1935-88)
Alvarez Kelly '66
The Crimson Kimono '59
The Eddy Duchin Story '56

Vinessa Shaw (1976-)
Two Lovers '09
Badland '07
3:10 to Yuma '07
The Hills Have Eyes '06
40 Days and 40 Nights '02
Corky Romano '01
The '70s '00
The Weight of Water '00
Eyes Wide Shut '99
Coyote Summer '96
Fallen Angels 2 '93
Hocus Pocus '93
Ladybugs '92

Alia Shawkat (1989-)
The Runaways '10
Amreeka '09
Whip It '09
Bart Got a Room '08
Deck the Halls '06
Rebound '05
The Trial of Old Drum '00

Joan Shawlee (1929-87)
The Reluctant Astronaut '67
The Apartment '60
Some Like It Hot '59
Francis Joins the WACs '54
Prehistoric Women '50
Buck Privates Come Home '47
House of Horrors '46

Dick Shawn (1929-87)
Rented Lips '88
Maid to Order '87
Beer '85
Check Is in the Mail '85
Angel '84
The Emperor's New Clothes '84
The Secret Diary of Sigmund Freud '84
Young Warriors '83
Goodbye Cruel World '82
Love at First Bite '79
Evil Roy Slade '71
The Happy Ending '69
The Producers '68
What Did You Do in the War, Daddy? '66
It's a Mad, Mad, Mad, Mad World '63

Wallace Shawn (1943-)
Toy Story 3 '10 (V)
Kit Kittredge: An American Girl '08
Happily N'Ever After '07 (V)
Chicken Little '05 (V)
Melinda and Melinda '05
Disney's Teacher's Pet '04 (V)
The Incredibles '04 (V)
Duplex '03
The Haunted Mansion '03
Monte Walsh '03
Love Thy Neighbor '02
Mr. St. Nick '02
Personal Velocity: Three Portraits '02
Blonde '01
The Curse of the Jade Scorpion '01
The Prime Gig '00
Toy Story 2 '99 (V)
My Favorite Martian '98
Noah '98
Critical Care '97
Just Write '97
House Arrest '96
Just Like Dad '96
Vegas Vacation '96
All Dogs Go to Heaven 2 '95 (V)
Clueless '95
Toy Story '95 (V)
The Wife '95
Canadian Bacon '94
A Goofy Movie '94 (V)
Mrs. Parker and the Vicious Circle '94
Vanya on 42nd Street '94
The Cemetery Club '93
The Magic Bubble '93
The Double O Kid '92
Mom and Dad Save the World '92
Nickel & Dime '92
Shadows and Fog '92
Scenes from the Class Struggle in Beverly Hills '89
She's Out of Control '89
We're No Angels '89
The Moderns '88
The Bedroom Window '87
Nice Girls Don't Explode '87
Prick Up Your Ears '87
The Princess Bride '87
Radio Days '87
Heaven Help Us '85
The Bostonians '84
Crackers '84
The Hotel New Hampshire '84
Micki & Maude '84
Strong Medicine '84
Deal of the Century '83
Strange Invaders '83
First Time '82
A Little Sex '82
My Dinner with Andre '81
Simon '80
Manhattan '79

Michele Shay
Never Die Alone '04
He Got Game '98
Manhunter '86

Lin Shaye (1944-)
Snakes on a Plane '06
Bachelor Party Vegas '05
Drop Dead Sexy '05
A Cinderella Story '04
The Hillside Strangler '04
Boat Trip '03
Dumb and Dumberer: When Harry Met Lloyd '03
Attention Shoppers '99
Detroit Rock City '99
There's Something about Mary '98
Trading Favors '97
Kingpin '96
Dumb & Dumber '94
Brain Smasher... A Love Story '93
The Running Man '87
Brewster's Millions '85
Jekyll & Hyde... Together Again '82

Skyler Shaye
Bratz '07
Superbabies: Baby Geniuses 2 '04

Konstantin Shayne (1888-1974)
Song of Love '47
The Stranger '46
The Seventh Cross '44
Five Graves to Cairo '43

Robert Shayne (1900-92)
Teenage Caveman '58
The Giant Claw '57
The Indestructible Man '56
Marshal of Cedar Rock '53
Mr. Walkie Talkie '52
The Strange Mrs. Crane '48
The Spirit of West Point '47
Welcome Stranger '47
Behind the Mask '46
Christmas in Connecticut '45
Rhapsody in Blue '45

Tamara Shayne (1897-1983)
The Jolson Story '46
Somewhere I'll Find You '42

Elizabeth She
The Howling: New Moon Rising '95
Howling 5: The Rebirth '89

Gloria Shea (1910-95)
Last Days of Pompeii '35
Demon for Trouble '34
The Dude Bandit '33
The Fiddlin' Buckaroo '33
Phantom of the Air '33

John Shea (1948-)
The Insurgents '06
The Adventures of Sebastian Cole '99
Southie '98
The Apocalypse Watch '97
Backstreet Justice '93
Freejack '92
Honey, I Blew Up the Kid '92
Ladykiller '92
Magic Moments '89
Small Sacrifices '89
Light Years '88 (V)
A New Life '88
Stealing Home '88
Unsettled Land '88
Honeymoon '87
The Impossible Spy '87
A Case of Deadly Force '86
The Dining Room '86
Windy City '84
Kennedy '83
Missing '82
Hussy '80
Nativity '78

Katt Shea (1957-)
Barbarian Queen '85
Devastator '85
Hollywood Hot Tubs '84
Preppies '82

Al Shean (1868-1949)
Ziegfeld Girl '41
The Great Waltz '38
It Could Happen to You '37
Tim Tyler's Luck '37
San Francisco '36

Al Shearer (1977-)
Glory Road '06
How High '01

Harry Shearer (1943-)
The Simpsons Movie '07 (V)
For Your Consideration '06
Chicken Little '05 (V)
A Mighty Wind '03
Dick '99
EDtv '99
Godzilla '98
Small Soldiers '98 (V)
Almost Heroes '97 (V)
Little Giants '94
A League of Their Own '92 (V)
The Return of Spinal Tap '92
The Fisher King '91
Pure Luck '91
Blood & Concrete: A Love Story '90
Plain Clothes '88
Portrait of a White Marriage '88
This Is Spinal Tap '84
The Right Stuff '83
One Trick Pony '80
Prime Time '77

Moira Shearer (1926-2006)
Black Tights '60
Peeping Tom '60
The Story of Three Loves '53
The Tales of Hoffmann '51
The Red Shoes '48

Norma Shearer (1900-83)
We Were Dancing '42
Idiot's Delight '39
The Women '39
Marie Antoinette '38
Romeo and Juliet '36
The Barretts of Wimpole Street '34
Riptide '34
Smilin' Through '33
Strange Interlude '32
A Free Soul '31
Private Lives '31
The Divorcee '30
Let Us Be Gay '30
A Lady of Chance '28
The Student Prince in Old Heidelberg '27
He Who Gets Slapped '24

Alan Shearman
Mother Teresa: In the Name of God's Poor '97
Stoogemania '85
Bullshot '83

Ally Sheedy (1962-)
Life During Wartime '09
Perestroika '09
Harold '08
Day Zero '07
The Veteran '06
Shooting Livien '05
Shelter Island '03
I'll Take You There '99
Sugar Town '99
The Fury Within '98
High Art '98
Buried Alive 2 '97
Highball '97
Amnesia '96
One Night Stand '95
The Tin Soldier '95
The Haunting of Seacliff Inn '94
Parallel Lives '94
Chantilly Lace '93
Man's Best Friend '93
The Pickle '93
Red Shoe Diaries 4: Auto Erotica '93
Tattle Tale '92
Only the Lonely '91
Betsy's Wedding '90
Fear '90
The Lost Capone '90
The Heart of Dixie '89
Maid to Order '87
We Are the Children '87
Blue City '86
Short Circuit '86
The Breakfast Club '85
St. Elmo's Fire '85
Twice in a Lifetime '85
Oxford Blues '84
Bad Boys '83
WarGames '83
The Best Little Girl in the World '81

Gladys Sheehan
Hear My Song '91
Rawhead Rex '87

Charlie Sheen (1965-)
Scary Movie 4 '06
The Big Bounce '04
Scary Movie 3 '03
Good Advice '01
Lisa Picard Is Famous '01
Rated X '00
Being John Malkovich '99
Free Money '99
No Code of Conduct '98
Postmortem '98
Under Pressure '98
Money Talks '97
Sisters '97 (N)
The Arrival '96
The Shadow Conspiracy '96
All Dogs Go to Heaven 2 '95 (V)
Major League 2 '94
Terminal Velocity '94
The Chase '93
Deadfall '93
Hot Shots! Part Deux '93
National Lampoon's Loaded Weapon 1 '93
The Three Musketeers '93
Beyond the Law '92
Hot Shots! '91
Men at Work '90
Navy SEALS '90
The Rookie '90

Fire, Ice and Dynamite *'91*
Murder on Line One *'90*
Henry V *'89*

Steve John Shepherd (1973-)
Layer Cake *'05*
Me Without You *'01*
Forgive and Forget *'99*
Virtual Sexuality *'99*

Suzanne Shepherd
Harold *'08*
A Dirty Shame *'04*
Lolita *'97*
The Jerky Boys *'95*
Palookaville *'95*

W. Morgan Shepherd
See William Morgan Sheppard

Tiffany Shepis
Home Sick *'08*
Nightmare Man *'06*
The Hazing *'04*

Michael Shepley (1907-61)
Mine Own Executioner *'47*
Henry V *'44*
The Demi-Paradise *'43*
Housemaster *'38*
The Private Secretary *'35*
A Shot in the Dark *'33*

Delia Sheppard (1961-)
Dead Boyz Can't Fly *'93*
Animal Instincts *'92*
Night Rhythms *'92*
Secret Games *'92*
Sins of Desire *'92*
Mirror Images *'91*
Roots of Evil *'91*
Witchcraft 2: The Temptress *'90*

Mark Sheppard (1964-)
Evil Eyes *'04*
Megalodon *'03*
Lost Voyage *'01*
Out of the Cold *'99*
Soldier of Fortune Inc. *'97*
In the Name of the Father *'93*

Paula Sheppard (1957-)
Liquid Sky *'83*
Alice Sweet Alice *'76*

William Morgan Sheppard (1932-)
Over Her Dead Body *'08*
Transformers *'07*
Love's Abiding Joy *'06*
The Prestige *'06*
Love's Long Journey *'05*
Gods and Generals *'03*
Goldrush: A Real Life Alaskan Adventure *'98*
Sometimes They Come Back... Again *'96*
The Escape *'95*
Gettysburg *'93*
Needful Things *'93*
Wild at Heart *'90*
Elvira, Mistress of the Dark *'88*
Lassiter *'84*
The Keep *'83*
Hawk the Slayer *'81*
Sea Wolves *'81*
Shogun *'80*
The Duellists *'77*

Anthony Sher (1949-)
God on Trial *'08*
The Miracle Maker: The Story of Jesus *'00 (V)*
Horatio Hornblower *'99*
Shakespeare in Love *'98*
Mrs. Brown *'97*
The Moonstone *'97*
Alive and Kicking *'96*
Mr. Toad's Wild Ride *'96*
The Young Poisoner's Handbook *'94*
Genghis Cohn *'93*
Tartuffe *'90*
Erik the Viking *'89*
Shadey *'87*

Peter Sherayko
Retribution Road *'07*
Black Snow *'89*

Maurice Sherbanee
Forty Days of Musa Dagh *'85*
Mausoleum *'83*
Jud *'71*

Rade Sherbedgia
See Rade Serbedzija
Battle in Seattle *'07*

Ann Sheridan (1915-67)
The Opposite Sex *'56*
Appointment in Honduras *'53*
I Was a Male War Bride *'49*
Good Sam *'48*
Silver River *'48*
Nora Prentiss *'47*
Edge of Darkness *'43*
Thank Your Lucky Stars *'43*
George Washington Slept Here *'42*
Juke Girl *'42*
Kings Row *'41*
The Man Who Came to Dinner *'41*
Castle on the Hudson *'40*
City for Conquest *'40*
They Drive by Night *'40*
Torrid Zone *'40*
Dodge City *'39*
They Made Me a Criminal *'39*
Angels with Dirty Faces *'38*
Letter of Introduction *'38*
The Black Legion *'37*
San Quentin *'37*
Wine, Women and Horses *'37*
The Fighting Westerner *'35*
Murder at the Vanities *'34*

Dave Sheridan (1969-)
The Devil's Rejects *'05*
Frank McKlusky, C.I. *'02*
Bubble Boy *'01*
Corky Romano *'01*
Ghost World *'01*
Scary Movie *'00*

Dinah Sheridan (1920-)
Thirteenth Reunion *'81*
The Railway Children *'70*
Genevieve *'53*
The Sound Barrier *'52*
Blackout *'50*
No Trace *'50*
Calling Paul Temple *'48*
Salute John Citizen *'42*

Jamey Sheridan (1951-)
Video Voyeur: The Susan Wilson Story *'02*
Desert Saints *'01*
Hamlet *'01*
Life as a House *'01*
The Lost Child *'00*
Luminous Motion *'00*
The Cradle Will Rock *'99*
Let the Devil Wear Black *'99*
The Simian Line *'99*
The Echo of Thunder *'98*
The Ice Storm *'97*
Wild America *'97*
Stephen King's The Stand *'94*
A Stranger Among Us *'92*
Whispers in the Dark *'92*
All I Want for Christmas *'91*
Talent for the Game *'91*
Quick Change *'90*
Stanley and Iris *'90*
Jumpin' Jack Flash *'86*

Jim Sheridan (1949-)
Moll Flanders *'96*
Way of the West *'35*

Margaret Sheridan (1926-82)
One Minute to Zero *'52*
The Thing *'51*

Nicolette Sheridan (1963-)
Fly Me to the Moon *'08 (V)*
Code Name: The Cleaner *'07*
Possessed *'05*
Karate Dog *'04 (V)*
Raw Nerve *'99*
Dead Husbands *'98*
Beverly Hills Ninja *'96*
Spy Hard *'96*
Silver Strand *'95*
Noises Off *'92*
Deceptions *'90*
The Sure Thing *'85*

Bobby Sherman (1943-)
Get Crazy *'83*
He Is My Brother *'75*

Daniel Stewart Sherman
The Brooklyn Heist *'08*
Redacted *'07*

Hiram Sherman
Oh Dad, Poor Dad (Momma's Hung You in the Closet & I'm Feeling So Sad) *'67*
Mary, Mary *'63*

Lowell Sherman (1885-1934)
False Faces *'32*
Three Broadway Girls *'32*
What Price Hollywood? *'32*
Bachelor Apartment *'31*
The Royal Bed *'31*
The Garden of Eden *'28*
A Lady of Chance *'28*
Monsieur Beaucaire *'24*
Way Down East *'20*

J. Barney Sherry (1872-1944)
The White Sister *'23*
The Bargain *'15*

Anthony Sherwood
Honey *'03*
Blue Hill Avenue *'01*
Closer and Closer *'96*
Eddie and the Cruisers 2: Eddie Lives! *'89*
Terror Train *'80*

David Sherwood
Curse of the Crystal Eye *'93*
River of Diamonds *'90*

Madeline Sherwood (1922-)
Broken Vows *'87*
Teachers *'84*
Pendulum *'69*
Sweet Bird of Youth *'62*
Parrish *'61*

Robin Sherwood
Love Butcher *'82*
Tourist Trap *'79*

Sheetal Sheth
Looking for Comedy in the Muslim World *'06*
Dancing in Twilight *'05*
ABCD *'99*

George Shevtsov
Ike: Countdown to D-Day *'04*
Japanese Story *'03*
Love Serenade *'96*

Vladek Sheybal (1923-92)
Running Blind *'78*
The Wind and the Lion *'75*
S*P*Y*S *'74*
Scorpio *'73*
The Boy Friend *'71*
Women in Love *'70*
Billion Dollar Brain *'67*
Kanal *'56*

Kou Shibasaki
Dororo *'07*
One Missed Call *'03*

Kiyohiko Shibukawa
9 Souls *'03*
Ichi the Killer *'01*

Arthur Shields (1896-1970)
Enchanted Island *'58*
The Daughter of Dr. Jekyll *'57*
The King and Four Queens *'56*
The Quiet Man *'52*
The River *'51*
Tarzan and the Slave Girl *'50*
She Wore a Yellow Ribbon *'49*
Fighting Father Dunne *'48*
The Fabulous Dorseys *'47*
The Corn Is Green *'45*
The Keys of the Kingdom *'44*
The White Cliffs of Dover *'44*
Gentleman Jim *'42*
How Green Was My Valley *'41*
Drums Along the Mohawk *'39*

Brooke Shields (1965-)
Furry Vengeance *'10*
The Midnight Meat Train *'08*
Bob the Butler *'05*
Our Italian Husband *'04*
Widows *'02*
The Weekend *'00*
The Bachelor *'99*
Black and White *'99*
Born Wild *'95*
Freeway *'95*
Freaked *'93*
The Seventh Floor *'93*
Stalking Laura *'93*
The Diamond Trap *'91*
Backstreet Dreams *'90*
Speed Zone *'88*
Brenda Starr *'86*
The Muppets Take Manhattan *'84*
Wet Gold *'84*
Sahara *'83*
Endless Love *'81*
The Blue Lagoon *'80*
Wanda Nevada *'79*
King of the Gypsies *'78*
Pretty Baby *'78*
Tilt *'78*
The Prince of Central Park *'77*
Alice Sweet Alice *'76*

Nicholas Shields
Liar's Edge *'92*
Lost in the Barrens *'91*
Princes in Exile *'90*

James Shigeta (1933-)
Brother *'00*
Mulan *'98 (V)*
Drive *'96*
Space Marines *'96*
Blood for Blood *'95*
China Cry *'91*
The Cage *'89*
Die Hard *'88*
Tomorrow's Child *'82*
Enola Gay: The Men, the Mission, the Atomic Bomb *'80*
Midway *'76*
Paradise, Hawaiian Style *'66*
Flower Drum Song *'61*
The Crimson Kimono *'59*

Etsuko (Sue) Shihomi (1956-)
Shogun's Ninja *'83*
Shogun's Samurai—The Yagyu Clan Conspiracy *'78*
The Bodyguard *'76*
Sister Street Fighter *'76*
The Street Fighter's Last Revenge *'74*

Eihi Shiina
Tokyo Gore Police *'08*
Audition *'99*

Kippei Shiina
Reincarnation *'05*
Shinobi *'05*

Marion Shilling (1910-2004)
Cavalcade of the West *'36*
The Clutching Hand *'36*
Gun Play *'36*
I'll Name the Murderer *'36*
Captured in Chinatown *'35*
Rio Rattler *'35*
A Shot in the Dark *'35*
Stone of Silver Creek *'35*
Inside Information *'34*
Thunder Over Texas *'34*
Curtain at Eight *'33*
Man's Land *'32*
Shop Angel *'32*

Shmuel Shilo
Double Edge *'92*
Goodbye, New York *'85*
Noa at Seventeen *'82*

Joseph Shiloah
The Lion of Africa *'87*
Private Manoeuvres *'83*
I Love You Rosa *'72*
Eagles Attack at Dawn *'70*

Hye-Jin Shim (1967-)
White Badge *'97*
White Badge *'92*

Yoko Shimada (1953-)
The Hunted *'94*
My Champion *'81*
Shogun *'80*

Armin Shimerman (1949-)
Insanitarium *'08*
The Shadow *'94*
Arena *'89*
Stoogemania *'85*

Jenny Shimizu
Itty Bitty Titty Committee *'07*
Foxfire *'96*

Kazuya Shimizu
Azumi *'03*
Returner *'02*

Kiriko Shimizu
Dark Water *'02*
Ju-On 2 *'00*
Ringu *'98*

Misa Shimizu (1970-)
The Sea is Watching *'02*
The Eel *'96*
Okoge *'93*

Joanna Shimkus (1943-)
The Virgin and the Gypsy *'70*
The Lost Man *'69*
Boom! *'68*
Six in Paris *'68*
Zita *'68*
The Last Adventure *'67*

Sadie Shimmin
Wallander: Firewall *'08*
Wallander: One Step Behind *'08*
Wallander: Sidetracked *'08*

Sab Shimono (1943-)
Robot Stories *'03*
Life Tastes Good *'99*
The Big Hit *'98*
Paradise Road *'97*
Waterworld *'95*
The Shadow *'94*
3 Ninjas Kick Back *'94*
Suture *'93*
Teenage Mutant Ninja Turtles 3 *'93*
Come See the Paradise *'90*
Hiroshima: Out of the Ashes *'90*
Presumed Innocent *'90*
The Wash *'88*
Blind Date *'87*
Gung Ho *'85*
When Hell Was in Session *'82*

Cheech and Chong's Nice Dreams *'81*
Rabbit Test *'78*
Midway *'76*
Loving *'70*

Takashi Shimura (1905-82)
Love and Faith *'78*
Last Days of Planet Earth *'74*
Ghidrah the Three Headed Monster *'65*
Kwaidan *'64*
Attack Squadron *'63*
Gorath *'62*
Mothra *'62*
Yojimbo *'61*
The Bad Sleep Well *'60*
The Hidden Fortress *'58*
The Mysterians *'58*
Throne of Blood *'57*
Godzilla, King of the Monsters *'56*
I Live in Fear *'55*
Seven Samurai *'54*
Ikiru *'52*
The Idiot *'51*
Rashomon *'51*
Scandal *'50*
A Quiet Duel *'49*
Stray Dog *'49*
Drunken Angel *'48*
The Men Who Tread on the Tiger's Tail *'45*
Sanshiro Sugata *'43*

Eun-Kyung Shin
Uzumaki *'00*
The Ring Virus *'99*

Ha-Kyun Shin (1974-)
Thirst *'09*
Save the Green Planet *'03*
Sympathy for Mr. Vengeance *'02*
JSA: Joint Security Area *'00*

Yi Shin
The Ghost *'04*
Whispering Corridors *'98*

Toru Shinagawa
Flower & Snake 2 *'05*
Dark Water *'02*

Sofia Shinas (1968-)
Dilemma *'97*
Hostile Intent *'97*
Hourglass *'95*
The Crow *'93*

Eitaro Shindo (1899-1977)
The Crucified Lovers *'54*
Sansho the Bailiff *'54*
A Geisha *'53*
Sisters of the Gion *'36*

David Shiner
Man of the House *'95*
Silent Tongue *'92*

Ronald Shiner (1903-66)
Up to His Neck *'54*
Bees in Paradise *'44*
Butler's Dilemma *'43*
Thursday's Child *'43*

Chen Shing
The Amsterdam Connection *'78*
The Two Great Cavaliers *'73*

Fui-On Shing (1955-)
The Untold Story *'93*
The Killer *'90*

Masayuki Shionoya
Pulse *'01*
Charisma *'99*
Okoge *'93*

Tokitoshi Shiota
The Great Yokai War *'05*
The Happiness of the Katakuris *'01*

Toshi Shioya
Mr. Baseball *'92*
Prisoners of the Sun *'91*

John Wesley Shipp (1956-)
Karma Police *'08*
Christie's Revenge *'07*
Soft Deceit *'94*
Baby of the Bride *'91*
NeverEnding Story 2: The Next Chapter *'91*
The Flash *'90*

Yumi Shirakawa (1936-)
Gorath *'62*
The Secret of the Telegian *'61*
H-Man *'59*
The Mysterians *'58*
Rodan *'56*

Talia Shire (1946-)
Dim Sum Funeral *'08*
Blue Smoke *'07*
The Whole Shebang *'01*
The Visit *'00*
The Landlady *'98*
Lured Innocence *'97*
A River Made to Drown In *'97*
Chantilly Lace *'93*
Bed & Breakfast *'92*
Cold Heaven *'92*
For Richer, for Poorer *'92*
Mark Twain and Me *'91*
The Godfather, Part 3 *'90*
Rocky 5 *'90*
New York Stories *'89*
Blood Vows: The Story of a Mafia Wife *'87*
Lionheart *'87*
Hyper-Sapien: People from Another Star *'86*
Rad *'86*
Rip van Winkle *'85*
Rocky 4 *'85*
Rocky 3 *'82*
The Godfather 1902-1959: The Complete Epic *'81*
Windows *'80*
Old Boyfriends *'79*
Prophecy *'79*
Rocky 2 *'79*
Rich Man, Poor Man *'76*
Rocky *'76*
The Godfather, Part 2 *'74*
The Godfather *'72*
The Dunwich Horror *'70*
Gas-s-s-s! *'70*
Murderer's Keep *'70*

Bill Shirk
Ballbuster *'89*
Escapist *'83*

Anne Shirley (1918-93)
Murder, My Sweet *'44*
Bombardier *'43*
The Devil & Daniel Webster *'41*
Four Jacks and a Jill *'41*
A Man to Remember *'39*
Law of the Underworld *'38*
Stella Dallas *'37*
Steamboat Round the Bend *'35*
Anne of Green Gables *'34*
Rasputin and the Empress *'33*
Young America *'32*

Bill (William) Shirley (1921-89)
Sleeping Beauty *'59 (V)*
Abbott and Costello Meet Captain Kidd *'52*
I Dream of Jeannie *'52*

Cathie Shirriff
Star Trek 3: The Search for Spock *'84*
Covergirl *'83*

Joe Shishido (1933-)
Flower & Snake 2 *'05*
Branded to Kill *'67*
Gate of Flesh *'64*
Youth of the Beast *'63*

Kai Shishido
Azumi 2 *'05*
Remembering the Cosmos Flower *'99*

Stephan Shkurat
Guerilla Brigade *'39*
Chapayev *'34*
Earth *'30*

Samia Shoaib
Pi *'98*
subUrbia *'96*

William Shockley (1963-)
Welcome to Paradise *'07*
Madison *'01*
Girl in the Cadillac *'94*
Dream Lover *'93*
Howling 5: The Rebirth *'89*

Ann Shoemaker (1891-1978)
Sunrise at Campobello *'60*
Thirty Seconds Over Tokyo *'44*
My Favorite Wife *'40*
Alice Adams *'35*

Craig Shoemaker (1962-)
Safe House *'99*
Acting on Impulse *'93*

Hristo Naumov Shopov
Command Performance *'09*
I Am David *'04*
The Passion of the Christ *'04*
Target of Opportunity *'04*

Dan Shor (1961-)
Red Rock West *'93*
Bill & Ted's Excellent Adventure *'89*
Daddy's Boys *'87*
Mesmerized *'84*
Mike's Murder *'84*
Strangers Kiss *'83*
Tron *'82*
Strange Behavior *'81*
A Rumor of War *'80*

Miriam Shor (1971-)
The Cake Eaters *'07*
Pizza *'05*
Bedazzled *'00*
Hedwig and the Angry Inch *'00*
Let It Snow *'99*

Dinah Shore (1917-94)
Oh, God! *'77*
Fun & Fancy Free *'47 (N)*
Till the Clouds Roll By *'46*
Up in Arms *'44*
Thank Your Lucky Stars *'43*

Pauly Shore (1968-)
The Wash *'01*
The Bogus Witch Project *'00*
Bio-Dome *'96*
The Curse of Inferno *'96*
Jury Duty *'95*
In the Army Now *'94*
Dream Date *'93*
Son-in-Law *'93*
Encino Man *'92*
Phantom of the Mall: Eric's Revenge *'89*
18 Again! *'88*

Bobby Short (1924-2005)
For Love or Money *'93*
Hardhat & Legs *'80*

Columbus Short (1982-)
Death at a Funeral *'10*
The Losers *'10*
Armored *'09*
Whiteout *'09*
Cadillac Records *'08*
Quarantine *'08*
Stomp the Yard *'07*
This Christmas *'07*
Accepted *'06*

Dorothy Short (1915-63)
The Phantom Pinto *'41*
Trail of the Silver Spurs *'41*
Pony Post *'40*
Daughter of the Tong *'39*
Phantom Rancher *'39*
Wild Horse Canyon *'39*
Reefer Madness *'38*
Brothers of the West *'37*
Assassin of Youth *'35*
Savage Fury *'35*

Florence Short (1889-1946)
The Love Flower *'20*
Way Down East *'20*

Martin Short (1950-)
Hoodwinked Too! Hood vs. Evil *'10 (V)*
The Spiderwick Chronicles *'08 (V)*
The Santa Clause 3: The Escape Clause *'06*
Jiminy Glick in LaLa Wood *'05*
Treasure Planet *'02 (V)*
Get Over It! *'01*
Jimmy Neutron: Boy Genius *'01 (V)*
Alice in Wonderland *'99*
Mumford *'99*
Merlin *'98*
Prince of Egypt *'98 (V)*
A Simple Wish *'97*
Jungle 2 Jungle *'96*
Mars Attacks! *'96*
Father of the Bride Part 2 *'95*
The Pebble and the Penguin *'94 (V)*
We're Back! A Dinosaur's Story *'93 (V)*
Captain Ron *'92*
Clifford *'92*
The Return of Spinal Tap *'92*
Father of the Bride *'91*
Pure Luck *'91*
The Big Picture *'89*
Three Fugitives *'89*
Cross My Heart *'88*
Innerspace *'87*
Johnny Appleseed *'86*
Really Weird Tales *'86*
Three Amigos *'86*
Sunset Limousine *'83*
The Family Man *'79*
Lost and Found *'79*

Ken Shorter (1945-)
Dragonheart: A New Beginning *'00*
Ned Kelly *'70*

Robin Shou (1960-)
Street Fighter: The Legend of Chun-Li *'09*
DOA: Dead or Alive *'06*
18 Fingers of Death *'05*
Mortal Kombat 2: Annihilation *'97*
Beverly Hills Ninja *'96*
Fatal Chase *'92*
Honor and Glory *'92*
Interpol Connection *'92*

Frida Show
Contract Killers *'08*
Cyclops *'08*
Lost Colony: The Legend of Roanoke *'07*

Grant Show (1962-)
The Natalee Holloway Story *'09*
Encrypt *'03*
The Alchemists *'99*
Texas *'94*
Treacherous Crossing *'92*
A Woman, Her Men and Her Futon *'92*

Max (Casey Adams) Showalter (1917-2000)
Racing with the Moon *'84*
Sixteen Candles *'84*
Lord Love a Duck *'66*
Move Over, Darling *'63*
Summer and Smoke *'61*
The Monster That Challenged the World *'57*
Bus Stop *'56*
The Indestructible Man *'56*
Dangerous Crossing *'53*
Niagara *'52*
What Price Glory? *'52*

Michael Showalter (1970-)
The Baxter *'05*
Four and a Half Women *'05*
Wet Hot American Summer *'01*

Kathy Shower (1953-)
Hindsight *'97*
To the Limit *'95*
Improper Conduct *'94*
Married People, Single Sex 2: For Better or Worse *'94*
American Kickboxer 2: To the Death *'93*
Sexual Malice *'93*
L.A. Goddess *'92*
Wild Cactus *'92*
Bedroom Eyes 2 *'89*
Out on Bail *'89*
Robo-Chic *'89*
Frankenstein General Hospital *'88*
The Further Adventures of Tennessee Buck *'88*
Commando Squad *'87*

John Shrapnel (1942-)
Mirrors *'08*
Elizabeth: The Golden Age *'07*
Troy *'04*
K-19: The Widowmaker *'02*
The Body *'01*
Gladiator *'00*
Fatherland *'94*
Two Deaths *'94*
Tragedy of Flight 103: The Inside Story *'91*
How to Get Ahead in Advertising *'89*

Kin Shriner (1953-)
Hoot *'06*
The Corporation *'96*
The Crying Child *'96*
Subliminal Seduction *'96*
Cyberzone *'95*
Escape *'90*
Angel 3: The Final Chapter *'88*
Manhunter *'86*
Vendetta *'85*
Obsessive Love *'84*

Jackie Shroff
Devdas *'02*
Mission Kashmir *'00*

Sonny Shroyer (1935-)
A Love Song for Bobby Long *'04*
The Rosa Parks Story *'02*
The Runaway *'00*
The Gingerbread Man *'97*
John Grisham's The Rainmaker *'97*
Wild America *'97*
Bastard out of Carolina *'96*
Forrest Gump *'94*
The Ernest Green Story *'93*
Love Crimes *'92*
The Devil & Max Devlin *'81*
They Went That-a-Way & That-a-Way *'78*
Smokey and the Bandit *'77*
Gator *'76*
The Longest Yard *'74*
Payday *'73*

Qi Shu
Blood Brothers *'07*
Seoul Raiders *'05*
The Eye 2 *'04*
So Close *'02*
Gorgeous *'99*

Karin Shubert
See Karin Schubert

Andrew Shue (1967-)
Gracie *'07*
John Grisham's The Rainmaker *'97*
The Karate Kid *'84*

Elisabeth Shue (1963-)
Piranha 3D *'10*
Hamlet 2 *'08*
Gracie *'07*
Dreamer: Inspired by a True Story *'05*
Hide and Seek *'05*
Mysterious Skin *'04*
Leo *'02*
Tuck Everlasting *'02 (N)*
Hollow Man *'00*
Molly *'99*
Palmetto *'98*
Cousin Bette *'97*
Deconstructing Harry *'97*
The Saint *'97*
The Trigger Effect *'96*
Leaving Las Vegas *'95*
The Underneath *'95*
Blind Justice *'94*
Radio Inside *'94*
Heart and Souls *'93*
Twenty Bucks *'93*
The Marrying Man *'91*
Soapdish *'91*
Back to the Future, Part 3 *'90*
Back to the Future, Part 2 *'89*
Cocktail *'88*
Adventures in Babysitting *'87*
Link *'86*
Call to Glory *'84*
The Karate Kid *'84*

Richard B. Shull (1929-99)
Trapped in Paradise *'94*
Housesitter *'92*
Splash *'84*
Unfaithfully Yours *'84*
Heartbeeps *'81*
Dreamer *'79*
The Pack *'77*
The Big Bus *'76*
Cockfighter *'74*
Hail *'73*
Slither *'73*
Sssssss *'73*
The Anderson Tapes *'71*

Constance Shulman (1958-)
Doug's 1st Movie *'99 (V)*
Sweet and Lowdown *'99*

Michael Shulman
Sherman's Way *'08*
The Perfect Daughter *'96*

Lee Shumway (1884-1959)
Sundown Fury *'42*
Hollywood Cowboy *'37*
Go-Get-'Em-Haines *'35*

Iris Shunn
See Iris Meredith

Antonina Shuranova (1936-)
An Unfinished Piece for a Player Piano *'77*
Tchaikovsky *'71*
War and Peace *'68*

Daryl Shuttleworth
On the Other Hand, Death *'08*
Shock to the System *'06*

M. Night Shyamalan (1970-)
Lady in the Water *'06*
Signs *'02*

Christopher Shyer
Fierce People *'05*
Category 6 : Day of Destruction *'04*
The Invitation *'03*
K-9 3: P.I. *'01*

Sabrina Siani (1963-)
El Barbaro *'84*
Ator the Fighting Eagle *'83*
Conquest *'83*
Throne of Fire *'82*

Jane Sibbett (1961-)
The Town That Banned Christmas *'06*
Au Pair *'99*
The Arrival 2 *'98*
Noah *'98*
It Takes Two *'95*
The Resurrected *'91*

Clement Sibony (1976-)
He Loves Me ... He Loves Me Not *'02*
Dad On the Run *'00*
Deep in the Woods *'00*

Alexander Siddig (1965-)
Cairo Time *'09*
Doomsday *'08*
The Last Legion *'07*
The Nativity Story *'06*
Kingdom of Heaven *'05*
Syriana *'05*
Reign of Fire *'02*
Vertical Limit *'00*
A Dangerous Man: Lawrence after Arabia *'91*

George Sidney (1916-2002)
Manhattan Melodrama *'34*
Rafter Romance *'34*

Sylvia Sidney (1910-99)
Mars Attacks! *'96*
Used People *'92*
Beetlejuice *'88*
Pals *'87*
An Early Frost *'85*
Come Along with Me *'84*
Corrupt *'84*
Finnegan Begin Again *'84*
Hammett *'82*
Having It All *'82*
A Small Killing *'81*
The Shadow Box *'80*
Damien: Omen 2 *'78*
I Never Promised You a Rose Garden *'77*
Raid on Entebbe *'77*
Snowbeast *'77*
God Told Me To *'76*
Death at Love House *'75*
Summer Wishes, Winter Dreams *'73*
Love from a Stranger *'47*
Mr. Ace *'46*
Blood on the Sun *'45*
The Wagons Roll at Night *'41*
One Third of a Nation *'39*
You and Me *'38*
Dead End *'37*
You Only Live Once *'37*
Fury *'36*
Sabotage *'36*
The Trail of the Lonesome Pine *'36*
Thirty Day Princess *'34*
Merrily We Go to Hell *'32*
An American Tragedy *'31*
Street Scene *'31*

Drew Sidora (1985-)
Never Die Alone *'04*
White Chicks *'04*

Charles Siebert (1938-)
A Cry for Love *'80*
Blue Sunshine *'78*
Tarantulas: The Deadly Cargo *'77*

Jim Siedow (1920-2003)
The Texas Chainsaw Massacre 2 *'86*
The Texas Chainsaw Massacre *'74*

Donald Siegel (1912-91)
Into the Night *'85*
Invasion of the Body Snatchers *'78*
Play Misty for Me *'71*
Invasion of the Body Snatchers *'56*

Jake Siegel
American Pie Presents: Beta House *'07*
American Pie Presents: The Naked Mile *'06*

George Siegmann (1882-1928)
Hotel Imperial '27
The Man Who Laughs '27
The Red Mill '27
Uncle Tom's Cabin '27
Anna Christie '23
Scaramouche '23
Oliver Twist '22
The Three Musketeers '21
The Birth of a Nation '15

Casey Siemaszko (1961-)
Waltzing Anna '06
The Crew '00
Chameleon 2: Death Match '99
Limbo '99
Stephen King's The Storm of the Century '99
Rose Hill '97
Bliss '96
Mistrial '96
Black Scorpion '95
Milk Money '94
My Life's in Turnaround '94
Teresa's Tattoo '94
Of Mice and Men '92
The Chase '91
Near Misses '91
The Big Slice '90
Back to the Future, Part 2 '89
Breaking In '89
Biloxi Blues '88
Young Guns '88
Gardens of Stone '87
Three o'Clock High '87
Miracle of the Heart: A Boys Town Story '86
Stand by Me '86
Amazing Stories '85
Back to the Future '85
Secret Admirer '85
Silence of the Heart '84
Class '83

Nina Siemaszko (1970-)
The Haunting of Molly Hartley '08
Mystery Woman: Mystery Weekend '05
Sleep Easy, Hutch Rimes '00
Goodbye, Lover '99
Jakob the Liar '99
Armistead Maupin's More Tales of the City '97
Suicide Kings '97
The American President '95
Sawbones '95
Airheads '94
Power of Attorney '94
Red Shoe Diaries 3: Another Woman's Lipstick '93
The Saint of Fort Washington '93
Twenty Bucks '93
Bed & Breakfast '92
Sinatra '92
Wild Orchid 2: Two Shades of Blue '92
Tucker: The Man and His Dream '88

Gregory Sierra (1941-)
Blood Money '99
Mafia! '98
The Wonderful Ice Cream Suit '98
Hot Shots! Part Deux '93
Deep Cover '92
Honey, I Blew Up the Kid '92
Dynamite and Gold '88
Code Name: Dancer '87
Let's Get Harry '87
Miami Vice '84
Mean Dog Blues '78
The Clones '73
The Thief Who Came to Dinner '73
Pocket Money '72

Rocco Siffredi (1964-)
Anatomy of Hell '04
Romance '99

Jamie-Lynn Sigler (1981-)
Call Me: The Rise and Fall of Heidi Fleiss '04
Extreme Dating '04

Tom Signorelli (1939-)
Robot in the Family '94
Crossover Dreams '85
One Down, Two to Go! '82
Alice Sweet Alice '76
Big Bad Mama '74
The Last Porno Flick '74
Kelly's Heroes '70
The St. Valentine's Day Massacre '67
The Trip '67

Simone Signoret (1921-85)
I Sent a Letter to My Love '81
Madame Rosa '77
Le Chat '75
Widow Couderc '74
Army of Shadows '69
Games '67
Is Paris Burning? '66
Ship of Fools '65
The Day and the Hour '63
Term of Trial '63
Le Joli Mai '62 (N)
Room at the Top '59
The Crucible '57
Death in the Garden '56
Diabolique '55
Casque d'Or '52
La Ronde '51
Dedee d'Anvers '49
Against the Wind '48

Caroline Sihol (1949-)
A Girl Cut in Two '07
Tous les Matins du Monde '92
Confidentially Yours '83

Cynthia Sikes (1951-)
Going Shopping '05
Possums '99
Love Hurts '91
Oceans of Fire '86
The Man Who Loved Women '83
Goodbye Cruel World '82
Ladies and Gentlemen, the Fabulous Stains '82

James B. Sikking (1934-)
Made of Honor '08
Fever Pitch '05
Nowhere to Land '00
Mutiny '99
In Pursuit of Honor '95
Tyson '95
Dead Badge '94
Seduced by Evil '94
The Pelican Brief '93
Doing Time on Maple Drive '92
Final Approach '91
Narrow Margin '90
Around the World in 80 Days '89
The Brotherhood of the Rose '89
Ollie Hopnoodle's Haven of Bliss '88
Dress Gray '86
Morons from Outer Space '85
Star Trek 3: The Search for Spock '84
Up the Creek '84
The Star Chamber '83
Outland '81
The Competition '80
Ordinary People '80
The Electric Horseman '79
Black Force 2 '78
Man on the Run '74
The Terminal Man '74
Scorpio '73
The New Centurions '72
The Night God Screamed '71
Charro! '69
Daddy's Gone A-Hunting '69
Point Blank '67

Von Ryan's Express '65
The Strangler '64

Joe Sikora
Night Skies '07
Normal '03
The Watcher '00

Vic Silayan
The Last Reunion '80
Project: Kill! '77

Tusse Silberg
Citizen X '95
Hidden City '87
The Company of Wolves '85

Johannes Silberschneider (1958-)
Bride of the Wind '01
The Girl of Your Dreams '99

Vira (Vera) Silenti (1931-)
Son of Samson '62
Atlas in the Land of the Cyclops '61
Maciste in Hell '60

Caroline Silhol
See Caroline Sihol

Karen Sillas (1965-)
Reach the Rock '98
Sour Grapes '98
The Beast '96
Female Perversions '96
Risk '94
What Happened Was... '94
Simple Men '92

Douglas Sills (1960-)
Deuce Bigalow: European Gigolo '05
The Swan Princess 2: Escape from Castle Mountain '97 (V)

Milton Sills (1882-1930)
Burning Daylight '28
The Sea Hawk '24

Darien Sills-Evans (1974-)
Preaching to the Choir '05
The Reception '05

David Silva (1917-76)
Sisters of Satan '75
The First Texan '56
Senora Tentacion '49

Geno Silva (1948-)
A Man Apart '03
Geronimo '93
Drug Wars 2: The Cocaine Cartel '92
Night Eyes 2 '91

Henry Silva (1928-)
Ocean's Eleven '01
Backlash '99
Ghost Dog: The Way of the Samurai '99
The End of Violence '97
Trigger Happy '96
The Prince '95
Possessed by the Night '93
The Harvest '92
The Colombian Connection '91
Three Days to a Kill '91
Above the Law '88
Bulletproof '88
Trained to Kill '88
Code of Silence '85
Escape from the Bronx '85
Lust in the Dust '85
Cannonball Run 2 '84
Chained Heat '83
Violent Breed '83
Megaforce '82
Wrong Is Right '82
Day of the Assassin '81
Sharky's Machine '81
Alligator '80
Almost Human '79
Buck Rogers in the 25th Century '79
Crimebusters '79
Love and Bullets '79
Thirst '79

Shoot '76
Deadly Sting '73
Hired to Kill '73
Hit Men '73
Killer '73
Killing in the Sun '73
Manhunt '73
Cry of a Prostitute: Love Kills '72
Man & Boy '71
The Desperados '70
Never a Dull Moment '68
Hail Mafia '65
The Secret Invasion '64
A Gathering of Eagles '63
The Manchurian Candidate '62
Sergeants 3 '62
Cinderfella '60
Ocean's 11 '60
Green Mansions '59
The Jayhawkers '59
The Bravados '58
The Law and Jake Wade '58
The Tall T '57

Maria Silva (1941-)
Devil's Kiss '75
Curse of the Devil '73
The Mummy's Revenge '73
Tombs of the Blind Dead '72
The Awful Dr. Orloff '62

Simone Silva (1928-57)
Big Deadly Game '54
The Shadow Man '53

Trinidad Silva (1950-88)
UHF '89
Colors '88
The Night Before '88
Crackers '84
The Jerk '79

Aldo Silvani (1891-1964)
Nights of Cabiria '57
La Strada '54
Valley of the Kings '54

Leonor Silveira (1970-)
I'm Going Home '00
Party '96
Voyage to the Beginning of the World '96
The Convent '95
Abraham's Valley '93

Fawn Silver
Terror in the Jungle '68
Orgy of the Dead '65

Joe Silver (1922-89)
Switching Channels '88
Mr. Nice Guy '86
Almost You '85
The Gig '85
Rabid '77
You Light Up My Life '77
They Came from Within '75
The Apprenticeship of Duddy Kravitz '74

Ron Silver (1946-2009)
The Ten '07
Find Me Guilty '06
Red Mercury '05
Spliced '03
Festival at Cannes '02
Master Spy: The Robert Hanssen Story '02
Ali '01
American Tragedy '00
Cutaway '00
Black & White '99
In the Company of Spies '99
Ratz '99
The White Raven '98
The Beneficiary '97
The Arrival '96
Deadly Outbreak '96
Girl 6 '96
Kissinger and Nixon '96
ShadowZone: The Undead Express '96
Skeletons '96
Danger Zone '95
Timecop '94
A Woman of Independent Means '94

Blind Side '93
Lifepod '93
Married to It '93
Live Wire '92
Mr. Saturday Night '92
Blue Steel '90
Forgotten Prisoners '90
Reversal of Fortune '90
Enemies, a Love Story '89
Fellow Traveler '89
A Father's Revenge '88
Billionaire Boys Club '87
Eat and Run '86
Trapped in Silence '86
Garbo Talks '84
Oh, God! You Devil '84
Romancing the Stone '84
The Entity '83
The Goodbye People '83
Lovesick '83
Silkwood '83
Best Friends '82
Silent Rage '82
Betrayal '78
Semi-Tough '77
Tunnelvision '76

Veronique Silver (1931-)
Life Is a Bed of Roses '83
Toute Une Nuit '82
The Woman Next Door '81
This Sweet Sickness '77

Frank Silvera (1914-70)
Valdez Is Coming '71
The St. Valentine's Day Massacre '67
Toys in the Attic '63
Crime and Punishment, USA '59
Death Tide '58
Killer's Kiss '55
The Fighter '52
Miracle of Our Lady of Fatima '52
White Mane '52

Jay Silverheels (1912-80)
Man Who Loved Cat Dancing '73
Santee '73
True Grit '69
Indian Paint '64
Justice of the West '61
Alias Jesse James '59
Lone Ranger '56
Walk the Proud Land '56
War Arrow '53
Broken Arrow '50
Lust for Gold '49

Daniela Silverio
Oriana '85
Identification of a Woman '82

David Michael Silverman (1966-)
Metro '96
Copycat '95

Jonathan Silverman (1966-)
Beethoven's Big Break '08
Coffee Date '06
Jam '06
The Cookout '04
Bobbie's Girl '02
The Medicine Show '01
These Old Broads '01
The Inspectors 2: A Shred of Evidence '00
Lip Service '00
Just a Little Harmless Sex '99
The Inspectors '98
Neil Simon's The Odd Couple 2 '98
Something About Sex '98
French Exit '97
At First Sight '95
Little Big League '94
Sketch Artist 2: Hands That See '94
Teresa's Tattoo '94
12:01 '93
Weekend at Bernie's 2 '93
Breaking the Rules '92

Broadway Bound '92
Death Becomes Her '92
For Richer, for Poorer '92
Little Sister '92
Age Isn't Everything '91
Class Action '91
Traveling Man '89
Weekend at Bernie's '89
Caddyshack 2 '88
Stealing Home '88
Brighton Beach Memoirs '86
Challenge of a Lifetime '85

Robert A. Silverman
Naked Lunch '91
Scanners '81
The Brood '79

Sarah Silverman (1970-)
Saint John of Las Vegas '09
I Want Someone to Eat Cheese With '06
School for Scoundrels '06
Sarah Silverman: Jesus Is Magic '05
School of Rock '03
What Planet Are You From? '00

Mary Silvers
See Maria Silva

Phil Silvers (1912-85)
The Happy Hooker Goes Hollywood '80
Racquet '79
The Cheap Detective '78
The Chicken Chronicles '77
The Strongest Man in the World '75
The Boatniks '70
Buona Sera, Mrs. Campbell '68
Follow That Camel '67
A Guide for the Married Man '67
A Funny Thing Happened on the Way to the Forum '66
It's a Mad, Mad, Mad, Mad World '63
40 Pounds of Trouble '62
Lucky Me '54
Summer Stock '50
If I'm Lucky '46
A Thousand and One Nights '45
Cover Girl '44
Four Jills in a Jeep '44
Something for the Boys '44
Lady Takes a Chance '43
All Through the Night '42
Footlight Serenade '42
Just Off Broadway '42
Roxie Hart '42
Lady Be Good '41
Tom, Dick, and Harry '41

Sid Silvers (1904-76)
Born to Dance '36
Broadway Melody of 1936 '35

Andrew (Dice Clay) Silverstein (1957-)
One Night at McCool's '01
My 5 Wives '00
Foolish '99
Jury Duty '95
National Lampoon's Favorite Deadly Sins '95
No Contest '94
Brain Smasher... A Love Story '93
The Adventures of Ford Fairlane '90
Casual Sex? '88
Amazon Women on the Moon '87
Pretty in Pink '86
Night Patrol '85
Making the Grade '84
Private Resort '84
Wacko '83

Alicia Silverstone (1976-)
Alex Rider: Operation Stormbreaker '06
Beauty Shop '05

Scooby-Doo 2: Monsters Unleashed '04
Rock My World '02
Scorched '02
Love's Labour's Lost '00
Blast from the Past '98
Batman and Robin '97
Excess Baggage '96
The Babysitter '95
Clueless '95
New World '95
True Crime '95
Cool and the Crazy '94
Hideaway '94
The Crush '93

Ben Silverstone (1979-)
Get Real '99
Lolita '97
The Browning Version '94

Armando Silvestre (1926-)
The Killing Zone '90
The Last Riders '90
Night of the Bloody Apes '68
Doctor of Doom '62
Geronimo '62
Neutron vs. the Death Robots '62
Neutron and the Black Mask '61
Neutron vs. the Amazing Dr. Caronte '61
Wrestling Women vs. the Aztec Mummy '59
The White Orchid '54

Victoria Silvstedt (1974-)
Boat Trip '03
Out Cold '01

Alastair Sim (1900-76)
The Littlest Horse Thieves '76
Rogue Male '76
Royal Flash '75
The Ruling Class '72
Cold Comfort Farm '71
The Millionairess '60
School for Scoundrels '60
Blue Murder at St. Trinian's '56
Escapade '55
Geordie '55
The Belles of St. Trinian's '53
Innocents in Paris '53
A Christmas Carol '51
The Happiest Days of Your Life '50
Stage Fright '50
Captain Boycott '47
Green for Danger '47
Hue and Cry '47
Cottage to Let '41
Inspector Hornleigh '39
The Terror '38
Gangway '37
Late Extra '35
The Private Secretary '35

Gerald Sim (1925-)
No Sex Please—We're British '73
Dr. Jekyll and Sister Hyde '71
Long Ago Tomorrow '71
Oh! What a Lovely War '69
King Rat '65

Sheila Sim (1922-)
Pandora and the Flying Dutchman '51
The Guinea Pig '48
Great Day '46
A Canterbury Tale '44

Silvio Simac (1973-)
DOA: Dead or Alive '06
Black Mask 2: City of Masks '02

Jon Simanton
The Creeps '97
Turbo: A Power Rangers Movie '96

John Simm (1970-)
Brothers of the Head '06
State of Play '03
Miranda '01
24 Hour Party People '01
Forgive and Forget '99
Human Traffic '99
Wonderland '99
Boston Kickout '95
Cracker: Best Boys '95

Chelan Simmons (1982-)
Good Luck Chuck '07
Final Destination 3 '06
Chupacabra Terror '05
Snakehead Terror '04

Dick Simmons (1913-2003)
Men of the Fighting Lady '54
Above and Beyond '53
Battle Circus '53

Gene Simmons (1949-)
Extract '09
The New Guy '02
Wish You Were Dead '00
Detroit Rock City '99
Red Surf '90
Decline of Western Civilization 2: The Metal Years '88
Never Too Young to Die '86
Trick or Treat '86
Wanted Dead or Alive '86
Runaway '84
KISS Meets the Phantom of the Park '78

Henry Simmons (1970-)
World's Greatest Dad '09
South of Pico '07
The Insurgents '06
Madea's Family Reunion '06
Taxi '04
A Gentleman's Game '01
Let It Snow '99

Jaason Simmons (1970-)
Frankenstein Reborn '98
Highway Hitcher '98
Nowhere '96

Jean Simmons (1929-)
Howl's Moving Castle '04 (V)
Final Fantasy: The Spirits Within '01 (V)
How to Make an American Quilt '95
Great Expectations '89
The Dawning '88
A Friendship in Vienna '88 (N)
Going Undercover '88
Perry Mason: The Case of the Lost Love '87
North and South Book 2 '86
North and South Book 1 '85
December Flower '84
The Thorn Birds '83
A Small Killing '81
Dominique Is Dead '79
The Dain Curse '78
Mr. Sycamore '74
Say Hello to Yesterday '71
The Happy Ending '69
Divorce American Style '67
Heidi '67
Rough Night in Jericho '67
Soldier in Love '67
The Grass Is Greener '61
Elmer Gantry '60
Spartacus '60
The Big Country '58
This Could Be the Night '57
Until They Sail '57
Guys and Dolls '55
A Bullet Is Waiting '54
Desiree '54
The Egyptian '54
The Actress '53
The Robe '53
Young Bess '53
Androcles and the Lion '52
Angel Face '52
She Couldn't Say No '52
The Clouded Yellow '51
Trio '50
Hamlet '48
Black Narcissus '47
Inheritance '47
Great Expectations '46

J.K. Simmons (1955-)
Crazy on the Outside '10
Aliens in the Attic '09 (V)
Extract '09
I Love You, Man '09
Jennifer's Body '09
New in Town '09
Up in the Air '09
The Vicious Kind '09
Burn After Reading '08
The Way of War '08
The Astronaut Farmer '07
Bury My Heart at Wounded Knee '07
First Snow '07
Juno '07
Postal '07
Spider-Man 3 '07
Thank You for Smoking '06
Harsh Times '05
Hidalgo '04
The Ladykillers '04
Spider-Man 2 '04
Off the Map '03
Spider-Man '02
Hit and Runway '01
The Mexican '01
The Gift '00
The Cider House Rules '99
For Love of the Game '99
Celebrity '98
Face Down '97
The Jackal '97
Love Walked In '97
Extreme Measures '96
The First Wives Club '96
Pom Poko '94 (V)
The Ref '93

Johnny Simmons
Hotel for Dogs '09
Jennifer's Body '09

Kimora Lee Simmons (1975-)
Waist Deep '06
Beauty Shop '05

Pat Simmons
My Science Project '85
The Giant Gila Monster '59

Peter Simmons
Sand '00
Best of the Best 3: No Turning Back '95
Renaissance Man '94

Joey Simmrin (1981-)
Star Kid '97
Nine Months '95
Little Giants '94

Ginny Simms (1913-94)
Night and Day '46
Broadway Rhythm '44
Hit the Ice '43
Seven Days' Leave '42
Playmates '41

Heather Alicia Simms
You Belong to Me '07
Broken Flowers '05

Larry Simms (1934-)
Blondie Hits the Jackpot '49
Blondie Knows Best '46
Footlight Glamour '43
It's a Great Life '43
Blondie for Victory '42
Blondie Goes Latin '42
Blondie Goes to College '42
Blondie's Blessed Event '42
Blondie in Society '41
Blondie Has Trouble '40
Blondie On a Budget '40
Blondie Plays Cupid '40
Blondie Brings Up Baby '39
Blondie Meets the Boss '39
Blondie Takes a Vacation '39
Blondie '38

Adam Simon (1962-)
The Haunting in Connecticut '09

Bob Roberts '92

Francois Simon (1917-82)
Christ Stopped at Eboli '79
Lumiere '76
Charles: Dead or Alive '69

Michel Simon (1895-1975)
The Two of Us '68
The Train '65
The Head '59
Femmes de Paris '53
Beauty and the Devil '50
Fabiola '48
Panique '47
Bizarre Bizarre '39
Circonstances Attenuantes '36
L'Atalante '34
Boudu Saved from Drowning '32
La Chienne '31
Passion of Joan of Arc '28

Paul Simon (1941-)
Mother Goose Rock 'n' Rhyme '90
One Trick Pony '80
All You Need Is Cash '78
Annie Hall '77

Robert F. Simon (1908-92)
Chinese Web '78
Spiderman: The Deadly Dust '78
The Man Who Shot Liberty Valance '62
Compulsion '59
Gunman's Walk '58
The Nine Lives of Elfego Baca '58
Edge of the City '57
The Catered Affair '56
The Court Martial of Billy Mitchell '55
Where the Sidewalk Ends '50

Simone Simon (1911-2005)
Le Plaisir '52
La Ronde '51
Women in Prison '49
Curse of the Cat People '44
Mademoiselle Fifi '44
Cat People '42
The Devil & Daniel Webster '41
La Bete Humaine '38
Girl's Dormitory '36

David Simonds
Amateur '94
The Refrigerator '91

Martine Simonet
The Last Metro '80
Simone Barbes '80

Mathieu Simonet (1975-)
Days of Glory '06
Merci pour le Chocolat '00

Nikolai Simonov
Peter the First: Part 2 '38
Peter the First: Part 1 '37
Chapayev '34

Ryan Simpkins
A Single Man '09
Gardens of the Night '08
Surveillance '08
Sherrybaby '06

Ivan Simpson (1875-1951)
Disraeli '30
Inside the Lines '30
The Sea God '30

Jessica Simpson (1980-)
Private Valentine: Blonde & Dangerous '08
Blonde Ambition '07
Employee of the Month '06
The Dukes of Hazzard '05

Jimmi Simpson (1975-)
Stay Alive '06
Herbie: Fully Loaded '05
D.E.B.S. '04
Stephen King's Rose Red '02
Loser '00

O.J. Simpson (1947-)
Naked Gun 33 1/3: The Final Insult '94
No Place to Hide '93
C.I.A.: Code Name Alexa '92
Naked Gun 2 1/2: The Smell of Fear '91
The Naked Gun: From the Files of Police Squad '88
Hambone & Hillie '84
Firepower '79
Capricorn One '78
Roots '77
The Cassandra Crossing '76
The Klansman '74
The Towering Inferno '74

Russell Simpson (1880-1959)
The Horse Soldiers '59
The Sun Shines Bright '53
Ma and Pa Kettle at the Fair '52
Coroner Creek '48
Saddle Tramp '47
My Dog Shep '46
They Were Expendable '45
Texas Masquerade '44
Border Patrol '43
The Grapes of Wrath '40
Three Faces West '40
San Francisco '36
Motive for Revenge '35
Sixteen Fathoms Deep '34
Ridin' for Justice '32
The Riding Tornado '32
Abraham Lincoln '30
The Lone Star Ranger '30
The First Auto '27
The Virginian '23
Human Hearts '22
Peg o' My Heart '22

Joan Sims (1930-2001)
The Last of the Blonde Bombshells '00
The Canterville Ghost '96
Carry On Behind '75
Carry On Dick '75
One of Our Dinosaurs Is Missing '75
Carry On Abroad '72
Carry On Matron '72
Carry On at Your Convenience '71
Carry On Camping '71
Carry On Henry VIII '71
Carry On Loving '70
Carry On Up the Jungle '70
Carry On Again Doctor '69
Carry On Up the Khyber '68
Carry On Cowboy '66
Carry On Screaming '66
Doctor in Clover '66
Don't Lose Your Head '66
Carry On Cleo '65
Carry On Regardless '61
Carry On Constable '60
Carry On Admiral '57
The Belles of St. Trinian's '53

Molly Sims (1973-)
Fired Up! '09
Yes Man '08
The Benchwarmers '06
Starsky & Hutch '04

Robin Sims
The Channeler '89
Shooters '89

Frank Sinatra (1915-98)
Who Framed Roger Rabbit '88 (V)
Cannonball Run 2 '84
The First Deadly Sin '80
That's Entertainment '74
The Detective '68
Lady in Cement '68
Tony Rome '67
Assault on a Queen '66
Cast a Giant Shadow '66
The Oscar '66
Marriage on the Rocks '65
None But the Brave '65
Von Ryan's Express '65
Paris When It Sizzles '64
Robin and the 7 Hoods '64
Come Blow Your Horn '63
Four for Texas '63
The List of Adrian Messenger '63
The Manchurian Candidate '62
Sergeants 3 '62
The Devil at 4 O'Clock '61
Can-Can '60
Ocean's 11 '60
A Hole in the Head '59
Never So Few '59
Kings Go Forth '58
Some Came Running '58
Pal Joey '57
The Pride and the Passion '57
Around the World in 80 Days '56
High Society '56
Meet Me in Las Vegas '56
Guys and Dolls '55
The Man with the Golden Arm '55
Not as a Stranger '55
The Tender Trap '55
Suddenly '54
Young at Heart '54
From Here to Eternity '53
Meet Danny Wilson '52
Double Dynamite '51
On the Town '49
Take Me Out to the Ball Game '49
The Kissing Bandit '48
The Miracle of the Bells '48
It Happened in Brooklyn '47
Till the Clouds Roll By '46
Anchors Aweigh '45
Higher and Higher '44
Step Lively '44
Strictly G.I. '44

Frank Sinatra, Jr. (1944-)
Hollywood Homicide '03
Cool World '92
Code Name: Zebra '84
Pepper and His Wacky Taxi '72
A Man Called Adam '66

Nancy Sinatra (1940-)
Speedway '68
Ghost in the Invisible Bikini '66
The Wild Angels '66
Marriage on the Rocks '65

Richard Sinatra
The Beast from Haunted Cave '60
Ski Troop Attack '60

Sinbad (1956-)
Crazy as Hell '02
Good Burger '97
The Cherokee Kid '96
First Kid '96
Homeward Bound 2: Lost in San Francisco '96 (V)
Jingle All the Way '96
Houseguest '94
Coneheads '93
The Meteor Man '93
Necessary Roughness '91

Gordon John Sinclair (1962-)
The Brylcreem Boys '96
Erik the Viking '89
Gregory's Girl '80

Hugh Sinclair (1903-62)
No Trace '50
The Gay Lady '49
The Rocking Horse Winner '49
The Secret Four '40

Madge Sinclair (1938-95)
The Lion King *'94 (V)*
Queen *'93*
The End of Innocence *'90*
Coming to America *'88*
Convoy *'78*
One in a Million: The Ron LeFlore Story *'78*
Cornbread, Earl & Me *'75*
Conrack *'74*

Donald Sinden (1923-)
The Canterville Ghost *'96*
The Children *'90*
The Island at the Top of the World *'74*
Rentadick *'72*
The Captain's Table *'60*
The Siege of Sidney Street *'60*
Doctor at Large *'57*
Above Us the Waves *'56*
Simba *'55*
Doctor in the House *'53*
Mogambo *'53*

Jeremy Sinden (1950-96)
The Innocent *'93*
Fortunes of War *'87*
Danger UXB *'81*

Ngai Sing
See Collin Chou

Campbell Singer (1909-76)
The Hands of Orlac *'60*
The Square Peg *'58*
The Young and the Guilty *'58*
Scotland Yard Inspector *'52*

Linda Singer
Junior *'86*
Zombie Nightmare *'86*

Lori Singer (1962-)
The Last Ride *'94*
Equinox *'93*
Short Cuts *'93*
Sunset Grill *'92*
Warlock *'91*
Storm and Sorrow *'90*
Made in USA *'88*
Summer Heat *'87*
Trouble in Mind *'86*
The Falcon and the Snowman *'85*
The Man with One Red Shoe *'85*
Footloose *'84*
Born Beautiful *'82*

Marc Singer (1948-)
Eagle Eye *'08*
L.A.P.D.: To Protect and Serve *'01*
Street Corner Justice *'96*
Beastmaster 3: The Eye of Braxus *'95*
Cyberzone *'95*
The Fighter *'95*
Silk Degrees *'94*
Victim of Desire *'94*
Sweet Justice *'92*
Beastmaster 2: Through the Portal of Time *'91*
The Berlin Conspiracy *'91*
Deadly Game *'91*
Ultimate Desires *'91*
Beyond the Silhouette *'90*
Body Chemistry *'90*
Dead Space *'90*
High Desert Kill *'90*
A Man Called Sarge *'90*
The Red Raven Kiss-Off *'90*
Watchers 2 *'90*
In the Cold of the Night *'89*
Born to Race *'88*
V: The Final Battle *'84*
Her Life as a Man *'83*
V *'83*
Beastmaster *'82*
If You Could See What I Hear *'82*
For Ladies Only *'81*
Roots: The Next Generation *'79*
The Two Worlds of Jenny Logan *'79*
Go Tell the Spartans *'78*
Sergeant Matlovich vs. the U.S. Air Force *'78*
Things in Their Season *'74*

Richard Singer
American Pop *'81 (V)*
Girls Next Door *'79*

Steve Singer
Palindromes *'04*
Hit and Runway *'01*
Ms. 45 *'81*

Joseph Singleton (1879-1946)
The Mad Whirl *'25*
The Toll Gate *'20*
Reggie Mixes In *'16*

Penny Singleton (1908-2003)
Jetsons: The Movie *'90 (V)*
Blondie Hits the Jackpot *'49*
Blondie Knows Best *'46*
Footlight Glamour *'43*
It's a Great Life *'43*
Blondie for Victory *'42*
Blondie Goes Latin *'42*
Blondie Goes to College *'42*
Blondie's Blessed Event *'42*
Blondie in Society *'41*
Blondie Has Trouble *'40*
Blondie On a Budget *'40*
Blondie Plays Cupid *'40*
Blondie Brings Up Baby *'39*
Blondie Meets the Boss *'39*
Blondie Takes a Vacation *'39*
Blondie *'38*
Boy Meets Girl *'38*
Hard to Get *'38*
Vogues of 1938 *'37*

Linda Sini (1926-)
Sartana's Here... Trade Your Pistol for a Coffin *'70*
Venus Against the Son of Hercules *'62*

Gary Sinise (1955-)
Open Season *'06 (V)*
The Big Bounce *'04*
The Forgotten *'04*
Fallen Angel *'03*
The Human Stain *'03*
Impostor *'02*
Path to War *'02*
A Gentleman's Game *'01*
Mission to Mars *'00*
Reindeer Games *'00*
The Dress Code *'99*
The Green Mile *'99*
It's the Rage *'99*
That Championship Season *'99*
Snake Eyes *'98*
George Wallace *'97*
Albino Alligator *'96*
Ransom *'96*
Apollo 13 *'95*
The Quick and the Dead *'95*
Truman *'95*
Forrest Gump *'94*
Stephen King's The Stand *'94*
Jack the Bear *'93*
A Midnight Clear *'92*
Of Mice and Men *'92*
My Name Is Bill W. *'89*
True West *'86*

Karolin Siol
See Caroline Sihol

Sir Lancelot (1903-2001)
Zombies on Broadway *'44*
I Walked with a Zombie *'43*

Joseph Siravo
Wisegirls *'02*
Walking and Talking *'96*
Carlito's Way *'93*

G. Anthony "Tony" Sirico (1942-)
It Had to Be You *'00*
Mob Queen *'98*
Gotti *'96*
Goodfellas *'90*
Backtrack *'89*
Cookie *'89*
The Pick-Up Artist *'87*

Joseph Sirola (1929-)
Seizure *'74*
Hail *'73*

Marina Sirtis (1960-)
Green Street Hooligans 2 *'09*
The Grudge 3 *'09*
InAlienable *'08*
Net Games *'03*
Star Trek: Nemesis *'02*
Terminal Error *'02*
Star Trek: Insurrection *'98*
Star Trek: First Contact *'96*
Gargoyles, The Movie: The Heroes Awaken *'94 (V)*
Star Trek: Generations *'94*
Waxwork 2: Lost in Time *'91*
Death Wish 3 *'85*
Blind Date *'84*

Sisqo (1978-)
Pieces of April *'03*
Snow Dogs *'02*
Get Over It! *'01*

Noble Sissle (1889-1975)
Junction 88 *'47*
Murder with Music *'45*
Mistaken Identity *'41*

Jeremy Sisto (1974-)
Into Temptation *'09*
Gardens of the Night *'08*
Waitress *'07*
Population 436 *'06*
The Thirst *'06*
A Lot Like Love *'05*
The Nickel Children *'05*
In Enemy Hands *'04*
Paranoia 1.0 *'04*
Thirteen *'03*
Wrong Turn *'03*
May *'02*
Now You Know *'02*
Angel Eyes *'01*
Dead Dog *'00*
Jesus *'00*
The '60s *'99*
Bongwater *'98*
Playing by Heart *'98*
Suicide Kings *'97*
Without Limits *'97*
White Squall *'96*
Clueless *'95*
The Crew *'95*
Moonlight and Valentino *'95*
Hideaway *'94*
Grand Canyon *'91*

Rocco Sisto (1953-)
Innocent Blood *'92*
Red Riding Hood *'88*
Truth or Die *'86*
After Hours *'85*

Tim Sitarz
Axe *'06*
Outta Time *'01*

Emil Sitka (1915-98)
The Outlaws Is Coming! *'65*
Three Stooges in Orbit *'62*
Carolina Cannonball *'55*

Olivier Sitruk
Coco Chanel *'08*
L'Appat *'94*

Phomsit Sitthijamroenkhun
The Iron Ladies 2 *'03*
The Iron Ladies *'00*

Sutthipong Sitthijamroenkhun
The Iron Ladies 2 *'03*
The Iron Ladies *'00*

Frank Sivero (1952-)
Foolish *'99*
Cop and a Half *'93*
Fist of Honor *'92*
Goodfellas *'90*
Ratings Game *'84*
The Godfather, Part 2 *'74*

Jamie Sives (1973-)
Mister Foe *'07*
Love and Other Disasters *'06*
On a Clear Day *'05*
Wilbur Wants to Kill Himself *'02*

Eva Six
Beach Party *'63*
Operation Bikini *'63*

Sean Six
Alien Nation: Millennium *'96*
Alien Nation: The Enemy Within *'96*
Alien Nation: Body and Soul *'95*
Alien Nation: Dark Horizon *'94*

Tom Sizemore (1964-)
American Son *'08*
Red *'08*
Stiletto *'08*
A Broken Life *'07*
Protecting the King *'07*
Splinter *'06*
Born Killers *'05*
The Nickel Children *'05*
Hustle *'04*
Paparazzi *'04*
Dreamcatcher *'03*
Big Trouble *'02*
Swindle *'02*
Black Hawk Down *'01*
Pearl Harbor *'01*
Sins of the Father *'01*
Ticker *'01*
Red Planet *'00*
Bringing Out the Dead *'99*
The Match *'99*
Play It to the Bone *'99*
Witness Protection *'99*
Enemy of the State *'98*
The Florentine *'98*
Saving Private Ryan *'98*
Witness to the Mob *'98*
The Relic *'96*
Bad Love *'95*
Devil in a Blue Dress *'95*
Heat *'95*
Strange Days *'95*
Natural Born Killers *'94*
Wyatt Earp *'94*
Heart and Souls *'93*
Striking Distance *'93*
True Romance *'93*
Watch It *'93*
An American Story *'92*
Passenger 57 *'92*
Guilty by Suspicion *'91*
Harley Davidson and the Marlboro Man *'91*
Point Break *'91*
Where Sleeping Dogs Lie *'91*
Blue Steel *'90*
Flight of the Intruder *'90*
A Matter of Degrees *'90*
Born on the Fourth of July *'89*

Gunnar Sjoberg (1909-71)
Brink of Life *'57*
June Night *'40*

Victor Sjostrom (1879-1960)
Wild Strawberries *'57*
To Joy *'50*
Walpurgis Night *'41*
Thomas Graal's First Child *'18*
The Outlaw and His Wife *'17*
Thomas Graal's Best Film *'17*

George Skaff (1930-95)
Frogs *'72*
The Incredible Petrified World *'58*
Man Beast *'55*

Jimmie F. Skaggs (1944-2004)
Backlash: Oblivion 2 *'95*
Tecumseh: The Last Warrior *'95*
Thousand Pieces of Gold *'91*
The Lost Capone *'90*
Puppet Master *'89*
Ghost Town *'88*

Norman Skaggs
Getting Out *'94*
Chrome Soldiers *'92*

Lilia Skala (1900-94)
House of Games *'87*
Flashdance *'83*
Testament *'83*
Heartland *'81*
Deadly Hero *'75*
Probe *'72*
Charly *'68*
Caprice *'67*
Lilies of the Field *'63*

Alexander Skarsgard (1976-)
Generation Kill *'08*
Kill Your Darlings *'06*
The Last Drop *'05*

Stellan Skarsgard (1951-)
Angels & Demons *'09*
God on Trial *'08*
Mamma Mia! *'08*
The Killing Gene *'07*
Pirates of the Caribbean: At World's End *'07*
Beowulf & Grendel *'06*
Goya's Ghosts *'06*
Kill Your Darlings *'06*
Pirates of the Caribbean: Dead Man's Chest *'06*
Dominion: Prequel to the Exorcist *'05*
Exorcist: The Beginning *'04*
King Arthur *'04*
City of Ghosts *'03*
Dogville *'03*
Helen of Troy *'03*
No Good Deed *'02*
The Glass House *'01*
Taking Sides *'01*
Aberdeen *'00*
Harlan County War *'00*
Passion of Mind *'00*
Signs & Wonders *'00*
Time Code *'00*
Deep Blue Sea *'99*
Ronin *'98*
Savior *'98*
Amistad *'97*
Good Will Hunting *'97*
Insomnia *'97*
My Son the Fanatic *'97*
Breaking the Waves *'95*
Zero Degrees Kelvin *'95*
Good Evening, Mr. Wallenberg *'93*
The Slingshot *'93*
Wind *'92*
The Ox *'91*
The Women on the Roof *'89*
The Unbearable Lightness of Being *'88*
Hip Hip Hurrah! *'87*
Noon Wine *'84*

Jackie Skarvellis
The Rats Are Coming! The Werewolves Are Here! *'72*
The Body Beneath *'70*

Brigitte Skay
Four Times That Night *'69*
Zeta One *'69*

Hal Skelly (1891-1934)
Struggle *'31*
Dance of Life *'29*

Red Skelton (1913-97)
Those Magnificent Men in Their Flying Machines *'65*
Ocean's 11 *'60*
Around the World in 80 Days *'56*
Clown *'53*
Lovely to Look At *'52*
Texas Carnival *'51*
The Fuller Brush Girl *'50*
Three Little Words *'50*
Watch the Birdie *'50*
The Yellow Cab Man *'50*
Neptune's Daughter *'49*
The Fuller Brush Man *'48*
A Southern Yankee *'48*
Merton of the Movies *'47*
The Show-Off *'46*
Ziegfeld Follies *'46*
Bathing Beauty *'44*
Du Barry Was a Lady *'43*
I Dood It *'43*
Thousands Cheer *'43*
Whistling in Brooklyn *'43*
Panama Hattie *'42*
Ship Ahoy *'42*
Whistling in Dixie *'42*
Lady Be Good *'41*
Whistling in the Dark *'41*
Having a Wonderful Time *'38*
Having Wonderful Time *'38*

Tom Skerritt (1933-)
For Sale by Owner *'09*
Whiteout *'09*
Beer for My Horses *'08*
Dr. Jekyll and Mr. Hyde *'08*
The Trojan Horse *'08*
Killer Wave *'07*
Bonneville *'06*
Mammoth *'06*
Category 7 : The End of the World *'05*
Tears of the Sun *'03*
Path to War *'02*
Greenmail *'01*
Texas Rangers *'01*
High Noon *'00*
Trial by Media *'00*
Aftershock: Earthquake in New York *'99*
The Other Sister *'98*
Smoke Signals *'98*
What the Deaf Man Heard *'98*
Contact *'97*
Two for Texas *'97*
Divided by Hate *'96*
Knight Moves *'93*
Getting Up and Going Home *'92*
Poison Ivy *'92*
A River Runs Through It *'92*
Singles *'92*
Wild Orchid 2: Two Shades of Blue *'92*
Nightmare at Bittercreek *'91*
Child in the Night *'90*
The China Lake Murders *'90*
The Rookie *'90*
Big Man on Campus *'89*
The Heist *'89*
Red King, White Knight *'89*
Steel Magnolias *'89*
Poltergeist 3 *'88*
Big Town *'87*
Maid to Order *'87*
Opposing Force *'87*
Poker Alice *'87*
Wisdom *'87*
Miles to Go *'86*
SpaceCamp *'86*
Top Gun *'86*
Calendar Girl Murders *'84*
Dead Zone *'83*
Dangerous Summer *'82*
Fighting Back *'82*
Silence of the North *'81*
Alien *'79*
Cheech and Chong's Up in Smoke *'79*
Ice Castles *'79*
The Turning Point *'77*
Devil's Rain *'75*
Big Bad Mama *'74*
Thieves Like Us *'74*
Fuzz *'72*
Wild Rovers *'71*
M*A*S*H *'70*

Anita Skinner
Sole Survivor *'84*
Girlfriends *'78*

Carole Skinner
Napoleon *'96 (V)*
Adventures of Eliza Fraser *'76*

Claire Skinner (1965-)
Sense & Sensibility *'07*

When Did You Last See Your Father? '07
Almost Strangers '01
Second Sight '99
Sleepy Hollow '99
Catherine Cookson's The Wingless Bird '97
A Dance to the Music of Time '97
The Return of the Native '94
Naked '93
Life Is Sweet '90

Cornelia Otis Skinner (1899-1979)
The Girl in the Red Velvet Swing '55
The Uninvited '44

Keith Skinner (1949-)
The Slipper and the Rose '76
Mademoiselle '66

Pat Skipper
Ed Gein '01
Chain of Command '00
Trade Off '95
Dancing with Danger '93

Alison Skipworth (1863-1952)
Wide Open Faces '38
The Princess Comes Across '36
Satan Met a Lady '36
Dangerous '35
The Devil Is a Woman '35
Doubting Thomas '35
Here is My Heart '34
Six of a Kind '34
The Song of Songs '33
Night After Night '32
Tonight or Never '31
Dubarry '30
Raffles '30

Espen Skjonberg (1924-)
O'Horten '09
The Last Lieutenant '94
One Day in the Life of Ivan Denisovich '71

Jerzy Skolimowski (1938-)
Eastern Promises '07
Big Shots '87
White Nights '85
Hands Up '81
Innocent Sorcerers '60

Helgi Skulason (1938-96)
Pathfinder '87
Revenge of the Barbarians '85

Sigurdur Skulason
Eleven Men Out '05
The Sea '02

Jennifer Sky (1977-)
Meet Market '08
Never Die Alone '04

Azura Skye (1981-)
One Missed Call '08
20 Years After '08
What We Do Is Secret '07
Heavens Fall '06
Love and Debate '06
Wristcutters: A Love Story '06
The Wendell Baker Story '05
Carolina '03
Red Dragon '02
The Salton Sea '02
Bandits '01
28 Days '00
Dementia '98

Ione Skye (1971-)
The Lather Effect '06
Fever Pitch '05
Tower of the Firstborn '98
Went to Coney Island on a Mission from God... Be Back by Five '98
One Night Stand '97
Dream for an Insomniac '96
The Color of Evening '95
Four Rooms '95
Girls in Prison '94
Gas Food Lodging '92
Guncrazy '92
Samantha '92
Mindwalk: A Film for Passionate Thinkers '91
The Rachel Papers '89
Say Anything '89
A Night in the Life of Jimmy Reardon '88
River's Edge '87
Stranded '87

Tristen Skylar (1971-)
Book of Shadows: Blair Witch 2 '00
Cadillac Man '90
Kidco '83

Demian Slade (1972-)
Back to the Beach '87
Better Off Dead '85

Max Elliott Slade (1980-)
Apollo 13 '95
3 Ninjas Knuckle Up '95
3 Ninjas Kick Back '94
3 Ninjas '92

Jeremy Slate (1926-2006)
The Lawnmower Man '92
Dream Machine '91
Voyage of the Heart '90
Dead Pit '89
Goodnight, Sweet Marilyn '89
Mr. Horn '79
Summer of Fear '78
The Centerfold Girls '74
Alligator Alley '72
Hell's Angels '69 '69
Hell's Belles '69
The Hooked Generation '69
True Grit '69
The Devil's Brigade '68
Born Losers '67
I'll Take Sweden '65
Girls! Girls! Girls! '62
G.I. Blues '60

Christian Slater (1969-)
Lies and Illusions '09
Igor '08 (V)
He Was a Quiet Man '07
Love Lies Bleeding '07
Slipstream '07
Bobby '06
Hollow Man 2 '06
Alone in the Dark '05
The Deal '05
Mindhunters '05
The Confessor '04
Who is Cletis Tout? '02
Windtalkers '02
Hard Cash '01
3000 Miles to Graceland '01
The Contender '00
Basil '98
Very Bad Things '98
Hard Rain '97
Julian Po '97
Bed of Roses '95
Broken Arrow '95
Murder in the First '95
Interview with the Vampire '94
Jimmy Hollywood '94
True Romance '93
Untamed Heart '93
Ferngully: The Last Rain Forest '92 (V)
Kuffs '92
Where the Day Takes You '92
Mobsters '91
Robin Hood: Prince of Thieves '91
Star Trek 6: The Undiscovered Country '91
Pump Up the Volume '90
Tales from the Darkside: The Movie '90
Young Guns 2 '90
Beyond the Stars '89
Gleaming the Cube '89
Heathers '89
The Wizard '89
Tucker: The Man and His Dream '88
The Name of the Rose '86
Twisted '86
Legend of Billie Jean '85
Living Proof: The Hank Williams Jr. Story '83

Helen Slater (1963-)
Seeing Other People '04
Nowhere in Sight '01
Toothless '97
No Way Back '96
Lassie '94
Parallel Lives '94
Chantilly Lace '93
A House in the Hills '93
12:01 '93
Betrayal of the Dove '92
City Slickers '91
Happy Together '89
Sticky Fingers '88
The Secret of My Success '87
Ruthless People '86
Legend of Billie Jean '85
Supergirl '84

Ryan Slater (1983-)
Home Team '98
Hell's Kitchen NYC '97
The Amazing Panda Adventure '95

John Slattery (1963-)
The Adjustment Bureau '10
Iron Man 2 '10
Charlie Wilson's War '07
Reservation Road '07
Underdog '07
Flags of Our Fathers '06
The Situation '06
Dirty Dancing: Havana Nights '04
Mona Lisa Smile '03
Bad Company '02
A Death in the Family '02
Cash Crop '01
From the Earth to the Moon '98
Harvest '98
The Naked Man '98
Red Meat '98
Where's Marlowe? '98
Lily Dale '96

Richard X. Slattery (1925-97)
Zebra Force '76
Trained to Kill, U.S.A. '75

Tony Slattery (1959-)
Heaven's a Drag '94
Peter's Friends '92

Tod Slaughter (1885-1956)
The Greed of William Hart '48
Crimes at the Dark House '39
The Face at the Window '39
The Hooded Terror '38
Sexton Blake and the Hooded Terror '38
Never Too Late to Mend '37
Ticket of Leave Man '37
The Crimes of Stephen Hawke '36
Demon Barber of Fleet Street '36
Murder in the Old Red Barn '36

Darla Slavens
See Darla Haun

Jonathan Slavin
Hard Pill '05
Free Enterprise '98

Millie Slavin
One Night Stand '95
The People vs. Jean Harris '81

Bobby Slayton (1955-)
The Third Wheel '02
Bandits '01
The Rat Pack '98
Get Shorty '95

Tommy Sledge
Movie... In Your Face '90
Lobster Man from Mars '89

Victor Slezak (1957-)
Happy Tears '09
The Notorious Bettie Page '06
The Cat's Meow '01
Lost Souls '00
One Tough Cop '98
The Siege '98
Beyond Rangoon '95
The Bridges of Madison County '95
Bed & Breakfast '92

Walter Slezak (1902-83)
Treasure Island '72
Black Beauty '71
Caper of the Golden Bulls '67
Emil and the Detectives '64
The Wonderful World of the Brothers Grimm '62
Come September '61
Ten Thousand Bedrooms '57
Bedtime for Bonzo '51
People Will Talk '51
Abbott and Costello in the Foreign Legion '50
The Yellow Cab Man '50
The Inspector General '49
The Pirate '48
Born to Kill '47
Riff-Raff '47
Sinbad, the Sailor '47
Cornered '45
Salome, Where She Danced '45
The Spanish Main '45
Lifeboat '44
The Princess and the Pirate '44
Step Lively '44
The Fallen Sparrow '43
This Land Is Mine '43
Once Upon a Honeymoon '42

Grace Slick (1939-)
Jackie's Back '99
Gimme Shelter '70

Everett Sloane (1909-65)
Hercules and the Princess of Troy '65
Disorderly Orderly '64
The Patsy '64
Home from the Hill '60
Marjorie Morningstar '58
Lust for Life '56
Patterns '56
Somebody Up There Likes Me '56
The Big Knife '55
The Enforcer '51
Sirocco '51
The Men '50
Prince of Foxes '49
The Lady from Shanghai '48
Citizen Kane '41

Lindsay Sloane (1977-)
The Other Guys '10
She's Out of My League '10
The Accidental Husband '08
Over Her Dead Body '08
The TV Set '06
Dog Gone Love '03
The In-Laws '03
Bring It On '00

Olive Sloane (1896-1963)
Curtain Up '53
Seven Days to Noon '50
Trapped by the Mormons '22

Joey Slotnick (1968-)
I Want Someone to Eat Cheese With '06
Hollow Man '00
The Pirates of Silicon Valley '99
Blast from the Past '98
Dinner and Driving '97
Since You've Been Gone '97
Twister '96
A League of Their Own '92

Georgia Slowe (1966-)
The Company of Wolves '85
The Black Arrow '84

James Sloyan (1941-)
Danielle Steel's Changes '91
Deadline Assault '90
Billionaire Boys Club '87
Code Name: Dancer '87
Amos '85
Prime Suspect '82
Callie and Son '81
The Disappearance of Aimee '76

Errol Slue
Baby on Board '92
Murder One '88

Marya Small
Zapped! '82
American Pop '81 (V)

Sharon Small (1967-)
Dear Frankie '04
Inspector Lynley Mysteries: A Great Deliverance '01

Phillips Smalley (1865-1939)
The Taxi Mystery '26
Charley's Aunt '25

Jimmy Smallhorne
When the Sky Falls '99
2 by 4 '98

Amy Smart (1976-)
Crank: High Voltage '09
Mirrors '08
Seventh Moon '08
Crank '06
Peaceful Warrior '06
Bigger Than the Sky '05
Just Friends '05
Blind Horizon '04
The Butterfly Effect '04
Starsky & Hutch '04
Win a Date with Tad Hamilton! '04
The Battle of Shaker Heights '03
Interstate 60 '02
Scotland, PA '02
Rat Race '01
Road Trip '00
The '70s '00
Outside Providence '99
Campfire Tales '98
Dee Snider's Strangeland '98
High Voltage '98
Varsity Blues '98
Starship Troopers '97

Dee Smart
Welcome to Woop Woop '97
Back of Beyond '95
Blackwater Trail '95

Jean Smart (1959-)
Youth in Revolt '10
Hero Wanted '08
Lucky You '07
Garden State '04
Audrey's Rain '03
Bringing Down the House '03
Sweet Home Alabama '02
Disney's The Kid '00
Snow Day '00
Guinevere '99
Change of Heart '98
Neil Simon's The Odd Couple 2 '98
The Brady Bunch Movie '95
Edie & Pen '95
A Stranger in Town '95
Scarlett '94
The Yarn Princess '94
The Yearling '94
Homeward Bound: The Incredible Journey '93
Mistress '91
A Fight for Jenny '90
Maximum Security '87
Project X '87
Fire with Fire '86
Piaf '81

Rebecca Smart (1976-)
Blackrock '97
Celia: Child of Terror '89

Sarah Smart
Wallander: Firewall '08
Wallander: One Step Behind '08
Wallander: Sidetracked '08
Five Days '07

Richard Smedley
The Abductors '72
A Place Called Today '72
Brain of Blood '71

Hana Smekalova
See Florence Marly

Ron Smerczak
Queen's Messenger II '01
Jackie Chan's Who Am I '98
Return of the Family Man '89
Hunted '88

Laura Smet (1983-)
Frontier of Dawn '08
The Bridesmaid '04

Robert Smigel (1960-)
Little Nicky '00 (V)
Happy Gilmore '96

Tava Smiley (1971-)
Timecop 2: The Berlin Decision '03
A Girl, 3 Guys and a Gun '01
Outta Time '01

Yakov Smirnoff (1951-)
Up Your Alley '89
Heartburn '86
The Money Pit '86
Brewster's Millions '85
The Adventures of Buckaroo Banzai Across the Eighth Dimension '84

Kodi Smit-McPhee (1996-)
The Road '09
Romulus, My Father '07

Alexis Smith (1921-93)
The Age of Innocence '93
Dress Gray '86
Tough Guys '86
La Truite '83
Casey's Shadow '78
The Little Girl Who Lives down the Lane '76
Once Is Not Enough '75
The Young Philadelphians '59
This Happy Feeling '58
The Sleeping Tiger '54
Split Second '53
Here Comes the Groom '51
Montana '50
Any Number Can Play '49
South of St. Louis '48
The Two Mrs. Carrolls '47
Night and Day '46
Conflict '45
The Horn Blows at Midnight '45
Rhapsody in Blue '45
San Antonio '45
The Adventures of Mark Twain '44
Hollywood Canteen '44
Gentleman Jim '42
Dive Bomber '41

Allison Smith (1969-)
Terror Tract '00
At First Sight '95
A Reason to Believe '95
Jason Goes to Hell: The Final Friday '93
Wildflower '91

Amanda Smith
The Cradle '06
Fall from Innocence '88

Amber Smith (1972-)
Def Jam's How to Be a Player '97

L.A. Confidential *'97*
Laws of Deception *'97*
Mars *'96*
Private Parts *'96*
Red Shoe Diaries 7: Burning Up *'96*

Anna Deavere Smith (1950-)
Rachel Getting Married *'08*
Life Support *'07*
Cry_Wolf *'05*
The Human Stain *'03*
The American President *'95*
Dave *'93*
Philadelphia *'93*

Anna Nicole Smith (1967-2007)
Skyscraper *'95*
To the Limit *'95*

Arjay Smith (1983-)
Be Kind Rewind *'08*
Vacancy 2: The First Cut *'08*
Masters of Horror: The V Word *'05*
The Day After Tomorrow *'04*

Art Smith (1899-1973)
The Painted Hills *'51*
In a Lonely Place *'50*
The Next Voice You Hear *'50*
Caught *'49*
Letter from an Unknown Woman *'48*
Mr. Peabody & the Mermaid *'48*

Benjamin Smith (1995-)
Bob the Butler *'05*
Second Sight *'99*

Brandon Smith (1952-)
Paradise, Texas *'05*
The Alamo *'04*
Slap Her, She's French *'02*
Jeepers Creepers *'01*
Powder *'95*

Britta Smith
Bloom *'03*
The Magdalene Sisters *'02*
American Women *'00*
A Certain Justice *'99*
Moll Flanders *'96*
The Summer House *'94*
In the Name of the Father *'93*

Brooke Smith (1967-)
In Her Shoes *'05*
Bad Company *'02*
Series 7: The Contenders *'01*
Last Summer In the Hamptons *'96*
Kansas City *'95*
Vanya on 42nd Street *'94*
The Night We Never Met *'93*
The Silence of the Lambs *'91*

Bubba Smith (1945-)
Silence of the Hams *'93*
Fist of Honor *'92*
My Samurai *'92*
Police Academy 6: City under Siege *'89*
Police Academy 5: Assignment Miami Beach *'88*
Police Academy 4: Citizens on Patrol *'87*
The Wild Pair *'87*
Police Academy 3: Back in Training *'86*
Police Academy 2: Their First Assignment *'85*
Police Academy *'84*
Stroker Ace *'83*
Escape from DS-3 *'81*

Sir C. Aubrey Smith (1863-1948)
An Ideal Husband *'47*
Unconquered *'47*
And Then There Were None *'45*
The Adventures of Mark Twain *'44*
Sensations of 1945 *'44*
The White Cliffs of Dover *'44*
Forever and a Day *'43*
Madame Curie *'43*
Beyond Tomorrow *'40*
Rebecca *'40*
Waterloo Bridge *'40*
Another Thin Man *'39*
Balalaika *'39*
East Side of Heaven *'39*
Eternally Yours *'39*
Five Came Back *'39*
The Four Feathers *'39*
Four Men and a Prayer *'38*
The Hurricane *'37*
Prisoner of Zenda *'37*
Thoroughbreds Don't Cry *'37*
Wee Willie Winkie *'37*
The Garden of Allah *'36*
Little Lord Fauntleroy *'36*
Lloyds of London *'36*
China Seas *'35*
The Crusades *'35*
The Lives of a Bengal Lancer *'35*
Transatlantic Tunnel *'35*
Cleopatra *'34*
Scarlet Empress *'34*
The Barbarian *'33*
Bombshell *'33*
Curtain at Eight *'33*
Queen Christina *'33*
Trouble in Paradise *'32*
The Phantom of Paris *'31*
Trader Horn *'31*

Carolyn Smith
Perfect Lies *'97*
Small Time *'91*
Something Weird *'68*

Cedric Smith (1943-)
The Gospel of John *'03*
Sea People *'00*
Jack Higgins' Thunder Point *'97*
Witchboard 3: The Possession *'95*
JFK: Reckless Youth *'93*
The Penthouse *'92*
Love and Hate: A Marriage Made in Hell *'90*
Anne of Green Gables *'85*
Who Has Seen the Wind? *'77*

Chad Smith
Hostage *'05*
Tears of the Sun *'03*

Charles Martin Smith (1953-)
Jack and Jill vs. the World *'08*
Lucky You *'07*
P.T. Barnum *'99*
Apartment Complex *'98*
Deep Impact *'98*
The Beast *'96*
Dead Silence *'96*
The Final Cut *'96*
Wedding Bell Blues *'96*
Larry McMurtry's Streets of Laredo *'95*
The Road Home *'95*
I Love Trouble *'94*
Roswell: The U.F.O. Cover-Up *'94*
Speechless *'94*
And the Band Played On *'93*
Boris and Natasha: The Movie *'92*
Deep Cover *'92*
The Hot Spot *'90*
The Experts *'89*
The Untouchables *'87*
Starman *'84*
Never Cry Wolf *'83*
Cotton Candy *'82*
Herbie Goes Bananas *'80*
More American Graffiti *'79*
The Buddy Holly Story *'78*
The Campus Corpse *'77*
Law of the Land *'76*
No Deposit, No Return *'76*
Rafferty & the Gold Dust Twins *'75*
American Graffiti *'73*
Pat Garrett & Billy the Kid *'73*
Culpepper Cattle Co. *'72*
Fuzz *'72*

Cheryl "Rainbeaux" Smith (1955-2002)
Independence Day *'83*
Parasite *'82*
Vice Squad *'82*
Melvin and Howard *'80*
Cheech and Chong's Up in Smoke *'79*
Laserblast *'78*
Incredible Melting Man *'77*
Drum *'76*
Massacre at Central High *'76*
Pom Pom Girls *'76*
Revenge of the Cheerleaders *'76*
Slumber Party '57 *'76*
Farewell, My Lovely *'75*
Caged Heat *'74*
The Swinging Cheerleaders *'74*
Lemora, Lady Dracula *'73*

Connie Smith (1941-)
Hell on Wheels *'67*
Road to Nashville *'67*
Treasure of the Golden Condor *'53*
Room to Let *'49*

Constance Smith (1928-2003)
Impulse *'55*
Man in the Attic *'53*

Cotter Smith (1949-)
X2: X-Men United *'03*
Ride the Wild Fields *'00*
Lifeform *'96*
Midnight's Child *'93*
The Last Prostitute *'91*
Cameron's Closet *'89*
K-9 *'89*
Lady Beware *'87*
Broken Badge *'85*
A Bunny's Tale *'85*

Cynthia Smith
For the Love of Benji *'77*
Benji *'74*

Cyril Smith (1892-1963)
John and Julie *'55*
A Stolen Face *'52*
Old Mother Riley, Headmistress *'50*
Appointment with Crime *'45*
Sidewalks of London *'38*

Daniel E. Smith
John Q *'02*
Heimat 2 *'92*

David Anthony Smith
Terror in Paradise *'90*
Judgment Day *'88*

David Lee Smith
The Man from Earth *'07*
Divine Secrets of the Ya-Ya Sisterhood *'02*

Douglas Smith (1985-)
Remember the Daze *'07*
Rock the Paint *'05*
Hangman's Curse *'03*

Ebbe Roe Smith
Tapeheads *'89*
Big Bad Mama 2 *'87*
The Big Easy *'87*

Eddie Bo Smith, Jr.
The Courage to Love *'00*
Stir of Echoes *'99*

Ethel Smith (1910-96)
Melody Time *'48 (V)*
Bathing Beauty *'44*

Geraldine Smith (1949-)
Spike of Bensonhurst *'88*
Mixed Blood *'84*
Flesh *'68*

Gregory Edward Smith (1983-)
Guns *'08*
Closing the Ring *'07*
The Seeker: The Dark Is Rising *'07*
Kids in America *'05*
Nearing Grace *'05*
Book of Love *'04*
American Outlaws *'01*
The Patriot *'00*
Krippendorf's Tribe *'98*
My Teacher Ate My Homework *'98*
Small Soldiers *'98*
The Climb *'97*
Harriet the Spy *'96*
Spellbreaker: Secret of the Leprechauns *'96*
Leapin' Leprechauns *'95*

Hillary Bailey Smith (1957-)
Last Breath *'96*
Love Potion #9 *'92*

Howard Smith (1893-1968)
The Brass Bottle *'63*
I Bury the Living *'58*
No Time for Sergeants *'58*
Call Northside 777 *'48*
State of the Union *'48*

Howard K. Smith (1914-2002)
Dawn of the Dead *'78*
Nasty Habits *'77*

J. Augustus Smith (1891-1964)
Junction 88 *'47*
Drums O'Voodoo *'34*

Jaclyn Smith (1947-)
Charlie's Angels: Full Throttle *'03*
My Very Best Friend *'96*
Lies Before Kisses *'92*
Danielle Steel's Kaleidoscope *'90*
The Bourne Identity *'88*
Windmills of the Gods *'88*
The Night They Saved Christmas *'87*
Rage of Angels: The Story Continues *'86*
Florence Nightingale *'85*
Deja Vu *'84*
George Washington *'84*
Rage of Angels *'83*
Jacqueline Bouvier Kennedy *'81*
Nightkill *'80*
Users *'78*
Probe *'72*
The Adventurers *'70*
Goodbye Columbus *'69*

Jacob Smith (1990-)
Cheaper by the Dozen 2 *'05*
Cheaper by the Dozen *'03*
Dragonfly *'02*

Jaden Smith
The Karate Kid *'10*
The Day the Earth Stood Still *'08*
The Pursuit of Happyness *'06*

James Todd Smith
See LL Cool J

Jamie Renee Smith (1987-)
MVP (Most Valuable Primate) *'00*
Dante's Peak *'97*
Children of the Corn 4: The Gathering *'96*
Magic in the Mirror: Fowl Play *'96*

John Smith (1932-95)
The Kettles on Old MacDonald's Farm *'57*
Hot Rod Girl *'56*
We're No Angels *'55*

Julie K. Smith (1967-)
Return to Savage Beach *'97*
The Dallas Connection *'94*

Kavan Smith (1970-)
Stark Raving Mad *'02*
Mission to Mars *'00*

Kellita Smith (1969-)
Feel the Noise *'07*
Three Can Play That Game *'07*
King's Ransom *'05*
Roll Bounce *'05*
Hair Show *'04*

Ken Smith
Santa Claus *'59 (N)*
Nora Prentiss *'47*

Kent Smith (1907-85)
Die Sister, Die! *'74*
The Affair *'73*
Pete 'n' Tillie *'72*
Probe *'72*
The Night Stalker *'71*
Death of a Gunfighter *'69*
Games *'67*
The Balcony *'63*
Strangers When We Meet *'60*
The Badlanders *'58*
Party Girl *'58*
Sayonara *'57*
The Damned Don't Cry *'50*
The Fountainhead *'49*
My Foolish Heart *'49*
Magic Town *'47*
The Spiral Staircase *'46*
Curse of the Cat People *'44*
Cat People *'42*
Back Door to Heaven *'39*

Kerr Smith (1972-)
My Bloody Valentine 3D *'09*
Cruel Intentions 3 *'04*
Pressure *'02*
The Forsaken *'01*
Hit and Runway *'01*
Final Destination *'00*

Kevin Smith (1963-2002)
Beyond Justice *'01*
Dead Evidence *'00*
Young Hercules *'97*
Desperate Remedies *'93*

Kevin Smith (1970-)
Catch and Release *'07*
Live Free or Die Hard *'07*
Clerks 2 *'06*
Comic Book: The Movie *'04*
Daredevil *'03*
Jay and Silent Bob Strike Back *'01*
Scream 3 *'00*
Dogma *'99*
Chasing Amy *'97*
Mallrats *'95*
Clerks *'94*

Kim Smith (1983-)
Catwoman *'04*
National Lampoon's Van Wilder *'02*
Oh! What a Lovely War *'69*

Kurtwood Smith (1943-)
Entry Level *'07*
A Bright Shining Lie *'98*
The Magnificent Seven *'98*
Safety Patrol *'98*
Shelter *'98*
Citizen Ruth *'96*
Prefontaine *'96*
A Time to Kill *'96*
The Last of the Dogmen *'95*
To Die For *'95*
Dead on Sight *'94*
Boxing Helena *'93*
The Crush *'93*
Fortress *'93*
Shadows and Fog *'92*
Company Business *'91*
Star Trek 6: The Undiscovered Country *'91*
Quick Change *'90*
Dead Poets Society *'89*
The Heart of Dixie *'89*
The Nightmare Years *'89*
True Believer *'89*
Rambo 3 *'88*
RoboCop *'87*

Lane Smith (1936-)
Winds of Terror *'01*
The Legend of Bagger Vance *'00*
Inherit the Wind *'99*
From the Earth to the Moon *'98*
The Hi-Lo Country *'98*
Why Do Fools Fall in Love? *'98*
The Scout *'94*
The Spy Within *'94*
Son-in-Law *'93*
The Distinguished Gentleman *'92*
Duplicates *'92*
False Arrest *'92*
The Mighty Ducks *'92*
My Cousin Vinny *'92*
Air America *'90*
Blind Vengeance *'90*
The Final Days *'89*
Night Game *'89*
Prison *'88*
Weeds *'87*
Dress Gray *'86*
Frances *'82*
Prime Suspect *'82*
The Solitary Man *'82*
A Rumor of War *'80*
Blue Collar *'78*
Network *'76*
The Last American Hero *'73*

Lauren Lee Smith (1980-)
Pathology *'08*
Trick 'r Treat *'08*
Normal *'07*
The Last Kiss *'06*
One Way *'06*

Lewis Smith (1958-)
Wyatt Earp *'94*
Diary of a Hitman *'91*
Fulfillment *'89*
North and South Book 2 *'86*
The Heavenly Kid *'85*
The Adventures of Buckaroo Banzai Across the Eighth Dimension *'84*
The Final Terror *'83*
Southern Comfort *'81*

Linda Smith
Taken *'99*
The Phone Call *'89*

Lionel Mark Smith (1946-2008)
Edmond *'05*
Spartan *'04*
King of the Ants *'03*
Galaxina *'80*

Liz Smith (1925-)
Charlie and the Chocolate Factory *'05*
Keeping Mum *'05*
Oliver Twist *'05*
Wallace & Gromit in The Curse of the Were-Rabbit *'05 (V)*
Dead Cool *'04*
A Christmas Carol *'99*
Sweet Revenge *'98*
A Merry War *'97*
Apartment Zero *'88*
We Think the World of You *'88*
A Private Function *'84*

Lois Smith (1930-)
Diminished Capacity *'08*
Turn the River *'07*
Griffin & Phoenix *'06*
Hollywoodland *'06*
Little Fugitive *'06*
Sweet Land *'05*
P.S. *'04*
2 Brothers & a Bride *'03*
Minority Report *'02*
The Pledge *'00*
The Eternal *'99*
Tumbleweeds *'98*
Larger Than Life *'96*

Twister '96
Dead Man Walking '95
How to Make an American Quilt '95
Truman '95
Holy Matrimony '94
Falling Down '93
Sarah, Plain and Tall: Skylark '93
Hard Promises '92
Keep the Change '92
Fried Green Tomatoes '91
Switched at Birth '91
Green Card '90
Black Widow '87
Twisted '86
Reckless '84
Reuben, Reuben '83
Five Easy Pieces '70

Loring Smith (1895-1981)

Ma and Pa Kettle at Waikiki '55
Shadow of the Thin Man '41

Madeleine Smith (1952-)

Frankenstein and the Monster from Hell '74
Live and Let Die '73
The Vampire Lovers '70

Madolyn Smith (1957-)

Final Approach '91
The Super '91
The Rose and the Jackal '90
Funny Farm '88
The Caller '87
All of Me '84
Ernie Kovacs: Between the Laughter '84
2010: The Year We Make Contact '84
Sadat '83
Pray TV '82
Rehearsal for Murder '82
Urban Cowboy '80

Maggie Smith (1934-)

Nanny McPhee 2 '10
Harry Potter and the Half-Blood Prince '09
Becoming Jane '07
Harry Potter and the Order of the Phoenix '07
Harry Potter and the Goblet of Fire '05
Keeping Mum '05
Harry Potter and the Prisoner of Azkaban '04
Ladies in Lavender '04
My House in Umbria '03
Divine Secrets of the Ya-Ya Sisterhood '02
Harry Potter and the Chamber of Secrets '02
Gosford Park '01
Harry Potter and the Sorcerer's Stone '01
All the King's Men '99
David Copperfield '99
The Last September '99
Tea with Mussolini '99
Curtain Call '97
Washington Square '97
The First Wives Club '96
Richard III '95
The Secret Garden '93
Sister Act 2: Back in the Habit '93
Sister Act '92
Hook '91
The Lonely Passion of Judith Hearne '87
A Room with a View '86
Lily in Love '85
Mrs. Silly '85
A Private Function '84
Better Late Than Never '83
Evil under the Sun '82
The Missionary '82
Clash of the Titans '81
Quartet '81
California Suite '78
Death on the Nile '78
Murder by Death '76
Love and Pain and the Whole Damn Thing '73
Travels with My Aunt '72
Oh! What a Lovely War '69
The Prime of Miss Jean Brodie '69
Hot Millions '68
The Honey Pot '67
Othello '65
The Pumpkin Eater '64
The V.I.P.'s '63

Mamie Smith

Murder on Lenox Avenue '41
Paradise in Harlem '40

Matt Smith

The Shadow in the North '07
Outsourced '06
Ruby in the Smoke '06

Maurice Smith

Double Whammy '01
Fist of Glory '95
Bloodfist 2 '90

Mel Smith (1952-)

The Riddle '07
Twelfth Night '96
Brain Donors '92
The Misadventures of Mr. Wilt '90
The Princess Bride '87
Morons from Outer Space '85
National Lampoon's European Vacation '85
Slayground '84

Melanie Smith (1962-)

Night Hunter '95
The Baby Doll Murders '92
Trancers 3: Deth Lives '92

Michael Bailey Smith (1957-)

The Hills Have Eyes 2 '07
The Hills Have Eyes '06
In Hell '03
Monster Man '03
Black Mask 2: City of Masks '02
Ice '93

Oliver Smith

Hellbound: Hellraiser 2 '88
Hellraiser '87

Patricia Smith (1930-)

Diary of a Teenage Hitchhiker '82
I Love You, Goodbye '74
Save the Tiger '73
Spirit of St. Louis '57

Paul Smith (1939-)

Maverick '94
Desert Kickboxer '92
Caged Fury '90
Crossing the Line '90
Gor '88
Death Chase '87
Outlaw Force '87
Sonny Boy '87
Haunted Honeymoon '86
Platypus Cove '86
Crimewave '85
The Fire in the Stone '85
Red Sonja '85
Sno-Line '85
Dune '84
Jungle Warriors '84
Pieces '83
The Salamander '82
Mortuary '81
Popeye '80
Midnight Express '78
Return of the Tiger '78
Madron '70
Loving You '57
Men of the Fighting Lady '54

Pete Smith

The Boys '98
Once Were Warriors '94

Queenie Smith

The Great Rupert '50
Mississippi '35

Quinn Smith

The Bad News Bears in Breaking Training '77
The Bad News Bears '76

Rachele Brooke Smith

Bring It On: Fight to the Finish '09
Center Stage: Turn It Up '08

Rebekah Louise Smith

No Sleep 'Til Madison '02
The Watcher '00

Rex Smith (1956-)

Collier & Co.: Hot Pursuit '06
Pope Dreams '06
A Passion to Kill '94
The Trial of the Incredible Hulk '89
Transformations '88
The Pirates of Penzance '83
Snow White and the Seven Dwarfs '83
Sooner or Later '78

Riley Smith (1978-)

Make It Happen '08
Graduation '07
New York Minute '04
Radio '03
Eight Legged Freaks '02
Full Ride '02
Not Another Teen Movie '01
Voodoo Academy '00
Wild Grizzly '99

Robin Smith

Never Say Die '94
Bopha! '93
Lights! Camera! Murder! '89

Roger Smith (1932-)

Never Steal Anything Small '59
Auntie Mame '58
Man of a Thousand Faces '57
Operation Mad Ball '57

Roger Guenveur Smith (1959-)

Fighting '09
Cover '08
The Take '07
Shade '03
All About the Benjamins '02
Hamlet '01
Final Destination '00
Summer of Sam '99
The Color of Courage '98
Get On the Bus '96
Tales from the Hood '95
Deep Cover '92

Russell Smith

Botched '07
Bloom '03

Sam Smith

Wondrous Oblivion '06
Oliver Twist '00

Samantha Smith

Love's Unending Legacy '07
Love's Unfolding Dream '07
Transformers '07

Savannah Smith

Everybody's All American '88
Code of Honor '84
The Long Riders '80

Sean Smith (1987-)

Children of the Corn: Revelation '01
Atomic Train '99
The King and I '99 (V)

Seth Smith (1982-)

The Climb '97
Home Alone 3 '97

Shawn Smith (1922-95)

It! The Terror from Beyond Space '58
The Land Unknown '57

Shawnee Smith (1970-)

The Grudge 3 '09
Saw 6 '09
Saw 5 '08
Saw 3 '06
The Island '05
Saw 2 '05
Saw '04
A Slipping Down Life '99
Breakfast of Champions '98
Carnival of Souls '98
Bombshell '97
Dogtown '97
The Low Life '95
Stephen King's The Stand '94
Desperate Hours '90
Who's Harry Crumb? '89
The Blob '88
Summer School '87

Shelley Smith (1952-)

The Fantastic World of D.C. Collins '84
National Lampoon's Class Reunion '82
The Night the City Screamed '80

Stuart Smith

Ninja Hunt '86
Joe's Bed-Stuy Barbershop: We Cut Heads '83
Ninja Destroyer '70

Sydney Smith (1909-78)

The Gallant Hours '60
No Time for Sergeants '58

Tasha Smith (1971-)

Tyler Perry's Why Did I Get Married Too? '10
Couples Retreat '09
The Longshots '08
Daddy's Little Girls '07
Love and Other Four Letter Words '07
Tyler Perry's Why Did I Get Married? '07
The Whole Ten Yards '04
The Corner '00
Chameleon 2: Death Match '99

Will Smith (1968-)

Hancock '08
Seven Pounds '08
I Am Legend '07
The Pursuit of Happyness '06
Hitch '05
I, Robot '04
Jersey Girl '04
Shark Tale '04 (V)
Bad Boys 2 '03
Men in Black 2 '02
Ali '01
The Legend of Bagger Vance '00
Wild Wild West '99
Enemy of the State '98
Men in Black '97
Independence Day '96
Bad Boys '95
Made in America '93
Six Degrees of Separation '93
Where the Day Takes You '92

William (Bill) Smith (1934-)

Broken Vessels '98
The Shooter '97
Taken Alive '95
Cartel '90
The Last Riders '90
Slow Burn '90
Spirit of the Eagle '90
Terror in Beverly Hills '90
Action U.S.A. '89
Deadly Breed '89
East L.A. Warriors '89
Emperor of the Bronx '89
Evil Altar '89
Jungle Assault '89
L.A. Vice '89
B.O.R.N. '88
Hell on the Battleground '88
Maniac Cop '88
Memorial Valley Massacre '88
Commando Squad '87
Platoon Leader '87
Eye of the Tiger '86
Moon in Scorpio '86
Fever Pitch '85
Mean Season '85
Red Dawn '84
Conan the Barbarian '82
Any Which Way You Can '80
The Frisco Kid '79
The Rebels '79
Seven '79
Blackjack '78
Fast Company '78
Twilight's Last Gleaming '77
Hollywood Man '76
Scorchy '76
The Ultimate Warrior '75
Boss '74
The Deadly Trackers '73
Gentle Savage '73
Invasion of the Bee Girls '73
A Taste of Hell '73
Grave of the Vampire '72
Chrome and Hot Leather '71
Angels Die Hard '70
C.C. & Company '70
Darker than Amber '70
The Losers '70
Run, Angel, Run! '69
Mail Order Bride '63
Atlantis, the Lost Continent '61

Willow Smith

Kit Kittredge: An American Girl '08
I Am Legend '07

Yeardley Smith (1964-)

The Simpsons Movie '07 (V)
As Good As It Gets '97
Just Write '97
We're Back! A Dinosaur's Story '93 (V)
City Slickers '91
Ginger Ale Afternoon '89
Maximum Overdrive '86
Heaven Help Us '85
Legend of Billie Jean '85

J. Smith-Cameron

The Rage: Carrie 2 '99
In and Out '97
Harriet the Spy '96

Jamie Smith-Jackson

Bug '75
Satan's School for Girls '73

Jan Smithers (1949-)

Mr. Nice Guy '86
Where the Lilies Bloom '74

William (Bill) Smithers (1927-)

Death Sport '78
Scorpio '73
Attack! '56

Bill Smitrovich (1947-)

Eagle Eye '08
Flash of Genius '08
Iron Man '08
Seven Pounds '08
The Contract '07
Heavens Fall '06
The Game of Their Lives '05
Mrs. Harris '05
The Reagans '04
The Golden Spiders: A Nero Wolfe Mystery '00
Kiss Toledo Goodbye '00
Thirteen Days '00
The '60s '99
Around the Fire '98
Dean Koontz's Mr. Murder '98
Futuresport '98
Air Force One '97
Ghosts of Mississippi '96
Independence Day '96
The Trigger Effect '96
Bodily Harm '95
Nick of Time '95
Crazy People '90
Renegades '89
Manhunter '86
A Killing Affair '85
Silver Bullet '85
Overdrawn at the Memory Bank '83

Jimmy Smits (1956-)

Mother and Child '09
The Jane Austen Book Club '07
Star Wars: Episode 3—Revenge of the Sith '05
Star Wars: Episode 2—Attack of the Clones '02
Bless the Child '00
Price of Glory '00
The Million Dollar Hotel '99
Murder in Mind '97
Marshal Law '96
The Last Word '95
The Cisco Kid '94
My Family '94
Gross Misconduct '93
Stephen King's The Tommyknockers '93
Fires Within '91
Switch '91
Vital Signs '90
Old Gringo '89
Glitz '88
The Believers '87
Stamp of a Killer '87
L.A. Law '86
Running Scared '86

Sonja Smits (1958-)

One Way '06
A Different Loyalty '04
Siblings '04
How to Deal '03
Owning Mahowny '03
Life with Judy Garland—Me and My Shadows '01
That's My Baby! '88
Videodrome '83
The Pit '81
War Brides '80

Jurnee Smollett (1986-)

The Great Debaters '07
Roll Bounce '05
Ruby's Bucket of Blood '01
Selma, Lord, Selma '99
Eve's Bayou '97

JB Smoove

Mr. Deeds '02
Pootie Tang '01

Dick Smothers (1939-)

Casino '95
Tales of the Unexpected '91
Speed Zone '88

Tom Smothers (1937-)

Speed Zone '88
Pandemonium '82
Serial '80
The Kids Are Alright '79
A Pleasure Doing Business '79
Silver Bears '78
Get to Know Your Rabbit '72
Alice Through the Looking Glass '66

Victoria Smurfit (1974-)

Bulletproof Monk '03
About a Boy '02
Berkeley Square '98
Ivanhoe '97
Romance and Rejection '96
The Run of the Country '95

Kasia Smutniak

From Paris With Love '10
Carnera: The Walking Mountain '08
Quiet Chaos '08

Ann Smyrner (1934-)

Beyond the Law '68
The House of 1000 Dolls '67
Reptilicus '62

Sam Snead

The Caddy '53
Follow the Sun '51

David Snedeker

If You Only Knew '00
Detour '99

Wesley Snipes (1962-)

Brooklyn's Finest '09
Art of War 2: The Betrayal '08
The Contractor '07

The Detonator '06
Seven Seconds '05
Blade: Trinity '04
Blade 2 '02
Liberty Stands Still '02
Undisputed '02
ZigZag '02
The Art of War '00
Disappearing Acts '00
Blade '98
Down in the Delta '98
Futuresport '98
U.S. Marshals '98
Murder at 1600 '97
One Night Stand '97
The Fan '96
America's Dream '95
Money Train '95
To Wong Foo, Thanks for Everything, Julie Newmar '95
Waiting to Exhale '95
Drop Zone '94
Sugar Hill '94
Boiling Point '93
Demolition Man '93
Rising Sun '93
Passenger 57 '92
White Men Can't Jump '92
Jungle Fever '91
New Jack City '91
The Waterdance '91
King of New York '90
Mo' Better Blues '90
Major League '89
Streets of Gold '86
Wildcats '86

Carrie Snodgress (1946-2004)

Bartleby '01
Ed Gein '01
The Forsaken '01
A Stranger in the Kingdom '98
Wild Things '98
Death Benefit '96
Phantom 2040 Movie: The Ghost Who Walks '95 (V)
White Man's Burden '95
8 Seconds '94
The Ballad of Little Jo '93
Woman with a Past '92
Blue Sky '91
Mission of the Shark '91
Chill Factor '90
The Rose and the Jackal '90
Across the Tracks '89
Blueberry Hill '88
Murphy's Law '86
L.A. Bad '85
Pale Rider '85
Nadia '84
A Night in Heaven '83
The Solitary Man '82
Trick or Treats '82
The Attic '80
The Fury '78
Diary of a Mad Housewife '70
Silent Night, Lonely Night '69

Snoop Dogg (1971-)

The Tenants '06
Racing Stripes '05 (V)
Soul Plane '04
Starsky & Hutch '04
Malibu's Most Wanted '03 (V)
Old School '03
Baby Boy '01
Bones '01
Training Day '01
The Wash '01
Urban Menace '99
The Wrecking Crew '99
Caught Up '98
Ride '98
Half-Baked '97

Brittany Snow (1986-)

The Vicious Kind '09
Finding Amanda '08
Prom Night '08
All the Good Ones Are Married '07
Hairspray '07
On the Doll '07
John Tucker Must Die '06
The Pacifier '05

Raven Snow

Delta of Venus '95
Red Shoe Diaries 6: How I Met My Husband '95

Victoria Snow

Waking Up Wally '05
My Husband's Double Life '01
Buffalo Jump '90
Love and Hate: A Marriage Made in Hell '90

Arlen Dean Snyder (1933-)

Cora Unashamed '00
Mommy 2: Mommy's Day '96
Running Cool '93
Internal Affairs '90
Marked for Death '90
Wheels of Terror '90
Heartbreak Ridge '86
Deadly Force '83
Night Partners '83
No Place to Hide '81
Red Flag: The Ultimate Game '81
Yanks '79
Young Love, First Love '79
Dear Detective '78
Scalpel '76

Drew Snyder (1946-)

Blindfold: Acts of Obsession '94
Separate Lives '94
Dance with Death '91
Project: Eliminator '91
Izzy & Moe '85
Firestarter '84
Night School '81

Suzanne Snyder (1962-)

Killer Klowns from Outer Space '88
The Night Before '88
Retribution '88
Return of the Living Dead 2 '88
Prettykill '87

Michele (Michael) Soavi (1957-)

Demons '86
Creepers '85
A Blade in the Dark '83
Gates of Hell '80

Barry Sobel (1959-)

That Thing You Do! '96
I Love Trouble '94
L.A. Rules: The Pros and Cons of Breathing '94
Doc Hollywood '91
Martians Go Home! '90
Punchline '88

Leelee Sobieski (1982-)

Night Train '09
Public Enemies '09
88 Minutes '08
In the Name of the King: A Dungeon Siege Tale '08
The Elder Son '06
Heavens Fall '06
The Wicker Man '06
Dangerous Liaisons '03
Max '02
The Glass House '01
Joy Ride '01
My First Mister '01
Uprising '01
Here on Earth '00
Eyes Wide Shut '99
Joan of Arc '99
Never Been Kissed '99
Deep Impact '98
A Soldier's Daughter Never Cries '98
Jungle 2 Jungle '96
A Horse for Danny '95

Ron Soble (1932-2002)

The Beast Within '82
True Grit '69

Maria Socas

Deathstalker 2: Duel of the Titans '87
Soldier's Revenge '84
The Warrior & the Sorceress '84

Kristina Soderbaum (1912-2001)

Night Train to Venice '93
Kolberg '45
Jud Suess '40

Steven Soderbergh (1963-)

Waking Life '01
Schizopolis '97

Camilla Soeberg (1966-)

The Empty Mirror '99
Mouse Hunt '97
Erotique '94
A Night of Love '87
Twist & Shout '84

Abraham Sofaer (1896-1988)

Demon with a Glass Hand '64
Captain Sinbad '63
Bhowani Junction '56
Elephant Walk '54
Naked Jungle '54
Quo Vadis '51
Calling Paul Temple '48
Dual Alibi '47

Rena Sofer (1968-)

Carrie '02
Keeping the Faith '00
Traffic '00
The Stepsister '97
Twinsitters '95

Sonja Sohn

Step Up 2 the Streets '08
Slam '98

Hans Sohnker (1903-81)

The Phantom of Soho '64
Sherlock Holmes and the Deadly Necklace '62
For the First Time '59
Die Grosse Freiheit Nr. 7 '45

Sojin (1884-1954)

Seven Samurai '54
The Thief of Baghdad '24

Marilyn Sokol

Something Short of Paradise '79
Foul Play '78
The Goodbye Girl '77

Marla Sokoloff (1980-)

Maneater '09
Meteor '09
Crazylove '05
Freshman Orientation '04
Love on the Side '04
The Tollbooth '04
Sugar & Spice '01
Dude, Where's My Car? '00
Whatever It Takes '00

Vladimir Sokoloff (1889-1962)

Taras Bulba '62
Mr. Sardonicus '61
Beyond the Time Barrier '60
I Was a Teenage Werewolf '57
Baron of Arizona '51
Cloak and Dagger '46
A Scandal in Paris '46
For Whom the Bell Tolls '43
Crossroads '42
The Road to Morocco '42
Comrade X '40
The Real Glory '39
Conquest '37
The Lower Depths '36

Kyung-gu Sol

Another Public Enemy '05
Public Enemy '02

Miguel Angel Sola (1950-)

Tango '98
A Shadow You Soon Will Be '94
Mayalunta '86
Funny, Dirty Little War '83

Silvia Solar (1940-)

Devil's Kiss '75
Night of the Howling Beast '75
The Gentleman Killer '69
Finger on the Trigger '65
As If It Were Raining '63

Domingo Soler

The Monster Demolisher '60
The Illusion Travels by Streetcar '53

Fernando Soler (1896-1979)

Susana '51
The Great Madcap '49

Paul Soles (1930-)

The Score '01
The Lotus Eaters '93
Beethoven Lives Upstairs '92
The Gunrunner '84
Ticket to Heaven '81

P.J. Soles (1955-)

The Tooth Fairy '06
The Devil's Rejects '05
Jawbreaker '98
Little Bigfoot '96
Out There '95
Soldier's Fortune '91
Alienator '89
B.O.R.N. '88
Innocent Prey '88
Saigon Commandos '88
Sweet Dreams '85
Stripes '81
Rock 'n' Roll High School '79
Halloween '78
The Possessed '77
The Boy in the Plastic Bubble '76
Carrie '76

Cristian Solimeno

Mother of Tears '08
Perfect Hideout '08
Highlander: The Source '07

Yulia Solntseva (1901-89)

Earth '30
Aelita: Queen of Mars '24
The Cigarette Girl of Mosselprom '24

Bruce Solomon (1944-)

Auto Focus '02
Night of the Creeps '86
Foul Play '78
Children Shouldn't Play with Dead Things '72

Charles Solomon

Witchcraft 4: Virgin Heart '92
Witchcraft 2: The Temptress '90
Witchcraft 3: The Kiss of Death '90
The Channeler '89

Todd Solondz (1960-)

As Good As It Gets '97
Fear, Anxiety and Depression '89

Anatoli (Otto) Solonitzin (1934-82)

Stalker '79
Solaris '72
Andrei Rublev '66

Elena Solovei (1947-)

Oblomov '81
A Slave of Love '78
An Unfinished Piece for a Player Piano '77

Yanti Somer

Metallica '85
Cosmos: War of the Planets '80
Reactor '78

Ian Somerhalder (1978-)

The Tournament '09
The Lost Samaritan '08
Marco Polo '07
Pulse '06
The Sensation of Sight '06
In Enemy Hands '04
The Rules of Attraction '02
Life as a House '01

Kristi Somers (1962-)

Tomboy '85
Hardbodies '84

Suzanne Somers (1946-)

Say It Isn't So '01
No Laughing Matter '97
Seduced by Evil '94
Serial Mom '94
Happily Ever After '82
Nothing Personal '80
Yesterday's Hero '79
Ants '77
Sky Hei$t '75
American Graffiti '73
Magnum Force '73

Bonnie Somerville (1974-)

Wedding Wars '06
Without a Paddle '04
Sleep Easy, Hutch Rimes '00

Geraldine Somerville (1967-)

Daphne '07
Gosford Park '01
The Aristocrats '99
Cracker: Best Boys '95
Cracker: Brotherly Love '95
Cracker: True Romance '95
Haunted '95
Cracker: Men Should Weep '94
Cracker: To Be a Somebody '94
Catherine Cookson's The Black Velvet Gown '92

Phyllis Somerville

The Brooklyn Heist '08
The Curious Case of Benjamin Button '08
Little Children '06
Swimfan '02

Julie Sommars (1941-)

Sex and the Single Parent '82
Herbie Goes to Monte Carlo '77
I'm the Girl He Wants to Kill '74

Elke Sommer (1940-)

Severed Ties '92
Adventures Beyond Belief '87
Anastasia: The Mystery of Anna '86
Jenny's War '85
Lily in Love '85
No One Cries Forever '85
Inside the Third Reich '82
The Big Scam '79
The Double McGuffin '79
Fantastic Seven '79
Prisoner of Zenda '79
The Treasure Seekers '79
Left for Dead '78
Swiss Conspiracy '77
The Invisible Strangler '76
One Away '76
Carry On Behind '75
Lisa and the Devil '75
Ten Little Indians '75
It's Not the Size That Counts '74
Probe '72
Torture Chamber of Baron Blood '72
Zeppelin '71
The Invincible Six '68
The Wrecking Crew '68
The Corrupt Ones '67
Deadlier Than the Male '67
Boy, Did I Get a Wrong Number! '66
The Oscar '66
The Money Trap '65
A Shot in the Dark '64
The Prize '63
The Victors '63
Sweet Ecstasy '62
Daniella by Night '61

Josef Sommer (1934-)

Stop-Loss '08
The Invasion '07
The Elephant King '06
X-Men: The Last Stand '06
Searching for Paradise '02
The Sum of All Fears '02
Family Man '00
The Next Best Thing '00
Shaft '00
Patch Adams '98
The Proposition '97
Hidden in America '96
Mistrial '96
Letter to My Killer '95
Moonlight and Valentino '95
Strange Days '95
The Enemy Within '94
Nobody's Fool '94
Hostages '93
Malice '93
An American Story '92
The Mighty Ducks '92
Shadows and Fog '92
A Woman Named Jackie '91
Forced March '90
Bloodhounds of Broadway '89
Bridge to Silence '89
Chances Are '89
Dracula's Widow '88
The Betty Ford Story '87
The Rosary Murders '87
Yuri Nosenko, KGB '86
Execution of Raymond Graham '85
Target '85
Witness '85
Iceman '84
Agatha Christie's Sparkling Cyanide '83
Independence Day '83
Silkwood '83
Still of the Night '82
Absence of Malice '81
Reds '81
Rollover '81
Hide in Plain Sight '80
The Scarlet Letter '79
Dirty Harry '71

Helga Sommerfeld (1941-91)

Code Name Alpha '67
The Phantom of Soho '64

Jennifer Sommerfield

Megalodon '03
Destination Vegas '95

Sommore (1966-)

Friday After Next '02
Queens of Comedy '01

Byeong-ho Son

R-Point '04
Spider Forest '04
Tube '03

Gale Sondergaard (1899-1985)

Echoes '83
The Return of a Man Called Horse '76
Savage Intruder '68
East Side, West Side '49
The Road to Rio '47
Anna and the King of Siam '46
The Time of Their Lives '46
The Climax '44
The Invisible Man's Revenge '44
Spider Woman '44
Isle of Forgotten Sins '43
My Favorite Blonde '42
A Night to Remember '42
The Black Cat '41
The Blue Bird '40
The Letter '40
The Mark of Zorro '40
Juarez '39

Never Say Die '39
The Life of Emile Zola '37
Anthony Adverse '36

Brenda Song (1988-)
College Road Trip '08
Get a Clue '02
Like Mike '02

Kang-ho Song (1967-)
Thirst '09
The Host '06
Sympathy for Mr. Vengeance '02
The Foul King '00
JSA: Joint Security Area '00
Shiri '99
The Quiet Family '98
No. 3 '97

Steph Song
The Thaw '09
Dim Sum Funeral '08
Everything's Gone Green '06

Paul Sonkkila
The Hard Word '02
The Interview '98
Mr. Reliable: A True Story '95

Michael Sonye
Sorority Babes in the Slimeball Bowl-A-Rama '87 (V)
Surf Nazis Must Die '87

Jack Soo (1916-79)
Return from Witch Mountain '78
The Green Berets '68
Flower Drum Song '61

Brandon Soo Hoo (1995-)
G.I. Joe: The Rise of Cobra '09
Tropic Thunder '08

Veena Sood
Nina's Heavenly Delights '06
Touch of Pink '04

Nikki SooHoo (1988-)
Bring It On: Fight to the Finish '09
Stick It '06

Michael Sopkiw (1954-)
After the Fall of New York '85
Blastfighter '85
Massacre in Dinosaur Valley '85
Devilfish '84

Agnes Soral (1960-)
Window to Paris '95
Blitz '85
Tchao Pantin '84
One Wild Moment '78

Kevin Sorbo (1958-)
Meet the Spartans '08
Never Cry Werewolf '08
Prairie Fever '08
Avenging Angel '07
Something Beneath '07
Walking Tall: Lone Justice '07
Kull the Conqueror '97
Hercules the Legendary Journeys, Vol. 1: And the Amazon Women '94
Hercules the Legendary Journeys, Vol. 2: The Lost Kingdom '94
Hercules the Legendary Journeys, Vol. 3: The Circle of Fire '94
Hercules the Legendary Journeys, Vol. 4: In the Underworld '94

Alberto Sordi (1920-2003)
Those Magnificent Men in Their Flying Machines '65
Mafioso '62
And the Wild, Wild Women '59
The Great War '59
A Farewell to Arms '57
Two Nights with Cleopatra '54
I Vitelloni '53
The White Sheik '52

Guy Sorel (1914-94)
Mayflower: The Pilgrims' Adventure '79
Honeymoon Killers '70

Jean Sorel (1934-)
A Lizard in a Woman's Skin '71
Short Night of Glass Dolls '71
Belle de Jour '67
Sandra of a Thousand Delights '65

Louise Sorel (1940-)
Mazes and Monsters '82
When Every Day Was the Fourth of July '78
Get Christie Love! '74
Plaza Suite '71
The President's Plane Is Missing '71

Nancy Sorel (1964-)
I Love You, Don't Touch Me! '97
In the Lake of the Woods '96

Ted (Theodore) Sorel (1936-)
Me and the Mob '94
Basket Case 2 '90
From Beyond '86
Network '76

Linda Sorensen (1942-)
Relative Fear '95
Family Reunion '88
Joshua Then and Now '85
Kavik the Wolf Dog '80
Stone Cold Dead '80

Ricky Sorenson (1946-94)
The Sword in the Stone '63 (V)
Tarzan and the Trappers '58
Tarzan's Fight for Life '58

Charo Soriano (1928-)
Orgy of the Vampires '73
Dracula's Great Love '72
The Garden of Delights '70

Arleen (Arlene) Sorkin (1956-)
Comic Book: The Movie '04
It's Pat: The Movie '94
I Don't Buy Kisses Anymore '92
From Here to Maternity '85

Lodovico Sorret
See Tom Noonan

Mira Sorvino (1967-)
The Last Templar '09
The Hades Factor '06
Human Trafficking '05
The Final Cut '04
Gods and Generals '03
Angel of Death '02
Between Strangers '02
Wisegirls '02
The Great Gatsby '01
The Grey Zone '01
The Triumph of Love '01
Free Money '99
Summer of Sam '99
At First Sight '98
Lulu on the Bridge '98
The Replacement Killers '98
Mimic '97
Romy and Michele's High School Reunion '97
Beautiful Girls '96
Sweet Nothing '96
Blue in the Face '95
The Buccaneers '95
Mighty Aphrodite '95
Norma Jean and Marilyn '95
Tarantella '95
Barcelona '94
New York Cop '94
Parallel Lives '94
Quiz Show '94
Amongst Friends '93
Tales of Erotica '93

Paul Sorvino (1939-)
Last Hour '08
Repo! The Genetic Opera '08
Mr. Fix It '06
Mr. 3000 '04
The Cooler '03
Mambo Italiano '03
Hey Arnold! The Movie '02 (V)
Perfume '01
See Spot Run '01
Cheaters '00
The Thin Blue Lie '00
Dead Broke '99
Houdini '99
That Championship Season '99
Bulworth '98
Knock Off '98
Dogwatch '97
Joe Torre: Curveballs Along the Way '97
Money Talks '97
Most Wanted '97
Escape Clause '96
Love Is All There Is '96
William Shakespeare's Romeo and Juliet '96
Cover Me '95
Nixon '95
Parallel Lives '94
Backstreet Justice '93
The Firm '93
Age Isn't Everything '91
Nightmare '91
The Rocketeer '91
Dick Tracy '90
Goodfellas '90
Almost Partners '87
A Fine Mess '86
Jailbait: Betrayed By Innocence '86
Vasectomy: A Delicate Matter '86
The Stuff '85
Turk 182! '85
My Mother's Secret Life '84
Very Close Quarters '84
Chiefs '83
I, the Jury '82
Melanie '82
Off the Wall '82
That Championship Season '82
Reds '81
Cruising '80
Question of Honor '80
Lost and Found '79
Bloodbrothers '78
Brink's Job '78
Oh, God! '77
I Will, I Will for Now '76
The Gambler '74
Shoot It Black, Shoot It Blue '74
Tell Me Where It Hurts '74
The Day of the Dolphin '73
A Touch of Class '73
Cry Uncle '71
Panic in Needle Park '71
Where's Poppa? '70

Roberto Sosa (1970-)
Hombres Armados '97
Optic Fiber '97
Lolo '92
Highway Patrolman '91
Cabeza de Vaca '90

Nina Sosanya
Wide Sargasso Sea '06
Casanova '05
Manderlay '05

Shannyn Sossamon (1979-)
Life is Hot in Cracktown '08
One Missed Call '08
Catacombs '07
The Holiday '06
Wristcutters: A Love Story '06
Chasing Ghosts '05
Devour '05
Kiss Kiss Bang Bang '05
Undiscovered '05
The Order '03
40 Days and 40 Nights '02
The Rules of Attraction '02
A Knight's Tale '01

Paul Soter (1972-)
Beerfest '06
Club Dread '04
Super Troopers '01

Ann Sothern (1909-2001)
The Whales of August '87
Little Dragons '80
The Manitou '78
Crazy Mama '75
The Killing Kind '73
The Best Man '64
Lady in a Cage '64
The Blue Gardenia '53
Nancy Goes to Rio '50
The Judge Steps Out '49
A Letter to Three Wives '49
Words and Music '48
Panama Hattie '42
Lady Be Good '41
Brother Orchid '40
Hell-Ship Morgan '36
Kid Millions '34

Fernando Soto
See Fernando Soto Mantequilla

Hugo Soto (1954-94)
Man Facing Southeast '86
Times to Come '81

Talisa Soto (1967-)
Ballistic: Ecks vs. Sever '02
Pinero '01
Island of the Dead '00
The Corporate Ladder '97
Flypaper '97
Mortal Kombat 2: Annihilation '97
Sunchaser '96
Vampirella '96
Mortal Kombat 1: The Movie '95
Don Juan DeMarco '94
Hostage '92
The Mambo Kings '92
Prison Stories: Women on the Inside '91
Silhouette '91
License to Kill '89
Spike of Bensonhurst '88

Zinedine Soualem
Roman de Gare '07
When the Cat's Away '96

Kath Soucie (1967-)
Space Chimps '08 (V)
Happily N'Ever After '07 (V)
Pooh's Heffalump Movie '05 (V)
Clifford's Really Big Movie '04 (V)
Piglet's Big Movie '03 (V)
Rugrats Go Wild! '03 (V)
Return to Never Land '02 (V)
Rugrats in Paris: The Movie '00 (V)
The Rugrats Movie '98 (V)

Masami Souda
Rica 3: Juvenile's Lullaby '73
Rica '72

David Soul (1943-)
Starsky & Hutch '04
Pentathlon '94
Grave Secrets: The Legacy of Hilltop Drive '92
Tides of War '90
In the Cold of the Night '89
Appointment with Death '88
In the Line of Duty: The FBI Murders '88
Hanoi Hilton '87
Through Naked Eyes '87
World War III '86
The Key to Rebecca '85
The Manions of America '81
Homeward Bound '80
Rage '80
Salem's Lot '79
Little Ladies of the Night '77
The Stick-Up '77
Dog Pound Shuffle '75
Magnum Force '73
Johnny Got His Gun '71

Renee Soutendijk (1957-)
Keeper of the City '92
Eve of Destruction '90
Forced March '90
Grave Secrets '89
Murderers Among Us: The Simon Wiesenthal Story '89
Second Victory '87
Cold Room '84
Out of Order '84
Inside the Third Reich '82
Spetters '80
The 4th Man '79

Eve Southern (1898-)
Law of the Sea '32
Morocco '30

Charles Southwood (1937-)
Guns for Dollars '73
Fistful of Lead '70
Sartana's Here... Trade Your Pistol for a Coffin '70

Ben Soutten
The Mutiny of the Elsinore '39
The Crimes of Stephen Hawke '36

Catherine Spaak (1945-)
Honey '81
The Cat o' Nine Tails '71
Counter Punch '71
The Libertine '69
Hotel '67
Circle of Love '64
Empty Canvas '64
The Easy Life '63
Le Trou '59

Arthur Space (1908-83)
Terror at Red Wolf Inn '72
Night Riders of Montana '50
The Vanishing Westerner '50
Miss Grant Takes Richmond '49
A Southern Yankee '48
The Red House '47
Magnificent Doll '46
Riot Squad '41

Sissy Spacek (1949-)
Get Low '09
Four Christmases '08
Lake City '08
Hot Rod '07
Pictures of Hollis Woods '07
Gray Matters '06
An American Haunting '05
Nine Lives '05
North Country '05
The Ring 2 '05
A Home at the End of the World '04
Last Call: The Final Chapter of F. Scott Fitzgerald '02
Tuck Everlasting '02
In the Bedroom '01
The Straight Story '99
Blast from the Past '98
Affliction '97
Beyond the Call '96
If These Walls Could Talk '96
The Good Old Boys '95
The Grass Harp '95
Larry McMurtry's Streets of Laredo '95
A Place for Annie '94
Trading Mom '94
Hard Promises '92
A Private Matter '92
JFK '91
The Long Walk Home '89
Crimes of the Heart '86
'night, Mother '86
Violets Are Blue '86
Marie '85
The River '84
The Man with Two Brains '83 (V)
Missing '82
Raggedy Man '81
Coal Miner's Daughter '80
Heart Beat '80
3 Women '77
Welcome to L.A. '77
Carrie '76
Katherine '75
Badlands '74
The Migrants '74
Ginger in the Morning '73
The Girls of Huntington House '73
Prime Cut '72

Kevin Spacey (1959-)
The Men Who Stare at Goats '09
Moon '09 (V)
Shrink '09
Recount '08
21 '08
Fred Claus '07
Superman Returns '06
Edison Force '05
Beyond the Sea '04
The Life of David Gale '03
United States of Leland '03
Austin Powers In Goldmember '02
K-PAX '01
The Shipping News '01
The Big Kahuna '00
Pay It Forward '00
American Beauty '99
Ordinary Decent Criminal '99
A Bug's Life '98 (V)
Hurlyburly '98
The Negotiator '98
L.A. Confidential '97
Midnight in the Garden of Good and Evil '97
Looking for Richard '96
A Time to Kill '96
Seven '95
The Usual Suspects '95
Doomsday Gun '94
Outbreak '94
Swimming with Sharks '94
Iron Will '93
The Ref '93
Consenting Adults '92
Glengarry Glen Ross '92
Henry & June '90
Dad '89
See No Evil, Hear No Evil '89
Long Day's Journey into Night '88
Rocket Gibraltar '88
Working Girl '88
The Murder of Mary Phagan '87

David Spade (1964-)
Grown Ups '10
The Benchwarmers '06
Grandma's Boy '06
Racing Stripes '05 (V)
Dickie Roberts: Former Child Star '03
Joe Dirt '01
The Emperor's New Groove '00 (V)
Loser '00
Lost and Found '99
The Rugrats Movie '98 (V)
Senseless '98
Beavis and Butt-Head Do America '96 (V)
Black Sheep '96
8 Heads in a Duffel Bag '96
A Very Brady Sequel '96
Tommy Boy '95
P.C.U. '94
Coneheads '93

James Spader (1961-)
Shorts: The Adventures of the Wishing Rock '09
I Witness '03
Secretary '02
The Stickup '01
Slow Burn '00
The Watcher '00
Supernova '99

Critical Care '97
Curtain Call '97
Keys to Tulsa '96
Two Days in the Valley '96
Crash '95
Stargate '94
Wolf '94
Dream Lover '93
The Music of Chance '93
Bob Roberts '92
Storyville '92
True Colors '91
Bad Influence '90
White Palace '90
The Rachel Papers '89
sex, lies and videotape '89
Baby Boom '87
Jack's Back '87
Less Than Zero '87
Mannequin '87
Wall Street '87
Pretty in Pink '86
The New Kids '85
Tuff Turf '85
Family Secrets '84
Endless Love '81

Joshua Spafford (1972-)

Robot Stories '03
XX/XY '02

Douglas Spain (1974-)

Still Green '07
The Reading Room '05
44 Minutes: The North Hollywood Shootout '03
Nightstalker '02
What's Cooking? '00
The Last Best Sunday '98
Ricochet River '98
Star Maps '97
Twelve Angry Men '97
Riot in the Streets '96

Fay Spain (1932-83)

The Godfather, Part 2 '74
Flight to Fury '66
Hercules and the Captive Women '63
Al Capone '59
God's Little Acre '58
Dragstrip Girl '57
Teenage Doll '57

Rafe Spall (1983-)

A Room With a View '08
Hot Fuzz '07
The Chatterley Affair '06
Dracula '06
Wide Sargasso Sea '06
Green Street Hooligans '05

Timothy Spall (1957-)

The Damned United '09
Harry Potter and the Half-Blood Prince '09
Appaloosa '08
A Room With a View '08
Death Defying Acts '07
Enchanted '07
Oliver Twist '07
Sweeney Todd: The Demon Barber of Fleet Street '07
Harry Potter and the Goblet of Fire '05
Harry Potter and the Prisoner of Azkaban '04
Lemony Snicket's A Series of Unfortunate Events '04
The Last Samurai '03
My House in Umbria '03
All or Nothing '02
Nicholas Nickleby '02
Lucky Break '01
Rock Star '01
Vacuuming Completely Nude in Paradise '01
Vanilla Sky '01
Chicken Run '00 (V)
Intimacy '00
Love's Labour's Lost '00
Vatel '00
Shooting the Past '99
Topsy Turvy '99
Immortality '98
Our Mutual Friend '98
Still Crazy '98
Hamlet '96
Secrets and Lies '95
Life Is Sweet '90
The Sheltering Sky '90
White Hunter, Black Heart '90
Crusoe '89
Dream Demon '88
Dutch Girls '87
Gothic '87
Home Sweet Home '82

Ignazio Spalla

See Pedro Sanchez
Adios, Sabata '71
Return of Sabata '71
Sabata '69
Cjamango '67

Laurette Spang (1951-)

Battlestar Galactica '78
Mission Galactica: The Cylon Attack '78

Joe Spano (1946-)

Hollywoodland '06
Hart's War '02
Texas Rangers '01
From the Earth to the Moon '98
A Call to Remember '97
Primal Fear '96
Apollo 13 '95
Rave Review '95
Fever '91
Cast the First Stone '89
Disaster at Silo 7 '88
Brotherhood of Justice '86
The Dunera Boys '85
Terminal Choice '85
Northern Lights '79
The Enforcer '76
American Graffiti '73
Warlock Moon '73

Vincent Spano (1962-)

Lone Rider '08
Nevermore '07
Pandemic '07
The Prince and the Pauper '07
Deathlands: Homeward Bound '03
The Rats '01
Texas Rangers '01
The Prophecy 3: The Ascent '99
No Strings Attached '98
A Brooklyn State of Mind '97
Downdraft '96
The Tie That Binds '95
The Ascent '94
Alive '93
Indian Summer '93
Afterburn '92
City of Hope '91
Oscar '91
And God Created Woman '88
High Frequency '88
Blood Ties '87
Good Morning, Babylon '87
Creator '85
Alphabet City '84
Maria's Lovers '84
The Black Stallion Returns '83
Rumble Fish '83
Baby It's You '82
Senior Trip '81
The Double McGuffin '79
Over the Edge '79

Paul Sparer (1923-99)

Mayflower: The Pilgrims' Adventure '79
Loving '70

Adrian Sparks

It Came from Outer Space 2 '95
My Stepmother Is an Alien '88
Roanoak '86

Jeany Sparks

Wallander: Firewall '08
Wallander: One Step Behind '08
Wallander: Sidetracked '08

Ned Sparks (1883-1957)

Hawaii Calls '38
The Bride Walks Out '36
One in a Million '36
Sweet Adeline '35
Imitation of Life '34
Marie Galante '34
Sing and Like It '34
42nd Street '33
Going Hollywood '33
Gold Diggers of 1933 '33
Lady for a Day '33
The Crusader '32
Corsair '31
Kept Husbands '31

Camilla Sparv (1943-)

Survival Zone '84
Downhill Racer '69
Dead Heat on a Merry-Go-Round '66
Murderers' Row '66

Tracy Spaulding

Stormy Nights '97
The Deadly Secret '94
Striking Point '94

Dan Speaker

Wizards of the Demon Sword '94
Glitch! '88

Jeff Speakman (1958-)

The Gunman '03
Running Red '99
Timelock '99
Land of the Free '98
Memorial Day '98
Escape from Atlantis '97
Scorpio One '97
Deadly Outbreak '96
Plato's Run '96
The Expert '95
Street Knight '93
The Perfect Weapon '91

Bernard Spear (1919-2003)

Yentl '83
Bedazzled '68

Hannah Spearritt (1981-)

Agent Cody Banks 2: Destination London '04
Seed of Chucky '04

Aaron Spears

Makin' Baby '02
Blue Hill Avenue '01

Aries Spears (1975-)

Jiminy Glick in LaLa Wood '05
The Pest '96

Britney Spears (1981-)

Austin Powers In Goldmember '02
Crossroads '02

Eddie Spears (1982-)

Black Cloud '04
The Slaughter Rule '01

David Speck

Crazy in Alabama '99
Other Voices, Other Rooms '95

Carol Speed (1945-)

Avenging Disco Godfather '76
Bummer '73
The Mack '73
Savage! '73
The Big Bird Cage '72

Scott Speedman (1975-)

Adoration '08
The Strangers '08
Anamorph '07
Weirdsville '07
Underworld: Evolution '05
XXX: State of the Union '05
The 24th Day '04
Dark Blue '03
My Life Without Me '03
Underworld '03
Duets '00
Rescuers: Stories of Courage—Two Couples '98
Dead Silence '96

Hermann Speelmanns (1904-60)

Baron Munchausen '43
F.P. 1 Doesn't Answer '33

Hugo Speer (1969-)

Fanny Hill '07
The Interpreter '05
The Debt '03
Warrior Queen '03
Deathwatch '02
Do or Die '01
Mainline Run '98
Swing '98
The Full Monty '96

Martin Speer

The Dark Ride '78
The Hills Have Eyes '77

Richard Speight, Jr. (1970-)

Love for Rent '05
Band of Brothers '01
Speed 2: Cruise Control '97
Independence Day '96
Menno's Mind '96
Amanda and the Alien '95
Dead Weekend '95
Out There '95
Demonic Toys '90
Goodbye, Miss 4th of July '88
Ernest Goes to Camp '87
Love Leads the Way '84

Dona Speir (1964-)

Fit to Kill '93
Hard Hunted '92
Do or Die '91
Guns '90
Picasso Trigger '89
Savage Beach '89
Hard Ticket to Hawaii '87

George Spell (1958-)

All God's Children '80
A Dream for Christmas '73
Man & Boy '71

Tori Spelling (1973-)

Cthulhu '08
Kiss the Bride '07
The Family Plan '05
How to Lose Your Lover '04
Evil Alien Conquerors '02
Scary Movie 2 '01
Sol Goode '01
Trick '99
Perpetrators of the Crime '98
The House of Yes '97
Scream 2 '97
Last Action Hero '93

Peter Spellos

Men in Black 2 '02
Bound '96
Dinosaur Island '93

Sharon Spelman

Twirl '81
Deadly Game '77

Georgina Spelvin (1936-)

Next Year in Jerusalem '98
Police Academy '84
Honkytonk Nights '78
I Spit on Your Corpse '74

Bruce Spence (1945-)

Australia '08
Aquamarine '06
Solo '06
Star Wars: Episode 3—Revenge of the Sith '05
Finding Nemo '03 (V)
The Matrix Revolutions '03
Inspector Gadget 2 '02
Queen of the Damned '02
Moby Dick '98
Dark City '97
Sweet Talker '91
...Almost '90
The Shrimp on the Barbie '90
Rikky and Pete '88
The Year My Voice Broke '87
Mad Max: Beyond Thunderdome '85
Midnite Spares '85
Where the Green Ants Dream '84
The Road Warrior '82

Paul J. Spence

Freezer Burn: The Invasion of Laxdale '08
It's All Gone, Pete Tong '04

Peter Spence (1963-)

Unfinished Business '89
Crazy Moon '87

Sebastian Spence (1969-)

Daniel's Daughter '08
On the Other Hand, Death '08
Shock to the System '06
Category 7 : The End of the World '05
Third Man Out: A Donald Strachey Mystery '05
Family of Cops 3 '98
Family of Cops 2: Breach of Faith '97
Firestorm '97
Family of Cops '95
The Boys of St. Vincent '93

Bud Spencer (1929-)

Troublemakers '94
Aladdin '86
Miami Supercops '85
Go for It '83
Crime Busters '78
Flatfoot '78
Odds and Evens '78
Trinity Is Still My Name '75
All the Way, Boys '73
A Reason to Live, a Reason to Die '73
Four Flies on Grey Velvet '72
They Call Me Trinity '72
Today We Kill, Tomorrow We Die '71
Boot Hill '69
Ace High '68
Beyond the Law '68

Chaske Spencer

The Twilight Saga: Eclipse '10
The Twilight Saga: New Moon '09
Skins '02

Chris Spencer (1968-)

Sin '02
All About You '01
The Sixth Man '97
Don't Be a Menace to South Central While Drinking Your Juice in the Hood '95

Danielle Spencer

The Crossing '92
What the Moon Saw '90

Douglas Spencer (1910-60)

Saddle the Wind '58
River of No Return '54
Trouble along the Way '53
The Thing '51

Jesse Spencer (1979-)

Flourish '06
P.D. James: Death in Holy Orders '03
Swimming Upstream '03
Uptown Girls '03

John Spencer (1946-)

Ravenous '99
The Negotiator '98
Twilight '98
Cafe Society '97
Cold Around the Heart '97
Cop Land '97
Albino Alligator '96
The Rock '96
Forget Paris '95
Presumed Innocent '90
Black Rain '89
Simple Justice '89
Echoes '83

Tara Spencer-Nairn (1978-)

Final Draft '07
Waking Up Wally '05
Wishmaster 4: The Prophecy Fulfilled '02
New Waterford Girl '99
Don't Look Down '98

Volker Spengler (1939-)

The Ogre '96
Chinese Roulette '86
Veronika Voss '82
Despair '78
In a Year of 13 Moons '78
The Stationmaster's Wife '77
Satan's Brew '76

Jeremy Spenser (1937-)

The Prince and the Showgirl '57
Escapade '55
Summertime '55
Devil on Horseback '54
Kind Hearts and Coronets '49

Tony Sperandeo (1953-)

La Scorta '94
Acla's Descent into Floristella '87

Wendie Jo Sperber (1958-2005)

Mr. Write '92
Back to the Future, Part 3 '90
Stewardess School '86
Back to the Future '85
Moving Violations '85
Bachelor Party '84
First Time '82
Used Cars '80
1941 '79
I Wanna Hold Your Hand '78

Alessandro Sperduti

I Am David '04
Heaven '01

Scott Spiegel (1957-)

Red '91
Darkman '90
The Dead Next Door '89
Skinned Alive '89
Evil Dead 2: Dead by Dawn '87
Thou Shalt Not Kill...Except '87
Evil Dead '83

David Spielberg (1939-)

Silent Predators '99
Alice '90
The Stranger '87
Christine '84
Policewoman Centerfold '83
The Best Little Girl in the World '81
The Henderson Monster '80
Sergeant Matlovich vs. the U.S. Air Force '78
Prime Time '77
Force Five '75

Steven Spielberg (1947-)

Austin Powers In Goldmember '02
The Blues Brothers '80

Laurent Spielvogel (1955-)

The Monster '96
French Kiss '95

Riva Spier

Syngenor '90
Ghost Keeper '80

Jacques Spiesser (1947-)
Baxter '89
La Truite '83
Black and White in Color '76

Mickey Spillane (1918-2006)
Mommy 2: Mommy's Day '96
Mommy '95
Girl Hunters '63

Maria Grazia Spina (1936-)
Revolt of the Barbarians '64
Tiger of the Seven Seas '62

Joe Spinell (1938-89)
Operation Warzone '89
Rapid Fire '89
The Pick-Up Artist '87
The Children of Times Square '86
Hollywood Harry '86
The Whoopee Boys '86
Big Score '83
Vigilante '83
Walking the Edge '83
Fanatic '82
The Last Fight '82
Night Shift '82
One Down, Two to Go! '82
The Godfather 1902-1959: The Complete Epic '81
Nighthawks '81
Cruising '80
Forbidden Zone '80
Little Dragons '80
Maniac '80
Winter Kills '79
One Man Jury '78
Star Crash '78
Rocky '76
Taxi Driver '76
The Godfather, Part 2 '74
Cops and Robbers '73
The Godfather '72

Stephen Spinella (1956-)
Milk '08
And Then Came Love '07
Connie and Carla '04
Our Town '03
Bubble Boy '01
Ravenous '99
What the Deaf Man Heard '98
David Searching '97
Great Expectations '97
The Jackal '97
Love! Valour! Compassion! '96
Tarantella '95
Virtuosity '95
And the Band Played On '93

Brent Spiner (1949-)
Material Girls '06
The Aviator '04
Master of Disguise '02
Star Trek: Nemesis '02
A Girl Thing '01
Gepetto '00
Introducing Dorothy Dandridge '99
South Park: Bigger, Longer and Uncut '99 (V)
Star Trek: Insurrection '98
Out to Sea '97
Independence Day '96
Phenomenon '96
Star Trek: First Contact '96
Star Trek: Generations '94
Crazy from the Heart '91
Family Sins '87

Victor Spinetti (1932-)
The Krays '90
Voyage of the Damned '76
The Little Prince '74
Return of the Pink Panther '74
Start the Revolution without Me '70
Magical Mystery Tour '67
Help! '65
A Hard Day's Night '64

Jordana Spiro (1977-)
The Goods: Live Hard, Sell Hard '09
Alone With Her '07
Living & Dying '07
Must Love Dogs '05

Kevin Blair Spirtas (1962-)
Green Plaid Shirt '96
Bloodlust: Subspecies 3 '93
Bloodstone: Subspecies 2 '92
Friday the 13th, Part 7: The New Blood '88
The Hills Have Eyes, Part 2 '84

Angelo Spizzirri (1974-2007)
The Pleasure Drivers '05
Underclassman '05
The Rookie '02

Gregory Sporleder (1964-)
Black Hawk Down '01
Clay Pigeons '98
Uncorked '98
The Rock '96
Twister '96
True Romance '93
A League of Their Own '92

Greg Spottiswood (1964-)
DC 9/11: Time of Crisis '04
Ice Men '04
The Snow Walker '03
JFK: Reckless Youth '93
Looking for Miracles '90

G.D. Spradlin (1920-)
Dick '99
The Long Kiss Goodnight '96
Riders of the Purple Sage '96
Nick of Time '95
Canadian Bacon '94
Ed Wood '94
Carolina Skeletons '92
The War of the Roses '89
Nutcracker: Money, Madness & Murder '87
Call to Glory '84
The Lords of Discipline '83
Tank '83
Wrong Is Right '82
The Godfather 1902-1959: The Complete Epic '81
The Formula '80
The Jayne Mansfield Story '80
Apocalypse Now '79
North Dallas Forty '79
And I Alone Survived '78
One on One '77
The Godfather, Part 2 '74
The Only Way Home '72
Zabriskie Point '70
Hell's Angels '69 '69

Charlie Spradling (1968-)
Spent '00
Johnny Skidmarks '97
Angel of Destruction '94
Bad Channels '92
To Sleep with a Vampire '92
Meridian: Kiss of the Beast '90
Mirror, Mirror '90
Puppet Master 2 '90
Wild at Heart '90

Elizabeth Spriggs (1929-)
Is Anybody There? '08
A Christmas Carol '99
Paradise Road '97
The Secret Agent '96
Sense and Sensibility '95
Impromptu '90
Oranges Are Not the Only Fruit '89
Thirteenth Day of Christmas '85
Parker '84

Jerry Springer (1944-)
Austin Powers 2: The Spy Who Shagged Me '99
Ringmaster '98

Rick Springfield (1949-)
Legion '98
A Change of Place '94
Silent Motive '91
Dead Reckoning '89
Nick Knight '89
Hard to Hold '84

Bruce Springsteen (1949-)
High Fidelity '00
Chuck Berry: Hail! Hail! Rock 'n' Roll '87

Pamela Springsteen (1962-)
The Gumshoe Kid '89
Sleepaway Camp 3: Teenage Wasteland '89
Dixie Lanes '88
Sleepaway Camp 2: Unhappy Campers '88
My Science Project '85
Reckless '84
Fast Times at Ridgemont High '82

Ove Sprogoe (1919-2004)
You Are Not Alone '78
Famous Five Get into Trouble '70

Cole Sprouse (1992-)
The Prince and the Pauper '07
The Heart Is Deceitful Above All Things '04
Big Daddy '99

Dylan Sprouse (1992-)
Snow Buddies '08 (V)
The Prince and the Pauper '07
The Heart Is Deceitful Above All Things '04
Big Daddy '99

Dina Spybey (1965-)
Just like Heaven '05
Freaky Friday '03
The Haunted Mansion '03
Full Frontal '02
Isn't She Great '00
An Alan Smithee Film: Burn, Hollywood, Burn '97
Julian Po '97
The First Wives Club '96
Striptease '96
subUrbia '96
Big Night '95

June Squibb (1935-)
A Stranger's Heart '07
Welcome to Mooseport '04
About Schmidt '02

Katherine Squire (1903-95)
Ride in the Whirlwind '66
Studs Lonigan '60

Ronald Squire (1886-1958)
Sea Wife '57
Encore '52
No Highway in the Sky '51
Woman Hater '49
Action for Slander '38

Rebecca Staab (1961-)
Safe Harbour '07
The Substitute 3: Winner Takes All '99
Stray Bullet '98
T.N.T. '98
Love Potion #9 '92

Kelly Stables (1984-)
Together Again for the First Time '08
Telling Lies '06
The Ring 2 '05

Ivano Staccioli (1927-95)
SS Girls '77
Gunslinger '70

Chris Stack
School of Rock '03
Roger Dodger '02

Robert Stack (1919-2003)
Killer Bud '00
Mumford '99
BASEketball '98
Beavis and Butt-Head Do America '96 (V)
The Return of Eliot Ness '91
Joe Versus the Volcano '90
Caddyshack 2 '88
Dangerous Curves '88
Plain Clothes '88
Big Trouble '86
Transformers: The Movie '86 (V)
George Washington '84
Uncommon Valor '83
Strike Force '81
Airplane! '80
1941 '79
Most Wanted '76
Murder on Flight 502 '75
A Strange and Deadly Occurrence '74
Action Man '67
The Corrupt Ones '67
Is Paris Burning? '66
Scarface Mob '62
The Last Voyage '60
John Paul Jones '59
Tarnished Angels '57
Great Day in the Morning '56
Written on the Wind '56
House of Bamboo '55
The High and the Mighty '54
Conquest of Cochise '53
Sabre Jet '53
My Outlaw Brother '51
Bullfighter & the Lady '50
Mr. Music '50
A Date with Judy '48
Miss Tatlock's Millions '48
To Be or Not to Be '42
Nice Girl? '41
The Mortal Storm '40
First Love '39

William Stack (1882-1949)
Mary of Scotland '36
Pennies from Heaven '36

James Stacy (1936-)
Matters of the Heart '90
Something Wicked This Way Comes '83
Double Exposure '82
The Dark Side of Love '79
Posse '75
Paper Man '71
A Swingin' Summer '65

John Stacy
The Big Game '72
Too Bad She's Bad '54

Lewis J. Stadlen (1947-)
The Imposters '98
In and Out '97
Windy City '84
Between the Lines '77
Savages '72

Michael Stadvec
The Chosen One: Legend of the Raven '98
The Dentist '96

Ann Stafford
Keep My Grave Open '80
Poor White Trash 2 '75

Frederick Stafford (1928-79)
The Legend of the Wolf Woman '77
Eagles Over London '69
Topaz '69
The Battle of El Alamein '68

Jim Stafford (1944-)
Kid Colter '85
E.S.P. '83

Jon Stafford
Crossing the Line '90
Full Metal Jacket '87
Munchies '87

Carola Stagnaro (1957-)
Dial Help '88
Unsane '82

Nick Stahl (1979-)
My One and Only '09
Quid Pro Quo '08
Sleepwalking '08
How to Rob a Bank '07
The Night of the White Pants '06
Sin City '05
Bookies '03
Terminator 3: Rise of the Machines '03
Twist '03
Taboo '02
Bully '01
In the Bedroom '01
The Sleepy Time Gal '01
Lover's Prayer '99
Soundman '99
Sunset Strip '99
Disturbing Behavior '98
The Thin Red Line '98
Eye of God '97
Blue River '95
Tall Tale: The Unbelievable Adventures of Pecos Bill '95
Safe Passage '94
The Man Without a Face '93

Richard Stahl (1932-2006)
Private School '83
Beware! The Blob '72
Five Easy Pieces '70
The Student Nurses '70

Philip Stainton (1908-61)
Who Done It? '56
Mogambo '53

Brent Stait (1959-)
Sea Beast '08
Born to Run '93
Call of the Wild '93

Marion Stalens
Trois Couleurs: Rouge '94
The Lovers on the Bridge '91

James Staley (1948-)
Robot Wars '93
Sweet Dreams '85
American Dreamer '84
Protocol '84

Joan Staley (1940-)
The Ghost and Mr. Chicken '66
Roustabout '64

Frank Stallone (1950-)
Total Force '98
Public Enemies '96
Taken Alive '95
Hudson Hawk '91
Lethal Games '90
Masque of the Red Death '90
Terror in Beverly Hills '90
Death Feud '89
Easy Kill '89
Heart of Midnight '89
Order of the Eagle '89
Ten Little Indians '89
Fear '88
Midnight Cop '88
Prime Suspect '88
Barfly '87
Death Blow '87
Outlaw Force '87
Take Two '87
The Pink Chiquitas '86

Sage Stallone (1976-)
Moscow Zero '06
Chaos '05

Daylight '96
Fatally Yours '95
Rocky 5 '90

Sylvester Stallone (1946-)
The Expendables '10
Rambo '08
Rocky Balboa '06
Shade '03
Spy Kids 3-D: Game Over '03
Avenging Angelo '02
Driven '01
Eye See You '01
Get Carter '00
Antz '98 (V)
An Alan Smithee Film: Burn, Hollywood, Burn '97
Cop Land '97
Daylight '96
Assassins '95
Judge Dredd '95
The Specialist '94
Cliffhanger '93
Demolition Man '93
Stop! or My Mom Will Shoot '92
Oscar '91
Rocky 5 '90
Lock Up '89
Tango and Cash '89
Rambo 3 '88
Cobra '86
Over the Top '86
Rambo: First Blood, Part 2 '85
Rocky 4 '85
Rhinestone '84
First Blood '82
Rocky 3 '82
Nighthawks '81
Victory '81
Rocky 2 '79
F.I.S.T. '78
Paradise Alley '78
Cannonball '76
Rocky '76
Death Race 2000 '75
Farewell, My Lovely '75
The Lords of Flatbush '74
Prisoner of Second Avenue '74
The Italian Stallion '73
Bananas '71
Rebel '70

Anne Stallybrass (1940-)
Diana: Her True Story '93
The Strauss Family '73
Six Wives of Henry VIII '71

Lynn Stalmaster
Flying Leathernecks '51
The Steel Helmet '51

David Stambaugh (1961-)
The Bad News Bears Go to Japan '78
Breaking Up '78
The Bad News Bears in Breaking Training '77
The Bad News Bears '76

Lauren Stamile (1976-)
The Blue Tooth Virgin '09
Midnight Bayou '09

John Stamos (1963-)
A Raisin in the Sun '08
Wedding Wars '06
Knots '05
The Reagans '04
The Disappearance of Christina '93
Born to Ride '91
Never Too Young to Die '86
Alice in Wonderland '85

Terence Stamp (1940-)
The Adjustment Bureau '10
Get Smart '08
Valkyrie '08
Wanted '08
Yes Man '08
September Dawn '07
These Foolish Things '06
Elektra '05
Dead Fish '04

Fellini: I'm a Born Liar '03
The Haunted Mansion '03
My Boss's Daughter '03
My Wife is an Actress '01
Red Planet '00
Bowfinger '99
The Limey '99
Star Wars: Episode 1—The Phantom Menace '99
Kiss the Sky '98
Love Walked In '97
Bliss '96
The Adventures of Priscilla, Queen of the Desert '94
The Real McCoy '93
Genuine Risk '89
Alien Nation '88
Young Guns '88
The Sicilian '87
Wall Street '87
Alamut Ambush '86
Cold War Killers '86
Deadly Recruits '86
Legal Eagles '86
Link '86
The Hit '85
Vatican Conspiracy '81
Superman 2 '80
Meetings with Remarkable Men '79
Together? '79
Superman: The Movie '78
The Thief of Baghdad '78
Insanity '76
Divine Nymph '71
Blue '68
Iron Cowboy '68
Spirits of the Dead '68
Teorema '68
Far from the Madding Crowd '67
Modesty Blaise '66
The Collector '65
Term of Trial '63
Billy Budd '62

Sebastian Stan (1983-)

Hot Tub Time Machine '10
Spread '09
The Architect '06
The Covenant '06
Red Doors '05

George Stanchev

Shark Attack 3: Megalodon '02
U.S. SEALs: Dead or Alive '02

Wadeck Stanczak (1961-)

Scene of the Crime '87
Rendez-vous '85

Lionel Stander (1908-94)

The Last Good Time '94
Cookie '89
Wicked Stepmother '89
The Squeeze '80
1941 '79
New York, New York '77
The Cassandra Crossing '76
Black Bird '75
The Sensual Man '74
Black Hand '73
1931: Once Upon a Time in New York '72
Pulp '72
Sting of the West '72
Treasure Island '72
Boot Hill '69
Beyond the Law '68
Dandy in Aspic '68
Once Upon a Time in the West '68
Cul de Sac '66
Promise Her Anything '66
The Loved One '65
Blast of Silence '61 (N)
St. Benny the Dip '51
Call Northside 777 '48
Unfaithfully Yours '48
The Sin of Harold Diddlebock '47
Spectre of the Rose '46
Guadalcanal Diary '43
Ice Follies of 1939 '39
The Last Gangster '37
A Star Is Born '37
If You Could Only Cook '36
Mr. Deeds Goes to Town '36
They Met in a Taxi '36
I Live My Life '35

Guy Standing (1873-1937)

Bulldog Drummond Comes Back '37
Bulldog Drummond Escapes '37
I'd Give My Life '36
Lloyds of London '36
The Lives of a Bengal Lancer '35
Death Takes a Holiday '34
Now and Forever '34
The Eagle and the Hawk '33

Joan Standing (1903-79)

Cricket on the Hearth '23
Oliver Twist '22

John Standing (1934-)

Before the Rains '07
I Want Candy '07
The Shadow in the North '07
Lassie '05
A Good Woman '04
Longitude '00
8 1/2 Women '99
Rogue Trader '98
The Man Who Knew Too Little '97
Mrs. Dalloway '97
The Woman in White '97
The Choir '95
Gulliver's Travels '95
Chaplin '92
The Endless Game '89
Riders '88
Nightflyers '87
To Catch a King '84
The Legacy '79
Rogue Male '76
Walk, Don't Run '66
King Rat '65

Aaron Stanford (1976-)

The Cake Eaters '07
Flakes '07
The Hills Have Eyes '06
X-Men: The Last Stand '06
Runaway '05
Standing Still '05
Spartan '04
Winter Solstice '04
Rick '03
X2: X-Men United '03
Tadpole '02

Arnold Stang (1918-2009)

Dennis the Menace '93
Ghost Dad '90
Marco Polo, Jr. '72 (V)
Hercules in New York '70
The Wonderful World of the Brothers Grimm '62
Dondi '61
The Man with the Golden Arm '55
Seven Days' Leave '42

Maya Stange

Garage Days '03
XX/XY '02
In a Savage Land '99

Florence Stanley (1924-2003)

Down With Love '03
Atlantis: The Lost Empire '01 (V)
Neil Simon's The Odd Couple 2 '98
A Goofy Movie '94 (V)
Trapped in Paradise '94
Trouble Bound '92
A Perfect Little Murder '90

Forrest Stanley (1889-1969)

Outlaws of the Desert '41
The Rider of Death Valley '32
Bare Knees '28
Up the Ladder '25

Helene Stanley (1929-90)

Dial Red O '55
The Snows of Kilimanjaro '52
Bandit King of Texas '49

Jack Stanley (1991-)

The Hitchhiker's Guide to the Galaxy '05
Carrie's War '04

Kim Stanley (1925-2001)

Cat on a Hot Tin Roof '84
The Right Stuff '83
Frances '82
The Three Sisters '65
Seance on a Wet Afternoon '64
To Kill a Mockingbird '62 (N)
The Goddess '58

Louise Stanley (1915-82)

Pinto Canyon '40
Sky Bandits '40
Yukon Flight '40
Danger on the Air '38
Gun Packer '38
Gunsmoke Trail '38
Thunder in the Desert '38
Gun Lords of Stirrup Basin '37
Riders of the Rockies '37
Sing, Cowboy, Sing '37

Paul Stanley (1952-)

Detroit Rock City '99
KISS Meets the Phantom of the Park '78
I Heard the Owl Call My Name '73

Rebecca Stanley

Body Double '84
Eyes of Fire '84

Don Stannard (1916-49)

The Temptress '49
Dick Barton, Special Agent '48
Dick Barton Strikes Back '48
Pink String and Sealing Wax '45

Claire Stansfield (1964-)

Sweepers '99
Darkdrive '98
Red Shoe Diaries 5: Weekend Pass '95
Wes Craven Presents Mind Ripper '95
Drop Zone '94
Sensation '94
Best of the Best 2 '93
The Swordsman '92

Andrew Stanton (1965-)

Finding Nemo '03 (V)
Toy Story 2 '99 (V)

Harry Dean Stanton (1926-)

Alice '09
The Open Road '09
The Good Life '07
Alpha Dog '06
Inland Empire '06
You, Me and Dupree '06
The Wendell Baker Story '05
The Big Bounce '04
Anger Management '03
Ginostra '02
Sonny '02
The Man Who Cried '00
The Pledge '00
Sand '00
The Green Mile '99
The Straight Story '99
Fear and Loathing in Las Vegas '98
The Mighty '98
Fire Down Below '97
She's So Lovely '97
Down Periscope '96
Larry McMurtry's Dead Man's Walk '96
Midnight Blue '96
Never Talk to Strangers '95
Playback '95
Against the Wall '94
Blue Tiger '94
Hostages '93
Hotel Room '93
Man Trouble '92
Twin Peaks: Fire Walk with Me '92
Payoff '91
The Fourth War '90
Wild at Heart '90
Dream a Little Dream '89
Twister '89
The Last Temptation of Christ '88
Mr. North '88
Stars and Bars '88
Slamdance '87
Fool for Love '86
Pretty in Pink '86
One Magic Christmas '85
Rip van Winkle '85
Christine '84
Red Dawn '84
Paris, Texas '83
Repo Man '83
One from the Heart '82
Young Doctors in Love '82
Escape from New York '81
The Godfather 1902-1959: The Complete Epic '81
Uforia '81
Death Watch '80
Oldest Living Graduate '80
Private Benjamin '80
Alien '79
The Black Marble '79
Flatbed Annie and Sweetiepie: Lady Truckers '79
The Rose '79
Wise Blood '79
Straight Time '78
Missouri Breaks '76
92 in the Shade '76
Farewell, My Lovely '75
Rafferty & the Gold Dust Twins '75
Rancho Deluxe '75
Cockfighter '74
The Godfather, Part 2 '74
Where the Lilies Bloom '74
Zandy's Bride '74
Dillinger '73
Pat Garrett & Billy the Kid '73
Two Lane Blacktop '71
Kelly's Heroes '70
Rebel Rousers '69
Cool Hand Luke '67
The Hostage '67
Ride in the Whirlwind '66
The Adventures of Huckleberry Finn '60
Proud Rebel '58

John Stanton (1944-)

Day of the Panther '88
Rent-A-Cop '88
Great Expectations: The Untold Story '87
Tai-Pan '86
Dusty '85
The Naked Country '85
Bellamy '81

Paul Stanton (1884-1955)

Across the Pacific '42
Night of January 16th '41
Whistling in the Dark '41
Stanley and Livingstone '39

Robert Stanton (1963-)

Confessions of a Shopaholic '09
Find Me Guilty '06
Head of State '03
The Quiet American '02
Mercury Rising '98
Next Stop, Wonderland '98
Red Corner '97
Washington Square '97
Dennis the Menace '93
Bob Roberts '92
I Eat Your Skin '64
Abbott and Costello in Hollywood '45

Barbara Stanwyck (1907-90)

The Thorn Birds '83
The Night Walker '64
Roustabout '64
Walk on the Wild Side '62
Crime of Passion '57
Forty Guns '57
Escape to Burma '55
The Maverick Queen '55
The Violent Men '55
Blowing Wild '54
Cattle Queen of Montana '54
Executive Suite '54
All I Desire '53
Jeopardy '53
The Moonlighter '53
Titanic '53
Clash by Night '52
The Furies '50
To Please a Lady '50
East Side, West Side '49
Sorry, Wrong Number '48
Cry Wolf '47
The Two Mrs. Carrolls '47
My Reputation '46
The Strange Love of Martha Ivers '46
Christmas in Connecticut '45
Double Indemnity '44
Hollywood Canteen '44
Lady of Burlesque '43
The Great Man's Lady '42
Ball of Fire '41
The Lady Eve '41
Meet John Doe '41
Remember the Night '40
Golden Boy '39
Union Pacific '39
Mad Miss Manton '38
Breakfast for Two '37
Internes Can't Take Money '37
Stella Dallas '37
The Bride Walks Out '36
Annie Oakley '35
Red Salute '35
Baby Face '33
The Bitter Tea of General Yen '33
Ladies They Talk About '33
The Purchase Price '32
Illicit '31
The Miracle Woman '31
Night Nurse '31

Huub Stapel (1954-)

Amsterdamned '88
The Attic: The Hiding of Anne Frank '88
The Lift '85

Jean Stapleton (1923-)

Pursuit of Happiness '01
Baby '00
You've Got Mail '98
Lily Dale '96
Michael '96
The Habitation of Dragons '91
Mother Goose Rock 'n' Rhyme '90
Grown Ups '86
Cinderella '84
The Buddy System '83
Jack & the Beanstalk '83
Eleanor: First Lady of the World '82
Cold Turkey '71
Klute '71
Up the Down Staircase '67
Bells Are Ringing '60
Damn Yankees '58

Kevin Stapleton

Cyclops '08
Carver's Gate '96

Maureen Stapleton (1925-2006)

Dead Silence '98
Addicted to Love '96
The Last Good Time '94
Trading Mom '94
Miss Rose White '92
Passed Away '92
Cocoon: The Return '88
Doin' Time on Planet Earth '88
Made in Heaven '87
Nuts '87
Sweet Lorraine '87
Heartburn '86
The Money Pit '86
Cocoon '85
Family Secrets '84
Johnny Dangerously '84
Little Gloria... Happy at Last '84
The Fan '81
On the Right Track '81
Reds '81
The Gathering: Part 2 '79
Lost and Found '79
The Runner Stumbles '79
Interiors '78
The Gathering '77
Queen of the Stardust Ballroom '75
Tell Me Where It Hurts '74
The Cosmic Eye '71 (V)
Plaza Suite '71
Airport '70
Bye, Bye, Birdie '63
The Fugitive Kind '60
Lonelyhearts '58

Nicola Stapleton (1974-)

Urban Ghost Story '98
Courage Mountain '89

Sullivan Stapleton

December Boys '07
Darkness Falls '03
River Street '95

Richard Stapley (1934-)

D-Day, the Sixth of June '56
The Strange Door '51

Don Stark (1954-)

Double Edge '97
Santa with Muscles '96
Bloodfist 5: Human Target '93
Evilspeak '82
Switchblade Sisters '75

Graham Stark (1922-)

Adventures Beyond Belief '87
Blind Date '87
Bloodbath at the House of Death '85
Salt & Pepper '68
Alfie '66

Jonathan Stark (1952-)

House 2: The Second Story '87
Project X '87
Fright Night '85

Koo Stark (1956-)

Eat the Rich '87
Electric Dreams '84
Emily '77
The Rocky Horror Picture Show '75

Anthony Starke (1963-)

Baby on Board '08
Inferno '98
The Magnificent Seven '98
Repossessed '90
18 Again! '88
Return of the Killer Tomatoes! '88

Pauline Starke (1901-77)

The Viking '28
Dante's Inferno '24
Little Church Around the Corner '23
Until They Get Me '18

Beau Starr (1944-)

Masters of Horror: Jenifer '05
Where the Truth Lies '05
The Golden Spiders: A Nero Wolfe Mystery '00
Mercy '00
The Thin Blue Lie '00
Mean Streak '99
Prisoner of Love '99
Hoodlum '96

Devil in a Blue Dress '95
Never Talk to Strangers '95
Dead Air '94
Trial by Jury '94
Goodfellas '90
Halloween 5: The Revenge of Michael Myers '89
Halloween 4: The Return of Michael Myers '88
Summer School '87
Manhunt for Claude Dallas '86
Fletch '85

Fredro Starr (1970-)
A Day in the Life '09
My Brother '06
Torque '04
Save the Last Dance '01
Light It Up '99
Ride '98
Sunset Park '96
The Addiction '95

Martin Starr (1982-)
Adventureland '09
Knocked Up '07
Walk Hard: The Dewey Cox Story '07

Mike Starr
I Hate Valentine's Day '09
Jesse Stone: Night Passage '06

Mike Starr (1950-)
Doughboys '08
Lone Rider '08
The Black Dahlia '06
Hot Tamale '06
Elvis Has Left the Building '04
Jersey Girl '04
The Next Big Thing '02
Tempted '01
3 A.M. '01
The Lady in Question '99
Murder in a Small Town '99
Frogs for Snakes '98
Gloria '98
The Deli '97
Path to Paradise '97
A River Made to Drown In '97
Flipping '96
Hoodlum '96
Just Your Luck '96
Two If by Sea '95
Dumb & Dumber '94
Ed Wood '94
Trial by Jury '94
Mad Dog and Glory '93
Mardi Gras for the Devil '93
The Bodyguard '92
Billy Bathgate '91
Goodfellas '90
Nasty Hero '89
The Money Pit '86
Cruising '80

Ringo Starr (1940-)
Alice in Wonderland '85
Water '85
Give My Regards to Broad Street '84
Princess Daisy '83
Caveman '81
The Kids Are Alright '79
Sextette '78
Lisztomania '75
That'll Be the Day '73
Born to Boogie '72
The Point '71 (N)
200 Motels '71
Let It Be '70
The Magic Christian '69
Candy '68
Yellow Submarine '68 (V)
Magical Mystery Tour '67
Help! '65
A Hard Day's Night '64

Charles Starrett (1903-86)
Bonanza Town '51
Blazing Across the Pecos '48
Lawless Plainsmen '42
The Durango Kid '40
Make a Million '35
A Shot in the Dark '35
Sons of Steel '35
Dangerous Appointment '34
Green Eyes '34
The Return of Casey Jones '34
The Silver Streak '34
Jungle Bride '33
Mr. Skitch '33
The Mask of Fu Manchu '32

Jack Starrett (1936-89)
Nightwish '89
Brothers in Arms '88
Death Chase '87
First Blood '82
Mr. Horn '79
Hell's Bloody Devils '70
The Losers '70
Angels from Hell '68

David Starzyk
Bring It On: Fight to the Finish '09
A Boyfriend for Christmas '04

Jason Statham (1972-)
The Expendables '10
Crank: High Voltage '09
The Bank Job '08
Death Race '08
In the Name of the King: A Dungeon Siege Tale '08
Transporter 3 '08
War '07
Crank '06
London '05
Revolver '05
Transporter 2 '05
Cellular '04
The Italian Job '03
The Transporter '02
John Carpenter's Ghosts of Mars '01
Mean Machine '01
The One '01
Snatch '00
Turn It Up '00
Lock, Stock and 2 Smoking Barrels '98

Chelsea Staub (1988-)
Minutemen '08
Bratz '07

Liz Stauber (1979-)
The Tollbooth '04
The Village '04
Almost Famous '00
Kitchen Privileges '00
Teaching Mrs. Tingle '99
Three Kings '99

Imelda Staunton (1956-)
Return to Cranford '09
Taking Woodstock '09
Cranford '08
Freedom Writers '07
Harry Potter and the Order of the Phoenix '07
How About You '07
Nanny McPhee '06
Shadow Man '06
Vera Drake '04
Cambridge Spies '03
I'll Be There '03
Crush '02
Another Life '01
Chicken Run '00 (V)
David Copperfield '99
Shakespeare in Love '98
Twelfth Night '96
Citizen X '95
Sense and Sensibility '95
Deadly Advice '93
Much Ado about Nothing '93
Peter's Friends '92
Antonia and Jane '91

Mary Stavin (1957-)
The Opponent '89
House '86
Open House '86

Eddie Stazak
Day of the Panther '88
Fists of Blood '87

Alison Steadman (1946-)
Fanny Hill '07
Pride and Prejudice '95
Secrets and Lies '95
Blame It on the Bellboy '92
Life Is Sweet '90
The Misadventures of Mr. Wilt '90
Tartuffe '90
The Adventures of Baron Munchausen '89
Shirley Valentine '89
Clockwise '86
Coming Through '85
Champions '84
A Private Function '84
Kipperbang '82
Abigail's Party '77
Nuts in May '76
Hard Labour '73

John Steadman (1909-93)
Fade to Black '80
The Hills Have Eyes '77
Poco '77

Ken Steadman (1969-96)
Hindsight '97
I Like to Play Games '95

Red Steagall (1937-)
Big Bad John '90
Dark Before Dawn '89
Benji the Hunted '87

Rick Stear (1972-)
Astoria '00
Went to Coney Island on a Mission from God... Be Back by Five '98

Michael Stearns (1940-)
Battle for the Planet of the Apes '73
Chain Gang Women '72
Chrome and Hot Leather '71

Peter Stebbings
Defendor '09
Jack and Jill vs. the World '08
Never Cry Werewolf '08
S.I.S. '08
Re-Generation '04
No Alibi '00

Ray Dennis Steckler (1939-)
Las Vegas Weekend '85
The Thrill Killers '65
Incredibly Strange Creatures Who Stopped Living and Became Mixed-Up Zombies '63
Eegah! '62
Wild Guitar '62
Wild Ones on Wheels '62

Myrtle Stedman (1885-1938)
The Mad Whirl '25
Sex '20
In the Days of the Thundering Herd & the Law & the Outlaw '14

Alan Steel
Hercules against the Moon Men '64
Samson and His Mighty Challenge '64
The Fury of Hercules '61
Samson '61

Amy Steel (1963-)
What Ever Happened To... '93
Walk Like a Man '87
April Fool's Day '86
Friday the 13th, Part 2 '81

Anthony Steel (1920-2001)
Perfect Crime '79
The Story of O '75
I'm the Girl He Wants to Kill '74
Massacre in Rome '73
Tiger of the Seven Seas '62
48 Hours to Live '60
Revenge of the Barbarians '60
Harry Black and the Tiger '58
Malta Story '53
The Master of Ballantrae '53
Another Man's Poison '52
Wooden Horse '50

Barbara Steele (1937-)
The Capitol Conspiracy '99
The Winds of War '83
Silent Scream '80
Piranha '78
Pretty Baby '78
They Came from Within '75
Caged Heat '74
The Crimson Cult '68
An Angel for Satan '66
Terror Creatures from the Grave '66
Nightmare Castle '65
The She-Beast '65
Castle of Blood '64
The Monocle '64
8 1/2 '63
The Ghost '63
The Horrible Dr. Hichcock '62
The Pit and the Pendulum '61
Black Sunday '60
La Dolce Vita '60

Bob Steele (1907-88)
Atomic Submarine '59
Pork Chop Hill '59
Rio Bravo '59
Giant from the Unknown '58
Pardners '56
The Enforcer '51
Ambush Trail '46
The Big Sleep '46
Northwest Trail '46
Rio Grande Raiders '46
Wildfire '45
Arizona Whirlwind '44
Death Valley Rangers '44
Marked Trails '44
Outlaw Trail '44
Sonora Stagecoach '44
Westward Bound '44
Riders of the Rio Grande '43
Code of the Outlaw '42
Shadows on the Sage '42
Billy the Kid in Santa Fe '41
Gangs of Sonora '41
Gauchos of El Dorado '41
Outlaws of the Cherokee Trail '41
Texas Trouble '41
Trigger Men '41
Twilight on the Rio Grande '41
West of Cimarron '41
Battling Outlaw '40
Billy the Kid in Texas '40
Carson City Kid '40
City for Conquest '40
Pinto Canyon '40
Wild Horse Valley '40
El Diablo Rides '39
Mesquite Buckaroo '39
Of Mice and Men '39
Durango Valley Raiders '38
Feud Maker '38
Thunder in the Desert '38
Arizona Gunfighter '37
Border Phantom '37
Doomed at Sundown '37
Gun Lords of Stirrup Basin '37
Lightning Bill Crandall '37
Paroled to Die '37
The Red Rope '37
Ridin' the Lone Trail '37
Brand of the Outlaws '36
Cavalry '36
Kid Ranger '36
Last of the Warrens '36
The Law Rides '36
Smokey Smith '36
Sundown Saunders '36
Alias John Law '35
Big Calibre '35
Kid Courageous '35
No Man's Range '35
Powdersmoke Range '35
Rider of the Law '35
Trail of Terror '35
Western Justice '35
Brand of Hate '34
Demon for Trouble '34
The Gun Ranger '34
Tombstone Terror '34
Breed of the Border '33
Fighting Champ '33
The Gallant Fool '33
Galloping Romeo '33
Mystery Squadron '33
Young Blood '33
Hidden Valley '32
Man from Hell's Edges '32
Riders of the Desert '32
South of Santa Fe '32
Texas Buddies '32
The Nevada Buckaroo '31
The Ridin' Fool '31
Sunrise Trail '31
Near the Rainbow's End '30
Oklahoma Cyclone '30

Brian Steele
Hellboy II: The Golden Army '08
Doom '05
Underworld: Evolution '05

Don Steele (1936-97)
Eating Raoul '82
Rock 'n' Roll High School '79
Death Race 2000 '75

Fred Steele
Nevil Shute's The Far Country '85
Demolition '77

Freddie (Fred) Steele (1912-84)
Call Northside 777 '48
A Foreign Affair '48
Black Angel '46
The Story of G.I. Joe '45
Hail the Conquering Hero '44

Jadrien Steele (1974-)
The Secret Garden '87
The Mosquito Coast '86

Karen Steele (1931-)
Trap on Cougar Mountain '72
The Rise and Fall of Legs Diamond '60
Ride Lonesome '59
Westbound '58
Bail Out at 43,000 '57
Decision at Sundown '57
Marty '55

Marjorie Steele (1930-)
Face to Face '52
Tough Assignment '49

Pippa Steele (1948-92)
Lust for a Vampire '71
The Vampire Lovers '70
Oh! What a Lovely War '69

Sarah Steele
The Good Student '08
Spanglish '04

Tommy Steele (1936-)
Finian's Rainbow '68
Half a Sixpence '67
The Happiest Millionaire '67
G-Men Never Forget '48

Jessica Steen (1965-)
Vipers '08
Slap Shot 2: Breaking the Ice '02
Smart House '00
Armageddon '98
The Principal Takes a Holiday '98
Dogwatch '97
Trial and Error '96
Still Life '92
Sing '89
John and the Missus '87
Striker's Mountain '87
The Housekeeper '86
Dream to Believe '85

Paprika Steen (1964-)
Adam's Apples '05
Forty Shades of Blue '05
Mifune '99
The Celebration '98

Mary Steenburgen (1953-)
Did You Hear About the Morgans? '09
The Open Road '09
The Proposal '09
Four Christmases '08
In the Electric Mist '08
Nobel Son '08
Step Brothers '08
The Brave One '07
Numb '07
The Dead Girl '06
Marilyn Hotchkiss' Ballroom Dancing & Charm School '06
Casa de los Babys '03
Elf '03
Sunshine State '02
I Am Sam '01
Life as a House '01
Nobody's Baby '01
The Trumpet of the Swan '01 (V)
Wish You Were Dead '00
Noah's Ark '99
The Grass Harp '95
Gulliver's Travels '95
Nixon '95
Powder '95
My Family '94
My Summer Story '94
Pontiac Moon '94
Philadelphia '93
What's Eating Gilbert Grape '93
Clifford '92
The Butcher's Wife '91
Back to the Future, Part 3 '90
The Long Walk Home '89 (N)
Miss Firecracker '89
Parenthood '89
The Attic: The Hiding of Anne Frank '88
End of the Line '88
Dead of Winter '87
The Whales of August '87
One Magic Christmas '85
Cross Creek '83
Little Red Riding Hood '83
Romantic Comedy '83
A Midsummer Night's Sex Comedy '82
Ragtime '81
Melvin and Howard '80
Time After Time '79
Goin' South '78

Eddie Steeples
I Know Who Killed Me '07
Wristcutters: A Love Story '06

Simonetta Stefanelli (1954-)
Three Brothers '80
The Godfather '72

Leslie Stefanson (1971-)
The Hunted '03
Desert Saints '01
Jackie, Ethel, Joan: The Kennedy Women '01
The Stickup '01
Beautiful '00
Unbreakable '00
The General's Daughter '99
Delivered '98
An Alan Smithee Film: Burn, Hollywood, Burn '97

Anthony Steffen (1929-2006)
Savage Island '85
Escape from Hell '79
The Night Evelyn Came Out of the Grave '71
Garringo '69
The Gentleman Killer '69
Stranger in Paso Bravo '68
An Angel for Satan '66

The Last Tomahawk *'65*

Bernice Stegers

My Life in Ruins *'09*
Little Lord Fauntleroy *'95*
A Dark Adapted Eye *'93*
To Play the King *'93*
The Girl *'86*
Xtro *'83*
City of Women *'81*
Macabre *'80*

Edgar Stehli (1884-1973)

Loving *'70*
No Name on the Bullet *'59*

Rod Steiger (1925-2002)

Poolhall Junkies *'02*
The Hollywood Sign *'01*
Frozen in Fear *'00*
Crazy in Alabama *'99*
Cypress Edge *'99*
End of Days *'99*
The Hurricane *'99*
Shiloh 2: Shiloh Season *'99*
Body and Soul *'98*
Modern Vampires *'98*
Incognito *'97*
The Kid *'97*
The Real Thing *'97*
Shiloh *'97*
Truth or Consequences, N.M. *'97*
Carpool *'96*
Mars Attacks! *'96*
Captain Nuke and the Bomber Boys *'95*
Dalva *'95*
In Pursuit of Honor *'95*
Out There *'95*
Black Water *'94*
The Specialist *'94*
Armistead Maupin's Tales of the City *'93*
The Neighbor *'93*
Guilty as Charged *'92*
The Player *'92*
Sinatra *'92*
The Ballad of the Sad Cafe *'91*
Midnight Murders *'91*
That Summer of White Roses *'90*
The January Man *'89*
Passion in Paradise *'89*
American Gothic *'88*
Catch the Heat *'87*
The Kindred *'87*
Sword of Gideon *'86*
The Glory Boys *'84*
The Naked Face *'84*
The Chosen *'81*
Lion of the Desert *'81*
The Amityville Horror *'79*
Klondike Fever *'79*
Love and Bullets *'79*
Wolf Lake *'79*
Breakthrough *'78*
F.I.S.T. *'78*
The Last Contract *'77*
Last Four Days *'77*
Portrait of a Hitman *'77*
Innocents with Dirty Hands *'76*
Hennessy *'75*
Lucky Luciano *'74*
A Fistful of Dynamite *'72*
Waterloo *'71*
The Illustrated Man *'69*
No Way to Treat a Lady *'68*
The Sergeant *'68*
In the Heat of the Night *'67*
Doctor Zhivago *'65*
The Loved One *'65*
The Pawnbroker *'65*
Time of Indifference *'64*
The Longest Day *'62*
The Mark *'61*
Seven Thieves *'60*
Al Capone *'59*
Across the Bridge *'57*
Unholy Wife *'57*
Back from Eternity *'56*
The Harder They Fall *'56*
Jubal *'56*
Run of the Arrow *'56*
The Big Knife *'55*
The Court Martial of Billy Mitchell *'55*
Oklahoma! *'55*
On the Waterfront *'54*

Ben Stein (1944-)

Casper *'95*
Miami Rhapsody *'95*
The Mask *'94*
My Girl 2 *'94*
North *'94*
Dave *'93*
Honeymoon in Vegas *'92*
Mastergate *'92*
Mr. Write *'92*
Ghostbusters 2 *'89*
Planes, Trains & Automobiles *'87*
Ferris Bueller's Day Off *'86*

June Stein

Bob Roberts *'92*
High Stakes *'89*

Margaret Sophie Stein (1956-)

Sarah, Plain and Tall: Skylark *'93*
Sarah, Plain and Tall *'91*
Enemies, a Love Story *'89*

Saul Stein

Open Water *'03*
Grind *'96*
Illtown *'96*
New Jersey Drive *'95*

David Steinberg (1942-)

Transylmania *'09*
The Marx Brothers in a Nutshell *'90*
Something Short of Paradise *'79*
The End *'78*
The Lost Man *'69*

John Steiner (1941-)

Sinbad of the Seven Seas *'89*
The Lone Runner *'88*
Operation 'Nam *'85*
Dagger Eyes *'83*
Yor, the Hunter from the Future *'83*
Ark of the Sun God *'82*
Hunters of the Golden Cobra *'82*
Unsane *'82*
Caligula *'80*
The Last Hunter *'80*
Blood and Guns *'79*
Shock *'79*
Massacre in Rome *'73*

Sherry Steiner (1948-)

Heaven Help Us *'85*
Asylum of Satan *'72*
Three on a Meathook *'72*

Jake Steinfeld (1958-)

Tough Guys *'86*
Home Sweet Home *'80*

Richard Steinmetz (1959-)

The One *'01*
Skyscraper *'95*
Liquid Dreams *'92*

Robert J. Steinmiller, Jr. (1978-)

Jack the Bear *'93*
The Ref *'93*
Rudy *'93*
Bingo *'91*

William (Bill) Steis (1945-95)

Raiders of the Sun *'92*
Demon of Paradise *'87*
Eye of the Eagle *'87*
Equalizer 2000 *'86*

Anna Sten (1908-93)

Soldier of Fortune *'55*
So Ends Our Night *'41*
The Girl with the Hat Box *'27*

Yutte Stensgaard (1946-)

Lust for a Vampire *'71*
Scream and Scream Again *'70*
Zeta One *'69*

Karel Stepanek (1899-1981)

Second Best Secret Agent in the Whole Wide World *'65*
Devil Doll *'64*
Brainwashed *'60*
Sink the Bismarck *'60*
Never Let Me Go *'53*
The Fallen Idol *'49*
Counterblast *'48*
Secret Mission *'42*

Idwig Stephane (1944-)

The Butterfly *'02*
Pauline and Paulette *'01*
Daens *'92*

Nicole Stephane (1923-2007)

Carve Her Name with Pride *'58*
Les Enfants Terrible *'50*
La Silence de la Mer *'47*

Daniel Stephen

2020 Texas Gladiators *'85*
Warbus *'85*

Susan Stephen (1931-2000)

White Huntress *'57*
Heat Wave *'54*
A Stolen Face *'52*

Ann Stephens

The Franchise Affair *'52*
The Upturned Glass *'47*

Darryl Stephens

Noah's Arc: Jumping the Broom *'08*
Boy Culture *'06*

Harvey Stephens (1901-86)

The Girl in the Red Velvet Swing *'55*
The Lady Is Willing *'42*
Sergeant York *'41*
Abe Lincoln in Illinois *'40*
The Fighting 69th *'40*
The Texas Rangers Ride Again *'40*
Beau Geste *'39*
Oklahoma Kid *'39*
The Texans *'38*
Forlorn River *'37*
Let 'Em Have It *'35*
Whipsaw *'35*
Evelyn Prentice *'34*
The Cheat *'31*

Heather Stephens

Messengers 2: The Scarecrow *'09*
Tomcats *'01*
Blue Ridge Fall *'99*
Forever Love *'98*
With Friends Like These *'98*
The Disappearance of Kevin Johnson *'95*

James Stephens (1951-)

Pancho Barnes *'88*
Mysterious Two *'82*
First Monday in October *'81*

Martin Stephens (1949-)

The Innocents *'61*
Village of the Damned *'60*

Nancy Stephens (1945-)

Halloween: H20 *'98*
Halloween *'78*

Perry Stephens (1958-2005)

Grizzly Mountain *'97*
Norma Jean and Marilyn *'95*
Two Bits & Pepper *'95*

Robert Stephens (1931-95)

Century *'94*
The Secret Rapture *'94*
Searching for Bobby Fischer *'93*
Afraid of the Dark *'92*
Chaplin *'92*
The Bonfire of the Vanities *'90*
The Children *'90*
Henry V *'89*
American Roulette *'88*
High Season *'88*
Wonderland *'88*
Empire of the Sun *'87*
Fortunes of War *'87*
Luther *'74*
The Asphyx *'72*
Travels with My Aunt *'72*
The Private Life of Sherlock Holmes *'70*
The Prime of Miss Jean Brodie *'69*
Morgan: A Suitable Case for Treatment *'66*
A Taste of Honey *'61*

Toby Stephens (1969-)

Dark Corners *'06*
Jane Eyre *'06*
Severance *'06*
Sharpe's Challenge *'06*
The Queen's Sister *'05*
Cambridge Spies *'03*
Napoleon *'03*
Die Another Day *'02*
Possession *'02*
Almost Strangers *'01*
The Great Gatsby *'01*
Onegin *'99*
Cousin Bette *'97*
Photographing Fairies *'97*
The Tenant of Wildfell Hall *'96*
Twelfth Night *'96*
The Camomile Lawn *'92*

Bob Stephenson

The Ex *'07*
Friends with Money *'06*

Henry Stephenson (1871-1956)

Challenge to Lassie *'49*
Oliver Twist *'48*
Song of Love *'47*
Heartbeat *'46*
Mr. Lucky *'43*
Lady from Louisiana *'42*
This Above All *'42*
Down Argentine Way *'40*
It's a Date *'40*
Spring Parade *'40*
The Old Maid *'39*
Tarzan Finds a Son *'39*
Marie Antoinette *'38*
Conquest *'37*
The Prince and the Pauper *'37*
The Charge of the Light Brigade *'36*
Mutiny on the Bounty *'35*
Stingaree *'34*
Thirty Day Princess *'34*
Double Harness *'33*
Tomorrow at Seven *'33*
The Animal Kingdom *'32*
A Bill of Divorcement *'32*
Red Headed Woman *'32*

James Stephenson (1889-1941)

The Letter *'40*
The Sea Hawk *'40*
Beau Geste *'39*
Boy Meets Girl *'38*
Nancy Drew—Detective *'38*

Mark Kinsey Stephenson

The Unnamable 2: The Statement of Randolph Carter *'92*
The Unnamable *'88*

Michael Stephenson (1978-)

Beyond Darkness *'92*
Troll 2 *'92*

Pamela Stephenson (1950-)

Les Patterson Saves the World *'90*
Ghosts Can Do It *'87*
Bloodbath at the House of Death *'85*
Finders Keepers *'84*
Scandalous *'84*
History of the World: Part 1 *'81*
The Comeback *'77*

Craig Stepp

Indecent Behavior 2 *'94*
Married People, Single Sex 2: For Better or Worse *'94*
Play Time *'94*

Ilse Steppat (1917-69)

On Her Majesty's Secret Service *'69*
Naked in the Night *'58*

Ford Sterling (1883-1939)

Headline Woman *'35*
Show Girl in Hollywood *'30*
Sally *'29*
The Show Off *'26*
He Who Gets Slapped *'24*
Yankee Doodle in Berlin *'19*

Jan Sterling (1923-2004)

First Monday in October *'81*
Backstairs at the White House *'79*
The Dark Side of Love *'79*
The Incident *'67*
High School Confidential *'58*
The Harder They Fall *'56*
1984 *'56*
The High and the Mighty *'54*
Pony Express *'53*
Split Second *'53*
Ace in the Hole *'51*
Rhubarb *'51*
Caged *'50*
Gunfire *'50*
Mystery Street *'50*
Union Station *'50*
Johnny Belinda *'48*
Tycoon *'47*

Maury Sterling

Smokin' Aces *'07*
Come as You Are *'05*

Mindy Sterling (1954-)

The Dog Who Saved Christmas *'09*
Ice Age: The Meltdown *'06 (V)*
Nanny Insanity *'06*
The Twelve Dogs of Christmas *'05*
Austin Powers In Goldmember *'02*
Totally Blonde *'01*
Austin Powers 2: The Spy Who Shagged Me *'99*
Drop Dead Gorgeous *'99*
Austin Powers: International Man of Mystery *'97*

Philip Sterling (1922-98)

My Giant *'98*
Death of the Incredible Hulk *'90*
Baby Broker *'81*

Robert Sterling (1917-2006)

A Global Affair *'63*
Return to Peyton Place *'61*
Voyage to the Bottom of the Sea *'61*
Johnny Eager *'42*
Somewhere I'll Find You *'42*
Two-Faced Woman *'41*

Tisha Sterling (1944-)

The Whales of August *'87*
The Killer Inside Me *'76*
Betrayal *'74*
Snatched *'72*
Defiant *'70*
Powder Keg *'70*
Coogan's Bluff *'68*
Village of the Giants *'65*

Daniel Stern (1957-)

Whip It *'09*
The Last Time *'06*
Bachelor Party Vegas *'05*
Dead Simple *'01*
Tourist Trap *'98*
Very Bad Things *'98*
Celtic Pride *'96*
Bushwhacked *'95*
City Slickers 2: The Legend of Curly's Gold *'94*
Rookie of the Year *'93*
Home Alone 2: Lost in New York *'92*
City Slickers *'91*
Coupe de Ville *'90*
The Court Martial of Jackie Robinson *'90*
Home Alone *'90*
My Blue Heaven *'90*
Friends, Lovers & Lunatics *'89*
Leviathan *'89*
Little Monsters *'89*
D.O.A. *'88*
The Milagro Beanfield War *'88*
Weekend War *'88*
Born in East L.A. *'87*
The Boss' Wife *'86*
Hannah and Her Sisters *'86*
Key Exchange *'85*
C.H.U.D. *'84*
Frankenweenie *'84*
Ratings Game *'84*
Blue Thunder *'83*
Get Crazy *'83*
Diner *'82*
I'm Dancing as Fast as I Can *'82*
It's My Turn *'80*
One Trick Pony *'80*
Stardust Memories *'80*
Breaking Away *'79*
Starting Over *'79*

Howard Stern (1954-)

Private Parts *'96*
Ryder P.I. *'86*

Miroslava Stern

The Criminal Life of Archibaldo de la Cruz *'55*
Stranger on Horseback *'55*

Selma Stern

Made of Honor *'08*
Smother *'08*

Tom Stern (1965-)

Freaked *'93*
Hell's Angels '69 *'69*
Angels from Hell *'68*
The Devil's Brigade *'68*

Wes Stern (1947-)

Three in the Cellar *'70*
The First Time *'69*

Frances Sternhagen (1930-)

Julie & Julia *'09*
The Con *'98*
Curtain Call *'97*
Raising Cain *'92*
Doc Hollywood *'91*
Stephen King's Golden Years *'91*
Misery *'90*
Sibling Rivalry *'90*
Communion *'89*
See You in the Morning *'89*
Bright Lights, Big City *'88*
The Dining Room *'86*
Independence Day *'83*
Prototype *'83*
Romantic Comedy *'83*
Who'll Save Our Children? *'82*
Outland *'81*
Mother & Daughter: A Loving War *'80*
Starting Over *'79*

Robyn Stevan

Stepping Out *'91*
Bye Bye Blues *'89*

Jean-Francois Stevenin (1944-)

The Limits of Control *'09*
On Guard! *'03*
The Man on the Train *'02*
Brotherhood of the Wolf *'01*

Total Western '00
For Sale '98
Olivier, Olivier '92
Small Change '76

Robinson Stevenin (1981-)
La Petite Lili '03
Transfixed '01
Bad Company '99

Sagamore Stevenin
Coco Chanel '08
Romance '99

Salome Stevenin (1985-)
Cold Showers '05
The Green House '96

Andrew Stevens (1955-)
Black Horizon '01
The Shooter '97
The Corporation '96
Scorned 2 '96
Subliminal Seduction '96
Body Chemistry 4: Full Exposure '95
Night Eyes 4: Fatal Passion '95
Illicit Dreams '94
The Skateboard Kid 2 '94
Body Chemistry 3: Point of Seduction '93
Eyewitness to Murder '93
Night Eyes 3 '93
Scorned '93
Deadly Rivals '92
Double Threat '92
Munchie '92
Night Eyes 2 '91
The Terror Within 2 '91
Night Eyes '90
Red Blooded American Girl '90
Down the Drain '89
Tusks '89
Deadly Innocence '88
Fine Gold '88
The Ranch '88
The Terror Within '88
Counterforce '87
Scared Stiff '87
Ten to Midnight '83
Forbidden Love '82
The Seduction '82
Death Hunt '81
Miracle on Ice '81
The Rebels '79
The Bastard '78
The Fury '78
The Boys in Company C '77
Day of the Animals '77
Secrets '77
Las Vegas Lady '76
Massacre at Central High '76

Brinke Stevens (1954-)
Demon Lust '01
Mom's Outta Sight '01
Witchouse 3: Demon Fire '01
American Nightmare '00
The Kid with the X-Ray Eyes '99
Hybrid '97
Mommy 2: Mommy's Day '96
Cyberzone '95
Jack-O '95
Masseuse '95
Mommy '95
Acting on Impulse '93
Teenage Exorcist '93
Haunting Fear '91
Bad Girls from Mars '90
Spirits '90
Phantom of the Mall: Eric's Revenge '89
Transylvania Twist '89
Grandma's House '88
Warlords '88
Nightmare Sisters '87
Slave Girls from Beyond Infinity '87
Sorority Babes in the Slimeball Bowl-A-Rama '87
Sole Survivor '84
Slumber Party Massacre '82

Charles Stevens (1893-1964)
Buffalo Bill Rides Again '47
Border Bandits '46
Overland Mail '42
The Lives of a Bengal Lancer '35
The California Trail '33
The Three Musketeers '21
Mark of Zorro '20

Connie Stevens (1938-)
James Dean: Live Fast, Die Young '97
Love Is All There Is '96
Tapeheads '89
Back to the Beach '87
Side Show '84
Scruples '80
Love's Savage Fury '79
Scorchy '76
Playmates '72
The Grissom Gang '71
The Littlest Angel '69
Never Too Late '65
Palm Springs Weekend '63
Parrish '61
Susan Slade '61
Rock-A-Bye Baby '57

Craig Stevens (1918-2000)
La Truite '83
S.O.B. '81
Secrets of Three Hungry Wives '78
Buchanan Rides Alone '58
The Deadly Mantis '57
The French Line '54
Abbott and Costello Meet Dr. Jekyll and Mr. Hyde '52
Phone Call from a Stranger '52
Drums in the Deep South '51
Blues Busters '50
Where the Sidewalk Ends '50
Humoresque '46
The Man I Love '46
God is My Co-Pilot '45
Since You Went Away '44
Dive Bomber '41

Dan Stevens (1982-)
Sense & Sensibility '07
Dracula '06
The Line of Beauty '06

Fisher Stevens (1963-)
Awake '07
Factotum '06
Kettle of Fish '06
Undiscovered '05
Undisputed '02
The Tic Code '99
Cold Fever '95
Hackers '95
The Right to Remain Silent '95
Nina Takes a Lover '94
Only You '94
Super Mario Bros. '93
Bob Roberts '92
The Marrying Man '91
Mystery Date '91
When the Party's Over '91
Reversal of Fortune '90
Short Circuit 2 '88
Short Circuit '86
My Science Project '85
The Flamingo Kid '84
The Burning '82

Inger Stevens (1934-70)
Savage Run '70
A Dream of Kings '69
Firecreek '68
Five Card Stud '68
Madigan '68
A Guide for the Married Man '67
Hang 'Em High '67
The Buccaneer '58

Joe Stevens
The Alamo '04
American Outlaws '01

K.T. Stevens (1919-94)
They're Playing with Fire '84
Missile to the Moon '59
Jungle Hell '55
Harriet Craig '50
Port of New York '49

Mark Stevens (1915-94)
The Fury of the Wolfman '70
Frozen Alive '64
Cry Vengeance '54
Torpedo Alley '53
Mutiny '52
The Snake Pit '48
The Street with No Name '48
Dark Corner '46
Objective, Burma! '45

Morgan Stevens (1951-)
Survival Zone '84
Up River '79

Onslow Stevens (1902-77)
Tribute to a Bad Man '56
Fangs of the Wild '54
Them! '54
A Lion in the Streets '53
A Lion Is in the Streets '53
One Too Many '51
Motor Patrol '50
The Creeper '48
Angel on My Shoulder '46
O.S.S. '46
House of Dracula '45
Hands Across the Border '43
The Monster and the Girl '41
Flight from Glory '37
Murder With Pictures '36
Three on the Trail '36
Yellow Dust '36
The Three Musketeers '35
Bombay Mail '34
I Can't Escape '34
Counsellor-at-Law '33

Paul Stevens (1921-86)
Get Christie Love! '74
Rage '72
Patton '70
Hercules and the Princess of Troy '65
The Mask '61
Exodus '60

Rise Stevens (1913-)
Going My Way '44
The Chocolate Soldier '41

Ronnie Stevens (1925-2002)
The Parent Trap '98
Dentist In the Chair '60

Shadoe Stevens (1947-)
The Death Artist '95
Traxx '87

Stella Stevens (1936-)
The Glass Trap '04
The Long Ride Home '01
By Dawn's Early Light '00
The Corporation '96
In Cold Blood '96
Invisible Mom '96
Subliminal Seduction '96
Body Chemistry 4: Full Exposure '95
The Nutt House '95
Star Hunter '95
Virtual Combat '95
The Granny '94
Hard Drive '94
Illicit Dreams '94
Molly and Gina '94
National Lampoon's Attack of the 5 Ft. 2 Women '94
Eye of the Stranger '93
The Terror Within 2 '91
Exiled in America '90
Last Call '90
Down the Drain '89
Mom '89
Adventures Beyond Belief '87
The Longshot '86
Monster in the Closet '86
The Amazons '84
Chained Heat '83
Power, Passion & Murder '83
Wacko '83
Twirl '81
Make Me an Offer '80
Express to Terror '79
Cruise into Terror '78
The Manitou '78
Las Vegas Lady '76
Cleopatra Jones & the Casino of Gold '75
Arnold '73
Slaughter '72
A Town Called Hell '72
Ballad of Cable Hogue '70
Where Angels Go, Trouble Follows '68
The Silencers '66
The Nutty Professor '63
The Courtship of Eddie's Father '62
Girls! Girls! Girls! '62
Li'l Abner '59

Warren Stevens (1919-)
No Name on the Bullet '59
Man or Gun '58
Forbidden Planet '56
The Barefoot Contessa '54
Shark River '53

Cynthia Stevenson (1963-)
Case 39 '10
I Love You, Beth Cooper '09
Snow Buddies '08
Full of It '07
Agent Cody Banks 2: Destination London '04
Agent Cody Banks '03
Air Bud 5: Buddy Spikes Back '03
Air Bud 4: Seventh Inning Fetch '02
Air Bud 2: Golden Receiver '98
From the Earth to the Moon '98
Happiness '98
Forget Paris '95
Home for the Holidays '95
Live Nude Girls '95
Watch It '93
The Player '92
The Reluctant Agent '89

Houseley Stevenson
The Sun Sets at Dawn '50
Kidnapped '48
Somewhere in the Night '46

Jessica Stevenson (1972-)
Son of Rambow '07
Confetti '06
Four Last Songs '06
Pinochet's Last Stand '06
Bridget Jones: The Edge of Reason '04
Shaun of the Dead '04

Juliet Stevenson (1956-)
Place of Execution '09
When Did You Last See Your Father? '07
Breaking and Entering '06
Infamous '06
Red Mercury '05
Being Julia '04
Mona Lisa Smile '03
Bend It Like Beckham '02
Food of Love '02
Nicholas Nickleby '02
The Road from Coorain '02
The Search for John Gissing '01
Cider with Rosie '99
Emma '96
The Secret Rapture '94
The Trial '93
Truly, Madly, Deeply '91
Drowning by Numbers '87

McLean Stevenson (1929-96)
Armistead Maupin's Tales of the City '93
The Cat from Outer Space '78
Win, Place, or Steal '72

Parker Stevenson (1952-)
Legion '98
Not of This Earth '96
Official Denial '93
Are You Lonesome Tonight '92
North and South Book 2 '86
Shooting Stars '85
Stitches '85
Stroker Ace '83
Lifeguard '76
Our Time '74
A Separate Peace '73

Ray Stevenson (1964-)
The Book of Eli '10
Cirque du Freak: The Vampire's Assistant '09
Punisher: War Zone '08
King Arthur '04
The Theory of Flight '98
Catherine Cookson's The Tide of Life '96
The Return of the Native '94

Robert Stevenson (1905-86)
One of Our Dinosaurs Is Missing '75
Zero Hour! '57
Fangs of the Wild '54

Tom Stevenson (1910-)
Gaslight '44
Across the Pacific '42

Venetia Stevenson (1938-)
Horror Hotel '60
The Day of the Outlaw '59
Darby's Rangers '58

Joe Stewardson
City of Blood '88
Follow That Rainbow '79
Flatfoot '78

Alexandra Stewart (1939-)
Under the Sand '00
Son of Gascogne '95
Sans Soleil '82 (N)
The Agency '81
Last Chase '81
In Praise of Older Women '78
Because of the Cats '74
The Destructors '74
Day for Night '73
Zeppelin '71
Kemek '70
Mickey One '65
The Fire Within '64
RoGoPaG '62
Exodus '60
Tarzan the Magnificent '60

Amy Stewart
Trucks '97
Another Woman '94
Mark Twain and Me '91

Athole Stewart (1879-1940)
Accused '36
The Speckled Band '31

Byron Stewart (1956-)
How U Like Me Now? '92
Grambling's White Tiger '81

Catherine Mary Stewart (1959-)
Sharpshooter '07
The Attic '06
Dead Silent '99
The Reaper '97
Number One Fan '94
Out of Annie's Past '94
Ordeal in the Arctic '93
Samurai Cowboy '93
The Sea Wolf '93
Cafe Romeo '91
Perfect Harmony '91
Psychic '91
Passion in Paradise '89
Weekend at Bernie's '89
World Gone Wild '88
Dudes '87
Murder by the Book '87
Nightflyers '87
Scenes from the Goldmine '87
Mischief '85
Sins '85
The Last Starfighter '84
Night of the Comet '84
Nighthawks '81
The Apple '80

Charlotte Stewart (1941-)
Tremors 3: Back to Perfection '01
Dark Angel: The Ascent '94
Tremors '89
Eraserhead '78

David J. Stewart
Murder, Inc. '60
Carnival Rock '57

Don Stewart (1935-2006)
Lost '83
The Doomsday Flight '66

Elaine Stewart (1929-)
The Rise and Fall of Legs Diamond '60
Night Passage '57
Meet Me in Las Vegas '56
Brigadoon '54
Riders of the Timberline '41

Eleanor Stewart (1913-2007)
Mystery Man '44
Flaming Lead '39
The Painted Trail '38
Arizona Days '37
The Rangers Step In '37
Where Trails Divide '37
Headin' for the Rio Grande '36
The Gun Ranger '34

Evelyn Stewart (1942-)
The Psychic '78
Django Shoots First '74
The Scorpion's Tail '71
Murder Mansion '70
Blood for a Silver Dollar '66

Ewan Stewart (1957-)
Conspiracy '01
American Women '00
The Big Brass Ring '99
Stella Does Tricks '96
Rob Roy '95

Frank Stewart
Cemetery High '89
Sexpot '88
Galactic Gigolo '87
Psychos in Love '87
Sensations '87

French Stewart (1964-)
Dog Gone '08
Surveillance '08
The Flock '07
Grindin' '07
Pandemic '07
Duck '05
Clockstoppers '02
Inspector Gadget 2 '02
Love Stinks '99
McHale's Navy '97
Glory Daze '96
Magic Island '95

James Stewart (1908-97)
An American Tail: Fievel Goes West '91 (V)
North and South Book 2 '86
Right of Way '84
Green Horizon '80
The Big Sleep '78
Magic of Lassie '78
Airport '77 '77

The Shootist *'76*
The Cheyenne Social Club *'70*
Bandolero! *'68*
Firecreek *'68*
The Rare Breed *'66*
Dear Brigitte *'65*
The Flight of the Phoenix *'65*
Shenandoah *'65*
Cheyenne Autumn *'64*
How the West Was Won *'63*
The Man Who Shot Liberty Valance *'62*
Mr. Hobbs Takes a Vacation *'62*
Two Rode Together *'61*
The Mountain Road *'60*
Anatomy of a Murder *'59*
The FBI Story *'59*
Bell, Book and Candle *'58*
Vertigo *'58*
Night Passage *'57*
Spirit of St. Louis *'57*
The Man Who Knew Too Much *'56*
Far Country *'55*
The Man from Laramie *'55*
Strategic Air Command *'55*
The Glenn Miller Story *'54*
Rear Window *'54*
The Naked Spur *'53*
Thunder Bay *'53*
Bend of the River *'52*
The Greatest Show on Earth *'52*
No Highway in the Sky *'51*
Broken Arrow *'50*
Harvey *'50*
The Jackpot *'50*
Winchester '73 *'50*
Malaya *'49*
The Stratton Story *'49*
Call Northside 777 *'48*
On Our Merry Way *'48*
Rope *'48*
You Gotta Stay Happy *'48*
Magic Town *'47*
It's a Wonderful Life *'46*
Pot o' Gold *'41*
Ziegfeld Girl *'41*
The Mortal Storm *'40*
The Philadelphia Story *'40*
The Shop Around the Corner *'40*
Destry Rides Again *'39*
Ice Follies of 1939 *'39*
Made for Each Other *'39*
Mr. Smith Goes to Washington *'39*
Of Human Hearts *'38*
Shopworn Angel *'38*
Vivacious Lady *'38*
You Can't Take It with You *'38*
The Last Gangster *'37*
Navy Blue and Gold *'37*
After the Thin Man *'36*
Born to Dance *'36*
The Gorgeous Hussy *'36*
Next Time We Love *'36*
Rose Marie *'36*
Wife Versus Secretary *'36*

John Stewart (1934-)
Boots Malone *'52*
Last of the Comanches *'52*

Johna Stewart (1979-)
Young Hercules *'97*
Address Unknown *'96*
Galgameth *'96*

Jon Stewart (1962-)
Death to Smoochy *'02*
Jay and Silent Bob Strike Back *'01*
Big Daddy *'99*
The Faculty *'98*
Playing by Heart *'98*
Half-Baked *'97*
Since You've Been Gone *'97*
Wishful Thinking *'96*

Josh Stewart (1977-)
The Collector *'09*
Law Abiding Citizen *'09*
Full Count *'06*

Kate McGregor Stewart
See Kate McGregor-Stewart

Kristen Stewart (1990-)
The Runaways *'10*
The Twilight Saga: Eclipse *'10*
Adventureland *'09*
The Twilight Saga: New Moon *'09*
Twilight *'08*
What Just Happened *'08*
The Yellow Handkerchief *'08*
The Cake Eaters *'07*
Into the Wild *'07*
The Messengers *'07*
In the Land of Women *'06*
Fierce People *'05*
Zathura *'05*
Catch That Kid *'04*
Speak *'04*
Cold Creek Manor *'03*
Panic Room *'02*
The Safety of Objects *'01*

Malcolm Stewart
Grace *'09*
Dr. Dolittle 4: Tail to the Chief *'08*
Deadlocked *'00*
Screwed *'00*
Fatal Error *'99*
Titanic *'96*
Timecop *'94*

Martha Stewart
Men in Black 2 *'02*
Daisy Kenyon *'47*

Mel Stewart (1928-2002)
Bride of Re-Animator *'89*
The Kid with the 200 I.Q. *'83*

Nils Allen Stewart
Undisputed *'02*
The Jesse Ventura Story *'99*

Pamela Stewart
The Reception *'05*
100 Proof *'96*
Amateur *'94*

Patrick Stewart (1940-)
The Invention of Lying *'09 (N)*
TMNT (Teenage Mutant Ninja Turtles) *'07 (V)*
Bambi II *'06 (V)*
X-Men: The Last Stand *'06*
Chicken Little *'05 (V)*
The Game of Their Lives *'05*
Steamboy *'05 (V)*
The Lion in Winter *'03*
X2: X-Men United *'03*
King of Texas *'02*
Star Trek: Nemesis *'02*
Jimmy Neutron: Boy Genius *'01 (V)*
X-Men *'00*
Animal Farm *'99 (V)*
A Christmas Carol *'99*
Safe House *'99*
Moby Dick *'98*
Prince of Egypt *'98 (V)*
Star Trek: Insurrection *'98*
Conspiracy Theory *'97*
Dad Savage *'97*
The Canterville Ghost *'96*
Masterminds *'96*
Star Trek: First Contact *'96*
Jeffrey *'95*
The Pagemaster *'94 (V)*
Star Trek: Generations *'94*
Detonator *'93*
Gunmen *'93*
L.A. Story *'91*
Code Name: Emerald *'85*
The Doctor and the Devils *'85*
Lady Jane *'85*
Lifeforce *'85*
Dune *'84*
The Plague Dogs *'82 (V)*
Smiley's People *'82*
Excalibur *'81*
Tinker, Tailor, Soldier, Spy *'80*
Hedda *'75*

Paul Stewart (1908-86)
Seduced *'85*
The Tempest *'82*
Opening Night *'77*
Bite the Bullet *'75*
Murph the Surf *'75*
How to Commit Marriage *'69*
In Cold Blood *'67*
King Creole *'58*
Top Secret Affair *'57*
The Cobweb *'55*
Kiss Me Deadly *'55*
The Joe Louis Story *'53*
Loan Shark *'52*
Walk Softly, Stranger *'50*
Champion *'49*
Easy Living *'49*
Twelve o'Clock High *'49*
Mr. Lucky *'43*
Citizen Kane *'41*

Peggy Stewart (1923-)
The Black Lash *'52*
The Fighting Redhead *'50*
Son of Zorro *'47*
Trail to San Antone *'47*
Alias Billy the Kid *'46*
The Phantom Rider *'46*
Stagecoach to Denver *'46*
Vigilantes of Boom Town *'46*
Rough Riders of Cheyenne *'45*
Silver City Kid *'45*
The Tiger Woman *'45*
The Vampire's Ghost *'45*
Girls in Chains *'43*

Penelope Stewart
Boulevard of Broken Dreams *'88*
Vigil *'84*

Rob Stewart
Demons from Her Past *'07*
Broken Lullaby *'94*

Robert Stewart (1961-)
Devour *'05*
Motel Blue *'98*
Annie O *'95*
Someone to Die For *'95*

Robin Stewart
The Legend of the 7 Golden Vampires *'73*
Masters of Venus *'62*

Roy Stewart (1883-1933)
Rustler's Roundup *'33*
Come on Tarzan *'32*
Sparrows *'26*
With Kit Carson over the Great Divide *'25*

Sara Stewart (1966-)
London Voodoo *'04*
Drop Dead Gorgeous *'99*
The Winslow Boy *'98*

Sophie Stewart (1908-77)
Devil Girl from Mars *'54*
Made in Heaven *'52*
My Son, My Son *'40*
Murder in the Old Red Barn *'36*

Tonea Stewart
The Rosa Parks Story *'02*
A Time to Kill *'96*

Trish Stewart (1946-)
Breaking Up Is Hard to Do *'79*
Wild Times *'79*

Dorothy Stickney (1900-98)
I Never Sang for My Father *'70*
Miss Tatlock's Millions *'48*
The Uninvited *'44*
Murder at the Vanities *'34*

Phyllis Stickney
The Inkwell *'94*
What's Love Got to Do with It? *'93*
Jungle Fever *'91*
Talkin' Dirty after Dark *'91*

Ethan Stiefel
Center Stage: Turn It Up *'08*
Center Stage *'00*

David Ogden Stiers (1942-)
Hoodwinked Too! Hood vs. Evil *'10 (V)*
Together Again for the First Time *'08*
Lady in the Water *'06 (N)*
Hoodwinked *'05 (V)*
Lilo & Stitch 2: Stitch Has a Glitch *'05 (V)*
Disney's Teacher's Pet *'04 (V)*
The Dead Zone *'02*
Lilo & Stitch *'02 (V)*
Atlantis: The Lost Empire *'01 (V)*
The Curse of the Jade Scorpion *'01*
The Majestic *'01*
Spirited Away *'01 (V)*
Tomcats *'01*
Krippendorf's Tribe *'98*
Meet Wally Sparks *'97*
Everyone Says I Love You *'96*
The Hunchback of Notre Dame *'96 (V)*
Jungle 2 Jungle *'96*
Mighty Aphrodite *'95*
Pocahontas *'95 (V)*
Steal Big, Steal Little *'95*
Bad Company *'94*
Past Tense *'94*
Iron Will *'93*
The Last of His Tribe *'92*
Mastergate *'92*
Shadows and Fog *'92*
Beauty and the Beast *'91 (V)*
Doc Hollywood *'91*
The Kissing Place *'90*
Day One *'89*
The Final Days *'89*
Final Notice *'89*
The Accidental Tourist *'88*
Another Woman *'88*
J. Edgar Hoover *'87*
Perry Mason: The Case of the Lost Love *'87*
The Bad Seed *'85*
Better Off Dead *'85*
Creator *'85*
The Man with One Red Shoe *'85*
North and South Book 1 *'85*
The First Olympics: Athens 1896 *'84*
Harry's War *'84*
The Innocents Abroad *'84*
M*A*S*H: Goodbye, Farewell & Amen *'83*
Damien: The Leper Priest *'80*
Oldest Living Graduate *'80*
Breaking Up Is Hard to Do *'79*
Magic *'78*
Sergeant Matlovich vs. the U.S. Air Force *'78*
Oh, God! *'77*

Hugo Stiglitz (1940-)
Naked Lies *'98*
Counterforce *'87*
City of the Walking Dead *'80*
Hostages *'80*
Fantastic Balloon Voyage *'76*
Night of a Thousand Cats *'72*
Robinson Crusoe & the Tiger *'72*

Julia Stiles (1981-)
Gospel Hill *'08*
The Bourne Ultimatum *'07*
The Omen *'06*
Edmond *'05*
A Little Trip to Heaven *'05*
The Bourne Supremacy *'04*
The Prince & Me *'04*
Carolina *'03*
A Guy Thing *'03*
Mona Lisa Smile *'03*
The Bourne Identity *'02*
The Business of Strangers *'01*
O *'01*
Save the Last Dance *'01*
Down to You *'00*
Hamlet *'00*
State and Main *'00*
The '60s *'99*
Ten Things I Hate about You *'99*
Wicked *'98*

Robin Stille (1961-96)
American Ninja 4: The Annihilation *'91*
Slumber Party Massacre *'82*

Amy Stiller (1961-)
Tropic Thunder *'08*
The Visit *'00*
Vampire's Kiss *'88*

Ben Stiller (1965-)
Greenberg *'10*
The Marc Pease Experience *'09*
Night at the Museum: Battle of the Smithsonian *'09*
Madagascar: Escape 2 Africa *'08 (V)*
Tropic Thunder *'08*
The Heartbreak Kid *'07*
Danny Roane: First Time Director *'06*
Night at the Museum *'06*
School for Scoundrels *'06*
Tenacious D in the Pick of Destiny *'06*
Madagascar *'05 (V)*
Along Came Polly *'04*
Anchorman: The Legend of Ron Burgundy *'04*
Dodgeball: A True Underdog Story *'04*
Envy *'04*
Meet the Fockers *'04*
Starsky & Hutch *'04*
Duplex *'03*
The Royal Tenenbaums *'01*
Zoolander *'01*
The Independent *'00*
Keeping the Faith *'00*
Meet the Parents *'00*
Black and White *'99*
Mystery Men *'99*
The Suburbans *'99*
Permanent Midnight *'98*
There's Something about Mary *'98*
Your Friends & Neighbors *'98*
Zero Effect *'97*
The Cable Guy *'96*
Happy Gilmore *'96*
Flirting with Disaster *'95*
If Lucy Fell *'95*
Heavyweights *'94*
Reality Bites *'94*
Next of Kin *'89*
Stella *'89*
Fresh Horses *'88*
Empire of the Sun *'87*
Hot Pursuit *'87*

Brett Stiller
The Alice *'04*
Garage Days *'03*

Jerry Stiller (1927-)
Hairspray *'07*
The Heartbreak Kid *'07*
Disney's Teacher's Pet *'04 (V)*
The Lion King 1 1/2 *'04 (V)*
Serving Sara *'02*
On the Line *'01*
Zoolander *'01*
The Independent *'00*
My 5 Wives *'00*
The Suburbans *'99*
A Rat's Tale *'98*
Secre of the Andes *'98*
The Deli *'97*
Stag *'97*
Subway Stories *'97*
Heavyweights *'94*
The Pickle *'93*
Women & Men: In Love There Are No Rules *'91*
Little Vegas *'90*
That's Adequate *'90*
Hairspray *'88*
Hot Pursuit *'87*
Nadine *'87*
Seize the Day *'86*
The McGuffin *'85*
Those Lips, Those Eyes *'80*
Nasty Habits *'77*
The Ritz *'76*
The Taking of Pelham One Two Three *'74*

Diane Stilwell
Earth Girls Are Easy *'89*
Perfect Match *'88*

Brett Stimely
Cannibal Women in the Avocado Jungle of Death *'89*
Bloodstone *'88*

Sting (1951-)
Bee Movie *'07 (V)*
Lock, Stock and 2 Smoking Barrels *'98*
Grave Indiscretions *'96*
The Adventures of Baron Munchausen *'89*
Stormy Monday *'88*
Julia and Julia *'87*
The Bride *'85*
Plenty *'85*
Dune *'84*
Brimstone & Treacle *'82*
The Secret Policeman's Other Ball *'82*
Quadrophenia *'79*

Colin Stinton (1947-)
The Bourne Ultimatum *'07*
The Winslow Boy *'98*
In Love and War *'96*

Linda Stirling (1921-97)
Jesse James Rides Again *'47*
Cyclotrode "X" *'46*
Rio Grande Raiders *'46*
D-Day on Mars *'45*
Manhunt of Mystery Island *'45*
The Purple Monster Strikes *'45*
The Topeka Terror *'45*
Perils of the Darkest Jungle *'44*
Zorro's Black Whip *'44*

Rachael Stirling (1977-)
The Haunted Airman *'06*
Freeze Frame *'04*
Bait *'02*
Tipping the Velvet *'02*
Another Life *'01*
The Triumph of Love *'01*
Maybe Baby *'99*
Retribution *'98*
Still Crazy *'98*

Brian Stirner
Poldark 2 *'75*
All Creatures Great and Small *'74*

Barbara Stock (1956-)
Verne Miller *'88*
Long Time Gone *'86*

Nigel Stock (1919-86)
The Lion in Winter *'68*
The Great Escape *'63*
Victim *'61*
The Silent Enemy *'58*
Brighton Rock *'47*

Amy Stock-Poynton (1958-)
Beanstalk *'94*
Bill & Ted's Bogus Journey *'91*
Bill & Ted's Excellent Adventure *'89*

Sara Stockbridge (1966-)
Spider *'02*
24 Hours in London *'00*

Carl Stockdale (1874-1953)
Condemned to Live *'35*
The Crimson Trail *'35*

Adventures Beyond Belief '87
Flight of Dragons '82 (V)
S.O.B. '81
Sweet 16 '81
Better Late Than Never '79
The Adventures of Huckleberry Finn '78
The Incredible Rocky Mountain Race '77
Airport '75 '75
The Woman Hunter '72
Hard Frame '70
That Funny Feeling '65
Sex and the Single Girl '64
Captain Newman, M.D. '63
40 Pounds of Trouble '62

June Storey (1918-91)

The Strange Woman '46
End of the Road '44
Dance Hall '41
Gaucho Serenade '40
First Love '39
South of the Border '39

Adam Storke (1962-)

Johnson County War '02
Rough Riders '97
National Lampoon's Attack of the 5 Ft. 2 Women '94
Stephen King's The Stand '94
Lifepod '93
Death Becomes Her '92
Highway to Hell '92
The Phantom of the Opera '90
Mystic Pizza '88

Dirk Storm

See Kevin Nealon

Gale Storm (1922-2009)

The Texas Rangers '51
The Underworld Story '50
The Dude Goes West '48
Abandoned '47
It Happened on 5th Avenue '47
Swing Parade of 1946 '46
Revenge of the Zombies '43
Rhythm Parade '43
Lure of the Islands '42
Man from Cheyenne '42
Smart Alecks '42
Let's Go Collegiate '41

James Storm (1943-)

Bone Eater '07
Firetrap '01
Ants '77
Trilogy of Terror '75
Scream of the Wolf '74
Night of Dark Shadows '71

Jim Storm

Chain Link '08
Dark Mirror '07

Lauren Storm (1987-)

I Love You, Beth Cooper '09
Together Again for the First Time '08

T.J. Storm

Doomsdayer '99
Urban Menace '99

Peter Stormare (1953-)

Horsemen '09
The Killing Room '09
Witless Protection '08
Anamorph '07
Premonition '07
Nacho Libre '06
The Brothers Grimm '05
Constantine '05
Birth '04
Bad Boys 2 '03
Hitler: The Rise of Evil '03
Bad Company '02
Minority Report '02
Spun '02
13 Moons '02
The Tuxedo '02
Windtalkers '02
Happy Campers '01
Bruiser '00
Chocolat '00
Circus '00
Dancer in the Dark '99
The Million Dollar Hotel '99
Purgatory '99
Armageddon '98
8mm '98
Mercury Rising '98
The Big Lebowski '97
The Lost World: Jurassic Park 2 '97
Somewhere in the City '97
Fargo '96
Le Polygraphe '96
Playing God '96
Damage '92
Awakenings '90

Raymond Storti

Decay '98
Amazon Warrior '97

Ludwig Stossel (1883-1973)

G.I. Blues '60
Song of Love '47
Cloak and Dagger '46
House of Dracula '45
Casablanca '42
Pittsburgh '42

Ken Stott (1955-)

Charlie Wilson's War '07
Casanova '05
The Girl in the Cafe '05
The Mighty Celt '05
King Arthur '04
I'll Sleep When I'm Dead '03
The Miracle Maker: The Story of Jesus '00 (V)
Plunkett & Macleane '98
The Boxer '97
Rhodes '97
Fever Pitch '96
Saint-Ex: The Story of the Storyteller '95
Star Hunter '95
Shallow Grave '94

George Stover

Attack of the 60-Foot Centerfold '95
Deadly Neighbor '91
Dracula's Widow '88
Hairspray '88
Fiend '83
Night Beast '83
Polyester '81
The Alien Factor '78
Desperate Living '77
Female Trouble '74

Madeleine Stowe (1958-)

Pulse '03
Avenging Angelo '02
Impostor '02
The Magnificent Ambersons '02
We Were Soldiers '02
The General's Daughter '99
Playing by Heart '98
The Proposition '97
12 Monkeys '95
Bad Girls '94
Another Stakeout '93
Blink '93
Short Cuts '93
The Last of the Mohicans '92
Unlawful Entry '92
China Moon '91
Closet Land '90
Revenge '90
The Two Jakes '90
Worth Winning '89
Tropical Snow '88
Stakeout '87
The Amazons '84
Gangster Wars '81
Nativity '78

Michael Stoyanov (1970-)

Restaurant '98
Freaked '93

Anthony Strachan

Sylvia '03
The Trench '99

Rose Stradner

The Keys of the Kingdom '44
The Last Gangster '37

Beatrice Straight (1918-2001)

Deceived '91
Robert Kennedy and His Times '90
Power '86
The Princess and the Pea '83
Two of a Kind '83
Poltergeist '82
Endless Love '81
The Formula '80
The Promise '79
Sidney Sheldon's Bloodline '79
The Dain Curse '78
Killer on Board '77
Network '76
The Nun's Story '59
Patterns '56

Julie Strain (1962-)

Blood Gnome '02
How to Make a Monster '01
Heavy Metal 2000 '00 (V)
The Rowdy Girls '00
Battle Queen 2020 '99
St. Patrick's Day '99
Lethal Seduction '97
Return to Savage Beach '97
Day of the Warrior '96
Red Line '96
Dark Secrets '95
Midnight Confessions '95
The Mosaic Project '95
Virtual Desire '95
The Dallas Connection '94
Money to Burn '94
Play Time '94
Psycho Cop 2 '94
Sorceress '94
Victim of Desire '94
Enemy Gold '93
Fit to Kill '93
Night Rhythms '92
The Unnamable 2: The Statement of Randolph Carter '92
Witchcraft 4: Virgin Heart '92
Mirror Images '91
Out for Justice '91
Psycho Cop '88

Steven Strait (1986-)

10,000 B.C. '08
The Covenant '06
Sky High '05
Undiscovered '05

Harry Strang (1983-72)

The Lone Star Trail '43
The Fighting Sullivans '42
Phantom Ranger '38

Glenn Strange (1899-1973)

Jailhouse Rock '57
The Lawless Breed '52
Comin' Round the Mountain '51
Master Minds '49
Abbott and Costello Meet Frankenstein '48
The Wistful Widow of Wagon Gap '47
House of Dracula '45
Silver City Kid '45
House of Frankenstein '44
Sonora Stagecoach '44
Action in the North Atlantic '43
The Black Raven '43
The Return of the Rangers '43
Billy the Kid Trapped '42
Boot Hill Bandits '42
The Mad Monster '42
Romance on the Range '42
Stagecoach Buckaroo '42
Sunset on the Desert '42
Arizona Cyclone '41
The Driftin' Kid '41
Fugitive Valley '41
Covered Wagon Trails '40
Across the Plains '39
Days of Jesse James '39
Law of the Pampas '39
Ghost Town Riders '38
Gun Packer '38
The Painted Trail '38
Border Vengeance '35
Border Law '31
Hard Hombre '31

Philip Strange

Behind That Curtain '29
Nevada '27

Robert Strange (1882-1952)

Far Frontier '48
Dead Men Walk '43
Arizona Cyclone '41
The Saint Strikes Back '39
Misleading Lady '32
The Cheat '31
The Smiling Lieutenant '31

Sarah Strange

Stargate: The Ark of Truth '08
.45 '06
White Noise '05

Lee Strasberg (1901-82)

The Godfather 1902-1959: The Complete Epic '81
And Justice for All '79
Going in Style '79
The Cassandra Crossing '76
The Godfather, Part 2 '74

Susan Strasberg (1938-99)

The Light in the Jungle '91
The Runnin' Kind '89
Prime Suspect '88
Delta Force '86
Mazes and Monsters '82
Sweet 16 '81
Bloody Birthday '80
In Praise of Older Women '78
The Manitou '78
Rollercoaster '77
Frankenstein '73
The Legend of Hillbilly John '73
The Sibling '72
The Brotherhood '68
Psych-Out '68
The Trip '67
Scream of Fear '61
Kapo '59
Stage Struck '57
The Cobweb '55
Picnic '55

Marcia Strassman (1948-)

Another Stakeout '93
Honey, I Blew Up the Kid '92
Mastergate '92
And You Thought Your Parents Were Weird! '91
Fast Getaway '91
Honey, I Shrunk the Kids '89
The Aviator '85
Soup for One '82
Changes '69

David Strathairn (1949-)

The Uninvited '09
The Spiderwick Chronicles '08
The Bourne Ultimatum '07
Fracture '07
My Blueberry Nights '07
Racing Daylight '07
Heavens Fall '06
The Notorious Bettie Page '06
The Sensation of Sight '06
We Are Marshall '06
Good Night, and Good Luck '05
Twisted '04
Blue Car '03
Harrison's Flowers '02
The Lathe of Heaven '02
Master Spy: The Robert Hanssen Story '02
Freedom Song '00
The Miracle Worker '00
A Good Baby '99
Limbo '99
A Map of the World '99
William Shakespeare's A Midsummer Night's Dream '99
Bad Manners '98
Simon Birch '98
With Friends Like These '98
The Climb '97
Evidence of Blood '97
In the Gloaming '97
L.A. Confidential '97
Beyond the Call '96
Mother Night '96
Home for the Holidays '95
Dolores Claiborne '94
Losing Isaiah '94
The River Wild '94
A Dangerous Woman '93
The Firm '93
Lost in Yonkers '93
Stand Off '93
Big Girls Don't Cry... They Get Even '92
Bob Roberts '92
A League of Their Own '92
Passion Fish '92
Sneakers '92
City of Hope '91
O Pioneers! '91
Son of the Morning Star '91
Without Warning: The James Brady Story '91
The Feud '90
Heat Wave '90
Judgment '90
Memphis Belle '90
Day One '89
Dominick & Eugene '88
Eight Men Out '88
Broken Vows '87
Matewan '87
At Close Range '86
The Brother from Another Planet '84
Iceman '84
Enormous Changes '83
Silkwood '83
Trumps '83
Return of the Secaucus 7 '80

Dorothy Stratten (1960-80)

They All Laughed '81
Galaxina '80
Americathon '79
Autumn Born '79

Charles Stratton

Notes from Underground '95
Munchies '87
Summer Camp Nightmare '86

John Stratton (1925-91)

Frankenstein and the Monster from Hell '74
Abandon Ship '57

Peter Strauss (1947-)

License to Wed '07
XXX: State of the Union '05
Strange Frequency 2 '01
A Father's Choice '00
Joan of Arc '99
In the Lake of the Woods '96
Keys to Tulsa '96
Nick of Time '95
The Yearling '94
Fugitive Among Us '92
Flight of Black Angel '91
The Brotherhood of the Rose '89
Peter Gunn '89
Proud Men '87
Penalty Phase '86
Spacehunter: Adventures in the Forbidden Zone '83
The Secret of NIMH '82 (V)
Masada '81
Whale for the Killing '81
Angel on My Shoulder '80
The Jericho Mile '79
The Last Tycoon '76
Rich Man, Poor Man '76
The Man Without a Country '73
Trial of the Catonsville Nine '72
Man of Legend '71
Soldier Blue '70
Hail, Hero! '69

Robert Strauss (1913-75)

The Noah '75
Family Jewels '65
Frankie and Johnny '65
That Funny Feeling '65
Girls! Girls! Girls! '62
Dondi '61
The 4D Man '59
I, Mobster '58
Attack! '56
The Bridges at Toko-Ri '55
The Man with the Golden Arm '55
The Seven Year Itch '55
The Atomic Kid '54
Here Come the Girls '53
The Redhead from Wyoming '53
Stalag 17 '53
Jumping Jacks '52
Sailor Beware '52

Meryl Streep (1949-)

Fantastic Mr. Fox '09 (V)
It's Complicated '09
Julie & Julia '09
Doubt '08
Mamma Mia! '08
Dark Matter '07
Evening '07
Lions for Lambs '07
Rendition '07
The Ant Bully '06 (V)
The Devil Wears Prada '06
A Prairie Home Companion '06
Prime '05
Lemony Snicket's A Series of Unfortunate Events '04
The Manchurian Candidate '04
Angels in America '03
Adaptation '02
The Hours '02
A. I.: Artificial Intelligence '01 (V)
Music of the Heart '99
Dancing at Lughnasa '98
One True Thing '98
First Do No Harm '97
Marvin's Room '96
Before and After '95
The Bridges of Madison County '95
The River Wild '94
The House of the Spirits '93
Death Becomes Her '92
Defending Your Life '91
Postcards from the Edge '90
She-Devil '89
A Cry in the Dark '88
Ironweed '87
Heartburn '86
Out of Africa '85
Plenty '85
Falling in Love '84
Silkwood '83
Sophie's Choice '82
Still of the Night '82
The French Lieutenant's Woman '81
Kramer vs. Kramer '79
Manhattan '79
The Seduction of Joe Tynan '79
The Deer Hunter '78
Holocaust '78
Julia '77

Elliot Street (1943-)

Melvin Purvis: G-Man '74
Harrad Experiment '73
Paper Man '71

Russell Streiner (1940-)

The Majorettes '87
Night of the Living Dead '68

Grave Indiscretions '96
Fair Game '89
Poldark 2 '75

Krystyna Stypulkowska (1939-)
Trace of Stones '66
Innocent Sorcerers '60

Emma Suarez (1964-)
Tierra '95
The Red Squirrel '93
Vacas '91
Against the Wind '90

Jeremy Suarez (1990-)
Brother Bear 2 '06 (V)
The Ladykillers '04
Brother Bear '03 (V)

Jose Suarez (1919-81)
Texas, Adios '66
Carthage in Flames '60

Tara Subkoff (1973-)
The Notorious Bettie Page '06
Anchorman: The Legend of Ron Burgundy '04
Undermind '03
Teenage Caveman '01
The Cell '00
American Pie '99
The Last Days of Disco '98
As Good As It Gets '97
Black Circle Boys '97
Lover Girl '97
All Over Me '96
Freeway '95

Michel Subor (1935-)
The Intruder '04
Beau Travail '98
Please Not Now! '61
Le Petit Soldat '60

Marla Sucharetza
Pipe Dream '02
Whore 2 '94

David Suchet (1946-)
The Bank Job '08
Flood '07
Dracula '06
Flushed Away '06 (V)
The In-Laws '03
Live from Baghdad '03
Pinocchio '02 (V)
The Way We Live Now '02
Victoria & Albert '01
RKO 281 '99
Wing Commander '99
A Perfect Murder '98
Solomon '98
Deadly Voyage '96
Executive Decision '96
Moses '96
Sunday '96
Don't Hang Up '90
To Kill a Priest '89
When the Whales Came '89
A World Apart '88
Cause Celebre '87
Harry and the Hendersons '87
The Last Innocent Man '87
Iron Eagle '86
Murrow '86
Agatha Christie's Thirteen at Dinner '85
Crime of Honor '85
The Falcon and the Snowman '85
Gulag '85

Koh1 Sudduth (1974-)
Jesse Stone: Thin Ice '09
Jesse Stone: Sea Change '07
Jesse Stone: Death in Paradise '06
Jesse Stone: Night Passage '06
Jesse Stone: Stone Cold '05
Cora Unashamed '00

Skipp (Robert L.) Sudduth (1956-)
Flawless '99
54 '98
Ronin '98

George Wallace '97
Money Train '95

Jason Sudeikis
The Bounty Hunter '10
Going the Distance '10
The Rocker '08
What Happens in Vegas '08
Meet Bill '07
Watching the Detectives '07

Lam Suet
Breaking News '04
Kung Fu Hustle '04
Tsui Hark's Vampire Hunters '02
The Mission '99

Ichiro Sugai (1907-73)
Sansho the Bailiff '54
Early Summer '51

Shun Sugata (1955-)
Marebito '04
The Last Samurai '03
Ichi the Killer '01
Pulse '01

Bunta Sugawara
The Great Yokai War '05
Distant Justice '92

Aya Sugimoto
Flower & Snake 2 '05
Flower & Snake '04

Haruko Sugimura (1905-97)
Drifting Weeds '59
Late Chrysanthemums '54
Tokyo Story '53
Early Summer '51
Late Spring '49
No Regrets for Our Youth '46

Viktor Sukhorukov (1951-)
Of Freaks and Men '98
Brother '97
Sideburns '91

Barbara Sukowa (1950-)
Thirteen Conversations About One Thing '01
Urbania '00
The Cradle Will Rock '99
The Lady in Question '99
The Third Miracle '99
Office Killer '97
Johnny Mnemonic '95
M. Butterfly '93
Zentropa '92
Voyager '91
The Sicilian '87
Rosa Luxemburg '86
Deadly Game '83
Marianne and Juliane '82
Berlin Alexanderplatz '80

Ania Suli
Stuart Bliss '98
Fun '94
Hold Me, Thrill Me, Kiss Me '93

Ali Suliman
Lemon Tree '08
The Kingdom '07
Paradise Now '05

Margaret Sullavan (1911-60)
Back Street '41
So Ends Our Night '41
The Mortal Storm '40
The Shop Around the Corner '40
The Shining Hour '38
Shopworn Angel '38
Three Comrades '38
The Moon's Our Home '36
Next Time We Love '36
The Good Fairy '35

Barry Sullivan (1912-94)
Casino '80
The Bastard '78
No Room to Run '78
Oh, God! '77
Washington Affair '77
The Human Factor '75
Take a Hard Ride '75
Earthquake '74
Hurricane '74
Kung Fu '72
Yuma '70
Night Gallery '69
Tell Them Willie Boy Is Here '69
Buckskin '68
Shark! '68
My Blood Runs Cold '65
Planet of the Vampires '65
A Gathering of Eagles '63
Another Time, Another Place '58
The Legend of the Sea Wolf '58
Forty Guns '57
Texas Lady '56
The Maverick Queen '55
Queen Bee '55
Strategic Air Command '55
Loophole '54
Jeopardy '53
The Bad and the Beautiful '52
Skirts Ahoy! '52
Cause for Alarm '51
Mr. Imperium '51
Payment on Demand '51
Three Guys Named Mike '51
A Life of Her Own '50
Nancy Goes to Rio '50
Tension '50
Any Number Can Play '49
The Great Gatsby '49
Smart Woman '48
The Gangster '47
Getting Gertie's Garter '45
The Woman of the Town '44

Billy L. Sullivan (1980-)
The Big Green '95
Little Big League '94

Brad Sullivan (1931-)
Bushwhacked '95
The Jerky Boys '95
Sister Act 2: Back in the Habit '93
Guilty by Suspicion '91
Orpheus Descending '91
The Prince of Tides '91
True Colors '91
Funny Farm '88
Cold River '81
Slap Shot '77

Camille Sullivan
Sea Beast '08
Normal '07

David Sullivan
Karma Police '08
Primer '04

Don Sullivan (1936-)
The Giant Gila Monster '59
The Rebel Set '59
Teenage Zombies '58
The Monster of Piedras Blancas '57

Elliott Sullivan (1907-74)
Vampyres '74
Action in the North Atlantic '43

Erik Per Sullivan (1991-)
Christmas With the Kranks '04
Finding Nemo '03 (V)
Unfaithful '02
Joe Dirt '01
Wendigo '01
The Cider House Rules '99
Armageddon '98

Francis L. Sullivan (1903-56)
The Prodigal '55
Behave Yourself! '52
Night and the City '50
Christopher Columbus '49
Oliver Twist '48
Caesar and Cleopatra '46
Great Expectations '46
Butler's Dilemma '43
The Day Will Dawn '42
Pimpernel Smith '42
The Secret Four '40
Action for Slander '38
Non-Stop New York '37
21 Days '37
Spy of Napoleon '36
The Mystery of Edwin Drood '35
Great Expectations '34
Power '34

Jean Sullivan (1923-2003)
Squirm '76
Uncertain Glory '44

Jenny Sullivan (1947-)
Katherine '75
The Other '72

Matthew Sullivan
Dementia '98
Max Is Missing '95

Michael Sullivan (1945-)
Great Ride '78
Greaser's Palace '72

Nicole Sullivan (1970-)
Black Dynamite '09
Meet the Robinsons '07 (V)
The Ant Bully '06 (V)
Guess Who '05
The Third Wheel '02
Bar Hopping '00

Paul Sullivan
I'll Believe You '07
Shoot the Living, Pray for the Dead '70

Sean Gregory Sullivan
RFK '02
Howling 6: The Freaks '90

Susan Sullivan (1942-)
My Best Friend's Wedding '97
Rage of Angels: The Story Continues '86
City in Fear '80
Marriage Is Alive and Well '80
The Ordeal of Dr. Mudd '80
The Dark Ride '78
Deadman's Curve '78
The Incredible Hulk '77
Midway '76

Frank Sully (1908-75)
The Tender Trap '55
Inside the Law '42

Cree Summer (1969-)
Clifford's Really Big Movie '04 (V)
Rugrats Go Wild! '03 (V)
Atlantis: The Lost Empire '01 (V)
The Rugrats Movie '98 (V)

Diane Summerfield (1949-2001)
Blackjack '78
Black Godfather '74

Eleanor Summerfield (1921-2001)
Black Glove '54
Blackout '54
Man on the Run '49

Roy Summerset
Cold Heat '90
Overkill '86

Slim Summerville (1892-1946)
I'm from Arkansas '44
Western Union '41
Jesse James '39
Rebecca of Sunnybrook Farm '38
Love Is News '37
Captain January '36
The Farmer Takes a Wife '35
Life Begins at Forty '35
All Quiet on the Western Front '30
Under Montana Skies '30
King of the Rodeo '28
The Beloved Rogue '27

Bart Sumner (1964-)
Video Violence '87
Video Violence Part 2... The Exploitation! '87

Peter Sumner (1942-)
The Chant of Jimmie Blacksmith '78
Ned Kelly '70

Donald (Don) Sumpter (1943-)
Eastern Promises '07
The Constant Gardener '05
K-19: The Widowmaker '02
Enigma '01
The Blackheath Poisonings '92
The Buddha of Suburbia '92
Rosencrantz & Guildenstern Are Dead '90
Black Panther '77
He Kills Night After Night After Night '69

Jeremy Sumpter (1989-)
The Sasquatch Gang '06
Peter Pan '03
Frailty '02
Local Boys '02

Chien Sun
Human Lanterns '82
House of Traps '81
Sword Masters: Two Champions of Shaolin '80
Heaven & Hell '78

Daolin Sun (1921-2007)
The Go-Masters '82
Crows and Sparrows '49

Honglei Sun (1970-)
Blood Brothers '07
Mongol '07
Zhou Yu's Train '02
The Road Home '01

Hideo Sunazuka
Blind Woman's Curse '70
Godzilla vs. the Sea Monster '66

Clinton Sundberg (1906-87)
The Thief and the Cobbler '96 (V)
Main Street to Broadway '53
The Belle of New York '52
As Young As You Feel '51
Annie Get Your Gun '50
Two Weeks with Love '50
In the Good Old Summertime '49
Mr. Peabody & the Mermaid '48
Undercurrent '46

Par Sundberg (1957-)
Pippi in the South Seas '70
Pippi on the Run '70
Pippi Goes on Board '69
Pippi Longstocking '69

Bjorn Sundquist (1948-)
Dead Snow '09
The Other Side of Sunday '96
Zero Degrees Kelvin '95
The Last Lieutenant '94
Shipwrecked '90
The Dive '89

Gerry Sundquist (1955-)
Don't Open Till Christmas '84
Great Expectations '81
Alexandria... Why? '78

Daniel Sunjata (1971-)
Ghosts of Girlfriends Past '09
The Bronx Is Burning '07
The Devil Wears Prada '06
Brother to Brother '04
Anne Rice's The Feast of All Saints '01

Ethan Suplee (1976-)
Art School Confidential '06
Clerks 2 '06
The Butterfly Effect '04
Without a Paddle '04
Cold Mountain '03
The First $20 Million is Always the Hardest '02
John Q '02
Blow '01
Evolution '01
Remember the Titans '00
Road Trip '00
American History X '98
Desert Blue '98
Chasing Amy '97
Mallrats '95

Helene Surgere (1928-)
Intimate Strangers '04
My Life on Ice '02

Cristina Suriani
Horror Rises from the Tomb '72
The Saga of the Draculas '72

Nicolas Surovy (1944-)
All Over the Guy '01
When Danger Follows You Home '97
The Man Who Captured Eichmann '96
Breaking Free '95
The Undercover Kid '95
12:01 '93
Forever Young '92
Anastasia: The Mystery of Anna '86
Stark '85
The Act '82

Tammin Sursok (1983-)
Spectacular '09
Aquamarine '06

Todd Susman (1947-)
Bodily Harm '95
The Invaders '95
Only the Strong '93
Beverly Hills Cop 2 '87
Star Spangled Girl '71

Kevin Sussman (1970-)
Killers '10
Insanitarium '08
Made of Honor '08
Heavy Petting '07
Little Black Book '04
Wet Hot American Summer '01

Matthew Sussman
13 Moons '02
Illuminata '98

David Sutcliffe (1969-)
Sticks and Stones '08
Towards Darkness '07
Cake '05
Happy Endings '05
Testosterone '03
Under the Tuscan Sun '03

Paul Sutera (1979-)
A Very Brady Sequel '96
The Brady Bunch Movie '95
Problem Child 2 '91

Catherine Sutherland (1974-)
The Cell '00
Turbo: A Power Rangers Movie '96

Donald Sutherland (1934-)
Astro Boy '09 (V)
Fool's Gold '08
Reign Over Me '07
Ask the Dust '06
Aurora Borealis '06
Beerfest '06
Land of the Blind '06
American Gun '05
An American Haunting '05
Fierce People '05
Human Trafficking '05

Pride and Prejudice '05
Salem's Lot '04
Cold Mountain '03
Fellini: I'm a Born Liar '03
The Italian Job '03
Path to War '02
Big Shot's Funeral '01
Final Fantasy: The Spirits Within '01 (V)
Uprising '01
The Art of War '00
Panic '00
Space Cowboys '00
Behind the Mask '99
Free Money '99
The Hunley '99
Instinct '99
Virus '98
The Assignment '97
Fallen '97
Without Limits '97
Natural Enemy '96
The Shadow Conspiracy '96
A Time to Kill '96
Citizen X '95
Hollow Point '95
Oldest Confederate Widow Tells All '95
Red Hot '95
Disclosure '94
Outbreak '94
The Puppet Masters '94
Younger & Younger '94
Benefit of the Doubt '93
Six Degrees of Separation '93
Buffy the Vampire Slayer '92
The Railway Station Man '92
Shadow of the Wolf '92
Backdraft '91
Eminent Domain '91
JFK '91
Long Road Home '91
Quicksand: No Escape '91
Dr. Bethune '90
A Dry White Season '89
Lock Up '89
Lost Angels '89
Apprentice to Murder '88
The Rosary Murders '87
The Trouble with Spies '87
The Wolf at the Door '87
Heaven Help Us '85
Revolution '85
Crackers '84
Ordeal by Innocence '84
Max Dugan Returns '83
Threshold '83
Disappearance '81
Eye of the Needle '81
Gas '81
Bear Island '80
Nothing Personal '80
Ordinary People '80
The Great Train Robbery '79
A Man, a Woman, and a Bank '79
Murder by Decree '79
Invasion of the Body Snatchers '78
National Lampoon's Animal House '78
Bethune '77
Blood Relatives '77
The Eagle Has Landed '77
Kentucky Fried Movie '77
1900 '76
The Day of the Locust '75
S*P*Y*S '74
Dan Candy's Law '73
Don't Look Now '73
Lady Ice '73
Steelyard Blues '73
Johnny Got His Gun '71
Klute '71
Little Murders '71
Alex in Wonderland '70
Kelly's Heroes '70
M*A*S*H '70
Start the Revolution without Me '70
Sebastian '68
The Dirty Dozen '67
Bedford Incident '65
Die! Die! My Darling! '65
Dr. Terror's House of Horrors '65
Castle of the Living Dead '64

Grant Sutherland
Nine Men '43
Edge of the World '37

Kiefer Sutherland (1966-)
Twelve '10 (N)
Monsters vs. Aliens '09 (V)
Mirrors '08
24 : Redemption '08
The Sentinel '06
The Wild '06 (V)
Jiminy Glick in LaLa Wood '05
River Queen '05
Taking Lives '04
Behind the Red Door '02
Phone Booth '02
Dead Heat '01
Desert Saints '01
To End All Wars '01
Beat '00
Cowboy Up '00
The Right Temptation '00
Eye of the Killer '99
Picking Up the Pieces '99
The Break Up '98
Ground Control '98
A Soldier's Sweetheart '98
Woman Wanted '98
Dark City '97
Truth or Consequences, N.M. '97
The Last Days of Frankie the Fly '96
A Time to Kill '96
An Eye for an Eye '95
Freeway '95
The Cowboy Way '94
Teresa's Tattoo '94
Last Light '93
The Three Musketeers '93
The Vanishing '93
Article 99 '92
A Few Good Men '92
Twin Peaks: Fire Walk with Me '92
The Nutcracker Prince '91 (V)
Chicago Joe & the Showgirl '90
Flatliners '90
Young Guns 2 '90
Flashback '89
1969 '89
Renegades '89
Bright Lights, Big City '88
Promised Land '88
Young Guns '88
Crazy Moon '87
The Killing Time '87
The Lost Boys '87
At Close Range '86
Brotherhood of Justice '86
Stand by Me '86
Trapped in Silence '86
Amazing Stories '85
The Bay Boy '85
Max Dugan Returns '83

Rossif Sutherland
Poor Man's Game '06
Red Doors '05

James Sutorius (1944-)
On Wings of Eagles '86
My Mother's Secret Life '84
Windy City '84
Prototype '83
A Question of Love '78

Dolores Sutton (1927-)
F. Scott Fitzgerald in Hollywood '76
Where Angels Go, Trouble Follows '68

Dudley Sutton (1933-)
Edward II '92
Orlando '92
Cry of the Penguins '71
The Devils '71
The Leather Boys '63

Frank Sutton (1923-74)
Hurricane '74
Town without Pity '61
Marty '55

Grady Sutton (1908-95)
Paradise, Hawaiian Style '66
Last of the Wild Horses '49
My Dog Shep '46
Goin' to Town '44
The More the Merrier '43
The Bashful Bachelor '42
Flying Blind '41
The Bank Dick '40
Dangerous Holiday '37
Waikiki Wedding '37
Alice Adams '35
Bachelor Bait '34
Pharmacist '32

John Sutton (1908-63)
The Bat '59
Beloved Infidel '59
Return of the Fly '59
Five Fingers '52 (N)
David and Bathsheba '51
Payment on Demand '51
The Second Woman '51
Bagdad '49
Mickey '48
Captain from Castile '47
Jane Eyre '44
Thunder Birds '42
A Yank in the R.A.F. '41
The Invisible Man Returns '40
Bulldog Drummond's Bride '39
Charlie McCarthy, Detective '39
The Tower of London '39
Arrest Bulldog Drummond '38

Kay Sutton (1915-88)
Sergeant York '41
The Saint in New York '38

Michael Sutton (1970-)
Dracula: The Dark Prince '01
Wanted '98

Paul Sutton
Shadows over Shanghai '38
The Sunset Murder Case '38
Rio Grande Ranger '37

Mena Suvari (1979-)
The Mysteries of Pittsburgh '08
Sex & Lies in Sin City: The Ted Binion Scandal '08
Brooklyn Rules '07
Stuck '07
Caffeine '06
The Dog Problem '06
Factory Girl '06
Beauty Shop '05
Domino '05
Edmond '05
Rumor Has It... '05
Standing Still '05
Trauma '04
Sonny '02
Spun '02
American Pie 2 '01
The Musketeer '01
Sugar & Spice '01
Loser '00
American Beauty '99
American Pie '99
Atomic Train '99
The Rage: Carrie 2 '99
American Virgin '98
Nowhere '96

Taro Suwa
The Machine Girl '07
Ju-On 2 '00
Uzumaki '00
Ringu 2 '99

Janet Suzman (1939-)
The Color of Magic '08
Max '02
Leon the Pig Farmer '93
Nuns on the Run '90
A Dry White Season '89
Mountbatten: The Last Viceroy '86
The Singing Detective '86
The Zany Adventures of Robin Hood '84
And the Ship Sails On '83
The Draughtsman's Contract '82
Priest of Love '81
Nijinsky '80
The House on Garibaldi Street '79
Voyage of the Damned '76
The Black Windmill '74
A Day in the Death of Joe Egg '71
Nicholas and Alexandra '71
Macbeth '70

Anne Suzuki (1987-)
Steamboy '05 (V)
Hana & Alice '04
Returner '02

Shogo Suzuki
Samurai Fiction '99
Cure '97

Semyon Svashenko (1904-69)
Earth '30
Arsenal '29
Zvenigora '28

Tore Svennberg
A Woman's Face '38
The Phantom Chariot '20

Bo Svenson (1941-)
Inglourious Basterds '09
Kill Bill Vol. 2 '04
Crackerjack 3 '00
Speed 2: Cruise Control '97
Private Obsession '94
Savage Land '94
Steel Frontier '94
Beyond the Door 3 '91
Steele's Law '91
Three Days to a Kill '91
Primal Rage '90
Tides of War '90
Andy and the Airwave Rangers '89
The Kill Reflex '89
Curse 2: The Bite '88
Deep Space '87
Delta Force Commando '87
The Dirty Dozen: The Deadly Mission '87
White Phantom: Enemy of Darkness '87
Choke Canyon '86
Delta Force '86
Heartbreak Ridge '86
The Manhunt '86
Thunder Warrior '85
Thunder Warrior 2 '85
Wizards of the Lost Kingdom '85
Deadly Impact '84
Jealousy '84
Night Warning '82
Virus '82
Gold of the Amazon Women '79
North Dallas Forty '79
Deadly Mission '78
The Inglorious Bastards '78
The Last Contract '77
Portrait of a Hitman '77
Snowbeast '77
Walking Tall: The Final Chapter '77
Special Delivery '76
The Great Waldo Pepper '75
Walking Tall: Part 2 '75
Big Mo '73
Frankenstein '73
The Bravos '72

Zdenek Sverak (1936-)
Kolya '96
The Elementary School '91

Bob Swaim (1943-)
Spies Like Us '85
La Balance '82

Dominique Swain (1980-)
Stuntmen '09
The Brooklyn Heist '08
Prairie Fever '08
Stiletto '08
The Pacific and Eddy '07
All In '06
Alpha Dog '06
Devour '05
Plain Dirty '04
The Job '03
New Best Friend '02
Pumpkin '02
Dead in the Water '01
Happy Campers '01
Tart '01
Intern '00
The Smokers '00
Girl '98
Face/Off '97
Lolita '97

Howard Swain
Night of the Scarecrow '95
Jon Jost's Frameup '93

Mack Swain (1876-1935)
The Chaplin Revue '58
The Beloved Rogue '27
Hands Up '26
The Nervous Wreck '26
The Gold Rush '25
Three Charlies and One Phoney! '18
Tillie's Punctured Romance '14

Darwyn Swalve (1946-99)
Deadly Reactor '89
Take Two '87

Hilary Swank (1974-)
Amelia '09
Birds of America '08
Freedom Writers '07
P.S. I Love You '07
The Reaping '07
The Black Dahlia '06
Million Dollar Baby '04
The Core '03
11:14 '03
Insomnia '02
The Affair of the Necklace '01
The Gift '00
Boys Don't Cry '99
Heartwood '98
Quiet Days in Hollywood '97
Kounterfeit '96
Sometimes They Come Back... Again '96
The Next Karate Kid '94
Buffy the Vampire Slayer '92

Brenda Swanson
Scanners: The Showdown '94
Secret Games 3 '94
Prototype X29A '92

Gary Swanson
Coldfire '90
The Guardian '90
Witchfire '86
TripleCross '85
Vice Squad '82

Gloria Swanson (1897-1983)
Airport '75 '75
The Love Goddesses '65
Three for Bedroom C '52
Sunset Boulevard '50
Indiscreet '31
Tonight or Never '31
Queen Kelly '29
Sadie Thompson '28
Manhandled '24
Beyond the Rocks '22
Affairs of Anatol '21
Why Change Your Wife? '20
Male and Female '19
Shifting Sands '18
Teddy at the Throttle '16

Jackie Swanson (1963-)
Oblivion '94
Lethal Weapon '87

Kristy Swanson (1969-)
Bound by Lies '05
Red Water '01
Soul Assassin '01
Zebra Lounge '01
Dude, Where's My Car? '00
Big Daddy '99
Supreme Sanction '99
Ground Control '98
Meeting Daddy '98
Lover Girl '97
Tinseltown '97
8 Heads in a Duffel Bag '96
Marshal Law '96
The Phantom '96
Getting In '94
Higher Learning '94
The Chase '93
The Program '93
Buffy the Vampire Slayer '92
Highway to Hell '92
Hot Shots! '91
Mannequin 2: On the Move '91
Diving In '90
Dream Trap '90
Flowers in the Attic '87
Deadly Friend '86
Ferris Bueller's Day Off '86
Pretty in Pink '86

Maureen Swanson (1932-)
Robbery under Arms '57
The Spanish Gardener '57
Moulin Rouge '52

Rochelle Swanson
On the Border '98
Mutual Needs '97
Deadly Outbreak '96
Cyberzone '95
Hard Bounty '94
Indecent Behavior 2 '94
Night Fire '94
Secret Games 3 '94

Nick Swardson (1976-)
You Don't Mess with the Zohan '08
Blades of Glory '07
I Now Pronounce You Chuck and Larry '07
Reno 911! Miami '07
Art School Confidential '06
The Benchwarmers '06
Click '06
Grandma's Boy '06

Rufus Swart (1959-94)
Dust Devil '93
The House of Usher '88

Don Swayze (1958-)
Prairie Fever '08
Lady Jayne Killer '03
The Prophet's Game '99
Money to Burn '94
Beach Babes from Beyond '93
Body of Influence '93
Broken Trust '93
Death Ring '93
Eye of the Stranger '93
Forced to Kill '93
Sexual Malice '93
Edge of Honor '91
Payback '90
Trapper County War '89
Driving Force '88
The Tracker '88
Death Blow '87
Shy People '87

Patrick Swayze (1952-2009)
Powder Blue '09
Christmas in Wonderland '07
The Fox and the Hound 2 '06 (V)
Frederick Forsyth's Icon '05
Keeping Mum '05
Dirty Dancing: Havana Nights '04
George and the Dragon '04
11:14 '03
Waking Up in Reno '02
Donnie Darko '01
Green Dragon '01
Along for the Ride '00
Black Dog '98
Letters from a Killer '98
Tall Tale: The Unbelievable Adventures of Pecos Bill '95
Three Wishes '95

To Wong Foo, Thanks for Everything, Julie Newmar *'95*
Father Hood *'93*
City of Joy *'92*
Point Break *'91*
Ghost *'90*
Next of Kin *'89*
Road House *'89*
Dirty Dancing *'87*
Steel Dawn *'87*
Tiger Warsaw *'87*
North and South Book 2 *'86*
Youngblood *'86*
North and South Book 1 *'85*
Grandview U.S.A. *'84*
Red Dawn *'84*
The Outsiders *'83*
Uncommon Valor *'83*
Return of the Rebels *'81*

Heidi Swedberg (1964-)
75 Degrees *'00*
The Ticket *'97*
Father and Scout *'94*
Hot Shots! *'91*

Bob Sweeney (1918-92)
Toby Tyler *'59*
A Christmas Carol *'54*
South Sea Woman *'53*

D.B. Sweeney (1961-)
Miracle at St. Anna *'08*
Stiletto *'08*
Entry Level *'07*
Two Tickets to Paradise *'06*
Yellow *'06*
Speak *'04*
Brother Bear *'03 (V)*
SuperFire *'02*
Greenmail *'01*
Hardball *'01*
Dinosaur *'00 (V)*
The Weekend *'00*
The Book of Stars *'99*
Introducing Dorothy Dandridge *'99*
Spawn *'97*
Roommates *'95*
Fire in the Sky *'93*
Hear No Evil *'93*
The Cutting Edge *'92*
A Day in October *'92*
Miss Rose White *'92*
Blue Desert *'91*
Heaven Is a Playground *'91*
Leather Jackets *'90*
Memphis Belle *'90*
Lonesome Dove *'89*
Sons *'89*
Eight Men Out *'88*
Gardens of Stone *'87*
No Man's Land *'87*
Fire with Fire *'86*

Dominic Sweeney
In Too Deep *'90*
Jigsaw *'90*

Garry Sweeney
The Acid House *'98*
Small Faces *'95*

Joseph Sweeney (1884-1963)
Twelve Angry Men *'57*
The Man in the Gray Flannel Suit *'56*

Julia Sweeney (1961-)
Don't Come Knocking *'05*
Clockstoppers *'02*
Beethoven's 4th *'01*
Beethoven's 3rd *'00*
Whatever It Takes *'00*
God Said "Ha!" *'99*
Stuart Little *'99*
Thick as Thieves *'99*
Vegas Vacation *'96*
It's Pat: The Movie *'94*
Pulp Fiction *'94*
Stuart Saves His Family *'94*
Coneheads *'93*
Honey, I Blew Up the Kid *'92*

Steve Sweeney
Beautiful People *'99*
Lock, Stock and 2 Smoking Barrels *'98*

Nil by Mouth *'96*

Blanche Sweet (1895-1986)
Show Girl in Hollywood *'30*
The Silver Horde *'30*
Anna Christie *'23*
Avenging Conscience *'14*
Home Sweet Home *'14*
Judith of Bethulia *'14*

Dolph Sweet (1920-85)
Acorn People *'82*
Jacqueline Bouvier Kennedy *'81*
Reds *'81*
Wanderers *'79*
Deathmoon *'78*
Go Tell the Spartans *'78*
The Bad News Bears in Breaking Training *'77*
Amazing Grace *'74*
The Migrants *'74*
Cops and Robbers *'73*
Sisters *'73*
The Lost Man *'69*
Finian's Rainbow *'68*

Gary Sweet (1957-)
Macbeth *'06*
What the Moon Saw *'90*
Fever *'88*
The Lighthorsemen *'87*
An Indecent Obsession *'85*
Stage Fright *'83*

Vonte Sweet
Restaurant *'98*
American Strays *'96*
Marshal Law *'96*
The Walking Dead *'94*
Laurel Avenue *'93*
Menace II Society *'93*

Rod Sweitzer
The Malibu Beach Vampires *'91*
The Invisible Maniac *'90*
Psycho Cop *'88*

Inga Swenson (1932-)
Nutcracker: Money, Madness & Murder *'87*
North and South Book 1 *'85*
Earth II *'71*
The Miracle Worker *'62*

Jeep Swenson (1957-97)
Batman and Robin *'97*
Bulletproof *'96*

Karl Swenson (1908-78)
Brighty of the Grand Canyon *'67*
Seconds *'66*
The Sword in the Stone *'63 (V)*
Lonely Are the Brave *'62*
Judgment at Nuremberg *'61*
Flaming Star *'60*
The Gallant Hours *'60*
The Hanging Tree *'59*
No Name on the Bullet *'59*

Tommy Swerdlow (1962-)
Child's Play *'88*
Hamburger Hill *'87*
Howard the Duck *'86*
Real Genius *'85*

William Swetland (1913-2003)
Mirrors *'78*
The Seagull *'75*

Joel Swetow
Lord of Illusions *'95*
Sex, Love and Cold Hard Cash *'93*

Josef Swickard (1866-1940)
Custer's Last Stand *'36*
The Lone Defender *'32*
Old San Francisco *'27*
The Night Patrol *'26*
The Wizard of Oz *'25*
Dante's Inferno *'24*

The Four Horsemen of the Apocalypse *'21*

Clive Swift (1936-)
The Aristocrats *'99*
Pack of Lies *'87*
Frenzy *'72*
Raw Meat *'72*

David Swift (1919-2001)
No Sex Please—We're British *'73*
Good Neighbor Sam *'64*

Francie Swift
The Great Gatsby *'01*
Fall *'97*
Last Breath *'96*

Jeremy Swift
Fred Claus *'07*
Oliver Twist *'05*
Gosford Park *'01*
Vanity Fair *'99*

Paul Swift (1934-94)
Female Trouble *'74*
Pink Flamingos *'72*
Multiple Maniacs *'70*

Nora Swinburne (1902-2000)
Strange Awakening *'58*
Helen of Troy *'56*
Betrayed *'54*
Quo Vadis *'51*
The River *'51*
Man of Evil *'48*

Tilda Swinton (1961-)
The Limits of Control *'09*
Burn After Reading *'08*
The Chronicles of Narnia: Prince Caspian *'08*
The Curious Case of Benjamin Button *'08*
Julia *'08*
Michael Clayton *'07*
Stephanie Daley *'06*
Broken Flowers *'05*
The Chronicles of Narnia: The Lion, the Witch and the Wardrobe *'05*
Constantine *'05*
Thumbsucker *'05*
The Statement *'03*
Young Adam *'03*
Adaptation *'02*
The Deep End *'01*
Vanilla Sky *'01*
The Beach *'00*
Love Is the Devil *'98*
The War Zone *'98*
Conceiving Ada *'97*
Female Perversions *'96*
Blue *'93 (N)*
Wittgenstein *'93*
Edward II *'92*
Orlando *'92*
The Garden *'90*
The Last of England *'87*
Caravaggio *'86*

Amanda Swisten (1978-)
The Girl Next Door *'04*
American Wedding *'03*

Loretta Swit (1937-)
Miracle at Moreaux *'86*
Beer *'85*
The Execution *'85*
First Affair *'83*
M*A*S*H: Goodbye, Farewell & Amen *'83*
S.O.B. *'81*
Race with the Devil *'75*
Freebie & the Bean *'74*

Bill Switzer
Mail to the Chief *'00*
Mr. Rice's Secret *'00*

Carl "Alfalfa" Switzer (1926-59)
Motorcycle Gang *'57*
Between Heaven and Hell *'56*
The High and the Mighty *'54*
Island in the Sky *'53*

Pat and Mike *'52*
Cause for Alarm *'51*
Redwood Forest Trail *'50*
Underworld Scandal *'47*
It's a Wonderful Life *'46*
The Great Mike *'44*
Reg'lar Fellers *'41*
General Spanky *'36*

Ken Swofford (1932-)
Disney's Teacher's Pet *'04 (V)*
The Taking of Beverly Hills *'91*
Black Roses *'88*
All God's Children *'80*
Sky Hei$t *'75*
Bless the Beasts and Children *'71*

Topo Swope (1948-)
My Old Man's Place *'71*
The Hot Rock *'70*

Tracy Brooks Swope (1952-)
Counter Measures *'99*
White Wolves 3: Cry of the White Wolf *'98*
Inner Sanctum 2 *'94*
The Power of One *'92*
The Big Picture *'89*

Souleymane Sy Savane
Behind the Wall *'08*
Goodbye Solo *'08*

Meera Syal (1961-)
Jekyll *'07*
Forgive and Forget *'99*
Sammy & Rosie Get Laid *'87*

Sabrina Syan
See Sabrina Siani

Basil Sydney (1894-1968)
The Hands of Orlac *'60*
The Devil's Disciple *'59*
John Paul Jones *'59*
The Three Worlds of Gulliver *'59*
Sea Wife *'57*
Dam Busters *'55*
Salome *'53*
Angel with the Trumpet *'50*
Treasure Island *'50*
Hamlet *'48*
The Secret Four *'40*
Accused *'36*
Rhodes *'36*

Robin Sydney
Wicked Lake *'08*
Masters of Horror: Right to Die *'07*

Brenda Sykes (1949-)
Mandingo *'75*
Cleopatra Jones *'73*
Black Gunn *'72*
Honky *'71*

Eric Sykes (1923-)
The Others *'01*
Those Daring Young Men in Their Jaunty Jalopies *'69*
Heavens Above *'63*
Very Important Person *'61*

Wanda Sykes (1964-)
Evan Almighty *'07*
Barnyard *'06 (V)*
Brother Bear 2 *'06 (V)*
Clerks 2 *'06*
My Super Ex-Girlfriend *'06*
Over the Hedge *'06 (V)*
Monster-in-Law *'05*
Pootie Tang *'01*

Harold Sylvester (1949-)
Missing Brendan *'03*
Trippin' *'99*
The Sixth Man *'97*
In the Deep Woods *'91*
In the Line of Duty: A Cop for the Killing *'90*
The Reluctant Agent *'89*

Innerspace *'87*
Vision Quest *'85*
Uncommon Valor *'83*
Fast Break *'79*

William Sylvester (1923-95)
2001: A Space Odyssey *'68*
Beast of Morocco *'66*
Devil Doll *'64*
Gorgo *'61*
Postmark for Danger *'56*
Unholy Four *'54*

Kari Sylway (1940-)
Face to Face *'76*
Cries and Whispers *'72*

Peter Symonds
Sharpe's Challenge *'06*
Lawless Heart *'01*

Robert Symonds (1926-2007)
Mandroid *'93*
Rumpelstiltskin *'86*
Ice Pirates *'84*

Sylvia Syms (1934-)
I'll Sleep When I'm Dead *'03*
What a Girl Wants *'03*
Catherine Cookson's The Glass Virgin *'95*
Shining Through *'92*
A Chorus of Disapproval *'89*
Shirley Valentine *'89*
Intimate Contact *'87*
Murders at Lynch Cross *'85*
The Tamarind Seed *'74*
Asylum *'72*
Desperados *'69*
Fiction Makers *'67*
The Quare Fellow *'62*
Victim *'61*
Conspiracy of Hearts *'60*
The World of Suzie Wong *'60*
Expresso Bongo *'59*
Ferry to Hong Kong *'59*
Teenage Bad Girl *'59*
Bachelor of Hearts *'58*
The Moonraker *'58*

Del Synnott
Othello *'01*
Princess of Thieves *'01*

Clancy Syrko
Black Bikers from Hell *'70*
The Outlaw Bikers—Gang Wars *'70*

Laszlo Szabo (1936-)
Esther Kahn *'00*
The Unbearable Lightness of Being *'88*
Passion *'82*
The Last Metro *'80*
Bad Guys *'79*
Nice Neighbor *'79*
Adoption *'75*
Alphaville *'65*
Le Petit Soldat *'60*

Pawel Szajda (1982-)
Generation Kill *'08*
Venom *'05*
Under the Tuscan Sun *'03*

Grazyna Szapolowska (1953-)
Flowers of Reverie *'84*
No End *'84*
Another Way *'82*

Keith Szarabajka (1952-)
We Were Soldiers *'02*
Andre *'94*
A Perfect World *'93*
Stephen King's Golden Years *'91*
Unnatural Pursuits *'91*
Nightlife *'90*
The Misfit Brigade *'87*
Billy Galvin *'86*
Wanted: The Perfect Guy *'86*
Marie *'85*
Protocol *'84*

Adam Szirtes
The Girl *'68*
Cold Days *'66*

Stephanie Szostak
Dinner for Schmucks *'10*
Motherhood *'09*

Magda Szubanski (1961-)
Happy Feet *'06 (V)*
The Crocodile Hunter: Collision Course *'02*
Babe: Pig in the City *'98*
Babe *'95*

Oleg Tabakov (1935-)
Taking Sides *'01*
Oblomov *'81*
An Unfinished Piece for a Player Piano *'77*

Jasmin Tabatabai (1967-)
Unveiled *'05*
Bandits *'99*

Kristopher Tabori (1952-)
Last Summer In the Hamptons *'96*
Marilyn & Bobby: Her Final Affair *'94*
Girlfriends *'78*
The Glass House *'72*
Journey Through Rosebud *'72*

Jorma Taccone (1977-)
Land of the Lost *'09*
Hot Rod *'07*

Hiroshi Tachikawa
Attack of the Mushroom People *'63*
Matango *'63*
Yojimbo *'61*

Ljuba Tadic
Black and White As Day and Night *'78*
Ward Six *'78*
Siberian Lady Macbeth *'61*

Yutaka Tadokoro
Lost in Translation *'03*
Tokyo Pop *'88*

Sydney Tafler (1916-79)
The Adventurers *'70*
Alfie *'66*
Sink the Bismarck *'60*
Carve Her Name with Pride *'58*
Fire Maidens from Outer Space *'56*
The Way Out *'56*
Uneasy Terms *'48*
It Always Rains on Sunday *'47*

Cary-Hiroyuki Tagawa (1950-)
Hachiko: A Dog's Tale *'09*
Elektra *'05*
Memoirs of a Geisha *'05*
Planet of the Apes *'01*
The Art of War *'00*
Bridge of Dragons *'99*
Tom Clancy's Netforce *'98*
Double Edge *'97*
John Carpenter's Vampires *'97*
Top of the World *'97*
The Phantom *'96*
Provocateur *'96*
Danger Zone *'95*
Mortal Kombat 1: The Movie *'95*
Soldier Boyz *'95*
White Tiger *'95*
Natural Causes *'94*
Picture Bride *'94*
Nemesis *'93*
Rising Sun *'93*
American Me *'92*
Showdown in Little Tokyo *'91*
The Last Warrior *'89*

A House in the Hills '93
Article 99 '92
Crossing the Bridge '92
Scott Turow's The Burden of Proof '92
City Slickers '91
Life Stinks '91
Pastime '91
Lisa '90
A Perfect Little Murder '90
Three o'Clock High '87
Brenda Starr '86
Desert Hearts '86
The Man Who Wasn't There '83
Mr. Mom '83
Sadat '83
Take Your Best Shot '82
Awakening of Candra '81
A Gun in the House '81
Saturday the 14th '81
And Justice for All '79

Jenny Tamburi (1952-2006)
Bloody Avenger '80
Women in Cell Block 7 '77

Zoe Tamerlis (1962-99)
Exquisite Corpses '88
Special Effects '85
Ms. 45 '81

Akim Tamiroff (1899-1972)
Don Quixote '92
Deadly Sanctuary '68
Then Came Bronson '68
Vulture '67
Hotel Paradiso '66
Lt. Robin Crusoe, U.S.N. '66
Alphaville '65
Lord Jim '65
Topkapi '64
The Bacchantes '63
The Trial '63
Panic Button '62
Ocean's 11 '60
Me and the Colonel '58
Touch of Evil '58
Anastasia '56
Battle Hell '56
The Black Sleep '56
Mr. Arkadin '55
Black Magic '49
Outpost in Morocco '49
My Girl Tisa '48
The Gangster '47
A Scandal in Paris '46
Can't Help Singing '45
The Bridge of San Luis Rey '44
Dragon Seed '44
His Butler's Sister '44
Miracle of Morgan's Creek '44
Five Graves to Cairo '43
For Whom the Bell Tolls '43
The Corsican Brothers '42
Tortilla Flat '42
The Great McGinty '40
The Texas Rangers Ride Again '40
Union Pacific '39
Spawn of the North '38
Desire '36
The General Died at Dawn '36
The Story of Louis Pasteur '36
China Seas '35
The Last Outpost '35
The Lives of a Bengal Lancer '35
The Merry Widow '34

Mary Tamm (1950-)
The Assassination Run '84
The Odessa File '74
Tales That Witness Madness '73

Takahiro Tamura (1928-2006)
The Silk Road '92
Forest of Little Bear '87
The Empire of Passion '76
Tora! Tora! Tora! '70

Haruo Tanaka
The Pornographers '66
Snow Country '57

Ken Tanaka (1951-)
Godzilla 1985 '85
Phoenix '78

Kinuyo Tanaka (1910-77)
Sandakan No. 8 '74
Equinox Flower '58
Sansho the Bailiff '54
Ugetsu '53
Life of Oharu '52
Mother '52
Utamaro and His Five Women '46

Miki Tanaka
Kibakichi '04
Kibakichi 2 '04

Min Tanaka (1945-)
The Hidden Blade '04
The Twilight Samurai '02

Sara Tanaka (1978-)
Rushmore '98
Race the Sun '96

Toru Tanaka (1930-2000)
3 Ninjas '92
Tax Season '90
The Running Man '87

Yoji Tanaka
Pistol Opera '02
Ringu 0 '01
Charisma '99
Shark Skin Man and Peach Hip Girl '98

Yoshiko Tanaka (1956-)
Ringu 0 '01
Godzilla vs. Biollante '89
Black Rain '88

Jessica Tandy (1909-94)
Camilla '94
Nobody's Fool '94
The Story Lady '93
To Dance with the White Dog '93
Used People '92
Fried Green Tomatoes '91
Driving Miss Daisy '89
Cocoon: The Return '88
The House on Carroll Street '88
*batteries not included '87
Foxfire '87
Cocoon '85
The Bostonians '84
Gin Game '84
Best Friends '82
Still of the Night '82
The World According to Garp '82
The Birds '63
The Light in the Forest '58
The Desert Fox '51
September Affair '50
Forever Amber '47
The Valley of Decision '45
The Seventh Cross '44

Mark Tandy (1957-)
The Buccaneers '95
The Railway Station Man '92
Maurice '87

Naomi Tani
Flower & Snake '74 '74
Madame O '67

Yoko Tani (1932-99)
Koroshi '67
Invasion '65
Samson and the 7 Miracles of the World '62
First Spaceship on Venus '60

Shosuke Tanihara
The Sky Crawlers '08
Fudoh: The New Generation '96

William Tannen (1911-76)
Jupiter's Darling '55
Roaring City '51
Riders of the Range '50
Mysterious Desperado '49
Whistling in the Dark '41

Antwon Tanner (1975-)
Coach Carter '05
Ganked '05
Never Die Alone '04
Sunset Park '96

Gordon Tanner (1918-83)
Hybrid '07
Something Beneath '07
Dr. Strangelove, or: How I Learned to Stop Worrying and Love the Bomb '64
Time Lock '57

Warhawk Tanzania
Black Force '75
Gang Wars '75

Guo Tao
So Close to Paradise '98
To Live '94

Colin Tapley
The Last Outpost '35
The Lives of a Bengal Lancer '35

Zoe Tapper
Affinity '08
A Harlot's Progress '06
These Foolish Things '06
Mrs. Palfrey at the Claremont '05
Stage Beauty '04

Amanda Tapping (1965-)
The Void '01
Terror Train '80

Brian Tarantina (1959-)
City by the Sea '02
Personal Velocity: Three Portraits '02

Quentin Tarantino (1963-)
Sukiyaki Western Django '08
Death Proof '07
Planet Terror '07
The Muppets' Wizard of Oz '05
Little Nicky '00
Kisses in the Dark '97
Girl 6 '96
Desperado '95
Destiny Turns on the Radio '95
Four Rooms '95
From Dusk Till Dawn '95
Pulp Fiction '94
Sleep with Me '94
Somebody to Love '94
Eddie Presley '92
Reservoir Dogs '92

Andrew Tarbet (1971-)
Between Strangers '02
Terminal Invasion '02
Cafe Ole '00

Mikhail Tarkanov
Peter the First: Part 2 '38
Peter the First: Part 1 '37

Rockne Tarkington (1932-)
Zebra Force '76
Trained to Kill, U.S.A. '75
Black Starlet '74
Clarence, the Cross-eyed Lion '65

Lilyan Tashman (1899-1934)
Riptide '34
Scarlet Dawn '32
Millie '31
Bulldog Drummond '29
So This Is Paris '26
Manhandled '24

Coralina Cataldi Tassoni
See Coralina Cataldi-Tassoni

Jun Tatara
The Human Condition: Road to Eternity '59
Seven Samurai '54

Catherine Tate (1968-)
Love and Other Disasters '06
Scenes of a Sexual Nature '06
Starter for Ten '06

Lahmard Tate (1970-)
Rocky Balboa '06
Back in the Day '05
Barbershop '02
Sabretooth '01
Don't Be a Menace to South Central While Drinking Your Juice in the Hood '95

Larenz Tate (1975-)
Waist Deep '06
Crash '05
Ray '04
Biker Boyz '03
A Man Apart '03
Love Come Down '00
Why Do Fools Fall in Love? '98
The Postman '97
Love Jones '96
Dead Presidents '95
The Inkwell '94
Menace II Society '93

Laura Tate
Dead Space '90
Subspecies '90

Nick (Nicholas) Tate (1942-)
The Junction Boys '02
A Cry in the Dark '88
Space: 1999—Alien Attack '79
The Devil's Playground '76
Destination Moonbase Alpha '75

Reginald Tate (1896-1955)
The King's Rhapsody '55
Immortal Battalion '44

Sharon Tate (1943-69)
12 Plus 1 '70
Ciao Federico! Fellini Directs Satyricon '69
The Wrecking Crew '68
The Fearless Vampire Killers '67
Valley of the Dolls '67

Jacques Tati (1908-82)
Parade '74
Traffic '71
Playtime '67
Mon Oncle '58
Mr. Hulot's Holiday '53
Jour de Fete '48
Sylvia and the Phantom '45

Bradford Tatum (1965-)
Standing on Fishes '99
Not in This Town '97
Pronto '97
Down Periscope '96
Within the Rock '96
Powder '95
Cool and the Crazy '94

Channing Tatum (1980-)
Dear John '10
Fighting '09
G.I. Joe: The Rise of Cobra '09
Public Enemies '09
Step Up 2 the Streets '08
Stop-Loss '08
Battle in Seattle '07
A Guide to Recognizing Your Saints '06
She's the Man '06
Step Up '06
Coach Carter '05
Supercross: The Movie '05

Sven-Bertil Taube (1934-)
The Girl With the Dragon Tattoo '09
London Voodoo '04
Jerusalem '96
Codename Kyril '91
Puppet on a Chain '72
The Buttercup Chain '70
Vibration '68

Audrey Tautou (1978-)
Coco Before Chanel '09
The Da Vinci Code '06
Priceless '06
Russian Dolls '05
A Very Long Engagement '04
Dirty Pretty Things '03
He Loves Me ... He Loves Me Not '02
L'Auberge Espagnole '02
Amelie '01
Happenstance '00
Venus Beauty Institute '98

Jay Tavare
Pathfinder '07
The Missing '03
Adaptation '02

Dino Tavarone (1942-)
Cafe Ole '00
2 Seconds '98

Nils (Niels) Tavernier (1965-)
After Sex '97
Revenge of the Musketeers '94
Mina Tannenbaum '93
L.627 '92
Beatrice '88
The Story of Women '88

Doron Tavory
Lemon Tree '08
Hide and Seek '80

Arthur Taxier
Home Room '02
Donnie Darko '01
Open Fire '94

Vic Tayback (1930-90)
The Horseplayer '91
All Dogs Go to Heaven '89 *(V)*
Beverly Hills Bodysnatchers '89
Criminal Act '88
The Underachievers '88
Weekend Warriors '86
Mysterious Two '82
Tut & Tuttle '81
Great American Traffic Jam '80
The Night the City Screamed '80
Rage '80
Portrait of a Stripper '79
The Cheap Detective '78
The Choirboys '77
The Big Bus '76
Special Delivery '76
Lepke '75
Alice Doesn't Live Here Anymore '74
Emperor of the North Pole '73
They Call It Murder '71
Murderer's Keep '70
With Six You Get Eggroll '68
Dead Heat on a Merry-Go-Round '66
Door to Door Maniac '61

Al Taylor
Ghost Valley '32
Quick Trigger Lee '31

Benedict Taylor (1960-)
Charles & Diana: A Palace Divided '93
Duel of Hearts '92
A Perfect Spy '88
Every Time We Say Goodbye '86
The Black Arrow '84
The Far Pavilions '84

Buck Taylor (1938-)
The Wendell Baker Story '05
Jericho '01
Tombstone '93
Conagher '91
Gunsmoke: Return to Dodge '87
Pony Express Rider '76
And Now Miguel '66

Christine Taylor (1971-)
Tropic Thunder '08
Dedication '07
License to Wed '07
Dodgeball: A True Underdog Story '04
Zoolander '01
Kiss Toledo Goodbye '00
Campfire Tales '98
Something About Sex '98
The Wedding Singer '97
The Craft '96
Overnight Delivery '96
A Very Brady Sequel '96
The Brady Bunch Movie '95
Breaking Free '95
Night of the Demons 2 '94

Courtney Taylor
Cover Me '95
Tracks of a Killer '95
Prom Night 3: The Last Kiss '89

Delores Taylor (1939-)
The Trial of Billy Jack '74
Billy Jack '71

Don Taylor (1920-98)
Men of Sherwood Forest '57
I'll Cry Tomorrow '55
Stalag 17 '53
Father's Little Dividend '51
Flying Leathernecks '51
Father of the Bride '50
Battleground '49
For the Love of Mary '48
The Naked City '48
Song of the Thin Man '47

Dub Taylor (1908-94)
Maverick '94
Falling from Grace '92
Conagher '91
My Heroes Have Always Been Cowboys '91
Back to the Future, Part 3 '90
Texas Guns '90
Soggy Bottom U.S.A. '84
1941 '79
Moonshine County Express '77
Creature from Black Lake '76
Gator '76
Great Smokey Roadblock '76
Pony Express Rider '76
Flash & Firecat '75
On the Run '73
Poor Pretty Eddie '73
This Is a Hijack '73
The Getaway '72
Support Your Local Gunfighter '71
A Man Called Horse '70
Death of a Gunfighter '69
The Wild Bunch '69
The Shakiest Gun in the West '68
Bonnie & Clyde '67
Spencer's Mountain '63
Parrish '61
Them! '54
Riding High '50
Brand of Fear '49
Range Renegades '48
You Can't Take It with You '38

Elayne J. Taylor
Rules of Engagement '00
The Wood '99

Elizabeth Taylor (1932-)
These Old Broads *'01*
The Flintstones *'94*
Sweet Bird of Youth *'89*
Poker Alice *'87*
The Rumor Mill *'86*
North and South Book 1 *'85*
Between Friends *'83*
The Mirror Crack'd *'80*
Winter Kills *'79*
Return Engagement *'78*
A Little Night Music *'77*
Victory at Entebbe *'76*
Ash Wednesday *'73*
Driver's Seat *'73*
Under Milk Wood *'73*
Divorce His, Divorce Hers *'72*
Hammersmith Is Out *'72*
Night Watch *'72*
X, Y & Zee *'72*
Secret Ceremony *'69*
Boom! *'68*
Doctor Faustus *'68*
The Comedians *'67*
Reflections in a Golden Eye *'67*
The Taming of the Shrew *'67*
Who's Afraid of Virginia Woolf? *'66*
The Love Goddesses *'65*
The Sandpiper *'65*
Cleopatra *'63*
The V.I.P.'s *'63*
Butterfield 8 *'60*
Suddenly, Last Summer *'59*
Cat on a Hot Tin Roof *'58*
Raintree County *'57*
Giant *'56*
Beau Brummel *'54*
Elephant Walk *'54*
The Last Time I Saw Paris *'54*
Rhapsody *'54*
The Girl Who Had Everything *'53*
Ivanhoe *'52*
Love Is Better Than Ever *'52*
Father's Little Dividend *'51*
A Place in the Sun *'51*
Quo Vadis *'51*
The Big Hangover *'50*
Father of the Bride *'50*
Conspirator *'49*
Little Women *'49*
A Date with Judy *'48*
Julia Misbehaves *'48*
Cynthia *'47*
Life with Father *'47*
Courage of Lassie *'46*
Jane Eyre *'44*
National Velvet *'44*
The White Cliffs of Dover *'44*
Lassie, Come Home *'43*

Estelle Taylor (1899-1958)
The Southerner *'45*
Cimarron *'31*
Street Scene *'31*
Where East Is East *'29*
Don Juan *'26*
Monte Cristo *'22*

Forrest Taylor (1883-1965)
Iron Mountain Trail *'53*
Border Saddlemates *'52*
Colorado Serenade *'46*
Driftin' River *'46*
Mystery Man *'44*
Shake Hands with Murder *'44*
Land of Hunted Men *'43*
Rangers Take Over *'42*
Sons of the Pioneers *'42*
Trail Riders *'42*
Trigger Men *'41*
Arizona Gangbusters *'40*
The Durango Kid *'40*
Chip of the Flying U *'39*
Outlaw's Paradise *'39*
Texas Wildcats *'39*
Ghost Town Riders *'38*
Lightnin' Carson Rides Again *'38*
The Phantom of the Range *'38*
The Red Rope *'37*
The Roamin' Cowboy *'37*
Tex Rides with the Boy Scouts *'37*
A Face in the Fog *'36*
Kelly of the Secret Service *'36*
Prison Shadows *'36*
West of Nevada *'36*
Trail of Terror *'35*
Riders of Destiny *'33*

Frank Hoyt Taylor
Junebug *'05*
A Lesson Before Dying *'99*
Matewan *'87*

Grant Taylor (1917-71)
Long John Silver *'54*
His Majesty O'Keefe *'53*
The Fighting Rats of Tobruk *'44*
Forty Thousand Horsemen *'41*

Grigor Taylor
Innocent Prey *'88*
La Notte *'60*

Holland Taylor (1943-)
Baby Mama *'08*
The Wedding Date *'05*
D.E.B.S. *'04*
Spy Kids 3-D: Game Over *'03*
Home Room *'02*
Spy Kids 2: The Island of Lost Dreams *'02*
The Day Reagan Was Shot *'01*
Legally Blonde *'01*
Happy Accidents *'00*
Keeping the Faith *'00*
Mail to the Chief *'00*
Next Stop, Wonderland *'98*
The Truman Show *'98*
Betty *'97*
George of the Jungle *'97*
Just Write *'97*
Last Summer In the Hamptons *'96*
One Fine Day *'96*
Steal Big, Steal Little *'95*
To Die For *'95*
Cop and a Half *'93*
The Favor *'92*
Alice *'90*
She's Having a Baby *'88*
The Jewel of the Nile *'85*

Jack Taylor (1936-)
The Ninth Gate *'99*
Panther Squad *'84*
Icebox Murders *'82*
Where Time Began *'77*
Horror of the Zombies *'74*
Female Vampire *'73*
The Mummy's Revenge *'73*
Orgy of the Vampires *'73*
Dr. Jekyll and the Wolfman *'71*
Night of the Sorcerers *'70*
Black Tide *'58*

James Taylor (1948-)
TMNT (Teenage Mutant Ninja Turtles) *'07 (V)*
Two Lane Blacktop *'71*

Jana Taylor
Dreamscape *'84*
Hell's Angels on Wheels *'67*

Jayceon Taylor
See The Game

Joan Taylor (1925-)
Omar Khayyam *'57*
20 Million Miles to Earth *'57*
Earth vs. the Flying Saucers *'56*
Girls in Prison *'56*
Apache Woman *'55*
Rose Marie *'54*

John Taylor (1960-)
The Ringer *'05*
Four Dogs Playing Poker *'00*
Sugar Town *'99*
The Seventh Sign *'88*
Foxstyle *'73*

Joseph Lyle Taylor (1964-)
The Breakup Artist *'04*
Borough of Kings *'98*

Joyce Taylor (1932-)
Atlantis, the Lost Continent *'61*
The FBI Story *'59*

Kent Taylor (1906-87)
I Spit on Your Corpse *'74*
Angels' Wild Women *'72*
Blood of Ghastly Horror *'72*
Brain of Blood *'71*
Hell's Bloody Devils *'70*
Satan's Sadists *'69*
Brides of the Beast *'68*
The Crawling Hand *'63*
The Phantom from 10,000 Leagues *'56*
Slightly Scarlet *'56*
Payment on Demand *'51*
Western Pacific Agent *'51*
Gang Busters *'42*
I Take This Woman *'40*
Escape to Paradise *'39*
Five Came Back *'39*
The Gracie Allen Murder Case *'39*
The Jury's Secret *'38*
Sky Parade *'36*
David Harum *'34*
Death Takes a Holiday *'34*
Mrs. Wiggs of the Cabbage Patch *'34*
Badmen of Nevada *'33*
I'm No Angel *'33*
The Mysterious Rider *'33*

Kimberly Taylor
Beauty School *'93*
Party Incorporated *'89*

Kit Taylor (1942-)
Innocent Prey *'88*
Cassandra *'87*
Long John Silver *'54*

Lawrence Taylor (1959-)
The Comebacks *'07*
In Hell *'03*
Mercy Streets *'00*

Lili Taylor (1967-)
Brooklyn's Finest *'09*
The Promotion *'08*
The Secret *'07*
Starting Out in the Evening *'07*
Factotum *'06*
The Notorious Bettie Page *'06*
Casa de los Babys *'03*
Live from Baghdad *'03*
Anne Frank: The Whole Story *'01*
Gaudi Afternoon *'01*
High Fidelity *'00*
The Haunting *'99*
A Slipping Down Life *'99*
The Imposters *'98*
Pecker *'98*
Kicked in the Head *'97*
Subway Stories *'97*
I Shot Andy Warhol *'96*
Illtown *'96*
Ransom *'96*
Things I Never Told You *'96*
The Addiction *'95*
Cold Fever *'95*
Four Rooms *'95*
Girls Town *'95*
Arizona Dream *'94*
Mrs. Parker and the Vicious Circle *'94*
Ready to Wear *'94*
Household Saints *'93*
Rudy *'93*
Short Cuts *'93*
Watch It *'93*
Bright Angel *'91*
Dogfight *'91*
Say Anything *'89*
Mystic Pizza *'88*

Lindsay Taylor
Hellraiser 5: Inferno *'00*
Hard to Die *'90*

Marjorie Taylor
The Face at the Window *'39*
Never Too Late to Mend *'37*
Ticket of Leave Man *'37*
The Crimes of Stephen Hawke *'36*

Mark L. Taylor (1954-)
Color of Justice *'97*
Eight Days a Week *'97*
Arachnophobia *'90*

Meshach Taylor (1947-)
Friends and Family *'01*
The Secret of NIMH 2 *'98 (V)*
Virtual Seduction *'96*
Double Double Toil and Trouble *'94*
Ultra Warrior *'92*
Class Act *'91*
Inside Out *'91*
Mannequin 2: On the Move *'91*
House of Games *'87*
Mannequin *'87*
Explorers *'85*
The Beast Within *'82*
The Howling *'81*
Damien: Omen 2 *'78*

Natascha Taylor
See Natascha (Natasha) McElhone

Noah Taylor (1969-)
Charlie and the Chocolate Factory *'05*
The New World *'05*
The Proposition *'05*
Lara Croft Tomb Raider: The Cradle of Life *'03*
Max *'02*
The Sleeping Dictionary *'02*
He Died With a Felafel in His Hand *'01*
Lara Croft: Tomb Raider *'01*
Vanilla Sky *'01*
Almost Famous *'00*
Life in the Fast Lane *'00*
Shine *'95*
One Crazy Night *'93*
The Nostradamus Kid *'92*
Flirting *'89*
The Year My Voice Broke *'87*

Rachael Taylor (1984-)
Bottle Shock *'08*
Deception *'08*
The Legend of Bloody Mary *'08*
Shutter *'08*
Transformers *'07*
See No Evil *'06*

Regina Taylor (1960-)
Cora Unashamed *'00*
Strange Justice: The Clarence Thomas and Anita Hill Story *'99*
The Negotiator *'98*
Hostile Waters *'97*
Courage Under Fire *'96*
A Family Thing *'96*
The Keeper *'96*
Spirit Lost *'96*
A Good Day to Die *'95*
Lean on Me *'89*

Renee Taylor (1935-)
Life During Wartime *'09*
Pandemic *'07*
Ice Age: The Meltdown *'06 (V)*
The Boynton Beach Club *'05*
Alfie *'04*
National Lampoon's Gold Diggers *'04*
61* *'01*
Love Is All There Is *'96*
Forever: A Ghost of a Love Story *'92*
Delirious *'91*
The End of Innocence *'90*
That's Adequate *'90*
White Palace *'90*
Last of the Red Hot Lovers *'72*
The Detective *'68*
The Errand Boy *'61*

Rip Taylor (1934-)
Alex & Emma *'03*
Private Obsession *'94*
Indecent Proposal *'93*
Silence of the Hams *'93*
Tom and Jerry: The Movie *'93 (V)*
Wayne's World 2 *'93*
DuckTales the Movie: Treasure of the Lost Lamp *'90 (V)*
Cheech and Chong: Things Are Tough All Over *'82*

Robert Taylor
The Hard Word *'02*
Vertical Limit *'00*
The Matrix *'99*
Saddle the Wind *'58*
Many Rivers to Cross *'55*

Robert Taylor (1911-69)
The Hot Line *'69*
Where Angels Go, Trouble Follows *'68*
Johnny Tiger *'66*
The Night Walker *'64*
The Miracle of the White Stallions *'63*
The Law and Jake Wade *'58*
Party Girl *'58*
D-Day, the Sixth of June *'56*
The Last Hunt *'56*
Quentin Durward *'55*
Valley of the Kings *'54*
Above and Beyond *'53*
All the Brothers Were Valiant *'53*
I Love Melvin *'53*
Knights of the Round Table *'53*
Ivanhoe *'52*
Quo Vadis *'51*
Westward the Women *'51*
Conspirator *'49*
The Bribe *'48*
Undercurrent *'46*
Bataan *'43*
Johnny Eager *'42*
Billy the Kid *'41*
When Ladies Meet *'41*
Waterloo Bridge *'40*
Three Comrades *'38*
Broadway Melody of 1938 *'37*
Personal Property *'37*
Camille *'36*
The Gorgeous Hussy *'36*
Broadway Melody of 1936 *'35*
Magnificent Obsession *'35*

Rod Taylor (1929-)
Inglourious Basterds *'09*
Welcome to Woop Woop *'97*
Open Season *'95*
Danielle Steel's Palomino *'91*
Marbella *'85*
On the Run *'83*
Time to Die *'83*
Jacqueline Bouvier Kennedy *'81*
Cry of the Innocent *'80*
The Treasure Seekers *'79*
Hell River *'75*
Germicide *'74*
The Deadly Trackers *'73*
Train Robbers *'73*
Darker than Amber *'70*
Man Who Had Power Over Women *'70*
Powder Keg *'70*
Zabriskie Point *'70*
Dark of the Sun *'68*
Chuka *'67*
Hotel *'67*
The Glass Bottom Boat *'66*
Do Not Disturb *'65*
Colossus and the Amazon Queen *'64*
36 Hours *'64*
The Birds *'63*
A Gathering of Eagles *'63*
Sunday in New York *'63*
The V.I.P.'s *'63*
101 Dalmatians *'61 (V)*
The Time Machine *'60*
Ask Any Girl *'59*
Separate Tables *'58*
Raintree County *'57*
The Catered Affair *'56*
Giant *'56*
Long John Silver *'54*

Russi Taylor (1944-)
Babe: Pig in the City *'98 (V)*
DuckTales the Movie: Treasure of the Lost Lamp *'90 (V)*
Jetsons: The Movie *'90 (V)*

Sandra Taylor (1966-)
Keeping Up with the Steins *'06*
The Student Affair *'97*

Tamara Taylor (1970-)
Diary of a Mad Black Woman *'05*
Introducing Dorothy Dandridge *'99*
Senseless *'98*
Nightstalker *'81*

Tammy Taylor
Lovelines *'84*
Meatballs 2 *'84*

Vanessa Taylor
Femalien 2 *'98*
Femalien *'96*

Vaughn Taylor (1910-83)
The Gallant Hours *'60*
The Lineup *'58*
Jailhouse Rock *'57*
Meet Danny Wilson *'52*
Francis Goes to the Races *'51*

Veronica Taylor
Pokemon 3: The Movie *'01 (V)*
Pokemon: The First Movie *'99 (V)*

Wally Taylor (1930-)
Hidden Fears *'93*
Night of the Creeps *'86*
Shaft's Big Score *'72*

Zack Taylor
The Young Nurses *'73*
Group Marriage *'72*

Scout Taylor-Compton (1989-)
The Runaways *'10*
Halloween II *'09*
Obsessed *'09*
April Fool's Day *'08*
Halloween *'07*
Love's Unfolding Dream *'07*
Sleepover *'04*

Leigh Taylor-Young (1944-)
Coffee Date *'06*
Klepto *'03*
Slackers *'02*
Bliss *'96*
Honeymoon Academy *'90*
Accidents *'89*
The Jagged Edge *'85*
Secret Admirer *'85*
Looker *'81*
Can't Stop the Music *'80*
Marathon *'80*
Soylent Green *'73*
The Adventurers *'70*
The Buttercup Chain *'70*
The Horsemen *'70*
The Big Bounce *'69*
I Love You, Alice B. Toklas! *'68*

Jun Tazaki (1910-85)
Ran *'85*
War of the Gargantuas *'70*
Destroy All Monsters *'68*
Godzilla vs. Monster Zero *'68*
King Kong vs. Godzilla *'63*
Seven Samurai *'54*

Ludmilla Tcherina (1924-2004)
Sins of Rome *'54*
The Red Shoes *'48*

Kiri Te Kanawa (1944-)
Meeting Venus *'91 (V)*
The Ring *'52*

Phil Tead (1893-1974)
Fangs of the Wild *'54*
Music in My Heart *'40*

Anthony Teague (1940-89)
The Trouble with Girls (and How to Get into It) *'69*
How to Succeed in Business without Really Trying *'67*

Marshall Teague
Special Forces *'03*
U.S. Seals 2 *'01*
What Matters Most *'01*
Across the Line *'00*
Crime and Punishment in Suburbia *'00*
The Bad Pack *'98*
The Colony *'95*
Fists of Iron *'94*
Guardian Angel *'94*
Super Force *'90*
Road House *'89*
Trained to Kill *'88*
The Shadow Riders *'82*

Ray Teal (1902-76)
Judgment at Nuremberg *'61*
Saddle the Wind *'58*
Band of Angels *'57*
The Command *'54*
Lucky Me *'54*
Ambush at Tomahawk Gap *'53*
Carrie *'52*
Cattle Town *'52*
Jumping Jacks *'52*
Montana Belle *'52*
Ace in the Hole *'51*
Distant Drums *'51*
Rusty's Birthday *'49*
The Best Years of Our Lives *'46*
Hollywood Canteen *'44*

Owen Teale (1961-)
The Last Legion *'07*
Conspiracy *'01*
Cleopatra *'99*
Wilderness *'96*
The Hawk *'93*
Robin Hood *'91*
Catherine Cookson's The Fifteen Streets *'90*

Conway Tearle (1878-1938)
Klondike Annie *'36*
Headline Woman *'35*
Sing Sing Nights *'35*
Stingaree *'34*
Held for Murder *'32*
Hurricane Express *'32*
The King Murder *'32*
Vanity Fair *'32*
Morals for Women *'31*
Pleasure *'31*
Lost Zeppelin *'29*
Dancing Mothers *'26*
Stella Maris *'18*

Godfrey Tearle (1884-1953)
One of Our Aircraft Is Missing *'41*
The 39 Steps *'35*

Verree Teasdale (1904-87)
I Take This Woman *'40*
Milky Way *'36*
Goodbye Love *'34*
Skyscraper Souls *'32*

Sandor Tecsy (1946-)
Fever *'99*
Angel Blue *'97*
'68 *'87*

Paola Tedesco
Watch Me When I Kill *'77*
New Mafia Boss *'72*

Travis Tedford (1988-)
Slappy and the Stinkers *'97*
The Little Rascals *'94*

Irene Tedrow (1908-95)
The Two Worlds of Jenny Logan *'79*
Special Olympics *'78*

Jill Teed
X2: X-Men United *'03*
Mission to Mars *'00*
Impolite *'92*

Maureen Teefy (1954-)
Star Time *'92*
Supergirl *'84*
Legs *'83*
Fame *'80*

Blair Tefkin (1959-)
Dream Lover *'93*
A Sinful Life *'89*

Aaron Teich (1961-)
Darkroom *'90*
Bloodspell *'87*

Virgilio Teixeira (1917-)
Tricheurs *'84*
The Magnificent Two *'67*
Saul and David *'64*

Fernando Tejero
Chef's Special *'08*
Torremolinos 73 *'03*

April Telek
Man in the Mirror: The Michael Jackson Story *'04*
The Immortal *'01*

Zoe Telford
Place of Execution *'09*
Beau Brummell: This Charming Man *'06*

Rut Tellefsen (1930-)
Kristin Lavransdatter *'95*
The Last Lieutenant *'94*

Teller (1948-)
Penn and Teller Get Killed *'90*
Light Years *'88 (V)*
Long Gone *'87*

Sybil Temchen (1970-)
Lip Service *'00*
Body Shots *'99*
Nice Guys Sleep Alone *'99*
The Passion of Ayn Rand *'99*
Restaurant *'98*
Ten Benny *'98*
Floating *'97*

Hedi Temessy (1925-2001)
Almanac of Fall *'85*
The Revolt of Job *'84*

Juno Temple
Greenberg *'10*
The Other Boleyn Girl *'08*
Wild Child *'08*
Atonement *'07*
St. Trinian's *'07*
Notes on a Scandal *'06*

Lew Temple
Waitress *'07*
The Texas Chainsaw Massacre: The Beginning *'06*
The Devil's Rejects *'05*
Domino *'05*

Shirley Temple (1928-)
The Story of Seabiscuit *'49*
Fort Apache *'48*
The Bachelor and the Bobby-Soxer *'47*
I'll Be Seeing You *'44*
Since You Went Away *'44*
Miss Annie Rooney *'42*
The Blue Bird *'40*
Young People *'40*
The Little Princess *'39*
Susannah of the Mounties *'39*
Just Around the Corner *'38*
Little Miss Broadway *'38*
Rebecca of Sunnybrook Farm *'38*
Heidi *'37*
Wee Willie Winkie *'37*
Captain January *'36*
Dimples *'36*
The Poor Little Rich Girl *'36*
Stowaway *'36*
Curly Top *'35*
The Little Colonel *'35*
The Littlest Rebel *'35*
Our Little Girl *'35*
Baby, Take a Bow *'34*
Bright Eyes *'34*
Little Miss Marker *'34*
Now and Forever *'34*
Stand Up and Cheer *'34*
Kid 'n' Hollywood and Polly Tix in Washington *'33*
To the Last Man *'33*

Harry Tenbrook (1887-1960)
They Were Expendable *'45*
Oklahoma Frontier *'39*
A Slight Case of Murder *'38*

John Tench
The Ticket *'97*
Dead Ahead *'96*

David Tennant (1971-)
Casanova *'05*
Harry Potter and the Goblet of Fire *'05*
Secret Smile *'05*
Bright Young Things *'03*
The Last September *'99*

Victoria Tennant (1953-)
Bram Stoker's The Mummy *'97*
Edie & Pen *'95*
L.A. Story *'91*
The Handmaid's Tale *'90*
War & Remembrance: The Final Chapter *'89*
Whispers *'89*
War & Remembrance *'88*
Best Seller *'87*
Flowers in the Attic *'87*
The Holcroft Covenant *'85*
All of Me *'84*
Chiefs *'83*
Dempsey *'83*
Strangers Kiss *'83*
The Winds of War *'83*
The Dogs of War *'81*
Inseminoid *'80*
Little Lord Fauntleroy *'80*

Anne Tenney
The Castle *'97*
Dead Heart *'96*

Jon Tenney (1961-)
The Stepfather *'09*
Looking for Comedy in the Muslim World *'06*
Masters of Horror: Homecoming *'05*
Entropy *'99*
You Can Count On Me *'99*
With Friends Like These *'98*
Fools Rush In *'97*
Homegrown *'97*
Lovelife *'97*
Music from Another Room *'97*
The Twilight of the Golds *'97*
The Phantom *'96*
Free Willy 2: The Adventure Home *'95*
Lassie *'94*
Tombstone *'93*
Watch It *'93*
Guilty by Suspicion *'91*
Nasty Hero *'89*

Julius Tennon
Lone Justice 2 *'93*
Riverbend *'89*

Judy Tenuta (1956-)
Material Girls *'06*
White Hot *'88*

William Tepper (1948-)
Bachelor Party *'84*
Miss Right *'81*

Johanna Ter Steege (1961-)
Paradise Road *'97*
Immortal Beloved *'94*

Meeting Venus *'91*
Vincent & Theo *'90*
The Vanishing *'88*

Susumu Terajima (1963-)
Black House *'07*
Gamera the Brave *'06*
Steamboy *'05 (V)*
Cursed *'04*
Flower & Snake *'04*
A Snake of June *'02*
Ichi the Killer *'01*
Brother *'00*
After Life *'98*
Shark Skin Man and Peach Hip Girl *'98*
Fireworks *'97*

Akira Terao (1947-)
Black House *'07*
Akira Kurosawa's Dreams *'90*
Ran *'85*

Lee Tergesen (1965-)
Generation Kill *'08*
The Texas Chainsaw Massacre: The Beginning *'06*
Extreme Dating *'04*
A Thief of Time *'04*
Monster *'03*
Bark! *'02*
Shot in the Heart *'01*
Wild Iris *'01*
Shaft *'00*
Point Break *'91*

Max Terhune (1891-1973)
Black Market Rustlers *'43*
Cowboy Commandos *'43*
Haunted Ranch *'43*
Land of Hunted Men *'43*
Two-Fisted Justice *'43*
Arizona Stagecoach *'42*
Boot Hill Bandits *'42*
Rock River Renegades *'42*
Texas to Bataan *'42*
Thunder River Feud *'42*
Trail Riders *'42*
Fugitive Valley *'41*
Kid's Last Ride *'41*
Saddle Mountain Roundup *'41*
Tonto Basin Outlaws *'41*
Trail of the Silver Spurs *'41*
Tumbledown Ranch in Arizona *'41*
Underground Rustlers *'41*
Range Busters *'40*
Trailing Double Trouble *'40*
West of Pinto Basin *'40*
Three Texas Steers *'39*
Call the Mesquiteers *'38*
Heroes of the Hills *'38*
Outlaws of Sonora *'38*
Overland Stage Raiders *'38*
Pals of the Saddle *'38*
Purple Vigilantes *'38*
Santa Fe Stampede *'38*
Come on, Cowboys *'37*
Heart of the Rockies *'37*
Hit the Saddle *'37*
Riders of the Whistling Skull *'37*
Roarin' Lead *'37*
The Trigger Trio *'37*
Wild Horse Rodeo *'37*
Ghost Town Gold *'36*
Ride, Ranger, Ride *'36*

Studs Terkel (1912-)
Eight Men Out *'88*
Long Shadows *'86*

John Terlesky (1961-)
Battling for Baby *'92*
Damned River *'89*
When He's Not a Stranger *'89*
The Allnighter *'87*
Deathstalker 2: Duel of the Titans *'87*
Chopping Mall *'86*

Leonard Termo
Midnight Cabaret *'90*
Year of the Dragon *'85*

Scott Terra (1987-)
Daredevil *'03*
Eight Legged Freaks *'02*
Shadrach *'98*

John Canada Terrell
The Five Heartbeats *'91*
Def by Temptation *'90*
She's Gotta Have It *'86*

Ken Terrell (1907-66)
Attack of the 50 Foot Woman *'58*
The Brain from Planet Arous *'57*
The Indestructible Man *'56*
Son of Zorro *'47*
In Old New Mexico *'45*

Steven Terrell
Dragstrip Girl *'57*
Invasion of the Saucer Men *'57*
Motorcycle Gang *'57*

Alice Terry
Scaramouche *'23*
The Prisoner of Zenda *'22*
The Four Horsemen of the Apocalypse *'21*

Bob Terry
Danger Ahead *'40*
Lightning Strikes West *'40*
Down the Wyoming Trail *'39*
Outlaw's Paradise *'39*
Six Gun Trail *'38*
The Stranger from Arizona *'38*
Brothers of the West *'37*
Stormy Trails *'36*

Don Terry (1902-88)
Don Winslow of the Coast Guard *'43*
Don Winslow of the Navy *'43*
Overland Mail *'42*
Hard to Hold *'37*
Border Romance *'30*

Harry Terry
The Face at the Window *'39*
Broken Melody *'34*

John Terry (1944-)
The Way of War *'08*
Zodiac *'07*
Change of Heart *'98*
The Big Green *'95*
Reflections in the Dark *'94*
A Dangerous Woman *'93*
Iron Will *'93*
Of Mice and Men *'92*
The Resurrected *'91*
Silhouette *'91*
A Killing in a Small Town *'90*
In Country *'89*
Full Metal Jacket *'87*
Hawk the Slayer *'81*

Kim Terry
Rushmore *'98*
Slugs *'87*

Nigel Terry (1945-)
Red Mercury *'05*
Feardotcom *'02*
The Emperor's New Clothes *'01*
The Ebb-Tide *'97*
Far from the Madding Crowd *'97*
Blue *'93 (N)*
Christopher Columbus: The Discovery *'92*
Edward II *'92*
Caravaggio *'86*
Sylvia *'86*
Deja Vu *'84*
Excalibur *'81*
The Lion in Winter *'68*

Phillip Terry (1909-93)
The Leech Woman *'59*
To Each His Own *'46*
George White's Scandals *'45*
The Lost Weekend *'45*
Bataan *'43*
Wake Island *'42*

The Monster and the Girl *'41*

Ruth Terry (1920-)
Hands Across the Border *'43*
Texas Legionnaires *'43*
Blondie Goes Latin *'42*
Call of the Canyon *'42*
Heart of the Golden West *'42*
Alexander's Ragtime Band *'38*

Sheila Terry (1910-57)
Go-Get-'Em-Haines *'35*
Lawless Frontier *'35*
Social Error *'35*
'Neath the Arizona Skies *'34*
The Sphinx *'33*
Haunted Gold *'32*
Scarlet Dawn *'32*

Terry-Thomas (1911-89)
The Bawdy Adventures of Tom Jones *'76*
Robin Hood *'73 (V)*
Vault of Horror *'73*
Doctor Phibes Rises Again *'72*
The Abominable Dr. Phibes *'71*
12 Plus 1 *'70*
Those Daring Young Men in Their Jaunty Jalopies *'69*
Danger: Diabolik *'68*
Don't Raise the Bridge, Lower the River *'68*
How Sweet It Is! *'68*
How to Kill 400 Duponts *'68*
Where Were You When the Lights Went Out? *'68*
A Guide for the Married Man *'67*
Those Fantastic Flying Fools *'67*
La Grande Vadrouille *'66*
Munster, Go Home! *'66*
Strange Bedfellows *'65*
Those Magnificent Men in Their Flying Machines *'65*
How to Murder Your Wife *'64*
It's a Mad, Mad, Mad, Mad World *'63*
A Matter of WHO *'62*
The Mouse on the Moon *'62*
The Wonderful World of the Brothers Grimm *'62*
Make Mine Mink *'60*
School for Scoundrels *'60*
Carlton Browne of the F.O. *'59*
I'm All Right Jack *'59*
Too Many Crooks *'59*
Lucky Jim *'58*
The Naked Truth *'58*
Tom Thumb *'58*
Brothers in Law *'57*
Blue Murder at St. Trinian's *'56*

Laurent Terzieff (1935-)
Fiesta *'95*
Germinal *'93*
Detective *'85*
Red Kiss *'85*
Medea *'70*
The Milky Way *'68*
A Coeur Joie *'67*
Head Over Heels *'67*
Vanina Vanini *'61*
Kapo *'59*

Venus Terzo
Masters of Horror: The Washingtonians *'07*
Meltdown *'06*

Ingrid Tesch
Masters of Horror: We All Scream for Ice Cream *'07*
Suspicious River *'00*

Robert Tessier (1934-2000)
Future Force *'89*
Nightwish *'89*
No Safe Haven *'87*
Avenging Angel *'85*
The Last of the Mohicans *'85*

The Fix '84
The Lost Empire '83
Sword & the Sorcerer '82
The Villain '79
Star Crash '78
The Longest Yard '74
The Velvet Vampire '71
Cry Blood, Apache '70
Born Losers '67
The Glory Stompers '67

Desmond Tester (1919-2002)
Non-Stop New York '37
Nine Days a Queen '36
Sabotage '36

Fabio Testi (1941-)
Iguana '89
Mussolini & I '85
The Ambassador '84
Contraband '80
Gunfire '78
The Uranium Conspiracy '78
The Inheritance '76
Stateline Motel '75
'Tis a Pity She's a Whore '73
The Garden of the Finzi-Continis '71

Sylvie Testud (1971-)
La Vie en Rose '07
A Loving Father '02
The Chateau '01
Beyond Silence '96

Lauren Tewes (1954-)
Nowhere '96
The Doom Generation '95
It Came from Outer Space 2 '95
National Lampoon's Attack of the 5 Ft. 2 Women '94
Magic Kid '92
Camp Cucamonga: How I Spent My Summer Vacation '90
The China Lake Murders '90
Eyes of a Stranger '81

Tia Texada (1971-)
Spartan '04
Crazy as Hell '02
Phone Booth '02
Glitter '01
Thirteen Conversations About One Thing '01
Bait '00
Nurse Betty '00
The Thirteenth Floor '99
Paulie '98
From Dusk Till Dawn '95

Gilda Texter (1946-)
Angels Hard As They Come '71
Vanishing Point '71

Katsumi Tezuka (1912-)
King Kong vs. Godzilla '63
Matango '63

Elizabeth Thai (1979-)
Mr. Troop Mom '09
Saved! '04

Eric Thal (1965-)
The Shaft '01
Prisoner of Love '99
Snow Falling on Cedars '99
Mixing Nia '98
Samson and Delilah '96
Wishful Thinking '96
The Puppet Masters '94
Six Degrees of Separation '93
The Gun in Betty Lou's Handbag '92
A Stranger Among Us '92

Katharina Thalbach (1954-)
King of Thieves '04
Good Evening, Mr. Wallenberg '93
Kaspar Hauser '93
The Tin Drum '79
The Second Awakening of Christa Klages '78

Byron Thames (1969-)
84 Charlie MoPic '89
Seven Minutes in Heaven '86
Blame It on the Night '84

Heather Thatcher (1896-1987)
The Moon and Sixpence '43
Son of Fury '42
The Undying Monster '42
Beau Geste '39
If I Were King '38

Torin Thatcher (1905-81)
Dr. Jekyll and Mr. Hyde '68
Holy Terror '65
From Hell to Borneo '64
Drums of Africa '63
Jack the Giant Killer '62
Darby's Rangers '58
The Seventh Voyage of Sinbad '58
Band of Angels '57
Istanbul '57
Witness for the Prosecution '57
Helen of Troy '56
Diane '55
Lady Godiva '55
Love Is a Many-Splendored Thing '55
The Black Shield of Falworth '54
The Desert Rats '53
Houdini '53
The Robe '53
Affair in Trinidad '52
Crimson Pirate '52
The Snows of Kilimanjaro '52
Great Expectations '46
Young and Innocent '37
Sabotage '36

Hilmar Thate (1931-)
The Ninth Day '04
Veronika Voss '82
Divided Heaven '64
The Gleiwitz Case '61

John Thaw (1942-2002)
Goodnight, Mr. Tom '99
The Waiting Time '99
Into the Blue '97
Chaplin '92
A Year in Provence '89
Business As Usual '88
Cry Freedom '87
Killing Heat '84
Macbeth '70

Phyllis Thaxter (1921-)
Three Sovereigns for Sarah '85
Superman: The Movie '78
The World of Henry Orient '64
Springfield Rifle '52
Jim Thorpe: All American '51
Act of Violence '48
Weekend at the Waldorf '45
Thirty Seconds Over Tokyo '44

Brynn Thayer (1949-)
Hero and the Terror '88
The Tracker '88
The Game of Love '87

Maria Thayer (1975-)
Forgetting Sarah Marshall '08
Accepted '06
Strangers with Candy '06

Max (Michael) Thayer (1946-)
No Retreat, No Surrender 2 '89
No Dead Heroes '87
The Dolls '83
Retrievers '82
Planet of the Dinosaurs '80
Ilsa, Harem Keeper of the Oil Sheiks '76

Tina Thayer
Jive Junction '43
The Payoff '43

Marcello Thedford
Freedom Song '00
An Alan Smithee Film: Burn, Hollywood, Burn '97

Ulrich Thein (1930-95)
Anton, the Magician '78
Five Cartridges '60

Darryl Theirse (1967-)
Crocodile 2: Death Swamp '01
I Love You, Don't Touch Me! '97

Brooke Theiss (1969-)
Quicksand '01
A Nightmare on Elm Street 4: Dream Master '88

Brother Theodore (1906-2001)
That's Adequate '90
The 'Burbs '89
The Invisible Kid '88
The Hobbit '78 (V)

Charlize Theron (1975-)
Astro Boy '09 (N)
The Road '09
The Burning Plain '08
Hancock '08
Sleepwalking '08
Battle in Seattle '07
In the Valley of Elah '07
Aeon Flux '05
North Country '05
Head in the Clouds '04
The Italian Job '03
Monster '03
Trapped '02
Waking Up in Reno '02
The Curse of the Jade Scorpion '01
15 Minutes '01
Sweet November '01
The Legend of Bagger Vance '00
Men of Honor '00
Reindeer Games '00
The Yards '00
The Astronaut's Wife '99
The Cider House Rules '99
Celebrity '98
Mighty Joe Young '98
The Devil's Advocate '97
Hollywood Confidential '97
That Thing You Do! '96
Trial and Error '96
Two Days in the Valley '96

Justin Theroux (1971-)
John Adams '08
Tropic Thunder '08
Broken English '07
The Ten '07
Inland Empire '06
The Legend of Lucy Keyes '06
Miami Vice '06
Strangers with Candy '06
The Baxter '05
Charlie's Angels: Full Throttle '03
Duplex '03
Mulholland Drive '01
The Broken Hearts Club '00
American Psycho '99
Dead Broke '99
Sirens '99
Frogs for Snakes '98
Body Count '97

Ernest Thesiger (1879-1961)
The Battle of the Sexes '60
Who Done It? '56
Quentin Durward '55
The Robe '53
A Christmas Carol '51
Beware of Pity '46
Henry V '44
The Bride of Frankenstein '35
The Ghoul '34
The Old Dark House '32

David Thewlis (1963-)
Harry Potter and the Half-Blood Prince '09
The Boy in the Striped Pajamas '08
Harry Potter and the Order of the Phoenix '07
Basic Instinct 2 '06
The Omen '06
Kingdom of Heaven '05
The New World '05
Harry Potter and the Prisoner of Azkaban '04
Timeline '03
Dinotopia '02
Gangster No. 1 '00
The Miracle Maker: The Story of Jesus '00 (V)
Besieged '98
The Big Lebowski '97
Seven Years in Tibet '97
Dragonheart '96
The Island of Dr. Moreau '96
James and the Giant Peach '96 (V)
Total Eclipse '95
Black Beauty '94
Restoration '94
Naked '93
Life Is Sweet '90
The Life and Adventures of Nicholas Nickleby '81

Jack Thibeau
Lethal Weapon '87
Sudden Impact '83
Ms. 45 '81
Apocalypse Now '79
Escape from Alcatraz '79

Debi Thibeault
Cemetery High '89
Galactic Gigolo '87
Psychos in Love '87

Sean Thibodeau
Luster '02
The Ladies Man '00

Alan Thicke (1947-)
The Goods: Live Hard, Sell Hard '09
National Lampoon Presents RoboDoc '08
Carolina '03
Hollywood North '03
Any Place But Home '97
Jack Higgins' The Windsor Protocol '97
Demolition High '95
Open Season '95
The Great American Sex Scandal '94
Rubdown '93
Betrayal of the Dove '92
Stepmonster '92
Still Not Quite Human '92
And You Thought Your Parents Were Weird! '91 (V)
Not Quite Human 2 '89
Obsessed '88
Not Quite Human '87
Scene of the Crime '85
Club Med '83

Hertha Thiele
Kuhle Wampe, Or Who Owns the World? '32
Maedchen in Uniform '31

Max Thieriot (1988-)
Chloe '09
Jumper '08
Kit Kittredge: An American Girl '08
The Astronaut Farmer '07
Nancy Drew '07
The Pacifier '05
Catch That Kid '04

Melanie Thierry
Babylon A.D. '08
Chrysalis '07
The Legend of 1900 '98

Rose Thiery
The Green House '96
Beau Pere '81

Tiffani(-Amber) Thiessen (1974-)
Cyborg Soldier '08
Pandemic '07
Hollywood Ending '02
The Ladies Man '00
Shriek If You Know What I Did Last Friday the 13th '00
Love Stinks '99
Speedway Junky '99
From Dusk Till Dawn 2: Texas Blood Money '98
Son-in-Law '93

Kevin Thigpen
Tar '97
Just Another Girl on the I.R.T. '93

Lynne Thigpen (1948-2003)
Anger Management '03
Novocaine '01
Shaft '00
Trial by Media '00
Bicentennial Man '99
The Insider '99
Night Ride Home '99
Random Hearts '99
The Boys Next Door '96
Just Cause '94
The Paper '94
Naked in New York '93
Article 99 '92
Bob Roberts '92
Separate but Equal '91
Impulse '90
Lean on Me '89
Rockabye '86
Streets of Fire '84
The Warriors '79
Godspell '73

Chief Ted Thin Elk (1919-97)
Walking Thunder '94
Thunderheart '92

Roy Thinnes (1936-)
Bar Hopping '00
Robin Cook's Terminal '96
The Invaders '95
Rush Week '88
Sizzle '81
From Here to Eternity '79
Code Name: Diamond Head '77
Secrets '77
Airport '75 '75
The Hindenburg '75
The Norliss Tapes '73
Satan's School for Girls '73
Journey to the Far Side of the Sun '69

Olivia Thirlby (1986-)
The Answer Man '09
New York, I Love You '09
What Goes Up '09
The Wackness '08
Juno '07
The Secret '07
Snow Angels '07

Victorie Thivisol (1991-)
Chocolat '00
Ponette '95

Alex Thomas
The Wash '01
The Players Club '98

Bernard B. Thomas
Pillow of Death '45
Dead Man's Eyes '44

Betty Thomas (1949-)
Prison for Children '93
Troop Beverly Hills '89
When Your Lover Leaves '83
Homework '82
Jackson County Jail '76

Damien Thomas (1942-)
Pirates '86
Shogun '80
The Message '77
Twins of Evil '71

Danny Thomas (1914-91)
Side by Side '88
Journey Back to Oz '71 (V)
I'll See You in My Dreams '51

Dave Thomas (1949-)
Brother Bear 2 '06 (V)
Love on the Side '04
White Coats '04
Beethoven's 5th '03
Brother Bear '03 (V)
Cold Sweat '93
Coneheads '93
Boris and Natasha: The Movie '92
Moving '88
Love at Stake '87
My Man Adam '86
Sesame Street Presents: Follow That Bird '85
Strange Brew '83
Stripes '81

Eddie Kaye Thomas (1980-)
Harold & Kumar Escape from Guantanamo Bay '08
Nature of the Beast '07
Blind Dating '06
Wasted '06
Dirty Love '05
Harold and Kumar Go to White Castle '04
American Wedding '03
Stolen Summer '02
Taboo '02
Winter Break '02
American Pie 2 '01
Freddy Got Fingered '01
More Dogs Than Bones '00
American Pie '99
Black and White '99
The Rage: Carrie 2 '99

Frank M. Thomas, Sr. (1889-1989)
Sunset on the Desert '42
A Man to Remember '39
Law of the Underworld '38
Breakfast for Two '37
Charlie Chan in Egypt '35

Frankie Thomas, Jr. (1921-2006)
The Major and the Minor '42
Nancy Drew and the Hidden Staircase '39
Nancy Drew, Reporter '39
Nancy Drew—Trouble Shooter '39
Boys Town '38
Nancy Drew—Detective '38
Tim Tyler's Luck '37

Heather Thomas (1957-)
My Giant '98
Hidden Obsession '92
Red Blooded American Girl '90
The Dirty Dozen: The Fatal Mission '88
Cyclone '87
Ford: The Man & the Machine '87
Zapped! '82

Henry Thomas (1971-)
Dear John '10
Dead Birds '04
Plain Dirty '04
11:14 '03
Gangs of New York '02
I Capture the Castle '02
I'm with Lucy '02
Dead in the Water '01
The Quickie '01
All the Pretty Horses '00
Fever '99
A Good Baby '99
The Happy Face Murders '99
Moby Dick '98
Bombshell '97
Hijacking Hollywood '97
Niagara, Niagara '97
Suicide Kings '97
Riders of the Purple Sage '96
Indictment: The McMartin Trial '95
Curse of the Starving Class '94

Legends of the Fall *'94*
Fire in the Sky *'93*
A Taste for Killing *'92*
Psycho 4: The Beginning *'90*
Valmont *'89*
Murder One *'88*
The Quest *'86*
Cloak & Dagger *'84*
Misunderstood *'84*
E.T.: The Extra-Terrestrial *'82*
Raggedy Man *'81*

Jake Thomas (1990-)

Aces 'n Eights *'08*
The Lizzie McGuire Movie *'03*
National Lampoon's Christmas Vacation 2: Cousin Eddie's Big Island Adventure *'03*
A. I.: Artificial Intelligence *'01*

James Thomas

Behind the Wall *'08*
Ice Men *'04*
Charlie Chan in Egypt *'35*

Jameson Thomas (1888-1939)

Sing Sing Nights *'35*
Beggars in Ermine *'34*
Jane Eyre *'34*
The Moonstone *'34*
Convicted *'32*
Night Birds *'31*
Night Life in Reno *'31*
The Farmer's Wife *'28*

Jay Thomas (1948-)

The Santa Clause 3: The Escape Clause *'06*
Disney's Teacher's Pet *'04 (V)*
Dragonfly *'02*
The Santa Clause 2 *'02*
Trial by Media *'00*
Killing Mr. Griffin *'97*
A Smile Like Yours *'96*
Mr. Holland's Opus *'95*
Straight Talk *'92*
Little Vegas *'90*
The Gig *'85*
C.H.U.D. *'84*

Jonathan Taylor Thomas (1981-)

Common Ground *'00*
Speedway Junky *'99*
I'll Be Home for Christmas *'98*
Wild America *'97*
The Adventures of Pinocchio *'96*
Man of the House *'95*
Tom and Huck *'95*
The Lion King *'94 (V)*
Pom Poko *'94 (V)*

Khleo Thomas (1989-)

Hurricane Season *'08*
Dirty *'05*
Roll Bounce *'05*
Walking Tall *'04*
Baadasssss! *'03*
Holes *'03*

Larry Thomas

Postal *'07*
Surface to Air *'98*
Night Ripper *'86*

Lyn Thomas (1929-2004)

Space Master X-7 *'58*
Missourians *'50*

Marcus Thomas

You Kill Me *'07*
Bigger Than the Sky *'05*
Noel *'04*
Cowboy Up *'00*
Drowning Mona *'00*

Marlo Thomas (1938-)

Playing Mona Lisa *'00*
The Real Blonde *'97*
Held Hostage *'91*
In the Spirit *'90*
Consenting Adult *'85*
Act of Passion: The Lost Honor of Kathryn Beck *'83*
Jenny *'70*

Melissa Thomas

Swimming Upstream *'03*
Brides of Christ *'91*

Michelle Rene Thomas (1970-)

National Lampoon's Van Wilder *'02*
The Last Don 2 *'98*
The Last Don *'97*
Midnight in Saint Petersburg *'97*
The Last Word *'95*
Major League 2 *'94*
Coneheads *'93*
Dazed and Confused *'93*

Patrick Thomas

The Witness *'99*
Eddie Presley *'92*

Philip Michael Thomas (1949-)

A Fight for Jenny *'90*
False Witness *'89*
The Wizard of Speed and Time *'88*
Miami Vice *'84*
Death Drug *'83*
Fist *'76*
Sparkle *'76*
Homeboy *'75*
Streetfight *'75*
Stigma *'73*

Richard Thomas (1951-)

Wonder Boys *'00*
The Million Dollar Kid *'99*
Big and Hairy *'98*
Flood: A River's Rampage *'97*
The Christmas Box *'95*
Down, Out and Dangerous *'95*
The Invaders *'95*
Linda *'93*
Stalking Laura *'93*
A Thousand Heroes *'92*
Mission of the Shark *'91*
Glory! Glory! *'90*
Stephen King's It *'90*
Andy and the Airwave Rangers *'89*
Hobson's Choice *'83*
Living Proof: The Hank Williams Jr. Story *'83*
Johnny Belinda *'82*
Berlin Tunnel 21 *'81*
Battle Beyond the Stars *'80*
All Quiet on the Western Front *'79*
Roots: The Next Generation *'79*
September 30, 1955 *'77*
Cactus in the Snow *'72*
You'll Like My Mother *'72*
Homecoming: A Christmas Story *'71*
The Todd Killings *'71*
Last Summer *'69*
Winning *'69*
A Doll's House *'59*

Robin Thomas (1953-)

Missing Brendan *'03*
The Banger Sisters *'02*
Clockstoppers *'02*
Halloweentown 2: Kalabar's Revenge *'01*
Halloweentown *'98*
Star Maps *'97*
Amityville Dollhouse *'96*
Chameleon *'95*
Memories of Murder *'90*
Personals *'90*
From the Dead of Night *'89*
Summer School *'87*
About Last Night... *'86*

Ron Thomas

Night Screams *'87*
The Big Bet *'85*

Ross Thomas

Shelter *'07*
American Pie Presents: The Naked Mile *'06*
The Cutting Edge: Going for the Gold *'05*

Rufus Thomas (1917-2001)

Cookie's Fortune *'99*
Mystery Train *'89*

Sean Patrick Thomas (1970-)

A Raisin in the Sun *'08*
Barbershop 2: Back in Business *'04*
Barbershop *'02*
Halloween: Resurrection *'02*
Save the Last Dance *'01*
Dracula 2000 *'00*
Cruel Intentions *'98*

Sian Thomas (1953-)

Half Broken Things *'07*
A Mind to Murder *'96*
The Wedding Gift *'93*

William Thomas

Solomon and Gaenor *'98*
Twin Town *'97*

Marsha Thomason (1976-)

Into the Blue 2: The Reef *'09*
Caffeine *'06*
The Nickel Children *'05*
My Baby's Daddy *'04*
The Haunted Mansion *'03*
Pure *'02*
Black Knight *'01*

William Thomason

The Devil's Sleep *'51*
Test Tube Babies *'48*

Florence Thomassin (1966-)

Cold Showers *'05*
Beaumarchais the Scoundrel *'96*
Elisa *'94*
Mina Tannenbaum *'93*

Tim Thomerson (1945-)

Wicked Lake *'08*
Bottoms Up *'06*
Christmas Do-Over *'06*
Forget About It *'06*
Left in Darkness *'06*
The Strange Case of Dr. Jekyll and Mr. Hyde *'06*
Final Approach *'04*
Shoot or Be Shot *'02*
The Devil's Prey *'01*
Gale Force *'01*
They Crawl *'01*
Gangland *'00*
Submerged *'00*
The Crimson Code *'99*
Detour *'99*
Unseen Evil *'99*
Crossfire *'98*
Fear and Loathing in Las Vegas *'98*
Escape from Atlantis *'97*
When Time Expires *'97*
Blast *'96*
Nemesis 3: Time Lapse *'96*
The Cisco Kid *'94*
Dominion *'94*
Fleshtone *'94*
Hong Kong '97 *'94*
Natural Causes *'94*
Spitfire *'94*
Trancers 5: Sudden Deth *'94*
Brain Smasher... A Love Story *'93*
Die Watching *'93*
Dollman vs Demonic Toys *'93*
Nemesis *'93*
Trancers 4: Jack of Swords *'93*
Bad Channels *'92*
Eddie Presley *'92*
The Harvest *'92*
Prime Time Murder *'92*
Trancers 3: Deth Lives *'92*
Intimate Stranger *'91*
Air America *'90*
Dollman *'90*
Trancers 2: The Return of Jack Deth *'90*
Vietnam, Texas *'90*
Who's Harry Crumb? *'89*
Cherry 2000 *'88*
The Wrong Guys *'88*
Glory Years *'87*
Near Dark *'87*
A Tiger's Tale *'87*
Iron Eagle *'86*
The Legend of Sleepy Hollow *'86*
Volunteers *'85*
Rhinestone *'84*
Trancers *'84*
Zone Troopers *'84*
Metalstorm: The Destruction of Jared Syn *'83*
Uncommon Valor *'83*
Jekyll & Hyde... Together Again *'82*
Some Kind of Hero *'82*
Fade to Black *'80*
A Wedding *'78*
Terraces *'77*

Vendela Thommessen (1967-)

Model Behavior *'00*
Batman and Robin *'97*

Al Thompson

Love Don't Cost a Thing *'03*
A Season on the Brink *'02*

Alina Thompson

Dead Cold *'96*
The Fiance *'96*
Marked Man *'96*
Seduce Me: Pamela Principle 2 *'94*

Andrea Thompson (1962-)

A Gun, a Car, a Blonde *'97*
Doin' Time on Planet Earth *'88*

Anna Thompson

See Anna Thomson

Bill Thompson (1913-71)

The Aristocats *'70 (V)*
Lady and the Tramp *'55 (V)*
Peter Pan *'53 (V)*

Bobb'e J. Thompson

Columbus Day *'08*
Role Models *'08*
Snow *'04*

Brian Thompson (1959-)

Epoch: Evolution *'03*
Epoch *'00*
Jason and the Argonauts *'00*
Perfect Target *'98*
Mortal Kombat 2: Annihilation *'97*
Dragonheart *'96*
Rage and Honor *'92*
Hired to Kill *'91*
Doctor Mordrid: Master of the Unknown *'90*
Lionheart *'90*
Moon 44 *'90*
Nightwish *'89*
Fright Night 2 *'88*
Commando Squad *'87*

Christopher Thompson (1969-)

La Buche *'00*
The Luzhin Defence *'00*
The Count of Monte Cristo *'99*

Derek Thompson (1948-)

Resurrection Man *'97*
Belfast Assassin *'84*
The Long Good Friday *'80*

Edward Thompson

Double Deal *'39*
The Duke Is Tops *'38*

Elizabeth Thompson

Metropolitan *'90*
The Car *'77*
Free Grass *'69*

Emma Thompson (1959-)

Nanny McPhee 2 *'10*
An Education *'09*
Pirate Radio *'09*
Brideshead Revisited *'08*
Last Chance Harvey *'08*
Harry Potter and the Order of the Phoenix *'07*
Nanny McPhee *'06*
Stranger Than Fiction *'06*
Harry Potter and the Prisoner of Azkaban *'04*
Imagining Argentina *'04*
Angels in America *'03*
Love Actually *'03*
Treasure Planet *'02 (V)*
Wit *'01*
Maybe Baby *'99*
Judas Kiss *'98*
Primary Colors *'98*
The Winter Guest *'97*
Carrington *'95*
Sense and Sensibility *'95*
Junior *'94*
In the Name of the Father *'93*
Much Ado about Nothing *'93*
My Father the Hero *'93*
The Remains of the Day *'93*
Howard's End *'92*
Peter's Friends *'92*
Dead Again *'91*
Impromptu *'90*
Henry V *'89*
Look Back in Anger *'89*
The Tall Guy *'89*
Fortunes of War *'87*

Fred Dalton Thompson (1942-)

Bury My Heart at Wounded Knee *'07*
Looking for Comedy in the Muslim World *'06*
Racing Stripes *'05 (V)*
Baby's Day Out *'94*
Barbarians at the Gate *'93*
Born Yesterday *'93*
In the Line of Fire *'93*
Aces: Iron Eagle 3 *'92*
Keep the Change *'92*
Thunderheart *'92*
White Sands *'92*
Cape Fear *'91*
Class Action *'91*
Curly Sue *'91*
Days of Thunder *'90*
Die Hard 2: Die Harder *'90*
The Hunt for Red October *'90*
Feds *'88*
No Way Out *'87*
Marie *'85*

Greg Thompson

Dark Remains *'05*
Ghost of the Needle *'03*

Hal Thompson

Lassie from Lancashire *'38*
Animal Crackers *'30*

Hugh Thompson

The Memory Keeper's Daughter *'08*
The Christmas Blessing *'05*
The Christmas Shoes *'02*
Recipe for Revenge *'98*
What Happened to Rosa? *'21*

Jack Thompson (1940-)

Australia *'08*
Leatherheads *'08*
December Boys *'07*
The Good German *'06*
The Assassination of Richard Nixon *'05*
Feed *'05*
Star Wars: Episode 2—Attack of the Clones *'02*
Original Sin *'01*
Rodgers & Hammerstein's South Pacific *'01*
Midnight in the Garden of Good and Evil *'97*
Under the Lighthouse Dancing *'97*
Excess Baggage *'96*
Last Dance *'96*
The Thorn Birds: The Missing Years *'96*
The Sum of Us *'94*
A Far Off Place *'93*
Deception *'92*
The Killing Beach *'92*
Resistance *'92*
Wind *'92*
Ground Zero *'88*
Shadow on the Sun *'88*
Trouble in Paradise *'88*
Burke & Wills *'85*
Flesh and Blood *'85*
Merry Christmas, Mr. Lawrence *'83*
Waterfront *'83*
The Man from Snowy River *'82*
Bad Blood *'81*
The Club *'81*
Breaker Morant *'80*
Earthling *'80*
The Chant of Jimmie Blacksmith *'78*
Love Under Pressure *'78*
Caddie *'76*
Jock Petersen *'74*
Sunday Too Far Away *'74*

Kay Thompson (1903-98)

Funny Face *'57*
Manhattan Merry-Go-Round *'37*

Kenan Thompson (1978-)

Stan Helsing *'09*
Space Chimps *'08 (V)*
Snakes on a Plane *'06*
Barbershop 2: Back in Business *'04*
Fat Albert *'04*
Love Don't Cost a Thing *'03*
My Boss's Daughter *'03*
The Adventures of Rocky & Bullwinkle *'00*
Good Burger *'97*
D2: The Mighty Ducks *'94*
Heavyweights *'94*

Larry Thompson

Bobby Jones: Stroke of Genius *'04*
King of the Forest Rangers *'46*

Lea Thompson (1962-)

Exit Speed *'08*
Final Approach *'08*
Senior Skip Day *'08*
Spy School *'08*
California Dreaming *'07*
The Right to Remain Silent *'95*
The Substitute Wife *'94*
The Beverly Hillbillies *'93*
Dennis the Menace *'93*
Article 99 *'92*
Back to the Future, Part 3 *'90*
Montana *'90*
Back to the Future, Part 2 *'89*
Nightbreaker *'89*
Casual Sex? *'88*
Going Undercover *'88*
The Wizard of Loneliness *'88*
Some Kind of Wonderful *'87*
Howard the Duck *'86*
SpaceCamp *'86*
Back to the Future *'85*
Red Dawn *'84*
The Wild Life *'84*
All the Right Moves *'83*
Jaws 3 *'83*

Marshall Thompson (1925-92)

Bog *'84*
The Turning Point *'77*
George! *'70*
Clarence, the Cross-eyed Lion *'65*
To the Shores of Hell *'65*
Mighty Jungle *'64*
No Man Is an Island *'62*
First Man into Space *'59*
Fiend without a Face *'58*

It! The Terror from Beyond Space '58
East of Kilimanjaro '57
Crashout '55
Cult of the Cobra '55
To Hell and Back '55
The Caddy '53
Mystery Street '50
Stars in My Crown '50 (N)
Battleground '49
Words and Music '48
The Show-Off '46
The Clock '45
They Were Expendable '45
The Purple Heart '44

Miles Thompson
Foreign Exchange '08
Me and You and Everyone We Know '05

Peter Thompson (1920-2001)
Santa Fe '51
The Happy Years '50
The Wistful Widow of Wagon Gap '47

Reece Thompson (1988-)
Afterwards '08
Rocket Science '07
The Sandlot 2 '05
Dreamcatcher '03
National Lampoon's Holiday Reunion '03

Rex Thompson (1942-)
All Mine to Give '56
The Eddy Duchin Story '56
The King and I '56
Young Bess '53

Sada Thompson (1929-)
Indictment: The McMartin Trial '95
Queen '93
The Adventures of Huckleberry Finn '85
Our Town '77
Desperate Characters '71

Sarah Thompson
Break '09
A Christmas Proposal '08
Dear Me: A Blogger's Tale '08
The Pink Conspiracy '07
Cruel Intentions 2 '99

Scott Thompson (1959-)
The Pacifier '05
My Baby's Daddy '04
Prom Queen '04
Tart '01
Loser '00
Mickey Blue Eyes '99
Armistead Maupin's More Tales of the City '97
Hijacking Hollywood '97
Kids in the Hall: Brain Candy '96

Shawn Thompson
Bram Stoker's Shadow-builder '98
Future Fear '97
Sleeping with Strangers '94
Hairspray '88

Shelley Thompson
Just Like a Woman '95
Labyrinth '86

Sophie Thompson (1962-)
A Room With a View '08
A Harlot's Progress '06
Gosford Park '01
Relative Values '99
Dancing at Lughnasa '98
Emma '96
Persuasion '95
Four Weddings and a Funeral '94
Twenty-One '91

Susanna Thompson (1958-)
The Ballad of Jack and Rose '05
Dragonfly '02
High Noon '00
Random Hearts '99
Ghosts of Mississippi '96
America's Dream '95
Little Giants '94

Teri Thompson
Breakaway '95
Married People, Single Sex '93

Tessa Thompson (1983-)
Make It Happen '08
The Initiation of Sarah '06
When a Stranger Calls '06
Cracker: Brotherly Love '95

Victoria Thompson (1946-)
Harrad Summer '74
Harrad Experiment '73

Wesley Thompson
Infestation '09
Smiling Fish & Goat on Fire '99

Tracie Thoms (1975-)
Death Proof '07
Sex and Breakfast '07
The Devil Wears Prada '06
Rent '05

Ulrich Thomsen (1963-)
Season of the Witch '10
The International '09
The Broken '08
The Company '07
Hitman '07
Opium: Diary of a Madwoman '07
Adam's Apples '05
Allegro '05
Kingdom of Heaven '05
Brothers '04
Max '02
Flickering Lights '01
Killing Me Softly '01
Mostly Martha '01
The Weight of Water '00
The World Is Not Enough '99
Angel of the Night '98
The Celebration '98
The Inheritance '76

Sally Thomsett (1950-)
Straw Dogs '72
The Railway Children '70

Anna Thomson (1957-)
Intern '00
Six Ways to Sunday '99
Water Drops on Burning Rocks '99
Fiona '98
Cafe Society '97
Drunks '96
I Shot Andy Warhol '96
Jaded '96
Angus '95
Other Voices, Other Rooms '95
Outside the Law '95
Angela '94
The Crow '93
Unforgiven '92

Erik Thomson
The Black Balloon '09
The Boys Are Back '09
The Alice '04
Somersault '04

Gordon Thomson (1945-)
The Fiance '96
The Donor '94
Explosion '69

Helen Thomson
Nowhere to Land '00
Bloodmoon '90

Kenneth Thomson (1899-1967)
Hopalong Cassidy '35
In Old Santa Fe '34
Daring Daughters '33
Jungle Bride '33
The Little Giant '33
Held for Murder '32
Broadway Melody '29
Say It With Songs '29
White Gold '28

Kim Thomson (1960-)
The Princess Diaries 2: Royal Engagement '04
Murder 101 '91
Hands of a Murderer '90
Jekyll and Hyde '90
The Tall Guy '89
Stealing Heaven '88

R.H. Thomson (1947-)
Chloe '09
Population 436 '06
Bugs '03
P.T. Barnum '99
Bone Daddy '97
The Twilight of the Ice Nymphs '97
The Lotus Eaters '93
The Quarrel '93
Glory Enough for All: The Discovery of Insulin '92
Mark Twain and Me '91
Love and Hate: A Marriage Made in Hell '90
Heaven on Earth '89
And Then You Die '88
Ford: The Man & the Machine '87
Canada's Sweetheart: The Saga of Hal C. Banks '85
Surfacing '84
If You Could See What I Hear '82
Ticket to Heaven '81
Charlie Grant's War '80

Scott Thomson
Ghoulies '84
Fast Times at Ridgemont High '82

Jon Mikl Thor
Zombie Nightmare '86
Rock 'n' Roll Nightmare '85

Jim Thorburn
Merlin and the Book of Beasts '09
The Deal '05

Kelly Thordsen (1917-78)
The Parallax View '74
Bad Charleston Charlie '73
Charley and the Angel '73
Now You See Him, Now You Don't '72
The Boatniks '70
Smoke '70
Blackbeard's Ghost '67
Good Times '67
Boy, Did I Get a Wrong Number! '66
Texas Across the River '66
Shenandoah '65
The Ugly Dachshund '65
The Misadventures of Merlin Jones '63
Sweet Bird of Youth '62
Invasion of the Saucer Men '57

Frankie Thorn (1964-)
Bad Blood '94
Bad Lieutenant '92
Liquid Dreams '92

Bill Thornbury (1952-)
Phantasm 4: Oblivion '98
Phantasm 3: Lord of the Dead '94
Phantasm '79

Russell Thorndike (1885-1972)
Henry V '44
A Shot in the Dark '33

Sybil Thorndike (1882-1976)
Shake Hands with the Devil '59
The Prince and the Showgirl '57
Stage Fright '50
Nicholas Nickleby '46
Major Barbara '41
Nine Days a Queen '36

Angela Thorne (1939-)
The Lady's Not for Burning '87
Poor Girl, a Ghost Story '74
Oh! What a Lovely War '69

Callie (Calliope) Thorne (1969-)
Watching the Detectives '07
Delirious '06
Four and a Half Women '05
Analyze That '02
Washington Heights '02
Revolution #9 '01
Sidewalks of New York '01
Double Parked '00
Homicide: The Movie '00
Whipped '00
Giving It Up '99
Wirey Spindell '99
Ed's Next Move '96

Dyanne Thorne (1932-)
Hellhole '85
Ilsa, the Tigress of Siberia '79
Ilsa, the Wicked Warden '78
Ilsa, Harem Keeper of the Oil Sheiks '76
Wham-Bam, Thank You Spaceman '75
Ilsa, She-Wolf of the SS '74
Point of Terror '71

Courtney Thorne-Smith (1967-)
Chairman of the Board '97
Breach of Conduct '94
Side Out '90
Revenge of the Nerds 2: Nerds in Paradise '87
Summer School '87
Welcome to 18 '87
Lucas '86

Billy Bob Thornton (1955-)
The Informers '09
Eagle Eye '08
The Astronaut Farmer '07
Mr. Woodcock '07
School for Scoundrels '06
The Bad News Bears '05
The Ice Harvest '05
The Alamo '04
Friday Night Lights '04
Bad Santa '03
Intolerable Cruelty '03
Levity '03
Love Actually '03
The Badge '02
Waking Up in Reno '02
Bandits '01
The Man Who Wasn't There '01
Monster's Ball '01
South of Heaven, West of Hell '00
Daddy & Them '99
Pushing Tin '99
Armageddon '98
Primary Colors '98
Princess Mononoke '98 (V)
A Simple Plan '98
An Alan Smithee Film: Burn, Hollywood, Burn '97
The Apostle '97
A Gun, a Car, a Blonde '97
Homegrown '97
U-Turn '97
Sling Blade '96
The Winner '96
Dead Man '95
Out There '95
Floundering '94
On Deadly Ground '94
Some Folks Call It a Sling Blade '94
The Ghost Brigade '93
Indecent Proposal '93
Tombstone '93
Chopper Chicks in Zombietown '91
One False Move '91

David Thornton (1953-)
Alpha Dog '06
John Q '02
100 Mile Rule '02
Swept Away '02
XX/XY '02
Dead Dog '00
High Art '98
Hush '98
The Last Days of Disco '98
Home Alone 3 '97
Office Killer '97
She's So Lovely '97
Breathing Room '96
Unhook the Stars '96
Diamond Run '90
Off and Running '90

Edith Thornton (1896-1984)
Lightning Hutch '26
Virtue's Revolt '24

Frank Thornton (1921-)
Auntie '73
Tomb of Ligeia '64

Noley Thornton (1983-)
Heidi '93
Danielle Steel's Fine Things '90

Sigrid Thornton (1959-)
Inspector Gadget 2 '02
Trapped in Space '94
Over the Hill '93
Return to Snowy River '88
Great Expectations: The Untold Story '87
The Lighthorsemen '87
Slate, Wyn & Me '87
Best Enemies '86
Nevil Shute's The Far Country '85
All the Rivers Run '84
Street Hero '84
The Man from Snowy River '82
1915 '82
The Night After Halloween '79

Jim Thorpe (1888-1953)
My Pal, the King '32
White Eagle '32
Battling with Buffalo Bill '31

Sven-Ole Thorsen (1944-)
In Enemy Hands '04
The Sum of All Fears '02
Gladiator '00
Foolish '99
Kull the Conqueror '97
Fatal Combat '96
Mallrats '95
The Undercover Kid '95
The Viking Sagas '95
Dragon: The Bruce Lee Story '93
Abraxas: Guardian of the Universe '90

Linda Thorson (1947-)
Straight into Darkness '04
Half Past Dead '02
The Other Sister '98
Walls of Glass '85

Russ Thorson
My Blood Runs Cold '65
36 Hours '64

William Thourlby (1924-)
Castle of Evil '66
Creeping Terror '64

Cyrille Thouvenin (1976-)
Dangerous Liaisons '03
Confusion of Genders '00

David Threlfall (1953-)
Nowhere Boy '09
Elizabeth: The Golden Age '07
The Queen's Sister '05
Master and Commander: The Far Side of the World '03
Conspiracy '01
Mary, Mother of Jesus '99
The Summer House '94
Diana: Her True Story '93
A Casualty of War '90
A Murder of Quality '90
The Russia House '90
When the Whales Came '89
Kiss of Death '77

Frank Thring, Jr. (1926-94)
Howling 3: The Marsupials '87
Mad Max: Beyond Thunderdome '85
Alvin Rides Again '74

Michelle Thrush
Skins '02
Ebenezer '97

Luc Thuillier
The Old Lady Who Walked in the Sea '91
Monsieur Hire '89

Ingrid Thulin (1926-2003)
Control '87
After the Rehearsal '84
The Cassandra Crossing '76
Moses '76
Cries and Whispers '72
Short Night of Glass Dolls '71
The Damned '69
The Rite '69
Hour of the Wolf '68
La Guerre Est Finie '66
The Silence '63
The Winter Light '62
The Magician '58
Brink of Life '57
Wild Strawberries '57

Chief Thundercloud (1899-1955)
Call of the Forest '49
Blazing Across the Pecos '48
The Phantom Rider '46
Renegade Girl '46
Outlaw Trail '44
Sonora Stagecoach '44
King of the Stallions '42
Ride, Ranger, Ride '36
Annie Oakley '35
Rustlers of Red Dog '35

Bill (Billy) Thurman (1920-95)
Mountaintop Motel Massacre '86
Creature from Black Lake '76
Slumber Party '57 '76
The Florida Connection '74
Gator Bait '73
The Last Picture Show '71
It's Alive! '68
Curse of the Swamp Creature '66

Dechen Thurman (1973-)
Hamlet '00
I Think I Do '97

Uma Thurman (1970-)
Percy Jackson & The Olympians: The Lightning Thief '10
Motherhood '09
The Accidental Husband '08
My Zinc Bed '08
The Life Before Her Eyes '07
My Super Ex-Girlfriend '06
Be Cool '05
Prime '05
The Producers '05
Kill Bill Vol. 2 '04
Kill Bill Vol. 1 '03

Paycheck *'03*
Hysterical Blindness *'02*
Chelsea Walls *'01*
Tape *'01*
The Golden Bowl *'00*
Vatel *'00*
Sweet and Lowdown *'99*
The Avengers *'98*
Batman and Robin *'97*
Gattaca *'97*
Les Miserables *'97*
Beautiful Girls *'96*
The Truth about Cats and Dogs *'96*
A Month by the Lake *'95*
Even Cowgirls Get the Blues *'94*
Pulp Fiction *'94*
Mad Dog and Glory *'93*
Final Analysis *'92*
Jennifer 8 *'92*
Robin Hood *'91*
Henry & June *'90*
Where the Heart Is *'90*
The Adventures of Baron Munchausen *'89*
Dangerous Liaisons *'88*
Johnny Be Good *'88*
Kiss Daddy Goodnight *'87*

Sophie Thursfield

Sister My Sister *'94*
Oranges Are Not the Only Fruit *'89*

Carol Thurston (1923-69)

Apache Chief *'50*
Swamp Fire *'46*
China Sky *'44*
The Story of Dr. Wassell *'44*

Greta Thyssen

Three Blondes in His Life *'61*
Terror Is a Man *'59*

Lung Ti

The Water Margin *'72*
Have Sword, Will Travel *'69*

Ben Tibber (1990-)

I Am David *'04*
A Christmas Carol *'99*

Gerard Tichy (1920-92)

Ricco *'74*
The Hanging Woman *'72*
Hatchet for the Honeymoon *'70*
The Hot Line *'69*
Four Dollars of Revenge *'66*
Doctor Zhivago *'65*
Gladiators 7 *'62*

Nancy Ticotin

The Tavern *'00*
Ransom *'96*

Rachel Ticotin (1959-)

The Burning Plain *'08*
The Eye *'08*
Sisterhood of the Traveling Pants *'05*
Man on Fire *'04*
Something's Gotta Give *'03*
Desert Saints *'01*
Warden of Red Rock *'01*
Forever Together *'00*
Full Disclosure *'00*
Aftershock: Earthquake in New York *'99*
Malicious Intent *'99*
Con Air *'97*
First Time Felon *'97*
Turbulence *'96*
Steal Big, Steal Little *'95*
The Wharf Rat *'95*
Deconstructing Sarah *'94*
Don Juan DeMarco *'94*
Natural Born Killers *'94*
Falling Down *'93*
Keep the Change *'92*
Where the Day Takes You *'92*
F/X 2: The Deadly Art of Illusion *'91*
One Good Cop *'91*
Prison Stories: Women on the Inside *'91*
Spies, Lies and Naked Thighs *'91*
Total Recall *'90*
Critical Condition *'86*
Rockabye *'86*
When the Bough Breaks *'86*
Fort Apache, the Bronx *'81*
King of the Gypsies *'78*

Max Tidof

The Harmonists *'99*
Burning Life *'94*

Andrea Tidona

The Listening *'06*
Best of Youth *'03*

Dov Tiefenbach (1981-)

Detention *'03*
Jason X *'01*

Feng Tien

A Time to Live and a Time to Die *'85*
King Boxer *'72*
The Shadow Whip *'71*
Sword Masters: Brothers Five *'70*

James Tien

Half a Loaf of Kung Fu *'78*
Chinese Connection *'73*

Andrew Tiernan (1965-)

300 *'07*
The Criminal *'00*
Horatio Hornblower *'99*
Face *'97*
The Scarlet Tunic *'97*
Playing God *'96*
Edward II *'92*

Patricia Tiernan

Zero Hour! *'57*
Battle Circus *'53*

Brigid Tierney

Twist *'03*
Affliction *'97*
The Paperboy *'94*

Gene Tierney (1920-91)

Scruples *'80*
Toys in the Attic *'63*
Advise and Consent *'62*
The Left Hand of God *'55*
Black Widow *'54*
The Egyptian *'54*
Never Let Me Go *'53*
Close to My Heart *'51*
Night and the City *'50*
Where the Sidewalk Ends *'50*
Whirlpool *'49*
That Wonderful Urge *'48*
The Ghost and Mrs. Muir *'47*
Dragonwyck *'46*
The Razor's Edge *'46*
Leave Her to Heaven *'45*
Laura *'44*
Heaven Can Wait *'43*
The Shanghai Gesture *'42*
Son of Fury *'42*
Thunder Birds *'42*
Sundown *'41*
Return of Frank James *'40*

Jacob Tierney (1979-)

Poor White Trash *'00*
The Life Before This *'99*
This Is My Father *'99*
Dead End *'98*
The Neon Bible *'95*
Josh and S.A.M. *'93*
Pin... *'88*

Lawrence Tierney (1919-2002)

Southie *'98*
A Kiss Goodnight *'94*
Wizards of the Demon Sword *'94*
Casualties of Love: The "Long Island Lolita" Story *'93*
Eddie Presley *'92*
Reservoir Dogs *'92*
City of Hope *'91*
The Death Merchant *'91*
Red *'91*
Why Me? *'90*
The Offspring *'87*
Tough Guys Don't Dance *'87*
Murphy's Law *'86*
Prizzi's Honor *'85*
Silver Bullet *'85*
Midnight *'81*
The Prowler *'81*
Never Pick Up a Stranger *'79*
Andy Warhol's Bad *'77*
Abduction *'75*
The Female Jungle *'56*
The Bushwackers *'52*
The Greatest Show on Earth *'52*
The Hoodlum *'51*
Best of the Badmen *'50*
Born to Kill *'47*
The Devil Thumbs a Ride *'47*
Back to Bataan *'45*
Dillinger *'45*
Those Endearing Young Charms *'45*
The Ghost Ship *'43*

Malcolm Tierney

The Apocalypse Watch *'97*
House of Cards *'90*

Maura Tierney (1965-)

Baby Mama *'08*
Finding Amanda *'08*
Semi-Pro *'08*
All the Good Ones Are Married *'07*
Danny Roane: First Time Director *'06*
Diggers *'06*
Welcome to Mooseport *'04*
Melvin Goes to Dinner *'03*
Insomnia *'02*
Scotland, PA *'02*
Forces of Nature *'99*
Instinct *'99*
Oxygen *'99*
Primary Colors *'98*
Liar Liar *'97*
Primal Fear *'96*
Fly by Night *'93*
The Temp *'93*
White Sands *'92*
Dead Women in Lingerie *'90*

Angelo Tiffe

Sword of Honor *'94*
3 Ninjas Kick Back *'94*

Jerry Tiffe

Sword of Honor *'94*
Hollywood in Trouble *'87*

Pamela Tiffin (1942-)

Viva Max *'69*
Harper *'66*
The Hallelujah Trail *'65*
State Fair *'62*
One, Two, Three *'61*
Summer and Smoke *'61*

Marie Tifo (1949-)

Prom Queen *'04*
Pouvoir Intime *'87*
Les Bons Debarras *'81*

Ken Tigar (1942-)

The Underground *'97*
Hollywood Safari *'96*
Little Bigfoot *'96*
Rage *'95*
Phantasm 2 *'88*
The Betty Ford Story *'87*

Kevin Tighe (1944-)

My Bloody Valentine 3D *'09*
The Deal *'05*
Stephen King's Rose Red *'02*
The Big Day *'99*
The Darwin Conspiracy *'99*
Mumford *'99*
Winchell *'98*
In Cold Blood *'96*
Race the Sun *'96*
The Avenging Angel *'95*
Better Off Dead *'94*
Double Cross *'94*
Men of War *'94*
Caught in the Act *'93*
Geronimo: An American Legend *'93*
A Man in Uniform *'93*
What's Eating Gilbert Grape *'93*
Newsies *'92*
School Ties *'92*
Bright Angel *'91*
City of Hope *'91*
Another 48 Hrs. *'90*
K-9 *'89*
Lost Angels *'89*
Road House *'89*
Eight Men Out *'88*
Matewan *'87*

Ramon Tikaram

Ruby in the Smoke *'06*
Kama Sutra: A Tale of Love *'96*

Zeffie Tilbury (1863-1950)

Sheriff of Tombstone *'41*
The Grapes of Wrath *'40*
Werewolf of London *'35*
The Single Standard *'29*

Lucas Till

Hannah Montana: The Movie *'09*
Dance of the Dead *'08*

Nadja Tiller (1929-)

Wanted: Babysitter *'75*
Dead Are Alive *'72*
How I Learned to Love Women *'66*
Tonio Kroger *'65*
The Burning Court *'62*
The Rough and the Smooth *'59*

Mel Tillis (1932-)

Uphill All the Way *'85*
Smokey and the Bandit 2 *'80*
The Villain *'79*

Grant Tilly (1937-)

Brilliant Lies *'96*
Treasure of the Yankee Zephyr *'83*
Carry Me Back *'82*
Beyond Reasonable Doubt *'80*

Jennifer Tilly (1963-)

American Girl: Chrissa Stands Strong *'09*
Bart Got a Room *'08*
Deal *'08*
The Initiation of Sarah *'06*
Bailey's Billion$ *'05*
Second Best *'05*
Tideland *'05*
Home on the Range *'04 (V)*
Love on the Side *'04*
Saint Ralph *'04*
Seed of Chucky *'04 (V)*
The Haunted Mansion *'03*
Hollywood North *'03*
Jericho Mansions *'03*
The Magnificent Ambersons *'02*
The Cat's Meow *'01*
Fast Sofa *'01*
Monsters, Inc. *'01 (V)*
The Crew *'00*
Dancing at the Blue Iguana *'00*
Hide and Seek *'00*
The Dress Code *'99*
The Muse *'99*
Silent Witness *'99*
Stuart Little *'99 (V)*
Bride of Chucky *'98*
Hoods *'98*
Relax... It's Just Sex! *'98*
Bella Mafia *'97*
Liar Liar *'97*
Music from Another Room *'97*
American Strays *'96*
Bound *'96*
House Arrest *'96*
The Wrong Guy *'96*
Bird of Prey *'95*
Edie & Pen *'95*
Embrace of the Vampire *'95*
Man with a Gun *'95*
The Pompatus of Love *'95*
At Home with the Webbers *'94*
Bullets over Broadway *'94*
Double Cross *'94*
The Getaway *'93*
Heads *'93*
Made in America *'93*
Scorchers *'92*
Shadow of the Wolf *'92*
Inside Out *'91*
The Fabulous Baker Boys *'89*
Far from Home *'89*
Let It Ride *'89*
High Spirits *'88*
Remote Control *'88*
Rented Lips *'88*
He's My Girl *'87*
Moving Violations *'85*
No Small Affair *'84*

Meg Tilly (1960-)

Journey *'95*
Primal Secrets *'94*
Sleep with Me *'94*
Body Snatchers *'93*
Fallen Angels 2 *'93*
Leaving Normal *'92*
The Two Jakes *'90*
The Girl in a Swing *'89*
Valmont *'89*
Masquerade *'88*
Off Beat *'86*
Agnes of God *'85*
Impulse *'84*
The Big Chill *'83*
Psycho 2 *'83*
One Dark Night *'82*
Tex *'82*

Charlene Tilton (1958-)

Totally Blonde *'01*
Safety Patrol *'98*
Silence of the Hams *'93*
Center of the Web *'92*
Deadly Bet *'91*
Problem Child 2 *'91*
Border Shootout *'90*
Ragin' Cajun *'90*
Diary of a Teenage Hitchhiker *'82*
The Fall of the House of Usher *'80*
Sweater Girls *'78*
Freaky Friday *'76*

Martha Tilton (1915-2006)

The Benny Goodman Story *'55*
Sunny *'41*

Justin Timberlake (1981-)

Shrek Forever After *'10 (V)*
The Open Road *'09*
The Love Guru *'08*
Black Snake Moan *'07*
Shrek the Third *'07 (V)*
Alpha Dog *'06*
Southland Tales *'06*
Edison Force *'05*
Model Behavior *'00*

Corbin Timbrook

Alien 3000 *'04*
Forbidden Sins *'99*

Filippo Timi

The Double Hour *'09*
Saturn in Opposition *'07*

Addison Timlin

Afterschool *'08*
Derailed *'05*

Cali Timmins (1963-)

Heaven's Fire *'99*
The Heist *'96*
Hard Evidence *'94*
The Takeover *'94*

Patrick Timsit (1959-)

Pedale Douce *'96*
Little Indian, Big City *'95*

Charles "Bud" Tingwell (1923-)

Irresistible *'06*
Ned Kelly *'03*
Innocence *'00*
The Castle *'97*
A Cry in the Dark *'88*
Miracle Down Under *'87*
Malcolm *'86*
Windrider *'86*
All the Rivers Run *'84*
Freedom *'82*
Breaker Morant *'80*
Money Movers *'78*
Gone to Ground *'76*
Endplay *'75*
Dracula, Prince of Darkness *'66*
Murder Most Foul *'65*
Murder Ahoy *'64*
Murder at the Gallop *'63*
Murder She Said *'62*
The Desert Rats *'53*

Gabriele Tinti (1932-91)

Women's Prison Massacre *'85*
Caged Women *'84*
Love Camp *'81*
Emmanuelle, the Queen *'79*
Emmanuelle's Daughter *'79*
Emmanuelle in the Country *'78*
Naked Paradise *'78*
Trap Them & Kill Them *'77*
Delusions of Grandeur *'76*
Lisa and the Devil *'75*
M'Lady's Court *'73*
Web of Deception *'71*
Journey Beneath the Desert *'61*

Jamie Tirelli (1945-)

Sugar *'09*
Bella *'06*
The Groomsmen *'06*
Yellow *'06*
Girlfight *'99*
Lotto Land *'95*
Sudden Death *'85*

Ashley Tisdale (1985-)

Aliens in the Attic *'09*
High School Musical 3: Senior Year *'08*
Picture This! *'08*
High School Musical 2 *'07*

Jennifer Tisdale

Bring It On: In It to Win It *'07*
Rollin' Plains *'38*

Jean Tissier (1896-1973)

Please Not Now! *'61*
The Hunchback of Notre Dame *'57*

Chapman To

The Beautiful Country *'04*
Infernal Affairs 2 *'03*
Infernal Affairs 3 *'03*
The Cave of the Silken Web *'67*

James Toback (1944-)

Never Down *'06*
When Will I Be Loved *'04*
Black and White *'99*
Giving It Up *'99*
Fingers *'78*

Joel Tobeck (1971-)

Eagle vs. Shark *'07*
Little Fish *'05*
Perfect Strangers *'03*

Kenneth Tobey (1919-2002)

Body Shot *'93*
Desire and Hell at Sunset Motel *'92*
Honey, I Blew Up the Kid *'92*
Single White Female *'92*
Gremlins 2: The New Batch *'90*
Freeway *'88*
Innerspace *'87*
Night of the Creeps *'86*
The Lost Empire *'83*
Strange Invaders *'83*
The Howling *'81*
Missiles of October *'74*
Ben *'72*
Gunfight at the O.K. Corral *'57*
Wings of Eagles *'57*
The Great Locomotive Chase *'56*

The Wild Thornberrys Movie '02 (V)
In the Bedroom '01
King of the Jungle '01
Someone Like You '01
Happy Accidents '00
The Watcher '00
What Women Want '00
My Own Country '98
Only Love '98
Slums of Beverly Hills '98
A Brother's Kiss '97
Since You've Been Gone '97
Welcome to Sarajevo '97
Unhook the Stars '96
Four Rooms '95
Only You '94
The Paper '94
The Perez Family '94
Equinox '93
Untamed Heart '93
Chaplin '92
My Cousin Vinny '92
Oscar '91
Zandalee '91

Frances Tomelty (1948-)

Cheri '09
The Field '90
Bellman and True '88
A Perfect Spy '88
Lamb '85
Blue Money '84
Bullshot '83

Joseph Tomelty (1911-95)

A Night to Remember '58
The Atomic Man '56
John and Julie '55
Devil Girl from Mars '54
The Sound Barrier '52

Akihiro Tomikawa (1968-)

Shogun Assassin 2: Lightning Swords of Death '73
Lone Wolf and Cub '72
Lone Wolf and Cub 4 '72
Lone Wolf and Cub: Baby Cart at the River Styx '72
Lone Wolf and Cub: Baby Cart to Hades '72

Tamlyn Tomita (1966-)

Pandemic '07
Only the Brave '06
The Day After Tomorrow '04
Robot Stories '03
Life Tastes Good '99
Soundman '99
The Killing Jar '96
Four Rooms '95
Picture Bride '94
The Joy Luck Club '93
Come See the Paradise '90
Hiroshima: Out of the Ashes '90
Vietnam, Texas '90
Hiroshima Maiden '88
The Karate Kid: Part 2 '86

Lily Tomlin (1939-)

The Pink Panther 2 '09
Ponyo '08 (V)
The Walker '07
The Ant Bully '06 (V)
A Prairie Home Companion '06
I Heart Huckabees '04
Orange County '02
Disney's The Kid '00
Tea with Mussolini '99
Krippendorf's Tribe '98
Getting Away With Murder '96
Blue in the Face '95
The Celluloid Closet '95 (N)
Flirting with Disaster '95
And the Band Played On '93
The Beverly Hillbillies '93
Short Cuts '93
The Player '92
Shadows and Fog '92
Search for Signs of Intelligent Life in the Universe '91
Big Business '88
All of Me '84
The Incredible Shrinking Woman '81
9 to 5 '80
The Late Show '77
Nashville '75

David Tomlinson (1917-2000)

The Fiendish Plot of Dr. Fu Manchu '80
Water Babies '79
Wombling Free '77
Bedknobs and Broomsticks '71
Mary Poppins '64
Tom Jones '63
Up the Creek '58
Carry On Admiral '57
Three Men in a Boat '56
Made in Heaven '52
Wooden Horse '50
Fame Is the Spur '47
Sleeping Car to Trieste '45
Pimpernel Smith '42

Ricky Tomlinson (1939-)

Once Upon a Time in the Midlands '02
Formula 51 '01
Preaching to the Perverted '97
Cracker: Best Boys '95
Cracker: Brotherly Love '95
Cracker: True Romance '95
Butterfly Kiss '94
Raining Stones '93
Riff Raff '92

Angel Tompkins (1943-)

Crack House '89
Relentless '89
A Tiger's Tale '87
Murphy's Law '86
Naked Cage '86
Alligator '80
The Bees '78
Walking Tall: Part 2 '75
The Teacher '74
The Don Is Dead '73
Prime Cut '72
Probe '72
I Love My... Wife '70

Matthew Tompkins

Missionary Man '07
G. Whilliker! '93

Stephen Tompkinson (1965-)

Oktober '98
Brassed Off '96
And a Nightingale Sang '91

Kate Toncray (1867-1927)

The Country Kid '23
The Lamb '15

Franchot Tone (1905-68)

In Harm's Way '65
Mickey One '65
Advise and Consent '62
Here Comes the Groom '51
Jigsaw '49
Every Girl Should Be Married '48
Man on the Eiffel Tower '48
Her Husband's Affairs '47
Lost Honeymoon '47
Because of Him '45
Dark Waters '44
His Butler's Sister '44
Phantom Lady '44
Five Graves to Cairo '43
Nice Girl? '41
Three Comrades '38
The Bride Wore Red '37
Quality Street '37
The Gorgeous Hussy '36
Love on the Run '36
Suzy '36
Dangerous '35
The Lives of a Bengal Lancer '35
Mutiny on the Bounty '35
Reckless '35
The Girl from Missouri '34
Sadie McKee '34
The World Moves On '34
Bombshell '33
Dancing Lady '33
Gabriel Over the White House '33
Today We Live '33

Tone Loc (1966-)

Rhapsody '01
They Crawl '01
Titan A.E. '00 (V)
Freedom Strike '98
Heat '95
Ace Ventura: Pet Detective '93
Blank Check '93
Posse '93
Surf Ninjas '93
Bebe's Kids '92 (V)
Ferngully: The Last Rain Forest '92 (V)
The Adventures of Ford Fairlane '90

Philip Tonge (1897-1959)

Invisible Invaders '59
Witness for the Prosecution '57
Love from a Stranger '47

Eijiro Tono (1907-94)

Tora! Tora! Tora! '70
Yojimbo '61
The Human Condition: No Greater Love '58

Taiji Tonoyama (1915-89)

Tokyo Pop '88
Rica 2: Lonely Wanderer '73
Rica 3: Juvenile's Lullaby '73
The Island '61

Regis Toomey (1902-91)

Change of Habit '69
Warlock '59
The Curfew Breakers '57
Great Day in the Morning '56
Guys and Dolls '55
The High and the Mighty '54
Island in the Sky '53
Never Wave at a WAC '52
Dynamite Pass '50
Beyond the Forest '49
Come to the Stable '49
I Wouldn't Be in Your Shoes '48
The Bishop's Wife '47
Magic Town '47
The Big Sleep '46
Spellbound '45
Strange Illusion '45
Betrayal from the East '44
Dark Mountain '44
Phantom Lady '44
Raiders of Ghost City '44
Destroyer '43
I Was Framed '42
Dive Bomber '41
Meet John Doe '41
They Died with Their Boots On '41
Arizona '40
The Phantom Creeps '39
Union Pacific '39
Shadows of the Orient '37
Bulldog Edition '36
"G" Men '35
Skull & Crown '35
Laughing at Life '33
They Never Come Back '32
Wayne Murder Case '32
Other Men's Women '31
Touchdown '31
The Light of Western Stars '30
Alibi '29

Geoffrey Toone

The Terror of the Tongs '61
Zero Hour! '57

Fred "Snowflake" Toones (1906-62)

Social Error '35
Single Handed Sanders '32

Gordon Tootoosis

Bury My Heart at Wounded Knee '07
Hybrid '07
Open Season '06 (V)
That Beautiful Somewhere '06
Now & Forever '02
Black Point '01
The Doe Boy '01
Nobody's Baby '01
Zoe '01
Big Bear '98
Coyote Summer '96
Crazy Horse '96
Pocahontas '95 (V)
Pocahontas: The Legend '95
Legends of the Fall '94
Call of the Wild '93
Spirit Rider '93
Stone Fox '87
Dan Candy's Law '73

Shawn Toovey (1983-)

Flash '98
The Fire Next Time '93

Jean Topart

Cop Au Vin '85
Action Man '67
The Testament of Dr. Cordelier '59

Chaim Topol (1935-)

Left Luggage '98
War & Remembrance: The Final Chapter '89
War & Remembrance '88
Queenie '87
The Winds of War '83
For Your Eyes Only '81
Flash Gordon '80
The House on Garibaldi Street '79
Fiddler on the Roof '71
Gun Crazy '69
Cast a Giant Shadow '66
Sallah '63

Peta Toppano (1952-)

Which Way Home '90
Echoes of Paradise '86

Amanda Topping

Stargate: Continuum '08
Stargate: The Ark of Truth '08

Sahaphap Tor

The Iron Ladies 2 '03
The Iron Ladies '00

Dan Toren

Year Zero '04
Atalia '85

Marta Toren (1926-57)

Paris Express '53
Casbah '48

Hal Torey (1915-89)

Invisible Invaders '59
Earth vs. the Spider '58

Sarah Torgov

American Gothic '88
If You Could See What I Hear '82
Drying Up the Streets '76

Peter Tork (1942-)

The Brady Bunch Movie '95
Head '68

Mel Torme (1925-99)

The Return of Spinal Tap '92
Naked Gun 2 1/2: The Smell of Fear '91
A Man Called Adam '66
Girls' Town '59
Words and Music '48
Good News '47

John Tormey (1937-)

Joe Gould's Secret '00
Ghost Dog: The Way of the Samurai '99

Angelica Torn (1964-)

The Golden Boys '08
Domestic Disturbance '01
Ruby's Bucket of Blood '01
Wrestling with Alligators '98

Rip Torn (1931-)

Happy Tears '09
August '08
The Golden Boys '08
Bee Movie '07 (V)
Three Days to Vegas '07
Turn the River '07
Marie Antoinette '06
Zoom '06
Forty Shades of Blue '05
The Sisters '05
Yours, Mine & Ours '05
Dodgeball: A True Underdog Story '04
Eulogy '04
Welcome to Mooseport '04
Men in Black 2 '02
Freddy Got Fingered '01
Wonder Boys '00
The Insider '99
Passing Glory '99
Senseless '98
Balloon Farm '97
Hercules '97 (V)
Men in Black '97
Down Periscope '96
Trial and Error '96
For Better or Worse '95
How to Make an American Quilt '95
Letter to My Killer '95
Canadian Bacon '94
Where the Rivers Flow North '94
Beautiful Dreamers '92
Beyond the Law '92
Dead Ahead: The Exxon Valdez Disaster '92
Dolly Dearest '92
Hard Promises '92
T Bone N Weasel '92
Another Pair of Aces: Three of a Kind '91
Defending Your Life '91
RoboCop 3 '91
Pair of Aces '90
Silence Like Glass '90
By Dawn's Early Light '89
Cold Feet '89
Sweet Bird of Youth '89
The Hit List '88
Extreme Prejudice '87
J. Edgar Hoover '87
Laguna Heat '87
Nadine '87
Manhunt for Claude Dallas '86
Beer '85
The Execution '85
Summer Rental '85
Cat on a Hot Tin Roof '84
City Heat '84
Flashpoint '84
Misunderstood '84
Songwriter '84
Cross Creek '83
Airplane 2: The Sequel '82
Beastmaster '82
Jinxed '82
A Stranger Is Watching '82
Heartland '81
One Trick Pony '80
Rape and Marriage: The Rideout Case '80
Blind Ambition '79
The Seduction of Joe Tynan '79
A Shining Season '79
Betrayal '78
The Birch Interval '78
Coma '78
Steel Cowboy '78
Nasty Habits '77
The Private Files of J. Edgar Hoover '77
The Man Who Fell to Earth '76
Payday '73
Cotter '72
Slaughter '72
The President's Plane Is Missing '71
Tropic of Cancer '70
Coming Apart '69
You're a Big Boy Now '66
The Cincinnati Kid '65
Critic's Choice '63
Sweet Bird of Youth '62
The King of Kings '61
24 Hours in a Woman's Life '61
Pork Chop Hill '59
Baby Doll '56

Mari Torocsik (1935-)

The Bachelor '93
Daniel Takes a Train '83
Love '71

Ingrid Torrance

Impulse '08
Act of War '96

David Torrence (1864-1951)

Jane Eyre '34
The Mask of Fu Manchu '32
Disraeli '30
Raffles '30
Tess of the Storm Country '22

Ernest Torrence (1878-1933)

I Cover the Waterfront '33
Fighting Caravans '31
Desert Nights '29
Speedway '29
Across to Singapore '28
Steamboat Bill, Jr. '28
King of Kings '27
Mantrap '26
The Pony Express '25
Peter Pan '24
The Covered Wagon '23
The Hunchback of Notre Dame '23
Tol'able David '21

Nate Torrence (1977-)

She's Out of My League '10
Get Smart '08
My Best Friend's Girl '08

Pip Torrens (1960-)

Easy Virtue '08
Miss Austen Regrets '07
Pinochet's Last Stand '06
Valiant '05 (V)
Shackleton '02
To End All Wars '01
Incognito '97
A Dark Adapted Eye '93
A Handful of Dust '88

Ana Torrent (1966-)

The Other Boleyn Girl '08
Thesis '96
Vacas '91
Blood and Sand '89
The Nest '80
Cria '76
Cria Cuervos '76
Spirit of the Beehive '73

Fernanda Torres (1965-)

House of Sand '05
Four Days in September '97
Foreign Land '95
Savage Capitalism '93
One Man's War '90

Gina Torres (1969-)

I Think I Love My Wife '07
South of Pico '07
Five Fingers '06
Jam '06
Serenity '05
Hair Show '04
The Matrix Reloaded '03
The Matrix Revolutions '03

Liz Torres (1947-)

Storm Chasers: Revenge of the Twister '98
The Wonderful Ice Cream Suit '98
A Million to Juan '94
National Lampoon's Attack of the 5 Ft. 2 Women '94
Bloodfist 4: Die Trying '92
Lena's Holiday '90
America '86

Raquel Torres (1908-87)

Duck Soup '33
So This Is Africa '33

White Shadows in the South Seas '29

Philippe Torreton (1965-)
District 13: Ultimatum '09
Monsieur N. '03
Capitaine Conan '96
L.627 '92

Guy Torry (1969-)
Runaway Jury '03
The Animal '01
Don't Say a Word '01
Pearl Harbor '01
The '70s '00
Life '99
Trippin' '99
American History X '98
Ride '98

Joe Torry (1965-)
The Dog Who Saved Christmas '09
The Boston Strangler: The Untold Story '08
Getting Played '05
Hair Show '04
Motives '03
The Flamingo Rising '01
Lockdown '00
Back in Business '96
Sprung '96
Tales from the Hood '95
Poetic Justice '93

Silvia Tortosa (1947-)
When the Screaming Stops '73
Horror Express '72

Jose Torvay (1910-73)
Battle Shock '56
Green Fire '55
The Hitch-Hiker '53
My Outlaw Brother '51
Borderline '50
Border Incident '49

Luis Tosar (1971-)
The Limits of Control '09
Miami Vice '06
Take My Eyes '03
Angel of Death '02
Mondays in the Sun '02
Jealousy '99

Luigi Tosi
The Black Devils of Kali '55
The Treasure of Bengal '53

Leslie Toth
Buying Time '89
Unfinished Business '89

Toto (1898-1967)
The Hawks & the Sparrows '67
Passionate Thief '60
Big Deal on Madonna Street '58

Merle Tottenham (1901-59)
Room to Let '49
This Happy Breed '47
Night Must Fall '37
Cavalcade '33

Audrey Totter (1918-)
The Carpetbaggers '64
Man or Gun '58
FBI Girl '52
Tension '50
Any Number Can Play '49
The Set-Up '49
Lady in the Lake '46
The Postman Always Rings Twice '46

Shaun Toub
The Last Airbender '10
Iron Man '08
The Kite Runner '07
The Nativity Story '06
Crash '05
Land of Plenty '04
Maryam '00

Elias Toufexis
Sand Serpents '09
Decoys '04

George Touliatos
36 Hours to Die '99
Tracks of a Killer '95
Red Scorpion 2 '94
Robbers of the Sacred Mountain '83
Firebird 2015 A.D. '81

Tamara Toumanova (1919-96)
The Private Life of Sherlock Holmes '70
Invitation to the Dance '56
Days of Glory '43

Sheila Tousey
Coyote Waits '03
Skinwalker '02
Christmas in the Clouds '01
Grand Avenue '96
Medicine River '94
Slaughter of the Innocents '93
Silent Tongue '92
Thunderheart '92

Beth Toussaint (1962-)
Breach of Conduct '94
Night Siege Project: Shadowchaser 2 '94
Blackmail '91

Lorraine Toussaint (1960-)
The Soloist '09
If These Walls Could Talk '96
Jaded '96
Nightjohn '96
America's Dream '95
Dangerous Minds '95
Bleeding Hearts '94
Mother's Boys '94
Point of No Return '93
Breaking In '89
A Case of Deadly Force '86

Roland Toutain (1905-77)
Eternal Return '43
The Rules of the Game '39
Liliom '35

Lupita Tovar (1911-)
The Westerner '40
South of the Border '39
Old Spanish Custom '36
Border Law '31
Dracula (Spanish Version) '31

Russell Tovey
Little Dorrit '08
The History Boys '06

Harry Towb (1925-)
Pictures '81
The Blue Max '66

Constance Towers (1933-)
A Perfect Murder '98
On Wings of Eagles '86
Sylvester '85
Naked Kiss '64
Shock Corridor '63
Sergeant Rutledge '60
The Horse Soldiers '59

Tom Towler
Home Sick '08
The Devil's Rejects '05
House of 1000 Corpses '03
Groom Lake '02
Mercenary 2: Thick and Thin '97
Gridlock'd '96
Normal Life '96
Girls in Prison '94
Blood In ... Blood Out: Bound by Honor '93
Mad Dog and Glory '93
The Pit & the Pendulum '91
Henry: Portrait of a Serial Killer '90
Night of the Living Dead '90
The Borrower '89

Aline Towne (1929-96)
Trader Tom of the China Seas '54
Radar Men from the Moon '52
Zombies of the Stratosphere '52
Don Daredevil Rides Again '51
The Invisible Monster '50
The Vanishing Westerner '50

Katharine Towne (1978-)
Something New '06
Lethal Dose '03
Evolution '01
Mulholland Drive '01
Sol Goode '01
Town and Country '01
What Lies Beneath '00
She's All That '99

Robert Towne (1936-)
The Pick-Up Artist '87
Villa Rides '68

Jill Townsend (1945-)
The Awakening '80
Oh, Alfie '75
Poldark '75
Poldark 2 '75
The Golden Bowl '72

Najarra Townsend
Supernova '09
Me and You and Everyone We Know '05

Patrice Townsend
Always '85
Sitting Ducks '80

Robert Kevin Townsend (1957-)
Black Listed '03
Love Songs '99
The Taxman '98
Mercenary 2: Thick and Thin '97
The Meteor Man '93
The Five Heartbeats '91
That's Adequate '90
The Mighty Quinn '89
I'm Gonna Git You Sucka '88
Hollywood Shuffle '87
Ratboy '86
American Flyers '85
Odd Jobs '85
A Soldier's Story '84
Streets of Fire '84
The Warriors '79

Stanley Townsend
The Nativity Story '06
Wondrous Oblivion '06

Stuart Townsend (1972-)
Chaos Theory '08
Head in the Clouds '04
The League of Extraordinary Gentlemen '03
Shade '03
Queen of the Damned '02
Trapped '02
About Adam '00
Wonderland '99
Shooting Fish '98
Resurrection Man '97
Under the Skin '97
Trojan Eddie '96

Pete Townshend (1945-)
The Secret Policeman's Other Ball '82
Secret Policeman's Private Parts '81
The Kids Are Alright '79
Tommy '75

Etsushi Toyokawa (1962-)
Hula Girls '06
The Great Yokai War '05
No Way Back '96
When I Close My Eyes '95

Fausto Tozzi (1921-78)
Street War '76
Escape from Death Row '73
Sicilian Connection '72
The Valachi Papers '72
Knives of the Avenger '65
The Return of Dr. Mabuse '61
East of Kilimanjaro '57

Giorgio Tozzi (1923-)
Torn Between Two Lovers '79
South Pacific '58 (V)

Ian Tracey (1964-)
Civic Duty '06
Call Me: The Rise and Fall of Heidi Fleiss '04
Ice Men '04
Emile '03
Owning Mahowny '03
Liberty Stands Still '02
Rupert's Land '98
Bloodhounds 2 '96
Man with a Gun '95
Incident at Deception Ridge '94
Timecop '94
The Comrades of Summer '92

Jeff Trachta (1960-)
Poison '01
Interlocked '98
Night Eyes 4: Fatal Passion '95

Michelle Trachtenberg (1985-)
17 Again '09
The Circuit '08
Kickin' It Old Skool '07
Beautiful Ohio '06
Black Christmas '06
Ice Princess '05
Eurotrip '04
Mysterious Skin '04
A Father's Choice '00
Forever Together '00
Inspector Gadget '99
Harriet the Spy '96

Keegan Connor Tracy (1971-)
The Net 2.0 '06
Final Destination 2 '03
Blackwoods '02

Lee Tracy (1898-1968)
The Best Man '64
Betrayal from the East '44
The Payoff '43
Power of the Press '43
Bombshell '33
Dinner at Eight '33
Blessed Event '32
Doctor X '32
The Half Naked Truth '32
The Strange Love of Molly Louvain '32

Spencer Tracy (1900-67)
Guess Who's Coming to Dinner '67
How the West Was Won '63
It's a Mad, Mad, Mad, Mad World '63
The Devil at 4 O'Clock '61
Judgment at Nuremberg '61
Inherit the Wind '60
Last Hurrah '58
The Old Man and the Sea '58
Desk Set '57
The Mountain '56
Bad Day at Black Rock '54
Broken Lance '54
The Actress '53
Pat and Mike '52
Father's Little Dividend '51
Adam's Rib '50
Father of the Bride '50
Malaya '49
State of the Union '48
Cass Timberlane '47
Without Love '45
A Guy Named Joe '44
The Seventh Cross '44
Thirty Seconds Over Tokyo '44
Keeper of the Flame '42
Tortilla Flat '42
Woman of the Year '42
Dr. Jekyll and Mr. Hyde '41
Men of Boys Town '41
Boom Town '40
Edison the Man '40
I Take This Woman '40
Northwest Passage '40
Stanley and Livingstone '39
Boys Town '38
Test Pilot '38
Captains Courageous '37
Mannequin '37
Fury '36
Libeled Lady '36
San Francisco '36
Riff Raff '35
Whipsaw '35
Marie Galante '34
20,000 Years in Sing Sing '33
Young America '32
Up the River '30

Steve Tracy (1952-86)
Desperate Moves '86
Beneath the Valley of the Ultra-Vixens '79

William Tracy (1917-67)
Mr. Walkie Talkie '52
As You Were '51
George Washington Slept Here '42
To the Shores of Tripoli '42
Tanks a Million '41
Strike Up the Band '40

Mary Ellen Trainor (1950-)
Amy's O '02
Anywhere But Here '99
Lethal Weapon 4 '98
Hope '97
Executive Decision '96
Congo '95
Forrest Gump '94
Greedy '94
Little Giants '94
Death Becomes Her '92
Kuffs '92
Lethal Weapon 3 '92
Grand Canyon '91
Ricochet '91
Fire Birds '90
Ghostbusters 2 '89
Lethal Weapon 2 '89
Tales from the Crypt '89
Action Jackson '88
Die Hard '88
Scrooged '88
Lethal Weapon '87
The Monster Squad '87
The Goonies '85
Romancing the Stone '84
The Stone Boy '84

Sam Trammell (1971-)
Aliens vs. Predator: Requiem '07
Anonymous Rex '04
Undermind '03
Beat '00
Wrestling with Alligators '98

Billinger C. Tran
We Were Soldiers '02
Green Dragon '01

Silvano Tranquilli (1925-97)
Castle of Blood '64
The Horrible Dr. Hichcock '62

Cordula Trantow (1942-)
The Castle '68
Hitler '62
The Bridge '59

Sophie Traub
Tenderness '08
Daltry Calhoun '05

Helen Traubel (1899-1972)
The Ladies' Man '61
Deep in My Heart '54

Daniel J. Travanti (1940-)
The Wasp Woman '96
Eyes of a Witness '94
Just Cause '94
Weep No More My Lady '93
Megaville '91
Tagget '90
Fellow Traveler '89
Millennium '89
Skin '89
Midnight Crossing '87
Murrow '86
Aurora '84
Adam '83
A Case of Libel '83
St. Ives '76

Bill Travers (1922-94)
The First Olympics: Athens 1896 '84
Christian the Lion '76
An Elephant Called Slowly '69
Ring of Bright Water '69
A Midsummer Night's Dream '68
Born Free '66
Duel at Diablo '66
Gorgo '61
The Smallest Show on Earth '57
Bhowani Junction '56
Geordie '55
Romeo and Juliet '54
The Browning Version '51
Trio '50

Henry Travers (1874-1965)
It's a Wonderful Life '46
The Yearling '46
The Bells of St. Mary's '45
The Naughty Nineties '45
Thrill of a Romance '45
Dragon Seed '44
Madame Curie '43
Shadow of a Doubt '43
Mrs. Miniver '42
Random Harvest '42
Ball of Fire '41
A Girl, a Guy and a Gob '41
High Sierra '41
Edison the Man '40
Primrose Path '40
Dark Victory '39
Dodge City '39
On Borrowed Time '39
The Rains Came '39
Stanley and Livingstone '39
The Sisters '38
The Invisible Man '33

Linden Travers (1913-2001)
Beware of Pity '46
The Lady Vanishes '38
The Terror '38

Susan Travers (1939-)
The Abominable Dr. Phibes '71
The Snake Woman '61
Peeping Tom '60

June Travis (1914-)
Monster a Go-Go! '65
The Star '52
The Gladiator '38
Exiled to Shanghai '37
Earthworm Tractors '36
Ceiling Zero '35

Kylie Travis (1970-)
Gia '98
Sanctuary '98
Retroactive '97
Eyes of the Beholder '92

Nancy Travis (1961-)
The Jane Austen Book Club '07
Sisterhood of the Traveling Pants '05
Stephen King's Rose Red '02
Beyond Suspicion '00
Running Mates '00
Bogus '96
Body Language '95
Destiny Turns on the Radio '95
Fluke '95
Greedy '94
Fallen Angels 1 '93

So I Married an Axe Murderer '93
The Vanishing '93
Chaplin '92
Passed Away '92
Air America '90
Internal Affairs '90
Loose Cannons '90
Three Men and a Little Lady '90
Eight Men Out '88
Married to the Mob '88
Three Men and a Baby '87
Harem '86

Randy Travis (1959-)
The Long Ride Home '01
Texas Rangers '01
John John in the Sky '00
The Trial of Old Drum '00
The Million Dollar Kid '99
White River '99
Black Dog '98
T.N.T. '98
Boys Will Be Boys '97
Fire Down Below '97
John Grisham's The Rainmaker '97
The Shooter '97
Edie & Pen '95
Frank and Jesse '94
Texas '94
Dead Man's Revenge '93

Richard Travis (1913-89)
Missile to the Moon '59
The Girl in the Red Velvet Swing '55
Mesa of Lost Women '52
Danger Zone '51
Fingerprints Don't Lie '51
Mask of the Dragon '51
One Too Many '51
Pier 23 '51
Roaring City '51
Motor Patrol '50
Operation Haylift '50
Sky Liner '49
Big Town After Dark '47
Spy Train '43
Dive Bomber '41
The Man Who Came to Dinner '41

Stacey Travis
The Great Buck Howard '09
Venom '05
Soul Plane '04
Intolerable Cruelty '03
Two Days '03
Bandits '01
Ghost World '01
Heartbreakers '01
Sleep Easy, Hutch Rimes '00
Submerged '00
Traffic '00
What Planet Are You From? '00
The Muse '99
Mystery Men '99
The Only Thrill '97
Playing God '96
Suspect Device '95
National Lampoon's Attack of the 5 Ft. 2 Women '94
Caroline at Midnight '93
Dracula Rising '93
Only the Strong '93
The Super '91
Hardware '90
Earth Girls Are Easy '89
Dr. Hackenstein '88

Tony Travis
Flesh Gordon 2: Flesh Gordon Meets the Cosmic Cheerleaders '90
The Beatniks '60

Ellen Travolta (1940-)
The Basket '99
Detour '99

Joey Travolta (1952-)
To the Limit '95
Beach Babes from Beyond '93
DaVinci's War '92
Wilding '90

American Born '89
Ghost Writer '89
Sinners '89
Amazon Women on the Moon '87
The Prodigal '83
Rosie: The Rosemary Clooney Story '82
Car Crash '80
Sunnyside '79

John Travolta (1954-)
From Paris With Love '10
Old Dogs '09
The Taking of Pelham 123 '09
Bolt '08 (V)
Hairspray '07
Wild Hogs '07
Lonely Hearts '06
Be Cool '05
Ladder 49 '04
A Love Song for Bobby Long '04
The Punisher '04
Basic '03
Austin Powers In Goldmember '02
Domestic Disturbance '01
Swordfish '01
Battlefield Earth '00
Lucky Numbers '00
The General's Daughter '99
A Civil Action '98
Primary Colors '98
The Thin Red Line '98
Face/Off '97
Mad City '97
She's So Lovely '97
Michael '96
Phenomenon '96
Broken Arrow '95
Get Shorty '95
White Man's Burden '95
Pulp Fiction '94
Look Who's Talking Now '93
Boris and Natasha: The Movie '92
Chains of Gold '92
Eyes of an Angel '91
Shout '91
Look Who's Talking, Too '90
The Experts '89
Look Who's Talking '89
Dumb Waiter '87
Perfect '85
Staying Alive '83
Two of a Kind '83
Blow Out '81
Urban Cowboy '80
Grease '78
Saturday Night Fever '77
The Boy in the Plastic Bubble '76
Carrie '76
Devil's Rain '75

Susan Traylor
Broken Vessels '98
She's So Lovely '97
Bastard out of Carolina '96
To Die For '95
The New Age '94
Sleep with Me '94

Joel Thomas Traywick
Sub Down '97
Nightjohn '96

Treach (1970-)
Connor's War '06
Conviction '02
Empire '02
Jason's Lyric '94

Arthur Treacher (1894-1975)
Delightfully Dangerous '45
In Society '44
National Velvet '44
The Amazing Mrs. Holiday '43
Star Spangled Rhythm '42
The Little Princess '39
Mad About Music '38
My Lucky Star '38
Heidi '37
Thin Ice '37
Satan Met a Lady '36
Stowaway '36

Curly Top '35
David Copperfield '35
I Live My Life '35
Magnificent Obsession '35
A Midsummer Night's Dream '35
Splendor '35
Hollywood Party '34

Emerson Treacy (1900-67)
A Star Is Born '54
Prowler '51
Give Me a Sailor '38
California Straight Ahead! '37
Champagne for Breakfast '35

Harry Treadway
Fish Tank '09
City of Ember '08
The Disappeared '08
Control '07
Brothers of the Head '06

Michael Treanor (1979-)
3 Ninjas Knuckle Up '95
3 Ninjas '92

Terri Treas (1959-)
Lady Killer '97
Alien Nation: Millennium '96
Alien Nation: The Enemy Within '96
Alien Nation: Body and Soul '95
Yankee Zulu '95
Alien Nation: Dark Horizon '94
Home for Christmas '93
Rage and Honor '92
House 4: Home Deadly Home '91
Frankenstein Unbound '90 (V)
Deathstalker 3 '89
The Nest '88
The Terror Within '88

Robert Trebor (1953-)
Jiminy Glick in LaLa Wood '05
Raise Your Voice '04
Hercules the Legendary Journeys, Vol. 2: The Lost Kingdom '94
52 Pick-Up '86
Out of the Darkness '85

David Tree (1915-)
Clouds over Europe '39
Drums '38
Pygmalion '38

Dorothy Tree (1906-92)
Hitler: Dead or Alive '43
Abe Lincoln in Illinois '40
Charlie Chan in City of Darkness '39
Confessions of a Nazi Spy '39
Mystery of Mr. Wong '39

Mary Treen (1907-89)
Paradise, Hawaiian Style '66
I Married a Monster from Outer Space '58
The Sad Sack '57
Clipped Wings '53
It's a Wonderful Life '46
Strange Impersonation '46
Casanova Brown '44
Hands Across the Border '43
So Proudly We Hail '43
First Love '39
Swing It, Sailor! '37

Yann Tregouet (1975-)
Born in 68 '08
Artemisia '97
Trois Couleurs: Bleu '93

Guy Trejan (1921-2001)
I Married a Dead Man '82
The Beast '75

Danny Trejo (1944-)
The Expendables '10
Predators '10
The Line '08

Delta Farce '07
Halloween '07
Urban Justice '07
Danny Roane: First Time Director '06
Sherrybaby '06
Slayer '06
All Souls Day '05
Chasing Ghosts '05
The Crow: Wicked Prayer '05
The Devil's Rejects '05
Lost '05
Anchorman: The Legend of Ron Burgundy '04
The Big Empty '04
Once Upon a Time in Mexico '03
Spy Kids 3-D: Game Over '03
Nightstalker '02
The Salton Sea '02
Spy Kids 2: The Island of Lost Dreams '02
13 Moons '02
XXX '02
Bubble Boy '01
Spy Kids '01
Animal Factory '00
Reindeer Games '00
Desert Heat '99
From Dusk Till Dawn 3: The Hangman's Daughter '99
Soundman '99
From Dusk Till Dawn 2: Texas Blood Money '98
Point Blank '98
The Replacement Killers '98
Six Days, Seven Nights '98
Con Air '97
Dilemma '97
Los Locos Posse '97
Anaconda '96
From Dusk Till Dawn '95
Undercover Cop '94

Christine Tremarco (1977-)
Five Days '07
Under the Skin '97
Priest '94

Les Tremayne (1913-2003)
Fangs '75
Creature of Destruction '67
King Kong vs. Godzilla '63 (N)
The Slime People '63
The Gallant Hours '60
The Angry Red Planet '59
The Monolith Monsters '57
The Monster of Piedras Blancas '57
Forbidden Planet '56 (N)
A Man Called Peter '55
Dream Wife '53
I Love Melvin '53
The War of the Worlds '53
Francis Goes to West Point '52

Johanne-Marie Tremblay (1950-)
The Barbarian Invasions '03
Jesus of Montreal '89
Straight for the Heart '88

Ken Tremblett (1965-)
The Betrayed '08
The Guilty '99
Tourist Trap '98

Anne Tremko
The Member of the Wedding '97
My Antonia '94

John Trent (1906-66)
Mystery Plane '39
Stunt Pilot '39
Blossoms on Broadway '37

Adam Trese (1969-)
2B Perfectly Honest '04
40 Days and 40 Nights '02
Cowboys and Angels '00
Polish Wedding '97
Illtown '96
Palookaville '95
The Underneath '95

The Good Fight '92
Laws of Gravity '92

Noel Trevarthen
Dusty '85
The Vengeance of Fu Manchu '67

Frederick Treves (1925-)
A Certain Justice '99
Shameless '94
Paper Mask '91
Flame to the Phoenix '85
Charlie Muffin '79

Leonardo Treviglio
Stealing Beauty '96
Sebastiane '79

Roger Treville (1902-2005)
The Green Glove '52
Mr. Peek-A-Boo '50

Vic Trevino
Firehawk '92
Born in East L.A. '87

Austin Trevor (1897-1978)
Abandon Ship '57
Night Train to Munich '40
Sabotage '36
Mimi '35
The Silent Passenger '35
Broken Melody '34

Claire Trevor (1909-2000)
Breaking Home Ties '87
Kiss Me Goodbye '82
How to Murder Your Wife '64
The Stripper '63
Two Weeks in Another Town '62
Marjorie Morningstar '58
The Mountain '56
Man Without a Star '55
The High and the Mighty '54
The Stranger Wore a Gun '53
Hoodlum Empire '52
Hard, Fast and Beautiful '51
Best of the Badmen '50
Borderline '50
Babe Ruth Story '48
Key Largo '48
Raw Deal '48
Velvet Touch '48
Born to Kill '47
Crack-Up '46
Johnny Angel '45
Murder, My Sweet '44
The Woman of the Town '44
The Desperadoes '43
Crossroads '42
Honky Tonk '41
Texas '41
Dark Command '40
Allegheny Uprising '39
Stagecoach '39
Amazing Dr. Clitterhouse '38
Dead End '37
Second Honeymoon '37
Baby, Take a Bow '34

Jack Trevor (1890-1976)
Champagne '28
Secrets of a Soul '25

Paula Trickey (1966-)
The Base '99
A Kiss Goodnight '94
Carnal Crimes '91

Ivan Triesault (1898-1980)
Von Ryan's Express '65
The Amazing Transparent Man '60
Jet Pilot '57
Five Fingers '52
Border River '47
Golden Earrings '47
Cry of the Werewolf '44

Leopoldo Trieste (1917-2003)
Cinema Paradiso '88
Henry IV '85
Quo Vadis '85
Loose in New York '74
Don't Look Now '73
Seduced and Abandoned '64
Divorce—Italian Style '62
I Vitelloni '53
The White Sheik '52

Sergej Trifunovic (1972-)
Love '05
3 A.M. '01
Savior '98
Someone Else's America '96

Sarah Trigger
Good Luck '96
Things to Do in Denver When You're Dead '95
Don't Do It '94
P.C.U. '94
Deadfall '93
Sleepless in Seattle '93
Pet Sematary 2 '92
Bill & Ted's Bogus Journey '91
Grand Canyon '91
Paradise '91
El Diablo '90
Kid '90

Zoe Trilling (1966-)
Last Exit to Earth '96
Night of the Demons 2 '94

Jerry Trimble (1963-)
Stranglehold '94
Full Contact '93
One Man Army '93
Breathing Fire '91

Jasmine Trinca (1981-)
Best of Youth '03
The Son's Room '00

Jean-Louis Trintignant (1930-)
Those Who Love Me Can Take the Train '98
The City of Lost Children '95 (V)
Fiesta '95
A Self-Made Hero '95
Trois Couleurs: Rouge '94
A Man and a Woman: 20 Years Later '86
Rendez-vous '85
Next Summer '84
Confidentially Yours '83
Under Fire '83
La Nuit de Varennes '82
Passion of Love '82
I Love You All '80
The Desert of the Tartars '76
Intruder '76
The Last Train '74
Le Secret '74
Les Violons du Bal '74
Act of Aggression '73
The Outside Man '73
And Hope to Die '72
The Conformist '71
The Libertine '69
My Night at Maud's '69
Z '69
Les Biches '68
Ramparts of Clay '68
Is Paris Burning? '66
A Man and a Woman '66
The Easy Life '63
Il Sorpasso '63
Journey Beneath the Desert '61
Dangerous Liaisons '60
And God Created Woman '57

Marie Trintignant (1962-2003)
Harrison's Flowers '02
Portraits Chinois '96
Ponette '95
Alberto Express '92
Betty '92
The Story of Women '88

Hostage '05
Criminal '04
Stateside '04
The Texas Chainsaw Massacre '03
The Deep End '01
100 Girls '00
The Virgin Suicides '99
Sleepers '96
Two If by Sea '95

Larry Tucker (1933-2001)
Angels Hard As They Come '71
Shock Corridor '63
Blast of Silence '61

Martin Tucker
Death Screams '83
House of Death '82

Michael Tucker (1944-)
Til There Was You '96
D2: The Mighty Ducks '94
For Love or Money '93
Too Young to Die '90
Checking Out '89
Day One '89
Spy '89
Assault and Matrimony '87
Radio Days '87
Tin Men '87
L.A. Law '86
The Purple Rose of Cairo '85
Diner '82
Eyes of Laura Mars '78

Richard Tucker (1884-1942)
Delinquent Parents '38
Convicted '32
The Bat Whispers '30
King of the Kongo '29
Wings '27
Captain Swagger '25
The Worldly Madonna '22

Rocky Tucker
Steps from Hell '92
Lunatic '91

Sophie Tucker (1884-1966)
Sensations of 1945 '44
Broadway Melody of 1938 '37
Thoroughbreds Don't Cry '37

Tanya Tucker (1958-)
Hard Country '81
Follow That Car '80
The Rebels '79

Alan Tudyk (1971-)
Meet Market '08
Death at a Funeral '07
Knocked Up '07
3:10 to Yuma '07
Ice Age: The Meltdown '06 (V)
Serenity '05
Dodgeball: A True Underdog Story '04
I, Robot '04
Ice Age '02 (V)
Hearts in Atlantis '01
A Knight's Tale '01
28 Days '00
Patch Adams '98

Sonny Tufts (1911-70)
Easy Come, Easy Go '67
The Seven Year Itch '55
Serpent Island '54
Cat Women of the Moon '53
The Gift Horse '52
Easy Living '49
The Virginian '46
Here Come the Waves '45
So Proudly We Hail '43

Ulrich Tukur (1957-)
The White Ribbon '09
North Face '08
Seraphine '08
The Lives of Others '06
Operation Valkyrie '04
Amen '02

Solaris '02
Taking Sides '01
My Mother's Courage '95

Dirkan Tulane
The Librarian: Curse of the Judas Chalice '08
Murder on Line One '90

Patricia Tulasne (1959-)
King of the Airwaves '94
The Savage Woman '91

Tom Tully (1908-82)
Coogan's Bluff '68
McHale's Navy Joins the Air Force '65
Ten North Frederick '58
Love Me or Leave Me '55
Soldier of Fortune '55
The Caine Mutiny '54
The Moon Is Blue '53
Trouble along the Way '53
Love Is Better Than Ever '52
Texas Carnival '51
Tomahawk '51
Where the Sidewalk Ends '50
June Bride '48
Killer McCoy '47
Lady in the Lake '46
Till the End of Time '46
The Virginian '46
Adventure '45
I'll Be Seeing You '44
Destination Tokyo '43
Northern Pursuit '43

Frans Tumbuan
Without Mercy '95
Rage and Honor 2: Hostile Takeover '93

Tommy Tune (1939-)
The Boy Friend '71
Hello, Dolly! '69

Bill Tung (1933-2006)
Jackie Chan's First Strike '96
Rumble in the Bronx '96
Police Story '85

Tamara Tunie (1959-)
The Caveman's Valentine '01
Snake Eyes '98
The Devil's Advocate '97
Eve's Bayou '97 (N)
Rebound: The Legend of Earl "The Goat" Manigault '96

Robin Tunney (1972-)
August '08
The Burning Plain '08
Hollywoodland '06
Open Window '06
Runaway '05
The Zodiac '05
Paparazzi '04
The In-Laws '03
Cherish '02
The Secret Lives of Dentists '02
Intimate Affairs '01
Vertical Limit '00
End of Days '99
Supernova '99
Naked City: Justice with a Bullet '98
Julian Po '97
Montana '97
Niagara, Niagara '97
The Craft '96
Riders of the Purple Sage '96
Empire Records '95
JFK: Reckless Youth '93
Encino Man '92

James Tupper
The Gambler, the Girl and the Gunslinger '09
Me and Orson Welles '09
Pictures of Hollis Woods '07
Invisible '06
Love's Abiding Joy '06
Love's Long Journey '05

Robert Turano
Brooklyn Rules '07
One Way Out '95
Federal Hill '94

Paige Turco (1965-)
Taking Chance '09
The Game Plan '07
Invincible '06
Waltzing Anna '06
Astoria '00
Dead Dog '00
Urbania '00
November Conspiracy '96
The Feminine Touch '95
The Pompatus of Love '95
Dead Funny '94
Vibrations '94
Teenage Mutant Ninja Turtles 3 '93
Teenage Mutant Ninja Turtles 2: The Secret of the Ooze '91

Paolo Turco
Bread and Chocolate '73
The Lickerish Quartet '70

Ann Turkel (1942-)
The Fear '94
Deep Space '87
Death Ray 2000 '81
Humanoids from the Deep '80
Golden Rendezvous '77
The Last Contract '77
Portrait of a Hitman '77
The Cassandra Crossing '76
99 & 44/100 Dead '74
Paper Lion '68

Joe Turkel (1927-)
Dark Side of the Moon '90
Blade Runner '82
The Shining '80
Cycle Psycho '72
The Desperados '70
The Sand Pebbles '66
King Rat '65
Village of the Giants '65
Paths of Glory '57
The Killing '56

Glynn Turman (1946-)
Sahara '05
Freedom Song '00
Men of Honor '00
The Visit '00
Light It Up '99
Subterfuge '98
Buffalo Soldiers '97
Rebound: The Legend of Earl "The Goat" Manigault '96
Race to Freedom: The Story of the Underground Railroad '94
Deep Cover '92
Charlotte Forten's Mission: Experiment in Freedom '85
Gremlins '84
Secrets of a Married Man '84
Penitentiary 2 '82
Centennial '78
A Hero Ain't Nothin' but a Sandwich '78
J.D.'s Revenge '76
The River Niger '76
The Blue Knight '75
Cooley High '75

John Turnbull (1880-1956)
The Happiest Days of Your Life '50
Man of Evil '48
Make-Up '37
Nine Days a Queen '36
The Passing of the Third Floor Back '36
The 39 Steps '35
The Private Life of Henry VIII '33

Bree Turner (1977-)
The Ugly Truth '09
Firehouse Dog '07
Just My Luck '06

Bring It On Again '03

Elizabeth Turner
Cannibal Apocalypse '80
Truck Stop '78

Florence Turner (1885-1946)
The Ridin' Fool '31
Pace That Kills '28
Walking Back '26

George Turner (1902-68)
Son of Zorro '47
Vigilantes of Boom Town '46

Guinevere Turner (1968-)
Itty Bitty Titty Committee '07
Pipe Dream '02
American Psycho '99
Dogma '99
Chasing Amy '97
Preaching to the Perverted '97
The Watermelon Woman '97
Go Fish '94

Janine Turner (1963-)
Miracle Dogs Too '06
The Night of the White Pants '06
Dr. T & the Women '00
Fatal Error '99
Leave It to Beaver '97
The Curse of Inferno '96
Cliffhanger '93
The Ambulance '90
Steel Magnolias '89
Monkey Shines '88
Knights of the City '85
Young Doctors in Love '82

Jessica Turner
Karma Police '08
All or Nothing at All '93

Jim Turner
Bewitched '05
Off the Lip '04
Joe's Apartment '96
The Ref '93
My Samurai '92
Kid Colter '85

John Turner (1932-)
The Slipper and the Rose '76
Captain Nemo and the Underwater City '69
Estate of Insanity '64

Kathleen Turner (1954-)
Marley & Me '08
Monster House '06 (V)
Beautiful '00
Prince of Central Park '00
Love and Action in Chicago '99
The Virgin Suicides '99
Baby Geniuses '98
Legalese '98
The Real Blonde '97
A Simple Wish '97
Moonlight and Valentino '95
Serial Mom '94
Naked in New York '93
Undercover Blues '93
House of Cards '92
V.I. Warshawski '91
Honey, I Shrunk the Kids '89 (V)
The War of the Roses '89
The Accidental Tourist '88
Switching Channels '88
Who Framed Roger Rabbit '88 (V)
Julia and Julia '87
Peggy Sue Got Married '86
The Jewel of the Nile '85
Prizzi's Honor '85
A Breed Apart '84
Crimes of Passion '84
Romancing the Stone '84
The Man with Two Brains '83
Body Heat '81

Kristopher Turner
Without a Paddle: Nature's Calling '09
An Old-Fashioned Thanksgiving '08
The Brotherhood 3: The Young Demons '02

Lana Turner (1920-95)
Witches' Brew '79
Bittersweet Love '76
The Graveyard '74
Bachelor in Paradise '69
Madame X '66
Love Has Many Faces '65
Who's Got the Action? '63
By Love Possessed '61
Portrait in Black '60
Imitation of Life '59
Another Time, Another Place '58
Peyton Place '57
Diane '55
The Prodigal '55
Sea Chase '55
Betrayed '54
Latin Lovers '53
The Bad and the Beautiful '52
The Merry Widow '52
Mr. Imperium '51
A Life of Her Own '50
Homecoming '48
The Three Musketeers '48
Cass Timberlane '47
Green Dolphin Street '47
The Postman Always Rings Twice '46
Weekend at the Waldorf '45
Johnny Eager '42
Somewhere I'll Find You '42
Dr. Jekyll and Mr. Hyde '41
Honky Tonk '41
Ziegfeld Girl '41
Love Finds Andy Hardy '38
The Great Garrick '37
They Won't Forget '37

Ted Turner (1938-)
Gods and Generals '03
Gettysburg '93

Tina Turner (1939-)
Mad Max: Beyond Thunderdome '85
Tommy '75
Gimme Shelter '70

Tyrin Turner (1971-)
Belly '98
Little Boy Blue '97
Soldier Boyz '95
Menace II Society '93

Zara Turner (1968-)
The Waiting Time '99
Resurrection Man '97
Sliding Doors '97

Ben Turpin (1874-1940)
Saps at Sea '40
Law of the Wild '34
Yankee Doodle in Berlin '19
Burlesque on Carmen '16

Kett Turton (1982-)
Firewall '06
A Simple Curve '05
Show Me '04
Falling Angels '03
Heart of America '03
Gypsy 83 '01

Aida Turturro (1962-)
Romance & Cigarettes '05
2B Perfectly Honest '04
Crocodile Dundee in Los Angeles '01
Sidewalks of New York '01
Bringing Out the Dead '99
Deep Blue Sea '99
Hitman's Journal '99
The 24 Hour Woman '99
24 Nights '99
Celebrity '98
Illuminata '98
Sleepers '96
Denise Calls Up '95
Money Train '95
Angie '94
Junior '94

Tales of Erotica '93
Jersey Girl '92
True Love '89

John Turturro (1957-)
The Taking of Pelham 123 '09
Transformers: Revenge of the Fallen '09
Miracle at St. Anna '08
What Just Happened '08
You Don't Mess with the Zohan '08
The Bronx Is Burning '07
Margot at the Wedding '07
Slipstream '07
Transformers '07
A Few Days in September '06
The Good Shepherd '06
Secret Window '04
She Hate Me '04
2B Perfectly Honest '04
Anger Management '03
Fear X '03
Collateral Damage '02
Mr. Deeds '02
Monday Night Mayhem '02
Monkeybone '01 (V)
Thirteen Conversations About One Thing '01
Company Man '00
The Luzhin Defence '00
The Man Who Cried '00
O Brother Where Art Thou? '00
The Cradle Will Rock '99
He Got Game '98
Illuminata '98
Rounders '98
The Big Lebowski '97
Box of Moonlight '96
Girl 6 '96
Grace of My Heart '96
The Search for One-Eye Jimmy '96
The Truce '96
Clockers '95
Sugartime '95
Unstrung Heroes '95
Being Human '94
Quiz Show '94
Search and Destroy '94
Fearless '93
Mac '93
Brain Donors '92
Barton Fink '91
Jungle Fever '91
Men of Respect '91
Miller's Crossing '90
Mo' Better Blues '90
State of Grace '90
Backtrack '89
Do the Right Thing '89
Five Corners '88
The Sicilian '87
The Color of Money '86
Hannah and Her Sisters '86
Off Beat '86
Desperately Seeking Susan '85
Gung Ho '85
To Live & Die in L.A. '85

Nicholas Turturro (1962-)
I Now Pronounce You Chuck and Larry '07
Trapped '06
The Longest Yard '05
The Hillside Strangler '04
The Hollow '04
Big Shot: Confessions of a Campus Bookie '02
Monday Night Mayhem '02
Hellraiser 5: Inferno '00
Witness to the Mob '98
Mercenary 2: Thick and Thin '97
Excess Baggage '96
The Search for One-Eye Jimmy '96
The Shadow Conspiracy '96
Cosmic Slop '94
Federal Hill '94
Mac '93
Jungle Fever '91
Mo' Better Blues '90

Rita Tushingham (1942-)
Being Julia '04
Swing '98
Under the Skin '97
An Awfully Big Adventure '94
Paper Marriage '93
The Housekeeper '86
Dream to Believe '85
Mysteries '84
Spaghetti House '82
Slaughterday '77
Green Eyes '76
The Human Factor '75
Rachel's Man '75
Dressed for Death '74
Loose in New York '74
Smashing Time '67
Trap '66
Doctor Zhivago '65
The Knack '65
Girl with Green Eyes '64
The Leather Boys '63
A Taste of Honey '61

Dorothy Tutin (1930-2001)
Alive and Kicking '96
Scarlett '94
Body & Soul '93
Shades of Fear '93
Agatha Christie's Murder with Mirrors '85
The Shooting Party '85
Sister Dora '77
Savage Messiah '72
Six Wives of Henry VIII '71
A Tale of Two Cities '58
Beggar's Opera '54
The Importance of Being Earnest '52

Tracy Tutor
No Vacancy '99
Expose '97

Lurene Tuttle (1906-86)
Testament '83
White Mama '80
The Manitou '78
The Fortune Cookie '66
The Ghost and Mr. Chicken '66
Ma Barker's Killer Brood '60
Untamed Youth '57
The Glass Slipper '55
The Affairs of Dobie Gillis '53
Don't Bother to Knock '52
Niagara '52
Goodbye My Fancy '51
Room for One More '51
Homecoming '48

Shannon Tweed (1957-)
Dead Sexy '01
The Rowdy Girls '00
Wish You Were Dead '00
Forbidden Sins '99
Naked Lies '98
Face the Evil '97
Human Desires '97
Shadow Warriors '97
Shadow Warriors 2: Hunt for the Death Merchant '97
Stormy Nights '97
White Cargo '96
Body Chemistry 4: Full Exposure '95
The Dark Dancer '95
Electra '95
Indecent Behavior 3 '95
Hard Vice '94
Illicit Dreams '94
Indecent Behavior 2 '94
Model by Day '94
Night Fire '94
No Contest '94
Vegas Vice '94
Victim of Desire '94
Cold Sweat '93
Indecent Behavior '93
Night Eyes 3 '93
Possessed by the Night '93
Scorned '93
Liar's Edge '92
Sexual Response '92
The Firing Line '91
The Last Hour '91
Night Eyes 2 '91
Last Call '90
Cannibal Women in the Avocado Jungle of Death '89
In the Cold of the Night '89
Night Visitor '89
Twisted Justice '89
Lethal Woman '88
Surrogate '88
Codename: Vengeance '87
Meatballs 3 '87
The Last Fling '86
Hot Dog... The Movie! '83
Of Unknown Origin '83

Terry Tweed
Night Rhythms '92
The Reincarnate '71

Helen Twelvetrees (1907-58)
Panama Flo '32
Millie '31
Painted Desert '31
State's Attorney '31

Twiggy (1949-)
Body Bags '93
The Diamond Trap '91
Istanbul '90
Madame Sousatzka '88
Young Charlie Chaplin '88
Club Paradise '86
The Doctor and the Devils '85
The Blues Brothers '80
Butterfly Ball '76
W '74
The Boy Friend '71

Archie Twitchell (1906-57)
Kentucky Jubilee '51
Thundering Trail '51
Young Bill Hickok '40

Anne Twomey (1951-)
The Confession '98
Rear Window '98
Picture Perfect '96
The Scout '94
Orpheus Descending '91
Last Rites '88
Deadly Friend '86
Behind Enemy Lines '85

Alexandra Tydings (1972-)
Red Shoe Diaries 7: Burning Up '96
Sunchaser '96

Aisha Tyler (1970-)
Bedtime Stories '08
Meet Market '08
Balls of Fury '07
Death Sentence '07
.45 '06
The Santa Clause 3: The Escape Clause '06
Never Die Alone '04
The Santa Clause 2 '02

Harry Tyler (1888-1961)
Bedtime for Bonzo '51
I Married a Witch '42
Pennies from Heaven '36

Liv Tyler (1977-)
The Incredible Hulk '08
Smother '08
The Strangers '08
Reign Over Me '07
Lonesome Jim '06
Jersey Girl '04
Lord of the Rings: The Return of the King '03
Lord of the Rings: The Two Towers '02
Lord of the Rings: The Fellowship of the Ring '01
One Night at McCool's '01
Dr. T & the Women '00
Cookie's Fortune '99
Onegin '99
Armageddon '98
Plunkett & Macleane '98
Inventing the Abbotts '97
U-Turn '97
Stealing Beauty '96
That Thing You Do! '96
Empire Records '95
Heavy '94
Silent Fall '94

Tom Tyler (1903-54)
Guns of Justice '50
Last Bullet '50
Outlaw Fury '50
Rangeland Empire '50
Riders of the Range '50
Sudden Death '50
Outlaw Gang '49
She Wore a Yellow Ribbon '49
Boss of Boomtown '44
Riders of the Rio Grande '43
Code of the Outlaw '42
Shadows on the Sage '42
Valley of the Sun '42
The Adventures of Captain Marvel '41
Gauchos of El Dorado '41
Outlaws of the Cherokee Trail '41
Riders of the Timberline '41
West of Cimarron '41
The Mummy's Hand '40
The Westerner '40
Stagecoach '39
Cheyenne Rides Again '38
The Phantom of the Range '38
Brothers of the West '37
Feud of the Trail '37
Riding On '37
Santa Fe Bound '37
Fast Bullets '36
Last Outlaw '36
Pinto Rustlers '36
Rip Roarin' Buckaroo '36
Coyote Trails '35
Laramie Kid '35
Powdersmoke Range '35
Ridin' Thru '35
Rio Rattler '35
Silent Code '35
Silent Valley '35
Unconquered Bandit '35
Fighting Hero '34
The Silver Bullet '34
Deadwood Pass '33
Phantom of the Air '33
When a Man Rides Alone '33
The Forty-Niners '32
Single Handed Sanders '32
Battling with Buffalo Bill '31
Phantom of the West '31
Two Fisted Justice '31

Judy Tylor
What Love Is '07
Freshman Orientation '04
My 5 Wives '00

George Tyne (1911-)
Sands of Iwo Jima '49
Call Northside 777 '48
Open Secret '48
A Walk in the Sun '46
Objective, Burma! '45

Charles Tyner (1925-)
Pulse '88
Planes, Trains & Automobiles '87
The Longest Yard '74
Emperor of the North Pole '73
Jeremiah Johnson '72
Harold and Maude '71
The Cheyenne Social Club '70
Cool Hand Luke '67

Tyrese
See Tyrese Gibson

Susan Tyrrell (1946-)
Buddy Boy '99
Relax... It's Just Sex! '98
The Demolitionist '95
Powder '95
Motorama '91
Cry-Baby '90
Rockula '90
Thompson's Last Run '90
Far from Home '89
Tapeheads '89
Big Top Pee-wee '88
The Underachievers '88
Windmills of the Gods '88
The Offspring '87
Poker Alice '87
Avenging Angel '85
Flesh and Blood '85
Angel '84
Fire and Ice '83 (V)
Tales of Ordinary Madness '83
Fast Walking '82
Liar's Moon '82
Night Warning '82
Forbidden Zone '80
Lady of the House '78
Andy Warhol's Bad '77
Another Man, Another Chance '77
Islands in the Stream '77
September 30, 1955 '77
The Killer Inside Me '76
Zandy's Bride '74
Fat City '72
Shoot Out '71

Barbara Tyson (1964-)
K-9 3: P.I. '01
Beautiful Joe '00
Ratz '99
Resurrection '99
Baby Monitor: Sound of Fear '97

Cathy Tyson (1965-)
Band of Gold '95
Priest '94
The Lost Language of Cranes '92
Business As Usual '88
The Serpent and the Rainbow '87
Mona Lisa '86

Cicely Tyson (1933-)
Tyler Perry's Why Did I Get Married Too? '10
Madea's Family Reunion '06
Because of Winn-Dixie '05
Diary of a Mad Black Woman '05
The Rosa Parks Story '02
Aftershock: Earthquake in New York '99
A Lesson Before Dying '99
Life '99
Always Outnumbered Always Outgunned '98
Mama Flora's Family '98
Ms. Scrooge '97
Hoodlum '96
Riot in the Streets '96
The Road to Galveston '96
Oldest Confederate Widow Tells All '95
Duplicates '92
Fried Green Tomatoes '91
Heat Wave '90
The Kid Who Loved Christmas '90
The Women of Brewster Place '89
Acceptable Risks '86
Samaritan: The Mitch Snyder Story '86
Bustin' Loose '81
The Concorde: Airport '79 '79
A Hero Ain't Nothin' but a Sandwich '78
King '78
A Woman Called Moses '78
Roots '77
Wilma '77
The River Niger '76
The Autobiography of Miss Jane Pittman '74
Sounder '72
The Heart Is a Lonely Hunter '68
A Man Called Adam '66

Mike Tyson (1966-)
The Hangover '09
Tyson '08
Crocodile Dundee in Los Angeles '01
Black and White '99

Pamela Tyson
Last Dance '96
What's Love Got to Do with It? '93
Jungle Fever '91

Richard Tyson (1961-)
Lost Treasure of the Maya '08
Flight of the Living Dead: Outbreak on a Plane '07
When I Find the Ocean '06
Black Hawk Down '01
Firetrap '01
Battlefield Earth '00
Lethal Force '00
Operation Sandman: Warriors in Hell '00
Desert Thunder '99
Liar's Poker '99
Beneath the Bermuda Triangle '98
Tales of the Kama Sutra 2: Monsoon '98
There's Something about Mary '98
Monsoon '97
The Glass Cage '96
Kingpin '96
Pharoah's Army '95
Dark Tide '93
Red Shoe Diaries 3: Another Woman's Lipstick '93
The Babe '92
Kindergarten Cop '90
Two Moon Junction '88
Three o'Clock High '87

Galina Tyunina
Day Watch '06
Night Watch '04

Margaret Tyzack (1933-)
Match Point '05
Our Mutual Friend '98
Mrs. Dalloway '97
The King's Whore '90
Mr. Love '86
Quatermass Conclusion '79
2001: A Space Odyssey '68

Asher Tzarfati
Secret of Yolanda '82
Shell Shock '63

Alanna Ubach (1977-)
Still Waiting '08
Waiting '05
Meet the Fockers '04
Legally Blonde 2: Red White & Blonde '03
Crazy Little Thing '02
Legally Blonde '01
Blue Moon '00
Clockwatchers '97
Trading Favors '97
johns '96
Just Your Luck '96
Denise Calls Up '95
Freeway '95
Airborne '93

Ryohei Uchida
Rica '72
Blind Woman's Curse '70
The Human Condition: Road to Eternity '59

Fabiana Udenio (1964-)
The Godson '98
Austin Powers: International Man of Mystery '97
Bride of Re-Animator '89
Summer School '87
Hardbodies 2 '86

Claudia Udy (1960-)
Captive Rage '88
The Pink Chiquitas '86
Out of Control '85

Helene Udy (1962-)
Sweet Murder '93
The Hollywood Detective '89
Pin... '88

Bob Uecker (1935-)
Major League 3: Back to the Minors '98
Homeward Bound 2: Lost in San Francisco '96 (V)
Major League 2 '94
Major League '89

Kichijiro Ueda (1904-72)
Gamera vs. Gaos '67
The Hidden Fortress '58
Seven Samurai '54
Rashomon '51

Misa(ko) Uehara (1937-)
Ju-On: The Grudge '03
I Bombed Pearl Harbor '60
Saga of the Vagabond '59
The Hidden Fortress '58

Kenjiro Uemura (1914-79)
The Human Condition: Road to Eternity '59
A Quiet Duel '49

Aya Ueto
Azumi 2 '05
Azumi '03

Leslie Uggams (1943-)
Sugar Hill '94
Sizzle '81
Backstairs at the White House '79
Roots '77
Poor Pretty Eddie '73
Two Weeks in Another Town '62

Nadja Uhl (1972-)
The Baader Meinhof Complex '08
Cherry Blossoms '08
What to Do in Case of Fire '02
The Legend of Rita '99

Gisela Uhlen (1919-2007)
Toto le Heros '91
The Marriage of Maria Braun '79
The Indian Scarf '63

Gaspard Ulliel (1984-)
Hannibal Rising '07
Paris, je t'aime '06
A Very Long Engagement '04
Strayed '03

Raviv (Ricky) Ullman (1986-)
Havoc 2: Normal Adolescent Behavior '07
The Big Bad Swim '06

Tracey Ullman (1961-)
The Tale of Despereaux '08 (V)
I Could Never Be Your Woman '06
Tim Burton's Corpse Bride '05 (V)
A Dirty Shame '04
Panic '00
Small Time Crooks '00
Bullets over Broadway '94
Ready to Wear '94
Happily Ever After '93 (V)
Household Saints '93
I'll Do Anything '93
Robin Hood: Men in Tights '93
I Love You to Death '90
Happy Since I Met You '89
Jumpin' Jack Flash '86
Plenty '85
Give My Regards to Broad Street '84

Liv Ullmann (1939-)
Saraband '03
Mindwalk: A Film for Passionate Thinkers '91
The Ox '91
The Rose Garden '89
Gaby: A True Story '87
The Bay Boy '85
Dangerous Moves '84
The Wild Duck '84
Richard's Things '80
Autumn Sonata '78
The Serpent's Egg '78

A Bridge Too Far '77
Face to Face '76
Leonor '75
Zandy's Bride '74
Forty Carats '73
The New Land '73
Scenes from a Marriage '73
Cries and Whispers '72
The Emigrants '72
Cold Sweat '71
The Night Visitor '70
The Passion of Anna '70
Hour of the Wolf '68
The Shame '68
Persona '66

Tristan Ulloa (1970-)
The 4 Musketeers '05
Sex and Lucia '01
Km. 0 '00

Lenore Ulric (1892-1970)
Northwest Outpost '47
Camille '36

Skeet Ulrich (1969-)
Armored '09
For Sale by Owner '09
Chilly Dogs '01
Nobody's Baby '01
Soul Assassin '01
Chill Factor '99
Ride with the Devil '99
A Soldier's Sweetheart '98
As Good As It Gets '97
The Newton Boys '97
Albino Alligator '96
The Craft '96
Last Dance '96
Scream '96
Touch '96
Boys '95

Mikhail Ulyanov (1927-2007)
Private Life '82
The Theme '79

Margaret Umbers
The Bridge to Nowhere '86
Death Warmed Up '85

Mark Umbers (1973-)
These Foolish Things '06
A Good Woman '04

Miyoshi Umeki (1929-2007)
The Horizontal Lieutenant '62
Flower Drum Song '61
Sayonara '57

Yoko Umemura
The Story of the Late Chrysanthemum '39
Sisters of the Gion '36

Claudio Undari (1935-)
Bronson's Revenge '72
Fighting Fists of Shanghai Joe '65

Edward Underdown (1908-89)
Beast of Morocco '66
Pattern for Plunder '62
Beat the Devil '53
Recoil '53
The Shadow Man '53
The Voice of Merrill '52
Man on the Run '49
Inspector Hornleigh '39
Wings of the Morning '37

Blair Underwood (1964-)
The Hades Factor '06
The Hit '06
Madea's Family Reunion '06
Something New '06
Malibu's Most Wanted '03
Full Frontal '02
G '02
Rules of Engagement '00
Asunder '99
Deep Impact '98
Mama Flora's Family '98
Mistrial '96
Set It Off '96
Soul of the Game '96
Just Cause '94
Dangerous Relations '93
Posse '93
Heat Wave '90
Krush Groove '85

Jay Underwood (1968-)
Dancing in September '00
Possums '99
Stalker '98
Afterglow '97
The Nurse '97
A Reason to Believe '95
The Raffle '94
Sleepstalker: The Sandman's Last Rites '94
Stalked '94
Wyatt Earp: Return to Tombstone '94
Still Not Quite Human '92
To Die For 2: Son of Darkness '91
The Gumshoe Kid '89
Not Quite Human 2 '89
Uncle Buck '89
The Invisible Kid '88
Promised Land '88
Not Quite Human '87
The Boy Who Could Fly '86
Desert Bloom '86

Birol Unel
Soul Kitchen '09
Head On '04

Deborah Kara Unger (1966-)
Angel and the Badman '09
88 Minutes '08
Lies & Alibis '06
Silent Hill '06
White Noise '05
A Love Song for Bobby Long '04
Paranoia 1.0 '04
Emile '03
Fear X '03
Hollywood North '03
Stander '03
Thirteen '03
Between Strangers '02
Leo '02
The Salton Sea '02
Luminous Motion '00
Signs & Wonders '00
The Weekend '00
The Hurricane '99
Sunshine '99
Payback '98
The Rat Pack '98
The Game '97
Keys to Tulsa '96
No Way Home '96
Crash '95
Highlander: The Final Dimension '94
Hotel Room '93
Whispers in the Dark '92
Prisoners of the Sun '91
Till There Was You '91

Joe Unger
Leatherface: The Texas Chainsaw Massacre 3 '89
Go Tell the Spartans '78

Gabrielle Union (1973-)
Cadillac Records '08
Meet Dave '08
The Box '07
Daddy's Little Girls '07
The Perfect Holiday '07
Running with Scissors '06
The Honeymooners '05
Say Uncle '05
Breakin' All The Rules '04
Bad Boys 2 '03
Cradle 2 the Grave '03
Deliver Us from Eva '03
Abandon '02
Welcome to Collinwood '02
The Brothers '01
Two Can Play That Game '01
Bring It On '00
She's All That '99
Ten Things I Hate about You '99

Johann Urb
The Hottie and the Nottie '08
Strictly Sexual '08
All In '06

Karl Urban (1972-)
Star Trek '09
Comanche Moon '08
Pathfinder '07
Doom '05
The Bourne Supremacy '04
The Chronicles of Riddick '04
Lord of the Rings: The Return of the King '03
Ghost Ship '02
Lord of the Rings: The Two Towers '02
The Price of Milk '00

James Urbaniak (1963-)
Fay Grim '06
Fortunes '05
Plain Dirty '04
American Splendor '03
Sweet and Lowdown '99
Henry Fool '98
The Sticky Fingers of Time '97

Mary Ure (1933-75)
A Reflection of Fear '72
Where Eagles Dare '68
The Mind Benders '63
Look Back in Anger '58
Windom's Way '57

Minerva Urecal (1894-1966)
Niagara '52
Kid Sister '45
Mr. Muggs Rides Again '45
The Ape Man '43

Fabio Urena
Return of the Living Dead 3 '93
The Bronx War '90

Justin Urich
Serial Killing 101 '04
Monster Man '03
Winter Break '02
The Rage: Carrie 2 '99

Robert Urich (1946-2002)
The Lazarus Man '96
Captains Courageous '95
A Horse for Danny '95
Spenser: A Savage Place '94
Spenser: Pale Kings & Princes '94
Spenser: The Judas Goat '94
Hit Woman: The Double Edge '93
Spenser: Ceremony '93
In a Stranger's Hand '92
Revolver '92
Blind Man's Bluff '91
A Perfect Little Murder '90
Lonesome Dove '89
Murder by Night '89
Scandal Sheet '85
Turk 182! '85
Ice Pirates '84
Invitation to Hell '84
Mistral's Daughter '84
Endangered Species '82
Take Your Best Shot '82
Killing at Hell's Gate '81
The Shadow Box '80
Vegas '78
Bunco '77
Magnum Force '73

Robert Urquhart (1922-95)
The Kitchen Toto '87
Playing Away '87
Children of the Full Moon '84
Sharma & Beyond '84
The Curse of Frankenstein '57
White Huntress '57
The House of the Arrow '53

Benny "The Jet" Urquidez (1952-)
Grosse Pointe Blank '97
Bloodmatch '91
The Kick Fighter '91
Down the Drain '89

Susan Ursitti
Defense Play '88
Teen Wolf '85

Jun Usami (1911-81)
Tora! Tora! Tora! '70
Late Spring '49

Usher
See Usher Raymond

Guy Usher
West of Cimarron '41
Danger Ahead '40
Prison Break '38
Justice of the Range '35
Make a Million '35

Peter Ustinov (1921-2004)
Luther '03
Victoria & Albert '01
Alice in Wonderland '99
Animal Farm '99 (V)
The Bachelor '99
Stiff Upper Lips '96
The Phoenix and the Magic Carpet '95
The Old Curiosity Shop '94
Lorenzo's Oil '92
Around the World in 80 Days '89
Appointment with Death '88
Agatha Christie's Thirteen at Dinner '85
Evil under the Sun '82
Grendel, Grendel, Grendel '82 (V)
Charlie Chan and the Curse of the Dragon Queen '81
The Great Muppet Caper '81
Ashanti, Land of No Mercy '79
Death on the Nile '78
The Thief of Baghdad '78
The Last Remake of Beau Geste '77
Mouse and His Child '77 (V)
The Purple Taxi '77
Logan's Run '76
The Treasure of Matecumbe '76
One of Our Dinosaurs Is Missing '75
Robin Hood '73 (V)
Hammersmith Is Out '72
Viva Max '69
Hot Millions '68
Blackbeard's Ghost '67
The Comedians '67
Barefoot in Athens '66
Lady L '65
Topkapi '64
Billy Budd '62
Spartacus '60
The Sundowners '60
The Man Who Wagged His Tail '57
Lola Montes '55
We're No Angels '55
Beau Brummel '54
The Egyptian '54
Le Plaisir '52 (N)
Quo Vadis '51
Immortal Battalion '44
One of Our Aircraft Is Missing '41

Kari Vaananen (1953-)
Ambush '99
La Vie de Boheme '93
Night on Earth '91
Amazon '90
Leningrad Cowboys Go America '89

Brenda Vaccaro (1939-)
The Boynton Beach Club '05
Sonny '02
The Mirror Has Two Faces '96
Love Affair '94
Lethal Games '90
Masque of the Red Death '90
Cookie '89
Heart of Midnight '89
Ten Little Indians '89
Water '85
Supergirl '84
A Long Way Home '81
Pride of Jesse Hallum '81
Zorro, the Gay Blade '81
The First Deadly Sin '80
The Guyana Tragedy: The Story of Jim Jones '80
Capricorn One '78
Dear Detective '78
Airport '77 '77
Death Weekend '76
Once Is Not Enough '75
Honor Thy Father '73
Summertree '71
I Love My... Wife '70
Midnight Cowboy '69

Annette (Stroyberg) Vadim (1936-2005)
Blood and Roses '61
Dangerous Liaisons '60

David Vadim (1972-)
Exit Wounds '01
Air Force One '97
Little Odessa '94

Roger Vadim (1928-2000)
Into the Night '85
Edie in Ciao! Manhattan '72

Dan Vadis (1938-87)
Seven Magnificent Gladiators '84
Bronco Billy '80
Fort Yuma Gold '66
The Triumph of Hercules '66
Son of Hercules in the Land of Darkness '63

Vera Vague
See Barbara Jo Allen

Lester Vail (1900-59)
Consolation Marriage '31
Dance Fools Dance '31

Myrtle Vail (1888-1978)
Little Shop of Horrors '60
Myrt and Marge '33

Charlotte Valandrey (1968-)
My Life and Times with Antonin Artaud '93
Orlando '92
Red Kiss '85

Birgitta Valberg (1916-)
The Shame '68
The Virgin Spring '59

Serge-Henri Valcke (1946-)
No Man's Land '01
Soul Assassin '01
The Quarry '98
Amsterdamned '88

Wilmer Valderrama (1980-)
Columbus Day '08
The Dead One '07
The Darwin Awards '06
Fast Food Nation '06
Unaccompanied Minors '06
Clifford's Really Big Movie '04 (V)
Party Monster '03
Summer Catch '01

Jerry Vale (1932-)
Casino '95
Goodfellas '90

Virginia Vale (1920-2006)
Blonde Comet '41
Panama Menace '41
Bullet Code '40
Legion of the Lawless '40

Nancy Valen (1965-)
Black Thunder '98
Final Embrace '92

Carlos Valencia
Towards Darkness '07
In the Blood '06
Ratas, Ratones, Rateros '99

Vladimir Valenta (1923-2001)
The Unbearable Lightness of Being '88
Vengeance Is Mine '74
Closely Watched Trains '66

Barbara Valentin (1940-2002)
Carmen, Baby '66
Horrors of Spider Island '59

Anthony Valentine (1939-)
Two Men Went to War '02
Body & Soul '93
Riders '88
Robin Hood... The Legend: Robin Hood and the Sorcerer '83
The Carpathian Eagle '81

Karen Valentine (1947-)
The Power Within '95
Children in the Crossfire '84
Jane Doe '83
Skeezer '82
The North Avenue Irregulars '79
Hot Lead & Cold Feet '78
Return to Fantasy Island '77

Scott Valentine (1958-)
Paranoia '98
Carnosaur 3: Primal Species '96
Mars '96
Object of Obsession '95
Phantom 2040 Movie: The Ghost Who Walks '95 (V)
Out of Annie's Past '94
Till the End of the Night '94
The Unborn 2 '94
Double Obsession '93
Homicidal Impulse '92
The Secret Passion of Robert Clayton '92
To Sleep with a Vampire '92
Write to Kill '91
After the Shock '90
Dangerous Pursuit '89
My Demon Lover '87
Deadtime Stories '86
True Stories '86

Rudolph Valentino (1895-1926)
Son of the Sheik '26
Cobra '25
The Eagle '25
Monsieur Beaucaire '24
Beyond the Rocks '22
Blood and Sand '22
Moran of the Lady Letty '22
Camille '21
The Four Horsemen of the Apocalypse '21
The Sheik '21
The Eyes of Youth '19
All Night '18
The Married Virgin '18

Tasia Valenza (1968-)
The Hillside Strangler '89
Rappin' '85
Crackers '84

Daniel Valenzuela
La Leon '07
The Road '00

Laura Valenzuela
Make Your Bets Ladies '65
Madame Sans-Gene '62

Jeanne Valerie (1941-)
Desert Commandos '67
Dangerous Liaisons '60

Joan Valerie (1911-83)
Roaring City '51
Charlie Chan at the Wax Museum '40
Michael Shayne: Private Detective '40
Day-Time Wife '39

Children of the Wild '37

Fanny Valette

Moliere '07
La Petite Jerusalem '05

Rosa Valetti (1878-1937)

M '31
The Blue Angel '30
Tartuffe '25

Frederick Valk (1895-1956)

Frenzy '46
Dead of Night '45
Hotel Reserve '44
Dangerous Moonlight '41
Night Train to Munich '40

Kitty Vallacher

The Legend of Frank Woods '77
Grave of the Vampire '72

Riccardo Valle

Hercules vs. the Sons of the Sun '64
The Awful Dr. Orloff '62

Marcel Vallee (1880-1957)

Topaze '33
The Crazy Ray '22

Rudy Vallee (1901-86)

Slashed Dreams '74
Live a Little, Love a Little '68
How to Succeed in Business without Really Trying '67
The Admiral Was a Lady '50
The Beautiful Blonde from Bashful Bend '49
Father Was a Fullback '49
My Dear Secretary '49
I Remember Mama '48
Unfaithfully Yours '48
The Bachelor and the Bobby-Soxer '47
The Sin of Harold Diddlebock '47
People Are Funny '46
The Palm Beach Story '42
Second Fiddle '39
Gold Diggers in Paris '38
International House '33
Glorifying the American Girl '30
Vagabond Lover '29

Nick Vallelonga (1959-)

The Prince and the Pauper '07
In the Kingdom of the Blind the Man with One Eye Is King '94

Amber Valletta (1974-)

The Spy Next Door '10
Gamer '09
Dead Silence '07
Premonition '07
The Last Time '06
Hitch '05
Transporter 2 '05
Duplex '03
Max Keeble's Big Move '01
Family Man '00
What Lies Beneath '00

Mark Valley (1964-)

Jericho '01
The Next Best Thing '00
The Siege '98
George Wallace '97

Alida Valli (1921-2006)

Angel of Death '02
A Month by the Lake '95
Le Jupon Rouge '87
Beyond Erotica '79
Perfect Crime '79
Berlinguer I Love You '77
Suspiria '77
The Cassandra Crossing '76
1900 '76
Lisa and the Devil '75
The Tempter '74
The Spider's Stratagem '70
Oedipus Rex '67
The Castilian '63
The Horror Chamber of Dr. Faustus '59
Il Grido '57
The Night Heaven Fell '57
The Wide Blue Road '57
Senso '54
Walk Softly, Stranger '50
The Third Man '49
The Miracle of the Bells '48
The Paradine Case '47
We the Living '42

Frankie Valli (1937-)

Witness to the Mob '98
Eternity '90
Modern Love '90
Dirty Laundry '87

Romolo Valli (1925-80)

Bobby Deerfield '77
A Fistful of Dynamite '72
The Garden of the Finzi-Continis '71
Boom! '68
The Leopard '63
The Girl with a Suitcase '60

Virginia Valli (1898-1968)

Night Life in Reno '31
Lost Zeppelin '29
Up the Ladder '25
The Shock '23

Rick Vallin (1919-77)

Dial Red O '55
The Last of the Redmen '47
Corregidor '43
Riders of the Rio Grande '43
King of the Stallions '42
The Panther's Claw '42

Raf Vallone (1917-2002)

The Godfather, Part 3 '90
Christopher Columbus '85
The Scarlet & the Black '83
Time to Die '83
Lion of the Desert '81
An Almost Perfect Affair '79
The Greek Tycoon '78
The Other Side of Midnight '77
The Girl in Room 2A '76
The Human Factor '75
Rosebud '75
That Lucky Touch '75
Ricco '74
Honor Thy Father '73
A Gunfight '71
The Italian Job '69
Nevada Smith '66
Harlow '65
The Secret Invasion '64
El Cid '61
Phaedra '61
Two Women '61
Anna '51
The Forbidden Christ '50
Bitter Rice '49

Vampira (1921-2008)

Night of the Ghouls '59
Plan 9 from Outer Space '56

Bobby Van (1930-80)

Bunco '77
Escape from Planet Earth '67
Navy vs. the Night Monsters '66
The Affairs of Dobie Gillis '53
Kiss Me Kate '53
Small Town Girl '53

Willeke Van Ammelrooy (1944-)

The Lake House '06
Antonia's Line '95
The Lift '85
Fatal Error '83
On Top of the Whale '82
A Flight of Rainbirds '81

Joan Van Ark (1943-)

Net Games '03
When the Dark Man Calls '95
Tainted Blood '93
Red Flag: The Ultimate Game '81
Frogs '72

Ingrid van Bergen (1931-)

The Vampire Happening '71
The Avenger '60

Lewis Van Bergen

Pinocchio's Revenge '96
The Relic '96
Street Knight '93
False Arrest '92
Bugsy '91
Rage of Honor '87
South of Reno '87
Overthrow '82

Mabel van Buren (1878-47)

Beyond the Rocks '22
The Four Horsemen of the Apocalypse '21

Emily Van Camp (1986-)

Black Irish '07
The Ring 2 '05
A Different Loyalty '04

Lee Van Cleef (1925-89)

Thieves of Fortune '89
Speed Zone '88
Armed Response '86
Jungle Raiders '85
Codename: Wildgeese '84
Escape from New York '81
Hard Way '80
Octagon '80
The Squeeze '80
The Rip Off '78
Fatal Chase '77
Perfect Killer '77
The Stranger and the Gunfighter '76
God's Gun '75
Kid Vengeance '75
Mean Frank and Crazy Tony '75
Take a Hard Ride '75
Commandos '73
Escape from Death Row '73
The Grand Duel '73
Bad Man's River '72
New Mafia Boss '72
Captain Apache '71
Return of Sabata '71
El Condor '70
Sabata '69
Beyond the Law '68
The Good, the Bad and the Ugly '67
For a Few Dollars More '65
The Man Who Shot Liberty Valance '62
Ride Lonesome '59
The Bravados '58
The Young Lions '58
China Gate '57
Gunfight at the O.K. Corral '57
The Tin Star '57
The Conqueror '56
It Conquered the World '56
Pardners '56
Tribute to a Bad Man '56
Big Combo '55
A Man Alone '55
Gypsy Colt '54
The Beast from 20,000 Fathoms '53
High Noon '52
Kansas City Confidential '52
The Lawless Breed '52

Ron Van Clief (1943-)

Way of the Black Dragon '81
Fist of Fear, Touch of Death '80

Jean-Claude Van Damme (1961-)

Universal Soldier: Regeneration '09
The Shepherd: Border Patrol '08
Second in Command '05
In Hell '03
Derailed '02
Replicant '01
Desert Heat '99
Universal Soldier: The Return '99
Knock Off '98
Legionnaire '98
Double Team '97
Maximum Risk '96
The Quest '96
Sudden Death '95
Street Fighter '94
Timecop '94
Hard Target '93
Last Action Hero '93
Nowhere to Run '93
Universal Soldier '92
Double Impact '91
Death Warrant '90
Lionheart '90
Cyborg '89
Kickboxer '89
Black Eagle '88
Bloodsport '88
No Retreat, No Surrender '86
Monaco Forever '83

Monique Van De Ven (1952-)

The Man Inside '90
Paint It Black '89
Amsterdamned '88
The Assault '86
Katie Tippel '75
Turkish Delight '73

Sylvie van den Elsen

La Vie de Boheme '93
L'Argent '83

James Van Der Beek (1977-)

Eye of the Beast '07
Final Draft '07
Danny Roane: First Time Director '06
Standing Still '05
The Rules of Attraction '02
Cash Crop '01
Jay and Silent Bob Strike Back '01
Texas Rangers '01
Harvest '98
Varsity Blues '98
I Love You, I Love You Not '97
Angus '95

Nadine Van Der Velde (1962-)

After Midnight '89
Shadow Dancing '88
Munchies '87
Critters '86

Diana Van Der Vlis (1935-2001)

Lovespell '79
The Incident '67
X: The Man with X-Ray Eyes '63
Girl in Black Stockings '57

Frederique van der Wal (1967-)

Wild Wild West '99
Two Girls and a Guy '98

Trish Van Devere (1945-)

Deadly Currents '93
Messenger of Death '88
Hollywood Vice Sqaud '86
Uphill All the Way '85
All God's Children '80
The Changeling '80
The Hearse '80
Mayflower: The Pilgrims' Adventure '79
Movie, Movie '78
Stalk the Wild Child '76
Savage Is Loose '74
The Day of the Dolphin '73
Where's Poppa? '70

Casper Van Dien (1968-)

Aces 'n Eights '08
Starship Troopers 3: Marauder '08
Meltdown '06
Slayer '06
Maiden Voyage: Ocean Hijack '04
The Vector File '03
Danger Beneath the Sea '02
Road Rage '01
Sanctimony '01
Under Heavy Fire '01
Chasing Destiny '00
Cutaway '00
Python '00
The Collectors '99
The Omega Code '99
Partners '99
Shark Attack '99
Sleepy Hollow '99
Thrill Seekers '99
Modern Vampires '98
On the Border '98
Tarzan and the Lost City '98
James Dean: Live Fast, Die Young '97
NightScreams '97
Starship Troopers '97
Beastmaster 3: The Eye of Braxus '95
Night Eyes 4: Fatal Passion '95

Mamie Van Doren (1931-)

Slackers '02
Voyage to the Planet of Prehistoric Women '68
Las Vegas Hillbillys '66
Navy vs. the Night Monsters '66
Three Nuts in Search of a Bolt '64
Born Reckless '59
Girls' Town '59
High School Confidential '58
Teacher's Pet '58
Girl in Black Stockings '57
Untamed Youth '57
Francis Joins the WACs '54

John van Dreelen (1922-92)

Becoming Colette '92
Too Hot to Handle '76
Von Ryan's Express '65
13 Ghosts '60
A Time to Love & a Time to Die '58

Granville Van Dusen (1944-)

The Rose and the Jackal '90
Hotline '82
The Wild and the Free '80
Breaking Up '78
Dynasty '76
War Between the Tates '76

Jennifer Van Dyck (1962-)

Michael Clayton '07
Series 7: The Contenders '01
States of Control '98

Barry Van Dyke (1951-)

Foxfire Light '82
Ants '77

Conny Van Dyke (1945-)

Framed '75
Hell's Angels '69 '69

Dick Van Dyke (1925-)

Furry Vengeance '10
Night at the Museum: Battle of the Smithsonian '09
Curious George '06 (V)
Night at the Museum '06
Dick Tracy '90
Country Girl '82
The Runner Stumbles '79
Cold Turkey '71
The Comic '69
Chitty Chitty Bang Bang '68
Never a Dull Moment '68
Divorce American Style '67
Lt. Robin Crusoe, U.S.N. '66
Mary Poppins '64
Bye, Bye, Birdie '63

Jerry Van Dyke (1932-)

Death Blow '87
Run If You Can '87
McLintock! '63
The Courtship of Eddie's Father '62

Phillip Van Dyke

Halloweentown 2: Kalabar's Revenge '01
The Modern Adventures of Tom Sawyer '99
Halloweentown '98

Peter Van Eyck (1911-69)

The Spy Who Came in from the Cold '65
Dr. Mabuse vs. Scotland Yard '64
The Brain '62
The Thousand Eyes of Dr. Mabuse '60
A Bullet for Joey '55
Wages of Fear '55
Five Graves to Cairo '43

John Van Eyssen (1922-95)

The Horror of Dracula '58
Men of Sherwood Forest '57
Quatermass 2 '57
Four Sided Triangle '53

Jo Van Fleet (1919-96)

The Tenant '76
Satan's School for Girls '73
I Love You, Alice B. Toklas! '68
Cool Hand Luke '67
Gunfight at the O.K. Corral '57
The King and Four Queens '56
I'll Cry Tomorrow '55
The Rose Tattoo '55
East of Eden '54

Harry Van Gorkum

The Foreigner '03
Avenging Angelo '02
Dragonheart: A New Beginning '00
Escape under Pressure '00
Face the Music '00

Kevin Van Hentenryck

Basket Case 3: The Progeny '92
Basket Case 2 '90
Brain Damage '88
Basket Case '82

Brian Van Holt (1969-)

House of Wax '05
Man of the House '05
Basic '03
Confidence '03
S.W.A.T. '03
Windtalkers '02
Black Hawk Down '01
Whipped '00

Patrick Van Horn (1969-)

Pursuit of Happiness '01
Three to Tango '99
Free Enterprise '98
Ivory Tower '97
Swingers '96

Carice van Houten (1976-)

Repo Men '10
Body of Lies '08
Valkyrie '08
Black Book '06

Fedja Van Huet (1973-)

Rosenstrasse '03
The Delivery '99
Character '97

Merete Van Kamp (1962-)

Lethal Woman '88
Princess Daisy '83

Erland van Lidth (1953-87)

The Running Man '87
Stir Crazy '80

Wanderers '79

Jon Van Ness

Hospital Massacre '81
Tourist Trap '79

Peter Van Norden (1950-)

Casualties of Love: The "Long Island Lolita" Story '93
The Accused '88
Scandal in a Small Town '88

Rik van Nutter (1929-2005)

Thunderball '65
Tharus Son of Attila '62
Assignment Outer Space '61

Nina Van Pallandt (1932-)

Jungle Warriors '84
Sword & the Sorcerer '82
Cutter's Way '81
American Gigolo '79
Diary of a Young Comic '79
Quintet '79
A Wedding '78
Assault on Agathon '75
The Long Goodbye '73

Dick Van Patten (1928-)

Groom Lake '02
The Santa Trap '02
Big Brother Trouble '00
Love Is All There Is '96
Demolition High '95
A Dangerous Place '94
Robin Hood: Men in Tights '93
Body Trouble '92
Final Embrace '92
The New Adventures of Pippi Longstocking '88
Spaceballs '87
The Midnight Hour '86
Diary of a Teenage Hitchhiker '82
High Anxiety '77
Freaky Friday '76
Gus '76
The Strongest Man in the World '75
Soylent Green '73
Superdad '73
Westworld '73
Beware! The Blob '72
Joe Kidd '72
Zachariah '70
Charly '68
Psychomania '63

James Van Patten (1956-)

Hyper Space '89
Twisted Justice '89
The Dirty Dozen: The Deadly Mission '87
Nightforce '86
Young Warriors '83
Roller Boogie '79
Tennessee Stallion '78
Freaky Friday '76

Joyce Van Patten (1934-)

Grown Ups '10
Breathing Lessons '94
Trust Me '89
Monkey Shines '88
Billy Galvin '86
Crawlspace '86
The Rumor Mill '86
The Falcon and the Snowman '85
St. Elmo's Fire '85
Eleanor: First Lady of the World '82
The Bad News Bears '76
Mame '74
The Stranger Within '74
Winter Kill '74
Housewife '72
Thumb Tripping '72
The Trouble with Girls (and How to Get into It) '69
I Love You, Alice B. Toklas! '68

Nels Van Patten (1955-)

Mirror Images '91
One Last Run '89
Grotesque '87
Summer School '87

Timothy Van Patten (1959-)

Curse 4: The Ultimate Sacrifice '90
Catacombs '89
The Wrong Guys '88
Dress Gray '86
Zone Troopers '84
Escape from El Diablo '83
Class of 1984 '82

Vincent Van Patten (1957-)

The Break '95
Payback '90
The Dirty Dozen: The Deadly Mission '87
Rooster: Spurs of Death! '83
Hell Night '81
The Victory '81
Survival Run '80
Rock 'n' Roll High School '79
Chino '75
Charley and the Angel '73
The Bravos '72

Mario Van Peebles (1958-)

Sharpshooter '07
Carlito's Way: Rise to Power '05
Baadasssss! '03
44 Minutes: The North Hollywood Shootout '03
Ali '01
Guardian '01
The Guardian '00
Sally Hemings: An American Scandal '00
Blowback '99
Judgment Day '99
Raw Nerve '99
Crazy Six '98
Love Kills '98
Mama Flora's Family '98
Los Locos Posse '97
Protector '97
Stag '97
Gang in Blue '96
Riot in the Streets '96
Solo '96
Panther '95
Highlander: The Final Dimension '94
Urban Crossfire '94
Full Eclipse '93
Gunmen '93
Posse '93
New Jack City '91
Identity Crisis '90
Jaws: The Revenge '87
Heartbreak Ridge '86
Hot Shot '86
Last Resort '86
Rappin' '85
South Bronx Heroes '85
Delivery Boys '84
Exterminator 2 '84
Sophisticated Gents '81
Sweet Sweetback's Baadasssss Song '71

Megan Van Peebles (1958-2006)

South Bronx Heroes '85
Sweet Sweetback's Baadasssss Song '71

Melvin Van Peebles (1932-)

Love Kills '98
Calm at Sunset '96
Gang in Blue '96
Riot in the Streets '96
Fist of the North Star '95
Terminal Velocity '94
Posse '93
Boomerang '92
O.C. and Stiggs '87
Sophisticated Gents '81
Sweet Sweetback's Baadasssss Song '71

Edward Van Sloan (1881-1964)

The Mask of Diijon '46
Riders of the Rio Grande '43
Before I Hang '40
Danger on the Air '38
Dracula's Daughter '36
A Shot in the Dark '35
Death Takes a Holiday '34
Manhattan Melodrama '34
The Death Kiss '33
Deluge '33
The Mummy '32
Dracula '31
Frankenstein '31

Alan Van Sprang (1971-)

Guns '08
Do or Die '03
The Gospel of John '03
Narc '02
Steal This Movie! '00

Deborah Van Valkenburgh (1952-)

Backwoods '08
The Devil's Rejects '05
Mystery Woman: Mystery Weekend '05
Firestarter 2: Rekindled '02
Chasing Destiny '00
Free Enterprise '98
Mean Guns '97
Brain Smasher... A Love Story '93
Erik '90
One Man Out '89
Phantom of the Ritz '88
Python Wolf '88
Rampage '87
A Bunny's Tale '85
Going for the Gold: The Bill Johnson Story '85
Streets of Fire '84
King of the Mountain '81
The Warriors '79

Monique Van Vooren (1933-)

Sugar Cookies '77
Andy Warhol's Frankenstein '74
Ash Wednesday '73
There Goes Barder '54
Tarzan and the She-Devil '53

Yorick Van Wageningen (1964-)

Winter in Wartime '10
The New World '05
The Chronicles of Riddick '04
Beyond Borders '03

Travis Van Winkle (1982-)

Friday the 13th '09
Meet the Spartans '08
Transformers '07
Accepted '06

Steve Van Wormer

Groove '00
The Extreme Adventures of Super Dave '98
Meet the Deedles '98

Philip Van Zandt (1904-58)

The Pride and the Passion '57
Clipped Wings '53
Ghost Chasers '51
Where Danger Lives '50
Woman in Brown '48
Decoy '46
A Thousand and One Nights '45
Sherlock Holmes and the Secret Weapon '42
Wake Island '42
Citizen Kane '41

Louis Vanaria

Searching for Bobby D '05
This Thing of Ours '03

A Soldier's Sweetheart '98

Karine Vanasse (1983-)

Head in the Clouds '04
Set Me Free '99

Courtney B. Vance (1960-)

Extraordinary Measures '10
Nothing But the Truth '08
Whitewash: The Clarence Brandley Story '02
Eye See You '01
Space Cowboys '00
Cookie's Fortune '99
Love and Action in Chicago '99
Blind Faith '98
Naked City: A Killer Christmas '98
Naked City: Justice with a Bullet '98
Twelve Angry Men '97
The Boys Next Door '96
The Last Supper '96
The Preacher's Wife '96
The Affair '95
Dangerous Minds '95
Panther '95
The Tuskegee Airmen '95
Holy Matrimony '94
The Piano Lesson '94
Race to Freedom: The Story of the Underground Railroad '94
The Adventures of Huck Finn '93
Percy & Thunder '93
Beyond the Law '92
The Hunt for Red October '90
Hamburger Hill '87

Danitra Vance (1959-94)

Jumpin' at the Boneyard '92
Little Man Tate '91
Limit Up '89
The War of the Roses '89
Sticky Fingers '88

Jim Vance

Blood Cult '85
How to Make a Doll '68

Joe Vance

Deadly Breed '89
L.A. Crackdown 2 '88

Musetta Vander (1969-)

Breaking Point '09
Transylmania '09
Kicking & Screaming '05
Mosquitoman '05
What's Up, Scarlet? '05
O Brother Where Art Thou? '00
Wild Wild West '99
Gunshy '98
Mortal Kombat 2: Annihilation '97
Backlash: Oblivion 2 '95
Project Shadowchaser 3000 '95
Under the Hula Moon '95

Jean Vander Pyl (1919-99)

The Flintstones '94
Jetsons: The Movie '90 (V)

Alexandra Vandernoot (1965-)

The Crown Prince '06
The Closet '00
The Dinner Game '98
Blood of the Hunter '94
Highlander: The Gathering '92

Titos Vandis (1917-2003)

Piece of the Action '77
Smile '75
Once Upon a Scoundrel '73
Never on Sunday '60

Pierre Vaneck (1931-)

The Science of Sleep '06
The Proprietor '96
Othello '95

Sweet Country '87
Erendira '83
Is Paris Burning? '66

Charles Vanel (1892-1989)

Three Brothers '80
Death in the Garden '56
Diabolique '55
To Catch a Thief '55
Wages of Fear '55

Vanilla Ice (1967-)

The New Guy '02
Cool As Ice '91
Teenage Mutant Ninja Turtles 2: The Secret of the Ooze '91

Vanity (1959-)

DaVinci's War '92
Highlander: The Gathering '92
South Beach '92
Neon City '91
Memories of Murder '90
Action Jackson '88
Deadly Illusion '87
52 Pick-Up '86
Never Too Young to Die '86
The Last Dragon '85
Tanya's Island '81
Terror Train '80

Renata Vanni (1909-2004)

Wait until Spring, Bandini '90
The Lady in White '88
Westward the Women '51

Joanne Vannicola (1968-)

Common Ground '00
Iron Eagle 4 '95
Love and Human Remains '93

Luigi Vannucchi (1930-78)

Lovers Like Us '75
The Savage '75
Red Tent '69

Victor Varconi (1891-1976)

Unconquered '47
For Whom the Bell Tolls '43
My Favorite Blonde '42
Mr. Moto Takes a Vacation '39
Mr. Takes a Vacation '39
Dancing Pirate '36
The Black Camel '31
The Divine Lady '29
King of Kings '27

Nia Vardalos (1962-)

I Hate Valentine's Day '09
My Life in Ruins '09
Connie and Carla '04
My Big Fat Greek Wedding '02

Evelyn Varden (1895-1958)

The Bad Seed '56
The Night of the Hunter '55
Athena '54
When Willie Comes Marching Home '50

Norma Varden (1898-1989)

The Sound of Music '65
Witness for the Prosecution '57
Jupiter's Darling '55
Fancy Pants '50
Forever Amber '47
National Velvet '44
The White Cliffs of Dover '44

Leonor Varela (1972-)

Balls Out: Gary the Tennis Coach '09
Hell Ride '08
Goal 2: Living the Dream '07
Where God Left His Shoes '07
Americano '05
Innocent Voices '04

Blade 2 '02
Texas Rangers '01
The Tailor of Panama '00
Cleopatra '99

Antonio Vargas

Strictly Ballroom '92
Whore '91

Daniele Vargas

Jungle Inferno '72
Terror of the Steppes '64

Jacob Vargas (1971-)

Death Race '08
Bobby Z '07
The Hills Have Eyes 2 '07
Love Lies Bleeding '07
Bobby '06
Jarhead '05
The Wendell Baker Story '05
Flight of the Phoenix '04
RFK '02
Dr. Dolittle 2 '01 (V)
Next Friday '00
Traffic '00
The Hi-Lo Country '98
Romy and Michele's High School Reunion '97
Selena '96
Mi Vida Loca '94
My Family '94
Airborne '93
Gas Food Lodging '92
The Principal '87
The Children of Times Square '86

John Vargas (1958-)

Primary Colors '98
In Dark Places '97
Seduced by Evil '94
Unnatural Causes '86

Valentina Vargas (1964-)

Hellraiser 4: Bloodline '95
The Tigress '93
Dirty Games '89

Beatrice Varley (1896-1964)

Room at the Top '59
Death Goes to School '53
Bedelia '46
Great Day '46
Bees in Paradise '44
Waterloo Road '44
Young and Innocent '37

John Varley (1915-)

Meet Sexton Blake '44
In Which We Serve '43
The Life and Death of Colonel Blimp '43
Nine Men '43

Indira Varma (1973-)

Basic Instinct 2 '06
Bride & Prejudice '04
Kama Sutra: A Tale of Love '96

Jim Varney (1949-2000)

Atlantis: The Lost Empire '01 (V)
Daddy & Them '99
Toy Story 2 '99 (V)
Treehouse Hostage '99
Ernest Goes to Africa '97
Ernest in the Army '97
3 Ninjas: High Noon at Mega Mountain '97
100 Proof '96
Snowboard Academy '96
The Expert '95
Slam Dunk Ernest '95
Toy Story '95 (V)
Ernest Goes to School '94
The Beverly Hillbillies '93
Ernest Rides Again '93
Wilder Napalm '93
Ernest Scared Stupid '91
Ernest Goes to Jail '90
The Rousters '90
Fast Food '89
Ernest Saves Christmas '88
Ernest Goes to Camp '87
Dr. Otto & the Riddle of the Gloom Beam '86

Roland Varno (1908-96)
Return of the Vampire '43
To Be or Not to Be '42
The Fighting 69th '40
Gunga Din '39

Diane Varsi (1937-92)
I Never Promised You a Rose Garden '77
Johnny Got His Gun '71
The People '71
Bloody Mama '70
Wild in the Streets '68
Sweet Love, Bitter '67
Compulsion '59
Ten North Frederick '58
Peyton Place '57

Michael Vartan (1968-)
Rogue '07
Monster-in-Law '05
One Hour Photo '02
Mists of Avalon '01
It Had to Be You '00
The Next Best Thing '00
Sand '00
Never Been Kissed '99
The Curve '97
The Myth of Fingerprints '97
The Pallbearer '95
Fiorile '93

Vagelis Vartan
Emmanuelle, the Queen '79
Emmanuelle's Daughter '79

Luiz Carlos Vasconcelos (1954-)
Carandiru '03
Behind the Sun '01
Me You Them '00

Razvan Vasilescu (1954-)
The Oak '93
Trahir '93

Nelson Vasquez
El Cantante '06
Pinero '01

Roberta Vasquez (1963-)
Fit to Kill '93
Hard Hunted '92
Do or Die '91
The Rookie '90
Street Asylum '90
Easy Wheels '89
Picasso Trigger '89

Yolanda Vasquez
Pinochet's Last Stand '06
Maria's Child '93

Liz Vassey (1972-)
Man of the House '05
Pursuit of Happiness '01

Sofia Vassilieva (1992-)
Hurt '09
My Sister's Keeper '09
Day Zero '07
Eloise at the Plaza '03

Robert Vattier (1906-82)
Letters from My Windmill '54
The Baker's Wife '33

Dorothy Vaughan
Slander House '38
Hoosier Schoolboy '37

Frankie Vaughan (1928-99)
Let's Make Love '60
Dangerous Youth '58

Greg Vaughan (1973-)
Children of the Corn 5: Fields of Terror '98
Poison Ivy 3: The New Seduction '97

Paris Vaughan (1961-)
Les Miserables '97
Buffy the Vampire Slayer '92
Heat Wave '90

Peter Vaughan (1923-)
Is Anybody There? '08
Death at a Funeral '07
The Mother '03
Lorna Doone '01
Longitude '00
An Ideal Husband '99
Our Mutual Friend '98
Face '97
The Crucible '96
The Secret Agent '96
The Choir '95
Circle of Deceit '94
Fatherland '94
Heart of Darkness '93
The Remains of the Day '93
Codename Kyril '91
Porridge '91
Prisoner of Honor '91
Mountains of the Moon '90
Haunted Honeymoon '86
Bleak House '85
Brazil '85
Forbidden '85
The Razor's Edge '84
Coming Out of the Ice '82
Time Bandits '81
Valentino '77
Blockhouse '73
Mackintosh Man '73
Pied Piper '72
Savage Messiah '72
Straw Dogs '72
The Man Outside '68
Die! Die! My Darling! '65
The Victors '63

Vanessa Vaughan
His Bodyguard '98
Dead Silence '96
Crazy Moon '87

Alberta Vaughn (1904-92)
Laramie Kid '35
The Live Wire '34
Randy Rides Alone '34
Daring Danger '32
Wild Horse '31
The Dropkick '27

Ned Vaughn (1964-)
Life '99
Courage Under Fire '96
Wind '92
Chips, the War Dog '90

Robert Vaughn (1932-)
2B Perfectly Honest '04
Happy Hour '03
Hoodlum & Son '03
Pootie Tang '01
Lethal Force '00
An American Affair '99
BASEketball '98
Motel Blue '98
The Sender '98
Joe's Apartment '96
Menno's Mind '96
Blind Vision '91
Going Under '91
Nobody's Perfect '90
River of Death '90
That's Adequate '90
Brutal Glory '89
Buried Alive '89
C.H.U.D. 2: Bud the Chud '89
Emissary '89
Skeleton Coast '89
Transylvania Twist '89
Captive Rage '88
Nightstick '87
Prince of Bel Air '87
Black Moon Rising '86
Delta Force '86
Hour of the Assassin '86
Murrow '86
The Last Bastion '84
Return of the Man from U.N.C.L.E. '83
Superman 3 '83
Inside the Third Reich '82
Virus '82
S.O.B. '81
Battle Beyond the Stars '80
City in Fear '80
Hangar 18 '80
Kill Castro '80
The Mercenaries '80
Question of Honor '80
Backstairs at the White House '79
The Rebels '79
The Shaming '79
Brass Target '78
Centennial '78
The Lucifer Complex '78
Demon Seed '77 (V)
Starship Invasions '77
Blue Jeans and Dynamite '76
Wanted: Babysitter '75
The Towering Inferno '74
The Woman Hunter '72
The Statue '71
Julius Caesar '70
The Bridge at Remagen '69
Bullitt '68
The Glass Bottom Boat '66
The Magnificent Seven '60
The Young Philadelphians '59
Good Day for a Hanging '58
Teenage Caveman '58

Terri J. Vaughn
Dirty Laundry '07
Three Can Play That Game '07

Vince Vaughn (1970-)
Couples Retreat '09
Four Christmases '08
Fred Claus '07
Into the Wild '07
The Break-Up '06
Vince Vaughn's Wild West Comedy Show '06
Be Cool '05
Mr. & Mrs. Smith '05
Thumbsucker '05
Wedding Crashers '05
Anchorman: The Legend of Ron Burgundy '04
Dodgeball: A True Underdog Story '04
Paparazzi '04
Starsky & Hutch '04
I Love Your Work '03
Old School '03
Domestic Disturbance '01
Made '01
The Cell '00
The Prime Gig '00
South of Heaven, West of Hell '00
Clay Pigeons '98
A Cool, Dry Place '98
Psycho '98
Return to Paradise '98
The Locusts '97
The Lost World: Jurassic Park 2 '97
Swingers '96
Rudy '93

Emmanuelle Vaugier (1976-)
Bachelor Party 2: The Last Temptation '08
Blonde and Blonder '07
Unearthed '07
House of the Dead 2: Dead Aim '05
Masters of Horror: Pro-Life '05
Saw 2 '05
Call Me: The Rise and Fall of Heidi Fleiss '04
Secondhand Lions '03
Water's Edge '03
40 Days and 40 Nights '02
Mindstorm '01
Return to Cabin by the Lake '01
Ripper: Letter from Hell '01
My 5 Wives '00
The Fear: Halloween Night '99
The Halfback of Notre Dame '96

Sophie Vavasseur (1992-)
Northanger Abbey '07
Resident Evil: Apocalypse '04
Evelyn '02

Dana Vavrova (1967-)
The Harmonists '99
Brother of Sleep '95

Ron Vawter (1949-94)
King of the Hill '93
Philadelphia '93
Mastergate '92
The Silence of the Lambs '91
Swoon '91
Internal Affairs '90
sex, lies and videotape '89
Sudden Death '77

Yul Vazquez
The Box '07
Music Within '07
The Take '07
War of the Worlds '05
Bad Boys 2 '03
Runaway Bride '99
Fresh '94
Fly by Night '93

Alex Veadov
We Own the Night '07
Black Horizon '01

Alexa Vega (1988-)
Repo! The Genetic Opera '08
Remember the Daze '07
Sleepover '04
Spy Kids 3-D: Game Over '03
Spy Kids 2: The Island of Lost Dreams '02
Follow the Stars Home '01
Spy Kids '01
Ride the Wild Fields '00
The Deep End of the Ocean '98
Tom Clancy's Netforce '98
Ghosts of Mississippi '96
The Glimmer Man '96
Twister '96
Nine Months '95
Little Giants '94

Isela Vega (1940-)
Blood Screams '88
Barbarosa '82
Bordello '79
Drum '76
Joshua '76
Bring Me the Head of Alfredo Garcia '74
The Fear Chamber '68

Makenzie Vega (1994-)
In the Land of Women '06
Just My Luck '06
X-Men: The Last Stand '06
Sin City '05
Saw '04

Paz Vega (1976-)
The Human Contract '08
The Spirit '08
10 Items or Less '06
Spanglish '04
Carmen '03
Sex and Lucia '01

Conrad Veidt (1893-1943)
Above Suspicion '43
All Through the Night '42
Casablanca '42
Whistling in the Dark '41
A Woman's Face '41
Contraband '40
The Thief of Bagdad '40
Spy in Black '39
Dark Journey '37
King of the Damned '36
The Passing of the Third Floor Back '36
Under the Red Robe '36
Power '34
F.P. 1 '33
Congress Dances '31
The Beloved Rogue '27
The Man Who Laughs '27
Napoleon '27
The Hands of Orlac '25
Waxworks '24
Cesare Borgia '23
The Indian Tomb '21
The Cabinet of Dr. Caligari '19

Patricia Velasquez (1971-)
Mindhunters '05
The Twelve Days of Christmas Eve '04
Fidel '02
The Mummy Returns '01
Committed '99
The Mummy '99
No Vacancy '99
Beowulf '98

Pilar Velasquez
Ace of Hearts '85
Fury '78

Nadine Velazquez
Kings of South Beach '07
War '07

Teresa Velazquez (1942-98)
The Killer Must Kill Again '75
Night of a Thousand Cats '72

Eddie Velez (1958-)
Black Dawn '05
White Chicks '04
The Hunted '03
A Father's Choice '00
Running Woman '98
Under Oath '97
Bitter Vengeance '94
Drug Wars: The Camarena Story '90
Romero '89
Rooftops '89
Split Decisions '88
Women's Club '87
Doin' Time '85

Lauren Velez (1964-)
Prince of Central Park '00
I Think I Do '97
I Like It Like That '94

Lupe Velez (1908-44)
Mexican Spitfire at Sea '42
Playmates '41
Mexican Spitfire '40
Mad About Money '37
Hollywood Party '34
Palooka '34
The Half Naked Truth '32
Hell Harbor '30
Where East Is East '29
Stand and Deliver '28
The Gaucho '27

Reginald VelJohnson (1952-)
The Great American Sex Scandal '94
Posse '93
Die Hard 2: Die Harder '90
Die Hard '88
Plain Clothes '88
Remo Williams: The Adventure Begins '85
Ghostbusters '84

Evelyn Venable (1913-93)
Lucky Cisco Kid '40
Pinocchio '40 (V)
The Frontiersmen '38
Hollywood Stadium Mystery '38
Alice Adams '35
Harmony Lane '35
The Little Colonel '35
David Harum '34
Death Takes a Holiday '34
Mrs. Wiggs of the Cabbage Patch '34

Veronique Vendell (1942-)
Cross of Iron '76
Barbarella '68

Amy Veness (1876-1960)
Madeleine '50
Man of Evil '48
This Happy Breed '47

Ingrid Veninger
Re-Generation '04
Hush Little Baby '93
Hide and Seek '77

Lenny Venito
The Brave One '07
The Wild '06 (V)
Duane Hopwood '05
War of the Worlds '05
Shark Tale '04 (V)
Gigli '03
Men in Black 2 '02
Just the Ticket '98
Rounders '98
Witness to the Mob '98
Money for Nothing '93

Chick Vennera (1952-)
The Glass Trap '04
Active Stealth '99
Tycus '98
Alone in the Woods '95
Body Chemistry 4: Full Exposure '95
Night Eyes 4: Fatal Passion '95
Double Threat '92
The Terror Within 2 '91
Last Rites '88
The Milagro Beanfield War '88
Kidnapped '87
High Risk '81
Yanks '79
Thank God It's Friday '78

Diane Venora (1952-)
All Good Things '09
Stiletto '08
Touched '05
Stateside '04
Hamlet '00
The Insider '99
Looking for an Echo '99
The 13th Warrior '99
True Crime '99
The Young Girl and the Monsoon '99
The Jackal '97
The Substitute '96
Surviving Picasso '96
William Shakespeare's Romeo and Juliet '96
Heat '95
Three Wishes '95
Bird '88
Ironweed '87
F/X '86
A.D. '85
Terminal Choice '85
The Cotton Club '84
Wolfen '81

Wanda Ventham (1939-)
Asylum '05
Out of the Shadows '88
Captain Kronos: Vampire Hunter '74
Blood Beast Terror '67

John Ventimiglia (1963-)
The War Within '05
Personal Velocity: Three Portraits '02 (N)
Mickey Blue Eyes '99
Row Your Boat '98
The Funeral '96
Girls Town '95
Angela '94

Milo Ventimiglia (1977-)
Armored '09
Gamer '09
Pathology '08
Rocky Balboa '06
Cursed '04
Winter Break '02
She's All That '99

Vincent Ventresca (1965-)
Mammoth '06
The Learning Curve '01
Madison '01
Love & Sex '00

Clyde Ventura (1936-90)
Gator Bait '73
Bury Me an Angel '71

Jesse Ventura (1951-)
Demolition Man *'93*
Ricochet *'91*
Abraxas: Guardian of the Universe *'90*
Boxcar Blues *'90*
Repossessed *'90*
Thunderground *'89*
Predator *'87*
The Running Man *'87*

Lino Ventura (1919-87)
Sword of Gideon *'86*
The Medusa Touch *'78*
Pain in the A— *'77*
The Slap *'76*
The French Detective *'75*
Happy New Year *'73*
The Valachi Papers *'72*
Army of Shadows *'69*
The Last Adventure *'67*
Le Deuxieme Souffle *'66*
Jailbird's Vacation *'65*
The Three Penny Opera *'62*
Classe Tous Risque *'60*
Mistress of the World *'59*
Modigliani *'58*
Grisbi *'53*

Richard Venture (1923-)
Series 7: The Contenders *'01*
Red Corner *'97*
Truman *'95*
Scent of a Woman *'92*
Heartbreak Ridge *'86*
Missing *'82*
The Onion Field *'79*
The Effect of Gamma Rays on Man-in-the-Moon Marigolds *'73*

Silvana Venturelli
The Lickerish Quartet *'70*
Camille 2000 *'69*
A Long Ride From Hell *'68*

Massimo Venturiello
My Wonderful Life *'90*
Rorret *'87*

Billy Vera (1944-)
The Doors *'91*
Finish Line *'89*
The Adventures of Buckaroo Banzai Across the Eighth Dimension *'84*

Victoria Vera (1953-)
A Man of Passion *'88*
Monster Dog *'82*

Vera-Ellen (1920-81)
White Christmas *'54*
The Belle of New York *'52*
Happy Go Lovely *'51*
Love Happy *'50*
Three Little Words *'50*
On the Town *'49*
Words and Music *'48*
Wonder Man *'45*

Eduardo Verastegui
Bella *'06*
Chasing Papi *'03*

Natalia Verbeke (1975-)
Guantanamero *'07*
The Method *'05*
Dot the I *'03*
The Son of the Bride *'01*

Gwen Verdon (1925-2000)
The Dress Code *'99*
In Cold Blood *'96*
Marvin's Room *'96*
Oldest Confederate Widow Tells All *'95*
Alice *'90*
Cocoon: The Return *'88*
Nadine *'87*
Cocoon *'85*
The Cotton Club *'84*
Legs *'83*
Damn Yankees *'58*
The Farmer Takes a Wife *'53*
The Merry Widow *'52*

Carlo Verdone (1950-)
Iris Blond *'98*
Acqua e Sapone *'83*

Maribel Verdu (1970-)
Tetro *'09*
Pan's Labyrinth *'06*
Jericho Mansions *'03*
Y Tu Mama Tambien *'01*
Goya in Bordeaux *'99*
Belle Epoque *'92*
Lovers: A True Story *'90*

Elena Verdugo (1926-)
Boss' Son *'78*
Cyrano de Bergerac *'50*
The Big Sombrero *'49*
Little Giant *'46*
House of Frankenstein *'44*
Weird Woman *'44*
The Moon and Sixpence *'43*

Peter Vere-Jones
Meet the Feebles *'89 (V)*
Bad Taste *'88*

Ben Vereen (1946-)
And Then Came Love *'07*
Idlewild *'06*
Anne Rice's The Feast of All Saints *'01*
I'll Take You There *'99*
Why Do Fools Fall in Love? *'98*
Once Upon a Forest *'93 (V)*
Intruders *'92*
The Kid Who Loved Christmas *'90*
Mother Goose Rock 'n' Rhyme *'90*
Buy & Cell *'89*
A.D. *'85*
The Zoo Gang *'85*
Breakin' Through *'84*
The Jesse Owens Story *'84*
Puss 'n Boots *'84*
Pippin *'81*
All That Jazz *'79*
Roots *'77*
Funny Lady *'75*
Gas-s-s-s! *'70*

Sofia Vergara (1972-)
Tyler Perry's Meet the Browns *'08*
Grilled *'06*
Four Brothers *'05*
The 24th Day *'04*
Chasing Papi *'03*
Big Trouble *'02*

Tom Verica (1964-)
Princess Protection Program *'09*
Red Dragon *'02*
From the Earth to the Moon *'98*
Lost in the Bermuda Triangle *'98*
The Assassination File *'96*
Breach of Conduct *'94*
800 Leagues Down the Amazon *'93*
Die Hard 2: Die Harder *'90*

Dany Verissimo
Gradiva *'06*
District B13 *'04*

Bernard Verley (1939-)
Lucie Aubrac *'98*
Helas pour Moi *'94*
Pas Tres Catholique *'93*
Phantom of Liberty *'74*
Chloe in the Afternoon *'72*
The Milky Way *'68*

Francoise Verley
The Monkey's Mask *'00*
Chloe in the Afternoon *'72*

Harold Vermilyea (1889-1958)
Emperor Waltz *'48*
Sorry, Wrong Number *'48*

Denise Vernac (1916-84)
Unnatural *'52*
The Mask of Diijon *'46*

Karen Verne (1918-67)
The Seventh Cross *'44*
All Through the Night *'42*
Sherlock Holmes and the Secret Weapon *'42*
Kings Row *'41*
Underground *'41*

Guy Verney (1915-70)
Martin Luther *'53*
Fame Is the Spur *'47*
This Happy Breed *'47*

Adam Vernier (1972-)
Bring It On: In It to Win It *'07*
Black Cadillac *'03*

Pierre Vernier (1931-)
Under the Sand *'00*
Betty *'92*
Mama, There's a Man in Your Bed *'89*

Jerry Verno (1895-1975)
The Belles of St. Trinian's *'53*
Sidewalks of London *'38*
Non-Stop New York *'37*
Young and Innocent *'37*
The 39 Steps *'35*

Anne Vernon (1925-)
Therese & Isabelle *'67*
Umbrellas of Cherbourg *'64*

Conrad Vernon (1968-)
Madagascar: Escape 2 Africa *'08 (V)*
Shrek the Third *'07 (V)*
Shrek 2 *'04 (V)*
Shrek *'01 (V)*

Glenn Vernon (1923-99)
I Bury the Living *'58*
Bedlam *'45*

Howard Vernon (1914-96)
Faceless *'88*
Revenge in the House of Usher *'82*
Zombie Lake *'80*
The Demons *'74*
The Perverse Countess *'73*
Dr. Orloff and the Invisible Man *'72*
Rites of Frankenstein *'72*
The Screaming Dead *'72*
Virgin among the Living Dead *'71*
Orloff and the Invisible Man *'70*
Castle of the Creeping Flesh *'68*
Triple Cross *'67*
Alphaville *'65*
The Diabolical Dr. Z *'65*
The Train *'65*
The Awful Dr. Orloff *'62*
Bob le Flambeur *'55*
La Silence de la Mer *'47*

John Vernon (1932-2005)
Malicious *'95*
Hostage for a Day *'94*
Sodbusters *'94*
Bail Out *'90*
Mob Story *'90*
Terminal Exposure *'89*
War Bus Commando *'89*
Deadly Stranger *'88*
Dixie Lanes *'88*
I'm Gonna Git You Sucka *'88*
Killer Klowns from Outer Space *'88*
Blue Monkey *'87*
Ernest Goes to Camp *'87*
Nightstick *'87*
Doin' Time *'85*
Fraternity Vacation *'85*
The Blood of Others *'84*
Jungle Warriors *'84*
Chained Heat *'83*
Curtains *'83*
Savage Streets *'83*
Herbie Goes Bananas *'80*
National Lampoon's Animal House *'78*
Angela *'77*
Golden Rendezvous *'77*
A Special Day *'77*
The Outlaw Josey Wales *'76*
The Virginia Hill Story *'76*
Brannigan *'75*
Sweet Movie *'75*
The Barbary Coast *'74*
The Black Windmill *'74*
W *'74*
Charley Varrick *'73*
Hunter *'73*
Journey *'72*
Dirty Harry *'71*
Justine *'69*
Tell Them Willie Boy Is Here *'69*

Kate Vernon (1961-)
Battlestar Galactica: The Plan *'09*
School of Life *'06*
The Family Plan *'05*
The Secret Life of Girls *'99*
Blackjack *'97*
Flood: A River's Rampage *'97*
Downdraft *'96*
Bloodknot *'95*
Probable Cause *'95*
The Sister-in-Law *'95*
Dangerous Touch *'94*
Soft Deceit *'94*
Malcolm X *'92*
Mob Story *'90*
Hostile Takeover *'88*
The Last of Philip Banter *'87*
Alphabet City *'84*
Roadhouse 66 *'84*

Richard Vernon (1925-97)
The Return of the Borrowers *'96*
The Human Factor *'79*
The Duchess of Duke Street *'78*
The Satanic Rites of Dracula *'73*
A Hard Day's Night *'64*
Tomb of Ligeia *'64*
The Servant *'63*
Village of the Damned *'60*

Wally Vernon (1905-70)
Bloodhounds of Broadway *'52*
Square Dance Jubilee *'51*
Gunfire *'50*
Silver City Kid *'45*
California Joe *'43*
Broadway Serenade *'39*
Happy Landing *'38*

Christine Veronica
Party Incorporated *'89*
Love Notes *'88*

Cec Verrell
Three of Hearts *'93*
Mad at the Moon *'92*
Hell Comes to Frogtown *'88*
Eye of the Eagle *'87*
Silk *'86*

Marie Versini
Escape from the KGB *'87*
Brides of Fu Manchu *'66*

Odile Versois (1930-80)
Le Crabe Tambour *'77*
Cartouche *'62*
To Paris with Love *'55*

Veruschka (1939-)
The Bride *'85*
Blow-Up *'66*

Arie Verveen (1966-)
Sin City *'05*
Plain Dirty *'04*
Cabin Fever *'03*
Red Roses and Petrol *'03*
Sin *'02*
Running Free *'00*
The Thin Red Line *'98*
Caught *'96*

Charlotte Very
Trois Couleurs: Bleu *'93*
A Tale of Winter *'92*

Viktor Verzhbitsky
Day Watch *'06*
Night Watch *'04*

Bruno VeSota (1922-76)
Hell's Angels on Wheels *'67*
The Wild World of Batwoman *'66*
The Haunted Palace *'63*
Night Tide *'63*
The Choppers *'61*
Creature of the Walking Dead *'60*
Attack of the Giant Leeches *'59*
A Bucket of Blood *'59*
The Wasp Woman *'59*
Carnival Rock *'57*
Rock All Night *'57*
Teenage Doll *'57*
The Undead *'57*
The Female Jungle *'56*
The Gunslinger *'56*
Daughter of Horror *'55*
The Wild One *'54*

Edy Vessel (1940-)
The Trojan Horse *'62*
Passionate Thief *'60*

Tricia Vessey (1972-)
Town and Country *'01*
On the Edge *'00*
Coming Soon *'99*
Ghost Dog: The Way of the Samurai *'99*
The Alarmist *'98*
Bean *'97*
Standoff *'97*

Ondrej Vetchy (1962-)
Dark Blue World *'01*
Martha and I *'91*

Victoria Vetri (1944-)
Invasion of the Bee Girls *'73*
Group Marriage *'72*
When Dinosaurs Ruled the Earth *'70*

Karin Viard (1966-)
Time Out *'01*
Children of the Century *'99*
La Separation *'98*
The New Eve *'98*
The Separation *'94*
Delicatessen *'92*

Ronan Vibert (1964-)
Tristan & Isolde *'06*
The Cat's Meow *'01*
Shadow of the Vampire *'00*
The Scarlet Pimpernel *'99*
The Scarlet Pimpernel 2: Mademoiselle Guillotine *'99*
The Scarlet Pimpernel 3: The Kidnapped King *'99*
The Buccaneers *'95*

Sid Vicious (1957-79)
The Filth and the Fury *'99*
Mr. Mike's Mondo Video *'79*

Nicole Vicius
Itty Bitty Titty Committee *'07*
Last Days *'05*

Martha Vickers (1925-71)
Four Fast Guns *'59*
Big Bluff *'55*
The Big Sleep *'46*
The Man I Love *'46*

Yvette Vickers (1936-)
Evil Spirits *'91*
Beach Party *'63*
Attack of the Giant Leeches *'59*
Attack of the 50 Foot Woman *'58*
Reform School Girl *'57*

John Vickery (1950-)
Deconstructing Sarah *'94*
Rapid Fire *'92*

Charles Victor (1896-1965)
The Pit and the Pendulum *'61*
The Frightened Man *'52*
Made in Heaven *'52*
Those People Next Door *'52*
Motor Patrol *'50*
The Woman in Question *'50*
San Demetrio, London *'47*
The Foreman Went to France *'42*
Seven Days' Leave *'42*
Contraband *'40*

Henry Victor (1892-1945)
Blue, White and Perfect *'42*
Sherlock Holmes and the Secret Weapon *'42*
To Be or Not to Be *'42*
Underground Agent *'42*
King of the Zombies *'41*
Freaks *'32*
The Mummy *'32*
Seas Beneath *'31*
The Beloved Rogue *'27*

Katherine Victor (1923-2004)
SuperGuy: Behind the Cape *'02*
The Wild World of Batwoman *'66*
House of the Black Death *'65*
Curse of the Stone Hand *'64*
Creature of the Walking Dead *'60*
Teenage Zombies *'58*
Mesa of Lost Women *'52*

Christina Vidal (1981-)
See No Evil *'06*
Freaky Friday *'03*
Brink *'98*
Life with Mikey *'93*

Gil Vidal (1931-)
Rape *'76*
Night of the Howling Beast *'75*

Gore Vidal (1925-)
Gattaca *'97*
The Shadow Conspiracy *'96*
With Honors *'94*
Bob Roberts *'92*
Fellini's Roma *'72*

Henri Vidal (1919-59)
Voulez-Vous Danser avec Moi? *'59*
Just Another Pretty Face *'58*
Sois Belle et Tais-Toi *'58*
Une Parisienne *'58*
Attila *'54*
Fabiola *'48*

Lisa Vidal (1965-)
Dark Mirror *'07*
Chasing Papi *'03*
Active Stealth *'99*
Naked City: A Killer Christmas *'98*
The Wonderful Ice Cream Suit *'98*
Fall *'97*
I Like It Like That *'94*

Gala Videnovic (1969-)
Happy Hell Night *'92*
Hey, Babu Riba *'88*

Steven Vidler (1960-)
See No Evil *'06*
Salem's Lot *'04*
The Crocodile Hunter: Collision Course *'02*
Child Star: The Shirley Temple Story *'01*
Two Hands *'98*
Napoleon *'96 (V)*
Encounter at Raven's Gate *'88*
Wrangler *'88*
The Good Wife *'86*
The Dunera Boys *'85*
Three's Trouble *'85*

Susan Vidler
Wilbur Wants to Kill Himself '02
The Woman in White '97
Naked '93

Florence Vidor (1895-1977)
Doomsday '28
The Grand Duchess and the Waiter '26
Are Parents People? '25
The Coming of Amos '25
The Marriage Circle '24
The Virginian '23
Beau Revel '21

Asia Vieira (1982-)
Omen 4: The Awakening '91
The Good Mother '88

Vince Vieluf (1970-)
Firewall '06
Death Valley '04
Grind '03
Rat Race '01
Clay Pigeons '98
An American Werewolf in Paris '97

Vesa Vierikko (1956-)
The Match Factory Girl '90
The Winter War '89

Abe Vigoda (1921-)
Crime Spree '03
Just the Ticket '98
Witness to the Mob '98
A Brooklyn State of Mind '97
Good Burger '97
Love Is All There Is '96
Underworld '96
Jury Duty '95
Home of Angels '94
North '94
Sugar Hill '94
Batman: Mask of the Phantasm '93 (V)
Fist of Honor '92
Joe Versus the Volcano '90
Keaton's Cop '90
Look Who's Talking '89
Prancer '89
Plain Clothes '88
Vasectomy: A Delicate Matter '86
The Stuff '85
The Godfather 1902-1959: The Complete Epic '81
Great American Traffic Jam '80
The Cheap Detective '78
How to Pick Up Girls '78
The Godfather, Part 2 '74
Newman's Law '74
The Godfather '72

Herb Vigran (1910-86)
The Star '52
Bedtime for Bonzo '51

Robert Viharo (1939-)
Coldfire '90
Romero '89
Night Stalker '87
Happy Birthday, Gemini '80
Hide in Plain Sight '80
Kid from Not-So-Big '78
Bare Knuckles '77
Villa Rides '68
Valley of the Dolls '67

Henri Vilbert (1904-97)
Ali Baba and the 40 Thieves '54
Manon '50

Jordi Vilches (1979-)
Two Tough Guys '03
Nico and Dani '00

Marthe Villalonga (1932-)
Ma Saison Preferee '93
Three Men and a Cradle '85
The Big Red One '80

Soledad Villamil
The Secret in Their Eyes '09
Life According to Muriel '97

Frank Villard
Duke of the Derby '62
Seven Deadly Sins '53

Tom Villard (1954-94)
My Girl '91
Popcorn '89
Swimsuit '89
The Trouble with Dick '88
Heartbreak Ridge '86
One Crazy Summer '86
Weekend Warriors '86

Carlos Villarias
The California Trail '33
Dracula (Spanish Version) '31

Daniel Villarreal (1960-)
Speed '94
American Me '92

J.R. Villarreal (1992-)
Bobby Z '07
Akeelah and the Bee '06

Astrid Villaume (1923-95)
Pelle the Conqueror '88
Famous Five Get into Trouble '70

Herve Villechaize (1943-93)
Two Moon Junction '88
Rumpelstiltskin '82
Forbidden Zone '80
The One and Only '78
Return to Fantasy Island '77
The Man with the Golden Gun '74
Seizure '74
Greaser's Palace '72

James Villemaire
Dead Silence '96
Gate 2 '92
Matinee '92

Fernando Villena
Earthquake in Chile '74
Planet of the Vampires '65

Jacques Villeret (1951-)
The Dinner Game '98
The Favor, the Watch, & the Very Big Fish '92
Edith & Marcel '83
Bolero '82
Robert et Robert '78

Christopher Villiers (1960-)
First Knight '95
Top Secret! '84

James Villiers (1933-98)
Wavelength '96
Uncovered '94
Let Him Have It '91
House of Cards '90
Mountains of the Moon '90
Fortunes of War '87
Death by Prescription '86
Mrs. Silly '85
The Scarlet Pimpernel '82
Asylum '72
The Ruling Class '72
Blood from the Mummy's Tomb '71
Nice Girl Like Me '69
The Nanny '65
Repulsion '65
King and Country '64
Eva '62

Jay Villiers (1961-)
The Sculptress '97
Henry V '89

Pruitt Taylor Vince (1960-)
In the Electric Mist '08
Captivity '07
When a Man Falls in the Forest '07
Constantine '05
Drop Dead Sexy '05
Identity '03
Monster '03
Simone '02
13 Moons '02
Trapped '02
The Cell '00
Nurse Betty '00
Mumford '99
The Legend of 1900 '98
The Break '97
The End of Violence '97
Beautiful Girls '96
Under the Hula Moon '95
City Slickers 2: The Legend of Curly's Gold '94
Heavy '94
Natural Born Killers '94
Nobody's Fool '94
Come See the Paradise '90
Jacob's Ladder '90
Mississippi Burning '88
Barfly '87
Shy People '87

Alex Vincent (1982-)
My Family Treasure '93
Child's Play 2 '90
Wait until Spring, Bandini '90
Child's Play '88

Allen Vincent (1903-79)
After Midnight '33
Carnival Lady '33
Daring Daughters '33
Mystery of the Wax Museum '33

Brian Vincent (1970-)
Blue Moon '00
Under Hellgate Bridge '99
Black Dog '98
Animal Room '95

Cerina Vincent (1979-)
Everybody Wants to Be Italian '08
Return to House on Haunted Hill '07
It Waits '05
Cabin Fever '03
Not Another Teen Movie '01

Frank Vincent (1940-)
The Last Request '06
A Tale of Two Pizzas '03
This Thing of Ours '03
Snipes '01
The Crew '00
Gun Shy '00
If You Only Knew '00
Entropy '99
Under Hellgate Bridge '99
Undercurrent '99
Ten Benny '98
Tom Clancy's Netforce '98
Witness to the Mob '98
Cop Land '97
The Deli '97
Gotti '96
Grind '96
She's the One '96
West New York '96
Federal Hill '94
Jungle Fever '91
Goodfellas '90
Street Hunter '90
Raging Bull '80

Helene Vincent (1940-)
The Count of Monte Cristo '99
Ma Vie en Rose '97
Trois Couleurs: Bleu '93
I Don't Kiss '91
Life Is a Long Quiet River '88

Jan-Michael Vincent (1944-)
Buffalo 66 '97
Deadly Heroes '96
Red Line '96
Body Count '95
Ice Cream Man '95
Abducted 2: The Reunion '94
Indecent Behavior '93
Midnight Witness '93
Animal Instincts '92
Beyond the Call of Duty '92
Hidden Obsession '92
Sins of Desire '92
The Divine Enforcer '91
Hangfire '91
Haunting Fear '91
In Gold We Trust '91
Raw Nerve '91
Xtro 2: The Second Encounter '91
Alienator '89
Demonstone '89
Dirty Games '89
Deadly Embrace '88
The Hit List '88
Born in East L.A. '87
Enemy Territory '87
Last Plane Out '83
The Winds of War '83
Hard Country '81
The Return '80
Defiance '79
Big Wednesday '78
Hooper '78
Damnation Alley '77
Bite the Bullet '75
White Line Fever '75
Buster and Billie '74
The World's Greatest Athlete '73
The Mechanic '72
Tribes '70
The Undefeated '69
The Bandits '67

June Vincent (1924-)
Clipped Wings '53
Colorado Sundown '52
Counterspy Meets Scotland Yard '50
The Creeper '48
Black Angel '46
Can't Help Singing '45
Here Come the Co-Eds '45
The Climax '44
Honeymoon Lodge '43

Russ Vincent
Twilight in the Sierras '50
Heading for Heaven '47

Virginia Vincent (1924-)
The Hills Have Eyes '77
The Baby '72
Sweet November '68
Love with the Proper Stranger '63
Never Steal Anything Small '59
I Want to Live! '58
Return of Dracula '58

Yves Vincent (1921-)
Her and She and Him '69
Sins of Rome '54

Lee Ving (1950-)
Grave Secrets '89
Dudes '87
Scenes from the Goldmine '87
Clue '85
Streets of Fire '84
The Wild Life '84
Flashdance '83
Get Crazy '83

Steve Vinovich (1945-)
The Swan Princess '94 (V)
Hollywood Boulevard 2 '89

Helen Vinson (1907-99)
The Thin Man Goes Home '44
Torrid Zone '40
Vogues of 1938 '37
King of the Damned '36
Reunion '36
Transatlantic Tunnel '35
Broadway Bill '34
The Little Giant '33
I Am a Fugitive from a Chain Gang '32
They Call It Sin '32

Alan Vint (1944-)
Ballad of Gregorio Cortez '83
Sniper '75
Badlands '74
Macon County Line '74
Unholy Rollers '72
Panic in Needle Park '71
The McMasters '70

Bill Vint (1942-)
Marilyn: The Untold Story '80
Summertree '71

Jesse Vint (1940-)
I Come in Peace '90
Merchants of War '90
Dempsey '83
On the Line '83
Forbidden World '82
Death Sport '78
Black Oak Conspiracy '77
Bobbie Jo and the Outlaw '76
Bug '75
Macon County Line '74
Pigs '73

Gustav Vintas
Zero Tolerance '93
Drug Wars 2: The Cocaine Cartel '92
And You Thought Your Parents Were Weird! '91
Midnight '89
Tales from the Crypt '89
Vampire at Midnight '88
Lethal Weapon '87
Welcome Back Mr. Fox '83

Arthur Vinton (1889-1963)
Circumstantial Evidence '35
Gambling Ship '33

Bobby Vinton (1935-)
Train Robbers '73
Big Jake '71
Surf Party '64

Ultra Violet (1935-)
Superstar: The Life and Times of Andy Warhol '90
Simon, King of the Witches '71

Ian Virgo (1981-)
Extreme Dating '04
Band of Brothers '01
Black Hawk Down '01

Denise Virieux
Diamond Girl '98
Northern Extremes '93

Michael Visaroff (1892-1951)
Charlie Chan at the Wax Museum '40
Arizona Terror '31
Last Command '28

Sal Viscuso (1948-)
Spaceballs '87
The Taking of Pelham One Two Three '74
M*A*S*H '70 (V)

Nana Visitor
Friday the 13th '09
Swing Vote '08

Goran Visnjic (1972-)
The Courageous Heart of Irena Sendler '09
Elektra '05
Close Your Eyes '02
Ice Age '02 (V)
The Deep End '01
Committed '99
Practical Magic '98
Rounders '98
Welcome to Sarajevo '97

Angela Visser (1966-)
Hot Under the Collar '91
Killer Tomatoes Eat France '91

Alex Vitale
Beyond the Door 3 '91
Urban Warriors '87

Antonella Vitale
The Church '98
Opera '88

Joseph (Joe) Vitale (1901-94)
Alias Jesse James '59
A Bullet for Joey '55
The Stranger Wore a Gun '53
Zombies on Broadway '44

Milly Vitale (1932-2006)
Revak the Rebel '60
Missiles from Hell '58
War and Peace '56
The Seven Little Foys '55

Elisabeth Vitali
Paris 36 '08
Western '96

Keith Vitali
American Kickboxer 1 '91
No Retreat, No Surrender 3: Blood Brothers '91
Revenge of the Ninja '83

Vitamin C
See Colleen (Ann) Fitzpatrick

Joe (Johnny) Viterelli (1941-2004)
Analyze That '02
Serving Sara '02
See Spot Run '01
Shallow Hal '01
Wannabes '01
Mickey Blue Eyes '99
Analyze This '98
Facade '98
Mafia! '98
Out to Sea '97
American Strays '96
Eraser '96
Heaven's Prisoners '95
Machine Gun Blues '95
Bullets over Broadway '94
The Crossing Guard '94
The Firm '93
Ruby '92
Mobsters '91
State of Grace '90

Antoine Vitez (1930-90)
The Green Room '78
My Night at Maud's '69

Michel Vitold (1915-94)
Basileus Quartet '82
The Testament of Dr. Cordelier '59

Ray Vitte (1949-83)
Grambling's White Tiger '81
Sky Hei$t '75

Monica Vitti (1931-)
Immortal Bachelor '80
Tigers in Lipstick '80
An Almost Perfect Affair '79
Blonde in Black Leather '77
Phantom of Liberty '74
The Eclipse '66
Modesty Blaise '66
The Red Desert '64
La Notte '60
L'Avventura '60

Kelly Vitz (1988-)
Nancy Drew '07
Sky High '05

Viva (1942-)
Superstar: The Life and Times of Andy Warhol '90
State of Things '82
Forbidden Zone '80
Edie in Ciao! Manhattan '72
Play It Again, Sam '72

Sal Viviano (1960-)
Black Roses '88
The Jitters '88

Floyd Vivino (1951-)
Crazy People '90
Good Morning, Vietnam '87

Marina Vlady (1938-)
Son of Gascogne '95
Chimes at Midnight '67
Two or Three Things I Know about Her '66
The Unfaithfuls '60
Double Agents '59

Sam Vlahos
Christmas in the Clouds '01
The Big Squeeze '96

Powwow Highway '89

Sandra Voe (1936-)

Janice Beard '99
The Winter Guest '97
Breaking the Waves '95
Body & Soul '93

Emmett Vogan (1893-1969)

Down Dakota Way '49
The Lady Confesses '45
Robot Pilot '41
San Quentin '37

Frederick Vogeding

Mr. Moto Takes a Chance '38
Mysterious Mr. Moto '38

Darlene Vogel (1962-)

Decoy '95
Ring of Steel '94
Back to the Future, Part 2 '89

Jack Vogel

Presumed Guilty '91
Lock 'n' Load '90

Mike Vogel (1979-)

Blue Valentine '10
Cloverfield '08
The Deaths of Ian Stone '07
Caffeine '06
Poseidon '06
Sisterhood of the Traveling Pants '05
Supercross: The Movie '05
Grind '03
MTV's Wuthering Heights '03
The Texas Chainsaw Massacre '03

Mitch Vogel (1956-)

Texas Detour '77
Born Innocent '74

Karl Michael Vogler (1928-)

Deep End '70
The Blue Max '66

Ruediger Vogler (1942-)

A Woman in Berlin '08
Lisbon Story '94
Faraway, So Close! '93
Until the End of the World '91
Night Sun '90
Marianne and Juliane '82
The Wrong Move '78
Kings of the Road—In the Course of Time '76
Alice in the Cities '74

Giannis Voglis (1937-)

Hero Bunker '71
The Brave Bunch '70

Joan Vohs (1931-2001)

Cry Vengeance '54
As You Were '51

Jon Voight (1938-)

An American Carol '08
Four Christmases '08
Pride and Glory '08
Tropic Thunder '08
24 : Redemption '08
Bratz '07
National Treasure: Book of Secrets '07
September Dawn '07
Transformers '07
Glory Road '06
Karate Dog '04
The Manchurian Candidate '04
National Treasure '04
Superbabies: Baby Geniuses 2 '04
Holes '03
Jasper, Texas '03
Ali '01
Jack and the Beanstalk: The Real Story '01
Lara Croft: Tomb Raider '01
Pearl Harbor '01
Uprising '01
Zoolander '01
A Dog of Flanders '99
Noah's Ark '99
Enemy of the State '98
The General '98
Varsity Blues '98
Boys Will Be Boys '97
The Fixer '97
John Grisham's The Rainmaker '97
Most Wanted '97
U-Turn '97
Anaconda '96
Mission: Impossible '96
Rosewood '96
Convict Cowboy '95
Heat '95
The Tin Soldier '95
Rainbow Warrior '94
Return to Lonesome Dove '93
The Last of His Tribe '92
Eternity '90
Final Warning '90
Desert Bloom '86
Runaway Train '85
Table for Five '83
Lookin' to Get Out '82
The Champ '79
Coming Home '78
Conrack '74
The Odessa File '74
Deliverance '72
Catch-22 '70
Midnight Cowboy '69
Hour of the Gun '67

Vicki Volante

Angels' Wild Women '72
Brain of Blood '71
Hell's Bloody Devils '70
Horror of the Blood Monsters '70
Blood of Dracula's Castle '69

Katie Volding

Au Pair 3: Adventure in Paradise '09
Au Pair 2: The Fairy Tale Continues '01
Au Pair '99

Gian Marie Volonte (1933-94)

Open Doors '89
Christ Stopped at Eboli '79
Lucky Luciano '74
Sacco & Vanzetti '71
Le Cercle Rouge '70
A Bullet for the General '68
The Witch '66
For a Few Dollars More '65
A Fistful of Dollars '64
Journey Beneath the Desert '61
The Girl with a Suitcase '60

Philippe Volter (1959-2005)

Resistance '03
The Five Senses '99
Trois Couleurs: Bleu '93
The Double Life of Veronique '91
Cyrano de Bergerac '90
The Music Teacher '88

Daniel von Bargen (1950-)

Coastlines '02
Simone '02
The Majestic '01
Super Troopers '01
Disney's The Kid '00
O Brother Where Art Thou? '00
Shaft '00
The General's Daughter '99
Universal Soldier: The Return '99
Inferno '98
The Postman '97
Stephen King's Thinner '96
Before and After '95
Lord of Illusions '95
Truman '95
Philadelphia '93
Rising Sun '93
The Silence of the Lambs '91

Wilhelm von Brinken (1881-1946)

Hidden Enemy '40
International Crime '37
King Kelly of the U.S.A. '34
Inside the Lines '30

Tomas von Bromssen (1943-)

All Things Fair '95
My Life As a Dog '85
Man from Mallorca '84

Erik von Detten (1982-)

The Princess Diaries '01
Brink '98
Leave It to Beaver '97
Top Dog '95
Toy Story '95 (V)

Lenny Von Dohlen (1958-)

Teeth '07
Home Alone 3 '97
Entertaining Angels: The Dorothy Day Story '96
Bird of Prey '95
One Good Turn '95
Tollbooth '94
Eyes of the Beholder '92
Leaving Normal '92
Blind Vision '91
Love Kills '91
Dracula's Widow '88
Billy Galvin '86
Under the Biltmore Clock '85
Electric Dreams '84
Tender Mercies '83

Theodore von Eltz (1894-1964)

California Straight Ahead! '37
Confidential '35
Trails of the Wild '35
High Gear '33
Drifting Souls '32
The Midnight Lady '32
Strangers of the Evening '32
No Man's Law '27

Clement von Franckenstein

Command Performance '09
Body Parts '94

Loni von Friedl (1943-)

Journey to the Far Side of the Sun '69
The Blue Max '66

Wilhelm von Homburg (1940-2004)

In the Mouth of Madness '95
Silence of the Hams '93
Diggstown '92
Eye of the Storm '91
Night of the Warrior '91
Midnight Cabaret '90
Ghostbusters 2 '89
The Package '89
Die Hard '88
Stroszek '77
The Devil's Brigade '68
The Wrecking Crew '68

Joel von Ornsteiner

Slashdance '89
Robot Holocaust '87

Heidi von Palleske

Cybercity '99
Shepherd '99
Falling Fire '97
Strip Search '97
2103: Deadly Wake '97
White Light '90
Blind Fear '89
Dead Ringers '88

Stefanie von Pfetten

Christmas Caper '07
Termination Point '07
Meltdown '06
One Way '06
Decoys '04
The Twelve Days of Christmas Eve '04
The Invitation '03
Posers '02

Gustav von Seyffertitz (1863-1943)

She '35
Mystery Liner '34
Rasputin and the Empress '33
Ambassador Bill '31
Dishonored '31
The Mysterious Lady '28
The Gaucho '27
The Bells '26
Don Juan '26
Sparrows '26
Sherlock Holmes '22
Down to Earth '17

Erich von Stroheim (1885-1957)

Napoleon '55
Unnatural '52
Sunset Boulevard '50
Portrait of an Assassin '49
The Mask of Diijon '46
Great Flamarion '45
Five Graves to Cairo '43
The North Star '43
So Ends Our Night '41
Grand Illusion '37
The Crime of Dr. Crespi '35
Crimson Romance '34
Fugitive Road '34
As You Desire Me '32
Lost Squadron '32
The Great Gabbo '29
The Wedding March '28
Foolish Wives '22
Blind Husbands '19
Heart of Humanity '18
Hearts of the World '18
Intolerance '16
The Birth of a Nation '15

Max von Sydow (1929-)

Shutter Island '09
Autumn Hearts: A New Beginning '07
The Diving Bell and the Butterfly '07
Rush Hour 3 '07
Minority Report '02
Druids '01
Intacto '01
Sleepless '01
Nuremberg '00
Snow Falling on Cedars '99
Private Confessions '98
Solomon '98
What Dreams May Come '98
Hostile Waters '97
Hamsun '96
Jerusalem '96
Citizen X '95
Judge Dredd '95
The Silent Touch '94
The Bachelor '93
Needful Things '93
The Best Intentions '92
Zentropa '92 (N)
A Kiss Before Dying '91
The Ox '91
Until the End of the World '91
Awakenings '90
Father '90
Hiroshima: Out of the Ashes '90
Red King, White Knight '89
Pelle the Conqueror '88
Second Victory '87
The Wolf at the Door '87
Duet for One '86
Hannah and Her Sisters '86
Christopher Columbus '85
Code Name: Emerald '85
Kojak: The Belarus File '85
The Last Place on Earth '85
Quo Vadis '85
Dreamscape '84
Dune '84
Samson and Delilah '84
Target Eagle '84
Never Say Never Again '83
Strange Brew '83
Conan the Barbarian '82
Flight of the Eagle '82
Victory '81
Death Watch '80
Flash Gordon '80
Hurricane '79
Brass Target '78
The Exorcist 2: The Heretic '77
March or Die '77
The Desert of the Tartars '76
Foxtrot '76
Voyage of the Damned '76
Three Days of the Condor '75
The Ultimate Warrior '75
Steppenwolf '74
The Exorcist '73
The New Land '73
Embassy '72
The Emigrants '72
The Touch '71
The Night Visitor '70
The Passion of Anna '70
Hour of the Wolf '68
The Shame '68
Hawaii '66
The Quiller Memorandum '66
The Greatest Story Ever Told '65
The Winter Light '62
Through a Glass Darkly '61
The Virgin Spring '59
The Magician '58
Brink of Life '57
Wild Strawberries '57
The Seventh Seal '56
Miss Julie '50

Margarethe von Trotta (1942-)

Coup de Grace '78
Beware of a Holy Whore '70
An Occurrence at Owl Creek Bridge/Coup de Grace '62

Hans von Twardowski (1898-1958)

Dawn Express '42
Hangmen Also Die '42
The Cabinet of Dr. Caligari '19

Gustav von Wagenheim (1895-1975)

Woman in the Moon '29
Nosferatu '22

Gila von Weitershausen (1944-)

Schnelles Geld '84
Black and White As Day and Night '78

Florence Marly von Wurmbrand

See Florence Marly

Harry von Zell (1906-81)

Son of Paleface '52
The Strange Affair of Uncle Harry '45

Danielle von Zerneck (1966-)

Acceptable Risk '01
Living in Oblivion '94
Under the Boardwalk '89
Dangerous Curves '88
La Bamba '87
My Science Project '85

Peter Von Zerneck (1908-92)

A Foreign Affair '48
13 Rue Madeleine '46

Kurt Vonnegut, Jr. (1922-2007)

Never Down '06
Breakfast of Champions '98
Back to School '86

Lark Voorhies (1974-)

Civil Brand '02
Widows '02
How High '01
Def Jam's How to Be a Player '97

Zandor Vorkov

Brain of Blood '71
Dracula vs. Frankenstein '71

Anthony (Tony) Vorno

Sweet Trash '70
Help Wanted Female '68
Hollywood after Dark '65

George Voskovec (1905-81)

The Iceman Cometh '73
The Boston Strangler '68
The Bravados '58
Twelve Angry Men '57
The 27th Day '57

Arnold Vosloo (1962-)

G.I. Joe: The Rise of Cobra '09
Living & Dying '07
Blood Diamond '06
American Meltdown '04
Agent Cody Banks '03
Endangered Species '02
Anti-Terrorist Cell: Manhunt '01
The Mummy Returns '01
The Mummy '99
Progeny '98
Diary of a Serial Killer '97
Zeus and Roxanne '96
Darkman 3: Die Darkman Die '95
Darkman 2: The Return of Durant '94
Hard Target '93
The Finishing Touch '92
Red Shoe Diaries 2: Double Dare '92
Living to Die '91
Reason to Die '90
The Rutanga Tapes '90
Act of Piracy '89
Steel Dawn '87

Frank Vosper (1899-1937)

Secret of Stamboul '36
Spy of Napoleon '36
The Man Who Knew Too Much '34
Power '34
Red Ensign '34

Jan Vostrcil (1903-85)

Intimate Lighting '65
Black Peter '63

Yorgo Voyagis (1945-)

Swept Away '02
Courage Mountain '89
The Bourne Identity '88
Frantic '88
The Little Drummer Girl '84
The Adventurers '70

Vlasta Vrana

Human Trafficking '05
Secret Window '04
Protection '01
Varian's War '01
Escape from Wildcat Canyon '99
Fallen Angel '99
Grey Owl '99
The Assignment '97
Night of the Demons 3 '97
The Reaper '97
Stranger in the House '97
Hawk's Vengeance '96
Deadly Surveillance '91
Scanners 2: The New Order '91
Keeping Track '86

Ron Vreeken

Deathfight '93
Rage and Honor 2: Hostile Takeover '93

Frederick Vroom (1857-1942)

Eyes Right! '26
The General '26
The Navigator '24

Spencer Vrooman (1981-)

Man of the House '95
Pet Shop '94

Robert Walden (1943-)
Perry Mason: The Case of the Lost Love *'87*
Memorial Day *'83*
Enola Gay: The Men, the Mission, the Atomic Bomb *'80*
Blue Sunshine *'78*
Larry *'74*
Our Time *'74*
Everything You Always Wanted to Know about Sex (But Were Afraid to Ask) *'72*
Bloody Mama *'70*
Murderer's Keep *'70*

Katie Walder
Safe Harbour *'07*
Shelter *'07*

Shawna Waldron (1982-)
Poison Ivy 4: The Secret Society *'08*
Change of Heart *'98*
Mr. Headmistress *'98*
The American President *'95*
Little Giants *'94*

Ethel Wales (1898-1952)
Border Vigilantes *'41*
The Gladiator *'38*
Under Montana Skies *'30*
Made for Love *'26*

Wally Wales (1895-1980)
Fighting Seabees *'44*
Bad Man of Deadwood *'41*
In Old Cheyenne *'41*
Sheriff of Tombstone *'41*
Adventures of Red Ryder *'40*
Carson City Kid *'40*
The Trigger Trio *'37*
Gun Play *'36*
Danger Trails *'35*
Fighting Caballero *'35*
The Miracle Rider *'35*
Pecos Kid *'35*
Powdersmoke Range *'35*
Rustlers of Red Dog *'35*
Silent Valley *'35*
Swifty *'35*
Way of the West *'35*
The Fighting Rookie *'34*
Deadwood Pass *'33*
Law and Lawless *'33*
Lone Bandit *'33*
Sagebrush Trail *'33*
Desert of the Lost *'27*

Sonya Walger (1974-)
Sweet Nothing in My Ear *'08*
Caffeine *'06*
The Librarian: Quest for the Spear *'04*
The Search for John Gissing *'01*
All the King's Men *'99*
Heat of the Sun *'99*
Noah's Ark *'99*

Christopher Walken (1943-)
$5 a Day *'08*
The Maiden Heist *'08*
Balls of Fury *'07*
Hairspray *'07*
Click *'06*
Man of the Year *'06*
Domino *'05*
Romance & Cigarettes *'05*
Wedding Crashers *'05*
Around the Bend *'04*
Envy *'04*
Man on Fire *'04*
The Stepford Wives *'04*
Gigli *'03*
The Rundown *'03*
Catch Me If You Can *'02*
The Country Bears *'02*
Kangaroo Jack *'02*
Poolhall Junkies *'02*
Scotland, PA *'02*
The Affair of the Necklace *'01*
America's Sweethearts *'01*
Joe Dirt *'01*
Kiss Toledo Goodbye *'00*
The Eternal *'99*
The External *'99*
The Prophecy 3: The Ascent *'99*
Sarah, Plain and Tall: Winter's End *'99*
Sleepy Hollow *'99*
Vendetta *'99*
Antz *'98 (V)*
Blast from the Past *'98*
Illuminata *'98*
New Rose Hotel *'98*
Mouse Hunt *'97*
The Prophecy 2: Ashtown *'97*
Suicide Kings *'97*
Basquiat *'96*
Excess Baggage *'96*
The Funeral *'96*
Last Man Standing *'96*
Touch *'96*
The Addiction *'95*
Nick of Time *'95*
The Prophecy *'95*
Things to Do in Denver When You're Dead *'95*
Wild Side *'95*
Pulp Fiction *'94*
Search and Destroy *'94*
A Business Affair *'93*
Day of Atonement *'93*
Sarah, Plain and Tall: Skylark *'93*
Scam *'93*
True Romance *'93*
Wayne's World 2 *'93*
Batman Returns *'92*
All-American Murder *'91*
The Comfort of Strangers *'91*
McBain *'91*
Mistress *'91*
Sarah, Plain and Tall *'91*
King of New York *'90*
Communion *'89*
Biloxi Blues *'88*
Homeboy *'88*
The Milagro Beanfield War *'88*
Deadline *'87*
At Close Range *'86*
A View to a Kill *'85*
Brainstorm *'83*
Dead Zone *'83*
Who Am I This Time? *'82*
The Dogs of War *'81*
Heaven's Gate *'81*
Pennies from Heaven *'81*
Shoot the Sun Down *'81*
Last Embrace *'79*
The Deer Hunter *'78*
Annie Hall *'77*
Roseland *'77*
Next Stop, Greenwich Village *'76*
The Sentinel *'76*
Mind Snatchers *'72*
The Anderson Tapes *'71*

Ally Walker (1961-)
Wonderful World *'09*
Happy, Texas *'99*
Kazaam *'96*
Bed of Roses *'95*
Someone to Die For *'95*
While You Were Sleeping *'95*
When the Bough Breaks *'93*
The Seventh Coin *'92*
Singles *'92*
Universal Soldier *'92*

Amanda Walker
Charles & Diana: A Palace Divided *'93*
Heat and Dust *'82*

Arnetia Walker (1961-)
Love Crimes *'92*
Scenes from the Class Struggle in Beverly Hills *'89*
The Wizard of Speed and Time *'88*

Bill Walker (1896-1992)
The Mask *'61*
No Time for Romance *'48*

Catherine Walker
Northanger Abbey *'07*
Conspiracy of Silence *'03*

Charlotte Walker
Annapolis *'28*
Midnight Girl *'25*

Cheryl Walker (1918-71)
Three on a Ticket *'47*
Larceny in her Heart *'46*
Murder Is My Business *'46*
Identity Unknown *'45*
Stage Door Canteen *'43*
Shadows on the Sage *'42*

Clint Walker (1927-)
Small Soldiers *'98 (V)*
The Gambler Returns: The Luck of the Draw *'93*
Mysterious Island of Beautiful Women *'79*
Snowbeast *'77*
The White Buffalo *'77*
Baker's Hawk *'76*
Scream of the Wolf *'74*
The Bounty Man *'72*
Deadly Harvest *'72*
Pancho Villa *'72*
Yuma *'70*
Sam Whiskey *'69*
More Dead Than Alive *'68*
The Dirty Dozen *'67*
Maya *'66*
Night of the Grizzly *'66*
None But the Brave *'65*
Gold of the Seven Saints *'61*

Eamonn Walker (1959-)
The Messenger *'09*
Cadillac Records *'08*
Duma *'05*
Lord of War *'05*
Tears of the Sun *'03*
Whitewash: The Clarence Brandley Story *'02*
Othello *'01*
Once in the Life *'00*
Unbreakable *'00*

Eric Walker (1970-)
Kicking & Screaming *'05*
And You Thought Your Parents Were Weird! *'91*
The Ewoks: Battle for Endor *'85*
The Ewok Adventure *'84*

Fiona Walker (1944-)
The Norman Conquests, Part 1: Table Manners *'78*
The Norman Conquests, Part 2: Living Together *'78*
The Norman Conquests, Part 3: Round and Round the Garden *'78*
The Asphyx *'72*
Jude the Obscure *'71*

Helen Walker (1920-68)
Big Combo *'55*
Impact *'49*
Call Northside 777 *'48*
Nightmare Alley *'47*
People Are Funny *'46*
Brewster's Millions *'45*
Murder, He Says *'45*
Abroad with Two Yanks *'44*

Jimmie Walker (1947-)
Frankenstein Sings... The Movie *'95*
Open Season *'95*
Invasion of the Space Preachers *'90*
Going Bananas *'88*
My African Adventure *'87*
Doin' Time *'85*
Water *'85*
Airplane! *'80*
B.A.D. Cats *'80*
The Concorde: Airport '79 *'79*
Let's Do It Again *'75*

Johnnie Walker (1894-1949)
Bare Knees *'28*
Broken Hearts of Broadway *'23*

Jonathan Walker (1967-)
Finding North *'97 (V)*
American Blue Note *'89*

Justin Walker
Boltneck *'98*
Born Bad *'97*

Kathryn Walker (1943-)
Dangerous Game *'90*
The Murder of Mary Phagan *'87*
Uncle Tom's Cabin *'87*
Private Contentment *'83*
Special Bulletin *'83*
Neighbors *'81*
Whale for the Killing *'81*
Rich Kids *'79*
Girlfriends *'78*
The Winds of Kitty Hawk *'78*
Slap Shot *'77*
Blade *'72*
A House Without a Christmas Tree *'72*

Kerry Walker (1948-)
A Little Bit of Soul *'97*
Road to Nhill *'97*
Cosi *'95*
The Piano *'93*

Kim Walker (1968-2001)
Heathers *'89*
Deadly Weapon *'88*

Liza Walker (1972-)
Wavelength *'96*
Buddy's Song *'91*
Twisted Obsession *'90*

Maggie Walker
Three Days of Rain *'02*
The House that Vanished *'73*

Marcy Walker (1961-)
Talking about Sex *'94*
Midnight's Child *'93*

Mark Walker
Random Encounter *'98*
Disconnected *'87*

Matthew (Matt) Walker (1942-)
Alone in the Dark *'05*
Ginger Snaps Back: The Beginning *'04*
The Princess Diaries 2: Royal Engagement *'04*
Blackwoods *'02*
Dead in a Heartbeat *'02*
Misbegotten *'98*
Intimate Relations *'95*
Child's Play 3 *'91*

Michael Walker (1941-)
Eating Out 3: All You Can Eat *'09*
Hell's Belles *'69*
Daring Game *'68*

Nancy Walker (1921-92)
Murder by Death *'76*
Death Scream *'75*
Thursday's Game *'74*
Forty Carats *'73*
Lucky Me *'54*
Broadway Rhythm *'44*
Best Foot Forward *'43*
Girl Crazy *'43*

Nicholas Walker
Body Count *'97*
Amnesia *'96*

Nicola Walker
Shooting Dogs *'05*
Thunderbirds *'04*
Shiner *'00*
Touching Evil *'97*

Paul Walker (1973-)
Takers *'10*
Fast & Furious *'09*
The Lazarus Project *'08*
Bobby Z *'07*
Eight Below *'06*
Flags of Our Fathers *'06*
Running Scared *'06*
Into the Blue *'05*
Noel *'04*
Timeline *'03*
2 Fast 2 Furious *'03*
The Fast and the Furious *'01*
Joy Ride *'01*
The Skulls *'00*
She's All That *'99*
Meet the Deedles *'98*
Pleasantville *'98*
Varsity Blues *'98*
Tammy and the T-Rex *'94*

Polly Walker (1966-)
Caprica *'09*
Scenes of a Sexual Nature *'06*
The Mayor of Casterbridge *'03*
State of Play *'03*
Savage Messiah *'02*
Eye See You *'01*
8 1/2 Women *'99*
Eye of the Killer *'99*
Dark Harbor *'98*
Brute *'97*
Curtain Call *'97*
The Gambler *'97*
Emma *'96*
For Roseanna *'96*
Robinson Crusoe *'96*
Talk of Angels *'96*
Restoration *'94*
Sliver *'93*
The Trial *'93*
Enchanted April *'92*
Patriot Games *'92*
A Dangerous Man: Lawrence after Arabia *'91*
Lorna Doone *'90*

Ray Walker (1904-80)
The Blue Gardenia *'53*
Rogue's Gallery *'44*
House of Errors *'42*
Bulldog Edition *'36*
The Dark Hour *'36*
Goodbye Love *'34*

Robert Walker (1888-1954)
El Diablo Rides *'39*
Fast Bullets *'36*
Fighting Caballero *'35*
Rough Riding Ranger *'35*

Robert Walker (1918-51)
Strangers on a Train *'51*
Vengeance Valley *'51*
One Touch of Venus *'48*
Song of Love *'47*
Till the Clouds Roll By *'46*
The Clock *'45*
Since You Went Away *'44*
Thirty Seconds Over Tokyo *'44*
Bataan *'43*
Madame Curie *'43*
The Crimson Trail *'35*

Robert Walker, Jr. (1940-)
Evil Town *'87*
Hambone & Hillie *'84*
Devonsville Terror *'83*
Olivia *'83*
AngKor: Cambodia Express *'81*
The Shrieking *'73*
The Spectre of Edgar Allen Poe *'73*
Beware! The Blob *'72*
Easy Rider *'69*
Road to Salina *'68*
The Savage Seven *'68*
The War Wagon *'67*
Ensign Pulver *'64*

Sarah Walker
Housekeeping *'87*
Man of Flowers *'84*

Terry Walker
Battling Outlaw *'40*
Take Me Back to Oklahoma *'40*
Delinquent Parents *'38*
Renfrew on the Great White Trail *'38*
23 1/2 Hours Leave *'37*

Tippy Walker (1947-)
The Challenge *'05*
The Jesus Trip *'71*
The World of Henry Orient *'64*

Walter Walker (1901-75)
Sons of Steel *'35*
American Madness *'32*
No Man of Her Own *'32*

Katie Wall
Introducing the Dwights *'07*
Marking Time *'03*

Max Wall (1894-1990)
Strike It Rich *'90*
Little Dorrit, Film 1: Nobody's Fault *'88*
Little Dorrit, Film 2: Little Dorrit's Story *'88*
We Think the World of You *'88*
Jabberwocky *'77*
A Killer in Every Corner *'74*

Basil Wallace
Blood Diamond *'06*
Joy Ride *'01*
Caught Up *'98*
Return of the Living Dead 3 *'93*
Deadlock *'91*
Marked for Death *'90*

Beryl Wallace (1910-48)
The Kansan *'43*
Sunset on the Desert *'42*
Rough Ridin' Rhythm *'37*

Bill Wallace (1949-)
Manchurian Avenger *'84*
Force of One *'79*

David Wallace (1957-)
Money to Burn *'83*
Humongous *'82*
Mazes and Monsters *'82*
The Babysitter *'80*

Dee Wallace
The House of the Devil *'09*
Bone Dry *'07*

Dee Wallace (1948-)
Extraordinary Measures *'10*
Halloween *'07*
Boo! *'05*
Voodoo Moon *'05*
Headspace *'02*
Out of the Black *'01*
Killer Instinct *'00*
Invisible Mom 2 *'99*
Black Circle Boys *'97*
Mutual Needs *'97*
Nevada *'97*
The Corporation *'96*
The Frighteners *'96*
Invisible Mom *'96*
Skeletons *'96*
Subliminal Seduction *'96*
Best of the Best 3: No Turning Back *'95*
The Phoenix and the Magic Carpet *'95*
The Road Home *'95*
Temptress *'95*
Runaway Daughters *'94*
The Skateboard Kid 2 *'94*
Discretion Assured *'93*
Huck and the King of Hearts *'93*
My Family Treasure *'93*
Rescue Me *'93*
Alligator 2: The Mutation *'90*
I'm Dangerous Tonight *'90*
Popcorn *'89*
Miracle Down Under *'87*
Club Life *'86*
Critters *'86*
Shadow Play *'86*
Secret Admirer *'85*
Cujo *'83*
Wait Till Your Mother Gets Home *'83*

E.T.: The Extra-Terrestrial '82
Jimmy the Kid '82
Skeezer '82
The Five of Me '81
The Howling '81
Whale for the Killing '81
10 '79
The Hills Have Eyes '77
The Stepford Wives '75

George Wallace (1952-)
The Ladykillers '04
The Wash '01
Three Strikes '00
Batman Forever '95

George D. Wallace (1917-2005)
Bicentennial Man '99
Forces of Nature '99
Diggstown '92
Defending Your Life '91
A Rage in Harlem '91
The Swinging Cheerleaders '74
Forbidden Planet '56
Radar Men from the Moon '52
Border River '47

Jack Wallace (1933-)
Edmond '05
Breakaway '02
Lakeboat '00
The Fixer '97
The Bear '89
Things Change '88
Assignment Outer Space '61 (N)

Jean Wallace (1923-90)
Sword of Lancelot '63
Big Combo '55
Native Son '51
Jigsaw '49

Marcia Wallace (1942-)
Big Stan '07
The Simpsons Movie '07 (V)
My Mom's a Werewolf '89
Pray TV '80

Morgan Wallace (1881-1953)
Honky Tonk '41
In Old Colorado '41
Star Reporter '39
Delinquent Parents '38
Gang Bullets '38
The House of Secrets '37
Confidential '35
Thunder Mountain '35
Up the River '30

William Wallace (1971-)
The Vector File '03
Cover Story '93

Dee Wallace Stone
See Dee Wallace

Eli Wallach (1915-)
The Ghost Writer '10
New York, I Love You '09
Mama's Boy '07
The Holiday '06
King of the Corner '04
Monday Night Mayhem '02
Keeping the Faith '00
Naked City: Justice with a Bullet '98
The Associate '96
Two Much '96
Article 99 '92
Legacy of Lies '92
Night and the City '92
Teamster Boss: The Jackie Presser Story '92
A Family Matter '91
Mistress '91
The Godfather, Part 3 '90
The Two Jakes '90
The Impossible Spy '87
Nuts '87
Rocket to the Moon '86
Something in Common '86
Tough Guys '86
Christopher Columbus '85
Embassy '85
My Sweet Victim '85
Sam's Son '84
The Executioner's Song '82
The Salamander '82
Pride of Jesse Hallum '81
The Hunter '80
Winter Kills '79
Circle of Iron '78
Girlfriends '78
Movie, Movie '78
The Deep '77
The Domino Principle '77
Nasty Habits '77
The Sentinel '76
Stateline Motel '75
Cinderella Liberty '73
Romance of a Horsethief '71
The Angel Levine '70
The People Next Door '70
The Brain '69
MacKenna's Gold '69
Ace High '68
The Good, the Bad and the Ugly '67
How to Steal a Million '66
The Poppy Is Also a Flower '66
Lord Jim '65
Kisses for My President '64
The Moon-Spinners '64
How the West Was Won '63
The Victors '63
The Misfits '61
The Magnificent Seven '60
Seven Thieves '60
The Lineup '58
Baby Doll '56

Roberta Wallach (1955-)
The Hollywood Knights '80
The Effect of Gamma Rays on Man-in-the-Moon Marigolds '73

Sigurd Wallen (1884-1947)
Swedenhielms '35
The Count of the Old Town '34

Eddy (Eddie, Ed) Waller (1889-1977)
El Paso Stampede '53
Marshal of Cedar Rock '53
Bandit King of Texas '49
Wild Frontier '47
Rough Riders of Cheyenne '45
Legion of the Lawless '40
Call the Mesquiteers '38

Deborah Walley (1943-2001)
Benji '74
The Severed Arm '73
Dr. Goldfoot and the Bikini Machine '66
Ghost in the Invisible Bikini '66
Spinout '66
Beach Blanket Bingo '65
Ski Party '65
Summer Magic '63
Bon Voyage! '62
Gidget Goes Hawaiian '61

David Walliams
Stardust '07
Stoned '05
Tristram Shandy: A Cock and Bull Story '05

William Walling (1842-1932)
Range Feud '31
Two Fisted Justice '31
Great K & A Train Robbery '26

Shani Wallis (1941-)
The Pebble and the Penguin '94 (N)
Round Numbers '91
Arnold '73
Oliver! '68

Tom Walls (1883-1949)
Maytime in Mayfair '49
While I Live '47
Johnny Frenchman '46

Jon Walmsley (1956-)
A Day for Thanks on Walton's Mountain '82
The Waltons: The Christmas Carol '80

Amanda Walsh (1981-)
WarGames 2: The Dead Code '08
Full of It '07
These Girls '05

Angela Walsh
Catherine Cookson's The Man Who Cried '93
Distant Voices, Still Lives '88

Arthur Walsh (1923-95)
Mystic Pizza '88
Last Hurrah '58
You Gotta Stay Happy '48
Courage of Lassie '46
They Were Expendable '45

Dermot Walsh (1924-2002)
The Great Armored Car Swindle '64
The Flesh and the Fiends '60
The Tell-Tale Heart '60
It Takes a Thief '59
Bond of Fear '56
Ghost Ship '53
The Frightened Man '52
Murder on the Campus '52

Dylan Walsh (1963-)
The Stepfather '09
Just Add Water '07
The Lake House '06
Edmond '05
Blood Work '02
Power Play '02
We Were Soldiers '02
Final Voyage '99
Eden '98
Men '97
Changing Habits '96
Divided by Hate '96
Congo '95
Nobody's Fool '94
Radio Inside '94
Arctic Blue '93
Betsy's Wedding '90
Where the Heart Is '90

Eileen Walsh (1977-)
The Magdalene Sisters '02
Janice Beard '99

George Walsh (1889-1981)
Pinto Rustlers '36
The Live Wire '34
The Broadway Drifter '27
Test of Donald Norton '26
American Pluck '25

Gwynyth Walsh
Sea Beast '08
MXP: Most Xtreme Primate '03
2103: Deadly Wake '97
The Limbic Region '96
Soft Deceit '94
The Crush '93
The Challengers '89
Blue Monkey '87

Jack Walsh
A Simple Plan '98
Multiple Maniacs '70

J.T. Walsh (1943-98)
Hidden Agenda '99
The Negotiator '98
Pleasantville '98
Hope '97
Breakdown '96
Crime of the Century '96
Executive Decision '96
Gang in Blue '96
Persons Unknown '96
Sling Blade '96
The Babysitter '95
Black Day Blue Night '95
The Little Death '95
The Low Life '95
Nixon '95
Blue Chips '94
The Client '94
The Last Seduction '94
Miracle on 34th Street '94
Outbreak '94
Silent Fall '94
Some Folks Call It a Sling Blade '94
Morning Glory '93
National Lampoon's Loaded Weapon 1 '93
Needful Things '93
Red Rock West '93
A Few Good Men '92
Hoffa '92
Sniper '92
Backdraft '91
Defenseless '91
Iron Maze '91
Crazy People '90
The Grifters '90
Narrow Margin '90
The Russia House '90
Why Me? '90
The Big Picture '89
Dad '89
Wired '89
Tequila Sunrise '88
Things Change '88
Good Morning, Vietnam '87
House of Games '87
Tin Men '87
Power '86
Hard Choices '84

Kate Walsh (1967-)
Legion '10
Bewitched '05
Inside Out '05
Kicking & Screaming '05
After the Sunset '04
Under the Tuscan Sun '03
Family Man '00
Henry: Portrait of a Serial Killer 2: Mask of Sanity '96
Normal Life '96

Kay Walsh (1914-2005)
The Witches '66
Greyfriars Bobby '61
Tunes of Glory '60
The Horse's Mouth '58
Cast a Dark Shadow '55
Young Bess '53
Encore '52
Last Holiday '50
The Magnet '50
Stage Fright '50
The October Man '48
Oliver Twist '48
This Happy Breed '47
In Which We Serve '43
Secret of Stamboul '36

Ken Walsh
Conspiracy of Fear '96
Straight Line '88

M. Emmet Walsh (1935-)
Youth in Revolt '10
Sherman's Way '08
Sundown: The Vampire in Retreat '08
Big Stan '07
Racing Stripes '05
Christmas With the Kranks '04
Snow Dogs '02
Christmas in the Clouds '01
Poor White Trash '00
The Iron Giant '99 (V)
Me & Will '99
Wild Wild West '99
Twilight '98
Chairman of the Board '97
My Best Friend's Wedding '97
Retroactive '97
Albino Alligator '96
The Killing Jar '96
A Time to Kill '96
William Shakespeare's Romeo and Juliet '96
Criminal Hearts '95
The Glass Shield '95
Panther '95
Portraits of a Killer '95
Probable Cause '95
Relative Fear '95
Camp Nowhere '94
Dead Badge '94
Bitter Harvest '93
Equinox '93
Four Eyes and Six Guns '93
The Music of Chance '93
Wilder Napalm '93
Killer Image '92
White Sands '92
Wildcard '92
Boxcar Blues '90
Fourth Story '90
Narrow Margin '90
The Brotherhood of the Rose '89
Catch Me... If You Can '89
Chattahoochee '89
The Mighty Quinn '89
Red Scorpion '89
Thunderground '89
War Party '89
Clean and Sober '88
The Milagro Beanfield War '88
Sunset '88
The Abduction of Kari Swenson '87
Broken Vows '87
Harry and the Hendersons '87
Murder Ordained '87
Raising Arizona '87
Back to School '86
The Best of Times '86
Critters '86
The Deliberate Stranger '86
Wildcats '86
Blood Simple '85
Fletch '85
Grandview U.S.A. '84
Missing in Action '84
The Pope of Greenwich Village '84
Raw Courage '84
Scandalous '84
Night Partners '83
Blade Runner '82
Cannery Row '82
Fast Walking '82
Reds '81
Brubaker '80
East of Eden '80
Ordinary People '80
The Jerk '79
Dear Detective '78
Straight Time '78
Slap Shot '77
The Invasion of Johnson County '76
The Gambler '74
Escape from the Planet of the Apes '71
They Might Be Giants '71
Alice's Restaurant '69
Stiletto '69

Mary Walsh (1952-)
Mambo Italiano '03
New Waterford Girl '99

Matt Walsh
Cyrus '10
Semi-Pro '08

Percy Walsh (1888-1952)
The Golden Salamander '51
Thursday's Child '43
Secret Mission '42
King of the Damned '36

Raoul Walsh (1887-1980)
Sadie Thompson '28
The Birth of a Nation '15

Susan Walsh
Female Trouble '74
Pink Flamingos '72
Multiple Maniacs '70

Sydney Walsh (1961-)
MacArthur Park '01
Danger of Love '95
A Kiss Goodnight '94
Homewrecker '92
Point Break '91
Three Men and a Little Lady '90
To Die For '89
A Nightmare on Elm Street 2: Freddy's Revenge '85

Vincent Walsh
Bridal Fever '08
Shattered City: The Halifax Explosion '03

Leanna (Leeanna) Walsman (1979-)
$9.99 '08 (V)
Star Wars: Episode 2—Attack of the Clones '02

Ray Walston (1918-2001)
Get a Clue! '98
My Favorite Martian '98
Tricks '97
House Arrest '96
Stephen King's The Stand '94
Of Mice and Men '92
The Player '92
Blood Salvage '90
Popcorn '89
Ski Patrol '89
Fine Gold '88
A Man of Passion '88
Paramedics '88
Saturday the 14th Strikes Back '88
Blood Relations '87
O.C. and Stiggs '87
From the Hip '86
Amos '85
For Love or Money '84
Johnny Dangerously '84
Private School '83
Fast Times at Ridgemont High '82
The Kid with the Broken Halo '82
O'Hara's Wife '82
Galaxy of Terror '81
The Fall of the House of Usher '80
Popeye '80
The Happy Hooker Goes to Washington '77
Silver Streak '76
The Sting '73
Caprice '67
Kiss Me, Stupid! '64
Who's Minding the Store? '63
The Apartment '60
Portrait in Black '60
Tall Story '60
Damn Yankees '58
South Pacific '58

Harriet Walter (1950-)
Cheri '09
The Young Victoria '09
Atonement '07
Ballet Shoes '07
Onegin '99
Bedrooms and Hallways '98
The Governess '98
A Merry War '97
Sense and Sensibility '95
The Advocate '93
May Fools '90
The Good Father '87

Jessica Walter (1940-)
Unaccompanied Minors '06
Dummy '02
Slums of Beverly Hills '98
Temptress '95
P.C.U. '94
Ghost in the Machine '93
Tapeheads '89
The Execution '85
The Flamingo Kid '84
Going Ape! '81
Miracle on Ice '81
Spring Fever '81
Goldengirl '79
She's Dressed to Kill '79
Dr. Strange '78
Secrets of Three Hungry Wives '78
Wild & Wooly '78
Victory at Entebbe '76
Hurricane '74
Home for the Holidays '72
Play Misty for Me '71

They Call It Murder '71
Bye Bye Braverman '67
The Group '66
Lilith '64

Lisa Ann Walter (1963-)
Entry Level '07
War of the Worlds '05
Shall We Dance? '04
Bruce Almighty '03
The Parent Trap '98
Eddie '96

Tracey Walter (1942-)
How High '01
Drowning Mona '00
Erin Brockovich '00
Wild America '97
Drive '96
Larger Than Life '96
Matilda '96
Buffalo Girls '95
Destiny Turns on the Radio '95
Philadelphia '93
Liquid Dreams '92
City Slickers '91
Delusion '91
Mortuary Academy '91
The Silence of the Lambs '91
Pacific Heights '90
The Two Jakes '90
Young Guns 2 '90
Batman '89
Under the Boardwalk '89
Married to the Mob '88
Out of the Dark '88
At Close Range '86
Something Wild '86
Conan the Destroyer '84
Repo Man '83
Timerider '83
Raggedy Man '81
Mad Bull '77

Desmond Walter-Ellis (1914-94)
The Great St. Trinian's Train Robbery '66
The Hellfire Club '61

Ashley Walters (1982-)
The Killing Gene '07
Sugarhouse '07
Goal! The Dream Begins '06
Get Rich or Die Tryin' '05
House of 9 '05

Hal Walters (1891-1941)
The Four Feathers '39
Sabotage '36

Julie Walters (1950-)
Harry Potter and the Half-Blood Prince '09
Filth '08
Mamma Mia! '08
Becoming Jane '07
Harry Potter and the Order of the Phoenix '07
Driving Lessons '06
Ruby in the Smoke '06
Wah-Wah '05
Harry Potter and the Prisoner of Azkaban '04
Calendar Girls '03
Harry Potter and the Chamber of Secrets '02
Strange Relations '02
Harry Potter and the Sorcerer's Stone '01
Billy Elliot '00
Oliver Twist '00
Lover's Prayer '99
Girls' Night '97
Melissa '97
Intimate Relations '95
Just Like a Woman '95
Sister My Sister '94
The Summer House '94
The Wedding Gift '93
Stepping Out '91
Happy Since I Met You '89
Mack the Knife '89
Buster '88
Personal Services '87
Prick Up Your Ears '87
Car Trouble '86
She'll Be Wearing Pink Pajamas '84
Educating Rita '83

Laurie Walters (1950-)
The Taking of Flight 847: The Uli Derickson Story '88
Harrad Summer '74
Harrad Experiment '73
Warlock Moon '73

Luana Walters (1912-63)
Shoot to Kill '47
The Corpse Vanishes '42
Inside the Law '42
Lawless Plainsmen '42
Arizona Bound '41
Kid's Last Ride '41
Misbehaving Husbands '41
Blondie Plays Cupid '40
The Durango Kid '40
Range Busters '40
Aces and Eights '36
Shadow of Chinatown '36
Speed Reporter '36
Assassin of Youth '35
Fighting Texans '33

Melora Walters (1968-)
Hurt '09
Brothers Three '07
The Big Empty '04
The Butterfly Effect '04
Cold Mountain '03
Wisegirls '02
Desert Saints '01
Magnolia '99
Boogie Nights '97
Los Locos Posse '97
American Strays '96
Hard Eight '96
Twenty Bucks '93
America's Deadliest Home Video '91

Susan Walters (1963-)
Framed for Murder '07
Where the Truth Lies '99
I Married a Monster '98
Galaxies Are Colliding '92
Defending Your Life '91
Elvis and Me '88
Russkies '87

Thorley Walters (1913-91)
In the Secret State '85
The Little Drummer Girl '84
The Sign of Four '83
The Adventures of Sherlock Holmes' Smarter Brother '78
The People That Time Forgot '77
Cry of the Penguins '71
Vampire Circus '71
Bartleby '70
Frankenstein Must Be Destroyed '69
Oh! What a Lovely War '69
Dracula, Prince of Darkness '66
Frankenstein Created Woman '66
Murder She Said '62
The Phantom of the Opera '62
Sherlock Holmes and the Deadly Necklace '62
The Pure Hell of St. Trinian's '61
Blue Murder at St. Trinian's '56
Who Done It? '56

Henry B. Walthall (1878-1936)
Last Outlaw '36
A Tale of Two Cities '36
Beggars in Ermine '34
Judge Priest '34
Men in White '34
The Scarlet Letter '34
Viva Villa! '34
Flaming Signal '33
Laughing at Life '33
Somewhere in Sonora '33
The Cabin in the Cotton '32
Chandu the Magician '32
Police Court '32
Ride Him, Cowboy '32
Strange Interlude '32
Abraham Lincoln '30
The Phantom in the House '29
Wings '27
The Plastic Age '25
With Kit Carson over the Great Divide '25
The Confession '20
False Faces '18
The Birth of a Nation '15
The Raven '15
Avenging Conscience '14
Home Sweet Home '14
Judith of Bethulia '14

Bill Walton (1952-)
Little Nicky '00
Celtic Pride '96

Douglas Walton (1910-61)
Murder, My Sweet '44
Sundown Fury '42
Bad Lands '39
Wallaby Jim of the Islands '37
I Conquer the Sea '36
Mary of Scotland '36
The Bride of Frankenstein '35
Charlie Chan in London '34
The Lost Patrol '34

John Walton (1953-)
The Lighthorsemen '87
Kangaroo '86

Mark Walton
Bolt '08 (V)
Home on the Range '04 (V)

Christoph Waltz
Inglourious Basterds '09
Jacob '94

Lisa Waltz
Starry Night '99
Neil Simon's The Odd Couple 2 '98
Pet Sematary 2 '92
Brighton Beach Memoirs '86

Patrick Waltz
Queen of Outer Space '58
The Sun Sets at Dawn '50

Chi Keung Wan
Infernal Affairs 2 '03
Infernal Affairs 3 '03

Lau Ching Wan (1964-)
Running out of Time '99
Black Mask '96

Siu-Lun Wan (1964-)
So Close '02
Legend of the Liquid Sword '93

Sam Wanamaker (1919-93)
Covert Assassin '94
City of Joy '92
Secret Ingredient '92
Guilty by Suspicion '91
Pure Luck '91
Running Against Time '90
The Shell Seekers '89
Judgment in Berlin '88
Baby Boom '87
Superman 4: The Quest for Peace '87
Raw Deal '86
The Aviator '85
Embassy '85
Detective Sadie & Son '84
Ghostwriter '84
Irreconcilable Differences '84
Our Family Business '81
The Competition '80
Private Benjamin '80
Charlie Muffin '79
From Hell to Victory '79
Sell Out '76
Voyage of the Damned '76
Spiral Staircase '75
The Spy Who Came in from the Cold '65
Those Magnificent Men in Their Flying Machines '65
Taras Bulba '62
The Battle of the Sexes '60 (N)
My Girl Tisa '48

Zoe Wanamaker (1949-)
The Old Curiosity Shop '07
Harry Potter and the Sorcerer's Stone '01
David Copperfield '99
The Magical Legend of the Leprechauns '99
A Dance to the Music of Time '97
Swept from the Sea '97
Wilde '97
The Widowing of Mrs. Holroyd '95
The Blackheath Poisonings '92
Prime Suspect '92
Tales of the Unexpected '91
The Raggedy Rawney '90
Poor Little Rich Girl: The Barbara Hutton Story '87

Carter Wang (1947-)
Hardcase and Fist '89
Way of the Black Dragon '81

Chung Wang
The Water Margin '72
Have Sword, Will Travel '69

Faye Wang
See Faye Wong

Hongwei Wang
The World '04
Balzac and the Little Chinese Seamstress '02

Lung-Wai Wang
Shaolin & Wu Tang '81
Master of the Flying Guillotine '75

Lung Wei Wang
Life Gamble '04
The Master '80

Peter Wang
The Laserman '90
A Great Wall '86
Chan Is Missing '82

Yu-Wen Wang
Eat Drink Man Woman '94
Rebels of the Neon God '92

Zhiwen Wang (1966-)
Together '02
The Emperor and the Assassin '99
Blush '95

Haruko Wanibuchi
One Missed Call 2 '05
One-Eyed Swordsman '63

Percy Waram (1881-1961)
The Big Hangover '50
Ministry of Fear '44

David Warbeck (1941-97)
Razor Blade Smile '98
Miami Horror '87
Formula for a Murder '85
Tiger Joe '85
Ark of the Sun God '82
The Beyond '82
Hunters of the Golden Cobra '82
The Black Cat '81
The Last Hunter '80
Panic '76
Blacksnake! '73
Twins of Evil '71

John Warburton (1887-1981)
King Rat '65
Secret File of Hollywood '62
Saratoga Trunk '45
Nothing But Trouble '44
The White Cliffs of Dover '44
Cavalcade '33

Patrick Warburton (1964-)
Hoodwinked Too! Hood vs. Evil '10 (V)
Get Smart '08
Space Chimps '08 (V)
Bee Movie '07 (V)
Happily N'Ever After '07 (V)
I'll Believe You '07
Underdog '07
Open Season '06 (V)
The Wild '06 (V)
Chicken Little '05 (V)
Hoodwinked '05 (V)
Rebound '05
Sky High '05 (V)
Home on the Range '04 (V)
Big Trouble '02
Men in Black 2 '02
Joe Somebody '01
Angels in the Infield '00
The Dish '00
The Emperor's New Groove '00 (V)
Scream 3 '00
Apartment Complex '98
Dragonard '88

Amelita Ward
Jungle Captive '45
Seven Days Ashore '44
Clancy Street Boys '43

B.J. Ward
The Opposite Sex and How to Live With Them '93
Pound Puppies and the Legend of Big Paw '88 (V)

Brendan Ward
South Bronx Heroes '85
Taps '81

Burt Ward (1945-)
Assault of the Party Nerds 2: Heavy Petting Detective '95
Beach Babes from Beyond '93
Smooth Talker '90
Virgin High '90
Killcrazy '89
Robo-Chic '89
Batman '66

Donal Lardner Ward (1964-)
The Suburbans '99
My Life's in Turnaround '94

Fred Ward (1943-)
Armored '09
Management '09
Exit Speed '08
Feast of Love '07
Coast to Coast '04
Abandon '02
Enough '02
Sweet Home Alabama '02
Corky Romano '01
Joe Dirt '01
Summer Catch '01
Wild Iris '01
Chaos Factor '00
Circus '00
The Crow: Salvation '00
Full Disclosure '00
Road Trip '00
The Crimson Code '99
Best Men '98
Dangerous Beauty '98
Forgotten City '98
Invasion: Earth '98
First Do No Harm '97
Chain Reaction '96
Tremors 2: Aftershocks '96
Naked Gun 33 1/3: The Final Insult '94
Equinox '93
Four Eyes and Six Guns '93
Short Cuts '93
Two Small Bodies '93
Bob Roberts '92
The Player '92
Thunderheart '92
Cast a Deadly Spell '91
Henry & June '90
Miami Blues '90
Backtrack '89
Tremors '89
Big Business '88
Prince of Pennsylvania '88
Florida Straits '87
Off Limits '87
Remo Williams: The Adventure Begins '85
Secret Admirer '85
Noon Wine '84
Swing Shift '84
The Right Stuff '83
Silkwood '83
Timerider '83
Uncommon Valor '83
Southern Comfort '81
Uforia '81
Escape from Alcatraz '79

John Ward (1924-95)
Holt of the Secret Service '42
Ridin' the Trail '40
Robinson Crusoe of Clipper Island '36

Jonathan Ward (1970-)
Ferngully: The Last Rain Forest '92 (V)
Mac and Me '88
White Water Summer '87

Kelly Ward (1956-)
The Big Red One '80
Grease '78

Larry Ward (1915-85)
Deathhead Virgin '74
Macabre '69

Lucille Ward (1907-69)
California Straight Ahead '25
A Woman of the World '25

Lyman Ward (1941-)
Independence Day '96
The Secret Agent Club '96
Serial Killer '95
Mikey '92
Sleepwalkers '92
The Taking of Beverly Hills '91
Perfect Victims '87
Planes, Trains & Automobiles '87
Ferris Bueller's Day Off '86
Creature '85
Great Smokey Roadblock '76

Maitland Ward (1977-)
White Chicks '04
Dish Dogs '98

Mary B. Ward
Operation Sandman: Warriors in Hell '00
Hangin' with the Homeboys '91
Surviving Desire '91

Megan Ward (1969-)
Murder Without Conviction '04
Rated X '00
Tick Tock '00
Don't Look Down '98
Glory Daze '96
Joe's Apartment '96
P.C.U. '94
Arcade '93
Freaked '93
Amityville 1992: It's About Time '92
Encino Man '92
Trancers 3: Deth Lives '92
Trancers 2: The Return of Jack Deth '90

Paddy Ward
Casanova '05
Waking Ned Devine '98

Penelope Dudley Ward (1919-82)
The Demi-Paradise '43
The Case of the Frightened Lady '39
The Citadel '38
I Stand Condemned '36

Rachel Ward (1957-)
Bobbie's Girl '02
Johnson County War '02

On the Beach '00
Twisted '96
The Ascent '94
Black Magic '92
Christopher Columbus: The Discovery '92
Double Jeopardy '92
Wide Sargasso Sea '92
After Dark, My Sweet '90
How to Get Ahead in Advertising '89
Hotel Colonial '88
The Good Wife '86
Fortress '85
Against All Odds '84
The Final Terror '83
The Thorn Birds '83
Dead Men Don't Wear Plaid '82
Night School '81
Sharky's Machine '81

Rich Ward
Vampires of Sorority Row: Kickboxers From Hell '99
Things 2 '97

Richard Ward (1915-79)
The Jerk '79
Mandingo '75
Across 110th Street '72

Robin Ward (1944-)
Mark of Cain '84
Thrillkill '84
When Angels Fly '82

Roger Ward (1936-)
Quigley Down Under '90
Mad Max '80

Roy Ward
The Ugly '96
The Forbidden Quest '93

Sandy Ward (1926-2005)
Blue Desert '91
Delta Force 3: The Killing Game '91
The Chinatown Murders: Man against the Mob '89
Cujo '83
Tank '83
The Velvet Vampire '71

Sela Ward (1957-)
The Stepfather '09
The Guardian '06
The Day After Tomorrow '04
Dirty Dancing: Havana Nights '04
The Badge '02
Runaway Bride '99
54 '98
Rescuers: Stories of Courage "Two Women" '97
My Fellow Americans '96
The Fugitive '93
Double Jeopardy '92
Child of Darkness, Child of Light '91
Rainbow Drive '90
Haunting of Sarah Hardy '89
Hello Again '87
Steele Justice '87
Nothing in Common '86

Simon Ward (1941-)
The Monster Club '85
Supergirl '84
Deadly Strangers '82
Dominique Is Dead '79
Zulu Dawn '79
The Four Feathers '78
The Chosen '77
Children of Rage '75
The Four Musketeers '75
All Creatures Great and Small '74
The Three Musketeers '74
Dracula '73
Hitler: The Last Ten Days '73
Young Winston '72
Frankenstein Must Be Destroyed '69

Sophie Ward (1965-)
Clive Barker's Book of Blood '08
The Big Fall '96
A Village Affair '95
A Dark Adapted Eye '93
Class of '61 '92
A Demon in My View '92
Emily Bronte's Wuthering Heights '92
Waxwork 2: Lost in Time '91
The Shell Seekers '89
Little Dorrit, Film 1: Nobody's Fault '88
Little Dorrit, Film 2: Little Dorrit's Story '88
A Summer Story '88
Casanova '87
Young Sherlock Holmes '85

Susan Ward (1976-)
Cruel World '05
Wild Things 2 '04
Shallow Hal '01
The In Crowd '00

Tom Ward (1971-)
The Lost World '02
Moll Flanders '96

Vincent Ward (1956-)
One Night Stand '97
The Shot '96

Wally Ward
See Wallace (Wally) Langham

Warwick Ward (1891-1967)
The Informer '29
Variety '25

Zack (Zach) Ward (1973-)
The Devil's Tomb '09
BloodRayne 2: Deliverance '07
Postal '07
Transformers '07
Hollywood Kills '06
L.A. Twister '04
Resident Evil: Apocalypse '04
April's Shower '03
Almost Famous '00
Brotherhood of Murder '99
Malicious Intent '99
Ed '96
Star Hunter '95
The Club '94
A Christmas Story '83

Jennifer Ward-Lealand
The Ugly '96
Desperate Remedies '93
Dangerous Orphans '86

Anthony Warde (1908-75)
Roaring City '51
Radar Patrol vs. Spy King '49
The Black Widow '47
King of the Forest Rangers '46
There Goes Kelly '45
The Ghost and the Guest '43
The Spider Returns '41
Chip of the Flying U '39

Harlan Warde (1917-80)
Above and Beyond '53
Loan Shark '52
Flying Leathernecks '51
Money Madness '47

Jack Warden (1920-2006)
The Replacements '00
A Dog of Flanders '99
Bulworth '98
Chairman of the Board '97
Dirty Work '97
The Island on Bird Street '97
Ed '96
Mighty Aphrodite '95
Things to Do in Denver When You're Dead '95
While You Were Sleeping '95
Bullets over Broadway '94
Guilty as Sin '93
Night and the City '92
Passed Away '92
Problem Child 2 '91
Everybody Wins '90
Judgment '90
Problem Child '90
Robert Kennedy and His Times '90
Dead Solid Perfect '88
The Presidio '88
September '88
A.D. '85
Alice in Wonderland '85
The Aviator '85
Crackers '84
Hobson's Choice '83
The Verdict '82
Carbon Copy '81
Chu Chu & the Philly Flash '81
The Great Muppet Caper '81
So Fine '81
Used Cars '80
And Justice for All '79
Being There '79
Beyond the Poseidon Adventure '79
The Champ '79
Dreamer '79
Death on the Nile '78
Heaven Can Wait '78
Raid on Entebbe '77
The White Buffalo '77
Shampoo '75
The Apprenticeship of Duddy Kravitz '74
Billy Two Hats '74
Man Who Loved Cat Dancing '73
The Sporting Club '72
Brian's Song '71
Man on a String '71
Summertree '71
Who Is Harry Kellerman and Why Is He Saying Those Terrible Things About Me? '71
Bye Bye Braverman '67
The Thin Red Line '64
Donovan's Reef '63
Darby's Rangers '58
Run Silent, Run Deep '58
Edge of the City '57
Twelve Angry Men '57
From Here to Eternity '53

Geoffrey Wardwell (1900-55)
Crimes at the Dark House '39
The Challenge '38

Herta Ware (1917-2005)
St. Patrick's Day '99
Top Dog '95
Crazy in Love '92
Dakota '88
Cocoon '85

Irene Ware (1910-93)
The Dark Hour '36
Federal Agent '36
The Raven '35
King Kelly of the U.S.A. '34
Chandu the Magician '32

Chris Warfield (1927-96)
Diary of a Madman '63
Dangerous Charter '62

Emily Warfield (1972-)
Bonanza: The Return '93
Calendar Girl '93
The Man in the Moon '91
Pair of Aces '90

Marsha Warfield (1954-)
The Whoopee Boys '86
Mask '85
D.C. Cab '84

William Warfield (1920-2002)
Old Explorers '90
Show Boat '51

Andy Warhol (1928-87)
Cocaine Cowboys '79
Driver's Seat '73

Raymond Waring (1977-)
Yes '04
Lucky Break '01

Todd Waring (1955-)
Sinatra '92
Love & Murder '91

Billy Warlock (1961-)
Steel Sharks '97
Opposite Corners '96
Panic in the Skies '96
Honor Thy Father and Mother: The True Story of the Menendez Brothers '94
Society '92
Swimsuit '89
Hot Shot '86

Kimberly Warnat
Papa's Angels '00
Silver Wolf '98

Gordon Warnecke (1963-)
A Fatal Inversion '92
London Kills Me '91
My Beautiful Laundrette '85

Amelia Warner (1982-)
Alpha Male '06
Aeon Flux '05
Stoned '05
Winter Passing '05
Lorna Doone '01

David Warner (1941-)
Wallander: Sidetracked '08
Hogfather '06
Perfect Parents '06
Ladies in Lavender '04
Straight into Darkness '04
Back to the Secret Garden '01
Horatio Hornblower: The Adventure Continues '01
Planet of the Apes '01
Houdini '99
Wing Commander '99
Money Talks '97
Scream 2 '97
Titanic '97
The Leading Man '96
Rasputin: Dark Servant of Destiny '96
Beastmaster 3: The Eye of Braxus '95
The Choir '95
Final Equinox '95
Ice Cream Man '95
In the Mouth of Madness '95
Naked Souls '95
Inner Sanctum 2 '94
Tryst '94
Body Bags '93
H.P. Lovecraft's Necronomicon: Book of the Dead '93
Quest of the Delta Knights '93
Return to the Lost World '93
Wild Palms '93
The Lost World '92
The Unnamable 2: The Statement of Randolph Carter '92
Cast a Deadly Spell '91
Star Trek 6: The Undiscovered Country '91
Teenage Mutant Ninja Turtles 2: The Secret of the Ooze '91
Blue Tornado '90
Code Name: Chaos '90
Mortal Passions '90
Spymaker: The Secret Life of Ian Fleming '90
Grave Secrets '89
Star Trek 5: The Final Frontier '89
Tripwire '89
Hanna's War '88
Hostile Takeover '88
Magdalene '88
Mr. North '88
My Best Friend Is a Vampire '88
Waxwork '88
The Company of Wolves '85
A Christmas Carol '84
The Man with Two Brains '83
Frankenstein '82
Tron '82
The Boy Who Left Home to Find Out About the Shivers '81
Disappearance '81
Masada '81
Time Bandits '81
The Island '80
The Concorde: Airport '79 '79
Nightwing '79
S.O.S. Titanic '79
The Thirty-Nine Steps '79
Time After Time '79
Holocaust '78
Silver Bears '78
Providence '77
Cross of Iron '76
The Omen '76
The Old Curiosity Shop '75
A Doll's House '73
From Beyond the Grave '73
Straw Dogs '72
Ballad of Cable Hogue '70
The Fixer '68
A Midsummer Night's Dream '68
Morgan: A Suitable Case for Treatment '66
Tom Jones '63

H.B. Warner (1876-1958)
The Ten Commandments '56
Savage Drums '51
The Judge Steps Out '49
It's a Wonderful Life '46
Strange Impersonation '46
Action in Arabia '44
Enemy of Women '44
Rogue's Gallery '44
Boss of Big Town '43
Hitler's Children '43
The Corsican Brothers '42
Yank in Libya '42
The Devil & Daniel Webster '41
Topper Returns '41
Bulldog Drummond's Bride '39
Bulldog Drummond's Secret Police '39
Let Freedom Ring '39
Mr. Smith Goes to Washington '39
The Rains Came '39
The Adventures of Marco Polo '38
Arrest Bulldog Drummond '38
You Can't Take It with You '38
Lost Horizon '37
Mr. Deeds Goes to Town '36
A Tale of Two Cities '36
Night Alarm '34
Supernatural '33
Cross Examination '32
The Crusader '32
The Divine Lady '29
King of Kings '27
Big Stakes '22

Jack Warner (1895-1981)
Carve Her Name with Pride '58
The Quatermass Experiment '56
The Ladykillers '55
Those People Next Door '52
A Christmas Carol '51
Valley of the Eagles '51
The Blue Lamp '49
Train of Events '49
Against the Wind '48
Captive Heart '47
Dear Murderer '47
Hue and Cry '47
It Always Rains on Sunday '47
The Dummy Talks '43

Julie Warner (1965-)
Forever Strong '08
Stick It '06
Dean Koontz's Mr. Murder '98
Wedding Bell Blues '96
Tommy Boy '95
The Puppet Masters '94
Indian Summer '93
Mr. Saturday Night '92
Doc Hollywood '91

Malcolm Jamal Warner (1970-)
Fool's Gold '08
Restaurant '98
The Tuskegee Airmen '95
Tyson '95
Drop Zone '94
The Father Clements Story '87

Barry Warren (1933-)
Frankenstein Created Woman '66
The Devil-Ship Pirates '64
Kiss of the Vampire '62

Bruce Warren
Held for Ransom '38
Mother and Son '31

C. Denier Warren (1889-1971)
Lolita '62
The Body Vanished '39

E. Alyn (Fred) Warren (1874-1940)
Get That Man '35
Mysterious Mr. Wong '35
Tarzan the Fearless '33
Abraham Lincoln '30
Medicine Man '30

Estella Warren (1978-)
The Cooler '03
Kangaroo Jack '02
Driven '01
Planet of the Apes '01
Tangled '01

Jennifer Warren (1941-)
The Amazons '84
Mutant '83
The Choice '81
Intruder Within '81
Angel City '80
Ice Castles '79
Steel Cowboy '78
Another Man, Another Chance '77
Slap Shot '77
Banjo Hackett '76
Night Moves '75
The Swap '71

Jennifer Leigh Warren
Matter of Trust '98
Sour Grapes '98
Grace of My Heart '96
The Crossing Guard '94

Katherine Warren (1905-65)
The Caine Mutiny '54
Prowler '51

Kenneth J. Warren (1929-73)
The Creeping Flesh '72
Demons of the Mind '72
I, Monster '71
Fiction Makers '67

Kiersten Warren (1965-)
The Christmas Cottage '08
Hoot '06
Black Cadillac '03
The Snow Walker '03
Circuit '02
Divine Secrets of the Ya-Ya Sisterhood '02
Duets '00
Bicentennial Man '99
Liberty Heights '99
Independence Day '96

Lesley Ann Warren (1946-)
Miracle Dogs Too '06
10th & Wolf '06

Deepwater '05
When Do We Eat? '05
Recipe for Disaster '03
Secretary '02
The Quickie '01
Trixie '00
The Limey '99
Twin Falls Idaho '99
Love Kills '98
Going All the Way '97
Natural Enemy '96
Bird of Prey '95
Joseph '95
Color of Night '94
Pure Country '92
Life Stinks '91
A Fight for Jenny '90
Worth Winning '89
Cop '88
Baja Oklahoma '87
Burglar '87
Apology '86
Clue '85
Choose Me '84
The Dancing Princesses '84
Songwriter '84
A Night in Heaven '83
Treasure of the Yankee Zephyr '83
Portrait of a Showgirl '82
Victor/Victoria '82
Beulah Land '80
Portrait of a Stripper '79
Betrayal '78
Pearl '78
Harry & Walter Go to New York '76
Legend of Valentino '75
Where the Eagle Flies '72
The One and Only, Genuine, Original Family Band '68
The Happiest Millionaire '67
Cinderella '64

Marc Warren (1967-)

Wanted '08
Ballet Shoes '07
Dracula '06
Hogfather '06
Green Street Hooligans '05
Hellraiser: Deader '05
State of Play '03
Band of Brothers '01
Dad Savage '97
Boston Kickout '95

Michael Warren (1946-)

Species 3 '04
Trippin' '99
Buffalo Soldiers '97
A Passion to Kill '94
Storyville '92
Heaven Is a Playground '91
The Kid Who Loved Christmas '90
Norman, Is That You? '76

Harold Warrender (1903-53)

Pandora and the Flying Dutchman '51
Conspirator '49
Contraband '40
Mimi '35

Ruth Warrick (1915-2005)

Deathmask '69
One Too Many '51
Let's Dance '50
Three Husbands '50
Great Dan Patch '49
Arch of Triumph '48
China Sky '44
Guest in the House '44
Mr. Winkle Goes to War '44
The Iron Major '43
The Corsican Brothers '42
Citizen Kane '41

David Warrilow (1934-95)

Barton Fink '91
Bright Lights, Big City '88
Strong Medicine '84

Dan Warry-Smith (1982-)

My Teacher Ate My Homework '98
The Legend of Gator Face '96

David Warshofsky (1959-)

Running Scared '06
Personal Velocity: Three Portraits '02
Suffering Bastards '90

John Warwick (1905-72)

While I Live '47
The Face at the Window '39
Ticket of Leave Man '37

Richard Warwick (1945-97)

Sebastiane '79
If... '69

Robert Warwick (1878-1964)

It Started with a Kiss '59
The Star '52
Tarzan and the Slave Girl '50
I Married a Witch '42
Sullivan's Travels '41
A Woman's Face '41
The Spy Ring '38
The Awful Truth '37
The Trigger Trio '37
The Bold Caballero '36
Bulldog Edition '36
Hopalong Cassidy '35
A Shot in the Dark '35
Whipsaw '35
Whispering Shadow '33
The Secrets of Wu Sin '32
The Royal Bed '31
A Girl's Folly '17

Mona Washbourne (1903-88)

December Flower '84
Brideshead Revisited '81
Therese Raquin '80
Stevie '78
Driver's Seat '73
O Lucky Man! '73
If... '69
Mrs. Brown, You've Got a Lovely Daughter '68
The Collector '65
My Fair Lady '64
The Brides of Dracula '60
Stranger in Town '57
Cast a Dark Shadow '55

Beverly Washburn (1943-)

When the Line Goes Through '73
Pit Stop '67
Spider Baby '64
Old Yeller '57

Bryant Washburn (1889-1963)

Shadows on the Sage '42
The Spider Returns '41
Savage Fury '35
The Throwback '35
Drifting Souls '32
Kept Husbands '31
The Wizard of Oz '25

Rick Washburne (1946-)

The Outfit '93
Comrades in Arms '91
Covert Action '88
Hangmen '87

Denzel Washington (1954-)

The Book of Eli '10
The Taking of Pelham 123 '09
American Gangster '07
The Great Debaters '07
Deja Vu '06
Inside Man '06
Man on Fire '04
The Manchurian Candidate '04
Out of Time '03
Antwone Fisher '02
John Q '02
Training Day '01
Remember the Titans '00
The Bone Collector '99
The Hurricane '99
He Got Game '98
The Siege '98
Fallen '97
Courage Under Fire '96
The Preacher's Wife '96
Crimson Tide '95
Devil in a Blue Dress '95
Virtuosity '95
Much Ado about Nothing '93
The Pelican Brief '93
Philadelphia '93
Malcolm X '92
Mississippi Masala '92
Ricochet '91
Heart Condition '90
Mo' Better Blues '90
Glory '89
The Mighty Quinn '89
Cry Freedom '87
Hard Lessons '86
Power '86
License to Kill '84
A Soldier's Story '84
Carbon Copy '81
Wilma '77

Fredi Washington (1903-94)

Imitation of Life '34
Emperor Jones '33

Gene Washington (1947-)

Lady Cocoa '75
The Black Six '74

Isaiah Washington, IV (1963-)

Hurricane Season '08
The Moguls '05
Dead Birds '04
Wild Things 2 '04
Hollywood Homicide '03
This Girl's Life '03
Ghost Ship '02
Welcome to Collinwood '02
Exit Wounds '01
Dancing in September '00
Romeo Must Die '00
A Texas Funeral '99
True Crime '99
Always Outnumbered Always Outgunned '98
Bulworth '98
Mixing Nia '98
Out of Sight '98
Joe Torre: Curveballs Along the Way '97
Get On the Bus '96
Girl 6 '96
Love Jones '96
Mr. & Mrs. Loving '96
Clockers '95
Crooklyn '94

Jascha Washington (1989-)

Last Holiday '06
My Sister's Keeper '02
Big Momma's House '00

Ken Washington

Laboratory '80
She Devils in Chains '76

Kerry Washington (1977-)

Mother and Child '09
Lakeview Terrace '08
Life is Hot in Cracktown '08
Miracle at St. Anna '08
Fantastic Four: Rise of the Silver Surfer '07
I Think I Love My Wife '07
The Dead Girl '06
The Last King of Scotland '06
Little Man '06
Fantastic Four '05
Mr. & Mrs. Smith '05
Against the Ropes '04
Ray '04
She Hate Me '04
The Human Stain '03
United States of Leland '03
Bad Company '02
Sin '02
Lift '01
Our Song '01
Save the Last Dance '01

Shirley Washington

Darktown Strutters '74
The Deadly and the Beautiful '73

Machiko Washio

The Black House '00
The Red Spectacles '87

Mia Wasikowska (1989-)

Alice in Wonderland '10
The Kids Are All Right '10
Amelia '09
That Evening Sun '09
Defiance '08
Rogue '07

Ted Wass (1952-)

Danielle Steel's Star '93
Fine Gold '88
Pancho Barnes '88
The Longshot '86
TripleCross '85
Oh, God! You Devil '84
Sheena '84
Curse of the Pink Panther '83
The Triangle Factory Fire Scandal '79

Rebecca Wassem

See Sheila Darcy

Jerry Wasserman (1945-)

A Cooler Climate '99
Quarantine '89

Craig Wasson (1954-)

Puerto Vallarta Squeeze '04
Boa '02
Epoch '00
Escape under Pressure '00
The Pornographer '00
Velocity Trap '99
The Last Best Sunday '98
Harvest of Fire '95
The Sister-in-Law '95
Trapped in Space '94
Strapped '93
Malcolm X '92
Midnight Fear '90
A Nightmare on Elm Street 3: Dream Warriors '87
The Men's Club '86
Body Double '84
The Innocents Abroad '84
Second Thoughts '83
Four Friends '81
Ghost Story '81
Carny '80
Schizoid '80
Skag '79
Go Tell the Spartans '78
The Boys in Company C '77
Rollercoaster '77

Atsuro Watabe

Three ... Extremes '04
Zebraman '04
Inugami '01

Gedde Watanabe (1955-)

Forgetting Sarah Marshall '08
Two for the Money '05
Alfie '04
EDtv '99
Guinevere '99
Mulan '98 (V)
Booty Call '96
Nick and Jane '96
That Thing You Do! '96
The Spring '89
UHF '89
Vamp '86
Gung Ho '85
Volunteers '85
Sixteen Candles '84

Ken(saku) Watanabe (1959-)

Inception '10
Cirque du Freak: The Vampire's Assistant '09
Letters from Iwo Jima '06
Batman Begins '05
Memoirs of a Geisha '05
The Last Samurai '03
Karate Warrior '88
Commando Invasion '87
Tampopo '86
MacArthur's Children '85

Tetsu Watanabe (1951-)

Fireworks '97
Sonatine '96

Tsunehiko Watase (1944-)

The Silk Road '92
Heaven & Earth '90
Sympathy for the Underdog '71

Dennis Waterman (1948-)

Back in Business '06
Circle of Deceit '94
Cold Justice '89
Fright '71
Man in the Wilderness '71
The Scars of Dracula '70

Felicity Waterman

Freedom Strike '98
Titanic '96
Hard Bounty '94
Unlawful Passage '94
Miracle Beach '92
Lena's Holiday '90

Ida Waterman (1852-1941)

Amarilly of Clothesline Alley '18
Stella Maris '18

Willard Waterman (1915-95)

Hail '73
Hollywood or Bust '56
Rhubarb '51

Cheryl Waters

Didn't You Hear? '83
Image of Death '77
Macon County Line '74

Dina Waters

See Dina Spybey

Ethel Waters (1896-1977)

The Member of the Wedding '52
Pinky '49
Cabin in the Sky '43
Stage Door Canteen '43
Cairo '42
Tales of Manhattan '42

Harry Waters, Jr.

Back to the Future, Part 2 '89
Back to the Future '85

John Waters (1946-)

Seed of Chucky '04
Sweet and Lowdown '99
Pecker '98 (V)
Serial Mom '94 (V)
Hairspray '88
Something Wild '86
Pink Flamingos '72 (N)

John Waters (1948-)

Ebbtide '94
Heaven Tonight '93
Which Way Home '90
Grievous Bodily Harm '89
Boulevard of Broken Dreams '88
Miracle Down Under '87
True Colors '87
Alice to Nowhere '86
Three's Trouble '85
All the Rivers Run '84
Attack Force Z '84
Breaker Morant '80
Cass '78
Demolition '77
The Getting of Wisdom '77
Scalp Merchant '77
Weekend of Shadows '77
Endplay '75

Nick Waters (1951-)

The Big Hurt '87
The Lighthorsemen '87

Sam Waterston (1940-)

Le Divorce '03
A House Divided '00
Miracle at Midnight '98
The Proprietor '96
The Shadow Conspiracy '96
The Journey of August King '95
Assault at West Point: The Court-Martial of Johnson Whittaker '94
The Enemy Within '94
Serial Mom '94
A Captive in the Land '91
The Man in the Moon '91
Mindwalk: A Film for Passionate Thinkers '91
Lantern Hill '90
Crimes & Misdemeanors '89
The Nightmare Years '89
Welcome Home '89
Gore Vidal's Lincoln '88
September '88
Hannah and Her Sisters '86
Just Between Friends '86
Trade Secrets '86
Warning Sign '85
The Boy Who Loved Trolls '84
Finnegan Begin Again '84
The Killing Fields '84
Dempsey '83
Heaven's Gate '81
Hopscotch '80
Eagle's Wing '79
Friendly Fire '79
Sweet William '79
Capricorn One '78
Interiors '78
Rancho Deluxe '75
The Great Gatsby '74
Journey into Fear '74
Reflections of Murder '74
Savages '72
Who Killed Mary What's 'Er Name? '71
Generation '69

Gwen Watford (1927-94)

The Body in the Library '84
In This House of Brede '75
Taste the Blood of Dracula '70
The Very Edge '63
The Fall of the House of Usher '49

Ian Watkin (1940-)

Dead Alive '93
Nutcase '83
Beyond Reasonable Doubt '80

Pierre Watkin (1889-1960)

The Stranger Wore a Gun '53
Atom Man vs. Superman '50
Redwood Forest Trail '50
The Strange Mrs. Crane '48
Wild Frontier '47
Little Giant '46
Murder Is My Business '46
Sioux City Sue '46
Swamp Fire '46
End of the Road '44
The Great Mike '44
The Magnificent Dope '42
Nevada City '41
The Road to Singapore '40
Wall Street Cowboy '39
Larceny On the Air '37
Country Gentlemen '36

Gerard Watkins

Taken '08
Love Me if You Dare '03

Joanne Watkins

The Big Sweat '90
Cold Heat '90

Royale Watkins (1969-)

Deliver Us from Eva '03
Speed 2: Cruise Control '97

Pals of the Saddle '38
Santa Fe Stampede '38
California Straight Ahead! '37
King of the Pecos '36
The Lawless Nineties '36
Winds of the Wasteland '36
Dawn Rider '35
Desert Trail '35
Lawless Frontier '35
Lawless Range '35
The New Frontier '35
Paradise Canyon '35
Texas Terror '35
Westward Ho '35
Blue Steel '34
Lucky Texan '34
Man from Utah '34
'Neath the Arizona Skies '34
Randy Rides Alone '34
The Star Packer '34
Trail Beyond '34
Baby Face '33
His Private Secretary '33
Man from Monterey '33
Riders of Destiny '33
Sagebrush Trail '33
Somewhere in Sonora '33
Telegraph Trail '33
The Three Musketeers '33
West of the Divide '33
The Big Stampede '32
Haunted Gold '32
Hurricane Express '32
Ride Him, Cowboy '32
Shadow of the Eagle '32
Texas Cyclone '32
Two-Fisted Law '32
Maker of Men '31
Range Feud '31
Big Trail '30
The Dropkick '27

John Ethan Wayne (1961-)

The Manhunt '86
Escape from El Diablo '83
Scream '83

Michael Wayne (1934-2003)

Rapid Fire '89
Alley Cat '84

Naunton Wayne (1901-70)

The Hidden Room '49
Obsession '49
Passport to Pimlico '49
A Girl in a Million '46
Dead of Night '45
Night Train to Munich '40
The Lady Vanishes '38

Nina Wayne (1943-)

The Comic '69
Dead Heat on a Merry-Go-Round '66

Patricia Wayne (1926-74)

The Long Dark Hall '51
Eye Witness '49

Patrick Wayne (1939-)

Chill Factor '90
Her Alibi '88
Young Guns '88
Revenge '86
Rustler's Rhapsody '85
The People That Time Forgot '77
Sinbad and the Eye of the Tiger '77
Texas Detour '77
The Bears & I '74
Beyond Atlantis '73
The Gatling Gun '72
Big Jake '71
Ride to Glory '71
The Green Berets '68
Talion '66
Shenandoah '65
McLintock! '63
The Alamo '60
The Young Land '59
The Searchers '56
Mister Roberts '55

Randy Wayne

To Save a Life '10
Foreign Exchange '08

Michael Weatherly (1968-)

Cabin by the Lake '00
The Substitute 4: Failure is Not an Option '00
The Colony '98
The Last Days of Disco '98
Asteroid '97

Shawn Weatherly (1960-)

Rustin '01
Amityville 1992: It's About Time '92
Mind Games '89
Shadowzone '89
Thieves of Fortune '89
Party Line '88
Police Academy 3: Back in Training '86

Carl Weathers (1948-)

The Comebacks '07
The Sasquatch Gang '06
Alien Siege '05
Little Nicky '00
Shadow Warriors '97
Shadow Warriors 2: Hunt for the Death Merchant '97
Happy Gilmore '96
Dangerous Passion '95
Hurricane Smith '92
Action Jackson '88
Predator '87
Fortune Dane '86
Rocky 4 '85
Rocky 3 '82
Death Hunt '81
Rocky 2 '79
The Bermuda Depths '78
Force 10 from Navarone '78
Semi-Tough '77
Rocky '76
Bucktown '75
Friday Foster '75

Blayne Weaver (1976-)

Weather Girl '09
Return to Never Land '02 (V)
Manic '01

Dennis Weaver (1924-2006)

Home on the Range '04 (V)
High Noon '00
Submerged '00
Escape from Wildcat Canyon '99
The Virginian '99
Two Bits & Pepper '95
Mastergate '92
Disaster at Silo 7 '88
Bluffing It '87
A Winner Never Quits '86
Going for the Gold: The Bill Johnson Story '85
Cocaine: One Man's Seduction '83
Amber Waves '82
Don't Go to Sleep '82
The Ordeal of Dr. Mudd '80
Centennial '78
Pearl '78
Intimate Strangers '77
Duel '71
A Man Called Sledge '71
What's the Matter with Helen? '71
Mission Batangas '69
Gentle Giant '67
Duel at Diablo '66
The Gallant Hours '60
Touch of Evil '58
Law and Order '53
The Redhead from Wyoming '53
War Arrow '53
Horizons West '52
The Lawless Breed '52

Doodles Weaver (1911-83)

Way He Was '76
Runaways '75
Cancel My Reservation '72
Road to Nashville '67
The Errand Boy '61
The Ladies' Man '61

Fritz Weaver (1926-)

The Thomas Crown Affair '99
Rescuers: Stories of Courage "Two Women" '97
Broken Trust '95
Blind Spot '93
Ironclads '90
My Name Is Bill W. '89
Power '86
The Hearst and Davies Affair '85
Creepshow '82
Jaws of Satan '81
The Martian Chronicles: Part 2 '79
The Martian Chronicles: Part 3 '79
The Big Fix '78
Holocaust '78
Black Sunday '77
Demon Seed '77
Marathon Man '76
The Day of the Dolphin '73
Hunter '73
Walk in the Spring Rain '70
Fail-Safe '64

Jacki Weaver (1947-)

Cosi '95
Three's Trouble '85
Squizzy Taylor '84
Caddie '76
Picnic at Hanging Rock '75

Jason Weaver (1979-)

Jada '08
ATL '06
The Ladykillers '04
Drumline '02
Freedom Song '00
The Jacksons: An American Dream '92

Lee Weaver (1930-)

The Box '03
O Brother Where Art Thou? '00
My Brother's Wife '89

Loretta Weaver

Heroes of the Saddle '40
Jeepers Creepers '39

Marjorie Weaver (1913-94)

Just Off Broadway '42
The Man Who Wouldn't Die '42
Charlie Chan's Murder Cruise '40
Michael Shayne: Private Detective '40
Murder over New York '40
Young Mr. Lincoln '39
The Gentleman from California '37
Second Honeymoon '37

Michael Weaver (1971-)

The Greatest Game Ever Played '05
Club Dread '04
Super Troopers '01

Sigourney Weaver (1949-)

Crazy on the Outside '10
Avatar '09
Baby Mama '08
Be Kind Rewind '08
The Tale of Despereaux '08 (N)
Vantage Point '08
WALL-E '08 (V)
Happily N'Ever After '07 (V)
Infamous '06
Snow Cake '06
The TV Set '06
Imaginary Heroes '05
The Village '04
Holes '03
Big Bad Love '02 (V)
The Guys '02
Tadpole '02
Heartbreakers '01
Company Man '00
Galaxy Quest '99
A Map of the World '99
Alien: Resurrection '97
The Ice Storm '97
Snow White: A Tale of Terror '97
Copycat '95
Jeffrey '95
Death and the Maiden '94
Dave '93
Alien 3 '92
1492: Conquest of Paradise '92
Ghostbusters 2 '89
Gorillas in the Mist '88
Working Girl '88
Aliens '86
Half Moon Street '86
One Woman or Two '85
Ghostbusters '84
Deal of the Century '83
The Year of Living Dangerously '82
Eyewitness '81
Alien '79
Madman '79
Sorrows of Gin '79

Hugo Weaving (1959-)

The Wolfman '09
Transformers '07 (V)
Happy Feet '06 (V)
V for Vendetta '06
Little Fish '05
After the Deluge '03
Lord of the Rings: The Return of the King '03
The Matrix Reloaded '03
The Matrix Revolutions '03
Lord of the Rings: The Two Towers '02
Lord of the Rings: The Fellowship of the Ring '01
The Matrix '99
Strange Planet '99
Bedrooms and Hallways '98
The Interview '98
Babe '95 (V)
The Adventures of Priscilla, Queen of the Desert '94
The Custodian '94
Frauds '93
Reckless Kelly '93
Proof '91
The Right Hand Man '87
For Love Alone '86

Alan Webb (1906-82)

Deadly Game '82
The Great Train Robbery '79
King Lear '71
Entertaining Mr. Sloane '70
King Rat '65
The Pumpkin Eater '64
Challenge to Lassie '49

Chloe Webb (1960-)

The Newton Boys '97
She's So Lovely '97
Love Affair '94
Armistead Maupin's Tales of the City '93
A Dangerous Woman '93
The Belly of an Architect '91
Queens Logic '91
Heart Condition '90
China Beach '88
Twins '88
Sid & Nancy '86

Clifton Webb (1889-1966)

The Man Who Never Was '55
Three Coins in the Fountain '54
A Woman's World '54
Titanic '53
Stars and Stripes Forever '52
Cheaper by the Dozen '50
Sitting Pretty '48
Dark Corner '46
The Razor's Edge '46
Laura '44

Danny (Daniel) Webb (1958-)

Attack Force '06
The Hound of the Baskervilles '02
Take Me '01
Shiner '00
Frenchman's Creek '98
Love and Death on Long Island '97
A Woman's Guide to Adultery '93
Alien 3 '92
Henry V '89
Death Wish 4: The Crackdown '87
The Unapproachable '82

Greg Webb

Puppet Master 2 '90
Running Mates '86

Jack Webb (1920-82)

The Commies Are Coming, the Commies Are Coming '57
D.I. '57
Pete Kelly's Blues '55
Dragnet '54
The Halls of Montezuma '50
The Men '50
Sunset Boulevard '50
He Walked by Night '48

Richard Webb (1915-93)

Beware! The Blob '72
Hell Raiders '68
Git! '65
Attack of the Mayan Mummy '63
Carson City '52
This Woman Is Dangerous '52
Distant Drums '51
I Was a Communist for the FBI '51
Starlift '51
The Invisible Monster '50
Sands of Iwo Jima '49
Out of the Past '47
O.S.S. '46

Rita Webb (1904-81)

Frenzy '72
Zeta One '69

Veronica Webb (1965-)

In Too Deep '99
Jungle Fever '91

Diane Webber (1932-)

Sinthia: The Devil's Doll '70
The Mermaids of Tiburon '62

Mark Webber (1980-)

Shrink '09
The Good Life '07
The Hottest State '06
Bomb the System '05
Broken Flowers '05
Dear Wendy '05
Winter Solstice '04
Hollywood Ending '02
The Laramie Project '02
People I Know '02
The Rising Place '02
Chelsea Walls '01
Storytelling '01
Snow Day '00
Drive Me Crazy '99
White Boyz '99

Robert Webber (1924-89)

Nuts '87
Assassin '86
Wild Geese 2 '85
Starflight One '83
Don't Go to Sleep '82
The Final Option '82
Wrong Is Right '82
S.O.B. '81
Private Benjamin '80
The Streets of L.A. '79
10 '79
Casey's Shadow '78
Revenge of the Pink Panther '78
The Choirboys '77
Midway '76
Soldat Duroc... Ca Va Etre Ta Fete! '75
Bring Me the Head of Alfredo Garcia '74
Death Stalk '74
Dollars '71
Thief '71
The Great White Hope '70
The Big Bounce '69
Manon '68
The Dirty Dozen '67
Dead Heat on a Merry-Go-Round '66
The Silencers '66
The Sandpiper '65
Hysteria '64
The Stripper '63
Twelve Angry Men '57

Timothy Webber

Cypher '02
The Boys of St. Vincent '93
That's My Baby! '88
Toby McTeague '87
The Grey Fox '83
Terror Train '80

Amy Weber (1970-)

Crackerjack 3 '00
Kolobos '99
Art House '98
Forbidden Games '95

Dewey Weber (1971-)

Ulee's Gold '97
Chain of Desire '93

Jacques Weber (1949-)

Beaumarchais the Scoundrel '96
Northern Passage '95
The Elegant Criminal '92
Cyrano de Bergerac '90

Jake Weber (1964-)

The Haunting of Molly Hartley '08
Dawn of the Dead '04
Leo '02
Love Thy Neighbor '02
100 Mile Rule '02
Wendigo '01
The Cell '00
U-571 '00
Pushing Tin '99
Dangerous Beauty '98
Meet Joe Black '98
What the Deaf Man Heard '98
Skin Art '93

Steven Weber (1961-)

My One and Only '09
Farmhouse '08
Choose Connor '07
Inside Out '05
Masters of Horror: Jenifer '05
The Twelve Days of Christmas Eve '04
Club Land '01
Common Ground '00
Sleep Easy, Hutch Rimes '00
Time Code '00
Late Last Night '99
Love Letters '99
At First Sight '98
The Break Up '98
Sour Grapes '98
Dracula: Dead and Loving It '95
Jeffrey '95
The Kennedys of Massachusetts '95
Leaving Las Vegas '95
The Temp '93
Single White Female '92
In the Line of Duty: A Cop for the Killing '90
Hamburger Hill '87
Pudd'nhead Wilson '84

Derek Webster

Flight of the Living Dead: Outbreak on a Plane '07
Josh Kirby... Time Warrior: Chapter 5, Journey to the Magic Cavern '96
Josh Kirby... Time Warrior: Chapter 6, Last Battle for the Universe '96
Josh Kirby. . .Time Warrior: Chapter 1, Planet of the Dino-Knights '95

Josh Kirby... Time Warrior: Chapter 3, Trapped on Toyworld '95
Josh Kirby... Time Warrior: Chapter 4, Eggs from 70 Million B.C. '95

Victor Webster (1973-)
Dirty Love '05
Wishmaster 4: The Prophecy Fulfilled '02

Nick Wechsler
Fling '08
Chicks, Man '99

Chris Wedge (1957-)
Ice Age: Dawn of the Dinosaurs '09 (V)
Ice Age '02 (V)

Ann Wedgeworth (1935-)
The Hawk Is Dying '06
Hunter's Moon '97
The Whole Wide World '96
Love and a .45 '94
Cooperstown '93
Hard Promises '92
Green Card '90
Miss Firecracker '89
Steel Magnolias '89
Far North '88
Made in Heaven '87
A Tiger's Tale '87
My Science Project '85
Sweet Dreams '85
No Small Affair '84
Soggy Bottom U.S.A. '84
Killjoy '81
Bogie: The Last Hero '80
The Birch Interval '78
Citizens Band '77
One Summer Love '76
War Between the Tates '76
The Catamount Killing '74
Law and Disorder '74
Bang the Drum Slowly '73
Scarecrow '73

Barbara Weeks (1913-2003)
The Violent Years '56
Hell's Headquarters '32
White Eagle '32
Palmy Days '31
Two Fisted Justice '31

Honeysuckle Weeks
Red Mercury '05
Catherine Cookson's The Rag Nymph '96

Jimmie Ray Weeks (1942-)
Buffalo Soldiers '01
Analyze This '98
The Siege '98
Dead Man '95
The Abyss '89
Frantic '88
Apology '86
The Manhattan Project '86
Kennedy '83

Kim Weeks (1962-)
Family of Cops 3 '98
Family of Cops 2: Breach of Faith '97

Perdita Weeks (1985-)
Catherine Cookson's The Rag Nymph '96
Cold Light of Day '95

Rollo Weeks (1987-)
The Thief Lord '06
George and the Dragon '04
The Little Vampire '00

Paul Wegener (1874-1948)
Kolberg '45
One Arabian Night '21
The Golem '20
Student of Prague '13

Tang Wei
Lust, Caution '07
Dynasty '77

Virginia Weidler (1926-68)
Best Foot Forward '43
Babes on Broadway '41
All This and Heaven Too '40
The Philadelphia Story '40
Young Tom Edison '40
The Great Man Votes '38
Too Hot to Handle '38

Paul Weigel (1867-1951)
The Great Dictator '40
For Heaven's Sake '26

Rafer Weigel (1969-)
Rated X '00
Free Enterprise '98

Teri Weigel (1962-)
Auntie Lee's Meat Pies '92
Marked for Death '90
Predator 2 '90
The Banker '89
Savage Beach '89
Cheerleader Camp '88
Glitch! '88
Return of the Killer Tomatoes! '88

Robin Weigert (1969-)
My One and Only '09
The Private Lives of Pippa Lee '09
Fragments '08
Things We Lost in the Fire '07
The Good German '06
Loggerheads '05

Liza Weil (1977-)
Stir of Echoes '99
Whatever '98

Mike Weinberg (1993-)
Stolen Summer '02
Life as a House '01

Isabelle Weingarten
State of Things '82
The Mother and the Whore '73

Scott Weinger (1975-)
Aladdin and the King of Thieves '96 (V)
The Return of Jafar '94 (V)
Aladdin '92 (V)

Harvey Weinstein (1952-)
An Alan Smithee Film: Burn, Hollywood, Burn '97
Forgotten Silver '96

Josh Weinstein (1966-)
Personal Velocity: Three Portraits '02
Boys Life '94

Carl Weintraub (1946-)
Sorry, Wrong Number '89
Oliver & Company '88 (V)

Cindy Weintraub
The Prowler '81
Humanoids from the Deep '80

Heidelinde Weis (1940-)
Something for Everyone '70
The Man Outside '68

Kevin Weisman (1970-)
Space Buddies '08
Clerks 2 '06
More Dogs Than Bones '00

Robin Weisman (1984-)
Thunder in Paradise '93
Three Men and a Little Lady '90

Florence Weiss
Overture to Glory '40
The Singing Blacksmith '38
The Cantor's Son '37

Michael T. Weiss (1962-)
Iowa '05
Bones '01

Freeway 2: Confessions of a Trickbaby '99
Freeway '95
Jeffrey '95
Howling 4: The Original Nightmare '88

Roberta Weiss (1958-)
Abducted '86
Autumn Born '79

Shaun Weiss (1978-)
D3: The Mighty Ducks '96
D2: The Mighty Ducks '94
Heavyweights '94
The Mighty Ducks '92

Morgan Weisser (1971-)
Murder Without Conviction '04
Mother '94
Long Road Home '91
Prayer of the Rollerboys '91

Norbert Weisser (1946-)
Nemesis 4: Cry of Angels '97
Adrenalin: Fear the Rush '96
Nemesis 3: Time Lapse '96
Omega Doom '96
Riders of the Purple Sage '96
Heatseeker '95
Children of Fury '94
My Antonia '94
The Road to Wellville '94
Arcade '93
Schindler's List '93
Midnight Cabaret '90
Deceit '89
Secret of the Ice Cave '89
Sweet Lies '88
Android '82

Jeffrey Weissman (1958-)
Back to the Future, Part 3 '90
Back to the Future, Part 2 '89

Johnny Weissmuller (1904-84)
Swamp Fire '46
Stage Door Canteen '43
Tarzan's New York Adventure '42
Tarzan's Secret Treasure '41
Tarzan Finds a Son '39
Tarzan Escapes '36
Tarzan and His Mate '34
Tarzan, the Ape Man '32

Lucinda Weist (1963-)
The Silencers '95
The Haunting of Seacliff Inn '94

Rachel Weisz (1971-)
The Brothers Bloom '09
The Lovely Bones '09
Definitely, Maybe '08
Fred Claus '07
My Blueberry Nights '07
Eragon '06 (V)
The Fountain '06
The Constant Gardener '05
Constantine '05
Envy '04
Confidence '03
Runaway Jury '03
The Shape of Things '03
About a Boy '02
The Mummy Returns '01
Beautiful Creatures '00
Enemy at the Gates '00
The Mummy '99
Sunshine '99
I Want You '98
The Land Girls '98
Going All the Way '97
Swept from the Sea '97
Chain Reaction '96
Stealing Beauty '96

Bruce Weitz (1943-)
Half Past Dead '02
Joe and Max '02
Shot '01

Facing the Enemy '00
Mach 2 '00
Velocity Trap '99
Deep Impact '98
The Landlady '98
Memorial Day '98
Breaking the Surface: The Greg Louganis Story '96
Coyote Summer '96
Prehysteria 3 '95
Molly and Gina '94
The O.J. Simpson Story '94
Windrunner '94
The Liar's Club '93
No Place to Hide '93
The Queen of Mean '90
Rainbow Drive '90
Death of a Centerfold '81

Chris Weitz (1969-)
Mr. & Mrs. Smith '05
Chuck & Buck '00

Jess Weixler
Peter and Vandy '09
Teeth '07
The Big Bad Swim '06

Zoe Weizenbaum (1991-)
Memoirs of a Geisha '05
12 and Holding '05

Justin Welborn
The Final Destination '09
Dance of the Dead '08

Christopher Evan Welch
Vicky Cristina Barcelona '08 (V)
The Interpreter '05

Elisabeth Welch (1904-2003)
Dead of Night '45
Big Fella '37
Song of Freedom '36

Michael Welch (1987-)
The Twilight Saga: Eclipse '10
The Twilight Saga: New Moon '09
Twilight '08
United States of Leland '03
Wilderness Love '02

Niles Welch (1888-1976)
Riding Wild '35
Stone of Silver Creek '35
Badmen of Nevada '33
The Lone Avenger '33
Come on Tarzan '32
Cornered '32

Raquel Welch (1940-)
Forget About It '06
Legally Blonde '01
Tortilla Soup '01
Chairman of the Board '97
Naked Gun 33 1/3: The Final Insult '94
Tainted Blood '93
Scandal in a Small Town '88
Trouble in Paradise '88
Legend of Walks Far Woman '82
Stuntwoman '81
The Prince and the Pauper '78
Mother, Jugs and Speed '76
The Four Musketeers '75
The Three Musketeers '74
Wild Party '74
The Last of Sheila '73
Bluebeard '72
Fuzz '72
Hannie Caulder '72
Restless '72
Myra Breckinridge '70
The Magic Christian '69
100 Rifles '69
Bandolero! '68
Bedazzled '68
Lady in Cement '68
Fathom '67
Oldest Profession '67
Fantastic Voyage '66
One Million Years B.C. '66

Shoot Loud, Louder, I Don't Understand! '66
A Swingin' Summer '65
Roustabout '64

Tahnee Welch (1961-)
Johnny 2.0 '99
Blacklight '98
Body and Soul '98
I Shot Andy Warhol '96
Improper Conduct '94
The Criminal Mind '93
Night Train to Venice '93
Sleeping Beauty '89
Cocoon: The Return '88
Lethal Obsession '87
Cocoon '85

Tuesday Weld (1943-)
Chelsea Walls '01
Intimate Affairs '01
Feeling Minnesota '96
Falling Down '93
Mistress '91
Heartbreak Hotel '88
Something in Common '86
Once Upon a Time in America '84
Author! Author! '82
Thief '81
Mother & Daughter: A Loving War '80
Serial '80
A Question of Guilt '78
Who'll Stop the Rain? '78
Looking for Mr. Goodbar '77
F. Scott Fitzgerald in Hollywood '76
Reflections of Murder '74
A Safe Place '71
I Walk the Line '70
Pretty Poison '68
Lord Love a Duck '66
The Cincinnati Kid '65
I'll Take Sweden '65
Soldier in the Rain '63
Return to Peyton Place '61
Wild in the Country '61
The Five Pennies '59
Rally 'Round the Flag, Boys! '58
Rock, Rock, Rock '56

Ben Welden (1901-97)
Tales of Robin Hood '52
Tough Assignment '49
Fighting Seabees '44
Smashing the Rackets '38
The Mystery of the Mary Celeste '35

Charles Weldon
Stir Crazy '80
Dynasty '76

Joan Weldon (1933-)
The Command '54
Them! '54
So This Is Love '53
The Stranger Wore a Gun '53

Frank Welker (1946-)
Toy Story 3 '10 (V)
The Ant Bully '06 (V)
Curious George '06 (V)
Doug's 1st Movie '99 (V)
Mulan '98 (V)
Cats Don't Dance '97 (V)
Aladdin and the King of Thieves '96 (V)
Pocahontas '95 (V)
Gargoyles, The Movie: The Heroes Awaken '94 (V)
The Pagemaster '94 (V)
Aladdin '92 (V)
The Rescuers Down Under '90 (V)
My Neighbor Totoro '88 (V)
How to Frame a Figg '71

Frederick Weller (1966-)
Southern Belles '05
When Will I Be Loved '04
The Shape of Things '03
The Business of Strangers '01
Cash Crop '01
Aftershock: Earthquake in New York '99

Harvest '98
Stonewall '95

Mary Louise Weller (1946-)
Forced Vengeance '82
Q (The Winged Serpent) '82
The Evil '78
National Lampoon's Animal House '78

Peter Weller (1947-)
Undiscovered '05
The Order '03
The Contaminated Man '01
Dracula: The Dark Prince '01
Styx '00
Diplomatic Siege '99
Tower of the Firstborn '98
End of Summer '97
Top of the World '97
Screamers '96
Beyond the Clouds '95
Decoy '95
Mighty Aphrodite '95
The New Age '94
The Substitute Wife '94
Sunset Grill '92
Naked Lunch '91
Road to Ruin '91
Cat Chaser '90
Rainbow Drive '90
RoboCop 2 '90
Women & Men: Stories of Seduction '90
Leviathan '89
The Tunnel '89
Shakedown '88
RoboCop '87
Apology '86
A Killing Affair '85
Two Kinds of Love '85
The Adventures of Buckaroo Banzai Across the Eighth Dimension '84
The Dancing Princesses '84
First Born '84
Of Unknown Origin '83
Shoot the Moon '82
Butch and Sundance: The Early Days '79
The Man Without a Country '73

Gwen Welles (1949-93)
Boys Life '94
Eating '90
New Year's Day '89
Sticky Fingers '88
Desert Hearts '86
The Men's Club '86
Nobody's Fool '86
Nashville '75
Hit! '73
A Safe Place '71

Mel Welles (1924-2005)
Wizards of the Lost Kingdom 2 '89
Rented Lips '88
Commando Squad '87
Chopping Mall '86
Dr. Heckyl and Mr. Hype '80
The She-Beast '65
Little Shop of Horrors '60
Rock All Night '57
The Undead '57
Abbott and Costello Meet the Mummy '55

Orson Welles (1915-85)
Don Quixote '92
Someone to Love '87
Tales of the Klondike: In a Far Country '87 (N)
Tales of the Klondike: Race for Number One '87 (N)
Tales of the Klondike: The Scorn of Women '87 (N)
Tales of the Klondike: The Unexpected '87 (N)
Transformers: The Movie '86 (V)
Scene of the Crime '85 (N)
Slapstick of Another Kind '84
Butterfly '82
History of the World: Part 1 '81 (N)
Shogun '80 (N)

Blood and Guns *'79*
The Double McGuffin *'79 (V)*
Hot Money *'79*
The Muppet Movie *'79*
Battleforce *'78 (N)*
America at the Movies *'76*
Voyage of the Damned *'76*
Ten Little Indians *'75*
Get to Know Your Rabbit *'72*
Ten Days Wonder *'72*
Treasure Island *'72*
The Witching *'72*
A Safe Place *'71*
Waterloo *'71*
Catch-22 *'70*
Start the Revolution without Me *'70*
12 Plus 1 *'70*
Battle of Neretva *'69*
Casino Royale *'67*
Chimes at Midnight *'67*
I'll Never Forget What's 'Isname *'67*
Is Paris Burning? *'66*
A Man for All Seasons *'66*
The Trial *'63*
The V.I.P.'s *'63*
RoGoPaG *'62*
The King of Kings *'61 (N)*
The Battle of Austerlitz *'60*
Compulsion *'59*
Ferry to Hong Kong *'59*
The Long, Hot Summer *'58*
Touch of Evil *'58*
The Vikings *'58 (N)*
Man in the Shadow *'57*
Moby Dick *'56*
Mr. Arkadin *'55*
Napoleon *'55*
Three Cases of Murder *'55*
Trouble in the Glen *'54*
Othello *'52*
Little World of Don Camillo *'51 (N)*
The Black Rose *'50*
Black Magic *'49*
Prince of Foxes *'49*
The Third Man *'49*
The Lady from Shanghai *'48*
Macbeth *'48*
The Stranger *'46*
Tomorrow Is Forever *'46*
Jane Eyre *'44*
Journey into Fear *'42*
Citizen Kane *'41*

Virginia Welles (1925-)
Francis in the Haunted House *'56*
Dynamite *'49*
To Each His Own *'46*

Tom Welling (1977-)
Cheaper by the Dozen 2 *'05*
The Fog *'05*
Cheaper by the Dozen *'03*

Titus Welliver (1961-)
Gone Baby Gone *'07*
Assault on Precinct 13 *'05*
Twisted *'04*
Biker Boyz *'03*
Blonde *'01*
Once in the Life *'00*
Rough Riders *'97*
The Big Fall *'96*
Zero Tolerance *'93*
The Lost Capone *'90*

William Wellman, Jr. (1937-)
Curfew *'88*
The Prodigal Planet *'88*
It's Alive *'74*
The Trial of Billy Jack *'74*
Born Losers *'67*
A Swingin' Summer *'65*
Macumba Love *'60*
High School Confidential *'58*
Lafayette Escadrille *'58*

William A. Wellman (1896-1975)
Wings *'27*
The Boob *'26*

Carole Wells (1942-)
Funny Lady *'75*
The House of Seven Corpses *'73*

David Wells
Inherit the Wind *'99*
Wild Cactus *'92*

Dawn Wells (1938-)
Super Sucker *'03*
Evil Lives *'92*
Rescue from Gilligan's Island *'78*
Return to Boggy Creek *'77*
Town That Dreaded Sundown *'76*
Winterhawk *'76*

Dolores Wells (1937-)
Bikini Beach *'64*
Muscle Beach Party *'64*
The Time Travelers *'64*
Beach Party *'63*

Jacqueline Wells
See Julie Bishop

John Wells (1936-98)
Princess Caraboo *'94*
Consuming Passions *'88*
Rentadick *'72*

Stuart Wells (1982-)
The Reckoning *'03*
Billy Elliot *'00*

Tico Wells
All About You *'01*
The Five Heartbeats *'91*

Tracy Wells (1971-)
Mirror, Mirror 2: Raven Dance *'94*
After Midnight *'89*

Vernon Wells (1945-)
The Strange Case of Dr. Jekyll and Mr. Hyde *'06*
King of the Ants *'03*
Beneath Loch Ness *'01*
Space Truckers *'97*
Hard Justice *'95*
Bounty Hunter 2002 *'94*
Plughead Rewired: Circuitry Man 2 *'94*
Stranglehold *'94*
Sexual Response *'92*
Enemy Unseen *'91*
Undeclared War *'91*
American Eagle *'90*
Circuitry Man *'90*
Crossing the Line *'90*
The Shrimp on the Barbie *'90*
Circle of Fear *'89*
Nam Angels *'88*
Circle Man *'87*
Innerspace *'87*
Last Man Standing *'87*
Commando *'85*
The Road Warrior *'82*

John Welsh (1904-85)
The Duchess of Duke Street *'78*
The Moonstone *'72*
Lucky Jim *'58*
The Revenge of Frankenstein *'58*

Kenneth Welsh (1942-)
Survival of the Dead *'09*
Adoration *'08*
Silk *'07*
The Hades Factor *'06*
Bailey's Billion$ *'05*
The Exorcism of Emily Rose *'05*
The Fog *'05*
Four Brothers *'05*
The Aviator *'04*
The Day After Tomorrow *'04*
Miracle *'04*
Eloise at the Plaza *'03*
The Day Reagan Was Shot *'01*
Deliberate Intent *'01*
Focus *'01*
The Sign of Four *'01*
The Hound of the Baskervilles *'00*
Love Come Down *'00*
Vendetta *'99*
Habitat *'97*
Jack Higgins' Thunder Point *'97*
Joe Torre: Curveballs Along the Way *'97*
Dead Silence *'96*
Escape Clause *'96*
Kissinger and Nixon *'96*
Rowing Through *'96*
The Wrong Guy *'96*
Hiroshima *'95*
Margaret's Museum *'95*
Portraits of a Killer *'95*
Another Woman *'94*
Death Wish 5: The Face of Death *'94*
Getting Gotti *'94*
Legends of the Fall *'94*
The Spider and the Fly *'94*
Timecop *'94*
Whale Music *'94*
Adrift *'93*
Dead Ahead: The Exxon Valdez Disaster *'92*
The Good Fight *'92*
Love, Lies and Murder *'91*
Perfectly Normal *'91*
The Big Slice *'90*
The Last Best Year *'90*
Love and Hate: A Marriage Made in Hell *'90*
And Then You Die *'88*
Another Woman *'88*
Crocodile Dundee 2 *'88*
The Climb *'87*
Lost *'86*
Loyalties *'86*
Screwball Academy *'86*
The War Boy *'85*
Reno and the Doc *'84*
Of Unknown Origin *'83*

Margaret Welsh
American Heart *'92*
Mr. & Mrs. Bridge *'90*
Smooth Talk *'85*

William Welsh (1870-1946)
20,000 Leagues under the Sea *'16*
Traffic in Souls *'13*

Ariadne Welter (1931-99)
The Brainiac *'61*
The Devil's Hand *'61*
The Vampire's Coffin *'58*
The Vampire *'57*
The Criminal Life of Archibaldo de la Cruz *'55*

Hsueh-erh Wen
The Master *'80*
Sword Masters: Two Champions of Shaolin *'80*

Jiang Wen
Warriors of Heaven and Earth *'03*
Devils on the Doorstep *'00*
The Emperor's Shadow *'96*
Red Sorghum *'87*

Lara Wendel (1965-)
Ghosthouse *'88*
Intervista *'87*
Unsane *'82*

Alan J. Wendl
Serial Mom *'94*
Hairspray *'88*

George Wendt (1948-)
Santa Buddies *'09*
Santa Baby *'06*
Edmond *'05*
Kids in America *'05*
Masters of Horror: Family *'05*
King of the Ants *'03*
Strange Relations *'02*
Lakeboat *'00*
The Prime Gig *'00*
Alice in Wonderland *'99*
Outside Providence *'99*
The Pooch and the Pauper *'99*
Rupert's Land *'98*
Space Truckers *'97*
Spice World: The Movie *'97*
Alien Avengers *'96*
Bye Bye Birdie *'95*
Man of the House *'95*
Hostage for a Day *'94*
Forever Young *'92*
Guilty by Suspicion *'91*
The Masters of Menace *'90*
Never Say Die *'90*
Plain Clothes *'88*
House *'86*
Fletch *'85*
Gung Ho *'85*
Dreamscape *'84*
No Small Affair *'84*
Ratings Game *'84*
Thief of Hearts *'84*
Jekyll & Hyde... Together Again *'82*
My Bodyguard *'80*

John Wengraf (1897-1974)
Return of Dracula *'58*
The Pride and the Passion *'57*
Five Fingers *'52*
The Razor's Edge *'46*
The Seventh Cross *'44*
U-Boat Prisoner *'44*
Sahara *'43*

David Wenham (1965-)
Public Enemies *'09*
Australia *'08*
The Children of Huang Shi *'08*
Married Life *'07*
300 *'07*
The Proposition *'05*
Van Helsing *'04*
After the Deluge *'03*
Lord of the Rings: The Return of the King *'03*
The Crocodile Hunter: Collision Course *'02*
Lord of the Rings: The Two Towers *'02*
Pure *'02*
The Bank *'01*
Dust *'01*
Moulin Rouge *'01*
Better Than Sex *'00*
Molokai: The Story of Father Damien *'99*
The Boys *'98*
A Little Bit of Soul *'97*
Cosi *'95*

Jann Wenner
Almost Famous *'00*
Perfect *'85*

Alexandra Wentworth (1965-)
It's Complicated *'09*
American Virgin *'98*
Meeting Daddy *'98*
Office Space *'98*
The Love Bug *'97*
Trial and Error *'96*

Martha Wentworth (1889-1974)
The Sword in the Stone *'63 (V)*
Jupiter's Darling *'55*
Homesteaders of Paradise Valley *'47*
Santa Fe Uprising *'46*
Stagecoach to Denver *'46*
The Stranger *'46*
Vigilantes of Boom Town *'46*
Clancy Street Boys *'43*

Fritz Wepper (1941-)
Le Dernier Combat *'84*
Cabaret *'72*
The Bridge *'59*

Jan Werich (1905-80)
Fabulous Adventures of Baron Munchausen *'61*
The Original Fabulous Adventures of Baron Munchausen *'61*

Barbara Werle
Charro! *'69*
Krakatoa East of Java *'69*
Battle of the Bulge *'65*

Oskar Werner (1922-84)
Voyage of the Damned *'76*
The Shoes of the Fisherman *'68*
Fahrenheit 451 *'66*
Ship of Fools *'65*
The Spy Who Came in from the Cold *'65*
Jules and Jim *'62*
The Life and Loves of Mozart *'59*
Lola Montes *'55*
Angel with the Trumpet *'50*

Roy Werner (1957-)
In Enemy Hands *'04*
Loco Love *'03*

Otto Wernicke (1893-1965)
Crimes of Dr. Mabuse *'32*
M *'31*

Gary Werntz
Pay It Forward *'00*
Deep Impact *'98*
The Peacemaker *'97*
The Art of Dying *'90*

Doug Wert (1961-)
Baby Face Nelson *'97*
The Wasp Woman *'96*
Haunted Symphony *'94*
Roswell: The U.F.O. Cover-Up *'94*
Dracula Rising *'93*
The Assassination Game *'92*

Massimo Wertmuller (1956-)
Summer Night with Greek Profile, Almond Eyes & Scent of Basil *'87*
Sotto, Sotto *'85*

Paul Wesley (1982-)
Killer Movie *'08*
That Russell Girl *'08*
Full Count *'06*
Peaceful Warrior *'06*
Roll Bounce *'05*

Dick Wessel (1913-65)
Corky of Gasoline Alley *'51*
Flying Leathernecks *'51*
Gasoline Alley *'51*
Starlift *'51*
Pitfall *'48*
Dick Tracy vs. Cueball *'46*
X Marks the Spot *'42*
Tanks a Million *'41*
They Died with Their Boots On *'41*

Dick Wesson (1919-79)
The Errand Boy *'61*
Calamity Jane *'53*
The Desert Song *'53*
Jim Thorpe: All American *'51*
Destination Moon *'50*

Adam West (1928-)
Super Capers *'09*
Meet the Robinsons *'07 (V)*
Chicken Little *'05 (V)*
Baadasssss! *'03*
Drop Dead Gorgeous *'99*
American Vampire *'97*
Joyride *'97*
The New Age *'94*
Maxim Xul *'91*
Night of the Kickfighters *'91*
Mad About You *'90*
Omega Cop *'90*
Doin' Time on Planet Earth *'88*
Return Fire *'88*
Zombie Nightmare *'86*
Young Lady Chatterly 2 *'85*
Hellriders *'84*
One Dark Night *'82*
For the Love of It *'80*
The Happy Hooker Goes Hollywood *'80*
Hooper *'78*
Hell River *'75*
The Specialist *'75*
Batman *'66*
The Outlaws Is Coming! *'65*
Robinson Crusoe on Mars *'64*
Geronimo *'62*

Billy West (1950-)
Queer Duck: The Movie *'06 (V)*
Comic Book: The Movie *'04*
Popeye's Voyage: The Quest for Pappy *'04*
Looney Tunes: Back in Action *'03 (V)*
Joe's Apartment *'96 (V)*

Chandra West (1970-)
Badland *'07*
I Now Pronounce You Chuck and Larry *'07*
The Tooth Fairy *'06*
The Long Weekend *'05*
White Noise *'05*
Category 6 : Day of Destruction *'04*
Water's Edge *'03*
The Salton Sea *'02*
The Perfect Son *'00*
The '70s *'00*
Something More *'99*
Universal Soldier 2: Brothers in Arms *'98*
Universal Soldier 3: Unfinished Business *'98*
The Waiting Game *'98*
Puppet Master 5: The Final Chapter *'94*
Puppet Master 4 *'93*

Dominic West (1969-)
Punisher: War Zone *'08*
Hannibal Rising *'07*
300 *'07*
The Forgotten *'04*
Mona Lisa Smile *'03*
Chicago *'02*
Rock Star *'01*
28 Days *'00*
A Christmas Carol *'99*
William Shakespeare's A Midsummer Night's Dream *'99*
The Gambler *'97*
Wavelength *'96*

Gregory West
The Surgeon *'94*
Class of 1999 2: The Substitute *'93*

Jeremy West
Curse 4: The Ultimate Sacrifice *'90*
Catacombs *'89*

Joel West (1975-)
Blood Surf *'00*
The Smokers *'00*

Kevin West (1965-)
Bio-Dome *'96*
Killer Tomatoes Eat France *'91*
Killer Tomatoes Strike Back *'90*

Lockwood West (1905-89)
Bedazzled *'68*
The Leather Boys *'63*

Mae West (1893-1980)
Sextette *'78*
Myra Breckinridge *'70*
The Love Goddesses *'65*
The Heat's On *'43*
My Little Chickadee *'40*
Every Day's a Holiday *'38*
Go West, Young Man *'36*
Klondike Annie *'36*
Goin' to Town *'35*
Belle of the Nineties *'34*
I'm No Angel *'33*
She Done Him Wrong *'33*
Night After Night *'32*

Martin West
Assault on Precinct 13 *'76*
Sweet November *'68*
Lord Love a Duck *'66*
A Swingin' Summer *'65*

Nathan West (1978-)
Forever Strong *'08*
Miracle *'04*
Home Room *'02*
The Skulls 2 *'02*

Norma West (1943-)
Cause Celebre *'87*
And the Ship Sails On *'83*

Red West (1936-)
Goodbye Solo *'08*
Forty Shades of Blue *'05*
John Grisham's The Rainmaker *'97*
The P.A.C.K. *'96*
The Expert *'95*
Grizzly Adams: The Legend Continues *'90*
Proud Men *'87*
Hard Knox *'83*
Will: G. Gordon Liddy *'82*

Samuel West (1966-)
Van Helsing *'04*
Cambridge Spies *'03*
Iris *'01*
Longitude *'00*
Pandaemonium *'00*
Horatio Hornblower *'99*
Retribution *'98*
Rupert's Land *'98*
The Ripper *'97*
Stiff Upper Lips *'96*
Carrington *'95*
Persuasion *'95*
The Vacillations of Poppy Carew *'94*
Howard's End *'92*
Reunion *'88*

Shane West (1978-)
Echelon Conspiracy *'09*
The Lodger *'09*
Red Sands *'09*
What We Do Is Secret *'07*
The Elder Son *'06*
The League of Extraordinary Gentlemen *'03*
A Walk to Remember *'02*
Get Over It! *'01*
A Time for Dancing *'00*
Whatever It Takes *'00*
Get a Clue! *'98*

Tegan West
Hi-Life *'98*
Sleep with Me *'94*
Hamburger Hill *'87*

Timothy West (1934-)
Endgame *'09*
A Room With a View *'08*
Bleak House *'05*
Beyond Borders *'03*
Sinbad: Legend of the Seven Seas *'03 (V)*
The Fourth Angel *'01*
Iris *'01*
Station Jim *'01*
102 Dalmatians *'00*
Ever After: A Cinderella Story *'98*
King Lear *'98*
Hiroshima *'95*
Framed *'93*
Tragedy of Flight 103: The Inside Story *'91*
Consuming Passions *'88*
Cry Freedom *'87*
Death by Prescription *'86*
The Last Bastion *'84*
Oliver Twist *'82*
Churchill and the Generals *'81*
Rough Cut *'80*
Agatha *'79*
Edward the King *'75*
Hedda *'75*

Simon Westaway (1958-)
Alien Cargo *'99*
Chameleon 2: Death Match *'99*
When Love Comes *'98*
The Thorn Birds: The Missing Years *'96*

John Westbrook (1922-89)
Masque of the Red Death *'65*
Tomb of Ligeia *'64*
Room at the Top *'59*

Helen Westcott (1927-98)
The Invisible Avenger *'58*
Abbott and Costello Meet Dr. Jekyll and Mr. Hyde *'52*
With a Song in My Heart *'52*
The Gunfighter *'50*
Thunder Over Texas *'34*

Travis Wester (1977-)
All Souls Day *'05*
Eurotrip *'04*
The Paper Brigade *'96*

James Westerfield (1913-71)
Born in America *'90*
True Grit *'69*
That Funny Feeling *'65*
Homicidal *'61*
The Gunfight at Dodge City *'59*

Hakan Westergren (1899-1981)
Dollar *'38*
Swedenhielms *'35*

Carlie Westerman
Me and You and Everyone We Know *'05*
King of the Ants *'03*

Floyd "Red Crow" Westerman (1936-2007)
Comanche Moon *'08*
Swing Vote *'08*
Hidalgo *'04*
The Last Assassins *'96*
Buffalo Girls *'95*
Lakota Woman: Siege at Wounded Knee *'94*
The Broken Chain *'93*
Walker: Texas Ranger: One Riot, One Ranger *'93*
Clearcut *'92*
Dances with Wolves *'90*

Jennifer Westfeldt (1970-)
Ira & Abby *'06*
How to Lose Your Lover *'04*
Kissing Jessica Stein *'02*

Dr. Ruth Westheimer (1928-)
Forever, Lulu *'87*
One Woman or Two *'85*

Helen Westley (1875-1942)
Lady from Louisiana *'42*
Sunny *'41*
All This and Heaven Too *'40*
Lillian Russell *'40*
Alexander's Ragtime Band *'38*
Rebecca of Sunnybrook Farm *'38*
Cafe Metropole *'37*
Heidi *'37*
Dimples *'36*
Stowaway *'36*
Splendor *'35*
Anne of Green Gables *'34*
Death Takes a Holiday *'34*

Nydia Westman (1902-70)
Velvet Touch *'48*
The Chocolate Soldier *'41*
Bulldog Drummond's Revenge *'37*
One Night of Love *'34*
King of the Jungle *'33*

Matt Westmore
Charlotte Sometimes *'02*
Shakedown *'02*
Hard As Nails *'01*

James Westmoreland (1935-)
Don't Answer the Phone *'80*
Stacey *'73*
The Undertaker and His Pals *'67*
Journey Beneath the Desert *'61*

Cecil Weston
Belles on Their Toes *'52*
Money Madness *'47*

Celia Weston (1951-)
The Invasion *'07*
Joshua *'07*
No Reservations *'07*
Junebug *'05*
The Village *'04*
Hulk *'03*
Undermind *'03*
Far from Heaven *'02*
Hearts in Atlantis *'01*
In the Bedroom *'01*
K-PAX *'01*
Joe Gould's Secret *'00*
Ride with the Devil *'99*
Snow Falling on Cedars *'99*
Dead Man Walking *'95*
Flirting with Disaster *'95*
Little Man Tate *'91*
Lost Angels *'89*

David Weston (1938-)
The Heroes of Telemark *'65*
Masque of the Red Death *'65*

Doris Weston (1917-60)
Chip of the Flying U *'39*
Born to Be Wild *'38*
Delinquent Parents *'38*

Jack Weston (1924-96)
Short Circuit 2 *'88*
Dirty Dancing *'87*
Ishtar *'87*
The Longshot *'86*
Rad *'86*
High Road to China *'83*
The Four Seasons *'81*
Cuba *'79*
Gator *'76*
The Ritz *'76*
Marco *'73*
Fuzz *'72*
A New Leaf *'71*
Cactus Flower *'69*
The Thomas Crown Affair *'68*
Wait until Dark *'67*
Mirage *'66*
The Cincinnati Kid *'65*
The Incredible Mr. Limpet *'64*
Palm Springs Weekend *'63*
The Honeymoon Machine *'61*
Please Don't Eat the Daisies *'60*

Jeff Weston (1960-)
Demonic Toys *'90*
Puppet Master 2 *'90*

Michael Weston (1973-)
Pathology *'08*
The Last Kiss *'06*
The Dukes of Hazzard *'05*
Garden State *'04*
Hart's War *'02*
Coyote Ugly *'00*
Lucky Numbers *'00*

Ed Westwick (1987-)
S. Darko: A Donnie Darko Tale *'09*
100 Feet *'08*
Son of Rambow *'07*

Jack Wetherall
Third Man Out: A Donald Strachey Mystery *'05*
The Victory *'81*

Virginia Wetherell (1943-)
Dracula *'73*
Demons of the Mind *'72*
Disciple of Death *'72*
The Big Switch *'70*
The Crimson Cult *'68*

Patricia Wettig (1951-)
Bongwater *'98*
Dancer, Texas—Pop. 81 *'98*
Stephen King's The Langoliers *'95*
City Slickers 2: The Legend of Curly's Gold *'94*
Parallel Lives *'94*
Me & Veronica *'93*
City Slickers *'91*
Guilty by Suspicion *'91*
Silent Motive *'91*

Merritt Wever
Series 7: The Contenders *'01*
All I Wanna Do *'98*

Marius Weyers (1945-)
Charlie *'04*
Stander *'03*
Bopha! *'93*
The Power of One *'92*
Deepstar Six *'89*
Farewell to the King *'89*
Happy Together *'89*
The Gods Must Be Crazy *'84*
African Rage *'78*

Ruth Weyher
Secrets of a Soul *'25*
Warning Shadows *'23*

Michael Whalen (1902-74)
Missile to the Moon *'59*
The Phantom from 10,000 Leagues *'56*
G.I. Jane *'51*
Kentucky Jubilee *'51*
King of the Bullwhip *'51*
Mask of the Dragon *'51*
Omoo Omoo, the Shark God *'49*
Shep Comes Home *'49*
Sky Liner *'49*
Thunder in the Pines *'49*
Tough Assignment *'49*
Highway 13 *'48*
Dawn Express *'42*
Wee Willie Winkie *'37*
The Poor Little Rich Girl *'36*

Sean M. Whalen (1965-)
Employee of the Month *'06*
Chasing Ghosts *'05*
The Last Shot *'04*
Charlie's Angels *'00*
Perfect Murder, Perfect Town *'00*
Idle Hands *'99*
Never Been Kissed *'99*
Suicide Kings *'97*
The Cable Guy *'96*
That Thing You Do! *'96*
Twister *'96*
Waterworld *'95*
The People under the Stairs *'91*

Frank Whaley (1963-)
The Cell 2 *'09*
Cherry Crush *'07*
Vacancy *'07*
Crazy Eights *'06*
Mrs. Harris *'05*
Red Dragon *'02*
Chelsea Walls *'01*
The Jimmy Show *'01*
Pursuit of Happiness *'01*
The Wall *'99*
Went to Coney Island on a Mission from God... Be Back by Five *'98*
When Trumpets Fade *'98*
Bombshell *'97*
Cafe Society *'97*
Curtain Call *'97*
Glam *'97*
Retroactive *'97*
The Winner *'96*
Broken Arrow *'95*
Homage *'95*
The Desperate Trail *'94*
I.Q. *'94*
Pulp Fiction *'94*
Swimming with Sharks *'94*
Swing Kids *'93*
To Dance with the White Dog *'93*
Back in the USSR *'92*
Hoffa *'92*
A Midnight Clear *'92*
Career Opportunities *'91*
The Doors *'91*
JFK *'91*
The Freshman *'90*
Born on the Fourth of July *'89*
Field of Dreams *'89*
Little Monsters *'89*
Ironweed *'87*

Justin Whalin (1974-)
Super Capers *'09*
Dungeons and Dragons *'00*
Final Encounter *'00*
Miracle at Midnight *'98*
Serial Mom *'94*
White Wolves 2: Legend of the Wild *'94*
The Fire Next Time *'93*
Child's Play 3 *'91*
Perfect Harmony *'91*
The Dead Pool *'88*

Joanne Whalley (1964-)
Flood *'07*
Played *'06*
Breathtaking *'00*
Ride the Wild Fields *'00*
The Guilty *'99*
A Texas Funeral *'99*
The Man Who Knew Too Little *'97*
A Good Man in Africa *'94*
Mother's Boys *'94*
Scarlett *'94*
The Secret Rapture *'94*
Trial by Jury *'94*
Storyville *'92*
The Big Man: Crossing the Line *'91*
Shattered *'91*
Navy SEALS *'90*
Kill Me Again *'89*
Scandal *'89*
To Kill a Priest *'89*
Willow *'88*
The Good Father *'87*
Edge of Darkness *'86*
No Surrender *'86*
The Singing Detective *'86*
Dance with a Stranger *'85*
Pink Floyd: The Wall *'82*

Kevin Whately (1951-)
Plain Jane *'01*
The English Patient *'96*

Liem Whatley
Heaven and Earth *'93*
The Iron Triangle *'89*

Alan Wheatley (1907-91)
Robin Hood: The Movie *'55*
The Limping Man *'53*
Home to Danger *'51*
Calling Paul Temple *'48*
Counterblast *'48*
Brighton Rock *'47*
Appointment with Crime *'45*

Thomas Wheatley (1951-)
Piglet's Big Movie *'03 (V)*
Where Angels Fear to Tread *'91*

Wil Wheaton (1972-)
Star Trek: Nemesis *'02*
Deep Core *'00*
Python *'00*
Flubber *'97*
Mr. Stitch *'95*
Pie in the Sky *'95*
The Liar's Club *'93*
December *'91*
The Last Prostitute *'91*
Toy Soldiers *'91*
The Curse *'87*
Long Time Gone *'86*
Stand by Me *'86*
The Last Starfighter *'84*
The Buddy System *'83*
The Secret of NIMH *'82 (V)*

Bert Wheeler (1895-1968)
Cockeyed Cavaliers *'34*
Hips, Hips, Hooray *'34*
Kentucky Kernels *'34*
Diplomaniacs *'33*
So This Is Africa *'33*
Hold 'Em Jail *'32*
Dixiana *'30*
Half-Shot at Sunrise *'30*
Hook, Line and Sinker *'30*
Rio Rita *'29*

Jane Wheeler
The Kid *'97*
Marked Man *'96*
The Neighbor *'93*

John Wheeler
Lucy and Desi: Before the Laughter *'91*
Bad Georgia Road *'77*

Dana Wheeler-Nicholson (1960-)
Living in Peril *'97*
Nick and Jane *'96*
Denise Calls Up *'95*
The Pompatus of Love *'95*
Bye Bye, Love *'94*
My Life's in Turnaround *'94*
The Night We Never Met *'93*
Tombstone *'93*
Circuitry Man *'90*
Fletch *'85*
Mrs. Soffel *'84*

Arleen Whelan (1916-93)
The Sun Shines Bright *'53*
Never Wave at a WAC *'52*
Ramrod *'47*
Castle in the Desert *'42*
Charley's Aunt *'41*
Young People *'40*
Young Mr. Lincoln *'39*
Thanks for Everything *'38*

Lisa Whelchel (1963-)
Where the Red Fern Grows: Part 2 *'92*
Twirl *'81*
The Double McGuffin *'79*
The Magician of Lublin *'79*

Shea Whigham (1969-)
Bad Lieutenant: Port of Call New Orleans *'09*
The Killing Room *'09*
Pride and Glory *'08*
First Snow *'07*
Wristcutters: A Love Story *'06*
Man of the House *'05*
All the Real Girls *'03*
Tigerland *'00*

Manning Whiley (1915-75)
Meet Sexton Blake *'44*
The Dummy Talks *'43*

Barbara Whinnery
Hot to Trot! *'88*
Crawlspace *'86*

Joseph Whipp (1941-)
Red Shoe Diaries: Luscious Lola *'00*
A Place Called Truth *'98*
Amazons *'86*

Sam Whipple (1961-2002)
The Rock *'96*
Airheads *'94*
T Bone N Weasel *'92*
Archie: Return to Riverdale *'90*
Jekyll & Hyde... Together Again *'82*
Grad Night *'81*

Shannon Whirry (1964-)
Mach 2 *'00*
Me, Myself, and Irene *'00*
The Prophet's Game *'99*
Retroactive *'97*
Omega Doom *'96*
Dangerous Prey *'95*
Exit *'95*
Playback *'95*
Animal Instincts 2 *'94*
The Granny *'94*
Lady in Waiting *'94*

Private Obsession '94
Body of Influence '93
Mirror Images 2 '93
Animal Instincts '92

Ben Whishaw (1980-)
Bright Star '09
Brideshead Revisited '08
I'm Not There '07
Perfume: The Story of a Murderer '06
Layer Cake '05
Stoned '05

Charles "Slim" Whitaker (1893-1960)
Outlaw of the Plains '46
Raiders of Red Gap '43
The Mysterious Rider '42
Battling Outlaw '40
Bullet Code '40
Cheyenne Rides Again '38
Phantom Gold '38
Melody of the Plains '37
Roaring Six Guns '37
Santa Fe Bound '37
Everyman's Law '36
Fast Bullets '36
Pinto Rustlers '36
Border Vengeance '35
Silent Valley '35
The Man from Hell '34
The Silver Bullet '34
Deadwood Pass '33
The Fiddlin' Buckaroo '33
Man from Monterey '33
Ghost Valley '32
The Saddle Buster '32
Desert of the Lost '27

Christina Whitaker
Assault of the Killer Bimbos '88
Vampire at Midnight '88
Naked Cage '86

Damon Whitaker (1970-)
Saints and Sinners '95
Bird '88

Denzel Whitaker
Bad Lieutenant: Port of Call New Orleans '09
The Great Debaters '07

Duane Whitaker (1959-)
Feast '06
The Devil's Rejects '05
From Dusk Till Dawn 2: Texas Blood Money '98
Spoiler '98
Tales from the Hood '95
Pulp Fiction '94
Eddie Presley '92

Forest Whitaker (1961-)
Our Family Wedding '10
Repo Men '10
Powder Blue '09
Where the Wild Things Are '09 (V)
Fragments '08
Hurricane Season '08
Street Kings '08
Vantage Point '08
The Air I Breathe '07
The Great Debaters '07
Ripple Effect '07
Even Money '06
Everyone's Hero '06 (V)
The Last King of Scotland '06
American Gun '05
Jiminy Glick in LaLa Wood '05
A Little Trip to Heaven '05
First Daughter '04 (N)
Panic Room '02
Phone Booth '02
Anne Rice's The Feast of All Saints '01
The Fourth Angel '01
Green Dragon '01
Battlefield Earth '00
Four Dogs Playing Poker '00
Ghost Dog: The Way of the Samurai '99
Light It Up '99
Witness Protection '99
Body Count '97
Phenomenon '96
Rebound: The Legend of Earl "The Goat" Manigault '96
Smoke '95
Species '95
Blown Away '94
The Enemy Within '94
Jason's Lyric '94
Lush Life '94
Ready to Wear '94
Bank Robber '93
Body Snatchers '93
Last Light '93
Article 99 '92
Consenting Adults '92
The Crying Game '92
Diary of a Hitman '91
A Rage in Harlem '91
Criminal Justice '90
Downtown '89
Johnny Handsome '89
Bird '88
Bloodsport '88
Good Morning, Vietnam '87
Stakeout '87
The Color of Money '86
Platoon '86
Vision Quest '85
Fast Times at Ridgemont High '82

Johnny Whitaker (1959-)
Tom Sawyer '73
Napoleon and Samantha '72
The Littlest Angel '69

Slim Whitaker
The Drifter '44
The Silver Bullet '42
Rio Grande Ranger '37
Unconquered Bandit '35

Alice White (1904-83)
Flamingo Road '49
Employees' Entrance '33
Picture Snatcher '33
Murder at Midnight '31
Playing Around '30
Show Girl in Hollywood '30

Bernie (Bernard) White (1959-)
American Dreamz '06
Land of Plenty '04
Killing Obsession '94
The Abduction of Allison Tate '92
Twenty Dollar Star '91
No Way Back '90
Ain't No Way Back '89
Body Count '87

Betty White (1922-)
The Proposal '09
Ponyo '08 (V)
Bringing Down the House '03
Whispers: An Elephant's Tale '00 (V)
Lake Placid '99
The Story of Us '99
Dennis the Menace Strikes Again '98
Hard Rain '97
A Weekend in the Country '96
Advise and Consent '62

Brian White (1973-)
Fighting '09
I Can Do Bad All By Myself '09
12 Rounds '09
In the Name of the King: A Dungeon Siege Tale '08
The Game Plan '07
Stomp the Yard '07
Brick '06
DOA: Dead or Alive '06
The Family Stone '05
Mr. 3000 '04

Bridget Ann White
Depth Charge '08
A Boyfriend for Christmas '04
The Apostate '98

Carol White (1942-91)
The Squeeze '77
Some Call It Loving '73
Man Who Had Power Over Women '70
Daddy's Gone A-Hunting '69
The Fixer '68
I'll Never Forget What's 'Is-name '67
Prehistoric Women '67
A Matter of WHO '62
Never Let Go '60

Dan(iel) White (1908-80)
Attack of the Giant Leeches '59
The Last Hunt '56
Outlaw Country '49

David White (1916-90)
The Amazing Spider-Man '77
The Tender Trap '55

David A.R. White (1970-)
Six: The Mark Unleashed '04
Mercy Streets '00

De'voreaux White
Die Hard '88
The Children of Times Square '86

Diz White
Stoogemania '85
Bullshot '83

Earl White
Omega Doom '96
Nemesis 2: Nebula '94

Harriet White (1914-2005)
The Ghost '63
Paisan '46

Harrison White
I Got the Hook-Up '98
Doom Asylum '88

Jack White (1975-)
It Might Get Loud '09
Walk Hard: The Dewey Cox Story '07
Coffee and Cigarettes '03
Cold Mountain '03

Jacqueline White (1922-)
The Narrow Margin '52
The Capture '50
Riders of the Range '50
Return of the Bad Men '48
The Show-Off '46
Thirty Seconds Over Tokyo '44
Air Raid Wardens '43

Jaleel White (1976-)
Beach Kings '08
Miracle Dogs Too '06
Who Made the Potatoe Salad? '05
Quest for Camelot '98 (V)
Silence of the Heart '84

Jeremy White
Twelve '10
Afterschool '08

Jesse White (1919-97)
Matinee '92
Monster in the Closet '86
Bless the Beasts and Children '71
Togetherness '70
The Reluctant Astronaut '67
Ghost in the Invisible Bikini '66
Pajama Party '64
Three Blondes in His Life '61
The Rise and Fall of Legs Diamond '60
Tomboy & the Champ '58
Designing Woman '57
The Bad Seed '56
Forever Female '53
Gunsmoke '53
Million Dollar Mermaid '52
Bedtime for Bonzo '51
Francis Goes to the Races '51
Harvey '50

John White (1981-)
American Pie Presents: Beta House '07
American Pie Presents: The Naked Mile '06
The Legend of Gator Face '96

Julie White
Monsters vs. Aliens '09 (V)
Transformers '07
Slap Her, She's French '02
The Heidi Chronicles '95

Lee White (1888-1949)
Red Rock Outlaw '47
In Old New Mexico '45
Oklahoma Renegades '40

Lillias White
Game 6 '05
Pieces of April '03

Marjorie White
Diplomaniacs '33
The Black Camel '31

Michael Jai White (1967-)
Tyler Perry's Why Did I Get Married Too? '10
Black Dynamite '09
The Dark Knight '08
Tyler Perry's Why Did I Get Married? '07
Undisputed II: Last Man Standing '06
Silver Hawk '04
Exit Wounds '01
Freedom Song '00
Mutiny '99
Thick as Thieves '99
Universal Soldier: The Return '99
Ringmaster '98
Spawn '97
City of Industry '96
Tyson '95

Mike White (1970-)
Gentlemen Broncos '09
Smother '08
School of Rock '03
The Good Girl '02
Chuck & Buck '00

Patricia White
See Patricia Barry

Peter White (1937-)
Thirteen Days '00
Mother '96

Ron White
Jasper, Texas '03
A House Divided '00
Locked in Silence '99
The Wall '99
Blood Brothers '97
Kissinger and Nixon '96
Screamers '96
ShadowZone: The Undead Express '96
Frame by Frame '95
Johnny's Girl '95
Race to Freedom: The Story of the Underground Railroad '94
Treacherous Beauties '94
Guilty as Sin '93
Love & Murder '91
Cowboys Don't Cry '88

Ruth White
Up the Down Staircase '67
Edge of the City '57

Slappy (Melvin) White (1920-95)
Mr. Saturday Night '92
Amazing Grace '74

Steve White (1961-)
Get On the Bus '96
Just for the Hell of It '68
She-Devils on Wheels '68

Thelma White (1910-2005)
Spy Train '43
Reefer Madness '38

Vanna White (1957-)
Gypsy Angels '94
Graduation Day '81

Charles White Eagle
Altered States '80
Three Warriors '77

O.Z. Whitehead (1911-98)
The Man Who Shot Liberty Valance '62
The Horse Soldiers '59
Rally 'Round the Flag, Boys! '58
Beware, My Lovely '52
Road House '48
The Grapes of Wrath '40

Paxton Whitehead (1937-)
Kate & Leopold '01
The Adventures of Huck Finn '93
My Boyfriend's Back '93
Boris and Natasha: The Movie '92
Child of Darkness, Child of Light '91
Chips, the War Dog '90
Baby Boom '87
Back to School '86
Jumpin' Jack Flash '86

Billie Whitelaw (1932-)
Hot Fuzz '07
The Last of the Blonde Bombshells '00
The Lost Son '98
Merlin '98
Jane Eyre '96
Duel of Hearts '92
Freddie the Frog '92 (V)
Catherine Cookson's The Fifteen Streets '90
The Krays '90
Lorna Doone '90
A Murder of Quality '90
The Dressmaker '89
Maurice '87
The Secret Garden '87
Shadey '87
Murder Elite '86
Slayground '84
Tangiers '83
Unsuitable Job for a Woman '82
A Tale of Two Cities '80
Water Babies '79
Leopard in the Snow '78
The Omen '76
Frenzy '72
Gumshoe '72
Night Watch '72
Start the Revolution without Me '70
Strange Case of Dr. Jekyll & Mr. Hyde '68
The Flesh and the Fiends '60
Make Mine Mink '60
No Love for Johnnie '60
Small Hotel '57

Arkie Whiteley (1965-2001)
The Last Musketeer '00
Gallowglass '95
Princess Caraboo '94
Razorback '84

Jon Whiteley (1945-)
The Spanish Gardener '57
Moonfleet '55

Paul Whiteman (1890-1967)
Lady Frankenstein '72
The Fabulous Dorseys '47
Strike Up the Band '40
King of Jazz '30

Charles Malik Whitfield
Bound by Lies '05
Behind Enemy Lines '01
The Temptations '98

Dondre T. Whitfield (1969-)
The Salon '05
Mr. 3000 '04
Two Can Play That Game '01
Alien Fury: Countdown to Invasion '00

June Whitfield (1925-)
Catherine Cookson's The Secret '00
The Last of the Blonde Bombshells '00
Carry On Columbus '92
Carry On Abroad '72

Lynn Whitfield (1953-)
The Women '08
The Cheetah Girls 2 '06
Madea's Family Reunion '06
The Cheetah Girls '03
Head of State '03
A Girl Thing '01
A Time for Dancing '00
Dangerous Evidence: The Lori Jackson Story '99
Love Songs '99
The Color of Courage '98
Stepmom '98
Eve's Bayou '97
Gone Fishin' '97
Junior's Groove '97
A Thin Line Between Love and Hate '96
State of Emergency '94
Taking the Heat '93
The Josephine Baker Story '90
Jaws: The Revenge '87
Johnnie Gibson F.B.I. '87
Hard Lessons '86
The Slugger's Wife '85
Doctor Detroit '83

Mitchell Whitfield (1968-)
TMNT (Teenage Mutant Ninja Turtles) '07 (V)
Amy's O '02
Lost and Found '99
Best Men '98
I Love You, Don't Touch Me! '97
My Cousin Vinny '92
Dogfight '91

Bradley Whitford (1959-)
Bottle Shock '08
An American Crime '07
Little Manhattan '05
Sisterhood of the Traveling Pants '05
Kate & Leopold '01
Behind the Mask '99
Bicentennial Man '99
The Muse '99
Red Corner '97
Masterminds '96
My Fellow Americans '96
Billy Madison '94
The Client '94
My Life '93
A Perfect World '93
Philadelphia '93
Scent of a Woman '92
Awakenings '90
Presumed Innocent '90
Vital Signs '90
Young Guns 2 '90
The Betty Ford Story '87
Dead As a Doorman '85

Peter Whitford (1939-)
Strictly Ballroom '92
Warm Nights on a Slow-Moving Train '87
Dead End Drive-In '86
My Brilliant Career '79
Cass '78

Jack Whiting (1901-61)
Give Me a Sailor '38
Sailing Along '38

Adventureland *'09*
All Good Things *'09*
Extract *'09*
Whip It *'09*
Ghost Town *'08*
The Brothers Solomon *'07*
Knocked Up *'07*
Meet Bill *'07*
Walk Hard: The Dewey Cox Story *'07*

Carlton Wilborn (1964-)
Grief *'94*
Dance *'90*

Crane Wilbur (1886-1973)
Crime School *'38*
Captain Calamity *'36*

George P. Wilbur
Halloween 6: The Curse of Michael Myers *'95*
Halloween 4: The Return of Michael Myers *'88*

James Wilby (1958-)
Little Devil *'07*
Gradiva *'06*
De-Lovely *'04*
Gosford Park *'01*
Cotton Mary *'99*
Behind the Lines *'97*
The Woman in White *'97*
Howard's End *'92*
Lady Chatterley *'92*
Conspiracy *'89*
A Tale of Two Cities *'89*
A Handful of Dust *'88*
A Summer Story *'88*
Maurice *'87*
Dreamchild *'85*

Frank Wilcox (1907-74)
Man From God's Country *'58*
Beginning of the End *'57*
A Majority of One *'56*
Seventh Cavalry *'56*
Carolina Cannonball *'55*
Abbott and Costello Meet the Keystone Kops *'54*
The Clay Pigeon *'49*
Mysterious Desperado *'49*
Infamous Crimes *'47*
Across the Pacific *'42*
They Died with Their Boots On *'41*
The Wagons Roll at Night *'41*

Larry Wilcox (1947-)
National Lampoon's Loaded Weapon 1 *'93*
Mission Manila *'87*
The Dirty Dozen: The Next Mission *'85*
The Last Ride of the Dalton Gang *'79*
The Last Hard Men *'76*
Sky Hei$t *'75*

Lisa Wilcox (1964-)
Watchers Reborn *'98*
A Nightmare on Elm Street 5: Dream Child *'89*
A Nightmare on Elm Street 4: Dream Master *'88*

Mary Wilcox (1944-)
Love Me Deadly *'73*
Beast of the Yellow Night *'70*

Robert Wilcox (1910-55)
Doctor Satan's Robot *'40*
Dreaming Out Loud *'40*
Mysterious Doctor Satan *'40*
Blondie Takes a Vacation *'39*
Buried Alive *'39*
The Man They Could Not Hang *'39*

Shannon Wilcox
A Boyfriend for Christmas *'04*
Hollywood Harry *'86*
When Your Lover Leaves *'83*

Collin Wilcox-Paxton (1937-2009)
The Crying Child *'96*
Fluke *'95*
Wildflower *'91*
Jaws 2 *'78*
Fury on Wheels *'71*
The Baby Maker *'70*
Catch-22 *'70*
To Kill a Mockingbird *'62*

Henry Wilcoxon (1905-84)
Caddyshack *'80*
Enola Gay: The Men, the Mission, the Atomic Bomb *'80*
The Two Worlds of Jenny Logan *'79*
When Every Day Was the Fourth of July *'78*
Pony Express Rider *'76*
Against a Crooked Sky *'75*
Man in the Wilderness *'71*
Escape from Planet Earth *'67*
The War Lord *'65*
The Ten Commandments *'56*
Scaramouche *'52*
Samson and Delilah *'50*
A Connecticut Yankee in King Arthur's Court *'49*
Unconquered *'47*
The Corsican Brothers *'42*
The Man Who Wouldn't Die *'42*
Mrs. Miniver *'42*
That Hamilton Woman *'41*
Tarzan Finds a Son *'39*
If I Were King *'38*
Jericho *'38*
Mysterious Mr. Moto *'38*
Souls at Sea *'37*
The Last of the Mohicans *'36*
The President's Mystery *'36*
The Crusades *'35*
Cleopatra *'34*

Jack Wild (1952-2006)
Robin Hood: Prince of Thieves *'91*
Pied Piper *'72*
Melody *'71*
Pufnstuf *'70*
Oliver! *'68*

Andrew Wilde
Murder on Line One *'90*
1984 *'84*

Cornel Wilde (1915-89)
The Fifth Musketeer *'79*
Norseman *'78*
Sharks' Treasure *'75*
The Comic *'69*
The Naked Prey *'66*
Sword of Lancelot *'63*
Omar Khayyam *'57*
Big Combo *'55*
Passion *'54*
A Woman's World *'54*
Main Street to Broadway *'53*
Treasure of the Golden Condor *'53*
The Greatest Show on Earth *'52*
At Sword's Point *'51*
Shockproof *'49*
Road House *'48*
Forever Amber *'47*
Leave Her to Heaven *'45*
A Song to Remember *'45*
A Thousand and One Nights *'45*
Wintertime *'43*
High Sierra *'41*

Lois Wilde (1907-95)
Brothers of the West *'37*
Stormy Trails *'36*
Undersea Kingdom *'36*

Olivia Wilde (1984-)
Year One *'09*
Bobby Z *'07*
Alpha Dog *'06*
Bickford Shmeckler's Cool Ideas *'06*
Turistas *'06*

Conversations with Other Women *'05*

Gene Wilder (1935-)
Alice in Wonderland *'99*
The Lady in Question *'99*
Murder in a Small Town *'99*
Another You *'91*
Funny About Love *'90*
See No Evil, Hear No Evil *'89*
Haunted Honeymoon *'86*
The Woman in Red *'84*
Hanky Panky *'82*
Stir Crazy *'80*
The Frisco Kid *'79*
The Adventures of Sherlock Holmes' Smarter Brother *'78*
World's Greatest Lover *'77*
Silver Streak *'76*
Blazing Saddles *'74*
The Little Prince *'74*
Thursday's Game *'74*
Young Frankenstein *'74*
Everything You Always Wanted to Know about Sex (But Were Afraid to Ask) *'72*
Willy Wonka & the Chocolate Factory *'71*
Quackser Fortune Has a Cousin in the Bronx *'70*
Start the Revolution without Me *'70*
The Producers *'68*
Bonnie & Clyde *'67*

Glenn Wilder (1933-)
Zebra Force *'76*
The Sand Pebbles *'66*

James Wilder (1963-)
Burning Down the House *'01*
Heart of Stone *'01*
First Degree *'98*
The Last Don 2 *'98*
Allie & Me *'97*
Flypaper *'97*
Ivory Tower *'97*
Kisses in the Dark *'97*
Nevada *'97*
Our Mother's Murder *'97*
Tollbooth *'94*
Scorchers *'92*
Prey of the Chameleon *'91*
Murder One *'88*
Zombie High *'87*

Webb Wilder
Heroes of the Heart *'94*
The Thing Called Love *'93*

Yvonne Wilder (1937-)
Honeyboy *'82*
Bloodbrothers *'78*
The Return of Count Yorga *'71*
West Side Story *'61*

Michael Wilding (1912-79)
Waterloo *'71*
The Naked Edge *'61*
The World of Suzie Wong *'60*
The Glass Slipper *'55*
The Egyptian *'54*
Torch Song *'53*
Stage Fright *'50*
Maytime in Mayfair *'49*
Under Capricorn *'49*
The Courtney Affair *'47*
An Ideal Husband *'47*
In Which We Serve *'43*
Secret Mission *'42*
Cottage to Let *'41*
Kipps *'41*
Convoy *'40*
Late Extra *'35*

Michael Wilding, Jr. (1953-)
Sweet Bird of Youth *'89*
A.D. *'85*

John Wildman (1961-)
American Boyfriends *'89*
Lethal Pursuit *'88*
Sorority Babes in the Slimeball Bowl-A-Rama *'87*

My American Cousin *'85*

Valerie Wildman (1953-)
Inner Sanctum *'91*
Neon City *'91*
Salvador *'86*

Dawn Wildsmith
Jack-O *'95*
Wizards of the Demon Sword *'94*
Alienator *'89*
Hollywood Chainsaw Hookers *'88*
Terminal Force *'88*
Warlords *'88*
Cyclone *'87*
Evil Spawn *'87*
Phantom Empire *'87*
Surf Nazis Must Die *'87*

Jason Wiles (1970-)
The Stepfather *'09*
Organizm *'08*
Kicking and Screaming *'95*
Higher Learning *'94*
Roadracers *'94*
Windrunner *'94*

Michael Shamus Wiles
Hydra *'09*
The Gene Generation *'07*
Rock Star *'01*

Mike Wiles
Held Up *'00*
Cole Justice *'89*
Terror at Tenkiller *'86*

Ed Wiley
The Canterville Ghost *'96*
Class of '61 *'92*

Jan Wiley (1916-93)
She Wolf of London *'46*
There Goes Kelly *'45*
Lawmen *'44*
Master Key *'44*
Jive Junction *'43*
Rhythm Parade *'43*
So Proudly We Hail *'43*
The Underdog *'43*
Dawn on the Great Divide *'42*
Thunder River Feud *'42*
Tonto Basin Outlaws *'41*
Zis Boom Bah *'41*

John Wilford
Ninja: American Warrior *'90*
Ninja Death Squad *'87*

Dianne Wilhite
Flesh Feast *'69*
Gruesome Twosome *'67*

Kathleen Wilhoite (1964-)
Audrey's Rain *'03*
My Sister's Keeper *'02*
Quicksand *'01*
Drowning Mona *'00*
Nurse Betty *'00*
Breast Men *'97*
Color of Night *'94*
Getting Even with Dad *'94*
Lorenzo's Oil *'92*
Bad Influence *'90*
Everybody Wins *'90*
Dream Demon *'88*
Angel Heart *'87*
Campus Man *'87*
Undercover *'87*
Witchboard *'87*
The Morning After *'86*
Murphy's Law *'86*
Quarterback Princess *'85*
Private School *'83*

Robert J. Wilke (1915-89)
The Cheyenne Social Club *'70*
Never Steal Anything Small *'59*
Night Passage *'57*
Tarnished Angels *'57*
Canyon River *'56*
20,000 Leagues under the Sea *'54*

From Here to Eternity *'53*
Cattle Town *'52*
High Noon *'52*
Kill the Umpire *'50*

Jose Wilker (1945-)
Medicine Man *'92*
Bye Bye Brazil *'79*
Dona Flor and Her Two Husbands *'78*
Xica *'76*

Guy Wilkerson (1899-1971)
Man of the West *'58*
Comin' Round the Mountain *'51*
Flaming Bullets *'45*
Frontier Fugitives *'45*
Marked for Murder *'45*
Boss of Rawhide *'44*
Dead or Alive *'44*
Guns of the Law *'44*
Outlaw Roundup *'44*
Fighting Valley *'43*
The Return of the Rangers *'43*
Rangers Take Over *'42*
Sergeant York *'41*

Donna Wilkes (1959-)
Grotesque *'87*
Angel *'84*
Blood Song *'82*
Baby Broker *'81*
Hard Knocks *'79*
Mid Knight Rider *'79*
Fyre *'78*

Elaine Wilkes (1965-)
Killer Party *'86*
Roommate *'84*

Barbara Wilkin
Six in Paris *'68*
The Flesh Eaters *'64*

Adrienne Wilkinson
Interceptor Force 2 *'02*
Death on the Set *'35*

Elizabeth Wilkinson
Suburban Roulette *'67*
A Taste of Blood *'67*

June Wilkinson (1940-)
Vasectomy: A Delicate Matter *'86*
Sno-Line *'85*
Frankenstein's Great Aunt Tillie *'83*
The Florida Connection *'74*
The Bellboy and the Playgirls *'62*
Macumba Love *'60*

Linden Wilkinson
The Monkey's Mask *'00*
The Wedding Party *'97*

Richard Wilkinson
The Butterfly Effect 3: Revelation *'09*
Nine Men *'43*

Scott Wilkinson
Benji: Off the Leash! *'04*
Wish upon a Star *'96*

Tom Wilkinson (1948-)
The Ghost Writer *'10*
Duplicity *'09*
John Adams *'08*
Recount *'08*
RocknRolla *'08*
Cassandra's Dream *'07*
Dedication *'07*
Michael Clayton *'07*
The Last Kiss *'06*
The Night of the White Pants *'06*
Batman Begins *'05*
The Exorcism of Emily Rose *'05*
Eternal Sunshine of the Spotless Mind *'04*
A Good Woman *'04*
If Only *'04*
Stage Beauty *'04*
Girl with a Pearl Earring *'03*
Normal *'03*
The Gathering Storm *'02*

The Importance of Being Earnest *'02*
Another Life *'01*
Black Knight *'01*
In the Bedroom *'01*
Chain of Fools *'00*
The Patriot *'00*
David Copperfield *'99 (N)*
Essex Boys *'99*
Molokai: The Story of Father Damien *'99*
Ride with the Devil *'99*
The Governess *'98*
Rush Hour *'98*
Shakespeare in Love *'98*
Oscar and Lucinda *'97*
Wilde *'97*
The Full Monty *'96*
The Ghost and the Darkness *'96*
Smilla's Sense of Snow *'96*
Martin Chuzzlewit *'94*
Priest *'94*
Royal Deceit *'94*
Prime Suspect *'92*
Paper Mask *'91*
Sylvia *'86*

Lee Wilkof (1951-)
Afterschool *'08*
Private Parts *'96*
Chattahoochee *'89*

Fred Willard (1939-)
Youth in Revolt *'10*
Harold *'08*
WALL-E *'08 (V)*
Epic Movie *'07*
I'll Believe You *'07*
Date Movie *'06*
For Your Consideration *'06*
I Could Never Be Your Woman *'06*
Ira & Abby *'06*
Monster House *'06 (V)*
Chicken Little *'05 (V)*
Anchorman: The Legend of Ron Burgundy *'04*
Harold and Kumar Go to White Castle *'04*
How to Lose Your Lover *'04*
Killer Diller *'04*
American Wedding *'03*
A Mighty Wind *'03*
National Lampoon's Christmas Vacation 2: Cousin Eddie's Big Island Adventure *'03*
How High *'01*
The Wedding Planner *'01*
Best in Show *'00*
Austin Powers 2: The Spy Who Shagged Me *'99*
Idle Hands *'99*
The Pooch and the Pauper *'99*
Permanent Midnight *'98*
Waiting for Guffman *'96*
Prehysteria 3 *'95*
Sodbusters *'94*
The Return of Spinal Tap *'92*
High Strung *'91*
Portrait of a White Marriage *'88*
Roxanne *'87*
Lots of Luck *'85*
Moving Violations *'85*
This Is Spinal Tap *'84*
How to Beat the High Cost of Living *'80*
Americathon *'79*
Salem's Lot *'79*
Chesty Anderson USN *'76*

Toyah Willcox (1958-)
Ebony Tower *'86*
Murder: Ultimate Grounds for Divorce *'84*
Quadrophenia *'79*

Jean Willes (1923-89)
The FBI Story *'59*
Invasion of the Body Snatchers *'56*
Abbott and Costello Go to Mars *'53*
So Proudly We Hail *'43*

Peter Willes
Dawn Patrol *'38*
Call It a Day *'37*

Chad Willet
Carolina Moon '07
The Locket '02
Outlaw Justice '98
Annie O '95

will.i.am
X-Men Origins: Wolverine '09
Madagascar: Escape 2 Africa '08 (V)

Warren William (1895-1948)
Black Tower '50
The Private Affairs of Bel Ami '47
Fear '46
Strange Illusion '45
The Wolf Man '41
Arizona '40
Lillian Russell '40
Day-Time Wife '39
The Gracie Allen Murder Case '39
The Man in the Iron Mask '39
Wives under Suspicion '38
The Firefly '37
Madame X '37
Go West, Young Man '36
Satan Met a Lady '36
The Case of the Lucky Legs '35
Cleopatra '34
Imitation of Life '34
Employees' Entrance '33
Gold Diggers of 1933 '33
Lady for a Day '33
Skyscraper Souls '32
Three on a Match '32

Adam Williams (1922-2006)
Gunfight at Comanche Creek '64
North by Northwest '59
Fear Strikes Out '57
Crashout '55
Without Warning '52
Flying Leathernecks '51
Queen for a Day '51

Allen Williams
Scorpion '86
The Two Worlds of Jenny Logan '79

Ashley Williams
Snow 2: Brain Freeze '08
Montana Sky '07
Snow '04

Barbara Williams (1953-)
Every Second Counts '08
Love Come Down '00
Family of Cops 3 '98
Krippendorf's Tribe '98
Naked City: A Killer Christmas '98
Naked City: Justice with a Bullet '98
Bone Daddy '97
Family of Cops 2: Breach of Faith '97
Inventing the Abbotts '97
Joe Torre: Curveballs Along the Way '97
Family of Cops '95
Digger '94
Spenser: Pale Kings & Princes '94
Spenser: Ceremony '93
Indecency '92
Oh, What a Night '92
City of Hope '91
Peter Gunn '89
Watchers '88
Tiger Warsaw '87
Jo Jo Dancer, Your Life Is Calling '86
Tell Me That You Love Me '84
Thief of Hearts '84

Barry Williams (1954-)
The Brady Bunch Movie '95
A Very Brady Christmas '88
Wild in the Streets '68

Bill Williams (1916-92)
Flight of the Grey Wolf '76
The Giant Spider Invasion '75
Buckskin '68
Space Master X-7 '58
Storm Rider '57
Torpedo Alley '53
Son of Paleface '52
Cavalry Charge '51
The Cariboo Trail '50
Operation Haylift '50
The Clay Pigeon '49
The Stratton Story '49
A Woman's Secret '49
Deadline at Dawn '46
Till the End of Time '46

Billy Dee Williams (1937-)
iMurders '08
Epoch: Evolution '03
Undercover Brother '02
The Ladies Man '00
The Visit '00
Fear Runs Silent '99
The Contract '98
Mask of Death '97
Steel Sharks '97
Moving Target '96
Dangerous Passion '95
The Prince '95
Triplecross '95
Alien Intruder '93
Percy & Thunder '93
Giant Steps '92
The Jacksons: An American Dream '92
Driving Me Crazy '91
Batman '89
Secret Agent 00-Soul '89
Deadly Illusion '87
Number One with a Bullet '87
Courage '86
Oceans of Fire '86
Fear City '85
Shooting Stars '85
Christmas Lilies of the Field '84
The Impostor '84
Marvin & Tige '84
Chiefs '83
Return of the Jedi '83
Nighthawks '81
Children of Divorce '80
The Empire Strikes Back '80
The Hostage Tower '80
Bingo Long Traveling All-Stars & Motor Kings '76
Mahogany '75
Hit! '73
Final Comedown '72
The Glass House '72
Lady Sings the Blues '72
Brian's Song '71
The Out-of-Towners '70
Black Brigade '69

Billy "Sly" Williams (1968-)
Mission of Justice '92
Voodoo Dawn '89

Brook Williams (1938-)
Absolution '81
Where Eagles Dare '68
Plague of the Zombies '66

Cara Williams (1925-)
The White Buffalo '77
Never Steal Anything Small '59
The Defiant Ones '58
The Helen Morgan Story '57
Meet Me in Las Vegas '56
The Girl Next Door '53
Boomerang '47

Caroline Williams (1957-)
Leprechaun 3 '95
Stepfather 2: Make Room for Daddy '89
The Texas Chainsaw Massacre 2 '86

Charles Williams (1909-75)
Born to Be Wild '38
Hollywood Stadium Mystery '38

Chris(topher) Williams
The Joneses '10
The World's Fastest Indian '05
Dodgeball: A True Underdog Story '04
The Courage to Love '00
Cremains '00

Chuck Williams
Dark Rider '91
Soultaker '90

Cindy Williams (1947-)
The Biggest Fan '02
Meet Wally Sparks '97
Bingo '91
Big Man on Campus '89
Rude Awakening '89
Tricks of the Trade '88
The Creature Wasn't Nice '81
Spaceship '81
Uforia '81
More American Graffiti '79
The First Nudie Musical '75
The Conversation '74
The Migrants '74
American Graffiti '73
The Killing Kind '73
Beware! The Blob '72
Travels with My Aunt '72
Gas-s-s-s! '70

Clara Williams (1888-1928)
Hell's Hinges '16
The Bargain '15
The Italian '15

Clarence Williams, III (1939-)
American Gangster '07
Mystery Woman: Mystery Weekend '05
Blue Hill Avenue '01
Mindstorm '01
Reindeer Games '00
The General's Daughter '99
Life '99
Malicious Intent '99
Frogs for Snakes '98
The Legend of 1900 '98
George Wallace '97
Half-Baked '97
The Love Bug '97
Hoodlum '96
Rebound: The Legend of Earl "The Goat" Manigault '96
The Road to Galveston '96
Sprung '96
The Immortals '95
The Silencers '95
Tales from the Hood '95
Against the Wall '94
Sugar Hill '94
Dangerous Relations '93
Deep Cover '92
My Heroes Have Always Been Cowboys '91
Maniac Cop 2 '90
The House of Dies Drear '88
I'm Gonna Git You Sucka '88
The Last Innocent Man '87
Perfect Victims '87
Tough Guys Don't Dance '87
52 Pick-Up '86
Purple Rain '84

Cole Williams
Mammoth '06
North Country '05
Harry and Max '04

Cynda Williams (1966-)
When Do We Eat? '05
MacArthur Park '01
The Courage to Love '00
Introducing Dorothy Dandridge '99
Caught Up '98
Relax... It's Just Sex! '98
Gang in Blue '96
Spirit Lost '96
Condition Red '95
Machine Gun Blues '95
The Sweeper '95
The Tie That Binds '95
Armistead Maupin's Tales of the City '93
The Ghost Brigade '93
Tales of Erotica '93
One False Move '91
Mo' Better Blues '90

Darnell Williams (1955-)
Firestarter 2: Rekindled '02
Detour '99
How U Like Me Now? '92

Dick Anthony Williams (1938-)
Black Listed '03
The Players Club '98
Edward Scissorhands '90
Mo' Better Blues '90
Tap '89
For Us, the Living '88
Gardens of Stone '87
Keeping On '81
Sophisticated Gents '81
The Night the City Screamed '80
An Almost Perfect Affair '79
A Woman Called Moses '78
Dog Day Afternoon '75
The Anderson Tapes '71

D.J. Williams (1868-1949)
The Courageous Mr. Penn '41
Mr. Reeder in Room 13 '38
The Crimes of Stephen Hawke '36
Murder in the Old Red Barn '36

Edy Williams (1942-)
Bad Girls from Mars '90
Rented Lips '88
Mankillers '87
Hellhole '85
Bad Manners '84
Hollywood Hot Tubs '84
Beyond the Valley of the Dolls '70
Secret Life of an American Wife '68
Good Times '67
Naked Kiss '64

Emlyn Williams (1905-87)
Deadly Game '82
The L-Shaped Room '62
The Wreck of the Mary Deare '59
Another Man's Poison '52
The Last Days of Dolwyn '49
This England '42
The Girl in the News '41
The Stars Look Down '39
The Citadel '38
The Iron Duke '34

Esther Williams (1923-)
That's Entertainment '74
Jupiter's Darling '55
Dangerous When Wet '53
Easy to Love '53
Million Dollar Mermaid '52
Skirts Ahoy! '52
Texas Carnival '51
The Duchess of Idaho '50
Pagan Love Song '50
Neptune's Daughter '49
Take Me Out to the Ball Game '49
On an Island with You '48
Easy to Wed '46
Ziegfeld Follies '46
Thrill of a Romance '45
Bathing Beauty '44
A Guy Named Joe '44
Andy Hardy's Double Life '42

Finty Williams (1972-)
The Importance of Being Earnest '02
The Mystery of Edwin Drood '93

Gareth Williams
13 Moons '02
Hard Luck '01
The Cell '00
From the Earth to the Moon '98
Palookaville '95
Blessing '94

Gary Anthony Williams (1966-)
Jiminy Glick in LaLa Wood '05
Undercover Brother '02

Genelle Williams
The Note 2: Taking a Chance on Love '09
Saving God '08

Grant Williams (1930-85)
Brain of Blood '71
Escape from Planet Earth '67
Susan Slade '61
The Leech Woman '59
The Incredible Shrinking Man '57
The Monolith Monsters '57
Written on the Wind '56

Gregory Alan Williams
Be Cool '05
Acts of Betrayal '98
In the Line of Fire '93

Guinn "Big Boy" Williams (1899-1962)
The Alamo '60
Hidden Guns '56
Springfield Rifle '52
Rocky Mountain '50
Nevada '44
The Desperadoes '43
Hands Across the Border '43
Lure of the Islands '42
Mr. Wise Guy '42
Billy the Kid '41
Castle on the Hudson '40
The Fighting 69th '40
Virginia City '40
Bad Lands '39
Mutiny on the Blackhawk '39
Dangerous Holiday '37
Feud of the Trail '37
You Only Live Once '37
Gun Play '36
Kelly the Second '36
The Vigilantes Are Coming '36
Danger Trails '35
Powdersmoke Range '35
Village Tale '35
Dangerous Appointment '34
Rafter Romance '34
Heritage of the Desert '33
Mystery Squadron '33
The Phantom Broadcast '33
When the West Was Young '32
The Phantom '31
Lucky Star '29
Burning Daylight '28
Wolfheart's Revenge '25
Rounding Up the Law '22

Guy Williams (1924-89)
Captain Sinbad '63
The Prince and the Pauper '62
The Sign of Zorro '60
I Was a Teenage Werewolf '57
The Secret of El Zorro '57
Savage Wilderness '55

Hal Williams (1938-)
Snow 2: Brain Freeze '08
Guess Who '05
Don't Look Back: The Story of Leroy "Satchel" Paige '81
On the Nickel '80

Harcourt Williams (1880-1957)
The Obsessed '51
Henry V '44

Harland Williams (1967-)
My Life in Ruins '09
Bachelor Party 2: The Last Temptation '08
Meet the Robinsons '07 (V)
Employee of the Month '06
Robots '05 (V)
Sorority Boys '02
Freddy Got Fingered '01
The Whole Nine Yards '00
Superstar '99
Dog Park '98
Mr. Headmistress '98
There's Something about Mary '98
Half-Baked '97
RocketMan '97
Down Periscope '96
Dumb & Dumber '94

Heathcote Williams (1941-)
Basic Instinct 2 '06
The Odyssey '97
The Tango Lesson '97
Blue Juice '95
Cold Light of Day '95
Orlando '92

Hugh Williams (1904-69)
Khartoum '66
Elizabeth of Ladymead '48
An Ideal Husband '47
A Girl in a Million '46
The Day Will Dawn '42
Secret Mission '42
One of Our Aircraft Is Missing '41
The Human Monster '39
Inspector Hornleigh '39
Wuthering Heights '39
Bitter Sweet '33

Ian Patrick Williams
Heaven's a Drag '94
Bad Channels '92
Bloodmoon '90
Dolls '87

Jason Williams (1952-)
Danger Zone 3: Steel Horse War '90
Danger Zone 2 '89
Vampire at Midnight '88
Danger Zone '87
Cheerleaders' Wild Weekend '85
Cop Killers '73
Flesh Gordon '72

Jermaine Williams
World's Greatest Dad '09
The Comebacks '07
The Great Debaters '07
Fat Albert '04

Jim Williams
Ex-Cop '93
Living to Die '91
The Newlydeads '87
Island of Blood '82
The Executioner '78

JoBeth Williams (1953-)
In the Land of Women '06
Crazylove '05
Fever Pitch '05
Into the Fire '05
The Ponder Heart '01
Backlash '99
Jackie's Back '99
From the Earth to the Moon '98
It Came from the Sky '98
Just Write '97
Little City '97
When Danger Follows You Home '97
Jungle 2 Jungle '96
Ruby Jean and Joe '96
Parallel Lives '94
Wyatt Earp '94
Chantilly Lace '93
Final Appeal '93
Sex, Love and Cold Hard Cash '93
Me, Myself & I '92

Stop! or My Mom Will Shoot '92
Dutch '91
Switch '91
Victim of Love '91
Child in the Night '90
My Name Is Bill W. '89
Welcome Home '89
Memories of Me '88
Murder Ordained '87
Desert Bloom '86
Poltergeist 2: The Other Side '86
American Dreamer '84
Teachers '84
Adam '83
The Big Chill '83
The Day After '83
Endangered Species '82
Poltergeist '82
The Dogs of War '81
Stir Crazy '80
Kramer vs. Kramer '79

John Williams (1903-83)

The Secret War of Harry Frigg '68
Double Trouble '67
Dear Brigitte '65
24 Hours in a Woman's Life '61
The Young Philadelphians '59
Island in the Sun '57
Will Success Spoil Rock Hunter? '57
Witness for the Prosecution '57
D-Day, the Sixth of June '56
To Catch a Thief '55
Dial "M" for Murder '54
Sabrina '54

Katt Micah Williams (1973-)

First Sunday '08
Internet Dating '08
Norbit '07
The Perfect Holiday '07
Ganked '05
Friday After Next '02

Kelli Williams (1970-)

A Boyfriend for Christmas '04
Flowers for Algernon '00
Sweetwater: A True Rock Story '99
Wavelength '96
Snowbound: The Jim and Jennifer Stolpa Story '94
Lifepod '93
There Goes My Baby '92
Till Murder Do Us Part '92
Zapped Again '89

Kenneth Williams (1926-88)

The Thief and the Cobbler '96 (V)
Carry On Emmanuelle '78
Carry On Behind '75
Carry On Abroad '72
Carry On Matron '72
Carry On at Your Convenience '71
Carry On Camping '71
Carry On Henry VIII '71
Carry On Loving '70
Carry On Again Doctor '69
Carry On Doctor '68
Carry On Up the Khyber '68
Follow That Camel '67
Carry On Cowboy '66
Carry On Screaming '66
Don't Lose Your Head '66
Carry On Cleo '65
Carry On Spying '64
Carry On Jack '63
Carry On Cruising '62
Carry On Regardless '61
Carry On Constable '60
Carry On Sergeant '58

Kiely Williams (1986-)

The Cheetah Girls: One World '08
The House Bunny '08
The Cheetah Girls 2 '06
The Cheetah Girls '03

Kimberly Williams (1971-)

How to Eat Fried Worms '06
How to Go Out on a Date in Queens '06
We Are Marshall '06
Lucky Seven '03
The Christmas Shoes '02
Follow the Stars Home '01
The 10th Kingdom '00
Just a Little Harmless Sex '99
Safe House '99
Simpatico '99
The War at Home '96
Father of the Bride Part 2 '95
Coldblooded '94
Indian Summer '93
Father of the Bride '91

Lee Williams (1974-)

The Debt '03
In His Life: The John Lennon Story '00
The Wolves of Kromer '98

Lia Williams (1964-)

The King Is Alive '00
Shot Through the Heart '98
Firelight '97

Malinda Williams (1975-)

A Day in the Life '09
First Sunday '08
Daddy's Little Girls '07
Idlewild '06
Dancing in September '00
Uninvited Guest '99
The Wood '99
High School High '96
A Thin Line Between Love and Hate '96
Laurel Avenue '93

Mark Williams (1959-)

Harry Potter and the Half-Blood Prince '09
A Room With a View '08
Harry Potter and the Order of the Phoenix '07
Harry Potter and the Goblet of Fire '05
Tristram Shandy: A Cock and Bull Story '05
Harry Potter and the Chamber of Secrets '02
High Heels and Low Lifes '01
The Borrowers '97
101 Dalmatians '96
Kill Line '91

Mary Parker Williams

Sarah's Child '96
Wish upon a Star '96

Michael Williams (1935-2001)

The Blair Witch Project '99
A Dance to the Music of Time '97
Murder by Night '89
Educating Rita '83

Michael K. Williams

Brooklyn's Finest '09
A Day in the Life '09
Life During Wartime '09
The Road '09
Wonderful World '09
Gone Baby Gone '07
I Think I Love My Wife '07

Michelle Williams (1980-)

Blue Valentine '10
Mammoth '09
Shutter Island '09
Deception '08
Incendiary '08
Synecdoche, New York '08
Wendy and Lucy '08
I'm Not There '07
The Hawk Is Dying '06
The Hottest State '06
The Baxter '05
Brokeback Mountain '05
Imaginary Heroes '05
A Hole in One '04
Land of Plenty '04
The Station Agent '03
United States of Leland '03
Me Without You '01
Perfume '01
Prozac Nation '01
If These Walls Could Talk 2 '00
Dick '99
Halloween: H20 '98
Killing Mr. Griffin '97
A Thousand Acres '97
Species '95
Timemaster '95
Lassie '94

Olivia Williams (1968-)

The Ghost Writer '10
Sex & Drugs & Rock & Roll '10
An Education '09
Flashbacks of a Fool '08
Miss Austen Regrets '07
X-Men: The Last Stand '06
Tara Road '05
Valiant '05 (V)
Agatha Christie: A Life in Pictures '04
Peter Pan '03
To Kill a King '03
Below '02
The Heart of Me '02
The Body '01
Lucky Break '01
The Man from Elysian Fields '01
Born Romantic '00
Four Dogs Playing Poker '00
Jason and the Argonauts '00
The Sixth Sense '99
Rushmore '98
Emma '97
The Postman '97

Oren Williams (1992-)

Rebound '05
Clifford's Really Big Movie '04 (V)
The Devil's Mistress '68

Paul Williams (1940-)

The Princess Diaries 2: Royal Engagement '04
Headless Body in Topless Bar '96
A Million to Juan '94
The Doors '91
Chill Factor '90
The Night They Saved Christmas '87
Zombie High '87
Best Enemies '86
Smokey and the Bandit, Part 3 '83
Smokey and the Bandit 2 '80
Stone Cold Dead '80
The Muppet Movie '79
The Cheap Detective '78
Smokey and the Bandit '77
Phantom of the Paradise '74
Battle for the Planet of the Apes '73
Watermelon Man '70
The Loved One '65

Paul W. Williams (1943-)

Mirage '94
The November Men '93

Peter Williams (1933-)

Love Come Down '00
Jungleground '95
Soul Survivor '95
Robin Hood... The Legend: Robin Hood and the Sorcerer '83
Destroy All Planets '68
The Bridge on the River Kwai '57

Rhys Williams (1897-1969)

Skullduggery '70
The Restless Breed '58
Fastest Gun Alive '56
Battle Cry '55
The Black Shield of Falworth '54
Man in the Attic '53
Kiss Tomorrow Goodbye '50
The Showdown '50
The Corn Is Green '45
Mrs. Miniver '42
Underground Agent '42
How Green Was My Valley '41

Robert Williams (1897-1931)

Devotion '31
Platinum Blonde '31

Robert B. Williams (1904-78)

Revenge of the Creature '55
Mysterious Desperado '49

Robin Williams (1952-)

Night at the Museum: Battle of the Smithsonian '09
Old Dogs '09
Shrink '09
World's Greatest Dad '09
August Rush '07
License to Wed '07
Everyone's Hero '06 (V)
Happy Feet '06 (V)
Man of the Year '06
Night at the Museum '06
The Night Listener '06
RV '06
The Big White '05
Robots '05 (V)
The Final Cut '04
House of D '04
Noel '04
Death to Smoochy '02
Insomnia '02
One Hour Photo '02
A. I.: Artificial Intelligence '01 (V)
Bicentennial Man '99
Jakob the Liar '99
Patch Adams '98
What Dreams May Come '98
Deconstructing Harry '97
Flubber '97
Good Will Hunting '97
Aladdin and the King of Thieves '96 (V)
Father's Day '96
Hamlet '96
Jack '96
The Secret Agent '96
The Birdcage '95
Jumanji '95
Nine Months '95
To Wong Foo, Thanks for Everything, Julie Newmar '95
Being Human '94
Mrs. Doubtfire '93
Aladdin '92 (V)
Ferngully: The Last Rain Forest '92 (V)
Shakes the Clown '92
Toys '92
Dead Again '91
The Fisher King '91
Hook '91
Awakenings '90
Cadillac Man '90
The Adventures of Baron Munchausen '89
Dead Poets Society '89
Good Morning, Vietnam '87
The Best of Times '86
Club Paradise '86
Seize the Day '86
Moscow on the Hudson '84
Survivors '83
The Tale of the Frog Prince '83
The World According to Garp '82
Popeye '80
Can I Do It... Till I Need Glasses? '77

Roger Williams (1889-1939)

Code of the Fearless '39
Cheyenne Rides Again '38
Feud Maker '38
Valley of Terror '38
Aces Wild '37
Brothers of the West '37
Heroes of the Alamo '37
The Roamin' Cowboy '37
Trailing Trouble '37
Gun Grit '36
Phantom Patrol '36
Pinto Rustlers '36
Stormy Trails '36
Pecos Kid '35
Social Error '35
Toll of the Desert '35
Wagon Trail '35

Samm-Art Williams (1946-)

A Rage in Harlem '91
The Adventures of Huckleberry Finn '85
Blood Simple '85

Saul Williams (1972-)

K-PAX '01
Slam '98

Scot Williams (1972-)

The Crew '08
In His Life: The John Lennon Story '00
Swing '98
Backbeat '94

Simon Williams (1946-)

The Fiendish Plot of Dr. Fu Manchu '80
The Blood on Satan's Claw '71

Spencer Williams, Jr. (1893-1969)

Juke Joint '47
Dirty Gertie from Harlem U.S.A. '46
Blood of Jesus '41
Go Down Death '41
Son of Ingagi '40
Bronze Buckaroo '39
Harlem Rides the Range '39

Steven Williams (1949-)

Adventures of Power '08
Darkwolf '03
Firetrap '01
Route 666 '01
Crash & Byrnes '99
The Sender '98
Bloodfist 7: Manhunt '95
Jason Goes to Hell: The Final Friday '93
Revolver '92
Better Off Dead '85
Missing in Action 2: The Beginning '85
Silent Witness '85
Twilight Zone: The Movie '83
The Blues Brothers '80

Treat Williams (1952-)

Front of the Class '08
What Happens in Vegas '08
Moola '07
Miss Congeniality 2: Armed and Fabulous '05
Hollywood Ending '02
Extreme Limits '01
The Fraternity '01
Gale Force '01
Venomous '01
Critical Mass '00
Skeletons in the Closet '00
The Substitute 4: Failure is Not an Option '00
Journey to the Center of the Earth '99
The Substitute 3: Winner Takes All '99
36 Hours to Die '99
The Deep End of the Ocean '98
Deep Rising '98
Escape: Human Cargo '98
The Substitute 2: School's Out '97
The Devil's Own '96
The Late Shift '96
The Phantom '96
Johnny's Girl '95
Mulholland Falls '95
Things to Do in Denver When You're Dead '95
Parallel Lives '94
Where the Rivers Flow North '94
Hand Gun '93
Till Death Do Us Part '92
The Water Engine '92
Final Verdict '91
Drug Wars: The Camarena Story '90
Max and Helen '90
The Heart of Dixie '89
Third Degree Burn '89
Third Solution '89
Dead Heat '88
Sweet Lies '88
Echoes in the Darkness '87
J. Edgar Hoover '87
Night of the Sharks '87
The Men's Club '86
Smooth Talk '85
Flashpoint '84
Once Upon a Time in America '84
A Streetcar Named Desire '84
Dempsey '83
Prince of the City '81
The Pursuit of D.B. Cooper '81
Hair '79
1941 '79
The Eagle Has Landed '77
The Ritz '76
Deadly Hero '75

Vanessa Williams (1963-)

Flirting with Forty '09
Imagine That '09
Ice Spiders '07
Black Listed '03
Like Mike '02
Our America '02
Incognito '99
Mother '96
DROP Squad '94
New Jack City '91

Vanessa L(ynne) Williams (1963-)

And Then Came Love '07
My Brother '06
Johnson Family Vacation '04
Winds of Terror '01
The Courage to Love '00
Don Quixote '00
Shaft '00
Light It Up '99
Dance with Me '98
Futuresport '98
The Odyssey '97
Soul Food '97
Eraser '96
Hoodlum '96
Bye Bye Birdie '95
Candyman '92
The Jacksons: An American Dream '92
Another You '91
Harley Davidson and the Marlboro Man '91
The Kid Who Loved Christmas '90
Full Exposure: The Sex Tape Scandals '89
Under the Gun '88
The Pick-Up Artist '87

Wade Andrew Williams (1961-)

I Witness '03
Bark! '02
Terror Tract '00
K-911 '99
Route 9 '98

Zelda Williams

Were the World Mine '08
House of D '04

Kimberly Williams-Paisley

See Kimberly Williams

Alister Williamson (1918-99)

Murder on the Midnight Express '74
The Oblong Box '69

Clayton Williamson
Clowning Around 2 *'93*
Clowning Around *'92*

Felix Williamson
Dirty Deeds *'02*
Strange Planet *'99*

Fred Williamson (1938-)
Starsky & Hutch *'04*
On the Edge *'02*
Rhapsody *'01*
The Independent *'00*
Submerged *'00*
Active Stealth *'99*
Children of the Corn 5: Fields of Terror *'98*
Blackjack *'97*
Night Vision *'97*
Original Gangstas *'96*
From Dusk Till Dawn *'95*
Silent Hunter *'94*
South Beach *'92*
Steele's Law *'91*
Three Days to a Kill *'91*
Black Cobra 3: The Manila Connection *'90*
Delta Force Commando 2 *'90*
Black Cobra 2 *'89*
The Kill Reflex *'89*
Deadly Intent *'88*
The Black Cobra *'87*
Delta Force Commando *'87*
The Messenger *'87*
Foxtrap *'85*
Deadly Impact *'84*
White Fire *'84*
Big Score *'83*
The New Gladiators *'83*
1990: The Bronx Warriors *'83*
Vigilante *'83*
Warriors of the Wasteland *'83*
The Last Fight *'82*
One Down, Two to Go! *'82*
Fear in the City *'81*
Fist of Fear, Touch of Death *'80*
Express to Terror *'79*
Blind Rage *'78*
Deadly Mission *'78*
The Inglorious Bastards *'78*
Mister Mean *'77*
Death Journey *'76*
Joshua *'76*
Adios Amigo *'75*
Bucktown *'75*
Mean Johnny Barrows *'75*
Take a Hard Ride *'75*
Boss *'74*
No Way Back *'74*
Three the Hard Way *'74*
Black Caesar *'73*
Hell Up in Harlem *'73*
That Man Bolt *'73*
M*A*S*H *'70*

Mykelti Williamson (1960-)
Black Dynamite *'09*
The Final Destination *'09*
Vice *'08*
ATL *'06*
Fatwa *'06*
Lucky Number Slevin *'06*
The Assassination of Richard Nixon *'05*
After the Sunset *'04*
Our America *'02*
Ali *'01*
Holiday Heart *'00*
Gideon *'99*
Having Our Say: The Delany Sisters' First 100 Years *'99*
Three Kings *'99*
Double Tap *'98*
Primary Colors *'98*
Species 2 *'98*
Buffalo Soldiers *'97*
Con Air *'97*
Truth or Consequences, N.M. *'97*
Twelve Angry Men *'97*
Soul of the Game *'96*
Heat *'95*
How to Make an American Quilt *'95*
Waiting to Exhale *'95*
Forrest Gump *'94*
The First Power *'89*
Miracle Mile *'89*
Number One with a Bullet *'87*
Streets of Fire *'84*

Nicol Williamson (1938-)
Spawn *'97*
Mr. Toad's Wild Ride *'96*
The Advocate *'93*
Exorcist 3: Legion *'90*
Black Widow *'87*
Mountbatten: The Last Viceroy *'86*
Passion Flower *'86*
Christopher Columbus *'85*
Return to Oz *'85*
I'm Dancing as Fast as I Can *'82*
Venom *'82*
Excalibur *'81*
The Human Factor *'79*
The Cheap Detective *'78*
The Word *'78*
Robin and Marian *'76*
The Seven-Per-Cent Solution *'76*
The Wilby Conspiracy *'75*
Hamlet *'69*

Amanda Williford
See Willa Ford

Noble Willingham (1930-2004)
Up Close and Personal *'96*
City Slickers 2: The Legend of Curly's Gold *'94*
Ace Ventura: Pet Detective *'93*
Article 99 *'92*
Career Opportunities *'91*
City Slickers *'91*
The Last Boy Scout *'91*
Pastime *'91*
Blind Fury *'90*
The Heist *'89*
Good Morning, Vietnam *'87*
Coward of the County *'81*
First Monday in October *'81*
Kenny Rogers as the Gambler *'80*
Backstairs at the White House *'79*
The Boys in Company C *'77*
Aloha, Bobby and Rose *'74*
Big Bad Mama *'74*
My Sweet Charlie *'70*

Bruce Willis (1955-)
The Expendables *'10*
Surrogates *'09*
What Just Happened *'08*
The Astronaut Farmer *'07*
Live Free or Die Hard *'07*
Perfect Stranger *'07*
Planet Terror *'07*
Alpha Dog *'06*
Fast Food Nation *'06*
Lucky Number Slevin *'06*
Over the Hedge *'06 (V)*
16 Blocks *'06*
Hostage *'05*
Sin City *'05*
The Whole Ten Yards *'04*
Rugrats Go Wild! *'03 (V)*
Tears of the Sun *'03*
Hart's War *'02*
Bandits *'01*
Disney's The Kid *'00*
Unbreakable *'00*
The Whole Nine Yards *'00*
The Sixth Sense *'99*
The Story of Us *'99*
Armageddon *'98*
Breakfast of Champions *'98*
Mercury Rising *'98*
The Siege *'98*
The Fifth Element *'97*
The Jackal *'97*
Beavis and Butt-Head Do America *'96 (V)*
Last Man Standing *'96*
Die Hard: With a Vengeance *'95*
Four Rooms *'95*
12 Monkeys *'95*
Color of Night *'94*
Nobody's Fool *'94*
North *'94*
Pulp Fiction *'94*
Striking Distance *'93*
Death Becomes Her *'92*
The Player *'92*
Billy Bathgate *'91*
Hudson Hawk *'91*
The Last Boy Scout *'91*
Mortal Thoughts *'91*
The Bonfire of the Vanities *'90*
Die Hard 2: Die Harder *'90*
Look Who's Talking, Too *'90 (V)*
That's Adequate *'90*
In Country *'89*
Look Who's Talking *'89 (V)*
Die Hard *'88*
Sunset *'88*
Blind Date *'87*
Moonlighting *'85*

Dave Willis
Aqua Teen Hunger Force Colon Movie Film for Theaters *'07 (V)*
There Will Be Blood *'07*

Matt Willis (1913-89)
Shep Comes Home *'49*
The Noose Hangs High *'48*
Blonde Savage *'47*
A Walk in the Sun *'46*
Behind Prison Walls *'43*
Return of the Vampire *'43*

Norman Willis (1903-88)
In Old New Mexico *'45*
Gauchos of El Dorado *'41*
Legion of the Lawless *'40*
Tim Tyler's Luck *'37*

Rumer Willis (1988-)
Sorority Row *'09*
The House Bunny *'08*
Hostage *'05*
Striptease *'96*

Susan Willis
The Majestic *'01*
What about Bob? *'91*

Noel Willman (1917-88)
21 Hours at Munich *'76*
The Odessa File *'74*
The Reptile *'66*
Doctor Zhivago *'65*
Kiss of the Vampire *'62*
Abandon Ship *'57*
Across the Bridge *'57*
The Warriors *'55*
Beau Brummel *'54*

Chill Wills (1903-78)
Mr. Billion *'77*
Poco *'77*
Pat Garrett & Billy the Kid *'73*
Over the Hill Gang *'69*
Fireball 500 *'66*
The Rounders *'65*
McLintock! *'63*
The Wheeler Dealers *'63*
Deadly Companions *'61*
Gold of the Seven Saints *'61*
The Alamo *'60*
Where the Boys Are *'60*
Gun Glory *'57*
Giant *'56*
Kentucky Rifle *'55*
Francis Joins the WACs *'54 (V)*
City That Never Sleeps *'53*
Francis Covers the Big Town *'53 (V)*
Man from the Alamo *'53*
Ride the Man Down *'53*
Small Town Girl *'53*
Francis Goes to West Point *'52 (V)*
Francis Goes to the Races *'51 (V)*
High Lonesome *'50*
Rio Grande *'50*
Francis the Talking Mule *'49 (V)*
Tulsa *'49*
That Wonderful Urge *'48*
Heartaches *'47*
The Harvey Girls *'46*
The Yearling *'46*
I'll Be Seeing You *'44*
Tarzan's New York Adventure *'42*
Billy the Kid *'41*
Honky Tonk *'41*
Western Union *'41*
Boom Town *'40*
The Westerner *'40*
Allegheny Uprising *'39*
Racketeers of the Range *'39*

Maury Wills (1932-)
The Sandlot *'93*
The Black Six *'74*

Paul Willson (1945-)
Office Space *'98*
My Best Friend Is a Vampire *'88*
Devonsville Terror *'83*

Douglas Wilmer (1920-)
The Adventures of Sherlock Holmes' Smarter Brother *'78*
The Incredible Sarah *'76*
Golden Voyage of Sinbad *'73*
The Vampire Lovers *'70*
The Vengeance of Fu Manchu *'67*
Brides of Fu Manchu *'66*
Woman of Straw *'64*
Jason and the Argonauts *'63*
Men of Sherwood Forest *'57*

Gary Wilmes
I Hate Valentine's Day *'09*
Birds of America *'08*
A Mighty Heart *'07*

Andre Wilms (1947-)
La Vie de Boheme *'93*
L'Enfer *'93*
Monsieur Hire *'89*
Life Is a Long Quiet River *'88*

Channing Wilroy
Desperate Living *'77*
Female Trouble *'74*
Pink Flamingos *'72*

Jay Wilsey
See Buffalo Bill Jr.
Westward Bound *'30*

Shannon Wilsey (1971-94)
Sorority House Massacre 2: Nighty Nightmare *'92*
The Invisible Maniac *'90*

Ajita Wilson (1950-87)
Savage Island *'85*
Escape from Hell *'79*

Andreas Wilson
Kill Your Darlings *'06*
Evil *'03*

Andrew Wilson (1964-)
The Big Bounce *'04*
Bottle Rocket *'95*

Anthony H. Wilson
Tristram Shandy: A Cock and Bull Story *'05*
The Outcast *'84*

Barbara Wilson
Invasion of the Animal People *'62*
Lost, Lonely, and Vicious *'59*
Teenage Doll *'57*

Brad Wilson
Pterodactyl Woman from Beverly Hills *'97*
Grotesque *'87*

Brian Wilson (1942-)
Beach Blanket Bingo *'65*
Beach Party *'63*

Charles C. Wilson (1894-1948)
Blazing Across the Pecos *'48*
Larceny in her Heart *'46*
The Spider's Web *'38*
Pennies from Heaven *'36*

Clarence Wilson (1876-1941)
Bachelor Bait *'34*
Badmen of Nevada *'33*
Night Life in Reno *'31*

Claude Wilson
The Boys in Company C *'77*
Combat Killers *'68*

Daniel Wilson
Things to Do *'06*
Wait until Spring, Bandini *'90*

David Wilson (1949-)
The Inside Man *'84*
Eddie and the Cruisers *'83*
Hometown U.S.A. *'79*

Don Wilson (1900-82)
The Last Sentinel *'07*
Niagara *'52*
The Chase *'46*
The Roundup *'41*

Don "The Dragon" Wilson (1955-)
18 Fingers of Death *'05*
Sci-Fighter *'04*
Moving Target *'00*
The Capitol Conspiracy *'99*
Bloodfist 8: Hard Way Out *'96*
Hollywood Safari *'96*
Terminal Rush *'96*
Batman Forever *'95*
Bloodfist 7: Manhunt *'95*
Cyber-Tracker 2 *'95*
Night Hunter *'95*
Virtual Combat *'95*
Bloodfist 6: Ground Zero *'94*
Red Sun Rising *'94*
Ring of Fire 3: Lion Strike *'94*
Bloodfist 5: Human Target *'93*
Cyber-Tracker *'93*
Out for Blood *'93*
Black Belt *'92*
Bloodfist 3: Forced to Fight *'92*
Bloodfist 4: Die Trying *'92*
Magic Kid *'92*
Ring of Fire 2: Blood and Steel *'92*
Futurekick *'91*
Ring of Fire *'91*
Bloodfist 2 *'90*
Bloodfist *'89*
Born on the Fourth of July *'89*
Say Anything *'89*
Sailor Beware *'52*

Dooley Wilson (1894-1953)
Seven Days Ashore *'44*
Stormy Weather *'43*
Casablanca *'42*

Dorothy Wilson (1909-98)
In Old Kentucky *'35*
Last Days of Pompeii *'35*
When a Man's a Man *'35*
Dangerous Appointment *'34*
His Greatest Gamble *'34*
Lucky Devils *'33*
Men of America *'32*

Earl Wilson (1907-87)
Beach Blanket Bingo *'65*
Night of Evil *'62 (N)*
Copacabana *'47*

Elizabeth Wilson (1921-)
The Boys Next Door *'96*
Quiz Show *'94*
Scarlett *'94*
Queen *'93*
Sarah, Plain and Tall: Skylark *'93*
The Addams Family *'91*
Regarding Henry *'91*
The Believers *'87*
A Conspiracy of Love *'87*
Nutcracker: Money, Madness & Murder *'87*
Where Are the Children? *'85*
Grace Quigley *'84*
You Can't Take It with You *'84*
Sanctuary of Fear *'79*
Miles to Go Before I Sleep *'74*
Prisoner of Second Avenue *'74*
Little Murders *'71*
Catch-22 *'70*
Jenny *'70*
The Graduate *'67*
The Tunnel of Love *'58*
Patterns *'56*

Flip Wilson (1933-98)
Zora Is My Name! *'90*
The Fish that Saved Pittsburgh *'79*
Uptown Saturday Night *'74*
Cancel My Reservation *'72*

Frank Wilson (1885-1956)
Beware *'46*
Paradise in Harlem *'40*
Green Pastures *'36*
Emperor Jones *'33*
Girl from Chicago *'32*

Georges Wilson (1921-)
Nudo di Donna *'83*
Make Room for Tomorrow *'81*
Attack of the Killer Tomatoes *'77*

Kristen Wilson (1969-)
Soccer Mom *'08*
Twitches Too *'07*
Crossover *'06*
Dr. Dolittle 3 *'06*
Twitches *'05*
Walking Tall *'04*
Confessions of a Dangerous Mind *'02*
Dr. Dolittle 2 *'01*
Dungeons and Dragons *'00*
Bulletproof *'96*
Girl 6 *'96*
The Pompatus of Love *'95*
Tyson *'95*

Lambert Wilson (1959-)
Babylon A.D. *'08*
Dante 01 *'08*
The Lazarus Project *'08*
Flawless *'07*
Private Fears in Public Places *'06*
Sahara *'05*
Catwoman *'04*
People *'04*
The Matrix Reloaded *'03*
The Matrix Revolutions *'03*
Timeline *'03*
Don Quixote *'00*
The Last September *'99*
Same Old Song *'97*
The Leading Man *'96*
Frankenstein *'93*
The Belly of an Architect *'91*
The Possessed *'88*
Red Kiss *'85*
Rendez-vous *'85*
The Blood of Others *'84*
Sahara *'83*
Five Days One Summer *'82*
Julia *'77*

Lois Wilson (1896-1983)
Bright Eyes *'34*
In the Money *'34*
Ticket to a Crime *'34*
Female *'33*
Laughing at Life *'33*
Drifting Souls *'32*
The Rider of Death Valley *'32*
The Secrets of Wu Sin *'32*
The Show Off *'26*
The Vanishing American *'25*
Monsieur Beaucaire *'24*
The Covered Wagon *'23*

Luke Wilson (1971-)
Death at a Funeral *'10*
Battle for Terra *'09 (V)*
Henry Poole Is Here *'08*
Blonde Ambition *'07*
Vacancy *'07*
You Kill Me *'07*
Hoot *'06*
Idiocracy *'06*
My Super Ex-Girlfriend *'06*
The Family Stone *'05*
The Wendell Baker Story *'05*
Anchorman: The Legend of Ron Burgundy *'04*
Around the World in 80 Days *'04*
Alex & Emma *'03*
Charlie's Angels: Full Throttle *'03*
Legally Blonde 2: Red White & Blonde *'03*
Masked and Anonymous *'03*
Old School *'03*
The Third Wheel *'02*
Legally Blonde *'01*
The Royal Tenenbaums *'01*
Soul Survivors *'01*
Bad Seed *'00*
Charlie's Angels *'00*
Blue Streak *'99*
Committed *'99*
My Dog Skip *'99*
Best Men *'98*
Bongwater *'98*
Dog Park *'98*
Home Fries *'98*
Telling Lies in America *'96*
Bottle Rocket *'95*

Mara Wilson (1987-)
Thomas and the Magic Railroad *'00*
Balloon Farm *'97*
A Simple Wish *'97*
Matilda *'96*
Miracle on 34th Street *'94*
Mrs. Doubtfire *'93*

Marie Wilson (1916-72)
Mr. Hobbs Takes a Vacation *'62*
A Girl in Every Port *'52*
Never Wave at a WAC *'52*
My Friend Irma *'49*
Fabulous Joe *'47*
The Private Affairs of Bel Ami *'47*
Flying Blind *'41*
Waterfront *'39*
Boy Meets Girl *'38*
The Great Garrick *'37*
Satan Met a Lady *'36*
March of the Wooden Soldiers *'34*

Mary Louise Wilson (1932-)
Searching for Paradise *'02*
A Season for Miracles *'99*
24 Nights *'99*
Stepmom *'98*
The Adventures of Huck Finn *'93*
Cheap Shots *'91*
Green Card *'90*

Owen Wilson (1968-)
Marmaduke *'10 (V)*
Fantastic Mr. Fox *'09 (V)*
Night at the Museum: Battle of the Smithsonian *'09*
Drillbit Taylor *'08*
Marley & Me *'08*
The Darjeeling Limited *'07*
Cars *'06 (V)*
Night at the Museum *'06*
You, Me and Dupree *'06*
Wedding Crashers *'05*
The Wendell Baker Story *'05*
Around the World in 80 Days *'04*
The Big Bounce *'04*
The Life Aquatic with Steve Zissou *'04*
Meet the Fockers *'04*
Starsky & Hutch *'04*
Shanghai Knights *'03*
I Spy *'02*
Behind Enemy Lines *'01*
The Royal Tenenbaums *'01*
Zoolander *'01*
Meet the Parents *'00*
Shanghai Noon *'00*
The Haunting *'99*
The Minus Man *'99*
Armageddon *'98*
Breakfast of Champions *'98*
Permanent Midnight *'98*
Anaconda *'96*
The Cable Guy *'96*
Bottle Rocket *'95*

Patrick Wilson (1973-)
The A-Team *'10*
Morning Glory *'10*
The Switch *'10*
Watchmen *'09*
Lakeview Terrace *'08*
Passengers *'08*
Brothers Three *'07*
Evening *'07*
Purple Violets *'07*
Hard Candy *'06*
Little Children *'06*
Running with Scissors *'06*
The Alamo *'04*
The Phantom of the Opera *'04*
Angels in America *'03*

Perry Wilson
The Matchmaker *'58*
Fear Strikes Out *'57*

Peta Wilson (1970-)
The League of Extraordinary Gentlemen *'03*
Joe and Max *'02*
Mercy *'00*
Loser *'97*

Rachel Wilson
Winter Break *'02*
Mystery, Alaska *'99*

Rainn Wilson (1968-)
Hesher *'10*
Monsters vs. Aliens *'09 (V)*
The Rocker *'08*
The Last Mimzy *'07*
My Super Ex-Girlfriend *'06*
Sahara *'05*
Baadasssss! *'03*

Reno Wilson (1970-)
Transformers *'07 (V)*
Crank *'06*
R.S.V.P. *'02*
She Creature *'01*
City of Industry *'96*

Richard Wilson (1936-)
The Proposition *'05*
The Man Who Knew Too Little *'97*
Unnatural Pursuits *'91*
How to Get Ahead in Advertising *'89*

Rita Wilson (1958-)
It's Complicated *'09*
Old Dogs *'09*
Beautiful Ohio *'06*
The Chumscrubber *'05*
Raise Your Voice *'04*
Auto Focus *'02*
The Glass House *'01*
Perfume *'01*
Invisible Child *'99*
Runaway Bride *'99*
The Story of Us *'99*
From the Earth to the Moon *'98*
Psycho *'98*
If These Walls Could Talk *'96*
Jingle All the Way *'96*
That Thing You Do! *'96*
Now and Then *'95*
Mixed Nuts *'94*
Sleepless in Seattle *'93*
Volunteers *'85*
The Day It Came to Earth *'77*

Robert Wilson
Day of Triumph *'54*
I Beheld His Glory *'53*

Rod Wilson
Widows *'02*
Madonna: Innocence Lost *'95*
Darkman 2: The Return of Durant *'94*

Roger Wilson (1958-)
Power of Attorney *'94*
The Ghost Brigade *'93*
Thunder Alley *'85*
Second Time Lucky *'84*
Porky's 2: The Next Day *'83*
Overthrow *'82*
Porky's *'82*

Ruth Wilson
The Prisoner *'09*
Jane Eyre *'06*

Scott Wilson (1942-)
Big Stan *'07*
The Heartbreak Kid *'07*
Come Early Morning *'06*
Open Window *'06*
Saving Shiloh *'06*
The Sensation of Sight *'06*
Junebug *'05*
The Last Samurai *'03*
Monster *'03*
Bark! *'02*
Coastlines *'02*
Pearl Harbor *'01*
Way of the Gun *'00*
The Jack Bull *'99*
Shiloh 2: Shiloh Season *'99*
Clay Pigeons *'98*
G.I. Jane *'97*
Shiloh *'97*
Dead Man Walking *'95*
Flesh and Bone *'93*
Pure Luck *'91*
Exorcist 3: Legion *'90*
Femme Fatale *'90*
Young Guns 2 *'90*
Johnny Handsome *'89*
Jesse *'88*
The Tracker *'88*
Malone *'87*
Blue City *'86*
The Aviator *'85*
Year of the Quiet Sun *'84*
On the Line *'83*
The Right Stuff *'83*
The Ninth Configuration *'79*
The Passover Plot *'75*
The New Centurions *'72*
The Grissom Gang *'71*
Castle Keep *'69*
The Gypsy Moths *'69*
In Cold Blood *'67*

Sheree J. Wilson (1958-)
Hellbound *'94*
Past Tense *'94*
Walker: Texas Ranger: One Riot, One Ranger *'93*
News at Eleven *'86*
Crimewave *'85*
Fraternity Vacation *'85*

Stuart Wilson (1946-)
Hot Fuzz *'07*
Fascination *'04*
The Rundown *'03*
Dinotopia *'02*
Princess of Thieves *'01*
Here on Earth *'00*
The Luzhin Defence *'00*
Slow Burn *'00*
Vertical Limit *'00*
Second Sight *'99*
Enemy of the State *'98*
The Mask of Zorro *'98*
Crossworlds *'96*
The Rock *'96*
Edie & Pen *'95*
Death and the Maiden *'94*
Exit to Eden *'94*
No Escape *'94*
The Age of Innocence *'93*
Teenage Mutant Ninja Turtles 3 *'93*
Lethal Weapon 3 *'92*
Lethal Charm *'90*
Secret Weapon *'90*
Romance on the Orient Express *'89*
The Highest Honor *'84*
Running Blind *'78*
The Strauss Family *'73*

Teddy Wilson (1943-91)
Life Stinks *'91*
Kiss Shot *'89*
The Mighty Pawns *'87*
The Ambush Murders *'82*
Cotton Comes to Harlem *'70*

Thick Wilson
The Thief and the Cobbler *'96 (V)*
Adventures Beyond Belief *'87*

Thomas F. Wilson (1959-)
Larry the Cable Guy: Health Inspector *'06*
Zoom *'06*
That Darn Cat *'96*
Andersonville *'95*
Born to Be Wild *'95*
Camp Nowhere *'94*
Blood In ... Blood Out: Bound by Honor *'93*
Caroline at Midnight *'93*
Mr. Write *'92*
High Strung *'91*
Back to the Future, Part 3 *'90*
Back to the Future, Part 2 *'89*
Action Jackson *'88*
Let's Get Harry *'87*
April Fool's Day *'86*
Back to the Future *'85*

Tom Wilson (1880-1965)
Battling Butler *'26*
California Straight Ahead *'25*
The Americano *'17*

Trey Wilson (1948-89)
Great Balls of Fire *'89*
Miss Firecracker *'89*
Welcome Home *'89*
Bull Durham *'88*
End of the Line *'88*
Married to the Mob *'88*
Twins *'88*
Raising Arizona *'87*
Kennedy *'83*
The Vampire Hookers *'78*
Three Warriors *'77*

Bridgette Wilson-Sampras (1973-)
Shopgirl *'05*
Buying the Cow *'02*
Extreme Ops *'02*
Just Visiting *'01*
The Wedding Planner *'01*
Beautiful *'00*
House on Haunted Hill *'99*
Love Stinks *'99*
The Suburbans *'99*
I Know What You Did Last Summer *'97*
Nevada *'97*
The Real Blonde *'97*
The Stepsister *'97*
Mortal Kombat 1: The Movie *'95*
Sweet Evil *'95*
Billy Madison *'94*
Last Action Hero *'93*

Penelope Wilton (1946-)
Five Days *'07*
Half Broken Things *'07*
The History Boys *'06*
Match Point *'05*
Pride and Prejudice *'05*
Shaun of the Dead *'04*
Calendar Girls *'03*
Iris *'01*
Victoria & Albert *'01*
Wives and Daughters *'01*
The Return of the Borrowers *'96*
Carrington *'95*
The Secret Rapture *'94*
The Borrowers *'93*
Blame It on the Bellboy *'92*
Cry Freedom *'87*
Clockwise *'86*
Singleton's Pluck *'84*
The Norman Conquests, Part 1: Table Manners *'78*
The Norman Conquests, Part 2: Living Together *'78*
The Norman Conquests, Part 3: Round and Round the Garden *'78*

Juliana Wimbles
Snakehead Terror *'04*
Restless Spirits *'99*

Mary Wimbush
Poldark *'75*
Oh! What a Lovely War *'69*

Brian Wimmer (1959-)
Outlaw Trail *'06*
Attack of the Sabretooth *'05*
Beneath Loch Ness *'01*
Bitter Sweet *'98*
Final Justice *'98*
The Maddening *'95*
Dead Badge *'94*
Tank Girl *'94*
Blue Flame *'93*
Kiss of a Killer *'93*
Lipstick Camera *'93*
The World's Oldest Living Bridesmaid *'92*
Late for Dinner *'91*
Dangerous Pursuit *'89*
China Beach *'88*

Troy Winbush
Backwoods *'08*
The Last Shot *'04*
Six: The Mark Unleashed *'04*
Sniper 3 *'04*
United States of Leland *'03*
A Light in the Darkness *'02*
What About Your Friends: Weekend Getaway *'02*
Carmen: A Hip Hopera *'01*
Gabriela *'01*
The Replacements *'00*
Mutiny *'99*
The Principal *'87*

Paul Winchell (1922-2005)
The Fox and the Hound *'81 (V)*
The Many Adventures of Winnie the Pooh *'77 (V)*
The Aristocats *'70 (V)*

Walter Winchell (1897-1972)
Scarface Mob *'62 (N)*
Dondi *'61*
The Bellboy *'60*

Philip Winchester (1981-)
Alice *'09*
Maneater *'09*
Flyboys *'06*
Thunderbirds *'04*
Lethal Dose *'03*

Jeff Wincott (1957-)
The Invasion *'07*
Battle Queen 2020 *'99*
Paper Bullets *'99*
Universal Soldier 2: Brothers in Arms *'98*
Universal Soldier 3: Unfinished Business *'98*
Future Fear *'97*
The Undertaker's Wedding *'97*
Fatal Combat *'96*
Profile for Murder *'96*
When the Bullet Hits the Bone *'96*
Last Man Standing *'95*
Street Law *'95*
The Donor *'94*
The Killing Man *'94*
Open Fire *'94*
Martial Outlaw *'93*
Mission of Justice *'92*
Deadly Bet *'91*
Martial Law 2: Undercover *'91*

Michael Wincott (1959-)
What Just Happened *'08*
Seraphim Falls *'06*
The Assassination of Richard Nixon *'05*
The Count of Monte Cristo *'02*
Treasure Planet *'02 (V)*
Along Came a Spider *'01*
Anti-Terrorist Cell: Manhunt *'01*
Before Night Falls *'00*
Hidden Agenda *'99*
Gunshy *'98*
Alien: Resurrection *'97*
Basquiat *'96*
Metro *'96*
Dead Man *'95*
Strange Days *'95*
The Crow *'93*
Romeo Is Bleeding *'93*
The Three Musketeers *'93*
1492: Conquest of Paradise *'92*
The Doors *'91*
Robin Hood: Prince of Thieves *'91*
Tragedy of Flight 103: The Inside Story *'91*
Talk Radio *'88*
Wild Horse Hank *'79*

William Windom (1923-)
Children of the Corn 4: The Gathering *'96*
Fugitive X *'96*
Miracle on 34th Street *'94*
Attack of the 50 Ft. Woman *'93*
Dennis the Menace: Dinosaur Hunter *'93*
Sommersby *'93*
Committed *'91*
Back to Hannibal: The Return of Tom Sawyer and Huckleberry Finn *'90*
Funland *'89*
Street Justice *'89*
She's Having a Baby *'88*
Planes, Trains & Automobiles *'87*
Grandview U.S.A. *'84*
Last Plane Out *'83*
Desperate Lives *'82*
Leave 'Em Laughing *'81*
Blind Ambition *'79*
Mean Dog Blues *'78*
Abduction of St. Anne *'75*
The Girls of Huntington House *'73*
Pursuit *'72*
Escape from the Planet of the Apes *'71*
The Mephisto Waltz *'71*
Brewster McCloud *'70*
The Gypsy Moths *'69*
The Detective *'68*
Columbo: Prescription Murder *'67*
The Americanization of Emily *'64*
For Love or Money *'63*
One Man's Way *'63*
To Kill a Mockingbird *'62*

Barbara Windsor (1937-)
Carry On Abroad *'72*
Carry On Matron *'72*
Carry On Camping *'71*
Carry On Henry VIII *'71*
Carry On Again Doctor *'69*
Carry On Doctor *'68*
Carry On Spying *'64*

Claire Windsor (1897-1972)
The Claw *'27*
The Blot *'21*
Too Wise Wives *'21*

Marie Windsor (1922-2000)
Commando Squad *'87*
Salem's Lot *'79*
Cahill: United States Marshal *'73*
Wild Women *'70*
Bedtime Story *'63*
Critic's Choice *'63*
Mail Order Bride *'63*
Girl in Black Stockings *'57*

Unholy Wife '57
The Killing '56
Abbott and Costello Meet the Mummy '55
Silver Star '55
Swamp Women '55
Cat Women of the Moon '53
City That Never Sleeps '53
Tall Texan '53
Trouble along the Way '53
Jungle '52
The Narrow Margin '52
Outlaw Women '52
The Sniper '52
Little Big Horn '51
Double Deal '50
The Showdown '50
The Fighting Kentuckian '49
Force of Evil '49
Outpost in Morocco '49
Hellfire '48
Smart Alecks '42

Romy Windsor

The Howling: New Moon Rising '95
Big Bad John '90
The House of Usher '88
Howling 4: The Original Nightmare '88

Paul Winfield (1940-2004)

Catfish in Black Bean Sauce '00
Strange Justice: The Clarence Thomas and Anita Hill Story '99
Relax... It's Just Sex! '98
The Assassination File '96
The Legend of Gator Face '96
Mars Attacks! '96
Original Gangstas '96
Tyson '95
White Dwarf '95
Breathing Lessons '94
In the Kingdom of the Blind the Man with One Eye Is King '94
Scarlett '94
Cliffhanger '93
Dennis the Menace '93
Queen '93
Back to Hannibal: The Return of Tom Sawyer and Huckleberry Finn '90
Presumed Innocent '90
The Women of Brewster Place '89
For Us, the Living '88
Big Shots '87
Death Before Dishonor '87
Guilty of Innocence '87
The Mighty Pawns '87
The Serpent and the Rainbow '87
Blue City '86
Go Tell It on the Mountain '84
Mike's Murder '84
The Terminator '84
On the Run '83
Star Trek 2: The Wrath of Khan '82
White Dog '82
Carbon Copy '81
Sophisticated Gents '81
Angel City '80
Backstairs at the White House '79
Roots: The Next Generation '79
A Hero Ain't Nothin' but a Sandwich '78
King '78
Damnation Alley '77
The Greatest '77
Twilight's Last Gleaming '77
Green Eyes '76
High Velocity '76
Conrack '74
Huckleberry Finn '74
It's Good to Be Alive '74
Gordon's War '73
Sounder '72
Brother John '70
R.P.M.* (*Revolutions Per Minute) '70

The Lost Man '69

Oprah Winfrey (1954-)

The Princess and the Frog '09 (V)
Bee Movie '07 (V)
Charlotte's Web '06 (V)
Beloved '98
The Women of Brewster Place '89
Native Son '86
The Color Purple '85

Leslie Wing

Retribution '88
The Cowboy & the Ballerina '84
Dungeonmaster '83

Toby Wing (1915-2001)

Mr. Boggs Steps Out '38
Murder at the Vanities '34
Search for Beauty '34

Mark Wing-Davey (1948-)

One Against the Wind '91
The Hitchhiker's Guide to the Galaxy '81

Debra Winger (1955-)

Rachel Getting Married '08
Sometimes in April '05
Eulogy '04
Radio '03
Big Bad Love '02
Forget Paris '95
A Dangerous Woman '93
Shadowlands '93
Wilder Napalm '93
Leap of Faith '92
Everybody Wins '90
The Sheltering Sky '90
Betrayed '88
Black Widow '87
Made in Heaven '87
Legal Eagles '86
Mike's Murder '84
Terms of Endearment '83
Cannery Row '82
E.T.: The Extra-Terrestrial '82 (V)
An Officer and a Gentleman '82
Urban Cowboy '80
French Postcards '79
Special Olympics '78
Thank God It's Friday '78
Slumber Party '57 '76

Peter Wingfield (1962-)

Highlander: The Source '07
Catwoman '04
Superbabies: Baby Geniuses 2 '04
X2: X-Men United '03
Edge of Madness '02
Highlander: Endgame '00
Uncovered '94

Angela Winkler (1944-)

Benny's Video '92
Sheer Madness '84
Danton '82
The Tin Drum '79
Knife in the Head '78
The Lost Honor of Katharina Blum '75

Henry Winkler (1945-)

The Most Wonderful Time of the Year '08
A Plumm Summer '08
Click '06
I Could Never Be Your Woman '06
Berkeley '05
The Kid and I '05
Holes '03
Down to You '00
Little Nicky '00
Ground Control '98
P.U.N.K.S. '98
The Waterboy '98
Hostage High '97
National Lampoon's Dad's Week Off '97
Scream '96
One Christmas '95
Night Shift '82
An American Christmas Carol '79

The One and Only '78
Heroes '77
Katherine '75
The Lords of Flatbush '74

Mel Winkler

City Hall '95
Devil in a Blue Dress '95
Laurel Avenue '93

Kitty Winn (1944-)

Mirrors '78
The Exorcist 2: The Heretic '77
Miles to Go Before I Sleep '74
The Exorcist '73
Man on a String '71
Panic in Needle Park '71
They Might Be Giants '71

Vic Winner

The Rue Morgue Massacres '73
Horror Rises from the Tomb '72

Olof Winnerstrand (1875-1956)

Night Is My Future '47
Torment '44

Katheryn Winnick (1978-)

Killers '10
Cold Souls '09
Amusement '08
Failure to Launch '06
Hellraiser: Hellworld '05
Satan's Little Helper '04
Fabled '02

Lucyna Winnicka (1928-)

25 Fireman's Street '73
First Spaceship on Venus '60
Mother Joan of the Angels '60

Charles Winninger (1884-1969)

The Sun Shines Bright '53
Torpedo Alley '53
Something in the Wind '47
She Wouldn't Say Yes '45
State Fair '45
Broadway Rhythm '44
Lady Takes a Chance '43
Pot o' Gold '41
Ziegfeld Girl '41
Beyond Tomorrow '40
If I Had My Way '40
Little Nellie Kelly '40
Babes in Arms '39
Destry Rides Again '39
Three Smart Girls Grow Up '39
Every Day's a Holiday '38
Hard to Get '38
Cafe Metropole '37
Nothing Sacred '37
Show Boat '36
Three Smart Girls '36
Flying High '31
Gun Smoke '31
Night Nurse '31
The Sin of Madelon Claudet '31

Mare Winningham (1959-)

Brothers '09
Swing Vote '08
The Maldonado Miracle '03
Snap Decision '01
Sally Hemings: An American Scandal '00
Everything That Rises '98
Under Pressure '98
George Wallace '97
The Boys Next Door '96
Georgia '95
Letter to My Killer '95
Better Off Dead '94
Teresa's Tattoo '94
The War '94
Wyatt Earp '94
Hard Promises '92
Intruders '92

Eye on the Sparrow '91
Fatal Exposure '91
Miracle Mile '89
Turner and Hooch '89
God Bless the Child '88
Made in Heaven '87
Shy People '87
Nobody's Fool '86
A Winner Never Quits '86
St. Elmo's Fire '85
Single Bars, Single Women '84
The Thorn Birds '83
Threshold '83
Amber Waves '82
One Trick Pony '80
Special Olympics '78
The Young Pioneers '76

Marissa Jaret Winokur (1973-)

Fever Pitch '05
On Edge '03

Kate Winslet (1975-)

The Reader '08
Revolutionary Road '08
All the King's Men '06
Flushed Away '06 (V)
The Holiday '06
Little Children '06
Romance & Cigarettes '05
Eternal Sunshine of the Spotless Mind '04
Finding Neverland '04
The Life of David Gale '03
Enigma '01
Iris '01
Quills '00
Hideous Kinky '99
Holy Smoke '99
Titanic '97
Hamlet '96
Jude '96
A Kid in King Arthur's Court '95
Sense and Sensibility '95
Heavenly Creatures '94

George Winslow (1946-)

Artists and Models '55
Gentlemen Prefer Blondes '53
Monkey Business '52

Michael Winslow (1960-)

National Lampoon Presents RoboDoc '08
Police Academy 7: Mission to Moscow '94
Going Under '91
Buy & Cell '89
Far Out Man '89
Police Academy 6: City under Siege '89
Police Academy 5: Assignment Miami Beach '88
Police Academy 4: Citizens on Patrol '87
Spaceballs '87
Police Academy 3: Back in Training '86
Police Academy 2: Their First Assignment '85
Alphabet City '84
Lovelines '84
Police Academy '84
Tag: The Assassination Game '82
Cheech and Chong's Nice Dreams '81

Mary Elizabeth Winstead (1984-)

Scott Pilgrim vs. the World '10
Make It Happen '08
Death Proof '07
Live Free or Die Hard '07
Black Christmas '06
Bobby '06
Final Destination 3 '06
Sky High '05

Hattie Winston (1945-)

True Crime '99
Jackie Brown '97
Clara's Heart '88

Helen Winston (1925-72)

Tobor the Great '54
Battle Circus '53
I Love Melvin '53

Helene Winston (1922-2004)

Utilities '83
The Devil & Max Devlin '81
Killjoy '81
Return from Witch Mountain '78
The Shaggy D.A. '76
A Boy and His Dog '75
Our Time '74
The Brotherhood of Satan '71
The Trouble with Girls (and How to Get into It) '69
The Witchmaker '69
The Shakiest Gun in the West '68
Double Trouble '67

Jaime Winstone

Donkey Punch '08
Cravings '06

Ray Winstone (1957-)

Edge of Darkness '10
Sex & Drugs & Rock & Roll '10
The Devil's Tomb '09
Fool's Gold '08
Indiana Jones and the Kingdom of the Crystal Skull '08
Beowulf '07 (V)
Breaking and Entering '06
The Departed '06
The Chronicles of Narnia: The Lion, the Witch and the Wardrobe '05 (V)
Doogal '05 (V)
The Proposition '05
King Arthur '04
Cold Mountain '03
Ripley's Game '02
Last Orders '01
Love, Honour & Obey '00
Sexy Beast '00
Agnes Browne '99
Darkness Falls '98
Final Cut '98
The Sea Change '98
The Very Thought of You '98
The War Zone '98
Face '97
Nil by Mouth '96
Ladybird, Ladybird '93
Ladies and Gentlemen, the Fabulous Stains '82
Quadrophenia '79
Scum '79

Maurice Dean Wint

The Circuit '08
Hedwig and the Angry Inch '00
Cube '98
Curtis's Charm '96
Rude '96

Alex Winter (1965-)

Freaked '93
Bill & Ted's Bogus Journey '91
Bill & Ted's Excellent Adventure '89
Rosalie Goes Shopping '89
Haunted Summer '88
The Lost Boys '87
Death Wish 3 '85

Edward Winter (1938-2001)

Held Hostage '91
The Buddy System '83
Mother & Daughter: A Loving War '80

Eric Winter (1976-)

The Ugly Truth '09
Harold & Kumar Escape from Guantanamo Bay '08

Vincent Winter (1947-98)

The Horse Without a Head '63

Almost Angels '62
Gorgo '61
Time Lock '57

Dean Winters (1964-)

Winter of Frozen Dreams '08
Hellraiser: Hellseeker '02
Snipes '01
Undercover Angel '99

Deborah Winters (1955-)

The Outing '87
Blue Sunshine '78
Tarantulas: The Deadly Cargo '77
Class of '44 '73
Kotch '71
The People Next Door '70
Hail, Hero! '69

Jonathan Winters (1925-)

National Lampoon Presents Cattle Call '06
Comic Book: The Movie '04
The Adventures of Rocky & Bullwinkle '00
The Thief and the Cobbler '96 (V)
The Flintstones '94
The Shadow '94
Tiny Toon Adventures: How I Spent My Vacation '91 (V)
Moon over Parador '88
The Longshot '86
Say Yes! '86
Alice in Wonderland '85
More Wild, Wild West '80
The Fish that Saved Pittsburgh '79
Viva Max '69
Eight on the Lam '67
Oh Dad, Poor Dad (Momma's Hung You in the Closet & I'm Feeling So Sad) '67
The Russians Are Coming, the Russians Are Coming '66
The Loved One '65
It's a Mad, Mad, Mad, Mad World '63

Kristoffer Ryan Winters (1978-)

Hot Blooded '98
Saint Maybe '98
Red Blooded 2 '96

Roland Winters (1904-89)

Loving '70
Blue Hawaii '62
Cash McCall '60
The Iceman Cometh '60
Jet Pilot '57
Top Secret Affair '57
Follow the Sun '51
Guilty of Treason '50
To Please a Lady '50
The Underworld Story '50
The West Point Story '50
Abbott and Costello Meet the Killer, Boris Karloff '49
Malaya '49
Kidnapped '48
Riders of the Whistling Skull '37

Shelley Winters (1922-2006)

Gideon '99
Portrait of a Lady '96
Jury Duty '95
Mrs. Munck '95
Raging Angels '95
Backfire! '94
Heavy '94
The Pickle '93
Silence of the Hams '93
Weep No More My Lady '93
Stepping Out '91
Superstar: The Life and Times of Andy Warhol '90
An Unremarkable Life '89
Purple People Eater '88
Delta Force '86
Witchfire '86

Alice in Wonderland *'85*
Deja Vu *'84*
Ellie *'84*
Very Close Quarters *'84*
Fanny Hill *'83*
Over the Brooklyn Bridge *'83*
S.O.B. *'81*
The Visitor *'80*
Elvis: The Movie *'79*
The Magician of Lublin *'79*
City on Fire *'78*
Initiation of Sarah *'78*
King of the Gypsies *'78*
Pete's Dragon *'77*
Tentacles *'77*
Next Stop, Greenwich Village *'76*
The Tenant *'76*
That Lucky Touch *'75*
Journey into Fear *'74*
Blume in Love *'73*
Cleopatra Jones *'73*
Poor Pretty Eddie *'73*
Diamonds *'72*
The Poseidon Adventure *'72*
Shattered *'72*
What's the Matter with Helen? *'71*
Who Slew Auntie Roo? *'71*
Bloody Mama *'70*
Buona Sera, Mrs. Campbell *'68*
The Scalphunters *'68*
Wild in the Streets *'68*
Enter Laughing *'67*
Alfie *'66*
Harper *'66*
The Greatest Story Ever Told *'65*
A Patch of Blue *'65*
The Three Sisters *'65*
Time of Indifference *'64*
The Balcony *'63*
Lolita *'62*
The Young Savages *'61*
Let No Man Write My Epitaph *'60*
The Diary of Anne Frank *'59*
Odds Against Tomorrow *'59*
The Big Knife *'55*
I Am a Camera *'55*
I Died a Thousand Times *'55*
Mambo *'55*
The Night of the Hunter *'55*
Treasure of Pancho Villa *'55*
Executive Suite *'54*
Behave Yourself! *'52*
Meet Danny Wilson *'52*
Phone Call from a Stranger *'52*
A Place in the Sun *'51*
South Sea Sinner *'50*
Winchester '73 *'50*
The Great Gatsby *'49*
A Double Life *'47*
The Gangster *'47*

Jane Winton (1905-59)

Hell's Angels *'30*
Bare Knees *'28*
The Patsy *'28*

Estelle Winwood (1883-1984)

Murder by Death *'76*
The Producers *'68*
Games *'67*
Dead Ringer *'64*
The Magic Sword *'62*
The Notorious Landlady *'62*
The Misfits *'61*
Darby O'Gill & the Little People *'59*
This Happy Feeling *'58*
The Swan *'56*
23 Paces to Baker Street *'56*
The Glass Slipper *'55*
Quality Street *'37*

Billy Wirth (1962-)

The Talent Given Us *'04*
Me & Will *'99*
Last Lives *'98*
Relax... It's Just Sex! *'98*
Starlight *'97*
Space Marines *'96*
A Good Day to Die *'95*
Venus Rising *'95*
The Fence *'94*
Judicial Consent *'94*
Body Snatchers *'93*
Final Mission *'93*
Red Shoe Diaries *'92*
War Party *'89*
The Lost Boys *'87*

Robert Wisden

The Snow Queen *'02*
Every Mother's Worst Fear *'98*
Outrage *'98*
Excess Baggage *'96*
Captains Courageous *'95*
Glory Enough for All: The Discovery of Insulin *'92*
Impolite *'92*
Blood Clan *'91*

Norman Wisdom (1920-)

The Night They Raided Minsky's *'69*
What's Good for the Goose *'69*
The Square Peg *'58*
Trouble in Store *'53*

Robert Wisdom (1953-)

Sex and Death 101 *'07*
The Hawk Is Dying *'06*
Mozart and the Whale *'05*
Barbershop 2: Back in Business *'04*
Crazy Like a Fox *'04*
The Forgotten *'04*
Haven *'04*
Killer Diller *'04*
Ray *'04*
Duplex *'03*
Live from Baghdad *'03*
Coastlines *'02*
Storytelling *'01*
Dancing at the Blue Iguana *'00*

Tom Wisdom (1973-)

Pirate Radio *'09*
The Sisterhood of the Traveling Pants 2 *'08*
300 *'07*

Greg Wise (1966-)

Place of Execution *'09*
Return to Cranford *'09*
Cranford *'08*
The Disappeared *'08*
Johnny English *'03*
Sirens *'02*
Madame Bovary *'00*
Judas Kiss *'98*
The Moonstone *'97*
The Buccaneers *'95*
Feast of July *'95*
Sense and Sensibility *'95*

Ray Wise (1947-)

Infestation *'09*
Pandemic *'09*
Stuntmen *'09*
One Missed Call *'08*
American East *'07*
The Flock *'07*
Strike *'07*
Cyxork 7 *'06*
Peaceful Warrior *'06*
Good Night, and Good Luck *'05*
The Battle of Shaker Heights *'03*
Jeepers Creepers 2 *'03*
Two Can Play That Game *'01*
The Garbage-Picking, Field Goal-Kicking Philadelphia Phenomenon *'98*
Powder *'95*
Body Shot *'93*
The Chase *'93*
The Ghost Brigade *'93*
Rising Sun *'93*
Bob Roberts *'92*
Sunstroke *'92*
Twin Peaks: Fire Walk with Me *'92*
Write to Kill *'91*
Endless Descent *'90*
Season of Fear *'89*
The Taking of Flight 847: The Uli Derickson Story *'88*
RoboCop *'87*
The Journey of Natty Gann *'85*
Swamp Thing *'82*

William Wise

In the Bedroom *'01*
Thirteen Conversations About One Thing *'01*
Farewell to the King *'89*

Joseph Wiseman (1918-2009)

Lady Mobster *'88*
Seize the Day *'86*
Ghostwriter *'84*
Jaguar Lives *'79*
Zalmen or the Madness of God *'75*
Pursuit *'72*
The Valachi Papers *'72*
Lawman *'71*
Stiletto *'69*
Bye Bye Braverman *'67*
Dr. No *'62*
The Unforgiven *'60*
The Garment Jungle *'57*
The Prodigal *'55*
The Silver Chalice *'54*
Viva Zapata! *'52*
Detective Story *'51*

Andreas Wisniewski (1959-)

Urban Ghost Story *'98*
The Living Daylights *'87*

Googie Withers (1917-)

Country Life *'95*
Shine *'95*
Northanger Abbey *'87*
Hotel du Lac *'86*
Devil on Horseback *'54*
Night and the City *'50*
It Always Rains on Sunday *'47*
Dead of Night *'45*
Pink String and Sealing Wax *'45*
On Approval *'44*
One of Our Aircraft Is Missing *'41*
Action for Slander *'38*
The Lady Vanishes *'38*
Accused *'36*

Grant Withers (1904-59)

Iron Mountain Trail *'53*
Hoodlum Empire *'52*
Oklahoma Annie *'51*
Bells of Coronado *'50*
Trigger, Jr. *'50*
The Fighting Kentuckian *'49*
Night Time in Nevada *'48*
Tycoon *'47*
My Darling Clementine *'46*
Bells of Rosarita *'45*
Fighting Seabees *'44*
The Yellow Rose of Texas *'44*
Billy the Kid *'41*
The Masked Rider *'41*
Doomed to Die *'40*
The Fatal Hour *'40*
Phantom of Chinatown *'40*
Tomboy *'40*
Boy's Reformatory *'39*
Daughter of the Tong *'39*
Irish Luck *'39*
Mr. Wong in Chinatown *'39*
Mystery of Mr. Wong *'39*
Held for Ransom *'38*
Mr. Wong, Detective *'38*
Radio Patrol *'37*
Fighting Marines *'36*
Let's Sing Again *'36*
Sky Parade *'36*
Valley of Wanted Men *'35*
Tailspin Tommy *'34*
The Secrets of Wu Sin *'32*
Other Men's Women *'31*
The Road to Ruin *'28*

Jane Withers (1926-)

Captain Newman, M.D. *'63*
Giant *'56*
The Holy Terror *'37*
The Farmer Takes a Wife *'35*
Bright Eyes *'34*

Cora Witherspoon (1890-1957)

Just for You *'52*
Colonel Effingham's Raid *'45*
The Bank Dick *'40*
Charlie Chan's Murder Cruise *'40*
Just Around the Corner *'38*
Marie Antoinette *'38*
On the Avenue *'37*
Personal Property *'37*
Quality Street *'37*
Libeled Lady *'36*

Jimmy Witherspoon (1921-97)

Georgia *'95*
Black Godfather *'74*

John Witherspoon (1942-)

Little Man *'06*
Friday After Next *'02*
The Ladies Man *'00*
Next Friday *'00*
I Got the Hook-Up *'98*
Ride *'98*
Sprung *'96*
Friday *'95*
Vampire in Brooklyn *'95*
Boomerang *'92*
Killer Tomatoes Strike Back *'90*

Reese Witherspoon (1976-)

Monsters vs. Aliens *'09 (V)*
Four Christmases *'08*
Rendition *'07*
Penelope *'06*
Just like Heaven *'05*
Walk the Line *'05*
Vanity Fair *'04*
Legally Blonde 2: Red White & Blonde *'03*
The Importance of Being Earnest *'02*
Sweet Home Alabama *'02*
Legally Blonde *'01*
The Trumpet of the Swan *'01 (V)*
Little Nicky *'00*
American Psycho *'99*
Best Laid Plans *'99*
Election *'99*
Cruel Intentions *'98*
Pleasantville *'98*
Twilight *'98*
Fear *'96*
Overnight Delivery *'96*
Freeway *'95*
S.F.W. *'94*
A Far Off Place *'93*
Jack the Bear *'93*
Return to Lonesome Dove *'93*
The Man in the Moon *'91*
Wildflower *'91*

Glenn Withrow (1953-)

Naked Lie *'89*
Pass the Ammo *'88*
Dudes *'87*
The Hollywood Knights *'80*
Lady in Red *'79*

Michael Witney (1931-83)

Darling Lili *'70*
The Way West *'67*

Alicia Witt (1975-)

88 Minutes *'08*
Blue Smoke *'07*
Last Holiday *'06*
The Upside of Anger *'05*
Two Weeks Notice *'02*
Vanilla Sky *'01*
Cecil B. Demented *'00*
Playing Mona Lisa *'00*
Bongwater *'98*
Urban Legend *'98*
Citizen Ruth *'96*
Four Rooms *'95*
Mr. Holland's Opus *'95*
Fun *'94*
Bodies, Rest & Motion *'93*
Hotel Room *'93*

Kathryn Witt (1950-)

Mickey Blue Eyes *'99*
Los Locos Posse *'97*
Buffalo Girls *'95*
Trapped in Paradise *'94*
Philadelphia *'93*
The Silence of the Lambs *'91*
Demon of Paradise *'87*
Cocaine Wars *'86*

Karen Witter (1961-)

Buried Alive *'89*
Midnight *'89*
Popcorn *'89*
The Vineyard *'89*
Perfect Match *'88*

Meg Wittner

Born Yesterday *'93*
Higher Ground *'88*

James Wlcek

Hydra *'09*
Don't Tell *'05*

Stefan Wodoslowsky

Mindfield *'89*
90 Days *'86*

David Wohl (1953-)

The Wackness *'08*
Joe Gould's Secret *'00*
Saving Private Ryan *'98*
Chillers *'88*
Armed and Dangerous *'86*

Johanna Wokalek

The Baader Meinhof Complex *'08*
North Face *'08*
Aimee & Jaguar *'98*

Fred Wolf (1964-)

Little Nicky *'00*
Dirty Work *'97*
Black Sheep *'96*

Hillary Wolf (1977-)

Big Girls Don't Cry... They Get Even *'92*
Home Alone 2: Lost in New York *'92*

Kelly Wolf

A Day in October *'92*
Graveyard Shift *'90*
Triumph of the Spirit *'89*

Scott Wolf (1968-)

Killing Emmett Young *'02*
Go *'99*
The Evening Star *'96*
White Squall *'96*
Double Dragon *'94*
Teenage Bonnie & Klepto Clyde *'93*

Sheldon Peters Wolfchild

Crazy Horse *'96*
The Scarlet Letter *'95*
Miracle in the Wilderness *'91*

David Wolfe (1915-94)

Salt of the Earth *'54*
Five Fingers *'52*
Bagdad *'49*

Ian Wolfe (1896-1992)

Games *'67*
Diary of a Madman *'63*
One Man's Way *'63*
Witness for the Prosecution *'57*
Moonfleet *'55*
The Actress *'53*
Houdini *'53*
The Great Caruso *'51*
The Magnificent Yankee *'50*
The Judge Steps Out *'49*
Bedlam *'45*
The White Cliffs of Dover *'44*
Zombies on Broadway *'44*
Mrs. Miniver *'42*
Mutiny on the Bounty *'35*
The Barretts of Wimpole Street *'34*

Jim Wolfe

Invasion of the Space Preachers *'90*
Chillers *'88*

Kedrick Wolfe

Smokey Bites the Dust *'81*
Dr. Heckyl and Mr. Hype *'80*

Traci Wolfe (1961-)

Lethal Weapon 4 *'98*
Lethal Weapon 3 *'92*
Lethal Weapon 2 *'89*
Lethal Weapon *'87*

Austin Wolff

A Death in the Family *'02*
Master of Disguise *'02*
13 Moons *'02*

Frank Wolff (1928-71)

The Lickerish Quartet *'70*
When Women Had Tails *'70*
Villa Rides *'68*
The Awful Dr. Orloff *'62*
Atlas *'60*
The Beast from Haunted Cave *'60*
Ski Troop Attack *'60*
The Wasp Woman *'59*
The King's Rhapsody *'55*

Donald Wolfit (1902-68)

The Charge of the Light Brigade *'68*
Becket *'64*
Lawrence of Arabia *'62*
The Mark *'61*
The Hands of Orlac *'60*
Room at the Top *'59*
The Rough and the Smooth *'59*
Blood of the Vampire *'58*
Svengali *'55*
Late Extra *'35*
The Silent Passenger *'35*

Wolfman Jack (1938-95)

Mortuary Academy *'91*
Midnight *'89*
Motel Hell *'80*
Deadman's Curve *'78*
Hanging on a Star *'78*
American Graffiti *'73*
A Session with The Committee *'68*

Louis Wolheim (1880-1931)

All Quiet on the Western Front *'30*
Danger Lights *'30*
The Silver Horde *'30*
Condemned *'29*
Square Shoulders *'29*
Across to Singapore *'28*
Tempest *'28*
America *'24*
Little Old New York *'23*
Sherlock Holmes *'22*
Dr. Jekyll and Mr. Hyde *'20*

Kirk B.R. Woller (1962-)

Urban Justice *'07*
Midnight Clear *'06*
Locusts: The 8th Plague *'05*
Hometown Legend *'02*
Killer Me *'01*

Sven Wollter (1934-)

Kira's Reason—A Love Story *'01*
A Song for Martin *'01*
The 13th Warrior *'99*
House of Angels *'92*
The Sacrifice *'86*
Man from Mallorca *'84*
The Man on the Roof *'76*

Ilya Woloshyn (1981-)

Hush Little Baby *'93*
Beethoven Lives Upstairs *'92*

Stevie Wonder (1950-)

Bikini Beach *'64*
Muscle Beach Party *'64*

Spring Fever '27
Paths to Paradise '25

Blake Woodruff

Whisper '07
Cheaper by the Dozen '03

Kurt Woodruff

Moving Target '89
Party Incorporated '89

Largo Woodruff

Bill: On His Own '83
Bill '81
The Choice '81
Coward of the County '81
The Funhouse '81

Barbara Alyn Woods (1962-)

I Downloaded a Ghost '04
The Wild Card '03
Dead Weekend '95
Eden '93
Eden 2 '93
Eden 3 '93
Eden 4 '93
Ghoulies 4 '93
Circuitry Man '90

Carol Woods

The Honeymooners '05
Stepping Out '91

Donald Woods (1909-98)

True Grit '69
Kissin' Cousins '64
Door to Door Maniac '61
13 Ghosts '60
The Beast from 20,000 Fathoms '53
Mr. Music '50
Bells of San Fernando '47
Never Say Goodbye '46
Roughly Speaking '45
The Bridge of San Luis Rey '44
Enemy of Women '44
Corregidor '43
Watch on the Rhine '43
If I Had My Way '40
Mexican Spitfire '40
Beauty for the Asking '39
The Black Doll '38
Danger on the Air '38
Sea Devils '37
The Story of Louis Pasteur '36
A Tale of Two Cities '36
Sweet Adeline '35

Edward (Eddie) Woods (1903-89)

Shadows over Shanghai '38
Tarzan the Fearless '33
Hot Saturday '32
They Never Come Back '32
Public Enemy '31

Harry Woods (1889-1968)

Colorado Territory '49
She Wore a Yellow Ribbon '49
Silver City Kid '45
West of the Pecos '45
Nevada '44
Westward Bound '44
Bordertown Gunfighters '43
Dawn on the Great Divide '42
Riders of the West '42
Romance on the Range '42
Today I Hang '42
Boss of Bullion City '41
Sheriff of Tombstone '41
Bullet Code '40
Winners of the West '40
Beau Geste '39
Days of Jesse James '39
In Old Caliente '39
Come on Rangers '38
Hawaiian Buckaroo '38
Last Outlaw '36
The Lawless Nineties '36
The Phantom Rider '36
The Unknown Ranger '36
Rustlers of Red Dog '35
Savage Fury '35
When a Man's a Man '35
Belle of the Nineties '34
Haunted Gold '32
Texas Gunfighter '32
Monkey Business '31
Palmy Days '31
Range Feud '31
Pardon My Gun '30
The Viking '28
Dynamite Dan '24

James Woods (1947-)

Surf's Up '07 (V)
End Game '06
Be Cool '05
Pretty Persuasion '05
Northfork '03
Rudy: The Rudy Giulani Story '03
This Girl's Life '03
John Q '02
Stuart Little 2 '02 (V)
Final Fantasy: The Spirits Within '01 (V)
Race to Space '01
Riding in Cars with Boys '01
Scary Movie 2 '01
Dirty Pictures '00
Any Given Sunday '99
The General's Daughter '99
True Crime '99
The Virgin Suicides '99
Another Day in Paradise '98
Contact '97
Hercules '97 (V)
John Carpenter's Vampires '97
Kicked in the Head '97
Ghosts of Mississippi '96
The Summer of Ben Tyler '96
Casino '95
For Better or Worse '95
Indictment: The McMartin Trial '95
Killer: A Journal of Murder '95
Nixon '95
Curse of the Starving Class '94
Next Door '94
The Specialist '94
Fallen Angels 1 '93
The Getaway '93
Chaplin '92
Citizen Cohn '92
Diggstown '92
Straight Talk '92
The Hard Way '91
In Love and War '91
The Gift of Love '90
Women & Men: Stories of Seduction '90
Immediate Family '89
My Name Is Bill W. '89
True Believer '89
The Boost '88
Cop '88
Best Seller '87
Salvador '86
Badge of the Assassin '85
Cat's Eye '85
Joshua Then and Now '85
Against All Odds '84
Once Upon a Time in America '84
Videodrome '83
Fast Walking '82
Split Image '82
Eyewitness '81
The Black Marble '79
The Incredible Journey of Dr. Meg Laurel '79
The Onion Field '79
Holocaust '78
The Choirboys '77
The Disappearance of Aimee '76
F. Scott Fitzgerald in Hollywood '76
Night Moves '75
The Gambler '74
The Way We Were '73

Michael Woods (1957-)

Demons from Her Past '07
Shock to the System '06
Rudy: The Rudy Giulani Story '03
Red Shoe Diaries: Swimming Naked '00
Blindfold: Acts of Obsession '94
Hit Woman: The Double Edge '93
Omen 4: The Awakening '91
Haunting of Sarah Hardy '89
War & Remembrance: The Final Chapter '89
War & Remembrance '88
Lady Beware '87
Agatha Christie's Sparkling Cyanide '83

Nan Woods (1966-)

China Beach '88
The Betty Ford Story '87
One More Saturday Night '86

Ren Woods (1958-)

Hostage High '97
The Brother from Another Planet '84

Robert Woods (1936-)

Chase '85
White Fang and the Hunter '85
The Perverse Countess '73
Challenge of McKenna '70
Four Dollars of Revenge '66

Simon Woods (1980-)

Cranford '08
Penelope '06
Pride and Prejudice '05
The Queen's Sister '05

DB Woodside (1969-)

More Dogs Than Bones '00
Romeo Must Die '00
The Temptations '98

Peter Woodthorpe (1931-2004)

The Charge of the Light Brigade '68
The Blue Max '66
The Skull '65
The Evil of Frankenstein '64

Kate Woodville (1938-)

Computer Wizard '77
Where's Willie? '77
Posse '75
Sex Through a Window '72

John Woodvine (1929-)

The Other Boleyn Girl '03
Persuasion '95
Dragonworld '94
Fatherland '94
Glory Enough for All: The Discovery of Insulin '92
And a Nightingale Sang '91
Edge of Darkness '86
Agatha Christie's Murder with Mirrors '85
An American Werewolf in London '81
The Life and Adventures of Nicholas Nickleby '81
Assault on Agathon '75

Edward Woodward (1930-2009)

Five Days '07
Hot Fuzz '07
Gulliver's Travels '95
A Christmas Reunion '93
Codename Kyril '91
Mister Johnson '91
Hands of a Murderer '90
Uncle Tom's Cabin '87
King David '85
Merlin and the Sword '85
Champions '84
A Christmas Carol '84
The Appointment '82
The Final Option '82
Breaker Morant '80
The Wicker Man '75
Young Winston '72
The Bloodsuckers '70

Joanne Woodward (1930-)

Empire Falls '05
Breathing Lessons '94
The Age of Innocence '93 (N)
Blind Spot '93
Foreign Affairs '93
Philadelphia '93
Mr. & Mrs. Bridge '90
The Glass Menagerie '87
Harry & Son '84
Crisis at Central High '80
The Shadow Box '80
The Streets of L.A. '79
A Christmas to Remember '78
The End '78
See How She Runs '78
Sybil '76
The Drowning Pool '75
The Effect of Gamma Rays on Man-in-the-Moon Marigolds '73
Summer Wishes, Winter Dreams '73
They Might Be Giants '71
Winning '69
Rachel, Rachel '68
A Big Hand for the Little Lady '66
A Fine Madness '66
A New Kind of Love '63
The Stripper '63
Paris Blues '61
From the Terrace '60
The Fugitive Kind '60
The Long, Hot Summer '58
Rally 'Round the Flag, Boys! '58
The Three Faces of Eve '57

Jonathan M. Woodward (1973-)

The Notorious Bettie Page '06
Wit '01

Morgan Woodward (1925-)

Dark Before Dawn '89
Girls Just Want to Have Fun '85
Battle Beyond the Stars '80
Speedtrap '78
Deadly Game '77
Moonshine County Express '77
Walking Tall: The Final Chapter '77
Which Way Is Up? '77
The Killing of a Chinese Bookie '76
The Longest Drive '76
Ride in a Pink Car '74
Running Wild '73
Death of a Gunfighter '69
Cool Hand Luke '67

Peter Woodward (1956-)

Hard Cash '01
Testament of Youth '79

Shannon Marie Woodward

The Shortcut '09
The Haunting of Molly Hartley '08

Tim Woodward (1953-)

K-19: The Widowmaker '02
Heat of the Sun '99
RKO 281 '99
B. Monkey '97
Some Mother's Son '96
The Scarlet Letter '95
The Dark Angel '91
Piece of Cake '88
Personal Services '87
The Europeans '79

Marjorie Woodworth (1919-2000)

Broadway Limited '41
Road Show '41

Emily Woof (1970-)

Wondrous Oblivion '06
Oliver Twist '00
Pandaemonium '00
Passion '99
Velvet Goldmine '98
Photographing Fairies '97
The Full Monty '96

Norman Wooland (1910-89)

Saul and David '64
Masters of Venus '62
The Rough and the Smooth '59
Teenage Bad Girl '59
Angel with the Trumpet '50
Madeleine '50

Susan Wooldridge (1952-)

Just Like a Woman '95
Twenty-One '91
How to Get Ahead in Advertising '89
Hope and Glory '87
Loyalties '86
The Last Place on Earth '85
The Jewel in the Crown '84

Sheb Wooley (1921-2003)

Hoosiers '86
Bugles in the Afternoon '52
High Noon '52

Charles Woolf (1927-94)

No Way Back '74
Private Parts '72

Eric Woolfe

Survival of the Dead '09
The Strauss Family '73

Fenella Woolgar (1973-)

Jekyll '07
St. Trinian's '07
Scoop '06
Wah-Wah '05
Bright Young Things '03

Monty Woolley (1888-1963)

As Young As You Feel '51
Miss Tatlock's Millions '48
The Bishop's Wife '47
Night and Day '46
Since You Went Away '44
The Man Who Came to Dinner '41
Man About Town '39
Never Say Die '39
Everybody Sing '38
Three Comrades '38

Robert Woolsey (1889-1938)

Cockeyed Cavaliers '34
Hips, Hips, Hooray '34
Kentucky Kernels '34
Diplomaniacs '33
So This Is Africa '33
Hold 'Em Jail '32
Dixiana '30
Half-Shot at Sunrise '30
Hook, Line and Sinker '30
Rio Rita '29

Michael Woolson

Au Pair '99
Widow's Kiss '94

Gordon Michael Woolvett (1970-)

Everything's Gone Green '06
The Highway Man '99
Bride of Chucky '98
The Legend of Gator Face '96

Jaimz Woolvett (1967-)

Power Play '02
Rock My World '02
Red Water '01
Under Heavy Fire '01
The Stepdaughter '00
The Guilty '99
Rites of Passage '99
Tail Lights Fade '99
Y2K '99
Boogie Boy '98
Sanctuary '98
The Assistant '97
Rosewood '96
The Dark '94
The Pathfinder '94
Unforgiven '92

Tom Wopat (1951-)

Taking Chance '09
The Hive '08
Bonneville '06
Contagious '96
Christmas Comes to Willow Creek '87
Burning Rage '84

Hank Worden (1901-92)

Almost an Angel '90
Scream '83
Uforia '81
Smokey and the Bandit '77
Zachariah '70
True Grit '69
The Alamo '60
The Horse Soldiers '59
The Searchers '56
Red River '48
Ghost Town Riders '38
The Stranger from Arizona '38

Marc Worden

Sky Blue '03 (V)
The Lesser Evil '97

Richard Wordsworth (1915-93)

Time Without Pity '57
The Quatermass Experiment '56

Jimmy Workman (1980-)

As Good As It Gets '97
Addams Family Values '93
The Addams Family '91

Jo Anne Worley (1937-)

A Goofy Movie '94 (V)
Beauty and the Beast '91 (V)
Tut & Tuttle '81

Frederick Worlock (1886-1973)

101 Dalmatians '61 (V)
The Woman in Green '49
The Last of the Redmen '47
Love from a Stranger '47
She Wolf of London '46
International Lady '41
Strange Cargo '40

Mary Woronov (1943-)

The House of the Devil '09
The Devil's Rejects '05
Invisible Mom 2 '99
Sweet Jane '98
Glory Daze '96
Invisible Mom '96
Good Girls Don't '95
Grief '94
Shake, Rattle & Rock! '94
Acting on Impulse '93
Mortuary Academy '91
Motorama '91
Rock 'n' Roll High School Forever '91
Warlock '91
Club Fed '90
Let It Ride '89
Scenes from the Class Struggle in Beverly Hills '89
Black Widow '87
Chopping Mall '86
Nomads '86
Terrorvision '86
Challenge of a Lifetime '85
Hellhole '85
Night of the Comet '84
The Princess Who Never Laughed '84
Get Crazy '83
Angel of H.E.A.T. '82
Eating Raoul '82
Heartbeeps '81
Lady in Red '79
Rock 'n' Roll High School '79
The Movie House Massacre '78

Margaret Wycherly (1881-1956)
White Heat *'49*
Forever Amber *'47*
Something in the Wind *'47*
The Yearling *'46*
Crossroads *'42*
Hangmen Also Die *'42*
Keeper of the Flame *'42*
Random Harvest *'42*
Sergeant York *'41*
Midnight *'34*

Katya Wyeth (1949-)
Dressed for Death *'74*
Twins of Evil *'71*

Michael Wyle
God's Lonely Man *'96*
Appointment with Fear *'85*

Noah Wyle (1971-)
An American Affair *'09*
The Librarian: Curse of the Judas Chalice *'08*
Nothing But the Truth *'08*
W. *'08*
The Librarian: Return to King Solomon's Mines *'06*
The Librarian: Quest for the Spear *'04*
Enough *'02*
White Oleander *'02*
Donnie Darko *'01*
Fail Safe *'00*
The Pirates of Silicon Valley *'99*
The Myth of Fingerprints *'97*
Swing Kids *'93*
A Few Good Men *'92*
There Goes My Baby *'92*
Crooked Hearts *'91*

Gretchen Wyler (1932-2007)
The Marrying Man *'91*
The Devil's Brigade *'68*

Adam Wylie (1984-)
Daybreak *'01*
Can of Worms *'00*
The King and I *'99 (V)*
Children of the Corn 5: Fields of Terror *'98*
Balloon Farm *'97*
Santa with Muscles *'96*
All Dogs Go to Heaven 2 *'95 (V)*
Breaking Free *'95*

John Wylie (1925-2004)
Robot in the Family *'94*
An Empty Bed *'90*

Daniel Wyllie
Unconditional Love *'03*
Chopper *'00*
Holy Smoke *'99*
Romper Stomper *'92*

Bill Wyman (1936-)
Eat the Rich *'87*
Gimme Shelter *'70*

Jane Wyman (1917-2007)
The Incredible Journey of Dr. Meg Laurel *'79*
How to Commit Marriage *'69*
Bon Voyage! *'62*
Pollyanna *'60*
All That Heaven Allows *'55*
Magnificent Obsession *'54*
Just for You *'52*
Here Comes the Groom *'51*
Three Guys Named Mike *'51*
Stage Fright *'50*
It's a Great Feeling *'49*
Johnny Belinda *'48*
Magic Town *'47*
Night and Day *'46*
The Yearling *'46*
The Lost Weekend *'45*
Princess O'Rourke *'43*
Footlight Serenade *'42*
Larceny, Inc. *'42*
The Spy Ring *'38*
Wide Open Faces *'38*
My Man Godfrey *'36*

John Wyman
Tuxedo Warrior *'82*
For Your Eyes Only *'81*

Patrick Wymark (1926-70)
The Blood on Satan's Claw *'71*
Battle of Britain *'69*
Journey to the Far Side of the Sun *'69*
The Conqueror Worm *'68*
Where Eagles Dare *'68*
Woman Times Seven *'67*
Repulsion *'65*
The Skull *'65*

Patrice Wymore (1926-)
The King's Rhapsody *'55*
Big Trees *'52*
I'll See You in My Dreams *'51*
Rocky Mountain *'50*
Tea for Two *'50*

Geraint Wyn Davies (1957-)
American Psycho 2: All American Girl *'02*
Cube 2: Hypercube *'02*
Trilogy of Terror 2 *'96*
Hush Little Baby *'93*
Terror Stalks the Class Reunion *'93*

H.M. Wynant (1927-)
The Big Empty *'98*
Conquest of the Planet of the Apes *'72*
Run Silent, Run Deep *'58*
Run of the Arrow *'56*

George Wyner (1945-)
How to be a Serial Killer *'08*
For Richer, for Poorer *'92*
The Taking of Beverly Hills *'91*
Fletch Lives *'89*
Spaceballs *'87*
Fletch *'85*
The Bad News Bears Go to Japan *'78*
Missiles of October *'74*

Joel Wyner (1969-)
Random Encounter *'98*
Listen *'96*
The Club *'94*

Peter Wyngarde (1923-)
Double Cross *'92*
Burn Witch, Burn! *'62*
The Innocents *'61*
The Siege of Sidney Street *'60*

Mick Wynhoff
5 Dark Souls *'96*
America's Deadliest Home Video *'91*

Joel D. Wynkoop (1960-)
Addicted to Murder 2: Tainted Blood *'97*
The Alien Agenda: Endangered Species *'97*

Ed Wynn (1886-1966)
The Gnome-Mobile *'67*
Dear Brigitte *'65*
The Greatest Story Ever Told *'65*
Those Calloways *'65*
Mary Poppins *'64*
The Absent-Minded Professor *'61*
Babes in Toyland *'61*
Cinderfella *'60*
The Diary of Anne Frank *'59*
Marjorie Morningstar *'58*
Requiem for a Heavyweight *'56*
Alice in Wonderland *'51 (V)*

Keenan Wynn (1916-86)
Hyper-Sapien: People from Another Star *'86*
Call to Glory *'84*
Wavelength *'83*
Best Friends *'82*
The Capture of Grizzly Adams *'82*
The Last Unicorn *'82 (V)*
A Piano for Mrs. Cimino *'82*
Just Tell Me What You Want *'80*
Mission to Glory *'80*
Mom, the Wolfman and Me *'80*
The Clonus Horror *'79*
The Dark *'79*
Hard Knocks *'79*
Mid Knight Rider *'79*
The Treasure Seekers *'79*
The Bastard *'78*
Coach *'78*
Laserblast *'78*
The Lucifer Complex *'78*
Monster *'78*
Piranha *'78*
Orca *'77*
High Velocity *'76*
The Killer Inside Me *'76*
The Longest Drive *'76*
The Shaggy D.A. *'76*
Devil's Rain *'75*
He Is My Brother *'75*
The Man Who Would Not Die *'75*
Nashville *'75*
Herbie Rides Again *'74*
Hit Lady *'74*
Legend of Earl Durand *'74*
Internecine Project *'73*
Cancel My Reservation *'72*
The Mechanic *'72*
Snowball Express *'72*
Manipulator *'71*
The Desperados *'70*
Loving *'70*
MacKenna's Gold *'69*
Smith! *'69*
Viva Max *'69*
Finian's Rainbow *'68*
Once Upon a Time in the West *'68*
Point Blank *'67*
The War Wagon *'67*
Promise Her Anything *'66*
Around the World Under the Sea *'65*
The Great Race *'65*
The Americanization of Emily *'64*
Bikini Beach *'64*
Dr. Strangelove, or: How I Learned to Stop Worrying and Love the Bomb *'64*
The Patsy *'64*
Son of Flubber *'63*
Pattern for Plunder *'62*
The Absent-Minded Professor *'61*
The King of the Roaring '20s: The Story of Arnold Rothstein *'61*
The Crowded Sky *'60*
A Hole in the Head *'59*
The Perfect Furlough *'59*
Deep Six *'58*
A Time to Love & a Time to Die *'58*
Don't Go Near the Water *'57*
The Man in the Gray Flannel Suit *'56*
Naked Hills *'56*
Requiem for a Heavyweight *'56*
The Glass Slipper *'55*
Shack Out on 101 *'55*
The Long, Long Trailer *'54*
Men of the Fighting Lady *'54*
All the Brothers Were Valiant *'53*
Battle Circus *'53*
Kiss Me Kate *'53*
The Belle of New York *'52*
Phone Call from a Stranger *'52*
Angels in the Outfield *'51*
It's a Big Country *'51*
Royal Wedding *'51*
Texas Carnival *'51*
Annie Get Your Gun *'50*
Three Little Words *'50*
My Dear Secretary *'49*
Neptune's Daughter *'49*
That Midnight Kiss *'49*
The Three Musketeers *'48*
The Hucksters *'47*
Song of the Thin Man *'47*
Easy to Wed *'46*
The Clock *'45*
Weekend at the Waldorf *'45*
Without Love *'45*
Since You Went Away *'44*
For Me and My Gal *'42*
Somewhere I'll Find You *'42*

May Wynn (1931-)
The Violent Men *'55*
The Caine Mutiny *'54*
The Farmer Takes a Wife *'53*

Christopher Wynne
1969 *'89*
Remote Control *'88*

Gilbert Wynne
He Kills Night After Night After Night *'69*
Night Slasher *'69*

Dana Wynter (1930-)
Backstairs at the White House *'79*
Lovers Like Us *'75*
The Savage *'75*
The Connection *'73*
Santee *'73*
Airport *'70*
Dead Right *'68*
The List of Adrian Messenger *'63*
Sink the Bismarck *'60*
Shake Hands with the Devil *'59*
Something of Value *'57*
D-Day, the Sixth of June *'56*
Invasion of the Body Snatchers *'56*

Sarah Wynter (1973-)
Circadian Rhythm *'05*
L.A. Dicks *'05*
Shooting Livien *'05*
Coastlines *'02*
Bride of the Wind *'01*
Lost Souls *'00*
Race Against Time *'00*
The 6th Day *'00*

Charlotte Wynters (1899-1991)
Harvest Melody *'43*
Tomboy *'40*
Hopalong Cassidy: Renegade Trail *'39*
Nancy Drew—Trouble Shooter *'39*
Panama Patrol *'39*
Renegade Trail *'39*
Sinners in Paradise *'38*
The Ivory Handled Gun *'35*
Struggle *'31*

Diana Wynyard (1906-64)
An Ideal Husband *'47*
Gaslight *'40*
Cavalcade *'33*
Rasputin and the Empress *'33*

Amanda Wyss (1960-)
Desert Steel *'94*
Bloodfist 4: Die Trying *'92*
Black Magic Woman *'91*
To Die For 2: Son of Darkness *'91*
Powwow Highway *'89*
Shakma *'89*
To Die For *'89*
Deadly Innocence *'88*
Better Off Dead *'85*
My Mother's Secret Life *'84*
A Nightmare on Elm Street *'84*
Fast Times at Ridgemont High *'82*

Nelson Xavier (1941-)
At Play in the Fields of the Lord *'91*
Gabriela *'84*

Xin-Xin Xiong (1965-)
Once Upon a Time in China III *'93*
Once Upon a Time in China II *'92*

Zhu Xu
Shower *'00*
The King of Masks *'99*

Wang Xueqi
Warriors of Heaven and Earth *'03*
Yellow Earth *'89*

Salvator Xuereb (1965-)
Lewis and Clark and George *'97*
My Brother's War *'97*
Ravager *'97*
Blood Ties *'92*

Xzibit (1974-)
American Violet *'09*
Bad Lieutenant: Port of Call New Orleans *'09*
The X Files: I Want to Believe *'08*
Gridiron Gang *'06*
Derailed *'05*
Hoodwinked *'05 (V)*
XXX: State of the Union *'05*

Kaoru Yachigusa (1931-)
Snow Country *'57*
Samurai 3: Duel at Ganryu Island *'56*
Samurai 1: Musashi Miyamoto *'55*
Samurai 2: Duel at Ichijoji Temple *'55*

Frank Yaconelli (1898-1965)
Riding the California Trail *'47*
South of Monterey *'47*
Lone Star Law Men *'42*
Western Mail *'42*
The Driftin' Kid *'41*
Riding the Sunset Trail *'41*
Dr. Cyclops *'40*
Across the Plains *'39*
Escape to Paradise *'39*
Wild Horse Canyon *'39*
Gun Play *'36*
Western Frontier *'35*
The Barber Shop *'33*

Raghuvir Yadav
Water *'05*
Lagaan: Once upon a Time in India *'01*
Bandit Queen *'94*
Salaam Bombay! *'88*

Jeff Yagher (1962-)
My Fellow Americans *'96*
Madonna: Innocence Lost *'95*
Lower Level *'91*
Shag: The Movie *'89*
Big Bad Mama 2 *'87*

Kenichi Yajima
Inugami *'01*
Onmyoji *'01*
Sonatine *'96*

Koji Yakusho (1956-)
Tokyo Sonata *'09*
Silk *'07*
Babel *'06*
Retribution *'06*
Memoirs of a Geisha *'05*
Pulse *'01*
Seance *'00*
Charisma *'99*
Cure *'97*
The Eel *'96*
Shall We Dance? *'96*
Tampopo *'86*

Simon Yam (1955-)
Exiled *'06*
Breaking News *'04*
Lara Croft Tomb Raider: The Cradle of Life *'03*
Full Time Killer *'01*
The Mission *'99*
Full Contact *'92*
Naked Killer *'92*
A Bullet in the Head *'90*
Tongs: An American Nightmare *'88*

Isuzu Yamada (1917-)
Shogun's Samurai—The Yagyu Clan Conspiracy *'78*
Yojimbo *'61*
The Lower Depths *'57*
Throne of Blood *'57*
Osaka Elegy *'36*
Sisters of the Gion *'36*

Mame Yamada
The Great Yokai War *'05*
9 Souls *'03*

Isao Yamagata (1915-96)
Shogun Assassin 2: Lightning Swords of Death *'73*
Warning from Space *'56*
Gate of Hell *'54*

Sayaka Yamaguchi
Pistol Opera *'02*
Rebirth of Mothra 2 *'97*
Rebirth of Mothra *'96*

Yoshiko (Shirley) Yamaguchi (1920-)
House of Bamboo *'55*
Scandal *'50*

Kenji Yamaki
Onmyoji 2 *'03*
Onmyoji *'01*

Fujiko Yamamoto (1931-)
An Actor's Revenge *'63*
Being Two Isn't Easy *'62*
Golden Demon *'53*

So Yamamura (1910-2000)
Gung Ho *'85*
Last Days of Planet Earth *'74*
Tora! Tora! Tora! *'70*
Barbarian and the Geisha *'58*
The Human Condition: No Greater Love *'58*
Princess Yang Kwei Fei *'55*
Tokyo Story *'53*

Hal Yamanouchi (1946-)
The Lone Runner *'88*
Endgame *'85*
2020 Texas Gladiators *'85*

Shingo Yamashiro (1938-)
Graveyard of Honor *'02*
Snake Woman's Curse *'68*

Tsutomu Yamazaki (1936-)
Departures *'08*
Doing Time *'02*
Rikyu *'90*
A Taxing Woman *'87*
Tampopo *'86*
The Funeral *'84*
Kagemusha *'80*

Yurei Yanagi
Ju-On 2 *'00*
Ringu 2 *'99*
Ringu *'98*

Emily Yancy (1939-)
Jasper, Texas *'03*
Blacula *'72*
Cotton Comes to Harlem *'70*

Eduardo Yanez (1960-)
The Punisher *'04*
Held Up *'00*

Kuei-Mei Yang
The Hole *'98*
Eat Drink Man Woman *'94*

Tony Yang
Blood Brothers *'07*
Formula 17 *'04*

Edward Yankie
The Sign of Four '01
Deadline '00

Weird Al Yankovic (1959-)
Naked Gun 33 1/3: The Final Insult '94
Naked Gun 2 1/2: The Smell of Fear '91
Tapeheads '89
UHF '89
The Naked Gun: From the Files of Police Squad '88

Jean Yanne (1933-2003)
Brotherhood of the Wolf '01
Beaumarchais the Scoundrel '96
The Horseman on the Roof '95
Victory '95
A la Mode '94
Indochine '92
Madame Bovary '91
Quicker Than the Eye '88
The Wolf at the Door '87
Bandits '86
Hanna K. '83
Cobra '71
This Man Must Die '70
Le Boucher '69
Weekend '67
Life Upside Down '64

Rossana Yanni (1938-)
The Rue Morgue Massacres '73
Dracula's Great Love '72
Fangs of the Living Dead '68
White Comanche '67

Atta Yaqub
Nina's Heavenly Delights '06
A Fond Kiss '04

Lillian Yarbo
Way Down South '39
You Can't Take It with You '38

Cedric Yarbrough
Black Dynamite '09
Entry Level '07
Reno 911! Miami '07
Mulligan '00

Margaret Yarde (1878-1944)
Thursday's Child '43
Crimes at the Dark House '39
The Deputy Drummer '35

Claire Yarlett (1965-)
Black Out '96
The Disappearance of Christina '93

Michael Yarmush (1982-)
Crown Heights '02
Little Men '98
First Do No Harm '97

Celeste Yarnall (1944-)
Born Yesterday '93
Midnight Kiss '93
Scorpio '73
The Velvet Vampire '71

Amy Yasbeck (1963-)
Dead Husbands '98
Something About Sex '98
Bloodhounds 2 '96
Dracula: Dead and Loving It '95
The Nutt House '95
The Mask '94
Robin Hood: Men in Tights '93
Problem Child 2 '91
Problem Child '90
House 2: The Second Story '87

Miki Yashiro
Attack of the Mushroom People '63
Matango '63

Rikiya Yasuoka (1947-)
The Toxic Avenger, Part 2 '89
Tampopo '86

Cassie Yates (1951-)
Perry Mason Returns '85
Unfaithfully Yours '84
Agatha Christie's A Caribbean Mystery '83
St. Helen's, Killer Volcano '82
Who'll Save Our Children? '82
Of Mice and Men '81
Father Figure '80
Convoy '78
The Evil '78
F.I.S.T. '78
FM '78

Marjorie Yates (1941-)
The Long Day Closes '92
Legend of the Werewolf '75
The Optimists '73

Isao Yatsu
Dark Water '02
Ringu 2 '99

Chingmy Yau
Meltdown '95
Legend of the Liquid Sword '93
Naked Killer '92

Jose Maria Yazpik (1970-)
Beverly Hills Chihuahua '08
The Burning Plain '08
Sueno '05
Cronicas '04
Innocent Voices '04
Nicotina '03

Liu Ye (1978-)
Curse of the Golden Flower '06
Balzac and the Little Chinese Seamstress '02
Lan Yu '01

Biff Yeager
Headless Body in Topless Bar '96
Straight to Hell '87
Sid & Nancy '86
Girls Just Want to Have Fun '85
Repo Man '83
Black Samurai '77

Steve Yeager (1948-)
Major League 3: Back to the Minors '98
Polyester '81
Pink Flamingos '72

Richard Yearwood
Webs '03
Breakaway '02
Dangerous Evidence: The Lori Jackson Story '99
Blood Brothers '97

Kelvin Han Yee
Lucky You '07
Life Tastes Good '99
A Great Wall '86

Sally Yeh (1961-)
The Killer '90
The Laserman '90

Anton Yelchin (1989-)
New York, I Love You '09
Star Trek '09
Terminator Salvation '09
Charlie Bartlett '07
Alpha Dog '06
Fierce People '05
House of D '04
Along Came a Spider '01
Hearts in Atlantis '01
A Time for Dancing '00

Hannah Yelland (1976-)
Dinotopia '02
Catherine Cookson's The Secret '00

Peter Yellen
Ms. 45 '81
Driller Killer '79

Donnie Yen (1963-)
Flash Point '07
Hero '03
Shanghai Knights '03
Blade 2 '02
Highlander: Endgame '00
Wing Chun '94
Iron Monkey '93

Tran Nu Yen-Khe (1968-)
The Vertical Ray of the Sun '00
Cyclo '95
The Scent of Green Papaya '93

Gwendoline Yeo
Night Skies '07
Broken Trail '06

Michelle Yeoh (1962-)
Babylon A.D. '08
The Children of Huang Shi '08
The Mummy: Tomb of the Dragon Emperor '08
Far North '07
Sunshine '07
Memoirs of a Geisha '05
Silver Hawk '04
Crouching Tiger, Hidden Dragon '00
Tomorrow Never Dies '97
Wing Chun '94
The Executioners '93
The Heroic Trio '93
Supercop 2 '93
Twin Warriors '93
Supercop '92
Royal Warriors '86

Don Yesso (1954-)
Out of Sync '95
The Hard Truth '94
Hero '92

Bolo Yeung (1938-)
Shootfighter 2: Kill or Be Killed! '96
Fearless Tiger '94
Shootfighter: Fight to the Death '93
TC 2000 '93
Ironheart '92
Breathing Fire '91
Tiger Claws '91
Bloodsport '88
Legacy of Rage '86
The Three Avengers '80
The Young Bruce Lee '80
King Boxer '72
The Wandering Swordsman '70

Charlie Yeung
Bangkok Dangerous '08
New Police Story '04

Serra Yilmaz (1954-)
Saturn in Opposition '07
Facing Windows '03
His Secret Life '01

Da(nniel) Ying
The White Countess '05
Big Shot's Funeral '01
Farewell My Concubine '93

Cecilia Yip (1962-)
What Time Is It There? '01
Organized Crime & Triad Bureau '93
Hong Kong 1941 '84

Francoise Yip (1972-)
Dim Sum Funeral '08
The Deal '05
Blade: Trinity '04
Romeo Must Die '00
Futuresport '98
Black Mask '96
Rumble in the Bronx '96

Richard Yniguez (1946-)
Stalking Laura '93
World War III '86
Boulevard Nights '79
Sniper '75

Kimiko Yo
The Ramen Girl '08
Gonin 2 '96

Dwight Yoakam (1956-)
Crank: High Voltage '09
Four Christmases '08
Crank '06
The Three Burials of Melquiades Estrada '05
Wedding Crashers '05
3-Way '04
Hollywood Homicide '03
Panic Room '02
South of Heaven, West of Hell '00
The Minus Man '99
When Trumpets Fade '98
The Newton Boys '97
Don't Look Back '96
Sling Blade '96
The Little Death '95
Painted Hero '95
Roswell: The U.F.O. Cover-Up '94
Red Rock West '93

Malik Yoba (1967-)
Tyler Perry's Why Did I Get Married Too? '10
Tyler Perry's Why Did I Get Married? '07
Kids in America '05
Personals '00
Ride '98
Cop Land '97
Blue in the Face '95
Smoke '95
Cool Runnings '93

Erica Yohn
Corrina, Corrina '94
An American Tail: Fievel Goes West '91 (V)
A Streetcar Named Desire '84

You Yong
Red Cliff '08
Breaking News '04

Aaron Yoo
The Good Guy '10
Friday the 13th '09
Nick & Norah's Infinite Playlist '08
21 '08
Disturbia '07

Wladimir Yordanoff
I Do '06
The Taste of Others '00
Un Air de Famille '96
Vincent & Theo '90

Dick York (1929-92)
Inherit the Wind '60
They Came to Cordura '59
Cowboy '58
Operation Mad Ball '57
My Sister Eileen '55

Francine York (1938-)
Flood! '76
The Centerfold Girls '74
The Doll Squad '73
Curse of the Swamp Creature '66
Space Monster '64
Secret File of Hollywood '62
Wild Ones on Wheels '62

Jeff York (1912-95)
Savage Sam '63
Old Yeller '57
Davy Crockett and the River Pirates '56
Westward Ho, the Wagons! '56
The Lady Says No '51
Kill the Umpire '50
The Yearling '46
They Were Expendable '45

Kathleen York
Front of the Class '08
Sublime '07
Shelter Island '03
The Big Day '99
Cries of Silence '97
Dead Men Can't Dance '97
Nightjohn '96
Dream Lover '93
Wild Hearts Can't Be Broken '91
Thompson's Last Run '90
Checking Out '89
Cold Feet '89
Winners Take All '87

Michael York (1942-)
Frederick Forsyth's Icon '05
Austin Powers In Goldmember '02
Borstal Boy '00
Austin Powers 2: The Spy Who Shagged Me '99
The Haunting of Hell House '99
The Omega Code '99
54 '98
A Knight in Camelot '98
The Treat '98
Wrongfully Accused '98
Austin Powers: International Man of Mystery '97
Dark Planet '97
The Ripper '97
True Women '97
Not of This Earth '96
A Young Connecticut Yankee in King Arthur's Court '95
Fall from Grace '94
Gospa '94
Discretion Assured '93
Duel of Hearts '92
Wide Sargasso Sea '92
The Heat of the Day '91
Night of the Fox '90
The Lady and the Highwayman '89
The Return of the Musketeers '89
The Four Minute Mile '88
Midnight Cop '88
Lethal Obsession '87
Phantom of Death '87
Sword of Gideon '86
Nevil Shute's The Far Country '85
Success Is the Best Revenge '84
Weather in the Streets '84
Final Assignment '80
The Riddle of the Sands '79
The Island of Dr. Moreau '77
The Last Remake of Beau Geste '77
Logan's Run '76
Conduct Unbecoming '75
The Four Musketeers '75
Murder on the Orient Express '74
The Three Musketeers '74
Cabaret '72
Zeppelin '71
Something for Everyone '70
Justine '69
Romeo and Juliet '68
Accident '67
Smashing Time '67
The Taming of the Shrew '67

Morgan York (1993-)
Cheaper by the Dozen 2 '05
The Pacifier '05
Cheaper by the Dozen '03

Rachel York (1971-)
Au Pair 2: The Fairy Tale Continues '01
Terror Tract '00
One Fine Day '96
Dead Center '94
Killer Instinct '92

Susannah York (1941-)
Visitors '03
St. Patrick: The Irish Legend '00
Romance and Rejection '96
Devices and Desires '91
Fate '90
The Man from the Pru '89
American Roulette '88
Diamond's Edge '88
A Summer Story '88
The Land of Faraway '87
Prettykill '87
Superman 4: The Quest for Peace '87 (V)
Alice '86
A Christmas Carol '84
Loophole '83
Yellowbeard '83
We'll Meet Again '82
The Awakening '80
Falling in Love Again '80
Second Chance '80
Superman 2 '80
The Shout '78
The Silent Partner '78
Superman: The Movie '78
Adventures of Eliza Fraser '76
Sky Riders '76
Conduct Unbecoming '75
That Lucky Touch '75
Images '72
X, Y & Zee '72
Battle of Britain '69
The Killing of Sister George '69
Oh! What a Lovely War '69
They Shoot Horses, Don't They? '69
Sebastian '68
Kaleidoscope '66
A Man for All Seasons '66
The Seventh Dawn '64
Tom Jones '63
Tunes of Glory '60

Jade Yorker
America '09
Bomb the System '05

Bud Yorkin (1926-)
For the Boys '91
Inspector Clouseau '68

Teruo Yoshida
Body Snatcher from Hell '69
Horrors of Malformed Men '69

Jitsuko Yoshimura (1943-)
Onibaba '64
The Insect Woman '63

Hidetaka Yoshioka
The Hidden Blade '04
The Sea is Watching '02

Ge You (1957-)
Big Shot's Funeral '01
The Emperor's Shadow '96
To Live '94
Farewell My Concubine '93

Aden Young (1972-)
The Starter Wife '07
After the Deluge '03
The Crocodile Hunter: Collision Course '02
The War Bride '01
In the Shadows '98
Cousin Bette '97
Hotel de Love '96
Cosi '95
River Street '95
Metal Skin '94
Sniper '92
Black Robe '91

Alan Young (1919-)
The Time Machine '02
Beverly Hills Cop 3 '94
DuckTales the Movie: Treasure of the Lost Lamp '90 (V)
The Great Mouse Detective '86 (V)
Baker's Hawk '76
The Time Machine '60
Androcles and the Lion '52

Artie Young
Bronze Buckaroo '39
Harlem Rides the Range '39

Bellamy Young
The Freebie '10
Mission '00

Bill Young (1950-)
Japanese Story '03
Chopper '00
Road to Nhill '97

Bruce A. Young (1956-)
Into Temptation '09
Jurassic Park 3 '01
Normal Life '96
The War '94
Blink '93
What Ever Happened To... '93
Basic Instinct '92

Burt Young (1940-)
Camera: The Walking Mountain '08
Hack! '07
Rocky Balboa '06
Carlito's Way: Rise to Power '05
Shut Up and Kiss Me '05
Transamerica '05
Land of Plenty '04
The Adventures of Pluto Nash '02
Blue Moon '00
Table One '00
Mickey Blue Eyes '99
Hot Blooded '98
Kicked in the Head '97
She's So Lovely '97
The Undertaker's Wedding '97
Heaven Before I Die '96
North Star '96
Red Blooded 2 '96
Excessive Force '93
Bright Angel '91
A Family Matter '91
Backstreet Dreams '90
Betsy's Wedding '90
Club Fed '90
Diving In '90
Last Exit to Brooklyn '90
Rocky 5 '90
Wait until Spring, Bandini '90
Beverly Hills Brats '89
Going Overboard '89
Blood Red '88
Back to School '86
Rocky 4 '85
Once Upon a Time in America '84
The Pope of Greenwich Village '84
A Summer to Remember '84
Over the Brooklyn Bridge '83
Amityville 2: The Possession '82
Lookin' to Get Out '82
Rocky 3 '82
...All the Marbles '81
Blood Beach '81
Rocky 2 '79
Convoy '78
The Choirboys '77
Twilight's Last Gleaming '77
Harry & Walter Go to New York '76
Rocky '76
The Killer Elite '75
Chinatown '74
The Gambler '74
Cinderella Liberty '73
Carnival of Blood '71

Carleton Young (1907-71)
The Man Who Shot Liberty Valance '62
Armored Command '61
The Gallant Hours '60
Sergeant Rutledge '60
The Horse Soldiers '59
Battle Cry '55
20,000 Leagues under the Sea '54
From Here to Eternity '53
Kansas City Confidential '52
Flying Leathernecks '51
Hard, Fast and Beautiful '51
People Will Talk '51
Thunder River Feud '42
Texas Trouble '41
Trigger Men '41
Adventures of Red Ryder '40
Battling Outlaw '40
Billy the Kid in Texas '40
Up in the Air '40
El Diablo Rides '39
Zorro's Fighting Legion '39
Heroes of the Hills '38
Outlaw Express '38
Reefer Madness '38

Chris Young (1971-)
Killing Mr. Griffin '97
Deep Down '94
P.C.U. '94
Runaway Daughters '94
Warlock: The Armageddon '93
Book of Love '91
December '91
The Runestone '91
The Great Outdoors '88

Clara Kimball Young (1890-1960)
The Frontiersmen '38
Oh Susannah '38
Rogue's Tavern '36
Chandu on the Magic Island '34
I Can't Escape '34
Return of Chandu '34
Murder on the High Seas '32
Probation '32
Kept Husbands '31
Mother and Son '31
The Worldly Madonna '22
Mid-Channel '20
The Eyes of Youth '19
Trilby '17

Damian Young
Kill the Poor '06
Amateur '94

David Young
Double Exposure '82
Banjo Hackett '76
Mary, Mary, Bloody Mary '76

Dey Young (1955-)
Protecting the King '07
The Mod Squad '99
True Heart '97
The Shadow Conspiracy '96
Letter to My Killer '95
Pie in the Sky '95
No Place to Hide '93
Back in the USSR '92
Conflict of Interest '92
Frankie and Johnny '91
Murder 101 '91
Spontaneous Combustion '89
Doin' Time '85
Strange Invaders '83
Strange Behavior '81
Rock 'n' Roll High School '79

Faron Young (1932-96)
Daniel Boone: Trail Blazer '56
Hidden Guns '56

Gig Young (1913-78)
The Hindenburg '75
The Killer Elite '75
Bring Me the Head of Alfredo Garcia '74
Lovers and Other Strangers '70
They Shoot Horses, Don't They? '69
Blood Island '68
Strange Bedfellows '65
For Love or Money '63
Kid Galahad '62
That Touch of Mink '62
Ask Any Girl '59
Teacher's Pet '58
The Tunnel of Love '58
Desk Set '57
Desperate Hours '55
Young at Heart '54
City That Never Sleeps '53
The Girl Who Had Everything '53
Torch Song '53
Slaughter Trail '51
Hunt the Man Down '50
Only the Valiant '50
Lust for Gold '49
Tell It to the Judge '49
Wake of the Red Witch '49
The Three Musketeers '48
Escape Me Never '47
Air Force '43
Sergeant York '41
They Died with Their Boots On '41

Harrison Young (1930-2005)
The Pleasure Drivers '05
House of 1000 Corpses '03
The Adventures of Rocky & Bullwinkle '00
Reptilian '99
Saving Private Ryan '98

Karen Young (1958-)
Factotum '06
Heading South '05
Mercy '00
Joe the King '99
Daylight '96
The Wife '95
Drug Wars 2: The Cocaine Cartel '92
Hoffa '92
The Ten Million Dollar Getaway '91
Little Sweetheart '90
Criminal Law '89
Night Game '89
Torch Song Trilogy '88
Heat '87
Jaws: The Revenge '87
9 1/2 Weeks '86
Almost You '85
Birdy '84
Maria's Lovers '84
Deep in the Heart '83

Keone Young (1947-)
Return to Halloweentown '06
Uncorked '98
Beverly Hills Bodysnatchers '89

Lee Thompson Young (1984-)
The Hills Have Eyes 2 '07
Akeelah and the Bee '06
Friday Night Lights '04

Loretta Young (1913-2000)
Because of You '52
Cause for Alarm '51
Key to the City '50
Come to the Stable '49
The Accused '48
Rachel and the Stranger '48
The Bishop's Wife '47
The Farmer's Daughter '47
The Perfect Marriage '46
The Stranger '46
Along Came Jones '45
China '43
A Night to Remember '42
Doctor Takes a Wife '40
Eternally Yours '39
The Story of Alexander Graham Bell '39
Four Men and a Prayer '38
Cafe Metropole '37
Love Is News '37
Second Honeymoon '37
The Crusades '35
Employees' Entrance '33
Heroes for Sale '33
Midnight Mary '33
They Call It Sin '32
Big Business Girl '31
Platinum Blonde '31

Mary (Marsden) Young (1880-1971)
Alias Jesse James '59
The Lost Weekend '45
Watch on the Rhine '43

Nedrick Young (1913-68)
Terror in a Texas Town '58
Crime Wave '54
Captain Scarlett '53
Gun Crazy '49
Dead Men Walk '43

Neil Young (1945-)
Love at Large '89
Made in Heaven '87
'68 '87

Noah Young (1887-1958)
For Heaven's Sake '26
Battling Orioles '24
Safety Last '23

Otis Young (1932-2001)
Blood Beach '81
The Capture of Bigfoot '79
The Last Detail '73

Paul Young (1944-)
The Girl in the Picture '86
Another Time, Another Place '83
Geordie '55

Polly Ann Young (1908-97)
The Invisible Ghost '41
Road Show '41
Murder on the Yukon '40
Mystery Plane '39
The Story of Alexander Graham Bell '39
The Crimson Trail '35
His Fighting Blood '35
Sons of Steel '35
Man from Utah '34

Ray Young (1940-99)
The Return of the Beverly Hillbillies '81
Blue Sunshine '78
Blood of Dracula's Castle '69

Ric Young
Long Life, Happiness and Prosperity '02
The Transporter '02
The Lost Empire '01
Chain of Command '00
The Corruptor '99
Dragon: The Bruce Lee Story '93
Drachenfutter '87
The Last Emperor '87
Ping Pong '87

Richard Young (1951-)
An Innocent Man '89
Inferno in Paradise '88
Saigon Commandos '88
Assassin '86
Love at the Top '86
Friday the 13th, Part 5: A New Beginning '85
Ninja Master of Death '85
Final Mission '84
Cocaine Cowboys '79
Banjo Hackett '76
Night Call Nurses '72

Robert Young (1907-98)
A Conspiracy of Love '87
Little Women '78
Goodbye My Fancy '51
The Half-Breed '51
The Second Woman '51
That Forsyte Woman '50
Sitting Pretty '48
Crossfire '47
They Won't Believe Me '47
The Enchanted Cottage '45
Those Endearing Young Charms '45
The Canterville Ghost '44
Sweet Rosie O'Grady '43
Cairo '42
Journey for Margaret '42
H.M. Pulham Esquire '41
Lady Be Good '41
Western Union '41
The Mortal Storm '40
Northwest Passage '40
Honolulu '39
The Shining Hour '38
Three Comrades '38
The Bride Wore Red '37
Navy Blue and Gold '37
The Bride Walks Out '36
It's Love Again '36
The Secret Agent '36
Stowaway '36
Red Salute '35
Hollywood Party '34
Spitfire '34
Today We Live '33
Tugboat Annie '33
Kid from Spain '32
Strange Interlude '32
The Black Camel '31
The Sin of Madelon Claudet '31

Roland Young (1887-1953)
St. Benny the Dip '51
Let's Dance '50
The Great Lover '49
You Gotta Stay Happy '48
And Then There Were None '45
Forever and a Day '43
They All Kissed the Bride '42
The Flame of New Orleans '41
Topper Returns '41
Two-Faced Woman '41
No, No Nanette '40
The Philadelphia Story '40
The Night of Nights '39
Topper Takes a Trip '39
Sailing Along '38
The Young in Heart '38
Call It a Day '37
King Solomon's Mines '37
The Man Who Could Work Miracles '37
Topper '37
One Rainy Afternoon '36
David Copperfield '35
Ruggles of Red Gap '35
Here is My Heart '34
His Double Life '33
One Hour with You '32
Wedding Rehearsal '32
The Guardsman '31
Madam Satan '30
Sherlock Holmes '22

Sean Young (1959-)
The Man Who Came Back '08
Jesse Stone: Sea Change '07
The Drop '06
Ghosts Never Sleep '05
Third Man Out: A Donald Strachey Mystery '05
Before I Say Goodbye '03
Headspace '02
Threat of Exposure '02
The House Next Door '01
Mockingbird Don't Sing '01
Sugar & Spice '01
Poor White Trash '00
Motel Blue '98
Men '97
Evil Has a Face '96
The Invader '96
The Proprietor '96
Dr. Jekyll and Ms. Hyde '95
Even Cowgirls Get the Blues '94
Mirage '94
Model by Day '94
Rebel Run '94
Witness to the Execution '94
Ace Ventura: Pet Detective '93
Fatal Instinct '93
Hold Me, Thrill Me, Kiss Me '93
Blue Ice '92
Forever: A Ghost of a Love Story '92
Love Crimes '92
Once Upon a Crime '92
Sketch Artist '92
A Kiss Before Dying '91
Fire Birds '90
Cousins '89
The Boost '88
No Way Out '87
Wall Street '87
Baby... Secret of the Lost Legend '85
Under the Biltmore Clock '85
Dune '84
Blade Runner '82
Young Doctors in Love '82
Stripes '81
Jane Austen in Manhattan '80

Stephen Young (1931-)
The Last Debate '00
Execution of Justice '99
Scorned '93
Who's Harry Crumb? '89
Deadline '82
Spring Fever '81
Lifeguard '76
Soylent Green '73
Rage '72
Patton '70

Tammany Young
It's a Gift '34
Tugboat Annie '33

Tony Young (1932-2002)
Policewomen '73
Chrome and Hot Leather '71

Victor Young (1901-66)
Charlie Chan at Treasure Island '39
Charlie Chan in Honolulu '38

William Allen Young (1953-)
Fear X '03
Serving in Silence: The Margarethe Cammermeyer Story '95
Stalking Laura '93
Johnnie Gibson F.B.I. '87
Outrage! '86

Jack Youngblood (1950-)
Python Wolf '88
Stalking Danger '86

Barrie Youngfellow (1950-)
Lady from Yesterday '85
It Came Upon a Midnight Clear '84
Nightmare in Blood '75

Henny Youngman (1906-98)
Goodfellas '90
Amazon Women on the Moon '87
History of the World: Part 1 '81
National Lampoon Goes to the Movies '81
The Gore-Gore Girls '72
The Unkissed Bride '66

Gail Youngs (1953-)
Timestalkers '87
Belizaire the Cajun '86
Last Days of Frank & Jesse James '86
Hockey Night '84
A Rumor of War '80

Jim Youngs (1956-)
Skeeter '93
You Talkin' to Me? '87
Hot Shot '86
Nobody's Fool '86
Wanderers '79

Chief Yowlachie (1891-1966)
Rose Marie '54
Red River '48
Bowery Buckaroos '47
Wild West '46
King of the Stallions '42

Ji-tae Yu
Natural City '03
Nightmare '00
Attack the Gas Station '99

Kelvin Yu
Milk '08
The Utopian Society '03

Rongguang Yu (1958-)
Jet Li's The Enforcer '95
Iron Monkey '93
Supercop 2 '93

Eugenia Yuan
The Eye 2 '04
Mail Order Wife '04
Charlotte Sometimes '02

Joe Zaso (1970-)
Addicted to Murder 3: Bloodlust *'99*
The Alien Agenda: Endangered Species *'97*

David Zayas
The Expendables *'10*
16 Blocks *'06*
Angel Rodriguez *'05*
The Interpreter *'05*
Washington Heights *'02*

Edmund Zayenda
A Brivele der Mamen *'38*
Mamele *'38*

Robert Z'Dar (1950-)
Decay *'98*
American Chinatown *'96*
Equal Impact *'96*
Fugitive X *'96*
Red Line *'96*
The Mosaic Project *'95*
In a Moment of Passion *'93*
Maniac Cop 3: Badge of Silence *'93*
The Legend of Wolf Mountain *'92*
Return to Frogtown *'92*
Wild Cactus *'92*
Beastmaster 2: Through the Portal of Time *'91*
The Divine Enforcer *'91*
Quiet Fire *'91*
The Big Sweat *'90*
Dragonfight *'90*
The Killer's Edge *'90*
Maniac Cop 2 *'90*
Soultaker *'90*
Evil Altar *'89*
Final Sanction *'89*
Tango and Cash *'89*
Dead End City *'88*
Maniac Cop *'88*
Trained to Kill *'88*
Grotesque *'87*
Night Stalker *'87*
Code Name: Zebra *'84*

Rosel Zech (1942-)
Salmonberries *'91*
The Oppermann Family *'82*
Veronika Voss *'82*

Kevin Zegers (1984-)
Frozen *'10*
Fifty Dead Men Walking *'08*
Gardens of the Night *'08*
The Jane Austen Book Club *'07*
Normal *'07*
The Stone Angel *'07*
It's a Boy Girl Thing *'06*
Zoom *'06*
Transamerica *'05*
Dawn of the Dead *'04*
The Hollow *'04*
The Incredible Mrs. Ritchie *'03*
Wrong Turn *'03*
Air Bud 4: Seventh Inning Fetch *'02*
Fear of the Dark *'02*
Air Bud 3: World Pup *'00*
MVP (Most Valuable Primate) *'00*
Four Days *'99*
Komodo *'99*
Treasure Island *'99*
Air Bud 2: Golden Receiver *'98*
Bram Stoker's Shadowbuilder *'98*
It Came from the Sky *'98*
Air Bud *'97*
A Call to Remember *'97*

Nora Zehetner
Princess: A Modern Fairytale *'08*
Beneath *'07*
Brick *'06*
Conversations with Other Women *'05*

Renee Zellweger (1969-)
Case 39 *'10*
Monsters vs. Aliens *'09 (V)*
My One and Only *'09*
New in Town *'09*
Appaloosa *'08*
Leatherheads *'08*
Bee Movie *'07 (V)*
Miss Potter *'06*
Cinderella Man *'05*
Bridget Jones: The Edge of Reason *'04*
Shark Tale *'04 (V)*
Cold Mountain *'03*
Down With Love *'03*
Chicago *'02*
White Oleander *'02*
Bridget Jones's Diary *'01*
Me, Myself, and Irene *'00*
Nurse Betty *'00*
The Bachelor *'99*
One True Thing *'98*
Deceiver *'97*
A Price above Rubies *'97*
Jerry Maguire *'96*
The Whole Wide World *'96*
Empire Records *'95*
The Low Life *'95*
The Texas Chainsaw Massacre 4: The Next Generation *'95*
Love and a .45 *'94*
Shake, Rattle & Rock! *'94*

Michael Zelniker
Stuart Bliss *'98*
Glory Enough for All: The Discovery of Insulin *'92*
Naked Lunch *'91*
Bird *'88*
The Terry Fox Story *'83*
Pick-Up Summer *'79*

Roschdy Zem (1965-)
The Girl From Monaco *'08*
Days of Glory *'06*
Le Petit Lieutenant *'05*
Monsieur N. *'03*
Change My Life *'01*
I Don't Kiss *'91*

Suzanne Zenor
The Baby *'72*
Get to Know Your Rabbit *'72*

Eracio Zepeda
El Norte *'83*
Reed: Insurgent Mexico *'73*

Anthony Zerbe (1936-)
The Matrix Reloaded *'03*
The Matrix Revolutions *'03*
True Crime *'99*
Star Trek: Insurrection *'98*
Asteroid *'97*
Touch *'96*
License to Kill *'89*
See No Evil, Hear No Evil *'89*
Onassis *'88*
Opposing Force *'87*
Private Investigations *'87*
Steel Dawn *'87*
A.D. *'85*
Soggy Bottom U.S.A. *'84*
Dead Zone *'83*
Attica *'80*
Question of Honor *'80*
Centennial *'78*
Child of Glass *'78*
KISS Meets the Phantom of the Park *'78*
Who'll Stop the Rain? *'78*
Farewell, My Lovely *'75*
Rooster Cogburn *'75*
The Parallax View *'74*
Papillon *'73*
Omega Man *'71*
The Liberation of L.B. Jones *'70*
They Call Me Mr. Tibbs! *'70*
Cool Hand Luke *'67*
Will Penny *'67*

Catherine Zeta-Jones (1969-)
Death Defying Acts *'07*
No Reservations *'07*
The Legend of Zorro *'05*
Ocean's Twelve *'04*
The Terminal *'04*
Intolerable Cruelty *'03*
Sinbad: Legend of the Seven Seas *'03 (V)*
Chicago *'02*
America's Sweethearts *'01*
High Fidelity *'00*
Traffic *'00*
Entrapment *'99*
The Haunting *'99*
The Mask of Zorro *'98*
The Phantom *'96*
Titanic *'96*
Blue Juice *'95*
Catherine the Great *'95*
Catherine Cookson's The Cinder Path *'94*
The Return of the Native *'94*
Splitting Heirs *'93*
Christopher Columbus: The Discovery *'92*

Mai Zetterling (1925-94)
Hidden Agenda *'90*
The Witches *'90*
Only Two Can Play *'62*
Pattern for Plunder *'62*
Truth about Women *'58*
Abandon Ship *'57*
Frieda *'47*
Night Is My Future *'47*
Torment *'44*

Monica Zetterlund (1937-2005)
The New Land *'73*
The Emigrants *'72*

Fengyi Zhang (1956-)
Red Cliff *'08*
The Emperor and the Assassin *'99*
Temptation of a Monk *'94*
Farewell My Concubine *'93*

Ziyi Zhang (1979-)
Horsemen *'09*
Purple Butterfly *'03*
The Warrior *'01*

Vicki Zhao
Red Cliff *'08*
Shaolin Soccer *'01*

Mikhail Zharov
Peter the First: Part 2 *'38*
Peter the First: Part 1 *'37*

Malik Zidi (1975-)
Changing Times *'04*
Almost Peaceful *'02*
Water Drops on Burning Rocks *'99*

Joseph Ziegler
Amreeka *'09*
Whitewash: The Clarence Brandley Story *'02*
Focus *'01*

Sonja Ziemann (1926-)
A Matter of WHO *'62*
Made in Heaven *'52*
The Merry Wives of Windsor *'50*

Chip Zien (1947-)
Breakfast of Champions *'98*
The Siege *'98*
Howard the Duck *'86 (V)*
Grace Quigley *'84*

Ian Ziering (1966-)
Domino *'05*
The Corporation *'96*
No Way Back *'96*
Subliminal Seduction *'96*
The Fighter *'95*

Madeline Zima (1985-)
The Collector *'09*
A Cinderella Story *'04*
The Sandy Bottom Orchestra *'00*
Second Chances *'98*
Mr. Nanny *'93*
The Hand that Rocks the Cradle *'92*

Vanessa Zima (1986-)
Zoe *'01*
Wicked *'98*
Ulee's Gold *'97*

Yvonne Zima (1989-)
A Father's Choice *'00*
Storm Catcher *'99*
The Long Kiss Goodnight *'96*

Efrem Zimbalist, Jr. (1918-)
Batman: Mask of the Phantasm *'93 (V)*
The Avenging *'92*
Hot Shots! *'91*
Shooting Stars *'85*
Scruples *'80*
The Gathering: Part 2 *'79*
Family Upside Down *'78*
Terror Out of the Sky *'78*
Airport '75 *'75*
Who Is the Black Dahlia? *'75*
Wait until Dark *'67*
By Love Possessed *'61*
The Crowded Sky *'60*
Deep Six *'58*
Band of Angels *'57*
Bombers B-52 *'57*
House of Strangers *'49*

Stephanie Zimbalist (1956-)
The Prophet's Game *'99*
Prison of Secrets *'97*
Dead Ahead *'96*
The Great Elephant Escape *'95*
Jericho Fever *'93*
The Story Lady *'93*
Caroline? *'90*
The Killing Mind *'90*
Personals *'90*
Love on the Run *'85*
Tomorrow's Child *'82*
The Awakening *'80*
The Babysitter *'80*
The Triangle Factory Fire Scandal *'79*
Centennial *'78*
Forever *'78*
Long Journey Back *'78*
Magic of Lassie *'78*
The Gathering *'77*

Constance Zimmer (1970-)
Chaos Theory *'08*
Home Room *'02*
Warm Blooded Killers *'01*

Joey Zimmerman (1986-)
Return to Halloweentown *'06*
Halloweentown High *'04*
Halloweentown 2: Kalabar's Revenge *'01*
Treehouse Hostage *'99*
Halloweentown *'98*
Very Bad Things *'98*
Mother's Boys *'94*

Luca Zingaretti (1961-)
Jesus *'00*
Artemisia *'97*

Victoria Zinny
Beyond the Door 3 *'91*
Shoot the Living, Pray for the Dead *'70*
Viridiana *'61*

William Zipp
Future Force *'89*
Jungle Assault *'89*
Operation Warzone *'89*
Death Chase *'87*
Mankillers *'87*

August Zirner (1956-)
The Counterfeiters *'07*
A Sound of Thunder *'05*
Mostly Martha *'01*
Taking Sides *'01*
The Promise *'94*
Voyager *'91*

Hanns Zischler (1947-)
Munich *'05*
Taking Sides *'01*
The Cement Garden *'93*
Francesco *'93*
Club Extinction *'89*
A Woman in Flames *'84*
Doktor Faustus *'82*
Les Rendez-vous D'Anna *'78*
Kings of the Road—In the Course of Time *'76*

Dan Ziskie
Satan's Little Helper *'04*
Dangerous Passion *'95*
Zebrahead *'92*
Twisted *'86*

Zhang Ziyi
Memoirs of a Geisha *'05*
House of Flying Daggers *'04*
2046 *'04*
Hero *'03*
The Road Home *'01*
Rush Hour 2 *'01*
Zu Warriors *'01*
Crouching Tiger, Hidden Dragon *'00*

Adrian Zmed (1954-)
Storm Chasers: Revenge of the Twister *'98*
Improper Conduct *'94*
Eyewitness to Murder *'93*
The Other Woman *'92*
Bachelor Party *'84*
The Final Terror *'83*
Grease 2 *'82*
For the Love of It *'80*

Moses Znaimer (1942-)
Abraxas: Guardian of the Universe *'90*
Best Revenge *'83*

Jean-Pierre Zola (1916-79)
The Train *'65*
Mon Oncle *'58*

Michael Zorek (1960-)
Hot Moves *'84*
Private School *'83*

Louis Zorich (1924-)
Commandments *'96*
Cheap Shots *'91*
City of Hope *'91*
Death of a Salesman *'86*
The Seagull *'75*
Newman's Law *'74*
Vengeance Is Mine *'74*

Vera Zorina (1917-2003)
Follow the Boys *'44*
Louisiana Purchase *'41*
The Goldwyn Follies *'38*

Zouzou (1943-)
S*P*Y*S *'74*
Chloe in the Afternoon *'72*

Rod Zuanic (1968-)
Danny Deckchair *'03*
Fast Talking *'86*
Mad Max: Beyond Thunderdome *'85*

George Zucco (1886-1960)
David and Bathsheba *'51*
Madame Bovary *'49*
The Pirate *'48*
Who Killed Doc Robbin? *'48*
Lured *'47*
Where There's Life *'47*
Scared to Death *'46*
Fog Island *'45*
Having Wonderful Crime *'45*
House of Frankenstein *'44*
The Mummy's Ghost *'44*
Return of the Ape Man *'44*
The Seventh Cross *'44*
The Black Raven *'43*
Dead Men Walk *'43*
The Mad Ghoul *'43*
Sherlock Holmes in Washington *'43*
The Black Swan *'42*
Dr. Renault's Secret *'42*
The Mad Monster *'42*
The Mummy's Tomb *'42*
My Favorite Blonde *'42*
International Lady *'41*
The Monster and the Girl *'41*
A Woman's Face *'41*
The Mummy's Hand *'40*
The Adventures of Sherlock Holmes *'39*
The Hunchback of Notre Dame *'39*
Arrest Bulldog Drummond *'38*
Charlie Chan in Honolulu *'38*
Marie Antoinette *'38*
Three Comrades *'38*
The Bride Wore Red *'37*
The Firefly *'37*
Saratoga *'37*
Souls at Sea *'37*

David Zucker (1947-)
Airplane! *'80*
Kentucky Fried Movie *'77*

Jerry Zucker (1950-)
Airplane! *'80*
Kentucky Fried Movie *'77*

Alex Zuckerman
Freaked *'93*
Me and the Kid *'93*

Josh Zuckerman
Sex Drive *'08*
Surviving Christmas *'04*

Mark Zuelzke
I Got the Hook-Up *'98*
Sinful Intrigue *'95*

Daphne Zuniga (1962-)
Mail Order Bride *'08*
Christmas Do-Over *'06*
Enemies of Laughter *'00*
Stand-Ins *'97*
Pandora's Clock *'96*
Degree of Guilt *'95*
Charlie's Ghost: The Secret of Coronado *'94*
800 Leagues Down the Amazon *'93*
Prey of the Chameleon *'91*
Eyes of the Panther *'90*
The Fly 2 *'89*
Gross Anatomy *'89*
Staying Together *'89*
Last Rites *'88*
Spaceballs *'87*
Modern Girls *'86*
Quarterback Princess *'85*
The Sure Thing *'85*
Vision Quest *'85*
The Initiation *'84*

Jose Zuniga
Next *'07*
Tortilla Heaven *'07*
Mission: Impossible 3 *'06*
Constantine *'05*
The Hunted *'03*
The Crew *'00*
For Love or Country: The Arturo Sandoval Story *'00*
Gun Shy *'00*
Happy Accidents *'00*
For Which He Stands *'98*
Next Stop, Wonderland *'98*
Con Air *'97*
Hurricane Streets *'96*
Ransom *'96*
Blue in the Face *'95*
Money Train *'95*
Smoke *'95*
Crooklyn *'94*

Dianik Zurakowska
Orgy of the Vampires *'73*
The Hanging Woman *'72*
Cauldron of Blood *'67*

Ayelet Zurer
Angels & Demons *'09*
Adam Resurrected *'08*
Vantage Point *'08*
Munich *'05*

Jahi JJ Zuri
Omega Doom *'96*
Nemesis 2: Nebula *'94*

Yoshitaka Zushi (1955-)
Akira Kurosawa's Dreams *'90*
Dodes 'ka-den *'70*

Brad Zutaut (1961-)
Knock Outs *'92*
Nudity Required *'90*
Hardbodies 2 *'86*

Noam Zylberman

Love and Hate: A Marriage Made in Hell *'90*
Outside Chance of Maximilian Glick *'88*

Elsa Zylberstein
(1969-)

I've Loved You So Long *'08*
La Petite Jerusalem *'05*
Modigliani *'04*
Monsieur N. *'03*
Three Blind Mice *'02*
Time Regained *'99*
Metroland *'97*
Portraits Chinois *'96*
Farinelli *'94*
Mina Tannenbaum *'93*

The Director Index provides a complete videography for any director with more than one video credit. The listings for the director names follow an alphabetical sort by last name (although the names appear in a first name-last name format). The videographies are listed chronologically, from most recent film to directorial debut. If a director helmed more than one film in the same year, these movies are listed alphabetically within the year. Use this index in conjunction with the **Cast** (immediately preceding this index), **Writer**, and **Cinematographer** indexes (immediately following) to see where some of today's hottest directors got their starts.

Paul Aaron
In Love and War *'91*
Maxie *'85*
Deadly Force *'83*
Force of One *'79*
The Miracle Worker *'79*
Different Story *'78*

George Abbott(1887-1995)
Damn Yankees *'58*
The Pajama Game *'57*
Too Many Girls *'40*
The Cheat *'31*
The Sea God *'30*

Derwin Abrahams(1903-74)
Northwest Trail *'46*
Border Vigilantes *'41*

Jim Abrahams(1944-)
Mafia! *'98*
First Do No Harm *'97*
Hot Shots! Part Deux *'93*
Hot Shots! *'91*
Welcome Home, Roxy Carmichael *'90*
Big Business *'88*
Ruthless People *'86*
Top Secret! *'84*
Airplane! *'80*

J.J. (Jeffrey) Abrams(1966-)
Star Trek *'09*
Mission: Impossible 3 *'06*

Neil Abramson
American Son *'08*
Ringmaster *'98*

Robert Allan Ackerman
The Ramen Girl *'08*
The Reagans *'04*
The Roman Spring of Mrs. Stone *'03*
Life with Judy Garland—Me and My Shadows *'01*
Baby *'00*
Double Platinum *'99*
Outrage *'98*
Safe Passage *'94*

David Acomba
Night Life *'90*
Slipstream *'73*

Daniel Adams
The Golden Boys *'08*
Primary Motive *'92*
A Fool and His Money *'88*

Al Adamson(1929-95)
Lost *'83*
Black Eliminator *'78*
Cinderella 2000 *'78*
Hospital of Terror *'78*
Kill Factor *'78*
Black Samurai *'77*
Black Heat *'76*
Blazing Stewardesses *'75*
Jessi's Girls *'75*
The Dynamite Brothers *'74*
I Spit on Your Corpse *'74*
Angels' Wild Women *'72*
Blood of Ghastly Horror *'72*
Brain of Blood *'71*
Dracula vs. Frankenstein *'71*
Horror of the Blood Monsters *'70*
Blood of Dracula's Castle *'69*
The Female Bunch *'69*
Gun Riders *'69*
Satan's Sadists *'69*

Andrew Adamson(1966-)
The Chronicles of Narnia: Prince Caspian *'08*
The Chronicles of Narnia: The Lion, the Witch and the Wardrobe *'05*
Shrek 2 *'04*
Shrek *'01*

Victor Adamson(1890-1972)
Boss Cowboy *'35*
Lightning Bill *'35*
Rawhide Romance *'34*
Circle Canyon *'33*
Fighting Cowboy *'33*
Lightning Range *'33*

Michael Addis
Heckler *'08*
Poor White Trash *'00*

Joseph Adler(1950-)
Scream, Baby, Scream *'69*
Sex and the College Girl *'64*

Lou Adler
Ladies and Gentlemen, the Fabulous Stains *'82*
Cheech and Chong's Up in Smoke *'79*

Zackary Adler
Familiar Strangers *'08*
I'm Reed Fish *'06*

Percy Adlon(1935-)
Younger & Younger *'94*
Salmonberries *'91*
Rosalie Goes Shopping *'89*
Bagdad Cafe *'88*
Sugarbaby *'85*
The Last Five Days *'82*
Celeste *'81*

Alejandro Agresti(1961-)
The Lake House *'06*
Valentin *'02*

Javier Aguirre(1935-)
The Rue Morgue Massacres *'73*
Dracula's Great Love *'72*

Joe Ahearne
Perfect Parents *'06*
Ultraviolet *'98*

Mac Ahlberg(1931-)
Gangsters *'79*
I, a Woman *'66*

Byeong-ki Ahn
Apartment 1303 *'07*
Phone *'02*
Nightmare *'00*

Alexandre Aja(1978-)
Piranha 3D *'10*
Mirrors *'08*
The Hills Have Eyes *'06*
High Tension *'03*

Jonas Akerlund
Horsemen *'09*
Spun *'02*

Chantal Akerman(1950-)
A Couch in New York *'95*
Night and Day *'91*
Window Shopping *'86*
The Eighties *'83*
Toute Une Nuit *'82*
Les Rendez-vous D'Anna *'78*
News from Home *'76*
Je Tu Il Elle *'74*

Fatih Akin(1973-)
New York, I Love You *'09*
Soul Kitchen *'09*
The Edge of Heaven *'07*
Head On *'04*

Moustapha Akkad(1933-2005)
Lion of the Desert *'81*
The Message *'77*

Jordan Alan(1967-)
Kiss & Tell *'99*
Terminal Bliss *'91*

Benito Alazraki(1923-)
Invasion of the Zombies *'61*
Spiritism *'61*

Bitto Albertini
Escape from Galaxy Three *'81*
Jungle Inferno *'72*

Felix Alcala(1951-)
Taken *'02*
Fire Down Below *'97*

Alan Alda(1936-)
Betsy's Wedding *'90*
A New Life *'88*
Sweet Liberty *'86*
M*A*S*H: Goodbye, Farewell & Amen *'83*
The Four Seasons *'81*

Robert Aldrich(1918-83)
...All the Marbles *'81*
The Frisco Kid *'79*
The Choirboys *'77*
Twilight's Last Gleaming *'77*
The Hustle *'75*
The Longest Yard *'74*
Emperor of the North Pole *'73*
Ulzana's Raid *'72*
The Grissom Gang *'71*
Too Late the Hero *'70*
The Killing of Sister George *'69*
The Dirty Dozen *'67*
The Flight of the Phoenix *'65*
Hush, Hush, Sweet Charlotte *'65*
Four for Texas *'63*
Sodom and Gomorrah *'62*
What Ever Happened to Baby Jane? *'62*
Attack! *'56*
Autumn Leaves *'56*
The Big Knife *'55*
Kiss Me Deadly *'55*
Apache *'54*
Vera Cruz *'53*

Jason Alexander(1959-)
Just Looking *'99*
For Better or Worse *'95*

Lexi Alexander
Punisher: War Zone *'08*
Green Street Hooligans *'05*

Grigori Alexandrov(1903-83)
Ten Days That Shook the World *'27*
The Battleship Potemkin *'25*

James Nelson Algar(1913-98)
Fantasia/2000 *'00*
Legend of Lobo *'62*
The Adventures of Ichabod and Mr. Toad *'49*
The Legend of Sleepy Hollow *'49*
Fantasia *'40*

Dan Algrant(1959-)
People I Know *'02*
Naked in New York *'93*

Dean Alioto
Shadowheart *'09*
L.A. Dicks *'05*

Marc Allegret(1900-73)
Sois Belle et Tais-Toi *'58*
Plucking the Daisy *'56*
Lady Chatterley's Lover *'55*
The Love of Three Queens *'54*
Blanche Fury *'48*
Zou Zou *'34*
Fanny *'32*

Yves Allegret(1907-87)
The Proud Ones *'53*
Seven Deadly Sins *'53*
Dedee d'Anvers *'49*
Johnny Apollo *'40*

Billy Allen
See William Allen Castleman

Corey Allen(1934-)
The Ann Jillian Story *'88*
The Last Fling *'86*
Brass *'85*
Codename: Foxfire *'85*
Return of Frank Cannon *'80*
The Man in the Santa Claus Suit *'79*

Avalanche '78
Thunder and Lightning '77

Dave Allen(1944-99)
Puppet Master 2 '90
Dungeonmaster '83

Debbie Allen(1950-)
The Old Settler '01
Out of Sync '95

Fred Allen(1896-1955)
Badmen of Nevada '33
The Mysterious Rider '33
Beyond the Rockies '32
Ghost Valley '32
Ride Him, Cowboy '32
The Saddle Buster '32

Irwin Allen(1916-91)
Beyond the Poseidon Adventure '79
The Swarm '78
The Towering Inferno '74
City Beneath the Sea '71
Five Weeks in a Balloon '62
Voyage to the Bottom of the Sea '61

Kevin Allen(1962-)
Agent Cody Banks 2: Destination London '04
The Big Tease '99
Twin Town '97

Lewis Allen(1905-2000)
Another Time, Another Place '58
A Bullet for Joey '55
Illegal '55
Suddenly '54
At Sword's Point '51
The Perfect Marriage '46
Those Endearing Young Charms '45
The Uninvited '44

Woody Allen(1935-)
Whatever Works '09
Vicky Cristina Barcelona '08
Cassandra's Dream '07
Scoop '06
Match Point '05
Melinda and Melinda '05
Anything Else '03
Hollywood Ending '02
The Curse of the Jade Scorpion '01
Small Time Crooks '00
Sweet and Lowdown '99
Celebrity '98
Deconstructing Harry '97
Everyone Says I Love You '96
Mighty Aphrodite '95
Bullets over Broadway '94
Manhattan Murder Mystery '93
Husbands and Wives '92
Shadows and Fog '92
Alice '90
Crimes & Misdemeanors '89
New York Stories '89
Another Woman '88
September '88
Radio Days '87
Hannah and Her Sisters '86
The Purple Rose of Cairo '85
Broadway Danny Rose '84
Zelig '83
A Midsummer Night's Sex Comedy '82
Stardust Memories '80
Manhattan '79
Interiors '78
Annie Hall '77
Love and Death '75
Sleeper '73
Everything You Always Wanted to Know about Sex (But Were Afraid to Ask) '72
Bananas '71
Take the Money and Run '69
What's Up, Tiger Lily? '66

Roger Allers
Open Season '06
The Lion King '94

Michael Almereyda(1960-)
Hamlet '00
The Eternal '99
The External '99
Nadja '95
Twister '89

Pedro Almodovar(1951-)
Broken Embraces '09
Volver '06
Bad Education '04
Talk to Her '02
All About My Mother '99
Live Flesh '97
The Flower of My Secret '95
Kika '94
High Heels '91
Tie Me Up! Tie Me Down! '90
Women on the Verge of a Nervous Breakdown '88
Law of Desire '86
Matador '86
What Have I Done to Deserve This? '85
Dark Habits '84
Labyrinth of Passion '82
Pepi, Luci, Bom and Other Girls on the Heap '80

Paul Almond(1931-)
The Dance Goes On '92
Captive Hearts '87
Prep School '81
Final Assignment '80
Journey '72

John A. Alonzo(1934-2001)
Blinded by the Light '82
Portrait of a Stripper '79
FM '78

Emmett Alston
Little Ninjas '92
Force of the Ninja '88
Demonwarp '87
Tigershark '87
Nine Deaths of the Ninja '85
Three Way Weekend '81
New Year's Evil '78

Robert Altman(1925-2006)
A Prairie Home Companion '06
Tanner on Tanner '04
The Company '03
Gosford Park '01
Dr. T & the Women '00
Cookie's Fortune '99
The Gingerbread Man '97
Kansas City '95
Ready to Wear '94
Short Cuts '93
The Player '92
Vincent & Theo '90
Aria '88
The Caine Mutiny Court Martial '88
Tanner '88 '88
Dumb Waiter '87
O.C. and Stiggs '87
The Room '87
Beyond Therapy '86
Fool for Love '86
Secret Honor '85
Streamers '83
Come Back to the Five & Dime Jimmy Dean, Jimmy Dean '82
Popeye '80
Quintet '79
A Wedding '78
3 Women '77
Buffalo Bill & the Indians '76
Nashville '75
Thieves Like Us '74
The Long Goodbye '73
Images '72
McCabe & Mrs. Miller '71
Brewster McCloud '70
M*A*S*H '70
That Cold Day in the Park '69
Countdown '68

Robert Alton(1906-57)
Pagan Love Song '50
Merton of the Movies '47

Christian Alvart
Case 39 '10
Pandorum '09
Antibodies '05

Keito Amamiya(1959-)
Moon over Tao '97
Cyber Ninja '94
Zeram 2 '94

Rod Amateau(1923-2003)
The Garbage Pail Kids Movie '87
High School USA '84
Lovelines '84
The Seniors '78
Drive-In '76
The Statue '71
The Bushwackers '52

Gianni Amelio(1945-)
Lamerica '95
The Stolen Children '92
Open Doors '89

Alejandro Amenabar(1972-)
The Sea Inside '04
The Others '01
Open Your Eyes '97
Thesis '96

Pino Amenta(1952-)
Heaven Tonight '93
What the Moon Saw '90
Boulevard of Broken Dreams '88
True Colors '87
My Brother Tom '86
All the Rivers Run '84

Jon Amiel(1948-)
Creation '09
The Core '03
Entrapment '99
The Man Who Knew Too Little '97
Copycat '95
Sommersby '93
Tune in Tomorrow '90
Queen of Hearts '89
The Singing Detective '86

Gideon Amir
Accidents '89
The P.O.W. Escape '86

Franco Amurri(1958-)
Monkey Trouble '94
Flashback '89

Julian Amyes(1917-92)
The Lady's Not for Burning '87
Jane Eyre '83
Great Expectations '81

Dominic Anciano(1959-)
Love, Honour & Obey '00
Final Cut '98

Allison Anders(1954-)
Things Behind the Sun '01
Sugar Town '99
Grace of My Heart '96
Four Rooms '95
Mi Vida Loca '94
Gas Food Lodging '92
Border Radio '88

Andy Anderson(1947-)
Positive I.D. '87
Interface '84

Bill Anderson
Warrior Queen '03
Sword of Honour '01
Melissa '97

Brad Anderson(1964-)
Transsiberian '08
Masters of Horror: Sounds Like '06
The Machinist '04
Session 9 '01
Happy Accidents '00

Next Stop, Wonderland '98

Clyde (Claudio Fragasso) Anderson(1951-)
Beyond Darkness '92
Monster Dog '82

Jane Anderson(1954-)
The Prize Winner of Defiance, Ohio '05
Normal '03
If These Walls Could Talk 2 '00
The Baby Dance '98

Kurt Anderson
The Killing Grounds '97
Dead Cold '96
Open Fire '94
Bounty Tracker '93
Martial Outlaw '93
Martial Law 2: Undercover '91

Lindsay Anderson(1923-94)
Glory! Glory! '90
The Whales of August '87
Britannia Hospital '82
Look Back in Anger '80
In Celebration '75
O Lucky Man! '73
If... '69
This Sporting Life '63

Michael Anderson, Sr.(1920-)
Summer of the Monkeys '98
20,000 Leagues Under the Sea '97
The Sea Wolf '93
Young Catherine '91
The Jeweller's Shop '90
Millennium '89
Separate Vacations '86
Sword of Gideon '86
Second Time Lucky '84
Murder by Phone '82
Dominique Is Dead '79
The Martian Chronicles: Part 1 '79
The Martian Chronicles: Part 2 '79
The Martian Chronicles: Part 3 '79
Orca '77
Logan's Run '76
Conduct Unbecoming '75
Doc Savage '75
The Shoes of the Fisherman '68
The Quiller Memorandum '66
Operation Crossbow '65
The Naked Edge '61
Shake Hands with the Devil '59
The Wreck of the Mary Deare '59
Around the World in 80 Days '56
Battle Hell '56
1984 '56
Dam Busters '55
The House of the Arrow '53

Paul Thomas Anderson(1970-)
There Will Be Blood '07
Punch-Drunk Love '02
Magnolia '99
Boogie Nights '97
Hard Eight '96

Paul W.S. Anderson(1965-)
Death Race '08
Alien vs. Predator '04
Resident Evil '02
Soldier '98
Event Horizon '97
Mortal Kombat 1: The Movie '95
Shopping '93

Steve (Stephen M.) Anderson
Dead Men Can't Dance '97
South Central '92

Wes Anderson(1969-)
Fantastic Mr. Fox '09
The Darjeeling Limited '07
The Life Aquatic with Steve Zissou '04
The Royal Tenenbaums '01
Rushmore '98
Bottle Rocket '95

Mario Andreacchio(1955-)
The Real Macaw '98
Napoleon '96
Fair Game '85

Jay Andrews
See Jim Wynorski

Peter Andrews
See Steven Soderbergh

Roger Andrieux(1940-)
La Petite Sirene '80
L'Amour en Herbe '77

Chris Angel(1972-)
Wishmaster 4: The Prophecy Fulfilled '02
Wishmaster 3: Beyond the Gates of Hell '01
Beyond Redemption '99
The Fear: Halloween Night '99

Robert Angelo
Dead Sexy '01
Forbidden Sins '99
Mutual Needs '97

Theo Angelopoulos(1935-)
Eternity and a Day '97
Ulysses' Gaze '95
Landscape in the Mist '88
The Travelling Players '75

Ken Annakin(1914-)
The New Adventures of Pippi Longstocking '88
Pirate Movie '82
Cheaper to Keep Her '80
The Fifth Musketeer '79
Paper Tiger '74
Call of the Wild '72
Those Daring Young Men in Their Jaunty Jalopies '69
Battle of the Bulge '65
Those Magnificent Men in Their Flying Machines '65
The Longest Day '62
The Swiss Family Robinson '60
Third Man on the Mountain '59
Across the Bridge '57
Three Men in a Boat '56
Land of Fury '55
The Sword & the Rose '53
The Story of Robin Hood & His Merrie Men '52
Trio '50

Jean-Jacques Annaud(1943-)
Two Brothers '04
Enemy at the Gates '00
Seven Years in Tibet '97
The Lover '92
The Bear '89
The Name of the Rose '86
Quest for Fire '82
Hothead '78
Black and White in Color '76

Paul Annett
The Witching of Ben Wagner '95
Tales of the Unexpected '91
The Beast Must Die '75
Poldark '75

Reverge Anselmo(1962-)
Stateside '04
Lover's Prayer '99

David Anspaugh(1946-)
The Game of Their Lives '05
Wisegirls '02
Moonlight and Valentino '95
Rudy '93

Fresh Horses '88
Hoosiers '86

Nimrod Antal(1973-)
Predators '10
Armored '09
Vacancy '07
Kontroll '03

Franz Antel
M'Lady's Court '73
Tower of Screaming Virgins '68

Joseph Anthony(1912-93)
Tomorrow '72
All in a Night's Work '61
Career '59
The Matchmaker '58
The Rainmaker '56

Manuel Antin(1926-)
Far Away and Long Ago '74
Don Segundo Sombra '69

Pedrag (Peter) Antonijevic(1959-)
Hard Cash '01
Savior '98

Lou Antonio(1934-)
Lies Before Kisses '92
A Taste for Killing '92
The Last Prostitute '91
This Gun for Hire '90
Mayflower Madam '87
Pals '87
Agatha Christie's Thirteen at Dinner '85
Between Friends '83
Breaking Up Is Hard to Do '79
Silent Victory: The Kitty O'Neil Story '79
The Gypsy Warriors '78
A Real American Hero '78
Someone I Touched '75

Michelangelo Antonioni(1912-2007)
Eros '04
Beyond the Clouds '95
Identification of a Woman '82
The Passenger '75
Zabriskie Point '70
Blow-Up '66
The Eclipse '66
The Red Desert '64
La Notte '60
L'Avventura '60
Il Grido '57
The Lady Without Camelias '53
Love in the City '53
Story of a Love Affair '50

Judd Apatow(1967-)
Funny People '09
Knocked Up '07
The 40 Year Old Virgin '05

Michael Apted(1941-)
Amazing Grace '06
Enough '02
Enigma '01
The World Is Not Enough '99
Always Outnumbered Always Outgunned '98
Extreme Measures '96
Nell '94
Blink '93
Incident at Oglala: The Leonard Peltier Story '92
Thunderheart '92
Class Action '91
Gorillas in the Mist '88
Critical Condition '86
First Born '84
Gorky Park '83
Kipperbang '82
Continental Divide '81
Coal Miner's Daughter '80
Agatha '79
The Squeeze '77
Triple Echo '77
Poor Girl, a Ghost Story '74

Manuel Gutierrez Aragon(1942-)
Half of Heaven *'86*
Demons in the Garden *'82*

Gregg Araki(1959-)
Smiley Face *'07*
Mysterious Skin *'04*
Splendor *'99*
Nowhere *'96*
The Doom Generation *'95*
Totally F***ed Up *'94*
The Living End *'92*

Vicente Aranda(1926-)
Carmen *'03*
Mad Love *'01*
Jealousy *'99*
Intruso *'93*
Lovers: A True Story *'90*
If They Tell You I Fell *'89*
The Blood Spattered Bride *'72*

Alfonso Arau(1932-)
A Painted House *'03*
The Magnificent Ambersons *'02*
Picking Up the Pieces *'99*
A Walk in the Clouds *'95*
Like Water for Chocolate *'93*

Denys Arcand(1941-)
The Barbarian Invasions *'03*
Stardom *'00*
Love and Human Remains *'93*
Jesus of Montreal *'89*
The Decline of the American Empire *'86*

George Archainbaud(1890-1959)
Last of the Pony Riders *'53*
On Top of Old Smoky *'53*
Winning of the West *'53*
Blue Canadian Rockies *'52*
Night Stage to Galveston *'52*
Hunt the Man Down *'50*
Hopalong Cassidy: Borrowed Trouble *'48*
Hopalong Cassidy: Dangerous Venture *'48*
Hopalong Cassidy: False Paradise *'48*
Hopalong Cassidy: Silent Conflict *'48*
Hopalong Cassidy: Sinister Journey *'48*
Hopalong Cassidy: The Dead Don't Dream *'48*
Hopalong Cassidy: Hoppy's Holiday *'47*
Hopalong Cassidy: The Marauders *'47*
Hopalong Cassidy: Unexpected Guest *'47*
The Millerson Case *'47*
Hopalong Cassidy: The Devil's Playground *'46*
Mystery Man *'44*
Texas Masquerade *'44*
The Woman of the Town *'44*
False Colors *'43*
Hoppy Serves a Writ *'43*
The Kansan *'43*
Rhythm Romance *'39*
Campus Confessions *'38*
Thanks for the Memory *'38*
Lost Squadron *'32*
The Lady Refuses *'31*
State's Attorney *'31*
The Silver Horde *'30*

Emile Ardolino(1943-93)
George Balanchine's The Nutcracker *'93*
Gypsy *'93*
Sister Act *'92*
Three Men and a Little Lady *'90*
Chances Are *'89*
Dirty Dancing *'87*
The Rise & Rise of Daniel Rocket *'86*
Rumpelstiltskin *'82*

Mats Arehn(1946-)
Istanbul *'90*
The Assignment *'78*

Asia Argento(1975-)
The Heart Is Deceitful Above All Things *'04*
Scarlet Diva *'00*

Dario Argento(1940-)
Mother of Tears *'08*
Masters of Horror: Pelts *'06*
Masters of Horror: Jenifer *'05*
Sleepless *'01*
The Phantom of the Opera *'98*
The Stendahl Syndrome *'95*
Dario Argento's Trauma *'93*
Two Evil Eyes *'90*
Opera *'88*
Creepers *'85*
Unsane *'82*
Inferno *'80*
Suspiria *'77*
Deep Red: Hatchet Murders *'75*
Four Flies on Grey Velvet *'72*
The Cat o' Nine Tails *'71*
The Bird with the Crystal Plumage *'70*

Adolfo Aristarain(1943-)
Martin (Hache) *'97*
A Place in the World *'92*
The Stranger *'87*
Time for Revenge *'82*
The Lion's Share *'79*

Allan Arkush(1948-)
Elvis Meets Nixon *'98*
The Temptations *'98*
Shake, Rattle & Rock! *'94*
Caddyshack 2 *'88*
Get Crazy *'83*
Heartbeeps *'81*
Rock 'n' Roll High School *'79*
Death Sport *'78*
Hollywood Boulevard *'76*

Leslie Arliss(1901-87)
A Man About the House *'47*
The Man in Grey *'45*
The Wicked Lady *'45*
The Night Has Eyes *'42*
Jack Ahoy *'34*

Montxo Armendariz(1949-)
Broken Silence *'01*
Secrets of the Heart *'97*
Letters from Alou *'90*

George Armitage(1942-)
The Big Bounce *'04*
Grosse Pointe Blank *'97*
Miami Blues *'90*
Hot Rod *'79*
Private Duty Nurses *'71*

Gillian Armstrong(1950-)
Death Defying Acts *'07*
Charlotte Gray *'01*
Oscar and Lucinda *'97*
Little Women *'94*
The Last Days of Chez Nous *'92*
Fires Within *'91*
High Tide *'87*
Mrs. Soffel *'84*
Starstruck *'82*
My Brilliant Career *'79*

Moira Armstrong(1930-)
A Village Affair *'95*
Body & Soul *'93*
How Many Miles to Babylon? *'82*
Testament of Youth *'79*

Gwen Arner
Necessary Parties *'88*
A Matter of Principle *'83*
My Champion *'81*

Andrea Arnold
Fish Tank *'09*
Red Road *'06*

Frank Arnold(1938-)
Josh Kirby... Time Warrior: Chapter 6, Last Battle for the Universe *'96*
Josh Kirby... Time Warrior: Chapter 2, The Human Pets *'95*
Josh Kirby... Time Warrior: Chapter 3, Trapped on Toyworld *'95*
A Waltz Through the Hills *'88*

Jack Arnold(1916-92)
Marilyn: The Untold Story *'80*
Swiss Conspiracy *'77*
Games Girls Play *'75*
Boss *'74*
Bachelor in Paradise *'69*
Hello Down There *'69*
A Global Affair *'63*
Monster on the Campus *'59*
The Mouse That Roared *'59*
No Name on the Bullet *'59*
High School Confidential *'58*
The Incredible Shrinking Man *'57*
Man in the Shadow *'57*
Revenge of the Creature *'55*
Tarantula *'55*
Creature from the Black Lagoon *'54*
It Came from Outer Space *'53*

Newton Arnold(1928-2000)
Bloodsport *'88*
Blood Thirst *'65*
Hands of a Stranger *'62*

Darren Aronofsky(1969-)
The Wrestler *'08*
The Fountain *'06*
Requiem for a Dream *'00*
Pi *'98*

Miguel Arteta(1965-)
Youth in Revolt *'10*
The Good Girl *'02*
Chuck & Buck *'00*
Star Maps *'97*

Karen Arthur(1941-)
The Christmas Blessing *'05*
The Locket *'02*
The Song of the Lark *'01*
The Lost Child *'00*
True Women *'97*
The Disappearance of Christina *'93*
The Secret *'93*
The Jacksons: An American Dream *'92*
Bridge to Silence *'89*
Lady Beware *'87*
Broken Badge *'85*
A Bunny's Tale *'85*
My Sister, My Love *'78*

Dorothy Arzner(1897-1979)
Dance, Girl, Dance *'40*
The Bride Wore Red *'37*
Craig's Wife *'36*
Christopher Strong *'33*
Merrily We Go to Hell *'32*

Kelly Asbury(1960-)
Shrek 2 *'04*
Spirit: Stallion of the Cimarron *'02*

Anthony Ascot
See Giuliano Carnimeo

Ash(1964-)
This Girl's Life *'03*
Pups *'99*
Bang *'95*

Hal Ashby(1930-88)
8 Million Ways to Die *'85*
The Slugger's Wife *'85*
Lookin' to Get Out *'82*
Being There *'79*
Coming Home *'78*
Bound for Glory *'76*
Shampoo *'75*
The Last Detail *'73*
Harold and Maude *'71*

John Mallory Asher(1971-)
Dirty Love *'05*
Diamonds *'99*
Kounterfeit *'96*

William Asher(1921-)
Movers and Shakers *'85*
Night Warning *'82*
Fireball 500 *'66*
Beach Blanket Bingo *'65*
How to Stuff a Wild Bikini *'65*
Bikini Beach *'64*
Muscle Beach Party *'64*
Beach Party *'63*
The 27th Day *'57*

Peter Askin
Trumbo *'07*
Company Man *'00*

Anthony Asquith(1902-68)
The V.I.P.'s *'63*
The Millionairess *'60*
Carrington, V.C. *'54*
The Importance of Being Earnest *'52*
The Browning Version *'51*
The Woman in Question *'50*
Man of Evil *'48*
The Winslow Boy *'48*
The Demi-Paradise *'43*
We Dive at Dawn *'43*
Cottage to Let *'41*
Pygmalion *'38*
I Stand Condemned *'36*

Olivier Assayas(1955-)
Summer Hours *'08*
Boarding Gate *'07*
Paris, je t'aime *'06*
Clean *'04*
Demonlover *'02*
Les Destinees *'00*
Late August, Early September *'98*
Irma Vep *'96*

Ovidio G. Assonitis(1943-)
Madhouse *'87*
Desperate Moves *'86*
Tentacles *'77*
Beyond the Door *'75*
Forever Emmanuelle *'75*

Doug Atchison
Akeelah and the Bee *'06*
The Pornographer *'00*

Francisco Athie(1956-)
Optic Fiber *'97*
Lolo *'92*

Mark Atkins
Evil Eyes *'04*
Night Orchid *'97*

Yvan Attal(1965-)
New York, I Love You *'09*
Happily Ever After *'04*
My Wife is an Actress *'01*

Richard Attenborough(1923-)
Closing the Ring *'07*
Grey Owl *'99*
In Love and War *'96*
Shadowlands *'93*
Chaplin *'92*
Cry Freedom *'87*
A Chorus Line *'85*
Gandhi *'82*
Magic *'78*
A Bridge Too Far *'77*
Young Winston *'72*
Oh! What a Lovely War *'69*

David Attwood(1952-)
Fidel *'02*
The Hound of the Baskervilles *'02*
Shot Through the Heart *'98*
Moll Flanders *'96*
Wild West *'93*

Jacques Audiard(1952-)
A Prophet *'09*
The Beat My Heart Skipped *'05*
Read My Lips *'01*
A Self-Made Hero *'95*

John H. Auer(1906-75)
City That Never Sleeps *'53*
Seven Days Ashore *'44*
Wheel of Fortune *'41*
Circus Girl *'37*
The Crime of Dr. Crespi *'35*

Bille August(1948-)
The Color of Freedom *'07*
Convicted *'04*
A Song for Martin *'01*
Les Miserables *'97*
Jerusalem *'96*
Smilla's Sense of Snow *'96*
The House of the Spirits *'93*
The Best Intentions *'92*
Pelle the Conqueror *'88*
Twist & Shout *'84*

Carlos Aured(1937-)
Curse of the Devil *'73*
House of Psychotic Women *'73*
The Mummy's Revenge *'73*
Horror Rises from the Tomb *'72*

Jean Aurel(1925-96)
Manon *'68*
The Women *'68*

Paul Auster(1947-)
Lulu on the Bridge *'98*
Blue in the Face *'95*

Sam Auster
Bounty Hunter 2002 *'94*
Screen Test *'85*

Ray Austin(1932-)
Highlander: The Gathering *'92*
The Zany Adventures of Robin Hood *'84*
Return of the Man from U.N.C.L.E. *'83*
House of the Living Dead *'73*
The Virgin Witch *'70*

Steve Austin
American Streetfighter *'96*
Expert Weapon *'93*

Claude Autant-Lara(1901-2000)
Oldest Profession *'67*
The Red and the Black *'57*
Four Bags Full *'56*
Seven Deadly Sins *'53*
The Red Inn *'51*
Devil in the Flesh *'46*
Sylvia and the Phantom *'45*

Igor Auzins(1949-)
The Gold & Glory *'88*
We of the Never Never *'82*
Death Train *'79*
High Rolling in a Hot Corvette *'77*
Night Nurse *'77*

Aram Avakian(1926-87)
11 Harrowhouse *'74*
Cops and Robbers *'73*
End of the Road *'70*

Roger Avary(1965-)
The Rules of Attraction *'02*
Mr. Stitch *'95*
Killing Zoe *'94*

Pupi Avati(1938-)
Incantato *'03*
The Best Man *'97*
The Story of Boys & Girls *'91*
Bix *'90*
Revenge of the Dead *'84*
Zeder *'83*

Howard (Hikmet) Avedis
Kidnapped *'87*
They're Playing with Fire *'84*
Separate Ways *'82*
Mortuary *'81*
The Fifth Floor *'80*
Texas Detour *'77*
Scorchy *'76*
The Specialist *'75*
The Teacher *'74*
The Stepmother *'71*

Joe Mari Avellana
Fist of Glory *'95*
Blackbelt 2: Fatal Force *'93*

Brian Avenet-Bradley
Dark Remains *'05*
Ghost of the Needle *'03*

Hy Averback(1925-97)
Where the Boys Are '84 *'84*
She's in the Army Now *'81*
A Guide for the Married Woman *'78*
Pearl *'78*
Suppose They Gave a War and Nobody Came? *'70*
I Love You, Alice B. Toklas! *'68*
Where Were You When the Lights Went Out? *'68*

Rick Avery
Deadly Outbreak *'96*
The Expert *'95*

John G. Avildsen(1935-)
8 Seconds *'94*
The Power of One *'92*
Rocky 5 *'90*
The Karate Kid: Part 3 *'89*
Lean on Me *'89*
For Keeps *'88*
Happy New Year *'87*
The Karate Kid: Part 2 *'86*
The Karate Kid *'84*
A Night in Heaven *'83*
Neighbors *'81*
The Formula *'80*
Rocky *'76*
Foreplay *'75*
Save the Tiger *'73*
Cry Uncle *'71*
Guess What We Learned in School Today? *'70*
Joe *'70*

Meiert Avis
Undiscovered *'05*
Far from Home *'89*

Jon Avnet(1949-)
88 Minutes *'08*
Righteous Kill *'08*
The Starter Wife *'07*
Uprising *'01*
Red Corner *'97*
Up Close and Personal *'96*
The War *'94*
Fried Green Tomatoes *'91*
Between Two Women *'86*

Gabriel Axel(1918-)
Royal Deceit *'94*
Babette's Feast *'87*

George Axelrod(1922-2003)
Secret Life of an American Wife *'68*
Lord Love a Duck *'66*

David Ayer(1972-)
Street Kings *'08*
Harsh Times *'05*

Steven Ayromlooi
Love and Other Four Letter Words *'07*
Leprechaun 6: Back 2 Tha Hood *'03*

Mario Azzopardi(1950-)
Savage Messiah *'02*
Stiletto Dance *'01*
Thrill Seekers *'99*
Total Recall 2070: Machine Dreams *'99*

Bone Daddy '97
Nowhere to Hide '83
Deadline '82

Beth B(1955-)
Two Small Bodies '93
Salvation! '87
Vortex '81

Jamie Babbit(1970-)
Itty Bitty Titty Committee '07
The Quiet '05
But I'm a Cheerleader '99

Hector Babenco(1946-)
Carandiru '03
At Play in the Fields of the Lord '91
Ironweed '87
Kiss of the Spider Woman '85
Pixote '81

Kevin Bacon(1958-)
Loverboy '05
Losing Chase '96

Lloyd Bacon(1890-1955)
The French Line '54
She Couldn't Say No '52
The Fuller Brush Girl '50
Kill the Umpire '50
It Happens Every Spring '49
Miss Grant Takes Richmond '49
Action in the North Atlantic '43
The Fighting Sullivans '42
Larceny, Inc. '42
Silver Queen '42
Footsteps in the Dark '41
Brother Orchid '40
Knute Rockne: All American '40
Invisible Stripes '39
Oklahoma Kid '39
Boy Meets Girl '38
A Slight Case of Murder '38
Marked Woman '37
San Quentin '37
Cain and Mabel '36
Gold Diggers of 1937 '36
Devil Dogs of the Air '35
Wonder Bar '34
Footlight Parade '33
42nd Street '33
Picture Snatcher '33
Kept Husbands '31
Say It With Songs '29
The Singing Fool '28

Clarence Badger(1880-1964)
It '27
Hands Up '26
Paths to Paradise '25
Teddy at the Throttle '16

John Badham(1939-)
Footsteps '03
Brother's Keeper '02
The Last Debate '00
The Jack Bull '99
Incognito '97
Nick of Time '95
Drop Zone '94
Another Stakeout '93
Point of No Return '93
The Hard Way '91
Bird on a Wire '90
Stakeout '87
Short Circuit '86
American Flyers '85
Blue Thunder '83
WarGames '83
Whose Life Is It Anyway? '81
Dracula '79
Saturday Night Fever '77
Bingo Long Traveling All-Stars & Motor Kings '76
Reflections of Murder '74

Reza Badiyi(1936-)
Blade in Hong Kong '85
Policewoman Centerfold '83
Of Mice and Men '81

Max Baer, Jr.(1937-)
Hometown U.S.A. '79
Ode to Billy Joe '76
The McCullochs '75

King Baggot(1879-1948)
The Notorious Lady '27
Tumbleweeds '25
Human Hearts '22

Charles "Chuck" Bail
Street Corner Justice '96
Choke Canyon '86
Gumball Rally '76
Cleopatra Jones & the Casino of Gold '75

Fenton Bailey
Inside Deep Throat '05
Party Monster '03
The Eyes of Tammy Faye '00

John Bailey(1942-)
Brief Interviews With Hideous Men '09
China Moon '91
Search for Signs of Intelligent Life in the Universe '91

Stuart Baird(1947-)
Vantage Point '08
Star Trek: Nemesis '02
U.S. Marshals '98
Executive Decision '96

David Baker(1931-)
Best Enemies '86
Air Hawk '84

Graham Baker
Beowulf '98
Born to Ride '91
Alien Nation '88
Impulse '84
The Final Conflict '81

Robert S. Baker(1916-)
The Hellfire Club '61
Jack the Ripper '60
The Siege of Sidney Street '60
Blackout '50

Roy Ward Baker(1916-)
Masks of Death '86
The Monster Club '85
Danger UXB '81
The Flame Trees of Thika '81
And Now the Screaming Starts '73
The Legend of the 7 Golden Vampires '73
Vault of Horror '73
Asylum '72
Dr. Jekyll and Sister Hyde '71
The Scars of Dracula '70
The Vampire Lovers '70
The Anniversary '68
Fiction Makers '67
A Night to Remember '58
One That Got Away '57
Don't Bother to Knock '52
I'll Never Forget You '51
Morning Departure '50
The Weaker Sex '49
The October Man '48

Ralph Bakshi(1938-)
Cool and the Crazy '94
Cool World '92
Fire and Ice '83
Hey Good Lookin' '82
American Pop '81
The Lord of the Rings '78
Wizards '77
Streetfight '75
Heavy Traffic '73
Fritz the Cat '72

Bob Balaban(1945-)
Bernard and Doris '08
Subway Stories '97
The Last Good Time '94
My Boyfriend's Back '93
Parents '89
The Stranger from Venus '54

Alexsei Balabanov(1959-)
Of Freaks and Men '98
Brother '97

Jaume Balaguero
Rec '07
Darkness '02

Josiane Balasko(1952-)
French Twist '95
Hotel America '81

Marius Balchunas
The Elder Son '06
No Vacancy '99

Gianfranco Baldanello(1928-)
The Uranium Conspiracy '78
Great Adventure '75
Death Ray '67

Ferdinando Baldi(1917-2007)
Treasure of the Four Crowns '82
Sicilian Connection '72
Texas, Adios '66
Duel of Champions '61

Marcello Baldi
Saul and David '64
Venus Against the Son of Hercules '62

Richard Balducci(1929-)
Too Pretty to Be Honest '72
Scandal Man '67
L'Odeur des Fauves '66

Peter Baldwin(1929-)
Meet Wally Sparks '97
A Very Brady Christmas '88
Lots of Luck '85

Rafael Baledon, Sr. (1919-95)
The Man and the Monster '65
Swamp of the Lost Monster '65
The Curse of the Crying Woman '61

Carroll Ballard(1937-)
Duma '05
Fly Away Home '96
Wind '92
Nutcracker: The Motion Picture '86
Never Cry Wolf '83
The Black Stallion '79

Albert Band(1924-2002)
Prehysteria 2 '94
Prehysteria '93
Robot Wars '93
Doctor Mordrid: Master of the Unknown '90
Ghoulies 2 '87
Zoltan... Hound of Dracula '78
She Came to the Valley '77
Tramplers '66
Hercules and the Princess of Troy '65
I Bury the Living '58

Charles Band(1952-)
The Creeps '97
Hideous '97
Dollman vs Demonic Toys '93
Prehysteria '93
Crash and Burn '90
Doctor Mordrid: Master of the Unknown '90
Meridian: Kiss of the Beast '90
Trancers 2: The Return of Jack Deth '90
Trancers '84
Dungeonmaster '83
Metalstorm: The Destruction of Jared Syn '83
Parasite '82
The Alchemist '81

Mirra Bank
Enormous Changes '83
Trumps '83

Montague (Monty) Banks(1897-1950)
Great Guns '41
The Church Mouse '34

Norberto Barba(1963-)
Lost in the Bermuda Triangle '98
Solo '96
Blue Tiger '94

Ernie Barbarash
Hardwired '09
Meteor '09
Stir of Echoes 2: The Homecoming '07
Cube: Zero '04

Uri Barbash
Unsettled Land '88
Beyond the Walls '84

Randy Barbato
Inside Deep Throat '05
Party Monster '03
The Eyes of Tammy Faye '00

Joseph Barbera(1911-)
Jetsons: The Movie '90
Hey There, It's Yogi Bear '64

Paris Barclay(1956-)
The Cherokee Kid '96
America's Dream '95
Don't Be a Menace to South Central While Drinking Your Juice in the Hood '95

Clive Barker(1952-)
Lord of Illusions '95
Nightbreed '90
Hellraiser '87

Mike Barker(1966-)
Shattered '07
A Good Woman '04
To Kill a King '03
Lorna Doone '01
Best Laid Plans '99
The Tenant of Wildfell Hall '96

Reginald Barker(1886-1945)
Healer '36
The Moonstone '34
Seven Keys to Baldpate '29
Civilization '16
The Bargain '15
The Italian '15
On the Night Stage '15
The Wrath of the Gods '14

Boris Barnet(1902-65)
The Patriots '33
The Girl with the Hat Box '27

Steve Barnett(1955-)
Scanner Cop 2: Volkin's Revenge '94
Scanners: The Showdown '94
Mission of Justice '92
Mindwarp '91
Hollywood Boulevard 2 '89
Emmanuelle 5 '87

Neema Barnette(1949-)
Civil Brand '02
Run for the Dream: The Gail Devers Story '96
Spirit Lost '96
Better Off Dead '94
Sin and Redemption '94
Zora Is My Name! '90

Daniel Barnz
Beastly '10
Phoebe in Wonderland '08

Allen Baron(1935-)
Foxfire Light '82
Red, White & Busted '75
Blast of Silence '61

Douglas Barr(1949-)
The Note 2: Taking a Chance on Love '09
The Note '07
Frame by Frame '95
Dead Badge '94

Christophe Barratier
Paris 36 '08
The Chorus '04

Bruno Barreto(1955-)
View from the Top '03
Bossa Nova '99
One Tough Cop '98
Four Days in September '97
Carried Away '95
A Show of Force '90
The Story of Fausta '88
Happily Ever After '86
Gabriela '84
Amor Bandido '79
Dona Flor and Her Two Husbands '78

Fabio Barreto(1957-)
O Quatrilho '95
Luzia '88

Steven Barron(1956-)
Arabian Nights '00
Merlin '98
The Adventures of Pinocchio '96
Coneheads '93
Teenage Mutant Ninja Turtles: The Movie '90
Electric Dreams '84

Zelda Barron(1929-2006)
Forbidden Sun '89
Shag: The Movie '89
Bulldance '88
Secret Places '85

Mariano Barroso
In the Time of the Butterflies '01
Extasis '96

Ian Barry
The Diamond of Jeru '01
Joey '98
Robo Warriors '96
Blackwater Trail '95
Crime Broker '94
Crimebroker '93
The Seventh Floor '93
Wrangler '88
Chain Reaction '80

Paul Bartel(1938-2000)
Scenes from the Class Struggle in Beverly Hills '89
The Longshot '86
Lust in the Dust '85
Not for Publication '84
Eating Raoul '82
Cannonball '76
Death Race 2000 '75
Private Parts '72
Paul Bartel's The Secret Cinema '69

Andrzej Bartkowiak(1950-)
Street Fighter: The Legend of Chun-Li '09
Doom '05
Cradle 2 the Grave '03
Exit Wounds '01
Romeo Must Die '00

Hall Bartlett(1922-93)
Children of Sanchez '79
Jonathan Livingston Seagull '73
Defiant '70
Changes '69
All the Young Men '60
Zero Hour! '57

Richard Bartlett(1922-94)
Ollie Hopnoodle's Haven of Bliss '88
Rock, Pretty Baby '56
Lonesome Trail '55
Silver Star '55

Charles T. Barton(1902-81)
The Shaggy Dog '59
Toby Tyler '59
Dance with Me, Henry '56
Ma and Pa Kettle at the Fair '52
Double Crossbones '51
Abbott and Costello Meet the Killer, Boris Karloff '49
Africa Screams '49
Abbott and Costello Meet Frankenstein '48
Mexican Hayride '48
The Noose Hangs High '48
Buck Privates Come Home '47
The Wistful Widow of Wagon Gap '47
The Time of Their Lives '46
Louisiana Hayride '44
Harmon of Michigan '41
Helltown '38
Forlorn River '37
Thunder Pass '37
Thunder Trail '37
Desert Gold '36
Murder With Pictures '36
The Last Outpost '35
Wagon Wheels '34

Paolo Barzman
Dr. Jekyll and Mr. Hyde '08
Autumn Hearts: A New Beginning '07
For Better and for Worse '92

K.C. Bascombe
Hide '08
Fear of the Dark '02
Swindle '02
The Contract '98

Harry Basil
Soul's Midnight '06
The 4th Tenor '02

Jules Bass(1935-)
Flight of Dragons '82
The Last Unicorn '82
The Return of the King '80
The Hobbit '78
Mad Monster Party '68

Lawrence Bassoff
Hunk '87
Weekend Pass '84

Bradley Battersby(1953-)
Red Letters '00
Blue Desert '91

Roy Battersby
Red Mercury '05
Catherine Cookson's The Moth '96
Cracker: Brotherly Love '95
Catherine Cookson's The Black Candle '92
Mr. Love '86
Winter Flight '84

Giacomo Battiato(1943-)
Blood Ties '87
Hearts & Armour '83

Noah Baumbach(1969-)
Greenberg '10
Margot at the Wedding '07
The Squid and the Whale '05
Mr. Jealousy '98
Highball '97
Kicking and Screaming '95

Lamberto Bava(1944-)
Ghost Son '06
Demons 2 '87
Demons '86
Blastfighter '85
Devilfish '84
A Blade in the Dark '83
Macabre '80

Mario Bava(1914-80)
Shock '79
Lisa and the Devil '75
Torture Chamber of Baron Blood '72
Twitch of the Death Nerve '71
Five Dolls for an August Moon '70

Hatchet for the Honeymoon '70
Four Times That Night '69
Danger: Diabolik '68
Kill, Baby, Kill '66
Knives of the Avenger '65
Planet of the Vampires '65
Black Sabbath '64
Blood and Black Lace '64
Hercules in the Haunted World '64
The Girl Who Knew Too Much '63
The Invaders '63
The Whip and the Body '63
The Wonders of Aladdin '61
Black Sunday '60

Craig R. Baxley(1949-)

Aces 'n Eights '08
The Diary of Ellen Rimbauer '03
Sniper 2 '02
Stephen King's Rose Red '02
Stephen King's The Storm of the Century '99
Under Pressure '98
Twilight Man '96
The Avenging Angel '95
Deconstructing Sarah '94
Deep Red '94
Stone Cold '91
I Come in Peace '90
Action Jackson '88

John Baxter(1896-1975)

Love on the Dole '41
Old Mother Riley's Ghosts '41

Michael Bay(1965-)

Transformers: Revenge of the Fallen '09
Transformers '07
The Island '05
Bad Boys 2 '03
Pearl Harbor '01
Armageddon '98
The Rock '96
Bad Boys '95

Rolf Bayer

Pacific Inferno '85
The Kill '73

Stephen Bayly(1942-)

Diamond's Edge '88
Coming Up Roses '87

Camillo Bazzoni

Black Lemons '70
A Long Ride From Hell '68

David Beaird(1952-)

Scorchers '92
It Takes Two '88
Pass the Ammo '88
My Chauffeur '86
Party Animal '83
Octavia '82

Henry Bean(1945-)

Noise '07
The Believer '01

Alan Beattie

Stand Alone '85
Delusion '80

Warren Beatty(1937-)

Bulworth '98
Dick Tracy '90
Reds '81
Heaven Can Wait '78

William Beaudine(1892-1970)

Billy the Kid Versus Dracula '66
Jesse James Meets Frankenstein's Daughter '65
Lassie's Great Adventure '62
Ten Who Dared '60
Westward Ho, the Wagons! '56
Bela Lugosi Meets a Brooklyn Gorilla '52
Here Come the Marines '52
Ghost Chasers '51
Blues Busters '50
Kidnapped '48
Smugglers' Cove '48
Spook Buckaroos '48
Bowery Buckaroos '47
Hard-Boiled Mahoney '47
Infamous Crimes '47
Mom & Dad '47
Too Many Winners '47
Follow the Leader '44
Ghost Crazy '44
The Ape Man '43
Clancy Street Boys '43
Ghost on the Loose '43
Here Comes Kelly '43
Spotlight Scandals '43
Spotlight Scandals '43
Miracle Kid '42
The Panther's Claw '42
Phantom Killer '42
Turf Boy '42
Blonde Comet '41
Desperate Cargo '41
Misbehaving Husbands '41
Robot Pilot '41
Sparrows '26
Little Annie Rooney '25
The Country Kid '23

Gabrielle Beaumont(1942-)

Beastmaster 3: The Eye of Braxus '95
Riders '88
He's My Girl '87
Gone Are the Days '84
Death of a Centerfold '81
The Godsend '79

Harry Beaumont(1888-1966)

The Show-Off '46
When's Your Birthday? '37
Dance Fools Dance '31
Laughing Sinners '31
Broadway Melody '29
Speedway '29
Our Dancing Daughters '28
Beau Brummel '24

Gorman Bechard(1959-)

Cemetery High '89
Disconnected '87
Galactic Gigolo '87
Psychos in Love '87

Martin Beck

Last Game '80
Challenge '74

Steve Beck

Ghost Ship '02
13 Ghosts '01

Harold Becker(1950-)

Domestic Disturbance '01
Mercury Rising '98
City Hall '95
Malice '93
Sea of Love '89
The Boost '88
Big Town '87
Vision Quest '85
Taps '81
The Black Marble '79
The Onion Field '79

Jacques Becker(1906-60)

Le Trou '59
Modigliani '58
Ali Baba and the 40 Thieves '54
Grisbi '53
Casque d'Or '52
Rendez-vous de Juillet '49
Antoine et Antoinette '47

Jean Becker(1938-)

Elisa '94
One Deadly Summer '83

Josh Becker(1958-)

Lunatics: A Love Story '92
Thou Shalt Not Kill...Except '87

Walt Becker(1968-)

Old Dogs '09
Wild Hogs '07
Buying the Cow '02
National Lampoon's Van Wilder '02

James Becket(1936-)

Final Approach '04
Plato's Run '96
Natural Causes '94
Ulterior Motives '92

James Gavin Bedford

The Street King '02
Red Shoe Diaries 8: Night of Abandon '97

Ford Beebe(1888-1978)

King of the Wild Stallions '59
Red Desert '50
Outlaw Gang '49
Shep Comes Home '49
The Lion Hunters '47
My Dog Shep '46
The Invisible Man's Revenge '44
Don Winslow of the Coast Guard '43
Don Winslow of the Navy '43
Night Monster '42
Overland Mail '42
The Masked Rider '41
Riders of Death Valley '41
Fantasia '40
Flash Gordon Conquers the Universe '40
Junior G-Men '40
Space Soldiers Conquer the Universe '40
Winners of the West '40
Buck Rogers Conquers the Universe '39
Destination Saturn '39
Flash Gordon: Mars Attacks the World '39
The Green Hornet '39
Oklahoma Frontier '39
The Phantom Creeps '39
Red Barry '38
Radio Patrol '37
Tim Tyler's Luck '37
Ace Drummond '36
The Man from Gun Town '36
Laughing at Life '33
The Last of the Mohicans '32
Shadow of the Eagle '32

Greg Beeman(1962-)

Miracle in Lane Two '00
Brink '98
Bushwhacked '95
Mom and Dad Save the World '92
License to Drive '88

Charles Beeson

Cider with Rosie '99
Second Sight '99
Agatha Christie's The Pale Horse '96

Jean-Jacques Beineix(1946-)

Mortal Transfer '01
Betty Blue '86
Moon in the Gutter '83
Diva '82

Timur Bekmambetov

Wanted '08
Day Watch '06
Night Watch '04

Arnold Belgard(1907-67)

Mighty Jungle '64
East of Kilimanjaro '57

Martin Bell

Brotherhood of Murder '99
Hidden in America '96
American Heart '92
Streetwise '84

Monta Bell(1891-1958)

Personal Maid '31
The King on Main Street '25

Earl Bellamy(1917-2003)

Magic on Love Island '80
Desperate Women '78
Speedtrap '78
Fire '77
Sidewinder One '77
Flood! '76
Against a Crooked Sky '75
Seven Alone '75
Walking Tall: Part 2 '75
The Trackers '71
Munster, Go Home! '66
Justice of the West '61
The Desperate Mission '60
Seminole Uprising '55

Donald P. Bellisario(1935-)

JAG '95
Last Rites '88

Marco Bellocchio(1939-)

The Wedding Director '06
My Mother's Smile '02
Devil in the Flesh '87
Henry IV '85
The Eyes, the Mouth '83

Jerry Belson(1938-2006)

Surrender '87
Jekyll & Hyde... Together Again '82

Maria-Luisa Bemberg(1922-95)

I Don't Want to Talk About It '94
I, the Worst of All '90
Miss Mary '86
Camila '84

Jack Bender

My Little Assassin '99
The Tempest '99
It Came from the Sky '98
A Call to Remember '97
Killing Mr. Griffin '97
Lone Justice 3: Showdown at Plum Creek '96
Lone Justice 2 '93
Child's Play 3 '91
My Brother's Wife '89
Side by Side '88
Tricks of the Trade '88
The Midnight Hour '86
Letting Go '85
Two Kinds of Love '85
Shattered Vows '84
In Love with an Older Woman '82

Joel Bender

Karla '06
Midnight Kiss '93
Rich Girl '91
The Immortalizer '89
Gas Pump Girls '79

Laszlo Benedek(1907-92)

Assault on Agathon '75
The Night Visitor '70
Daring Game '68
Namu, the Killer Whale '66
The Wild One '54
Death of a Salesman '51
Port of New York '49
The Kissing Bandit '48

Roberto Benigni(1952-)

The Tiger and the Snow '05
Pinocchio '02
Life Is Beautiful '98
The Monster '96
Johnny Stecchino '92

Richard Benjamin(1938-)

Marci X '03
The Pentagon Wars '98
Tourist Trap '98
Mrs. Winterbourne '96
Milk Money '94
Made in America '93
Mermaids '90
Downtown '89
Little Nikita '88
My Stepmother Is an Alien '88
The Money Pit '86
City Heat '84
Racing with the Moon '84
My Favorite Year '82

Richard Benner(1943-90)

Happy Birthday, Gemini '80
Outrageous! '77

Spencer Gordon Bennet(1893-1987)

Atomic Submarine '59
Submarine Seahawk '59
King of the Congo '52
Atom Man vs. Superman '50
Pirates of the High Seas '50
The Black Widow '47
Son of Zorro '47
Daughter of Don Q '46
King of the Forest Rangers '46
The Phantom Rider '46
D-Day on Mars '45
Manhunt of Mystery Island '45
The Purple Monster Strikes '45
Perils of the Darkest Jungle '44
Zorro's Black Whip '44
California Joe '43
Calling Wild Bill Elliott '43
Manhunt in the African Jungles '43
The Masked Marvel '43
The Secret Code '42
Arizona Bound '41
Gunman from Bodie '41
Across the Plains '39
The Rangers Step In '37
Rio Grande Ranger '37
The Unknown Ranger '36
Get That Man '35
The Fighting Rookie '34
Last Frontier '32
Midnight Warning '32
Rogue of the Rio Grande '30
Marked Money '28

Bill Bennett(1953-)

Bollywood Hero '09
The Nugget '02
Tempted '01
In a Savage Land '99
Kiss or Kill '97
Two If by Sea '95
Backlash '86

Compton Bennett(1900-74)

The Gift Horse '52
King Solomon's Mines '50
That Forsyte Woman '50
The Seventh Veil '46

Edward Bennett(1950-)

The Scarlet Pimpernel 3: The Kidnapped King '99
A Woman at War '94

Rodney Bennett

Monsignor Quixote '91
Sense & Sensibility '85
Edwin '84
The Lost Boys '78

Spencer Gordon Bennett

Federal Operator 99 '45
Night Alarm '34
Jaws of Justice '33

Richard Benson(1924-)

Werewolf in a Girl's Dormitory '61
The Day the Sky Exploded '57

Robby Benson(1956-)

Modern Love '90
White Hot '88

Steve Benson

See Joe D'Amato

Thomas Bentley(1880-1950)

Murder at the Baskervilles '37
The Old Curiosity Shop '35
The Living Dead '33

Robert Benton(1932-)

Feast of Love '07
The Human Stain '03
Twilight '98
Nobody's Fool '94
Billy Bathgate '91
Nadine '87
Places in the Heart '84
Still of the Night '82
Kramer vs. Kramer '79
The Late Show '77
Bad Company '72

Luca Bercovici(1957-)

Luck of the Draw '00
Bitter Sweet '98
Convict 762 '98
The Granny '94
Dark Tide '93
Rockula '90
Ghoulies '84

Bruce Beresford(1940-)

The Contract '07
And Starring Pancho Villa as Himself '03
Evelyn '02
Bride of the Wind '01
Double Jeopardy '99
Paradise Road '97
Last Dance '96
A Good Man in Africa '94
Silent Fall '94
Rich in Love '93
Black Robe '91
Mister Johnson '91
Driving Miss Daisy '89
Aria '88
Her Alibi '88
Crimes of the Heart '86
The Fringe Dwellers '86
King David '85
Tender Mercies '83
The Club '81
Puberty Blues '81
Breaker Morant '80
Money Movers '78
The Getting of Wisdom '77
Don's Party '76
Barry McKenzie Holds His Own '74

Peter Berg(1964-)

Hancock '08
The Kingdom '07
Friday Night Lights '04
The Rundown '03
Very Bad Things '98

Pamela Berger

The Magic Stone '95
The Imported Bridegroom '89

Andrew Bergman(1945-)

Isn't She Great '00
Striptease '96
It Could Happen to You '94
Honeymoon in Vegas '92
The Freshman '90
So Fine '81

Daniel Bergman(1962-)

Expectations '97
Sunday's Children '94

Ingmar Bergman(1918-2007)

Saraband '03
After the Rehearsal '84
Fanny and Alexander '83
From the Life of the Marionettes '80
Autumn Sonata '78
The Serpent's Egg '78
Face to Face '76
The Magic Flute '73
Scenes from a Marriage '73
Cries and Whispers '72
The Touch '71
The Passion of Anna '70
The Rite '69
Hour of the Wolf '68
The Shame '68
Persona '66
The Silence '63
The Winter Light '62
Through a Glass Darkly '61
The Devil's Eye '60

The Virgin Spring '59
The Magician '58
Brink of Life '57
Wild Strawberries '57
The Seventh Seal '56
Dreams '55
Smiles of a Summer Night '55
Lesson in Love '54
Sawdust & Tinsel '53
Monika '52
Secrets of Women '52
Summer Interlude '50
To Joy '50
Devil's Wanton '49
Three Strange Loves '49
Port of Call '48
Night Is My Future '47

Robert Bergman

Skull: A Night of Terror '88
A Whisper to a Scream '88

William Berke(1903-58)

The Lost Missile '58
The Marshal's Daughter '53
FBI Girl '52
Jungle '52
Bandit Queen '51
Pier 23 '51
Roaring City '51
Savage Drums '51
Border Rangers '50
Deputy Marshal '50
Gunfire '50
I Shot Billy the Kid '50
Operation Haylift '50
Treasure of Monte Cristo '50
Sky Liner '49
Highway 13 '48
Rolling Home '48
Shoot to Kill '47
Renegade Girl '46
Dick Tracy, Detective '45
Betrayal from the East '44
Dangerous Passage '44
Dark Mountain '44
The Falcon in Mexico '44
Navy Way '44
That's My Baby! '44
Lawless Plainsmen '42
Gun Grit '36
Toll of the Desert '35

Busby Berkeley(1895-1976)

Take Me Out to the Ball Game '49
The Gang's All Here '43
For Me and My Gal '42
Babes on Broadway '41
Strike Up the Band '40
Babes in Arms '39
They Made Me a Criminal '39
Hollywood Hotel '37
Stage Struck '36
Gold Diggers of 1935 '35

Abby Berlin(1907-65)

Double Deal '50
Blondie Knows Best '46

Alain Berliner(1963-)

Passion of Mind '00
Ma Vie en Rose '97

Joe Berlinger(1961-)

Metallica: Some Kind of Monster '04
Book of Shadows: Blair Witch 2 '00
Brother's Keeper '92

Monty Berman(1912-2006)

The Hellfire Club '61
Jack the Ripper '60
The Siege of Sidney Street '60

Shari Springer Berman

The Nanny Diaries '07
American Splendor '03

Ted Berman(1920-2001)

The Black Cauldron '85
The Fox and the Hound '81

Zev Berman

Borderland '07
Plain Dirty '04

Edward L. Bernds(1905-2000)

Gunfight at Comanche Creek '64
Three Stooges in Orbit '62
The Three Stooges Meet Hercules '61
Return of the Fly '59
Queen of Outer Space '58
Space Master X-7 '58
Reform School Girl '57
Storm Rider '57
Bowery Boys Meet the Monsters '54
Clipped Wings '53
Corky of Gasoline Alley '51
Gasoline Alley '51
Gold Raiders '51
Blondie Hits the Jackpot '49

Jack Bernhard(1913-)

Unknown Island '48
Violence '47
Decoy '46

Curtis Bernhardt(1899-1981)

Kisses for My President '64
Interrupted Melody '55
Beau Brummel '54
Miss Sadie Thompson '53
The Merry Widow '52
Payment on Demand '51
Sirocco '51
The Possessed '47
My Reputation '46
A Stolen Life '46
Conflict '45
Juke Girl '42

Adam Bernstein(1960-)

Six Ways to Sunday '99
It's Pat: The Movie '94

Armyan Bernstein

Cross My Heart '88
Windy City '84

Walter Bernstein(1919-)

Women & Men: In Love There Are No Rules '91
Little Miss Marker '80

Claude Berri(1934-)

The Housekeeper '02
Lucie Aubrac '98
Germinal '93
Uranus '91
Jean de Florette '87
Manon of the Spring '87
Tchao Pantin '84
I Love You All '80
One Wild Moment '78
Le Sex Shop '73
Marry Me, Marry Me '69
The Two of Us '68

Bill Berry

Off the Mark '87
Brotherhood of Death '76

John Berry(1917-99)

Boesman & Lena '00
A Captive in the Land '91
Honeyboy '82
Angel on My Shoulder '80
The Bad News Bears Go to Japan '78
Maya '66
Tamango '59
Pantaloons '57
There Goes Barder '54
Tension '50
Casbah '48

Tom Berry

Twin Sisters '91
The Amityville Curse '90
Blind Fear '89

Bernardo Bertolucci(1940-)

The Dreamers '03
Besieged '98
Stealing Beauty '96
Little Buddha '93
The Sheltering Sky '90
The Last Emperor '87
The Tragedy of a Ridiculous Man '81
1900 '76
Last Tango in Paris '73
The Conformist '71
The Spider's Stratagem '70
Partner '68
Before the Revolution '65
The Grim Reaper '62

Irvin Berwick(1914-)

Malibu High '79
The 7th Commandment '61
The Monster of Piedras Blancas '57

Carl Bessai

Normal '07
Emile '03

Luc Besson(1959-)

Arthur and the Invisibles '06
Angel-A '05
The Messenger: The Story of Joan of Arc '99
The Fifth Element '97
The Professional '94
La Femme Nikita '91
The Big Blue '88
Subway '85
Le Dernier Combat '84

Nicole Bettauer

Duck '05
Zack & Reba '98

Gil Bettman

Night Vision '97
Crystal Heart '87
Never Too Young to Die '86

Jonathan Betuel(1949-)

Theodore Rex '95
My Science Project '85

Eddie Beverly, Jr.

Ballbuster '89
Amateur Night '85
Escapist '83

Frank Beyer(1932-2006)

Jacob the Liar '74
Trace of Stones '66
Carbide and Sorrel '63
Five Cartridges '60

Troy Beyer(1965-)

Love Don't Cost a Thing '03
Let's Talk About Sex '98

Thomas Bezucha

The Family Stone '05
Big Eden '00

Radha Bharadwaj

Basil '98
Closet Land '90

Andrea Bianchi(1925-)

Burial Ground '85
Cry of a Prostitute: Love Kills '72
What the Peeper Saw '72

Edward Bianchi(1942-)

Off and Running '90
The Fan '81

Roberto Bianchi

See Robert Bianchi Montero

Herbert Biberman(1900-71)

Salt of the Earth '54
The Master Race '44

Antonio Bido(1949-)

The Bloodstained Shadow '78
Watch Me When I Kill '77

Fabian Bielinsky(1959-2006)

The Aura '05
Nine Queens '00

Marc Bienstock

Indiscreet '98
The Beneficiary '97

Suzanne (Susanne) Bier(1960-)

Things We Lost in the Fire '07
After the Wedding '06
Brothers '04
Like It Never Was Before '95
Freud Leaving Home '91

Robert Bierman

A Merry War '97
The Moonstone '97
Clarissa '91
Vampire's Kiss '88
Apology '86

Kathryn Bigelow(1952-)

The Hurt Locker '08
K-19: The Widowmaker '02
The Weight of Water '00
Strange Days '95
Wild Palms '93
Point Break '91
Blue Steel '90
Near Dark '87
Loveless '83

Tony Bill(1940-)

Pictures of Hollis Woods '07
Flyboys '06
Whitewash: The Clarence Brandley Story '02
Harlan County War '00
Oliver Twist '97
Beyond the Call '96
One Christmas '95
Next Door '94
A Home of Our Own '93
Untamed Heart '93
Crazy People '90
Five Corners '88
The Princess and the Pea '83
Six Weeks '82
My Bodyguard '80

Bruce Bilson(1928-)

Chattanooga Choo Choo '84
The North Avenue Irregulars '79

Danny Bilson(1956-)

The Wrong Guys '88
Zone Troopers '84

Charles Biname

The Trojan Horse '08
Street Heart '98

Mike Binder(1958-)

Reign Over Me '07
The Upside of Anger '05
The Search for John Gissing '01
The Sex Monster '99
Blankman '94
Indian Summer '93
Crossing the Bridge '92

Steve Binder

Give 'Em Hell, Harry! '75
The T.A.M.I. Show '64

William Bindley

Madison '01
The Eighteenth Angel '97
Judicial Consent '94
Freeze Frame '92

Josh Binney(1889-1956)

Boardinghouse Blues '48
Killer Diller '48
Hi-De-Ho '35

Antonia Bird(1959-)

The Hamburg Cell '04
Ravenous '99
Face '97
Mad Love '95
Priest '94

Brad Bird(1957-)

Ratatouille '07
The Incredibles '04
The Iron Giant '99

Richard Bird(1895-1986)

Men of Ireland '38
The Terror '38

Andrew Birkin(1945-)

The Cement Garden '93
Desire '93
Burning Secret '89

Alan Birkinshaw

Masque of the Red Death '90
Ten Little Indians '89
The House of Usher '88

Daniel Birt(1907-55)

Robin Hood: The Movie '55
Big Deadly Game '54
Interrupted Journey '49
The Three Weird Sisters '48

Larry Bishop(1947-)

Hell Ride '08
Trigger Happy '96

Bill Bixby(1934-93)

The Woman Who Loved Elvis '93
Another Pair of Aces: Three of a Kind '91
Baby of the Bride '91
Death of the Incredible Hulk '90
The Trial of the Incredible Hulk '89
The Barbary Coast '74

Herbert Blache(1882-1953)

Head Winds '25
The Untamable '23
The Saphead '21

Noel Black(1937-)

Eyes of the Panther '90
A Conspiracy of Love '87
Quarterback Princess '85
Private School '83
Prime Suspect '82
A Man, a Woman, and a Bank '79
Mirrors '78
Pretty Poison '68

David Blair

Tess of the D'Urbervilles '08
Wax, or the Discovery of Television among the Bees '93

David Blair

Anna Karenina '00
Split Second '99

George Blair(1905-70)

Jaguar '56
Silver City Bonanza '51
Thunder in God's Country '51
Missourians '50
G.I. War Brides '46
End of the Road '44

Alfonso Corona Blake(1919-99)

Samson in the Wax Museum '63
Samson vs. the Vampire Women '61

Michael Blakemore(1928-)

Country Life '95
Privates on Parade '84

John Blanchard

Shriek If You Know What I Did Last Friday the 13th '00
Really Weird Tales '86
The Last Polka '84

Jamie Blanks

Nature's Grave '08
Valentine '01
Urban Legend '98

Alessandro Blasetti(1900-87)

Simon Bolivar '69
What a Woman! '56
Too Bad She's Bad '54
Fabiola '48
The Iron Crown '41
1860 '33

William Peter Blatty(1928-)

Exorcist 3: Legion '90
The Ninth Configuration '79

Jeff Bleckner(1943-)

Loving Leah '09
That Russell Girl '08
Have No Fear: The Life of Pope John Paul II '05
Dean Koontz's Black River '01
Flowers for Algernon '00
Rear Window '98
The Beast '96
Serving in Silence: The Margarethe Cammermeyer Story '95
Target: Favorite Son '87
White Water Summer '87
Brotherly Love '85
When Your Lover Leaves '83

Bernard Blier(1916-89)

How Much Do You Love Me? '05
Notre Histoire '84

Bertrand Blier(1939-)

Mon Homme '96
Too Beautiful for You '88
Menage '86
My Best Friend's Girl '84
Beau Pere '81
Buffet Froid '79
Get Out Your Handkerchiefs '78
Going Places '74

Jeffrey Blitz(1969-)

Rocket Science '07
Spellbound '02

Jason Bloom

Dead Simple '01
Bio-Dome '96
Overnight Delivery '96

Jeffrey Bloom

Flowers in the Attic '87
Jealousy '84
Blood Beach '81
The Stick-Up '77
Dog Pound Shuffle '75

George Bloomfield(1930-)

Jacob Two Two Meets the Hooded Fang '99
The Awakening '95
The Double Negative '80
Nothing Personal '80
Riel '79
To Kill a Clown '72
Jenny '70

Philippe Blot

Running Wild '94
Hot Blood '89

Ralph Bluemke

Kid and the Killers '74
Robby '68

Don Bluth(1938-)

Titan A.E. '00
Anastasia '97
The Pebble and the Penguin '94
Thumbelina '94
A Troll in Central Park '94
Rock-a-Doodle '92
All Dogs Go to Heaven '89
The Land Before Time '88
An American Tail '86
The Secret of NIMH '82

John Blystone(1892-1938)

Block-heads '38
Swiss Miss '38
23 1/2 Hours Leave '37
Great Guy '36
Too Busy to Work '32
Dick Turpin '25
Our Hospitality '23

David Blyth(1956-)

Hot Blooded '98
Red Blooded 2 '96

My Grandpa Is a Vampire '92
Red Blooded American Girl '90
Death Warmed Up '85

Tanio Boccia
Terror of the Steppes '64
Caesar the Conqueror '63

Hart Bochner(1956-)
Just Add Water '07
High School High '96
P.C.U. '94

Sergei Bodrov(1948-)
Mongol '07
The Quickie '01
Running Free '00
Prisoner of the Mountains '96
Freedom Is Paradise '89

Christoffer Boe
Allegro '05
Reconstruction '03

Budd Boetticher(1916-2001)
Comanche Station '60
The Rise and Fall of Legs Diamond '60
Ride Lonesome '59
Buchanan Rides Alone '58
Westbound '58
Decision at Sundown '57
The Tall T '57
The Magnificent Matador '55
Man from the Alamo '53
Horizons West '52
Red Ball Express '52
Bullfighter & the Lady '50
Behind Locked Doors '48
Human Gorilla '48

Paul Bogart(1919-)
The Heidi Chronicles '95
Broadway Bound '92
Torch Song Trilogy '88
Nutcracker: Money, Madness & Murder '87
Oh, God! You Devil '84
Power, Passion & Murder '83
Tell Me Where It Hurts '74
Class of '44 '73
Cancel My Reservation '72
A House Without a Christmas Tree '72
Skin Game '71
Marlowe '69
The Three Sisters '65

Yurek Bogayevicz(1948-)
Exit in Red '97
Three of Hearts '93
Anna '87

Peter Bogdanovich(1939-)
Hustle '04
The Cat's Meow '01
A Saintly Switch '99
Naked City: A Killer Christmas '98
Rescuers: Stories of Courage "Two Women" '97
The Thing Called Love '93
Noises Off '92
Texasville '90
Illegally Yours '87
Mask '85
They All Laughed '81
Saint Jack '79
Daisy Miller '74
Paper Moon '73
What's Up, Doc? '72
The Last Picture Show '71
Targets '68
Voyage to the Planet of Prehistoric Women '68

Willy Bogner(1942-)
Fire, Ice and Dynamite '91
Fire and Ice '87

Michel Boisrond(1921-2002)
Catherine & Co. '76
Voulez-Vous Danser avec Moi? '59
Mam'zelle Pigalle '58
That Naughty Girl '58
Une Parisienne '58

Yves Boisset(1939-)
Double Identity '89
Prize of Peril '84
Dog Day '83
The Purple Taxi '77
Dupont Lajoie '74
Cobra '71

Jerome Boivin(1954-)
Barjo '93
Baxter '89

Richard Boleslawski(1889-1937)
The Last of Mrs. Cheyney '37
The Garden of Allah '36
Theodora Goes Wild '36
Les Miserables '35
Hollywood Party '34
Men in White '34
Operator 13 '34
The Painted Veil '34
Rasputin and the Empress '33

Uwe Boll(1965-)
In the Name of the King: A Dungeon Siege Tale '08
Seed '08
Tunnel Rats '08
BloodRayne 2: Deliverance '07
Postal '07
BloodRayne '06
Alone in the Dark '05
Heart of America '03
House of the Dead '03
Blackwoods '02
Sanctimony '01

Mauro Bolognini(1922-2001)
Husbands and Lovers '91
The Inheritance '76
La Grande Bourgeoise '74
Oldest Profession '67
Il Bell'Antonio '60

Craig Bolotin(1954-)
Light It Up '99
That Night '93

Ben Bolt(1952-)
The Turn of the Screw '99
Wilderness '96
Big Town '87

James Bolton
The Graffiti Artist '04
Eban and Charley '01

Timothy Bond(1942-)
Running Wild '99
Diamond Girl '98
Loving Evangeline '98
Night of the Twisters '95
Return to the Lost World '93
The Lost World '92
One Night Only '84
Deadly Harvest '72

Sergei Bondarchuk(1920-94)
Waterloo '71
War and Peace '68

Peter Bonerz(1938-)
Police Academy 6: City under Siege '89
Nobody's Perfekt '79

Joon-ho Bong
Madeo '09
Tokyo! '09
The Host '06

Mario Bonnard(1889-1965)
The Mercenaries '62
The Last Days of Pompeii '60

Rene Bonniere(1928-)
The Halfback of Notre Dame '96
Dream Man '94
Islands '87
Perfect Timing '84
Hide and Seek '77

J.R. Bookwalter(1966-)
Witchouse 3: Demon Fire '01
Witchouse 2: Blood Coven '00
The Dead Next Door '89

John Boorman(1933-)
The Tiger's Tale '06
In My Country '04
The Tailor of Panama '00
The General '98
Beyond Rangoon '95
Picture Windows '95
Where the Heart Is '90
Hope and Glory '87
The Emerald Forest '85
Excalibur '81
The Exorcist 2: The Heretic '77
Zardoz '73
Deliverance '72
Hell in the Pacific '69
Point Blank '67

H. Gordon Boos(1958-2004)
Forgotten City '98
Perfect Assassins '98
Red Surf '90

Lizzie Borden(1958-)
Erotique '94
Love Crimes '92
Working Girls '87

Michael Borden
No Way Back '90
Ain't No Way Back '89

Bernard Borderie(1924-78)
Angelique and the Sultan '68
Untamable Angelique '67
Angelique and the King '66
Angelique: The Road to Versailles '65
Angelique '64
Your Turn Darling '63
Ladies' Man '62
Dishonorable Discharge '57

Robert Boris(1945-)
Frank and Jesse '94
Buy & Cell '89
Steele Justice '87
Oxford Blues '84

Ole Bornedal
Just Another Love Story '08
Nightwatch '96

Achim Bornhak
Eight Miles High '08
Eight Miles High '07

Walerian Borowczyk(1923-2006)
Emmanuelle 5 '87
The Beast '75

Clay Borris(1950-)
Someone to Die For '95
Suspicious Agenda '94
Prom Night 4: Deliver Us from Evil '91
The Gunfighters '87
Quiet Cool '86

Phillip Borsos(1954-95)
Far from Home: The Adventures of Yellow Dog '94
Dr. Bethune '90
Mean Season '85
One Magic Christmas '85
The Grey Fox '83

Frank Borzage(1893-1962)
Journey Beneath the Desert '61
The Smallest Show on Earth '48
I've Always Loved You '46
Magnificent Doll '46
The Spanish Main '45
His Butler's Sister '44
Stage Door Canteen '43
Smilin' Through '41
The Mortal Storm '40
Strange Cargo '40
The Shining Hour '38
Three Comrades '38
History Is Made at Night '37
Mannequin '37
Desire '36
Shipmates Forever '35
Flirtation Walk '34
After Tomorrow '32
A Farewell to Arms '32
Young America '32
Bad Girl '31
Song o' My Heart '30
Lucky Star '29
Song o' My Heart '29
They Had to See Paris '29
Street Angel '28
7th Heaven '27
Lazybones '25
Until They Get Me '18

Rick Bota
Hellraiser: Deader '05
Hellraiser: Hellworld '05
Hellraiser: Hellseeker '02

John Boulting(1913-85)
Heavens Above '63
I'm All Right Jack '59
Lucky Jim '58
Seven Days to Noon '50
Brighton Rock '47

Roy Boulting(1913-2001)
There's a Girl in My Soup '70
Heavens Above '63
Carlton Browne of the F.O. '59
Lucky Jim '58
Brothers in Law '57
Sailor of the King '53
Seven Days to Noon '50
The Guinea Pig '48
Fame Is the Spur '47

Serge Bourguignon(1928-)
A Coeur Joie '67
Head Over Heels '67
Sundays & Cybele '62

Darren Lynn Bousman(1979-)
Repo! The Genetic Opera '08
Saw 4 '07
Saw 3 '06
Saw 2 '05

Jenny (H. Anne Riley) Bowen
Animal Behavior '89
The Wizard of Loneliness '88
Street Music '81

John Bowen(1948-)
Hindsight '97
Dark Secrets '95
Knock Outs '92
Lethal Games '90

David Bowers
Astro Boy '09
Flushed Away '06

George Bowers(1944-)
Private Resort '84
My Tutor '82
Body & Soul '81
The Hearse '80

Chuck Bowman
The Tooth Fairy '06
Threshold '03

Rob Bowman(1960-)
Elektra '05
Reign of Fire '02
The X-Files '98
Airborne '93

Muriel Box(1905-91)
Rattle of a Simple Man '64
Truth about Women '58

Tim Boxell
Valley of the Heart's Delight '07
Chasing Destiny '00
Aberration '97

Daniel Boyd(1956-)
Heroes of the Heart '94
Invasion of the Space Preachers '90
Chillers '88

Don Boyd(1948-)
Kleptomania '94
Twenty-One '91
Goldeneye: The Secret Life of Ian Fleming '89
East of Elephant Rock '76

Jean Boyer(1901-65)
Fernandel the Dressmaker '57
Dressmaker '56
The French Touch '54
Femmes de Paris '53
Crazy for Love '52
Mr. Peek-A-Boo '50
Circonstances Attenuantes '36

Danny Boyle(1956-)
Slumdog Millionaire '08
Sunshine '07
Millions '05
28 Days Later '02
Vacuuming Completely Nude in Paradise '01
The Beach '00
A Life Less Ordinary '97
Trainspotting '95
Shallow Grave '94

Steve Boyum(1952-)
Supercross: The Movie '05
Timecop 2: The Berlin Decision '03
Slap Shot 2: Breaking the Ice '02
Meet the Deedles '98

Bruno Bozzetto(1933-)
VIP, My Brother Superman '90
Allegro Non Troppo '76

Charles Brabin(1883-1957)
The Beast of the City '32
The Mask of Fu Manchu '32
Twinkletoes '26
The Raven '15

Robert North Bradbury(1886-1949)
Forbidden Trails '41
God's Country and the Man '37
Hittin' the Trail '37
Riders of the Rockies '37
Sing, Cowboy, Sing '37
Trouble in Texas '37
Where Trails Divide '37
Brand of the Outlaws '36
Cavalry '36
Headin' for the Rio Grande '36
Kid Ranger '36
Last of the Warrens '36
The Law Rides '36
Smokey Smith '36
Sundown Saunders '36
Valley of the Lawless '36
Alias John Law '35
Between Men '35
Big Calibre '35
Courageous Avenger '35
Dawn Rider '35
Desert Trail '35
Kid Courageous '35
Lawless Frontier '35
Lawless Range '35
No Man's Range '35
Rider of the Law '35
Texas Terror '35
Trail of Terror '35
Western Justice '35
Westward Ho '35
Blue Steel '34
The Gun Ranger '34
Lucky Texan '34
Man from Utah '34
The Star Packer '34
Tombstone Terror '34
Trail Beyond '34
Breed of the Border '33
The Gallant Fool '33
Galloping Romeo '33
Riders of Destiny '33
West of the Divide '33
Hidden Valley '32
Man from Hell's Edges '32
Riders of the Desert '32
Texas Buddies '32
Behind Two Guns '24

Al (Alfonso Brescia) Bradley(1930-2001)
Cross Mission '89
Miami Cops '89
Iron Warrior '87
Metallica '85
White Fang and the Hunter '85
Bloody Avenger '80
Cosmos: War of the Planets '80
Captive Planet '78

John Bradshaw(1952-)
Darwin's Darkest Hour '09
Every Second Counts '08
Triggermen '02
Full Disclosure '00
Killing Moon '00
Breakout '98
The Reaper '97
Specimen '97
The Undertaker's Wedding '97
Lethal Tender '96
The Big Slice '90
That's My Baby! '88

Randy Bradshaw
Cold Blooded '00
Song Spinner '95
Blades of Courage '88

Eugene Brady
Missing Brendan '03
The Nephew '97

Jordan Brady(1964-)
The Third Wheel '02
Waking Up in Reno '02

Tom Brady
The Comebacks '07
The Hot Chick '02

Carlo L. Bragaglia(1894-1988)
The Loves of Hercules '60
The Sword and the Cross '58

John Brahm(1893-1982)
Face to Face '52
Miracle of Our Lady of Fatima '52
Singapore '47
Hangover Square '45
Guest in the House '44
Wintertime '43
The Undying Monster '42

Marco Brambilla(1960-)
Dinotopia '02
Excess Baggage '96
Demolition Man '93

Bill Brame(1928-)
Miss Melody Jones '73
Free Grass '69

Kenneth Branagh(1960-)
Sleuth '07
As You Like It '06
Love's Labour's Lost '00
Hamlet '96
A Midwinter's Tale '95
Mary Shelley's Frankenstein '94
Much Ado about Nothing '93
Peter's Friends '92
Dead Again '91
Henry V '89

Larry Brand
Paranoia '98
Till the End of the Night '94
Overexposed '90
Masque of the Red Death '89

The Drifter '88

Charlotte Brandstrom(1959-)

A Business Affair '93
Road to Ruin '91
Sweet Revenge '90

Fred Brannon(1901-53)

Jungle Drums of Africa '53
Radar Men from the Moon '52
Zombies of the Stratosphere '52
Don Daredevil Rides Again '51
Government Agents vs. Phantom Legion '51
The Invisible Monster '50
Night Riders of Montana '50
Bandit King of Texas '49
Federal Agents vs. Underworld, Inc. '49
King of the Rocketmen '49
Lost Planet Airmen '49
Radar Patrol vs. Spy King '49
G-Men Never Forget '48
Jesse James Rides Again '47
Son of Zorro '47
Cyclotrode "X" '46
Daughter of Don Q '46
King of the Forest Rangers '46
The Phantom Rider '46
D-Day on Mars '45
The Purple Monster Strikes '45

Michel Brault(1928-)

Mon Amie Max '94
A Paper Wedding '89

Joseph (Jose Ramon Larraz) Braunstein(1929-)

Edge of the Axe '89
Rest in Pieces '87

Charles Braverman(1944-)

Final Shot: The Hank Gathers Story '92
Prince of Bel Air '87
Brotherhood of Justice '86
Hit & Run '82

Kevin Bray

Linewatch '08
Walking Tall '04
All About the Benjamins '02

William Brayne

Cold War Killers '86
Flame to the Phoenix '85
Running Blind '78

George Breakston(1920-73)

The Manster '59
White Huntress '57
Scarlet Spear '54
Geisha Girl '52

Paddy Breathnach(1964-)

Shrooms '07
Blow Dry '00
I Went Down '97

Michael Scott Bregman

Carlito's Way: Rise to Power '05
Table One '00

Catherine Breillat(1948-)

Anatomy of Hell '04
Sex is Comedy '02
Romance '99
Perfect Love '96
36 Fillete '88
A Real Young Girl '75

Valerie Breiman

Love & Sex '00
Going Overboard '89

Herbert Brenon(1880-1958)

Black Eyes '39
Housemaster '38
Dancing Mothers '26
Peter Pan '24

Alfonso Brescia

Reactor '78
War in Space '77
Special Forces '68

Robert Bresson(1907-99)

L'Argent '83
The Devil, Probably '77
Lancelot of the Lake '74
A Gentle Woman '69
Mouchette '67
Pickpocket '59
A Man Escaped '57
Diary of a Country Priest '50
The Ladies of the Bois de Bologne '44

Martin Brest(1951-)

Gigli '03
Meet Joe Black '98
Scent of a Woman '92
Midnight Run '88
Beverly Hills Cop '84
Going in Style '79

Howard Bretherton(1896-1969)

The Prince of Thieves '48
Trail of the Mounties '47
Where the North Begins '47
The Topeka Terror '45
Bordertown Gunfighters '43
Rhythm Parade '43
Riders of the Rio Grande '43
Below the Border '42
Dawn on the Great Divide '42
Down Texas Way '42
Ghost Town Law '42
Riders of the West '42
West of the Law '42
In Old Colorado '41
Outlaws of the Desert '41
Twilight on the Trail '41
Hidden Enemy '40
Midnight Limited '40
The Showdown '40
Up in the Air '40
Boy's Reformatory '39
Irish Luck '39
Star Reporter '39
Tough Kid '39
Western Gold '37
Three on the Trail '36
Wild Brian Kent '36
Hopalong Cassidy '35
Ladies They Talk About '33

Craig Brewer(1971-)

Black Snake Moan '07
Hustle & Flow '05

Salome Breziner

Fast Sofa '01
An Occasional Hell '96
Tollbooth '94

Marshall Brickman(1941-)

The Manhattan Project '86
Lovesick '83
Simon '80

Paul Brickman(1949-)

Men Don't Leave '89
Risky Business '83

Alan Bridges(1927-)

The Shooting Party '85
Pudd'nhead Wilson '84
Return of the Soldier '82
Out of Season '75
Invasion '65

Beau Bridges(1941-)

Seven Hours to Judgment '88
The Wild Pair '87

James Bridges(1936-93)

Bright Lights, Big City '88
Perfect '85
Mike's Murder '84
Urban Cowboy '80
The China Syndrome '79
September 30, 1955 '77
The Paper Chase '73
The Baby Maker '70

Stephen Bridgewater

Prairie Fever '08
The Christmas Card '06

Matthew Bright(1952-)

Freeway 2: Confessions of a Trickbaby '99
Freeway '95

Steven Brill(1962-)

Drillbit Taylor '08
Without a Paddle '04
Mr. Deeds '02
Little Nicky '00
Late Last Night '99
Heavyweights '94

Burt Brinckerhoff(1936-)

A Girl of the Limberlost '90
The Day the Women Got Even '80
Mother & Daughter: A Loving War '80
Can You Hear the Laughter? The Story of Freddie Prinze '79
The Cracker Factory '79
Acapulco Gold '78
The Invasion of Carol Enders '74

Deborah Brock

Rock 'n' Roll High School Forever '91
Andy and the Airwave Rangers '89
Slumber Party Massacre 2 '87

John Broderick(1942-2001)

The Warrior & the Sorceress '84
Bad Georgia Road '77

Kevin Brodie(1952-)

A Dog of Flanders '99
Mugsy's Girls '85

Henry Bromell(1947-)

Last Call: The Final Chapter of F. Scott Fitzgerald '02
Panic '00

Rex Bromfield

Cafe Romeo '91
Home Is Where the Hart Is '88
Melanie '82
Love at First Sight '76

Harry Bromley-Davenport(1950-)

Mockingbird Don't Sing '01
Xtro 3: Watch the Skies '95
Xtro 2: The Second Encounter '91
Xtro '83

Peter Brook(1925-)

The Mahabharata '89
Meetings with Remarkable Men '79
King Lear '71
Lord of the Flies '63

Adam Brooks(1956-)

Definitely, Maybe '08
Invisible Circus '00
Red Riding Hood '88
Almost You '85

Albert Brooks(1947-)

Looking for Comedy in the Muslim World '06
The Muse '99
Mother '96
Defending Your Life '91
Lost in America '85
Modern Romance '81
Real Life '79

James L. Brooks(1940-)

Spanglish '04
As Good As It Gets '97
I'll Do Anything '93
Broadcast News '87
Terms of Endearment '83
Thursday's Game '74

Joseph Brooks(1938-)

If Ever I See You Again '78
You Light Up My Life '77
Invitation to the Wedding '73

Mel Brooks(1926-)

Dracula: Dead and Loving It '95
Robin Hood: Men in Tights '93
Life Stinks '91
Spaceballs '87
History of the World: Part 1 '81
High Anxiety '77
Silent Movie '76
Blazing Saddles '74
Young Frankenstein '74
The Twelve Chairs '70
The Producers '68

Richard Brooks(1912-92)

Fever Pitch '85
Wrong Is Right '82
Looking for Mr. Goodbar '77
Bite the Bullet '75
Dollars '71
The Happy Ending '69
In Cold Blood '67
The Professionals '66
Lord Jim '65
Sweet Bird of Youth '62
Elmer Gantry '60
The Brothers Karamazov '58
Cat on a Hot Tin Roof '58
Something of Value '57
The Catered Affair '56
The Last Hunt '56
Blackboard Jungle '55
The Last Time I Saw Paris '54
Battle Circus '53
Crisis '50

Sue Brooks(1953-)

Japanese Story '03
Road to Nhill '97

Nick Broomfield(1948-)

Aileen: Life and Death of a Serial Killer '03
Monster in a Box '92
Dark Obsession '90

Eric Bross(1964-)

Vacancy 2: The First Cut '08
On the Line '01
Stranger than Fiction '99
Restaurant '98
Ten Benny '98

Hilary Brougher

Stephanie Daley '06
The Sticky Fingers of Time '97

Otto Brower(1895-1946)

Postal Inspector '36
The Outlaw Deputy '35
The Phantom Empire '35
I Can't Escape '34
Mystery Mountain '34
Devil Horse '32
Law of the Sea '32
Local Badman '32
Spirit of the West '32
Clearing the Range '31
Fighting Caravans '31
Hard Hombre '31
Pleasure '31
The Light of Western Stars '30

Alan Brown

Superheroes '07
Book of Love '04

Arvin Brown(1940-)

Change of Heart '98
Diary of the Dead '76

Barry Alexander Brown(1960-)

Winning Girls Through Psychic Mind Control '02
Lonely in America '90

Bruce Brown(1938-)

The Endless Summer 2 '94
The Endless Summer '66

Clarence Brown(1890-1987)

Angels in the Outfield '51
It's a Big Country '51
To Please a Lady '50
Intruder in the Dust '49
Song of Love '47
The Yearling '46
National Velvet '44
The White Cliffs of Dover '44
The Human Comedy '43
They Met in Bombay '41
Edison the Man '40
Idiot's Delight '39
The Rains Came '39
Of Human Hearts '38
Conquest '37
The Gorgeous Hussy '36
Wife Versus Secretary '36
Ah, Wilderness! '35
Anna Karenina '35
Chained '34
Sadie McKee '34
Night Flight '33
Emma '32
A Free Soul '31
Possessed '31
Anna Christie '30
Romance '30
The Trail of '98 '28
A Woman of Affairs '28
The Flesh and the Devil '27
The Eagle '25
Smouldering Fires '25
The Light of Faith '22
The Last of the Mohicans '20

Dana Brown

Dust to Glory '05
Step Into Liquid '03

Ewing Miles Brown

Killers '88
Whale of a Tale '76

Georg Stanford Brown(1943-)

The Reading Room '05
Dangerous Relations '93
Alone in the Neon Jungle '87
Miracle of the Heart: A Boys Town Story '86
Grambling's White Tiger '81

Gregory Brown(1954-)

See No Evil '06
Stranger by Night '94
Street Asylum '90
Dead Man Walking '88

Harry Joe Brown(1890-1972)

The Fighting Legion '30
Mountain Justice '30
One-Punch O'Day '26

Karl Brown(1896-1990)

The Port of Missing Girls '38
The White Legion '36
Fire Alarm '32

Larry G. Brown

Final Cut '88
Psychopath '73

Mark Brown

The Salon '05
Two Can Play That Game '01

Melville Brown(1887-1938)

Mad About Money '37
Champagne for Breakfast '35
Behind Office Doors '31
Check & Double Check '30

Mende Brown

Nowhere to Hide '83
On the Run '83

Christopher Browne

League of Ordinary Gentlemen '04
Third World Cop '99

Ricou Browning(1930-)

Salty '73
Island of the Lost '68

Tod Browning(1882-1962)

Devil Doll '36
Mark of the Vampire '35
Freaks '32
Dracula '31
Where East Is East '29
West of Zanzibar '28
The Unknown '27
The Unholy Three '25
White Tiger '23
Outside the Law '21

S.F. Brownrigg(1937-96)

Thinkin' Big '87
Keep My Grave Open '80
Poor White Trash 2 '75
Don't Open the Door! '74
Don't Look in the Basement '73

James Bruce

Whacked! '02
Love to Kill '97
Headless Body in Topless Bar '96

Clyde Bruckman(1894-1955)

Feet First '30
The General '26

Franco Brusati(1922-93)

The Sleazy Uncle '89
To Forget Venice '79
Bread and Chocolate '73

James Bryan

Lady Street Fighter '86
Hellriders '84
Don't Go in the Woods '81

Zbynek Brynych(1927-95)

Transport from Paradise '65
The Fifth Horseman Is Fear '64

Larry Buchanan(1923-2004)

Goodnight, Sweet Marilyn '89
The Loch Ness Horror '82
Mistress of the Apes '79
Hughes & Harlow: Angels in Hell '77
Goodbye, Norma Jean '75
Hell Raiders '68
It's Alive! '68
Creature of Destruction '67
Curse of the Swamp Creature '66
Mars Needs Women '66
Zontar, the Thing from Venus '66
The Eye Creatures '65
The Naked Witch '64
Free, White, and 21 '62

Amnon Buchbinder

Whole New Thing '05
The Fishing Trip '98

Dimitri Buchowetzki(1885-1932)

The Swan '25
Othello '22

Chris Buck

Surf's Up '07
Tarzan '99

Bethel Buckalew

My Boys Are Good Boys '78
Summer School '77
Dirty Mind of Young Sally '72

Allan A. Buckhantz

The Last Contract '77
Portrait of a Hitman '77

Colin Bucksey(1946-)

Midnight's Child '93
Curiosity Kills '90

Manhunt of Mystery Island '45

Giorgio Capitani(1927-)

I Hate Blondes '83
Lobster for Breakfast '82
Lady of the Evening '75
The Ruthless Four '70
Samson and His Mighty Challenge '64

Frank Cappello

No Way Back '96
American Yakuza '94

Frank Capra(1897-1991)

Pocketful of Miracles '61
A Hole in the Head '59
Here Comes the Groom '51
Riding High '50
State of the Union '48
It's a Wonderful Life '46
Arsenic and Old Lace '44
Prelude to War '42
Meet John Doe '41
Mr. Smith Goes to Washington '39
You Can't Take It with You '38
Lost Horizon '37
Mr. Deeds Goes to Town '36
Broadway Bill '34
It Happened One Night '34
The Bitter Tea of General Yen '33
Lady for a Day '33
American Madness '32
The Miracle Woman '31
Platinum Blonde '31
That Certain Thing '28
Long Pants '27
Strong Man '26

Luigi Capuano

The Snake Hunter Strangler '66
Cold Steel for Tortuga '65
Marauder '65
The Conqueror & the Empress '64
Tiger of the Seven Seas '62

Leos Carax(1960-)

Tokyo! '09
Pola X '99
The Lovers on the Bridge '91
Mauvais Sang '86
Boy Meets Girl '84

Costa Carayiannis(1932-93)

Land of the Minotaur '77
The Brave Bunch '70

Lamar Card(1942-)

Shadow Warriors '95
The Clones '73

Jack Cardiff(1914-)

The Freakmaker '73
Dark of the Sun '68
The Girl on a Motorcycle '68
The Long Ships '64
My Geisha '62

Roger Cardinal

Dead Silent '99
Malarek '89
Snowballin' '71

Rene Cardona, Sr.(1906-88)

Doctor of Doom '62
Santa Claus '59
Wrestling Women vs. the Aztec Mummy '59

Rene Cardona, Jr.(1939-2003)

Beaks: The Movie '87
The Treasure of the Amazon '84
Hostages '80
Tintorera... Tiger Shark '78
Fantastic Balloon Voyage '76
Night of a Thousand Cats '72
Robinson Crusoe & the Tiger '72

Night of the Bloody Apes '68

J.S. Cardone(1946-)

The Forsaken '01
True Blue '01
Outside Ozona '98
Black Day Blue Night '95
Shadowhunter '93
A Climate for Killing '91
Shadowzone '89
Thunder Alley '85
The Slayer '82

John Cardos(1928-)

Act of Piracy '89
Skeleton Coast '89
Outlaw of Gor '87
Mutant '83
Day Time Ended '80
The Dark '79
Kingdom of the Spiders '77
The Female Bunch '69

Christian Carion(1963-)

Joyeux Noel '05
The Girl from Paris '02

Gilles Carle(1929-)

The Other Side of the Law '95
Blood of the Hunter '94
Maria Chapdelaine '84
The Red Half-Breed '70
In Trouble '67

Carlo Carlei(1960-)

Fluke '95
Flight of the Innocent '93

Lewis John Carlino(1932-)

Class '83
The Great Santini '80
The Sailor Who Fell from Grace with the Sea '76

Henning Carlsen(1927-)

The Wolf at the Door '87
Hunger '66
A World of Strangers '62

Joe Carnahan(1969-)

The A-Team '10
Smokin' Aces '07
Narc '02
Blood, Guts, Bullets and Octane '99

Marcel Carne(1906-96)

La Merveilleuse Visite '74
Les Assassins de L'Ordre '71
Children of Paradise '44
Les Visiteurs du Soir '42
Bizarre Bizarre '39
Le Jour Se Leve '39

Charles Robert Carner(1957-)

Witless Protection '08
Breakaway '02
Red Water '01
Echo of Murder '00
The Fixer '97

John Carney

Once '06
On the Edge '00

Giuliano Carnimeo(1932-)

Guns for Dollars '73
The Case of the Bloody Iris '72
Fistful of Lead '70
Gunslinger '70
Sartana's Here... Trade Your Pistol for a Coffin '70

Marc Caro(1956-)

Dante 01 '08
The City of Lost Children '95
Delicatessen '92

Niki Caro(1967-)

North Country '05
Whale Rider '02

Glenn Gordon Caron(1954-)

Picture Perfect '96
Love Affair '94

Wilder Napalm '93
Clean and Sober '88

Heiner Carow(1929-97)

The Mistake '91
Coming Out '89
The Legend of Paul and Paula '73

John Carpenter(1948-)

Masters of Horror: Cigarette Burns '05
John Carpenter's Ghosts of Mars '01
John Carpenter's Vampires '97
Escape from L.A. '96
In the Mouth of Madness '95
Village of the Damned '95
Body Bags '93
Memoirs of an Invisible Man '92
They Live '88
Prince of Darkness '87
Big Trouble in Little China '86
Christine '84
Starman '84
The Thing '82
Escape from New York '81
Elvis: The Movie '79
The Fog '78
Halloween '78
Assault on Precinct 13 '76
Dark Star '74

Stephen Carpenter

Soul Survivors '01
The Kindred '87
Dorm That Dripped Blood '82
The Power '80

Bernard Carr(1911-2005)

Who Killed Doc Robbin? '48
Curley '47

John Carr

Death Wish Club '83
Runaways '75

Steve Carr

Paul Blart: Mall Cop '09
Are We Done Yet? '07
Rebound '05
Daddy Day Care '03
Dr. Dolittle 2 '01
Next Friday '00

Thomas Carr(1907-97)

Dino '57
Captain Scarlett '53
Blazing Guns '50
Guns of Justice '50
Last Bullet '50
Marshal of Heldorado '50
Outlaw Fury '50
Pirates of the High Seas '50
Rangeland Empire '50
Sudden Death '50
Jesse James Rides Again '47
Alias Billy the Kid '46
Rio Grande Raiders '46
The Undercover Woman '46
Rough Riders of Cheyenne '45

Anthony Carras

Fearmaker '71
Operation Bikini '63

Michael Carreras(1927-94)

Call Him Mr. Shatter '74
Prehistoric Women '67
Maniac '63

Willard Carroll(1955-)

Marigold '07
Playing by Heart '98
The Runestone '91

David Carson

Blue Smoke '07
Carrie '02
In His Life: The John Lennon Story '00
The 10th Kingdom '00
From the Earth to the Moon '98

Letters from a Killer '98
Star Trek: Generations '94
This Lightning Always Strikes Twice '85

Jack Paddy Carstairs(1910-70)

The Square Peg '58
Up to His Neck '54
Trouble in Store '53
Made in Heaven '52
Tony Draws a Horse '51
Sleeping Car to Trieste '45
He Found a Star '41
The Saint in London '39
Lassie from Lancashire '38

John Carter

The Way of War '08
Fatwa '06

Peter Carter(1933-82)

Intruder Within '81
Highpoint '80
Kavik the Wolf Dog '80
Klondike Fever '79
Rituals '79
High Ballin' '78

Thomas Carter(1953-)

Gifted Hands: The Ben Carson Story '09
Coach Carter '05
Save the Last Dance '01
Metro '96
Swing Kids '93
Call to Glory '84
Miami Vice '84

D.J. Caruso(1965-)

Eagle Eye '08
Disturbia '07
Two for the Money '05
Taking Lives '04
The Salton Sea '02
Black Cat Run '98

Steve Carver(1945-)

The Wolves '95
Dead Center '94
River of Death '90
Bulletproof '88
Jocks '87
Oceans of Fire '86
Lone Wolf McQuade '83
An Eye for an Eye '81
Steel '80
Drum '76
Big Bad Mama '74
The Arena '73

Robert Cary

Save Me '07
Ira & Abby '06
Anything But Love '02

Kimberly Casey

Deadly Dancer '90
Born Killer '89

Richard Casey

Hellbent '88
Horror House on Highway 5 '86

David S. Cass, Sr.

Love Finds a Home '09
Lone Rider '08
Prairie Fever '08
Avenging Angel '07
The Family Plan '05
Johnson County War '02

Henry Cass(1902-89)

The Hand '60
Blood of the Vampire '58
Bond of Fear '56
No Smoking '55
Last Holiday '50

Jon Cassar(1958-)

24 : Redemption '08
Danger Beneath the Sea '02
Shadow Warriors '97
Shadow Warriors 2: Hunt for the Death Merchant '97
The Ultimate Weapon '97
The Final Goal '94

John Cassavetes(1929-89)

Big Trouble '86
Love Streams '84

Gloria '80
Opening Night '77
The Killing of a Chinese Bookie '76
A Woman under the Influence '74
Minnie and Moskowitz '71
Husbands '70
Faces '68
A Child Is Waiting '63
Shadows '60
Saddle the Wind '58

Nick Cassavetes(1959-)

Alpha Dog '06
The Notebook '04
John Q '02
She's So Lovely '97
Unhook the Stars '96

Renato Castellani(1913-85)

Life of Verdi '82
And the Wild, Wild Women '59
Romeo and Juliet '54

Enzo G. Castellari(1938-)

Sinbad of the Seven Seas '89
Escape from the Bronx '85
Lightblast '85
Day of the Cobra '84
1990: The Bronx Warriors '83
Warriors of the Wasteland '83
Shark Hunter '79
Deadly Mission '78
The Inglorious Bastards '78
Loves & Times of Scaramouche '76
Spaghetti Western '75
Street Law '74
High Crime '73
Sting of the West '72
Cold Eyes of Fear '70
Eagles Over London '69
Go Kill and Come Back '68
Any Gun Can Play '67

Nick Castle(1947-)

Connor's War '06
Major Payne '95
Mr. Wrong '95
Dennis the Menace '93
Tap '89
The Boy Who Could Fly '86
The Last Starfighter '84
Tag: The Assassination Game '82

William Castle(1914-77)

The Busy Body '67
The Night Walker '64
Strait-Jacket '64
Zotz! '62
Homicidal '61
Mr. Sardonicus '61
13 Ghosts '60
The Tingler '59
House on Haunted Hill '58
Americano '55
Conquest of Cochise '53
The Law Rides Again '43

William Allen Castleman(1922-2006)

Johnny Firecloud '75
Bummer '73

Joe Catalanotto

French Quarter Undercover '85
Terror in the Swamp '85

Gil Cates, Jr.

Deal '08
Spent '00

Gilbert Cates(1934-)

Collected Stories '02
A Death in the Family '02
Backfire '88
Consenting Adult '85
Burning Rage '84
Goldilocks & the Three Bears '83

Hobson's Choice '83
Rapunzel '82
The Last Married Couple in America '80
Oh, God! Book 2 '80
The Promise '79
Johnny We Hardly Knew Ye '77
One Summer Love '76
The Affair '73
Summer Wishes, Winter Dreams '73
To All My Friends on Shore '71
I Never Sang for My Father '70

Michael Caton-Jones(1958-)

Basic Instinct 2 '06
Shooting Dogs '05
City by the Sea '02
The Jackal '97
Rob Roy '95
This Boy's Life '93
Doc Hollywood '91
Memphis Belle '90
Scandal '89

Peter Cattaneo(1964-)

The Rocker '08
Lucky Break '01
The Full Monty '96

Alberto Cavalcanti(1897-1982)

They Made Me a Fugitive '47
Nicholas Nickleby '46
Dead of Night '45

Liliana Cavani(1937-)

Ripley's Game '02
Francesco '93
The Berlin Affair '85
Beyond Obsession '82
The Night Porter '74

Joseph Cedar

Beaufort '07
Time of Favor '00

Jeff Celentano

Breaking Point '09
Gunshy '98
Under the Hula Moon '95

Nuri Bilge Ceylan

Three Monkeys '08
Climates '06

Claude Chabrol(1930-)

A Girl Cut in Two '07
Comedy of Power '06
The Bridesmaid '04
Merci pour le Chocolat '00
The Swindle '97
La Ceremonie '95
L'Enfer '93
Betty '92
Madame Bovary '91
Quiet Days in Clichy '90
Club Extinction '89
The Story of Women '88
The Cry of the Owl '87
Cop Au Vin '85
The Blood of Others '84
The Horse of Pride '80
Violette '78
Blood Relatives '77
Innocents with Dirty Hands '76
Twist '76
A Piece of Pleasure '74
Wedding in Blood '74
High Heels '72
Ten Days Wonder '72
Just Before Nightfall '71
La Rupture '70
This Man Must Die '70
La Femme Infidele '69
Le Boucher '69
Les Biches '68
Six in Paris '68
Bluebeard '63
Les Bonnes Femmes '60
The Cousins '59
Le Beau Serge '58

Alan Clarke(1935-90)
Rita, Sue & Bob Too *'87*
Scum *'79*

James Kenelm Clarke(1941-)
Going Undercover *'88*
Funny Money *'82*
The House on Straw Hill *'76*

Malcolm Clarke
Prisoner of Paradise *'02*
Chasing Holden *'01*
Voices from a Locked Room *'95*

Shirley Clarke(1919-97)
The Cool World *'63*
The Connection *'61*

Zoe Clarke-Williams(1974-)
New Best Friend *'02*
Men *'97*

James Clavell(1925-94)
The Last Valley *'71*
To Sir, with Love *'67*

William Claxton(1914-96)
The Canterville Ghost *'91*
Night of the Lepus *'72*
Fangs of the Wild *'54*

Jack Clayton(1921-95)
The Lonely Passion of Judith Hearne *'87*
Something Wicked This Way Comes *'83*
The Great Gatsby *'74*
The Pumpkin Eater *'64*
The Innocents *'61*
Room at the Top *'59*

Marc Clebanoff
Break *'09*
The Pink Conspiracy *'07*

Tom Clegg(1927-)
Sharpe's Challenge *'06*
Sharpe's Justice *'97*
Sharpe's Revenge *'97*
Sharpe's Waterloo *'97*
Sharpe's Mission *'96*
Sharpe's Regiment *'96*
Sharpe's Siege *'96*
Sharpe's Battle *'94*
Sharpe's Company *'94*
Sharpe's Enemy *'94*
Sharpe's Gold *'94*
Sharpe's Honour *'94*
Sharpe's Sword *'94*
Sharpe's Eagle *'93*
Sharpe's Rifles *'93*
Any Man's Death *'90*
A Casualty of War *'90*
Stroke of Midnight *'90*
Mountbatten: The Last Viceroy *'86*
Children of the Full Moon *'84*
The Inside Man *'84*
The House that Bled to Death *'81*
McVicar *'80*
Destination Moonbase Alpha *'75*

Brian Clemens(1931-)
Anatomy of Terror *'74*
Captain Kronos: Vampire Hunter *'74*

William Clemens(1905-80)
Night of January 16th *'41*
Nancy Drew and the Hidden Staircase *'39*
Nancy Drew, Reporter *'39*
Nancy Drew—Trouble Shooter *'39*
Nancy Drew—Detective *'38*

Dick Clement(1937-)
Porridge *'91*
Water *'85*
Bullshot *'83*
Catch Me a Spy *'71*

Rene Clement(1913-96)
Wanted: Babysitter *'75*
And Hope to Die *'72*
The Deadly Trap *'71*
Rider on the Rain *'70*
Is Paris Burning? *'66*
Joy House *'64*
The Day and the Hour *'63*
Purple Noon *'60*
Gervaise *'56*
Forbidden Games *'52*
The Walls of Malapaga *'49*
Battle of the Rails *'46*

Ron Clements(1953-)
The Princess and the Frog *'09*
Treasure Planet *'02*
Hercules *'97*
Aladdin *'92*
The Little Mermaid *'89*
The Great Mouse Detective *'86*

Graeme Clifford(1942-)
Redeemer *'02*
Caracara *'00*
The Last Don 2 *'98*
My Husband's Secret Life *'98*
The Last Don *'97*
Past Tense *'94*
Deception *'92*
Gleaming the Cube *'89*
The Turn of the Screw *'89*
Burke & Wills *'85*
Little Red Riding Hood *'83*
Frances *'82*
The Boy Who Left Home to Find Out About the Shivers *'81*

Elmer Clifton(1892-1949)
Silver Bandit *'50*
The Judge *'49*
Streets of Sin *'49*
Red Rock Outlaw *'47*
Marked for Murder *'45*
Boss of Rawhide *'44*
Dead or Alive *'44*
Gangsters of the Frontier *'44*
Guns of the Law *'44*
Seven Doors to Death *'44*
Youth Aflame *'44*
Frontier Law *'43*
The Return of the Rangers *'43*
Sundown Kid *'43*
Law of the Texan *'38*
The Stranger from Arizona *'38*
Roaring Speedboats *'37*
Slaves in Bondage *'37*
Custer's Last Stand *'36*
Assassin of Youth *'35*
Captured in Chinatown *'35*
Cyclone of the Saddle *'35*
Fighting Caballero *'35*
Pals of the Range *'35*
Rough Riding Ranger *'35*
Skull & Crown *'35*
Let 'er Go Gallegher *'28*
Down to the Sea in Ships *'22*

Edward F. (Eddie) Cline(1892-1961)
Slightly Terrific *'44*
Crazy House *'43*
Swingtime Johnny *'43*
Private Buckaroo *'42*
Snuffy Smith, Yard Bird *'42*
Cracked Nuts *'41*
Never Give a Sucker an Even Break *'41*
The Villain Still Pursued Her *'41*
The Bank Dick *'40*
My Little Chickadee *'40*
Breaking the Ice *'38*
Hawaii Calls *'38*
Peck's Bad Boy with the Circus *'38*
Cowboy Millionaire *'35*
Dude Ranger *'34*
Peck's Bad Boy *'34*
So This Is Africa *'33*
Hook, Line and Sinker *'30*
Three Ages *'23*

Hayley Cloake
Impact Point *'08*
The House of Usher *'06*

George Clooney(1961-)
Good Night, and Good Luck *'05*
Confessions of a Dangerous Mind *'02*

Robert Clouse(1929-97)
Ironheart *'92*
China O'Brien 2 *'89*
China O'Brien *'88*
Gymkata *'85*
Deadly Eyes *'82*
Force: Five *'81*
The Big Brawl *'80*
Game of Death *'79*
The Amsterdam Kill *'78*
The Pack *'77*
The Ultimate Warrior *'75*
Black Belt Jones *'74*
Enter the Dragon *'73*
Darker than Amber *'70*

Henri-Georges Clouzot(1907-77)
Diabolique *'55*
Wages of Fear *'55*
Manon *'50*
Jenny Lamour *'47*
Le Corbeau *'43*

E.B. (Enzo Barboni) Clucher(1922-2002)
Sons of Trinity *'95*
The Odd Squad *'86*
Go for It *'83*
Crime Busters *'78*
Trinity Is Still My Name *'75*
They Call Me Trinity *'72*

Craig Clyde
The Derby Stallion *'05*
Miracle Dogs *'03*
Walking Thunder *'94*
The Legend of Wolf Mountain *'92*
Little Heroes *'91*

Lewis (Luigi Cozzi) Coates(1947-)
Black Cat *'90*
Hercules 2 *'85*
Hercules *'83*
Alien Contamination *'81*
Star Crash *'78*

Stacy Cochran
Boys *'95*
My New Gun *'92*

Jean Cocteau(1889-1963)
The Testament of Orpheus *'59*
Orpheus *'49*
The Eagle Has Two Heads *'48*
The Storm Within *'48*
Beauty and the Beast *'46*
The Blood of a Poet *'30*

Ethan Coen(1957-)
A Serious Man *'09*
Burn After Reading *'08*
No Country for Old Men *'07*
Paris, je t'aime *'06*
The Ladykillers *'04*

Joel Coen(1954-)
A Serious Man *'09*
Burn After Reading *'08*
No Country for Old Men *'07*
Paris, je t'aime *'06*
The Ladykillers *'04*
Intolerable Cruelty *'03*
The Man Who Wasn't There *'01*
O Brother Where Art Thou? *'00*
The Big Lebowski *'97*
Fargo *'96*
The Hudsucker Proxy *'93*
Barton Fink *'91*
Miller's Crossing *'90*
Raising Arizona *'87*
Blood Simple *'85*

Dan Cohen
Corporate Affairs *'07*
Madman *'79*

Eli Cohen(1940-)
Under the Domim Tree *'95*
The Soft Kill *'94*
The Quarrel *'93*
The Summer of Aviya *'88*

Gary P. Cohen
Video Violence *'87*
Video Violence Part 2... The Exploitation! *'87*

Howard R. Cohen(1942-99)
Deathstalker 4: Match of Titans *'92*
Saturday the 14th Strikes Back *'88*
Time Trackers *'88*
Space Raiders *'83*
Saturday the 14th *'81*

Larry Cohen(1947-)
Original Gangstas *'96*
As Good as Dead *'95*
The Ambulance *'90*
Wicked Stepmother *'89*
Deadly Illusion *'87*
It's Alive 3: Island of the Alive *'87*
Return to Salem's Lot *'87*
Special Effects *'85*
The Stuff *'85*
Perfect Strangers *'84*
Q (The Winged Serpent) *'82*
It's Alive 2: It Lives Again *'78*
The Private Files of J. Edgar Hoover *'77*
God Told Me To *'76*
It's Alive *'74*
Black Caesar *'73*
Hell Up in Harlem *'73*
Housewife *'72*

Rob Cohen(1949-)
The Mummy: Tomb of the Dragon Emperor *'08*
Stealth *'05*
XXX *'02*
The Fast and the Furious *'01*
The Skulls *'00*
The Rat Pack *'98*
Daylight *'96*
Dragonheart *'96*
Dragon: The Bruce Lee Story *'93*
Scandalous *'84*
A Small Circle of Friends *'80*

Steve Cohen
Bar Hopping *'00*
Devil in the Flesh *'98*
Tough and Deadly *'94*

Michael Cohn
Snow White: A Tale of Terror *'97*
When the Bough Breaks *'93*
Interceptor *'92*

Isabel Coixet(1960-)
Elegy *'08*
Paris, je t'aime *'06*
My Life Without Me *'03*
Things I Never Told You *'96*

Cyril Coke(1914-93)
Pride and Prejudice *'85*
Flickers *'80*
The Duchess of Duke Street *'78*

Harley Cokliss(1945-)
Inferno *'99*
Hercules the Legendary Journeys, Vol. 2: The Lost Kingdom *'94*
Dream Demon *'88*
Malone *'87*
Black Moon Rising *'86*
Warlords of the 21st Century *'82*

Marcus Cole
The Christmas Box *'95*
From the Mixed-Up Files of Mrs. Basil E. Frankweiler *'95*

Nigel Cole
$5 a Day *'08*
A Lot Like Love *'05*
Calendar Girls *'03*
Saving Grace *'00*

Randel Cole
Real Time *'08*
2B Perfectly Honest *'04*

John David Coles
The Good Fight *'92*
Rising Son *'90*
Signs of Life *'89*

Duilio Coletti(1906-99)
Submarine Attack *'54*
Lure of the Sila *'49*

Giuseppe Colizzi(1925-78)
All the Way, Boys *'73*
Boot Hill *'69*
Ace High *'68*

Richard A. Colla(1936-)
Blind Witness *'89*
Naked Lie *'89*
The Prize Pulitzer *'89*
Don't Look Back: The Story of Leroy "Satchel" Paige *'81*
Battlestar Galactica *'78*
Olly Olly Oxen Free *'78*
Fuzz *'72*

Robert Collector
Believe in Me *'06*
Red Heat *'85*

Jaume Collet-Serra
Orphan *'09*
Goal 2: Living the Dream *'07*
House of Wax *'05*

James F. Collier(1929-91)
China Cry *'91*
Beyond the Next Mountain *'87*
A Cry from the Mountain *'85*
Joni *'79*
The Hiding Place *'75*

Boon Collins
Abducted 2: The Reunion *'94*
Spirit of the Eagle *'90*
Abducted *'86*

Lewis D. Collins(1899-1954)
The Fighting Redhead *'50*
Jungle Goddess *'49*
Heading for Heaven *'47*
Killer Dill *'47*
Lost City of the Jungle *'45*
Master Key *'44*
Mystery of the Riverboat *'44*
Raiders of Ghost City *'44*
Junior G-Men of the Air *'42*
The Great Plane Robbery *'40*
Doughnuts & Society *'36*
Make a Million *'35*
Sing Sing Nights *'35*
Brand of Hate *'34*
The Man from Hell *'34*
Ticket to a Crime *'34*
Gun Law *'33*
Trouble Busters *'33*

Max Allan Collins(1948-)
Real Time: Siege at Lucas Street Market *'00*
Mommy 2: Mommy's Day *'96*
Mommy *'95*

Robert E. Collins(1943-)
J. Edgar Hoover *'87*
Mafia Princess *'86*
Our Family Business *'81*
Gideon's Trumpet *'80*
The Life and Assassination of the Kingfish *'76*

Peter Collinson(1936-80)
Earthling *'80*
The House on Garibaldi Street *'79*
African Rage *'78*
Tomorrow Never Comes *'77*
Sell Out *'76*
Spiral Staircase *'75*
Ten Little Indians *'75*
Dressed for Death *'74*
Fright *'71*
The Italian Job *'69*

Walter Colmes
Accomplice *'46*
Identity Unknown *'45*
The Woman Who Came Back *'45*

Fernando Colomo(1942-)
Star Knight *'85*
Skyline *'84*

Carl Colpaert(1963-)
Drowning on Dry Land *'00*
Facade *'98*
The Crew *'95*
Delusion *'91*
In the Aftermath: Angels Never Sleep *'87*

Chris Columbus(1958-)
Percy Jackson & The Olympians: The Lightning Thief *'10*
I Love You, Beth Cooper *'09*
Rent *'05*
Harry Potter and the Chamber of Secrets *'02*
Harry Potter and the Sorcerer's Stone *'01*
Bicentennial Man *'99*
Stepmom *'98*
Nine Months *'95*
Mrs. Doubtfire *'93*
Home Alone 2: Lost in New York *'92*
Only the Lonely *'91*
Home Alone *'90*
Heartbreak Hotel *'88*
Adventures in Babysitting *'87*

Ryan Combs(1974-)
Animal 2 *'07*
The Hit *'06*
I Accidentally Domed Your Son *'04*
Straight out of Compton *'99*

Luigi Comencini(1916-2007)
Misunderstood *'87*
Till Marriage Do Us Part *'74*
Bread, Love and Dreams *'53*
Heidi *'52*

Lance Comfort(1908-66)
The Great Armored Car Swindle *'64*
Great Day *'46*
Hotel Reserve *'44*
The Courageous Mr. Penn *'41*

Don Como
Unknown Powers *'80*
Aliens from Spaceship Earth *'77*

Richard Compton(1938-2007)
Super Force *'90*
Wild Times *'79*
Deadman's Curve *'78*
Maniac *'77*
Return to Macon County *'75*
Macon County Line *'74*
Angels Die Hard *'70*

Bill Condon(1955-)
Dreamgirls *'06*
Kinsey *'04*
Gods and Monsters *'98*
Candyman 2: Farewell to the Flesh *'94*
Dead in the Water *'91*
Murder 101 *'91*
White Lie *'91*
Sister, Sister *'87*

W. Merle Connell(1905-63)
The Devil's Sleep *'51*
Test Tube Babies *'48*

Jason Connery(1962-)
The Devil's Tomb *'09*
Pandemic *'09*

Kevin Connor(1940-)
Marco Polo *'07*
Nanny Insanity *'06*
A Boyfriend for Christmas *'04*
Murder Without Conviction *'04*
Mary, Mother of Jesus *'99*
The Apocalypse Watch *'97*
Mother Teresa: In the Name of God's Poor *'97*
The Old Curiosity Shop *'94*
Diana: Her True Story *'93*
Sunset Grill *'92*
Iran: Days of Crisis *'91*
Great Expectations *'89*
The Hollywood Detective *'89*
The Lion of Africa *'87*
House Where Evil Dwells *'82*
Goliath Awaits *'81*
Motel Hell *'80*
The People That Time Forgot *'77*
At the Earth's Core *'76*
Choice of Weapons *'76*
The Land That Time Forgot *'75*
From Beyond the Grave *'73*

William Conrad(1920-94)
Side Show *'84*
My Blood Runs Cold *'65*
Man From Galveston *'63*

James A. Contner
Shark Swarm *'08*
The Cover Girl Murders *'93*
The Return of Eliot Ness *'91*
The Ten Million Dollar Getaway *'91*
Hitler's Daughter *'90*

Gary Conway(1936-)
The Fire in the Stone *'85*
Bellamy *'81*
Sara Dane *'81*

Jack Conway(1887-1952)
Julia Misbehaves *'48*
The Hucksters *'47*
Dragon Seed *'44*
Crossroads *'42*
Honky Tonk *'41*
Love Crazy *'41*
Boom Town *'40*
Let Freedom Ring *'39*
Too Hot to Handle *'38*
Saratoga *'37*
Libeled Lady *'36*
A Tale of Two Cities *'36*
The Girl from Missouri *'34*
Tarzan and His Mate *'34*
Viva Villa! *'34*
Red Headed Woman *'32*
The Easiest Way *'31*
The Unholy Three *'30*
Our Modern Maidens *'29*
The Smart Set *'28*

James L. Conway(1950-)
The Last of the Mohicans *'85*
Donner Pass: The Road to Survival *'84*
The Fall of the House of Usher *'80*
Hangar 18 *'80*
The Incredible Rocky Mountain Race *'77*

Bruce Cook, Jr.
Nightwish *'89*
Husbands, Wives, Money, and Murder *'86*

Fielder Cook(1923-2003)
The Member of the Wedding *'97*
Seize the Day *'86*
I Know Why the Caged Bird Sings *'79*
Love Affair: The Eleanor & Lou Gehrig Story *'77*
Judge Horton and the Scottsboro Boys *'76*
Miles to Go Before I Sleep *'74*
The Hideaways *'73*
Homecoming: A Christmas Story *'71*
A Big Hand for the Little Lady *'66*
Patterns *'56*

Phillip Cook
Invader *'91*
Star Quest *'89*

Troy Cook
Phoenix *'95*
The Takeover *'94*

Martha Coolidge(1946-)
American Girl: Chrissa Stands Strong *'09*
Tribute *'09*
Material Girls *'06*
The Prince & Me *'04*
The Twelve Days of Christmas Eve *'04*
The Flamingo Rising *'01*
The Ponder Heart *'01*
If These Walls Could Talk 2 *'00*
Introducing Dorothy Dandridge *'99*
Out to Sea *'97*
Three Wishes *'95*
Angie *'94*
Lost in Yonkers *'93*
Crazy in Love *'92*
Bare Essentials *'91*
Rambling Rose *'91*
Plain Clothes *'88*
Real Genius *'85*
Joy of Sex *'84*
Valley Girl *'83*

Michael Cooney(1967-)
Jack Frost 2: Revenge of the Mutant Killer Snowman *'00*
Jack Frost *'97*

Jackie Cooper(1922-)
The Night They Saved Christmas *'87*
Izzy & Moe *'85*
Go for the Gold *'84*
Rosie: The Rosemary Clooney Story *'82*
Sex and the Single Parent *'82*
Leave 'Em Laughing *'81*
Marathon *'80*
Rodeo Girl *'80*
White Mama *'80*
Rainbow *'78*

Merian C. Cooper(1893-1973)
King Kong *'33*
Chang: A Drama of the Wilderness *'27*

Stuart Cooper(1942-)
Chameleon *'98*
The Hunted *'98*
The Ticket *'97*
Bloodhounds 2 *'96*
Dead Ahead *'96*
Bitter Vengeance *'94*
Out of Annie's Past *'94*
Dancing with Danger *'93*
Rubdown *'93*
Payoff *'91*
The Long, Hot Summer *'86*
A.D. *'85*
Disappearance *'81*

Christopher Coppola(1962-)
Gunfighter *'98*
Deadfall *'93*
Dracula's Widow *'88*

Francis Ford Coppola(1939-)
Tetro *'09*
Youth Without Youth *'07*
John Grisham's The Rainmaker *'97*
Jack *'96*
Bram Stoker's Dracula *'92*
The Godfather, Part 3 *'90*
New York Stories *'89*
Tucker: The Man and His Dream *'88*
Gardens of Stone *'87*
Peggy Sue Got Married *'86*
Rip van Winkle *'85*
The Cotton Club *'84*
The Outsiders *'83*
Rumble Fish *'83*
One from the Heart *'82*
The Godfather 1902-1959: The Complete Epic *'81*
Apocalypse Now *'79*
The Conversation *'74*
The Godfather, Part 2 *'74*
The Godfather *'72*
The Rain People *'69*
Finian's Rainbow *'68*
You're a Big Boy Now *'66*
Battle Beyond the Sun *'63*
Dementia 13 *'63*
The Terror *'63*
The Bellboy and the Playgirls *'62*
Tonight for Sure *'61*

Sofia Coppola(1971-)
Marie Antoinette *'06*
Lost in Translation *'03*
The Virgin Suicides *'99*

Frank Coraci(1965-)
Click *'06*
Around the World in 80 Days *'04*
The Waterboy *'98*
The Wedding Singer *'97*
Murdered Innocence *'94*

Gregory Corarito
Delinquent School Girls *'84*
Wanda, the Sadistic Hypnotist *'67*

Gerard Corbiau(1941-)
Farinelli *'94*
The Music Teacher *'88*

Bruno Corbucci(1931-96)
Aladdin *'86*
Miami Supercops *'85*
Cop in Blue Jeans *'78*

Sergio Corbucci(1927-90)
Super Fuzz *'81*
The Con Artists *'80*
Odds and Evens *'78*
The Switch *'76*
Sonny and Jed *'73*
Companeros *'70*
Django *'68*
Hellbenders *'67*
Navajo Joe *'67*
Minnesota Clay *'65*

Bill Corcoran
Outlaw Justice *'98*
Portraits of a Killer *'95*
Sherlock Holmes and the Incident at Victoria Falls *'91*

Sebastian Cordero(1972-)
Cronicas *'04*
Ratas, Ratones, Rateros *'99*

Nicholas J. Corea(1943-99)
The Incredible Hulk Returns *'88*
Archer: The Fugitive from the Empire *'81*

David Corley
Angel's Dance *'99*
Executive Power *'98*

Roger Corman(1926-)
Frankenstein Unbound *'90*
Bloody Mama *'70*
Gas-s-s-s! *'70*
The St. Valentine's Day Massacre *'67*
The Trip *'67*
The Wild Angels *'66*
Masque of the Red Death *'65*
The Secret Invasion *'64*
Tomb of Ligeia *'64*
The Haunted Palace *'63*
The Raven *'63*
The Terror *'63*
X: The Man with X-Ray Eyes *'63*
Premature Burial *'62*
Tales of Terror *'62*
Tower of London *'62*
The Last Woman on Earth *'61*
The Pit and the Pendulum *'61*
Shame *'61*
Atlas *'60*
Creature from the Haunted Sea *'60*
The Fall of the House of Usher *'60*
Little Shop of Horrors *'60*
Ski Troop Attack *'60*
A Bucket of Blood *'59*
The Wasp Woman *'59*
I, Mobster *'58*
Machine Gun Kelly *'58*
Teenage Caveman *'58*
Carnival Rock *'57*
Rock All Night *'57*
Sorority Girl *'57*
Teenage Doll *'57*
The Undead *'57*
The Gunslinger *'56*
It Conquered the World *'56*
She Gods of Shark Reef *'56*
Apache Woman *'55*
Day the World Ended *'55*
Swamp Women *'55*

Gerald Cormier
See Alan Rudolph

Alain Corneau(1943-)
New World *'95*
Tous les Matins du Monde *'92*
Fort Saganne *'84*
Choice of Arms *'83*

Henry Cornelius(1913-58)
I Am a Camera *'55*
Genevieve *'53*
Passport to Pimlico *'49*

John Cornell(1941-)
Almost an Angel *'90*
Crocodile Dundee 2 *'88*

Hubert Cornfield(1929-2006)
The Night of the Following Day *'69*
Pressure Point *'62*
Angel Baby *'61*
Plunder Road *'57*

Stephen Cornwell
Marshal Law *'96*
Philadelphia Experiment 2 *'93*
Killing Streets *'91*

Charles Correll(1944-)
Deadly Desire *'91*
In the Deep Woods *'91*
Writer's Block *'91*

Michael Corrente(1960-)
Brooklyn Rules *'07*
A Shot at Glory *'00*
Outside Providence *'99*
American Buffalo *'95*
Federal Hill *'94*

Lloyd Corrigan(1900-69)
Dancing Pirate *'36*
No One Man *'32*
Daughter of the Dragon *'31*

Don A. Coscarelli(1954-)
Bubba Ho-Tep *'03*
Phantasm 4: Oblivion *'98*
Phantasm 3: Lord of the Dead *'94*
Survival Quest *'89*
Phantasm 2 *'88*
Beastmaster *'82*
Phantasm *'79*

George P. Cosmatos(1941-2005)
The Shadow Conspiracy *'96*
Tombstone *'93*
Leviathan *'89*
Cobra *'86*
Rambo: First Blood, Part 2 *'85*
Of Unknown Origin *'83*
Escape to Athena *'79*
The Cassandra Crossing *'76*
Massacre in Rome *'73*
Restless *'72*

Mario Costa(1904-95)
Rough Justice *'70*
Gladiator of Rome *'63*

Constantin Costa-Gavras(1933-)
Amen *'02*
Mad City *'97*
Music Box *'89*
Betrayed *'88*
Conseil de Famille *'86*
Hanna K. *'83*
Missing *'82*
State of Siege *'73*
Z *'69*

Kevin Costner(1955-)
Open Range *'03*
The Postman *'97*
Dances with Wolves *'90*

Manny Coto
Star Kid *'97*
Dr. Giggles *'92*
Cover-Up *'91*
Playroom *'90*

Vittorio Cottafavi(1914-98)
Hercules and the Captive Women *'63*
Goliath and the Dragon *'61*

Jack Couffer(1924-)
Living Free *'72*
Ring of Bright Water *'69*
Nikki, the Wild Dog of the North *'61*

Allen Coulter
Remember Me *'10*
Hollywoodland *'06*
Stephen King's Golden Years *'91*

Alex Cox(1954-)
The Winner *'96*
Highway Patrolman *'91*
Straight to Hell *'87*
Walker *'87*
Sid & Nancy *'86*
Repo Man *'83*

C. Jay Cox(1962-)
Kiss the Bride *'07*
Latter Days *'04*

James Cox(1975-)
Wonderland *'03*
Highway *'01*

Nell Cox
Konrad *'85*
Roommate *'84*

Paul Cox(1940-)
Innocence *'00*
Molokai: The Story of Father Damien *'99*
Lust and Revenge *'95*
A Woman's Tale *'92*
Vincent: The Life and Death of Vincent van Gogh *'87*
Cactus *'86*
Man of Flowers *'84*
My First Wife *'84*
Lonely Hearts *'82*
Kostas *'79*

John T. Coyle(1890-1970)
I Beheld His Glory *'53*
Call of the Yukon *'38*

Arthur Crabtree(1900-75)
Fiend without a Face *'58*
Dear Murderer *'47*

William Crain(1949-)
Midnight Fear *'90*
Kid from Not-So-Big *'78*
Dr. Black, Mr. Hyde *'76*
Blacula *'72*

Kenneth Crane
The Manster *'59*
Monster from Green Hell *'58*
When Hell Broke Loose *'58*

Jay Craven
Disappearances *'06*
A Stranger in the Kingdom *'98*
Where the Rivers Flow North *'94*

Wes Craven(1939-)
Paris, je t'aime *'06*
Red Eye *'05*
Cursed *'04*
Scream 3 *'00*
Music of the Heart *'99*
Scream 2 *'97*
Scream *'96*
Vampire in Brooklyn *'95*
Wes Craven's New Nightmare *'94*
The People under the Stairs *'91*
Shocker *'89*
The Serpent and the Rainbow *'87*
Deadly Friend *'86*
The Hills Have Eyes, Part 2 *'84*
Invitation to Hell *'84*
A Nightmare on Elm Street *'84*
Swamp Thing *'82*
Deadly Blessing *'81*
Summer of Fear *'78*
The Hills Have Eyes *'77*
Last House on the Left *'72*

Guy Crawford
Autopsy: A Love Story *'02*
The Catcher *'98*
Starved *'97*

Wayne Crawford
American Cop *'94*
Crime Lords *'91*

Alfredo B. Crevenna(1914-96)
Neutron vs. the Maniac *'62*
The New Invisible Man *'58*

Charles Crichton(1910-99)
A Fish Called Wanda *'88*
The Battle of the Sexes *'60*
The Lavender Hill Mob *'51*
Train of Events *'49*
Against the Wind *'48*
Hue and Cry *'47*
Dead of Night *'45*

Michael Crichton(1942-2008)
The 13th Warrior *'99*
Physical Evidence *'89*
Runaway *'84*
Looker *'81*
The Great Train Robbery *'79*
Coma *'78*
Westworld *'73*
Pursuit *'72*

Donald Crisp(1880-1974)
Saddle the Wind *'58*
Dr. Ehrlich's Magic Bullet *'40*
Stand and Deliver *'28*
Sunny Side Up *'28*

Dress Parade '27
The Fighting Eagle '27
Don Q., Son of Zorro '25
The Navigator '24

Armando Crispino(1925-)
Autopsy '74
Commandos '73
Dead Are Alive '72

Michael Cristofer(1945-)
Original Sin '01
Body Shots '99
Gia '98

Emma-Kate Croghan(1972-)
Strange Planet '99
Love and Other Catastrophes '95

Donald Crombie(1942-)
Kitty and the Bagman '82
Killing of Angel Street '81
The Irishman '78
Caddie '76

John Cromwell(1888-1979)
The Goddess '58
The Racket '51
Caged '50
Dead Reckoning '47
Anna and the King of Siam '46
The Enchanted Cottage '45
Since You Went Away '44
Son of Fury '42
So Ends Our Night '41
Abe Lincoln in Illinois '40
In Name Only '39
Made for Each Other '39
Algiers '38
Prisoner of Zenda '37
Little Lord Fauntleroy '36
I Dream Too Much '35
Village Tale '35
Of Human Bondage '34
Spitfire '34
Ann Vickers '33
Double Harness '33
Vice Squad '31
Tom Sawyer '30
Dance of Life '29

David Cronenberg(1943-)
Eastern Promises '07
A History of Violence '05
Spider '02
eXistenZ '99
Crash '95
M. Butterfly '93
Naked Lunch '91
Dead Ringers '88
The Fly '86
Dead Zone '83
Videodrome '83
Scanners '81
The Brood '79
Fast Company '78
Rabid '77
They Came from Within '75

Alan Crosland(1894-1936)
Massacre '34
Big Boy '30
On with the Show '29
The Jazz Singer '27
Old San Francisco '27
When a Man Loves '27
Don Juan '26

Avery Crounse(1946-)
Cries of Silence '97
The Invisible Kid '88
Eyes of Fire '84

Cameron Crowe(1957-)
Elizabethtown '05
Vanilla Sky '01
Almost Famous '00
Jerry Maguire '96
Singles '92
Say Anything '89

Christopher Crowe(1948-)
Whispers in the Dark '92
Off Limits '87

John Crowley
Is Anybody There? '08
Boy A '07

James Cruze(1884-1942)
The Wrong Road '37
David Harum '34
I Cover the Waterfront '33
Mr. Skitch '33
The Great Gabbo '29
Old Ironsides '26
The Pony Express '25
The Covered Wagon '23
Leap Year '21
Hawthorne of the USA '19
The Roaring Road '19

Billy Crystal(1947-)
61* '01
Forget Paris '95
Mr. Saturday Night '92

Alfonso Cuaron(1961-)
Children of Men '06
Paris, je t'aime '06
Harry Potter and the Prisoner of Azkaban '04
Y Tu Mama Tambien '01
Great Expectations '97
A Little Princess '95
Fallen Angels 1 '93

Michael Cuesta(1963-)
12 and Holding '05
L.I.E. '01

George Cukor(1899-1983)
Rich and Famous '81
The Corn Is Green '79
Love Among the Ruins '75
Travels with My Aunt '72
Justine '69
My Fair Lady '64
Heller in Pink Tights '60
Let's Make Love '60
Song Without End '60
Les Girls '57
Bhowani Junction '56
It Should Happen to You '54
A Star Is Born '54
The Actress '53
The Marrying Kind '52
Pat and Mike '52
Adam's Rib '50
Born Yesterday '50
A Life of Her Own '50
A Double Life '47
Gaslight '44
Keeper of the Flame '42
Two-Faced Woman '41
A Woman's Face '41
The Philadelphia Story '40
Susan and God '40
The Women '39
Holiday '38
Camille '36
Romeo and Juliet '36
David Copperfield '35
Sylvia Scarlett '35
Dinner at Eight '33
Little Women '33
A Bill of Divorcement '32
One Hour with You '32
What Price Hollywood? '32

Jeremiah Cullinane
Dangerous Curves '99
Spacejacked '98

Mark Cullingham(1942-95)
Dead on the Money '91
Gryphon '88
Cinderella '84

Irving Cummings(1888-1959)
Double Dynamite '51
The Dolly Sisters '46
Sweet Rosie O'Grady '43
Springtime in the Rockies '42
Louisiana Purchase '41
That Night in Rio '41
Down Argentine Way '40
Everything Happens at Night '39
Hollywood Cavalcade '39
The Story of Alexander Graham Bell '39
Just Around the Corner '38
Little Miss Broadway '38
Vogues of 1938 '37
Girl's Dormitory '36
The Poor Little Rich Girl '36
Curly Top '35
Behind That Curtain '29
Broken Hearts of Broadway '23
Flesh and Blood '22

Rusty Cundieff(1965-)
Sprung '96
Tales from the Hood '95
Fear of a Black Hat '94

Richard Cunha(1922-2005)
Missile to the Moon '59
Frankenstein's Daughter '58
Giant from the Unknown '58
She Demons '58

Sean S. Cunningham(1941-)
Terminal Invasion '02
Deepstar Six '89
The New Kids '85
Spring Break '83
A Stranger Is Watching '82
Friday the 13th '80
Manny's Orphans '78

Terry Cunningham
Earthstorm '06
Chaos Factor '00

Frederick Curiel(1917-85)
Genie of Darkness '62
Neutron vs. the Death Robots '62
Neutron and the Black Mask '61
Neutron vs. the Amazing Dr. Caronte '61
Curse of Nostradamus '60
The Monster Demolisher '60

John Curran
The Painted Veil '06
We Don't Live Here Anymore '04
Praise '98

Dan Curtis(1928-2006)
The Love Letter '98
Trilogy of Terror 2 '96
Me and the Kid '93
Intruders '92
War & Remembrance: The Final Chapter '89
War & Remembrance '88
The Winds of War '83
The Long Days of Summer '80
Express to Terror '79
The Last Ride of the Dalton Gang '79
Mrs. R's Daughter '79
When Every Day Was the Fourth of July '78
Curse of the Black Widow '77
Dead of Night '77
Burnt Offerings '76
Trilogy of Terror '75
Melvin Purvis: G-Man '74
Nightmare at 43 Hillcrest '74
Scream of the Wolf '74
The Turn of the Screw '74
Dracula '73
The Norliss Tapes '73
The Night Strangler '72
Night of Dark Shadows '71
House of Dark Shadows '70

Douglas Curtis(1947-)
The Sleeping Car '90
The Campus Corpse '77

Richard Curtis(1956-)
Pirate Radio '09
Love Actually '03

Simon Curtis
Return to Cranford '09
Cranford '08
Five Days '07
David Copperfield '99

Vondie Curtis-Hall(1956-)
Waist Deep '06
Glitter '01
Gridlock'd '96

Michael Curtiz(1888-1962)
The Comancheros '61
The Adventures of Huckleberry Finn '60
Breath of Scandal '60
King Creole '58
Proud Rebel '58
The Helen Morgan Story '57
We're No Angels '55
The Egyptian '54
White Christmas '54
Trouble along the Way '53
I'll See You in My Dreams '51
Jim Thorpe: All American '51
Bright Leaf '50
Young Man with a Horn '50
Flamingo Road '49
My Dream Is Yours '49
Romance on the High Seas '48
Life with Father '47
The Unsuspected '47
Night and Day '46
Mildred Pierce '45
Roughly Speaking '45
Passage to Marseilles '44
Mission to Moscow '43
This Is the Army '43
Captains of the Clouds '42
Casablanca '42
Yankee Doodle Dandy '42
Dive Bomber '41
The Sea Wolf '41
Santa Fe Trail '40
The Sea Hawk '40
Virginia City '40
Dodge City '39
The Private Lives of Elizabeth & Essex '39
The Adventures of Robin Hood '38
Angels with Dirty Faces '38
Four Daughters '38
Four's a Crowd '38
Kid Galahad '37
The Charge of the Light Brigade '36
Black Fury '35
Captain Blood '35
Female '33
The Kennel Murder Case '33
Mystery of the Wax Museum '33
20,000 Years in Sing Sing '33
The Cabin in the Cotton '32
Doctor X '32
The Strange Love of Molly Louvain '32

Catherine Cyran
The Prince & Me 3: A Royal Honeymoon '08
Christmas Do-Over '06
The Prince & Me 2: Royal Wedding '06
True Heart '97
Sawbones '95
Hostile Intentions '94
In the Heat of Passion 2: Unfaithful '94

Paul Czinner(1890-1972)
Dreaming Lips '37
As You Like It '36
Catherine the Great '34

Renee Daalder(1944-)
Habitat '97
Massacre at Central High '76

Morton DaCosta(1914-89)
The Music Man '62
Auntie Mame '58

Olivier Dahan(1967-)
La Vie en Rose '07
Crimson Rivers 2: Angels of the Apocalypse '05
La Vie Promise '02

John Dahl(1956-)
The Great Raid '05
Joy Ride '01
Rounders '98
Unforgettable '96
The Last Seduction '94
Red Rock West '93
Kill Me Again '89

Stephen Daldry(1960-)
The Reader '08
The Hours '02
Billy Elliot '00

Zale Dalen(1947-)
Call of the Wild '04
Expect No Mercy '95
Deadly Business '77

Massimo Dallamano(1917-76)
Super Bitch '73
Dorian Gray '70
A Black Veil for Lisa '68

Joe D'Amato(1936-99)
Passion '92
Quest for the Mighty Sword '90
Endgame '85
Blade Master '84
Ator the Fighting Eagle '83
Black Cobra '83
Buried Alive '81
Grim Reaper '81
Trap Them & Kill Them '77
Heroes in Hell '73

Michael Damian
Moondance Alexander '07
Hot Tamale '06

Damiano Damiani(1922-)
The Inquiry '87
The Sicilian Connection '85
Amityville 2: The Possession '82
The Warning '80
Confessions of a Police Captain '72
A Bullet for the General '68
The Witch '66
Empty Canvas '64
The Hit Man '60

Mel Damski(1946-)
Wildcard '92
A Connecticut Yankee in King Arthur's Court '89
Happy Together '89
Murder by the Book '87
A Winner Never Quits '86
Badge of the Assassin '85
Mischief '85
Yellowbeard '83
Legend of Walks Far Woman '82
American Dream '81
For Ladies Only '81
Long Journey Back '78

Rod Daniel(1942-)
Alley Cats Strike '00
Beethoven's 2nd '93
The Super '91
K-9 '89
Like Father, Like Son '87
Teen Wolf '85

Harold Daniels(1903-71)
House of the Black Death '65
Terror in the Haunted House '58
Poor White Trash '57
Sword of Venus '53

Jeff Daniels(1955-)
Super Sucker '03
Escanaba in da Moonlight '01

Lee Daniels
Precious: Based on the Novel by Sapphire '09
Shadowboxer '06

Marc Daniels(1912-89)
Vengeance '89
Planet Earth '74

Joe Dante(1946-)
Masters of Horror: The Screwfly Solution '06
Masters of Horror: Homecoming '05
Looney Tunes: Back in Action '03
Small Soldiers '98
The Second Civil War '97
Picture Windows '95
Runaway Daughters '94
Matinee '92
Gremlins 2: The New Batch '90
The 'Burbs '89
Amazon Women on the Moon '87
Innerspace '87
Explorers '85
Gremlins '84
Twilight Zone: The Movie '83
The Howling '81
Piranha '78
Hollywood Boulevard '76

Ray Danton(1931-92)
Tales of the Unexpected '91
Psychic Killer '75
Crypt of the Living Dead '73

Frank Darabont(1959-)
The Mist '07
The Majestic '01
The Green Mile '99
The Shawshank Redemption '94
Buried Alive '90

Jonathan Darby
Hush '98
The Enemy Within '94

Jean-Pierre Dardenne(1951-)
Lorna's Silence '08
The Child '05
Rosetta '99
La Promesse '96

Luc Dardenne(1954-)
Lorna's Silence '08
The Child '05
Rosetta '99
La Promesse '96

Gregory Dark
See Gregory Brown
Sins of the Night '93

Joan Darling(1935-)
Hiroshima Maiden '88
Check Is in the Mail '85
Willa '79
First Love '77

Eric Darnell
Madagascar: Escape 2 Africa '08
Madagascar '05
Antz '98

Harry D'Abbadie D'Arrast(1897-1968)
Topaze '33
Raffles '30

Julie Dash(1952-)
The Rosa Parks Story '02
Love Song '00
Incognito '99
Subway Stories '97
Daughters of the Dust '91

Jules Dassin(1911-2008)
Circle of Two '80
A Dream of Passion '78
Topkapi '64
Phaedra '61
Never on Sunday '60

Where the Hot Wind Blows '59
Rififi '54
Night and the City '50
The Naked City '48
Brute Force '47
The Canterville Ghost '44
Reunion in France '42

Dorothy Davenport

See Dorothy Davenport Reid

Delmer Daves(1904-77)

Spencer's Mountain '63
Rome Adventure '62
Parrish '61
Susan Slade '61
The Hanging Tree '59
A Summer Place '59
The Badlanders '58
Cowboy '58
Kings Go Forth '58
3:10 to Yuma '57
Jubal '56
Demetrius and the Gladiators '54
Drum Beat '54
Never Let Me Go '53
Treasure of the Golden Condor '53
Broken Arrow '50
Task Force '49
Dark Passage '47
The Red House '47
Pride of the Marines '45
Hollywood Canteen '44
Destination Tokyo '43

Lorena David

Extreme Dating '04
Outta Time '01
Eastside '99

Pierre David(1944-)

Serial Killer '95
Scanner Cop '94

Boaz Davidson(1943-)

Outside the Law '95
American Cyborg: Steel Warrior '94
Solar Force '94
Going Bananas '88
Salsa '88
Dutch Treat '86
Last American Virgin '82
Hospital Massacre '81
Hot Bubblegum '81

Gordon Davidson(1933-)

The Trial of Lee Harvey Oswald '77
Trial of the Catonsville Nine '72

Martin Davidson(1939-)

Looking for an Echo '99
Follow the River '95
Hard Promises '92
The Heart of Dixie '89
Long Gone '87
Eddie and the Cruisers '83
Hero at Large '80
The Lords of Flatbush '74

Gareth Davies

A Mind to Murder '96
Unexplained Laughter '89
Oliver Twist '85

John Davies(1953-)

Devices and Desires '91
Kim '84
A Married Man '84

Terence Davies(1945-)

Of Time and the City '08
House of Mirth '00
The Neon Bible '95
The Long Day Closes '92
Distant Voices, Still Lives '88

Andrew Davis(1946-)

The Guardian '06
Holes '03
Collateral Damage '02
A Perfect Murder '98
Chain Reaction '96
Steal Big, Steal Little '95
The Fugitive '93
Under Siege '92
The Package '89
Above the Law '88
Code of Silence '85
The Final Terror '83

B.J. Davis

Forget About It '06
White Ghost '88

Charles Davis

Die Watching '93
Hazel's People '73

Desmond Davis(1928-)

Ordeal by Innocence '84
The Sign of Four '83
Clash of the Titans '81
Nice Girl Like Me '69
Smashing Time '67
Girl with Green Eyes '64

John A. Davis

The Ant Bully '06
Jimmy Neutron: Boy Genius '01

Julie Davis(1969-)

Amy's O '02
All Over the Guy '01
I Love You, Don't Touch Me! '97
Witchcraft 6: The Devil's Mistress '94

Lee Davis

Christmas at Water's Edge '04
3 A.M. '01

Michael Davis(1961-)

Shoot 'Em Up '07
Monster Man '03
100 Girls '00
Eight Days a Week '97
Beanstalk '94

Mick Davis(1961-)

Modigliani '04
The Match '99

Nick Davis

1999 '98
The Survivor '98

Ossie Davis(1917-2005)

Gordon's War '73
Cotton Comes to Harlem '70

Tamra Davis(1962-)

Crossroads '02
Skipped Parts '00
Best Men '98
Half-Baked '97
Billy Madison '94
CB4: The Movie '93
Guncrazy '92

Norman Dawn(1884-1975)

Wild Women '53
Two Lost Worlds '50
Orphans of the North '40
Tundra '36

Anthony M. Dawson(1930-2002)

Indio '90
Jungle Raiders '85
Tiger Joe '85
Codename: Wildgeese '84
Tornado '83
Yor, the Hunter from the Future '83
Ark of the Sun God '82
Hunters of the Golden Cobra '82
Cannibal Apocalypse '80
The Last Hunter '80
The Squeeze '80
Killer Fish '79
The Rip Off '78
Death Rage '77
The Stranger and the Gunfighter '76
Take a Hard Ride '75
Andy Warhol's Dracula '74
Mr. Superinvisible '73
Seven Deaths in the Cat's Eye '72
Web of the Spider '70
And God Said to Cain '69
Lightning Bolt '67
Planet on the Prowl '65
The Virgin of Nuremberg '65
Wild, Wild Planet '65
Castle of Blood '64
Hercules, Prisoner of Evil '64
Assignment Outer Space '61
Battle of the Worlds '61

Ernest Day(1927-2006)

Waltz across Texas '83
Green Ice '81

Robert Day(1922-)

Higher Ground '88
The Quick and the Dead '87
Lady from Yesterday '85
Your Place or Mine '83
Peter and Paul '81
The Man with Bogart's Face '80
Walking Through the Fire '80
Murder by Natural Causes '79
The Grass Is Always Greener Over the Septic Tank '78
Initiation of Sarah '78
A Home of Our Own '75
Death Stalk '74
The Big Game '72
She '65
Tarzan the Magnificent '60
Two-Way Stretch '60
First Man into Space '59
Corridors of Blood '58
The Haunted Strangler '58

Josee Dayan(1943-)

Dangerous Liaisons '03
Balzac: A Life of Passion '99
The Count of Monte Cristo '99
Hot Chocolate '92

Lyman Dayton

The Avenging '92
Dream Machine '91
The Red Fury '84
Baker's Hawk '76

Fabrizio de Angelis(1940-)

Karate Warrior '88
Thunder Warrior 3 '88
The Manhunt '86
Operation 'Nam '85
Thunder Warrior '85
Thunder Warrior 2 '85
Deadly Impact '84
Overthrow '82

Jan De Bont(1943-)

Lara Croft Tomb Raider: The Cradle of Life '03
The Haunting '99
Speed 2: Cruise Control '97
Twister '96
Speed '94

Philippe de Broca(1933-2004)

On Guard! '03
The Green House '96
Louisiana '87
Jupiter's Thigh '81
Le Cavaleur '78
Dear Detective '77
Le Magnifique '76
Oldest Profession '67
The King of Hearts '66
That Man from Rio '64
Cartouche '62

Fred de Cordova(1910-2001)

Frankie and Johnny '65
I'll Take Sweden '65
Here Come the Nelsons '52
Yankee Buccaneer '52
Bedtime for Bonzo '51
Buccaneer's Girl '50
For the Love of Mary '48

Andy de Emmony

Filth '08
God on Trial '08

Frank De Felitta(1921-)

Scissors '91
Dark Night of the Scarecrow '81
The Two Worlds of Jenny Logan '79

Raymond De Felitta(1964-)

The Thing About My Folks '05
Two Family House '99
Cafe Society '97

Eduardo de Filippo(1900-84)

Shoot Loud, Louder, I Don't Understand! '66
Seven Deadly Sins '53

Michael de Gaetano

The Haunted '79
UFO: Target Earth '74

Rolf de Heer(1951-)

Dance Me to My Song '98
The Quiet Room '96
Alien Visitor '95
Bad Boy Bubby '93
Dingo '90
Encounter at Raven's Gate '88

Ate De Jong(1953-)

Highway to Hell '92
Drop Dead Fred '91
A Flight of Rainbirds '81

Hubert de la Bouillerie(1951-)

The Apocalypse '96
The Right to Remain Silent '95

Alex de la Iglesia(1965-)

El Crimen Perfecto '04
Dance with the Devil '97
The Day of the Beast '95

Eloy De La Iglesia(1944-)

El Diputado '78
Cannibal Man '71

Jose Antonio De La Loma(1924-2004)

Fine Gold '88
A Man of Passion '88
Counterforce '87
Target Eagle '84
Street Warriors, Part 2 '79
The Barcelona Kill '77
Street Warriors '77
The Boldest Job in the West '71
Surprise Attack '70

Gerardo (Gerry) De Leon(1913-81)

Brides of the Beast '68
Mad Doctor of Blood Island '68
The Vampire People '66
The Walls of Hell '64
Terror Is a Man '59

Marcus De Leon

The Big Squeeze '96
Kiss Me a Killer '91

Paul de Lussanet

Mysteries '84
Dear Boys '80

Alberto De Martino(1929-)

Miami Horror '87
Bloodlink '86
Formula for a Murder '85
The Puma Man '80
The Chosen '77
Strange Shadows in an Empty Room '76
Django Shoots First '74
The Tempter '74
New Mafia Boss '72
Scenes from a Murder '72
Dirty Heroes '71
Secret Agent 00 '67
The Triumph of Hercules '66
The Invincible Gladiator '62
Medusa Against the Son of Hercules '62

Pierre De Moro

Hellhole '85
Savannah Smiles '82
Story of a Cowboy Angel '81

Robert De Niro(1943-)

The Good Shepherd '06
A Bronx Tale '93

Manoel de Oliveira(1908-)

Belle Toujours '06
I'm Going Home '00
Party '96
Voyage to the Beginning of the World '96
The Convent '95
Abraham's Valley '93

Armando de Ossorio(1926-2001)

Night of the Death Cult '75
People Who Own the Dark '75
Return of the Evil Dead '75
Terror Beach '75
Horror of the Zombies '74
When the Screaming Stops '73
Tombs of the Blind Dead '72
Night of the Sorcerers '70
Fangs of the Living Dead '68

Brian De Palma(1941-)

Redacted '07
The Black Dahlia '06
Femme Fatale '02
Mission to Mars '00
Snake Eyes '98
Mission: Impossible '96
Carlito's Way '93
Raising Cain '92
The Bonfire of the Vanities '90
Casualties of War '89
The Untouchables '87
Wise Guys '86
Body Double '84
Scarface '83
Blow Out '81
Dressed to Kill '80
Home Movies '79
The Fury '78
Carrie '76
Obsession '76
Phantom of the Paradise '74
Sisters '73
Get to Know Your Rabbit '72
Hi, Mom! '70
The Wedding Party '69
Greetings '68

Jean De Segonzac

Mimic 2 '01
Homicide: The Movie '00

Vittorio De Sica(1902-74)

The Garden of the Finzi-Continis '71
Woman Times Seven '67
After the Fox '66
Marriage Italian Style '64
Yesterday, Today and Tomorrow '64
Boccaccio '70 '62
Two Women '61
It Happened in the Park '56
The Roof '56
Umberto D '55
The Gold of Naples '54
Indiscretion of an American Wife '54
Miracle in Milan '51
The Bicycle Thief '48
Shoeshine '47
The Children Are Watching Us '44
Teresa Venerdi '41

Tom De Simone(1939-)

Angel 3: The Final Chapter '88
Reform School Girls '86
The Concrete Jungle '82
Hell Night '81
Chatterbox '76
Terror in the Jungle '68

Steven E. de Souza(1947-)

Possessed '00
Street Fighter '94

Andre de Toth(1912-2002)

The Mongols '60
Morgan the Pirate '60
The Day of the Outlaw '59
The Indian Fighter '55
Crime Wave '54
House of Wax '53
The Stranger Wore a Gun '53
Carson City '52
Last of the Comanches '52
Springfield Rifle '52
Man in the Saddle '51
Pitfall '48
Ramrod '47
Dark Waters '44

Geoffrey De Vallois

Vampire Centerfolds '98
Sorority House Vampires '95

Alfredo de Villa

Nothing Like the Holidays '08
Adrift in Manhattan '07
Yellow '06
Washington Heights '02

Basil Dean(1888-1978)

21 Days '37
Lorna Doone '34

William Dear(1944-)

Free Style '09
Mr. Troop Mom '09
The Sandlot 3: Heading Home '07
Simon Says '07
The Foursome '06
School of Life '06
Balloon Farm '97
Wild America '97
Angels in the Outfield '94
If Looks Could Kill '91
Harry and the Hendersons '87
Timerider '83
Northville Cemetery Massacre '76

Basil Dearden(1911-71)

The Man Who Haunted Himself '70
The Assassination Bureau '69
Khartoum '66
Woman of Straw '64
The Mind Benders '63
Victim '61
The League of Gentlemen '60
Sapphire '59
The Smallest Show on Earth '57
Who Done It? '56
The Blue Lamp '49
Train of Events '49
Captive Heart '47
Frieda '47
Dead of Night '45

James Dearden(1949-)

Rogue Trader '98
A Kiss Before Dying '91
Pascali's Island '88
Cold Room '84

John DeBello(1952-)

Killer Tomatoes Eat France '91
Killer Tomatoes Strike Back '90
Return of the Killer Tomatoes! '88
Happy Hour '87
Attack of the Killer Tomatoes '77

Dean DeBlois

How to Train Your Dragon '10
Lilo & Stitch '02

James D. Deck(1964-)

Silent Partner '05
Two Shades of Blue '98

Ravager '97

David DeCoteau(1962-)

Grizzly Rage '07
The Raven '07
Witches of the Caribbean '05
Ring of Darkness '04
The Brotherhood 3: The Young Demons '02
Brotherhood 2: The Young Warlocks '01
Ancient Evil: Scream of the Mummy '00
Voodoo Academy '00
Curse of the Puppet Master: The Human Experiment '98
Femalien 2 '98
Frankenstein Reborn '98
Leather Jacket Love Story '98
Talisman '98
Femalien '96
Prey of the Jaguar '96
Skeletons '96
Beach Babes 2: Cave Girl Island '95
Prehysteria 3 '95
Beach Babes from Beyond '93
Test Tube Teens from the Year 2000 '93
Puppet Master 3: Toulon's Revenge '90
Lady Avenger '89
Deadly Embrace '88
Dr. Alien '88
Creepozoids '87
Nightmare Sisters '87
Sorority Babes in the Slimeball Bowl-A-Rama '87

Miles Deem

See Demofilo Fidani

Allessandro DeGaetano

Project Metalbeast: DNA Overload '94
Bloodbath in Psycho Town '89

Philip DeGuere(1944-2005)

Misfits of Science '85
Dr. Strange '78

Edward Dein(1907-84)

Curse of the Undead '59
The Leech Woman '59
Shack Out on 101 '55

Donna Deitch(1945-)

Common Ground '00
The Devil's Arithmetic '99
A Change of Place '94
Prison Stories: Women on the Inside '91
The Women of Brewster Place '89
Desert Hearts '86

Steve DeJarnatt

Miracle Mile '89
Cherry 2000 '88

Fred Dekker(1959-)

RoboCop 3 '91
The Monster Squad '87
Night of the Creeps '86

Peter Del Monte(1943-)

Traveling Companion '96
Julia and Julia '87
Invitation au Voyage '82

Deborah Del Prete

Ricochet River '98
Simple Justice '89

Roy Del Ruth(1893-1961)

Why Must I Die? '60
Three Sailors and a Girl '53
On Moonlight Bay '51
Starlift '51
The West Point Story '50
Babe Ruth Story '48
It Happened on 5th Avenue '47
Broadway Rhythm '44
Du Barry Was a Lady '43
The Chocolate Soldier '41
Topper Returns '41
Happy Landing '38
My Lucky Star '38
Broadway Melody of 1938 '37
On the Avenue '37
Born to Dance '36
Broadway Melody of 1936 '35
Kid Millions '34
Bureau of Missing Persons '33
Employees' Entrance '33
Lady Killer '33
The Little Giant '33
Blessed Event '32
Blonde Crazy '31
The Maltese Falcon '31
The First Auto '27

Guillermo del Toro(1964-)

Hellboy II: The Golden Army '08
Pan's Labyrinth '06
Hellboy '04
Blade 2 '02
The Devil's Backbone '01
Mimic '97
Cronos '94

Jean Delannoy(1908-)

Bernadette '90
Action Man '67
This Special Friendship '67
Imperial Venus '63
Love and the Frenchwoman '60
The Hunchback of Notre Dame '57
La Symphonie Pastorale '46
Eternal Return '43

Dom DeLuise(1933-2009)

Boys Will Be Boys '97
Hot Stuff '80

Tulio Demicheli(1915-92)

Mean Machine '73
Dracula vs. Frankenstein '69
Son of Captain Blood '62

Cecil B. DeMille(1881-1959)

The Ten Commandments '56
The Greatest Show on Earth '52
Samson and Delilah '50
Unconquered '47
The Story of Dr. Wassell '44
Reap the Wild Wind '42
Union Pacific '39
The Plainsman '37
The Crusades '35
Cleopatra '34
The Sign of the Cross '33
Madam Satan '30
King of Kings '27
The Road to Yesterday '25
The Ten Commandments '23
Affairs of Anatol '21
Why Change Your Wife? '20
Male and Female '19
The Little American '17
The Cheat '15

Jonathan Demme(1944-)

Rachel Getting Married '08
Neil Young: Heart of Gold '06
The Manchurian Candidate '04
The Truth About Charlie '02
Beloved '98
Subway Stories '97
Philadelphia '93
The Silence of the Lambs '91
Married to the Mob '88
Swimming to Cambodia '87
Something Wild '86
Stop Making Sense '84
Swing Shift '84
Who Am I This Time? '82
Melvin and Howard '80
Last Embrace '79
Citizens Band '77
Fighting Mad '76
Crazy Mama '75
Caged Heat '74

Ted (Edward) Demme(1964-2002)

A Decade Under the Influence '02
Blow '01
Life '99
Monument Ave. '98
Subway Stories '97
Beautiful Girls '96
The Ref '93
Who's the Man? '93

Jacques Demy(1931-90)

A Slightly Pregnant Man '79
Pied Piper '72
Peau D'Ane '71
Donkey Skin '70
Model Shop '69
The Young Girls of Rochefort '68
Umbrellas of Cherbourg '64
Lola '61

Claire Denis(1948-)

35 Shots of Rum '08
The Intruder '04
Friday Night '02
Beau Travail '98
Nenette and Boni '96
I Can't Sleep '93
No Fear, No Die '90
Chocolat '88

Pen Densham(1947-)

Houdini '99
Moll Flanders '96
The Kiss '88
The Zoo Gang '85

Ruggero Deodato(1939-)

Dial Help '88
The Lone Runner '88
The Barbarians '87
Phantom of Death '87
Cut and Run '85
House on the Edge of the Park '84
Cannibal Holocaust '80

Gerard Depardieu(1948-)

Paris, je t'aime '06
The Bridge '00
Tartuffe '84

Jacques Deray(1929-2003)

The Outside Man '73
Borsalino '70
Swimming Pool '70
La Piscine '69

John Derek(1926-98)

Ghosts Can't Do It '90
Bolero '84
Tarzan, the Ape Man '81
Fantasies '73
Confessions of Tom Harris '72
Once Before I Die '65

Scott Derrickson

The Day the Earth Stood Still '08
The Exorcism of Emily Rose '05
Hellraiser 5: Inferno '00

Dominique Deruddere(1957-)

Everybody's Famous! '00
Hombres Complicados '97
Suite 16 '94
Wait until Spring, Bandini '90

Caleb Deschanel(1941-)

Crusoe '89
The Escape Artist '82

Arnaud Desplechin(1960-)

A Christmas Tale '08
Kings and Queen '04
Esther Kahn '00
My Sex Life... Or How I Got into an Argument '96
La Sentinelle '92

Howard Deutch(1950-)

My Best Friend's Girl '08
The Whole Ten Yards '04
The Replacements '00
Neil Simon's The Odd Couple 2 '98
Grumpier Old Men '95
Getting Even with Dad '94
Article 99 '92
The Great Outdoors '88
Some Kind of Wonderful '87
Pretty in Pink '86

Geoffrey DeVallois

See Geoffrey De Vallois

Ross Devenish(1939-)

A Certain Justice '99
Over Indulgence '87
Bleak House '85

Michel DeVille(1931-)

Almost Peaceful '02
La Lectrice '88
Peril '85
Voyage en Douce '81

David Devine

Bailey's Billion$ '05
Beethoven Lives Upstairs '92

Dennis Devine

Bloodstream '00
Merchants of Death '99
Vampires of Sorority Row: Kickboxers From Hell '99
Haunted '98
Amazon Warrior '97
Things 2 '97
Things '93
Dead Girls '90
Fatal Images '89

Danny DeVito(1944-)

The Oh in Ohio '06
Duplex '03
Death to Smoochy '02
Matilda '96
Hoffa '92
The War of the Roses '89
Throw Momma from the Train '87
Amazing Stories '85
Ratings Game '84

John Dexter(1925-90)

I Want What I Want '72
The Virgin Soldiers '69

Maury Dexter(1927-)

Hell's Belles '69
Surf Party '64

Tom Dey

Marmaduke '10
Failure to Launch '06
Showtime '02
Shanghai Noon '00

Fernando Di Leo(1932-2003)

Violent Breed '83
Big Boss '77
Mr. Scarface '77
Kidnap Syndicate '76
Rulers of the City '76
Loaded Guns '75
Hired to Kill '73
Hit Men '73
Manhunt '73
Slaughter Hotel '71

Rino Di Silvestro(1932-)

The Legend of the Wolf Woman '77
Women in Cell Block 7 '77

Matthew Diamond

Camp Rock '08
These Old Broads '01

Jose Diaz Morales(1908-)

Loyola, the Soldier Saint '52
Senora Tentacion '49

Saul Dibb

The Duchess '08
The Line of Beauty '06

Tom DiCillo(1954-)

Delirious '06
Double Whammy '01
The Real Blonde '97
Box of Moonlight '96
Living in Oblivion '94
Johnny Suede '92

Kirby Dick

Outrage '09
This Film Is Not Yet Rated '06

Nigel Dick(1953-)

Dead Connection '94
Final Combination '93
Deadly Intent '88
P.I. Private Investigations '87
Private Investigations '87

Ernest R. Dickerson(1952-)

Masters of Horror: The V Word '05
Never Die Alone '04
Good Fences '03
Big Shot: Confessions of a Campus Bookie '02
Monday Night Mayhem '02
Our America '02
Bones '01
Strange Justice: The Clarence Thomas and Anita Hill Story '99
Blind Faith '98
Futuresport '98
Bulletproof '96
Surviving the Game '94
Tales from the Crypt Presents Demon Knight '94
Juice '92

Thorold Dickinson(1903-84)

Hill 24 Doesn't Answer '55
The Queen of Spades '49
Men of Two Worlds '46
Gaslight '40
The Arsenal Stadium Mystery '39
High Command '37

Katherine Dieckmann

Motherhood '09
Diggers '06
A Good Baby '99

Samuel Diege(1902-39)

Ride 'Em Cowgirl '41
The Singing Cowgirl '39
Water Rustlers '39
King of the Sierras '38

Carlos Diegues(1940-)

Orfeu '99
Tieta of Agreste '96
Subway to the Stars '87
Quilombo '84
Bye Bye Brazil '79
Xica '76

William Dieterle(1893-1972)

Quick, Let's Get Married '71
Mistress of the World '59
Omar Khayyam '57
Elephant Walk '54
Salome '53
Boots Malone '52
September Affair '50
The Accused '48
Portrait of Jennie '48
Love Letters '45
I'll Be Seeing You '44
The Devil & Daniel Webster '41
Dr. Ehrlich's Magic Bullet '40
The Hunchback of Notre Dame '39
Juarez '39
The Life of Emile Zola '37
Satan Met a Lady '36
The Story of Louis Pasteur '36
A Midsummer Night's Dream '35
Fashions of 1934 '34
Female '33
Scarlet Dawn '32

Erwin C. Dietrich

Inn of Temptation '73
Sex Adventures of the Three Musketeers '71

Erin Dignam

Loved '97
Denial: The Dark Side of Passion '91

John Francis Dillon(1887-1934)

Millie '31
Sally '29
Suds '20

Steve DiMarco

Prisoner of Love '99
Back in Action '94

Ross Dimsey(1943-)

Death Games '80
Blue Fire Lady '78

Mark Dindal

Chicken Little '05
The Emperor's New Groove '00
Cats Don't Dance '97

Paul Dinello(1962-)

Gym Teacher: The Movie '08
Strangers with Candy '06

Michael Dinner

The Crew '00
Hot to Trot! '88
Off Beat '86
Heaven Help Us '85

Mark Dippe(1958-)

Frankenfish '04
Halloweentown High '04
Spawn '97

Mark DiSalle

The Perfect Weapon '91
Kickboxer '89

Denver Dixon

See Victor Adamson

Ivan Dixon(1931-2008)

Percy & Thunder '93
The Spook Who Sat by the Door '73

Jamie Dixon

Bats: Human Harvest '07
Bram Stoker's Shadowbuilder '98

Edward Dmytryk(1908-99)

He Is My Brother '75
The Human Factor '75
Bluebeard '72
Anzio '68
Shalako '68
Alvarez Kelly '66
Mirage '66
The Carpetbaggers '64
Where Love Has Gone '64
Walk on the Wild Side '62
Warlock '59
The Young Lions '58
Raintree County '57
The Mountain '56
End of the Affair '55
The Left Hand of God '55
Soldier of Fortune '55
Broken Lance '54
The Caine Mutiny '54
Mutiny '52
The Sniper '52
The Hidden Room '49
Obsession '49
Crossfire '47
Till the End of Time '46
Back to Bataan '45
Cornered '45
Murder, My Sweet '44
Behind the Rising Sun '43
Captive Wild Woman '43
Hitler's Children '43
Tender Comrade '43
Golden Gloves '40
Her First Romance '40
Trail of the Hawk '37

Francois Dupeyron(1950-)
Monsieur Ibrahim *'03*
The Machine *'96*

Jay Duplass
Cyrus *'10*
Baghead *'08*

Mark Duplass
Cyrus *'10*
Baghead *'08*

David E. Durston(1921-)
Stigma *'73*
I Drink Your Blood *'71*

Charles S. Dutton(1951-)
Against the Ropes *'04*
The Corner *'00*
First Time Felon *'97*

Robert Duvall(1931-)
Assassination Tango *'03*
The Apostle *'97*
Angelo My Love *'83*

Julien Duvivier(1896-1967)
Diabolically Yours *'67*
The Burning Court *'62*
The Man in the Raincoat *'57*
Captain Blackjack *'51*
Little World of Don Camillo *'51*
Anna Karenina *'48*
Panique *'47*
Heart of a Nation *'43*
Tales of Manhattan *'42*
Lydia *'41*
The Great Waltz *'38*
Pepe Le Moko *'37*
Maria Chapdelaine *'34*
Poil de Carotte *'31*

Allan Dwan(1885-1981)
Enchanted Island *'58*
The Restless Breed *'58*
Slightly Scarlet *'56*
Escape to Burma *'55*
Pearl of the South Pacific *'55*
Tennessee's Partner *'55*
Cattle Queen of Montana *'54*
Passion *'54*
Silver Lode *'54*
I Dream of Jeannie *'52*
Montana Belle *'52*
Sands of Iwo Jima *'49*
Northwest Outpost *'47*
Brewster's Millions *'45*
Getting Gertie's Garter *'45*
Abroad with Two Yanks *'44*
Around the World *'43*
Here We Go Again! *'42*
Look Who's Laughing *'41*
Young People *'40*
The Gorilla *'39*
The Three Musketeers *'39*
Rebecca of Sunnybrook Farm *'38*
Heidi *'37*
Hollywood Party *'34*
The Iron Mask *'29*
Manhandled *'24*
Robin Hood *'22*

H. Kaye Dyal
Project: Eliminator *'91*
Trained to Kill *'88*
Memory of Us *'74*

Robert Dyke
InAlienable *'08*
Moontrap *'89*

Jesse Dylan(1966-)
Kicking & Screaming *'05*
American Wedding *'03*
How High *'01*

Bill Eagles
Dracula *'06*
The Riverman *'04*
Beautiful Creatures *'00*

B. Reeves Eason(1886-1956)
Rimfire *'49*
'Neath Canadian Skies *'46*
Call of the Yukon *'38*
Darkest Africa *'36*
Fighting Marines *'36*
Red River Valley *'36*
Undersea Kingdom *'36*
The Miracle Rider *'35*
The Phantom Empire *'35*
Hollywood Mystery *'34*
Law of the Wild *'34*
Mystery Mountain *'34*
Cornered *'32*
The Last of the Mohicans *'32*
Sunset Trail *'32*
The Galloping Ghost *'31*
Vanishing Legion *'31*
Roaring Ranch *'30*
Spurs *'30*
Trigger Tricks *'30*
The Prairie King *'27*
Test of Donald Norton *'26*

Eric Eason
Journey to the End of the Night *'06*
Manito *'03*

Allan Eastman(1950-)
Danger Zone *'95*
Crazy Moon *'87*
Ford: The Man & the Machine *'87*
The War Boy *'85*
Snapshot *'77*

Clint Eastwood(1930-)
Invictus *'09*
Changeling *'08*
Gran Torino *'08*
Flags of Our Fathers *'06*
Letters from Iwo Jima *'06*
Million Dollar Baby *'04*
Mystic River *'03*
Blood Work *'02*
Space Cowboys *'00*
True Crime *'99*
Absolute Power *'97*
Midnight in the Garden of Good and Evil *'97*
The Bridges of Madison County *'95*
A Perfect World *'93*
Unforgiven *'92*
The Rookie *'90*
White Hunter, Black Heart *'90*
Bird *'88*
Heartbreak Ridge *'86*
Pale Rider *'85*
Sudden Impact *'83*
Firefox *'82*
Honkytonk Man *'82*
Bronco Billy *'80*
The Gauntlet *'77*
The Outlaw Josey Wales *'76*
The Eiger Sanction *'75*
High Plains Drifter *'73*
Play Misty for Me *'71*

Thom Eberhardt(1947-)
Ratz *'99*
Face Down *'97*
Captain Ron *'92*
Gross Anatomy *'89*
The Night Before *'88*
Without a Clue *'88*
Night of the Comet *'84*
Sole Survivor *'84*

Uli Edel(1947-)
The Baader Meinhof Complex *'08*
King of Texas *'02*
Mists of Avalon *'01*
The Little Vampire *'00*
Purgatory *'99*
Rasputin: Dark Servant of Destiny *'96*
Tyson *'95*
Confessions of Sorority Girls *'94*
Body of Evidence *'92*
Last Exit to Brooklyn *'90*
Christiane F. *'82*

Don Edmonds(1937-)
Terror on Tour *'83*
Bare Knuckles *'77*
Ilsa, Harem Keeper of the Oil Sheiks *'76*
Ilsa, She-Wolf of the SS *'74*
Tender Loving Care *'73*

Blake Edwards(1922-)
Son of the Pink Panther *'93*
Switch *'91*
Peter Gunn *'89*
Skin Deep *'89*
Sunset *'88*
Blind Date *'87*
A Fine Mess *'86*
That's Life! *'86*
Micki & Maude *'84*
Curse of the Pink Panther *'83*
The Man Who Loved Women *'83*
Trail of the Pink Panther *'82*
Victor/Victoria *'82*
S.O.B. *'81*
10 *'79*
Revenge of the Pink Panther *'78*
The Pink Panther Strikes Again *'76*
Return of the Pink Panther *'74*
The Tamarind Seed *'74*
Wild Rovers *'71*
Darling Lili *'70*
The Party *'68*
What Did You Do in the War, Daddy? *'66*
The Great Race *'65*
The Pink Panther *'64*
A Shot in the Dark *'64*
Days of Wine and Roses *'62*
Experiment in Terror *'62*
Breakfast at Tiffany's *'61*
Operation Petticoat *'59*
The Perfect Furlough *'59*
This Happy Feeling *'58*

Henry Edwards(1882-1952)
Juggernaut *'37*
The Private Secretary *'35*
Scrooge *'35*

Robert Edwards
Land of the Blind *'06*
Thunder in the Pines *'49*

Christine Edzard(1945-)
Little Dorrit, Film 1: Nobody's Fault *'88*
Little Dorrit, Film 2: Little Dorrit's Story *'88*

Colin Eggleston(1941-2002)
The Wicked *'89*
Innocent Prey *'88*
Cassandra *'87*
Sky Pirates *'87*

Jan Egleson(1946-)
Coyote Waits *'03*
The Last Hit *'93*
A Shock to the System *'90*
Roanoak *'86*
The Tender Age *'84*

Atom Egoyan(1960-)
Chloe *'09*
Adoration *'08*
Where the Truth Lies *'05*
Ararat *'02*
Felicia's Journey *'99*
The Sweet Hereafter *'96*
Exotica *'94*
Calendar *'93*
The Adjuster *'91*
Speaking Parts *'89*
Family Viewing *'87*
Next of Kin *'84*

Franz Eichhorn
River of Evil *'64*
The Violent Years *'56*

Rafael Eisenman
Red Shoe Diaries: Swimming Naked *'00*
A Place Called Truth *'98*
Red Shoe Diaries 8: Night of Abandon *'97*
Business for Pleasure *'96*
Red Shoe Diaries 7: Burning Up *'96*
Red Shoe Diaries: Four on the Floor *'96*
Red Shoe Diaries: Strip Poker *'96*
Red Shoe Diaries 3: Another Woman's Lipstick *'93*
Lake Consequence *'92*

Sergei Eisenstein(1898-1948)
Ivan the Terrible, Part 2 *'46*
Ivan the Terrible, Part 1 *'44*
Alexander Nevsky *'38*
Que Viva Mexico *'32*
The General Line *'29*
Ten Days That Shook the World *'27*
The Battleship Potemkin *'25*
Strike *'24*

Breck Eisner(1970-)
The Crazies *'09*
Sahara *'05*
Taken *'02*

Clifford S. Elfelt
$50,000 Reward *'25*
Big Stakes *'22*

Richard Elfman(1942-)
Modern Vampires *'98*
Shrunken Heads *'94*
Forbidden Zone *'80*

Harry Elfont(1968-)
Josie and the Pussycats *'01*
Can't Hardly Wait *'98*

Michael Elias(1940-)
No Laughing Matter *'97*
Lush Life *'94*

Larry Elikann(1923-2004)
Robin Cook's Terminal *'96*
An Unexpected Family *'96*
Blue River *'95*
A Mother's Prayer *'95*
Tecumseh: The Last Warrior *'95*
Kiss of a Killer *'93*
The Story Lady *'93*
Fever *'91*
The Great Los Angeles Earthquake *'91*
An Inconvenient Woman *'91*
One Against the Wind *'91*
Last Flight Out: A True Story *'90*
Disaster at Silo 7 *'88*
God Bless the Child *'88*
Hands of a Stranger *'87*
Stamp of a Killer *'87*
Poison Ivy *'85*
Spraggue *'84*
Charlie and the Great Balloon Chase *'82*
The Great Wallendas *'78*

Ellory Elkayem(1972-)
Without a Paddle: Nature's Calling *'09*
Return of the Living Dead: Rave to the Grave *'05*
Eight Legged Freaks *'02*

Doug Ellin(1968-)
Kissing a Fool *'98*
Phat Beach *'96*

Lang Elliott(1950-)
Cage 2: The Arena of Death *'94*
The Private Eyes *'80*

Stephan Elliott(1963-)
Eye of the Beholder *'99*
Welcome to Woop Woop *'97*
The Adventures of Priscilla, Queen of the Desert *'94*
Frauds *'93*

Bob Ellis(1942-)
The Nostradamus Kid *'92*
Warm Nights on a Slow-Moving Train *'87*

David R. Ellis(1952-)
The Final Destination *'09*
Snakes on a Plane *'06*
Cellular *'04*
Final Destination 2 *'03*
Homeward Bound 2: Lost in San Francisco *'96*

Sean Ellis
The Broken *'08*
Cashback *'06*

Joseph Ellison(1948-)
Joey *'85*
Don't Go in the House *'80*

Jose Maria Elorrieta(1921-)
Feast for the Devil *'71*
Emerald of Artama *'67*
Hawk and Castile *'67*

Maurice Elvey(1887-1967)
The Gay Dog *'54*
The Obsessed *'51*
Beware of Pity *'46*
Salute John Citizen *'42*
Spy of Napoleon *'36*
Phantom Fiend *'35*
Transatlantic Tunnel *'35*
The Evil Mind *'34*
Lily of Killarney *'34*

Bob Emenegger
Escape from DS-3 *'81*
Killings at Outpost Zeta *'80*
Laboratory *'80*

John Emerson(1874-1956)
The Americano *'17*
Down to Earth *'17*
Reaching for the Moon *'17*
His Picture in the Papers *'16*
The Social Secretary *'16*

Robert Emery
The Florida Connection *'74*
Ride in a Pink Car *'74*
My Brother Has Bad Dreams *'72*
Scream Bloody Murder *'72*

Roland Emmerich(1955-)
2012 *'09*
10,000 B.C. *'08*
The Day After Tomorrow *'04*
The Patriot *'00*
Godzilla *'98*
Independence Day *'96*
Stargate *'94*
Universal Soldier *'92*
Moon 44 *'90*
Ghost Chase *'88*
Making Contact *'86*

Cy Endfield(1914-95)
Zulu *'64*
Mysterious Island *'61*
Impulse *'55*
Try and Get Me *'50*
The Underworld Story *'50*

John English(1903-69)
Hills of Utah *'51*
Valley of Fire *'51*
Cow Town *'50*
Riders of the Whistling Pines *'49*
Rim of the Canyon *'49*
Loaded Pistols *'48*
Trail to San Antone *'47*
Don't Fence Me In *'45*
Silver City Kid *'45*
Utah *'45*
Captain America *'44*
San Fernando Valley *'44*
Death Valley Manhunt *'43*
Fighting Devil Dogs *'43*
Man from Thunder River *'43*
Raiders of Sunset Pass *'43*
Code of the Outlaw *'42*
Code of the Outlaw *'42*
Gangs of Sonora *'41*
King of the Texas Rangers *'41*
Adventures of Red Ryder *'40*
Doctor Satan's Robot *'40*
Drums of Fu Manchu *'40*
Mysterious Doctor Satan *'40*
Zorro's Fighting Legion *'39*
Call the Mesquiteers *'38*
Daredevils of the Red Circle *'38*
The Lone Ranger *'38*
Arizona Days *'37*
Dick Tracy *'37*
Zorro Rides Again *'37*
Whistling Bullets *'36*
His Fighting Blood *'35*

George Englund(1926-)
Dixie: Changing Habits *'85*
The Vegas Strip Wars *'84*
A Christmas to Remember *'78*
Zachariah *'70*
The Ugly American *'63*

Robert Englund(1947-)
Killer Pad *'06*
976-EVIL *'88*

Robert Enrico(1931-2001)
Old Gun *'76*
Le Secret *'74*
Zita *'68*
The Last Adventure *'67*
Jailbird's Vacation *'65*
An Occurrence at Owl Creek Bridge/Coup de Grace *'62*

Ray Enright(1896-1965)
Man from Cairo *'54*
Montana *'50*
Coroner Creek *'48*
Return of the Bad Men *'48*
South of St. Louis *'48*
Trail Street *'47*
China Sky *'44*
Gung Ho! *'43*
The Iron Major *'43*
The Spoilers *'42*
The Wagons Roll at Night *'41*
Gold Diggers in Paris *'38*
Hard to Get *'38*
Sing Me a Love Song *'37*
Earthworm Tractors *'36*
Alibi Ike *'35*
Dames *'34*
Havana Widows *'33*
Tomorrow at Seven *'33*
Golden Dawn *'30*

Ildiko Enyedi(1955-)
Simon the Magician *'99*
Magic Hunter *'96*
My Twentieth Century *'90*

Nora Ephron(1941-)
Julie & Julia *'09*
Bewitched *'05*
Lucky Numbers *'00*
You've Got Mail *'98*
Michael *'96*
Mixed Nuts *'94*
Sleepless in Seattle *'93*
This Is My Life *'92*

Robert Epstein(1955-)
The Celluloid Closet *'95*
Common Threads: Stories from the Quilt *'89*
Times of Harvey Milk *'83*

Rene Eram
Sweet Evil *'95*
Voodoo *'95*

Rainer Erler
Nuclear Conspiracy *'85*
Spare Parts *'79*

John Erman(1935-)
Victoria & Albert *'01*
Only Love *'98*
Ellen Foster *'97*
The Boys Next Door *'96*
The Sunshine Boys *'95*
Breathing Lessons *'94*
Scarlett *'94*
Queen *'93*
Carolina Skeletons *'92*
Our Sons *'91*
When the Time Comes *'91*
The Last Best Year *'90*
Stella *'89*
The Attic: The Hiding of Anne Frank *'88*
An Early Frost *'85*
A Streetcar Named Desire *'84*
Eleanor: First Lady of the World *'82*

My Old Man *'79*
Roots: The Next Generation *'79*
Child of Glass *'78*
Alexander: The Other Side of Dawn *'77*
Roots *'77*
Green Eyes *'76*

George Erschbamer(1954-)
Christmas Town *'08*
Bounty Hunters 2: Hardball *'97*
Bounty Hunters *'96*
Flinch *'94*
Final Round *'93*
SnakeEater 3: His Law *'92*
SnakeEater *'89*
SnakeEater 2: The Drug Buster *'89*

Joakim (Jack) Ersgard
Rancid *'04*
Backlash *'99*
Acts of Betrayal *'98*
Living in Peril *'97*
Invisible: The Chronicles of Benjamin Knight *'93*
Mandroid *'93*
The Visitors *'89*

Chester Erskine(1905-86)
Androcles and the Lion *'52*
A Girl in Every Port *'52*
Egg and I *'47*
Frankie and Johnny *'36*
Midnight *'34*

Dwain Esper(1893-1982)
Marihuana *'36*
Maniac *'34*

Harry Essex(1910-97)
The Cremators *'72*
Octaman *'71*

Emilio Estevez(1962-)
Bobby *'06*
Rated X *'00*
The War at Home *'96*
Men at Work *'90*
Wisdom *'87*

Paul Etheredge-Ouzts(1968-)
Angel of Death *'09*
Hellbent *'04*

Corey Michael Eubanks
Two Bits & Pepper *'95*
Bigfoot: The Unforgettable Encounter *'94*

Bruce A. Evans
Mr. Brooks *'07*
Kuffs *'92*

David Mickey Evans(1962-)
Ace Ventura Jr.: Pet Detective *'08*
The Final Season *'07*
The Sandlot 2 *'05*
Beethoven's 4th *'01*
Beethoven's 3rd *'00*
First Kid *'96*
The Sandlot *'93*

John Evans(1934-)
Blackjack *'78*
Black Godfather *'74*
Speeding Up Time *'71*

Marc Evans
Snow Cake *'06*
Trauma *'04*
Resurrection Man *'97*
Thicker Than Water *'93*

Roger Evans
Forever Evil *'87*
Jet Benny Show *'86*

Tim Everitt
Too Fast, Too Young *'96*
Fatally Yours *'95*

Valie Export(1940-)
The Practice of Love *'84*
Invisible Adversaries *'77*

Chris Eyre(1969-)
A Thief of Time *'04*
Skins *'02*
Skinwalker *'02*
Smoke Signals *'98*

Richard Eyre(1943-)
The Other Man *'08*
Notes on a Scandal *'06*
Stage Beauty *'04*
Iris *'01*
King Lear *'98*
Loose Connections *'87*
Singleton's Pluck *'84*
The Ploughman's Lunch *'83*

John Eyres
Irish Jam *'05*
Ripper: Letter from Hell *'01*
Octopus *'00*
Conspiracy of Fear *'96*
Judge & Jury *'96*
Project Shadowchaser 3000 *'95*
Night Siege Project: Shadowchaser 2 *'94*
Monolith *'93*
Project: Shadowchaser *'92*
Slow Burn *'90*

Christian Faber
The Next Step *'95*
Bail Jumper *'89*

Roberto Faenza(1943-)
The Bachelor *'93*
Corrupt *'84*

Peter Faiman
Dutch *'91*
Crocodile Dundee *'86*

William Fairchild(1919-2000)
Horsemasters *'61*
The Silent Enemy *'58*
John and Julie *'55*

Ferdinand Fairfax(1944-)
Frenchman's Creek *'98*
The Choir *'95*
Spymaker: The Secret Life of Ian Fleming *'90*
The Rescue *'88*
The Last Place on Earth *'85*
Nate and Hayes *'83*
Danger UXB *'81*

Harry Falk(1933-)
High Desert Kill *'90*
Sophisticated Gents *'81*
Beulah Land *'80*
The Night the City Screamed *'80*
Centennial *'78*
Abduction of St. Anne *'75*
The Death Squad *'73*

Jim Fall(1962-)
Wedding Wars *'06*
The Lizzie McGuire Movie *'03*
Trick *'99*

Rick Famuyiwa(1973-)
Our Family Wedding *'10*
Brown Sugar *'02*
The Wood *'99*

Jamaa Fanaka(1942-)
Street Wars *'91*
Penitentiary 3 *'87*
Penitentiary 2 *'82*
Penitentiary *'79*
Black Sister's Revenge *'76*
Soul Vengeance *'75*

James Fargo(1938-)
Second Chances *'98*
Born to Race *'88*
Voyage of the Rock Aliens *'87*
Game for Vultures *'86*
Forced Vengeance *'82*
Every Which Way But Loose *'78*
The Enforcer *'76*

Ernest Farino
Josh Kirby... Time Warrior: Chapter 5, Journey to the Magic Cavern *'96*
Josh Kirby. . .Time Warrior: Chapter 1, Planet of the Dino-Knights *'95*
Steel and Lace *'90*

Julian Farino
Byron *'03*
Our Mutual Friend *'98*

Leonard Farlinger
All Hat *'07*
The Perfect Son *'00*

Donald Farmer(1954-)
Vampire Cop *'90*
Scream Dream *'89*
Demon Queen *'80*

Bobby Farrelly(1958-)
The Heartbreak Kid *'07*
Fever Pitch *'05*
Stuck On You *'03*
Osmosis Jones *'01*
Shallow Hal *'01*
Me, Myself, and Irene *'00*
There's Something about Mary *'98*
Kingpin *'96*

Peter Farrelly(1957-)
The Heartbreak Kid *'07*
Fever Pitch *'05*
Stuck On You *'03*
Osmosis Jones *'01*
Shallow Hal *'01*
Me, Myself, and Irene *'00*
There's Something about Mary *'98*
Kingpin *'96*
Dumb & Dumber *'94*

John Farrow(1904-63)
John Paul Jones *'59*
Unholy Wife *'57*
Back from Eternity *'56*
Sea Chase *'55*
A Bullet Is Waiting *'54*
Botany Bay *'53*
Hondo *'53*
His Kind of Woman *'51*
Copper Canyon *'50*
Where Danger Lives *'50*
The Big Clock *'48*
Calcutta *'47*
The Saint Strikes Back: Criminal Court *'46*
Two Years before the Mast *'46*
China *'43*
Commandos Strike at Dawn *'43*
Wake Island *'42*
Five Came Back *'39*
The Saint Strikes Back *'39*

John Fasano
Black Roses *'88*
The Jitters *'88*
Rock 'n' Roll Nightmare *'85*

Rainer Werner Fassbinder(1946-82)
Chinese Roulette *'86*
Querelle *'83*
Veronika Voss *'82*
Berlin Alexanderplatz *'80*
The Marriage of Maria Braun *'79*
Despair *'78*
Germany in Autumn *'78*
In a Year of 13 Moons *'78*
The Stationmaster's Wife *'77*
I Only Want You to Love Me *'76*
Mother Kusters Goes to Heaven *'76*
Satan's Brew *'76*
Fear of Fear *'75*
Fox and His Friends *'75*
Ali: Fear Eats the Soul *'74*
Effi Briest *'74*
The Bitter Tears of Petra von Kant *'72*
The Merchant of Four Seasons *'71*
The American Soldier *'70*
Beware of a Holy Whore *'70*
Whity *'70*
Gods of the Plague *'69*
Love Is Colder Than Death *'69*
Why Does Herr R. Run Amok? *'69*

Don E. Fauntleroy
Anacondas: Trail of Blood *'09*
Anaconda 3: The Offspring *'08*
Urban Justice *'07*
Seven Days of Grace *'06*
The Perfect Wife *'00*

Jon Favreau(1966-)
Iron Man 2 *'10*
Iron Man *'08*
Zathura *'05*
Elf *'03*
Made *'01*

John Fawcett(1968-)
Taken *'02*
Ginger Snaps *'01*
The Boys Club *'96*

Neill Fearnley
Daniel's Daughter *'08*
Escape from Mars *'99*
Johnny 2.0 *'99*
Black Ice *'92*

Xie Fei(1942-)
A Mongolian Tale *'94*
Women from the Lake of Scented Souls *'94*
Girl from Hunan *'86*

Michael Feifer
The Dog Who Saved Christmas *'09*
The Boston Strangler: The Untold Story *'08*
Bundy: A Legacy of Evil *'08*
A Christmas Proposal *'08*
Dear Me: A Blogger's Tale *'08*
A Dead Calling *'06*

Paul Feig(1962-)
Unaccompanied Minors *'06*
I Am David *'04*

Beda Docampo Feijoo(1948-)
What Your Eyes Don't See *'99*
The Perfect Husband *'92*
Under the Earth *'86*

Felix Feist(1910-65)
Donovan's Brain *'53*
Big Trees *'52*
This Woman Is Dangerous *'52*
Guilty of Treason *'50*
Threat *'49*
The Devil Thumbs a Ride *'47*
George White's Scandals *'45*
Golden Gloves *'40*
Deluge *'33*

John Feldman(1954-)
Dead Funny *'94*
Alligator Eyes *'90*

Marty Feldman(1933-82)
In God We Trust *'80*
The Last Remake of Beau Geste *'77*

Sam Fell
The Tale of Despereaux *'08*
Flushed Away *'06*

Federico Fellini(1920-93)
Intervista *'87*
Ginger & Fred *'86*
And the Ship Sails On *'83*
City of Women *'81*
Orchestra Rehearsal *'78*
Amarcord *'74*
Fellini's Roma *'72*
The Clowns *'71*
Fellini Satyricon *'69*
Spirits of the Dead *'68*
Juliet of the Spirits *'65*
8 1/2 *'63*
Boccaccio '70 *'62*
La Dolce Vita *'60*
Nights of Cabiria *'57*
Il Bidone *'55*
La Strada *'54*
I Vitelloni *'53*
Love in the City *'53*
The White Sheik *'52*
Variety Lights *'51*

Georg Fenady(1930-)
Arnold *'73*
Terror in the Wax Museum *'73*

Leslie Fenton(1902-78)
On Our Merry Way *'48*
Saigon *'47*
Tomorrow the World *'44*

Larry Ferguson(1940-)
Gunfighter's Moon *'96*
Beyond the Law *'92*

Guy Ferland(1966-)
Dirty Dancing: Havana Nights *'04*
After the Storm *'01*
Delivered *'98*
Telling Lies in America *'96*
The Babysitter *'95*

Emilio Fernandez(1904-86)
Flor Silvestre *'58*
The Torch *'50*
The Pearl *'48*
Maria Candelaria *'46*

Abel Ferrara(1952-)
'R Xmas *'01*
New Rose Hotel *'98*
The Blackout *'97*
Subway Stories *'97*
The Funeral *'96*
The Addiction *'95*
Body Snatchers *'93*
Dangerous Game *'93*
Bad Lieutenant *'92*
Cat Chaser *'90*
King of New York *'90*
China Girl *'87*
The Gladiator *'86*
Fear City *'85*
Ms. 45 *'81*
Driller Killer *'79*

Davide Ferrario(1956-)
After Midnight *'04*
Children of Hannibal *'98*

Jose Ferrer(1909-92)
State Fair *'62*
Return to Peyton Place *'61*

Marco Ferreri(1928-97)
Tales of Ordinary Madness *'83*
La Grande Bouffe *'73*
L'Udienza *'71*
Dillinger Is Dead *'69*
El Cochecito *'60*

Darin Ferriola(1970-)
Mr. Fix It *'06*
Ivory Tower *'97*

Giorgio Ferroni(1908-81)
The Battle of El Alamein *'68*
Blood for a Silver Dollar *'66*
Fort Yuma Gold *'66*
Secret Agent Super Dragon *'66*
Coriolanus, Man without a Country *'64*
The Lion of Thebes *'64*
The Bacchantes *'63*
Conquest of Mycene *'63*
Hero of Rome *'63*
The Trojan Horse *'62*
Mill of the Stone Women *'60*

Larry Fessenden(1963-)
The Last Winter *'06*
Wendigo *'01*
Habit *'97*

Louis Feuillade(1873-1925)
Judex *'16*
Les Vampires *'15*

Jacques Feyder(1885-1948)
Knight Without Armour *'37*
Carnival in Flanders *'35*
The Kiss *'29*
Crainquebille *'23*

Andy Fickman
Race to Witch Mountain *'09*
The Game Plan *'07*
She's the Man *'06*

Demofilo Fidani(1913-94)
Jungle Master *'72*
Fistful of Death *'71*

Sally Field(1946-)
Beautiful *'00*
From the Earth to the Moon *'98*

Todd Field(1964-)
Little Children *'06*
In the Bedroom *'01*

Michael Fields
Bright Angel *'91*
Noon Wine *'84*

Mike Figgis(1948-)
Cold Creek Manor *'03*
Hotel *'01*
Time Code *'00*
Miss Julie *'99*
The Loss of Sexual Innocence *'98*
One Night Stand *'97*
Leaving Las Vegas *'95*
The Browning Version *'94*
Mr. Jones *'93*
Liebestraum *'91*
Women & Men: In Love There Are No Rules *'91*
Internal Affairs *'90*
Stormy Monday *'88*

Ivan Fila(1956-)
King of Thieves *'04*
Lea *'96*

Charles Finch(1962-)
Circle of Passion *'97*
Where Sleeping Dogs Lie *'91*
Priceless Beauty *'90*

Nigel Finch(1950-95)
Stonewall *'95*
The Lost Language of Cranes *'92*
The Vampyr *'92*

David Fincher(1963-)
The Curious Case of Benjamin Button *'08*
Zodiac *'07*
Panic Room *'02*
Fight Club *'99*
The Game *'97*
Seven *'95*
Alien 3 *'92*

Roberta Findlay
Lurkers *'88*
Prime Evil *'88*
Blood Sisters *'86*
The Oracle *'85*

Kenneth Fink
Tricks *'97*
Tall, Dark and Deadly *'95*
Stephen King's Golden Years *'91*

Ken Finkleman(1946-)
Head Office *'86*
Airplane 2: The Sequel *'82*

Edward Finney(1903-83)
Queen of the Amazons *'47*
King of the Stallions *'42*
Riot Squad *'41*
Silver Stallion *'41*

Laurent Firode
My First Wedding *'04*
Happenstance *'00*

Sam Firstenberg(1950-)
Quicksand *'01*

Spiders 2: Breeding Ground '01
Agent of Death '99
Motel Blue '98
Operation: Delta Force '97
Cyborg Soldier '94
Blood Warriors '93
Cyborg Cop '93
American Samurai '92
Delta Force 3: The Killing Game '91
One More Chance '90
Riverbend '89
American Ninja 2: The Confrontation '87
My African Adventure '87
Avenging Force '86
American Ninja '85
Breakin' 2: Electric Boogaloo '84
Ninja 3: The Domination '84
Revenge of the Ninja '83

Michael Firth
Sylvia '86
Heart of the Stag '84
The Lazarus Syndrome '79

Michael Fischa(1952-)
Delta Heat '92
Crack House '89
My Mom's a Werewolf '89
Death Spa '87

Max Fischer(1929-)
Taken '99
Psychopath '97
Entangled '93
Killing 'Em Softly '85

Chris Fisher(1973-)
S. Darko: A Donnie Darko Tale '09
Dirty '05
Rampage: The Hillside Strangler Murders '04
Nightstalker '02

David Fisher(1948-)
Toy Soldiers '84
Liar's Moon '82

Terence Fisher(1904-80)
Frankenstein and the Monster from Hell '74
Frankenstein Must Be Destroyed '69
The Devil Rides Out '68
Island of the Burning Doomed '67
Dracula, Prince of Darkness '66
Frankenstein Created Woman '66
Island of Terror '66
The Gorgon '64
The Phantom of the Opera '62
Sherlock Holmes and the Deadly Necklace '62
The Curse of the Werewolf '61
The Brides of Dracula '60
The Stranglers of Bombay '60
Sword of Sherwood Forest '60
The Two Faces of Dr. Jekyll '60
The Hound of the Baskervilles '59
The Mummy '59
The Horror of Dracula '58
The Revenge of Frankenstein '58
The Curse of Frankenstein '57
Kill Me Tomorrow '57
Race for Life '55
Robin Hood: The Movie '55
Black Glove '54
Blackout '54
Unholy Four '54
Four Sided Triangle '53
Spaceways '53
Three Stops to Murder '53
Man Bait '52
A Stolen Face '52
Home to Danger '51

Bill Fishman
Car 54, Where Are You? '94
Tapeheads '89

Jack Fisk(1945-)
Final Verdict '91
Daddy's Dyin'... Who's Got the Will? '90
Violets Are Blue '86
Raggedy Man '81

Christopher Fitchett(1951-)
Fair Game '82
Blood Money '80

Thom Fitzgerald(1968-)
The Event '03
Beefcake '99
The Hanging Garden '97

George Fitzmaurice(1885-1940)
The Last of Mrs. Cheyney '37
Suzy '36
As You Desire Me '32
Mata Hari '32
Raffles '30
Son of the Sheik '26

Cash Flagg
See Ray Dennis Steckler

Paul Flaherty(1945-)
Clifford '92
Who's Harry Crumb? '89
18 Again! '88

Robert Flaherty(1884-1951)
Louisiana Story '48
Elephant Boy '37
Man of Aran '34
Tabu: A Story of the South Seas '31
Moana, a Romance of the Golden Age '26

Ryan Fleck
Sugar '09
Half Nelson '06

Gary Fleder(1963-)
The Express '08
Runaway Jury '03
Impostor '02
Don't Say a Word '01
From the Earth to the Moon '98
Kiss the Girls '97
Things to Do in Denver When You're Dead '95
The Companion '94

Dave Fleischer(1894-1979)
Hoppity Goes to Town '41
Gulliver's Travels '39

Richard Fleischer(1916-2006)
Million Dollar Mystery '87
Red Sonja '85
Conan the Destroyer '84
Amityville 3: The Demon '83
Tough Enough '83
The Jazz Singer '80
Ashanti, Land of No Mercy '79
The Prince and the Pauper '78
The Incredible Sarah '76
Mandingo '75
Mr. Majestyk '74
The Don Is Dead '73
Soylent Green '73
The New Centurions '72
See No Evil '71
10 Rillington Place '71
Tora! Tora! Tora! '70
The Boston Strangler '68
Doctor Dolittle '67
Fantastic Voyage '66
Barabbas '62
Compulsion '59
The Vikings '58
Between Heaven and Hell '56
The Girl in the Red Velvet Swing '55
20,000 Leagues under the Sea '54
The Narrow Margin '52
Armored Car Robbery '50
The Clay Pigeon '49
Follow Me Quietly '49
Trapped '49

Andrew Fleming(1964-)
Hamlet 2 '08
Nancy Drew '07
The In-Laws '03
Dick '99
The Craft '96
Threesome '94
Bad Dreams '88

Victor Fleming(1883-1949)
Joan of Arc '48
Adventure '45
A Guy Named Joe '44
Tortilla Flat '42
Dr. Jekyll and Mr. Hyde '41
Gone with the Wind '39
The Wizard of Oz '39
Test Pilot '38
Captains Courageous '37
The Farmer Takes a Wife '35
Reckless '35
Treasure Island '34
Bombshell '33
Red Dust '32
The Virginian '29
Hula '28
Mantrap '26
The Mollycoddle '20
When the Clouds Roll By '19

Gordon Flemyng(1934-95)
Cloud Waltzing '87
Philby, Burgess and MacLean: Spy Scandal of the Century '84
Daleks—Invasion Earth 2150 A.D. '66

Rodman Flender(1964-)
Nature of the Beast '07
Idle Hands '99
Leprechaun 2 '94
In the Heat of Passion '91
The Unborn '91

Anne Fletcher
The Proposal '09
27 Dresses '08
Step Up '06

Clive Fleury
Big City Blues '99
Tunnel Vision '95
Fatal Past '94

Theodore J. Flicker(1930-)
Soggy Bottom U.S.A. '84
Playmates '72
Three in the Cellar '70
The President's Analyst '67

James T. Flocker
Ground Zero '88
Ghosts That Still Walk '77
The Secret of Navajo Cave '76

John Florea(1916-2000)
Hot Child in the City '87
Computer Wizard '77
Where's Willie? '77
The Invisible Strangler '76
Where the Eagle Flies '72
Island of the Lost '68

Isaac Florentine
Undisputed II: Last Man Standing '06
Special Forces '03
U.S. Seals 2 '01
Bridge of Dragons '99
Cold Harvest '98
High Voltage '98
The Fighter '95
Desert Kickboxer '92

David Flores
Lake Placid 2 '07
Crimson Force '05

Robert Florey(1900-79)
Outpost in Morocco '49
The Beast with Five Fingers '46
God is My Co-Pilot '45
King of Alcatraz '38
Ex-Lady '33
Murders in the Rue Morgue '32
The Cocoanuts '29

John Flynn(1932-2007)
Protection '01
Absence of the Good '99
Brainscan '94
Scam '93
Nails '92
Out for Justice '91
Lock Up '89
Best Seller '87
Touched '82
Marilyn: The Untold Story '80
Defiance '79
Rolling Thunder '77
The Sergeant '68

Lawrence Foldes(1959-)
Finding Home '03
Pre-Madonnas: Rebels Without a Clue '95
Nightforce '86
Young Warriors '83
The Great Skycopter Rescue '82
Nightstalker '81

Peter Foldy
Seeds of Doubt '96
Tryst '94
Widow's Kiss '94
Midnight Witness '93

Brendan Foley
Legend of the Bog '08
The Riddle '07

James Foley(1953-)
Perfect Stranger '07
Confidence '03
The Corruptor '99
The Chamber '96
Fear '96
Two Bits '96
Glengarry Glen Ross '92
After Dark, My Sweet '90
Who's That Girl? '87
At Close Range '86
Reckless '84

Sheree Folkson
Casanova '05
A Royal Scandal '96

Peter Fonda(1939-)
Wanda Nevada '79
Idaho Transfer '73
Hired Hand '71

Leo Fong(1928-)
Showdown '93
24 Hours to Midnight '92
Hawkeye '88

Jorge Fons(1939-)
Midaq Alley '95
Jory '72

Anne Fontaine(1959-)
Coco Before Chanel '09
The Girl From Monaco '08
How I Killed My Father '03
Nathalie '03
Dry Cleaning '97
Augustin '95

Bryan Forbes(1926-)
The Endless Game '89
The Naked Face '84
Better Late Than Never '83
International Velvet '78
The Slipper and the Rose '76
The Stepford Wives '75
Long Ago Tomorrow '71
The Madwoman of Chaillot '69
The Wrong Box '66
King Rat '65
Seance on a Wet Afternoon '64
The L-Shaped Room '62
Whistle down the Wind '61

John Ford(1895-1973)
December 7th: The Movie '91
Cheyenne Autumn '64
Donovan's Reef '63
How the West Was Won '63
The Man Who Shot Liberty Valance '62
Two Rode Together '61
Sergeant Rutledge '60
The Horse Soldiers '59
Last Hurrah '58
Wings of Eagles '57
The Searchers '56
The Long Gray Line '55
Mister Roberts '55
Mogambo '53
The Sun Shines Bright '53
The Quiet Man '52
What Price Glory? '52
Rio Grande '50
Wagon Master '50
When Willie Comes Marching Home '50
She Wore a Yellow Ribbon '49
Fort Apache '48
The Fugitive '48
Three Godfathers '48
My Darling Clementine '46
They Were Expendable '45
How Green Was My Valley '41
The Grapes of Wrath '40
The Long Voyage Home '40
Drums Along the Mohawk '39
Stagecoach '39
Young Mr. Lincoln '39
Four Men and a Prayer '38
The Hurricane '37
Wee Willie Winkie '37
Mary of Scotland '36
The Prisoner of Shark Island '36
The Informer '35
Steamboat Round the Bend '35
The Whole Town's Talking '35
Judge Priest '34
The Lost Patrol '34
The World Moves On '34
Doctor Bull '33
Pilgrimage '33
Arrowsmith '32
Seas Beneath '31
Up the River '30
Four Sons '28
Hangman's House '28
The Iron Horse '24
Straight Shootin' '17

Philip Ford(1900-76)
Rodeo King and the Senorita '51
Redwood Forest Trail '50
The Vanishing Westerner '50
Outcasts of the Trail '49
Pioneer Marshal '49
Wild Frontier '47
The Inner Circle '46
The Tiger Woman '45

Ron Ford(1958-)
Witchcraft 11: Sisters in Blood '00
The Alien Agenda: Endangered Species '97

Eugene Forde
Sleepers West '41
Charlie Chan's Murder Cruise '40
Michael Shayne: Private Detective '40
Inspector Hornleigh '39
Charlie Chan at Monte Carlo '37
Charlie Chan on Broadway '37
Charlie Chan in London '34

Walter Forde(1896-1984)
The Ghost Train '41
The Secret Four '40
King of the Damned '36
Bulldog Jack '35

Milos Forman(1932-)
Goya's Ghosts '06
Man on the Moon '99
The People vs. Larry Flynt '96
Valmont '89
Amadeus '84
Ragtime '81
Hair '79
One Flew Over the Cuckoo's Nest '75
The Firemen's Ball '68
Loves of a Blonde '65
Black Peter '63

Tom Forman(1893-1926)
The Fighting American '24
The Virginian '23
Shadows '22

Jose Maria Forque
Beyond Erotica '79
Autopsy '74

Marc Forster(1969-)
The Kite Runner '07
Stranger Than Fiction '06
Stay '05
Finding Neverland '04
Monster's Ball '01
Everything Put Together '00

Bill Forsyth(1948-)
Being Human '94
Breaking In '89
Housekeeping '87
Comfort and Joy '84
Local Hero '83
Gregory's Girl '80
That Sinking Feeling '79

Ed Forsyth(1920-2004)
Inferno in Paradise '88
Chesty Anderson USN '76
Superchick '71

John Fortenberry
A Night at the Roxbury '98
Jury Duty '95

Bob Fosse(1927-87)
Star 80 '83
All That Jazz '79
Lenny '74
Cabaret '72
Sweet Charity '69

Giles Foster
The Prince and the Pauper '01
Relative Strangers '99
Coming Home '98
The Rector's Wife '94
Innocent Victim '90
Consuming Passions '88
Dutch Girls '87
Northanger Abbey '87
Hotel du Lac '86
Silas Marner '85

Jodie Foster(1963-)
Home for the Holidays '95
Little Man Tate '91

Lewis R. Foster(1898-1974)
The Sign of Zorro '60
Tonka '58
Dakota Incident '56
Crashout '55
Cavalry Charge '51
El Paso '49
Laurel & Hardy: Blotto '30
Laurel & Hardy: Berth Marks '29
Laurel & Hardy: Men O'War '29

Norman Foster(1900-76)
Crazy Horse and Custer: "The Untold Story" '90
Deathhead Virgin '74

Brighty of the Grand Canyon '67
Indian Paint '64
The Sign of Zorro '60
The Nine Lives of Elfego Baca '58
Davy Crockett and the River Pirates '56
Davy Crockett, King of the Wild Frontier '55
Tell It to the Judge '49
Rachel and the Stranger '48
Journey into Fear '42
Charlie Chan at Treasure Island '39
Mr. Moto Takes a Vacation '39
Mr. Moto's Last Warning '39
Mr. Takes a Vacation '39
Mr. Moto Takes a Chance '38
Mysterious Mr. Moto '38
Thank you, Mr. Moto '37
Think Fast, Mr. Moto '37

Alastair Fothergill
Earth '07
Deep Blue '03

Claude Fournier(1931-)
Tales of the Klondike: The Scorn of Women '87
Dan Candy's Law '73

Gene Fowler, Jr.(1917-98)
The Rebel Set '59
I Married a Monster from Outer Space '58
Showdown at Boot Hill '58
I Was a Teenage Werewolf '57

Eytan Fox(1964-)
The Bubble '06
Yossi & Jagger '02

Wallace Fox(1895-1958)
Guns of Fury '49
Bad Men of the Border '45
Mr. Muggs Rides Again '45
Pillow of Death '45
Dead Man's Eyes '44
The Great Mike '44
Million Dollar Kid '44
Ghost Rider '43
Kid Dynamite '43
Bowery at Midnight '42
The Corpse Vanishes '42
Let's Get Tough '42
'Neath Brooklyn Bridge '42
Smart Alecks '42
Bowery Blitzkrieg '41
Gun Packer '38
Yellow Dust '36
Powdersmoke Range '35

William A. Fraker(1923-)
Legend of the Lone Ranger '81
A Reflection of Fear '72
Monte Walsh '70

Jonathan Frakes(1952-)
The Librarian: Curse of the Judas Chalice '08
The Librarian: Return to King Solomon's Mines '06
Thunderbirds '04
Clockstoppers '02
Star Trek: Insurrection '98
Star Trek: First Contact '96

Freddie Francis(1917-2007)
Dark Tower '87
The Doctor and the Devils '85
The Ghoul '75
Legend of the Werewolf '75
Craze '74
Tales That Witness Madness '73
The Creeping Flesh '72
Tales from the Crypt '72
The Vampire Happening '71
Girly '70
Dracula Has Risen from the Grave '68
They Came from Beyond Space '67
Torture Garden '67
Dr. Terror's House of Horrors '65
The Skull '65
The Evil of Frankenstein '64
Hysteria '64
Day of the Triffids '63
Nightmare '63
The Brain '62
Paranoiac '62

Pietro Francisci(1906-77)
Hercules Unchained '59
Hercules '58
Roland the Mighty '56
Attila '54

Jess (Jesus) Franco(1930-)
Devil Hunter '08
Tender Flesh '97
Faceless '88
Angel of Death '86
Bloody Moon '83
Oasis of the Zombies '82
Revenge in the House of Usher '82
Sex Is Crazy '79
Ilsa, the Wicked Warden '78
Jack the Ripper '76
The Demons '74
Female Vampire '73
The Perverse Countess '73
Rites of Frankenstein '72
The Screaming Dead '72
Count Dracula '71
Virgin among the Living Dead '71
Venus in Furs '70
99 Women '69
The Castle of Fu Manchu '68
Deadly Sanctuary '68
Kiss and Kill '68
Attack of the Robots '66
The Diabolical Dr. Z '65
Dr. Orloff's Monster '64
The Awful Dr. Orloff '62

Ricardo Franco(1949-98)
Berlin Blues '89
In 'n Out '86

Georges Franju(1912-87)
Judex '64
The Horror Chamber of Dr. Faustus '59
The Shadow Man '53

Christopher Frank(1943-93)
L'Annee des Meduses '86
Josepha '82

Hubert Frank(1925-)
The Dolls '83
Melody in Love '78

Melvin Frank(1913-88)
Walk Like a Man '87
Lost and Found '79
The Duchess and the Dirtwater Fox '76
Prisoner of Second Avenue '74
A Touch of Class '73
Buona Sera, Mrs. Campbell '68
Strange Bedfellows '65
The Facts of Life '60
The Jayhawkers '59
Li'l Abner '59
Court Jester '56
Above and Beyond '53

Cyril Frankel(1921-)
Permission To Kill '75
The Trygon Factor '66
The Witches '66
The Very Edge '63
On the Fiddle '61
Make Me an Offer '55
Devil on Horseback '54

David Frankel(1960-)
Marley & Me '08
The Devil Wears Prada '06
Band of Brothers '01
From the Earth to the Moon '98
Miami Rhapsody '95

John Frankenheimer(1930-2002)
Path to War '02
Reindeer Games '00
Ronin '98
George Wallace '97
The Island of Dr. Moreau '96
Andersonville '95
Against the Wall '94
The Burning Season '94
Year of the Gun '91
The Fourth War '90
Dead Bang '89
52 Pick-Up '86
The Holcroft Covenant '85
The Challenge '82
Prophecy '79
Black Sunday '77
French Connection 2 '75
99 & 44/100 Dead '74
The Iceman Cometh '73
The Story of a Love Story '73
The Horsemen '70
I Walk the Line '70
The Gypsy Moths '69
The Fixer '68
Grand Prix '66
Seconds '66
The Train '65
Seven Days in May '64
All Fall Down '62
Birdman of Alcatraz '62
The Manchurian Candidate '62
The Young Savages '61
Days of Wine and Roses '58

Carl Franklin(1949-)
Out of Time '03
High Crimes '02
One True Thing '98
Devil in a Blue Dress '95
Laurel Avenue '93
One False Move '91
Full Fathom Five '90
Eye of the Eagle 2 '89
Nowhere to Run '88

Howard Franklin
Larger Than Life '96
The Public Eye '92
Quick Change '90

Jeff Franklin(1955-)
Love Stinks '99
Double Double Toil and Trouble '94
To Grandmother's House We Go '94

Richard Franklin(1948-)
Visitors '03
Brilliant Lies '96
Sorrento Beach '95
Running Delilah '93
F/X 2: The Deadly Art of Illusion '91
Link '86
Cloak & Dagger '84
Psycho 2 '83
Road Games '81
Patrick '78

Sidney Franklin(1893-1972)
The Good Earth '37
The Dark Angel '35
The Barretts of Wimpole Street '34
Smilin' Through '33
The Guardsman '31
Private Lives '31
Wild Orchids '28
The Duchess of Buffalo '26
The Forbidden City '18
The Primitive Lover '16

Harry Fraser(1889-1974)
Chained for Life '51
Ambush Trail '46
People's Choice '46
Enemy of the Law '45
Flaming Bullets '45
Frontier Fugitives '45
Three in the Saddle '45
Outlaw Roundup '44
Lightning Strikes West '40
Phantom Rancher '39
Six Shootin' Sheriff '38
Aces Wild '37
Galloping Dynamite '37
Ghost Town '37
Heroes of the Alamo '37
The Spirit of Youth '37
Cavalcade of the West '36
The Riding Avenger '36
Feud of the West '35
Fighting Parson '35
Pecos Kid '35
Rustler's Paradise '35
Saddle Aces '35
Social Error '35
The Tonto Kid '35
Wagon Trail '35
Wild Mustang '35
'Neath the Arizona Skies '34
Randy Rides Alone '34
Diamond Trail '33
Rainbow Ranch '33
Wolf Dog '33
Broadway to Cheyenne '32
Ghost City '32
Mason of the Mounted '32
The Savage Girl '32
Texas Pioneers '32
The Wildcat '26

James Frawley(1937-)
Mr. Headmistress '98
Sins of the Mind '97
Spies, Lies and Naked Thighs '91
Assault and Matrimony '87
Fraternity Vacation '85
Hansel and Gretel '82
Great American Traffic Jam '80
The Muppet Movie '79
The Big Bus '76

Stephen Frears(1941-)
Cheri '09
The Queen '06
Mrs. Henderson Presents '05
Dirty Pretty Things '03
Fail Safe '00
High Fidelity '00
Liam '00
The Hi-Lo Country '98
Mary Reilly '95
The Van '95
The Snapper '93
Hero '92
The Grifters '90
Dangerous Liaisons '88
Prick Up Your Ears '87
Saigon: Year of the Cat '87
Sammy & Rosie Get Laid '87
The Hit '85
My Beautiful Laundrette '85
December Flower '84
Gumshoe '72

Riccardo Freda(1909-99)
Double Face '70
The Ghost '63
Devil of the Desert Against the Son of Hercules '62
The Horrible Dr. Hichcock '62
Samson and the 7 Miracles of the World '62
The Giants of Thessaly '60
Maciste in Hell '60
The Mongols '60
I, Vampiri '56
Sins of Rome '54
Les Miserables '52

Herb Freed
Subterfuge '98
Survival Game '87
Tomboy '85
Graduation Day '81
Beyond Evil '80
Haunts '77

Jerrold Freedman(1927-)
Thompson's Last Run '90
Best Kept Secrets '88
Family Sins '87
Native Son '86
Seduced '85
Legs '83
Borderline '80
The Streets of L.A. '79
He Who Walks Alone '78

Thornton Freeland(1898-1987)
Jericho '38
Accused '36
Flying Down to Rio '33
They Call It Sin '32
Be Yourself '30
Whoopee! '30

Joan Freeman(1941-)
Satisfaction '88
Streetwalkin' '85

Morgan Freeman(1937-)
Just Like the Son '06
Bopha! '93

Morgan J. Freeman(1969-)
Homecoming '09
Born Killers '05
American Psycho 2: All American Girl '02
Desert Blue '98
Hurricane Streets '96

Hugo Fregonese(1908-87)
Dracula vs. Frankenstein '69
Apache's Last Battle '64
Harry Black and the Tiger '58
Blowing Wild '54
Decameron Nights '53
Man in the Attic '53
Saddle Tramp '47

Harold French(1900-97)
Paris Express '53
Rob Roy—The Highland Rogue '53
Encore '52
Trio '50
Mr. Emmanuel '44
The Day Will Dawn '42
Secret Mission '42

Charles Frend(1909-77)
The Third Key '57
The Cruel Sea '53
Scott of the Antarctic '48
San Demetrio, London '47
Johnny Frenchman '46
The Foreman Went to France '42

Robert M. Fresco(1928-)
Dirty Little Secret '98
Evil Has a Face '96
Small Kill '93

Juan Carlos Fresnadillo(1967-)
28 Weeks Later '07
Intacto '01

Thor Freudenthal
Diary of a Wimpy Kid '10
Hotel for Dogs '09

Karl Freund(1890-1969)
Mad Love '35
The Mummy '32

Bart Freundlich(1970-)
Trust the Man '06
Catch That Kid '04
World Traveler '01
The Myth of Fingerprints '97

Fridrik Thor Fridriksson(1953-)
Devil's Island '96
Cold Fever '95
Children of Nature '91

Jason Friedberg
Disaster Movie '08
Meet the Spartans '08
Epic Movie '07

Rick Friedberg
Spy Hard '96
Off the Wall '82
Pray TV '80

Richard Friedenberg
Snow in August '01
The Education of Little Tree '97
Mr. & Mrs. Loving '96
The Deerslayer '78
The Adventures of Frontier Fremont '75
Life & Times of Grizzly Adams '74

William Friedkin(1939-)
Bug '06
The Hunted '03
Rules of Engagement '00
Twelve Angry Men '97
Jade '95
Blue Chips '94
Jailbreakers '94
The Guardian '90
Python Wolf '88
Rampage '87
Stalking Danger '86
To Live & Die in L.A. '85
Deal of the Century '83
Cruising '80
Brink's Job '78
Sorcerer '77
The Exorcist '73
The French Connection '71
The Boys in the Band '70
The Night They Raided Minsky's '69
Good Times '67

Lee Friedlander
Out at the Wedding '07
Girl Play '04

Louis Friedlander
See Lew Landers

Jeffrey Friedman
The Celluloid Closet '95
Common Threads: Stories from the Quilt '89

Richard Friedman
Darkwolf '03
Forever Together '00
Phantom of the Mall: Eric's Revenge '89
Doom Asylum '88
Scared Stiff '87
Deathmask '69

Seymour Friedman(1917-)
I'll Get You '53
Loan Shark '52
Counterspy Meets Scotland Yard '50
Rusty's Birthday '49

Harvey Frost
All I Want for Christmas '07
A Grandpa for Christmas '07
Recipe for Disaster '03
National Lampoon's Golf Punks '99
Midnight Heat '95
Tracks of a Killer '95

Lee Frost(1935-2007)
Private Obsession '94
Dixie Dynamite '76
Black Gestapo '75
Policewomen '73
Chain Gang Women '72
The Thing with Two Heads '72
Chrome and Hot Leather '71
Rebel Vixens '69
Love Desperados '68

William Fruet(1933-)
Blue Monkey '87
Bedroom Eyes '86
Killer Party '86
Funeral Home '82

Spasms *'82*
Search and Destroy *'81*
Death Weekend *'76*
Wedding in White *'72*

Robert Fuest(1927-)
Revenge of the Stepford Wives *'80*
Devil's Rain *'75*
The Final Programme *'73*
Doctor Phibes Rises Again *'72*
The Abominable Dr. Phibes *'71*
And Soon the Darkness *'70*
Wuthering Heights *'70*

Kinji Fukasaku(1930-2003)
Fall Guy *'82*
Virus *'82*
Samurai Reincarnation *'81*
Shogun's Samurai—The Yagyu Clan Conspiracy *'78*
Under the Flag of the Rising Sun *'72*
Sympathy for the Underdog *'71*
Tora! Tora! Tora! *'70*
Black Lizard *'68*
The Green Slime *'68*

Jun Fukuda(1924-2000)
Godzilla vs. Megalon *'76*
Godzilla vs. the Cosmic Monster *'74*
Godzilla on Monster Island *'72*
Godzilla vs. the Sea Monster *'66*
Son of Godzilla *'66*
The Secret of the Telegian *'61*

Shozin Fukui
Rubber's Lover *'97*
Pinocchio 964 *'92*

Lucio Fulci(1927-96)
Demonia *'90*
Voices from Beyond *'90*
Dangerous Obsession *'88*
Challenge to White Fang *'86*
El Barbaro *'84*
Conquest *'83*
The House by the Cemetery *'83*
The New Gladiators *'83*
The Beyond *'82*
Manhattan Baby *'82*
New York Ripper *'82*
The Black Cat *'81*
Contraband *'80*
Gates of Hell *'80*
Zombie *'80*
The Psychic *'78*
Don't Torture a Duckling *'72*
A Lizard in a Woman's Skin *'71*

Samuel Fuller(1911-97)
White Dog *'82*
The Big Red One *'80*
Dead Pigeon on Beethoven Street *'72*
Shark! *'68*
The Meanest Men in the West *'67*
Naked Kiss *'64*
Shock Corridor *'63*
Merrill's Marauders *'62*
Underworld USA *'61*
Underworld, U.S.A. *'60*
The Crimson Kimono *'59*
Verboten! *'59*
China Gate *'57*
Forty Guns *'57*
Run of the Arrow *'56*
House of Bamboo *'55*
Pickup on South Street *'53*
Baron of Arizona *'51*
Fixed Bayonets! *'51*
The Steel Helmet *'51*
I Shot Jesse James *'49*

Keith Fulton(1965-)
Brothers of the Head *'06*
Lost in La Mancha *'03*

Antoine Fuqua(1966-)
Brooklyn's Finest *'09*
Shooter *'07*
King Arthur *'04*
Lighting in a Bottle *'04*
Tears of the Sun *'03*
Training Day *'01*
Bait *'00*
The Replacement Killers *'98*

Sidney J. Furie(1933-)
The Veteran *'06*
American Soldiers *'05*
Rock My World *'02*
The Fraternity *'01*
Road Rage *'01*
Under Heavy Fire *'01*
Hide and Seek *'00*
My 5 Wives *'00*
The Collectors *'99*
Top of the World *'97*
The Rage *'96*
Hollow Point *'95*
Iron Eagle 4 *'95*
Ladybugs *'92*
The Taking of Beverly Hills *'91*
Iron Eagle 2 *'88*
Superman 4: The Quest for Peace *'87*
Iron Eagle *'86*
Purple Hearts *'84*
The Entity *'83*
The Boys in Company C *'77*
Hit! *'73*
Lady Sings the Blues *'72*
The Appaloosa *'66*
The Ipcress File *'65*
The Leather Boys *'63*
Doctor Blood's Coffin *'62*
The Snake Woman *'61*
A Dangerous Age *'57*

Stephen Furst(1955-)
Dragon Storm *'04*
Magic Kid 2 *'94*

Tim Fywell(1951-)
Affinity *'08*
Half Broken Things *'07*
Ice Princess *'05*
Cambridge Spies *'03*
I Capture the Castle *'02*
Madame Bovary *'00*
The Ice House *'97*
The Woman in White *'97*
Cracker: Best Boys *'95*
Cracker: True Romance *'95*
Gallowglass *'95*
Norma Jean and Marilyn *'95*
Cracker: To Be a Somebody *'94*
A Dark Adapted Eye *'93*
A Fatal Inversion *'92*

Richard Gabai(1964-)
Miracle Dogs Too *'06*
Virtual Girl *'00*
Vice Girls *'96*
Assault of the Party Nerds 2: Heavy Petting Detective *'95*
Hot Under the Collar *'91*
Virgin High *'90*
Assault of the Party Nerds *'89*

Pal Gabor(1932-87)
Brady's Escape *'84*
Angi Vera *'78*

Radu Gabrea(1937-)
Secret of the Ice Cave *'89*
A Man Like Eva *'83*

Mike Gabriel
Pocahontas *'95*
The Rescuers Down Under *'90*

Stephen Gaghan(1965-)
Syriana *'05*
Abandon *'02*

Rene Gainville(1941-)
The Associate *'79*
Le Complot *'73*

John Gale
The Firing Line *'91*
Commando Invasion *'87*
Slash *'87*

Richard Gale
Pressure *'02*
The Proposal *'00*

Timothy Galfas
Sunnyside *'79*
Fist *'76*
Homeboy *'75*

John A. Gallagher
Blue Moon *'00*
The Deli *'97*
Street Hunter *'90*
Beach House *'82*

Fred Gallo(1965-)
Termination Man *'97*
Machine Gun Blues *'95*
Lady in Waiting *'94*
Dracula Rising *'93*
The Finishing Touch *'92*
Dead Space *'90*

George Gallo(1956-)
My Mom's New Boyfriend *'08*
Local Color *'06*
Double Take *'01*
Trapped in Paradise *'94*
29th Street *'91*

Vincent Gallo(1961-)
The Brown Bunny *'03*
Buffalo 66 *'97*

Samuel Gallu(1918-91)
The Man Outside *'68*
Theatre of Death *'67*

Nisha Ganatra
Cake *'05*
Chutney Popcorn *'99*

Abel Gance(1889-1981)
The Battle of Austerlitz *'60*
J'Accuse *'37*
Beethoven *'36*
Napoleon *'27*
La Roue *'23*
J'accuse! *'19*
The Torture of Silence *'17*

Pierre Gang
Armistead Maupin's More Tales of the City *'97*
Sous Sol *'96*

Albert C. Gannaway(1920-)
Man or Gun *'58*
Daniel Boone: Trail Blazer *'56*
Hidden Guns *'56*

Christophe Gans(1960-)
Silent Hill *'06*
Brotherhood of the Wolf *'01*
H.P. Lovecraft's Necronomicon: Book of the Dead *'93*

Robert Ben Garant(1970-)
Balls of Fury *'07*
Reno 911! Miami *'07*

Nicole Garcia(1946-)
Place Vendome *'98*
The Favorite Son *'94*
Every Other Weekend *'91*

Rodrigo Garcia(1959-)
Mother and Child *'09*
Passengers *'08*
Things You Can Tell Just by Looking at Her *'00*

Yolanda Garcia Serrano(1958-)
Km. 0 *'00*
Amor de Hombre *'97*

Herb Gardner(1934-2003)
I'm Not Rappaport *'96*
The Goodbye People *'83*

Richard Harding Gardner(1949-)
Sherlock: Undercover Dog *'94*
Deadly Daphne's Revenge *'93*

Mario Gariazzo(1930-2002)
White Slave *'86*
Eyes Behind the Stars *'72*

Lee Garmes(1898-1978)
Actors and Sin *'52*
Angels Over Broadway *'40*
Dreaming Lips *'37*

Tay Garnett(1898-1977)
Challenge To Be Free *'76*
The Big Push *'75*
Main Street to Broadway *'53*
One Minute to Zero *'52*
Cause for Alarm *'51*
A Connecticut Yankee in King Arthur's Court *'49*
The Postman Always Rings Twice *'46*
The Valley of Decision *'45*
Mrs. Parkington *'44*
Bataan *'43*
Cheers for Miss Bishop *'41*
Seven Sinners *'40*
Slightly Honorable *'40*
Eternally Yours *'39*
Joy of Living *'38*
Love Is News *'37*
Stand-In *'37*
China Seas *'35*
One Way Passage *'32*
The Flying Fool *'29*

Otis Garrett(1893-1941)
The Black Doll *'38*
Danger on the Air *'38*

Roy Garrett
See Mario Gariazzo

Mick Garris(1951-)
Masters of Horror: Valerie on the Stairs *'06*
Riding the Bullet *'04*
Quicksilver Highway *'98*
Stephen King's The Stand *'94*
Sleepwalkers *'92*
Psycho 4: The Beginning *'90*
Critters 2: The Main Course *'88*

Matteo Garrone
Gomorrah *'08*
The Embalmer *'03*

Harry Garson(1882-1938)
The Worldly Madonna *'22*
Mid-Channel *'20*

Jerome Gary
Traxx *'87*
Stripper *'86*

Louis Gasnier(1875-1963)
Murder on the Yukon *'40*
Reefer Madness *'38*
The Sunset Murder Case *'38*
The Last Outpost *'35*
Gambling Ship *'33*
Topaze *'33*
Parisian Love *'25*
Kismet *'20*

Leon Gast
When We Were Kings *'96*
Hell's Angels Forever *'83*

Robert Gaston
2 Minutes Later *'07*
Open Cam *'05*

Tony Gatlif(1948-)
The Crazy Stranger *'98*
Mondo *'96*

Nils Gaup(1955-)
North Star *'96*
Shipwrecked *'90*
Pathfinder *'87*

Joe Gayton
Sweet Jane *'98*
Wes Craven Presents Mind Ripper *'95*
Warm Summer Rain *'89*

Armand Gazarian
Prison Planet *'92*
Game of Survival *'89*

Gyula Gazdag(1947-)
Stand Off *'89*
A Hungarian Fairy Tale *'87*

Glenn Gebhard
Desert Steel *'94*
One Last Run *'89*
Blood Screams *'88*

Augusto Genina(1892-1957)
Prix de Beaute *'30*
Cyrano de Bergerac *'25*

John Gentil
Battle of Valiant *'63*
Pirates of Blood River *'62*

Giacomo Gentilomo(1909-2001)
Hercules against the Moon Men *'64*
Young Caruso *'51*

Terry George(1952-)
Reservation Road *'07*
Hotel Rwanda *'04*
A Bright Shining Lie *'98*
Some Mother's Son *'96*

Fred Gerber
Prison of Secrets *'97*
Closer and Closer *'96*
Rent-A-Kid *'95*

Marion Gering
Thunder in the City *'37*
Thirty Day Princess *'34*
The Devil and the Deep *'32*

Pietro Germi(1904-74)
Alfredo, Alfredo *'72*
Seduced and Abandoned *'64*
Divorce—Italian Style *'62*
Four Ways Out *'57*

Clyde Geronimi(1901-89)
101 Dalmatians *'61*
Sleeping Beauty *'59*
Lady and the Tramp *'55*
Alice in Wonderland *'51*
The Adventures of Ichabod and Mr. Toad *'49*
The Legend of Sleepy Hollow *'49*
Melody Time *'48*

Peter Gerretsen
Kidnapping of Baby John Doe *'88*
Night Friend *'87*

Theodore Gershuny
Silent Night, Bloody Night *'73*
Kemek *'70*

Nicolas Gessner(1931-)
Black Water *'94*
Quicker Than the Eye *'88*
It Rained All Night the Day I Left *'78*
The Little Girl Who Lives down the Lane *'76*
Someone Behind the Door *'71*
12 Plus 1 *'70*
The Peking Blond *'68*

Steven Gethers(1922-89)
The Hillside Strangler *'89*
Jenny's War *'85*
Jacqueline Bouvier Kennedy *'81*
Damien: The Leper Priest *'80*
Billy: Portrait of a Street Kid *'77*

Bahman Ghobadi(1968-)
Turtles Can Fly *'04*
Marooned in Iraq *'02*

Francis Giacobetti
Emmanuelle 4 *'84*
Emmanuelle, the Joys of a Woman *'76*

David Giancola(1969-)
Diamond Run *'00*
Peril *'00*
Time Chasers *'95*

Ettore Giannini
Neapolitan Carousel *'54*
Neapolitan Carousel *'54*

Duncan Gibbins(1952-93)
A Case for Murder *'93*
Eve of Destruction *'90*
Fire with Fire *'86*

Cedric Gibbons(1893-1960)
Desert Nights *'29*
A Lady of Chance *'28*

Rodney Gibbons
The Sign of Four *'01*
The Hound of the Baskervilles *'00*
Wilder *'00*
The Pact *'99*
Little Men *'98*
Captive *'97*
Stranger in the House *'97*
The Neighbor *'93*

Gwyneth Gibby
Isaac Asimov's Nightfall *'00*
Marquis de Sade *'96*

Alex Gibney
Gonzo: The Life and Work of Dr. Hunter S. Thompson *'08*
Taxi to the Dark Side *'07*
Enron: The Smartest Guys in the Room *'05*

Alan Gibson(1938-87)
The Charmer *'87*
Martin's Day *'85*
Silent Scream *'84*
The Two Faces of Evil *'82*
A Woman Called Golda *'82*
Churchill and the Generals *'81*
The Satanic Rites of Dracula *'73*
Dracula A.D. 1972 *'72*
Twinsanity *'70*
Crescendo *'69*

Brian Gibson(1944-2004)
Still Crazy *'98*
The Juror *'96*
What's Love Got to Do with It? *'93*
Drug Wars: The Camarena Story *'90*
The Josephine Baker Story *'90*
Murderers Among Us: The Simon Wiesenthal Story *'89*
Poltergeist 2: The Other Side *'86*
Breaking Glass *'80*

Mel Gibson(1956-)
Apocalypto *'06*
The Passion of the Christ *'04*
Braveheart *'95*
The Man Without a Face *'93*

Coky Giedroyc
Wuthering Heights *'09*
Oliver Twist *'07*
Carrie's War *'04*
Stella Does Tricks *'96*

Gregory Gieras
Centipede *'05*
Dark Asylum *'01*
The Prince and the Surfer *'99*
The Whispering *'94*

Tony Giglio(1971-)
In Enemy Hands *'04*
Soccer Dog: The Movie *'98*

Tormented '60
Attack of the Puppet People '58
Earth vs. the Spider '58
The War of the Colossal Beast '58
The Amazing Colossal Man '57
Beginning of the End '57
Cyclops '56
King Dinosaur '55

Bette Gordon(1950-)
Luminous Motion '00
Variety '83

Bryan Gordon
Pie in the Sky '95
Career Opportunities '91
The Discovery Program '89

Dennie Gordon
New York Minute '04
What a Girl Wants '03
Joe Dirt '01

Josh Gordon
The Switch '10
Blades of Glory '07

Keith Gordon(1961-)
The Singing Detective '03
Waking the Dead '00
Mother Night '96
Wild Palms '93
A Midnight Clear '92
The Chocolate War '88

Michael Gordon(1911-93)
The Impossible Years '68
Texas Across the River '66
For Love or Money '63
Move Over, Darling '63
Boys' Night Out '62
Portrait in Black '60
Pillow Talk '59
Cyrano de Bergerac '50
Underground Agent '42

Robert Gordon(1895-1971)
The Gatling Gun '72
It Came from Beneath the Sea '55
The Joe Louis Story '53

Seth Gordon
Four Christmases '08
The King of Kong: A Fistful of Quarters '07

Stuart Gordon(1947-)
Stuck '07
Edmond '05
Masters of Horror: Dreams in the Witch House '05
King of the Ants '03
The Wonderful Ice Cream Suit '98
Space Truckers '97
Castle Freak '95
Fortress '93
The Pit & the Pendulum '91
Robot Jox '90
Daughter of Darkness '89
Dolls '87
From Beyond '86
Re-Animator '84

Laurence Gordon Clark
See Lawrence Gordon-Clark

Lawrence Gordon-Clark
Jack Higgins' Midnight Man '96
Jack Higgins' On Dangerous Ground '95
Monkey Boy '90
Magic Moments '89
Romance on the Orient Express '89
Belfast Assassin '84
Jamaica Inn '82
Flambards '78

Lisa Gornick
Tick Tock Lullaby '07
Do I Love You? '02

John Gorrie(1932-)
Like A Bride '94
Cause Celebre '87
Edward the King '75
Macbeth '70

Marleen Gorris(1948-)
Carolina '03
The Luzhin Defence '00
Mrs. Dalloway '97
Antonia's Line '95
Broken Mirrors '85
Question of Silence '83

Hideo Gosha(1929-92)
The Wolves '82
Hunter in the Dark '80
Goyokin '69

Jurgen Goslar(1927-)
Slavers '77
Albino '76

Raja Gosnell(1968-)
Beverly Hills Chihuahua '08
Yours, Mine & Ours '05
Scooby-Doo 2: Monsters Unleashed '04
Scooby-Doo '02
Big Momma's House '00
Never Been Kissed '99
Home Alone 3 '97

Andrew Goth
Cold and Dark '05
B.U.S.T.E.D. '99

Carl Gottlieb(1938-)
Amazon Women on the Moon '87
Caveman '81

Franz Gottlieb(1930-2006)
The Phantom of Soho '64
The Black Abbot '63
Curse of the Yellow Snake '63

Lisa Gottlieb
Cadillac Ranch '96
Across the Moon '94
Just One of the Guys '85

Michael Gottlieb
A Kid in King Arthur's Court '95
Mr. Nanny '93
Mannequin '87

Heywood Gould
Double Bang '01
Mistrial '96
Trial by Jury '94
One Good Cop '91

Alfred Goulding(1896-1972)
Dick Barton, Special Agent '48
A Yank in Australia '43
A Chump at Oxford '40

Edmund Goulding(1891-1959)
We're Not Married '52
Nightmare Alley '47
The Razor's Edge '46
Forever and a Day '43
The Great Lie '41
Dark Victory '39
The Old Maid '39
Dawn Patrol '38
That Certain Woman '37
Riptide '34
Grand Hotel '32
Reaching for the Moon '31

Anne Goursaud
Another 9 1/2 Weeks '96
Embrace of the Vampire '95
Poison Ivy 2: Lily '95
Red Shoe Diaries 6: How I Met My Husband '95

David S. Goyer(1965-)
The Unborn '09
The Invisible '07
Blade: Trinity '04
ZigZag '02

Marc Gracie
Jigsaw '90
A Kink in the Picasso '90

Gustavo Graef-Marino
Instinct to Kill '01
Diplomatic Siege '99
Johnny 100 Pesos '93

Todd Graff(1959-)
Bandslam '09
Camp '03

William A. Graham(1930-)
Blood Crime '02
Acceptable Risk '01
The Man Who Captured Eichmann '96
Return to the Blue Lagoon '91
Montana '90
Gore Vidal's Billy the Kid '89
Proud Men '87
George Washington: The Forging of a Nation '86
Last Days of Frank & Jesse James '86
Calendar Girl Murders '84
Secrets of a Married Man '84
Harry Tracy '83
M.A.D.D.: Mothers Against Drunk Driving '83
The Guyana Tragedy: The Story of Jim Jones '80
Rage '80
Orphan Train '79
And I Alone Survived '78
One in a Million: The Ron LeFlore Story '78
The Amazing Howard Hughes '77
21 Hours at Munich '76
Beyond the Bermuda Triangle '75
Get Christie Love! '74
Larry '74
Mr. Inside, Mr. Outside '74
Where the Lilies Bloom '74
Birds of Prey '72
Deadly Encounter '72
Honky '71
Jigsaw '71
Thief '71
Change of Habit '69
Then Came Bronson '68
Waterhole Number 3 '67
The Doomsday Flight '66

Pierre Granier-Deferre(1927-2007)
A Woman at Her Window '77
The French Detective '75
Le Chat '75
The Last Train '74
Widow Couderc '74

Debra Granik
Winter's Bone '10
Down to the Bone '04

Brian Grant
The Immortals '95
Sensation '94
Love Kills '91
Sweet Poison '91

Darren Grant
Make It Happen '08
Diary of a Mad Black Woman '05

Julian Grant
Airborne '98
Electra '95

Lee Grant(1927-)
The Loretta Claiborne Story '00
Staying Together '89
Tell Me a Riddle '80

Alex Grasshof(1930-)
A Billion for Boris '90
Pepper and His Wacky Taxi '72

Jorge Grau(1930-)
Let Sleeping Corpses Lie '74
The Legend of Blood Castle '72

Walter Grauman(1922-)
Nightmare on the 13th Floor '90
Outrage! '86
Scene of the Crime '85
Pleasure Palace '80
To Race the Wind '80
Are You in the House Alone? '78
Most Wanted '76
Force Five '75
Manhunter '74
The Streets of San Francisco '72
Paper Man '71
They Call It Murder '71
Lady in a Cage '64
633 Squadron '64

Gary Graver(1938-2006)
The Escort '97
Sexual Roulette '96
Evil Spirits '91
Roots of Evil '91
Crossing the Line '90
Party Camp '87
Moon in Scorpio '86
Trick or Treats '82
Texas Lightning '81

Alex Graves
Casualties '97
The Crude Oasis '95

F. Gary Gray(1969-)
Law Abiding Citizen '09
Be Cool '05
The Italian Job '03
A Man Apart '03
The Negotiator '98
Set It Off '96
Friday '95

James Gray(1969-)
Two Lovers '09
We Own the Night '07
The Yards '00
Little Odessa '94

John Gray
Brian's Song '01
The Seventh Stream '01
The Hunley '99
The Glimmer Man '96
Born to Be Wild '95
A Place for Annie '94
An American Story '92
The Lost Capone '90
When He's Not a Stranger '89
Billy Galvin '86

Godfrey Grayson(1913-98)
Room to Let '49
Dick Barton Strikes Back '48

Kjell Grede(1936-)
Good Evening, Mr. Wallenberg '93
Hip Hip Hurrah! '87

Alfred E. Green(1889-1960)
Invasion U.S.A. '52
The Jackie Robinson Story '50
Four Faces West '48
Copacabana '47
The Fabulous Dorseys '47
The Jolson Story '46
A Thousand and One Nights '45
Mr. Winkle Goes to War '44
South of Pago Pago '40
The Gracie Allen Murder Case '39
The Duke of West Point '38
Thoroughbreds Don't Cry '37
Colleen '36
They Met in a Taxi '36
Dangerous '35
Baby Face '33
Union Depot '32
Smart Money '31
Disraeli '30
Ella Cinders '26

Bruce Seth Green
In Self Defense '93

The Hunt for the Night Stalker '91
Running Against Time '90
Rags to Riches '87

David Green(1948-)
Breathtaking '00
Fire Birds '90
Buster '88
Car Trouble '86
Car Trouble '85
Code of Honor '84

David Gordon Green(1975-)
Pineapple Express '08
Snow Angels '07
Undertow '04
All the Real Girls '03

Guy Green(1913-2005)
Strong Medicine '84
The Incredible Journey of Dr. Meg Laurel '79
Once Is Not Enough '75
Luther '74
Walk in the Spring Rain '70
A Patch of Blue '65
Diamond Head '62
The Mark '61
S.O.S. Pacific '60
Sea of Sand '58
Postmark for Danger '56
River Beat '54

Jack N. Green(1946-)
Seduced: Pretty When You Cry '01
Traveller '96

Joseph Green(1900-96)
The Brain that Wouldn't Die '63
A Brivele der Mamen '38
Mamele '38
Der Purimshpiler '37
Yidl Mitn Fidl '36

Terry Green
Heavens Fall '06
Cold Justice '89

Peter Greenaway(1942-)
8 1/2 Women '99
The Pillow Book '95
The Belly of an Architect '91
Prospero's Books '91
The Cook, the Thief, His Wife & Her Lover '90
A Zed & Two Noughts '88
Drowning by Numbers '87
The Draughtsman's Contract '82

David Greene(1921-2003)
Bella Mafia '97
Family of Cops 2: Breach of Faith '97
A Good Day to Die '95
What Ever Happened To... '93
In a Stranger's Hand '92
The Penthouse '92
Small Sacrifices '89
Vanishing Act '88
After the Promise '87
The Betty Ford Story '87
Miles to Go '86
World War III '86
Guilty Conscience '85
TripleCross '85
Fatal Vision '84
The Guardian '84
Prototype '83
Rehearsal for Murder '82
Take Your Best Shot '82
The Choice '81
Hard Country '81
Friendly Fire '79
Gray Lady Down '77
Roots '77
The Count of Monte Cristo '74
Godspell '73
Madame Sin '71
The People Next Door '70
Blood Island '68
Sebastian '68

Martin Greene
Undercover Cop '94
Dark Sanity '82

Luke Greenfield(1972-)
The Girl Next Door '04
The Animal '01

Paul Greengrass(1955-)
Green Zone '10
The Bourne Ultimatum '07
United 93 '06
The Bourne Supremacy '04
Bloody Sunday '01
The Murder of Stephen Lawrence '99
The Theory of Flight '98
The One That Got Away '96

Maggie Greenwald(1955-)
Get a Clue '02
Songcatcher '99
The Ballad of Little Jo '93
The Kill-Off '90
Home Remedy '88

Robert Greenwald(1948-)
Wal-Mart: The High Cost of Low Price '05
Outfoxed: Rupert Murdoch's War on Journalism '04
Uncovered: The War on Iraq '04
Steal This Movie! '00
Breaking Up '97
A Woman of Independent Means '94
Hear No Evil '93
Forgotten Prisoners '90
Sweet Hearts Dance '88
Shattered Spirits '86
The Burning Bed '85
In the Custody of Strangers '82
Xanadu '80
Flatbed Annie and Sweetiepie: Lady Truckers '79

David Greenwalt(1949-)
Rude Awakening '89
Secret Admirer '85

William Grefe(1930-)
Whiskey Mountain '77
Jaws of Death '76
Impulse '74
Alligator Alley '72
Stanley '72
Wild Rebels '71
The Hooked Generation '69
The Death Curse of Tartu '66
The Checkered Flag '63

Colin Gregg(1947-)
We Think the World of You '88
Lamb '85
To the Lighthouse '83
Trespasser '81

Ezio Greggio(1954-)
Screw Loose '99
Silence of the Hams '93

Jean Gremillon(1901-59)
Pattes Blanches '49
Stormy Waters '41

Marc S. Grenier
Hidden Agenda '01
Cause of Death '00
Fallen Angel '99
Stalker '98

Edmond T. Greville(1906-66)
The Liars '64
Beat Girl '60
The Hands of Orlac '60
Princess Tam Tam '35

John Greyson(1960-)
Lilies '96
Zero Patience '94

Sergio Grieco(1917-82)
Mad Dog '84
Mad Dog Killer '77

The Devil's Disciple *'59*
The Colditz Story *'55*

John Hamilton

Codename: Jaguar *'00*
Perpetrators of the Crime *'98*
The Kid *'97*

Strathford Hamilton(1952-)

Escape from Atlantis *'97*
The Proposition *'96*
The Set Up *'95*
Temptation *'94*
Betrayal of the Dove *'92*
Diving In *'90*
Blueberry Hill *'88*

Nick Hamm(1957-)

Godsend *'04*
The Hole *'01*
The Very Thought of You *'98*
Talk of Angels *'96*

Peter Hammond(1923-)

The Dark Angel *'91*
The Maze *'85*
Cold Comfort Farm *'71*

Christopher Hampton(1946-)

Imagining Argentina *'04*
The Secret Agent *'96*
Carrington *'95*

Robert Hampton

See Riccardo Freda

Sanaa Hamri

The Sisterhood of the Traveling Pants 2 *'08*
Something New *'06*

Victor Hanbury(1954-)

Hotel Reserve *'44*
The Avenging Hand *'36*

John Hancock(1939-)

Suspended Animation *'02*
Prancer *'89*
Steal the Sky *'88*
Weeds *'87*
California Dreaming *'79*
Bang the Drum Slowly *'73*
Let's Scare Jessica to Death *'71*

John Lee Hancock(1957-)

The Blind Side *'09*
The Alamo *'04*
The Rookie *'02*

David Hand(1900-86)

Bambi *'42*
Snow White and the Seven Dwarfs *'37*

Michael Haneke(1942-)

The White Ribbon *'09*
Funny Games *'07*
Hidden *'05*
Time of the Wolf *'03*
The Piano Teacher *'01*
Code Unknown *'00*
Funny Games *'97*
Benny's Video *'92*

Susumu Hani

Green Horizon *'80*
She and He *'63*

Tom Hanks(1956-)

Band of Brothers *'01*
From the Earth to the Moon *'98*
That Thing You Do! *'96*
Fallen Angels 2 *'93*

William Hanna(1910-2001)

Jetsons: The Movie *'90*
Hey There, It's Yogi Bear *'64*

Ken Hannam(1929-2004)

The Assassination Run *'84*
Dawn! *'83*
Sunday Too Far Away *'74*

Marion Hansel(1949-)

The Quarry *'98*
Between Heaven and Earth *'93*
Dust *'85*

Ed Hansen(1937-)

Hell's Belles *'95*
The Bikini Car Wash Company *'90*
Party Plane *'90*
Party Favors *'89*
Robo-Chic *'89*

Curtis Hanson(1945-)

Lucky You *'07*
In Her Shoes *'05*
8 Mile *'02*
Wonder Boys *'00*
L.A. Confidential *'97*
The River Wild *'94*
The Hand that Rocks the Cradle *'92*
Bad Influence *'90*
The Bedroom Window *'87*
The Children of Times Square *'86*
Losin' It *'82*
Little Dragons *'80*
The Arousers *'70*

John Hanson(1922-98)

Wildrose *'85*
Northern Lights *'79*

Masato Harada

Inugami *'01*
Rowing Through *'96*

Tomoo Haraguchi

Kibakichi *'04*
Kibakichi 2 *'04*

C.B. Harding

Bait Shop *'08*
Delta Farce *'07*

Sarah Harding

Dead Gorgeous *'02*
Reckless *'97*

Gary Hardwick

Deliver Us from Eva *'03*
The Brothers *'01*

Catherine Hardwicke(1955-)

Twilight *'08*
The Nativity Story *'06*
Lords of Dogtown *'05*
Thirteen *'03*

Joseph Hardy(1929-90)

To Love Again *'80*
Love's Savage Fury *'79*
Return Engagement *'78*
Users *'78*
Man of Destiny *'73*

Robin Hardy(1929-)

The Fantasist *'89*
The Wicker Man *'75*

Rod Hardy(1949-)

December Boys *'07*
High Noon *'00*
Two for Texas *'97*
Buffalo Girls *'95*
The Yearling *'94*
Under Capricorn *'82*
Sara Dane *'81*
Thirst *'79*

David Hare(1947-)

The Designated Mourner *'97*
Strapless *'90*
Wetherby *'85*

Tsui Hark(1951-)

Black Mask 2: City of Masks *'02*
Zu Warriors *'01*
Time and Tide *'00*
Knock Off *'98*
Double Team *'97*
Green Snake *'93*
Once Upon a Time in China III *'93*
Once Upon a Time in China II *'92*
Twin Dragons *'92*
Once Upon a Time in China *'91*
A Better Tomorrow, Part 3 *'89*
Mad Mission 3 *'84*
Zu: Warriors from the Magic Mountain *'83*

Veit Harlan(1899-1964)

The Third Sex *'57*
Kolberg *'45*
Jud Suess *'40*

Renny Harlin(1959-)

12 Rounds *'09*
Cleaner *'07*
The Covenant *'06*
Mindhunters *'05*
Exorcist: The Beginning *'04*
Driven *'01*
Deep Blue Sea *'99*
The Long Kiss Goodnight *'96*
Cutthroat Island *'95*
Cliffhanger *'93*
The Adventures of Ford Fairlane *'90*
Die Hard 2: Die Harder *'90*
A Nightmare on Elm Street 4: Dream Master *'88*
Prison *'88*
Born American *'86*

John Harlow(1896-1977)

Those People Next Door *'52*
Old Mother Riley, Headmistress *'50*
Old Mother Riley's New Venture *'49*
While I Live *'47*
Appointment with Crime *'45*
Echo Murders *'45*
Candles at Nine *'44*
Meet Sexton Blake *'44*
Spellbound *'41*

Robert Harmon

Jesse Stone: Thin Ice *'09*
Jesse Stone: Sea Change *'07*
Jesse Stone: Death in Paradise *'06*
Jesse Stone: Night Passage *'06*
Jesse Stone: Stone Cold *'05*
Ike: Countdown to D-Day *'04*
Highwaymen *'03*
Wes Craven Presents: They *'02*
The Crossing *'00*
Gotti *'96*
Nowhere to Run *'93*
Eyes of an Angel *'91*
The Hitcher *'86*

Curtis Harrington(1928-2007)

Devil Dog: The Hound of Hell *'78*
Ruby *'77*
The Dead Don't Die *'75*
The Killing Kind *'73*
What's the Matter with Helen? *'71*
Who Slew Auntie Roo? *'71*
Games *'67*
Planet of Blood *'66*
Voyage to the Prehistoric Planet *'65*
Night Tide *'63*

Damian Harris(1958-)

Gardens of the Night *'08*
Mercy *'00*
Bad Company *'94*
Deceived *'91*
The Discovery Program *'89*
The Rachel Papers *'89*

Ed Harris(1949-)

Appaloosa *'08*
Pollock *'00*

Frank Harris

Lockdown *'90*
Aftershock *'88*
The Patriot *'86*
Killpoint *'84*

Harry Harris(1922-)

Alice in Wonderland *'85*
A Day for Thanks on Walton's Mountain *'82*
The Runaways *'75*

James B. Harris(1928-)

Boiling Point *'93*
Cop *'88*
Fast Walking *'82*
Some Call It Loving *'73*
Black Box Affair *'66*
Bedford Incident *'65*

Trent Harris(1952-)

Plan 10 from Outer Space *'95*
Rubin & Ed *'92*

Greg Harrison(1969-)

November *'05*
Groove *'00*

John Harrison

Clive Barker's Book of Blood *'08*
Dune *'00*
The Assassination File *'96*
Donor Unknown *'95*
Tales from the Darkside: The Movie *'90*

John Kent Harrison

The Courageous Heart of Irena Sendler *'09*
Helen of Troy *'03*
In Love and War *'01*
A House Divided *'00*
You Know My Name *'99*
What the Deaf Man Heard *'98*
William Faulkner's Old Man *'97*
Hole in the Sky *'95*
Johnny's Girl *'95*
City Boy *'93*
The Sound and the Silence *'93*
Beautiful Dreamers *'92*

Ken Harrison(1942-)

On Valentine's Day *'86*
1918 *'85*

Matthew Harrison(1960-)

Kicked in the Head *'97*
Rhythm Thief *'94*
Spare Me *'92*

Mary Harron(1953-)

The Notorious Bettie Page *'06*
American Psycho *'99*
I Shot Andy Warhol *'96*

Lee Harry

Street Soldiers *'91*
Silent Night, Deadly Night 2 *'87*

Harvey Hart(1928-89)

Passion in Paradise *'89*
Stone Fox *'87*
Beverly Hills Madam *'86*
Reckless Disregard *'84*
Utilities *'83*
Born Beautiful *'82*
High Country *'81*
Aliens Are Coming *'80*
East of Eden *'80*
Standing Tall *'78*
Goldenrod *'77*
The Prince of Central Park *'77*
The City *'76*
Shoot *'76*
Murder or Mercy *'74*
Panic on the 5:22 *'74*
The Pyx *'73*
Fortune and Men's Eyes *'71*

William S. Hart(1864-1946)

The Cradle of Courage *'20*
Blue Blazes Rawden *'18*
Narrow Trail *'17*
Hell's Hinges *'16*
Return of Draw Egan *'16*
The Disciple *'15*
The Fugitive: Taking of Luke McVane *'15*

Kenneth Hartford

Hell Squad *'85*
The Lucifer Complex *'78*

Robert Hartford-Davis(1923-77)

Black Gunn *'72*
The Fiend *'71*
The Bloodsuckers *'70*
Estate of Insanity *'64*

Karl Hartl(1898-1978)

The Life and Loves of Mozart *'59*
The Mozart Story *'48*
F.P. 1 *'33*
F.P. 1 Doesn't Answer *'33*

Hal Hartley(1959-)

Fay Grim *'06*
No Such Thing *'01*
Henry Fool *'98*
Flirt *'95*
Amateur *'94*
Simple Men *'92*
Surviving Desire *'91*
Trust *'91*
The Unbelievable Truth *'90*

Don Hartman(1900-58)

Mr. Imperium *'51*
Holiday Affair *'49*
Every Girl Should Be Married *'48*

Anthony Harvey(1931-)

Grace Quigley *'84*
Svengali *'83*
Richard's Things *'80*
Eagle's Wing *'79*
Players *'79*
The Disappearance of Aimee *'76*
The Abdication *'74*
They Might Be Giants *'71*
The Lion in Winter *'68*
Dutchman *'67*

Grant Harvey(1966-)

Freezer Burn: The Invasion of Laxdale *'08*
Ginger Snaps Back: The Beginning *'04*

Byron Haskin(1899-1984)

Demon with a Glass Hand *'64*
Robinson Crusoe on Mars *'64*
Captain Sinbad *'63*
Armored Command *'61*
Jet Over the Atlantic *'59*
From the Earth to the Moon *'58*
The First Texan *'56*
Conquest of Space *'55*
Long John Silver *'54*
Naked Jungle *'54*
His Majesty O'Keefe *'53*
The War of the Worlds *'53*
The Denver & Rio Grande *'51*
Tarzan's Peril *'51*
Treasure Island *'50*
Too Late for Tears *'49*

Masanori Hata

The Adventures of Milo & Otis *'89*
Milo & Otis *'89*

Henry Hathaway(1898-1985)

Raid on Rommel *'71*
Shoot Out *'71*
True Grit *'69*
Five Card Stud *'68*
The Last Safari *'67*
Nevada Smith *'66*
Sons of Katie Elder *'65*
Circus World *'64*
Of Human Bondage *'64*
How the West Was Won *'63*
North to Alaska *'60*
Seven Thieves *'60*
Legend of the Lost *'57*
23 Paces to Baker Street *'56*
The Racers *'55*
Garden of Evil *'54*
Prince Valiant *'54*
Diplomatic Courier *'52*
Niagara *'52*
The Desert Fox *'51*
The Black Rose *'50*
Rawhide *'50*
Call Northside 777 *'48*
Kiss of Death *'47*
Dark Corner *'46*
13 Rue Madeleine *'46*
House on 92nd Street *'45*
A Wing and a Prayer *'44*
The Shepherd of the Hills *'41*
Sundown *'41*
Brigham Young: Frontiersman *'40*
The Real Glory *'39*
Spawn of the North *'38*
Souls at Sea *'37*
Go West, Young Man *'36*
The Trail of the Lonesome Pine *'36*
The Lives of a Bengal Lancer *'35*
Now and Forever *'34*
Buffalo Stampede *'33*
Heritage of the Desert *'33*
Man of the Forest *'33*
To the Last Man *'33*
When the West Was Young *'32*

Jeff Hathcock

Three Bad Men *'05*
Night Ripper *'86*

Wings Hauser(1948-)

Gang Boys *'97*
Living to Die *'91*
The Art of Dying *'90*
Coldfire *'90*

Mary Haverstick

Home *'08*
Shades of Black *'93*

James Hawes

Fanny Hill *'07*
The Chatterley Affair *'06*

Ethan Hawke(1971-)

The Hottest State *'06*
Chelsea Walls *'01*

Howard Hawks(1896-1977)

Rio Lobo *'70*
El Dorado *'67*
Red Line 7000 *'65*
Man's Favorite Sport? *'63*
Hatari! *'62*
Rio Bravo *'59*
Land of the Pharaohs *'55*
Gentlemen Prefer Blondes *'53*
The Big Sky *'52*
Monkey Business *'52*
The Thing *'51*
I Was a Male War Bride *'49*
Red River *'48*
A Song Is Born *'48*
The Big Sleep *'46*
To Have & Have Not *'44*
Air Force *'43*
Ball of Fire *'41*
Sergeant York *'41*
His Girl Friday *'40*
Only Angels Have Wings *'39*
Bringing Up Baby *'38*
Come and Get It *'36*
Barbary Coast *'35*
Ceiling Zero *'35*
Twentieth Century *'34*
Today We Live *'33*
Tiger Shark *'32*
Criminal Code *'31*
Scarface *'31*
A Girl in Every Port *'28*

Richard Haydn(1905-85)

Mr. Music *'50*
Dear Wife *'49*
Miss Tatlock's Millions *'48*

Sidney Hayers(1921-2000)

Deadly Strangers *'82*
The Seekers *'79*
Bananas Boat *'78*
One Away *'76*
King Arthur, the Young Warlord *'75*

Revenge '71
Assault '70
Trap '66
Burn Witch, Burn! '62
Circus of Horrors '60

John Hayes(1930-2000)

End of the World '76
Mama's Dirty Girls '74
Grave of the Vampire '72
Tomb of the Undead '72
All the Lovin' Kinfolk '70
Corruption '70
Dream No Evil '70
Sweet Trash '70
The Cut Throats '69
Five Minutes to Love '63

John Patrick Hayes(1930-2000)

The Farmer's Other Daughter '65
Hollywood after Dark '65

David Hayman(1950-)

The Hawk '93
A Woman's Guide to Adultery '93

Peter Hayman

Cybercity '99
Shepherd '99

Gregory C. Haynes(1968-)

Cowboys and Angels '00
Heaven or Vegas '98
Magenta '96

Todd Haynes(1961-)

I'm Not There '07
Far from Heaven '02
Velvet Goldmine '98
Safe '95
Poison '91

Jimmy Hayward

Jonah Hex '10
Dr. Seuss' Horton Hears a Who! '08

Jonathan Heap

Greenmail '01
Past Perfect '98
Hostile Intent '97
Benefit of the Doubt '93

David Heavener(1958-)

Fugitive X '96
Dragon Fury '95
Eye of the Stranger '93
Prime Target '91
Deadly Reactor '89
Killcrazy '89
Twisted Justice '89
Outlaw Force '87

Ben Hecht(1894-1964)

Actors and Sin '52
Spectre of the Rose '46
Angels Over Broadway '40

Amy Heckerling(1954-)

I Could Never Be Your Woman '06
Loser '00
Clueless '95
Look Who's Talking, Too '90
Look Who's Talking '89
National Lampoon's European Vacation '85
Johnny Dangerously '84
Fast Times at Ridgemont High '82

Rob Hedden(1954-)

Alien Fury: Countdown to Invasion '00
Kidnapped in Paradise '98
Any Place But Home '97
The Colony '95
Friday the 13th, Part 8: Jason Takes Manhattan '89

Peter Hedges(1962-)

Dan in Real Life '07
Pieces of April '03

Richard T. Heffron(1930-2007)

Tagget '90
Broken Angel '88
Pancho Barnes '88
Convicted: A Mother's Story '87
Guilty of Innocence '87
Samaritan: The Mitch Snyder Story '86
V: The Final Battle '84
I, the Jury '82
Whale for the Killing '81
Foolin' Around '80
A Rumor of War '80
See How She Runs '78
Outlaw Blues '77
Futureworld '76
Death Scream '75
I Will Fight No More Forever '75
The California Kid '74
Newman's Law '74

Chris Hegedus(1952-)

Only the Strong Survive '03
Moon over Broadway '98
The War Room '93

Yosif Heifitz(1905-95)

The Lady with the Dog '59
Baltic Deputy '37

Stuart Heisler(1894-1979)

Hitler '62
The Burning Hills '56
Lone Ranger '56
I Died a Thousand Times '55
Island of Desire '52
Storm Warning '51
Chain Lightning '50
Tokyo Joe '49
Tulsa '49
Smash-Up: The Story of a Woman '47
Blue Skies '46
Along Came Jones '45
The Glass Key '42
The Monster and the Girl '41

Mats Helge

The Russian Terminator '90
Ninja Mission '84

Brian Helgeland(1961-)

The Order '03
A Knight's Tale '01
Payback '98

Martin Hellberg(1905-99)

Minna von Barnhelm or The Soldier's Fortune '62
Intrigue and Love '59

Olle Hellbom(1925-82)

Brothers Lionheart '77
Pippi in the South Seas '70
Pippi on the Run '70
Pippi Goes on Board '69
Pippi Longstocking '69

Monte Hellman(1932-)

Iguana '89
Silent Night, Deadly Night 3: Better Watch Out! '89
Gunfire '78
Cockfighter '74
Two Lane Blacktop '71
Flight to Fury '66
Ride in the Whirlwind '66
The Shooting '66
The Terror '63
The Beast from Haunted Cave '60
Creature from the Haunted Sea '60

Oliver Hellman

See Ovidio G. Assonitis

Ralph Hemecker

Midnight Bayou '09
Double Edge '97
Dead On '93

David Hemmings(1941-2003)

Lone Justice 3: Showdown at Plum Creek '96
A Christmas Reunion '93
Dark Horse '92
The Key to Rebecca '85
Treasure of the Yankee Zephyr '83
Survivor '80
Just a Gigolo '79

Joseph Henabery(1888-1976)

Leather Burners '43
Cobra '25
His Majesty, the American '19
The Man from Painted Post '17

Eric Hendershot

The Robin Hood Gang '98
Clubhouse Detectives '96

Clark Henderson(1951-)

Circle of Fear '89
Primary Target '89
Saigon Commandos '88
Warlords from Hell '87

Don Henderson(1931-97)

The Touch of Satan '70
Weekend with the Babysitter '70

John Henderson(1949-)

Two Men Went to War '02
The Magical Legend of the Leprechauns '99
The Return of the Borrowers '96
Loch Ness '95
The Borrowers '93

Stewart Hendler

Sorority Row '09
Whisper '07

Frank Henenlotter(1950-)

Basket Case 3: The Progeny '92
Basket Case 2 '90
Frankenhooker '90
Brain Damage '88
Basket Case '82

Paul Henreid(1908-92)

Ballad in Blue '66
Dead Ringer '64
Battle Shock '56
Tall Lie '53

Buck Henry(1930-)

First Family '80
Heaven Can Wait '78

Brian Henson(1963-)

Jack and the Beanstalk: The Real Story '01
Muppet Treasure Island '96
The Muppet Christmas Carol '92

Jim Henson(1936-90)

Labyrinth '86
The Dark Crystal '82
The Great Muppet Caper '81

Robby Henson

Thr3e '07
The Badge '02
Pharoah's Army '95

Henry Herbert(1939-2003)

Forbidden Passion: The Oscar Wilde Movie '85
Danger UXB '81
Emily '77

Stephen Herek(1958-)

Into the Blue 2: The Reef '09
Picture This! '08
Man of the House '05
Life or Something Like It '02
Rock Star '01
Holy Man '98
101 Dalmatians '96
Mr. Holland's Opus '95
The Three Musketeers '93
The Mighty Ducks '92
Don't Tell Mom the Babysitter's Dead '91
Bill & Ted's Excellent Adventure '89
Critters '86

Al(bert) Herman(1887-1967)

The Missing Corpse '45
The Phantom of 42nd Street '45
Delinquent Daughters '44
Rogue's Gallery '44
Shake Hands with Murder '44
Dawn Express '42
Rangers Take Over '42
Yank in Libya '42
Gentleman from Dixie '41
The Pioneers '41
Take Me Back to Oklahoma '40
Down the Wyoming Trail '39
Man from Texas '39
Roll, Wagons, Roll '39
Renfrew on the Great White Trail '38
Rollin' Plains '38
Utah Trail '38
Valley of Terror '38
Renfrew of the Royal Mounted '37
The Clutching Hand '36
Gun Play '36
Outlaws of the Range '36
Cowboy & the Bandit '35
Western Frontier '35
Whispering Shadow '33
Beyond the Trail '26

Jean Herman(1933-)

Butterfly Affair '71
Queen of Diamonds '70
Honor Among Thieves '68

Mark Herman(1954-)

The Boy in the Striped Pajamas '08
Little Voice '98
Brassed Off '96
Blame It on the Bellboy '92

Charles Herman-Wurmfeld(1966-)

The Hammer '07
Legally Blonde 2: Red White & Blonde '03
Kissing Jessica Stein '02
Fanci's Persuasion '95

Jaime Humberto Hermosillo(1942-)

Esmeralda Comes by Night '98
Forbidden Homework '92
Homework '90
The Summer of Miss Forbes '88
Dona Herlinda & Her Son '86
Mary, My Dearest '83

Denis Heroux(1940-)

The Uncanny '78
Born for Hell '76

Rowdy Herrington(1951-)

Bobby Jones: Stroke of Genius '04
I Witness '03
The Stickup '01
A Murder of Crows '99
Striking Distance '93
Gladiator '92
Road House '89
Jack's Back '87

W(illiam) Blake Herron

A Texas Funeral '99
Skin Art '93

Joel Hershman(1958-)

Greenfingers '00
Hold Me, Thrill Me, Kiss Me '93

Marshall Herskovitz(1952-)

Dangerous Beauty '98
Jack the Bear '93

Michael Herz(1949-)

Sgt. Kabukiman N.Y.P.D. '94
The Toxic Avenger, Part 2 '89
The Toxic Avenger, Part 3: The Last Temptation of Toxie '89
Troma's War '88
The Toxic Avenger '86
Stuck on You '84
First Turn On '83
Sugar Cookies '77

John Herzfeld

S.I.S. '08
Bobby Z '07
15 Minutes '01
Don King: Only in America '97
Two Days in the Valley '96
Casualties of Love: The "Long Island Lolita" Story '93
The Preppie Murder '89
A Father's Revenge '88
Two of a Kind '83

Brian Herzinger

Baby on Board '08
My Date With Drew '05

Werner Herzog(1942-)

Bad Lieutenant: Port of Call New Orleans '09
Encounters at the End of the World '07
Rescue Dawn '06
Grizzly Man '05
The White Diamond '04
Invincible '01
Cobra Verde '88
Where the Green Ants Dream '84
Fitzcarraldo '82
Nosferatu the Vampyre '79
Woyzeck '78
Stroszek '77
Every Man for Himself & God Against All '75
Heart of Glass '74
Aguirre, the Wrath of God '72
Signs of Life '68

Jared Hess(1979-)

Gentlemen Broncos '09
Nacho Libre '06
Napoleon Dynamite '04

Jon Hess

Crash & Byrnes '99
Legion '98
Mars '96
Excessive Force '93
Alligator 2: The Mutation '90
Assassin '89
The Lawless Land '88
Watchers '88

Gordon Hessler(1930-)

Journey of Honor '91
Tales of the Unexpected '91
The Girl in a Swing '89
Out on Bail '89
The Misfit Brigade '87
Rage of Honor '87
Pray for Death '85
Escape from El Diablo '83
KISS Meets the Phantom of the Park '78
Puzzle '78
Secrets of Three Hungry Wives '78
Blue Jeans and Dynamite '76
Betrayal '74
Medusa '74
Golden Voyage of Sinbad '73
Embassy '72
Murders in the Rue Morgue '71
Cry of the Banshee '70
Scream and Scream Again '70
The Oblong Box '69

Charlton Heston(1924-2008)

A Man for All Seasons '88
Mother Lode '82
Antony and Cleopatra '73

Fraser Heston(1955-)

Alaska '96
Needful Things '93
The Crucifer of Blood '91
Treasure Island '89

David L. Hewitt(1939-)

The Lucifer Complex '78
Alien Massacre '67
Gallery of Horrors '67
Journey to the Center of Time '67
Monsters Crash the Pajama Party '65
Horrors of the Red Planet '64

Peter Hewitt(1962-)

The Maiden Heist '08
Zoom '06
Garfield: The Movie '04
Princess of Thieves '01
The Borrowers '97
Tom and Huck '95
Wild Palms '93
Bill & Ted's Bogus Journey '91

Rod Hewitt

The Debt '98
Strip Search '97
The Dangerous '95
Verne Miller '88

Douglas Heyes(1919-93)

Powder Keg '70
Kitten with a Whip '64

Laurent Heynemann(1948-)

The Old Lady Who Walked in the Sea '91
Birgitt Haas Must Be Killed '83

Jesse Hibbs(1906-85)

Walk the Proud Land '56
To Hell and Back '55
Ride Clear of Diablo '54

Jochen Hick(1960-)

No One Sleeps '01
Via Appia '92

George Hickenlooper(1964-)

Factory Girl '06
Mayor of the Sunset Strip '03
The Man from Elysian Fields '01
The Big Brass Ring '99
Dogtown '97
Persons Unknown '96
The Low Life '95
Some Folks Call It a Sling Blade '94
The Ghost Brigade '93
Hearts of Darkness: A Filmmaker's Apocalypse '91

Steve Hickner

Bee Movie '07
Prince of Egypt '98

Anthony Hickox(1959-)

Sundown: The Vampire in Retreat '08
Submerged '05
Blast '04
Federal Protection '02
The Contaminated Man '01
Last Run '01
Jill the Ripper '00
Storm Catcher '99
Prince Valiant '97
Invasion of Privacy '96
Payback '94
Full Eclipse '93
Warlock: The Armageddon '93
Hellraiser 3: Hell on Earth '92
Sundown '91
Waxwork 2: Lost in Time '91
Waxwork '88

Douglas Hickox(1929-88)

Blackout '85
Sins '85
Mistral's Daughter '84
The Hound of the Baskervilles '83

Zulu Dawn *'79*
Sky Riders *'76*
Brannigan *'75*
Theatre of Blood *'73*
Entertaining Mr. Sloane *'70*

James D.R. Hickox

Sabretooth *'01*
Blood Surf *'00*
Children of the Corn 3: Urban Harvest *'95*

Scott Hicks(1953-)

The Boys Are Back *'09*
No Reservations *'07*
Hearts in Atlantis *'01*
Snow Falling on Cedars *'99*
Shine *'95*
Freedom *'82*

Howard Higgin(1891-1938)

Carnival Lady *'33*
Hell's House *'32*
Painted Desert *'31*
High Voltage *'29*
The Racketeer *'29*
The Leatherneck *'28*
Power *'28*

Colin Higgins(1941-88)

The Best Little Whorehouse in Texas *'82*
9 to 5 *'80*
Foul Play *'78*

Mikey Hilb

Deep Winter *'08*
Dishdogz *'05*

George Hill(1895-1934)

The Big House *'30*
Min & Bill *'30*

George Roy Hill(1922-2002)

Funny Farm *'88*
The Little Drummer Girl *'84*
The World According to Garp *'82*
A Little Romance *'79*
Slap Shot *'77*
The Great Waldo Pepper *'75*
The Sting *'73*
Slaughterhouse Five *'72*
Butch Cassidy and the Sundance Kid *'69*
Thoroughly Modern Millie *'67*
Hawaii *'66*
The World of Henry Orient *'64*
Toys in the Attic *'63*
Period of Adjustment *'62*

Jack Hill(1933-)

Switchblade Sisters *'75*
Foxy Brown *'74*
The Swinging Cheerleaders *'74*
Coffy *'73*
The Big Bird Cage *'72*
The Big Doll House *'71*
The Fear Chamber *'68*
The Sinister Invasion *'68*
Pit Stop *'67*
Portrait in Terror *'66*
Track of the Vampire *'66*
Spider Baby *'64*
The Terror *'63*

James Hill(1919-94)

The Wild and the Free *'80*
The Belstone Fox *'73*
Black Beauty *'71*
Captain Nemo and the Underwater City *'69*
An Elephant Called Slowly *'69*
The Corrupt Ones *'67*
Born Free *'66*
A Study in Terror *'66*
Seaside Swingers *'65*
Trial & Error *'62*

Jody Hill

Observe and Report *'09*
The Foot Fist Way *'08*

Robert F. "Bob" Hill(1886-1966)

East Side Kids *'40*
Flash Gordon: Mars Attacks the World *'39*
Wild Horse Canyon *'39*
Cheyenne Rides Again *'38*
Man's Country *'38*
The Painted Trail *'38*
The Phantom of the Range *'38*
Whirlwind Horseman *'38*
Feud of the Trail *'37*
The Roamin' Cowboy *'37*
Blake of Scotland Yard *'36*
A Face in the Fog *'36*
Kelly of the Secret Service *'36*
Prison Shadows *'36*
Rip Roarin' Buckaroo *'36*
Rogue's Tavern *'36*
Shadow of Chinatown *'36*
West of Nevada *'36*
Danger Trails *'35*
Queen of the Jungle *'35*
Demon for Trouble *'34*
Inside Information *'34*
Cheyenne Kid *'33*
Tarzan the Fearless *'33*
Come on Danger! *'32*
Murder on the High Seas *'32*
The Adventures of Tarzan *'21*

Terence Hill(1941-)

Lucky Luke *'94*
Troublemakers *'94*

Tim Hill

Alvin and the Chipmunks *'07*
Garfield: A Tail of Two Kitties *'06*

Timothy Hill

Max Keeble's Big Move *'01*
Muppets from Space *'99*

Walter Hill(1942-)

Broken Trail *'06*
Undisputed *'02*
Supernova *'99*
Last Man Standing *'96*
Wild Bill *'95*
Geronimo: An American Legend *'93*
Trespass *'92*
Another 48 Hrs. *'90*
Johnny Handsome *'89*
Tales from the Crypt *'89*
Red Heat *'88*
Extreme Prejudice *'87*
Crossroads *'86*
Brewster's Millions *'85*
Streets of Fire *'84*
48 Hrs. *'82*
Southern Comfort *'81*
The Long Riders *'80*
The Warriors *'79*
The Driver *'78*
Hard Times *'75*

John Hillcoat

The Road *'09*
The Proposition *'05*

David Hillenbrand

Transylmania *'09*
Gamebox 1.0 *'04*
Survival Island *'02*
King Cobra *'98*

Scott Hillenbrand

Transylmania *'09*
Gamebox 1.0 *'04*
Survival Island *'02*
King Cobra *'98*

Arthur Hiller(1923-)

An Alan Smithee Film: Burn, Hollywood, Burn *'97*
Carpool *'96*
Married to It *'93*
The Babe *'92*
Taking Care of Business *'90*
See No Evil, Hear No Evil *'89*
Outrageous Fortune *'87*
The Lonely Guy *'84*
Teachers *'84*
Romantic Comedy *'83*
Author! Author! *'82*
Making Love *'82*
The In-Laws *'79*
Nightwing *'79*
Silver Streak *'76*
The Man in the Glass Booth *'75*
Man of La Mancha *'72*
The Hospital *'71*
Plaza Suite *'71*
Love Story *'70*
The Out-of-Towners *'70*
Popi *'69*
Promise Her Anything *'66*
Tobruk *'66*
The Americanization of Emily *'64*
The Miracle of the White Stallions *'63*
The Wheeler Dealers *'63*

Richard Hilliard

Psychomania *'63*
The Lonely Sex *'59*

William B. Hillman

Quigley *'03*
Ragin' Cajun *'90*
Double Exposure *'82*
Photographer *'75*

Lambert Hillyer(1889-1969)

Range Renegades *'48*
Sundown Riders *'48*
Hat Box Mystery *'47*
Land of the Lawless *'47*
Border Bandits *'46*
Gentleman from Texas *'46*
South of the Rio Grande *'45*
The Stranger from Pecos *'45*
Lawmen *'44*
Partners of the Trail *'44*
Range Law *'44*
Six Gun Gospel *'43*
Texas Kid *'43*
The Durango Kid *'40*
Gang Bullets *'38*
Dracula's Daughter *'36*
The Invisible Ray *'36*
The California Trail *'33*
Fighting Fool *'32*
Hello Trouble *'32*
White Eagle *'32*
The Shock *'23*
Three Word Brand *'21*
The Cradle of Courage *'20*
The Toll Gate *'20*
Wagon Tracks *'19*

Arthur Hilton(1897-1979)

Big Chase *'54*
Cat Women of the Moon *'53*
Return of Jesse James *'50*

Gregory Hines(1946-2003)

The Red Sneakers *'01*
Bleeding Hearts *'94*

Bill (William Heinzman) Hinzman(1936-)

Revenge of the Living Zombies *'88*
The Majorettes *'87*

Alexander Gregory (Gregory Dark) Hippolyte(1954-)

Animal Instincts 3: The Seductress *'95*
Object of Obsession *'95*
Animal Instincts 2 *'94*
Secret Games 3 *'94*
Undercover *'94*
Mirror Images 2 *'93*
Secret Games 2: The Escort *'93*
Animal Instincts *'92*
Night Rhythms *'92*
Secret Games *'92*
Carnal Crimes *'91*
Mirror Images *'91*

Oliver Hirschbiegel(1957-)

Five Minutes of Heaven *'09*
The Invasion *'07*
Downfall *'04*
The Experiment *'01*

Leslie Hiscott(1894-1968)

The Time of His Life *'55*
Butler's Dilemma *'43*
She Shall Have Music *'36*
Death on the Set *'35*
Department Store *'35*
The Triumph of Sherlock Holmes *'35*

Alfred Hitchcock(1899-1980)

Family Plot *'76*
Frenzy *'72*
Topaz *'69*
Torn Curtain *'66*
Marnie *'64*
The Birds *'63*
Psycho *'60*
North by Northwest *'59*
Vertigo *'58*
The Man Who Knew Too Much *'56*
The Wrong Man *'56*
To Catch a Thief *'55*
The Trouble with Harry *'55*
Dial "M" for Murder *'54*
Rear Window *'54*
I Confess *'53*
Strangers on a Train *'51*
Stage Fright *'50*
Under Capricorn *'49*
Rope *'48*
The Paradine Case *'47*
Notorious *'46*
Spellbound *'45*
Lifeboat *'44*
Shadow of a Doubt *'43*
Saboteur *'42*
Mr. & Mrs. Smith *'41*
Suspicion *'41*
Foreign Correspondent *'40*
Rebecca *'40*
Jamaica Inn *'39*
The Lady Vanishes *'38*
Young and Innocent *'37*
Sabotage *'36*
The Secret Agent *'36*
The 39 Steps *'35*
The Man Who Knew Too Much *'34*
No. 17 *'32*
Rich and Strange *'32*
Skin Game *'31*
Juno and the Paycock *'30*
Murder *'30*
Blackmail *'29*
The Manxman *'29*
Champagne *'28*
The Farmer's Wife *'28*
Three by Hitchcock *'28*
Easy Virtue *'27*
The Ring *'27*
The Lodger *'26*

Rupert Hitzig(1942-)

Nowhere Land *'98*
Backstreet Dreams *'90*
Night Visitor *'89*

Jack B. Hively(1910-95)

California Gold Rush *'81*
The Adventures of Huckleberry Finn *'78*
Starbird and Sweet William *'73*
Lassie: Well of Love *'70*
Lassie: Adventures of Neeka *'68*
Four Jacks and a Jill *'41*
The Saint Takes Over *'40*
The Saint's Double Trouble *'40*
Panama Lady *'39*

Godfrey Ho(1948-)

Undefeatable *'94*
Honor and Glory *'92*
Lethal Panther *'90*
Ninja: American Warrior *'90*
Full Metal Ninja *'89*
Ninja of the Magnificence *'89*
Vampire Raiders—Ninja Queen *'89*
Ninja Death Squad *'87*
Ninja Phantom Heroes *'87*
Ninja Fantasy *'86*
Ninja, the Violent Sorcerer *'86*
Bionic Ninja *'85*
Ninja Masters of Death *'85*
Ninja Champion *'80*
Ninja Destroyer *'70*

Meng Hua Ho

The Mighty Peking Man *'77*
Vengeance is a Golden Blade *'69*
The Cave of the Silken Web *'67*

Gregory Hoblit(1944-)

Untraceable *'08*
Fracture *'07*
Hart's War *'02*
Frequency *'00*
Fallen *'97*
Primal Fear *'96*
Class of '61 *'92*
Roe vs. Wade *'89*
L.A. Law *'86*

Victoria Hochberg

Dawg *'02*
Sweet 15 *'90*
Jacob Have I Loved *'88*

Mike Hodges(1932-)

I'll Sleep When I'm Dead *'03*
Croupier *'97*
Black Rainbow *'91*
Florida Straits *'87*
Prayer for the Dying *'87*
Morons from Outer Space *'85*
Missing Pieces *'83*
Flash Gordon *'80*
The Terminal Man *'74*
Pulp *'72*
Get Carter *'71*

Jeno Hodi

Triplecross *'95*
American Kickboxer 2: To the Death *'93*
Deadly Obsession *'88*

Christopher Hodson

Like A Bride *'94*
We'll Meet Again *'82*

Mark Hoeger

Full Ride *'02*
The Little Match Girl *'84*

Paul Hoen

The Cheetah Girls: One World *'08*
Jump In! *'07*

Arthur Hoerl(1891-1968)

Drums O'Voodoo *'34*
Before Morning *'33*

Ernest Hofbauer

Secrets of Sweet Sixteen *'74*
Code Name Alpha *'67*

Herman Hoffman(1909-89)

The Invisible Boy *'57*
It's a Dog's Life *'55*

Jerzy Hoffman(1932-)

Leper *'76*
The Deluge *'73*
Colonel Wolodyjowski *'69*

John Hoffman

Good Boy! *'03*
Strange Confession *'45*

Michael Hoffman(1956-)

The Last Station *'09*
Game 6 *'05*
The Emperor's Club *'02*
William Shakespeare's A Midsummer Night's Dream *'99*
One Fine Day *'96*
Restoration *'94*
Soapdish *'91*
Promised Land *'88*
Some Girls *'88*

Yvette Hoffman

The Catcher *'98*
Starved *'97*

Tamar Simon Hoffs(1934-)

Red Roses and Petrol *'03*
The Allnighter *'87*

Gray Hofmeyr

Yankee Zulu *'95*
The Light in the Jungle *'91*
Dirty Games *'89*
The Outcast *'84*

Jack Hofsiss(1950-)

Cat on a Hot Tin Roof *'84*
Family Secrets *'84*
I'm Dancing as Fast as I Can *'82*
Oldest Living Graduate *'80*
Sorrows of Gin *'79*

David Hogan

Most Wanted *'97*
Barb Wire *'96*

James Hogan(1891-1943)

The Mad Ghoul *'43*
Power Dive *'41*
The Texas Rangers Ride Again *'40*
Bulldog Drummond's Bride *'39*
Bulldog Drummond's Secret Police *'39*
Arrest Bulldog Drummond *'38*
Bulldog Drummond's Peril *'38*
The Texans *'38*
Bulldog Drummond Escapes *'37*
Arizona Mahoney *'36*
The Broken Mask *'28*

P.J. Hogan(1962-)

Confessions of a Shopaholic *'09*
Peter Pan *'03*
Unconditional Love *'03*
My Best Friend's Wedding *'97*
Muriel's Wedding *'94*

Rod Holcomb(1924-)

Convict Cowboy *'95*
Dead to Rights *'93*
Royce *'93*
Chains of Gold *'92*
China Beach *'88*
Blind Justice *'86*
Chase *'85*
Stark *'85*
Two Fathers' Justice *'85*
Cartier Affair *'84*
The Red Light Sting *'84*
Captain America *'79*

William Hole, Jr.

The Devil's Hand *'61*
Four Fast Guns *'59*
The Ghost of Dragstrip Hollow *'59*

Agnieszka Holland(1948-)

The Healer *'02*
Shot in the Heart *'01*
The Third Miracle *'99*
Washington Square *'97*
Total Eclipse *'95*
The Secret Garden *'93*
Olivier, Olivier *'92*
Europa, Europa *'91*
To Kill a Priest *'89*
Angry Harvest *'85*
Fever *'81*
Provincial Actors *'79*

Savage Steve Holland(1960-)

Shredderman Rules *'07*
Safety Patrol *'98*
How I Got into College *'89*
One Crazy Summer *'86*
Better Off Dead *'85*

Todd Holland(1961-)

Firehouse Dog *'07*
Krippendorf's Tribe *'98*
The Wizard *'89*

Tom Holland(1943-)
Masters of Horror: We All Scream for Ice Cream *'07*
Stephen King's Thinner *'96*
Stephen King's The Langoliers *'95*
The Temp *'93*
Child's Play *'88*
Fatal Beauty *'87*
Fright Night *'85*

Allan Holleb
School Spirit *'85*
Candy Stripe Nurses *'74*

Ben Holmes(1890-1943)
Maid's Night Out *'38*
The Saint in New York *'38*

Fred Holmes
Harley *'90*
Dakota *'88*

Nicole Holofcener(1960-)
Friends with Money *'06*
Lovely & Amazing *'02*
Walking and Talking *'96*

Jason Holt
Swindle *'92*
Wager of Love *'90*

Seth Holt(1923-71)
Blood from the Mummy's Tomb *'71*
The Nanny *'65*
Scream of Fear *'61*

Allan Holzman(1946-)
Intimate Stranger *'91*
Programmed to Kill *'86*
Grunt! The Wrestling Movie *'85*
Out of Control *'85*
Forbidden World *'82*

Edward Holzman
Body Strokes *'95*
Forbidden Games *'95*
Friend of the Family *'95*
Sinful Intrigue *'95*
Seduce Me: Pamela Principle 2 *'94*

Inoshiro Honda(1911-93)
Terror of Mechagodzilla *'78*
Yog, Monster from Space *'71*
War of the Gargantuas *'70*
Godzilla's Revenge *'69*
Destroy All Monsters *'68*
Godzilla vs. Monster Zero *'68*
Dagora, the Space Monster *'65*
Ghidrah the Three Headed Monster *'65*
Godzilla vs. Mothra *'64*
Attack of the Mushroom People *'63*
King Kong vs. Godzilla *'63*
Gorath *'62*
Mothra *'62*
Varan the Unbelievable *'61*
H-Man *'59*
Half Human *'58*
The Mysterians *'58*
Godzilla, King of the Monsters *'56*
Rodan *'56*

Ishio Honda
Latitude Zero *'69*
King Kong Escapes *'67*
Frankenstein Conquers the World *'64*
Matango *'63*

Elliot Hong
Retrievers *'82*
They Call Me Bruce? *'82*
Kill the Golden Goose *'79*

James Hong(1929-)
The Vineyard *'89*
Girls Next Door *'79*

Christophe Honore(1970-)
Love Songs *'07*
Inside Paris *'06*
Close to Leo *'02*

Gavin Hood(1963-)
X-Men Origins: Wolverine *'09*
Rendition *'07*
Tsotsi *'05*
In Desert and Wilderness *'01*

Harry Hook(1960-)
St. Ives *'98*
The Last of His Tribe *'92*
Lord of the Flies *'90*
The Kitchen Toto *'87*

Kevin Hooks(1958-)
Mutiny *'99*
Black Dog *'98*
Glory & Honor *'98*
Fled *'96*
Murder Without Motive *'92*
Passenger 57 *'92*
Strictly Business *'91*
Heat Wave *'90*
Roots: The Gift *'88*

Lance Hool(1948-)
One Man's Hero *'98*
Steel Dawn *'87*
Missing in Action 2: The Beginning *'85*

Tobe Hooper(1946-)
Mortuary *'05*
Taken *'02*
Crocodile *'00*
Apartment Complex *'98*
The Mangler *'94*
Body Bags *'93*
I'm Dangerous Tonight *'90*
Spontaneous Combustion *'89*
Invaders from Mars *'86*
The Texas Chainsaw Massacre 2 *'86*
Lifeforce *'85*
Poltergeist *'82*
The Funhouse *'81*
Salem's Lot *'79*
Eaten Alive *'76*
The Texas Chainsaw Massacre *'74*

Tom Hooper
The Damned United *'09*
John Adams *'08*
Longford *'06*
Elizabeth I *'05*
Daniel Deronda *'02*

Claudia Hoover
Gideon *'99*
Double Exposure *'93*

Anthony Hopkins(1937-)
Slipstream *'07*
August *'95*

Stephen Hopkins(1958-)
The Reaping *'07*
The Reaping *'07*
Under Suspicion *'00*
Lost in Space *'98*
The Ghost and the Darkness *'96*
Blown Away *'94*
Judgment Night *'93*
Dangerous Game *'90*
Predator 2 *'90*
A Nightmare on Elm Street 5: Dream Child *'89*

Dennis Hopper(1936-)
Chasers *'94*
The Hot Spot *'90*
Backtrack *'89*
Colors *'88*
Out of the Blue *'80*
The Last Movie *'71*
Easy Rider *'69*

E. Mason Hopper(1885-1967)
Hong Kong Nights *'35*
Curtain at Eight *'33*
Held for Murder *'32*
Shop Angel *'32*
Square Shoulders *'29*
Getting Gertie's Garter *'27*

Jerry Hopper(1907-88)
Bull of the West *'71*
Madron *'70*
Missouri Traveler *'58*
The Private War of Major Benson *'55*
Pony Express *'53*
The Atomic City *'52*

Russell Hopton(1900-45)
Black Gold *'36*
Song of the Trail *'36*

James W. Horne(1880-1942)
Holt of the Secret Service *'42*
The Spider Returns *'41*
Green Archer *'40*
The Spider's Web *'38*
All Over Town *'37*
Way Out West *'37*
Bohemian Girl *'36*
Bonnie Scotland *'35*
Laurel & Hardy: Chickens Come Home *'31*
Laurel & Hardy: Brats *'30*
College *'27*
The Cruise of the Jasper B *'26*
Laughing at Danger *'24*

Harry Horner(1910-94)
New Faces of 1952 *'54*
Beware, My Lovely *'52*
Red Planet Mars *'52*

Robert J. Horner
Apache Kid's Escape *'30*
The Walloping Kid *'26*

Peter Horton(1953-)
The Cure *'95*
Amazon Women on the Moon *'87*

Robert Hossein(1927-)
I Killed Rasputin *'67*
Double Agents *'59*

Chien Hsiao Hou
See Hou Hsiao-Hsien

Hsiao-Hsien Hou
See Hou Hsiao-Hsien
A Time to Live and a Time to Die *'85*

Joy Houck, Jr.(1942-2003)
Creature from Black Lake *'76*
Night of the Strangler *'73*
Mind Warp *'72*
Night of Bloody Horror *'69*

John Hough(1941-)
Hell's Gate *'01*
Duel of Hearts *'92*
The Lady and the Highwayman *'89*
American Gothic *'88*
Howling 4: The Original Nightmare *'88*
The Dying Truth *'86*
Biggles *'85*
The Black Arrow *'84*
Triumphs of a Man Called Horse *'83*
Incubus *'82*
The Watcher in the Woods *'81*
Brass Target *'78*
Return from Witch Mountain *'78*
Escape to Witch Mountain *'75*
Dirty Mary Crazy Larry *'74*
The Legend of Hell House *'73*
Treasure Island *'72*
Twins of Evil *'71*
Eye Witness *'70*

Bobby Houston
Caged Fear *'92*
Trust Me *'89*
Bad Manners *'84*

Adrian Hoven(1922-81)
Dandelions *'74*
Mark of the Devil 2 *'72*

David Howard(1896-1941)
Bullet Code *'40*
Legion of the Lawless *'40*
Hollywood Stadium Mystery *'38*
Park Avenue Logger *'37*
Thunder Mountain *'35*
Crimson Romance *'34*
Daniel Boone *'34*
In Old Santa Fe *'34*
The Lost Jungle *'34*
Mystery Ranch *'34*

Leslie Howard(1893-1943)
Pimpernel Smith *'42*
Spitfire *'42*
Pygmalion *'38*

Ron Howard(1954-)
Angels & Demons *'09*
Frost/Nixon *'08*
The Da Vinci Code *'06*
Cinderella Man *'05*
The Missing *'03*
A Beautiful Mind *'01*
Dr. Seuss' How the Grinch Stole Christmas *'00*
EDtv *'99*
Ransom *'96*
Apollo 13 *'95*
The Paper *'94*
Far and Away *'92*
Backdraft *'91*
Parenthood *'89*
Willow *'88*
Cocoon *'85*
Gung Ho *'85*
Splash *'84*
Cotton Candy *'82*
Night Shift *'82*
Tut & Tuttle *'81*
Grand Theft Auto *'77*

Sandy Howard
One Step to Hell *'67*
Tarzan and the Trappers *'58*

William K. Howard(1899-1954)
Johnny Come Lately *'43*
Back Door to Heaven *'39*
Fire Over England *'37*
The Princess Comes Across *'36*
The Cat and the Fiddle *'34*
Evelyn Prentice *'34*
White Gold *'28*
Let's Go! *'23*

C. Thomas Howell(1966-)
The Land That Time Forgot *'09*
The Big Fall *'96*
Pure Danger *'96*
Hourglass *'95*

Peter Howitt(1957-)
Laws of Attraction *'04*
Johnny English *'03*
Antitrust *'00*
Sliding Doors *'97*

Frank Howson(1952-)
Flynn *'96*
The Hunting *'92*

Harry Hoyt(1885-1961)
Jungle Bride *'33*
The Return of Boston Blackie *'27*
The Lost World *'25*

Jan Hrebejk(1967-)
Up and Down *'04*
Divided We Fall *'00*

Hou Hsiao-Hsien(1947-)
Flight of the Red Balloon *'08*
Cafe Lumiere *'05*
Three Times *'05*
Flowers of Shanghai *'98*
Goodbye South, Goodbye *'96*

Talun Hsu
Body Count *'95*
Witchcraft 5: Dance with the Devil *'92*

King Hu(1931-97)
Painted Skin *'93*
Come Drink with Me *'65*

Shan Hua
Infra-Man *'76*
Super Inframan *'76*

George Huang
How to Make a Monster *'01*
Trojan War *'97*
Swimming with Sharks *'94*

Jean-Loup Hubert(1949-)
Le Grand Chemin *'87*
Next Year If All Goes Well *'83*

John Huddles
Uncorked *'98*
Far Harbor *'96*

Reginald (Reggie) Hudlin(1961-)
Serving Sara *'02*
The Ladies Man *'00*
The Great White Hype *'96*
Cosmic Slop *'94*
Boomerang *'92*
House Party *'90*

Hugh Hudson(1936-)
I Dreamed of Africa *'00*
My Life So Far *'98*
Lost Angels *'89*
Revolution *'85*
Greystoke: The Legend of Tarzan, Lord of the Apes *'84*
Chariots of Fire *'81*

Brent Huff(1961-)
Welcome to Paradise *'07*
100 Mile Rule *'02*
The Bad Pack *'98*
Final Justice *'94*

R. John Hugh(1924-85)
The Meal *'75*
You've Ruined Me, Eddie *'58*
Naked in the Sun *'57*
Yellowneck *'55*

Albert Hughes(1972-)
The Book of Eli *'10*
From Hell *'01*
Dead Presidents *'95*
Menace II Society *'93*

Allen Hughes(1972-)
The Book of Eli *'10*
New York, I Love You *'09*
Knights of the South Bronx *'05*
From Hell *'01*
Dead Presidents *'95*
Menace II Society *'93*

Bronwen Hughes
Stander *'03*
Forces of Nature *'99*
Harriet the Spy *'96*

Howard Hughes(1905-76)
The Outlaw *'43*
Hell's Angels *'30*

John Hughes(1950-2009)
Curly Sue *'91*
Uncle Buck *'89*
She's Having a Baby *'88*
Planes, Trains & Automobiles *'87*
Ferris Bueller's Day Off *'86*
The Breakfast Club *'85*
Weird Science *'85*
Sixteen Candles *'84*

Ken Hughes(1922-2001)
Night School *'81*
Sextette *'78*
Oh, Alfie *'75*
Internecine Project *'73*
Cromwell *'70*
Chitty Chitty Bang Bang *'68*
Casino Royale *'67*
Arrivederci, Baby! *'66*
Of Human Bondage *'64*
The Trials of Oscar Wilde *'60*
The Long Haul *'57*
The Atomic Man *'56*
Heat Wave *'54*

Robert C. Hughes
St. Patrick: The Irish Legend *'00*
Down the Drain *'89*
Memorial Valley Massacre *'88*
Hunter's Blood *'87*

Terry Hughes
Mrs. Santa Claus *'96*
The Butcher's Wife *'91*
For Love or Money *'84*
Sunset Limousine *'83*

Ann Hui(1947-)
Summer Snow *'94*
Song of the Exile *'90*

Don Hulette(1937-)
Great Ride *'78*
Greedy Terror *'78*
Tennessee Stallion *'78*
Breaker! Breaker! *'77*

Steven A. Hull
Devil Wears White *'86*
Ten Speed *'76*

H. Bruce Humberstone(1903-84)
Tarzan and the Trappers *'58*
Tarzan's Fight for Life *'58*
Tarzan and the Lost Safari *'57*
Tarzan's Hidden Jungle *'55*
Ten Wanted Men *'54*
The Desert Song *'53*
Happy Go Lovely *'51*
South Sea Sinner *'50*
Wonder Man *'45*
Pin-Up Girl *'44*
Hello, Frisco, Hello *'43*
Iceland *'42*
To the Shores of Tripoli *'42*
I Wake Up Screaming *'41*
Sun Valley Serenade *'41*
Lucky Cisco Kid *'40*
Charlie Chan in Honolulu *'38*
Charlie Chan at the Opera *'36*
Charlie Chan at the Race Track *'36*
King of the Jungle *'33*
The Crooked Circle *'32*
Strangers of the Evening *'32*

Sammo Hung(1952-)
Mr. Nice Guy *'98*
Dragons Forever *'88*
Eastern Condors *'87*
The Millionaire's Express *'86*
Heart of Dragon *'85*
The Prodigal Son *'82*
Spooky Encounters *'80*

Tran Anh Hung(1963-)
The Vertical Ray of the Sun *'00*
Cyclo *'95*
The Scent of Green Papaya *'93*

Tom Hunsinger(1952-)
Lawless Heart *'01*
Boyfriends *'96*

Ed(ward) Hunt
The Brain *'88*
Alien Warrior *'85*
Bloody Birthday *'80*
Starship Invasions *'77*

Paul Hunt(1943-)
Merlin *'92*
Twisted Nightmare *'87*
The Great Gundown *'75*
The Clones *'73*

Peter Hunt(1925-2002)
Assassination *'87*

Hyper-Sapien: People from Another Star *'86*
Wild Geese 2 *'85*
Death Hunt *'81*
The Private History of a Campaign That Failed *'81*
Gulliver's Travels *'77*
Shout at the Devil *'76*
On Her Majesty's Secret Service *'69*

Peter H. Hunt(1938-)
The Adventures of Huckleberry Finn *'85*
It Came Upon a Midnight Clear *'84*
The Mysterious Stranger *'82*
Skeezer *'82*
1776 *'72*

Neil Hunter
Lawless Heart *'01*
Boyfriends *'96*

Simon Hunter(1969-)
Mutant Chronicles *'08*
Dead of Night *'99*

Tim Hunter(1947-)
Kings of South Beach *'07*
The Far Side of Jericho *'06*
Video Voyeur: The Susan Wilson Story *'02*
Mean Streak *'99*
The Maker *'98*
Rescuers: Stories of Courage—Two Couples *'98*
The Saint of Fort Washington *'93*
Lies of the Twins *'91*
Paint It Black *'89*
River's Edge *'87*
Sylvester *'85*
Tex *'82*

Lawrence Huntington(1900-68)
Vulture *'67*
Eight Witnesses *'54*
The Franchise Affair *'52*
Man on the Run *'49*
The Upturned Glass *'47*
Tower of Terror *'42*

Nick Hurran(1959-)
The Prisoner *'09*
It's a Boy Girl Thing *'06*
Little Black Book *'04*
Virtual Sexuality *'99*
Girls' Night *'97*

Brian Desmond Hurst(1900-86)
Playboy of the Western World *'62*
Simba *'55*
Malta Story *'53*
A Christmas Carol *'51*
The Gay Lady *'49*
Dangerous Moonlight *'41*
The Lion Has Wings *'40*
River of Unrest *'36*

Michael Hurst(1973-)
Pumpkinhead 4: Blood Feud *'07*
House of the Dead 2: Dead Aim *'05*
New Blood *'99*

Paul Hurst(1888-1953)
Battling Bunyon *'24*
Branded a Bandit *'24*

Harry Hurwitz(1938-95)
Fleshtone *'94*
That's Adequate *'90*
Rosebud Beach Hotel *'85*
Safari 3000 *'82*
The Projectionist *'71*

Waris Hussein(1938-)
Fall from Grace *'94*
The Summer House *'94*
Switched at Birth *'91*
The Shell Seekers *'89*
Onassis *'88*
Intimate Contact *'87*
When the Bough Breaks *'86*
Arch of Triumph *'85*
Little Gloria... Happy at Last *'84*
Princess Daisy *'83*
Coming Out of the Ice *'82*
Callie and Son *'81*
Edward and Mrs. Simpson *'80*
The Henderson Monster *'80*
And Baby Makes Six *'79*
Divorce His, Divorce Hers *'72*
The Possession of Joel Delaney *'72*
Melody *'71*
Quackser Fortune Has a Cousin in the Bronx *'70*

Anjelica Huston(1951-)
Agnes Browne *'99*
Bastard out of Carolina *'96*

Danny Huston(1962-)
The Maddening *'95*
Becoming Colette *'92*
Mr. Corbett's Ghost *'90*
Mr. North *'88*

Jimmy Huston
The Wharf Rat *'95*
My Best Friend Is a Vampire *'88*
Final Exam *'81*
Death Driver *'78*

John Huston(1906-87)
The Dead *'87*
Prizzi's Honor *'85*
Under the Volcano *'84*
Annie *'82*
Victory *'81*
Phobia *'80*
Wise Blood *'79*
The Man Who Would Be King *'75*
Mackintosh Man *'73*
Fat City *'72*
Life & Times of Judge Roy Bean *'72*
Casino Royale *'67*
Reflections in a Golden Eye *'67*
The Bible *'66*
The Night of the Iguana *'64*
The List of Adrian Messenger *'63*
The Misfits *'61*
The Unforgiven *'60*
Barbarian and the Geisha *'58*
Heaven Knows, Mr. Allison *'57*
Moby Dick *'56*
Beat the Devil *'53*
Moulin Rouge *'52*
The African Queen *'51*
The Red Badge of Courage *'51*
The Asphalt Jungle *'50*
Key Largo *'48*
Treasure of the Sierra Madre *'48*
Across the Pacific *'42*
In This Our Life *'42*
The Maltese Falcon *'41*
Dr. Ehrlich's Magic Bullet *'40*

Charles (Hutchison) Hutchinson(1879-1949)
Children of the Wild *'37*
Phantom Patrol *'36*
Found Alive *'34*
Lightning Hutch *'26*

Clint Hutchison
Conjurer *'08*
Terror Tract *'00*

Brian G. Hutton(1935-)
High Road to China *'83*
The First Deadly Sin *'80*
Night Watch *'72*
X, Y & Zee *'72*
Kelly's Heroes *'70*
Where Eagles Dare *'68*

Willard Huyck(1945-)
Howard the Duck *'86*
Best Defense *'84*
French Postcards *'79*
Messiah of Evil *'74*

Peter Hyams(1943-)
Beyond a Reasonable Doubt *'09*
A Sound of Thunder *'05*
The Musketeer *'01*
End of Days *'99*
The Relic *'96*
Sudden Death *'95*
Timecop *'94*
Stay Tuned *'92*
Narrow Margin *'90*
The Presidio *'88*
Running Scared *'86*
2010: The Year We Make Contact *'84*
Death Target *'83*
The Star Chamber *'83*
Outland *'81*
Hanover Street *'79*
Capricorn One *'78*
Busting *'74*
Our Time *'74*

Nicholas Hytner(1957-)
The History Boys *'06*
Center Stage *'00*
The Object of My Affection *'98*
The Crucible *'96*
The Madness of King George *'94*

Juan Ibanez(1938-2000)
Dance of Death *'68*
The Fear Chamber *'68*
The Sinister Invasion *'68*

Juan Luis Iborra(1959-)
Valentin *'03*
Km. 0 *'00*
Amor de Hombre *'97*

Leon Ichaso(1948-)
El Cantante *'06*
Pinero *'01*
Hendrix *'00*
Execution of Justice *'99*
Free of Eden *'98*
Bitter Sugar *'96*
Zooman *'95*
Sugar Hill *'94*
The Fear Inside *'92*
The Take *'90*
Crossover Dreams *'85*
Power, Passion & Murder *'83*
El Super *'79*

Kon Ichikawa(1915-2008)
The Makioka Sisters *'83*
Phoenix *'78*
Tokyo Olympiad *'66*
An Actor's Revenge *'63*
Being Two Isn't Easy *'62*
Odd Obsession *'60*
Fires on the Plain *'59*
Enjo *'58*
The Burmese Harp *'56*

Eric Idle(1943-)
The Tale of the Frog Prince *'83*
All You Need Is Cash *'78*

Miguel Iglesias
Rape *'76*
Kilma, Queen of the Amazons *'75*
Green Inferno *'72*
The Sword of El Cid *'62*

Joji Iida
Rasen *'98*
Battle Heater *'89*

Toshiharu Ikeda
Beautiful Beast *'95*
Evil Dead Trap *'88*

Kazuo Ikehiro(1928-)
Zatoichi: Master Ichi and a Chest of Gold *'64*
Zatoichi: Zatoichi's Flashing Sword *'64*

Dennis Iliadis
The Last House on the Left *'09*
Hardcore *'04*

Mark Illsley(1958-)
Bookies *'03*
Happy, Texas *'99*

Shohei Imamura(1926-2006)
Dr. Akagi *'98*
The Eel *'96*
Black Rain *'88*
The Ballad of Narayama *'83*
Eijanaika *'81*
Vengeance Is Mine *'79*
The Pornographers *'66*
The Insect Woman *'63*

Hiroshi Inagaki(1905-80)
Kojiro *'67*
Rikisha-Man *'58*
Samurai 3: Duel at Ganryu Island *'56*
Samurai 1: Musashi Miyamoto *'55*
Samurai 2: Duel at Ichijoji Temple *'55*

Alejandro Gonzalez Inarritu(1963-)
Babel *'06*
21 Grams *'03*
Amores Perros *'00*

Ralph Ince(1887-1937)
Lucky Devils *'33*
Men of America *'32*

Franco Indovina(1932-72)
Catch as Catch Can *'68*
Oldest Profession *'67*

Lloyd Ingraham(1885-1956)
Eyes of Julia Deep *'18*
American Aristocracy *'17*
Hoodoo Ann *'16*

Rex Ingram(1892-1950)
Scaramouche *'23*
The Prisoner of Zenda *'22*
The Four Horsemen of the Apocalypse *'21*

Terry Ingram
Angel and the Badman *'09*
All the Good Ones Are Married *'07*

Boris Ingster(1904-78)
The Judge Steps Out *'49*
Stranger on the Third Floor *'40*

J. Christian Ingvordsen(1957-)
Blood Relic *'05*
Airboss *'97*
The Outfit *'93*
Comrades in Arms *'91*
Covert Action *'88*
Mob War *'88*
Search and Destroy *'88*
Firehouse *'87*
Hangmen *'87*

Dan Ireland(1958-)
Living Proof *'08*
Mrs. Palfrey at the Claremont *'05*
The Velocity of Gary *'98*
The Whole Wide World *'96*

O'Dale Ireland(1928-81)
Date Bait *'60*
High School Caesar *'60*

Matthew Irmas
Sleep Easy, Hutch Rimes *'00*
Edie & Pen *'95*
When the Party's Over *'91*

John Irvin(1940-)
The Moon & the Stars *'07*
Dot.Kill *'05*
The Boys and Girl From County Clare *'03*
The Fourth Angel *'01*
Shiner *'00*
Noah's Ark *'99*
When Trumpets Fade *'98*
City of Industry *'96*
Crazy Horse *'96*
A Month by the Lake *'95*
Firefall *'94*
Widow's Peak *'94*
Eminent Domain *'91*
Robin Hood *'91*
Next of Kin *'89*
Hamburger Hill *'87*
Raw Deal *'86*
Turtle Diary *'86*
Champions *'84*
The Dogs of War *'81*
Ghost Story *'81*
Tinker, Tailor, Soldier, Spy *'80*
Haunted: The Ferryman *'74*

Sam Irvin(1956-)
Too Cool for Christmas *'04*
Elvira's Haunted Hills *'02*
Backlash: Oblivion 2 *'95*
Magic Island *'95*
Out There *'95*
Oblivion *'94*
Acting on Impulse *'93*
Guilty as Charged *'92*

David Irving(1949-)
Night of the Cyclone *'90*
C.H.U.D. 2: Bud the Chud *'89*
Rumpelstiltskin *'86*
Goodbye Cruel World *'82*

Richard Irving(1917-90)
The Jesse Owens Story *'84*
The Art of Crime *'75*
Columbo: Prescription Murder *'67*

James Isaac(1960-)
Skinwalkers *'07*
Jason X *'01*
The Horror Show *'89*

Antonio (Isasi-Isasmendi) Isasi(1927-)
Vengeance *'86*
Ricco *'74*

Robert Iscove(1947-)
Spectacular *'09*
From Justin to Kelly *'03*
Firestarter 2: Rekindled *'02*
Boys and Girls *'00*
She's All That *'99*
Cinderella *'97*
Mission of the Shark *'91*
Shattered Dreams *'90*
The Lawrenceville Stories *'88*
Puss 'n Boots *'84*

Katushito Ishii
Funky Forest: The First Contact *'06*
The Taste of Tea *'04*
Party 7 *'00*
Shark Skin Man and Peach Hip Girl *'98*

Sogo Ishii
Electric Dragon 80,000V *'01*
Angel Dust *'96*

Takashi Ishii
Flower & Snake 2 *'05*
Flower & Snake *'04*
Gonin 2 *'96*

Teru Ishii
The Street Fighter's Last Revenge *'74*
Bohachi Bushido: Code of the Forgotten Eight *'73*
Blind Woman's Curse *'70*

Neal Israel(1945-)
National Lampoon's Holiday Reunion *'03*
National Lampoon's Dad's Week Off *'97*
Surf Ninjas *'93*
Breaking the Rules *'92*
Combat Academy *'86*
Moving Violations *'85*
Bachelor Party *'84*
Americathon *'79*
Tunnelvision *'76*

Juzo Itami(1933-97)
Minbo—Or the Gentle Art of Japanese Extortion *'92*
A Taxing Woman's Return *'88*
A Taxing Woman *'87*
Tampopo *'86*
The Funeral *'84*

James Ivory(1928-)
The White Countess *'05*
Le Divorce *'03*
The Golden Bowl *'00*
A Soldier's Daughter Never Cries *'98*
Surviving Picasso *'96*
Jefferson in Paris *'94*
The Remains of the Day *'93*
Howard's End *'92*
Mr. & Mrs. Bridge *'90*
Slaves of New York *'89*
Maurice *'87*
A Room with a View *'86*
The Courtesans of Bombay *'85*
The Bostonians *'84*
Heat and Dust *'82*
Quartet *'81*
Jane Austen in Manhattan *'80*
The Europeans *'79*
Hullabaloo over Georgie & Bonnie's Pictures *'78*
Roseland *'77*
Autobiography of a Princess *'75*
Wild Party *'74*
Savages *'72*
Bombay Talkie *'70*
Shakespeare Wallah *'65*
The Householder *'63*

Shunji Iwai(1963-)
New York, I Love You *'09*
Hana & Alice *'04*
All About Lily Chou-Chou *'01*
When I Close My Eyes *'95*

David Jablin
National Lampoon's The Don's Analyst *'97*
National Lampoon's Favorite Deadly Sins *'95*

Fred W. Jackman(1881-1959)
No Man's Law *'27*
King of the Wild Horses *'24*

David S. Jackson
Return to Halloweentown *'06*
Do or Die *'03*
Atomic Train *'99*
The Jesse Ventura Story *'99*
Wolverine *'96*
Detonator 2: Night Watch *'95*
Detonator *'93*
Mystery Mansion *'83*

Donald G. Jackson(1943-2003)
Return to Frogtown *'92*
Roller Blade Warriors: Taken By Force *'90*
Hell Comes to Frogtown *'88*
Roller Blade *'85*
The Demon Lover *'77*

Douglas Jackson(1938-)
Christie's Revenge *'07*
Demons from Her Past *'07*
Framed for Murder *'07*
Nowhere in Sight *'01*
The Witness Files *'00*
Requiem for Murder *'99*
Dead End *'98*
Random Encounter *'98*
Twists of Terror *'98*
Natural Enemy *'96*
The Wrong Woman *'95*
The Paperboy *'94*
Stalked *'94*
Deadbolt *'92*
Whispers *'89*

G. Philip Jackson
2103: Deadly Wake *'97*
Replikator: Cloned to Kill *'94*

Mick Jackson(1943-)
The Memory Keeper's Daughter *'08*
The Hades Factor *'06*
Live from Baghdad *'03*

The First $20 Million is Always the Hardest '02
Tuesdays with Morrie '99
Volcano '97
Indictment: The McMartin Trial '95
Clean Slate '94
The Bodyguard '92
L.A. Story '91
Chattahoochee '89
A Very British Coup '88
Yuri Nosenko, KGB '86
Threads '85

Pat Jackson(1916-)
King Arthur, the Young Warlord '75
What a Carve-Up! '62
Encore '52

Peter Jackson(1961-)
The Lovely Bones '09
King Kong '05
Lord of the Rings: The Return of the King '03
Lord of the Rings: The Two Towers '02
Lord of the Rings: The Fellowship of the Ring '01
Forgotten Silver '96
The Frighteners '96
Heavenly Creatures '94
Dead Alive '93
Meet the Feebles '89
Bad Taste '88

Wilfred Jackson(1906-88)
Lady and the Tramp '55
Alice in Wonderland '51
Cinderella '50
Melody Time '48
Fantasia '40

Alan Jacobs
American Gun '02
Just One Night '00
Diary of a Serial Killer '97
Nina Takes a Lover '94

Gregory Jacobs
Wind Chill '07
Criminal '04

Jerry P. Jacobs
Running Red '99
Freedom Strike '98
A Dangerous Place '94

John Jacobs(1924-2001)
The First to Go '97
Rocket to the Moon '86

Lawrence-Hilton Jacobs(1953-)
Quiet Fire '91
Angels of the City '89

David Jacobson
Down in the Valley '05
Dahmer '02

Rick Jacobson
Black Thunder '98
Interlocked '98
Night Hunter '95
Suspect Device '95
Bloodfist 6: Ground Zero '94
Ring of Fire 3: Lion Strike '94
Star Quest '94
The Unborn 2 '94
Full Contact '93

Joseph Jacoby(1942-)
Great Bank Hoax '78
Hurry Up or I'll Be Thirty '73

Gualtiero Jacopetti(1919-)
Mondo Cane 2 '64
Mondo Cane '63

Benoit Jacquot(1947-)
Sade '00
Seventh Heaven '98
A Single Girl '96
The Disenchanted '90

Just Jaeckin(1940-)
The Perils of Gwendoline '84
Lady Chatterley's Lover '81
The French Woman '79
The Story of O '75
Emmanuelle '74

Henry Jaglom(1943-)
Going Shopping '05
Festival at Cannes '02
Deja Vu '98
Last Summer In the Hamptons '96
Babyfever '94
Venice, Venice '92
Eating '90
New Year's Day '89
Someone to Love '87
Always '85
Can She Bake a Cherry Pie? '83
National Lampoon Goes to the Movies '81
Sitting Ducks '80
Tracks '76
A Safe Place '71

Thomas Jahn
80 Minutes '08
The Lost Samaritan '08

Alan James(1890-1952)
Red Barry '38
Dick Tracy '37
Dick Tracy: The Spider Strikes '37
S.O.S. Coast Guard '37
Lucky Terror '36
Swifty '35
Valley of Wanted Men '35
When a Man Sees Red '34
The Lone Avenger '33
Phantom Thunderbolt '33
Trail Drive '33
Come on Tarzan '32
Fargo Express '32
Justice Rides Again '32
Tombstone Canyon '32
The Phantom '31
Backfire '22

Steve James
Reel Paradise '05
Joe and Max '02
Passing Glory '99
Prefontaine '96
Hoop Dreams '94

Jerry Jameson
Anti-Terrorist Cell: Manhunt '01
Land of the Free '98
Bonanza: The Return '93
Fire and Rain '89
The Cowboy & the Ballerina '84
Starflight One '83
Hotline '82
Killing at Hell's Gate '81
High Noon: Part 2 '80
Raise the Titanic '80
The Invasion of Johnson County '76
Sniper '75
The Bat People '74
Hurricane '74
Terror on the 40th Floor '74
Dirt Gang '71

Miklos Jancso(1921-)
Hungarian Rhapsody '78
The Red and the White '68
The Round Up '66

Conrad Janis(1928-)
November Conspiracy '96
The Feminine Touch '95

Annabel Jankel(1955-)
Super Mario Bros. '93
D.O.A. '88

Agnes Jaoui(1964-)
Look at Me '04
The Taste of Others '00

Andrew Jarecki
All Good Things '09
Capturing the Friedmans '03

Derek Jarman(1942-94)
Blue '93
Wittgenstein '93
Edward II '92
The Garden '90
Aria '88
The Last of England '87
Caravaggio '86
Sebastiane '79

Jim Jarmusch(1953-)
The Limits of Control '09
Broken Flowers '05
Coffee and Cigarettes '03
Ghost Dog: The Way of the Samurai '99
Year of the Horse '97
Dead Man '95
Night on Earth '91
Mystery Train '89
Down by Law '86
Permanent Vacation '84
Stranger than Paradise '84

Julian Jarrold
Brideshead Revisited '08
Becoming Jane '07
Kinky Boots '06
Anonymous Rex '04
All the King's Men '99
Great Expectations '99
The Painted Lady '97
Touching Evil '97
Cracker: The Big Crunch '94

Charles Jarrott(1927-)
At the Midnight Hour '95
Treacherous Beauties '94
Danielle Steel's Changes '91
Lucy and Desi: Before the Laughter '91
Night of the Fox '90
The Woman He Loved '88
Poor Little Rich Girl: The Barbara Hutton Story '87
Boy in Blue '86
The Amateur '82
Condorman '81
The Last Flight of Noah's Ark '80
The Other Side of Midnight '77
The Littlest Horse Thieves '76
The Dove '74
Mary, Queen of Scots '71
Anne of the Thousand Days '69
Dr. Jekyll and Mr. Hyde '68
Strange Case of Dr. Jekyll & Mr. Hyde '68

Ilkka Jarvilaturi(1961-)
Spy Games '99
City Unplugged '95

Steve Jarvis
Bloodstream '00
Chain of Souls '00
Things 2 '97

Vojtech Jasny(1925-)
The Great Land of Small '86
All My Good Countrymen '68

Leigh Jason(1904-79)
The Choppers '61
The Go-Getter '54
Lost Honeymoon '47
Out of the Blue '47
Lady for a Night '42
The Flying Irishman '39
Mad Miss Manton '38
The Bride Walks Out '36
That Girl from Paris '36
High Gear '33

Vadim Jean(1963-)
The Color of Magic '08
Hogfather '06
Jiminy Glick in LaLa Wood '05
One More Kiss '99
The Real Howard Spitz '98
Leon the Pig Farmer '93
Nightscare '93

Tom Jeffrey(1938-)
The Odd Angry Shot '79
Weekend of Shadows '77

Lionel Jeffries(1926-)
Water Babies '79
Wombling Free '77
Amazing Mr. Blunden '72
The Railway Children '70
No Smoking '55

Christine Jeffs(1963-)
Sunshine Cleaning '09
Sylvia '03
Rain '01

Michael Jenkins(1946-)
Sweet Talker '91
Rebel '85

Tamara Jenkins
The Savages '07
Slums of Beverly Hills '98

Garth Jennings
Son of Rambow '07
The Hitchhiker's Guide to the Galaxy '05

Anders Thomas Jensen(1972-)
Adam's Apples '05
The Green Butchers '03
Flickering Lights '01

Victoria Jenson
Post Grad '09
Shark Tale '04
Shrek '01

Alain Jessua(1932-)
The Killing Game '67
Life Upside Down '64

Jean-Pierre Jeunet(1955-)
Micmacs '09
A Very Long Engagement '04
Amelie '01
Alien: Resurrection '97
The City of Lost Children '95
Delicatessen '92

Norman Jewison(1926-)
The Statement '03
Dinner with Friends '01
The Hurricane '99
Bogus '96
Only You '94
Other People's Money '91
In Country '89
Moonstruck '87
Agnes of God '85
A Soldier's Story '84
Best Friends '82
And Justice for All '79
F.I.S.T. '78
Rollerball '75
Jesus Christ, Superstar '73
Fiddler on the Roof '71
The Thomas Crown Affair '68
In the Heat of the Night '67
The Russians Are Coming, the Russians Are Coming '66
The Cincinnati Kid '65
Send Me No Flowers '64
The Thrill of It All! '63
40 Pounds of Trouble '62

Sut Jhally(1955-)
Hijacking Catastrophe: 9/11, Fear and the Selling of America '04
Peace, Propaganda & the Promised Land '04

Phil Joanou(1961-)
Gridiron Gang '06
Entropy '99
Heaven's Prisoners '95
Fallen Angels 2 '93
Wild Palms '93
Final Analysis '92
State of Grace '90
U2: Rattle and Hum '88
Three o'Clock High '87

Richard Jobson(1960-)
The Purifiers '04
16 Years of Alcohol '03

Arthur Joffe(1953-)
Alberto Express '92
Harem '85

Mark Joffe(1956-)
The Matchmaker '97
Cosi '95
The Efficiency Expert '92
Grievous Bodily Harm '89
Night Master '87

Roland Joffe(1945-)
Captivity '07
Vatel '00
Goodbye, Lover '99
The Scarlet Letter '95
City of Joy '92
Fat Man and Little Boy '89
The Mission '86
The Killing Fields '84

Sande N. Johnsen
Teenage Gang Debs '66
The Beautiful, the Bloody and the Bare '64

Alan Johnson
Solarbabies '86
To Be or Not to Be '83

Clark Johnson(1954-)
The Sentinel '06
Sleeper Cell '05
S.W.A.T. '03
Boycott '02

Emory Johnson(1894-1960)
Phantom Express '32
West-Bound Limited '23

Irvin Johnson
Blood Ring '93
Fist of Steel '93

Jesse Johnson(1971-)
Green Street Hooligans 2 '09
Alien Agent '07
The Butcher '07

Jesse Johnson(1982-)
The Last Sentinel '07
Pit Fighter '05

Kenneth Johnson(1942-)
Steel '97
Alien Nation: Millennium '96
Alien Nation: The Enemy Within '96
Alien Nation: Body and Soul '95
Alien Nation: Dark Horizon '94
Short Circuit 2 '88
Hot Pursuit '84
V '83
Senior Trip '81
The Incredible Hulk '77

Lamont Johnson(1922-)
The Kennedys of Massachusetts '95
The Broken Chain '93
A Thousand Heroes '92
Escape '90
Gore Vidal's Lincoln '88
Unnatural Causes '86
Ernie Kovacs: Between the Laughter '84
Jack & the Beanstalk '83
Spacehunter: Adventures in the Forbidden Zone '83
Crisis at Central High '80
One on One '77
Lipstick '76
The Execution of Private Slovik '74
The Last American Hero '73
The Groundstar Conspiracy '72
You'll Like My Mother '72
A Gunfight '71
McKenzie Break '70
My Sweet Charlie '70

Mark Steven Johnson(1964-)
When in Rome '09
Ghost Rider '07
Daredevil '03
Simon Birch '98

Nunnally Johnson(1897-1977)
The Three Faces of Eve '57
The Man in the Gray Flannel Suit '56
Black Widow '54

Patrick Read Johnson(1964-)
When Good Ghouls Go Bad '01
Angus '95
Baby's Day Out '94
Spaced Invaders '90

Raymond K. Johnson
See Bernard B. Ray

Rian Johnson
The Brothers Bloom '09
Brick '06

Tim Johnson
Over the Hedge '06
Sinbad: Legend of the Seven Seas '03
Antz '98

Aaron Kim Johnston
For the Moment '94
The Last Winter '89

Joe Johnston(1950-)
The Wolfman '09
Hidalgo '04
Jurassic Park 3 '01
October Sky '99
Jumanji '95
The Pagemaster '94
The Rocketeer '91
Honey, I Shrunk the Kids '89

Amy Holden Jones(1953-)
The Rich Man's Wife '96
Maid to Order '87
Love Letters '83
Slumber Party Massacre '82

Brian Thomas Jones
Posed for Murder '89
Escape from Safehaven '88
The Rejuvenator '88
Ocean Drive Weekend '85

Chuck Jones(1912-2002)
Looney Looney Looney Bugs Bunny Movie '81
Phantom Tollbooth '69

David Hugh Jones(1934-)
A Christmas Carol '99
The Confession '98
An Unexpected Life '97
Is There Life Out There? '94
The Trial '93
Jacknife '89
Look Back in Anger '89
The Christmas Wife '88
84 Charing Cross Road '86
Betrayal '83

Donald M. Jones(1953-)
Lethal Pursuit '88
Murderlust '86
Project: Nightmare '85
Deadly Sunday '82
Love Butcher '82
Sweater Girls '78

F. Richard Jones(1894-1930)
Bulldog Drummond '29
The Gaucho '27
Extra Girl '23
Yankee Doodle in Berlin '19

Gary Jones
Boogeyman 3 '08
Ghouls '07
Crocodile 2: Death Swamp '01
Spiders '00
Mosquito '95
Stay Tuned for Murder '88

Harmon Jones(1911-72)
Bullwhip '58
The Legend of the Sea Wolf '58
Canyon River '56

Bloodhounds of Broadway '52
Pride of St. Louis '52
As Young As You Feel '51

James Cellan Jones(1931-)
The Vacillations of Poppy Carew '94
Fortunes of War '87
The Golden Bowl '72
Portrait of a Lady '67

Jon Jones
The Diary of Anne Frank '08
Northanger Abbey '07
The Secret Life of Mrs. Beeton '06
Archangel '05
The Debt '03

Kirk Jones(1963-)
Everybody's Fine '09
Nanny McPhee '06
Waking Ned Devine '98

Mark Jones(1953-)
Rumpelstiltskin '96
Leprechaun '93

Pete Jones
Outing Riley '04
Stolen Summer '02

Philip Jones(1963-2003)
Asylum of the Damned '03
Backflash '01
Wish Me Luck '95
Cause of Death '90

Simon Cellan Jones
Generation Kill '08
The Queen's Sister '05

Terry Jones(1942-)
Mr. Toad's Wild Ride '96
Erik the Viking '89
Personal Services '87
Monty Python's The Meaning of Life '83
Monty Python's Life of Brian '79
Monty Python and the Holy Grail '75

Tommy Lee Jones(1946-)
The Three Burials of Melquiades Estrada '05
The Good Old Boys '95

Spike Jonze(1969-)
Where the Wild Things Are '09
Adaptation '02
Being John Malkovich '99

Glenn Jordan(1936-)
Night Ride Home '99
Sarah, Plain and Tall: Winter's End '99
Legalese '98
My Brother's Keeper '95
A Streetcar Named Desire '95
Barbarians at the Gate '93
To Dance with the White Dog '93
O Pioneers! '91
Sarah, Plain and Tall '91
Jesse '88
Echoes in the Darkness '87
Dress Gray '86
Something in Common '86
Toughlove '85
Mass Appeal '84
The Buddy System '83
Lois Gibbs and the Love Canal '82
Only When I Laugh '81
The Family Man '79
Les Miserables '78
One of My Wives Is Missing '76
Picture of Dorian Gray '74
Frankenstein '73

Gregor Jordan(1967-)
The Informers '09
Ned Kelly '03
Buffalo Soldiers '01

Two Hands '98
Twisted '96

Kevin Jordan(1974-)
Brooklyn Lobster '05
Smiling Fish & Goat on Fire '99

Neil Jordan(1950-)
The Brave One '07
The Good Thief '03
The End of the Affair '99
In Dreams '98
The Butcher Boy '97
Michael Collins '96
Interview with the Vampire '94
The Crying Game '92
The Miracle '91
We're No Angels '89
High Spirits '88
Mona Lisa '86
The Company of Wolves '85
Danny Boy '82

Jon Jost(1943-)
The Bed You Sleep In '93
Jon Jost's Frameup '93
All the Vermeers in New York '91
Sure Fire '90
Slow Moves '84

C. Courtney Joyner
Lurking Fear '94
Trancers 3: Deth Lives '92

Mike Judge(1962-)
Extract '09
Idiocracy '06
Office Space '98
Beavis and Butt-Head Do America '96

Rupert Julian(1889-1943)
Yankee Clipper '27
Walking Back '26
The Phantom of the Opera '25
Merry-Go-Round '23

Gil Junger(1954-)
If Only '04
Black Knight '01
Ten Things I Hate about You '99

Nathan "Jerry" Juran(1907-2002)
Land Raiders '69
First Men in the Moon '64
Jack the Giant Killer '62
Attack of the 50 Foot Woman '58
Good Day for a Hanging '58
The Seventh Voyage of Sinbad '58
The Brain from Planet Arous '57
The Deadly Mantis '57
Hellcats of the Navy '57
20 Million Miles to Earth '57
Gunsmoke '53
Law and Order '53
The Black Castle '52

Paul Justman
Standing in the Shadows of Motown '02
Gimme an F '85

Claude Jutra(1930-86)
My Father, My Rival '85
Surfacing '84
By Design '82
Mon Oncle Antoine '71

Karel Kachyna(1924-2004)
The Cow '93
The Last Butterfly '92

George Kaczender(1933-)
Maternal Instincts '96
Vanished '95
Prettykill '87
Your Ticket Is No Longer Valid '84
The Agency '81

Chanel Solitaire '81
In Praise of Older Women '78
The Girl in Blue '74

Jan Kadar(1918-79)
Freedom Road '79
Lies My Father Told Me '75
The Angel Levine '70
The Shop on Main Street '65
Death Is Called Engelchen '63

Ellis Kadison(1928-98)
The Cat '66
Git! '65

Jeremy Paul Kagan(1945-)
Bobbie's Girl '02
Crown Heights '02
Taken '02
Color of Justice '97
Roswell: The U.F.O. Cover-Up '94
By the Sword '93
Descending Angel '90
Big Man on Campus '89
Conspiracy: The Trial of the Chicago Eight '87
Courage '86
The Journey of Natty Gann '85
The Sting 2 '83
The Chosen '81
The Big Fix '78
Heroes '77
Katherine '75

Cedric Kahn(1966-)
Red Lights '04
L'Ennui '98

Harvey Kahn
The Deal '05
Water's Edge '03

Richard C. Kahn(1897-1960)
Guns Don't Argue '57
The Phantom Pinto '41
Buzzy Rides the Range '40
Son of Ingagi '40
Bronze Buckaroo '39
Harlem Rides the Range '39
Two-Gun Man from Harlem '38

Chen Kaige(1952-)
The Promise '05
Together '02
Killing Me Softly '01
The Emperor and the Assassin '99
Temptress Moon '96
Farewell My Concubine '93
Life on a String '90
Yellow Earth '89

Mikhail Kalatozov(1903-73)
Red Tent '69
I Am Cuba '64
The Cranes Are Flying '57

Tom Kalin
Savage Grace '07
Swoon '91

Max Kalmanowicz
Dreams Come True '84
The Children '80

Scott Kalvert
Deuces Wild '02
The Basketball Diaries '95

Deborah Kampmeier
Hounddog '08
Virgin '03

Joseph Kane(1897-1975)
Smoke in the Wind '75
He Lives: The Search for the Evil One '67
The Maverick Queen '55
Jubilee Trail '54
Ride the Man Down '53
Hoodlum Empire '52
The Cheaters '45

Dakota '45
Flame of the Barbary Coast '45
Cowboy & the Senorita '44
Song of Nevada '44
The Yellow Rose of Texas '44
Hands Across the Border '43
Idaho '43
King of the Cowboys '43
Silver Spurs '43
Song of Texas '43
Texas Legionnaires '43
Texas Legionnaires '43
Heart of the Golden West '42
Man from Cheyenne '42
Ridin' Down the Canyon '42
Romance on the Range '42
Sons of the Pioneers '42
South of Santa Fe '42
Sunset on the Desert '42
Sunset Serenade '42
Bad Man of Deadwood '41
In Old Cheyenne '41
Jesse James at Bay '41
Nevada City '41
Red River Valley '41
Robin Hood of the Pecos '41
Sheriff of Tombstone '41
The Border Legion '40
Carson City Kid '40
Colorado '40
Ranger and the Lady '40
Young Bill Hickok '40
Young Buffalo Bill '40
Arizona Kid '39
Days of Jesse James '39
Frontier Pony Express '39
In Old Caliente '39
Rough Riders' Roundup '39
Saga of Death Valley '39
Southward Ho! '39
Wall Street Cowboy '39
Billy the Kid Returns '38
Born to Be Wild '38
Come on Rangers '38
Oh Susannah '38
Old Barn Dance '38
Shine on, Harvest Moon '38
Boots & Saddles '37
Come on, Cowboys '37
Git Along Little Dogies '37
Heart of the Rockies '37
Public Cowboy No. 1 '37
Round-Up Time in Texas '37
Springtime in the Rockies '37
Yodelin' Kid from Pine Ridge '37
Darkest Africa '36
Fighting Marines '36
Ghost Town Gold '36
King of the Pecos '36
The Lawless Nineties '36
Old Corral '36
Ride, Ranger, Ride '36
Melody Trail '35
In Old Santa Fe '34

Rolfe Kanefsky(1969-)
The Hazing '04
My Family Treasure '93
There's Nothing out There '90

Shusuke (Shu) Kaneko(1955-)
Death Note 2: The Last Name '07
Azumi 2 '05
H.P. Lovecraft's Necronomicon: Book of the Dead '93
Summer Vacation: 1999 '88

Jeff Kanew(1944-)
National Lampoon's Adam & Eve '05
V.I. Warshawski '91
Troop Beverly Hills '89
Tough Guys '86
Gotcha! '85
Revenge of the Nerds '84
Eddie Macon's Run '83
Natural Enemies '79

Woo-suk Kang
Another Public Enemy '05
Public Enemy '02

Charles Kanganis
Impulse '08
K-911 '99
Dennis the Menace Strikes Again '98
Race the Sun '96
3 Ninjas Kick Back '94
No Escape, No Return '93
A Time to Die '91
Chance '89
Deadly Breed '89
Sinners '89

Marek Kanievska(1952-)
A Different Loyalty '04
Where the Money Is '00
Less Than Zero '87
Another Country '84

Garson Kanin(1912-99)
Tom, Dick, and Harry '41
My Favorite Wife '40
They Knew What They Wanted '40
Bachelor Mother '39
A Man to Remember '39
The Great Man Votes '38
Next Time I Marry '38

Hal Kanter(1918-)
For the Love of It '80
Loving You '57
I Married a Woman '56

Asif Kapadia(1972-)
Far North '07
The Return '06
The Warrior '81

Deborah Kaplan
Josie and the Pussycats '01
Can't Hardly Wait '98

Ed Kaplan
Primal Secrets '94
Chips, the War Dog '90
Walking on Air '87

Jonathan Kaplan(1947-)
Brokedown Palace '99
In Cold Blood '96
Bad Girls '94
Fallen Angels 1 '93
Unlawful Entry '92
Love Field '91
Immediate Family '89
The Accused '88
Project X '87
Girls of the White Orchid '85
Heart Like a Wheel '83
Gentleman Bandit '81
Over the Edge '79
Mr. Billion '77
White Line Fever '75
Truck Turner '74
The Student Teachers '73
Night Call Nurses '72

Nelly Kaplan(1934-)
Charles et Lucie '79
Nea '78
A Very Curious Girl '69

Shekhar Kapur(1945-)
New York, I Love You '09
Elizabeth: The Golden Age '07
The Four Feathers '02
Elizabeth '98
Bandit Queen '94

Wong Kar-Wai(1958-)
Ashes of Time Redux '08
My Blueberry Nights '07
Eros '04
2046 '04
In the Mood for Love '00
Happy Together '96
Chungking Express '95
Fallen Angels '95
Ashes of Time '94

Michael Karbelnikoff
The Last Ride '94
Mobsters '91

Phil Karlson(1908-85)
Framed '75
Walking Tall '73

Ben '72
Hornet's Nest '70
The Wrecking Crew '68
The Silencers '66
Kid Galahad '62
Scarface Mob '62
Hell to Eternity '60
Gunman's Walk '58
The Brothers Rico '57
5 Against the House '55
Tight Spot '55
Kansas City Confidential '52
Scandal Sheet '52
The Texas Rangers '51
The Big Cat '49
Ladies of the Chorus '49
Behind the Mask '46
Swing Parade of 1946 '46
The Shanghai Cobra '45
There Goes Kelly '45

Bill Karn(1913-66)
Door to Door Maniac '61
Ma Barker's Killer Brood '60
Guns Don't Argue '57
Gang Busters '55

Matia Karrell
Once Upon a Wedding '05
Behind the Red Door '02

Eric Karson
Angel Town '89
Black Eagle '88
Opposing Force '87
Octagon '80

Jake Kasdan(1975-)
Walk Hard: The Dewey Cox Story '07
The TV Set '06
Orange County '02
Zero Effect '97

Lawrence Kasdan(1949-)
Dreamcatcher '03
Mumford '99
French Kiss '95
Wyatt Earp '94
Grand Canyon '91
I Love You to Death '90
The Accidental Tourist '88
Silverado '85
The Big Chill '83
Body Heat '81

Sam Henry Kass
Body and Soul '98
The Search for One-Eye Jimmy '96

Mathieu Kassovitz(1967-)
Babylon A.D. '08
Gothika '03
The Crimson Rivers '01
Hate '95
Cafe au Lait '94

Peter Kassovitz(1938-)
Jakob the Liar '99
Make Room for Tomorrow '81

Jeremy Kasten
The Wizard of Gore '07
The Thirst '06
All Souls Day '05

Brian Katkin
Shakedown '02
Hard As Nails '01
If I Die Before I Wake '98

Michael Katleman
Primeval '07
Bloodhounds '96
The Spider and the Fly '94

Milton Katselas(1933-)
Strangers: The Story of a Mother and Daughter '79
Report to the Commissioner '74
Forty Carats '73
Butterflies Are Free '72

Lee H. Katzin(1935-2002)
Restraining Order '99
The Break '95

The Dirty Dozen: The Fatal Mission '88
World Gone Wild '88
The Dirty Dozen: The Deadly Mission '87
Death Ray 2000 '81
Space: 1999—Alien Attack '79
The Bastard '78
Terror Out of the Sky '78
The Man from Atlantis '77
The Captive: The Longest Drive 2 '76
The Longest Drive '76
Savages '75
Sky Hei$t '75
The Stranger '73
The Salzburg Connection '72
The Voyage of the Yes '72
Le Mans '71
Whatever Happened to Aunt Alice? '69

Jonathan Kaufer(1955-)
Bad Manners '98
Soup for One '82

Charles Kaufman
Jakarta '88
When Nature Calls '85
Mother's Day '80

Jim Kaufman
Nightwaves '03
Time at the Top '99
Night of the Demons 3 '97
Whiskers '96
Backstab '90

Lloyd Kaufman(1945-)
Citizen Toxie: The Toxic Avenger 4 '01
Tromeo & Juliet '95
Sgt. Kabukiman N.Y.P.D. '94
The Toxic Avenger, Part 2 '89
The Toxic Avenger, Part 3: The Last Temptation of Toxie '89
Troma's War '88
Class of Nuke 'Em High '86
The Toxic Avenger '86
Stuck on You '84
First Turn On '83
Waitress '81
Squeeze Play '79

Philip Kaufman(1936-)
Twisted '04
Quills '00
Rising Sun '93
Henry & June '90
The Unbearable Lightness of Being '88
The Right Stuff '83
Wanderers '79
Invasion of the Body Snatchers '78
The White Dawn '75
The Great Northfield Minnesota Raid '72
Goldstein '64

Aki Kaurismaki(1957-)
Lights in the Dusk '06
The Man Without a Past '02
La Vie de Boheme '93
The Match Factory Girl '90
Ariel '89
Leningrad Cowboys Go America '89

Mika Kaurismaki(1955-)
Condition Red '95
Zombie and the Ghost Train '91
Amazon '90

Helmut Kautner(1908-80)
The Captain from Koepenick '56
The Last Bridge '54
Die Grosse Freiheit Nr. 7 '45

Denis Kavanagh(1906-84)
Flight from Vienna '56

The Ghost of Rashmon Hall '47

Anwar Kawadri(1953-)
Claudia '85
Nutcracker Sweet '84

Yoshiaki Kawajiri
Wicked City '89
Lensman '84

Jerzy Kawalerowicz(1922-2007)
Pharaoh '66
Mother Joan of the Angels '60
Shadow '56

Koji Kawano(1972-)
Cruel Restaurant '08
Attack Girls' Swim Team vs. the Undead '07

Kikuo Kawasaki
Lured Innocence '97
Private Passions '85

Minoru Kawasaki
Executive Koala '06
The Rug Cop '06
The World Sinks Except Japan '06
The Calamari Wrestler '04

Stephen Kay
Boogeyman '05
Get Carter '00
The Last Time I Committed Suicide '96

Richard Kaye
Fist '76
Homeboy '75

Robert Kaylor(1934-)
Nobody's Perfect '90
Carny '80
Derby '71

Elia Kazan(1909-2003)
The Last Tycoon '76
The Arrangement '69
Splendor in the Grass '61
A Face in the Crowd '57
Baby Doll '56
East of Eden '54
On the Waterfront '54
Viva Zapata! '52
A Streetcar Named Desire '51
Panic in the Streets '50
Pinky '49
Boomerang '47
Gentleman's Agreement '47
A Tree Grows in Brooklyn '45

James Keach(1948-)
Blind Dating '06
Camouflage '00
The Stars Fell on Henrietta '94
Praying Mantis '93
Sunstroke '92
False Identity '90
The Forgotten '89

Kevin Keating
Giuliani Time '05
Hell's Angels Forever '83

Buster Keaton(1895-1966)
Battling Butler '26
The General '26
Seven Chances '25
The Navigator '24
Sherlock, Jr. '24
Our Hospitality '23
Three Ages '23

Diane Keaton(1946-)
Hanging Up '99
Unstrung Heroes '95
Wildflower '91
Heaven '87

Bob Keen(1960-)
Sir Arthur Conan Doyle's The Lost World '98
Proteus '95

To Catch a Yeti '95

Don Keeslar
Bog '84
The Capture of Grizzly Adams '82

Worth Keeter
Last Lives '98
Memorial Day '98
Snapdragon '93
Illicit Behavior '91
L.A. Bounty '89
Trapper County War '89
Order of the Black Eagle '87
Unmasking the Idol '86
Dogs of Hell '83
Lady Grey '82
The Wolfman '82

Jon Keeyes
Living & Dying '07
Mad Bad '07
American Nightmare '00

Peter Keglevic(1950-)
Kill Cruise '90
The Cop & the Girl '86

William Keighley(1889-1972)
The Master of Ballantrae '53
Close to My Heart '51
Rocky Mountain '50
The Street with No Name '48
George Washington Slept Here '42
The Bride Came C.O.D. '41
The Man Who Came to Dinner '41
The Fighting 69th '40
Torrid Zone '40
Each Dawn I Die '39
Bullets or Ballots '38
The Prince and the Pauper '37
Varsity Show '37
Green Pastures '36
The Singing Kid '36
"G" Men '35
Ladies They Talk About '33

David Keith(1954-)
The Further Adventures of Tennessee Buck '88
The Curse '87

Harvey Keith
Stand-Ins '97
Jezebel's Kiss '90

Frederick King Keller
Vamping '84
The Eyes of the Amaryllis '82

Harry Keller(1913-87)
The Brass Bottle '63
Tammy and the Doctor '63
Texas John Slaughter: Stampede at Bitter Creek '62
Geronimo's Revenge '60
Texas John Slaughter: Geronimo's Revenge '60
Phantom Stallion '54
El Paso Stampede '53
Marshal of Cedar Rock '53

Albert Kelley(1894-1989)
Motorcycle Squad '41
Jungle Bride '33
Campus Knights '29

Roy Kellino(1912-56)
Charade '53
I Met a Murderer '39

Nick Kellis
Endangered '94
Uncivilized '94

Bob Kelljan(1930-82)
Black Oak Conspiracy '77
Act of Vengeance '74
Scream Blacula Scream '73
The Return of Count Yorga '71
Count Yorga, Vampire '70

Barnet Kellman(1947-)
Slappy and the Stinkers '97
Straight Talk '92
Key Exchange '85

David Kellogg(1952-)
Inspector Gadget '99
Cool As Ice '91

Ray Kellogg(1905-76)
The Giant Gila Monster '59
The Killer Shrews '59

Gene Kelly(1912-96)
That's Entertainment, Part 2 '76
The Cheyenne Social Club '70
Hello, Dolly! '69
A Guide for the Married Man '67
The Tunnel of Love '58
Invitation to the Dance '56
Singin' in the Rain '52
On the Town '49

Richard Kelly(1975-)
The Box '09
Southland Tales '06
Donnie Darko '01

Sarah Kelly
The Lather Effect '06
Full Tilt Boogie '97

Gil Kenan
City of Ember '08
Monster House '06

Nicholas (Nick) Kendall(1949-)
Mr. Rice's Secret '00
Cadillac Girls '93

Burt Kennedy(1922-2001)
Suburban Commando '91
Big Bad John '90
Texas Guns '90
Dynamite and Gold '88
The Trouble with Spies '87
More Wild, Wild West '80
The Concrete Cowboys '79
Wild, Wild West Revisited '79
Wolf Lake '79
The Killer Inside Me '76
All the Kind Strangers '74
Train Robbers '73
Hannie Caulder '72
Ride to Glory '71
Support Your Local Gunfighter '71
The Good Guys and the Bad Guys '69
Support Your Local Sheriff '69
The War Wagon '67
Return of the Magnificent Seven '66
The Money Trap '65
The Rounders '65
Mail Order Bride '63

Chris Kennedy
Doing Time for Patsy Cline '97
Glass '90

Ken Kennedy
Grizzly Adams: The Legend Continues '90
Mission to Glory '80
Iron Angel '64

Michael Kennedy(1954-)
The Heist '96
Robin of Locksley '95
Broken Lullaby '94
Hard Evidence '94
Red Scorpion 2 '94
The Swordsman '92
Talons of the Eagle '92
Erik '90
One Man Out '89
Caribe '87

Billy Kent
Endgame '09
The Oh in Ohio '06

Larry Kent(1900-67)
The Victory '81
The Apprentice '71

Chris Kentis(1962-)
Open Water '03
Grind '96

Erle C. Kenton(1896-1980)
One Too Many '51
House of Dracula '45
House of Frankenstein '44
It Ain't Hay '43
The Ghost of Frankenstein '42
Pardon My Sarong '42
Who Done It? '42
Melody for Three '41
They Meet Again '41
Remedy for Riches '40
Escape to Paradise '39
Frolics on Ice '39
Search for Beauty '34
Island of Lost Souls '32
Bare Knees '28

James V. Kern(1909-66)
The Second Woman '51
Two Tickets to Broadway '51
Never Say Goodbye '46

Sarah Kernochan(1947-)
All I Wanna Do '98
Marjoe '72

Lodge Kerrigan(1964-)
Keane '04
Claire Dolan '97
Clean, Shaven '93

Irvin Kershner(1923-)
RoboCop 2 '90
Traveling Man '89
Never Say Never Again '83
The Empire Strikes Back '80
Eyes of Laura Mars '78
Raid on Entebbe '77
The Return of a Man Called Horse '76
S*P*Y*S '74
Up the Sandbox '72
Loving '70
Flim-Flam Man '67
A Fine Madness '66
A Face in the Rain '63
The Hoodlum Priest '61

Harry Kerwin(1930-79)
Barracuda '78
God's Bloody Acre '75
Cheering Section '73

Alek Keshishian(1964-)
Love and Other Disasters '06
With Honors '94
Truth or Dare '91

Bruce Kessler(1936-)
Cruise into Terror '78
Deathmoon '78
Simon, King of the Witches '71
The Gay Deceivers '69
Angels from Hell '68

Stephen Kessler
The Independent '00
Vegas Vacation '96

Michael Keusch(1955-)
Attack Force '06
Shadow Man '06
Double Cross '94
Anything for Love '93
Huck and the King of Hearts '93
Just One of the Girls '93
Samurai Cowboy '93
Lena's Holiday '90

Callie Khouri(1957-)
Mad Money '08
Divine Secrets of the Ya-Ya Sisterhood '02

Kim Ki Duk
Spring, Summer, Fall, Winter... and Spring '03

Bad Guy '01

Abbas Kiarostami(1940-)
The Taste of Cherry '96
Through the Olive Trees '94
Life and Nothing More ... '92
Where Is My Friend's House? '87

Dylan Kidd(1969-)
P.S. '04
Roger Dodger '02

Beeban Kidron(1961-)
Bridget Jones: The Edge of Reason '04
Swept from the Sea '97
To Wong Foo, Thanks for Everything, Julie Newmar '95
Shades of Fear '93
Used People '92
Antonia and Jane '91
Oranges Are Not the Only Fruit '89

Fritz Kiersch(1951-)
The Stranger '95
Shattered Image '93
Into the Sun '92
Under the Boardwalk '89
Gor '88
Winners Take All '87
Tuff Turf '85
Children of the Corn '84

Krzysztof Kieslowski(1941-96)
Trois Couleurs: Blanc '94
Trois Couleurs: Rouge '94
Trois Couleurs: Bleu '93
The Double Life of Veronique '91
The Decalogue '88
No End '84
Camera Buff '79

Gerard Kikoine(1946-)
Buried Alive '89
Edge of Sanity '89
Dragonard '88

Edward Killy
West of the Pecos '45
Nevada '44

Clare Kilner
American Virgin '09
The Wedding Date '05
How to Deal '03
Janice Beard '99

Ji-woon Kim
A Tale of Two Sisters '03
3 Extremes 2 '02
The Foul King '00
The Quiet Family '98

Ki-Duk Kim
Time '06
Samaritan Girl '04
The Isle '01

Bruce Kimmel(1947-)
The Creature Wasn't Nice '81
Spaceship '81
The First Nudie Musical '75

Anthony Kimmins(1910-62)
Captain's Paradise '53
Bonnie Prince Charlie '48
Mine Own Executioner '47

John Kincade
Back to Back '90
Terminal Entry '87

Tim Kincaid(1952-)
The Occultist '89
Maximum Thrust '88
She's Back '88
Mutant Hunt '87
Necropolis '87
Robot Holocaust '87
Breeders '86
Bad Girls Dormitory '84

Allan King(1930-)
By Way of the Stars '92

Kurt Vonnegut's Monkey House *'91*
One Night Stand *'78*
Who Has Seen the Wind? *'77*

Burton King(1877-1944)
When Lightning Strikes *'34*
The Adorable Cheat *'28*
The Man from Beyond *'22*
The Houdini Serial *'20*

George King(1899-1966)
The Case of the Frightened Lady *'39*
Crimes at the Dark House *'39*
The Face at the Window *'39*
The Hooded Terror *'38*
Sexton Blake and the Hooded Terror *'38*
Ticket of Leave Man *'37*
The Crimes of Stephen Hawke *'36*
Demon Barber of Fleet Street *'36*
Matinee Idol *'33*

Henry King(1888-1982)
Beloved Infidel *'59*
The Bravados *'58*
Carousel *'56*
Love Is a Many-Splendored Thing *'55*
The Snows of Kilimanjaro *'52*
David and Bathsheba *'51*
I'd Climb the Highest Mountain *'51*
The Gunfighter *'50*
Prince of Foxes *'49*
Twelve o'Clock High *'49*
Captain from Castile *'47*
Wilson *'44*
The Song of Bernadette *'43*
The Black Swan *'42*
A Yank in the R.A.F. *'41*
Jesse James *'39*
Stanley and Livingstone *'39*
Alexander's Ragtime Band *'38*
In Old Chicago *'37*
Lloyds of London *'36*
Marie Galante *'34*
Hell Harbor *'30*
She Goes to War *'29*
The Winning of Barbara Worth *'26*
Romola *'25*
The White Sister *'23*
Tol'able David *'21*

Jeff King
Ruslan *'09*
Kill Switch *'08*

Louis King(1898-1962)
Massacre *'56*
Dangerous Mission *'54*
Sabre Jet *'53*
Mrs. Mike *'49*
Bulldog Drummond Comes Back *'37*
Bulldog Drummond's Revenge *'37*
Wine, Women and Horses *'37*
Special Investigator *'36*
Charlie Chan in Egypt *'35*
Drifting Souls *'32*
Police Court *'32*
Border Law *'31*
The Fighting Sheriff *'31*

Michael Patrick King
Sex and the City 2 *'10*
Sex and the City: The Movie *'08*

Rick King
Catherine's Grove *'98*
Road Ends *'98*
Terminal Justice: Cybertech P.D. *'95*
A Passion to Kill *'94*
Quick *'93*
Kickboxer 3: The Art of War *'92*
Prayer of the Rollerboys *'91*
Forced March *'90*
The Killing Time *'87*
Hot Shot *'86*
Hard Choices *'84*

Robert King
Angels in the Infield *'00*
The Principal Takes a Holiday *'98*

Robert Lee King
Psycho Beach Party *'00*
Boys Life *'94*

Zalman King(1941-)
Red Shoe Diaries: Luscious Lola *'00*
Red Shoe Diaries: Swimming Naked *'00*
In God's Hands *'98*
Shame, Shame, Shame *'98*
Red Shoe Diaries: Four on the Floor *'96*
Red Shoe Diaries: Strip Poker *'96*
Delta of Venus *'95*
Red Shoe Diaries 3: Another Woman's Lipstick *'93*
Red Shoe Diaries 4: Auto Erotica *'93*
Red Shoe Diaries *'92*
Red Shoe Diaries 2: Double Dare *'92*
Wild Orchid 2: Two Shades of Blue *'92*
Wild Orchid *'90*
Two Moon Junction *'88*
Wildfire *'88*

Jack Kinney(1909-92)
1001 Arabian Nights *'59*
The Legend of Sleepy Hollow *'49*
Melody Time *'48*
Fun & Fancy Free *'47*

Brian Kirk(1968-)
My Boy Jack *'07*
Middletown *'06*

Karey Kirkpatrick
Imagine That *'09*
Over the Hedge *'06*

Ralf Kirsten(1930-)
Under the Pear Tree *'73*
On the Sunny Side *'62*

Ryuhei Kitamura
The Midnight Meat Train *'08*
Azumi *'03*
Versus *'00*

Takeshi "Beat" Kitano(1948-)
Zatoichi *'03*
Dolls *'02*
Brother *'00*
Kikujiro *'99*
Fireworks *'97*
Sonatine *'96*
Boiling Point *'90*
Violent Cop *'89*

Martin Kitrosser
Daddy's Girl *'96*
The Fiance *'96*
Silent Night, Deadly Night 5: The Toymaker *'91*

Robert J. Kizer(1952-)
Death Ring *'93*
Hell Comes to Frogtown *'88*
Godzilla 1985 *'85*

Alf Kjellin(1920-88)
The Girls of Huntington House *'73*
The McMasters *'70*

Robert Klane(1941-)
Weekend at Bernie's 2 *'93*
Thank God It's Friday *'78*

Cedric Klapisch(1961-)
Russian Dolls *'05*
L'Auberge Espagnole *'02*
Un Air de Famille *'96*
When the Cat's Away *'96*

Josh Klausner
Date Night *'10*
The 4th Floor *'99*

Randal Kleiser(1946-)
Shadow of Doubt *'98*
It's My Party *'95*
Honey, I Blew Up the Kid *'92*
White Fang *'91*
Getting It Right *'89*
Big Top Pee-wee *'88*
Flight of the Navigator *'86*
Grandview U.S.A. *'84*
Summer Lovers *'82*
The Blue Lagoon *'80*
Grease *'78*
The Gathering *'77*
The Boy in the Plastic Bubble *'76*

Walter Klenhard
Disappearance *'02*
The Haunting of Seacliff Inn *'94*

Richard Kletter
The Android Affair *'95*
Dangerous Indiscretion *'94*

Max Kleven(1933-)
Fugitive Champion *'99*
Bail Out *'90*
Deadly Stranger *'88*
Ruckus *'81*

Elem Klimov(1933-2003)
Come and See *'85*
Rasputin *'85*

Leon Klimovsky(1907-96)
The Devil's Possessed *'74*
Orgy of the Vampires *'73*
The Saga of the Draculas *'72*
Vengeance of the Zombies *'72*
Dr. Jekyll and the Wolfman *'71*
Challenge of McKenna *'70*
The Werewolf vs. the Vampire Woman *'70*
Rattler Kid *'68*
Commando Attack *'67*

Herbert Kline(1909-99)
The Fighter *'52*
The Kid From Cleveland *'49*

Werner Klingler(1903-72)
Secret of the Black Trunk *'62*
Testament of Dr. Mabuse *'62*

Glenn Klinker
The Nickel Children *'05*
Dark Justice *'00*

Dan Klores
Crazy Love *'07*
The Boys of 2nd Street Park *'03*

Elmar Klos(1910-93)
The Shop on Main Street *'65*
Death Is Called Engelchen *'63*

Nicolas Klotz
Heartbeat Detector *'07*
The Bengali Night *'88*

Steve Kloves(1960-)
Flesh and Bone *'93*
The Fabulous Baker Boys *'89*

Robert Knights(1942-)
The Man Who Made Husbands Jealous *'98*
Mosley *'98*
Double Vision *'92*
And a Nightingale Sang *'91*
The Dawning *'88*
A Dedicated Man *'86*
Ebony Tower *'86*
Miss A & Miss M *'86*
Lovers of Their Time *'85*

Bernard Knowles(1900-75)
Frozen Alive *'64*
Murder on Approval *'56*
Norman Conquest *'53*
The Magic Bow *'47*

Philip Ko
Interpol Connection *'92*
Platoon the Warriors *'88*

Masaki Kobayashi(1916-96)
Samurai Rebellion *'67*
Kwaidan *'64*
Harakiri *'62*
The Human Condition: A Soldier's Prayer *'61*
The Human Condition: Road to Eternity *'59*
The Human Condition: No Greater Love *'58*

Chris Koch
A Guy Thing *'03*
Snow Day *'00*

Howard W. Koch(1916-2001)
Badge 373 *'73*
Born Reckless *'59*
Frankenstein 1970 *'58*
Girl in Black Stockings *'57*
Untamed Youth *'57*

David Koepp(1964-)
Ghost Town *'08*
Secret Window *'04*
Stir of Echoes *'99*
The Trigger Effect *'96*

Ana Kokkinos(1959-)
Head On *'98*
Only the Brave *'94*

Amos Kollek(1947-)
Fiona *'98*
Whore 2 *'94*
Double Edge *'92*
High Stakes *'89*
Forever, Lulu *'87*
Goodbye, New York *'85*

Xavier Koller(1944-)
Cowboy Up *'00*
Squanto: A Warrior's Tale *'94*
Journey of Hope *'90*

Lajos Koltai(1946-)
Evening *'07*
Fateless *'05*

Andrei Konchalovsky(1937-)
The Lion in Winter *'03*
House of Fools *'02*
The Odyssey *'97*
The Inner Circle *'91*
Homer and Eddie *'89*
Tango and Cash *'89*
Shy People *'87*
Duet for One *'86*
Runaway Train *'85*
Maria's Lovers *'84*
Siberiade *'79*

Jackie Kong(1954-)
The Underachievers *'88*
Blood Diner *'87*
Night Patrol *'85*
The Being *'83*

Masaura Konuma
Beautiful Hunter *'94*
Flower & Snake *'74 '74*

Brian Koppelman
Solitary Man *'10*
Knockaround Guys *'01*

Barbara Kopple(1946-)
Fallen Champ: The Untold Story of Mike Tyson *'93*
Keeping On *'81*
Harlan County, U.S.A. *'76*

Alexander Korda(1893-1956)
An Ideal Husband *'47*
That Hamilton Woman *'41*
The Thief of Bagdad *'40*
Rembrandt *'36*
Private Life of Don Juan *'34*
The Private Life of Henry VIII *'33*
Wedding Rehearsal *'32*
Marius *'31*

Zoltan Korda(1895-1961)
Cry, the Beloved Country *'51*
Sahara *'43*
The Jungle Book *'42*
The Thief of Bagdad *'40*
The Four Feathers *'39*
Drums *'38*
Elephant Boy *'37*
Sanders of the River *'35*
If I Were Rich *'33*

Hirokazu Kore-eda(1962-)
Nobody Knows *'04*
After Life *'98*
Maborosi *'95*

Harmony Korine(1974-)
Mister Lonely *'07*
Julien Donkey-boy *'99*
Gummo *'97*

Baltasar Kormakur(1966-)
A Little Trip to Heaven *'05*
The Sea *'02*
101 Reykjavik *'00*

John Korty(1936-)
Ms. Scrooge *'97*
Redwood Curtain *'95*
Getting Out *'94*
They Watch *'93*
Eye on the Sparrow *'91*
Long Road Home *'91*
Cast the First Stone *'89*
Baby Girl Scott *'87*
Deadly Business *'86*
The Ewok Adventure *'84*
The Haunting Passion *'83*
A Christmas Without Snow *'80*
Forever *'78*
Oliver's Story *'78*
The Autobiography of Miss Jane Pittman *'74*
Class of '63 *'73*
Silence *'73*
The People *'71*

Peter Kosminsky(1956-)
White Oleander *'02*
Emily Bronte's Wuthering Heights *'92*

Henry Koster(1905-88)
The Singing Nun *'66*
Dear Brigitte *'65*
Mr. Hobbs Takes a Vacation *'62*
Flower Drum Song *'61*
The Story of Ruth *'60*
The Naked Maja *'59*
My Man Godfrey *'57*
D-Day, the Sixth of June *'56*
A Man Called Peter *'55*
The Virgin Queen *'55*
Desiree *'54*
The Robe *'53*
Stars and Stripes Forever *'52*
No Highway in the Sky *'51*
Harvey *'50*
My Blue Heaven *'50*
Come to the Stable *'49*
The Inspector General *'49*
The Luck of the Irish *'48*
The Bishop's Wife *'47*
It Started with Eve *'41*
Spring Parade *'40*
First Love *'39*
Three Smart Girls Grow Up *'39*
The Rage of Paris *'38*
100 Men and a Girl *'37*
Three Smart Girls *'36*

Tom Kotani
The Bushido Blade *'80*
The Bermuda Depths *'78*

Ted Kotcheff(1931-)
Family of Cops *'95*
Red Shoe Diaries 5: Weekend Pass *'95*
Hidden Assassin *'94*
Red Shoe Diaries 3: Another Woman's Lipstick *'93*
Folks! *'92*
Weekend at Bernie's *'89*
Winter People *'89*
Switching Channels *'88*
Joshua Then and Now *'85*
Uncommon Valor *'83*
First Blood *'82*
Split Image *'82*
North Dallas Forty *'79*
Who Is Killing the Great Chefs of Europe? *'78*
Fun with Dick and Jane *'77*
The Apprenticeship of Duddy Kravitz *'74*
Billy Two Hats *'74*
Tiara Tahiti *'62*

Jim Kouf(1951-)
Gang Related *'96*
Disorganized Crime *'89*
Miracles *'86*

Bernard L. Kowalski(1929-2007)
Nashville Beat *'89*
B.A.D. Cats *'80*
Marciano *'79*
Nativity *'78*
Sssssss *'73*
The Woman Hunter *'72*
Macho Callahan *'70*
Krakatoa East of Java *'69*
Stiletto *'69*
Attack of the Giant Leeches *'59*
Night of the Blood Beast *'58*

Karl Kozak(1964-)
Clawed: The Legend of Sasquatch *'05*
Out of the Black *'01*

Soeren Kragh-Jacobsen(1947-)
Mifune *'99*
Emma's Shadow *'88*

Stanley Kramer(1913-2001)
The Runner Stumbles *'79*
The Domino Principle *'77*
Oklahoma Crude *'73*
Bless the Beasts and Children *'71*
R.P.M.* (*Revolutions Per Minute) *'70*
The Secret of Santa Vittoria *'69*
Guess Who's Coming to Dinner *'67*
Ship of Fools *'65*
It's a Mad, Mad, Mad, Mad World *'63*
Judgment at Nuremberg *'61*
Inherit the Wind *'60*
On the Beach *'59*
The Defiant Ones *'58*
The Pride and the Passion *'57*
Not as a Stranger *'55*

Wayne Kramer(1965-)
Crossing Over *'09*
Running Scared *'06*
The Cooler *'03*

Norman Krasna(1909-84)
The Ambassador's Daughter *'56*
The Big Hangover *'50*
Princess O'Rourke *'43*

Paul Krasny(1935-2001)
Drug Wars 2: The Cocaine Cartel *'92*
Back to Hannibal: The Return of Tom Sawyer and Huckleberry Finn *'90*
When Hell Was in Session *'82*
Centennial *'78*
Joe Panther *'76*
Christina *'74*

John Krish(1923-)
Man Who Had Power Over Women *'70*

The Unearthly Stranger '64

Suri Krishnamma(1961-)

MTV's Wuthering Heights '03
A Respectable Trade '98
A Man of No Importance '94

Allen Kroeker

Showdown at Williams Creek '91
Age Old Friends '89
Heaven on Earth '89
Tramp at the Door '87

Karl Krogstad

The Last Ride '91
The Last Ride '91

Jon Kroll

Menno's Mind '96
Amanda and the Alien '95

Steve Kroschel

Avalanche '99
Running Free '94

Lisa Krueger(1961-)

Committed '99
Manny & Lo '96

Michael Krueger(1951-90)

Mindkiller '87
Night Vision '87

Stanley Kubrick(1928-99)

Eyes Wide Shut '99
Full Metal Jacket '87
The Shining '80
Barry Lyndon '75
A Clockwork Orange '71
2001: A Space Odyssey '68
Dr. Strangelove, or: How I Learned to Stop Worrying and Love the Bomb '64
Lolita '62
Spartacus '60
Paths of Glory '57
The Killing '56
Killer's Kiss '55
The Seafarers '53

Buzz Kulik(1923-99)

Around the World in 80 Days '89
Code Name: Dancer '87
Women of Valor '86
Rage of Angels '83
The Hunter '80
From Here to Eternity '79
The Lindbergh Kidnapping Case '76
Babe! '75
Bad Ronald '74
Pioneer Woman '73
Shamus '73
Brian's Song '71
Riot '69
Sergeant Ryker '68
Villa Rides '68

Edward Kull(1886-1946)

Tarzan and the Green Goddess '38
The New Adventures of Tarzan '35

Kei Kumai(1929-2007)

The Sea is Watching '02
Love and Faith '78
Sandakan No. 8 '74

Roger Kumble(1966-)

Furry Vengeance '10
College Road Trip '08
Just Friends '05
The Sweetest Thing '02
Cruel Intentions 2 '99
Cruel Intentions '98

Joachim Kunert

The Adventures of Werner Holt '65
The Second Track '62

Koreyoshi Kurahara

Hiroshima '95
Antarctica '84

Yoshiyuki Kuroda

Along with Ghosts '69
Spook Warfare '68

Akira Kurosawa(1910-98)

Rhapsody in August '91
Akira Kurosawa's Dreams '90
Ran '85
Kagemusha '80
Dersu Uzala '75
Dodes 'ka-den '70
Red Beard '65
High & Low '62
Sanjuro '62
Yojimbo '61
The Bad Sleep Well '60
The Hidden Fortress '58
The Lower Depths '57
Throne of Blood '57
I Live in Fear '55
Seven Samurai '54
Ikiru '52
The Idiot '51
Rashomon '51
Scandal '50
A Quiet Duel '49
Stray Dog '49
Drunken Angel '48
One Wonderful Sunday '47
No Regrets for Our Youth '46
The Men Who Tread on the Tiger's Tail '45
Sanshiro Sugata '43

Kiyoshi Kurosawa(1955-)

Tokyo Sonata '09
Retribution '06
Bright Future '03
Pulse '01
Seance '00
Charisma '99
Cure '97

Robert Kurtzman(1964-)

Wishmaster '97
The Demolitionist '95

Diane Kurys(1948-)

Children of the Century '99
Love After Love '94
Six Days, Six Nights '94
A Man in Love '87
Entre-Nous '83
Peppermint Soda '77

Karyn Kusama(1968-)

Jennifer's Body '09
Aeon Flux '05
Girlfight '99

Emir Kusturica(1954-)

Black Cat, White Cat '98
Underground '95
Arizona Dream '94
Time of the Gypsies '90
When Father Was Away on Business '85

Fran Rubel Kuzui

Buffy the Vampire Slayer '92
Tokyo Pop '88

Ken Kwapis(1957-)

He's Just Not That Into You '09
License to Wed '07
Sisterhood of the Traveling Pants '05
Noah '98
The Beautician and the Beast '97
Dunston Checks In '95
He Said, She Said '91
Vibes '88
Sesame Street Presents: Follow That Bird '85
The Beniker Gang '83

Richard Kwietniowski(1957-)

Owning Mahowny '03
Love and Death on Long Island '97

Jeff Kwitny(1951-)

Beyond the Door 3 '91
Iced '88

Paul Kyriazi

Omega Cop '90
Crazed Cop '88
Death Machines '76

Gregory La Cava(1892-1952)

Primrose Path '40
Fifth Avenue Girl '39
Stage Door '37
My Man Godfrey '36
Gabriel Over the White House '33
The Half Naked Truth '32
Smart Woman '31
Big News '29
His First Command '29
Feel My Pulse '28
Running Wild '27

Steven La Rocque

Above Suspicion '00
Samantha '92

Eriq La Salle(1962-)

Crazy as Hell '02
Rebound: The Legend of Earl "The Goat" Manigault '96

Neil LaBute(1963-)

Death at a Funeral '10
Lakeview Terrace '08
The Wicker Man '06
The Shape of Things '03
Possession '02
Nurse Betty '00
Your Friends & Neighbors '98
In the Company of Men '96

Gregory LaCava

See Gregory La Cava

Harry Lachman(1886-1975)

Castle in the Desert '42
Dr. Renault's Secret '42
The Loves of Edgar Allen Poe '42
Charlie Chan in Rio '41
Dead Men Tell '41
Murder over New York '40
It Happened in Hollywood '37
Charlie Chan at the Circus '36
Our Relations '36
Baby, Take a Bow '34

Aldo Lado(1934-)

Night Train Murders '75
Torture Train '75
Who Saw Her Die? '72
Short Night of Glass Dolls '71

Edward Laemmle

Texas Bad Man '32
The Drake Case '29

John Lafia

The Rats '01
Chameleon 3: Dark Angel '00
Man's Best Friend '93
Child's Play 2 '90
Blue Iguana '88

Jean LaFleur

Ilsa, the Tigress of Siberia '79
Mystery of the Million Dollar Hockey Puck '75

Ron Lagomarsino

Snowglobe '07
My Sister's Keeper '02
Running Mates '00
Dinner at Eight '89

Richard LaGravenese(1959-)

Freedom Writers '07
P.S. I Love You '07
Paris, je t'aime '06
A Decade Under the Influence '02
Living Out Loud '98

Craig Lahiff

Heaven's Burning '97
Ebbtide '94

Strangers '90
Deadly Possession '88
Fever '88

Joseph Lai

Ninja Powerforce '90
Ninja Showdown '90
Ninja Strike Force '88
The Power of the Ninjitsu '88
Ninja Commandments '87
Ninja Operation: Licensed to Terminate '87
Ninja Hunt '86

Harvey Laidman(1942-)

The Boy Who Loved Trolls '84
Steel Cowboy '78

John Laing

Absent Without Leave '95
The Lost Tribe '89
Dangerous Orphans '86
Beyond Reasonable Doubt '80

Frank Laloggia(1954-)

Mother '94
The Lady in White '88
Fear No Evil '80

Ringo Lam(1954-)

In Hell '03
Replicant '01
Maximum Risk '96
Full Contact '92
Twin Dragons '92
Prison on Fire 2 '91
Undeclared War '91
City on Fire '87
Prison on Fire '87

Bruce Lambert

See Godfrey Ho

Mary Lambert(1951-)

The Attic '06
Urban Legends: Bloody Mary '05
Halloweentown 2: Kalabar's Revenge '01
The In Crowd '00
Dragstrip Girl '94
Grand Isle '92
Pet Sematary 2 '92
Pet Sematary '89
Siesta '87

Charles Lamont(1895-1993)

Francis in the Haunted House '56
The Kettles in the Ozarks '56
Abbott and Costello Meet the Mummy '55
Carolina Cannonball '55
Carolina Cannonball '55
Abbott and Costello Meet the Keystone Kops '54
Ma and Pa Kettle at Home '54
Abbott and Costello Go to Mars '53
Ma and Pa Kettle on Vacation '53
Abbott and Costello Meet Captain Kidd '52
Abbott and Costello Meet Dr. Jekyll and Mr. Hyde '52
Abbott and Costello Meet the Invisible Man '51
Comin' Round the Mountain '51
Flame of Araby '51
Abbott and Costello in the Foreign Legion '50
Ma and Pa Kettle Go to Town '50
Bagdad '49
Ma and Pa Kettle '49
Salome, Where She Danced '45
Hit the Ice '43
Panama Patrol '39
Shadows over Shanghai '38
Slander House '38
International Crime '37
Wallaby Jim of the Islands '37

Bulldog Edition '36
The Dark Hour '36
Little Red Schoolhouse '36
Circumstantial Evidence '35
A Shot in the Dark '35
Sons of Steel '35
The World Accuses '35
Kid 'n' Hollywood and Polly Tix in Washington '33

Albert Lamorisse(1922-70)

Circus Angel '65
Voyage en Balloon '59
The Red Balloon '56
White Mane '52

Lew Landers(1901-62)

Torpedo Alley '53
Dynamite Pass '50
The Adventures of Gallant Bess '48
Inner Sanctum '48
Son of Rusty '47
Death Valley '46
The Mask of Diijon '46
The Enchanted Forest '45
Trouble Chasers '45
I'm from Arkansas '44
U-Boat Prisoner '44
Power of the Press '43
Return of the Vampire '43
The Boogie Man Will Get You '42
Junior Army '42
Back in the Saddle '41
Ridin' on a Rainbow '41
Wagons Westward '40
Bad Lands '39
Law of the Underworld '38
Smashing the Rackets '38
Flight from Glory '37
Living on Love '37
Without Orders '36
The Raven '35
Rustlers of Red Dog '35
Savage Fury '35
Tailspin Tommy '34

James Landis(1926-91)

Deadwood '65
Nasty Rabbit '64
The Sadist '63
Stakeout '62

John Landis(1950-)

Masters of Horror: Deer Woman '05
Masters of Horror: Family '05
Blues Brothers 2000 '98
Dying to Get Rich '98
The Stupids '95
Beverly Hills Cop 3 '94
Innocent Blood '92
Oscar '91
Coming to America '88
Amazon Women on the Moon '87
Three Amigos '86
Into the Night '85
Spies Like Us '85
Trading Places '83
Twilight Zone: The Movie '83
An American Werewolf in London '81
The Blues Brothers '80
National Lampoon's Animal House '78
Kentucky Fried Movie '77
Schlock '73

Jeffrey Scott Lando(1969-)

Decoys: The Second Seduction '07
Insecticidal '05
Savage Island '03

Michael Landon(1936-91)

Sam's Son '84
Killing Stone '78
The Loneliest Runner '76
It's Good to Be Alive '74
Little House on the Prairie '74

Michael Landon, Jr.(1964-)

Saving Sarah Cain '07
Love's Abiding Joy '06
Love's Long Journey '05
Love's Enduring Promise '04
Love Comes Softly '03

Paul Landres(1912-2001)

Flipper's Odyssey '66
Go, Johnny Go! '59
Man From God's Country '58
Return of Dracula '58
Square Dance Jubilee '51

Andrew Lane(1951-)

Trade Off '95
The Secretary '94
Desperate Motives '92
Mortal Passions '90
Jake Speed '86

Eric Laneuville(1952-)

Pandora's Clock '96
The Ernest Green Story '93
The Mighty Pawns '87
Hard Lessons '86

Sidney Lanfield(1898-1972)

Skirts Ahoy! '52
Follow the Sun '51
The Lemon Drop Kid '51
Sorrowful Jones '49
Station West '48
Where There's Life '47
My Favorite Blonde '42
You'll Never Get Rich '41
The Hound of the Baskervilles '39
Second Fiddle '39
Thin Ice '37
One in a Million '36
Red Salute '35

Fritz Lang(1890-1976)

The Thousand Eyes of Dr. Mabuse '60
The Indian Tomb '59
Tiger of Eschnapur '59
Journey to the Lost City '58
Beyond a Reasonable Doubt '56
While the City Sleeps '56
Moonfleet '55
Human Desire '54
The Big Heat '53
The Blue Gardenia '53
Clash by Night '52
Rancho Notorious '52
Secret Beyond the Door '48
Cloak and Dagger '46
Scarlet Street '45
Ministry of Fear '44
Woman in the Window '44
Hangmen Also Die '42
Man Hunt '41
Western Union '41
Return of Frank James '40
You and Me '38
You Only Live Once '37
Fury '36
Liliom '35
Crimes of Dr. Mabuse '32
M '31
Woman in the Moon '29
Spies '28
Metropolis '26
Kriemhilde's Revenge '24
Siegfried '24
Dr. Mabuse, The Gambler '22
Destiny '21
Spiders '18

Michael (Michel) Lang(1939-)

The Gift '82
Holiday Hotel '77

Perry Lang(1959-)

Men of War '94
Little Vegas '90

Richard Lang

Texas '94
Christmas Comes to Willow Creek '87

Kung Fu: The Movie '86
Shooting Stars '85
Don't Go to Sleep '82
Strike Force '81
A Change of Seasons '80
The Mountain Men '80
Night Cries '78
Vegas '78
The Word '78
Force of Evil '77
The Hunted Lady '77
Fantasy Island '76

Rocky Lang

Nervous Ticks '93
Race for Glory '89

Samantha Lang(1967-)

The Monkey's Mask '00
The Well '97
Twisted '96

Walter Lang(1898-1972)

Snow White and the Three Stooges '61
Can-Can '60
But Not for Me '59
Desk Set '57
The King and I '56
There's No Business Like Show Business '54
With a Song in My Heart '52
Cheaper by the Dozen '50
The Jackpot '50
Sitting Pretty '48
Mother Wore Tights '47
State Fair '45
Greenwich Village '44
The Magnificent Dope '42
Song of the Islands '42
Moon over Miami '41
Week-End in Havana '41
The Blue Bird '40
Tin Pan Alley '40
The Little Princess '39
Second Honeymoon '37
Red Kimono '25

Noel Langley(1911-80)

The Search for Bridey Murphy '56
The Adventures of Sadie '55
Svengali '55
The Pickwick Papers '54

Simon Langton(1941-)

Pride and Prejudice '95
Catherine Cookson's The Cinder Path '94
Casanova '87
Laguna Heat '87
The Whistle Blower '87
Anna Karenina '85
Act of Passion: The Lost Honor of Kathryn Beck '83
Smiley's People '82
Danger UXB '81
Therese Raquin '80
Love for Lydia '79
The Duchess of Duke Street '78

Lawrence Lanoff

The Chosen One: Legend of the Raven '98
Miami Hustle '95
Playing Dangerous '95
Temptress '95
Indecent Behavior '93

Yelena Lanskaya

Hybrid '07
Hidden Places '06

Anthony M. Lanza

The Incredible Two-Headed Transplant '71
The Glory Stompers '67

James Lapine(1949-)

Earthly Possessions '99
Life with Mikey '93
Impromptu '90
Sunday in the Park with George '86

Joseph (Jose Ramon) Larraz(1929-)

Golden Lady '79
Vampyres '74
The House that Vanished '73

Sheldon Larry(1949-)

Trial by Media '00
Family of Cops 3 '98
Family of Strangers '93
Behind Enemy Lines '85
Terminal Choice '85

Keith Larsen(1924-2006)

Whitewater Sam '78
Young & Free '78
Trap on Cougar Mountain '72
Mission Batangas '69

John Lasseter(1957-)

Cars '06
Toy Story 2 '99
A Bug's Life '98
Toy Story '95

Stan Lathan(1945-)

Uncle Tom's Cabin '87
Beat Street '84
Go Tell It on the Mountain '84
Amazing Grace '74

Steve Latshaw(1959-)

Death Mask '98
Biohazard: The Alien Force '95
Jack-O '95
Dark Universe '93

Alberto Lattuada(1913-2005)

Christopher Columbus '85
La Cicada '83
Stay As You Are '78
Mafioso '62
Love in the City '53
Anna '51
Variety Lights '51

Andrew Lau

See Wai Keung (Andrew) Lau
The Flock '07

Patrick Lau

The Scarlet Pimpernel '99
The Scarlet Pimpernel 2: Mademoiselle Guillotine '99
Invasion: Earth '98
Murders at Lynch Cross '85
Thirteenth Day of Christmas '85

Wai Keung (Andrew) Lau(1960-)

Infernal Affairs 2 '03
Infernal Affairs 3 '03
Infernal Affairs '02

Nicholas Laughland

Like Father Like Son '05
Under the Greenwood Tree '05
Sirens '02

Michael Laughlin

Mesmerized '84
Strange Invaders '83
Strange Behavior '81

Tom Laughlin(1939-)

The Trial of Billy Jack '74
Billy Jack '71
Born Losers '67

Frank Launder(1907-97)

The Great St. Trinian's Train Robbery '66
The Pure Hell of St. Trinian's '61
Blue Murder at St. Trinian's '56
Geordie '55
The Belles of St. Trinian's '53
The Happiest Days of Your Life '50
Captain Boycott '47
I See a Dark Stranger '46

Fabrizio Laurenti(1956-)

The Crawlers '93
Witchery '88

Georges Lautner(1926-)

La Cage aux Folles 3: The Wedding '86
My Other Husband '85
Le Professionnel '81
Icy Breasts '75
No Problem '75
Road to Salina '68
The Monocle '64

Jean-Claude Lauzon(1953-97)

Leolo '92
Night Zoo '87

Arnold Laven(1922-)

Sam Whiskey '69
Rough Night in Jericho '67
Geronimo '62
The Monster That Challenged the World '57
Without Warning '52

Martin Lavut(1939-)

Smokescreen '90
Palais Royale '88
Charlie Grant's War '80
War Brides '80

Clara Law(1957-)

Floating Life '95
Erotique '94
Temptation of a Monk '94
Autumn Moon '92
The Reincarnation of Golden Lotus '89

Diarmuid Lawrence

Little Dorrit '08
P.D. James: The Murder Room '04
Heat of the Sun '99
Emma '97

Francis Lawrence

I Am Legend '07
Constantine '05

John Lawrence(1931-92)

Savage Abduction '73
Cycle Psycho '72

Marc Lawrence(1959-)

Did You Hear About the Morgans? '09
Music & Lyrics '07
Two Weeks Notice '02

Ray Lawrence(1948-)

Jindabyne '06
Lantana '01
Bliss '85

J.F. Lawton(1960-)

The Hunted '94
Pizza Man '91
Cannibal Women in the Avocado Jungle of Death '89

Richard Laxton

An Englishman in New York '09
Inspector Lynley Mysteries: A Great Deliverance '01
Invasion: Earth '98
Poldark '96
Band of Gold '95

Wilford Leach(1929-88)

The Pirates of Penzance '83
The Wedding Party '69

Philip Leacock(1917-90)

Three Sovereigns for Sarah '85
Angel City '80
The Curse of King Tut's Tomb '80
Wild & Wooly '78
Killer on Board '77
Dying Room Only '73
Baffled '72
Shattered Silence '71
War Lover '62
Let No Man Write My Epitaph '60
The Spanish Gardener '57
Escapade '55

David Lean(1908-91)

A Passage to India '84
Ryan's Daughter '70
Doctor Zhivago '65
Lawrence of Arabia '62
The Bridge on the River Kwai '57
Summertime '55
Hobson's Choice '53
The Sound Barrier '52
Madeleine '50
Oliver Twist '48
This Happy Breed '47
Brief Encounter '46
Great Expectations '46
Blithe Spirit '45
In Which We Serve '43

Reginald LeBorg(1902-89)

The Sibling '72
House of the Black Death '65
Diary of a Madman '63
The Black Sleep '56
Sins of Jezebel '54
The White Orchid '54
G.I. Jane '51
Great Jesse James Raid '49
Dead Man's Eyes '44
Jungle Woman '44
The Mummy's Ghost '44
Weird Woman '44
Calling Dr. Death '43

Jean-Paul LeChanois(1909-85)

Le Cas du Dr. Laurent '57
Les Miserables '57
Passion for Life '48

Patrice Leconte(1947-)

My Best Friend '06
Intimate Strangers '04
The Man on the Train '02
The Widow of Saint-Pierre '00
The Girl on the Bridge '98
Ridicule '96
The Perfume of Yvonne '94
The Hairdresser's Husband '92
Monsieur Hire '89
French Fried Vacation '79

Jacques LeCotier

See Jerry Warren

John L'Ecuyer

Prom Queen '04
Curtis's Charm '96

Mimi Leder(1952-)

The Code '09
Pay It Forward '00
Deep Impact '98
The Peacemaker '97
Woman with a Past '92

Paul Leder(1926-96)

Killing Obsession '94
Molly and Gina '94
The Abduction of Allison Tate '92
The Baby Doll Murders '92
Deadly Conspiracy '91
Frame Up '91
Twenty Dollar Star '91
Exiled in America '90
Murder by Numbers '89
Body Count '87
Vultures '84
Sketches of a Strangler '78
A*P*E* '76
I Dismember Mama '74

David Ross Lederman(1894-1972)

Cooking Up Trouble '44
I Was Framed '42
Shadows on the Stairs '41
Racketeers of the Range '39
Adventure in Sahara '38
Tarzan's Revenge '38
I Promise to Pay '37
Alibi for Murder '36
Hell-Ship Morgan '36
Daring Danger '32
The Fighting Marshal '32
Ridin' for Justice '32
The Riding Tornado '32
Texas Cyclone '32
Two-Fisted Law '32
Phantom of the West '31
Range Feud '31

Richard Ledes

The Caller '08
A Hole in One '04

Paul Leduc(1942-)

Frida '84
Reed: Insurgent Mexico '73

Ang Lee(1954-)

Taking Woodstock '09
Lust, Caution '07
Brokeback Mountain '05
Hulk '03
Crouching Tiger, Hidden Dragon '00
Ride with the Devil '99
The Ice Storm '97
Sense and Sensibility '95
Eat Drink Man Woman '94
The Wedding Banquet '93
Pushing Hands '92

Damian Lee

Hearts of War '07
Agent Red '00
Trail of a Serial Killer '98
Fatal Combat '96
Moving Target '96
Terminal Rush '96
When the Bullet Hits the Bone '96
Street Law '95
The Donor '94
Ski School '91
Abraxas: Guardian of the Universe '90
Boxcar Blues '90
Food of the Gods: Part 2 '88
Circle Man '87
Last Man Standing '87

Daniel Lee

The Kumite '03
Black Mask '96

DeWitt Lee

The Legend of Jedediah Carver '76
Ransom Money '70

Jack Lee(1913-2002)

The Captain's Table '60
Robbery under Arms '57
Wooden Horse '50

Malcolm Lee(1970-)

Soul Men '08
Welcome Home Roscoe Jenkins '08
Roll Bounce '05
Undercover Brother '02
The Best Man '99

Norman Lee(1898-1964)

Chamber of Horrors '40
Mr. Reeder in Room 13 '38
Bulldog Drummond at Bay '37

Robert Lee

The Silencer '99
Dead Fire '98
Crackerjack 2 '97
Act of War '96
Virtual Assassin '95

Rowland V. Lee(1891-1975)

Captain Kidd '45
The Bridge of San Luis Rey '44
The Son of Monte Cristo '40
Son of Frankenstein '39
The Tower of London '39
Service De Luxe '38
Love from a Stranger '37
Toast of New York '37
One Rainy Afternoon '36
The Three Musketeers '35
The Count of Monte Cristo '34
The Return of Dr. Fu Manchu '30
The Mysterious Dr. Fu Manchu '29
Doomsday '28
The Sea Lion '21

Spike Lee(1957-)

Miracle at St. Anna '08
Inside Man '06
Sucker Free City '05
She Hate Me '04
25th Hour '02
Bamboozled '00
Summer of Sam '99
He Got Game '98
Get On the Bus '96
Girl 6 '96
Clockers '95
Crooklyn '94
Malcolm X '92
Jungle Fever '91
Mo' Better Blues '90
Do the Right Thing '89
School Daze '88
She's Gotta Have It '86
Joe's Bed-Stuy Barbershop: We Cut Heads '83

Herbert I. Leeds(1900-54)

Blue, White and Perfect '42
Just Off Broadway '42
The Man Who Wouldn't Die '42
Time to Kill '42
Charlie Chan in City of Darkness '39

Doug Lefler

The Last Legion '07
Dragonheart: A New Beginning '00
Hercules the Legendary Journeys, Vol. 3: The Circle of Fire '94

Michael Lehmann(1957-)

Because I Said So '07
Flakes '07
40 Days and 40 Nights '02
My Giant '98
The Truth about Cats and Dogs '96
Airheads '94
Hudson Hawk '91
The Applegates '89
Heathers '89

Neil Leifer

Trading Hearts '87
Yesterday's Hero '79

Mike Leigh(1943-)

Happy-Go-Lucky '08
Vera Drake '04
All or Nothing '02
Topsy Turvy '99
Career Girls '97
Secrets and Lies '95
Naked '93
Life Is Sweet '90
High Hopes '88
Four Days in July '85
Home Sweet Home '82
Meantime '81
Grown Ups '80
Who's Who '78
Abigail's Party '77
Kiss of Death '77
Nuts in May '76
Hard Labour '73
Bleak Moments '71

Danny Leiner

Balls Out: Gary the Tennis Coach '09
The Great New Wonderful '06
Harold and Kumar Go to White Castle '04
Dude, Where's My Car? '00

Mitchell Leisen(1898-1972)

The Girl Most Likely '57
Golden Earrings '47
To Each His Own '46
Frenchman's Creek '44
The Lady Is Willing '42

Remember the Night *'40*
Midnight *'39*
The Big Broadcast of 1938 *'38*
Easy Living *'37*
Swing High, Swing Low *'37*
Hands Across the Table *'35*
Death Takes a Holiday *'34*
Murder at the Vanities *'34*

Christopher Leitch
I've Been Waiting for You *'98*
Courage Mountain *'89*
Teen Wolf Too *'87*
The Hitter *'79*

David Leland(1947-)
Virgin Territory *'07*
Band of Brothers *'01*
The Land Girls *'98*
The Big Man: Crossing the Line *'91*
Checking Out *'89*
Wish You Were Here *'87*

Claude Lelouch(1937-)
Roman de Gare *'07*
And Now Ladies and Gentlemen *'02*
Les Miserables *'95*
Bandits *'86*
A Man and a Woman: 20 Years Later *'86*
Edith & Marcel *'83*
Bolero *'82*
Cat and Mouse *'78*
Robert et Robert *'78*
Another Man, Another Chance *'77*
And Now My Love *'74*
Happy New Year *'73*
A Man and a Woman *'66*

Michael Lembeck(1948-)
Tooth Fairy *'10*
The Clique *'08*
The Santa Clause 3: The Escape Clause *'06*
Connie and Carla *'04*
The Santa Clause 2 *'02*

James (Momel) Lemmo(1949-)
Bodily Harm *'95*
Dream a Little Dream 2 *'94*
Relentless 3 *'93*
We're Talkin' Serious Money *'92*
Tripwire *'89*
Heart *'87*

Kasi Lemmons(1961-)
Talk to Me *'07*
The Caveman's Valentine *'01*
Eve's Bayou *'97*

Rusty Lemorande
The Turn of the Screw *'92*
Journey to the Center of the Earth *'88*

Paul Leni(1885-1929)
The Cat and the Canary *'27*
The Man Who Laughs *'27*
Waxworks *'24*

Umberto Lenzi(1931-)
Welcome to Spring Break *'88*
Bridge to Hell *'87*
Thundersquad *'85*
Ironmaster *'82*
City of the Walking Dead *'80*
Emerald Jungle *'80*
Almost Human *'79*
From Hell to Victory *'79*
Battleforce *'78*
Eyeball *'78*
Man from Deep River *'77*
Bruce Lee Fights Back from the Grave *'76*
Battle of the Commandos *'71*
Paranoia *'69*
Desert Commandos *'67*
Messalina vs. the Son of Hercules *'64*
Pirates of the Seven Seas *'62*

Arthur Leonard
Sepia Cinderella *'47*
Boy! What a Girl *'45*
The Devil's Daughter *'39*

Brett Leonard
Highlander: The Source *'07*
Feed *'05*
Virtuosity *'95*
Hideaway *'94*
The Lawnmower Man *'92*
Dead Pit *'89*

Robert Z. Leonard(1889-1968)
The King's Thief *'55*
Clown *'53*
Everything I Have is Yours *'52*
The Duchess of Idaho *'50*
Nancy Goes to Rio *'50*
In the Good Old Summertime *'49*
The Bribe *'48*
Cynthia *'47*
Weekend at the Waldorf *'45*
We Were Dancing *'42*
When Ladies Meet *'41*
Ziegfeld Girl *'41*
New Moon *'40*
Pride and Prejudice *'40*
Broadway Serenade *'39*
Girl of the Golden West *'38*
The Firefly *'37*
Maytime *'37*
The Great Ziegfeld *'36*
Dancing Lady *'33*
Strange Interlude *'32*
Susan Lenox: Her Fall and Rise *'31*
The Divorcee *'30*
Let Us Be Gay *'30*
A Lady of Chance *'28*
A Lady of Chance *'28*
A Mormon Maid *'17*

Anthony Leondis
Igor *'08*
Lilo & Stitch 2: Stitch Has a Glitch *'05*

Sergio Leone(1929-89)
Once Upon a Time in America *'84*
A Fistful of Dynamite *'72*
Once Upon a Time in the West *'68*
The Good, the Bad and the Ugly *'67*
For a Few Dollars More *'65*
A Fistful of Dollars *'64*

John R. Leonetti
The Butterfly Effect 2 *'06*
Mortal Kombat 2: Annihilation *'97*

Po Chih Leong
See Po-Chih Leung
The Detonator *'06*

Antonio Leonviola(1913-95)
Tor *'64*
Atlas in the Land of the Cyclops *'61*
Mole Men Against the Son of Hercules *'61*
Angel in a Taxi *'59*

Robert Lepage(1957-)
Far Side of the Moon *'03*
No *'98*
Le Polygraphe *'96*
The Confessional *'95*

Dan Lerner
Direct Contact *'09*
Finding Rin Tin Tin *'07*
Target of Opportunity *'04*
Lone Justice 3: Showdown at Plum Creek *'96*
Shame *'92*

Irving Lerner(1909-76)
Cry of Battle *'63*
Studs Lonigan *'60*
City of Fear *'59*
Murder by Contract *'58*

Jeff Leroy
Alien 3000 *'04*
Crystal's Diary *'99*
Crack Up *'97*

Mervyn LeRoy(1900-87)
Moment to Moment *'66*
Mary, Mary *'63*
Gypsy *'62*
The Devil at 4 O'Clock *'61*
The FBI Story *'59*
No Time for Sergeants *'58*
The Bad Seed *'56*
A Majority of One *'56*
Mister Roberts *'55*
Rose Marie *'54*
Latin Lovers *'53*
Lovely to Look At *'52*
Million Dollar Mermaid *'52*
Quo Vadis *'51*
Any Number Can Play *'49*
East Side, West Side *'49*
Little Women *'49*
Homecoming *'48*
Without Reservations *'46*
Thirty Seconds Over Tokyo *'44*
Madame Curie *'43*
Johnny Eager *'42*
Random Harvest *'42*
Blossoms in the Dust *'41*
Waterloo Bridge *'40*
They Won't Forget *'37*
Anthony Adverse *'36*
Three Men on a Horse *'36*
Sweet Adeline *'35*
Happiness Ahead *'34*
Gold Diggers of 1933 *'33*
Tugboat Annie *'33*
I Am a Fugitive from a Chain Gang *'32*
Three on a Match *'32*
Two Seconds *'32*
Tonight or Never *'31*
Little Caesar *'30*
Playing Around *'30*
Show Girl in Hollywood *'30*

Mark L. Lester(1949-)
Stealing Candy *'04*
Lady Jayne Killer *'03*
Sacrifice *'00*
The Base *'99*
Blowback *'99*
Hitman's Run *'99*
Misbegotten *'98*
Double Take *'97*
The Ex *'96*
Public Enemies *'96*
Night of the Running Man *'94*
Extreme Justice *'93*
Showdown in Little Tokyo *'91*
Class of 1999 *'90*
Armed and Dangerous *'86*
Commando *'85*
Firestarter *'84*
Class of 1984 *'82*
Gold of the Amazon Women *'79*
Roller Boogie *'79*
Stunts *'77*
Bobbie Jo and the Outlaw *'76*
Way He Was *'76*
Truck Stop Women *'74*
Steel Arena *'72*

Richard Lester(1932-)
The Return of the Musketeers *'89*
Finders Keepers *'84*
Superman 3 *'83*
Superman 2 *'80*
Butch and Sundance: The Early Days *'79*
Cuba *'79*
The Ritz *'76*
Robin and Marian *'76*
The Four Musketeers *'75*
Royal Flash *'75*
Juggernaut *'74*
The Three Musketeers *'74*
Petulia *'68*
How I Won the War *'67*
A Funny Thing Happened on the Way to the Forum *'66*
Help! *'65*
The Knack *'65*
A Hard Day's Night *'64*
The Mouse on the Moon *'62*

Louis Leterrier(1973-)
Clash of the Titans *'10*
The Incredible Hulk *'08*
Transporter 2 *'05*
Unleashed *'05*

Rob Letterman
Monsters vs. Aliens *'09*
Shark Tale *'04*

Sheldon Lettich(1962-)
The Last Warrior *'99*
Perfect Target *'98*
Only the Strong *'93*
Double Impact *'91*
Lionheart *'90*

Po-Chih Leung(1939-)
Return to Cabin by the Lake *'01*
Cabin by the Lake *'00*
Immortality *'98*
Ping Pong *'87*
Hong Kong 1941 *'84*

Brian Levant(1952-)
The Spy Next Door *'10*
Are We There Yet? *'05*
Snow Dogs *'02*
The Flintstones in Viva Rock Vegas *'00*
Jingle All the Way *'96*
The Flintstones *'94*
Beethoven *'92*
Problem Child 2 *'91*

Jeremy Leven(1941-)
My Sister's Keeper *'09*
Don Juan DeMarco *'94*

Joseph Levering
Phantom Gold *'38*
Defenders of the Law *'31*
Sea Devils *'31*

Michel Levesque
Sweet Sugar *'72*
Werewolves on Wheels *'71*

William A. Levey(1943-)
Committed *'91*
Hellgate *'89*
Lightning: The White Stallion *'86*
Monaco Forever *'83*
The Happy Hooker Goes to Washington *'77*
Slumber Party '57 *'76*
Wham-Bam, Thank You Spaceman *'75*
Blackenstein *'73*

Alan J. Levi
Dead Man's Revenge *'93*
Blood Song *'82*
Last Song *'80*
Riding with Death *'76*

Henry Levin(1901-80)
Scout's Honor *'80*
The Treasure Seekers *'79*
Run for the Roses *'78*
That Man Bolt *'73*
Desperados *'69*
The Ambushers *'67*
Murderers' Row *'66*
The Wonderful World of the Brothers Grimm *'62*
The Wonders of Aladdin *'61*
Where the Boys Are *'60*
Journey to the Center of the Earth *'59*
Lonely Man *'57*
The Warriors *'55*
The Farmer Takes a Wife *'53*
Belles on Their Toes *'52*
Jolson Sings Again *'49*
Man from Colorado *'49*
Cry of the Werewolf *'44*

Marc Levin
Nim's Island *'08*
Little Manhattan *'05*
Protocols of Zion *'05*
White Boyz *'99*
Slam *'98*

Peter Levin
Queen Sized *'08*
A Perfect Day *'06*
A Stranger in Town *'95*
Take Down *'92*
Washington Mistress *'81*
Comeback Kid *'80*
Rape and Marriage: The Rideout Case *'80*
Zalmen or the Madness of God *'75*

Paul Levine
Spider's Web *'01*
Deal of a Lifetime *'99*
Operation Intercept *'95*

Barry Levinson(1942-)
What Just Happened *'08*
Man of the Year *'06*
Envy *'04*
Bandits *'01*
An Everlasting Piece *'00*
Liberty Heights *'99*
Sphere *'97*
Wag the Dog *'97*
Sleepers *'96*
Disclosure *'94*
Jimmy Hollywood *'94*
Toys *'92*
Bugsy *'91*
Avalon *'90*
Rain Man *'88*
Good Morning, Vietnam *'87*
Tin Men *'87*
Young Sherlock Holmes *'85*
The Natural *'84*
Diner *'82*

Israeli Nadav Levitan(1945-)
The Seventeenth Bride *'84*
Intimate Story *'81*

Kristian Levring(1957-)
The Intended *'02*
The King Is Alive *'00*

Dani Levy
My Fuhrer *'07*
Go for Zucker *'05*

Eugene Levy(1946-)
Sodbusters *'94*
Once Upon a Crime *'92*

I. Robert Levy
Can I Do It.. Till I Need Glasses? *'77*
If You Don't Stop It.. You'll Go Blind *'77*

Jefery Levy(1958-)
S.F.W. *'94*
Inside Monkey Zetterland *'93*

Ralph Levy(1919-2001)
Do Not Disturb *'65*
Bedtime Story *'63*
A Christmas Carol *'54*

Raoul Levy
The Defector *'66*
Hail Mafia *'65*

Scott Levy
Beneath the Bermuda Triangle *'98*
Baby Face Nelson *'97*
Spectre *'96*
Piranha *'95*
Unknown Origin *'95*
Midnight Tease *'94*

Shawn Levy
Date Night *'10*
Night at the Museum: Battle of the Smithsonian *'09*
Night at the Museum *'06*
The Pink Panther *'06*
Cheaper by the Dozen *'03*
Just Married *'03*
Big Fat Liar *'02*
Address Unknown *'96*

Shuki Levy
Aussie and Ted's Great Adventure *'09*
Turbo: A Power Rangers Movie *'96*
Blind Vision *'91*
Perfect Victims *'87*

Albert Lewin(1916-96)
Pandora and the Flying Dutchman *'51*
The Private Affairs of Bel Ami *'47*
Picture of Dorian Gray *'45*
The Moon and Sixpence *'43*

Ben Lewin(1946-)
Paperback Romance *'96*
The Favor, the Watch, & the Very Big Fish *'92*
Georgia *'87*

Christopher Lewis(1944-)
The Red Raven Kiss-Off *'90*
Revenge *'86*
The Ripper *'86*
Blood Cult *'85*

Everet Lewis
Luster *'02*
The Natural History of Parking Lots *'90*

Herschell Gordon Lewis(1926-)
The Gore-Gore Girls *'72*
This Stuff'll Kill Ya! *'71*
The Wizard of Gore *'70*
How to Make a Doll *'68*
Just for the Hell of It *'68*
The Psychic *'68*
She-Devils on Wheels *'68*
Something Weird *'68*
Blast-Off Girls *'67*
The Girl, the Body and the Pill *'67*
Gruesome Twosome *'67*
Suburban Roulette *'67*
A Taste of Blood *'67*
Jimmy, the Boy Wonder *'66*
Monster a Go-Go! *'65*
Color Me Blood Red *'64*
Moonshine Mountain *'64*
2000 Maniacs *'64*
Blood Feast *'63*
Scum of the Earth *'63*
Nature's Playmates *'62*
The Prime Time *'60*

Jerry Lewis(1926-)
Cracking Up *'83*
Hardly Working *'81*
One More Time *'70*
Which Way to the Front? *'70*
Big Mouth *'67*
Family Jewels *'65*
The Patsy *'64*
The Nutty Professor *'63*
The Errand Boy *'61*
The Ladies' Man *'61*
The Bellboy *'60*

Joseph H. Lewis(1907-2000)
Terror in a Texas Town *'58*
Seventh Cavalry *'56*
Big Combo *'55*
A Lawless Street *'55*
Retreat, Hell! *'52*
Gun Crazy *'49*
The Silver Bullet *'42*
Criminals Within *'41*
The Invisible Ghost *'41*
Pride of the Bowery *'41*
Boys of the City *'40*
That Gang of Mine *'40*
The Spy Ring *'38*

Kevin Lewis
Dark Heart *'06*
The Drop *'06*

Mark Lewis
The Thaw *'09*
Gordy *'95*

Richard J. Lewis
K-9 3: P.I. *'01*
Whale Music *'94*

Robert Lewis(1909-97)
The Crying Child *'96*
Circumstances Unknown *'95*
Don't Talk to Strangers *'94*
Memories of Murder *'90*
Dead Reckoning *'89*
Ladykillers *'88*
City Killer *'87*
Embassy *'85*
A Summer to Remember *'84*
Agatha Christie's A Caribbean Mystery *'83*

Agatha Christie's Sparkling Cyanide '83
Desperate Lives '82
Child Bride of Short Creek '81
Fallen Angel '81
If Things Were Different '79
S*H*E '79
No Room to Run '78
Pray for the Wildcats '74

Peter Paul Liapis

The Stepdaughter '00
Alone with a Stranger '99
Captured '99

Mitchell Lichtenstein(1956-)

Happy Tears '09
Teeth '07

Carlo Liconti

Goodnight, Michelangelo '89
Concrete Angels '87

Jeff Lieberman(1947-)

Satan's Little Helper '04
Remote Control '88
Just Before Dawn '80
Blue Sunshine '78
Squirm '76

Robert Lieberman(1941-)

The Dead Zone '02
Tom Clancy's Netforce '98
D3: The Mighty Ducks '96
Titanic '96
Fire in the Sky '93
Table for Five '83
Will: G. Gordon Liddy '82

Jonathan Liebesman(1976-)

The Killing Room '09
The Texas Chainsaw Massacre: The Beginning '06
Darkness Falls '03

Peter Lilienthal(1929-)

Ruby's Dream '82
The Uprising '81
David '79

Edward Lilley(1896-1974)

Hi, Good Lookin'! '44
Honeymoon Lodge '43

Kevin Lima(1962-)

Enchanted '07
Eloise at the Plaza '03
102 Dalmatians '00
Tarzan '99
A Goofy Movie '94

Doug Liman(1965-)

Jumper '08
Mr. & Mrs. Smith '05
The Bourne Identity '02
Go '99
Swingers '96
Getting In '94

Justin Lin(1973-)

Fast & Furious '09
Annapolis '06
The Fast and the Furious: Tokyo Drift '06
Better Luck Tomorrow '02

Kevin J. Lindenmuth

Addicted to Murder 3: Bloodlust '99
Rage of the Werewolf '99
Addicted to Murder 2: Tainted Blood '97
The Alien Agenda: Endangered Species '97
The Alien Agenda: Under the Skin '97
The Alien Agenda: Out of the Darkness '96
Addicted to Murder '95

Maud Linder

Man in the Silk Hat '83
Man in the Silk Hat '15

Lance Lindsay

Real Bullets '90
Star Crystal '85

Michael Lindsay-Hogg(1940-)

Two of Us '00
Horton Foote's Alone '97
Frankie Starlight '95
Running Mates '92
The Habitation of Dragons '91
Murder by Moonlight '91
The Object of Beauty '91
Strange Case of Dr. Jekyll & Mr. Hyde '89
The Little Match Girl '87
As Is '85
Master Harold and the Boys '84
Sound of Murder '82
Thumbelina '82
Brideshead Revisited '81
Nasty Habits '77
Let It Be '70

Leopold Lindtberg(1902-84)

Four in a Jeep '51
The Last Chance '45

Caroline Link(1964-)

Nowhere in Africa '02
Beyond Silence '96

John F. Link

Call of the Forest '49
The Devil's Cargo '48

Richard Linklater(1961-)

Me and Orson Welles '09
Fast Food Nation '06
A Scanner Darkly '06
The Bad News Bears '05
Before Sunset '04
School of Rock '03
Tape '01
Waking Life '01
The Newton Boys '97
subUrbia '96
Before Sunrise '94
Dazed and Confused '93
Slacker '91

Art Linson(1942-)

The Wild Life '84
Where the Buffalo Roam '80

Aaron Lipstadt(1952-)

Blood Money '99
Pair of Aces '90
City Limits '85
Android '82

Steven Lisberger(1951-)

Slipstream '89
Hot Pursuit '87
Tron '82

David Lister

The Story of an African Farm '04
The Rutanga Tapes '90
Hunted '88

Peter MacKenzie Litten

Heaven's a Drag '94
Living Doll '90

Dwight Little(1947-)

Anacondas: The Hunt for the Blood Orchid '04
Papa's Angels '00
Boss of Bosses '99
Murder at 1600 '97
Free Willy 2: The Adventure Home '95
Rapid Fire '92
Marked for Death '90
The Phantom of the Opera '89
Bloodstone '88
Halloween 4: The Return of Michael Myers '88
Getting Even '86

Ryan Little

Forever Strong '08
Outlaw Trail '06
Everything You Want '05
Saints and Soldiers '03

Lynne Littman(1941-)

Having Our Say: The Delany Sisters' First 100 Years '99
Rescuers: Stories of Courage—Two Couples '98
Testament '83

Anatole Litvak(1902-74)

Night of the Generals '67
Goodbye Again '61
Anastasia '56
The Snake Pit '48
Sorry, Wrong Number '48
The Long Night '47
This Above All '42
Blues in the Night '41
Out of the Fog '41
All This and Heaven Too '40
Castle on the Hudson '40
City for Conquest '40
Confessions of a Nazi Spy '39
Amazing Dr. Clitterhouse '38
The Sisters '38
Mayerling '36

Gerry Lively

The Art of War 3: Retribution '08
Finish Line '08
Body Armour '07
Darkness Falls '98
Body Moves '90

Carlo Lizzani(1922-)

House of the Yellow Carpet '84
Last Four Days '77
Love in the City '53

Luis Llosa(1951-)

Anaconda '96
The Specialist '94
800 Leagues Down the Amazon '93
Fire on the Amazon '93
Sniper '92
Crime Zone '88
Hour of the Assassin '86

Frank Lloyd(1886-1960)

The Last Command '55
Blood on the Sun '45
Forever and a Day '43
The Howards of Virginia '40
If I Were King '38
Mutiny on the Bounty '35
Cavalcade '33
Hoopla '33
The Divine Lady '29
The Sea Hawk '24
Oliver Twist '22

Wei Lo

The Shadow Whip '71
Sword Masters: Brothers Five '70

Ken Loach(1936-)

Looking for Eric '09
The Wind That Shakes the Barley '06
A Fond Kiss '04
Sweet Sixteen '02
The Navigators '01
Bread and Roses '00
My Name Is Joe '98
Carla's Song '97
Land and Freedom '95
Ladybird, Ladybird '93
Raining Stones '93
Riff Raff '92
Hidden Agenda '90
Singing the Blues in Red '87
Family Life '71

Rogelio Lobato

Valentina's Tango '07
Depraved '98

Victor Lobl

Eden '93
Eden 3 '93

Sondra Locke(1947-)

Trading Favors '97
Impulse '90

Ratboy '86

Bob Logan

Meatballs 4 '92
Repossessed '90
Up Your Alley '89

Joshua Logan(1908-88)

Paint Your Wagon '69
Camelot '67
Ensign Pulver '64
Fanny '61
Tall Story '60
South Pacific '58
Sayonara '57
Bus Stop '56
Picnic '55

Tom Logan(1954-)

Dream Trap '90
The Night Brings Charlie '90

Dimitri Logothetis

The Lost Angel '04
Body Shot '93
The Closer '91
Slaughterhouse Rock '88
Pretty Smart '87

J. Anthony Loma

See Jose Antonio De La Loma

Lou Lombardo(1932-2002)

P.K. and the Kid '85
Russian Roulette '75

Ulli Lommel(1944-)

Son of Sam '08
BTK Killer '06
The Big Sweat '90
Cold Heat '90
Warbirds '88
Overkill '86
Strangers in Paradise '84
Devonsville Terror '83
Olivia '83
Brainwaves '82
The Boogey Man '80
Cocaine Cowboys '79
Tenderness of the Wolves '73

Richard Loncraine(1946-)

My One and Only '09
Firewall '06
Wimbledon '04
My House in Umbria '03
The Gathering Storm '02
Band of Brothers '01
Richard III '95
The Wedding Gift '93
Bellman and True '88
Deep Cover '88
Brimstone & Treacle '82
The Missionary '82
Full Circle '77

Jerry London(1937-)

Counterstrike '03
Take Me Home: The John Denver Story '00
Victim of Love '91
Haunting of Sarah Hardy '89
Kiss Shot '89
Rent-A-Cop '88
Manhunt for Claude Dallas '86
Chiefs '83
The Scarlet & the Black '83
Father Figure '80
Shogun '80

Stanley Long(1933-)

Adventures of a Private Eye '77
Adventures of a Taxi Driver '76

Harry S. Longstreet

The Perfect Daughter '96
A Vow to Kill '94
Sex, Love and Cold Hard Cash '93

Temistocles Lopez(1947-)

Bird of Prey '95
Chain of Desire '93

Exquisite Corpses '88

Del Lord(1894-1970)

I Love a Bandleader '45
Vengeance '37

Jean-Claude Lord(1943-)

Landslide '92
Eddie and the Cruisers 2: Eddie Lives! '89
Mindfield '89
Toby McTeague '87
The Vindicator '85
Covergirl '83
Visiting Hours '82

Joseph Losey(1909-84)

Steaming '86
La Truite '83
Roads to the South '78
Mr. Klein '76
Romantic Englishwoman '75
A Doll's House '73
Assassination of Trotsky '72
The Go-Between '71
Secret Ceremony '69
Boom! '68
Accident '67
Modesty Blaise '66
King and Country '64
The Servant '63
Eva '62
Time Without Pity '57
The Sleeping Tiger '54
Prowler '51
The Boy with the Green Hair '48

Eb Lottimer(1950-)

Twisted Love '95
Love Matters '93

Ye Lou

Summer Palace '06
Purple Butterfly '03

Todd Louiso(1970-)

The Marc Pease Experience '09
Love Liza '02

Pavel (Lungin) Lounguine(1949-)

Luna Park '91
Taxi Blues '90

John Lounsbery

The Many Adventures of Winnie the Pooh '77
The Rescuers '77

Eugene Lourie(1903-91)

Gorgo '61
The Beast from 20,000 Fathoms '53

Eric Louzil(1951-)

Class of Nuke 'Em High 3: The Good, the Bad and the Subhumanoid '94
Class of Nuke 'Em High 2: Subhumanoid Meltdown '91
Wilding '90
Fortress of Amerikka '89
Lust for Freedom '87

Nick Love

Outlaw '07
The Business '05

Charles Loventhal

Meet Market '08
Mr. Write '92
My Demon Lover '87
First Time '82

Otho Lovering(1892-1968)

Drift Fence '36
Sky Parade '36

Steven Lovy

Plughead Rewired: Circuitry Man 2 '94
Circuitry Man '90

Lucas Lowe

American Shaolin: King of the Kickboxers 2 '92

The King of the Kickboxers '91
No Retreat, No Surrender 3: Blood Brothers '91

Richard Lowenstein(1959-)

He Died With a Felafel in His Hand '01
Dogs in Space '87

Dick Lowry(1944-)

Category 7 : The End of the World '05
Category 6 : Day of Destruction '04
Little John '02
Attila '01
The Diamond of Jeru '01
Follow the Stars Home '01
Atomic Train '99
Dean Koontz's Mr. Murder '98
Last Stand at Saber River '96
A Horse for Danny '95
Urban Crossfire '94
The Gambler Returns: The Luck of the Draw '93
In the Line of Duty: Ambush in Waco '93
Till Murder Do Us Part '92
Midnight Murders '91
Archie: Return to Riverdale '90
In the Line of Duty: A Cop for the Killing '90
In the Line of Duty: The FBI Murders '88
Kenny Rogers as the Gambler, Part 3: The Legend Continues '87
Agatha Christie's Murder with Mirrors '85
Wet Gold '84
Wild Horses '84
Kenny Rogers as the Gambler, Part 2: The Adventure Continues '83
Living Proof: The Hank Williams Jr. Story '83
Smokey and the Bandit, Part 3 '83
Coward of the County '81
The Jayne Mansfield Story '80
Kenny Rogers as the Gambler '80

Sam Lowry

See Steven Soderbergh

Nanni Loy(1925-95)

Where's Piccone '84
Cafe Express '83
Head of the Family '71

Arthur Lubin(1898-1995)

The Incredible Mr. Limpet '64
Thief of Baghdad '61
Escapade in Japan '57
Francis in the Navy '55
Lady Godiva '55
Francis Joins the WACs '54
Francis Covers the Big Town '53
South Sea Woman '53
Francis Goes to West Point '52
Francis Goes to the Races '51
Queen for a Day '51
Rhubarb '51
Francis the Talking Mule '49
Impact '49
New Orleans '47
Delightfully Dangerous '45
Ali Baba and the Forty Thieves '43
The Phantom of the Opera '43
Ride 'Em Cowboy '42
Buck Privates '41
Hold That Ghost '41
In the Navy '41
Keep 'Em Flying '41
Black Friday '40
Prison Break '38

Rob Malenfant
Facing the Enemy *'00*
The Perfect Nanny *'00*
The Landlady *'98*
The Night Caller *'97*
The Nurse *'97*

Terrence Malick(1943-)
The New World *'05*
The Thin Red Line *'98*
Days of Heaven *'78*
Badlands *'74*

Laurence Malkin
Five Fingers *'06*
Soul Assassin *'01*

Louis Malle(1932-95)
Vanya on 42nd Street *'94*
Damage *'92*
May Fools *'90*
Au Revoir les Enfants *'87*
Alamo Bay *'85*
Crackers *'84*
Atlantic City *'81*
My Dinner with Andre *'81*
Pretty Baby *'78*
Murmur of the Heart *'71*
Spirits of the Dead *'68*
The Thief of Paris *'67*
Viva Maria! *'65*
The Fire Within *'64*
A Very Private Affair *'62*
The Lovers *'59*
Frantic *'58*

James "Jim" Mallon
Mystery Science Theater 3000: The Movie *'96*
Blood Hook *'86*

Bruce Malmuth(1937-)
Pentathlon *'94*
Hard to Kill *'89*
Where Are the Children? *'85*
The Man Who Wasn't There *'83*
Nighthawks *'81*
Foreplay *'75*

Mark Malone
Dead Heat *'01*
The Last Stop *'99*
Hoods *'98*
Bulletproof Heart *'95*

William Malone(1953-)
Masters of Horror: Fair Haired Child *'06*
Feardotcom *'02*
House on Haunted Hill *'99*
Creature *'85*
Scared to Death *'80*

David Mamet(1947-)
Redbelt *'08*
Spartan *'04*
Heist *'01*
State and Main *'00*
The Winslow Boy *'98*
The Spanish Prisoner *'97*
Oleanna *'94*
Homicide *'91*
Things Change *'88*
House of Games *'87*

Yuri Mamin(1946-)
Window to Paris *'95*
Sideburns *'91*

Rouben Mamoulian(1897-1987)
Silk Stockings *'57*
Summer Holiday *'48*
Blood and Sand *'41*
The Mark of Zorro *'40*
Golden Boy *'39*
The Gay Desperado *'36*
Becky Sharp *'35*
Queen Christina *'33*
The Song of Songs *'33*
Dr. Jekyll and Mr. Hyde *'32*
Applause *'29*

Milcho Manchevski(1959-)
Shadows *'07*
Dust *'01*
Before the Rain *'94*

Jeffrey Mandel
Elves *'89*
Robo-Chic *'89*

Robert Mandel
A Season on the Brink *'02*
Winds of Terror *'01*
Thin Air *'00*
The Substitute *'96*
School Ties *'92*
Perfect Witness *'89*
Big Shots *'87*
F/X *'86*
Touch and Go *'86*
Independence Day *'83*

Artie Mandelberg
His Bodyguard *'98*
Where's the Money, Noreen? *'95*

Luis Mandoki(1954-)
Innocent Voices *'04*
Trapped *'02*
Angel Eyes *'01*
Message in a Bottle *'98*
When a Man Loves a Woman *'94*
Born Yesterday *'93*
White Palace *'90*
Gaby: A True Story *'87*

Neil Mandt(1969-)
Last Stop for Paul *'08*
Arthur's Quest *'99*
The Million Dollar Kid *'99*
Hijacking Hollywood *'97*

Joseph Manduke
The Gumshoe Kid *'89*
Omega Syndrome *'87*
Beatlemania! The Movie *'81*
Cornbread, Earl & Me *'75*
Kid Vengeance *'75*
Fury on Wheels *'71*

James Mangold(1964-)
Knight and Day *'10*
3:10 to Yuma *'07*
Walk the Line *'05*
Identity *'03*
Kate & Leopold *'01*
Girl, Interrupted *'99*
Cop Land *'97*
Heavy *'94*

Francis Mankiewicz(1944-93)
Love and Hate: A Marriage Made in Hell *'90*
And Then You Die *'88*
Les Bons Debarras *'81*

Joseph L. Mankiewicz(1909-93)
Sleuth *'72*
There Was a Crooked Man *'70*
The Honey Pot *'67*
Cleopatra *'63*
Suddenly, Last Summer *'59*
Guys and Dolls *'55*
The Barefoot Contessa *'54*
Julius Caesar *'53*
Five Fingers *'52*
People Will Talk *'51*
All About Eve *'50*
No Way Out *'50*
House of Strangers *'49*
A Letter to Three Wives *'49*
The Ghost and Mrs. Muir *'47*
Dragonwyck *'46*
Somewhere in the Night *'46*

Tom Mankiewicz(1942-)
Taking the Heat *'93*
Delirious *'91*
Dragnet *'87*

Anthony Mann(1906-67)
Dandy in Aspic *'68*
The Heroes of Telemark *'65*
The Fall of the Roman Empire *'64*
El Cid *'61*
Cimarron *'60*
God's Little Acre *'58*
Man of the West *'58*
Men in War *'57*
The Tin Star *'57*
Far Country *'55*
The Man from Laramie *'55*
Savage Wilderness *'55*
Strategic Air Command *'55*
The Glenn Miller Story *'54*
The Naked Spur *'53*
Thunder Bay *'53*
Bend of the River *'52*
The Furies *'50*
Side Street *'50*
Winchester '73 *'50*
Border Incident *'49*
Reign of Terror *'49*
He Walked by Night *'48*
Raw Deal *'48*
Desperate *'47*
Railroaded *'47*
T-Men *'47*
The Bamboo Blonde *'46*
Strange Impersonation *'46*
Great Flamarion *'45*

Daniel Mann(1912-91)
The Man Who Broke 1,000 Chains *'87*
Playing for Time *'80*
Matilda *'78*
Journey into Fear *'74*
Big Mo *'73*
Interval *'73*
Willard *'71*
A Dream of Kings *'69*
For Love of Ivy *'68*
Our Man Flint *'66*
Who's Got the Action? *'63*
Butterfield 8 *'60*
The Mountain Road *'60*
The Last Angry Man *'59*
Hot Spell *'58*
The Teahouse of the August Moon *'56*
I'll Cry Tomorrow *'55*
The Rose Tattoo *'55*
Come Back, Little Sheba *'52*

Delbert Mann(1920-2007)
Lily in Winter *'94*
Ironclads *'90*
The Last Days of Patton *'86*
Love Leads the Way *'84*
The Member of the Wedding *'83*
Night Crossing *'81*
All Quiet on the Western Front *'79*
Home to Stay *'79*
Torn Between Two Lovers *'79*
The Birch Interval *'78*
Breaking Up *'78*
Francis Gary Powers: The True Story of the U-2 Spy *'76*
The Man Without a Country *'73*
No Place to Run *'72*
She Waits *'71*
David Copperfield *'70*
The Pink Jungle *'68*
Heidi *'67*
A Gathering of Eagles *'63*
That Touch of Mink *'62*
Lover Come Back *'61*
Desire Under the Elms *'58*
Separate Tables *'58*
Marty *'55*

Edward Andrew (Santos Alcocer) Mann(1923-95)
Hooch *'76*
Cauldron of Blood *'67*
Hallucination *'67*
Hothead *'63*

Farhad Mann
The Lost Treasure of the Grand Canyon *'08*
Lawnmower Man 2: Beyond Cyberspace *'95*
Return to Two Moon Junction *'93*
Nick Knight *'89*

Michael Mann(1943-)
Public Enemies *'09*
Miami Vice *'06*
Collateral *'04*
Ali *'01*
The Insider *'99*
Heat *'95*
The Last of the Mohicans *'92*
Manhunter *'86*
The Keep *'83*
Thief *'81*
The Jericho Mile *'79*

Peter Manoogian
Soldiers of Change *'06*
Seedpeople *'92*
Demonic Toys *'90*
Arena *'89*
Enemy Territory *'87*
The Eliminators *'86*
Dungeonmaster *'83*

Mark Manos
Josh Kirby... Time Warrior: Chapter 4, Eggs from 70 Million B.C. *'95*
Liquid Dreams *'92*

Rene Manzor(1959-)
Red Shoe Diaries 8: Night of Abandon *'97*
Legends of the North *'95*
Warrior Spirit *'94*

Robert Marcarelli
The Long Ride Home *'01*
The Omega Code *'99*
I Don't Buy Kisses Anymore *'92*
Original Intent *'91*

Terry Marcel(1942-)
The Last Seduction 2 *'98*
Jane & the Lost City *'87*
Prisoners of the Lost Universe *'84*
Hawk the Slayer *'81*

Siro Marcellini
Gangster's Law *'86*
The Beast of Babylon Against the Son of Hercules *'63*

Alex March(1921-89)
Master Mind *'73*
Firehouse *'72*
The Big Bounce *'69*
Paper Lion *'68*

Rafael Romero Marchent(1926-)
Heat of the Flame *'76*
Garringo *'69*

Max Marcin(1879-1948)
Gambling Ship *'33*
King of the Jungle *'33*

Greg Marcks
Echelon Conspiracy *'09*
11:14 *'03*

Adam Marcus(1968-)
Let It Snow *'99*
Jason Goes to Hell: The Final Friday *'93*

Mitch Marcus
The Haunting of Hell House *'99*
Knocking on Death's Door *'99*
Boltneck *'98*
A Boy Called Hate *'95*

Paul Marcus(1955-)
Eye of the Killer *'99*
The Break Up *'98*

Andreas Marfori
Desperate Crimes *'93*
Evil Clutch *'89*

Antonio Margheriti
See Anthony M. Dawson
Car Crash *'80*
Giants of Rome *'63*

Stuart Margolin(1940-)
The Sweetest Gift *'98*
How the West Was Fun *'95*
Medicine River *'94*
Paramedics *'88*
The Glitter Dome *'84*
Dirkham Detective Agency *'83*
A Shining Season *'79*

A. L. Mariaux
See Jess (Jesus) Franco

Edwin L. Marin(1899-1951)
The Cariboo Trail *'50*
Christmas Eve *'47*
Abilene Town *'46*
Mr. Ace *'46*
Nocturne *'46*
Johnny Angel *'45*
Show Business *'44*
Tall in the Saddle *'44*
Invisible Agent *'42*
Miss Annie Rooney *'42*
A Christmas Carol *'38*
Everybody Sing *'38*
Listen, Darling *'38*
I'd Give My Life *'36*
Bombay Mail *'34*
The Death Kiss *'33*
A Study in Scarlet *'33*

Lex Marinos(1949-)
An Indecent Obsession *'85*
Remember Me *'85*

Peter Maris
Diplomatic Immunity *'91*
Hangfire *'91*
Ministry of Vengeance *'89*
True Blood *'89*
Viper *'88*
Terror Squad *'87*
Land of Doom *'84*
Delirium *'77*

Chris Marker(1921-)
Sans Soleil *'82*
Le Joli Mai *'62*

Anthony Markes
Bikini Island *'91*
Last Dance *'91*

Monte Markham(1935-)
Neon City *'91*
Defense Play *'88*

Fletcher Markle(1921-91)
The Incredible Journey *'63*
Jigsaw *'49*

Peter Markle(1946-)
High Noon *'09*
The Tenth Circle *'08*
The Last Days of Frankie the Fly *'96*
White Dwarf *'95*
Wagons East *'94*
Through the Eyes of a Killer *'92*
El Diablo *'90*
Nightbreaker *'89*
Bat 21 *'88*
Youngblood *'86*
Hot Dog... The Movie! *'83*
The Personals *'83*

Robert Markowitz(1935-)
The Great Gatsby *'01*
The Pilot's Wife *'01*
Small Vices: A Spenser Mystery *'99*
David *'97*
Into Thin Air: Death on Everest *'97*
The Tuskegee Airmen *'95*
Afterburn *'92*
Love, Lies and Murder *'91*
Decoration Day *'90*
Too Young to Die *'90*
Dangerous Life *'89*
Kojak: The Belarus File *'85*
My Mother's Secret Life *'84*
Pray TV *'82*
A Long Way Home *'81*

Arthur Marks(1927-)
Monkey Hustle *'77*
J.D.'s Revenge *'76*
Bucktown *'75*
Friday Foster *'75*
Bonnie's Kids *'73*
Detroit 9000 *'73*
Togetherness *'70*

Ross Kagen Marks
The Twilight of the Golds *'97*
Homage *'95*

Christian Marquand(1927-2000)
Candy *'68*
Attila *'54*

Richard Marquand(1938-87)
Hearts of Fire *'87*
The Jagged Edge *'85*
Until September *'84*
Return of the Jedi *'83*
Eye of the Needle *'81*
The Legacy *'79*

David Marsh
Stormswept *'95*
Lords of Magick *'88*

Philip Marshak
Cataclysm *'81*
Dracula Sucks *'79*

Frank Marshall(1954-)
Eight Below *'06*
From the Earth to the Moon *'98*
Congo *'95*
Alive *'93*
Arachnophobia *'90*

Garry Marshall(1934-)
Valentine's Day *'10*
Georgia Rule *'07*
The Princess Diaries 2: Royal Engagement *'04*
Raising Helen *'04*
The Princess Diaries *'01*
Runaway Bride *'99*
The Other Sister *'98*
Dear God *'96*
Exit to Eden *'94*
Frankie and Johnny *'91*
Pretty Woman *'90*
Beaches *'88*
Overboard *'87*
Nothing in Common *'86*
The Flamingo Kid *'84*
Young Doctors in Love *'82*

George Marshall(1891-1975)
Eight on the Lam *'67*
Boy, Did I Get a Wrong Number! *'66*
How the West Was Won *'63*
Papa's Delicate Condition *'63*
The Gazebo *'59*
It Started with a Kiss *'59*
The Mating Game *'59*
The Sheepman *'58*
The Sad Sack *'57*
Red Garters *'54*
Houdini *'53*
Money from Home *'53*
Off Limits *'53*
Scared Stiff *'53*
Fancy Pants *'50*
Never a Dull Moment *'50*
My Friend Irma *'49*
The Perils of Pauline *'47*
Variety Girl *'47*
The Blue Dahlia *'46*
Monsieur Beaucaire *'46*
Murder, He Says *'45*
Star Spangled Rhythm *'42*
Valley of the Sun *'42*
Pot o' Gold *'41*
Texas *'41*
The Ghost Breakers *'40*
Destry Rides Again *'39*
You Can't Cheat an Honest Man *'39*
The Goldwyn Follies *'38*
In Old Kentucky *'35*
Life Begins at Forty *'35*
Show Them No Mercy *'35*
365 Nights in Hollywood *'34*
Pack Up Your Troubles *'32*

Neil Marshall(1970-)
Doomsday *'08*
The Descent *'05*
Dog Soldiers *'01*

Penny Marshall(1947-)
Riding in Cars with Boys *'01*
The Preacher's Wife *'96*
Renaissance Man *'94*
A League of Their Own *'92*

Awakenings '90
Big '88
Jumpin' Jack Flash '86

Rob Marshall(1960-)
Nine '09
Memoirs of a Geisha '05
Chicago '02
Annie '99

Scott Marshall
Blonde Ambition '07
Keeping Up with the Steins '06

Tonie Marshall
Venus Beauty Institute '98
Pas Tres Catholique '93

William Marshall(1924-2003)
The Phantom Planet '61
Adventures of Captain Fabian '51

Joshua Marston(1968-)
New York, I Love You '09
Maria Full of Grace '04

Charles Martin(1910-83)
One Man Jury '78
How to Seduce a Woman '74
Dead Right '68
Death of a Scoundrel '56
My Dear Secretary '49

Darnell Martin
Cadillac Records '08
I Like It Like That '94

D'Urville Martin(1938-84)
Fass Black '77
Dolemite '75

Eugenio (Gene) Martin(1935-)
Bad Man's River '72
Horror Express '72
Pancho Villa '72
It Happened at Nightmare Inn '70

Frank Martin
Elvis in Hollywood '93
Doctor Butcher M.D. '80

Gregory Mars Martin
See Mars Callahan

Philip Martin
Wallander: Sidetracked '08
Bloodlines '05

Richard Martin(1956-)
Air Bud 2: Golden Receiver '98
Wounded '97
White Tiger '95
Elizabeth R '72

Jacques Martineau(1963-)
Born in 68 '08
Cote d'Azur '05
My Life on Ice '02
The Adventures of Felix '99
Jeanne and the Perfect Guy '98

Renzo Martinelli
Carnera: The Walking Mountain '08
The Stone Merchant '06

Richard Martini(1955-)
Cannes Man '96
Limit Up '89
You Can't Hurry Love '88

Raymond Martino
Skyscraper '95
To the Limit '95
DaVinci's War '92
American Born '89

Sergio Martino(1938-)
American Tiger '89
Casablanca Express '89
The Opponent '89
Hands of Steel '86
After the Fall of New York '85
Scorpion with Two Tails '82
The Great Alligator '81
Screamers '80
Mountain of the Cannibal God '79
Day of the Maniac '77
The Cheaters '76
Sex with a Smile '76
Torso '73
Violent Professionals '73
Your Vice is a Closed Room and Only I Have the Key '72
The Case of the Scorpion's Tail '71
The Next Victim '71
The Scorpion's Tail '71
Blade of the Ripper '70

Leslie Martinson(1915-)
Return to Africa '89
The Fantastic World of D.C. Collins '84
The Kid with the 200 I.Q. '83
The Kid with the Broken Halo '82
Rescue from Gilligan's Island '78
Fathom '67
Batman '66
PT 109 '63
Hot Rod Girl '56
The Atomic Kid '54

Andrew Marton(1904-92)
Africa Texas Style '67
Around the World Under the Sea '65
Clarence, the Cross-eyed Lion '65
The Thin Red Line '64
The Longest Day '62
Green Fire '55
Gypsy Colt '54
Men of the Fighting Lady '54
Secret of Stamboul '36

Mike Marvin
Sunstorm '01
Wishman '93
The Wraith '87
Hamburger... The Motion Picture '86

Francesco Maselli(1930-)
Time of Indifference '64
Love in the City '53

Noel Mason Smith(1895-1955)
Fighting Pilot '35
The Night Patrol '26

Stelvio Massi(1929-2004)
Black Cobra 2 '89
The Black Cobra '87
Fearless '77

Joe Massot
Space Riders '83
Wonderwall: The Movie '69

Master P(1967-)
Internet Dating '08
No Tomorrow '99

Quentin Masters(1946-)
Dangerous Summer '82
The Stud '78
Thumb Tripping '72

Peter Masterson(1934-)
Lost Junction '03
West of Here '02
Mermaid '00
The Only Thrill '97
Lily Dale '96
Arctic Blue '93
Night Game '89
Blood Red '88
Full Moon in Blue Water '88
The Trip to Bountiful '85

Nico Mastorakis(1941-)
Hired to Kill '91
Ninja Academy '90
In the Cold of the Night '89
Terminal Exposure '89
Glitch! '88
Nightmare at Noon '87
The Wind '87
Zero Boys '86
Blind Date '84
Next One '84
Sky High '84

Camillo Mastrocinque(1901-69)
An Angel for Satan '66
Full Hearts & Empty Pockets '63

Armand Mastroianni(1948-)
Final Approach '08
The Pledge '08
Pandemic '07
Sharpshooter '07
The Celestine Prophecy '06
Though None Go With Me '06
Nowhere to Land '00
Fatal Error '99
First Daughter '99
One of Her Own '97
Robin Cook's Invasion '97
Cameron's Closet '89
Double Revenge '89
Distortions '87
The Supernaturals '86
Killing Hour '84
He Knows You're Alone '80

Toshio Masuda(1927-)
Zero '84
Last Days of Planet Earth '74
Tora! Tora! Tora! '70

Eddy Matalon
Sweet Killing '93
Blackout '78
Cathy's Curse '77

Rudolph Mate(1898-1964)
The 300 Spartans '62
Revak the Rebel '60
For the First Time '59
Deep Six '58
Three Violent People '57
The Far Horizons '55
The Violent Men '55
The Black Shield of Falworth '54
Second Chance '53
The Green Glove '52
When Worlds Collide '51
Branded '50
Union Station '50
The Dark Past '49
D.O.A. '49

Ted Mather
Faith '90
Body Beat '88

Tim Matheson(1947-)
Behind Enemy Lines 3: Colombia '08
True Confessions of a Hollywood Starlet '08
In the Company of Spies '99
Buried Alive 2 '97
Tails You Live, Heads You're Dead '95
Breach of Conduct '94

Shue Matsubayashi(1920-)
Last War '68
Attack Squadron '63
I Bombed Pearl Harbor '60

Bruno Mattei(1931-2007)
Strike Commando '87
Caged Women '84
Seven Magnificent Gladiators '84
Hell of the Living Dead '83
Rats '83
SS Girls '77

Charles Matthau(1964-)
The Grass Harp '95
Doin' Time on Planet Earth '88

Paul Matthews
Hooded Angels '00
Breeders '97
Grim '95

Arne Mattson(1920-95)
The Girl '86
The Doll '62

Norman Maurer(1926-86)
The Outlaws Is Coming! '65
Around the World in a Daze '63

Robert (Roberto) Mauri(1924-)
Animal Called Man '72
Island of Lost Girls '68
Invincible Gladiators '64
The Slaughter of the Vampires '62

Garth Maxwell(1963-)
When Love Comes '98
Jack Be Nimble '94

Peter Maxwell(1924-)
Platypus Cove '86
The Highest Honor '84
Run, Rebecca, Run '81
Touch & Go '80
Plunge Into Darkness '77

Ronald F. Maxwell(1947-)
Gods and Generals '03
Gettysburg '93
Kidco '83
The Night the Lights Went Out in Georgia '81
Little Darlings '80

Bradford May
Ring of Death '08
The Devil's Prey '01
Gargantua '98
Asteroid '97
Darkman 3: Die Darkman Die '95
Madonna: Innocence Lost '95
Darkman 2: The Return of Durant '94
Marilyn & Bobby: Her Final Affair '94
Lethal Lolita—Amy Fisher: My Story '92
Mortal Sins '92

Elaine May(1932-)
Ishtar '87
Mikey & Nicky '76
The Heartbreak Kid '72
A New Leaf '71

Joe May(1880-1954)
The House of the Seven Gables '40
The Invisible Man Returns '40
Homecoming '28
The Indian Tomb '21

Russ Mayberry
Challenge of a Lifetime '85
A Matter of Life and Death '81
The $5.20 an Hour Dream '80
Marriage Is Alive and Well '80
The Rebels '79
Unidentified Flying Oddball '79
Fer-De-Lance '74
Probe '72
The Jesus Trip '71

John Maybury(1958-)
The Edge of Love '08
The Jacket '05
Love Is the Devil '98

Daisy von Scherler Mayer(1965-)
The Guru '02
Madeline '98
Woo '97
Party Girl '94

Michael Mayer(1960-)
Graduation '07
Flicka '06
A Home at the End of the World '04

Paul Mayersberg(1941-)
The Last Samurai '90
Nightfall '88
Captive '87

Les Mayfield
Code Name: The Cleaner '07
The Man '05
American Outlaws '01
Blue Streak '99
Flubber '97
Miracle on 34th Street '94
Encino Man '92

Tony Maylam(1943-)
Split Second '92
The Burning '82
The Sins of Dorian Gray '82
The Riddle of the Sands '79

Ken Maynard(1895-1973)
Honor of the Range '34
The Fiddlin' Buckaroo '33
Strawberry Roan '33

Archie Mayo(1891-1968)
Angel on My Shoulder '46
A Night in Casablanca '46
Crash Dive '43
Moontide '42
Orchestra Wives '42
Charley's Aunt '41
The Great American Broadcast '41
House Across the Bay '40
They Shall Have Music '39
The Adventures of Marco Polo '38
The Black Legion '37
Call It a Day '37
Petrified Forest '36
Bordertown '35
The Case of the Lucky Legs '35
Go Into Your Dance '35
The Man with Two Faces '34
The Mayor of Hell '33
Night After Night '32
Illicit '31
Svengali '31

Melanie Mayron(1952-)
Slap Her, She's French '02
The Baby-Sitters' Club '95

Michael Mazo
Crackerjack '94
Time Runner '92
Possession: Until Death Do You Part '90
Maniac Warriors '88

Paul Mazursky(1930-)
Coast to Coast '04
Winchell '98
Faithful '95
The Pickle '93
Scenes from a Mall '91
Enemies, a Love Story '89
Moon over Parador '88
Down and Out in Beverly Hills '86
Moscow on the Hudson '84
The Tempest '82
Willie & Phil '80
An Unmarried Woman '78
Next Stop, Greenwich Village '76
Harry and Tonto '74
Blume in Love '73
Alex in Wonderland '70
Bob & Carol & Ted & Alice '69

Des McAnuff
The Adventures of Rocky & Bullwinkle '00
Cousin Bette '97

Don McBrearty
Luna: Spirit of the Whale '07
Chasing Freedom '04
Race to Freedom: The Story of the Underground Railroad '94
Really Weird Tales '86
Coming Out Alive '84
American Nightmare '81

Jim McBride(1941-)
Meat Loaf: To Hell and Back '00
The Informant '97
Pronto '97
Uncovered '94
The Wrong Man '93
Blood Ties '92
Great Balls of Fire '89
The Big Easy '87
Breathless '83
Hot Times '74
Glen and Randa '71
David Holzman's Diary '67

Jon McBride
Terror House '97
Feeders '96
Woodchipper Massacre '89
Cannibal Campout '88

Howard McCain
Outlander '08
Shadow of a Scream '97
No Dessert Dad, 'Til You Mow the Lawn '94

Rod McCall
Lewis and Clark and George '97
Cheatin' Hearts '93

James McCalmont
Escape from Safehaven '88
Underground Terror '88

Tim McCanlies(1953-)
Secondhand Lions '03
Dancer, Texas—Pop. 81 '98

Tim McCann(1968-)
The Poker Club '08
Runaway '05
Revolution #9 '01
Desolation Angels '95

Leo McCarey(1898-1969)
Rally 'Round the Flag, Boys! '58
An Affair to Remember '57
Good Sam '48
The Bells of St. Mary's '45
Going My Way '44
Once Upon a Honeymoon '42
Love Affair '39
The Awful Truth '37
Milky Way '36
Ruggles of Red Gap '35
Belle of the Nineties '34
Six of a Kind '34
Duck Soup '33
Kid from Spain '32
Indiscreet '31

Ray McCarey(1898-1948)
So This Is Washington '43
You Can't Fool Your Wife '40
Devil's Party '38
Hot Tip '35
The Mystery Man '35
Sunset Range '35

John P. McCarthy(1884-1962)
Marked Trails '44
Raiders of the Border '44
The Lion Man '36
Song of the Gringo '36
The Return of Casey Jones '34
Fighting Champ '33
The Forty-Niners '32
Cavalier of the West '31
Mother and Son '31
The Nevada Buckaroo '31
The Ridin' Fool '31
Sunrise Trail '31
Oklahoma Cyclone '30

Michael McCarthy(1917-59)
Operation Amsterdam '60
Crow Hollow '52

Thomas (Tom) McCarthy(1969-)
The Visitor *'07*
The Station Agent *'03*

John McCauley
Deadly Intruder *'84*
Rattlers *'76*

Michael McClary
Annie O *'95*
Curse of the Starving Class *'94*

Gregory McClatchy
Soccer Mom *'08*
Vampire at Midnight *'88*

Michael (Mick) McCleery
Track 16 *'02*
The Alien Agenda: Out of the Darkness *'96*

Bret McCormick(1958-)
Time Tracers *'97*
Rumble in the Streets *'96*
Blood on the Badge *'92*
Tabloid! *'88*

Nelson McCormick
The Stepfather *'09*
Prom Night *'08*
Operation Sandman: Warriors in Hell *'00*
Where the Truth Lies *'99*
For Which He Stands *'98*

George McCowan(1927-95)
July Group *'81*
Return to Fantasy Island *'77*
Murder on Flight 502 *'75*
Frogs *'72*
Savage Run *'70*
The Ballad of Andy Crocker *'69*
Black Brigade *'69*

Ian McCrudden
Islander *'06*
The Big Day *'99*
Trailer, the Movie *'99*

Bruce McCulloch(1961-)
Stealing Harvard *'02*
Superstar *'99*
Dog Park *'98*

Jim McCullough, Sr.
The St. Tammany Miracle *'94*
Where the Red Fern Grows: Part 2 *'92*
Video Murders *'87*
Mountaintop Motel Massacre *'86*
The Aurora Encounter *'85*
Charge of the Model T's *'76*

Bruce McDonald(1959-)
Pontypool *'09*
Killer Wave *'07*
The Tracey Fragments *'07*
Picture Claire *'01*
Hard Core Logo *'96*
Dance Me Outside *'95*
Highway 61 *'91*
Roadkill *'89*

Frank McDonald(1899-1980)
Wyatt Earp: Return to Tombstone *'94*
Gunfight at Comanche Creek *'64*
Thunder Pass *'54*
Apache Chief *'50*
The Big Sombrero *'49*
Ringside *'49*
Lights of Old Santa Fe *'47*
My Pal Trigger *'46*
Rainbow over Texas *'46*
Sioux City Sue *'46*
Song of Arizona *'46*
Under Nevada Skies *'46*
Along the Navaho Trail *'45*
Bells of Rosarita *'45*
Sunset in El Dorado *'45*
Treasure of Fear *'45*
Gambler's Choice *'44*
One Body Too Many *'44*
Take It Big *'44*
Timber Queen *'44*
Wildcat *'42*
Flying Blind *'41*
Twilight on the Rio Grande *'41*
Gaucho Serenade *'40*
Jeepers Creepers *'39*

Michael James McDonald(1964-)
The Death Artist *'95*
The Crazysitter *'94*

Rodney McDonald
Deep Core *'00*
Nautilus *'99*
Sonic Impact *'99*
Surface to Air *'98*
Steel Sharks *'97*
Scorned 2 *'96*
Desire *'95*
Night Eyes 4: Fatal Passion *'95*
Night Eyes 2 *'91*

Edward T. McDougal
The Prodigy *'98*
One for the Road *'82*

Charles McDougall
Call Me: The Rise and Fall of Heidi Fleiss *'04*
Heart *'99*

Francine McDougall
Cow Belles *'06*
Sugar & Spice *'01*

Ross McElwee(1947-)
Time Indefinite *'93*
Sherman's March *'86*

Bernard McEveety(1924-2004)
Roughnecks *'80*
Centennial *'78*
The Bears & I *'74*
One Little Indian *'73*
Napoleon and Samantha *'72*
The Brotherhood of Satan *'71*

Vincent McEveety
Gunsmoke: Return to Dodge *'87*
Amy *'81*
Herbie Goes Bananas *'80*
The Apple Dumpling Gang Rides Again *'79*
Herbie Goes to Monte Carlo *'77*
Gus *'76*
The Treasure of Matecumbe *'76*
The Castaway Cowboy *'74*
Charley and the Angel *'73*
Superdad *'73*
Million Dollar Duck *'71*
Menace on the Mountain *'70*
Smoke *'70*
Firecreek *'68*

McG(1968-)
Terminator Salvation *'09*
We Are Marshall *'06*
Charlie's Angels: Full Throttle *'03*
Charlie's Angels *'00*

William F. McGaha
Iron Horsemen *'71*
The Speed Lovers *'68*

William McGann(1893-1977)
American Empire *'42*
In Old California *'42*
Dr. Christian Meets the Women *'40*

Scott McGehee
Bee Season *'05*
The Deep End *'01*
Suture *'93*

Robert McGinley
Jimmy Zip *'00*
Shredder Orpheus *'89*

Sean McGinly
The Great Buck Howard *'09*
Two Days *'03*

Scott McGinnis(1958-)
The Last Gasp *'94*
Caroline at Midnight *'93*

J(ohn) P(aterson) McGowan(1880-1952)
Roaring Six Guns *'37*
Rough Ridin' Rhythm *'37*
Deadwood Pass *'33*
Drum Taps *'33*
Lone Bandit *'33*
The Outlaw Tamer *'33*
When a Man Rides Alone *'33*
Hurricane Express *'32*
Mark of the Spur *'32*
Quick Trigger Lee *'31*
Near the Rainbow's End *'30*
Below the Deadline *'29*
Red Signals *'27*
Road Agent *'26*
Blood and Steel *'25*

Robert McGowan(1882-1955)
Old Swimmin' Hole *'40*
Tomboy *'40*
Frontier Justice *'35*

Stuart E. McGowan(1904-99)
The Billion Dollar Hobo *'78*
The Showdown *'50*

Tom McGowan(1921-)
Savage Journey *'83*
Cataclysm *'81*

Douglas McGrath(1958-)
Infamous *'06*
Nicholas Nickleby *'02*
Company Man *'00*
Emma *'96*

Joseph McGrath(1930-)
The Strange Case of the End of Civilization As We Know It *'93*
Great McGonagall *'75*
Digby, the Biggest Dog in the World *'73*
The Magic Christian *'69*
The Bliss of Mrs. Blossom *'68*
30 Is a Dangerous Age, Cynthia *'68*
Casino Royale *'67*

Tom McGrath
Madagascar: Escape 2 Africa *'08*
Madagascar *'05*

Sean McGregor
Devil Times Five *'74*
Gentle Savage *'73*

Mary McGuckian(1963-)
The Bridge of San Luis Rey *'05*
This Is the Sea *'96*

Paul McGuigan(1963-)
Push *'09*
Lucky Number Slevin *'06*
Wicker Park *'04*
The Reckoning *'03*
Gangster No. 1 *'00*
The Acid House *'98*

Doug McHenry
Kingdom Come *'01*
Jason's Lyric *'94*
House Party 2: The Pajama Jam *'91*

Christian McIntire(1964-)
Antibody *'02*
Lost Voyage *'01*

Chris T. McIntyre
Backstreet Justice *'93*
Border Shootout *'90*

Adam McKay(1968-)
The Other Guys *'10*
Step Brothers *'08*
Talladega Nights: The Ballad of Ricky Bobby *'06*
Anchorman: The Legend of Ron Burgundy *'04*

Cole McKay
The Underground *'97*
Star Hunter *'95*
The Secret of the Golden Eagle *'91*

Jim McKay
Angel Rodriguez *'05*
Our Song *'01*
Girls Town *'95*

Lucky McKee(1975-)
Red *'08*
Masters of Horror: Sick Girl *'06*
The Woods *'03*
May *'02*

Duncan McLachlan
Rudyard Kipling's the Second Jungle Book: Mowgli and Baloo *'97*
Born Wild *'95*
The Double O Kid *'92*
Scavengers *'87*

Andrew V. McLaglen(1920-)
On Wings of Eagles *'86*
The Dirty Dozen: The Next Mission *'85*
Sahara *'83*
The Blue and the Gray *'82*
The Shadow Riders *'82*
Sea Wolves *'81*
ffolkes *'80*
Breakthrough *'78*
Wild Geese *'78*
Banjo Hackett *'76*
The Last Hard Men *'76*
Mitchell *'75*
Cahill: United States Marshal *'73*
Chisum *'70*
The Undefeated *'69*
Bandolero! *'68*
The Devil's Brigade *'68*
Hellfighters *'68*
The Way West *'67*
Monkeys, Go Home! *'66*
The Rare Breed *'66*
Shenandoah *'65*
McLintock! *'63*
Man in the Vault *'56*

Greg Mclean
Rogue *'07*
Wolf Creek *'05*

Don McLennan(1949-)
Slate, Wyn & Me *'87*
Hard Knocks *'80*

Norman Z. McLeod(1898-1964)
Alias Jesse James *'59*
Casanova's Big Night *'54*
Never Wave at a WAC *'52*
Let's Dance *'50*
The Paleface *'48*
The Road to Rio *'47*
The Secret Life of Walter Mitty *'47*
Kid from Brooklyn *'46*
Panama Hattie *'42*
Lady Be Good *'41*
Little Men *'40*
Topper Takes a Trip *'39*
Topper *'37*
Pennies from Heaven *'36*
Here Comes Cookie *'35*
It's a Gift *'34*
Horse Feathers *'32*
Monkey Business *'31*
Touchdown *'31*

Tom McLoughlin(1950-)
Murder in Greenwich *'02*
The Unsaid *'01*
Behind the Mask *'99*
Journey *'95*
The Yarn Princess *'94*
The Fire Next Time *'93*
Sometimes They Come Back *'91*
Date with an Angel *'87*
Friday the 13th, Part 6: Jason Lives *'86*
One Dark Night *'82*

David McNally
Kangaroo Jack *'02*
Coyote Ugly *'00*

Sean McNamara(1963-)
Bratz *'07*
The Cutting Edge: Going for the Gold *'05*
Raise Your Voice *'04*
Race to Space *'01*
The Trial of Old Drum *'00*
Treehouse Hostage *'99*
Wild Grizzly *'99*
P.U.N.K.S. *'98*
3 Ninjas: High Noon at Mega Mountain *'97*
Galgameth *'96*
Hollywood Chaos *'89*

Bob McNaught
Sea Wife *'57*
Grand National Night *'53*

John McNaughton(1950-)
Lansky *'99*
Wild Things *'98*
Normal Life *'96*
Girls in Prison *'94*
Mad Dog and Glory *'93*
Sex, Drugs, Rock & Roll: Eric Bogosian *'91*
Henry: Portrait of a Serial Killer *'90*
The Borrower *'89*

John McPherson(1941-2007)
Incident at Deception Ridge *'94*
Fade to Black *'93*
Dirty Work *'92*
Strays *'91*

James McTeigue
Ninja Assassin *'09*
V for Vendetta *'06*

John McTiernan(1951-)
Basic *'03*
Rollerball *'02*
The 13th Warrior *'99*
The Thomas Crown Affair *'99*
Die Hard: With a Vengeance *'95*
Last Action Hero *'93*
Medicine Man *'92*
The Hunt for Red October *'90*
Die Hard *'88*
Predator *'87*
Nomads *'86*

Nick Mead
Swing *'98*
Bank Robber *'93*

Shane Meadows(1972-)
This Is England *'06*
Dead Man's Shoes *'04*
Once Upon a Time in the Midlands *'02*
24-7 *'97*

Nancy Meckler
Alive and Kicking *'96*
Sister My Sister *'94*

Peter Medak(1940-)
Sex & Lies in Sin City: The Ted Binion Scandal *'08*
Masters of Horror: The Washingtonians *'07*
Anne Rice's The Feast of All Saints *'01*
Species 2 *'98*
The Hunchback *'97*
Pontiac Moon *'94*
Romeo Is Bleeding *'93*
Let Him Have It *'91*
The Krays *'90*
The Men's Club *'86*
Breakin' Through *'84*
The Dancing Princesses *'84*
The Emperor's New Clothes *'84*
Pinocchio *'83*
The Snow Queen *'83*
Snow White and the Seven Dwarfs *'83*
Zorro, the Gay Blade *'81*
The Babysitter *'80*
The Changeling *'80*
The Odd Job *'78*
Ghost in the Noonday Sun *'74*
The Ruling Class *'72*
A Day in the Death of Joe Egg *'71*
Negatives *'68*

Julio Medem(1958-)
Sex and Lucia *'01*
Lovers of the Arctic Circle *'98*
Tierra *'95*
The Red Squirrel *'93*
Vacas *'91*

Don Medford(1917-)
Sizzle *'81*
The Organization *'71*

Cary Medoway(1949-)
The Heavenly Kid *'85*
Paradise Motel *'84*

Alexander Medvedkin
Happiness *'32*
Happiness *'32*

Francis Megahy(1937-)
The Disappearance of Kevin Johnson *'95*
Red Sun Rising *'94*
Taffin *'88*
Flashpoint Africa *'84*
The Carpathian Eagle *'81*
The House that Bled to Death *'81*
The Great Riviera Bank Robbery *'79*
Freelance *'71*

Alan Mehrez
Bloodsport 3 *'97*
Bloodsport 2: The Next Kumite *'95*

Deepa Mehta(1950-)
Water *'05*
The Republic of Love *'03*
Earth *'98*
Fire *'96*
Camilla *'94*

Gus Meins(1893-1940)
The Gentleman from California *'37*
Roll Along Cowboy *'37*
Kelly the Second *'36*
March of the Wooden Soldiers *'34*

Fernando Meirelles(1955-)
Blindness *'08*
The Constant Gardener *'05*
City of God *'02*

Norbert Meisel(1930-)
Night Children *'89*
Walking the Edge *'83*
The Adultress *'77*

Ib Melchior(1917-)
The Time Travelers *'64*
The Angry Red Planet *'59*

Bill Melendez(1916-2008)
Bon Voyage, Charlie Brown *'80*
Race for Your Life, Charlie Brown *'77*

George Melford(1877-1961)
Cowboy Counselor *'33*
The Dude Bandit *'33*
Man of Action *'33*
Boiling Point *'32*
Dracula (Spanish Version) *'31*
East of Borneo *'31*
The Charlatan *'29*
Moran of the Lady Letty *'22*
The Sheik *'21*

James Melkonian
The Jerky Boys *'95*
The Stoned Age *'94*

Jean-Pierre Melville(1917-73)
Le Cercle Rouge *'70*
Army of Shadows *'69*
Le Samourai *'67*
Le Deuxieme Souffle *'66*
Le Doulos *'61*
Leon Morin, Priest *'61*
Bob le Flambeur *'55*
Les Enfants Terrible *'50*
La Silence de la Mer *'47*

Stevan Mena
Brutal Massacre: A Comedy *'07*
Malevolence *'04*

Christopher Menaul
See No Evil: The Moors Murders *'06*
Secret Smile *'05*
One Kill *'00*
The Passion of Ayn Rand *'99*
Feast of July *'95*
Fatherland *'94*
Prime Suspect *'92*
A Dangerous Man: Lawrence after Arabia *'91*

George Mendeluk(1948-)
Men of Means *'99*
Meatballs 3 *'87*
Doin' Time *'85*
The Kidnapping of the President *'80*
Stone Cold Dead *'80*

Lothar Mendes(1894-1974)
Moonlight Sonata *'38*
The Man Who Could Work Miracles *'37*
Power *'34*
Strangers in Love *'32*
Personal Maid *'31*

Sam Mendes(1965-)
Away We Go *'09*
Revolutionary Road *'08*
Jarhead *'05*
Road to Perdition *'02*
American Beauty *'99*

Fernando Mendez(1908-66)
The Living Coffin *'58*
The Vampire's Coffin *'58*
The Vampire *'57*
Black Pit of Dr. M *'47*

Ramon Menendez
Money for Nothing *'93*
Stand and Deliver *'88*

Chris Menges(1940-)
The Lost Son *'98*
Second Best *'94*
Crisscross *'92*
A World Apart *'88*

Jiri Menzel(1938-)
I Served the King of England *'07*
My Sweet Little Village *'86*
Larks on a String *'68*
Closely Watched Trains *'66*

William Cameron Menzies(1896-1957)
Invaders from Mars *'53*
Drums in the Deep South *'51*
The Thief of Bagdad *'40*
The Green Cockatoo *'37*
Things to Come *'36*
Chandu the Magician *'32*

Ismail Merchant(1936-2005)
The Mystic Masseur *'01*
Cotton Mary *'99*
The Proprietor *'96*
In Custody *'94*
The Courtesans of Bombay *'85*

Burgess Meredith(1908-97)
Yin & Yang of Mr. Go *'71*
Man on the Eiffel Tower *'48*

Michael Meredith
The Open Road *'09*
Three Days of Rain *'02*

James Merendino(1967-)
SLC Punk! *'99*
The Real Thing *'97*
A River Made to Drown In *'97*
Hard Drive *'94*
Terrified *'94*
Witchcraft 4: Virgin Heart *'92*

Joseph Merhi(1953-)
Executive Target *'97*
Riot *'96*
Last Man Standing *'95*
Rage *'95*
The Sweeper *'95*
Direct Hit *'93*
To Be the Best *'93*
Zero Tolerance *'93*
C.I.A.: Code Name Alexa *'92*
Magic Kid *'92*
Maximum Force *'92*
Final Impact *'91*
The Last Riders *'90*
Night of the Wilding *'90*
Repo Jake *'90*
Emperor of the Bronx *'89*
L.A. Vice *'89*
Midnight Warrior *'89*
The Glass Jungle *'88*
L.A. Crackdown 2 *'88*
L.A. Heat *'88*
Fresh Kill *'87*
Heat Street *'87*
Hollywood in Trouble *'87*
The Killing Game *'87*
L.A. Crackdown *'87*
Mayhem *'87*
The Newlydeads *'87*

Edmund Elias Merhige(1964-)
Suspect Zero *'04*
Shadow of the Vampire *'00*

Jose Luis Merino(1927-)
The Hanging Woman *'72*
Scream of the Demon Lover *'71*
Hell Commandos *'69*

Agnes Merlet(1959-)
Artemisia *'97*
The Son of the Shark *'93*

Laurence Merrick(1926-77)
Black Bikers from Hell *'70*
The Outlaw Bikers—Gang Wars *'70*

Keith Merrill(1940-)
The Twelve Dogs of Christmas *'05*
Harry's War *'84*
Windwalker *'81*
Take Down *'79*
Three Warriors *'77*

William Mesa
DNA *'97*
The Black Gate *'95*
Galaxis *'95*

Marta Meszaros(1931-)
Adoption *'75*
The Girl *'68*
The Girl *'68*

Alan Metter
Billboard Dad *'98*
Police Academy 7: Mission to Moscow *'94*
Moving *'88*
Back to School *'86*
Girls Just Want to Have Fun *'85*

Alan Metzger
My Husband's Double Life *'01*
Snap Decision *'01*
New Eden *'94*
Fatal Exposure *'91*
Red Wind *'91*
The China Lake Murders *'90*

Radley Metzger(1929-)
The Princess & the Call Girl *'84*
The Cat and the Canary *'79*
Score *'72*
Little Mother *'71*
The Lickerish Quartet *'70*
Camille 2000 *'69*
Therese & Isabelle *'67*
Carmen, Baby *'66*
The Alley Cats *'65*
The Dirty Girls *'64*
Dark Odyssey *'57*

Andrew Meyer(1943-87)
Tidal Wave *'75*
Night of the Cobra Woman *'72*

Kevin Meyer
Perfect Alibi *'94*
Under Investigation *'93*
Invasion of Privacy *'92*
Civil War Diary *'90*

Nicholas Meyer(1945-)
Vendetta *'99*
Company Business *'91*
Star Trek 6: The Undiscovered Country *'91*
The Deceivers *'88*
Volunteers *'85*
The Pied Piper of Hamelin *'84*
The Day After *'83*
Star Trek 2: The Wrath of Khan *'82*
Time After Time *'79*

Russ Meyer(1922-2004)
Beneath the Valley of the Ultra-Vixens *'79*
Supervixens *'75*
Blacksnake! *'73*
Beyond the Valley of the Dolls *'70*
Faster, Pussycat! Kill! Kill! *'65*
Motor Psycho *'65*
Fanny Hill: Memoirs of a Woman of Pleasure *'64*

Turi Meyer(1964-)
Candyman 3: Day of the Dead *'98*
Sleepstalker: The Sandman's Last Rites *'94*

Janet Meyers
The Ripper *'97*
Letter to My Killer *'95*

Nancy Meyers(1949-)
It's Complicated *'09*
The Holiday *'06*
Something's Gotta Give *'03*
What Women Want *'00*
The Parent Trap *'98*

Menno Meyjes(1954-)
Martian Child *'07*
Max *'02*

Eric Meza
The Breaks *'99*
House Party 3 *'94*

Richard Michaels(1936-)
Father and Scout *'94*
Backfield in Motion *'91*
Lethal Charm *'90*
The Queen of Mean *'90*
Indiscreet *'88*
Rockabye *'86*
Heart of a Champion: The Ray Mancini Story *'85*
Silence of the Heart *'84*
Blue Skies Again *'83*
One Cooks, the Other Doesn't *'83*
Sadat *'83*
Plutonium Incident *'82*
Berlin Tunnel 21 *'81*
Homeward Bound *'80*

Oscar Micheaux(1884-1951)
Lying Lips *'39*
Girl from Chicago *'32*
Body and Soul *'24*

Roger Michell(1957-)
Venus *'06*
Enduring Love *'04*
The Mother *'03*
Changing Lanes *'02*
Notting Hill *'99*
The Buddha of Suburbia *'92*

Anne-Marie Mieville(1945-)
Soft and Hard *'85*
Scenario du Film Passion *'82*
Comment Ca Va? *'76*

Radu Mihaileanu(1958-)
Train of Life *'98*
Trahir *'93*

George Mihalka(1952-)
Sticks and Stones *'08*
Cruel and Unusual *'01*
Jack Higgins' The Windsor Protocol *'97*
Jack Higgins' Thunder Point *'97*
Bullet to Beijing *'95*
Relative Fear *'95*
Deceptions 2: Edge of Deception *'94*
Psychic *'91*
Hostile Takeover *'88*
Straight Line *'88*
Eternal Evil *'87*
My Bloody Valentine *'81*
Pick-Up Summer *'79*

Takashi Miike(1960-)
Sukiyaki Western Django *'08*
The Great Yokai War *'05*
Masters of Horror: Imprint *'05*
Three ... Extremes *'04*
Zebraman *'04*
Gozu *'03*
One Missed Call *'03*
Graveyard of Honor *'02*
The Happiness of the Katakuris *'01*
Ichi the Killer *'01*
Visitor Q *'01*
Andromedia *'00*
Audition *'99*
Fudoh: The New Generation *'96*
The Way To Fight *'96*

Ted V. Mikels(1929-)
WarCat *'88*
Aftermath *'85*
10 Violent Women *'79*
Cruise Missile *'78*
Hustler Squad *'76*
Blood Orgy of the She-Devils *'74*
The Doll Squad *'73*
The Corpse Grinders *'71*
Girl in Gold Boots *'69*
The Astro-Zombies *'67*
The Black Klansman *'66*

Nikita Mikhalkov(1945-)
12 *'07*
Burnt by the Sun *'94*
Anna *'93*
Close to Eden *'90*
Dark Eyes *'87*
Oblomov *'81*
A Slave of Love *'78*
An Unfinished Piece for a Player Piano *'77*

Christopher Miles(1939-)
Priest of Love *'81*
That Lucky Touch *'75*
The Virgin and the Gypsy *'70*

Lewis Milestone(1895-1980)
Mutiny on the Bounty *'62*
Ocean's 11 *'60*
Pork Chop Hill *'59*
The Halls of Montezuma *'50*
The Red Pony *'49*
Arch of Triumph *'48*
The Strange Love of Martha Ivers *'46*
A Walk in the Sun *'46*
The Purple Heart *'44*
Edge of Darkness *'43*
The North Star *'43*
Lucky Partners *'40*
The Night of Nights *'39*
Of Mice and Men *'39*
The General Died at Dawn *'36*
Paris in Spring *'35*
Hallelujah, I'm a Bum *'33*
Rain *'32*
The Front Page *'31*
All Quiet on the Western Front *'30*
The Garden of Eden *'28*

John Milius(1944-)
Rough Riders *'97*
Flight of the Intruder *'90*
Farewell to the King *'89*
Red Dawn *'84*
Conan the Barbarian *'82*
Big Wednesday *'78*
The Wind and the Lion *'75*
Dillinger *'73*

Gerry Mill
Second Chance *'80*
The Duchess of Duke Street *'78*

Ray Milland(1905-86)
Panic in the Year Zero! *'62*
Lisbon *'56*
A Man Alone *'55*
Rhubarb *'51*

Catherine Millar
Twisted *'96*
Darlings of the Gods *'90*

Gavin Millar(1938-)
Retribution *'98*
The Crow Road *'96*
Catherine Cookson's The Dwelling Place *'94*
My Friend Walter *'93*
A Murder of Quality *'90*
Tidy Endings *'88*
Dreamchild *'85*
Secrets *'82*

Stuart Millar(1929-)
Rooster Cogburn *'75*
When the Legends Die *'72*

Nick Millard
Terrorists *'88*
Gunblast *'74*

Chris Miller(1942-)
Cloudy with a Chance of Meatballs *'09*
Shrek the Third *'07*

Claude Miller(1942-)
A Secret *'07*
La Petite Lili *'03*
Alias Betty *'01*
The Accompanist *'93*
The Little Thief *'89*
This Sweet Sickness *'77*
The Best Way *'76*

David Miller(1909-92)
Bittersweet Love *'76*
Executive Action *'73*
Hail, Hero! *'69*
Captain Newman, M.D. *'63*
Lonely Are the Brave *'62*
Back Street *'61*
Midnight Lace *'60*
The Story of Esther Costello *'57*
The Opposite Sex *'56*
Diane *'55*
Sudden Fear *'52*
Love Happy *'50*
Our Very Own *'50*
Flying Tigers *'42*
Billy the Kid *'41*

Frank Miller
The Spirit *'08*
Sin City *'05*

George Miller(1943-)
Happy Feet *'06*
Attack of the Sabretooth *'05*
Journey to the Center of the Earth *'99*
In the Doghouse *'98*
Zeus and Roxanne *'96*
The Great Elephant Escape *'95*
Andre *'94*
Gross Misconduct *'93*
Over the Hill *'93*
Frozen Assets *'92*
NeverEnding Story 2: The Next Chapter *'91*
Les Patterson Saves the World *'90*
Goodbye, Miss 4th of July *'88*
Anzacs: The War Down Under *'85*
The Aviator *'85*
Nevil Shute's The Far Country *'85*
All the Rivers Run *'84*
The Man from Snowy River *'82*

George Miller(1945-)
Cybermutt *'02*
Babe: Pig in the City *'98*
Robinson Crusoe *'96*
Silver Strand *'95*
Lorenzo's Oil *'92*
Miracle Down Under *'87*
The Witches of Eastwick *'87*
Mad Max: Beyond Thunderdome *'85*
Twilight Zone: The Movie *'83*
The Road Warrior *'82*
Mad Max *'80*

Harvey Miller(1936-99)
Getting Away With Murder *'96*
Bad Medicine *'85*

Michael Miller
Dangerous Passion *'95*
Danielle Steel's Heartbeat *'93*
Danielle Steel's Star *'93*
Danielle Steel's Daddy *'91*
Danielle Steel's Palomino *'91*
Blown Away *'90*
A Case of Deadly Force *'86*
Can You Feel Me Dancing? *'85*
Silent Witness *'85*
National Lampoon's Class Reunion *'82*
Silent Rage *'82*
Outside Chance *'78*
Jackson County Jail *'76*
Street Girls *'75*

Neal Miller
Raising Flagg *'06*
Under the Biltmore Clock *'85*

Percy Miller
See Master P

Randall Miller
Bottle Shock *'08*
Nobel Son *'08*
Marilyn Hotchkiss' Ballroom Dancing & Charm School *'06*
The Sixth Man *'97*
Houseguest *'94*
Class Act *'91*

Rebecca Miller(1962-)
The Private Lives of Pippa Lee *'09*
The Ballad of Jack and Rose *'05*
Personal Velocity: Three Portraits *'02*
Angela *'94*

Robert Ellis Miller(1932-)
Bed & Breakfast *'92*
Hawks *'89*
Brenda Starr *'86*
Her Life as a Man *'83*
Reuben, Reuben *'83*
The Baltimore Bullet *'80*

The Girl from Petrovka *'74*
The Buttercup Chain *'70*
The Heart Is a Lonely Hunter *'68*
Sweet November *'68*
Any Wednesday *'66*

Sharron Miller
The Woman Who Willed a Miracle *'83*
House of the Dead *'78*

Troy Miller
Dumb and Dumberer: When Harry Met Lloyd *'03*
Jack Frost *'98*
Beverly Hills Family Robinson *'97*

Andy Milligan(1929-91)
The Weirdo *'89*
Carnage *'84*
Legacy of Horror *'78*
Man with Two Heads *'72*
The Rats Are Coming! The Werewolves Are Here! *'72*
Fleshpot on 42nd Street *'71*
The Body Beneath *'70*
Torture Dungeon *'70*
The Ghastly Ones *'68*

Bill Milling
Body Trouble *'92*
Caged Fury *'90*
Lauderdale *'89*

Alec Mills(1932-)
Dead Sleep *'91*
Bloodmoon *'90*

Dan Milner
The Oh in Ohio *'06*
The Phantom from 10,000 Leagues *'56*

Tom Milo
Kiss and Be Killed *'91*
Smooth Talker *'90*

Ilias Milonakos(1941-)
Emmanuelle, the Queen *'79*
Operation Orient *'78*

Sergio Mimica-Gezzan
The Legend of Butch & Sundance *'04*
Taken *'02*

Allen Miner
Black Patch *'57*
The Ride Back *'57*

Michael Miner
The Book of Stars *'99*
Deadly Weapon *'88*

Steve Miner(1951-)
Private Valentine: Blonde & Dangerous *'08*
Texas Rangers *'01*
Lake Placid *'99*
Halloween: H20 *'98*
Big Bully *'95*
My Father the Hero *'93*
Forever Young *'92*
Warlock *'91*
Wild Hearts Can't Be Broken *'91*
House *'86*
Soul Man *'86*
Friday the 13th, Part 3 *'82*
Friday the 13th, Part 2 *'81*

Wu Ming
See Xiaoshuai Wang

Anthony Minghella(1954-2008)
Breaking and Entering *'06*
Cold Mountain *'03*
The Talented Mr. Ripley *'99*
The English Patient *'96*
Mr. Wonderful *'93*
Truly, Madly, Deeply *'91*

Rob Minkoff
The Forbidden Kingdom *'08*
The Haunted Mansion *'03*
Stuart Little 2 *'02*
Stuart Little *'99*
The Lion King *'94*
Honey, I Shrunk the Kids *'89*

Vincente Minnelli(1903-86)
A Matter of Time *'76*
On a Clear Day You Can See Forever *'70*
The Sandpiper *'65*
Goodbye Charlie *'64*
The Courtship of Eddie's Father *'62*
The Four Horsemen of the Apocalypse *'62*
Two Weeks in Another Town *'62*
Bells Are Ringing *'60*
Home from the Hill *'60*
Gigi *'58*
The Reluctant Debutante *'58*
Some Came Running *'58*
Designing Woman *'57*
Lust for Life *'56*
Tea and Sympathy *'56*
The Cobweb *'55*
Kismet *'55*
Brigadoon *'54*
The Long, Long Trailer *'54*
The Band Wagon *'53*
The Story of Three Loves *'53*
The Bad and the Beautiful *'52*
An American in Paris *'51*
Father's Little Dividend *'51*
Father of the Bride *'50*
Madame Bovary *'49*
The Pirate *'48*
Undercurrent *'46*
Ziegfeld Follies *'46*
The Clock *'45*
Yolanda and the Thief *'45*
Meet Me in St. Louis *'44*
Cabin in the Sky *'43*
I Dood It *'43*

Emilio P. Miraglio(1924-)
Halloween Night *'90*
Night Eyes *'90*
The Night Evelyn Came Out of the Grave *'71*

David Mirkin(1955-)
Heartbreakers *'01*
Romy and Michele's High School Reunion *'97*

Bob Misiorowski
Derailed *'02*
Shark Attack *'99*
On the Border *'98*
Beyond Forgiveness *'94*
Point of Impact *'93*
Blink of an Eye *'92*

Kenji Misumi(1921-75)
Shogun Assassin 2: Lightning Swords of Death *'73*
Lone Wolf and Cub *'72*
Lone Wolf and Cub: Baby Cart at the River Styx *'72*
Lone Wolf and Cub: Baby Cart to Hades *'72*
The Razor: Sword of Justice *'72*
Wrath of Daimajin *'66*
Zatoichi: The Blind Swordsman and the Chess Expert *'65*
Zatoichi: The Life and Opinion of Masseur Ichi *'62*

Bruce Mitchell(1880-1952)
The Phantom Flyer *'28*
Dynamite Dan *'24*

David Mitchell
UKM: The Ultimate Killing Machine *'06*
Mask of Death *'97*
Downhill Willie *'96*
The Killing Man *'94*
Ski School 2 *'94*
Thunderground *'89*
City of Shadows *'86*
Club Med *'83*

Mike Mitchell
Shrek Forever After *'10*
Sky High *'05*
Surviving Christmas *'04*
Deuce Bigalow: Male Gigolo *'99*

Oswald Mitchell(1890-1949)
The Temptress *'49*
The Greed of William Hart *'48*
House of Darkness *'48*
Mysterious Mr. Nicholson *'47*
The Dummy Talks *'43*

Roger Mitchell
Morning Glory *'10*
Persuasion *'95*

Sollace Mitchell
Row Your Boat *'98*
Call Me *'88*

Hayao Miyazaki(1941-)
Ponyo *'08*
Howl's Moving Castle *'04*
Spirited Away *'01*
Kiki's Delivery Service *'98*
Princess Mononoke *'98*
My Neighbor Totoro *'88*
The Castle of Cagliostro *'80*

Kenji Mizoguchi(1898-1956)
Street of Shame *'56*
Princess Yang Kwei Fei *'55*
Shin Heike Monogatari *'55*
The Crucified Lovers *'54*
Sansho the Bailiff *'54*
A Geisha *'53*
Ugetsu *'53*
Life of Oharu *'52*
Utamaro and His Five Women *'46*
47 Ronin, Part 1 *'42*
47 Ronin, Part 2 *'42*
The Story of the Late Chrysanthemum *'39*
Osaka Elegy *'36*
Sisters of the Gion *'36*

Moshe Mizrahi(1931-)
Every Time We Say Goodbye *'86*
War & Love *'84*
La Vie Continue *'82*
I Sent a Letter to My Love *'81*
Madame Rosa *'77*
Rachel's Man *'75*
The House on Chelouche Street *'73*
I Love You Rosa *'72*

Juan Lopez Moctezuma(1932-95)
To Kill a Stranger *'84*
Mary, Mary, Bloody Mary *'76*
Dr. Tarr's Torture Dungeon *'75*
Sisters of Satan *'75*

Richard (Dick) Moder(1906-94)
The Bionic Woman *'75*
Lassie: Adventures of Neeka *'68*

Leonide Moguy(1899-1976)
Whistle Stop *'46*
Action in Arabia *'44*

Jose Mojica Marins(1929-)
Hallucinations of a Deranged Mind *'78*
Awakenings of the Beast *'68*
Strange World of Coffin Joe *'68*
At Midnight, I'll Take Your Soul *'63*

Hans Petter Moland(1955-)
The Beautiful Country *'04*
Aberdeen *'00*
Zero Degrees Kelvin *'95*
The Last Lieutenant *'94*

Gustaf Molander(1888-1973)
Only One Night *'42*
Dollar *'38*
A Woman's Face *'38*
Intermezzo *'36*
Swedenhielms *'35*

Ron Moler
Local Boys *'02*
The Runner *'99*

Jacinto (Jack) Molina
See Paul Naschy

William H. Molina
The Last Assassins *'96*
Where Truth Lies *'96*

Edouard Molinaro(1928-)
Beaumarchais the Scoundrel *'96*
Just the Way You Are *'84*
La Cage aux Folles 2 *'81*
La Cage aux Folles *'78*
Pain in the A— *'77*
Dracula and Son *'76*
Ravishing Idiot *'64*
Back to the Wall *'56*

Dominik Moll(1962-)
Lemming *'05*
With a Friend Like Harry *'00*

Karen Moncrieff(1963-)
The Dead Girl *'06*
Blue Car *'03*

Andrew Mondshein(1962-)
An Unfinished Life *'05*
Evidence of Blood *'97*

Paul Mones(1955-)
Saints and Sinners *'95*
Fathers and Sons *'92*

Christopher Monger(1950-)
The Englishman Who Went up a Hill But Came down a Mountain *'95*
Just Like a Woman *'95*
Waiting for the Light *'90*

Mario Monicelli(1915-)
Lovers and Liars *'81*
Casanova '70 *'65*
The Organizer *'64*
Joyful Laughter *'60*
Passionate Thief *'60*
The Unfaithfuls *'60*
The Great War *'59*
Big Deal on Madonna Street *'58*

Stephen R. Monroe
Wyvern *'09*
Storm Cell *'08*
House of 9 *'05*
It Waits *'05*

Carl Monson(1932-88)
Death Feud *'89*
Blood Legacy *'73*
Please Don't Eat My Mother *'72*

Edward Montagne(1912-2003)
They Went That-a-Way & That-a-Way *'78*
The Reluctant Astronaut *'67*
McHale's Navy Joins the Air Force *'65*
McHale's Navy *'64*

Guiliano Montaldo(1930-)
Time to Kill *'89*
Control *'87*
Fifth Day of Peace *'72*
Sacco & Vanzetti *'71*

Robert Bianchi Montero(1907-86)
The Slasher *'72*
Mondo Balordo *'64*
Tharus Son of Attila *'62*
Island Monster *'53*

Jorge Montesi
Call of the Wild *'04*
Turbulence 3: Heavy Metal *'00*
Bloodknot *'95*
Soft Deceit *'94*
Hush Little Baby *'93*
Omen 4: The Awakening *'91*

George Montgomery(1916-2000)
From Hell to Borneo *'64*
Samar *'62*
The Steel Claw *'61*

Robert Montgomery(1904-81)
The Gallant Hours *'60*
Eye Witness *'49*
Lady in the Lake *'46*

Dito Montiel
Fighting *'09*
A Guide to Recognizing Your Saints *'06*

Vincent Monton(1949-)
The Hit *'01*
Fatal Bond *'91*
Windrider *'86*

Lukas Moodysson
Mammoth *'09*
Show Me Love *'99*

Charles Philip Moore
Angel of Destruction *'94*
Black Belt *'92*
Dance with Death *'91*
Demon Wind *'90*

John Moore(1970-)
Max Payne *'08*
The Omen *'06*
Flight of the Phoenix *'04*
Behind Enemy Lines *'01*

Michael Moore(1954-)
Capitalism: A Love Story *'09*
Sicko *'07*
Fahrenheit 9/11 *'04*
Bowling for Columbine *'02*
The Big One *'98*
Canadian Bacon *'94*
Roger & Me *'89*

Michael D. Moore(1914-)
Buckskin *'68*
Fastest Guitar Alive *'68*
Paradise, Hawaiian Style *'66*
Talion *'66*

Robert Moore(1927-84)
Chapter Two *'79*
The Cheap Detective *'78*
Murder by Death *'76*

Tom (Thomas R.) Moore
Gepetto *'00*
Danielle Steel's Fine Things *'90*
'night, Mother *'86*
Return to Boggy Creek *'77*

Jocelyn Moorhouse(1960-)
A Thousand Acres *'97*
How to Make an American Quilt *'95*
Proof *'91*

Philippe Mora(1949-)
Burning Down the House *'01*
Mercenary 2: Thick and Thin *'97*
Pterodactyl Woman from Beverly Hills *'97*
Back in Business *'96*
Precious Find *'96*
Communion *'89*
Howling 3: The Marsupials *'87*
Death of a Soldier *'85*
Howling 2: Your Sister Is a Werewolf *'85*
A Breed Apart *'84*
Return of Captain Invincible *'83*
The Beast Within *'82*
Screams of a Winter Night *'79*
Mad Dog Morgan *'76*

Andrew Morahan
Murder in Mind *'97*
Highlander: The Final Dimension *'94*

Christopher Morahan(1929-)
Element of Doubt *'96*
Paper Mask *'91*
After Pilkington *'88*
Troubles *'88*
Clockwise *'86*
In the Secret State *'85*
The Jewel in the Crown *'84*

Gael Morel
Apres Lui *'07*
Full Speed *'96*

Pierre Morel
From Paris With Love *'10*
Taken *'08*
District B13 *'04*

David Moreton
Testosterone *'03*
Edge of Seventeen *'99*

Nanni Moretti(1953-)
The Son's Room *'00*
Caro Diario *'93*
Palombella Rossa *'89*

Glen Morgan
Black Christmas *'06*
Willard *'03*

William M. Morgan(1899-1964)
The Violent Years *'56*
Fun & Fancy Free *'47*
Bells of Capistrano *'42*
Heart of the Rio Grande *'42*
Mr. District Attorney *'41*

Brett Morgen
Chicago 10 *'07*
The Kid Stays in the Picture *'02*

Louis Morneau
Joy Ride 2: Dead Ahead *'08*
The Hitcher 2: I've Been Waiting *'03*
Bats *'99*
Made Men *'99*
Retroactive *'97*
Soldier Boyz *'95*
Carnosaur 2 *'94*
Final Judgment *'92*
Quake *'92*
To Die Standing *'91*

David Burton Morris(1948-)
The Three Lives of Karen *'97*
Hometown Boy Makes Good *'93*
Jersey Girl *'92*
Patti Rocks *'88*

Ernest Morris
Masters of Venus *'62*
The Tell-Tale Heart *'60*

Errol Morris(1948-)
Standard Operating Procedure *'08*
The Fog of War: Eleven Lessons from the Life of Robert S. McNamara *'03*
Fast, Cheap & Out of Control *'97*
A Brief History of Time *'92*
The Dark Wind *'91*
The Thin Blue Line *'88*

Howard Morris(1919-2005)
Goin' Coconuts *'78*
Don't Drink the Water *'69*
With Six You Get Eggroll *'68*
Who's Minding the Mint? *'67*

Betsan Morris-Evans
Lady Audley's Secret *'00*
Dad Savage *'97*

Bruce Morrison
Tearaway *'87*
Shaker Run *'85*

Paul Morrison
Wondrous Oblivion *'06*
Solomon and Gaenor *'98*

Paul Morrissey(1939-)
Beethoven's Nephew *'88*
Spike of Bensonhurst *'88*
Mixed Blood *'84*
The Hound of the Baskervilles *'77*
Andy Warhol's Dracula *'74*
Andy Warhol's Frankenstein *'74*
Heat *'72*
Trash *'70*
Flesh *'68*

Hollingsworth Morse(1910-88)
Justin Morgan Had a Horse *'81*
Daughters of Satan *'72*
Pufnstuf *'70*
Rocky Jones, Space Ranger: Renegade Satellite *'54*

Terry Morse(1906-84)
Godzilla, King of the Monsters *'56*
Unknown World *'51*
Bells of San Fernando *'47*
Danny Boy *'46*
The Verdict *'46*
Fog Island *'45*
British Intelligence *'40*
Waterfront *'39*
Crime School *'38*

Catherine Morshead
Me & Mrs. Jones *'02*
The Railway Children *'00*

Edmund Mortimer(1874-1944)
The Prairie Pirate *'25*
County Fair *'20*

Rocky Morton(1955-)
Super Mario Bros. *'93*
D.O.A. *'88*

Gilbert Moses(1943-95)
A Fight for Jenny *'90*
The Fish that Saved Pittsburgh *'79*
Roots *'77*

Gregory Mosher
The Prime Gig *'00*
A Life in the Theater *'93*
Our Town *'89*

Elijah Moshinsky(1946-)
Genghis Cohn *'93*
The Green Man *'91*

Donny Most(1953-)
Moola *'07*
The Last Best Sunday *'98*

Jonathan Mostow(1961-)
Surrogates *'09*
Terminator 3: Rise of the Machines *'03*
U-571 *'00*
From the Earth to the Moon *'98*
Breakdown *'96*
Flight of Black Angel *'91*
Beverly Hills Bodysnatchers *'89*

Greg Mottola(1964-)
Adventureland *'09*
Superbad *'07*
The Daytrippers *'96*

Emmanuel Mouret
Shall We Kiss *'09*
Shall We Kiss? *'07*

Malcolm Mowbray(1961-)
Sweet Revenge *'98*
Don't Tell Her It's Me *'90*
Out Cold *'89*
A Private Function *'84*

John Llewellyn Moxey(1925-)
Lady Mobster *'88*
Through Naked Eyes *'87*
Detective Sadie & Son *'84*
The Cradle Will Fall *'83*
The Solitary Man *'82*
Killjoy *'81*
Mating Season *'81*
No Place to Hide *'81*
The Children of An Lac *'80*
The Power Within *'79*
Sanctuary of Fear *'79*
President's Mistress *'78*
Intimate Strangers *'77*
Panic in Echo Park *'77*
Nightmare in Badham County *'76*
Conspiracy of Terror *'75*
A Strange and Deadly Occurrence *'74*
Where Have All the People Gone? *'74*
Genesis II *'73*
The Bounty Man *'72*
Home for the Holidays *'72*
The Night Stalker *'71*
Circus of Fear *'67*
Horror Hotel *'60*

Allan Moyle(1947-)
Weirdsville *'07*
Man in the Mirror: The Michael Jackson Story *'04*
Say Nothing *'01*
Jailbait! *'00*
Xchange *'00*
New Waterford Girl *'99*
Empire Records *'95*
The Gun in Betty Lou's Handbag *'92*
Pump Up the Volume *'90*
Times Square *'80*

Gabriele Muccino(1967-)
Seven Pounds *'08*
The Pursuit of Happyness *'06*
The Last Kiss *'01*

Russell Mulcahy(1953-)
The Scorpion King 2: Rise of a Warrior *'08*
Crash and Burn *'07*
Resident Evil: Extinction *'07*
The Sitter *'07*
Swimming Upstream *'03*
Lost Battalion *'01*
On the Beach *'00*
Resurrection *'99*
Russell Mulcahy's Tale of the Mummy *'99*
Silent Trigger *'97*
The Shadow *'94*
The Real McCoy *'93*
Blue Ice *'92*
Highlander 2: The Quickening *'91*
Ricochet *'91*
Highlander *'86*
Razorback *'84*

Peter Mullan(1954-)
The Magdalene Sisters *'02*
Orphans *'97*

Edward (Edoardo Mulargia) Muller(1925-)
Savage Island *'85*
Escape from Hell *'79*

Robert Mulligan(1925-2008)
The Man in the Moon *'91*
Clara's Heart *'88*
Kiss Me Goodbye *'82*
Bloodbrothers *'78*
Same Time, Next Year *'78*
The Other *'72*
Summer of '42 *'71*
The Pursuit of Happiness *'70*
The Stalking Moon *'69*
Up the Down Staircase *'67*
Inside Daisy Clover *'65*
Baby, the Rain Must Fall *'64*
Love with the Proper Stranger *'63*
To Kill a Mockingbird *'62*
Come September *'61*
The Great Impostor *'61*
The Rat Race *'60*
Fear Strikes Out *'57*

Claude Mulot(-1986)
Black Venus *'83*
The Immoral One *'80*

Christopher Munch(1962-)
Harry and Max *'04*
The Sleepy Time Gal *'01*
Color of a Brisk and Leaping Day *'95*
The Hours and Times *'92*

Richard W. Munchkin
Evil Obsession *'96*
Texas Payback *'95*
Fists of Iron *'94*
Guardian Angel *'94*
Out for Blood *'93*
Ring of Fire 2: Blood and Steel *'92*
Deadly Bet *'91*
Ring of Fire *'91*
Dance or Die *'87*

Marc Munden
Miranda *'01*
Vanity Fair *'99*
Touching Evil *'97*

Jag Mundhra(1946-)
Tales of the Kama Sutra 2: Monsoon *'98*
Tales of the Kama Sutra: The Perfumed Garden *'98*
Monsoon *'97*
Irresistible Impulse *'95*
Improper Conduct *'94*
Eyewitness to Murder *'93*
Sexual Malice *'93*
Tropical Heat *'93*
L.A. Goddess *'92*
The Other Woman *'92*
Wild Cactus *'92*
Last Call *'90*
Legal Tender *'90*
Jigsaw Murders *'89*
Hack O'Lantern *'87*
Open House *'86*

Ian Mune(1941-)
The Bridge to Nowhere *'86*
Came a Hot Friday *'85*

Chris Munger
Kiss of the Tarantula *'75*
Black Starlet *'74*

Lance Mungia(1972-)
The Crow: Wicked Prayer *'05*
Six-String Samurai *'98*

Robert Munic(1968-)
They Call Me Sirr *'00*
In a Class of His Own *'99*
Timelock *'99*
L.A. Rules: The Pros and Cons of Breathing *'94*

Jimmy T. Murakami(1933-)
When the Wind Blows *'86*
Battle Beyond the Stars *'80*

Ryu Murakami(1952-)
Because of You *'95*
Tokyo Decadence *'91*

Toru Murakawa
New York Cop *'94*
Distant Justice *'92*

John Murlowski
Black Cadillac *'03*
Terminal Error *'02*
Santa with Muscles *'96*
The Secret Agent Club *'96*
Automatic *'94*
Amityville: A New Generation *'93*
Return of the Family Man *'89*

F.W. Murnau(1888-1931)
Tabu: A Story of the South Seas *'31*
City Girl *'30*
Sunrise *'27*
Faust *'26*
Tartuffe *'25*
The Finances of the Grand Duke *'24*
The Last Laugh *'24*
Nosferatu *'22*
Phantom *'22*
The Haunted Castle *'21*

David Murphy
Border Lost *'08*
Lost Treasure of the Maya *'08*

Dudley Murphy(1897-1968)
One Third of a Nation *'39*
Emperor Jones *'33*

Edward Murphy
Heated Vengeance *'87*
Raw Force *'81*

Geoff Murphy(1938-)
Race Against Time *'00*
Fortress 2: Re-Entry *'99*
The Magnificent Seven *'98*
Don't Look Back *'96*
Under Siege 2: Dark Territory *'95*
Blind Side *'93*
The Last Outlaw *'93*
Freejack *'92*
Never Say Die *'90*
Young Guns 2 *'90*
Red King, White Knight *'89*
The Quiet Earth *'85*
Utu *'83*
Goodbye Pork Pie *'81*

Maurice Murphy(1939-)
15 Amore *'98*
Wet and Wild Summer *'92*
Fatty Finn *'84*
Doctors and Nurses *'82*

Ralph Murphy(1895-1967)
The Black Devils of Kali *'55*
Mickey *'48*
The Spirit of West Point *'47*
Panama Flo *'32*

Ryan Murphy
Eat, Pray, Love *'10*
Running with Scissors *'06*

Tab Murphy
Dark Country *'09*
The Last of the Dogmen *'95*

Robin Murray
Season of Change *'94*
Dance *'90*

John Musker(1953-)
The Princess and the Frog *'09*
Treasure Planet *'02*
Hercules *'97*
Aladdin *'92*
The Little Mermaid *'89*
The Great Mouse Detective *'86*

Victoria Muspratt
White Wolves 3: Cry of the White Wolf *'98*
Inhumanoid *'96*

Floyd Mutrux(1941-)
There Goes My Baby *'92*
The Hollywood Knights *'80*
Aloha, Bobby and Rose *'74*
Dusty and Sweets Mcgee *'71*

Zion Myers(1898-1948)
Sidewalks of New York *'31*
Dogville Shorts *'30*

Alan Myerson
Holiday Affair *'96*
Police Academy 5: Assignment Miami Beach *'88*
Bayou Romance *'86*
Private Lessons *'75*
Steelyard Blues *'73*

Daniel Myrick
The Objective *'08*
Believers *'07*
The Blair Witch Project *'99*

Petter Naess(1960-)
Mozart and the Whale *'05*
Elling *'01*

Ivan Nagy(1938-)
Skinner *'93*
Jane Doe *'83*
A Gun in the House *'81*
Captain America 2: Death Too Soon *'79*
Deadly Hero *'75*
Bad Charleston Charlie *'73*

Chris Nahon
Blood: The Last Vampire *'09*
Empire of the Wolves *'05*
Kiss of the Dragon *'01*

Mira Nair(1957-)
Amelia *'09*
New York, I Love You *'09*
The Namesake *'06*
Vanity Fair *'04*
Hysterical Blindness *'02*
Monsoon Wedding *'01*
My Own Country *'98*
Kama Sutra: A Tale of Love *'96*
The Perez Family *'94*
Mississippi Masala *'92*
Salaam Bombay! *'88*

Nobuo Nakagawa
Legends of the Poisonous Seductress 2: Quick Draw Okatsu *'69*
Legends of the Poisonous Seductress 3: Okatsu the Fugitive *'69*
Snake Woman's Curse *'68*
The Ghost of Yotsuya *'58*

Ko Nakahira
Rica 2: Lonely Wanderer *'73*
Rica *'72*

Hideo Nakata(1961-)
Death Note 3: L, Change the World *'08*
The Ring 2 *'05*
Dark Water *'02*
Ringu 2 *'99*
Ringu *'98*

Rodion Nakhapetov
Border Blues *'03*
Stir *'98*

Bharat Nalluri(1965-)
Miss Pettigrew Lives for a Day *'08*
The Crow: Salvation *'00*
Killing Time *'97*

Silvio Narizzano(1927-)
The Body in the Library *'84*
Why Shoot the Teacher *'79*
The Class of Miss MacMichael *'78*
Bloodbath *'76*
Redneck *'73*
Loot... Give Me Money, Honey! *'70*
Blue *'68*
Georgy Girl *'66*
Die! Die! My Darling! *'65*
24 Hours in a Woman's Life *'61*

Mikio Naruse(1905-69)
When a Woman Ascends the Stairs *'60*
Late Chrysanthemums *'54*
Mother *'52*

Paul Naschy(1934-)
The Craving *'80*
Human Beasts *'80*
Inquisition *'76*

Vincenzo Natali(1969-)
Splice *'09*
Paris, je t'aime *'06*
Cypher *'02*
Cube *'98*

Mort Nathan
National Lampoon's Van Wilder 2: The Rise of Taj *'06*
Boat Trip *'03*

Bill Naud
Ricky 1 *'88*
Whodunit *'82*

Gregory Nava(1949-)
Bordertown *'06*
Why Do Fools Fall in Love? *'98*
Selena *'96*
My Family *'94*
A Time of Destiny *'88*
El Norte *'83*

Ray Nazarro(1902-86)
Dog Eat Dog *'64*
Kansas Pacific *'53*
Indian Uprising *'51*
David Harding, Counterspy *'50*
Blazing Across the Pecos *'48*

Ronald Neame(1911-)
Foreign Body *'86*
First Monday in October *'81*
Hopscotch *'80*
Meteor *'79*
The Odessa File *'74*
The Poseidon Adventure *'72*
Scrooge *'70*
The Prime of Miss Jean Brodie *'69*
Gambit *'66*
The Chalk Garden *'64*
I Could Go on Singing *'63*
Tunes of Glory *'60*
The Horse's Mouth *'58*
Windom's Way *'57*
The Man Who Never Was *'55*
The Promoter *'52*
The Golden Salamander *'51*

Hal Needham(1931-)
Hostage Hotel *'00*
Body Slam *'87*
Rad *'86*
Cannonball Run 2 *'84*
Stroker Ace *'83*
Megaforce *'82*
Cannonball Run *'81*
Smokey and the Bandit 2 *'80*
The Villain *'79*
Hooper *'78*
Smokey and the Bandit *'77*

Alberto Negrin(1940-)
Tower of the Firstborn *'98*
Voyage of Terror: The Achille Lauro Affair *'90*
Mussolini & I *'85*

Jean Negulesco(1900-93)
The Invincible Six *'68*
The Best of Everything *'59*
Daddy Long Legs *'55*
Three Coins in the Fountain *'54*
A Woman's World *'54*
How to Marry a Millionaire *'53*
Titanic *'53*
Phone Call from a Stranger *'52*
Three Came Home *'50*
Johnny Belinda *'48*
Road House *'48*
Humoresque *'46*
The Mask of Dimitrios *'44*

Marshall Neilan(1891-1958)
Swing It, Professor *'37*
Vagabond Lover *'29*
Daddy Long Legs *'19*
Amarilly of Clothesline Alley *'18*
Stella Maris *'18*
Rebecca of Sunnybrook Farm *'17*

Roy William Neill(1886-1946)
The Woman in Green *'49*
Black Angel *'46*
Dressed to Kill *'46*
Terror by Night *'46*
House of Fear *'45*

Pursuit to Algiers '45
The Pearl of Death '44
Scarlet Claw '44
Spider Woman '44
Sherlock Holmes Faces Death '43
Sherlock Holmes in Washington '43
Frankenstein Meets the Wolfman '42
Sherlock Holmes and the Secret Weapon '42
Dr. Syn '37
The Black Room '35
The Viking '28

James Neilson(1910-79)

The Adventures of Tom Sawyer '73
The First Time '69
Where Angels Go, Trouble Follows '68
Gentle Giant '67
The Adventures of Bullwhip Griffin '66
Dr. Syn, Alias the Scarecrow '64
The Moon-Spinners '64
Johnny Shiloh '63
Summer Magic '63
Bon Voyage! '62
Moon Pilot '62
Mooncussers '62
Night Passage '57

Frans Nel

American Kickboxer 1 '91
Lights! Camera! Murder! '89

David Nelson(1936-)

Last Plane Out '83
House of Death '82
A Rare Breed '81
Confessions of Tom Harris '72

Dusty Nelson

Inferno '01
Necromancer: Satan's Servant '88
White Phantom: Enemy of Darkness '87

Gary Nelson

Melanie Darrow '97
Revolver '92
The Lookalike '90
Get Smart, Again! '89
Noble House '88
Allan Quatermain and the Lost City of Gold '86
The Baron and the Kid '84
Murder in Coweta County '83
Jimmy the Kid '82
Pride of Jesse Hallum '81
The Black Hole '79
Freaky Friday '76
Santee '73
Molly & Lawless John '72

Gene Nelson(1920-96)

Harum Scarum '65
Kissin' Cousins '64

Jessie Nelson

I Am Sam '01
Corrina, Corrina '94

Ralph Nelson(1916-87)

Christmas Lilies of the Field '84
A Hero Ain't Nothin' but a Sandwich '78
Lady of the House '78
Love Under Pressure '78
Embryo '76
The Wilby Conspiracy '75
Soldier Blue '70
Charly '68
Duel at Diablo '66
Father Goose '64
Lilies of the Field '63
Soldier in the Rain '63
Requiem for a Heavyweight '62
Requiem for a Heavyweight '56

Tim Blake Nelson(1965-)

The Grey Zone '01
O '01
Eye of God '97

Jan Nemec(1936-)

The Report on the Party and the Guests '66
Diamonds of the Night '64

Avi Nesher(1953-)

The Secrets '07
Raw Nerve '99
The Taxman '98
Mercenary '96
Savage '96
Timebomb '91
Doppelganger: The Evil Within '90
She '83

Kurt Neumann(1906-58)

The Fly '58
Kronos '57
Mohawk '56
They Were So Young '55
Carnival Story '54
Party Girls for Sale '54
Tarzan and the She-Devil '53
The Ring '52
Rocketship X-M '50
The Dude Goes West '48
Bad Boy '39
Wide Open Faces '38
Make a Wish '37
It Happened in New Orleans '36
Let's Sing Again '36
My Pal, the King '32

Mark Neveldine

Crank: High Voltage '09
Gamer '09
Crank '06

Mike Newell(1942-)

Prince of Persia: The Sands of Time '10
Love in the Time of Cholera '07
Harry Potter and the Goblet of Fire '05
Mona Lisa Smile '03
Pushing Tin '99
Donnie Brasco '96
An Awfully Big Adventure '94
Four Weddings and a Funeral '94
Enchanted April '92
Into the West '92
Amazing Grace & Chuck '87
The Good Father '87
Dance with a Stranger '85
Bad Blood '81
The Awakening '80
The Man in the Iron Mask '77

Sam Newfield(1899-1964)

The Gambler & the Lady '52
Outlaw Women '52
Scotland Yard Inspector '52
Fingerprints Don't Lie '51
Leave It to the Marines '51
The Lost Continent '51
Sky High '51
Western Pacific Agent '51
Hi-Jacked '50
Motor Patrol '50
Radar Secret Service '50
Three Desperate Men '50
She Shoulda Said No '49
State Department File 649 '49
The Strange Mrs. Crane '48
Adventure Island '47
Money Madness '47
Three on a Ticket '47
Blonde for a Day '46
Larceny in her Heart '46
Murder Is My Business '46
Outlaw of the Plains '46
Border Badmen '45
Gangster's Den '45
His Brother's Ghost '45
I Accuse My Parents '45
Kid Sister '45
The Lady Confesses '45
Lightning Raiders '45
Shadows of Death '45
White Pongo '45
Death Rides the Plains '44
Devil Riders '44
The Drifter '44
Frontier Outlaws '44
The Monster Maker '44
Nabonga '44
Oath of Vengeance '44
Rustler's Hideout '44
Thundering Gunslingers '44
Wild Horse Phantom '44
The Black Raven '43
Dead Men Walk '43
Harvest Melody '43
Raiders of Red Gap '43
Tiger Fangs '43
Along the Sundown Trail '42
Billy the Kid Trapped '42
Jungle Siren '42
Law and Order '42
The Lone Rider in Cheyenne '42
The Mad Monster '42
The Mysterious Rider '42
Prairie Pals '42
Texas Justice '42
Tumbleweed Trail '42
Billy the Kid in Santa Fe '41
Border Roundup '41
The Lone Rider Crosses the Rio '41
The Lone Rider in Frontier Fury '41
The Lone Rider in Ghost Town '41
Outlaws of the Rio Grande '41
Texas Trouble '41
Trigger Men '41
Arizona Gangbusters '40
Battling Outlaw '40
Billy the Kid in Texas '40
Death Rides the Range '40
Gun Code '40
I Take This Oath '40
The Invisible Killer '40
Fighting Mad '39
Fighting Renegade '39
Flaming Lead '39
Outlaw's Paradise '39
Six Gun Rhythm '39
Texas Wildcats '39
Trigger Pals '39
Durango Valley Raiders '38
Feud Maker '38
Frontier Scout '38
Gunsmoke Trail '38
Harlem on the Prairie '38
Lightnin' Carson Rides Again '38
Phantom Ranger '38
The Rangers' Roundup '38
Six Gun Trail '38
Songs and Bullets '38
Terror of Tiny Town '38
Thunder in the Desert '38
Arizona Gunfighter '37
Boothill Brigade '37
Doomed at Sundown '37
The Gambling Terror '37
Gun Lords of Stirrup Basin '37
Guns in the Dark '37
A Lawman Is Born '37
Lightning Bill Crandall '37
Melody of the Plains '37
Paroled to Die '37
Ridin' the Lone Trail '37
Roarin' Lead '37
Windjammer '37
Aces and Eights '36
Border Caballero '36
Federal Agent '36
Ghost Patrol '36
Lightnin' Bill Carson '36
Lion's Den '36
Roaring Guns '36
Stormy Trails '36
The Traitor '36
Branded a Coward '35
Bulldog Courage '35
Go-Get-'Em-Haines '35
Racing Luck '35
Range Riders '35
Trails of the Wild '35
Frontier Days '34

John Newland(1917-2000)

Don't Be Afraid of the Dark '73
The Legend of Hillbilly John '73

Anthony Newley(1931-99)

Summertree '71
Those People Next Door '52

Joseph M. Newman(1909-2006)

The George Raft Story '61
The King of the Roaring '20s: The Story of Arnold Rothstein '61
The Big Circus '59
The Gunfight at Dodge City '59
This Island Earth '55
Dangerous Crossing '53
Love Nest '51
Great Dan Patch '49
Jungle Patrol '48
Abandoned '47

Kyle Newman

Fanboys '09
The Hollow '04

Paul Newman(1925-2008)

The Glass Menagerie '87
Harry & Son '84
The Shadow Box '80
The Effect of Gamma Rays on Man-in-the-Moon Marigolds '73
Sometimes a Great Notion '71
Rachel, Rachel '68

Fred Newmeyer(1888-1967)

Rodeo Rhythm '42
General Spanky '36
They Never Come Back '32
The Freshman '25
The Perfect Clown '25
Girl Shy '24
Safety Last '23

Phil Nibbelink

We're Back! A Dinosaur's Story '93
An American Tail: Fievel Goes West '91

Fred Niblo(1874-1948)

Ben-Hur '26
The Temptress '26
Blood and Sand '22
Camille '21
The Three Musketeers '21
Mark of Zorro '20
Sex '20
Dangerous Hours '19

Andrew Niccol(1964-)

Lord of War '05
Simone '02
Gattaca '97

Maurizio Nichetti(1948-)

Luna e L'Altra '96
Stephano Quantestorie '93
Volere Volare '92
The Icicle Thief '89

Paul Nicholas(1945-)

Luckytown '00
Naked Cage '86
Chained Heat '83
Daughter of Death '82

George Nicholls, Jr. (1897-1939)

The Return of Peter Grimm '35
Anne of Green Gables '34
Finishing School '33

Mike Nichols(1931-)

Charlie Wilson's War '07
Closer '04
Angels in America '03
Wit '01
What Planet Are You From? '00
Primary Colors '98
The Birdcage '95
Wolf '94
Regarding Henry '91
Postcards from the Edge '90
Biloxi Blues '88
Working Girl '88
Heartburn '86
Gin Game '84
Silkwood '83
The Day of the Dolphin '73
Carnal Knowledge '71
Catch-22 '70
The Graduate '67
Who's Afraid of Virginia Woolf? '66

Arch Nicholson(1941-90)

Dark Age '88
Fortress '85
Deadline '81

Jack Nicholson(1937-)

The Two Jakes '90
Goin' South '78
The Terror '63

Alex Nicol(1919-2001)

Point of Terror '71
The Screaming Skull '58

Ted Nicolaou

Bloodstorm: Subspecies 4 '98
Magic in the Mirror: Fowl Play '96
Spellbreaker: Secret of the Leprechauns '96
Vampire Journals '96
Leapin' Leprechauns '95
Dragonworld '94
Bloodlust: Subspecies 3 '93
Remote '93
Bad Channels '92
Bloodstone: Subspecies 2 '92
Subspecies '90
Terrorvision '86
Dungeonmaster '83

John Nicolella(1946-98)

Kull the Conqueror '97
Sunset Heat '92
Runaway Father '91
Finish Line '89

Sebastian Niemann(1968-)

Ancient Relic '02
Seven Days to Live '01

William Nigh(1881-1955)

I Wouldn't Be in Your Shoes '48
Riding the California Trail '47
South of Monterey '47
Corregidor '43
The Ghost and the Guest '43
The Underdog '43
The Black Dragons '42
Mr. Wise Guy '42
The Strange Case of Dr. Rx '42
Zis Boom Bah '41
The Ape '40
Doomed to Die '40
The Fatal Hour '40
The Abe Lincoln of Ninth Avenue '39
Mr. Wong in Chinatown '39
Mutiny in the Big House '39
Mystery of Mr. Wong '39
Mr. Wong, Detective '38
Rose of Rio Grande '38
Hoosier Schoolboy '37
The Thirteenth Man '37
Headline Woman '35
Mysterious Mr. Wong '35
House of Mystery '34
Monte Carlo Nights '34
Mystery Liner '34
Border Devils '32
Night Rider '32
Without Honors '32
Fightin' Ranch '30
Fighting Thru '30
Desert Nights '29
Across to Singapore '28

Rob Nilsson(1940-)

Heat and Sunlight '87
On the Edge '86
Signal 7 '83
Northern Lights '79

Leonard Nimoy(1931-)

Holy Matrimony '94
Funny About Love '90
The Good Mother '88
Three Men and a Baby '87
Star Trek 4: The Voyage Home '86
Star Trek 3: The Search for Spock '84

Marcus Nispel(1964-)

Friday the 13th '09
Pathfinder '07
The Texas Chainsaw Massacre '03

Gaspar Noe(1963-)

Irreversible '02
I Stand Alone '98

Christopher Nolan(1970-)

Inception '10
The Dark Knight '08
The Prestige '06
Batman Begins '05
Insomnia '02
Memento '00
Following '99

Chris Noonan(1952-)

Miss Potter '06
Babe '95
Cass '78

Tom Noonan(1951-)

The House of the Devil '09
The Wife '95
What Happened Was... '94

Stephen Norrington(1965-)

The League of Extraordinary Gentlemen '03
The Last Minute '01
Blade '98
Death Machine '95

Aaron Norris(1951-)

Forest Warrior '95
Top Dog '95
Hellbound '94
Sidekicks '93
The Hitman '91
Delta Force 2: Operation Stranglehold '90
Braddock: Missing in Action 3 '88
Platoon Leader '87

Bill W.L. Norton(1943-)

Every Mother's Worst Fear '98
Our Mother's Murder '97
Hercules the Legendary Journeys, Vol. 1: And the Amazon Women '94
Hercules the Legendary Journeys, Vol. 4: In the Underworld '94
False Arrest '92
Three for the Road '87
Tour of Duty '87
Baby... Secret of the Lost Legend '85
More American Graffiti '79

Max Nosseck(1902-72)

The Hoodlum '51
Korea Patrol '47
Black Beauty '46
Brighton Strangler '45
Dillinger '45

Noel Nosseck(1943-)

Another Woman's Husband '00
Silent Predators '99
The Fury Within '98

Cliff Owen(1919-93)
The Bawdy Adventures of Tom Jones *'76*
No Sex Please—We're British *'73*
The Vengeance of She *'68*
The Magnificent Two *'67*
The Wrong Arm of the Law *'63*

Frank Oz(1944-)
Death at a Funeral *'07*
The Stepford Wives *'04*
The Score *'01*
Bowfinger *'99*
In and Out *'97*
The Indian in the Cupboard *'95*
Housesitter *'92*
What about Bob? *'91*
Dirty Rotten Scoundrels *'88*
Little Shop of Horrors *'86*
The Muppets Take Manhattan *'84*
The Dark Crystal *'82*

Sakae Ozawa
See Shigehiro (Sakae) Ozawa

Shigehiro (Sakae) Ozawa
Return of the Street Fighter *'74*
The Street Fighter *'74*

Francois Ozon(1967-)
Time to Leave *'05*
5x2 *'04*
Swimming Pool *'03*
8 Women *'02*
Under the Sand *'00*
Criminal Lovers *'99*
Water Drops on Burning Rocks *'99*
Sitcom *'97*

Ferzan Ozpetek(1959-)
Saturn in Opposition *'07*
Facing Windows *'03*
His Secret Life *'01*
Harem *'99*
Steam: A Turkish Bath *'96*

Yasujiro Ozu(1903-63)
An Autumn Afternoon *'62*
Drifting Weeds *'59*
Good Morning *'59*
Equinox Flower *'58*
Tokyo Story *'53*
Early Summer *'51*
Late Spring *'49*
Record of a Tenement Gentleman *'47*
I Was Born But... *'32*

G.W. Pabst(1885-1967)
Don Quixote *'35*
Kameradschaft *'31*
The Threepenny Opera *'31*
Westfront 1918 *'30*
Diary of a Lost Girl *'29*
Pandora's Box *'28*
The Love of Jeanne Ney *'27*
Joyless Street *'25*
Secrets of a Soul *'25*

Anthony Page(1935-)
My Zinc Bed *'08*
Human Bomb *'97*
Middlemarch *'93*
Final Warning *'90*
The Nightmare Years *'89*
Scandal in a Small Town *'88*
Pack of Lies *'87*
Heartbreak House *'86*
Monte Carlo *'86*
Forbidden *'85*
My Sweet Victim *'85*
Bill: On His Own *'83*
The Grace Kelly Story *'83*
Johnny Belinda *'82*
Absolution *'81*
Bill *'81*
The Lady Vanishes *'79*
I Never Promised You a Rose Garden *'77*
F. Scott Fitzgerald in Hollywood *'76*
Missiles of October *'74*
Alpha Beta *'73*
Pueblo Affair *'73*

Teddy Page
Blood Debts *'83*
Fireback *'78*

Marcel Pagnol(1895-1974)
Letters from My Windmill *'54*
Topaze *'51*
Well-Digger's Daughter *'46*
Le Schpountz *'38*
Harvest *'37*
Cesar *'36*
Angele *'34*
The Baker's Wife *'33*

Peter Paige
Leaving Barstow *'08*
Say Uncle *'05*

John Paizs
Invasion! *'99*
The Big Crimewave *'86*

Alan J. Pakula(1928-98)
The Devil's Own *'96*
The Pelican Brief *'93*
Consenting Adults *'92*
Presumed Innocent *'90*
See You in the Morning *'89*
Orphans *'87*
Dream Lover *'85*
Sophie's Choice *'82*
Rollover *'81*
Starting Over *'79*
Comes a Horseman *'78*
All the President's Men *'76*
The Parallax View *'74*
Love and Pain and the Whole Damn Thing *'73*
Klute *'71*
The Sterile Cuckoo *'69*

George Pal(1908-80)
7 Faces of Dr. Lao *'63*
The Wonderful World of the Brothers Grimm *'62*
Atlantis, the Lost Continent *'61*
The Time Machine *'60*
Tom Thumb *'58*

Euzhan Palcy(1957-)
The Killing Yard *'01*
Ruby Bridges *'98*
A Dry White Season *'89*
Sugar Cane Alley *'83*

Jean Marie Pallardy(1940-)
White Fire *'84*
Truck Stop *'78*

Anders Palm(1949-)
Dead Certain *'92*
Murder on Line One *'90*
Unmasked Part 25 *'88*

Tony Palmer
The Children *'90*
Wagner: The Complete Epic *'85*
Wagner: The Movie *'85*

Chazz Palminteri(1952-)
Noel *'04*
Women vs. Men *'02*

Conrad Palmisano(1948-)
Busted Up *'86*
Space Rage *'86*

Bruce Paltrow(1943-2002)
Duets *'00*
A Little Sex *'82*

Jafar Panahi(1960-)
Crimson Gold *'03*
The Circle *'00*
The White Balloon *'95*

Norman Panama(1914-2003)
Barnaby and Me *'77*
I Will, I Will for Now *'76*
How to Commit Marriage *'69*
The Road to Hong Kong *'62*
The Trap *'59*
Court Jester *'56*
Above and Beyond *'53*

Danny Pang(1965-)
Bangkok Dangerous *'08*
The Messengers *'07*
Re-Cycle *'06*
The Eye 3 *'05*
The Eye 2 *'04*
The Eye *'02*
Bangkok Dangerous *'00*

Oxide Pang(1965-)
Bangkok Dangerous *'08*
The Messengers *'07*
The Eye *'02*

Hsueh Li Pao
Sword Masters: The Battle Wizard *'77*
The Water Margin *'72*

Domenico Paolella(1918-2002)
Challenge of the Gladiator *'65*
Samson Against the Sheik *'62*
Pirates of the Coast *'61*

Phedon Papamichael(1962-)
Dark Side of Genius *'94*
Sketch Artist *'92*

Sven Pape
Hollywood Kills *'06*
L.A. Twister *'04*

Giullo Paradisi(1934-)
Spaghetti House *'82*
The Visitor *'80*

Roger Paradiso
Tony n' Tina's Wedding *'07*
Kisses in the Dark *'97*

Sergei Paradjanov(1924-90)
Ashik Kerib *'88*
The Legend of Suram Fortress *'85*
The Color of Pomegranates *'69*
Shadows of Forgotten Ancestors *'64*

John Paragon(1954-)
Twinsitters *'95*
Ring of the Musketeers *'93*
Double Trouble *'91*

Paul S. Parco
Pucker Up and Bark Like a Dog *'89*
Deadly Alliance *'78*

Chuck Parello
The Hillside Strangler *'04*
Ed Gein *'01*
Henry: Portrait of a Serial Killer 2: Mask of Sanity *'96*

Domonic Paris
Splitz *'84*
Dracula's Last Rites *'79*

Jerry Paris(1925-86)
Police Academy 3: Back in Training *'86*
Police Academy 2: Their First Assignment *'85*
Make Me an Offer *'80*
How to Break Up a Happy Divorce *'76*
Only with Married Men *'74*
Evil Roy Slade *'71*
Star Spangled Girl *'71*
The Passing of Evil *'70*
The Grasshopper *'69*
Viva Max *'69*
Don't Raise the Bridge, Lower the River *'68*
How Sweet It Is! *'68*
Never a Dull Moment *'68*

Dean Parisot
Fun With Dick and Jane *'05*
Galaxy Quest *'99*
Home Fries *'98*
Framed *'90*

Chan-wook Park(1963-)
Thirst *'09*
Lady Vengeance *'05*
Three ... Extremes *'04*
Oldboy *'03*
Sympathy for Mr. Vengeance *'02*
JSA: Joint Security Area *'00*

Chul-Soo Park
301/302 *'95*
301/302 *'95*
301, 302 *'94*

Nick Park(1958-)
Wallace & Gromit in The Curse of the Were-Rabbit *'05*
Chicken Run *'00*

Richard W. Park
American Chinatown *'96*
Gang Justice *'94*

Young-hoon Park
Addicted *'02*
Addicted *'02*

Alan Parker(1944-)
The Life of David Gale *'03*
Angela's Ashes *'99*
Evita *'96*
The Road to Wellville *'94*
The Commitments *'91*
Come See the Paradise *'90*
Mississippi Burning *'88*
Angel Heart *'87*
Birdy *'84*
Pink Floyd: The Wall *'82*
Shoot the Moon *'82*
Fame *'80*
Midnight Express *'78*
Bugsy Malone *'76*

Albert Parker(1887-1974)
Late Extra *'35*
The Black Pirate *'26*
Sherlock Holmes *'22*
The Eyes of Youth *'19*
Shifting Sands *'18*

Jonathan Parker
(Untitled) *'09*
Bartleby *'01*

Norton S. Parker
Pace That Kills *'28*
The Road to Ruin *'28*

Oliver Parker(1960-)
I Really Hate My Job *'07*
St. Trinian's *'07*
The Importance of Being Earnest *'02*
An Ideal Husband *'99*
Othello *'95*

Trey Parker(1969-)
Team America: World Police *'04*
South Park: Bigger, Longer and Uncut *'99*
Orgazmo *'98*
Cannibal! The Musical *'96*

Eric Parkinson
Future Shock *'93*
Terror Eyes *'87*

Gordon Parks(1912-2006)
Half Slave, Half Free *'85*
Three the Hard Way *'74*
Shaft's Big Score *'72*
Shaft *'71*
The Learning Tree *'69*

Gordon Parks, Jr. (1934-79)
Aaron Loves Angela *'75*
Superfly *'72*

Hugh Parks
Fatal Passion *'94*
Shoot *'92*
King's Ransom *'91*
Dream Trap *'90*
Shakma *'89*
Deadly Innocence *'88*

Gianfranco Parolini(1930-)
God's Gun *'75*
This Time I'll Make You Rich *'75*
Adios, Sabata *'71*
Return of Sabata *'71*
Sabata *'69*
Five for Hell *'67*
The Fury of Hercules *'61*
Samson *'61*

John H. Parr
Prey for the Hunter *'92*
Pursuit *'90*

Robert Parrish(1916-95)
The Destructors *'74*
A Town Called Hell *'72*
Journey to the Far Side of the Sun *'69*
The Bobo *'67*
Casino Royale *'67*
Saddle the Wind *'58*
Fire Down Below *'57*
Cry Danger *'51*

James Parrott
Laurel & Hardy: Be Big *'31*
Pardon Us *'31*
Laurel & Hardy: Another Fine Mess *'30*
Laurel & Hardy: Below Zero *'30*
Laurel & Hardy: Hog Wild *'30*
Laurel & Hardy: Night Owls *'30*
Laurel & Hardy: Perfect Day *'29*
Laurel & Hardy: The Hoose-Gow *'29*

Gordon Parry(1908-81)
Tread Softly Stranger *'58*
Innocents in Paris *'53*
Tom Brown's School Days *'51*

Gabriel Pascal(1894-1954)
Caesar and Cleopatra *'46*
Major Barbara *'41*

Goran Paskalyevic(1947-)
How Harry Became a Tree *'01*
Cabaret Balkan *'98*
Someone Else's America *'96*

Pier Paolo Pasolini(1922-75)
Salo, or the 120 Days of Sodom *'75*
Arabian Nights *'74*
The Canterbury Tales *'71*
The Decameron *'70*
Medea *'70*
Porcile *'69*
Teorema *'68*
The Hawks & the Sparrows *'67*
Oedipus Rex *'67*
The Gospel According to St. Matthew *'64*
Love Meetings *'64*
Mamma Roma *'62*
RoGoPaG *'62*
Accatone! *'61*

John Pasquin
Miss Congeniality 2: Armed and Fabulous *'05*
Joe Somebody *'01*
Jungle 2 Jungle *'96*
The Santa Clause *'94*
Nightmare *'91*

Ivan Passer(1933-)
Kidnapped *'95*
Stalin *'92*
Fourth Story *'90*
Haunted Summer *'88*
Creator *'85*
The Nightingale *'83*
Cutter's Way *'81*
Silver Bears *'78*
Crime & Passion *'75*
Law and Disorder *'74*
Born to Win *'71*
Intimate Lighting *'65*

Giovanni Pastrone(1883-1959)
Cabiria *'14*
Salammbo *'14*

Jonas Pate(1970-)
Shrink *'09*
Deceiver *'97*
The Grave *'95*

Stuart Paton(1883-1944)
Silent Code *'35*
Mystery Trooper *'32*
Chinatown After Dark *'31*
20,000 Leagues under the Sea *'16*

Nigel Patrick(1913-81)
Johnny Nobody *'61*
The Sound Barrier *'52*

Giuseppe Patroni-Griffi(1921-2005)
Collector's Item *'89*
Driver's Seat *'73*
'Tis a Pity She's a Whore *'73*
Divine Nymph *'71*

John D. Patterson(1940-2005)
Grave Secrets: The Legacy of Hilltop Drive *'92*
The Spring *'89*
Taken Away *'89*
Deadly Innocence *'88*
Legend of Earl Durand *'74*

Richard Patterson
The Marx Brothers in a Nutshell *'90*
J-Men Forever! *'79*

Willi Patterson(1949-)
Out of the Shadows *'88*
Dreams Lost, Dreams Found *'87*

Michael Pattinson(1957-)
The Limbic Region *'96*
One Crazy Night *'93*
...Almost *'90*
Ground Zero *'88*
Street Hero *'84*
Moving Out *'83*

Robert Patton-Spruill
Body Count *'97*
Squeeze *'97*

Peter Patzak(1945-)
Midnight Cop *'88*
Lethal Obsession *'87*
The Uppercrust *'81*
Slaughterday *'77*

Don Michael Paul(1963-)
Who's Your Caddy? *'07*
Half Past Dead *'02*

Steven Paul(1954-)
Eternity *'90*
Slapstick of Another Kind *'84*
Falling in Love Again *'80*

Stuart Paul
Fate *'90*
Emanon *'86*

David Paulsen
Savage Weekend *'80*
Schizoid *'80*

George Pavlou(1953-)
Rawhead Rex *'87*
Transmutations *'85*

Bill Paxton(1955-)
The Greatest Game Ever Played *'05*
Frailty *'02*

Alexander Payne(1961-)
Paris, je t'aime *'06*
Sideways *'04*

About Schmidt '02
Election '99
Citizen Ruth '96

Dave Payne
Under Oath '97
Not Like Us '96
Alien Terminator '95
Criminal Hearts '95
Concealed Weapon '94

Richard Pearce(1943-)
Fatal Contact: Bird Flu in America '06
Rodgers & Hammerstein's South Pacific '01
Witness Protection '99
A Family Thing '96
Leap of Faith '92
Dead Man Out '89
The Final Days '89
The Long Walk Home '89
No Mercy '86
Country '84
Sessions '83
Threshold '83
Heartland '81

Steven Pearl
The Substitute 2: School's Out '97
At First Sight '95

George Pearson(1875-1973)
Midnight at the Wax Museum '36
A Shot in the Dark '33

Peter Pearson(1938-)
Tales of the Klondike: The Unexpected '87
Paperback Hero '73

Max Pecas(1925-2003)
I Am Frigid... Why? '72
The Sensuous Teenager '70
Her and She and Him '69
Erotic Touch of Hot Skin '65
Sweet Ecstasy '62
Daniella by Night '61

Raoul Peck(1953-)
Sometimes in April '05
Lumumba '01

Ron Peck(1948-)
Empire State '87
Nighthawks '78

Sam Peckinpah(1925-84)
The Osterman Weekend '83
Convoy '78
Cross of Iron '76
The Killer Elite '75
Bring Me the Head of Alfredo Garcia '74
Pat Garrett & Billy the Kid '73
The Getaway '72
Junior Bonner '72
Straw Dogs '72
Ballad of Cable Hogue '70
The Wild Bunch '69
Major Dundee '65
Ride the High Country '62
Deadly Companions '61

Larry Peerce(1935-)
The Abduction '96
Murder So Sweet '93
Prison for Children '93
A Woman Named Jackie '91
The Court Martial of Jackie Robinson '90
The Neon Empire '89
Wired '89
Elvis and Me '88
Queenie '87
Hard to Hold '84
Love Child '82
The Bell Jar '79
The Other Side of the Mountain, Part 2 '78
Two Minute Warning '76
The Other Side of the Mountain '75
The Stranger Who Looks Like Me '74
Ash Wednesday '73

A Separate Peace '73
The Sporting Club '72
Goodbye Columbus '69
The Incident '67

Barbara Peeters
Humanoids from the Deep '80
Starhops '78
Summer School Teachers '75
Bury Me an Angel '71

Kimberly Peirce
Stop-Loss '08
Boys Don't Cry '99

Anthony Pelissier(1912-88)
Encore '52
The Rocking Horse Winner '49

Jean Pellerin
Daybreak '01
Escape under Pressure '00
Laserhawk '99
For Hire '98

Mark Pellington(1965-)
Henry Poole Is Here '08
The Mothman Prophecies '02
Arlington Road '99
Going All the Way '97

Arthur Penn(1922-)
Inside '96
The Portrait '93
Penn and Teller Get Killed '90
Dead of Winter '87
Target '85
Four Friends '81
Missouri Breaks '76
Night Moves '75
Little Big Man '70
Alice's Restaurant '69
Bonnie & Clyde '67
The Chase '66
Mickey One '65
The Miracle Worker '62
The Left-Handed Gun '58

Leo Penn(1921-98)
Judgment in Berlin '88
The Dark Secret of Harvest Home '78
A Man Called Adam '66

Sean Penn(1960-)
Into the Wild '07
The Pledge '00
The Crossing Guard '94
The Indian Runner '91

D.A. Pennebaker(1925-)
Only the Strong Survive '03
Moon over Broadway '98
The War Room '93
Monterey Pop '68

Eagle Pennell(1952-2002)
Ice House '89
Last Night at the Alamo '83
The Whole Shootin' Match '79

C.M. Pennington-Richards(1911-2005)
A Challenge for Robin Hood '68
Ladies Who Do '63
Black Tide '58
Hour of Decision '57

Louis Pepe(1966-)
Brothers of the Head '06
Lost in La Mancha '03

Richard Pepin
The Box '03
Mindstorm '01
Y2K '99
The Sender '98
Dark Breed '96
Cyber-Tracker 2 '95
Hologram Man '95
The Silencers '95
T-Force '94

Cyber-Tracker '93
Firepower '93
Fist of Honor '92

Clare Peploe(1942-)
The Triumph of Love '01
Rough Magic '95
High Season '88

Mark Peploe(1943-)
Victory '95
Afraid of the Dark '92

Brian Percival
The Old Curiosity Shop '07
Ruby in the Smoke '06

Daniel Percival
Place of Execution '09
The State Within '06

Hope Perello
St. Patrick's Day '99
Pet Shop '94
Howling 6: The Freaks '90

Vadim Perelman
The Life Before Her Eyes '07
House of Sand and Fog '03

Jesse Peretz(1968-)
The Ex '07
The Chateau '01
First Love, Last Rites '98

Jack Perez
Mega Shark Vs. Giant Octopus '09
Wild Things 2 '04
La Cucaracha '99
The Big Empty '98
America's Deadliest Home Video '91

Etienne Perier(1931-)
Investigation '79
When Eight Bells Toll '71
Zeppelin '71
The Hot Line '69
Murder at 45 R.P.M. '65

Anthony Perkins(1932-92)
Lucky Stiff '88
Psycho 3 '86

Jacques Perrin(1941-)
Oceans '09
Winged Migration '01

Frank Perry(1930-95)
Hello Again '87
Compromising Positions '85
Monsignor '82
Mommie Dearest '81
Skag '79
Rancho Deluxe '75
Diary of a Mad Housewife '70
Last Summer '69
The Swimmer '68
ABC Stage 67: Truman Capote's A Christmas Memory '66
David and Lisa '62

Nickolas Perry(1967-)
The Hunting of the President '04
Speedway Junky '99

Tyler Perry(1969-)
Tyler Perry's Why Did I Get Married Too? '10
I Can Do Bad All By Myself '09
Madea Goes to Jail '09
Tyler Perry's Meet the Browns '08
Daddy's Little Girls '07
Tyler Perry's Why Did I Get Married? '07
Madea's Family Reunion '06

Bill Persky(1931-)
Wait Till Your Mother Gets Home '83
Serial '80
How to Pick Up Girls '78

P.J. Pesce(1961-)
Smokin' Aces 2: Assassins' Ball '10

Lost Boys: The Tribe '08
Sniper 3 '04
From Dusk Till Dawn 3: The Hangman's Daughter '99
The Desperate Trail '94
Body Waves '92

Brooke L. Peters
See Boris L. Petroff

Charlie Peters
Music from Another Room '97
Passed Away '92

Wolfgang Petersen(1941-)
Poseidon '06
Troy '04
The Perfect Storm '00
Air Force One '97
Outbreak '94
In the Line of Fire '93
Shattered '91
Enemy Mine '85
The NeverEnding Story '84
Das Boot '81
For Your Love Only '79
Black and White As Day and Night '78

Kristine Peterson
Slaves to the Underground '96
Redemption: Kickboxer 5 '95
The Hard Truth '94
Eden 2 '93
Eden 4 '93
Critters 3 '91
Lower Level '91
Body Chemistry '90
Deadly Dreams '88

Christopher Petit(1949-)
Chinese Boxes '84
Unsuitable Job for a Woman '82

Daniel Petrie(1920-2004)
Walter and Henry '01
Wild Iris '01
Inherit the Wind '99
The Assistant '97
Calm at Sunset '96
Kissinger and Nixon '96
Lassie '94
Mark Twain and Me '91
My Name Is Bill W. '89
Cocoon: The Return '88
Rocket Gibraltar '88
Square Dance '87
Half a Lifetime '86
The Bay Boy '85
Execution of Raymond Graham '85
The Dollmaker '84
Six Pack '82
Fort Apache, the Bronx '81
Resurrection '80
The Betsy '78
Eleanor & Franklin '76
Lifeguard '76
Sybil '76
Buster and Billie '74
Neptune Factor '73
Moon of the Wolf '72
Silent Night, Lonely Night '69
Spy with a Cold Nose '66
Stolen Hours '63
A Raisin in the Sun '61
The Bramble Bush '60
Bang the Drum Slowly '56

Daniel Petrie, Jr.(1952-)
Dead Silence '96
In the Army Now '94
Toy Soldiers '91

Donald Petrie(1954-)
My Life in Ruins '09
Just My Luck '06
Welcome to Mooseport '04
How to Lose a Guy in 10 Days '03
Miss Congeniality '00
My Favorite Martian '98
The Associate '96
Richie Rich '94

Grumpy Old Men '93
The Favor '92
Opportunity Knocks '90
Mystic Pizza '88

Boris L. Petroff(1894-1972)
Anatomy of a Psycho '61
Outcasts of the City '58
The Unearthly '57
Hats Off '37

Vladimir Petrov(1896-1966)
The Inspector General '52
Peter the First: Part 2 '38
Peter the First: Part 1 '37

J.T. Petty
Mimic 3: Sentinel '03
Soft for Digging '01

Joseph Pevney(1920-)
Mysterious Island of Beautiful Women '79
Who Is the Black Dahlia? '75
Night of the Grizzly '66
Cash McCall '60
The Crowded Sky '60
The Plunderers '60
Torpedo Run '58
Istanbul '57
Man of a Thousand Faces '57
Tammy and the Bachelor '57
Away All Boats '56
Because of You '52
Meet Danny Wilson '52
The Strange Door '51

John Peyser(1916-2002)
Fantastic Seven '79
The Centerfold Girls '74
Four Rode Out '69
Kashmiri Run '69

Lee Philips(1927-99)
Silent Motive '91
Blind Vengeance '90
Windmills of the Gods '88
Barnum '86
The Blue Lightning '86
Mae West '84
Samson and Delilah '84
On the Right Track '81
Hardhat & Legs '80
Special Olympics '78
The Spell '77
Dynasty '76
War Between the Tates '76
Sweet Hostage '75
The Stranger Within '74

Lou Diamond Phillips(1962-)
Love Takes Wing '09
Dangerous Touch '94
Sioux City '94

Maurice Phillips
Another You '91
Enid Is Sleeping '90
Riders of the Storm '88

Nick (Steve Millard) Phillips(1941-)
Death Nurse '87
Crazy Fat Ethel II '85
Criminally Insane '75

Toby Phillips
See Paul Thomas

Todd Phillips(1970-)
The Hangover '09
School for Scoundrels '06
Starsky & Hutch '04
Old School '03
Road Trip '00

Maurice Pialat(1925-2003)
Van Gogh '92
Under Satan's Sun '87
Police '85
A Nos Amours '84
Loulou '80

Rex Piano
Trapped '06
Hope Ranch '02

Giuseppe Piccioni(1953-)
Light of My Eyes '01
Not of This World '99

Irving Pichel(1891-1954)
Day of Triumph '54
Martin Luther '53
Santa Fe '51
Destination Moon '50
The Great Rupert '50
Quicksand '50
The Miracle of the Bells '48
Mr. Peabody & the Mermaid '48
Something in the Wind '47
They Won't Believe Me '47
O.S.S. '46
Tomorrow Is Forever '46
Colonel Effingham's Raid '45
Dance Hall '41
The Great Commandment '41
Larceny On the Air '37
She '35
The Most Dangerous Game '32
An American Tragedy '31

Andrew Piddington
The Killing of John Lennon '07
The Fall '98

Arthur C. Pierce(1923-87)
Las Vegas Hillbillys '66
Women of the Prehistoric Planet '66

Charles B. Pierce(1938-)
Hawken's Breed '87
Boggy Creek II '83
Sacred Ground '83
The Evictors '79
Norseman '78
Grayeagle '77
Town That Dreaded Sundown '76
Winterhawk '76
Legend of Boggy Creek '75

Carl Pierson(1891-1977)
The New Frontier '35
Paradise Canyon '35

Frank Pierson(1925-)
Soldier's Girl '03
Conspiracy '01
Dirty Pictures '00
Truman '95
Lakota Woman: Siege at Wounded Knee '94
Citizen Cohn '92
Somebody Has to Shoot the Picture '90
King of the Gypsies '78
A Star Is Born '76
The Looking Glass War '69

Alex Pillai
Take Me '01
The Wyvern Mystery '00

Sam Pillsbury
Audrey's Rain '03
Morgan's Ferry '99
Free Willy 3: The Rescue '97
Into the Badlands '92
Zandalee '91
Starlight Hotel '90

William H. Pine(1896-1955)
Dynamite '49
Seven Were Saved '47
Swamp Fire '46

Marcelo Pineyro(1953-)
The Method '05
Burnt Money '00
Wild Horses '95

He Ping(1957-)
Warriors of Heaven and Earth '03
Red Firecracker, Green Firecracker '93

Yuen Woo Ping(1945-)
Wing Chun '94
Eagle's Shadow '84

Sidney W. Pink(1916-2002)
The Christmas Kid '68
Finger on the Trigger '65
Reptilicus '62

Steve Pink(1966-)
Hot Tub Time Machine '10
Accepted '06

Efren C. Pinon
Blind Rage '78
Enforcer from Death Row '78

Claude Pinoteau(1925-)
La Boum '81
The Slap '76

Gordon Pinsent(1930-)
John and the Missus '87
Far Cry from Home '81

Lucian Pintilie(1933-)
An Unforgettable Summer '94
The Oak '93
Ward Six '78

Ernest Pintoff(1931-2002)
St. Helen's, Killer Volcano '82
Lunch Wagon '81
Jaguar Lives '79
Blade '72
Who Killed Mary What's 'Er Name? '71
Dynamite Chicken '70

Bret Piper
Screaming Dead '03
They Bite '95
A Nymphoid Barbarian in Dinosaur Hell '94

Robert Pirosh(1910-89)
Valley of the Kings '54
Go for Broke! '51

Massimo Pirri(1945-)
Fatal Fix '80
Could It Happen Here? '77

Mark Pirro(1956-)
Buford's Beach Bunnies '92
Deathrow Gameshow '88
Curse of the Queerwolf '87
A Polish Vampire in Burbank '80

Peter Pistor
In Pursuit '00
The Fence '94

Glen Pitre
The Man Who Came Back '08
The Home Front '02
Time Served '99
Belizaire the Cajun '86

Bruce Pittman(1950-)
Shattered City: The Halifax Explosion '03
No Alibi '00
Locked in Silence '99
Blood Brothers '97
Flood: A River's Rampage '97
Kurt Vonnegut's Harrison Bergeron '95
Where the Spirit Lives '89
Hello Mary Lou: Prom Night 2 '87
Confidential '86
Mark of Cain '84

Mark Piznarski
Here on Earth '00
The '60s '99
Death Benefit '96

Lucas Platt
Subway Stories '97
Girl in the Cadillac '94

Allen Plone
Sweet Justice '92
Phantom of the Ritz '88
Night Screams '87

Jeremy Podeswa(1962-)
The Five Senses '99
Eclipse '94

Amos Poe
Frogs for Snakes '98
Dead Weekend '95
Alphabet City '84
The Foreigner '78

Jean-Marie Poire(1945-)
Just Visiting '01
The Visitors '95

Sidney Poitier(1924-)
Ghost Dad '90
Fast Forward '84
Hanky Panky '82
Stir Crazy '80
Piece of the Action '77
Let's Do It Again '75
Uptown Saturday Night '74
Buck and the Preacher '72

James Polakof
The Vals '85
Balboa '82
Demon Rage '82
Swim Team '79
Midnight Auto Supply '78
Slashed Dreams '74

Roman Polanski(1933-)
The Ghost Writer '10
Oliver Twist '05
The Pianist '02
The Ninth Gate '99
Death and the Maiden '94
Bitter Moon '92
Frantic '88
Pirates '86
Tess '79
The Tenant '76
Chinatown '74
Diary of Forbidden Dreams '73
Macbeth '71
Rosemary's Baby '68
The Fearless Vampire Killers '67
Cul de Sac '66
Repulsion '65
Knife in the Water '62
Two Men & a Wardrobe '58

Stephen Poliakoff(1952-)
Friends & Crocodiles '05
Gideon's Daughter '05
Almost Strangers '01
Shooting the Past '99
Century '94
Close My Eyes '91
Hidden City '87

Michael Polish(1972-)
The Astronaut Farmer '07
Northfork '03
Jackpot '01
Twin Falls Idaho '99

Jeff Pollack(1959-)
Lost and Found '99
Booty Call '97
Above the Rim '94

Sydney Pollack(1934-2008)
The Interpreter '05
Random Hearts '99
Sabrina '95
The Firm '93
Havana '90
Out of Africa '85
Tootsie '82
Absence of Malice '81
The Electric Horseman '79
Bobby Deerfield '77
Three Days of the Condor '75
The Yakuza '75
The Way We Were '73
Jeremiah Johnson '72
Castle Keep '69
They Shoot Horses, Don't They? '69
The Scalphunters '68
This Property Is Condemned '66
The Slender Thread '65

Bud Pollard(1886-1952)
Look Out Sister '48
Beware '46
Tall, Tan and Terrific '46
The Black King '32

Harry A. Pollard(1883-1934)
Undertow '30
Uncle Tom's Cabin '27
California Straight Ahead '25

George Pollock(1907-79)
Murder Most Foul '65
Murder Ahoy '64
Murder at the Gallop '63
Murder She Said '62
Broth of a Boy '59
Stranger in Town '57

John Polonia
Razorteeth '05
Terror House '97
Feeders '96

Mark Alan Polonia
Terror House '97
Feeders '96

Abraham Polonsky(1910-99)
Romance of a Horsethief '71
Tell Them Willie Boy Is Here '69
Force of Evil '49

John Polson(1965-)
Tenderness '08
Hide and Seek '05
Swimfan '02
Siam Sunset '99

Ventura Pons(1945-)
Food of Love '02
Beloved/Friend '99
To Die (Or Not) '99
Caresses '97
What It's All About '95

Gillo Pontecorvo(1919-2006)
Burn! '70
The Battle of Algiers '66
Kapo '59
The Wide Blue Road '57

Maurizio Ponzi(1939-)
Aurora '84
Pool Hustlers '83

DJ Pooh
The Wash '01
Three Strikes '00

Lea Pool(1950-)
The Blue Butterfly '04
Lost and Delirious '01
Set Me Free '99
Mouvements du Desir '94
The Savage Woman '91
Straight for the Heart '88

Angela Pope(1945-)
Hollow Reed '95
Captives '94

Leo Popkin(1914-)
The Well '51
Gang War '40

Jeffrey Porter
All I Want '02
The Liar's Club '93

Rafael Portillo(1916-95)
Broken Trust '93
The Curse of the Aztec Mummy '59
The Robot vs. the Aztec Mummy '59

Ralph Portillo
One of Them '03
Big Brother Trouble '00
Bloody Murder '99
Naked Lies '98
Stolen Hearts '95
Hollywood Dreams '94

P.J. Posner
The Next Big Thing '02
Last Breath '96

Ted Post(1918-)
The Human Shield '92
Stagecoach '86
Diary of a Teenage Hitchhiker '82
Nightkill '80
Go Tell the Spartans '78
Good Guys Wear Black '78
Whiffs '75
Harrad Experiment '73
Magnum Force '73
The Baby '72
The Bravos '72
Beneath the Planet of the Apes '70
Yuma '70
Hang 'Em High '67
Legend of Tom Dooley '59

H.C. Potter(1904-77)
Top Secret Affair '57
Three for the Show '55
The Miniver Story '50
Mr. Blandings Builds His Dream House '48
The Time of Your Life '48
You Gotta Stay Happy '48
The Farmer's Daughter '47
Mr. Lucky '43
Second Chorus '40
The Story of Vernon and Irene Castle '39
The Cowboy and the Lady '38
Shopworn Angel '38
Beloved Enemy '36

Sally Potter(1947-)
Yes '04
The Man Who Cried '00
The Tango Lesson '97
Orlando '92

Gerald Potterton(1931-)
Heavy Metal '81
The Rainbow Gang '73
Railrodder '65

Michel Poulette
Bonanno: A Godfather's Story '99
King of the Airwaves '94

Dick Powell(1904-63)
The Hunters '58
Enemy Below '57
The Conqueror '56
Split Second '53

Michael Powell(1905-90)
Age of Consent '69
Peeping Tom '60
Night Ambush '57
Pursuit of the Graf Spee '57
The Tales of Hoffmann '51
The Elusive Pimpernel '50
The Small Back Room '49
The Red Shoes '48
Black Narcissus '47
Stairway to Heaven '46
I Know Where I'm Going '45
A Canterbury Tale '44
The Life and Death of Colonel Blimp '43
The Forty-Ninth Parallel '41
One of Our Aircraft Is Missing '41
Contraband '40
The Lion Has Wings '40
The Thief of Bagdad '40
Spy in Black '39
Edge of the World '37
The Phantom Light '35
Red Ensign '34

Paul Powell(1881-1944)
Pollyanna '20
Matrimaniac '16

Tristam Powell(1940-)
American Friends '91
Ghostwriter '84

John Power(1930-)
Goldrush: A Real Life Alaskan Adventure '98
Charles & Diana: A Palace Divided '93
Stephen King's The Tommyknockers '93
Father '90
Alice to Nowhere '86
All My Sons '86
Great Gold Swindle '84
Sound of Love '78

Wayne Powers
Out of Order '03
Skeletons in the Closet '00

Manuel Pradal
Ginostra '02
Marie Baie des Anges '97

Stanley Prager(1917-72)
Bang Bang Kid '67
Madigan's Millions '67

Udayan Prasad(1953-)
The Yellow Handkerchief '08
Gabriel & Me '01
My Son the Fanatic '97
Brothers in Trouble '95

Michael Preece
Beretta's Island '92
Prize Fighter '79

Otto Preminger(1906-86)
The Human Factor '79
Rosebud '75
In Harm's Way '65
The Cardinal '63
Advise and Consent '62
Exodus '60
Anatomy of a Murder '59
Bonjour Tristesse '57
Saint Joan '57
The Court Martial of Billy Mitchell '55
The Man with the Golden Arm '55
Carmen Jones '54
River of No Return '54
The Moon Is Blue '53
Angel Face '52
Where the Sidewalk Ends '50
Whirlpool '49
Daisy Kenyon '47
Forever Amber '47
Laura '44

Andrew Prendergast
Hydra '09
Parasite '03

Emeric Pressburger(1902-88)
Night Ambush '57
The Tales of Hoffmann '51
The Small Back Room '49
The Red Shoes '48
Black Narcissus '47
Stairway to Heaven '46
I Know Where I'm Going '45
A Canterbury Tale '44
The Life and Death of Colonel Blimp '43
One of Our Aircraft Is Missing '41

Michael Pressman(1950-)
A Season for Miracles '99
Saint Maybe '98
To Gillian on Her 37th Birthday '96
Quicksand: No Escape '91
Teenage Mutant Ninja Turtles 2: The Secret of the Ooze '91
Dark River: A Father's Revenge '90
Capone '89
The Chinatown Murders: Man against the Mob '89
To Heal a Nation '88
Secret Passions '87
The Impostor '84
Doctor Detroit '83
Some Kind of Hero '82
Those Lips, Those Eyes '80
Boulevard Nights '79
The Bad News Bears in Breaking Training '77
The Great Texas Dynamite Chase '76

Gaylene Preston
Perfect Strangers '03
Dark of the Night '85

Ruben Preuss
The Art of Murder '99
Almost Dead '94
Dead on Sight '94
Blackmail '91
Write to Kill '91
Deceptions '90
In Dangerous Company '88

Steve Previn(1925-93)
Waltz King '63
Almost Angels '62
Escapade in Florence '62

David F. Price(1961-)
Dr. Jekyll and Ms. Hyde '95
Children of the Corn 2: The Final Sacrifice '92
To Die For 2: Son of Darkness '91

Joseph Prieto
Savages from Hell '68
Shanty Tramp '67

Prince(1958-)
Graffiti Bridge '90
Under the Cherry Moon '86

Harold Prince(1928-)
Sweeney Todd: The Demon Barber of Fleet Street '84
A Little Night Music '77
Something for Everyone '70

Gina Prince-Bythewood(1969-)
The Secret Life of Bees '08
Disappearing Acts '00
Love and Basketball '00

David A. Prior
Felony '95
Mutant Species '95
Mardi Gras for the Devil '93
Raw Justice '93
Center of the Web '92
Double Threat '92
Future Zone '90
Invasion Force '90
Lock 'n' Load '90
Lock 'n' Load '90
White Fury '90
Final Sanction '89
Future Force '89
Jungle Assault '89
The Lost Platoon '89
Operation Warzone '89
Rapid Fire '89
Hell on the Battleground '88
Night Wars '88
Deadly Prey '87
Death Chase '87
Mankillers '87
Killer Workout '86
Killzone '85
Sledgehammer '83

Franco Prosperi(1928-)
The Wild Beasts '85
Invincible Barbarian '83
Throne of Fire '82
Counter Punch '71
Mondo Cane 2 '64

Alex Proyas(1965-)
Knowing '09
I, Robot '04
Garage Days '03
Dark City '97
The Crow '93

Craig Pryce
The Good Witch '08
The Dark '94
Revenge of the Radioactive Reporter '91

Alexander Ptushko(1900-73)
Sword & the Dragon '56
The Magic Voyage of Sinbad '52

Vsevolod Pudovkin(1893-1953)
Storm over Asia '28

The End of St. Petersburg *'27*
Mother *'26*

Luis Puenzo(1946-)
The Plague *'92*
Old Gringo *'89*
The Official Story *'85*

Evelyn Purcell
Borderline *'02*
Woman Undone *'95*
Nobody's Fool *'86*

Jon Purdy
Joshua *'02*
Star Portal *'97*
Dillinger and Capone *'95*
Reflections in the Dark *'94*

John Putch(1961-)
Route 30 *'08*
BachelorMan *'03*
A Time to Remember *'03*
Pursuit of Happiness *'01*
Tycus *'98*
My Magic Dog *'97*
Alone in the Woods *'95*

Joe Pytka(1938-)
Space Jam *'96*
Let It Ride *'89*

Albert Pyun(1954-)
Ticker *'01*
Corrupt *'99*
Urban Menace *'99*
The Wrecking Crew *'99*
Crazy Six *'98*
Postmortem *'98*
Mean Guns *'97*
Nemesis 4: Cry of Angels *'97*
Adrenalin: Fear the Rush *'96*
Blast *'96*
Nemesis 3: Time Lapse *'96*
Omega Doom *'96*
Heatseeker *'95*
Ravenhawk *'95*
Hong Kong '97 *'94*
Kickboxer 4: The Aggressor *'94*
Nemesis 2: Nebula *'94*
Spitfire *'94*
Arcade *'93*
Brain Smasher... A Love Story *'93*
Knights *'93*
Nemesis *'93*
Bloodmatch *'91*
Dollman *'90*
Kickboxer 2: The Road Back *'90*
Captain America *'89*
Cyborg *'89*
Deceit *'89*
Down Twisted *'89*
Alien from L.A. *'87*
Dangerously Close *'86*
Radioactive Dreams *'86*
Sword & the Sorcerer *'82*

James Quattrochi(1961-)
The Prince and the Pauper *'07*
True Friends *'98*

Stephen Quay(1947-)
Piano Tuner of Earthquakes *'05*
Institue Benjamenta or This Dream People Call Human Life *'95*

Timothy Quay(1947-)
Piano Tuner of Earthquakes *'05*
Institue Benjamenta or This Dream People Call Human Life *'95*

George P. Quigley
Junction 88 *'47*
Murder with Music *'45*
Mistaken Identity *'41*

Richard Quine(1920-89)
Prisoner of Zenda *'79*
W *'74*
Gun Crazy *'69*
Hotel *'67*
Oh Dad, Poor Dad (Momma's Hung You in the Closet & I'm Feeling So Sad) *'67*
How to Murder Your Wife *'64*
Paris When It Sizzles *'64*
Sex and the Single Girl *'64*
The Notorious Landlady *'62*
Strangers When We Meet *'60*
The World of Suzie Wong *'60*
Bell, Book and Candle *'58*
Operation Mad Ball *'57*
Full of Life *'56*
Solid Gold Cadillac *'56*
My Sister Eileen *'55*
Pushover *'54*

John Quinn
Total Exposure *'91*
Cheerleader Camp *'88*

Gene Quintano(1946-)
National Lampoon's Loaded Weapon 1 *'93*
Honeymoon Academy *'90*
Why Me? *'90*

Eduardo Quiroz
The Damned *'06*
San Franpsycho *'06*
I Got Five on It *'05*

Jose Quiroz
The Damned *'06*
San Franpsycho *'06*
I Got Five on It *'05*

Marcus Raboy
Janky Promoters *'09*
Friday After Next *'02*

Fons Rademakers(1920-2007)
The Rose Garden *'89*
The Assault *'86*
Because of the Cats *'74*

Peter Rader
Hired to Kill *'91*
Grandma's House *'88*

Michael Radford(1946-)
Flawless *'07*
The Merchant of Venice *'04*
Dancing at the Blue Iguana *'00*
B. Monkey *'97*
The Postman *'94*
White Mischief *'88*
1984 *'84*
Another Time, Another Place *'83*

Robert Radler
The Substitute 4: Failure is Not an Option *'00*
The Substitute 3: Winner Takes All *'99*
T.N.T. *'98*
Soldier of Fortune Inc. *'97*
Best of the Best 2 *'93*
Showdown *'93*
Best of the Best *'89*

Eric Radomski
Todd McFarlane's Spawn *'97*
Batman: Mask of the Phantasm *'93*

Michael Raeburn(1943-)
Jit *'94*
Killing Heat *'84*
Laserblast *'78*

Bob Rafelson(1933-)
No Good Deed *'02*
Poodle Springs *'98*
Blood & Wine *'96*
Picture Windows *'95*
Tales of Erotica *'93*
Man Trouble *'92*
Mountains of the Moon *'90*
Black Widow *'87*
The Postman Always Rings Twice *'81*
Stay Hungry *'76*
The King of Marvin Gardens *'72*
Five Easy Pieces *'70*
Head *'68*

Stewart Raffill(1945-)
Croc *'07*
Grizzly Falls *'99*
Tammy and the T-Rex *'94*
Mannequin 2: On the Move *'91*
Mac and Me *'88*
Ice Pirates *'84*
The Philadelphia Experiment *'84*
High Risk *'81*
Sea Gypsies *'78*
Across the Great Divide *'76*
The Adventures of the Wilderness Family *'76*
When the North Wind Blows *'74*
The Tender Warrior *'71*

Alan Rafkin(1928-2001)
How to Frame a Figg *'71*
The Shakiest Gun in the West *'68*
The Ghost and Mr. Chicken *'66*
Ski Party *'65*

Sam Raimi(1959-)
Drag Me to Hell *'09*
Spider-Man 3 *'07*
Spider-Man 2 *'04*
Spider-Man *'02*
The Gift *'00*
For Love of the Game *'99*
A Simple Plan *'98*
The Quick and the Dead *'95*
Army of Darkness *'92*
Darkman *'90*
Evil Dead 2: Dead by Dawn *'87*
Crimewave *'85*
Evil Dead *'83*

Frank Rainone
A Brooklyn State of Mind *'97*
Me and the Mob *'94*

Alvin Rakoff(1927-)
A Dance to the Music of Time *'97*
A Voyage 'Round My Father *'89*
The First Olympics: Athens 1896 *'84*
Dirty Tricks *'81*
Death Ship *'80*
City on Fire *'78*
King Solomon's Treasure *'76*
Say Hello to Yesterday *'71*
Hoffman *'70*
Room 43 *'58*

Harold Ramis(1944-)
Year One *'09*
The Ice Harvest *'05*
Analyze That *'02*
Bedazzled *'00*
Analyze This *'98*
Multiplicity *'96*
Stuart Saves His Family *'94*
Groundhog Day *'93*
Club Paradise *'86*
National Lampoon's Vacation *'83*
Caddyshack *'80*

Lynne Ramsay(1969-)
Morvern Callar *'02*
Ratcatcher *'99*

Shyam Ramsay
Bandh Darwaza *'90*
Purana Mandir *'84*

Tulsi Ramsay
Bandh Darwaza *'90*
Purana Mandir *'84*

Addison Randall(1949-)
The Killing Zone *'90*
Chance *'89*
East L.A. Warriors *'89*
Payback *'89*

Tony Randel(1956-)
Rattled *'96*
Fist of the North Star *'95*
One Good Turn *'95*
Ticks *'93*
Amityville 1992: It's About Time *'92*
Children of the Night *'92*
Hellbound: Hellraiser 2 *'88*

Arthur Rankin, Jr.(1924-)
Flight of Dragons *'82*
The Return of the King *'80*
The Hobbit *'78*

Kyle Rankin
Infestation *'09*
The Battle of Shaker Heights *'03*

Mark Rappaport
From the Journals of Jean Seberg *'95*
Rock Hudson's Home Movies *'92*
Impostors *'80*

Jean-Paul Rappeneau(1932-)
Bon Voyage *'03*
The Horseman on the Roof *'95*
Cyrano de Bergerac *'90*
Swashbuckler *'84*
Lovers Like Us *'75*
The Savage *'75*

Irving Rapper(1898-1999)
Born Again *'78*
Marjorie Morningstar *'58*
The Brave One *'56*
Forever Female *'53*
Another Man's Poison *'52*
Deception *'46*
The Corn Is Green *'45*
Rhapsody in Blue *'45*
The Adventures of Mark Twain *'44*
Now, Voyager *'42*

Steve Rash
Road Trip: Beer Pong *'09*
Bring It On: In It to Win It *'07*
Bring It On: All or Nothing *'06*
American Pie Presents Band Camp *'05*
Good Advice *'01*
Held Up *'00*
Eddie *'96*
Son-in-Law *'93*
Queens Logic *'91*
Can't Buy Me Love *'87*
Under the Rainbow *'81*
The Buddy Holly Story *'78*

Ian Iqbal Rashid
How She Move *'08*
Touch of Pink *'04*

Daniel Raskov
A Kiss Goodnight *'94*
The Masters of Menace *'90*
Wedding Band *'89*

Pen-ek Ratanaruang
Last Life in the Universe *'03*
6ixtynin9 *'99*

Brett Ratner(1969-)
New York, I Love You *'09*
Rush Hour 3 *'07*
X-Men: The Last Stand *'06*
After the Sunset *'04*
Red Dragon *'02*
Rush Hour 2 *'01*
Family Man *'00*
Rush Hour *'98*
Money Talks *'97*

Gregory Ratoff(1897-1960)
Abdulla the Great *'56*
Black Magic *'49*
The Heat's On *'43*
The Corsican Brothers *'42*
Footlight Serenade *'42*
Adam Had Four Sons *'41*
Day-Time Wife *'39*
Intermezzo *'39*
Rose of Washington Square *'39*

John Rawlins(1902-97)
Shark River *'53*
Dick Tracy Meets Gruesome *'47*
Dick Tracy's Dilemma *'47*
Arabian Nights *'42*
Overland Mail *'42*
Sherlock Holmes: The Voice of Terror *'42*
Junior G-Men *'40*

Albert Ray(1897-1944)
Everyman's Law *'36*
Undercover Man *'36*
Dancing Man *'33*
Shriek in the Night *'33*
13th Guest *'32*

Bernard B. Ray(1895-1964)
Movie Stuntmen *'53*
Buffalo Bill Rides Again *'47*
House of Errors *'42*
Broken Strings *'40*
Covered Wagon Trails *'40*
Pinto Canyon *'40*
Ridin' the Trail *'40*
Code of the Fearless *'39*
Daughter of the Tong *'39*
In Old Montana *'39*
Two-Gun Troubador *'37*
I'll Name the Murderer *'36*
The Reckless Way *'36*
Speed Reporter *'36*
Coyote Trails *'35*
Kentucky Blue Streak *'35*
The Midnight Phantom *'35*
Silent Valley *'35*
Suicide Squad *'35*
Texas Jack *'35*
The Silver Bullet *'34*

Billy Ray
Breach *'07*
Shattered Glass *'03*

Fred Olen Ray(1954-)
Silent Venom *'08*
The Glass Trap *'04*
Air Rage *'01*
Black Horizon *'01*
Kept *'01*
Venomous *'01*
Critical Mass *'00*
Mach 2 *'00*
Submerged *'00*
Active Stealth *'99*
The Capitol Conspiracy *'99*
Fugitive Mind *'99*
Invisible Mom 2 *'99*
The Kid with the X-Ray Eyes *'99*
Rapid Assault *'99*
Mom, Can I Keep Her? *'98*
Death and Desire *'97*
Hybrid *'97*
Invisible Dad *'97*
Night Shade *'97*
The Shooter *'97*
Friend of the Family 2 *'96*
Fugitive Rage *'96*
Invisible Mom *'96*
Attack of the 60-Foot Centerfold *'95*
Cyberzone *'95*
Over the Wire *'95*
Bikini Drive-In *'94*
Inner Sanctum 2 *'94*
Wizards of the Demon Sword *'94*
Dinosaur Island *'93*
Mind Twister *'93*
Possessed by the Night *'93*
Haunting Fear *'91*
Inner Sanctum *'91*
Bad Girls from Mars *'90*
Evil Toons *'90*
Mob Boss *'90*
Spirits *'90*
Alienator *'89*
Beverly Hills Vamp *'88*
Hollywood Chainsaw Hookers *'88*
Terminal Force *'88*
Warlords *'88*
Commando Squad *'87*
Cyclone *'87*
Deep Space *'87*
Phantom Empire *'87*
Star Slammer *'87*
Armed Response *'86*
Tomb *'86*
Bio Hazard *'85*
Alien Dead *'79*

Nicholas Ray(1911-79)
55 Days at Peking *'63*
The King of Kings *'61*
Party Girl *'58*
Rebel without a Cause *'55*
Johnny Guitar *'53*
The Lusty Men *'52*
Flying Leathernecks *'51*
On Dangerous Ground *'51*
Born to Be Bad *'50*
In a Lonely Place *'50*
Knock on Any Door *'49*
They Live by Night *'49*
A Woman's Secret *'49*

Satyajit Ray(1921-92)
The Stranger *'92*
The Home and the World *'84*
The Middleman *'76*
Distant Thunder *'73*
The Adversary *'71*
Days and Nights in the Forest *'70*
Charulata *'64*
The Big City *'63*
Two Daughters *'61*
Devi *'60*
The World of Apu *'59*
Aparajito *'58*
Jalsaghar *'58*
Pather Panchali *'54*

Ed Raymond
See Fred Olen Ray

David Raynr
Whatever It Takes *'00*
Trippin' *'99*

Spiro Razatos(1960-)
Class of 1999 2: The Substitute *'93*
Fast Getaway *'91*

Bill Rebane(1937-)
The Capture of Bigfoot *'79*
The Alpha Incident *'76*
The Giant Spider Invasion *'75*
Rana: The Legend of Shadow Lake *'75*
Monster a Go-Go! *'65*

Eric Red(1961-)
100 Feet *'08*
Bad Moon *'96*
Undertow *'95*
Body Parts *'91*
Cohen and Tate *'88*

Robert Redford(1937-)
Lions for Lambs *'07*
The Legend of Bagger Vance *'00*
The Horse Whisperer *'97*
Quiz Show *'94*
A River Runs Through It *'92*
The Milagro Beanfield War *'88*
Ordinary People *'80*

Carol Reed(1906-76)
Oliver! *'68*
The Agony and the Ecstasy *'65*
Our Man in Havana *'59*
The Key *'58*
Trapeze *'56*
A Kid for Two Farthings *'55*
The Fallen Idol *'49*
The Third Man *'49*
Odd Man Out *'47*
Immortal Battalion *'44*
The Girl in the News *'41*
Kipps *'41*
Night Train to Munich *'40*
The Stars Look Down *'39*

Joel M. Reed(1933-)
Night of the Zombies *'81*
Bloodsucking Freaks *'75*

G.I. Executioner '71

Luther Reed(1888-1961)

Convention Girl '35
Dixiana '30
Rio Rita '29

Peyton Reed(1964-)

Yes Man '08
The Break-Up '06
Down With Love '03
Bring It On '00
The Love Bug '97

Roland D. Reed(1894-1974)

The House of Secrets '37
Red Lights Ahead '36

Theodore Reed(1887-1959)

What a Life '39
Double or Nothing '37
The Nut '21

Tripp Reed

Walking Tall: Lone Justice '07
Manticore '05

Clive Rees

When the Whales Came '89
Blockhouse '73

Christopher Reeve(1952-2004)

Everyone's Hero '06
In the Gloaming '97

Geoffrey Reeve(1932-)

Souvenir '88
Caravan to Vaccares '74
Puppet on a Chain '72

Matt Reeves(1966-)

Cloverfield '08
The Pallbearer '95
Future Shock '93

Michael Reeves(1944-69)

The Conqueror Worm '68
The She-Beast '65

Nicolas Winding Refn(1970-)

Bronson '09
Valhalla Rising '09
Fear X '03
Pusher '96

Godfrey Reggio(1940-)

Powaqqatsi: Life in Transformation '88
Koyaanisqatsi '83

Kelly Reichardt

Wendy and Lucy '08
Old Joy '06
River of Grass '94

Alastair Reid(1939-)

Nostromo '96
Armistead Maupin's Tales of the City '93
Teamster Boss: The Jackie Presser Story '92
Traffik '90
Shattered '72
Baby Love '69

Dorothy Reid

See Dorothy Davenport Reid

Dorothy Davenport Reid(1895-1977)

Sucker Money '34
Woman Condemned '33
Linda '29

Tim Reid(1944-)

For Real '02
Asunder '99
Once Upon a Time ... When We Were Colored '95
The Little Mermaid '75

Roel Reine

The Marine 2 '09
Pistol Whipped '08
Black Ops '07
The Delivery '99

Carl Reiner(1922-)

That Old Feeling '96
Fatal Instinct '93
Sibling Rivalry '90
Bert Rigby, You're a Fool '89
Summer School '87
Summer Rental '85
All of Me '84
The Man with Two Brains '83
Dead Men Don't Wear Plaid '82
The Jerk '79
The One and Only '78
Oh, God! '77
Where's Poppa? '70
The Comic '69
Enter Laughing '67

Jeff Reiner

Caprica '09
Wilderness Love '02
Deadly Game '98
Smalltime '96
Serpent's Lair '95
Trouble Bound '92
Blood & Concrete: A Love Story '90

Rob Reiner(1945-)

The Bucket List '07
Rumor Has It... '05
Alex & Emma '03
The Story of Us '99
Ghosts of Mississippi '96
The American President '95
North '94
A Few Good Men '92
Misery '90
When Harry Met Sally... '89
The Princess Bride '87
Stand by Me '86
The Sure Thing '85
This Is Spinal Tap '84

Gottfried Reinhardt(1911-94)

Town without Pity '61
Betrayed '54
The Story of Three Loves '53
Invitation '51

John Reinhardt

Open Secret '48
Captain Calamity '36

Harald Reinl(1908-86)

Fight for Gold '86
Hell Hounds of Alaska '73
The Torture Chamber of Dr. Sadism '69
The Last Tomahawk '65
Carpet of Horror '64
Strangler of Blackmoor Castle '63
The Invisible Dr. Mabuse '62
Forger of London '61
The Return of Dr. Mabuse '61

Irving Reis(1906-53)

Three Husbands '50
All My Sons '48
The Bachelor and the Bobby-Soxer '47
Crack-Up '46
Big Street '42
The Falcon Takes Over '42

Walter Reisch(1903-83)

Song of Scheherazade '47
Men Are Not Gods '37

Charles Reisner(1887-1962)

Train to Tombstone '50
The Traveling Saleswoman '50
The Cobra Strikes '48
Lost in a Harem '44
Big Store '41
Manhattan Merry-Go-Round '37
Politics '31
Reducing '31
Hollywood Revue of 1929 '29
Steamboat Bill, Jr. '28
The Better 'Ole '26

The Man on the Box '25

Karel Reisz(1926-2002)

Everybody Wins '90
Sweet Dreams '85
The French Lieutenant's Woman '81
Who'll Stop the Rain? '78
The Gambler '74
Isadora '68
Morgan: A Suitable Case for Treatment '66
Saturday Night and Sunday Morning '60

Wolfgang Reitherman(1909-85)

The Many Adventures of Winnie the Pooh '77
The Rescuers '77
Robin Hood '73
The Aristocats '70
The Jungle Book '67
The Sword in the Stone '63
101 Dalmatians '61
Sleeping Beauty '59

Ivan Reitman(1946-)

My Super Ex-Girlfriend '06
Evolution '01
Six Days, Seven Nights '98
Father's Day '96
Junior '94
Dave '93
Kindergarten Cop '90
Ghostbusters 2 '89
Twins '88
Legal Eagles '86
Ghostbusters '84
Stripes '81
Meatballs '79

Jason Reitman

Up in the Air '09
Juno '07
Thank You for Smoking '06

Edgar Reitz(1932-)

Heimat 2 '92
Heimat 1 '84
Germany in Autumn '78

Pierre-Paul Renderss

Mr. Average '06
Thomas in Love '01

Norman Rene(1951-96)

Reckless '95
Prelude to a Kiss '92
Longtime Companion '90

Jeff Renfroe

Sand Serpents '09
Civic Duty '06
Paranoia 1.0 '04

Jean Renoir(1894-1979)

The Little Theatre of Jean Renoir '71
The Elusive Corporal '62
Picnic on the Grass '59
The Testament of Dr. Cordelier '59
Elena and Her Men '56
French Can-Can '55
The Golden Coach '52
The River '51
A Day in the Country '46
Diary of a Chambermaid '46
The Southerner '45
This Land Is Mine '43
The Rules of the Game '39
La Bete Humaine '38
Grand Illusion '37
La Marseillaise '37
The Crime of Monsieur Lange '36
The Lower Depths '36
Madame Bovary '34
Toni '34
Boudu Saved from Drowning '32
La Chienne '31
Tournament '29
Renoir Shorts '27
Charleston '26

Nicholas Renton(1946-)

A Room With a View '08
Bait '02

Wives and Daughters '01
The Ebb-Tide '97
Far from the Madding Crowd '97

Alain Resnais(1922-)

Private Fears in Public Places '06
Same Old Song '97
Smoking/No Smoking '94
I Want to Go Home '89
Melo '86
Life Is a Bed of Roses '83
Mon Oncle d'Amerique '80
Providence '77
Stavisky '74
La Guerre Est Finie '66
Muriel '63
Last Year at Marienbad '61
Hiroshima, Mon Amour '59

Dale Resteghini(1968-)

Da Hip Hop Witch '00
Colorz of Rage '97

Harry Revier(1889-1957)

The Lost City '34
When Lightning Strikes '34

Franc Reyes

Illegal Tender '07
Empire '02

Burt Reynolds(1936-)

The Final Hit '02
The Man from Left Field '93
Stick '85
Sharky's Machine '81
The End '78
Gator '76

Kevin Reynolds(1950-)

Tristan & Isolde '06
The Count of Monte Cristo '02
187 '97
Waterworld '95
Rapa Nui '93
Robin Hood: Prince of Thieves '91
The Beast '88
Fandango '85

Lynn F. Reynolds(1889-1927)

Riders of the Purple Sage '25
Sky High '22
Trailin' '21

Scott Reynolds(1968-)

Heaven '99
The Ugly '96

Phillip Rhee(1960-)

Best of the Best: Without Warning '98
Best of the Best 3: No Turning Back '95

Michael Rhodes(1935-)

Christy '94
Heidi '93
The Killing Mind '90
Matters of the Heart '90

Michael Ray Rhodes

Entertaining Angels: The Dorothy Day Story '96
Fourth Wise Man '85
Shooting '82

Tonino Ricci(1927-)

Buck and the Magic Bracelet '97
Rush '84
Great Treasure Hunt '72
Liberators '69

David Lowell Rich(1923-)

Choices '86
Convicted '86
The Hearst and Davies Affair '85
Scandal Sheet '85
Chu Chu & the Philly Flash '81
Enola Gay: The Men, the Mission, the Atomic Bomb '80

Nurse '80
The Concorde: Airport '79 '79
Family Upside Down '78
Little Women '78
Satan's School for Girls '73
That Man Bolt '73
Northeast of Seoul '72
Madame X '66
Have Rocket Will Travel '59

John Rich(1925-)

Easy Come, Easy Go '67
Boeing Boeing '65
Roustabout '64

Matty Rich(1971-)

The Inkwell '94
Straight out of Brooklyn '91

Richard Rich

The Trumpet of the Swan '01
The King and I '99
The Swan Princess 2: Escape from Castle Mountain '97
The Swan Princess '94
The Black Cauldron '85
The Fox and the Hound '81

Jefferson (Jeff) Richard(1946-)

Berserker '87
In Search of a Golden Sky '84

Pierre Richard(1934-)

Too Shy to Try '78
The Daydreamer '75

Cybil (Sybil) Richards

Femalien 2 '98
Erotic House of Wax '97
Lolida 2000 '97
Femalien '96
Virtual Encounters '96

David Richards

Little Devil '07
Reckless: The Sequel '98
Reckless '97
Kiss and Tell '96

Dick Richards(1934-)

Man, Woman & Child '83
Death Valley '81
March or Die '77
Farewell, My Lovely '75
Rafferty & the Gold Dust Twins '75
Culpepper Cattle Co. '72

Lloyd Richards(1919-2006)

The Piano Lesson '94
Paul Robeson '77

Peter Richardson(1951-)

The Pope Must Diet '91
Eat the Rich '87
Supergrass '87

Tony Richardson(1928-91)

Blue Sky '91
The Phantom of the Opera '90
Women & Men: Stories of Seduction '90
Shadow on the Sun '88
Penalty Phase '86
The Hotel New Hampshire '84
The Border '82
Joseph Andrews '77
Ned Kelly '70
Hamlet '69
The Charge of the Light Brigade '68
Mademoiselle '66
The Loved One '65
Tom Jones '63
The Loneliness of the Long Distance Runner '62
A Taste of Honey '61
The Entertainer '60
Look Back in Anger '58

William Richert(1944-)

The Man in the Iron Mask '97

A Night in the Life of Jimmy Reardon '88
Winter Kills '79

Anthony Richmond(1942-)

Night of the Sharks '87
Days of Hell '84
Deja Vu '84
A Man Called Rage '84

Roland Suso Richter

Dresden '06
The Tunnel '01

W.D. Richter(1945-)

Late for Dinner '91
The Adventures of Buckaroo Banzai Across the Eighth Dimension '84

Thomas (Tom) Rickman

Crash Course '00
The River Rat '84

Philip Ridley

The Passion of Darkly Noon '95
The Reflecting Skin '91

Leni Riefenstahl(1902-2003)

Tiefland '44
Triumph of the Will '34
The Blue Light '32

Charles Riesner

Meet the People '44
Flying High '31

Adam Rifkin(1966-)

National Lampoon's The Stoned Aged '07
Night at the Golden Eagle '02
Welcome to Hollywood '00
Detroit Rock City '99
Something About Sex '98
The Nutt House '95
Psycho Cop 2 '94
The Chase '93
The Dark Backward '91
The Invisible Maniac '90
Tale of Two Sisters '89
Never on Tuesday '88

Ned Rifle

See Hal Hartley

Eran Riklis(1954-)

Lemon Tree '08
The Syrian Bride '04
Cup Final '92

Wolf Rilla(1920-2005)

Village of the Damned '60
Bachelor of Hearts '58
The Scamp '57
Roadhouse Girl '53

Arthur Ripley(1895-1961)

Thunder Road '58
The Chase '46
The Barber Shop '33
Pharmacist '32

Maria Ripoli

Tortilla Soup '01
Twice upon a Yesterday '98

Arturo Ripstein(1943-)

Deep Crimson '96
Foxtrot '76

Dino Risi(1916-)

Running Away '89
How Funny Can Sex Be? '76
The Scent of a Woman '75
Tiger and the Pussycat '67
The Easy Life '63
Il Sorpasso '63
Love in the City '53

Michael Rissi

Soultaker '90
Terror Eyes '87

Guy Ritchie(1968-)

Sherlock Holmes '09
RocknRolla '08

Revolver '05
Swept Away '02
Snatch '00
Lock, Stock and 2 Smoking Barrels '98

Michael Ritchie(1938-2001)
A Simple Wish '97
The Fantasticks '95
Cops and Robbersons '94
The Scout '94
The Positively True Adventures of the Alleged Texas Cheerleader-Murdering Mom '93
Diggstown '92
Fletch Lives '89
The Couch Trip '87
The Golden Child '86
Wildcats '86
Fletch '85
Survivors '83
The Island '80
An Almost Perfect Affair '79
Semi-Tough '77
The Bad News Bears '76
Smile '75
The Candidate '72
Prime Cut '72
Downhill Racer '69

Martin Ritt(1914-90)
Stanley and Iris '90
Nuts '87
Murphy's Romance '85
Cross Creek '83
Back Roads '81
Norma Rae '79
Casey's Shadow '78
The Front '76
Conrack '74
Pete 'n' Tillie '72
Sounder '72
The Great White Hope '70
Molly Maguires '70
The Brotherhood '68
Hombre '67
The Spy Who Came in from the Cold '65
The Outrage '64
Hud '63
Paris Blues '61
Black Orchid '59
The Long, Hot Summer '58
Edge of the City '57

Tim Ritter
The Alien Agenda: Endangered Species '97
Truth or Dare? '86

Lance Rivera
The Perfect Holiday '07
The Cookout '04

Jacques Rivette(1928-)
The Duchess of Langeais '07
The Story of Marie and Julien '03
Va Savoir '01
Up/Down/Fragile '95
Jeanne la Pucelle '94
La Belle Noiseuse '90
Celine and Julie Go Boating '74
The Nun '66
Paris Belongs to Us '60

Hal Roach(1892-1992)
Road Show '41
One Million B.C. '40
The Devil's Brother '33

Jay Roach(1957-)
Dinner for Schmucks '10
Recount '08
Meet the Fockers '04
Austin Powers In Goldmember '02
Meet the Parents '00
Austin Powers 2: The Spy Who Shagged Me '99
Mystery, Alaska '99
Austin Powers: International Man of Mystery '97

Seymour Robbie(1919-2004)
Marco '73
C.C. & Company '70

Brian Robbins(1964-)
Meet Dave '08
Norbit '07
The Shaggy Dog '06
The Perfect Score '04
Hardball '01
Ready to Rumble '00
Varsity Blues '98
Good Burger '97
The Show '95

Matthew Robbins(1945-)
Bingo '91
*batteries not included '87
Legend of Billie Jean '85
Dragonslayer '81
Corvette Summer '78

Tim Robbins(1958-)
The Cradle Will Rock '99
Dead Man Walking '95
Bob Roberts '92

Mike Robe
Montana Sky '07
The Junction Boys '02
Emma's Wish '98
Degree of Guilt '95
Return to Lonesome Dove '93
Scott Turow's The Burden of Proof '92
Son of the Morning Star '91
Child in the Night '90
Murder Ordained '87
News at Eleven '86
Urge to Kill '84

Yves Robert(1920-2002)
My Father's Glory '91
My Mother's Castle '91
Pardon Mon Affaire, Too! '77
Pardon Mon Affaire '76
Return of the Tall Blond Man with One Black Shoe '74
Salut l'Artiste '74
The Tall Blond Man with One Black Shoe '72

Alan Roberts
Save Me '93
Round Trip to Heaven '92
Karate Cop '91
Young Lady Chatterly 2 '85
The Happy Hooker Goes Hollywood '80

Charles E. Roberts(1894-1951)
Hurry, Charlie, Hurry '41
Roaring Roads '35
Flaming Signal '33

Daryll Roberts
How U Like Me Now? '92
Sweet Perfection '90

John Roberts
Station Jim '01
Paulie '98
War of the Buttons '95

Stephen Roberts(1917-99)
Ex-Mrs. Bradford '36
Star of Midnight '35
Romance in Manhattan '34
One Sunday Afternoon '33

John S. Robertson(1878-1964)
Our Little Girl '35
His Greatest Gamble '34
One Man's Journey '33
Little Orphan Annie '32
The Phantom of Paris '31
The Single Standard '29
Shore Leave '25
Soul-Fire '25
Tess of the Storm Country '22
Dr. Jekyll and Mr. Hyde '20

Angela Robinson(1971-)
Herbie: Fully Loaded '05
D.E.B.S. '04

Bruce Robinson(1946-)
Jennifer 8 '92
How to Get Ahead in Advertising '89
Withnail and I '87

Chris Robinson(1938-)
Sunshine Run '79
Thunder County '74
Women's Prison Escape '74

John Mark Robinson
All Tied Up '92
Kid '90
Roadhouse 66 '84

Phil Alden Robinson(1950-)
The Sum of All Fears '02
Band of Brothers '01
Freedom Song '00
Sneakers '92
Field of Dreams '89
In the Mood '87

Richard Robinson
Poor Pretty Eddie '73
Bloody Trail '72

Arthur Robison(1883-1935)
The Informer '29
Warning Shadows '23

Mark Robson(1913-)
Avalanche Express '79
Earthquake '74
Daddy's Gone A-Hunting '69
Valley of the Dolls '67
The Lost Command '66
Von Ryan's Express '65
The Prize '63
From the Terrace '60
The Inn of the Sixth Happiness '58
Peyton Place '57
The Harder They Fall '56
The Bridges at Toko-Ri '55
Phffft! '54
Return to Paradise '53
I Want You '51
Champion '49
Home of the Brave '49
My Foolish Heart '49
Bedlam '45
Isle of the Dead '45
The Ghost Ship '43
The Seventh Victim '43

Marc Rocco(1965-)
Murder in the First '95
Where the Day Takes You '92
Dream a Little Dream '89
Scenes from the Goldmine '87

Glauce Rocha(1930-73)
Antonio Das Mortes '68
Earth Entranced '66
Black God, White Devil '64

Eric Rochant(1961-)
Total Western '00
Love Without Pity '91
The Fifth Monkey '90

Chris Rock(1966-)
I Think I Love My Wife '07
Head of State '03

Alexandre Rockwell(1957-)
13 Moons '02
Four Rooms '95
Somebody to Love '94
In the Soup '92
Sons '89

Franc Roddam(1946-)
Cleopatra '99
Moby Dick '98
K2: The Ultimate High '92
War Party '89
Aria '88
The Bride '85
The Lords of Discipline '83
Quadrophenia '79

Serge Rodnunsky
Chill '06
Dead Lenny '06
Newsbreak '00
TripFall '00
Cypress Edge '99
Fear Runs Silent '99
Paper Bullets '99
Silicon Towers '99
Bomb Squad '97
Dead Tides '97
Powder Burn '96
Final Equinox '95
Lovers' Lovers '94

Joao Pedro Rodrigues(1966-)
Two Drifters '05
O Fantasma '00

Hugo Rodriguez
Nicotina '03
In the Middle of Nowhere '93

Ismael Rodriguez(1917-2004)
Autopsy of a Ghost '67
Daniel Boone: Trail Blazer '56

Robert Rodriguez(1968-)
Shorts: The Adventures of the Wishing Rock '09
Planet Terror '07
The Adventures of Sharkboy and Lavagirl in 3-D '05
Sin City '05
Once Upon a Time in Mexico '03
Spy Kids 3-D: Game Over '03
Spy Kids 2: The Island of Lost Dreams '02
Spy Kids '01
The Faculty '98
Desperado '95
Four Rooms '95
From Dusk Till Dawn '95
Roadracers '94
El Mariachi '93

Nicolas Roeg(1928-)
Samson and Delilah '96
Full Body Massage '95
Two Deaths '94
Heart of Darkness '93
Cold Heaven '92
The Witches '90
Sweet Bird of Youth '89
Aria '88
Track 29 '88
Castaway '87
Insignificance '85
Eureka! '81
The Man Who Fell to Earth '76
Don't Look Now '73
Walkabout '71
Performance '70

Michael Roemer(1928-)
Pilgrim, Farewell '82
The Plot Against Harry '69
Nothing but a Man '64

Albert Rogell(1901-88)
The Admiral Was a Lady '50
War of the Wildcats '43
The Black Cat '41
Argentine Nights '40
Li'l Abner '40
Murder in Greenwich Village '37
No More Women '34
The Rider of Death Valley '32
Suicide Fleet '31
The Tip-Off '31
The Red Raiders '27
Cyclone Cavalier '25

Charles R. Rogers(1887-1956)
March of the Wooden Soldiers '34
The Devil's Brother '33

James B. Rogers
American Pie 2 '01
Say It Isn't So '01

Maclean Rogers(1899-1962)
Down Among the Z Men '52
Goon Movie '52
Old Mother Riley's Jungle Treasure '51
Calling Paul Temple '48
Murder in the Footlights '46

Eric Rohmer(1920-2010)
The Romance of Astrea and Celadon '07
Triple Agent '04
The Lady and the Duke '01
Autumn Tale '98
A Summer's Tale '96
Rendezvous in Paris '95
A Tale of Winter '92
Four Adventures of Reinette and Mirabelle '89
A Tale of Springtime '89
Boyfriends & Girlfriends '88
Summer '86
Full Moon in Paris '84
Pauline at the Beach '83
Le Beau Mariage '82
The Aviator's Wife '80
Perceval '78
The Marquise of O '76
Chloe in the Afternoon '72
Claire's Knee '71
My Night at Maud's '69
Six in Paris '68
La Collectionneuse '67

Sutton Roley(1922-2007)
Loners '72
Snatched '72

Jean Rollin(1938-)
Emmanuelle 6 '88
The Living Dead Girl '82
Zombie Lake '80
Lips of Blood '75

Phil Roman(1930-)
Tom and Jerry: The Movie '93
Race for Your Life, Charlie Brown '77

Mark Romanek(1959-)
One Hour Photo '02
Static '87

Eddie Romero(1924-)
WhiteForce '88
Beyond Atlantis '73
Twilight People '72
Woman Hunt '72
Beast of the Yellow Night '70
Brides of the Beast '68
Mad Doctor of Blood Island '68
The Ravagers '65
The Walls of Hell '64
Cavalry Command '63
Raiders of Leyte Gulf '63

George A. Romero(1940-)
Survival of the Dead '09
Diary of the Dead '07
George A. Romero's Land of the Dead '05
Bruiser '00
The Dark Half '91
Two Evil Eyes '90
Monkey Shines '88
Day of the Dead '85
Creepshow '82
Knightriders '81
Dawn of the Dead '78
Martin '77
The Crazies '73
Season of the Witch '73
Night of the Living Dead '68

Charles R. Rondeau(1917-96)
The Girl in Lover's Lane '60
The Devil's Partner '58

Darrell Roodt(1963-)
Lullaby '08
Queen's Messenger II '01
Second Skin '00
Dangerous Ground '96
Cry, the Beloved Country '95
Father Hood '93
To the Death '93
Sarafina! '92
City of Blood '88
Place of Weeping '86

Don Roos(1959-)
Happy Endings '05
Bounce '00
The Opposite of Sex '98

Tom Ropelewski
Look Who's Talking Now '93
Madhouse '90

Mark Roper(1958-)
Queen's Messenger II '01
Operation Delta Force 3: Clear Target '98
Alien Chaser '96
Warhead '96
Live Wire: Human Timebomb '95

Cliff Roquemore(1948-2002)
Devil's Son-in-Law '77
Dolemite 2: Human Tornado '76

Giuseppe Rosati
Perfect Crime '79
Street War '76

Bernard Rose(1960-)
The Kreutzer Sonata '08
Leo Tolstoy's Anna Karenina '96
Immortal Beloved '94
Candyman '92
Chicago Joe & the Showgirl '90
Paperhouse '89
Smart Money '88

Lee Rose
A Girl Thing '01
The Truth About Jane '00
The Color of Courage '98

Les Rose
Gas '81
Title Shot '81
Hog Wild '80

Barry Rosen
The Yum-Yum Girls '78
Gang Wars '75

Martin Rosen
Stacking '87
The Plague Dogs '82
Watership Down '78

Phil Rosen(1888-1951)
In Old New Mexico '45
The Jade Mask '45
The Scarlet Clue '45
Charlie Chan in the Secret Service '44
The Chinese Cat '44
Meeting at Midnight '44
Return of the Ape Man '44
Wings over the Pacific '43
I Killed That Man '42
The Man with Two Lives '42
Gangs, Inc. '41
Spooks Run Wild '41
Phantom of Chinatown '40
It Could Happen to You '37
Youth on Parole '37
Mistaken Identity '36
The President's Mystery '36
Tango '36
Beggars in Ermine '34
Dangerous Corner '34
Woman in the Shadows '34
The Phantom Broadcast '33
The Sphinx '33
Young Blood '33
The Gay Buckaroo '32
Man's Land '32
Texas Gunfighter '32
Whistlin' Dan '32
Arizona Terror '31
Branded Men '31
The Pocatello Kid '31
Range Law '31
Two Gun Man '31
The Peacock Fan '29
The Phantom in the House '29

Craig Rosenberg(1965-)
Half Light '05
Hotel de Love '96

Rick Rosenberg
Southern Man '99
Distant Thunder '88

Stuart Rosenberg(1927-2007)
My Heroes Have Always Been Cowboys '91
The Pope of Greenwich Village '84
Brubaker '80
The Amityville Horror '79
Love and Bullets '79
Voyage of the Damned '76
The Drowning Pool '75
The Laughing Policeman '74
Pocket Money '72
April Fools '69
Cool Hand Luke '67
Murder, Inc. '60

Seth Zvi Rosenfeld
King of the Jungle '01
A Brother's Kiss '97
Subway Stories '97

Rick Rosenthal(1949-)
Nearing Grace '05
Halloween: Resurrection '02
Just a Little Harmless Sex '99
The Birds 2: Land's End '94
Devlin '92
Russkies '87
American Dreamer '84
Bad Boys '83
Halloween 2: The Nightmare Isn't Over! '81

Robert J. Rosenthal
Zapped! '82
Malibu Beach '78

Francesco Rosi(1922-)
The Truce '96
The Palermo Connection '91
Three Brothers '80
Christ Stopped at Eboli '79
Lucky Luciano '74

Mark Rosman(1959-)
Princess: A Modern Fairytale '08
Snow 2: Brain Freeze '08
The Perfect Man '05
A Cinderella Story '04
Life-Size '00
Model Behavior '00
The Invader '96
Evolver '94
The Force '94
The Blue Yonder '86
The House on Sorority Row '83

Milton Rosmer(1881-1971)
The Challenge '38
Murder in the Old Red Barn '36
The Secret of the Loch '34

Craig Ross, Jr.
Motives '03
Blue Hill Avenue '01

Gary Ross(1956-)
Seabiscuit '03
Pleasantville '98

Herbert Ross(1927-2001)
Boys on the Side '94
Undercover Blues '93
True Colors '91
My Blue Heaven '90
Steel Magnolias '89
Dancers '87
The Secret of My Success '87
Footloose '84
Protocol '84
Max Dugan Returns '83
I Ought to Be in Pictures '82
Pennies from Heaven '81
Nijinsky '80
California Suite '78
The Goodbye Girl '77
The Turning Point '77
The Seven-Per-Cent Solution '76
Funny Lady '75
The Sunshine Boys '75
The Last of Sheila '73
Play It Again, Sam '72
The Owl and the Pussycat '70
Goodbye, Mr. Chips '69
Goodbye Love '34

Roberto Rossellini(1906-77)
The Messiah '75
Augustine of Hippo '72
Blaise Pascal '71
The Rise of Louis XIV '66
RoGoPaG '62
Vanina Vanini '61
Era Notte a Roma '60
Generale Della Rovere '60
Seven Deadly Sins '53
Voyage in Italy '53
Europa '51 '52
The Flowers of St. Francis '50
Stromboli '50
Amore '48
Machine to Kill Bad People '48
The Miracle '48
Deutschland im Jahre Null '47
Paisan '46
Open City '45
Man with a Cross '43

Robert Rossen(1908-66)
Lilith '64
The Hustler '61
They Came to Cordura '59
Island in the Sun '57
Alexander the Great '55
Mambo '55
All the King's Men '49
Body and Soul '47

Arthur Rosson(1886-1960)
Boots of Destiny '37
Trailing Trouble '37
Hidden Gold '33
The Concentratin' Kid '30
Trailing Trouble '30
The Last Outlaw '27

Bobby Roth(1950-)
Berkeley '05
Brave New Girl '04
Keeper of the City '92
The Man Inside '90
Rainbow Drive '90
Dead Solid Perfect '88
Baja Oklahoma '87
The Game of Love '87
Heartbreakers '84
Circle of Power '83
Boss' Son '78

Eli Roth(1972-)
Hostel: Part 2 '07
Hostel '06
Cabin Fever '03

Joe Roth(1948-)
Freedomland '06
Christmas With the Kranks '04
America's Sweethearts '01
Coupe de Ville '90
Revenge of the Nerds 2: Nerds in Paradise '87
Streets of Gold '86

Phillip J. Roth(1959-)
Boa '02
Interceptor Force 2 '02
Interceptor Force '99
Velocity Trap '99
Darkdrive '98
Total Reality '97
A.P.E.X. '94
Digital Man '94
Prototype X29A '92
Red Snow '91

Stephanie Rothman(1936-)
Working Girls '75
Terminal Island '73
Group Marriage '72
The Velvet Vampire '71
The Student Nurses '70
Track of the Vampire '66

William Rotsler(1926-97)
Mantis in Lace '68
Agony of Love '66

Nick Rotundo
G2: Mortal Conquest '99
Gladiator Cop: The Swordsman 2 '95

Brigitte Rouan(1965-)
After Sex '97
Overseas: Three Women with Man Trouble '90

Russell Rouse(1913-87)
Caper of the Golden Bulls '67
The Oscar '66
Fastest Gun Alive '56
The Thief '52
The Well '51

Peter Rowe(1947-)
Treasure Island '99
Personal Exemptions '88
Take Two '87
Lost '86

Roy Rowland(1902-95)
Girl Hunters '63
The Seven Hills of Rome '58
Gun Glory '57
Meet Me in Las Vegas '56
Hit the Deck '55
Many Rivers to Cross '55
The 5000 Fingers of Dr. T '53
The Moonlighter '53
Bugles in the Afternoon '52
Two Weeks with Love '50
Killer McCoy '47
Our Vines Have Tender Grapes '45

William Rowland(1898-)
Flight to Nowhere '46
Follies Girl '43

Christopher Rowley
Bonneville '06
Soul Patrol '80

Jean-Claude Roy
Deadly Sting '73
Killer '73

Patricia Rozema(1958-)
Kit Kittredge: An American Girl '08
Mansfield Park '99
When Night Is Falling '95
I've Heard the Mermaids Singing '87

John Ruane(1952-)
Dead Letter Office '98
That Eye, the Sky '94
Death in Brunswick '90

Andy Ruben
Club Vampire '98
Streets '90

J. Walter Ruben(1899-1942)
Java Head '35
Riff Raff '35
Ace of Aces '33
No Marriage Ties '33
No Other Woman '33

Joseph Ruben(1951-)
The Forgotten '04
Return to Paradise '98
Money Train '95
The Good Son '93
Sleeping with the Enemy '91
True Believer '89
The Stepfather '87
Dreamscape '84
Gorp '80
Joyride '77
Pom Pom Girls '76

Percival Rubens
Sweet Murder '93
Wild Zone '89
Survival Zone '84
The Demon '81
Mr. Kingstreet's War '71

Saul Rubinek(1949-)
Club Land '01
Jerry and Tom '98

Sergio Rubini(1959-)
The Blonde '92
The Station '92

Alan Rudolph(1943-)
The Secret Lives of Dentists '02
Intimate Affairs '01
Trixie '00
Breakfast of Champions '98
Afterglow '97
Mrs. Parker and the Vicious Circle '94
Equinox '93
Mortal Thoughts '91
Love at Large '89
The Moderns '88
Made in Heaven '87
Trouble in Mind '86
Choose Me '84
Songwriter '84
Endangered Species '82
Roadie '80
Welcome to L.A. '77
Barn of the Naked Dead '73
Premonition '71

Wesley Ruggles(1889-1972)
Somewhere I'll Find You '42
Arizona '40
Too Many Husbands '40
College Humor '33
I'm No Angel '33
No Man of Her Own '32
Cimarron '31
Condemned '29
The Plastic Age '25
The Leopard Woman '20

Raul Ruiz(1941-)
Klimt '06
Comedy of Innocence '00
Time Regained '99
Shattered Image '98
Genealogies of a Crime '97
Three Lives and Only One Death '96
On Top of the Whale '82
The Hypothesis of the Stolen Painting '78

Richard Rush(1930-)
Color of Night '94
The Stunt Man '80
Freebie & the Bean '74
Getting Straight '70
Psych-Out '68
The Savage Seven '68
Hell's Angels on Wheels '67
Thunder Alley '67

Josef Rusnak
Art of War 2: The Betrayal '08
The Contractor '07
The Thirteenth Floor '99
No Strings Attached '98
Quiet Days in Hollywood '97

Chuck Russell(1952-)
The Scorpion King '02
Bless the Child '00
Eraser '96
The Mask '94
The Blob '88
A Nightmare on Elm Street 3: Dream Warriors '87

David O. Russell(1959-)
I Heart Huckabees '04
Three Kings '99
Flirting with Disaster '95
Spanking the Monkey '94

Jay Russell(1960-)
The Water Horse: Legend of the Deep '07
Ladder 49 '04
Tuck Everlasting '02
My Dog Skip '99
End of the Line '88

Ken Russell(1927-)
Tracked '98
Tales of Erotica '93
Lady Chatterley '92
Prisoner of Honor '91
Whore '91
Women & Men: Stories of Seduction '90
The Rainbow '89
Aria '88
The Lair of the White Worm '88
Salome's Last Dance '88
Gothic '87
Crimes of Passion '84
Altered States '80
Valentino '77
Lisztomania '75
Tommy '75
Mahler '74
Savage Messiah '72
The Boy Friend '71
The Devils '71
The Music Lovers '71
Women in Love '70
Dante's Inferno: Life of Dante Gabriel Rossetti '69
Billion Dollar Brain '67

William D. Russell(1908-68)
Best of the Badmen '50
The Green Promise '49

Anthony Russo
You, Me and Dupree '06
Welcome to Collinwood '02

Joe Russo
You, Me and Dupree '06
Welcome to Collinwood '02

John A. Russo(1939-)
Midnight 2: Sex, Death, and Videotape '93
Heartstopper '92
Midnight '81

Marti Rustam
James Dean: Live Fast, Die Young '97
Evils of the Night '85

Stefan Ruzowitzky(1961-)
The Counterfeiters '07
All the Queen's Men '02
Anatomy '00
The Inheritors '98

Frank Ryan(1947-)
Can't Help Singing '45
Call Out the Marines '42

James Ryan
Bachelor Party 2: The Last Temptation '08
The Young Girl and the Monsoon '99

Terence Ryan
The Brylcreem Boys '96
Going Home '86

Edgar Ryazanov(1927-)
A Forgotten Tune for the Flute '88
Private Life '82

Mark Rydell(1934-)
Even Money '06
James Dean '01
Crime of the Century '96
Intersection '93
For the Boys '91
The River '84
On Golden Pond '81
The Rose '79
Harry & Walter Go to New York '76
Cinderella Liberty '73
The Cowboys '72
The Reivers '69

Renny Rye(1947-)
Oliver Twist '00
Lipstick on Your Collar '94

Michael Rymer(1963-)
Queen of the Damned '02
Perfume '01
In Too Deep '99
Allie & Me '97
Angel Baby '95

Seung-wan Ryoo
The City of Violence '06
No Blood No Tears '02

Ira Sachs(1965-)
Married Life '07
Forty Shades of Blue '05
The Delta '97

William Sachs
The Last Hour '91
Hitz '89
Galaxina '80
Van Nuys Blvd. '79
Incredible Melting Man '77
South of Hell Mountain '70

Daniel Sackheim
The Glass House '01
Grand Avenue '96

James Sadwith(1952-)
Sinatra '92
Bluffing It '87

Henri Safran(1932-)
The Wild Duck '84
Prince and the Great Race '83
Norman Loves Rose '82

Boris Sagal(1917-81)
Masada '81
Angela '77
The Runaway Barge '75
Omega Man '71
Night Gallery '69
Girl Happy '65
Made in Paris '65
Guns of Diablo '64

Malcolm St. Clair(1897-1952)
Bullfighters '45
Two Weeks to Live '43
The Bashful Bachelor '42
The Grand Duchess and the Waiter '26
The Show Off '26
Are Parents People? '25

Gene Saks(1921-)
Bye Bye Birdie '95
Brighton Beach Memoirs '86
Mame '74
Last of the Red Hot Lovers '72
Cactus Flower '69
The Odd Couple '68
Barefoot in the Park '67

Luciano Salce
The Innocents Abroad '84
How I Learned to Love Women '66

Carlos Saldanha
Ice Age: Dawn of the Dinosaurs '09
Ice Age: The Meltdown '06

Richard Sale(1911-93)
Abandon Ship '57
The Girl Next Door '53
Let's Make It Legal '51
Ticket to Tomahawk '50
Spoilers of the North '47

Sidney Salkow(1909-2000)
The Last Man on Earth '64
Twice-Told Tales '63
Sitting Bull '54
City Without Men '43

Walter Salles(1956-)
Paris, je t'aime '06
The Motorcycle Diaries '04
Dark Water '02
Behind the Sun '01
Central Station '98
Foreign Land '95

Mikael Salomon(1945-)
Flirting with Forty '09
The Natalee Holloway Story '09
The Andromeda Strain '08
Beer for My Horses '08
The Company '07

Salem's Lot '04
Benedict Arnold: A Question of Honor '03
Band of Brothers '01
A Glimpse of Hell '01
Aftershock: Earthquake in New York '99
Hard Rain '97
A Far Off Place '93

Victor Salva(1958-)
Peaceful Warrior '06
Jeepers Creepers 2 '03
Jeepers Creepers '01
Rites of Passage '99
Powder '95
Nature of the Beast '94
Clownhouse '88

Pierre Salvadori(1964-)
Priceless '06
Apres-Vous '03
Les Apprentis '95

Gabriele Salvatores(1950-)
I'm Not Scared '03
Nirvana '97
Mediterraneo '91

Emmimo Salvi
Ali Baba and the Seven Saracens '64
Vulcan God of Fire '62

Salvatore Samperi(1944-)
Ernesto '79
Submission '77
Malicious '74

Keith Samples
Love Lies Bleeding '07
Single White Female 2: The Psycho '05
A Smile Like Yours '96

Barry Samson
Bloodfist 8: Hard Way Out '96
Yesterday's Target '96
The Ice Runner '93
Ice Pawn '92

Yann Samuell
My Sassy Girl '08
Love Me if You Dare '03

Rachel Samuels
Dark Streets '08
Robert Louis Stevenson's The Game of Death '99
Running Woman '98

Eduardo Sanchez
Seventh Moon '08
The Blair Witch Project '99

Christopher Sanders(1960-)
How to Train Your Dragon '10
Lilo & Stitch '02

Denis Sanders(1929-87)
Invasion of the Bee Girls '73
One Man's Way '63
Crime and Punishment, USA '59

Scott Sanders
Black Dynamite '09
Thick as Thieves '99

Helma Sanders-Brahms
Under the Pavement Lies the Strand '75
Earthquake in Chile '74

Helmer Sanders-Brahms
The Future of Emily '85
Germany, Pale Mother '80

Allan Sandler
Killings at Outpost Zeta '80
Laboratory '80

Jay Sandrich(1932-)
For Richer, for Poorer '92
Seems Like Old Times '80

Mark Sandrich(1900-45)
Here Come the Waves '45
So Proudly We Hail '43
Holiday Inn '42
Buck Benny Rides Again '40
Man About Town '39
Carefree '38
Shall We Dance '37
Follow the Fleet '36
A Woman Rebels '36
Top Hat '35
Cockeyed Cavaliers '34
The Gay Divorcee '34
Hips, Hips, Hooray '34
Aggie Appleby, Maker of Men '33
Melody Cruise '32

Arlene Sanford
Frank McKlusky, C.I. '02
I'll Be Home for Christmas '98
A Very Brady Sequel '96

Jonathan Sanger
Down Came a Blackbird '94
Code Name: Emerald '85

Jimmy Sangster(1924-)
Dynasty of Fear '72
Lust for a Vampire '71
The Horror of Frankenstein '70

Alfred Santell(1895-1981)
That Brennan Girl '46
The Hairy Ape '44
Jack London '44
Having a Wonderful Time '38
Having Wonderful Time '38
Breakfast for Two '37
Internes Can't Take Money '37
Winterset '36

Cirio H. Santiago(1936-)
Caged Heat 3000 '95
Caged Heat 2: Stripped of Freedom '94
Stranglehold '94
Fast Gun '93
One Man Army '93
Beyond the Call of Duty '92
Field of Fire '92
Firehawk '92
Raiders of the Sun '92
Dune Warriors '91
Eye of the Eagle 3 '91
The Expendables '89
Silk 2 '89
Future Hunters '88
Nam Angels '88
The Sisterhood '88
Demon of Paradise '87
Eye of the Eagle '87
Equalizer 2000 '86
Silk '86
Devastator '85
Naked Vengeance '85
Final Mission '84
Wheels of Fire '84
Stryker '83
Firecracker '81
Caged Fury '80
Death Force '78
The Vampire Hookers '78
Fighting Mad '77
The Muthers '76
She Devils in Chains '76
Cover Girl Models '75
TNT Jackson '75
Savage! '73

Joseph Santley(1889-1971)
Call of the Canyon '42
Down Mexico Way '41
Melody Ranch '40
Music in My Heart '40
Harmony Lane '35
The Cocoanuts '29

Damon Santostefano
Another Cinderella Story '08
Bring It On Again '03
Three to Tango '99
Severed Ties '92

Ken Sanzel
Lone Hero '02
Scarred City '98

David Saperstein(1937-)
Beyond the Stars '89
A Killing Affair '85

Deran Sarafian(1968-)
The Road Killers '95
Terminal Velocity '94
Gunmen '93
Back in the USSR '92
Death Warrant '90
To Die For '89
Interzone '88
Interzone '88
Alien Predators '80

Richard Sarafian(1935-)
Solar Crisis '92
Street Justice '89
Eye of the Tiger '86
Gangster Wars '81
Sunburn '79
The Arab Conspiracy '76
Man Who Loved Cat Dancing '73
Man in the Wilderness '71
Vanishing Point '71

Joseph Sargent(1925-)
Sweet Nothing in My Ear '08
Out of the Ashes '03
Bojangles '01
For Love or Country: The Arturo Sandoval Story '00
Dostoevsky's Crime and Punishment '99
A Lesson Before Dying '99
The Wall '99
Mandela and de Klerk '97
Miss Evers' Boys '97
Larry McMurtry's Streets of Laredo '95
Abraham '94
My Antonia '94
World War II: When Lions Roared '94
Sarah, Plain and Tall: Skylark '93
Miss Rose White '92
Never Forget '91
Caroline? '90
Ivory Hunters '90
Day One '89
The Incident '89
Jaws: The Revenge '87
Passion Flower '86
Memorial Day '83
Nightmares '83
Amber Waves '82
Tomorrow's Child '82
The Manions of America '81
Coast to Coast '80
Goldengirl '79
MacArthur '77
Hustling '75
The Taking of Pelham One Two Three '74
White Lightning '73
Man on a String '71
Maybe I'll Come Home in the Spring '71
Colossus: The Forbin Project '70
Maybe I'll Be Home in the Spring '70
Tribes '70

Marina Sargenti
Child of Darkness, Child of Light '91
Mirror, Mirror '90

Vic Sarin(1945-)
Partition '07
Love on the Side '04
Sea People '00
Hard to Forget '98
The Waiting Game '98
In His Father's Shoes '97
The Legend of Gator Face '96
Spenser: Pale Kings & Princes '94
Cold Comfort '90

Michael J. Sarna
Doomsdayer '01
Doomsdayer '99

Peter Sasdy(1935-)
The Lonely Lady '83
The Two Faces of Evil '82
Rude Awakening '81
Thirteenth Reunion '81
Visitor from the Grave '81
Welcome to Blood City '77
The Devil's Undead '75
I Don't Want to Be Born '75
King Arthur, the Young Warlord '75
Young Warlord '75
Doomwatch '72
Nothing But the Night '72
Hands of the Ripper '71
Taste the Blood of Dracula '70

Oley Sassone
Playback '95
Fast Getaway 2 '94
Relentless 4 '94
Future Shock '93
Bloodfist 3: Forced to Fight '92
Final Embrace '92

Sasuke Sasuga
Chain Gang Girls '08
Female Prisoner Sigma '06

Ron Satlof
Perry Mason: The Case of the Lost Love '87
Perry Mason Returns '85
Waikiki '80
Spiderman: The Deadly Dust '78

Hajime Sato(1929-95)
Body Snatcher from Hell '69
Terror Beneath the Sea '66

Junya Sato(1932-)
The Silk Road '92
The Go-Masters '82
Proof of the Man '77

Ernest G. Sauer
Broadcast Bombshells '95
Bikini Bistro '94
Beauty School '93

Charles Saunders(1904-97)
The Womaneater '59
Meet Mr. Callaghan '54
Love in Pawn '53

Carlos Saura(1932-)
Goya in Bordeaux '99
Tango '98
Outrage '93
Ay, Carmela! '90
El Amor Brujo '86
The Stilts '84
Carmen '83
Blood Wedding '81
Mama Turns a Hundred '79
Elisa, Vida Mia '77
Cria '76
Cria Cuervos '76
The Garden of Delights '70
The Hunt '65

Claude Sautet(1924-2000)
Nelly et Monsieur Arnaud '95
Un Coeur en Hiver '93
A Simple Story '79
Mado '76
Vincent, Francois, Paul and the Others '76
Cesar & Rosalie '72
The Things of Life '70
Classe Tous Risque '60

Philip Saville(1930-)
The Gospel of John '03
My Uncle Silas '01
Deacon Brodie '98
Metroland '97
The Buccaneers '95
Family Pictures '93
Max and Helen '90
Fellow Traveler '89
Wonderland '88
Mandela '87
Shadey '87
Those Glory, Glory Days '83
Count Dracula '77
Secrets '71

Victor Saville(1897-1979)
The Silver Chalice '54
Kim '50
Conspirator '49
Green Dolphin Street '47
Tonight and Every Night '45
Forever and a Day '43
Dark Journey '37
South Riding '37
Storm in a Teacup '37
It's Love Again '36
First a Girl '35
Evergreen '34
The Iron Duke '34

Nancy Savoca(1960-)
The 24 Hour Woman '99
If These Walls Could Talk '96
Household Saints '93
Dogfight '91
True Love '89

Geoffrey Sax
Alex Rider: Operation Stormbreaker '06
White Noise '05
Tipping the Velvet '02
Widows '02
Othello '01
Doctor Who '96
Ruby Jean and Joe '96
Broken Trust '95
Framed '93

John Sayles(1950-)
Honeydripper '07
Silver City '04
Casa de los Babys '03
Sunshine State '02
Limbo '99
Hombres Armados '97
Lone Star '95
The Secret of Roan Inish '94
Passion Fish '92
City of Hope '91
Eight Men Out '88
Matewan '87
The Brother from Another Planet '84
Lianna '83
Baby It's You '82
Return of the Secaucus 7 '80

Stefan Scaini
Anne of Green Gables: The Continuing Story '99
Double Play '96
Under the Piano '95

Joseph L. Scanlan
Spenser: A Savage Place '94
Spenser: The Judas Goat '94
The World's Oldest Living Bridesmaid '92
Nightstick '87
Spring Fever '81

Steven Schachter
The Deal '08
A Slight Case of Murder '99
The Con '98
Above Suspicion '95
Getting Up and Going Home '92
The Water Engine '92

Armand Schaefer(1898-1967)
The Miracle Rider '35
Law of the Wild '34
The Lost Jungle '34
Sixteen Fathoms Deep '34
Fighting Texans '33
Fighting with Kit Carson '33
Law and Lawless '33
Sagebrush Trail '33
Terror Trail '33
The Three Musketeers '33
Hurricane Express '32
Outlaw Justice '32
Lightning Warrior '31

George Schaefer(1920-97)
The Man Upstairs '93
Children in the Crossfire '84
Right of Way '84
Deadly Game '82
A Piano for Mrs. Cimino '82
Who'll Save Our Children? '82
The People vs. Jean Harris '81
Blind Ambition '79
Mayflower: The Pilgrims' Adventure '79
An Enemy of the People '77
Lost Legacy: A Girl Called Hatter Fox '77
The Last of Mrs. Lincoln '76
In This House of Brede '75
Once Upon a Scoundrel '73
Doctors' Wives '70
Generation '69
Pendulum '69
Elizabeth, the Queen '68
Soldier in Love '67
Barefoot in Athens '66
Lamp at Midnight '66
Holy Terror '65
Invincible Mr. Disraeli '63
The Tempest '63
Victoria Regina '61
A Doll's House '59

Eric Schaeffer(1962-)
Mind the Gap '04
Never Again '01
Wirey Spindell '99
Fall '97
If Lucy Fell '95
My Life's in Turnaround '94

Francis Schaeffer
Baby on Board '92
Rebel Storm '90
Headhunter '89
Wired to Kill '86

Franklin J. Schaffner(1920-89)
Welcome Home '89
Lionheart '87
Yes, Giorgio '82
Sphinx '81
The Boys from Brazil '78
Islands in the Stream '77
Our Town '77
Papillon '73
Nicholas and Alexandra '71
Patton '70
Planet of the Apes '68
The War Lord '65
The Best Man '64
The Stripper '63

Don Schain
Too Hot to Handle '76
Girls Are for Loving '73
The Abductors '72
Ginger '72
A Place Called Today '72

Jerry Schatzberg(1927-)
Blood Money: The Story of Clinton and Nadine '88
Reunion '88
Street Smart '87
Misunderstood '84
No Small Affair '84
Honeysuckle Rose '80
The Seduction of Joe Tynan '79
Scarecrow '73
Panic in Needle Park '71

Robert Scheerer(1929-)
Happily Ever After '82
How to Beat the High Cost of Living '80
Ants '77
The World's Greatest Athlete '73
Adam at 6 a.m. '70
Hans Brinker '69

Maximilian Schell(1930-)
The Pedestrian '73
First Love '70

Henning Schellerup
The Adventures of Nellie Bly '81
The Legend of Sleepy Hollow '79
Time Machine '78

Carl Schenkel(1948-2003)
Missing Pieces '00
Tarzan and the Lost City '98
In the Lake of the Woods '96
The Surgeon '94
Knight Moves '93
Silhouette '91
Silence Like Glass '90
The Mighty Quinn '89
Eye of the Demon '87
Out of Order '84
Strike Back '80

Richard Schenkman(1958-)
And Then Came Love '07
The Man from Earth '07
Went to Coney Island on a Mission from God.. Be Back by Five '98
The Pompatus of Love '95

Fred Schepisi(1939-)
Empire Falls '05
It Runs in the Family '03
Last Orders '01
Fierce Creatures '96
I.Q. '94
Six Degrees of Separation '93
Mr. Baseball '92
The Russia House '90
A Cry in the Dark '88
Roxanne '87
Plenty '85
Iceman '84
Barbarosa '82
The Chant of Jimmie Blacksmith '78
The Devil's Playground '76

Lone Scherfig(1959-)
An Education '09
Wilbur Wants to Kill Himself '02
Italian for Beginners '01

Victor Schertzinger(1890-1941)
Birth of the Blues '41
The Road to Zanzibar '41
Rhythm on the River '40
The Road to Singapore '40
Something to Sing About '36
One Night of Love '34
Uptown New York '32
What Happened to Rosa? '21
Clodhopper '17

Lawrence Schiller(1936-)
Master Spy: The Robert Hanssen Story '02
American Tragedy '00
Perfect Murder, Perfect Town '00
Double Jeopardy '92
Double Exposure: The Story of Margaret Bourke-White '89
The Executioner's Song '82
Marilyn: The Untold Story '80

Thomas Schlamme(1950-)
Kingfish: A Story of Huey P. Long '95
You So Crazy '94
So I Married an Axe Murderer '93
Crazy from the Heart '91
Miss Firecracker '89
Spalding Gray: Terrors of Pleasure '88

John Schlesinger(1926-2003)
The Next Best Thing '00
An Eye for an Eye '95
Cold Comfort Farm '94
The Innocent '93
A Question of Attribution '91
Pacific Heights '90
Madame Sousatzka '88
The Believers '87
The Falcon and the Snowman '85
An Englishman Abroad '83
Separate Tables '83
Honky Tonk Freeway '81
Yanks '79
Marathon Man '76
The Day of the Locust '75
Sunday, Bloody Sunday '71
Midnight Cowboy '69
Far from the Madding Crowd '67
Darling '65
Billy Liar '63
A Kind of Loving '62

Volker Schlondorff(1939-)
The Ninth Day '04
The Legend of Rita '99
Palmetto '98
The Ogre '96
Murder on the Bayou '91
Voyager '91
The Handmaid's Tale '90
Death of a Salesman '86
Swann in Love '84
The Tin Drum '79
Coup de Grace '78
Germany in Autumn '78
The Lost Honor of Katharina Blum '75
An Occurrence at Owl Creek Bridge/Coup de Grace '62

Rob Schmidt(1965-)
The Alphabet Killer '08
Masters of Horror: Right to Die '07
Wrong Turn '03
Crime and Punishment in Suburbia '00
Speed of Life '99

Wolfgang Schmidt
See Ray Dennis Steckler

David Schmoeller(1947-)
The Arrival '90
Curse 4: The Ultimate Sacrifice '90
Netherworld '90
Catacombs '89
Puppet Master '89
Crawlspace '86
The Seduction '82
Tourist Trap '79

Julian Schnabel(1951-)
The Diving Bell and the Butterfly '07
Before Night Falls '00
Basquiat '96

Paul Schneider(1973-)
Behind the Wall '08
Can of Worms '00
Honor Thy Father and Mother: The True Story of the Menendez Brothers '94
Roseanne: An Unauthorized Biography '94
Babycakes '89
Something Special '86

Robert Allen Schnitzer
Kandyland '87
The Premonition '75
Rebel '70

Ernest B. Schoedsack(1893-1979)
Mighty Joe Young '49
Dr. Cyclops '40
Last Days of Pompeii '35
King Kong '33
Son of Kong '33
The Most Dangerous Game '32
Chang: A Drama of the Wilderness '27

Pierre Schoendoerffer(1928-)
Le Crabe Tambour '77
The 317th Platoon '65

Paul Schrader(1946-)
Adam Resurrected '08
The Walker '07
Dominion: Prequel to the Exorcist '05
Auto Focus '02
Forever Mine '99
Affliction '97
Touch '96
Witch Hunt '94
Light Sleeper '92
The Comfort of Strangers '91
Patty Hearst '88
Light of Day '87
Mishima: A Life in Four Chapters '85
Cat People '82
American Gigolo '79
Hardcore '79
Blue Collar '78

Myrl A. Schreibman(1945-)
Liberty & Bash '90
Angel of H.E.A.T. '82

Barbet Schroeder(1941-)
Murder by Numbers '02
Our Lady of the Assassins '01
Desperate Measures '98
Before and After '95
Kiss of Death '94
Single White Female '92
Reversal of Fortune '90
Barfly '87
Tricheurs '84
Maitresse '76
The Valley Obscured by the Clouds '70
More '69

Michael Schroeder(1952-)
The Glass Cage '96
Cover Me '95
Cyborg 3: The Recycler '95
Cyborg 2 '93
Mortuary Academy '91
Relentless 2: Dead On '91
Damned River '89
Out of the Dark '88

Carl Schultz(1939-)
To Walk with Lions '99
Deadly Currents '93
Which Way Home '90
The Seventh Sign '88
Travelling North '87
Careful, He Might Hear You '84
Blue Fin '78

John Schultz
Aliens in the Attic '09
The Honeymooners '05
Like Mike '02
Drive Me Crazy '99
Bandwagon '95

Michael A. Schultz(1938-)
Woman, Thou Art Loosed '04
The Great American Sex Scandal '94
Livin' Large '91
For Us, the Living '88
Disorderlies '87
Timestalkers '87
Krush Groove '85
The Last Dragon '85
Carbon Copy '81
Scavenger Hunt '79
Sgt. Pepper's Lonely Hearts Club Band '78
Greased Lightning '77
Which Way Is Up? '77
Car Wash '76
Cooley High '75
Honeybaby '74

Joel Schumacher(1942-)
Twelve '10
Blood Creek '09
The Number 23 '07
The Phantom of the Opera '04
Veronica Guerin '03
Bad Company '02
Phone Booth '02
Tigerland '00
Flawless '99
8mm '98
Batman and Robin '97
A Time to Kill '96
Batman Forever '95
The Client '94
Falling Down '93
Dying Young '91
Flatliners '90
Cousins '89
The Lost Boys '87
St. Elmo's Fire '85
D.C. Cab '84
The Incredible Shrinking Woman '81
The Virginia Hill Story '76

Reinhold Schunzel(1886-1954)
Balalaika '39
Ice Follies of 1939 '39
Fortune's Fool '21

Harold Schuster(1902-86)
Courage of Black Beauty '57
Portland Expose '57
The Finger Man '55
Loophole '54
Kid Monk Baroni '52
So Dear to My Heart '49
The Tender Years '47
Breakfast in Hollywood '46
Marine Raiders '43
My Friend Flicka '43
On the Sunny Side '42
Dinner at the Ritz '37
Wings of the Morning '37

Douglas Schwartz
Baywatch the Movie: Forbidden Paradise '95
Thunder in Paradise 2 '94
Thunder in Paradise 3 '94
Thunder in Paradise '93
Peacekillers '71

Robert Schwentke
The Time Traveler's Wife '09
Flightplan '05

David Schwimmer(1966-)
Run, Fatboy, Run '07
Since You've Been Gone '97

Alberto Sciamma
Jericho Mansions '03
Killer Tongue '96

Ettore Scola(1931-)
The Family '87
Macaroni '85
La Nuit de Varennes '82
Le Bal '82
Passion of Love '82
A Special Day '77
We All Loved Each Other So Much '77
Down & Dirty '76

Martin Scorsese(1942-)
Shutter Island '09
Shine a Light '08
The Departed '06
The Aviator '04
Gangs of New York '02
Bringing Out the Dead '99
Kundun '97
Casino '95
The Age of Innocence '93
Cape Fear '91
Goodfellas '90
New York Stories '89
The Last Temptation of Christ '88
The Color of Money '86
After Hours '85
King of Comedy '82
Raging Bull '80
The Last Waltz '78
New York, New York '77
Taxi Driver '76
Alice Doesn't Live Here Anymore '74
Mean Streets '73
Boxcar Bertha '72
Who's That Knocking at My Door? '68

Campbell Scott(1962-)
Off the Map '03
Final '01
Hamlet '01
Big Night '95

George C. Scott(1927-99)
Descending Angel '90
Don't Look Back: The Story of Leroy "Satchel" Paige '81
Savage Is Loose '74
Rage '72
The Andersonville Trial '70

Michael Scott
Gradiva '06
Possessed '05
Heck's Way Home '95
Sharon's Secret '95
Dangerous Heart '93
Spirit Rider '93
Ladykiller '92
Lost in the Barrens '91

Oz Scott(1950-)
The Cheetah Girls '03
Spanish Judges '99
Bustin' Loose '81

Peter Graham Scott
Subterfuge '68
Let's Get Married '60

Ridley Scott(1939-)
Robin Hood '10
Body of Lies '08
American Gangster '07
A Good Year '06
Kingdom of Heaven '05
Matchstick Men '03
Black Hawk Down '01
Hannibal '01
Gladiator '00
RKO 281 '99
G.I. Jane '97
White Squall '96
1492: Conquest of Paradise '92
Thelma & Louise '91
Black Rain '89
Someone to Watch Over Me '87
Legend '86
Blade Runner '82
Alien '79
The Duellists '77

Sherman Scott
See Fred Olen Ray

T.J. Scott
Young Hercules '97
TC 2000 '93

Tony Scott(1944-)
The Taking of Pelham 123 '09
Deja Vu '06
Domino '05
Man on Fire '04
Spy Game '01
Enemy of the State '98
The Fan '96
Crimson Tide '95
True Romance '93
The Last Boy Scout '91
Days of Thunder '90
Revenge '90
Beverly Hills Cop 2 '87
Top Gun '86
The Hunger '83

James Seale
Juncture '07
Momentum '03
Scorcher '02
Asylum '97

Francis Searle(1909-2002)
Profile '54
Someone at the Door '50
Things Happen at Night '48
A Girl in a Million '46

Fred F. Sears(1913-57)
The Giant Claw '57
Earth vs. the Flying Saucers '56
Teenage Crime Wave '55
Ambush at Tomahawk Gap '53
Bonanza Town '51

George Seaton(1911-79)
Showdown '73
Airport '70
36 Hours '64
The Counterfeit Traitor '62
Teacher's Pet '58
Country Girl '54
The Big Lift '50
Miracle on 34th Street '47

Beverly Sebastian
Running Cool '93
The American Angels: Baptism of Blood '89
Gator Bait 2: Cajun Justice '88
Delta Fox '77
Gator Bait '73

Ferd Sebastian
Running Cool '93
The American Angels: Baptism of Blood '89
Gator Bait 2: Cajun Justice '88
Rocktober Blood '85
On the Air Live with Captain Midnight '79
Delta Fox '77
Flash & Firecat '75
Gator Bait '73
Hitchhikers '72

Mike Sedan
Naked Wishes '00
Lap Dancing '95
Married People, Single Sex 2: For Better or Worse '94
Night Fire '94
Married People, Single Sex '93

Edward Sedgwick(1892-1953)
Ma and Pa Kettle Back On the Farm '51
A Southern Yankee '48
Air Raid Wardens '43
The Gladiator '38
Fit for a King '37
Pick a Star '37
Riding on Air '37
What! No Beer? '33
Speak Easily '32
Maker of Men '31
Parlor, Bedroom and Bath '31
Doughboys '30
Free and Easy '30
Spite Marriage '29
The Cameraman '28
Spring Fever '27
The Phantom of the Opera '25

Paul Seed(1947-)
Strange Relations '02
Dr. Bell and Mr. Doyle: The Dark Beginnings of Sherlock Holmes '00
Every Woman Knows a Secret '99
Heat of the Sun '99
A Rather English Marriage '98
The Affair '95
To Play the King '93
Dead Ahead: The Exxon Valdez Disaster '92
House of Cards '90

Charles Seeling
Wolfheart's Revenge '25
Rounding Up the Law '22

Alex Segal(1915-77)
The Story of David '76
My Father's House '75

Peter Segal(1962-)
Get Smart '08
The Longest Yard '05
50 First Dates '04
Anger Management '03
Nutty Professor 2: The Klumps '00
My Fellow Americans '96
Tommy Boy '95
Naked Gun 33 1/3: The Final Insult '94

Stu Segall
Illegal in Blue '95
Cassie '83
Drive-In Massacre '74

Peter Sehr(1951-)
Love the Hard Way '01
Obsession '97
Kaspar Hauser '93

Arthur Allan Seidelman
The Sisters '05
Puerto Vallarta Squeeze '04
By Dawn's Early Light '00
The Runaway '00
Sex & Mrs. X '00
Grace & Glorie '98
The Summer of Ben Tyler '96
Harvest of Fire '95
Trapped in Space '94
Dying to Remember '93
Rescue Me '93
Body Language '92
The Kid Who Loved Christmas '90
False Witness '89
A Friendship in Vienna '88
The Caller '87
Glory Years '87
Poker Alice '87
Echoes '83
Children of Rage '75
Hercules in New York '70

Susan Seidelman(1952-)
The Boynton Beach Club '05
Power and Beauty '02
Gaudi Afternoon '01
A Cooler Climate '99
Tales of Erotica '93
Cookie '89
She-Devil '89
Making Mr. Right '86
Desperately Seeking Susan '85
Smithereens '82

Joseph Seiden(1892-1974)
God, Man and Devil '49
Eli Eli '40
Paradise in Harlem '40

Lewis Seiler(1890-1964)
The Winning Team '52
Doll Face '46
If I'm Lucky '46
Something for the Boys '44
Guadalcanal Diary '43
Pittsburgh '42
Crime School '38
Charlie Chan in Paris '35
Great K & A Train Robbery '26

William A. Seiter(1890-1964)
Make Haste to Live '54
Borderline '50
One Touch of Venus '48
Up in Central Park '48
I'll Be Yours '47
Little Giant '46
It's a Pleasure '45
Four Jills in a Jeep '44
Destroyer '43
Lady Takes a Chance '43
Broadway '42
You Were Never Lovelier '42
Nice Girl? '41
It's a Date '40
Allegheny Uprising '39
Susannah of the Mounties '39
Room Service '38
Thanks for Everything '38
Dimples '36
If You Could Only Cook '36
The Moon's Our Home '36
Stowaway '36
In Person '35
Roberta '35
Rafter Romance '34
Sing and Like It '34
Diplomaniacs '33
Sons of the Desert '33
Hot Saturday '32
Way Back Home '32
Big Business Girl '31
The Cheerful Fraud '27
Skinner's Dress Suit '26
The Mad Whirl '25
The White Sin '24
Little Church Around the Corner '23

George B. Seitz(1888-1944)
Andy Hardy's Double Life '42
Andy Hardy's Private Secretary '41
Life Begins for Andy Hardy '41
Andy Hardy Meets Debutante '40
Kit Carson '40
Love Finds Andy Hardy '38
The Last of the Mohicans '36
Treason '33
Drums of Jeopardy '31
Danger Lights '30
The Ice Flood '26
The Vanishing American '25

Steve Sekely(1899-1979)
Day of the Triffids '63
The Scar '48
Blonde Savage '47
Lady in the Death House '44
Waterfront '44
Behind Prison Walls '43
Revenge of the Zombies '43

Andrzej Sekula(1954-)
The Pleasure Drivers '05
Cube 2: Hypercube '02
Voodoo Dawn '99

Lesley Selander(1900-79)
Arizona Bushwackers '67
The Texican '66
Shotgun '55
Dragonfly Squadron '54
Fighter Attack '53
Flat Top '52
Flight to Mars '52
Gunplay '51
Rider from Tucson '50
Riders of the Range '50
Storm over Wyoming '50
Mysterious Desperado '49
Panhandle '48
The Red Stallion '47
Robin Hood of Texas '47
The Vampire's Ghost '45
Call of the Rockies '44
Border Patrol '43
Buckskin Frontier '43
Colt Comrades '43
Hopalong Cassidy: Riders of the Deadline '43
Lost Canyon '43
Doomed Caravan '41
Riders of the Timberline '41
The Roundup '41
Knights of the Range '40
The Light of Western Stars '40
Santa Fe Marshal '40
Hopalong Cassidy: Renegade Trail '39
Renegade Trail '39
The Frontiersmen '38
The Mysterious Rider '38
Sandflow '37

Henry Selick(1952-)
Coraline '09
Monkeybone '01
James and the Giant Peach '96
The Nightmare Before Christmas '93

Jack M. Sell(1954-)
The Psychotronic Man '91
Deadly Spygames '89

Michael D. Sellers
Eye of the Dolphin '06
Vlad '03

Charles E. Sellier
The Annihilators '85
Snowballing '85
Silent Night, Deadly Night '84

David Selman
Prescott Kid '36
Fighting Shadows '35
Justice of the Range '35
The Revenge Rider '35
Riding Wild '35
Square Shooter '35

Aaron Seltzer
Disaster Movie '08
Meet the Spartans '08
Date Movie '06

David Seltzer(1940-)
Nobody's Baby '01
Shining Through '92
Punchline '88
Lucas '86

Edgar Selwyn(1875-1944)
Skyscraper Souls '32
The Sin of Madelon Claudet '31

Ousmane Sembene
Moolaade '04
Xala '75
Mandabi '68
Black Girl '66
Borom Sarret '66

David Semel
Lone Star State of Mind '02
Campfire Tales '98

Dean Semler(1943-)
The Patriot '99
Firestorm '97

Dominic Sena(1949-)
Whiteout '09
Swordfish '01
Gone in 60 Seconds '00
Kalifornia '93

Ralph Senensky(1923-)
Death Cruise '74
A Dream for Christmas '73

Ron Senkowski
Wicked Ways '99
Let's Kill All the Lawyers '93

Lorraine Senna
Paradise, Texas '05
Sweetwater: A True Rock Story '99

Mack Sennett(1880-1960)
Mickey '17
Tillie's Punctured Romance '14

Mario Sequi(1910-)
The Cobra '68
Tramplers '66

Yahoo Serious(1954-)
Mr. Accident '99
Reckless Kelly '93
Young Einstein '89

Coline Serreau(1947-)
Chaos '01
Mama, There's a Man in Your Bed '89
Three Men and a Cradle '85

Alex Sessa(1928-98)
Stormquest '87
Amazons '86

Javier Seto
Macabre '69
The Castilian '63

Vernon Sewell(1903-2001)
Ghost Keeper '80
Horrors of Burke & Hare '71
The Crimson Cult '68
Blood Beast Terror '67
Missiles from Hell '58
Rogue's Yarn '56
Where There's a Will '55
Radio Cab Murder '54
Terror Ship '54
Ghost Ship '53
Uneasy Terms '48
Ghosts of Berkeley Square '47
The World Owes Me a Living '47
Frenzy '46

Nicholas Sgarro
Fortune Dane '86
The Happy Hooker '75

Tom Shadyac(1960-)
Evan Almighty '07
Bruce Almighty '03
Dragonfly '02
Patch Adams '98
Liar Liar '97
The Nutty Professor '96
Ace Ventura: Pet Detective '93

Krishna Shah(1938-)
Hard Rock Zombies '85
Deadly Thief '78
The River Niger '76
Rivals '72

Steven Shainberg(1963-)
Fur: An Imaginary Portrait of Diane Arbus '06
Secretary '02
Hit Me '96

Adam Shankman(1964-)
Bedtime Stories '08
Hairspray '07
Cheaper by the Dozen 2 '05
The Pacifier '05
Bringing Down the House '03
A Walk to Remember '02
The Wedding Planner '01

John Patrick Shanley(1950-)
Doubt '08
Joe Versus the Volcano '90

Alan Shapiro(1957-)
Flipper '96
The Crush '93
Tiger Town '83

Ken Shapiro(1943-)
Modern Problems '81
The Groove Tube '72

Paul Shapiro(1955-)
Plain Truth '04
Murder at Devil's Glen '99
Dead Husbands '98
The Invaders '95
Heads '93
The Lotus Eaters '93
Kurt Vonnegut's Monkey House '91
Miracle at Moreaux '86
Hockey Night '84

Jim Sharman(1945-)
Shock Treatment '81
The Rocky Horror Picture Show '75

Don Sharp(1922-)
Tears in the Rain '88
Hold the Dream '86
A Woman of Substance '84
What Waits Below '83
Guardian of the Abyss '82
Bear Island '80
The Thirty-Nine Steps '79
The Four Feathers '78
Hennessy '75
Dark Places '73
Psychomania '73
Those Fantastic Flying Fools '67
Brides of Fu Manchu '66
Rasputin the Mad Monk '66
The Devil-Ship Pirates '64
Kiss of the Vampire '62

Ian Sharp(1946-)
Tess of the D'Urbervilles '98
R.P.M. '97
Codename Kyril '91
Secret Weapon '90
Robin Hood... The Legend: Robin Hood and the Sorcerer '83
The Final Option '82

Ben Sharpsteen(1895-1980)
Dumbo '41
Fantasia '40
Pinocchio '40

William Shatner(1931-)
Groom Lake '02
TekWar '94
Star Trek 5: The Final Frontier '89

Alfred Shaughnessy(1916-2005)
Cat Girl '57
Suspended Alibi '56

Melville Shavelson(1917-2007)
Ike '79
Legend of Valentino '75
Yours, Mine & Ours '68
Cast a Giant Shadow '66
A New Kind of Love '63
It Started in Naples '60
The Five Pennies '59
Houseboat '58
The Seven Little Foys '55

Helen Shaver(1952-)
Due East '02
Summer's End '99

Larry Shaw
Jackie, Ethel, Joan: The Kennedy Women '01
Don't Look Down '98

Robert Shaye(1939-)
The Last Mimzy '07
Book of Love '91

Linda Shayne
The Undercover Kid '95
Purple People Eater '88

Bashar Shbib
Lana in Love '92
Julia Has Two Lovers '91

Andrew Shea
Forfeit '07
Santa Fe '97

Katt Shea(1957-)
The Rage: Carrie 2 '99
Last Exit to Earth '96
Poison Ivy '92
Streets '90
Stripped to Kill II: Live Girls '89
Dance of the Damned '88
Stripped to Kill '87

Barry Shear(1923-79)
The Crash of Flight 401 '78
Strike Force '75
The Deadly Trackers '73
Across 110th Street '72
The Todd Killings '71
Wild in the Streets '68

Donald Shebib(1938-)
The Ascent '94
The Pathfinder '94
The Little Kidnappers '90
The Climb '87
Heartaches '82
Fish Hawk '79
Men of Steel '77
Second Wind '76

Todd Sheets
Goblin '93
Prehistoric Bimbos in Armageddon City '93

Riki Shelach
Mercenary Fighters '88
The Last Winter '84

Forrest Sheldon
Between Fighting Men '32
Dynamite Ranch '32
Hell Fire Austin '32

Adrienne Shelly(1966-2006)
Waitress '07
I'll Take You There '99
Sudden Manhattan '96

Lynn Shelton
Humpday '09
My Effortless Brilliance '08

Ron Shelton(1945-)
Dark Blue '03
Hollywood Homicide '03
Play It to the Bone '99
Tin Cup '96
Cobb '94
White Men Can't Jump '92
Blaze '89
Bull Durham '88

Richard Shepard
The Hunting Party '07
The Matador '06
Mexico City '00
Oxygen '99
Mercy '96
The Linguini Incident '92
Cool Blue '88

Sam Shepard(1943-)
Silent Tongue '92
Far North '88

John Shepphird
Chupacabra Terror '05
The Santa Trap '02
Snowboard Academy '96
Teenage Bonnie & Klepto Clyde '93

Adrian Shergold
Persuasion '07
Heat of the Sun '99
Stalag Luft '93
Christabel '89

Jim Sheridan(1949-)
Brothers '09
Get Rich or Die Tryin' '05
In America '02
The Boxer '97
In the Name of the Father '93
The Field '90
My Left Foot '89

Kristen Sheridan
August Rush '07
Disco Pigs '01

Edwin Sherin(1930-)
The Father Clements Story '87
My Old Man's Place '71
Valdez Is Coming '71

Gary Sherman(1945-)
Murderous Vision '91
After the Shock '90
Lisa '90
Poltergeist 3 '88
Wanted Dead or Alive '86
Mysterious Two '82
Vice Squad '82
Dead and Buried '81
Raw Meat '72

George Sherman(1908-91)
Big Jake '71
Panic Button '62
Treasure of Pancho Villa '55
War Arrow '53
Against All Flags '52

Tomahawk '51
Comanche Territory '50
Border River '47
The Last of the Redmen '47
The Sombrero Kid '42
Sundown Fury '42
X Marks the Spot '42
Covered Wagon Days '40
Rocky Mountain Rangers '40
Cowboys from Texas '39
Frontier Horizon '39
The Kansas Terrors '39
South of the Border '39
Three Texas Steers '39
Wyoming Outlaw '39
Heroes of the Hills '38
Outlaws of Sonora '38
Overland Stage Raiders '38
Pals of the Saddle '38
Purple Vigilantes '38
Santa Fe Stampede '38
Wild Horse Rodeo '37

Jon Sherman
I'm with Lucy '02
Breathing Room '96

Lowell Sherman(1885-1934)
Morning Glory '33
She Done Him Wrong '33
False Faces '32
Three Broadway Girls '32
Bachelor Apartment '31
The Royal Bed '31
A Lady of Chance '28

Vincent Sherman(1906-2006)
Bogie: The Last Hero '80
Ice Palace '60
The Young Philadelphians '59
The Garment Jungle '57
Affair in Trinidad '52
Lone Star '52
Goodbye My Fancy '51
The Damned Don't Cry '50
Harriet Craig '50
Adventures of Don Juan '49
Nora Prentiss '47
Mr. Skeffington '44
All Through the Night '42
Underground '41
Crime School '38

John Sherwood(1959-)
The Monolith Monsters '57
The Creature Walks among Us '56

Dominic Shiach
Dark Side '02
Blackheart '98

Brent Shields(1963-)
Brush with Fate '03
Cupid & Cate '00
Durango '99

Frank Shields(1908-75)
Project: Alien '89
Savage Attraction '83

Barry Shils
Wigstock: The Movie '95
Motorama '91

Hyung Rae Shim
Dragon Wars '07
Reptilian '99

Koji Shima(1901-86)
Warning from Space '56
Golden Demon '53

Takashi Shimizu(1972-)
The Grudge 2 '06
Reincarnation '05
The Grudge '04
Marebito '04
Ju-On: The Grudge '03
Ju-On 2 '00

Kaneto Shindo(1912-)
Onibaba '64
The Island '61

Masahiro Shinoda(1931-)
Gonza the Spearman '86
MacArthur's Children '85

Double Suicide '69

Akihiko Shiota
Dororo '07
Moonlight Whispers '99

Kohi Shiraishi
Carved '07
Ju-Rei: The Uncanny '04

Jack Sholder(1945-)
Arachnid '01
Wishmaster 2: Evil Never Dies '98
Sketch Artist 2: Hands That See '94
12:01 '93
By Dawn's Early Light '89
Renegades '89
The Hidden '87
A Nightmare on Elm Street 2: Freddy's Revenge '85
Alone in the Dark '82

Lee Sholem(1913-2000)
Escape from Planet Earth '67
Hell Ship Mutiny '57
Ma and Pa Kettle at Waikiki '55
Tobor the Great '54
The Redhead from Wyoming '53
Superman & the Mole Men '51
Tarzan and the Slave Girl '50
Tarzan's Magic Fountain '48

Lindsay Shonteff(1935-2006)
The Killing Edge '86
Number 1 of the Secret Service '77
Big Zapper '73
Fast Kill '73
He Kills Night After Night After Night '69
Night Slasher '69
Second Best Secret Agent in the Whole Wide World '65
Devil Doll '64

Sig Shore(1919-2006)
The Survivalist '87
Sudden Death '85
The Act '82
Shining Star '75

Lynn Shores(1893-1949)
Charlie Chan at the Wax Museum '40
Here's Flash Casey '38
A Million to One '37
The Shadow Strikes '37
The Glory Trail '36

Cate Shortland
The Silence '06
Somersault '04

Mina Shum
Long Life, Happiness and Prosperity '02
Double Happiness '94

M. Night Shyamalan(1970-)
The Last Airbender '10
The Happening '08
Lady in the Water '06
The Village '04
Signs '02
Unbreakable '00
The Sixth Sense '99
Wide Awake '97

Charles Shyer(1941-)
Alfie '04
The Affair of the Necklace '01
Father of the Bride Part 2 '95
I Love Trouble '94
Father of the Bride '91
Baby Boom '87
Irreconcilable Differences '84

Melville Shyer(1895-1968)
Mad Youth '40
Sucker Money '34

James Shyman
Slashdance '89
Hollywood's New Blood '88

Alex Sichel(1963-)
If These Walls Could Talk 2 '00
All Over Me '96

Andy Sidaris(1933-)
Return to Savage Beach '97
Day of the Warrior '96
The Dallas Connection '94
Fit to Kill '93
Hard Hunted '92
Do or Die '91
Guns '90
Picasso Trigger '89
Savage Beach '89
Hard Ticket to Hawaii '87
Malibu Express '85
Seven '79
Stacey '73

George Sidney(1916-2002)
Half a Sixpence '67
Bye, Bye, Birdie '63
Viva Las Vegas '63
Pal Joey '57
The Eddy Duchin Story '56
Jupiter's Darling '55
Kiss Me Kate '53
Young Bess '53
Scaramouche '52
Show Boat '51
Annie Get Your Gun '50
Key to the City '50
The Three Musketeers '48
Cass Timberlane '47
The Harvey Girls '46
Holiday in Mexico '46
Anchors Aweigh '45
Bathing Beauty '44
Thousands Cheer '43

Scott Sidney(1872-1928)
The Nervous Wreck '26
Charley's Aunt '25
Tarzan of the Apes '17

Marcos Siega(1969-)
Chaos Theory '08
Pretty Persuasion '05
Underclassman '05

David Siegel
Bee Season '05
The Deep End '01
Suture '93

Donald Siegel(1912-91)
Jinxed '82
Rough Cut '80
Escape from Alcatraz '79
Telefon '77
The Shootist '76
The Black Windmill '74
Charley Varrick '73
Dirty Harry '71
The Beguiled '70
Two Mules for Sister Sara '70
Death of a Gunfighter '69
Coogan's Bluff '68
Madigan '68
The Killers '64
Hell Is for Heroes '62
Flaming Star '60
The Lineup '58
Invasion of the Body Snatchers '56
An Annapolis Story '55
Private Hell 36 '54
Riot in Cell Block 11 '54
Duel at Silver Creek '52
Big Steal '49

Robert Siegel
Big Fan '09
Swimming '00
The Line '80

Robert Sigl(1964-)
School's Out '99
Tales from a Parallel Universe: Giga Shadow '97

James Signorelli
Hotel Room '93

Elvira, Mistress of the Dark '88
Easy Money '83

Dai Sijie(1954-)
Balzac and the Little Chinese Seamstress '02
China, My Sorrow '89

Joel Silberg(1927-)
Lambada '89
Catch the Heat '87
Bad Guys '86
Rappin' '85
Breakin' '84
Secret of Yolanda '82
Kuni Lemel in Tel Aviv '77

Brad Silberling(1962-)
Land of the Lost '09
10 Items or Less '06
Lemony Snicket's A Series of Unfortunate Events '04
Moonlight Mile '02
City of Angels '98
Casper '95

Joan Micklin Silver(1935-)
Charms for the Easy Life '02
Invisible Child '99
In the Presence of Mine Enemies '97
Big Girls Don't Cry... They Get Even '92
A Private Matter '92
Prison Stories: Women on the Inside '91
Loverboy '89
Crossing Delancey '88
Finnegan Begin Again '84
Chilly Scenes of Winter '79
Between the Lines '77
Hester Street '75

Marisa Silver(1960-)
Indecency '92
He Said, She Said '91
Vital Signs '90
Permanent Record '88
Old Enough '84

Scott Silver
The Mod Squad '99
johns '96

Elliot Silverstein(1937-)
Flashfire '94
Jailbait: Betrayed By Innocence '86
The Car '77
A Man Called Horse '70
Cat Ballou '65

Lloyd A. Simandl(1948-)
Crackerjack 3 '00
Escape Velocity '99
Dangerous Prey '95
Chained Heat 2 '92
Ultimate Desires '91
Beyond the Silhouette '90
Possession: Until Death Do You Part '90
Maniac Warriors '88
Ladies of the Lotus '87
Autumn Born '79

Lawrence L. Simeone(1954-2002)
Blindfold: Acts of Obsession '94
Eyes of the Beholder '92
Cop-Out '91
Presumed Guilty '91

Anthony Simmons
Little Sweetheart '90
The Optimists '73

Adam Simon(1962-)
Carnosaur '93
Body Chemistry 2: Voice of a Stranger '91
Brain Dead '89

J(uan) Piquer Simon(1934-)
Cthulhu Mansion '91
Endless Descent '90
Slugs '87

Pieces '83
Supersonic Man '78
Where Time Began '77

Rainer Simon(1941-)
The Woman and the Stranger '84
Jadup and Boel '81

Roger L. Simon
Lies and Whispers '98
My Man Adam '86

S. Sylvan Simon(1910-51)
Lust for Gold '49
Her Husband's Affairs '47
Abbott and Costello in Hollywood '45
Son of Lassie '45
Whistling in Brooklyn '43
Grand Central Murder '42
Rio Rita '42
Whistling in Dixie '42
Whistling in the Dark '41

Yves Simoneau(1955-)
America '09
Bury My Heart at Wounded Knee '07
44 Minutes: The North Hollywood Shootout '03
Napoleon '03
Ignition '01
Nuremberg '00
Free Money '99
36 Hours to Die '99
Larry McMurtry's Dead Man's Walk '96
Amelia Earhart: The Final Flight '94
Mother's Boys '94
Till Death Do Us Part '92
Memphis '91
Perfectly Normal '91
Pouvoir Intime '87

Jane Simpson
Little Witches '96
Number One Fan '94

John Simpson
Amusement '08
Freeze Frame '04

Megan Simpson
Dating the Enemy '95
Alex '92

Michael A. Simpson
Fast Food '89
Funland '89
Sleepaway Camp 3: Teenage Wasteland '89
Sleepaway Camp 2: Unhappy Campers '88
Impure Thoughts '86
Cyrano de Bergerac '85

Andrew Sinclair(1935-)
Tuxedo Warrior '82
Blue Blood '73
Under Milk Wood '73

Gerald Seth Sindell(1944-)
H.O.T.S. '79
Teenager '74

Alexander Singer(1932-)
Pearl '78
Bunco '77
Captain Apache '71
Love Has Many Faces '65

Bryan Singer(1966-)
Valkyrie '08
Superman Returns '06
X2: X-Men United '03
X-Men '00
Apt Pupil '97
The Usual Suspects '95
Public Access '93

Tarsem Singh
See Tarsem

John Singleton(1968-)
Four Brothers '05
2 Fast 2 Furious '03
Baby Boy '01

Shaft '00
Rosewood '96
Higher Learning '94
Poetic Justice '93
Boyz N the Hood '91

Gary Sinise(1955-)
Of Mice and Men '92
Miles from Home '88

Bruce Sinofsky(1956-)
Metallica: Some Kind of Monster '04
Brother's Keeper '92

Gary Sinyor(1962-)
In Your Dreams '07
Bob the Butler '05
The Bachelor '99
Stiff Upper Lips '96
Solitaire for 2 '94
Leon the Pig Farmer '93

Robert Siodmak(1900-73)
The Rough and the Smooth '59
Crimson Pirate '52
Criss Cross '48
Dark Mirror '46
The Killers '46
The Spiral Staircase '46
The Strange Affair of Uncle Harry '45
Cobra Woman '44
Phantom Lady '44
Son of Dracula '43

Douglas Sirk(1900-87)
Imitation of Life '59
A Time to Love & a Time to Die '58
Battle Hymn '57
Tarnished Angels '57
Written on the Wind '56
All That Heaven Allows '55
Magnificent Obsession '54
All I Desire '53
First Legion '51
Shockproof '49
Lured '47
A Scandal in Paris '46

Rob Sitch(1962-)
The Dish '00
The Castle '97

Santosh Sivan
Before the Rains '07
The Terrorist '98

Alf Sjoberg(1903-80)
Miss Julie '50
Torment '44

John Sjogren(1966-)
Choke '00
Red Line '96
The Mosaic Project '95
Money to Burn '94

Victor Sjostrom(1879-1960)
Under the Red Robe '36
The Wind '28
He Who Gets Slapped '24
The Phantom Chariot '20
The Outlaw and His Wife '17

Erik Skjoldbjaerg
Prozac Nation '01
Insomnia '97

Keri Skogland
Fifty Dead Men Walking '08
The Stone Angel '07
Banshee '06
Liberty Stands Still '02
Zebra Lounge '01
The Courage to Love '00
Children of the Corn 666: Isaac's Return '99
White Lies '98

Jerzy Skolimowski(1938-)
Torrents of Spring '90
The Lightship '86
Success Is the Best Revenge '84
Moonlighting '82
Hands Up '81

The Shout '78
King, Queen, Knave '72
Deep End '70

David Slade
The Twilight Saga: Eclipse '10
30 Days of Night '07
Hard Candy '06

Bohdan Slama(1967-)
The Country Teacher '08
Something Like Happiness '05

Bob Slatzer(1927-2005)
Big Foot '72
Hellcats '68

John Sledge
The Invisible Avenger '58
New Orleans After Dark '58

Brian Sloan
I Think I Do '97
Boys Life '94

Holly Goldberg Sloan(1958-)
The Secret Life of Girls '99
The Big Green '95

Paul Sloane(1893-1963)
The Sun Sets at Dawn '50
Consolation Marriage '31
Half-Shot at Sunrise '30
Made for Love '26
The Coming of Amos '25

Rick Sloane(1961-)
Good Girls Don't '95
Mind, Body & Soul '92
Vice Academy 3 '91
Vice Academy 2 '90
Marked for Murder '89
Vice Academy '88
Hobgoblins '87
Visitants '87
The Movie House Massacre '78

Edward Sloman(1886-1972)
The Jury's Secret '38
Gun Smoke '31
Lost Zeppelin '29
Up the Ladder '25

Karl Slovin
On Edge '03
Sex and the Other Man '95

George Sluizer(1932-)
Crimetime '96
Utz '93
The Vanishing '93
The Vanishing '88
Red Desert Penitentiary '83
Twice a Woman '79

Ralph Smart(1908-2001)
Robin Hood: The Movie '55
Curtain Up '53

Robert J. Smawley
American Eagle '90
River of Diamonds '90
Murphy's Fault '88

Jack Smight(1926-2003)
Intimate Power '89
Number One with a Bullet '87
Holocaust Survivors... Remembrance of Love '83
Loving Couples '80
Fast Break '79
Roll of Thunder, Hear My Cry '78
Airport '77 '77
Damnation Alley '77
Midway '76
Airport '75 '75
The Illustrated Man '69
No Way to Treat a Lady '68
The Secret War of Harry Frigg '68
Harper '66
Kaleidoscope '66

Brian J. Smith
Tarzan 2 '05
Body of Influence 2 '96

Bruce Smith
The Proud Family Movie '05
Bebe's Kids '92

Charles Martin Smith(1953-)
Frederick Forsyth's Icon '05
The Snow Walker '03
Air Bud '97
Boris and Natasha: The Movie '92
Trick or Treat '86

Chris Smith(1970-)
Collapse '09
Severance '06
The Yes Men '03
American Movie '99

Cliff(ord) Smith(1894-1937)
Radio Patrol '37
The Phantom Bullet '26
The Fugitive: Taking of Luke McVane '15

John N. Smith(1943-)
A Cool, Dry Place '98
Dangerous Minds '95
Sugartime '95
The Boys of St. Vincent '93

Kevin Smith(1970-)
Zack and Miri Make a Porno '08
Clerks 2 '06
Jersey Girl '04
Jay and Silent Bob Strike Back '01
Dogma '99
Chasing Amy '97
Mallrats '95
Clerks '94

Mark Smith
Seance '06
Overnight '03

Mel Smith(1952-)
High Heels and Low Lifes '01
Bean '97
Radioland Murders '94
The Tall Guy '89

Noel Mason Smith(1895-1955)
Cattle Town '52
Gang Busters '42
Burma Convoy '41

Peter Smith
The Alchemists '99
No Surrender '86

Richard Curson Smith
Pinochet's Last Stand '06
Agatha Christie: A Life in Pictures '04

Roy Allen Smith(1954-)
The Land Before Time 4: Journey Through the Mists '96
The Land Before Time 3: The Time of the Great Giving '95
The Land Before Time 2: The Great Valley Adventure '94

Alan Smithee
Sub Down '97
Hellraiser 4: Bloodline '95
Raging Angels '95
Gypsy Angels '94
The O.J. Simpson Story '94
Call of the Wild '93
Fatal Charm '92
Solar Crisis '92
Bloodsucking Pharoahs of Pittsburgh '90
The Shrimp on the Barbie '90
Ghost Fever '87
I Love N.Y. '87
Let's Get Harry '87

Morgan Stewart's Coming Home '87
Appointment with Fear '85
Stitches '85
City in Fear '80
Iron Cowboy '68

Stephen Smoke
Street Crimes '92
Final Impact '91

Skott Snider
Midnight Blue '96
Miracle Beach '92

Zack Snyder(1966-)
Watchmen '09
300 '07
Dawn of the Dead '04

Michele (Michael) Soavi(1957-)
The Church '98
Cemetery Man '95
The Devil's Daughter '91
Stagefright '87

Mark Sobel(1956-)
Storm Chasers: Revenge of the Twister '98
Ordeal in the Arctic '93
Trial and Error '92
Sweet Revenge '87
Access Code '84

Steven Soderbergh(1963-)
The Girlfriend Experience '09
The Informant! '09
Che '08
Ocean's Thirteen '07
Bubble '06
The Good German '06
Eros '04
Ocean's Twelve '04
Full Frontal '02
Solaris '02
Ocean's Eleven '01
Erin Brockovich '00
Traffic '00
The Limey '99
Out of Sight '98
Schizopolis '97
Gray's Anatomy '96
The Underneath '95
Fallen Angels 2 '93
King of the Hill '93
Kafka '91
sex, lies and videotape '89

Iain Softley(1958-)
Inkheart '09
The Skeleton Key '05
K-PAX '01
The Wings of the Dove '97
Hackers '95
Backbeat '94

Alexander Sokurov(1951-)
Father and Son '03
Mother and Son '97

Russell Solberg
Raven '97
Forced to Kill '93
Payback '90

Silvio Soldini(1958-)
Days and Clouds '07
Agata and the Storm '04
Bread and Tulips '01

Alfred Sole(1943-)
Pandemonium '82
Tanya's Island '81
Alice Sweet Alice '76

Peter Sollett
Nick & Norah's Infinite Playlist '08
Raising Victor Vargas '03

Courtney Solomon(1971-)
An American Haunting '05
Dungeons and Dragons '00

Todd Solondz(1960-)
Life During Wartime '09
Palindromes '04

Storytelling '01
Happiness '98
Welcome to the Dollhouse '95
Fear, Anxiety and Depression '89

Ola Solum(1943-96)
The Polar Bear King '94
Turnaround '87

Stephen Sommers(1962-)
G.I. Joe: The Rise of Cobra '09
Van Helsing '04
The Mummy Returns '01
The Mummy '99
Deep Rising '98
Rudyard Kipling's The Jungle Book '94
The Adventures of Huck Finn '93
Catch Me... If You Can '89
Terror Eyes '87

Barry Sonnenfeld(1953-)
RV '06
Big Trouble '02
Men in Black 2 '02
Wild Wild West '99
Men in Black '97
Get Shorty '95
Addams Family Values '93
For Love or Money '93
The Addams Family '91

Lodovico Sorret
See Tom Noonan

Jim Sotos(1935-)
Hot Moves '84
Sweet 16 '81
Forced Entry '75

Kevin Spacey(1959-)
Beyond the Sea '04
Albino Alligator '96

Robert Sparr(1915-69)
More Dead Than Alive '68
A Swingin' Summer '65

Will Speck
The Switch '10
Blades of Glory '07

Greg Spence
The Prophecy 2: Ashtown '97
Children of the Corn 4: The Gathering '96

Richard Spence(1957-)
New World Disorder '99
Different for Girls '96
Blind Justice '94

Brenton Spencer
Never Cry Werewolf '08
Call of the Wild '04
The Club '94
Blown Away '93

Robert Spera
Bloody Murder 2 '03
Leprechaun 5: In the Hood '99
Stray Bullet '98
Witchcraft '88

Penelope Spheeris(1945-)
The Kid and I '05
Senseless '98
Black Sheep '96
The Little Rascals '94
The Beverly Hillbillies '93
Wayne's World '92
Prison Stories: Women on the Inside '91
Thunder & Mud '89
Decline of Western Civilization 2: The Metal Years '88
Dudes '87
Hollywood Vice Sqaud '86
The Boys Next Door '85
Suburbia '83
Decline of Western Civilization 1 '81

Bryan Spicer
Taken '02
For Richer or Poorer '97
McHale's Navy '97
Mighty Morphin Power Rangers: The Movie '95

Marcus Spiegel
Devil in the Flesh 2 '00
Eye of the Storm '98

Scott Spiegel(1957-)
From Dusk Till Dawn 2: Texas Blood Money '98
Intruder '88

Steven Spielberg(1947-)
Indiana Jones and the Kingdom of the Crystal Skull '08
Munich '05
War of the Worlds '05
The Terminal '04
Catch Me If You Can '02
Minority Report '02
A. I.: Artificial Intelligence '01
Saving Private Ryan '98
Amistad '97
The Lost World: Jurassic Park 2 '97
Jurassic Park '93
Schindler's List '93
Hook '91
Always '89
Indiana Jones and the Last Crusade '89
Empire of the Sun '87
Amazing Stories '85
The Color Purple '85
Indiana Jones and the Temple of Doom '84
Twilight Zone: The Movie '83
E.T.: The Extra-Terrestrial '82
Raiders of the Lost Ark '81
1941 '79
Close Encounters of the Third Kind '77
Jaws '75
The Sugarland Express '74
Columbo: Murder by the Book '71
Duel '71
Night Gallery '69

Michael Spierig
Daybreakers '09
Undead '05

Peter Spierig
Daybreakers '09
Undead '05

Bob Spiers
Chilly Dogs '01
Spice World: The Movie '97
That Darn Cat '96

Philip Spink
The Duke '99
Big and Hairy '98
Ronnie and Julie '97

Tony Spiridakis(1959-)
Tinseltown '97
The Last Word '95

Lev L. Spiro
The Wizards of Waverly Place: The Movie '09
Minutemen '08
Alien Avengers '96

Roger Spottiswoode(1945-)
The Children of Huang Shi '08
Noriega: God's Favorite '00
The 6th Day '00
Tomorrow Never Dies '97
Hiroshima '95
Mesmer '94
And the Band Played On '93
Stop! or My Mom Will Shoot '92
Air America '90
Third Degree Burn '89
Turner and Hooch '89
Shoot to Kill '88
The Last Innocent Man '87

The Best of Times '86
Under Fire '83
The Pursuit of D.B. Cooper '81
Terror Train '80

G.D. Spradlin(1920-)
Red, White & Busted '75
The Only Way Home '72

Jill Sprecher
Thirteen Conversations About One Thing '01
Clockwatchers '97

Tim Spring
Raw Target '95
Reason to Die '90

R.G. Springsteen(1904-89)
Hostile Guns '67
Apache Uprising '66
Johnny Reno '66
King of the Wild Stallions '59
When Gangland Strikes '56
Oklahoma Annie '51
Hills of Oklahoma '50
Arizona Cowboy '49
The Red Menace '49
Hellfire '48
Son of God's Country '48
Homesteaders of Paradise Valley '47
Under Colorado Skies '47
Santa Fe Uprising '46
Stagecoach to Denver '46
Vigilantes of Boom Town '46

Robin Spry(1939-)
A Cry in the Night '93
Obsessed '88
Keeping Track '86
Suzanne '80
Drying Up the Streets '76

Morgan Spurlock
Where in the World Is Osama Bin Laden? '06
Super Size Me '04

Pasquale Squitieri(1938-)
Third Solution '89
Corleone '79
The Sniper '78
Blood Brothers '74

Salvatore Stabile
Where God Left His Shoes '07
Gravesend '97

Stephen Stafford
The Color of Evening '95
Hit Woman: The Double Edge '93
I Posed for Playboy '91

Nick Stagliano
The Florentine '98
Home of Angels '94

C. Ray Stahl(1921-59)
Scarlet Spear '54
Geisha Girl '52

Eric Steven Stahl(1959-)
I-See-You.Com '06
Safe House '99
Final Approach '91

John M. Stahl(1886-1950)
Father Was a Fullback '49
Leave Her to Heaven '45
The Keys of the Kingdom '44
Immortal Sergeant '43
Letter of Introduction '38
Imitation of Life '34

Sylvester Stallone(1946-)
The Expendables '10
Rambo '08
Rocky Balboa '06
Rocky 4 '85
Staying Alive '83
Rocky 3 '82
Rocky 2 '79

Paradise Alley '78

Richard Standeven

Falling for a Dancer '98
Band of Gold '95

Sean Stanek

Played '06
A Crack in the Floor '00

Jeremy Stanford

Watchers 3 '94
Stepmonster '92

Paul Stanley(1952-)

The Ultimate Imposter '79
Cotter '72

Richard Stanley(1966-)

Fly Boy '99
Dust Devil '93
Hardware '90

Andrew Stanton(1965-)

WALL-E '08
Finding Nemo '03
A Bug's Life '98

Jeff Stanzler

Sorry, Haters '05
Jumpin' at the Boneyard '92

Ringo Starr(1940-)

Born to Boogie '72
Magical Mystery Tour '67

Jack Starrett(1936-89)

Kiss My Grits '82
Mr. Horn '79
On the Edge: The Survival of Dana '79
Fatal Chase '77
Walking Tall: The Final Chapter '77
Hollywood Man '76
A Small Town in Texas '76
Race with the Devil '75
Cleopatra Jones '73
Slaughter '72
Cry Blood, Apache '70
The Losers '70
Run, Angel, Run! '69

Ralph Staub(1899-1969)

Danger Ahead '40
Sky Bandits '40
Yukon Flight '40
Prairie Moon '38
The Mandarin Mystery '37
Country Gentlemen '36

Wolfgang Staudte(1906-84)

The Three Penny Opera '62
The Kaiser's Lackey '51
The Murderers Are Among Us '46

Ray Dennis Steckler(1939-)

Las Vegas Serial Killer '86
The Hollywood Strangler Meets the Skid Row Slasher '79
The Hollywood Strangler Meets the Skid Row Slasher '79
Sinthia: The Devil's Doll '70
Rat Pfink a Boo-Boo '66
The Thrill Killers '65
Incredibly Strange Creatures Who Stopped Living and Became Mixed-Up Zombies '63
Wild Guitar '62

Burr Steers(1966-)

17 Again '09
Igby Goes Down '02

Giorgio Stegani(1928-)

The Gentleman Killer '69
Beyond the Law '68

Mark Steilen

Wieners '08
The Settlement '99

Darren Stein(1973-)

Sparkler '99
Jawbreaker '98

Herbert Stein

Escape to Love '82
Isle of Secret Passion '82

Ken Stein

Killer Instinct '92
The Rain Killer '90

Paul Stein(1892-1951)

Counterblast '48
Black Limelight '38
Heart's Desire '37
Mimi '35
Lottery Bride '30
Sin Takes a Holiday '30

David Steinberg(1942-)

The Wrong Guy '96
Going Berserk '83
Paternity '81

Michael Steinberg(1959-)

Wicked '98
Bodies, Rest & Motion '93
The Waterdance '91

Danny Steinmann

Friday the 13th, Part 5: A New Beginning '85
Savage Streets '83

Jos Stelling(1945-)

The Pointsman '86
Rembrandt—1669 '77

Steno(1915-88)

Flatfoot '78
How to Kill 400 Duponts '68
The Unfaithfuls '60
Uncle Was a Vampire '59

Frederick Stephani

Flash Gordon: Rocketship '40
Rocketship '36

A.C. (Stephen Apostoloff) Stephen(-2005)

Lady Godiva Rides '68
Orgy of the Dead '65

Jason Robert Stephens

Merchants of Death '99
Decay '98

James D. Stern

Every Little Step '08
It's the Rage '99

Noah Stern

The Invisibles '99
Pyrates '91

Sandor Stern(1936-)

Jericho Fever '93
Duplicates '92
Web of Deceit '90
Amityville 4: The Evil Escapes '89
Dangerous Pursuit '89
Glitz '88
Pin... '88
Assassin '86
John & Yoko: A Love Story '85

Steven Hilliard Stern(1937-)

Breaking the Surface: The Greg Louganis Story '96
Black Fox: Blood Horse '94
Black Fox: Good Men and Bad '94
Black Fox: The Price of Peace '94
Morning Glory '93
Love & Murder '91
Personals '90
Final Notice '89
Weekend War '88
Not Quite Human '87
Rolling Vengeance '87
Murder in Space '85
The Park Is Mine '85
Undergrads '85
Getting Physical '84
Obsessive Love '84
The Ambush Murders '82
Forbidden Love '82
Mazes and Monsters '82
Portrait of a Showgirl '82
The Devil & Max Devlin '81
Draw! '81
Miracle on Ice '81
A Small Killing '81
Anatomy of a Seduction '79
Young Love, First Love '79
I Wonder Who's Killing Her Now? '76
Harrad Summer '74

Patrick Stettner

The Night Listener '06
The Business of Strangers '01

Andrew Stevens(1955-)

The White Raven '98
The Corporation '96
Crash Dive '96
Subliminal Seduction '96
Virtual Combat '95
Illicit Dreams '94
The Skateboard Kid 2 '94
Night Eyes 3 '93
Scorned '93
The Terror Within 2 '91

David Stevens(1940-)

Kansas '88
A Town Like Alice '85
Roses Bloom Twice '77

George Stevens(1904-75)

The Greatest Story Ever Told '65
The Diary of Anne Frank '59
Giant '56
Shane '53
A Place in the Sun '51
I Remember Mama '48
The More the Merrier '43
Talk of the Town '42
Woman of the Year '42
Penny Serenade '41
Gunga Din '39
Vivacious Lady '38
A Damsel in Distress '37
Quality Street '37
Swing Time '36
Alice Adams '35
Annie Oakley '35
Bachelor Bait '34
Kentucky Kernels '34

Leslie Stevens(1924-98)

Three Kinds of Heat '87
Incubus '65

Robert Stevenson(1905-86)

The Shaggy D.A. '76
One of Our Dinosaurs Is Missing '75
Herbie Rides Again '74
The Island at the Top of the World '74
Bedknobs and Broomsticks '71
My Dog, the Thief '69
The Love Bug '68
Blackbeard's Ghost '67
The Gnome-Mobile '67
Monkey's Uncle '65
That Darn Cat '65
Mary Poppins '64
The Misadventures of Merlin Jones '63
Son of Flubber '63
In Search of the Castaways '62
The Absent-Minded Professor '61
Kidnapped '60
Darby O'Gill & the Little People '59
Johnny Tremain & the Sons of Liberty '58
Old Yeller '57
The Las Vegas Story '52
My Forbidden Past '51
Walk Softly, Stranger '50
The Woman on Pier 13 '50
Dishonored Lady '47
Jane Eyre '44
Forever and a Day '43
Joan of Paris '42
Back Street '41
Tom Brown's School Days '40
King Solomon's Mines '37
Non-Stop New York '37
The Man Who Lived Again '36
Nine Days a Queen '36

Alan L. Stewart(1951-)

Ghetto Blaster '89
Ghostriders '87

Douglas Day Stewart

Listen to Me '89
Thief of Hearts '84

Jean Stewart

Butterfly Collectors '99
Cracker: Men Should Weep '94

John Stewart(1934-)

Hidden Obsession '92
Cartel '90
Action U.S.A. '89

Robert Stewart(1961-)

Rock & Roll Cowboys '92
Mark of the Beast '87

Alex Steyermark

One Last Thing '05
Prey for Rock and Roll '03

Ben Stiller(1965-)

Tropic Thunder '08
Zoolander '01
The Cable Guy '96
Reality Bites '94

Mauritz Stiller(1883-1928)

Hotel Imperial '27
The Atonement of Gosta Berling '24
Treasure of Arne '19
Thomas Graal's First Child '18
Thomas Graal's Best Film '17

Whit Stillman(1952-)

The Last Days of Disco '98
Barcelona '94
Metropolitan '90

John Stockwell(1961-)

Turistas '06
Into the Blue '05
Blue Crush '02
crazy/beautiful '01
Cheaters '00
Undercover '87

Bryan Michael Stoller(1960-)

Miss Cast Away '04
Undercover Angel '99
Turn of the Blade '97
Dragon Fury 2 '96

Nicholas Stoller

Get Him to the Greek '10
Forgetting Sarah Marshall '08

Ben Stoloff(1895-1960)

It's a Joke, Son! '47
The Affairs of Annabel '38
Sea Devils '37
Palooka '34
Transatlantic Merry-Go-Round '34
Night of Terror '33
Justice Rides Again '32

Victor Stoloff(1913-)

Washington Affair '77
The 300 Year Weekend '71

Andrew L. Stone(1902-99)

Song of Norway '70
The Last Voyage '60
A Blueprint for Murder '53
Sensations of 1945 '44
Hi Diddle Diddle '43
Stormy Weather '43
The Girl Said No '37
Hell's Headquarters '32

Charles Stone, III(1966-)

Mr. 3000 '04
Drumline '02
Paid in Full '02

Norman Stone

Catherine Cookson's The Gambling Man '98
Catherine Cookson's The Black Velvet Gown '92
The Vision '87
Shadowlands '85

Oliver Stone(1946-)

Wall Street 2: Money Never Sleeps '10
W. '08
World Trade Center '06
Alexander '04
Any Given Sunday '99
U-Turn '97
Nixon '95
Natural Born Killers '94
Heaven and Earth '93
The Doors '91
JFK '91
Born on the Fourth of July '89
Talk Radio '88
Wall Street '87
Platoon '86
Salvador '86
The Hand '81
Seizure '74

Virginia Lively Stone

Run If You Can '87
Money to Burn '83
The Treasure of Jamaica Reef '74

Lynne Stopkewich(1964-)

Suspicious River '00
Kissed '96

Michael Storey

Before I Say Goodbye '03
We'll Meet Again '02
Blacklight '98

Esben Storm(1950-)

Subterano '01
In Search of Anna '79

Howard Storm(1939-)

Once Bitten '85
The Three Little Pigs '84

Jerome Storm(1890-1958)

Courtin' Wildcats '29
Sweet Adeline '26
The Busher '19

Tim Story(1970-)

Hurricane Season '08
Fantastic Four: Rise of the Silver Surfer '07
Fantastic Four '05
Taxi '04
Barbershop '02

Mark Stouffer

Dog Gone '08
Man Outside '88

Frank Strayer(1891-1964)

Footlight Glamour '43
It's a Great Life '43
Blondie for Victory '42
Blondie Goes Latin '42
Blondie Goes to College '42
Blondie's Blessed Event '42
Blondie in Society '41
Blondie Has Trouble '40
Blondie On a Budget '40
Blondie Plays Cupid '40
Blondie Brings Up Baby '39
Blondie Meets the Boss '39
Blondie Takes a Vacation '39
Blondie '38
Death from a Distance '36
Condemned to Live '35
Dangerous Appointment '34
Fugitive Road '34
The Ghost Walks '34
In the Money '34
The Crusader '32
The Monster Walks '32
Tangled Destinies '32
The Vampire Bat '32
Murder at Midnight '31

Barbra Streisand(1942-)

The Mirror Has Two Faces '96
The Prince of Tides '91
Yentl '83

Joseph Strick(1923-)

James Joyce: A Portrait of the Artist as a Young Man '77
Road Movie '72
Tropic of Cancer '70
Ulysses '67
The Balcony '63

Wesley Strick(1954-)

Hitched '01
The Tie That Binds '95

Herbert L. Strock(1918-2005)

Witches' Brew '79
Monster '78
Man on the Run '74
The Crawling Hand '63
How to Make a Monster '58
Teenage Frankenstein '58
Blood of Dracula '57

Mel Stuart(1928-)

Sophia Loren: Her Own Story '80
The Chisholms '79
The Triangle Factory Fire Scandal '79
Mean Dog Blues '78
Willy Wonka & the Chocolate Factory '71
I Love My... Wife '70
If It's Tuesday, This Must Be Belgium '69

John Sturges(1910-92)

The Eagle Has Landed '77
Chino '75
McQ '74
Joe Kidd '72
Marooned '69
Ice Station Zebra '68
Hour of the Gun '67
The Hallelujah Trail '65
The Great Escape '63
Sergeants 3 '62
By Love Possessed '61
The Magnificent Seven '60
Last Train from Gun Hill '59
Never So Few '59
The Law and Jake Wade '58
The Old Man and the Sea '58
Gunfight at the O.K. Corral '57
Underwater! '55
Bad Day at Black Rock '54
Escape from Fort Bravo '53
Jeopardy '53
It's a Big Country '51
The Capture '50
The Magnificent Yankee '50
Mystery Street '50

Preston Sturges(1898-1959)

The Beautiful Blonde from Bashful Bend '49
Unfaithfully Yours '48
The Sin of Harold Diddlebock '47
The Great Moment '44
Hail the Conquering Hero '44
Miracle of Morgan's Creek '44
The Palm Beach Story '42
The Lady Eve '41
Sullivan's Travels '41
Christmas in July '40
The Great McGinty '40

Charles Sturridge(1951-)

Lassie '05
Shackleton '02
Longitude '00
FairyTale: A True Story '97

Gulliver's Travels '95
A Foreign Field '93
Where Angels Fear to Tread '91
Aria '88
A Handful of Dust '88
Brideshead Revisited '81

Eric Styles(1967-)
Miss Conception '08
Dreaming of Joseph Lees '99
Relative Values '99

Richard Styles
Midnight Tease 2 '95
Escape '90
Shallow Grave '87

Bobby Suarez
Warriors of the Apocalypse '85
American Commandos '84
Pay or Die '83

Gonzalo Suarez(1934-)
Rowing with the Wind '88
House of the Damned '71

Eliseo Subiela(1944-)
The Dark Side of the Heart '92
Man Facing Southeast '86

Sara Sugarman(1962-)
Confessions of a Teenage Drama Queen '04
Very Annie Mary '00

Kevin Sullivan(1955-)
Cosmic Slop '94
Lantern Hill '90
Looking for Miracles '90
Anne of Avonlea '87
Anne of Green Gables '85
Wild Pony '83

Kevin Rodney Sullivan(1958-)
Guess Who '05
Barbershop 2: Back in Business '04
Conviction '02
How Stella Got Her Groove Back '98
Soul of the Game '96
America's Dream '95

Jeremy Summers(1931-)
Danger UXB '81
Five Golden Dragons '67
The House of 1000 Dolls '67
The Vengeance of Fu Manchu '67

Walter Summers(1896-1973)
House of Mystery '41
The Human Monster '39

Cedric Sundstrom
American Ninja 4: The Annihilation '91
The Revenger '90
American Ninja 3: Blood Hunt '89
Captive Rage '88

Stephen Surjik
I Want Candy '07
Weapons of Mass Distraction '97
Wayne's World 2 '93

Edward Sutherland(1895-1974)
Having Wonderful Crime '45
Follow the Boys '44
The Navy Comes Through '42
Sing Your Worries Away '42
Beyond Tomorrow '40
The Invisible Woman '40
One Night in the Tropics '40
The Flying Deuces '39
Every Day's a Holiday '38
Mississippi '35
International House '33
Murders in the Zoo '33
Mr. Robinson Crusoe '32
Palmy Days '31
Behind the Front '26
It's the Old Army Game '26

Kiefer Sutherland(1966-)
Woman Wanted '98
Truth or Consequences, N.M. '97
Last Light '93

Junichi Suzuki
Haunted Highway '05
Remembering the Cosmos Flower '99

Noribumi Suzuki
Shogun's Ninja '83
Sex and Fury '73

Seijun Suzuki(1923-)
Pistol Opera '02
Branded to Kill '67
Fighting Elegy '66
Tokyo Drifter '66
Story of a Prostitute '65
Gate of Flesh '64
Youth of the Beast '63

Peter Svatek
The Christmas Choir '08
The Rendering '02
Silver Wolf '98
Bleeders '97
Jack London's The Call of the Wild '97
Sci-Fighters '96
Witchboard 3: The Possession '95
Mystery of the Million Dollar Hockey Puck '75

Jan Sverak(1965-)
Dark Blue World '01
Kolya '96
The Elementary School '91

E.W. Swackhamer(1927-94)
Are You Lonesome Tonight '92
Perfect Family '92
The Secret Passion of Robert Clayton '92
The Rousters '90
Terror at London Bridge '85
Long Shot Kids '81
The Dain Curse '78
The Winds of Kitty Hawk '78
The Amazing Spider-Man '77
Night Terror '76
Death at Love House '75
Death Sentence '74
Man & Boy '71

Bob Swaim(1943-)
The Climb '97
Masquerade '88
Half Moon Street '86

Joe Swanberg
Nights and Weekends '08
Hannah Takes the Stairs '07

Bruce Sweeney
American Venus '07
Live Bait '95

David Swift(1919-2001)
How to Succeed in Business without Really Trying '67
Good Neighbor Sam '64
Under the Yum-Yum Tree '63
The Interns '62
The Parent Trap '61
Pollyanna '60

Saul Swimmer(1936-2007)
Mrs. Brown, You've Got a Lovely Daughter '68
Force of Impulse '60

Michael Switzer
Fallen Angel '03
Forever Love '98
Unlikely Angel '97
Past the Bleachers '95
Fergie & Andrew: Behind Palace Doors '93
Stalking Laura '93
Undesirable '92
The Lightning Incident '91
Nitti: The Enforcer '88

Peter Sykes(1939-)
Jesus '79
To the Devil, a Daughter '76
Night of the Laughing Dead '75
Demons of the Mind '72

Istvan Szabo(1938-)
Being Julia '04
Taking Sides '01
Sunshine '99
Meeting Venus '91
Hanussen '88
Mephisto '81
25 Fireman's Street '73
Love Film '70
Father '67

William Szarka
Phantom Brother '88
South Bronx Heroes '85

Janos Szasz
Opium: Diary of a Madwoman '07
Woyzeck '94

Boris Szulzinger
Mama Dracula '80
Shame of the Jungle '75

Jeannot Szwarc(1937-)
Grand Larceny '92
The Murders in the Rue Morgue '86
Santa Claus: The Movie '85
Supergirl '84
Enigma '82
Somewhere in Time '80
Jaws 2 '78
Code Name: Diamond Head '77
Bug '75
Sex Through a Window '72

Juan Carlos Tabio
Guantanamera '95
Strawberry and Chocolate '93

Jean-Charles Tacchella(1925-)
Blue Country '77
Cousin, Cousine '76
The Last Winters '71

Kidlat Tahimik(1942-)
Perfumed Nightmare '89
Turumba '84

Tibor Takacs(1954-)
Lies and Illusions '09
Ice Spiders '07
Megasnake '07
Kraken: Tentacles of the Deep '06
Sanctuary '98
Redline '97
Sabotage '96
Sabrina the Teenage Witch '96
Deadly Past '95
Bad Blood '94
Gate 2 '92
Red Shoe Diaries 2: Double Dare '92
I, Madman '89
The Gate '87

Isao Takahata
Pom Poko '94
Grave of the Fireflies '88

Beat Takeshi
See Takeshi "Beat" Kitano

Yojiro Takita
Departures '08
Onmyoji 2 '03
When the Last Sword is Drawn '02
Onmyoji '01

Rachel Talalay
Tank Girl '94
Ghost in the Machine '93
Freddy's Dead: The Final Nightmare '91

Igor Talankin
Tchaikovsky '71
A Summer to Remember '61

Paul Talbot
Hellblock 13 '97
Freakshow '95

Gregg Tallas(1915-)
Cataclysm '81
Espionage in Tangiers '65
Prehistoric Women '50
Summer Storm '44

Richard Talmadge(1892-1981)
Project Moon Base '53
Detour to Danger '45
Devil Horse '32

Lee Tamahori(1950-)
Next '07
XXX: State of the Union '05
Die Another Day '02
Along Came a Spider '01
The Edge '97
Mulholland Falls '95
Once Were Warriors '94

Harry (Hurwitz) Tampa(1938-95)
Nocturna '79
Fairy Tales '76

Tokuzo Tanaka(1925-2007)
Zatoichi: The Blind Swordsman's Vengeance '66
Sleepy Eyes of Death: The Chinese Jade '63

Senkichi Taniguchi(1912-2007)
What's Up, Tiger Lily? '66
The Gambling Samurai '60

Terrell Tannen
Shadows in the Storm '88
A Minor Miracle '83

William (Bill) Tannen
Hero and the Terror '88
Deadly Illusion '87
Flashpoint '84

Alain Tanner(1929-)
In the White City '83
Messidor '77
Jonah Who Will Be 25 in the Year 2000 '76
La Salamandre '71
Charles: Dead or Alive '69

Robert Emmett Tansey(1897-1951)
The Caravan Trail '46
Colorado Serenade '46
Driftin' River '46
God's Country '46
Wild West '46
Song of Old Wyoming '45
Wildfire '45
Arizona Whirlwind '44
Death Valley Rangers '44
Outlaw Trail '44
Sonora Stagecoach '44
Westward Bound '44
Haunted Ranch '43
Two-Fisted Justice '43
Arizona Roundup '42
Lone Star Law Men '42
Texas to Bataan '42
Trail Riders '42
Western Mail '42
Where Trails End '42
The Driftin' Kid '41
Dynamite Canyon '41
Riding the Sunset Trail '41
Courage of the North '35
Way of the West '35

Daniel Taplitz
Breakin' All The Rules '04
Commandments '96
Black Magic '92
Nightlife '90

Michael Tarantini
Massacre in Dinosaur Valley '85
Crimebusters '79

Quentin Tarantino(1963-)
Inglourious Basterds '09
Death Proof '07
Kill Bill Vol. 2 '04
Kill Bill Vol. 1 '03
Jackie Brown '97
Four Rooms '95
Pulp Fiction '94
Reservoir Dogs '92

Andrei Tarkovsky(1932-86)
The Sacrifice '86
Nostalghia '83
Stalker '79
The Mirror '75
Solaris '72
Andrei Rublev '66
My Name Is Ivan '62

Tarsem(1961-)
The Fall '06
The Cell '00

Frank Tashlin(1913-72)
Private Navy of Sgt. O'Farrell '68
Caprice '67
The Glass Bottom Boat '66
The Alphabet Murders '65
Disorderly Orderly '64
Who's Minding the Store? '63
Cinderfella '60
The Geisha Boy '58
Rock-A-Bye Baby '57
Will Success Spoil Rock Hunter? '57
The Girl Can't Help It '56
Hollywood or Bust '56
Artists and Models '55
Susan Slept Here '54
Son of Paleface '52
The Fuller Brush Man '48

Nadia Tass(1956-)
Child Star: The Shirley Temple Story '01
The Miracle Worker '00
Amy '98
Mr. Reliable: A True Story '95
Pure Luck '91
Rikky and Pete '88
Malcolm '86

Jacques Tati(1908-82)
Parade '74
Traffic '71
Playtime '67
Mon Oncle '58
Mr. Hulot's Holiday '53
Jour de Fete '48

John Tatoulis
Zone 39 '96
The Silver Stallion: King of the Wild Brumbies '93

Norman Taurog(1899-1981)
Live a Little, Love a Little '68
Speedway '68
Double Trouble '67
Dr. Goldfoot and the Bikini Machine '66
Spinout '66
Tickle Me '65
It Happened at the World's Fair '63
Palm Springs Weekend '63
Blue Hawaii '62
Girls! Girls! Girls! '62
G.I. Blues '60
Birds & the Bees '56
Bundle of Joy '56
Pardners '56
The Caddy '53
Jumping Jacks '52
Rich, Young and Pretty '51
Room for One More '51
The Stooge '51
The Toast of New Orleans '50
That Midnight Kiss '49
Words and Music '48
Girl Crazy '43
Presenting Lily Mars '43
Men of Boys Town '41
Broadway Melody of 1940 '40
Little Nellie Kelly '40
Young Tom Edison '40
The Adventures of Tom Sawyer '38
Boys Town '38
Mad About Music '38
Rhythm on the Range '36
Strike Me Pink '36
Mrs. Wiggs of the Cabbage Patch '34
We're Not Dressing '34
Hold 'Em Jail '32
Sunny Skies '30

David Tausik
Haunted Symphony '94
Homicidal Impulse '92

Bertrand Tavernier(1941-)
In the Electric Mist '08
Capitaine Conan '96
L'Appat '94
Revenge of the Musketeers '94
L.627 '92
Daddy Nostalgia '90
Life and Nothing But '89
Beatrice '88
Round Midnight '86
A Sunday in the Country '84
Coup de Torchon '81
Death Watch '80
Spoiled Children '77
The Judge and the Assassin '75
The Clockmaker '73

Paolo Taviani(1931-)
Elective Affinities '96
Fiorile '93
Night Sun '90
Good Morning, Babylon '87
Kaos '85
The Night of the Shooting Stars '82
Padre Padrone '77
Allonsanfan '73
St. Michael Had a Rooster '72

Vittorio Taviani(1929-)
Elective Affinities '96
Fiorile '93
Night Sun '90
Good Morning, Babylon '87
Kaos '85
The Night of the Shooting Stars '82
Padre Padrone '77
Allonsanfan '73
St. Michael Had a Rooster '72

Alan Taylor(1965-)
Kill the Poor '06
The Emperor's New Clothes '01
Palookaville '95

Baz Taylor(1944-)
Shooting Elizabeth '92
Tattle Tale '92
Near Misses '91
Happy Since I Met You '89

Brian Taylor
Crank: High Voltage '09
Gamer '09
Crank '06

Don Taylor(1920-98)
The Diamond Trap '91
Going for the Gold: The Bill Johnson Story '85
Secret Weapons '85
My Wicked, Wicked Ways '84
Listen to Your Heart '83
September Gun '83
Red Flag: The Ultimate Game '81
The Final Countdown '80
Damien: Omen 2 '78
The Island of Dr. Moreau '77
Great Scout & Cathouse Thursday '76
Tom Sawyer '73
Escape from the Planet of the Apes '71

Wild Women *'70*
Ride the Wild Surf *'64*

Finn Taylor(1958-)
The Darwin Awards *'06*
Cherish *'02*
Dream with the Fishes *'97*

Jud Taylor(1940-)
Secrets *'94*
Danielle Steel's Kaleidoscope *'90*
The Old Man and the Sea *'90*
The Great Escape 2: The Untold Story *'88*
Broken Vows *'87*
Foxfire *'87*
Out of the Darkness *'85*
License to Kill *'84*
Packin' It In *'83*
Lovey: A Circle of Children 2 *'82*
Question of Honor *'80*
The Christmas Coal Mine Miracle *'77*
Mary White *'77*
Future Cop *'76*
Return to Earth *'76*
Search for the Gods *'75*
Winter Kill *'74*
Say Goodbye, Maggie Cole *'72*

Malcolm Taylor
A Killer in Every Corner *'74*
Murder Motel *'74*

Ray Taylor(1888-1952)
Outlaw Country *'49*
Black Hills *'48*
Check Your Guns *'48*
The Hawk of Powder River *'48*
Return of Wildfire *'48*
Stage to Mesa City *'48*
The Tioga Kid *'48*
Border Feud *'47*
Cheyenne Takes Over *'47*
Fighting Vigilantes *'47*
Ghost Town Renegades *'47*
Law of the Lash *'47*
Return of the Lash *'47*
West to Glory *'47*
Wild Country *'47*
Lost City of the Jungle *'45*
Boss of Boomtown *'44*
Master Key *'44*
Mystery of the Riverboat *'44*
Raiders of Ghost City *'44*
Adventures of Smilin' Jack *'43*
Don Winslow of the Coast Guard *'43*
Don Winslow of the Navy *'43*
The Lone Star Trail *'43*
Gang Busters *'42*
Junior G-Men of the Air *'42*
Stagecoach Buckaroo *'42*
Boss of Bullion City *'41*
Bury Me Not on the Lone Prairie *'41*
Man from Montana *'41*
Riders of Death Valley *'41*
Flash Gordon Conquers the Universe *'40*
Law and Order *'40*
Pony Post *'40*
Riders of Pasco Basin *'40*
Space Soldiers Conquer the Universe *'40*
Winners of the West *'40*
The Green Hornet *'39*
Flaming Frontiers *'38*
Hawaiian Buckaroo *'38*
Panamint's Bad Man *'38*
Rawhide *'38*
The Spider's Web *'38*
Dick Tracy *'37*
Dick Tracy: The Spider Strikes *'37*
Mystery of the Hooded Horseman *'37*
The Painted Stallion *'37*
Tex Rides with the Boy Scouts *'37*
The Phantom Rider *'36*
The Three Mesquiteers *'36*
The Vigilantes Are Coming *'36*
The Ivory Handled Gun *'35*
Law for Tombstone *'35*
Stone of Silver Creek *'35*
The Throwback *'35*
Chandu on the Magic Island *'34*
The Fighting Trooper *'34*
The Perils of Pauline *'34*
Return of Chandu *'34*
Phantom of the Air *'33*
Battling with Buffalo Bill *'31*

S. Lee Taylor
See Steve Taylor

Sam Taylor(1895-1958)
Nothing But Trouble *'44*
Ambassador Bill *'31*
Dubarry *'30*
Coquette *'29*
The Taming of the Shrew *'29*
Tempest *'28*
My Best Girl *'27*
Exit Smiling *'26*
For Heaven's Sake *'26*
The Freshman *'25*
Safety Last *'23*

Steve Taylor(1957-)
The Second Chance *'06*
Social Intercourse *'01*

Julie Taymor(1952-)
Across the Universe *'07*
Frida *'02*
Titus *'99*

Colin Teague(1970-)
The Last Drop *'05*
Shooters *'00*

Lewis Teague(1941-)
The Triangle *'01*
Saved by the Light *'95*
T Bone N Weasel *'92*
Deadlock *'91*
Navy SEALS *'90*
Collision Course *'89*
Cat's Eye *'85*
The Jewel of the Nile *'85*
Cujo *'83*
Fighting Back *'82*
Alligator *'80*
Lady in Red *'79*

Andre Techine(1943-)
The Girl on the Train *'09*
The Witnesses *'07*
Changing Times *'04*
Strayed *'03*
Alice et Martin *'98*
Les Voleurs *'96*
Wild Reeds *'94*
Ma Saison Preferee *'93*
I Don't Kiss *'91*
Scene of the Crime *'87*
Rendez-vous *'85*
Hotel America *'81*
Barocco *'76*

Julien Temple(1953-)
Pandaemonium *'00*
The Filth and the Fury *'99*
Bullet *'94*
Earth Girls Are Easy *'89*
Aria *'88*
Absolute Beginners *'86*
Running out of Luck *'86*
The Secret Policeman's Other Ball *'82*
Secret Policeman's Private Parts *'81*

Andy Tennant(1955-)
The Bounty Hunter *'10*
Fool's Gold *'08*
Hitch *'05*
Sweet Home Alabama *'02*
Anna and the King *'99*
Ever After: A Cinderella Story *'98*
Fools Rush In *'97*
It Takes Two *'95*
The Amy Fisher Story *'93*
Keep the Change *'92*

Del Tenney(1930-)
Curse of the Living Corpse *'64*
Horror of Party Beach *'64*
I Eat Your Skin *'64*

Kevin S. Tenney(1955-)
Endangered Species *'02*
Tick Tock *'00*
The Arrival 2 *'98*
Pinocchio's Revenge *'96*
Witchboard 2: The Devil's Doorway *'93*
The Cellar *'90*
Peacemaker *'90*
WitchTrap *'89*
Night of the Demons *'88*
Witchboard *'87*

John Terlesky(1961-)
Smoke Jumpers *'08*
Fire Serpent *'07*
Cerberus *'05*
Guardian *'01*
Chain of Command *'00*
The Guardian *'00*
Judgment Day *'99*
Supreme Sanction *'99*

Hiroshi Teshigahara(1927-2001)
Rikyu *'90*
Face of Another *'66*
Woman in the Dunes *'64*

Duccio Tessari(1926-94)
Beyond Justice *'92*
Blood at Sundown *'88*
Zorro *'74*
Sundance and the Kid *'69*

Ted Tetzlaff(1903-95)
The Young Land *'59*
Son of Sinbad *'55*
The White Tower *'50*
The Window *'49*
Fighting Father Dunne *'48*
Riff-Raff *'47*

Joan Tewkesbury(1936-)
Strangers *'91*
Sudie & Simpson *'90*
Cold Sassy Tree *'89*
Acorn People *'82*
Old Boyfriends *'79*
Tenth Month *'79*

Peter Tewkesbury(1923-2003)
The Trouble with Girls (and How to Get into It) *'69*
Stay Away, Joe *'68*
Emil and the Detectives *'64*
Sunday in New York *'63*

David Thacker
The Mayor of Casterbridge *'03*
Broken Glass *'96*

Graham Theakston
Sherlock: Case of Evil *'02*
Seeing Red *'99*
Money Kings *'98*
The Mill on the Floss *'97*
Tripods: The White Mountains *'84*

Betty Thomas(1949-)
Alvin and the Chipmunks: The Squeakuel *'09*
John Tucker Must Die *'06*
I Spy *'02*
28 Days *'00*
Dr. Dolittle *'98*
The Late Shift *'96*
Private Parts *'96*
The Brady Bunch Movie *'95*

Dave Thomas(1949-)
The Experts *'89*
Strange Brew *'83*

Gerald Thomas(1920-93)
Carry On Columbus *'92*
Second Victory *'87*
Carry On Emmanuelle *'78*
Carry On England *'76*
Carry On Behind *'75*
Carry On Dick *'75*
Carry On Abroad *'72*
Carry On Matron *'72*
Carry On at Your Convenience *'71*
Carry On Camping *'71*
Carry On Henry VIII *'71*
Carry On Loving *'70*
Carry On Up the Jungle *'70*
Carry On Again Doctor *'69*
Carry On Doctor *'68*
Carry On Up the Khyber *'68*
Follow That Camel *'67*
Carry On Cowboy *'66*
Carry On Screaming *'66*
Don't Lose Your Head *'66*
Carry On Cleo *'65*
Carry On Spying *'64*
Carry On Cabby *'63*
Carry On Jack *'63*
Carry On Cruising *'62*
Carry On Regardless *'61*
Carry On Constable *'60*
No Kidding *'60*
Carry On Nurse *'59*
Carry On Sergeant *'58*
Time Lock *'57*
The Vicious Circle *'57*

John G. Thomas(1948-)
Arizona Heat *'87*
Banzai Runner *'86*
Tin Man *'83*

Paul Thomas(1947-)
Killer Looks *'94*
The Pamela Principle *'91*

Ralph Thomas(1915-2001)
The Big Scam *'79*
It's Not the Size That Counts *'74*
Quest for Love *'71*
Deadlier Than the Male *'67*
Doctor in Clover *'66*
Doctor in Distress *'63*
Conspiracy of Hearts *'60*
Doctor in Love *'60*
No Love for Johnnie *'60*
A Tale of Two Cities *'58*
Doctor at Large *'57*
Above Us the Waves *'56*
Doctor at Sea *'56*
Doctor in the House *'53*
The Clouded Yellow *'51*

Ralph L. (R.L.) Thomas(1939-)
A Young Connecticut Yankee in King Arthur's Court *'95*
Young Ivanhoe *'95*
Apprentice to Murder *'88*
The Terry Fox Story *'83*
Ticket to Heaven *'81*
Carry On Regardless *'61*

Scott Thomas
Flight of the Living Dead: Outbreak on a Plane *'07*
Latin Dragon *'03*
Deranged *'01*
Silent Assassins *'88*

William C. Thomas(1903-84)
Big Town *'47*
Big Town After Dark *'47*
Underworld Scandal *'47*
Dark Mountain *'44*

Harry Z. Thomason(1940-)
The Hunting of the President *'04*
The Day It Came to Earth *'77*
Encounter with the Unknown *'75*
Hootch Country Boys *'75*
Visions of Evil *'75*

Caroline Thompson(1956-)
Snow White: The Fairest of Them All *'02*
Buddy *'97*
Black Beauty *'94*

Daniele Thompson(1942-)
Avenue Montaigne *'06*
Jet Lag *'02*
La Buche *'00*

Donald W. Thompson
Blood on the Mountain *'88*
The Prodigal Planet *'88*

Ernest Thompson(1949-)
Out of Time *'00*
1969 *'89*

J. Lee Thompson(1914-2002)
Kinjite: Forbidden Subjects *'89*
Messenger of Death *'88*
Death Wish 4: The Crackdown *'87*
Firewalker *'86*
Murphy's Law *'86*
King Solomon's Mines *'85*
The Ambassador *'84*
The Evil That Men Do *'84*
Ten to Midnight *'83*
Cabo Blanco *'81*
Happy Birthday to Me *'81*
The Greek Tycoon *'78*
The White Buffalo *'77*
St. Ives *'76*
The Widow *'76*
The Blue Knight *'75*
The Reincarnation of Peter Proud *'75*
Huckleberry Finn *'74*
Battle for the Planet of the Apes *'73*
Conquest of the Planet of the Apes *'72*
The Chairman *'69*
MacKenna's Gold *'69*
Kings of the Sun *'63*
Taras Bulba *'62*
Cape Fear *'61*
The Guns of Navarone *'61*
Flame Over India *'60*
Tiger Bay *'59*

Chris Thomson(1945-)
Trucks *'97*
Swimsuit *'89*
The Empty Beach *'85*
Three's Trouble *'85*
The Last Bastion *'84*
Waterfront *'83*
1915 *'82*

Youngyooth Thongkonthun
The Iron Ladies 2 *'03*
The Iron Ladies *'00*

Michael Thornhill(1941-)
The Everlasting Secret Family *'88*
Robbery *'85*
Between Wars *'74*

Billy Bob Thornton(1955-)
All the Pretty Horses *'00*
Daddy & Them *'99*
Sling Blade *'96*

Jerry Thorpe(1930-)
All God's Children *'80*
For Heaven's Sake *'79*
A Question of Love *'78*
The Possessed *'77*
Wonderland Cove *'75*
Smile, Jenny, You're Dead *'74*
Kung Fu *'72*

Richard Thorpe(1896-1986)
That Funny Feeling *'65*
Fun in Acapulco *'63*
The Horizontal Lieutenant *'62*
The Honeymoon Machine *'61*
Jailhouse Rock *'57*
Ten Thousand Bedrooms *'57*
The Prodigal *'55*
Quentin Durward *'55*
Athena *'54*
The Student Prince *'54*
All the Brothers Were Valiant *'53*
The Girl Who Had Everything *'53*
Knights of the Round Table *'53*
Ivanhoe *'52*
Prisoner of Zenda *'52*
The Great Caruso *'51*
It's a Big Country *'51*
Vengeance Valley *'51*
The Black Hand *'50*
Three Little Words *'50*
Challenge to Lassie *'49*
Malaya *'49*
The Sun Comes Up *'49*
A Date with Judy *'48*
On an Island with You *'48*
Thrill of a Romance *'45*
The Thin Man Goes Home *'44*
Two Girls and a Sailor *'44*
Above Suspicion *'43*
Tarzan's New York Adventure *'42*
White Cargo *'42*
Tarzan's Secret Treasure *'41*
The Adventures of Huckleberry Finn *'39*
Tarzan Finds a Son *'39*
Double Wedding *'37*
Night Must Fall *'37*
Tarzan Escapes *'36*
Green Eyes *'34*
After Midnight *'33*
Rainbow over Broadway *'33*
Cross Examination *'32*
The King Murder *'32*
The Lone Defender *'32*
The Midnight Lady *'32*
Probation *'32*
The Secrets of Wu Sin *'32*
Wild Horse *'31*
Border Romance *'30*
Under Montana Skies *'30*
King of the Kongo *'29*
Desert of the Lost *'27*

Rawson Marshall Thurber(1975-)
The Mysteries of Pittsburgh *'08*
Dodgeball: A True Underdog Story *'04*

Antonio Tibaldi
Kiss of Fire *'98*
Little Boy Blue *'97*
On My Own *'92*

Eric Till(1929-)
Luther *'03*
The Girl Next Door *'98*
Glory Enough for All: The Discovery of Insulin *'92*
Oh, What a Night *'92*
To Catch a Killer *'92*
Clarence *'91*
Buffalo Jump *'90*
A Case of Libel *'83*
If You Could See What I Hear *'82*
Improper Channels *'82*
An American Christmas Carol *'79*
Mary and Joseph: A Story of Faith *'79*
Wild Horse Hank *'79*
Bethune *'77*
Hot Millions *'68*

George Tillman, Jr. (1969-)
Notorious *'09*
Men of Honor *'00*
Soul Food *'97*

James Tinling(1889-1967)
Tales of Robin Hood *'52*
Mr. Moto's Gamble *'38*
The Holy Terror *'37*
Charlie Chan in Shanghai *'35*
Under the Pampas Moon *'35*

Robert Tinnell(1961-)
Believe *'99*
Frankenstein and Me *'96*

Peter Ustinov(1921-2004)
Hammersmith Is Out '72
Lady L '65
Billy Budd '62

Jamie Uys(1921-96)
The Gods Must Be Crazy 2 '89
The Gods Must Be Crazy '84
Dingaka '65

Roger Vadim(1928-2000)
And God Created Woman '88
Beauty and the Beast '83
Hot Touch '82
Night Games '80
Game of Seduction '76
Don Juan (Or If Don Juan Were a Woman) '73
Barbarella '68
Spirits of the Dead '68
The Game Is Over '66
Circle of Love '64
Le Repos du Guerrier '62
Love on a Pillow '62
Blood and Roses '61
Please Not Now! '61
Dangerous Liaisons '60
And God Created Woman '57
The Night Heaven Fell '57

Ladislao Vajda(1906-65)
The Man Who Wagged His Tail '57
The Miracle of Marcelino '55

Luis Valdez(1940-)
The Cisco Kid '94
La Bamba '87
Zoot Suit '81

Frank (Pierluigi Ciriaci) Valenti
Delta Force Commando 2 '90
War Bus Commando '89
Delta Force Commando '87

Tonino Valerii(1934-)
My Name Is Nobody '74
A Reason to Live, a Reason to Die '73

Amir Valinia
Lords of the Street '08
Mutants '08

Jean-Marc Vallee
The Young Victoria '09
Los Locos Posse '97

Nick Vallelonga(1959-)
Stiletto '08
All In '06
The Corporate Ladder '97
In the Kingdom of the Blind the Man with One Eye Is King '94
A Brilliant Disguise '93

Franklin A. Vallette
U.S. Navy SEALS: Dead or Alive '02
U.S. SEALs: Dead or Alive '02

Rudolf Van Den Berg(1949-)
Snapshots '02
Cold Light of Day '95

Jaco Van Dormael(1957-)
The Eighth Day '95
Toto le Heros '91

Woodbridge S. Van Dyke(1889-1943)
Cairo '42
I Married an Angel '42
Journey for Margaret '42
Shadow of the Thin Man '41
Bitter Sweet '40
I Love You Again '40
Andy Hardy Gets Spring Fever '39
Another Thin Man '39
Marie Antoinette '38
Rosalie '38
Sweethearts '38
Personal Property '37
After the Thin Man '36
The Devil Is a Sissy '36
Love on the Run '36
Rose Marie '36
San Francisco '36
Forsaking All Others '35
I Live My Life '35
Naughty Marietta '35
Hide-Out '34
Manhattan Melodrama '34
The Thin Man '34
Penthouse '33
The Prizefighter and the Lady '33
Tarzan, the Ape Man '32
Trader Horn '31
White Shadows in the South Seas '29

Andre Van Heerden(1971-)
Revelation '00
Tribulation '00

Buddy Van Horn(1929-)
Pink Cadillac '89
The Dead Pool '88
Any Which Way You Can '80

Mario Van Peebles(1958-)
Baadasssss! '03
Love Kills '98
Gang in Blue '96
Panther '95
Posse '93
New Jack City '91

Melvin Van Peebles(1932-)
Gang in Blue '96
Tales of Erotica '93
Identity Crisis '90
Sweet Sweetback's Baadasssss Song '71
Watermelon Man '70
The Story of a Three Day Pass '68

Gus Van Sant(1952-)
Milk '08
Paranoid Park '07
Paris, je t'aime '06
Last Days '05
Elephant '03
Gerry '02
Finding Forrester '00
Psycho '98
Good Will Hunting '97
To Die For '95
Even Cowgirls Get the Blues '94
My Own Private Idaho '91
Drugstore Cowboy '89

Andrew Van Slee(1965-)
Net Games '03
Totally Blonde '01

Norman Thaddeus Vane
Taxi Dancers '93
Midnight '89
Club Life '86
The Black Room '82
Frightmare '81

Carlo Vanzina(1952-)
Millions '90
My Wonderful Life '90
The Gamble '88
Nothing Underneath '85
Dagger Eyes '83

Agnes Varda(1928-)
One Hundred and One Nights '95
Jacquot '91
Le Petit Amour '87
Vagabond '85
One Sings, the Other Doesn't '77
Le Bonheur '65
Cleo from 5 to 7 '61

Giuseppe Vari(1916-93)
The Legend of Sea Wolf '75
Shoot the Living, Pray for the Dead '70
Place in Hell '69
Conquest of the Normans '62
Revenge of the Barbarians '60

Marcel Varnel(1894-1947)
Hey! Hey! USA! '38
Oh, Mr. Porter '37
Chandu the Magician '32

Joseph B. Vasquez(1962-95)
Manhattan Merenque! '95
Street Hitz '92
Hangin' with the Homeboys '91
The Bronx War '90

Tom Vaughan
Extraordinary Measures '10
What Happens in Vegas '08
Starter for Ten '06

Matthew Vaughn(1971-)
Kick-Ass '10
Stardust '07
Layer Cake '05

Francis Veber(1937-)
The Valet '06
The Closet '00
The Dinner Game '98
Out on a Limb '92
Three Fugitives '89
Les Comperes '83
La Chevre '81

Gore Verbinski(1964-)
Pirates of the Caribbean: At World's End '07
Pirates of the Caribbean: Dead Man's Chest '06
The Weather Man '05
Pirates of the Caribbean: The Curse of the Black Pearl '03
The Ring '02
The Mexican '01
Mouse Hunt '97

Carlo Verdone(1950-)
Iris Blond '98
Acqua e Sapone '83

Michael Verhoeven(1929-)
My Mother's Courage '95
The Nasty Girl '90
Blitz '85
The White Rose '83

Paul Verhoeven(1938-)
Black Book '06
Hollow Man '00
Starship Troopers '97
Showgirls '95
Basic Instinct '92
Total Recall '90
RoboCop '87
Flesh and Blood '85
Spetters '80
The 4th Man '79
Soldier of Orange '78
Katie Tippel '75
Turkish Delight '73
Business is Business '71
The Eternal Waltz '54

Henri Verneuil(1920-2002)
Night Flight from Moscow '73
Any Number Can Win '63
Un Singe en Hiver '62
Just Another Pretty Face '58
The Sheep Has Five Legs '54
Forbidden Fruit '52

Conrad Vernon(1968-)
Monsters vs. Aliens '09
Shrek 2 '04

Stephen Verona(1940-)
Talking Walls '85
Pipe Dreams '76
The Lords of Flatbush '74

Todd Verow(1966-)
Between Something & Nothing '08
Little Shots of Happiness '97
Frisk '95

Bruno VeSota(1922-76)
Invasion of the Star Creatures '63
The Brain Eaters '58
The Female Jungle '56

Marco Vicario(1925-)
Wifemistress '79
The Sensual Man '74

Charles Vidor(1900-59)
Song Without End '60
A Farewell to Arms '57
The Swan '56
Love Me or Leave Me '55
Rhapsody '54
Hans Christian Andersen '52
It's a Big Country '51
The Loves of Carmen '48
Gilda '46
A Song to Remember '45
Cover Girl '44
The Desperadoes '43
The Tuttles of Tahiti '42
The Lady in Question '40
My Son, My Son '40

King Vidor(1894-1982)
Solomon and Sheba '59
War and Peace '56
Man Without a Star '55
Ruby Gentry '52
Beyond the Forest '49
The Fountainhead '49
On Our Merry Way '48
Duel in the Sun '46
Together Again '43
H.M. Pulham Esquire '41
Comrade X '40
Northwest Passage '40
The Citadel '38
Stella Dallas '37
The Texas Rangers '36
Our Daily Bread '34
Bird of Paradise '32
The Champ '32
Street Scene '31
Hallelujah! '29
The Crowd '28
The Patsy '28
Show People '28
Bardelys the Magnificent '26
The Big Parade '25
Peg o' My Heart '22
The Sky Pilot '21
The Jack Knife Man '20

Berthold Viertel(1885-1954)
The Passing of the Third Floor Back '36
Rhodes '36

Joel Viertel
Strictly Sexual '08
Devil's Pond '03

Daniel Vigne(1942-)
One Woman or Two '85
The Return of Martin Guerre '83
Killing in the Sun '73

Jean Vigo(1905-34)
L'Atalante '34
Zero for Conduct '33
A Propos de Nice '29

Camilo Vila
Unlawful Passage '94
Options '88
The Unholy '88

Reynaldo Villalobos(1940-)
Hollywood Confidential '97
Conagher '91

Joseph Vilsmaier(1939-)
The Harmonists '99
Brother of Sleep '95
Stalingrad '94

Robert Vince
Santa Buddies '09
Snow Buddies '08
Space Buddies '08
Air Bud 6: Air Buddies '06
MXP: Most Xtreme Primate '03
Air Bud 4: Seventh Inning Fetch '02
MVP2: Most Vertical Primate '01
MVP (Most Valuable Primate) '00

Christian Vincent(1955-)
La Separation '98
The Separation '94
La Discrete '90

Chuck Vincent(1940-91)
A Woman Obsessed '93
Enrapture '90
Wildest Dreams '90
Bedroom Eyes 2 '89
Cleo/Leo '89
Party Incorporated '89
Young Nurses in Love '89
Sexpot '88
Student Affairs '88
Thrilled to Death '88
Deranged '87
New York's Finest '87
Sensations '87
Slammer Girls '87
Warrior Queen '87
Wimps '87
If Looks Could Kill '86
Hollywood Hot Tubs '84
C.O.D. '83
Preppies '82
Hot T-Shirts '79
A Matter of Love '78
American Tickler '76

Thomas Vinterberg(1969-)
Dear Wendy '05
It's All About Love '03
The Celebration '98

Albert T. Viola
Preacherman '83
Cry of the Penguins '71

Joe Viola
Hot Box '72
Angels Hard As They Come '71

Norton Virgien
Rugrats Go Wild! '03
The Rugrats Movie '98

Clement Virgo(1966-)
Love Come Down '00
Junior's Groove '97
Rude '96

Luchino Visconti(1906-76)
The Innocent '76
Conversation Piece '75
Ludwig '72
Death in Venice '71
The Damned '69
Sandra of a Thousand Delights '65
The Leopard '63
Boccaccio '70 '62
Rocco and His Brothers '60
White Nights '57
Senso '54
Bellissima '51
La Terra Trema '48
Ossessione '42

Tony Vitale
One Last Ride '03
Kiss Me, Guido '97

Virgil W. Vogel(1920-96)
Walker: Texas Ranger: One Riot, One Ranger '93
Portrait of a Rebel: Margaret Sanger '82
Beulah Land '80
Centennial '78
Law of the Land '76
Invasion of the Animal People '62
The Kettles on Old MacDonald's Farm '57
The Land Unknown '57
The Mole People '56

Alfred Vohrer(1918-86)
Creature with the Blue Hand '70
The Mysterious Magician '65
The Squeaker '65
The Indian Scarf '63
Door with the Seven Locks '62
Inn on the River '62
Dead Eyes of London '61

Marc Voizard
Escape from Wildcat Canyon '99
Hawk's Vengeance '96
Marked Man '96

Paul G. Volk
Steel Frontier '94
Sunset Strip '91

Josef von Baky(1902-66)
The Strange Countess '61
Baron Munchausen '43

Katja von Garnier(1966-)
Blood & Chocolate '07
Bandits '99

Josef von Sternberg(1894-1969)
Jet Pilot '57
Macao '52
The Shanghai Gesture '42
Crime and Punishment '35
The Devil Is a Woman '35
Scarlet Empress '34
Blonde Venus '32
Shanghai Express '32
An American Tragedy '31
Dishonored '31
The Blue Angel '30
Morocco '30
Docks of New York '28
Last Command '28
It '27
Underworld '27

Erich von Stroheim(1885-1957)
Queen Kelly '29
The Wedding March '28
Greed '24
Merry-Go-Round '23
Foolish Wives '22
Blind Husbands '19

Ernst R. von Theumer
Hell Hunters '87
Jungle Warriors '84

Lars von Trier(1956-)
Antichrist '09
The Boss of It All '06
Manderlay '05
Dogville '03
Dancer in the Dark '99
The Idiots '99
The Kingdom 2 '97
Breaking the Waves '95
The Kingdom '95
Zentropa '92
Medea '88
The Element of Crime '84

Margarethe von Trotta(1942-)
Rosenstrasse '03
The Promise '94
Rosa Luxemburg '86
Sheer Madness '84
Marianne and Juliane '82
Sisters, Or the Balance of Happiness '79
The Second Awakening of Christa Klages '78
The Lost Honor of Katharina Blum '75

Linda Voorhees
California Dreaming '07
Raising Genius '04

Bernard Vorhaus(1904-2000)
The Amazing Mr. X *'48*
Lady from Louisiana *'42*
Courageous Dr. Christian *'40*
Three Faces West *'40*
Fisherman's Wharf *'39*
Meet Dr. Christian *'39*
Way Down South *'39*
Cotton Queen *'37*
Broken Melody *'34*
The Ghost Camera *'33*

Kurt Voss(1963-)
Sugar Town *'99*
Highway Hitcher *'98*
Body Count *'97*
Poison Ivy 3: The New Seduction *'97*
Amnesia *'96*
Baja *'95*
The Horseplayer *'91*
Genuine Risk *'89*
Border Radio *'88*

Andy Wachowski(1967-)
Speed Racer *'08*
The Matrix Reloaded *'03*
The Matrix Revolutions *'03*
The Matrix *'99*
Bound *'96*

Larry Wachowski(1965-)
Speed Racer *'08*
The Matrix Reloaded *'03*
The Matrix Revolutions *'03*
The Matrix *'99*
Bound *'96*

Jonathan Wacks
Ed and His Dead Mother *'93*
Mystery Date *'91*
Powwow Highway *'89*

Andrucha Waddington(1970-)
House of Sand *'05*
Me You Them *'00*

Michael Wadleigh(1941-)
Wolfen *'81*
Woodstock *'70*

Jeff Wadlow
Never Back Down *'08*
Cry_Wolf *'05*

George Waggner(1894-1984)
The Commies Are Coming, the Commies Are Coming *'57*
The Fighting Kentuckian *'49*
The Climax *'44*
Horror Island *'41*
Man Made Monster *'41*
The Wolf Man *'41*
Mystery Plane *'39*
Stunt Pilot *'39*
Wolf Call *'39*
Ghost Town Riders *'38*
Outlaw Express *'38*
Western Trails *'38*

Andrew Wagner
Starting Out in the Evening *'07*
The Talent Given Us *'04*

David Wain
Role Models *'08*
The Ten *'07*
Wet Hot American Summer *'01*

Rupert Wainwright(1961-)
The Fog *'05*
Stigmata *'99*
Blank Check *'93*
Dillinger *'91*
The Discovery Program *'89*

Andrzej Wajda(1927-)
Katyn *'07*
Zemsta *'02*
Korczak *'90*
The Possessed *'88*
A Love in Germany *'84*
Danton *'82*
Man of Iron *'81*
The Conductor *'80*
Maids of Wilko *'79*
Without Anesthesia *'78*
Man of Marble *'76*
Land of Promise *'74*
Landscape After Battle *'70*
Everything for Sale *'68*
Lotna *'64*
Siberian Lady Macbeth *'61*
Innocent Sorcerers *'60*
Ashes and Diamonds *'58*
Kanal *'56*
A Generation *'54*

Chris Walas(1953-)
The Vagrant *'92*
The Fly 2 *'89*

Grant Austin Waldman
Teenage Exorcist *'93*
The Channeler *'89*
Gator King *'70*

Chuck Walker
Retribution Road *'07*
Ryder P.I. *'86*

Dorian Walker
Teen Witch *'89*
Making the Grade *'84*

Giles Walker(1946-)
Ordinary Magic *'93*
Princes in Exile *'90*
90 Days *'86*

Hal Walker(1896-1972)
The Road to Bali *'53*
Sailor Beware *'52*
At War with the Army *'50*
The Road to Utopia *'46*
The Stork Club *'45*

Pete Walker(1939-)
Home Before Midnight *'84*
House of the Long Shadows *'82*
The Comeback *'77*
Schizo *'77*
The Confessional *'75*
House of Whipcord *'75*
Tiffany Jones *'75*
Frightmare *'74*
Die Screaming, Marianne *'73*
Flesh and Blood Show *'73*
Man of Violence *'71*
The Big Switch *'70*

Stuart Walker(1887-1941)
The Mystery of Edwin Drood *'35*
Werewolf of London *'35*
Great Expectations *'34*
The Eagle and the Hawk *'33*
Misleading Lady *'32*

Gary Walkow
Crashing *'07*
Beat *'00*
Notes from Underground *'95*
The Trouble with Dick *'88*

Randall Wallace(1949-)
We Were Soldiers *'02*
The Man in the Iron Mask *'98*

Richard Wallace(1894-1951)
Sinbad, the Sailor *'47*
Tycoon *'47*
Because of Him *'45*
It's in the Bag *'45*
Bombardier *'43*
The Fallen Sparrow *'43*
A Night to Remember *'42*
A Girl, a Guy and a Gob *'41*
Captain Caution *'40*
The Young in Heart *'38*
Blossoms on Broadway *'37*
Wedding Present *'36*
Little Minister *'34*
Man of the World *'31*

Rick Wallace
Acceptable Risks *'86*
A Time to Live *'85*
California Girls *'84*

Stephen Wallace(1943-)
The Killing Beach *'92*
Prisoners of the Sun *'91*
For Love Alone *'86*
Winner Takes All *'84*

Tommy Lee Wallace(1949-)
John Carpenter Presents Vampires: Los Muertos *'02*
Final Justice *'98*
The Spree *'96*
Witness to the Execution *'94*
The Comrades of Summer *'92*
Stephen King's It *'90*
Aloha Summer *'88*
Fright Night 2 *'88*
Halloween 3: Season of the Witch *'82*

Anthony Waller(1959-)
The Guilty *'99*
An American Werewolf in Paris *'97*
Mute Witness *'95*

Raoul Walsh(1887-1980)
A Distant Trumpet *'64*
Esther and the King *'60*
The Sheriff of Fractured Jaw *'59*
The Naked and the Dead *'58*
Band of Angels *'57*
The King and Four Queens *'56*
Battle Cry *'55*
The Tall Men *'55*
Gun Fury *'53*
A Lion in the Streets *'53*
A Lion Is in the Streets *'53*
Sea Devils *'53*
Blackbeard the Pirate *'52*
The Lawless Breed *'52*
The World in His Arms *'52*
Along the Great Divide *'51*
Captain Horatio Hornblower *'51*
Distant Drums *'51*
The Enforcer *'51*
Colorado Territory *'49*
White Heat *'49*
Silver River *'48*
Pursued *'47*
The Man I Love *'46*
The Horn Blows at Midnight *'45*
Objective, Burma! *'45*
Salty O'Rourke *'45*
Uncertain Glory *'44*
Background to Danger *'43*
Northern Pursuit *'43*
Desperate Journey *'42*
Gentleman Jim *'42*
High Sierra *'41*
Manpower *'41*
Strawberry Blonde *'41*
They Died with Their Boots On *'41*
Dark Command *'40*
They Drive by Night *'40*
The Roaring Twenties *'39*
College Swing *'38*
O.H.M.S. *'37*
When Thief Meets Thief *'37*
Big Brown Eyes *'36*
Klondike Annie *'36*
The Bowery *'33*
Going Hollywood *'33*
Women of All Nations *'31*
Big Trail *'30*
Sadie Thompson *'28*
The Thief of Baghdad *'24*
Regeneration *'15*

Charles Walters(1911-82)
Walk, Don't Run *'66*
The Unsinkable Molly Brown *'64*
Billy Rose's Jumbo *'62*
Please Don't Eat the Daisies *'60*
Ask Any Girl *'59*
Don't Go Near the Water *'57*
High Society *'56*
The Glass Slipper *'55*
The Tender Trap *'55*
Dangerous When Wet *'53*
Easy to Love *'53*
Lili *'53*
Torch Song *'53*
The Belle of New York *'52*
Texas Carnival *'51*
Three Guys Named Mike *'51*
Summer Stock *'50*
The Barkleys of Broadway *'49*
Easter Parade *'48*
Good News *'47*

Fred Walton
The Courtyard *'95*
Dead Air *'94*
When a Stranger Calls Back *'93*
Homewrecker *'92*
Trapped *'89*
The Rosary Murders *'87*
April Fool's Day *'86*
Hadley's Rebellion *'84*
When a Stranger Calls *'79*

James Wan(1977-)
Dead Silence *'07*
Death Sentence *'07*
Saw *'04*

Sam Wanamaker(1919-93)
Killing of Randy Webster *'81*
The Dark Side of Love *'79*
Sinbad and the Eye of the Tiger *'77*
Catlow *'71*
The Executioner *'70*

Peter Wang
The Laserman *'90*
A Great Wall *'86*

Steve Wang
Drive *'96*
Guyver 2: Dark Hero *'94*
The Guyver *'91*

Wayne Wang(1949-)
The Princess of Nebraska *'07*
A Thousand Years of Good Prayers *'07*
Last Holiday *'06*
Because of Winn-Dixie *'05*
Maid in Manhattan *'02*
The Center of the World *'01*
Anywhere But Here *'99*
Chinese Box *'97*
Blue in the Face *'95*
Smoke *'95*
The Joy Luck Club *'93*
Eat a Bowl of Tea *'89*
Slamdance *'87*
Dim Sum: A Little Bit of Heart *'85*
Chan Is Missing *'82*

Xiaoshuai Wang(1966-)
In Love We Trust *'07*
Beijing Bicycle *'01*
Frozen *'98*
So Close to Paradise *'98*

David S. Ward(1947-)
Down Periscope *'96*
Major League 2 *'94*
The Program *'93*
King Ralph *'91*
Major League *'89*
Cannery Row *'82*

Donal Lardner Ward(1964-)
The Suburbans *'99*
My Life's in Turnaround *'94*

Vincent Ward(1956-)
River Queen *'05*
What Dreams May Come *'98*
Map of the Human Heart *'93*
The Navigator *'88*
Vigil *'84*

Clyde Ware(1936-)
Bad Jim *'89*
The Hatfields & the McCoys *'75*
When the Line Goes Through *'73*
No Drums, No Bugles *'71*

Regis Wargnier(1948-)
East-West *'99*
Indochine *'92*

Charles Marquis Warren(1912-90)
Macbeth *'88*
Charro! *'69*
Tension at Table Rock *'56*
Arrowhead *'53*
Hellgate *'52*
Little Big Horn *'51*
Red Desert *'50*

Deryn Warren
Black Magic Woman *'91*
Bloodspell *'87*
Mirror of Death *'87*

Jennifer Warren(1941-)
Partners in Crime *'99*
Forbidden Choices *'94*

Jerry Warren(1921-88)
Frankenstein Island *'81*
The Wild World of Batwoman *'66*
Curse of the Stone Hand *'64*
Attack of the Mayan Mummy *'63*
Invasion of the Animal People *'62*
Terror of the Bloodhunters *'62*
Creature of the Walking Dead *'60*
Face of the Screaming Werewolf *'59*
The Incredible Petrified World *'58*
Teenage Zombies *'58*
Man Beast *'55*

John Warren(1953-)
Major League 3: Back to the Minors *'98*
The Curse of Inferno *'96*

Norman J. Warren(1942-)
Bloody New Year *'87*
Gunpowder *'87*
Inseminoid *'80*
Spaced Out *'80*
The Terror *'79*
Alien Prey *'78*

Denzel Washington(1954-)
The Great Debaters *'07*
Antwone Fisher *'02*

Daniel Waters(1962-)
Sex and Death 101 *'07*
Happy Campers *'01*

John Waters(1946-)
A Dirty Shame *'04*
Cecil B. Demented *'00*
Pecker *'98*
Serial Mom *'94*
Cry-Baby *'90*
Divine *'90*
Hairspray *'88*
Polyester *'81*
Desperate Living *'77*
Female Trouble *'74*
Pink Flamingos *'72*
Multiple Maniacs *'70*
Mondo Trasho *'69*

Mark S. Waters(1964-)
Ghosts of Girlfriends Past *'09*
The Spiderwick Chronicles *'08*
Just like Heaven *'05*
Mean Girls *'04*
Freaky Friday *'03*
Head Over Heels *'01*
The House of Yes *'97*

Frederick P. Watkins
Lethal Seduction *'97*
A Matter of Honor *'95*
Brutal Fury *'92*

Peter Watkins(1935-)
Edvard Munch *'74*
The Gladiators *'70*
Privilege *'67*

John Watson
The Zoo Gang *'85*
Deathstalker *'83*

Harry Watt(1906-87)
Eureka Stockade *'49*
Overlanders *'46*

Nate Watt(1889-1968)
Frontier Vengeance *'40*
Law of the Pampas *'39*
Borderland *'37*
Rustler's Valley *'37*
Hopalong Cassidy Returns *'36*

Ric Roman Waugh(1968-)
Felon *'08*
In the Shadows *'01*
Exit *'95*

Al Waxman(1935-2001)
Diamond Fleece *'92*
White Light *'90*
My Pleasure Is My Business *'74*

Keoni Waxman(1968-)
The Keeper *'09*
The Highway Man *'99*
I Shot a Man in Vegas *'96*
Serial Bomber *'96*
Almost Blue *'93*

Keenen Ivory Wayans(1958-)
Little Man *'06*
White Chicks *'04*
Scary Movie 2 *'01*
Scary Movie *'00*
A Low Down Dirty Shame *'94*
I'm Gonna Git You Sucka *'88*

John Wayne(1907-79)
The Green Berets *'68*
The Alamo *'60*

David Weaver
Charlie & Me *'08*
Siblings *'04*

Harry S. Webb(1896-1959)
Mesquite Buckaroo *'39*
Riding On *'37*
Santa Fe Bound *'37*
Fast Bullets *'36*
Pinto Rustlers *'36*
Laramie Kid *'35*
Ridin' Thru *'35*
Unconquered Bandit *'35*
Fighting Hero *'34*
The Live Wire *'34*
Westward Bound *'30*
The Man From Oklahoma *'26*

Ira Webb(1899-1971)
Wild Horse Valley *'40*
El Diablo Rides *'39*

Jack Webb(1920-82)
D.I. *'57*
Pete Kelly's Blues *'55*
Dragnet *'54*

Lewin Webb
The Confessor *'04*
Gone Dark *'03*

Millard Webb(1893-1935)
Glorifying the American Girl *'30*
The Dropkick *'27*

Robert D. Webb(1903-90)
The Jackals *'67*
Love Me Tender *'56*
Seven Cities of Gold *'55*
Beneath the 12-Mile Reef *'53*

William Webb
The Hit List *'93*
The Banker *'89*

Party Line '88
Dirty Laundry '87
Sunset Strip '85

Peter Webber(1968-)
Hannibal Rising '07
Girl with a Pearl Earring '03

Lois Weber(1881-1939)
The Blot '21
Too Wise Wives '21
Discontent '16

Nicholas Webster(1912-2006)
Mission Mars '67
Santa Claus Conquers the Martians '64
Gone Are the Days '63
Purlie Victorious '63

David Wechter(1956-)
Malibu Bikini Shop '86
Midnight Madness '80

Chris Wedge(1957-)
Robots '05
Ice Age '02

Stephen Weeks(1948-)
Sword of the Valiant '83
Madhouse Mansion '74
I, Monster '71

Paul Wegener(1874-1948)
The Golem '20
Student of Prague '13

Lo Wei(1918-96)
New Fist of Fury '76
Chinese Connection '73
Fists of Fury '73

John Weidner
Space Marines '96
Blood for Blood '95
Private Wars '93

Samuel Weil
See Lloyd Kaufman

Paul Weiland(1953-)
Made of Honor '08
For Roseanna '96
City Slickers 2: The Legend of Curly's Gold '94
Bernard and the Genie '91
Leonard Part 6 '87

Claudia Weill(1947-)
Critical Choices '97
Once a Hero '88
It's My Turn '80
Girlfriends '78

Yossi Wein
Octopus 2: River of Fear '02
Shark Attack 2 '00
U.S. Seals '98
Mission of Death '97
Operation Delta Force 2: Mayday '97
Terminal Impact '95
Never Say Die '94
Lethal Ninja '93

Peter Weir(1944-)
Master and Commander: The Far Side of the World '03
The Truman Show '98
Fearless '93
Green Card '90
Dead Poets Society '89
The Mosquito Coast '86
Witness '85
The Year of Living Dangerously '82
Gallipoli '81
Plumber '79
The Last Wave '77
Picnic at Hanging Rock '75
The Cars That Ate Paris '74

Don Weis(1922-2000)
The Munsters' Revenge '81
Zero to Sixty '78
Ghost in the Invisible Bikini '66
Billie '65
Pajama Party '64
Critic's Choice '63
The Gene Krupa Story '59
The Affairs of Dobie Gillis '53
I Love Melvin '53
It's a Big Country '51

Gary Weis
Wholly Moses! '80
Diary of a Young Comic '79
All You Need Is Cash '78

Jack Weis
Mardi Gras Massacre '78
Crypt of Dark Secrets '76
Storyville '74

Sam Weisman
Dickie Roberts: Former Child Star '03
What's the Worst That Could Happen? '01
The Out-of-Towners '99
George of the Jungle '97
Bye Bye, Love '94
D2: The Mighty Ducks '94

Jiri Weiss(1913-2004)
Martha and I '91
Murder Czech Style '66
The Coward '62
Sweet Light in a Dark Room '60
Wolf Trap '57

Michael Cole Weiss(1979-)
Deceit '06
Standing Still '05

Adam Weissman
Infected '08
The Modern Adventures of Tom Sawyer '99

Chris Weitz(1969-)
The Twilight Saga: New Moon '09
The Golden Compass '07
About a Boy '02
Down to Earth '01
American Pie '99

Paul Weitz(1965-)
Cirque du Freak: The Vampire's Assistant '09
American Dreamz '06
In Good Company '04
About a Boy '02
Down to Earth '01
American Pie '99

Mel Welles(1924-2005)
Joy Ride to Nowhere '78
Lady Frankenstein '72

Orson Welles(1915-85)
It's All True '93
Don Quixote '92
Chimes at Midnight '67
The Trial '63
Touch of Evil '58
Mr. Arkadin '55
Othello '52
The Lady from Shanghai '48
Macbeth '48
The Stranger '46
The Magnificent Ambersons '42
Citizen Kane '41

David Wellington(1963-)
Restless Spirits '99
Long Day's Journey Into Night '96
A Man in Uniform '93
The Carpenter '89

William A. Wellman(1896-1975)
Darby's Rangers '58
Lafayette Escadrille '58
Goodbye, My Lady '56
Blood Alley '55
The High and the Mighty '54
Island in the Sky '53
Across the Wide Missouri '51
It's a Big Country '51
Westward the Women '51
The Happy Years '50
The Next Voice You Hear '50
Battleground '49
Magic Town '47
The Story of G.I. Joe '45
Buffalo Bill '44
Lady of Burlesque '43
The Ox-Bow Incident '43
The Great Man's Lady '42
Roxie Hart '42
Thunder Birds '42
Beau Geste '39
Nothing Sacred '37
A Star Is Born '37
Stingaree '34
Heroes for Sale '33
Midnight Mary '33
Wild Boys of the Road '33
Frisco Jenny '32
The Purchase Price '32
Night Nurse '31
Other Men's Women '31
Public Enemy '31
Beggars of Life '28
Wings '27
The Boob '26
The Boob '26

Audrey Wells(1960-)
Under the Tuscan Sun '03
Guinevere '99

Simon Wells(1961-)
The Time Machine '02
Prince of Egypt '98
Balto '95
We're Back! A Dinosaur's Story '93
An American Tail: Fievel Goes West '91

Wim Wenders(1945-)
Don't Come Knocking '05
Land of Plenty '04
Buena Vista Social Club '99
The Million Dollar Hotel '99
The End of Violence '97
Beyond the Clouds '95
Lisbon Story '94
Faraway, So Close! '93
Until the End of the World '91
Wings of Desire '88
Tokyo-Ga '85
Paris, Texas '83
Hammett '82
State of Things '82
The Wrong Move '78
The American Friend '77
Kings of the Road—In the Course of Time '76
Alice in the Cities '74
The Scarlet Letter '73
The Goalie's Anxiety at the Penalty Kick '71

Paul Wendkos(1922-)
The Chase '91
White Hot: The Mysterious Murder of Thelma Todd '91
Deadline Assault '90
The Flight '89
From the Dead of Night '89
The Great Escape 2: The Untold Story '88
The Taking of Flight 847: The Uli Derickson Story '88
Blood Vows: The Story of a Mafia Wife '87
Rage of Angels: The Story Continues '86
The Bad Seed '85
Celebrity '85
The Execution '85
Cocaine: One Man's Seduction '83
Awakening of Candra '81
The Five of Me '81
A Cry for Love '80
The Ordeal of Dr. Mudd '80
Betrayal '78
A Woman Called Moses '78
Secrets '77
The Death of Richie '76
Special Delivery '76
Honor Thy Father '73
Haunts of the Very Rich '72
The Mephisto Waltz '71
The Tattered Web '71
Guns of the Magnificent Seven '69
Johnny Tiger '66
Gidget Goes to Rome '63
Angel Baby '61
Gidget Goes Hawaiian '61
Gidget '59

Richard Wenk(1956-)
Just the Ticket '98
National Lampoon's Attack of the 5 Ft. 2 Women '94
Vamp '86

Alfred Werker(1896-1975)
At Gunpoint '55
Devil's Canyon '53
Lost Boundaries '49
He Walked by Night '48
Shock! '46
The Adventures of Sherlock Holmes '39
It Could Happen to You '39

Sandra Werneck(1951-)
Possible Loves '00
Boca '94

Byron Werner
Death Valley: The Revenge of Bloody Bill '04
Starkweather '04

Jeff Werner
Cheerleaders' Wild Weekend '85
Die Laughing '80

Peter Werner(1947-)
A Dog Named Christmas '09
The Circuit '08
Front of the Class '08
Gracie's Choice '04
Call Me Claus '01
Ruby's Bucket of Blood '01
The '70s '00
Mama Flora's Family '98
The Substitute Wife '94
Lone Justice '93
Hiroshima: Out of the Ashes '90
The Image '89
LBJ: The Early Years '88
The Alamo: Thirteen Days to Glory '87
No Man's Land '87
I Married a Centerfold '84
Hard Knox '83
Don't Cry, It's Only Thunder '82
In the Region of Ice '76

Lina Wertmuller(1928-)
The Worker and the Hairdresser '96
Ciao, Professore! '94
Summer Night with Greek Profile, Almond Eyes & Scent of Basil '87
Camorra: The Naples Connection '85
Sotto, Sotto '85
A Joke of Destiny, Lying in Wait Around the Corner Like a Bandit '84
Belle Starr '79
Blood Feud '79
A Night Full of Rain '78
Seven Beauties '76
Swept Away... '75
All Screwed Up '74
Love and Anarchy '73
Seduction of Mimi '72

Jake West
Pumpkinhead 3: Ashes to Ashes '06
Razor Blade Smile '98

Roland West(1885-1952)
Corsair '31
The Bat Whispers '30
Alibi '29
The Bat '26
The Monster '25

Simon West(1961-)
When a Stranger Calls '06
Lara Croft: Tomb Raider '01
The General's Daughter '99
Con Air '97

William West
Double Trouble '41
Flying Wild '41

Eric Weston
To Protect and Serve '92
The Iron Triangle '89
Marvin & Tige '84
Evilspeak '82

Haskell Wexler(1926-)
Latino '85
Medium Cool '69

James Whale(1896-1957)
The Man in the Iron Mask '39
Sinners in Paradise '38
Wives under Suspicion '38
The Great Garrick '37
Show Boat '36
The Bride of Frankenstein '35
The Invisible Man '33
The Old Dark House '32
Frankenstein '31

Frank Whaley(1963-)
The Jimmy Show '01
Joe the King '99

George Whaley(1949-)
Clowning Around 2 '93
Clowning Around '92

Tony Wharmby
Covert Assassin '94
Like A Bride '94
Seduced by Evil '94
Treacherous Crossing '92
The Kissing Place '90
Sorry, Wrong Number '89
Love for Lydia '79

Claude Whatham(1927-2008)
Buddy's Song '91
Murder Elite '86
Agatha Christie's Murder is Easy '82
Disraeli '79
Sweet William '79
All Creatures Great and Small '74
That'll Be the Day '73
Elizabeth R '72

Jim Wheat(1952-)
Pitch Black '00
After Midnight '89
The Ewoks: Battle for Endor '85
Lies '83

Ken Wheat(1950-)
Pitch Black '00
After Midnight '89
The Ewoks: Battle for Endor '85
Lies '83

David Wheatley(1950-)
Catherine Cookson's The Wingless Bird '97
Catherine Cookson's The Girl '96
Catherine Cookson's The Rag Nymph '96
Catherine Cookson's The Tide of Life '96
Hostages '93
Catherine Cookson's The Fifteen Streets '90

Anne Wheeler(1946-)
The Gambler, the Girl and the Gunslinger '09
Mail Order Bride '08
Edge of Madness '02
Better Than Chocolate '99
Angel Square '92
Bye Bye Blues '89
Cowboys Don't Cry '88
Loyalties '86

Tim Whelan(1893-1957)
Texas Lady '56
Rage at Dawn '55
Badman's Territory '46
Higher and Higher '44
Step Lively '44
Seven Days' Leave '42
Twin Beds '42
International Lady '41
The Thief of Bagdad '40
Clouds over Europe '39
Action for Slander '38
The Divorce of Lady X '38
Sidewalks of London '38
The Mill on the Floss '37

Forest Whitaker(1961-)
First Daughter '04
Hope Floats '98
Waiting to Exhale '95
Strapped '93

Alan White
Risk '00
Erskinville Kings '99

Andrew White
See Andrea Bianchi

Jules White(1900-85)
The Robert Benchley Miniatures Collection '35
Sidewalks of New York '31
Dogville Shorts '30

Susanna White
Nanny McPhee 2 '10
Generation Kill '08
Jane Eyre '06
Bleak House '05

Sylvain White
The Losers '10
Stomp the Yard '07

Mat Whitecross
Sex & Drugs & Rock & Roll '10
The Road to Guantanamo '06

Alexander Whitelaw
Vicious Circles '97
Lifespan '75

John Whitesell
Big Momma's House 2 '06
Deck the Halls '06
Malibu's Most Wanted '03
See Spot Run '01
Calendar Girl '93

Philip H. (Phil, P.H.) Whitman(1893-1935)
His Private Secretary '33
Girl from Calgary '32
Wayne Murder Case '32

Preston A. Whitmore, II(1962-)
This Christmas '07
Crossover '06
The Walking Dead '94

William Whitney
Heroes of the Saddle '40
S.O.S. Coast Guard '37

Tom Whitus
The Wild Card '03
Threat of Exposure '02

Richard Whorf(1906-66)
Champagne for Caesar '50
Luxury Liner '48
It Happened in Brooklyn '47
Love from a Stranger '47
Till the Clouds Roll By '46
Blues in the Night '41

Michael Whyte
Catherine Cookson's The Man Who Cried '93
The Railway Station Man '92

William Wiard(1928-87)
Kicks '85
Help Wanted: Male '82
Tom Horn '80
Snowblind '78

David Wickes
Frankenstein '93
Jekyll and Hyde '90
Jack the Ripper '88

Silver Dream Racer '83

Bernhard Wicki(1919-2000)
Morituri '65
The Longest Day '62
The Bridge '59

Bo Widerberg(1930-97)
All Things Fair '95
Man from Mallorca '84
The Man on the Roof '76
Elvira Madigan '67

Ken Wiederhorn
A House in the Hills '93
Return of the Living Dead 2 '88
Dark Tower '87
Meatballs 2 '84
Eyes of a Stranger '81
Shock Waves '77

Robert Wiemer(1938-)
The Night Train to Kathmandu '88
Somewhere Tomorrow '85
Anna to the Infinite Power '84

Robert Wiene(1881-1938)
The Hands of Orlac '25
The Cabinet of Dr. Caligari '19

Crane Wilbur(1886-1973)
The Bat '59
The Devil on Wheels '47
Crime School '38
We're in the Legion Now '37
Yellow Cargo '36
Tomorrow's Children '34

Fred M. Wilcox(1905-64)
Forbidden Planet '56
The Secret Garden '49
The Hills of Home '48
Three Daring Daughters '48
Courage of Lassie '46
Lassie, Come Home '43

Herbert Wilcox(1892-1977)
Teenage Bad Girl '59
Dangerous Youth '58
The King's Rhapsody '55
Let's Make Up '55
Trouble in the Glen '54
Maytime in Mayfair '49
Elizabeth of Ladymead '48
The Courtney Affair '47
I Live in Grosvenor Square '46
Forever and a Day '43
Sunny '41
No, No Nanette '40
Nurse Edith Cavell '39
London Melody '37
Bitter Sweet '33

Cornel Wilde(1915-89)
Sharks' Treasure '75
The Naked Prey '66
Sword of Lancelot '63

Ted Wilde(1893-1929)
Speedy '28
The Kid Brother '27
Battling Orioles '24

Billy Wilder(1906-2002)
Buddy Buddy '81
The Front Page '74
Avanti! '72
The Private Life of Sherlock Holmes '70
The Fortune Cookie '66
Kiss Me, Stupid! '64
Irma La Douce '63
One, Two, Three '61
The Apartment '60
Some Like It Hot '59
Love in the Afternoon '57
Spirit of St. Louis '57
Witness for the Prosecution '57
The Seven Year Itch '55
Sabrina '54
Stalag 17 '53
Ace in the Hole '51
Sunset Boulevard '50
Emperor Waltz '48
A Foreign Affair '48
The Lost Weekend '45
Double Indemnity '44
Five Graves to Cairo '43
The Major and the Minor '42
Mauvaise Graine '33

Gene Wilder(1935-)
Haunted Honeymoon '86
The Woman in Red '84
The Adventures of Sherlock Holmes' Smarter Brother '78
World's Greatest Lover '77

W. Lee Wilder(1904-82)
Fright '56
Manfish '56
Big Bluff '55
Killers from Space '54
The Snow Creature '54
Phantom from Space '53
Woman in Brown '48

Georg Wildhagen(1920-)
The Merry Wives of Windsor '50
The Marriage of Figaro '49

Gavin Wilding
Spliced '03
Christina's House '99
Premonition '98
Stag '97
Listen '96
The Raffle '94

Gordon Wiles(1902-50)
The Gangster '47
Mr. Boggs Steps Out '38
Prison Train '38
Lady from Nowhere '36
Charlie Chan's Secret '35

Ethan Wiley
Children of the Corn 5: Fields of Terror '98
House 2: The Second Story '87

Charles Wilkinson
Breach of Trust '95
Blood Clan '91
Quarantine '89

Irvin Willat(1890-1976)
The Michigan Kid '28
False Faces '18

Anson Williams(1949-)
Dream Date '93
All-American Murder '91
A Perfect Little Murder '90
Little White Lies '89

Elmo Williams(1913-)
Hell Ship Mutiny '57
Tall Texan '53

Lester Williams
See William Berke

Matt Williams
Walker Payne '06
Where the Heart Is '00

Oscar Williams(1944-)
Death Drug '83
Hot Potato '76
Final Comedown '72

Paul Williams(1940-)
Miss Right '81
Dealing: Or the Berkeley-to-Boston Forty-Brick Lost-Bag Blues '72

Paul W. Williams(1943-)
Mirage '94
The November Men '93

Rob Williams
Make the Yuletide Gay '09
Long-Term Relationship '06

Spencer Williams, Jr.(1893-1969)
Juke Joint '47
Dirty Gertie from Harlem U.S.A. '46
Blood of Jesus '41
Go Down Death '41

Stephen Williams
A Killing Spring '02
Verdict in Blood '02
My Teacher Ate My Homework '98
ShadowZone: The Undead Express '96
Soul Survivor '95

Tod Williams(1968-)
The Door in the Floor '04
The Adventures of Sebastian Cole '99

Tony Williams(1942-)
Next of Kin '82
Solo '77

Fred Williamson(1938-)
On the Edge '02
Silent Hunter '94
South Beach '92
Steele's Law '91
Three Days to a Kill '91
The Kill Reflex '89
The Messenger '87
Foxtrap '85
Big Score '83
The Last Fight '82
One Down, Two to Go! '82
Mister Mean '77
Death Journey '76
Adios Amigo '75
Mean Johnny Barrows '75
No Way Back '74

Nick Willing(1961-)
Alice '09
The River King '05
Close Your Eyes '02
Jason and the Argonauts '00
Alice in Wonderland '99
Photographing Fairies '97

J. Elder Wills(1900-70)
Big Fella '37
Song of Freedom '36

Ben F. Wilson
The Fighting Stallion '26
Wild Horse Canyon '25

Dean Wilson
Blind Faith '89
Free Amerika Broadcasting '89
Clayton County Line '78

Hugh Wilson(1943-)
Dudley Do-Right '99
Blast from the Past '98
The First Wives Club '96
Guarding Tess '94
Burglar '87
Rustler's Rhapsody '85
Police Academy '84

Jim Wilson
Whirlygirl '04
Head Above Water '96
Movie Maker '86
Stacy's Knights '83

Richard Wilson(1915-91)
It's All True '93
Three in the Attic '68
Invitation to a Gunfighter '64
Al Capone '59

Sandy Wilson(1947-)
American Boyfriends '89
My American Cousin '85

Sheldon Wilson
Screamers: The Hunting '09
Shallow Ground '04

Kurt Wimmer(1964-)
Ultraviolet '06
Equilibrium '02
One Man's Justice '95

James R. Winburn
Miami Beach Cops '93
The Death Merchant '91
Evil Altar '89

Simon Wincer(1943-)
Comanche Moon '08
Monte Walsh '03
Crocodile Dundee in Los Angeles '01
Crossfire Trail '01
P.T. Barnum '99
The Echo of Thunder '98
Escape: Human Cargo '98
Flash '98
Murder She Purred: A Mrs. Murphy Mystery '98
The Phantom '96
Operation Dumbo Drop '95
Lightning Jack '94
Free Willy '93
Harley Davidson and the Marlboro Man '91
Quigley Down Under '90
Lonesome Dove '89
The Lighthorsemen '87
The Girl Who Spelled Freedom '86
D.A.R.Y.L. '85
Phar Lap '84
Dark Forces '83
The Night After Halloween '79

Bretaigne Windust(1906-60)
The Pied Piper of Hamelin '57
The Enforcer '51
Perfect Strangers '50
Pretty Baby '50
June Bride '48
Winter Meeting '48

Harry Winer(1947-)
Lucky Seven '03
Jeremiah '98
House Arrest '96
JFK: Reckless Youth '93
SpaceCamp '86
Mirrors '85
Single Bars, Single Women '84

Jonathan Winfrey
Legend of the Lost Tomb '97
Black Scorpion 2: Ground Zero '96
Carnosaur 3: Primal Species '96
Black Scorpion '95
Bloodfist 7: Manhunt '95
Excessive Force 2: Force on Force '95
The Assassination Game '92

Gary Winick(1961-)
Letters to Juliet '10
Bride Wars '09
Charlotte's Web '06
13 Going on 30 '04
Tadpole '02
The Tic Code '99
Sweet Nothing '96
Out of the Rain '90
Curfew '88

Charles Winkler
Streets of Blood '09
The Net 2.0 '06
At Any Cost '00
Rocky Marciano '99
Disturbed '90
You Talkin' to Me? '87

David Winkler
Christmas Caper '07
Devour '05
Finding Graceland '98

Henry Winkler(1945-)
The Most Wonderful Time of the Year '08
Cop and a Half '93
Memories of Me '88
A Smoky Mountain Christmas '86

Irwin Winkler(1934-)
Home of the Brave '06
De-Lovely '04
Life as a House '01
At First Sight '98
The Net '95
Night and the City '92
Guilty by Suspicion '91

Terence H. Winkless
Get a Clue! '98
Lady Killer '97
Not of This Earth '96
White Wolves 2: Legend of the Wild '94
Rage and Honor '92
The Berlin Conspiracy '91
Corporate Affairs '90
Bloodfist '89
The Nest '88

Michael Winner(1935-)
Parting Shots '98
Bullseye! '90
A Chorus of Disapproval '89
Appointment with Death '88
Scream for Help '86
Death Wish 3 '85
The Wicked Lady '83
Death Wish 2 '82
Firepower '79
The Big Sleep '78
The Sentinel '76
Death Wish '74
Scorpio '73
The Stone Killer '73
The Mechanic '72
The Nightcomers '72
Chato's Land '71
Lawman '71
I'll Never Forget What's 'Isname '67
The Girl Getters '66
Cool Mikado '63
Murder on the Campus '52

David Winning(1961-)
Swamp Devil '08
Black Swarm '07
Something Beneath '07
Call of the Wild '04
He Sees You When You're Sleeping '02
Profile for Murder '96
Turbo: A Power Rangers Movie '96
Killer Image '92
Storm '87

Peter Winograd
One Last Run '89
Flicks '85

Terry Winsor
In the Spider's Web '07
Essex Boys '99
The Magician '93
Fool's Gold: The Story of the Brink's-Mat Robbery '92
Party! Party! '83

Stan Winston(1946-2008)
The Adventures of a Gnome Named Gnorm '93
Pumpkinhead '88

Alex Winter(1965-)
Fever '99
Freaked '93

Michael Winterbottom(1961-)
The Killer Inside Me '10
A Mighty Heart '07
The Road to Guantanamo '06
Tristram Shandy: A Cock and Bull Story '05
Code 46 '03
In This World '03
24 Hour Party People '01
The Claim '00
Wonderland '99
I Want You '98
Welcome to Sarajevo '97
Go Now '96
Jude '96
Butterfly Kiss '94
Family '94

David Winters(1939-)
Rage to Kill '88
Space Mutiny '88
Codename: Vengeance '87
Thrashin' '86
Mission... Kill '85
Fanatic '82
Racquet '79
Dr. Jekyll and Mr. Hyde '73

Peter Winther
Touch the Top of the World '06
The Librarian: Quest for the Spear '04

Scott Wiper(1970-)
The Condemned '07
A Better Way to Die '00

Frank Wisbar(1899-1967)
The Devil Bat's Daughter '46
Strangler of the Swamp '46

Herbert Wise(1924-)
The 10th Kingdom '00
Breaking the Code '95
Strange Interlude '90
Woman in Black '89
Pope John Paul II '84
The Norman Conquests, Part 1: Table Manners '78
The Norman Conquests, Part 2: Living Together '78
The Norman Conquests, Part 3: Round and Round the Garden '78
The Gathering Storm '74
Elizabeth R '72
Castle of the Living Dead '64
Alone Against Rome '62

Kirk Wise(1963-)
Atlantis: The Lost Empire '01
The Hunchback of Notre Dame '96
Beauty and the Beast '91

Robert Wise(1914-2005)
Rooftops '89
Star Trek: The Motion Picture '79
Audrey Rose '77
The Hindenburg '75
The Andromeda Strain '71
Star! '68
The Sand Pebbles '66
The Sound of Music '65
The Haunting '63
Two for the Seesaw '62
West Side Story '61
Odds Against Tomorrow '59
I Want to Live! '58
Run Silent, Run Deep '58
This Could Be the Night '57
Until They Sail '57
Helen of Troy '56
Somebody Up There Likes Me '56
Tribute to a Bad Man '56
Executive Suite '54
The Desert Rats '53
The Day the Earth Stood Still '51
Three Secrets '50
The Set-Up '49
Blood on the Moon '48
Born to Kill '47
Criminal Court '46
The Body Snatcher '45
Curse of the Cat People '44
Mademoiselle Fifi '44
The Magnificent Ambersons '42

Carol Wiseman
Face the Music '92
Does This Mean We're Married? '90
May Wine '90
The Little Princess '87

Len Wiseman(1973-)
Live Free or Die Hard '07
Underworld: Evolution '05
Underworld '03

Doris Wishman(1920-2002)
Double Agent 73 '80
The Amazing Transplant '70
Deadly Weapons '70
Bad Girls Go to Hell '65
Nude on the Moon '61

William Witney(1915-2002)
Darktown Strutters *'74*
Arizona Raiders *'65*
Master of the World *'61*
The Outcast *'54*
Iron Mountain Trail *'53*
Shadows of Tombstone *'53*
Border Saddlemates *'52*
Colorado Sundown *'52*
Heart of the Rockies *'51*
Bells of Coronado *'50*
North of the Great Divide *'50*
Sunset in the West *'50*
Trail of Robin Hood *'50*
Trigger, Jr. *'50*
Twilight in the Sierras *'50*
Down Dakota Way *'49*
The Golden Stallion *'49*
Susanna Pass *'49*
Eyes of Texas *'48*
Far Frontier *'48*
Grand Canyon Trail *'48*
Night Time in Nevada *'48*
Under California Stars *'48*
Apache Rose *'47*
Bells of San Angelo *'47*
Home in Oklahoma *'47*
On the Old Spanish Trail *'47*
Springtime in the Sierras *'47*
Cyclotrode "X" *'46*
Helldorado *'46*
Roll on Texas Moon *'46*
Fighting Devil Dogs *'43*
G-Men vs. the Black Dragon *'43*
The Gay Ranchero *'42*
Nyoka and the Tigermen *'42*
Spy Smasher *'42*
Spy Smasher Returns *'42*
The Adventures of Captain Marvel *'41*
Dick Tracy vs. Crime Inc. *'41*
King of the Texas Rangers *'41*
Adventures of Red Ryder *'40*
Doctor Satan's Robot *'40*
Drums of Fu Manchu *'40*
Mysterious Doctor Satan *'40*
Zorro's Fighting Legion *'39*
Daredevils of the Red Circle *'38*
Dick Tracy Returns *'38*
Hawk of the Wilderness *'38*
The Lone Ranger *'38*
The Painted Stallion *'37*
The Trigger Trio *'37*
Zorro Rides Again *'37*

Peter Wittman
Ellie *'84*
Play Dead *'81*

Jay Woelfel(1962-)
Unseen Evil *'99*
Things *'93*
Beyond Dream's Door *'88*

Fred Wolf(1915-2004)
Mouse and His Child *'77*
The Point *'71*

Fred Wolf(1964-)
The House Bunny *'08*
Strange Wilderness *'08*

Konrad Wolf(1925-82)
Solo Sunny *'80*
I Was Nineteen *'68*
Divided Heaven *'64*

Andy Wolk
A Stranger's Heart *'07*
The Christmas Shoes *'02*
Deliberate Intent *'01*
Mr. Rock 'n' Roll: The Alan Freed Story *'99*
The Defenders: Taking the First *'98*
The Defenders: Payback *'97*
Traces of Red *'92*
Criminal Justice *'90*

Dan Wolman(1941-)
Soldier of the Night *'84*
Baby Love *'83*
Nana *'82*
Hide and Seek *'80*
My Michael *'75*

M. Wallace Wolodarsky
Seeing Other People *'04*
Sorority Boys *'02*
Coldblooded *'94*

James Wong(1940-2004)
Dragonball: Evolution *'09*
Final Destination 3 *'06*
The One *'01*
Final Destination *'00*

Kar-Wai Wong
Days of Being Wild *'91*
As Tears Go By *'88*

Kirk Wong(1949-)
The Big Hit *'98*
Crime Story *'93*
Organized Crime & Triad Bureau *'93*

John Woo(1948-)
Red Cliff *'08*
Paycheck *'03*
Windtalkers *'02*
Mission: Impossible 2 *'00*
Blackjack *'97*
Face/Off *'97*
Once a Thief *'96*
Broken Arrow *'95*
Hard Target *'93*
Hard-Boiled *'92*
A Bullet in the Head *'90*
The Killer *'90*
Once a Thief *'90*
A Better Tomorrow, Part 2 *'88*
A Better Tomorrow, Part 1 *'86*
Heroes Shed No Tears *'86*
Last Hurrah for Chivalry *'78*

Edward D. Wood, Jr. (1924-78)
The Sinister Urge *'60*
Night of the Ghouls *'59*
Plan 9 from Outer Space *'56*
The Violent Years *'56*
Bride of the Monster *'55*
Jail Bait *'54*
Glen or Glenda? *'53*

Sam Wood(1883-1949)
The Stratton Story *'49*
Command Decision *'48*
Heartbeat *'46*
Guest Wife *'45*
Saratoga Trunk *'45*
Casanova Brown *'44*
For Whom the Bell Tolls *'43*
The Pride of the Yankees *'42*
The Devil & Miss Jones *'41*
Kings Row *'41*
Kitty Foyle *'40*
Our Town *'40*
Goodbye, Mr. Chips *'39*
A Day at the Races *'37*
Madame X *'37*
Navy Blue and Gold *'37*
Let 'Em Have It *'35*
A Night at the Opera *'35*
Whipsaw *'35*
The Barbarian *'33*
Hold Your Man *'33*
It's a Great Life *'29*
Beyond the Rocks *'22*
Peck's Bad Boy *'21*

Bille Woodruff
Bring It On: Fight to the Finish *'09*
Beauty Shop *'05*
Honey *'03*

John Woods
Plain Jane *'01*
Kings in Grass Castles *'97*

Rowan Woods(1959-)
Fragments *'08*
Little Fish *'05*
Do or Die *'01*
The Boys *'98*

Skip Woods
Hitman *'07*
Thursday *'98*

Jeff Woolnough
Celine *'08*
Taken *'02*

Strange Frequency 2 *'01*
Universal Soldier 2: Brothers in Arms *'98*
Universal Soldier 3: Unfinished Business *'98*
First Degree *'95*

Chuck Workman
Superstar: The Life and Times of Andy Warhol *'90*
Stoogemania *'85*
Kill Castro *'80*
The Mercenaries *'80*
The Money *'75*

Duke Worne(1888-1933)
Man from Headquarters *'28*
Ships in the Night *'28*

Wallace Worsley, II(1878-1944)
The Hunchback of Notre Dame *'23*
The Penalty *'20*

David Worth
Honor *'06*
Shark Attack 3: Megalodon *'02*
Time Lapse *'01*
Shark Attack 2 *'00*
The Prophet's Game *'99*
True Vengeance *'97*
Chain of Command *'95*
Lady Dragon 2 *'93*
Lady Dragon *'92*
Soldier's Revenge *'84*
Warrior of the Lost World *'84*
Mid Knight Rider *'79*

William Worthington
The Dragon Painter *'19*
The Tong Man *'19*

Soenke Wortmann(1959-)
The Hollywood Sign *'01*
Maybe... Maybe Not *'94*

John Griffith Wray(1896-1929)
Anna Christie *'23*
Soul of the Beast *'23*
Soul of the Beast *'23*
Beau Revel *'21*

Casper Wrede(1929-98)
The Terrorists *'74*
One Day in the Life of Ivan Denisovich *'71*

Alexander Wright
Styx *'00*
The First 9 1/2 Weeks *'98*
Fast Money *'96*

Edgar Wright(1974-)
Scott Pilgrim vs. the World *'10*
Hot Fuzz *'07*
Shaun of the Dead *'04*

Geoffrey Wright(1959-)
Macbeth *'06*
Cherry Falls *'00*
Terror Tract *'00*
Metal Skin *'94*
Romper Stomper *'92*

Joe Wright
The Soloist *'09*
Atonement *'07*
Pride and Prejudice *'05*

Mack V. Wright(1895-1965)
Sea Hound *'47*
Rootin' Tootin' Rhythm *'38*
Big Show *'37*
Hit the Saddle *'37*
Riders of the Whistling Skull *'37*
Roarin' Lead *'37*
Robinson Crusoe of Clipper Island *'36*
Robinson Crusoe of Mystery Island *'36*
The Vigilantes Are Coming *'36*
Winds of the Wasteland *'36*
Man from Monterey *'33*

Somewhere in Sonora *'33*
Haunted Gold *'32*

Tenny Wright(1885-1971)
Telegraph Trail *'33*
The Big Stampede *'32*

Thomas J. Wright
Taken *'02*
Unspeakable *'02*
Chrome Soldiers *'92*
Highlander: The Gathering *'92*
Deadly Game *'91*
The Fatal Image *'90*
Snow Kill *'90*
No Holds Barred *'89*
Torchlight *'85*

Donald Wrye
Range of Motion *'00*
Not in This Town *'97*
Ice Castles *'79*
Death Be Not Proud *'75*
Born Innocent *'74*

David Wu
Merlin's Apprentice *'06*
Webs *'03*
The Snow Queen *'02*
Formula 51 *'01*
The Bride with White Hair 2 *'93*

Ma Wu
Exorcist Master *'93*
The Water Margin *'72*

William Wyler(1902-81)
The Liberation of L.B. Jones *'70*
Funny Girl *'68*
How to Steal a Million *'66*
The Collector *'65*
The Children's Hour *'61*
Ben-Hur *'59*
The Big Country *'58*
Friendly Persuasion *'56*
Desperate Hours *'55*
Roman Holiday *'53*
Carrie *'52*
Detective Story *'51*
The Heiress *'49*
The Best Years of Our Lives *'46*
Mrs. Miniver *'42*
The Little Foxes *'41*
The Letter *'40*
The Westerner *'40*
Wuthering Heights *'39*
Jezebel *'38*
Dead End *'37*
Come and Get It *'36*
Dodsworth *'36*
These Three *'36*
The Good Fairy *'35*
Counsellor-at-Law *'33*
The Love Trap *'29*

Paul Wynne
Barrio Wars *'02*
Makin' Baby *'02*
Bombshell *'97*
Destination Vegas *'95*

Jim Wynorski(1950-)
Bone Eater *'07*
Extreme Limits *'01*
Gale Force *'01*
Poison *'01*
Ablaze *'00*
Rangers *'00*
Desert Thunder *'99*
Final Voyage *'99*
Militia *'99*
Stealth Fighter *'99*
Against the Law *'98*
Storm Trooper *'98*
Vampirella *'96*
The Wasp Woman *'96*
Body Chemistry 4: Full Exposure *'95*
Demolition High *'95*
Hard Bounty *'94*
Sorceress *'94*
Victim of Desire *'94*
Body Chemistry 3: Point of Seduction *'93*
Dinosaur Island *'93*
Ghoulies 4 *'93*

Home for Christmas *'93*
Munchie *'92*
Sins of Desire *'92*
Sorority House Massacre 2: Nighty Nightmare *'92*
The Haunting of Morella *'91*
976-EVIL 2: The Astral Factor *'91*
Hard to Die *'90*
The Return of Swamp Thing *'89*
Transylvania Twist *'89*
Not of This Earth *'88*
Big Bad Mama 2 *'87*
Deathstalker 2: Duel of the Titans *'87*
Chopping Mall *'86*
The Lost Empire *'83*

Greg Yaitanes(1970-)
Children of Dune *'03*
Double Tap *'98*
Hard Justice *'95*

Boaz Yakin(1944-)
Uptown Girls *'03*
Remember the Titans *'00*
A Price above Rubies *'97*
Fresh *'94*

Yoji Yamada(1931-)
Kabei: Our Mother *'08*
The Hidden Blade *'04*
The Twilight Samurai *'02*

Kazuhiko Yamaguchi
Sister Street Fighter *'76*
Delinquent Girl Boss: Blossoming Night Dreams *'70*

Yudai Yamaguchi
Battlefield Baseball *'03*
Shogun's Samurai—The Yagyu Clan Conspiracy *'78*

Satsuo Yamamoto(1910-83)
Nomugi Pass *'79*
Shinobi no Mono 2: Vengeance *'63*
Shinobi no Mono *'62*

Mitsuo Yanagimachi(1944-)
Shadow of China *'91*
Himatsuri *'85*

Jean Yarbrough(1900-75)
Over the Hill Gang *'69*
Hillbillies in a Haunted House *'67*
Jack & the Beanstalk *'52*
Lost in Alaska *'52*
Holiday in Havana *'49*
Master Minds *'49*
Pirate Ship *'49*
The Creeper *'48*
The Brute Man *'46*
House of Horrors *'46*
She Wolf of London *'46*
Here Come the Co-Eds *'45*
The Naughty Nineties *'45*
In Society *'44*
Law of the Jungle *'42*
Lure of the Islands *'42*
Meet the Mob *'42*
The Devil Bat *'41*
King of the Zombies *'41*
Let's Go Collegiate *'41*
Panama Menace *'41*
The Gang's All Here *'40*
Under Western Stars *'38*

Kimiyoshi Yasuda
Along with Ghosts *'69*
100 Monsters *'68*
Zatoichi: The Blind Swordsman and the Fugitives *'68*
Daimajin *'66*

David Yates(1963-)
Harry Potter and the Half-Blood Prince *'09*
Harry Potter and the Order of the Phoenix *'07*
The Girl in the Cafe *'05*
State of Play *'03*
The Way We Live Now *'02*

Gary Yates
Eye of the Beast *'07*
Maneater *'07*

Peter Yates(1929-)
A Separate Peace *'04*
Don Quixote *'00*
Curtain Call *'97*
Roommates *'95*
The Run of the Country *'95*
Year of the Comet *'92*
An Innocent Man *'89*
The House on Carroll Street *'88*
Suspect *'87*
Eleni *'85*
The Dresser *'83*
Krull *'83*
Eyewitness *'81*
Breaking Away *'79*
The Deep *'77*
Mother, Jugs and Speed *'76*
For Pete's Sake *'74*
Murphy's War *'71*
Bullitt *'68*
Koroshi *'67*
Robbery *'67*

Irvin S. Yeaworth, Jr. (1926-2004)
Dinosaurus! *'60*
The 4D Man *'59*
The Blob *'58*
The Flaming Teen-Age *'56*

Linda Yellen(1949-)
The Simian Line *'99*
End of Summer *'97*
Parallel Lives *'94*
Chantilly Lace *'93*

Wilson (Wai-Shun) Yip
Flash Point *'07*
Special Unit 2002 *'01*
Biozombie *'98*

Jeff Yonis
Born Bad *'97*
Humanoids from the Deep *'96*
Bloodfist 5: Human Target *'93*

Bud Yorkin(1926-)
Love Hurts *'91*
Arthur 2: On the Rocks *'88*
Twice in a Lifetime *'85*
The Thief Who Came to Dinner *'73*
Start the Revolution without Me *'70*
Divorce American Style *'67*
Never Too Late *'65*
Come Blow Your Horn *'63*

Yaky Yosha(1951-)
Sexual Response *'92*
Dead End Street *'83*

Hiroaki Yoshida
Iron Maze *'91*
Twilight of the Cockroaches *'90*

Harold Young(1897-1972)
Jungle Captive *'45*
Weird Woman *'44*
Spy Train *'43*
The Mummy's Tomb *'42*
Dreaming Out Loud *'40*
Little Tough Guys *'38*
The Scarlet Pimpernel *'34*

James L. Young(1872-1948)
The Bells *'26*
The Unchastened Woman *'25*

John G. Young
The Reception *'05*
Parallel Sons *'95*

Robert Young(1933-)
Blood Monkey *'07*
Mad Death *'83*

Robert M. Young(1924-)
One Special Night *'99*
Captain Jack *'98*

The Writer Index provides a videography for any writer with more than one video credit. The listings for the writer names follow an alphabetical sort by last name (although the names appear in a first name-last name format). The videographies are listed chronologically, from most recent film to their first. If a writer wrote more than one film in the same year, these movies are listed alphabetically within the year. Used in conjunction with the **Cast** index, this index will let you find actors and actresses who wrote themselves juicy parts (with varying degrees of success). Directors also tend to show up here, either before their directorial ambitions surfaced, or after they'd gained enough clout to get one of their scripts to the screen.

Douglas Aarniokoski
Puppet Master 5: The Final Chapter *'94*
Puppet Master 4 *'93*

Paul Aaron
In Too Deep *'99*
Laurel Avenue *'93*
Octagon *'80*

George Abbott(1887-1995)
The Pajama Game *'57*
All Quiet on the Western Front *'30*
The Sea God *'30*

Paul Abbott(1960-)
State of Play *'03*
Butterfly Collectors *'99*
Reckless: The Sequel *'98*
Reckless *'97*
Touching Evil *'97*
Cracker: Best Boys *'95*
Cracker: True Romance *'95*

Scott Abbott
Queen of the Damned *'02*
Introducing Dorothy Dandridge *'99*
The Wall *'99*
Winchell *'98*
Run for the Dream: The Gail Devers Story *'96*
Breach of Conduct *'94*

Kobe Abe(1924-93)
Face of Another *'66*
Woman in the Dunes *'64*

Keith Aberdein(1943-)
Iris *'89*
Utu *'83*
Carry Me Back *'82*

Lewis Abernathy
Terminal Invasion *'02*
Deepstar Six *'89*

Dustin Lee Abraham
How High *'01*
The Runner *'99*

Jim Abrahams(1944-)
Scary Movie 4 *'06*
Mafia! *'98*
Hot Shots! Part Deux *'93*
Hot Shots! *'91*
The Naked Gun: From the Files of Police Squad *'88*
Top Secret! *'84*
Airplane! *'80*
Kentucky Fried Movie *'77*

J.J. (Jeffrey) Abrams(1966-)
Mission: Impossible 3 *'06*
Joy Ride *'01*
Armageddon *'98*
Gone Fishin' *'97*
Forever Young *'92*
Regarding Henry *'91*
Taking Care of Business *'90*

Peter Ackerman
Ice Age: Dawn of the Dinosaurs *'09*
Ice Age *'02*

Rodney Ackland(1908-91)
Thursday's Child *'43*
Dangerous Moonlight *'41*
The Forty-Ninth Parallel *'41*

Allen Actor
Dungeonmaster *'83*
Terror at Red Wolf Inn *'72*

Daniel Adams
The Golden Boys *'08*
Primary Motive *'92*
A Fool and His Money *'88*

Douglas Adams(1952-2001)
The Hitchhiker's Guide to the Galaxy *'05*
The Hitchhiker's Guide to the Galaxy *'81*

Gerald Drayson Adams(1900-88)
Harum Scarum *'65*
Duel at Silver Creek *'52*
Flame of Araby *'51*
Armored Car Robbery *'50*
Big Steal *'49*

Andrew Adamson(1966-)
The Chronicles of Narnia: Prince Caspian *'08*
The Chronicles of Narnia: The Lion, the Witch and the Wardrobe *'05*
Shrek 2 *'04*

Ewart Adamson(1882-1945)
House of Errors *'42*
Circumstantial Evidence *'35*
Inside the Lines *'30*

Lisa Addario(1968-)
Surf's Up *'07*
Lover Girl *'97*

Milo Addica
The King *'05*
Birth *'04*
Monster's Ball *'01*

Bear Aderhold
Bait Shop *'08*
Delta Farce *'07*

Robert Adetuyi
Code Name: The Cleaner *'07*
Stomp the Yard *'07*
Turn It Up *'00*

Alan J. Adler
Metalstorm: The Destruction of Jared Syn *'83*
The Concrete Jungle *'82*
Parasite *'82*
The Alchemist *'81*

Duane Adler
Make It Happen *'08*
Step Up *'06*
Save the Last Dance *'01*

Gilbert Adler
Tales from the Crypt Presents Bordello of Blood *'96*
Children of the Corn 2: The Final Sacrifice *'92*

Eleonore Adlon
Rosalie Goes Shopping *'89*
Bagdad Cafe *'88*

Felix Adlon
Eat Your Heart Out *'96*
Younger & Younger *'94*
Salmonberries *'91*

Percy Adlon(1935-)
Younger & Younger *'94*
Salmonberries *'91*
Rosalie Goes Shopping *'89*
Bagdad Cafe *'88*
Sugarbaby *'85*
Celeste *'81*

Ed Adlum(1944-)
Shriek of the Mutilated *'74*
Invasion of the Blood Farmers *'72*

Frank (Franklyn) Adreon(1902-79)
Son of Zorro *'47*
Adventures of Red Ryder *'40*
Drums of Fu Manchu *'40*
Mysterious Doctor Satan *'40*
Zorro's Fighting Legion *'39*
S.O.S. Coast Guard *'37*

Gilles Adrien
The City of Lost Children *'95*
Delicatessen *'92*

Ben Affleck(1972-)
Gone Baby Gone *'07*
Good Will Hunting *'97*

James Agee(1909-55)
The Night of the Hunter *'55*
The African Queen *'51*

Joe Ahearne
Perfect Parents *'06*
Ultraviolet *'98*

Kamal Ahmed
Rapturious *'07*
The Jerky Boys *'95*

Byeong-ki Ahn
Apartment 1303 *'07*
Nightmare *'00*

Jonathan Aibel
Alvin and the Chipmunks: The Squeakuel *'09*
Monsters vs. Aliens *'09*
Kung Fu Panda *'08*

Karim Ainouz(1966-)
Madame Sata *'02*
Behind the Sun *'01*

Mary Ainslee(1919-91)
Desert Nights *'29*
Desert Nights *'29*

Alexandre Aja(1978-)
Piranha 3D *'10*
Mirrors *'08*
P2 *'07*
High Tension *'03*

Chantal Akerman(1950-)
A Couch in New York *'95*
Night and Day *'91*
Window Shopping *'86*
The Eighties *'83*
Les Rendez-vous D'Anna *'78*
News from Home *'76*

Yasushi Akimoto
One Missed Call 2 *'05*
One Missed Call *'03*

Fatih Akin(1973-)
New York, I Love You *'09*
Soul Kitchen *'09*
The Edge of Heaven *'07*
Head On *'04*

Jeff Albert
The Base *'99*
Warhead *'96*
Danger Zone *'95*
Live Wire: Human Timebomb *'95*
Terminal Impact *'95*
Never Say Die *'94*

Luis Alcoriza(1918-92)
The Exterminating Angel *'62*
Death in the Garden *'56*
El *'52*

Todd Alcott(1961-)
Antz *'98*
Curtain Call *'97*

Alan Alda(1936-)
Betsy's Wedding *'90*
A New Life *'88*
Sweet Liberty *'86*
M*A*S*H: Goodbye, Farewell & Amen *'83*
The Four Seasons *'81*
The Seduction of Joe Tynan *'79*

Robert Alden
Uncaged *'91*
Streetwalkin' *'85*

Will Aldis
Black Cadillac *'03*
Avenging Angelo *'02*
Clifford *'92*
Stealing Home *'88*
The Couch Trip *'87*
Back to School *'86*

Robert Aldrich(1918-83)
Too Late the Hero *'70*
Four for Texas *'63*

David Alexander
A Grandpa for Christmas *'07*
The Ticket *'97*
Dead Ahead *'96*

J. Grubb Alexander(1887-1932)
Svengali *'31*
County Fair *'20*

Scott M. Alexander(1963-)
1408 *'07*
Agent Cody Banks *'03*
Screwed *'00*
Man on the Moon *'99*
The People vs. Larry Flynt *'96*
That Darn Cat *'96*
Ed Wood *'94*
Problem Child 2 *'91*
Problem Child *'90*

Grigori Alexandrov(1903-83)
Que Viva Mexico *'32*
Ten Days That Shook the World *'27*

Sherman Alexie(1966-)
The Business of Fancydancing *'02*
Smoke Signals *'98*

Richard Alfieri(1952-)
The Sisters *'05*
Puerto Vallarta Squeeze *'04*
Harvest of Fire *'95*
A Friendship in Vienna *'88*
Echoes *'83*
Children of Rage *'75*

Dean Alioto
Shadowheart *'09*
L.A. Dicks *'05*

Ted Allan(1916-95)
Dr. Bethune *'90*
Love Streams *'84*
Falling in Love Again *'80*
Lies My Father Told Me *'75*

James Allardice
Money from Home *'53*
Sailor Beware *'52*

Chris Allen
In God We Trust *'80*
The Last Remake of Beau Geste *'77*

Curt Allen
Alligator 2: The Mutation *'90*
Blind Vengeance *'90*
Bloodstone *'88*
Hollywood Harry *'86*
Walking the Edge *'83*

Irwin Allen(1916-91)
Five Weeks in a Balloon *'62*
Voyage to the Bottom of the Sea *'61*
The Big Circus *'59*

Janis Allen
The Double Negative *'80*
Meatballs *'79*

Jay Presson Allen(1922-2006)
Year of the Gun *'91*
Deathtrap *'82*
Prince of the City *'81*
Just Tell Me What You Want *'80*
Funny Lady *'75*
Forty Carats *'73*
Cabaret *'72*
Travels with My Aunt *'72*
The Prime of Miss Jean Brodie *'69*
Marnie *'64*

Jim Allen(1926-99)
Land and Freedom *'95*
Raining Stones *'93*
Hidden Agenda *'90*

J.T. Allen
Jesse Stone: Death in Paradise *'06*
The Good Old Boys *'95*
Geronimo *'93*

Woody Allen(1935-)
Whatever Works *'09*
Vicky Cristina Barcelona *'08*
Cassandra's Dream *'07*
Scoop *'06*
Match Point *'05*
Melinda and Melinda *'05*
Anything Else *'03*
Hollywood Ending *'02*
The Curse of the Jade Scorpion *'01*
Small Time Crooks *'00*
Sweet and Lowdown *'99*
Celebrity *'98*
Deconstructing Harry *'97*
Everyone Says I Love You *'96*
Mighty Aphrodite *'95*
Bullets over Broadway *'94*
Manhattan Murder Mystery *'93*
Husbands and Wives *'92*
Shadows and Fog *'92*
Alice *'90*
Crimes & Misdemeanors *'89*
New York Stories *'89*
Another Woman *'88*
September *'88*
Radio Days *'87*
Hannah and Her Sisters *'86*
The Purple Rose of Cairo *'85*
Broadway Danny Rose *'84*
Zelig *'83*
A Midsummer Night's Sex Comedy *'82*
Stardust Memories *'80*
Manhattan *'79*
Interiors *'78*
Annie Hall *'77*
Love and Death *'75*
Sleeper *'73*
Everything You Always Wanted to Know about Sex (But Were Afraid to Ask) *'72*
Play It Again, Sam *'72*
Bananas *'71*
Take the Money and Run *'69*
What's Up, Tiger Lily? *'66*
What's New Pussycat? *'65*

Bradley Allenstein
Who's Your Caddy? *'07*
Juwanna Mann *'02*

Gila Almagor(1939-)
Under the Domim Tree *'95*
The Summer of Aviya *'88*

Michael Almereyda(1960-)
Hamlet *'00*
The Eternal *'99*
Nadja *'95*
Search and Destroy *'94*
Twister *'89*
Cherry 2000 *'88*

Pedro Almodovar(1951-)
Broken Embraces *'09*
Volver *'06*
Bad Education *'04*
Talk to Her *'02*
All About My Mother *'99*
Live Flesh *'97*
The Flower of My Secret *'95*
Kika *'94*
High Heels *'91*
Tie Me Up! Tie Me Down! *'90*
Women on the Verge of a Nervous Breakdown *'88*
Law of Desire *'86*
Matador *'86*
What Have I Done to Deserve This? *'85*
Dark Habits *'84*
Labyrinth of Passion *'82*
Pepi, Luci, Bom and Other Girls on the Heap *'80*

Arthur Alsberg(1917-2004)
Hot Lead & Cold Feet *'78*
Herbie Goes to Monte Carlo *'77*
Gus *'76*
No Deposit, No Return *'76*

Emmett Alston
Hunter's Blood *'87*
Nine Deaths of the Ninja *'85*
New Year's Evil *'78*

Eric Alter
The Experts *'89*
Hardbodies 2 *'86*
Hardbodies *'84*

Daniel Altiere
Dr. Dolittle: Million Dollar Mutts *'09*
Gym Teacher: The Movie *'08*

Steven Altiere
Dr. Dolittle: Million Dollar Mutts *'09*
Gym Teacher: The Movie *'08*

Sergio D. Altieri(1952-)
Silent Trigger *'97*
Little Sister *'92*
Blind Fear *'89*

Mark Altman
All Souls Day *'05*
House of the Dead *'03*
Free Enterprise *'98*

Robert Altman(1925-2006)
Kansas City *'95*
Ready to Wear *'94*
Short Cuts *'93*
Aria *'88*
Beyond Therapy *'86*
Quintet *'79*
A Wedding *'78*
3 Women *'77*
Buffalo Bill & the Indians *'76*
Thieves Like Us *'74*
Images *'72*
McCabe & Mrs. Miller *'71*

Christian Alvart
Case 39 *'10*
Pandorum *'09*
Antibodies *'05*

D. Alvelo(1965-2004)
Bound by Lies *'05*
Spider's Web *'01*

Silvio Amadio(1926-95)
Assassination in Rome *'65*
The Inveterate Bachelor *'58*

David Amann
The Rendering *'02*
Dead Air *'94*

Rod Amateau(1923-2003)
Sunset *'88*
The Garbage Pail Kids Movie *'87*
The Wilby Conspiracy *'75*
Hook, Line and Sinker *'30*

Dail Ambler(1925-)
He Kills Night After Night After Night *'69*
Night Slasher *'69*
Beat Girl *'60*

Eric Ambler(1909-98)
The Wreck of the Mary Deare *'59*
A Night to Remember *'58*
Battle Hell *'56*
The Cruel Sea *'53*
Encore *'52*
The Promoter *'52*
The Clouded Yellow *'51*
The October Man *'48*
Immortal Battalion *'44*

David Ambrose(1943-)
Year of the Gun *'91*
Taffin *'88*
Blackout *'85*
D.A.R.Y.L. *'85*
Amityville 3: The Demon *'83*
Dangerous Summer *'82*
The Final Countdown *'80*
Survivor *'80*
The Fifth Musketeer *'79*

Gianni Amelio(1945-)
Lamerica *'95*
The Stolen Children *'92*
Open Doors *'89*

Deborah Amelon(1955-)
Tricks *'97*
Exit to Eden *'94*

Alejandro Amenabar(1972-)
The Sea Inside *'04*
The Others *'01*
Open Your Eyes *'97*
Thesis *'96*

Sergio Amidei(1904-81)
Tales of Ordinary Madness *'83*
Generale Della Rovere *'60*
Shoeshine *'47*
Open City *'45*

Jack Amiel
The Shaggy Dog *'06*
The Prince & Me *'04*
Raising Helen *'04*

Cesar Amigo
The Ravagers *'65*
The Walls of Hell *'64*

Santiago Amigorena
A Few Days in September *'06*
After Sex *'97*

Mark Amin
The Prince & Me *'04*
Diplomatic Siege *'99*
The Principal Takes a Holiday *'98*

Hossein Amini(1966-)
Killshot *'09*
Shanghai *'09*
The Four Feathers *'02*
The Wings of the Dove *'97*
Jude *'96*

Dominic Anciano(1959-)
Love, Honour & Obey *'00*
Final Cut *'98*

Allison Anders(1954-)
Things Behind the Sun *'01*
Sugar Town *'99*
Grace of My Heart *'96*
Four Rooms *'95*
Mi Vida Loca *'94*
Gas Food Lodging *'92*
Border Radio *'88*

Sean Anders
She's Out of My League *'10*
Sex Drive *'08*
Never Been Thawed *'05*

Brad Anderson(1964-)
Session 9 *'01*
Happy Accidents *'00*
Next Stop, Wonderland *'98*

Edward A. Anderson
Shuttle *'09*
Flawless *'07*

Elizabeth Anderson
Three Wishes *'95*
Lassie *'94*

Gerry Anderson
Blonde and Blonder *'07*
Journey to the Far Side of the Sun *'69*

Hesper Anderson(1934-)
Grand Isle *'92*
Children of a Lesser God *'86*
Touched by Love *'80*

Jace Anderson
Mother of Tears *'08*
Mortuary *'05*
Derailed *'02*
Crocodile 2: Death Swamp *'01*
Crocodile *'00*

Jane Anderson(1954-)
The Prize Winner of Defiance, Ohio *'05*
Normal *'03*
If These Walls Could Talk 2 *'00*
The Baby Dance *'98*
How to Make an American Quilt *'95*
It Could Happen to You *'94*
The Positively True Adventures of the Alleged Texas Cheerleader-Murdering Mom *'93*

Josef Anderson
Stephen King's Golden Years *'91*
Shooting *'82*

Maxwell Anderson(1888-1959)
A Christmas Carol *'54*
Death Takes a Holiday *'34*
Rain *'32*
Women of All Nations *'31*
All Quiet on the Western Front *'30*

Paul Thomas Anderson(1970-)
There Will Be Blood *'07*
Punch-Drunk Love *'02*
Magnolia *'99*
Boogie Nights *'97*
Hard Eight *'96*

Paul W.S. Anderson(1965-)
Death Race *'08*
Resident Evil: Extinction *'07*
Alien vs. Predator *'04*
Resident Evil: Apocalypse *'04*
Resident Evil *'02*
Shopping *'93*

Robert Anderson(1923-)
I Never Sang for My Father *'70*
The Sand Pebbles *'66*
The Nun's Story *'59*
Until They Sail *'57*
Tea and Sympathy *'56*

Wes Anderson(1969-)
Fantastic Mr. Fox *'09*
The Darjeeling Limited *'07*
The Life Aquatic with Steve Zissou *'04*
The Royal Tenenbaums *'01*
Rushmore *'98*
Bottle Rocket *'95*

Guy Andrews
Lost in Austen *'08*
The Infiltrator *'95*
Lie Down with Lions *'94*
All or Nothing at All *'93*

Jay Andrews
See Jim Wynorski

Peter Andrews
See Steven Soderbergh

Robert D. (Robert Hardy) Andrews(1903-76)
Girls' Town *'59*
The Woman on Pier 13 *'50*
Bataan *'43*
Power of the Press *'43*
Before I Hang *'40*

Tina Andrews(1951-)
Sally Hemings: An American Scandal *'00*
Why Do Fools Fall in Love? *'98*

Roger Andrieux(1940-)
La Petite Sirene *'80*
L'Amour en Herbe *'77*

James Andronica(1945-)
Mirage *'94*
The November Men *'93*

Mark Andrus
Georgia Rule *'07*
Divine Secrets of the Ya-Ya Sisterhood *'02*
Life as a House *'01*
As Good As It Gets *'97*
Late for Dinner *'91*

Mikel Angel
Evil Spirits *'91*
Grotesque *'87*
Psychic Killer *'75*

Michael Angeli
Killing Mr. Griffin *'97*
Sketch Artist 2: Hands That See *'94*
Conflict of Interest *'92*
Sketch Artist *'92*

Theo Angelopoulos(1935-)
Eternity and a Day *'97*
Ulysses' Gaze *'95*
Landscape in the Mist *'88*
The Travelling Players *'75*

Edward Anhalt(1914-2000)
The Take *'90*
Peter the Great *'86*
The Holcroft Covenant *'85*
Green Ice *'81*
Escape to Athena *'79*
Fatal Chase *'77*
The Man in the Glass Booth *'75*
Luther *'74*
QB VII *'74*
Jeremiah Johnson *'72*
The Madwoman of Chaillot *'69*
The Boston Strangler *'68*
Hour of the Gun *'67*
Boeing Boeing *'65*
Becket *'64*
Girls! Girls! Girls! *'62*
The Sins of Rachel Cade *'61*
The Young Savages *'61*
The Young Lions *'58*
The Pride and the Passion *'57*
Not as a Stranger *'55*
The Member of the Wedding *'52*
Panic in the Streets *'50*

Erik Anjou(1961-)
The Cool Surface *'92*
976-EVIL 2: The Astral Factor *'91*
The Road to Ruin *'28*

Ken Annakin(1914-)
The New Adventures of Pippi Longstocking *'88*
Those Daring Young Men in Their Jaunty Jalopies *'69*
Those Magnificent Men in Their Flying Machines *'65*
Very Important Person *'61*

Jean-Jacques Annaud(1943-)
Two Brothers *'04*
Enemy at the Gates *'00*
The Lover *'92*
Black and White in Color *'76*

Jean Anouilh(1910-87)
Circle of Love *'64*
Monsieur Vincent *'47*

Reverge Anselmo(1962-)
Stateside *'04*
Lover's Prayer *'99*

Joseph Anthony(1912-93)
Wedding Present *'36*
Crime and Punishment *'35*

Stuart Anthony(1891-1942)
The Monster and the Girl *'41*

The Shepherd of the Hills '41
Helltown '38
Arizona Mahoney '36
Drift Fence '36
Motive for Revenge '35
Police Court '32
Border Law '31
The Fighting Sheriff '31

Walter Anthony
Tarzan the Fearless '33
Golden Dawn '30

Steve Antin(1956-)
Chasing Papi '03
Gloria '98
Inside Monkey Zetterland '93

Michelangelo Antonioni(1912-2007)
Eros '04
Beyond the Clouds '95
Identification of a Woman '82
The Passenger '75
Zabriskie Point '70
Blow-Up '66
The Eclipse '66
The Red Desert '64
La Notte '60
L'Avventura '60
Il Grido '57
The Lady Without Camelias '53
Story of a Love Affair '50

Judd Apatow(1967-)
Funny People '09
You Don't Mess with the Zohan '08
Knocked Up '07
Walk Hard: The Dewey Cox Story '07
The 40 Year Old Virgin '05
Fun With Dick and Jane '05
The Cable Guy '96
Celtic Pride '96
Heavyweights '94

Max Apple
Roommates '95
The Air Up There '94
Smokey Bites the Dust '81

William Applegate, Jr. (1972-)
The Big Fall '96
Pure Danger '96
Riot '96
Tiger Heart '96
Skyscraper '95
The Sweeper '95

Gregg Araki(1959-)
Mysterious Skin '04
Splendor '99
Nowhere '96
The Doom Generation '95
Totally F***ed Up '94
The Living End '92

Shimon Arama(1941-)
Triumph of the Spirit '89
Black Eagle '88

Vicente Aranda(1926-)
Carmen '03
Mad Love '01
Jealousy '99
Intruso '93
Lovers: A True Story '90
If They Tell You I Fell '89
The Blood Spattered Bride '72

David Arata
Spy Game '01
Brokedown Palace '99

Denys Arcand(1941-)
The Barbarian Invasions '03
Stardom '00
Jesus of Montreal '89
The Decline of the American Empire '86

Manuel Arce
Crossover Dreams '85
El Super '79

Jeffrey Arch
Iron Will '93
Sleepless in Seattle '93

William Archibald(1917-70)
The Innocents '61
I Confess '53

Robert Ardrey(1908-80)
Khartoum '66
Quentin Durward '55
Song of Love '47

Asia Argento(1975-)
The Heart Is Deceitful Above All Things '04
Scarlet Diva '00

Dario Argento(1940-)
Mother of Tears '08
Sleepless '01
The Church '98
The Phantom of the Opera '98
The Stendahl Syndrome '95
Dario Argento's Trauma '93
The Devil's Daughter '91
Two Evil Eyes '90
Opera '88
Demons 2 '87
Demons '86
Creepers '85
Unsane '82
Inferno '80
Suspiria '77
Deep Red: Hatchet Murders '75
Commandos '73
Four Flies on Grey Velvet '72
The Cat o' Nine Tails '71
The Bird with the Crystal Plumage '70
Once Upon a Time in the West '68

Adolfo Aristarain(1943-)
Martin (Hache) '97
A Place in the World '92
The Lion's Share '79

Alice Arlen
Then She Found Me '07
The Weight of Water '00
Cookie '89
Alamo Bay '85
Silkwood '83

Giorgio Arlorio(1929-)
Zorro '74
Burn! '70

Montxo Armendariz(1949-)
Broken Silence '01
Secrets of the Heart '97
Letters from Alou '90

George Armitage(1942-)
The Late Shift '96
The Last of the Finest '90
Miami Blues '90
Night Call Nurses '72
Private Duty Nurses '71
Gas-s-s-s! '70

Steve Armogida
Death and Desire '97
Attack of the 60-Foot Centerfold '95
Masseuse '95

Michael Armstrong(1944-)
House of the Long Shadows '82
Adventures of a Private Eye '77
Black Panther '77

Mike Armstrong
Monument Ave. '98
Two If by Sea '95

Scot Armstrong(1970-)
Semi-Pro '08
The Heartbreak Kid '07
School for Scoundrels '06

Starsky & Hutch '04
Old School '03
Road Trip '00

Adam Armus
Final Approach '08
Frederick Forsyth's Icon '05

Michael Arndt
Toy Story 3 '10
Little Miss Sunshine '06

Andrea Arnold
Fish Tank '09
Red Road '06

Elliott Arnold
Alvarez Kelly '66
Kings of the Sun '63

Jack Arnold(1916-92)
The Monolith Monsters '57
Tarantula '55

David Arnott(1976-)
Last Action Hero '93
The Adventures of Ford Fairlane '90

Darren Aronofsky(1969-)
The Fountain '06
Below '02
Requiem for a Dream '00
Pi '98

Suha Arraf
Lemon Tree '08
The Syrian Bride '04

Guillermo Arriaga(1958-)
The Burning Plain '08
Babel '06
The Three Burials of Melquiades Estrada '05
21 Grams '03
Amores Perros '00

Emmanuelle Arsan(1932-)
Good-bye, Emmanuelle '77
Forever Emmanuelle '75

Art Arthur
Day-Time Wife '39
Everything Happens at Night '39

Brooks Arthur
I Now Pronounce You Chuck and Larry '07
Adam Sandler's 8 Crazy Nights '02

Ash(1964-)
This Girl's Life '03
Pups '99
Bang '95

William Asher(1921-)
Fireball 500 '66
Beach Blanket Bingo '65
How to Stuff a Wild Bikini '65
Bikini Beach '64
Muscle Beach Party '64

Piers Ashworth
St. Trinian's '07
Sherlock: Case of Evil '02
Nostradamus '93

Peter Askin
Company Man '00
Smithereens '82

Olivier Assayas(1955-)
Summer Hours '08
Boarding Gate '07
Paris, je t'aime '06
Clean '04
Demonlover '02
Les Destinees '00
Alice et Martin '98
Late August, Early September '98
Irma Vep '96
Scene of the Crime '87
Rendez-vous '85

Ovidio G. Assonitis(1943-)
Red Riding Hood '03
Beyond the Door '75

Tom J. Astle
Get Smart '08
Failure to Launch '06

Doug Atchison
The Longshots '08
Akeelah and the Bee '06
The Pornographer '00

Francisco Athie(1956-)
Optic Fiber '97
Lolo '92

David Atkins
Novocaine '01
Arizona Dream '94

Peter Atkins(1955-)
Wishmaster '97
Hellraiser 4: Bloodline '95
Hellraiser 3: Hell on Earth '92
Hellbound: Hellraiser 2 '88

Leopold Atlas(1907-54)
Raw Deal '48
The Story of G.I. Joe '45
Tomorrow the World '44

Yvan Attal(1965-)
New York, I Love You '09
Happily Ever After '04
My Wife is an Actress '01

Paul Attanasio
The Good German '06
The Sum of All Fears '02
Sphere '97
Donnie Brasco '96
Disclosure '94
Quiz Show '94
Rapid Fire '92

Kin-Yee Au
Running Out of Time 2 '06
Running on Karma '03

David Auburn(1970-)
The Lake House '06
Proof '05

Jacques Audiard(1952-)
A Prophet '09
The Beat My Heart Skipped '05
Read My Lips '01
A Self-Made Hero '95
Barjo '93
Baxter '89

Michel Audiard(1920-85)
Jupiter's Thigh '81
Le Professionnel '81
Dear Detective '77
Any Number Can Win '63

Bille August(1948-)
A Song for Martin '01
Jerusalem '96
The House of the Spirits '93
Pelle the Conqueror '88
Twist & Shout '84

John August(1970-)
The Nines '07
Charlie and the Chocolate Factory '05
Tim Burton's Corpse Bride '05
Big Fish '03
Charlie's Angels: Full Throttle '03
Charlie's Angels '00
Titan A.E. '00
Go '99

Joe Augustyn
Exit '95
Night of the Demons 2 '94
Night Angel '90
Night of the Demons '88

Jean Aurel(1925-96)
Confidentially Yours '83
Manon '68
The Women '68
Le Trou '59
Une Parisienne '58

Jean Aurenche(1904-92)
The Judge and the Assassin '75

The Clockmaker '73
The Hunchback of Notre Dame '57
Forbidden Games '52
The Red Inn '51
The Walls of Malapaga '49
Devil in the Flesh '46

Robert Alan Aurthur(1922-78)
All That Jazz '79
Warlock '59
Edge of the City '57

Paul Auster(1947-)
Lulu on the Bridge '98
Blue in the Face '95
Smoke '95

Sam Auster
Bounty Hunter 2002 '94
Screen Test '85

Carl Austin(1968-)
Telling Lies '06
Improper Conduct '94
Sexual Malice '93
Wild Cactus '92

Michael Austin
Princess Caraboo '94
Greystoke: The Legend of Tarzan, Lord of the Apes '84
Five Days One Summer '82
The Shout '78

Phillip Avalon(1955-)
Fatal Bond '91
Summer City '77

Roger Avary(1965-)
Beowulf '07
Silent Hill '06
The Rules of Attraction '02
Mr. Stitch '95
Killing Zoe '94
Pulp Fiction '94

Antonio Avati
Bix '90
Zeder '83
Macabre '80

Pupi Avati(1938-)
Incantato '03
The Best Man '97
The Story of Boys & Girls '91
Bix '90
Zeder '83
The Boss Is Served '76

Howard (Hikmet) Avedis
Kidnapped '87
They're Playing with Fire '84
Mortuary '81
The Fifth Floor '80
Scorchy '76
The Specialist '75

Brian Avenet-Bradley
Dark Remains '05
Ghost of the Needle '03

Belle Avery
The Keeper: The Legend of Omar Khayyam '05
Malevolence '95

Robert J. Avrech(1950-)
Brotherhood of Murder '99
The Devil's Arithmetic '99
Into Thin Air: Death on Everest '97
A Stranger Among Us '92
Dark Tower '87
Body Double '84

George Axelrod(1922-2003)
The Fourth Protocol '87
The Holcroft Covenant '85
The Lady Vanishes '79
Secret Life of an American Wife '68
Lord Love a Duck '66
How to Murder Your Wife '64
Paris When It Sizzles '64

The Manchurian Candidate '62
Breakfast at Tiffany's '61
Rally 'Round the Flag, Boys! '58
Bus Stop '56
The Seven Year Itch '55
Phffft! '54

Alan Ayckbourn(1939-)
Private Fears in Public Places '06
A Chorus of Disapproval '89
The Norman Conquests, Part 1: Table Manners '78
The Norman Conquests, Part 2: Living Together '78
The Norman Conquests, Part 3: Round and Round the Garden '78

David Ayer(1972-)
Harsh Times '05
Dark Blue '03
S.W.A.T. '03
The Fast and the Furious '01
Training Day '01
U-571 '00

Frederick Ayeroff
Ace of Hearts '08
Soccer Mom '08

Clay Ayers
The Watcher '00
Sword of Honor '94

Dan Aykroyd(1952-)
Blues Brothers 2000 '98
Coneheads '93
Nothing But Trouble '91
Ghostbusters 2 '89
Dragnet '87
Spies Like Us '85
Ghostbusters '84
The Blues Brothers '80

Gerald Ayres
Crazy in Love '92
Rich and Famous '81
Foxes '80

Rafael Azcona(1926-)
The Girl of Your Dreams '99
Butterfly '98
Belle Epoque '92
Ay, Carmela! '90
Blood and Sand '89
Autopsy '74
La Grande Bouffe '73
Mafioso '62
El Cochecito '60

Beth B(1955-)
Two Small Bodies '93
Salvation! '87
Vortex '81

Thom Babbes(1958-)
Body Chemistry '90
Deadly Dreams '88

Dwight V. Babcock(1909-79)
Loophole '54
Jungle Captive '45
Pillow of Death '45
Dead Man's Eyes '44

Hector Babenco(1946-)
Carandiru '03
At Play in the Fields of the Lord '91
Pixote '81

Michael Bacall
Scott Pilgrim vs. the World '10
Bookies '03
Manic '01

Danilo Bach
Escape Clause '96
April Fool's Day '86
Beverly Hills Cop '84

Jean-Pierre Bacri(1951-)
Look at Me '04
The Taste of Others '00
Same Old Song '97

Un Air de Famille '96
Smoking/No Smoking '94

Tom Badal
Vietnam, Texas '90
Out on Bail '89

Nicola Badalucco
Escape from Death Row '73
Death in Venice '71

Randall Badat
The Cutting Edge 3: Chasing the Dream '08
WarGames 2: The Dead Code '08
Born to Run '93
Hear No Evil '93
Surf 2 '84

Phillip Badger
Retroactive '97
The Forgotten One '89

Nicholas E. Baehr
The Invasion of Johnson County '76
The Incident '67

Geoffrey Baere
Corporate Affairs '90
Campus Man '87
School Spirit '85

Michael Bafaro
Behind the Wall '08
Act of War '96
Listen '96
Crackerjack '94

Fax Bahr
Malibu's Most Wanted '03
Jury Duty '95
In the Army Now '94
Son-in-Law '93
Hearts of Darkness: A Filmmaker's Apocalypse '91

Steven Baigelman
Brother's Keeper '02
Feeling Minnesota '96

Fenton Bailey
Inside Deep Throat '05
Party Monster '03

Frederick Bailey
Threat of Exposure '02
Terminal Justice: Cybertech P.D. '95
Fast Gun '93
Quick '93
Raiders of the Sun '92
Desert Warrior '88
Demon of Paradise '87

Sandra K. Bailey
False Identity '90
Prettykill '87
The KGB: The Secret War '86
Hambone & Hillie '84

John Baines(1909-)
The Hands of Orlac '60
Dead of Night '45

Jon Robin Baitz(1961-)
People I Know '02
The Substance of Fire '96
Fallen Angels 1 '93

Bart Baker
Supercross: The Movie '05
Any Place But Home '97
Live Wire '92
Baby of the Bride '91

C. Graham Baker
You Only Live Once '37
The Singing Fool '28

Elliott Baker(1922-2007)
Breakout '75
A Fine Madness '66

Herbert Baker(1920-83)
The Jazz Singer '80
Sextette '78
The Ambushers '67
Oh Dad, Poor Dad (Momma's Hung You in the Closet & I'm Feeling So Sad) '67
Murderers' Row '66
King Creole '58
The Girl Can't Help It '56
Artists and Models '55
Dream Wife '53

Ralph Bakshi(1938-)
Cool and the Crazy '94
Fire and Ice '83
Hey Good Lookin' '82
Wizards '77
Streetfight '75
Heavy Traffic '73
Fritz the Cat '72

Alexsei Balabanov(1959-)
Of Freaks and Men '98
Brother '97

Jaume Balaguero
Rec '07
Darkness '02

Josiane Balasko(1952-)
French Twist '95
Hotel America '81

Bela Balazs(1884-1949)
The Blue Light '32
The Threepenny Opera '31

Jaime Jesus Balcazar
The Gentleman Killer '69
Twice a Judas '69
Four Dollars of Revenge '66

Nigel Balchin
Barabbas '62
23 Paces to Baker Street '56

Marius Balchunas
The Elder Son '06
No Vacancy '99

John Lloyd Balderston(1889-1954)
Red Planet Mars '52
Gaslight '44
Prisoner of Zenda '37
The Bride of Frankenstein '35
The Lives of a Bengal Lancer '35
Mad Love '35
The Mystery of Edwin Drood '35
The Mummy '32
Frankenstein '31

Ferdinando Baldi(1917-2007)
Sicilian Connection '72
Texas, Adios '66

Richard Balducci(1929-)
Scandal Man '67
The Gendarme of Saint-Tropez '64

Earl Baldwin
The Go-Getter '54
South Sea Woman '53
Africa Screams '49
Greenwich Village '44
Gold Diggers in Paris '38
A Slight Case of Murder '38
Go Into Your Dance '35
Wonder Bar '34
Havana Widows '33
Wild Boys of the Road '33
Doctor X '32

Alan Ball(1957-)
Towelhead '07
American Beauty '99

Peter Baloff
Near Misses '91
Quicksand: No Escape '91

Albert Band(1924-2002)
She Came to the Valley '77
Gunfight at Red Sands '63
The Red Badge of Courage '51

Beatrice Banyard(1897-1968)
Myrt and Marge '33
Reducing '31

Jack Baran
Uncovered '94
Great Balls of Fire '89
Band of the Hand '86

Steve Barancik(1961-)
Domino '05
No Good Deed '02
The Last Seduction '94

Ernie Barbarash
Stir of Echoes 2: The Homecoming '07
Cube: Zero '04

Bob Barbash(1919-95)
The Gambler, the Girl and the Gunslinger '09
The Plunderers '60

Randy Barbato
Inside Deep Throat '05
Party Monster '03

Neal Barbera
P.K. and the Kid '85
Too Scared to Scream '85
The Prowler '81

Malcolm Barbour
Deadly Sins '95
The P.O.W. Escape '86

Ann Louise Bardach
Backtrack '89
Sorry, Wrong Number '89

Richard Bare
The Joe McDoakes Collection '42
Two-Gun Troubador '37

David Barenbaum
Elf '03
The Haunted Mansion '03

Frank Barhydt
Kansas City '95
Short Cuts '93
Quintet '79

Leora Barish
Basic Instinct 2 '06
Venus Rising '95
Desperately Seeking Susan '85

Clive Barker(1952-)
Lord of Illusions '95
Nightbreed '90
Hellraiser '87
Rawhead Rex '87
Transmutations '85

Kim Barker
All About Steve '09
License to Wed '07

Jeff Barmash(1957-)
Bounty Hunters 2: Hardball '97
Power of Attorney '94

Joseph John Barmettler, Jr.
Timelock '99
Pure Danger '96
Riot '96
Rage '95
Witchcraft 8: Salem's Ghost '95

Peter Barnes(1931-2004)
The Moon & the Stars '07
Arabian Nights '00
Alice in Wonderland '99
A Christmas Carol '99
The Magical Legend of the Leprechauns '99
Noah's Ark '99
Voices from a Locked Room '95
Enchanted April '92
The Ruling Class '72

Daniel Barnz
Beastly '10
Phoebe in Wonderland '08

Alexander Baron(1917-99)
Oliver Twist '85
Poldark 2 '75

Allen Baron(1935-)
Red, White & Busted '75
Blast of Silence '61

Jessica Barondes
Lucky Seven '03
Little Secrets '02
Wish upon a Star '96

Douglas Barr(1949-)
The Note 2: Taking a Chance on Love '09
Frame by Frame '95
Dead Badge '94
The Cover Girl Murders '93
Fade to Black '93

Jackson Barr
Body Chemistry 3: Point of Seduction '93
800 Leagues Down the Amazon '93
Mandroid '93
Bad Channels '92
Seedpeople '92
Body Chemistry 2: Voice of a Stranger '91
Body Chemistry '90

Christophe Barratier
Paris 36 '08
The Chorus '04

Bruno Barreto(1955-)
Gabriela '84
Dona Flor and Her Two Husbands '78

James Lee Barrett(1929-89)
Warden of Red Rock '01
Ruby Jean and Joe '96
Poker Alice '87
Angel City '80
Mayflower: The Pilgrims' Adventure '79
The Green Berets '68
The Greatest Story Ever Told '65
Shenandoah '65

Simon Barrett
Red Sands '09
Dead Birds '04
Frankenfish '04

H.E. Barrie
Missile to the Moon '59
She Demons '58

J.M. Barrie(1860-1937)
Quality Street '37
As You Like It '36

Michael Barrie
Bad Boys '95
National Lampoon's Favorite Deadly Sins '95
Oscar '91
Amazon Women on the Moon '87
Ratings Game '84

Michael Barringer
Butler's Dilemma '43
The Dummy Talks '43
Death on the Set '35

Barry Barrington
Held for Ransom '38
Valley of Wanted Men '35
Dynamite Ranch '32

Fred Barron
Something Short of Paradise '79
Between the Lines '77

Janet Barron
The Tenant of Wildfell Hall '96
Clarissa '91

Nicholas T. Barrows
That's My Baby! '44
Dangerous Holiday '37

Julian Barry(1931-)
Me, Myself & I '92
The River '84
Lenny '74

Odile Barski
The Girl on the Train '09
Comedy of Power '06
The Cry of the Owl '87
Violette '78

Peter Barsocchini
High School Musical 3: Senior Year '08
High School Musical 2 '07
Drop Zone '94

Paul Bartel(1938-2000)
Not for Publication '84
Eating Raoul '82
Cannonball '76
Paul Bartel's The Secret Cinema '69

Phillip J. Bartell
Eating Out 3: All You Can Eat '09
Eating Out 2: Sloppy Seconds '06

Hall Bartlett(1922-93)
Children of Sanchez '79
All the Young Men '60
Zero Hour! '57

Richard Bartlett(1922-94)
Lonesome Trail '55
Silver Star '55

Sy Bartlett(1900-78)
Beloved Infidel '59
The Big Country '58
Twelve o'Clock High '49
13 Rue Madeleine '46

Hal Barwood
Warning Sign '85
Dragonslayer '81
Corvette Summer '78
MacArthur '77
Bingo Long Traveling All-Stars & Motor Kings '76
The Sugarland Express '74

Ben Barzman(1911-89)
The Blue Max '66
The Heroes of Telemark '65
Time Without Pity '57
The Lady in Question '40

K.C. Bascombe
Fear of the Dark '02
Swindle '02

Ron Base
Deadline '00
First Degree '95
Heavenly Bodies '84

Harry Basil
The 4th Tenor '02
My 5 Wives '00
Meet Wally Sparks '97

Ronald Bass(1942-)
Amelia '09
Mozart and the Whale '05
Passion of Mind '00
Entrapment '99
Snow Falling on Cedars '99
How Stella Got Her Groove Back '98
Stepmom '98
What Dreams May Come '98
My Best Friend's Wedding '97
Dangerous Minds '95
Waiting to Exhale '95
The Enemy Within '94
When a Man Loves a Woman '94
The Joy Luck Club '93
Sleeping with the Enemy '91
Rain Man '88
Black Widow '87
Gardens of Stone '87
Code Name: Emerald '85

Seth Bass
Martian Child '07
The Twilight of the Golds '97

Lawrence Bassoff
Hunk '87
Weekend Pass '84

William Bast(1931-)
Power and Beauty '02
The Betsy '78
James Dean '76
The Valley of Gwangi '69

Joe Batteer
Windtalkers '02
Blown Away '94
Chasers '94
Curiosity Kills '90

Bradley Battersby(1953-)
Red Letters '00
Blue Desert '91

Lucio Battistrada
Autopsy '74
Commandos '73
Dead Are Alive '72
Stranger in Paso Bravo '68
Autopsy of a Ghost '67

Hans Bauer
The Flock '07
Highwaymen '03
Komodo '99
Anaconda '96

Thomas Baum
Journey to the Center of the Earth '08
Dracula: The Dark Prince '01
Journey to the Center of the Earth '99
Witness to the Execution '94
The Manhattan Project '86
The Sender '82
Carny '80
Simon '80
Hugo the Hippo '76

Noah Baumbach(1969-)
Greenberg '10
Fantastic Mr. Fox '09
Margot at the Wedding '07
The Squid and the Whale '05
The Life Aquatic with Steve Zissou '04
Mr. Jealousy '98
Highball '97
Kicking and Screaming '95

Lamberto Bava(1944-)
Ghost Son '06
Demons 2 '87
Demons '86
Macabre '80
Shock '79

Mario Bava(1914-80)
Lisa and the Devil '75
Twitch of the Death Nerve '71
Hatchet for the Honeymoon '70
Danger: Diabolik '68
Kill, Baby, Kill '66
Knives of the Avenger '65
Planet of the Vampires '65
Black Sabbath '64
Blood and Black Lace '64
The Girl Who Knew Too Much '63
Black Sunday '60

George L. Baxt(1923-2003)
Burn Witch, Burn! '62
Circus of Horrors '60
Horror Hotel '60

Sergio Bazzini
Husbands and Lovers '91
The Inheritance '76
Dillinger Is Dead '69

Wayne Beach
Slow Burn '05
The Art of War '00
Murder at 1600 '97
The Shadow Conspiracy '96

Peter S. Beagle(1939-)
The Last Unicorn '82
The Lord of the Rings '78
The Dove '74

The Shame '68
Persona '66
The Silence '63
The Winter Light '62
Through a Glass Darkly '61
The Devil's Eye '60
The Magician '58
Wild Strawberries '57
The Seventh Seal '56
Dreams '55
Smiles of a Summer Night '55
Lesson in Love '54
Sawdust & Tinsel '53
Monika '52
Secrets of Women '52
Summer Interlude '50
To Joy '50
Devil's Wanton '49
Torment '44

Linda J. Bergman

The Lookalike '90
Matters of the Heart '90

Robert Bergman

Skull: A Night of Terror '88
A Whisper to a Scream '88

Eric Bergren

The Dark Wind '91
Frances '82
The Elephant Man '80

Eleanor Bergstein(1938-)

Dirty Dancing '87
It's My Turn '80

Martin Berkeley(1904-79)

The Deadly Mantis '57
Revenge of the Creature '55
Tarantula '55
A Stolen Face '52

Shari Springer Berman

The Nanny Diaries '07
American Splendor '03

Steven H. Berman

Prairie Fever '08
Sharpshooter '07

Patrick Bermel

The Invitation '03
Ripper: Letter from Hell '01

Paul Bern

The Beloved Rogue '27
The Marriage Circle '24

Carlo Bernard

Prince of Persia: The Sands of Time '10
The Sorcerer's Apprentice '10
The Uninvited '09
The Great Raid '05

James Bernard(1925-2001)

She '65
The Stranglers of Bombay '60
Seven Days to Noon '50

Judd Bernard(1927-)

Enter the Ninja '81
The Class of Miss MacMichael '78
The Destructors '74

Sam Bernard

Blood Surf '00
Diplomatic Siege '99
Payback '94
Warlock: The Armageddon '93
Rad '86
3:15—The Moment of Truth '86

Paul Bernbaum(1957-)

Next '07
Hollywoodland '06
In the Doghouse '98
Rent-A-Kid '95
Royce '93

Edward L. Bernds(1905-2000)

Return of the Fly '59
Reform School Girl '57
Storm Rider '57
Corky of Gasoline Alley '51
Blondie Knows Best '46

Peter Berneis(1910-)

My Man Godfrey '57
Portrait of Jennie '48

Kevin Bernhardt(1961-)

Peaceful Warrior '06
Jill the Ripper '00
Diplomatic Siege '99
Sweepers '99
Turbulence 2: Fear of Flying '99
Natural Enemy '96
The Immortals '95

Emmanuele Bernheim

5x2 '04
Swimming Pool '03
Friday Night '02
Under the Sand '00

Gisella Bernice

The Simian Line '99
Parallel Lives '94

Armyan Bernstein

The Hurricane '99
Cross My Heart '88
Windy City '84
One from the Heart '82
Thank God It's Friday '78

Jon Bernstein

Meet the Robinsons '07
Larry the Cable Guy: Health Inspector '06
Max Keeble's Big Move '01
Beautiful '00
Ringmaster '98

Marcos Bernstein(1970-)

Central Station '98
Foreign Land '95

Richard Bernstein(1922-83)

The Oh in Ohio '06
Force of Impulse '60
Why Must I Die? '60

Sarah Bernstein

Call Me Claus '01
Trial and Error '96

Walter Bernstein(1919-)

Fail Safe '00
Durango '99
Miss Evers' Boys '97
Doomsday Gun '94
The House on Carroll Street '88
Little Miss Marker '80
An Almost Perfect Affair '79
Yanks '79
The Betsy '78
Semi-Tough '77
The Front '76
Molly Maguires '70
The Money Trap '65
The Train '65
Fail-Safe '64
Paris Blues '61
Heller in Pink Tights '60

Eric Bernt

The Hitcher '07
Bachelor Party Vegas '05
Romeo Must Die '00
Virtuosity '95
Surviving the Game '94

Claude Berri(1934-)

The Housekeeper '02
Lucie Aubrac '98
Germinal '93
Uranus '91
Jean de Florette '87
Manon of the Spring '87
I Love You All '80
One Wild Moment '78
The Two of Us '68

John Berry(1917-99)

Boesman & Lena '00
There Goes Barder '54

Michael Berry

Blue Streak '99
Short Time '90

Peter Berry

The Last Enemy '08
The Incredible Journey of Mary Bryant '05
The Luzhin Defence '00

Tom Berry

Decoys '04
Crazy Moon '87

Bernardo Bertolucci(1940-)

The Triumph of Love '01
Besieged '98
Stealing Beauty '96
The Sheltering Sky '90
The Last Emperor '87
The Tragedy of a Ridiculous Man '81
1900 '76
Last Tango in Paris '73
The Conformist '71
The Spider's Stratagem '70
Once Upon a Time in the West '68
Before the Revolution '65

Giuseppe Bertolucci(1947-)

Berlinguer I Love You '77
1900 '76

Jean-Louis Bertucelli

The Desert of the Tartars '76
Ramparts of Clay '68

Andrew Rai Berzins

Beowulf & Grendel '06
Blood & Donuts '95

Jean-Marie Besset

The Girl on the Train '09
The Proprietor '96

Luc Besson(1959-)

District 13: Ultimatum '09
Taken '08
Transporter 3 '08
Arthur and the Invisibles '06
Angel-A '05
Crimson Rivers 2: Angels of the Apocalypse '05
Transporter 2 '05
Unleashed '05
District B13 '04
The Transporter '02
Kiss of the Dragon '01
Wasabi '01
The Messenger: The Story of Joan of Arc '99
The Fifth Element '97
The Professional '94
La Femme Nikita '91
The Big Blue '88
Subway '85
Le Dernier Combat '84

Jonathan Betuel(1949-)

Theodore Rex '95
My Science Project '85
The Last Starfighter '84

Alberto Bevilacqua(1934-)

Planet of the Vampires '65
Black Sabbath '64
Atom Age Vampire '61

Troy Beyer(1965-)

Love Don't Cost a Thing '03
Let's Talk About Sex '98
B.A.P.'s '97

Thomas Bezucha

The Family Stone '05
Big Eden '00

A(lbert) I(saac) Bezzerides(1908-2007)

A Bullet for Joey '55
Kiss Me Deadly '55
Beneath the 12-Mile Reef '53
Action in the North Atlantic '43
Juke Girl '42

Thomas Bidegain

A Prophet '09
The Chateau '01

Ann Biderman

Public Enemies '09
Primal Fear '96
Smilla's Sense of Snow '96
Copycat '95

Antonio Bido(1949-)

The Bloodstained Shadow '78
Watch Me When I Kill '77

James Biederman

Cash Crop '01
Harvest '98

Fabian Bielinsky(1959-2006)

The Aura '05
Nine Queens '00

Kathryn Bigelow(1952-)

Undertow '95
Blue Steel '90
Near Dark '87
Loveless '83

Danny Bilson(1956-)

The Rocketeer '91
Arena '89
The Wrong Guys '88
The Eliminators '86
Trancers '84
Zone Troopers '84
Future Cop '76

Carl Binder

He Sees You When You're Sleeping '02
Pocahontas '95

John Binder(1940-)

Endangered Species '82
Uforia '81
Honeysuckle Rose '80

Mike Binder(1958-)

Reign Over Me '07
The Upside of Anger '05
The Search for John Gissing '01
The Sex Monster '99
Indian Summer '93
Crossing the Bridge '92
Coupe de Ville '90

William Bindley

Madison '01
Judicial Consent '94
Freeze Frame '92

Steve Bing(1965-)

Kangaroo Jack '02
Every Breath '93
Missing in Action 2: The Beginning '85

Charlotte Bingham

Magic Moments '89
Riders '88

Joe Bini

The Tillman Story '10
Roman Polanski: Wanted and Desired '08

Claude Binyon(1905-78)

Rally 'Round the Flag, Boys! '58
A Woman's World '54
My Blue Heaven '50
Arizona '40
Too Many Husbands '40
Mississippi '35
Search for Beauty '34
College Humor '33

Brad Bird(1957-)

Ratatouille '07
The Incredibles '04
*batteries not included '87

Brian Bird

Not Easily Broken '09
Saving Sarah Cain '07
Bopha! '93

Sarah Bird

The Oh in Ohio '06
Don't Tell Her It's Me '90

Andrew Birkin(1945-)

Perfume: The Story of a Murderer '06
The Messenger: The Story of Joan of Arc '99
The Cement Garden '93
Burning Secret '89
The Name of the Rose '86
King David '85
The Final Conflict '81
The Lost Boys '78
Pied Piper '72

Lajos Biro(1880-)

An Ideal Husband '47
The Thief of Bagdad '40
The Four Feathers '39
The Scarlet Pimpernel '34
The Private Life of Henry VIII '33

John Bishop(1929-2006)

Drop Zone '94
The Package '89

Larry Bishop(1947-)

Hell Ride '08
Trigger Happy '96
Underworld '96

Wes Bishop(1933-93)

Dixie Dynamite '76
Black Gestapo '75
Race with the Devil '75

Wesley Bishop

The Christmas Blessing '05
The Christmas Shoes '02
Dream Chasers '82

Shem Bitterman

Full Count '06
Off the Lip '04
Peephole '93
Out of the Rain '90
Halloween 5: The Revenge of Michael Myers '89

Emerson Bixby(1963-)

Bikini Island '91
Disturbed '90

Jerome Bixby(1923-98)

The Man from Earth '07
It! The Terror from Beyond Space '58

David Black(1945-)

The Confession '98
Legacy of Lies '92

Dustin Lance Black

Milk '08
The Journey of Jared Price '00

Jennifer Black

Recipe for Revenge '98
The Waiting Game '98

Michael Ian Black(1971-)

Run, Fatboy, Run '07
Wedding Daze '06

Shane Black(1961-)

Kiss Kiss Bang Bang '05
The Long Kiss Goodnight '96
Last Action Hero '93
The Last Boy Scout '91
Lethal Weapon '87
The Monster Squad '87

Stephen Black

Eden '93
Eden 2 '93
Love Among Thieves '86

Richard Blackburn

Eating Raoul '82
Lemora, Lady Dracula '73

Tom Blackburn

Orwell Rolls in His Grave '03
Cattle Town '52

Dirk Blackman

Underworld: Rise of the Lycans '09
Outlander '08

Ken Blackwell

Dark Tower '87
Triumphs of a Man Called Horse '83

April Blair

Private Valentine: Blonde & Dangerous '08
Christmas Caper '07

Michael Blake(1945-)

Dances with Wolves '90
Stacy's Knights '83

Michael Blankfort(1907-82)

Tribute to a Bad Man '56
The Caine Mutiny '54
The Halls of Montezuma '50

Philippe Blasband(1964-)

Irina Palm '07
Thomas in Love '01
An Affair of Love '99

Joel Blasberg

Family of Cops 2: Breach of Faith '97
Family of Cops '95

Vera Blasi

Tortilla Soup '01
Woman on Top '00

William Peter Blatty(1928-)

Exorcist 3: Legion '90
The Ninth Configuration '79
The Exorcist '73
Darling Lili '70
Promise Her Anything '66
What Did You Do in the War, Daddy? '66
A Shot in the Dark '64

Barry W. Blaustein(1955-)

The Honeymooners '05
Nutty Professor 2: The Klumps '00
The Nutty Professor '96
Boomerang '92
Coming to America '88
Police Academy 2: Their First Assignment '85

Alan Bleasdale(1946-)

Oliver Twist '00
Melissa '97
No Surrender '86

Corey Blechman

Free Willy 2: The Adventure Home '95
Free Willy '93
Max and Helen '90
Dominick & Eugene '88

Robert Blees(1925-)

Doctor Phibes Rises Again '72
Frogs '72
Who Slew Auntie Roo? '71
From the Earth to the Moon '58
High School Confidential '58
The Black Scorpion '57
Autumn Leaves '56
Slightly Scarlet '56
Cattle Queen of Montana '54
Magnificent Obsession '54
All I Desire '53

Lee Blessing

Steal Big, Steal Little '95
Cooperstown '93

Bernard Blier(1916-89)

How Much Do You Love Me? '05
Notre Histoire '84

Bertrand Blier(1939-)

Mon Homme '96
Too Beautiful for You '88
Menage '86
My Best Friend's Girl '84
Beau Pere '81
Buffet Froid '79
Get Out Your Handkerchiefs '78
Going Places '74

William Blinn(1938-)

Brian's Song '01
The Boys Next Door '96

Purple Rain '84
For Heaven's Sake '79
The Lazarus Syndrome '79
Roots '77
Brian's Song '71

Robert Bloch(1917-94)

Asylum '72
The House that Dripped Blood '71
Torture Garden '67
The Night Walker '64
Strait-Jacket '64

Larry Block(1943-)

My Blueberry Nights '07
The Funhouse '81

Michael Blodgett(1940-2007)

The White Raven '98
Run '91
Turner and Hooch '89
Hero and the Terror '88
Rent-A-Cop '88

George Arthur Bloom

The Man Who Guards the Greenhouse '88
The Last Flight of Noah's Ark '80

Harold Jack Bloom(1925-99)

A Gunfight '71
Land of the Pharaohs '55
The Naked Spur '53

Jeffrey Bloom

Flowers in the Attic '87
Nightmares '83
Blood Beach '81
The Stick-Up '77
Swashbuckler '76
Dog Pound Shuffle '75
11 Harrowhouse '74

Steven L. Bloom

Jack Frost '98
Overnight Delivery '96
Tall Tale: The Unbelievable Adventures of Pecos Bill '95
Like Father, Like Son '87
The Sure Thing '85

Jill Blotevogel

That Russell Girl '08
Wilderness Love '02

Edwin Blum(1906-95)

Pearl of the South Pacific '55
South Sea Woman '53
Stalag 17 '53
Down to Earth '47
The Canterville Ghost '44
The Boogie Man Will Get You '42
Young People '40
The Adventures of Sherlock Holmes '39

Len Blum

Over the Hedge '06
The Pink Panther '06
Private Parts '96
Beethoven's 2nd '93
Feds '88
Spacehunter: Adventures in the Forbidden Zone '83
Heavy Metal '81
Stripes '81
Meatballs '79

Stuart Blumberg(1969-)

The Kids Are All Right '10
The Girl Next Door '04
Keeping the Faith '00

John Blumenthal

Blue Streak '99
Short Time '90

Don Bluth(1938-)

Thumbelina '94
All Dogs Go to Heaven '89
The Secret of NIMH '82

Henry Blyth

Very Important Person '61
The Square Peg '58

Jeffrey Boam(1949-2000)

The Phantom '96
Lethal Weapon 3 '92
Indiana Jones and the Last Crusade '89
Lethal Weapon 2 '89
Funny Farm '88
Innerspace '87
The Lost Boys '87
Dead Zone '83
Straight Time '78

Paul Harris Boardman

The Exorcism of Emily Rose '05
Hellraiser 5: Inferno '00
Urban Legends 2: Final Cut '00

Al Boasberg(1892-1937)

A Night at the Opera '35
Myrt and Marge '33
Freaks '32
Hollywood Revue of 1929 '29
It's a Great Life '29
Battling Butler '26
The General '26

Sam Bobrick(1932-)

Jimmy the Kid '82
Norman, Is That You? '76

Steven Bochco(1943-)

Columbo: Murder by the Book '71
Silent Running '71

DeWitt Bodeen(1908-88)

Mrs. Mike '49
I Remember Mama '48
Cat People '42

Anna Boden

Sugar '09
Half Nelson '06

Sergei Bodrov(1948-)

Mongol '07
Schizo '04
The Quickie '01
East-West '99
Prisoner of the Mountains '96
Somebody to Love '94
Freedom Is Paradise '89

Christoffer Boe

Allegro '05
Reconstruction '03

Sydney (Sidney) Boehm(1908-90)

Rough Night in Jericho '67
Seven Thieves '60
The Tall Men '55
The Big Heat '53
Second Chance '53
When Worlds Collide '51
Mystery Street '50
Side Street '50

Peter Bogdanovich(1939-)

Texasville '90
They All Laughed '81
Saint Jack '79
The Last Picture Show '71
Targets '68
The Wild Angels '66

Nicholas Bogner

No Strings Attached '98
The Little Death '95

Eric Bogosian(1953-)

subUrbia '96
Sex, Drugs, Rock & Roll: Eric Bogosian '91
Talk Radio '88

Roger Bohbot

Lady Chatterley '06
Kings and Queen '04
Since Otar Left... '03
The Dreamlife of Angels '98

Endre Bohem(1900-90)

Twenty Bucks '93
Monster from Green Hell '58

Leslie Bohem(1952-)

The Alamo '04
Taken '02
Dante's Peak '97
Daylight '96
Nowhere to Run '93
Twenty Bucks '93
The Horror Show '89
A Nightmare on Elm Street 5: Dream Child '89

Charles F. Bohl

Swimfan '02
He's My Girl '87

Don Bohlinger

The Experiment '01
Women '97
The Killing Time '87

Tewd A. Bohus

This Thing of Ours '03
Vampire Vixens from Venus '94

Jerome Boivin(1954-)

Barjo '93
Baxter '89

Jon Bokenkamp

Taking Lives '04
Bad Seed '00

Bridget Boland(1913-88)

Anne of the Thousand Days '69
War and Peace '56
He Found a Star '41
Gaslight '40

Uwe Boll(1965-)

Seed '08
Tunnel Rats '08
Postal '07
Heart of America '03
Blackwoods '02
Sanctimony '01

Joseph Bologna(1938-)

Love Is All There Is '96
Lovers and Other Strangers '70

Craig Bolotin(1954-)

Light It Up '99
That Night '93
Straight Talk '92
Black Rain '89

Troy Bolotnick

Cyborg 3: The Recycler '95
Red Scorpion 2 '94

Robert Bolt(1924-95)

Without Warning: The James Brady Story '91
The Mission '86
The Bounty '84
Lady Caroline Lamb '73
Ryan's Daughter '70
A Man for All Seasons '66
Doctor Zhivago '65
Lawrence of Arabia '62

Guy Bolton(1884-1979)

Weekend at the Waldorf '45
Angel '37
The Love Parade '29

James Bolton

The Graffiti Artist '04
Eban and Charley '01

Adriano Bolzoni

Your Vice is a Closed Room and Only I Have the Key '72
Place in Hell '69
Diary of a Rebel '68

Mark Bomback

Race to Witch Mountain '09
Deception '08
Live Free or Die Hard '07
Godsend '04

Julian Bond(1930-)

Lie Down with Lions '94
The Whistle Blower '87
The Shooting Party '85
Love for Lydia '79

The Duchess of Duke Street '78
Choice of Weapons '76

Joon-ho Bong

Madeo '09
Tokyo! '09
The Host '06

Vittorio Bonicelli(1919-94)

Moses '76
Waterloo '71
Barbarella '68
The Bible '66

Pascal Bonitzer(1946-)

The Duchess of Langeais '07
Changing Times '04
The Story of Marie and Julien '03
Lumumba '01
Va Savoir '01
Genealogies of a Crime '97
Three Lives and Only One Death '96
Jeanne la Pucelle '94
Night and Day '91
La Belle Noiseuse '90

Taro Bonten

Rica 2: Lonely Wanderer '73
Rica 3: Juvenile's Lullaby '73
Sex and Fury '73
Rica '72

John Boorman(1933-)

The Tiger's Tale '06
The Tailor of Panama '00
The General '98
Where the Heart Is '90
Hope and Glory '87
Excalibur '81
Zardoz '73

Telsche Boorman(1957-97)

French Twist '95
Where the Heart Is '90

James Booth(1927-2005)

American Ninja 2: The Confrontation '87
Avenging Force '86
Pray for Death '85
Sunburn '79

Teena Booth

The Natalee Holloway Story '09
Sex & Lies in Sin City: The Ted Binion Scandal '08

Lizzie Borden(1958-)

Erotique '94
Working Girls '87

Bernard Borderie(1924-78)

Angelique and the Sultan '68
Angelique and the King '66
Your Turn Darling '63
Ladies' Man '62
Dishonorable Discharge '57

Allen Boretz(1900-86)

Copacabana '47
Where There's Life '47
It Ain't Hay '43

Robert Boris(1945-)

Diplomatic Siege '99
Frank and Jesse '94
Extreme Justice '93
Steele Justice '87
Oxford Blues '84
Doctor Detroit '83
Some Kind of Hero '82
Electra Glide in Blue '73

Ole Bornedal

Just Another Love Story '08
Nightwatch '96

Christopher Borrelli

The Marine 2 '09
Whisper '07

Michael Bortman

Resurrecting the Champ '07
Chain Reaction '96
Crooked Hearts '91
The Good Mother '88

Aida Bortnik(1938-)

Wild Horses '95
Old Gringo '89
The Official Story '85

Pierre Bost(1901-75)

The Judge and the Assassin '75
The Clockmaker '73
Forbidden Games '52
The Red Inn '51
The Walls of Malapaga '49
Devil in the Flesh '46

Daniel Boulanger(1922-)

Game of Seduction '76
Spirits of the Dead '68
The King of Hearts '66
Love Play '60

Roy Boulting(1913-2001)

Carlton Browne of the F.O. '59
Brothers in Law '57
Seven Days to Noon '50
The Guinea Pig '48

Emmanuel Bourdieu

A Christmas Tale '08
Esther Kahn '00
My Sex Life... Or How I Got into an Argument '96

David Bourla

Push '09
When Time Expires '97

Jason Bourque

Wyvern '09
Art of War 2: The Betrayal '08

Kate Boutilier

Rugrats Go Wild! '03
The Wild Thornberrys Movie '02
Rugrats in Paris: The Movie '00

Nouri Bouzid(1945-)

The Silences of the Palace '94
Man of Ashes '86

Andrew Bovell(1962-)

Edge of Darkness '10
Lantana '01
Head On '98

Susan Bowen

The Power Within '95
Storybook '95

T.R. Bowen(1942-)

Catherine Cookson's The Secret '00
Catherine Cookson's The Gambling Man '98
Catherine Cookson's The Round Tower '98
Catherine Cookson's The Rag Nymph '96
The Body in the Library '84

William Bowers(1916-87)

Support Your Local Sheriff '69
Alias Jesse James '59
The Sheepman '58
My Man Godfrey '57
5 Against the House '55
Tight Spot '55
Split Second '53
Abandoned '47
Something in the Wind '47

Douglas Bowie

Must Be Santa '99
Boy in Blue '86

Mike Bowler

Things 2 '97
Things '93

Fatal Images '89

Brandon Boyce

Venom '05
Wicker Park '04
Apt Pupil '97

Frank Cottrell Boyce

God on Trial '08
Millions '05

Daniel Boyd(1956-)

Heroes of the Heart '94
Invasion of the Space Preachers '90
Chillers '88

Don Boyd(1948-)

Kleptomania '94
Twenty-One '91
East of Elephant Rock '76

William Boyd(1952-)

Sword of Honour '01
The Trench '99
A Good Man in Africa '94
Chaplin '92
Mister Johnson '91
Tune in Tomorrow '90
Stars and Bars '88

Philippa Boyens

The Lovely Bones '09
King Kong '05
Lord of the Rings: The Return of the King '03
Lord of the Rings: The Two Towers '02
Lord of the Rings: The Fellowship of the Ring '01

Malcolm Stuart Boylan(1897-1967)

One Too Many '51
Son of Rusty '47
Mr. District Attorney '41
Red River Valley '41
Hangman's House '28

Bruno Bozzetto(1933-)

VIP, My Brother Superman '90
Allegro Non Troppo '76

Bill Bozzone

Ivory Hunters '90
Full Moon in Blue Water '88

Gerard Brach(1927-2006)

The Phantom of the Opera '98
Bitter Moon '92
The Lover '92
The Bear '89
Frantic '88
Jean de Florette '87
Manon of the Spring '87
Shy People '87
The Name of the Rose '86
Pirates '86
Maria's Lovers '84
My Best Friend's Girl '84
Identification of a Woman '82
Quest for Fire '82
I Sent a Letter to My Love '81
Tess '79
The Tenant '76
Diary of Forbidden Dreams '73
The Fearless Vampire Killers '67
Cul de Sac '66
Repulsion '65

Charles Brackett(1892-1969)

Journey to the Center of the Earth '59
The Girl in the Red Velvet Swing '55
Titanic '53
Niagara '52
Sunset Boulevard '50
Emperor Waltz '48
A Foreign Affair '48
Miss Tatlock's Millions '48
To Each His Own '46
The Lost Weekend '45

Five Graves to Cairo '43
The Major and the Minor '42
Ball of Fire '41
Midnight '39
What a Life '39
Bluebeard's Eighth Wife '38
The Last Outpost '35

Leigh Brackett(1915-78)

The Empire Strikes Back '80
The Long Goodbye '73
Hatari! '62
Gold of the Seven Saints '61
Rio Bravo '59
The Big Sleep '46

Jacob Brackman(1943-)

Times Square '80
The King of Marvin Gardens '72

Malcolm Bradbury(1932-2000)

Cold Comfort Farm '94
The Green Man '91

Ray Bradbury(1920-)

The Wonderful Ice Cream Suit '98
Something Wicked This Way Comes '83
Moby Dick '56
It Came from Outer Space '53

Robert North Bradbury(1886-1949)

Rangeland Empire '50
Valley of the Lawless '36
Kid Courageous '35
Texas Terror '35
Western Justice '35
Lucky Texan '34
The Star Packer '34
Tombstone Terror '34
The Gallant Fool '33
Riders of Destiny '33
West of the Divide '33
Texas Buddies '32
Behind Two Guns '24

Sue Bradford

The Atomic Brain '64
The Indestructible Man '56

Al (Alfonso Brescia) Bradley(1930-2001)

Iron Warrior '87
Metallica '85

Clive Bradley

The Killing Gene '07
A Harlot's Progress '06

John Bradshaw(1952-)

The Undertaker's Wedding '97
The Big Slice '90

Pam Brady

Hamlet 2 '08
Hot Rod '07
Team America: World Police '04
South Park: Bigger, Longer and Uncut '99

Tom Brady

The Hot Chick '02
The Animal '01

Brannon Braga(1965-)

Star Trek: First Contact '96
Star Trek: Generations '94

Melvyn Bragg(1939-)

Jesus Christ, Superstar '73
The Music Lovers '71
Isadora '68

Kenneth Branagh(1960-)

As You Like It '06
Love's Labour's Lost '00
Hamlet '96
A Midwinter's Tale '95
Much Ado about Nothing '93
Henry V '89

Chris Brancato

Species 2 '98
Hoodlum '96

John Brancato

Surrogates '09
Terminator Salvation '09
Primeval '07
Catwoman '04
Terminator 3: Rise of the Machines '03
The Game '97
The Net '95
Interceptor '92
Into the Sun '92
Flight of Black Angel '91
Mindwarp '91
The Unborn '91
Femme Fatale '90

Benjamin Brand

Bollywood Hero '09
November '05

Larry Brand

Halloween: Resurrection '02
Paranoia '98
Till the End of the Night '94
Overexposed '90
Masque of the Red Death '89
Backfire '88
The Drifter '88

David Brandes

The Quarrel '93
Dirt Bike Kid '86

Richard Brandes

Devil in the Flesh 2 '00
The Nurse '97
Dead Cold '96
Martial Law 2: Undercover '91
Martial Law '90
Party Line '88

Michael Brandman

Jesse Stone: Death in Paradise '06
Jesse Stone: Stone Cold '05
Monte Walsh '03

Gary Brandner(1933-)

Cameron's Closet '89
Howling 2: Your Sister Is a Werewolf '85

Clark Brandon(1958-)

Skeeter '93
Fast Food '89

Michael Brandt(1968-)

The A-Team '10
Wanted '08
3:10 to Yuma '07
Catch That Kid '04
2 Fast 2 Furious '03

Caliope Brattlestreet

Murder So Sweet '93
Showdown in Little Tokyo '91

Irving Brecher(1914-2008)

Bye, Bye, Birdie '63
Best Foot Forward '43
Du Barry Was a Lady '43
Ship Ahoy '42
Go West '40
At the Circus '39

Andy Breckman(1955-)

Rat Race '01
Sgt. Bilko '95
I.Q. '94
True Identity '91
Arthur 2: On the Rocks '88
Moving '88

Don Bredes

A Stranger in the Kingdom '98
Where the Rivers Flow North '94

Richard L. Breen(1918-67)

Tony Rome '67
Do Not Disturb '65
Mary, Mary '63
The FBI Story '59
Stopover Tokyo '57
Titanic '53
A Foreign Affair '48
Miss Tatlock's Millions '48

Martin Bregman(1931-)

A Weekend in the Country '96
Peter's Friends '92

Michael Scott Bregman

Carlito's Way: Rise to Power '05
Table One '00

Catherine Breillat(1948-)

Anatomy of Hell '04
Sex is Comedy '02
Romance '99
Perfect Love '96
36 Fillete '88
Police '85
A Real Young Girl '75

J. Robert Bren(1903-81)

Underground Agent '42
Without Orders '36

Frederick Hazlitt Brennan(1901-62)

Follow the Sun '51
Killer McCoy '47
Adventure '45

Alfonso Brescia

Reactor '78
War in Space '77
Two Gladiators '64

Lou Breslow(1900-87)

Bedtime for Bonzo '51
On Our Merry Way '48
Merton of the Movies '47
Murder, He Says '45
Follow the Boys '44
Blondie Goes to College '42
Sleepers West '41
Mr. Moto Takes a Chance '38
The Holy Terror '37
No More Women '34

Eric Bress

The Final Destination '09
The Butterfly Effect '04
Final Destination 2 '03

Robert Bresson(1907-99)

L'Argent '83
The Devil, Probably '77
Lancelot of the Lake '74
A Gentle Woman '69
Pickpocket '59
A Man Escaped '57
Diary of a Country Priest '50
The Ladies of the Bois de Bologne '44

Martin Brest(1951-)

Gigli '03
Going in Style '79

Jonathan Brett

Turbulence '96
Tales of Erotica '93

Craig Brewer(1971-)

Black Snake Moan '07
Hustle & Flow '05
Water's Edge '03
Pressure '02

Jameson Brewer(1916-2003)

Arnold '73
Terror in the Wax Museum '73
Over the Hill Gang '69
The Incredible Mr. Limpet '64

Salome Breziner

Fast Sofa '01
Tollbooth '94

Mitch Brian(1961-)

The '70s '00
Transformations '88

Monte Brice

Variety Girl '47
We're in the Navy Now '27

George Bricker(1898-1955)

Loophole '54
Heartaches '47
The Brute Man '46
House of Horrors '46
If I'm Lucky '46
She Wolf of London '46
Pillow of Death '45
Dead Man's Eyes '44

Marshall Brickman(1941-)

Intersection '93
Manhattan Murder Mystery '93
For the Boys '91
The Manhattan Project '86
Lovesick '83
Simon '80
Manhattan '79
Annie Hall '77
Sleeper '73

Paul Brickman(1949-)

Uprising '01
True Crime '99
Men Don't Leave '89
Deal of the Century '83
Risky Business '83
The Bad News Bears in Breaking Training '77
Citizens Band '77

Leslie Bricusse(1931-)

Bullseye! '90
Scrooge '70
Doctor Dolittle '67
Bachelor of Hearts '58

James Bridges(1936-93)

White Hunter, Black Heart '90
Perfect '85
Mike's Murder '84
Urban Cowboy '80
The China Syndrome '79
September 30, 1955 '77
The Paper Chase '73
The Baby Maker '70
Colossus: The Forbin Project '70
The Appaloosa '66

Elisa Briganti

The New Gladiators '83
Manhattan Baby '82
Zombie '80

John Bright(1908-89)

The Kid From Cleveland '49
Broadway '42
San Quentin '37
She Done Him Wrong '33
Union Depot '32
Public Enemy '31
Smart Money '31

Matthew Bright(1952-)

Freeway 2: Confessions of a Trickbaby '99
Modern Vampires '98
Freeway '95
Dark Angel: The Ascent '94
Shrunken Heads '94
Guncrazy '92
Wildfire '88
Forbidden Zone '80

John Briley(1925-)

Molokai: The Story of Father Damien '99
Christopher Columbus: The Discovery '92
Cry Freedom '87
Tai-Pan '86
Marie '85
Enigma '82
Gandhi '82
Eagle's Wing '79
The Medusa Touch '78
That Lucky Touch '75
Children of the Damned '63
Postman's Knock '62

Steven Brill(1962-)

Little Nicky '00
Ready to Rumble '00
D3: The Mighty Ducks '96
D2: The Mighty Ducks '94
Heavyweights '94
The Mighty Ducks '92

Ron L. Brinkerhoff

The Guardian '06
Eye See You '01

Mort Briskin(1919-2000)

Framed '75
Walking Tall '73
The Second Woman '51

Eduardo Brochero(1919-)

The Case of the Scorpion's Tail '71
Blade of the Ripper '70

Deborah Brock

Rock 'n' Roll High School Forever '91
Slumber Party Massacre 2 '87

Jeremy Brock(1959-)

Brideshead Revisited '08
Driving Lessons '06
The Last King of Scotland '06
Charlotte Gray '01
Mrs. Brown '97

Tricia Brock

Killer Diller '04
Due East '02

Q. Allan Brocka

Boy Culture '06
Eating Out 2: Sloppy Seconds '06

Kevin Brodbin(1964-)

Constantine '05
Mindhunters '05
The Glimmer Man '96

Brendan Broderick

Turbulence 2: Fear of Flying '99
Route 9 '98
Spacejacked '98
Spectre '96
Bloodfist 7: Manhunt '95
The Death Artist '95
Bloodfist 6: Ground Zero '94

Oscar Brodney(1906-)

Ghost Fever '87
The Brass Bottle '63
Tammy and the Doctor '63
When Hell Broke Loose '58
Tammy and the Bachelor '57
Lady Godiva '55
The Black Shield of Falworth '54
The Glenn Miller Story '54
Francis Covers the Big Town '53
Francis Goes to West Point '52
Double Crossbones '51
Francis Goes to the Races '51
Comanche Territory '50
Harvey '50
South Sea Sinner '50
For the Love of Mary '48
Mexican Hayride '48

Henry Bromell(1947-)

Last Call: The Final Chapter of F. Scott Fitzgerald '02
Panic '00

Dan Bronson

A Taste for Killing '92
The Last Innocent Man '87

Peter Brook(1925-)

Swann in Love '84
Lord of the Flies '63

Ralph Brooke(1920-63)

Bloodlust '59
Giant from the Unknown '58

William Brookfield

Close Your Eyes '02
Rough Magic '95

Adam Brooks(1956-)

Definitely, Maybe '08
Bridget Jones: The Edge of Reason '04
Wimbledon '04
Invisible Circus '00
Beloved '98
Practical Magic '98
Subway Stories '97
French Kiss '95
Heads '93

Albert Brooks(1947-)

Looking for Comedy in the Muslim World '06
The Muse '99
Mother '96
The Scout '94
Defending Your Life '91
Lost in America '85
Modern Romance '81
Real Life '79

Carlos Brooks

Quid Pro Quo '08
American Cop '94

James L. Brooks(1940-)

The Simpsons Movie '07
Spanglish '04
As Good As It Gets '97
I'll Do Anything '93
Broadcast News '87
Terms of Endearment '83
Starting Over '79
Thursday's Game '74

Joseph Brooks(1938-)

If Ever I See You Again '78
You Light Up My Life '77

Mel Brooks(1926-)

The Producers '05
Dracula: Dead and Loving It '95
Robin Hood: Men in Tights '93
Life Stinks '91
Spaceballs '87
History of the World: Part 1 '81
High Anxiety '77
Silent Movie '76
Blazing Saddles '74
Young Frankenstein '74
The Twelve Chairs '70
The Producers '68

Richard Brooks(1912-92)

Fever Pitch '85
Wrong Is Right '82
Looking for Mr. Goodbar '77
Bite the Bullet '75
Dollars '71
The Happy Ending '69
In Cold Blood '67
The Professionals '66
Lord Jim '65
Sweet Bird of Youth '62
Elmer Gantry '60
The Brothers Karamazov '58
Cat on a Hot Tin Roof '58
Something of Value '57
The Last Hunt '56
Blackboard Jungle '55
The Last Time I Saw Paris '54
Battle Circus '53
Storm Warning '51
Crisis '50
Mystery Street '50
Any Number Can Play '49
Key Largo '48
Brute Force '47
Cobra Woman '44

Stephen Brooks

Spiders 2: Breeding Ground '01
The Mangler '94

Larry Brothers

Two for Texas '97
Fever '91
An Innocent Man '89

Hilary Brougher

Stephanie Daley '06
The Sticky Fingers of Time '97

The Road to Zanzibar *'41*
The Road to Singapore *'40*
Never Say Die *'39*
Give Me a Sailor *'38*
Waikiki Wedding *'37*
The Princess Comes Across *'36*
Strike Me Pink *'36*
March of the Wooden Soldiers *'34*
Search for Beauty *'34*
College Humor *'33*

Hugo Butler(1914-68)
A Face in the Rain *'63*
Eva *'62*
The Young One *'61*
Autumn Leaves *'56*
Torero *'56*
Prowler *'51*
The Southerner *'45*
Young Tom Edison *'40*

John K. Butler(1908-64)
Rodeo King and the Senorita *'51*
G.I. War Brides *'46*

Michael Butler
Execution of Justice *'99*
Pronto *'97*
White Mile *'94*
Code of Silence *'85*
Pale Rider *'85*
Flashpoint *'84*
Murder by Phone *'82*
The Car *'77*
The Gauntlet *'77*
Brannigan *'75*
The Don Is Dead *'73*

William Butler
Return of the Living Dead: Rave to the Grave *'05*
Madhouse *'04*

Jez Butterworth(1969-)
The Last Legion *'07*
Birthday Girl *'02*

Tom Butterworth(1967-)
The Last Legion *'07*
Birthday Girl *'02*

Jorg Buttgereit(1963-)
Nekromantik 2 *'91*
Der Todesking *'89*
Nekromantik *'87*

Floyd Byars
Masterminds *'96*
Mindwalk: A Film for Passionate Thinkers *'91*
Making Mr. Right *'86*

Jim Byrnes(1948-)
The Pledge *'08*
Dead Man's Revenge *'93*
Miracle in the Wilderness *'91*
The Shadow Riders *'82*

John Byrum(1947-)
Duets *'00*
The Razor's Edge *'84*
Scandalous *'84*
Sphinx *'81*
Heart Beat *'80*
Valentino *'77*
Harry & Walter Go to New York *'76*
Inserts *'76*
Mahogany *'75*

Reggie Rock Bythewood(1965-)
Notorious *'09*
Biker Boyz *'03*
Dancing in September *'00*
Get On the Bus *'96*

Sun Ryong Byun
301/302 *'95*
301/302 *'95*

Won-mi Byun
Addicted *'02*
Addicted *'02*

Scott Caan(1976-)
The Dog Problem *'06*
Dallas 362 *'03*

Michael Cacoyannis(1927-)
Iphigenia *'77*
A Matter of Dignity *'57*
Girl in Black *'56*
Stella *'55*

Jerome Cady(1903-48)
Call Northside 777 *'48*
A Wing and a Prayer *'44*
Guadalcanal Diary *'43*
Mr. Moto's Gamble *'38*
Charlie Chan at Monte Carlo *'37*

David Caesar
Dirty Deeds *'02*
Idiot Box *'97*

Mario Caiano(1933-)
Erik, the Viking *'65*
Two Gladiators *'64*
Medusa Against the Son of Hercules *'62*

Alan Caillou(1914-2006)
Kingdom of the Spiders *'77*
The Losers *'70*
Clarence, the Cross-eyed Lion *'65*
Village of the Giants *'65*

Bill Cain
Papa's Angels *'00*
Nightjohn *'96*

Jeffrey Caine
The Constant Gardener *'05*
Rory O'Shea Was Here *'04*
Goldeneye *'95*

Yule Caise(1964-)
Way Past Cool *'00*
Free of Eden *'98*

Joseph M. Cala(1932-)
Avenging Angel *'85*
Angel *'84*

H. H. Caldwell
The Boob *'26*
The Boob *'26*

Neil Callaghan
Return Fire *'88*
Return Fire *'88*

David Callaham
The Expendables *'10*
Horsemen *'09*
Doom *'05*

Mars Callahan(1972-)
What Love Is *'07*
Poolhall Junkies *'02*
Double Down *'01*

Gian Paolo Callegari(1912-)
The Beast of Babylon Against the Son of Hercules *'63*
Samson Against the Sheik *'62*
The Treasure of Bengal *'53*

Dayton Callie
Executive Target *'97*
The Last Days of Frankie the Fly *'96*

Paul Callisi
Josh Kirby. . .Time Warrior: Chapter 1, Planet of the Dino-Knights *'95*
Josh Kirby... Time Warrior: Chapter 2, The Human Pets *'95*

Art Camacho
Confessions of a Pit Fighter *'05*
Little Bigfoot 2: The Journey Home *'97*

James Cameron(1954-)
Avatar *'09*
Titanic *'97*
Strange Days *'95*
True Lies *'94*
Terminator 2: Judgment Day *'91*
The Abyss *'89*
Aliens *'86*
Rambo: First Blood, Part 2 *'85*
The Terminator *'84*

Ken Cameron(1946-)
Fast Talking *'86*
Monkey Grip *'82*

Lorne Cameron
Over the Hedge *'06*
Brother Bear *'03*
Deadly Game *'98*
The Extreme Adventures of Super Dave *'98*
Clarence *'91*
Like Father, Like Son *'87*

China Cammell
Wild Side *'95*
White of the Eye *'88*

Donald Cammell(1939-96)
Wild Side *'95*
White of the Eye *'88*
Tilt *'78*
Performance *'70*

Brandon Camp
Love Happens *'09*
Dragonfly *'02*

Joe Camp(1939-)
Benji: Off the Leash! *'04*
Benji the Hunted *'87*
Oh, Heavenly Dog! *'80*
For the Love of Benji *'77*
Benji *'74*

Juan J. Campanella(1959-)
The Secret in Their Eyes *'09*
The Son of the Bride *'01*
Love Walked In *'97*

Pasquale Festa Campanile(1927-86)
The Sex Machine *'75*
Rocco and His Brothers *'60*

Alan Campbell(1904-63)
Tales of Manhattan *'42*
The Moon's Our Home *'36*

Darren O. Campbell
Black Dawn *'05*
The Foreigner *'03*

Robert W(right) Campbell(1927-2000)
Captain Nemo and the Underwater City *'69*
Hell's Angels on Wheels *'67*
Masque of the Red Death *'65*
Machine Gun Kelly *'58*
Teenage Caveman *'58*

Robin Campillo
The Class *'08*
Heading South *'05*
They Came Back *'04*
Time Out *'01*

Anna Campion(1952-)
Holy Smoke *'99*
Loaded *'94*

Jane Campion(1954-)
Bright Star *'09*
In the Cut *'03*
Holy Smoke *'99*
The Piano *'93*
Sweetie *'89*

Christopher Canaan
No Good Deed *'02*
The Apocalypse Watch *'97*
Robinson Crusoe *'96*
The Great Elephant Escape *'95*
The Ten Million Dollar Getaway *'91*
Drug Wars: The Camarena Story *'90*

Cuca Canals
The Chambermaid on the Titanic *'97*
Jamon, Jamon *'93*

Guillaume Canet(1973-)
Tell No One *'06*
Whatever You Say *'02*

Stephen J. Cannell(1942-)
The Tooth Fairy *'06*
It Waits *'05*
The Rousters *'90*

Laurent Cantet(1961-)
The Class *'08*
Heading South *'05*
Time Out *'01*

Leon Capetanos
Fletch Lives *'89*
Moon over Parador *'88*
Down and Out in Beverly Hills *'86*
Moscow on the Hudson *'84*
Silent Rebellion *'82*
The Tempest *'82*
Greased Lightning *'77*
Gumball Rally *'76*

Truman Capote(1924-84)
ABC Stage 67: Truman Capote's A Christmas Memory *'66*
The Innocents *'61*
Indiscretion of an American Wife *'54*
Beat the Devil *'53*

Frank Cappello
Constantine *'05*
No Way Back *'96*
Suburban Commando *'91*

James (Jim) Carabatsos
Lost Battalion *'01*
Hamburger Hill *'87*
Heartbreak Ridge *'86*
No Mercy *'86*
Underground Aces *'80*
Heroes *'77*

Steven W. Carabatsos
Hot Pursuit *'87*
The Last Flight of Noah's Ark *'80*
Tentacles *'77*
El Condor *'70*

Leos Carax(1960-)
Tokyo! *'09*
Pola X *'99*
The Lovers on the Bridge *'91*
Mauvais Sang *'86*
Boy Meets Girl *'84*

Julien Carbon
Running Out of Time 2 *'06*
Black Mask 2: City of Masks *'02*

Frank Cardea
Kiss Me Deadly *'08*
Dying to Remember *'93*

Rene Cardona, Jr.(1939-2003)
Hostages *'80*
Night of the Bloody Apes *'68*

J.S. Cardone(1946-)
The Stepfather *'09*
Prom Night *'08*
The Covenant *'06*
Sniper 3 *'04*
The Forsaken *'01*
True Blue *'01*
Outside Ozona *'98*
Black Day Blue Night *'95*
Shadowhunter *'93*
A Climate for Killing *'91*
Crash and Burn *'90*
Shadowzone *'89*
Thunder Alley *'85*
The Slayer *'82*

Mark Patrick Carducci(1955-97)
Buried Alive *'90*
Pumpkinhead *'88*

Topper Carew(1943-)
Talkin' Dirty after Dark *'91*
D.C. Cab *'84*

Peter Carey(1943-)
Until the End of the World *'91*
Bliss *'85*

Christian Carion(1963-)
Joyeux Noel *'05*
Plain Dirty *'04*
The Girl from Paris *'02*

Carlo Carlei(1960-)
Fluke *'95*
Flight of the Innocent *'93*

John Carlen
Sonny *'02*
Blind Side *'93*

Lewis John Carlino(1932-)
Haunted Summer *'88*
The Great Santini *'80*
Resurrection *'80*
I Never Promised You a Rose Garden *'77*
The Sailor Who Fell from Grace with the Sea *'76*
The Mechanic *'72*
A Reflection of Fear *'72*
The Brotherhood *'68*
Seconds *'66*

Jim Carlson(1932-2007)
Pound Puppies and the Legend of Big Paw *'88*
Mission Galactica: The Cylon Attack *'78*

Roy Carlson
China Moon *'91*
Stand Alone *'85*

Don Carmody
Whispers *'89*
Junior *'86*

Joe Carnahan(1969-)
Pride and Glory *'08*
Smokin' Aces *'07*
Narc *'02*
Blood, Guts, Bullets and Octane *'99*

Matthew Carnahan
State of Play *'09*
The Kingdom *'07*
Lions for Lambs *'07*
Black Circle Boys *'97*

Charles Robert Carner(1957-)
Witless Protection *'08*
Breakaway *'02*
Crossfire Trail *'01*
Echo of Murder *'00*
The Fixer *'97*
Eyes of a Witness *'94*
Blind Fury *'90*
Let's Get Harry *'87*
Gymkata *'85*

Michael Carnes
Furry Vengeance *'10*
Mr. Woodcock *'07*

John Carney
Once *'06*
On the Edge *'00*

Marc Caro(1956-)
The City of Lost Children *'95*
Delicatessen *'92*

Glenn Gordon Caron(1954-)
Picture Perfect *'96*
Moonlighting *'85*
Condorman *'81*

A.J. Carothers(1931-2007)
The Secret of My Success *'87*
Hero at Large *'80*
Never a Dull Moment *'68*
The Happiest Millionaire *'67*
Emil and the Detectives *'64*
The Miracle of the White Stallions *'63*

John Carpenter(1948-)
John Carpenter's Ghosts of Mars *'01*
Silent Predators *'99*
John Carpenter's Vampires *'97*
Escape from L.A. *'96*
Village of the Damned *'95*
El Diablo *'90*
They Live *'88*
Prince of Darkness *'87*
Black Moon Rising *'86*
Escape from New York *'81*
Halloween 2: The Nightmare Isn't Over! *'81*
Eyes of Laura Mars *'78*
The Fog *'78*
Halloween *'78*
Assault on Precinct 13 *'76*
Dark Star *'74*

Richard Carpenter(1933-)
The Scarlet Pimpernel *'99*
The Scarlet Pimpernel 2: Mademoiselle Guillotine *'99*
The Scarlet Pimpernel 3: The Kidnapped King *'99*
The Return of the Borrowers *'96*
The Borrowers *'93*

Stephen Carpenter
The Man *'05*
Soul Survivors *'01*
Blue Streak *'99*
Servants of Twilight *'91*
The Kindred *'87*
Dorm That Dripped Blood *'82*
The Power *'80*

Fabio Carpi
Buck and the Magic Bracelet *'97*
Basileus Quartet *'82*

Tito Carpi
Shark Hunter *'79*
Tentacles *'77*
Sting of the West *'72*
Cold Eyes of Fear *'70*
Fistful of Lead *'70*
Sartana's Here... Trade Your Pistol for a Coffin *'70*
Eagles Over London *'69*
Revenge of the Musketeers *'63*
Beauty on the Beach *'61*

Allan Carr(1937-99)
Can't Stop the Music *'80*
Grease *'78*

Benjamin Carr
Retro Puppet Master *'99*
Curse of the Puppet Master: The Human Experiment *'98*
Talisman *'98*
The Creeps *'97*
Hideous *'97*
Shrieker *'97*
Head of the Family *'96*
Zarkorr! The Invader *'96*

Caleb Carr(1955-)
Dominion: Prequel to the Exorcist *'05*
Exorcist: The Beginning *'04*

Richard Carr(1929-88)
Americana *'81*
Hell Is for Heroes *'62*

Joan Carr-Wiggin
My First Wedding *'04*
Sleeping with Strangers *'94*

Michael Carreras(1927-94)
Creatures the World Forgot *'70*
Unholy Four *'54*

Jean-Claude Carriere(1931-)
Goya's Ghosts *'06*
Birth *'04*

Cheech and Chong's Up in Smoke '79

Elie Chouraqui(1953-)

O Jerusalem '07
Harrison's Flowers '02
Love Songs '84

Chris Chow

Blood: The Last Vampire '09
Jet Li's Fearless '06

Matt Chow

Dog Bite Dog '06
3 Extremes 2 '02

Stephen (Chiau) Chow(1962-)

Kung Fu Hustle '04
Shaolin Soccer '01

Ronnie Christensen

Passengers '08
Chameleon 3: Dark Angel '00

Christian-Jaque(1904-94)

Madame Sans-Gene '62
Nana '55
Fanfan la Tulipe '51
La Chartreuse de Parme '48

Mark Christopher

Pizza '05
54 '98

Tien-wen Chu(1956-)

Flowers of Shanghai '98
Goodbye South, Goodbye '96

Oxide Pang Chun

Diary '06
Re-Cycle '06
The Eye 3 '05
The Tesseract '03
Bangkok Dangerous '00

Gerard Ciccoritti(1956-)

Skull: A Night of Terror '88
A Whisper to a Scream '88
Psycho Girls '86

Cynthia Cidre

The Mambo Kings '92
Fires Within '91
In Country '89

Santo Cilauro(1962-)

The Dish '00
The Castle '97

Matt Cimber(1936-)

Yellow Hair & the Fortress of Gold '84
Butterfly '82

Michael Cimino(1943-)

Year of the Dragon '85
Heaven's Gate '81
The Deer Hunter '78
Thunderbolt & Lightfoot '74
Magnum Force '73
Silent Running '71

Tony Cinciripini

Hell's Kitchen NYC '97
Confessions of a Hit Man '94
The Lawless Land '88

Patrick Cirillo

Tears of the Sun '03
The Surgeon '94
Dangerous Heart '93
Homer and Eddie '89

Louis CK(1967-)

I Think I Love My Wife '07
Down to Earth '01
Pootie Tang '01

John Claflin

Fool's Gold '08
Anacondas: The Hunt for the Blood Orchid '04

Rene Clair(1898-1981)

Les Grandes Manoeuvres '55
Beauties of the Night '52
Beauty and the Devil '50
And Then There Were None '45
It Happened Tomorrow '44
A Nous la Liberte '31
Under the Roofs of Paris '29

Bob (Benjamin) Clark(1941-2007)

Baby Geniuses '98
My Summer Story '94
Loose Cannons '90
From the Hip '86
A Christmas Story '83
Porky's 2: The Next Day '83
Porky's '82
Children Shouldn't Play with Dead Things '72

Bruce (B.D.) Clark(1945-)

Galaxy of Terror '81
The Naked Angels '69

Dennis Lynton Clark

In Pursuit of Honor '95
The Court Martial of Jackie Robinson '90
The Keep '83
Comes a Horseman '78

Frank Howard Clark(1888-1962)

The Prairie King '27
$50,000 Reward '25
Big Stakes '22

Greydon Clark(1943-)

Dance Macabre '91
Skinheads: The Second Coming of Hate '88
Final Justice '84
Angel's Brigade '79
Satan's Cheerleaders '77
Psychic Killer '75

Richard Clark

Double Play '96
The Halfback of Notre Dame '96

Ron Clark(1933-)

The Funny Farm '82
Revenge of the Pink Panther '78
High Anxiety '77
Norman, Is That You? '76
Silent Movie '76

Arthur C. Clarke(1917-2008)

2010: The Year We Make Contact '84
2001: A Space Odyssey '68

Frank Clarke(1956-)

Wonderland '88
Letter to Brezhnev '86

John Clarke(1948-)

Lust and Revenge '95
Lonely Hearts '82

Roy Clarke(1930-)

A Foreign Field '93
Hawks '89
Pictures '81
Flickers '80

T.E.B. Clarke(1907-89)

Who Done It? '56
The Lavender Hill Mob '51
The Magnet '50
Johnny Frenchman '46
Dead of Night '45

James Clavell(1925-94)

The Last Valley '71
To Sir, with Love '67
King Rat '65
633 Squadron '64
The Great Escape '63
The Fly '58

Christian Clavier(1952-)

Just Visiting '01
The Visitors '95

Elliot J. Clawson

The Leatherneck '28
The Phantom of the Opera '25

Thomas McKelvey Cleaver

Field of Fire '92
Raiders of the Sun '92
Immortal Sins '91
Heroes Stand Alone '89
The Terror Within '88

Marc Clebanoff

Break '09
The Pink Conspiracy '07

John Cleese(1939-)

Fierce Creatures '96
The Strange Case of the End of Civilization As We Know It '93
A Fish Called Wanda '88
Monty Python's The Meaning of Life '83
Monty Python's Life of Brian '79
Monty Python and the Holy Grail '75
And Now for Something Completely Different '72
Rentadick '72
The Magic Christian '69

Brian Clemens(1931-)

The Watcher in the Woods '81
Cry Terror '76
If It's a Man, Hang Up '75
Captain Kronos: Vampire Hunter '74
Death in Deep Water '74
The Devil's Web '74
I'm the Girl He Wants to Kill '74
In the Steps of a Dead Man '74
A Killer in Every Corner '74
Killer with Two Faces '74
Murder Motel '74
Murder on the Midnight Express '74
One Deadly Owner '74
Screamer '74
Golden Voyage of Sinbad '73
Dr. Jekyll and Sister Hyde '71
See No Evil '71
And Soon the Darkness '70
The Corrupt Ones '67
The Tell-Tale Heart '60

Dick Clement(1937-)

The Bank Job '08
Across the Universe '07
Flushed Away '06
Goal! The Dream Begins '06
Archangel '05
Still Crazy '98
Excess Baggage '96
The Commitments '91
Vice Versa '88
Water '85
Prisoner of Zenda '79
Catch Me a Spy '71

Rene Clement(1913-96)

Joy House '64
Purple Noon '60
Forbidden Games '52
Battle of the Rails '46

Ron Clements(1953-)

The Princess and the Frog '09
Treasure Planet '02
Hercules '97
Aladdin '92
The Little Mermaid '89
The Great Mouse Detective '86

Gianfranco Clerici

Devilfish '84
New York Ripper '82
Cannibal Holocaust '80

Rick Cleveland

Runaway Jury '03
Jerry and Tom '98

Denison Clift(1885-1961)

End of the Road '44
The Mystery of the Mary Celeste '35

Elmer Clifton(1892-1949)

Kid from Gower Gulch '50
Silver Bandit '50
Red Rock Outlaw '47
Lightning Raiders '45
Marked for Murder '45
Boss of Rawhide '44
Captain America '44
Gangsters of the Frontier '44
Guns of the Law '44
Teenage '44
Youth Aflame '44
Frontier Law '43
The Return of the Rangers '43
Rangers Take Over '42
Fighting Caballero '35
Pals of the Range '35
Rough Riding Ranger '35

Harry Clork(1888-1978)

Ma and Pa Kettle at Waikiki '55
Painting the Clouds With Sunshine '51
Broadway Rhythm '44
Ship Ahoy '42
Whistling in the Dark '41

Robert Clouse(1929-97)

China O'Brien '88
Force: Five '81
The Big Brawl '80
The Amsterdam Kill '78
The Pack '77
The Ultimate Warrior '75

Henri-Georges Clouzot(1907-77)

L'Enfer '93
Diabolique '55
Wages of Fear '55

Daniel Clowes(1961-)

Art School Confidential '06
Ghost World '01

Craig Clyde

Miracle Dogs '03
Walking Thunder '94
The Legend of Wolf Mountain '92
Little Heroes '91

Lewis (Luigi Cozzi) Coates(1947-)

Black Cat '90
Hercules '83
Alien Contamination '81
Star Crash '78

Stacy Cochran

Boys '95
My New Gun '92

Jay Cocks(1944-)

De-Lovely '04
Gangs of New York '02
Strange Days '95
The Age of Innocence '93

Jean Cocteau(1889-1963)

The Testament of Orpheus '59
Les Enfants Terrible '50
Orpheus '49
The Eagle Has Two Heads '48
Ruyblas '48
The Storm Within '48
Beauty and the Beast '46
The Ladies of the Bois de Bologne '44
Eternal Return '43
The Blood of a Poet '30

Diablo Cody

Jennifer's Body '09
Juno '07

Ethan Coen(1957-)

A Serious Man '09
Burn After Reading '08
No Country for Old Men '07
Paris, je t'aime '06
The Ladykillers '04
Intolerable Cruelty '03
The Man Who Wasn't There '01
O Brother Where Art Thou? '00
The Naked Man '98
The Big Lebowski '97
Fargo '96
The Hudsucker Proxy '93
Barton Fink '91
Miller's Crossing '90
Raising Arizona '87
Blood Simple '85
Crimewave '85

Franklin Coen(1912-90)

Black Gunn '72
Alvarez Kelly '66
The Train '65
Living on Love '37

Joel Coen(1954-)

A Serious Man '09
Burn After Reading '08
No Country for Old Men '07
Paris, je t'aime '06
The Ladykillers '04
Intolerable Cruelty '03
The Man Who Wasn't There '01
O Brother Where Art Thou? '00
The Big Lebowski '97
Fargo '96
The Hudsucker Proxy '93
Barton Fink '91
Miller's Crossing '90
Raising Arizona '87
Blood Simple '85
Crimewave '85

Lenore Coffee(1896-1984)

Cash McCall '60
End of the Affair '55
Sudden Fear '52
My Son, My Son '40
Four Daughters '38
Evelyn Prentice '34
Torch Singer '33

Charlie Coffey

National Lampoon's Attack of the 5 Ft. 2 Women '94
Earth Girls Are Easy '89

Barney Cohen

Doom Runners '97
Sabrina the Teenage Witch '96
Next Door '94
Killer Party '86
Friday the 13th, Part 4: The Final Chapter '84

Bennett Cohen

Chameleon 2: Death Match '99
The Hunted '98
Rainbow Drive '90

Bennett Cohen(1890-1964)

Sagebrush Law '43
Man from Montana '41
Frontier Vengeance '40
Melody of the Plains '37
Skull & Crown '35
The Three Musketeers '33
Come on Danger! '32
Sunset Trail '32
Texas Gunfighter '32
Midnight Faces '26

Charles Cohen(1948-)

The Gambler '97
Beyond Forgiveness '94

Charles Zev Cohen

Eddie and the Cruisers 2: Eddie Lives! '89
Lady Beware '87

David Aaron Cohen

Friday Night Lights '04
The Devil's Own '96
V.I. Warshawski '91

David M. Cohen

Hollywood Zap '86
Friday the 13th, Part 5: A New Beginning '85

Etan Cohen

Tropic Thunder '08
Idiocracy '06

Howard R. Cohen(1942-99)

Barbarian Queen 2: The Empress Strikes Back '89
Deathstalker 3 '89
Lords of the Deep '89
Saturday the 14th Strikes Back '88
Time Trackers '88
Barbarian Queen '85
Deathstalker '83
Space Raiders '83
Stryker '83
Saturday the 14th '81
The Young Nurses '73

Joel Cohen

Garfield: A Tail of Two Kitties '06
Garfield: The Movie '04
Cheaper by the Dozen '03
Goodbye, Lover '99
Money Talks '97
Toy Story '95
Pass the Ammo '88
Sister, Sister '87
Hot Money '79

Larry Cohen(1947-)

The Gambler, the Girl and the Gunslinger '09
Captivity '07
Cellular '04
Phone Booth '02
Misbegotten '98
The Ex '96
Invasion of Privacy '96
Uncle Sam '96
As Good as Dead '95
Guilty as Sin '93
Maniac Cop 3: Badge of Silence '93
The Ambulance '90
Maniac Cop 2 '90
Wicked Stepmother '89
Maniac Cop '88
Best Seller '87
Deadly Illusion '87
It's Alive 3: Island of the Alive '87
Return to Salem's Lot '87
Into Thin Air '85
Special Effects '85
The Stuff '85
Perfect Strangers '84
Scandalous '84
I, the Jury '82
Q (The Winged Serpent) '82
It's Alive 2: It Lives Again '78
The Private Files of J. Edgar Hoover '77
God Told Me To '76
It's Alive '74
Black Caesar '73
Hell Up in Harlem '73
Housewife '72
El Condor '70
Daddy's Gone A-Hunting '69
Return of the Magnificent Seven '66

Lawrence D. Cohen

Rodgers & Hammerstein's South Pacific '01
Stephen King's The Tommyknockers '93
Ghost Story '81
Carrie '76

Lawrence J. Cohen

Delirious '91
The Big Bus '76
S*P*Y*S '74
Start the Revolution without Me '70

Lester Cohen(1901-63)

Of Human Bondage '34
One Man's Journey '33

Martin B. Cohen

Humanoids from the Deep '80
Rebel Rousers '69

Neil Cohen

The Disappearance of Garcia Lorca '96
Pass the Ammo '88
Hot Money '79

Rob Cohen(1949-)
Dragon: The Bruce Lee Story '93
Scandalous '84

Ronald M. Cohen(1939-98)
Aces 'n Eights '08
Last Stand at Saber River '96
Twilight's Last Gleaming '77
The Good Guys and the Bad Guys '69
Blue '68

Sacha Baron Cohen(1971-)
Bruno '09
Borat: Cultural Learnings of America for Make Benefit Glorious Nation of Kazakhstan '06

Steve Cohen
The Bachelor '99
Tough and Deadly '94

Art Cohn(1909-58)
The Seven Hills of Rome '58
Ten Thousand Bedrooms '57
Men of the Fighting Lady '54
The Set-Up '49

Isabel Coixet(1960-)
Paris, je t'aime '06
My Life Without Me '03
Things I Never Told You '96

Brandon Cole
Illuminata '98
Mac '93
Sons '89

Lester Cole(1904-85)
Born Free '66
Blood on the Sun '45
Objective, Burma! '45
Footsteps in the Dark '41
The Invisible Man Returns '40
The Jury's Secret '38

Randel Cole
Real Time '08
2B Perfectly Honest '04

Tom Cole(1933-2009)
High Stakes '93
Streets of Gold '86
Smooth Talk '85

Duilio Coletti(1906-99)
Sicilian Connection '72
Operation Crossbow '65

Lewis Colick
Beyond the Sea '04
Ladder 49 '04
Domestic Disturbance '01
October Sky '99
Bulletproof '96
Ghosts of Mississippi '96
Judgment Night '93
Unlawful Entry '92
Dirt Bike Kid '86

Sid Colin
It's Not the Size That Counts '74
Carry On Spying '64

Bill Collage
Accepted '06
New York Minute '04

Dave Collard
Annapolis '06
Out of Time '03

Michael Colleary
Firehouse Dog '07
Face/Off '97
Darkman 3: Die Darkman Die '95

Robert Collector
Believe in Me '06
Memoirs of an Invisible Man '92

John Collee(1955-)
Creation '09
Happy Feet '06
Master and Commander: The Far Side of the World '03
Paper Mask '91

Peter Colley
Illusions '91
Mark of Cain '84

John Collier
The War Lord '65
Sylvia Scarlett '35

Boon Collins
Abducted 2: The Reunion '94
Spirit of the Eagle '90

Jackie Collins(1941-)
The World Is Full of Married Men '80
Yesterday's Hero '79
The Stud '78

Max Allan Collins(1948-)
Real Time: Siege at Lucas Street Market '00
Mommy 2: Mommy's Day '96
The Expert '95
Mommy '95

Monte (Monty) Collins, Jr.(1898-1951)
Utopia '51
The Green Promise '49
Heartaches '47

Harry Colomby
Touch and Go '86
Johnny Dangerously '84

Carl Colpaert(1963-)
Facade '98
The Crew '95
Delusion '91

John Colton(1891-1946)
The Invisible Ray '36
Werewolf of London '35

Chris Columbus(1958-)
Christmas With the Kranks '04
Nine Months '95
Little Nemo: Adventures in Slumberland '92
Only the Lonely '91
Heartbreak Hotel '88
The Goonies '85
Young Sherlock Holmes '85
Gremlins '84
Reckless '84

Adele Comandini(1898-1987)
Strange Illusion '45
Beyond Tomorrow '40
Her First Romance '40
Three Smart Girls '36
Jane Eyre '34

Ryan Combs(1974-)
The Hit '06
I Accidentally Domed Your Son '04
Straight out of Compton '99

Betty Comden(1915-2006)
Bells Are Ringing '60
Auntie Mame '58
It's Always Fair Weather '55
The Band Wagon '53
Singin' in the Rain '52
The Barkleys of Broadway '49
On the Town '49
Good News '47

Bob Comfort
Good Luck '96
Dogfight '91

Kevin Commins
Every Second Counts '08
Cybermutt '02

Jacques Companeez(1906-56)
Casque d'Or '52
Forbidden Fruit '52

Richard Compton(1938-2007)
Return to Macon County '75
The California Kid '74
Angels Die Hard '70

Georges Conchon(1925-90)
The Elegant Criminal '92
Black and White in Color '76

Bill Condon(1955-)
Dreamgirls '06
Kinsey '04
Chicago '02
Gods and Monsters '98
F/X 2: The Deadly Art of Illusion '91
Murder 101 '91
Sister, Sister '87
Strange Invaders '83
Strange Behavior '81

Heather Conkie
Bailey's Billion$ '05
Beethoven Lives Upstairs '92

Shane Connaughton(1947-)
Tara Road '05
The Run of the Country '95
The Playboys '92
My Left Foot '89

Richard Connell
Luxury Liner '48
Nice Girl? '41

Jon Connolly
Eddie '96
The Dream Team '89

Ray Connolly
Forever Young '85
That'll Be the Day '73

Barry Connors
Pilgrimage '33
Too Busy to Work '32
The Black Camel '31

Jean Conover
Jesus of Nazareth '28
Midnight Girl '25

Steve Conrad(1968-)
The Promotion '08
The Pursuit of Happyness '06
The Weather Man '05
Wrestling Ernest Hemingway '93

Christine Conradt(1973-)
Christie's Revenge '07
Demons from Her Past '07
Framed for Murder '07
Ghetto Dawg 2: Out of the Pits '05
The Perfect Nanny '00

William Conselman
East Side of Heaven '39
Bright Eyes '34
365 Nights in Hollywood '34

Robert Conte
The Breed '06
Who's Harry Crumb? '89
Odd Jobs '85

Alessandro Continenza(1920-96)
Deadly Mission '78
Let Sleeping Corpses Lie '74
The Loves of Hercules '60
What a Woman! '56
Too Bad She's Bad '54

Ernie Contreras
FairyTale: A True Story '97
The Pagemaster '94

Gary Conway(1936-)
American Ninja 3: Blood Hunt '89
American Ninja 2: The Confrontation '87
Over the Top '86

Tim Conway(1933-)
The Longshot '86
The Private Eyes '80
Prize Fighter '79
They Went That-a-Way & That-a-Way '78

Douglas S. Cook
Double Jeopardy '99
Holy Matrimony '94
Payoff '91

Peter Cook(1937-95)
Yellowbeard '83
The Hound of the Baskervilles '77
Bedazzled '68

T.S. Cook(1947-)
The Hive '08
High Noon '00
High Desert Kill '90
Nightbreaker '89
Out of the Darkness '85
The China Syndrome '79

Jon Cooksey
Before I Say Goodbye '03
Halloweentown 2: Kalabar's Revenge '01
Halloweentown '98

Greg Coolidge(1972-)
Employee of the Month '06
Sorority Boys '02

Gene L. Coon(1924-73)
The Killers '64
No Name on the Bullet '59
Man in the Shadow '57

Michael Cooney(1967-)
Identity '03
Jack Frost 2: Revenge of the Mutant Killer Snowman '00
Jack Frost '97
Murder in Mind '97
Tracks of a Killer '95

Adam Cooper
Accepted '06
New York Minute '04

Barry Michael Cooper
Above the Rim '94
Sugar Hill '94
New Jack City '91

John C. Cooper(1907-94)
First Man into Space '59
The Haunted Strangler '58

Olive Cooper(1892-1987)
Hills of Oklahoma '50
Bandit King of Texas '49
Outcasts of the Trail '49
Sioux City Sue '46
In Old Cheyenne '41
Sheriff of Tombstone '41
The Border Legion '40
Young Bill Hickok '40
Hot Tip '35

Paul Cooper
The Maldonado Miracle '03
Once Upon a Time ... When We Were Colored '95

Robert Cooper(1968-)
Stargate: The Ark of Truth '08
The Club '94
The Dark '94
No Contest '94
Blown Away '93

Scott Cooper
Crazy Heart '09
For Sale by Owner '09

Susan Cooper
George Balanchine's The Nutcracker '93
To Dance with the White Dog '93

Willis Cooper
Son of Frankenstein '39
Thank you, Mr. Moto '37

Martin Copeland
Texas Rangers '01
The Heavenly Kid '85

Alec Coppel(-1972)
Moment to Moment '66
Captain's Paradise '53
The Hidden Room '49
Obsession '49

Francis Ford Coppola(1939-)
Tetro '09
Youth Without Youth '07
John Grisham's The Rainmaker '97
The Godfather, Part 3 '90
New York Stories '89
The Cotton Club '84
Rumble Fish '83
One from the Heart '82
The Godfather 1902-1959: The Complete Epic '81
Apocalypse Now '79
The Conversation '74
The Godfather, Part 2 '74
The Great Gatsby '74
The Godfather '72
Patton '70
The Rain People '69
Is Paris Burning? '66
This Property Is Condemned '66
You're a Big Boy Now '66
Dementia 13 '63
The Bellboy and the Playgirls '62
Tonight for Sure '61
The Magic Voyage of Sinbad '52

Roman Coppola(1965-)
The Darjeeling Limited '07
CQ '01

Sofia Coppola(1971-)
Marie Antoinette '06
Lost in Translation '03
The Virgin Suicides '99
New York Stories '89

Sergio Corbucci(1927-90)
Super Fuzz '81
Companeros '70
Django '68

Sebastian Cordero(1972-)
Cronicas '04
Ratas, Ratones, Rateros '99

Laurence Coriat
A Mighty Heart '07
Me Without You '01
Wonderland '99

David Corley
Second in Command '05
Angel's Dance '99
Executive Power '98
Solo '96

Roger Corman(1926-)
The Skateboard Kid '93
Frankenstein Unbound '90
The Terror '63

Gerald Cormier
See Alan Rudolph

Alain Corneau(1943-)
Tous les Matins du Monde '92
Fort Saganne '84

Stephen Cornwell
Marshal Law '96
Killing Streets '91

Eugene Corr
Prefontaine '96
Getting Out '94
Desert Bloom '86
Wildrose '85

Michael Corrente(1960-)
Outside Providence '99
Federal Hill '94

Lloyd Corrigan(1900-69)
Campus Confessions '38
The Return of Dr. Fu Manchu '30
The Mysterious Dr. Fu Manchu '29

John W. Corrington(1932-88)
Isaac Asimov's Nightfall '00
The Arena '73
Battle for the Planet of the Apes '73
Boxcar Bertha '72
Omega Man '71

Joyce H. Corrington
The Arena '73
Battle for the Planet of the Apes '73
Boxcar Bertha '72
Omega Man '71

Catherine Corsini
Born in 68 '08
The New Eve '98
Full Speed '96

Laurent Cortiaud
Running Out of Time 2 '06
Black Mask 2: City of Masks '02

Bill Cosby(1937-)
Fat Albert '04
Leonard Part 6 '87

Don A. Coscarelli(1954-)
Bubba Ho-Tep '03
Phantasm 4: Oblivion '98
Phantasm 3: Lord of the Dead '94
Survival Quest '89
Phantasm 2 '88
Beastmaster '82
Phantasm '79

George P. Cosmatos(1941-2005)
The Cassandra Crossing '76
Massacre in Rome '73

Jean Cosmos(1923-)
On Guard! '03
Capitaine Conan '96
Colonel Chabert '94

Francis Cosne
Angelique and the Sultan '68
Untamable Angelique '67
Angelique and the King '66
Angelique: The Road to Versailles '65
Angelique '64

Constantin Costa-Gavras(1933-)
Amen '02
Conseil de Famille '86
Missing '82
Z '69

Maurizio Costanzo(1938-)
Zeder '83
A Special Day '77

James Costigan(1926-2007)
Mr. North '88
King David '85
S.O.S. Titanic '79

Manny Coto
Hostile Intent '97
Star Kid '97
Dr. Giggles '92

Richard Cottan
Wallander: Firewall '08
Wallander: One Step Behind '08
Wallander: Sidetracked '08

William Cottrell(1906-95)
Peter Pan '53
Pinocchio '40

Frank Cottrell-Boyce(1961-)
Code 46 '03
24 Hour Party People '01

The Claim '00
Pandaemonium '00
Hilary and Jackie '98
Welcome to Sarajevo '97
Saint-Ex: The Story of the Storyteller '95
Butterfly Kiss '94
A Woman's Guide to Adultery '93

Daniel P. Coughlin
Farmhouse '08
Lake Dead '07

Bob Couttie
Doomsdayer '01
Doomsdayer '99

Suzette Couture
The Last Templar '09
The Terrorist Next Door '08
Jesus '00
Love and Hate: A Marriage Made in Hell '90

Allen Covert(1964-)
The Benchwarmers '06
Grandma's Boy '06
Adam Sandler's 8 Crazy Nights '02

Noel Coward(1899-1973)
This Happy Breed '47
Brief Encounter '46
Blithe Spirit '45
In Which We Serve '43
Bitter Sweet '40
Bitter Sweet '33

Alex Cox(1954-)
Fear and Loathing in Las Vegas '98
Straight to Hell '87
Sid & Nancy '86
Repo Man '83

Brian Cox(1946-)
Scorpion Spring '96
Deadly Obsession '88

C. Jay Cox(1962-)
New in Town '09
Latter Days '04
Sweet Home Alabama '02

Deb Cox
After the Deluge '03
Dead Letter Office '98

Jim Cox
Murder She Purred: A Mrs. Murphy Mystery '98
Ferngully: The Last Rain Forest '92
The Rescuers Down Under '90
Oliver & Company '88

Morgan Cox(1900-68)
Raiders of Ghost City '44
Gang Busters '42
Desperate Cargo '41
The Spider Returns '41
Drums of Fu Manchu '40
Zorro's Fighting Legion '39

Paul Cox(1940-)
Innocence '00
Lust and Revenge '95
A Woman's Tale '92
Vincent: The Life and Death of Vincent van Gogh '87
Cactus '86
Man of Flowers '84
My First Wife '84
Lonely Hearts '82

Kerry Crabbe
Innocent Lies '95
The Playboys '92

Peter Crabbe
McHale's Navy '97
Car 54, Where Are You? '94

Dean Craig
Death at a Funeral '10
Death at a Funeral '07
Caffeine '06

H.A.L. Craig(1921-78)
Lion of the Desert '81
The Message '77

Waterloo '71
Anzio '68

Laurie Craig
Ramona and Beezus '10
Ella Enchanted '04
Paulie '98
Modern Girls '86

Frank Craven(1875-1945)
Our Town '40
Sons of the Desert '33

Jay Craven
Disappearances '06
A Stranger in the Kingdom '98
Where the Rivers Flow North '94

Jonathan Craven(1965-)
The Hills Have Eyes 2 '07
Wes Craven Presents Mind Ripper '95

Wes Craven(1939-)
The Hills Have Eyes 2 '07
Paris, je t'aime '06
Pulse '06
Wes Craven's New Nightmare '94
The People under the Stairs '91
Shocker '89
A Nightmare on Elm Street 3: Dream Warriors '87
The Hills Have Eyes, Part 2 '84
A Nightmare on Elm Street '84
Swamp Thing '82
Deadly Blessing '81
The Hills Have Eyes '77
Last House on the Left '72

Joanna Crawford
Sophia Loren: Her Own Story '80
The Birch Interval '78

Wayne Crawford
Jake Speed '86
Valley Girl '83

James A. Creelman(1901-41)
King Kong '33
The Most Dangerous Game '32
Vagabond Lover '29

James Cresson(1934-2004)
Defenseless '91
Chattahoochee '89
The Morning After '86

John Cresswell
Cast a Dark Shadow '55
The Woman in Question '50

Michael Crichton(1942-2008)
The 13th Warrior '99
Twister '96
Jurassic Park '93
Rising Sun '93
Runaway '84
Looker '81
The Great Train Robbery '79
Coma '78
Westworld '73
Sex Through a Window '72

Armando Crispino(1925-)
Autopsy '74
Commandos '73
Dead Are Alive '72
Autopsy of a Ghost '67

Michael Cristofer(1945-)
Original Sin '01
Gia '98
Breaking Up '97
Mr. Jones '93
The Bonfire of the Vanities '90

The Witches of Eastwick '87
Falling in Love '84

Keith Critchlow
New Jack City '91
Night Life '90

Thomas J. Crizer(1888-1963)
My Pal, the King '32
The Perfect Clown '25

Emma-Kate Croghan(1972-)
Strange Planet '99
Love and Other Catastrophes '95

David Cronenberg(1943-)
eXistenZ '99
Crash '95
Naked Lunch '91
Dead Ringers '88
The Fly '86
Videodrome '83
Scanners '81
The Brood '79
Fast Company '78
Rabid '77
They Came from Within '75

Allison Cross
Blood & Wine '96
Serving in Silence: The Margarethe Cammermeyer Story '95

Beverley Cross(1932-98)
Clash of the Titans '81
Sinbad and the Eye of the Tiger '77
Half a Sixpence '67
The Long Ships '64
Jason and the Argonauts '63

Avery Crounse(1946-)
Cries of Silence '97
The Invisible Kid '88
Eyes of Fire '84

Bill Crounse
American Cyborg: Steel Warrior '94
9 1/2 Ninjas '90

Lance Crouther
Good Hair '09
Down to Earth '01

Cameron Crowe(1957-)
Elizabethtown '05
Vanilla Sky '01
Almost Famous '00
Jerry Maguire '96
Singles '92
Say Anything '89
The Wild Life '84
Fast Times at Ridgemont High '82

Christopher Crowe(1948-)
Fear '96
The Last of the Mohicans '92
Whispers in the Dark '92
Off Limits '87
Mean Season '85
Nightmares '83
Last Chase '81

John Crowther
Damned River '89
The Evil That Men Do '84
Kill and Kill Again '81

Jim Cruickshank
Christmas in Wonderland '07
Man of the House '95
Sister Act 2: Back in the Habit '93
Mr. Destiny '90
Three Men and a Baby '87
Tough Guys '86
Breaking All the Rules '85

Jon Cryer(1965-)
Went to Coney Island on a Mission from God.. Be Back by Five '98

The Pompatus of Love '95

Billy Crystal(1947-)
America's Sweethearts '01
Forget Paris '95
City Slickers 2: The Legend of Curly's Gold '94
Mr. Saturday Night '92
Memories of Me '88

Alfonso Cuaron(1961-)
Children of Men '06
Paris, je t'aime '06
Y Tu Mama Tambien '01

Carlos Cuaron
Rudo y Cursi '09
Y Tu Mama Tambien '01

Allan Cubitt
The Boys Are Back '09
The Hound of the Baskervilles '02
Anna Karenina '00
St. Ives '98

Milo G. Cuccia
Count Dracula '71
Venus in Furs '70

Tom Cudworth
Restaurant '98
Ten Benny '98

Alma Cullen
All the King's Men '99
A Village Affair '95
Intimate Contact '87

Mike Cullen
Bloodlines '05
Horatio Hornblower '99

Carmen Culver
The Last Prostitute '91
Agatha Christie's Murder is Easy '82

David Cummings
Kevin & Perry Go Large '00
The Last Seduction 2 '98

Hugh Cummings
Hot Tip '35
Pardon My Gun '30

Rusty Cundieff(1965-)
Sprung '96
Tales from the Hood '95
Fear of a Black Hat '94
House Party 2: The Pajama Jam '91

Jack Cunningham(1882-1941)
Mississippi '35
It's a Gift '34
The Rider of Death Valley '32
The Viking '28
The Black Pirate '26
Don Q., Son of Zorro '25
Beyond the Rocks '22

Jere P. Cunningham
Boss of Bosses '99
The Last of the Finest '90

Michael Cunningham(1952-)
Evening '07
A Home at the End of the World '04
Splatter University '84

Terry Cunningham
The Stray '00
Y2K '99
Land of the Free '98

Pat Cupo
One Last Ride '03
Smalltime '96

Tim Curnen
Ghostwarrior '86
Forbidden World '82

Ian Curteis(1935-)
The Choir '95
Philby, Burgess and MacLean: Spy Scandal of the Century '84

Valerie Curtin(1945-)
Toys '92
Unfaithfully Yours '84
Best Friends '82
Inside Moves '80
And Justice for All '79

Dan Curtis(1928-2006)
Trilogy of Terror 2 '96
Burnt Offerings '76

Nathaniel Curtis(1909-83)
Jack & the Beanstalk '52
Blood on the Sun '45

Richard Curtis(1956-)
Pirate Radio '09
The Girl in the Cafe '05
Bridget Jones: The Edge of Reason '04
Love Actually '03
Bridget Jones's Diary '01
Notting Hill '99
Bean '97
Four Weddings and a Funeral '94
The Tall Guy '89

Vondie Curtis-Hall(1956-)
Waist Deep '06
Gridlock'd '96

Stephen J. Curwick(1960-)
Police Academy 6: City under Siege '89
Police Academy 5: Assignment Miami Beach '88

John Cusack(1966-)
War, Inc. '08
High Fidelity '00
Grosse Pointe Blank '97

Neil Cuthbert
The Adventures of Pluto Nash '02
Mystery Men '99
Hocus Pocus '93

Ron Cutler
Article 99 '92
Blood Red '88

Catherine Cyran
True Heart '97
Hostile Intentions '94
Fire on the Amazon '93
Futurekick '91
Uncaged '91
Bloodfist 2 '90
A Cry in the Wild '90
Slumber Party Massacre 3 '90

Renee Daalder(1944-)
Habitat '97
Massacre at Central High '76

Jean-Loup Dabadie(1938-)
Vincent, Francois, Paul and the Others '76
The Savage '75
Cesar & Rosalie '72

Ingram D'Abbes
Big Fella '37
Song of Freedom '36

Don DaGradi
Bedknobs and Broomsticks '71
Blackbeard's Ghost '67
Lady and the Tramp '55

John Dahl(1956-)
Red Rock West '93
Kill Me Again '89
P.I. Private Investigations '87
Private Investigations '87

Julia Dahl
Flirting with Forty '09
Uptown Girls '03

Roald Dahl(1916-90)
Willy Wonka & the Chocolate Factory '71

Chitty Chitty Bang Bang '68
You Only Live Twice '67
36 Hours '64

Minako Daira
One Missed Call 2 '05
One Missed Call '03

Salvador Dali(1904-89)
L'Age D'Or '30
Un Chien Andalou '28

Walter Dallenbach
Greedy Terror '78
Las Vegas Lady '76

Ian Dalrymple(1903-89)
Three Cases of Murder '55
Clouds over Europe '39
Pygmalion '38
South Riding '37

Darren Dalton(1965-)
The Land That Time Forgot '09
Hourglass '95

Joe D'Amato(1936-99)
Endgame '85
Trap Them & Kill Them '77
Heroes in Hell '73

Janeen Damian
Moondance Alexander '07
Hot Tamale '06

Michael Damian
Moondance Alexander '07
Hot Tamale '06

Damiano Damiani(1922-)
The Sicilian Connection '85
Confessions of a Police Captain '72
The Hit Man '60

Suso Cecchi D'Amico(1914-)
The Sky Is Falling '00
Jesus of Nazareth '77
The Innocent '76
Conversation Piece '75
Sandra of a Thousand Delights '65
The Leopard '63
Joyful Laughter '60
Rocco and His Brothers '60
Big Deal on Madonna Street '58
White Nights '57
What a Woman! '56
Too Bad She's Bad '54
The Lady Without Camelias '53
Bellissima '51

Matt Damon(1970-)
Gerry '02
Good Will Hunting '97

Oniroku Dan
Flower & Snake 2 '05
Flower & Snake '04
Flower & Snake '74 '74

Clemence Dane(1888-1965)
Salute John Citizen '42
Sidewalks of London '38
Fire Over England '37
Anna Karenina '35

Rodney Dangerfield(1921-2004)
The 4th Tenor '02
My 5 Wives '00
Meet Wally Sparks '97
Easy Money '83

Damon "Coke" Daniels
Who Made the Potatoe Salad? '05
My Baby's Daddy '04

Jeff Daniels(1955-)
Super Sucker '03
Escanaba in da Moonlight '01

Stan Daniels(1934-2007)
The Substitute Wife '94
For Richer, for Poorer '92

Blondie Plays Cupid *'40*
Doughnuts & Society *'36*

Annie de Young
MTV's Wuthering Heights *'03*
The Day the World Ended *'01*
Earth vs. the Spider *'01*

Geoff Deane
It's a Boy Girl Thing *'06*
Kinky Boots *'06*

Nick Dear(1955-)
Byron *'03*
The Turn of the Screw *'99*
The Gambler *'97*
Persuasion *'95*

William Dear(1944-)
Simon Says *'07*
Harry and the Hendersons *'87*
Timerider *'83*

James Dearden(1949-)
Rogue Trader *'98*
A Kiss Before Dying *'91*
Pascali's Island *'88*
Fatal Attraction *'87*

Frank Deasy
Prozac Nation *'01*
The Rats *'01*
Captives *'94*

John DeBello(1952-)
Killer Tomatoes Eat France *'91*
Killer Tomatoes Strike Back *'90*
Return of the Killer Tomatoes! *'88*
Happy Hour *'87*
Attack of the Killer Tomatoes *'77*

Dean DeBlois
How to Train Your Dragon *'10*
Lilo & Stitch *'02*

James D. Deck(1964-)
Silent Partner *'05*
Ravager *'97*

Denise DeClue
The Cherokee Kid *'96*
For Keeps *'88*
About Last Night... *'86*

Didier Decoin(1945-)
The Crown Prince *'06*
Napoleon *'03*
Balzac: A Life of Passion *'99*
The Count of Monte Cristo *'99*
Jakob the Liar *'99*

David DeCoteau(1962-)
Femalien 2 *'98*
Femalien *'96*

Edward Decter(1959-)
The Santa Clause 3: The Escape Clause *'06*
The Wild *'06*
The Lizzie McGuire Movie *'03*
The Santa Clause 2 *'02*
There's Something about Mary *'98*
Options *'88*

Miles Deem
See Demofilo Fidani

Frank Deese
Josh and S.A.M. *'93*
The Principal *'87*

David DeFalco
Chaos *'05*
Gangland *'00*

Christopher DeFaria(1959-)
Amityville: A New Generation *'93*
Amityville 1992: It's About Time *'92*

James DeFelice
Angel Square *'92*
Out of the Dark *'88*

Why Shoot the Teacher *'79*

Michael DeForrest
The Lickerish Quartet *'70*
Camille 2000 *'69*

Brian Degas(1935-)
Barbarella *'68*
Danger: Diabolik *'68*

Michael deGuzman
Hidden in America *'96*
Jaws: The Revenge *'87*

Paul Dehn(1912-76)
Murder on the Orient Express *'74*
Conquest of the Planet of the Apes *'72*
Escape from the Planet of the Apes *'71*
Beneath the Planet of the Apes *'70*
The Spy Who Came in from the Cold *'65*
Goldfinger *'64*
Seven Days to Noon *'50*

Len Deighton(1929-)
Oh! What a Lovely War *'69*
Billion Dollar Brain *'67*

Edward Dein(1907-84)
Curse of the Undead *'59*
Shack Out on 101 *'55*
Jungle Woman *'44*
Slightly Terrific *'44*
Calling Dr. Death *'43*

Mildred Dein
Curse of the Undead *'59*
Shack Out on 101 *'55*

Steve DeJarnatt
Miracle Mile *'89*
Strange Brew *'83*

Fred Dekker(1959-)
If Looks Could Kill *'91*
RoboCop 3 *'91*
The Monster Squad *'87*
Night of the Creeps *'86*

Alvaro del Amo
Jealousy *'99*
Intruso *'93*
Lovers: A True Story *'90*

Remigio del Grosso(1912-)
Coriolanus, Man without a Country *'64*
Conquest of Mycene *'63*
Mill of the Stone Women *'60*
Neapolitan Carousel *'54*

Peter Del Monte(1943-)
Traveling Companion *'96*
Julia and Julia *'87*

Guillermo del Toro(1964-)
Hellboy II: The Golden Army *'08*
Pan's Labyrinth *'06*
Hellboy *'04*
The Devil's Backbone *'01*
Cronos *'94*

Shelagh Delaney(1939-)
The Railway Station Man *'92*
Dance with a Stranger *'85*
A Taste of Honey *'61*

Jean Delannoy(1908-)
Action Man *'67*
Imperial Venus *'63*

Walter DeLeon(1884-1947)
Little Giant *'46*
Birth of the Blues *'41*
Pot o' Gold *'41*
The Ghost Breakers *'40*
Union Pacific *'39*
The Big Broadcast of 1938 *'38*
College Swing *'38*
Waikiki Wedding *'37*
The Princess Comes Across *'36*
Rhythm on the Range *'36*

Strike Me Pink *'36*
Ruggles of Red Gap *'35*
Six of a Kind *'34*
Union Depot *'32*
Lonely Wives *'31*

Francis Delia
Trouble Bound *'92*
Freeway *'88*

William F. Delligan(1944-95)
A Passion to Kill *'94*
Praying Mantis *'93*

Jeffrey Delman
Double Obsession *'93*
Voodoo Dawn *'89*

Vina Delmar
The Awful Truth *'37*
Make Way for Tomorrow *'37*

Julie Delpy(1969-)
2 Days in Paris *'07*
Before Sunset *'04*

Rudy DeLuca
Screw Loose *'99*
Dracula: Dead and Loving It *'95*
Life Stinks *'91*
Million Dollar Mystery *'87*
Transylvania 6-5000 *'85*
Caveman *'81*
High Anxiety *'77*
Silent Movie *'76*

Paul DeMeo
The Rocketeer *'91*
Arena *'89*
The Wrong Guys *'88*
The Eliminators *'86*
Zone Troopers *'84*
Future Cop *'76*

William DeMeo
Searching for Bobby D *'05*
Wannabes *'01*

Jonathan Demme(1944-)
The Truth About Charlie *'02*
Fighting Mad *'76*
Caged Heat *'74*
Hot Box *'72*
Angels Hard As They Come *'71*

James DeMonaco(1968-)
Skinwalkers *'07*
Assault on Precinct 13 *'05*
The Negotiator *'98*
Jack *'96*

Albert DeMond(1901-73)
Marshal of Cedar Rock *'53*
Border Saddlemates *'52*
Wild Frontier *'47*
Cyclotrode "X" *'46*
Daughter of Don Q *'46*
King of the Forest Rangers *'46*
Federal Operator 99 *'45*
Manhunt of Mystery Island *'45*
The Purple Monster Strikes *'45*
Riders of the Rio Grande *'43*
Ridin' Down the Canyon *'42*
Gangs of Sonora *'41*
Gauchos of El Dorado *'41*
Outlaws of the Cherokee Trail *'41*
West of Cimarron *'41*
The Great Plane Robbery *'40*
The Love Trap *'29*

Jacques Demy(1931-90)
A Slightly Pregnant Man *'79*
Pied Piper *'72*
Model Shop *'69*
The Young Girls of Rochefort *'68*
Umbrellas of Cherbourg *'64*

Claire Denis(1948-)
35 Shots of Rum *'08*
The Intruder *'04*

Friday Night *'02*
Beau Travail *'98*
Nenette and Boni *'96*
I Can't Sleep *'93*
No Fear, No Die *'90*
Chocolat *'88*

Wilton Denmark
Johnny Firecloud *'75*
Cain's Cutthroats *'71*

Gill Dennis
Walk the Line *'05*
Riders of the Purple Sage *'96*
Without Evidence *'96*
Return to Oz *'85*

Pen Densham(1947-)
Houdini *'99*
Moll Flanders *'96*
Lifepod *'93*
Robin Hood: Prince of Thieves *'91*
The Zoo Gang *'85*

Alan Dent(1905-78)
Hamlet *'48*
Henry V *'44*

Greg DePaul
Saving Silverman *'01*
Killer Bud *'00*

Jacques Deray(1929-2003)
Borsalino *'70*
La Piscine *'69*

Everett DeRoche
See Everett De Roche
Link *'86*
Razorback *'84*
Road Games *'81*

Bob DeRosa
Killers *'10*
The Air I Breathe *'07*

Scott Derrickson
The Exorcism of Emily Rose *'05*
Hellraiser 5: Inferno *'00*
Urban Legends 2: Final Cut *'00*

Dominique Deruddere(1957-)
Everybody's Famous! *'00*
Hombres Complicados *'97*
Wait until Spring, Bandini *'90*

Georges des Esseintes
Animal Instincts *'92*
Secret Games *'92*

Arnaud Desplechin(1960-)
A Christmas Tale *'08*
Kings and Queen *'04*
Esther Kahn *'00*
My Sex Life... Or How I Got into an Argument *'96*
La Sentinelle *'92*

Helen Deutsch(1906-92)
Valley of the Dolls *'67*
It's a Big Country *'51*
King Solomon's Mines *'50*
Shockproof *'49*
The Loves of Carmen *'48*
Golden Earrings *'47*
National Velvet *'44*
The Seventh Cross *'44*

Jacques Deval
Balalaika *'39*
Cafe Metropole *'37*

Michel DeVille(1931-)
La Lectrice *'88*
Peril *'85*

D.V. DeVincentis
High Fidelity *'00*
Grosse Pointe Blank *'97*

Dennis Devine
Bloodstream *'00*
Chain of Souls *'00*
Merchants of Death *'99*
Vampires of Sorority Row: Kickboxers From Hell *'99*

Things 2 *'97*
Things *'93*
Fatal Images *'89*

Scott Devine(1969-)
Shark Attack 3: Megalodon *'02*
Shark Attack 2 *'00*
Shark Attack *'99*

Dean Devlin(1962-)
Godzilla *'98*
Independence Day *'96*
Stargate *'94*
Universal Soldier *'92*

Christopher DeVore
Hamlet *'90*
Frances *'82*
The Elephant Man *'80*

Jack DeWitt(1900-81)
Triumphs of a Man Called Horse *'83*
The Return of a Man Called Horse *'76*
Sky Riders *'76*
Neptune Factor *'73*
Man in the Wilderness *'71*
A Man Called Horse *'70*
The Legend of the Sea Wolf *'58*
Portland Expose *'57*
Sitting Bull *'54*
Bells of San Fernando *'47*

Karen DeWolf
Getting Gertie's Garter *'45*
Pioneers of the West *'40*

Pete Dexter
Michael *'96*
Mulholland Falls *'95*
Paris Trout *'91*
Rush *'91*

Annie DeYoung
Princess Protection Program *'09*
Return to Halloweentown *'06*

Elize D'Haene
Red Shoe Diaries: Luscious Lola *'00*
Red Shoe Diaries: Strip Poker *'96*

Fernando Di Leo(1932-2003)
Rulers of the City *'76*
Hired to Kill *'73*
Hit Men *'73*

Edward Di Lorenzo
Lady Frankenstein *'72*
A Place Called Glory *'66*

Vince Di Meglio
Marmaduke *'10*
Smother *'08*

Catherine Di Napoli
(Untitled) *'09*
Bartleby *'01*

Mario di Nardo
Mean Machine *'73*
Five Dolls for an August Moon *'70*

Gerald Di Pego(1941-)
The Forgotten *'04*
Angel Eyes *'01*
Instinct *'99*
Message in a Bottle *'98*
Phenomenon *'96*
Keeper of the City *'92*
Sharky's Machine *'81*

David Diamond
Old Dogs *'09*
When in Rome *'09*
The Tenants *'06*
Evolution *'01*
Family Man *'00*
Body Count *'97*

I.A.L. Diamond(1920-88)
Buddy Buddy *'81*
The Front Page *'74*
Avanti! *'72*
The Private Life of Sherlock Holmes *'70*

Cactus Flower *'69*
The Fortune Cookie *'66*
Kiss Me, Stupid! *'64*
Irma La Douce *'63*
One, Two, Three *'61*
The Apartment *'60*
Some Like It Hot *'59*
Love in the Afternoon *'57*
Monkey Business *'52*
Let's Make It Legal *'51*
Love Nest *'51*
Never Say Goodbye *'46*

Agustin Diaz Yanes(1950-)
No News from God *'01*
Baton Rouge *'88*

Tom DiCillo(1954-)
Delirious *'06*
Double Whammy *'01*
The Real Blonde *'97*
Box of Moonlight *'96*
Living in Oblivion *'94*
Johnny Suede *'92*

Basil Dickey(1880-1958)
Brand of Fear *'49*
Son of Zorro *'47*
Daughter of Don Q *'46*
King of the Forest Rangers *'46*
The Phantom Rider *'46*
Federal Operator 99 *'45*
Manhunt of Mystery Island *'45*
The Purple Monster Strikes *'45*
Manhunt in the African Jungles *'43*
Flash Gordon Conquers the Universe *'40*
Junior G-Men *'40*
Space Soldiers Conquer the Universe *'40*
The Green Hornet *'39*
Brothers of the West *'37*
The Phantom Rider *'36*

Joan Didion(1934-)
Up Close and Personal *'96*
Broken Trust *'95*
True Confessions *'81*
A Star Is Born *'76*
Panic in Needle Park *'71*

Katherine Dieckmann
Motherhood *'09*
A Good Baby *'99*

Carlos Diegues(1940-)
Orfeu *'99*
Tieta of Agreste *'96*
Quilombo *'84*
Bye Bye Brazil *'79*

Anton Diether
Cleopatra *'99*
Moby Dick *'98*

Erwin C. Dietrich
Ilsa, the Wicked Warden *'78*
Inn of Temptation *'73*
Sex Adventures of the Three Musketeers *'71*

Frank Dietz
Cold Harvest *'98*
Magic in the Mirror: Fowl Play *'96*
Naked Souls *'95*

John Dighton(1909-89)
The Devil's Disciple *'59*
The Happiest Days of Your Life *'50*
Kind Hearts and Coronets *'49*
The Foreman Went to France *'42*

Erin Dignam
The Yellow Handkerchief *'08*
Loved *'97*
Denial: The Dark Side of Passion *'91*

Richard Dilello
Riot in the Streets *'96*
Bad Boys *'83*

Flint Dille(1955-)
Venom *'05*

An American Tail: Fievel Goes West '91

Constantine Dillon(1953-)
Killer Tomatoes Eat France '91
Killer Tomatoes Strike Back '90
Return of the Killer Tomatoes! '88

Robert Dillon(1889-1944)
Waking the Dead '00
Deception '92
Flight of the Intruder '90
The Survivalist '87
Revolution '85
The River '84
French Connection 2 '75
99 & 44/100 Dead '74
Prime Cut '72
Bikini Beach '64
Muscle Beach Party '64
X: The Man with X-Ray Eyes '63
City of Fear '59

Robert A.(R.A.) Dillon(1889-1944)
Slaves in Bondage '37
The Last of the Mohicans '20

Howard Dimsdale(1914-44)
The Sheriff of Fractured Jaw '59
Abbott and Costello Meet Dr. Jekyll and Mr. Hyde '52
The Traveling Saleswoman '50
Somewhere in the Night '46

Dennis Dimster-Denk(1965-)
Outside the Law '95
Terminal Impact '95

Brian DiMuccio
Moonbase '97
Little Witches '96
The Demolitionist '95
Voodoo '95

Mel Dinelli
Jeopardy '53
The Spiral Staircase '46

Leslie Dixon
Hairspray '07
The Heartbreak Kid '07
Just like Heaven '05
Freaky Friday '03
Pay It Forward '00
The Thomas Crown Affair '99
That Old Feeling '96
Look Who's Talking Now '93
Mrs. Doubtfire '93
Loverboy '89
Outrageous Fortune '87
Overboard '87

Peter Dixon
Unlawful Passage '94
Down the Wyoming Trail '39

Peter Dobai(1944-)
Hanussen '88
Colonel Redl '84
Mephisto '81

Frank Q. Dobbs(1939-2006)
The Magnificent Seven '98
Hotwire '80

Lem Dobbs(1961-)
The Score '01
The Limey '99
Dark City '97
The Hard Way '91
Kafka '91

Neal Dobrofsky
$5 a Day '08
Mail Order Bride '08
The Donor '94

Tippi Dobrofsky
$5 a Day '08
Mail Order Bride '08
The Donor '94

Frances Doel
Cyclops '08
Big Bad Mama '74

Donald M. Dohler(1946-2006)
Galaxy Invader '85
The Alien Factor '78

Jacques Doillon(1944-)
Petits Freres '00
Ponette '95
La Vèngeance d'une Femme '89

Bob Dolman
How to Eat Fried Worms '06
The Banger Sisters '02
Far and Away '92
Willow '88

Henry Dominic
See John Brancato

Andrew Dominik
The Assassination of Jesse James by the Coward Robert Ford '07
Chopper '00

Patrick G. Donahue
Savage Instinct '89
Code of Honor '82
Kill Squad '81

Simon Donald
Beautiful Creatures '00
Deacon Brodie '98
My Life So Far '98
The Ebb-Tide '97

Sergio Donati(1933-)
North Star '96
Beyond Justice '92
Orca '77
Spaghetti Western '75
Escape from Death Row '73
The Good, the Bad and the Ugly '67

Thomas Dean Donnelly
Sahara '05
A Sound of Thunder '05

Thomas Michael Donnelly
Bonanno: A Godfather's Story '99
A Soldier's Sweetheart '98
The Garden of Redemption '97
Talent for the Game '91
Quicksilver '86
Defiance '79

Mary Agnes Donoghue
Veronica Guerin '03
White Oleander '02
Deceived '91
Paradise '91
Beaches '88
The Buddy System '83

Martin Donovan(1950-)
Somebody Is Waiting '96
Death Becomes Her '92
Mad at the Moon '92
Apartment Zero '88

Paul Donovan(1954-)
Tales from a Parallel Universe: Eating Pattern '97
Tales from a Parallel Universe: Giga Shadow '97
Tales from a Parallel Universe: I Worship His Shadow '97
Tales from a Parallel Universe: Super Nova '97
Tomcat: Dangerous Desires '93
Self-Defense '83

Mark Donskoi(1901-81)
My Universities '40
My Apprenticeship '39

Anita Doohan
Whispers '89
Embryo '76

Matt Dorff
Category 6 : Day of Destruction '04
Mr. Rock 'n' Roll: The Alan Freed Story '99
Requiem for Murder '99
Silent Predators '99
Random Encounter '98
The Reaper '97
The Stepsister '97
Closer and Closer '96

David Dorfman(1993-)
Anger Management '03
My Boss's Daughter '03

Douglas Z. Doty(1874-1935)
Dress Parade '27
The Fighting Eagle '27
The King on Main Street '25

Gil Doud(1914-57)
Walk the Proud Land '56
To Hell and Back '55

Ziad Doueiri
Lila Says '04
West Beirut '98

Joseph Dougherty
Witch Hunt '94
Attack of the 50 Ft. Woman '93
Cast a Deadly Spell '91
Steel and Lace '90

Michael Dougherty
Superman Returns '06
Urban Legends: Bloody Mary '05
X2: X-Men United '03

Lorenzo Doumani(1962-)
Storybook '95
Amore! '93

Richard D'Ovidio
Exit Wounds '01
13 Ghosts '01

Alexander Dovzhenko(1849-1956)
Earth '30
Arsenal '29

Nancy Dowd(1945-)
Let It Ride '89
Ladies and Gentlemen, the Fabulous Stains '82
Slap Shot '77

Allison Louise Downe
Just for the Hell of It '68
She-Devils on Wheels '68
The Girl, the Body and the Pill '67
Gruesome Twosome '67
Blood Feast '63

Robert Downey(1936-)
Greaser's Palace '72
Putney Swope '69

Carol Doyle
Human Trafficking '05
Veronica Guerin '03
Washington Square '97

Laird Doyle
Cain and Mabel '36
Bordertown '35
Sing and Like It '34

Larry Doyle
I Love You, Beth Cooper '09
Duplex '03
Looney Tunes: Back in Action '03

Roddy Doyle(1958-)
When Brendan Met Trudy '00
The Van '95
Family '94
The Snapper '93
The Commitments '91

Brian Doyle-Murray(1945-)
Club Paradise '86
Caddyshack '80

Srdjan Dragojevic(1963-)
The Wounds '98
Pretty Village, Pretty Flame '96

Oliver Drake(1903-91)
Fighting Valley '43
The Lone Star Trail '43
Trailing Double Trouble '40
Cowboys from Texas '39
Purple Vigilantes '38
Public Cowboy No. 1 '37
Roarin' Lead '37
Law and Lawless '33
The Drifter '32
Rogue of the Rio Grande '30

Peter Draper
Poldark '75
The Buttercup Chain '70
I'll Never Forget What's 'Isname '67
The Girl Getters '66

Jay Dratler(1911-68)
Impact '49
Call Northside 777 '48
That Wonderful Urge '48
Dark Corner '46
Laura '44

Hal Dresner
The Eiger Sanction '75
Sssssss '73

Carl Theodor Dreyer(1889-1968)
Medea '88
Gertrud '64
Ordet '55
Day of Wrath '43
Vampyr '31
Passion of Joan of Arc '28
Master of the House '25

Karim Dridi(1961-)
Bye-Bye '96
Pigalle '95

Robin Driscoll
Mr. Bean's Holiday '07
Bean '97

Kevin Droney(1948-)
Wing Commander '99
Mortal Kombat 1: The Movie '95
Down Came a Blackbird '94

Michael B. Druxman(1941-)
The Doorway '00
Isaac Asimov's Nightfall '00
Battle Queen 2020 '99
Dillinger and Capone '95
Cheyenne Warrior '94

Lee Drysdale
Sweet Nothing '96
Leather Jackets '90

Olivier Ducastel(1962-)
Born in 68 '08
Cote d'Azur '05
My Life on Ice '02
The Adventures of Felix '99
Jeanne and the Perfect Guy '98

James Duff(1955-)
The War at Home '96
Doing Time on Maple Drive '92

Warren Duff(1904-73)
Step Lively '44
Invisible Stripes '39
Angels with Dirty Faces '38
Gold Diggers in Paris '38
Varsity Show '37
Gold Diggers of 1937 '36
The Singing Kid '36
Last Command '28

Jesse Duffy(1894-1952)
Son of Zorro '47
Daughter of Don Q '46

King of the Forest Rangers '46
The Phantom Rider '46
Federal Operator 99 '45
Manhunt of Mystery Island '45
Manhunt in the African Jungles '43

Jo Duffy
Puppet Master 5: The Final Chapter '94
Puppet Master 4 '93

Troy Duffy
The Boondock Saints II: All Saints Day '09
Boondock Saints '99

Martine Dugowson(1958-)
Portraits Chinois '96
Mina Tannenbaum '93

John Duigan(1949-)
Head in the Clouds '04
The Leading Man '96
Sirens '94
Wide Sargasso Sea '92
Flirting '89
The Year My Voice Broke '87

Bruno Dumont(1958-)
Flanders '06
Twentynine Palms '03
Humanity '99
The Life of Jesus '96

Don Carlos Dunaway
Impulse '84
Cujo '83

David Duncan(1913-99)
The Time Machine '60
The Leech Woman '59
Monster on the Campus '59

Patrick Duncan(1963-)
Nick of Time '95
A Home of Our Own '93

Patrick Sheane Duncan(1947-)
A Painted House '03
The Wall '99
Courage Under Fire '96
Mr. Holland's Opus '95
Live! From Death Row '92
84 Charlie MoPic '89

Peter Duncan(1954-)
A Little Bit of Soul '97
Children of the Revolution '95

Phil Dunham(1885-1972)
The Duke Is Tops '38
Trailing Trouble '37
Two-Gun Troubador '37
Stormy Trails '36

Winifred Dunn
The Dropkick '27
Sparrows '26
Twinkletoes '26

John Gregory Dunne(1932-2003)
Up Close and Personal '96
Broken Trust '95
True Confessions '81
A Star Is Born '76
Panic in Needle Park '71

Philip Dunne(1908-92)
The Agony and the Ecstasy '65
Ten North Frederick '58
Demetrius and the Gladiators '54
The Egyptian '54
The Robe '53
David and Bathsheba '51
Pinky '49
The Luck of the Irish '48
Forever Amber '47
The Ghost and Mrs. Muir '47
Son of Fury '42
How Green Was My Valley '41

Johnny Apollo '40
The Rains Came '39
The Count of Monte Cristo '34

John Dunning
SnakeEater 3: His Law '92
The Victory '81

Marcus Dunstan
The Collector '09
Hellraiser '09
Saw 6 '09
Feast 2: Sloppy Seconds '08
Saw 5 '08
Saw 4 '07
Feast '06

Francois Dupeyron(1950-)
Monsieur Ibrahim '03
The Machine '96

Jay Duplass
Cyrus '10
Baghead '08

Mark Duplass
Cyrus '10
Baghead '08

Carl DuPre
Hellraiser: Hellworld '05
Hellraiser: Hellseeker '02
Detroit Rock City '99
The Prophecy 3: The Ascent '99

Marguerite Duras(1914-96)
Nathalie Granger '72
Hiroshima, Mon Amour '59

Brooke Durham
Merlin and the Book of Beasts '09
Showdown at Area 51 '07
Mammoth '06

Arnaud d'Usseau(1916-90)
Psychomania '73
Horror Express '72
Just Off Broadway '42

Robert Duvall(1931-)
Assassination Tango '03
The Apostle '97

Julien Duvivier(1896-1967)
Anna Karenina '48
Pepe Le Moko '37

Jim Dwyer(1970-)
Little Shots of Happiness '97
Frisk '95

H. Kaye Dyal
Project: Eliminator '91
Trained to Kill '88
Lone Wolf McQuade '83

Eric Eason
Journey to the End of the Night '06
Manito '03

Robert Easter(1945-2002)
Kiss Toledo Goodbye '00
Sworn to Justice '97
The Toolbox Murders '78

Thom Eberhardt(1947-)
Ratz '99
Face Down '97
Captain Ron '92
Honey, I Blew Up the Kid '92
All I Want for Christmas '91
The Night Before '88
Night of the Comet '84

Roger Ebert(1942-)
Beneath the Valley of the Ultra-Vixens '79
Beyond the Valley of the Dolls '70

Marriott Edgar
Bees in Paradise '44
The Ghost Train '41
Hey! Hey! USA! '38

Patrick Edgeworth(1942-)
Driving Force '88
Raw Deal '86
BMX Bandits '83

Dave Edison
Cast a Deadly Spell '91
Steel and Lace '90

Blake Edwards(1922-)
Son of the Pink Panther '93
Switch '91
Skin Deep '89
Sunset '88
A Fine Mess '86
That's Life! '86
City Heat '84
Curse of the Pink Panther '83
The Man Who Loved Women '83
Trail of the Pink Panther '82
Victor/Victoria '82
S.O.B. '81
10 '79
Revenge of the Pink Panther '78
Return of the Pink Panther '74
The Tamarind Seed '74
Wild Rovers '71
Darling Lili '70
The Party '68
What Did You Do in the War, Daddy? '66
The Pink Panther '64
A Shot in the Dark '64
Soldier in the Rain '63
The Notorious Landlady '62
This Happy Feeling '58
Operation Mad Ball '57
My Sister Eileen '55
The Atomic Kid '54
Panhandle '48

Cheryl Edwards
Against the Ropes '04
Save the Last Dance '01

Cory Edwards
Hoodwinked Too! Hood vs. Evil '10
Hoodwinked '05

Paul F. Edwards
Tecumseh: The Last Warrior '95
Ordeal in the Arctic '93
Fire Birds '90
High Ballin' '78

Todd Edwards
Hoodwinked Too! Hood vs. Evil '10
Hoodwinked '05

Christine Edzard(1945-)
Little Dorrit, Film 1: Nobody's Fault '88
Little Dorrit, Film 2: Little Dorrit's Story '88

Karl-Georg Egel
Anton, the Magician '78
Trace of Stones '66

Dave Eggers
Away We Go '09
Where the Wild Things Are '09

Atom Egoyan(1960-)
Adoration '08
Where the Truth Lies '05
Ararat '02
Felicia's Journey '99
The Sweet Hereafter '96
Exotica '94
Calendar '93
The Adjuster '91
Speaking Parts '89
Family Viewing '87
Next of Kin '84

Kerry Ehrin
Inspector Gadget '99
Mr. Wrong '95

Max Ehrlich(1909-83)
The Reincarnation of Peter Proud '75
Zero Population Growth '72

Bernd Eichinger(1949-)
The Baader Meinhof Complex '08
Perfume: The Story of a Murderer '06
Downfall '04

Robert Eisele
Hurricane Season '08
The Great Debaters '07
Lily in Winter '94

Sergei Eisenstein(1898-1948)
Ivan the Terrible, Part 2 '46
Ivan the Terrible, Part 1 '44
Alexander Nevsky '38
Que Viva Mexico '32
Ten Days That Shook the World '27
The Battleship Potemkin '25
Strike '24

Jo Eisinger(1909-91)
The Rover '67
Crime of Passion '57
Night and the City '50
Gilda '46

Philip Eisner
Mutant Chronicles '08
Firestarter 2: Rekindled '02
Event Horizon '97

John (Anthony Hinds) Elder(1922-)
Frankenstein and the Monster from Hell '74
The Scars of Dracula '70
Taste the Blood of Dracula '70
Dracula Has Risen from the Grave '68
Dracula, Prince of Darkness '66
Frankenstein Created Woman '66
Plague of the Zombies '66
Rasputin the Mad Monk '66
The Reptile '66
The Evil of Frankenstein '64
Kiss of the Vampire '62
The Phantom of the Opera '62
The Curse of the Werewolf '61

Lonnie Elder, III(1926-96)
Bustin' Loose '81
A Woman Called Moses '78
Sounder '72

Kevin Elders
Echelon Conspiracy '09
Ravenhawk '95
Iron Eagle 2 '88
Iron Eagle '86

Laurice Elehwany
The Amazing Panda Adventure '95
The Brady Bunch Movie '95
My Girl '91

Harry Elfont(1968-)
Leap Year '10
Made of Honor '08
Surviving Christmas '04
Josie and the Pussycats '01
The Flintstones in Viva Rock Vegas '00
Can't Hardly Wait '98
A Very Brady Sequel '96

Caroline Eliacheff
Merci pour le Chocolat '00
La Ceremonie '95

Michael Elias(1940-)
No Laughing Matter '97
Lush Life '94
Young Doctors in Love '82
Serial '80
The Frisco Kid '79
The Jerk '79

Joyce Eliason(1934-)
America '09
A Perfect Day '06
Gracie's Choice '04
Blonde '01
The Last Don 2 '98
The Last Don '97
Titanic '96
A Good Day to Die '95
Oldest Confederate Widow Tells All '95
Small Sacrifices '89
Tell Me a Riddle '80

Doug Ellin(1968-)
Kissing a Fool '98
Phat Beach '96

David Elliot
Catacombs '07
Four Brothers '05

Michael Elliot
Brown Sugar '02
Carmen: A Hip Hopera '01
Fatal Games '84

Pearse Elliott
Shrooms '07
The Mighty Celt '05

Stephan Elliott(1963-)
Eye of the Beholder '99
The Adventures of Priscilla, Queen of the Desert '94
Frauds '93

Ted Elliott(1961-)
Pirates of the Caribbean: At World's End '07
Pirates of the Caribbean: Dead Man's Chest '06
Pirates of the Caribbean: The Curse of the Black Pearl '03
Shrek '01
The Road to El Dorado '00
The Mask of Zorro '98
Small Soldiers '98
The Puppet Masters '94
Aladdin '92
Little Monsters '89

Bob Ellis(1942-)
Ebbtide '94
Warm Nights on a Slow-Moving Train '87
Cactus '86
Man of Flowers '84
My First Wife '84

Kirk Ellis
John Adams '08
Anne Frank: The Whole Story '01

Michael Ellis
The Wedding Planner '01
Bounty Hunters 2: Hardball '97

Robert Ellis(1892-1974)
If I'm Lucky '46
Four Jills in a Jeep '44
Something for the Boys '44
Hello, Frisco, Hello '43
Iceland '42
Lucky Cisco Kid '40
Tin Pan Alley '40
Charlie Chan in City of Darkness '39
Charlie Chan at the Olympics '37
Charlie Chan at the Circus '36
Charlie Chan at the Race Track '36
Charlie Chan in Egypt '35
Dangerous Appointment '34

Sean Ellis
The Broken '08
Cashback '06

Trey Ellis(1962-)
Good Fences '03
The Tuskegee Airmen '95
Cosmic Slop '94
The Inkwell '94

Harlan Ellison
The Oscar '66
Demon with a Glass Hand '64

Joseph Ellison(1948-)
Joey '85
Don't Go in the House '80

Carl Ellsworth
The Last House on the Left '09
Disturbia '07
Red Eye '05

Guy Elmes
The Big Scam '79
Serious Charge '59

Jose Maria Elorrieta(1921-)
Feast for the Devil '71
Emerald of Artama '67
Hawk and Castile '67

Matt Ember
Get Smart '08
Failure to Launch '06

John Emerson(1874-1956)
The Girl from Missouri '34
Struggle '31
His Picture in the Papers '16

Robert Emery
The Florida Connection '74
My Brother Has Bad Dreams '72

Roland Emmerich(1955-)
2012 '09
10,000 B.C. '08
The Day After Tomorrow '04
Godzilla '98
Independence Day '96
Stargate '94
Ghost Chase '88

Toby Emmerich(1963-)
The Last Mimzy '07
Frequency '00

E.V.H. Emmett(1902-71)
Non-Stop New York '37
Sabotage '36

Robert Emmett(1921-2000)
Riding the Sunset Trail '41
Gun Packer '38
God's Country and the Man '37

Frank Encarnacao
A Young Connecticut Yankee in King Arthur's Court '95
Young Ivanhoe '95

Cy Endfield(1914-95)
Zulu '64
Impulse '55
Try and Get Me '50

Guy Endore(1900-70)
Captain Sinbad '63
The Story of G.I. Joe '45
Devil Doll '36
Mad Love '35
Mark of the Vampire '35

Samuel G. Engel(1904-84)
My Darling Clementine '46
Blue, White and Perfect '42
Johnny Apollo '40

Otto Englander(1906-69)
Fantasia '40
Pinocchio '40
Snow White and the Seven Dwarfs '37

Diane English
The Women '08
The Lathe of Heaven '80

Richard English(1910-57)
A Thousand and One Nights '45
Larceny On the Air '37

Ken Englund(1914-93)
The Secret Life of Walter Mitty '47
Springtime in the Rockies '42

Robert Enrico(1931-2001)
Old Gun '76
The Last Adventure '67

Don Enright
Spasms '82
Acapulco Gold '78

Nick Enright(1950-2003)
Blackrock '97
Lorenzo's Oil '92

Max Enscoe
Return to Halloweentown '06
MTV's Wuthering Heights '03
The Day the World Ended '01
Earth vs. the Spider '01

Ildiko Enyedi(1955-)
Simon the Magician '99
My Twentieth Century '90

Delia Ephron
Bewitched '05
Sisterhood of the Traveling Pants '05
Hanging Up '99
Michael '96
Mixed Nuts '94
This Is My Life '92

Henry Ephron(1911-92)
Desk Set '57
Carousel '56
There's No Business Like Show Business '54
Belles on Their Toes '52
Look for the Silver Lining '49
John Loves Mary '48

Nora Ephron(1941-)
Julie & Julia '09
Bewitched '05
Hanging Up '99
You've Got Mail '98
Michael '96
Mixed Nuts '94
Sleepless in Seattle '93
This Is My Life '92
My Blue Heaven '90
Cookie '89
When Harry Met Sally... '89
Heartburn '86
Silkwood '83

Phoebe Ephron(1914-71)
Desk Set '57
Carousel '56
There's No Business Like Show Business '54
Belles on Their Toes '52
Look for the Silver Lining '49
John Loves Mary '48

Tom Epperson
Jesse Stone: Night Passage '06
Camouflage '00
The Gift '00
A Gun, a Car, a Blonde '97
Don't Look Back '96
A Family Thing '96
One False Move '91

Jack Epps, Jr.(1949-)
The Flintstones in Viva Rock Vegas '00
Anaconda '96
Dick Tracy '90
Turner and Hooch '89
The Secret of My Success '87
Legal Eagles '86
Top Gun '86

Adam Jay Epstein
Extreme Movie '08
Not Another Teen Movie '01

Julius J. Epstein(1909-2000)
Reuben, Reuben '83
Cross of Iron '76
Once Is Not Enough '75
Pete 'n' Tillie '72
Any Wednesday '66
Send Me No Flowers '64
Fanny '61
Tall Story '60
The Tender Trap '55
The Last Time I Saw Paris '54
Young at Heart '54
Forever Female '53
My Foolish Heart '49
Romance on the High Seas '48
Arsenic and Old Lace '44
Casablanca '42
The Male Animal '42
The Bride Came C.O.D. '41
The Man Who Came to Dinner '41
Strawberry Blonde '41
Four Daughters '38

Philip G. Epstein(1909-52)
The Last Time I Saw Paris '54
Forever Female '53
My Foolish Heart '49
Arsenic and Old Lace '44
Casablanca '42
The Male Animal '42
The Bride Came C.O.D. '41
The Man Who Came to Dinner '41
Strawberry Blonde '41

Greg Erb
Senseless '98
RocketMan '97

Dave Erickson
Murder in Greenwich '02
Power and Beauty '02

Rainer Erler
Nuclear Conspiracy '85
Spare Parts '79

George Erschbamer(1954-)
Bounty Hunters 2: Hardball '97
Bounty Hunters '96
Power of Attorney '94

Joakim (Jack) Ersgard
Rancid '04
Living in Peril '97

Patrick Ersgard
Rancid '04
Backlash '99
Living in Peril '97

Chester Erskine(1905-86)
All My Sons '48
Midnight '34

John Eskow
The Mask of Zorro '98
Pink Cadillac '89

John Esposito
Russell Mulcahy's Tale of the Mummy '99
Graveyard Shift '90

Harry Essex(1910-97)
Octaman '71
Sons of Katie Elder '65
Creature from the Black Lagoon '54
It Came from Outer Space '53
Kansas City Confidential '52
The Killer That Stalked New York '47

Howard Estabrook(1884-1978)
Lone Star '52
The Bridge of San Luis Rey '44
International Lady '41
David Copperfield '35
The Bowery '33
Hell's Angels '30

Julian Esteban
Devil Hunter '08
Zombie Lake '80

Jacob Aaron Estes
Nearing Grace '05
Mean Creek '04

Joseph Fields(1895-1966)
The Farmer Takes a Wife '53
A Night in Casablanca '46
My Sister Eileen '42
Louisiana Purchase '41
Mexican Spitfire '40

W.C. Fields(1879-1946)
Never Give a Sucker an Even Break '41
The Bank Dick '40
My Little Chickadee '40
The Dentist '32
Pool Sharks '15

Harvey Fierstein(1954-)
Common Ground '00
Tidy Endings '88
Torch Song Trilogy '88

Jacques Fieschi
The Girl From Monaco '08
How I Killed My Father '03
Nathalie '03
Les Destinees '00
Sade '00
Place Vendome '98
Nelly et Monsieur Arnaud '95
Un Coeur en Hiver '93
Every Other Weekend '91

Mike Figgis(1948-)
Hotel '01
Time Code '00
The Loss of Sexual Innocence '98
One Night Stand '97
Leaving Las Vegas '95
Liebestraum '91
Stormy Monday '88

Ivan Fila(1956-)
King of Thieves '04
Lea '96

Jason Filardi
17 Again '09
Bringing Down the House '03

Peter Filardi(1962-)
Salem's Lot '04
The Craft '96
Flatliners '90

Hal Fimberg(1907-74)
In Like Flint '67
Our Man Flint '66
In Society '44
Big Store '41

Brian Finch(1936-2007)
Goodbye, Mr. Chips '02
Goodnight, Mr. Tom '99

Scot (Scott) Finch
Catlow '71
Shalako '68

Diane Fine
Art Heist '05
Firetrap '01

Anthony Fingleton
Swimming Upstream '03
Drop Dead Fred '91

Abem Finkel(1889-1948)
God is My Co-Pilot '45
Sergeant York '41
Jezebel '38
The Black Legion '37

Fred Finklehoffe(1910-77)
The Stooge '51
At War with the Army '50
Mr. Ace '46

Melanie Finn
Red Shoe Diaries: Swimming Naked '00
Lake Consequence '92

Alan Finney
Alvin Rides Again '74
Alvin Purple '73

Augusto Finochi
Hit Men '73
Count Dracula '71

Odoardo Fiory
They Paid with Bullets: Chicago 1929 '69
Rattler Kid '68

Tim Firth(1964-)
Confessions of a Shopaholic '09
G-Force '09
Kinky Boots '06
Calendar Girls '03

Antwone Fisher(1959-)
ATL '06
Antwone Fisher '02

Bob Fisher
Wedding Crashers '05
Eight on the Lam '67
I'll Take Sweden '65
A Global Affair '63

Carrie Fisher(1956-)
These Old Broads '01
Postcards from the Edge '90

Chris Fisher(1973-)
Dirty '05
Rampage: The Hillside Strangler Murders '04
Nightstalker '02
Taboo '02

Michael Fisher
Nowhere to Hide '83
On the Run '83

Steve Fisher(1912-80)
Hostile Guns '67
Johnny Reno '66
Terror Street '54
I Wouldn't Be in Your Shoes '48
Dead Reckoning '47
I Wake Up Screaming '41

Steve(n) Fisher
Alien Trespass '09
Profile for Murder '96
Brothers in Arms '88
The Woman Inside '83

Jeffrey Alladin Fiskin
The '60s '99
From the Earth to the Moon '98
Cutter's Way '81
Angel Unchained '70

Benedict Fitzgerald(1949-)
The Passion of the Christ '04
In Cold Blood '96
Heart of Darkness '93

Ed Fitzgerald
Dead Silent '99
Blue Movies '88

F. Scott Fitzgerald(1896-1940)
Marie Antoinette '38
Three Comrades '38

Thom Fitzgerald(1968-)
The Event '03
Beefcake '99
The Hanging Garden '97

Peter Fitzpatrick
Brilliant Lies '96
Sorrento Beach '95

Jennifer Flacket
Little Manhattan '05
Wimbledon '04
Madeline '98

Jennifer Flackett
Journey to the Center of the Earth '08
Nim's Island '08

Cash Flagg
See Ray Dennis Steckler

Ennio Flaiano(1910-72)
Sundance and the Kid '69
Juliet of the Spirits '65
10th Victim '65
8 1/2 '63
Boccaccio '70 '62
La Dolce Vita '60
La Notte '60
Nights of Cabiria '57
What a Woman! '56
Il Bidone '55
La Strada '54
Too Bad She's Bad '54
I Vitelloni '53
The White Sheik '52
Variety Lights '51

Sara Flanigan(1931-2006)
Other Voices, Other Rooms '95
Wildflower '91

Harvey Flaxman(1939-)
Preacherman '83
Grizzly '76

Ryan Fleck
Sugar '09
Half Nelson '06

Hugh Fleetwood
The Bachelor '93
Corrupt '84

Andrew Fleming(1964-)
Hamlet 2 '08
Nancy Drew '07
Dick '99
The Craft '96
Threesome '94
Every Breath '93
Bad Dreams '88

R. Lee Fleming, Jr.(1970-)
Get Over It! '01
She's All That '99

Charlie Fletcher
Mean Machine '01
Fair Game '95

Lucille Fletcher(1912-2000)
The Hitch-Hiker '53
Sorry, Wrong Number '48

Clive Fleury
Big City Blues '99
Tunnel Vision '95

Richard Flournoy(1901-67)
Blondie Goes Latin '42
Blondie's Blessed Event '42
Blondie Has Trouble '40
Blondie On a Budget '40
Blondie Plays Cupid '40
Blondie Brings Up Baby '39
Blondie Meets the Boss '39
Blondie Takes a Vacation '39
Blondie '38

George "Buck" Flower(1936-)
Hell's Belles '95
Drive-In Massacre '74

Ladislas Fodor(1989-78)
Apache's Last Battle '64
Strangler of Blackmoor Castle '63
Testament of Dr. Mabuse '62
Tom Thumb '58

Dan Fogelman
Bolt '08
Fred Claus '07
Cars '06

Lawrence Foldes(1959-)
Finding Home '03
Young Warriors '83
Nightstalker '81

Peter Foldy
Tryst '94
Widow's Kiss '94
Midnight Witness '93

Brendan Foley
Legend of the Bog '08
The Riddle '07
Johnny Was '05

Dave Foley(1963-)
Suck '09
The Wrong Guy '96

James Foley(1953-)
S.F.W. '94
After Dark, My Sweet '90

Marcello Fondato(1924-)
Black Sabbath '64
Blood and Black Lace '64

Naomi Foner(1946-)
Bee Season '05
Losing Isaiah '94
A Dangerous Woman '93
Running on Empty '88
Violets Are Blue '86

Eddie Ling-Ching Fong(1954-)
Floating Life '95
Erotique '94
Temptation of a Monk '94

Leo Fong(1928-)
Showdown '93
Enforcer from Death Row '78

Anne Fontaine(1959-)
Coco Before Chanel '09
The Girl From Monaco '08
How I Killed My Father '03
Nathalie '03
Dry Cleaning '97
Augustin '95

Tom Fontana
Homicide: The Movie '00
Fourth Wise Man '85

Dennis Foon
Long Life, Happiness and Prosperity '02
Torso '01
White Lies '98

Bradbury Foote(1894-1995)
Young Tom Edison '40
Of Human Hearts '38

Horton Foote(1916-2009)
Horton Foote's Alone '97
William Faulkner's Old Man '97
Lily Dale '96
Of Mice and Men '92
The Habitation of Dragons '91
On Valentine's Day '86
1918 '85
The Trip to Bountiful '85
Tender Mercies '83
Tomorrow '72
The Chase '66
Baby, the Rain Must Fall '64
To Kill a Mockingbird '62

John Taintor Foote(1881-1950)
Great Dan Patch '49
The Mark of Zorro '40

Bryan Forbes(1926-)
Chaplin '92
The Endless Game '89
The Slipper and the Rose '76
Eye Witness '70
The Man Who Haunted Himself '70
King Rat '65
Of Human Bondage '64
The L-Shaped Room '62

Maya Forbes
Monsters vs. Aliens '09
The Rocker '08
Seeing Other People '04

Christian Ford
Merlin's Apprentice '06
Category 7 : The End of the World '05
Slow Burn '00
Kazaam '96

Derek Ford
Auntie '73
Estate of Insanity '64

Ron Ford(1958-)
Witchcraft 11: Sisters in Blood '00
The Alien Agenda: Endangered Species '97
The Fear '94

Carl Foreman(1914-84)
High Noon '00
MacKenna's Gold '69
The Victors '63
The Guns of Navarone '61
The Key '58
The Bridge on the River Kwai '57
The Sleeping Tiger '54
High Noon '52
Cyrano de Bergerac '50
Champion '49
The Clay Pigeon '49
Home of the Brave '49
Spooks Run Wild '41

Milos Forman(1932-)
Goya's Ghosts '06
The Firemen's Ball '68
Loves of a Blonde '65
Black Peter '63

Larry Forrester
Tora! Tora! Tora! '70
Hercules and the Princess of Troy '65

Bengt Forslund
The New Land '73
The Emigrants '72

Bill Forsyth(1948-)
Being Human '94
Housekeeping '87
Comfort and Joy '84
Local Hero '83
Gregory's Girl '80
That Sinking Feeling '79

Frederick Forsyth(1938-)
A Casualty of War '90
The Fourth Protocol '87

Garrett Fort(1900-45)
Devil Doll '36
Dracula's Daughter '36
The Lost Patrol '34
Panama Flo '32
Dracula (Spanish Version) '31
Dracula '31
Frankenstein '31

Will Forte(1970-)
MacGruber '10
The Brothers Solomon '07

Bob Fosse(1927-87)
Star 80 '83
All That Jazz '79

Lewis R. Foster(1898-1974)
El Paso '49
Never Say Goodbye '46
Can't Help Singing '45
Golden Gloves '40
Rhythm Romance '39

Norman Foster(1900-76)
Mr. Moto Takes a Vacation '39
Mr. Takes a Vacation '39
Mysterious Mr. Moto '38
Thank you, Mr. Moto '37
Think Fast, Mr. Moto '37

Robert Foster
The Contractor '07
Dead Bang '89

Alastair Fothergill
Earth '07
Deep Blue '03

Vincent Fotre
Torture Chamber of Baron Blood '72
Missile to the Moon '59
The Commies Are Coming, the Commies Are Coming '57

Alyson Fouse
Bring It On: Fight to the Finish '09
Bring It On: In It to Win It '07
Bring It On: All or Nothing '06
Scary Movie 2 '01

Gene Fowler, Sr.(1890-1960)
Billy the Kid '41
Rhythm Romance '39
What Price Hollywood? '32
State's Attorney '31

Dana Fox
Couples Retreat '09
What Happens in Vegas '08
The Wedding Date '05

Victoria Foyt
Going Shopping '05
Deja Vu '98
Last Summer In the Hamptons '96
Babyfever '94

Claudio Fragasso(1951-)
Hell of the Living Dead '83
Rats '83

Randall Frakes
Instinct to Kill '01
Blowback '99
The Force '94
Roller Blade Warriors: Taken By Force '90
Hell Comes to Frogtown '88

Michael France(1962-)
Fantastic Four '05
The Punisher '04
Hulk '03
Goldeneye '95
Cliffhanger '93

Dan Franck
One Day You'll Understand '08
La Separation '98
The Separation '94

Jess (Jesus) Franco(1930-)
Devil Hunter '08
Tender Flesh '97
Bloody Moon '83
Oasis of the Zombies '82
Zombie Lake '80
Ilsa, the Wicked Warden '78
Jack the Ripper '76
The Demons '74
Rites of Frankenstein '72
Count Dracula '71
Venus in Furs '70
The Diabolical Dr. Z '65
The Awful Dr. Orloff '62

Ricardo Franco(1949-98)
Blood and Sand '89
In 'n Out '86

Debra Frank
The Muppets' Wizard of Oz '05
Mr. St. Nick '02

Frederic M. Frank(1911-77)
The Ten Commandments '56
Unconquered '47

Harriet Frank, Jr.(1917-)
Stanley and Iris '90
Murphy's Romance '85
Norma Rae '79
Conrack '74
The Cowboys '72
The Reivers '69
Hombre '67
Hud '63
Home from the Hill '60
The Long, Hot Summer '58
Ten Wanted Men '54
Silver River '48

Laurie Frank
Love Crimes '92
Making Mr. Right '86

Melvin Frank(1913-88)
A Funny Thing Happened on the Way to the Forum '66

Parenthood '89
Vibes '88
Gung Ho '85
Spies Like Us '85
Splash '84
Night Shift '82

Robert Ben Garant(1970-)
Night at the Museum: Battle of the Smithsonian '09
Balls of Fury '07
Reno 911! Miami '07
Let's Go to Prison '06
Night at the Museum '06
Herbie: Fully Loaded '05
The Pacifier '05

Nicole Garcia(1946-)
Place Vendome '98
The Favorite Son '94
Every Other Weekend '91

Rodrigo Garcia(1959-)
Mother and Child '09
Nine Lives '05
Things You Can Tell Just by Looking at Her '00

Gabriel Garcia Marquez(1927-)
The Fable of the Beautiful Pigeon Fancier '88
Letters from the Park '88
Miracle in Rome '88
Erendira '83
Mary, My Dearest '83

Yolanda Garcia Serrano(1958-)
Km. 0 '00
Between Your Legs '99
Amor de Hombre '97

Louis Gardel
East-West '99
Indochine '92
Fort Saganne '84

Eric Gardner
Race to Space '01
Breakaway '95

Herb Gardner(1934-2003)
I'm Not Rappaport '96
The Goodbye People '83
A Thousand Clowns '65

Pierce Gardner
Dan in Real Life '07
Lost Souls '00

Richard Harding Gardner(1949-)
Sherlock: Undercover Dog '94
Deadly Daphne's Revenge '93

Louis Garfinkle(1928-2005)
The Deer Hunter '78
I Bury the Living '58

Alex Garland(1970-)
Sunshine '07
The Tesseract '03
28 Days Later '02

Robert Garland
No Way Out '87
The Electric Horseman '79

Helen Garner(1942-)
The Last Days of Chez Nous '92
Two Friends '86

Tony Garnett(1936-)
Fat Man and Little Boy '89
Deep in the Heart '83

David Garrett
Deuce Bigalow: European Gigolo '05
Corky Romano '01

Oliver H.P. Garrett(1894-1952)
Dead Reckoning '47
Duel in the Sun '46
The Hurricane '37
Manhattan Melodrama '34
Night Flight '33
A Farewell to Arms '32

Mick Garris(1951-)
Riding the Bullet '04
Quicksilver Highway '98
Hocus Pocus '93
The Fly 2 '89
Critters 2: The Main Course '88

Matteo Garrone
Gomorrah '08
The Embalmer '03

Harold Gast(1918-2003)
The Jesse Owens Story '84
A Woman Called Golda '82
From Here to Eternity '79

Ernesto Gastaldi(1934-)
The Sicilian Connection '85
Scorpion with Two Tails '82
The Great Alligator '81
Lady of the Evening '75
The Grand Duel '73
Torso '73
The Case of the Bloody Iris '72
Your Vice is a Closed Room and Only I Have the Key '72
The Case of the Scorpion's Tail '71
The Scorpion's Tail '71
Blade of the Ripper '70
Giants of Rome '63
The Whip and the Body '63
Venus Against the Son of Hercules '62

Robert Gaston
2 Minutes Later '07
Open Cam '05

Harvey Gates(1894-1948)
Mr. Muggs Rides Again '45
Clancy Street Boys '43
Zis Boom Bah '41
Badmen of Nevada '33

Tudor Gates(1930-2007)
The Optimists '73
Fright '71
Lust for a Vampire '71
Twins of Evil '71
The Vampire Lovers '70
Barbarella '68
Danger: Diabolik '68

John Gatins
Coach Carter '05
Dreamer: Inspired by a True Story '05
Hardball '01
Summer Catch '01

Tony Gatlif(1948-)
The Crazy Stranger '98
Mondo '96

Nate Gatzert(1890-1959)
Rio Grande Ranger '37
Western Courage '35
The Fiddlin' Buckaroo '33
Trail Drive '33

Massimo Gaudioso
Gomorrah '08
The Embalmer '03

Emile Gaudreault(1964-)
Mambo Italiano '03
King of the Airwaves '94

Peter Gaulke
Strange Wilderness '08
Ice Age: The Meltdown '06
Black Knight '01
Say It Isn't So '01

Nils Gaup(1955-)
Shipwrecked '90
Pathfinder '87

Eleanor Gaver
Dead in the Water '91
Slipping into Darkness '88

Bart Gavigan
End of the Spear '06
Luther '03

John Gay(1924-)
Final Notice '89
Windmills of the Gods '88
Manhunt for Claude Dallas '86
Fatal Vision '84
A Tale of Two Cities '80
Hennessy '75
Sometimes a Great Notion '71
Soldier Blue '70
No Way to Treat a Lady '68
The Last Safari '67
The Hallelujah Trail '65
The Courtship of Eddie's Father '62
The Four Horsemen of the Apocalypse '62
Run Silent, Run Deep '58
Separate Tables '58

Joe Gayton
The Shepherd: Border Patrol '08
Sweet Jane '98
Bulletproof '96

Tony Gayton(1959-)
Murder by Numbers '02
The Salton Sea '02

Paul Gegauff(1922-83)
A Piece of Pleasure '74
This Man Must Die '70
Purple Noon '60

Larry Gelbart(1928-2009)
And Starring Pancho Villa as Himself '03
Bedazzled '00
Weapons of Mass Distraction '97
Barbarians at the Gate '93
Mastergate '92
Blame It on Rio '84
Tootsie '82
Neighbors '81
Rough Cut '80
Movie, Movie '78
Oh, God! '77
The Wrong Box '66
The Notorious Landlady '62

Stephen Geller
Slaughterhouse Five '72
The Valachi Papers '72

Milton S. Gelman(1919-90)
One Man's Hero '98
Cabo Blanco '81

Erwin Gelsey(1900-88)
Double or Nothing '37
Scarlet Dawn '32
The Strange Love of Molly Louvain '32

Jonathan Gems
The Treat '98
Mars Attacks! '96

Pierre Gendron(1896-1956)
Fog Island '45
Bluebeard '44
The Monster Maker '44

Michael Genet(1958-)
Talk to Me '07
She Hate Me '04

Robert Geoffrion
Cruel and Unusual '01
The Peacekeeper '98
Eternal Evil '87

Dean Georgaris
Tristan & Isolde '06
The Manchurian Candidate '04
Lara Croft Tomb Raider: The Cradle of Life '03
Paycheck '03

Nelson George
Life Support '07
CB4: The Movie '93

Terry George(1952-)
Hart's War '02
A Bright Shining Lie '98
The Boxer '97
Some Mother's Son '96
In the Name of the Father '93

Gerald Geraghty(1906-54)
Phantom Stallion '54
Iron Mountain Trail '53
Shadows of Tombstone '53
Sunset in the West '50
Trigger, Jr. '50
Rainbow over Texas '46
Along the Navaho Trail '45
Carson City Kid '40
Pioneers of the West '40
In Old Caliente '39
South of the Border '39
Southward Ho! '39
Wall Street Cowboy '39
Come on Rangers '38

Maurice Geraghty(1908-87)
Mohawk '56
Tomahawk '51
Who Killed Doc Robbin? '48

Tom Geraghty
Wings of the Morning '37
The Church Mouse '34

Gary Gerani
Vampirella '96
Pumpkinhead '88

Pietro Germi(1904-74)
Alfredo, Alfredo '72
Seduced and Abandoned '64
Divorce—Italian Style '62

Chris Gerolmo
Citizen X '95
Miles from Home '88
Mississippi Burning '88

Glen Gers
Mad Money '08
Fracture '07
Brother's Keeper '02
Off Season '01

Sacha Gervasi
The Terminal '04
The Big Tease '99

Greta Gerwig
Nights and Weekends '08
Hannah Takes the Stairs '07

Nicolas Gessner(1931-)
Black Water '94
Someone Behind the Door '71
The Peking Blond '68

Robert Getchell
The Client '94
Point of No Return '93
This Boy's Life '93
Stella '89
Sweet Dreams '85
Mommie Dearest '81
Bound for Glory '76
Alice Doesn't Live Here Anymore '74

Steven Gethers(1922-89)
Jenny's War '85
A Woman Called Golda '82

Russell Gewirtz
Righteous Kill '08
Inside Man '06

Bahman Ghobadi(1968-)
Turtles Can Fly '04
Marooned in Iraq '02

Ettore Giannini
Neapolitan Carousel '54
Neapolitan Carousel '54

Robert Gianviti
Don't Torture a Duckling '72
A Lizard in a Woman's Skin '71
Gunslinger '70
The Triumph of Hercules '66
Revenge of the Musketeers '63

Daniel Giat
Bury My Heart at Wounded Knee '07
Path to War '02

Andrea Gibb
Nina's Heavenly Delights '06
Dear Frankie '04

Duncan Gibbins(1952-93)
A Case for Murder '93
Eve of Destruction '90

Rodney Gibbons
Captive '97
Digger '94

Stuart Gibbs(1969-)
Repli-Kate '01
Silk Degrees '94

Alex Gibney
Gonzo: The Life and Work of Dr. Hunter S. Thompson '08
Taxi to the Dark Side '07
Enron: The Smartest Guys in the Room '05

Channing Gibson
Walking Tall '04
Lethal Weapon 4 '98

Mark Gibson
The Wild '06
Snow Dogs '02
Lush '01
The In Crowd '00

Mel Gibson(1956-)
Apocalypto '06
The Passion of the Christ '04

Nelson Gidding(1919-2004)
The Mummy Lives '93
The Hindenburg '75
The Andromeda Strain '71
The Haunting '63
Odds Against Tomorrow '59
I Want to Live! '58
The Helen Morgan Story '57

Raynold Gideon
Mr. Brooks '07
Jungle 2 Jungle '96
The River Wild '94
Kuffs '92
Made in Heaven '87
Stand by Me '86
Starman '84
A Man, a Woman, and a Bank '79

Gregory Gieras
Centipede '05
Dark Asylum '01

Adam Gierasch
Night of the Demons '09
Mother of Tears '08
Derailed '02
Crocodile 2: Death Swamp '01
Crocodile '00

Barry Gifford(1946-)
City of Ghosts '03
Dance with the Devil '97
Lost Highway '96
Hotel Room '93

Jaime Comas Gil
Iguana '89
Panic '76

Mateo Gil(1972-)
The Sea Inside '04
Open Your Eyes '97
Thesis '96

Josh Gilbert
Furry Vengeance '10
Mr. Woodcock '07

Lewis Gilbert(1920-)
Haunted '95
Carve Her Name with Pride '58
Cosh Boy '52
Little Ballerina '47

Berne Giler
Tarzan the Magnificent '60
Tarzan's Greatest Adventure '59
Westbound '58

David Giler
Undisputed '02
The Money Pit '86
Southern Comfort '81
Fun with Dick and Jane '77
The Parallax View '74
Myra Breckinridge '70

David Giles
Paradise Road '97
Under the Lighthouse Dancing '97

Stuart Gillard(1950-)
Teenage Mutant Ninja Turtles 3 '93
Spring Fever '81

Terry Gilliam(1940-)
The Imaginarium of Doctor Parnassus '09
Tideland '05
Fear and Loathing in Las Vegas '98
The Adventures of Baron Munchausen '89
Brazil '85
Monty Python's The Meaning of Life '83
Time Bandits '81
Monty Python's Life of Brian '79
Jabberwocky '77
Monty Python and the Holy Grail '75
And Now for Something Completely Different '72

Sidney Gilliat(1908-94)
Endless Night '71
Geordie '55
The Belles of St. Trinian's '53
Waterloo Road '44
The Girl in the News '41
Night Train to Munich '40
Jamaica Inn '39
The Lady Vanishes '38
King of the Damned '36

Vince Gilligan(1967-)
Hancock '08
Home Fries '98
Wilder Napalm '93

John Gilling(1912-85)
The Mummy's Shroud '67
The Gorgon '64
The Flesh and the Fiends '60
It Takes a Thief '59
Bond of Fear '56
Recoil '53
The Frightened Man '52
The Voice of Merrill '52
House of Darkness '48

Rob Gilmer
Out of Time '00
The Crying Child '96

Dan Gilroy(1959-)
The Fall '06
Two for the Money '05
Chasers '94
Freejack '92

Frank D. Gilroy(1925-)
The Gig '85
Jinxed '82
Once in Paris... '79
From Noon Till Three '76
Desperate Characters '71
The Subject Was Roses '68
The Gallant Hours '60
Fastest Gun Alive '56

Henry Gilroy
Star Wars: The Clone Wars '08

Bionicle 3: Web of Shadows '05

Tom Gilroy
Bait '00
Spring Forward '99

Tony Gilroy(1956-)
State of Play '09
The Bourne Ultimatum '07
Michael Clayton '07
The Cutting Edge: Going for the Gold '05
The Bourne Supremacy '04
The Bourne Identity '02
Proof of Life '00
The Devil's Advocate '97
Extreme Measures '96
Dolores Claiborne '94
The Cutting Edge '92
For Better and for Worse '92

Milton Moses Ginsberg(1943-)
Werewolf of Washington '73
Coming Apart '69

Mario Giordano
The Experiment '01
Car Crash '80

Jose Giovanni(1923-2004)
Le Gitan '75
La Scoumoune '72
Le Deuxieme Souffle '66
Classe Tous Risque '60
Le Trou '59

Buddy Giovinazzo(1957-)
Life is Hot in Cracktown '08
No Way Home '96
Combat Shock '84

Bernard Girard(1918-97)
Dead Heat on a Merry-Go-Round '66
A Public Affair '62
The Rebel Set '59

Francois Girard(1963-)
Silk '07
The Red Violin '98
32 Short Films about Glenn Gould '93

Michael Paul Girard(1954-)
Bikini Med School '98
Sweet Evil '98
Bikini House Calls '96
Illegal Affairs '96
The Perfect Gift '95
Body Parts '94

William Girdler(1947-78)
The Manitou '78
Sheba, Baby '75
Asylum of Satan '72
Three on a Meathook '72

Francis Girod(1944-)
Transfixed '01
The Elegant Criminal '92

Marino Girolami
You've Got to Have Heart '77
Girl Under the Sheet '61

Francoise Giroud(1916-2003)
Where the Hot Wind Blows '59
Antoine et Antoinette '47

Karin Gist
Camp Rock '08
Jump In! '07

Amos Gitai(1950-)
Free Zone '05
Kippur '00
Kadosh '99

Kubec Glasmon
Union Depot '32
Public Enemy '31
Smart Money '31

Robert Glass
Death Dreams '92
Running Against Time '90

Handel Glassberg
The Day My Parents Ran Away '93
The Take '90

Richard Glatzer
Quinceanera '06
Grief '94

Benjamin Glazer(1887-1956)
A Farewell to Arms '32
No Man of Her Own '32
Beggars of Life '28
The Trail of '98 '28
7th Heaven '27

Mitch Glazer(1953-)
The Recruit '03
Great Expectations '97
Scrooged '88
Mr. Mike's Mondo Video '79
Moon over Miami '41

David Gleeson
The Front Line '06
Cowboys & Angels '04

Tom Gleisner
The Dish '00
The Castle '97

John Glenn
Eagle Eye '08
The Lazarus Project '08

Peter Glenville(1913-96)
Hotel Paradiso '66
Term of Trial '63

James Glickenhaus(1950-)
Timemaster '95
Slaughter of the Innocents '93
McBain '91
Shakedown '88
Exterminator '80

Greg Glienna(1963-)
Relative Strangers '06
A Guy Thing '03

Jean-Luc Godard(1930-)
Our Music '04
In Praise of Love '01
For Ever Mozart '96
Helas pour Moi '94
Nouvelle Vague '90
Aria '88
Hail Mary '85
Passion '82
Every Man for Himself '79
Comment Ca Va? '76
Here and Elsewhere '76
Numero Deux '75
Six in Paris '68
La Chinoise '67
Oldest Profession '67
Weekend '67
Two or Three Things I Know about Her '66
Alphaville '65
The Joy of Knowledge '65
A Married Woman '65
Pierrot le Fou '65
Band of Outsiders '64
Contempt '64
Une Femme Mariee '64
Les Carabiniers '63
My Life to Live '62
RoGoPaG '62
Le Petit Soldat '60
A Woman Is a Woman '60
Breathless '59

Ivan Goff(1910-99)
Legend of the Lone Ranger '81
Midnight Lace '60
Portrait in Black '60
Shake Hands with the Devil '59
Band of Angels '57
Man of a Thousand Faces '57

Green Fire '55
Captain Horatio Hornblower '51
Goodbye My Fancy '51
White Heat '49

Menahem Golan(1929-)
Hanna's War '88
The Apple '80
Eagles Attack at Dawn '70
What's Good for the Goose '69

Sandra Goldbacher(1960-)
Me Without You '01
The Governess '98

Willis Goldbeck(1898-1979)
The Man Who Shot Liberty Valance '62
Sergeant Rutledge '60
The Secret of Dr. Kildare '39
Freaks '32
Peter Pan '24
Scaramouche '23

Adam F. Goldberg(1976-)
Aliens in the Attic '09
Fanboys '09
The Muppets' Wizard of Oz '05

Brent Goldberg
Underclassman '05
The Girl Next Door '04
My Baby's Daddy '04
National Lampoon's Van Wilder '02

Dan Goldberg
Feds '88
Heavy Metal '81

Evan Goldberg
Pineapple Express '08
Superbad '07

Gary David Goldberg(1944-)
Must Love Dogs '05
Bye Bye, Love '94
Dad '89

Harris Goldberg(1972-)
Numb '07
Without a Paddle '04
Master of Disguise '02
Deuce Bigalow: Male Gigolo '99
I'll Be Home for Christmas '98

Howard Goldberg
Eden '98
Spontaneous Combustion '89

Marshall Goldberg
Where the Truth Lies '99
The Abduction '96

Michael Goldberg
Harry Potter and the Order of the Phoenix '07
Snow Dogs '02
Bushwhacked '95
Little Giants '94
Cool Runnings '93

Paula Goldberg
Out at the Wedding '07
In Her Line of Fire '06

Kenny Golde
The Job '03
The Smokers '00

Dan Golden
Venomous '01
Wizards of the Demon Sword '94

Ray Golden(1906-87)
Big Store '41
Argentine Nights '40

Jeffrey Goldenberg
Blowback '99
Looking for an Echo '99

Jorge Goldenberg
I Don't Want to Talk About It '94

Eversmile New Jersey '89
Miss Mary '86

Michael Goldenberg(1965-)
Peter Pan '03
Contact '97
Bed of Roses '95

Joshua Goldin
Wonderful World '09
Darkman '90

Marilyn Goldin
The Triumph of Love '01
Camille Claudel '89
Barocco '76

Bo Goldman(1932-)
Meet Joe Black '98
City Hall '95
Scent of a Woman '92
Little Nikita '88
Swing Shift '84
Shoot the Moon '82
Melvin and Howard '80
One Flew Over the Cuckoo's Nest '75

Gary Goldman(1944-)
Next '07
Navy SEALS '90
Total Recall '90
Big Trouble in Little China '86

James Goldman(1927-98)
The Lion in Winter '03
Anastasia: The Mystery of Anna '86
Oliver Twist '82
Nicholas and Alexandra '71
They Might Be Giants '71
The Lion in Winter '68

Jane Goldman
Kick-Ass '10
Stardust '07

William Goldman(1931-)
Dreamcatcher '03
Hearts in Atlantis '01
The General's Daughter '99
Absolute Power '97
The Chamber '96
The Ghost and the Darkness '96
Maverick '94
Chaplin '92
Year of the Comet '92
Misery '90
Casual Sex? '88
Heat '87
The Princess Bride '87
Mr. Horn '79
Magic '78
A Bridge Too Far '77
All the President's Men '76
Marathon Man '76
The Great Waldo Pepper '75
The Stepford Wives '75
Butch Cassidy and the Sundance Kid '69
Harper '66

Akiva Goldsman(1963-)
Angels & Demons '09
I Am Legend '07
The Da Vinci Code '06
Cinderella Man '05
I, Robot '04
A Beautiful Mind '01
Lost in Space '98
Practical Magic '98
Batman and Robin '97
A Time to Kill '96
Batman Forever '95
The Client '94
Silent Fall '94

John Goldsmith
Darwin's Darkest Hour '09
The Gospel of John '03
Victoria & Albert '01
Agnes Browne '99
Coming Home '98
The Apocalypse Watch '97
The Island on Bird Street '97
Catherine the Great '95

Kidnapped '95
The Old Curiosity Shop '94

Josh Goldsmith(1970-)
13 Going on 30 '04
What Women Want '00

Martin Goldsmith
The Gunfight at Dodge City '59
Detour '46

Allan Goldstein
Snakeman '05
Jungle Boy '96
Death Wish 5: The Face of Death '94
Rooftops '89

Mark Goldstein
Pet Shop '94
Prehysteria '93

Bob(cat) Goldthwait(1962-)
World's Greatest Dad '09
Sleeping Dogs Lie '06
Shakes the Clown '92

Larry Golin
Rocky Marciano '99
Hostage High '97
Love Walked In '97
Rebound: The Legend of Earl "The Goat" Manigault '96
Final Combination '93

Bryan Goluboff
The Affair '95
The Basketball Diaries '95

Sy Gomberg(1918-2001)
Three Warriors '77
Bloodhounds of Broadway '52
Summer Stock '50

Nick Gomez(1963-)
Illtown '96
New Jersey Drive '95
Laws of Gravity '92

Manuel Gomez Pereira(1958-)
Between Your Legs '99
Love Can Seriously Damage Your Health '96
Mouth to Mouth '95
Why Do They Call It Love When They Mean Sex? '92

Michel Gondry(1963-)
Tokyo! '09
Be Kind Rewind '08
The Science of Sleep '06
Eternal Sunshine of the Spotless Mind '04

Noam Gonick(1973-)
Stryker '04
Hey, Happy! '01

Reuben Gonzalez
Once Upon a Wedding '05
Mambo Cafe '00

Gregory Goodell
Don't Look Down '98
My Brother's Keeper '95
Shattered Spirits '86

William Goodhart(1925-99)
Cloud Dancer '80
The Exorcist 2: The Heretic '77
Generation '69

Philip Goodhew
Another Life '01
Intimate Relations '95

J. Mills Goodloe
Pride '07
A Gentleman's Game '01

David Zelag Goodman
Monte Walsh '03
Fighting Back '82
Eyes of Laura Mars '78

March or Die '77
Logan's Run '76
Farewell, My Lovely '75
Straw Dogs '72
Lovers and Other Strangers '70
Monte Walsh '70
The Stranglers of Bombay '60

Frances Goodrich(1890-1984)
The Long, Long Trailer '54
Seven Brides for Seven Brothers '54
Father's Little Dividend '51
Father of the Bride '50
Easter Parade '48
It's a Wonderful Life '46
The Virginian '46
The Thin Man '34

Alex Gordon(1922-2003)
Bride of the Monster '55
Jail Bait '54

Bernard Gordon(1918-2007)
Krakatoa East of Java '69
The Thin Red Line '64
Day of the Triffids '63
Hellcats of the Navy '57
Earth vs. the Flying Saucers '56
Crime Wave '54
The Lawless Breed '52

Bert I. Gordon(1922-)
Empire of the Ants '77
The Witching '72
Tormented '60
The Amazing Colossal Man '57
King Dinosaur '55

Bryan Gordon
Pie in the Sky '95
The Discovery Program '89

Dan Gordon
The Celestine Prophecy '06
The Hurricane '99
Murder in the First '95
New Eden '94
Wyatt Earp '94
Surf Ninjas '93
Taking the Heat '93
Highlander: The Gathering '92
Passenger 57 '92
Gotcha! '85
Tank '83
Gulliver's Travels '39

Keith Gordon(1961-)
A Midnight Clear '92
The Chocolate War '88
Static '87

Leo Gordon(1922-2000)
The Terror '63
Tower of London '62
Attack of the Giant Leeches '59
The Wasp Woman '59
Black Patch '57

Leon Gordon(1894-1960)
White Cargo '42
They Met in Bombay '41
Balalaika '39
Tarzan and His Mate '34
Freaks '32

Richard Gordon
Death by Prescription '86
The Lion Man '36

Robert Gordon
Lemony Snicket's A Series of Unfortunate Events '04
Men in Black 2 '02
Galaxy Quest '99
Addicted to Love '96

Rose Gordon
Coyote Trails '35
Kentucky Blue Streak '35

Silent Valley '35
Fighting Hero '34

Ruth Gordon(1896-1985)

Hardhat & Legs '80
It Should Happen to You '54
The Actress '53
The Marrying Kind '52
Pat and Mike '52
Adam's Rib '50
A Double Life '47
Dr. Ehrlich's Magic Bullet '40

Stuart Gordon(1947-)

The Dentist '96
Body Snatchers '93
Honey, I Shrunk the Kids '89
Re-Animator '84

Christopher Gore

Coco Before Chanel '09
Fame '09

Lisa Gornick

Tick Tock Lullaby '07
Do I Love You? '02

Laszlo Gorog(1903-97)

Earth vs. the Spider '58
The Land Unknown '57
The Mole People '56

Marleen Gorris(1948-)

Antonia's Line '95
Broken Mirrors '85

Rene Goscinny

Lucky Luke '94
The Holes '72

Hideo Gosha(1929-92)

The Wolves '82
Goyokin '69

Carl Gottlieb(1938-)

Doctor Detroit '83
Jaws 3 '83
Caveman '81
The Jerk '79
Jaws 2 '78
Which Way Is Up? '77
Jaws '75

Alfred Gough(1967-)

The Mummy: Tomb of the Dragon Emperor '08
Herbie: Fully Loaded '05
Spider-Man 2 '04
Shanghai Knights '03
Showtime '02
Shanghai Noon '00

Heywood Gould

Double Bang '01
Mistrial '96
Trial by Jury '94
One Good Cop '91
Cocktail '88
Streets of Gold '86
Fort Apache, the Bronx '81
The Boys from Brazil '78
Rolling Thunder '77

Peter Gould

Meeting Daddy '98
Double Dragon '94

Edmund Goulding(1891-1959)

That Certain Woman '37
Riptide '34
No Man of Her Own '32
Tol'able David '21

David S. Goyer(1965-)

The Unborn '09
Jumper '08
Batman Begins '05
Blade: Trinity '04
Blade 2 '02
ZigZag '02
Blade '98
Dark City '97
The Crow 2: City of Angels '96
The Puppet Masters '94
Arcade '93
Death Warrant '90

Jean-Francois Goyet

Western '96

La Vengeance d'une Femme '89

Todd Graff(1959-)

Bandslam '09
Camp '03
Coyote Ugly '00
The Beautician and the Beast '97
Angie '94
Fly by Night '93
The Vanishing '93
Used People '92

Benoit Graffin

The Girl From Monaco '08
Priceless '06
Apres-Vous '03
The New Yorker '98

Sue Grafton(1940-)

The Game of Love '87
Agatha Christie's A Caribbean Mystery '83
Agatha Christie's Sparkling Cyanide '83

Bruce Graham

Gradiva '06
Steal This Movie! '00
Anastasia '97
Dunston Checks In '95

Ronny Graham(1919-99)

Spaceballs '87
Finders Keepers '84
To Be or Not to Be '83

Michael Grais

Cool World '92
Marked for Death '90
Poltergeist 2: The Other Side '86
Poltergeist '82
Death Hunt '81

Jean-Christophe Grange(1961-)

Crimson Rivers 2: Angels of the Apocalypse '05
Empire of the Wolves '05
The Crimson Rivers '01

Derek Granger

Where Angels Fear to Tread '91
A Handful of Dust '88

Pierre Granier-Deferre(1927-2007)

A Woman at Her Window '77
The Last Train '74

Debra Granik

Winter's Bone '10
Down to the Bone '04

James Edward Grant(1905-66)

Support Your Local Gunfighter '71
Circus World '64
Donovan's Reef '63
McLintock! '63
The Alamo '60
The Sheepman '58
Three Violent People '57
Hondo '53
Flying Leathernecks '51
Sands of Iwo Jima '49
Angel and the Badman '47
Gambler's Choice '44
Johnny Eager '42
The Lady Is Willing '42

John Grant(1891-1955)

Abbott and Costello Meet the Mummy '55
Abbott and Costello Meet the Keystone Kops '54
Abbott and Costello Go to Mars '53
Abbott and Costello Meet Dr. Jekyll and Mr. Hyde '52
Ma and Pa Kettle at the Fair '52
Abbott and Costello Meet the Invisible Man '51

Comin' Round the Mountain '51
Abbott and Costello in the Foreign Legion '50
Abbott and Costello Meet the Killer, Boris Karloff '49
Abbott and Costello Meet Frankenstein '48
Buck Privates Come Home '47
Here Come the Co-Eds '45
In Society '44
It Ain't Hay '43
Buck Privates '41
Hold That Ghost '41
In the Navy '41

Susannah Grant(1963-)

The Soloist '09
Catch and Release '07
Charlotte's Web '06
In Her Shoes '05
Erin Brockovich '00
28 Days '00
Ever After: A Cinderella Story '98
Pocahontas '95

Robert Grasmere

Baby Geniuses '98
A Million to Juan '94

Alex Graves

Casualties '97
The Crude Oasis '95

Beverly Gray

Haunted Symphony '94
Full Contact '93

James Gray(1969-)

Two Lovers '09
We Own the Night '07
The Yards '00
Little Odessa '94

John Gray

Brian's Song '01
The Seventh Stream '01
The Hunley '99
An American Story '92
Showdown at Williams Creek '91
The Lost Capone '90
Billy Galvin '86

Mike Gray

Code of Silence '85
Wavelength '83
The China Syndrome '79

Pamela Gray

Music of the Heart '99
A Walk on the Moon '99
Calm at Sunset '96

Simon Gray(1936-)

Unnatural Pursuits '91
A Month in the Country '87

William Gray

Killer Wave '07
Humongous '82
The Changeling '80
Prom Night '80

Charles Grayson(1903-73)

Battle Hymn '57
The Woman on Pier 13 '50
Outpost in Morocco '49
Underground '41
One Night in the Tropics '40

Brian Grazer(1951-)

Housesitter '92
Armed and Dangerous '86

Claudio Grazioso

Are We There Yet? '05
Bring It On Again '03

Kjell Grede(1936-)

Good Evening, Mr. Wallenberg '93
Hip Hip Hurrah! '87

Adolph Green(1915-2002)

Bells Are Ringing '60
Auntie Mame '58
It's Always Fair Weather '55
Singin' in the Rain '52

The Barkleys of Broadway '49
On the Town '49

Clifford Green

Bless the Child '00
Mystery Island '81
Picnic at Hanging Rock '75

David Gordon Green(1975-)

Snow Angels '07
Undertow '04
All the Real Girls '03

Howard J. Green(1893-1965)

George White's Scandals '45
Having Wonderful Crime '45
Take It Big '44
Harmon of Michigan '41
If You Could Only Cook '36
They Met in a Taxi '36
Blessed Event '32
I Am a Fugitive from a Chain Gang '32
They Call It Sin '32
Maker of Men '31

Lewis Green

Never Talk to Strangers '95
Dead on Sight '94
The Spy Within '94

Paul Green

Doctor Bull '33
The Cabin in the Cotton '32

Terry Green

Heavens Fall '06
Cold Justice '89

Walon Green(1936-)

The Hi-Lo Country '98
Eraser '96
RoboCop 2 '90
Crusoe '89
Solarbabies '86
The Border '82
Brink's Job '78
Sorcerer '77
The Wild Bunch '69

Peter Greenaway(1942-)

8 1/2 Women '99
The Pillow Book '95
The Belly of an Architect '91
Prospero's Books '91
The Cook, the Thief, His Wife & Her Lover '90
A Zed & Two Noughts '88
Drowning by Numbers '87
The Draughtsman's Contract '82

Everett Greenbaum(1920-99)

The Shakiest Gun in the West '68
The Reluctant Astronaut '67
Good Neighbor Sam '64

Dan Greenberg

The Guardian '90
Oh! Calcutta! '72

Matt Greenberg

1408 '07
Reign of Fire '02
Halloween: H20 '98
The Prophecy 2: Ashtown '97
The Ghost Brigade '93

Stanley R. Greenberg(1928-2002)

Blind Ambition '79
Soylent Green '73

Anthony Laurence Greene

Dead Sexy '01
Number One Fan '94

Clarence Greene(1913-95)

The Oscar '66
D.O.A. '49

Eve Greene

Operator 13 '34
Tugboat Annie '33

Graham Greene(1904-91)

The Comedians '67
Our Man in Havana '59
Saint Joan '57
The Fallen Idol '49
The Third Man '49
Brighton Rock '47
21 Days '37

Harold Greene(1915-2000)

Texas Across the River '66
Kansas City Confidential '52
Counterspy Meets Scotland Yard '50
The House of the Seven Gables '40

Paul Greengrass(1955-)

United 93 '06
Bloody Sunday '01
The Murder of Stephen Lawrence '99
The One That Got Away '96

Matt Greenhalgh

Nowhere Boy '09
Control '07

Seth Greenland

My Teacher's Wife '95
Who's the Man? '93

Maggie Greenwald(1955-)

Songcatcher '99
The Ballad of Little Jo '93

Edwin Greenwood(1895-1939)

Young and Innocent '37
The Man Who Knew Too Much '34

James Greer

The Spy Next Door '10
Larry the Cable Guy: Health Inspector '06
Max Keeble's Big Move '01

William Grefe(1930-)

The Hooked Generation '69
The Death Curse of Tartu '66
The Checkered Flag '63

Clark Gregg(1964-)

Choke '08
What Lies Beneath '00

Andre Gregory(1934-)

Vanya on 42nd Street '94
My Dinner with Andre '81

Nick Gregory

Love Thy Neighbor '02
Marshal Law '96

Frederic Grendel(1924-2001)

Violette '78
Diabolique '55

Sergio Grieco(1917-82)

Deadly Mission '78
The Inglorious Bastards '78
Mad Dog Killer '77

Tom Gries(1922-77)

Will Penny '67
King Dinosaur '55

Maurice Griffe

Grisbi '53
Rendez-vous de Juillet '49
Antoine et Antoinette '47

Ted Griffin(1970-)

Killers '10
Matchstick Men '03
Ocean's Eleven '01
Best Laid Plans '99
Ravenous '99

Charles B. Griffith(1930-2007)

Not of This Earth '88
Dr. Heckyl and Mr. Hype '80
Eat My Dust '76
Death Race 2000 '75

Devil's Angels '67
The Wild Angels '66
Atlas '60
The Beast from Haunted Cave '60
Creature from the Haunted Sea '60
Little Shop of Horrors '60
Ski Troop Attack '60
A Bucket of Blood '59
Rock All Night '57
Teenage Doll '57
The Undead '57
The Gunslinger '56
It Conquered the World '56

D.W. Griffith(1875-1948)

Struggle '31
Isn't Life Wonderful '24
Orphans of the Storm '21
The Love Flower '20
Way Down East '20
Broken Blossoms '19
Hoodoo Ann '16
Intolerance '16
The Birth of a Nation '15
Judith of Bethulia '14

Thomas Ian Griffith(1962-)

Mr. Troop Mom '09
Black Point '01
Excessive Force '93
Night of the Warrior '91

David Griffiths(1952-)

The Hunted '03
Collateral Damage '02

Leon Griffiths(1928-92)

Piece of Cake '88
The Grissom Gang '71
The Flesh and the Fiends '60

Peter Griffiths(1950-)

The Hunted '03
Collateral Damage '02

Trevor Griffiths(1935-)

Singing the Blues in Red '87
The Last Place on Earth '85

Aurelio Grimaldi(1957-)

Nerolio '96
Acla's Descent into Floristella '87

Pierre Grimblat

Slogan '69
It Means That to Me '60

Christopher Grimm

Rhythm Thief '94
Spare Me '92

Maria Grimm

November Conspiracy '96
The Feminine Touch '95

Tony Grisoni

Death Defying Acts '07
Brothers of the Head '06
Tideland '05
In This World '03
Fear and Loathing in Las Vegas '98
The Island on Bird Street '97

Ferde Grofe, Jr.

The Day of the Wolves '71
Warkill '65
The Walls of Hell '64

Adam Gross

DOA: Dead or Alive '06
Devour '05

Jerry Gross(1940-2002)

Teenage Mother '67
Girl on a Chain Gang '65

Joel Gross

No Escape '94
Blind Man's Bluff '91

Larry Gross(1953-)

The Beautiful Country '04
We Don't Live Here Anymore '04
Crime and Punishment in Suburbia '00

Dust '85

Curtis Hanson(1945-)

Lucky You '07
L.A. Confidential '97
The Bedroom Window '87
The Children of Times Square '86
Never Cry Wolf '83
White Dog '82
The Silent Partner '78
The Arousers '70
The Dunwich Horror '70

Marla Hanson

The Blackout '97
Subway Stories '97

Kenchiro Hara

47 Ronin, Part 1 '42
47 Ronin, Part 2 '42

Masato Harada

Inugami '01
Rowing Through '96

Robert Harari

Day-Time Wife '39
Everything Happens at Night '39

Carl Harbaugh(1886-1960)

Three Legionnaires '37
Steamboat Bill, Jr. '28
College '27
Regeneration '15

Patrick Harbinson

Place of Execution '09
Horatio Hornblower '99
The Waiting Time '99
Frenchman's Creek '98

Gary Hardwick

Deliver Us from Eva '03
The Brothers '01
Trippin' '99
Todd McFarlane's Spawn '97

David Hare(1947-)

My Zinc Bed '08
The Reader '08
The Hours '02
The Secret Rapture '94
Damage '92
Strapless '90
Saigon: Year of the Cat '87
Plenty '85
Wetherby '85

Lance Z. Hargreaves

Devil Doll '64
First Man into Space '59

Marion Hargrove(1919-2003)

40 Pounds of Trouble '62
The Music Man '62
Cash McCall '60

Tsui Hark(1951-)

Black Mask 2: City of Masks '02
Tsui Hark's Vampire Hunters '02
Zu Warriors '01
Time and Tide '00
Black Mask '96
Iron Monkey '93
Once Upon a Time in China III '93
Once Upon a Time in China II '92
Twin Dragons '92
Wicked City '92
Once Upon a Time in China '91

Eric Harlacher

Murder at Devil's Glen '99
Homewrecker '92

Robert Harling(1951-)

Laws of Attraction '04
The Evening Star '96
The First Wives Club '96
Soapdish '91
Steel Magnolias '89

John Harlow(1896-1977)

Those People Next Door '52
Appointment with Crime '45
Echo Murders '45
Meet Sexton Blake '44

Julian Harmon(1908-66)

Danger Zone '51
Pier 23 '51
Roaring City '51

Phil Harnage

Inspector Gadget's Biggest Caper Ever '05
Banzai Runner '86

Patricia Harper

The Topeka Terror '45
The Drifter '44

Sam Harper

Cheaper by the Dozen 2 '05
Cheaper by the Dozen '03
Just Married '03
Rookie of the Year '93

Stephen Harrigan

King of Texas '02
Take Me Home: The John Denver Story '00
Cleopatra '99
Lone Justice 3: Showdown at Plum Creek '96
The O.J. Simpson Story '94

Curtis Harrington(1928-2007)

Planet of Blood '66
Night Tide '63

Damian Harris(1958-)

Gardens of the Night '08
Mercy '00
The Rachel Papers '89

Daniel P. "Dan" Harris(1979-)

Superman Returns '06
Imaginary Heroes '05
X2: X-Men United '03

Elmer Harris(1878-1966)

Red Salute '35
The Barbarian '33
Tess of the Storm Country '22

Eoghan Harris

Sharpe's Revenge '97
Sharpe's Mission '96
Sharpe's Regiment '96
Sharpe's Siege '96
Sharpe's Enemy '94
Sharpe's Sword '94
Sharpe's Eagle '93
Sharpe's Rifles '93

James B. Harris(1928-)

Boiling Point '93
Cop '88

Joe Harris

The Tripper '06
Darkness Falls '03

Kirk Harris

Hard Luck '01
Loser '97

Timothy Harris(1946-)

Astro Boy '09
Pure Luck '91
Kindergarten Cop '90
My Stepmother Is an Alien '88
Twins '88
Brewster's Millions '85
Trading Places '83
Cheaper to Keep Her '80

Trent Harris(1952-)

Plan 10 from Outer Space '95
Rubin & Ed '92

Vernon Harris(1905-99)

Oliver! '68
Carve Her Name with Pride '58
The Admirable Crichton '57
Three Men in a Boat '56

Jim Harrison(1937-)

Dalva '95
Wolf '94
Revenge '90
Cold Feet '89

Joan Harrison(1911-94)

Dark Waters '44
Foreign Correspondent '40
Rebecca '40
Jamaica Inn '39

John Harrison

Clive Barker's Book of Blood '08
Experiment '05
Children of Dune '03
Dinosaur '00
Dune '00
Donor Unknown '95

John Kent Harrison

The Courageous Heart of Irena Sendler '09
You Know My Name '99
Calm at Sunset '96
City Boy '93
The Sound and the Silence '93
Beautiful Dreamers '92
Memories of Murder '90
Murder by Phone '82
Shock Waves '77

Matthew Harrison(1960-)

Kicked in the Head '97
Rhythm Thief '94

Mary Harron(1953-)

The Notorious Bettie Page '06
American Psycho '99
I Shot Andy Warhol '96

Jacobsen Hart

Raven '97
The Power Within '95
Rage '95
Steel Frontier '94
Cyber-Tracker '93
Direct Hit '93
Zero Tolerance '93

James V. Hart

August Rush '07
Sahara '05
Tuck Everlasting '02
Jack and the Beanstalk: The Real Story '01
Muppet Treasure Island '96
Bram Stoker's Dracula '92

Moss Hart(1904-61)

A Star Is Born '54
Hans Christian Andersen '52
Gentleman's Agreement '47

Hal Hartley(1959-)

Fay Grim '06
No Such Thing '01
Henry Fool '98
Flirt '95
Amateur '94
Simple Men '92
Trust '91
The Unbelievable Truth '90

Don Hartman(1900-58)

Mr. Imperium '51
Wonder Man '45
The Princess and the Pirate '44
My Favorite Blonde '42
The Road to Morocco '42
The Road to Zanzibar '41
The Road to Singapore '40
Never Say Die '39
Waikiki Wedding '37
The Princess Comes Across '36
Here Comes Cookie '35

Edmund Hartmann(1911-2003)

Casanova's Big Night '54
The Lemon Drop Kid '51
Variety Girl '47
In Society '44
Ali Baba and the Forty Thieves '43

Steven Hartov

Mars '96
Mercenary '96

Jack Harvey(1881-1954)

Last of the Wild Horses '49
Unknown Island '48

Johanna Harwood

Call Me Bwana '63
From Russia with Love '63
Dr. No '62

Ronald Harwood(1934-)

Australia '08
The Diving Bell and the Butterfly '07
Love in the Time of Cholera '07
Oliver Twist '05
Being Julia '04
The Statement '03
The Pianist '02
Taking Sides '01
The Browning Version '94
A Fine Romance '92
The Doctor and the Devils '85
The Dresser '83
One Day in the Life of Ivan Denisovich '71

Claude Harz

Find the Lady '76
It Seemed Like a Good Idea at the Time '75

Izo Hashimoto

Oh! My Zombie Mermaid '04
Akira '89

Shinobu Hashimoto(1918-)

Dodes 'ka-den '70
Samurai Rebellion '67
Attack Squadron '63
Harakiri '62
The Bad Sleep Well '60
I Bombed Pearl Harbor '60
The Hidden Fortress '58
Throne of Blood '57
I Live in Fear '55
Seven Samurai '54
Ikiru '52
Rashomon '51

Michael Hastings(1938-)

The American '01
Tom & Viv '94
The Nightcomers '72

Jeffrey Hatcher

The Duchess '08
Casanova '05
Stage Beauty '04

Richard Hatem(1966-)

The Mothman Prophecies '02
Under Siege 2: Dark Territory '95

Jeffrey Hause

BachelorMan '03
Once Bitten '85

Wings Hauser(1948-)

Gang Boys '97
No Safe Haven '87

Chris Hauty

Never Back Down '08
Homeward Bound 2: Lost in San Francisco '96

Anthony Havelock-Allan(1904-2003)

Brief Encounter '46
Blithe Spirit '45

Jean C. Havez(1870-1925)

Seven Chances '25
The Navigator '24
Sherlock, Jr. '24
Our Hospitality '23
Safety Last '23

Ethan Hawke(1971-)

The Hottest State '06
Before Sunset '04

John Hawkesworth(1920-2003)

Forbidden Passion: The Oscar Wilde Movie '85
The Flame Trees of Thika '81
The Duchess of Duke Street '78
Tiger Bay '59

J.G. Hawks(1874-1940)

The Charlatan '29
The Sea Hawk '24

Christopher Hawthorne

Whiskers '96
The Courtyard '95
Parents '89

Ian Hay(1876-1952)

Sabotage '36
The 39 Steps '35

Phil Hay

Clash of the Titans '10
Aeon Flux '05
crazy/beautiful '01

Carey Hayes(1961-)

Whiteout '09
The Reaping '07
The Reaping '07
House of Wax '05
First Daughter '99
Down, Out and Dangerous '95

Chad Hayes(1961-)

Whiteout '09
The Reaping '07
The Reaping '07
House of Wax '05
First Daughter '99
Down, Out and Dangerous '95

John Hayes(1930-2000)

All the Lovin' Kinfolk '70
Corruption '70
Dream No Evil '70
The Cut Throats '69

John Michael Hayes(1919-)

Iron Will '93
Pancho Barnes '88
Winter Kill '74
Nevada Smith '66
Harlow '65
The Carpetbaggers '64
The Chalk Garden '64
Where Love Has Gone '64
The Children's Hour '61
Butterfield 8 '60
But Not for Me '59
The Matchmaker '58
Peyton Place '57
The Man Who Knew Too Much '56
It's a Dog's Life '55
To Catch a Thief '55
The Trouble with Harry '55
Rear Window '54
Thunder Bay '53
War Arrow '53
Red Ball Express '52

Joseph Hayes(1918-2006)

Desperate Hours '90
Stolen Hours '63

Steve Hayes

The Muppets' Wizard of Oz '05
Mr. St. Nick '02
Fantastic Planet '73

Terry Hayes(1951-)

From Hell '01
Vertical Limit '00
Payback '98
Mr. Reliable: A True Story '95
Dead Calm '89
Mad Max: Beyond Thunderdome '85
The Road Warrior '82

Gregory C. Haynes(1968-)

Cowboys and Angels '00
Heaven or Vegas '98
Magenta '96

Todd Haynes(1961-)

I'm Not There '07
Far from Heaven '02
Velvet Goldmine '98
Office Killer '97
Safe '95
Poison '91

David Hayter(1969-)

Watchmen '09
The Scorpion King '02
X-Men '00

Justin Haythe

Revolutionary Road '08
The Clearing '04

Lillie Hayward(1891-1977)

Proud Rebel '58
Tarzan and the Lost Safari '57
Tarzan's Hidden Jungle '55
On the Sunny Side '42
The Undying Monster '42
Lady Killer '33
They Call It Sin '32

Ping He(1957-)

Rhapsody of Spring '98
Swordsmen in Double Flag Town '91

Gary Heacock

Alien Massacre '67
Gallery of Horrors '67

Percy Heath(1884-1933)

Dr. Jekyll and Mr. Hyde '32
No One Man '32

David Heavener(1958-)

Fugitive X '96
Eye of the Stranger '93
Prime Target '91
Killcrazy '89
Twisted Justice '89

Julie Hebert

Ruby's Bucket of Blood '01
Female Perversions '96

Ben Hecht(1894-1964)

Circus World '64
Walk on the Wild Side '62
A Farewell to Arms '57
The Indian Fighter '55
Actors and Sin '52
Monkey Business '52
The Thing '51
Where the Sidewalk Ends '50
Whirlpool '49
Notorious '46
Spectre of the Rose '46
Spellbound '45
The Black Swan '42
Tales of Manhattan '42
Angels Over Broadway '40
Comrade X '40
Gunga Din '39
Let Freedom Ring '39
Wuthering Heights '39
Nothing Sacred '37
Twentieth Century '34
Viva Villa! '34
Hallelujah, I'm a Bum '33
The Great Gabbo '29

Amy Heckerling(1954-)

I Could Never Be Your Woman '06
Loser '00
Clueless '95
Look Who's Talking, Too '90
Look Who's Talking '89

Rob Hedden(1954-)

The Condemned '07
Clockstoppers '02
Alien Fury: Countdown to Invasion '00
The Colony '95
Friday the 13th, Part 8: Jason Takes Manhattan '89

Roger Hedden
Hi-Life *'98*
Sleep with Me *'94*
Bodies, Rest & Motion *'93*

Peter Hedges(1962-)
Dan in Real Life *'07*
Pieces of April *'03*
About a Boy *'02*
A Map of the World *'99*
What's Eating Gilbert Grape *'93*

Victor Heerman(1893-1977)
Golden Boy *'39*
Stella Dallas *'37*
Break of Hearts *'35*
Magnificent Obsession *'35*
Little Minister *'34*
Little Women *'33*
My Boy *'21*

Kevin Heffernan(1968-)
Beerfest *'06*
Preaching to the Choir *'05*
Club Dread *'04*
Super Troopers *'01*

Carol Heikkinen(1966-)
Center Stage *'00*
Empire Records *'95*
The Thing Called Love *'93*

Adelaide Heilbron(1892-1974)
Misleading Lady *'32*
Personal Maid *'31*

Jo Heims(1930-78)
You'll Like My Mother *'72*
Play Misty for Me *'71*
Double Trouble *'67*

Robert Heinlein(1907-88)
Project Moon Base *'53*
Destination Moon *'50*

Ross Helford
Single White Female 2: The Psycho *'05*
Sniper 3 *'04*
Wild Things 2 *'04*

Brian Helgeland(1961-)
Green Zone *'10*
Robin Hood *'10*
Salt *'10*
Cirque du Freak: The Vampire's Assistant *'09*
The Taking of Pelham 123 *'09*
Man on Fire *'04*
Mystic River *'03*
The Order *'03*
Blood Work *'02*
A Knight's Tale *'01*
Payback *'98*
Conspiracy Theory *'97*
L.A. Confidential *'97*
The Postman *'97*
Assassins *'95*
A Nightmare on Elm Street 4: Dream Master *'88*
976-EVIL *'88*

Lukas Heller(1930-88)
Monte Walsh *'03*
Blue City *'86*
Damnation Alley *'77*
The Killing of Sister George *'69*
The Dirty Dozen *'67*
Hush, Hush, Sweet Charlotte *'65*
What Ever Happened to Baby Jane? *'62*

Lillian Hellman(1905-84)
The Chase *'66*
The North Star *'43*
Watch on the Rhine *'43*
The Little Foxes *'41*
Dead End *'37*
These Three *'36*
The Dark Angel *'35*

Oliver Hellman
See Ovidio G. Assonitis

Sam Hellman(1885-1950)
My Darling Clementine *'46*
The Three Musketeers *'39*
In Old Kentucky *'35*
Little Miss Marker *'34*
Murder at the Vanities *'34*
Thirty Day Princess *'34*

Axel Hellstenius
Elling *'01*
The Last Lieutenant *'94*

Zach Helm
Mr. Magorium's Wonder Emporium *'07*
Stranger Than Fiction *'06*

Chris Henchy
The Other Guys *'10*
Land of the Lost *'09*

Frank Henenlotter(1950-)
Basket Case 3: The Progeny *'92*
Basket Case 2 *'90*
Frankenhooker *'90*
Brain Damage *'88*
Basket Case *'82*

James Henerson
Mutiny *'99*
The Tempest *'99*
The Love Letter *'98*
Getting Gotti *'94*
The Fire Next Time *'93*

Liu Heng
The Story of Qiu Ju *'91*
Ju Dou *'90*

Paul Hengge
The Rose Garden *'89*
Double Face *'70*

Kim Henkel
The Texas Chainsaw Massacre 4: The Next Generation *'95*
Eaten Alive *'76*
The Texas Chainsaw Massacre *'74*

Hilary Henkin(1962-)
Wag the Dog *'97*
Romeo Is Bleeding *'93*
Fatal Beauty *'87*

Beth Henley(1952-)
Miss Firecracker *'89*
Crimes of the Heart *'86*
Nobody's Fool *'86*
True Stories *'86*

Jack Henley(1896-1958)
Ma and Pa Kettle at Waikiki *'55*
Ma and Pa Kettle on Vacation *'53*
Ma and Pa Kettle Back On the Farm *'51*
Blondie Hits the Jackpot *'49*
A Thousand and One Nights *'45*
Zis Boom Bah *'41*

Paul Henning(1911-2005)
Dirty Rotten Scoundrels *'88*
The Return of the Beverly Hillbillies *'81*

Buck Henry(1930-)
Town and Country *'01*
To Die For *'95*
Protocol *'84*
First Family *'80*
The Day of the Dolphin *'73*
What's Up, Doc? *'72*
Catch-22 *'70*
The Owl and the Pussycat *'70*
Candy *'68*
The Graduate *'67*

Todd Henschell
Puppet Master 5: The Final Chapter *'94*
Puppet Master 4 *'93*

Jim Henshaw
Escape from Mars *'99*
Another Woman *'94*
Broken Lullaby *'94*
A Change of Place *'94*
Treacherous Beauties *'94*

Jonathan Hensleigh
Next *'07*
The Punisher *'04*
Armageddon *'98*
The Saint *'97*
The Rock *'96*
Die Hard: With a Vengeance *'95*
Jumanji *'95*
A Far Off Place *'93*

Robby Henson
The Badge *'02*
Pharoah's Army *'95*

F. Hugh Herbert(1897-1958)
Let's Make It Legal *'51*
Our Very Own *'50*
Sitting Pretty *'48*
Together Again *'43*
Colleen *'36*
The Great Gabbo *'29*

Ron Herbst
Warlords 3000 *'93*
Deadly Diamonds *'91*

Tim Herlihy(1966-)
Bedtime Stories *'08*
Mr. Deeds *'02*
Little Nicky *'00*
Big Daddy *'99*
The Waterboy *'98*
The Wedding Singer *'97*
Happy Gilmore *'96*

Mark Herman(1954-)
The Boy in the Striped Pajamas *'08*
Little Voice *'98*
Brassed Off *'96*
Blame It on the Bellboy *'92*

Pee-wee Herman
See Paul (Pee-wee Herman) Reubens

Jaime Humberto Hermosillo(1942-)
Esmeralda Comes by Night *'98*
Forbidden Homework *'92*
Homework *'90*
Dona Herlinda & Her Son *'86*
Mary, My Dearest *'83*

Gyula Hernadi(1926-2005)
Adoption *'75*
The Red and the White *'68*
The Round Up *'66*

Michael Herr(1940-)
John Grisham's The Rainmaker *'97*
Full Metal Jacket *'87*
Apocalypse Now *'79*

Rowdy Herrington(1951-)
Bobby Jones: Stroke of Genius *'04*
The Stickup *'01*
A Murder of Crows *'99*
Striking Distance *'93*
Jack's Back *'87*

W(illiam) Blake Herron
The Bourne Identity *'02*
A Texas Funeral *'99*
Skin Art *'93*

Joel Hershman(1958-)
Greenfingers *'00*
Hold Me, Thrill Me, Kiss Me *'93*

Marshall Herskovitz(1952-)
The Last Samurai *'03*
Glory *'89*
Special Bulletin *'83*

Harry Hervey
His Greatest Gamble *'34*
The Cheat *'31*

Adam Herz(1973-)
American Wedding *'03*
American Pie 2 *'01*
American Pie *'99*

Michael Herz(1949-)
Stuck on You *'84*
First Turn On *'83*

Jim Herzfeld
Meet the Fockers *'04*
Meet the Parents *'00*
Meet the Deedles *'98*

John Herzfeld
S.I.S. *'08*
15 Minutes *'01*
Two Days in the Valley *'96*
Casualties of Love: The "Long Island Lolita" Story *'93*

Sid Herzig(1897-1985)
Meet the People *'44*
They Made Me a Criminal *'39*
Four's a Crowd *'38*
Sing Me a Love Song *'37*
Varsity Show *'37*
Colleen *'36*

Werner Herzog(1942-)
Encounters at the End of the World *'07*
Rescue Dawn *'06*
Invincible *'01*
Cobra Verde *'88*
Fitzcarraldo *'82*
Nosferatu the Vampyre *'79*
Woyzeck *'78*
Stroszek *'77*
Every Man for Himself & God Against All *'75*
Heart of Glass *'74*
Aguirre, the Wrath of God *'72*
Signs of Life *'68*

Eugene Hess
Streets of Blood *'09*
Cruel World *'05*
Don't Do It *'94*

Jared Hess(1979-)
Gentlemen Broncos *'09*
Nacho Libre *'06*
Napoleon Dynamite *'04*

Jerusha Hess(1980-)
Gentlemen Broncos *'09*
Nacho Libre *'06*
Napoleon Dynamite *'04*

Fraser Heston(1955-)
Treasure Island *'89*
The Mountain Men *'80*

Peter Hewitt(1962-)
I Want Candy *'07*
Thunderbirds *'04*

Rod Hewitt
The Debt *'98*
Sworn Enemies *'96*
The Dangerous *'95*

Douglas Heyes(1919-93)
Ice Station Zebra *'68*
Kitten with a Whip *'64*

Louis M. Heyward(1920-2002)
The Conqueror Worm *'68*
Ghost in the Invisible Bikini *'66*
Planet of the Vampires *'65*
Pajama Party *'64*

Guy Hibbert
Five Minutes of Heaven *'09*
Shot Through the Heart *'98*

Winston Hibler(1910-76)
Charlie the Lonesome Cougar *'67*
Nikki, the Wild Dog of the North *'61*

Peter Pan *'53*
The Adventures of Ichabod and Mr. Toad *'49*

Jochen Hick(1960-)
No One Sleeps *'01*
Via Appia *'92*

George Hickenlooper(1964-)
Mayor of the Sunset Strip *'03*
The Big Brass Ring *'99*
Dogtown *'97*
The Low Life *'95*
Hearts of Darkness: A Filmmaker's Apocalypse *'91*

Anthony Hickox(1959-)
Sundown: The Vampire in Retreat *'08*
Submerged *'05*
Last Run *'01*
Prince Valiant *'97*
Waxwork 2: Lost in Time *'91*
Waxwork *'88*

Regina Hicks
Camp Rock *'08*
Jump In! *'07*

Scott Hicks(1953-)
The Boys Are Back *'09*
Snow Falling on Cedars *'99*

Julie Hickson
Snow White: The Fairest of Them All *'02*
Homeward Bound 2: Lost in San Francisco *'96*

Colin Higgins(1941-88)
Foul Play *'78*
Silver Streak *'76*
Harold and Maude *'71*

John C. Higgins(1908-95)
Robinson Crusoe on Mars *'64*
Untamed Youth *'57*
The Black Sleep *'56*
Border Incident *'49*
He Walked by Night *'48*
Raw Deal *'48*
Railroaded *'47*
T-Men *'47*

Patrick Highsmith
Acts of Betrayal *'98*
Mars *'96*
Savage *'96*
Automatic *'94*

Charles Higson(1958-)
King of the Ants *'03*
Suite 16 *'94*

David Hill
Shattered Dreams *'90*
Too Young to Die *'90*
Promised a Miracle *'88*

Debra Hill(1950-2005)
Escape from L.A. *'96*
Jailbreakers *'94*
Halloween 2: The Nightmare Isn't Over! *'81*
The Fog *'78*
Halloween *'78*

Elizabeth Hill
H.M. Pulham Esquire *'41*
Our Daily Bread *'34*

Ethel Hill
The Little Princess *'39*
It Happened in Hollywood *'37*

Jack Hill(1933-)
Foxy Brown *'74*
Coffy *'73*
The Big Bird Cage *'72*
The Fear Chamber *'68*
Pit Stop *'67*
Spider Baby *'64*
The Terror *'63*

Jody Hill
Observe and Report *'09*
The Foot Fist Way *'08*

John Hill
Griffin & Phoenix *'06*
Quigley Down Under *'90*

Little Nikita *'88*
Heartbeeps *'81*

Robert F. "Bob" Hill(1886-1966)
West of Nevada *'36*
Murder on the High Seas *'32*
The Cat and the Canary *'27*
The Adventures of Tarzan *'21*

Robert J. Hill
Fanny Hill: Memoirs of a Woman of Pleasure *'64*
Battle Shock *'56*

Walter Hill(1942-)
Undisputed *'02*
Last Man Standing *'96*
Wild Bill *'95*
The Getaway *'93*
Red Heat *'88*
Aliens *'86*
Blue City *'86*
Streets of Fire *'84*
48 Hrs. *'82*
Southern Comfort *'81*
The Warriors *'79*
The Driver *'78*
The Drowning Pool *'75*
Hard Times *'75*
Mackintosh Man *'73*
The Thief Who Came to Dinner *'73*
The Getaway *'72*

David Hillenbrand
Survival Island *'02*
King Cobra *'98*

Scott Hillenbrand
Survival Island *'02*
King Cobra *'98*

Richard Hilliard
Horror of Party Beach *'64*
The Lonely Sex *'59*

Katherine Hilliker
The Boob *'26*
The Boob *'26*

Lambert Hillyer(1889-1969)
The California Trail *'33*
The Cradle of Courage *'20*
The Toll Gate *'20*

David Hilton
The Delivery *'99*
The Young Americans *'93*

James Hilton(1900-54)
Mrs. Miniver *'42*
Foreign Correspondent *'40*
Camille *'36*

David Himmelstein
Soul of the Game *'96*
Village of the Damned *'95*
Talent for the Game *'91*
Power *'86*

Alan Hines
Save Me *'07*
My Husband's Double Life *'01*
Breaking the Surface: The Greg Louganis Story *'96*
Square Dance *'87*

David Hines
BachelorMan *'03*
Once Bitten *'85*

Kenya Hirata
Shinobi *'05*
Returner *'02*

Roger O. Hirson(1926-)
A Woman Named Jackie *'91*
The Old Man and the Sea *'90*
A Christmas Carol *'84*
Pippin *'81*
Demon Seed *'77*

Michael Hirst(1952-)
Elizabeth: The Golden Age *'07*
Have No Fear: The Life of Pope John Paul II *'05*

Elizabeth *'98*
Uncovered *'94*
The Ballad of the Sad Cafe *'91*
Meeting Venus *'91*
Fools of Fortune *'90*

Alfred Hitchcock(1899-1980)
Saboteur *'42*
No. 17 *'32*
Rich and Strange *'32*
Skin Game *'31*
Juno and the Paycock *'30*
Murder *'30*
Blackmail *'29*
Champagne *'28*
The Farmer's Wife *'28*
The Ring *'27*
The Lodger *'26*

Michael Hitchcock(1958-)
House Arrest *'96*
Where the Day Takes You *'92*

Carl K. Hittleman(1907-99)
Billy the Kid Versus Dracula *'66*
Jesse James Meets Frankenstein's Daughter *'65*
36 Hours *'64*
Tough Assignment *'49*

Ken Hixon
City by the Sea *'02*
Inventing the Abbotts *'97*
Incident at Deception Ridge *'94*
Caught in the Act *'93*

Godfrey Ho(1948-)
Bionic Ninja *'85*
Ninja Champion *'80*
Ninja Destroyer *'70*

Danny Hoch(1970-)
White Boyz *'99*
Subway Stories *'97*

John Hodge(1964-)
The Seeker: The Dark Is Rising *'07*
The Beach *'00*
A Life Less Ordinary *'97*
Trainspotting *'95*
Shallow Grave *'94*

Adrian Hodges
The History of Mr. Polly *'07*
The Shadow in the North *'07*
Ruby in the Smoke *'06*
The Lost World *'02*
Lorna Doone *'01*
David Copperfield *'99*
Amongst Women *'98*
Metroland *'97*
Tom & Viv *'94*

Mike Hodges(1932-)
Black Rainbow *'91*
Damien: Omen 2 *'78*
The Terminal Man *'74*
Pulp *'72*
Get Carter *'71*

Erich Hoeber
Whiteout *'09*
Montana *'97*

Jon Hoeber
Whiteout *'09*
Montana *'97*

Arthur Hoerl(1891-1968)
Blind Fools *'40*
The Singing Cowgirl *'39*
Reefer Madness *'38*
The Sunset Murder Case *'38*
The Spirit of Youth *'37*
Cross Examination *'32*
They Never Come Back *'32*
Wayne Murder Case *'32*
Night Life in Reno *'31*
The Peacock Fan *'29*
Man from Headquarters *'28*
Ships in the Night *'28*

Samuel Hoffenstein(1890-1947)
His Butler's Sister *'44*
Laura *'44*
The Phantom of the Opera *'43*
Tales of Manhattan *'42*
Paris in Spring *'35*
The Song of Songs *'33*
Dr. Jekyll and Mr. Hyde *'32*
Sinners in the Sun *'32*
An American Tragedy *'31*

Charles Hoffman
The Blue Gardenia *'53*
The West Point Story *'50*

Joseph Hoffman(1909-97)
At Sword's Point *'51*
Buccaneer's Girl *'50*
The Man with Two Lives *'42*

Michael Hoffman(1956-)
The Last Station *'09*
William Shakespeare's A Midsummer Night's Dream *'99*
Promised Land *'88*

Tamar Simon Hoffs(1934-)
Red Roses and Petrol *'03*
The Allnighter *'87*

Gray Hofmeyr
Yankee Zulu *'95*
The Outcast *'84*

Michael Hogan
Forever and a Day *'43*
Arabian Nights *'42*
King Solomon's Mines *'37*

Paul Hogan(1939-)
Lightning Jack *'94*
Almost an Angel *'90*
Crocodile Dundee 2 *'88*
Crocodile Dundee *'86*

P.J. Hogan(1962-)
Peter Pan *'03*
Unconditional Love *'03*
Muriel's Wedding *'94*

Brian Hohlfield
Pooh's Heffalump Movie *'05*
Piglet's Big Movie *'03*
The Mighty Ducks *'92*
He Said, She Said *'91*

Michael Holden
No Strings Attached *'98*
The Little Death *'95*

Jeremy Hole
A Killing Spring *'02*
Verdict in Blood *'02*

Agnieszka Holland(1948-)
The Healer *'02*
Trois Couleurs: Bleu *'93*
Olivier, Olivier *'92*
Europa, Europa *'91*
Korczak *'90*
To Kill a Priest *'89*
The Possessed *'88*
Anna *'87*
Angry Harvest *'85*
A Love in Germany *'84*
Danton *'82*
Without Anesthesia *'78*

Mandel Holland
Love and Other Four Letter Words *'07*
The Other Brother *'02*

Savage Steve Holland(1960-)
One Crazy Summer *'86*
Better Off Dead *'85*

Tom Holland(1943-)
Stephen King's Thinner *'96*
Stephen King's The Langoliers *'95*
Child's Play *'88*
Scream for Help *'86*
Fright Night *'85*

Cloak & Dagger *'84*
Psycho 2 *'83*
The Beast Within *'82*
Class of 1984 *'82*

David Hollander
Personal Effects *'09*
Rated X *'00*

Cliff Hollingsworth
Cinderella Man *'05*
Too Good to Be True *'98*

Jean Holloway(1917-89)
Madame X *'66*
Till the Clouds Roll By *'46*

Mat Holloway
Iron Man *'08*
Punisher: War Zone *'08*

Brown Holmes
Castle on the Hudson *'40*
20,000 Years in Sing Sing *'33*
The Strange Love of Molly Louvain *'32*

Geoffrey Holmes
See Daniel Mainwaring

Milton Holmes(1907-87)
Boots Malone *'52*
Salty O'Rourke *'45*

Nicole Holofcener(1960-)
Friends with Money *'06*
Lovely & Amazing *'02*
Walking and Talking *'96*

Edward Holzman
Forbidden Games *'95*
Friend of the Family *'95*

Geoffrey Homes
See Daniel Mainwaring

Inoshiro Honda(1911-93)
War of the Gargantuas *'70*
Destroy All Monsters *'68*
Godzilla, King of the Monsters *'56*

Christophe Honore(1970-)
Apres Lui *'07*
Love Songs *'07*
Inside Paris *'06*
Close to Leo *'02*
Girls Can't Swim *'99*

Brendan William Hood
The Deaths of Ian Stone *'07*
Wes Craven Presents: They *'02*

Gavin Hood(1963-)
Tsotsi *'05*
In Desert and Wilderness *'01*

Sean Hood(1966-)
The Crow: Wicked Prayer *'05*
Cube 2: Hypercube *'02*
Halloween: Resurrection *'02*

William Hooke
Shark Attack 3: Megalodon *'02*
Shark Attack 2 *'00*
Shark Attack *'99*

Tobe Hooper(1946-)
The Mangler *'94*
Spontaneous Combustion *'89*
The Texas Chainsaw Massacre *'74*

Arthur Hopcraft(1932-2004)
Rebecca *'97*
A Tale of Two Cities *'89*
A Perfect Spy *'88*
Tinker, Tailor, Soldier, Spy *'80*

Edward Hope(1986-58)
The Long Gray Line *'55*
Three for the Show *'55*

Alan Hopgood(1934-)
Alvin Rides Again *'74*
Alvin Purple *'73*

John Hopkins
Dunston Checks In *'95*
Hiroshima *'95*
Codename Kyril *'91*
The Holcroft Covenant *'85*
Torment *'85*
Smiley's People *'82*
Murder by Decree *'79*
The Offence *'73*
The Virgin Soldiers *'69*
Thunderball *'65*

Karen Leigh Hopkins
Because I Said So *'07*
A Woman's a Helluva Thing *'01*
Stepmom *'98*

Robert Hopkins
Saratoga *'37*
Flying High *'31*
Hollywood Revue of 1929 *'29*

Arthur T. Horman(1905-64)
I Beheld His Glory *'53*
Here Come the Co-Eds *'45*
Buck Privates *'41*
In the Navy *'41*
Argentine Nights *'40*

Nick Hornby(1957-)
An Education *'09*
Fever Pitch *'96*

Israel Horovitz(1939-)
James Dean *'01*
Sunshine *'99*
North Shore Fish *'97*
A Man in Love *'87*
Author! Author! *'82*
The Strawberry Statement *'70*

Anthony Horowitz(1955-)
Alex Rider: Operation Stormbreaker *'06*
The Gathering *'02*
Diamond's Edge *'88*

Ed Horowitz
Exit Wounds *'01*
K-9 3: P.I. *'01*
On Deadly Ground *'94*

Jason Horwitch
Joe and Max *'02*
Finding Graceland *'98*

David Hoselton
Over the Hedge *'06*
Brother Bear *'03*
Deadly Game *'98*

Coleman Hough
Bubble *'06*
Full Frontal *'02*

Don Houghton(1930-91)
The Legend of the 7 Golden Vampires *'73*
The Satanic Rites of Dracula *'73*
Dracula A.D. 1972 *'72*

Lionel Houser(1908-49)
First Love *'39*
Smashing the Rackets *'38*
I Promise to Pay *'37*

Dianne Houston
Take the Lead *'06*
Knights of the South Bronx *'05*
Run for the Dream: The Gail Devers Story *'96*

Norman Houston(1887-1958)
Riders of the Range *'50*
Mysterious Desperado *'49*
In Old Caliente *'39*

Cy Howard(1915-93)
Marriage on the Rocks *'65*
My Friend Irma *'49*

Elizabeth Jane Howard(1923-)
Getting It Right *'89*
The Very Edge *'63*

Karin Howard
The Tigress *'93*
NeverEnding Story 2: The Next Chapter *'91*

Rance Howard(1929-)
Tut & Tuttle *'81*
Grand Theft Auto *'77*

Ron Howard(1954-)
Parenthood *'89*
Cotton Candy *'82*
Grand Theft Auto *'77*

Sidney Howard(1891-1939)
Gone with the Wind *'39*
Dodsworth *'36*
Raffles *'30*
Bulldog Drummond *'29*
Condemned *'29*

C. Thomas Howell(1966-)
Hope Ranch *'02*
Hourglass *'95*

Dorothy Howell(1899-1971)
The Miracle Woman *'31*
Platinum Blonde *'31*

Frank Howson(1952-)
Flynn *'96*
The Hunting *'92*
What the Moon Saw *'90*

Perry Howze
Chances Are *'89*
Mystic Pizza *'88*
Maid to Order *'87*

Rita Hsiao
Toy Story 2 *'99*
Mulan *'98*

King Hu(1931-97)
Painted Skin *'93*
Come Drink with Me *'65*

George Huang
How to Make a Monster *'01*
Swimming with Sharks *'94*

Lucien Hubbard
Smart Money *'31*
The Vanishing American *'25*
Outside the Law *'21*

Tom Hubbard(1919-74)
Daniel Boone: Trail Blazer *'56*
Thunder Pass *'54*
Two Lost Worlds *'50*

Tom Huckabee
Deep in the Heart (of Texas) *'98*
Deathfight *'93*

John Huddles
Uncorked *'98*
Far Harbor *'96*

Norman Hudis
Carry On Constable *'60*
No Kidding *'60*
Bond of Fear *'56*

Reginald (Reggie) Hudlin(1961-)
Bebe's Kids *'92*
House Party *'90*

Brent Huff(1961-)
Welcome to Paradise *'07*
Power Play *'02*
Final Justice *'94*

John Huff
Cyxork 7 *'06*
Hunter's Moon *'97*

Clair Huffaker(1926-90)
Chino *'75*
Hellfighters *'68*
The War Wagon *'67*
Flaming Star *'60*

Roy Huggins(1914-2002)
Pushover *'54*
Too Late for Tears *'49*

Gwyneth Hughes
Five Days *'07*
Miss Austen Regrets *'07*

John Hughes(1950-2009)
Just Visiting *'01*
Reach the Rock *'98*
Flubber *'97*
Home Alone 3 *'97*
101 Dalmatians *'96*
Baby's Day Out *'94*
Miracle on 34th Street *'94*
Dennis the Menace *'93*
Beethoven *'92*
Home Alone 2: Lost in New York *'92*
Career Opportunities *'91*
Curly Sue *'91*
Dutch *'91*
Home Alone *'90*
National Lampoon's Christmas Vacation *'89*
Uncle Buck *'89*
The Great Outdoors *'88*
She's Having a Baby *'88*
Planes, Trains & Automobiles *'87*
Some Kind of Wonderful *'87*
Ferris Bueller's Day Off *'86*
Pretty in Pink *'86*
The Breakfast Club *'85*
National Lampoon's European Vacation *'85*
Weird Science *'85*
Sixteen Candles *'84*
Mr. Mom *'83*
National Lampoon's Vacation *'83*
National Lampoon's Class Reunion *'82*

Ken Hughes(1922-2001)
Oh, Alfie *'75*
Cromwell *'70*
Chitty Chitty Bang Bang *'68*
Arrivederci, Baby! *'66*
The Trials of Oscar Wilde *'60*
Heat Wave *'54*

Russell S. Hughes
Savage Wilderness *'55*
The Command *'54*

Tom Hughes
Red Letters *'00*
Breathing Room *'96*

Jojo Hui
Warlords *'08*
The Eye 2 *'04*
The Eye *'02*
3 Extremes 2 *'02*

William Humble
Every Woman Knows a Secret *'99*
The Vacillations of Poppy Carew *'94*

Cyril Hume(1900-66)
The Invisible Boy *'57*
Forbidden Planet *'56*
Tarzan's Savage Fury *'52*
The Great Gatsby *'49*
Trader Horn *'31*

Steve Humphrey
The Game of Love *'87*
Agatha Christie's A Caribbean Mystery *'83*
Agatha Christie's Sparkling Cyanide *'83*

Ted Humphrey
The Code *'09*
The Triangle *'01*

Sammo Hung(1952-)
The Millionaire's Express *'86*
Spooky Encounters *'80*

Tran Anh Hung(1963-)
The Vertical Ray of the Sun *'00*

Cyclo '95
The Scent of Green Papaya '93

Tom Hunsinger(1952-)
Lawless Heart '01
Boyfriends '96

Ed(ward) Hunt
Bloody Birthday '80
Starship Invasions '77

Evan Hunter(1926-2005)
The Birds '63
High & Low '62

Ian McLellan Hunter(1915-91)
Captain Sinbad '63
The Amazing Mr. X '48

John Hunter(1911-)
Hollywood North '03
The Grey Fox '83
Hard Part Begins '73
Pirates of Blood River '62

Neil Hunter
Lawless Heart '01
Boyfriends '96

Tim Hunter(1947-)
Tex '82
Over the Edge '79

Lawrence Huntington(1900-68)
The Oblong Box '69
Man on the Run '49

William Hurlbut(1878-1957)
It Happened in New Orleans '36
The Bride of Frankenstein '35
Imitation of Life '34

Andy Hurst
Are You Scared? '06
Single White Female 2: The Psycho '05
Wild Things 2 '04

Michael Hurst(1973-)
Hardwired '09
Pumpkinhead 4: Blood Feud '07
Mosquitoman '05
New Blood '99

Harry Hurwitz(1938-95)
Fleshtone '94
That's Adequate '90
Under the Rainbow '81
The Projectionist '71

Jon Hurwitz
Harold & Kumar Escape from Guantanamo Bay '08
Harold and Kumar Go to White Castle '04

Rich Husky
Children of Fury '94
Nightmare '91

John Huston(1906-87)
Mr. North '88
The Man Who Would Be King '75
The Night of the Iguana '64
Heaven Knows, Mr. Allison '57
Moby Dick '56
Beat the Devil '53
Moulin Rouge '52
The African Queen '51
Key Largo '48
Treasure of the Sierra Madre '48
The Killers '46
High Sierra '41
The Maltese Falcon '41
Sergeant York '41
Dr. Ehrlich's Magic Bullet '40
Amazing Dr. Clitterhouse '38
Jezebel '38
Murders in the Rue Morgue '32

Paul Huston
Junior G-Men of the Air '42
Overland Mail '42

Ron Hutchinson
Marco Polo '07
The Island of Dr. Moreau '96
The Tuskegee Airmen '95
Against the Wall '94
The Burning Season '94
Fatherland '94
Blue Ice '92

Clint Hutchison
Conjurer '08
Terror Tract '00

Willard Huyck(1945-)
Radioland Murders '94
Howard the Duck '86
Best Defense '84
Indiana Jones and the Temple of Doom '84
French Postcards '79
More American Graffiti '79
Messiah of Evil '74
American Graffiti '73

David Henry Hwang(1957-)
Possession '02
The Lost Empire '01
Golden Gate '93
M. Butterfly '93

Peter Hyams(1943-)
Beyond a Reasonable Doubt '09
Narrow Margin '90
2010: The Year We Make Contact '84
The Star Chamber '83
Outland '81
The Hunter '80
Hanover Street '79
Capricorn One '78
Telefon '77
Busting '74

Chris Hyde
Chained Heat 3: Hell Mountain '98
Crackerjack 2 '97
Chained Heat 2 '92

Marc Hyman
The Perfect Score '04
Osmosis Jones '01

Jeremy Iacone
The Bone Collector '99
One Tough Cop '98
Blood In ... Blood Out: Bound by Honor '93

Juan Luis Iborra(1959-)
Valentin '03
Km. 0 '00
Between Your Legs '99
Amor de Hombre '97
Mouth to Mouth '95

Rustam Ibragimbekov(1939-)
East-West '99
Burnt by the Sun '94
Close to Eden '90

Ice Cube(1969-)
Janky Promoters '09
All About the Benjamins '02
Friday After Next '02
Next Friday '00
The Players Club '98
Friday '95

Leon Ichaso(1948-)
El Cantante '06
Pinero '01
Bitter Sugar '96
Crossover Dreams '85
El Super '79

Masato Ide(1922-)
Ran '85
Kagemusha '80

Eric Idle(1943-)
Splitting Heirs '93
National Lampoon's European Vacation '85
Monty Python's The Meaning of Life '83
The Tale of the Frog Prince '83
Monty Python's Life of Brian '79

All You Need Is Cash '78
Monty Python and the Holy Grail '75
And Now for Something Completely Different '72

Miguel Iglesias
Rape '76
Kilma, Queen of the Amazons '75

Joji Iida
Black Belt '07
Rasen '98

Bakuto Ijuin
Chain Gang Girls '08
Female Prisoner Sigma '06

W. Peter Iliff
Under Suspicion '00
Varsity Blues '98
Patriot Games '92
Point Break '91
Prayer of the Rollerboys '91

Shohei Imamura(1926-2006)
Dr. Akagi '98
The Eel '96
Black Rain '88
The Ballad of Narayama '83

Hiroshi Inagaki(1905-80)
Samurai 3: Duel at Ganryu Island '56
Samurai 1: Musashi Miyamoto '55
Samurai 2: Duel at Ichijoji Temple '55

Thomas Ince(1882-1924)
The Bargain '15
The Disciple '15
The Italian '15
The Wrath of the Gods '14

Agenore Incrocci(1919-2005)
The Good, the Bad and the Ugly '67
Mafioso '62
Joyful Laughter '60

Don Ingalls
Airport '75 '75
Bull of the West '71

William Inge(1913-73)
All Fall Down '62
Splendor in the Grass '61

Raul Inglis
Sand Serpents '09
Vice '08
Cerberus '05
Greenmail '01
Premonition '98
The Final Cut '96
Breach of Trust '95

Boris Ingster(1904-78)
Happy Landing '38
Thin Ice '37

J. Christian Ingvordsen(1957-)
Blood Relic '05
The Outfit '93
Comrades in Arms '91
Mob War '88
Search and Destroy '88
Firehouse '87
Hangmen '87

Sheldon Inkol
Dark Side '02
Specimen '97
Carver's Gate '96

Christopher Isherwood(1904-86)
The Loved One '65
Diane '55
Forever and a Day '43

Toshiro Ishido(1932-)
Hiroshima '95
Black Rain '88

Kazuo Ishiguro(1954-)
The White Countess '05

The Saddest Music in the World '03

Katushito Ishii
Funky Forest: The First Contact '06
The Taste of Tea '04
Party 7 '00
Shark Skin Man and Peach Hip Girl '98

Sogo Ishii
Electric Dragon 80,000V '01
Angel Dust '96

Takashi Ishii
Flower & Snake 2 '05
Flower & Snake '04
Gonin 2 '96
Evil Dead Trap '88

Teru Ishii
Blind Woman's Curse '70
Horrors of Malformed Men '69

Ira Israel(1966-)
American Virgin '98
Dilemma '97

Neal Israel(1945-)
National Lampoon's Dad's Week Off '97
All I Want for Christmas '91
Look Who's Talking, Too '90
Real Genius '85
Police Academy '84
Americathon '79

Juzo Itami(1933-97)
Minbo—Or the Gentle Art of Japanese Extortion '92
A Taxing Woman's Return '88
A Taxing Woman '87
Tampopo '86
The Funeral '84

Daisuke Ito(1898-1981)
Zatoichi: The Blind Swordsman and the Chess Expert '65
An Actor's Revenge '63

Junji Ito
Uzumaki '00
Tomie '99

Kazunori Ito(1954-)
Pistol Opera '02
Ghost in the Shell '95
H.P. Lovecraft's Necronomicon: Book of the Dead '93
The Red Spectacles '87

James Ivory(1928-)
A Soldier's Daughter Never Cries '98
Maurice '87
Shakespeare Wallah '65

Shunji Iwai(1963-)
New York, I Love You '09
Hana & Alice '04
All About Lily Chou-Chou '01
When I Close My Eyes '95

Renato Izzo
Night Train Murders '75
Adios, Sabata '71
Return of Sabata '71
Sabata '69

David S. Jackson
Do or Die '03
Detonator 2: Night Watch '95
Detonator '93
Mystery Mansion '83

Felix Jackson(1902-92)
Broadway '42
Back Street '41
Spring Parade '40
Destry Rides Again '39
Three Smart Girls Grow Up '39
Mad About Music '38

Horace Jackson(1898-1952)
We're Not Dressing '34
The Animal Kingdom '32

Joseph Jackson
Smart Money '31
Say It With Songs '29
The Singing Fool '28

Peter Jackson(1961-)
The Lovely Bones '09
King Kong '05
Lord of the Rings: The Return of the King '03
Lord of the Rings: The Two Towers '02
Lord of the Rings: The Fellowship of the Ring '01
Forgotten Silver '96
The Frighteners '96
Heavenly Creatures '94
Jack Brown, Genius '94
Dead Alive '93
Meet the Feebles '89
Bad Taste '88

Tracey Jackson
Confessions of a Shopaholic '09
The Other End of the Line '08
The Guru '02

Alan Jacobs
American Gun '02
Just One Night '00
Nina Takes a Lover '94

Alexander Jacobs
An Enemy of the People '77
Hell in the Pacific '69

Harrison Jacobs(1892-1968)
Wagons Westward '40
Renegade Trail '39
Borderland '37
Three on the Trail '36

Jon Jacobs(1966-)
Welcome Says the Angel '01
The Girl with the Hungry Eyes '94

Matthew Jacobs(1956-)
Doctor Who '96
Lassie '94
Lorna Doone '90
Paperhouse '89
Smart Money '88

Robert Nelson Jacobs
Extraordinary Measures '10
The Water Horse: Legend of the Deep '07
The Shipping News '01
Chocolat '00
Dinosaur '00
Out to Sea '97

Andrew Jacobson
Extreme Movie '08
Not Another Teen Movie '01

Danny Jacobson
The Honeymooners '05
Out to Sea '97

David Jacobson
Down in the Valley '05
Dahmer '02

Hans Jacoby
The Stranger from Venus '54
Tarzan's Savage Fury '52
Tarzan and the Slave Girl '50

John Jacoby
She Wouldn't Say Yes '45
The Amazing Mrs. Holiday '43

Michael Jacoby
The Undying Monster '42
The Charge of the Light Brigade '36

Benoit Jacquot(1947-)
Seventh Heaven '98
A Single Girl '96
The Disenchanted '90

Rick Jaffa
The Relic '96
An Eye for an Eye '95

Robert Jaffe
Motel Hell '80
Demon Seed '77

Henry Jaglom(1943-)
Going Shopping '05
Festival at Cannes '02
Deja Vu '98
Last Summer In the Hamptons '96
Babyfever '94
Venice, Venice '92
Eating '90
New Year's Day '89
Someone to Love '87
Always '85
Can She Bake a Cherry Pie? '83
Sitting Ducks '80
Tracks '76
A Safe Place '71

Randall Jahnson
See J. Randall Johnson

Don Jakoby
Evolution '01
Double Team '97
Arachnophobia '90
Invaders from Mars '86
Lifeforce '85
The Philadelphia Experiment '84
Blue Thunder '83

Alan James(1890-1952)
The Lone Avenger '33
Trail Drive '33
Come on Tarzan '32

Daniel James
On the Edge '00
Gorgo '61

Polly James
The Redhead from Wyoming '53
Mrs. Parkington '44

Rian James(1899-1953)
Down Argentine Way '40
Internes Can't Take Money '37
42nd Street '33

Steve Jankowski
Chupacabra Terror '05
Demolition High '95

Susan Estelle Jansen
Bratz '07
The Lizzie McGuire Movie '03

Karen Janszen
Gracie '07
Duma '05
A Walk to Remember '02
Digging to China '98
From the Earth to the Moon '98
The Matchmaker '97

Michael January
The Heist '96
C.I.A. 2: Target Alexa '94
Deadly Target '94
Firepower '93
To Be the Best '93

Agnes Jaoui(1964-)
Look at Me '04
The Taste of Others '00
Same Old Song '97
Un Air de Famille '96
Smoking/No Smoking '94

Sebastien Japrisot(1931-2003)
The Story of O '75
Honor Among Thieves '68

Petr Jarchovsky(1966-)
Zelary '03
Divided We Fall '00

Pascal Jardin(1934-80)
A Coeur Joie '67
Classe Tous Risque '60

Derek Jarman(1942-94)
Blue '93
Wittgenstein '93

Edward II '92
The Garden '90
Aria '88
The Last of England '87
Caravaggio '86
Sebastiane '79

Jim Jarmusch(1953-)
The Limits of Control '09
Broken Flowers '05
Coffee and Cigarettes '03
Ghost Dog: The Way of the Samurai '99
Dead Man '95
Night on Earth '91
Mystery Train '89
Down by Law '86
Permanent Vacation '84
Stranger than Paradise '84

Kevin Jarre
The Devil's Own '96
Tombstone '93
Glory '89

John Jarrell
Terminal Invasion '02
Romeo Must Die '00
Restraining Order '99

Daniel Jarrett(1894-1938)
Hollywood Cowboy '37
Thunder Mountain '35

Rollin Jarrett
American Vampire '97
Laws of Deception '97

Paul Jarrico(1915-97)
Messenger of Death '88
The Girl Most Likely '57
Paris Express '53
The Las Vegas Story '52
The White Tower '50
The Search '48
Thousands Cheer '43
Tom, Dick, and Harry '41

Steve Jarvis
Bloodstream '00
Haunted '98
Amazon Warrior '97
Things 2 '97
Things '93
Dead Girls '90
Fatal Images '89

Griffin Jay(1905-54)
The Devil Bat's Daughter '46
The Mask of Diijon '46
The Mummy's Ghost '44
Captive Wild Woman '43
Return of the Vampire '43
Junior G-Men of the Air '42
The Mummy's Tomb '42
The Mummy's Hand '40

Vadim Jean(1963-)
The Color of Magic '08
Hogfather '06
Nightscare '93

Henri Jeanson(1900-70)
Modigliani '58
Nana '55
Pepe Le Moko '37

Richard Jefferies
Organizm '08
Cold Creek Manor '03

L.V. Jefferson(1873-1959)
Lightning Bill '35
Rawhide Romance '34
Lightning Range '33

Erik Jendresen
Sublime '07
Crazy as Hell '02
Band of Brothers '01
Deadlocked '00

Dan Jenkins
The Break '95
Dead Solid Perfect '88

Tamara Jenkins
The Savages '07
Slums of Beverly Hills '98

Jim Jennewein
The Flintstones '94
Getting Even with Dad '94
Richie Rich '94

Talbot Jennings(1894-1985)
The Black Rose '50
Anna and the King of Siam '46
Frenchman's Creek '44
Spawn of the North '38
Mutiny on the Bounty '35

Anders Thomas Jensen(1972-)
The Duchess '08
After the Wedding '06
Adam's Apples '05
Brothers '04
The Green Butchers '03
Wilbur Wants to Kill Himself '02
Flickering Lights '01
The King Is Alive '00
Mifune '99

Seo-gyeong Jeong
Thirst '09
Lady Vengeance '05

Jean-Pierre Jeunet(1955-)
Micmacs '09
Amelie '01
The City of Lost Children '95
Delicatessen '92

Jack Jevne(1892-1972)
Wonder Man '45
Wintertime '43

Ruth Prawer Jhabvala(1927-)
Le Divorce '03
The Golden Bowl '00
A Soldier's Daughter Never Cries '98
Surviving Picasso '96
Jefferson in Paris '94
The Remains of the Day '93
Howard's End '92
Mr. & Mrs. Bridge '90
Madame Sousatzka '88
A Room with a View '86
The Bostonians '84
Heat and Dust '82
Quartet '81
Jane Austen in Manhattan '80
The Europeans '79
Hullabaloo over Georgie & Bonnie's Pictures '78
Roseland '77
Autobiography of a Princess '75
Bombay Talkie '70
Shakespeare Wallah '65
The Householder '63

Neal Jimenez(1960-)
Desperate Measures '98
Hideaway '94
Sleep with Me '94
For the Boys '91
The Waterdance '91
River's Edge '87

Wong Jing(1955-)
Her Name Is Cat '99
Meltdown '95

Peter Jobin(1944-)
Queen's Messenger II '01
Happy Birthday to Me '81

Richard Jobson(1960-)
The Purifiers '04
16 Years of Alcohol '03

Tim John
Call of the Wild '04
Dr. Jekyll and Ms. Hyde '95

Bayard Johnson
Tarzan and the Lost City '98
Rudyard Kipling's the Second Jungle Book: Mowgli and Baloo '97

Charles Johnson
Beyond Atlantis '73
Slaughter's Big Ripoff '73

Charles Eric Johnson
Steele's Law '91
Hard Lessons '86

David C(lark) Johnson(1962-)
Animal '05
Woo '97
DROP Squad '94

Denis Johnson
Dog Gone '08
Hit Me '96

J. Randall Johnson
Sunset Strip '99
The Doors '91

Jesse Johnson(1982-)
The Last Sentinel '07
Pit Fighter '05

Kenneth Johnson(1942-)
Steel '97
Alien Nation: Millennium '96
Hot Pursuit '84
V '83

Kristine Johnson
I Am Sam '01
Imaginary Crimes '94

Mark Steven Johnson(1964-)
Ghost Rider '07
Daredevil '03
Jack Frost '98
Simon Birch '98
Big Bully '95
Grumpier Old Men '95
Grumpy Old Men '93

Matt Johnson
Into the Blue '05
Torque '04

Monica Johnson(1956-)
The Muse '99
Mother '96
The Scout '94
Lost in America '85
Jekyll & Hyde... Together Again '82
Modern Romance '81
Americathon '79
Real Life '79

Niall Johnson
Keeping Mum '05
White Noise '05

Nunnally Johnson(1897-1977)
The Dirty Dozen '67
The World of Henry Orient '64
Mr. Hobbs Takes a Vacation '62
Flaming Star '60
The Three Faces of Eve '57
Black Widow '54
How to Marry a Millionaire '53
Phone Call from a Stranger '52
We're Not Married '52
Three Came Home '50
Mr. Peabody & the Mermaid '48
Along Came Jones '45
Casanova Brown '44
The Keys of the Kingdom '44
Woman in the Window '44
Roxie Hart '42
The Grapes of Wrath '40
Jesse James '39
Rose of Washington Square '39
The Prisoner of Shark Island '36

Rian Johnson
The Brothers Bloom '09
Brick '06

Robert P. Johnson
Bojangles '01
The Temptations '98

Tyson '95

Toni Johnson
Step Up 2 the Streets '08
Crown Heights '02
The Courage to Love '00
Ruby Bridges '98

Kurt Johnstad
300 '07
True Vengeance '97

Aaron Kim Johnston
For the Moment '94
The Last Winter '89

Agnes Christine Johnston(1896-1978)
When a Man's a Man '35
Lucky Devils '33
Daddy Long Legs '19

Becky Johnston
Seven Years in Tibet '97
The Prince of Tides '91

Rory Johnston
Prey of the Jaguar '96
The Secret Agent Club '96

Stephen Johnston
Starkweather '04
Ed Gein '01

Tony Johnston(1960-)
Hollywood North '03
Triggermen '02
Full Disclosure '00
Killing Moon '00
Replikator: Cloned to Kill '94

Amy Holden Jones(1953-)
The Relic '96
The Rich Man's Wife '96
The Getaway '93
Indecent Proposal '93
Beethoven '92
Indecency '92
Mystic Pizza '88
Love Letters '83

Ed Jones
Carried Away '95
Ninja in the U.S.A. '88

Evan Jones(1927-)
Shadow of the Wolf '92
A Show of Force '90
Kangaroo '86
Champions '84
Killing of Angel Street '81
Funeral in Berlin '66
Modesty Blaise '66
King and Country '64
Eva '62

Grover Jones(1893-1940)
The Shepherd of the Hills '41
Souls at Sea '37
The Trail of the Lonesome Pine '36
The Lives of a Bengal Lancer '35
One Sunday Afternoon '33
Strangers in Love '32
Trouble in Paradise '32
Gun Smoke '31
Touchdown '31

Ian Jones(1931-)
The Lighthorsemen '87
Ned Kelly '70

Jerry Jones
Dolemite 2: Human Tornado '76
Dolemite '75

Kirk Jones(1963-)
Everybody's Fine '09
Waking Ned Devine '98

Laura Jones(1951-)
Possession '02
Angela's Ashes '99
Oscar and Lucinda '97
A Thousand Acres '97
The Well '97
Portrait of a Lady '96
An Angel at My Table '89

High Tide '87
Cass '78

Mark Jones(1953-)
Rumpelstiltskin '96
Leprechaun '93

Pete Jones
Outing Riley '04
Stolen Summer '02

Robert C. Jones
P.D. James: The Murder Room '04
P.D. James: Death in Holy Orders '03
Coming Home '78

Terry Jones(1942-)
Mr. Toad's Wild Ride '96
Erik the Viking '89
Labyrinth '86
Monty Python's The Meaning of Life '83
Monty Python's Life of Brian '79
Monty Python and the Holy Grail '75
And Now for Something Completely Different '72

Gregor Jordan(1967-)
Buffalo Soldiers '01
Two Hands '98

Kevin Jordan(1974-)
Brooklyn Lobster '05
Smiling Fish & Goat on Fire '99

Neil Jordan(1950-)
The Good Thief '03
The End of the Affair '99
In Dreams '98
The Butcher Boy '97
Michael Collins '96
The Crying Game '92
The Miracle '91
High Spirits '88
Mona Lisa '86
The Company of Wolves '85
Danny Boy '82

Robert L. Joseph(1923-2002)
World War III '86
The Hitch-Hiker '53

Jon Jost(1943-)
The Bed You Sleep In '93
Jon Jost's Frameup '93
All the Vermeers in New York '91
Sure Fire '90
Slow Moves '84

Adrien (Carole Eastman) Joyce(1934-2004)
Man Trouble '92
Five Easy Pieces '70
Model Shop '69
The Shooting '66

Odette Joyeux(1917-2000)
The Bride Is Much Too Beautiful '58
Sois Belle et Tais-Toi '58

C. Courtney Joyner
Stealing Candy '04
Lady Jayne Killer '03
Nautilus '99
Public Enemies '96
Lurking Fear '94
Desperate Motives '92
Trancers 3: Deth Lives '92
Class of 1999 '90
Puppet Master 3: Toulon's Revenge '90
Vietnam, Texas '90
Catacombs '89
Prison '88
The Offspring '87

Mike Judge(1962-)
Extract '09
Idiocracy '06
Office Space '98
Beavis and Butt-Head Do America '96

Jerry Juhl(1938-2005)
Muppets from Space '99
Muppet Treasure Island '96
The Muppet Movie '79

Lenny Juliano
Desert Thunder '99
Stealth Fighter '99

Harry Junkin
Vendetta for the Saint '68
Fiction Makers '67

Karel Kachyna(1924-2004)
The Cow '93
The Last Butterfly '92

Cedric Kahn(1966-)
Red Lights '04
L'Ennui '98

Gordon Kahn(1902-62)
Lights of Old Santa Fe '47
Cowboy & the Senorita '44

Chen Kaige(1952-)
The Promise '05
Together '02
The Emperor and the Assassin '99
Life on a String '90

David Kajganich
Blood Creek '09
The Invasion '07

Kengo Kaji
Tokyo Gore Police '08
Uzumaki '00

Masahiro Kakefuda
Sex and Fury '73
Horrors of Malformed Men '69

Michael Kalesniko(1961-)
How to Kill Your Neighbor's Dog '01
Spoiler '98
Private Parts '96

Tom Kalin
Office Killer '97
Swoon '91

Bert Kalmar(1884-1947)
A Night at the Opera '35
Duck Soup '33
Horse Feathers '32
Kid from Spain '32

Laeta Kalogridis(1965-)
Shutter Island '09
Pathfinder '07
Alexander '04

Steven Kaman
The Outfit '93
Firehouse '87
Hangmen '87

Karl Kamb(1903-88)
Tarzan and the She-Devil '53
Luxury Liner '48
Pitfall '48
Carnegie Hall '47

Robert Mark Kamen
Taken '08
Transporter 3 '08
Transporter 2 '05
The Transporter '02
Kiss of the Dragon '01
A Walk in the Clouds '95
Gladiator '92
Lethal Weapon 3 '92
The Power of One '92
The Karate Kid: Part 3 '89
The Karate Kid: Part 2 '86
The Karate Kid '84
Split Image '82
Taps '81

Kazuo Kamimura
The Princess Blade '02
Lady Snowblood '73

Steven Kampmann(1947-)
Clifford '92
Stealing Home '88

The Couch Trip '87
Back to School '86

Deborah Kampmeier
Hounddog '08
Virgin '03

John Kamps
Ghost Town '08
Zathura '05
The Borrowers '97
Mighty Morphin Power Rangers: The Movie '95

Aben Kandel(1897-1993)
Blood of Dracula '57
I Was a Teenage Werewolf '57
The Fighter '52
They Won't Forget '37

David Kane
The River King '05
Born Romantic '00

Michael Kane
The Cisco Kid '94
The Bear '89
All the Right Moves '83
Hard Country '81
Legend of the Lone Ranger '81
Southern Comfort '81
Foolin' Around '80
Hot Stuff '80
Smokey and the Bandit 2 '80

Rolfe Kanefsky(1969-)
Blonde and Blonder '07
The Hazing '04
Red Line '96
There's Nothing out There '90

Charles Kanganis
Impulse '08
No Escape, No Return '93
Fist of Honor '92
A Time to Die '91

Fay Kanin(1917-)
Teacher's Pet '58
The Opposite Sex '56
Rhapsody '54

Garson Kanin(1912-99)
It Should Happen to You '54
The Marrying Kind '52
Pat and Mike '52
Adam's Rib '50
A Double Life '47

Michael Kanin(1910-93)
How to Commit Marriage '69
The Outrage '64
Teacher's Pet '58
The Opposite Sex '56
Rhapsody '54
Woman of the Year '42
Panama Lady '39

Hal Kanter(1918-)
Bachelor in Paradise '69
Dear Brigitte '65
Move Over, Darling '63
Blue Hawaii '62
Pocketful of Miracles '61
Loving You '57
Artists and Models '55
The Rose Tattoo '55
Casanova's Big Night '54
Here Come the Girls '53
Money from Home '53
The Road to Bali '53

Asif Kapadia(1972-)
Far North '07
The Warrior '81

Deborah Kaplan
Leap Year '10
Made of Honor '08
Surviving Christmas '04
Josie and the Pussycats '01
The Flintstones in Viva Rock Vegas '00
Can't Hardly Wait '98
A Very Brady Sequel '96

Jonathan Kaplan(1947-)
Mr. Billion '77
White Line Fever '75

Marty Kaplan
Striking Distance '93
The Distinguished Gentleman '92
Noises Off '92

Mitchell Kapner
Into the Blue 2: The Reef '09
The Whole Ten Yards '04
The Whole Nine Yards '00

Wong Kar-Wai(1958-)
Ashes of Time Redux '08
My Blueberry Nights '07
Eros '04
2046 '04
In the Mood for Love '00
Happy Together '96
Chungking Express '95
Fallen Angels '95
Ashes of Time '94

Luca Karall
Maria's Day '84
25 Fireman's Street '73

Larry Karaszewski(1961-)
1408 '07
Agent Cody Banks '03
Screwed '00
Man on the Moon '99
The People vs. Larry Flynt '96
That Darn Cat '96
Ed Wood '94
Problem Child 2 '91
Problem Child '90

Kazuo Kasahara
Ronin Gai '90
Father of the Kamikaze '74

Jake Kasdan(1975-)
Walk Hard: The Dewey Cox Story '07
The TV Set '06
Zero Effect '97

Lawrence Kasdan(1949-)
Dreamcatcher '03
Mumford '99
Wyatt Earp '94
The Bodyguard '92
Grand Canyon '91
The Accidental Tourist '88
Silverado '85
The Big Chill '83
Return of the Jedi '83
Body Heat '81
Continental Divide '81
The Empire Strikes Back '80

Sam Henry Kass
Body and Soul '98
The Search for One-Eye Jimmy '96

Mathieu Kassovitz(1967-)
Babylon A.D. '08
The Crimson Rivers '01
Hate '95
Cafe au Lait '94

Brian Katkin
Vipers '08
Shakedown '02
Hard As Nails '01
If I Die Before I Wake '98

A.L. Katz
Tales from the Crypt Presents Bordello of Blood '96
Children of the Corn 2: The Final Sacrifice '92

Gloria Katz
Radioland Murders '94
Howard the Duck '86
Best Defense '84
Indiana Jones and the Temple of Doom '84
French Postcards '79
More American Graffiti '79
Messiah of Evil '74
American Graffiti '73

Jordan Katz(1960-)
Valiant '05
Incognito '97
Trial by Jury '94

Stephen Katz(1946-2005)
The Contract '07
From the Earth to the Moon '98
Satan's Princess '90

Steven Katz
Wind Chill '07
Shadow of the Vampire '00
Fallen Angels 1 '93

Charles Kaufman
Ferocious Female Freedom Fighters '88
Waitress '81
Mother's Day '80
Squeeze Play '79
Cynthia '47
Breakfast for Two '37

Charles A. Kaufman(1904-91)
The Story of Esther Costello '57
Return to Paradise '53

Charlie Kaufman(1958-)
Synecdoche, New York '08
Eternal Sunshine of the Spotless Mind '04
Adaptation '02
Confessions of a Dangerous Mind '02
Human Nature '02
Being John Malkovich '99

George S. Kaufman(1889-1961)
Star Spangled Rhythm '42
A Night at the Opera '35
The Cocoanuts '29

Ken Kaufman(1963-)
Curious George '06
The Missing '03
Space Cowboys '00
In the Army Now '94

Lloyd Kaufman(1945-)
Citizen Toxie: The Toxic Avenger 4 '01
Class of Nuke 'Em High 3: The Good, the Bad and the Subhumanoid '94
Sgt. Kabukiman N.Y.P.D. '94
Class of Nuke 'Em High 2: Subhumanoid Meltdown '91
The Toxic Avenger, Part 2 '89
The Toxic Avenger, Part 3: The Last Temptation of Toxie '89
Troma's War '88
Class of Nuke 'Em High '86
Stuck on You '84
First Turn On '83

Millard Kaufman(1917-)
Living Free '72
The War Lord '65

Philip Kaufman(1936-)
Rising Sun '93
Henry & June '90
The Unbearable Lightness of Being '88
The Right Stuff '83
Raiders of the Lost Ark '81
Wanderers '79
The Outlaw Josey Wales '76
The Great Northfield Minnesota Raid '72
Goldstein '64

Robert Kaufman
Love at First Bite '79
Ski Party '65

Aki Kaurismaki(1957-)
Lights in the Dusk '06
The Man Without a Past '02
La Vie de Boheme '93
The Match Factory Girl '90
Ariel '89
Leningrad Cowboys Go America '89

Helmut Kautner(1908-80)
The Last Bridge '54
Die Grosse Freiheit Nr. 7 '45

Frances Kavanaugh
Driftin' River '46
Wild West '46
Westward Bound '44
Trail Riders '42
The Driftin' Kid '41
Dynamite Canyon '41
Riding the Sunset Trail '41

Jerzy Kawalerowicz(1922-2007)
Pharaoh '66
Mother Joan of the Angels '60

Kikuo Kawasaki
Lured Innocence '97
Private Passions '85

Minoru Kawasaki
Executive Koala '06
The Rug Cop '06
The World Sinks Except Japan '06
The Calamari Wrestler '04

Stephen Kay
The Mod Squad '99
The Last Time I Committed Suicide '96

Tony Kayden
When Justice Fails '98
Slipstream '89

John Kaye
Along for the Ride '00
Where the Buffalo Roam '80

Elia Kazan(1909-2003)
The Arrangement '69
Blues in the Night '41

Nicholas Kazan(1950-)
Enough '02
Bicentennial Man '99
Fallen '97
Homegrown '97
Matilda '96
Dream Lover '93
Mobsters '91
Reversal of Fortune '90
Patty Hearst '88
At Close Range '86
Impulse '84
Frances '82

Tim Kazurinsky(1950-)
Strange Relations '02
The Cherokee Kid '96
For Keeps '88
About Last Night... '86

James Keach(1948-)
The Forgotten '89
Armed and Dangerous '86
The Long Riders '80
Slashed Dreams '74

Gene R. Kearney
The Invasion of Carol Enders '74
Night of the Lepus '72
Games '67

Joe Keenan(1958-)
Flushed Away '06
Sleep with Me '94

Jon Keeyes
Living & Dying '07
American Nightmare '00

Harvey Keith
Stand-Ins '97
Jezebel's Kiss '90

Woody Keith
Dementia '98
Bride of Re-Animator '89

Ed Kelleher(1944-2005)
Stand-Ins '97
Lurkers '88
Shriek of the Mutilated '74
Invasion of the Blood Farmers '72

Sean Keller
Kraken: Tentacles of the Deep '06
Mammoth '06

Cindy Kelley
Love's Unfolding Dream '07
Saving Sarah Cain '07
Love's Enduring Promise '04
Love Comes Softly '03

David E. Kelley(1956-)
Lake Placid '99
Mystery, Alaska '99
To Gillian on Her 37th Birthday '96

Nick Kellis
Endangered '94
Uncivilized '94

Bob Kelljan(1930-82)
The Return of Count Yorga '71
Count Yorga, Vampire '70

Bill Kelly
Enchanted '07
Premonition '07
Blast from the Past '98

Karen Kelly
The Last Best Sunday '98
Poison Ivy 3: The New Seduction '97
The Corporation '96
Body Chemistry 4: Full Exposure '95
Hard Bounty '94
Illicit Dreams '94

Patrick Smith Kelly
Don't Say a Word '01
A Perfect Murder '98

Richard Kelly(1975-)
The Box '09
Southland Tales '06
Domino '05
Donnie Darko '01

Tim Kelly(1931-98)
Fist '76
Homeboy '75
Cry of the Banshee '70

Edmond Kelso(1910-69)
King of the Zombies '41
Up in the Air '40
Roll, Wagons, Roll '39
Tex Rides with the Boy Scouts '37

Kurt Kempler
Telegraph Trail '33
The Big Stampede '32
Two-Fisted Law '32

David Kendall
Nature of the Beast '07
The New Guy '02

James Kennaway
Battle of Britain '69
The Mind Benders '63

Anne Kennedy(1959-)
The Monkey's Mask '00
Crush '93

Burt Kennedy(1922-2001)
Texas Guns '90
White Hunter, Black Heart '90
Dynamite and Gold '88
The Trouble with Spies '87
Train Robbers '73
Hannie Caulder '72
The Rounders '65
Mail Order Bride '63
Comanche Station '60
Ride Lonesome '59
The Tall T '57
Man in the Vault '56

Chris Kennedy
Doing Time for Patsy Cline '97
Glass '90

Jane Kennedy(1964-)
The Dish '00
The Castle '97

Kerry Kennedy
Baby '00
Hope '97

Michael Kennedy(1954-)
The Swordsman '92
Erik '90

William Kennedy(1928-)
Ironweed '87
The Cotton Club '84

Troy Kennedy-Martin(1932-)
Hostile Waters '97
Kelly's Heroes '70

Doug Kenney
Caddyshack '80
National Lampoon's Animal House '78

Gary Kent(1933-)
Street Corner Justice '96
L.A. Bad '85

Robert E. Kent
Diary of a Madman '63
Twice-Told Tales '63
Seminole Uprising '55
Dick Tracy vs. Cueball '46
Zombies on Broadway '44
Gildersleeve on Broadway '43
The Spider's Web '38
Hard to Hold '37

Willis Kent(1878-1966)
Mad Youth '40
Sucker Money '34
Woman Condemned '33

Chris Kentis(1962-)
Open Water '03
Grind '96

Earl Kenton
Invisible: The Chronicles of Benjamin Knight '93
Mandroid '93

Charles Kenyon(1880-1961)
100 Men and a Girl '37
Think Fast, Mr. Moto '37
A Midsummer Night's Dream '35
The Iron Horse '24
The Penalty '20

Curtis Kenyon(1914-)
Twin Beds '42
Thanks for Everything '38

Bill Kerby
On the Beach '00
Dead Men Can't Dance '97
Lakota Woman: Siege at Wounded Knee '94
Hooper '78

Rob Kerchner
Heaven's Fire '99
Turbulence 2: Fear of Flying '99
Route 9 '98
Bloodfist 7: Manhunt '95
Bloodfist 6: Ground Zero '94

Ronni Kern
Jesse Stone: Thin Ice '09
Blue Smoke '07
Jesse Stone: Sea Change '07
Helen of Troy '03
American Pop '81

Sarah Kernochan(1947-)
All I Wanna Do '98
Sommersby '93
Impromptu '90

Lodge Kerrigan(1964-)
Keane '04
Claire Dolan '97

Clean, Shaven '93

Wendy Kesselman

A Separate Peace '04
I Love You, I Love You Not '97
Sister My Sister '94

Lyle Kessler

The Saint of Fort Washington '93
Gladiator '92
Orphans '87

Larry Ketron

The Only Thrill '97
Freeway '88
Permanent Record '88

Michael Keusch(1955-)

Samurai Cowboy '93
Lena's Holiday '90

Edward Khmara

Merlin '98
Dragon: The Bruce Lee Story '93
Enemy Mine '85
Ladyhawke '85

Callie Khouri(1957-)

Divine Secrets of the Ya-Ya Sisterhood '02
Something to Talk About '95
Thelma & Louise '91

Abbas Kiarostami(1940-)

Crimson Gold '03
The Taste of Cherry '96
The White Balloon '95
Through the Olive Trees '94
Life and Nothing More ... '92
Where Is My Friend's House? '87

Roland Kibbee(1914-84)

The Devil's Disciple '59
Top Secret Affair '57
The Desert Song '53
Three Sailors and a Girl '53
Vera Cruz '53
Painting the Clouds With Sunshine '51
A Night in Casablanca '46

David Kidd

Yours, Mine & Ours '05
Head Over Heels '01

Dylan Kidd(1969-)

P.S. '04
Roger Dodger '02

Krzysztof Kieslowski(1941-96)

Heaven '01
Trois Couleurs: Blanc '94
Trois Couleurs: Rouge '94
Trois Couleurs: Bleu '93
The Double Life of Veronique '91
The Decalogue '88
No End '84
Camera Buff '79

Ryuzo Kikushima

Tora! Tora! Tora! '70
High & Low '62
Sanjuro '62
Yojimbo '61
The Bad Sleep Well '60
The Hidden Fortress '58
Throne of Blood '57
Scandal '50

Jeong-min Kim

The City of Violence '06
Tube '03

Ji-woon Kim

A Tale of Two Sisters '03
3 Extremes 2 '02
The Foul King '00
The Quiet Family '98

Ki-Duk Kim

Time '06
Samaritan Girl '04
The Isle '01

Lawrence Kimble(1904-77)

Seven Days Ashore '44
Zombies on Broadway '44
Bells of Capistrano '42

Bruce Kimmel(1947-)

The Creature Wasn't Nice '81
The First Nudie Musical '75

Takeshi Kimura

King Kong Escapes '67
Frankenstein Conquers the World '64
Matango '63

Takeshi Kimura(1912-88)

War of the Gargantuas '70
Destroy All Monsters '68
Attack of the Mushroom People '63
Gorath '62

Judson Kinberg

To Catch a Killer '92
Sell Out '76
Vampire Circus '71

Simon Kinberg(1973-)

Sherlock Holmes '09
Jumper '08
X-Men: The Last Stand '06
Fantastic Four '05
Mr. & Mrs. Smith '05
XXX: State of the Union '05

Tim Kincaid(1952-)

The Occultist '89
Mutant Hunt '87
Robot Holocaust '87
Breeders '86

Bradley King

Under the Pampas Moon '35
Hoopla '33

Brian King

Night Train '09
Cypher '02

Chloe King

Red Shoe Diaries: Luscious Lola '00
Red Shoe Diaries: Swimming Naked '00
B. Monkey '97
Poison Ivy 2: Lily '95
Red Shoe Diaries 3: Another Woman's Lipstick '93

I. Marlene King

Just My Luck '06
If These Walls Could Talk '96
National Lampoon's Senior Trip '95
Now and Then '95

Jonathan King

The Tattooist '07
Black Sheep '06

Michael Patrick King

Sex and the City 2 '10
Sex and the City: The Movie '08

Robert King

Vertical Limit '00
Red Corner '97
Cutthroat Island '95
Clean Slate '94
Speechless '94
Bloodfist '89
Phantom of the Mall: Eric's Revenge '89
The Nest '88

Robert Lee King

Slap Her, She's French '02
Boys Life '94

Stephen King(1947-)

Stephen King's Rose Red '02
Stephen King's The Storm of the Century '99
Stephen King's The Stand '94
Sleepwalkers '92
Stephen King's Golden Years '91
Graveyard Shift '90
Stephen King's It '90
Pet Sematary '89
Maximum Overdrive '86
Cat's Eye '85
Silver Bullet '85
Creepshow '82

Zalman King(1941-)

Red Shoe Diaries: Swimming Naked '00
In God's Hands '98
Business for Pleasure '96
Red Shoe Diaries: Strip Poker '96
Red Shoe Diaries 3: Another Woman's Lipstick '93
Lake Consequence '92
Wild Orchid 2: Two Shades of Blue '92
Wild Orchid '90
Two Moon Junction '88
Wildfire '88
9 1/2 Weeks '86

Dorothy Kingsley(1909-97)

Valley of the Dolls '67
Green Mansions '59
Don't Go Near the Water '57
Pal Joey '57
Seven Brides for Seven Brothers '54
Angels in the Outfield '51
It's a Big Country '51
Easy to Wed '46
Broadway Rhythm '44

Ernest Kinoy(1925-)

Rescuers: Stories of Courage "Two Women" '97
Gore Vidal's Lincoln '88
Murrow '86
Roots '77
The Story of David '76
Victory at Entebbe '76
The Story of Jacob & Joseph '74

Teinosuke Kinugasa(1896-1982)

An Actor's Revenge '63
Gate of Hell '54

Isao Kiriyama

Azumi '03
Battlefield Baseball '03

Jack Kirkland

The Golden Coach '52
Wings in the Dark '35

Karey Kirkpatrick

The Spiderwick Chronicles '08
Flakes '07
Charlotte's Web '06
Over the Hedge '06
Chicken Run '00
The Little Vampire '00
Honey, We Shrunk Ourselves '97
The Rescuers Down Under '90

Ralf Kirsten(1930-)

Under the Pear Tree '73
On the Sunny Side '62

Takeshi "Beat" Kitano(1948-)

Zatoichi '03
Dolls '02
Brother '00
Kikujiro '99
Fireworks '97
Sonatine '96

Martin Kitrosser

Facing the Enemy '00
Silent Night, Deadly Night 5: The Toymaker '91
Friday the 13th, Part 5: A New Beginning '85
Friday the 13th, Part 3 '82

Robert Klane(1941-)

Weekend at Bernie's 2 '93
Weekend at Bernie's '89
National Lampoon's European Vacation '85
Unfaithfully Yours '84
Where's Poppa? '70

Cedric Klapisch(1961-)

Russian Dolls '05
L'Auberge Espagnole '02
Un Air de Famille '96
When the Cat's Away '96

David Klass

Walking Tall '04
In the Time of the Butterflies '01
Desperate Measures '98
Kiss the Girls '97

Josh Klausner

Date Night '10
Shrek Forever After '10
The 4th Floor '99

Andrew Klavan

One Missed Call '08
A Shock to the System '90

Marc Klein

Suburban Girl '07
A Good Year '06
Serendipity '01

Nicholas Klein

The Million Dollar Hotel '99
The End of Violence '97

Philip Klein

Pilgrimage '33
Too Busy to Work '32
The Black Camel '31
Four Sons '28
Street Angel '28

Robert Dean Klein

Heart of America '03
Blackwoods '02

Harry Kleiner(1916-2007)

Le Mans '71
Fantastic Voyage '66
The Garment Jungle '57
House of Bamboo '55
Carmen Jones '54

Dan Kleinman

Ultra Warrior '92
Rage '72

Walter Klenhard

Disappearance '02
Buried Alive 2 '97
The Haunting of Seacliff Inn '94
The Last Hit '93
Dead in the Water '91

Richard Kletter

Queen Sized '08
Missing Pieces '00
The Colony '98
The Android Affair '95
Dangerous Indiscretion '94

Harald Kloser(1956-)

2012 '09
10,000 B.C. '08

Claude Klotz(1932-)

The Man on the Train '02
The Hairdresser's Husband '92

Steve Kloves(1960-)

Harry Potter and the Half-Blood Prince '09
Harry Potter and the Goblet of Fire '05
Harry Potter and the Prisoner of Azkaban '04
Harry Potter and the Chamber of Secrets '02
Harry Potter and the Sorcerer's Stone '01
Wonder Boys '00
Flesh and Bone '93
The Fabulous Baker Boys '89
Racing with the Moon '84

Nigel Kneale(1922-2006)

Sharpe's Gold '94
Woman in Black '89
The Witches '66
First Men in the Moon '64
Damn the Defiant '62
The Entertainer '60
Look Back in Anger '58
Quatermass and the Pit '58
The Abominable Snowman '57
Quatermass 2 '57

Andrew Knight

After the Deluge '03
Siam Sunset '99
The Efficiency Expert '92

Steven Knight(1959-)

Eastern Promises '07
Amazing Grace '06
Dirty Pretty Things '03

Patricia Louisianna Knop

Red Shoe Diaries: Strip Poker '96
Delta of Venus '95
Siesta '87
9 1/2 Weeks '86

Christopher Knopf

Not My Kid '85
Peter and Paul '81
Emperor of the North Pole '73
The Bravos '72
20 Million Miles to Earth '57
The King's Thief '55

Hirohoshi Kobayashi

Death Note 3: L, Change the World '08
Cursed '04

Masaki Kobayashi(1916-96)

The Human Condition: Road to Eternity '59
The Human Condition: No Greater Love '58

Arthur Kober

Having a Wonderful Time '38
Hollywood Party '34

Howard Koch(1901-95)

War Lover '62
Rhapsody in Blue '45
Mission to Moscow '43
Casablanca '42
Sergeant York '41
The Letter '40
The Sea Hawk '40

Laird Koenig

Black Water '94
The Little Girl Who Lives down the Lane '76

David Koepp(1964-)

Angels & Demons '09
Ghost Town '08
Indiana Jones and the Kingdom of the Crystal Skull '08
War of the Worlds '05
Zathura '05
Secret Window '04
Panic Room '02
Spider-Man '02
Stir of Echoes '99
Snake Eyes '98
The Lost World: Jurassic Park 2 '97
Mission: Impossible '96
The Trigger Effect '96
The Paper '94
The Shadow '94
Carlito's Way '93
Jurassic Park '93
Death Becomes Her '92
Apartment Zero '88

Wolfgang Kohlhaase(1931-)

The Legend of Rita '99
Solo Sunny '80

Abby Kohn

Valentine's Day '10
He's Just Not That Into You '09
Never Been Kissed '99

Kazuo Koike

The Princess Blade '02
Shogun Assassin '80
Bohachi Bushido: Code of the Forgotten Eight '73
Lady Snowblood '73
Shogun Assassin 2: Lightning Swords of Death '73

Goseki Kojima(1928-)

Bohachi Bushido: Code of the Forgotten Eight '73
Shogun Assassin 2: Lightning Swords of Death '73

Vincent Kok

Special Unit 2002 '01
Gorgeous '99

Ana Kokkinos(1959-)

Head On '98
Only the Brave '94

Emil Kolbe

American Kickboxer 1 '91
Lights! Camera! Murder! '89

Stefan Kolditz

Dresden '06
Burning Life '94

Amos Kollek(1947-)

Fiona '98
Whore 2 '94
Double Edge '92
High Stakes '89

Todd Komarnicki

Perfect Stranger '07
Resistance '03

Andrei Konchalovsky(1937-)

House of Fools '02
The Odyssey '97
The Inner Circle '91
Runaway Train '85
Maria's Lovers '84
Siberiade '79
Andrei Rublev '66

Kate Kondell(1973-)

First Daughter '04
Legally Blonde 2: Red White & Blonde '03

Larry Konner

Flicka '06
Mona Lisa Smile '03
Planet of the Apes '01
Mercury Rising '98
Mighty Joe Young '98
The Beverly Hillbillies '93
For Love or Money '93
Sometimes They Come Back '91
Desperate Hours '90
The Jewel of the Nile '85

Chuck Konzelman

The Insatiable '06
Earth vs. the Spider '01

Peter Koper

Island of the Dead '00
Headless Body in Topless Bar '96

Arthur Kopit(1937-)

Roswell: The U.F.O. Cover-Up '94
The Phantom of the Opera '90
Hands of a Stranger '87

Brian Koppelman

Solitary Man '10
The Girlfriend Experience '09
Ocean's Thirteen '07
Walking Tall '04
Runaway Jury '03
Knockaround Guys '01
Rounders '98

Howard Korder(1957-)

Lakeview Terrace '08
Stealing Sinatra '04
My Little Assassin '99
The Passion of Ayn Rand '99

Hirokazu Kore-eda(1962-)
Nobody Knows *'04*
After Life *'98*

Steve Koren
Click *'06*
Bruce Almighty *'03*
Superstar *'99*
A Night at the Roxbury *'98*

Harmony Korine(1974-)
Mister Lonely *'07*
Julien Donkey-boy *'99*
Gummo *'97*
Kids *'95*

Baltasar Kormakur(1966-)
A Little Trip to Heaven *'05*
The Sea *'02*
101 Reykjavik *'00*

David A. Korn
Cash Crop *'01*
Harvest *'98*

Randy Kornfield
Jingle All the Way *'96*
Bloodknot *'95*
Incident at Deception Ridge *'94*

Mari Kornhauser
Kitchen Privileges *'00*
The Last Ride *'94*
Zandalee *'91*

Scott Kosar
The Crazies *'09*
The Machinist *'04*
The Texas Chainsaw Massacre *'03*

Ron Koslow
Last Dance *'96*
Running Delilah *'93*
Into the Night *'85*
Lifeguard *'76*

Jim Kouf(1951-)
National Treasure *'04*
Taxi *'04*
Snow Dogs *'02*
Rush Hour *'98*
Gang Related *'96*
Operation Dumbo Drop *'95*
Another Stakeout *'93*
Disorganized Crime *'89*
The Hidden *'87*
Stakeout *'87*
Class *'83*

Edward Kovach
Blink of an Eye *'92*
Jailbird Rock *'88*

Paul Koval
Dead Silent *'99*
Psychic *'91*
Blue Movies *'88*

Janet Kovalcik
My Girl 2 *'94*
Married to It *'93*

Yu Koyama
Azumi 2 *'05*
Azumi *'03*

Karl Kozak(1964-)
Clawed: The Legend of Sasquatch *'05*
Out of the Black *'01*

Olaf Kraemer
Eight Miles High *'08*
Eight Miles High *'07*

John Krafft
Here's Flash Casey *'38*
Slander House *'38*

Soeren Kragh-Jacobsen(1947-)
Mifune *'99*
Emma's Shadow *'88*

Andrzej Krakowski(1946-)
Eminent Domain *'91*
Triumph of the Spirit *'89*

Hans Kraly(1884-1950)
Private Lives *'31*
The Garden of Eden *'28*
The Duchess of Buffalo *'26*

Richard Kramer
Armistead Maupin's Tales of the City *'93*
All I Want for Christmas *'91*

Wayne Kramer(1965-)
Crossing Over *'09*
Running Scared *'06*
Mindhunters *'05*
The Cooler *'03*

Norman Krasna(1909-84)
Sunday in New York *'63*
Let's Make Love *'60*
Indiscreet *'58*
The Ambassador's Daughter *'56*
The Big Hangover *'50*
Princess O'Rourke *'43*
The Flame of New Orleans *'41*
It Started with Eve *'41*
Mr. & Mrs. Smith *'41*
It's a Date *'40*
Wife Versus Secretary *'36*
Hands Across the Table *'35*
So This Is Africa *'33*

Stu Krieger(1952-)
Cow Belles *'06*
In the Army Now *'94*
Monkey Trouble *'94*
A Troll in Central Park *'94*
The Land Before Time *'88*

Peter Krikes
Anna and the King *'99*
Star Trek 4: The Voyage Home *'86*

Milton Krims(1904-88)
Mohawk *'56*
Tennessee's Partner *'55*
Prince of Foxes *'49*
Confessions of a Nazi Spy *'39*

Henry Krinkle
Friend of the Family 2 *'96*
Night Eyes 4: Fatal Passion *'95*

John Krizanc
The Summit *'08*
Men with Brooms *'02*

Jerzy Kromolowski
In the Electric Mist *'08*
The Pledge *'00*

Sandy Kroopf
Contagious *'96*
Birdy *'84*

Lisa Krueger(1961-)
Committed *'99*
Manny & Lo *'96*

Ehren Kruger(1972-)
Transformers: Revenge of the Fallen *'09*
Blood & Chocolate *'07*
The Brothers Grimm *'05*
The Ring 2 *'05*
The Skeleton Key *'05*
Impostor *'02*
The Ring *'02*
Reindeer Games *'00*
Scream 3 *'00*
Arlington Road *'99*
New World Disorder *'99*

Carl Krusada(1879-1951)
Wild Horse Valley *'40*
El Diablo Rides *'39*
Fast Bullets *'36*
Silent Valley *'35*
Skull & Crown *'35*
Fighting Hero *'34*
Mystery Trooper *'32*
Westward Bound *'30*

John Kruse
Vendetta for the Saint *'68*
Fiction Makers *'67*

Stanley Kubrick(1928-99)
Eyes Wide Shut *'99*
Full Metal Jacket *'87*
The Shining *'80*
Barry Lyndon *'75*
A Clockwork Orange *'71*
2001: A Space Odyssey *'68*
Dr. Strangelove, or: How I Learned to Stop Worrying and Love the Bomb *'64*
Paths of Glory *'57*
The Killing *'56*
Killer's Kiss *'55*

Kankuro Kudo
Zebraman *'04*
Ping Pong *'02*

Robert Kuhn
Mickey Blue Eyes *'99*
The Cure *'95*
High Strung *'91*

Sid Kuller(1910-93)
Big Store *'41*
Argentine Nights *'40*

Roger Kumble(1966-)
Cruel Intentions 2 *'99*
Cruel Intentions *'98*
National Lampoon's Senior Trip *'95*
Unveiled *'94*

Hanif Kureishi(1954-)
Venus *'06*
The Mother *'03*
My Son the Fanatic *'97*
The Buddha of Suburbia *'92*
London Kills Me *'91*
Sammy & Rosie Get Laid *'87*
My Beautiful Laundrette *'85*

Harry Kurnitz(1908-68)
How to Steal a Million *'66*
Goodbye Charlie *'64*
Witness for the Prosecution *'57*
Pretty Baby *'50*
The Inspector General *'49*
One Touch of Venus *'48*
Something in the Wind *'47*
The Heavenly Body *'44*
They Got Me Covered *'43*
Ship Ahoy *'42*

Akira Kurosawa(1910-98)
The Sea is Watching *'02*
Rhapsody in August *'91*
Akira Kurosawa's Dreams *'90*
Ran *'85*
Kagemusha *'80*
Dersu Uzala *'75*
Dodes 'ka-den *'70*
High & Low *'62*
Sanjuro *'62*
Yojimbo *'61*
The Bad Sleep Well *'60*
The Hidden Fortress *'58*
The Lower Depths *'57*
Throne of Blood *'57*
I Live in Fear *'55*
Seven Samurai *'54*
Ikiru *'52*
Rashomon *'51*
Scandal *'50*
A Quiet Duel *'49*
One Wonderful Sunday *'47*
No Regrets for Our Youth *'46*
The Men Who Tread on the Tiger's Tail *'45*

Kiyoshi Kurosawa(1955-)
Tokyo Sonata *'09*
Retribution *'06*
Bright Future *'03*
Pulse *'01*
Seance *'00*
Charisma *'99*
Cure *'97*

Alex Kurtzman(1973-)
Star Trek *'09*
Transformers: Revenge of the Fallen *'09*
Transformers *'07*
Mission: Impossible 3 *'06*
The Island *'05*
The Legend of Zorro *'05*

Andrew Kurtzman
Down Periscope *'96*
Camp Nowhere *'94*
See No Evil, Hear No Evil *'89*
Number One with a Bullet *'87*

Diane Kurys(1948-)
Children of the Century *'99*
Love After Love *'94*
Six Days, Six Nights *'94*
A Man in Love *'87*
Entre-Nous *'83*
Peppermint Soda *'77*

Tony Kushner(1956-)
Munich *'05*
Angels in America *'03*

Alex Kustanovich
Mirror Wars: Reflection One *'05*
Out of the Cold *'99*

Emir Kusturica(1954-)
Underground *'95*
Arizona Dream *'94*

Richard Kwietniowski(1957-)
Owning Mahowny *'03*
Love and Death on Long Island *'97*

Christopher Kyle
Alexander *'04*
K-19: The Widowmaker *'02*
The Weight of Water *'00*

Gregory La Cava(1892-1952)
My Man Godfrey *'36*
The Half Naked Truth *'32*

Ian La Frenais(1937-)
The Bank Job *'08*
Across the Universe *'07*
Flushed Away *'06*
Goal! The Dream Begins *'06*
Archangel *'05*
Still Crazy *'98*
Excess Baggage *'96*
The Commitments *'91*
Vice Versa *'88*
Water *'85*
Prisoner of Zenda *'79*
It's Not the Size That Counts *'74*
Catch Me a Spy *'71*

Lynda La Plante(1946-)
Widows *'02*
Bella Mafia *'97*
Framed *'93*
Prime Suspect *'92*

Michael LaBash
Lilo & Stitch 2: Stitch Has a Glitch *'05*
Home on the Range *'04*

Jeanne Labrune(1950-)
Vatel *'00*
Sand and Blood *'87*

Neil LaBute(1963-)
The Wicker Man *'06*
The Shape of Things *'03*
Possession *'02*
Your Friends & Neighbors *'98*
In the Company of Men *'96*

Gregory LaCava
See Gregory La Cava

Kathleen Laccinole
Dr. Dolittle 4: Tail to the Chief *'08*
A Dennis the Menace Christmas *'07*

Antoine Lacomblez
Wolves in the Snow *'02*
Love After Love *'94*
Six Days, Six Nights *'94*
Oriana *'85*

Preston Lacy
The Life of Lucky Cucumber *'08*
Jackass Number Two *'06*

Aldo Lado(1934-)
Night Train Murders *'75*
Torture Train *'75*
Who Saw Her Die? *'72*
Short Night of Glass Dolls *'71*

John Lafia
Man's Best Friend *'93*
Child's Play *'88*

Ian LaFrenais
See Ian La Frenais

Jacques Lagrange
Traffic *'71*
Mon Oncle *'58*
Mr. Hulot's Holiday *'53*

Richard LaGravenese(1959-)
Freedom Writers *'07*
P.S. I Love You *'07*
Paris, je t'aime *'06*
Beloved *'98*
Living Out Loud *'98*
The Horse Whisperer *'97*
The Mirror Has Two Faces *'96*
The Bridges of Madison County *'95*
A Little Princess *'95*
Unstrung Heroes *'95*
The Ref *'93*
The Fisher King *'91*
Rude Awakening *'89*

Don Lake(1956-)
Return to Me *'00*
The Extreme Adventures of Super Dave *'98*

Frank Laloggia(1954-)
The Lady in White *'88*
Fear No Evil *'80*

Paul LaLonde
Revelation *'00*
Tribulation *'00*

Peter LaLonde(1960-)
Revelation *'00*
Tribulation *'00*

Oi Wah Lam
Warlords *'08*
Perhaps Love *'05*

Ross LaManna
Rush Hour *'98*
Titanic *'96*
Arctic Blue *'93*

John Lamb
Postmortem *'98*
The Mermaids of Tiburon *'62*

Bruce Lambert
See Godfrey Ho

Gavin Lambert(1924-2005)
Dead on the Money *'91*
Sweet Bird of Youth *'89*
I Never Promised You a Rose Garden *'77*
Inside Daisy Clover *'65*
Roman Spring of Mrs. Stone *'61*

Ken Lamplugh
Body Armour *'07*
Midnight Kiss *'93*
Private Wars *'93*

Bill Lancaster(1947-97)
The Bad News Bears *'05*
The Thing *'82*
The Bad News Bears Go to Japan *'78*
The Bad News Bears *'76*

Richard H. Landau(1914-93)
Frankenstein 1970 *'58*
Race for Life *'55*
Blackout *'54*
Sins of Jezebel *'54*
Spaceways *'53*
A Stolen Face *'52*
The Lost Continent *'51*

James Landis(1926-91)
The Sadist *'63*
Stakeout *'62*

John Landis(1950-)
Blues Brothers 2000 *'98*
Dying to Get Rich *'98*
Clue *'85*
Twilight Zone: The Movie *'83*
An American Werewolf in London *'81*
The Blues Brothers *'80*
Schlock *'73*

Christopher Landon(1975-)
Blood & Chocolate *'07*
Disturbia *'07*
Another Day in Paradise *'98*

Joseph Landon
Von Ryan's Express *'65*
The Hoodlum Priest *'61*

Michael Landon(1936-91)
Sam's Son *'84*
Killing Stone *'78*

Michael Landon, Jr.(1964-)
Love's Unfolding Dream *'07*
Love's Abiding Joy *'06*
Love's Long Journey *'05*
Love's Enduring Promise *'04*
Love Comes Softly *'03*

Fritz Lang(1890-1976)
The Thousand Eyes of Dr. Mabuse *'60*
M *'31*
Metropolis *'26*
Dr. Mabuse, The Gambler *'22*
The Indian Tomb *'21*

Harry Langdon(1884-1944)
Road Show *'41*
The Flying Deuces *'39*

John Langley
Deadly Sins *'95*
The P.O.W. Escape *'86*

Lee Langley
Another Woman *'94*
A Woman of Substance *'84*

Noel Langley(1911-80)
Snow White and the Three Stooges *'61*
The Search for Bridey Murphy *'56*
The Adventures of Sadie *'55*
Svengali *'55*
Ivanhoe *'52*
A Christmas Carol *'51*
They Made Me a Fugitive *'47*
The Wizard of Oz *'39*
Maytime *'37*
King of the Damned *'36*

Arlette Langmann
Frontier of Dawn *'08*
Germinal *'93*
A Nos Amours *'84*
Loulou *'80*

Kate Lanier
Beauty Shop *'05*
Glitter *'01*
The Mod Squad *'99*
Set It Off *'96*
What's Love Got to Do with It? *'93*

T.L. Lankford
Storm Trooper *'98*
Hollywood Chainsaw Hookers *'88*
Phantom Empire *'87*

Ring Lardner, Jr.(1915-2000)
The Greatest *'77*
M*A*S*H *'70*

The Cincinnati Kid '65
Forever Amber '47
Cloak and Dagger '46
Laura '44
Tomorrow the World '44
Woman of the Year '42

John Larkin

The Dolly Sisters '46
Castle in the Desert '42
Dead Men Tell '41
Charlie Chan at Treasure Island '39

Glen Larson(1937-)

The Darwin Conspiracy '99
Magnum P.I.: Don't Eat the Snow in Hawaii '80
Battlestar Galactica '78
Mission Galactica: The Cylon Attack '78

Louis LaRusso, II(1935-2003)

The Closer '91
Hell Hunters '87

James Lasdun(1958-)

Signs & Wonders '00
Sunday '96

Alex Lasker

Tears of the Sun '03
Beyond Rangoon '95

Lawrence Lasker(1949-)

Sneakers '92
Project X '87
WarGames '83

Andrew Laskos

A Face to Kill For '99
A Prayer in the Dark '97

Jesse Lasky, Jr.(1910-88)

John Paul Jones '59
The Ten Commandments '56
Unconquered '47
Reap the Wild Wind '42
Back in the Saddle '41
Union Pacific '39

Louise Lasser(1939-)

Just Me & You '78
What's Up, Tiger Lily? '66

Aaron Latham

The Program '93
Perfect '85
Urban Cowboy '80

Jonathan Latimer(1906-83)

The Big Clock '48
Nocturne '46
The Glass Key '42
Topper Returns '41

Steve Latshaw(1959-)

Command Performance '09
Scorcher '02
U.S. Navy SEALS: Dead or Alive '02
U.S. SEALs: Dead or Alive '02
Black Horizon '01
Ablaze '00
Mach 2 '00
Rangers '00
Submerged '00
Counter Measures '99
Militia '99
Invisible Dad '97
Scorpio One '97

Greg Latter

The Color of Freedom '07
Dangerous Ground '96
Cyborg Cop '93

Michael Laughlin

Town and Country '01
Mesmerized '84
Strange Behavior '81

Tom Laughlin(1939-)

The Trial of Billy Jack '74
Billy Jack '71
Born Losers '67

Frank Launder(1907-97)

Geordie '55
The Belles of St. Trinian's '53
The Happiest Days of Your Life '50
Captain Boycott '47
Night Train to Munich '40
The Lady Vanishes '38

Dale Launer(1952-)

Love Potion #9 '92
My Cousin Vinny '92
Dirty Rotten Scoundrels '88
Blind Date '87

Salvatore Laurani(1924-)

Confessions of a Police Captain '72
A Bullet for the General '68

Guillaume Laurant

Micmacs '09
Amelie '01

S.K. Lauren(1893-1979)

When Ladies Meet '41
Crime and Punishment '35

Christine Laurent(1948-)

The Story of Marie and Julien '03
Va Savoir '01
Jeanne la Pucelle '94
La Belle Noiseuse '90

Arthur Laurents(1918-)

Gypsy '93
The Turning Point '77
The Way We Were '73
Gypsy '62
Bonjour Tristesse '57
Anastasia '56
Rope '48

Peter Lauterman

Recipe for Revenge '98
This Matter of Marriage '98
The Waiting Game '98

Russell Lavalle

Secret Games 2: The Escort '93
Sins of the Night '93

Paul Laverty(1957-)

Looking for Eric '09
The Wind That Shakes the Barley '06
Sweet Sixteen '02
Bread and Roses '00
My Name Is Joe '98
Carla's Song '97

George LaVoo

Blood Monkey '07
Real Women Have Curves '02
Frisk '95

Evan Law

Hero Wanted '08
Hero Wanted '08

William Lawlor

Mexican Blow '02
The Underground '97

Bruno Lawrence(1941-95)

The Quiet Earth '85
Smash Palace '82

John Lawrence(1931-92)

Cycle Psycho '72
The Incredible Two-Headed Transplant '71

Marc Lawrence(1959-)

Did You Hear About the Morgans? '09
Music & Lyrics '07
Miss Congeniality 2: Armed and Fabulous '05
Two Weeks Notice '02
Miss Congeniality '00
Forces of Nature '99
The Out-of-Towners '99
Life with Mikey '93

Martin Lawrence(1965-)

A Thin Line Between Love and Hate '96
You So Crazy '94

Vincent Lawrence(1890-1946)

Adventure '45
Hands Across the Table '35
Now and Forever '34
Night After Night '32
Sinners in the Sun '32

John Lawson

Fatal Combat '96
Jungle Boy '96

John Howard Lawson(1894-1977)

Cry, the Beloved Country '51
Smash-Up: The Story of a Woman '47
Action in the North Atlantic '43
Sahara '43
Bachelor Apartment '31

J.F. Lawton(1960-)

DOA: Dead or Alive '06
Chain Reaction '96
Blankman '94
The Hunted '94
Under Siege '92
Mistress '91
Pizza Man '91
Pretty Woman '90
Cannibal Women in the Avocado Jungle of Death '89

Beirne Lay, Jr.(1909-82)

The Gallant Hours '60
Above and Beyond '53
Twelve o'Clock High '49

Cooper Layne

The Fog '05
The Core '03

Charles Lazar

Diamond Girl '98
Loving Evangeline '98

Michael Lazarou

Possessed '00
Heat Wave '90

Martin Lazarus

Deep Core '00
Interceptor Force '99

Philip LaZebnik

Mulan '98
Pocahontas '95

Alain Le Henry

A Self-Made Hero '95
Subway '85

Didier Le Pecheur(1959-)

Harrison's Flowers '02
Don't Let Me Die on a Sunday '98

Paul Leadon

Back of Beyond '95
Around the World in 80 Ways '86

Larry Leahy

Confessions of a Hit Man '94
The Lawless Land '88

David Lean(1908-91)

A Passage to India '84
Summertime '55
Oliver Twist '48
This Happy Breed '47
Brief Encounter '46
Great Expectations '46

Norman Lear(1922-)

Cold Turkey '71
The Night They Raided Minsky's '69
Divorce American Style '67
Come Blow Your Horn '63

Charles Leavitt

The Express '08
Blood Diamond '06
K-PAX '01
The Mighty '98
Sunchaser '96

Keith Ross Leckie

Shattered City: The Halifax Explosion '03
To Walk with Lions '99
Lost in the Barrens '91
Where the Spirit Lives '89

Patrice Leconte(1947-)

My Best Friend '06
Intimate Strangers '04
The Perfume of Yvonne '94
The Hairdresser's Husband '92
Monsieur Hire '89

Jacques LeCotier

See Jerry Warren

Paul Leder(1926-96)

Killing Obsession '94
The Baby Doll Murders '92
Exiled in America '90
Murder by Numbers '89
A*P*E* '76

Reuben Leder(1950-)

Molly and Gina '94
A*P*E* '76

Charles Lederer(1911-76)

A Global Affair '63
Mutiny on the Bounty '62
Follow That Dream '61
Ocean's 11 '60
Kismet '55
Gentlemen Prefer Blondes '53
Monkey Business '52
The Thing '51
I Was a Male War Bride '49
Comrade X '40
His Girl Friday '40
Broadway Serenade '39
Double or Nothing '37

Richard Ledes

The Caller '08
A Hole in One '04

Ang Lee(1954-)

Eat Drink Man Woman '94
The Wedding Banquet '93
Pushing Hands '92

Bruce Lee(1940-73)

Circle of Iron '78
Fists of Fury '73
Return of the Dragon '73

Connie Lee

Footlight Glamour '43
It's a Great Life '43
Blondie for Victory '42
Blondie's Blessed Event '42

Damian Lee

Agent Red '00
Specimen '97
Deadly Heroes '96
Fatal Combat '96
Jungle Boy '96
When the Bullet Hits the Bone '96
Electra '95
Street Law '95
The Killing Man '94
Abraxas: Guardian of the Universe '90
Circle Man '87

Gregory Lee

I'll Believe You '07
Deadly Heroes '96

Lilian Lee

Three ... Extremes '04
Farewell My Concubine '93

Malcolm Lee(1970-)

Welcome Home Roscoe Jenkins '08
The Best Man '99

Mark Lee(1958-)

Fortunes of War '94
The Next Karate Kid '94

Mu-yeong Lee

Sympathy for Mr. Vengeance '02
JSA: Joint Security Area '00

Robert N. Lee(1890-1964)

The Tower of London '39
Badmen of Nevada '33
The Kennel Murder Case '33
The Charlatan '29

Spike Lee(1957-)

She Hate Me '04
Bamboozled '00
Summer of Sam '99
He Got Game '98
Clockers '95
Malcolm X '92
Jungle Fever '91
Mo' Better Blues '90
Do the Right Thing '89
School Daze '88
She's Gotta Have It '86
Joe's Bed-Stuy Barbershop: We Cut Heads '83

Suh-Goon Lee

301/302 '95
301/302 '95
301, 302 '94

Timothy Lee

2103: Deadly Wake '97
Street Gun '96

William Lee

The Pact '99
Psychopath '97

Won-jae Lee

The City of Violence '06
Blood Rain '05

Tony Leech

Hoodwinked Too! Hood vs. Evil '10
Hoodwinked '05

Robert Lees(1912-2004)

Abbott and Costello Meet the Invisible Man '51
Comin' Round the Mountain '51
Abbott and Costello Meet Frankenstein '48
Buck Privates Come Home '47
Crazy House '43
The Black Cat '41
Hold That Ghost '41
The Invisible Woman '40

Michael Leeson

The Tuxedo '02
What Planet Are You From? '00
I.Q. '94
The War of the Roses '89
Survivors '83
Jekyll & Hyde... Together Again '82

Peter Lefcourt

Danielle Steel's Fine Things '90
May Wine '90

Philippe Lefebvre

Tell No One '06
Whatever You Say '02

Ernest Lehman(1915-2005)

Black Sunday '77
Family Plot '76
Portnoy's Complaint '72
Hello, Dolly! '69
Who's Afraid of Virginia Woolf? '66
The Sound of Music '65
The Prize '63
West Side Story '61
From the Terrace '60
North by Northwest '59
Sweet Smell of Success '57
The King and I '56
Somebody Up There Likes Me '56
Executive Suite '54
Sabrina '54

Gladys Lehman(1892-1993)

Luxury Liner '48
Nice Girl? '41
Blondie Brings Up Baby '39
Death Takes a Holiday '34
Little Miss Marker '34

Jerry Leichtling(1948-)

Blue Sky '91
Peggy Sue Got Married '86

Mike Leigh(1943-)

Happy-Go-Lucky '08
Vera Drake '04
All or Nothing '02
Topsy Turvy '99
Career Girls '97
Secrets and Lies '95
Naked '93
Life Is Sweet '90
High Hopes '88
Home Sweet Home '82
Grown Ups '80
Who's Who '78
Kiss of Death '77
Nuts in May '76
Bleak Moments '71

Rowland Leigh

The Master Race '44
Summer Storm '44
The Charge of the Light Brigade '36

Warren Leight

Dear God '96
The Night We Never Met '93
Mother's Day '80

David Leland(1947-)

Virgin Territory '07
White River '99
The Land Girls '98
Personal Services '87
Wish You Were Here '87
Mona Lisa '86

Claude Lelouch(1937-)

Roman de Gare '07
And Now Ladies and Gentlemen '02
Les Miserables '95
Bandits '86
A Man and a Woman: 20 Years Later '86
Bolero '82
Cat and Mouse '78
Robert et Robert '78
Another Man, Another Chance '77
And Now My Love '74
Happy New Year '73
A Man and a Woman '66

Alan LeMay(1899-1964)

High Lonesome '50
Rocky Mountain '50
The Adventures of Mark Twain '44
The Story of Dr. Wassell '44
Reap the Wild Wind '42

Jonathan Lemkin

Shooter '07
Red Planet '00
The Devil's Advocate '97

Steve Lemme(1973-)

Beerfest '06
Club Dread '04
Super Troopers '01

James (Momel) Lemmo(1949-)

Nowhere in Sight '01
Bodily Harm '95
Relentless 3 '93
We're Talkin' Serious Money '92

Kay Lenard(1911-97)

The Kettles in the Ozarks '56
Ma and Pa Kettle at Home '54

Vicente Lenero(1933-)

The Crime of Father Amaro '02
Midaq Alley '95

Nathan Long
The Sender '98
Guyver 2: Dark Hero '94

Sheryl Longin
Dick '99
Lies and Whispers '98

Harry S. Longstreet
Wounded '97
A Vow to Kill '94
Sex, Love and Cold Hard Cash '93

Renee Longstreet
Double Platinum '99
A Vow to Kill '94
Undesirable '92

Stephen Longstreet(1907-2002)
The Helen Morgan Story '57
Silver River '48

Anita Loos(1888-1981)
I Married an Angel '42
They Met in Bombay '41
When Ladies Meet '41
Susan and God '40
The Women '39
Saratoga '37
San Francisco '36
The Girl from Missouri '34
The Barbarian '33
Hold Your Man '33
Red Headed Woman '32
Struggle '31
His Picture in the Papers '16
Matrimaniac '16

Mary Loos(1910-2004)
A Woman's World '54
Ticket to Tomahawk '50
When Willie Comes Marching Home '50
Father Was a Fullback '49
The Dude Goes West '48

Matt Lopez
The Sorcerer's Apprentice '10
Race to Witch Mountain '09
Bedtime Stories '08

Phillips Lord(1902-75)
Guns Don't Argue '57
Gang Busters '42

Robert Lord(1900-76)
Stage Struck '36
Heroes for Sale '33
The Little Giant '33
20,000 Years in Sing Sing '33
Frisco Jenny '32
One Way Passage '32
The Purchase Price '32
Big Business Girl '31
On with the Show '29

Dean Lorey(1967-)
Major Payne '95
Jason Goes to Hell: The Final Friday '93
My Boyfriend's Back '93

Hope Loring(1894-1959)
It '27
My Best Girl '27
Wings '27
Shadows '22

Ye Lou
Summer Palace '06
Purple Butterfly '03

David Loucka
Borderline '02
Eddie '96
The Dream Team '89

David Loughery
Obsessed '09
Lakeview Terrace '08
Money Train '95
Tom and Huck '95
The Three Musketeers '93
Passenger 57 '92
Star Trek 5: The Final Frontier '89

Pavel (Lungin) Lounguine(1949-)
Luna Park '91
Taxi Blues '90

Eric Louzil(1951-)
Class of Nuke 'Em High 2: Subhumanoid Meltdown '91
Fortress of Amerikka '89

Nick Love
Outlaw '07
The Business '05

Robert Lovy
Plughead Rewired: Circuitry Man 2 '94
Circuitry Man '90

Steven Lovy
Plughead Rewired: Circuitry Man 2 '94
Circuitry Man '90

Edward T. Lowe(1890-1973)
House of Dracula '45
House of Frankenstein '44
Bulldog Drummond Escapes '37
Charlie Chan at the Race Track '36
Charlie Chan in Shanghai '35
Curtain at Eight '33
The Crusader '32
The Midnight Lady '32
Tangled Destinies '32
The Vampire Bat '32
Undertow '30
Head Winds '25
The Hunchback of Notre Dame '23

Sherman Lowe(1894-1968)
The Undercover Woman '46
Yank in Libya '42
Arizona Cyclone '41
Bury Me Not on the Lone Prairie '41
The Masked Rider '41
Law and Order '40
Pony Post '40
Frolics on Ice '39
Devil Diamond '37
They Never Come Back '32

Jeff Lowell
Hotel for Dogs '09
Over Her Dead Body '08
John Tucker Must Die '06

Richard Lowenstein(1959-)
He Died With a Felafel in His Hand '01
Dogs in Space '87

Andrew Lowery(1970-)
Boys and Girls '00
Simon Sez '99

Sam Lowry
See Steven Soderbergh

John Loy
Beethoven's 4th '01
The Land Before Time 6: The Secret of Saurus Rock '98
The Land Before Time 5: The Mysterious Island '97
The Land Before Time 3: The Time of the Great Giving '95

Ernst Lubitsch(1892-1947)
To Be or Not to Be '42
The Smiling Lieutenant '31

Craig Lucas(1950-)
The Dying Gaul '05
The Secret Lives of Dentists '02
Reckless '95
Prelude to a Kiss '92
Longtime Companion '90

George Lucas(1944-)
Star Wars: Episode 3—Revenge of the Sith '05
Star Wars: Episode 2—Attack of the Clones '02
Star Wars: Episode 1—The Phantom Menace '99
Return of the Jedi '83
Raiders of the Lost Ark '81
Star Wars '77
American Graffiti '73
THX 1138 '71

Jon Lucas
Ghosts of Girlfriends Past '09
The Hangover '09
Four Christmases '08
Full of It '07
Rebound '05
Rustin '01

Ralph Lucas
Planet of the Dinosaurs '80
The Child '76

Daniele Luchetti(1960-)
My Brother Is an Only Child '07
Ginger and Cinnamon '03

Werner Jorg Luddecke
The Indian Tomb '59
Tiger of Eschnapur '59

John Ludin
The Land Before Time 3: The Time of the Great Giving '95
The Land Before Time 2: The Great Valley Adventure '94

Graham Ludlow
Storm Cell '08
Jack London's The Call of the Wild '97

William Ludwig(1912-99)
Gun Glory '57
Ten Thousand Bedrooms '57
Interrupted Melody '55
Oklahoma! '55
Athena '54
The Merry Widow '52
It's a Big Country '51
The Sun Comes Up '49
The Hills of Home '48

Kurt Luedtke
Random Hearts '99
Out of Africa '85
Absence of Malice '81

Baz Luhrmann(1962-)
Australia '08
Moulin Rouge '01
William Shakespeare's Romeo and Juliet '96
Strictly Ballroom '92

Eric Luke
Gargoyles, The Movie: The Heroes Awaken '94
Still Not Quite Human '92
Explorers '85

Sergei Lukyanenko
Day Watch '06
Night Watch '04

Jenny Lumet(1967-)
Remember Me '10
Rachel Getting Married '08

Sidney Lumet(1924-)
Find Me Guilty '06
Night Falls on Manhattan '96
Q & A '90
Prince of the City '81

Bigas Luna(1946-)
The Chambermaid on the Titanic '97
Jamon, Jamon '93
Anguish '88
Reborn '81

Dolph Lundgren(1959-)
Command Performance '09
Missionary Man '07

Ida Lupino(1914-95)
Private Hell 36 '54
The Hitch-Hiker '53
Streets of Sin '49

Rod Lurie(1962-)
Nothing But the Truth '08
The Contender '00
Deterrence '00

Patrick Lussier
Dracula 3: Legacy '05
Dracula 2: Ascension '03

Arnost Lustig
A Prayer for Katarina Horovitzova '69
Diamonds of the Night '64

Jan Lustig(1902-79)
The Story of Three Loves '53
Young Bess '53
Homecoming '48
The White Cliffs of Dover '44

Karen McCullah Lutz
The House Bunny '08
She's the Man '06
Ella Enchanted '04
Legally Blonde '01
Ten Things I Hate about You '99

David Lynch(1946-)
Inland Empire '06
Mulholland Drive '01
Lost Highway '96
Twin Peaks: Fire Walk with Me '92
Wild at Heart '90
Blue Velvet '86
Dune '84
The Elephant Man '80
Eraserhead '78

Barre Lyndon(1896-1972)
Man in the Attic '53
The War of the Worlds '53
To Please a Lady '50
Hangover Square '45
House on 92nd Street '45

Jonathan Lynn(1943-)
Nuns on the Run '90
Clue '85

Fibe Ma
Mr. Nice Guy '98
Rumble in the Bronx '96
Supercop '92

Jingle Ma
Seoul Raiders '05
Silver Hawk '04

Dick Maas(1951-)
The Shaft '01
Amsterdamned '88

John Maass(1960-)
The Last Debate '00
Curdled '95

Charles MacArthur(1895-1956)
Wuthering Heights '39
Twentieth Century '34
Rasputin and the Empress '33

Richard Macaulay
Across the Pacific '42
Manpower '41
Out of the Fog '41
Torrid Zone '40
The Roaring Twenties '39
Hard to Get '38
Hollywood Hotel '37
Varsity Show '37

Ruggero Maccari
The Family '87
A Special Day '77
Down & Dirty '76
The Scent of a Woman '75

Nora MacCoby
Buffalo Soldiers '01
Bongwater '98

Ian MacDonald(1914-78)
Silver Star '55
Montana '50

Philip MacDonald(1901-80)
Love from a Stranger '47
The Body Snatcher '45
Mr. Moto Takes a Vacation '39
Mr. Takes a Vacation '39
Mysterious Mr. Moto '38
River of Unrest '36
The Last Outpost '35
Charlie Chan in London '34

Sharman MacDonald
The Edge of Love '08
The Winter Guest '97

Ranald MacDougall(1915-73)
Queen Bee '55
We're No Angels '55
I'll Never Forget You '51
Bright Leaf '50
June Bride '48
The Unsuspected '47
Mildred Pierce '45
Objective, Burma! '45

Willard Mack
It's a Great Life '29
The Monster '25

Aeneas MacKenzie(1889-1962)
The Ten Commandments '56
Fighting Seabees '44
They Died with Their Boots On '41

David Mackenzie(1966-)
Mister Foe '07
Young Adam '03

Billy Mackinnon
Hideous Kinky '99
Small Faces '95

Patricia MacLachlan(1938-)
Baby '00
Journey '95
Sarah, Plain and Tall: Skylark '93

Bernard MacLaverty(1942-)
Hostages '93
The Real Charlotte '91
Lamb '85
Cal '84

Alistair MacLean(1922-87)
Breakheart Pass '76
When Eight Bells Toll '71
Where Eagles Dare '68

Andrew Maclear
The Man Who Made Husbands Jealous '98
Dealers '89

Angus MacPhail(1903-62)
Dead of Night '45
The Foreman Went to France '42

Don MacPherson
The Avengers '98
The Big Man: Crossing the Line '91
Absolute Beginners '86

Jeanie Macpherson
Male and Female '19
The Little American '17

Earl MacRauch
Wired '89
The Adventures of Buckaroo Banzai Across the Eighth Dimension '84

William H. Macy(1950-)
A Slight Case of Murder '99
The Con '98

Guy Maddin(1956-)
Brand Upon the Brain! '06
The Saddest Music in the World '03
Careful '92
Tales from the Gimli Hospital '88

Brent Maddock
Wild Wild West '99
Tremors 2: Aftershocks '96
Heart and Souls '93
Ghost Dad '90
Tremors '89
Short Circuit 2 '88
*batteries not included '87
Short Circuit '86

Ben Maddow(1909-92)
The Chairman '69
The Secret of Santa Vittoria '69
The Balcony '63
Men in War '57
The Asphalt Jungle '50

Robert Madero
All Tied Up '92
Mausoleum '83

Jose Maesso
Blue Jeans and Dynamite '76
Django '68

David Magee(1962-)
Miss Pettigrew Lives for a Day '08
Finding Neverland '04

Doug Magee
Beyond the Call '96
Cold Light of Day '95
Somebody Has to Shoot the Picture '90

Maria Maggenti(1962-)
Puccini for Beginners '06
The Love Letter '99
The Incredibly True Adventure of Two Girls in Love '95

Joe Maggio
Milk and Honey '03
Virgil Bliss '01

Jeff Maguire
Gridiron Gang '06
Timeline '03
In the Line of Fire '93
Victory '81

Redge Mahaffey
First Encounter '97
Life 101 '95
Quest of the Delta Knights '93
Deadly Rivals '92

John Lee Mahin(1902-84)
Moment to Moment '66
The Horse Soldiers '59
No Time for Sergeants '58
Heaven Knows, Mr. Allison '57
The Bad Seed '56
Mogambo '53
Johnny Eager '42
Dr. Jekyll and Mr. Hyde '41
Boom Town '40
The Last Gangster '37
The Devil Is a Sissy '36
Love on the Run '36
Wife Versus Secretary '36
The Beast of the City '32
Red Dust '32

Wilkie Mahoney(1897-1976)
Whistling in Brooklyn '43
Whistling in Dixie '42

Richard Maibaum(1909-91)
License to Kill '89
The Living Daylights '87
S*H*E '79
The Spy Who Loved Me '77
On Her Majesty's Secret Service '69

Thunderball '65
Goldfinger '64
From Russia with Love '63
Dr. No '62
The Great Gatsby '49
O.S.S. '46

Norman Mailer(1923-2007)
Master Spy: The Robert Hanssen Story '02
American Tragedy '00
King Lear '87
Tough Guys Don't Dance '87

David Main
Find the Lady '76
It Seemed Like a Good Idea at the Time '75
Vengeance Is Mine '74

Daniel Mainwaring(1902-77)
Atlantis, the Lost Continent '61
The George Raft Story '61
Space Master X-7 '58
Invasion of the Body Snatchers '56
An Annapolis Story '55
A Bullet for Joey '55
The Hitch-Hiker '53
Bugles in the Afternoon '52
This Woman Is Dangerous '52
Cavalry Charge '51
Big Steal '49
Big Town '47
Out of the Past '47
Swamp Fire '46
Treasure of Fear '45
Dangerous Passage '44

Arduino (Dino) Maiuri(1916-84)
Chino '75
Street Law '74
Companeros '70
Danger: Diabolik '68

Majid Majidi(1959-)
Baran '01
The Color of Paradise '99
Children of Heaven '98

Siu Fai Mak
Infernal Affairs 2 '03
Infernal Affairs 3 '03

Dusan Makavejev(1932-)
Montenegro '81
Sweet Movie '75
WR: Mysteries of the Organism '71
Innocence Unprotected '68
The Love Affair, or The Case of the Missing Switchboard Operator '67
Man Is Not a Bird '65

Mohsen Makhmalbaf(1957-)
Kandahar '01
Gabbeh '96

James Makichuk
Maiden Voyage: Ocean Hijack '04
Greenmail '01

Terrence Malick(1943-)
The New World '05
The Thin Red Line '98
Days of Heaven '78
Badlands '74
Pocket Money '72

Robert Malkani
The Chaos Experiment '09
Dot.Kill '05

Laurence Malkin
Five Fingers '06
Soul Assassin '01

Louis Malle(1932-95)
May Fools '90
Au Revoir les Enfants '87
Murmur of the Heart '71
Spirits of the Dead '68
The Thief of Paris '67

Viva Maria! '65
The Fire Within '64
Zazie dans le Metro '61
The Lovers '59

Miles Malleson(1888-1969)
The Thief of Bagdad '40
Nine Days a Queen '36
Lorna Doone '34
Night Birds '31

Tom Malloy
The Alphabet Killer '08
The Attic '06

Mark Malone
Dead Heat '01
Hoods '98
Bulletproof Heart '95
Signs of Life '89
Dead of Winter '87

H.F. Maltby(1880-1963)
Crimes at the Dark House '39
Ticket of Leave Man '37

Albert (John B. Sherry) Maltz(1908-85)
The Beguiled '70
Two Mules for Sister Sara '70
The Robe '53
Broken Arrow '50
The Naked City '48
Cloak and Dagger '46
Pride of the Marines '45
This Gun for Hire '42

David Mamet(1947-)
Redbelt '08
Edmond '05
Spartan '04
Hannibal '01
Heist '01
Lakeboat '00
State and Main '00
Lansky '99
Ronin '98
The Winslow Boy '98
The Edge '97
The Spanish Prisoner '97
Wag the Dog '97
American Buffalo '95
Oleanna '94
Vanya on 42nd Street '94
A Life in the Theater '93
Glengarry Glen Ross '92
Hoffa '92
The Water Engine '92
Homicide '91
We're No Angels '89
Things Change '88
House of Games '87
The Untouchables '87
The Verdict '82
The Postman Always Rings Twice '81

Chan Man-keung
Kung Fu Hustle '04
Summer Snow '94

Milcho Manchevski(1959-)
Shadows '07
Dust '01
Before the Rain '94

Don Mancini(1963-)
Seed of Chucky '04
Bride of Chucky '98
Child's Play 3 '91
Child's Play 2 '90
Child's Play '88

Babaloo Mandel(1949-)
Fever Pitch '05
Robots '05
Where the Heart Is '00
EDtv '99
Father's Day '96
Multiplicity '96
Forget Paris '95
City Slickers 2: The Legend of Curly's Gold '94
Greedy '94
A League of Their Own '92
Mr. Saturday Night '92
City Slickers '91

Parenthood '89
Vibes '88
Gung Ho '85
Spies Like Us '85
Splash '84
Night Shift '82

David Mandel(1971-)
Eurotrip '04
Dr. Seuss' The Cat in the Hat '03

Neil Mandt(1969-)
Last Stop for Paul '08
Hijacking Hollywood '97

Matt Manfredi
Clash of the Titans '10
Aeon Flux '05
crazy/beautiful '01

James Mangold(1964-)
Walk the Line '05
Kate & Leopold '01
Girl, Interrupted '99
Cop Land '97
Heavy '94
Oliver & Company '88

Herman J. Mankiewicz(1897-1953)
Pride of St. Louis '52
A Woman's Secret '49
The Pride of the Yankees '42
Citizen Kane '41
Dinner at Eight '33
Lost Squadron '32

Joseph L. Mankiewicz(1909-93)
The Honey Pot '67
Cleopatra '63
Guys and Dolls '55
The Barefoot Contessa '54
Julius Caesar '53
People Will Talk '51
All About Eve '50
No Way Out '50
A Letter to Three Wives '49
Dragonwyck '46
Somewhere in the Night '46
The Keys of the Kingdom '44
Forsaking All Others '35
I Live My Life '35
Manhattan Melodrama '34
Diplomaniacs '33

Tom Mankiewicz(1942-)
Dragnet '87
Ladyhawke '85
The Eagle Has Landed '77
The Cassandra Crossing '76
Mother, Jugs and Speed '76
The Man with the Golden Gun '74
Live and Let Die '73
Diamonds Are Forever '71

Wolf Mankowitz(1925-98)
Casino Royale '67
Waltz of the Toreadors '62
The Day the Earth Caught Fire '61
The Two Faces of Dr. Jekyll '60
Expresso Bongo '59
A Kid for Two Farthings '55

Abby Mann(1927-2008)
Whitewash: The Clarence Brandley Story '02
Indictment: The McMartin Trial '95
Murderers Among Us: The Simon Wiesenthal Story '89
King '78
Report to the Commissioner '74
The Detective '68
Ship of Fools '65
A Child Is Waiting '63
Judgment at Nuremberg '61

Edward Andrew (Santos Alcocer) Mann(1923-95)
Seizure '74
The Freakmaker '73

Cauldron of Blood '67
Hallucination '67

Michael Mann(1943-)
Miami Vice '06
Ali '01
The Insider '99
Heat '95
The Last of the Mohicans '92
Manhunter '86
The Keep '83
Thief '81
Vegas '78

Stanley Mann(1928-)
Conan the Destroyer '84
Firestarter '84
Eye of the Needle '81
Meteor '79
The Collector '65
Woman of Straw '64
The Mouse That Roared '59

Albert Mannheimer(1913-72)
Born Yesterday '50
Three Daring Daughters '48
Whistling in the Dark '41

Bruce Manning(1902-65)
Back Street '41
Spring Parade '40
First Love '39
Three Smart Girls Grow Up '39
Mad About Music '38
That Certain Age '38
100 Men and a Girl '37

Graeme Manson
Cube '98
Rupert's Land '98

John Mantley(1920-2003)
My Blood Runs Cold '65
The 27th Day '57

Braulio Mantovani
The Year My Parents Went on Vacation '07
City of God '02

Guido Manuli
Volere Volare '92
Allegro Non Troppo '76

Russell V. Manzatt
Trapper County War '89
Rush Week '88
Long Shot Kids '81

Rene Manzor(1959-)
Monsieur N. '03
Legends of the North '95

Patrick Marber(1964-)
Notes on a Scandal '06
Asylum '05
Closer '04

Joseph Moncure March(1899-1977)
Wagons Westward '40
Two Alone '34
Hoopla '33
Hell's Angels '30

Gilles Marchand(1963-)
Lemming '05
Bon Voyage '03
With a Friend Like Harry '00

Francesca Marciano(1955-)
Don't Tell '05
I'm Not Scared '03
Iris Blond '98

Max Marcin(1879-1948)
Gambling Ship '33
King of the Jungle '33

David Marconi
Enemy of the State '98
The Harvest '92

Art Marcum
Iron Man '08
Punisher: War Zone '08

Lawrence B. Marcus(1917-2001)
The Stunt Man '80
Justine '69
Petulia '68

Mitch Marcus
The Haunting of Hell House '99
A Boy Called Hate '95
The Force '94

Andreas Marfori
Desperate Crimes '93
Evil Clutch '89

Antonio Margheriti
See Anthony M. Dawson

Herbert Margolis
The Kettles on Old MacDonald's Farm '57
Francis in the Haunted House '56
Pier 23 '51
Roaring City '51
Ma and Pa Kettle '49
Smart Woman '48

Paul B. Margolis
Dr. Jekyll and Mr. Hyde '08
Ticker '01

Donald Margulies
Collected Stories '02
Dinner with Friends '01

A. L. Mariaux
See Jess (Jesus) Franco

Richard "Cheech" Marin(1946-)
Born in East L.A. '87
Cheech and Chong's The Corsican Brothers '84
Cheech and Chong: Still Smokin' '83
Cheech and Chong: Things Are Tough All Over '82
Cheech and Chong's Nice Dreams '81
Cheech and Chong's Next Movie '80
Cheech and Chong's Up in Smoke '79

Ken Marino(1968-)
Role Models '08
The Ten '07

Frances Marion(1888-1973)
Camille '36
Dinner at Eight '33
The Champ '32
The Big House '30
Let Us Be Gay '30
The Wind '28
The Red Mill '27
Son of the Sheik '26
The Winning of Barbara Worth '26
Lazybones '25
The Love Light '21
Pollyanna '20
Amarilly of Clothesline Alley '18
Stella Maris '18
Tillie Wakes Up '17

Petros Markaris(1937-)
Weeping Meadow '04
Ulysses' Gaze '95

Gene Markey(1895-1980)
On the Avenue '37
Girl's Dormitory '36
Baby Face '33
Female '33
Midnight Mary '33

Mitch Markowitz
Crazy People '90
Good Morning, Vietnam '87

Clarence Marks(1893-1972)
Terror of Tiny Town '38
The Love Trap '29

Jack Marks(1895-1987)
Old Mother Riley, Headmistress '50

Old Mother Riley's New Venture '49

Ben Markson(1892-1971)
Lady Killer '33
Lucky Devils '33
What Price Hollywood? '32

Christopher Markus
The Chronicles of Narnia: Prince Caspian '08
You Kill Me '07
The Chronicles of Narnia: The Lion, the Witch and the Wardrobe '05

Russell P. Marleau(1965-)
The Curiosity of Chance '06
3-Way '04

Andrew Marlowe
Hollow Man '00
End of Days '99
Air Force One '97

Brad (Sean) Marlowe
Object of Obsession '95
At Home with the Webbers '94

Malcolm Marmorstein
Dead Men Don't Die '91
Konrad '85
Return from Witch Mountain '78
Pete's Dragon '77
Mary, Mary, Bloody Mary '76
Whiffs '75
S*P*Y*S '74

Franco Marotta
The Sicilian Connection '85
Deadly Mission '78

Henri Marquet
Mr. Hulot's Holiday '53
Jour de Fete '48

Garry Marshall(1934-)
The Other Sister '98
The Flamingo Kid '84
Evil Roy Slade '71
The Grasshopper '69

Neil Marshall(1970-)
Doomsday '08
The Descent '05
Dog Soldiers '01
Killing Time '97
The Flamingo Kid '84

Roger Marshall(1934-)
And Now the Screaming Starts '73
Theatre of Death '67

Steve Marshall
Revenge of the Nerds 2: Nerds in Paradise '87
Laboratory '80

Tonie Marshall
Venus Beauty Institute '98
Pas Tres Catholique '93

Joshua Marston(1968-)
New York, I Love You '09
Maria Full of Grace '04

William Martell
The Base '99
Black Thunder '98
Steel Sharks '97
Crash Dive '96
Invisible Mom '96
Cyberzone '95
Virtual Combat '95
Hard Evidence '94
Victim of Desire '94

Peter Marthesheimer
Veronika Voss '82
The Marriage of Maria Braun '79

Al Martin(1897-1971)
Invasion of the Saucer Men '57
Money Madness '47
Blondie Knows Best '46
Stagecoach Buckaroo '42

Flying Wild '41
The Invisible Ghost '41
The Shadow Strikes '37
Kelly of the Secret Service '36
The Law Rides '36
Prison Shadows '36

Charles Martin(1910-83)
How to Seduce a Woman '74
Dead Right '68
My Dear Secretary '49

Darnell Martin
Cadillac Records '08
I Like It Like That '94

Donald Martin
Celine '08
The Christmas Choir '08
Dim Sum Funeral '08
Ebenezer '97
Spenser: A Savage Place '94

Francis Martin
One Night in the Tropics '40
The Big Broadcast of 1938 '38
College Swing '38
Waikiki Wedding '37
The Princess Comes Across '36
Rhythm on the Range '36
Strike Me Pink '36
Mississippi '35
We're Not Dressing '34

Gregory Mars Martin
See Mars Callahan

Helen Martin(1909-2000)
The Lady Confesses '45
The Invisible Ghost '41

John Benjamin Martin
Before I Say Goodbye '03
We'll Meet Again '02
Wishmaster 4: The Prophecy Fulfilled '02
The House Next Door '01

Mardik Martin(1937-)
Raging Bull '80
New York, New York '77
Valentino '77
Mean Streets '73

Robert Martin(1948-)
Basket Case 3: The Progeny '92
Frankenhooker '90

Steve Martin(1945-)
The Pink Panther 2 '09
The Pink Panther '06
Shopgirl '05
Bowfinger '99
A Simple Twist of Fate '94
L.A. Story '91
Roxanne '87
Three Amigos '86
The Man with Two Brains '83
Dead Men Don't Wear Plaid '82
The Jerk '79

Jacques Martineau(1963-)
Born in 68 '08
Cote d'Azur '05
My Life on Ice '02
The Adventures of Felix '99
Jeanne and the Perfect Guy '98

Renzo Martinelli
Camera: The Walking Mountain '08
The Stone Merchant '06

Derick Martini
Lymelife '08
Smiling Fish & Goat on Fire '99

Richard Martini(1955-)
My Faraway Bride '06
My Champion '81

Steven Martini(1978-)
Lymelife '08
Smiling Fish & Goat on Fire '99

Luciano Martino(1933-)
Your Vice is a Closed Room and Only I Have the Key '72
Giants of Rome '63
The Whip and the Body '63

Raymond Martino
To the Limit '95
DaVinci's War '92
American Born '89
Angels of the City '89

Sergio Martino(1938-)
The Great Alligator '81
Torso '73

Mike Marvin
Wishman '93
The Wraith '87

Arthur Marx(1921-)
Cancel My Reservation '72
Eight on the Lam '67
I'll Take Sweden '65
A Global Affair '63

Rick Marx(1955-)
Firehouse '87
Warrior Queen '87

R.J. Marx
Double Obsession '93
Master of Dragonard Hill '89
Dead Man Walking '88
Dragonard '88
Gor '88
Outlaw of Gor '87
Platoon Leader '87
C.O.D. '83

Sarah Y. Mason(1896-1980)
Golden Boy '39
Stella Dallas '37
Magnificent Obsession '35
Little Women '33

Elan Mastai
Alone in the Dark '05
MVP2: Most Vertical Primate '01

Master P(1967-)
Internet Dating '08
Foolish '99

Ed Masterson
Storm Catcher '99
No Code of Conduct '98

Nico Mastorakis(1941-)
Hired to Kill '91
In the Cold of the Night '89
Bloodstone '88
Glitch! '88
The Wind '87
Zero Boys '86
Blind Date '84
Blood Tide '82

William Mastrosimone
Benedict Arnold: A Question of Honor '03
The Burning Season '94
With Honors '94
Sinatra '92
The Beast '88
Extremities '86

Berkely Mather(1909-96)
The Long Ships '64
Dr. No '62

Ted Mather
Faith '90
Body Beat '88

Ali Matheson
Before I Say Goodbye '03
Halloweentown 2: Kalabar's Revenge '01
Halloweentown '98

Chris Matheson
Evil Alien Conquerors '02
Mr. Wrong '95
A Goofy Movie '94
Bill & Ted's Bogus Journey '91
Bill & Ted's Excellent Adventure '89

Richard Matheson(1926-)
Trilogy of Terror 2 '96
Jaws 3 '83
Twilight Zone: The Movie '83
Young Warriors '83
Somewhere in Time '80
Trilogy of Terror '75
Scream of the Wolf '74
Dracula '73
Dying Room Only '73
The Legend of Hell House '73
The Night Strangler '72
Duel '71
The Night Stalker '71
The Devil Rides Out '68
Die! Die! My Darling! '65
The Comedy of Terrors '64
The Last Man on Earth '64
The Raven '63
Burn Witch, Burn! '62
Tales of Terror '62
Master of the World '61
The Pit and the Pendulum '61
The Fall of the House of Usher '60
The Incredible Shrinking Man '57

Richard Christian Matheson(1953-)
It Waits '05
Full Eclipse '93
Loose Cannons '90
It Takes Two '88
Three o'Clock High '87

Temple Mathews
Picture This! '08
Return to Never Land '02

June Mathis(1892-1927)
Blood and Sand '22
The Four Horsemen of the Apocalypse '21
The Saphead '21

Melissa Mathison(1950-)
Kundun '97
The Indian in the Cupboard '95
The Escape Artist '82
E.T.: The Extra-Terrestrial '82
The Black Stallion '79

Francisca Matos
Baby Geniuses '98
A Million to Juan '94

Hiro Matsuda
Shogun's Samurai—The Yagyu Clan Conspiracy '78
Sympathy for the Underdog '71

Zenzo Matsuyama
Proof of the Man '77
The Human Condition: Road to Eternity '59
The Human Condition: No Greater Love '58

Paul Matthews
Hooded Angels '00
Breeders '97
The Proposition '96
Grim '95

John Mattson
Free Willy 3: The Rescue '97
Free Willy 2: The Adventure Home '95
Milk Money '94

Nat Mauldin
The Perfect Holiday '07
The In-Laws '03
Dr. Dolittle '98
The Preacher's Wife '96

J. Stephen Maunder
The Veteran '06
Expect No Mercy '95
Talons of the Eagle '92
Tiger Claws '91

Armistead Maupin(1944-)
The Night Listener '06
The Celluloid Closet '95

Joseph Maurer
The Song of the Lark '01
The Sandy Bottom Orchestra '00

Robert (Roberto) Mauri(1924-)
Animal Called Man '72
The Slaughter of the Vampires '62

Captain Mauzner
Factory Girl '06
Wonderland '03

Garth Maxwell(1963-)
When Love Comes '98
Jack Be Nimble '94

Richard Maxwell
Shadow of China '91
The Serpent and the Rainbow '87
The Challenge '82

Ronald F. Maxwell(1947-)
Gods and Generals '03
Gettysburg '93

Elaine May(1932-)
Primary Colors '98
The Birdcage '95
Ishtar '87
Heaven Can Wait '78
Mikey & Nicky '76
A New Leaf '71

Carl Mayer(1894-1944)
Tartuffe '25
The Last Laugh '24
Shattered '21
The Cabinet of Dr. Caligari '19

Edwin Justus Mayer(1896-1960)
To Be or Not to Be '42
They Met in Bombay '41
Desire '36
Thirty Day Princess '34
Merrily We Go to Hell '32

Paul Mayersberg(1941-)
Croupier '97
Merry Christmas, Mr. Lawrence '83
The Man Who Fell to Earth '76

Wendell Mayes(1918-92)
Monsignor '82
Love and Bullets '79
Go Tell the Spartans '78
Bank Shot '74
Death Wish '74
The Poseidon Adventure '72
Hotel '67
In Harm's Way '65
Von Ryan's Express '65
Advise and Consent '62
Anatomy of a Murder '59
The Hanging Tree '59
The Hunters '58
Spirit of St. Louis '57

Craig Mazin(1971-)
Scary Movie 4 '06
Scary Movie 3 '03
Senseless '98
RocketMan '97

Stephen Mazur
Without a Paddle: Nature's Calling '09
Wedding Wars '06
Heartbreakers '01
Liar Liar '97
The Little Rascals '94

Paul Mazursky(1930-)
The Pickle '93
Scenes from a Mall '91
Enemies, a Love Story '89
Moon over Parador '88
Down and Out in Beverly Hills '86
Moscow on the Hudson '84
The Tempest '82
Willie & Phil '80
An Unmarried Woman '78
Next Stop, Greenwich Village '76
Harry and Tonto '74
Blume in Love '73
Alex in Wonderland '70
Bob & Carol & Ted & Alice '69
I Love You, Alice B. Toklas! '68

Danny McBride
Underworld: Rise of the Lycans '09
The Foot Fist Way '08
Underworld: Evolution '05
Underworld '03

Jim McBride(1941-)
Uncovered '94
Great Balls of Fire '89
Breathless '83
Hot Times '74
Glen and Randa '71
David Holzman's Diary '67

Richard McBrien
Wallander: Firewall '08
The Debt '03

Howard McCain
Underworld: Rise of the Lycans '09
Outlander '08

Mary C. McCall(1904-86)
The Fighting Sullivans '42
Breaking the Ice '38
I Promise to Pay '37
A Midsummer Night's Dream '35

Tim McCanlies(1953-)
Secondhand Lions '03
The Iron Giant '99
Dancer, Texas—Pop. 81 '98
Dennis the Menace Strikes Again '98

Tim McCann(1968-)
Revolution #9 '01
Desolation Angels '95

Leo McCarey(1898-1969)
Move Over, Darling '63
Rally 'Round the Flag, Boys! '58
An Affair to Remember '57
Going My Way '44
My Favorite Wife '40
Love Affair '39
Laurel & Hardy: Blotto '30
Laurel & Hardy: Brats '30
Laurel & Hardy: Berth Marks '29
Laurel & Hardy: Men O'War '29

John P. McCarthy(1884-1962)
Marked Trails '44
Beyond the Rockies '32

Peter McCarthy
Car 54, Where Are You? '94
Floundering '94
Tapeheads '89

Thomas (Tom) McCarthy(1969-)
The Visitor '07
The Station Agent '03

Michael (Mick) McCleery
Track 16 '02
The Alien Agenda: Out of the Darkness '96

Bernard McConville
King of the Pecos '36
Monte Cristo '22

Jonas McCord(1952-)
The Body '01
Class of '61 '92

Mark McCorkle
Hotel for Dogs '09
Sky High '05
Aladdin and the King of Thieves '96

Pete McCormack
The Blue Butterfly '04
Whirlygirl '04

John McCormick
Living on Tokyo Time '87
Victim '61

Nelson McCormick
Operation Sandman: Warriors in Hell '00
For Which He Stands '98

Pat McCormick(1927-2005)
Under the Rainbow '81
Oh Dad, Poor Dad (Momma's Hung You in the Closet & I'm Feeling So Sad) '67

Randall McCormick
The Scorpion King 2: Rise of a Warrior '08
Speed 2: Cruise Control '97

Horace McCoy(1897-1955)
Rage at Dawn '55
The Texas Rangers Ride Again '40
Postal Inspector '36
The Trail of the Lonesome Pine '36

Michael McCullers
Baby Mama '08
Thunderbirds '04
Austin Powers In Goldmember '02
Undercover Brother '02
Austin Powers 2: The Spy Who Shagged Me '99

Bruce McCulloch(1961-)
Dog Park '98
Kids in the Hall: Brain Candy '96

Jim McCullough, Jr.
The St. Tammany Miracle '94
Video Murders '87
Mountaintop Motel Massacre '86
The Aurora Encounter '85
Creature from Black Lake '76

Michael James McDonald(1964-)
Alien Avengers '96
The Death Artist '95
The Crazysitter '94
Revenge of the Red Baron '93

Rodney McDonald
Steel Sharks '97
Desire '95

Michael McDowell(1950-99)
Stephen King's Thinner '96
The Nightmare Before Christmas '93
Tales from the Darkside: The Movie '90
Beetlejuice '88

Alan B. McElroy
Thr3e '07
The Marine '06
Wrong Turn '03
Ballistic: Ecks vs. Sever '02
Left Behind: The Movie '00
Spawn '97

Todd McFarlane's Spawn '97
Rapid Fire '92
Halloween 4: The Return of Michael Myers '88

Ross McElwee(1947-)
Time Indefinite '93
Sherman's March '86

Donald McEnery
A Bug's Life '98
Hercules '97

Ian McEwan(1948-)
The Good Son '93
The Innocent '93

Stephen McFeely
The Chronicles of Narnia: Prince Caspian '08
You Kill Me '07
The Chronicles of Narnia: The Lion, the Witch and the Wardrobe '05

Mark Thomas McGee
Sorceress '94
Sins of Desire '92
Bad Girls from Mars '90

Ron McGee
Christmas Town '08
Finish Line '08
On the Other Hand, Death '08
Fatal Contact: Bird Flu in America '06
Shock to the System '06
Maiden Voyage: Ocean Hijack '04
Meat Loaf: To Hell and Back '00

Scott McGehee
The Deep End '01
Suture '93

Kathleen McGhee-Anderson
The Color of Courage '98
Sunset Park '96

Josann McGibbon
The Starter Wife '07
Runaway Bride '99
The Favor '92
Three Men and a Little Lady '90
Worth Winning '89

David McGillivray(1947-)
The Terror '79
House of Whipcord '75
Frightmare '74

Sean McGinley(1956-)
Venomous '01
Fugitive Mind '99
Scorned 2 '96
Sexual Roulette '96

Sean McGinly
The Great Buck Howard '09
Two Days '03

Jimmy McGovern(1949-)
Liam '00
Heart '99
Go Now '96
Cracker: Brotherly Love '95
Cracker: Men Should Weep '94
Cracker: The Big Crunch '94
Cracker: To Be a Somebody '94
Priest '94

Dorrell McGowan(1899-1997)
The Showdown '50
Don't Fence Me In '45
San Fernando Valley '44
Jeepers Creepers '39
King of the Pecos '36

Stuart E. McGowan(1904-99)
The Showdown '50
Don't Fence Me In '45
San Fernando Valley '44
Jeepers Creepers '39
King of the Pecos '36

Douglas McGrath(1958-)
Infamous '06
Nicholas Nickleby '02
Company Man '00
Emma '96
Bullets over Broadway '94
Born Yesterday '93

Patrick McGrath(1950-)
Spider '02
Grave Indiscretions '96

Tom McGrath
Madagascar: Escape 2 Africa '08
Madagascar '05

John McGreevey
Ms. Scrooge '97
Captains Courageous '95
Consenting Adult '85
Night Crossing '81
The Disappearance of Aimee '76
Hello Down There '69
Hot Rod Girl '56

Thomas McGuane(1939-)
Cold Feet '89
Tom Horn '80
Missouri Breaks '76
92 in the Shade '76
Rancho Deluxe '75

Frank McGuinness
Dancing at Lughnasa '98
Talk of Angels '96

James Kevin McGuinness(1893-1950)
Rio Grande '50
I Take This Woman '40
China Seas '35
Tarzan and His Mate '34

Don McGuire(1919-99)
Tootsie '82
Suppose They Gave a War and Nobody Came? '70
The Delicate Delinquent '56
Meet Danny Wilson '52

William Anthony McGuire(1881-1640)
Lillian Russell '40
The Great Ziegfeld '36
Kid from Spain '32

Jay McInerney(1955-)
Gia '98
Hotel Room '93

Douglas Lloyd McIntosh
Love's Abiding Joy '06
Love's Long Journey '05
Disaster at Silo 7 '88

Daniel McIvor
Whole New Thing '05
Marion Bridge '02

Adam McKay(1968-)
The Other Guys '10
Step Brothers '08
Talladega Nights: The Ballad of Ricky Bobby '06
Anchorman: The Legend of Ron Burgundy '04

Jim McKay
Life Support '07
Angel Rodriguez '05
Our Song '01
Girls Town '95

Steven McKay
Darkman 2: The Return of Durant '94
Diggstown '92
Hard to Kill '89

Michael McKean(1947-)
The Return of Spinal Tap '92
The Big Picture '89
This Is Spinal Tap '84

Grace McKeaney
The Loretta Claiborne Story '00
Range of Motion '00
Grace & Glorie '98

Lucky McKee(1975-)
Roman '06
May '02

Don McKellar(1963-)
Blindness '08
Last Night '98
The Red Violin '98
Dance Me Outside '95
32 Short Films about Glenn Gould '93
Highway 61 '91
Roadkill '89

Aline Brosh McKenna(1967-)
Morning Glory '10
27 Dresses '08
The Devil Wears Prada '06
Laws of Attraction '04
Three to Tango '99

David McKenna(1968-)
S.W.A.T. '03
Blow '01
Get Carter '00
Body Shots '99
American History X '98

Charles McKeown
The Imaginarium of Doctor Parnassus '09
Ripley's Game '02
Plunkett & Macleane '98
The Adventures of Baron Munchausen '89
Brazil '85

Vince McKewin
The Replacements '00
The Climb '97
Fly Away Home '96

Mark McKinney(1959-)
Slings & Arrows: Season 2 '05
Kids in the Hall: Brain Candy '96

Rob McKittrick
Still Waiting '08
Waiting '05

Duncan McLachlan
Born Wild '95
The Double O Kid '92

Sean McLain
I-See-You.Com '06
Safe House '99

John McLaughlin
Man of the House '05
The Great Gatsby '01
The Last Good Time '94

Greg Mclean
Rogue '07
Wolf Creek '05

Victor McLeod
Gang Busters '42
Boss of Bullion City '41
Bury Me Not on the Lone Prairie '41
The Masked Rider '41
Law and Order '40

Tom McLoughlin(1950-)
Date with an Angel '87
Friday the 13th, Part 6: Jason Lives '86

John McMahon
Rip It Off '02
Broken Vessels '98

James McManus
ABCD '99
La Cucaracha '99
The Big Empty '98

Larry McMurtry(1936-)
Comanche Moon '08
Brokeback Mountain '05
Johnson County War '02
Larry McMurtry's Dead Man's Walk '96
Larry McMurtry's Streets of Laredo '95
Falling from Grace '92
Memphis '91
Montana '90
The Last Picture Show '71

Terrance McNally(1939-)
Common Ground '00
Love! Valour! Compassion! '96
Frankie and Johnny '91
Earth Girls Are Easy '89

Eoin McNamee
I Want You '98
Resurrection Man '97

Dennis McNicholas
Land of the Lost '09
The Ladies Man '00

William Slavens McNutt(1885-1938)
The Lives of a Bengal Lancer '35
One Sunday Afternoon '33
Strangers in Love '32
Touchdown '31

Christopher McQuarrie(1968-)
Valkyrie '08
Way of the Gun '00
The Usual Suspects '95
Public Access '93

Will McRobb
Alvin and the Chipmunks: The Squeakuel '09
Angus, Thongs and Perfect Snogging '08
Alvin and the Chipmunks '07
Snow Day '00

Anna McRoberts
Santa Buddies '09
Snow Buddies '08
Space Buddies '08
Air Bud 6: Air Buddies '06
MXP: Most Xtreme Primate '03

Nick Mead
Parting Shots '98
Swing '98
Bank Robber '93

Herb Meadow(1912-95)
Lone Ranger '56
Stranger on Horseback '55
The Redhead from Wyoming '53
The Strange Woman '46

Shane Meadows(1972-)
This Is England '06
Dead Man's Shoes '04
Once Upon a Time in the Midlands '02
24-7 '97

Irene Mecchi
Annie '99
Hercules '97
The Hunchback of Notre Dame '96
The Lion King '94

Julio Medem(1958-)
Sex and Lucia '01
Lovers of the Arctic Circle '98
Tierra '95
The Red Squirrel '93
Vacas '91

Harold Medford(1911-77)
Brainwashed '60
The Damned Don't Cry '50

Enrico Medioli(1925-)
Coco Chanel '08
Once Upon a Time in America '84
The Innocent '76
Conversation Piece '75
The Leopard '63
Rocco and His Brothers '60

Mark Medoff(1940-)
Santa Fe '97
Homage '95
City of Joy '92
Clara's Heart '88
Apology '86
Children of a Lesser God '86
Off Beat '86
Good Guys Wear Black '78

John Meehan(1890-1954)
Three Daring Daughters '48
The Valley of Decision '45
Seven Sinners '40
Madame X '37

Thomas Meehan
Hairspray '07
The Producers '05
Spaceballs '87
One Magic Christmas '85
Annie '82

Steve Meerson
Anna and the King '99
Star Trek 4: The Voyage Home '86

Leslie Megahey
Earth '07
The Advocate '93

Robert T. Megginson
Wolverine '96
F/X '86

Deepa Mehta(1950-)
The Republic of Love '03
Earth '98
Fire '96

Gordon Melbourne
Bulletproof Heart '95
White Tiger '95

Ib Melchior(1917-)
Planet of the Vampires '65
Robinson Crusoe on Mars '64
Reptilicus '62
The Angry Red Planet '59

Kay Mellor(1950-)
Girls' Night '97
Jane Eyre '97
Band of Gold '95

Greg Mellott
American Soldiers '05
Black Point '01
Road Rage '01
Under Heavy Fire '01
Jackie Chan's First Strike '96
The Rage '96
Shootfighter 2: Kill or Be Killed! '96

Patrick Melton
The Collector '09
Hellraiser '09
Saw 6 '09
Feast 2: Sloppy Seconds '08
Saw 5 '08
Saw 4 '07
Feast '06

Lewis Meltzer(1911-95)
High School Confidential '58
The Brothers Rico '57
Autumn Leaves '56
The Man with the Golden Arm '55
Shark River '53
Comanche Territory '50

Jean-Pierre Melville(1917-73)
Le Cercle Rouge '70
Army of Shadows '69
Le Samourai '67
Bob le Flambeur '55
Les Enfants Terrible '50
La Silence de la Mer '47

Stevan Mena
Brutal Massacre: A Comedy '07
Malevolence '04

Aaron Mendelsohn(1966-)
Air Bud 2: Golden Receiver '98
Change of Heart '98
Air Bud '97

George Mendeluk(1948-)
Doin' Time '85
Stone Cold Dead '80

Ramon Menendez
Tortilla Soup '01
Money for Nothing '93
Stand and Deliver '88

Joe Menosky
Anonymous Rex '04
Hiding Out '87

Jiri Menzel(1938-)
I Served the King of England '07
Larks on a String '68
Closely Watched Trains '66

David Mercer(1928-80)
Providence '77
Morgan: A Suitable Case for Treatment '66

Anne Meredith
Out of the Ashes '03
Rated X '00
Bastard out of Carolina '96
Losing Chase '96

Michael Meredith
The Open Road '09
Land of Plenty '04

Bess Meredyth(1890-1969)
That Night in Rio '41
When a Man Loves '27
Don Juan '26
The Red Lily '24

James Merendino(1967-)
SLC Punk! '99
The Real Thing '97
Hard Drive '94
Terrified '94

Joseph Merhi(1953-)
Last Man Standing '95
Angels of the City '89
Emperor of the Bronx '89
Hollywood in Trouble '87
Mayhem '87
The Newlydeads '87

Agnes Merlet(1959-)
Artemisia '97
The Son of the Shark '93

Monte Merrick
The Miracle Worker '00
Miracle at Midnight '98
Oliver Twist '97
8 Seconds '94
Mr. Baseball '92
Memphis Belle '90
Staying Together '89

Brett Merryman
Impact Point '08
Glass House: The Good Mother '06

Roger Merton
Queen of the Amazons '47
Down the Wyoming Trail '39
Roll, Wagons, Roll '39

Marta Meszaros(1931-)
Adoption '75
The Girl '68

Alex Metcalf
An American Affair '09
The Crimson Code '99

Stephen Metcalfe
Beautiful Joe '00
Roommates '95
Cousins '89
Jacknife '89
Florida Straits '87

Half a Lifetime '86

Tim Metcalfe(1956-)

44 Minutes: The North Hollywood Shootout '03
Killer: A Journal of Murder '95
Kalifornia '93
Iron Maze '91
Fright Night 2 '88
Million Dollar Mystery '87
Three for the Road '87
Revenge of the Nerds '84

Radley Metzger(1929-)

The Cat and the Canary '79
The Alley Cats '65
Dark Odyssey '57

Kevin Meyer

A Smile Like Yours '96
Under Investigation '93
Invasion of Privacy '92
Civil War Diary '90

Nicholas Meyer(1945-)

Elegy '08
The Human Stain '03
The Informant '97
Sommersby '93
Company Business '91
Star Trek 6: The Undiscovered Country '91
Star Trek 4: The Voyage Home '86
Time After Time '79
The Seven-Per-Cent Solution '76
Invasion of the Bee Girls '73

Russ Meyer(1922-2004)

Beneath the Valley of the Ultra-Vixens '79
Supervixens '75
Blacksnake! '73
Faster, Pussycat! Kill! Kill! '65
Motor Psycho '65

Turi Meyer(1964-)

Wrong Turn 2: Dead End '07
Candyman 3: Day of the Dead '98
Chairman of the Board '97
Leprechaun 2 '94

Nancy Meyers(1949-)

It's Complicated '09
The Holiday '06
Something's Gotta Give '03
The Parent Trap '98
Father of the Bride Part 2 '95
I Love Trouble '94
Father of the Bride '91
Baby Boom '87
Irreconcilable Differences '84
Protocol '84
Private Benjamin '80

Menno Meyjes(1954-)

Max '02
The Siege '98
Foreign Student '94
Empire of the Sun '87
The Color Purple '85

Boleslaw Michalek(1925-97)

A Love in Germany '84
Danton '82

Dave Michener

The Great Mouse Detective '86
The Fox and the Hound '81

William Mickelberry

Black Dog '98
Escape: Human Cargo '98
Woman Undone '95

Elizabeth (Lizzie) Mickery

The State Within '06
Inspector Lynley Mysteries: A Great Deliverance '01
Love or Money '01
The Ice House '97

Anne-Marie Mieville(1945-)

First Name: Carmen '83
Every Man for Himself '79
Comment Ca Va? '76
Numero Deux '75

Masakazu Migita

Executive Koala '06
The World Sinks Except Japan '06
The Calamari Wrestler '04

Romano Migliorini

Deadly Mission '78
The Bloody Pit of Horror '65

Radu Mihaileanu(1958-)

Train of Life '98
Trahir '93

Gordan Mihic(1938-)

Black Cat, White Cat '98
Someone Else's America '96

Takashi Miike(1960-)

Sukiyaki Western Django '08
The Great Yokai War '05

Ted V. Mikels(1929-)

10 Violent Women '79
Blood Orgy of the She-Devils '74
The Doll Squad '73
The Corpse Grinders '71
The Astro-Zombies '67

Nikita Mikhalkov(1945-)

12 '07
Burnt by the Sun '94
Anna '93

Jean-Louis Milesi(1956-)

The Town Is Quiet '00
Marius and Jeannette '97

Lewis Milestone(1895-1980)

Arch of Triumph '48
Lucky Partners '40

Djordje Milicevic(1942-)

Iron Will '93
Toby McTeague '87
Runaway Train '85
Victory '81

Frank Military

Blind Faith '98
Buffalo Soldiers '97

John Milius(1944-)

Rough Riders '97
Clear and Present Danger '94
Geronimo: An American Legend '93
Farewell to the King '89
Red Dawn '84
Conan the Barbarian '82
Apocalypse Now '79
1941 '79
Big Wednesday '78
The Wind and the Lion '75
Dillinger '73
Magnum Force '73
Evel Knievel '72
Jeremiah Johnson '72
Life & Times of Judge Roy Bean '72

Miles Millar(1970-)

The Mummy: Tomb of the Dragon Emperor '08
Herbie: Fully Loaded '05
Spider-Man 2 '04
Shanghai Knights '03
Shanghai Noon '00

Ronald Millar(1919-98)

Never Let Me Go '53
The Miniver Story '50

Nick Millard

Terrorists '88
Gunblast '74

Oscar Millard(1908-90)

Dead Ringer '64
The Conqueror '56
Second Chance '53
Angel Face '52
No Highway in the Sky '51
Come to the Stable '49

Alice Duer Miller(1874-1942)

Wife Versus Secretary '36
Are Parents People? '25

Andrew Miller

Boys and Girls '00
Simon Sez '99

Arthur Miller(1915-2005)

The Crucible '96
Everybody Wins '90
The Misfits '61

Chris Miller(1942-)

Multiplicity '96
National Lampoon's Animal House '78

Claude Miller(1942-)

A Secret '07
Alias Betty '01
The Accompanist '93
The Little Thief '89
This Sweet Sickness '77
The Best Way '76

David Keith Miller

The Glass Cage '96
I Like to Play Games '95

Eric Miller

Ice Spiders '07
Night Skies '07

Frank Miller

The Spirit '08
RoboCop 3 '91
The Living Dead '33
Trapped by the Mormons '22

George Miller(1945-)

Babe '95
Lorenzo's Oil '92
Mad Max: Beyond Thunderdome '85
The Road Warrior '82
Mad Max '80

Harvey Miller(1936-99)

Getting Away With Murder '96
Bad Medicine '85
Cannonball Run 2 '84
Protocol '84
Jekyll & Hyde... Together Again '82
Private Benjamin '80

J(ames) P(inckney) Miller(1919-2001)

Helter Skelter '76
The Lindbergh Kidnapping Case '76
The People Next Door '70
Behold a Pale Horse '64
Days of Wine and Roses '62

Jeff Miller

Eye of the Killer '99
Hellblock 13 '97

Jennifer Miller

Cupid & Cate '00
Family Pictures '93
The Dark Secret of Harvest Home '78

Percy Miller

See Master P

Randall Miller

Bottle Shock '08
Nobel Son '08
Marilyn Hotchkiss' Ballroom Dancing & Charm School '06

Rebecca Miller(1962-)

The Private Lives of Pippa Lee '09
The Ballad of Jack and Rose '05
Personal Velocity: Three Portraits '02
Angela '94

Seton I. Miller(1902-74)

Istanbul '57
Calcutta '47
Singapore '47
Two Years before the Mast '46
Ministry of Fear '44
The Black Swan '42
Here Comes Mr. Jordan '41
Castle on the Hudson '40
The Adventures of Robin Hood '38
Bullets or Ballots '38
Dawn Patrol '38
Kid Galahad '37
"G" Men '35
The Eagle and the Hawk '33
Murders in the Zoo '33
Hot Saturday '32
A Girl in Every Port '28

Tim Miller

Far North '07
The Warrior '81

Winston Miller(1910-94)

The Far Horizons '55
Carson City '52
Cavalry Charge '51
Rocky Mountain '50
My Darling Clementine '46
One Body Too Many '44
Man from Cheyenne '42
Dick Tracy: The Spider Strikes '37
S.O.S. Coast Guard '37

Worm Miller

Transylmania '09
Gamebox 1.0 '04

Bertram Millhauser(1892-1958)

The Woman in Green '49
The Invisible Man's Revenge '44
The Texans '38

Andy Milligan(1929-91)

Man with Two Heads '72
The Rats Are Coming! The Werewolves Are Here! '72
The Ghastly Ones '68

Bill Milling

Body Trouble '92
Lauderdale '89

Travis Milloy

Pandorum '09
Street Gun '96

Hugh Mills(1913-71)

Blanche Fury '48
Personal Property '37

Mark Mills

The Reckoning '03
Rock My World '02
The Lost Son '98

Paula Milne

I Dreamed of Africa '00
Second Sight '99
Hollow Reed '95
Mad Love '95

Peter Milne(1896-1968)

The Most Wonderful Time of the Year '08
Painting the Clouds With Sunshine '51
God is My Co-Pilot '45
Step Lively '44
San Quentin '37
Colleen '36
The Kennel Murder Case '33

Waturu Mimura

Godzilla 2000 '99
Orochi, the Eight Headed Dragon '94

Daniel Minahan

Series 7: The Contenders '01
I Shot Andy Warhol '96

Seishi Minakimi

Paprika '06
Paprika '06

Michael Miner

Anacondas: The Hunt for the Blood Orchid '04
Deadly Weapon '88
RoboCop '87

Pang Ming

Frozen '98
So Close to Paradise '98

Wu Ming

See Xiaoshuai Wang

Anthony Minghella(1954-2008)

New York, I Love You '09
Nine '09
Breaking and Entering '06
Cold Mountain '03
The Talented Mr. Ripley '99
The English Patient '96
Truly, Madly, Deeply '91

Joe Minion(1957-)

Motorama '91
Vampire's Kiss '88
Julia and Julia '87
After Hours '85

Susan Minot(1956-)

Evening '07
Stealing Beauty '96

Sam Mintz(1897-1957)

Here Comes Cookie '35
Rafter Romance '34
No Marriage Ties '33

Brad Mirman(1953-)

The Confessor '04
Crime Spree '03
Joshua '02
The Target '02
Gideon '99
Resurrection '99
Truth or Consequences, N.M. '97
Knight Moves '93
Body of Evidence '92

Doug Miro

Prince of Persia: The Sands of Time '10
The Sorcerer's Apprentice '10
The Uninvited '09
The Great Raid '05

C. Gaby Mitchell

Get Low '09
Fallen Angels 2 '93

Craig Mitchell

The Flock '07
Highwaymen '03
Komodo '99
Milo '98

David Mitchell

Dead Fish '04
The Killing Man '94
Circle Man '87

Gene Mitchell

Flipping '96
The Takeover '94

Joseph A. Mitchell

Seven Chances '25
The Navigator '24
Sherlock, Jr. '24
Our Hospitality '23

Julian Mitchell(1935-)

Wilde '97
August '95
Vincent & Theo '90
Another Country '84
Elizabeth R '72
Persuasion '71

Keith Mitchell(1967-)

The Sandlot 3: Heading Home '07
Mr. 3000 '04
Eddie '96

Steve Mitchell

Tin Man '07
Against the Law '98
Chopping Mall '86

Hayao Miyazaki(1941-)

Ponyo '08
Howl's Moving Castle '04
Spirited Away '01
Kiki's Delivery Service '98
My Neighbor Totoro '88

Wilson Mizner(1876-1933)

Heroes for Sale '33
The Little Giant '33
20,000 Years in Sing Sing '33
Frisco Jenny '32
One Way Passage '32

Moshe Mizrahi(1931-)

Every Time We Say Goodbye '86
La Vie Continue '82
I Sent a Letter to My Love '81
Madame Rosa '77
I Love You Rosa '72

Patrick Modiano(1945-)

Bon Voyage '03
Son of Gascogne '95

Ivan Moffat(1918-2002)

They Came to Cordura '59
Bhowani Junction '56
Giant '56

Peter Moffatt

Criminal Justice '08
Cambridge Spies '03

Jordan Moffet

Like Mike '02
Whispers: An Elephant's Tale '00

John Moffitt

Double or Nothing '37
Murder With Pictures '36
Rhythm on the Range '36

Deborah Moggach

The Diary of Anne Frank '08
Pride and Prejudice '05

Jose Mojica Marins(1929-)

Hallucinations of a Deranged Mind '78
Awakenings of the Beast '68
Strange World of Coffin Joe '68
At Midnight, I'll Take Your Soul '63

Hans Petter Moland(1955-)

Aberdeen '00
Zero Degrees Kelvin '95
The Last Lieutenant '94

Gustaf Molander(1888-1973)

Intermezzo '36
Treasure of Arne '19

Jacinto (Jack) Molina

See Paul Naschy

Edouard Molinaro(1928-)

Beaumarchais the Scoundrel '96
La Cage aux Folles '78
Pain in the A— '77
Dracula and Son '76

Dominik Moll(1962-)

Lemming '05
With a Friend Like Harry '00

William Monahan(1960-90)

Edge of Darkness '10
Body of Lies '08
The Departed '06
Kingdom of Heaven '05

Paul Monash(1917-2003)

The Golden Spiders: A Nero Wolfe Mystery '00
Rescuers: Stories of Courage—Two Couples '98
George Wallace '97
Kingfish: A Story of Huey P. Long '95
Stalin '92

The Way To Fight '96

Desmond Nakano(1953-)
White Man's Burden '95
American Me '92

Hideo Nakata(1961-)
Death Note 3: L, Change the World '08
The Ring 2 '05
Dark Water '02
Ringu 2 '99

Rodion Nakhapetov
Border Blues '03
Stir '98

Yin Nam
Full Contact '92
Prison on Fire '87

Michael Nankin(1955-)
Gate 2 '92
The Gate '87

Paul Naschy(1934-)
Human Beasts '80
Inquisition '76
Night of the Howling Beast '75
Exorcism '74
Curse of the Devil '73
House of Psychotic Women '73
The Mummy's Revenge '73
Dracula's Great Love '72
Horror Rises from the Tomb '72
Dr. Jekyll and the Wolfman '71
The Fury of the Wolfman '70
The Werewolf vs. the Vampire Woman '70
Dracula vs. Frankenstein '69

Gustin Nash
Youth in Revolt '10
Charlie Bartlett '07

N. Richard Nash(1913-2000)
One Summer Love '76
Helen of Troy '56
The Rainmaker '56
Nora Prentiss '47

Roberto Natale(1921-)
A Long Ride From Hell '68
The Bloody Pit of Horror '65

Vincenzo Natali(1969-)
Splice '09
Paris, je t'aime '06
Cube '98

Mort Nathan
Boat Trip '03
Kingpin '96

Jeff Nathanson
New York, I Love You '09
Rush Hour 3 '07
The Last Shot '04
The Terminal '04
Catch Me If You Can '02
Rush Hour 2 '01
Bait '00
Speed 2: Cruise Control '97
For Better or Worse '95

Maria Nation
The Tenth Circle '08
A Season for Miracles '99
Ellen Foster '97
The Awakening '95
Blue River '95

Rick Natkin
Gang in Blue '96
Necessary Roughness '91
The Boys in Company C '77

Jack Natteford(1894-1970)
Trail to San Antone '47
Double Trouble '41
Heroes of the Saddle '40
Pioneers of the West '40
Come on Rangers '38
Roarin' Lead '37
The Three Mesquiteers '36
The Crimson Trail '35
Rider of the Law '35
Demon for Trouble '34
Cowboy Counselor '33
The Dude Bandit '33
My Pal, the King '32
Arizona Terror '31
Border Romance '30
Lightning Hutch '26

William T. Naud
Necromancer: Satan's Servant '88
Island of Blood '82

Gregory Nava(1949-)
Bordertown '06
Frida '02
Selena '96
My Family '94
A Time of Destiny '88
El Norte '83
End of August '82

Christopher Neame(1947-)
Feast of July '95
Zeta One '69

Ronald Neame(1911-)
This Happy Breed '47
Brief Encounter '46
Great Expectations '46

Hal Needham(1931-)
Stroker Ace '83
Smokey and the Bandit '77

Troy Neighbors
Fortress 2: Re-Entry '99
Fortress '93

Paul Jan Nelissen
Winter in Wartime '10
Nothing to Lose '08

Hank Nelken
Are We Done Yet? '07
Mama's Boy '07
Saving Silverman '01
Killer Bud '00

B.J. Nelson
Alien Chaser '96
Scanners 2: The New Order '91

Brian Nelson
30 Days of Night '07
Hard Candy '06

Jessie Nelson
Because I Said So '07
I Am Sam '01
The Story of Us '99
Stepmom '98
Corrina, Corrina '94

John Allen Nelson(1959-)
American Yakuza '94
Best of the Best 2 '93

Peter Nelson
Getting Up and Going Home '92
The Lonely Passion of Judith Hearne '87

Sean Nelson(1980-)
My Effortless Brilliance '08
Godmoney '97

Tim Blake Nelson(1965-)
The Grey Zone '01
Eye of God '97

Dennis Nemec
The Avenging Angel '95
God Bless the Child '88
Murder in Coweta County '83

Jan Nemec(1936-)
The Report on the Party and the Guests '66
Diamonds of the Night '64

Vladimir Nemirovsky
Hangman '00
Indiscreet '98
The Beneficiary '97

Claude Neron(1927-91)
Vincent, Francois, Paul and the Others '76
Cesar & Rosalie '72

Avi Nesher(1953-)
The Secrets '07
The Taxman '98
Mercenary '96
Timebomb '91
Doppelganger: The Evil Within '90

Kurt Neumann(1906-58)
Party Girls for Sale '54
Rocketship X-M '50

Edward Neumeier
Starship Troopers 3: Marauder '08
Anacondas: The Hunt for the Blood Orchid '04
Starship Troopers 2: Hero of the Federation '04
Starship Troopers '97
RoboCop '87

Scott Neustadter
(500) Days of Summer '09
The Pink Panther 2 '09

Mark Neveldine
Jonah Hex '10
Gamer '09
Crank '06

John Thomas "Jack" Neville(1886-1970)
The Devil Bat '41
Never Give a Sucker an Even Break '41
Lion's Den '36
The Midnight Phantom '35
Ticket to a Crime '34
Trader Horn '31
The Dawn Trail '30

Craig J. Nevius
Baby Face Nelson '97
Lady Killer '97
Black Scorpion 2: Ground Zero '96
Marquis de Sade '96
Black Scorpion '95

David Newman(1954-)
Santa Claus: The Movie '85
Sheena '84
Superman 3 '83
Jinxed '82
Still of the Night '82
Superman 2 '80
Superman: The Movie '78
Bad Company '72
What's Up, Doc? '72
There Was a Crooked Man '70
Bonnie & Clyde '67

Samuel Newman
Invisible Invaders '59
Tarzan's Peril '51

Walter Newman(1916-93)
The Interns '62
Crime and Punishment, USA '59
The Man with the Golden Arm '55
Ace in the Hole '51

Kuang Ni
Life Gamble '04
Five Element Ninjas '82
Human Lanterns '82
House of Traps '81
The Master '80
Sword Masters: Two Champions of Shaolin '80
Heaven & Hell '78
The 36th Chamber of Shaolin '78
Sword Masters: The Battle Wizard '77
Infra-Man '76
Super Inframan '76
The Water Margin '72
Duel of Fists '71
The Shadow Whip '71
Sword Masters: Brothers Five '70
The Wandering Swordsman '70
Have Sword, Will Travel '69

Sloan Nibley(1908-90)
Hostile Guns '67
Carson City '52
Far Frontier '48

Andrew Niccol(1964-)
Lord of War '05
The Terminal '04
Simone '02
The Truman Show '98
Gattaca '97

Maurizio Nichetti(1948-)
Luna e L'Altra '96
Stephano Quantestorie '93
Volere Volare '92
The Icicle Thief '89
Allegro Non Troppo '76

David Nicholls
Tess of the D'Urbervilles '08
When Did You Last See Your Father? '07
Starter for Ten '06
Simpatico '99

Dudley Nichols(1895-1960)
Prince Valiant '54
Pinky '49
The Fugitive '48
And Then There Were None '45
The Bells of St. Mary's '45
It Happened Tomorrow '44
Air Force '43
For Whom the Bell Tolls '43
Man Hunt '41
Stagecoach '39
Bringing Up Baby '38
The Hurricane '37
The Crusades '35
The Informer '35
She '35
The Lost Patrol '34
Pilgrimage '33
Seas Beneath '31

Jack Nicholson(1937-)
Head '68
The Trip '67
Flight to Fury '66
Ride in the Whirlwind '66

William Nicholson(1948-)
Gladiator '00
Grey Owl '99
Firelight '97
Crime of the Century '96
First Knight '95
Nell '94
Shadowlands '93
A Private Matter '92
Sarafina! '92

Nicholas Niciphor
Fatal Charm '92
Death Sport '78

Ted Nicolaou
Bloodstorm: Subspecies 4 '98
Spellbreaker: Secret of the Leprechauns '96
Vampire Journals '96
Leapin' Leprechauns '95
Dragonworld '94
Bloodlust: Subspecies 3 '93
Bloodstone: Subspecies 2 '92
Assault of the Killer Bimbos '88
Terrorvision '86

Rob Nilsson(1940-)
Heat and Sunlight '87
On the Edge '86
Signal 7 '83
Northern Lights '79

Brian Nissen
The Swan Princess 2: Escape from Castle Mountain '97
The Swan Princess '94

Gaspar Noe(1963-)
Irreversible '02
I Stand Alone '98

Marie Noelle
Love the Hard Way '01
Obsession '97

Tatsuo Nogami
Shogun's Samurai—The Yagyu Clan Conspiracy '78
Father of the Kamikaze '74

David Nokes
The Tenant of Wildfell Hall '96
Clarissa '91

Christopher Nolan(1970-)
Inception '10
The Dark Knight '08
The Prestige '06
Batman Begins '05
Memento '00
Following '99

Jonathan Nolan
The Dark Knight '08
The Prestige '06

Ken Nolan
The Company '07
Black Hawk Down '01

William F. Nolan(1928-)
Trilogy of Terror 2 '96
The Norliss Tapes '73

George Nolfi
The Adjustment Bureau '10
The Bourne Ultimatum '07
The Sentinel '06
Ocean's Twelve '04
Timeline '03

William Nolte(1889-1965)
Square Dance Jubilee '51
Two-Fisted Justice '43

Tom Noonan(1951-)
The House of the Devil '09
The Wife '95
What Happened Was... '94

Eric Norden
Blood Legacy '73
Please Don't Eat My Mother '72

Marc Norman(1941-)
Shakespeare in Love '98
Cutthroat Island '95
Waterworld '95
Bat 21 '88
The Aviator '85
Breakout '75
The Killer Elite '75
Zandy's Bride '74
Oklahoma Crude '73

Marsha Norman(1947-)
The Audrey Hepburn Story '00
A Cooler Climate '99
'night, Mother '86

Stephen Norrington(1965-)
The Last Minute '01
Death Machine '95

Edmund H. North(1911-90)
Patton '70
Damn the Defiant '62
Sink the Bismarck '60
Cowboy '58
The Far Horizons '55
The Day the Earth Stood Still '51
Colorado Territory '49
Flamingo Road '49

Bill W.L. Norton(1943-)
Back to the Beach '87
Losin' It '82

William W. Norton, Sr.(1925-)
Dirty Tricks '81
Night of the Juggler '80
Day of the Animals '77
Gator '76
Moving Violation '76
A Small Town in Texas '76
Brannigan '75
Big Bad Mama '74
I Dismember Mama '74
White Lightning '73
McKenzie Break '70
Sam Whiskey '69
The Scalphunters '68

Frank Norwood
Past Midnight '92
Driven to Kill '90

Jonathan Nossiter(1961-)
Signs & Wonders '00
Sunday '96

Louis Nowra(1950-)
Radiance '98
Heaven's Burning '97
The Matchmaker '97
Cosi '95
Map of the Human Heart '93

Betsy Giffen Nowrasteh
The Stoning of Soraya M. '08
Under Pressure '98

Cyrus Nowrasteh
The Stoning of Soraya M. '08
The Day Reagan Was Shot '01

Frank Nugent(1908-66)
Donovan's Reef '63
Gunman's Walk '58
Last Hurrah '58
The Searchers '56
Mister Roberts '55
The Tall Men '55
Angel Face '52
The Quiet Man '52
She Wore a Yellow Ribbon '49
Fort Apache '48

Victor Nunez(1945-)
Coastlines '02
Ulee's Gold '97
Ruby in Paradise '93
A Flash of Green '85
Gal Young 'Un '79

Tom Nursall
Without a Paddle '04
I'll Be Home for Christmas '98

Raphael Nussbaum(1932-93)
Speak of the Devil '90
The Invisible Terror '63

Colin Nutley(1944-)
Under the Sun '98
The Last Dance '93

Ron Nyswaner(1956-)
The Painted Veil '06
Soldier's Girl '03
Philadelphia '93
Love Hurts '91
Gross Anatomy '89
Prince of Pennsylvania '88
Mrs. Soffel '84
Purple Hearts '84
Swing Shift '84
Smithereens '82

Tsugumi Oba
Death Note 3: L, Change the World '08
Death Note 2: The Last Name '07
Death Note '06

Dan O'Bannon(1946-2009)
Alien vs. Predator '04
Bleeders '97
Screamers '96
Total Recall '90
Invaders from Mars '86
Lifeforce '85
Return of the Living Dead '85

Blue Thunder *'83*
Dead and Buried *'81*
Alien *'79*
Dark Star *'74*

Rockne S. O'Bannon(1955-)
Fatal Error *'99*
Robin Cook's Invasion *'97*
Alien Nation *'88*

Sean O'Bannon
Air Rage *'01*
Mom's Outta Sight *'01*
Poison *'01*
Invisible Mom 2 *'99*
The Kid with the X-Ray Eyes *'99*
Mom, Can I Keep Her? *'98*
The Escort *'97*
Hybrid *'97*
Night Shade *'97*
Invisible Mom *'96*

Takeshi Obata
Death Note 3: L, Change the World *'08*
Death Note 2: The Last Name *'07*
Death Note *'06*

Margaret Grieco Oberman
The American Mall *'08*
The Man *'05*
Troop Beverly Hills *'89*

Arch Oboler
One Plus One *'61*
Five *'51*

Edna O'Brien(1930-)
X, Y & Zee *'72*
Girl with Green Eyes *'64*

Jeff O'Brien(1965-)
Insecticidal *'05*
Blind Heat *'00*

John O'Brien(1962-)
Starsky & Hutch *'04*
Cradle 2 the Grave *'03*
The Big Dis *'89*

Liam O'Brien(1913-96)
Young at Heart *'54*
Chain Lightning *'50*

Richard O'Brien(1942-)
Shock Treatment *'81*
The Rocky Horror Picture Show *'75*

Robert O'Brien(1918-2005)
By the Light of the Silvery Moon *'53*
The Lemon Drop Kid *'51*
Lady on a Train *'45*

Jeffrey Obrow
Bram Stoker's The Mummy *'97*
The Kindred *'87*
The Power *'80*

James O'Connolly(1924-87)
Tower of Evil *'72*
Night Caller from Outer Space *'66*

Gavin O'Connor
Pride and Glory *'08*
Tumbleweeds *'98*

David Odell
Masters of the Universe *'87*
Supergirl *'84*
The Dark Crystal *'82*
Dealing: Or the Berkeley-to-Boston Forty-Brick Lost-Bag Blues *'72*
Cry Uncle *'71*

Clifford Odets(1906-63)
Wild in the Country *'61*
Sweet Smell of Success *'57*
Deadline at Dawn *'46*
Humoresque *'46*
None But the Lonely Heart *'44*

The General Died at Dawn *'36*

Jerome Odlum(1905-54)
The Fast and the Furious *'54*
I Was Framed *'42*

Joseph O'Donnell(1891-1963)
Manhunt in the African Jungles *'43*
Raiders of Red Gap *'43*
Billy the Kid in Santa Fe *'41*
Battling Outlaw *'40*
Billy the Kid in Texas *'40*
Border Caballero *'36*
Lightnin' Bill Carson *'36*
Racing Blood *'36*
The Traitor *'36*
His Fighting Blood *'35*
Trails of the Wild *'35*

Michael O'Donoghue(1940-94)
Scrooged *'88*
Shame of the Jungle *'75*

Steve Oedekerk(1961-)
Evan Almighty *'07*
Barnyard *'06*
Bruce Almighty *'03*
Kung Pow! Enter the Fist *'02*
Jimmy Neutron: Boy Genius *'01*
Nutty Professor 2: The Klumps *'00*
Patch Adams *'98*
Nothing to Lose *'96*
The Nutty Professor *'96*
Ace Ventura: When Nature Calls *'95*
High Strung *'91*

Mo Ogrodnik(1966-)
Uptown Girls *'03*
Ripe *'97*

Hideo Oguni(1904-96)
Ran *'85*
Dodes 'ka-den *'70*
Tora! Tora! Tora! *'70*
High & Low *'62*
Sanjuro *'62*
Yojimbo *'61*
The Bad Sleep Well *'60*
The Hidden Fortress *'58*
The Lower Depths *'57*
Throne of Blood *'57*
I Live in Fear *'55*
Seven Samurai *'54*
Ikiru *'52*

Colo Tavernier O'Hagan
L'Appat *'94*
Daddy Nostalgia *'90*
Beatrice *'88*
The Story of Women *'88*
A Sunday in the Country *'84*

James O'Hanlon(1910-69)
Calamity Jane *'53*
Destination Moon *'50*
Sahara *'43*

Brian O'Hara
Apartment 1303 *'07*
Nightmare *'00*

Mary O'Hara
Braveheart *'25*
The Prisoner of Zenda *'22*

Tommy O'Haver(1968-2005)
An American Crime *'07*
Billy's Hollywood Screen Kiss *'98*

Paul Ohl
North Star *'96*
Highlander: The Final Dimension *'94*

Ataru Oikawa
The Black House *'00*
Tomie *'99*

Tetsuya Oishi
Death Note 2: The Last Name *'07*

Death Note *'06*

Mark O'Keefe
Click *'06*
Bruce Almighty *'03*

Barbara O'Kelly
The Waiting Game *'98*
Skin Deep *'94*

Pedro Olea(1938-)
Zafarinas *'94*
The Fencing Master *'92*

Joel Oliansky(1935-2002)
Bird *'88*
The Todd Killings *'71*

Deanna Oliver
My Favorite Martian *'98*
Casper *'95*

Ron Oliver
Liar's Edge *'92*
Prom Night 3: The Last Kiss *'89*
Hello Mary Lou: Prom Night 2 *'87*

Hector Olivera(1931-)
The Road *'00*
A Shadow You Soon Will Be *'94*
Funny, Dirty Little War *'83*

Ermanno Olmi(1931-)
The Tree of Wooden Clogs *'78*
Fiances *'63*

Arne Olsen
Grizzly Rage *'07*
Hybrid *'07*
Escape from Atlantis *'97*
All Dogs Go to Heaven 2 *'95*
Mighty Morphin Power Rangers: The Movie *'95*
Cop and a Half *'93*
Final Round *'93*
Red Scorpion *'89*

Dana Olsen
George of the Jungle *'97*
The 'Burbs *'89*

David C. Olson
Anacondas: Trail of Blood *'09*
Anaconda 3: The Offspring *'08*

Josh Olson
A History of Violence *'05*
Infested: Invasion of the Killer Bugs *'02*
On the Border *'98*

David O'Malley(1944-)
Dark Honeymoon *'08*
Fatal Instinct *'93*
Edge of Honor *'91*
Easy Wheels *'89*
Kid Colter *'85*
Hangar 18 *'80*
House of the Dead *'78*
Mountain Man *'77*

Kazuki Omori(1952-)
Godzilla vs. King Ghidora *'91*
Godzilla vs. Biollante *'89*

Charles "Blackie" O'Neal(1904-96)
Lassie's Great Adventure *'62*
Montana *'50*
Return of the Bad Men *'48*
Cry of the Werewolf *'44*
The Seventh Victim *'43*

Robert Vincent O'Neil
Jailbait *'93*
Deadly Force *'83*
Vice Squad *'82*
The Baltimore Bullet *'80*

Ella O'Neill
The Phantom Rider *'36*
Battling with Buffalo Bill *'31*

Max Ophuls(1902-57)
Modigliani *'58*
Lola Montes *'55*

The Earrings of Madame De... *'54*
Le Plaisir *'52*

George Oppenheimer(1900-77)
Undercurrent *'46*
A Day at the Races *'37*
Libeled Lady *'36*

Joshua Oppenheimer
Sahara *'05*
A Sound of Thunder *'05*

Timothy O'Rawe
Midnight Confessions *'95*
Ghoul School *'90*

Roberto Orci
Star Trek *'09*
Transformers: Revenge of the Fallen *'09*
Transformers *'07*
Mission: Impossible 3 *'06*
The Island *'05*
The Legend of Zorro *'05*

Joaquin Oristrell(1958-)
Between Your Legs *'99*
Extasis *'96*
Mouth to Mouth *'95*

Arthur Orloff
Thunder in God's Country *'51*
Missourians *'50*

John Orloff
A Mighty Heart *'07*
Band of Brothers *'01*

Ron Ormond(1911-81)
Kentucky Jubilee *'51*
Square Dance Jubilee *'51*
Yes, Sir, Mr. Bones *'51*
Last Bullet *'50*
Outlaw Fury *'50*
Rangeland Empire *'50*
Red Desert *'50*
Sudden Death *'50*
Rimfire *'49*
Ringside *'49*

Alan Ormsby(1944-)
The Substitute *'96*
High Stakes *'93*
Indecency *'92*
Popcorn *'89*
Porky's 2: The Next Day *'83*
Cat People *'82*
Little Dragons *'80*
My Bodyguard *'80*
Touch & Go *'80*
Deranged *'74*
Children Shouldn't Play with Dead Things *'72*
Deathdream *'72*

Samuel Ornitz
One Man's Journey *'33*
Men of America *'32*

Gertrude Orr
Call of the Yukon *'38*
Slander House *'38*

James Orr(1953-)
Christmas in Wonderland *'07*
Man of the House *'95*
Sister Act 2: Back in the Habit *'93*
Mr. Destiny *'90*
Three Men and a Baby *'87*
Tough Guys *'86*
Breaking All the Rules *'85*

Marion Orth
Tomboy *'40*
Street Angel *'28*

J.O.C. Orton(1889-1962)
The Ghost Train *'41*
Hey! Hey! USA! *'38*
Non-Stop New York *'37*

Paul Osborn(1901-88)
South Pacific *'58*
Sayonara *'57*
East of Eden *'54*
Invitation *'51*

Homecoming *'48*
Portrait of Jennie *'48*
The Young in Heart *'38*

Ron Osborn
Meet Joe Black *'98*
Radioland Murders *'94*

Andrew Osborne
On_Line *'01*
Behind Enemy Lines *'96*

John Osborne(1929-94)
Look Back in Anger *'80*
Luther *'74*
Tom Jones *'63*
The Entertainer *'60*
Look Back in Anger *'58*

Ken Osborne
Escape from Cell Block 3 *'74*
Wild Wheels *'69*

Kent Osborne
Hannah Takes the Stairs *'07*
Women Unchained *'72*

William Osborne
Thunderbirds *'04*
The Scorpion King *'02*
Chilly Dogs *'01*
Dr. Jekyll and Ms. Hyde *'95*
Ghost in the Machine *'93*
The Real McCoy *'93*
Stop! or My Mom Will Shoot *'92*
Twins *'88*

Mamoru Oshii
Talking Head *'92*
Stray Dog *'91*
The Red Spectacles *'87*

Nagisa Oshima(1932-)
Taboo *'99*
Max, Mon Amour *'86*
Merry Christmas, Mr. Lawrence *'83*
In the Realm of the Senses *'76*
The Cruel Story of Youth *'60*

Diana Ossana
Comanche Moon *'08*
Brokeback Mountain *'05*
Johnson County War *'02*
Larry McMurtry's Dead Man's Walk *'96*
Larry McMurtry's Streets of Laredo *'95*

Hawk Ostby
Iron Man *'08*
First Snow *'07*

Olatunde Osunsanmi(1977-)
The Fourth Kind *'09*
The Cavern *'05*

Katsuhiro Otomo(1954-)
Steamboy *'05*
Akira *'89*

Idrissa Ouedraogo(1954-)
Tilai *'90*
Yaaba *'89*

Jean-Paul Ouellette
The Unnamable 2: The Statement of Randolph Carter *'92*
The Unnamable *'88*

Richard Outten
Last Rites *'98*
Little Nemo: Adventures in Slumberland *'92*
Pet Sematary 2 *'92*
Lionheart *'87*

Eric Overmyer(1951-)
Homicide: The Movie *'00*
Rear Window *'98*

Satoshi Owada
Cruel Restaurant *'08*
Attack Girls' Swim Team vs. the Undead *'07*

Alun Owen
Unexplained Laughter *'89*
A Hard Day's Night *'64*

Francois Ozon(1967-)
Time to Leave *'05*
5x2 *'04*
Swimming Pool *'03*
8 Women *'02*
Under the Sand *'00*
Criminal Lovers *'99*
Water Drops on Burning Rocks *'99*
Sitcom *'97*

Ferzan Ozpetek(1959-)
Saturn in Opposition *'07*
Facing Windows *'03*
His Secret Life *'01*
Harem *'99*
Steam: A Turkish Bath *'96*

Yasujiro Ozu(1903-63)
An Autumn Afternoon *'62*
Good Morning *'59*
Tokyo Story *'53*

William R. Pace(1958-)
Charming Billy *'98*
Blades *'89*

Ernest Pagano
Greenwich Village *'44*
The Flying Irishman *'39*

Jo Pagano(1906-82)
Try and Get Me *'50*
The Man I Love *'46*

Marcel Pagnol(1895-1974)
Nais *'45*
Le Schpountz *'38*
Harvest *'37*
Cesar *'36*
The Baker's Wife *'33*
Topaze *'33*
Fanny *'32*
Marius *'31*

Nick Paine
Josh Kirby... Time Warrior: Chapter 3, Trapped on Toyworld *'95*
Philadelphia Experiment 2 *'93*

Melissa Painter
Fishtales *'07*
Wildflowers *'99*

Alan J. Pakula(1928-98)
The Pelican Brief *'93*
Presumed Innocent *'90*
See You in the Morning *'89*
Sophie's Choice *'82*

Euzhan Palcy(1957-)
A Dry White Season *'89*
Sugar Cane Alley *'83*

Michael Palin(1943-)
American Friends *'91*
Consuming Passions *'88*
Monty Python's The Meaning of Life *'83*
The Missionary *'82*
The Secret Policeman's Other Ball *'82*
Time Bandits *'81*
Monty Python's Life of Brian *'79*
Monty Python and the Holy Grail *'75*
And Now for Something Completely Different *'72*

Rospo Pallenberg
Druids *'01*
The Emerald Forest *'85*
Excalibur *'81*

Anders Palm(1949-)
Dead Certain *'92*
Murder on Line One *'90*

Chazz Palminteri(1952-)
Faithful *'95*
A Bronx Tale *'93*

Norman Panama(1914-2003)
I Will, I Will for Now *'76*
The Road to Hong Kong *'62*
The Facts of Life *'60*
Li'l Abner *'59*
The Trap *'59*
Court Jester *'56*
White Christmas *'54*
Above and Beyond *'53*
Mr. Blandings Builds His Dream House *'48*
Monsieur Beaucaire *'46*
The Road to Utopia *'46*
Thank Your Lucky Stars *'43*
Star Spangled Rhythm *'42*

Danny Pang(1965-)
Re-Cycle *'06*
The Eye 3 *'05*
The Eye *'02*
Bangkok Dangerous *'00*

Thomas Pang
Diary *'06*
Re-Cycle *'06*

Alan Pao
Loaded *'08*
Chasing Ghosts *'05*

Dennis Paoli
The Dentist *'96*
Castle Freak *'95*
Body Snatchers *'93*
Mortal Sins *'92*
The Pit & the Pendulum *'91*
Meridian: Kiss of the Beast *'90*
From Beyond *'86*
Re-Animator *'84*

Jaroslav Papousek(1929-95)
The Firemen's Ball *'68*
Intimate Lighting *'65*
Loves of a Blonde *'65*
Black Peter *'63*

Roger Paradiso
Tony n' Tina's Wedding *'07*
Kisses in the Dark *'97*

John Paragon(1954-)
Elvira's Haunted Hills *'02*
Twinsitters *'95*
Elvira, Mistress of the Dark *'88*

Edward Paramore(1895-1956)
Three Comrades *'38*
The Bitter Tea of General Yen *'33*

Gail Parent
Confessions of a Teenage Drama Queen *'04*
All I Want for Christmas *'91*

Chan-wook Park(1963-)
Thirst *'09*
Lady Vengeance *'05*
Three ... Extremes *'04*
Oldboy *'03*
Sympathy for Mr. Vengeance *'02*
JSA: Joint Security Area *'00*

Alan Parker(1944-)
Evita *'96*
The Road to Wellville *'94*
Come See the Paradise *'90*
Angel Heart *'87*
Bugsy Malone *'76*
Melody *'71*

David Parker(1947-)
House of the Dead *'03*
Amy *'98*
Rikky and Pete *'88*
Malcolm *'86*

Dorothy Parker(1893-1967)
A Star Is Born *'37*
The Moon's Our Home *'36*

Joan H. Parker
Spenser: Pale Kings & Princes *'94*
Spenser: Ceremony *'93*

Jonathan Parker
(Untitled) *'09*
Bartleby *'01*

Norton S. Parker
Rio Grande Raiders *'46*
Young Bill Hickok *'40*

Oliver Parker(1960-)
The Importance of Being Earnest *'02*
An Ideal Husband *'99*
Othello *'95*

Robert B. Parker(1932-)
Monte Walsh *'03*
Thin Air *'00*
Small Vices: A Spenser Mystery *'99*
Spenser: Ceremony *'93*

Ronald Parker
Joan of Arc *'99*
Gargantua *'98*

Scott Parker
Die Laughing *'80*
He Knows You're Alone *'80*

Tom S. Parker
The Flintstones *'94*
Getting Even with Dad *'94*
Richie Rich *'94*
Stay Tuned *'92*

Trey Parker(1969-)
Team America: World Police *'04*
South Park: Bigger, Longer and Uncut *'99*
Orgazmo *'98*
Cannibal! The Musical *'96*

William Parker(1886-1941)
The Nut *'21*
The Jack Knife Man *'20*

Walter F. Parkes
Sneakers *'92*
WarGames *'83*

Gianfranco Parolini(1930-)
Adios, Sabata *'71*
Return of Sabata *'71*
Sabata *'69*
Island of Lost Girls *'68*

Sara Parriott
The Starter Wife *'07*
Runaway Bride *'99*
The Favor *'92*
Three Men and a Little Lady *'90*
Worth Winning *'89*

Marion Parsonnet
Gilda *'46*
I'll Be Seeing You *'44*

Lindsley Parsons(1905-92)
Rollin' Plains *'38*
Desert Trail *'35*
Paradise Canyon *'35*
Man from Utah *'34*
Randy Rides Alone *'34*
Trail Beyond *'34*
Sagebrush Trail *'33*

Michael Part(1949-)
A Kid in Aladdin's Palace *'97*
A Kid in King Arthur's Court *'95*

Frank Partos(1901-56)
The Snake Pit *'48*
The Uninvited *'44*
Honolulu *'39*
The Last Outpost *'35*
Wings in the Dark *'35*
Thirty Day Princess *'34*

Ernest Pascal(1896-1966)
Canyon Passage *'46*
Hollywood Cavalcade *'39*
Lloyds of London *'36*
Under the Pampas Moon *'35*

Goran Paskalyevic(1947-)
How Harry Became a Tree *'01*
Cabaret Balkan *'98*

Pier Paolo Pasolini(1922-75)
Salo, or the 120 Days of Sodom *'75*
Arabian Nights *'74*
The Canterbury Tales *'71*
The Decameron *'70*
Porcile *'69*
The Hawks & the Sparrows *'67*
The Gospel According to St. Matthew *'64*
Love Meetings *'64*
The Grim Reaper *'62*
Mamma Roma *'62*
RoGoPaG *'62*
Accatone! *'61*
Il Bell'Antonio *'60*
That Long Night in '43 *'60*

Ivan Passer(1933-)
Law and Disorder *'74*
Born to Win *'71*
The Firemen's Ball *'68*
Intimate Lighting *'65*
Loves of a Blonde *'65*

Jonas Pate(1970-)
The Take *'07*
Deceiver *'97*
The Grave *'95*

Josh Pate(1970-)
The Take *'07*
Deceiver *'97*
The Grave *'95*

David Paterson(1966-)
Bridge to Terabithia *'07*
Love, Ludlow *'05*

John Patrick(1905-95)
Daniel Boone: Trail Blazer *'56*
Love Is a Many-Splendored Thing *'55*
Mr. Moto Takes a Chance *'38*
The Holy Terror *'37*

Vincent Patrick
The Devil's Own *'96*
Family Business *'89*
The Pope of Greenwich Village *'84*

Cinco Paul
Despicable Me *'10*
Dr. Seuss' Horton Hears a Who! *'08*
The Santa Clause 2 *'02*
Bubble Boy *'01*

Don Michael Paul(1963-)
Who's Your Caddy? *'07*
Half Past Dead *'02*
Harley Davidson and the Marlboro Man *'91*

Elliot Paul(1891-1958)
New Orleans *'47*
It's a Pleasure *'45*
A Woman's Face *'41*

Steven Paul(1954-)
Karate Dog *'04*
Baby Geniuses *'98*

David Paulsen
Savage Weekend *'80*
The Uranium Conspiracy *'78*

John Paxton(1911-85)
On the Beach *'59*
The Wild One *'54*
Murder, My Sweet *'44*

Alexander Payne(1961-)
I Now Pronounce You Chuck and Larry *'07*
Paris, je t'aime *'06*
Sideways *'04*
About Schmidt *'02*
Jurassic Park 3 *'01*
Election *'99*
Citizen Ruth *'96*

Dave Payne
Boltneck *'98*
Criminal Hearts *'95*

Don Payne
Fantastic Four: Rise of the Silver Surfer *'07*
My Super Ex-Girlfriend *'06*

Keith Payson
Puppet Master 5: The Final Chapter *'94*
Puppet Master 4 *'93*

Senel Paz
A Paradise Under the Stars *'99*
Strawberry and Chocolate *'93*

Steve Peace(1953-)
Killer Tomatoes Eat France *'91*
Return of the Killer Tomatoes! *'88*

Ann Peacock
The Killing Room *'09*
Kit Kittredge: An American Girl *'08*
Nights in Rodanthe *'08*
Pictures of Hollis Woods *'07*
The Chronicles of Narnia: The Lion, the Witch and the Wardrobe *'05*
In My Country *'04*
Cora Unashamed *'00*
A Lesson Before Dying *'99*

Craig Pearce
Moulin Rouge *'01*
William Shakespeare's Romeo and Juliet *'96*
Strictly Ballroom *'92*

Humphrey Pearson(1894-1937)
Red Salute *'35*
Lost Squadron *'32*
Men of America *'32*

Raoul Peck(1953-)
Sometimes in April *'05*
Lumumba *'01*

Anthony Peckham
The Book of Eli *'10*
Invictus *'09*
Sherlock Holmes *'09*
Don't Say a Word *'01*

David Peckinpah(1951-2006)
The Paperboy *'94*
The Diamond Trap *'91*

Sam Peckinpah(1925-84)
Bring Me the Head of Alfredo Garcia *'74*
Straw Dogs *'72*
The Wild Bunch *'69*
Villa Rides *'68*
Invasion of the Body Snatchers *'56*

Quinton Peeples
The Circuit *'08*
Joyride *'97*

Bill Peet(1915-2002)
The Sword in the Stone *'63*
101 Dalmatians *'61*
Peter Pan *'53*
Fantasia *'40*
Call of the Yukon *'38*

Simon Pegg(1970-)
Hot Fuzz *'07*
Shaun of the Dead *'04*

Kimberly Peirce
Stop-Loss *'08*
Boys Don't Cry *'99*

Louis Pelletier(1907-2000)
Smith! *'69*
The Horse in the Gray Flannel Suit *'68*
Follow Me, Boys! *'66*
Those Calloways *'65*
Big Red *'62*

Joe Penhall
The Road *'09*
Enduring Love *'04*

Sean Penn(1960-)
Into the Wild *'07*
The Crossing Guard *'94*
The Indian Runner *'91*

Zak Penn(1968-)
The Incredible Hulk *'08*
X-Men: The Last Stand *'06*
Elektra *'05*
Suspect Zero *'04*
Behind Enemy Lines *'01*
Inspector Gadget *'99*
P.C.U. *'94*

Erdman Penner(1905-56)
Lady and the Tramp *'55*
Peter Pan *'53*
The Adventures of Ichabod and Mr. Toad *'49*
Pinocchio *'40*

John Penney
The Contaminated Man *'01*
The Enemy *'01*
In Pursuit *'00*
Matter of Trust *'98*
Past Perfect *'98*
Perfect Assassins *'98*
Return of the Living Dead 3 *'93*
The Kindred *'87*
The Power *'80*

Phil Penningroth
In the Line of Duty: Ambush in Waco *'93*
Silence of the Heart *'84*

David Peoples(1940-)
Soldier *'98*
12 Monkeys *'95*
Deadfall *'93*
Hero *'92*
Unforgiven *'92*
The Blood of Heroes *'89*
Leviathan *'89*
Blade Runner *'82*

Clare Peploe(1942-)
The Triumph of Love *'01*
Besieged *'98*
Rough Magic *'95*
High Season *'88*
Zabriskie Point *'70*

Mark Peploe(1943-)
Victory *'95*
Little Buddha *'93*
Afraid of the Dark *'92*
The Sheltering Sky *'90*
High Season *'88*
The Last Emperor *'87*
The Passenger *'75*
Pied Piper *'72*

Stacy Peralta(1957-)
Lords of Dogtown *'05*
Riding Giants *'04*

S.J. Perelman(1904-79)
Around the World in 80 Days *'56*
Horse Feathers *'32*
Monkey Business *'31*

Jesse Peretz(1968-)
The Chateau *'01*
First Love, Last Rites *'98*

Jack Perez
Mega Shark Vs. Giant Octopus *'09*
America's Deadliest Home Video *'91*

Mark Perez
Accepted *'06*
The Country Bears *'02*
Frank McKlusky, C.I. *'02*

Frank Ray Perilli
Alligator *'80*
Laserblast *'78*
Zoltan... Hound of Dracula *'78*
The Doberman Gang *'72*

Ivo Perilli(1902-94)
Barabbas *'62*
The Unfaithfuls *'60*
War and Peace *'56*

Lynn Perkins
Daughter of Don Q *'46*
King of the Forest Rangers *'46*
The Phantom Rider *'46*
The Purple Monster Strikes *'45*

Jacques Perrin(1941-)
Oceans *'09*
Winged Migration *'01*

Nat Perrin(1905-98)
I'll Take Sweden *'65*
Whistling in Brooklyn *'43*
Whistling in Dixie *'42*
The Gracie Allen Murder Case *'39*
Dimples *'36*
Duck Soup *'33*

Eleanor Perry(1914-81)
Man Who Loved Cat Dancing *'73*
David and Lisa *'62*

Fred C. Perry
The Wind *'87*
Zero Boys *'86*

Nickolas Perry(1967-)
The Hunting of the President *'04*
Speedway Junky *'99*

Tyler Perry(1969-)
Tyler Perry's Why Did I Get Married Too? *'10*
I Can Do Bad All By Myself *'09*
Madea Goes to Jail *'09*
Tyler Perry's Meet the Browns *'08*
Daddy's Little Girls *'07*
Tyler Perry's Why Did I Get Married? *'07*
Madea's Family Reunion *'06*
Diary of a Mad Black Woman *'05*

Michael Pertwee(1916-91)
One More Time *'70*
Salt & Pepper *'68*
A Funny Thing Happened on the Way to the Forum *'66*
Strange Bedfellows *'65*
Ladies Who Do *'63*
The Mouse on the Moon *'62*

Roland Pertwee(1885-1963)
The Magic Bow *'47*
King Solomon's Mines *'37*
Non-Stop New York *'37*
The Ghoul *'34*

P.J. Pesce(1961-)
Smokin' Aces 2: Assassins' Ball *'10*
The Desperate Trail *'94*

Steve Pesce(1960-)
Stranger in the House *'97*
Daddy's Girl *'96*

Charlie Peters
My One and Only *'09*
Krippendorf's Tribe *'98*
Music from Another Room *'97*
My Father the Hero *'93*
Passed Away *'92*
Three Men and a Little Lady *'90*
Her Alibi *'88*
Hot to Trot! *'88*
Blame It on Rio *'84*
Kiss Me Goodbye *'82*
Paternity *'81*

Stephen Peters(1947-)
Wild Things *'98*
The Wolves *'95*

Wolfgang Petersen(1941-)
Shattered '91
The NeverEnding Story '84
Das Boot '81

Bob Peterson
Up '09
Finding Nemo '03

Cassandra Peterson(1951-)
Elvira's Haunted Hills '02
Elvira, Mistress of the Dark '88

Sandro Petraglia(1947-)
The Girl by the Lake '07
My Brother Is an Only Child '07
Best of Youth '03
The Truce '96
Fiorile '93
The Stolen Children '92
Forever Mary '89
Julia and Julia '87

Daniel Petrie, Jr.(1952-)
In the Army Now '94
Toy Soldiers '91
Shoot to Kill '88
The Big Easy '87
Beverly Hills Cop '84

Michael Petroni
Possession '09
The Dangerous Lives of Altar Boys '02
Till Human Voices Wake Us '02

Vladimir Petrov(1896-1966)
The Inspector General '52
Peter the First: Part 1 '37

Pamela Pettler
9 '09
Monster House '06
Tim Burton's Corpse Bride '05

J.T. Petty
Mimic 3: Sentinel '03
Soft for Digging '01

Harley Peyton
Bandits '01
Elmore Leonard's Gold Coast '97
Keys to Tulsa '96
Heaven's Prisoners '95
Less Than Zero '87

Chuck Pfarrer
Red Planet '00
Virus '98
The Jackal '97
Barb Wire '96
Darkman 2: The Return of Durant '94
Hard Target '93
Darkman '90

Anna Hamilton Phelan
Amelia '09
Girl, Interrupted '99
In Love and War '96
Gorillas in the Mist '88
Mask '85

Brian Phelan
In the Secret State '85
Little Mother '71

Bill Phillips(1908-57)
Forbidden Choices '94
El Diablo '90
Rainbow Drive '90
Rising Son '90
Physical Evidence '89
Fire with Fire '86
Christine '84

Jeff Phillips
I Downloaded a Ghost '04
Treehouse Hostage '99
3 Ninjas: High Noon at Mega Mountain '97

Lou Diamond Phillips(1962-)
Ambition '91
Trespasses '86

Patrick Phillips
Good People, Bad Things '08
Dragon Storm '04
Interceptor Force 2 '02

Todd Phillips(1970-)
School for Scoundrels '06
Starsky & Hutch '04
Old School '03
Road Trip '00

Robert Phippeny
Simon, King of the Witches '71
The Night of the Following Day '69

Nicholas Phipps(1913-80)
Doctor in Love '60
Captain's Paradise '53
Madeleine '50

Maurice Pialat(1925-2003)
Van Gogh '92
Under Satan's Sun '87
A Nos Amours '84
Loulou '80

Fabio Piccioni
Cjamango '67
Thor and the Amazon Women '60

Giuseppe Piccioni(1953-)
Light of My Eyes '01
Not of This World '99

Francesco Piccolo(1964-)
Quiet Chaos '08
Days and Clouds '07
Agata and the Storm '04

Jim Piddock(1956-)
The Man '05
One Good Turn '95
Traces of Red '92

John Pielmeier
Gifted Hands: The Ben Carson Story '09
The Memory Keeper's Daughter '08
Hitler: The Rise of Evil '03
Dodson's Journey '01
Sins of the Father '01
Flowers for Algernon '00
The Happy Face Murders '99
Through the Eyes of a Killer '92
An Inconvenient Woman '91
The Shell Seekers '89
Agnes of God '85

Arthur C. Pierce(1923-87)
The Invisible Strangler '76
Invasion of the Animal People '62
The Cosmic Man '59

Charles B. Pierce(1938-)
Boggy Creek II '83
Sacred Ground '83
The Evictors '79
Norseman '78
Grayeagle '77
Winterhawk '76

Shirley Pierce
For Real '02
Incognito '99

Frank Pierson(1925-)
Presumed Innocent '90
In Country '89
King of the Gypsies '78
A Star Is Born '76
Dog Day Afternoon '75
The Anderson Tapes '71

The Looking Glass War '69
Cool Hand Luke '67
Cat Ballou '65

Krzysztof Piesiewicz(1945-)
Heaven '01
Trois Couleurs: Blanc '94
Trois Couleurs: Rouge '94
Trois Couleurs: Bleu '93
The Double Life of Veronique '91
The Decalogue '88
No End '84

Tseng Pik-Yin
The Bride with White Hair '93
Iron Monkey '93

Jeremy Pikser
War, Inc. '08
Bulworth '98
The Lemon Sisters '90

Nicholas Pileggi(1933-)
Kings of South Beach '07
Casino '95
City Hall '95
Goodfellas '90

Michael Piller(1948-2005)
The Dead Zone '02
Star Trek: Insurrection '98

Tullio Pinelli(1908-)
Ginger & Fred '86
Juliet of the Spirits '65
8 1/2 '63
Boccaccio '70 '62
La Dolce Vita '60
Nights of Cabiria '57
Il Bidone '55
La Strada '54
Love in the City '53
The White Sheik '52
Variety Lights '51

Marcelo Pineyro(1953-)
The Method '05
Wild Horses '95

Sidney W. Pink(1916-2002)
The Castilian '63
Reptilicus '62
The Angry Red Planet '59

Steve Pink(1966-)
High Fidelity '00
Grosse Pointe Blank '97

Harold Pinter(1930-2008)
Sleuth '07
The Trial '93
The Comfort of Strangers '91
The Heat of the Day '91
The Handmaid's Tale '90
Reunion '88
Dumb Waiter '87
The Room '87
Turtle Diary '86
Betrayal '83
The French Lieutenant's Woman '81
The Last Tycoon '76
The Go-Between '71
Accident '67
The Quiller Memorandum '66
The Pumpkin Eater '64
The Servant '63

Lucian Pintilie(1933-)
An Unforgettable Summer '94
The Oak '93
Ward Six '78

Bret Piper
Screaming Dead '03
They Bite '95
A Nymphoid Barbarian in Dinosaur Hell '94

David Pirie(1953-)
Dr. Bell and Mr. Doyle: The Dark Beginnings of Sherlock Holmes '00

The Wyvern Mystery '00
The Woman in White '97

Robert Pirosh(1910-89)
Hell Is for Heroes '62
Valley of the Kings '54
Go for Broke! '51
Battleground '49
I Married a Witch '42
Night of January 16th '41
A Day at the Races '37

Mark Pirro(1956-)
Buford's Beach Bunnies '92
My Mom's a Werewolf '89
Deathrow Gameshow '88
Curse of the Queerwolf '87

Glen Pitre
The Man Who Came Back '08
The Home Front '02
Belizaire the Cajun '86

Montgomery Pittman
Tarzan and the Lost Safari '57
Tarzan's Hidden Jungle '55

Angelo Pizzo
The Game of Their Lives '05
Rudy '93
Hoosiers '86

Alan Plater(1935-)
The Last of the Blonde Bombshells '00
A Merry War '97
A Very British Coup '88
Fortunes of War '87
Coming Through '85
The Inside Man '84
Priest of Love '81
The Virgin and the Gypsy '70

Jonathan Platnick
End of Summer '97
Silent Victim '92

Polly Platt(1939-)
A Map of the World '99
Pretty Baby '78

David Pliler
Forever Strong '08
Outlaw Trail '06

George Plympton(1889-1972)
Trouble Chasers '45
Gang Busters '42
Junior G-Men of the Air '42
Outlaws of the Rio Grande '41
Flash Gordon Conquers the Universe '40
Junior G-Men '40
Space Soldiers Conquer the Universe '40
The Green Hornet '39
Texas Wildcats '39
Feud Maker '38
The Rangers' Roundup '38
The Spider's Web '38
Doomed at Sundown '37
Paroled to Die '37
The Red Rope '37
Crooked Trail '36
The Phantom Rider '36
Range Riders '35
Murder on the High Seas '32
Battling with Buffalo Bill '31
Blood and Steel '25

Jeremy Podeswa(1962-)
The Five Senses '99
Eclipse '94

Amos Poe
The Guitar '08
Frogs for Snakes '98
Rocket Gibraltar '88
Alphabet City '84
The Foreigner '78

James Poe(1921-80)
The Nightman '93
Riot '69
They Shoot Horses, Don't They? '69

Lilies of the Field '63
Toys in the Attic '63
Cat on a Hot Tin Roof '58
Around the World in 80 Days '56
Attack! '56
Scandal Sheet '52

Charles Edward Pogue
Kull the Conqueror '97
Dragonheart '96
Hands of a Murderer '90
D.O.A. '88
The Fly '86
Psycho 3 '86
The Hound of the Baskervilles '83
The Sign of Four '83

John Pogue
Ghost Ship '02
Rollerball '02
The Skulls '00
U.S. Marshals '98

Jean-Marie Poire(1945-)
Just Visiting '01
The Visitors '95
No Problem '75

Gregory Poirier
A Sound of Thunder '05
Tomcats '01
Gossip '99
Rosewood '96
The Stranger '95

Joseph Poland(1892-1962)
Federal Operator 99 '45
Manhunt of Mystery Island '45
The Purple Monster Strikes '45
Manhunt in the African Jungles '43
Mysterious Doctor Satan '40
Winds of the Wasteland '36
The Sea Lion '21

Roman Polanski(1933-)
The Ghost Writer '10
The Ninth Gate '99
Bitter Moon '92
Frantic '88
Pirates '86
Tess '79
The Tenant '76
Diary of Forbidden Dreams '73
Macbeth '71
Rosemary's Baby '68
The Fearless Vampire Killers '67
Cul de Sac '66
Repulsion '65
Knife in the Water '62

Stephen Poliakoff(1952-)
Friends & Crocodiles '05
Gideon's Daughter '05
Almost Strangers '01
Shooting the Past '99
Century '94
Close My Eyes '91

Mark Polish(1972-)
The Astronaut Farmer '07
Northfork '03
Jackpot '01
Twin Falls Idaho '99

Michael Polish(1972-)
The Astronaut Farmer '07
Northfork '03
Jackpot '01
Twin Falls Idaho '99

Jack Pollexfen(1908-2003)
The Atomic Brain '64
The Daughter of Dr. Jekyll '57
The Man from Planet X '51

Gene Pollock
The Thrill Killers '65
Incredibly Strange Creatures Who Stopped Living and Became Mixed-Up Zombies '63

Vicki Polon
Mr. Wonderful '93
Girlfriends '78

Mark Alan Polonia
Terror House '97
Feeders '96

Abraham Polonsky(1910-99)
Monsignor '82
Avalanche Express '79
Tell Them Willie Boy Is Here '69
Madigan '68
Odds Against Tomorrow '59
Force of Evil '49
Body and Soul '47
Golden Earrings '47

Abe Polsky
The Baby '72
Rebel Rousers '69

Darryl Ponicsan
The Enemy Within '94
School Ties '92
The Boost '88
Nuts '87
Vision Quest '85
Taps '81
Cinderella Liberty '73

Ventura Pons(1945-)
Food of Love '02
To Die (Or Not) '99
Caresses '97
What It's All About '95

Gillo Pontecorvo(1919-2006)
The Battle of Algiers '66
Kapo '59
The Wide Blue Road '57

DJ Pooh
The Wash '01
Three Strikes '00
Friday '95

Lea Pool(1950-)
Set Me Free '99
Mouvements du Desir '94

Robert Roy Pool
Outbreak '94
Dead to Rights '93
Big Town '87

Duane Poole
Moonlight & Mistletoe '08
I Married a Monster '98
I've Been Waiting for You '98
Shattered Image '98
One Christmas '95
The Man in the Attic '94
Praying Mantis '93
Sunstroke '92

Marty Poole
Diamond Run '00
Reptilian '99

Aaron Pope
Pandemic '09
Rampage: The Hillside Strangler Murders '04

Elaine Pope
Alfie '04
These Old Broads '01

Jeff Pope
Essex Boys '99
The Magician '93
Fool's Gold: The Story of the Brink's-Mat Robbery '92

Tom Pope
The Manitou '78
Don't Look in the Basement '73

Eric Poppen
Borderland '07
Virtual Assassin '95

Joel Posner
The Next Big Thing '02
Last Breath '96

Getting In *'94*

P.J. Posner

The Next Big Thing *'02*
Last Breath *'96*
Getting In *'94*

Dennis Potter(1935-94)

The Singing Detective *'03*
Lipstick on Your Collar *'94*
Mesmer *'94*
Christabel *'89*
Track 29 *'88*
Dreamchild *'85*
Gorky Park *'83*
Brimstone & Treacle *'82*
Pennies from Heaven *'81*

Sally Potter(1947-)

The Man Who Cried *'00*
The Tango Lesson *'97*
Orlando *'92*

Gerald Potterton(1931-)

The Rainbow Gang *'73*
Railrodder *'65*

Michel W. Potts(1946-)

Night Eyes 3 *'93*
Tropical Heat *'93*

Michael Powell(1905-90)

The Elusive Pimpernel *'50*
The Red Shoes *'48*
Black Narcissus *'47*
Stairway to Heaven *'46*
I Know Where I'm Going *'45*
Contraband *'40*
Edge of the World *'37*
Red Ensign *'34*

Donna Powers

The Italian Job *'03*
Out of Order *'03*
Valentine *'01*
Skeletons in the Closet *'00*
Deep Blue Sea *'99*

Wayne Powers

The Italian Job *'03*
Out of Order *'03*
Valentine *'01*
Skeletons in the Closet *'00*
Deep Blue Sea *'99*

Manuel Pradal

Ginostra *'02*
Marie Baie des Anges *'97*

Tim Prager

Quicksand *'01*
Heat of the Sun *'99*
Vendetta *'99*
Haunted *'95*

Leonard Praskins

So This Is Washington *'43*
Ice Follies of 1939 *'39*
One in a Million *'36*
Emma *'32*

Dennis Pratt

Depth Charge *'08*
Leprechaun 4: In Space *'96*

John Prebble(1915-2001)

Elizabeth R *'72*
Zulu *'64*
Mysterious Island *'61*

David Prentiss

Alien Massacre *'67*
Gallery of Horrors *'67*

Robert Presnell, Jr. (1914-86)

Conspiracy of Hearts *'60*
Let No Man Write My Epitaph *'60*
Man in the Attic *'53*

Robert Presnell, Sr. (1894-1969)

Second Chance *'53*
Meet John Doe *'41*
The Real Glory *'39*
They Shall Have Music *'39*
Postal Inspector *'36*
Bureau of Missing Persons *'33*
Employees' Entrance *'33*
The Kennel Murder Case *'33*
What Price Hollywood? *'32*

Emeric Pressburger(1902-88)

The Elusive Pimpernel *'50*
The Red Shoes *'48*
Black Narcissus *'47*
Stairway to Heaven *'46*
I Know Where I'm Going *'45*
The Forty-Ninth Parallel *'41*

Steven Pressfield(1943-)

Army of One *'94*
Separate Lives *'94*
Freejack *'92*
Above the Law *'88*
King Kong Lives *'86*

Gaylene Preston

Perfect Strangers *'03*
Dark of the Night *'85*

Jason Preston

Trapped *'06*
The Utopian Society *'03*

Richard Preston, Jr.

Final Move *'06*
Firetrap *'01*
The Sender *'98*
Recoil *'97*
Little Bigfoot *'96*
Cyber-Tracker 2 *'95*

Trevor Preston

I'll Sleep When I'm Dead *'03*
Thicker Than Water *'93*
Parker *'84*

Jacques Prevert(1900-77)

The Hunchback of Notre Dame *'57*
Children of Paradise *'44*
Les Visiteurs du Soir *'42*
Bizarre Bizarre *'39*
The Crime of Monsieur Lange *'36*

Jeffrey Price(1949-)

Shrek the Third *'07*
Last Holiday *'06*
Dr. Seuss' How the Grinch Stole Christmas *'00*
Wild Wild West *'99*
Doc Hollywood *'91*
Who Framed Roger Rabbit *'88*
Trenchcoat *'83*

Richard Price(1949-)

Freedomland *'06*
Shaft *'00*
Ransom *'96*
Clockers *'95*
Kiss of Death *'94*
Mad Dog and Glory *'93*
Night and the City *'92*
New York Stories *'89*
Sea of Love *'89*
The Color of Money *'86*
Streets of Gold *'86*

Stanley Price(1892-1955)

A Royal Scandal *'96*
Genghis Cohn *'93*

Tim Rose Price

The Serpent's Kiss *'97*
Rapa Nui *'93*
A Dangerous Man: Lawrence after Arabia *'91*
Dark Obsession *'90*

J.B. Priestley(1894-1984)

Last Holiday *'50*
Dangerous Corner *'34*

Peter Prince

Waterland *'92*
The Hit *'85*

Gina Prince-Bythewood(1969-)

The Secret Life of Bees *'08*
Love and Basketball *'00*

David A. Prior

Felony *'95*
Mutant Species *'95*
Mardi Gras for the Devil *'93*
Raw Justice *'93*
Raw Nerve *'91*
Deadly Dancer *'90*
Lock 'n' Load *'90*
Final Sanction *'89*
Future Force *'89*
Operation Warzone *'89*
Hell on the Battleground *'88*
Deadly Prey *'87*
Sledgehammer *'83*

Ted Prior(1959-)

The Last Ride *'91*
Operation Warzone *'89*

David Pritchard

Violent Zone *'89*
Slashed Dreams *'74*

Pat Proft(1947-)

Scary Movie 3 *'03*
Wrongfully Accused *'98*
Mr. Magoo *'97*
High School High *'96*
Naked Gun 33 1/3: The Final Insult *'94*
Hot Shots! Part Deux *'93*
Brain Donors *'92*
Hot Shots! *'91*
Naked Gun 2 1/2: The Smell of Fear *'91*
Lucky Stiff *'88*
The Naked Gun: From the Files of Police Squad *'88*
Moving Violations *'85*
Real Genius *'85*
Bachelor Party *'84*
Police Academy *'84*

Biagio Proietti

The Black Cat *'81*
Taste of Death *'68*

Chip Proser

Innerspace *'87*
Iceman *'84*

Giorgio Prosperi

The Naked Maja *'59*
The Seven Hills of Rome *'58*

Mark Protosevich(1961-)

I Am Legend *'07*
Poseidon *'06*
The Cell *'00*

Monique Proulx(1952-)

Street Heart *'98*
Le Sexe des Etoiles *'93*

Alex Proyas(1965-)

Garage Days *'03*
Dark City *'97*

Richard Pryor(1940-2005)

Jo Jo Dancer, Your Life Is Calling *'86*
Bustin' Loose *'81*
Blazing Saddles *'74*

Robert Pucci

The Corruptor *'99*
The Spider and the Fly *'94*

Luis Puenzo(1946-)

Old Gringo *'89*
The Official Story *'85*

Frank Pugliese

Undefeated *'03*
Shot in the Heart *'01*

Jack Pulman(1925-79)

Poldark *'75*
War and Peace *'73*
The Golden Bowl *'72*
Portrait of a Lady *'67*

Daniella Purcell

Spacejacked *'98*
Not Like Us *'96*
The Wasp Woman *'96*
Midnight Tease *'94*

Gertrude Purcell(1895-1963)

Follow the Boys *'44*
The Invisible Woman *'40*
One Night in the Tropics *'40*
Destry Rides Again *'39*
Service De Luxe *'38*
If You Could Only Cook *'36*

Charles Purpura(1945-2005)

Satisfaction *'88*
Heaven Help Us *'85*

David Pursall

The Blue Max *'66*
The Longest Day *'62*

Neal Purvis(1961-)

Quantum of Solace *'08*
Casino Royale *'06*
Stoned *'05*
Convicted *'04*
Johnny English *'03*
Die Another Day *'02*
The World Is Not Enough *'99*
Plunkett & Macleane *'98*
Let Him Have It *'91*

Mario Puzo(1920-99)

Christopher Columbus: The Discovery *'92*
The Godfather, Part 3 *'90*
The Cotton Club *'84*
The Godfather 1902-1959: The Complete Epic *'81*
Superman 2 *'80*
Superman: The Movie *'78*
Earthquake *'74*
The Godfather, Part 2 *'74*
The Godfather *'72*

Daniel Pyne

Fracture *'07*
The Manchurian Candidate *'04*
The Sum of All Fears *'02*
Where's Marlowe? *'98*
White Sands *'92*
Doc Hollywood *'91*
The Hard Way *'91*
Pacific Heights *'90*

Albert Pyun(1954-)

Nemesis 4: Cry of Angels *'97*
Adrenalin: Fear the Rush *'96*
Nemesis 3: Time Lapse *'96*
Spitfire *'94*
Brain Smasher... A Love Story *'93*
Knights *'93*
Down Twisted *'89*
Alien from L.A. *'87*
Radioactive Dreams *'86*
Sword & the Sorcerer *'82*

John Quaintance

Aquamarine *'06*
Material Girls *'06*

Paris Qualles

A Raisin in the Sun *'08*
The Rosa Parks Story *'02*
A House Divided *'00*
Blood Brothers *'97*
The Tuskegee Airmen *'95*
The Inkwell *'94*

Darryl Quarles(1954-)

Black Knight *'01*
Big Momma's House *'00*
Soldier Boyz *'95*

Paul Quarrington(1953-)

Camilla *'94*
Whale Music *'94*
Giant Steps *'92*
Perfectly Normal *'91*

Jonas Quastel

Sasquatch *'02*
Listen *'96*
Crackerjack *'94*

Stephen Quay(1947-)

Piano Tuner of Earthquakes *'05*
Institue Benjamenta or This Dream People Call Human Life *'95*

Timothy Quay(1947-)

Piano Tuner of Earthquakes *'05*
Institue Benjamenta or This Dream People Call Human Life *'95*

Florence Quentin(1946-)

Le Bonheur Est Dans le Pre *'95*
Life Is a Long Quiet River *'88*

Pascal Quignard

A Pure Formality *'94*
Tous les Matins du Monde *'92*

Gene Quintano(1946-)

The Musketeer *'01*
Outlaw Justice *'98*
Operation Dumbo Drop *'95*
Sudden Death *'95*
National Lampoon's Loaded Weapon 1 *'93*
Honeymoon Academy *'90*
Police Academy 4: Citizens on Patrol *'87*
Allan Quatermain and the Lost City of Gold *'86*
Police Academy 3: Back in Training *'86*
King Solomon's Mines *'85*
Making the Grade *'84*

Eduardo Quiroz

The Damned *'06*
San Franpsycho *'06*
I Got Five on It *'05*

Jose Quiroz

The Damned *'06*
San Franpsycho *'06*
I Got Five on It *'05*

David Rabe(1940-)

Hurlyburly *'98*
Casualties of War *'89*
Streamers *'83*
I'm Dancing as Fast as I Can *'82*

Martin Rackin(1918-76)

Revak the Rebel *'60*
The Horse Soldiers *'59*
Long John Silver *'54*
Loan Shark *'52*
Sailor Beware *'52*
The Enforcer *'51*
The Stooge *'51*

Michael Radford(1946-)

The Merchant of Venice *'04*
Dancing at the Blue Iguana *'00*
The Postman *'94*
White Mischief *'88*
Another Time, Another Place *'83*

Niklas Radstrom

Everlasting Moments *'08*
Speak Up! It's So Dark *'93*

Edward A. Radtke(1962-)

A Loving Father *'02*
The Dream Catcher *'99*

Bob Rafelson(1933-)

Tales of Erotica *'93*
Mountains of the Moon *'90*
Stay Hungry *'76*
Five Easy Pieces *'70*
Head *'68*

Stewart Raffill(1945-)

Mac and Me *'88*
Ice Pirates *'84*
High Risk *'81*
Sea Gypsies *'78*
Across the Great Divide *'76*
The Adventures of the Wilderness Family *'76*
Napoleon and Samantha *'72*

John Raffo

Johnny Skidmarks *'97*
The Relic *'96*
Dragon: The Bruce Lee Story *'93*

Martin Ragaway(1923-89)

Lost in Alaska *'52*
Abbott and Costello in the Foreign Legion *'50*
Ma and Pa Kettle Go to Town *'50*

Philip Railsback

Flash of Genius *'08*
The Stars Fell on Henrietta *'94*

Ivan Raimi(1956-)

Drag Me to Hell *'09*
Spider-Man 3 *'07*
Army of Darkness *'92*
Darkman *'90*
Easy Wheels *'89*

Sam Raimi(1959-)

Drag Me to Hell *'09*
Spider-Man 3 *'07*
The Nutt House *'95*
The Hudsucker Proxy *'93*
Army of Darkness *'92*
Darkman *'90*
Evil Dead 2: Dead by Dawn *'87*
Crimewave *'85*
Evil Dead *'83*

Norman Reilly Raine(1894-1971)

Captain Kidd *'45*
The Fighting 69th *'40*
Each Dawn I Die *'39*
The Adventures of Robin Hood *'38*
The Life of Emile Zola *'37*

Frank Rainone

A Brooklyn State of Mind *'97*
Me and the Mob *'94*

Milton Raison(1930-82)

Spoilers of the North *'47*
Underworld Scandal *'47*
Motorcycle Squad *'41*

Ron Raley

The Locket *'02*
Cupid & Cate *'00*
The Runaway *'00*
Edge of Sanity *'89*

Gilbert Ralston(1912-99)

Ben *'72*
Willard *'71*

Rick Ramage

Stigmata *'99*
The Proposition *'97*

Hans Rameau

We Were Dancing *'42*
Waterloo Bridge *'40*

Harold Ramis(1944-)

Year One *'09*
Analyze That *'02*
Bedazzled *'00*
Analyze This *'98*
Multiplicity *'96*
Groundhog Day *'93*
Rover Dangerfield *'91*
Ghostbusters 2 *'89*
Caddyshack 2 *'88*
Armed and Dangerous *'86*
Back to School *'86*
Club Paradise *'86*
Ghostbusters *'84*
National Lampoon's Vacation *'83*
Stripes *'81*
Caddyshack *'80*
Meatballs *'79*
National Lampoon's Animal House *'78*

Lynne Ramsay(1969-)

Morvern Callar *'02*
Ratcatcher *'99*

Robert Ramsey(1962-)

Soul Men *'08*
Man of the House *'05*
Intolerable Cruelty *'03*
Big Trouble *'02*
Life *'99*
Destiny Turns on the Radio *'95*

Charles Randolph

The Interpreter *'05*
The Life of David Gale *'03*

Day for Night *'73*
The Bride Wore Black *'68*
Fahrenheit 451 *'66*
The Soft Skin *'64*

Pierre Richard(1934-)
Too Shy to Try *'78*
The Daydreamer *'75*

Cybil (Sybil) Richards
Femalien 2 *'98*
Femalien *'96*

John C. Richards(1957-)
Sahara *'05*
Nurse Betty *'00*

Robert L. Richards
Gorgo *'61*
The Indian Fighter *'55*
Act of Violence *'48*

Doug Richardson
Hostage *'05*
Welcome to Mooseport *'04*
Money Train *'95*
Die Hard 2: Die Harder *'90*

Tony Richardson(1928-91)
The Hotel New Hampshire *'84*
Ned Kelly *'70*
A Taste of Honey *'61*

William Richert(1944-)
The Man in the Iron Mask *'97*
A Night in the Life of Jimmy Reardon *'88*
Winter Kills *'79*
Law and Disorder *'74*

Mordecai Richler(1931-2001)
Joshua Then and Now *'85*
Fun with Dick and Jane *'77*
The Apprenticeship of Duddy Kravitz *'74*
No Love for Johnnie *'60*

Maurice Richlin(1930-90)
For Pete's Sake *'74*
Come September *'61*
Operation Petticoat *'59*
Pillow Talk *'59*

Jason Richman
Bangkok Dangerous *'08*
Swing Vote *'08*
Bad Company *'02*

W.D. Richter(1945-)
Stealth *'05*
Home for the Holidays *'95*
Needful Things *'93*
Big Trouble in Little China *'86*
All Night Long *'81*
Brubaker *'80*
Dracula *'79*
Invasion of the Body Snatchers *'78*
Slither *'73*

Thomas (Tom) Rickman
Front of the Class *'08*
The Reagans *'04*
Bless the Child *'00*
Tuesdays with Morrie *'99*
Truman *'95*
Hooper *'78*

Tom Ricostronza
See Trey Ellis

Brad Riddell
Road Trip: Beer Pong *'09*
American Pie Presents Band Camp *'05*

John Ridley(1965-)
Undercover Brother *'02*
Cold Around the Heart *'97*
U-Turn *'97*

Philip Ridley
The Passion of Darkly Noon *'95*
The Reflecting Skin *'91*
The Krays *'90*

Leni Riefenstahl(1902-2003)
Triumph of the Will *'34*
The Blue Light *'32*

August Rieger(1914-84)
The Uranium Conspiracy *'78*
The Vampire Happening *'71*

Dean Riesner(1918-2002)
Fatal Beauty *'87*
Charley Varrick *'73*
High Plains Drifter *'73*
Dirty Harry *'71*
Play Misty for Me *'71*
Coogan's Bluff *'68*
Man From Galveston *'63*
The Helen Morgan Story *'57*
Operation Haylift *'50*

Adam Rifkin(1966-)
National Lampoon's The Stoned Aged *'07*
Underdog *'07*
Zoom *'06*
Night at the Golden Eagle *'02*
Small Soldiers *'98*
Something About Sex *'98*
Mouse Hunt *'97*
The Chase *'93*
The Dark Backward *'91*
The Invisible Maniac *'90*
Never on Tuesday *'88*

Ned Rifle
See Hal Hartley

Ray Rigby
The Hill *'65*
Operation Crossbow *'65*

Lawrence Riggins
Replicant *'01*
Ironheart *'92*

Sharon Riis
Savage Messiah *'02*
Loyalties *'86*

Eran Riklis(1954-)
Lemon Tree *'08*
The Syrian Bride *'04*

Wolf Rilla(1920-2005)
Village of the Damned *'60*
The Scamp *'57*
Roadhouse Girl *'53*

Joe Rinaldi(1914-74)
Peter Pan *'53*
The Adventures of Ichabod and Mr. Toad *'49*

Frederic Rinaldo(1913-92)
Abbott and Costello Meet the Invisible Man *'51*
Comin' Round the Mountain *'51*
Abbott and Costello Meet Frankenstein *'48*
Buck Privates Come Home *'47*
The Black Cat *'41*
Hold That Ghost *'41*
The Invisible Woman *'40*

David W. Rintels(1938-)
A Season on the Brink *'02*
Nuremberg *'00*
The Member of the Wedding *'97*
Andersonville *'95*
World War II: When Lions Roared *'94*
The Last Best Year *'90*
Not Without My Daughter *'90*
Day One *'89*
Scorpio *'73*

Robert Riskin(1897-1955)
Riding High *'50*
Meet John Doe *'41*
You Can't Take It with You *'38*
Lost Horizon *'37*
Mr. Deeds Goes to Town *'36*
The Whole Town's Talking *'35*
It Happened One Night *'34*
Lady for a Day *'33*
American Madness *'32*

Steven Ritch
City of Fear *'59*
Plunder Road *'57*

Guy Ritchie(1968-)
Sherlock Holmes *'09*
RocknRolla *'08*
Revolver *'05*
Swept Away *'02*
Snatch *'00*
Lock, Stock and 2 Smoking Barrels *'98*

Tim Ritter
The Alien Agenda: Endangered Species *'97*
Truth or Dare? *'86*

Thomas Ritz
The Killing Grounds *'97*
Marked Man *'96*
Open Fire *'94*
Martial Outlaw *'93*

Stephen J. Rivele(1949-)
Ali *'01*
Nixon *'95*

Jose Rivera
Letters to Juliet *'10*
Trade *'07*
The Motorcycle Diaries *'04*

Jacques Rivette(1928-)
The Duchess of Langeais *'07*
The Story of Marie and Julien *'03*
Va Savoir *'01*
La Belle Noiseuse *'90*
Celine and Julie Go Boating *'74*
Paris Belongs to Us *'60*

Allen Rivkin(1903-90)
It's a Big Country *'51*
Tension *'50*
Dead Reckoning *'47*
Dancing Lady *'33*
Picture Snatcher *'33*
What Price Hollywood? *'32*

Janet Roach
Mr. North *'88*
Prizzi's Honor *'85*

Alain Robbe-Grillet(1922-2008)
Gradiva *'06*
Last Year at Marienbad *'61*

Matthew Robbins(1945-)
Mimic *'97*
*batteries not included *'87*
Warning Sign *'85*
Dragonslayer *'81*
Corvette Summer *'78*
MacArthur *'77*
Bingo Long Traveling All-Stars & Motor Kings *'76*
The Sugarland Express *'74*

Tim Robbins(1958-)
The Cradle Will Rock *'99*
Dead Man Walking *'95*
Bob Roberts *'92*

Jacques Robert
Make Your Bets Ladies *'65*
The Monocle *'64*

Ben Roberts(1916-84)
Portrait in Black *'60*
Green Fire *'55*
Goodbye My Fancy *'51*
White Heat *'49*

Charles E. Roberts(1894-1951)
Goin' to Town *'44*
Mexican Spitfire *'40*
Roaring Roads *'35*
Social Error *'35*
Flaming Signal *'33*

Jonathan Roberts
Jack Frost *'98*
The Hunchback of Notre Dame *'96*
The Lion King *'94*
Once Bitten *'85*
The Sure Thing *'85*

Jordan Roberts
March of the Penguins *'05*
Around the Bend *'04*

June Roberts
Mermaids *'90*
Experience Preferred... But Not Essential *'83*

Marguerite Roberts(1905-89)
Shoot Out *'71*
True Grit *'69*
Five Card Stud *'68*
Ivanhoe *'52*
The Bribe *'48*
Undercurrent *'46*
Somewhere I'll Find You *'42*

Scott Roberts
The Hard Word *'02*
K2: The Ultimate High *'92*
Riders of the Storm *'88*

Stanley Roberts(1916-82)
Made in Paris *'65*
The Caine Mutiny *'54*
Death of a Salesman *'51*
Prairie Moon *'38*

William Roberts(1913-97)
Ten to Midnight *'83*
Legend of the Lone Ranger *'81*
Posse *'75*
The Last American Hero *'73*
Red Sun *'71*
The Bridge at Remagen *'69*
The Devil's Brigade *'68*
The Wonderful World of the Brothers Grimm *'62*
The Magnificent Seven *'60*
The Mating Game *'59*
The Private War of Major Benson *'55*
Easy to Love *'53*

Mira Robertson
Head On *'98*
Only the Brave *'94*

R.J. Robertson
Home for Christmas *'93*
Final Embrace *'92*
The Haunting of Morella *'91*
Think Big *'90*
Transylvania Twist *'89*
Not of This Earth *'88*
Big Bad Mama 2 *'87*
Forbidden World *'82*

John Robins
Hot Resort *'85*
Death Ship *'80*

Bruce Robinson(1946-)
In Dreams *'98*
Return to Paradise *'98*
Jennifer 8 *'92*
Fat Man and Little Boy *'89*
How to Get Ahead in Advertising *'89*
Withnail and I *'87*
The Killing Fields *'84*

Butch Robinson
Crazy as Hell *'02*
DROP Squad *'94*

Casey Robinson(1903-79)
The Egyptian *'54*
The Snows of Kilimanjaro *'52*
Father Was a Fullback *'49*
Saratoga Trunk *'45*
Now, Voyager *'42*
Dark Victory *'39*
Four's a Crowd *'38*
Call It a Day *'37*
Captain Blood *'35*

David Robinson
Just Business *'08*
Exit *'95*

James Robinson
The League of Extraordinary Gentlemen *'03*
Cyber Bandits *'94*

Matt Robinson
The Invention of Lying *'09*
Nanny McPhee *'06*
Amazing Grace *'74*
The Possession of Joel Delaney *'72*

Phil Alden Robinson(1950-)
Freedom Song *'00*
The Chamber *'96*
Sneakers *'92*
Field of Dreams *'89*
In the Mood *'87*
All of Me *'84*
Rhinestone *'84*

Sally Robinson
Follow the Stars Home *'01*
Princess of Thieves *'01*
The Lost Child *'00*
A Far Off Place *'93*

Todd Robinson
Lonely Hearts *'06*
Mermaid *'00*
White Squall *'96*

Marc Rocco(1965-)
Where the Day Takes You *'92*
Dream a Little Dream *'89*

Glauce Rocha(1930-73)
Antonio Das Mortes *'68*
Earth Entranced *'66*
Black God, White Devil *'64*

Eric Rochant(1961-)
Total Western *'00*
Love Without Pity *'91*
The Fifth Monkey *'90*

Chris Rock(1966-)
Good Hair *'09*
I Think I Love My Wife *'07*
Head of State *'03*
Down to Earth *'01*
CB4: The Movie *'93*

Kevin Rock
Raging Angels *'95*
Suspicious Agenda *'94*
Philadelphia Experiment 2 *'93*
Warlock: The Armageddon *'93*

Alexandre Rockwell(1957-)
13 Moons *'02*
Four Rooms *'95*
Somebody to Love *'94*
In the Soup *'92*
Sons *'89*

Robert Rodat(1953-)
The Patriot *'00*
36 Hours to Die *'99*
Saving Private Ryan *'98*
The Ripper *'97*
Fly Away Home *'96*
Tall Tale: The Unbelievable Adventures of Pecos Bill *'95*
The Comrades of Summer *'92*

Franc Roddam(1946-)
Moby Dick *'98*
Aria *'88*
Quadrophenia *'79*

Franz Rodenkirchen(1963-)
Nekromantik 2 *'91*
Der Todesking *'89*
Nekromantik *'87*

Hans Rodionoff
Lost Boys: The Tribe *'08*
The Hollow *'04*
The Skulls 2 *'02*

Geoff Rodkey
Daddy Day Camp *'07*
RV *'06*
The Shaggy Dog *'06*
Daddy Day Care *'03*

Howard Rodman(1920-85)
Scandal Sheet *'85*
Winning *'69*

Howard A. Rodman
August *'08*
Savage Grace *'07*
Joe Gould's Secret *'00*

Serge Rodnunsky
Chill *'06*
Dead Lenny *'06*
Newsbreak *'00*
TripFall *'00*
Cypress Edge *'99*
Fear Runs Silent *'99*
Paper Bullets *'99*
Silicon Towers *'99*
Bomb Squad *'97*
Dead Tides *'97*
Powder Burn *'96*
Final Equinox *'95*
Lovers' Lovers *'94*

Joao Pedro Rodrigues(1966-)
Two Drifters *'05*
O Fantasma *'00*

Robert Rodriguez(1968-)
Shorts: The Adventures of the Wishing Rock *'09*
Planet Terror *'07*
The Adventures of Sharkboy and Lavagirl in 3-D *'05*
Once Upon a Time in Mexico *'03*
Spy Kids 3-D: Game Over *'03*
Spy Kids 2: The Island of Lost Dreams *'02*
Spy Kids *'01*
Desperado *'95*
Four Rooms *'95*
Roadracers *'94*
El Mariachi *'93*

Michael Roemer(1928-)
The Plot Against Harry *'69*
Nothing but a Man *'64*

Michael Roesch(1974-)
Brotherhood of Blood *'08*
Alone in the Dark *'05*
House of the Dead 2: Dead Aim *'05*

Seth Rogen(1982-)
Drillbit Taylor *'08*
Pineapple Express *'08*
Superbad *'07*

Howard Emmett Rogers(1890-1971)
Gambler's Choice *'44*
Libeled Lady *'36*
Whipsaw *'35*
Tarzan and His Mate *'34*
Hold Your Man *'33*

Ivan Rogers(1954-)
Two Wrongs Make a Right *'89*
Tigershark *'87*

John Rogers
Catwoman *'04*
The Core *'03*
American Outlaws *'01*

Peter Rogers
Time Lock *'57*
The Gay Dog *'54*

Roswell Rogers
So This Is Washington *'43*
Two Weeks to Live *'43*

Steven Rogers
P.S. I Love You *'07*
Kate & Leopold *'01*
Earthly Possessions *'99*

Hope Floats '98
Stepmom '98

Eric Rohmer(1920-2010)
The Romance of Astrea and Celadon '07
Triple Agent '04
The Lady and the Duke '01
Autumn Tale '98
A Summer's Tale '96
Rendezvous in Paris '95
A Tale of Winter '92
Four Adventures of Reinette and Mirabelle '89
A Tale of Springtime '89
Boyfriends & Girlfriends '88
Summer '86
Full Moon in Paris '84
Pauline at the Beach '83
Le Beau Mariage '82
The Aviator's Wife '80
Perceval '78
The Marquise of O '76
Chloe in the Afternoon '72
Claire's Knee '71
My Night at Maud's '69
Six in Paris '68
La Collectionneuse '67

Sam Rolfe
Law of the Land '76
They Call It Murder '71
The Naked Spur '53

Mark Romanek(1959-)
One Hour Photo '02
Static '87

John Romano(1948-)
Nights in Rodanthe '08
The Third Miracle '99

Eddie Romero(1924-)
Brides of the Beast '68
The Ravagers '65
The Walls of Hell '64
Cavalry Command '63

George A. Romero(1940-)
Survival of the Dead '09
Diary of the Dead '07
George A. Romero's Land of the Dead '05
Bruiser '00
The Dark Half '91
Night of the Living Dead '90
Tales from the Darkside: The Movie '90
Two Evil Eyes '90
Monkey Shines '88
Creepshow 2 '87
Day of the Dead '85
Knightriders '81
Dawn of the Dead '78
Martin '77
The Crazies '73
Season of the Witch '73
Night of the Living Dead '68

Gianni Romoli(1948-)
Facing Windows '03
His Secret Life '01
Harem '99
Cemetery Man '95

Brunello Rondi(1924-89)
Naked Paradise '78
Orchestra Rehearsal '78
Juliet of the Spirits '65
8 1/2 '63
La Dolce Vita '60
La Strada '54

David Ronn
Norbit '07
Guess Who '05
National Security '03
I Spy '02
Serving Sara '02

Don Roos(1959-)
Marley & Me '08
Happy Endings '05
Bounce '00
The Opposite of Sex '98
Diabolique '96
Boys on the Side '94
Single White Female '92

Love Field '91

Wells Root(1900-93)
Texas Across the River '66
Prisoner of Zenda '37
Tiger Shark '32
Politics '31

Tom Ropelewski
The Next Best Thing '00
Look Who's Talking Now '93
Madhouse '90
Loverboy '89
The Kiss '88

Bradford Ropes(1905-66)
Redwood Forest Trail '50
Hi, Good Lookin'! '44
Gaucho Serenade '40
Circus Girl '37

Giuseppe Rosati
Perfect Crime '79
Street War '76

Bernard Rose(1960-)
The Kreutzer Sonata '08
Leo Tolstoy's Anna Karenina '96
Immortal Beloved '94
Candyman '92

Jack Rose(1911-95)
The Great Muppet Caper '81
Lost and Found '79
A Touch of Class '73
Papa's Delicate Condition '63
Who's Got the Action? '63
It Started in Naples '60
The Five Pennies '59
Houseboat '58
The Seven Little Foys '55
Trouble along the Way '53
April in Paris '52
I'll See You in My Dreams '51
On Moonlight Bay '51
Room for One More '51
Riding High '50
The Great Lover '49
Sorrowful Jones '49
My Favorite Brunette '47
The Road to Rio '47

Lee Rose
The Truth About Jane '00
An Unexpected Life '97
An Unexpected Family '96
A Mother's Prayer '95
Deconstructing Sarah '94

Louisa Rose
Monique '76
Sisters '73

Mickey Rose(1935-)
Student Bodies '81
I Wonder Who's Killing Her Now? '76
Bananas '71
Take the Money and Run '69
What's Up, Tiger Lily? '66

Reginald Rose(1920-2002)
Twelve Angry Men '97
Wild Geese 2 '85
The Final Option '82
Sea Wolves '81
Whose Life Is It Anyway? '81
Wild Geese '78
Man of the West '58
Twelve Angry Men '57

Ruth Rose(1896-1978)
She '35
King Kong '33

William Rose(1914-87)
Dr. Frankenstein's Castle of Freaks '74
The Secret of Santa Vittoria '69
Guess Who's Coming to Dinner '67
It's a Mad, Mad, Mad, Mad World '63
The Smallest Show on Earth '57

The Ladykillers '55
Genevieve '53

Gualtiero Rosella
Not of This World '99
Flight of the Innocent '93

Dan Rosen(1963-)
The Curve '97
The Last Supper '96

Gary Rosen
Sink or Swim '97
Major Payne '95

Martin Rosen
The Plague Dogs '82
Watership Down '78

Henry Rosenbaum
Get Crazy '83
The Dunwich Horror '70

Craig Rosenberg(1965-)
Half Light '05
After the Sunset '04
Hotel de Love '96

Jeanne Rosenberg
Running Free '00
Heidi '93
White Fang '91
The Journey of Natty Gann '85
The Black Stallion '79

Marc Rosenberg
December Boys '07
Serpent's Lair '95
Dingo '90

Melissa Rosenberg
The Twilight Saga: Eclipse '10
The Twilight Saga: New Moon '09
Twilight '08
Step Up '06

Philip Rosenberg(1942-)
Missing Pieces '00
Joe Torre: Curveballs Along the Way '97
Death Benefit '96
In the Lake of the Woods '96
In the Line of Duty: A Cop for the Killing '90

Scott Rosenberg(1963-)
Kangaroo Jack '02
Highway '01
Gone in 60 Seconds '00
High Fidelity '00
Disturbing Behavior '98
Con Air '97
Beautiful Girls '96
Things to Do in Denver When You're Dead '95

Dale Rosenbloom(1964-)
Saving Shiloh '06
Shiloh 2: Shiloh Season '99
Shiloh '97

Seth Zvi Rosenfeld
King of the Jungle '01
A Brother's Kiss '97
Subway Stories '97
Sunset Park '96

Jack Rosenthal(1931-2004)
Captain Jack '98
The Wedding Gift '93
The Duchess of Duke Street '78

Mark Rosenthal
Flicka '06
Mona Lisa Smile '03
Planet of the Apes '01
Mercury Rising '98
Mighty Joe Young '98
The Beverly Hillbillies '93
For Love or Money '93
Sometimes They Come Back '91

Desperate Hours '90
The In Crowd '88
Superman 4: The Quest for Peace '87
The Jewel of the Nile '85
Legend of Billie Jean '85

Francesco Rosi(1922-)
The Truce '96
The Palermo Connection '91
Three Brothers '80
Christ Stopped at Eboli '79
Bellissima '51

David Rosiak
Ring of Death '08
Shark Swarm '08

Mark Rosman(1959-)
Sorority Row '09
Dead in a Heartbeat '02
Life-Size '00
The Invader '96
Evolver '94
The House on Sorority Row '83

Arthur Ross
Brubaker '80
Satan's School for Girls '73
The Three Worlds of Gulliver '59
The Creature Walks among Us '56
Creature from the Black Lagoon '54
Star Spangled Rhythm '42

Brian Ross
Dying to Remember '93
Body Language '92
The Secret Passion of Robert Clayton '92

David Ross
The Babysitters '07
The Woods '03

Dev Ross
The Land Before Time 4: Journey Through the Mists '96
The Land Before Time 3: The Time of the Great Giving '95
The Land Before Time 2: The Great Valley Adventure '94

Gary Ross(1956-)
The Tale of Despereaux '08
Seabiscuit '03
Pleasantville '98
Lassie '94
Dave '93
Mr. Baseball '92
Big '88

Kenneth Ross(1941-)
Out of the Body '88
The Odessa File '74
The Day of the Jackal '73

Kevin Ross
Vernie '04
Mulligan '00

Roberto Rossellini(1906-77)
The Messiah '75
Blaise Pascal '71
RoGoPaG '62
Era Notte a Roma '60
Generale Della Rovere '60
Voyage in Italy '53
The Flowers of St. Francis '50
Machine to Kill Bad People '48
Paisan '46
Man with a Cross '43

Robert Rossen(1908-66)
Lilith '64
Billy Budd '62
The Hustler '61
All the King's Men '49
The Strange Love of Martha Ivers '46
A Walk in the Sun '46
Edge of Darkness '43

Blues in the Night '41
Out of the Fog '41
The Sea Wolf '41
The Roaring Twenties '39
They Won't Forget '37

Terry Rossio(1960-)
Pirates of the Caribbean: At World's End '07
Deja Vu '06
Pirates of the Caribbean: Dead Man's Chest '06
Pirates of the Caribbean: The Curse of the Black Pearl '03
Shrek '01
The Road to El Dorado '00
The Mask of Zorro '98
Small Soldiers '98
The Puppet Masters '94
Aladdin '92
Little Monsters '89

Leo Rosten(1908-97)
Velvet Touch '48
Lured '47
Dark Corner '46

Bobby Roth(1950-)
Berkeley '05
The Man Inside '90
Dead Solid Perfect '88
Baja Oklahoma '87
Heartbreakers '84
Boss' Son '78

Eli Roth(1972-)
Hostel: Part 2 '07
Hostel '06
Cabin Fever '03

Eric Roth(1945-)
The Curious Case of Benjamin Button '08
Lucky You '07
The Good Shepherd '06
Munich '05
Ali '01
The Insider '99
The Horse Whisperer '97
The Postman '97
Forrest Gump '94
Mr. Jones '93
Memories of Me '88
Suspect '87
The Concorde: Airport '79 '79
The Onion Field '79

Phillip J. Roth(1959-)
Boa '02
Interceptor Force '99
Velocity Trap '99
Total Reality '97
A.P.E.X. '94
Digital Man '94
Prototype X29A '92
Ghostwriter '84

Jeff Rothberg
The Whole Shebang '01
A Simple Wish '97
The Amazing Panda Adventure '95
Hiding Out '87

Stephanie Rothman(1936-)
Starhops '78
The Velvet Vampire '71

Talbot Rothwell(1916-81)
Carry On Abroad '72
Carry On Matron '72
Carry On Camping '71
Carry On Henry VIII '71
Carry On Loving '70
Carry On Up the Jungle '70
Carry On Again Doctor '69
Carry On Up the Khyber '68
Carry On Cowboy '66
Don't Lose Your Head '66
Carry On Spying '64
Carry On Cabby '63
Carry On Jack '63

Nick Rotundo
G2: Mortal Conquest '99
Gladiator Cop: The Swordsman 2 '95

Brigitte Rouan(1965-)
After Sex '97
Overseas: Three Women with Man Trouble '90

Russell Rouse(1913-87)
The Oscar '66
Fastest Gun Alive '56
The Thief '52
D.O.A. '49

Francois Olivier Rousseau
Change My Life '01
Children of the Century '99

Pierre Rouve(1915-98)
Cop-Out '67
Trial & Error '62

Jean Rouveral(1916-)
A Face in the Rain '63
Autumn Leaves '56

Kathleen Rowell
Video Voyeur: The Susan Wilson Story '02
Killing Mr. Griffin '97
Vanished '95
Hear No Evil '93
Tainted Blood '93
Joy of Sex '84
The Outsiders '83

Nick Rowntree
The Tournament '09
The Tournament '09

Charles Francis Royal(1880-1955)
Ridin' the Lone Trail '37
Shadows of the Orient '37
Courageous Avenger '35

Patricia Rozema(1958-)
Grey Gardens '09
Mansfield Park '99
When Night Is Falling '95

John Ruane(1952-)
That Eye, the Sky '94
Death in Brunswick '90

Andy Ruben
Club Vampire '98
Poison Ivy '92
Streets '90
Dance of the Damned '88
Stripped to Kill '87
The Patriot '86

J. Walter Ruben(1899-1942)
Bachelor Apartment '31
The Royal Bed '31

Bruce Joel Rubin(1943-)
The Time Traveler's Wife '09
The Last Mimzy '07
Stuart Little 2 '02
Deep Impact '98
My Life '93
Ghost '90
Jacob's Ladder '90
Deadly Friend '86
Brainstorm '83

Mann Rubin(1927-)
The First Deadly Sin '80
The Best of Everything '59

Stanley Rubin(1916-)
Violence '47
Burma Convoy '41

Sergio Rubini(1959-)
The Blonde '92
The Station '92

Cliff Ruby
Beethoven's 5th '03
Cats Don't Dance '97
Balto '95

Harry Ruby(1895-1974)
A Night at the Opera '35
Duck Soup '33
Horse Feathers '32
Kid from Spain '32

David Rudkin(1936-)
December Bride '91
Fahrenheit 451 '66

Rita Rudner(1955-)
A Weekend in the Country '96
Peter's Friends '92

Paul Rudnick(1957-)
The Stepford Wives '04
Marci X '03
Isn't She Great '00
In and Out '97
Jeffrey '95
Addams Family Values '93

Steve Rudnick
Kicking & Screaming '05
The Santa Clause '94

Alan Rudolph(1943-)
Intimate Affairs '01
Trixie '00
Breakfast of Champions '98
Afterglow '97
Equinox '93
Love at Large '89
The Moderns '88
Trouble in Mind '86
Choose Me '84
Endangered Species '82
Roadie '80
Welcome to L.A. '77
Buffalo Bill & the Indians '76
Barn of the Naked Dead '73
Premonition '71

Ed Rugoff
Double Take '97
Mr. Nanny '93
Mannequin 2: On the Move '91
Mannequin '87

Raul Ruiz(1941-)
Comedy of Innocence '00
Time Regained '99
Genealogies of a Crime '97
Three Lives and Only One Death '96
On Top of the Whale '82
The Hypothesis of the Stolen Painting '78

Mogens Rukov(1943-)
Reconstruction '03
The Celebration '98

Stefano Rulli(1949-)
My Brother Is an Only Child '07
Best of Youth '03
The Truce '96
The Stolen Children '92

Terry Runte(1960-94)
Super Mario Bros. '93
Mystery Date '91

Peter Ruric(1902-66)
Grand Central Murder '42
The Black Cat '34

Richard Rush(1930-)
Color of Night '94
Air America '90
The Stunt Man '80
Psych-Out '68

Harry Ruskin(1894-1969)
Lady Godiva '55
The Happy Years '50
The Postman Always Rings Twice '46
The Secret of Dr. Kildare '39
Six of a Kind '34

Josef Rusnak
The Thirteenth Floor '99
Quiet Days in Hollywood '97

Lou Rusoff(1911-63)
Beach Party '63
The Ghost of Dragstrip Hollow '59
Cat Girl '57
Motorcycle Gang '57
Shake, Rattle and Rock '57
It Conquered the World '56
The Phantom from 10,000 Leagues '56
Day the World Ended '55

Chuck Russell(1952-)
The Blob '88
A Nightmare on Elm Street 3: Dream Warriors '87
Dreamscape '84

David O. Russell(1959-)
I Heart Huckabees '04
Three Kings '99
Flirting with Disaster '95
Spanking the Monkey '94

Ken Russell(1927-)
Lady Chatterley '92
Whore '91
The Rainbow '89
Aria '88
The Lair of the White Worm '88
Salome's Last Dance '88
Valentino '77
Lisztomania '75
Tommy '75
Mahler '74
The Boy Friend '71
The Devils '71

Michael Russell
A Certain Justice '99
Tangiers '83

Ray Russell(1924-99)
X: The Man with X-Ray Eyes '63
Premature Burial '62
Zotz! '62
Mr. Sardonicus '61

Vivian Russell
The Rainbow '89
The Atomic Brain '64

Willy Russell(1947-)
Shirley Valentine '89
Educating Rita '83

John A. Russo(1939-)
Heartstopper '92
Night of the Living Dead '90
Voodoo Dawn '89
The Majorettes '87
Return of the Living Dead '85
Night of the Living Dead '68

Richard Russo(1949-)
Empire Falls '05
The Ice Harvest '05
Keeping Mum '05
Brush with Fate '03
The Flamingo Rising '01
Twilight '98

Marti Rustam
Evils of the Night '85
Eaten Alive '76

Neil Ruttenberg
Magic Island '95
Prehysteria 3 '95
Bad Blood '94

Morrie Ruvinsky
A Woman Hunted '03
Jack Higgins' Thunder Point '97

Stefan Ruzowitzky(1961-)
The Counterfeiters '07
Anatomy '00
The Inheritors '98

David Ryan(1964-)
Mean Streak '99
First Love, Last Rites '98

Frank Ryan(1947-)
Can't Help Singing '45
The Amazing Mrs. Holiday '43
Call Out the Marines '42

Tim Ryan(1899-1956)
Bela Lugosi Meets a Brooklyn Gorilla '52
Ghost Crazy '44

Florence Ryerson(1892-1965)
Ice Follies of 1939 '39
The Return of Dr. Fu Manchu '30
The Mysterious Dr. Fu Manchu '29

Michael Rymer(1963-)
Perfume '01
Allie & Me '97
Angel Baby '95

Seung-wan Ryoo
The City of Violence '06
No Blood No Tears '02

Morrie Ryskind(1895-1985)
Penny Serenade '41
Room Service '38
My Man Godfrey '36
A Night at the Opera '35
Palmy Days '31
Animal Crackers '30
The Cocoanuts '29

Joseph Sabo
Fantasia '40
Pinocchio '40

Dardano Sacchetti(1944-)
Specters '87
Demons '86
Devilfish '84
A Blade in the Dark '83
The House by the Cemetery '83
The New Gladiators '83
The Beyond '82
Manhattan Baby '82
New York Ripper '82
Cannibal Apocalypse '80
Gates of Hell '80
Zombie '80
Shock '79

Ira Sachs(1965-)
Married Life '07
Forty Shades of Blue '05
The Delta '97

William Sachs
Hitz '89
Galaxina '80

William Sackheim(1920-2004)
Barricade '49
Border River '47

Peter Sagal
Dirty Dancing: Havana Nights '04
Savage '96

Arthur St. Claire(1899-1950)
Rimfire '49
The Mask of Diijon '46
Yank in Libya '42
Boss of Bullion City '41

Adela Rogers St. John
Smart Woman '48
The Great Man's Lady '42

Nicholas St. John
The Funeral '96
The Addiction '95
Body Snatchers '93
Dangerous Game '93
King of New York '90
China Girl '87
Fear City '85
Ms. 45 '81
Driller Killer '79

Cecil Saint-Laurent(1919-2000)
Manon '68
The Women '68

Hiroshi Saito
Tetsujin 28 '04
Samurai Fiction '99
Rubber's Lover '97

Alfredo Salazar(1922-)
Doctor of Doom '62
The Robot vs. the Aztec Mummy '59
Wrestling Women vs. the Aztec Mummy '59

Richard Sale(1911-93)
Assassination '87
Abandon Ship '57
Suddenly '54
A Woman's World '54
Ticket to Tomahawk '50
When Willie Comes Marching Home '50
Father Was a Fullback '49
The Dude Goes West '48

Kario Salem
The Score '01
The Rat Pack '98
Don King: Only in America '97

Martin Salinas
Nicotina '03
Gaby: A True Story '87

Sidney Salkow(1909-2000)
Sitting Bull '54
Murder With Pictures '36
Rhythm on the Range '36

Walter Salles(1956-)
Paris, je t'aime '06
Behind the Sun '01
Foreign Land '95

Waldo Salt(1914-87)
Serpico '73
Midnight Cowboy '69
Mr. Winkle Goes to War '44
Shopworn Angel '38

Claudia Salter
Man in the Mirror: The Michael Jackson Story '04
Running Mates '00

Mark Saltzman
Third Man Out: A Donald Strachey Mystery '05
The Red Sneakers '01
Mrs. Santa Claus '96
Napoleon '96
3 Ninjas Kick Back '94
Iron & Silk '91
The Adventures of Milo & Otis '89
Milo & Otis '89

Victor Salva(1958-)
Peaceful Warrior '06
Jeepers Creepers 2 '03
Jeepers Creepers '01
Rites of Passage '99
Powder '95
Nature of the Beast '94

Pierre Salvadori(1964-)
Priceless '06
Apres-Vous '03
Les Apprentis '95

Hal Salwen
Denise Calls Up '95
Probable Cause '95

Todd Samovitz
Black Swarm '07
Wonderland '03

Jon Robert Samsel
Animal Instincts '92
Carnal Crimes '91

Lesser Samuels(1894-1980)
Ace in the Hole '51
No Way Out '50
Bitter Sweet '40
Strange Cargo '40
Gangway '37

Eduardo Sanchez
Seventh Moon '08
The Blair Witch Project '99

Duke Sandefur
The Phantom of the Opera '89
Ghost Town '88

Christopher Sanders(1960-)
How to Train Your Dragon '10
Lilo & Stitch '02
Mulan '98

Scott Sanders
Black Dynamite '09
Thick as Thieves '99

Helma Sanders-Brahms
Under the Pavement Lies the Strand '75
Earthquake in Chile '74

Helmer Sanders-Brahms
The Future of Emily '85
Germany, Pale Mother '80

Mark Sanderson
Silent Venom '08
I'll Remember April '99

Adam Sandler(1966-)
Grown Ups '10
You Don't Mess with the Zohan '08
Adam Sandler's 8 Crazy Nights '02
Little Nicky '00
Big Daddy '99
The Waterboy '98
Happy Gilmore '96
Billy Madison '94

Barry Sandler
All-American Murder '91
Crimes of Passion '84
Making Love '82
The Mirror Crack'd '80
The Duchess and the Dirtwater Fox '76
Loners '72

Anna Sandor
My Louisiana Sky '02
Amelia Earhart: The Final Flight '94
Family of Strangers '93
Miss Rose White '92

Jimmy Sangster(1924-)
The Devil & Max Devlin '81
Phobia '80
Dynasty of Fear '72
The Horror of Frankenstein '70
Crescendo '69
The Anniversary '68
Deadlier Than the Male '67
The Nanny '65
The Devil-Ship Pirates '64
Hysteria '64
Maniac '63
Nightmare '63
Paranoiac '62
The Hellfire Club '61
Scream of Fear '61
The Terror of the Tongs '61
The Brides of Dracula '60
The Siege of Sidney Street '60
The Mummy '59
Blood of the Vampire '58
The Crawling Eye '58
The Horror of Dracula '58
The Revenge of Frankenstein '58
The Curse of Frankenstein '57
X The Unknown '56

Marie-Jose Sanselme
Free Zone '05
Kippur '00

Nick Santora
Prison Break: The Final Break '09
The Longshots '08
Punisher: War Zone '08

Ken Sanzel
Lone Hero '02
The Replacement Killers '98
Scarred City '98

Alvin Sapinsley(1922-2002)
The Scarlet Letter '79
Moon of the Wolf '72

Tedi Sarafian(1966-)
The Road Killers '95
Tank Girl '94
Solar Crisis '92

Jan Sardi
The Notebook '04
Shine '95
Street Hero '84

Barney A. Sarecky(1895-1968)
Buffalo Bill Rides Again '47
The Phantom Rider '46
The Purple Monster Strikes '45
The Ape Man '43
Adventures of Red Ryder '40
Drums of Fu Manchu '40
Mysterious Doctor Satan '40
Zorro's Fighting Legion '39
Darkest Africa '36
Fighting Marines '36

Alvin Sargent(1931-)
Spider-Man 3 '07
Spider-Man 2 '04
Unfaithful '02
Anywhere But Here '99
Bogus '96
Other People's Money '91
What about Bob? '91
White Palace '90
Dominick & Eugene '88
Nuts '87
Ordinary People '80
Straight Time '78
Bobby Deerfield '77
Julia '77
Love and Pain and the Whole Damn Thing '73
Paper Moon '73
I Walk the Line '70
The Stalking Moon '69
The Sterile Cuckoo '69
Gambit '66

Arlene Sarner
The Healer '02
Blue Sky '91
Peggy Sue Got Married '86

Robert Sarno
Decoy '95
Howling 2: Your Sister Is a Werewolf '85

Jean-Paul Sartre(1905-80)
The Crucible '57
The Respectful Prostitute '52

Vaclav Sasek
The Firemen's Ball '68
Intimate Lighting '65
Loves of a Blonde '65

Oley Sassone
Playback '95
Wild Hearts Can't Be Broken '91

Oscar Saul(1912-94)
The Silencers '66
The Helen Morgan Story '57
Road House '48

George Saunders(1959-)
The Perfect Wife '00
Bloodsport 4: The Dark Kumite '98
The Landlady '98
Intimate Deception '96
Malicious '95
Scanner Cop '94

Carlos Saura(1932-)
Goya in Bordeaux '99
Tango '98
Outrage '93
Carmen '83
Blood Wedding '81
Elisa, Vida Mia '77
Cria '76
Cria Cuervos '76

Claude Sautet(1924-2000)
Nelly et Monsieur Arnaud '95
Vincent, Francois, Paul and the Others '76
Cesar & Rosalie '72
Borsalino '70
Classe Tous Risque '60

Jody Savin
Bottle Shock '08

Wild Wild West '99
Doc Hollywood '91
Who Framed Roger Rabbit '88
Trenchcoat '83

Phil Sears
Flyboys '06
Ripper Man '96

Ted Sears(1900-58)
Peter Pan '53
The Adventures of Ichabod and Mr. Toad '49
Pinocchio '40
Snow White and the Seven Dwarfs '37

Zelda Sears
Operator 13 '34
Dancing Lady '33
Tugboat Annie '33
Emma '32

George Seaton(1911-79)
Miracle on 34th Street '94
Airport '70
36 Hours '64
The Counterfeit Traitor '62
Country Girl '54
Miracle on 34th Street '47
Charley's Aunt '41
That Night in Rio '41
Doctor Takes a Wife '40
A Day at the Races '37

Cheryl Seban
Au Pair 2: The Fairy Tale Continues '01
Au Pair '99

Beverly Sebastian
Running Cool '93
Gator Bait 2: Cajun Justice '88
Gator Bait '73

Ferd Sebastian
Running Cool '93
Gator Bait 2: Cajun Justice '88
Gator Bait '73

Jack Seddon(1924-2001)
The Blue Max '66
The Longest Day '62

Manuel Seff(1895-1969)
Louisiana Hayride '44
Breaking the Ice '38
Love on the Run '36
Red Salute '35

Erich Segal(1937-)
Man, Woman & Child '83
A Change of Seasons '80
Oliver's Story '78
Love Story '70
R.P.M.* (*Revolutions Per Minute) '70
Yellow Submarine '68

Peter Sehr(1951-)
Love the Hard Way '01
Obsession '97
Kaspar Hauser '93

Susan Seidelman(1952-)
The Boynton Beach Club '05
Tales of Erotica '93

David Seidler
By Dawn's Early Light '00
The King and I '99
Goldrush: A Real Life Alaskan Adventure '98
Quest for Camelot '98
Tucker: The Man and His Dream '88
The Rumor Mill '86

Hillary Seitz
Eagle Eye '08
Insomnia '02

Michael Seitzman(1967-)
North Country '05
Here on Earth '00

Farmer & Chase '96

Shinichi Sekizawa(1921-92)
Godzilla vs. Megalon '76
Godzilla's Revenge '69
Latitude Zero '69
Godzilla vs. Monster Zero '68
Godzilla vs. the Sea Monster '66
Son of Godzilla '66
Dagora, the Space Monster '65
Ghidrah the Three Headed Monster '65
Godzilla vs. Mothra '64
King Kong vs. Godzilla '63
Mothra '62

Hubert Selby, Jr.(1928-2004)
Fear X '03
Requiem for a Dream '00

David Self
Road to Perdition '02
Thirteen Days '00
The Haunting '99

Michael D. Sellers
Lullaby '08
Eye of the Dolphin '06
Karla '06
Vlad '03

Aaron Seltzer
Disaster Movie '08
Meet the Spartans '08
Date Movie '06
Spy Hard '96

David Seltzer(1940-)
The Omen '06
Dragonfly '02
Nobody's Baby '01
My Giant '98
The Eighteenth Angel '97
Shining Through '92
Bird on a Wire '90
Punchline '88
Lucas '86
Table for Five '83
Prophecy '79
The Omen '76
My Father's House '75
The Other Side of the Mountain '75
King, Queen, Knave '72
The Hellstrom Chronicle '71

Terrel Seltzer
One Fine Day '96
How I Got into College '89
Dim Sum: A Little Bit of Heart '85
Chan Is Missing '82

David O. Selznick(1902-65)
The Paradine Case '47
Duel in the Sun '46
Since You Went Away '44
A Star Is Born '37

Ousmane Sembene
Moolaade '04
Xala '75
Black Girl '66

Lorenzo Semple, Jr.(1923-)
Never Say Never Again '83
Flash Gordon '80
King Kong '76
The Parallax View '74
Papillon '73
Pretty Poison '68
Fathom '67
Batman '66

Jorge Semprun(1923-)
Roads to the South '78
A Woman at Her Window '77
Stavisky '74
La Guerre Est Finie '66

Ron Senkowski
Wicked Ways '99
Let's Kill All the Lawyers '93

Mack Sennett(1880-1960)
Extra Girl '23
Yankee Doodle in Berlin '19

Al Septien(1966-)
Wrong Turn 2: Dead End '07
Candyman 3: Day of the Dead '98
Chairman of the Board '97
Leprechaun 2 '94

Yahoo Serious(1954-)
Mr. Accident '99
Reckless Kelly '93
Young Einstein '89

Rod Serling(1924-75)
A Town Has Turned to Dust '98
In the Presence of Mine Enemies '97
Night Gallery '69
Planet of the Apes '68
Assault on a Queen '66
The Doomsday Flight '66
Seven Days in May '64
Requiem for a Heavyweight '62
Saddle the Wind '58
Patterns '56
Requiem for a Heavyweight '56

Alexandra Seros
The Specialist '94
Point of No Return '93

Leopoldo Serran
Four Days in September '97
O Quatrilho '95

Coline Serreau(1947-)
Chaos '01
Mama, There's a Man in Your Bed '89
Three Men and a Cradle '85

Philippe Setbon(1957-)
Mr. Frost '89
Honeymoon '87
Detective '85

Mark Sevi
Arachnid '01
Dead Men Can't Dance '97
Moving Target '96
Sci-Fighters '96
Excessive Force 2: Force on Force '95
Serial Killer '95
Fast Getaway 2 '94
Relentless 4 '94
Scanner Cop 2: Volkin's Revenge '94
Scanners: The Showdown '94
Class of 1999 2: The Substitute '93
Ghoulies 4 '93

Vernon Sewell(1903-2001)
Where There's a Will '55
Radio Cab Murder '54
The World Owes Me a Living '47
Frenzy '46

Timothy J. Sexton
Children of Men '06
Live from Baghdad '03
Boycott '02
For Love or Country: The Arturo Sandoval Story '00

Alan Seymour(1927-)
Catherine Cookson's The Wingless Bird '97
Catherine Cookson's The Glass Virgin '95
Catherine Cookson's The Cinder Path '94

David Shaber(1929-99)
Nighthawks '81
The Warriors '79

Susan Shadburne(1945-)
Shadow Play '86

The Adventures of Mark Twain '85

Tom Shadyac(1960-)
The Nutty Professor '96
Ace Ventura: Pet Detective '93

Anthony Shaffer(1926-2001)
Appointment with Death '88
Evil under the Sun '82
Whodunit '82
Absolution '81
Death on the Nile '78
The Wicker Man '75
Frenzy '72
Sleuth '72
Cry of the Penguins '71

Peter Shaffer(1926-)
Amadeus '84
Equus '77

Steve Shagan(1927-)
Gotti '96
Primal Fear '96
The Sicilian '87
Nightwing '79
Voyage of the Damned '76

Robert Shallcross
Uncle Nino '03
Little Giants '94

Maxwell Shane(1905-83)
Big Town '47
Fear in the Night '47
Seven Were Saved '47
Treasure of Fear '45
Dark Mountain '44
Gambler's Choice '44
Navy Way '44
One Body Too Many '44
Wildcat '42
Flying Blind '41
Power Dive '41
Golden Gloves '40
The Mummy's Hand '40
Adventure in Sahara '38

Peter Shaner
Lover's Knot '96
Shootfighter 2: Kill or Be Killed! '96
Shootfighter: Fight to the Death '93

John Patrick Shanley(1950-)
Doubt '08
Live from Baghdad '03
Congo '95
Alive '93
We're Back! A Dinosaur's Story '93
Joe Versus the Volcano '90
The January Man '89
Five Corners '88
Moonstruck '87

Damian Shannon
Friday the 13th '09
Freddy vs. Jason '03

Alan Shapiro(1957-)
Flipper '96
The Crush '93

J. David Shapiro(1969-)
Battlefield Earth '00
Robin Hood: Men in Tights '93

Paul Shapiro(1955-)
Calendar Girl '93
Breaking the Rules '92

Stanley Shapiro(1925-90)
Dirty Rotten Scoundrels '88
Carbon Copy '81
For Pete's Sake '74
That Touch of Mink '62
Come September '61
Operation Petticoat '59
The Perfect Furlough '59
Pillow Talk '59
South Sea Woman '53

Jim Sharman(1945-)
Shock Treatment '81

The Rocky Horror Picture Show '75

Alan Sharp(1934-)
The Lathe of Heaven '02
Rob Roy '95
The Last Hit '93
Little Treasure '85
Damnation Alley '77
Night Moves '75
Billy Two Hats '74
Ulzana's Raid '72
Hired Hand '71

William Shatner(1931-)
Groom Lake '02
Star Trek 5: The Final Frontier '89

Alfred Shaughnessy(1916-2005)
Flesh and Blood Show '73
Crescendo '69

Melville Shavelson(1917-2007)
Yours, Mine & Ours '68
Cast a Giant Shadow '66
A New Kind of Love '63
It Started in Naples '60
The Five Pennies '59
Houseboat '58
The Seven Little Foys '55
Trouble along the Way '53
April in Paris '52
Double Dynamite '51
I'll See You in My Dreams '51
On Moonlight Bay '51
Room for One More '51
Riding High '50
The Great Lover '49
Sorrowful Jones '49
Where There's Life '47
Wonder Man '45
The Princess and the Pirate '44

Bob Shaw
A Bug's Life '98
Hercules '97

Irwin Shaw(1913-84)
Fire Down Below '57
War and Peace '56
I Want You '51
Commandos Strike at Dawn '43

Wallace Shawn(1943-)
The Fever '04
Marie and Bruce '04
The Designated Mourner '97
My Dinner with Andre '81

Katt Shea(1957-)
Last Exit to Earth '96
Poison Ivy '92
Stripped to Kill II: Live Girls '89
Dance of the Damned '88
Stripped to Kill '87
The Patriot '86

Harry Shearer(1943-)
The Return of Spinal Tap '92
This Is Spinal Tap '84
Real Life '79

Ally Sheedy(1962-)
Life During Wartime '09
Perestroika '09

Arthur Sheekman(1901-78)
Saigon '47
Welcome Stranger '47
Blue Skies '46
Dimples '36
Duck Soup '33
Monkey Business '31

Charlie Sheen(1965-)
No Code of Conduct '98
Tale of Two Sisters '89

David Sheffield
The Honeymooners '05
Nutty Professor 2: The Klumps '00
The Nutty Professor '96

Boomerang '92
Coming to America '88

Forrest Sheldon
The Fighting Trooper '34
The Lone Avenger '33

Sidney Sheldon(1917-2007)
Billy Rose's Jumbo '62
All in a Night's Work '61
Birds & the Bees '56
Pardners '56
Dream Wife '53
Rich, Young and Pretty '51
Three Guys Named Mike '51
Annie Get Your Gun '50
Nancy Goes to Rio '50
Easter Parade '48
The Bachelor and the Bobby-Soxer '47

Adrienne Shelly(1966-2006)
Waitress '07
I'll Take You There '99
Sudden Manhattan '96

Angela Shelton(1972-)
Charms for the Easy Life '02
Tumbleweeds '98

Lynn Shelton
Humpday '09
My Effortless Brilliance '08

Ron Shelton(1945-)
Bad Boys 2 '03
Hollywood Homicide '03
Play It to the Bone '99
The Great White Hype '96
Tin Cup '96
Blue Chips '94
Cobb '94
White Men Can't Jump '92
Blaze '89
Bull Durham '88
The Best of Times '86
Under Fire '83

Nina Shengold
Double Platinum '99
Blind Spot '93

Richard Shepard
The Hunting Party '07
The Matador '06
Mexico City '00
Oxygen '99
Mercy '96
The Linguini Incident '92

Sam Shepard(1943-)
Don't Come Knocking '05
Silent Tongue '92
Far North '88
Fool for Love '86
Paris, Texas '83
Oh! Calcutta! '72
Zabriskie Point '70

Jean Shepherd(1921-99)
My Summer Story '94
A Christmas Story '83

John Scott Shepherd(1964-)
Life or Something Like It '02
Joe Somebody '01

John Shepphird
Chupacabra Terror '05
The Santa Trap '02
Teenage Bonnie & Klepto Clyde '93

Eyal Sher
Axe '06
Under the Domim Tree '95

Jack Sher(1913-88)
Critic's Choice '63
Move Over, Darling '63
Paris Blues '61
The Three Worlds of Gulliver '59
Walk the Proud Land '56
Shane '53

Ted Sherdeman(1909-87)
Latitude Zero '69

Island of the Blue Dolphins '64
Misty '61
Away All Boats '56
Them! '54
Scandal Sheet '52

Bob Sheridan
Against the Law '98
Dinosaur Island '93
Sorority House Massacre 2: Nighty Nightmare '92

Jim Sheridan(1949-)
In America '02
The Boxer '97
Some Mother's Son '96
In the Name of the Father '93
Into the West '92
The Field '90
My Left Foot '89

Michael J. Sheridan
When the Sky Falls '99
That's Entertainment, Part 3 '93

Fenn Sherie(1896-1953)
Big Fella '37
Song of Freedom '36

David Sherman
Frankenstein and Me '96
Kids of the Round Table '96

Eric P. Sherman
Eastside '99
Carnival of Wolves '96

Gary Sherman(1945-)
After the Shock '90
Fire and Rain '89
Poltergeist 3 '88
Phobia '80

J. Michael Sherman
KISS Meets the Phantom of the Park '78
Too Hot to Handle '76

Jeffrey C. Sherman
Au Pair 3: Adventure in Paradise '09
Au Pair 2: The Fairy Tale Continues '01
Au Pair '99

Martin Sherman(1938-)
Mrs. Henderson Presents '05
The Roman Spring of Mrs. Stone '03
Callas Forever '02
Bent '97
Alive and Kicking '96
The Summer House '94

Teddi Sherman
Four for Texas '63
Tennessee's Partner '55

R.C. Sherriff(1896-1975)
No Highway in the Sky '51
Odd Man Out '47
This Above All '42
The Four Feathers '39
Goodbye, Mr. Chips '39
The Invisible Man '33
The Old Dark House '32

David Sherwin(1942-)
Britannia Hospital '82
If... '69

Robert Sherwood(1896-1955)
The Bishop's Wife '47
The Best Years of Our Lives '46
Abe Lincoln in Illinois '40
Rebecca '40
The Adventures of Marco Polo '38
The Ghost Goes West '36
The Scarlet Pimpernel '34

Susan Shilliday
I Dreamed of Africa '00
Legends of the Fall '94

Takashi Shimizu(1972-)
Reincarnation '05
The Grudge '04
Ju-On: The Grudge '03
Ju-On 2 '00

Kaneto Shindo(1912-)
Rica 2: Lonely Wanderer '73
Rica 3: Juvenile's Lullaby '73
Rica '72
Under the Flag of the Rising Sun '72

Barry Shipman(1912-94)
Carolina Cannonball '55
Code of the Outlaw '42
Code of the Outlaw '42
Flash Gordon Conquers the Universe '40
Frontier Vengeance '40
Space Soldiers Conquer the Universe '40
Dick Tracy: The Spider Strikes '37
S.O.S. Coast Guard '37

Ryan Shiraki
Spring Breakdown '08
Poster Boy '04

Jack Sholder(1945-)
Wishmaster 2: Evil Never Dies '98
Alone in the Dark '82

Del Shores(1957-)
Sordid Lives '00
Daddy's Dyin'... Who's Got the Will? '90

Michael Showalter(1970-)
The Baxter '05
Wet Hot American Summer '01

Dennis Shryack(1936-)
Aces 'n Eights '08
Pale Rider '85
The Car '77

Takeshi Shudo
Pokemon 3: The Movie '01
Pokemon the Movie 2000: The Power of One '00
Pokemon: The First Movie '99

Mina Shum
Long Life, Happiness and Prosperity '02
Double Happiness '94

Harold Shumate(1893-1983)
Buccaneer's Girl '50
Saddle Tramp '47
Abilene Town '46
The Kansan '43
The Roundup '41
Charlie McCarthy, Detective '39
Square Shooter '35
Ridin' for Justice '32
Through the Breakers '28

Ronald Shusett
Bleeders '97
Freejack '92
King Kong Lives '86
Dead and Buried '81
Phobia '80

M. Night Shyamalan(1970-)
The Last Airbender '10
The Happening '08
Lady in the Water '06
The Village '04
Signs '02
Unbreakable '00
The Sixth Sense '99
Stuart Little '99
Wide Awake '97

Charles Shyer(1941-)
Alfie '04
The Parent Trap '98
Father of the Bride Part 2 '95
I Love Trouble '94
Father of the Bride '91
Baby Boom '87
Irreconcilable Differences '84
Protocol '84
Private Benjamin '80
Goin' South '78
House Calls '78
Smokey and the Bandit '77

Sylvia Sichel
If These Walls Could Talk 2 '00
All Over Me '96

Andy Sidaris(1933-)
Return to Savage Beach '97
Day of the Warrior '96
Fit to Kill '93
Hard Hunted '92
Do or Die '91
Guns '90
Picasso Trigger '89
Hard Ticket to Hawaii '87

Lynn Siefert
Cousin Bette '97
Cool Runnings '93

David Siegel
The Deep End '01
Suture '93

Robert Siegel
Big Fan '09
The Wrestler '08
Swimming '00

Brian Sieve
Boogeyman 3 '08
Boogeyman 2 '07

Dai Sijie(1954-)
Balzac and the Little Chinese Seamstress '02
China, My Sorrow '89

Sean Silas(1970-)
The Perfect Daughter '96
A Vow to Kill '94

Brad Silberling(1962-)
10 Items or Less '06
Moonlight Mile '02

James R. Silke
Ninja 3: The Domination '84
Revenge of the Ninja '83
Sahara '83

Robert Silliphant(1937-99)
Creeping Terror '64
Incredibly Strange Creatures Who Stopped Living and Became Mixed-Up Zombies '63

Stirling Silliphant(1918-96)
The Grass Harp '95
Catch the Heat '87
Over the Top '86
When Time Ran Out '80
Circle of Iron '78
Pearl '78
The Swarm '78
Telefon '77
The Enforcer '76
Death Scream '75
The Killer Elite '75
The Towering Inferno '74
Shaft in Africa '73
The New Centurions '72
The Poseidon Adventure '72
Murphy's War '71
The Liberation of L.B. Jones '70
Walk in the Spring Rain '70
Marlowe '69
Charly '68
In the Heat of the Night '67
The Slender Thread '65
Village of the Damned '60
The Lineup '58
Nightfall '56
5 Against the House '55

Amanda Silver
The Relic '96
An Eye for an Eye '95
Fallen Angels 1 '93
The Hand that Rocks the Cradle '92

Joan Micklin Silver(1935-)
Chilly Scenes of Winter '79
Hester Street '75

Scott Silver
8 Mile '02
The Mod Squad '99
johns '96

Peter Silverman
Touch the Top of the World '06
Harlan County War '00
Hidden in America '96
American Heart '92

Nancy Silvers
One Special Night '99
Battling for Baby '92

Marc Silverstein
Valentine's Day '10
He's Just Not That Into You '09
Never Been Kissed '99

Lawrence L. Simeone(1954-2002)
Blindfold: Acts of Obsession '94
Eyes of the Beholder '92
Cop-Out '91
Presumed Guilty '91

David Simkins
Alien Raiders '08
Adventures in Babysitting '87

Michael L. Simmons
Two Weeks to Live '43
Mutiny on the Blackhawk '39
Murder in Greenwich Village '37

Jay Simms
Panic in the Year Zero! '62
The Giant Gila Monster '59
The Killer Shrews '59

Adam Simon(1962-)
Bones '01
Carnosaur '93
Brain Dead '89

Alex Simon(1967-)
My Brother's War '97
Bloodfist 8: Hard Way Out '96
Piranha '95
Suspect Device '95
Unknown Origin '95

Ellen Simon
One Fine Day '96
Moonlight and Valentino '95

J(uan) Piquer Simon(1934-)
Cthulhu Mansion '91
Slugs '87

Neil Simon(1927-)
Neil Simon's The Odd Couple 2 '98
The Sunshine Boys '95
Lost in Yonkers '93
Broadway Bound '92
The Marrying Man '91
Biloxi Blues '88
Brighton Beach Memoirs '86
The Slugger's Wife '85
Max Dugan Returns '83
I Ought to Be in Pictures '82
Only When I Laugh '81
Seems Like Old Times '80
Chapter Two '79
California Suite '78
The Cheap Detective '78
The Goodbye Girl '77
Murder by Death '76
The Sunshine Boys '75
Prisoner of Second Avenue '74
The Heartbreak Kid '72
Last of the Red Hot Lovers '72
Plaza Suite '71
Star Spangled Girl '71
The Out-of-Towners '70
The Odd Couple '68
Barefoot in the Park '67
After the Fox '66

Rainer Simon(1941-)
The Woman and the Stranger '84
Jadup and Boel '81

Giovanni Simonelli
Gunslinger '70
Assassination in Rome '65

Rocco Simonelli
The Substitute 3: Winner Takes All '99
The Substitute 2: School's Out '97
The Substitute '96

Albert Simonin(1905-80)
Cold Sweat '71
Any Number Can Win '63

Theodore Simonson
The 4D Man '59
The Blob '58

Stephen Sinclair
Lord of the Rings: The Two Towers '02
Dead Alive '93
Meet the Feebles '89

Bryan Singer(1966-)
Superman Returns '06
Public Access '93

Raymond Singer
Mulan '98
NightScreams '97

John Singleton(1968-)
Baby Boy '01
Higher Learning '94
Poetic Justice '93
Boyz N the Hood '91

Gary Sinyor(1962-)
In Your Dreams '07
Bob the Butler '05
Stiff Upper Lips '96
Solitaire for 2 '94
Leon the Pig Farmer '93

Curt Siodmak(1902-2000)
Bride of the Gorilla '51
Tarzan's Magic Fountain '48
The Beast with Five Fingers '46
The Climax '44
I Walked with a Zombie '43
Frankenstein Meets the Wolfman '42
Invisible Agent '42
The Wolf Man '41
Black Friday '40
The Invisible Man Returns '40
Non-Stop New York '37

Rosemary Anne Sisson(1923-)
The Bretts '88
Candleshoe '78
The Duchess of Duke Street '78
The Littlest Horse Thieves '76
Elizabeth R '72

Rob Sitch(1962-)
The Dish '00
The Castle '97

John Sjogren(1966-)
Red Line '96
The Mosaic Project '95
Money to Burn '94

Victor Sjostrom(1879-1960)
He Who Gets Slapped '24
The Phantom Chariot '20

Warren Skaaren(1946-90)
Batman '89
Beetlejuice '88
Beverly Hills Cop 2 '87

Vance Skarstedt(1922-84)
The Slime People '63
Man or Gun '58

Mark Skeet
Vanity Fair '04
Jason and the Argonauts '00

Keri Skogland
Fifty Dead Men Walking '08
Liberty Stands Still '02
John John in the Sky '00

Jerzy Skolimowski(1938-)
Success Is the Best Revenge '84
Hands Up '81
Deep End '70
Knife in the Water '62
Innocent Sorcerers '60

Bohdan Slama(1967-)
The Country Teacher '08
Something Like Happiness '05

Pete Slate
Over the Wire '95
Virtual Desire '95

Brian Sloan
I Think I Do '97
Boys Life '94

Douglas J. Sloan
Children On Their Birthdays '02
Silk Degrees '94

Holly Goldberg Sloan(1958-)
The Crocodile Hunter: Collision Course '02
Whispers: An Elephant's Tale '00
The Big Green '95
Angels in the Outfield '94
Made in America '93
Indecency '92

Paul Sloane(1893-1963)
The Sun Sets at Dawn '50
The Texans '38

Rick Sloane(1961-)
Good Girls Don't '95
Mind, Body & Soul '92
Vice Academy 3 '91
The Movie House Massacre '78

Trace Slobotkin
Kickin' It Old Skool '07
Serial Killing 101 '04

Karl Slovin
On Edge '03
Sex and the Other Man '95

Shawn Slovo(1950-)
Catch a Fire '06
Captain Corelli's Mandolin '01
A World Apart '88

George Sluizer(1932-)
The Vanishing '88
Twice a Woman '79

Adam Small
Malibu's Most Wanted '03
In the Army Now '94
Son-in-Law '93

Christopher Warre Smets
Cyborg Soldier '08
The Last Hit Man '08

Brian J. Smith
Flu Birds '08
Body of Influence 2 '96

Charles Henry Smith(1866-1942)
Battling Butler '26
The General '26

Craig Smith
Federal Protection '02
Caracara '00

Persons Unknown '96

Earl E. Smith
Shadow of Chikara '77
Town That Dreaded Sundown '76
Winterhawk '76
Legend of Boggy Creek '75

Ebbe Roe Smith
Car 54, Where Are You? '94
Falling Down '93

Harold Jacob Smith(1912-70)
Inherit the Wind '99
Inherit the Wind '60
The Defiant Ones '58

Kevin Smith(1970-)
Zack and Miri Make a Porno '08
Clerks 2 '06
Jersey Girl '04
Jay and Silent Bob Strike Back '01
Coyote Ugly '00
Dogma '99
Chasing Amy '97
Mallrats '95
Clerks '94

Kirsten Smith(1970-)
The Ugly Truth '09
The House Bunny '08
She's the Man '06
Ella Enchanted '04
Legally Blonde '01
Ten Things I Hate about You '99

Lance Smith
Facade '98
Munchies '87

Mark Smith
Vacancy '07
Seance '06
Dr. Frankenstein's Castle of Freaks '74

Martin Smith
Under the Rainbow '81
The Art of Crime '75

Murray Smith
Cold War Killers '86
Sell Out '76
Die Screaming, Marianne '73

Paul Girard Smith(1894-1968)
Hi, Good Lookin'! '44
Hurry, Charlie, Hurry '41
Battling Butler '26

Richard Curson Smith
Pinochet's Last Stand '06
Agatha Christie: A Life in Pictures '04
Trauma '04

Richard Dana Smith
Framed for Murder '07
Alone with a Stranger '99

Robert Smith
Platinum High School '60
Girls' Town '59
The Beast from 20,000 Fathoms '53
Invasion U.S.A. '52
Sudden Fear '52
The Second Woman '51
Quicksand '50

Scott B. Smith(1965-)
The Ruins '08
Ladder 49 '04
A Simple Plan '98

Scott Marshall Smith
The Score '01
Men of Honor '00

Sue Smith
The Road from Coorain '02
Brides of Christ '91

Wallace Smith(1888-1937)
The Gay Desperado '36
Bordertown '35
Lost Squadron '32
The Lady Refuses '31
The Silver Horde '30
Bulldog Drummond '29

Webb Smith
Fantasia '40
Pinocchio '40
Snow White and the Seven Dwarfs '37

Stephen Smoke
Magic Kid '92
Street Crimes '92

Earle Snell(1886-1965)
Homesteaders of Paradise Valley '47
Santa Fe Uprising '46
Cooking Up Trouble '44
Rock River Renegades '42
Thunder River Feud '42
Saddle Mountain Roundup '41
Oklahoma Renegades '40
West of Pinto Basin '40
Days of Jesse James '39
Everyman's Law '36
Rogue of the Range '36
Wild Brian Kent '36
Night Alarm '34
Tombstone Canyon '32
Range Law '31

Norman Snider
Call Me: The Rise and Fall of Heidi Fleiss '04
Rated X '00
Body Parts '91
Dead Ringers '88

Melinda M. Snodgrass
The Outer Limits: Sandkings '95
Trapped in Space '94

Michael Anthony Snowden
White Chicks '04
Scary Movie 2 '01

Blake Snyder
Blank Check '93
Stop! or My Mom Will Shoot '92

Howard Snyder
Abbott and Costello Meet the Killer, Boris Karloff '49
George White's Scandals '45

Michael Snyder
D.R.E.A.M. Team '99
Rescue Me '93

Elena Soarez
City of Men '07
House of Sand '05
Me You Them '00

Carol Sobieski(1939-90)
Money for Nothing '93
Fried Green Tomatoes '91
Sarah, Plain and Tall '91
Winter People '89
The Bourne Identity '88
The Toy '82
Honeysuckle Rose '80

Steven Soderbergh(1963-)
Criminal '04
Eros '04
Solaris '02
Mimic '97
Schizopolis '97
Nightwatch '96
The Underneath '95
King of the Hill '93
sex, lies and videotape '89

Gerard Soeteman(1936-)
Black Book '06
Flesh and Blood '85
The 4th Man '79
Soldier of Orange '78
Katie Tippel '75
Turkish Delight '73
Business is Business '71

Roger Soffer
Merlin's Apprentice '06
Category 7 : The End of the World '05
Slow Burn '00
Kazaam '96

Jerry Sohl(1913-2002)
Die, Monster, Die! '65
Frankenstein Conquers the World '64

Joel Soisson
Pulse 2: Afterlife '08
Hollow Man 2 '06
Dracula 3: Legacy '05
Hellraiser: Hellworld '05
Dracula 2: Ascension '03
Mimic 2 '01
Dracula 2000 '00
Highlander: Endgame '00
The Prophecy 3: The Ascent '99
Blue Tiger '94
Lower Level '91
Trick or Treat '86

Alec Sokolow
Garfield: A Tail of Two Kitties '06
Garfield: The Movie '04
Cheaper by the Dozen '03
Goodbye, Lover '99
Money Talks '97
Toy Story '95

Ken Solarz(1953-)
Croc '07
Supercross: The Movie '05
City of Industry '96

Silvio Soldini(1958-)
Days and Clouds '07
Agata and the Storm '04
Bread and Tulips '01

Franco Solinas(1927-82)
Mr. Klein '76
Burn! '70
A Bullet for the General '68
The Battle of Algiers '66
The Wide Blue Road '57

Cary Solomon
The Insatiable '06
Earth vs. the Spider '01

Edward Solomon(1961-)
Imagine That '09
The In-Laws '03
Levity '03
What Planet Are You From? '00
Men in Black '97
Super Mario Bros. '93
Leaving Normal '92
Bill & Ted's Bogus Journey '91
Bill & Ted's Excellent Adventure '89

Todd Solondz(1960-)
Life During Wartime '09
Palindromes '04
Storytelling '01
Happiness '98
Welcome to the Dollhouse '95
Fear, Anxiety and Depression '89

Andrew Solt(1916-90)
This Is Elvis '81
For the First Time '59
In a Lonely Place '50
Little Women '49
Whirlpool '49
They All Kissed the Bride '42

Edith Sommer
This Property Is Condemned '66
The Best of Everything '59
Perfect Strangers '50

Stephen Sommers(1962-)
Van Helsing '04
The Scorpion King '02
The Mummy Returns '01
The Mummy '99
Deep Rising '98
Tom and Huck '95
Rudyard Kipling's The Jungle Book '94
The Adventures of Huck Finn '93
Gunmen '93

Michael Sonye
Blood Diner '87
Star Slammer '87

Trish Soodik
Annie: A Royal Adventure '95
Shake, Rattle & Rock! '94

Aaron Sorkin(1961-)
Charlie Wilson's War '07
The American President '95
Malice '93
A Few Good Men '92

Lodovico Sorret
See Tom Noonan

Paul Soter(1972-)
Watching the Detectives '07
Beerfest '06
Club Dread '04
Super Troopers '01

Terry Southern(1926-95)
The Telephone '87
End of the Road '70
Easy Rider '69
The Magic Christian '69
Barbarella '68
The Cincinnati Kid '65
The Loved One '65
Dr. Strangelove, or: How I Learned to Stop Worrying and Love the Bomb '64

Charles Spaak(1903-75)
L'Idiot '46
Grand Illusion '37
The Lower Depths '36

David Spade(1964-)
Dickie Roberts: Former Child Star '03
Joe Dirt '01
Lost and Found '99

Esta Spalding(1966-)
Falling Angels '03
The Republic of Love '03

David Sparling
Operation Delta Force 3: Clear Target '98
Mission of Death '97
Operation: Delta Force '97
Operation Delta Force 2: Mayday '97

Greg Spence
The Prophecy 2: Ashtown '97
Children of the Corn 4: The Gathering '96

Ralph Spence(1890-1949)
Down Argentine Way '40
The Flying Deuces '39
Stand Up and Cheer '34
A Lady of Chance '28
A Lady of Chance '28
The Patsy '28

Don Spencer
The Big Doll House '71
The Student Nurses '70

Scott Spencer(1945-)
Father Hood '93
Act of Vengeance '86

Milton Sperling(1912-88)
Merrill's Marauders '62
Happy Landing '38
Thin Ice '37

Bella Spewack(1899-1990)
Weekend at the Waldorf '45
My Favorite Wife '40
Boy Meets Girl '38
The Cat and the Fiddle '34

Samuel Spewack(1899-1971)
Weekend at the Waldorf '45
My Favorite Wife '40
Boy Meets Girl '38
The Cat and the Fiddle '34

Penelope Spheeris(1945-)
The Little Rascals '94
Suburbia '83

Scott Spiegel(1957-)
From Dusk Till Dawn 2: Texas Blood Money '98
The Nutt House '95
Evil Dead 2: Dead by Dawn '87
Thou Shalt Not Kill...Except '87

Steven Spielberg(1947-)
A. I.: Artificial Intelligence '01
The Goonies '85
Poltergeist '82
Close Encounters of the Third Kind '77
The Sugarland Express '74

Michael Spierig
Daybreakers '09
Undead '05

Peter Spierig
Daybreakers '09
Undead '05

Leonard Spigelgass(1908-85)
Gypsy '62
Ten Thousand Bedrooms '57
A Majority of One '56
Athena '54
I Was a Male War Bride '49
The Perfect Marriage '46
Service De Luxe '38

Evan Spiliotopolos
Battle for Terra '09
Art Heist '05
Pooh's Heffalump Movie '05

Tony Spiridakis(1959-)
Tinseltown '97
If Lucy Fell '95
The Last Word '95
Queens Logic '91

Marian Spitzer(1899-1983)
Look for the Silver Lining '49
The Dolly Sisters '46

Frank Spotnitz
The X Files: I Want to Believe '08
The X-Files '98

Mark Spragg
An Unfinished Life '05
Everything That Rises '98

Jill Sprecher
Thirteen Conversations About One Thing '01
Clockwatchers '97

Karen Sprecher
Thirteen Conversations About One Thing '01
Clockwatchers '97

Robin Spry(1939-)
A Cry in the Night '93
Suzanne '80

Morgan Spurlock
Where in the World Is Osama Bin Laden? '06
Super Size Me '04

Salvatore Stabile
Where God Left His Shoes '07
Gravesend '97

Hildegarde Stadie
Marihuana '36
Maniac '34

Bima Stagg
Stander '03
Inside '96

C. Ray Stahl(1921-59)
Scarlet Spear '54
Geisha Girl '52

Eric Steven Stahl(1959-)
I-See-You.Com '06
Safe House '99

Jerry Stahl(1953-)
Bad Boys 2 '03
Dr. Caligari '89

Laurence Stallings(1894-1968)
She Wore a Yellow Ribbon '49
On Our Merry Way '48
Christmas Eve '47
The Jungle Book '42

Sylvester Stallone(1946-)
The Expendables '10
Rambo '08
Rocky Balboa '06
Driven '01
Cliffhanger '93
Rocky 5 '90
Rambo 3 '88
Cobra '86
Over the Top '86
Rambo: First Blood, Part 2 '85
Rocky 4 '85
Rhinestone '84
Staying Alive '83
First Blood '82
Rocky 3 '82
Rocky 2 '79
F.I.S.T. '78
Paradise Alley '78
Rocky '76
The Lords of Flatbush '74

Sean Stanek
Played '06
A Crack in the Floor '00

Zac Stanford
Sleepwalking '08
The Chumscrubber '05

Justin Stanley(1973-)
Beneath Loch Ness '01
The Last Assassins '96

Richard Stanley(1966-)
The Abandoned '06
The Island of Dr. Moreau '96
Dust Devil '93

Eliot Stannard(1888-1944)
The Manxman '29
The Lodger '26

Andrew Stanton(1965-)
WALL-E '08
Finding Nemo '03
Monsters, Inc. '01
Toy Story 2 '99
A Bug's Life '98

Jeff Stanzler
Sorry, Haters '05
Jumpin' at the Boneyard '92

Anthony Stark
The Art of Murder '99
The Dogfighters '95

Jim Stark
Factotum '06
Cold Fever '95

Lynn Starling(1888-1955)
It's a Pleasure '45
The Climax '44
Wintertime '43
Thanks for the Memory '38
Torch Singer '33

Ben Starr
How to Commit Marriage '69
The Busy Body '67
Our Man Flint '66

Poison Ivy 4: The Secret Society *'08*
Termination Point *'07*
Trapped *'06*

Tim Sullivan
Letters to Juliet *'10*
Jack and Sarah *'95*
Where Angels Fear to Tread *'91*
A Handful of Dust *'88*

Tom Sullivan
Bait Shop *'08*
Cocaine Cowboys *'79*

Lasse Summanen
The Ox *'91*
The Women on the Roof *'89*

Walter Summers(1896-1973)
The Human Monster *'39*
Black Limelight *'38*
She *'25*

Shirley Sun
Iron & Silk *'91*
A Great Wall *'86*

Madeline Sunshine
Call of the Wild *'04*
Say Nothing *'01*

Masayuki Suo(1956-)
Shall We Dance? *'04*
Shall We Dance? *'96*

Stephen Susco
Red *'08*
The Grudge 2 *'06*

Phoef Sutton
The Fan *'96*
Mrs. Winterbourne *'96*

Junichi Suzuki
Haunted Highway *'05*
Remembering the Cosmos Flower *'99*

Koji Suzuki
Dark Water *'02*
Ringu 0 *'01*
The Ring Virus *'99*
Ringu 2 *'99*
Rasen *'98*
Rasen *'98*
Ringu *'98*

Zdenek Sverak(1936-)
Dark Blue World *'01*
Kolya *'96*
The Elementary School *'91*
My Sweet Little Village *'86*

Gerry Swallow
Ice Age: The Meltdown *'06*
Black Knight *'01*
Say It Isn't So *'01*

Joe Swanberg
Nights and Weekends *'08*
Hannah Takes the Stairs *'07*

Francis Swann(1913-83)
Force of Impulse *'60*
Tarzan's Peril *'51*

Ron Swanson
Forest Warrior *'95*
Top Dog *'95*

Nick Swardson(1976-)
The Benchwarmers *'06*
Grandma's Boy *'06*
Malibu's Most Wanted *'03*

Roger E. Swaybill(1943-91)
Porky's 2: The Next Day *'83*
The Lathe of Heaven *'80*

Bruce Sweeney
American Venus *'07*
Live Bait *'95*

Julia Sweeney(1961-)
God Said "Ha!" *'99*
It's Pat: The Movie *'94*

John Sweet
The Affair of the Necklace *'01*

The Great Elephant Escape *'95*

Michael Swerdlick
Love Don't Cost a Thing *'03*
Can't Buy Me Love *'87*

Tommy Swerdlow(1962-)
Snow Dogs *'02*
Bushwhacked *'95*
Little Giants *'94*
Cool Runnings *'93*

Jo Swerling(1893-1964)
It's a Wonderful Life *'46*
Leave Her to Heaven *'45*
Lifeboat *'44*
Crash Dive *'43*
The Pride of the Yankees *'42*
Blood and Sand *'41*
The Westerner *'40*
Made for Each Other *'39*
The Real Glory *'39*
I Am the Law *'38*
Double Wedding *'37*
Pennies from Heaven *'36*
The Whole Town's Talking *'35*
Lady by Choice *'34*
The Miracle Woman *'31*
Platinum Blonde *'31*

Robin Swicord(1952-)
The Jane Austen Book Club *'07*
Memoirs of a Geisha *'05*
Practical Magic *'98*
Matilda *'96*
Little Women *'94*
The Perez Family *'94*
Shag: The Movie *'89*

David Swift(1919-2001)
The Parent Trap *'98*
Candleshoe *'78*
How to Succeed in Business without Really Trying *'67*
Good Neighbor Sam *'64*
Under the Yum-Yum Tree *'63*
The Interns *'62*
The Parent Trap *'61*
Pollyanna *'60*

Don Swift
Wild Brian Kent *'36*
Thunder Mountain *'35*

Mark Swift
Friday the 13th *'09*
Freddy vs. Jason *'03*

Joe Syracuse(1967-)
Surf's Up *'07*
Lover Girl *'97*

Istvan Szabo(1938-)
Sunshine *'99*
Meeting Venus *'91*
Hanussen *'88*
Mephisto *'81*
25 Fireman's Street *'73*
Love Film *'70*
Father *'67*

Kam-yeun Szeto
Flash Point *'07*
Exiled *'06*

Kam-yuen Szeto
Dog Bite Dog *'06*
Special Unit 2002 *'01*
Roseanne: An Unauthorized Biography *'94*

Roy Szeto
The Phantom Lover *'95*
Wicked City *'92*
Dragons Forever *'88*
Mr. Vampire *'86*

Thomas Szollosi
It Waits *'05*
Bone Daddy *'97*
Snow White: A Tale of Terror *'97*
It Takes Two *'88*
Three o'Clock High *'87*

Matthew Tabak
Plain Truth *'04*
Point of Origin *'02*

Beyond Suspicion *'00*

Paul Tabori(1908-74)
Paid to Kill *'54*
Four Sided Triangle *'53*
Spaceways *'53*

Jean-Charles Tacchella(1925-)
Blue Country *'77*
Cousin, Cousine *'76*

Massy Tadjedin
Last Night *'10*
The Jacket *'05*
Leo *'02*

Brian Taggert
Trucks *'97*
Dangerous Passion *'95*
What Ever Happened To... *'93*
Child of Darkness, Child of Light *'91*
Poltergeist 3 *'88*
Wanted Dead or Alive *'86*
The New Kids *'85*
Of Unknown Origin *'83*
Visiting Hours *'82*

Hajime Taikawa
Shinobi no Mono 2: Vengeance *'63*
Shinobi no Mono *'62*

Don Tait
The North Avenue Irregulars *'79*
Unidentified Flying Oddball *'79*
Hell's Angels '69 *'69*

Koji Takada(1934-)
Return of the Street Fighter *'74*
The Street Fighter *'74*
Legends of the Poisonous Seductress 2: Quick Draw Okatsu *'69*
Legends of the Poisonous Seductress 3: Okatsu the Fugitive *'69*
Legends of the Poisonous Seductress 1: Female Demon Ohyaku *'68*

Hiroshi Takahashi
Ringu 0 *'01*
Ringu 2 *'99*
Ringu *'98*

Isao Takahata
Pom Poko *'94*
Grave of the Fireflies *'88*

Beat Takeshi
See Takeshi "Beat" Kitano

Igor Talankin
Tchaikovsky *'71*
A Summer to Remember *'61*

Amy Talkington
The Night of the White Pants *'06*
Brave New Girl *'04*

Ted Tally(1952-)
Red Dragon *'02*
All the Pretty Horses *'00*
The Juror *'96*
Before and After *'95*
The Silence of the Lambs *'91*
White Palace *'90*

Paul Tamasy
Air Bud 2: Golden Receiver *'98*
Air Bud *'97*

Nat Tanchuck(1912-78)
Married Too Young *'62*
Chained for Life *'51*

Edward Tang(1946-)
Mr. Nice Guy *'98*
Rumble in the Bronx *'96*
The Legend of Drunken Master *'94*
Supercop *'92*
Operation Condor *'91*
Project A: Part 2 *'87*

Operation Condor 2: The Armour of the Gods *'86*
Project A *'83*

Alain Tanner(1929-)
In the White City *'83*
Messidor *'77*
Jonah Who Will Be 25 in the Year 2000 *'76*
La Salamandre *'71*
Charles: Dead or Alive *'69*

Robert Emmett Tansey(1897-1951)
The Driftin' Kid *'41*
Dynamite Canyon *'41*
The Painted Trail *'38*
Sing, Cowboy, Sing *'37*
Pinto Rustlers *'36*
Courage of the North *'35*
Paradise Canyon *'35*

Daniel Taplitz
Chaos Theory *'08*
Breakin' All The Rules *'04*
Dean Koontz's Black River *'01*
Winds of Terror *'01*
Little Richard *'00*
Commandments *'96*
Black Magic *'92*

Daniel Taradash(1913-2003)
The Other Side of Midnight *'77*
Doctors' Wives *'70*
Castle Keep *'69*
Hawaii *'66*
Morituri *'65*
Bell, Book and Candle *'58*
Picnic *'55*
Desiree *'54*
From Here to Eternity *'53*
Don't Bother to Knock *'52*
Rancho Notorious *'52*
Knock on Any Door *'49*
Golden Boy *'39*

Paul Tarantino
Headhunter *'05*
Newsbreak *'00*

Quentin Tarantino(1963-)
Inglourious Basterds *'09*
Death Proof *'07*
Kill Bill Vol. 2 *'04*
Kill Bill Vol. 1 *'03*
Jackie Brown *'97*
Four Rooms *'95*
From Dusk Till Dawn *'95*
Pulp Fiction *'94*
True Romance *'93*
Reservoir Dogs *'92*

Sooni Taraporevala
The Namesake *'06*
My Own Country *'98*
Such a Long Journey *'98*
Mississippi Masala *'92*
Salaam Bombay! *'88*

Andrei Tarkovsky(1932-86)
The Sacrifice *'86*
Nostalghia *'83*
The Mirror *'75*
Solaris *'72*
Andrei Rublev *'66*

Frank Tarloff(1916-99)
A Guide for the Married Man *'67*
Father Goose *'64*

Susan Tarr
My Sister's Keeper *'02*
Cousin Bette *'97*

Frank Tashlin(1913-72)
Private Navy of Sgt. O'Farrell *'68*
Caprice *'67*
Who's Minding the Store? *'63*
Cinderfella *'60*
Rock-A-Bye Baby *'57*
Will Success Spoil Rock Hunter? *'57*
The Girl Can't Help It *'56*

Artists and Models *'55*
Son of Paleface *'52*
The Lemon Drop Kid *'51*
The Fuller Brush Girl *'50*
Kill the Umpire *'50*
Love Happy *'50*
One Touch of Venus *'48*
Variety Girl *'47*
A Night in Casablanca *'46*

Robert Tasker(1898-1944)
San Quentin *'37*
Doctor X *'32*

Jacques Tati(1908-82)
Parade *'74*
Traffic *'71*
Mon Oncle *'58*
Mr. Hulot's Holiday *'53*
Jour de Fete *'48*

Gilles Taurand(1943-)
Strayed *'03*
Time Regained *'99*
Alice et Martin *'98*
Dry Cleaning *'97*
Les Voleurs *'96*
Wild Reeds *'94*
Hotel America *'81*

Catherine Tavel(1959-)
Night Fire *'94*
Married People, Single Sex *'93*

Bertrand Tavernier(1941-)
Capitaine Conan *'96*
L'Appat *'94*
L.627 *'92*
Life and Nothing But *'89*
Round Midnight *'86*
A Sunday in the Country *'84*
Coup de Torchon *'81*
Death Watch *'80*
Spoiled Children *'77*
The Judge and the Assassin *'75*
The Clockmaker *'73*

Paolo Taviani(1931-)
Elective Affinities *'96*
Fiorile *'93*
Night Sun *'90*
Good Morning, Babylon *'87*
Kaos *'85*
The Night of the Shooting Stars *'82*
Padre Padrone *'77*
Allonsanfan *'73*
St. Michael Had a Rooster *'72*

Vittorio Taviani(1929-)
Elective Affinities *'96*
Fiorile *'93*
Night Sun *'90*
Good Morning, Babylon *'87*
Kaos *'85*
The Night of the Shooting Stars *'82*
Padre Padrone *'77*
Allonsanfan *'73*
St. Michael Had a Rooster *'72*

Eli Tavor
Dead End Street *'83*
Secret of Yolanda *'82*
Hot Bubblegum *'81*

Alison Taylor
The Cheetah Girls 2 *'06*
The Cheetah Girls *'03*

Brian Taylor
Jonah Hex *'10*
Crank: High Voltage *'09*
Gamer *'09*
Crank *'06*

Bruce Taylor
The Brave One *'07*
At Any Cost *'00*
Inferno *'98*

David Taylor
Tracked *'98*
DROP Squad *'94*
Devlin *'92*
Get Crazy *'83*

Delores Taylor(1939-)
The Trial of Billy Jack *'74*
Billy Jack *'71*

Doug Taylor
Splice *'09*
In the Name of the King: A Dungeon Siege Tale *'08*
The Carpenter *'89*

Dwight Taylor(1902-86)
We're Not Married *'52*
I Wake Up Screaming *'41*
Rhythm on the River *'40*
Top Hat *'35*
Today We Live *'33*

Eric Taylor(1897-1952)
Dick Tracy Meets Gruesome *'47*
Dick Tracy, Detective *'45*
The Phantom of the Opera *'43*
Son of Dracula *'43*
The Black Cat *'41*
Black Friday *'40*

Finn Taylor(1958-)
The Darwin Awards *'06*
Cherish *'02*
Dream with the Fishes *'97*
Pontiac Moon *'94*

Greg Taylor
Prancer Returns *'01*
Santa and Pete *'99*
Summer of the Monkeys *'98*
The Christmas Box *'95*
Prancer *'89*

Jim Taylor(1962-)
I Now Pronounce You Chuck and Larry *'07*
About Schmidt *'02*
Jurassic Park 3 *'01*
Election *'99*
Citizen Ruth *'96*

Kenneth Taylor(1922-)
The Camomile Lawn *'92*
Cause Celebre *'87*
The Maze *'85*

Lawrence Taylor
The Jackie Robinson Story *'50*
The Spider Returns *'41*

Renee Taylor(1935-)
Love Is All There Is *'96*
Lovers and Other Strangers *'70*

Roderick Taylor
The Brave One *'07*
American Outlaws *'01*
At Any Cost *'00*
Inferno *'98*
The Star Chamber *'83*

S. Lee Taylor
See Steve Taylor

Sam Taylor(1895-1958)
Exit Smiling *'26*
The Freshman *'25*
Girl Shy *'24*
Safety Last *'23*

Samuel A. Taylor(1912-2000)
The Love Machine *'71*
Topaz *'69*
Goodbye Again *'61*
Vertigo *'58*
The Eddy Duchin Story *'56*

Steve Taylor(1957-)
The Second Chance *'06*
Social Intercourse *'01*
Sorority House Party *'92*

Pierre Tchernia
The Holes *'72*
Belle Americaine *'61*

Andre Techine(1943-)
The Girl on the Train *'09*
The Witnesses *'07*
Changing Times *'04*
Strayed *'03*
Alice et Martin *'98*
Les Voleurs *'96*

Dale Trevillion
Beyond Desire '94
One Man Force '89
Las Vegas Weekend '85

Lawrence Trilling
Delivered '98
Dinner and Driving '97

Dorothy Tristan(1942-)
Suspended Animation '02
Weeds '87

Victor Trivas(1896-1970)
The Head '59
The Stranger '46

Anne-Louise Trividic
Gabrielle '05
Intimacy '00

Pierre Trividic
Lady Chatterley '06
Those Who Love Me Can Take the Train '98

Rose Troche
The Safety of Objects '01
Go Fish '94

Jan Troell(1931-)
Everlasting Moments '08
The New Land '73
The Emigrants '72

Guy Trosper(1911-63)
The Spy Who Came in from the Cold '65
Birdman of Alcatraz '62
Darby's Rangers '58
Jailhouse Rock '57
Many Rivers to Cross '55
The Stratton Story '49
Crossroads '42

Lamar Trotti(1900-52)
With a Song in My Heart '52
I'd Climb the Highest Mountain '51
Cheaper by the Dozen '50
My Blue Heaven '50
Captain from Castile '47
Mother Wore Tights '47
The Razor's Edge '46
Wilson '44
Guadalcanal Diary '43
Immortal Sergeant '43
The Ox-Bow Incident '43
Thunder Birds '42
Brigham Young: Frontiersman '40
The Story of Alexander Graham Bell '39
Young Mr. Lincoln '39
Alexander's Ragtime Band '38
In Old Chicago '37
Life Begins at Forty '35
Steamboat Round the Bend '35

David Trueba
The Girl of Your Dreams '99
Dance with the Devil '97
Two Much '96

Guerdon (Gordon) Trueblood
The Chase '91
The Bastard '78
Terror Out of the Sky '78
Ants '77
Tarantulas: The Deadly Cargo '77
The Last Hard Men '76
The Savage Bees '76

Francois Truffaut(1932-84)
Confidentially Yours '83
The Last Metro '80
The Man Who Loved Women '77
Small Change '76
Day for Night '73
Two English Girls '72
Bed and Board '70
The Wild Child '70
Mississippi Mermaid '69
The Bride Wore Black '68
Stolen Kisses '68
Fahrenheit 451 '66
The Soft Skin '64
Jules and Jim '62
Shoot the Piano Player '62
The 400 Blows '59
Les Mistons '57

Christopher Trumbo
Trumbo '07
Naked City: A Killer Christmas '98

Dalton Trumbo(1905-76)
Papillon '73
Johnny Got His Gun '71
The Horsemen '70
The Fixer '68
Hawaii '66
Lonely Are the Brave '62
Exodus '60
Spartacus '60
Terror in a Texas Town '58
The Brave One '56
Roman Holiday '53
Prowler '51
Rocketship X-M '50
Gun Crazy '49
Our Vines Have Tender Grapes '45
A Guy Named Joe '44
Thirty Seconds Over Tokyo '44
The Flying Irishman '39
A Man to Remember '39

Alan R. Trustman(1930-)
The Arab Conspiracy '76
Hit! '73
Lady Ice '73
They Call Me Mr. Tibbs! '70
Bullitt '68
The Thomas Crown Affair '68

Glenn Tryon(1894-1970)
Lawmen '44
Small Town Boy '37
Bachelor Bait '34

Ming-liang Tsai
Goodbye, Dragon Inn '03
What Time Is It There? '01
The Hole '98
Rebels of the Neon God '92

Kan-Cheung (Sammy) Tsang
Kung Fu Hustle '04
Shaolin Soccer '01

Alex Tse
Watchmen '09
Sucker Free City '05

Shinya Tsukamoto(1960-)
Nightmare Detective '06
Tetsuo 2: Body Hammer '97
Tetsuo: The Iron Man '92

Slava Tsukerman
Perestroika '09
Liquid Sky '83

Yun Chih Tu
Vengeance is a Golden Blade '69
Golden Swallow '68

Stanley Tucci(1960-)
Joe Gould's Secret '00
The Imposters '98
Big Night '95

James Tucker
Steps from Hell '92
Lunatic '91

Larry Tucker(1933-2001)
Alex in Wonderland '70
Bob & Carol & Ted & Alice '69
I Love You, Alice B. Toklas! '68

Harry Tugend(1897-1989)
Who's Minding the Store? '63
Pocketful of Miracles '61
Take Me Out to the Ball Game '49
Star Spangled Rhythm '42
Birth of the Blues '41
Caught in the Draft '41
Seven Sinners '40
Second Fiddle '39
My Lucky Star '38
Thanks for Everything '38
Love Is News '37
Pigskin Parade '36

Jim Tully(1891-1947)
The Raven '35
Beggars of Life '28

Karl Tunberg(1909-92)
The Seventh Dawn '64
Ben-Hur '59
Beau Brummel '54
Valley of the Kings '54
Up in Central Park '48
You Gotta Stay Happy '48
Week-End in Havana '41
Down Argentine Way '40

William Tunberg
Old Yeller '57
That's My Baby! '44

Gary J. Tunnicliffe(1968-)
Megalodon '03
The Guardian '00
Within the Rock '96

Ann Turner(1960-)
Irresistible '06
The Killing Beach '92
Hammers over the Anvil '91

Barbara Turner
The Company '03
Pollock '00
Georgia '95
War Between the Tates '76

Bonnie Turner
The Brady Bunch Movie '95
Tommy Boy '95
Coneheads '93
Wayne's World 2 '93
Wayne's World '92

Brian Turner
Snowglobe '07
Santa Baby '06

Guinevere Turner(1968-)
BloodRayne '06
The Notorious Bettie Page '06
American Psycho '99
Go Fish '94

Sheldon Turner
Up in the Air '09
The Texas Chainsaw Massacre: The Beginning '06
The Longest Yard '05

Terry Turner
The Brady Bunch Movie '95
Tommy Boy '95
Coneheads '93
Wayne's World 2 '93
Wayne's World '92

Catherine Turney(1906-98)
Cry Wolf '47
The Man I Love '46
My Reputation '46

John Turturro(1957-)
Romance & Cigarettes '05
Illuminata '98
Mac '93

Derek Twist(1905-79)
Angels One Five '54
Non-Stop New York '37

John Twist(1898-1976)
A Distant Trumpet '64
The FBI Story '59
Band of Angels '57
Helen of Troy '56
King Richard and the Crusaders '54
Colorado Territory '49
Tycoon '47
Pittsburgh '42

David N. Twohy(1955-)
A Perfect Getaway '09
The Chronicles of Riddick '04
Below '02
Impostor '02
Pitch Black '00
G.I. Jane '97
The Arrival '96
Waterworld '95
Terminal Velocity '94
The Fugitive '93
Grand Tour: Disaster in Time '92
Warlock '91
Critters 2: The Main Course '88

Jonathan Tydor
The King's Guard '01
The Hard Truth '94

Tom Tykwer(1965-)
Paris, je t'aime '06
Perfume: The Story of a Murderer '06
The Princess and the Warrior '00
Run Lola Run '98
Winter Sleepers '97

Steve Tymon(1956-)
Hindsight '97
Mirror, Mirror 3: The Voyeur '96
Dark Secrets '95

Bob Tzudiker
Tarzan 2 '05
102 Dalmatians '00
Tarzan '99
Anastasia '97
The Hunchback of Notre Dame '96
Newsies '92

Keinosuke Uegusa
Drunken Angel '48
One Wonderful Sunday '47

Jim Uhls
Jumper '08
Fight Club '99

Alfred Uhry(1936-)
Rich in Love '93
Driving Miss Daisy '89
Mystic Pizza '88

Daniel Ullman(1918-79)
Wyatt Earp: Return to Tombstone '94
Mysterious Island '61
The Gunfight at Dodge City '59
Good Day for a Hanging '58
Canyon River '56
The First Texan '56
An Annapolis Story '55
Dial Red O '55
Square Dance Jubilee '51
Red Desert '50
Ringside '49

Elwood Ullman(1903-85)
Snow White and the Three Stooges '61
The Three Stooges Meet Hercules '61
Ma and Pa Kettle at Waikiki '55
The Stooge '51

Liv Ullmann(1939-)
Kristin Lavransdatter '95
Sofie '92

Gladys Unger(1885-1940)
The Mystery of Edwin Drood '35
Sylvia Scarlett '35
Great Expectations '34

Eve Unsell(1887-1937)
The Plastic Age '25
Shadows '22
Her Silent Sacrifice '18

Leon Uris(1924-2003)
Gunfight at the O.K. Corral '57
Battle Cry '55

Peter Ustinov(1921-2004)
Hot Millions '68
Lady L '65
Billy Budd '62
Immortal Battalion '44

Pierre Uytterhoeven
Roman de Gare '07
And Now Ladies and Gentlemen '02
Bandits '86
Happy New Year '73
A Man and a Woman '66

Rodney Vaccaro(1952-)
Bigger Than the Sky '05
Ride the Wild Fields '00
Three to Tango '99

Roger Vadim(1928-2000)
Game of Seduction '76
Barbarella '68
Spirits of the Dead '68
The Game Is Over '66
Love on a Pillow '62
Blood and Roses '61
Please Not Now! '61
Dangerous Liaisons '60
Sois Belle et Tais-Toi '58
And God Created Woman '57
The Night Heaven Fell '57
Plucking the Daisy '56

Laszlo Vadnay(1904-67)
Ten Thousand Bedrooms '57
The Great Rupert '50
Copacabana '47
Uncertain Glory '44

Ernest Vajda(1886-1954)
The Smiling Lieutenant '31
Tonight or Never '31
Monte Carlo '30
The Love Parade '29

Ladislao Vajda(1906-65)
The Miracle of Marcelino '55
The Threepenny Opera '31

Luis Valdez(1940-)
The Cisco Kid '94
La Bamba '87
Zoot Suit '81

Val Valentine(1895-1971)
The Belles of St. Trinian's '53
Grand National Night '53
My Son, the Vampire '52
Old Mother Riley's Jungle Treasure '51
We Dive at Dawn '43

Vincent Valentini
Sepia Cinderella '47
Murder on Lenox Avenue '41

Nick Vallelonga(1959-)
The Corporate Ladder '97
In the Kingdom of the Blind the Man with One Eye Is King '94
A Brilliant Disguise '93

Jean-Claude Van Damme(1961-)
Double Impact '91
Lionheart '90
Kickboxer '89

Jaco Van Dormael(1957-)
The Eighth Day '95
Toto le Heros '91

John Van Druten(1901-57)
Gaslight '44
Lucky Partners '40
Night Must Fall '37

Dale Van Every(1896-1976)
Souls at Sea '37
Wings in the Dark '35
Murders in the Rue Morgue '32
Trader Horn '31

Mario Van Peebles(1958-)
Baadasssss! '03
Love Kills '98
Los Locos Posse '97

Melvin Van Peebles(1932-)
Panther '95
Tales of Erotica '93
Sophisticated Gents '81
Greased Lightning '77
Sweet Sweetback's Baadasssss Song '71
The Story of a Three Day Pass '68

Gus Van Sant(1952-)
Paranoid Park '07
Paris, je t'aime '06
Last Days '05
Elephant '03
Gerry '02
Even Cowgirls Get the Blues '94
My Own Private Idaho '91
Drugstore Cowboy '89

Andrew Van Slee(1965-)
Net Games '03
Totally Blonde '01

Virginia Van Upp(1902-70)
She Wouldn't Say Yes '45
Together Again '43
Bahama Passage '42
Young and Willing '42
You and Me '38

Norman Vance, Jr.
Pride '07
Roll Bounce '05

James Vanderbilt
The Losers '10
Zodiac '07
Basic '03
Darkness Falls '03
The Rundown '03

Agnes Varda(1928-)
One Hundred and One Nights '95
Jacquot '91
Vagabond '85
One Sings, the Other Doesn't '77
Le Bonheur '65
Cleo from 5 to 7 '61

Nia Vardalos(1962-)
I Hate Valentine's Day '09
Connie and Carla '04
My Big Fat Greek Wedding '02

Ethlie Ann Vare
Swamp Devil '08
Black Swarm '07
Something Beneath '07

Michael Varhol
The Big Picture '89
Pee-wee's Big Adventure '85
The Last Word '80

John Varley(1947-)
Millennium '89
Overdrawn at the Memory Bank '83
Pleasure '31

Joseph B. Vasquez(1962-95)
Manhattan Merenque! '95
Hangin' with the Homeboys '91

Matthew Vaughn(1971-)
Kick-Ass '10
Stardust '07

Blackbeard's Ghost *'67*
Mary Poppins *'64*
The Absent-Minded Professor *'61*

Fran Walsh(1959-)
The Lovely Bones *'09*
King Kong *'05*
Lord of the Rings: The Return of the King *'03*
Lord of the Rings: The Two Towers *'02*
Lord of the Rings: The Fellowship of the Ring *'01*
The Frighteners *'96*
Heavenly Creatures *'94*
Jack Brown, Genius *'94*
Dead Alive *'93*
Meet the Feebles *'89*

Mary Walsh(1952-)
The Silence *'06*
Bailey's Billion$ *'05*

Matthew Jason Walsh(1970-)
The Raven *'07*
Ring of Darkness *'04*
Witchouse *'99*

Raoul Walsh(1887-1980)
Esther and the King *'60*
Big Brown Eyes *'36*
Sadie Thompson *'28*
Regeneration *'15*

Fred Walton
When a Stranger Calls Back *'93*
Trapped *'89*
The Rosary Murders *'87*
Hadley's Rebellion *'84*
When a Stranger Calls *'79*

Bin Wang
House of Flying Daggers *'04*
Hero *'03*

Hui-Ling Wang
Fleeing by Night *'00*
Eat Drink Man Woman *'94*

Peter Wang
The Laserman *'90*
A Great Wall *'86*

Wayne Wang(1949-)
The Center of the World *'01*
Chinese Box *'97*
Blue in the Face *'95*
Chan Is Missing *'82*

Xiaoshuai Wang(1966-)
In Love We Trust *'07*
Beijing Bicycle *'01*
Frozen *'98*
So Close to Paradise *'98*

David S. Ward(1947-)
Flyboys *'06*
The Program *'93*
Sleepless in Seattle *'93*
King Ralph *'91*
Major League *'89*
The Milagro Beanfield War *'88*
Saving Grace *'86*
The Sting 2 *'83*
Cannery Row *'82*
Steelyard Blues *'73*
The Sting *'73*

Donal Lardner Ward(1964-)
The Suburbans *'99*
My Life's in Turnaround *'94*

Edmund Ward(1928-93)
Prayer for the Dying *'87*
Twinsanity *'70*

Jason Ward
Deuce Bigalow: European Gigolo *'05*
Corky Romano *'01*

Kelly Ward(1956-)
All Dogs Go to Heaven 2 *'95*
Once Upon a Forest *'93*

Lucille Ward(1907-69)
Weird Woman *'44*
Texas Legionnaires *'43*

Lawless Plainsmen *'42*
Call the Mesquiteers *'38*
A Woman of the World *'25*

Morgan Ward
Riding in Cars with Boys *'01*
A Pyromaniac's Love Story *'95*

Vincent Ward(1956-)
River Queen *'05*
Map of the Human Heart *'93*
The Navigator *'88*
Vigil *'84*

David Warfield
Linewatch *'08*
Kiss of a Killer *'93*
Kill Me Again *'89*
P.I. Private Investigations *'87*
Private Investigations *'87*

Regis Wargnier(1948-)
East-West *'99*
Indochine *'92*

Dave Warner(1953-)
Garage Days *'03*
Cut *'00*

Charles Marquis Warren(1912-90)
Charro! *'69*
Hellgate *'52*

Jerry Warren(1921-88)
The Wild World of Batwoman *'66*
Terror of the Bloodhunters *'62*
Teenage Zombies *'58*

John Warren(1953-)
Major League 3: Back to the Minors *'98*
The Curse of Inferno *'96*
Flashfire *'94*
Girl in the Cadillac *'94*
Naked in New York *'93*

Deric Washburn
Extreme Prejudice *'87*
The Border *'82*
The Deer Hunter *'78*
Silent Running *'71*

Art Washington
Hendrix *'00*
Percy & Thunder *'93*

Wendy Wasserstein(1950-2006)
Trial by Media *'00*
The Object of My Affection *'98*
The Heidi Chronicles *'95*
Sorrows of Gin *'79*

Keith Waterhouse(1929-)
Charlie Muffin *'79*
Billy Liar *'63*
A Kind of Loving *'62*
Whistle down the Wind *'61*

Daniel Waters(1962-)
Sex and Death 101 *'07*
Happy Campers *'01*
Demolition Man *'93*
Batman Returns *'92*
Hudson Hawk *'91*
The Adventures of Ford Fairlane *'90*
Heathers *'89*

John Waters(1946-)
A Dirty Shame *'04*
Cecil B. Demented *'00*
Pecker *'98*
Serial Mom *'94*
Cry-Baby *'90*
Hairspray *'88*
Polyester *'81*
Desperate Living *'77*
Female Trouble *'74*
Pink Flamingos *'72*
Multiple Maniacs *'70*
Mondo Trasho *'69*

Lawrence Edward Watkin(1901-81)
Darby O'Gill & the Little People *'59*

The Great Locomotive Chase *'56*

Maurine Watkins(1896-1969)
Libeled Lady *'36*
No Man of Her Own *'32*
Up the River *'30*

Peter Watkins(1935-)
Edvard Munch *'74*
Privilege *'67*

Carol Watson
Crazylove *'05*
Friday the 13th, Part 3 *'82*

John Watson
Robin Hood: Prince of Thieves *'91*
The Zoo Gang *'85*

Kim Watson
Honey *'03*
What About Your Friends: Weekend Getaway *'02*

Ric Roman Waugh(1968-)
Felon *'08*
In the Shadows *'01*

Craig Wayans
Dance Flick *'09*
Scary Movie 2 *'01*

Damon Wayans(1960-)
Major Payne *'95*
Blankman *'94*
Mo' Money *'92*

Keenen Ivory Wayans(1958-)
Dance Flick *'09*
Little Man *'06*
White Chicks *'04*
Most Wanted *'97*
A Low Down Dirty Shame *'94*
The Five Heartbeats *'91*
I'm Gonna Git You Sucka *'88*
Hollywood Shuffle *'87*

Marlon Wayans(1972-)
Dance Flick *'09*
Little Man *'06*
White Chicks *'04*
Scary Movie 2 *'01*
Scary Movie *'00*
Don't Be a Menace to South Central While Drinking Your Juice in the Hood *'95*

Shawn Wayans(1971-)
Dance Flick *'09*
Little Man *'06*
White Chicks *'04*
Scary Movie 2 *'01*
Scary Movie *'00*
Don't Be a Menace to South Central While Drinking Your Juice in the Hood *'95*

Frank Wead(1895-1947)
They Were Expendable *'45*
Dive Bomber *'41*
Ceiling Zero *'35*

Blayne Weaver(1976-)
Weather Girl *'09*
The Prince & Me 3: A Royal Honeymoon *'08*
Manic *'01*

James R. Webb(1910-74)
The Organization *'71*
How the West Was Won *'63*
Kings of the Sun *'63*
Pork Chop Hill *'59*
The Big Country *'58*
Vera Cruz *'53*
The Iron Mistress *'52*
Close to My Heart *'51*
Montana *'50*
Bad Man of Deadwood *'41*
Nevada City *'41*

Michael H. Weber
(500) Days of Summer *'09*
The Pink Panther 2 *'09*

Steven Weber(1961-)
Masters of Horror: Jenifer *'05*
Club Land *'01*

M. Coates Webster(1903-55)
Night Riders of Montana *'50*
The Brute Man *'46*
Jungle Captive *'45*
Strange Confession *'45*

David Wechter(1956-)
Malibu Bikini Shop *'86*
Midnight Madness *'80*

Hugh Wedlock, Jr.
Abbott and Costello Meet the Killer, Boris Karloff *'49*
George White's Scandals *'45*

Bob Wehling(1919-83)
Eegah! *'62*
Wild Guitar *'62*

Lo Wei(1918-96)
New Fist of Fury *'76*
Chinese Connection *'73*
Fists of Fury *'73*

Lu Wei
To Live *'94*
Farewell My Concubine *'93*

John Weidner
Body Armour *'07*
Midnight Kiss *'93*
Private Wars *'93*

Samuel Weil
See Lloyd Kaufman

Herschel Weingrod(1947-)
Pure Luck *'91*
Kindergarten Cop *'90*
My Stepmother Is an Alien *'88*
Twins *'88*
Brewster's Millions *'85*
Trading Places *'83*
Cheaper to Keep Her *'80*

Peter Weir(1944-)
Master and Commander: The Far Side of the World *'03*
Green Card *'90*
The Year of Living Dangerously *'82*
Gallipoli *'81*
Plumber *'79*
The Last Wave *'77*
The Cars That Ate Paris *'74*

Brenda Weisberg
Rusty's Birthday *'49*
The Mummy's Ghost *'44*
Weird Woman *'44*
The Mad Ghoul *'43*

David Weisberg
Double Jeopardy *'99*
Holy Matrimony *'94*

Stanley Weiser
W. *'08*
Rudy: The Rudy Giulani Story *'03*
Freedom Song *'00*
Witness to the Mob *'98*
Fatherland *'94*
Project X *'87*
Wall Street *'87*

David Weisman(1942-)
Shogun Assassin *'80*
Edie in Ciao! Manhattan *'72*

Straw Weisman
Fight for Your Life *'77*
Toga Party *'77*

Allan Weiss
Paradise, Hawaiian Style *'66*
Sons of Katie Elder *'65*

David N. Weiss
Daddy Day Camp *'07*
Are We There Yet? *'05*
Shrek 2 *'04*
Clockstoppers *'02*

Jimmy Neutron: Boy Genius *'01*
Rugrats in Paris: The Movie *'00*
The Rugrats Movie *'98*
Rock-a-Doodle *'92*
All Dogs Go to Heaven *'89*

Eric Weiss
Buffalo Soldiers *'01*
Bongwater *'98*
Wicked *'98*

Jiri Weiss(1913-2004)
Martha and I *'91*
Murder Czech Style *'66*
The Coward *'62*
Wolf Trap *'57*

Michael D. Weiss
Journey to the Center of the Earth *'08*
The Butterfly Effect 2 *'06*
Octopus 2: River of Fear *'02*
U.S. Seals 2 *'01*
Crocodile *'00*
Octopus *'00*

David Weissman
Old Dogs *'09*
When in Rome *'09*
Evolution *'01*
Family Man *'00*
Dream a Little Dream 2 *'94*

Chris Weitz(1969-)
The Golden Compass *'07*
About a Boy *'02*
Nutty Professor 2: The Klumps *'00*
Antz *'98*
Madeline *'98*

Paul Weitz(1965-)
Cirque du Freak: The Vampire's Assistant *'09*
American Dreamz *'06*
In Good Company *'04*
About a Boy *'02*
Nutty Professor 2: The Klumps *'00*
Antz *'98*
Madeline *'98*

Peter Welbeck
See Harry Alan Towers

Robert L. Welch(1910-64)
Son of Paleface *'52*
Variety Girl *'47*

Sandy Welch
Emma *'09*
Jane Eyre *'06*
Our Mutual Friend *'98*
A Dark Adapted Eye *'93*
A Fatal Inversion *'92*

William Welch
The Brotherhood of Satan *'71*
Promises! Promises! *'63*

Les Weldon
Direct Contact *'09*
Target of Opportunity *'04*
Hidden Agenda *'01*
Replicant *'01*
Cause of Death *'00*

Colin Welland(1934-)
War of the Buttons *'95*
A Dry White Season *'89*
Twice in a Lifetime *'85*
Chariots of Fire *'81*
Yanks *'79*

Michael Weller(1943-)
Lost Angels *'89*
Ragtime *'81*
Hair *'79*

Halsted Welles
3:10 to Yuma *'07*
The Hanging Tree *'59*
3:10 to Yuma *'57*
Eight Witnesses *'54*

Orson Welles(1915-85)
Don Quixote *'92*
Treasure Island *'72*
Chimes at Midnight *'67*

The Trial *'63*
Touch of Evil *'58*
Mr. Arkadin *'55*
Othello *'52*
The Lady from Shanghai *'48*
The Magnificent Ambersons *'42*
Citizen Kane *'41*

William A. Wellman(1896-1975)
A Star Is Born *'37*
The Boob *'26*

Audrey Wells(1960-)
Under the Tuscan Sun *'03*
Disney's The Kid *'00*
Guinevere *'99*
George of the Jungle *'97*
The Truth about Cats and Dogs *'96*

George Wells(1909-2000)
The Impossible Years *'68*
The Horizontal Lieutenant *'62*
The Honeymoon Machine *'61*
Where the Boys Are *'60*
The Gazebo *'59*
Designing Woman *'57*
Don't Go Near the Water *'57*
Everything I Have is Yours *'52*
Angels in the Outfield *'51*
It's a Big Country *'51*
Show Boat *'51*
Summer Stock *'50*
Take Me Out to the Ball Game *'49*
The Hucksters *'47*
Merton of the Movies *'47*
The Show-Off *'46*

John Wells(1936-98)
Entertaining Angels: The Dorothy Day Story *'96*
Princess Caraboo *'94*

Peter Wells
First Love and Other Pains / One of Them *'99*
When Love Comes *'98*
Desperate Remedies *'93*

William K. Wells
Other Men's Women *'31*
Big Boy *'30*

Wim Wenders(1945-)
Don't Come Knocking *'05*
Land of Plenty *'04*
Beyond the Clouds *'95*
Lisbon Story *'94*
Faraway, So Close! *'93*
Until the End of the World *'91*
Wings of Desire *'88*
Tokyo-Ga *'85*
The American Friend *'77*
Kings of the Road—In the Course of Time *'76*
Alice in the Cities *'74*
The Goalie's Anxiety at the Penalty Kick *'71*

Gina Wendkos
The Perfect Man *'05*
The Princess Diaries *'01*
Coyote Ugly *'00*
Jersey Girl *'92*
Ginger Ale Afternoon *'89*

Richard Wenk(1956-)
16 Blocks *'06*
Just the Ticket *'98*
Vamp *'86*

Mike Werb
Firehouse Dog *'07*
Face/Off *'97*
Darkman 3: Die Darkman Die *'95*
The Mask *'94*
Machine Gun Kelly *'58*

Snag Werris
If I'm Lucky *'46*
If I'm Lucky *'46*
Four Jills in a Jeep *'44*

Lina Wertmuller(1928-)
The Worker and the Hair-dresser *'96*
Ciao, Professore! *'94*
Summer Night with Greek Profile, Almond Eyes & Scent of Basil *'87*
Camorra: The Naples Connection *'85*
Sotto, Sotto *'85*
A Joke of Destiny, Lying in Wait Around the Corner Like a Bandit *'84*
Blood Feud *'79*
A Night Full of Rain *'78*
Seven Beauties *'76*
Swept Away... *'75*
All Screwed Up *'74*
Love and Anarchy *'73*
Seduction of Mimi *'72*

Quentin Werty
That Man Bolt *'73*
Dark of the Sun *'68*

Richard Wesley(1945-)
Bojangles *'01*
Mandela and de Klerk *'97*
Native Son *'86*
Fast Forward *'84*
Let's Do It Again *'75*
Uptown Saturday Night *'74*

Claudine West(1890-1943)
The White Cliffs of Dover *'44*
Mrs. Miniver *'42*
Random Harvest *'42*
We Were Dancing *'42*
The Mortal Storm *'40*
Goodbye, Mr. Chips *'39*

Con West
Old Mother Riley, Headmistress *'50*
Old Mother Riley's New Venture *'49*
The Dummy Talks *'43*

Jake West
Pumpkinhead 3: Ashes to Ashes *'06*
Razor Blade Smile *'98*

Jessamyn West(1902-84)
Stolen Hours *'63*
The Big Country *'58*

Mae West(1893-1980)
My Little Chickadee *'40*
Every Day's a Holiday *'38*
Go West, Young Man *'36*
Klondike Annie *'36*
Goin' to Town *'35*
Belle of the Nineties *'34*
I'm No Angel *'33*
Night After Night *'32*

Roland West(1885-1952)
The Bat Whispers *'30*
Alibi *'29*
The Bat *'26*

Robert Westerby(1909-68)
Sea of Sand *'58*
War and Peace *'56*
The Spider and the Fly *'49*

Jennifer Westfeldt(1970-)
Ira & Abby *'06*
Kissing Jessica Stein *'02*

Donald E. Westlake(1933-)
The Grifters *'90*
Why Me? *'90*
The Stepfather *'87*
Hot Stuff *'80*
Cops and Robbers *'73*

Ellen Weston
Outrage *'98*
Sin and Redemption *'94*
Lies Before Kisses *'92*

Garnett Weston(1890-1980)
Bulldog Drummond's Bride *'39*
Bulldog Drummond's Secret Police *'39*
The White Zombie *'32*
Blackmail *'29*

Edwin Westrate(1894-1955)
Rolling Home *'48*
Shoot to Kill *'47*
Renegade Girl *'46*

Gerald Wexler
Hard to Forget *'98*
Margaret's Museum *'95*

Haskell Wexler(1926-)
Latino *'85*
Medium Cool *'69*

Norman Wexler(1926-99)
Saturday Night Fever *'77*
Mandingo *'75*
Serpico *'73*
Joe *'70*

John Wexley(1907-85)
The Long Night *'47*
Hangmen Also Die *'42*
Footsteps in the Dark *'41*
City for Conquest *'40*
Confessions of a Nazi Spy *'39*
Amazing Dr. Clitterhouse *'38*
Angels with Dirty Faces *'38*

Hannah Weyer
Life Support *'07*
Angel Rodriguez *'05*

Frank Whaley(1963-)
The Jimmy Show *'01*
Joe the King *'99*

Leigh Whannell(1977-)
Dead Silence *'07*
Saw 3 *'06*
Saw 2 *'05*
Saw *'04*

Jim Wheat(1952-)
Rattled *'96*
It Came from Outer Space 2 *'95*
The Birds 2: Land's End *'94*
After Midnight *'89*
The Fly 2 *'89*
Silent Scream *'80*

Ken Wheat(1950-)
Rattled *'96*
It Came from Outer Space 2 *'95*
The Birds 2: Land's End *'94*
After Midnight *'89*
The Fly 2 *'89*
Silent Scream *'80*

Mark Wheaton
Infected *'08*
The Messengers *'07*

John Whedon(1905-91)
The Bears & I *'74*
The Island at the Top of the World *'74*

Joss Whedon(1964-)
Serenity *'05*
Titan A.E. *'00*
Alien: Resurrection *'97*
Toy Story *'95*
Buffy the Vampire Slayer *'92*

Anne Wheeler(1946-)
Edge of Madness *'02*
Bye Bye Blues *'89*

Martin Wheeler
The Detonator *'06*
Black Dawn *'05*

Rene Wheeler(1912-2000)
Fanfan la Tulipe *'51*
Utopia *'51*

William Wheeler
The Hoax *'06*
The Prime Gig *'00*

Tim Whelan(1893-1957)
My Best Girl *'27*
Exit Smiling *'26*
Safety Last *'23*

Graeme Whifler(1951-)
Dr. Giggles *'92*
Sonny Boy *'87*

Duane Whitaker(1959-)
From Dusk Till Dawn 2: Texas Blood Money *'98*
Eddie Presley *'92*

Denis Whitburn(1944-)
Billy's Holiday *'95*
The Cursed Mountain Mystery *'93*
The Last Bastion *'84*

Cynthia Whitcomb(1951-)
Selma, Lord, Selma *'99*
Emma's Wish *'98*
Buffalo Girls *'95*
Degree of Guilt *'95*

David White(1916-90)
Undisputed II: Last Man Standing *'06*
Great Gold Swindle *'84*

Garry Michael White
The Promise *'79*
Sky Riders *'76*
Scarecrow *'73*

James Gordon White
The Thing with Two Heads *'72*
The Incredible Two-Headed Transplant *'71*
The Tormentors *'71*
Free Grass *'69*
Hell's Belles *'69*

J.B. White
The National Tree *'09*
The Twelve Days of Christmas Eve *'04*
Counterstrike *'03*
The Spring *'00*
The Beast *'96*

Mike White(1970-)
Gentlemen Broncos *'09*
Year of the Dog *'07*
Nacho Libre *'06*
School of Rock *'03*
The Good Girl *'02*
Orange County *'02*
Chuck & Buck *'00*
Dead Man on Campus *'97*

Noni White
Tarzan 2 *'05*
102 Dalmatians *'00*
Tarzan *'99*
Anastasia *'97*
The Hunchback of Notre Dame *'96*

Philip Graham White
Trailing Trouble *'37*
The Gay Buckaroo *'32*
Local Badman *'32*

Robb White(1909-)
Homicidal *'61*
13 Ghosts *'60*
The Tingler *'59*
House on Haunted Hill *'58*

Robertson White
Dick Tracy Meets Gruesome *'47*
Charlie Chan's Murder Cruise *'40*

Ted Whitehead
The Mayor of Casterbridge *'03*
Tess of the D'Urbervilles *'98*
Cracker: The Big Crunch *'94*

Hugh Whitemore(1936-)
My House in Umbria *'03*
The Gathering Storm *'02*
A Dance to the Music of Time *'97*
Jane Eyre *'96*
Breaking the Code *'95*
The Rector's Wife *'94*
Pack of Lies *'87*
84 Charing Cross Road *'86*
Office Romances *'86*
All Creatures Great and Small *'74*
Elizabeth R *'72*

Preston A. Whitmore, II(1962-)
This Christmas *'07*
Crossover *'06*
Blood Crime *'02*
Civil Brand *'02*
Lockdown *'00*
Fled *'96*
The Walking Dead *'94*

Cormac Wibberley(1959-)
G-Force *'09*
National Treasure: Book of Secrets *'07*
The Shaggy Dog *'06*
National Treasure *'04*
Charlie's Angels: Full Throttle *'03*
I Spy *'02*
The 6th Day *'00*
Motel Blue *'98*

Marianne S. Wibberley(1965-)
G-Force *'09*
National Treasure: Book of Secrets *'07*
The Shaggy Dog *'06*
National Treasure *'04*
Charlie's Angels: Full Throttle *'03*
I Spy *'02*
The 6th Day *'00*
Motel Blue *'98*

David Wickes
Frankenstein *'93*
Jekyll and Hyde *'90*
Jack the Ripper *'88*

Christopher Wicking(1943-)
To the Devil, a Daughter *'76*
Demons of the Mind *'72*
Blood from the Mummy's Tomb *'71*
Cry of the Banshee *'70*
Scream and Scream Again *'70*

Gregory Widen
The Prophecy *'95*
Backdraft *'91*
Highlander *'86*

Bo Widerberg(1930-97)
All Things Fair *'95*
Man from Mallorca *'84*
The Man on the Roof *'76*
Elvira Madigan *'67*

Ken Wiederhorn
A House in the Hills *'93*
Return of the Living Dead 2 *'88*
Shock Waves *'77*

Joe Wiesenfeld
A Killing Spring *'02*
Back to the Secret Garden *'01*
Child Star: The Shirley Temple Story *'01*
The Sign of Four *'01*
The Hound of the Baskervilles *'00*
A Knight in Camelot *'98*
20,000 Leagues Under the Sea *'97*
At the Midnight Hour *'95*
The Yearling *'94*
Anne of Green Gables *'85*

Crane Wilbur(1886-1973)
The George Raft Story *'61*
Mysterious Island *'61*
The Bat *'59*
Crime Wave *'54*
House of Wax *'53*
I Was a Communist for the FBI *'51*
The Devil on Wheels *'47*
Crime School *'38*
Captain Calamity *'36*
Yellow Cargo *'36*

Billy Wilder(1906-2002)
Buddy Buddy *'81*
The Front Page *'74*
Avanti! *'72*
The Private Life of Sherlock Holmes *'70*
The Fortune Cookie *'66*
Kiss Me, Stupid! *'64*
Irma La Douce *'63*
One, Two, Three *'61*
The Apartment *'60*
Some Like It Hot *'59*
Love in the Afternoon *'57*
Spirit of St. Louis *'57*
Witness for the Prosecution *'57*
The Seven Year Itch *'55*
Sabrina *'54*
Stalag 17 *'53*
Ace in the Hole *'51*
Sunset Boulevard *'50*
Emperor Waltz *'48*
A Foreign Affair *'48*
The Lost Weekend *'45*
Double Indemnity *'44*
Five Graves to Cairo *'43*
The Major and the Minor *'42*
Ball of Fire *'41*
Midnight *'39*
Ninotchka *'39*
Bluebeard's Eighth Wife *'38*
Mauvaise Graine *'33*

Gene Wilder(1935-)
Murder in a Small Town *'99*
See No Evil, Hear No Evil *'89*
Haunted Honeymoon *'86*
The Woman in Red *'84*
The Adventures of Sherlock Holmes' Smarter Brother *'78*
World's Greatest Lover *'77*
Young Frankenstein *'74*

John Wilder
Anne Rice's The Feast of All Saints *'01*
Return to Lonesome Dove *'93*
Breaking Home Ties *'87*
Centennial *'78*
Law of the Land *'76*

Robert Wilder(1901-74)
The Big Country *'58*
Flamingo Road *'49*

Thornton Wilder(1897-1975)
Our Town *'03*
Shadow of a Doubt *'43*

Georg Wildhagen(1920-)
The Merry Wives of Windsor *'50*
The Marriage of Figaro *'49*

Ethan Wiley
Black Ops *'07*
Children of the Corn 5: Fields of Terror *'98*
House 2: The Second Story *'87*
House *'86*

Rich Wilkes(1966-)
XXX *'02*
Glory Daze *'96*
The Jerky Boys *'95*
Airheads *'94*

Christopher Wilkinson(1950-)
Ali *'01*
Nixon *'95*

Bob Williams
20 Million Miles to Earth *'57*
Silver City Bonanza *'51*

Brock Williams
Black Tide *'58*
Meet Mr. Callaghan *'54*

Charles Williams(1909-75)
The Hot Spot *'90*
The Pink Jungle *'68*

Emlyn Williams(1905-87)
The Last Days of Dolwyn *'49*
Evergreen *'34*
The Man Who Knew Too Much *'34*

Rob Williams
Make the Yuletide Gay *'09*
Long-Term Relationship *'06*

Sarah Williams
Becoming Jane *'07*
The Secret Life of Mrs. Beeton *'06*

Spencer Williams, Jr.(1893-1969)
Blood of Jesus *'41*
Son of Ingagi *'40*
Harlem Rides the Range *'39*

Tennessee Williams(1911-83)
The Loss of a Teardrop Diamond *'08*
The Roman Spring of Mrs. Stone *'03*
Orpheus Descending *'91*
The Glass Menagerie *'87*
Cat on a Hot Tin Roof *'84*
Boom! *'68*
Baby Doll *'56*
The Rose Tattoo *'55*
A Streetcar Named Desire *'51*

Tod Williams(1968-)
The Door in the Floor *'04*
The Adventures of Sebastian Cole *'99*

David Williamson(1942-)
On the Beach *'00*
Dangerous Life *'89*
The Four Minute Mile *'88*
Travelling North *'87*
The Last Bastion *'84*
Phar Lap *'84*
The Year of Living Dangerously *'82*
The Club *'81*
Gallipoli *'81*
Don's Party *'76*

Fred Williamson(1938-)
Adios Amigo *'75*
Boss *'74*

Kevin Williamson(1965-)
Cursed *'04*
Teaching Mrs. Tingle *'99*
The Faculty *'98*
I Know What You Did Last Summer *'97*
Scream 2 *'97*
Scream *'96*

Nick Willing(1961-)
Alice *'09*
Close Your Eyes *'02*
Photographing Fairies *'97*

Calder Willingham(1922-95)
Rambling Rose *'91*
Thieves Like Us *'74*
Little Big Man *'70*
The Graduate *'67*
One-Eyed Jacks *'61*
The Vikings *'58*
Paths of Glory *'57*
The Strange One *'57*

F. McGrew Willis
Getting Gertie's Garter *'27*
Charley's Aunt *'25*

Tim Willocks
Sin *'02*
Swept from the Sea *'97*

Carey Wilson(1889-1962)
Mutiny on the Bounty *'35*
Gabriel Over the White House *'33*
Behind Office Doors *'31*

He Who Gets Slapped '24

David Wilson(1949-)

The Perfect Weapon '91
Strangers in Good Company '91

Erin Cressida Wilson(1964-)

Chloe '09
Fur: An Imaginary Portrait of Diane Arbus '06
Secretary '02

Gerald Wilson

Scorpio '73
Chato's Land '71
Lawman '71
Free Grass '69

Hugh Wilson(1943-)

Dudley Do-Right '99
Blast from the Past '98
Rough Riders '97
Down Periscope '96
Guarding Tess '94
Burglar '87
Rustler's Rhapsody '85
Police Academy '84
Stroker Ace '83

Michael Wilson(1914-78)

Planet of the Apes '68
Lawrence of Arabia '62
The Bridge on the River Kwai '57
Friendly Persuasion '56
Salt of the Earth '54
Five Fingers '52
A Place in the Sun '51

Michael G. Wilson(1943-)

License to Kill '89
The Living Daylights '87
A View to a Kill '85
Octopussy '83
For Your Eyes Only '81

Michael J. Wilson

Shark Tale '04
Ice Age '02
The Tuxedo '02

Owen Wilson(1968-)

The Royal Tenenbaums '01
Rushmore '98
Bottle Rocket '95

Sandy Wilson(1947-)

American Boyfriends '89
My American Cousin '85

S.S. Wilson

Wild Wild West '99
Tremors 2: Aftershocks '96
Heart and Souls '93
Ghost Dad '90
Tremors '89
Short Circuit 2 '88
*batteries not included '87
Short Circuit '86

Kurt Wimmer(1964-)

Law Abiding Citizen '09
Street Kings '08
Ultraviolet '06
The Recruit '03
Equilibrium '02
The Thomas Crown Affair '99
Relative Fear '95
The Neighbor '93

Arthur Wimperis(1874-1953)

Young Bess '53
Mrs. Miniver '42
Random Harvest '42
The Four Feathers '39
The Green Cockatoo '37
The Scarlet Pimpernel '34
The Private Life of Henry VIII '33

Michael Winder

Welcome to Blood City '77
The Beast Must Die '75

Jenny Wingfield

A Dog Named Christmas '09
The Outsider '02

Charles Winkler

Rocky Marciano '99
Disturbed '90
You Talkin' to Me? '87

Terence H. Winkless

Rage and Honor '92
Corporate Affairs '90
He's My Girl '87
The Howling '81

Michael Winner(1935-)

Parting Shots '98
Bullseye! '90
A Chorus of Disapproval '89
Appointment with Death '88
The Wicked Lady '83
Firepower '79
The Big Sleep '78
The Sentinel '76
Murder on the Campus '52

Terry Winsor

Essex Boys '99
Fool's Gold: The Story of the Brink's-Mat Robbery '92
Party! Party! '83

Alex Winter(1965-)

Fever '99
Freaked '93

Terence Winter

Brooklyn Rules '07
Get Rich or Die Tryin' '05

Scott Wiper(1970-)

The Condemned '07
A Better Way to Die '00

Mildred Wirt Benson

Nancy Drew and the Hidden Staircase '39
Nancy Drew—Trouble Shooter '39
Nancy Drew—Detective '38

Frank Wisbar(1899-1967)

Rimfire '49
Strangler of the Swamp '46

Aubrey Wisberg

Hercules in New York '70
The Man from Planet X '51
The Adventures of Rusty '45

Jerome Wish

The Gay Deceivers '69
Run, Angel, Run! '69

William Wisher

Dominion: Prequel to the Exorcist '05
Exorcist: The Beginning '04
Judge Dredd '95

Doris Wishman(1920-2002)

Double Agent 73 '80
The Amazing Transplant '70
Bad Girls Go to Hell '65
Nude on the Moon '61

Theodore Witcher

Body Count '97
Love Jones '96

Wolfram Witt

The Mistake '91
Coming Out '89

Dirk Wittenborn

The Lucky Ones '08
Fierce People '05

William D. Wittliff

The Perfect Storm '00
The Cowboy Way '94
Legends of the Fall '94
Lone Justice '93
Lone Justice 2 '93
Lonesome Dove '89
Red Headed Stranger '87
Country '84
Raggedy Man '81
Honeysuckle Rose '80
The Black Stallion '79

Dick Wolf(1946-)

School Ties '92
Masquerade '88
No Man's Land '87

Gas '81
Skateboard '77

Fred Wolf(1964-)

Grown Ups '10
Strange Wilderness '08
Without a Paddle '04
Dickie Roberts: Former Child Star '03
Joe Dirt '01
Dirty Work '97
Black Sheep '96

Jurgen Wolff(1948-)

The Real Howard Spitz '98
Jack Higgins' Midnight Man '96

P.J. Wolfson(1903-79)

They All Kissed the Bride '42
Mad Love '35
Dancing Lady '33
Picture Snatcher '33

Andy Wolk

The Defenders: Taking the First '98
From the Earth to the Moon '98
The Defenders: Payback '97
Criminal Justice '90

Peter Wolk

The Defenders: Taking the First '98
The Defenders: Payback '97

Dave Wollert

Near Misses '91
Quicksand: No Escape '91

M. Wallace Wolodarsky

The Rocker '08
Seeing Other People '04
Coldblooded '94

Barry Wong(1946-92)

Hard-Boiled '92
Twin Dragons '92
Heart of Dragon '85

James Wong(1940-2004)

Dragonball: Evolution '09
Final Destination 3 '06
The One '01
Final Destination '00
The Boys Next Door '85

Jing Wong

Naked Weapon '03
Legend of the Liquid Sword '93
Naked Killer '92
The Prodigal Son '82

Kar-Wai Wong

Days of Being Wild '91
As Tears Go By '88

Raymond Wong(1948-)

The Phantom Lover '95
Mad Mission 3 '84

John Woo(1948-)

Red Cliff '08
Hard-Boiled '92
A Bullet in the Head '90
The Killer '90
Once a Thief '90
A Better Tomorrow, Part 2 '88
A Better Tomorrow, Part 1 '86
Heroes Shed No Tears '86
Last Hurrah for Chivalry '78

Charles Wood(1932-)

The Other Man '08
Iris '01
An Awfully Big Adventure '94
Sharpe's Company '94
Cuba '79
The Charge of the Light Brigade '68
How I Won the War '67
Help! '65
The Knack '65

Christopher Wood(1935-)

Dangerous Curves '99
Stray Bullet '98

Remo Williams: The Adventure Begins '85
Moonraker '79
The Spy Who Loved Me '77

Edward D. Wood, Jr. (1924-78)

Class Reunion '72
Orgy of the Dead '65
The Sinister Urge '60
Night of the Ghouls '59
The Bride & the Beast '58
Plan 9 from Outer Space '56
The Violent Years '56
Bride of the Monster '55
Jail Bait '54
Glen or Glenda? '53

Christopher Wooden

The Showgirl Murders '95
Dinosaur Island '93
Body Chemistry 2: Voice of a Stranger '91

Jack Woods

Beware! The Blob '72
Equinox '71

Lotta Woods(1869-1957)

The Gaucho '27
The Three Musketeers '21

Skip Woods

The A-Team '10
G.I. Joe: The Rise of Cobra '09
X-Men Origins: Wolverine '09
Swordfish '01
Thursday '98

Walter Woods

David Harum '34
The Pony Express '25
Leap Year '21

Abbe Wool

Roadside Prophets '92
Sid & Nancy '86

Edgar Allen Woolf

Ice Follies of 1939 '39
Freaks '32

Linda Woolverton(1959-)

Alice in Wonderland '10
Homeward Bound: The Incredible Journey '93
Beauty and the Beast '91

Chuck Workman

Superstar: The Life and Times of Andy Warhol '90
Stoogemania '85

David Worth

Lady Dragon '92
Soldier's Revenge '84

Martin Worth

The Dying Truth '86
Poldark 2 '75

Ardel Wray(1907-83)

Isle of the Dead '45
I Walked with a Zombie '43
The Leopard Man '43

Alexander Wright

Wishmaster 3: Beyond the Gates of Hell '01
The First 9 1/2 Weeks '98
Fast Money '96

Brad Wright

Stargate: Continuum '08
Poltergeist: The Legacy '96

Edgar Wright(1974-)

Scott Pilgrim vs. the World '10
Hot Fuzz '07
Shaun of the Dead '04

Geoffrey Wright(1959-)

Macbeth '06
Metal Skin '94
Romper Stomper '92

Lawrence Wright

Noriega: God's Favorite '00
The Siege '98

Ralph Wright(1908-88)

Nikki, the Wild Dog of the North '61
Lady and the Tramp '55
Peter Pan '53

Ray Wright

Case 39 '10
The Crazies '09
Pulse '06

David Wu

The Bride with White Hair '93
The Bride with White Hair 2 '93

Rudy Wurlitzer(1938-)

Little Buddha '93
Shadow of the Wolf '92
Wind '92
Voyager '91
Candy Mountain '87
Walker '87
Pat Garrett & Billy the Kid '73
Glen and Randa '71
Two Lane Blacktop '71

Robert Wyler(1900-71)

The Big Country '58
Detective Story '51

Philip Wylie(1902-71)

Murders in the Zoo '33
Island of Lost Souls '32

J.H. Wyman(1967-)

The Mexican '01
Mr. Rice's Secret '00

Tracy Keenan Wynn(1945-)

Robinson Crusoe '96
Carolina Skeletons '92
Capone '89
In the Line of Duty: The FBI Murders '88
The Deep '77
The Drowning Pool '75
The Autobiography of Miss Jane Pittman '74
The Longest Yard '74

Paul Wynne

Barrio Wars '02
Bombshell '97
Destination Vegas '95

Jim Wynorski(1950-)

Bone Eater '07
Final Voyage '99
Home for Christmas '93
Final Embrace '92
The Haunting of Morella '91
Think Big '90
Not of This Earth '88
Big Bad Mama 2 '87
Deathstalker 2: Duel of the Titans '87
Chopping Mall '86
The Lost Empire '83
Screwballs '83
Forbidden World '82
Sorceress '82

Frank Yablans(1935-)

Mommie Dearest '81
North Dallas Forty '79

Jeff Yagher(1962-)

Guardian '01
The Guardian '00

Boaz Yakin(1944-)

Dirty Dancing: Havana Nights '04
A Price above Rubies '97
Fresh '94
The Punisher '90

Kazuo Yamada

Godzilla vs. the Sea Monster '66
What's Up, Tiger Lily? '66

Yoji Yamada(1931-)

Kabei: Our Mother '08
The Hidden Blade '04
The Twilight Samurai '02

Yudai Yamaguchi

Battlefield Baseball '03
Versus '00

Pi-ying Yang

What Time Is It There? '01
The Hole '98

Brock Yates

Cannonball Run '81
Smokey and the Bandit 2 '80

George Worthing Yates(1901-75)

Tormented '60
Attack of the Puppet People '58
Earth vs. the Spider '58
Frankenstein 1970 '58
Space Master X-7 '58
Earth vs. the Flying Saucers '56
This Woman Is Dangerous '52
Cavalry Charge '51

Nai-Hoi Yau

Running Out of Time 2 '06
Running on Karma '03
The Mission '99

Paul Yawitz

I Love a Bandleader '45
Breakfast for Two '37

Peter Yeldham

1915 '82
Age of Consent '69

Jack Yellen(1892-1991)

My Lucky Star '38
Love Is News '37
Pigskin Parade '36

Linda Yellen(1949-)

End of Summer '97
Chantilly Lace '93

Bennett Yellin

Joy Ride 2: Dead Ahead '08
The Pooch and the Pauper '99
Dumb & Dumber '94

Yevgeny Yevtushenko

Kindergarten '84
I Am Cuba '64

Valentin Yezhov(1921-2004)

Siberiade '79
Ballad of a Soldier '60

Rafael Yglesias

Dark Water '02
From Hell '01
Les Miserables '97
Death and the Maiden '94
Fearless '93

Tin-Shing Yip

Exiled '06
Running on Karma '03

Yoshikata Yoda(1909-)

Sansho the Bailiff '54
A Geisha '53
Ugetsu '53
Utamaro and His Five Women '46
47 Ronin, Part 1 '42
47 Ronin, Part 2 '42
Sisters of the Gion '36

Naoyuki Yokota

Carved '07
Ju-Rei: The Uncanny '04

Jeff Yonis

Humanoids from the Deep '96
Bloodfist 5: Human Target '93
Firehawk '92

Il-han Yoo

Hidden Floor '06
My Bloody Roommates '06

Philip Yordan(1914-2003)

The Unholy '88
Bloody Wednesday '87
Night Train to Terror '84
Bad Man's River '72
Captain Apache '71

Cinematographer Index

The Cinematographer Index provides a videography for any cinematographer, or Director of Photography, as they are also known, with a video credit. The listings for the cinematographer names follow an alphabetical sort by last name (although the names appear in a first name last name format). The videographies are listed chronologically, from oldest film to the most recent. If a cinematographer lensed more than one film in the same year, these movies are listed alphabetically within the year. Many of today's top directors started as cinematographers, the people responsible for the "look" of a movie.

David Abel(1884-1973)
Rafter Romance *'34*
Merrily We Go to Hell *'32*
The First Auto *'27*

Phil Abraham
I Love You, Beth Cooper *'09*
Annapolis *'06*

Michel Abramowicz
From Paris With Love *'10*
Taken *'08*
The Secrets *'07*
Empire of the Wolves *'05*

Bernie Abramson
Ants *'77*
Baker's Hawk *'76*

Thomas Ackerman
Fired Up! *'09*
Infestation *'09*
Superhero Movie *'08*
Balls of Fury *'07*
The Benchwarmers *'06*
Looking for Comedy in the Muslim World *'06*
Scary Movie 4 *'06*
Are We There Yet? *'05*
Anchorman: The Legend of Ron Burgundy *'04*
The Battle of Shaker Heights *'03*
Dickie Roberts: Former Child Star *'03*
Snow Dogs *'02*
Rat Race *'01*
The Adventures of Rocky & Bullwinkle *'00*
Beautiful Joe *'00*
The Muse *'99*
My Favorite Martian *'98*
The Eighteenth Angel *'97*
George of the Jungle *'97*
Jumanji *'95*
Baby's Day Out *'94*
Dennis the Menace *'93*
National Lampoon's Christmas Vacation *'89*
Beetlejuice *'88*
Back to School *'86*
Girls Just Want to Have Fun *'85*
Frankenweenie *'84*
Roadhouse 66 *'84*
Foxfire Light *'82*

Barry Ackroyd(1954-)
Green Zone *'10*
Looking for Eric *'09*
The Hurt Locker *'08*
Battle in Seattle *'07*
United 93 *'06*
The Wind That Shakes the Barley *'06*
Friends & Crocodiles *'05*
Gideon's Daughter *'05*
A Fond Kiss *'04*
Sweet Sixteen *'02*
Dust *'01*
The Navigators *'01*
Bread and Roses *'00*
Very Annie Mary *'00*
Beautiful People *'99*
The Lost Son *'98*
My Name Is Joe *'98*
Carla's Song *'97*
Under the Skin *'97*
Stella Does Tricks *'96*
Land and Freedom *'95*
Ladybird, Ladybird *'93*
Raining Stones *'93*

Lance Acord(1964-)
Where the Wild Things Are *'09*
Marie Antoinette *'06*
Lost in Translation *'03*
Adaptation *'02*
The Dangerous Lives of Altar Boys *'02*
Being John Malkovich *'99*
Buffalo 66 *'97*

Witold Adamek(1945-)
The Decalogue *'88*
The Possessed *'88*
Train to Hollywood *'86*
Hero of the Year *'85*

Steve Adcock
Night Skies *'07*
Facing the Enemy *'00*
Speedway Junky *'99*
Timelock *'99*
L.A. Rules: The Pros and Cons of Breathing *'94*

Remi Adefarasin(1948-)
Elizabeth: The Golden Age *'07*
Fred Claus *'07*
Amazing Grace *'06*
Scoop *'06*
Match Point *'05*
In Good Company *'04*
The Haunted Mansion *'03*
Johnny English *'03*
Unconditional Love *'03*
About a Boy *'02*
Band of Brothers *'01*
Arabian Nights *'00*
House of Mirth *'00*
Onegin *'99*
Elizabeth *'98*
Sliding Doors *'97*
Hollow Reed *'95*
Captives *'94*
Bitter Harvest *'93*
The Wedding Gift *'93*
The Lost Language of Cranes *'92*
Truly, Madly, Deeply *'91*
Christabel *'89*

Tom Agnello
Rapturious *'07*
Fresh Cut Grass *'04*

Philippe Agostini(1910-2001)
Rififi *'54*
Le Plaisir *'52*

Jose F. Aguayo(1911-99)
Tristana *'70*
Viridiana *'61*

Javier Aguirresarobe(1948-)
The Twilight Saga: Eclipse *'10*
The Road *'09*
The Twilight Saga: New Moon *'09*
Vicky Cristina Barcelona *'08*
Goya's Ghosts *'06*
The Bridge of San Luis Rey *'05*
The Sea Inside *'04*
Talk to Her *'02*
The Others *'01*
The Girl of Your Dreams *'99*
The Yellow Fountain *'99*
Secrets of the Heart *'97*
Fiesta *'95*
Tierra *'95*
Running Out of Time *'94*
Outrage *'93*

G. Magni Agustsson
The Last Winter *'06*
Eleven Men Out *'05*

Lloyd Ahern(1905-83)
Father Was a Fullback *'49*
Miracle on 34th Street *'47*

Lloyd Ahern, II(1942-)
Broken Trail *'06*
Kicking & Screaming *'05*
American Wedding *'03*
My Sister's Keeper *'02*
Undisputed *'02*
The Unsaid *'01*
Supernova *'99*
Can't Hardly Wait *'98*
Last Man Standing *'96*
Turbulence *'96*
Wild Bill *'95*
Geronimo: An American Legend *'93*
Trespass *'92*
Danielle Steel's Palomino *'91*

Mac Ahlberg(1931-)
King of the Ants *'03*
Groom Lake *'02*
Air Rage *'01*
The Wonderful Ice Cream Suit *'98*
Good Burger *'97*
The Second Civil War *'97*
Space Truckers *'97*
The Late Shift *'96*
A Very Brady Sequel *'96*
The Brady Bunch Movie *'95*
Beverly Hills Cop 3 *'94*
My Boyfriend's Back *'93*
Striking Distance *'93*
Innocent Blood *'92*
Oscar *'91*
Robot Jox *'90*
Deepstar Six *'89*
The Horror Show *'89*
Prison *'88*
House 2: The Second Story *'87*
From Beyond *'86*
Ghostwarrior *'86*
House *'86*
Ghoulies *'84*
Prime Risk *'84*
Re-Animator *'84*
Zone Troopers *'84*
Chained Heat *'83*
Metalstorm: The Destruction of Jared Syn *'83*
Young Warriors *'83*
My Tutor *'82*
Parasite *'82*
The Seduction *'82*
Hell Night *'81*
Nocturna *'79*
I, a Woman *'66*

Pierre Aim
Paris, je t'aime *'06*
Wah-Wah *'05*
Monsieur N. *'03*
He Loves Me ... He Loves Me Not *'02*
Madeline *'98*
Resurrection Man *'97*
Hate *'95*
Cafe au Lait *'94*

Yuzuru Aizawa
Godzilla vs. Megalon *'76*
The Bad Sleep Well *'60*

Shigeru Akatsuka
Legend of the Dinosaurs and Monster Birds *'77*
Horrors of Malformed Men *'69*

Robert Alazraki
American Women *'00*
Born Romantic *'00*
St. Ives *'98*
Another 9 1/2 Weeks *'96*
My Father's Glory *'91*
The Old Lady Who Walked in the Sea *'91*
Conseil de Famille *'86*
Love Songs *'85*
Love Songs *'84*

Romano Albani(1945-)
The Sleazy Uncle *'89*
Troll *'86*
Creepers *'85*
Inferno *'80*

Arthur Albert(1946-)
Puff, Puff, Pass *'06*
Max Keeble's Big Move *'01*
Saving Silverman *'01*
Behind the Mask *'99*
Dirty Work *'97*
Beverly Hills Ninja *'96*
Happy Gilmore *'96*
One Night Stand *'95*
You So Crazy *'94*
By the Sword *'93*
Surf Ninjas *'93*
Passed Away *'92*
Heart Condition *'90*
Miss Firecracker *'89*
The Principal *'87*
The Squeeze *'87*
Streets of Gold *'86*
The Boys Next Door *'85*
Odd Jobs *'85*

Night of the Comet '84

Maryse Alberti

Gonzo: The Life and Work of Dr. Hunter S. Thompson '08
The Wrestler '08
Taxi to the Dark Side '07
We Don't Live Here Anymore '04
The Guys '02
Get Over It! '01
Tape '01
Joe Gould's Secret '00
Happiness '98
Velvet Goldmine '98
I Love You, I Love You Not '97
Stag '97
Crumb '94
Deadfall '93
Tales of Erotica '93
Zebrahead '92
Poison '91

Giulio Albonico

The Sniper '78
Zorro '74

Jose Luis Alcaine(1938-)

My Life in Ruins '09
Volver '06
Bad Education '04
The Dancer Upstairs '02
Jealousy '99
Blast from the Past '98
Two Much '96
Jamon, Jamon '93
Belle Epoque '92
Ay, Carmela! '90
Lovers: A True Story '90
Tie Me Up! Tie Me Down! '90
Twisted Obsession '90
Women on the Verge of a Nervous Breakdown '88
Rustler's Rhapsody '85
Demons in the Garden '82

John Alcott(1931-86)

No Way Out '87
Under Fire '83
Beastmaster '82
Fort Apache, the Bronx '81
The Shining '80
Terror Train '80
Barry Lyndon '75
A Clockwork Orange '71
2001: A Space Odyssey '68

Robert Alcott

It's Alive! '68
Zontar, the Thing from Venus '66

Henri Alekan(1909-2001)

Wings of Desire '88
On Top of the Whale '82
Mayerling '68
Topkapi '64
The Would-Be Gentleman '58
Forbidden Fruit '52
Anna Karenina '48
Beauty and the Beast '46

Maxime Alexandre(1971-)

The Crazies '09
Mirrors '08
Catacombs '07
P2 '07
The Hills Have Eyes '06
The Last Drop '05
High Tension '03

Sepp Allgeier(1895-1968)

Triumph of the Will '34
Diary of a Lost Girl '29

Nestor Almendros(1930-92)

Billy Bathgate '91
New York Stories '89
Nadine '87
Heartburn '86
Places in the Heart '84
Confidentially Yours '83
Pauline at the Beach '83
Sophie's Choice '82
Still of the Night '82
The Blue Lagoon '80
The Last Metro '80
Kramer vs. Kramer '79
Days of Heaven '78
Goin' South '78
The Green Room '78
Love on the Run '78
Perceval '78
Madame Rosa '77
The Man Who Loved Women '77
Maitresse '76
The Marquise of O '76
The Story of Adele H. '75
Cockfighter '74
Chloe in the Afternoon '72
Two English Girls '72
Claire's Knee '71
Bed and Board '70
The Valley Obscured by the Clouds '70
The Wild Child '70
More '69
My Night at Maud's '69
Six in Paris '68
La Collectionneuse '67

Alan Almond

Little Dorrit '08
A Room With a View '08
Gabriel & Me '01
Kevin & Perry Go Large '00
Get Real '99
My Son the Fanatic '97
Kiss and Tell '96
Brothers in Trouble '95
Loaded '94

John A. Alonzo(1934-2001)

Deuces Wild '02
The Prime Gig '00
Lansky '99
Letters from a Killer '98
The Grass Harp '95
Star Trek: Generations '94
World War II: When Lions Roared '94
The Meteor Man '93
Clifford '92
Cool World '92
Housesitter '92
The Guardian '90
Internal Affairs '90
Navy SEALS '90
Physical Evidence '89
Steel Magnolias '89
Roots: The Gift '88
Overboard '87
Real Men '87
Jo Jo Dancer, Your Life Is Calling '86
Nothing in Common '86
The Hit '85
Out of Control '85
No Small Affair '84
Runaway '84
Blue Thunder '83
Cross Creek '83
Scarface '83
Back Roads '81
Zorro, the Gay Blade '81
Tom Horn '80
Norma Rae '79
Casey's Shadow '78
The Cheap Detective '78
Beyond Reason '77
Black Sunday '77
Which Way Is Up? '77
The Bad News Bears '76
I Will, I Will for Now '76
Farewell, My Lovely '75
Once Is Not Enough '75
Chinatown '74
Conrack '74
Get to Know Your Rabbit '72
Lady Sings the Blues '72
Pete 'n' Tillie '72
Sounder '72
Harold and Maude '71
Vanishing Point '71
Bloody Mama '70

Herbert S. Alpert(1918-)

The Mask '61
A Dangerous Age '57

Russ T. Alsobrook(1946-)

Paul Blart: Mall Cop '09
Forgetting Sarah Marshall '08
Role Models '08
Reign Over Me '07
Superbad '07

John Alton(1901-96)

Elmer Gantry '60
The Brothers Karamazov '58
Designing Woman '57
The Catered Affair '56
Slightly Scarlet '56
Tea and Sympathy '56
The Teahouse of the August Moon '56
Big Combo '55
Pearl of the South Pacific '55
Tennessee's Partner '55
Battle Circus '53
An American in Paris '51
Father's Little Dividend '51
It's a Big Country '51
Father of the Bride '50
Mystery Street '50
Border Incident '49
Reign of Terror '49
The Amazing Mr. X '48
He Walked by Night '48
Raw Deal '48
T-Men '47
Power Dive '41
Courageous Dr. Christian '40

Michel Amathieu

The Man of My Life '06
Paris, je t'aime '06
Spy Games '99

Samuel Ameen

Zoe '01
Spark '98

Alex Ameri(1937-86)

The Gore-Gore Girls '72
This Stuff'll Kill Ya! '71
The Wizard of Gore '70

Juan Amoros(1936-)

Between Your Legs '99
Love Can Seriously Damage Your Health '96
Mouth to Mouth '95
Sons of Trinity '95
How to Be a Woman and Not Die in the Attempt '91
If They Tell You I Fell '89

Mitchell Amundsen(1958-)

Jonah Hex '10
G.I. Joe: The Rise of Cobra '09
Jonas Brothers: The 3D Concert Experience '09
Wanted '08
Transformers '07
Transporter 2 '05

Juan Ruiz Anchia

See Juan Ruiz-Anchia
Sleepwalking '08
In 'n Out '86

Jack Anderson

The Morgue '07
Family Reunion '79

Jamie Anderson

Happy Tears '09
Art School Confidential '06
The Girl Next Door '04
Bad Santa '03
Jay and Silent Bob Strike Back '01
The Flintstones in Viva Rock Vegas '00
The Gift '00
Neil Simon's The Odd Couple 2 '98
Small Soldiers '98
The Temptations '98
Grosse Pointe Blank '97
The Juror '96
Man of the House '95
What's Love Got to Do with It? '93
Unlawful Entry '92
Malibu Beach '78
Piranha '78
The Great Texas Dynamite Chase '76
Hollywood Boulevard '76

M.A. Anderson

Slander House '38
Little Red Schoolhouse '36
Dangerous Appointment '34
Cross Examination '32
The Midnight Lady '32
Night Life in Reno '31
The Peacock Fan '29

Michael Anderson

Our Brand Is Crisis '05
Take It to the Limit '00

Shohei Ando

Hiroshima '95
Female Prisoner: Caged '83
Flower & Snake '74 '74

Peter Andrews

See Steven Soderbergh

Stephen F. Andrich

The Junction Boys '02
Killer Tomatoes Strike Back '90

Lucien N. Andriot(1892-1979)

Borderline '50
Outpost in Morocco '49
New Orleans '47
The Strange Woman '46
And Then There Were None '45
The Southerner '45
The Fighting Sullivans '42
Just Off Broadway '42
On the Sunny Side '42
Lucky Cisco Kid '40
Mr. Moto in Danger Island '39
Mr. Moto's Gamble '38
Thanks for Everything '38
Cafe Metropole '37
The Gay Desperado '36
Two Alone '34
The Cruise of the Jasper B '26
Monte Cristo '22

Theo Angell(1962-)

Silent Venom '08
Black Horizon '01
Kept '01
Mom's Outta Sight '01
Critical Mass '00
Fugitive Mind '99
The Kid with the X-Ray Eyes '99

Yves Angelo(1956-)

The Accompanist '93
Germinal '93
Un Coeur en Hiver '93
Tous les Matins du Monde '92
Baxter '89

Richard Angst

The Indian Tomb '59
Tiger of Eschnapur '59

Gregg Araki(1959-)

Totally F***ed Up '94
The Living End '92

Daniel Aranyo

High School Musical 3: Senior Year '08
High School Musical 2 '07
The Cheetah Girls 2 '06

Thierry Arbogast

Babylon A.D. '08
Arthur and the Invisibles '06
Angel-A '05
Catwoman '04
Swindled '04
Bon Voyage '03
Femme Fatale '02
The Crimson Rivers '01
Kiss of the Dragon '01
Woman on Top '00
The Messenger: The Story of Joan of Arc '99
Wing Commander '99
Black Cat, White Cat '98
The Fifth Element '97
She's So Lovely '97
Ridicule '96
The Horseman on the Roof '95
The Professional '94
Ma Saison Preferee '93
I Don't Kiss '91
La Femme Nikita '91

Arch Archambault

Little Men '98
Count Yorga, Vampire '70

Georges Archambault

Nightwaves '03
Fallen Angel '99
The Witness '99
Dead End '98
Random Encounter '98
Stalker '98

Simon Archer

Another Life '01
The Bachelor '99
Stiff Upper Lips '96

Fernando Arguelles

Anti-Terrorist Cell: Manhunt '01
Bloodhounds '96
Wes Craven Presents Mind Ripper '95
Hidden Assassin '94
Star Time '92

Arthur E. Arling(1906-91)

Ski Party '65
Strait-Jacket '64
The Notorious Landlady '62
Pillow Talk '59
Man in the Shadow '57
Three for the Show '55
The Farmer Takes a Wife '53
Belles on Their Toes '52
My Blue Heaven '50
Captain from Castile '47

Arledge Armenaki

Auntie Lee's Meat Pies '92
Club Fed '90
Crack House '89
Howling 5: The Rebirth '89
Blackout '88
Off the Mark '87
Crime Killer '85
Grad Night '81
Avenging Disco Godfather '76

David Armstrong

Last Resort '09
The Lodger '09
Next Day Air '09
Saw 6 '09
Saw 5 '08
Saw 4 '07
Skinwalkers '07
Saw 3 '06
Saw 2 '05
Saw '04
P.S. Your Cat is Dead! '02

Chuck (Charles G.) Arnold

The Chase '91
Assassin '86
The Lazarus Syndrome '79

John Arnold(1889-1964)

The Garden of Eden '28
The Big Parade '25

Steve Arnold

Disgrace '08
Highlander: The Source '07
Mr. Accident '99
Doom Runners '97
Dating the Enemy '95

Ricardo Aronovich(1930-)

Klimt '06
Moscow Zero '06
Time Regained '99
Celestial Clockwork '94
Christmas Evil '80
Providence '77
Lumiere '76
Murmur of the Heart '71

John Aronson

America '09
Gifted Hands: The Ben Carson Story '09
In Hell '03
Beethoven's 4th '01
Beethoven's 3rd '00
Trippin' '99
Gunshy '98
In God's Hands '98
The Haunted Sea '97
Murder in Mind '97
Bloodfist 8: Hard Way Out '96
The Glass Cage '96
Inhumanoid '96
Dillinger and Capone '95
Machine Gun Blues '95
Suspect Device '95
Carnosaur 2 '94
White Wolves 2: Legend of the Wild '94
Class of Fear '91

Fernando Arribas(1940-)

Cannibal Apocalypse '80
The Blood Spattered Bride '72

Yorgos Arvanitis(1941-)

Anatomy of Hell '04
Signs & Wonders '00
Romance '99
Train of Life '98
Bent '97
Eternity and a Day '97
Someone Else's America '96
Total Eclipse '95
Ulysses' Gaze '95
Landscape in the Mist '88
A Dream of Passion '78
Iphigenia '77
The Travelling Players '75

Jerome Ash(1892-1953)

Pillow of Death '45
Hi, Good Lookin'! '44
Swingtime Johnny '43
Stagecoach Buckaroo '42
Flash Gordon Conquers the Universe '40
Junior G-Men '40
Law and Order '40
Space Soldiers Conquer the Universe '40
The Green Hornet '39
Oklahoma Frontier '39
Rocketship '36
Undertow '30
The Drake Case '29

Jack Asher(1916-91)

The Brides of Dracula '60
The Two Faces of Dr. Jekyll '60
The Hound of the Baskervilles '59
The Mummy '59
The Horror of Dracula '58
The Curse of Frankenstein '57
Grand National Night '53
The Magic Bow '47

Monroe Askins(1915-2001)

Napoleon and Samantha '72
Thunder Alley '67
Blood of Dracula '57
Sorority Girl '57

William Asman

Sheba, Baby '75
Three on a Meathook '72

James Aspinall

Fanny Hill '07
The Chatterley Affair '06

Jacques Assuerus

Black Venus '83
Rendez-Moi Ma Peau '81
Blue Jeans '78

Sergei Astakhov(1953-)
In Tranzit '07
Of Freaks and Men '98
Brother '97

Yoram Astrakhan
Shakedown '02
Dark Justice '00
The Doorway '00
Moving Target '00
Plan B '97

Howard Atherton
When Did You Last See Your Father? '07
Color Me Kubrick '05
Lassie '05
Hanging Up '99
Deep Rising '98
Lolita '97
Bad Boys '95
Gulliver's Travels '95
Indecent Proposal '93
Mermaids '90
The Boost '88
Fatal Attraction '87

Mark Atkins
The Land That Time Forgot '09
Supernova '09
Evil Eyes '04

Yuuharu Atsuta(1905-93)
An Autumn Afternoon '62
Good Morning '59
Tokyo Story '53

Giorgio Attili
Awakenings of the Beast '68
At Midnight, I'll Take Your Soul '63

Joseph August(1890-1947)
Portrait of Jennie '48
They Were Expendable '45
Gunga Din '39
The Hunchback of Notre Dame '39
The Whole Town's Talking '35
The Black Camel '31
Seas Beneath '31
Up the River '30
The Beloved Rogue '27
The Cradle of Courage '20
The Toll Gate '20
The Bargain '15

Laurence Avenet-Bradley
Dark Remains '05
Ghost of the Needle '03

Gordon Avil(-1970)
Zotz! '62
The Black Sleep '56
King Dinosaur '55
On Our Merry Way '48

John G. Avildsen(1935-)
Cry Uncle '71
Joe '70

Joaquin Baca-Asay
Two Lovers '09
We Own the Night '07
Thumbsucker '05
P.S. '04
Roger Dodger '02
Super Troopers '01
Two Ninas '00
Coming Soon '99
Dead Broke '99

Jean Bachelet(1894-1977)
The Crime of Monsieur Lange '36
The Lower Depths '36

Jean Badal(1927-)
Good-bye, Emmanuelle '77
Germicide '74
A Very Curious Girl '69

Hanania Baer(1943-)
Going Shopping '05
Festival at Cannes '02
Bug Buster '99
Deja Vu '98
Last Summer In the Hamptons '96
The Prince '95
Babyfever '94
Rescue Me '93
Body Language '92
Venice, Venice '92
Ernest Scared Stupid '91
Diving In '90
Eating '90
The Kid Who Loved Christmas '90
The Queen of Mean '90
Elvira, Mistress of the Dark '88
Seven Hours to Judgment '88
Assassination '87
Masters of the Universe '87
Someone to Love '87
Bad Guys '86
Always '85
American Ninja '85
Night Patrol '85
Breakin' '84
Breakin' 2: Electric Boogaloo '84
Cartier Affair '84
Ninja 3: The Domination '84
Echoes '83
Choices '81

Christopher Baffa
Running with Scissors '06
Unaccompanied Minors '06
Beethoven's 5th '03
Next Friday '00
Idle Hands '99
Baby Face Nelson '97
Lady Killer '97
Suicide Kings '97
True Heart '97
Alien Avengers '96
Humanoids from the Deep '96
Sometimes They Come Back... Again '96
Spectre '96
Criminal Hearts '95
The Death Artist '95
Piranha '95
Sawbones '95
The Crazysitter '94

James R. Bagdonas(1951-)
National Lampoon's Van Wilder '02
Slackers '02
Brotherhood of Murder '99
Cruel Intentions 2 '99
Love Songs '99
Hidden in America '96
American Heart '92

King Baggot
Boiling Point '93
The Last Starfighter '84
Revenge of the Nerds '84
Some Kind of Hero '82
The Hand '81

John Bailey(1942-)
Ramona and Beezus '10
Brief Interviews With Hideous Men '09
He's Just Not That Into You '09
When in Rome '09
Mad Money '08
Over Her Dead Body '08
License to Wed '07
The Architect '06
Must Love Dogs '05
The Producers '05
Sisterhood of the Traveling Pants '05
Incident at Loch Ness '04
How to Lose a Guy in 10 Days '03
Divine Secrets of the Ya-Ya Sisterhood '02
The Kid Stays in the Picture '02
The Anniversary Party '01
Antitrust '00
For Love of the Game '99
Forever Mine '99
The Out-of-Towners '99
Always Outnumbered Always Outgunned '98
Living Out Loud '98
As Good As It Gets '97
Extreme Measures '96
Nobody's Fool '94
Groundhog Day '93
In the Line of Fire '93
A Brief History of Time '92
My Blue Heaven '90
The Accidental Tourist '88
Vibes '88
Light of Day '87
Swimming to Cambodia '87
Tough Guys Don't Dance '87
Brighton Beach Memoirs '86
Crossroads '86
Mishima: A Life in Four Chapters '85
Silverado '85
The Pope of Greenwich Village '84
Racing with the Moon '84
The Big Chill '83
Without a Trace '83
Cat People '82
That Championship Season '82
Continental Divide '81
Honky Tonk Freeway '81
Ordinary People '80
American Gigolo '79
Boulevard Nights '79
Premonition '71

Bob Bailin
Family Enforcer '76
Shoot It Black, Shoot It Blue '74
The Groove Tube '72

Anton Bakarski
The Grudge 3 '09
Lost Colony: The Legend of Roanoke '07

Lubomir Bakchev
2 Days in Paris '07
Games of Love and Chance '03

Brydon Baker(1898-1973)
The Oh in Ohio '06
Ballad of a Gunfighter '64
Space Master X-7 '58
The Phantom from 10,000 Leagues '56
Wetbacks '56
Riding Speed '35
Fighting Cowboy '33
Lightning Range '33

Ian Baker
Evan Almighty '07
Empire Falls '05
It Runs in the Family '03
Japanese Story '03
Queen of the Damned '02
The Chamber '96
Fierce Creatures '96
I.Q. '94
Six Degrees of Separation '93
Mr. Baseball '92
Everybody Wins '90
The Punisher '90
The Russia House '90
A Cry in the Dark '88
Roxanne '87
Plenty '85
Iceman '84
Barbarosa '82
The Chant of Jimmie Blacksmith '78
The Devil's Playground '76

Walter Bal(1939-)
Say Nothing '01
Pterodactyl Woman from Beverly Hills '97
Back in Business '96
Precious Find '96

Robert M. "Bob" Baldwin, Jr.(1933-)
Basket Case 2 '90
Frankenhooker '90
Exterminator '80
Diary of the Dead '76
Werewolf of Washington '73

Christopher Ball
Darwin's Darkest Hour '09
Whole New Thing '05

Lucien Ballard(1908-88)
Breakheart Pass '76
Drum '76
From Noon Till Three '76
Breakout '75
The Getaway '72
Junior Bonner '72
Ballad of Cable Hogue '70
True Grit '69
The Wild Bunch '69
How Sweet It Is! '68
The Party '68
Will Penny '67
Nevada Smith '66
Sons of Katie Elder '65
Ride the High Country '62
The Parent Trap '61
Susan Slade '61
City of Fear '59
Buchanan Rides Alone '58
Murder by Contract '58
I Married a Woman '56
The Killing '56
Diplomatic Courier '52
Don't Bother to Knock '52
Fixed Bayonets! '51
Let's Make It Legal '51
The Undying Monster '42
I Promise to Pay '37
The Devil Is a Woman '35

Antonio Ballesteros
Insanity '76
Cold Eyes of Fear '70

Florian Ballhaus(1965-)
Did You Hear About the Morgans? '09
The Time Traveler's Wife '09
Definitely, Maybe '08
Marley & Me '08
The Devil Wears Prada '06
The Secret Lives of Dentists '02
Intimate Affairs '01

Michael Ballhaus(1935-)
The Departed '06
Something's Gotta Give '03
Uptown Girls '03
Gangs of New York '02
The Legend of Bagger Vance '00
What Planet Are You From? '00
Wild Wild West '99
Primary Colors '98
Air Force One '97
Sleepers '96
Outbreak '94
Quiz Show '94
The Age of Innocence '93
I'll Do Anything '93
Bram Stoker's Dracula '92
The Mambo Kings '92
Guilty by Suspicion '91
What about Bob? '91
Goodfellas '90
Postcards from the Edge '90
The Fabulous Baker Boys '89
Big '88
Dirty Rotten Scoundrels '88
The House on Carroll Street '88
The Last Temptation of Christ '88
Working Girl '88
Baja Oklahoma '87
Broadcast News '87
The Glass Menagerie '87
Chinese Roulette '86
The Color of Money '86
Death of a Salesman '86
Under the Cherry Moon '86
After Hours '85
Heartbreakers '84
Old Enough '84
Reckless '84
Sheer Madness '84
Malou '83
Baby It's You '82
Ruby's Dream '82
The Marriage of Maria Braun '79
Despair '78
The Stationmaster's Wife '77
I Only Want You to Love Me '76
Mother Kusters Goes to Heaven '76
Satan's Brew '76
Cold Blood '75
Fox and His Friends '75
The Bitter Tears of Petra von Kant '72
Beware of a Holy Whore '70
Whity '70

Lionel Banes(1904-96)
Fiend without a Face '58
The Haunted Strangler '58
The Magnet '50

Larry Banks
The Substitute 2: School's Out '97
The Show '95
Erotique '94
Fly by Night '93
Juice '92

Diane Baratier
The Romance of Astrea and Celadon '07
Triple Agent '04
Satin Rouge '02
The Lady and the Duke '01
Autumn Tale '98
A Summer's Tale '96
Rendezvous in Paris '95

Charles L. Barbee
The Trip '02
Warm Blooded Killers '01
Free Enterprise '98

William Barber
Shredderman Rules '07
The Man in the Iron Mask '97

Enzo Barboni(1922-2002)
Kemek '70
Django '68
A Long Ride From Hell '68
Texas, Adios '66
Erik, the Viking '65
Hercules and the Princess of Troy '65

Leonida Barboni
The Rover '67
After the Fox '66
Divorce—Italian Style '62
Joyful Laughter '60
Passionate Thief '60
And the Wild, Wild Women '59
Submarine Attack '54

George Barnes(1892-1953)
The Road to Bali '53
The War of the Worlds '53
Riding High '50
Samson and Delilah '50
Force of Evil '49
Emperor Waltz '48
Sinbad, the Sailor '47
Sister Kenny '46
The Bells of St. Mary's '45
The Spanish Main '45
Spellbound '45
Frenchman's Creek '44
Jane Eyre '44
None But the Lonely Heart '44
Mr. Lucky '43
Broadway '42
Once Upon a Honeymoon '42
Meet John Doe '41
That Uncertain Feeling '41
Rebecca '40
Jesse James '39
Stanley and Livingstone '39
Gold Diggers in Paris '38
The Black Legion '37
Hollywood Hotel '37
Marked Woman '37
Varsity Show '37
Cain and Mabel '36
The Singing Kid '36
Gold Diggers of 1935 '35
Dames '34
Massacre '34
Footlight Parade '33
Street Scene '31
Raffles '30
Bulldog Drummond '29
Condemned '29
Our Dancing Daughters '28
Sadie Thompson '28
Son of the Sheik '26
The Eagle '25
Peg o' My Heart '22
Dangerous Hours '19

Will Barratt
Frozen '10
Spiral '07

Michael Barrett(1970-)
Takers '10
Bedtime Stories '08
The Mysteries of Pittsburgh '08
You Don't Mess with the Zohan '08
Bobby '06
Goal! The Dream Begins '06
Kiss Kiss Bang Bang '05
Crazy Little Thing '02
Lone Star State of Mind '02
75 Degrees '00
Skeletons in the Closet '00
The Suburbans '99
Safe Men '98
Finding North '97

Todd Barron
The Room '03
Boa '02
Interceptor Force 2 '02

Mario Barroso
The Convent '95
God's Comedy '95
Abraham's Valley '93

Michael Barrow
On the Borderline '01
A Slipping Down Life '99
Row Your Boat '98
Whatever '98
Caught '96
Sunday '96
Wigstock: The Movie '95
Heavy '94

Carl F. Bartels
Kiss the Bride '07
Adam & Steve '05
Boo! '05
Latter Days '04
A Light in the Darkness '02
Blue Hill Avenue '01
Deranged '01

Andrzej Bartkowiak(1950-)
Thirteen Days '00
Gossip '99
Lethal Weapon 4 '98
U.S. Marshals '98
Dante's Peak '97
The Devil's Advocate '97
The Mirror Has Two Faces '96
Jade '95
Species '95
A Good Man in Africa '94
Losing Isaiah '94
Speed '94
Falling Down '93
Guilty as Sin '93
A Stranger Among Us '92
Off and Running '90
Q & A '90
Family Business '89
Twins '88
Beyond Innocence '87
Nuts '87
The Morning After '86
Power '86
Prizzi's Honor '85
Garbo Talks '84
Daniel '83
Terms of Endearment '83
Deathtrap '82
The Verdict '82
Prince of the City '81

Deadly Hero '75

James Bartle

California Dreaming '07
Inherit the Wind '99
Dead Heart '96
Twisted '96
Hammers over the Anvil '91
Iris '89
My Best Friend Is a Vampire '88
The Good Wife '86
The Quiet Earth '85

John Bartley

Gray Matters '06
The Nickel Children '05
Wrong Turn '03
Eight Legged Freaks '02
Dean Koontz's Black River '01
See Spot Run '01
A Cooler Climate '99
Disturbing Behavior '98
Tricks '97

Adolfo Bartoli

Warbirds '08
Antibody '02
Queen's Messenger II '01
Final Encounter '00
The Horrible Dr. Bones '00
Octopus '00
Bloodstorm: Subspecies 4 '98
The Creeps '97
Rudyard Kipling's the Second Jungle Book: Mowgli and Baloo '97
Forbidden Zone: Alien Abduction '96
Head of the Family '96
Magic in the Mirror: Fowl Play '96
Spellbreaker: Secret of the Leprechauns '96
Vampire Journals '96
Puppet Master 5: The Final Chapter '94
Bad Channels '92
Netherworld '90
Puppet Master 3: Toulon's Revenge '90

J.E. Bash

Stealth Fighter '99
Storm Trooper '98

Miroslaw Baszak

The Boondock Saints II: All Saints Day '09
Pontypool '09
Celine '08
George A. Romero's Land of the Dead '05
The Gospel of John '03
Conviction '02
Picture Claire '01
Two of Us '00
Four Days '99
Naked City: Justice with a Bullet '98
Rescuers: Stories of Courage—Two Couples '98
Rescuers: Stories of Courage "Two Women" '97
Eclipse '94

Joe Batac

Raiders of the Sun '92
The Siege of Firebase Gloria '89
South Seas Massacre '74

Edson Batista

Massacre in Dinosaur Valley '85
Women in Fury '84

Gianlorenzo Battaglia

Men Men Men '95
Interzone '88
Demons 2 '87
Warrior Queen '87
Demons '86
Formula for a Murder '85
A Blade in the Dark '83

Brian Baugh

An American Carol '08
The Ultimate Gift '07

Jurgen Baum

What About Your Friends: Weekend Getaway '02
The Dentist 2: Brace Yourself '98
American Vampire '97
Flypaper '97
The Big Fall '96
Phat Beach '96
One Man's Justice '95
Open Fire '94
Slumber Party Massacre 3 '90

Hank Baumert, Jr.

The Dog Who Saved Christmas '09
The Boston Strangler: The Untold Story '08
Miracle Dogs Too '06

Peter Baumgartner

Jack the Ripper '76
Inn of Temptation '73
Sex Adventures of the Three Musketeers '71

Jeff Baustert

The Prince and the Pauper '07
All In '06
Mockingbird Don't Sing '01
True Friends '98

Mario Bava(1914-80)

Twitch of the Death Nerve '71
Hatchet for the Honeymoon '70
The Girl Who Knew Too Much '63
Black Sunday '60
The Giant of Marathon '60
Hercules '58
The Day the Sky Exploded '57
I, Vampiri '56
Roland the Mighty '56

Jeff Baynes

The Haunted Airman '06
Pinochet's Last Stand '06
Agatha Christie: A Life in Pictures '04

Bojan Bazelli

The Sorcerer's Apprentice '10
G-Force '09
Hairspray '07
Mr. & Mrs. Smith '05
The Ring '02
Dangerous Beauty '98
Sugar Hill '94
Surviving the Game '94
Body Snatchers '93
Boxing Helena '93
Kalifornia '93
Deep Cover '92
The Fear Inside '92
Fever '91
The Rapture '91
Curiosity Kills '90
King of New York '90
Somebody Has to Shoot the Picture '90
Big Man on Campus '89
Haunting of Sarah Hardy '89
Tapeheads '89
Patty Hearst '88
Pumpkinhead '88
China Girl '87

Frank Beasoechea

In the Line of Duty: A Cop for the Killing '90
Nick Knight '89

Alfonso Beato

Nights in Rodanthe '08
Love in the Time of Cholera '07
The Queen '06
Dot the I '03
The Fighting Temptations '03
View from the Top '03
Dark Water '02
Ghost World '01
Price of Glory '00
All About My Mother '99
Orfeu '99

The Informant '97
Live Flesh '97
Pronto '97
The Flower of My Secret '95
Uncovered '94
The Wrong Man '93
Enid Is Sleeping '90
Great Balls of Fire '89
The Big Easy '87
Happily Ever After '86
Circle of Power '83
Boss' Son '78
Antonio Das Mortes '68

Christophe Beaucarne

Coco Before Chanel '09
Irina Palm '07
A Few Days in September '06

Etienne Becker

Elisa '94
I Love You All '80
Old Gun '76

Jack Beckett

Desperate Target '80
Thunder County '74
Blood Legacy '73
Please Don't Eat My Mother '72

Terry Bedford(1943-)

Jabberwocky '77
Monty Python and the Holy Grail '75

Dion Beebe

Land of the Lost '09
Nine '09
Rendition '07
Miami Vice '06
Memoirs of a Geisha '05
Collateral '04
In the Cut '03
Chicago '02
Equilibrium '02
Charlotte Gray '01
Along for the Ride '00
Holy Smoke '99
Praise '98
Floating Life '95
Crush '93

Lloyd Beebe

Charlie the Lonesome Cougar '67
Nikki, the Wild Dog of the North '61

John-Paul Beeghly

River's End '05
Step Into Liquid '03

Paul Beeson(1921-2001)

Jane & the Lost City '87
Unidentified Flying Oddball '79
Candleshoe '78
The Littlest Horse Thieves '76
The Freakmaker '73
Crescendo '69
To Sir, with Love '67
Die, Monster, Die! '65
The Prince and the Pauper '62

Yves Belanger(1960-)

Wolves in the Snow '02
Cause of Death '00
The List '99

Peter Belcher

Octopus 2: River of Fear '02
Spiders 2: Breeding Ground '01
U.S. Seals 2 '01
Mission of Death '97
Operation Delta Force 2: Mayday '97

Andreas Bellis

In the Cold of the Night '89
The Wind '87

Ted C. Bemiller(1924-2003)

Heavy Traffic '73
Fritz the Cat '72

Youssef Ben Youssef

The Silences of the Palace '94
Man of Ashes '86

Robert Benavides

Garden Party '08
Thicker than Water '99

Richard Benda

Sworn to Justice '97
Slaughterhouse '87

Henning Bendtsen(1925-)

Gertrud '64
Ordet '55

Peter Benison

The Note 2: Taking a Chance on Love '09
A Broken Life '07
Maneater '07
Memory '06
Cruel and Unusual '01
Big and Hairy '98
Loving Evangeline '98
Jack Higgins' The Windsor Protocol '97
Jack Higgins' Thunder Point '97
Conspiracy of Fear '96
The Wrong Woman '95

Albert Benitz(1904-79)

Testament of Dr. Mabuse '62
The Challenge '38

Mark Benjamin

Protocols of Zion '05
White Boyz '99
Slam '98

David Bennett

Endgame '01
Human Traffic '99

Georges Benoit(1883-1942)

The Baker's Wife '33
Regeneration '15

Michael A. Benson

Universal Soldier: The Return '99
Nowhere to Run '93

Steve Benson

See Joe D'Amato

Roberto Benvenuti

Have No Fear: The Life of Pope John Paul II '05
Red Riding Hood '03

Andres Berenguer

The Story of O, Part 2 '87
Satan's Blood '77

Manuel Berenguer

Flying from the Hawk '86
Simon Bolivar '69
The Thin Red Line '64
The Inveterate Bachelor '58

Giovanni Bergamini

Buck and the Magic Bracelet '97
The Inglorious Bastards '78
Panic '76

Carl Berger

Portland Expose '57
One Too Many '51
Stop That Cab '51
Sky Liner '49

Christian Berger(1945-)

The White Ribbon '09
Hidden '05
The Piano Teacher '01

Kalle Bergholm

Pippi in the South Seas '70
Pippi on the Run '70
Pippi Goes on Board '69
Pippi Longstocking '69

Gabriel Beristain(1955-)

Street Kings '08
The Invisible '07
The Sentinel '06

The Shaggy Dog '06
The Ring 2 '05
Blade: Trinity '04
S.W.A.T. '03
Blade 2 '02
Molly '99
Russell Mulcahy's Tale of the Mummy '99
The Spanish Prisoner '97
Trial and Error '96
Dolores Claiborne '94
Greedy '94
Blood In ... Blood Out: Bound by Honor '93
The Distinguished Gentleman '92
Caravaggio '86

Monty Berman(1912-2006)

The Flesh and the Fiends '60
The Siege of Sidney Street '60
Bond of Fear '56
No Smoking '55
Love in Pawn '53
Recoil '53
The Frightened Man '52
The Voice of Merrill '52

Michael Bernard

Haven '04
On the Line '01

Kristian Bernier(1968-)

April's Shower '03
Dog Gone Love '03
Net Games '03
MacArthur Park '01
Enemies of Laughter '00
Partners '99
Sugar Town '99
Six-String Samurai '98

Steven Bernstein

Tortured '08
Little Man '06
White Chicks '04
Monster '03
Big Shot: Confessions of a Campus Bookie '02
Christmas in the Clouds '01
Corky Romano '01
The Forsaken '01
Scary Movie 2 '01
The Wood '99
Mr. Jealousy '98
The Waterboy '98
Half-Baked '97
Highball '97
Murder at 1600 '97
Bulletproof '96
Underworld '96
Curdled '95
Kicking and Screaming '95
Moondance '95
The Secretary '94
Like Water for Chocolate '93

Gonzalo F. Berridi

Two Tough Guys '03
Lovers of the Arctic Circle '98
The Red Squirrel '93

John Berrie

The Christmas Shoes '02
The Red Sneakers '01
The Peacekeeper '98
This Matter of Marriage '98
Hawk's Vengeance '96
A Young Connecticut Yankee in King Arthur's Court '95
Young Ivanhoe '95

Ross Berryman(1954-)

Pursuit of Happiness '01
Tycus '98
Living in Peril '97
The Thorn Birds: The Missing Years '96
Chameleon '95
Gold Diggers: The Secret of Bear Mountain '95
The Hard Truth '94
Playmaker '94
The Fire in the Stone '85
Prince and the Great Race '83

Renato Berta(1945-)

Kippur '00
Merci pour le Chocolat '00
Kadosh '99
Same Old Song '97
Party '96
Voyage to the Beginning of the World '96
May Fools '90
Twister '89
Au Revoir les Enfants '87
L'Annee des Meduses '86
Full Moon in Paris '84
L'Homme Blesse '83
Every Man for Himself '79
Messidor '77
Jonah Who Will Be 25 in the Year 2000 '76
Charles: Dead or Alive '69

Carl Bessai

Normal '07
Emile '03

Jacques Besse

Bamako '06
Hollow City '04

Thom Best

Men with Brooms '02
Ginger Snaps '01
Ride the Wild Fields '00
Grizzly Falls '99
Hidden Agenda '99
The Boys Club '96

Amit Bhattacharya

Pandemic '07
Though None Go With Me '06
A Boyfriend for Christmas '04
The Souler Opposite '97
Green Plaid Shirt '96

Pete Biagi

I Want Someone to Eat Cheese With '06
Outing Riley '04
Stolen Summer '02

Giulio Biccari

The Breed '06
Blast '04
Queen's Messenger II '01

Adrian Biddle(1952-2005)

V for Vendetta '06
An American Haunting '05
Bridget Jones: The Edge of Reason '04
Laws of Attraction '04
Shanghai Knights '03
Reign of Fire '02
The Mummy Returns '01
102 Dalmatians '00
The Weight of Water '00
The Mummy '99
The World Is Not Enough '99
Holy Man '98
The Butcher Boy '97
Event Horizon '97
Fierce Creatures '96
101 Dalmatians '96
Judge Dredd '95
Thelma & Louise '91
The Tall Guy '89
Willow '88
The Princess Bride '87
Aliens '86

Luca Bigazzi(1958-)

Il Divo '08
Bread and Tulips '01
Not of This World '99
Kiss of Fire '98
Luna e L'Altra '96
Lamerica '95

Ray Binger(1888-1970)

Stagecoach '39
Private Lives '31

Joseph Biroc(1903-96)

Airplane 2: The Sequel '82
Hammett '82
...All the Marbles '81
Airplane! '80
Beyond the Poseidon Adventure '79

The Choirboys '77
The Duchess and the Dirtwater Fox '76
The Hustle '75
Blazing Saddles '74
The Longest Yard '74
The Towering Inferno '74
Emperor of the North Pole '73
Ulzana's Raid '72
Brian's Song '71
Escape from the Planet of the Apes '71
The Grissom Gang '71
The Organization '71
Too Late the Hero '70
The Killing of Sister George '69
Whatever Happened to Aunt Alice? '69
The Detective '68
Lady in Cement '68
Enter Laughing '67
Tony Rome '67
Who's Minding the Mint? '67
The Russians Are Coming, the Russians Are Coming '66
The Flight of the Phoenix '65
Hush, Hush, Sweet Charlotte '65
Gunfight at Comanche Creek '64
Kitten with a Whip '64
Bye, Bye, Birdie '63
Promises! Promises! '63
Toys in the Attic '63
Under the Yum-Yum Tree '63
Viva Las Vegas '63
The Devil at 4 O'Clock '61
Gold of the Seven Saints '61
Ice Palace '60
13 Ghosts '60
The Bat '59
The FBI Story '59
Verboten! '59
The Amazing Colossal Man '57
China Gate '57
Forty Guns '57
The Garment Jungle '57
The Ride Back '57
Attack! '56
Run of the Arrow '56
Donovan's Brain '53
Tall Texan '53
Loan Shark '52
Cry Danger '51
Mrs. Mike '49
On Our Merry Way '48
Magic Town '47
It's a Wonderful Life '46

Billy (G.W.) Bitzer(1872-1944)
Battle of the Sexes '28
America '24
Orphans of the Storm '21
Way Down East '20
Broken Blossoms '19
Intolerance '16
The Birth of a Nation '15
Battle of Elderbush Gulch '13

Peter Biziou(1944-)
Ladies in Lavender '04
Festival Express '03
Unfaithful '02
The Truman Show '98
Richard III '95
The Road to Wellville '94
In the Name of the Father '93
City of Joy '92
Damage '92
Rosencrantz & Guildenstern Are Dead '90
Mississippi Burning '88
A World Apart '88
9 1/2 Weeks '86
Another Country '84
Pink Floyd: The Wall '82
Time Bandits '81
Monty Python's Life of Brian '79
Bugsy Malone '76

Stephen Blackman
Strictly Sinatra '01
The Cement Garden '93

Hilding Bladh(1906-82)
Invasion of the Animal People '62
Dreams '55

Rudolf Blahacek(1942-)
Real Time '08
Saving God '08
Do or Die '03
Crown Heights '02
Terminal Invasion '02
The Pilot's Wife '01
Doktor Faustus '82

Stephen Blake
Final Shot: The Hank Gathers Story '92
Beverly Hills Vamp '88
Hack O'Lantern '87
Sorority Babes in the Slimeball Bowl-A-Rama '87

Ken Blakey(1947-)
Conjurer '08
Christmas Do-Over '06
The 4th Tenor '02
Extreme Honor '01
Agent Red '00
Rangers '00
The Stray '00
Terror Tract '00
Final Voyage '99
Running Red '99
Land of the Free '98
Executive Target '97
Recoil '97
The Underground '97
Little Bigfoot '96
Pure Danger '96
Riot '96
Rage '95
The Sweeper '95
Cyber-Tracker '93
Firepower '93

Larry Blanford
Hero Wanted '08
Hurricane Season '08
Fantastic Four: Rise of the Silver Surfer '07
Operation Sandman: Warriors in Hell '00
For Which He Stands '98

Roberto Blasini
Forfeit '07
Gamers '06

Sebastian Blenkov
Adam's Apples '05
The Green Butchers '03

Regis Blondeau
I Do '06
Quartier Mozart '92

David Blood
Bad City '06
Steele's Law '91

Jonathan Bloom
Cravings '06
Inspector Lynley Mysteries: A Great Deliverance '01

Patrick Blossier(1949-)
The Girl From Monaco '08
Days of Glory '06
La Moustache '05
Red Lights '04
Amen '02
Jet Lag '02
The Chambermaid on the Titanic '97
Mad City '97
Innocent Lies '95
Revenge of the Musketeers '94
Jacquot '91
Dr. Petiot '90
Music Box '89
Betrayed '88
Sorceress '88
Vagabond '85

Nigel Bluck
Murderous Intent '06
Stickmen '01

Sydney Blythe
Juggernaut '37
She Shall Have Music '36
Scrooge '35

Sean Bobbitt
Sense & Sensibility '07
The Situation '06
Lawless Heart '01
Wonderland '99

Ralf Bode(1942-2001)
Boys and Girls '00
Annie '99
Sarah, Plain and Tall: Winter's End '99
A Simple Wish '97
Sink or Swim '97
The Big Green '95
A Streetcar Named Desire '95
Don Juan DeMarco '94
Safe Passage '94
George Balanchine's The Nutcracker '93
Gypsy '93
Made in America '93
Leaving Normal '92
Love Field '91
One Good Cop '91
Cousins '89
Uncle Buck '89
The Accused '88
Distant Thunder '88
Big Town '87
Critical Condition '86
Violets Are Blue '86
The Whoopee Boys '86
First Born '84
Gorky Park '83
A Little Sex '82
A Long Way Home '81
Raggedy Man '81
Coal Miner's Daughter '80
Dressed to Kill '80
Rich Kids '79
Saturday Night Fever '77
Foreplay '75
Saturday Night at the Baths '75

Jean Boffety(1925-88)
Vincent, Francois, Paul and the Others '76
Cesar & Rosalie '72
Zita '68
The Last Adventure '67

Kip Bogdahn
Bought and Sold '03
Camp '03

Hagen Bogdanski
Case 39 '10
The Young Victoria '09
The Lives of Others '06
Antibodies '05

Haskell Boggs(1909-2003)
Bonanza: The Return '93
The Bellboy '60
I Married a Monster from Outer Space '58
Teacher's Pet '58
Rock-A-Bye Baby '57

Ludek Bogner
Psychic '91
Erik '90
Circle Man '87

Oliver Bokelberg(1964-)
The Bounty Hunter '10
The Answer Man '09
Dark Matter '07
The Visitor '07
Strangers with Candy '06
Loggerheads '05
The Station Agent '03
The Next Big Thing '02
Cash Crop '01
Harvest '98
Long Time Since '97
Last Breath '96

Alun Bollinger
River Queen '05
Perfect Strangers '03
Forgotten Silver '96

The Frighteners '96
Heavenly Creatures '94
A Soldier's Tale '91
Came a Hot Friday '85
Goodbye Pork Pie '81

Balasz Bolygo
Fakers '04
It's All Gone, Pete Tong '04

Jean-Louis Bompoint
Grace Is Gone '07
The Science of Sleep '06

Michael Bonvillain
Zombieland '09
Cloverfield '08
Sniper 3 '04
A Texas Funeral '99
Saints and Sinners '95
The Desperate Trail '94
Amongst Friends '93
When the Bough Breaks '93

Lamar Boren(1917-86)
The Spy Who Loved Me '77
Brewster McCloud '70

Harlan Bosmajian
The Other End of the Line '08
Havoc 2: Normal Adolescent Behavior '07
Starting Out in the Evening '07
The Great New Wonderful '06
Ira & Abby '06
Kill the Poor '06
Shooting Livien '05
Brother to Brother '04
Saving Face '04
Winter Solstice '04
Lovely & Amazing '02
Virgil Bliss '01
Maryam '00
Spin the Bottle '97

Rick Bota
Valentine '01
House on Haunted Hill '99
Barb Wire '96
The Glimmer Man '96
The Companion '94
Tales from the Crypt Presents Demon Knight '94
Article 99 '92
Bloodfist 3: Forced to Fight '92
Pure Country '92
Wheels of Terror '90

Davis Boulton(1911-89)
Children of the Damned '63
The Haunting '63

Jacques Bouquin
Wall '04
Comedy of Innocence '00
The Man I Love '97

Jean (Yves, Georges) Bourgoin(1913-91)
The Counterfeit Traitor '62
The Longest Day '62
Black Orpheus '58
Mon Oncle '58
Mr. Arkadin '55
Dedee d'Anvers '49
Voyage Suprise '46
La Marseillaise '37

Richard Bowen
Head Above Water '96
A Smile Like Yours '96
Fair Game '95
Major Payne '95
The Little Rascals '94
Runaway Daughters '94
Animal Behavior '89
The Wizard of Loneliness '88
Stacking '87
Belizaire the Cajun '86
Street Music '81

David Boyd
Get Low '09
12 Rounds '09
Kit Kittredge: An American Girl '08
Full Count '06

Firestarter 2: Rekindled '02

Russell Boyd(1944-)
Ghost Rider '07
Master and Commander: The Far Side of the World '03
American Outlaws '01
Company Man '00
Dr. Dolittle '98
Liar Liar '97
Tin Cup '96
Operation Dumbo Drop '95
Cobb '94
Forever Young '92
The Killing Beach '92
White Men Can't Jump '92
Sweet Talker '91
Almost an Angel '90
In Country '89
Crocodile Dundee 2 '88
The Rescue '88
High Tide '87
Crocodile Dundee '86
Burke & Wills '85
Mrs. Soffel '84
Phar Lap '84
A Soldier's Story '84
Dawn! '83
Tender Mercies '83
Starstruck '82
The Year of Living Dangerously '82
Gallipoli '81
Chain Reaction '80
The Last Wave '77
Alternative '76
Gone to Ground '76
Picnic at Hanging Rock '75

Charles P. Boyle(1892-1968)
Old Yeller '57
The Great Locomotive Chase '56
Gunsmoke '53
Tomahawk '51
She Wore a Yellow Ribbon '49
Fun & Fancy Free '47
Saddle Tramp '47
We're in the Navy Now '27

Geoff Boyle
Dark Country '09
Street Fighter: The Legend of Chun-Li '09
Mutant Chronicles '08

John Boyle(1891-1959)
Carson City '52
Who Killed Doc Robbin? '48
The Bridge of San Luis Rey '44
Gang Busters '42
Mutiny on the Blackhawk '39
Treason '33

Kurt Brabbee
The Crow: Wicked Prayer '05
Dead Silence '98
Get a Clue! '98

William Bradford(1905-59)
Trail to San Antone '47
Along the Navaho Trail '45
Don't Fence Me In '45
Rough Riders of Cheyenne '45
End of the Road '44
Fighting Seabees '44
San Fernando Valley '44
Manhunt in the African Jungles '43

Julio Bragado
Slugs '87
Blue Jeans and Dynamite '76

Henry Braham(1965-)
Everybody's Fine '09
The Golden Compass '07
Flyboys '06
Nanny McPhee '06
Bright Young Things '03
Crush '02
Shackleton '02
Invisible Circus '00

The Land Girls '98
Shooting Fish '98
Waking Ned Devine '98
For Roseanna '96
Solitaire for 2 '94

Russ Brandt
The Haunting of Hell House '99
Don't Be a Menace to South Central While Drinking Your Juice in the Hood '95
Excessive Force 2: Force on Force '95
Playback '95
H.P. Lovecraft's Necronomicon: Book of the Dead '93

Ulf Brantas
Wuthering Heights '09
Show Me Love '99
The Women on the Roof '89

Denise Brassard
Seamless '00
Deal of a Lifetime '99
St. Patrick's Day '99

Sylvain Brault(1958-)
One Way Out '02
Hidden Agenda '01
2001: A Space Travesty '00
The Boys '97
Jack London's The Call of the Wild '97
Rowing Through '96
Sworn Enemies '96
A Paper Wedding '89

Elwood "Woody" Bredell(1884-1976)
The Female Jungle '56
The Inspector General '49
The Unsuspected '47
The Killers '46
Can't Help Singing '45
Lady on a Train '45
His Butler's Sister '44
Phantom Lady '44
The Amazing Mrs. Holiday '43
The Strange Case of Dr. Rx '42
Hold That Ghost '41
Horror Island '41
Man Made Monster '41
Argentine Nights '40
Black Friday '40
Boom Town '40
The Invisible Woman '40
The Mummy's Hand '40
Forbidden Valley '38

Brian J. Breheny
Aquamarine '06
The Hard Word '02
The Other Side of Heaven '02
When Good Ghouls Go Bad '01
Siam Sunset '99
That's the Way I Like It '99
Heaven's Burning '97
The Adventures of Priscilla, Queen of the Desert '94

Jochen Breitenstein
The Boogey Man '80
Cocaine Cowboys '79

Jules Brenner
1969 '89
Return of the Living Dead '85
Salem's Lot '79
Cornbread, Earl & Me '75
Dillinger '73
Johnny Got His Gun '71

Justin Brickle
Strange Planet '99
Love and Other Catastrophes '95

David Bridges
Submerged '05
What the #$*! Do We Know? '04
Rip It Off '02
Big City Blues '99
The Simian Line '99

End of Summer '97
Crosscut '95
Painted Hero '95
Payback '94
P.I. Private Investigations '87

Uta Briesewitz

Life Support '07
Walk Hard: The Dewey Cox Story '07
The TV Set '06
The Home Front '02
XX/XY '02
Session 9 '01
Love Stinks '99
Next Stop, Wonderland '98

Robert Brinkmann(1962-)

The Christmas Cottage '08
Tenacious D in the Pick of Destiny '06
Standing Still '05
The Rules of Attraction '02
Serving Sara '02
Sugar & Spice '01
Screwed '00
The Cable Guy '96
The Truth about Cats and Dogs '96
The Beverly Hillbillies '93
Encino Man '92
Shout '91
Mirror, Mirror '90
U2: Rattle and Hum '88
Kandyland '87

Cyril Bristow

House of Darkness '48
Big Fella '37

Anchise Brizzi

Othello '52
1860 '33

Norbert Brodine(1896-1970)

Sitting Pretty '48
Boomerang '47
Somewhere in the Night '46
13 Rue Madeleine '46
House on 92nd Street '45
Topper Returns '41
Of Mice and Men '39
Libeled Lady '36
The Good Fairy '35
Counsellor-at-Law '33
The Beast of the City '32
Let Us Be Gay '30
The Sea Hawk '24

Damian Bromley

The Business '05
Dot.Kill '05
House of 9 '05

Eric Broms

Horsemen '09
Spun '02

Robert J. Bronner(1907-69)

7 Faces of Dr. Lao '63
Pocketful of Miracles '61
Please Don't Eat the Daisies '60
Where the Boys Are '60
The Sheepman '58
Jailhouse Rock '57
Ten Thousand Bedrooms '57

Alice Brooks

Mulligans '08
Ten 'Til Noon '06

Robert Brooks

Who Shot Pat? '92
Snapshot '77

Edward R. Brown

Blind Ambition '79
Great Smokey Roadblock '76
Amazing Grace '74

James S. Brown, Jr. (1892-1949)

The Devil Bat's Daughter '46
Renegade Girl '46
Strangler of the Swamp '46
Kid Sister '45
Land of Hunted Men '43
The Great Plane Robbery '40
Rio Grande Ranger '37
Shadows of the Orient '37
The Fighting Rookie '34
Night Alarm '34

Jonathan Brown

Mama's Boy '07
The Pink Panther '06
School for Scoundrels '06
The Family Stone '05
Without a Paddle '04
Cheaper by the Dozen '03
Just Married '03
Big Fat Liar '02
The Third Wheel '02
Pros & Cons '99

Karl Brown(1896-1990)

Leap Year '21
Intolerance '16

Neal Brown

Miracle Dogs '03
The Santa Trap '02
Teenage Bonnie & Klepto Clyde '93

Joseph Brun(1907-98)

The 300 Year Weekend '71
The Fat Spy '66
Odds Against Tomorrow '59
Edge of the City '57
The Joe Louis Story '53
Martin Luther '53

Laurent Brunet

Seraphine '08
Grocer's Son '07
Free Zone '05
La Petite Jerusalem '05
Or (My Treasure) '04

Eigil Bryld

In Bruges '08
Becoming Jane '07
Kinky Boots '06
PU-239 '06
The King '05
To Kill a King '03

Michael Bucher(1939-)

The Mating Habits of the Earthbound Human '99
My Brother's War '97

Marc Bujard

The Chess Player '27
J'accuse! '19

Bobby Bukowski

The Messenger '09
The Guitar '08
Phoebe in Wonderland '08
The Stone Angel '07
Glass House: The Good Mother '06
The Hawk Is Dying '06
The Tripper '06
Boogeyman '05
The Dying Gaul '05
Saved! '04
Tangled '01
Crime and Punishment in Suburbia '00
Arlington Road '99
The Minus Man '99
Going All the Way '97
If These Walls Could Talk '96
The Last Time I Committed Suicide '96
Til There Was You '96
The Tie That Binds '95
Tom and Huck '95
Holy Matrimony '94
Search and Destroy '94
Golden Gate '93
Household Saints '93
Ethan Frome '92
Shakes the Clown '92
Men of Respect '91
Thousand Pieces of Gold '91
Anna '87
Kiss Daddy Goodnight '87

Miguel Bunster(1979-)

Pandemic '09
The Line '08

Alexander Buono

Bigger Stronger Faster '08
Shanghai Kiss '07
Green Street Hooligans '05
Snipes '01

Leonce-Henri Burel(1892-1977)

Pickpocket '59
A Man Escaped '57
Diary of a Country Priest '50
Napoleon '27
J'accuse! '19
The Torture of Silence '17

Don Burgess(1956-)

The Book of Eli '10
Aliens in the Attic '09
Fool's Gold '08
Enchanted '07
Eight Below '06
My Super Ex-Girlfriend '06
Christmas With the Kranks '04
The Polar Express '04
13 Going on 30 '04
Radio '03
Terminator 3: Rise of the Machines '03
Spider-Man '02
Cast Away '00
What Lies Beneath '00
Contact '97
The Evening Star '96
Forget Paris '95
Forrest Gump '94
Richie Rich '94
Josh and S.A.M. '93
Mo' Money '92
Blind Fury '90
The Court Martial of Jackie Robinson '90
Under the Boardwalk '89
World Gone Wild '88
Death Before Dishonor '87
Night Stalker '87
Summer Camp Nightmare '86
Fury to Freedom: The Life Story of Raul Ries '85
Ruckus '81

Robert Burks(1910-68)

Waterhole Number 3 '67
A Patch of Blue '65
Marnie '64
The Birds '63
The Music Man '62
The Great Impostor '61
The Rat Race '60
Black Orchid '59
But Not for Me '59
North by Northwest '59
Vertigo '58
Spirit of St. Louis '57
The Man Who Knew Too Much '56
The Wrong Man '56
To Catch a Thief '55
The Trouble with Harry '55
Dial "M" for Murder '54
Rear Window '54
The Desert Song '53
Hondo '53
I Confess '53
So This Is Love '53
Close to My Heart '51
The Enforcer '51
Room for One More '51
Strangers on a Train '51
Beyond the Forest '49
The Fountainhead '49

Hans Burman(1937-)

Open Your Eyes '97
Thesis '96
Guantanamera '95
Why Do They Call It Love When They Mean Sex? '92
Car Crash '80
City of the Walking Dead '80

Alexander Burov

The Italian '05
Father and Son '03

David Burr

The Crocodile Hunter: Collision Course '02
Crocodile Dundee in Los Angeles '01
Komodo '99
Paperback Hero '99
Escape: Human Cargo '98
Joey '98
Wild America '97
The Phantom '96
Race the Sun '96
Ghosts Can Do It '87

Dan Burstall(1951-)

Criminal Ways '03
Under the Gun '95
Crime Broker '94
Crimebroker '93
Ladybugs '92
Kangaroo '86
Squizzy Taylor '84

Thomas Burstyn

The Last Templar '09
Vipers '08
Marco Polo '07
Tin Man '07
Population 436 '06
The Boys and Girl From County Clare '03
Lost Junction '03
Deadlocked '00
Where the Money Is '00
When Trumpets Fade '98
City of Industry '96
Crazy Horse '96
Dead Silence '96
Magic in the Water '95
Andre '94
The Surgeon '94
Arctic Blue '93
Toy Soldiers '91
Cheetah '89
Cold Front '89
Promised a Miracle '88
Broken Vows '87
Ford: The Man & the Machine '87
Foxfire '87
Native Son '86
Dark of the Night '85
Heavenly Bodies '84

Geoff Burton(1946-)

After the Deluge '03
The Beast '96
Brilliant Lies '96
Sorrento Beach '95
Sirens '94
The Sum of Us '94
Frauds '93
Wide Sargasso Sea '92
Romero '89
The Time Guardian '87
The Year My Voice Broke '87
Midnite Spares '85
Winner Takes All '84
Blue Fin '78
Sound of Love '78
Fourth Wish '75
Sunday Too Far Away '74

Stephen Burum(1940-)

Confessions of a Teenage Drama Queen '04
Life or Something Like It '02
Mission to Mars '00
Mystery Men '99
Snake Eyes '98
Father's Day '96
Mission: Impossible '96
The Shadow '94
Carlito's Way '93
Hoffa '92
Man Trouble '92
Raising Cain '92
He Said, She Said '91
Casualties of War '89
The War of the Roses '89
Arthur 2: On the Rocks '88
The Untouchables '87
The Bride '85
8 Million Ways to Die '85
St. Elmo's Fire '85
Body Double '84
The Entity '83
The Outsiders '83
Rumble Fish '83
Something Wicked This Way Comes '83
Uncommon Valor '83
The Escape Artist '82
Death Valley '81
Wild Gypsies '69

Dick Bush(1931-97)

The Man in the Attic '94
Shadowhunter '93
Son of the Pink Panther '93
Switch '91
Little Monsters '89
Staying Together '89
The Lair of the White Worm '88
Assault and Matrimony '87
The Quick and the Dead '87
The Journey of Natty Gann '85
Crimes of Passion '84
The Philadelphia Experiment '84
Curse of the Pink Panther '83
Trail of the Pink Panther '82
Victor/Victoria '82
The Fan '81
One Trick Pony '80
The Legacy '79
Yanks '79
The Hound of the Baskervilles '77
Sorcerer '77
In Celebration '75
Tommy '75
Mahler '74
Phase 4 '74
Dracula A.D. 1972 '72
Savage Messiah '72
The Blood on Satan's Claw '71
Twins of Evil '71
When Dinosaurs Ruled the Earth '70

Bill Butler(1931-)

Redline '07
Frailty '02
Joe and Max '02
Passing Glory '99
Deceiver '97
Don King: Only in America '97
Anaconda '96
Flipper '96
Beethoven's 2nd '93
Cop and a Half '93
Sniper '92
Hot Shots! '91
Graffiti Bridge '90
Biloxi Blues '88
Child's Play '88
Wildfire '88
Big Trouble '86
Beer '85
Rocky 4 '85
A Streetcar Named Desire '84
The Sting 2 '83
The Thorn Birds '83
Rocky 3 '82
The Night the Lights Went Out in Georgia '81
Stripes '81
Can't Stop the Music '80
It's My Turn '80
Ice Castles '79
Rocky 2 '79
Capricorn One '78
Damien: Omen 2 '78
Grease '78
Demon Seed '77
Mary White '77
Raid on Entebbe '77
Bingo Long Traveling All-Stars & Motor Kings '76
Lipstick '76
Jaws '75
One Flew Over the Cuckoo's Nest '75
The Conversation '74
The Execution of Private Slovik '74
The Return of Count Yorga '71
The Rain People '69

Michael C. Butler

Cannonball Run '81
Smokey and the Bandit 2 '80
Jaws 2 '78
Harry and Tonto '74

Taylor Byars

Shame '61
Teenage Monster '57

Frank Byers

Illegal Tender '07
Jackie, Ethel, Joan: The Kennedy Women '01
Kiss Toledo Goodbye '00
Having Our Say: The Delany Sisters' First 100 Years '99
Ride '98
Shiloh '97
Trigger Happy '96
Archie: Return to Riverdale '90

Bobby Byrne

The Lemon Sisters '90
Bull Durham '88
Stealing Home '88
Sixteen Candles '84
The Villain '79
Blue Collar '78
The End '78
Hooper '78
Smokey and the Bandit '77

John Cabrera(1925-)

Hell of the Living Dead '83
Conan the Barbarian '82
Call of the Wild '72

Patrick Cady

The Lottery Ticket '10
The Stepfather '09
Private Valentine: Blonde & Dangerous '08
Kings of South Beach '07
Broken Bridges '06
The Far Side of Jericho '06
Marie and Bruce '04
Sunshine State '02
Girlfight '99

Sharon Calahan

Ratatouille '07
Finding Nemo '03
A Bug's Life '98

Duke Callaghan

Conan the Barbarian '82
The Last Hard Men '76
Jeremiah Johnson '72

Thomas Callaway

Without a Paddle: Nature's Calling '09
Exit Speed '08
Still Waiting '08
Undead or Alive '07
Who's Your Caddy? '07
Feast '06
Drop Dead Sexy '05
Cruel Intentions 3 '04
National Lampoon's Gold Diggers '04
Au Pair 2: The Fairy Tale Continues '01
Earth vs. the Spider '01
She Creature '01
Mach 2 '00
Submerged '00
Counter Measures '99
Caught Up '98
A River Made to Drown In '97
Amityville Dollhouse '96
Night of the Scarecrow '95
Eddie Presley '92
Cartel '90
Steel and Lace '90
Action U.S.A. '89
Lady Avenger '89
Assault of the Killer Bimbos '88
Slave Girls from Beyond Infinity '87
Slumber Party Massacre 2 '87

Tom Calloway

The Devil's Tomb '09
The Dead Hate the Living '99

Antonio Calvache

What Goes Up '09
Little Children '06

3-Way *'04*
Prey for Rock and Roll *'03*
Unspeakable *'02*
In the Bedroom *'01*
Broken Vessels *'98*
I Got the Hook-Up *'98*

Maurizio Calvesi(1954-)
Ginostra *'02*
Up at the Villa *'00*
Nerolio *'96*
Acla's Descent into Floristella *'87*

Tom Camarda
Eating Out 3: All You Can Eat *'09*
Dog Gone *'08*

Alistair Cameron
Surveillance 24/7 *'07*
Like It Is *'98*
Gunpowder *'87*

Paul Cameron(1958-)
Deja Vu *'06*
In the Land of Women *'06*
Collateral *'04*
Man on Fire *'04*
Swordfish *'01*
Gone in 60 Seconds *'00*
The Last Supper *'96*

Marcelo Camorino
Nine Queens *'00*
Autumn Sun *'98*

John Campbell
Just One Night *'00*
Change of Heart *'98*
Reach the Rock *'98*
Rough Magic *'95*
Even Cowgirls Get the Blues *'94*
Imaginary Crimes *'94*
My Own Private Idaho *'91*

Stephen Campbell
Beethoven's Big Break *'08*
National Lampoon Presents RoboDoc *'08*

Yves Cape(1960-)
Flanders *'06*
Buffalo Boy *'04*
Humanity *'99*
Ma Vie en Rose *'97*

Gary Capo
Cellular *'04*
Final Destination 2 *'03*

Michael Caporale
How You Look to Me *'05*
Ball of Wax *'03*

Marco Cappetta(1963-)
Dark Heart *'06*
Now You Know *'02*
Hard As Nails *'01*

Robert Caramico(1932-97)
KISS Meets the Phantom of the Park *'78*
Slithis *'78*
Eaten Alive *'76*
Blackenstein *'73*
Lemora, Lady Dracula *'73*
Octaman *'71*
Orgy of the Dead *'65*

Jack Cardiff(1914-)
Million Dollar Mystery *'87*
Tai-Pan *'86*
Cat's Eye *'85*
Rambo: First Blood, Part 2 *'85*
Conan the Destroyer *'84*
The Far Pavilions *'84*
Scandalous *'84*
The Wicked Lady *'83*
The Dogs of War *'81*
Ghost Story *'81*
The Awakening *'80*
Avalanche Express *'79*
The Fifth Musketeer *'79*
A Man, a Woman, and a Bank *'79*
Death on the Nile *'78*
The Prince and the Pauper *'78*
Ride a Wild Pony *'75*
The Girl on a Motorcycle *'68*
War and Peace *'68*
Fanny *'61*
The Vikings *'58*
Legend of the Lost *'57*
The Prince and the Showgirl *'57*
The Brave One *'56*
War and Peace *'56*
The Barefoot Contessa *'54*
The Master of Ballantrae *'53*
The African Queen *'51*
Pandora and the Flying Dutchman *'51*
The Black Rose *'50*
Under Capricorn *'49*
The Red Shoes *'48*
Black Narcissus *'47*
Stairway to Heaven *'46*
The Four Feathers *'39*
Wings of the Morning *'37*
As You Like It *'36*
Last Days of Pompeii *'35*

Carlo Carlini(1929-)
Autopsy *'74*
Street Law *'74*
Era Notte a Roma *'60*
Generale Della Rovere *'60*
I Vitelloni *'53*

James Carman
Otto: Or, Up with Dead People *'08*
Hustler White *'96*

Paolo Carnera(1957-)
Ginger and Cinnamon *'03*
Pizzicata *'96*

Russell Carpenter(1950-)
Killers *'10*
The Ugly Truth *'09*
21 *'08*
Awake *'07*
Monster-in-Law *'05*
Noel *'04*
Charlie's Angels: Full Throttle *'03*
Shallow Hal *'01*
Charlie's Angels *'00*
The Negotiator *'98*
Money Talks *'97*
Titanic *'97*
The Indian in the Cupboard *'95*
True Lies *'94*
Hard Target *'93*
The Lawnmower Man *'92*
Pet Sematary 2 *'92*
Solar Crisis *'92*
The Perfect Weapon *'91*
Death Warrant *'90*
Cameron's Closet *'89*
Critters 2: The Main Course *'88*
The Lady in White *'88*
The Wizard of Speed and Time *'88*
Sole Survivor *'84*

Ezequiel Carrasco(1900-78)
Wrestling Women vs. the Aztec Mummy *'59*
Senora Tentacion *'49*

Ellis W. Carter(1906-64)
Diary of a Madman *'63*
Twice-Told Tales *'63*
Curse of the Undead *'59*
The Incredible Shrinking Man *'57*
El Paso *'49*
Radar Patrol vs. Spy King *'49*
Big Town After Dark *'47*
Underworld Scandal *'47*

James L. Carter
Believe in Me *'06*
Walker Payne *'06*
Ladder 49 *'04*
Sleepover *'04*
The Shape of Things *'03*
Tuck Everlasting *'02*
ZigZag *'02*
My Dog Skip *'99*
Phoenix *'98*
Grand Avenue *'96*
Gunfighter's Moon *'96*
Ruby Jean and Joe *'96*
Convict Cowboy *'95*
Destiny Turns on the Radio *'95*
The Last Ride *'94*
One False Move *'91*
Back to Back *'90*
Playroom *'90*
Spaced Invaders *'90*
Leatherface: The Texas Chainsaw Massacre 3 *'89*
Deadly Weapon *'88*
In Dangerous Company *'88*
Terminal Entry *'87*
Paradise Motel *'84*
Don't Answer the Phone *'80*
Home Movies *'79*

Miki Carter
Tarzan and the Lost Safari *'57*
Tarzan's Hidden Jungle *'55*

Walter Carvalho(1947-)
Carandiru *'03*
Madame Sata *'02*
Behind the Sun *'01*
Possible Loves *'00*
Central Station *'98*
Foreign Land *'95*

Alan Caso
Comanche Moon *'08*
First Sunday *'08*
The Librarian: Quest for the Spear *'04*
Master Spy: The Robert Hanssen Story *'02*
Widows *'02*
Repli-Kate *'01*
Another Woman's Husband *'00*
Reindeer Games *'00*
Running Mates *'00*
Muppets from Space *'99*
George Wallace *'97*
Top of the World *'97*
Ed *'96*
The Good Old Boys *'95*
Caged Fear *'92*
Stepfather 3: Father's Day *'92*
84 Charlie MoPic *'89*

Darrell Cathcart(1935-2007)
House of Death *'82*
The Wolfman *'82*

Arnaldo Catinari(1964-)
Agata and the Storm *'04*
Caterina in the Big City *'03*
Light of My Eyes *'01*

Francois Catonne
How Much Do You Love Me? *'05*
My Life and Times with Antonin Artaud *'93*
Indochine *'92*

Alan Caudillo
A Day Without a Mexican *'04*
The Shot *'96*

Sarah Cawley
Oxygen *'99*
Mercy *'96*
Because of You *'95*
A Reason to Believe *'95*

Eric Cayla
The Christmas Choir *'08*
The Sign of Four *'01*
The Hound of the Baskervilles *'00*
Karmina *'96*
Le Sexe des Etoiles *'93*
Necromancer: Satan's Servant *'88*

Vanja Cernjul(1968-)
Diminished Capacity *'08*
Where God Left His Shoes *'07*
Wristcutters: A Love Story *'06*
The Mudge Boy *'03*
American Psycho 2: All American Girl *'02*
Ed Gein *'01*
I'll Take You There *'99*

Milan Chadima
Hostel: Part 2 *'07*
Hostel *'06*

Christopher Challis(1919-)
Top Secret! *'84*
Evil under the Sun *'82*
The Mirror Crack'd *'80*
S.O.S. Titanic *'79*
Force 10 from Navarone *'78*
The Deep *'77*
The Little Prince *'74*
Mary, Queen of Scots *'71*
The Private Life of Sherlock Holmes *'70*
Chitty Chitty Bang Bang *'68*
Two for the Road *'67*
Kaleidoscope *'66*
The Long Ships *'64*
A Shot in the Dark *'64*
The Victors *'63*
Damn the Defiant *'62*
The Grass Is Greener *'61*
Sink the Bismarck *'60*
Quentin Durward *'55*
Angels One Five *'54*
Genevieve *'53*

Douglas Chamberlain
Humble Pie *'07*
Moving McAllister *'07*
I'm Reed Fish *'06*

Giselle Chamma
Tony n' Tina's Wedding *'07*
Happy Hour *'03*

Caroline Champetier(1954-)
Tokyo! *'09*
One Day You'll Understand *'08*
Le Petit Lieutenant *'05*
Lush *'01*
Alice et Martin *'98*
Dry Cleaning *'97*
A Single Girl *'96*
Ponette *'95*
Helas pour Moi *'94*
La Sentinelle *'92*
The Disenchanted *'90*
Aria *'88*

Marc Champion
Out of the Blue *'80*
Vengeance Is Mine *'74*
Slipstream *'73*

Chi Ying Chan
DOA: Dead or Alive *'06*
Silver Hawk *'04*

Joe Chan
Tsui Hark's Vampire Hunters *'02*
Wicked City *'92*

Tom Chaney
Mosquito *'95*
Frostbiter: Wrath of the Wendigo *'94*

Gu Changwei(1957-)
Devils on the Doorstep *'00*
Hurlyburly *'98*
The Gingerbread Man *'97*
Farewell My Concubine *'93*
Ju Dou *'90*
Life on a String *'90*
Red Sorghum *'87*

Michael Chapman(1935-)
Bridge to Terabithia *'07*
Hoot *'06*
Eulogy *'04*
House of D *'04*
Suspect Zero *'04*
Evolution *'01*
The Watcher *'00*
The Story of Us *'99*
White River *'99*
Six Days, Seven Nights *'98*
Primal Fear *'96*
Space Jam *'96*
The Fugitive *'93*
Rising Sun *'93*
Whispers in the Dark *'92*
Doc Hollywood *'91*
Kindergarten Cop *'90*
Quick Change *'90*
Ghostbusters 2 *'89*
Gotham *'88*
Scrooged *'88*
Shoot to Kill *'88*
The Lost Boys *'87*
The Man with Two Brains *'83*
Dead Men Don't Wear Plaid *'82*
Personal Best *'82*
Raging Bull *'80*
Hardcore *'79*
Wanderers *'79*
Fingers *'78*
Invasion of the Body Snatchers *'78*
The Last Waltz *'78*
The Arab Conspiracy *'76*
The Front *'76*
Taxi Driver *'76*
The White Dawn *'75*
The Last Detail *'73*

Ron Chapman
Class of Nuke 'Em High 3: The Good, the Bad and the Subhumanoid *'94*
Class of Nuke 'Em High 2: Subhumanoid Meltdown *'91*
Shock 'Em Dead *'90*
Fortress of Amerikka *'89*

Robert Chappell
Standard Operating Procedure *'08*
The Fog of War: Eleven Lessons from the Life of Robert S. McNamara *'03*
The Thin Blue Line *'88*

Dominique Chapuis(1948-2001)
Mina Tannenbaum *'93*
Pas Tres Catholique *'93*
The Little Thief *'89*
Sugar Cane Alley *'83*

Marc Charlebois
Fear of the Dark *'02*
Protection *'01*
Treasure Island *'99*

Cliff Charles
Good Hair *'09*
30 Years to Life *'01*

Cesar Charlone(1958-)
Blindness *'08*
The Constant Gardener *'05*
City of God *'02*

Rodney Charters(1948-)
Intern *'00*
Blind Faith *'98*
Kull the Conqueror *'97*
Frame by Frame *'95*
Sleepwalkers *'92*
Psycho 4: The Beginning *'90*

Chuy Chavez
Youth in Revolt *'10*
Me and You and Everyone We Know *'05*
The Sisters *'05*
Puerto Vallarta Squeeze *'04*
Chuck & Buck *'00*
Star Maps *'97*

Claudio Chea
Behind Enemy Lines 3: Colombia *'08*
El Cantante *'06*
Yellow *'06*
MTV's Wuthering Heights *'03*
A Season on the Brink *'02*
Washington Heights *'02*
Pinero *'01*
Winds of Terror *'01*
Hendrix *'00*
Execution of Justice *'99*
Free of Eden *'98*
Bitter Sugar *'96*

Enrique Chediak
Repo Men *'10*
The Flock *'07*
28 Weeks Later *'07*
Lies & Alibis *'06*
Turistas *'06*
Down in the Valley *'05*
Cronicas *'04*
A Home at the End of the World *'04*
Undefeated *'03*
Brown Sugar *'02*
The Good Girl *'02*
The Safety of Objects *'01*
3 A.M. *'01*
Boiler Room *'00*
Songcatcher *'99*
Desert Blue *'98*
The Faculty *'98*
Frogs for Snakes *'98*
Hurricane Streets *'96*

Pierre Chemaly
Mexican Gangster *'08*
Fear Runs Silent *'99*
Powder Burn *'96*

Carolyn Chen
The Crow: Salvation *'00*
Entropy *'99*

Chin-Kui Chen
Downdraft *'96*
Half a Loaf of Kung Fu *'78*

Siu Keung Cheng
Running Out of Time 2 *'06*
Running on Karma *'03*
Full Time Killer *'01*

Man Po Cheung
Flash Point *'07*
Vampire Effect *'03*
Gorgeous *'99*

Yiu-tsou Cheung
The Legend of Drunken Master *'94*
Police Story *'85*

Remy Chevrin
Love Songs *'07*
Happily Ever After *'04*
Monsieur Ibrahim *'03*
Close to Leo *'02*
My Wife is an Actress *'01*
Doctor Chance *'97*

Michael G. Chin
Life Tastes Good *'99*
Chan Is Missing *'82*

Roger Chingirian
Loaded *'08*
Hack! *'07*

Steven Chivers
High Heels and Low Lifes *'01*
Highlander: The Final Dimension *'94*
Dust Devil *'93*

Yeong-hwon Choi
Blood Rain *'05*
No Blood No Tears *'02*
Take Care of My Cat *'01*

Chris Chomyn
Flying By *'09*
Lockdown *'00*
Phantasm 4: Oblivion *'98*

Alain Choquart
Boesman & Lena *'00*
Capitaine Conan *'96*
L.627 *'92*

Gordon Chou
Milk and Honey *'03*
Margarita Happy Hour *'01*

James Chressanthis
Living Proof *'08*
The Reagans *'04*
Eloise at the Plaza *'03*
Brian's Song *'01*
Life with Judy Garland—Me and My Shadows *'01*
Judas Kiss *'98*
Urban Legend *'98*

Dangerous Relations '93

T.C. Christensen

Forever Strong '08
The Robin Hood Gang '98

Vassilis Christomoglou

Love Camp '81
Emmanuelle, the Queen '79
Emmanuelle's Daughter '79

Chen Ching Chu

Chinese Connection '73
Fists of Fury '73

Bruce Chun(1963-)

WarGames 2: The Dead Code '08
Bon Cop Bad Cop '06
Swindle '02
The Reaper '97

Fabio Cianchetti

Shadows '07
Don't Tell '05
The Tiger and the Snow '05
The Dreamers '03
The Triumph of Love '01
Besieged '98

Luis Ciccarese

Demonia '90
Animal Called Man '72

Richard Ciupka(1950-)

Atlantic City '81
The Victory '81
Ilsa, the Tigress of Siberia '79

Josep Civit(1954-)

Shiver '08
People '04
Warriors '02
Gaudi Afternoon '01
The Sea Change '98
A House in the Hills '93
Iguana '89
Anguish '88

Ramiro Civita

Days and Clouds '07
The Girl by the Lake '07
Lost Embrace '04

Richard Clabaugh(1960-)

Deep Core '00
Escape under Pressure '00
Phantoms '97
The Prophecy 2: Ashtown '97
Children of the Corn 4: The Gathering '96
No Way Back '96
Plato's Run '96
The Prophecy '95
American Yakuza '94
Necromancer: Satan's Servant '88

David Claessen(1959-)

Bring It On: Fight to the Finish '09
Make It Happen '08
Diary of a Mad Black Woman '05
Love Song '00

Curtis Clark(1947-)

Dominick & Eugene '88
Extremities '86
Agatha Christie's Thirteen at Dinner '85
Sesame Street Presents: Follow That Bird '85

Daniel B. Clark(1890-1961)

Charlie Chan at Monte Carlo '37
Charlie Chan at the Olympics '37
Charlie Chan at the Circus '36
Charlie Chan in Egypt '35
Justice Rides Again '32
My Pal, the King '32
The Rider of Death Valley '32
The Black Camel '31

Matthew Clark

Day Zero '07
Never Forever '07
Bam Bam & Celeste '05
Evergreen '04
The Other Brother '02

Tony Clark(1966-)

Tempted '01
Innocence '00
Dance Me to My Song '98
The Quiet Room '96
Alien Visitor '95

Charles G. Clarke(1899-1983)

Flaming Star '60
The Hunters '58
Carousel '56
Black Widow '54
Suddenly '54
That Wonderful Urge '48
Captain from Castile '47
Miracle on 34th Street '47
Guadalcanal Diary '43
Moontide '42
Time to Kill '42
Dead Men Tell '41
Mr. Moto Takes a Vacation '39
Mr. Takes a Vacation '39
Charlie Chan in Honolulu '38
The Cat and the Fiddle '34
Tarzan and His Mate '34
Too Busy to Work '32

Ross Clarkson(1963-)

Direct Contact '09
Undisputed II: Last Man Standing '06
Derailed '02

Manuel Alberto Claro

Allegro '05
Reconstruction '03

Dominic Clemence

Like Father Like Son '05
Sirens '02

George T. Clemens(1902-93)

Big Brown Eyes '36
Klondike Annie '36

Denys Clerval

Erendira '83
Mississippi Mermaid '69
Stolen Kisses '68

Robert Cline

Thundering Gunslingers '44
The Return of the Rangers '43
Road Agent '26

Robert E. Cline(1898-1946)

Buffalo Bill Rides Again '47
Law of the Lash '47
Wild Country '47
Flaming Bullets '45
I Accuse My Parents '45
Three in the Saddle '45
Boss of Rawhide '44
The Drifter '44
The Monster Maker '44
The Black Raven '43
The Ghost and the Guest '43
Law of the Saddle '43
Raiders of Red Gap '43
Two-Fisted Justice '43
Rangers Take Over '42
Rock River Renegades '42
Thunder River Feud '42
Trail Riders '42
Saddle Mountain Roundup '41
The Duke Is Tops '38
Paroled to Die '37
The Spirit of Youth '37
The Lion Man '36
Stormy Trails '36
West of Nevada '36
Last of the Clintons '35
Roaring Roads '35
Wagon Trail '35

Wilfrid M. Cline(1903-76)

The Giant Gila Monster '59
The Killer Shrews '59
The First Texan '56
Calamity Jane '53
Bugles in the Afternoon '52
Painting the Clouds With Sunshine '51

Ghislan Cloquet(1925-82)

Four Friends '81
I Sent a Letter to My Love '81
Tess '79
Love and Death '75
Nathalie Granger '72
Donkey Skin '70
A Gentle Woman '69
Marry Me, Marry Me '69
The Young Girls of Rochefort '68
Mouchette '67
Mickey One '65
The Fire Within '64
Belle Americaine '61
Classe Tous Risque '60
Le Trou '59
Girl in His Pocket '57

William Clothier(1903-96)

Train Robbers '73
Big Jake '71
The Cheyenne Social Club '70
Chisum '70
Rio Lobo '70
The Undefeated '69
Bandolero! '68
The Devil's Brigade '68
Firecreek '68
Hellfighters '68
The War Wagon '67
The Way West '67
The Rare Breed '66
Shenandoah '65
Cheyenne Autumn '64
A Distant Trumpet '64
Donovan's Reef '63
McLintock! '63
The Man Who Shot Liberty Valance '62
Merrill's Marauders '62
The Comancheros '61
Deadly Companions '61
The Alamo '60
The Horse Soldiers '59
Darby's Rangers '58
Lafayette Escadrille '58
Bombers B-52 '57
Guns Don't Argue '57
Man in the Vault '56
Blood Alley '55
Sea Chase '55
Phantom from Space '53

Patrice Lucien Cochet

Player 5150 '08
The Good Life '07
L.A. Twister '04
Better Luck Tomorrow '02

Chuck Cohen

End Game '06
Love Don't Cost a Thing '03
Stark Raving Mad '02
In the Shadows '01
Hank Aaron: Chasing the Dream '95

Danny Cohen

Pirate Radio '09
Longford '06
This Is England '06
Dead Man's Shoes '04

Ted Cohen

Red Dirt '99
Yellow '98

Dominique Colin

Gradiva '06
Russian Dolls '05
L'Auberge Espagnole '02
I Stand Alone '98

Andy Collins(1961-)

David Copperfield '99
Little Voice '98
Brassed Off '96

Peter Lyons Collister(1956-)

Furry Vengeance '10
Alvin and the Chipmunks '07
Meet Bill '07
Garfield: A Tail of Two Kitties '06
The Amityville Horror '05
Win a Date with Tad Hamilton! '04
Master of Disguise '02
Mr. Deeds '02
The Animal '01
Deuce Bigalow: Male Gigolo '99
The Replacement Killers '98
The Beautician and the Beast '97
Dunston Checks In '95
Higher Learning '94
Poetic Justice '93
Livin' Large '91
Problem Child '90
All's Fair '89
Limit Up '89
Halloween 4: The Return of Michael Myers '88
Pulse '88
You Can't Hurry Love '88
Can't Buy Me Love '87
He's My Girl '87
Eye of the Tiger '86
Getting Even '86
The KGB: The Secret War '86
The Supernaturals '86
Avenging Angel '85
Odd Jobs '85

Roy Collodi

Just for the Hell of It '68
She-Devils on Wheels '68
The Girl, the Body and the Pill '67
Gruesome Twosome '67
Suburban Roulette '67

Ben Colman(1907-88)

Battlestar Galactica '78
The Norliss Tapes '73

Edward Colman(1905-95)

The Love Bug '68
The Ambushers '67
Blackbeard's Ghost '67
The Gnome-Mobile '67
The Happiest Millionaire '67
The Adventures of Bullwhip Griffin '66
Monkey's Uncle '65
That Darn Cat '65
Those Calloways '65
The Ugly Dachshund '65
Mary Poppins '64
The Misadventures of Merlin Jones '63
Savage Sam '63
Son of Flubber '63
Big Red '62
The Absent-Minded Professor '61
Babes in Toyland '61
The Shaggy Dog '59
Black Patch '57

Giovanni Fiore Coltellacci

Transporter 3 '08
O Jerusalem '07
Hostage '05
In Love and War '01

Fred Conde

Dolemite 2: Human Tornado '76
Too Hot to Handle '76
Deathhead Virgin '74
A Taste of Hell '73
The Big Doll House '71

David Connell

The Librarian: Curse of the Judas Chalice '08
December Boys '07
The Snow Walker '03
Disappearance '02
Sniper 2 '02
Stephen King's Rose Red '02
The Lost Empire '01
Don Quixote '00
Chameleon 2: Death Match '99
Cleopatra '99
Stephen King's The Storm of the Century '99
Moby Dick '98
Two for Texas '97
Robinson Crusoe '96
Stephen King's The Night Flier '96
Twilight Man '96
Zeus and Roxanne '96
Buffalo Girls '95
Silver Strand '95
The Ascent '94
Gross Misconduct '93
Heaven Tonight '93
Over the Hill '93
NeverEnding Story 2: The Next Chapter '91
Les Patterson Saves the World '90
What the Moon Saw '90
Slate, Wyn & Me '87
The Aviator '85
All the Rivers Run '84

John J. Connor

Kung Pow! Enter the Fist '02
A Night in the Life of Jimmy Reardon '88

Jack Conroy

Tick Tock '00
A Bright Shining Lie '98
Everything That Rises '98
The Magnificent Seven '98
The Nephew '97
Homeward Bound 2: Lost in San Francisco '96
Blind Justice '94
Broken Harvest '94
The Hunted '94
The Playboys '92
Silent Tongue '92
The Field '90
My Left Foot '89
Two by Forsyth '86

Alfio Contini(1927-)

Ripley's Game '02
Beyond the Clouds '95
The Night Porter '74
The Libertine '69

James A. Contner

Monkey Shines '88
The Last Dragon '85
The Flamingo Kid '84
Where the Boys Are '84 '84
Jaws 3 '83
Nighthawks '81
Cruising '80
Times Square '80

Fabio Conversi

Pedale Douce '96
Love After Love '94

Peter Coombs

The Norman Conquests, Part 1: Table Manners '78
The Norman Conquests, Part 2: Living Together '78

Denys Coop(1920-81)

And Now the Screaming Starts '73
Asylum '72
10 Rillington Place '71
King and Country '64
Billy Liar '63
The Mind Benders '63
This Sporting Life '63
A Kind of Loving '62

Arthur E. Cooper

Guns '08
Heater '99

Wilkie Cooper(1911-2001)

First Men in the Moon '64
Jason and the Argonauts '63
Maniac '63
The Mouse on the Moon '62
Mysterious Island '61
The Three Worlds of Gulliver '59
Sea of Sand '58
The Seventh Voyage of Sinbad '58
Abandon Ship '57
The Admirable Crichton '57
End of the Affair '55
Geordie '55
Captain Boycott '47
The Foreman Went to France '42

John Coquillon(1933-87)

Clockwise '86
Hold the Dream '86
The Last Place on Earth '85
Absolution '81
The Changeling '80
All Quiet on the Western Front '79
The Big Scam '79
Cross of Iron '76
Rentadick '72
Straw Dogs '72
Cry of the Banshee '70
Scream and Scream Again '70
Wuthering Heights '70
The Oblong Box '69
The Conqueror Worm '68

Gilles Corbeil

Balance of Power '96
Jungleground '95

Ericson Core

Invincible '06
Daredevil '03
The Fast and the Furious '01
Dancing at the Blue Iguana '00
Mumford '99
Payback '98
Exit in Red '97
187 '97
The Show '95

Charles Correll(1944-)

Revenge of the Nerds 2: Nerds in Paradise '87
Star Trek 3: The Search for Spock '84
Cheech and Chong's Nice Dreams '81
In God We Trust '80
National Lampoon's Animal House '78
The Last Contract '77

Stanley Cortez(1905-97)

The Bridge at Remagen '69
Ghost in the Invisible Bikini '66
Naked Kiss '64
They Saved Hitler's Brain '64
Shock Corridor '63
Dinosaurus! '60
The Angry Red Planet '59
The Three Faces of Eve '57
Top Secret Affair '57
The Night of the Hunter '55
Smart Woman '48
Since You Went Away '44
The Black Cat '41

Gianfilippo Corticelli

Saturn in Opposition '07
Facing Windows '03

Steve Cosens

The Tracey Fragments '07
Snow Cake '06

Andrew M. Costikyan

Bananas '71
The Beast from Haunted Cave '60
Ski Troop Attack '60

Paul Cotteret

The Twilight Girls '57
Mauvaise Graine '33

Michael Coulter

The Bank Job '08
Love Actually '03

Killing Me Softly *'01*
Mansfield Park *'99*
Notting Hill *'99*
My Giant *'98*
FairyTale: A True Story *'97*
The Neon Bible *'95*
Sense and Sensibility *'95*
Being Human *'94*
Four Weddings and a Funeral *'94*
Foreign Affairs *'93*
The Long Day Closes *'92*
Monster in a Box *'92*
Where Angels Fear to Tread *'91*
Dark Obsession *'90*
Breaking In *'89*
The Dressmaker *'89*
The Good Father *'87*
The Gospel According to Vic *'87*
Housekeeping *'87*
No Surrender *'86*
Gregory's Girl *'80*
That Sinking Feeling *'79*

Curt Courant

Monsieur Verdoux *'47*
De Mayerling a Sarajevo *'40*
La Bete Humaine *'38*
Spy of Napoleon *'36*
The Man Who Knew Too Much *'34*

Julian Court

Bloodlines *'05*
Carrie's War *'04*
Lady Audley's Secret *'00*
Heart *'99*

Raoul Coutard(1924-)

Dr. Bethune *'90*
Max, Mon Amour *'86*
Dangerous Moves *'84*
First Name: Carmen *'83*
Passion *'82*
Le Crabe Tambour *'77*
The Bride Wore Black *'68*
La Chinoise *'67*
The Defector *'66*
Two or Three Things I Know about Her *'66*
Alphaville *'65*
Hail Mafia *'65*
A Married Woman *'65*
Pierrot le Fou *'65*
The 317th Platoon *'65*
Band of Outsiders *'64*
Contempt *'64*
The Soft Skin *'64*
Une Femme Mariee *'64*
Les Carabiniers *'63*
Jules and Jim *'62*
My Life to Live *'62*
Shoot the Piano Player *'62*
Le Petit Soldat *'60*
A Woman Is a Woman *'60*
Breathless *'59*

Bernard Couture

Affinity *'08*
Picture This! *'08*
Sweetwater: A True Rock Story *'99*

Graeme Cowley

Utu *'83*
Carry Me Back *'82*

Jack Cox(1896-1960)

The Square Peg *'58*
Devil Girl from Mars *'54*
Mister Drake's Duck *'50*
The Magic Bow *'47*
We Dive at Dawn *'43*
The Ghost Train *'41*
The Lady Vanishes *'38*
No. 17 *'32*
Rich and Strange *'32*
Skin Game *'31*
Murder *'30*
Blackmail *'29*
The Manxman *'29*
The Farmer's Wife *'28*
The Ring *'27*

Vincent Cox

The Raven *'07*
Hooded Angels *'00*
Act of Piracy *'89*
Lethal Woman *'88*
The Demon *'81*
Chain Gang Killings *'80*

James A. Crabe(1931-89)

The Karate Kid: Part 2 *'86*
Night Shift *'82*
The China Syndrome *'79*
Sextette *'78*
The Disappearance of Aimee *'76*
Rocky *'76*
The Autobiography of Miss Jane Pittman *'74*

Arthur Crabtree(1900-75)

Waterloo Road *'44*
Hey! Hey! USA! *'38*

Jeff Cronenweth(1962-)

Down With Love *'03*
K-19: The Widowmaker *'02*
One Hour Photo *'02*
Fight Club *'99*

Jordan Cronenweth(1935-96)

Final Analysis *'92*
State of Grace *'90*
U2: Rattle and Hum *'88*
Gardens of Stone *'87*
Just Between Friends *'86*
Peggy Sue Got Married *'86*
Stop Making Sense *'84*
Best Friends *'82*
Blade Runner *'82*
Cutter's Way *'81*
Altered States *'80*
And I Alone Survived *'78*
One in a Million: The Ron LeFlore Story *'78*
Citizens Band *'77*
Rolling Thunder *'77*
The Front Page *'74*
Zandy's Bride *'74*
Birds of Prey *'72*
Brewster McCloud *'70*

Edward Cronjager(1904-60)

Beneath the 12-Mile Reef *'53*
Bloodhounds of Broadway *'52*
On Our Merry Way *'48*
Canyon Passage *'46*
Colonel Effingham's Raid *'45*
I Wake Up Screaming *'41*
Everything Happens at Night *'39*
No Other Woman *'33*
Lost Squadron *'32*

Henry Cronjager(1877-1967)

Ace of Aces *'33*
No Marriage Ties *'33*
The Love Light *'21*
Tol'able David *'21*
Daddy Long Legs *'19*

Henry Cronjager, Jr. (1906-91)

The Ballad of Andy Crocker *'69*
Over the Hill Gang *'69*
Hands of a Stranger *'62*

William Cronjager(1930-95)

Baby Broker *'81*
Dynasty *'76*
How to Seduce a Woman *'74*
Spitfire *'34*

Floyd Crosby(1899-1985)

Fireball 500 *'66*
Beach Blanket Bingo *'65*
How to Stuff a Wild Bikini *'65*
Bikini Beach *'64*
The Comedy of Terrors *'64*
Pajama Party *'64*
The Raven *'63*
Sallah *'63*
X: The Man with X-Ray Eyes *'63*
Premature Burial *'62*
Tales of Terror *'62*
The Pit and the Pendulum *'61*
The Fall of the House of Usher *'60*
Crime and Punishment, USA *'59*
I, Mobster *'58*
Machine Gun Kelly *'58*
The Old Man and the Sea *'58*
Teenage Caveman *'58*
Carnival Rock *'57*
Reform School Girl *'57*
Rock All Night *'57*
Teenage Doll *'57*
Shack Out on 101 *'55*
The Fast and the Furious *'54*
Monster from the Ocean Floor *'54*
The Fighter *'52*
High Noon *'52*
Tabu: A Story of the South Seas *'31*

Nat Crosby

Paper Mask *'91*
Northanger Abbey *'87*
In the Secret State *'85*

Eric Cross

Three Men in a Boat *'56*
Mr. Reeder in Room 13 *'38*
Song of Freedom *'36*
The Mystery of the Mary Celeste *'35*
Matinee Idol *'33*

Malcolm Cross

Range of Motion *'00*
Treacherous Beauties *'94*

Denis Crossan

The Pink Panther 2 *'09*
Agent Cody Banks 2: Destination London *'04*
Agent Cody Banks *'03*
The Hole *'01*
Me Without You *'01*
I Know What You Did Last Summer *'97*
Incognito *'97*
Killer Tongue *'96*
The Real McCoy *'93*
A Murder of Quality *'90*

Richard Crudo

Pistol Whipped *'08*
Brooklyn Rules *'07*
Bring It On Again *'03*
Grind *'03*
Down to Earth *'01*
Out Cold *'01*
In Pursuit *'00*
American Pie *'99*
Outside Providence *'99*
Bongwater *'98*
Music from Another Room *'97*
Persons Unknown *'96*
American Buffalo *'95*
The Low Life *'95*
Federal Hill *'94*

Luis Cuadrado(1934-80)

Spirit of the Beehive *'73*
Bronson's Revenge *'72*
What the Peeper Saw *'72*

R(aul) P. Cubero

The Grandfather *'98*
Icebox Murders *'82*
Shark Hunter *'79*

Dean Cundey(1946-)

The Spy Next Door *'10*
Whisper *'07*
The Holiday *'06*
Garfield: The Movie *'04*
Looney Tunes: Back in Action *'03*
What Women Want *'00*
Krippendorf's Tribe *'98*
The Parent Trap *'98*
Flubber *'97*
Apollo 13 *'95*
Casper *'95*
The Flintstones *'94*
Jurassic Park *'93*
Death Becomes Her *'92*
Hook *'91*
Nothing But Trouble *'91*
Back to the Future, Part 3 *'90*
Back to the Future, Part 2 *'89*
Road House *'89*
Big Business *'88*
Who Framed Roger Rabbit *'88*
Project X *'87*
Big Trouble in Little China *'86*
Back to the Future *'85*
Warning Sign *'85*
D.C. Cab *'84*
It Came Upon a Midnight Clear *'84*
Romancing the Stone *'84*
M.A.D.D.: Mothers Against Drunk Driving *'83*
Psycho 2 *'83*
Halloween 3: Season of the Witch *'82*
Separate Ways *'82*
The Thing *'82*
Escape from New York *'81*
Halloween 2: The Nightmare Isn't Over! *'81*
Jaws of Satan *'81*
Galaxina *'80*
Angel's Brigade *'79*
Rock 'n' Roll High School *'79*
Roller Boogie *'79*
The Fog *'78*
Halloween *'78*
Bare Knuckles *'77*
Satan's Cheerleaders *'77*
Ilsa, Harem Keeper of the Oil Sheiks *'76*
Trained to Kill, U.S.A. *'75*
Where the Red Fern Grows *'74*

Jan Curik

Transport from Paradise *'65*
The Gleiwitz Case *'61*

Alec Curtis

Horatio Hornblower *'99*
Hostile Waters *'97*
Rhodes *'97*

Oliver Curtis

American Virgin *'09*
Death at a Funeral *'07*
The Wedding Date *'05*
Owning Mahowny *'03*
Bait *'02*
Vanity Fair *'99*
Immortality *'98*
Love and Death on Long Island *'97*
Madagascar Skin *'95*

Jeff Cutter

A Nightmare on Elm Street *'10*
Orphan *'09*

Henryk Cymerman

Brothers Three *'07*
To the Limit *'95*

Stefan Czapsky

Fighting *'09*
Blades of Glory *'07*
Bulletproof Monk *'03*
Matilda *'96*
Ed Wood *'94*
Batman Returns *'92*
Prelude to a Kiss *'92*
Child's Play 2 *'90*
Edward Scissorhands *'90*
Last Exit to Brooklyn *'90*
Sons *'89*
The Thin Blue Line *'88*
Vampire's Kiss *'88*

Erik Daarstad

Zertigo Diamond Caper *'82*
The Exiles *'61*

Stephen Dade(1909-)

The Viking Queen *'67*
Night Caller from Outer Space *'66*
Zulu *'64*
Coast of Skeletons *'63*
The Obsessed *'51*

Francois Dagenais

The National Tree *'09*
Charlie & Me *'08*
Daniel's Daughter *'08*
Stir of Echoes 2: The Homecoming *'07*
Cube: Zero *'04*
The Rendering *'02*

Yves Dahan

Face the Music *'92*
For Better and for Worse *'92*
May Wine *'90*

Ake Dahlqvist

June Night *'40*
Intermezzo *'36*

Laurent Dailland(1956-)

The Taste of Others *'00*
East-West *'99*
Place Vendome *'98*
Train of Life *'98*
Perfect Love *'96*
36 Fillete *'88*

Massimo Dallamano(1917-76)

For a Few Dollars More *'65*
A Fistful of Dollars *'64*
Gunfight at Red Sands *'63*

John Daly

Lila Says *'04*
Me & Mrs. Jones *'02*
Greenfingers *'00*
The Railway Children *'00*
Essex Boys *'99*
A Royal Scandal *'96*
Persuasion *'95*

Arch R. Dalzell(1911-92)

The Boy in the Plastic Bubble *'76*
The Trip *'67*
Tower of London *'62*
Little Shop of Horrors *'60*

Dennis Dalzell

The Betty Ford Story *'87*
Bustin' Loose *'81*

Joe D'Amato(1936-99)

Endgame *'85*
Trap Them & Kill Them *'77*
The Arena *'73*
Escape from Death Row *'73*
Heroes in Hell *'73*
Fistful of Death *'71*

David Daniel

Love and Other Four Letter Words *'07*
The Night of the White Pants *'06*
Leprechaun 6: Back 2 Tha Hood *'03*

Lee Daniel(1962-)

Fast Food Nation *'06*
Before Sunset *'04*
Rift *'96*
subUrbia *'96*
...And God Spoke *'94*
Before Sunrise *'94*
Dazed and Confused *'93*
Slacker *'91*

Arthur Daniels

Terror House *'97*
Feeders *'96*

William H. Daniels(1895-1970)

Marlowe *'69*
In Like Flint *'67*
Valley of the Dolls *'67*
Assault on a Queen *'66*
Marriage on the Rocks *'65*
Von Ryan's Express *'65*
Robin and the 7 Hoods *'64*
Come Blow Your Horn *'63*
The Prize *'63*
Back Street *'61*
Come September *'61*
Can-Can *'60*
Ocean's 11 *'60*
A Hole in the Head *'59*
Never So Few *'59*
Cat on a Hot Tin Roof *'58*
Some Came Running *'58*
Istanbul *'57*
My Man Godfrey *'57*
Night Passage *'57*
Away All Boats *'56*
Far Country *'55*
Strategic Air Command *'55*
The Glenn Miller Story *'54*
Thunder Bay *'53*
Pat and Mike *'52*
Harvey *'50*
Three Came Home *'50*
Winchester '73 *'50*
For the Love of Mary *'48*
The Naked City *'48*
Brute Force *'47*
Lured *'47*
Girl Crazy *'43*
Keeper of the Flame *'42*
Back Street *'41*
So Ends Our Night *'41*
The Mortal Storm *'40*
The Shop Around the Corner *'40*
Idiot's Delight *'39*
Ninotchka *'39*
Marie Antoinette *'38*
Broadway Melody of 1938 *'37*
The Last Gangster *'37*
Camille *'36*
Romeo and Juliet *'36*
Rose Marie *'36*
Anna Karenina *'35*
Naughty Marietta *'35*
The Barretts of Wimpole Street *'34*
The Painted Veil *'34*
Dinner at Eight *'33*
Queen Christina *'33*
Rasputin and the Empress *'33*
Grand Hotel *'32*
Mata Hari *'32*
A Free Soul *'31*
Susan Lenox: Her Fall and Rise *'31*
Anna Christie *'30*
Romance *'30*
The Kiss *'29*
A Lady of Chance *'28*
A Lady of Chance *'28*
The Mysterious Lady *'28*
Wild Orchids *'28*
The Flesh and the Devil *'27*
Bardelys the Magnificent *'26*
The Boob *'26*
The Boob *'26*
The Temptress *'26*
Foolish Wives *'22*

Steve Danyluk

It's a Boy Girl Thing *'06*
The Skulls 2 *'02*

John Darbonne

Bone Dry *'07*
Perception *'06*
National Lampoon's Adam & Eve *'05*

Jeff Darling

The Crossing *'92*
Young Einstein *'89*

Tobias Datum

Amreeka *'09*
How the Garcia Girls Spent Their Summer *'05*

Allen Davey(1894-1946)

Hollywood Cavalcade *'39*
Eyes Right! *'26*

Allen Daviau(1942-)

Van Helsing *'04*
The Astronaut's Wife *'99*
Congo *'95*
Fearless *'93*
Bugsy *'91*
Defending Your Life *'91*
Avalon *'90*
Empire of the Sun *'87*
Harry and the Hendersons *'87*
The Color Purple *'85*
The Falcon and the Snowman *'85*

Harry Tracy '83
Legs '83
Twilight Zone: The Movie '83
E.T.: The Extra-Terrestrial '82
Rage '80
The Streets of L.A. '79

Zoltan David(1955-)
Hitman's Run '99
The Colony '98
Row Your Boat '98
Redline '97
Donor Unknown '95
The Last Word '95
My Teacher's Wife '95

Andrew Davis(1946-)
Over the Edge '79
Private Parts '72

Benjamin Davis
Kick-Ass '10
Incendiary '08
Hannibal Rising '07
Stardust '07
Virgin Territory '07
Imagine Me & You '06
Layer Cake '05
Miranda '01
Sleepaway Camp '83

Elliot Davis
Personal Effects '09
Surfer, Dude '08
Twilight '08
The Nativity Story '06
Lords of Dogtown '05
A Love Song for Bobby Long '04
Legally Blonde 2: Red White & Blonde '03
Thirteen '03
40 Days and 40 Nights '02
White Oleander '02
Happy Campers '01
I Am Sam '01
The Next Best Thing '00
Forces of Nature '99
Light It Up '99
Breakfast of Champions '98
Finding Graceland '98
Out of Sight '98
Get On the Bus '96
Larger Than Life '96
Lawn Dogs '96
Nightjohn '96
The Glass Shield '95
Things to Do in Denver When You're Dead '95
The Underneath '95
The Air Up There '94
Mother's Boys '94
Equinox '93
The Cutting Edge '92
Mr. Write '92
Shakes the Clown '92
Mortal Thoughts '91
Bloodhounds of Broadway '89
Love at Large '89
Signs of Life '89
Miles from Home '88
Summer Heat '87
Vamp '86

Michael J. Davis
A Woman, Her Men and Her Futon '92
Riders '88

Mohammad Davudi
Baran '01
The Color of Paradise '99

Ernest Day(1927-2006)
Parents '89
A Passage to India '84
Revenge of the Pink Panther '78

Acacio De Almeida(1938-)
Yerma '99
In the White City '83

Ricardo De Angelis(1948-)
A Place in the World '92
Man Facing Southeast '86

Gerard de Battista
Roman de Gare '07
A Secret '07
La Petite Lili '03
Venus Beauty Institute '98
French Twist '95
The Rascals '81

Jan De Bont(1943-)
Basic Instinct '92
Lethal Weapon 3 '92
Shining Through '92
Flatliners '90
The Hunt for Red October '90
Total Recall '90
Bert Rigby, You're a Fool '89
Black Rain '89
Die Hard '88
Leonard Part 6 '87
RoboCop '87
Who's That Girl? '87
The Clan of the Cave Bear '86
Jumpin' Jack Flash '86
Ruthless People '86
Flesh and Blood '85
The Jewel of the Nile '85
Bad Manners '84
All the Right Moves '83
Cujo '83
I'm Dancing as Fast as I Can '82
Spetters '80
The 4th Man '79
Soldier of Orange '78
Katie Tippel '75
Private Lessons '75
Turkish Delight '73
Business is Business '71

John de Borman(1954-)
An Education '09
Last Chance Harvey '08
Miss Pettigrew Lives for a Day '08
A Lot Like Love '05
Tara Road '05
Ella Enchanted '04
Shall We Dance? '04
The Guru '02
Pure '02
Serendipity '01
Hamlet '00
Saving Grace '00
Hideous Kinky '99
The Mighty '98
Photographing Fairies '97
The Full Monty '96
Trojan Eddie '96
Death Machine '95
The Passion of Darkly Noon '95
Small Faces '95

Cian de Buitlear
Blow Dry '00
I Went Down '97

Robert De Grasse(1900-71)
The Clay Pigeon '49
Home of the Brave '49
The Body Snatcher '45
George White's Scandals '45
Step Lively '44
Forever and a Day '43
The Leopard Man '43
Lucky Partners '40
Having a Wonderful Time '38

Bruno de Keyzer(1949-)
In the Electric Mist '08
About Adam '00
North Star '96
The Ogre '96
Victory '95
War of the Buttons '95
Afraid of the Dark '92
December Bride '91
Impromptu '90
Life and Nothing But '89
Beatrice '88
Little Dorrit, Film 1: Nobody's Fault '88
Little Dorrit, Film 2: Little Dorrit's Story '88
Reunion '88
The Murders in the Rue Morgue '86
Round Midnight '86
Sincerely Charlotte '86
A Sunday in the Country '84

Kiko de la Rica
Guantanamero '07
Torremolinos 73 '03
Sex and Lucia '01

Axel de Roche
The Nasty Girl '90
The White Rose '83

Pasqualino De Santis(1927-96)
The Truce '96
A Month by the Lake '95
The Palermo Connection '91
Salome '85
Misunderstood '84
Sheena '84
L'Argent '83
Immortal Bachelor '80
Three Brothers '80
Christ Stopped at Eboli '79
The Devil, Probably '77
A Special Day '77
The Innocent '76
Conversation Piece '75
Lancelot of the Lake '74
Lucky Luciano '74
Assassination of Trotsky '72
Death in Venice '71
Romeo and Juliet '68

Jean De Segonzac
Homicide: The Movie '00
Path to Paradise '97
Normal Life '96
Confessions of Sorority Girls '94
Girls in Prison '94
Shake, Rattle & Rock! '94
Laws of Gravity '92

Clyde De Vinna(1890-1953)
Jungle '52
Immortal Sergeant '43
Whistling in Dixie '42
Of Human Hearts '38
Ah, Wilderness! '35
Tarzan and His Mate '34
Treasure Island '34
Tarzan, the Ape Man '32
Politics '31
Trader Horn '31
White Shadows in the South Seas '29
Ben-Hur '26

Roger Deakins(1949-)
A Serious Man '09
Doubt '08
The Reader '08
Revolutionary Road '08
The Assassination of Jesse James by the Coward Robert Ford '07
In the Valley of Elah '07
No Country for Old Men '07
Jarhead '05
The Ladykillers '04
The Village '04
House of Sand and Fog '03
Intolerable Cruelty '03
Levity '03
A Beautiful Mind '01
The Man Who Wasn't There '01
O Brother Where Art Thou? '00
Anywhere But Here '99
The Hurricane '99
The Siege '98
The Big Lebowski '97
Kundun '97
Courage Under Fire '96
Fargo '96
Dead Man Walking '95
Rob Roy '95
The Shawshank Redemption '94
The Hudsucker Proxy '93
The Secret Garden '93
Passion Fish '92
Thunderheart '92
Barton Fink '91
Homicide '91
Air America '90
Mountains of the Moon '90
The Long Walk Home '89
Pascali's Island '88
Stormy Monday '88
White Mischief '88
The Kitchen Toto '87
Personal Services '87
Shadey '87
Sid & Nancy '86
Defense of the Realm '85
Return to Waterloo '85
1984 '84
Another Time, Another Place '83

Faxon M. Dean(1890-1965)
Texas Pioneers '32
The Nevada Buckaroo '31
Braveheart '25

Seamus Deasy
The Tiger's Tale '06
The Mighty Celt '05
In My Country '04
Benedict Arnold: A Question of Honor '03
The Seventh Stream '01
An Everlasting Piece '00
When the Sky Falls '99
The General '98

Benoit Debie
The Runaways '10
Carriers '09
New York, I Love You '09
Joshua '07
Day Night Day Night '06

Henri Decae(1915-87)
Exposed '83
Le Professionnel '81
The Island '80
The Boys from Brazil '78
Bobby Deerfield '77
Don Juan (Or If Don Juan Were a Woman) '73
Light at the Edge of the World '71
Joe '70
Le Cercle Rouge '70
Castle Keep '69
Le Samourai '67
The Thief of Paris '67
Viva Maria! '65
Joy House '64
Les Bonnes Femmes '60
Purple Noon '60
The 400 Blows '59
Frantic '58
Bob le Flambeur '55
La Silence de la Mer '47

Anghel Decca
Midnight Bayou '09
Hangin' with the Homeboys '91

Jackson Deerson
When the Line Goes Through '73
Two Lane Blacktop '71

Gina DeGirolamo
Gypsy 83 '01
Edge of Seventeen '99
Jerome '98

Thomas Del Ruth(1942-)
Kissing a Fool '98
Asteroid '97
Leave It to Beaver '97
JAG '95
Next Door '94
Barbarians at the Gate '93
Dead to Rights '93
The Mighty Ducks '92
T Bone N Weasel '92
Look Who's Talking, Too '90
The Running Man '87
Stand by Me '86
The Breakfast Club '85
Impulse '84
Get Crazy '83
Hysterical '83
Motel Hell '80

Bruno Delbonnel
Harry Potter and the Half-Blood Prince '09
Across the Universe '07
Infamous '06
Paris, je t'aime '06
A Very Long Engagement '04
Amelie '01
The Cat's Meow '01

Benoit Delhomme(1961-)
Shanghai '09
The Boy in the Striped Pajamas '08
1408 '07
Breaking and Entering '06
The Proposition '05
The Merchant of Venice '04
Mortal Transfer '01
What Time Is It There? '01
Sade '00
Miss Julie '99
The Loss of Sexual Innocence '98
The Winslow Boy '98
Artemisia '97
Un Air de Famille '96
When the Cat's Away '96
Cyclo '95
The Scent of Green Papaya '93

Franco Delli Colli(1929-2004)
Macabre '80
The Last Man on Earth '64

Tonino Delli Colli(1922-2005)
Life Is Beautiful '98
Death and the Maiden '94
Bitter Moon '92
Intervista '87
Ginger & Fred '86
The Name of the Rose '86
Once Upon a Time in America '84
Tales of Ordinary Madness '83
Lovers and Liars '81
Seven Beauties '76
Salo, or the 120 Days of Sodom '75
The Canterbury Tales '71
The Decameron '70
Porcile '69
Murder for Sale '68
Once Upon a Time in the West '68
Spirits of the Dead '68
The Good, the Bad and the Ugly '67
The Gospel According to St. Matthew '64
Love Meetings '64
Mamma Roma '62
Accatone! '61

Frank DeMarco
Peter and Vandy '09
Spring Breakdown '08
Beerfest '06
Delirious '06
Hedwig and the Angry Inch '00
Habit '97

Peter Deming(1957-)
Last Night '10
Drag Me to Hell '09
The Love Guru '08
Lucky You '07
Married Life '07
The Jacket '05
Rumor Has It... '05
I Heart Huckabees '04
Twisted '04
Austin Powers In Goldmember '02
People I Know '02
From Hell '01
Mulholland Drive '01
If These Walls Could Talk 2 '00
Scream 3 '00
Music of the Heart '99
Mystery, Alaska '99
Austin Powers: International Man of Mystery '97
Scream 2 '97
Joe's Apartment '96
Lost Highway '96
Cosmic Slop '94
National Lampoon's Loaded Weapon 1 '93
Son-in-Law '93
My Cousin Vinny '92
House Party '90
From Hollywood to Deadwood '89
It Takes Two '88
The Carrier '87
Evil Dead 2: Dead by Dawn '87
Hollywood Shuffle '87

John L. (Ndiaga) Demps, Jr.
Phat Girlz '06
Finding Buck McHenry '00
The Visit '00
The Three Lives of Karen '97
The Show '95
Fear of a Black Hat '94
The Inkwell '94
The Walking Dead '94
Street Wars '91

Austin Dempster(1921-75)
A Touch of Class '73
Bedazzled '68

Daniil Demutsky(1893-1954)
Earth '30
Arsenal '29

Jim Denault(1960-)
Dinner for Schmucks '10
She's Out of My League '10
Hounddog '08
Recount '08
The Sisterhood of the Traveling Pants 2 '08
Freedom Writers '07
The Night of the White Pants '06
Heights '04
Maria Full of Grace '04
City of Ghosts '03
Real Women Have Curves '02
The Believer '01
Our Song '01
Chasing Sleep '00
Double Parked '00
Boys Don't Cry '99
The Eternal '99
A Good Baby '99
The Taxman '98
Clockwatchers '97
Breathing Room '96
Illtown '96
Sudden Manhattan '96
Nadja '95
River of Grass '94

Simon Dennis
Octane '07
Nina's Heavenly Delights '06

Thomas Denove
Flexing with Monty '10
Secret Games '92
Puppet Master 2 '90
Fanatic '82

Hap Depew(1887-1940)
Man from Headquarters '28
Ships in the Night '28

Kamal Derkaoui
Santa Buddies '09
Poison Ivy 4: The Secret Society '08
Space Buddies '08
Firefight '03

Benjamin Dernbecker
Eight Miles High '08
Eight Miles High '07

Alain Derobe
We Will Not Enter the Forest '79

Sexus '64

Joe DeSalvo

The Alphabet Killer '08
Fever '99
Fall '97
All Over Me '96
The Wife '95
What Happened Was... '94
Joey Breaker '93

Paul Desatoff

Animal Instincts '92
Carnal Crimes '91

Caleb Deschanel(1941-)

Killshot '09
My Sister's Keeper '09
The Spiderwick Chronicles '08
Ask the Dust '06
National Treasure '04
The Passion of the Christ '04
The Hunted '03
Timeline '03
The Patriot '00
Anna and the King '99
The Haunting '99
Hope Floats '98
Message in a Bottle '98
Fly Away Home '96
It Could Happen to You '94
The Slugger's Wife '85
The Natural '84
The Right Stuff '83
Being There '79
The Black Stallion '79
More American Graffiti '79
A Woman under the Influence '74

Laurent Desmet

Shall We Kiss? '07
Shall We Kiss? '07

James Desmond

Only the Strong Survive '03
Moon over Broadway '98

Dennis Devine

Bloodstream '00
Chain of Souls '00
Vampire Night '00
Merchants of Death '99
Decay '98
Vampire Time Travelers '98

Franco Di Giacomo(1932-)

The Sky Is Falling '00
Foreign Student '94
The Postman '94
The Jeweller's Shop '90
Dark Eyes '87
Amityville 2: The Possession '82
Fighting Back '82
The Night of the Shooting Stars '82
The Sex Machine '75
Four Flies on Grey Velvet '72

Mario Di Leo

See Mario DiLeo

Carlo Di Palma(1925-2004)

Deconstructing Harry '97
Everyone Says I Love You '96
The Monster '96
Mighty Aphrodite '95
Bullets over Broadway '94
Manhattan Murder Mystery '93
Husbands and Wives '92
Shadows and Fog '92
Alice '90
September '88
Radio Days '87
The Secret of My Success '87
Hannah and Her Sisters '86
Off Beat '86
Gabriela '84
The Black Stallion Returns '83
The Appointment '82

Identification of a Woman '82
The Tragedy of a Ridiculous Man '81
Blow-Up '66
The Red Desert '64
Divorce—Italian Style '62
That Long Night in '43 '60

Dario Di Palma

Down & Dirty '76
Seduction of Mimi '72
The Clowns '71

Roxanne Di Santo

Frankenstein and Me '96
Kids of the Round Table '96

Gianni Di Venanzo(1920-66)

The Eclipse '66
Juliet of the Spirits '65
10th Victim '65
8 1/2 '63
Eva '62
La Notte '60
Big Deal on Madonna Street '58
Il Grido '57
Love in the City '53

James Diamond(1894-1936)

Circle of Death '36
Suicide Squad '35
Sucker Money '34
Woman Condemned '33
Night Rider '32
They Never Come Back '32
The Road to Ruin '28

Gabriel Diaz

En la Cama '05
The Sacred Family '04

Jimmy Dibling

Dreaming of Joseph Lees '99
Relative Values '99

Tom DiCillo(1954-)

Coffee and Cigarettes '03
Stranger than Paradise '84
Variety '83

Ernest R. Dickerson(1952-)

Our America '02
Jungle Fever '91
Def by Temptation '90
Mo' Better Blues '90
Do the Right Thing '89
School Daze '88
She's Gotta Have It '86
Joe's Bed-Stuy Barbershop: We Cut Heads '83

Desmond Dickinson(1902-86)

Tower of Evil '72
The Bloodsuckers '70
The Frightened City '61
The Hands of Orlac '60
Horror Hotel '60
Fire Down Below '57
The Importance of Being Earnest '52
Morning Departure '50
The Woman in Question '50
Hamlet '48
Thursday's Child '43

Billy Dickson

Halloween 6: The Curse of Michael Myers '95
Tainted Blood '93
Chrome Soldiers '92
The Secret Passion of Robert Clayton '92
Victim of Love '91

Mario DiLeo

When I Find the Ocean '06
Sudie & Simpson '90
Hell Hunters '87
Nightmares '83
The Evil '78
Breaker! Breaker! '77

Bill Dill

Dancing in September '00
B.A.P.'s '97

The Five Heartbeats '91

Phillip W. Dingeldein(1954-)

Real Time: Siege at Lucas Street Market '00
Mommy 2: Mommy's Day '96
Mommy '95

Andrew Dintenfass

Cowboy Up '00
Dancer, Texas—Pop. 81 '98
The Cure '95
About Last Night... '86

John Dirlam

On the Edge '02
Raven '97

George E. Diskant(1907-65)

Kansas City Confidential '52
David Harding, Counterspy '50
The Traveling Saleswoman '50
They Live by Night '49
Dick Tracy vs. Cueball '46

Irl Dixon

The Bone Yard '90
Trapper County War '89

Mark Doering-Powell

Seeing Other People '04
One Last Ride '03
The Trial of Old Drum '00
Treehouse Hostage '99
Telling You '98

Sergio d'Offizi(1934-)

Cannibal Holocaust '80
The Squeeze '80
Don't Torture a Duckling '72
Summer Affair '71

Mike Dolgetta

Throw Down '00
Final Exam '98

Raul Dominguez

The Fear Chamber '68
The Sinister Invasion '68

Peter Donahue

$5 a Day '08
Gigantic '08
Then She Found Me '07
Junebug '05
The Fog of War: Eleven Lessons from the Life of Robert S. McNamara '03

Harris Done(1963-)

Forbidden Games '95
Sinful Intrigue '95

Robert Doran

Children of the Wild '37
Racing Blood '36

Bruce Dorfman

Raw Target '95
An American Summer '90
Bloodfist 2 '90

Alan Dostie(1943-)

Silk '07
Nuremberg '00
The Red Violin '98
The Confessional '95
32 Short Films about Glenn Gould '93
Iron Eagle 2 '88

Dermott Downs

Sublime '07
Dracula: The Dark Prince '01

Christopher Doyle(1952-)

The Limits of Control '09
Ashes of Time Redux '08
Downloading Nancy '08
Paranoid Park '07
Lady in the Water '06
Paris, je t'aime '06
Perhaps Love '05
The White Countess '05
Eros '04
Three ... Extremes '04

2046 '04
Hero '03
Last Life in the Universe '03
The Quiet American '02
Rabbit-Proof Fence '02
3 Extremes 2 '02
Made '01
Andromedia '00
In the Mood for Love '00
Liberty Heights '99
Psycho '98
Happy Together '96
Temptress Moon '96
Chungking Express '95
Fallen Angels '95
Ashes of Time '94
Days of Being Wild '91

David Doyle

Into Temptation '09
Vernie '04

John Drake

My Faraway Bride '06
Hellraiser: Hellseeker '02

Rob Draper

Trucks '97
The Assassination File '96
The Spitfire Grill '95
Sex, Love and Cold Hard Cash '93
Stalking Laura '93
Dr. Giggles '92
Undesirable '92
Tales from the Darkside: The Movie '90
Halloween 5: The Revenge of Michael Myers '89

Roland Dressel(1932-)

The Woman and the Stranger '84
Jadup and Boel '81

Jean-Marie Dreujou

My Best Friend '06
Two Brothers '04
Balzac and the Little Chinese Seamstress '02
The Man on the Train '02
The Girl on the Bridge '98
Augustin '95

Randy Drummond

Series 7: The Contenders '01
Anima '98
Welcome to the Dollhouse '95

Stuart Dryburgh(1952-)

Amelia '09
Nim's Island '08
No Reservations '07
The Painted Veil '06
Aeon Flux '05
The Beautiful Country '04
The Recruit '03
Bridget Jones's Diary '01
Kate & Leopold '01
Shaft '00
Runaway Bride '99
Analyze This '98
Poodle Springs '98
Portrait of a Lady '96
Lone Star '95
Once Were Warriors '94
The Perez Family '94
The Piano '93
An Angel at My Table '89

Christopher Duddy

The Wizard of Gore '07
All Souls Day '05

Georges Dufaux(1927-)

Le Polygraphe '96
A Wind from Wyoming '94

Guy Dufaux(1943-)

The Barbarian Invasions '03
Napoleon '03
The Great Gatsby '01
Love the Hard Way '01
Stardom '00
Eye of the Beholder '99
One Special Night '99
Polish Wedding '97
Jesus of Montreal '89

Bryan Duggan

T.N.T. '98

Plan 10 from Outer Space '95
Rubin & Ed '92
Cold Feet '89
P.I. Private Investigations '87

Keith J. Duggan

Route 30 '08
Soul's Midnight '06
BachelorMan '03

Simon Duggan(1959-)

Knowing '09
The Mummy: Tomb of the Dragon Emperor '08
Restraint '08
Live Free or Die Hard '07
Underworld: Evolution '05
I, Robot '04
Garage Days '03
Risk '00
The Interview '98

Donald Duncan

The Cheetah Girls: One World '08
Jack Be Nimble '94

Albert J. Dunk

Dr. Dolittle: Million Dollar Mutts '09
Anonymous Rex '04
The Inspectors 2: A Shred of Evidence '00
Mail to the Chief '00
Trial by Media '00
The Happy Face Murders '99
Must Be Santa '99
The Pooch and the Pauper '99
The Inspectors '98
Flashfire '94
Class of 1984 '82
Incubus '82

David M. Dunlap

Griffin & Phoenix '06
Game 6 '05
Shaun of the Dead '04

Andrew Dunn

Extraordinary Measures '10
Precious: Based on the Novel by Sapphire '09
Good '08
Hot Rod '07
The History Boys '06
Miss Potter '06
Hitch '05
Mrs. Henderson Presents '05
Stage Beauty '04
The Company '03
What a Girl Wants '03
The Count of Monte Cristo '02
Sweet Home Alabama '02
Gosford Park '01
Monkeybone '01
Liam '00
Ordinary Decent Criminal '99
Ever After: A Cinderella Story '98
Hush '98
Practical Magic '98
Addicted to Love '96
The Crucible '96
Grave Indiscretions '96
The Madness of King George '94
The Bodyguard '92
L.A. Story '91
Strapless '90
Death by Prescription '86

Edwin DuPar(1885-1961)

Lone Ranger '56
I Was a Communist for the FBI '51
The Better 'Ole '26

Elmer Dyer(1892-1970)

Air Force '43
Lightning Strikes West '40
The Flying Deuces '39
Night Flight '33
Hell's Angels '30

Paul Eagler(1890-1961)

The Hurricane '37
Tess of the Storm Country '22

John Ealer

Towards Darkness '07
Pope Dreams '06

Mark Eberle

Flight of the Living Dead: Outbreak on a Plane '07
Latin Dragon '03

Pawel Edelman(1958-)

The Ghost Writer '10
New York, I Love You '09
Katyn '07
The Life Before Her Eyes '07
All the King's Men '06
Oliver Twist '05
Ray '04
The Pianist '02
Zemsta '02

Arthur Edeson(1891-1970)

The Mask of Dimitrios '44
Across the Pacific '42
Casablanca '42
The Male Animal '42
The Maltese Falcon '41
Castle on the Hudson '40
Each Dawn I Die '39
Gold Diggers of 1937 '36
The Invisible Man '33
The Old Dark House '32
Frankenstein '31
All Quiet on the Western Front '30
The Lost World '25
Robin Hood '22
The Three Musketeers '21
The Eyes of Youth '19

Sebastian Edscmid

The Last Station '09
Adam Resurrected '08

Eric Alan Edwards(1953-)

Couples Retreat '09
Love Happens '09
Management '09
Fragments '08
First Snow '07
Knocked Up '07
The Break-Up '06
The Heart Is Deceitful Above All Things '04
How to Deal '03
Crossroads '02
The Slaughter Rule '01
On the Edge '00
Another Day in Paradise '98
Clay Pigeons '98
Cop Land '97
Flirting with Disaster '95
Kids '95
To Die For '95
Even Cowgirls Get the Blues '94
My Own Private Idaho '91

David Eggby(1950-)

Underdog '07
The Marine '06
Racing Stripes '05
Eurotrip '04
Monte Walsh '03
Scooby-Doo '02
Crossfire Trail '01
Pitch Black '00
Blue Streak '99
Virus '98
Daylight '96
Dragonheart '96
Lightning Jack '94
Dragon: The Bruce Lee Story '93
Fortress '93
Harley Davidson and the Marlboro Man '91
Warlock '91
Quigley Down Under '90
The Blood of Heroes '89
Kansas '88
The Naked Country '85
Mad Max '80

Edgar Egger
Breakout '98
Hot Blooded '98
The Undertaker's Wedding '97
Red Blooded 2 '96
Gladiator Cop: The Swordsman 2 '95

Eagle Egilsson(1966-)
Red Shoe Diaries: Luscious Lola '00
Red Shoe Diaries: Swimming Naked '00
Sirens '99
American Virgin '98
Business for Pleasure '96
Red Shoe Diaries: Strip Poker '96
Delta of Venus '95

Mike Eley
Nanny McPhee 2 '10
Grey Gardens '09
Jane Eyre '06
Touching the Void '03
The Navigators '01

Ian Elkin
The Crimson Code '99
For the Moment '94
The Last Winter '89
Outside Chance of Maximillian Glick '88

Marcus Elliott
Never Forget '08
All the Good Ones Are Married '07
Harm's Way '07
UKM: The Ultimate Killing Machine '06

Paul Elliott
Beer for My Horses '08
Front of the Class '08
Spy School '08
Elvis Has Left the Building '04
Fat Albert '04
King of Texas '02
The Broken Hearts Club '00
If These Walls Could Talk 2 '00
Diamonds '99
Lost and Found '99
Santa Fe '97
Soul Food '97
Riot in the Streets '96
Truman '95
My Girl 2 '94
And the Band Played On '93
Citizen Cohn '92
And You Thought Your Parents Were Weird! '91
Final Verdict '91
My Girl '91
Daddy's Dyin'... Who's Got the Will? '90
The Lost Capone '90
Welcome Home, Roxy Carmichael '90
Far from Home '89
Friday the 13th, Part 7: The New Blood '88
976-EVIL '88
Cyclone '87
Stacking '87
Armed Response '86
Tomb '86

Frederick Elmes(1946-)
Bride Wars '09
Brothers '09
The Namesake '06
Broken Flowers '05
Coffee and Cigarettes '03
Hulk '03
Trapped '02
The Empty Mirror '99
Ride with the Devil '99
The Ice Storm '97
In the Gloaming '97
Reckless '95
Trial by Jury '94
The Saint of Fort Washington '93
Night on Earth '91
Wild at Heart '90
Permanent Record '88
River's Edge '87
Allan Quatermain and the Lost City of Gold '86
Blue Velvet '86
Valley Girl '83
Eraserhead '78
Opening Night '77
The Killing of a Chinese Bookie '76

John Else
The Crow Road '96
A Village Affair '95

Danny Elsen
The Memory of a Killer '03
The Red Dwarf '99

Robert Elswit(1950-)
Salt '10
Duplicity '09
The Men Who Stare at Goats '09
The Burning Plain '08
Redbelt '08
Michael Clayton '07
There Will Be Blood '07
American Dreamz '06
Good Night, and Good Luck '05
Syriana '05
Gigli '03
Runaway Jury '03
Behind the Red Door '02
Impostor '02
Punch-Drunk Love '02
Heist '01
Bounce '00
Magnolia '99
8mm '98
Boogie Nights '97
Tomorrow Never Dies '97
Hard Eight '96
Boys '95
The Pallbearer '95
The River Wild '94
A Dangerous Woman '93
The Hand that Rocks the Cradle '92
Waterland '92
Paris Trout '91
Bad Influence '90
A Killing in a Small Town '90
Double Exposure: The Story of Margaret Bourke-White '89
The Heart of Dixie '89
How I Got into College '89
Return of the Living Dead 2 '88
Amazing Grace & Chuck '87
Desert Hearts '86
Trick or Treat '86
Moving Violations '85
The Sure Thing '85
Tiger Town '83
Waltz across Texas '83
End of August '82

Dimitry Elyashkavich(1975-)
Jackass Number Two '06
Jackass: The Movie '02

Susan Emerson
First Degree '98
Men '97

Ross Emery
Underworld: Rise of the Lycans '09
The Condemned '07

Basil Emmott
Missiles from Hell '58
Where There's a Will '55

Bryan England
Robin Cook's Invasion '97
Raging Angels '95
The Judas Project: The Ultimate Encounter '94
Conflict of Interest '92
Gate 2 '92
The Water Engine '92
Sometimes They Come Back '91
Friday the 13th, Part 8: Jason Takes Manhattan '89
I, Madman '89
My Mom's a Werewolf '89
Wicked Stepmother '89
Cheerleader Camp '88
Hunk '87
Weekend Pass '84
Party Animal '83

Porfirio Enriquez
Valentin '03
Martin (Hache) '97

Michael Epp
Beaumarchais the Scoundrel '96
My Mother's Courage '95

Nils Erickson
Sticks '98
Mirror, Mirror 3: The Voyeur '96

Tom Erisman
Paid '06
Shooters '00
1-900 '94

Teodoro Escamilla(1940-97)
Carmen '83
Blood Wedding '81
The Nest '80
Cria '76
Cria Cuervos '76

Jean-Yves Escoffier(1951-2003)
The Human Stain '03
Possession '02
15 Minutes '01
Nurse Betty '00
The Cradle Will Rock '99
Rounders '98
Good Will Hunting '97
Gummo '97
The Crow 2: City of Angels '96
Excess Baggage '96
Grace of My Heart '96
Jack and Sarah '95
Dream Lover '93
The Lovers on the Bridge '91
Mauvais Sang '86
Three Men and a Cradle '85
Boy Meets Girl '84
Simone Barbes '80

Jesus Escosa(1959-)
Beloved/Friend '99
To Die (Or Not) '99
Caresses '97

Lukas Ettlin(1975-)
Fanboys '09
The Killing Room '09
Shrink '09
Never Back Down '08
The Take '07
The Texas Chainsaw Massacre: The Beginning '06

Blake T. Evans
The Prince & Me 2: Royal Wedding '06
All I Want '02
Comic Book Villains '02
Au Pair '99
3 Ninjas: High Noon at Mega Mountain '97
Behind Enemy Lines '96
Ripper Man '96
Body Count '95

Kelly Evans
Die Mommie Die! '03
Let's Talk About Sex '98

R. Kent Evans
The Abductors '72
Ginger '72

Nikos Evdemon
Blue Smoke '07
Dangerous Child '01
Torso '01
Lip Service '00

Jean-Marc Fabre(1964-)
Avenue Montaigne '06
Lemming '05
How I Killed My Father '03
Nathalie '03
A Soldier's Daughter Never Cries '98
A Self-Made Hero '95
Ivan and Abraham '94

Geoffrey Faithfull(1893-1979)
Naked Evil '66
Village of the Damned '60
First Man into Space '59
Black Tide '58
Corridors of Blood '58
Kill Me Tomorrow '57
Radio Cab Murder '54
Goon Movie '52
The Mystery of the Mary Celeste '35

Christopher Faloona
Beowulf '98
Dennis the Menace Strikes Again '98
Breaking Free '95
3 Ninjas Kick Back '94

Pasquale Fanetti
Invincible Barbarian '83
The Boss Is Served '76

George Fanto(1911-)
It's All True '93
Othello '52

Daniel F. Fapp(1901-86)
Marooned '69
Five Card Stud '68
Ice Station Zebra '68
Sweet November '68
Lord Love a Duck '66
Our Man Flint '66
I'll Take Sweden '65
Send Me No Flowers '64
The Unsinkable Molly Brown '64
Fun in Acapulco '63
The Great Escape '63
Move Over, Darling '63
A New Kind of Love '63
One, Two, Three '61
West Side Story '61
All the Young Men '60
Let's Make Love '60
The Five Pennies '59
Li'l Abner '59
On the Beach '59
Desire Under the Elms '58
Kings Go Forth '58
Artists and Models '55
The Far Horizons '55
Money from Home '53
Jumping Jacks '52
Sailor Beware '52
The Lemon Drop Kid '51
The Stooge '51
Union Station '50
Sorrowful Jones '49
Golden Earrings '47
To Each His Own '46

Marco Fargnoli
The Blue Tooth Virgin '09
The Gymnast '06

Frederic Fasano
Mother of Tears '08
Scarlet Diva '00

Mike Fash
Flowers for Algernon '00
The Golden Spiders: A Nero Wolfe Mystery '00
Take Me Home: The John Denver Story '00
Love Letters '99
The Confession '98
Grace & Glorie '98
Entertaining Angels: The Dorothy Day Story '96
Sarah, Plain and Tall: Skylark '93
Sarah, Plain and Tall '91
The Whales of August '87
Women of Valor '86
Success Is the Best Revenge '84
King of America '80

Brian Fass
Skinned Alive '08
Crutch '04

Etienne Fauduet
Red Shoe Diaries: Four on the Floor '96
Marquis '90

Don E. Fauntleroy
Anacondas: Trail of Blood '09
Anaconda 3: The Offspring '08
Urban Justice '07
Seven Days of Grace '06
Jeepers Creepers 2 '03
U.S. Navy SEALS: Dead or Alive '02
U.S. SEALs: Dead or Alive '02
Jeepers Creepers '01
The Perfect Nanny '00
Seven Girlfriends '00
Sex & Mrs. X '00
Rites of Passage '99
The Only Thrill '97
Lily Dale '96
Body Chemistry 3: Point of Seduction '93

Jim Fealy
Splendor '99
The Doom Generation '95

Gerald Feil
Friday the 13th, Part 3 '82
He Knows You're Alone '80

Jockey A. Feindel(1895-1971)
Day the World Ended '55
Revolt of the Zombies '36

Buzz Feitshans, IV
Dragonheart: A New Beginning '00
Black Dog '98
For Richer or Poorer '97
McHale's Navy '97
The Shadow Conspiracy '96

Maurice Fellous
Sweet Young Thing '79
The Monocle '64

Roger Fellous(1919-)
Faceless '88
White Fire '84
No Problem '75
Erotic Escape '72
Diary of a Chambermaid '64
The Three Penny Opera '62

Marc Felperlaan(1944-)
Deuce Bigalow: European Gigolo '05
Resistance '03
The Shaft '01
The Dress '96
Amsterdamned '88

Paco Femenia
Carmen '03
Mad Love '01
No News from God '01
Amor de Hombre '97
Zafarinas '94

John Fenner
Valiant '05
The Borrowers '97
Muppet Treasure Island '96
The Muppet Christmas Carol '92
Teenage Mutant Ninja Turtles: The Movie '90

Joao Fernandes
The Diary of Ellen Rimbauer '03
Lady Jayne Killer '03
Gideon '99
One Man's Hero '98
Sprung '96
Forest Warrior '95
Top Dog '95
Deconstructing Sarah '94
Sidekicks '93
The Hitman '91
Delta Force 2: Operation Stranglehold '90
Red Scorpion '89
Braddock: Missing in Action 3 '88
Prettykill '87
Invasion U.S.A. '85
Rosebud Beach Hotel '85
Friday the 13th, Part 4: The Final Chapter '84
Missing in Action '84
Big Score '83
The Nesting '80

Angel Luis Fernandez(1947-)
Km. 0 '00
Baton Rouge '88
Law of Desire '86
Matador '86
Dark Habits '84

Giancarlo Ferrando
The Messenger '87
Thundersquad '85
Devilfish '84
Ironmaster '82
Scorpion with Two Tails '82
The Great Alligator '81
Inhibition '76
Torso '73
Your Vice is a Closed Room and Only I Have the Key '72

David Ferrara
Harvard Man '01
Kill Me Later '01
Black and White '99

Michael Ferris
Bar Girls '95
I Don't Buy Kisses Anymore '92

Steven Fierberg
Twelve '10
Meet Market '08
Suburban Girl '07
Secretary '02
Attila '01
Red Letters '00
Atomic Train '99
A Horse for Danny '95
Aspen Extreme '93
29th Street '91
Criminal Justice '90
Scenes from the Class Struggle in Beverly Hills '89
A Nightmare on Elm Street 4: Dream Master '88
Spike of Bensonhurst '88
The Game of Love '87
Seven Minutes in Heaven '86
Streetwalkin' '85
Vortex '81

Gabriel Figueroa(1907-97)
Kelly's Heroes '70
Simon of the Desert '66
The Night of the Iguana '64
The Exterminating Angel '62
El '52

Vilko Filac(1950-)
Novocaine '01
Children of the Century '99
Chinese Box '97
Underground '95
Arizona Dream '94
When Father Was Away on Business '85

William Fildew
Outside the Law '21
Sold for Marriage '16

Michael Fimognari
Dare '09
Shuttle '09
Everybody Wants to Be Italian '08
Yonkers Joe '08
Black Irish '07
The Neighbor '07
Think Tank '06
Knots '05
The Twelve Dogs of Christmas '05

Roberta Findlay
Lurkers '88
Shriek of the Mutilated '74

Russell Fine
Sherrybaby *'06*
Ash Wednesday *'02*
The Grey Zone *'01*
O *'01*
Eye of God *'97*
Office Killer *'97*
Girls Town *'95*
The Pompatus of Love *'95*

Steven Finestone
Once Upon a Wedding *'05*
Dawg *'02*
How to Make a Monster *'01*
I Shot a Man in Vegas *'96*
Swimming with Sharks *'94*

Gerald Perry Finnerman(1931-)
Nightmares *'83*
Devil Dog: The Hound of Hell *'78*
Genesis II *'73*
Sssssss *'73*
That Man Bolt *'73*
Hard Frame *'70*
They Call Me Mr. Tibbs! *'70*
The Lost Man *'69*

Gavin Finney
The Color of Magic *'08*
St. Trinian's *'07*
The Flying Scotsman *'06*
Hogfather *'06*
These Foolish Things *'06*
Bailey's Billion$ *'05*
Keeping Mum *'05*
Alex & Emma *'03*
Gentlemen's Relish *'01*
Breathtaking *'00*
A Rather English Marriage *'98*
Dad Savage *'97*
The Sculptress *'97*

Mauro Fiore
The A-Team *'10*
Avatar *'09*
Avatar *'09*
The Kingdom *'07*
Smokin' Aces *'07*
The Island *'05*
Tears of the Sun *'03*
The Center of the World *'01*
Driven *'01*
Highway *'01*
Training Day *'01*
Get Carter *'00*
Lost Souls *'00*
Billboard Dad *'98*
An Occasional Hell *'96*

Mario Fioretti
The Big Game *'72*
Blaise Pascal *'71*
Beauty on the Beach *'61*

Harry Fischbeck(1879-1968)
Bulldog Drummond's Bride *'39*
The Big Broadcast of 1938 *'38*
Now and Forever *'34*
Search for Beauty *'34*
The Eagle and the Hawk *'33*
The Mysterious Dr. Fu Manchu *'29*
Sally of the Sawdust *'25*

Gunnar Fischer(1910-)
The Devil's Eye *'60*
Wild Strawberries *'57*
The Seventh Seal *'56*
To Joy *'50*

Jens Fischer(1946-)
The Girl With the Dragon Tattoo *'09*
Under the Sun *'98*
The Last Dance *'93*
More about the Children of Noisy Village *'87*

Garrett Fisher
Kitchen Privileges *'00*
The Debt *'98*

Gerry Fisher(1926-)
When Saturday Comes *'95*
Cops and Robbersons *'94*
Exorcist 3: Legion *'90*
Dead Bang *'89*
Running on Empty *'88*
Highlander *'86*
Lovesick *'83*
Yellowbeard *'83*
Victory *'81*
Wolfen *'81*
Roads to the South *'78*
The Island of Dr. Moreau *'77*
Mr. Klein *'76*
Brannigan *'75*
Juggernaut *'74*
The Go-Between *'71*
Accident *'67*

Cash Flagg
See Ray Dennis Steckler

Andre Fleuren
And Starring Pancho Villa as Himself *'03*
Evelyn *'02*

Ray Flin
Then Came Bronson *'68*
Monster from Green Hell *'58*

Pili Flores-Guerra
800 Leagues Down the Amazon *'93*
Fire on the Amazon *'93*

Brendan Flynt
Brutal Massacre: A Comedy *'07*
Remedy *'05*
Citizen Toxie: The Toxic Avenger 4 *'01*
Boricua's Bond *'00*
Tromeo & Juliet *'95*

George Folsey, Jr.
The Pink Panther *'06*
Housewife *'72*

George J. Folsey(1898-1988)
That's Entertainment, Part 2 *'76*
The Balcony *'63*
Cash McCall *'60*
Saddle the Wind *'58*
Torpedo Run *'58*
Fastest Gun Alive *'56*
Forbidden Planet *'56*
The Cobweb *'55*
Hit the Deck *'55*
Deep in My Heart *'54*
Executive Suite *'54*
Men of the Fighting Lady *'54*
Seven Brides for Seven Brothers *'54*
All the Brothers Were Valiant *'53*
Lovely to Look At *'52*
Million Dollar Mermaid *'52*
Mr. Imperium *'51*
Vengeance Valley *'51*
Adam's Rib *'50*
The Big Hangover *'50*
A Life of Her Own *'50*
Malaya *'49*
Take Me Out to the Ball Game *'49*
State of the Union *'48*
Green Dolphin Street *'47*
The Harvey Girls *'46*
The Clock *'45*
Meet Me in St. Louis *'44*
The White Cliffs of Dover *'44*
Thousands Cheer *'43*
Andy Hardy's Double Life *'42*
Grand Central Murder *'42*
Panama Hattie *'42*
Rio Rita *'42*
Lady Be Good *'41*
The Shining Hour *'38*
The Bride Wore Red *'37*
The Last of Mrs. Cheyney *'37*
Mannequin *'37*
The Gorgeous Hussy *'36*
Forsaking All Others *'35*
I Live My Life *'35*
Reckless *'35*
Chained *'34*
Men in White *'34*
Operator 13 *'34*
Going Hollywood *'33*
The Animal Kingdom *'32*
The Cheat *'31*
The Smiling Lieutenant *'31*
Animal Crackers *'30*
Applause *'29*
The Cocoanuts *'29*

Larry Fong
Watchmen *'09*
300 *'07*
Cape of Good Hope *'04*

Stephane Fontaine
A Prophet *'09*
What Just Happened *'08*
Talk to Me *'07*
The Beat My Heart Skipped *'05*
Look at Me *'04*

Harry Forbes
Tombstone Terror *'34*
Daring Daughters *'33*

David Foreman
Chameleon 3: Dark Angel *'00*
Cut *'00*
The Real Macaw *'98*

Emilio Foriscot
The Case of the Scorpion's Tail *'71*
They Paid with Bullets: Chicago 1929 *'69*

Tony Forsberg(1933-)
The White Lioness *'96*
Revenge of the Barbarians *'85*

Cinders Forshaw
Tipping the Velvet *'02*
Almost Strangers *'01*
Butterfly Collectors *'99*

Joey Forsyte
Off the Lip *'04*
Bad Seed *'00*
Me & Will *'99*
The Treat *'98*
The Curve *'97*
The Dark Backward *'91*

Ron Fortunato
Hachiko: A Dog's Tale *'09*
Before the Devil Knows You're Dead *'07*
Catch a Fire *'06*
Find Me Guilty *'06*
The Weekend *'00*
Sunset Strip *'99*
One Tough Cop *'98*
Basquiat *'96*
Nil by Mouth *'96*
If Lucy Fell *'95*
Mac *'93*
Fathers and Sons *'92*
Skin *'89*

Marc Fossard(1912-)
The Gendarme of Saint-Tropez *'64*
Beethoven *'36*

John Foster
Adrift in Manhattan *'07*
Rock the Paint *'05*
Keane *'04*
Tully *'00*
The Adventures of Sebastian Cole *'99*
Sunday *'96*

Crystal Fournier
Water Lilies *'07*
Carnage *'02*

Ian Fox
Urban Legends: Bloody Mary *'05*
No Turning Back *'01*
Don't Do It *'94*

Mike J. Fox
Florence Nightingale *'08*
Jiminy Glick in LaLa Wood *'05*
One More Kiss *'99*

Francisco Fraile
Mean Machine *'73*
Dr. Jekyll and the Wolfman *'71*

Robert Fraisse
The Color of Freedom *'07*
Alpha Dog *'06*
The Valet *'06*
Hotel Rwanda *'04*
The Notebook *'04*
Luther *'03*
Enemy at the Gates *'00*
La Buche *'00*
Vatel *'00*
Ronin *'98*
Seven Years in Tibet *'97*
Keys to Tulsa *'96*
Citizen X *'95*
The Lover *'92*
L'Addition *'85*
Lady Chatterley's Lover *'81*
Emmanuelle, the Joys of a Woman *'76*
The Story of O *'75*

Graham Frake
The Truth About Love *'04*
A Woman's Guide to Adultery *'93*

William A. Fraker(1923-)
Waking Up in Reno *'02*
Town and Country *'01*
Rules of Engagement *'00*
The Island of Dr. Moreau *'96*
Vegas Vacation *'96*
Father of the Bride Part 2 *'95*
Street Fighter *'94*
Tombstone *'93*
Honeymoon in Vegas *'92*
The Freshman *'90*
Chances Are *'89*
Baby Boom *'87*
Burglar *'87*
Protocol *'84*
WarGames *'83*
Sharky's Machine *'81*
The Hollywood Knights *'80*
1941 *'79*
Heaven Can Wait *'78*
The Exorcist 2: The Heretic *'77*
Looking for Mr. Goodbar *'77*
The Killer Inside Me *'76*
Lipstick *'76*
One Flew Over the Cuckoo's Nest *'75*
Rancho Deluxe *'75*
Streetfight *'75*
Aloha, Bobby and Rose *'74*
Dusty and Sweets Mcgee *'71*
Bullitt *'68*
Rosemary's Baby *'68*
Games *'67*
The President's Analyst *'67*

Freddie Francis(1917-2007)
The Straight Story *'99*
Princess Caraboo *'94*
School Ties *'92*
Cape Fear *'91*
Glory *'89*
Her Alibi *'88*
Brenda Starr *'86*
Dune *'84*
The French Lieutenant's Woman *'81*
The Elephant Man *'80*
The Innocents *'61*
The Battle of the Sexes *'60*
Saturday Night and Sunday Morning *'60*
Room at the Top *'59*
The Scamp *'57*
Time Without Pity *'57*

David Franco(1963-)
Bury My Heart at Wounded Knee *'07*
Code Name: The Cleaner *'07*
Banshee *'06*
Call Me: The Rise and Fall of Heidi Fleiss *'04*
44 Minutes: The North Hollywood Shootout *'03*
Mr. St. Nick *'02*
3000 Miles to Graceland *'01*
The Whole Nine Yards *'00*
Earthly Possessions *'99*
Free Money *'99*
Vendetta *'99*
The Last Don 2 *'98*
The Assignment *'97*
Silent Trigger *'97*
Long Day's Journey Into Night *'96*
Hollow Point *'95*
Soul Survivor *'95*
A Man in Uniform *'93*
The Carpenter *'89*

Silvio Fraschetti
Metallica *'85*
Reactor *'78*
War in Space *'77*

Greig Fraser(1975-)
The Boys Are Back *'09*
Bright Star *'09*

Tom Fraser
Chopper Chicks in Zombietown *'91*
Frankenstein General Hospital *'88*
The Unnamable *'88*
Alien from L.A. *'87*

Benito Frattari
Commandos *'73*
Taste of Death *'68*
Mondo Cane *'63*

David Frazee
Everything's Gone Green *'06*
Chained Heat 3: Hell Mountain *'98*

Ellsworth Fredericks(1904-93)
Picture Mommy Dead *'66*
Seven Days in May *'64*
Tall Story *'60*
The Light in the Forest *'58*
Sayonara *'57*
Friendly Persuasion *'56*
Invasion of the Body Snatchers *'56*
At Gunpoint *'55*
Shotgun *'55*

Neal Fredericks
Killer Me *'01*
The Blair Witch Project *'99*

Jonathan Freeman
Remember Me *'10*
The Edge of Love *'08*
Fifty Dead Men Walking *'08*
Hollywoodland *'06*
The Prize Winner of Defiance, Ohio *'05*
Good Fences *'03*
Monday Night Mayhem *'02*
Taken *'02*
Hitched *'01*
Ignition *'01*
Lost Battalion *'01*
The Courage to Love *'00*
Resurrection *'99*
Deadly Game *'98*
Falling Fire *'97*
Junior's Groove *'97*
Carver's Gate *'96*

Lloyd Freidus
Fight for Your Life *'77*
Toga Party *'77*

Robert Fresco
Go Further *'03*
At the Midnight Hour *'95*

Henry Freulich(1906-85)
Good Day for a Hanging *'58*
The 27th Day *'57*
Bonanza Town *'51*
Corky of Gasoline Alley *'51*
Son of Rusty *'47*
Blondie for Victory *'42*
Blondie Goes Latin *'42*
Blondie Goes to College *'42*
Blondie's Blessed Event *'42*
The Boogie Man Will Get You *'42*
Blondie in Society *'41*
Blondie Has Trouble *'40*
Blondie On a Budget *'40*
Blondie Plays Cupid *'40*
Blondie Brings Up Baby *'39*
Blondie Meets the Boss *'39*
Blondie Takes a Vacation *'39*
Blondie *'38*
Murder in Greenwich Village *'37*

Karl Freund(1890-1969)
Bright Leaf *'50*
Montana *'50*
Key Largo *'48*
South of St. Louis *'48*
Undercurrent *'46*
Without Love *'45*
A Guy Named Joe *'44*
The Seventh Cross *'44*
Du Barry Was a Lady *'43*
Tortilla Flat *'42*
The Chocolate Soldier *'41*
Pride and Prejudice *'40*
Balalaika *'39*
Rose of Washington Square *'39*
Letter of Introduction *'38*
Conquest *'37*
The Good Earth *'37*
Murders in the Rue Morgue *'32*
Dracula *'31*
Personal Maid *'31*
All Quiet on the Western Front *'30*
Metropolis *'26*
Tartuffe *'25*
Variety *'25*
The Finances of the Grand Duke *'24*
The Last Laugh *'24*
The Golem *'20*

Ron Fricke
Baraka *'93*
Koyaanisqatsi *'83*

Martin Fuhrer(1956-)
P.D. James: Death in Holy Orders *'03*
The Gathering *'02*
Goodbye, Mr. Chips *'02*
The Sleeping Dictionary *'02*
Wilde *'97*
Lord of the Flies *'90*

Hideo Fujii
The Adventures of Milo & Otis *'89*
Milo & Otis *'89*
Irezumi *'83*

Tak Fujimoto
The Great Buck Howard *'09*
The Happening *'08*
John Adams *'08*
Breach *'07*
The Final Cut *'04*
The Manchurian Candidate *'04*
Signs *'02*
The Truth About Charlie *'02*
The Replacements *'00*
The Sixth Sense *'99*
Beloved *'98*
A Thousand Acres *'97*
That Thing You Do! *'96*
Devil in a Blue Dress *'95*
Grumpier Old Men *'95*
Philadelphia *'93*
Gladiator *'92*
Night and the City *'92*
Crooked Hearts *'91*
The Silence of the Lambs *'91*
Miami Blues *'90*
Cocoon: The Return *'88*
Married to the Mob *'88*
Sweet Hearts Dance *'88*
Ferris Bueller's Day Off *'86*
Pretty in Pink *'86*
Something Wild *'86*
Swing Shift *'84*
Melvin and Howard *'80*
Where the Buffalo Roam *'80*
Cannonball *'76*
Death Race 2000 *'75*
Badlands *'74*
Caged Heat *'74*

Junichi Fujisawa
9 Souls *'03*
Inugami *'01*

Jonathan Furmanski
Descent *'07*
Trumbo *'07*
You Belong to Me *'07*

Takumi Furuya
Azumi *'03*
Versus *'00*

Steve Gainer(1962-)
Taking Chances *'09*
Punisher: War Zone *'08*
While She Was Out *'08*
Remember the Daze *'07*
Wassup Rockers *'06*
Black Cloud *'04*
A Dirty Shame *'04*
Mysterious Skin *'04*
Bully *'01*
Teenage Caveman *'01*
Foolish *'99*
Club Vampire *'98*

Ricardo Jacques Gale(1955-)
I-See-You.Com *'06*
Stalked *'99*
West Beirut *'98*
Bloodfist *'89*
The Nest *'88*

Michael Gallagher
Bloodfist 7: Manhunt *'95*
Bloodfist 6: Ground Zero *'94*

Tom Galligan
Trailing Trouble *'37*
The Dude Bandit *'33*
The Three Musketeers *'33*
Boiling Point *'32*
Local Badman *'32*

Mark Anthony Galluzzo
R.S.V.P. *'02*
Magenta *'96*

Brendan Galvin
Blood & Chocolate *'07*
Flight of the Phoenix *'04*
Thunderbirds *'04*
Bookies *'03*
Veronica Guerin *'03*
Behind Enemy Lines *'01*

Robert Gantz
Lake City *'08*
Assault on Precinct 13 *'05*
Mindhunters *'05*

Rodrigo Garcia(1959-)
Body Shots *'99*
Gia *'98*
Four Rooms *'95*
Indictment: The McMartin Trial *'95*

Ron Garcia
The First $20 Million is Always the Hardest *'02*
Deliberate Intent *'01*
Baby *'00*
The Runaway *'00*
Mutiny *'99*
Small Vices: A Spenser Mystery *'99*
The Great White Hype *'96*
Twin Peaks: Fire Walk with Me *'92*
El Diablo *'90*
Disorganized Crime *'89*

Greg Gardiner
Marmaduke *'10*
Race to Witch Mountain *'09*
Welcome Home Roscoe Jenkins *'08*
The Game Plan *'07*
She's the Man *'06*
Herbie: Fully Loaded *'05*
Son of the Mask *'05*
New York Minute *'04*
Biker Boyz *'03*
Elf *'03*
Big Trouble *'02*
Men in Black 2 *'02*
Orange County *'02*
To End All Wars *'01*
Dean Koontz's Mr. Murder *'98*
Where's Marlowe? *'98*
Homegrown *'97*
The Apocalypse *'96*
Somebody Is Waiting *'96*
Boys Life *'94*
Suture *'93*
The Unnamable 2: The Statement of Randolph Carter *'92*

James Gardner
Hustle *'04*
Naked City: A Killer Christmas *'98*

Mike Garfath
I'll Sleep When I'm Dead *'03*
The Enemy *'01*
Croupier *'97*
Nuns on the Run *'90*
Car Trouble *'85*
Lamb *'85*

Lee Garmes(1898-1978)
A Big Hand for the Little Lady *'66*
Misty *'61*
Abdulla the Great *'56*
D-Day, the Sixth of June *'56*
Desperate Hours *'55*
Land of the Pharaohs *'55*
Actors and Sin *'52*
The Lusty Men *'52*
Detective Story *'51*
Our Very Own *'50*
Caught *'49*
My Foolish Heart *'49*
Nightmare Alley *'47*
The Paradine Case *'47*
The Secret Life of Walter Mitty *'47*
Love Letters *'45*
Guest in the House *'44*
Since You Went Away *'44*
Forever and a Day *'43*
Footlight Serenade *'42*
The Jungle Book *'42*
Lydia *'41*
Angels Over Broadway *'40*
Dreaming Lips *'37*
Smilin' Through *'33*
Shanghai Express *'32*
Strange Interlude *'32*
An American Tragedy *'31*
Dishonored *'31*
Scarface *'31*
Disraeli *'30*
Morocco *'30*
Say It With Songs *'29*
The Show Off *'26*

Mark Garret
Amusement *'08*
Freeze Frame *'04*

Andres Garreton
Darkdrive *'98*
Total Reality *'97*
Intimate Relations *'95*

Romolo Garroni
Last Gun *'64*
Caesar the Conqueror *'63*

Marcello Gatti(1924-)
The Switch *'76*
The Black Belly of the Tarantula *'71*
Burn! *'70*
The Battle of Algiers *'66*

Gaetano Antonio "Tony" Gaudio(1885-1951)
The Red Pony *'49*
Love from a Stranger *'47*
I've Always Loved You *'46*
A Song to Remember *'45*
I'll Be Seeing You *'44*
Days of Glory *'43*
Larceny, Inc. *'42*
The Great Lie *'41*
High Sierra *'41*
The Man Who Came to Dinner *'41*
Brother Orchid *'40*
The Fighting 69th *'40*
The Letter *'40*
Juarez *'39*
The Old Maid *'39*
The Adventures of Robin Hood *'38*
Amazing Dr. Clitterhouse *'38*
Dawn Patrol *'38*
Kid Galahad *'37*
The Life of Emile Zola *'37*
Anthony Adverse *'36*
The Story of Louis Pasteur *'36*
Bordertown *'35*
Go Into Your Dance *'35*
Happiness Ahead *'34*
The Man with Two Faces *'34*
The Mask of Fu Manchu *'32*
Tiger Shark *'32*
Hell's Angels *'30*
Little Caesar *'30*
The Gaucho *'27*
The Notorious Lady *'27*
The Temptress *'26*
Kismet *'20*

Eric Gautier(1961-)
Taking Woodstock *'09*
A Christmas Tale *'08*
Summer Hours *'08*
Into the Wild *'07*
A Guide to Recognizing Your Saints *'06*
Paris, je t'aime *'06*
Private Fears in Public Places *'06*
Gabrielle *'05*
Clean *'04*
Kings and Queen *'04*
The Motorcycle Diaries *'04*
The Housekeeper *'02*
Esther Kahn *'00*
Intimacy *'00*
Les Destinees *'00*
Pola X *'99*
Those Who Love Me Can Take the Train *'98*
Irma Vep *'96*
Love, etc. *'96*
My Sex Life... Or How I Got into an Argument *'96*
One Hundred and One Nights *'95*
The Favorite Son *'94*

Carlos Gaviria
Undercurrent *'99*
A Gun, a Car, a Blonde *'97*

David Geddes(1949-)
Smokin' Aces 2: Assassins' Ball *'10*
The Messengers *'07*
Nearing Grace *'05*
A Simple Curve *'05*
Halloween: Resurrection *'02*
Fatal Error *'99*
Don't Look Down *'98*
My Husband's Secret Life *'98*
A Call to Remember *'97*
Killing Mr. Griffin *'97*
The Colony *'95*
Incident at Deception Ridge *'94*
Call of the Wild *'93*
When a Stranger Calls Back *'93*

Luke Geissbuhler(1970-)
Borat: Cultural Learnings of America for Make Benefit Glorious Nation of Kazakhstan *'06*
Alchemy *'05*
Mail Order Wife *'04*
Acts of Worship *'01*

Alessio Gelsini Torresi(1951-)
The Emperor's New Clothes *'01*
The Blonde *'92*

Lu Gengxin
The Emperor's Shadow *'96*
Ermo *'94*

Dominique Gentil
Moolaade *'04*
Winged Migration *'01*

Laszlo George
The Loretta Claiborne Story *'00*
Model Behavior *'00*
The Stepsister *'97*
Last Flight Out: A True Story *'90*
Swimsuit *'89*
Vanishing Act *'88*

Dejan Georgevich
Satan's Little Helper *'04*
Love Thy Neighbor *'02*

Roberto Gerardi(1919-)
Ring of Death *'69*
Madame Sans-Gene *'62*

Henry W. Gerrard(1894-)
Of Human Bondage *'34*
Little Women *'33*
The Most Dangerous Game *'32*
Beggars of Life *'28*

Merritt B. Gerstad(1900-74)
Watch on the Rhine *'43*
Bulldog Drummond's Secret Police *'39*
Girl's Dormitory *'36*
Strike Me Pink *'36*
A Night at the Opera *'35*
Imitation of Life *'34*
Freaks *'32*
Flying High *'31*
The Mad Whirl *'25*

Maury Gertsman(1907-99)
Invisible Invaders *'59*
The Creature Walks among Us *'56*
To Hell and Back *'55*
Red Ball Express *'52*
Double Crossbones *'51*
Singapore *'47*
The Brute Man *'46*
Dressed to Kill *'46*
She Wolf of London *'46*
Terror by Night *'46*
Jungle Captive *'45*

Ebraheem Ghafouri
Osama *'03*
Kandahar *'01*

Rodney Gibbons
Eye *'96*
Natural Enemy *'96*
Screamers *'96*
My Bloody Valentine *'81*

Gerald Gibbs(1907-90)
Devil Doll *'64*
The Leather Boys *'63*
Quatermass 2 *'57*
X The Unknown *'56*

Paul Gibson
Paris Is Burning *'91*
The Refrigerator *'91*

Sue Gibson(1952-)
The Search for John Gissing *'01*
Amongst Women *'98*
Mrs. Dalloway *'97*
Hear My Song *'91*

William Gibson(1914-)
Rogue *'07*
Macbeth *'06*
Wolf Creek *'05*

Peter Gilbert(1957-)
Prefontaine *'96*
Hoop Dreams *'94*

Alfred Gilks
The Secret of Dr. Kildare *'39*
Sky Parade *'36*
Beyond the Rocks *'22*

Pierre Gill
Outlander *'08*
The Covenant *'06*
The Rocket *'05*
Hitler: The Rise of Evil *'03*
Lost and Delirious *'01*
The Art of War *'00*
Joan of Arc *'99*
Street Heart *'98*
Los Locos Posse *'97*

Dan Gillham
The Thing About My Folks *'05*
Burning Down the House *'01*
Final *'01*
Hamlet *'01*
Notes from Underground *'95*
Voodoo *'95*

Paul Gilpin
The Natalee Holloway Story *'09*
In Desert and Wilderness *'01*
Tarzan and the Lost City *'98*
Dangerous Ground *'96*
Cry, the Beloved Country *'95*

Xavi Gimenez(1970-)
Transsiberian *'08*
The Abandoned *'06*
The Machinist *'04*
Darkness *'02*

Aldo Giordani(1914-)
Amuck! *'71*
Terror of the Steppes *'64*
Atom Age Vampire *'61*
Too Bad She's Bad *'54*

Blasco Giurato(1941-)
The Stone Merchant *'06*
Doctor Zhivago *'03*
The Worker and the Hairdresser *'96*
A Pure Formality *'94*
Cinema Paradiso *'88*

Irving Glassberg(1906-58)
Tarnished Angels *'57*
The Black Shield of Falworth *'54*
Ride Clear of Diablo *'54*
Duel at Silver Creek *'52*
The Lawless Breed *'52*
The Strange Door *'51*
Casbah *'48*

Ken Glassing
Brigham City *'01*
Southern Man *'99*

Hone Glendinning(1912-97)
Crimes at the Dark House *'39*
The Hooded Terror *'38*
Ticket of Leave Man *'37*

Pierre William Glenn(1943-)
And Now Ladies and Gentlemen *'02*
Le Choc *'82*
Coup de Torchon *'81*
Loulou *'80*
Avalanche *'78*
Small Change *'76*
The Judge and the Assassin *'75*
Day for Night *'73*

Bert Glennon(1893-1967)
Man From Galveston *'63*
Crime Wave *'54*
House of Wax *'53*
Rio Grande *'50*
Copacabana *'47*
The Red House *'47*
Mission to Moscow *'43*
Juke Girl *'42*
Dive Bomber *'41*
They Died with Their Boots On *'41*
Our Town *'40*
Stagecoach *'39*
The Hurricane *'37*
Dimples *'36*
Lloyds of London *'36*
The Prisoner of Shark Island *'36*
Scarlet Empress *'34*
The Half Naked Truth *'32*
Are Parents People? *'25*
A Woman of the World *'25*

James Glennon(1942-2006)
Good Boy! *'03*
United States of Leland *'03*
About Schmidt *'02*
Local Boys *'02*
Blonde *'01*
Dead Simple *'01*
Life Without Dick *'01*
Madison *'01*
Playing Mona Lisa *'00*
South of Heaven, West of Hell *'00*
Election *'99*
The Runner *'99*
Best Men *'98*
Citizen Ruth *'96*
Lifeform *'96*
Mojave Moon *'96*
My Very Best Friend *'96*
Mrs. Munck *'95*
High Stakes *'93*
In the Deep Woods *'91*
Smooth Talk *'85*

Paul Glickman
The Stuff *'85*
God Told Me To *'76*
Tracks *'76*
Dracula vs. Frankenstein *'71*

Richard C. Glouner(1932-98)
Awakening of Candra *'81*
The Savage Bees *'76*
Payday *'73*
Moon of the Wolf *'72*
The Dunwich Horror *'70*
The Gay Deceivers *'69*

Agnes Godard(1950-)
35 Shots of Rum *'08*
The Intruder *'04*
Strayed *'03*
Friday Night *'02*
Beau Travail *'98*
The Dreamlife of Angels *'98*
The New Eve *'98*
Nenette and Boni *'96*
I Can't Sleep *'93*

Michael Goi(1959-)
Witless Protection *'08*
Breakaway *'02*
Red Water *'01*
What Matters Most *'01*
Echo of Murder *'00*
Forbidden Sins *'99*
The Fixer *'97*

Stephen Goldblatt(1945-)
Percy Jackson & The Olympians: The Lightning Thief *'10*
Julie & Julia *'09*
Charlie Wilson's War *'07*
Rent *'05*
Closer *'04*
Angels in America *'03*
Path to War *'02*
Conspiracy *'01*
The Deep End of the Ocean *'98*
Batman and Robin *'97*
Striptease *'96*
Batman Forever *'95*
The Pelican Brief *'93*
For the Boys *'91*
The Prince of Tides *'91*
Joe Versus the Volcano *'90*
Lethal Weapon 2 *'89*
Lethal Weapon *'87*
The Cotton Club *'84*
The Hunger *'83*
Outland *'81*

Adriano Goldman
Sin Nombre *'09*
City of Men *'07*
The Year My Parents Went on Vacation *'07*

Paul Goldsmith
Soul Power *'08*
A Shock to the System *'90*

Eric Goldstein
Dr. Dolittle 3 *'06*
Break a Leg *'03*
Mr. Barrington *'03*
Shelter *'98*
Naked Souls *'95*

David Golia
Street Corner Justice *'96*
The Rosary Murders *'87*

Burnett Guffey(1905-83)
The Great White Hope '70
The Learning Tree '69
The Ambushers '67
Bonnie & Clyde '67
How to Succeed in Business without Really Trying '67
The Silencers '66
King Rat '65
Good Neighbor Sam '64
Birdman of Alcatraz '62
Kid Galahad '62
Homicidal '61
Mr. Sardonicus '61
Let No Man Write My Epitaph '60
Gidget '59
Me and the Colonel '58
The Brothers Rico '57
Decision at Sundown '57
The Strange One '57
The Harder They Fall '56
Tight Spot '55
The Violent Men '55
Human Desire '54
Private Hell 36 '54
From Here to Eternity '53
Scandal Sheet '52
The Sniper '52
Sirocco '51
In a Lonely Place '50
All the King's Men '49
Knock on Any Door '49
Reckless Moment '49

Eric Guichard
Paris, je t'aime '06
Himalaya '99
The Crazy Stranger '98
Mondo '96

Allen Guilford
The Legend of Johnny Lingo '03
Aberration '97
The Climb '97
Jack Brown, Genius '94

David Gurfinkel
Under the Domim Tree '95
Blink of an Eye '92
Delta Force '86
Secret of Yolanda '82

Brian Gurley
Fatwa '06
In the Flesh '97

Carlos Gusi
The Kovak Box '06
Take My Eyes '03
Vacas '91

Erich Gusko(1930-)
The Third '72
The Rabbit Is Me '65

Eugeny Guslinsky(1938-)
Termination Man '97
Marquis de Sade '96

Yevgeni Guslinsky
See Eugeny Guslinsky

Manfred Guthe
Jack and Jill vs. the World '08
Twitches Too '07
The Initiation of Sarah '06
Twitches '05
Poltergeist: The Legacy '96
The Awakening '95
The Stupids '95

Carl Guthrie(1905-67)
Dondi '61
The George Raft Story '61
Revak the Rebel '60
The Gunfight at Dodge City '59
King of the Wild Stallions '59
Frankenstein 1970 '58
House on Haunted Hill '58
Untamed Youth '57
Lady Godiva '55
Long John Silver '54
Francis Covers the Big Town '53
Three Sailors and a Girl '53
Francis Goes to West Point '52
Bedtime for Bonzo '51
Storm Warning '51
Caged '50
Barricade '49

Eric Haase
Extreme Movie '08
American Pie Presents: The Naked Mile '06
The Lather Effect '06

Shana Hagan
This Film Is Not Yet Rated '06
After Innocence '05

Ron Hagen(1947-)
Little Boy Blue '97
Talk '94
Romper Stomper '92

D. Gregor Hagey
Suck '09
Re-Generation '04

Rob Hahn
The Stepford Wives '04
The Score '01
Loser '00
In and Out '97

Bert Haines
Steamboat Bill, Jr. '28
College '27
Battling Butler '26
The General '26

Jacques Haitkin
Art Heist '05
Shut Up and Kiss Me '05
Hell's Gate '01
Faust: Love of the Damned '00
The Base '99
Blowback '99
Apartment Complex '98
Inferno '98
Wishmaster '97
The Big Squeeze '96
Fist of the North Star '95
One Good Turn '95
Two Bits & Pepper '95
Evolver '94
The Force '94
Silence of the Hams '93
The Ambulance '90
Shocker '89
To Die For '89
Cherry 2000 '88
The Hidden '87
A Nightmare on Elm Street 2: Freddy's Revenge '85
Making the Grade '84
A Nightmare on Elm Street '84
House Where Evil Dwells '82
Galaxy of Terror '81
Long Shot Kids '81
The Private Eyes '80

Conrad L. Hall(1926-2003)
Road to Perdition '02
American Beauty '99
A Civil Action '98
Without Limits '97
Searching for Bobby Fischer '93
Tequila Sunrise '88
Black Widow '87
Incubus '82
Marathon Man '76
The Day of the Locust '75
Smile '75
Electra Glide in Blue '73
Fat City '72
Butch Cassidy and the Sundance Kid '69
The Happy Ending '69
Hell in the Pacific '69
Tell Them Willie Boy Is Here '69
Cool Hand Luke '67
Divorce American Style '67
In Cold Blood '67
Harper '66
The Professionals '66
Incubus '65
Morituri '65

Conrad W. Hall(1958-)
The Longshots '08
Two for the Money '05
The Punisher '04
Panic Room '02
A Gentleman's Game '01

Geoffrey Hall
Shadow Man '06
Kidnapped '05
Dirty Deeds '02
Chopper '00

Jess Hall
The Switch '10
Creation '09
Brideshead Revisited '08
Hot Fuzz '07
Son of Rambow '07
Stander '03

Jonathan Hall
Green Street Hooligans 2 '09
InAlienable '08
Asian Stories '06

Harry Hallenberger(1877-1954)
The Virginian '46
Louisiana Purchase '41

Ernest Haller(1896-1970)
The Most Wonderful Time of the Year '08
Dead Ringer '64
Lilies of the Field '63
Married Too Young '62
What Ever Happened to Baby Jane? '62
Three Blondes in His Life '61
Why Must I Die? '60
Men in War '57
Plunder Road '57
Rebel without a Cause '55
Humoresque '46
Saratoga Trunk '45
Princess O'Rourke '43
Blues in the Night '41
The Bride Came C.O.D. '41
Manpower '41
Dark Victory '39
Invisible Stripes '39
The Roaring Twenties '39
Four Daughters '38
Four's a Crowd '38
Jezebel '38
Call It a Day '37
The Great Garrick '37
King of the Jungle '33

Doug Hallows
Catherine Cookson's The Gambling Man '98
Catherine Cookson's The Girl '96
Catherine Cookson's The Tide of Life '96
Catherine Cookson's The Glass Virgin '95

Takashi Hamada
Departures '08
When the Last Sword is Drawn '02
Adrenaline Drive '99

Fenton Hamilton
It's Alive 2: It Lives Again '78
It's Alive '74
Black Caesar '73
Hell Up in Harlem '73

Victor Hammer(1957-)
Big Stan '07
Firehouse Dog '07
Welcome to Mooseport '04
Sour Grapes '98
Down Periscope '96
Billy Madison '94
8 Seconds '94
Heavyweights '94
Major League 2 '94
House of Cards '92
Going Under '91
Lean on Me '89

Peter Hannan(1941-)
The Gathering Storm '02
Longitude '00
Not Without My Daughter '90
How to Get Ahead in Advertising '89
A Handful of Dust '88
The Lonely Passion of Judith Hearne '87
Withnail and I '87
Dance with a Stranger '85
Insignificance '85
Monty Python's The Meaning of Life '83
Dangerous Summer '82

Kazutami Hara
Akira Kurosawa's Dreams '90
Godzilla 1985 '85

Anthony Hardwick
Religulous '08
Borat: Cultural Learnings of America for Make Benefit Glorious Nation of Kazakhstan '06

Alain Hardy
Sensual Partners '87
Revenge in the House of Usher '82

Rob Hardy
Is Anybody There? '08
Boy A '07

Russell Harlan(1903-74)
Hatari! '62
To Kill a Mockingbird '62
Pollyanna '60
Sunrise at Campobello '60
The Day of the Outlaw '59
Operation Petticoat '59
Rio Bravo '59
King Creole '58
Run Silent, Run Deep '58
Witness for the Prosecution '57
Blackboard Jungle '55
The Thing '51
Tarzan and the Slave Girl '50
Gun Crazy '49
Red River '48
A Walk in the Sun '46
The Kansan '43
Twilight on the Trail '41
Renegade Trail '39

Virgil Harper
Sweet Insanity '06
Miracle at Sage Creek '05
Tremors 3: Back to Perfection '01
Tremors 2: Aftershocks '96
... And the Earth Did Not Swallow Him '94

Harvey Harrison
R.P.M. '97
The Witches '90
American Gothic '88
Salome's Last Dance '88
Castaway '87
Cheech and Chong's The Corsican Brothers '84
Cheech and Chong: Still Smokin' '83
The Burning '82

Thomas M. Harting
Ruslan '09
Deal '08
Impact Point '08
Kill Switch '08
Single White Female 2: The Psycho '05
Death Valley '04
The Event '03
No One Sleeps '01
Ripper: Letter from Hell '01
Beefcake '99
Defying Gravity '99

Irek Hartowicz(1951-)
Music Within '07
Kill Your Darlings '06
Mr. Fix It '06
The Iris Effect '04
The Badge '02
Bark! '02
Outside Ozona '98
Subterfuge '98
Lured Innocence '97
Perfect Crime '97
Mercenary '96

Walter J. (Jimmy W.) Harvey(1903-)
Race for Life '55
Big Deadly Game '54
Black Glove '54
Blackout '54
Heat Wave '54
Paid to Kill '54
Terror Street '54
Unholy Four '54
Three Stops to Murder '53
The Gambler & the Lady '52
Scotland Yard Inspector '52
A Stolen Face '52
River of Unrest '36

Kiyoshi Hasegawa
Samurai Reincarnation '81
Phoenix '78

Byron Haskin(1899-1984)
The First Texan '56
Colleen '36
The Singing Fool '28
When a Man Loves '27
Don Juan '26

Kim Haun
Body Strokes '95
Friend of the Family '95
I Like to Play Games '95

Robert B. Hauser(1919-94)
The Frisco Kid '79
Mean Dog Blues '78
Twilight's Last Gleaming '77
Walking Tall: The Final Chapter '77
Le Mans '71
Willard '71
A Man Called Horse '70
Soldier Blue '70
Hail, Hero! '69
The Odd Couple '68

Yuri Haviv
Double Agent 73 '80
I Spit on Your Grave '77

James Hawkinson(1962-)
The Unborn '09
The Hitcher '07
Progeny '98

Nick Hay
Circadian Rhythm '05
Manic '01

Junichiro Hayashi
Dark Water '02
Pulse '01
Charisma '99
Ringu '98

Robert Hayes
The Butcher '07
The Last Sentinel '07
Welcome to Paradise '07
Pit Fighter '05
Witches of the Caribbean '05
Devil's Knight '03
Body Armor '96
Werewolf '95
Mind, Body & Soul '92
Driven to Kill '90
Hardcase and Fist '89

James Hayman
Buffy the Vampire Slayer '92
Blades '89

George Heath
The Fighting Rats of Tobruk '44
Forty Thousand Horsemen '41

Brian R.R. Hebb
Humongous '82
July Group '81

Antoine Heberle
Paradise Now '05
The Girl from Paris '02
Under the Sand '00

Matthew Heckerling
Left in Darkness '06
Crazylove '05

Dan Heigh
Whacked! '02
The Basket '99
Matter of Trust '98
Laws of Deception '97
Navajo Blues '97

Bernd Heinl
Milwaukee, Minnesota '03
The Little Vampire '00
The Extreme Adventures of Super Dave '98
Wicked '98
Johnny Skidmarks '97
Julian Po '97
The Last of the High Kings '96
It's My Party '95
The Nutt House '95
Pie in the Sky '95
The Fear '94
Younger & Younger '94
Bodies, Rest & Motion '93
Bagdad Cafe '88

Wolfgang Held
American Teen '08
Crazy Love '07
Teeth '07
Disappearances '06
Slippery Slope '06
Poster Boy '04
Undermind '03
Fallout '01
Maze '01
The Tic Code '99
Floating '97
Ripe '97
Dogs: The Rise and Fall of an All-Girl Bookie Joint '96
Wigstock: The Movie '95

Otto Heller(1896-1970)
I'll Never Forget What's 'Isname '67
Alfie '66
Funeral in Berlin '66
The Ipcress File '65
Woman of Straw '64
Victim '61
Peeping Tom '60
The Rough and the Smooth '59
The Sheriff of Fractured Jaw '59
Who Done It? '56
The Ladykillers '55
They Made Me a Fugitive '47
Mr. Emmanuel '44
De Mayerling a Sarajevo '40

Peter Hendry
1915 '82
Love Under Pressure '78

Peter Hennessy(1916-)
The Quare Fellow '62
Cat Girl '57
Time Lock '57

David Hennings
Hannah Montana: The Movie '09
Strange Wilderness '08
Ice Princess '05
Underclassman '05
Breakin' All The Rules '04
You Got Served '04
Blue Crush '02
Boycott '02
Cheaters '00
Meet the Deedles '98
Tom Clancy's Netforce '98
Very Bad Things '98
Asteroid '97
D3: The Mighty Ducks '96
Titanic '96

Gilles Henry
Moliere '07
Priceless '06

Apres-Vous '03
Van Gogh '92

David Herrington

True Confessions of a Hollywood Starlet '08
Carry Me Home '04
A Killing Spring '02
Verdict in Blood '02
You Stupid Man '02
Blues Brothers 2000 '98

Karl Herrmann

Missing Pieces '00
Kounterfeit '96
America's Dream '95

John Herzog

Crackerjack 2 '97
Hello Mary Lou: Prom Night 2 '87

Gregg Heschong

A Cry in the Wild '90
Heavy Traffic '73

Sid Hickox(1895-1982)

Battle Cry '55
Them! '54
Colorado Territory '49
White Heat '49
The Big Sleep '46
God is My Co-Pilot '45
All Through the Night '42
Underground '41
The Wagons Roll at Night '41
A Slight Case of Murder '38
San Quentin '37
The Little Giant '33
Frisco Jenny '32

Ken Higgins

Hot Millions '68
Salt & Pepper '68
Cop-Out '67
Georgy Girl '66
Darling '65

David Higgs

Vampire Killers '09
Lost in Austen '08
RocknRolla '08
Cambridge Spies '03

Jack Hildyard(1908-90)

Florence Nightingale '85
Lion of the Desert '81
Emily '77
The Message '77
The Beast Must Die '75
Puppet on a Chain '72
Topaz '69
Villa Rides '68
Casino Royale '67
Modesty Blaise '66
Battle of the Bulge '65
Circus World '64
55 Days at Peking '63
The V.I.P.'s '63
The Road to Hong Kong '62
The Millionairess '60
The Sundowners '60
The Devil's Disciple '59
Suddenly, Last Summer '59
Another Time, Another Place '58
The Bridge on the River Kwai '57
Anastasia '56
Summertime '55
Hobson's Choice '53
The Sound Barrier '52

Richard Hilliard

Horror of Party Beach '64
The Lonely Sex '59

Erwin Hillier(1911-2005)

The Valley of Gwangi '69
School for Scoundrels '60
Happy Go Lovely '51
I Know Where I'm Going '45
Butler's Dilemma '43

Sinsaku Himeda(1916-97)

Vengeance Is Mine '79
Proof of the Man '77
Tora! Tora! Tora! '70

Harvey Hines

Kid from Gower Gulch '50
Silver Bandit '50

Milas C. Hinshaw

Mystery Mansion '83
Dream Chasers '82

Paul Hipp(1938-2006)

Psycho from Texas '75
The Incredible Two-Headed Transplant '71
Superchick '71
Corruption '70
Dream No Evil '70

Julien Hirsch(1964-)

The Girl on the Train '09
The Witnesses '07
Lady Chatterley '06
Changing Times '04
Our Music '04
In Praise of Love '01

Gerald Hirschfeld(1921-)

Coma '78
The Car '77
Two Minute Warning '76
Young Frankenstein '74
Cotton Comes to Harlem '70
The Incident '67
Fail-Safe '64

Daf Hobson(1951-)

Othello '01
Sword of Honour '01
Welcome to Sarajevo '97
Go Now '96
The Tenant of Wildfell Hall '96

Winton C. Hoch(1907-79)

The Witching '72
The Green Berets '68
Robinson Crusoe on Mars '64
Five Weeks in a Balloon '62
Sergeants 3 '62
Voyage to the Bottom of the Sea '61
Darby O'Gill & the Little People '59
The Young Land '59
Missouri Traveler '58
Jet Pilot '57
The Searchers '56
Mister Roberts '55
The Halls of Montezuma '50
She Wore a Yellow Ribbon '49
Tulsa '49
Melody Time '48
Three Godfathers '48
Dive Bomber '41
Dr. Cyclops '40

Zoran Hochstatter(1955-)

If I Die Before I Wake '98
The Last Best Sunday '98
Slaves to the Underground '96
Body Chemistry 4: Full Exposure '95
Demolition High '95
Almost Dead '94
Hard Bounty '94
Night Fire '94
Home for Christmas '93
Revenge of the Nerds 3: The Next Generation '92
Not of This Earth '88

Ken Hodges(1922-93)

No Sex Please—We're British '73
The Ruling Class '72

Carl Hoffmann

Faust '26
Dr. Mabuse, The Gambler '22

Florian Hoffmeister

The Prisoner '09
House of Saddam '08
Five Days '07
The Hamburg Cell '04

Henner Hofmann

Warden of Red Rock '01
Immortal Combat '94

Siegfried Hold

M'Lady's Court '73
Apache's Last Battle '64

Adam Holender(1937-)

Carlito's Way: Rise to Power '05
Stateside '04
Road to Riches '01
A Price above Rubies '97
Wide Awake '97
8 Heads in a Duffel Bag '96
I'm Not Rappaport '96
Smoke '95
Fresh '94
To Kill a Priest '89
Street Smart '87
Idolmaker '80
Panic in Needle Park '71
Midnight Cowboy '69

Keith Holland

One of Them '03
Blind Heat '00
Bloody Murder '99
Hindsight '97
Trucks '97
Dark Secrets '95
Carnosaur '93

John Holosko

The Jesse Ventura Story '99
Face Down '97

Bodo Holst

Beyond Fear '93
Pushed to the Limit '92

Ernest Holzman

Cora Unashamed '00
Double Edge '97
Love Jones '96

Kyung-Pyo Hong

Madeo '09
3 Extremes 2 '02

John Hooper

The Scarlet Pimpernel 3: The Kidnapped King '99
Catherine Cookson's The Dwelling Place '94
Buddy's Song '91

Nathan Hope

The Fog '05
Mimic 2 '01
Nice Guys Sleep Alone '99
The Prophecy 3: The Ascent '99

John Hora

God Said "Ha!" '99
Matinee '92
Gremlins 2: The New Batch '90
Gremlins '84
Twilight Zone: The Movie '83
The Howling '81

Louis Horvath

Mesmerized '84
Strange Invaders '83
Strange Behavior '81
Black Samurai '77
Brain of Blood '71

Alan Hostetter

The 24th Day '04
Orwell Rolls in His Grave '03

Byron Houck(1891-1969)

Seven Chances '25
The Navigator '24
Sherlock, Jr. '24

Tom Houghton

Finding Amanda '08
State Property 2 '05
The Cookout '04
Fire Down Below '97

James Wong Howe(1899-1976)

The Old Man and the Sea '90
Funny Lady '75
Molly Maguires '70
The Heart Is a Lonely Hunter '68
Hombre '67
Seconds '66
The Outrage '64
Hud '63
Song Without End '60
The Last Angry Man '59
Bell, Book and Candle '58
The Old Man and the Sea '58
Sweet Smell of Success '57
Picnic '55
The Rose Tattoo '55
Come Back, Little Sheba '52
The Fighter '52
Baron of Arizona '51
Mr. Blandings Builds His Dream House '48
Body and Soul '47
Nora Prentiss '47
Pursued '47
My Reputation '46
Objective, Burma! '45
Passage to Marseilles '44
Air Force '43
The North Star '43
Hangmen Also Die '42
Yankee Doodle Dandy '42
Kings Row '41
Out of the Fog '41
Strawberry Blonde '41
Abe Lincoln in Illinois '40
City for Conquest '40
Dr. Ehrlich's Magic Bullet '40
Torrid Zone '40
Oklahoma Kid '39
They Made Me a Criminal '39
The Adventures of Tom Sawyer '38
Algiers '38
Fire Over England '37
Prisoner of Zenda '37
Under the Red Robe '36
Mark of the Vampire '35
Whipsaw '35
Hollywood Party '34
Manhattan Melodrama '34
The Thin Man '34
After Tomorrow '32
Chandu the Magician '32
Desert Nights '29
Desert Nights '29
The King on Main Street '25
Peter Pan '24

Matt Howe

Blood Relic '05
Desolation Angels '95
Parallel Sons '95

Gil Hubbs

Flowers in the Attic '87
Terror at London Bridge '85
California Girls '84
This Is Elvis '81
The Guyana Tragedy: The Story of Jim Jones '80
Enter the Dragon '73
The Wrestler '73

Roger Hubert(1903-64)

Paris Holiday '57
Portrait of an Assassin '49
Children of Paradise '44
Eternal Return '43
Napoleon '27

Angus Hudson

The Broken '08
Cashback '06

Andrew Huebscher

Shadowheart '09
Believers '07
Crashing '07
The Elder Son '06
Chasing Ghosts '05
Window Theory '04

Michael Hugo

The Mountain Men '80
The Bastard '78
The Manitou '78
Terror Out of the Sky '78
Bug '75
Earth II '71
Model Shop '69
Head '68

Alan Hume(1924-)

20,000 Leagues Under the Sea '97
Annie: A Royal Adventure '95
Just Like a Woman '95
Carry On Columbus '92
Eve of Destruction '90
Shirley Valentine '89
A Fish Called Wanda '88
Lifeforce '85
Runaway Train '85
A View to a Kill '85
Supergirl '84
Octopussy '83
Return of the Jedi '83
Caveman '81
Eye of the Needle '81
For Your Eyes Only '81
The Watcher in the Woods '81
The People That Time Forgot '77
At the Earth's Core '76
The Land That Time Forgot '75
The Legend of Hell House '73
Carry On Abroad '72
Captain Nemo and the Underwater City '69
Carry On Cowboy '66
Don't Lose Your Head '66
Dr. Terror's House of Horrors '65
Carry On Spying '64
Carry On Cabby '63
Carry On Jack '63
Kiss of the Vampire '62
Carry On Regardless '61
No Kidding '60

Robert Humphreys

The Silence '06
Nora's Hair Salon '04
Dopamine '03
Charlotte Sometimes '02
Walking on Water '02
The Invisibles '99

John Huneck

Diamond Men '01
Big Brother Trouble '00
One Man's Justice '95
No Retreat, No Surrender 3: Blood Brothers '91
The Banker '89

J. Roy Hunt(1884-1972)

Gunplay '51
Riders of the Range '50
Storm over Wyoming '50
I Walked with a Zombie '43
Call Out the Marines '42
The Flying Irishman '39
A Man to Remember '39
Panama Lady '39
Room Service '38
Breakfast for Two '37
Without Orders '36
She '35
Double Harness '33
Dancing Mothers '26
Sherlock Holmes '22

W. Mott Hupfel, III

The Savages '07
The Notorious Bettie Page '06
Boys Life '94

Shane Hurlbut

Terminator Salvation '09
Semi-Pro '08
Swing Vote '08
Something New '06
Waist Deep '06
We Are Marshall '06
The Greatest Game Ever Played '05
Into the Blue '05
Mr. 3000 '04
11:14 '03
Drumline '02
crazy/beautiful '01
The Skulls '00
The Rat Pack '98

Philip Hurn

Six: The Mark Unleashed '04
Undercover '94

Tom Hurwitz

Our Brand Is Crisis '05
Subway Stories '97
Creepshow 2 '87
Wanted: The Perfect Guy '86

Seo-Shik Hwang

The Isle '01
Sorum '01

Peter Hyams(1943-)

Beyond a Reasonable Doubt '09
Universal Soldier: Regeneration '09
A Sound of Thunder '05
The Musketeer '01
End of Days '99
The Relic '96
Sudden Death '95
Timecop '94
Stay Tuned '92
Running Scared '86
2010: The Year We Make Contact '84

William (Bill) Hyer(1905-89)

Phantom Rancher '39
The Rangers' Roundup '38
Brothers of the West '37
Pinto Rustlers '36
Racing Blood '36
Kid Courageous '35
Range Riders '35
Texas Terror '35
Western Justice '35

Fred Iannone

Hot Tamale '06
Smiling Fish & Goat on Fire '99

Arthur Ibbetson(1922-97)

Santa Claus: The Movie '85
The Bounty '84
Sell Out '76
When Eight Bells Toll '71
Willy Wonka & the Chocolate Factory '71
The Railway Children '70
Inspector Clouseau '68
Where Eagles Dare '68
A Countess from Hong Kong '67
Die! Die! My Darling! '65
Murder at the Gallop '63
Whistle down the Wind '61
The Horse's Mouth '58

Slawomir Idziak(1945-)

Harry Potter and the Order of the Phoenix '07
King Arthur '04
Black Hawk Down '01
Proof of Life '00
The Last September '99
Love and Rage '99
I Want You '98
Gattaca '97
Hombres Armados '97
Commandments '96
The Journey of August King '95
Lilian's Story '95
Trois Couleurs: Bleu '93
The Double Life of Veronique '91
The Decalogue '88
From a Far Country: Pope John Paul II '81
Contract '80

Hiroshi Imai

Along with Ghosts '69
Spook Warfare '68

Tony Imi(1937-)

Lighthouse Hill '04
Chaos & Cadavers '03
Victoria & Albert '01
Rancid Aluminium '00
Dead of Night '99
Aimee & Jaguar '98

The Abduction '96
Dalva '95
Shopping '93
Carolina Skeletons '92
Wired '89
Enemy Mine '85
A Christmas Carol '84
The Slipper and the Rose '76
Edward the King '75
It's Not the Size That Counts '74

Ofer Inov
Beaufort '07
Time of Favor '00

David Insley
An American Affair '09
Cry-Baby '90
Hairspray '88
Polyester '81

John Inwood
Six Ways to Sunday '99
The Daytrippers '96

Silvano Ippoliti(1923-)
Caligula '80
Act of Aggression '73

Judy Irola(1943-)
Eban and Charley '01
The Settlement '99
Eat Your Heart Out '96
Working Girls '87

Louis Irving
The Alice '04
Howling 3: The Marsupials '87
The Last Bastion '84
Return of Captain Invincible '83

Matthew Irving
Table for Three '09
Waitress '07
Daltry Calhoun '05
Waiting '05
Monster Man '03
Groove '00

Mark Irwin
Dance Flick '09
Terror Eyes '87

Mark Irwin(1950-)
Ace Ventura Jr.: Pet Detective '08
Blonde Ambition '07
Sydney White '07
Big Momma's House 2 '06
Deck the Halls '06
Grandma's Boy '06
The Ringer '05
Malibu's Most Wanted '03
Old School '03
Scary Movie 3 '03
American Pie 2 '01
Freddy Got Fingered '01
Osmosis Jones '01
Say It Isn't So '01
Me, Myself, and Irene '00
Road Trip '00
Ten Things I Hate about You '99
Misbegotten '98
There's Something about Mary '98
Zack & Reba '98
Joe Torre: Curveballs Along the Way '97
Steel '97
Kingpin '96
Scream '96
The Avenging Angel '95
Vampire in Brooklyn '95
Dumb & Dumber '94
Wes Craven's New Nightmare '94
Extreme Justice '93
Passenger 57 '92
Showdown in Little Tokyo '91
Heat Wave '90
RoboCop 2 '90
Bat 21 '88
The Blob '88
Fright Night 2 '88
The Fly '86
Dead Zone '83
Videodrome '83
Night School '81
Scanners '81
The Brood '79

Levie Isaacks
Road Trip: Beer Pong '09
Sundown: The Vampire in Retreat '08
Bring It On: In It to Win It '07
Dead Men Can't Dance '97
North Shore Fish '97
The Dentist '96
Marshal Law '96
The Dogfighters '95
The Expert '95
The Texas Chainsaw Massacre 4: The Next Generation '95
The Wharf Rat '95
Leprechaun '93
Spontaneous Combustion '89
Saturday the 14th Strikes Back '88

Marco Isoli
Desperate Crimes '93
Evil Clutch '89

Takeo Ito
Drunken Angel '48
The Men Who Tread on the Tiger's Tail '45

Paul Ivano(1900-84)
The Naked Flame '68
Black Angel '46
Slightly Terrific '44
Honeymoon Lodge '43
The Shanghai Gesture '42
Hoosier Schoolboy '37
Queen Kelly '29

Stefan Ivanov(1954-)
Marion Bridge '02
Genealogies of a Crime '97

Tim Ives
Heavy Petting '07
Dinner Rush '00

Fred H. Jackman, Jr. (1913-82)
Viva Knievel '77
Harum Scarum '65
Earth vs. the Flying Saucers '56
Coroner Creek '48
The Prince of Thieves '48
Big Town '47
Swamp Fire '46
Wild West '46
Treasure of Fear '45
Dangerous Passage '44
Dark Mountain '44
Gambler's Choice '44
Navy Way '44
One Body Too Many '44
Take It Big '44
Wildcat '42
Flying Blind '41
Flying Wild '41
Phantom of Chinatown '40
Up in the Air '40
Stunt Pilot '39
Wolf Call '39

Fred W. Jackman(1881-1959)
Unknown Island '48
Yankee Doodle in Berlin '19

Andrew Jackson
The Strongest Man in the World '75
I Love You, Goodbye '74
Don't Be Afraid of the Dark '73
Death of a Gunfighter '69

Donald G. Jackson(1943-2003)
Roller Blade Warriors: Taken By Force '90
Hell Comes to Frogtown '88

Harry Jackson(1896-1953)
The Halls of Montezuma '50
Ticket to Tomahawk '50
Mother Wore Tights '47
Greenwich Village '44
Charlie Chan on Broadway '37
Think Fast, Mr. Moto '37
Charlie Chan at the Race Track '36
Life Begins at Forty '35
Jungle Bride '33

Igor Jadue-Lillo
The Kids Are All Right '10
Passengers '08
The Hitchhiker's Guide to the Galaxy '05
Disco Pigs '01
The Low Down '00

Julius Jaenzon
The Phantom Chariot '20
Treasure of Arne '19

Peter James(1947-)
27 Dresses '08
Cheaper by the Dozen 2 '05
The Pacifier '05
And Starring Pancho Villa as Himself '03
Bride of the Wind '01
Meet the Parents '00
Double Jeopardy '99
The Newton Boys '97
Paradise Road '97
Diabolique '96
Last Dance '96
Silent Fall '94
Alive '93
My Life '93
The Thing Called Love '93
Black Robe '91
Mister Johnson '91
Driving Miss Daisy '89
Echoes of Paradise '86
The Irishman '78
Caddie '76

Nyika Jancso(1952-)
Broken Lullaby '94
A Change of Place '94
Where '90

Andrew Janczak
The Undertaker and His Pals '67
Creeping Terror '64

Anthony C. "Tony" Jannelli
All I Wanna Do '98
Lovelife '97
Subway Stories '97

Maris Jansons
Double Play '96
The Halfback of Notre Dame '96
Heck's Way Home '95

Manfred O. Jelinski
Nekromantik 2 '91
Der Todesking '89

Devereaux Jennings(1884-1952)
Helltown '38
Public Enemy '31
Golden Dawn '30
Sally '29
Steamboat Bill, Jr. '28
Battling Butler '26
The General '26

Johnny E. Jensen
American Girl: Chrissa Stands Strong '09
Tribute '09
Material Girls '06
The Game of Their Lives '05
Wisegirls '02
The Flamingo Rising '01
The Ladies Man '00
Morgan's Ferry '99
Rosewood '96
Three Wishes '95
Grumpy Old Men '93
An American Story '92
Rambling Rose '91

Matthew Jensen
Killer Diller '04
Devil's Pond '03
Man of the Century '99
Ratas, Ratones, Rateros '99

Peter C. Jensen
Glitch! '88
Grandma's House '88

Jeong-hun Jeong
Thirst '09
Lady Vengeance '05
Three ... Extremes '04
Oldboy '03

Peter Jessop(1930-)
Band of Gold '95
Piece of Cake '88
Mountbatten: The Last Viceroy '86
Parker '84
Schizo '77
House of Whipcord '75
Frightmare '74
Flesh and Blood Show '73
The Harder They Come '72

Robert C. Jessup
Porky's Revenge '85
Silent Rage '82
Deadly Blessing '81
Race with the Devil '75
Creature of Destruction '67
Mars Needs Women '66

Thomas Jewett
Fast Money '96
Serial Killer '95
Scanner Cop 2: Volkin's Revenge '94
Mikey '92

Yong Duk Jhun
Shrek Forever After '10
Kung Fu Panda '08

Daniel Jobin(1949-)
Varian's War '01
It's My Turn, Laura Cadieux '98
The Hanging Garden '97
Lilies '96

Pierre Jodoin
The Cutting Edge 3: Chasing the Dream '08
Dr. Jekyll and Mr. Hyde '08
Flood '07
Killer Wave '07
Stiletto Dance '01

Jon Joffin(1963-)
Alice '09
Flirting with Forty '09
Another Cinderella Story '08
It Waits '05
Lucky Seven '03
The Snow Walker '03
Snow White: The Fairest of Them All '02
Mermaid '00
Aftershock: Earthquake in New York '99

Ron Johanson(1949-)
Freedom '82
Death Games '80

Jorgen Johansson(1960-)
Wilbur Wants to Kill Himself '02
Italian for Beginners '01
Kira's Reason—A Love Story '01

Bruce Douglas Johnson
Minutemen '08
Harold and Kumar Go to White Castle '04
Scorched '02
The Contaminated Man '01
Drowning Mona '00
Happy, Texas '99
Perfect Assassins '98
Road Ends '98
Cadillac Ranch '96
The Prophecy '95
Public Access '93

David Johnson
Resident Evil: Extinction '07
On a Clear Day '05

David C(lark) Johnson(1962-)
Alien vs. Predator '04
Resident Evil '02
An Ideal Husband '99
Hilary and Jackie '98
The Very Thought of You '98
The Mill on the Floss '97
Othello '95
Saint-Ex: The Story of the Storyteller '95

Frank Johnson
Alone in the Woods '95
Project: Kill! '77

Hugh Johnson
Eragon '06
The Chronicles of Riddick '04
G.I. Jane '97
White Squall '96

Kirsten Johnson
Darfur Now '07
This Film Is Not Yet Rated '06

Shelly Johnson
The Wolfman '09
The House Bunny '08
Sky High '05
Hidalgo '04
Jurassic Park 3 '01
The Last Castle '01
Durango '99
A Season for Miracles '99
Quicksilver Highway '98
Saint Maybe '98
Alien Nation: Millennium '96
Alien Nation: Body and Soul '95
Hitz '89
Jack's Back '87

Dusan Joksimovic
The Keeper: The Legend of Omar Khayyam '05
The Wounds '98
Pretty Village, Pretty Flame '96

Lawrence Jones
Strange Relations '02
In His Life: The John Lennon Story '00
The 10th Kingdom '00
Reckless: The Sequel '98

Richard A. Jones
Wanted '98
Turn of the Blade '97

Jon Jost(1943-)
The Bed You Sleep In '93
Slow Moves '84

Mario Garcia Joya
Strawberry and Chocolate '93
Alias, La Gringa '91
Letters from the Park '88

Ray June(1895-1958)
Court Jester '56
Above and Beyond '53
Invitation '51
It's a Big Country '51
Crisis '50
The Secret Garden '49
H.M. Pulham Esquire '41
Night Must Fall '37
Wife Versus Secretary '36
China Seas '35
Horse Feathers '32
The Bat Whispers '30
Alibi '29
Through the Breakers '28

Jeffrey Jur
The Eye '08
You Kill Me '07
Last Call: The Final Chapter of F. Scott Fitzgerald '02
My Big Fat Greek Wedding '02
Joy Ride '01
My First Mister '01
Panic '00
How Stella Got Her Groove Back '98
Horton Foote's Alone '97
Unforgettable '96
The Last Seduction '94
Dirty Dancing '87
Soul Man '86
Screen Test '85

Hans Jura
Little Mother '71
The Lickerish Quartet '70
Therese & Isabelle '67
Carmen, Baby '66

William B. Jurgensen
Mayday at 40,000 Feet '76
Arnold '73

Jurgen Jurges(1940-)
Time of the Wolf '03
Code Unknown '00
Funny Games '97
Faraway, So Close! '93
Germany, Pale Mother '80
Fear of Fear '75
Ali: Fear Eats the Soul '74
Effi Briest '74
Tenderness of the Wolves '73

Emmanuel (Manu) Kadosh
The Christmas Miracle of Jonathan Toomey '07
The Lost City '05
Modigliani '04

Mahmoud Kalari
Boutique '04
Gabbeh '96

Ernst W. Kalinke(1918-)
Mark of the Devil '69
Strangler of Blackmoor Castle '63

Milton Kam
ABCD '99
I Think I Do '97

Steven Kaman
Mob War '88
Search and Destroy '88
Firehouse '87
Hangmen '87

Janusz Kaminski(1959-)
Funny People '09
Indiana Jones and the Kingdom of the Crystal Skull '08
The Diving Bell and the Butterfly '07
Munich '05
War of the Worlds '05
The Terminal '04
Catch Me If You Can '02
Minority Report '02
A. I.: Artificial Intelligence '01
Saving Private Ryan '98
Amistad '97
The Lost World: Jurassic Park 2 '97
Jerry Maguire '96
How to Make an American Quilt '95
Tall Tale: The Unbelievable Adventures of Pecos Bill '95
Little Giants '94
The Adventures of Huck Finn '93
Schindler's List '93
Class of '61 '92
Homicidal Impulse '92
Cool As Ice '91
Wildflower '91
Grim Prairie Tales '89

Adam Kane
Resurrecting the Champ '07
Skinwalkers '07
The Man '05
Love & Sex '00
Boondock Saints '99
No Code of Conduct '98
Within the Rock '96

Taiichi Kankura
Yog, Monster from Space '71

Latitude Zero '69
Destroy All Monsters '68

Otto Kanturek

The Girl in the News '41
Night Train to Munich '40

Avi (Avraham) Karpik

Simon Sez '99
Sticks and Stones '96
Outside the Law '95
Solar Force '94
The Seventh Coin '92

Norimichi Kasamatsu

Electric Dragon 80,000V '01
Angel Dust '96

Norayr Kasper

The Terrorist Next Door '08
Redeemer '02
The Last Debate '00
The Life Before This '99
Calendar '93

Benjamin Kasulke

The Freebie '10
Humpday '09
My Effortless Brilliance '08
Nights and Weekends '08
Brand Upon the Brain! '06

Stephen M. Katz

A Death in the Family '02
Her Majesty '01
Return to Cabin by the Lake '01
Gepetto '00
I'll Remember April '99
Baby Geniuses '98
Gods and Monsters '98
Mrs. Santa Claus '96
Letter to My Killer '95
My Summer Story '94
18 Again! '88
Last Resort '86
The Blues Brothers '80
Kentucky Fried Movie '77
Las Vegas Lady '76
Pom Pom Girls '76
Switchblade Sisters '75

David Katznelson

Driving Lessons '06
The Queen's Sister '05

Boris Kaufman(1906-80)

The Brotherhood '68
Bye Bye Braverman '67
The Group '66
The Pawnbroker '65
The World of Henry Orient '64
Gone Are the Days '63
Purlie Victorious '63
Long Day's Journey into Night '62
The Fugitive Kind '60
Twelve Angry Men '57
Baby Doll '56
Patterns '56
On the Waterfront '54
L'Atalante '34
Zero for Conduct '33
A Propos de Nice '29

Lloyd Kaufman(1945-)

Stuck on You '84
First Turn On '83
Waitress '81
Squeeze Play '79

Judith Kaufmann(1962-)

Unveiled '05
Nico Icon '95

Taro Kawazu

The Neighbor No. Thirteen '05
The Princess Blade '02

Naoke Kayano

Onmyoji '01
Shall We Dance? '96

Naoki Kayano

Premonition '04
Onmyoji '01

Stephen Kazmierski

Homecoming '09
The Caller '08

Dedication '07
Beautiful Ohio '06
Two Weeks '06
Transamerica '05
A Hole in One '04
Love in the Time of Money '02
Skins '02
Tart '01
You Can Count On Me '99
The Bumblebee Flies Anyway '98
The Myth of Fingerprints '97
Grind '96
Blessing '94

Kevin Keating

Soul Power '08
Giuliani Time '05

Michel Kelber

Phedre '68
It Means That to Me '60
The Hunchback of Notre Dame '57
Beauty and the Devil '50
Devil in the Flesh '46

Alfred S. Keller(1911-89)

Homesteaders of Paradise Valley '47
Spoilers of the North '47
Under Colorado Skies '47
Wild Frontier '47
G.I. War Brides '46
Rio Grande Raiders '46

Wallace Kelley(1902-82)

Paradise, Hawaiian Style '66
The Nutty Professor '63
Who's Minding the Store? '63

Nina Kellgren

Wondrous Oblivion '06
Solomon and Gaenor '98

Roy Kellino(1912-56)

Johnny Frenchman '46
Nine Men '43
I Met a Murderer '39

Shane Kelly

A Scanner Darkly '06
Urbania '00
Delivered '98

Ken Kelsch

100 Feet '08
The Black Widow '05
Testosterone '03
'R Xmas '01
It Had to Be You '00
Invisible Child '99
Dying to Get Rich '98
The Imposters '98
New Rose Hotel '98
Rear Window '98
The Blackout '97
A Brooklyn State of Mind '97
Montana '97
Subway Stories '97
The Funeral '96
The Addiction '95
Big Night '95
Condition Red '95
Killer: A Journal of Murder '95
DROP Squad '94
Bad Lieutenant '92
Driller Killer '79

Victor Kemper(1927-)

American Pie Presents Band Camp '05
Eddie '96
Jingle All the Way '96
Tommy Boy '95
Beethoven '92
F/X 2: The Deadly Art of Illusion '91
See No Evil, Hear No Evil '89
Clue '85
Pee-wee's Big Adventure '85
The Lonely Guy '84
Mr. Mom '83
National Lampoon's Vacation '83

Xanadu '80
And Justice for All '79
The Jerk '79
Coma '78
Eyes of Laura Mars '78
Magic '78
Audrey Rose '77
Slap Shot '77
Dog Day Afternoon '75
The Reincarnation of Peter Proud '75
The Gambler '74
The Candidate '72
The Hospital '71
They Might Be Giants '71
Husbands '70

Nils Kenaston

Borough of Kings '98
Day at the Beach '98
Mob Queen '98

Francis Kenny

Cover '08
Edison Force '05
Getting Played '05
From Justin to Kelly '03
Finder's Fee '01
How High '01
Kingdom Come '01
Scary Movie '00
She's All That '99
A Night at the Roxbury '98
Something About Sex '98
Bean '97
Harriet the Spy '96
A Thin Line Between Love and Hate '96
Coneheads '93
Wayne's World 2 '93
New Jack City '91
Heathers '89

John Kenway

My Uncle Silas '01
Dr. Bell and Mr. Doyle: The Dark Beginnings of Sherlock Holmes '00
Pride and Prejudice '95
Bhaji on the Beach '94

Martin Kenzie

Easy Virtue '08
Back in Business '06

Glenn Kershaw

At First Sight '95
A Kiss Goodnight '94
Sins of the Night '93
Fatal Skies '90

Rolf Kestermann

Casual Sex? '88
Surf Nazis Must Die '87

Cheng Siu Keung

Breaking News '04
Running out of Time '99

Kwok-Man Keung

DOA: Dead or Alive '06
So Close '02

Scott Kevan(1972-)

The Losers '10
Fame '09
Death Race '08
Hell Ride '08
Nothing Like the Holidays '08
Borderland '07
Cleaner '07
Stomp the Yard '07
Deepwater '05
The Hollow '04
Plain Dirty '04
Cabin Fever '03
The Job '03
The Trip '02

Darius Khondji(1955-)

Cheri '09
The Ruins '08
Funny Games '07
My Blueberry Nights '07
The Interpreter '05
Wimbledon '04
Anything Else '03
Panic Room '02
The Beach '00
The Ninth Gate '99
In Dreams '98

Alien: Resurrection '97
Evita '96
Stealing Beauty '96
The City of Lost Children '95
Seven '95
Delicatessen '92

Gary B. Kibbe(1941-)

John Carpenter's Ghosts of Mars '01
John Carpenter's Vampires '97
Escape from L.A. '96
In the Mouth of Madness '95
Village of the Damned '95
Double Dragon '94
RoboCop 3 '91
They Live '88
Prince of Darkness '87

Jan Kiesser

The Thaw '09
Luna: Spirit of the Whale '07
Beowulf & Grendel '06
Fido '06
Now & Forever '02
Rare Birds '01
Dr. T & the Women '00
Holiday Heart '00
Trixie '00
The Dress Code '99
The Baby Dance '98
Such a Long Journey '98
National Lampoon's Dad's Week Off '97
Bad Moon '96
Georgia '95
Man with a Gun '95
Mrs. Parker and the Vicious Circle '94
Clean and Sober '88
Fright Night '85
Choose Me '84

Tokusho Kikumura

Death Note 3: L, Change the World '08
One Missed Call 2 '05
Ju-On: The Grudge '03
Cure '97

Laela Kilbourn

American Teen '08
Word Wars: Tiles and Tribulations on the Scrabble Circuit '04

Byeong-il Kim

Addicted '02
Addicted '02
Sympathy for Mr. Vengeance '02

Hoon-Gwang Kim

Hidden Floor '06
My Bloody Roommates '06

Hyung-ku Kim

The Host '06
The Warrior '01

Shawn Kim

Smiley Face '07
Ghetto Dawg '02

Sung-Bok Kim

Female Prisoner Sigma '06
JSA: Joint Security Area '00
Shiri '99

Yoon-soo Kim

Bloody Beach '00
Memento Mori '00

Jeffrey L. Kimball(1943-)

The Expendables '10
Old Dogs '09
Four Christmases '08
Bonneville '06
Glory Road '06
Be Cool '05
The Big Bounce '04
Paycheck '03
Star Trek: Nemesis '02
Windtalkers '02
Mission: Impossible 2 '00
Stigmata '99
Wild Things '98
The Specialist '94
True Romance '93
Jacob's Ladder '90

Beverly Hills Cop 2 '87
Top Gun '86

Adam Kimmel

Rudo y Cursi '09
Lars and the Real Girl '07
Capote '05
Beyond Suspicion '00
Jesus' Son '99
Monument Ave. '98
Almost Heroes '97
Subway Stories '97
Beautiful Girls '96
Bed of Roses '95
New Jersey Drive '95

Mike King

Don't Tell '05
The Manson Family '04

Rory King

Dirty Laundry '07
April's Shower '03

Sean Kirby

The Tillman Story '10
Cthulhu '08

Herbert Kirkpatrick

Motive for Revenge '35
Western Courage '35

Sven Kirsten(1955-)

School's Out '99
Beyond Desire '94
Play Time '94
Teresa's Tattoo '94
Mistress '91

Thomas Kist

Blind Date '08
Interview '07

Nattawut Kittihun

Ong-Bak '03
3 Extremes 2 '02

Alar Kivilo(1953-)

The Blind Side '09
Taking Chance '09
Year One '09
The Lookout '07
Aurora Borealis '06
The Lake House '06
The Ice Harvest '05
Normal '03
Hart's War '02
The Glass House '01
Frequency '00
A Simple Plan '98
Weapons of Mass Distraction '97
Gotti '96
Rebound: The Legend of Earl "The Goat" Manigault '96
The Invaders '95

Eugen Klagemann

The Merry Wives of Windsor '50
The Marriage of Figaro '49
The Murderers Are Among Us '46

Rainer Klausmann(1949-)

Soul Kitchen '09
The Baader Meinhof Complex '08
Lemon Tree '08
The Edge of Heaven '07
The Invasion '07
Downfall '04
Head On '04
The Experiment '01

David Klein(1972-)

Zack and Miri Make a Porno '08
Clerks 2 '06
Novel Romance '06
Tattoo, a Love Story '02
Wish You Were Dead '00
Chasing Amy '97
Mallrats '95
Clerks '94

Vladimir Klimov(1949-)

Out of the Cold '99
The Thief '97

Benjamin (Ben H.) Kline(1894-1974)

Bull of the West '71
Munster, Go Home! '66
Holiday Rhythm '50
Operation Haylift '50
Last of the Wild Horses '49
Tough Assignment '49
Rolling Home '48
Shoot to Kill '47
Trail of the Mounties '47
Detour '46
Lawless Plainsmen '42
Before I Hang '40
Riding Wild '35
The California Trail '33
Ridin' for Justice '32
Two-Fisted Law '32

Richard H. Kline(1926-)

Meet Wally Sparks '97
Double Impact '91
My Stepmother Is an Alien '88
Howard the Duck '86
All of Me '84
Death Wish 2 '82
Body Heat '81
Star Trek: The Motion Picture '79
The Fury '78
Who'll Stop the Rain? '78
I Wonder Who's Killing Her Now? '76
King Kong '76
Battle for the Planet of the Apes '73
Harrad Experiment '73
Soylent Green '73
Black Gunn '72
The Mechanic '72
The Andromeda Strain '71
Camelot '67
Hang 'Em High '67

Edward Klosinski(1943-2008)

Love Comes Lately '07
Gloomy Sunday '02
Trois Couleurs: Blanc '94
Kill Cruise '90
The Decalogue '88
Mother of Kings '82
Man of Iron '81
Illumination '73

Thomas Kloss(1956-)

Showtime '02
Palmetto '98
Fear '96

Douglas Knapp

Assault on Precinct 13 '76
The First Nudie Musical '75
Dark Star '74

David Knaus

Red Shoe Diaries: Swimming Naked '00
Bird of Prey '95

Nicholas D. Knowland

Piano Tuner of Earthquakes '05
Jesus Christ Superstar '00
Joseph and the Amazing Technicolor Dreamcoat '00
Institue Benjamenta or This Dream People Call Human Life '95
Barbarians at the Gate '93
Wild West '93

Bernard Knowles(1900-75)

Secret Mission '42
Gaslight '40
Young and Innocent '37
Sabotage '36
The Secret Agent '36
The 39 Steps '35

Cyril Knowles(1905-61)

Secret Mission '42
King Solomon's Mines '37

Gen Kobayashi

Nezulla the Rat Monster '02
Uzumaki '00

Setsuo Kobayashi(1920-)
Nomugi Pass '79
An Actor's Revenge '63
Fires on the Plain '59

Douglas Koch
The Bronx Is Burning '07
American Meltdown '04
The Republic of Love '03
Last Night '98
When Night Is Falling '95
Kidnapping of Baby John Doe '88

Fred W. Koenekamp(1922-)
Flight of the Intruder '90
Listen to Me '89
Welcome Home '89
Alice in Wonderland '85
The Adventures of Buckaroo Banzai Across the Eighth Dimension '84
Two of a Kind '83
Wrong Is Right '82
First Monday in October '81
The Hunter '80
When Time Ran Out '80
The Amityville Horror '79
The Champ '79
Love and Bullets '79
The Swarm '78
The Bad News Bears in Breaking Training '77
The Domino Principle '77
Fun with Dick and Jane '77
Islands in the Stream '77
The Other Side of Midnight '77
Embryo '76
Doc Savage '75
The McCullochs '75
White Line Fever '75
The Towering Inferno '74
Uptown Saturday Night '74
Papillon '73
Rage '72
Billy Jack '71
Beyond the Valley of the Dolls '70
Patton '70

Karl Kofler(1940-)
Echo Park '86
The Children of Theatre Street '77

Hajime Koizumi
War of the Gargantuas '70
Godzilla vs. Monster Zero '68
King Kong Escapes '67
Dagora, the Space Monster '65
Ghidrah the Three Headed Monster '65
Frankenstein Conquers the World '64
Godzilla vs. Mothra '64
Attack of the Mushroom People '63
King Kong vs. Godzilla '63
Gorath '62
Mothra '62

Lajos Koltai(1946-)
Being Julia '04
The Emperor's Club '02
Max '02
Taking Sides '01
Malena '00
Sunshine '99
The Legend of 1900 '98
Out to Sea '97
Mother '96
Home for the Holidays '95
Just Cause '94
When a Man Loves a Woman '94
Born Yesterday '93
Wrestling Ernest Hemingway '93
Meeting Venus '91
Mobsters '91
White Palace '90
Homer and Eddie '89
Hanussen '88
Gaby: A True Story '87
Colonel Redl '84
Time Stands Still '82
Mephisto '81
Angi Vera '78
Adoption '75

Takashi Komatsu
Flower & Snake 2 '05
Flower & Snake '04

Shigeru Komatsubara
Dr. Akagi '98
The Eel '96

Tanya Koop
Roman Polanski: Wanted and Desired '08
Little Chenier: A Cajun Story '06

Avi Koren
Chain of Command '95
The Mummy Lives '93

Petra Korner
The Informers '09
The Wackness '08

Carl F. Koschnick(1949-)
My Fuhrer '07
Go for Zucker '05
Agnes and His Brothers '04

Simon Kossoff
Dead Gorgeous '02
The Scarlet Pimpernel '99
The Scarlet Pimpernel 2: Mademoiselle Guillotine '99

Gabriel Kosuth(1958-)
Flu Birds '08
Hellraiser: Hellworld '05
Return of the Living Dead: Rave to the Grave '05

Laszlo Kovacs(1933-2007)
Two Weeks Notice '02
Miss Congeniality '00
Return to Me '00
Jack Frost '98
My Best Friend's Wedding '97
Multiplicity '96
Copycat '95
Free Willy 2: The Adventure Home '95
The Scout '94
Say Anything '89
Legal Eagles '86
Mask '85
Ghostbusters '84
Frances '82
The Toy '82
For Pete's Sake '74
Five Easy Pieces '70
Hell's Bloody Devils '70
Blood of Dracula's Castle '69
Easy Rider '69
Rebel Rousers '69
Mantis in Lace '68
Targets '68
Hell's Angels on Wheels '67
Incredibly Strange Creatures Who Stopped Living and Became Mixed-Up Zombies '63

Pete Kozachik
Coraline '09
Tim Burton's Corpse Bride '05
James and the Giant Peach '96
The Nightmare Before Christmas '93

Sergei Kozlov(1964-)
Border Blues '03
The Lion in Winter '03
House of Fools '02
The Quickie '01
Jason and the Argonauts '00
Merlin '98
The Odyssey '97

Gunther Krampf(1899-1950)
The Ghoul '34
Kuhle Wampe, Or Who Owns the World? '32
Pandora's Box '28
The Hands of Orlac '25
Nosferatu '22

Leland Krane
Confess '05
Giving It Up '99
Under Hellgate Bridge '99

Jon Kranhouse
Something More '99
Decoy '95
Kickboxer '89
Friday the 13th, Part 6: Jason Lives '86
Fourth Wise Man '85
Brainwaves '82

Robert Krasker(1913-81)
Trap '66
The Collector '65
The Heroes of Telemark '65
The Fall of the Roman Empire '64
Billy Budd '62
Birdman of Alcatraz '62
El Cid '61
The Story of Esther Costello '57
Trapeze '56
Alexander the Great '55
Romeo and Juliet '54
Senso '54
Another Man's Poison '52
Cry, the Beloved Country '51
The Third Man '49
Odd Man Out '47
Brief Encounter '46
Caesar and Cleopatra '46
Henry V '44

Milton Krasner(1904-88)
Beneath the Planet of the Apes '70
The Sterile Cuckoo '69
The St. Valentine's Day Massacre '67
The Singing Nun '66
Made in Paris '65
Red Line 7000 '65
The Sandpiper '65
Goodbye Charlie '64
How the West Was Won '63
Love with the Proper Stranger '63
The Courtship of Eddie's Father '62
The Four Horsemen of the Apocalypse '62
Sweet Bird of Youth '62
Two Weeks in Another Town '62
The King of Kings '61
Bells Are Ringing '60
Home from the Hill '60
An Affair to Remember '57
Bus Stop '56
23 Paces to Baker Street '56
The Girl in the Red Velvet Swing '55
The Seven Year Itch '55
Demetrius and the Gladiators '54
Desiree '54
Garden of Evil '54
Three Coins in the Fountain '54
Dream Wife '53
Monkey Business '52
Phone Call from a Stranger '52
People Will Talk '51
All About Eve '50
No Way Out '50
Rawhide '50
Three Came Home '50
House of Strangers '49
The Set-Up '49
The Accused '48
Up in Central Park '48
A Double Life '47
Egg and I '47
The Farmer's Daughter '47
Something in the Wind '47
Dark Mirror '46
Without Reservations '46
Along Came Jones '45
Scarlet Street '45
The Invisible Man's Revenge '44
Woman in the Window '44
Gung Ho! '43
The Mad Ghoul '43
Arabian Nights '42
A Gentleman After Dark '42
The Ghost of Frankenstein '42
Pardon My Sarong '42
The Spoilers '42
Buck Privates '41
The Bank Dick '40
The House of the Seven Gables '40
The Invisible Man Returns '40
You Can't Cheat an Honest Man '39
The Jury's Secret '38
Make a Million '35

Richard Kratina(1928-)
The Sentinel '76
Aaron Loves Angela '75
The Angel Levine '70
Love Story '70

Eric Kress
The Girl With the Dragon Tattoo '09
Flickering Lights '01
The Kingdom 2 '97
The Kingdom '95

Henning Kristiansen(1927-2006)
Royal Deceit '94
Babette's Feast '87
Parallel Corpse '83

Les Krizsan
Tales from a Parallel Universe: Eating Pattern '97
Tales from a Parallel Universe: Giga Shadow '97
Tales from a Parallel Universe: I Worship His Shadow '97
Tales from a Parallel Universe: Super Nova '97
Self-Defense '83

Svein Krovel
Mozart and the Whale '05
Elling '01

Tom Krueger
Committed '99
Manny & Lo '96

Jules Kruger(1891-1959)
Sidewalks of London '38
Pepe Le Moko '37
Napoleon '27

Howard Krupa
1999 '98
Kicked in the Head '97
Rhythm Thief '94

J. Henry Kruse
The Duke Is Tops '38
Silent Valley '35
Unconquered Bandit '35
Fighting Hero '34

Alwin Kuchler(1965-)
Morning Glory '10
Solitary Man '10
Sunshine '07
Proof '05
Code 46 '03
The Mother '03
Morvern Callar '02
Lucky Break '01
The Claim '00
Ratcatcher '99

Ben Kufrin
Jimmy & Judy '06
ESL: English as a Second Language '05
Cock & Bull Story '03
Gang of Roses '03
Players '03
The Prodigy '98

Toni Kuhn(1942-)
Like A Bride '94
Homework '90
The Vanishing '88

Martin Kukula(1957-)
Good Bye, Lenin! '03
The Trio '97

Edward Kull(1886-1946)
Rodeo Rhythm '42
Wild Horse Valley '40
El Diablo Rides '39
Carnival Lady '33
Mystery Trooper '32
Quick Trigger Lee '31

Mu-To Kung
Heaven & Hell '78
The Water Margin '72

Willy Kurant(1934-)
Pootie Tang '01
The Baby-Sitters' Club '95
White Man's Burden '95
A Business Affair '93
Day of Atonement '93
China Moon '91
Trade Secrets '86
Tuff Turf '85
French Intrigue '70

Ellen Kuras(1959-)
Away We Go '09
Be Kind Rewind '08
Dave Chappelle's Block Party '06
Neil Young: Heart of Gold '06
The Ballad of Jack and Rose '05
Eternal Sunshine of the Spotless Mind '04
Coffee and Cigarettes '03
Analyze That '02
Personal Velocity: Three Portraits '02
Blow '01
Bamboozled '00
The Mod Squad '99
Summer of Sam '99
Just the Ticket '98
I Shot Andy Warhol '96
If These Walls Could Talk '96
Postcards from America '95
Angela '94
Unzipped '94
Swoon '91

Toyomichi Kurita(1950-)
Tyler Perry's Why Did I Get Married Too? '10
The Family That Preys '08
Sukiyaki Western Django '08
Tyler Perry's Why Did I Get Married? '07
Madea's Family Reunion '06
First Daughter '04
Cookie's Fortune '99
Taboo '99
Afterglow '97
Crime of the Century '96
Homecoming '96
Infinity '96
Waiting to Exhale '95
Woman Undone '95
Lakota Woman: Siege at Wounded Knee '94
Grand Isle '92
Powwow Highway '89
Trouble in Mind '86

Robert B. Kurrle(1890-1932)
One Way Passage '32
Smart Money '31
Evangeline '29
Rio Rita '29
Sadie Thompson '28

Luigi Kuveiller(1927-)
New York Ripper '82
Deep Red: Hatchet Murders '75
Andy Warhol's Dracula '74
Andy Warhol's Frankenstein '74
A Lizard in a Woman's Skin '71

Ting Wo Kwong
Last Hour '08
Shaolin Soccer '01

Khasan Kydyraliyev
Schizo '04
Beshkempir the Adopted Son '98

Christopher La Vasseur
Descent '07
2B Perfectly Honest '04

Jules Labarthe
But I'm a Cheerleader '99
Stray Bullet '98

Flavio Labiano
See Flavio Martinez Labiano
Goal 2: Living the Dream '07
Timecrimes '07
Extasis '96

Daniel Lacambre
'68 '87
Saturday the 14th '81
Battle Beyond the Stars '80
Humanoids from the Deep '80
Lady in Red '79
The Velvet Vampire '71
The Arousers '70
Magical Mystery Tour '67

Edward Lachman(1948-)
Collapse '09
Life During Wartime '09
Hounddog '08
I'm Not There '07
A Prairie Home Companion '06
Stryker '04
Far from Heaven '02
Simone '02
Sweet November '01
Erin Brockovich '00
The Limey '99
The Virgin Suicides '99
Why Do Fools Fall in Love? '98
Selena '96
Touch '96
Theremin: An Electronic Odyssey '95
My Family '94
Light Sleeper '92
London Kills Me '91
Portfolio '88
Less Than Zero '87
True Stories '86
Desperately Seeking Susan '85
Union City '81

Serge Ladouceur(1952-)
Mambo Italiano '03
Rudy: The Rudy Giulani Story '03
Savage Messiah '02
Bonanno: A Godfather's Story '99
Armistead Maupin's More Tales of the City '97

Kjell Lagerros(1961-)
Rancid '04
Ambush '99
Like It Never Was Before '95
Dreaming of Rita '94

Ardy Lam
Crime Story '93
Supercop '92
A Bullet in the Head '90

Alex Lamarque
Sheitan '06
Crimson Rivers 2: Angels of the Apocalypse '05
La Vie Promise '02

Rick Lamb
Mexican Blow '02
Hell's Belles '95

Ken Lamkin
Big Bad John '90
Texas Guns '90

Sabine Lancelin

Belle Toujours '06
I'm Going Home '00

Giuseppe Lanci(1942-)

The Spectator '04
The Son's Room '00
Elective Affinities '96
Traveling Companion '96
Caro Diario '93
Fiorile '93
Francesco '93
Johnny Stecchino '92
Night Sun '90
Palombella Rossa '89
Devil in the Flesh '87
Kaos '85
Nostalghia '83

Charles Lang

Buck Benny Rides Again '40
Mississippi '35

Charles B(ryant) Lang, Jr.(1902-98)

Forty Carats '73
Butterflies Are Free '72
The Love Machine '71
Doctors' Wives '70
Walk in the Spring Rain '70
Bob & Carol & Ted & Alice '69
Cactus Flower '69
How to Commit Marriage '69
Flim-Flam Man '67
Hotel '67
Wait until Dark '67
How to Steal a Million '66
Inside Daisy Clover '65
Father Goose '64
Paris When It Sizzles '64
Sex and the Single Girl '64
Charade '63
Critic's Choice '63
How the West Was Won '63
One-Eyed Jacks '61
Summer and Smoke '61
The Facts of Life '60
The Magnificent Seven '60
Strangers When We Meet '60
Last Train from Gun Hill '59
Some Like It Hot '59
The Matchmaker '58
Separate Tables '58
Gunfight at the O.K. Corral '57
Loving You '57
Autumn Leaves '56
The Rainmaker '56
Solid Gold Cadillac '56
The Man from Laramie '55
Queen Bee '55
It Should Happen to You '54
Phffft! '54
Sabrina '54
The Big Heat '53
Salome '53
Sudden Fear '52
Ace in the Hole '51
Fancy Pants '50
September Affair '50
The Great Lover '49
A Foreign Affair '48
Miss Tatlock's Millions '48
The Ghost and Mrs. Muir '47
Blue Skies '46
The Uninvited '44
So Proudly We Hail '43
The Shepherd of the Hills '41
Sundown '41
The Ghost Breakers '40
Midnight '39
Spawn of the North '38
You and Me '38
Angel '37
Souls at Sea '37
The Lives of a Bengal Lancer '35
Death Takes a Holiday '34
Gambling Ship '33
She Done Him Wrong '33
The Devil and the Deep '32
A Farewell to Arms '32
No One Man '32
Vice Squad '31
Tom Sawyer '30

Martin Langer(1959-)

Sophie Scholl: The Final Days '05
The Tunnel '01

Bryan Langley

Lassie from Lancashire '38
No. 17 '32

Norman G. Langley(1935-)

Jekyll and Hyde '90
House of the Long Shadows '82
Die Screaming, Marianne '73

Reggie Lanning(1893-1965)

Carolina Cannonball '55
Abbott and Costello Meet the Keystone Kops '54
Sands of Iwo Jima '49
Lights of Old Santa Fe '47
Rainbow over Texas '46
Sioux City Sue '46
Silver City Kid '45
King of the Cowboys '43
Bells of Capistrano '42
Code of the Outlaw '42
Code of the Outlaw '42
Man from Cheyenne '42
Gauchos of El Dorado '41
Mr. District Attorney '41
Frontier Vengeance '40
Gaucho Serenade '40
Oklahoma Renegades '40
Days of Jesse James '39
Zorro's Fighting Legion '39
Heroes of the Hills '38

Roger Lanser

As You Like It '06
Strange Bedfellows '04
Till Human Voices Wake Us '02
Maybe Baby '99
Kings in Grass Castles '97
Prince Valiant '97
Billy's Holiday '95
A Midwinter's Tale '95
Much Ado about Nothing '93

Christopher Lanzenberg

Watching the Detectives '07
The Sensation of Sight '06

Vilis Lapenieks(1931-87)

Rainbow Bridge '71
Planet of Blood '66
Hollywood after Dark '65
Night Tide '63
Eegah! '62
Hideous Sun Demon '59

Jeanne Lapoirie

Time to Leave '05
They Came Back '04
8 Women '02
Confusion of Genders '00
Under the Sand '00
Set Me Free '99
Water Drops on Burning Rocks '99
Full Speed '96
Les Voleurs '96
Wild Reeds '94

Stevan Larner(1930-2005)

Partners in Crime '99
Forbidden Choices '94
Guilty Conscience '85
Fatal Vision '84
Twilight Zone: The Movie '83
Rehearsal for Murder '82
Caddyshack '80
A Rumor of War '80
The Buddy Holly Story '78
Roots '77
Badlands '74
The Student Nurses '70

Federico G. Larraya

A Place Called Glory '66
A Fistful of Dollars '64

Jean-Claude Larrieu

Elegy '08
Paris, je t'aime '06
My Life Without Me '03
Oriana '85

Joseph LaShelle(1905-89)

Barefoot in the Park '67
The Fortune Cookie '66
Kiss Me, Stupid! '64
The Honeymoon Machine '61
The Apartment '60
Career '59
The Long, Hot Summer '58
The Naked and the Dead '58
Crime of Passion '57
I Was a Teenage Werewolf '57
The Conqueror '56
Marty '55
River of No Return '54
Dangerous Crossing '53
Les Miserables '52
The Jackpot '50
Where the Sidewalk Ends '50
Come to the Stable '49
The Luck of the Irish '48
Road House '48
Hangover Square '45
Laura '44

Jacek Laskus(1951-)

The Whole Shebang '01
Common Ground '00
The Devil's Arithmetic '99
A Soldier's Sweetheart '98
Elmore Leonard's Gold Coast '97
The Garden of Redemption '97
The Undercover Kid '95
Stepfather 2: Make Room for Daddy '89
Parting Glances '86

Jeremy Lasky

WALL-E '08
Finding Nemo '03

Walter Lassally(1926-)

The Ballad of the Sad Cafe '91
The Deceivers '88
The Bostonians '84
Pudd'nhead Wilson '84
Private School '83
Heat and Dust '82
The Private History of a Campaign That Failed '81
Danger in the Skies '79
Great Bank Hoax '78
Hullabaloo over Georgie & Bonnie's Pictures '78
Wild Party '74
Run, Stranger, Run '73
Savages '72
Something for Everyone '70
Zorba the Greek '64
Tom Jones '63
The Loneliness of the Long Distance Runner '62
A Taste of Honey '61
Beat Girl '60
A Matter of Dignity '57
Girl in Black '56

Andrew Laszlo(1926-)

Star Trek 5: The Final Frontier '89
Poltergeist 2: The Other Side '86
Remo Williams: The Adventure Begins '85
Streets of Fire '84
Thief of Hearts '84
First Blood '82
The Funhouse '81
Southern Comfort '81
The Warriors '79
The Man Without a Country '73
The Owl and the Pussycat '70

Ernest Laszlo(1905-84)

Logan's Run '76
Showdown '73
Airport '70
Daddy's Gone A-Hunting '69
Star! '68
Luv '67
Fantastic Voyage '66
Ship of Fools '65
Baby, the Rain Must Fall '64
Four for Texas '63
It's a Mad, Mad, Mad, Mad World '63
Judgment at Nuremberg '61
Inherit the Wind '60
Tormented '60
Attack of the Puppet People '58
While the City Sleeps '56
The Big Knife '55
The Kentuckian '55
Kiss Me Deadly '55
Apache '54
Naked Jungle '54
Houdini '53
The Moon Is Blue '53
Stalag 17 '53
Vera Cruz '53
The Star '52
The Well '51
The Jackie Robinson Story '50
D.O.A. '49
Impact '49
On Our Merry Way '48
The Road to Rio '47
Two Years before the Mast '46
Pace That Kills '28

Philip Lathrop(1912-95)

Deadly Friend '86
Jekyll & Hyde... Together Again '82
National Lampoon's Class Reunion '82
Foolin' Around '80
Swashbuckler '76
Airport '75 '75
Hard Times '75
Earthquake '74
Mame '74
The Gypsy Moths '69
They Shoot Horses, Don't They? '69
I Love You, Alice B. Toklas! '68
The Cincinnati Kid '65
Never Too Late '65
The Pink Panther '64
36 Hours '64
Lonely Are the Brave '62
The Monster of Piedras Blancas '57

Andrew Lau

See Wai Keung (Andrew) Lau

Tom Lau

The Bodyguard from Beijing '94
The Heroic Trio '93
Twin Warriors '93

Wai Keung (Andrew) Lau(1960-)

Infernal Affairs 2 '03
Once Upon a Time in China III '93
Wicked City '92
As Tears Go By '88
City on Fire '87

Paul Laufer

The Cell '00
Frankie Starlight '95

Dan Laustsen(1954-)

Just Another Love Story '08
Wind Chill '07
Silent Hill '06
Darkness Falls '03
The League of Extraordinary Gentlemen '03
Brotherhood of the Wolf '01
Running Free '00
Heart of Light '97
Mimic '97
Nightwatch '96
Emma's Shadow '88

Charles Lawton, Jr.(1904-65)

A Raisin in the Sun '61
Comanche Station '60
Cowboy '58
Gunman's Walk '58
Last Hurrah '58
Operation Mad Ball '57
3:10 to Yuma '57
The Long Gray Line '55
Kill the Umpire '50
The Nevadan '50
Shockproof '49
The Lady from Shanghai '48
Getting Gertie's Garter '45
Big Store '41

Vernon Layton

My First Wedding '04
Seed of Chucky '04
Station Jim '01
I Still Know What You Did Last Summer '98
High School High '96
The Englishman Who Went up a Hill But Came down a Mountain '95
Under Suspicion '92

Jean-Yves Le Mener

The Visitors '95
The Fatal Image '90

Marcel Le Picard(1887-1952)

'Neath Canadian Skies '46
Trouble Chasers '45
Ghost Crazy '44
Westward Bound '44
The Invisible Ghost '41
The Pioneers '41
Zis Boom Bah '41
Roll, Wagons, Roll '39
Here's Flash Casey '38
Six Gun Trail '38
The Shadow Strikes '37
America '24

Yorick Le Saux(1968-)

Julia '08
Boarding Gate '07
5x2 '04
Swimming Pool '03
Sitcom '97

Philippe Le Sourd

Seven Pounds '08
A Good Year '06

Eric Leach

Organizm '08
Social Misfits '00

Sam Leavitt(1904-84)

The Man in the Glass Booth '75
Evil Roy Slade '71
Star Spangled Girl '71
The Passing of Evil '70
Desperados '69
The Grasshopper '69
The Wrecking Crew '68
Guess Who's Coming to Dinner '67
Murderers' Row '66
Major Dundee '65
My Blood Runs Cold '65
Advise and Consent '62
Diamond Head '62
Cape Fear '61
Seven Thieves '60
Anatomy of a Murder '59
The Crimson Kimono '59
Pork Chop Hill '59
The Defiant Ones '58
Hot Rod Girl '56
An Annapolis Story '55
The Court Martial of Billy Mitchell '55
The Man with the Golden Arm '55
Carmen Jones '54
A Star Is Born '54
The Thief '52

Pavel Lebeshev(1941-2003)

Prisoner of the Mountains '96
Anna '93
The Ascent '76

Henry Lebo

We'll Meet Again '02
Ebenezer '97

Claude Lecomte

Le Grand Chemin '87
The Women '68

Eun-ju Lee

301/302 '95
301/302 '95

Philip Lee

Protecting the King '07
Terminal Error '02
Route 666 '01
From Dusk Till Dawn 2: Texas Blood Money '98
Spoiler '98
Galaxies Are Colliding '92

Pin Bing Lee

See Mark Lee Ping-Bin
A Time to Live and a Time to Die '85

Seok-hyeon Lee

Apartment 1303 '07
Nightmare '00

Robert Lefebvre(1907-89)

I Am Frigid... Why? '72
Her and She and Him '69
Please Not Now! '61
Voulez-Vous Danser avec Moi? '59
Casque d'Or '52
Beethoven '36

Jason Lehel

Bob the Butler '05
Conspiracy of Silence '03

Richard Leiterman(1935-2005)

The Spree '96
Higher Ground '88
Watchers '88
Ticket to Heaven '81
Who Has Seen the Wind? '77

Claude Lelouch(1937-)

Les Miserables '95
A Man and a Woman '66

Jacques Lemare

Dishonorable Discharge '57
There Goes Barder '54

James (Momel) Lemmo(1949-)

Maniac Cop 2 '90
Maniac Cop '88
Fear City '85
Vigilante '83
Madman '82
One Down, Two to Go! '82
Ms. 45 '81

Ryszard Lenczewski(1948-)

My Summer of Love '05
Anna Karenina '00

Denis Lenoir

88 Minutes '08
Righteous Kill '08
The Clearing '04
Demonlover '02
Uprising '01
Meat Loaf: To Hell and Back '00
Steal This Movie! '00
Mean Streak '99
La Separation '98
Late August, Early September '98
Thursday '98
The Secret Agent '96
Carrington '95
The Separation '94
Daddy Nostalgia '90
Dingo '90

Dean Lent

Phat Girlz '06
Fast Sofa '01
Catfish in Black Bean Sauce '00
Drowning on Dry Land '00
Jack Frost '97
Lover Girl '97
When Time Expires '97

Acting on Impulse '93
Bound and Gagged: A Love Story '93
Gas Food Lodging '92

Miklos Lente

Ordeal in the Arctic '93
Happy Birthday to Me '81
Suzanne '80

Hanno Lentz

Cherry Blossoms '08
Guys and Balls '04

Don Lenzer

Rush It '77
Road Movie '72

John R. Leonetti

Dead Silence '07
Death Sentence '07
I Know Who Killed Me '07
The Perfect Man '05
Raise Your Voice '04
Honey '03
The Woods '03
The Scorpion King '02
Joe Dirt '01
Detroit Rock City '99
Spy Hard '96
Mortal Kombat 1: The Movie '95
The Mask '94

Matthew F. Leonetti(1941-)

Soul Men '08
What Happens in Vegas '08
The Heartbreak Kid '07
Pride '07
Accepted '06
Fever Pitch '05
The Butterfly Effect '04
Dawn of the Dead '04
2 Fast 2 Furious '03
Along Came a Spider '01
Rush Hour 2 '01
Species 2 '98
Star Trek: Insurrection '98
Mortal Kombat 2: Annihilation '97
Fled '96
Star Trek: First Contact '96
Strange Days '95
Angels in the Outfield '94
Dead Again '91
Another 48 Hrs. '90
Hard to Kill '89
Action Jackson '88
Red Heat '88
Dragnet '87
Commando '85
The Jagged Edge '85
Weird Science '85
Fast Times at Ridgemont High '82
Poltergeist '82
Breaking Away '79
Prime Time '77
The Bat People '74

Jean Lepine

Coast to Coast '04
A Different Loyalty '04
Charms for the Easy Life '02
Whitewash: The Clarence Brandley Story '02
To Walk with Lions '99
A Cool, Dry Place '98
Habitat '97
Woo '97
Beyond the Call '96
Ready to Wear '94
A Home of Our Own '93
JFK: Reckless Youth '93
Bob Roberts '92
The Player '92
Vincent & Theo '90

Andrew Lesnie(1956-)

The Last Airbender '10
The Lovely Bones '09
I Am Legend '07
King Kong '05
Lord of the Rings: The Return of the King '03
Lord of the Rings: The Two Towers '02
Lord of the Rings: The Fellowship of the Ring '01
Babe: Pig in the City '98
Doing Time for Patsy Cline '97
Babe '95
Two If by Sea '95
Temptation of a Monk '94
Fair Game '85

Elgin Lessley(1881-1944)

Tramp, Tramp, Tramp '26
Seven Chances '25
The Navigator '24
Sherlock, Jr. '24
Our Hospitality '23

Pierre Letarte

The Audrey Hepburn Story '00
Mafia! '98
First Do No Harm '97
Dangerous Minds '95
Sugartime '95
The Boys of St. Vincent '93

John Leuba

Friends and Family '01
Swimming '00

Alain Levent

Daughter of Keltoum '01
Franz '72

Moshe Levin

Axe '06
Motel Blue '98
Hard Justice '95

Peter Levy

The Reaping '07
The Reaping '07
Lonely Hearts '06
Torque '04
Under Suspicion '00
Lost in Space '98
The War at Home '96
Broken Arrow '95
Cutthroat Island '95
Judgment Night '93
Ricochet '91
Predator 2 '90
A Nightmare on Elm Street 5: Dream Child '89

Yaron Levy

Night of the Demons '09
Aces 'n Eights '08

Shawn Lewallen

The Last Confederate: The Story of Robert Adams '05
Sergio Lapel's Drawing Blood '99

David Lewis

Leprechaun 4: In Space '96
Leprechaun 3 '95
Fatal Pulse '88

David Lewis(1916-2000)

Killer Bud '00
Atomic Dog '98
Children of the Corn 5: Fields of Terror '98
Chairman of the Board '97
The Proposition '96
The Set Up '95
Witchboard 2: The Devil's Doorway '93
UHF '89
The Hills Have Eyes, Part 2 '84

Herschell Gordon Lewis(1926-)

The Psychic '68
Something Weird '68
Color Me Blood Red '64
Moonshine Mountain '64
2000 Maniacs '64
Blood Feast '63

Denis Lewiston

The Canterville Ghost '96
Nightmare '91
One Against the Wind '91
The Sign of Four '83
The House on Straw Hill '76

Pierre Lhomme(1930-)

Le Divorce '03
Cotton Mary '99
Mon Homme '96
Cyrano de Bergerac '90
Camille Claudel '89
Maurice '87
This Sweet Sickness '77
The Savage '75
Sweet Movie '75
The Mother and the Whore '73
Someone Behind the Door '71
Army of Shadows '69
The King of Hearts '66

Pen-jung Liao

The Hole '98
Vive l'Amour '94
Rebels of the Neon God '92

Matthew Libatique(1969-)

Iron Man 2 '10
Iron Man '08
Miracle at St. Anna '08
The Number 23 '07
The Fountain '06
Inside Man '06
Everything is Illuminated '05
Never Die Alone '04
She Hate Me '04
Gothika '03
Abandon '02
Phone Booth '02
Josie and the Pussycats '01
Requiem for a Dream '00
Tigerland '00
Speed of Life '99
Pi '98

Charlie Lieberman

Red Meat '98
South Central '92
Henry: Portrait of a Serial Killer '90

Stephen Lighthill

The Crying Child '96
Evil Has a Face '96
The Perfect Daughter '96
Open Season '95
Spirit of '76 '91
Break of Dawn '88

Doug Liman(1965-)

Go '99
Swingers '96

Jong Lin

Bend It Like Beckham '02
What's Cooking? '00
Eat Drink Man Woman '94
The Wedding Banquet '93
Pushing Hands '92

Kuo-Hsiang Lin

Vengeance is a Golden Blade '69
The Cave of the Silken Web '67

Patick Lin

Up '09
The Incredibles '04

Edward Linden(1891-1956)

Yank in Libya '42
Range Busters '40
Trailing Double Trouble '40
West of Pinto Basin '40
The Stranger from Arizona '38
Slaves in Bondage '37
Pals of the Range '35
Rough Riding Ranger '35
King Kong '33

Karl Walter Lindenlaub(1957-)

Ninja Assassin '09
The Chronicles of Narnia: Prince Caspian '08
Georgia Rule '07
Black Book '06
Because of Winn-Dixie '05
Guess Who '05
The Banger Sisters '02
City by the Sea '02
Maid in Manhattan '02
One Night at McCool's '01
The Princess Diaries '01
Isn't She Great '00
The Jackal '97
Red Corner '97
Independence Day '96
Up Close and Personal '96
The Last of the Dogmen '95
Rob Roy '95
Casualties of Love: The "Long Island Lolita" Story '93
Universal Soldier '92
Ghost Chase '88

John Lindley

The Last Song '10
Legion '10
Imagine That '09
Catch and Release '07
Mr. Brooks '07
Reservation Road '07
Bewitched '05
The Last Shot '04
The Core '03
The Sum of All Fears '02
Lucky Numbers '00
Pleasantville '98
You've Got Mail '98
Michael '96
Money Train '95
I Love Trouble '94
The Good Son '93
Sneakers '92
Father of the Bride '91
Field of Dreams '89
True Believer '89
Shakedown '88
The Serpent and the Rainbow '87
The Stepfather '87
Killer Party '86
Girls of the White Orchid '85

Lionel Lindon(1905-71)

Generation '69
Pendulum '69
The Meanest Men in the West '67
Boy, Did I Get a Wrong Number! '66
Dead Heat on a Merry-Go-Round '66
Grand Prix '66
The Trouble with Angels '66
McHale's Navy Joins the Air Force '65
All Fall Down '62
The Manchurian Candidate '62
The Young Savages '61
Alias Jesse James '59
I Want to Live! '58
Lonely Man '57
Around the World in 80 Days '56
Conquest of Space '55
A Man Alone '55
Casanova's Big Night '54
Rhubarb '51
Destination Moon '50
The Great Rupert '50
Only the Valiant '50
Quicksand '50
The Sun Sets at Dawn '50
My Favorite Brunette '47
Variety Girl '47
Welcome Stranger '47
The Blue Dahlia '46
Monsieur Beaucaire '46
O.S.S. '46
The Road to Utopia '46
Going My Way '44

Philip Linzey

Journey to the Center of the Earth '08
Cabin by the Lake '00
Life-Size '00
Turbulence 3: Heavy Metal '00
Evidence of Blood '97
Bloodknot '95

Jerzy Lipman(1922-83)

Dead Pigeon on Beethoven Street '72
Lotna '64
Knife in the Water '62
Kanal '56
Shadow '56
A Generation '54

Harold Lipstein(1898-1974)

Hell Is for Heroes '62
Heller in Pink Tights '60
No Name on the Bullet '59
Pal Joey '57
Walk the Proud Land '56
The Private War of Major Benson '55

Greg Littlewood

SLC Punk! '99
Sweet Jane '98
The Real Thing '97
Skinner '93

Gerry Lively

In Enemy Hands '04
Cutaway '00
DNA '97
The Brylcreem Boys '96
Friday '95
Showdown '94
Return of the Living Dead 3 '93
Warlock: The Armageddon '93
Hellraiser 3: Hell on Earth '92
Project: Eliminator '91
Waxwork 2: Lost in Time '91
Lobster Man from Mars '89
Waxwork '88

Guy Livneh

Eye of the Dolphin '06
Kids in America '05
Purple Heart '05

Art Lloyd(1896-1954)

The Flying Deuces '39
March of the Wooden Soldiers '34
Laurel & Hardy: Be Big '31

Walt Lloyd

Alien Raiders '08
Wieners '08
The Air I Breathe '07
The Librarian: Return to King Solomon's Mines '06
Superstar '99
Three to Tango '99
Dark Harbor '98
Feeling Minnesota '96
Private Parts '96
Empire Records '95
Frank and Jesse '94
The Santa Clause '94
Short Cuts '93
Kafka '91
Pump Up the Volume '90
To Sleep with Anger '90
Down Twisted '89
sex, lies and videotape '89
The Wash '88
Dangerously Close '86

Bryan Loftus

Botched '07
Jake Speed '86
The Company of Wolves '85

Bruce Logan

Kiss Tomorrow Goodbye '00
Tron '82
Zoltan... Hound of Dracula '78
I Never Promised You a Rose Garden '77
Jackson County Jail '76
Crazy Mama '75
Big Bad Mama '74
This Is a Hijack '73

Dietrich Lohmann(1943-97)

According to Greta '08
Deep Impact '98
The Peacemaker '97
Quiet Days in Hollywood '97
In the Lake of the Woods '96
The Machine '96
A Couch in New York '95
Color of Night '94
Knight Moves '93
Milo Milo '79
Earthquake in Chile '74
Effi Briest '74
The American Soldier '70
Love Is Colder Than Death '69

Paul Lohmann

Lust in the Dust '85
Mommie Dearest '81
Meteor '79
North Dallas Forty '79
An Enemy of the People '77
Nashville '75
Trilogy of Terror '75
Scream of the Wolf '74
Coffy '73
Hell's Angels '69 '69

Jacques Loiseleux

The Stranger: Kabloonak '95
A Nos Amours '84

Ulli Lommel(1944-)

Devonsville Terror '83
Brainwaves '82

James London

The Toxic Avenger, Part 2 '89
The Toxic Avenger, Part 3: The Last Temptation of Toxie '89
Troma's War '88
The Toxic Avenger '86

Bert Longenecker(1876-1940)

The Painted Trail '38
The Red Rope '37
The Law Rides '36
Fighting Caballero '35
$50,000 Reward '25
Behind Two Guns '24

Gordon C. Lonsdale

High School Musical '06
Houdini '99
The Last Don '97
A Girl of the Limberlost '90

Angelo Lotti

Venus in Furs '70
The Lion of Thebes '64

Sam Lowry

See Steven Soderbergh

Emmanuel Lubezki(1964-)

Burn After Reading '08
Children of Men '06
The Assassination of Richard Nixon '05
The New World '05
Lemony Snicket's A Series of Unfortunate Events '04
Dr. Seuss' The Cat in the Hat '03
Ali '01
Y Tu Mama Tambien '01
Things You Can Tell Just by Looking at Her '00
Sleepy Hollow '99
Meet Joe Black '98
Great Expectations '97
The Birdcage '95
A Little Princess '95
A Walk in the Clouds '95
Reality Bites '94
Twenty Bucks '93

William Lubtchansky(1937-)

The Duchess of Langeais '07
The Story of Marie and Julien '03
Va Savoir '01
New World '95
Jeanne la Pucelle '94
Every Other Weekend '91
La Belle Noiseuse '90
The Woman Next Door '81
Every Man for Himself '79
Comment Ca Va? '76

Fabrizio Lucci

Coco Chanel '08
Forgotten City '98

William Luff(1872-1960)

Juggernaut '37
She Shall Have Music '36

Death on the Set '35
Department Store '35
Scrooge '35

Yang Lun
Red Firecracker, Green Firecracker '93
Ju Dou '90

Franz Lustig(1967-)
Don't Come Knocking '05
Land of Plenty '04

Igor Luther(1942-)
The Legend of Suriyothai '02
The Handmaid's Tale '90
The Tin Drum '79

Bernard Lutic(1943-2000)
Lumumba '01
Winged Migration '01
I Dreamed of Africa '00
The Luzhin Defence '00
My Life So Far '98
The Quarry '98
Colonel Chabert '94
Boyfriends & Girlfriends '88
Entre-Nous '83
Le Beau Mariage '82
The Aviator's Wife '80

Chester Lyons(1885-1936)
Mad Love '35
Under the Pampas Moon '35
Bad Girl '31
Song o' My Heart '30
Lucky Star '29
They Had to See Paris '29

Edgar Lyons(1894-1950)
Shadows on the Sage '42
Dick Tracy: The Spider Strikes '37
The Fighting Trooper '34

Russell Lyster
Evil Alien Conquerors '02
Styx '00
Ringmaster '98

Jingle Ma
Tokyo Raiders '00
Mr. Magoo '97
Jackie Chan's First Strike '96
Rumble in the Bronx '96
The Legend of Drunken Master '94

Syd Macartney
Transmutations '85
Party! Party! '83

Julio Macat
Our Family Wedding '10
The Code '09
Columbus Day '08
Smother '08
Because I Said So '07
Blind Dating '06
Wedding Crashers '05
Catch That Kid '04
Bringing Down the House '03
Ballistic: Ecks vs. Sever '02
A Walk to Remember '02
Cats & Dogs '01
The Wedding Planner '01
Crazy in Alabama '99
Home Alone 3 '97
My Fellow Americans '96
The Nutty Professor '96
Moonlight and Valentino '95
Ace Ventura: Pet Detective '93
Home Alone 2: Lost in New York '92
Home Alone '90
Out of the Dark '88

John MacBurnie(1892-1956)
Border Saddlemates '52
Silver City Bonanza '51
Thunder in God's Country '51
Missourians '50
Night Riders of Montana '50
Pioneer Marshal '49
Son of God's Country '48
Sundown Fury '42

Joe MacDonald(1906-68)
MacKenna's Gold '69
Alvarez Kelly '66
The Sand Pebbles '66
The Carpetbaggers '64
Kings of the Sun '63
Walk on the Wild Side '62
The Gallant Hours '60
The Fiend Who Walked the West '58
The Young Lions '58
Will Success Spoil Rock Hunter? '57
House of Bamboo '55
Broken Lance '54
A Woman's World '54
How to Marry a Millionaire '53
Pickup on South Street '53
Niagara '52
Call Northside 777 '48
Dark Corner '46
My Darling Clementine '46
The Man Who Wouldn't Die '42

Peter Macdonald
Shag: The Movie '89
Hamburger Hill '87

Thierry Machado
Winged Migration '01
Microcosmos '96

Hiroshi Machida
Party 7 '00
Shark Skin Man and Peach Hip Girl '98

Laurent Machuel
Merci Docteur Rey '04
Sex is Comedy '02
Change My Life '01
Dad On the Run '00
Three Lives and Only One Death '96
Diary of a Seducer '95

Jack MacKenzie(1892-1979)
Return of Dracula '58
Isle of the Dead '45
Jungle Woman '44
Zombies on Broadway '44
Gildersleeve on Broadway '43
Two Weeks to Live '43
Timber! '42
Mexican Spitfire '40
Breaking the Ice '38
Hot Tip '35
One Man's Journey '33

Kenneth Macmillan(1939-)
Dancing at Lughnasa '98
Almost Heroes '97
Inventing the Abbotts '97
Mr. & Mrs. Loving '96
Circle of Friends '94
Lassie '94
Of Mice and Men '92
King Ralph '91
Rush '91
Henry V '89
A Month in the Country '87
Pack of Lies '87
Smiley's People '82

Glen MacPherson(1957-)
The Final Destination '09
One Missed Call '08
Rambo '08
Trick 'r Treat '08
16 Blocks '06
Rebound '05
My Baby's Daddy '04
Walking Tall '04
All About the Benjamins '02
Friday After Next '02
Exit Wounds '01
Camouflage '00
Romeo Must Die '00
The Real Howard Spitz '98
Wrongfully Accused '98
Behind the Lines '97
Calm at Sunset '96
Doctor Who '96
Captains Courageous '95
First Degree '95
The Amy Fisher Story '93

Glen MacWilliams(1898-1984)
If I'm Lucky '46
Lifeboat '44
A Wing and a Prayer '44
Blue, White and Perfect '42
King Solomon's Mines '37
First a Girl '35
Evergreen '34
Lazybones '25
Oliver Twist '22

Guy Maddin(1956-)
Careful '92
Tales from the Gimli Hospital '88

Eric Maddison
Criminal Justice '08
The Listening '06

Yonezo Maeda(1935-)
Pistol Opera '02
Minbo—Or the Gentle Art of Japanese Extortion '92
A Taxing Woman '87
The Funeral '84
The Family Game '83

Lon Magdich
Relax... It's Just Sex! '98
Equal Impact '96

Simon Maggs
Take Me '01
The Wyvern Mystery '00

Barry Mahon(1921-99)
Master's Revenge '71
The Beast That Killed Women '65

Paul Maibaum(1951-)
NightScreams '97
Tornado! '96
Down, Out and Dangerous '95
Stephen King's The Langoliers '95
Shooters '89

Rex Maidment
Cider with Rosie '99
Relative Strangers '99
Second Sight '99
Rebecca '97
Gallowglass '95
A Dark Adapted Eye '93
Enchanted April '92
Antonia and Jane '91

Christine A. Maier
Itty Bitty Titty Committee '07
Grbavica: The Land of My Dreams '06

David Makin
Princess Protection Program '09
The Wizards of Waverly Place: The Movie '09
Princess: A Modern Fairytale '08
Jump In! '07
Say Uncle '05
Touch of Pink '04
Held Up '00
Dog Park '98
Kids in the Hall: Brain Candy '96
The Wrong Guy '96

Harry Makin
Dark Side '02
It Seemed Like a Good Idea at the Time '75

Chishi Makiura
Shogun Assassin '80
Shogun Assassin 2: Lightning Swords of Death '73
Zatoichi: The Blind Swordsman and the Chess Expert '65

Mihai Malaimare, Jr.
Tetro '09
Youth Without Youth '07

Michael Maley
April Fool's Day '08
No One Sleeps '01
Farmer & Chase '96

Jira Maligool
The Iron Ladies 2 '03
The Iron Ladies '00

Jan Malir(1948-)
Up and Down '04
Divided We Fall '00

Max Malkin
Collapse '09
Step Up 2 the Streets '08
Blind Horizon '04

Denis Maloney
Baby on Board '08
Stuck '07
Open Window '06
Return to Halloweentown '06
Edmond '05
The Moguls '05
The Zodiac '05
Final Approach '04
Interstate 60 '02
Liberty Stands Still '02
The Contender '00
Luckytown '00
No Vacancy '99
One Small Hero '99
Bad Manners '98
Bikini Med School '98
Highway Hitcher '98
Body Count '97
Bikini House Calls '96
Illegal Affairs '96
The Winner '96
Wolverine '96
Baja '95
Desert Winds '95
Witchcraft 7: Judgement Hour '95
Witchcraft 8: Salem's Ghost '95
Floundering '94
Natural Causes '94

Yousuke Mamiya
Talking Head '92
Stray Dog '91
The Red Spectacles '87

Alvaro Mancori(1923-)
Espionage in Tangiers '65
Mole Men Against the Son of Hercules '61

Guglielmo Mancori
Black Cobra 2 '89
Manhattan Baby '82
His Name Was King '71
Thor and the Amazon Women '60

Sandro Mancori
Escape from Galaxy Three '81
Liberators '69

Joseph Mangine
Alligator 2: The Mutation '90
Sword & the Sorcerer '82
Alligator '80
Mother's Day '80

Teodoro Maniaci
The Perfect Holiday '07
.45 '06
Outsourced '06
Inside Deep Throat '05
Party Monster '03
Searching for Paradise '02
The Business of Strangers '01
Luminous Motion '00
The Tao of Steve '00
Claire Dolan '97
Tarantella '95
Clean, Shaven '93

Isidore Mankofsky
The Heidi Chronicles '95
Out of Sync '95
Nutcracker: Money, Madness & Murder '87
Hard Lessons '86
Better Off Dead '85
The Jazz Singer '80
Second Coming of Suzanne '80
Somewhere in Time '80
The Muppet Movie '79

Chris Manley
Gracie '07
The Big Empty '04
Dahmer '02
Endangered Species '02
The Stickup '01
Robert Louis Stevenson's The Game of Death '99
Running Woman '98

Laurence Manly
Dangerous Curves '99
Spacejacked '98

Anthony Dod Mantle(1955-)
Antichrist '09
Slumdog Millionaire '08
Wallander: One Step Behind '08
Wallander: Sidetracked '08
Brothers of the Head '06
The Last King of Scotland '06
Dear Wendy '05
Manderlay '05
Millions '05
Dogville '03
It's All About Love '03
28 Days Later '02
Vacuuming Completely Nude in Paradise '01
Julien Donkey-boy '99
Mifune '99
The Celebration '98

Aiter Mantxola
Lisboa '99
Butterfly Wings '91

Vincenzo Marano
Total Western '00
Lucie Aubrac '98
Portraits Chinois '96

Alain Marcoen
Lorna's Silence '08
The Child '05
A Model Employee '02
Rosetta '99
La Promesse '96

Gunter Marczinkowski(1927-2004)
Jacob the Liar '74
Trace of Stones '66
Carbide and Sorrel '63
Five Cartridges '60

Divis Marek(1964-)
The Country Teacher '08
Something Like Happiness '05

Michael D. Margulies(1936-)
Best of the Best: Without Warning '98
Moonlighting '85
Police Academy '84
My Bodyguard '80
The Dark Side of Love '79
The Baby '72

William Margulies(1906-88)
How to Frame a Figg '71
The Love God? '70
Clambake '67
The Ghost and Mr. Chicken '66
McHale's Navy '64

Pasquale Mari
The Wedding Director '06
My Mother's Smile '02
His Secret Life '01
Harem '99
Steam: A Turkish Bath '96

Francis Marin(1920-83)
The Gentleman Killer '69
Twice a Judas '69
The Texican '66

Barry Markowitz
Crazy Heart '09
Sonny '02
All the Pretty Horses '00
Daddy & Them '99
Two Girls and a Guy '98
The Apostle '97
Sling Blade '96

J. Peverell Marley(1901-64)
The Sins of Rachel Cade '61
Westbound '58
Perfect Strangers '50
Pretty Baby '50
John Loves Mary '48
Life with Father '47
Pride of the Marines '45
Four Jills in a Jeep '44
Charley's Aunt '41
Sleepers West '41
Day-Time Wife '39
The Count of Monte Cristo '34
It's a Great Life '29
A Lady of Chance '28
A Lady of Chance '28
Dress Parade '27
The Fighting Eagle '27
King of Kings '27

Brick Marquard
Foxy Brown '74
This Is Not a Test '62

Jacques "Jack" Marquette(1915-99)
Scandal Sheet '85
Halloween with the Addams Family '79
A Home of Our Own '75
More Dead Than Alive '68
Frankie and Johnny '65
Creature from the Haunted Sea '60
Attack of the 50 Foot Woman '58
The Brain from Planet Arous '57

Horacio Marquinez
World's Greatest Dad '09
Vacancy 2: The First Cut '08
Anything But Love '02
Dummy '02
G '02
In the Weeds '00
Loving Jezebel '99
Stranger than Fiction '99
Eye of the Storm '98
Restaurant '98
Ten Benny '98

Daniel Marracino
Capitalism: A Love Story '09
Where in the World Is Osama Bin Laden? '06
All Saint's Day '98

Oliver Marsh(1892-1941)
Ice Follies of 1939 '39
Dancing Lady '33
Night Flight '33
Emma '32
Rain '32
The Phantom of Paris '31
Sadie Thompson '28
The Smart Set '28
The Duchess of Buffalo '26

Charles A. Marshall(1898-1985)
Air Force '43
Night Flight '33

Michael Marshall
Eye of the Beast '07
Ginger Snaps Back: The Beginning '04
The Twilight of the Ice Nymphs '97

Michael Marszalek
2069: A Sex Odyssey '78
The Invisible Terror '63

Jack Marta(1903-91)
The Trial of Billy Jack '74
Walking Tall '73

You'll Like My Mother *'72*
Duel *'71*
Cat Ballou *'65*
Earth vs. the Spider *'58*
Beginning of the End *'57*
Sunset in the West *'50*
The Kid From Cleveland *'49*
Far Frontier *'48*
Bordertown Gunfighters *'43*
Texas Legionnaires *'43*
Red River Valley *'41*
Pioneers of the West *'40*
Southward Ho! *'39*
Wall Street Cowboy *'39*
Circus Girl *'37*
Larceny On the Air *'37*
Public Cowboy No. 1 *'37*
King of the Pecos *'36*

Otello Martelli(1902-2000)

Boccaccio '70 *'62*
Where the Hot Wind Blows *'59*
What a Woman! *'56*
Il Bidone *'55*
I Vitelloni *'53*
Anna *'51*
Variety Lights *'51*
The Flowers of St. Francis *'50*
Bitter Rice *'49*

Pascal Marti

Paris, je t'aime *'06*
L'Ennui *'98*

F. Smith Martin

Hard Vice *'94*
Zipperface *'92*

Arthur Martinelli(1881-1967)

In Old New Mexico *'45*
The Devil Bat *'41*
Double Trouble *'41*
Gangs, Inc. *'41*
Motorcycle Squad *'41*
Revolt of the Zombies *'36*
Supernatural *'33*
The White Zombie *'32*

Alejandro Martinez

Blackout *'07*
Stay Alive *'06*

Flavio Martinez Labiano(1962-)

800 Bullets *'02*
Bones *'01*
Harlan County War *'00*
Dance with the Devil *'97*
The Day of the Beast *'95*

Igor Martinovic

The Tillman Story *'10*
Man on Wire *'08*

Joseph Mascelli(1917-81)

The Thrill Killers *'65*
Incredibly Strange Creatures Who Stopped Living and Became Mixed-Up Zombies *'63*
Wild Guitar *'62*

Raffaele Masciocchi

Challenge of the Gladiator *'65*
The Ghost *'63*
Magnificent Adventurer *'63*
The Horrible Dr. Hichcock *'62*

Mario Masini

Padre Padrone *'77*
Allegro Non Troppo *'76*
Private Lessons *'75*
St. Michael Had a Rooster *'72*

Steve Mason(1954-)

Harsh Times *'05*
Venom *'05*
The Wendell Baker Story *'05*
Basic *'03*
Rollerball *'02*
Bootmen *'00*
BASEketball *'98*
Buddy *'97*
That Old Feeling *'96*
Strictly Ballroom *'92*

Stelvio Massi(1929-2004)

The Case of the Bloody Iris *'72*
Fistful of Lead *'70*
Gunslinger *'70*
Sartana's Here... Trade Your Pistol for a Coffin *'70*
Place in Hell *'69*

Peter Masterson(1934-)

The Cake Eaters *'07*
West of Here *'02*

Rudolph Mate(1898-1964)

Gilda *'46*
Cover Girl *'44*
Sahara *'43*
They Got Me Covered *'43*
The Pride of the Yankees *'42*
To Be or Not to Be *'42*
The Flame of New Orleans *'41*
It Started with Eve *'41*
My Favorite Wife *'40*
Seven Sinners *'40*
Love Affair *'39*
The Real Glory *'39*
Stella Dallas *'37*
Come and Get It *'36*
Dodsworth *'36*
Vampyr *'31*
Passion of Joan of Arc *'28*

Tibor Mathe(1943-)

Opium: Diary of a Madwoman *'07*
Simon the Magician *'99*
Woyzeck *'94*

James Mathers

Aussie and Ted's Great Adventure *'09*
American Crude *'07*
The U.S. Vs. John Lennon *'06*
St. Patrick: The Irish Legend *'00*
Sexual Malice *'93*
Snapdragon *'93*
Rock 'n' Roll High School Forever *'91*
Silent Night, Deadly Night 5: The Toymaker *'91*
The Forgotten One *'89*

John Mathieson(1958-)

Flashbacks of a Fool *'08*
August Rush *'07*
Kingdom of Heaven *'05*
Stoned *'05*
The Phantom of the Opera *'04*
Trauma *'04*
Matchstick Men *'03*
Hannibal *'01*
K-PAX *'01*
Gladiator *'00*
Love Is the Devil *'98*
Plunkett & Macleane *'98*
Twin Town *'97*
Bye-Bye *'96*
Pigalle *'95*

Clark Mathis

Meet Dave *'08*
Norbit *'07*
Rocky Balboa *'06*
Happy Endings *'05*
In the Mix *'05*
The Perfect Score *'04*
Ready to Rumble *'00*

Christian Matras(1903-77)

Lola Montes *'55*
Nana *'55*
The Earrings of Madame De... *'54*
Le Plaisir *'52*
Fanfan la Tulipe *'51*
L'Idiot *'46*
Grand Illusion *'37*

Thomas Mauch(1937-)

Fitzcarraldo *'82*
Stroszek *'77*
Under the Pavement Lies the Strand *'75*
Aguirre, the Wrath of God *'72*
Signs of Life *'68*

Shawn Maurer

Black Dynamite *'09*
Disaster Movie *'08*
Van Wilder: Freshman Year *'08*
Epic Movie *'07*
Caffeine *'06*
Date Movie *'06*
The Honeymooners *'05*
Johnson Family Vacation *'04*
Johnson Family Vacation *'04*
Boat Trip *'03*
Like Mike *'02*
Bring It On *'00*
La Cucaracha *'99*
The Big Empty *'98*
Bandwagon *'95*

Tim Maurice-Jones

Envy *'04*
Human Nature *'02*
Snatch *'00*
Lock, Stock and 2 Smoking Barrels *'98*

Joe C. Maxwell

Zarkorr! The Invader *'96*
Malevolence *'95*

Robert Maxwell(1923-78)

Sweet Sweetback's Baadasssss Song *'71*
Girl in Gold Boots *'69*
Rebel Vixens *'69*
The Astro-Zombies *'67*

Bradford May

Darkman 3: Die Darkman Die *'95*
Darkman 2: The Return of Durant *'94*
Target: Favorite Son *'87*

Harry J. May(1924-85)

J.D.'s Revenge *'76*
Friday Foster *'75*
Detroit 9000 *'73*

Mike Mayers

The Jimmy Show *'01*
Joe the King *'99*
Two Family House *'99*
Broadway Damage *'98*
Meeting Daddy *'98*
Whatever *'98*
Cafe Society *'97*
Lewis and Clark and George *'97*
Changing Habits *'96*
Denise Calls Up *'95*
Spanking the Monkey *'94*
Spare Me *'92*

Paul Mayne

The Family Holiday *'07*
Frank *'07*

Alfredo Mayo(1911-85)

The Method *'05*
Mondays in the Sun *'02*
Burnt Money *'00*
Women *'97*
Wild Horses *'95*
Kika *'94*
The Fencing Master *'92*
High Heels *'91*

Donald McAlpine(1934-)

X-Men Origins: Wolverine *'09*
The Chronicles of Narnia: The Lion, the Witch and the Wardrobe *'05*
Anger Management *'03*
Peter Pan *'03*
The Time Machine *'02*
Moulin Rouge *'01*
Stepmom *'98*
The Edge *'97*
William Shakespeare's Romeo and Juliet *'96*
Nine Months *'95*
Clear and Present Danger *'94*
Mrs. Doubtfire *'93*
Medicine Man *'92*
Patriot Games *'92*
Career Opportunities *'91*
Parenthood *'89*
Predator *'87*
Down and Out in Beverly Hills *'86*
Moscow on the Hudson *'84*
The Tempest *'82*
Breaker Morant *'80*
My Brilliant Career *'79*
The Odd Angry Shot *'79*
Don's Party *'76*

Lawrence McConkey

Tyson *'08*
When Will I Be Loved *'04*

Ted D. McCord(1900-76)

A Fine Madness *'66*
The Sound of Music *'65*
Proud Rebel *'58*
The Helen Morgan Story *'57*
South Sea Woman *'53*
Cattle Town *'52*
This Woman Is Dangerous *'52*
Goodbye My Fancy *'51*
Starlift *'51*
The Damned Don't Cry *'50*
Rocky Mountain *'50*
Treasure of the Sierra Madre *'48*
Action in the North Atlantic *'43*
I Was Framed *'42*
Trail Drive *'33*
Dynamite Ranch *'32*
Tombstone Canyon *'32*
The Dawn Trail *'30*
Fightin' Ranch *'30*

Malcolm McCulloch

Two Hands *'98*
Kiss or Kill *'97*

Sam McCurdy

Doomsday *'08*
The Hills Have Eyes 2 *'07*
Outlaw *'07*
Cold and Dark *'05*
The Descent *'05*
Preaching to the Perverted *'97*

David McDonald

Horror Hospital *'73*
The Harder They Come *'72*

Michael McDonough

Winter's Bone *'10*
Quid Pro Quo *'08*
The Babysitters *'07*
Diggers *'06*
Down to the Bone *'04*

Seamus McGarvey(1967-)

Nowhere Boy *'09*
The Soloist *'09*
Atonement *'07*
Charlotte's Web *'06*
World Trade Center *'06*
Sahara *'05*
Along Came Polly *'04*
The Hours *'02*
Enigma *'01*
Wit *'01*
High Fidelity *'00*
The Big Tease *'99*
A Map of the World *'99*
The War Zone *'98*
The Winter Guest *'97*
Butterfly Kiss *'94*

Barney McGill(1890-1942)

Charlie Chan in Shanghai *'35*
The Bowery *'33*
Bureau of Missing Persons *'33*
Employees' Entrance *'33*
The Mayor of Hell *'33*
Other Men's Women *'31*
Svengali *'31*

Walter McGill

Quicksand *'01*
Oliver Twist *'00*
Aldrich Ames: Traitor Within *'98*

Brendan McGinty

Octane *'07*
Soho Square *'00*

John McGlashan

Captain Jack *'98*
The Buddha of Suburbia *'92*
Clarissa *'91*

Ian Mcglocklin

Make the Yuletide Gay *'09*
Corporate Affairs *'07*

Jack McGowan

Deranged *'74*
Children Shouldn't Play with Dead Things *'72*
Deathdream *'72*

Patrick Mcgowan

Fire Serpent *'07*
A Lobster Tale *'06*
Show Me *'04*

Martin McGrath(1956-)

Irresistible *'06*
Danny Deckchair *'03*
My Boss's Daughter *'03*
Swimming Upstream *'03*
Do or Die *'01*
On the Beach *'00*
Passion *'99*
In the Winter Dark *'98*
Blackrock *'97*
A Little Bit of Soul *'97*
The Ripper *'97*
Children of the Revolution *'95*
River Street *'95*
Bullet Down Under *'94*
Muriel's Wedding *'94*

Kieran McGuigan

The Other Boleyn Girl *'08*
Bleak House *'05*

Austin McKinney

Rockin' Road Trip *'85*
Axe *'74*
Free Grass *'69*
The Fear Chamber *'68*
The Sinister Invasion *'68*
Alien Massacre *'67*
Gallery of Horrors *'67*
Pit Stop *'67*

Robert McLachlan

Dragonball: Evolution *'09*
Black Christmas *'06*
Final Destination 3 *'06*
King's Ransom *'05*
Cursed *'04*
Willard *'03*
The One *'01*
Final Destination *'00*
High Noon *'00*
Impolite *'92*

Nick McLean

Short Circuit *'86*
The Goonies *'85*
Cannonball Run 2 *'84*
Stroker Ace *'83*

Geary McLeod

Not Easily Broken *'09*
Who Made the Potatoe Salad? *'05*
Carmen: A Hip Hopera *'01*
Cement *'99*
Black Circle Boys *'97*
Dinner and Driving *'97*

Stephen McNutt

Battlestar Galactica: The Plan *'09*
Call of the Wild *'04*
Black Point *'01*
Out of Time *'00*
Inferno *'99*
Spanish Judges *'99*

Glen McPherson

See Glen MacPherson

John McPherson(1941-2007)

Short Circuit 2 *'88*
*batteries not included *'87*
Jaws: The Revenge *'87*
Hot Pursuit *'84*

Owen McPolin

Little Dorrit *'08*
The Mapmaker *'01*

Steve McWilliams(1954-)

No Safe Haven *'87*
Revenge *'86*

Terry Meade

Shooting *'82*
The California Kid *'74*

Graeme Mears

Cybercity *'99*
Future Fear *'97*

Suki Medencevic(1963-)

I Hope They Serve Beer in Hell *'09*
The Art of War 3: Retribution *'08*
Connor's War *'06*
The Great Water *'04*
Hunter's Moon *'97*
Embrace of the Vampire *'95*
Poison Ivy 2: Lily *'95*

Teresa Medina(1965-)

The 24 Hour Woman *'99*
Female Perversions *'96*
Things I Never Told You *'96*
Reflections in the Dark *'94*

George Meehan, Jr. (1891-1947)

The Desperadoes *'43*
Hard to Hold *'37*
Alibi for Murder *'36*
Justice of the Range *'35*
Square Shooter *'35*
Inside Information *'34*

Phil Meheux

Edge of Darkness *'10*
Casino Royale *'06*
The Legend of Zorro *'05*
Around the World in 80 Days *'04*
Beyond Borders *'03*
Bicentennial Man *'99*
Entrapment *'99*
The Mask of Zorro *'98*
The Saint *'97*
Goldeneye *'95*
No Escape *'94*
The Trial *'93*
Ruby *'92*
Highlander 2: The Quickening *'91*
Criminal Law *'89*
Renegades *'89*
The Fourth Protocol *'87*
Morons from Outer Space *'85*
Beyond the Limit *'83*
Experience Preferred... But Not Essential *'83*
The Final Option *'82*
The Final Conflict *'81*
The Long Good Friday *'80*

Anil Mehta

Marigold *'07*
Lagaan: Once upon a Time in India *'01*

Sharon Meir

The Last House on the Left *'09*
Dark Streets *'08*
The Haunting of Molly Hartley *'08*
Peaceful Warrior *'06*
Coach Carter *'05*
Mean Creek *'04*

Eloy Mella

The Invincible Gladiator *'62*
Medusa Against the Son of Hercules *'62*

William Mellor(1904-63)

The Greatest Story Ever Told *'65*
State Fair *'62*
Wild in the Country *'61*
The Best of Everything *'59*

Compulsion '59
The Diary of Anne Frank '59
Love in the Afternoon '57
Peyton Place '57
Back from Eternity '56
Giant '56
Bad Day at Black Rock '54
The Affairs of Dobie Gillis '53
The Naked Spur '53
Across the Wide Missouri '51
It's a Big Country '51
A Place in the Sun '51
Westward the Women '51
Love Happy '50
Too Late for Tears '49
The Senator Was Indiscreet '47
Commandos Strike at Dawn '43
The Great Man's Lady '42
My Favorite Blonde '42
The Road to Morocco '42
Wake Island '42
Birth of the Blues '41
The Great McGinty '40
The Road to Singapore '40
Make Way for Tomorrow '37
Sky Parade '36
Wings in the Dark '35

Mark Melville

Trapped '06
Attack of the Sabretooth '05
Asylum of the Damned '03
The Darwin Conspiracy '99
Dilemma '97

Erico Menczer(1926-)

The Innocents Abroad '84
Rulers of the City '76
Dead Are Alive '72
The Cat o' Nine Tails '71
How I Learned to Love Women '66

Chris Menges(1940-)

The Reader '08
Stop-Loss '08
The Yellow Handkerchief '08
Notes on a Scandal '06
North Country '05
The Three Burials of Melquiades Estrada '05
Criminal '04
Dirty Pretty Things '03
The Good Thief '03
The Pledge '00
The Boxer '97
Michael Collins '96
High Season '88
Shy People '87
Singing the Blues in Red '87
The Mission '86
Marie '85
Comfort and Joy '84
The Killing Fields '84
Local Hero '83
Danny Boy '82
Warlords of the 21st Century '82
Gumshoe '72
Black Beauty '71

Peter Menzies, Jr.

Clash of the Titans '10
The Incredible Hulk '08
Shooter '07
When a Stranger Calls '06
Four Brothers '05
The Great Raid '05
Man of the House '05
Miss Congeniality 2: Armed and Fabulous '05
Kangaroo Jack '02
Lara Croft: Tomb Raider '01
Bless the Child '00
Disney's The Kid '00
The General's Daughter '99
The 13th Warrior '99
Hard Rain '97
A Time to Kill '96
Die Hard: With a Vengeance '95
The Getaway '93
Posse '93
White Sands '92

Jacques Mercanton(1909-)

Mr. Hulot's Holiday '53
Jour de Fete '48

Manuel Merino(1918-2001)

Count Dracula '71
The Castle of Fu Manchu '68

Raffaele Mertes

Jesus '00
David '97
Moses '96
Samson and Delilah '96
Fluke '95
Joseph '95
Abraham '94

Mark Mervis

Alice Upside Down '07
Hellbent '04
Amy's O '02
Standing on Fishes '99
Billy's Hollywood Screen Kiss '98

John Mescall(1899-1962)

Dark Waters '44
Night of January 16th '41
The Bride of Frankenstein '35
Magnificent Obsession '35
The Black Cat '34
The Easiest Way '31
The Leatherneck '28

John Metcalfe

Rawhead Rex '87
Xtro '83
Trespasser '81
Inseminoid '80

Anthony C. Metchie

Angel and the Badman '09
Loch Ness Terror '07
Too Cool for Christmas '04
Crash & Byrnes '99

Russell Metty(1906-78)

Ben '72
Cancel My Reservation '72
Maybe I'll Come Home in the Spring '71
Omega Man '71
Change of Habit '69
Madigan '68
The Pink Jungle '68
The Secret War of Harry Frigg '68
Rough Night in Jericho '67
Thoroughly Modern Millie '67
The Appaloosa '66
Madame X '66
Texas Across the River '66
The War Lord '65
The Thrill of It All! '63
The Interns '62
That Touch of Mink '62
By Love Possessed '61
Flower Drum Song '61
The Misfits '61
Midnight Lace '60
Portrait in Black '60
Spartacus '60
Imitation of Life '59
A Time to Love & a Time to Die '58
Touch of Evil '58
Battle Hymn '57
Man of a Thousand Faces '57
Written on the Wind '56
All That Heaven Allows '55
Crashout '55
Magnificent Obsession '54
Because of You '52
The World in His Arms '52
Yankee Buccaneer '52
Flame of Araby '51
Buccaneer's Girl '50
Bagdad '49
All My Sons '48
Arch of Triumph '48
You Gotta Stay Happy '48
The Stranger '46
The Story of G.I. Joe '45

West of the Pecos '45
The Master Race '44
Seven Days Ashore '44
Forever and a Day '43
Dance, Girl, Dance '40
No, No Nanette '40
Frolics on Ice '39
Bringing Up Baby '38
The Great Man Votes '38
Sylvia Scarlett '35

Rexford Metz

The Midnight Hour '86
Every Which Way But Loose '78
The Gauntlet '77
The Invasion of Johnson County '76

Russ Meyer(1922-2004)

Beneath the Valley of the Ultra-Vixens '79
Supervixens '75
Motor Psycho '65

Richard Michalak(1954-)

Newcastle '08
Gordy '95
Children of the Night '92
Body Chemistry 2: Voice of a Stranger '91

Jan Michalik

18 Fingers of Death '05
Ghosts Never Sleep '05

Anastas Michos

Cadillac Records '08
Untraceable '08
The Women '08
Perfect Stranger '07
Freedomland '06
The Forgotten '04
Duplex '03
Mona Lisa Smile '03
Death to Smoochy '02
What's the Worst That Could Happen? '01
The Big Kahuna '00
Keeping the Faith '00
The Education of Little Tree '97

Gregory Middleton

Possession '09
Slither '06
Cake '05
Falling Angels '03
Moving Malcolm '03
Between Strangers '02
The Snow Queen '02
After the Storm '01
Mr. Rice's Secret '00
Suspicious River '00
Better Than Chocolate '99
The Five Senses '99
Rupert's Land '98
Wounded '97
The Invader '96
Kissed '96
White Tiger '95

Peter Middleton

The Alchemists '99
Extremely Dangerous '99
The Waiting Time '99
Body & Soul '93
Sebastiane '79

Pierre Mignot(1944-)

The Lathe of Heaven '02
Noriega: God's Favorite '00
The 6th Day '00
P.T. Barnum '99
No '98
Sous Sol '96
Hiroshima '95
Vanished '95
Mouvements du Desir '94
Ready to Wear '94
Dumb Waiter '87
The Room '87
Boy in Blue '86
Secret Honor '85

Elfi Mikesch(1940-)

Erotique '94
Virgin Machine '88

Tristan Milani

The Road from Coorain '02
The Bank '01

The Boys '98

Michael Mileham(1947-)

Falling in Love Again '80
Runaways '75

C. Kim Miles(1973-)

Wyvern '09
On the Other Hand, Death '08
Smoke Jumpers '08
Storm Cell '08
Alien Agent '07
Blonde and Blonder '07
A Dennis the Menace Christmas '07
Termination Point '07
Shock to the System '06
Chasing Christmas '05

Arthur C. Miller(1895-1970)

Prowler '51
The Gunfighter '50
A Letter to Three Wives '49
Whirlpool '49
Gentleman's Agreement '47
Anna and the King of Siam '46
Dragonwyck '46
The Razor's Edge '46
The Keys of the Kingdom '44
The Purple Heart '44
Immortal Sergeant '43
The Ox-Bow Incident '43
The Song of Bernadette '43
This Above All '42
How Green Was My Valley '41
Man Hunt '41
The Blue Bird '40
Brigham Young: Frontiersman '40
Johnny Apollo '40
The Mark of Zorro '40
The Little Princess '39
The Rains Came '39
Susannah of the Mounties '39
Little Miss Broadway '38
Rebecca of Sunnybrook Farm '38
Heidi '37
Wee Willie Winkie '37
Pigskin Parade '36
Stowaway '36
The Little Colonel '35
Bright Eyes '34
Panama Flo '32

David J. Miller

Shriek If You Know What I Did Last Friday the 13th '00
Footsteps '98
Virtual Combat '95

Ernest Miller(1885-1957)

Rocky Jones, Space Ranger: Renegade Satellite '54
Hellgate '52
Square Dance Jubilee '51
The Steel Helmet '51
Thundering Trail '51
Last Bullet '50
Motor Patrol '50
Outlaw Fury '50
Radar Secret Service '50
Rangeland Empire '50
Red Desert '50
Sudden Death '50
Outlaw Gang '49
Rimfire '49
Ringside '49
Shep Comes Home '49
Return of Wildfire '48
The Tiger Woman '45
California Joe '43
Riders of the Rio Grande '43
Sundown Kid '43
Back in the Saddle '41
Outlaws of the Cherokee Trail '41
West of Cimarron '41
Wagons Westward '40
Cowboys from Texas '39

Jeepers Creepers '39
Call of the Yukon '38
Purple Vigilantes '38
Come on, Cowboys '37
The Three Musketeers '33
Virtue's Revolt '24

Virgil Miller(1887-1974)

The Woman in Green '49
The Mummy's Curse '44
Calling Dr. Death '43
Castle in the Desert '42
Dr. Renault's Secret '42
Charlie Chan's Murder Cruise '40
Charlie Chan at Treasure Island '39
Charlie Chan in City of Darkness '39
Mr. Moto Takes a Chance '38
Mysterious Mr. Moto '38
Thank you, Mr. Moto '37
The Phantom of the Opera '25
The Trap '22

William J. Miller

Lost Boundaries '49
Carnegie Hall '47
Blind Fools '40

William M. Miller

Home Movie '08
Headspace '02

Andy Milligan(1929-91)

Man with Two Heads '72
The Rats Are Coming! The Werewolves Are Here! '72
The Ghastly Ones '68

Alec Mills(1932-)

Catherine Cookson's The Moth '96
Catherine Cookson's The Rag Nymph '96
License to Kill '89
The Living Daylights '87
On the Third Day '83

Charles Mills

Karla '06
Black Listed '03
Baby Boy '01
Jackie's Back '99
Body Count '97
How I Spent My Summer Vacation '97
Lily in Winter '94
Boyz N the Hood '91

Murray Milne

Dead Alive '93
Meet the Feebles '89

Victor Milner(1893-1972)

Jeopardy '53
Carrie '52
The Furies '50
Unfaithfully Yours '48
The Strange Love of Martha Ivers '46
Wonder Man '45
The Great Moment '44
The Princess and the Pirate '44
The Story of Dr. Wassell '44
The Palm Beach Story '42
Reap the Wild Wind '42
The Lady Eve '41
The Monster and the Girl '41
Union Pacific '39
What a Life '39
College Swing '38
Bulldog Drummond Escapes '37
The Plainsman '37
The General Died at Dawn '36
The Crusades '35
Cleopatra '34
One Sunday Afternoon '33
The Song of Songs '33
One Hour with You '32
Trouble in Paradise '32
Man of the World '31
Monte Carlo '30
The Love Parade '29
The Red Lily '24

Human Hearts '22

Pierre Milon

The Class '08
Heading South '05
Who Killed Bambi? '03
My Life on Ice '02
Time Out '01
The Troubles We've Seen '94

Doug Milsome

Dracula 3: Legacy '05
Second in Command '05
Dracula 2: Ascension '03
Johnson County War '02
Standing in the Shadows of Motown '02
Dungeons and Dragons '00
Highlander: Endgame '00
Legionnaire '98
Breakdown '96
Rumpelstiltskin '96
Sunchaser '96
The Old Curiosity Shop '94
Nowhere to Run '93
Body of Evidence '92
Desperate Hours '90
Hawks '89
The Beast '88
Full Metal Jacket '87

Dan Mindel

Star Trek '09
Mission: Impossible 3 '06
Domino '05
The Skeleton Key '05
Stuck On You '03
Spy Game '01
Shanghai Noon '00
Enemy of the State '98

Charles Minsky

Valentine's Day '10
Loving Leah '09
Post Grad '09
That Russell Girl '08
Keeping Up with the Steins '06
You, Me and Dupree '06
The Producers '05
The Princess Diaries 2: Royal Engagement '04
Raising Helen '04
Slap Her, She's French '02
Welcome to Collinwood '02
Tomcats '01
Guinevere '99
Looking for an Echo '99
Dear God '96
Kazaam '96
Pretty Woman '90
April Fool's Day '86

Virgil Marcus Mirano

Coastlines '02
Ulee's Gold '97

George Mitas

Searching for Bobby D '05
Lie Down with Dogs '95

Paul Mitchnick

The Gambler, the Girl and the Gunslinger '09
Every Second Counts '08
The Lost Angel '04

Subrata Mitra(1930-2001)

Shakespeare Wallah '65
Charulata '64
The Big City '63
Devi '60
Aparajito '58
Jalsaghar '58

Kazuo Miyagawa(1908-99)

Kagemusha '80
Tokyo Olympiad '66
Zatoichi: Master Ichi and a Chest of Gold '64
Yojimbo '61
Enjo '58
Ugetsu '53
Rashomon '51

Yoshio Miyajima(1910-)

Kwaidan '64
Harakiri '62

The Human Condition: Road to Eternity *'59*
The Human Condition: No Greater Love *'58*

Hal Mohr(1894-1974)

Underworld USA *'61*
The Last Voyage *'60*
Underworld, U.S.A. *'60*
The Lineup *'58*
The Wild One *'54*
The Member of the Wedding *'52*
Rancho Notorious *'52*
The Second Woman *'51*
I'll Be Yours *'47*
Lost Moment *'47*
Song of Scheherazade *'47*
Because of Him *'45*
Salome, Where She Danced *'45*
The Climax *'44*
The Phantom of the Opera *'43*
Watch on the Rhine *'43*
Twin Beds *'42*
International Lady *'41*
Pot o' Gold *'41*
Destry Rides Again *'39*
Bullets or Ballots *'38*
Green Pastures *'36*
Captain Blood *'35*
A Midsummer Night's Dream *'35*
David Harum *'34*
The Front Page *'31*
Big Boy *'30*
The Wedding March *'28*
The Jazz Singer *'27*
Old San Francisco *'27*
Sparrows *'26*
The Monster *'25*

Amir M. Mokri(1956-)

Season of the Witch *'10*
Fast & Furious *'09*
Vantage Point *'08*
National Treasure: Book of Secrets *'07*
Lord of War *'05*
Taking Lives *'04*
Bad Boys 2 *'03*
The Salton Sea *'02*
Don't Say a Word *'01*
Coyote Ugly *'00*
An Eye for an Eye *'95*
Freejack *'92*
Queens Logic *'91*
Pacific Heights *'90*
Eat a Bowl of Tea *'89*

Peter Mokrosinski(1953-)

Evil *'03*
Speak Up! It's So Dark *'93*

William H. Molina

The Last Assassins *'96*
Where Truth Lies *'96*
Destination Vegas *'95*

Mike Molloy(1940-)

The Fourth Angel *'01*
Shiner *'00*
Noah's Ark *'99*
All the Little Animals *'98*
Welcome to Woop Woop *'97*
Bliss *'96*
Scandal *'89*
Link *'86*
Return of Captain Invincible *'83*
Shock Treatment *'81*

Sandro Moncori

Adios, Sabata *'71*
Return of Sabata *'71*
Sabata *'69*

Carlos Montaner

Friends & Lovers *'99*
Breakaway *'95*
Lap Dancing *'95*

Pierre Montazel(1911-75)

Antoine et Antoinette *'47*
The Fantastic Night *'42*

Joe Montgomery

Bar Hopping *'00*
Hugo Pool *'97*

Felix Monti

The Secret in Their Eyes *'09*
Holy Girl *'04*
Assassination Tango *'03*
Four Days in September *'97*
O Quatrilho *'95*
Of Love and Shadows *'94*
A Shadow You Soon Will Be *'94*
I, the Worst of All *'90*

Vincent Monton(1949-)

Paperback Romance *'96*
Street Hero *'84*
Road Games *'81*
The Night After Halloween *'79*
Blue Fire Lady *'78*

Luc Montpellier

Cairo Time *'09*
Autumn Hearts: A New Beginning *'07*
Poor Man's Game *'06*
Confessions of a Sociopathic Social Climber *'05*
The Saddest Music in the World *'03*

Mario Montuori(1920-)

The Messiah *'75*
Goliath and the Dragon *'61*
The Wide Blue Road *'57*

George Mooradian

Heart of the Beholder *'05*
The Hitcher 2: I've Been Waiting *'03*
Crazy as Hell *'02*
Winter Break *'02*
Bats *'99*
K-911 *'99*
Made Men *'99*
Love Kills *'98*
Postmortem *'98*
Mean Guns *'97*
Nemesis 4: Cry of Angels *'97*
Retroactive *'97*
Adrenalin: Fear the Rush *'96*
Nemesis 3: Time Lapse *'96*
Omega Doom *'96*
Ravenhawk *'95*
Spitfire *'94*
Brain Smasher... A Love Story *'93*
Nemesis *'93*

Richard Moore(1925-)

Annie *'82*
Myra Breckinridge *'70*
Winning *'69*
Wild in the Streets *'68*
The Wild Angels *'66*

Ted Moore(1914-87)

Clash of the Titans *'81*
Priest of Love *'81*
Orca *'77*
Sinbad and the Eye of the Tiger *'77*
The Man with the Golden Gun *'74*
Golden Voyage of Sinbad *'73*
Live and Let Die *'73*
Psychomania *'73*
Diamonds Are Forever *'71*
The Chairman *'69*
The Prime of Miss Jean Brodie *'69*
Shalako *'68*
The Last Safari *'67*
A Man for All Seasons *'66*
The Amorous Adventures of Moll Flanders *'65*
Thunderball *'65*
Goldfinger *'64*
Day of the Triffids *'63*
From Russia with Love *'63*
Dr. No *'62*
Let's Get Married *'60*
The Trials of Oscar Wilde *'60*
The Gamma People *'56*

Pierre Morel

War *'07*
Love and Other Disasters *'06*
Unleashed *'05*
The Transporter *'02*

Adriano Moreno

Knocks at My Door *'93*
Shoot to Kill *'90*

Donald M. Morgan

Sweet Nothing in My Ear *'08*
Back in the Day *'05*
Out of the Ashes *'03*
Bojangles *'01*
For Love or Country: The Arturo Sandoval Story *'00*
Sally Hemings: An American Scandal *'00*
The Thin Blue Lie *'00*
A Lesson Before Dying *'99*
The Rage: Carrie 2 *'99*
The Wall *'99*
Kiss the Sky *'98*
Miss Evers' Boys *'97*
The Rage *'96*
Born to Be Wild *'95*
Excessive Force *'93*
Dillinger *'91*
Double-Crossed *'91*
Christine *'84*
Starman *'84*
Used Cars *'80*

Ira Morgan(1889-1959)

Fog Island *'45*
Mr. Muggs Rides Again *'45*
Girls in Chains *'43*
Three Legionnaires *'37*
Modern Times *'36*
Curtain at Eight *'33*
The Vampire Bat *'32*
The Great Gabbo *'29*
Spring Fever *'27*
West Point *'27*
Little Old New York *'23*

Ken Morgan

Catherine Cookson's The Black Candle *'92*
Catherine Cookson's The Fifteen Streets *'90*
The Maze *'85*

Kramer Morgenthau

The Express *'08*
Feast of Love *'07*
Fracture *'07*
Full of It *'07*
Godsend *'04*
Cuban Blood *'03*
Mayor of the Sunset Strip *'03*
Empire *'02*
Green Dragon *'01*
The Man from Elysian Fields *'01*
Cowboys and Angels *'00*
The Big Brass Ring *'99*
Wirey Spindell *'99*
Dogtown *'97*

Mark Moriarty

The Riddle *'07*
Johnny Was *'05*
The Fever *'04*

Fujio Morita

Rikyu *'90*
Daimajin *'66*

Rhett Morita

Get a Clue *'02*
Snap Decision *'01*
Gang in Blue *'96*
Prom Night 3: The Last Kiss *'89*

John Morrill

The Dark *'79*
Kingdom of the Spiders *'77*
A Boy and His Dog *'75*
The Brotherhood of Satan *'71*
The Exiles *'61*
Hideous Sun Demon *'59*

Mark Morris

Texas Payback *'95*
Hangfire *'91*

Nic Morris

The Criminal *'00*
Firelight *'97*
Masterminds *'96*

Oswald Morris(1915-)

The Dark Crystal *'82*
The Great Muppet Caper *'81*
Just Tell Me What You Want *'80*
The Wiz *'78*
Equus *'77*
The Seven-Per-Cent Solution *'76*
The Man Who Would Be King *'75*
The Odessa File *'74*
Dracula *'73*
Lady Caroline Lamb *'73*
Sleuth *'72*
Fiddler on the Roof *'71*
Scrooge *'70*
Goodbye, Mr. Chips *'69*
Oliver! *'68*
Reflections in a Golden Eye *'67*
The Taming of the Shrew *'67*
The Hill *'65*
The Spy Who Came in from the Cold *'65*
Of Human Bondage *'64*
The Pumpkin Eater *'64*
Lolita *'62*
The Guns of Navarone *'61*
The Entertainer *'60*
Our Man in Havana *'59*
The Key *'58*
Look Back in Anger *'58*
A Farewell to Arms *'57*
Heaven Knows, Mr. Allison *'57*
Moby Dick *'56*
The Man Who Never Was *'55*
Beau Brummel *'54*
Indiscretion of an American Wife *'54*
Beat the Devil *'53*
Moulin Rouge *'52*
The Golden Salamander *'51*
Captain Boycott *'47*

Reginald Morris

A Christmas Story *'83*
Porky's 2: The Next Day *'83*
Porky's *'82*
Empire of the Ants *'77*
Welcome to Blood City *'77*
Second Wind *'76*
Black Christmas *'75*

Kevin Morrisey

Headless Body in Topless Bar *'96*
Killer Tomatoes Eat France *'91*

David Rush Morrison

Stephanie Daley *'06*
Love for Rent *'05*
Double Bang *'01*
Fanci's Persuasion *'95*

Robert L. Morrison

Backstairs at the White House *'79*
Tarantulas: The Deadly Cargo *'77*

Paul Morrissey(1939-)

Heat *'72*
Trash *'70*
Flesh *'68*

Andrei Moskvin(1901-61)

Don Quixote *'57*
Ivan the Terrible, Part 2 *'46*

Ian Moss

The Diary of Anne Frank *'08*
The Secret Life of Mrs. Beeton *'06*

Edgar Moura

Tieta of Agreste *'96*
The Fable of the Beautiful Pigeon Fancier *'88*

David Moxness

Alien Trespass *'09*
Spectacular *'09*

Eric Moynier

The Boynton Beach Club *'05*
Snakeman *'05*
Sueno *'05*

Sead Muhtarevic

Brown's Requiem *'98*
The Beneficiary *'97*
American Strays *'96*
Hard Drive *'94*

David Muir

Neither the Sea Nor the Sand *'73*
And Now for Something Completely Different *'72*
Lust for a Vampire *'71*

M. David Mullen(1962-)

Jennifer's Body *'09*
The Astronaut Farmer *'07*
Akeelah and the Bee *'06*
Shadowboxer *'06*
The Quiet *'05*
When Do We Eat? *'05*
D.E.B.S. *'04*
Northfork *'03*
2 Brothers & a Bride *'03*
Infested: Invasion of the Killer Bugs *'02*
Jackpot *'01*
Devil in the Flesh 2 *'00*
Alone with a Stranger *'99*
Perfect Tenant *'99*
Twin Falls Idaho *'99*
The Night Caller *'97*
Cupid *'96*
Dead Cold *'96*
The Fiance *'96*
Shadow Warriors *'95*
Lipstick Camera *'93*

Robby Muller(1940-)

Coffee and Cigarettes *'03*
24 Hour Party People *'01*
Dancer in the Dark *'99*
Ghost Dog: The Way of the Samurai *'99*
Shattered Image *'98*
The Tango Lesson *'97*
Beyond the Clouds *'95*
Breaking the Waves *'95*
Dead Man *'95*
Mad Dog and Glory *'93*
When Pigs Fly *'93*
Until the End of the World *'91*
Mystery Train *'89*
Barfly *'87*
The Believers *'87*
Down by Law *'86*
Repo Man *'83*
Saint Jack *'79*
The American Friend *'77*
Kings of the Road—In the Course of Time *'76*
The Goalie's Anxiety at the Penalty Kick *'71*

Maximo Munzi

Meteor *'09*
Finish Line *'08*
Ring of Death *'08*
Avenging Angel *'07*
Crash and Burn *'07*
The Sitter *'07*
A Stranger's Heart *'07*
The Christmas Card *'06*
Bound by Lies *'05*
Mystery Woman: Mystery Weekend *'05*
Love's Enduring Promise *'04*
Momentum *'03*
Scorcher *'02*
Backflash *'01*
Out of the Black *'01*
They Crawl *'01*
The Guardian *'00*
The Stepdaughter *'00*
Judgment Day *'99*
Good Luck *'96*
Blondes Have More Guns *'95*

J.(James) Michael Muro

Cirque du Freak: The Vampire's Assistant *'09*
Traitor *'08*
The Last Mimzy *'07*
Rush Hour 3 *'07*
Flicka *'06*
Crash *'05*
Roll Bounce *'05*
Open Range *'03*

Fred Murphy(1942-)

Drillbit Taylor *'08*
Ghost Town *'08*
Anamorph *'07*
Trumbo *'07*
RV *'06*
Dreamer: Inspired by a True Story *'05*
Secret Window *'04*
Freddy vs. Jason *'03*
Auto Focus *'02*
The Mothman Prophecies *'02*
Soul Survivors *'01*
Stir of Echoes *'99*
Witness Protection *'99*
Dance with Me *'98*
A Family Thing *'96*
Metro *'96*
Faithful *'95*
The Fantasticks *'95*
Murder in the First *'95*
Jack the Bear *'93*
Scenes from a Mall *'91*
Enemies, a Love Story *'89*
Five Corners *'88*
Full Moon in Blue Water *'88*
Best Seller *'87*
The Dead *'87*
Hoosiers *'86*
The Trip to Bountiful *'85*
Eddie and the Cruisers *'83*
Q (The Winged Serpent) *'82*
Heartland *'81*
Impostors *'80*
Girlfriends *'78*

Michael D. Murphy

Beach Girls *'82*
Silent Scream *'80*

Paul Murphy(1954-)

October Sky *'99*
Under the Lighthouse Dancing *'97*
Mighty Morphin Power Rangers: The Movie *'95*
Tunnel Vision *'95*

Nicholas Musuraca(1892-1975)

The Blue Gardenia *'53*
The Hitch-Hiker *'53*
Where Danger Lives *'50*
The Woman on Pier 13 *'50*
Mysterious Desperado *'49*
Out of the Past *'47*
The Spiral Staircase *'46*
Bedlam *'45*
Forever and a Day *'43*
The Ghost Ship *'43*
Call Out the Marines *'42*
Cat People *'42*
Hurry, Charlie, Hurry *'41*
Smashing the Rackets *'38*
Living on Love *'37*
Village Tale *'35*
Cheyenne Kid *'33*
Smart Woman *'31*
Inside the Lines *'30*

Sead Mutarevic

See Sead Muhtarevic

Oleg Mutu

4 Months, 3 Weeks and 2 Days *'07*
The Death of Mr. Lazarescu *'05*

David Myers(1914-2004)

Hard Traveling *'85*
Uforia *'81*
FM *'78*

Jeffrey Mygatt

Prison Break: The Final Break *'09*
Stiletto *'08*

Yasatako Nagano

The Machine Girl *'07*
Executive Koala *'06*

Mutsuo Naganuma

Kabei: Our Mother *'08*
The Hidden Blade *'04*
The Twilight Samurai *'02*

Tetsuo Nagata
Micmacs '09
Splice '09
La Vie en Rose '07
Paris, je t'aime '06

Asakazu Nakai
Ran '85
Dersu Uzala '75
High & Low '62
Throne of Blood '57
I Live in Fear '55
Seven Samurai '54
Ikiru '52
One Wonderful Sunday '47
No Regrets for Our Youth '46

Anthony G. Nakonechnyi
The Gene Generation '07
Point of Origin '02

Armando Nannuzzi(1925-2001)
Frankenstein Unbound '90
Maximum Overdrive '86
Silver Bullet '85
La Cage aux Folles 2 '81
La Cage aux Folles '78
Chino '75
Ludwig '72
Waterloo '71
Porcile '69
Mafioso '62
Il Bell'Antonio '60

Choochart Nantitanyatada
Blood Monkey '07
Croc '07

Leon Narbey(1947-)
The Tattooist '07
Whale Rider '02
The Price of Milk '00
Desperate Remedies '93

Hiro Narita(1941-)
Valley of the Heart's Delight '07
The Darwin Awards '06
Dirty Pictures '00
I'll Be Home for Christmas '98
Shadrach '98
Conceiving Ada '97
Sub Down '97
The Arrival '96
James and the Giant Peach '96
The Rocketeer '91
Star Trek 6: The Undiscovered Country '91
Honey, I Shrunk the Kids '89
Never Cry Wolf '83

Toichiro Narushima
Merry Christmas, Mr. Lawrence '83
Double Suicide '69

Mohsen Nasr
An Egyptian Story '82
Alexandria.. Why? '78

Guillermo Navarro(1955-)
It Might Get Loud '09
Hellboy II: The Golden Army '08
Night at the Museum '06
Pan's Labyrinth '06
Zathura '05
Hellboy '04
Imagining Argentina '04
Broken Silence '01
The Devil's Backbone '01
Spy Kids '01
Stuart Little '99
Jackie Brown '97
Spawn '97
Dream for an Insomniac '96
The Long Kiss Goodnight '96
Desperado '95
Four Rooms '95
From Dusk Till Dawn '95
Cronos '94
Cabeza de Vaca '90

Ronald Neame(1911-)
This Happy Breed '47
Blithe Spirit '45
In Which We Serve '43

Andre Neau
Waiting for the Moon '87
The Return of Martin Guerre '83

Louis Nee
Utopia '51
Vampyr '31

Michael Negrin
My Mom's New Boyfriend '08
Senior Skip Day '08
Cyxork 7 '06
Local Color '06

Sol Negrin(1929-)
Happy Hell Night '92
Amazing Grace '74

Peter Nelson(1959-)
A Tale of Two Pizzas '03
Pipe Dream '02
Ed's Next Move '96

Jan Nemecek
Murder Czech Style '66
Who Wants to Kill Jessie? '65
Black Peter '63

Alex Nepomniaschy(1955-)
Take the Lead '06
10th & Wolf '06
The Prince & Me '04
Narc '02
A Time for Dancing '00
It's the Rage '99
Never Been Kissed '99
The Alarmist '98
The Associate '96
Mrs. Winterbourne '96
Safe '95
Lisa '90
Poltergeist 3 '88
Last Resort '86
Wanted Dead or Alive '86

Benedict Neuenfels
A Woman in Berlin '08
The Counterfeiters '07

Harry Neuman
See Harry Neumann
A Bullet for Joey '55

Harry Neumann(1891-1971)
The Wasp Woman '59
Man From God's Country '58
Flight to Mars '52
I Was an American Spy '51
Two Lost Worlds '50
Panhandle '48
Riding the California Trail '47
Lawmen '44
Marked Trails '44
Raiders of Ghost City '44
Raiders of the Border '44
The Man with Two Lives '42
The Fatal Hour '40
Tomboy '40
Mr. Wong, Detective '38
Prison Break '38
California Straight Ahead! '37
Wild Brian Kent '36
Mysterious Mr. Wong '35
The Dude Bandit '33
Tarzan the Fearless '33
Boiling Point '32
Local Badman '32
The Prairie King '27
The Phantom Bullet '26

Mathias Neumann(1965-)
In the Name of the King: A Dungeon Siege Tale '08
Seed '08
Tunnel Rats '08
Postal '07
BloodRayne '06

Alone in the Dark '05
Heart of America '03
House of the Dead '03
Blackwoods '02
Sanctimony '01

Thomas Neuwirth
The Locket '02
The Lost Child '00
True Women '97

Robert New
Stan Helsing '09
Joy Ride 2: Dead Ahead '08
Riding the Bullet '04
The Chosen One: Legend of the Raven '98
Lionheart '90
Big Bad Mama 2 '87
Night of the Creeps '86
Prom Night '80

Peter Newbrook(1920-)
Crucible of Terror '72
Estate of Insanity '64

John Newby
Desert Saints '01
Alien Fury: Countdown to Invasion '00
Santa and Pete '99
The Defenders: Taking the First '98
The Defenders: Payback '97
The Christmas Box '95
The Disappearance of Kevin Johnson '95
Operation Intercept '95
The Fence '94
Red Sun Rising '94

Harry Newmann
See Harry Neumann

Yuri Neyman
Civil Brand '02
Milo '98
Spirit Lost '96
Roseanne: An Unauthorized Biography '94
Back in the USSR '92
Red Riding Hood '88
Liquid Sky '83

Man-Ching Ng
Infernal Affairs 2 '03
Infernal Affairs 3 '03

Peter Ngor
Sex and Zen '93
Mr. Vampire '86
Operation Condor 2: The Armour of the Gods '86

Meredith Nicholson(1913-2005)
The Amazing Transparent Man '60
Missile to the Moon '59
Frankenstein's Daughter '58
She Demons '58

Rex Nicholson
Perfume '01
Allie & Me '97
Plump Fiction '97
A Modern Affair '94

Ramsay Nickell(1963-)
Endgame '09
Chaos Theory '08
Let's Go to Prison '06
The Oh in Ohio '06
Pretty Persuasion '05
The Medicine Show '01

John M. Nickolaus, Jr.(1913-85)
The Terror '63
Attack of the Giant Leeches '59
Four Fast Guns '59
Night of the Blood Beast '58
Showdown at Boot Hill '58

Guillermo Nieto
Lion's Den '08
Rolling Family '04

Alfonso Nieva
Stranger in Paso Bravo '68
Emerald of Artama '67

Hawk and Castile '67
Dr. Orloff's Monster '64

Tadashi Nishimoto
Super Inframan '76
Come Drink with Me '65
The Ghost of Yotsuya '58

William Nobles(1892-1968)
Romance on the Range '42
Bad Man of Deadwood '41
In Old Cheyenne '41
Nevada City '41
Sheriff of Tombstone '41
Adventures of Red Ryder '40
Carson City Kid '40
Drums of Fu Manchu '40
Heroes of the Saddle '40
Mysterious Doctor Satan '40
Young Bill Hickok '40
In Old Caliente '39
South of the Border '39
Call the Mesquiteers '38
Prairie Moon '38
Dangerous Holiday '37
Dick Tracy: The Spider Strikes '37
Roarin' Lead '37
S.O.S. Coast Guard '37
Wild Horse Rodeo '37
Doughnuts & Society '36
The Three Mesquiteers '36
Winds of the Wasteland '36
No Man's Range '35
Sucker Money '34
Law and Lawless '33
The Lone Avenger '33
The Drifter '32
Mystery Trooper '32
Westward Bound '30

Eric Van Haren Noman
Montana Sky '07
Brave New Girl '04
Brush with Fate '03
These Old Broads '01
The Truth About Jane '00
The Color of Courage '98
What the Deaf Man Heard '98
Robin Cook's Terminal '96
An Unexpected Family '96
Blue River '95
A Mother's Prayer '95
Too Young to Die '90
Hero and the Terror '88

Christopher Norr
What Doesn't Kill You '08
Trumbo '07
The Hottest State '06
Into the Fire '05
One Last Thing '05
Second Best '05
Guarding Eddy '04
Nick and Jane '96
Nueba Yol '95

Crescenzo G.P. Notarile
Timecop 2: The Berlin Decision '03
Bullet '94

Ben Nott
Daybreakers '09
The Company '07
See No Evil '06
Salem's Lot '04
Counterstrike '03
The Outsider '02

Jehane Noujaim(1974-)
Control Room '04
Only the Strong Survive '03

Vladimir Novotny(1914-97)
The Shop on Main Street '65
Lemonade Joe '64

Danny Nowak(1959-)
Dead in a Heartbeat '02
The Big Hit '98
Bone Daddy '97
Hard Core Logo '96
Probable Cause '95
Abducted 2: The Reunion '94

Crackerjack '94
Flesh Gordon 2: Flesh Gordon Meets the Cosmic Cheerleaders '90
Maniac Warriors '88

Victor Nunez(1945-)
Without Evidence '96
Gal Young 'Un '79

Giles Nuttgens(1960-)
Saint John of Las Vegas '09
The Loss of a Teardrop Diamond '08
The Good Night '07
Mister Foe '07
Asylum '05
Bee Season '05
Water '05
If Only '04
Young Adam '03
Swimfan '02
The Deep End '01
Battlefield Earth '00
Alice in Wonderland '99
Earth '98
A Merry War '97
Fire '96

Bruno Nuytten(1945-)
Jean de Florette '87
Manon of the Spring '87
Detective '85
Life Is a Bed of Roses '83
Hotel America '81
Possession '81
Barocco '76
The Best Way '76
Going Places '74

Sven Nykvist(1922-2006)
Celebrity '98
Private Confessions '98
Curtain Call '97
Kristin Lavransdatter '95
Something to Talk About '95
Only You '94
With Honors '94
Sleepless in Seattle '93
What's Eating Gilbert Grape '93
Chaplin '92
Crimes & Misdemeanors '89
New York Stories '89
Another Woman '88
The Unbearable Lightness of Being '88
The Sacrifice '86
Agnes of God '85
Dream Lover '85
After the Rehearsal '84
Swann in Love '84
Fanny and Alexander '83
Star 80 '83
Cannery Row '82
The Postman Always Rings Twice '81
From the Life of the Marionettes '80
Willie & Phil '80
Hurricane '79
Starting Over '79
Autumn Sonata '78
King of the Gypsies '78
Pretty Baby '78
The Serpent's Egg '78
Face to Face '76
The Tenant '76
The Dove '74
Scenes from a Marriage '73
Cries and Whispers '72
Siddhartha '72
One Day in the Life of Ivan Denisovich '71
The Touch '71
First Love '70
The Passion of Anna '70
The Rite '69
Hour of the Wolf '68
The Shame '68
Persona '66
The Silence '63
The Winter Light '62
Through a Glass Darkly '61
The Virgin Spring '59
The True and the False '55

Carl Oakwood
Human Desires '97
Mutual Needs '97

John O'Brien(1962-)
Vermont Is for Lovers '92
The Big Dis '89

P.H. O'Brien
War Tapes '06
Reel Paradise '05

L.W. O'Connell
Decoy '46
Return of the Vampire '43
Underground Agent '42
In Old Kentucky '35
Charlie Chan in London '34
Maker of Men '31
A Girl in Every Port '28
The Bells '26

David Odd
Filth '08
Half Broken Things '07
My Boy Jack '07
Persuasion '07
The Line of Beauty '06
Byron '03
The Lost World '02
All the King's Men '99
The Turn of the Screw '99
Our Mutual Friend '98
Retribution '98
Girls' Night '97
Touching Evil '97

Christophe Offenstein
Tell No One '06
Whatever You Say '02

Philip Ogaard
Kitchen Stories '03
Aberdeen '00
Zero Degrees Kelvin '95
Cross My Heart and Hope to Die '94

Rene Ohashi
Jesse Stone: Thin Ice '09
Jesse Stone: Sea Change '07
Jesse Stone: Stone Cold '05
Saint Ralph '04
Highwaymen '03
Shattered City: The Halifax Explosion '03
Wes Craven Presents: They '02
Club Land '01
Wild Iris '01
Rent-A-Kid '95
To Catch a Killer '92
Millennium '89
Where the Spirit Lives '89
Anne of Green Gables '85

Azusa Ohno
Body of Influence 2 '96
Hostile Intentions '94

Daryn Okada(1960-)
Ghosts of Girlfriends Past '09
The Goods: Live Hard, Sell Hard '09
Baby Mama '08
Harold & Kumar Escape from Guantanamo Bay '08
Sex and Death 101 '07
Stick It '06
Just like Heaven '05
Mean Girls '04
Paparazzi '04
Cradle 2 the Grave '03
Dr. Dolittle 2 '01
Good Advice '01
Joe Somebody '01
Texas Rangers '01
Lake Placid '99
Halloween: H20 '98
Senseless '98
Black Sheep '96
Leo Tolstoy's Anna Karenina '96
Big Bully '95
Phantasm 2 '88

Kozo Okazaki
The Wolves '82
Goyokin '69

Tristan Oliver
Fantastic Mr. Fox '09

Wallace & Gromit in The Curse of the Were-Rabbit *'05*

Peter Olsen

Robot Stories *'03*
Ultrachrist! *'03*
Kaaterskill Falls *'01*

Ruben O'Malley

Deceit *'06*
Love, Ludlow *'05*

David Omedes

Chef's Special *'08*
My Mother Likes Women *'02*

Woody Omens

Harlem Nights *'89*
Coming to America *'88*
History of the World: Part 1 *'81*

Miroslav Ondricek(1934-)

Riding in Cars with Boys *'01*
The Preacher's Wife *'96*
A League of Their Own *'92*
Funny Farm *'88*
F/X *'86*
Amadeus *'84*
Silkwood *'83*
The World According to Garp *'82*
Ragtime *'81*
Hair *'79*
Slaughterhouse Five *'72*
If... *'69*
The Firemen's Ball *'68*
Intimate Lighting *'65*
Loves of a Blonde *'65*

S.D. Onions(1905-68)

Sweet Beat *'59*
Mysterious Mr. Nicholson *'47*

Marco Onorato

Gomorrah *'08*
The Embalmer *'03*

Paul Onorato

Nowhere to Hide *'83*
On the Run *'83*
Tim *'79*

Yaron Orbach

The Joneses *'10*
An Englishman in New York *'09*
The Open Road *'09*
Birds of America *'08*
The Unmistaken Child *'08*
Holly *'07*
The Ten *'07*
Just Like the Son *'06*
Waltzing Anna *'06*
Fabled *'02*

Ronald Orieux

The War Bride *'01*
The Passion of Ayn Rand *'99*
Y2K *'99*
Family of Cops 2: Breach of Faith *'97*
Booty Call *'96*
Broken Trust *'95*
A Good Day to Die *'95*
The Tuskegee Airmen *'95*
Family of Strangers *'93*
Take Down *'92*

Arthur Ornitz(1916-85)

Wilma *'77*
Death Wish *'74*
Law and Disorder *'74*
Blacksnake! *'73*
Serpico *'73*
The Possession of Joel Delaney *'72*
Minnie and Moskowitz *'71*
House of Dark Shadows *'70*
A Thousand Clowns *'65*
Requiem for a Heavyweight *'62*

Jim Orr

A Family Affair *'01*
Totally Blonde *'01*

Tim Orr(1968-)

Observe and Report *'09*
Choke *'08*
Pineapple Express *'08*
Sex Drive *'08*
Snow Angels *'07*
Year of the Dog *'07*
Come Early Morning *'06*
Trust the Man *'06*
Imaginary Heroes *'05*
Little Manhattan *'05*
Undertow *'04*
All the Real Girls *'03*
Raising Victor Vargas *'03*

Julio Ortas

Rattler Kid *'68*
One Step to Hell *'67*
Hercules vs. the Sons of the Sun *'64*

Michael D. O'Shea

The New Guy *'02*
Sorority Boys *'02*
Big Momma's House *'00*
Here on Earth *'00*
The '60s *'99*
Dracula: Dead and Loving It *'95*

Roman Osin(1961-)

Vanilla Gorilla *'09*
Far North *'07*
Mr. Magorium's Wonder Emporium *'07*
The Return *'06*
Pride and Prejudice *'05*
The Warrior *'81*

H. Michael Otano

Familiar Strangers *'08*
How to be a Serial Killer *'08*
Turn the River *'07*
Corn *'02*

Tim Otholt

Break *'09*
The Pink Conspiracy *'07*

Michael Ozier

Bottle Shock *'08*
Nobel Son *'08*
The Sixth Man *'97*

Harald Gunnar Paalgard

Red *'08*
The Last Lieutenant *'94*
The Inheritance *'76*

Bianco Pacelli

Son of Sam *'08*
BTK Killer *'05*

Gerald Packer

Bridal Fever *'08*
Wisegal *'08*
Twist *'03*
Hangman *'00*
Jacob Two Two Meets the Hooded Fang *'99*
Conquest *'98*
The Wicked, Wicked West *'97*
Swann *'96*

Fred Paddock

All Roads Lead Home *'08*
Threat of Exposure *'02*

Gyula Pados(1969-)

Predators *'10*
The Duchess *'08*
Evening *'07*
Basic Instinct 2 *'06*
Fateless *'05*
Kontroll *'03*
The Heart of Me *'02*

Louis Page(1905-90)

Any Number Can Win *'63*
Duke of the Derby *'62*
The Bride Is Much Too Beautiful *'58*
Plucking the Daisy *'56*

Luc Pages

A Tale of Winter *'92*
A Tale of Springtime *'89*

Krysztof Pakulski

The Decalogue *'88*
I Like Bats *'85*

Riccardo (Pallton) Pallottini

Fearless *'77*
Emmanuelle on Taboo Island *'76*
The Killer Must Kill Again *'75*
Black Hand *'73*
Lady Frankenstein *'72*
1931: Once Upon a Time in New York *'72*
And God Said to Cain *'69*
Castle of Blood *'64*

Ernest Palmer(1885-1978)

The Womaneater *'59*
Broken Arrow *'50*
Uneasy Terms *'48*
The Dolly Sisters *'46*
Meet the Navy *'46*
Murder in the Footlights *'46*
Pin-Up Girl *'44*
Something for the Boys *'44*
Sweet Rosie O'Grady *'43*
Springtime in the Rockies *'42*
Thunder Birds *'42*
Blood and Sand *'41*
He Found a Star *'41*
Hollywood Cavalcade *'39*
Four Men and a Prayer *'38*
Love Is News *'37*
Second Honeymoon *'37*
Death on the Set *'35*
Stand Up and Cheer *'34*
Cavalcade *'33*
Hoopla *'33*
Street Angel *'28*
7th Heaven *'27*

Marius Panduru

Police, Adjective *'09*
Ryna *'05*

Cecilio Paniagua

Lisa and the Devil *'75*
Mission in Morocco *'59*

Bob Paone

Judge & Jury *'96*
Basket Case 3: The Progeny *'92*

Phedon Papamichael(1962-)

Knight and Day *'10*
W. *'08*
3:10 to Yuma *'07*
The Pursuit of Happyness *'06*
10 Items or Less *'06*
Walk the Line *'05*
The Weather Man *'05*
Sideways *'04*
Identity *'03*
Moonlight Mile *'02*
America's Sweethearts *'01*
The Million Dollar Hotel *'99*
Patch Adams *'98*
The Locusts *'97*
Mouse Hunt *'97*
Bio-Dome *'96*
Phenomenon *'96*
Unhook the Stars *'96*
Unstrung Heroes *'95*
While You Were Sleeping *'95*
Dark Side of Genius *'94*
Cool Runnings *'93*
Wild Palms *'93*
Love Crimes *'92*
Poison Ivy *'92*
Prayer of the Rollerboys *'91*
Body Chemistry *'90*
Dance of the Damned *'88*

Andrij Parekh(1971-)

Blue Valentine *'10*
Cold Souls *'09*
Sugar *'09*
August *'08*
Noise *'07*
Half Nelson *'06*
The Treatment *'06*
Speak *'04*

Andy Parke

Iowa *'05*
Grizzly Mountain *'97*
Future Force *'89*
Operation Warzone *'89*

David Parker(1947-)

Child Star: The Shirley Temple Story *'01*
The Miracle Worker *'00*
Amy *'98*
Mr. Reliable: A True Story *'95*
Malcolm *'86*

Dino Parks

Center Stage: Turn It Up *'08*
Killer Movie *'08*
How to Lose Your Lover *'04*

Phil Parmet(1942-)

Blue State *'07*
Halloween *'07*
The Dog Problem *'06*
Lonesome Jim *'06*
The Devil's Rejects *'05*
Dallas 362 *'03*
American Gun *'02*
13 Moons *'02*
Hard Cash *'01*
Animal Factory *'00*
Black & White *'99*
Love and Action in Chicago *'99*
Flipping *'96*
The Last Days of Frankie the Fly *'96*
Four Rooms *'95*
Under the Hula Moon *'95*
Nina Takes a Lover *'94*
Two Small Bodies *'93*
In the Soup *'92*
Street Hunter *'90*
Fatal Mission *'89*
Harlan County, U.S.A. *'76*

Feliks Parnell(1953-)

Wilderness Love *'02*
Lip Service *'00*
The Nurse *'97*
Poison Ivy 3: The New Seduction *'97*
Smalltime *'96*
Serpent's Lair *'95*

Aiace Parolini(1920-)

Alfredo, Alfredo *'72*
Sicilian Connection *'72*
Super Brother *'68*

Barry Parrell

A Woman's a Helluva Thing *'01*
Zebra Lounge *'01*
The Minion *'98*

Mark Parry

Military Intelligence and You! *'06*
Going Postal *'98*

Greg Patterson

TripFall *'00*
Paper Bullets *'99*
Fatal Passion *'94*

Peter Pau(1952-)

The Forbidden Kingdom *'08*
Shoot 'Em Up *'07*
Perhaps Love *'05*
The Promise *'05*
Crouching Tiger, Hidden Dragon *'00*
Bride of Chucky *'98*
Double Team *'97*
Warriors of Virtue *'97*
The Phantom Lover *'95*
The Bride with White Hair *'93*
Naked Killer *'92*
The Killer *'90*

Justo Paulino

Beyond Atlantis *'73*
Mad Doctor of Blood Island *'68*

Stanley Pavey

The Runaway Bus *'54*
The Belles of St. Trinian's *'53*
My Son, the Vampire *'52*
Dead of Night *'45*

Goran Paviceric

The Second Front *'05*
Amy's O *'02*
All Over the Guy *'01*
Dee Snider's Strangeland *'98*
American Vampire *'97*

Pier Ludovico Pavoni(1927-)

The Triumph of Hercules *'66*
Two Gladiators *'64*
The Beast of Babylon Against the Son of Hercules *'63*
The Hit Man *'60*
Mill of the Stone Women *'60*

Robert Paynter(1928-)

Strike It Rich *'90*
The Secret Garden *'87*
Little Shop of Horrors *'86*
Spies Like Us *'85*
The Muppets Take Manhattan *'84*
Superman 3 *'83*
An American Werewolf in London *'81*
The Final Conflict *'81*
Superman 2 *'80*
The Nightcomers *'72*
Chato's Land *'71*
Lawman *'71*

Homayun Payvar

Daughters of the Sun *'00*
The Taste of Cherry *'96*
Life and Nothing More ... *'92*

Kenneth Peach, Sr.(1903-88)

City Beneath the Sea *'71*
Pufnstuf *'70*
Demon with a Glass Hand *'64*
It! The Terror from Beyond Space *'58*
Sons of the Desert *'33*

Glen Pearcy

Outfoxed: Rupert Murdoch's War on Journalism *'04*
Uncovered: The War on Iraq *'04*

Daniel Pearl(1951-)

Friday the 13th *'09*
Aliens vs. Predator: Requiem *'07*
Captivity *'07*
Pathfinder *'07*
The Texas Chainsaw Massacre *'03*
Amazon Women on the Moon *'87*
Hiding Out *'87*
It's Alive 3: Island of the Alive *'87*
Return to Salem's Lot *'87*
Invaders from Mars *'86*
Getting Wasted *'80*
She Came to the Valley *'77*
The Texas Chainsaw Massacre *'74*

Brian Pearson(1967-)

My Bloody Valentine 3D *'09*
White Noise 2: The Light *'07*
The Butterfly Effect 2 *'06*
School of Life *'06*
Devour *'05*
The Long Weekend *'05*
Karate Dog *'04*
Stealing Sinatra *'04*
Urban Legends 2: Final Cut *'00*
Eye of the Killer *'99*
Tail Lights Fade *'99*
Bounty Hunters 2: Hardball *'97*
Listen *'96*

Christopher Pearson

Recipe for Disaster *'03*
Double Down *'01*
Sabretooth *'01*
Blood Surf *'00*

Nicola Pecorini(1957-)

The Imaginarium of Doctor Parnassus *'09*
Tideland *'05*
The Order *'03*
Harrison's Flowers *'02*
Rules of Engagement *'00*
Fear and Loathing in Las Vegas *'98*

Edward Pei

Primeval *'07*
Helen of Troy *'03*
Anne Rice's The Feast of All Saints *'01*
Little Richard *'00*
Possessed *'00*
Emma's Wish *'98*
Larry McMurtry's Dead Man's Walk *'96*
Overnight Delivery *'96*
Run for the Dream: The Gail Devers Story *'96*
Larry McMurtry's Streets of Laredo *'95*
Panther *'95*
Stephen King's The Stand *'94*
Night of the Warrior *'91*
Masque of the Red Death *'89*

David Pelletier

Mail Order Bride *'08*
American Venus *'07*
Hearts of War *'07*
The Tooth Fairy *'06*
Blood Angels *'05*
The Sandlot 2 *'05*
Before I Say Goodbye *'03*
He Sees You When You're Sleeping *'02*
Lone Hero *'02*
Jill the Ripper *'00*
New Blood *'99*
Bram Stoker's Shadowbuilder *'98*
Mask of Death *'97*
Act of War *'96*
Downhill Willie *'96*
Moving Target *'96*
Live Bait *'95*
The Killing Man *'94*

D.A. Pennebaker(1925-)

Only the Strong Survive *'03*
Moon over Broadway *'98*
The War Room *'93*

C.M. Pennington-Richards(1911-2005)

Tarzan and the Lost Safari *'57*
Tarzan's Hidden Jungle *'55*
A Christmas Carol *'51*
The Hidden Room *'49*
Obsession *'49*

Jean Penzer(1927-)

Notre Histoire *'84*
Buffet Froid *'79*
Get Out Your Handkerchiefs *'78*
The Two of Us *'68*
Love Play *'60*

Richard Pepin

Avalanche *'99*
Deadly Target *'94*
Repo Jake *'90*
Emperor of the Bronx *'89*
Mayhem *'87*
The Newlydeads *'87*

Richard Perez

Outfoxed: Rupert Murdoch's War on Journalism *'04*
Uncovered: The War on Iraq *'04*

Georges Perinal(1897-1965)

Serious Charge *'59*
Tom Thumb *'58*
Bonjour Tristesse *'57*
A King in New York *'57*
Saint Joan *'57*
Three Cases of Murder *'55*
I'll Never Forget You *'51*
The Fallen Idol *'49*
An Ideal Husband *'47*
Nicholas Nickleby *'46*
The Life and Death of Colonel Blimp *'43*
Spitfire *'42*
Dangerous Moonlight *'41*
The Thief of Bagdad *'40*
The Four Feathers *'39*
The Challenge *'38*

Rembrandt '36
Things to Come '36
Sanders of the River '35
Catherine the Great '34
Private Life of Don Juan '34
The Private Life of Henry VIII '33
A Nous la Liberte '31
The Blood of a Poet '30
Under the Roofs of Paris '29

David Perrault
The State Within '06
They Call Me Sirr '00
To Catch a Yeti '95

Harry Perry(1988-85)
Hell's Angels '30
Wings '27
The Vanishing American '25
Shadows '22

Henri Persin
Angelique and the Sultan '68
The Sergeant '68
Untamable Angelique '67
Angelique and the King '66
Angelique: The Road to Versailles '65
Angelique '64
Your Turn Darling '63
The Longest Day '62

Jorgen Persson(1936-)
A Song for Martin '01
Faithless '00
Digging to China '98
Les Miserables '97
Jerusalem '96
Smilla's Sense of Snow '96
The House of the Spirits '93
The Best Intentions '92
The Women on the Roof '89
My Life As a Dog '85
The Inside Man '84
Elvira Madigan '67

Reinhart Pesche
Fascination '04
Fascination '04
Woman, Thou Art Loosed '04
The Apostate '98

Jan Pester
Hogfather '06
Wild Country '05

Don Peterman
Dr. Seuss' How the Grinch Stole Christmas '00
Mighty Joe Young '98
Men in Black '97
Get Shorty '95
Speechless '94
Mr. Saturday Night '92
Point Break '91
She's Out of Control '89
She's Having a Baby '88
Planes, Trains & Automobiles '87
Star Trek 4: The Voyage Home '86
Splash '84
Flashdance '83
When a Stranger Calls '79

Dennis Peters
Faith '90
Body Beat '88

John Peters
Carolina '03
Family Tree '00
Campfire Tales '98
Double Tap '98
Sweethearts '97
Shameless '94

Curtis Petersen
Never Cry Werewolf '08
Lake Dead '07
Safe Harbour '07
The Wailer '06
Confessions of a Pit Fighter '05
The Confessor '04
Detention '03
Gone Dark '03
Rock My World '02
Road Rage '01

Under Heavy Fire '01
My 5 Wives '00
The Proposal '00
The Hunted '98
My Teacher Ate My Homework '98
Silver Wolf '98
The Ticket '97
Bloodhounds 2 '96
Dead Ahead '96
Sabotage '96
ShadowZone: The Undead Express '96
Expect No Mercy '95
Iron Eagle 4 '95
Death Wish 5: The Face of Death '94
Tiger Claws '91
Abraxas: Guardian of the Universe '90
Dragonfight '90

Barry Peterson
Jumper '08
Starsky & Hutch '04
Dark Blue '03
Hollywood Homicide '03
Zoolander '01

Dane Peterson
Love Finds a Home '09
Love Takes Wing '09
Depth Charge '08
Final Approach '08
Shark Swarm '08
All I Want for Christmas '07
Sharpshooter '07
Murder Without Conviction '04

Gus Peterson(1893-1969)
Lady in the Death House '44
Rollin' Plains '38
Sing, Cowboy, Sing '37
Tex Rides with the Boy Scouts '37
Rider of the Law '35
Charley's Aunt '25

Aleksandar Petkovic(1929-2000)
Vukovar '94
Man Is Not a Bird '65

Victor Petrashevich
Love Thrill Murders '71
The Projectionist '71

Jacek Petrycki
Dead Man's Bounty '06
The Healer '02
Shot in the Heart '01
Europa, Europa '91
The Interrogation '82
Fever '81

Wally Pfister
Inception '10
The Dark Knight '08
The Prestige '06
Batman Begins '05
Slow Burn '05
The Italian Job '03
Insomnia '02
Laurel Canyon '02
Scotland, PA '02
Rustin '01
Memento '00
A Kid in Aladdin's Palace '97
Object of Obsession '95
Secret Games 3 '94
Stranger by Night '94
Secret Games '92
Lower Level '91
The Unborn '91

Bruno Philip(1956-)
A Woman Hunted '03
Nowhere in Sight '01
Heavy Metal 2000 '00
Dead Silent '99
The Arrival 2 '98
Captive '97
Snowboard Academy '96
The Scorpio Factor '90

Alex Phillips, Jr.(1935-2007)
Luminarias '99
Dreaming About You '92

Forbidden Homework '92
Born in East L.A. '87
Number One with a Bullet '87
Murphy's Law '86
To Kill a Stranger '84
Cabo Blanco '81
High Risk '81
Fade to Black '80
Devil's Rain '75
Bring Me the Head of Alfredo Garcia '74
Fearmaker '71
The Swap '71
Remolino de Pasiones '68
Yanco '64

David Phillips
Beer League '06
Lift '01
The Basketball Diaries '95
The Little Death '95

Frank Phillips(1912-94)
Midnight Madness '80
The Black Hole '79
Pete's Dragon '77
The Island at the Top of the World '74
Bedknobs and Broomsticks '71

Garry Phillips
Candy '06
Catch a Fire '06
Better Than Sex '00
The Monkey's Mask '00

Roberto D'Ettorre Piazzoli
Curse 2: The Bite '88
Sonny Boy '87
Piranha 2: The Spawning '82
Tentacles '77
Forever Emmanuelle '75

Joseph Pickering
The Incredible Journey of Mary Bryant '05
Idiot Box '97

Andre Pienaar
How She Move '08
Restless Spirits '99
A Slight Case of Murder '99

Tony Pierce-Roberts(1945-)
Made of Honor '08
Home of the Brave '06
Doom '05
De-Lovely '04
Underworld '03
Dinotopia '02
The Importance of Being Earnest '02
The Golden Bowl '00
The Trench '99
Paulie '98
Jungle 2 Jungle '96
Surviving Picasso '96
Haunted '95
The Client '94
Disclosure '94
The Remains of the Day '93
Howard's End '92
The Dark Half '91
White Fang '91
Mr. & Mrs. Bridge '90
Slaves of New York '89
A Tiger's Tale '87
A Room with a View '86
A Private Function '84
Moonlighting '82
Tinker, Tailor, Soldier, Spy '80

Mark Lee Ping-Bin(1954-)
Afterwards '08
Flight of the Red Balloon '08
Three Times '05
In the Mood for Love '00
The Vertical Ray of the Sun '00
Flowers of Shanghai '98
Goodbye South, Goodbye '96
Summer Snow '94

Guiseppe Pinori(1928-)
Corrupt '84
The New Gladiators '83

Tomislav Pinter(1926-)
Transylvania 6-5000 '85
Montenegro '81
Steppenwolf '74

John Pirozzi
Broken English '07
The Hillside Strangler '04

Robert Pittack(1899-1976)
Queen of the Amazons '47
Strange Impersonation '46
Goin' to Town '44
That's My Baby! '44
Pennies from Heaven '36

Larry Pizer
The Proprietor '96
In Custody '94
Murder in Coweta County '83
Timerider '83
Phantom of the Paradise '74
The Optimists '73
Isadora '68
Morgan: A Suitable Case for Treatment '66

Tomas Pladevall
Rape '76
Night of the Howling Beast '75

Robert Planck(1894-1963)
Royal Wedding '51
Luxury Liner '48
The Heavenly Body '44
Above Suspicion '43
We Were Dancing '42
A Woman's Face '41
Strange Cargo '40
The Man in the Iron Mask '39
The Duke of West Point '38
Red Salute '35
Jane Eyre '34
The Moonstone '34
Our Daily Bread '34
The Bat Whispers '30
Be Yourself '30

Franz Planer(1894-1963)
Breakfast at Tiffany's '61
The Nun's Story '59
The Big Country '58
The Pride and the Passion '57
The Caine Mutiny '54
20,000 Leagues under the Sea '54
The 5000 Fingers of Dr. T '53
Death of a Salesman '51
Cyrano de Bergerac '50
Champion '49
Criss Cross '48
One Touch of Venus '48
I Love a Bandleader '45
Adventure in Sahara '38
The Finances of the Grand Duke '24

Aaron Platt
The Pacific and Eddy '07
Wild Tigers I Have Known '06

Karl Plintzner(1911-)
Intrigue and Love '59
The Merry Wives of Windsor '50
The Marriage of Figaro '49

Mark Plummer
A Perfect Getaway '09
Pulse '06
Head Over Heels '01
Albino Alligator '96
The Waterdance '91
After Dark, My Sweet '90
Two Moon Junction '88

Rui Pocas(1966-)
Two Drifters '05
O Fantasma '00

Gabor Pogany(1915-99)
Night Train Murders '75
Torture Train '75
Bluebeard '72
Double Face '70
Those Daring Young Men in Their Jaunty Jalopies '69
Imperial Venus '63
Two Women '61
The Forbidden Christ '50

Mathieu Poirot-Delpech(1959-)
Born in 68 '08
Paris, je t'aime '06
Cote d'Azur '05
My Life on Ice '02
With a Friend Like Harry '00
The Adventures of Felix '99
Jeanne and the Perfect Guy '98

Clifford Poland
Hello Down There '69
Force of Impulse '60

Gene Polito(1918-)
Cheech and Chong's Up in Smoke '79
The Bad News Bears Go to Japan '78
Westworld '73
Colossus: The Forbin Project '70
The Plunderers '60

Sol Polito(1892-1960)
Sorry, Wrong Number '48
The Long Night '47
Arsenic and Old Lace '44
Now, Voyager '42
Sergeant York '41
Santa Fe Trail '40
Confessions of a Nazi Spy '39
The Adventures of Robin Hood '38
Angels with Dirty Faces '38
Gold Diggers in Paris '38
Varsity Show '37
The Charge of the Light Brigade '36
Colleen '36
Petrified Forest '36
"G" Men '35
Shipmates Forever '35
Wonder Bar '34
42nd Street '33
Picture Snatcher '33
Two Seconds '32
Union Depot '32
Playing Around '30
Show Girl in Hollywood '30

Ekkehart Pollack
Gamer '09
Pathology '08

Christophe Pollock
Since Otar Left... '03
Alias Betty '01
In Praise of Love '01
Marie Baie des Anges '97
For Ever Mozart '96
Up/Down/Fragile '95

Gordon Pollock
City Lights '31
Queen Kelly '29

Marco Pontecorvo(1966-)
Letters to Juliet '10
My One and Only '09
The Last Legion '07
Firewall '06
Eros '04
My House in Umbria '03
The Truce '96

Hang-Seng Poon
Blood: The Last Vampire '09
Jet Li's Fearless '06
Kung Fu Hustle '04
Formula 51 '01
Pavilion of Women '01
Special Unit 2002 '01
Zu Warriors '01
Jackie Chan's Who Am I '98
The Executioners '93

The Heroic Trio '93

Bill Pope(1952-)
Scott Pilgrim vs. the World '10
The Spirit '08
Spider-Man 3 '07
Fur: An Imaginary Portrait of Diane Arbus '06
Spider-Man 2 '04
Team America: World Police '04
The Matrix Reloaded '03
The Matrix Revolutions '03
Bedazzled '00
The Matrix '99
Zero Effect '97
Bound '96
Gridlock'd '96
Clueless '95
Army of Darkness '92
Closet Land '90
Darkman '90

Dick Pope(1947-)
Happy-Go-Lucky '08
Honeydripper '07
The Illusionist '06
Man of the Year '06
Vera Drake '04
All or Nothing '02
Nicholas Nickleby '02
Thirteen Conversations About One Thing '01
Way of the Gun '00
Topsy Turvy '99
Career Girls '97
Swept from the Sea '97
Nothing Personal '95
Secrets and Lies '95
An Awfully Big Adventure '94
Naked '93
The Blackheath Poisonings '92
Fool's Gold: The Story of the Brink's-Mat Robbery '92
The Reflecting Skin '91
Wonderland '88

Richard Pope
Me and Orson Welles '09
Angus, Thongs and Perfect Snogging '08

Zoran Popovic
Grace '09
Lies and Illusions '09
War, Inc. '08
Sin '02

Gideon Porath
Special Forces '03
Power Play '02
Breach of Conduct '94
Hit Woman: The Double Edge '93

Itzik Portal
Bonjour Monsieur Shlomi '03
Pick a Card '97

Piero Portalupi
A Farewell to Arms '57
Neapolitan Carousel '54
Neapolitan Carousel '54
Bellissima '51

Christopher Porter
Noah's Arc: Jumping the Broom '08
Just Buried '07

Stephen Posey
Friday the 13th, Part 5: A New Beginning '85
Hellhole '85
Penitentiary 2 '82
Slumber Party Massacre '82

Nils Post(1960-)
For a Lost Soldier '93
To Play or to Die '91

Steven Poster(1944-)
Cats & Dogs: The Revenge of Kitty Galore '10
The Box '09
Spread '09
Southland Tales '06
Mrs. Harris '05
Daddy Day Care '03
Stuart Little 2 '02

Donnie Darko '01
Color of Justice '97
RocketMan '97
Roswell: The U.F.O. Cover-Up '94
The Cemetery Club '93
Life Stinks '91
Rocky 5 '90
Next of Kin '89
Big Top Pee-wee '88
Someone to Watch Over Me '87
The Boy Who Could Fly '86
Strange Brew '83
Blood Beach '81
Dead and Buried '81

Bert Pot

Nothing to Lose '08
Zus & Zo '01

Andreas Poulsson

We All Fall Down '00
Contagious '96
Canada's Sweetheart: The Saga of Hal C. Banks '85

Munn Powell

Gentlemen Broncos '09
The Sasquatch Gang '06
Napoleon Dynamite '04

Vinod Pradhan

Devdas '02
Mission Kashmir '00

Roger Pratt(1947-)

Inkheart '09
Closing the Ring '07
Harry Potter and the Goblet of Fire '05
Troy '04
Harry Potter and the Chamber of Secrets '02
Iris '01
Chocolat '00
The End of the Affair '99
Grey Owl '99
The Avengers '98
King Lear '98
In Love and War '96
12 Monkeys '95
Mary Shelley's Frankenstein '94
Shadowlands '93
The Fisher King '91
Batman '89
High Hopes '88
Mona Lisa '86
Brazil '85
Meantime '81

Robert Presley

A Christmas Carol '09
Beowulf '07
The Polar Express '04

Roland Price(1893-1966)

The Bride & the Beast '58
Son of Ingagi '40
Held for Ransom '38
Marihuana '36
Silent Code '35
Blood and Steel '25

Jack Priestley(1926-93)

Rage of Angels: The Story Continues '86
The First Deadly Sin '80
Across 110th Street '72
Born to Win '71
Where's Poppa? '70
Stiletto '69
No Way to Treat a Lady '68
The Subject Was Roses '68
A Man Called Adam '66

Tom Priestley

Delta Farce '07
The List '07
Three Days to Vegas '07
Barbershop 2: Back in Business '04
Surviving Christmas '04
Barbershop '02
New Best Friend '02
Undercover Brother '02
The In Crowd '00
The Thomas Crown Affair '99

This World, Then the Fireworks '97
Tales from the Crypt Presents Bordello of Blood '96
Dr. Jekyll and Ms. Hyde '95

Rodrigo Prieto(1965-)

Wall Street 2: Money Never Sleeps '10
State of Play '09
Lust, Caution '07
Babel '06
Brokeback Mountain '05
Alexander '04
21 Grams '03
8 Mile '02
Frida '02
25th Hour '02
Original Sin '01
Amores Perros '00
Optic Fiber '97

Robert Primes(1940-)

Bachelor Party Vegas '05
Sleeper Cell '05
Baadasssss! '03
The Sandy Bottom Orchestra '00
Money Talks '97
My Antonia '94
The Hard Way '91
Bird on a Wire '90
Crimewave '85
Rescue from Gilligan's Island '78

Frank Prinzi

Trumbo '07
Sidewalks of New York '01
The Best Man '99
No Looking Back '98
200 Cigarettes '98
Witness to the Mob '98
The Real Blonde '97
She's the One '96
The Grave '95
Sex and the Other Man '95
Living in Oblivion '94
Night of the Living Dead '90
Sleepwalk '88

Gareth Pritchard

In a Day '06
Experiment '05

Brian Probyn(1920-82)

Badlands '74
Frankenstein and the Monster from Hell '74
The Satanic Rites of Dracula '73

Fortunato Procopio

The Devil and Daniel Johnston '05
King of the Jungle '01
A Brother's Kiss '97

Francois Protat

Time at the Top '99
Whiskers '96
Johnny Mnemonic '95
The Stranger: Kabloonak '95
Tails You Live, Heads You're Dead '95
A Vow to Kill '94
Weekend at Bernie's '89
The Dog Who Stopped the War '84
Hot Touch '82
Dirty Dishes '78

Bryan Pryzpek

Blue Blood '07
You Are Here * '00

Anthony Pun

Robin-B-Hood '06
New Police Story '04

Ian Punter

Every Woman Knows a Secret '99
The Final Cut '95
House of Cards '90

Cynthia Pusheck(1964-)

Loving Annabelle '06
Three Days of Rain '02

Mark Putnam

I Love Your Work '03
The Fluffer '01
I Love You, Don't Touch Me! '97

Allan Pyrah

Catherine Cookson's The Secret '00
Prince of Poisoners: The Life and Crimes of William Palmer '98

David Quaid

Gold of the Amazon Women '79
Pretty Poison '68
Santa Claus Conquers the Martians '64

Dick Quinlan

Losing Chase '96
Moonshine Highway '96
Curse of the Starving Class '94
In the Spirit '90

Declan Quinn(1957-)

New York, I Love You '09
The Private Lives of Pippa Lee '09
The Lucky Ones '08
Pride and Glory '08
Rachel Getting Married '08
Get Rich or Die Tryin' '05
Vanity Fair '04
Cold Creek Manor '03
Hysterical Blindness '02
In America '02
Monsoon Wedding '01
28 Days '00
Flawless '99
This Is My Father '99
One True Thing '98
2 by 4 '98
One Night Stand '97
Kama Sutra: A Tale of Love '96
Carried Away '95
Leaving Las Vegas '95
Vanya on 42nd Street '94
The Ballad of Little Jo '93
Freddy's Dead: The Final Nightmare '91
Blood & Concrete: A Love Story '90

Pascal Rabaud

Idlewild '06
Paris, je t'aime '06
Bossa Nova '99
The End of Violence '97

Jean Rabier(1927-)

Quiet Days in Clichy '90
The Story of Women '88
The Cry of the Owl '87
Cop Au Vin '85
Violette '78
Wedding in Blood '74
Cold Sweat '71
Just Before Nightfall '71
This Man Must Die '70
La Femme Infidele '69
Le Bonheur '65
Umbrellas of Cherbourg '64
Cleo from 5 to 7 '61

Simon Raby(1961-)

Heaven '99
The Ugly '96

Pasquale Rachini

Incantato '03
The Best Man '97

Roger Racine

Seizure '74
Snowballin' '71

Martina Radwan

Flannel Pajamas '06
The Killing Floor '06

Kevin Rafferty

The War Room '93
Roger & Me '89

Elemer Ragalyi(1939-)

The Moon & the Stars '07
An American Rhapsody '01
Anne Frank: The Whole Story '01

Dostoevsky's Crime and Punishment '99
Jakob the Liar '99
Mary, Mother of Jesus '99
A Knight in Camelot '98
The Hunchback '97
Ms. Scrooge '97
Rasputin: Dark Servant of Destiny '96
Trilogy of Terror 2 '96
Catherine the Great '95
A Kid in King Arthur's Court '95
Never Talk to Strangers '95
Mesmer '94
The Phantom of the Opera '89
Flowers of Reverie '84
Daniel Takes a Train '83

John Raggett

When Evil Calls '06
The Witches Hammer '06

David Rakoczy

Doomsdayer '01
Doomsdayer '99
Asylum '97

Jose Ortiz Ramos(1911-)

The Brainiac '61
The Curse of the Crying Woman '61
Creature of the Walking Dead '60
My Outlaw Brother '51

Gangu Ramsay

Bandh Darwaza '90
Purana Mandir '84

Clark Ramsey

The Choppers '61
The Flaming Urge '53

Joel Ransom

Caprica '09
High Noon '09
The Stoning of Soraya M. '08
The Tenth Circle '08
Angels Fall '07
The Seeker: The Dark Is Rising '07
Slap Shot 2: Breaking the Ice '02
Taken '02
Freeway 2: Confessions of a Trickbaby '99

Xiaobing Rao

Diamond Dogs '07
Missionary Man '07

Claudia Raschke

Mad Hot Ballroom '05
Kiss Me, Guido '97
No Way Home '96
The Last Good Time '94
Thank You & Good Night '91

Earl Rath

Raid on Rommel '71
Shoot Out '71

Franz Rath(1932-)

The Promise '94
Marianne and Juliane '82
Sisters, Or the Balance of Happiness '79
The Second Awakening of Christa Klages '78

Ousama Rawi(1939-)

DC 9/11: Time of Crisis '04
Jasper, Texas '03
Avenging Angelo '02
The Pirates of Silicon Valley '99
Blackheart '98
Parting Shots '98
Charlie Muffin '79

Richard L. Rawlings(1916-92)

The Blue Knight '75
Kung Fu '72
The Killers '64

Andreu Rebes

Beyond Re-Animator '03
Nico and Dani '00

Don Reddy

Benji: Off the Leash! '04
For the Love of Benji '77
Benji '74

Frank Redman

Dick Tracy Meets Gruesome '47
Dick Tracy's Dilemma '47
Dick Tracy, Detective '45
Having Wonderful Crime '45

Arthur Reed

Fighting Renegade '39
Six Gun Rhythm '39
Held for Ransom '38
Swifty '35
Valley of Wanted Men '35
Sunset Trail '32
Arizona Terror '31
Range Law '31

Michael Reed(1929-)

The Groundstar Conspiracy '72
Zero Population Growth '72
McKenzie Break '70
The Busy Body '67
Fiction Makers '67
Prehistoric Women '67
Dracula, Prince of Darkness '66
Rasputin the Mad Monk '66
The Devil-Ship Pirates '64
The Gorgon '64

Tami Reiker

For One More Day '07
Mr. Woodcock '07
Pieces of April '03
Disappearing Acts '00
The Love Letter '99
Girl '98
High Art '98
Far Harbor '96

Arthur Reinhart(1965-)

Tristan & Isolde '06
Children of Dune '03
Brute '97
Crows '94

Stephen Reizes

Marked Man '96
Lana in Love '92

Ricardo Remias

Fast Gun '93
Nam Angels '88
Demon of Paradise '87

Peter Reniers

Bloodsucking Pharoahs of Pittsburgh '90
Two Evil Eyes '90

Ray Rennahan(1896-1980)

Terror in a Texas Town '58
Seventh Cavalry '56
A Lawless Street '55
Rage at Dawn '55
Stranger on Horseback '55
Arrowhead '53
Pony Express '53
At Sword's Point '51
Great Missouri Raid '51
A Connecticut Yankee in King Arthur's Court '49
The Paleface '48
The Perils of Pauline '47
Unconquered '47
Duel in the Sun '46
It's a Pleasure '45
A Thousand and One Nights '45
Up in Arms '44
For Whom the Bell Tolls '43
Blood and Sand '41
Louisiana Purchase '41
That Night in Rio '41
Down Argentine Way '40
Drums Along the Mohawk '39
Gone with the Wind '39
Wings of the Morning '37
Becky Sharp '35
The Cat and the Fiddle '34
Mystery of the Wax Museum '33
Doctor X '32

Claude Renoir(1914-93)

The Spy Who Loved Me '77
Game of Seduction '76
French Connection 2 '75
Barbarella '68
Spirits of the Dead '68
The Game Is Over '66
Blood and Roses '61
The Crucible '57
Elena and Her Men '56
The Golden Coach '52
The River '51
Rendez-vous de Juillet '49
Monsieur Vincent '47
Toni '34

Gayne Rescher(1925-2008)

Love Among Thieves '86
Star Trek 2: The Wrath of Khan '82
Pearl '78
Deadly Game '77
Murder, Inc. '60

Marc Reshovsky(1957-)

Most Wanted '97
Set It Off '96
Red Rock West '93
Sorority House Massacre '86

Scott Ressler

Hollywood Chainsaw Hookers '88
Sorority Babes in the Slimeball Bowl-A-Rama '87

William Rexer

The Accidental Husband '08
I Think I Love My Wife '07
Purple Violets '07
The Groomsmen '06
Fierce People '05
Prime '05
Book of Love '04
Looking for Kitty '04
Lisa Picard Is Famous '01

Brian Reynolds

Boss of Bosses '99
Murder at Devil's Glen '99
With Friends Like These '98
Gang Related '96
Guarding Tess '94

Buster Reynolds

Hoodlum & Son '03
Diamond Girl '98
Hard to Forget '98
The Gods Must Be Crazy '84

Mick Reynolds

Just Business '08
Final Draft '07

John Rhode

Devon's Ghost: Legend of the Bloody Boy '05
Born to Lose '99

John Rhodes

The Purifiers '04
16 Years of Alcohol '03

Edmond Richard(1927-)

That Obscure Object of Desire '77
Phantom of Liberty '74
The Discreet Charm of the Bourgeoisie '72
Manon '68
Chimes at Midnight '67
The Trial '63

Zack Richard(1975-)

Bram Stoker's Way of the Vampire '05
Up for Grabs '05

Jack L. Richards

The Beast Within '82
My Brother Has Bad Dreams '72

Robert Richardson(1955-)

Eat, Pray, Love '10
Inglourious Basterds '09

Shutter Island '09
Shine a Light '08
Standard Operating Procedure '08
The Good Shepherd '06
The Aviator '04
Kill Bill Vol. 2 '04
Kill Bill Vol. 1 '03
The Four Feathers '02
Bringing Out the Dead '99
Snow Falling on Cedars '99
Fast, Cheap & Out of Control '97
The Horse Whisperer '97
U-Turn '97
Wag the Dog '97
Casino '95
Nixon '95
Natural Born Killers '94
Heaven and Earth '93
A Few Good Men '92
City of Hope '91
The Doors '91
JFK '91
Born on the Fourth of July '89
Eight Men Out '88
Talk Radio '88
Wall Street '87
Platoon '86
Salvador '86

Ross Richardson

Deadline '09
Unearthed '07
Unearthed '07

Bob Richman

The September Issue '09
An Inconvenient Truth '06

Robert Richman

Metallica: Some Kind of Monster '04
My Architect: A Son's Journey '03

Anthony B. Richmond(1942-)

Alvin and the Chipmunks: The Squeakuel '09
Miss March '09
The Rocker '08
Sex & Lies in Sin City: The Ted Binion Scandal '08
The Comebacks '07
Good Luck Chuck '07
Employee of the Month '06
John Tucker Must Die '06
Just Friends '05
A Cinderella Story '04
Dirty Dancing: Havana Nights '04
Dumb and Dumberer: When Harry Met Lloyd '03
Shade '03
The Sweetest Thing '02
Legally Blonde '01
Someone Like You '01
Cherry Falls '00
Men of Honor '00
Agnes Browne '99
Ravenous '99
A Walk on the Moon '99
Rough Riders '97
Bastard out of Carolina '96
First Kid '96
Playing God '96
Full Body Massage '95
The Immortals '95
Tales from the Hood '95
The Sandlot '93
Candyman '92
Sunset '88
The Kids Are Alright '79
The Eagle Has Landed '77
The Man Who Fell to Earth '76
Don't Look Now '73

Tom Richmond

Nick & Norah's Infinite Playlist '08
Chapter 27 '07
The Ex '07
Right at Your Door '06
Palindromes '04
Tanner on Tanner '04
House of 1000 Corpses '03
The Singing Detective '03
I'm with Lucy '02
The Chateau '01
Chelsea Walls '01
Hardball '01
Knockaround Guys '01
Gun Shy '00
Waking the Dead '00
First Love, Last Rites '98
Slums of Beverly Hills '98
The Twilight of the Golds '97
johns '96
Mother Night '96
Homage '95
Killing Zoe '94
Little Odessa '94
Love and a .45 '94
A Midnight Clear '92
Heaven Is a Playground '91
Pastime '91
I'm Gonna Git You Sucka '88
Stand and Deliver '88
Straight to Hell '87
Chopping Mall '86

Antonio Rinaldi

Five Dolls for an August Moon '70
Danger: Diabolik '68
Kill, Baby, Kill '66
Planet of the Vampires '65

Lisa Rinzler

The Night Listener '06
The War Within '05
Lighting in a Bottle '04
Rick '03
Love Liza '02
Welcome to Collinwood '02
Pollock '00
Three Seasons '98
Tree's Lounge '96
Dead Presidents '95
Menace II Society '93
Guncrazy '92
True Love '89
I Was a Teenage TV Terrorist '87

Leif Rise

To the Shores of Hell '65
The Starfighters '63

Gunther Rittau(1893-1971)

The Blue Angel '30
Metropolis '26

Neil Roach

The Circuit '08
Queen Sized '08
Category 7 : The End of the World '05
Category 6 : Day of Destruction '04
Gracie's Choice '04
The Whole Ten Yards '04
The '70s '00
Mama Flora's Family '98
Lone Justice 3: Showdown at Plum Creek '96
The Summer of Ben Tyler '96
Harvest of Fire '95
The Substitute Wife '94
Lone Justice 2 '93
To Dance with the White Dog '93
Devlin '92
My Name Is Bill W. '89
Silent Rage '82

James Robb

Ernest Goes to Africa '97
Ernest in the Army '97
Thieves of Fortune '89
The Outcast '84

James Roberson

Tough and Deadly '94
Wyatt Earp: Return to Tombstone '94
Visions of Evil '75

Jim Roberson

The Hunting of the President '04
Shadow of Chikara '77
Town That Dreaded Sundown '76
Winterhawk '76

Jacques Robin

Life Upside Down '64
Double Agents '59

Jean-Francois Robin(1943-)

On Guard! '03
Belphegar: Phantom of the Louvre '01
Chaos '01
Nora '00
The Ice Rink '99
Rogue Trader '98
Metroland '97
The Serpent's Kiss '97
The Leading Man '96
Nelly et Monsieur Arnaud '95
Suite 16 '94
Betty Blue '86

George Robinson(1890-1958)

Francis in the Haunted House '56
Abbott and Costello Meet the Mummy '55
Abbott and Costello Meet Dr. Jekyll and Mr. Hyde '52
Jack & the Beanstalk '52
Abbott and Costello Meet the Invisible Man '51
Abbott and Costello in the Foreign Legion '50
House of Dracula '45
House of Frankenstein '44
Son of Dracula '43
The Falcon Takes Over '42
Frankenstein Meets the Wolfman '42
The Mummy's Tomb '42
Overland Mail '42
If I Had My Way '40
The Son of Monte Cristo '40
Charlie McCarthy, Detective '39
East Side of Heaven '39
Son of Frankenstein '39
The Tower of London '39
Service De Luxe '38
Dracula's Daughter '36
The Invisible Ray '36
Postal Inspector '36
The Mystery of Edwin Drood '35
Great Expectations '34
The Charlatan '29

Claudio Rocha

The Skeptic '09
Two Tickets to Paradise '06
Mrs. Palfrey at the Claremont '05
The Maldonado Miracle '03
Four Dogs Playing Poker '00
Skipped Parts '00
In the Shadows '98
The Velocity of Gary '98
The Whole Wide World '96
On the Air '95
Picture Bride '94

Eliot Rockett

The House of the Devil '09
Dirty '05
Frankenfish '04
Rampage: The Hillside Strangler Murders '04
Nightstalker '02
Crocodile '00
The Specials '00

Alexei Rodionov(1947-)

Yes '04
Passion in the Desert '97
Red Shoe Diaries: Strip Poker '96
Talk of Angels '96
Orlando '92
Come and See '85

Serge Rodnunsky

Chill '06
Dead Lenny '06

Robert Rodriguez(1968-)

Shorts: The Adventures of the Wishing Rock '09
Planet Terror '07
The Adventures of Sharkboy and Lavagirl in 3-D '05
Sin City '05
Once Upon a Time in Mexico '03
Spy Kids 3-D: Game Over '03
Spy Kids 2: The Island of Lost Dreams '02
El Mariachi '93

Bill Roe

For Sale by Owner '09
The X Files: I Want to Believe '08
Elektra '05
Where the Truth Lies '99
Hostage High '97

Guy Roe(1903-59)

Godzilla, King of the Monsters '56
Silver Star '55
Armored Car Robbery '50
Try and Get Me '50
Behind Locked Doors '48
Human Gorilla '48
Railroaded '47
A Scandal in Paris '46

Nicolas Roeg(1928-)

Walkabout '71
Performance '70
Petulia '68
Far from the Madding Crowd '67
Fahrenheit 451 '66
A Funny Thing Happened on the Way to the Forum '66
The Girl Getters '66
Masque of the Red Death '65

Derek Rogers

Resident Evil: Apocalypse '04
Crime Spree '03
Cypher '02
New Waterford Girl '99
Cube '98
The Fishing Trip '98

Julie Rogers

Kit Kittredge: An American Girl '08
Curious George '06

Owen Roizman(1936-)

French Kiss '95
Wyatt Earp '94
The Addams Family '91
Grand Canyon '91
Havana '90
I Love You to Death '90
Vision Quest '85
Tootsie '82
Absence of Malice '81
Taps '81
True Confessions '81
The Electric Horseman '79
Straight Time '78
Network '76
The Return of a Man Called Horse '76
The Stepford Wives '75
Three Days of the Condor '75
The Taking of Pelham One Two Three '74
The Exorcist '73
The Heartbreak Kid '72
Play It Again, Sam '72
The French Connection '71

Erich Roland

Waiting for Superman '10
It Might Get Loud '09
Raising Flagg '06

Glenn Roland

First Strike '85
Ilsa, Harem Keeper of the Oil Sheiks '76

Gernot Roll(1939-)

Nowhere in Africa '02
Beyond Silence '96
Maybe... Maybe Not '94
Kaspar Hauser '93
Terror Stalks the Class Reunion '93
Heimat 2 '92
Heimat 1 '84

Sonja Rom(1969-)

Attack Force '06
Extreme Dating '04
Tiptoes '03

Andy Romanoff

Something Weird '68
A Taste of Blood '67
Jimmy, the Boy Wonder '66

George A. Romero(1940-)

Season of the Witch '73
Night of the Living Dead '68

Jackson Rose

Texas Gunfighter '32
Up the Ladder '25

Ilan Rosenberg

Turbo: A Power Rangers Movie '96
Baby Love '83

John Christian Rosenlund

O'Horten '09
Factotum '06

Charles Rosher(1885-1974)

Jupiter's Darling '55
Kiss Me Kate '53
The Story of Three Loves '53
Young Bess '53
Scaramouche '52
Show Boat '51
Annie Get Your Gun '50
East Side, West Side '49
Neptune's Daughter '49
Song of the Thin Man '47
The Yearling '46
Ziegfeld Follies '46
Yolanda and the Thief '45
Hard to Get '38
Hollywood Hotel '37
Little Lord Fauntleroy '36
Broadway Melody of 1936 '35
What Price Hollywood? '32
Dance Fools Dance '31
Laughing Sinners '31
Tempest '28
My Best Girl '27
Sunrise '27
Sparrows '26
Little Annie Rooney '25
Tess of the Storm Country '22
The Love Light '21
Pollyanna '20
Daddy Long Legs '19

Charles Rosher, Jr. (1935-)

Heartbeeps '81
Nightwing '79
The Onion Field '79
3 Women '77

Ann T. Rossetti(1966-)

Voices from a Locked Room '95
Go Fish '94

Fausto Rossi

The Slasher '72
Special Forces '68

Harold Rosson(1895-1988)

No Time for Sergeants '58
The Bad Seed '56
The Actress '53
The Story of Three Loves '53
Singin' in the Rain '52
The Red Badge of Courage '51
Command Decision '48
The Hucksters '47
Thirty Seconds Over Tokyo '44
Boom Town '40
I Take This Woman '40
The Wizard of Oz '39
As You Like It '36
The Devil Is a Sissy '36
The Ghost Goes West '36
The Cat and the Fiddle '34
The Scarlet Pimpernel '34
The Barbarian '33
Red Headed Woman '32
Getting Gertie's Garter '27

Andrea V. Rossotto

The Hunt for Eagle One: Crash Point '06
Sci-Fighter '04
Extreme Limits '01
Poison '01
Venomous '01
Ablaze '00
Gangland '00
Against the Law '98
Carnosaur 3: Primal Species '96
Vampirella '96

Giuseppe Rotunno(1923-)

Sabrina '95
The Stendahl Syndrome '95
The Night and the Moment '94
Wolf '94
Regarding Henry '91
The Adventures of Baron Munchausen '89
Rent-A-Cop '88
Casanova '87
Julia and Julia '87
And the Ship Sails On '83
City of Women '81
All That Jazz '79
Orchestra Rehearsal '78
Amarcord '74
Love and Anarchy '73
Fellini's Roma '72
Carnal Knowledge '71
Fellini Satyricon '69
The Secret of Santa Vittoria '69
Anzio '68
Candy '68
Spirits of the Dead '68
The Bible '66
The Organizer '64
The Leopard '63
Boccaccio '70 '62
Rocco and His Brothers '60
White Nights '57

Denis Rouden

Deep in the Woods '00
Don't Let Me Die on a Sunday '98

Philippe Rousselot(1945-)

Sherlock Holmes '09
The Brave One '07
The Great Debaters '07
Lions for Lambs '07
Charlie and the Chocolate Factory '05
Constantine '05
Big Fish '03
Antwone Fisher '02
Planet of the Apes '01
Remember the Titans '00
The Tailor of Panama '00
Instinct '99
Random Hearts '99
The People vs. Larry Flynt '96
Mary Reilly '95
Interview with the Vampire '94
Queen Margot '94
Sommersby '93
A River Runs Through It '92
The Miracle '91
Henry & June '90
The Bear '89
We're No Angels '89
Dangerous Liaisons '88
Too Beautiful for You '88
Hope and Glory '87
The Emerald Forest '85
Moon in the Gutter '83
Diva '82
Peppermint Soda '77

Monty Rowan

Chronicle of the Raven '04
The Feminine Touch '95

Ashley Rowe(1959-)
Shattered '07
Starter for Ten '06
Alfie '04
Chasing Liberty '04
Calendar Girls '03
The Roman Spring of Mrs. Stone '03
The Affair of the Necklace '01
Mad About Mambo '00
When Brendan Met Trudy '00
Bedrooms and Hallways '98
The Governess '98
Still Crazy '98
B. Monkey '97
24-7 '97
Sister My Sister '94
Widow's Peak '94
Unexplained Laughter '89

Kevin Rowley
Forgive and Forget '99
Falling for a Dancer '98

Soumendu Roy
The Middleman '76
Distant Thunder '73
The Adversary '71
Days and Nights in the Forest '70
Two Daughters '61

Mauricio Rubinstein
New York, I Love You '09
Bernard and Doris '08
Love and Debate '06
Puccini for Beginners '06
Sorry, Haters '05
King of the Corner '04
Casa de los Babys '03

Danny Ruhlmann
Little Fish '05
The Night We Called It a Day '03
The Nugget '02
In a Savage Land '99

Juan Ruiz-Anchia(1949-)
September Dawn '07
Innocent Voices '04
Spartan '04
Confidence '03
Off the Map '03
No Good Deed '02
Focus '01
The Crew '00
The Corruptor '99
Mararia '98
The Adventures of Pinocchio '96
The Disappearance of Garcia Lorca '96
Two Bits '96
A Far Off Place '93
Mr. Jones '93
Glengarry Glen Ross '92
Dying Young '91
Liebestraum '91
The Seventh Sign '88
House of Games '87
Surrender '87
At Close Range '86
Where the River Runs Black '86
Maria's Lovers '84
The Stone Boy '84
Reborn '81

John L. "Jack" Russell
Psycho '60
Girls' Town '59
The Indestructible Man '56
The Beast from 20,000 Fathoms '53
Invasion U.S.A. '52
Government Agents vs. Phantom Legion '51
The Man from Planet X '51
The Green Promise '49
Golden Gloves '40

Ward Russell
Cruel World '05
The X-Files '98
Lawnmower Man 2: Beyond Cyberspace '95
The Last Boy Scout '91
Days of Thunder '90

Richard Rutkowski(1966-)
Home '08
How to Eat Fried Worms '06
Interview with the Assassin '02
Kill by Inches '99

Joseph Ruttenberg(1889-93)
Speedway '68
The Oscar '66
Harlow '65
A Global Affair '63
Butterfield 8 '60
Green Mansions '59
Gigi '58
The Reluctant Debutante '58
Somebody Up There Likes Me '56
The Swan '56
Kismet '55
The Prodigal '55
Brigadoon '54
The Last Time I Saw Paris '54
Julius Caesar '53
Prisoner of Zenda '52
The Great Caruso '51
It's a Big Country '51
The Miniver Story '50
Side Street '50
That Forsyte Woman '50
The Bribe '48
Killer McCoy '47
Adventure '45
The Valley of Decision '45
Gaslight '44
Mrs. Parkington '44
Madame Curie '43
Presenting Lily Mars '43
Crossroads '42
Mrs. Miniver '42
Random Harvest '42
Woman of the Year '42
Dr. Jekyll and Mr. Hyde '41
Two-Faced Woman '41
The Philadelphia Story '40
Waterloo Bridge '40
Ice Follies of 1939 '39
On Borrowed Time '39
The Women '39
The Great Waltz '38
Shopworn Angel '38
Three Comrades '38
A Day at the Races '37
Fury '36
Woman in the Shadows '34
Struggle '31

Viktor Ruzicka(1943-)
Martha and I '91
Cobra Verde '88

Giuseppe Ruzzolini(1930-)
Firestarter '84
Life of Verdi '82
Arabian Nights '74
Allonsanfan '73
Short Night of Glass Dolls '71
Porcile '69

Ellery Ryan(1949-)
Visitors '03
In Too Deep '99
Dead Letter Office '98
The Matchmaker '97
Angel Baby '95
Cosi '95
That Eye, the Sky '94
Running Delilah '93
Death in Brunswick '90

Paul Ryan
Her Best Move '07
Spin '04
Big Bad Love '02
Thomas and the Magic Railroad '00
Wildflowers '99
Box of Moonlight '96
Other Voices, Other Rooms '95
Where the Rivers Flow North '94
Fraternity Vacation '85

Robbie Ryan
Fish Tank '09
Red Road '06
This Is Not a Love Song '02

Robert Saad
Anne of Green Gables: The Continuing Story '99
Under the Piano '95
They Came from Within '75
Hard Part Begins '73
The Rainbow Gang '73

Eric Saarinen
Rooster: Spurs of Death! '83
Real Life '79
The Hills Have Eyes '77
You Light Up My Life '77
Eat My Dust '76

Farhad Saba
Through the Olive Trees '94
Where Is My Friend's House? '87

Felipe Sacdalan
TNT Jackson '75
The Big Bird Cage '72
The Walls of Hell '64
Raiders of Leyte Gulf '63

Odd Geir Saether(1941-)
Inland Empire '06
The Man on the Roof '76
Edvard Munch '74

Stephen St. John
The Guardian '06
Holes '03

Virginie Saint-Martin(1965-)
Mr. Average '06
Thomas in Love '01
An Affair of Love '99

Takao Saito(1920-)
Rhapsody in August '91
Akira Kurosawa's Dreams '90
Ran '85
Dodes 'ka-den '70
Attack Squadron '63
High & Low '62
Sanjuro '62

Yoshitaka Sakamoto
The Ramen Girl '08
Azumi 2 '05

Alik Sakharov(1959-)
Nothing But the Truth '08
Lulu on the Bridge '98
Love! Valour! Compassion! '96

Akira Sakoh
Ping Pong '02
Returner '02
Tomie '99

Anthony Salinas
Blood Orgy of the She-Devils '74
The Doll Squad '73

Timo Salminen(1952-)
Lights in the Dusk '06
The Man Without a Past '02
Ariel '89
Leningrad Cowboys Go America '89

Javier Salmones(1953-)
Four Last Songs '06
My Father, My Mother, My Brothers and My Sisters '99
Butterfly '98
Twice upon a Yesterday '98

Amnon Salomon
The Milky Way '97
The Mangler '94
Hot Bubblegum '81

Mikael Salomon(1945-)
Far and Away '92
Backdraft '91
Arachnophobia '90
The Abyss '89
Always '89
Torch Song Trilogy '88
Zelly & Me '88
Zero Population Growth '72
Famous Five Get into Trouble '70

Sergio Salvati(1938-)
Red Riding Hood '03
Wax Mask '97
Puppet Master '89
The House by the Cemetery '83
The Beyond '82
The Black Cat '81
Contraband '80
Gates of Hell '80
Zombie '80

Geno Salvatori
The Cell 2 '09
Daddy Day Camp '07
Outlaw Trail '06
Everything You Want '05

Berhard Salzmann
The Android Affair '95
The Color of Evening '95
Deadly Past '95
Bad Blood '94

Ryan Samul
Mulberry Street '06
Steel City '06

Francisco Sanchez(1925-)
Kilma, Queen of the Amazons '75
Terror Beach '75
Exorcism '74
Curse of the Devil '73
House of Psychotic Women '73
Challenge of McKenna '70

Rodolfo Sanchez
Beach Hotel '92
Kiss of the Spider Woman '85
Pixote '81

Gregory Sandor
Forty Days of Musa Dagh '85
Forbidden Zone '80
Sisters '73
Fury on Wheels '71
The Hooked Generation '69
Born Losers '67
Ride in the Whirlwind '66
The Shooting '66

Tino Santoni(1913-)
The Girl with a Suitcase '60
Verdi '53
Young Caruso '51

Sandor Sara
25 Fireman's Street '73
Sinbad '71

Vic Sarin(1945-)
Partition '07
Love on the Side '04
The Waiting Game '98
Margaret's Museum '95
Spenser: A Savage Place '94
Spenser: Pale Kings & Princes '94
Whale Music '94
Cold Comfort '90
Bye Bye Blues '89
Men of Steel '77

Paul Sarossy(1963-)
Chloe '09
Adoration '08
The Deal '08
All Hat '07
Charlie Bartlett '07
The Secret '07
One Way '06
The Wicker Man '06
The River King '05
Where the Truth Lies '05
Head in the Clouds '04
The Incredible Mrs. Ritchie '03
The Snow Walker '03
Soldier's Girl '03
Ararat '02
Paid in Full '02
Duets '00
Lakeboat '00
Rated X '00
Felicia's Journey '99
Rocky Marciano '99
Jerry and Tom '98
Pete's Meteor '98
Affliction '97
Mistrial '96
Picture Perfect '96
The Sweet Hereafter '96
Blood & Donuts '95
Exotica '94
Love and Human Remains '93
Giant Steps '92
The Adjuster '91
Speaking Parts '89

Hendrik Sartov(1885-1970)
The Red Mill '27
America '24
Orphans of the Storm '21
Way Down East '20

Yasushi Sasakibara
Gonin 2 '96
The Mystery of Rampo '94
Violent Cop '89
Rica 2: Lonely Wanderer '73

Kazuto Sato
Flower & Snake '04
Suicide Club '02

Masaru Sato(1928-99)
The Battle of the Japan Sea '70
Godzilla vs. the Sea Monster '66

Claude Saunier
Deadly Sting '73
Killer '73

Harris Savides(1957-)
Greenberg '10
Whatever Works '09
Milk '08
American Gangster '07
Margot at the Wedding '07
Zodiac '07
Last Days '05
Birth '04
Elephant '03
Gerry '02
Finding Forrester '00
The Yards '00
Illuminata '98
The Game '97
Heaven's Prisoners '95

Malik Hassan Sayeed
Belly '98
He Got Game '98
The Players Club '98
Cold Around the Heart '97
Girl 6 '96
Clockers '95

Edward Scaife(1912-94)
The Dirty Dozen '67
Khartoum '66
Trial & Error '62
On the Fiddle '61
Carry On Constable '60
Tarzan the Magnificent '60
Tarzan's Greatest Adventure '59
Curse of the Demon '57
Sea Wife '57
A Kid for Two Farthings '55
Captain's Paradise '53

Marco Scarpelli(1918-95)
The Mercenaries '62
Uncle Was a Vampire '59

Aldo Scavarda(1923-)
Before the Revolution '65
L'Avventura '60

Roberto Schaefer
Quantum of Solace '08
The Kite Runner '07
For Your Consideration '06
Stranger Than Fiction '06
Stay '05
Finding Neverland '04
Monster's Ball '01
Best in Show '00
Everything Put Together '00
Waiting for Guffman '96
Cool and the Crazy '94
Roadracers '94

Guillaume Schiffman
OSS 117: Cairo, Nest of Spies '06
Anatomy of Hell '04

Martin Schlesinger
The Mistake '91
Coming Out '89

Tobias Schliessler
The Taking of Pelham 123 '09
Hancock '08
Dreamgirls '06
Friday Night Lights '04
The Rundown '03
Bait '00
The Guilty '99
Hoods '98
Legalese '98
Outrage '98
Free Willy 3: The Rescue '97
Mandela and de Klerk '97
Volcano: Fire on the Mountain '97
The Limbic Region '96
Bulletproof Heart '95
The Escape '95
Candyman 2: Farewell to the Flesh '94
Double Cross '94
Sin and Redemption '94

Jens Schlosser
The Intended '02
The King Is Alive '00

Eric Schmidt(1966-)
Henry Poole Is Here '08
My Sassy Girl '08
Dead Dog '00

Ronn Schmidt
The Mist '07
Star Kid '97
Lord of Illusions '95
Men of War '94
The Terror Within '88
Time Trackers '88

Wolfgang Schmidt
See Ray Dennis Steckler

Jorge Schmidt-Reitwein(1939-)
Nosferatu the Vampyre '79
Woyzeck '78
Every Man for Himself & God Against All '75
Heart of Glass '74

Aaron Schneider
Get Low '09
Simon Birch '98
Kiss the Girls '97
Dead Girls '90

George Schneiderman(1894-1964)
Michael Shayne: Private Detective '40
The Devil Is a Sissy '36
Steamboat Round the Bend '35
The World Moves On '34
Doctor Bull '33
Pilgrimage '33
Young America '32
Four Sons '28
Hangman's House '28
Lazybones '25
The Iron Horse '24
A Fool There Was '14

Charles E. Schoenbaum(1893-1951)
Cynthia '47
Good News '47

Junior Army '42
It Happened in New Orleans '36
Sally '29
Nevada '27
The Vanishing American '25

Nancy Schreiber(1949-)
Motherhood '09
Flakes '07
The Nines '07
American Gun '05
Born Killers '05
Loverboy '05
November '05
Red Roses and Petrol '03
Buying the Cow '02
Path to War '02
Book of Shadows: Blair Witch 2 '00
Shadow Magic '00
Never 2 Big '98
Your Friends & Neighbors '98
Nevada '97
The Curse of Inferno '96
Scorpion Spring '96
The Celluloid Closet '95
Girl in the Cadillac '94
Chain of Desire '93
Visions of Light: The Art of Cinematography '93

Frederick Schroeder
Fling '08
Four Sheets to the Wind '07

Fred Schuler(1940-)
Just Looking '99
Haunted Honeymoon '86
Fletch '85
Amityville 3: The Demon '83
King of Comedy '82
Arthur '81
Stir Crazy '80

Howard Schwartz(1919-90)
The Devil & Max Devlin '81
Haywire '80
The Big Bounce '69
Batman '66
A Public Affair '62

Philip D. Schwartz
The Golden Boys '08
Gamebox 1.0 '04
Survival Island '02
High Voltage '98
King Cobra '98

John Schwartzman(1960-)
Night at the Museum: Battle of the Smithsonian '09
The Bucket List '07
National Treasure: Book of Secrets '07
Meet the Fockers '04
Seabiscuit '03
The Rookie '02
Pearl Harbor '01
EDtv '99
Armageddon '98
Conspiracy Theory '97
The Rock '96
Mr. Wrong '95
A Pyromaniac's Love Story '95
Airheads '94
Red Surf '90

Xaver Schwarzenberger(1946-)
Querelle '83
Veronika Voss '82
Berlin Alexanderplatz '80

Lawrence Schweich
Come as You Are '05
Tequila Body Shots '99
Wind River '98

Eric Scott(1958-)
The Dark Dancer '95
The House on Todville Road '95

Chris Seager
New in Town '09
The Merry Gentleman '08
Wild Child '08
Closure '07
The Walker '07
Alex Rider: Operation Stormbreaker '06
Archangel '05
White Noise '05
State of Play '03
Suspicion '03
The Way We Live Now '02
Lorna Doone '01
Frenchman's Creek '98
A Dance to the Music of Time '97
Alive and Kicking '96
Fever Pitch '96
Beautiful Thing '95
Stonewall '95
Cold Comfort Farm '94
The Vampyr '92

John Seale(1943-)
Prince of Persia: The Sands of Time '10
Poseidon '06
Spanglish '04
Cold Mountain '03
Dreamcatcher '03
Harry Potter and the Sorcerer's Stone '01
The Perfect Storm '00
The Talented Mr. Ripley '99
At First Sight '98
City of Angels '98
The English Patient '96
Ghosts of Mississippi '96
The American President '95
Beyond Rangoon '95
The Paper '94
The Firm '93
Lorenzo's Oil '92
The Doctor '91
Dead Poets Society '89
Gorillas in the Mist '88
Rain Man '88
Children of a Lesser God '86
The Hitcher '86
The Mosquito Coast '86
Witness '85
Careful, He Might Hear You '84

Robert E. Seaman
The Kid and I '05
Halloweentown High '04

Christian Sebaldt(1958-)
Bratz '07
Crossover '06
Resident Evil: Apocalypse '04
Starship Troopers 2: Hero of the Federation '04
Feardotcom '02
Race to Space '01
Galgameth '96
Illicit Dreams '94
Inevitable Grace '94
Revenge of the Red Baron '93

Edmond Sechan
Blue Country '77
Love on a Pillow '62

Jeffrey Seckendorf
Finding Home '03
Judy Berlin '99

Nanu Segal
Donkey Punch '08
Shrooms '07

Hiroshi Segawa
Under the Flag of the Rising Sun '72
Face of Another '66
Woman in the Dunes '64

John Seitz(1892-1979)
The Badlanders '58
Many Rivers to Cross '55
Invaders from Mars '53
The Iron Mistress '52
Sunset Boulevard '50
The Great Gatsby '49
The Big Clock '48
On Our Merry Way '48
The Lost Weekend '45
Double Indemnity '44
Five Graves to Cairo '43
This Gun for Hire '42
Sullivan's Travels '41
Across to Singapore '28
The Patsy '28
The Trail of '98 '28
Scaramouche '23
The Prisoner of Zenda '22
The Four Horsemen of the Apocalypse '21

Yoshinori Sekiguchi
Orochi, the Eight Headed Dragon '94
Godzilla vs. King Ghidora '91

Andrzej Sekula(1954-)
Armored '09
Vice '08
Vacancy '07
The Pleasure Drivers '05
American Psycho '99
The Break '97
Cousin Bette '97
Stand-Ins '97
Four Rooms '95
Hackers '95
Across the Moon '94
Oleanna '94
Pulp Fiction '94
Reservoir Dogs '92

Jonathan Sela
Law Abiding Citizen '09
Powder Blue '09
Max Payne '08
The Midnight Meat Train '08
Dreamland '06
Marilyn Hotchkiss' Ballroom Dancing & Charm School '06
The Omen '06
Soul Plane '04

Dean Semler(1943-)
Date Night '10
2012 '09
Appaloosa '08
Get Smart '08
I Now Pronounce You Chuck and Larry '07
Apocalypto '06
Click '06
Just My Luck '06
The Longest Yard '05
Stealth '05
The Alamo '04
Bruce Almighty '03
Dragonfly '02
We Were Soldiers '02
XXX '02
Eye See You '01
Heartbreakers '01
Nutty Professor 2: The Klumps '00
The Bone Collector '99
Gone Fishin' '97
Trojan War '97
Waterworld '95
The Cowboy Way '94
Last Action Hero '93
The Three Musketeers '93
The Power of One '92
City Slickers '91
Dances with Wolves '90
Young Guns 2 '90
Dead Calm '89
Farewell to the King '89
K-9 '89
Cocktail '88
Young Guns '88
The Lighthorsemen '87
Mad Max: Beyond Thunderdome '85
The Coca-Cola Kid '84
Razorback '84
The Road Warrior '82

Lorenzo Senatore(1974-)
Echelon Conspiracy '09
The Fourth Kind '09
Messengers 2: The Scarecrow '09
Wrong Turn 3: Left for Dead '09
Boogeyman 3 '08
Starship Troopers 3: Marauder '08
Lake Placid 2 '07
Return to House on Haunted Hill '07
Behind Enemy Lines 2: Axis of Evil '06
Alien Siege '05
Crimson Force '05
Locusts: The 8th Plague '05
Manticore '05
Darklight '04

Ken Seng
Step Up 3D '10
Obsessed '09
The Poker House '09
Sorority Row '09
Quarantine '08
League of Ordinary Gentlemen '04
Zombie Honeymoon '04

Jeong-min Seo
The Wishing Stairs '03
Piano Man '96

Enzo Serafin(1912-)
The Lady Without Camelias '53
Voyage in Italy '53
Story of a Love Affair '50
Musica Proibita '43

Ben Seresin
Transformers: Revenge of the Fallen '09
A Good Woman '04
Circus '00
Best Laid Plans '99

Michael Seresin(1942-)
All Good Things '09
Paris, je t'aime '06
Step Up '06
Harry Potter and the Prisoner of Azkaban '04
The Life of David Gale '03
Domestic Disturbance '01
Angela's Ashes '99
Mercury Rising '98
City Hall '95
Angel Heart '87
Midnight Express '78

Viorel Sergovici, Jr.
Transylmania '09
Devil's Den '06
Cerberus '05
Madhouse '04
Straight into Darkness '04
Vlad '03
Dark Asylum '01
Retro Puppet Master '99
Witchouse '99

Eduardo Serra(1943-)
Defiance '08
A Girl Cut in Two '07
Blood Diamond '06
Comedy of Power '06
Beyond the Sea '04
The Bridesmaid '04
Intimate Strangers '04
Girl with a Pearl Earring '03
Passion of Mind '00
Unbreakable '00
The Widow of Saint-Pierre '00
What Dreams May Come '98
The Swindle '97
The Wings of the Dove '97
The Jew '96
Jude '96
Grosse Fatigue '94
The Hairdresser's Husband '92

Byron Shah
An American Crime '07
Careless '07
The Go-Getter '07

Afshin Shahidi
The Man from Earth '07
Mulligan '00

Leon Shamroy(1901-74)
Justine '69
Planet of the Apes '68
Caprice '67
The Glass Bottom Boat '66
The Agony and the Ecstasy '65
Do Not Disturb '65
The Cardinal '63
Cleopatra '63
Snow White and the Three Stooges '61
North to Alaska '60
Beloved Infidel '59
The Bravados '58
Rally 'Round the Flag, Boys! '58
South Pacific '58
Desk Set '57
The Girl Can't Help It '56
The King and I '56
Daddy Long Legs '55
Love Is a Many-Splendored Thing '55
The Egyptian '54
There's No Business Like Show Business '54
The Girl Next Door '53
The Robe '53
The Snows of Kilimanjaro '52
With a Song in My Heart '52
David and Bathsheba '51
Cheaper by the Dozen '50
Prince of Foxes '49
Twelve o'Clock High '49
Daisy Kenyon '47
Forever Amber '47
Leave Her to Heaven '45
State Fair '45
A Tree Grows in Brooklyn '45
Buffalo Bill '44
Greenwich Village '44
Wilson '44
Crash Dive '43
Stormy Weather '43
The Black Swan '42
Roxie Hart '42
The Great American Broadcast '41
Moon over Miami '41
That Night in Rio '41
Down Argentine Way '40
Lillian Russell '40
Tin Pan Alley '40
The Adventures of Sherlock Holmes '39
Made for Each Other '39
The Story of Alexander Graham Bell '39
You Only Live Once '37
Wedding Present '36
Kiss and Make Up '34
Thirty Day Princess '34
Wayne Murder Case '32

Brian Shanley
A Grandpa for Christmas '07
Love's Unfolding Dream '07
Love's Abiding Joy '06
Love's Long Journey '05

Douglas W. Shannon
The Arrangement '99
Blowin' Smoke '99

Yaron Sharf
The Bubble '06
Yossi & Jagger '02

Henry Sharp(1892-1966)
The Young Land '59
It Happened on 5th Avenue '47
The Woman Who Came Back '45
Ministry of Fear '44
Tomorrow the World '44
Dr. Cyclops '40
Golden Gloves '40
Campus Confessions '38
It's a Gift '34
Six of a Kind '34
Duck Soup '33
Strangers in Love '32
The Iron Mask '29
Speedway '29
The Black Pirate '26
Don Q., Son of Zorro '25
Soul of the Beast '23

Steve (Steven) Shaw
Children On Their Birthdays '02
Sunstorm '01
The Tempest '99
Dangerous Passion '95
Lethal Charm '90
Zero Boys '86

Roger Shearman
Lone Wolf McQuade '83
An Eye for an Eye '81

Jas Shelton
Cyrus '10
Rest Stop: Don't Look Back '08
Walking Tall: Lone Justice '07

Lawrence Sher(1970-)
The Hangover '09
I Love You, Man '09
The Promotion '08
Trucker '08
Dan in Real Life '07
When a Man Falls in the Forest '07
Grilled '06
The Chumscrubber '05
The Dukes of Hazzard '05
Life of the Party '05
Club Dread '04
Garden State '04
Killing Emmett Young '02
Kissing Jessica Stein '02
Shark Attack '99
On the Border '98

Takahide Shibanushi
Reincarnation '05
Bright Future '03
Seance '00

Noboru Shinoda
Hana & Alice '04
All About Lily Chou-Chou '01
When I Close My Eyes '95

Eugene Shlugleit
3 Ninjas Knuckle Up '95
The Wolves '95
Twogether '94

Simon Shohet
Time Bomb '08
Grindstone Road '07

Eugen Shufftan(1893-1977)
Lilith '64
The Hustler '61
The Horror Chamber of Dr. Faustus '59
Bizarre Bizarre '39
Metropolis '26

Eugene Shufftan
See Eugen Shufftan

Eugene Shugleit
See Eugene Shlugleit

Daniel Shulman
Wonderful World '09
The Son of the Bride '01
Love Walked In '97

William Sickner(1890-1967)
The Undead '57
The Finger Man '55
Kidnapped '48
Boss of Boomtown '44
The Mummy's Ghost '44
Raiders of Ghost City '44
The Lone Star Trail '43
Gang Busters '42
Junior G-Men of the Air '42
Overland Mail '42
Flash Gordon Conquers the Universe '40
Space Soldiers Conquer the Universe '40
Chip of the Flying U '39
The Green Hornet '39
Savage Fury '35

Jerry Sidell
Sleep Easy, Hutch Rimes '00
Acts of Betrayal '98

Trading Favors '97

Allen Siegler(1892-1960)

The Spider's Web '38
The Black Room '35
Parisian Love '25
The Plastic Age '25

Newton Thomas (Tom) Sigel(1961-)

Leap Year '10
Leatherheads '08
Valkyrie '08
Towelhead '07
Superman Returns '06
The Brothers Grimm '05
X2: X-Men United '03
Confessions of a Dangerous Mind '02
X-Men '00
Brokedown Palace '99
Three Kings '99
Apt Pupil '97
Fallen '97
Blood & Wine '96
Foxfire '96
The Trigger Effect '96
The Usual Suspects '95
Blankman '94
Salmonberries '91

James Signorelli

Black Caesar '73
Superfly '72

Michael Simmonds

Big Fan '09
Goodbye Solo '08

Johnny (John W.) Simmons

Collected Stories '02
The Killing Yard '01
Three Strikes '00
Asunder '99
Once Upon a Time ... When We Were Colored '95

Geoffrey Simpson

Romulus, My Father '07
The Starter Wife '07
Last Holiday '06
Under the Tuscan Sun '03
Glitter '01
Center Stage '00
Life '99
Oscar and Lucinda '97
Some Mother's Son '96
Shine '95
Little Women '94
The War '94
Mr. Wonderful '93
Fried Green Tomatoes '91
Celia: Child of Terror '89

Andreas Sinanos

Weeping Meadow '04
Eternity and a Day '97

Peter Sinclair

Dealers '89
Adventures of a Private Eye '77

Geza Sinkovics

What's Up, Scarlet? '05
The Last Seduction 2 '98
French Exit '97
Undertow '95
Delusion '91

Sandi Sissel

Tyler Perry's Meet the Browns '08
Going Upriver: The Long War of John Kerry '04
Barney's Great Adventure '98
Soul of the Game '96
Camp Nowhere '94
Dragstrip Girl '94
Full Eclipse '93
The People under the Stairs '91
Drug Wars: The Camarena Story '90
Heavy Petting '89
Salaam Bombay! '88

Santosh Sivan

Before the Rains '07
The Mistress of Spices '05
Bride & Prejudice '04
The Terrorist '98

William V. Skall(1898-1976)

Everything I Have is Yours '52
Rope '48
Life with Father '47
Song of Scheherazade '47
Billy the Kid '41

Adam Sliwinski

Merlin and the Book of Beasts '09
The Lost Treasure of the Grand Canyon '08
Meltdown '06
The Deal '05
Possessed '05
Air Bud 5: Buddy Spikes Back '03
Mindstorm '01

Douglas Slocombe(1913-)

Indiana Jones and the Last Crusade '89
Indiana Jones and the Temple of Doom '84
Never Say Never Again '83
Raiders of the Lost Ark '81
Julia '77
Rollerball '75
Jesus Christ, Superstar '73
The Music Lovers '71
The Buttercup Chain '70
Boom! '68
Fathom '67
The Fearless Vampire Killers '67
The Blue Max '66
The Servant '63
The L-Shaped Room '62
Circus of Horrors '60
Tread Softly Stranger '58
The Smallest Show on Earth '57
Kind Hearts and Coronets '49
It Always Rains on Sunday '47
Dead of Night '45

Michael Slovis

Seven Seconds '05
The Foreigner '03
Half Past Dead '02
The 4th Floor '99
Halloweentown '98
Scarred City '98
The White Raven '98
Crash Dive '96
Breach of Trust '95
Malicious '95
Party Girl '94

Arturo Smith

Psycho Beach Party '00
Race '99
Body and Soul '98
Nowhere '96

C. Davis Smith(1930-)

The Amazing Transplant '70
Bad Girls Go to Hell '65

Chris Smith(1970-)

The Yes Men '03
American Movie '99

Doyle Smith

Scorpio One '97
Widow's Kiss '94

Gavin Smith

Ginger Snaps: Unleashed '04
Ice Men '04
My Louisiana Sky '02

Glen R. Smith

Rebel Rousers '69
Heroes Die Young '60

Graham Smith

Beau Brummell: This Charming Man '06
The Other Boleyn Girl '03

Jeffrey Smith

San Saba '08
Are You Scared? '06
Missing Brendan '03

Keith L. Smith

What Up? '08
The Wash '01
Luck of the Draw '00
The Sex Monster '99
Diary of a Serial Killer '97
Love to Kill '97

Larry Smith

Bronson '09
Elizabeth I '05
Fear X '03
The Target '02
Eyes Wide Shut '99

Leonard Smith(1894-1947)

National Velvet '44
Billy the Kid '41
Go West '40
At the Circus '39
Devil Doll '36
So This Is Africa '33
Reducing '31
The Wizard of Oz '25

Roland Smith

Savage Land '94
The New Adventures of Pippi Longstocking '88

S. Douglas Smith

The Net 2.0 '06
Black Cadillac '03
Joyride '97
Stormy Nights '97
The Secret Agent Club '96

Ben Smithard

The Damned United '09
Return to Cranford '09
Cranford '08

Reed Smoot

Jonas Brothers: The 3D Concert Experience '09
Homeward Bound: The Incredible Journey '93

Vladimir Smutny

King of Thieves '04
Dark Blue World '01
Kolya '96

Edward Snyder

Youth on Parole '37
Jaws of Justice '33
Lonely Wives '31

William E. Snyder(1901-84)

Smoke '70
Tarzan's Fight for Life '58
The Conqueror '56
Creature from the Black Lagoon '54
Second Chance '53
Flying Leathernecks '51
The Loves of Carmen '48

Piotr Sobocinski(1958-2001)

Trapped '02
Angel Eyes '01
Hearts in Atlantis '01
Twilight '98
Marvin's Room '96
Ransom '96
Trois Couleurs: Rouge '94
The Decalogue '88

Witold Sobocinski(1929-)

Frantic '88
Hands Up '81
Everything for Sale '68

Morten Soborg

Valhalla Rising '09
The Killing Gene '07
After the Wedding '06
Brothers '04
Pusher '96

Steven Soderbergh(1963-)

The Girlfriend Experience '09
Che '08
Ocean's Thirteen '07
Bubble '06
The Good German '06
Ocean's Twelve '04
Full Frontal '02
Solaris '02
Ocean's Eleven '01
Traffic '00
Schizopolis '97

Jaromir Sofr(1939-)

I Served the King of England '07
My Sweet Little Village '86
Closely Watched Trains '66

Yuri Sokol

Warm Nights on a Slow-Moving Train '87
Cactus '86
Man of Flowers '84
Lonely Hearts '82

Bing Sokolsky(1963-)

Mammoth '06
Black Cat Run '98
Doing Time on Maple Drive '92

Rosalio Solano(1914-)

Vintage Model '92
Slaughter '72

Juan Soler

Devil Hunter '08
Bloody Moon '83

Leonardo Solis

Jailbird Rock '88
Deathstalker 2: Duel of the Titans '87
Soldier's Revenge '84
Deathstalker '83
Funny, Dirty Little War '83

Tamas Somlo

The Girl '68
The Red and the White '68

Barry Sonnenfeld(1953-)

Misery '90
When Harry Met Sally... '89
Raising Arizona '87
Throw Momma from the Train '87
Blood Simple '85

Christopher Soos

Anvil! The Story of Anvil '09
Whiteout '09
Paranoia 1.0 '04

Jeri Sopanen

My Dinner with Andre '81
The Bermuda Depths '78

Leonard J. South(1913-2006)

The North Avenue Irregulars '79
Family Plot '76
Hang 'Em High '67

Mike Southon

Beneath '07
Air Bud 6: Air Buddies '06
Sorted '04
MXP: Most Xtreme Primate '03
Replicant '01
The Duke '99
RKO 281 '99
Air Bud 2: Golden Receiver '98
Air Bud '97
Snow White: A Tale of Terror '97
The Final Cut '96
Roommates '95
The Run of the Country '95
Emily Bronte's Wuthering Heights '92
Little Man Tate '91
Goldeneye: The Secret Life of Ian Fleming '89
Gothic '87

Peter Sova

Push '09
The Strangers '08
Lucky Number Slevin '06
Wicker Park '04
The Reckoning '03
Close Your Eyes '02
Gangster No. 1 '00
Perfect Murder, Perfect Town '00
The Proposition '97
Donnie Brasco '96
Feast of July '95
Sgt. Bilko '95
Fatherland '94
Jimmy Hollywood '94
Good Morning, Vietnam '87
Tin Men '87
Diner '82

Alberto Spagnoli(1936-85)

Cut and Run '85
Shock '79
Lady of the Evening '75

Thomas E. Spalding(1926-96)

Island of Blood '82
The Blob '58

Theodor Sparkuhl(1891-1946)

Blood on the Sun '45
Murder, He Says '45
Salty O'Rourke '45
The Glass Key '42
Star Spangled Rhythm '42
Wake Island '42
Beau Geste '39
If I Were King '38
Internes Can't Take Money '37
The Last Outpost '35

Milan Spasic(1946-)

How Harry Became a Tree '01
Cabaret Balkan '98

Scott Spears

Witchcraft 11: Sisters in Blood '00
Unseen Evil '99
Too Good to Be True '98

Glynn Speeckaert

The Scorpion King 2: Rise of a Warrior '08
Secret Society '00

Brenton Spencer

Something Beneath '07
Where's the Money, Noreen? '95
American Boyfriends '89

James Lawrence Spencer(1958-)

The Killing Club '01
100 Girls '00
Eight Days a Week '97
Hybrid '97
Night Shade '97
Magic Island '95

David Sperling

The Drifter '88
Street Trash '87
The Boogey Man '80

Michael Spiller(1961-)

No Such Thing '01
Drop Dead Gorgeous '99
Henry Fool '98
The House of Yes '97
Niagara, Niagara '97
Walking and Talking '96
Flirt '95
Amateur '94
Search and Destroy '94
Hand Gun '93
Simple Men '92
Age Isn't Everything '91
Surviving Desire '91
Trust '91
The Unbelievable Truth '90

Dante Spinotti(1943-)

Public Enemies '09
Deception '08
Flash of Genius '08
The Contract '07
Slipstream '07
X-Men: The Last Stand '06
After the Sunset '04
Pinocchio '02
Red Dragon '02
Bandits '01
Family Man '00
Wonder Boys '00
Goodbye, Lover '99
The Insider '99
The Other Sister '98
L.A. Confidential '97
The Mirror Has Two Faces '96
Heat '95
The Quick and the Dead '95
The Star Maker '95
Blink '93
The Last of the Mohicans '92
The Comfort of Strangers '91
Frankie and Johnny '91
Hudson Hawk '91
Fair Game '89
Beaches '88
Crimes of the Heart '86
From the Hip '86
Manhunter '86
Basileus Quartet '82

John Spooner

Freezer Burn: The Invasion of Laxdale '08
Decoys: The Second Seduction '07
Merlin's Apprentice '06
White Coats '04

Tony Spratling

Edge of Sanity '89
Fanny Hill '83
The Man Who Haunted Himself '70

Buddy Squires

After Innocence '05
The Boys of 2nd Street Park '03

Chris Squires

Love Comes Lately '07
On Edge '03
Lola and Billy the Kid '98
True Crime '95
Nam Angels '88

Decha Srimantra

Bangkok Dangerous '08
Re-Cycle '06
The Eye 3 '05
The Eye 2 '04
The Tesseract '03
Bangkok Dangerous '00

Terry Stacey

Dear John '10
Adventureland '09
The Nanny Diaries '07
P.S. I Love You '07
Friends with Money '06
In Her Shoes '05
Winter Passing '05
The Door in the Floor '04
American Splendor '03
Just a Kiss '02
The Laramie Project '02
Things Behind the Sun '01
Wendigo '01
World Traveler '01
Happy Accidents '00
The Dream Catcher '99
Spring Forward '99
Trick '99

Jorge Stahl, Jr.(1921-2003)

A Rumor of War '80
Zachariah '70
Battle Shock '56
Death in the Garden '56

John Stanier

If These Walls Could Talk '96
Rambo 3 '88
Spy Trap '88

Frank Stanley

10 '79
Car Wash '76
The Eiger Sanction '75
Thunderbolt & Lightfoot '74
Winter Kill '74

Magnum Force '73

Ron Stannett

Mr. Troop Mom '09
Dr. Dolittle 4: Tail to the Chief '08
Wedding Wars '06
Footsteps '03
Brother's Keeper '02
In a Class of His Own '99
The Sweetest Gift '98

Oliver Stapleton(1948-)

The Proposal '09
How to Lose Friends & Alienate People '08
The Water Horse: Legend of the Deep '07
The Hoax '06
Casanova '05
An Unfinished Life '05
Ned Kelly '03
Birthday Girl '02
Buffalo Soldiers '01
The Shipping News '01
Pay It Forward '00
State and Main '00
The Cider House Rules '99
William Shakespeare's A Midsummer Night's Dream '99
The Hi-Lo Country '98
The Object of My Affection '98
The Designated Mourner '97
One Fine Day '96
Kansas City '95
The Van '95
Restoration '94
Look Who's Talking Now '93
Hero '92
The Grifters '90
Earth Girls Are Easy '89
She-Devil '89
Aria '88
Prick Up Your Ears '87
Sammy & Rosie Get Laid '87
Absolute Beginners '86
My Beautiful Laundrette '85

Willy Stassen(1948-)

Everybody's Famous! '00
Balzac: A Life of Passion '99
The Count of Monte Cristo '99
Hombres Complicados '97
Antonia's Line '95

Pieter Stathis

Insecticidal '05
The House Next Door '01

Hannes Staudinger

Superbug Super Agent '76
Age of Consent '69

Robert Steadman

Dancing in Twilight '05
Blood Crime '02
At Any Cost '00
A Face to Kill For '99
The Man Who Captured Eichmann '96
Return to the Blue Lagoon '91
Above the Law '88
Acapulco Gold '78
Executive Action '73

Ray Dennis Steckler(1939-)

Rat Pfink a Boo-Boo '66
Wild Ones on Wheels '62

Eric Steelberg

Going the Distance '10
Bandslam '09
(500) Days of Summer '09
Up in the Air '09
Juno '07
Numb '07
Quinceanera '06

Jack Steely

Black Godfather '74
The Thing with Two Heads '72
The Incredible Two-Headed Transplant '71

Ueli Steiger(1954-)

The Maiden Heist '08
10,000 B.C. '08
The Day After Tomorrow '04
Stealing Harvard '02
Black Knight '01
Just Visiting '01
Rock Star '01
Austin Powers 2: The Spy Who Shagged Me '99
Bowfinger '99
Godzilla '98
House Arrest '96
Now and Then '95
Better Off Dead '94
Chasers '94
Singles '92
Soapdish '91
The Hot Spot '90

Peter Stein

The Con '98
Necessary Roughness '91
Graveyard Shift '90
Pet Sematary '89
C.H.U.D. '84
Friday the 13th, Part 2 '81

Matt Steinauer

Dear Me: A Blogger's Tale '08
Slayer '06
Voodoo Moon '05

Raymond N. Stella

The Thirst '06
House of the Dead 2: Dead Aim '05
Honey, We Shrunk Ourselves '97

Mack Stengler(1895-1962)

Hopalong Cassidy: Dangerous Venture '48
I Wouldn't Be in Your Shoes '48
The Ape Man '43
Clancy Street Boys '43
Spotlight Scandals '43
Spy Train '43
Bowery at Midnight '42
King of the Zombies '41
Sky Bandits '40
Yukon Flight '40
The Sunset Murder Case '38
Terror of Tiny Town '38
Captain Calamity '36

Alan Stensvold(1908-81)

The Invisible Strangler '76
Cotter '72
Private Navy of Sgt. O'Farrell '68
Eight on the Lam '67
Thunder Road '58

John Stephens

Sorcerer '77
Boxcar Bertha '72
Billy Jack '71
Run, Angel, Run! '69

Gerard Sterin

Paris, je t'aime '06
Wasabi '01

Tom Stern(1946-)

Invictus '09
Changeling '08
Gran Torino '08
Paris 36 '08
Tenderness '08
Rails & Ties '07
Things We Lost in the Fire '07
Flags of Our Fathers '06
The Last Kiss '06
Letters from Iwo Jima '06
The Exorcism of Emily Rose '05
Romance & Cigarettes '05
Bobby Jones: Stroke of Genius '04
Million Dollar Baby '04
Mystic River '03
Blood Work '02

George Stevens(1904-75)

Laurel & Hardy: Below Zero '30
Laurel & Hardy: Blotto '30
Laurel & Hardy: Brats '30
Laurel & Hardy: Night Owls '30
Laurel & Hardy: Men O'War '29
Laurel & Hardy: The Hoose-Gow '29

Jack Stevens

Laurel & Hardy: Chickens Come Home '31
Laurel & Hardy: Another Fine Mess '30
Laurel & Hardy: Hog Wild '30

Robert M. Stevens

Kickin' It Old Skool '07
Cecil B. Demented '00
Dude, Where's My Car? '00
Simply Irresistible '99
Pecker '98
Breast Men '97
The Man Who Knew Too Little '97
Serial Mom '94
Beyond the Law '92
Tune in Tomorrow '90
The 'Burbs '89

Ernest Steward

Carry On Matron '72
Carry On Loving '70
Carry On Up the Jungle '70
One More Time '70
Carry On Again Doctor '69
Carry On Up the Khyber '68
Deadlier Than the Male '67
The Magnificent Two '67
Brides of Fu Manchu '66
Very Important Person '61
Doctor in Love '60

Patrick Alexander Stewart

Hotel '01
Time Code '00

Rod Stewart

Alien Chaser '96
Warhead '96
Live Wire: Human Timebomb '95
Terminal Impact '95

Jacques Steyn(1954-)

Kill Me Again '89
The Mighty Quinn '89
Blitz '85

Clifford Stine(1906-86)

That Funny Feeling '65
The Brass Bottle '63
Abbott and Costello Go to Mars '53
It Came from Outer Space '53
Law and Order '53

Harold E. Stine(1903-77)

Crazy Horse and Custer: "The Untold Story" '90
The Poseidon Adventure '72
M*A*S*H '70
The Busy Body '67

Ken Stipe

Motives '03
Epoch '00

Rogier Stoffers(1961-)

Death at a Funeral '10
Balls Out: Gary the Tennis Coach '09
Lakeview Terrace '08
The Secret Life of Bees '08
Disturbia '07
Mongol '07
The Bad News Bears '05
Masked and Anonymous '03
School of Rock '03
Enough '02
John Q '02
Quills '00
Character '97

Witold Stok(1946-)

The Match '99
Among Giants '98
Century '94
Two Deaths '94
Close My Eyes '91
Eat the Rich '87
Foul Play '76

John Stokes(1961-)

Journey to the Center of the Earth '99
Silent Predators '99
Gargantua '98
Blackwater Trail '95

Dan Stoloff

The Butterfly Effect 3: Revelation '09
Labor Pains '09
College '08
Wedding Daze '06
Miracle '04
Tumbleweeds '98

Barry Stone(1945-)

Tweek City '05
Hollywood North '03
Cherish '02
Triggermen '02
Full Disclosure '00
The Perfect Son '00
Dream with the Fishes '97
Pale Saints '97
Rude '96
Understudy: The Graveyard Shift 2 '88

Vittorio Storaro(1940-)

Dominion: Prequel to the Exorcist '05
Exorcist: The Beginning '04
Dune '00
Goya in Bordeaux '99
Picking Up the Pieces '99
Bulworth '98
Tango '98
Little Buddha '93
Dick Tracy '90
The Sheltering Sky '90
Ishtar '87
The Last Emperor '87
Peter the Great '86
Ladyhawke '85
Reds '81
Apocalypse Now '79
1900 '76
Primal Impulse '74
Last Tango in Paris '73
The Conformist '71
The Bird with the Crystal Plumage '70

Michael Storey

Walter and Henry '01
No Alibi '00
One Kill '00
Locked in Silence '99
Blacklight '98
Elvis Meets Nixon '98
Recipe for Revenge '98
Summer of the Monkeys '98
In His Father's Shoes '97
Another Woman '94

Archie Stout(1886-1965)

The High and the Mighty '54
Hondo '53
Island in the Sky '53
The Sun Shines Bright '53
Big Jim McLain '52
The Quiet Man '52
Hard, Fast and Beautiful '51
Fort Apache '48
Angel and the Badman '47
Abilene Town '46
Captain Kidd '45
Dark Waters '44
It Happened Tomorrow '44
Summer Storm '44
Beau Geste '39
Borderland '37
The Hurricane '37
Hopalong Cassidy Returns '36
Three on the Trail '36
Desert Trail '35
Hopalong Cassidy '35
Paradise Canyon '35
Lucky Texan '34
Man from Utah '34
The Star Packer '34
Trail Beyond '34
Badmen of Nevada '33
Riders of Destiny '33
Sagebrush Trail '33
West of the Divide '33
Law of the Sea '32
Police Court '32
Riders of the Desert '32
Single Handed Sanders '32
The Ridin' Fool '31
Two Fisted Justice '31
The Return of Dr. Fu Manchu '30
The Sea God '30
The Ten Commandments '23

Harry Stradling, Sr. (1902-70)

On a Clear Day You Can See Forever '70
The Owl and the Pussycat '70
Hello, Dolly! '69
Funny Girl '68
Moment to Moment '66
How to Murder Your Wife '64
My Fair Lady '64
Mary, Mary '63
Gypsy '62
Parrish '61
The Crowded Sky '60
A Summer Place '59
The Young Philadelphians '59
Auntie Mame '58
Marjorie Morningstar '58
A Face in the Crowd '57
The Pajama Game '57
The Eddy Duchin Story '56
Helen of Troy '56
Guys and Dolls '55
Johnny Guitar '53
A Lion in the Streets '53
Androcles and the Lion '52
Angel Face '52
Hans Christian Andersen '52
I Want You '51
A Streetcar Named Desire '51
Tension '50
The Barkleys of Broadway '49
In the Good Old Summertime '49
Easter Parade '48
The Pirate '48
Song of Love '47
Holiday in Mexico '46
Till the Clouds Roll By '46
Picture of Dorian Gray '45
Bathing Beauty '44
The Human Comedy '43
The Corsican Brothers '42
The Devil & Miss Jones '41
Suspicion '41
The Lion Has Wings '40
My Son, My Son '40
They Knew What They Wanted '40
Clouds over Europe '39
Jamaica Inn '39
The Citadel '38
The Divorce of Lady X '38
Pygmalion '38
Knight Without Armour '37
South Riding '37
Carnival in Flanders '35

Harry Stradling, Jr. (1925-)

Caddyshack 2 '88
Blind Date '87
A Fine Mess '86
Micki & Maude '84
Buddy Buddy '81
The Pursuit of D.B. Cooper '81
S.O.B. '80
Carny '80
Prophecy '79
Born Again '78
Convoy '78
Go Tell the Spartans '78
Damnation Alley '77
The Greatest '77
The Big Bus '76
Midway '76
Special Delivery '76
Bite the Bullet '75
Mitchell '75
Rooster Cogburn '75
Bank Shot '74
McQ '74
Man Who Loved Cat Dancing '73
The Way We Were '73
1776 '72
Support Your Local Gunfighter '71
Little Big Man '70
There Was a Crooked Man '70
The Good Guys and the Bad Guys '69
Support Your Local Sheriff '69
With Six You Get Eggroll '68

Walter Stradling(1875-1918)

Amarilly of Clothesline Alley '18
Stella Maris '18

Ivan Strasburg

Generation Kill '08
A Raisin in the Sun '08
Fatal Contact: Bird Flu in America '06
The Hades Factor '06
Shooting Dogs '05
Live from Baghdad '03
The Mayor of Casterbridge '03
Bloody Sunday '01
The Corner '00
Britannic '99
The Murder of Stephen Lawrence '99
New World Disorder '99
Deacon Brodie '98
The Theory of Flight '98
Moll Flanders '96
The Affair '95
Sharpe's Eagle '93
Sharpe's Rifles '93
Rita, Sue & Bob Too '87

Christopher W. Strattan

Code of Honor '82
Kill Squad '81

Lukas Strebel

Little Dorrit '08
See No Evil: The Moors Murders '06
Sherlock: Case of Evil '02

Walter Strenge(1898-1974)

Mr. Walkie Talkie '52
Rodeo King and the Senorita '51
Before Morning '33

Karl Struss(1891-1981)

The Rebel Set '59
The Fly '58
Kronos '57
Mohawk '56
Tarzan and the She-Devil '53
Limelight '52
Mesa of Lost Women '52
Tarzan's Savage Fury '52
Tarzan's Peril '51
Rocketship X-M '50
The Dude Goes West '48
Tarzan's Magic Fountain '48
Mr. Ace '46
Journey into Fear '42
The Great Dictator '40
Rhythm Romance '39
Thanks for the Memory '38
Double or Nothing '37
Waikiki Wedding '37
Go West, Young Man '36
Rhythm on the Range '36
Goin' to Town '35
Belle of the Nineties '34
Dr. Jekyll and Mr. Hyde '32
Island of Lost Souls '32
Abraham Lincoln '30
Be Yourself '30

Coquette '29
The Taming of the Shrew '29
Battle of the Sexes '28
Sunrise '27
Sparrows '26
Affairs of Anatol '21
Dr. Jekyll and Mr. Hyde '20

Ian Struthers

The Seducer '69
Fire Maidens from Outer Space '56

Charles Stumar(1891-1935)

The Raven '35
Werewolf of London '35
Bombay Mail '34
The Mummy '32
Uncle Tom's Cabin '27

John Stumar(1892-1962)

Power of the Press '43
Return of the Vampire '43
The Durango Kid '40
If You Could Only Cook '36
The Claw '27
Head Winds '25

David G. Stump

What Love Is '07
Killer Pad '06
Daddy's Boys '87

Jens Sturup

How to Go Out on a Date in Queens '06
Two Days '03
Stuart Bliss '98
Fun '94
Witchcraft 2: The Temptress '90
Witchcraft '88

Ramon Suarez

The Silence of Neto '94
Private Passions '85
Red Kiss '85
L'Amour en Herbe '77
Memories of Underdevelopment '68
Death of a Bureaucrat '66

Aguri Sugita

Rica 2: Lonely Wanderer '73
Rica 3: Juvenile's Lullaby '73
Rica '72

Kohei Sugiyama(1899-1960)

Gate of Hell '54
47 Ronin, Part 1 '42
47 Ronin, Part 2 '42

Tim Suhrstedt

All About Steve '09
Extract '09
The Invention of Lying '09
The Marc Pease Experience '09
17 Again '09
The Brothers Solomon '07
Idiocracy '06
The Last Time '06
Little Miss Sunshine '06
Relative Strangers '06
Clockstoppers '02
Frank McKlusky, C.I. '02
The Hot Chick '02
Pumpkin '02
Summer Catch '01
Whatever It Takes '00
Major League 3: Back to the Minors '98
Office Space '98
The Wedding Singer '97
To Gillian on Her 37th Birthday '96
Getting Even with Dad '94
The Favor '92
Traces of Red '92
Don't Tell Mom the Babysitter's Dead '91
Men at Work '90
Rainbow Drive '90
Bill & Ted's Excellent Adventure '89
Capone '89
The Chinatown Murders: Man against the Mob '89

Mystic Pizza '88
Mannequin '87
Critters '86
Ratings Game '84
The House on Sorority Row '83
Suburbia '83
Android '82
Forbidden World '82

Bob Sullivan

Outfoxed: Rupert Murdoch's War on Journalism '04
Uncovered: The War on Iraq '04

Brian Sullivan

The Last Days of Summer '07
Little Secrets '02
Route 9 '98
Coyote Summer '96
Just Like Dad '96
Wish upon a Star '96

Igor Sunara(1955-)

Somewhere in the City '97
The Keeper '96
Tales of Erotica '93
For Love or Money '88

Bruce Surtees(1944-)

Joshua '02
American Tragedy '00
Dash and Lilly '99
Just a Little Harmless Sex '99
The Lady in Question '99
Murder in a Small Town '99
That Championship Season '99
The Substitute '96
Corrina, Corrina '94
The Stars Fell on Henrietta '94
The Crush '93
Run '91
The Super '91
Men Don't Leave '89
License to Drive '88
Back to the Beach '87
Out of Bounds '86
Psycho 3 '86
Ratboy '86
Pale Rider '85
Beverly Hills Cop '84
Tightrope '84
Risky Business '83
Sudden Impact '83
Firefox '82
Honkytonk Man '82
Ladies and Gentlemen, the Fabulous Stains '82
White Dog '82
Escape from Alcatraz '79
Three Warriors '77
The Outlaw Josey Wales '76
The Shootist '76
Night Moves '75
Lenny '74
Blume in Love '73
High Plains Drifter '73
Conquest of the Planet of the Apes '72
The Great Northfield Minnesota Raid '72
Joe Kidd '72
Dirty Harry '71
Play Misty for Me '71
The Beguiled '70

Robert L. Surtees(1906-85)

Thin Air '00
Bloodbrothers '78
Same Time, Next Year '78
The Turning Point '77
A Star Is Born '76
The Great Waldo Pepper '75
The Hindenburg '75
Oklahoma Crude '73
The Sting '73
The Cowboys '72
The Other '72
The Last Picture Show '71
Summer of '42 '71
The Arrangement '69
Sweet Charity '69
Doctor Dolittle '67
The Graduate '67

The Lost Command '66
The Collector '65
The Hallelujah Trail '65
Mutiny on the Bounty '62
Ben-Hur '59
Les Girls '57
Raintree County '57
The Swan '56
Oklahoma! '55
The Long, Long Trailer '54
Valley of the Kings '54
Escape from Fort Bravo '53
Mogambo '53
The Bad and the Beautiful '52
The Merry Widow '52
Quo Vadis '51
King Solomon's Mines '50
Intruder in the Dust '49
That Midnight Kiss '49
Act of Violence '48
A Date with Judy '48
The Kissing Bandit '48
Our Vines Have Tender Grapes '45
Meet the People '44
Thirty Seconds Over Tokyo '44
Two Girls and a Sailor '44

Adam Suschitzky

Emma '09
Jekyll '07
The Shadow in the North '07
Middletown '06

Peter Suschitzky(1941-)

Eastern Promises '07
A History of Violence '05
Shopgirl '05
Spider '02
eXistenZ '99
The Man in the Iron Mask '98
Mars Attacks! '96
Crash '95
Immortal Beloved '94
Naked Lunch '91
Where the Heart Is '90
Dead Ringers '88
Falling in Love '84
Krull '83
The Empire Strikes Back '80
Valentino '77
Lisztomania '75
The Rocky Horror Picture Show '75
All Creatures Great and Small '74
That'll Be the Day '73
Pied Piper '72
The Vengeance of She '68
Privilege '67

Wolfgang Suschitzky(1912-)

Theatre of Blood '73
Get Carter '71
Entertaining Mr. Sloane '70
Ring of Bright Water '69
Ulysses '67

Misha (Mikhail) Suslov

Suspended Animation '02
Prancer '89
Black Moon Rising '86
Nobody's Fool '86
Smokey & the Judge '80

Morgan Susser

Hesher '10
Rize '05

Maida Sussman

Stricken '98
Ivory Tower '97

Darko Suvak

Blood Creek '09
Keith '08
True Blue '01
The Landlady '98
Stir '98

Rob Sweeney

Canvas '06
Between '05
Harry and Max '04
Blue Car '03
The Street King '02

The Sleepy Time Gal '01
Big Eden '00
I'm Losing You '98
Color of a Brisk and Leaping Day '95

Adam Swica

The Haunting in Connecticut '09
Survival of the Dead '09
Diary of the Dead '07
Weirdsville '07
Bruiser '00

Attila Szalay(1961-)

Gym Teacher: The Movie '08
Touch the Top of the World '06
Dodson's Journey '01
The Void '01

Wojciech Szepel

God on Trial '08
Tess of the D'Urbervilles '08

Michel Taburiaux

Blood Brothers '07
The Great Challenge '04

Hubert Taczanowski(1960-)

Dragon Wars '07
National Lampoon's Van Wilder 2: The Rise of Taj '06
Deathwatch '02
Tadpole '02
How to Kill Your Neighbor's Dog '01
Turn It Up '00
Buddy Boy '99
Chicago Cab '98
Eden '98
The Maker '98
The Opposite of Sex '98
The Young Poisoner's Handbook '94

Carlo Tafani

Lucky Luke '94
Troublemakers '94

Renato Tafuri

The Church '98
Dial Help '88
Berlinguer I Love You '77

Wong Ngok Tai

Once Upon a Time in China II '92
Operation Condor '91

Yasukazu Takemura

100 Monsters '68
Shinobi no Mono '62

Ken Talbot(1920-93)

Doomwatch '72
Hands of the Ripper '71
Girl Hunters '63
The Time of His Life '55
The Stranger from Venus '54
Old Mother Riley, Headmistress '50

Fred Tammes(1937-)

Face '97
Mad Love '95
Priest '94
Catherine Cookson's The Man Who Cried '93
The Whistle Blower '87

Masaki Tamura(1939-)

Tampopo '86
Himatsuri '85
Lady Snowblood '73

Kaz Tanaka

Remembering the Cosmos Flower '99
Carnival of Wolves '96

Kazunari Tanaka

Masked Rider—The First '05
Zebraman '04
Gozu '03
Carnival of Wolves '96

Ciaran Tanham

Northanger Abbey '07
Bloom '03

Bobbie's Girl '02
Borstal Boy '00

Philip Tannura(1897-1973)

Counterspy Meets Scotland Yard '50
The Flying Saucer '50
Hi-Jacked '50
The Millerson Case '47
Strange Illusion '45
Footlight Glamour '43

Jean-Jacques Tarbes

My New Partner '84
Le Gitan '75
Borsalino '70
Queen of Diamonds '70
La Piscine '69
Honor Among Thieves '68

John Tarver

Screamers: The Hunting '09
Earthstorm '06
Serial Killing 101 '04
Shallow Ground '04
Seventeen Again '00
The Art of Murder '99
The First 9 1/2 Weeks '98
Stonebrook '98

David Tattersall(1960-)

Tooth Fairy '10
The Day the Earth Stood Still '08
Speed Racer '08
The Hunting Party '07
Next '07
The Matador '06
Zoom '06
Star Wars: Episode 3—Revenge of the Sith '05
XXX: State of the Union '05
Lara Croft Tomb Raider: The Cradle of Life '03
Die Another Day '02
Star Wars: Episode 2—Attack of the Clones '02
The Majestic '01
Vertical Limit '00
The Green Mile '99
Star Wars: Episode 1—The Phantom Menace '99
Soldier '98
Con Air '97
Mr. Toad's Wild Ride '96
Moll Flanders '96
Theodore Rex '95
Radioland Murders '94

Gale Tattersall(1948-)

Ghost Ship '02
13 Ghosts '01
The Jack Bull '99
Pushing Tin '99
From the Earth to the Moon '98
Virtuosity '95
Hideaway '94
Tank Girl '94
The Commitments '91
Wild Orchid '90
Aria '88

Alfred Taylor

Killer Klowns from Outer Space '88
Fatal Games '84
Mutant '83
The Swinging Cheerleaders '74
Spider Baby '64

Christopher Taylor

Nobody's Baby '01
Death Benefit '96
Glory Daze '96
Live Nude Girls '95
Inside Monkey Zetterland '93

Gilbert Taylor(1914-)

The Bedroom Window '87
Voyage of the Rock Aliens '87
Losin' It '82
Flash Gordon '80
Dracula '79
Star Wars '77

The Omen '76
Frenzy '72
Macbeth '71
Quackser Fortune Has a Cousin in the Bronx '70
Theatre of Death '67
Repulsion '65
Dr. Strangelove, or: How I Learned to Stop Worrying and Love the Bomb '64
A Hard Day's Night '64
Sailor of the King '53
Seven Days to Noon '50

J.O. Taylor(1887-1974)

King Kong '33
Song o' My Heart '30
The Sea Lion '21

Rodney Taylor

That Evening Sun '09
Save Me '07
Sparkler '99

Ronnie Taylor(1924-)

Sleepless '01
The Phantom of the Opera '98
Popcorn '89
Sea of Love '89
Opera '88
Cry Freedom '87
The Hound of the Baskervilles '83
Tommy '75

Manuel Teran

District B13 '04
Mercy '00
Petits Freres '00
Red Shoe Diaries: Four on the Floor '96
Before the Rain '94

Ubaldo Terzano

Black Sabbath '64
Blood and Black Lace '64
The Whip and the Body '63
Black Sunday '60

Ted Tetzlaff(1903-95)

Notorious '46
I Married a Witch '42
The Road to Zanzibar '41
Remember the Night '40
Easy Living '37
Murder With Pictures '36
My Man Godfrey '36
The Princess Comes Across '36
Hands Across the Table '35
His Greatest Gamble '34

Ellis Thackerey

See Bud Thackery

Bud Thackery(1903-90)

Jaguar '56
Phantom Stallion '54
Trader Tom of the China Seas '54
Iron Mountain Trail '53
Shadows of Tombstone '53
Outcasts of the Trail '49
Son of Zorro '47
Alias Billy the Kid '46
King of the Forest Rangers '46
The Phantom Rider '46
Santa Fe Uprising '46
Federal Operator 99 '45
Manhunt of Mystery Island '45
The Purple Monster Strikes '45
Gangs of Sonora '41

Gary Thieltges

Sticky Fingers '88
Eating Raoul '82

Armand Thirard(1899-1973)

Ladies' Man '62
Love on a Pillow '62
Sois Belle et Tais-Toi '58
And God Created Woman '57
The Night Heaven Fell '57
Diabolique '55
Wages of Fear '55

Beauties of the Night '52
Utopia '51

John Thomas
Sex and the City 2 '10
Sex and the City: The Movie '08
The Hunley '99
Hi-Life '98
The Last Days of Disco '98
Dead Man on Campus '97
Kicked in the Head '97
Still Breathing '97
Freeway '95
Norma Jean and Marilyn '95
Palookaville '95
Barcelona '94
Metropolitan '90

Jamie Thompson(1962-)
Eternal '04
Tracked '98
Cyborg 2 '93
Freaked '93
Desire and Hell at Sunset Motel '92
Circuitry Man '90

Stuart Thompson
At War with the Army '50
Variety Girl '47

William C. Thompson(1889-1963)
The Sinister Urge '60
Night of the Ghouls '59
The Astounding She-Monster '58
Plan 9 from Outer Space '56
The Violent Years '56
Bride of the Monster '55
Daughter of Horror '55
Jail Bait '54
Glen or Glenda? '53
Project Moon Base '53
Pin Down Girls '51
Demon for Trouble '34
Maniac '34

Alex Thomson(1929-2007)
Love's Labour's Lost '00
A Shot at Glory '00
Executive Decision '96
Hamlet '96
The Scarlet Letter '95
Black Beauty '94
Cliffhanger '93
Demolition Man '93
Alien 3 '92
The Krays '90
Leviathan '89
Date with an Angel '87
The Sicilian '87
Labyrinth '86
Raw Deal '86
The Keep '83
Excalibur '81
The Cat and the Canary '79
Doctor Phibes Rises Again '72
Raw Meat '72

Donald E. Thorin(1934-)
Head of State '03
Dudley Do-Right '99
Mickey Blue Eyes '99
The First Wives Club '96
Nothing to Lose '96
Ace Ventura: When Nature Calls '95
Boys on the Side '94
Scent of a Woman '92
Lock Up '89
Tango and Cash '89
Midnight Run '88
The Golden Child '86
Against All Odds '84
Purple Rain '84
Bad Boys '83
An Officer and a Gentleman '82
Thief '81

Erling Thurmann-Andersen(1945-2002)
Prozac Nation '01
Insomnia '97

Peter Thwaites
Janice Beard '99
Appetite '98

Clive Tickner
The Magical Legend of the Leprechauns '99
Ivanhoe '97
Spice World: The Movie '97
Twelfth Night '96
Loch Ness '95
The Borrowers '93
Split Second '92
Hidden Agenda '90
Traffik '90

Frank Tidy
The Boys Next Door '96
Chain Reaction '96
Getting Away With Murder '96
Hoodlum '96
Steal Big, Steal Little '95
Black Fox: Blood Horse '94
Black Fox: Good Men and Bad '94
Black Fox: The Price of Peace '94
Under Siege '92
The Butcher's Wife '91
Slipstream '89
Hot Pursuit '87
One Magic Christmas '85
The Grey Fox '83
Spacehunter: Adventures in the Forbidden Zone '83

Gary Tieche
Tribute '09
Menno's Mind '96
Bad Love '95
Dead Weekend '95
Out There '95

Seamus Tierney
The Good Guy '10
Adam '09

Augusto Tiezzi
Conquest of Mycene '63
Hero of Rome '63
Girl Under the Sheet '61

Jiri (George) Tirl(1947-)
Left Behind: The Movie '00
Revelation '00
Tribulation '00
The Heist '89
Steel Dawn '87

Romeo Tirone
Cry_Wolf '05
12 and Holding '05
L.I.E. '01

Gokhan Tiryaki
Three Monkeys '08
Climates '06

Eduard Tisse(1897-1961)
Ivan the Terrible, Part 2 '46
Ivan the Terrible, Part 1 '44
Alexander Nevsky '38
Que Viva Mexico '32
Ten Days That Shook the World '27
The Battleship Potemkin '25
Strike '24

Volker Tittel
The Front Line '06
Cowboys & Angels '04
Halfmoon '95

Arthur L. Todd(1895-1942)
The Verdict '46
Crime School '38
Sing Me a Love Song '37
Alibi Ike '35
Wild Boys of the Road '33
Hot Saturday '32
Monkey Business '31

Gregg Toland(1904-48)
A Song Is Born '48
The Bishop's Wife '47
The Best Years of Our Lives '46
Kid from Brooklyn '46
The Outlaw '43
Ball of Fire '41
Citizen Kane '41
The Little Foxes '41
The Grapes of Wrath '40
The Long Voyage Home '40
The Westerner '40
Intermezzo '39
They Shall Have Music '39
Wuthering Heights '39
The Cowboy and the Lady '38
The Goldwyn Follies '38
Dead End '37
History Is Made at Night '37
Beloved Enemy '36
Come and Get It '36
Strike Me Pink '36
These Three '36
The Dark Angel '35
Les Miserables '35
Mad Love '35
Splendor '35
Roman Scandals '33
Tugboat Annie '33
Kid from Spain '32
Palmy Days '31
Tonight or Never '31
Raffles '30
Bulldog Drummond '29
Condemned '29
The Winning of Barbara Worth '26

John Toll
The Adjustment Bureau '10
It's Complicated '09
Tropic Thunder '08
Gone Baby Gone '07
Rise: Blood Hunter '07
Seraphim Falls '06
Elizabethtown '05
The Last Samurai '03
Captain Corelli's Mandolin '01
Vanilla Sky '01
Almost Famous '00
Simpatico '99
The Thin Red Line '98
John Grisham's The Rainmaker '97
Jack '96
Braveheart '95
Legends of the Fall '94
Wind '92

Sokei Tomioka
War of the Wizards '83
Godzilla's Revenge '69

Shinji Tomita
The Adventures of Milo & Otis '89
Milo & Otis '89

Aldo Tonti(1910-88)
Escape from Death Row '73
The Valachi Papers '72
The Family '70
Cast a Giant Shadow '66
Barabbas '62
The Unfaithfuls '60
Nights of Cabiria '57
War and Peace '56
Attila '54
The Miracle '48
Ossessione '42

John Toon
Sunshine Cleaning '09
The Jane Austen Book Club '07
Glory Road '06
Sylvia '03
Rain '01
Broken English '96

Emil Topuzov
Cyclops '08
The Prince & Me 3: A Royal Honeymoon '08
Finding Rin Tin Tin '07
Megasnake '07
Mosquitoman '05

Bruce Torbet
Brain Damage '88
Basket Case '82

Carlos Torlaschi
Brain Drain '98
Condemned to Hell '84

Mario Tosi
The Stunt Man '80
The Betsy '78
MacArthur '77
Carrie '76
Red, White & Busted '75
Frogs '72

Roland H. Totheroh(1890-1967)
Monsieur Verdoux '47
The Great Dictator '40
Modern Times '36
City Lights '31
The Gold Rush '25
The Circus '19
One A.M. '16
Pawnshop '16

Salvatore Totino(1964-)
Angels & Demons '09
Frost/Nixon '08
The Da Vinci Code '06
Cinderella Man '05
The Missing '03
Changing Lanes '02
Any Given Sunday '99

Bert Tougas
Christie's Revenge '07
Demons from Her Past '07
Framed for Murder '07
Codename: Jaguar '00
Wilder '00
The Pact '99
The Ultimate Weapon '97

Jean Tournier(1926-2004)
The Fiendish Plot of Dr. Fu Manchu '80
Moonraker '79
The Day of the Jackal '73
The Holes '72
Start the Revolution without Me '70
The Train '65

Leo Tover(1902-64)
Strange Bedfellows '65
Island of the Blue Dolphins '64
Sunday in New York '63
Follow That Dream '61
Misty '61
From the Terrace '60
Journey to the Center of the Earth '59
Between Heaven and Hell '56
The Conqueror '56
Love Me Tender '56
Soldier of Fortune '55
The Tall Men '55
A Blueprint for Murder '53
Man in the Attic '53
Pride of St. Louis '52
We're Not Married '52
The Day the Earth Stood Still '51
Follow the Sun '51
Payment on Demand '51
When Willie Comes Marching Home '50
The Heiress '49
My Friend Irma '49
The Snake Pit '48
Dead Reckoning '47
China '43
Bahama Passage '42
The Major and the Minor '42
Star Spangled Rhythm '42
Young and Willing '42
Never Say Die '39
Bluebeard's Eighth Wife '38
Love in Bloom '35
Murder at the Vanities '34
College Humor '33
I'm No Angel '33
Lost Squadron '32
No Man of Her Own '32
Bachelor Apartment '31
The Lady Refuses '31
The Royal Bed '31
State's Attorney '31
The Silver Horde '30
Vagabond Lover '29

Luciano Tovoli
Murder by Numbers '02
The Closet '00
Titus '99
Desperate Measures '98
The Dinner Game '98
Before and After '95
Single White Female '92
Reversal of Fortune '90
Unsane '82
Suspiria '77
The Desert of the Tartars '76
Bread and Chocolate '73
Bandits of Orgosolo '61

Eric Trageser
Already Dead '07
The House of Usher '06

Luciano Trasatti
Season for Assassins '71
Rough Justice '70
And God Said to Cain '69
Diary of a Rebel '68
The Bloody Pit of Horror '65

Jan Troell(1931-)
Everlasting Moments '08
Hamsun '96
The New Land '73
The Emigrants '72

Sergei Trofimov(1961-)
Mongol '07
Day Watch '06
Night Watch '04

Oberdan Troiani
Tower of Screaming Virgins '68
Hercules against the Moon Men '64
Othello '52

William G. Troiano(1914-83)
She-Freak '67
The Wild World of Batwoman '66
The Slime People '63

Brandon Trost(1981-)
MacGruber '10
Crank: High Voltage '09
Halloween II '09
Weather Girl '09
Pulse 2: Afterlife '08
He Was a Quiet Man '07
Chaos '05
The Salon '05

Alan M. Trow
Grim '95
Chasing the Deer '94

David Trulli(1961-)
Bloody Murder 2 '03
Face the Music '00
Dementia '98

Hui-chi Tsao
Opium and Kung-Fu Master '84
House of Traps '81
Sword Masters: Two Champions of Shaolin '80

Shinya Tsukamoto(1960-)
Nightmare Detective '06
Tetsuo 2: Body Hammer '97
Tetsuo: The Iron Man '92

Brian Tufano(1939-)
My Zinc Bed '08
I Could Never Be Your Woman '06
Once Upon a Time in the Midlands '02
Last Orders '01
Billy Elliot '00
East Is East '99
Virtual Sexuality '99
A Life Less Ordinary '97
Element of Doubt '96
Trainspotting '95
Shallow Grave '94
Middlemarch '93
The Endless Game '89
War Party '89
Dreamscape '84

The Lords of Discipline '83
Agatha Christie's Murder is Easy '82
Heavy Metal '81
Quadrophenia '79

Christopher Tufty
The Theory of the Leisure Class '01
Jimmy Zip '00
To Cross the Rubicon '91
West Is West '87
Stoogemania '85

David Tumblety
Gospel Hill '08
The New Twenty '08
Brooklyn Lobster '05
Sweet Land '05
Hit and Runway '01

Andre Turpin(1966-)
Familia '05
Maelstrom '00
Because Why? '93

Gerry Turpin(1925-97)
The Last of Sheila '73
Hoffman '70
Oh! What a Lovely War '69

Masaharu Ueda(1938-)
Rhapsody in August '91
Akira Kurosawa's Dreams '90
Ran '85
Kagemusha '80
Murders in the Doll House '79

Matthew Uhry
Graduation '07
Mission '00
Trailer, the Movie '99

Frantisek Uldrich
The Perfect Husband '92
Adelheid '69

Alejandro Ulloa(1926-)
El Barbaro '84
Vatican Conspiracy '81
Fury '78
Spaghetti Western '75
Autopsy '74
Bad Man's River '72
Horror Express '72
Pancho Villa '72
Companeros '70
Eagles Over London '69
The Diabolical Dr. Z '65

Derick Underschultz
The Trojan Horse '08
Carolina Moon '07
Holiday in Handcuffs '07
The Note '07
Snowglobe '07
Santa Baby '06
Knights of the South Bronx '05
The Twelve Days of Christmas Eve '04
The Cheetah Girls '03
Danger Beneath the Sea '02
Power and Beauty '02
RFK '02
Jason X '01
Sins of the Father '01
Mr. Rock 'n' Roll: The Alan Freed Story '99
Thrill Seekers '99

Geoffrey Unsworth(1914-78)
The Great Train Robbery '79
Tess '79
Superman: The Movie '78
A Bridge Too Far '77
A Matter of Time '76
Royal Flash '75
The Abdication '74
Murder on the Orient Express '74
Return of the Pink Panther '74
Internecine Project '73
Love and Pain and the Whole Damn Thing '73
Zardoz '73
Cabaret '72

Cromwell '70
The Assassination Bureau '69
The Magic Christian '69
2001: A Space Odyssey '68
Half a Sixpence '67
Oh Dad, Poor Dad (Momma's Hung You in the Closet & I'm Feeling So Sad) '67
Othello '65
Becket '64
The 300 Spartans '62
Flame Over India '60
The World of Suzie Wong '60
A Night to Remember '58
Simba '55
The Sword & the Rose '53
Made in Heaven '52
The Clouded Yellow '51
Trio '50
Blanche Fury '48
Scott of the Antarctic '48
Meet the Navy '46

Sergei Urusevsky(1908-74)
I Am Cuba '64
The Cranes Are Flying '57

Jost Vacano
Hollow Man '00
Starship Troopers '97
Showgirls '95
Untamed Heart '93
The NeverEnding Story '84
Das Boot '81

Joseph Valentine(1900-49)
Joan of Arc '48
Rope '48
The Possessed '47
Heartbeat '46
Magnificent Doll '46
Tomorrow Is Forever '46
Guest Wife '45
Shadow of a Doubt '43
Saboteur '42
In the Navy '41
Nice Girl? '41
The Wolf Man '41
It's a Date '40
My Little Chickadee '40
Spring Parade '40
First Love '39
Mad About Music '38
The Rage of Paris '38
That Certain Age '38
100 Men and a Girl '37
The Moon's Our Home '36
Next Time We Love '36
Three Smart Girls '36
Myrt and Marge '33
Night of Terror '33

Charlie Van Damme
I Want to Go Home '89
Melo '86
One Sings, the Other Doesn't '77

Theo van de Sande(1947-)
Grown Ups '10
College Road Trip '08
Beauty Shop '05
Yours, Mine & Ours '05
Little Black Book '04
Out of Time '03
High Crimes '02
Double Take '01
Little Nicky '00
Big Daddy '99
Tuesdays with Morrie '99
Blade '98
Cruel Intentions '98
Volcano '97
Wayne's World '92
Body Parts '91
The First Power '89
Miracle Mile '89

Paul van den Bos
Diary of a Mad Old Man '88
A Flight of Rainbirds '81

Jules Van Den Steenhoven
The Gambler '97
Crimetime '96

Eddy van der Enden
Lie Down with Lions '94
Daughters of Darkness '71
Traffic '71

Charles Van Enger(1890-1980)
Sitting Bull '54
Bela Lugosi Meets a Brooklyn Gorilla '52
Abbott and Costello Meet the Killer, Boris Karloff '49
Abbott and Costello Meet Frankenstein '48
Buck Privates Come Home '47
It Ain't Hay '43
Night Monster '42
The Silver Bullet '42
Arizona Cyclone '41
Cracked Nuts '41
Man from Montana '41
Never Give a Sucker an Even Break '41
Half a Soldier '40
The Phantom of the Opera '25
The Marriage Circle '24
Seven Years Bad Luck '21
The Last of the Mohicans '20

Sean Van Hales
Love or Money '01
Different for Girls '96

Kees Van Oostrum(1953-)
The Last Word '08
A Perfect Day '06
Gods and Generals '03
Cupid & Cate '00
A House Divided '00
Drive Me Crazy '99
You Know My Name '99
William Faulkner's Old Man '97
Stephen King's Thinner '96
Degree of Guilt '95
Journey '95
Down Came a Blackbird '94
The Enemy Within '94
Gettysburg '93
Scott Turow's The Burden of Proof '92
Long Road Home '91

James Van Trees(1890-1973)
Angel on My Shoulder '46
A Night in Casablanca '46
Stingaree '34
Baby Face '33
Midnight Mary '33
Twinkletoes '26

Walther Vanden Ende(1947-)
Joyeux Noel '05
No Man's Land '01
A Dog of Flanders '99
Left Luggage '98
The Eighth Day '95
Farinelli '94
Toto le Heros '91

Gerard Vandenburg(1932-99)
Heimat 2 '92
Spring Symphony '86
The Vampire Happening '71

Checco Varese
Prom Night '08
Under the Same Moon '07
The Aura '05
A Separate Peace '04
Fidel '02
Night at the Golden Eagle '02

Henry Vargas
Tollbooth '94
Unlawful Passage '94

Mark Vargo
A Plumm Summer '08
Rest Stop '06
The Day the World Ended '01
Play It to the Bone '99

Carlo Varini
Badland '07
The Chorus '04
L'Eleve '95
The Big Blue '88
Subway '85
Le Dernier Combat '84

Jeff Venditti
Soccer Mom '08
Jam '06

Alex Vendler
The Hottie and the Nottie '08
Out at the Wedding '07
These Girls '05
Melvin Goes to Dinner '03
The Bible and Gun Club '96

Gordon Verheul
Ace of Hearts '08
Impulse '08
Heaven's Fire '99

Todd Verow(1966-)
Between Something & Nothing '08
Little Shots of Happiness '97

Rene Verzier
Eddie and the Cruisers 2: Eddie Lives! '89
Of Unknown Origin '83
Death Ship '80
Rabid '77
The Little Girl Who Lives down the Lane '76
By the Blood of Others '73

Jean-Louis Vialard
Inside Paris '06
Tropical Malady '04
The Sea '02

Mark Vicente
Slow Burn '00
Dish Dogs '98
Uncorked '98
Midnight Blue '96

Robin Vidgeon(1939-)
Lethal Dose '03
Pulse '03
Catherine Cookson's Tilly Trotter '99
Catherine Cookson's The Round Tower '98
August '95
The NeverEnding Story 3: Escape from Fantasia '94
Lady Chatterley '92
Mr. Corbett's Ghost '90
Nightbreed '90
The Fly 2 '89
Parents '89
Hellbound: Hellraiser 2 '88
Mr. North '88
Hellraiser '87

Ronald Vidor
Crossfire '98
Mortuary Academy '91

Sacha Vierny(1919-2001)
The Man Who Cried '00
8 1/2 Women '99
The Pillow Book '95
The Belly of an Architect '91
Prospero's Books '91
The Cook, the Thief, His Wife & Her Lover '90
A Zed & Two Noughts '88
Drowning by Numbers '87
The Future of Emily '85
Love Unto Death '84
The Draughtsman's Contract '82
Beau Pere '81
Mon Oncle d'Amerique '80
Stavisky '74
Belle de Jour '67
La Guerre Est Finie '66
Muriel '63
Last Year at Marienbad '61
Hiroshima, Mon Amour '59

Franco Villa
Hired to Kill '73
Hit Men '73
Jungle Master '72
Shoot the Living, Pray for the Dead '70

Reynaldo Villalobos(1940-)
One Long Night '07
Bordertown '06
Juwanna Mann '02
Not Another Teen Movie '01
Love and Basketball '00
Return to Paradise '98
An Alan Smithee Film: Burn, Hollywood, Burn '97
Hollywood Confidential '97
Loved '97
Romy and Michele's High School Reunion '97
Telling Lies in America '96
Roosters '95
A Bronx Tale '93
American Me '92
Sinatra '92
Major League '89
Punchline '88
Desert Bloom '86
Blame It on Rio '84
Ballad of Gregorio Cortez '83
Risky Business '83
Prime Suspect '82
9 to 5 '80
Urban Cowboy '80

Leopoldo Villasenor(1941-)
Hostages '80
The Werewolf vs. the Vampire Woman '70

Daniel Villeneuve
Infected '08
Decoys '04

Joseph Vilsmaier(1939-)
The Harmonists '99
Brother of Sleep '95
Stalingrad '94

Daniel Vincelette
Sticks and Stones '08
Swamp Devil '08
Black Swarm '07
Leaving Metropolis '02

Amy Vincent(1959-)
Black Snake Moan '07
This Film Is Not Yet Rated '06
Hustle & Flow '05
The Caveman's Valentine '01
Way Past Cool '00
Jawbreaker '98
Eve's Bayou '97

Ernest Vincze(1942-)
The Mystic Masseur '01
The Camomile Lawn '92
Business As Usual '88
A Very British Coup '88
A Woman of Substance '84
Kennedy '83
Tangiers '83

John Visconti
Junction 88 '47
Mistaken Identity '41

Paul Vogel(1899-1975)
Return of the Magnificent Seven '66
The Rounders '65
Village of the Giants '65
Drums of Africa '63
Mail Order Bride '63
The Wonderful World of the Brothers Grimm '62
The Time Machine '60
Wings of Eagles '57
High Society '56
Interrupted Melody '55
The Tender Trap '55
Rose Marie '54
The Student Prince '54
Clown '53
Angels in the Outfield '51
Go for Broke! '51
The Black Hand '50
The Happy Years '50
Battleground '49
Lady in the Lake '46
Wide Open Faces '38
Fit for a King '37

Ted Voightlander(1913-88)
Agatha Christie's A Caribbean Mystery '83
Agatha Christie's Sparkling Cyanide '83
Night of the Lepus '72

Peter von Haller(1961-)
Anatomy '00
The Inheritors '98

Wedigo von Schultzendorff
All the Queen's Men '02
Hollywood Ending '02
Igby Goes Down '02
The Hollywood Sign '01
The Thirteenth Floor '99
No Strings Attached '98

Wendigo von Schultzendorff
Pandorum '09
The Contractor '07

Nicholas Josef von Sternberg(1951-)
Killing Moon '00
Jungle Boy '96
American Cop '94
Body Shot '93
Out of Sight, Out of Her Mind '89
Final Justice '84
Tourist Trap '79
Kill Alex Kill '76
Dolemite '75

Mario Vulpiani
Castle Freak '95
The Bloodstained Shadow '78
Watch Me When I Kill '77
The Grand Duel '73
La Grande Bouffe '73
Dillinger Is Dead '69

Steven Wacks
Diplomatic Siege '99
Convict 762 '98
Terror at Tenkiller '86

Thaddeus Wadleigh(1964-)
Outrage '09
Who Killed the Electric Car? '06
Loco Love '03

William Wages
Supercross: The Movie '05
Fallen Angel '03
SuperFire '02
A Father's Choice '00
Down in the Delta '98
Buffalo Soldiers '97
Riders of the Purple Sage '96
Children of Fury '94
Love Potion #9 '92
A Thousand Heroes '92

Fritz Arno Wagner(1894-1958)
Kameradschaft '31
M '31
The Threepenny Opera '31
Diary of a Lost Girl '29
Warning Shadows '23
Nosferatu '22
Destiny '21

Roy Wagner
Streets of Blood '09
Bachelor Party 2: The Last Temptation '08
A Thief of Time '04
Coyote Waits '03
A Rumor of Angels '00
In the Company of Spies '99
The Pest '96
Nick of Time '95
Drop Zone '94
Another Stakeout '93
Mortuary Academy '91
Disaster at Silo 7 '88
A Nightmare on Elm Street 3: Dream Warriors '87
Return to Horror High '87
Witchboard '87

Sidney Wagner(1901-47)
The Postman Always Rings Twice '46
Bataan '43
Whistling in the Dark '41

Keith Wagstaff
The Gold & Glory '88
The Man from Snowy River '82

Ric Waite(1933-)
The Triangle '01
Ratz '99
Truth or Consequences, N.M. '97
Last Stand at Saber River '96
Andersonville '95
On Deadly Ground '94
Out for Justice '91
Marked for Death '90
The Great Outdoors '88
Adventures in Babysitting '87
Cobra '86
Brewster's Millions '85
Summer Rental '85
Volunteers '85
Red Dawn '84
Class '83
Tex '82
The Long Riders '80
The Day of the Wolves '71

Kent Wakeford
Last Lives '98
Loser '97
Power 98 '96
Wedding Bell Blues '96
Some Folks Call It a Sling Blade '94
The Ghost Brigade '93
Hold Me, Thrill Me, Kiss Me '93
China O'Brien '88
Alice Doesn't Live Here Anymore '74
Mean Streets '73

Ralph Waldo
Cain's Cutthroats '71
Wild Wheels '69

Brad Walker
The Deadbeat Club '04
American Nightmare '00

John Walker
A Winter Tan '88
The Body in the Library '84

Joseph Walker(1892-1985)
The Marrying Kind '52
Born Yesterday '50
Harriet Craig '50
It's a Wonderful Life '46
Roughly Speaking '45
She Wouldn't Say Yes '45
Mr. Winkle Goes to War '44
Together Again '43
My Sister Eileen '42
Tales of Manhattan '42
They All Kissed the Bride '42
Penny Serenade '41
His Girl Friday '40
Too Many Husbands '40
Only Angels Have Wings '39
Joy of Living '38
It Happened in Hollywood '37
Lost Horizon '37
Mr. Deeds Goes to Town '36
Theodora Goes Wild '36
It Happened One Night '34

Lady for a Day '33
American Madness '32
The Miracle Woman '31
The Fighting Stallion '26

Mandy Walker(1963-)
Beastly '10
Australia '08
Shattered Glass '03
Lantana '01
The Well '97
Love Serenade '96

Enrique Wallace
Doctor of Doom '62
The Robot vs. the Aztec Mummy '59

Chris Walling
Sol Goode '01
Blue Ridge Fall '99
Thick as Thieves '99
Wicked Ways '99
Crosswords '96
Solo '96

David M. Walsh
Carpool '96
Taking Care of Business '90
Fatal Beauty '87
Outrageous Fortune '87
Summer School '87
My Science Project '85
Romantic Comedy '83
Private Benjamin '80
Seems Like Old Times '80
California Suite '78
Foul Play '78
Rollercoaster '77
Murder by Death '76
My Father's House '75
Cleopatra Jones '73
Sleeper '73
Evel Knievel '72
Everything You Always Wanted to Know about Sex (But Were Afraid to Ask) '72
I Walk the Line '70

Yu Wang
Lost in Beijing '07
Purple Butterfly '03

John Ward
Love, Honour & Obey '00
Final Cut '98
Heaven's a Drag '94

Mark Wareham
Introducing the Dwights '07
Murder in Greenwich '02
Dr. Jekyll & Mr. Hyde '99
First Daughter '99

John F. Warren(1909-2000)
Torn Curtain '66
The Cosmic Man '59
The Daughter of Dr. Jekyll '57
Zero Hour! '57

Gilbert Warrenton(1894-1980)
Operation Bikini '63
Panic in the Year Zero! '62
Atomic Submarine '59
The Ghost of Dragstrip Hollow '59
Massacre '56
Sins of Jezebel '54
Mesa of Lost Women '52
Great Dan Patch '49
Here Comes Cookie '35
Sunset Range '35
Ticket to a Crime '34
The Love Trap '29
The Cat and the Canary '27
The Plastic Age '25
Little Old New York '23

Norman Warwick(1920-94)
The Final Programme '73
The Creeping Flesh '72
The Abominable Dr. Phibes '71
Dr. Jekyll and Sister Hyde '71

John Waters(1946-)
Female Trouble '74
Pink Flamingos '72
Multiple Maniacs '70
Mondo Trasho '69

Philip Alan Waters
Urban Menace '99
Cyborg '89

David Watkin(1925-2008)
Lover's Prayer '99
Tea with Mussolini '99
Gloria '98
Critical Care '97
Obsession '97
Bogus '96
Jane Eyre '96
Night Falls on Manhattan '96
This Boy's Life '93
The Object of Beauty '91
Hamlet '90
Memphis Belle '90
The Good Mother '88
Last Rites '88
Masquerade '88
Moonstruck '87
Out of Africa '85
Return to Oz '85
White Nights '85
The Hotel New Hampshire '84
Yentl '83
Chariots of Fire '81
Endless Love '81
Cuba '79
Hanover Street '79
Joseph Andrews '77
Robin and Marian '76
To the Devil, a Daughter '76
The Four Musketeers '75
Mahogany '75
The Three Musketeers '74
The Boy Friend '71
The Devils '71
Catch-22 '70
The Charge of the Light Brigade '68
How I Won the War '67
Mademoiselle '66
Help! '65
The Knack '65

Michael Watkins
Heart and Souls '93
Point of No Return '93

Harry Waxman(1912-84)
Find the Lady '76
The Pink Panther Strikes Again '76
The Wicker Man '75
Vampyres '74
Not Tonight Darling '72
What the Peeper Saw '72
Endless Night '71
Wonderwall: The Movie '69
The Trygon Factor '66
She '65
The Day the Earth Caught Fire '61
The Swiss Family Robinson '60
Meet Mr. Callaghan '54
The Gift Horse '52

Henry Waxman(1939-)
The Anniversary '68
The Nanny '65

Jesse Weathington
Tracks '05
Invisible Mom 2 '99
Interlocked '98
Mom, Can I Keep Her? '98

Michael Weaver(1971-)
The Clique '08
The Sender '98

George Webber
Sepia Cinderella '47
Murder on Lenox Avenue '41

Samuel Weil
See Lloyd Kaufman

Yossi Wein
Bridge of Dragons '99
Sweepers '99

Operation: Delta Force '97
Danger Zone '95
Cyborg Cop '93
Lethal Ninja '93
Point of Impact '93
The House of Usher '88
Soldier of the Night '84

Jan Weincke(1945-)
Inside '96
Twist & Shout '84

Ben Weinstein
Conspiracy '08
Wet Hot American Summer '01
Let It Snow '99

Charles S. Welbourne(1907-79)
The Three Stooges Meet Hercules '61
Revenge of the Creature '55
Creature from the Black Lagoon '54

James Welland(1961-)
The Hound of the Baskervilles '02
The Last Minute '01
Beautiful Creatures '00

Harold E. Wellman(1905-92)
Muscle Beach Party '64
Atlantis, the Lost Continent '61
The Invisible Boy '57

Philippe Welt
Le Bonheur Est Dans le Pre '95
Madame Butterfly '95

Harold Wenstrom
The Lost Patrol '34
The Saphead '21

Egon Werdin(1954-)
An American Werewolf in Paris '97
Mute Witness '95

Byron Werner
Death Valley: The Revenge of Bloody Bill '04
Starkweather '04
Sam & Janet '02

Brian West(1928-)
Ellen Foster '97
Treacherous Crossing '92
The Dying Truth '86
84 Charing Cross Road '86
Agatha Christie's Murder with Mirrors '85
Bloodbath at the House of Death '85
The Lonely Lady '83
Billy Two Hats '74

David West
Incognito '99
Winner Takes All '98

Frederick E. West(1903-84)
Terror in the Haunted House '58
Invasion of the Saucer Men '57
The Gunslinger '56
It Conquered the World '56
I Beheld His Glory '53

Ken Westbury
Jack Higgins' Midnight Man '96
Jack Higgins' On Dangerous Ground '95
Catherine Cookson's The Black Velvet Gown '92
Magic Moments '89
Bellman and True '88

Tony Westman
Cow Belles '06
The Muppets' Wizard of Oz '05
Call of the Wild '04
Halloweentown 2: Kalabar's Revenge '01

Off Season '01
The Last Stop '99
Alaska '96
Needful Things '93
The Deserters '83

Haskell Wexler(1926-)
Silver City '04
61* '01
Limbo '99
The Rich Man's Wife '96
Mulholland Falls '95
Canadian Bacon '94
The Secret of Roan Inish '94
The Babe '92
Other People's Money '91
Blaze '89
Three Fugitives '89
Colors '88
Matewan '87
The Man Who Loved Women '83
Coming Home '78
Bound for Glory '76
One Flew Over the Cuckoo's Nest '75
Gimme Shelter '70
Medium Cool '69
The Thomas Crown Affair '68
In the Heat of the Night '67
Who's Afraid of Virginia Woolf? '66
The Loved One '65
The Best Man '64
A Face in the Rain '63
Angel Baby '61
The Hoodlum Priest '61
Studs Lonigan '60

Howard Wexler
Coffee Date '06
Hope Ranch '02
Newsbreak '00
The Modern Adventures of Tom Sawyer '99
Curse of the Puppet Master: The Human Experiment '98
Leather Jacket Love Story '98
Return to Savage Beach '97
Prey of the Jaguar '96
Attack of the 60-Foot Centerfold '95
Over the Wire '95
Die Watching '93
Picasso Trigger '89
Hard Ticket to Hawaii '87
Banzai Runner '86
Reform School Girls '86

Charles F. Wheeler(1915-2004)
The Best of Times '86
Condorman '81
The Last Flight of Noah's Ark '80
The Cat from Outer Space '78
Truck Turner '74
Slaughter's Big Ripoff '73
Silent Running '71
C.C. & Company '70
Tora! Tora! Tora! '70
Yours, Mine & Ours '68

Des Whelan
How About You '07
This Is the Sea '96

James Whitaker
Crossing Over '09
King of California '07
Running Scared '06
Thank You for Smoking '06
The Cooler '03
The Book of Stars '99
Let the Devil Wear Black '99

Joseph White(1978-)
Repo! The Genetic Opera '08
Shelter '07

Lester White(1907-58)
The Monster That Challenged the World '57
5 Against the House '55
Pushover '54
Gasoline Alley '51

Guns of Fury '49
Whistling in Brooklyn '43
Sherlock Holmes and the Secret Weapon '42
Beyond Tomorrow '40

William F. Whitley
Queen of Outer Space '58
Cat Women of the Moon '53

Lisa Wiegand
Bob Funk '09
Eating Out 2: Sloppy Seconds '06
Little Athens '05
Fish in a Barrel '01
Outta Time '01
Eastside '99

Derek Wiesehahn
The Reception '05
Hell's Kitchen NYC '97

Joseph M. Wilcots(1939-)
Where the Red Fern Grows: Part 2 '92
Video Murders '87
Mountaintop Motel Massacre '86
Roots: The Next Generation '79
Roots '77

John Wilcox(1905-79)
The Legend of the 7 Golden Vampires '73
Au Pair Girls '72
The Last Valley '71
The Chairman '69
The Skull '65
The Evil of Frankenstein '64
Nightmare '63
Waltz of the Toreadors '62
Expresso Bongo '59
Carve Her Name with Pride '58

Harry Wild(1900-61)
The Conqueror '56
Gentlemen Prefer Blondes '53
Son of Paleface '52
His Kind of Woman '51
Big Steal '49
Pitfall '48
Tycoon '47
Nocturne '46
Murder, My Sweet '44
So This Is Washington '43
Stage Door Canteen '43
Legion of the Lawless '40

Donald Wilder
Spring Fever '81
Meatballs '79

Jo Willems
Confessions of a Shopaholic '09
Rocket Science '07
30 Days of Night '07
Hard Candy '06
London '05

Billy Williams(1929-)
The Rainbow '89
Stella '89
Suspect '87
The Manhattan Project '86
Dreamchild '85
Eleni '85
Ordeal by Innocence '84
Survivors '83
Gandhi '82
Monsignor '82
On Golden Pond '81
Saturn 3 '80
Eagle's Wing '79
The Silent Partner '78
Voyage of the Damned '76
The Wind and the Lion '75
The Exorcist '73
Night Watch '72
X, Y & Zee '72
Sunday, Bloody Sunday '71
Women in Love '70
Billion Dollar Brain '67

Frank D. Williams
The Dragon Painter '19

Tillie's Punctured Romance '14

Mahlon Todd Williams
Ba'al: The Storm God '08
Sea Beast '08

Matthew Williams
The American Mall '08
Boxboarders! '07
Saving Sarah Cain '07

Gordon Willis(1931-)
The Devil's Own '96
Malice '93
The Godfather, Part 3 '90
Presumed Innocent '90
Bright Lights, Big City '88
The Pick-Up Artist '87
The Money Pit '86
Perfect '85
The Purple Rose of Cairo '85
Broadway Danny Rose '84
Zelig '83
A Midsummer Night's Sex Comedy '82
Pennies from Heaven '81
Stardust Memories '80
Windows '80
Manhattan '79
Comes a Horseman '78
Interiors '78
Annie Hall '77
All the President's Men '76
The Drowning Pool '75
The Godfather, Part 2 '74
The Parallax View '74
The Paper Chase '73
Bad Company '72
The Godfather '72
Up the Sandbox '72
Klute '71
Little Murders '71
End of the Road '70
Loving '70

Mark Willis
One Way '06
Tiger Claws '91

Jack Willoughby
Bog '84
The Giant Spider Invasion '75

Nigel Willoughby
The Last Enemy '08
The History of Mr. Polly '07
The Magdalene Sisters '02

Willy
Le Schpountz '38
Harvest '37
The Chess Player '27

Barry M. Wilson
Nanny Insanity '06
The Substitute 3: Winner Takes All '99

Ian Wilson(1939-)
Niagara Motel '06
A Way of Life '04
I'll Be There '03
Below '02
Back to the Secret Garden '01
A Christmas Carol '99
Savior '98
Swing '98
The Island on Bird Street '97
Emma '96
A Midsummer Night's Dream '96
Backbeat '94
Doomsday Gun '94
The Secret Rapture '94
The Crying Game '92
Erik the Viking '89
Wish You Were Here '87
The Flame Trees of Thika '81
Captain Kronos: Vampire Hunter '74
Fright '71
And Soon the Darkness '70

James Wilson
The Gay Dog '54
Old Mother Riley's Jungle Treasure '51

Old Mother Riley's New Venture '49
Echo Murders '45
The Dummy Talks '43
Salute John Citizen '42
The Living Dead '33

Nathan Wilson
The Keeper '09
Alone With Her '07

Richard Wincenty
Bugs '03
Webs '03

Andreas Winding(1928-77)
A Slightly Pregnant Man '79
La Scoumoune '72
Ramparts of Clay '68

Romain Winding(1951-)
Seventh Heaven '98
Sweet Revenge '98

Stephen Windon(1959-)
The Fast and the Furious: Tokyo Drift '06
House of Wax '05
Anacondas: The Hunt for the Blood Orchid '04
The Tuxedo '02
The Diamond of Jeru '01
Rodgers & Hammerstein's South Pacific '01
Deep Blue Sea '99
The Patriot '99
Firestorm '97
The Postman '97
Hotel de Love '96
Country Life '95
In Pursuit of Honor '95

Zack Winestine
The Rook '99
Strawberry Fields '97
The Next Step '95

Glen Winter
MVP (Most Valuable Primate) '00
Horsey '99
Premonition '98

Peter Woeste
Stargate: Continuum '08
Stargate: The Ark of Truth '08
Video Voyeur: The Susan Wilson Story '02
Escape from Mars '99
Snowbound: The Jim and Jennifer Stolpa Story '94
Mortal Sins '92

Michael G. Wojciechowski
American East '07
Only the Brave '06
I Witness '03
Greenmail '01
Angel's Dance '99
Black Thunder '98
Candyman 3: Day of the Dead '98
Levitation '97
The Killing Jar '96
Bloodfist 5: Human Target '93

Jerzy Wojcik(1930-)
The Deluge '73
Pharaoh '66
Ashes and Diamonds '58

Ben Wolf
Virgin '03
The Young Girl and the Monsoon '99

Darius Wolski(1956-)
Alice in Wonderland '10
Pirates of the Caribbean: At World's End '07
Sweeney Todd: The Demon Barber of Fleet Street '07
Pirates of the Caribbean: Dead Man's Chest '06
Hide and Seek '05
Pirates of the Caribbean: The Curse of the Black Pearl '03
Bad Company '02
The Mexican '01
A Perfect Murder '98
Dark City '97
The Fan '96
Crimson Tide '95
The Crow '93
Romeo Is Bleeding '93
Nightfall '88

Arthur Wong
Warlords '08
The 36th Chamber of Shaolin '78

Bill Wong
Caracara '00
Invasion! '99
Blackjack '97
Once a Thief '96
Dream Lovers '86
Zu: Warriors from the Magic Mountain '83

Wing-Hung Wong
Black Mask 2: City of Masks '02
The Accidental Spy '01
Organized Crime & Triad Bureau '93
Twin Dragons '92
A Bullet in the Head '90
The Killer '90
A Better Tomorrow, Part 1 '86

Arthur Wong Ngok Tai
Ultraviolet '06
The Medallion '03
Double Vision '02
Gen-X Cops '99
Knock Off '98
Erotique '94
Crime Story '93
Iron Monkey '93
Once Upon a Time in China '91
Heart of Dragon '85

Graeme Wood
Subterano '01
The Dish '00

Oliver Wood
The Other Guys '10
Surrogates '09
Step Brothers '08
The Bourne Ultimatum '07
Talladega Nights: The Ballad of Ricky Bobby '06
Fantastic Four '05
The Bourne Supremacy '04
Scooby-Doo 2: Monsters Unleashed '04
Freaky Friday '03
National Security '03
The Adventures of Pluto Nash '02
The Bourne Identity '02
I Spy '02
U-571 '00
Mighty Joe Young '98
Face/Off '97
Switchback '97
Celtic Pride '96
Two Days in the Valley '96
Mr. Holland's Opus '95
Terminal Velocity '94
Rudy '93
Sister Act 2: Back in the Habit '93
Bill & Ted's Bogus Journey '91
Die Hard 2: Die Harder '90
Nasty Hero '89
Joey '85
Don't Go in the House '80
Honeymoon Killers '70

Ralph Woolsey
The Great Santini '80
The Iceman Cometh '73

Bruce Worrall
Deathlands: Homeward Bound '03
Innocents '00
Ronnie and Julie '97
The Heist '96
Profile for Murder '96
Circumstances Unknown '95
Tracks of a Killer '95
Hard Evidence '94

David Worth
Shark Attack 3: Megalodon '02
The Prophet's Game '99
True Vengeance '97
Lady Dragon 2 '93
Lady Dragon '92
Any Which Way You Can '80
Bronco Billy '80

Lothrop Worth(1903-2000)
Billy the Kid Versus Dracula '66
Jesse James Meets Frankenstein's Daughter '65

Walter Wottitz(1911-86)
The Last Train '74
Action Man '67
The Train '65
The Longest Day '62

James W. Wrenn
Backwoods '08
Lone Rider '08
The Pledge '08
Hidden Places '06
The Family Plan '05
The Reading Room '05
Audrey's Rain '03
Love Comes Softly '03
A Time to Remember '03
Dakota '88

Dewey Wrigley
Wings in the Dark '35
Hell's Angels '30

Peter Wunstorf(1959-)
Hollow Man 2 '06
Long Life, Happiness and Prosperity '02
Total Recall 2070: Machine Dreams '99
Invasion of Privacy '96
Double Happiness '94
Heartstrings '93
Tomcat: Dangerous Desires '93

Alvin Wyckoff(1877-1957)
Blood and Sand '22
Affairs of Anatol '21
Male and Female '19
The Little American '17

Reg Wyer(1901-70)
Burn Witch, Burn! '62
Masters of Venus '62
Dentist In the Chair '60
Four Sided Triangle '53
Spaceways '53
Home to Danger '51
Trio '50
The Upturned Glass '47

Manny Wynn(1928-75)
Smashing Time '67
Girl with Green Eyes '64

Steve Yaconelli(1941-2003)
The Temp '93
Blue Sky '91
The Phantom of the Opera '90
The Karate Kid: Part 3 '89

Kazuo Yamada
Samurai Banners '69
Son of Godzilla '66
What's Up, Tiger Lily? '66
I Bombed Pearl Harbor '60
Samurai 3: Duel at Ganryu Island '56

Hideo Yamamoto(1960-)
Big Man Japan '07
Hula Girls '06
The Great Yokai War '05
The Grudge '04
One Missed Call '03
Graveyard of Honor '02
The Happiness of the Katakuris '01
Ichi the Killer '01
Visitor Q '01
Andromedia '00
Audition '99
Ringu 2 '99
Fireworks '97
Fudoh: The New Generation '96
The Way To Fight '96

Yoshikazu Yamasawa
The Green Slime '68
Snake Woman's Curse '68

Kazuo Yamazaki
The Hidden Fortress '58
The Lower Depths '57

Yutaka Yamazaki
Nobody Knows '04
After Life '98

Hiro'o Yanagida
Flower & Snake 2 '05
Flower & Snake '04

Katsumi Yanagijima
Shutter '08
The Grudge 2 '06
Zatoichi '03
Dolls '02

Katsumi Yanagishima
Brother '00
Kikujiro '99
Sonatine '96
Boiling Point '90

Jun Yasumoto
Samurai 1: Musashi Miyamoto '55
Samurai 2: Duel at Ichijoji Temple '55

Herman Yau(1961-)
Tsui Hark's Vampire Hunters '02
Zu Warriors '01
Time and Tide '00

Steve Yedlin
American Violet '09
The Brothers Bloom '09
The Dead One '07
Lovely by Surprise '07
Brick '06
Conversations with Other Women '05
Dead Birds '04
May '02

Alexander Yellen
Mega Shark Vs. Giant Octopus '09
I Am Omega '07

Robert Yeoman(1951-)
Whip It '09
Yes Man '08
The Darjeeling Limited '07
Martian Child '07
Red Eye '05
The Squid and the Whale '05
The Life Aquatic with Steve Zissou '04
CQ '01
Double Whammy '01
The Royal Tenenbaums '01
Beautiful '00
Down to You '00
Dogma '99
The Pentagon Wars '98
Permanent Midnight '98
Rushmore '98
Dogwatch '97
The Substance of Fire '96
Bottle Rocket '95
Coldblooded '94
The Linguini Incident '92
Drugstore Cowboy '89
Dead Heat '88

Pyotr Yermolov
My Universities '40
My Apprenticeship '39
My Childhood '38

William Yim
Black Mask 2: City of Masks '02
Zu Warriors '01
Naked Killer '92

Hou Yong
The Road Home '01
Happy Times '00
Not One Less '99
The Day the Sun Turned Cold '94
The Horse Thief '87

Frederick A. (Freddie) Young(1902-98)
Sword of the Valiant '83
Richard's Things '80
Rough Cut '80
Sidney Sheldon's Bloodline '79
Stevie '78
Permission To Kill '75
Luther '74
The Tamarind Seed '74
The Asphyx '72
Nicholas and Alexandra '71
Ryan's Daughter '70
Battle of Britain '69
You Only Live Twice '67
Doctor Zhivago '65
Lord Jim '65
The Seventh Dawn '64
Lawrence of Arabia '62
Gorgo '61
Solomon and Sheba '59
Indiscreet '58
The Inn of the Sixth Happiness '58
Island in the Sun '57
Bhowani Junction '56
Betrayed '54
Knights of the Round Table '53
Ivanhoe '52
Treasure Island '50
Conspirator '49
The Winslow Boy '48
While I Live '47
Bedelia '46
Contraband '40
Goodbye, Mr. Chips '39
When Knights Were Bold '36
The Speckled Band '31

Robert M. Young(1924-)
The Plot Against Harry '69
Nothing but a Man '64

Lu Yue
Red Cliff '08
Xiu Xiu: The Sent Down Girl '97
Shanghai Triad '95
To Live '94

Vadim Yusov(1929-)
Anna '93
Solaris '72
Andrei Rublev '66

Fabio Zamarion
The Unknown Woman '06
Respiro '02

Haris Zambarloukos
Mamma Mia! '08
The Other Man '08
Death Defying Acts '07
Sleuth '07
Venus '06
Enduring Love '04

Wieslaw Zdort
The Decalogue '88
Without Love '80

Peter Zeitlinger(1960-)
Bad Lieutenant: Port of Call New Orleans '09
Encounters at the End of the World '07
Grizzly Man '05
Invincible '01

Massimo Zeri
Strike '07
Bottoms Up '06
National Lampoon Presents Cattle Call '06
Beretta's Island '92

Li Zhang
Red Cliff '08
Big Shot's Funeral '01

Fei Zhao(1961-)
Warriors of Heaven and Earth '03
The Curse of the Jade Scorpion '01
Small Time Crooks '00
The Emperor and the Assassin '99
Sweet and Lowdown '99
The Horse Thief '87

Xiaoding Zhao
The Children of Huang Shi '08
Curse of the Golden Flower '06
Riding Alone for Thousands of Miles '05
House of Flying Daggers '04

Yuri Zhelyabuzhsky
Aelita: Queen of Mars '24
The Cigarette Girl of Mosselprom '24

Howard Ziehm(1940-)
Cop Killers '73
Flesh Gordon '72

Jerzy Zielinski(1961-)
The Courageous Heart of Irena Sendler '09
The Lazarus Project '08
Fun With Dick and Jane '05
Dodgeball: A True Underdog Story '04
The SpongeBob SquarePants Movie '04
The Lizzie McGuire Movie '03
Who is Cletis Tout? '02
Bubble Boy '01
Galaxy Quest '99
Teaching Mrs. Tingle '99
The Third Miracle '99
Home Fries '98
Washington Square '97
That Darn Cat '96
Powder '95
Houseguest '94
Swing Kids '93
The January Man '89

Bernard Zitzermann
The Blood Oranges '97
Angels and Insects '95
La Ceremonie '95
L'Enfer '93
The Music of Chance '93
The Favor, the Watch, & the Very Big Fish '92
November Moon '85
I Married a Dead Man '82

Vilmos Zsigmond(1930-)
Cassandra's Dream '07
The Black Dahlia '06
Melinda and Melinda '05
Jersey Girl '04
The Body '01
Life as a House '01
Mists of Avalon '01
Playing by Heart '98
The Ghost and the Darkness '96
Assassins '95
The Crossing Guard '94
Maverick '94
Intersection '93
Sliver '93
Stalin '92
The Bonfire of the Vanities '90
The Two Jakes '90
The Witches of Eastwick '87
The River '84
Blow Out '81
Heaven's Gate '81
The Rose '79
Winter Kills '79
The Deer Hunter '78
Close Encounters of the Third Kind '77
Obsession '76
The Sugarland Express '74
Cinderella Liberty '73
The Long Goodbye '73
Scarecrow '73
Blood of Ghastly Horror '72
Deliverance '72

Composer Index

The Composer Index provides a videography for any composer, arranger, lyricist, or band that has provided an original music score for more than one film now on video. The listings for the composer names follow an alphabetical sort by last name (although the names appear in a first name, last name format). The videographies are listed chronologically, from most recent film to the first. If a composer provided music for more than one film in the same year, these movies are listed alphabetically within the year.

Temple Abady
Kill Me Tomorrow *'57*
Love in Pawn *'53*

Barron Abramovitch
Profile for Murder *'96*
Tracks of a Killer *'95*
Hard Evidence *'94*

Anton Abril(1933-)
Return of the Evil Dead *'75*
Terror Beach *'75*
Pancho Villa *'72*
Tombs of the Blind Dead *'72*
The Werewolf vs. the Vampire Woman *'70*

Andre Abujarrura
Innocent Voices *'04*
Carandiru *'03*

Neal Acree(1974-)
Juncture *'07*
Cerberus *'05*
They Crawl *'01*
Venomous *'01*
Ablaze *'00*
Critical Mass *'00*
Militia *'99*

Bryan Adams(1959-)
Color Me Kubrick *'05*
Spirit: Stallion of the Cimarron *'02*

Tree Adams
Keith *'08*
The Bronx Is Burning *'07*
Wasted *'06*
Poor White Trash *'00*
No Money Down *'97*

Barry Adamson(1958-)
Gas Food Lodging *'92*
Delusion *'91*

Ishai Adar
Beaufort *'07*
Year Zero *'04*

Richard Addinsell(1904-77)
Waltz of the Toreadors *'62*
A Christmas Carol *'51*
The Black Rose *'50*
Blithe Spirit *'45*
Dangerous Moonlight *'41*
Gaslight *'40*
Fire Over England *'37*
South Riding *'37*

John Addison(1920-98)
The Phantom of the Opera *'90*
Something in Common *'86*
Agatha Christie's Thirteen at Dinner *'85*
Code Name: Emerald *'85*
Grace Quigley *'84*
Strange Invaders *'83*
Eleanor: First Lady of the World *'82*
Love's Savage Fury *'79*
The Bastard *'78*
Pearl *'78*
A Bridge Too Far *'77*
Joseph Andrews *'77*
The Seven-Per-Cent Solution *'76*
Swashbuckler *'76*
Ride a Wild Pony *'75*
Luther *'74*
Sleuth *'72*
Cry of the Penguins *'71*
Start the Revolution without Me *'70*
The Charge of the Light Brigade *'68*
The Honey Pot *'67*
Smashing Time *'67*
A Fine Madness *'66*
Torn Curtain *'66*
The Amorous Adventures of Moll Flanders *'65*
The Loved One *'65*
Girl with Green Eyes *'64*
Guns at Batasi *'64*
Tom Jones *'63*
The Loneliness of the Long Distance Runner *'62*
A Taste of Honey *'61*
The Entertainer *'60*
School for Scoundrels *'60*
Carlton Browne of the F.O. *'59*
Look Back in Anger *'58*
Lucky Jim *'58*
Reach for the Sky *'56*
Three Men in a Boat *'56*
Seven Days to Noon *'50*

Brian Adler
Ordinary Sinner *'02*
Hostage High *'97*

Larry Adler(1914-2001)
King and Country *'64*
A Cry from the Streets *'57*
Genevieve *'53*

Mark Adler
Bottle Shock *'08*
Food, Inc. *'08*
Nobel Son *'08*
The Far Side of Jericho *'06*
Fatal Contact: Bird Flu in America *'06*
Marilyn Hotchkiss' Ballroom Dancing & Charm School *'06*
Life of the Party *'05*
When Do We Eat? *'05*
Leo *'02*
Focus *'01*
Cupid & Cate *'00*
Flowers for Algernon *'00*
Apartment Complex *'98*
The Rat Pack *'98*
Ernest in the Army *'97*
Decoy *'95*
Slam Dunk Ernest *'95*
Henry & June *'90*
Eat a Bowl of Tea *'89*
Break of Dawn *'88*
The Unbearable Lightness of Being *'88*
Heat and Sunlight *'87*

Chris Ainscough
The Foursome *'06*
Moving Malcolm *'03*

Yashushi Akutagawa(1925-89)
An Actor's Revenge *'63*
Fires on the Plain *'59*
Gate of Hell *'54*

Kays Al-Atrakchi
The Objective *'08*
Believers *'07*

Damon Albarn(1968-)
101 Reykjavik *'00*
Ordinary Decent Criminal *'99*
Ravenous *'99*

Robert Alcivar
Blind Witness *'89*
Naked Lie *'89*
Hysterical *'83*
One from the Heart *'82*
Olly Olly Oxen Free *'78*
Butterflies Are Free *'72*

Edesio Alejandro
Cuban Blood *'03*
Hello, Hemingway *'90*

Jeff Alexander(1910-89)
Clambake *'67*
The George Raft Story *'61*
The Sheepman *'58*
Gun Glory *'57*
Jailhouse Rock *'57*
Westward the Women *'51*

Van Alexander(1915-)
Strait-Jacket *'64*
Platinum High School *'60*
Girls' Town *'59*
Jaguar *'56*
When Gangland Strikes *'56*
The Atomic Kid *'54*

Hossein Alizadeh(1951-)
Turtles Can Fly *'04*
Gabbeh *'96*

Eric Allaman
The Note 2: Taking a Chance on Love *'09*
Witless Protection *'08*
The Note *'07*
Latter Days *'04*
Elvira's Haunted Hills *'02*
One Kill *'00*
Luminarias *'99*
True Heart *'97*
Midnight Blue *'96*
Down Twisted *'89*
Angel 3: The Final Chapter *'88*

Cameron Allan
The Nutt House *'95*
Jericho Fever *'93*
JFK: Reckless Youth *'93*
The Good Wife *'86*
Midnite Spares *'85*

Billy Allen
See William Allen Castleman

Peter Allen(1944-92)
On the Other Hand, Death *'08*
Kiss Me Goodbye *'82*
Arthur *'81*

Peter Allen(1952-)
Ruslan *'09*
Art of War 2: The Betrayal *'08*
Christmas Town *'08*
A Dennis the Menace Christmas *'07*
Shock to the System *'06*
Too Cool for Christmas *'04*
Ripper: Letter from Hell *'01*
Crackerjack 3 *'00*
Escape from Mars *'99*
Escape Velocity *'99*
The Silencer *'99*
Chained Heat 3: Hell Mountain *'98*
Dead Fire *'98*
Crackerjack 2 *'97*
Act of War *'96*
Dangerous Prey *'95*
Crackerjack *'94*
Cyborg 2 *'93*

John Altman(1949-)
The Queen's Sister *'05*
The Reagans *'04*
Shall We Dance? *'04*
The Roman Spring of Mrs. Stone *'03*
Fidel *'02*
King of Texas *'02*
Mr. St. Nick *'02*
The Lost Empire *'01*
Boss of Bosses *'99*
RKO 281 *'99*
Vendetta *'99*
Legionnaire *'98*
Little Voice *'98*
Tracked *'98*
The Garden of Redemption *'97*
The Matchmaker *'97*
Pronto *'97*
A Royal Scandal *'96*
Bhaji on the Beach *'94*
Funny Bones *'94*
Bad Behavior *'92*
Devlin *'92*
Hear My Song *'91*

Joseph (Joey) Altruda
Comic Book Villains *'02*
Slackers *'02*
Slaves of Hollywood *'99*
Shake, Rattle & Rock! *'94*

Elik Alvarez
The Proud Family Movie *'05*
Yu-Gi-Oh! The Movie: Pyramid of Light *'04*

William Alwyn(1905-85)
The Swiss Family Robinson *'60*

Carve Her Name with Pride '58
Geordie '55
I'll Never Forget You '51
Madeleine '50
The Magnet '50
Captain Boycott '47
Odd Man Out '47
Immortal Battalion '44
On Approval '44

Armand Amar(1953-)
Blame It on Fidel '06
Days of Glory '06
Amen '02

Alejandro Amenabar(1972-)
The Sea Inside '04
The Others '01
Butterfly '98
Open Your Eyes '97
Thesis '96

Daniele Amfitheatrof(1901-83)
Heller in Pink Tights '60
The Last Hunt '56
Storm Warning '51
The Damned Don't Cry '50
You Gotta Stay Happy '48
Singapore '47
O.S.S. '46
The Virginian '46
I'll Be Seeing You '44

David Amram(1930-)
The Arrangement '69
The Manchurian Candidate '62
Splendor in the Grass '61
The Young Savages '61

Chris Anderson
Trapped '06
The Box '03
Treasure Island '99

Lars Anderson
Hellraiser: Hellworld '05
Rancid '04
Deranged '01

Laurie Anderson(1947-)
Monster in a Box '92
Swimming to Cambodia '87
Something Wild '86

Michael Andrews
Cyrus '10
She's Out of My League '10
Funny People '09
Walk Hard: The Dewey Cox Story '07
Paris, je t'aime '06
The TV Set '06
Unaccompanied Minors '06
Me and You and Everyone We Know '05
Cypher '02
Orange County '02
Donnie Darko '01
Out Cold '01

Gerard Anfosso
Blue Country '77
Cousin, Cousine '76

George Antheil(1900-59)
The Pride and the Passion '57
Daughter of Horror '55
Actors and Sin '52
The Sniper '52
Make Way for Tomorrow '37

Pete Anthony
Love Songs '99
Run for the Dream: The Gail Devers Story '96

Paul Antonelli
China O'Brien '88
Out of the Dark '88
Princess Academy '87
Women's Club '87
Avenging Angel '85

Mar Degli Antoni
Roman Polanski: Wanted and Desired '08
Marie and Bruce '04

Louis Applebaum(1918-2000)
The Mask '61
Lost Boundaries '49
The Story of G.I. Joe '45

Philip Appleby
The Wyvern Mystery '00
Butterfly Collectors '99
Nothing Personal '95
Maria's Child '93

Tito Arevalo(1911-2000)
Mad Doctor of Blood Island '68
The Ravagers '65
The Walls of Hell '64
Raiders of Leyte Gulf '63

Dario Argento(1940-)
Dawn of the Dead '78
Suspiria '77

Steven Argila
The Thing About My Folks '05
Memron '04

Eddie Arkin
Pretty Smart '87
Hardbodies 2 '86
Modern Girls '86

Harold Arlen(1905-86)
Gay Purr-ee '62
A Star Is Born '54
The Farmer Takes a Wife '53
Cabin in the Sky '43
At the Circus '39
Gold Diggers of 1937 '36
Strike Me Pink '36

Martin Armiger
Introducing the Dwights '07
Marking Time '03
The Wedding Party '97
The Crossing '92
Sweetie '89
Young Einstein '89
Two Friends '86

Craig Armstrong(1959-)
Clash of the Titans '10
The Incredible Hulk '08
Elizabeth: The Golden Age '07
World Trade Center '06
Fever Pitch '05
Must Love Dogs '05
The Clearing '04
Ray '04
Love Actually '03
The Magdalene Sisters '02
The Quiet American '02
Kiss of the Dragon '01
Moulin Rouge '01
Best Laid Plans '99
The Bone Collector '99
Plunkett & Macleane '98
Orphans '97

Stefano Arnaldi
How Harry Became a Tree '01
Tea with Mussolini '99

David Arnold(1962-)
Morning Glory '10
How to Lose Friends & Alienate People '08
Quantum of Solace '08
Hot Fuzz '07
Amazing Grace '06
Casino Royale '06
Venus '06
Stoned '05
The Stepford Wives '04
2 Fast 2 Furious '03
Changing Lanes '02
Die Another Day '02
Enough '02
Baby Boy '01
The Musketeer '01
Zoolander '01
Shaft '00
The World Is Not Enough '99
Godzilla '98
A Life Less Ordinary '97
Tomorrow Never Dies '97
Independence Day '96
The Last of the Dogmen '95
Stargate '94
The Young Americans '93

Harry Arnold
Invasion of the Animal People '62
48 Hours to Live '60

Malcolm Arnold(1921-2006)
David Copperfield '70
Battle of Britain '69
Africa Texas Style '67
The Great St. Trinian's Train Robbery '66
The Heroes of Telemark '65
The Chalk Garden '64
The Thin Red Line '64
On the Fiddle '61
The Pure Hell of St. Trinian's '61
Whistle down the Wind '61
No Love for Johnnie '60
Tunes of Glory '60
Solomon and Sheba '59
Suddenly, Last Summer '59
The Inn of the Sixth Happiness '58
The Key '58
The Bridge on the River Kwai '57
Island in the Sun '57
Blue Murder at St. Trinian's '56
Trapeze '56
I Am a Camera '55
The Sea Shall Not Have Them '55
Devil on Horseback '54
The Sleeping Tiger '54
The Belles of St. Trinian's '53
Captain's Paradise '53
Curtain Up '53
Four Sided Triangle '53
Hobson's Choice '53
The Sound Barrier '52
A Stolen Face '52
Wings of Danger '52
Home to Danger '51
No Highway in the Sky '51
Eye Witness '49

Norman Arnold
War Tapes '06
Reel Paradise '05
Shot '01

Bruce Arntson
Ernest Rides Again '93
Ernest Scared Stupid '91
Ernest Goes to Jail '90

Leon Aronson(1945-)
Bounty Hunters 2: Hardball '97
Jack Higgins' Midnight Man '96
Jack Higgins' On Dangerous Ground '95
Eddie and the Cruisers 2: Eddie Lives! '89

Jorge Arriagada(1943-)
Klimt '06
Our Lady of the Assassins '01
Comedy of Innocence '00
Time Regained '99
Shattered Image '98
Genealogies of a Crime '97
Three Lives and Only One Death '96
It's All True '93
The Disenchanted '90
On Top of the Whale '82

Eduard Artemyev(1937-)
House of Fools '02
The Odyssey '97
Burnt by the Sun '94
Anna '93
Double Jeopardy '92
The Inner Circle '91
Close to Eden '90
Homer and Eddie '89
Siberiade '79
Stalker '79
A Slave of Love '78
The Mirror '75
Solaris '72

Bent Aserud(1950-)
Mendel '98
The Other Side of Sunday '96

Gary Ashiya
Ju-On 2 '00
Seance '00

Howard Ashman(1950-91)
Aladdin '92
Beauty and the Beast '91
The Little Mermaid '89
Little Shop of Horrors '86

Spring Aspers
The Unborn '09
Rebound '05
The Specials '00

Edwin Astley(1922-98)
Digby, the Biggest Dog in the World '73
Vendetta for the Saint '68
Fiction Makers '67
A Matter of WHO '62
The Phantom of the Opera '62
Let's Get Married '60
The Mouse That Roared '59
The Womaneater '59
To Paris with Love '55
Devil Girl from Mars '54

Tim Atack
The Invention of Lying '09
Among Giants '98

Michael Atkinson
Heaven's Burning '97
Backlash '86

Georges Auric(1899-1983)
Therese & Isabelle '67
The Mind Benders '63
The Innocents '61
The Testament of Orpheus '59
The Crucible '57
Heaven Knows, Mr. Allison '57
The Hunchback of Notre Dame '57
The Night Heaven Fell '57
The Story of Esther Costello '57
Abdulla the Great '56
Gervaise '56
Lola Montes '55
Wages of Fear '55
Rififi '54
Orpheus '49
It Always Rains on Sunday '47
Beauty and the Beast '46
Dead of Night '45
Eternal Return '43
A Nous la Liberte '31
The Blood of a Poet '30

William Axt(1888-1959)
Libeled Lady '36
Whipsaw '35
Men in White '34
Operator 13 '34
Tarzan and His Mate '34
Dinner at Eight '33
Midnight Mary '33
Laurel & Hardy: Hog Wild '30
Laurel & Hardy: The Hoose-Gow '29
Don Juan '26
The Big Parade '25

Alexandre Azaria
Transporter 3 '08
Love and Other Disasters '06
Transporter 2 '05

Charles Aznavour(1924-)
Mauvais Sang '86
Sweet Ecstasy '62
Daniella by Night '61
Dishonorable Discharge '57

Chris Babida
Fleeing by Night '00
The Phantom Lover '95

Luis Bacalov(1933-)
Assassination Tango '03
It Had to Be You '00
The Sky Is Falling '00
Woman on Top '00
Children of the Century '99
The Love Letter '99
Polish Wedding '97
The Truce '96
The Postman '94
Entre-Nous '83
City of Women '81
Rulers of the City '76
The Grand Duel '73
His Name Was King '71
A Bullet for the General '68
Catch as Catch Can '68
Django '68
Empty Canvas '64
The Gospel According to St. Matthew '64

Burt Bacharach(1928-)
Isn't She Great '00
Arthur 2: On the Rocks '88
Night Shift '82
Arthur '81
Together? '79
Butch Cassidy and the Sundance Kid '69
Casino Royale '67
After the Fox '66
Alfie '66
What's New Pussycat? '65
The Blob '58
The Sad Sack '57

Pierre Bachelet(1944-2005)
Emmanuelle 5 '87
The Perils of Gwendoline '84
Black and White in Color '76
Emmanuelle, the Joys of a Woman '76
The Story of O '75
Emmanuelle '74

Chris P. Bacon
Midnight Bayou '09
Space Chimps '08
Angels Fall '07
Blue Smoke '07

Michael Bacon(1949-)
Loverboy '05
Losing Chase '96

Angelo Badalamenti(1937-)
The Edge of Love '08
The Wicker Man '06
Dominion: Prequel to the Exorcist '05
Before the Fall '04
A Very Long Engagement '04
Dangerous Liaisons '03
Resistance '03
Auto Focus '02
Dark Water '02
The Lathe of Heaven '02
Secretary '02
Suspended Animation '02
Mulholland Drive '01
The Beach '00
Arlington Road '99
Forever Mine '99
Holy Smoke '99
The Straight Story '99
The Blood Oranges '97
The Last Don '97
Invasion of Privacy '96
Lost Highway '96
The City of Lost Children '95
Witch Hunt '94
Hotel Room '93
Naked in New York '93
Twin Peaks: Fire Walk with Me '92
The Comfort of Strangers '91
Wait until Spring, Bandini '90
Wild at Heart '90
Cousins '89
National Lampoon's Christmas Vacation '89
Parents '89
A Nightmare on Elm Street 3: Dream Warriors '87
Tough Guys Don't Dance '87
Weeds '87
Blue Velvet '86
Across the Great Divide '76
Law and Disorder '74
Gordon's War '73

Wally Badarou(1955-)
Boesman & Lena '00
Dancehall Queen '97
The Lunatic '92
Kiss of the Spider Woman '85

Klaus Badelt(1968-)
Killshot '09
The Scorpion King 2: Rise of a Warrior '08
Starship Troopers 3: Marauder '08
Premonition '07
TMNT (Teenage Mutant Ninja Turtles) '07
Poseidon '06
16 Blocks '06
Ultraviolet '06
Constantine '05
The Promise '05
Catwoman '04
Basic '03
Ned Kelly '03
Pirates of the Caribbean: The Curse of the Black Pearl '03
The Recruit '03
Equilibrium '02
K-19: The Widowmaker '02
The Time Machine '02
Invincible '01

David Baerwald(1960-)
Undiscovered '05
Around the Bend '04
Hurlyburly '98
Loved '97

Tom Bahler(1943-)
Gordy '95
The Object of Beauty '91
Cold Feet '89
Fast Forward '84
Mary, Mary, Bloody Mary '76

Tadeusz Baird(1928-81)
Lotna '64
Passenger '61

James Bairian
The Art of War 3: Retribution '08
Bats: Human Harvest '07

C. Bakaleinikoff
Dick Tracy vs. Cueball '46
Power Dive '41

Mischa Bakaleinikoff(1890-1960)
The Lineup '58
20 Million Miles to Earth '57
The 27th Day '57
Earth vs. the Flying Saucers '56
Blondie Hits the Jackpot '49
The Millerson Case '47
Jane Eyre '34

Alexander Baker
Route 30 '08
Tycus '98

Buddy (Norman Dale) Baker(1918-2002)
The Puppetoon Movie '87
The Devil & Max Devlin '81
The Fox and the Hound '81
The Apple Dumpling Gang Rides Again '79
Hot Lead & Cold Feet '78

School for Scoundrels '06
The Sentinel '06
We Are Marshall '06
Zoom '06
Elektra '05
Ice Princess '05
The Perfect Man '05
Two for the Money '05
Yours, Mine & Ours '05
A Cinderella Story '04
Garfield: The Movie '04
Little Black Book '04
Saved! '04
Taxi '04
Without a Paddle '04
American Wedding '03
Cheaper by the Dozen '03
Dickie Roberts: Former Child Star '03
The Event '03
Just Married '03
Under the Tuscan Sun '03
Interstate 60 '02
The Skulls 2 '02
Slap Her, She's French '02
Stealing Harvard '02
The Tuxedo '02
Bring It On '00
The Broken Hearts Club '00
Guinevere '99
Thick as Thieves '99
The Alarmist '98
Past Perfect '98
Bone Daddy '97
Hostile Intent '97
Killing Mr. Griffin '97
Crossworlds '96

Frank Becker

American Kickboxer 1 '91
Terminal Bliss '91

Hal Beckett

Call of the Wild '04
Power of Attorney '94

Herman Beeftink

Forbidden Sins '99
One Small Hero '99
Dish Dogs '98
I Like to Play Games '95

David Bell(1954-)

The Sandy Bottom Orchestra '00
Larry McMurtry's Dead Man's Walk '96
Sin and Redemption '94
Lone Justice 2 '93
There Goes the Neighborhood '92
Memphis '91
Final Justice '84
Killing at Hell's Gate '81

Wayne Bell

The Texas Chainsaw Massacre 4: The Next Generation '95
Last Night at the Alamo '83
Eaten Alive '76
The Texas Chainsaw Massacre '74

Andrew Belling

Starchaser: The Legend of Orin '85
The Deerslayer '78
Zoltan... Hound of Dracula '78
Wizards '77
End of the World '76
The Killing Kind '73

Richard Bellis(1946-)

One Special Night '99
How the West Was Fun '95
Where's the Money, Noreen? '95
The Spider and the Fly '94
Blind Man's Bluff '91
Double-Crossed '91
Stephen King's It '90
Fallen Angel '81
Breaking Up Is Hard to Do '79
A Shining Season '79

Roger Bellon(1953-)

The Christmas Card '06
Hidden Places '06
Murder Without Conviction '04
Break a Leg '03
Hitman's Run '99
The Last Don 2 '98
My Husband's Secret Life '98
The Last Don '97
The Unholy '88
Waxwork '88
Princess Academy '87

Marco Beltrami(1966-)

Repo Men '10
Knowing '09
Amusement '08
The Eye '08
The Hurt Locker '08
In the Electric Mist '08
Max Payne '08
Captivity '07
The Invisible '07
Live Free or Die Hard '07
3:10 to Yuma '07
The Omen '06
Red Eye '05
The Three Burials of Melquiades Estrada '05
Underworld: Evolution '05
XXX: State of the Union '05
Cursed '04
Flight of the Phoenix '04
Hellboy '04
I, Robot '04
Terminator 3: Rise of the Machines '03
Blade 2 '02
The Dangerous Lives of Altar Boys '02
The First $20 Million is Always the Hardest '02
Resident Evil '02
Angel Eyes '01
Joy Ride '01
The Crow: Salvation '00
Dracula 2000 '00
Scream 3 '00
The Watcher '00
The Minus Man '99
Tuesdays with Morrie '99
The Faculty '98
Mimic '97
Scream 2 '97
Inhumanoid '96
Scream '96

Gilad Benamram

Chaos Theory '08
Pretty Persuasion '05

Vassal Benford

Class Act '91
House Party 2: The Pajama Jam '91

Arthur Benjamin(1893-1960)

Fire Down Below '57
An Ideal Husband '47
Wings of the Morning '37
The Scarlet Pimpernel '34

Daryl Bennett

Decoys '04
Love on the Side '04
Wishmaster 4: The Prophecy Fulfilled '02
Big and Hairy '98

James Bennett

Poison '91
Swoon '91

Richard Rodney Bennett(1936-)

Swann '96
Four Weddings and a Funeral '94
Enchanted April '92
The Attic: The Hiding of Anne Frank '88
Poor Little Rich Girl: The Barbara Hutton Story '87
Ebony Tower '86
Agatha Christie's Murder with Mirrors '85
Return of the Soldier '82
Yanks '79
Brink's Job '78
Equus '77
Permission To Kill '75
Murder on the Orient Express '74
Lady Caroline Lamb '73
Nicholas and Alexandra '71
The Buttercup Chain '70
Secret Ceremony '69
Billion Dollar Brain '67
Far from the Madding Crowd '67
The Witches '66
The Nanny '65
Billy Liar '63
Heavens Above '63
The Wrong Arm of the Law '63
Only Two Can Play '62
The Mark '61
The Devil's Disciple '59
Indiscreet '58

Warren Bennett

Chaos & Cadavers '03
Wuthering Heights '98

David Benoit(1953-)

Perfect Game '00
The Stars Fell on Henrietta '94
Captive Hearts '87

Jean-Marie Benoit

Seducing Doctor Lewis '03
King of the Airwaves '94
Jesus of Montreal '89

David Bergeaud

Bollywood Hero '09
Thr3e '07
Anonymous Rex '04
The Badge '02
Prince Valiant '97
Donor Unknown '95
Twice Dead '88

Cary Berger

Eating Out 2: Sloppy Seconds '06
Cleopatra's Second Husband '00
Full Tilt Boogie '97
Suture '93

Tal Bergman

Sasquatch '02
Kill Me Later '01
Dancing at the Blue Iguana '00
Wedding Bell Blues '96

Michael Berkeley(1948-)

Twenty-One '91
Goldeneye: The Secret Life of Ian Fleming '89

Irving Berlin(1888-1989)

Le Bal '82
There's No Business Like Show Business '54
Annie Get Your Gun '50
Easter Parade '48
Second Fiddle '39
Alexander's Ragtime Band '38
Carefree '38
On the Avenue '37
Follow the Fleet '36
Top Hat '35
The Cocoanuts '29
Hallelujah! '29

James Bernard(1925-2001)

Frankenstein and the Monster from Hell '74
The Legend of the 7 Golden Vampires '73
The Scars of Dracula '70
Taste the Blood of Dracula '70
The Devil Rides Out '68
Dracula Has Risen from the Grave '68
Torture Garden '67
Dracula, Prince of Darkness '66
Plague of the Zombies '66
She '65
The Gorgon '64
Kiss of the Vampire '62
The Terror of the Tongs '61
The Stranglers of Bombay '60
The Hound of the Baskervilles '59
The Horror of Dracula '58
Across the Bridge '57
The Curse of Frankenstein '57
Quatermass 2 '57
The Quatermass Experiment '56
X The Unknown '56

Jean-Michel Bernard

Be Kind Rewind '08
The Science of Sleep '06

Charles Bernstein(1943-)

Darwin's Darkest Hour '09
Sweet Nothing in My Ear '08
After Innocence '05
Out of the Ashes '03
The Day the World Ended '01
Earth vs. the Spider '01
Miss Evers' Boys '97
The Ticket '97
When Danger Follows You Home '97
Bloodhounds 2 '96
Dead Ahead '96
Rumpelstiltskin '96
Excessive Force '93
Final Appeal '93
The Sea Wolf '93
Payoff '91
Caroline? '90
Drug Wars: The Camarena Story '90
Ivory Hunters '90
Too Young to Die '90
The Allnighter '87
Dudes '87
The Man Who Broke 1,000 Chains '87
April Fool's Day '86
Deadly Friend '86
The Last Fling '86
The Long, Hot Summer '86
The Rumor Mill '86
Chase '85
Secret Weapons '85
A Nightmare on Elm Street '84
Cujo '83
The Entity '83
Independence Day '83
Sadat '83
Bogie: The Last Hero '80
Coast to Coast '80
Foolin' Around '80
The Hunter '80
Scruples '80
The House on Garibaldi Street '79
Love at First Bite '79
Are You in the House Alone? '78
Steel Cowboy '78
Wild & Wooly '78
The Winds of Kitty Hawk '78
Outlaw Blues '77
Viva Knievel '77
Gator '76
Nightmare in Badham County '76
A Small Town in Texas '76
Mr. Majestyk '74
Invasion of the Bee Girls '73
Pigs '73
The Shrieking '73
That Man Bolt '73
White Lightning '73
The Arousers '70

Elmer Bernstein(1922-2004)

Far from Heaven '02
Keeping the Faith '00
Bringing Out the Dead '99
The Happy Face Murders '99
Introducing Dorothy Dandridge '99
Wild Wild West '99
The Deep End of the Ocean '98
Twilight '98
Buddy '97
John Grisham's The Rainmaker '97
Bulletproof '96
Hoodlum '96
Devil in a Blue Dress '95
Frankie Starlight '95
Roommates '95
Canadian Bacon '94
Search and Destroy '94
The Age of Innocence '93
The Cemetery Club '93
Fallen Angels 1 '93
The Good Son '93
Lost in Yonkers '93
Mad Dog and Glory '93
The Babe '92
Cape Fear '91
Oscar '91
A Rage in Harlem '91
Rambling Rose '91
The Field '90
The Grifters '90
My Left Foot '89
Slipstream '89
Da '88
Funny Farm '88
The Good Mother '88
A Night in the Life of Jimmy Reardon '88
Amazing Grace & Chuck '87
Leonard Part 6 '87
Hamburger... The Motion Picture '86
Legal Eagles '86
Three Amigos '86
The Black Cauldron '85
Gulag '85
Spies Like Us '85
Bolero '84
The Ewok Adventure '84
Ghostbusters '84
Class '83
Prince Jack '83
Spacehunter: Adventures in the Forbidden Zone '83
Trading Places '83
Airplane 2: The Sequel '82
Five Days One Summer '82
An American Werewolf in London '81
The Chosen '81
Going Ape! '81
Heavy Metal '81
Honky Tonk Freeway '81
Stripes '81
Airplane! '80
The Blues Brothers '80
The Great Santini '80
The Guyana Tragedy: The Story of Jim Jones '80
Saturn 3 '80
The Chisholms '79
Meatballs '79
Zulu Dawn '79
Bloodbrothers '78
Little Women '78
National Lampoon's Animal House '78
Slap Shot '77
From Noon Till Three '76
The Incredible Sarah '76
The Shootist '76
The Old Curiosity Shop '75
McQ '74
Report to the Commissioner '74
The Trial of Billy Jack '74
Cahill: United States Marshal '73
Amazing Mr. Blunden '72
Big Jake '71
See No Evil '71
Doctors' Wives '70
The Liberation of L.B. Jones '70
Walk in the Spring Rain '70
The Bridge at Remagen '69
Guns of the Magnificent Seven '69
The Gypsy Moths '69
True Grit '69
I Love You, Alice B. Toklas! '68
The Scalphunters '68
Thoroughly Modern Millie '67
Will Penny '67
Cast a Giant Shadow '66
Hawaii '66
Return of the Magnificent Seven '66
The Silencers '66
The Hallelujah Trail '65
Sons of Katie Elder '65
Baby, the Rain Must Fall '64
The Carpetbaggers '64
The World of Henry Orient '64
The Great Escape '63
Hud '63
Kings of the Sun '63
Love with the Proper Stranger '63
Birdman of Alcatraz '62
To Kill a Mockingbird '62
Walk on the Wild Side '62
By Love Possessed '61
The Comancheros '61
Summer and Smoke '61
From the Terrace '60
The Magnificent Seven '60
The Rat Race '60
The Buccaneer '58
Desire Under the Elms '58
God's Little Acre '58
Kings Go Forth '58
Saddle the Wind '58
Some Came Running '58
Fear Strikes Out '57
Men in War '57
Sweet Smell of Success '57
The Tin Star '57
The Ten Commandments '56
It's a Dog's Life '55
The Man with the Golden Arm '55
Make Haste to Live '54
Silent Raiders '54
Cat Women of the Moon '53
Robot Monster '53
Boots Malone '52
Never Wave at a WAC '52
Sudden Fear '52

Leonard Bernstein(1918-90)

On the Town '91
West Side Story '61
On the Waterfront '54
On the Town '49

Peter Bernstein(1951-)

Mail to the Chief '00
Atomic Dog '98
Dying to Get Rich '98
Rough Riders '97
Canadian Bacon '94
Nightbreaker '89
Remote Control '88
The Alamo: Thirteen Days to Glory '87
Morgan Stewart's Coming Home '87
Miracles '86
Broken Badge '85
The Ewoks: Battle for Endor '85
Kicks '85
My Science Project '85
Bolero '84
The Ewok Adventure '84
Summer Fantasy '84
Surf 2 '84
Club Med '83
Hot Dog... The Movie! '83
National Lampoon's Class Reunion '82
Silent Rage '82

Reinhard Besser

Heart of America '03
House of the Dead '03
Blackwoods '02

Peter Best(1943-)

Doing Time for Patsy Cline '97
Country Life '95
Muriel's Wedding '94
Crocodile Dundee 2 '88
High Tide '87
Crocodile Dundee '86
Sound of Love '78

Harry Betts

Cheech and Chong's Nice Dreams '81
Big Mouth '67

Ryan Beveridge
Boy Culture '06
L.A. Dicks '05
Frankenfish '04
Rampage: The Hillside Strangler Murders '04
Nightstalker '02
Taboo '02

Amin Bhatia
Detention '03
Under Heavy Fire '01
Once a Thief '96
The Awakening '95
Anything for Love '93
Just One of the Girls '93
Ordeal in the Arctic '93
Black Ice '92
Iron Eagle 2 '88
Storm '87

Nick Bicat(1949-)
Carrie's War '04
Suspicion '03
Relative Strangers '99
Stella Does Tricks '96
The Passion of Darkly Noon '95
Framed '93
The Hawk '93
The Reflecting Skin '91
Strapless '90
Stealing Heaven '88
Wetherby '85
A Christmas Carol '84
To Catch a King '84
Oliver Twist '82
The Scarlet Pimpernel '82

Arnold Bieber
Smoke '93
Small Time '91

Keith Bilderbeck
Stir '98
Voodoo '95

Edward Bilous
Just One Time '00
Dead Broke '99
Sleepaway Camp '83

Rene Marc Bini
Grosse Fatigue '94
Weep No More My Lady '93

Joseph Bishara
Night of the Demons '09
The Convent '00

Ulf Bjorlin(1933-93)
Vibration '68
Elvira Madigan '67

Karen Black(1942-)
The Blue Tooth Virgin '09
Can She Bake a Cherry Pie? '83

Stanley Black(1913-2002)
Maniac '63
The Day the Earth Caught Fire '61
The Battle of the Sexes '60
The Flesh and the Fiends '60
Jack the Ripper '60
The Siege of Sidney Street '60
Black Tide '58
The Crawling Eye '58
Time Lock '57
Bond of Fear '56
Recoil '53

Damon Blackman
Cradle 2 the Grave '03
Exit Wounds '01

Wendy Blackstone
Love Walked In '97
New Jersey Drive '95
Tales of Erotica '93
Only You '92
Eddie Macon's Run '83

Ruben Blades(1948-)
Empire '02
Q & A '90
The Story of Fausta '88

Alan Blaikley
The Body in the Library '84
The Flame Trees of Thika '81

Howard Blake(1938-)
My Life So Far '98
A Midsummer Night's Dream '96
A Month in the Country '87
Amityville 3: The Demon '83
The Lords of Discipline '83
Amityville 2: The Possession '82
Flash Gordon '80
The Riddle of the Sands '79
S.O.S. Titanic '79
The Odd Job '78
The Rainbow Gang '73
An Elephant Called Slowly '69

Peter Blake
Maiden Voyage: Ocean Hijack '04
Dead Evidence '00

Terence Blanchard(1962-)
Cadillac Records '08
Miracle at St. Anna '08
Talk to Me '07
Inside Man '06
Waist Deep '06
She Hate Me '04
Dark Blue '03
Barbershop '02
People I Know '02
25th Hour '02
Bojangles '01
The Caveman's Valentine '01
Glitter '01
Original Sin '01
Bamboozled '00
Love and Basketball '00
Next Friday '00
The Truth About Jane '00
Summer of Sam '99
The Color of Courage '98
Free of Eden '98
Gia '98
Eve's Bayou '97
Get On the Bus '96
Til There Was You '96
Clockers '95
Assault at West Point: The Court-Martial of Johnson Whittaker '94
Crooklyn '94
The Inkwell '94
Sugar Hill '94
Trial by Jury '94
Malcolm X '92
Jungle Fever '91

Ralph Blane(1914-95)
Athena '54
Good News '47

Larry Blank(1952-)
That Championship Season '99
Taxi Dancers '93

Arthur Bliss(1891-1975)
Abandon Ship '57
Beggar's Opera '54
Things to Come '36

George Blondheim
Summer of the Monkeys '98
The Halfback of Notre Dame '96
Man with a Gun '95
Red Scorpion 2 '94
Whale Music '94
Heartstrings '93
Gate 2 '92
Bye Bye Blues '89

Michael Bloomfield(1944-81)
Andy Warhol's Bad '77
Medium Cool '69

Frankie Blue
Redeemer '02
Dracula: The Dark Prince '01
Return to Cabin by the Lake '01
Cabin by the Lake '00
Out There '95

Chris Boardman(1954-)
My Mom's New Boyfriend '08
Senior Skip Day '08
Local Color '06
Blood Crime '02
The Dress Code '99
Payback '98
Tales from the Crypt Presents Bordello of Blood '96
Prime Target '91
The Color Purple '85

Michael Boddicker
Freejack '92
F/X 2: The Deadly Art of Illusion '91
The Adventures of Milo & Otis '89
Milo & Otis '89
White Water Summer '87
The Adventures of Buckaroo Banzai Across the Eighth Dimension '84
Get Crazy '83

Todd Boekelheide
Ballet Russes '05
Spin '04
The Outsider '02
Digger '94
Nina Takes a Lover '94
Exposure '91
Hearts of Darkness: A Filmmaker's Apocalypse '91
The Blood of Heroes '89
Dim Sum: A Little Bit of Heart '85

Ed Bogas
Bon Voyage, Charlie Brown '80
A Christmas Without Snow '80
Race for Your Life, Charlie Brown '77
Heavy Traffic '73
Payday '73
Fritz the Cat '72

Lazare Boghossian
Under the Bombs '07
The Man I Love '97

Geir Bohren(1951-)
Mendel '98
The Other Side of Sunday '96

William Bolcom(1938-)
Illuminata '98
Hester Street '75

Bill Boll(1965-)
The Low Life '95
Some Folks Call It a Sling Blade '94

Claude Bolling(1930-)
The Bay Boy '85
The Awakening '80
Willie & Phil '80
California Suite '78
Silver Bears '78
Intruder '76
L'Annee Sainte '76
Le Magnifique '76
Le Gitan '75
The Passenger '75
Catch Me a Spy '71
Borsalino '70
The Day and the Hour '63
The Hands of Orlac '60

Jay Bolton
Mom's Outta Sight '01
The Kid with the X-Ray Eyes '99
Stormy Nights '97

Scott Bomar
Gospel Hill '08
Black Snake Moan '07
Hustle & Flow '05

Bernardo Bonezzi(1964-)
Gaudi Afternoon '01
No News from God '01
Between Your Legs '99
Mouth to Mouth '95
All Tied Up '92
Don Juan, My Love '90
Women on the Verge of a Nervous Breakdown '88
Matador '86

Marc Bonilla
Caught Up '98
Hollywood Confidential '97
National Lampoon's Dad's Week Off '97

Bono(1960-)
The Million Dollar Hotel '99
In the Name of the Father '93

Simon Boswell(1956-)
My Zinc Bed '08
Tin Man '07
The River King '05
Close Your Eyes '02
The Sleeping Dictionary '02
Widows '02
Born Romantic '00
Circus '00
Jason and the Argonauts '00
William Shakespeare's A Midsummer Night's Dream '99
Deacon Brodie '98
The War Zone '98
Cousin Bette '97
Dad Savage '97
Dance with the Devil '97
Photographing Fairies '97
The Android Affair '95
Hackers '95
Jack and Sarah '95
Lord of Illusions '95
Second Best '94
Shallow Grave '94
Dust Devil '93
Love Matters '93
The Turn of the Screw '92
Hardware '90
Santa Sangre '90
Dangerous Obsession '88
Karate Warrior '88
Demons 2 '87
Creepers '85

Perry Botkin(1933-)
Windmills of the Gods '88
Weekend Warriors '86
Silent Night, Deadly Night '84
Tarzan, the Ape Man '81
Goin' South '78
Lady Ice '73
They Only Kill Their Masters '72
Bless the Beasts and Children '71
R.P.M.* (*Revolutions Per Minute) '70
Murder by Contract '58

Frederic Botton
The Housekeeper '02
Queen of Diamonds '70

Roddy Bottum
What Goes Up '09
Gigantic '08
I'm Reed Fish '06
Adam & Steve '05

Ned Bouhalassa
Infected '08
Banshee '06
These Girls '05
The Arrival 2 '98

Andres Boulton
The Dog Who Saved Christmas '09
The Boston Strangler: The Untold Story '08
Bundy: A Legacy of Evil '08
A Christmas Proposal '08

Roger Bourland(1952-)
New Jack City '91
Night Life '90
The Trouble with Dick '88
The Wolf at the Door '87

Richard Bowers
A Woman Hunted '03
Facing the Enemy '00
The Perfect Nanny '00
The Nurse '97
Dead Cold '96
The Fiance '96
Open Fire '94

David Bowie(1947-)
The Buddha of Suburbia '92
Labyrinth '86
Party! Party! '83
Christiane F. '82

Euel Box
Benji the Hunted '87
The Double McGuffin '79
For the Love of Benji '77
Hawmps! '76
Benji '74

Christopher Brady(1967-)
Pressure '02
Deadly Game '98

Reiner Bredemeyer
The Woman and the Stranger '84
Jadup and Boel '81
The Rabbit Is Me '65

Goran Bregovic(1950-)
The Lost Son '98
Train of Life '98
The Serpent's Kiss '97
A Chef in Love '96
Underground '95
Queen Margot '94

Danny Brenner
Rhythm Thief '94
Spare Me '92

Alan Brewer
Come Early Morning '06
Tokyo Pop '88

Peter Brewis
The Tall Guy '89
Morons from Outer Space '85

Ales Brezina(1965-)
I Served the King of England '07
Up and Down '04
Divided We Fall '00

Leslie Bricusse(1931-)
Tom and Jerry: The Movie '93
Babes in Toyland '86
Willy Wonka & the Chocolate Factory '71
Scrooge '70
Goodbye, Mr. Chips '69
Doctor Dolittle '67

David Bridie
Tempted '01
In a Savage Land '99
The Myth of Fingerprints '97
River Street '95
That Eye, the Sky '94

Jon Brion(1963-)
Step Brothers '08
Synecdoche, New York '08
The Break-Up '06
Eternal Sunshine of the Spotless Mind '04
Punch-Drunk Love '02
Magnolia '99
Hard Eight '96

Michi Britsch
Case 39 '10
Pandorum '09
Antibodies '05

Timothy Brock
Diary of a Lost Girl '29
Faust '26
The Show Off '26

David Broekman(1899-1958)
Frankenstein '31
All Quiet on the Western Front '30

Broken Social Scene
The Tracey Fragments '07
Snow Cake '06

Richard Bronskill
National Lampoon's Golf Punks '99
Body Strokes '95
Friend of the Family '95
The Perfect Bride '91

Michael Brook(1952-)
Sugar '09
Into the Wild '07
An Inconvenient Truth '06
Who Killed the Electric Car? '06
Charlotte Sometimes '02
Crime and Punishment in Suburbia '00
Buddy Boy '99
Affliction '97
Albino Alligator '96

Harvey Brooks(1899-1968)
The Duke Is Tops '38
I'm No Angel '33

Joseph Brooks(1938-)
If Ever I See You Again '78
You Light Up My Life '77
The Lords of Flatbush '74
Invitation to the Wedding '73

Mel Brooks(1926-)
The Producers '05
The Twelve Chairs '70

Bruce Broughton(1945-)
Bambi II '06
Eloise at the Plaza '03
Bobbie's Girl '02
The Locket '02
Krippendorf's Tribe '98
Lost in Space '98
One Tough Cop '98
A Simple Wish '97
True Women '97
House Arrest '96
Infinity '96
The Shadow Conspiracy '96
Carried Away '95
JAG '95
Baby's Day Out '94
Holy Matrimony '94
Miracle on 34th Street '94
For Love or Money '93
Homeward Bound: The Incredible Journey '93
So I Married an Axe Murderer '93
Tombstone '93
Honey, I Blew Up the Kid '92
Stay Tuned '92
All I Want for Christmas '91
Betsy's Wedding '90
Narrow Margin '90
The Old Man and the Sea '90
The Rescuers Down Under '90
Jacknife '89
Sorry, Wrong Number '89
Cross My Heart '88
Last Rites '88
The Presidio '88
The Rescue '88
Big Shots '87
Harry and the Hendersons '87
The Monster Squad '87
Square Dance '87
The Boy Who Could Fly '86
George Washington: The Forging of a Nation '86
Sweet Liberty '86
Silverado '85
Young Sherlock Holmes '85
The Cowboy & the Ballerina '84
The First Olympics: Athens 1896 '84
Ice Pirates '84
M.A.D.D.: Mothers Against Drunk Driving '83
The Prodigal '83
The Blue and the Gray '82
Desperate Lives '82
One Shoe Makes It Murder '82
Killjoy '81
Return of Frank Cannon '80

Leo Brouwer(1930-)
A Walk in the Clouds '95
Like Water for Chocolate '93
Up to a Certain Point '83
Death of a Bureaucrat '66

Bill Brown(1969-)
The Devil's Tomb '09
Scorcher '02

James Brown(1933-2006)
Black Caesar '73
Slaughter's Big Ripoff '73

Larry Brown
Don't Tell '05
The Wall '99
Elvis Meets Nixon '98
Gang in Blue '96
Rio Diablo '93

Nacio Herb Brown(1896-1964)
Singin' in the Rain '52
Broadway Melody of 1938 '37
Broadway Melody of 1936 '35
Broadway Melody '29

Christian Bruhn(1934-)
Pippi on the Run '70
Pippi Goes on Board '69

Andre Brummer(1916-2006)
Rat Pfink a Boo-Boo '66
The Thrill Killers '65
Incredibly Strange Creatures Who Stopped Living and Became Mixed-Up Zombies '63
Monster from the Ocean Floor '54

Robert F. Brunner(1938-)
Amy '81
The North Avenue Irregulars '79
Gus '76
The Strongest Man in the World '75
The Castaway Cowboy '74
Now You See Him, Now You Don't '72
Snowball Express '72
The Barefoot Executive '71
The Wild Country '71
The Boatniks '70
Smoke '70
The Computer Wore Tennis Shoes '69
Smith! '69
Never a Dull Moment '68
Blackbeard's Ghost '67
Lt. Robin Crusoe, U.S.N. '66
Monkeys, Go Home! '66
That Darn Cat '65

George Bruns(1914-83)
Herbie Rides Again '74
Robin Hood '73
The Aristocats '70
Daring Game '68
The Horse in the Gray Flannel Suit '68
Island of the Lost '68
The Love Bug '68
The Jungle Book '67
The Adventures of Bullwhip Griffin '66
The Fighting Prince of Donegal '66
Follow Me, Boys! '66
Man from Button Willow '65
The Ugly Dachshund '65
Son of Flubber '63
The Sword in the Stone '63
The Absent-Minded Professor '61
Babes in Toyland '61
101 Dalmatians '61
Sleeping Beauty '59
Davy Crockett and the River Pirates '56
Westward Ho, the Wagons! '56
Davy Crockett, King of the Wild Frontier '55

Gerald Brunskill
World's Greatest Dad '09
Deep Winter '08

Jerry Brunskill
Pistol Whipped '08
Soccer Mom '08
Sleeping Dogs Lie '06

Joanne Bruzdowicz(1943-)
Jacquot '91
Vagabond '85

BT (Brian Transeau)(1971-)
Catch and Release '07
Stealth '05
Underclassman '05
Monster '03
Driven '01
The Fast and the Furious '01

Chico Buarque(1944-)
Possible Loves '00
Bye Bye Brazil '79
Dona Flor and Her Two Husbands '78

Alexander Bubenheim(1962-)
In Hell '03
Night Train to Venice '93

David Buchbinder
Whole New Thing '05
Club Land '01
Jerry and Tom '98

David Buckley
From Paris With Love '10
Blood Creek '09
The Forbidden Kingdom '08

Paul Buckmaster
Mean Streak '99
The Maker '98
Murder in Mind '97
The Last Word '95
12 Monkeys '95
Diving In '90
The Spy Who Loved Me '77

Roy Budd(1947-93)
Sinbad and the Eye of the Tiger '77
Welcome to Blood City '77
Get Carter '71

Kenneth Burgomaster
The Wizards of Waverly Place: The Movie '09
Hero Wanted '08
Snow 2: Brain Freeze '08
Cow Belles '06
End Game '06
Return to Halloweentown '06
Halloweentown High '04

Geoffrey Burgon(1941-)
Longitude '00
Cider with Rosie '99
When Trumpets Fade '98
A Foreign Field '93
Robin Hood '91
Turtle Diary '86
Bleak House '85
Brideshead Revisited '81
The Dogs of War '81
Tinker, Tailor, Soldier, Spy '80
Monty Python's Life of Brian '79

Chris Burke
Search and Destroy '88
Splatter University '84

Johnny Burke(1908-64)
Welcome Stranger '47
The Road to Utopia '46
The Bells of St. Mary's '45
East Side of Heaven '39
Pennies from Heaven '36

Justin Caine Burnett(1973-)
Dungeons and Dragons '00
Possums '99

T-Bone Burnett(1948-)
Crazy Heart '09
Don't Come Knocking '05
Walk the Line '05
Divine Secrets of the Ya-Ya Sisterhood '02
O Brother Where Art Thou? '00
In 'n Out '86

Ralph Burns(1922-2001)
The Josephine Baker Story '90
All Dogs Go to Heaven '89
Bert Rigby, You're a Fool '89
Sweet Bird of Youth '89
After the Promise '87
In the Mood '87
Penalty Phase '86
A Chorus Line '85
Moving Violations '85
Perfect '85
Ernie Kovacs: Between the Laughter '84
The Muppets Take Manhattan '84
Side Show '84
National Lampoon's Vacation '83
Star 80 '83
Annie '82
Kiss Me Goodbye '82
My Favorite Year '82
Pennies from Heaven '81
First Family '80
Make Me an Offer '80
Urban Cowboy '80
All That Jazz '79
Movie, Movie '78
New York, New York '77
Lenny '74
Cabaret '72

George Burt(1929-)
Fool for Love '86
Secret Honor '85

Carter Burwell(1955-)
The Blind Side '09
A Serious Man '09
Where the Wild Things Are '09
Burn After Reading '08
In Bruges '08
Twilight '08
Before the Devil Knows You're Dead '07
No Country for Old Men '07
Fur: An Imaginary Portrait of Diane Arbus '06
The Hoax '06
The Alamo '04
Kinsey '04
The Ladykillers '04
Intolerable Cruelty '03
Adaptation '02
The Rookie '02
Searching for Paradise '02
Simone '02
A Knight's Tale '01
The Man Who Wasn't There '01
Before Night Falls '00
Book of Shadows: Blair Witch 2 '00
Hamlet '00
O Brother Where Art Thou? '00
What Planet Are You From? '00
Being John Malkovich '99
The Corruptor '99
The General's Daughter '99
Mystery, Alaska '99
Three Kings '99
Gods and Monsters '98
The Hi-Lo Country '98
Velvet Goldmine '98
The Big Lebowski '97
Conspiracy Theory '97
The Jackal '97
The Locusts '97
The Spanish Prisoner '97
The Chamber '96
Fargo '96
Fear '96
Picture Perfect '96
The Celluloid Closet '95
Rob Roy '95
Airheads '94
Bad Company '94
It Could Happen to You '94
And the Band Played On '93
A Dangerous Woman '93
The Hudsucker Proxy '93
Kalifornia '93
This Boy's Life '93
Wayne's World 2 '93
Buffy the Vampire Slayer '92
Storyville '92
Waterland '92
Barton Fink '91
Doc Hollywood '91
Miller's Crossing '90
Checking Out '89
The Beat '88
It Takes Two '88
Pass the Ammo '88
Raising Arizona '87
Psycho 3 '86
Blood Simple '85

Artie Butler(1942-)
Grease 2 '82
O'Hara's Wife '82
American Dream '81
She's in the Army Now '81
Sizzle '81
Angel on My Shoulder '80
Sextette '78
The Rescuers '77
Rafferty & the Gold Dust Twins '75
For Pete's Sake '74
Harrad Experiment '73
What's Up, Doc? '72
The Love Machine '71

Ben Butler
The Insurgents '06
Heights '04

Edmund Butt
Secret Smile '05
Do or Die '01
24 Hours in London '00

David Buttolph(1902-83)
Man From Galveston '63
The Horse Soldiers '59
Westbound '58
Lone Ranger '56
Crime Wave '54
Long John Silver '54
The Beast from 20,000 Fathoms '53
House of Wax '53
South Sea Woman '53
Carson City '52
This Woman Is Dangerous '52
Montana '50
Pretty Baby '50
Colorado Territory '49
John Loves Mary '48
Rope '48
Boomerang '47
My Darling Clementine '46
Somewhere in the Night '46
13 Rue Madeleine '46
House on 92nd Street '45
Crash Dive '43
Guadalcanal Diary '43
Immortal Sergeant '43
My Favorite Blonde '42
This Gun for Hire '42
Thunder Birds '42
Wake Island '42
Love Is News '37
Second Honeymoon '37

R. Dale Butts(1910-90)
Phantom Stallion '54
Trader Tom of the China Seas '54
Shadows of Tombstone '53
Too Late for Tears '49
Far Frontier '48
Son of God's Country '48
Sioux City Sue '46

David Byrne(1952-)
Pittsburgh '06
Young Adam '03
Married to the Mob '88
The Last Emperor '87
Something Wild '86
True Stories '86

Niall Byrne
Cairo Time '09
How About You '07
The Honeymooners '03
Amongst Women '98

John Cacavas(1930-)
Perfect Murder, Perfect Town '00
My Sweet Victim '85
Shooting '82
Silent Rebellion '82
Airport '75 '75
The Satanic Rites of Dracula '73

Eric Cadesky
Never Forget '08
Saving God '08
Grindstone Road '07
Harm's Way '07
A Lobster Tale '06

Emil Cadkin
Mission to Death '66
The Killer Shrews '59
Heartaches '47
Three on a Ticket '47

Sammy Cahn(1913-93)
Court Jester '56
Rich, Young and Pretty '51
The West Point Story '50
Anchors Aweigh '45

John Cale(1940-)
American Psycho '99
Somewhere in the City '97
Basquiat '96
I Shot Andy Warhol '96
Primary Motive '92
Something Wild '86
Who Am I This Time? '82
Caged Heat '74
Heat '72

John Califra
My Brother '06
Tarnation '03

Darrell Calker(1905-64)
The Oh in Ohio '06
The Amazing Transparent Man '60
Terror in the Haunted House '58
Savage Drums '51
The Flying Saucer '50
El Paso '49
Big Town '47
Big Town After Dark '47
Seven Were Saved '47
Shoot to Kill '47
Underworld Scandal '47
Renegade Girl '46

Sean Callery
24 : Redemption '08
Blowback '99

Gerard Calvi
The Holes '72
Belle Americaine '61

John Cameron(1944-)
To End All Wars '01
Mr. Corbett's Ghost '90
The Secret Garden '87
The Mirror Crack'd '80
A Touch of Class '73
The Ruling Class '72

Bruce Campbell
Plan 9 from Outer Space '56
Mister Drake's Duck '50

James Campbell(1946-)
Elvira, Mistress of the Dark '88
Please Not Now! '61

Paul Cantelon
The Other Boleyn Girl '08
W. '08
Superheroes '07

Xavier Capellas(1962-)
Beyond Re-Animator '03
Faust: Love of the Damned '00

John Caper, Jr.
Equinox '71

He Lives: The Search for the Evil One '67

Claudio Capponi
The Fever '04
My House in Umbria '03
Jane Eyre '96

Al Capps
Stroker Ace '83
Cannonball Run '81

David Carbonara
Giuliani Time '05
The Guru '02
The Young Girl and the Monsoon '99

Gerard Carbonara(1886-1959)
The Kansan '43
The Shepherd of the Hills '41
Dr. Cyclops '40

Sam Cardon
Little Secrets '02
Brigham City '01

Jeff Cardoni
Miss March '09
The Vicious Kind '09
Beer for My Horses '08
American Pie Presents: Beta House '07
Firehouse Dog '07
Save Me '07
American Pie Presents: The Naked Mile '06
Bonneville '06
Love and Debate '06
Just Friends '05
Love for Rent '05
April's Shower '03

Philip Carli
Evangeline '29
Peter Pan '24

Robert Carli
Survival of the Dead '09
The Terrorist Next Door '08
A Killing Spring '02
Verdict in Blood '02
Road Rage '01
Hide and Seek '00
My 5 Wives '00
Silver Wolf '98

Walter (Wendy) Carlos(1939-)
Tron '82
The Shining '80
The Odd Angry Shot '79
A Clockwork Orange '71

Hoagy Carmichael(1899-1981)
Hoppity Goes to Town '41
College Swing '38

Ralph Carmichael
The 4D Man '59
The Blob '58

Stefan Carow
The Mistake '91
Coming Out '89

John Carpenter(1948-)
John Carpenter's Ghosts of Mars '01
Halloween: H20 '98
John Carpenter's Vampires '97
Escape from L.A. '96
In the Mouth of Madness '95
Village of the Damned '95
Body Bags '93
Halloween 5: The Revenge of Michael Myers '89
Halloween 4: The Return of Michael Myers '88
They Live '88
Prince of Darkness '87
Big Trouble in Little China '86
Christine '84
Halloween 3: Season of the Witch '82
Escape from New York '81
Halloween 2: The Nightmare Isn't Over! '81

Operation: Delta Force '97

Ray Colcord

Wish upon a Star '96
Devonsville Terror '83

Lionel Cole

Asunder '99
Spirit Lost '96

Cy Coleman(1929-2004)

Family Business '89
Power '86
Garbo Talks '84
The Heartbreak Kid '72
Sweet Charity '69
Father Goose '64

Graeme Coleman

Better Than Chocolate '99
Breach of Trust '95
Bulletproof Heart '95
Malicious '95
White Tiger '95
Breaking Point '94
Double Cross '94
Dream Man '94
Final Round '93
Common Bonds '91

Jim Coleman

Acts of Worship '01
The Unbelievable Truth '90

Lisa Coleman(1960-)

Something New '06
Juwanna Mann '02
The Third Wheel '02
Foolish '99
Hav Plenty '97
Soul Food '97

Phil Collins(1951-)

Brother Bear '03
Tarzan '99

Michel Colombier(1939-2004)

Swept Away '02
Warden of Red Rock '01
Innocents '00
Screwed '00
Pros & Cons '99
How Stella Got Her Groove Back '98
Kiss of Fire '98
Color of Justice '97
Meet Wally Sparks '97
Woo '97
Barb Wire '96
Foxfire '96
Major League 2 '94
Posse '93
The Program '93
Deep Cover '92
Folks! '92
Diary of a Hitman '91
Fever '91
New Jack City '91
Strictly Business '91
Buried Alive '90
Impulse '90
Midnight Cabaret '90
Sudie & Simpson '90
Backtrack '89
Loverboy '89
Out Cold '89
Who's Harry Crumb? '89
Cop '88
Satisfaction '88
The Wizard of Loneliness '88
The Couch Trip '87
Florida Straits '87
Surrender '87
The Golden Child '86
The Money Pit '86
Ruthless People '86
White Nights '85
Against All Odds '84
Purple Rain '84
Steel '80
Autopsy '74
Paul and Michelle '74
Les Assassins de L'Ordre '71
Colossus: The Forbin Project '70

Alberto Colombo(1889-1954)

Go for Broke! '51
Call of the Yukon '38
Dangerous Holiday '37

Juan J. Colomer

Dark Honeymoon '08
A Day Without a Mexican '04

Eric Colvin

Monte Walsh '03
Bark! '02
Crossfire Trail '01
Life-Size '00
Model Behavior '00
Escape: Human Cargo '98

Betty Comden(1915-2006)

On the Town '91
It's Always Fair Weather '55

Joseph Conlan

For Sale by Owner '09
Behind Enemy Lines 3: Colombia '08
Mortuary '05
Mosquitoman '05
Finding Home '03
Miracle Dogs '03
The Santa Trap '02
Dodson's Journey '01
Big Eden '00
The Proposal '00
Sex & Mrs. X '00
Perfect Crime '97
Silver Strand '95
Mortal Sins '92
Nick Knight '89
Hot Pursuit '87
Chained Heat '83
Code of Honor '82
Kill Squad '81

David Connor

The Dark Dancer '95
The House on Todville Road '95

Rick Conrad

Watchers 2 '90
Amityville 4: The Evil Escapes '89
Crime Zone '88
The Drifter '88
The Nest '88
The Terror Within '88

Bill Conti(1942-)

Rocky Balboa '06
Coast to Coast '04
Avenging Angelo '02
G '02
Tortilla Soup '01
American Tragedy '00
Desert Heat '99
The Thomas Crown Affair '99
The Real Macaw '98
Winchell '98
Wrongfully Accused '98
Entertaining Angels: The Dorothy Day Story '96
Napoleon '96
Spy Hard '96
Bushwhacked '95
8 Seconds '94
The Next Karate Kid '94
The Scout '94
The Adventures of Huck Finn '93
Blood In ... Blood Out: Bound by Honor '93
By the Sword '93
Rookie of the Year '93
A Captive in the Land '91
Necessary Roughness '91
Year of the Gun '91
Backstreet Dreams '90
The Fourth War '90
Rocky 5 '90
The Bear '89
The Karate Kid: Part 3 '89
Lean on Me '89
Lock Up '89
Murderers Among Us: The Simon Wiesenthal Story '89
The Big Blue '88
Cohen and Tate '88
For Keeps '88
The Gold & Glory '88
A Night in the Life of Jimmy Reardon '88
Baby Boom '87
Broadcast News '87
Happy New Year '87
I Love N.Y. '87
Masters of the Universe '87
Prayer for the Dying '87
Big Trouble '86
The Boss' Wife '86
F/X '86
The Karate Kid: Part 2 '86
Nomads '86
North and South Book 2 '86
Beer '85
Gotcha! '85
North and South Book 1 '85
Rocky 4 '85
The Karate Kid '84
Mass Appeal '84
Unfaithfully Yours '84
Bad Boys '83
The Right Stuff '83
The Terry Fox Story '83
I, the Jury '82
Rocky 3 '82
Split Image '82
That Championship Season '82
Carbon Copy '81
For Your Eyes Only '81
Neighbors '81
Victory '81
The Formula '80
Gloria '80
Private Benjamin '80
Dreamer '79
Fantastic Seven '79
Goldengirl '79
A Man, a Woman, and a Bank '79
Rocky 2 '79
The Seduction of Joe Tynan '79
The Big Fix '78
F.I.S.T. '78
Paradise Alley '78
An Unmarried Woman '78
Citizens Band '77
Next Stop, Greenwich Village '76
Rocky '76
Harry and Tonto '74
Blume in Love '73
The Garden of the Finzi-Continis '71

Michael Convertino(1953-)

Straight into Darkness '04
Liberty Stands Still '02
Dance with Me '98
Where's Marlowe? '98
Critical Care '97
Jungle 2 Jungle '96
The Last of the High Kings '96
Mother Night '96
Bed of Roses '95
Things to Do in Denver When You're Dead '95
Guarding Tess '94
Milk Money '94
The Santa Clause '94
Aspen Extreme '93
Bodies, Rest & Motion '93
A Home of Our Own '93
Wrestling Ernest Hemingway '93
The Doctor '91
The Waterdance '91
The End of Innocence '90
Shattered Dreams '90
Queen of Hearts '89
Bull Durham '88
The Hidden '87
Mistress '87
Children of a Lesser God '86
Hollywood Vice Sqaud '86
Frankenweenie '84

Ry Cooder(1947-)

My Blueberry Nights '07
Primary Colors '98
The End of Violence '97
Last Man Standing '96
Geronimo: An American Legend '93
Trespass '92
Johnny Handsome '89
Tales from the Crypt '89
Blue City '86
Crossroads '86
Alamo Bay '85
Brewster's Millions '85
Streets of Fire '84
Paris, Texas '83
The Border '82
Southern Comfort '81
The Long Riders '80

Stewart Copeland(1952-)

I Am David '04
Deuces Wild '02
On the Line '01
Boys and Girls '00
Skipped Parts '00
Made Men '99
She's All That '99
Simpatico '99
Sunset Strip '99
Legalese '98
Pecker '98
Very Bad Things '98
West Beirut '98
Four Days in September '97
Good Burger '97
Little Boy Blue '97
Welcome to Woop Woop '97
Gridlock'd '96
The Leopard Son '96
Boys '95
The Pallbearer '95
Tyson '95
White Dwarf '95
Silent Fall '94
Surviving the Game '94
Airborne '93
Bank Robber '93
Raining Stones '93
Rapa Nui '93
Riff Raff '92
Wide Sargasso Sea '92
Highlander 2: The Quickening '91
Hidden Agenda '90
Men at Work '90
Taking Care of Business '90
The First Power '89
See No Evil, Hear No Evil '89
She's Having a Baby '88
Talk Radio '88
Wall Street '87
Out of Bounds '86
Rumble Fish '83

Aaron Copland(1900-90)

The Heiress '49
The Red Pony '49
The North Star '43
Our Town '40
Of Mice and Men '39

Carmine Coppola(1911-91)

The Godfather, Part 3 '90
New York Stories '89
Tucker: The Man and His Dream '88
Gardens of Stone '87
The Outsiders '83
Apocalypse Now '79
The Black Stallion '79
The Godfather, Part 2 '74
The People '71
Tonight for Sure '61
Napoleon '27

Tony Cora

Seventh Moon '08
The Blair Witch Project '99

Normand Corbeil

America '09
The Last Templar '09
Autumn Hearts: A New Beginning '07
The Contract '07
Killer Wave '07
White Noise 2: The Light '07
Human Trafficking '05
Before the Fall '04
A Different Loyalty '04
Hitler: The Rise of Evil '03
Lost Junction '03
The Statement '03
Extreme Ops '02
Seduced: Pretty When You Cry '01
The Art of War '00
Double Jeopardy '99
Stalker '98
The Assignment '97
The Boys '97
The Kid '97
Psychopath '97
Frankenstein and Me '96
Kids of the Round Table '96
Screamers '96

Frank Cordell(1918-80)

God Told Me To '76
Ring of Bright Water '69
Khartoum '66
The Voice of Merrill '52

Carlo Maria Cordio

Sonny Boy '87
Endgame '85

Lanny Cordola

Now You Know '02
Fish in a Barrel '01

Billy Corgan

When a Man Falls in the Forest '07
Spun '02

John Corigliano(1938-)

The Red Violin '98
Altered States '80

Dale Cornelius

Strange Bedfellows '04
Till Human Voices Wake Us '02

Michael Corriveau

Bon Cop Bad Cop '06
Wilder '00

Vladimir Cosma(1940-)

The Closet '00
The Dinner Game '98
The Favor, the Watch, & the Very Big Fish '92
My Father's Glory '91
My Mother's Castle '91
The Nightmare Years '89
Just the Way You Are '84
Mistral's Daughter '84
Les Comperes '83
Diva '82
Le Bal '82
La Boum '81
La Chevre '81
Too Shy to Try '78
Pardon Mon Affaire, Too! '77
Pardon Mon Affaire '76
The Daydreamer '75
Return of the Tall Blond Man with One Black Shoe '74
Salut l'Artiste '74
The Mad Adventures of Rabbi Jacob '73
The Tall Blond Man with One Black Shoe '72

Don Costa(1925-83)

Madigan '68
Rough Night in Jericho '67

Elvis Costello(1954-)

The Shape of Things '03
Oliver Twist '00
The Courier '88
Party! Party! '83

Bruno Coulais(1954-)

Coraline '09
Oceans '09
The Secret of Kells '09
Sometimes in April '05
The Chorus '04
Belphegar: Phantom of the Louvre '01
The Crimson Rivers '01
Winged Migration '01
Balzac: A Life of Passion '99
The Count of Monte Cristo '99
Himalaya '99
Microcosmos '96
The Son of the Shark '93

Jerome Coullet

He Loves Me ... He Loves Me Not '02
Deep in the Woods '00

James Covell

The List '07
Santa with Muscles '96

Michael Covertino(1953-)

Snow White: The Fairest of Them All '02
Pie in the Sky '95

Noel Coward(1899-1973)

The Grass Is Greener '61
This Happy Breed '47
In Which We Serve '43

Rick Cox

Bram Stoker's The Mummy '97
Bad Love '95
Corrina, Corrina '94
Inside Monkey Zetterland '93

Paul Cristo

Species 4: The Awakening '07
River's End '05

Carlo Crivelli(1953-)

The Spectator '04
Ginostra '02
Marie Baie des Anges '97
Elective Affinities '96
Devil in the Flesh '87

Michael Csanyi-Wills

The Thief Lord '06
The Little Vampire '00

Xavier Cugat(1900-90)

Bathing Beauty '44
The White Zombie '32

Stephen Cullo

Proximity '00
Belly '98

Douglas J. Cuomo(1958-)

Crazy Love '07
Revolution #9 '01
Homicide: The Movie '00
In the Weeds '00
Hand Gun '93

Michael Curb(1944-)

Family Tree '00
The Big Bounce '69
Thunder Alley '67
The Wild Angels '66

Hoyt Curtin(1922-2000)

KISS Meets the Phantom of the Park '78
Mesa of Lost Women '52

Michel Cusson(1957-)

The Rocket '05
My First Wedding '04
Cruel and Unusual '01

Miriam Cutler

Flexing with Monty '10
Stolen Childhoods '05
Lost in La Mancha '03
Bikini Med School '98
Bikini House Calls '96
Illegal Affairs '96
Witchcraft 7: Judgement Hour '95
Body Parts '94
Night Fire '94
Beyond Fear '93
Pushed to the Limit '92
Witchcraft 2: The Temptress '90

Richard Cuvillier

Humanity '99
The Life of Jesus '96

Dominique Dalcan

Stealth '06
Ma Vie en Rose '97

Burkhard Dallwitz(1959-)
Paperback Hero '99
The Truman Show '98
Zone 39 '96

Roger Daltrey(1945-)
Buddy's Song '91
The Kids Are Alright '79

Paul D'Amour(1967-)
Backwoods '08
Finish Line '08
Insanitarium '08
On the Doll '07

Ikuma Dan(1924-2001)
Attack Squadron '63
I Bombed Pearl Harbor '60
Samurai 3: Duel at Ganryu Island '56
Samurai 1: Musashi Miyamoto '55
Samurai 2: Duel at Ichijoji Temple '55

John D'Andrea
Boiling Point '93
Beyond the Law '92
Child's Play 3 '91
Swimsuit '89
Body Slam '87
Savage Streets '83
Grambling's White Tiger '81

Oswald D'Andrea
Capitaine Conan '96
Every Other Weekend '91

John Dankworth(1927-)
Gangster No. 1 '00
10 Rillington Place '71
Salt & Pepper '68
Accident '67
Fathom '67
Modesty Blaise '66
Morgan: A Suitable Case for Treatment '66
Darling '65
The Servant '63
Saturday Night and Sunday Morning '60

Jeff Danna(1964-)
The Boondock Saints II: All Saints Day '09
The Imaginarium of Doctor Parnassus '09
Lakeview Terrace '08
Chicago 10 '07
Closing the Ring '07
Fracture '07
Silent Hill '06
Tideland '05
Resident Evil: Apocalypse '04
The Gospel of John '03
The Kid Stays in the Picture '02
Green Dragon '01
The Grey Zone '01
O '01
Baby '00
Boondock Saints '99
New Blood '99
Uncorked '98
The Big Slice '90

Mychael Danna(1958-)
Chloe '09
(500) Days of Summer '09
The Imaginarium of Doctor Parnassus '09
Management '09
The Time Traveler's Wife '09
Adoration '08
Lakeview Terrace '08
Trucker '08
Breach '07
Fracture '07
Surf's Up '07
Aurora Borealis '06
Little Miss Sunshine '06
Lonely Hearts '06
The Nativity Story '06
Capote '05
Tideland '05
Water '05
Where the Truth Lies '05
Being Julia '04
Vanity Fair '04
Shattered Glass '03
The Snow Walker '03
Antwone Fisher '02
Ararat '02
Green Dragon '01
Hearts in Atlantis '01
Monsoon Wedding '01
Bounce '00
Felicia's Journey '99
Girl, Interrupted '99
Ride with the Devil '99
The Confession '98
8mm '98
Behind the Lines '97
The Ice Storm '97
Kama Sutra: A Tale of Love '96
Lilies '96
The Sweet Hereafter '96
Exotica '94
Still Life '92
The Adjuster '91
The Big Slice '90
Erik '90
Speaking Parts '89
Termini Station '89
Family Viewing '87

Carl Dante(1950-)
Cypress Edge '99
The Creeps '97
Cannibal Women in the Avocado Jungle of Death '89
Slave Girls from Beyond Infinity '87

Mason Daring(1949-)
Honeydripper '07
Walker Payne '06
Silver City '04
Casa de los Babys '03
Sunshine State '02
Say It Isn't So '01
Where the Heart Is '00
Limbo '99
Music of the Heart '99
A Walk on the Moon '99
The Opposite of Sex '98
Cold Around the Heart '97
Evidence of Blood '97
Hombres Armados '97
The Ripper '97
Hidden in America '96
Prefontaine '96
Letter to My Killer '95
Lone Star '95
Getting Out '94
The Old Curiosity Shop '94
The Secret of Roan Inish '94
Fathers and Sons '92
Passion Fish '92
City of Hope '91
Wild Hearts Can't Be Broken '91
The Laserman '90
Little Vegas '90
Off and Running '90
Day One '89
Eight Men Out '88
Matewan '87
Osa '85
The Brother from Another Planet '84
Lianna '83
Return of the Secaucus 7 '80

Mohammad Reza Darvishi(1955-)
Osama '03
Kandahar '01

Peter Dasent
Heavenly Creatures '94
Dead Alive '93
Meet the Feebles '89

Gerhard Daum
Felon '08
Hollywood Kills '06

Shaun Davey(1948-)
Ella Enchanted '04
The Tailor of Panama '00
Waking Ned Devine '98
Kings in Grass Castles '97
Twelfth Night '96

Martin Davich
Gifted Hands: The Ben Carson Story '09
Mad Money '08
Jackie, Ethel, Joan: The Kennedy Women '01
La Cucaracha '99

Hal David(1921-)
What's New Pussycat? '65
The Blob '58
The Sad Sack '57

Neil Davidge
Push '09
Gomorrah '08

Howard J. Davidson
Romance and Rejection '96
Death Games '80

Iva Davies
The Incredible Journey of Mary Bryant '05
Master and Commander: The Far Side of the World '03

Victor Davies(1939-)
For the Moment '94
The Last Winter '89

Carl Davis(1936-)
Return to Cranford '09
Cranford '08
The Great Gatsby '01
Topsy Turvy '99
A Dance to the Music of Time '97
Pride and Prejudice '95
The Return of the Native '94
Widow's Peak '94
The Trial '93
Catherine Cookson's The Black Velvet Gown '92
Frankenstein Unbound '90
The Rainbow '89
Scandal '89
Hotel du Lac '86
Murrow '86
Forbidden Passion: The Oscar Wilde Movie '85
King David '85
Silas Marner '85
Champions '84
The Far Pavilions '84
Sakharov '84
Weather in the Streets '84
Praying Mantis '83
The French Lieutenant's Woman '81
Man Friday '75
The Naked Civil Servant '75
Catholics '73
Rentadick '72
I, Monster '71
Naughty Knights '71
The Only Way '70
Napoleon '27
The Eagle '25
The Thief of Baghdad '24

Don Davis(1957-)
The Good Life '07
The Marine '06
The Matrix Reloaded '03
The Matrix Revolutions '03
Ballistic: Ecks vs. Sever '02
Murder in Greenwich '02
Wilderness Love '02
Behind Enemy Lines '01
Jurassic Park 3 '01
The Unsaid '01
Valentine '01
Antitrust '00
House on Haunted Hill '99
In the Company of Spies '99
The Matrix '99
Universal Soldier: The Return '99
Route 9 '98
The Lesser Evil '97
Not in This Town '97
Robin Cook's Invasion '97
Warriors of Virtue '97
Weapons of Mass Distraction '97
The Beast '96
Bound '96
In the Lake of the Woods '96
Pandora's Clock '96
The Perfect Daughter '96

Miles Davis(1926-91)
Dingo '90
Siesta '87
Street Smart '87
Frantic '58

Guido de Angelis(1944-)
Faith '90
Body Beat '88
Devilfish '84
A Blade in the Dark '83
Ironmaster '82
Mountain of the Cannibal God '79
Shark Hunter '79
Inhibition '76
Chino '75
The Legend of Sea Wolf '75
Spaghetti Western '75
Street Law '74
Zorro '74
Torso '73
Sicilian Connection '72
Sting of the West '72

Maurizio de Angelis(1947-)
Faith '90
Body Beat '88
Devilfish '84
A Blade in the Dark '83
Ironmaster '82
Mountain of the Cannibal God '79
Shark Hunter '79
Inhibition '76
Chino '75
The Legend of Sea Wolf '75
Spaghetti Western '75
Street Law '74
Zorro '74
Torso '73
Sicilian Connection '72
Sting of the West '72

Lex de Azevedo
The Swan Princess 2: Escape from Castle Mountain '97
The Swan Princess '94
Baker's Hawk '76
Where the Red Fern Grows '74
Fearmaker '71

Marcello De Francisci
The Butcher '07
The Last Sentinel '07
Pit Fighter '05

Luchi De Jesus(1923-84)
Friday Foster '75
Bad Charleston Charlie '73
Detroit 9000 '73
Slaughter '72

Christopher De Marco
The Toxic Avenger, Part 3: The Last Temptation of Toxie '89
Troma's War '88

Francesco De Masi(1930-2005)
Formula for a Murder '85
Lone Wolf McQuade '83
New York Ripper '82
The Inglorious Bastards '78
The Arena '73
The Big Game '72
Challenge of McKenna '70
Fistful of Lead '70
Sartana's Here... Trade Your Pistol for a Coffin '70
Eagles Over London '69
Island of Lost Girls '68
Rattler Kid '68
Taste of Death '68
An Angel for Satan '66
The Triumph of Hercules '66
The Lion of Thebes '64
Magnificent Adventurer '63
Son of Hercules in the Land of Darkness '63
Colossus of the Arena '62

Jessica de Rooij
In the Name of the King: A Dungeon Siege Tale '08
Seed '08
Tunnel Rats '08
BloodRayne 2: Deliverance '07
Postal '07

Francois de Roubaix(1939-)
Old Gun '76
La Scoumoune '72
Daughters of Darkness '71
Honor Among Thieves '68
Zita '68
The Last Adventure '67
Le Samourai '67

Aldo De Scalzi(1957-)
Carnera: The Walking Mountain '08
Harem '99
Steam: A Turkish Bath '96

Manuel De Sica(1949-)
Cemetery Man '95
Men Men Men '95
The Icicle Thief '89
Bye Bye Baby '88
Hostages '80
Twist '76
The Garden of the Finzi-Continis '71

Alfonso de Villalonga
Transsiberian '08
My Life Without Me '03

Marius De Vries
Kick-Ass '10
Easy Virtue '08
Eye of the Beholder '99

De Wolfe
Jabberwocky '77
Monty Python and the Holy Grail '75

John Debney(1956-)
Iron Man 2 '10
Predators '10
Valentine's Day '10
Aliens in the Attic '09
Hotel for Dogs '09
Old Dogs '09
Meet Dave '08
My Best Friend's Girl '08
The Stoning of Soraya M. '08
Swing Vote '08
Evan Almighty '07
Georgia Rule '07
The Ant Bully '06
Barnyard '06
Everyone's Hero '06
Idlewild '06
Keeping Up with the Steins '06
The Adventures of Sharkboy and Lavagirl in 3-D '05
Cheaper by the Dozen 2 '05
Chicken Little '05
Dreamer: Inspired by a True Story '05
The Pacifier '05
Sin City '05
Zathura '05
Christmas With the Kranks '04
The Passion of the Christ '04
The Princess Diaries 2: Royal Engagement '04
Raising Helen '04
Welcome to Mooseport '04
The Whole Ten Yards '04
Bruce Almighty '03
Elf '03
Dragonfly '02
The Hot Chick '02
The Scorpion King '02
Snow Dogs '02
Spy Kids 2: The Island of Lost Dreams '02
The Tuxedo '02
Cats & Dogs '01
Heartbreakers '01
Jimmy Neutron: Boy Genius '01
The Princess Diaries '01
See Spot Run '01
Spy Kids '01
The Emperor's New Groove '00
Running Mates '00
Dick '99
End of Days '99
Inspector Gadget '99
Komodo '99
Lost and Found '99
Relative Values '99
I'll Be Home for Christmas '98
My Favorite Martian '98
Paulie '98
I Know What You Did Last Summer '97
Liar Liar '97
Carpool '96
Doctor Who '96
Getting Away With Murder '96
The Lazarus Man '96
The Relic '96
Chameleon '95
Cutthroat Island '95
In Pursuit of Honor '95
Sudden Death '95
Houseguest '94
Little Giants '94
White Fang 2: The Myth of the White Wolf '94
Gunmen '93
Hocus Pocus '93
Praying Mantis '93
Jetsons: The Movie '90
The Further Adventures of Tennessee Buck '88
Seven Hours to Judgment '88
The Wild Pair '87

Marc David Decker(1951-)
Bikini Island '91
The Dark Backward '91
The Invisible Maniac '90
Tale of Two Sisters '89

Christopher Dedrick
A Broken Life '07
Waking Up Wally '05
The Saddest Music in the World '03
Shattered City: The Halifax Explosion '03
Torso '01
Walter and Henry '01
The Courage to Love '00
This Matter of Marriage '98
Junior's Groove '97
Under the Piano '95
Race to Freedom: The Story of the Underground Railroad '94

Georges Delerue(1925-92)
Rich in Love '93
Man Trouble '92
American Friends '91
Black Robe '91
Curly Sue '91
Mister Johnson '91
Joe Versus the Volcano '90
A Show of Force '90
Cadence '89
Steel Magnolias '89
To Kill a Priest '89
Beaches '88
Biloxi Blues '88
Heartbreak Hotel '88
Her Alibi '88
The House on Carroll Street '88
Memories of Me '88
A Summer Story '88
Twins '88
Code Name: Dancer '87
Escape from Sobibor '87
The Lonely Passion of Judith Hearne '87
Maid to Order '87
A Man in Love '87
The Pick-Up Artist '87
Queenie '87
Conseil de Famille '86
Crimes of the Heart '86
Platoon '86
Salvador '86
Sword of Gideon '86
Women of Valor '86

Agnes of God *'85*
Amos *'85*
Arch of Triumph *'85*
The Execution *'85*
Maxie *'85*
A Time to Live *'85*
Aurora *'84*
Mesmerized *'84*
Silence of the Heart *'84*
The Black Stallion Returns *'83*
Confidentially Yours *'83*
Exposed *'83*
La Passante *'83*
Man, Woman & Child *'83*
One Deadly Summer *'83*
Silkwood *'83*
The Escape Artist *'82*
La Vie Continue *'82*
A Little Sex *'82*
Partners *'82*
Rich and Famous *'81*
True Confessions *'81*
The Woman Next Door *'81*
The Last Metro *'80*
Richard's Things *'80*
An Almost Perfect Affair *'79*
A Little Romance *'79*
Dear Detective *'78*
Get Out Your Handkerchiefs *'78*
Le Cavaleur *'78*
Love on the Run *'78*
Dear Detective *'77*
Julia *'77*
The Slap *'76*
Dan Candy's Law *'73*
Day for Night *'73*
The Day of the Dolphin *'73*
The Day of the Jackal *'73*
Two English Girls *'72*
The Conformist *'71*
The Horsemen *'70*
Women in Love *'70*
Anne of the Thousand Days *'69*
The Brain *'69*
The Two of Us *'68*
The King of Hearts *'66*
A Man for All Seasons *'66*
Viva Maria! *'65*
Contempt *'64*
The Pumpkin Eater *'64*
The Soft Skin *'64*
That Man from Rio *'64*
Muriel *'63*
Cartouche *'62*
Jules and Jim *'62*
Shoot the Piano Player *'62*
Time Out for Love *'61*
Classe Tous Risque *'60*
Love and the Frenchwoman *'60*
Love Play *'60*
Hiroshima, Mon Amour *'59*

Joe Delia

Carlito's Way: Rise to Power *'05*
Bought and Sold *'03*
The Tao of Steve *'00*
Fever *'99*
No Looking Back *'98*
The Blackout *'97*
The Substitute 2: School's Out *'97*
Drunks *'96*
The Funeral *'96*
The Addiction *'95*
Body Snatchers *'93*
Bad Lieutenant *'92*
King of New York *'90*
Freeway *'88*
China Girl *'87*
Ms. 45 *'81*
Driller Killer *'79*

Eric Demarsen(1938-)

Le Cercle Rouge *'70*
Army of Shadows *'69*

Gary DeMichele

Off the Map *'03*
The Secret Lives of Dentists *'02*
The Imposters *'98*

Eumir Deodato(1942-)

Bossa Nova *'99*
The Onion Field *'79*

Thomas DeRenzo(1956-)

The Breakup Artist *'04*
Control Room *'04*

Claude Desjardins

Full Disclosure *'00*
Captains Courageous *'95*
Broken Lullaby *'94*

Alexandre Desplat(1961-)

The Ghost Writer *'10*
Cheri *'09*
Coco Before Chanel *'09*
Fantastic Mr. Fox *'09*
Julie & Julia *'09*
The Twilight Saga: New Moon *'09*
Afterwards *'08*
The Curious Case of Benjamin Button *'08*
The Golden Compass *'07*
Lust, Caution *'07*
Firewall *'06*
Lies & Alibis *'06*
The Painted Veil *'06*
The Queen *'06*
The Valet *'06*
Casanova *'05*
Hostage *'05*
Syriana *'05*
The Upside of Anger *'05*
Birth *'04*
Girl with a Pearl Earring *'03*
Read My Lips *'01*
Transfixed *'01*
The Luzhin Defence *'00*
Sweet Revenge *'98*
Love, etc. *'96*
Innocent Lies *'95*
A Self-Made Hero *'95*

Pierre Desrochers

Maelstrom *'00*
La Deroute *'98*

Adolph Deutsch(1897-1980)

The Apartment *'60*
Some Like It Hot *'59*
The Long, Long Trailer *'54*
It's a Big Country *'51*
Stars in My Crown *'50*
Little Women *'49*
The Mask of Dimitrios *'44*
Action in the North Atlantic *'43*
Across the Pacific *'42*
All Through the Night *'42*
Juke Girl *'42*
Larceny, Inc. *'42*
High Sierra *'41*
The Maltese Falcon *'41*
Manpower *'41*
Underground *'41*
The Fighting 69th *'40*
Torrid Zone *'40*
A Slight Case of Murder *'38*
The Great Garrick *'37*

Frank DeVol(1911-99)

The Longest Yard *'74*
Emperor of the North Pole *'73*
Ulzana's Raid *'72*
Krakatoa East of Java *'69*
Caprice *'67*
The Dirty Dozen *'67*
Guess Who's Coming to Dinner *'67*
Cat Ballou *'65*
Good Neighbor Sam *'64*
Under the Yum-Yum Tree *'63*
What Ever Happened to Baby Jane? *'62*
Murder, Inc. *'60*
Pillow Talk *'59*
The Ride Back *'57*
Attack! *'56*
Kiss Me Deadly *'55*

Barry DeVorzon(1934-)

Exorcist 3: Legion *'90*
Night of the Creeps *'86*
Jekyll & Hyde... Together Again *'82*
Xanadu *'80*
The Warriors *'79*

Hard Times *'75*
Dillinger *'73*

Von Dexter(1912-96)

Mr. Sardonicus *'61*
13 Ghosts *'60*
The Tingler *'59*
House on Haunted Hill *'58*

Paul Di Franco

Body Chemistry 4: Full Exposure *'95*
Masseuse *'95*

Ron Di Lulio

Mountaintop Motel Massacre *'86*
Honeymoon Horror *'82*

Joel Diamond

The Believer *'01*
Anima *'98*

Neil Diamond(1941-)

The Jazz Singer *'80*
Jonathan Livingston Seagull *'73*

Antonio Diaz Conde

Night of the Bloody Apes *'68*
Doctor of Doom *'62*
The Robot vs. the Aztec Mummy *'59*
Senora Tentacion *'49*

Andrew Dickson(1945-)

Vera Drake *'04*
All or Nothing *'02*
Someone Else's America *'96*
Secrets and Lies *'95*
Naked *'93*
Meantime *'81*

John Dickson

Lost Colony: The Legend of Roanoke *'07*
Showdown at Area 51 *'07*
Mammoth *'06*
Darklight *'04*

Vince DiCola

Sci-Fighter *'04*
Transformers: The Movie *'86*
Rocky 4 *'85*

Robert Diggs

See RZA

Loek Dikker(1944-)

Rosenstrasse *'03*
The Babysitter *'95*
The Escape *'95*
Body Parts *'91*
Pascali's Island *'88*
Slow Burn *'86*
The 4th Man *'79*

Jerome Dillon

The Collector *'09*
Vacancy 2: The First Cut *'08*

Ramin Djawadi(1974-)

The Unborn *'09*
Deception *'08*
Fly Me to the Moon *'08*
Iron Man *'08*
Mr. Brooks *'07*
Ask the Dust *'06*
Open Season *'06*
Blade: Trinity *'04*

DMX(1970-)

Last Hour *'08*
Never Die Alone *'04*

Robert Emmett Dolan(1906-72)

King Kong vs. Godzilla *'63*
The Three Faces of Eve *'57*
The Great Gatsby *'49*
My Favorite Brunette *'47*
Saigon *'47*
The Bells of St. Mary's *'45*
Murder, He Says *'45*
Salty O'Rourke *'45*
The Major and the Minor *'42*
Birth of the Blues *'41*

Thomas Dolby(1958-)

Gothic *'87*
Fever Pitch *'85*

Klaus Doldinger(1936-)

Palmetto *'98*
Me and Him *'89*

A Father's Revenge *'88*
The NeverEnding Story *'84*
Das Boot *'81*
Black and White As Day and Night *'78*
The Second Awakening of Christa Klages *'78*
Swiss Conspiracy *'77*

Francois Dompierre(1943-)

Stardom *'00*
It's My Turn, Laura Cadieux *'98*
Vanished *'95*
Jesus of Montreal *'89*

Pino Donaggio(1941-)

Winter in Wartime *'10*
Seed of Chucky *'04*
Up at the Villa *'00*
Rescuers: Stories of Courage—Two Couples *'98*
Backlash: Oblivion 2 *'95*
Never Talk to Strangers *'95*
Oblivion *'94*
Troublemakers *'94*
A Fine Romance *'92*
Indio 2: The Revolt *'92*
Raising Cain *'92*
The Devil's Daughter *'91*
Meridian: Kiss of the Beast *'90*
Two Evil Eyes *'90*
Catacombs *'89*
Night Game *'89*
Appointment with Death *'88*
Hotel Colonial *'88*
Kansas *'88*
Zelly & Me *'88*
The Barbarians *'87*
Dancers *'87*
Phantom of Death *'87*
Crawlspace *'86*
The Berlin Affair *'85*
Hercules 2 *'85*
The Assisi Underground *'84*
Body Double *'84*
Deja Vu *'84*
Ordeal by Innocence *'84*
Hercules *'83*
Over the Brooklyn Bridge *'83*
Tex *'82*
The Black Cat *'81*
Blow Out *'81*
The Fan *'81*
The Howling *'81*
Vatican Conspiracy *'81*
Beyond Evil *'80*
Dressed to Kill *'80*
Home Movies *'79*
Tourist Trap *'79*
Gunfire *'78*
Piranha *'78*
Haunts *'77*
Carrie *'76*
Don't Look Now *'73*

Marc Donahue(1953-2002)

After Midnight *'89*
Opposing Force *'87*
Murphy's Law *'86*
Lies *'83*

Donovan(1946-)

84 Charlie MoPic *'89*
Brother Sun, Sister Moon *'73*

James Dooley(1976-)

Obsessed *'09*
Bachelor Party 2: The Last Temptation *'08*
Daddy Day Camp *'07*
When a Stranger Calls *'06*

Steve Dorff(1949-)

The Junction Boys *'02*
Dudley Do-Right *'99*
Blast from the Past *'98*
Dancer, Texas—Pop. 81 *'98*
Coyote Summer *'96*
Breaking Free *'95*
The Undercover Kid *'95*
Murder So Sweet *'93*
Pure Country *'92*
Kiss Shot *'89*

Pink Cadillac *'89*
My Best Friend Is a Vampire *'88*
Back to the Beach *'87*
The Quick and the Dead *'87*
Convicted *'86*
Manhunt for Claude Dallas *'86*
Rustler's Rhapsody *'85*
Stick *'85*
Cannonball Run 2 *'84*
Honkytonk Man *'82*
Honky Tonk Freeway *'81*
Bronco Billy *'80*
Every Which Way But Loose *'78*
The Defiant Ones *'58*

Adam Dorn

Crazy Little Thing *'02*
The Doe Boy *'01*

Ivan Dorochuk

Universal Soldier 2: Brothers in Arms *'98*
Universal Soldier 3: Unfinished Business *'98*

Patrick Doyle(1953-)

Igor *'08*
Nim's Island *'08*
The Last Legion *'07*
Sleuth *'07*
As You Like It *'06*
Eragon *'06*
Nanny McPhee *'06*
Harry Potter and the Goblet of Fire *'05*
Wah-Wah *'05*
Calendar Girls *'03*
Secondhand Lions *'03*
Bridget Jones's Diary *'01*
Gosford Park *'01*
Killing Me Softly *'01*
Blow Dry *'00*
Love's Labour's Lost *'00*
East-West *'99*
Quest for Camelot *'98*
Great Expectations *'97*
Donnie Brasco *'96*
Hamlet *'96*
Mrs. Winterbourne *'96*
A Little Princess *'95*
Sense and Sensibility *'95*
Exit to Eden *'94*
Mary Shelley's Frankenstein *'94*
Carlito's Way *'93*
Much Ado about Nothing *'93*
Needful Things *'93*
Indochine *'92*
Into the West *'92*
Dead Again *'91*
Shipwrecked *'90*
Henry V *'89*

Carmen Dragon(1914-84)

Invasion of the Body Snatchers *'56*
The Strange Woman *'46*
Mr. Winkle Goes to War *'44*

Elizabeth Drake

Japanese Story *'03*
Road to Nhill *'97*

Robert Jackson Drasnin

Murder Once Removed *'71*
The Tattered Web *'71*
They Call It Murder *'71*
Ride in the Whirlwind *'66*

George Dreyfus(1928-)

The Fringe Dwellers *'86*
Tender Mercies *'83*

Ludek Drizhal(1966-)

Badland *'07*
Simon Says *'07*
Slayer *'06*
Voodoo Moon *'05*

Pete Droge

Tattoo, a Love Story *'02*
Tattoo, a Love Story *'02*

John Du Prez(1946-)

Fascination *'04*
Fascination *'04*

Mr. Toad's Wild Ride *'96*
Teenage Mutant Ninja Turtles 3 *'93*
Carry On Columbus *'92*
Mystery Date *'91*
Bullseye! *'90*
Teenage Mutant Ninja Turtles: The Movie *'90*
A Chorus of Disapproval *'89*
UHF *'89*
A Fish Called Wanda *'88*
Personal Services *'87*
Love with a Perfect Stranger *'86*
Once Bitten *'85*
Oxford Blues *'84*
A Private Function *'84*
She'll Be Wearing Pink Pajamas *'84*
Bullshot *'83*
Monty Python's The Meaning of Life *'83*

Al Dubin(1891-1945)

Stage Door Canteen *'43*
42nd Street *'33*

Joseph Dubin

G.I. War Brides *'46*
Silver City Kid *'45*

Jack Curtis Dubowsky

Redwoods *'09*
Rock Haven *'07*
Under One Roof *'02*

Anne Dudley(1956-)

The Walker *'07*
Black Book *'06*
Tristan & Isolde *'06*
Bright Young Things *'03*
A Man Apart *'03*
The Gathering *'02*
Lucky Break *'01*
Monkeybone *'01*
The Miracle Maker: The Story of Jesus *'00*
The 10th Kingdom *'00*
Pushing Tin *'99*
American History X *'98*
The Full Monty *'96*
Grave Indiscretions *'96*
Hollow Reed *'95*
When Saturday Comes *'95*
Knight Moves *'93*
The Crying Game *'92*
The Miracle *'91*
The Pope Must Diet *'91*
The Misadventures of Mr. Wilt *'90*
Silence Like Glass *'90*
The Mighty Quinn *'89*
Say Anything *'89*
Buster *'88*
Disorderlies *'87*
Hiding Out *'87*

Antoine Duhamel(1925-)

The Girl of Your Dreams *'99*
Ridicule *'96*
Belle Epoque *'92*
Daddy Nostalgia *'90*
Twisted Obsession *'90*
Bed and Board *'70*
The Wild Child *'70*
Mississippi Mermaid *'69*
Stolen Kisses *'68*
Weekend *'67*
Pierrot le Fou *'65*

George Duke(1946-)

Never Die Alone *'04*
Good Fences *'03*

Tan Dun(1957-)

Hero *'03*
Crouching Tiger, Hidden Dragon *'00*
Fallen *'97*

Robert Duncan

Into the Blue 2: The Reef *'09*
The Cutting Edge 3: Chasing the Dream *'08*
Shattered *'07*
Vampire Effect *'03*
Battle Queen 2020 *'99*

David Dundas(1945-)
How to Get Ahead in Advertising '89
Withnail and I '87

George Duning(1908-2000)
Goliath Awaits '81
The Man with Bogart's Face '80
Abduction of St. Anne '75
Arnold '73
Honor Thy Father '73
Pat Garrett & Billy the Kid '73
Terror in the Wax Museum '73
Yuma '70
Then Came Bronson '68
Any Wednesday '66
My Blood Runs Cold '65
Critic's Choice '63
The Notorious Landlady '62
That Touch of Mink '62
The Devil at 4 O'Clock '61
All the Young Men '60
Let No Man Write My Epitaph '60
1001 Arabian Nights '59
Bell, Book and Candle '58
Cowboy '58
Houseboat '58
Me and the Colonel '58
The Brothers Rico '57
Operation Mad Ball '57
3:10 to Yuma '57
The Eddy Duchin Story '56
5 Against the House '55
The Man from Laramie '55
Picnic '55
Queen Bee '55
Three for the Show '55
Tight Spot '55
From Here to Eternity '53
Salome '53
Scandal Sheet '52
Harriet Craig '50
The Dark Past '49
The Doolins of Oklahoma '49
Jolson Sings Again '49
Lust for Gold '49
Man from Colorado '49
Shockproof '49
Down to Earth '47
Her Husband's Affairs '47

Paul Dunlap(1919-)
Naked Kiss '64
Shock Corridor '63
The Three Stooges Meet Hercules '61
The Angry Red Planet '59
The Rebel Set '59
Blood of Dracula '57
Crime of Passion '57
Guns Don't Argue '57
I Was a Teenage Werewolf '57
Portland Expose '57
The Finger Man '55
Shack Out on 101 '55
Stranger on Horseback '55
Hellgate '52
The Lost Continent '51
The Steel Helmet '51
Hi-Jacked '50

Nick Dyer
Never Forget '08
Saving God '08
Grindstone Road '07
A Lobster Tale '06

Bob Dylan(1941-)
Masked and Anonymous '03
High Stakes '89

Kiril Dzajkovski
The Great Water '04
Dust '01

Arie Dzierlatka
Mon Oncle d'Amerique '80
Messidor '77
Chloe in the Afternoon '72

Brian Easdale(1909-95)
Peeping Tom '60
The Red Shoes '48
Black Narcissus '47

Clint Eastwood(1930-)
Changeling '08
Grace Is Gone '07
Flags of Our Fathers '06
Million Dollar Baby '04
Mystic River '03

Kyle Eastwood(1968-)
Gran Torino '08
Rails & Ties '07
Letters from Iwo Jima '06

Randy Edelman(1947-)
Leap Year '10
The Mummy: Tomb of the Dragon Emperor '08
27 Dresses '08
Balls of Fury '07
Underdog '07
The Last Time '06
Son of the Mask '05
Connie and Carla '04
Surviving Christmas '04
Gods and Generals '03
National Security '03
Shanghai Knights '03
Frank McKlusky, C.I. '02
A Season on the Brink '02
Who is Cletis Tout? '02
XXX '02
Black Knight '01
Corky Romano '01
Head Over Heels '01
Osmosis Jones '01
Passion of Mind '00
Shanghai Noon '00
The Skulls '00
The Whole Nine Yards '00
EDtv '99
The Hunley '99
Six Days, Seven Nights '98
For Richer or Poorer '97
Gone Fishin' '97
Leave It to Beaver '97
Anaconda '96
Daylight '96
Diabolique '96
Down Periscope '96
Dragonheart '96
The Quest '96
The Big Green '95
Citizen X '95
While You Were Sleeping '95
Angels in the Outfield '94
Billy Madison '94
Greedy '94
The Mask '94
Pontiac Moon '94
Beethoven's 2nd '93
Dragon: The Bruce Lee Story '93
Gettysburg '93
Beethoven '92
The Distinguished Gentleman '92
The Last of the Mohicans '92
My Cousin Vinny '92
Drop Dead Fred '91
Shout '91
V.I. Warshawski '91
Come See the Paradise '90
Kindergarten Cop '90
Quick Change '90
Ghostbusters 2 '89
Troop Beverly Hills '89
Feds '88
Twins '88
Scandal Sheet '85
When Your Lover Leaves '83
Red, White & Busted '75
Executive Action '73
Snatched '72

Roger Edens(1905-70)
Take Me Out to the Ball Game '49
Good News '47
Till the Clouds Roll By '46
Go West '40
Ice Follies of 1939 '39

Greg Edmonson
Luckytown '00
Blue Ridge Fall '99
Undercover Angel '99
Frog and Wombat '98
Last Lives '98
Turn of the Blade '97

Stephen (Steve) Edwards
Direct Contact '09
Lies and Illusions '09
Feast 2: Sloppy Seconds '08
Finding Rin Tin Tin '07
The Neighbor '07
Feast '06
Undisputed II: Last Man Standing '06
The Upside of Anger '05
Audrey's Rain '03
Special Forces '03
Hellraiser: Hellseeker '02
No Sleep 'Til Madison '02
Hard Cash '01
U.S. Seals 2 '01
Cowboys and Angels '00
Luck of the Draw '00
75 Degrees '00
The Substitute 4: Failure is Not an Option '00
Bridge of Dragons '99
K-911 '99
The Patriot '99
Cold Harvest '98
High Voltage '98
T.N.T. '98
Bloodsport 3 '97
Diary of a Serial Killer '97
Conspiracy of Fear '96
Illegal in Blue '95
Project Shadowchaser 3000 '95
Night Siege Project: Shadowchaser 2 '94
The Camomile Lawn '92

Robert Een
The Rook '99
Mr. Jealousy '98

Cliff Eidelman(1967-)
He's Just Not That Into You '09
Open Window '06
Sisterhood of the Traveling Pants '05
The Lizzie McGuire Movie '03
Harrison's Flowers '02
An American Rhapsody '01
Witness Protection '99
One True Thing '98
The Beautician and the Beast '97
Free Willy 3: The Rescue '97
Montana '97
If These Walls Could Talk '96
Now and Then '95
My Girl 2 '94
Picture Bride '94
A Simple Twist of Fate '94
Untamed Heart '93
Christopher Columbus: The Discovery '92
Leap of Faith '92
Delirious '91
Star Trek 6: The Undiscovered Country '91
Crazy People '90
Strike It Rich '90
Animal Behavior '89
Dead Man Out '89
To Die For '89
Triumph of the Spirit '89

Ludovico Einaudi(1955-)
This Is England '06
Doctor Zhivago '03
Light of My Eyes '01
Not of This World '99

Richard Einhorn
A House in the Hills '93
Closet Land '90
Blood Rage '87
Dead of Winter '87
Sister, Sister '87
Eyes of a Stranger '81
The Prowler '81
Don't Go in the House '80
Shock Waves '77

Hanns Eisler(1898-1962)
A Scandal in Paris '46
Hangmen Also Die '42
Kuhle Wampe, Or Who Owns the World? '32

Konrad Elfers
Pippi Longstocking '69
Funeral in Berlin '66

Danny Elfman(1953-)
Alice in Wonderland '10
Notorious '09
Taking Woodstock '09
Terminator Salvation '09
The Wolfman '09
Hellboy II: The Golden Army '08
Milk '08
Standard Operating Procedure '08
Wanted '08
The Kingdom '07
Meet the Robinsons '07
Charlotte's Web '06
Nacho Libre '06
Charlie and the Chocolate Factory '05
Tim Burton's Corpse Bride '05
Spider-Man 2 '04
Big Fish '03
Hulk '03
Chicago '02
Men in Black 2 '02
Red Dragon '02
Spider-Man '02
Planet of the Apes '01
Spy Kids '01
Family Man '00
Proof of Life '00
Anywhere But Here '99
Instinct '99
Sleepy Hollow '99
A Civil Action '98
Modern Vampires '98
A Simple Plan '98
Flubber '97
Good Will Hunting '97
Men in Black '97
Extreme Measures '96
The Frighteners '96
Mars Attacks! '96
Mission: Impossible '96
Dead Presidents '95
Freeway '95
To Die For '95
Dolores Claiborne '94
The Nightmare Before Christmas '93
Sommersby '93
Army of Darkness '92
Article 99 '92
Batman Returns '92
Darkman '90
Dick Tracy '90
Edward Scissorhands '90
The Flash '90
Nightbreed '90
Batman '89
Beetlejuice '88
Big Top Pee-wee '88
Hot to Trot! '88
Midnight Run '88
Scrooged '88
Summer School '87
Wisdom '87
Back to School '86
Pee-wee's Big Adventure '85
Forbidden Zone '80

Jonathan Elias
Fighting '09
Pathfinder '07
A Guide to Recognizing Your Saints '06
Leprechaun 2 '94
Morning Glory '93
Far from Home '89
Parents '89
Rude Awakening '89
Shakedown '88
Two Moon Junction '88
Vamp '86
Almost You '85
Key Exchange '85
Tuff Turf '85
Children of the Corn '84

Boris Elkis
A Perfect Getaway '09
The Godson '98
Bugged! '96

Duke Ellington(1899-1974)
Paris Blues '61
Anatomy of a Murder '59
Cabin in the Sky '43

Alan Elliott(1964-)
Let's Go to Prison '06
Seeing Other People '04
Borough of Kings '98

Bill Elliott
Carry Me Home '04
Sticks '98
Stand-Ins '97

Jack Elliott(1927-2001)
The Jerk '79
The Man Without a Country '73
Get to Know Your Rabbit '72
Support Your Local Gunfighter '71
Where's Poppa? '70

Don Ellis(1934-78)
Ruby '77
French Connection 2 '75
The French Connection '71

Marc Ellis
Adam Sandler's 8 Crazy Nights '02
Master of Disguise '02
Assault of the Killer Bimbos '88

Warren Ellis
The Assassination of Jesse James by the Coward Robert Ford '07
The Proposition '05

Timo Elliston
Rapturious '07
Blood Relic '05

Keith Emerson(1944-)
The Church '98
Best Revenge '83
Nighthawks '81
Inferno '80

Stephen Endelman
Free Style '09
Street Fighter: The Legend of Chun-Li '09
Streets of Blood '09
Redbelt '08
O Jerusalem '07
Home of the Brave '06
The Net 2.0 '06
Phat Girlz '06
Knights of the South Bronx '05
The Blue Butterfly '04
Evelyn '02
I'm with Lucy '02
Bride of the Wind '01
Blue Moon '00
Earthly Possessions '99
Two Family House '99
Finding Graceland '98
Witness to the Mob '98
Kicked in the Head '97
The Proposition '97
City of Industry '96
Ed '96
Keys to Tulsa '96
Cosi '95
The Englishman Who Went up a Hill But Came down a Mountain '95
Flirting with Disaster '95
Jeffrey '95
The Journey of August King '95
Postcards from America '95
Reckless '95
Tom and Huck '95
The Desperate Trail '94
Imaginary Crimes '94
Household Saints '93
Operation Condor '91

Koji Endo(1964-)
Sukiyaki Western Django '08
The Great Yokai War '05
Three ... Extremes '04
Zebraman '04
Gozu '03
One Missed Call '03
Graveyard of Honor '02
The Happiness of the Katakuris '01
Visitor Q '01
Audition '99

Paul Englishby
An Education '09
An Englishman in New York '09
Miss Pettigrew Lives for a Day '08
Confetti '06

Charles Engstrom
Coastlines '02
Ulee's Gold '97
Ruby in Paradise '93
A Flash of Green '85

Brian Eno(1948-)
Boarding Gate '07
The Jacket '05
Clean '04
Fear X '03
Buddy Boy '99
The Million Dollar Hotel '99
Neil Gaiman's NeverWhere '96
Dune '84
Sebastiane '79
Land of the Minotaur '77

John Entwhistle(1944-2002)
The Kids Are Alright '79
Quadrophenia '79
Tommy '75

Micky Erbe
Blackjack '97
Ticket to Heaven '81

Leo Erdody(1888-1949)
Detour '46
Larceny in her Heart '46
Strange Illusion '45
Dead Men Walk '43
Girls in Chains '43

Sebastien Erms
A Summer's Tale '96
Rendezvous in Paris '95
A Tale of Winter '92

Bengt Ernryd
The New Land '73
I Am Curious (Yellow) '67

Nicolas Errera
XIII '08
The Butterfly '02

Jim Ervin
Uncovered: The War on Iraq '04
The Man in the Iron Mask '97
Ripper Man '96

Harry Escott
A Mighty Heart '07
The Road to Guantanamo '06

Ilan Eshkeri
Ninja Assassin '09
The Young Victoria '09
The Disappeared '08
Closure '07
Hannibal Rising '07
Stardust '07
Virgin Territory '07
Layer Cake '05

Pascal Esteve(1961-)
Intimate Strangers '04
The Man on the Train '02
The Widow of Saint-Pierre '00
The Perfume of Yvonne '94

Asher Ettinger
Brave New Girl '04
Joan of Arc '99

Francois Eudes(1974-)
High Tension '03
Who Killed Bambi? '03

Evan Evans(1975-)
The Poker Club '08
Newsbreak '00
TripFall '00
Wicked Ways '99

Ray Evans(1915-2007)
Red Garters '54
The Lemon Drop Kid '51

Mark Oliver Everett
Yes Man '08
Levity '03

Harold Faltermeyer(1952-)
Kuffs '92
Fletch Lives '89
Tango and Cash '89
Beverly Hills Cop 2 '87
Fatal Beauty '87
Fire and Ice '87
The Running Man '87
Top Gun '86
Fletch '85
Beverly Hills Cop '84
Thief of Hearts '84

Sharon Farber
Dark Justice '00
They Call Me Sirr '00
In a Class of His Own '99

Guy Farley(1963-)
The Broken '08
Clive Barker's Book of Blood '08
The Christmas Miracle of Jonathan Toomey '07
The Flock '07
Cashback '06
Land of the Blind '06
Submerged '05
Modigliani '04
Sorted '04
Darkness Falls '98

Jim Farmer
Double Whammy '01
The Waiting Game '99
The Real Blonde '97
Box of Moonlight '96
Living in Oblivion '94
Johnny Suede '92

Robert Farnon(1917-2005)
Shalako '68
The Sheriff of Fractured Jaw '59

Kurt Farquhar
Not Easily Broken '09
Cover '08

Robert Farrar
Terror at Tenkiller '86
The Last Contract '77
Don't Look in the Basement '73

Chris Farrell
The Hazing '04
Shakedown '02
Hard As Nails '01

Christopher Farrell
Nightmare Man '06
Serial Slayer '03

Ricky Fataar(1952-)
The Efficiency Expert '92
High Tide '87

Louis Febre
Alien Trespass '09
Breakaway '02
Dead in a Heartbeat '02
Swimfan '02
A Woman's a Helluva Thing '01
First Daughter '99
Dean Koontz's Mr. Murder '98
Little Bigfoot '96
Last Man Standing '95
Rage '95
Serial Killer '95
Two Bits & Pepper '95
Fists of Iron '94
The Force '94
The Secretary '94

Jack Feldman
Thumbelina '94
Newsies '92

Tony Fennell
Megalodon '03
Within the Rock '96

George Fenton(1950-)
Looking for Eric '09
Fool's Gold '08
Earth '07
The History Boys '06
Last Holiday '06
The Wind That Shakes the Barley '06
Bewitched '05
Hitch '05
Mrs. Henderson Presents '05
Valiant '05
A Fond Kiss '04
Imagining Argentina '04
Stage Beauty '04
Deep Blue '03
Sweet Home Alabama '02
Sweet Sixteen '02
The Navigators '01
Summer Catch '01
Bread and Roses '00
Center Stage '00
Lucky Numbers '00
Anna and the King '99
Entropy '99
Grey Owl '99
Dangerous Beauty '98
Ever After: A Cinderella Story '98
Living Out Loud '98
My Name Is Joe '98
The Object of My Affection '98
You've Got Mail '98
Carla's Song '97
The Crucible '96
In Love and War '96
Multiplicity '96
Heaven's Prisoners '95
Land and Freedom '95
Mary Reilly '95
The Madness of King George '94
Mixed Nuts '94
Born Yesterday '93
Groundhog Day '93
Ladybird, Ladybird '93
Shadowlands '93
Final Analysis '92
Hero '92
China Moon '91
The Fisher King '91
Memphis Belle '90
White Palace '90
The Dressmaker '89
The Long Walk Home '89
We're No Angels '89
Dangerous Liaisons '88
A Handful of Dust '88
High Spirits '88
White Mischief '88
White of the Eye '88
Cry Freedom '87
Saigon: Year of the Cat '87
Clockwise '86
84 Charing Cross Road '86
The Company of Wolves '85
The Jewel in the Crown '84
An Englishman Abroad '83
Gandhi '82
Hussy '80

Allyn Ferguson
High Noon '00
All Quiet on the Western Front '79
The Man Without a Country '73
Get to Know Your Rabbit '72
Support Your Local Gunfighter '71

David Ferguson
Catherine Cookson's The Gambling Man '98
Hostile Waters '97
The Woman in White '97
A Dark Adapted Eye '93
Dead Ahead: The Exxon Valdez Disaster '92
A Fatal Inversion '92
Tailspin: Behind the Korean Airline Tragedy '89

Jay Ferguson(1943-)
Paradise, Texas '05
Tremors 2: Aftershocks '96
Double Dragon '94
Gleaming the Cube '89
A Nightmare on Elm Street 5: Dream Child '89
Race for Glory '89
Bad Dreams '88
Johnny Be Good '88
License to Drive '88
Pulse '88
Best Seller '87
The Patriot '86
Quiet Cool '86

Ralph Ferraro
Flesh Gordon '72
The She-Beast '65

Gianni Ferrio(1924-)
Sundance and the Kid '69
Blood for a Silver Dollar '66
Fort Yuma Gold '66
Fiances '63

Paul Ferris(1941-95)
The Conqueror Worm '68
Blood Beast Terror '67

Cy Feuer(1911-2006)
Sundown Fury '42
Bad Man of Deadwood '41
Mr. District Attorney '41
Nevada City '41
West of Cimarron '41
Adventures of Red Ryder '40
Carson City Kid '40
Drums of Fu Manchu '40
Pioneers of the West '40
Come on Rangers '38
Heroes of the Hills '38

Nico Fidenco(1933-)
Doctor Butcher M.D. '80
Trap Them & Kill Them '77
Diary of a Rebel '68

Brad Fiedel(1951-)
Eden '98
Mistrial '96
Rasputin: Dark Servant of Destiny '96
Johnny Mnemonic '95
True Lies '94
Blink '93
The Real McCoy '93
Striking Distance '93
Gladiator '92
Straight Talk '92
Terminator 2: Judgment Day '91
Blue Steel '90
Forgotten Prisoners '90
Cold Sassy Tree '89
Immediate Family '89
Perfect Witness '89
True Believer '89
The Accused '88
Fright Night 2 '88
Weekend War '88
The Big Easy '87
Bluffing It '87
Hostage '87
The Last Innocent Man '87
Let's Get Harry '87
The Serpent and the Rainbow '87
Brotherhood of Justice '86
Desert Bloom '86
The Midnight Hour '86
Compromising Positions '85
Fraternity Vacation '85
Fright Night '85
Girls of the White Orchid '85
Into Thin Air '85
The Baron and the Kid '84
Calendar Girl Murders '84
Children in the Crossfire '84
Eyes of Fire '84
Mae West '84
My Mother's Secret Life '84
Right of Way '84
The Terminator '84
Cocaine: One Man's Seduction '83
Murder in Coweta County '83
Nowhere to Hide '83
Born Beautiful '82
Hit & Run '82
Night School '81
The People vs. Jean Harris '81
The Day the Women Got Even '80
Hardhat & Legs '80
Just Before Dawn '80
Playing for Time '80
Deadly Hero '75

Jerry Fielding(1922-80)
Escape from Alcatraz '79
The Gauntlet '77
The Bad News Bears '76
The Enforcer '76
The Outlaw Josey Wales '76
The Killer Elite '75
Bring Me the Head of Alfredo Garcia '74
The Gambler '74
Junior Bonner '72
The Mechanic '72
The Nightcomers '72
Straw Dogs '72
Chato's Land '71
Johnny Got His Gun '71
Lawman '71
Hard Frame '70
The Wild Bunch '69

Adam Fields(1965-)
Meeting Daddy '98
Lovelife '97

Dorothy Fields(1905-74)
Joy of Living '38
Swing Time '36

Magnus Fiennes(1965-)
The Last Enemy '08
Five Days '07
Onegin '99
Preaching to the Perverted '97

Mike Figgis(1948-)
Cold Creek Manor '03
Hotel '01
Time Code '00
Miss Julie '99
The Loss of Sexual Innocence '98
One Night Stand '97
Leaving Las Vegas '95
Liebestraum '91
Internal Affairs '90
Stormy Monday '88

David Findlay
Nowhere in Sight '01
Dead Silent '99
Captive '97
Eye '96

Sylvia Fine(1913-91)
Court Jester '56
The Secret Life of Walter Mitty '47

Neil Finn(1958-)
Perfect Strangers '03
Rain '01

Chad Fischer
The Rocker '08
The Babysitters '07
Little Manhattan '05

Gunther Fischer(1944-)
Bear Ye One Another's Burden... '88
Solo Sunny '80

Peter Fish
A Tale of Two Pizzas '03
Intimate Betrayal '96
Wigstock: The Movie '95

Simon Fisher Turner(1954-)
I'll Sleep When I'm Dead '03
The Eternal '99
Claire Dolan '97
Croupier '97
Nadja '95
Loaded '94
Blue '93
Edward II '92
The Garden '90
The Last of England '87

Frank Fitzpatrick
Jump In! '07
Paid in Full '02
Love Song '00
The Pirates of Silicon Valley '99
Friday '95

Patrick Flynn
Caddie '76
Sunday Too Far Away '74

Claude Foisy
Pontypool '09
Wrong Turn 3: Left for Dead '09
Kiss Me Deadly '08
White Noise '05
We'll Meet Again '02
2001: A Space Travesty '00

Pierre Foldes
12 and Holding '05
From Other Worlds '04
L.I.E. '01

Ruy Folguera
A Painted House '03
Picking Up the Pieces '99

Robert Folk(1949-)
Beethoven's Big Break '08
National Lampoon's Van Wilder 2: The Rise of Taj '06
American Pie Presents Band Camp '05
Back in the Day '05
Boat Trip '03
National Lampoon's Holiday Reunion '03
Kung Pow! Enter the Fist '02
Held Up '00
Major League 3: Back to the Minors '98
Booty Call '96
Maximum Risk '96
Nothing to Lose '96
The Thief and the Cobbler '96
Ace Ventura: When Nature Calls '95
Lawnmower Man 2: Beyond Cyberspace '95
Theodore Rex '95
In the Army Now '94
Police Academy 7: Mission to Moscow '94
Trapped in Paradise '94
A Troll in Central Park '94
National Lampoon's Loaded Weapon 1 '93
Rock-a-Doodle '92
Beastmaster 2: Through the Portal of Time '91
A Climate for Killing '91
NeverEnding Story 2: The Next Chapter '91
Toy Soldiers '91
Honeymoon Academy '90
Happy Together '89
Police Academy 6: City under Siege '89
Wicked Stepmother '89
Miles from Home '88
Police Academy 5: Assignment Miami Beach '88
Can't Buy Me Love '87
Police Academy 4: Citizens on Patrol '87
Prince of Bel Air '87
Police Academy 3: Back in Training '86
Stewardess School '86
Odd Jobs '85
Bachelor Party '84
Police Academy '84
Purple Hearts '84
The Slayer '82

Mark Fontana
Axe '06
Dark Town '04

Sherman Foote
It Takes Two '95
Parents '89

Louis Forbes(1902-81)
The Bat '59
Slightly Scarlet '56
Pearl of the South Pacific '55
Tennessee's Partner '55
Pitfall '48
Made for Each Other '39

Lou Forestieri
Sherlock: Undercover Dog '94
Twin Sisters '91
Crazy Moon '87

Keith Forsey(1948-)
Wisegirls '02
The Breakfast Club '85

David Foster(1949-)
The Little Rascals '94
If Looks Could Kill '91
Listen to Me '89
Fresh Horses '88
Stealing Home '88
The Secret of My Success '87
St. Elmo's Fire '85

Charles Fox(1940-)
Collected Stories '02
A Death in the Family '02
The Song of the Lark '01
The Broken Chain '93
A Thousand Heroes '92
Repossessed '90
False Witness '89
The Gods Must Be Crazy 2 '89
Hard to Kill '89
One Man Force '89
Short Circuit 2 '88
Christmas Comes to Willow Creek '87
Love at Stake '87
The Longshot '86
Unnatural Causes '86
Doin' Time '85
National Lampoon's European Vacation '85
A Summer to Remember '84
Strange Brew '83
Trenchcoat '83
Love Child '82
Six Pack '82
Zapped! '82
The Last Married Couple in America '80
Little Darlings '80
9 to 5 '80
Oh, God! Book 2 '80
Better Late Than Never '79
Foul Play '78
Rainbow '78
One on One '77
The Duchess and the Dirtwater Fox '76
Two Minute Warning '76
Victory at Entebbe '76
Bug '75
The Drowning Pool '75
My Father's House '75
The Other Side of the Mountain '75
The Laughing Policeman '74
The Stranger Within '74
Dying Room Only '73
The Last American Hero '73
A Separate Peace '73
Star Spangled Girl '71
Pufnstuf '70
Goodbye Columbus '69
Barbarella '68
The Green Slime '68
The Incident '67

Neal Fox
Killer Tomatoes Strike Back '90
Return of the Killer Tomatoes! '88

Carlo Franci
Two Gladiators '64
The Invincible Gladiator '62

Carlo Franci(1927-)
Erik, the Viking '65
Hercules against the Moon Men '64

The Beast of Babylon Against the Son of Hercules '63
The Invincible Gladiator '62
Medusa Against the Son of Hercules '62
The Wide Blue Road '57
Young Caruso '51

Jess (Jesus) Franco(1930-)
Devil Hunter '08
Tender Flesh '97
The Diabolical Dr. Z '65

David Michael Frank
Sherman's Way '08
Slap Her, She's French '02
The Last Warrior '99
Billboard Dad '98
A Kid in Aladdin's Palace '97
A Prayer in the Dark '97
Volcano: Fire on the Mountain '97
Annie: A Royal Adventure '95
The Baby-Sitters' Club '95
The Prince '95
Tails You Live, Heads You're Dead '95
Bitter Vengeance '94
Best of the Best 2 '93
Casualties of Love: The "Long Island Lolita" Story '93
Extreme Justice '93
Linda '93
Poison Ivy '92
Going Under '91
Out for Justice '91
Showdown in Little Tokyo '91
Above the Law '88
Hero and the Terror '88
I'm Gonna Git You Sucka '88
Mirror of Death '87

Christopher Franke(1953-)
Berkeley '05
Green Street Hooligans '05
What the #$*! Do We Know? '04
Footsteps '03
Seventeen Again '00
Lost in the Bermuda Triangle '98
Tarzan and the Lost City '98
Menno's Mind '96
Public Enemies '96
Solo '96
Wolverine '96
The Surgeon '94
Stephen King's The Tommyknockers '93
Universal Soldier '92

Benjamin Frankel(1906-73)
Battle of the Bulge '65
The Night of the Iguana '64
End of the Affair '55
A Kid for Two Farthings '55
The Importance of Being Earnest '52

Michael Franks(1944-)
Cockfighter '74
Zandy's Bride '74

Ian Fraser
First Monday in October '81
Zorro, the Gay Blade '81

Jason Frederick(1970-)
Four and a Half Women '05
2B Perfectly Honest '04
Dawg '02

Arthur Freed(1894-1973)
Yolanda and the Thief '45
Broadway Melody of 1938 '37
Broadway Melody of 1936 '35
Broadway Melody '29

Terry Frewer
Christmas in Wonderland '07
Hybrid '07
Head in the Clouds '04
Black Point '01
The Inspectors 2: A Shred of Evidence '00
Out of Time '00
The Last Stop '99
The Inspectors '98

Gavin Friday(1959-)
Get Rich or Die Tryin' '05
In America '02
Disco Pigs '01
The Boxer '97

Gerald Fried(1928-)
Agatha Christie's Murder is Easy '82
Roots: The Next Generation '79
Rescue from Gilligan's Island '78
Roots '77
The Baby '72
The Grissom Gang '71
Too Late the Hero '70
The Killing of Sister George '69
Whatever Happened to Aunt Alice? '69
I Bury the Living '58
Machine Gun Kelly '58
Terror in a Texas Town '58
Paths of Glory '57
The Killing '56
Killer's Kiss '55

Hugo Friedhofer(1901-81)
Private Parts '72
Homicidal '61
Barbarian and the Geisha '58
The Young Lions '58
An Affair to Remember '57
Between Heaven and Hell '56
Soldier of Fortune '55
Above and Beyond '53
Hondo '53
Man in the Attic '53
Vera Cruz '53
The Marrying Kind '52
Ace in the Hole '51
Three Came Home '50
The Bishop's Wife '47
Body and Soul '47
Dead Reckoning '47
The Best Years of Our Lives '46
Lifeboat '44
A Wing and a Prayer '44
The Adventures of Marco Polo '38

David Friedman(1923-)
Bush's Brain '04
Trick '99

Marco Frisina(1954-)
Moses '96
Samson and Delilah '96
Joseph '95
Abraham '94
Jacob '94

John (Gianni) Frizzell(1966-)
Legion '10
The Lodger '09
Whiteout '09
Henry Poole Is Here '08
100 Feet '08
Wisegal '08
Beneath '07
Black Irish '07
Careless '07
Primeval '07
The Reaping '07
Stay Alive '06
Mrs. Harris '05
The Prize Winner of Defiance, Ohio '05
Wal-Mart: The High Cost of Low Price '05
Cradle 2 the Grave '03
Gods and Generals '03
The Woods '03
Ghost Ship '02
Scorched '02
Josie and the Pussycats '01
13 Ghosts '01
Beautiful '00
Lockdown '00
Possessed '00
The Empty Mirror '99
Teaching Mrs. Tingle '99
White River '99
I Still Know What You Did Last Summer '98
Mafia! '98
Office Space '98
Alien: Resurrection '97
Dante's Peak '97
Beavis and Butt-Head Do America '96
Crime of the Century '96
The Rich Man's Wife '96
Undertow '95

Fabio Frizzi(1951-)
Last Mercenary '84
Manhattan Baby '82
Scorpion with Two Tails '82
Contraband '80
Gates of Hell '80
Zombie '80

Dominic Frontiere(1931-)
Color of Night '94
Danielle Steel's Palomino '91
The Aviator '85
The Stunt Man '80
Brannigan '75
Hang 'Em High '67
Incubus '65
Seven Thieves '60

Gary Fry
Trancers 5: Sudden Deth '94
Trancers 4: Jack of Swords '93
Cease Fire '85

Shiro Fukai
47 Ronin, Part 1 '42
47 Ronin, Part 2 '42

Parmer Fuller
Get a Clue! '98
Spirit of the Eagle '90
Saturday the 14th Strikes Back '88
Time Trackers '88
Saturday the 14th '81

Darren Fung
Beyond Sherwood Forest '09
Just Buried '07

Lewis Furey(1949-)
The Peanut Butter Solution '85
American Dreamer '84
The Agency '81

Nathan Furst(1978-)
Shark Swarm '08
Already Dead '07
Lake Placid 2 '07
Magma: Volcanic Disaster '06
Though None Go With Me '06
Bionicle 3: Web of Shadows '05
Dust to Glory '05
National Lampoon's Christmas Vacation 2: Cousin Eddie's Big Island Adventure '03

Giovanni Fusco(1906-68)
The Eclipse '66
La Guerre Est Finie '66
The Red Desert '64
The Trojan Horse '62
L'Avventura '60
Hiroshima, Mon Amour '59
Il Grido '57
The Lady Without Camelias '53
Story of a Love Affair '50

Peter Gabriel(1950-)
Rabbit-Proof Fence '02
The Last Temptation of Christ '88
Birdy '84

Pascal Gaigne
Dark Blue Almost Black '06
Broken Silence '01

Serge Gainsbourg(1928-91)
Menage '86
I Love You All '80
The French Woman '79
Good-bye, Emmanuelle '77
Le Sex Shop '73
Too Pretty to Be Honest '72
French Intrigue '70
Slogan '69
Manon '68
The Defector '66

Michael Galasso
Seraphine '08
In the Mood for Love '00

Vincent Gallo(1961-)
Get Well Soon '01
Buffalo 66 '97

Douglas Gamley(1924-98)
The Beast Must Die '75
The Land That Time Forgot '75
And Now the Screaming Starts '73
And Now for Something Completely Different '72
Night Slasher '69
The Rough and the Smooth '59
Tarzan's Greatest Adventure '59
Tom Thumb '58
The Admirable Crichton '57
Fire Down Below '57

Russell Garcia(1916-)
Atlantis, the Lost Continent '61
The Time Machine '60
Radar Secret Service '50

Craig Stuart Garfinkle
Ghosts Never Sleep '05
Gabriela '01

Robert Garrett
Eye of the Stranger '93
Roller Blade Warriors: Taken By Force '90
Roller Blade '85

Mort Garson
To Kill a Stranger '84
Beware! The Blob '72

Georges Garvarentz(1931-93)
Someone Behind the Door '71
Carbon Copy '69
Daniella by Night '61

Giorgio Gaslini(1929-)
Deep Red: Hatchet Murders '75
The Slasher '72
La Notte '60

Christian Gaubert
A Wind from Wyoming '94
The Little Girl Who Lives down the Lane '76

Claude Gaudette
Virtual Combat '95
Illicit Dreams '94

Mark Geary
Steel City '06
Loggerheads '05

James Gelfand
The Christmas Choir '08
An Old-Fashioned Thanksgiving '08
Swamp Devil '08
The Rendering '02

Lynne Geller
The Adventures of Sebastian Cole '99
1999 '98
Denise Calls Up '95

Bernard Gerard
Deadly Sting '73
Killer '73
Le Deuxieme Souffle '66

Alexander Gerens
The Fast and the Furious '54
Korea Patrol '47

Lisa Gerrard(1961-)
Layer Cake '05
Salem's Lot '04
Whale Rider '02
Ali '01

Joseph Gershenson(1904-88)
Man in the Shadow '57
The Monolith Monsters '57
The Creature Walks among Us '56
Francis in the Haunted House '56
Abbott and Costello Meet the Mummy '55
All That Heaven Allows '55
Revenge of the Creature '55
Abbott and Costello Meet the Keystone Kops '54
The Black Shield of Falworth '54
Abbott and Costello Go to Mars '53
All I Desire '53
Francis Covers the Big Town '53
Francis Goes to West Point '52
The Lawless Breed '52
Saddle Tramp '47

George Gershwin(1898-1937)
The Goldwyn Follies '38
A Damsel in Distress '37
Shall We Dance '37

Ira Gershwin(1896-1983)
Funny Face '57
A Star Is Born '54
An American in Paris '51
The Barkleys of Broadway '49
Rhapsody in Blue '45
Cover Girl '44
Girl Crazy '43
Lady Be Good '41
The Goldwyn Follies '38
A Damsel in Distress '37
Shall We Dance '37

Irving Gertz(1915-)
Curse of the Undead '59
Plunder Road '57
I Beheld His Glory '53
It Came from Outer Space '53

Michael Giacchino(1967-)
Land of the Lost '09
Star Trek '09
Up '09
Speed Racer '08
Ratatouille '07
Looking for Comedy in the Muslim World '06
Mission: Impossible 3 '06
The Family Stone '05
Sky High '05
The Incredibles '04
Sin '02
Legal Deceit '95

Carlo Giacco
The Wedding Bros. '08
December Boys '07
Murderous Intent '06
15 Amore '98

Riccardo Giagni
The Wedding Director '06
My Mother's Smile '02

Jeff Gibbs
Capitalism: A Love Story '09
Fahrenheit 9/11 '04

Michael Gibbs(1937-)
Being Human '94
Century '94
Hard-Boiled '92
Close My Eyes '91
Iron & Silk '91
Breaking In '89
American Roulette '88
Heat '87
Housekeeping '87
Madame Sin '71
Secrets '71

Richard Gibbs(1955-)
Fired Up! '09
Cleaner '07
Valley of the Heart's Delight '07
John Tucker Must Die '06
The Honeymooners '05
Barbershop 2: Back in Business '04
Fat Albert '04
Johnson Family Vacation '04
Johnson Family Vacation '04
My Baby's Daddy '04
Love Don't Cost a Thing '03
Step Into Liquid '03
I Spy '02
Like Mike '02
Queen of the Damned '02
Big Momma's House '00
28 Days '00
The Book of Stars '99
The Jesse Ventura Story '99
Ten Things I Hate about You '99
Dr. Dolittle '98
Dirty Work '97
Music from Another Room '97
First Kid '96
That Darn Cat '96
At First Sight '95
Blind Justice '94
Dangerous Indiscretion '94
Amos and Andrew '93
Barbarians at the Gate '93
The Chase '93
Fatal Instinct '93
Son-in-Law '93
Three of Hearts '93
Clifford '92
The Gun in Betty Lou's Handbag '92
Ladybugs '92
Once Upon a Crime '92
Passed Away '92
Bingo '91
A Killing in a Small Town '90
Say Anything '89
Sweet Hearts Dance '88

Herschel Burke Gilbert(1918-2003)
I Dismember Mama '74
Sam Whiskey '69
Crime and Punishment, USA '59
Project Moon Base '53
The Thief '52

Glover Gill
Before Sunset '04
Waking Life '01

Vincent Gillioz
Seance '06
Headhunter '05

Scott Gilman
Extreme Dating '04
Outta Time '01

Marcello Giombini(1928-2003)
Metallica '85
Reactor '78
Mandinga '77
War in Space '77
Emmanuelle on Taboo Island '76
Panic '76
Jungle Inferno '72
Sabata '69
Knives of the Avenger '65

Lim Giong(1964-)
The World '04
Goodbye South, Goodbye '96

Ricky Giovinazzo
No Way Home '96
Combat Shock '84

Michael Paul Girard(1954-)
Sweet Evil '98
Witchcraft 9: Bitter Flesh '96
The Perfect Gift '95

Claudio Gizzi
Andy Warhol's Dracula '74
Andy Warhol's Frankenstein '74

Scott Glasgow
Taking Chances '09
Bone Dry '07
The Gene Generation '07
Hack! '07
Chasing Ghosts '05

Philip Glass(1937-)
Cassandra's Dream '07
No Reservations '07
The Illusionist '06
Notes on a Scandal '06
Going Upriver: The Long War of John Kerry '04
Secret Window '04
Taking Lives '04
Undertow '04
The Fog of War: Eleven Lessons from the Life of Robert S. McNamara '03
The Hours '02
The Truman Show '98
Bent '97
Kundun '97
The Secret Agent '96
Candyman 2: Farewell to the Flesh '94
A Brief History of Time '92
Candyman '92
Mindwalk: A Film for Passionate Thinkers '91
Powaqqatsi: Life in Transformation '88
The Thin Blue Line '88
Hamburger Hill '87
Mishima: A Life in Four Chapters '85
Koyaanisqatsi '83

Albert Glasser(1916-98)
Tormented '60
Attack of the Puppet People '58
Giant from the Unknown '58
Monster from Green Hell '58
Teenage Caveman '58
The Amazing Colossal Man '57
Beginning of the End '57
The Indestructible Man '56
Invasion U.S.A. '52
Guns of Fury '49
Tough Assignment '49
Law of the Lash '47
The Monster Maker '44

Richard Glasser(1947-)
Kickin' It Old Skool '07
Find Me Guilty '06
Poolhall Junkies '02

Patrick Gleeson
In Self Defense '93
The Bedroom Window '87
Deadly Illusion '87
Stacking '87
The Children of Times Square '86
The Zoo Gang '85
The Plague Dogs '82

Nick Glennie-Smith(1951-)
A Sound of Thunder '05
We Were Soldiers '02
Attila '01
The Man in the Iron Mask '98
Fire Down Below '97
Home Alone 3 '97
The Rock '96

Mort Glickman
Riders of the Rio Grande '43
Sundown Kid '43
Shadows on the Sage '42

The Goblins
Sleepless '01
Unsane '82
Alien Contamination '81
The Bloodstained Shadow '78
Dawn of the Dead '78
Suspiria '77
Deep Red: Hatchet Murders '75

Erik Godal
What Love Is '07
Axe '06
Subject Two '06

Lucio Godoy(1958-)
The Aura '05
Mondays in the Sun '02
Intacto '01

Ernest Gold(1921-99)
Gore Vidal's Lincoln '88
Safari 3000 '82
Tom Horn '80
Marciano '79
The Runner Stumbles '79
Fun with Dick and Jane '77
Cross of Iron '76
The McCullochs '75
Betrayal '74
The Secret of Santa Vittoria '69
Ship of Fools '65
A Child Is Waiting '63
It's a Mad, Mad, Mad, Mad World '63
Pressure Point '62
Judgment at Nuremberg '61
Exodus '60
Inherit the Wind '60
On the Beach '59
The Young Philadelphians '59
The Screaming Skull '58
Tarzan's Fight for Life '58
Unknown World '51
G.I. War Brides '46

Murray Gold
Hoodwinked Too! Hood vs. Evil '10
Death at a Funeral '07
I Want Candy '07
Perfect Parents '06
Casanova '05
Miranda '01
Beautiful Creatures '00

Barry Goldberg
Best of the Best 3: No Turning Back '95
Hometown Boy Makes Good '93
Return of the Living Dead 3 '93
Beverly Hills Brats '89
Flashback '89
Powwow Highway '89
Three for the Road '87
Thrashin' '86
The Trip '67

Stu Goldberg
Angel and the Badman '09
Impulse '08
Silent Venom '08
Afghan Knights '07

Billy Goldenberg(1936-)
18 Again! '88
Johnnie Gibson F.B.I. '87
Nutcracker: Money, Madness & Murder '87
Dress Gray '86
Rage of Angels: The Story Continues '86
Guilty Conscience '85
Love on the Run '85
For Love or Money '84
Dempsey '83
Memorial Day '83
Prototype '83
Rage of Angels '83
Reuben, Reuben '83
Rehearsal for Murder '82
Awakening of Candra '81
The Best Little Girl in the World '81
Callie and Son '81
Jacqueline Bouvier Kennedy '81
All God's Children '80
Crisis at Central High '80
Father Figure '80
Haywire '80
The Cracker Factory '79
The Family Man '79
The Miracle Worker '79
Scavenger Hunt '79
King '78
A Question of Love '78
The Domino Principle '77
Helter Skelter '76
James Dean '76
The Lindbergh Kidnapping Case '76
Queen of the Stardust Ballroom '75
Busting '74
I Love You, Goodbye '74
Reflections of Murder '74
Don't Be Afraid of the Dark '73
The Last of Sheila '73
Brand New Life '72
The Glass House '72
Play It Again, Sam '72
Up the Sandbox '72
Duel '71
The Passing of Evil '70
Change of Habit '69
The Grasshopper '69
Night Gallery '69
Silent Night, Lonely Night '69

Elliot Goldenthal(1954-)
Public Enemies '09
Across the Universe '07
The Good Thief '03
S.W.A.T. '03
Frida '02
Final Fantasy: The Spirits Within '01
Titus '99
In Dreams '98
Batman and Robin '97
The Butcher Boy '97
Sphere '97
Michael Collins '96
A Time to Kill '96
Batman Forever '95
Heat '95
Voices from a Locked Room '95
Interview with the Vampire '94
Roswell: The U.F.O. Cover-Up '94
Demolition Man '93
Golden Gate '93
Alien 3 '92
Drugstore Cowboy '89
Pet Sematary '89
Cocaine Cowboys '79

Alison Goldfrapp
Nowhere Boy '09
My Summer of Love '05

Jerry Goldsmith(1929-2004)
Looney Tunes: Back in Action '03
Star Trek: Nemesis '02
The Sum of All Fears '02
Along Came a Spider '01
The Last Castle '01
Disney's The Kid '00
Hollow Man '00
The Haunting '99
The Mummy '99
The 13th Warrior '99
Deep Rising '98
Mulan '98
Small Soldiers '98
Star Trek: Insurrection '98
U.S. Marshals '98
Air Force One '97
The Edge '97
L.A. Confidential '97
Chain Reaction '96
Executive Decision '96
Fierce Creatures '96
The Ghost and the Darkness '96
Star Trek: First Contact '96
City Hall '95
Congo '95
First Knight '95
Powder '95
Bad Girls '94
I.Q. '94
The River Wild '94
The Shadow '94
Dennis the Menace '93
Malice '93
Maniac Cop 3: Badge of Silence '93
Rudy '93
Six Degrees of Separation '93
The Vanishing '93
Basic Instinct '92
Forever Young '92
Matinee '92
Medicine Man '92
Mr. Baseball '92
Mom and Dad Save the World '92
Blue Desert '91
Love Field '91
Sleeping with the Enemy '91
Warlock '91
Gremlins 2: The New Batch '90
Not Without My Daughter '90
The Russia House '90
Total Recall '90
The 'Burbs '89
Criminal Law '89
Leviathan '89
Star Trek 5: The Final Frontier '89
Rambo 3 '88
Rent-A-Cop '88
Extreme Prejudice '87
Innerspace '87
Lionheart '87
Hoosiers '86
Legend '86
Link '86
Poltergeist 2: The Other Side '86
Explorers '85
King Solomon's Mines '85
Rambo: First Blood, Part 2 '85
Gremlins '84
The Lonely Guy '84
Runaway '84
Supergirl '84
Psycho 2 '83
Twilight Zone: The Movie '83
Under Fire '83
The Challenge '82
First Blood '82
Poltergeist '82
The Salamander '82
The Secret of NIMH '82
Cabo Blanco '81
The Final Conflict '81
Masada '81
Night Crossing '81
Outland '81
Raggedy Man '81
Alien '79
The Great Train Robbery '79
Players '79
Star Trek: The Motion Picture '79
The Boys from Brazil '78
Capricorn One '78
Coma '78
Damien: Omen 2 '78
Magic '78
The Swarm '78
Damnation Alley '77
Islands in the Stream '77
MacArthur '77
Twilight's Last Gleaming '77
Breakheart Pass '76
The Cassandra Crossing '76
High Velocity '76
The Last Hard Men '76
Logan's Run '76
The Omen '76
Babe! '75
Breakout '75
The Reincarnation of Peter Proud '75
Take a Hard Ride '75
The Wind and the Lion '75
Chinatown '74
QB VII '74
S*P*Y*S '74
The Terrorists '74
Winter Kill '74
The Don Is Dead '73
One Little Indian '73
Papillon '73
Shamus '73
Culpepper Cattle Co. '72
The Other '72
Pursuit '72
Escape from the Planet of the Apes '71
The Mephisto Waltz '71
Wild Rovers '71
Ballad of Cable Hogue '70
Patton '70
Rio Lobo '70
Tora! Tora! Tora! '70
The Chairman '69
The Illustrated Man '69
Justine '69
100 Rifles '69
Bandolero! '68
The Detective '68
Planet of the Apes '68
Sebastian '68
Flim-Flam Man '67
Hour of the Gun '67
In Like Flint '67
The Blue Max '66
Our Man Flint '66
The Sand Pebbles '66
Seconds '66
The Trouble with Angels '66
The Agony and the Ecstasy '65
In Harm's Way '65
Morituri '65
A Patch of Blue '65
Von Ryan's Express '65
Rio Conchos '64
Seven Days in May '64
A Gathering of Eagles '63
Lilies of the Field '63
The List of Adrian Messenger '63
The Prize '63
The Stripper '63
Lonely Are the Brave '62
Studs Lonigan '60
City of Fear '59
Black Patch '57
The Detective '54

Joel Goldsmith(1957-)
Stargate: Continuum '08
Helen of Troy '03
Chameleon 3: Dark Angel '00
Diamonds '99
Shiloh 2: Shiloh Season '99
Inferno '98
Double Edge '97
Kull the Conqueror '97
Shiloh '97
Vampirella '96
Blood for Blood '95
One Good Turn '95
Home for Christmas '93
Man's Best Friend '93
A Woman, Her Men and Her Futon '92
Across the Tracks '89
Ricky 1 '88
Watchers '88
Crystal Heart '87
No Safe Haven '87
Banzai Runner '86
The Man with Two Brains '83
Island of Blood '82
Laserblast '78

Jonathan Goldsmith
Tenderness '08
Eye of the Beast '07
Away From Her '06
Rare Birds '01
Lip Service '00
Dangerous Evidence: The Lori Jackson Story '99
Must Be Santa '99
Dead Silence '96
Kissinger and Nixon '96
Heads '93
Stand Off '93
Palais Royale '88
Miracle at Moreaux '86
The Guardian '84
Visiting Hours '82

Gil Goldstein
Simply Irresistible '99
I Love You, I Love You Not '97

John Goldstein
For Better and for Worse '92
Hot Chocolate '92

William Goldstein
The Miracle Worker '00
Just Like Dad '96
The Quarrel '93
Shocker '89
Blood Vows: The Story of a Mafia Wife '87
Hello Again '87
Bad Guys '86
Saving Grace '86
Lots of Luck '85
Getting Physical '84
Up the Creek '84
Holocaust Survivors... Remembrance of Love '83
Forced Vengeance '82
An Eye for an Eye '81
Force: Five '81
A Long Way Home '81
Aliens Are Coming '80
Marilyn: The Untold Story '80
Terror Out of the Sky '78
Terror Out of the Sky '78
Bingo Long Traveling All-Stars & Motor Kings '76
Norman, Is That You? '76

Vinnie Golia(1946-)
Highway Hitcher '98
Smalltime '96
Serpent's Lair '95
Trouble Bound '92
Blood & Concrete: A Love Story '90

Osvaldo Golijov
Tetro '09
Youth Without Youth '07
The Man Who Cried '00

Peter Golub
Outrage '09
Frozen River '08
The Great Debaters '07
Sublime '07
Wordplay '06
American Gun '05
Americano '05
The Laramie Project '02

John Gonzalez
The Underground '97
Tiger Heart '96
Hologram Man '95
Street Crimes '92
Bikini Summer '91
Final Impact '91
Sunset Strip '91
Repo Jake '90
Mayhem '87
The Newlydeads '87

Joseph Julian Gonzalez
Price of Glory '00
Curdled '95

Howard Goodall(1958-)
Mr. Bean's Holiday '07
Bean '97
The Return of the Borrowers '96
The Borrowers '93

Joel Goodman
Canvas '06
Disorder '06
Undermind '03

Miles Goodman(1949-96)
Larger Than Life '96
Sunset Park '96
Til There Was You '96
Dunston Checks In '95
For Better or Worse '95
The Indian in the Cupboard '95
Blankman '94
Getting Even with Dad '94

Indian Summer '93
Sister Act 2: Back in the Habit '93
Housesitter '92
The Muppet Christmas Carol '92
He Said, She Said '91
What about Bob? '91
Opportunity Knocks '90
Problem Child '90
Thompson's Last Run '90
Vital Signs '90
K-9 '89
Staying Together '89
Traveling Man '89
Dirty Rotten Scoundrels '88
La Bamba '87
Like Father, Like Son '87
Real Men '87
The Squeeze '87
About Last Night... '86
Blind Justice '86
Little Shop of Horrors '86
Passion Flower '86
Poison Ivy '85
Teen Wolf '85
Footloose '84
High School USA '84
The Man Who Wasn't There '83
Table for Five '83
Having It All '82
Jinxed '82
Lookin' to Get Out '82
Last Cry for Help '79
Slumber Party '57 '76
Wham-Bam, Thank You Spaceman '75

William Goodrum

Blonde and Blonder '07
Recipe for Disaster '03

Jim Goodwin

Darkdrive '98
A.P.E.X. '94

Ronald Goodwin(1925-2003)

Unidentified Flying Oddball '79
Candleshoe '78
Force 10 from Navarone '78
The Littlest Horse Thieves '76
The Little Mermaid '75
Frenzy '72
Battle of Britain '69
Those Daring Young Men in Their Jaunty Jalopies '69
Where Eagles Dare '68
The Magnificent Two '67
Murder at the Gallop '63
Postman's Knock '62
The Trials of Oscar Wilde '60
Village of the Damned '60

Alain Goraguer(1931-)

Beyond Fear '75
Fantastic Planet '73

Christopher Gordon

Daybreakers '09
Salem's Lot '04
Master and Commander: The Far Side of the World '03
When Good Ghouls Go Bad '01
Moby Dick '98

Mack Gordon(1904-59)

Mother Wore Tights '47
That Night in Rio '41
Down Argentine Way '40
We're Not Dressing '34

Michael Gore(1951-)

Superstar '99
Mr. Wonderful '93
The Butcher's Wife '91
Defending Your Life '91
Don't Tell Her It's Me '90
Broadcast News '87
Pretty in Pink '86
Terms of Endearment '83
Fame '80

Adam Gorgoni(1963-)

Starting Out in the Evening '07

The Dead Girl '06
Saving Shiloh '06
Waiting '05
In the Shadows '01
Tollbooth '94

Coriolano Gori(1927-82)

The Uranium Conspiracy '78
Jungle Master '72
Fistful of Death '71
Hercules vs. the Sons of the Sun '64

Louis F. Gottschalk(1864-1934)

The Four Horsemen of the Apocalypse '21
Orphans of the Storm '21
The Three Musketeers '21
Broken Blossoms '19

Gerald Gouriet

Men of War '94
Hit Woman: The Double Edge '93
Hold Me, Thrill Me, Kiss Me '93
The Innocent '93
Philadelphia Experiment 2 '93
Rubdown '93
The Substitute '93
They Watch '93
Madame Sousatzka '88

Mark Governor

Santa Fe '97
Uncle Sam '96
Notes from Underground '95
Masque of the Red Death '89

Terence Gowan

Hollywood North '03
Triggermen '02
Specimen '97

Patrick Gowers(1936-)

Comic Act '98
Smiley's People '82
Therese Raquin '80

Paul Grabowsky

Empire Falls '05
It Runs in the Family '03
Last Orders '01
Innocence '00
Shiner '00
Noah's Ark '99
Siam Sunset '99
Paperback Romance '96
Lust and Revenge '95
The Last Days of Chez Nous '92

Jeff Grace

The House of the Devil '09
The Last Winter '06

John Graham

My Brother's War '97
American Strays '96
Bloodfist 6: Ground Zero '94

Ron Grainer(1922-81)

Omega Man '71
Hoffman '70
To Sir, with Love '67
The Moon-Spinners '64
A Kind of Loving '62
The Mouse on the Moon '62
Trial & Error '62

Stephane Grappelli(1908-97)

May Fools '90
Going Places '74

Richard Grassby-Lewis

Owning Mahowny '03
Love and Death on Long Island '97

Allan Gray(1902-73)

Slow Burn '90
Stairway to Heaven '46
I Know Where I'm Going '45
The Challenge '38

Stephen Graziano(1954-)

Love Finds a Home '09
Depth Charge '08
All I Want for Christmas '07
Love's Unfolding Dream '07
Sharpshooter '07
What's Up, Scarlet? '05
Highlander: Endgame '00
Contagious '96
Ruby Jean and Joe '96

Adolph Green(1915-2002)

On the Town '91
It's Always Fair Weather '55

Bernard Green(1908-75)

The Brass Bottle '63
Zotz! '62

Johnny Green(1908-89)

They Shoot Horses, Don't They? '69
Alvarez Kelly '66
Bye, Bye, Birdie '63
The Great Caruso '51
Royal Wedding '51
The Inspector General '49
Something in the Wind '47
Easy to Wed '46

Philip Green(1911-82)

Girl Hunters '63
Victim '61
The Square Peg '58
Who Done It? '56

Walter Greene(1910-83)

The Brain from Planet Arous '57
Teenage Doll '57
Square Dance Jubilee '51
Thundering Trail '51
Last Bullet '50
Rangeland Empire '50
Rimfire '49
Shep Comes Home '49
Danny Boy '46

Johnny Greenwood

There Will Be Blood '07
Grand National Night '53

Richard Gregoire(1944-)

Napoleon '03
Nuremberg '00
Bonanno: A Godfather's Story '99
Street Heart '98
Armistead Maupin's More Tales of the City '97

Harry Gregson-Williams(1961-)

Prince of Persia: The Sands of Time '10
Shrek Forever After '10
Twelve '10
The Taking of Pelham 123 '09
X-Men Origins: Wolverine '09
The Chronicles of Narnia: Prince Caspian '08
Gone Baby Gone '07
The Number 23 '07
Shrek the Third '07
Deja Vu '06
Flushed Away '06
Seraphim Falls '06
The Chronicles of Narnia: The Lion, the Witch and the Wardrobe '05
Domino '05
Kingdom of Heaven '05
Bridget Jones: The Edge of Reason '04
Convicted '04
Man on Fire '04
Shrek 2 '04
Team America: World Police '04
The Rundown '03
Sinbad: Legend of the Seven Seas '03
Veronica Guerin '03
Phone Booth '02

King of the Jungle '01
Shrek '01
Spy Game '01
Chicken Run '00
Light It Up '99
The Match '99
Antz '98
Enemy of the State '98
The Replacement Killers '98
The Borrowers '97
Deceiver '97
Smilla's Sense of Snow '96
The Whole Wide World '96
Full Body Massage '95

Rupert Gregson-Williams(1966-)

Grown Ups '10
Bedtime Stories '08
Made of Honor '08
The Maiden Heist '08
You Don't Mess with the Zohan '08
Bee Movie '07
I Now Pronounce You Chuck and Larry '07
Click '06
Over the Hedge '06
Hotel Rwanda '04
Crime Spree '03
The Night We Called It a Day '03
What a Girl Wants '03
Strange Relations '02
Extremely Dangerous '99
Virtual Sexuality '99
Urban Ghost Story '98

Benoit Grey

Screamers: The Hunting '09
Jimmy & Judy '06

Philip Griffin

Table for Three '09
Gradiva '06

D.W. Griffith(1875-1948)

Struggle '31
The Birth of a Nation '15

Mario Grigorov

Precious: Based on the Novel by Sapphire '09
Tennessee '08
The Attic '06
The Insurgents '06
Shadowboxer '06

Anthony Grimaldi

The Jimmy Show '01
Joe the King '99

Dean Grinsfelder

P.S. Your Cat is Dead! '02
Stonebrook '98

David Grisman(1945-)

King of the Gypsies '78
Eat My Dust '76
Big Bad Mama '74

Ferde Grofe, Jr.

Valentino '77
Rocketship X-M '50

Andrew Gross(1969-)

Bring It On: Fight to the Finish '09
Dog Gone '08
The Prince & Me 3: A Royal Honeymoon '08
Forfeit '07
Christmas Do-Over '06
The Prince & Me 2: Royal Wedding '06
Shut Up and Kiss Me '05
Off the Lip '04
All I Want '02
Buying the Cow '02
Dead Simple '01
The Extreme Adventures of Super Dave '98
Bio-Dome '96
8 Heads in a Duffel Bag '96
Overnight Delivery '96

Charles Gross(1934-)

Eyes of a Witness '94
Air America '90
Turner and Hooch '89
Sweet Dreams '85

Prime Suspect '82
A Rumor of War '80
Blue Sunshine '78
Valdez Is Coming '71

Guy Gross

Cut '00
That's the Way I Like It '99
The Adventures of Priscilla, Queen of the Desert '94
Frauds '93

Lawrence Nash Groupe

Nothing But the Truth '08
Resurrecting the Champ '07
Clawed: The Legend of Sasquatch '05
Out of the Black '01
The Search for John Gissing '01
The Contender '00
Deterrence '00

Judith Gruber-Stitzer

Dumb Waiter '87
The Room '87

Louis Gruenberg(1883-1964)

Quicksand '50
All the King's Men '49
Smart Woman '48

Jean Jacques Grunenwald(1911-82)

Diary of a Country Priest '50
Antoine et Antoinette '47
Monsieur Vincent '47

Dave Grusin(1934-)

Recount '08
Even Money '06
Random Hearts '99
Hope Floats '98
In the Gloaming '97
Selena '96
The Cure '95
Mulholland Falls '95
The Firm '93
For the Boys '91
The Bonfire of the Vanities '90
Havana '90
A Dry White Season '89
The Fabulous Baker Boys '89
Clara's Heart '88
The Milagro Beanfield War '88
Tequila Sunrise '88
Ishtar '87
Lucas '86
The Goonies '85
Falling in Love '84
The Little Drummer Girl '84
The Pope of Greenwich Village '84
Racing with the Moon '84
Scandalous '84
Author! Author! '82
Tootsie '82
Absence of Malice '81
On Golden Pond '81
Reds '81
My Bodyguard '80
And Justice for All '79
The Champ '79
The Electric Horseman '79
Heaven Can Wait '78
Bobby Deerfield '77
The Goodbye Girl '77
Mr. Billion '77
The Front '76
Murder by Death '76
Eric '75
Three Days of the Condor '75
The Yakuza '75
Fuzz '72
The Great Northfield Minnesota Raid '72
Shoot Out '71
Generation '69
Tell Them Willie Boy Is Here '69
Winning '69
The Heart Is a Lonely Hunter '68
Divorce American Style '67

The Graduate '67
Waterhole Number 3 '67

Jay Gruska(1953-)

Outlaw Justice '98
Trapped in Space '94
Mo' Money '92
Wheels of Terror '90
Sing '89
Shadow Dancing '88
The Principal '87
Traxx '87

Barrie Guard

Shameless '94
The Toxic Avenger, Part 2 '89
Hold the Dream '86
Monster in the Closet '86

Anthony Guefen

Assassin '86
The Stuff '85

Andrea Guerra(1961-)

Extraordinary Measures '10
Letters to Juliet '10
Nine '09
The Accidental Husband '08
Coco Chanel '08
The Pursuit of Happyness '06
Hotel Rwanda '04
Facing Windows '03
Angel of Death '02
Angela '02
His Secret Life '01

Christopher Guest(1948-)

Waiting for Guffman '96
This Is Spinal Tap '84

Ivor Guest

Taxi to the Dark Side '07
The Business '05

Christopher Gunning(1944-)

La Vie en Rose '07
Lighthouse Hill '04
Prince of Poisoners: The Life and Crimes of William Palmer '98
Firelight '97
The Affair '95
Catherine Cookson's The Glass Virgin '95
Under Suspicion '92
When the Whales Came '89
Cold War Killers '86
Charlie Muffin '79
Running Blind '78
Hands of the Ripper '71
Twinsanity '70

Steve Gurevitch

Christie's Revenge '07
Demons from Her Past '07
Framed for Murder '07
Jill the Ripper '00

Steve Gutheinz

Infestation '09
Glass House: The Good Mother '06
The Pleasure Drivers '05

Joaquin Gutierrez Heras

Like A Bride '94
Mary, My Dearest '83

Joseph Gutowski

Echelon Conspiracy '09
All Souls Day '05

Jim Guttridge

Decoys '04
Wishmaster 4: The Prophecy Fulfilled '02
Big and Hairy '98

Omar Guzman

Esmeralda Comes by Night '98
Forbidden Homework '92

Todd Haberman

Killer Movie '08
The Hollow '04

Alexander Hacke

Eight Miles High '08
Eight Miles High '07

Manos Hadjidakis
Sweet Movie '75
The Pedestrian '73
Blue '68
Topkapi '64
The 300 Spartans '62
Never on Sunday '60
A Matter of Dignity '57
Girl in Black '56
Stella '55

Richard Hageman(1882-1966)
She Wore a Yellow Ribbon '49
Fort Apache '48
Angel and the Badman '47
The Shanghai Gesture '42
If I Were King '38

Francis Haines
Conspiracy of Silence '03
Another 9 1/2 Weeks '96
Split Second '92

Kuniaki Haishima
Retribution '06
Spriggan '98

Chris Hajian
Dr. Dolittle: Million Dollar Mutts '09
Yonkers Joe '08
The Take '07
The Pooch and the Pauper '99
Ten Benny '98
Chairman of the Board '97
Other Voices, Other Rooms '95

Karl Hajos(1889-1950)
Summer Storm '44
It Happened in New Orleans '36
The Song of Songs '33
Beggars of Life '28

Jim Halfpenny
Running Red '99
Dead Silence '98
Subterfuge '98
Little Bigfoot 2: The Journey Home '97
Riot '96
The Power Within '95
Skyscraper '95
Texas Payback '95
To the Limit '95
No Escape, No Return '93
Bikini Summer 2 '92
Magic Kid '92
Zipperface '92

Erwin Halletz(1923-)
Fanny Hill: Memoirs of a Woman of Pleasure '64
The Third Sex '57
Liane, Jungle Goddess '56

Dick Halligan
Fear City '85
Go Tell the Spartans '78
The Owl and the Pussycat '70

Marvin Hamlisch(1944-)
The Informant! '09
Every Little Step '08
The Mirror Has Two Faces '96
Open Season '95
Frankie and Johnny '91
When the Time Comes '91
The Experts '89
The January Man '89
Little Nikita '88
Three Men and a Baby '87
A Chorus Line '85
D.A.R.Y.L. '85
A Streetcar Named Desire '84
Romantic Comedy '83
I Ought to Be in Pictures '82
Sophie's Choice '82
The Devil & Max Devlin '81
Pennies from Heaven '81
Ordinary People '80
Seems Like Old Times '80
Ice Castles '79
Starting Over '79
Same Time, Next Year '78
The Spy Who Loved Me '77
Prisoner of Second Avenue '74
Save the Tiger '73
The Sting '73
The Way We Were '73
The World's Greatest Athlete '73
Fat City '72
Bananas '71
Kotch '71
April Fools '69
Take the Money and Run '69
The Swimmer '68

Jan Hammer(1948-)
The Corporate Ladder '97
Beastmaster 3: The Eye of Braxus '95
A Modern Affair '94
I Come in Peace '90
K-9000 '89

Wolfgang Hammerschmid
Mickey Blue Eyes '99
Mandragora '97

Oscar Hammerstein(1895-1960)
South Pacific '58
Carousel '56
The King and I '56
Oklahoma! '55
Carmen Jones '54
Show Boat '51
State Fair '45
Lady Be Good '41
Show Boat '36
Sweet Adeline '35

Jawe-kwon Han
Another Public Enemy '05
No Blood No Tears '02

Herbie Hancock(1940-)
Livin' Large '91
Harlem Nights '89
Action Jackson '88
Colors '88
Hard Lessons '86
Jo Jo Dancer, Your Life Is Calling '86
A Soldier's Story '84
Death Wish '74
The Spook Who Sat by the Door '73
Blow-Up '66

Habib Shehadeh Hanna
Lemon Tree '08
The Band's Visit '07

E.Y. Harburg(1896-1981)
Can't Help Singing '45
Cabin in the Sky '43

Hagood Hardy(1937-)
Anne of Avonlea '87
Anne of Green Gables '85
Wild Pony '83
Forbidden Love '82
Mazes and Monsters '82
Dirty Tricks '81
An American Christmas Carol '79
Anatomy of a Seduction '79
Home to Stay '79
Klondike Fever '79
Second Wind '76

John E.R. Hardy
Rancid Aluminium '00
Hedd Wyn '92

John Harle(1956-)
Take Me '01
Butterfly Kiss '94

Leigh Harline(1907-69)
Strange Bedfellows '65
7 Faces of Dr. Lao '63
The Honeymoon Machine '61
The Facts of Life '60
23 Paces to Baker Street '56
The Girl in the Red Velvet Swing '55
House of Bamboo '55
Savage Wilderness '55
Black Widow '54
Broken Lance '54
Money from Home '53
Pickup on South Street '53
Monkey Business '52
His Kind of Woman '51
I Want You '51
The Happy Years '50
Perfect Strangers '50
The Woman on Pier 13 '50
Big Steal '49
It Happens Every Spring '49
They Live by Night '49
Mr. Blandings Builds His Dream House '48
Tycoon '47
Nocturne '46
The Road to Utopia '46
Having Wonderful Crime '45
Isle of the Dead '45
They Got Me Covered '43
The Pride of the Yankees '42
Blondie Has Trouble '40
Snow White and the Seven Dwarfs '37

W. Franke Harling(1887-1958)
Penny Serenade '41
The Invisible Man '33
No Man of Her Own '32
Trouble in Paradise '32
Monte Carlo '30

Don Harper
The Lion King 1 1/2 '04
Beyond Suspicion '00
Houdini '99
The Magnificent Seven '98

Scott Harper
Roseanne: An Unauthorized Biography '94
Reborn '81

Johnny Harris
Ravenhawk '95
Baby Broker '81
Man in the Wilderness '71

Peter Harris
Happy, Texas '99
Elmore Leonard's Gold Coast '97

George Harrison(1943-2001)
Shanghai Surprise '86
Time Bandits '81
Let It Be '70
Wonderwall: The Movie '69
Yellow Submarine '68
Magical Mystery Tour '67
Help! '65

John Harrison
Day of the Dead '85
Creepshow '82

Deborah Harry(1945-)
Rock & Rule '83
Polyester '81

Jimmy Harry
Party Monster '03
Intern '00

Daniel Hart
Carmen, Baby '66
Nude on the Moon '61

Lorenz Hart(1895-1943)
I Married an Angel '42
Too Many Girls '40
Babes in Arms '39
Evergreen '34
The Merry Widow '34
Hallelujah, I'm a Bum '33

Hal Hartley(1959-)
Milk and Honey '03
No Such Thing '01
Henry Fool '98
Flirt '95
Amateur '94
Simple Men '92

Richard Hartley(1944-)
The Lion in Winter '03
Don Quixote '00
Mad About Mambo '00
When Brendan Met Trudy '00
Alice in Wonderland '99
All the Little Animals '98
Rogue Trader '98
Curtain Call '97
The Designated Mourner '97
A Thousand Acres '97
The Brylcreem Boys '96
Playing God '96
Stealing Beauty '96
Rough Magic '95
The Van '95
Victory '95
An Awfully Big Adventure '94
Princess Caraboo '94
The Rector's Wife '94
The Secret Rapture '94
Catherine Cookson's The Man Who Cried '93
The Good Father '87
The Impossible Spy '87
Dance with a Stranger '85
December Flower '84
Parker '84
Kennedy '83
Bad Blood '81
Shock Treatment '81
The Rocky Horror Picture Show '75

Richard Harvey(1953-)
Luther '03
The Legend of Suriyothai '02
Two Men Went to War '02
Arabian Nights '00
Animal Farm '99
The Magical Legend of the Leprechauns '99
Captain Jack '98
Jane Eyre '97
Melissa '97
Paper Mask '91
Cause Celebre '87
In the Secret State '85

Bo Harwood
Happy Birthday to Me '81
Opening Night '77

Gary Hashiya
Charisma '99
Cure '97

Jimmie Haskell(1936-)
The Dogfighters '95
L.A. Bad '85
Night of the Lepus '72
Zachariah '70

Paul Haslinger(1962-)
Takers '10
Underworld: Rise of the Lycans '09
Make It Happen '08
Prom Night '08
While She Was Out '08
Shoot 'Em Up '07
Vacancy '07
Crank '06
Turistas '06
Into the Blue '05
Sleeper Cell '05
The Girl Next Door '04
Bring It On Again '03
Underworld '03
Blue Crush '02
crazy/beautiful '01
Picture Claire '01
Cheaters '00

Harley Hatcher
Cain's Cutthroats '71
Satan's Sadists '69
Wild Wheels '69

Marvin Hatley(1905-86)
Who Killed Doc Robbin? '48
Laurel & Hardy: Night Owls '30

Tadashi Hattori
One Wonderful Sunday '47
No Regrets for Our Youth '46
The Men Who Tread on the Tiger's Tail '45

Takayuki Hattori
Train Man: Densha Otoko '05
Godzilla 2000 '99

Roy Hay(1961-)
Styx '00
Pterodactyl Woman from Beverly Hills '97
Precious Find '96

Fumio Hayasaka(1914-55)
I Live in Fear '55
Sansho the Bailiff '54
Seven Samurai '54
Ugetsu '53
Ikiru '52
Rashomon '51
Scandal '50
Drunken Angel '48

Todd Hayen
When Time Expires '97
The Invader '96
Panic in the Skies '96
Shooters '89

Isaac Hayes(1942-2008)
Shaft '00
Truck Turner '74
Shaft '71

Lennie Hayton(1908-71)
Battle Circus '53
Singin' in the Rain '52
It's a Big Country '51
Side Street '50
Battleground '49
The Hucksters '47
Till the Clouds Roll By '46

Richard Hazard(1921-2000)
Bela Lugosi Meets a Brooklyn Gorilla '52
Radar Secret Service '50

Alex Heffes
State of Play '09
Imagine Me & You '06
The Last King of Scotland '06
Dear Frankie '04
Trauma '04
Touching the Void '03

Neal Hefti(1922-)
Barefoot in the Park '67
Oh Dad, Poor Dad (Momma's Hung You in the Closet & I'm Feeling So Sad) '67
Lord Love a Duck '66
Sex and the Single Girl '64

Leonardo Heiblum
Trade '07
In the Pit '06
Maria Full of Grace '04
The Maldonado Miracle '03

Reinhold Heil(1954-)
The International '09
One Missed Call '08
Anamorph '07
Blackout '07
Blood & Chocolate '07
Paris, je t'aime '06
Perfume: The Story of a Murderer '06
The Cave '05
George A. Romero's Land of the Dead '05
Sophie Scholl: The Final Days '05
Swimming Upstream '03
Big Shot: Confessions of a Campus Bookie '02
One Hour Photo '02
Tangled '01
The Princess and the Warrior '00
Winter Sleepers '97

Nachum Heiman
The Milky Way '97
Neither the Sea Nor the Sand '73

Ray Heindorf(1908-80)
The Music Man '62
No Time for Sergeants '58
Goodbye My Fancy '51
Wonder Man '45
The Roaring Twenties '39
Four's a Crowd '38

Nona Hendryx(1944-)
Preaching to the Choir '05
Gospa '94

Ben Heneghan
Breeders '97
The Proposition '96

Joe Henry
Motherhood '09
Knocked Up '07
Jesus' Son '99

Christian Henson(1971-)
Pandemic '09
Lost in Austen '08
Miss Conception '08
It's a Boy Girl Thing '06
Severance '06
Chasing Liberty '04
The Great Challenge '04

Paul Hepker
Rendition '07
Tsotsi '05

Matthew Herbert
The Intended '02
Human Traffic '99

Jerry Herman(1931-)
Mrs. Santa Claus '96
Mame '74
Hello, Dolly! '69

Bernard Herrmann(1911-75)
Obsession '76
Taxi Driver '76
It's Alive '74
Sisters '73
Endless Night '71
The Bride Wore Black '68
Fahrenheit 451 '66
Marnie '64
The Birds '63
Jason and the Argonauts '63
Cape Fear '61
Mysterious Island '61
Psycho '60
Journey to the Center of the Earth '59
North by Northwest '59
The Three Worlds of Gulliver '59
The Seventh Voyage of Sinbad '58
Vertigo '58
The Man Who Knew Too Much '56
The Trouble with Harry '55
A Christmas Carol '54
Garden of Evil '54
Beneath the 12-Mile Reef '53
Five Fingers '52
The Snows of Kilimanjaro '52
The Day the Earth Stood Still '51
On Dangerous Ground '51
The Ghost and Mrs. Muir '47
Anna and the King of Siam '46
Hangover Square '45
Jane Eyre '44
The Magnificent Ambersons '42
Citizen Kane '41
The Devil & Daniel Webster '41

Nigel Hess
Ladies in Lavender '04
Love or Money '01
Every Woman Knows a Secret '99
A Woman of Substance '84

Boo Hewerdine

24-7 '97
Fever Pitch '96

Werner R. Heymann(1886-1961)

Together Again '43
They All Kissed the Bride '42
To Be or Not to Be '42
That Uncertain Feeling '41
The Shop Around the Corner '40
Bluebeard's Eighth Wife '38
Gambling Ship '33
Faust '26

Tom Hiel

Cyclops '08
A Plumm Summer '08
The Killing Club '01
Dark Side of Genius '94

Richard Hieronymous

The Invisible Strangler '76
Angels Hard As They Come '71
Bury Me an Angel '71

Mike Higham

Clash of the Titans '10
Dead Cool '04

John Hill

Tar '97
The Pompatus of Love '95

Hilmar Orn Hilmarsson(1958-)

Beowulf & Grendel '06
In the Cut '03
Devil's Island '96
Cold Fever '95
Children of Nature '91

Peter Himmelman(1960-)

A Face to Kill For '99
Liar's Poker '99
A Slipping Down Life '99
Dinner and Driving '97
The Souler Opposite '97

Dickon Hinchliffe

Winter's Bone '10
Cold Souls '09
Last Chance Harvey '08
Married Life '07
Forty Shades of Blue '05
Keeping Mum '05
Friday Night '02

Wilbert Hirsch(1961-)

An American Werewolf in Paris '97
Mute Witness '95

David Hirschfelder(1960-)

Australia '08
The Children of Huang Shi '08
Aquamarine '06
Irresistible '06
Kidnapped '05
Criminal Ways '03
Better Than Sex '00
The Weight of Water '00
Hanging Up '99
Elizabeth '98
The Interview '98
Sliding Doors '97
Dating the Enemy '95
Shine '95
Tunnel Vision '95
Strictly Ballroom '92

Joe Hisaishi(1950-)

Departures '08
Ponyo '08
Howl's Moving Castle '04
Dolls '02
When the Last Sword is Drawn '02
Spirited Away '01
Brother '00
Kikujiro '99
Princess Mononoke '98
Fireworks '97

John Hodian

101 Ways (The Things a Girl Will Do to Keep Her Volvo) '00
Blades '89
Girls School Screamers '86

Michael Hoenig

The Contaminated Man '01
Eye of the Killer '99
Terminal Justice: Cybertech P.D. '95
The Amy Fisher Story '93
Shattered Spirits '86
Koyaanisqatsi '83

Paul Hoffert(1947-)

Mr. Nice Guy '86
Fanny Hill '83
Outrageous! '77
Vengeance Is Mine '74
The Groundstar Conspiracy '72

Joachim Holbek(1957-)

Just Another Love Story '08
Wilbur Wants to Kill Himself '02
Heart of Light '97
Junk Mail '97
The Kingdom 2 '97
Nightwatch '96
Breaking the Waves '95
The Kingdom '95
Medea '88

Ben Holbrook

Kiss the Bride '07
Long-Term Relationship '06

Mark Holden

Body Armor '96
Ava's Magical Adventure '94
Beyond Desire '94

Lee Holdridge(1944-)

Puerto Vallarta Squeeze '04
Mists of Avalon '01
The Pilot's Wife '01
Take Me Home: The John Denver Story '00
Atomic Train '99
Love Letters '99
Mutiny '99
The Secret of NIMH 2 '98
The Twilight of the Golds '97
Two for Texas '97
Gunfighter's Moon '96
Holiday Affair '96
Soul of the Game '96
Buffalo Girls '95
Harvest of Fire '95
Prince Brat and the Whipping Boy '95
The Tuskegee Airmen '95
Texas '94
The Yearling '94
Call of the Wild '93
Heidi '93
Running Delilah '93
The Story Lady '93
One Against the Wind '91
Back to Hannibal: The Return of Tom Sawyer and Huckleberry Finn '90
Old Gringo '89
Higher Ground '88
Born in East L.A. '87
Moonlighting '85
Transylvania 6-5000 '85
Splash '84
Agatha Christie's A Caribbean Mystery '83
Mr. Mom '83
Beastmaster '82
American Pop '81
Winterhawk '76

Deborah Holland

Out There '95
Circuitry Man '90

Andrew Hollander

Labor Pains '09
Weather Girl '09
Waitress '07
Anything But Love '02
I'll Take You There '99
Wrestling with Alligators '98

Frederick "Friedrich" Hollander(1896-1976)

The Most Wonderful Time of the Year '08
We're No Angels '55
The 5000 Fingers of Dr. T '53
Born Yesterday '50
A Foreign Affair '48
Princess O'Rourke '43
Here Comes Mr. Jordan '41
Remember the Night '40
Too Many Husbands '40
Bluebeard's Eighth Wife '38
Angel '37
Desire '36
The Blue Angel '30

David Holmes

Five Minutes of Heaven '09
Ocean's Thirteen '07
The War Within '05
Ocean's Twelve '04
Code 46 '03
Stander '03
Analyze That '02
Buffalo Soldiers '01
Ocean's Eleven '01
Resurrection Man '97

Rupert Holmes

No Small Affair '84
The Desperados '70

Nigel Holton(1952-2006)

Cries of Silence '97
Naked Souls '95
Twogether '94
Carnosaur '93
Bloodfist 3: Forced to Fight '92
Homicidal Impulse '92
Body Chemistry 2: Voice of a Stranger '91
Bloodfist 2 '90
South of Reno '87

Toshiyuki Honda(1957-)

Minbo—Or the Gentle Art of Japanese Extortion '92
A Taxing Woman '87

Arthur Honegger(1892-1955)

Harvest '37
Crime and Punishment '35
Napoleon '27

Nicholas Hooper

Harry Potter and the Half-Blood Prince '09
Harry Potter and the Order of the Phoenix '07
The Chatterley Affair '06
Bloodlines '05
State of Play '03
The Heart of Me '02
The Way We Live Now '02

Tobe Hooper(1946-)

The Texas Chainsaw Massacre 2 '86
The Texas Chainsaw Massacre '74

Anthony Hopkins(1937-)

Slipstream '07
August '95

Kenyon Hopkins(1912-83)

Lilith '64
The Strange One '57
Twelve Angry Men '57

James Horner(1953-)

Avatar '09
The Boy in the Striped Pajamas '08
The Spiderwick Chronicles '08
The Life Before Her Eyes '07
All the King's Men '06
Apocalypto '06
The Chumscrubber '05
Flightplan '05
The Legend of Zorro '05
The New World '05
Bobby Jones: Stroke of Genius '04
The Forgotten '04
Troy '04
Beyond Borders '03
House of Sand and Fog '03
The Missing '03
Radio '03
The Four Feathers '02
Windtalkers '02
A Beautiful Mind '01
Iris '01
Dr. Seuss' How the Grinch Stole Christmas '00
Enemy at the Gates '00
Freedom Song '00
The Perfect Storm '00
Bicentennial Man '99
Deep Impact '98
The Mask of Zorro '98
Mighty Joe Young '98
Titanic '97
Courage Under Fire '96
The Devil's Own '96
Ransom '96
To Gillian on Her 37th Birthday '96
Apollo 13 '95
Balto '95
Braveheart '95
Casper '95
Jade '95
Jumanji '95
The Spitfire Grill '95
Clear and Present Danger '94
Legends of the Fall '94
The Pagemaster '94
Bopha! '93
A Far Off Place '93
Jack the Bear '93
The Man Without a Face '93
The Pelican Brief '93
Searching for Bobby Fischer '93
Swing Kids '93
Patriot Games '92
Sneakers '92
Thunderheart '92
Unlawful Entry '92
An American Tail: Fievel Goes West '91
Class Action '91
My Heroes Have Always Been Cowboys '91
Once Around '91
The Rocketeer '91
Another 48 Hrs. '90
I Love You to Death '90
Dad '89
Field of Dreams '89
Glory '89
Honey, I Shrunk the Kids '89
In Country '89
Cocoon: The Return '88
The Land Before Time '88
Red Heat '88
Vibes '88
Willow '88
*batteries not included '87
Project X '87
Aliens '86
An American Tail '86
The Name of the Rose '86
Off Beat '86
Where the River Runs Black '86
Cocoon '85
Commando '85
Heaven Help Us '85
The Journey of Natty Gann '85
P.K. and the Kid '85
Volunteers '85
Star Trek 3: The Search for Spock '84
The Stone Boy '84
Between Friends '83
Brainstorm '83
The Dresser '83
Gorky Park '83
Krull '83
Something Wicked This Way Comes '83
Testament '83
Uncommon Valor '83
48 Hrs. '82
A Piano for Mrs. Cimino '82
Star Trek 2: The Wrath of Khan '82
Deadly Blessing '81
The Hand '81
The Pursuit of D.B. Cooper '81
Wolfen '81
Battle Beyond the Stars '80
Humanoids from the Deep '80
Lady in Red '79
Up from the Depths '79

Richard Horowitz

Drowning on Dry Land '00
Three Seasons '98
Broken Trust '95
Lakota Woman: Siege at Wounded Knee '94
The Sheltering Sky '90

Vladimir Horunzhy(1949-)

Original Gangstas '96
Stephen King's The Langoliers '95
Point of Impact '93
Blink of an Eye '92

James Newton Howard(1951-)

The Last Airbender '10
Salt '10
Confessions of a Shopaholic '09
Duplicity '09
The Dark Knight '08
Defiance '08
The Happening '08
Mad Money '08
Charlie Wilson's War '07
The Great Debaters '07
I Am Legend '07
The Lookout '07
Michael Clayton '07
The Water Horse: Legend of the Deep '07
Blood Diamond '06
Freedomland '06
Lady in the Water '06
RV '06
Batman Begins '05
The Interpreter '05
King Kong '05
Collateral '04
Hidalgo '04
The Village '04
Dreamcatcher '03
Peter Pan '03
Unconditional Love '03
Big Trouble '02
The Emperor's Club '02
Signs '02
Treasure Planet '02
America's Sweethearts '01
Atlantis: The Lost Empire '01
Dinosaur '00
Unbreakable '00
Vertical Limit '00
Mumford '99
Runaway Bride '99
The Sixth Sense '99
Snow Falling on Cedars '99
Stir of Echoes '99
A Perfect Murder '98
The Devil's Advocate '97
My Best Friend's Wedding '97
The Postman '97
Father's Day '96
The Juror '96
One Fine Day '96
Primal Fear '96
Space Jam '96
The Trigger Effect '96
An Eye for an Eye '95
French Kiss '95
Waterworld '95
Junior '94
Just Cause '94
Outbreak '94
Restoration '94
Wyatt Earp '94
Alive '93
Dave '93
Falling Down '93
The Fugitive '93
Intersection '93
The Saint of Fort Washington '93
American Heart '92
Diggstown '92
Glengarry Glen Ross '92
Night and the City '92
Grand Canyon '91
Guilty by Suspicion '91
King Ralph '91
My Girl '91
The Prince of Tides '91
Coupe de Ville '90
Flatliners '90
Marked for Death '90
Pretty Woman '90
Somebody Has to Shoot the Picture '90
Three Men and a Little Lady '90
The Image '89
Major League '89
The Package '89
Tap '89
Everybody's All American '88
Five Corners '88
Promised Land '88
Some Girls '88
Campus Man '87
Off Limits '87
Russkies '87
Head Office '86
Never Too Young to Die '86
Nobody's Fool '86
Tough Guys '86
Wildcats '86
8 Million Ways to Die '85

Alan Howarth

Flu Birds '08
Ghouls '07
Alone with a Stranger '99
The Dentist 2: Brace Yourself '98
The Dentist '96
Halloween 6: The Curse of Michael Myers '95
Arcade '93
Halloween 5: The Revenge of Michael Myers '89
Halloween 4: The Return of Michael Myers '88
They Live '88
Big Trouble in Little China '86
Christine '84

David A. Hughes(1960-)

The Color of Magic '08
In Your Dreams '07
Hogfather '06
Bob the Butler '05
The Long Weekend '05
New Best Friend '02
The Bachelor '99
One More Kiss '99
Lock, Stock and 2 Smoking Barrels '98
Stiff Upper Lips '96
Solitaire for 2 '94
C.H.U.D. '84

Gary Hughes(1922-78)

A Challenge for Robin Hood '68
The Viking Queen '67
The Devil-Ship Pirates '64
Pirates of Blood River '62

Don Hulette(1937-)

Greedy Terror '78
Breaker! Breaker! '77
They Saved Hitler's Brain '64

Tony Humecke

American East '07
The Dead One '07
November Conspiracy '96
The Feminine Touch '95

Nina Humphreys

Wide Sargasso Sea '06
Warrior Queen '03
Sword of Honour '01

John Hunter(1911-)

American Virgin '09
Big Stan '07

Steve Hunter
Dead Weekend '95
Cyber Bandits '94

Robert Hurst
Brown Sugar '02
The Wood '99

Zakir Hussain
The Mystic Masseur '01
In Custody '94

Terry Huud
Civic Duty '06
Paranoia 1.0 '04

Jeehun Hwang
Midnight Clear '06
Tart '01

Tor Hyams
100 Mile Rule '02
The Substitute 3: Winner Takes All '99

Soren Hyldgaard
Red '08
Angel of the Night '98

Dick Hyman(1927-)
Sweet and Lowdown '99
Everyone Says I Love You '96
Mighty Aphrodite '95
Alan & Naomi '92
The Lemon Sisters '90
Leader of the Band '87
Moonstruck '87
The Purple Rose of Cairo '85

Abdullah Ibrahim(1934-)
No Fear, No Die '90
Tilai '90

Akira Ifukube(1914-2006)
Godzilla vs. King Ghidora '91
Terror of Mechagodzilla '78
Yog, Monster from Space '71
War of the Gargantuas '70
Latitude Zero '69
Destroy All Monsters '68
Godzilla vs. Monster Zero '68
King Kong Escapes '67
Daimajin '66
Return of Daimajin '66
Wrath of Daimajin '66
Ghidrah the Three Headed Monster '65
Zatoichi: The Blind Swordsman and the Chess Expert '65
Frankenstein Conquers the World '64
Godzilla vs. Mothra '64
King Kong vs. Godzilla '63
The Burmese Harp '56
Godzilla, King of the Monsters '56
A Quiet Duel '49

Alberto Iglesias(1955-)
Che '08
The Kite Runner '07
Volver '06
The Constant Gardener '05
Bad Education '04
Take My Eyes '03
The Dancer Upstairs '02
Talk to Her '02
Sex and Lucia '01
All About My Mother '99
Lovers of the Arctic Circle '98
The Chambermaid on the Titanic '97
Live Flesh '97
The Flower of My Secret '95
Tierra '95
Outrage '93
The Red Squirrel '93
Vacas '91

Shinichiro Ikebe(1943-)
The Eel '96
Rhapsody in August '91
Akira Kurosawa's Dreams '90
The Ballad of Narayama '83
Kagemusha '80
Vengeance Is Mine '79

Neil Innes(1944-)
Erik the Viking '89
All You Need Is Cash '78
Monty Python and the Holy Grail '75

Akira Inoue
Wind and Cloud: The Storm Riders '04
Lensman '84
Young Master '80

Ashley Irwin
Naked City: Justice with a Bullet '98
Entertaining Angels: The Dorothy Day Story '96
The Expert '95
Secret Games 3 '94
Stranger by Night '94
Undercover '94
Secret Games 2: The Escort '93
Sins of the Night '93
Deadly Rivals '92
Fair Game '85

Pat Irwin
Bam Bam & Celeste '05
But I'm a Cheerleader '99
Breathing Room '96
Sudden Manhattan '96
My New Gun '92

Bjorn Isfalt(1942-97)
What's Eating Gilbert Grape '93
My Life As a Dog '85

Mark Isham(1951-)
Bad Lieutenant: Port of Call New Orleans '09
Crossing Over '09
Fame '09
My One and Only '09
The Express '08
Pride and Glory '08
The Women '08
Freedom Writers '07
Gracie '07
In the Valley of Elah '07
Lions for Lambs '07
The Mist '07
Next '07
Reservation Road '07
The Black Dahlia '06
Bobby '06
Eight Below '06
Invincible '06
Running Scared '06
Crash '05
In Her Shoes '05
Kicking & Screaming '05
Racing Stripes '05
Miracle '04
Spartan '04
Twisted '04
The Cooler '03
Highwaymen '03
Impostor '02
Moonlight Mile '02
Don't Say a Word '01
Hardball '01
Life as a House '01
The Majestic '01
Save the Last Dance '01
Men of Honor '00
Rules of Engagement '00
Trixie '00
Where the Money Is '00
Body Shots '99
October Sky '99
At First Sight '98
Blade '98
Breakfast of Champions '98
The Defenders: Taking the First '98
Varsity Blues '98
Afterglow '97
The Defenders: Payback '97
The Education of Little Tree '97
The Gingerbread Man '97
Kiss the Girls '97
Fly Away Home '96
Gotti '96
Last Dance '96
Night Falls on Manhattan '96
Home for the Holidays '95
Miami Rhapsody '95
The Net '95
The Browning Version '94
Losing Isaiah '94
Mrs. Parker and the Vicious Circle '94
Quiz Show '94
Safe Passage '94
Timecop '94
Fire in the Sky '93
The Getaway '93
Made in America '93
Nowhere to Run '93
Romeo Is Bleeding '93
Short Cuts '93
Cool World '92
A Midnight Clear '92
Of Mice and Men '92
A River Runs Through It '92
Billy Bathgate '91
Crooked Hearts '91
Little Man Tate '91
Mortal Thoughts '91
Point Break '91
Reversal of Fortune '90
The Beast '88
The Moderns '88
Made in Heaven '87
The Hitcher '86
Trouble in Mind '86
Mrs. Soffel '84
Never Cry Wolf '83

Chu Ishikawa
Nightmare Detective '06
A Snake of June '02
Fudoh: The New Generation '96
Tetsuo: The Iron Man '92

Steve Isles
RocknRolla '08
Nina's Heavenly Delights '06

Peter Ivers(1946-83)
Eraserhead '78
Grand Theft Auto '77

Taro Iwashiro
Red Cliff '08
Shinobi '05
Azumi '03
Memories of Murder '03

Steve Jablonsky
A Nightmare on Elm Street '10
Friday the 13th '09
Transformers: Revenge of the Fallen '09
Dragon Wars '07
The Hitcher '07
Transformers '07
The Texas Chainsaw Massacre: The Beginning '06
The Amityville Horror '05
The Island '05
Steamboy '05
The Texas Chainsaw Massacre '03

Corey A. Jackson(1968-)
Storm Cell '08
Left in Darkness '06
It Waits '05

Howard Jackson(1900-66)
Merrill's Marauders '62
Gold of the Seven Saints '61
Sergeant Rutledge '60
A Slight Case of Murder '38
The Great Gabbo '29

Joe Jackson(1954-)
Queens Logic '91
Tucker: The Man and His Dream '88
Party! Party! '83

Sidney James
Strange Fruit '04
Bug Buster '99

Leos Janacek(1854-1928)
The Unbearable Lightness of Being '88
Don's Party '76

Chaz Jankel(1952-)
Sex & Drugs & Rock & Roll '10
The Rachel Papers '89
D.O.A. '88

Alaric Jans
The Winslow Boy '98
Things Change '88
House of Games '87

Pierre Jansen(1930-)
Violette '78
A Piece of Pleasure '74
Just Before Nightfall '71
La Rupture '70
La Femme Infidele '69
The 317th Platoon '65
Les Bonnes Femmes '60

Werner Janssen(1899-1990)
A Night in Casablanca '46
The Southerner '45
Guest in the House '44

Maurice Jarre(1924-2009)
Uprising '01
I Dreamed of Africa '00
Sunshine '99
Sunchaser '96
Fearless '93
Mr. Jones '93
School Ties '92
Solar Crisis '92
Fires Within '91
Only the Lonely '91
After Dark, My Sweet '90
Almost an Angel '90
Ghost '90
Jacob's Ladder '90
Chances Are '89
Dead Poets Society '89
Enemies, a Love Story '89
Prancer '89
Distant Thunder '88
Gorillas in the Mist '88
Moon over Parador '88
Wildfire '88
Fatal Attraction '87
Gaby: A True Story '87
Julia and Julia '87
The Murder of Mary Phagan '87
No Way Out '87
Apology '86
The Mosquito Coast '86
Solarbabies '86
Tai-Pan '86
The Bride '85
Enemy Mine '85
Mad Max: Beyond Thunderdome '85
Witness '85
Dreamscape '84
A Passage to India '84
Samson and Delilah '84
Top Secret! '84
Coming Out of the Ice '82
Don't Cry, It's Only Thunder '82
Firefox '82
The Year of Living Dangerously '82
Young Doctors in Love '82
Lion of the Desert '81
Taps '81
Enola Gay: The Men, the Mission, the Atomic Bomb '80
The Last Flight of Noah's Ark '80
Resurrection '80
Shogun '80
The Black Marble '79
The Magician of Lublin '79
The Tin Drum '79
Winter Kills '79
The Prince and the Pauper '78
Users '78
Jesus of Nazareth '77
March or Die '77
The Message '77
The Last Tycoon '76
Shout at the Devil '76
The Man Who Would Be King '75
Mandingo '75
Posse '75
The Island at the Top of the World '74
Mr. Sycamore '74
Ash Wednesday '73
Mackintosh Man '73
Life & Times of Judge Roy Bean '72
Plaza Suite '71
Red Sun '71
El Condor '70
Ryan's Daughter '70
The Damned '69
Topaz '69
Five Card Stud '68
The Fixer '68
Isadora '68
Villa Rides '68
Night of the Generals '67
Gambit '66
Grand Prix '66
Is Paris Burning? '66
The Professionals '66
The Collector '65
Doctor Zhivago '65
The Train '65
Behold a Pale Horse '64
Judex '64
Lawrence of Arabia '62
The Longest Day '62
Sundays & Cybele '62
The Horror Chamber of Dr. Faustus '59

Maurice Jaubert(1900-40)
The Green Room '78
The Man Who Loved Women '77
Small Change '76
The Story of Adele H. '75
Bizarre Bizarre '39
L'Atalante '34

Nelust Wyclef Jean(1972-)
The Manchurian Candidate '04
Life '99

Gordon Jenkins(1910-)
The First Deadly Sin '80
San Fernando Valley '44

Merrill Jenson
The Red Fury '84
Three Warriors '77

Geir Jenssen(1962-)
Kill by Inches '99
Insomnia '97

Jae-hyeong Jeong
Addicted '02
Addicted '02

Peter Jermyn
The Climb '87
Self-Defense '83

Yeong-wook Jo
Thirst '09
Blood Rain '05
Oldboy '03
Public Enemy '02
JSA: Joint Security Area '00

Johann Johannsson
Personal Effects '09
In the Arms of My Enemy '07

Elton John(1947-)
The Road to El Dorado '00
The Muse '99
The Lion King '94
Friends '71

Carl Johnson
Piglet's Big Movie '03
Gargoyles, The Movie: The Heroes Awaken '94

J.J. Johnson(1924-2001)
Cleopatra Jones '73
Shaft '71

Laurie Johnson(1927-)
The Lady and the Highwayman '89
It's Alive 3: Island of the Alive '87
Anatomy of Terror '74
Captain Kronos: Vampire Hunter '74
One Deadly Owner '74
And Soon the Darkness '70
Dr. Strangelove, or: How I Learned to Stop Worrying and Love the Bomb '64
First Men in the Moon '64
Tiger Bay '59

Nathan Johnson
The Brothers Bloom '09
Blue State '07
Brick '06

Adrian Johnston
Brideshead Revisited '08
Becoming Jane '07
My Boy Jack '07
Kinky Boots '06
Friends & Crocodiles '05
Gideon's Daughter '05
Lassie '05
The Mighty Celt '05
If Only '04
Byron '03
The Mayor of Casterbridge '03
Shackleton '02
This Is Not a Love Song '02
Tipping the Velvet '02
Almost Strangers '01
Lawless Heart '01
Me Without You '01
About Adam '00
All the King's Men '99
Robert Louis Stevenson's The Game of Death '99
The Turn of the Screw '99
I Want You '98
Our Mutual Friend '98
Touching Evil '97
Welcome to Sarajevo '97
Jude '96

Arthur Johnston(1898-1954)
Sidewalks of London '38
Pennies from Heaven '36
Belle of the Nineties '34
Murder at the Vanities '34
College Humor '33

Bobby Johnston
Humble Pie '07
Wristcutters: A Love Story '06
Edmond '05
I Walk the Line '70

Philip Johnston
Noise '07
The Music of Chance '93

Alain Jomy(1941-)
The Accompanist '93
The Little Thief '89
The Best Way '76

Dan (Danie!) Jones
In Tranzit '07
Four Last Songs '06
Jericho Mansions '03
Max '02
Shadow of the Vampire '00
The Weekend '00

Jeffrey Alan Jones
Serial Killing 101 '04
Crack Up '97

Kenneth V. Jones(1924-)
Tower of Evil '72
Tomb of Ligeia '64
Dentist In the Chair '60
The Horse's Mouth '58
Sea Wife '57

Quincy Jones(1933-)
Get Rich or Die Tryin' '05
The Color Purple '85
The Wiz '78
Roots '77
The Getaway '72

The New Centurions *'72*
The Anderson Tapes *'71*
Dollars *'71*
Honky *'71*
Man & Boy *'71*
Brother John *'70*
The Hot Rock *'70*
They Call Me Mr. Tibbs! *'70*
Bob & Carol & Ted & Alice *'69*
Cactus Flower *'69*
The Italian Job *'69*
The Lost Man *'69*
MacKenna's Gold *'69*
Dandy in Aspic *'68*
For Love of Ivy *'68*
Enter Laughing *'67*
In Cold Blood *'67*
In the Heat of the Night *'67*
Mirage *'66*
Walk, Don't Run *'66*
The Pawnbroker *'65*
The Slender Thread *'65*

Ralph Jones

Love Letters *'83*
Slumber Party Massacre *'82*

Rickie Lee Jones(1954-)

Friends with Money *'06*
Subway *'85*

Terry Jones(1942-)

Mr. Toad's Wild Ride *'96*
Monty Python's The Meaning of Life *'83*

Tim Jones

Smokin' Aces 2: Assassins' Ball *'10*
Bobby Z *'07*
Karla *'06*
I Downloaded a Ghost *'04*

Timothy S. (Tim) Jones(1971-)

Attack of the Sabretooth *'05*
Sniper 3 *'04*
Amazons and Gladiators *'01*
The Forsaken *'01*
True Blue *'01*
Killer Instinct *'00*

Trevor Jones(1949-)

Around the World in 80 Days *'04*
I'll Be There *'03*
The League of Extraordinary Gentlemen *'03*
Crossroads *'02*
Dinotopia *'02*
The Gathering Storm *'02*
From Hell *'01*
Thirteen Days *'00*
Cleopatra *'99*
Molly *'99*
Notting Hill *'99*
Desperate Measures *'98*
Merlin *'98*
The Mighty *'98*
Dark City *'97*
G.I. Jane *'97*
Brassed Off *'96*
For Roseanna *'96*
Lawn Dogs *'96*
Talk of Angels *'96*
Gulliver's Travels *'95*
Loch Ness *'95*
Richard III *'95*
Hideaway *'94*
Kiss of Death *'94*
Cliffhanger *'93*
In the Name of the Father *'93*
Blame It on the Bellboy *'92*
Chains of Gold *'92*
Crisscross *'92*
Freejack *'92*
The Last of the Mohicans *'92*
Defenseless *'91*
Murder by Moonlight *'91*
Arachnophobia *'90*
Bad Influence *'90*
By Dawn's Early Light *'89*
Sea of Love *'89*
Diamond's Edge *'88*
Dominick & Eugene *'88*
Mississippi Burning *'88*
Sweet Lies *'88*
Angel Heart *'87*
Labyrinth *'86*
The Last Place on Earth *'85*
Runaway Train *'85*
Nate and Hayes *'83*
Those Glory, Glory Days *'83*
The Dark Crystal *'82*
The Sender *'82*
Excalibur *'81*

Wilfred Josephs(1927-97)

All Creatures Great and Small *'74*
Die! Die! My Darling! *'65*

Phil Judd(1953-)

Amy *'98*
Mr. Reliable: A True Story *'95*
Rikky and Pete *'88*

David Julyan

The Killing Gene *'07*
Outlaw *'07*
The Prestige *'06*
The Descent *'05*
The Last Drop *'05*
Rory O'Shea Was Here *'04*
Insomnia *'02*
Memento *'00*
Following *'99*

Federico Jusid

The Secret in Their Eyes *'09*
Fermat's Room *'07*

Bill Justis(1926-82)

The Villain *'79*
Hooper *'78*
Smokey and the Bandit *'77*

Jeppe Kaas(1966-)

Adam's Apples *'05*
The Green Butchers *'03*
Flickering Lights *'01*

Hajime Kaburagi

Bohachi Bushido: Code of the Forgotten Eight *'73*
Blind Woman's Curse *'70*

Jan A.P. Kaczmarek(1953-)

The Courageous Heart of Irena Sendler *'09*
Get Low *'09*
Hachiko: A Dog's Tale *'09*
Horsemen *'09*
Evening *'07*
The Visitor *'07*
Finding Neverland *'04*
Soldier's Girl *'03*
Unfaithful *'02*
Lost Souls *'00*
The Third Miracle *'99*
Aimee & Jaguar *'98*
Washington Square *'97*
Bliss *'96*
Felony *'95*
Total Eclipse *'95*

Bert Kalmar(1884-1947)

Duck Soup *'33*
Animal Crackers *'30*

Peter Kam

Warlords *'08*
Perhaps Love *'05*
3 Extremes 2 *'02*
The Accidental Spy *'01*
Tokyo Raiders *'00*

Camara Kambon

The Cookout *'04*
Biker Boyz *'03*

Michael Kamen(1948-2003)

Against the Ropes *'04*
First Daughter *'04*
Open Range *'03*
Band of Brothers *'01*
Frequency *'00*
X-Men *'00*
The Iron Giant *'99*
From the Earth to the Moon *'98*
Lethal Weapon 4 *'98*
What Dreams May Come *'98*
Event Horizon *'97*
Inventing the Abbotts *'97*
The Winter Guest *'97*
Jack *'96*
101 Dalmatians *'96*
Die Hard: With a Vengeance *'95*
Mr. Holland's Opus *'95*
Stonewall *'95*
Circle of Friends *'94*
Don Juan DeMarco *'94*
Last Action Hero *'93*
Splitting Heirs *'93*
The Three Musketeers *'93*
Wilder Napalm *'93*
Blue Ice *'92*
Lethal Weapon 3 *'92*
Shining Through *'92*
Hudson Hawk *'91*
The Last Boy Scout *'91*
Robin Hood: Prince of Thieves *'91*
Die Hard 2: Die Harder *'90*
The Krays *'90*
The Raggedy Rawney *'90*
The Adventures of Baron Munchausen *'89*
Crusoe *'89*
Dead Bang *'89*
Lethal Weapon 2 *'89*
License to Kill *'89*
Renegades *'89*
Road House *'89*
Rooftops *'89*
Action Jackson *'88*
Die Hard *'88*
Homeboy *'88*
Adventures in Babysitting *'87*
Lethal Weapon *'87*
Rita, Sue & Bob Too *'87*
Someone to Watch Over Me *'87*
Suspect *'87*
Edge of Darkness *'86*
Highlander *'86*
Mona Lisa *'86*
Shanghai Surprise *'86*
Brazil *'85*
Lifeforce *'85*
Angelo My Love *'83*
Dead Zone *'83*
Pink Floyd: The Wall *'82*
Venom *'82*
Polyester *'81*
S*H*E *'79*
Between the Lines *'77*
Stunts *'77*
The Arab Conspiracy *'76*

John Kander(1927-)

Chicago *'02*
The Boys Next Door *'96*
I Want to Go Home *'89*

Artie Kane

Devil Dog: The Hound of Hell *'78*
The Bat People *'74*

Yoko Kanno

Kamikaze Girls *'04*
Orochi, the Eight Headed Dragon *'94*

Tuomas Kantelinen(1969-)

Skeleton Crew *'09*
Mongol *'07*
Mindhunters *'05*
Mother of Mine *'05*
Ambush *'99*

Bronislau Kaper(1902-83)

Lord Jim *'65*
Somebody Up There Likes Me *'56*
Quentin Durward *'55*
Them! *'54*
Lili *'53*
The Naked Spur *'53*
Invitation *'51*
It's a Big Country *'51*
Mr. Imperium *'51*
The Red Badge of Courage *'51*
Malaya *'49*
The Secret Garden *'49*
Act of Violence *'48*
Cynthia *'47*
The Stranger *'46*
Gaslight *'44*
The Heavenly Body *'44*
Above Suspicion *'43*
Bataan *'43*
Crossroads *'42*
Keeper of the Flame *'42*
We Were Dancing *'42*
White Cargo *'42*
H.M. Pulham Esquire *'41*
A Woman's Face *'41*
I Take This Woman *'40*
A Day at the Races *'37*

Elliot Kaplan

Cry Blood, Apache *'70*
Finnegan's Wake *'65*

Sol Kaplan(1919-90)

Over the Edge *'79*
The Spy Who Came in from the Cold *'65*
The Victors *'63*
Salt of the Earth *'54*
Niagara *'52*
The Halls of Montezuma *'50*
Tales of Manhattan *'42*

Dana Kaproff

Murder at Devil's Glen *'99*
Dead Air *'94*
When a Stranger Calls Back *'93*
Nightmare *'91*
Full Exposure: The Sex Tape Scandals *'89*
The Big Red One *'80*

Eleni Karaindrou(1939-)

Weeping Meadow *'04*
Eternity and a Day *'97*
Ulysses' Gaze *'95*
Landscape in the Mist *'88*

Fred Karger(1916-79)

Fastest Guitar Alive *'68*
Frankie and Johnny *'65*
Harum Scarum *'65*

Fred Karlin(1936-2004)

Lethal Charm *'90*
KISS Meets the Phantom of the Park *'78*
Greased Lightning *'77*
The Autobiography of Miss Jane Pittman *'74*
Born Innocent *'74*
Westworld *'73*
Yours, Mine & Ours *'68*

Steve Karmen

Teenage Mother *'67*
Teenage Gang Debs *'66*
The Beautiful, the Bloody and the Bare *'64*

Laura Karpman

The Tournament *'09*
Ace Ventura Jr.: Pet Detective *'08*
Center Stage: Turn It Up *'08*
Out at the Wedding *'07*
The Sandlot 2 *'05*
Carrie *'02*
Taken *'02*
Brotherhood of Murder *'99*
Dash and Lilly *'99*
Emma's Wish *'98*
Lover's Knot *'96*
Doing Time on Maple Drive *'92*

Al Kasha(1937-)

Rescue Me *'93*
The Closer *'91*
The Fat Spy *'66*

John Kastner

Suck *'09*
Universal Soldier 2: Brothers in Arms *'98*
Universal Soldier 3: Unfinished Business *'98*

Fred Katz(1919-)

Creature from the Haunted Sea *'60*
Ski Troop Attack *'60*
A Bucket of Blood *'59*
The Wasp Woman *'59*

Emilio Kauderer

Friends & Lovers *'99*
A Place in the World *'92*
Savage Instinct *'89*
Lost Diamond *'86*

Bernhard Kaun(1899-1980)

The Black Legion *'37*
Petrified Forest *'36*
Bureau of Missing Persons *'33*
Employees' Entrance *'33*
The Kennel Murder Case *'33*
20,000 Years in Sing Sing *'33*

Koichi Kawabe

Legends of the Poisonous Seductress 2: Quick Draw Okatsu *'69*
Legends of the Poisonous Seductress 3: Okatsu the Fugitive *'69*

Kenji Kawai

Death Note 3: L, Change the World *'08*
The Sky Crawlers *'08*
Death Note 2: The Last Name *'07*
Death Note *'06*
Reincarnation *'05*
Kibakichi *'04*
Kibakichi 2 *'04*
Dark Water *'02*
The Princess Blade *'02*
Ringu 2 *'99*
Ringu *'98*
Talking Head *'92*
Stray Dog *'91*
The Red Spectacles *'87*

Edward Kay(1898-1973)

I Was an American Spy *'51*
I Wouldn't Be in Your Shoes *'48*
Kidnapped *'48*
Decoy *'46*
Bowery at Midnight *'42*
King of the Zombies *'41*
Phantom of Chinatown *'40*
Tomboy *'40*
Up in the Air *'40*
Wolf Call *'39*

Norman Kaye(1927-2007)

Vincent: The Life and Death of Vincent van Gogh *'87*
Lonely Hearts *'82*

Samuel Kaylin

Charlie Chan at Treasure Island *'39*
Mr. Moto in Danger Island *'39*
Mr. Takes a Vacation *'39*
Mr. Moto Takes a Chance *'38*
Mr. Moto's Gamble *'38*
Mysterious Mr. Moto *'38*
Charlie Chan at Monte Carlo *'37*
Charlie Chan at the Olympics *'37*
Charlie Chan on Broadway *'37*
Thank you, Mr. Moto *'37*
Think Fast, Mr. Moto *'37*
Charlie Chan at the Circus *'36*
Charlie Chan at the Race Track *'36*
Charlie Chan in Egypt *'35*
Charlie Chan in Shanghai *'35*
Steamboat Round the Bend *'35*
Charlie Chan in London *'34*
365 Nights in Hollywood *'34*
Doctor Bull *'33*
The Black Camel *'31*

Brian Keane

Illtown *'96*
Stephen King's The Night Flier *'96*

John Keane

Mansfield Park *'07*
Tara Road *'05*
Bait *'02*
Horatio Hornblower: The Adventure Continues *'01*
Anna Karenina *'00*
The Last of the Blonde Bombshells *'00*
Hideous Kinky *'99*
The Break *'97*
Trojan Eddie *'96*
Small Faces *'95*
A Vow to Kill *'94*
Armistead Maupin's Tales of the City *'93*
Sex, Love and Cold Hard Cash *'93*
A Very British Coup *'88*
The Kitchen Toto *'87*

Toby Keith

Beer for My Horses *'08*
Broken Bridges *'06*

Dominic Kelly

The Lather Effect *'06*
Full Tilt Boogie *'97*

Paul Kelly(1955-)

Jindabyne *'06*
The Forgotten *'04*
Lantana *'01*

Victoria Kelly(1973-)

Black Sheep *'06*
Heaven *'99*
The Ugly *'96*

Arthur Kempel(1945-2004)

Stray Bullet *'98*
The Arrival *'96*
Behind Enemy Lines *'96*
Riders of the Purple Sage *'96*
Sensation *'94*
Windrunner *'94*
Double Impact *'91*
A Cry in the Wild *'90*
Fleshburn *'84*

Greg Kendall

Drive Me Crazy *'99*
Bandwagon *'95*

Rolfe Kent(1963-)

Ghosts of Girlfriends Past *'09*
The Men Who Stare at Goats *'09*
17 Again *'09*
Up in the Air *'09*
The Lucky Ones *'08*
The Hunting Party *'07*
Reign Over Me *'07*
Sex and Death 101 *'07*
Failure to Launch *'06*
The Matador *'06*
Thank You for Smoking *'06*
You, Me and Dupree *'06*
Just like Heaven *'05*
Wedding Crashers *'05*
The Last Shot *'04*
Mean Girls *'04*
Sideways *'04*
Freaky Friday *'03*
Legally Blonde 2: Red White & Blonde *'03*
About Schmidt *'02*
40 Days and 40 Nights *'02*
Happy Campers *'01*
Kate & Leopold *'01*
Legally Blonde *'01*
Someone Like You *'01*
Town and Country *'01*
Gun Shy *'00*
Nurse Betty *'00*
Election *'99*
Oxygen *'99*
Slums of Beverly Hills *'98*
The Theory of Flight *'98*
Citizen Ruth *'96*
Dead Connection *'94*
Final Combination *'93*

Jerome Kern(1885-1945)
Can't Help Singing '45
Cover Girl '44
You Were Never Lovelier '42
Lady Be Good '41
Joy of Living '38
Show Boat '36
Swing Time '36
Sweet Adeline '35
The Cat and the Fiddle '34

Wojciech Kilar(1932-)
We Own the Night '07
The Pianist '02
Zemsta '02
The Ninth Gate '99
Portrait of a Lady '96
Death and the Maiden '94
The Silent Touch '94
From a Far Country: Pope John Paul II '81
Contract '80
Land of Promise '74
Dracula '73
Illumination '73
Family Life '71

Mark Kilian
Traitor '08
Before the Rains '07
Tsotsi '05

Mark Killian
Rendition '07
Lover Girl '97

John Kimbrough
Pizza '05
Winter Passing '05
Winter Passing '05
A Decade Under the Influence '02

Bruce Kimmel(1947-)
Ratings Game '84
The Creature Wasn't Nice '81
The First Nudie Musical '75

Kevin Kiner
Final Approach '08
Star Wars: The Clone Wars '08
Love's Unending Legacy '07
I-See-You.Com '06
Love's Abiding Joy '06
Love's Long Journey '05
Love's Enduring Promise '04
The Legend of Johnny Lingo '03
The Other Side of Heaven '02
Madison '01
Tremors 3: Back to Perfection '01
Safe House '99
Wing Commander '99
Against the Law '98
Black Scorpion 2: Ground Zero '96
Carnosaur 3: Primal Species '96
Lifeform '96
The Pest '96
Black Scorpion '95
Demolition High '95
Excessive Force 2: Force on Force '95
Exit '95
Freaked '93

Chuji Kinoshita
The Human Condition: Road to Eternity '59
The Human Condition: No Greater Love '58

Basil Kirchin(1927-2005)
The Freakmaker '73
The Abominable Dr. Phibes '71

David Kitay
Mr. Troop Mom '09
Year One '09
My Sassy Girl '08
Over Her Dead Body '08
Wieners '08
Because I Said So '07
Shanghai Kiss '07
Smiley Face '07
Art School Confidential '06
Caffeine '06
The Darwin Awards '06
Date Movie '06
Relative Strangers '06
The Family Plan '05
The Ice Harvest '05
Elvis Has Left the Building '04
Harold and Kumar Go to White Castle '04
Bad Santa '03
How to Deal '03
I Witness '03
Ghost World '01
The Stickup '01
Tomcats '01
Dude, Where's My Car? '00
Loser '00
Scary Movie '00
Can't Hardly Wait '98
A Night at the Roxbury '98
Clueless '95
Roosters '95
Father and Scout '94
Trading Mom '94
Surf Ninjas '93
Breaking the Rules '92
Look Who's Talking, Too '90
Look Who's Talking '89

Leo Klatzkin(1914-92)
Lonesome Trail '55
Silver Star '55
Mr. Walkie Talkie '52

Larry Klein
Sugar Town '99
Grace of My Heart '96

Kevin Kliesch(1970-)
Dracula 3: Legacy '05
Dracula 2: Ascension '03

Johnny Klimek(1962-)
The International '09
One Missed Call '08
Anamorph '07
Blackout '07
Blood & Chocolate '07
Paris, je t'aime '06
Perfume: The Story of a Murderer '06
The Cave '05
George A. Romero's Land of the Dead '05
Sophie Scholl: The Final Days '05
Swimming Upstream '03
Big Shot: Confessions of a Campus Bookie '02
One Hour Photo '02
Tangled '01
The Princess and the Warrior '00
Winter Sleepers '97

Kevin Klinger
Aftershock '88
Necromancer: Satan's Servant '88

Harald Kloser(1956-)
2012 '09
10,000 B.C. '08
Dresden '06
Alien vs. Predator '04
The Day After Tomorrow '04
Rudy: The Rudy Giulani Story '03
RFK '02
Sins of the Father '01
The Tunnel '01
Kiss Tomorrow Goodbye '00
The Harmonists '99
The Thirteenth Floor '99
Quiet Days in Hollywood '97
Magenta '96
The O.J. Simpson Story '94

Thomas Knak
Allegro '05
Reconstruction '03

Jurgen Knieper(1941-)
The Promise '94
The Blonde '92
December Bride '91
Wings of Desire '88
River's Edge '87
The Future of Emily '85
Germany, Pale Mother '80
The American Friend '77
The Goalie's Anxiety at the Penalty Kick '71

Mark Knopfler(1949-)
A Shot at Glory '00
Metroland '97
Wag the Dog '97
The Princess Bride '87
Cal '84
Comfort and Joy '84
Local Hero '83

Leon Ko
Warlords '08
Perhaps Love '05

Johannes Kobilke
The Midnight Meat Train '08
Pathology '08

Gary Koftinoff
The Confessor '04
Prom Queen '04
G2: Mortal Conquest '99
Breakout '98

Krzysztof Komeda(1931-69)
Rosemary's Baby '68
The Fearless Vampire Killers '67
Knife in the Water '62
Innocent Sorcerers '60
The Dybbuk '37

Robbie Kondor
The Suburbans '99
Happiness '98

Zygmunt Konieczny(1937-)
The Possessed '88
Landscape After Battle '70

Joseph Koo
Fist of Legend '94
A Better Tomorrow, Part 2 '88
Return of the Dragon '73

Brian Koonin
Mr. Nanny '93
When Angels Fly '82

Herman Kopp
Nekromantik 2 '91
Der Todesking '89
Nekromantik '87

Rudolph Kopp(1887-1972)
Vengeance Valley '51
Mystery Street '50
The Crusades '35
The Sign of the Cross '33

Erich Wolfgang Korngold(1897-1957)
Kings Row '41
The Adventures of Robin Hood '38
The Prince and the Pauper '37
Anthony Adverse '36
Captain Blood '35

Mark Korven
Shake Hands With the Devil: The Journey of Romeo Dallaire '04
Cube '98
Curtis's Charm '96
I've Heard the Mermaids Singing '87

Abel Korzeniowski
Battle for Terra '09
A Single Man '09

Andrzej Korzynski(1940-)
Man of Iron '81
Possession '81
Man of Marble '76
In Desert and Wilderness '73
Everything for Sale '68

Richard Kosinski
Bloodstorm: Subspecies 4 '98
Magic in the Mirror: Fowl Play '96
Spellbreaker: Secret of the Leprechauns '96
Vampire Journals '96

Joseph Kosma(1905-69)
The Testament of Dr. Cordelier '59
Children of Paradise '44
Grand Illusion '37
The Crime of Monsieur Lange '36

Irwin Kostal(1911-94)
Pete's Dragon '77
Charlotte's Web '73

Ivan Koutikov
Undead or Alive '07
The Haunting of Hell House '99

Joe Kraemer
Lone Rider '08
Avenging Angel '07
Ten 'Til Noon '06
The Thirst '06
An Unreasonable Man '06
House of the Dead 2: Dead Aim '05
Mystery Woman: Mystery Weekend '05
The Hitcher 2: I've Been Waiting '03
A Time to Remember '03
Way of the Gun '00

Robert Kraft
The Mambo Kings '92
Hudson Hawk '91

Robert Kral
The Haunting in Connecticut '09
Maslin Beach '97

Raoul Kraushaar(1908-2001)
Billy the Kid Versus Dracula '66
Jesse James Meets Frankenstein's Daughter '65
Sitting Bull '54
The Blue Gardenia '53
Invaders from Mars '53
Sky Liner '49

Amanda Kravat(1966-)
Never Again '01
Wirey Spindell '99
Fall '97
If Lucy Fell '95

Jan Krenz(1926-)
Ashes and Diamonds '58
Kanal '56

Shigeru Kumebayashi
Onmyoji 2 '03
Onmyoji '01

Meyer Kupferman(1926-2003)
Black Like Me '64
Goldstein '64
Blast of Silence '61

Dan Kuramato
Only the Brave '06
Life Tastes Good '99

David Kurtz
Alien Nation: Millennium '96
Alien Nation: Body and Soul '95
Alien Nation: Dark Horizon '94

Teddy Robin Kwan
Full Contact '92
As Tears Go By '88
City on Fire '87

Milan Kymlicka(1936-)
Fallen Angel '99
Requiem for Murder '99
Dead End '98
Little Men '98
Sir Arthur Conan Doyle's The Lost World '98
Sci-Fighters '96
Legends of the North '95
Margaret's Museum '95
The Paperboy '94
Psychic '91

Simon Lacey
Good '08
Me & Mrs. Jones '02
The Railway Children '00

Yves Laferriere
Plain Truth '04
Jesus of Montreal '89

Francis Lai(1932-)
Les Miserables '95
Marie '85
My New Partner '84
Cat and Mouse '78
Emmanuelle, the Joys of a Woman '76
Insanity '76
By the Blood of Others '73
Killing in the Sun '73
Love Story '70
Mayerling '68
Action Man '67
I'll Never Forget What's 'Isname '67
Scandal Man '67
A Man and a Woman '66

Nick Laird-Clowes
Fierce People '05
Invisible Circus '00

Russ Landau
Lost '05
Killer Bud '00
Love and Action in Chicago '99
Nowhere Land '98
Telling You '98

Burton Lane(1912-97)
Royal Wedding '51
College Swing '38
Dancing Lady '33

Robert (Rob) Lane
John Adams '08
Tess of the D'Urbervilles '08
Jane Eyre '06
Longford '06
Archangel '05
Elizabeth I '05
Aileen: Life and Death of a Serial Killer '03
Daniel Deronda '02
The Hound of the Baskervilles '02
The Lost World '02
Breathtaking '00
David Copperfield '99
The Young Poisoner's Handbook '94

Jim Lang
Born Killers '05
Hey Arnold! The Movie '02
In the Mouth of Madness '95
Body Bags '93
For Love or Money '88

Arthur Lange(1889-1956)
Pride of St. Louis '52
Along Came Jones '45
It's a Pleasure '45
Casanova Brown '44
Woman in the Window '44
The Undying Monster '42
Golden Gloves '40
Girl's Dormitory '36
In Old Kentucky '35

Johnny Lange(1905-2006)
Flying Wild '41
Up in the Air '40
Six Gun Rhythm '39

Clive Langer
Brothers of the Head '06
Still Crazy '98

Bruce Langhorne
Fourth Wise Man '85
Melvin and Howard '80
Hired Hand '71

Brian Langsbard
The Specials '00
Johnny Skidmarks '97

Daniel Lanois(1951-)
The Million Dollar Hotel '99
Sling Blade '96
Camilla '94

Alphonse Lanza
The Last Hit Man '08
Time Bomb '08

Tito Larriva
Just a Little Harmless Sex '99
Dream with the Fishes '97
Repo Man '83

Nathan Larson(1970-)
The Kids Are All Right '10
The Messenger '09
August '08
Choke '08
Little Fish '05
A Love Song for Bobby Long '04
Palindromes '04
The Woodsman '04
Dirty Pretty Things '03
The Chateau '01
Prozac Nation '01
Storytelling '01
Tigerland '00
Boys Don't Cry '99

Richard LaSalle(1918-)
Alice Doesn't Live Here Anymore '74
Deathhead Virgin '74
City Beneath the Sea '71
Wild Gypsies '69
Boy, Did I Get a Wrong Number! '66
Twice-Told Tales '63
Why Must I Die? '60

Alexander Lasarenko
Pipe Dream '02
The Business of Strangers '01
Dinner Rush '00

Jeff Lass
Partners '99
Matter of Trust '98
Laws of Deception '97
The Student Affair '97
Hard Vice '94
Vegas Vice '94
DaVinci's War '92

Alexander Laszlo(1895-1970)
Atomic Submarine '59
Attack of the Giant Leeches '59
Night of the Blood Beast '58
Rocky Jones, Space Ranger: Renegade Satellite '54
Tarzan's Magic Fountain '48
Dangerous Passage '44
One Body Too Many '44

Jim Latham
Extreme Movie '08
Tweek City '05
On Edge '03

Ryan Latham
Just Business '08
The Devil's Mercy '07
Final Draft '07

William Lava(1911-71)
Dracula vs. Frankenstein '71
Cattle Town '52
Zorro's Fighting Legion '39

Angelo Francesco Lavagnino(1909-87)
Stranger in Paso Bravo '68
Chimes at Midnight '67
Four Dollars of Revenge '66
Hero of Rome '63
Imperial Venus '63
Madame Sans-Gene '62
Gorgo '61
Esther and the King '60
Roland the Mighty '56

Othello '52

Raul Lavista

Simon of the Desert '66
The Exterminating Angel '62
Daniel Boone: Trail Blazer '56

David Lawrence

The Cheetah Girls: One World '08
High School Musical 3: Senior Year '08
A Grandpa for Christmas '07
High School Musical 2 '07
The Cheetah Girls 2 '06
High School Musical '06
Getting Played '05
Jiminy Glick in LaLa Wood '05
Snow '04
National Lampoon's Van Wilder '02
American Pie 2 '01
Life Without Dick '01
Company Man '00
American Pie '99
Hi-Life '98
Steel Sharks '97
Moving Target '96
Alone in the Woods '95
Sleep with Me '94
Skeeter '93

Stephen Lawrence

Red Riding Hood '88
Alice Sweet Alice '76

Maury Laws

The Return of the King '80
The Bermuda Depths '78
The Hobbit '78

Alan Ari Lazar(1967-)

An American Crime '07
Duck '05
Two Days '03
Purpose '02
Billy's Hollywood Screen Kiss '98

Maurice Le Roux

See Maurice Leroux

Adrian Lee

The Medallion '03
The Reckoning '03

Bill Lee(1928-)

Mo' Better Blues '90
Do the Right Thing '89
School Daze '88
She's Gotta Have It '86

Byung-woo Lee

The Host '06
The Red Shoes '05
A Tale of Two Sisters '03
3 Extremes 2 '02

Dong-jun Lee

Save the Green Planet '03
Shiri '99
The Soul Guardians '98

Jon Lee

Afghan Knights '07
Who's Your Caddy? '07
Devil's Den '06
The Tooth Fairy '06

Tae-beon Lee

Apartment 1303 '07
Nightmare '00

Eric Leeds

Giant Steps '92
Giant Steps '92

Michel Legrand(1932-)

And Now Ladies and Gentlemen '02
La Buche '00
Madeline '98
Ready to Wear '94
The Pickle '93
Dingo '90
The Jeweller's Shop '90
Switching Channels '88
Love Songs '84
Never Say Never Again '83
Yentl '83
Atlantic City '81
Falling in Love Again '80
The Mountain Men '80
A Slightly Pregnant Man '79
Roads to the South '78
The Savage '75
It's Good to Be Alive '74
The Three Musketeers '74
Brian's Song '71
The Go-Between '71
Summer of '42 '71
Donkey Skin '70
Wuthering Heights '70
Castle Keep '69
La Piscine '69
Ice Station Zebra '68
Sweet November '68
The Young Girls of Rochefort '68
Band of Outsiders '64
Umbrellas of Cherbourg '64
Duke of the Derby '62
Eva '62
My Life to Live '62
Cleo from 5 to 7 '61
Keep Talking Baby '61
It Means That to Me '60
A Woman Is a Woman '60

Franz Lehar(1870-1948)

The Merry Widow '52
The Merry Widow '34

Jed Leiber

Blue Chips '94
Love Potion #9 '92

John Leipold(1888-1970)

The Desperadoes '43
Twilight on the Trail '41
Campus Confessions '38

Bruce Leitl

Man in the Mirror: The Michael Jackson Story '04
Ebenezer '97

Christopher Lennertz(1972-)

Cats & Dogs: The Revenge of Kitty Galore '10
Marmaduke '10
To Save a Life '10
Adam '09
The Open Road '09
Disaster Movie '08
Alvin and the Chipmunks '07
The Comebacks '07
The Perfect Holiday '07
Tortilla Heaven '07
Dr. Dolittle 3 '06
The Deal '05
Deathlands: Homeward Bound '03
The 4th Tenor '02
Undercurrent '99
Art House '98
Running Woman '98
Baby Face Nelson '97
Humanoids from the Deep '96
Spectre '96
Piranha '95
Suspect Device '95
Unknown Origin '95
Midnight Tease '94

John Lennon(1940-80)

Le Bal '82
Let It Be '70
Yellow Submarine '68
Magical Mystery Tour '67
Help! '65
A Hard Day's Night '64

Jack Lenz

Celine '08
Men with Brooms '02
Treacherous Beauties '94

Patrick Leonard

With Honors '94
Timebomb '91
At Close Range '86
Nothing in Common '86

Valentine Leone(1975-)

Asylum of the Damned '03
Backflash '01

Cory Lerios

Boiling Point '93
Beyond the Law '92
Child's Play 3 '91
One Crazy Summer '86

Alan Jay Lerner(1918-86)

The Little Prince '74
Paint Your Wagon '69
Camelot '67
My Fair Lady '64
Brigadoon '54

Cesar Lerner

Lost Embrace '04
Nine Queens '00

Maurice Leroux

Le Petit Soldat '60
Les Mistons '57

Oscar Levant(1906-72)

Nothing Sacred '37
In Person '35
Gambling Ship '33

Sylvester Levay

Flashfire '94
Dead to Rights '93
Hot Shots! '91
Stone Cold '91
Navy SEALS '90
Courage Mountain '89
The Tracker '88
Burglar '87
Mannequin '87
Cobra '86
Howard the Duck '86
Invaders from Mars '86
Creator '85
Where the Boys Are '84 '84

Alvin Levin

Railroaded '47
Too Many Winners '47

Andres Levin

Borderland '07
Feel the Noise '07
El Cantante '06

Geoff Levin

Flying By '09
Confessions of a Pit Fighter '05
Who Made the Potatoe Salad? '05
Darkwolf '03
One of Them '03
Extreme Honor '01
Jimmy Zip '00
Perfect Assassins '98
Gang Boys '97

James Levine

Delta Farce '07
Running with Scissors '06
A Little Inside '01

Michael A. Levine

Columbus Day '08
Adrift in Manhattan '07
Wonderland '03

Krishna Levy(1964-)

The Fall '06
8 Women '02
Dad On the Run '00
Artemisia '97
My Sex Life... Or How I Got into an Argument '96

Louis Levy(1894-1957)

The Girl in the News '41
The Lady Vanishes '38
Young and Innocent '37
The Secret Agent '36
The 39 Steps '35

Shuki Levy

Aussie and Ted's Great Adventure '09
Turbo: A Power Rangers Movie '96
Blindfold: Acts of Obsession '94
Trapper County War '89
Fatal Games '84

Herschell Gordon Lewis(1926-)

This Stuff'll Kill Ya! '71
Moonshine Mountain '64
2000 Maniacs '64
Blood Feast '63

John Lewis

Kemek '70
Odds Against Tomorrow '59

Laurie Lewis

Nowhere to Hide '83
On the Run '83

Mel Lewis

Final Engagement '07
The Hunt for Eagle One: Crash Point '06

Michael Lewis(1939-)

Deadly Target '94
The Hound of the Baskervilles '83
On the Third Day '83
Theatre of Blood '73
The Man Who Haunted Himself '70

Paul Lewis

The Maze '85
Murders at Lynch Cross '85

W. Michael Lewis

Hot Child in the City '87
Ballad of Gregorio Cortez '83
Revenge of the Ninja '83
Shogun Assassin '80
New Year's Evil '78

Blake Leyh

Outside the Law '95
True Crime '95

Daniel Licht

Maneater '09
Gym Teacher: The Movie '08
The Memory Keeper's Daughter '08
Frederick Forsyth's Icon '05
Video Voyeur: The Susan Wilson Story '02
Off Season '01
Soul Survivors '01
Cabin by the Lake '00
Cowboy Up '00
Hendrix '00
Splendor '99
Permanent Midnight '98
Bad Moon '96
Stephen King's Thinner '96
The Winner '96
Children of the Corn 3: Urban Harvest '95
Hellraiser 4: Bloodline '95
Woman Undone '95
Acting on Impulse '93
H.P. Lovecraft's Necronomicon: Book of the Dead '93
Final Embrace '92

Max Lichtenstein

The King '05
Puzzlehead '05
Tarnation '03
Margarita Happy Hour '01

Ivri Lider

The Bubble '06
Yossi & Jagger '02

Jacobo Lieberman

Trade '07
Maria Full of Grace '04
The Maldonado Miracle '03

Jimmy Lifton(1955-)

Powder Burn '96
Mirror, Mirror 2: Raven Dance '94
The Takeover '94
Mirror, Mirror '90

Joseph J. Lilley(1913-95)

How to Commit Marriage '69
Paradise, Hawaiian Style '66
Papa's Delicate Condition '63
Who's Minding the Store? '63
Girls! Girls! Girls! '62
Sailor Beware '52

Hal Lindes(1953-)

The Boys Are Back '09
Little Devil '07
Quicksand '01
Forgive and Forget '99
Gunshy '98
Reckless: The Sequel '98
Kiss and Tell '96
Band of Gold '95
The Infiltrator '95

Mort Lindsey(1923-)

Real Life '79
40 Pounds of Trouble '62

Michael Linn(1952-95)

Snapdragon '93
American Ninja '85

Michael Lipton

Heroes of the Heart '94
Invasion of the Space Preachers '90

Alan Lisk

Tess of the D'Urbervilles '98
R.P.M. '97

Zdenek Liska(1922-83)

Adelheid '69
Murder Czech Style '66
The Shop on Main Street '65
Death Is Called Engelchen '63
Fabulous Adventures of Baron Munchausen '61

Jack Livesey(1901-61)

Homecoming '09
The Yellow Handkerchief '08
Sherrybaby '06

Jay Livingston(1915-2001)

Red Garters '54
The Lemon Drop Kid '51

Andrew Lloyd Webber(1948-)

The Phantom of the Opera '04
Jesus Christ Superstar '00
Joseph and the Amazing Technicolor Dreamcoat '00
Evita '96
The Odessa File '74
Jesus Christ, Superstar '73
Gumshoe '72

Lowell Lo

Shaolin Soccer '01
Naked Killer '92
Prison on Fire 2 '91
The Killer '90
Prison on Fire '87

Brian Lock

The Land Girls '98
The Gambler '97

Robert Lockhart

Inspector Lynley Mysteries: A Great Deliverance '01
Vicious Circles '97
Cold Comfort Farm '94

Andrew Lockington(1974-)

City of Ember '08
How She Move '08
Journey to the Center of the Earth '08
Skinwalkers '07
Cake '05
Saint Ralph '04
Touch of Pink '04
Long Life, Happiness and Prosperity '02

Malcolm Lockyer

Deadlier Than the Male '67
The Vengeance of Fu Manchu '67

Joseph LoDuca(1958-)

Messengers 2: The Scarecrow '09
Boogeyman 3 '08
My Name Is Bruce '08
The Messengers '07
The Librarian: Return to King Solomon's Mines '06
Touch the Top of the World '06
Boogeyman '05
Devour '05
The Librarian: Quest for the Spear '04
Brotherhood of the Wolf '01
Young Hercules '97
Hercules the Legendary Journeys, Vol. 1: And the Amazon Women '94
Hercules the Legendary Journeys, Vol. 2: The Lost Kingdom '94
Hercules the Legendary Journeys, Vol. 3: The Circle of Fire '94
Hercules the Legendary Journeys, Vol. 4: In the Underworld '94
H.P. Lovecraft's Necronomicon: Book of the Dead '93
Army of Darkness '92
Lunatics: A Love Story '92
The Carrier '87
Evil Dead 2: Dead by Dawn '87
Thou Shalt Not Kill...Except '87
Crimewave '85
Evil Dead '83

Frank Loesser(1910-69)

How to Succeed in Business without Really Trying '67
Guys and Dolls '55
Hans Christian Andersen '52
The Perils of Pauline '47
Hoppity Goes to Town '41
College Swing '38

Frederick Loewe(1901-88)

The Little Prince '74
Paint Your Wagon '69
Camelot '67
My Fair Lady '64
Gigi '58
Brigadoon '54

J.M. Logan

Black Mask 2: City of Masks '02
Tsui Hark's Vampire Hunters '02

Henning Lohner(1961-)

Night Train '09
Shuttle '09
In the Name of the King: A Dungeon Siege Tale '08
Love Comes Lately '07
BloodRayne '06
Hellraiser: Deader '05
The Ring 2 '05
Incident at Loch Ness '04
Mimic 3: Sentinel '03

Frank London

A Brother's Kiss '97
Everything Relative '96

Steve London

Decoys: The Second Seduction '07
That Beautiful Somewhere '06
Shallow Ground '04

William Loose(1910-91)

Mystery Mansion '83
Dream Chasers '82
Johnny Firecloud '75
Supervixens '75
The Swinging Cheerleaders '74
Blacksnake! '73
The Big Bird Cage '72
Rebel Rousers '69
Mission to Death '66

Peter Lopez

Dirty '05
Dead Birds '04

Robert Lord(1900-76)

Pumpkinhead 4: Blood Feud '07
Pumpkinhead 3: Ashes to Ashes '06

Michael Lorenc

Brute '97
Exit in Red '97

Daktari Lorenz(1962-)
Nekromantik 2 *'91*
Der Todesking *'89*

Alexina Louie(1949-)
The Five Senses *'99*
Last Night *'98*

Jacques Loussier(1934-)
Dark of the Sun *'68*
Life Upside Down *'64*

Mundell Lowe(1922-)
Deadly Game *'77*
Tarantulas: The Deadly Cargo *'77*
Everything You Always Wanted to Know about Sex (But Were Afraid to Ask) *'72*
Billy Jack *'71*
Satan in High Heels *'61*

Richard Lowry(1964-)
Mommy 2: Mommy's Day *'96*
Mommy *'95*

Marcos Loya
... And the Earth Did Not Swallow Him *'94*
Hostile Intentions *'94*

Dario Lucantoni
Traveling Companion *'96*
Acla's Descent into Floristella *'87*

Eric Lundmark
Quigley *'03*
The Landlady *'98*
No Strings Attached *'98*

John Lunn(1956-)
Criminal Justice *'08*
Little Dorrit *'08*
The Shadow in the North *'07*
See No Evil: The Moors Murders *'06*
Bleak House *'05*
Like Father Like Son *'05*
Under the Greenwood Tree *'05*
P.D. James: The Murder Room *'04*
Cambridge Spies *'03*
Once Upon a Time in the Midlands *'02*
Sirens *'02*
Lorna Doone *'01*
Get Real *'99*
Immortality *'98*

Donal Lunny(1947-)
This Is My Father *'99*
Eat the Peach *'86*

Deborah Lurie
Dear John *'10*
9 *'09*
The Betrayed *'08*
Spring Breakdown *'08*
Sydney White *'07*
Drop Dead Sexy *'05*
Imaginary Heroes *'05*
Mozart and the Whale *'05*
Sleepover *'04*
Sleepover *'04*
Whirlygirl *'04*

Evan Lurie(1954-)
Interview *'07*
Lisa Picard Is Famous *'01*
The Whole Shebang *'01*
Happy Accidents *'00*
Joe Gould's Secret *'00*
Office Killer *'97*
The Monster *'96*
Tree's Lounge *'96*
The Night We Never Met *'93*
Johnny Stecchino *'92*
Doomed Love *'83*

John Lurie(1952-)
Animal Factory *'00*
Clay Pigeons *'98*
Excess Baggage *'96*
Manny & Lo *'96*
Get Shorty *'95*
Mystery Train *'89*
Down by Law *'86*
Permanent Vacation *'84*
Stranger than Paradise *'84*
Variety *'83*

Lelio Luttazzi(1923-)
The Switch *'76*
Joyful Laughter *'60*

Steven Lutvak
Mad Hot Ballroom *'05*
Anything But Love *'02*

Elisabeth Lutyens(1906-83)
Dr. Terror's House of Horrors *'65*
The Skull *'65*
Paranoiac *'62*

Danny Lux
The Circuit *'08*
Holiday in Handcuffs *'07*
Lucky Seven *'03*
Halloween: Resurrection *'02*
Stolen Summer *'02*

Allen Lynch
Mosquito *'95*
Rain Without Thunder *'93*

Bruce Lynch
The Vector File *'03*
Hope Ranch *'02*

Randall Lynch
Mosquito *'95*
Rain Without Thunder *'93*

Egisto Macchi(1928-92)
The Rose Garden *'89*
Diary of a Mad Old Man *'88*
Padre Padrone *'77*
Mr. Klein *'76*

Neil MacColl
24-7 *'97*
Fever Pitch *'96*

Galt MacDermot(1928-)
Mistress *'91*
Hair *'79*
Cotton Comes to Harlem *'70*

Don MacDonald
The Chaos Experiment *'09*
Dr. Dolittle 4: Tail to the Chief *'08*
Fido *'06*
Suspicious River *'00*
Kissed *'96*

Mader(1958-)
My Louisiana Sky *'02*
Steal This Movie! *'00*
Morgan's Ferry *'99*
Eat Drink Man Woman *'94*
In the Soup *'92*
Sons *'89*

Michel Magne(1930-84)
S.A.S. San Salvador *'84*
Cold Sweat *'71*
Angelique and the Sultan *'68*
The Sergeant *'68*
Untamable Angelique *'67*
Angelique and the King *'66*
Angelique *'64*
The Monocle *'64*
Any Number Can Win *'63*
Love on a Pillow *'62*

Cliff Magness
Body Shot *'93*
Beretta's Island *'92*

Stefano Mainetti(1957-)
Silent Trigger *'97*
Sub Down *'97*
Sons of Trinity *'95*
Hidden Assassin *'94*
Interzone *'88*

Hans-Martin Majewski(1911-97)
Brainwashed *'60*
The Bridge *'59*

William V. Malpede(1965-)
Dog Gone Love *'03*
Fast Sofa *'01*

Nikos Mamangakis(1929-)
Kaspar Hauser *'93*
Heimat 2 *'92*
Heimat 1 *'84*
Milo Milo *'79*

Bob Mamet
Lakeboat *'00*
Aftershock *'88*
Necromancer: Satan's Servant *'88*

Richiro Manabe
Godzilla vs. Megalon *'76*
Flower & Snake '74 *'74*

Mark Mancina(1957-)
Imagine That *'09*
August Rush *'07*
Shooter *'07*
Asylum *'05*
Tarzan 2 *'05*
Brother Bear *'03*
The Haunted Mansion *'03*
The Reckoning *'03*
Domestic Disturbance *'01*
Training Day *'01*
Bait *'00*
Beyond Suspicion *'00*
From the Earth to the Moon *'98*
Return to Paradise *'98*
Con Air *'97*
Speed 2: Cruise Control *'97*
Moll Flanders *'96*
Twister *'96*
Assassins *'95*
Bad Boys *'95*
Fair Game *'95*
Man of the House *'95*
Money Train *'95*
Monkey Trouble *'94*
Speed *'94*
True Romance *'93*
Future Force *'89*

Henry Mancini(1924-94)
Married to It *'93*
Son of the Pink Panther *'93*
Tom and Jerry: The Movie *'93*
Never Forget *'91*
Switch *'91*
Fear *'90*
Ghost Dad *'90*
Peter Gunn *'89*
Physical Evidence *'89*
Skin Deep *'89*
Welcome Home *'89*
Sunset *'88*
Without a Clue *'88*
Blind Date *'87*
The Glass Menagerie *'87*
A Fine Mess *'86*
The Great Mouse Detective *'86*
That's Life! *'86*
Lifeforce *'85*
Santa Claus: The Movie *'85*
That's Dancing! *'85*
Harry & Son *'84*
Better Late Than Never *'83*
Curse of the Pink Panther *'83*
The Man Who Loved Women *'83*
Second Thoughts *'83*
The Thorn Birds *'83*
Trail of the Pink Panther *'82*
Victor/Victoria *'82*
Back Roads *'81*
Condorman *'81*
Mommie Dearest *'81*
S.O.B. *'81*
A Change of Seasons *'80*
Little Miss Marker *'80*
The Shadow Box *'80*
Nightwing *'79*
Prisoner of Zenda *'79*
10 *'79*
Family Upside Down *'78*
House Calls *'78*
Revenge of the Pink Panther *'78*
Who Is Killing the Great Chefs of Europe? *'78*
Angela *'77*
The Pink Panther Strikes Again *'76*
Silver Streak *'76*
The Great Waldo Pepper *'75*
Once Is Not Enough *'75*
The White Dawn *'75*
The Girl from Petrovka *'74*
99 & 44/100 Dead *'74*
Return of the Pink Panther *'74*
That's Entertainment *'74*
Oklahoma Crude *'73*
The Thief Who Came to Dinner *'73*
Sometimes a Great Notion *'71*
Darling Lili *'70*
Molly Maguires *'70*
The Night Visitor *'70*
Bachelor in Paradise *'69*
The Party *'68*
Two for the Road *'67*
Wait until Dark *'67*
Arabesque *'66*
Moment to Moment *'66*
What Did You Do in the War, Daddy? *'66*
The Great Race *'65*
The Pink Panther *'64*
A Shot in the Dark *'64*
Charade *'63*
King Kong vs. Godzilla *'63*
Man's Favorite Sport? *'63*
Soldier in the Rain *'63*
Days of Wine and Roses *'62*
Experiment in Terror *'62*
Hatari! *'62*
Mr. Hobbs Takes a Vacation *'62*
Breakfast at Tiffany's *'61*
The Great Impostor *'61*
Never Steal Anything Small *'59*
Touch of Evil *'58*
The Land Unknown *'57*
The Creature Walks among Us *'56*
Rock, Pretty Baby *'56*
The Benny Goodman Story *'55*
Far Country *'55*
To Hell and Back *'55*
Creature from the Black Lagoon *'54*
The Glenn Miller Story *'54*
It Came from Outer Space *'53*
Law and Order *'53*
Horizons West *'52*
Lost in Alaska *'52*

Johnny Mandel(1925-)
Brenda Starr *'86*
Deathtrap *'82*
The Verdict *'82*
Caddyshack *'80*
Being There *'79*
The Last Detail *'73*
M*A*S*H *'70*
Pretty Poison *'68*
Harper *'66*
Drums of Africa *'63*
I Want to Live! *'58*

Harry Manfredini(1943-)
All In *'06*
Endangered Species *'02*
Hell's Gate *'01*
Jason X *'01*
Hidden Agenda *'99*
The Omega Code *'99*
Catherine's Grove *'98*
A Gun, a Car, a Blonde *'97*
Raven *'97*
Wishmaster *'97*
Dead on Sight *'94*
Jason Goes to Hell: The Final Friday *'93*
Deepstar Six *'89*
Friday the 13th, Part 6: Jason Lives *'86*
House *'86*
Swamp Thing *'82*
Friday the 13th, Part 2 *'81*
Friday the 13th *'80*

Barry Manilow(1943-)
The Pebble and the Penguin *'94*
Thumbelina *'94*

Hummie Mann
Meat Loaf: To Hell and Back *'00*
Thomas and the Magic Railroad *'00*
After the Rain *'99*
Naked City: A Killer Christmas *'98*
Rescuers: Stories of Courage—Two Couples *'98*
Rescuers: Stories of Courage "Two Women" *'97*
The Second Civil War *'97*
Sticks and Stones *'96*
Dracula: Dead and Loving It *'95*
Cool and the Crazy *'94*
Fall Time *'94*
Girls in Prison *'94*
Jailbreakers *'94*
Runaway Daughters *'94*
Benefit of the Doubt *'93*
Robin Hood: Men in Tights *'93*
Year of the Comet *'92*
In Gold We Trust *'91*
Stoogemania *'85*

Franco Mannino(1924-2005)
The Innocent *'76*
Conversation Piece *'75*
Driver's Seat *'73*
The Ghost *'63*
I, Vampiri *'56*
Beat the Devil *'53*

Clint Mansell(1963-)
Last Night *'10*
Blood: The Last Vampire *'09*
Moon *'09*
Definitely, Maybe *'08*
The Wrestler *'08*
Smokin' Aces *'07*
Wind Chill *'07*
The Fountain *'06*
Trust the Man *'06*
Doom *'05*
Sahara *'05*
Suspect Zero *'04*
11:14 *'03*
Abandon *'02*
Murder by Numbers *'02*
Sonny *'02*
The Hole *'01*
Knockaround Guys *'01*
World Traveler *'01*
Requiem for a Dream *'00*
Pi *'98*

David Mansfield(1956-)
The Guitar *'08*
Then She Found Me *'07*
Broken Trail *'06*
Diggers *'06*
Stephanie Daley *'06*
Transamerica *'05*
Get a Clue *'02*
A Good Baby *'99*
Songcatcher *'99*
Dark Harbor *'98*
Outrage *'98*
Road Ends *'98*
Tumbleweeds *'98*
The Apostle *'97*
Floating *'97*
Deep Crimson *'96*
A Streetcar Named Desire *'95*
Truman *'95*
The Ballad of Little Jo *'93*
Me & Veronica *'93*
Desperate Hours *'90*
Miss Firecracker *'89*
The Sicilian *'87*
Club Paradise *'86*

Kevin Manthei
The 24th Day *'04*
Milo *'98*

Jim Manzie
Blood Surf *'00*
Night of the Scarecrow *'95*
Lurking Fear *'94*
Night of the Demons 2 *'94*
Eddie Presley *'92*
Leatherface: The Texas Chainsaw Massacre 3 *'89*
The Offspring *'87*

Gianni Marchetti
SS Girls *'77*
Summer Affair *'71*
One Step to Hell *'67*

Veigar Margeirsson
How You Look to Me *'05*
Mind the Gap *'04*

Dario Marianelli
Eat, Pray, Love *'10*
Everybody's Fine *'09*
The Soloist *'09*
Atonement *'07*
The Brave One *'07*
The Color of Freedom *'07*
Far North *'07*
Shrooms *'07*
The Return *'06*
V for Vendetta *'06*
The Brothers Grimm *'05*
Pride and Prejudice *'05*
Shooting Dogs *'05*
In This World *'03*
I Capture the Castle *'02*
Pandaemonium *'00*
I Went Down *'97*
The Warrior *'81*

A. L. Mariaux
See Jess (Jesus) Franco

Mariano Marin(1959-)
Open Your Eyes *'97*
Thesis *'96*

Anthony Marinelli(1959-)
The Human Contract *'08*
Chapter 27 *'07*
Ripple Effect *'07*
Dreamland *'06*
Memory *'06*
Mayor of the Sunset Strip *'03*
American Gun *'02*
Borderline *'02*
Lone Hero *'02*
15 Minutes *'01*
Hotel *'01*
The Man from Elysian Fields *'01*
Quicksand *'01*
Just One Night *'00*
Slow Burn *'00*
Time Code *'00*
Gideon *'99*
God Said "Ha!" *'99*
The Runner *'99*
Hoods *'98*
Scarred City *'98*
Don King: Only in America *'97*
Sink or Swim *'97*
Flynn *'96*
Masterminds *'96*
Two Days in the Valley *'96*
Underworld *'96*
One Man's Justice *'95*
Young Guns *'88*

Richard Markowitz(1926-94)
Mayday at 40,000 Feet *'76*
The Hanged Man *'74*
The Shooting *'66*
A Face in the Rain *'63*

Andrzej Markowski
Shadow *'56*
A Generation *'54*

Rick Marotta
Moola *'07*
Just the Ticket *'98*
Painted Hero *'95*
The Cover Girl Murders *'93*

Branford Marsalis(1960-)
3 A.M. *'01*
Once in the Life *'00*
Mr. & Mrs. Loving *'96*
Sneakers *'92*
Mo' Better Blues *'90*

Jeff Marsh(1961-)
Unspeakable *'02*
Burning Down the House *'01*

Halloween with the Addams Family '79
How to Frame a Figg '71
The Love God? '70
The Busy Body '67
The Reluctant Astronaut '67
The Ghost and Mr. Chicken '66

Moby(1965-)

Southland Tales '06
Double Tap '98

Cyril Mockridge(1896-1979)

Donovan's Reef '63
The Man Who Shot Liberty Valance '62
Flaming Star '60
Tall Story '60
Rally 'Round the Flag, Boys! '58
Desk Set '57
Will Success Spoil Rock Hunter? '57
Bus Stop '56
I Married a Woman '56
Solid Gold Cadillac '56
Many Rivers to Cross '55
River of No Return '54
A Woman's World '54
The Farmer Takes a Wife '53
The Girl Next Door '53
Belles on Their Toes '52
We're Not Married '52
Follow the Sun '51
Let's Make It Legal '51
Love Nest '51
Cheaper by the Dozen '50
Ticket to Tomahawk '50
Where the Sidewalk Ends '50
Come to the Stable '49
Father Was a Fullback '49
I Was a Male War Bride '49
The Luck of the Irish '48
Road House '48
That Wonderful Urge '48
Miracle on 34th Street '47
Nightmare Alley '47
Dark Corner '46
My Darling Clementine '46
Colonel Effingham's Raid '45
The Ox-Bow Incident '43
The Fighting Sullivans '42
The Undying Monster '42
I Wake Up Screaming '41
Sleepers West '41
Brigham Young: Frontiersman '40
Johnny Apollo '40
Lucky Cisco Kid '40
Michael Shayne: Private Detective '40
Day-Time Wife '39
Everything Happens at Night '39

Mark Moffatt

Back of Beyond '95
High Tide '87

Charlie Mole

The Diary of Anne Frank '08
I Really Hate My Job '07
St. Trinian's '07
The Secret Life of Mrs. Beeton '06
The Importance of Being Earnest '02
High Heels and Low Lifes '01
An Ideal Husband '99
Othello '95

Fred Mollin

Inferno '99
Thrill Seekers '99
The Abduction '96
Spring Fever '81

Paddy Moloney(1938-)

Agnes Browne '99
Under the Sun '98

Thom Monahan

Hijacking Catastrophe: 9/11, Fear and the Selling of America '04
Peace, Propaganda & the Promised Land '04

Hugo Montenegro(1925-81)

Too Hot to Handle '76
Charro! '69
The Wrecking Crew '68
The Ambushers '67

Michael Montes

Whipped '00
Firehouse '87
Hangmen '87

Osvaldo Montes

Burnt Money '00
A Shadow You Soon Will Be '94
The Dark Side of the Heart '92

Bruce Montgomery(1921-78)

Brides of Fu Manchu '66
Carry On Regardless '61
Carry On Constable '60
Doctor in Love '60
No Kidding '60
Carry On Sergeant '58

Tim Montijo

Bob Funk '09
The Life of Lucky Cucumber '08

Guy Moon

These Old Broads '01
A Very Brady Sequel '96
The Brady Bunch Movie '95
Diving In '90
Sorority Babes in the Slimeball Bowl-A-Rama '87
Wild Thing '87

Hal Mooney(1911-95)

Bull of the West '71
Raid on Rommel '71
The Meanest Men in the West '67

Dudley Moore(1935-2002)

Six Weeks '82
The Hound of the Baskervilles '77
Bedazzled '68
30 Is a Dangerous Age, Cynthia '68

Mike Moran

Sherlock: Case of Evil '02
Bloodbath at the House of Death '85
Time Bandits '81

Lucien Moraweck

Two Weeks to Live '43
International Lady '41
The Man in the Iron Mask '39

Patrick Moraz(1948-)

The Stepfather '87
La Salamandre '71

Fernando Garcia Morcillo

Voodoo Black Exorcist '73
Hawk and Castile '67

Jaques Morelembaum

Paid '06
Central Station '98

Mark Morgan

Shark Attack 2 '00
Where the Day Takes You '92

Cyril Morin(1962-)

The Unmistaken Child '08
La Petite Jerusalem '05
The Syrian Bride '04

Sophia Morizet

Mosquitoman '05
Possessed '05

Angela Morley

When Eight Bells Toll '71
Captain Nemo and the Underwater City '69

Giorgio Moroder(1940-)

Fair Game '89
Let It Ride '89
The NeverEnding Story '84
Flashdance '83
Scarface '83
Cat People '82
American Gigolo '79
Midnight Express '78

Jerome Moross(1913-83)

The Valley of Gwangi '69
The Big Country '58
Proud Rebel '58

Andrea Morricone(1964-)

Capturing the Friedmans '03
Here on Earth '00
Liberty Heights '99

Ennio Morricone(1928-)

Baaria '09
The Unknown Woman '06
Fateless '05
Ripley's Game '02
Malena '00
Mission to Mars '00
Vatel '00
Bulworth '98
The Legend of 1900 '98
The Phantom of the Opera '98
Tower of the Firstborn '98
Lolita '97
U-Turn '97
Nostromo '96
The Star Maker '95
The Stendahl Syndrome '95
Abraham '94
Disclosure '94
La Scorta '94
Love Affair '94
The Night and the Moment '94
A Pure Formality '94
Wolf '94
The Bachelor '93
In the Line of Fire '93
Beyond Justice '92
City of Joy '92
The Big Man: Crossing the Line '91
Bugsy '91
Husbands and Lovers '91
The Palermo Connection '91
A Time to Die '91
Everybody's Fine '90
State of Grace '90
Tie Me Up! Tie Me Down! '90
Casualties of War '89
The Endless Game '89
Fat Man and Little Boy '89
Time to Kill '89
Cinema Paradiso '88
Frantic '88
Python Wolf '88
A Time of Destiny '88
Rampage '87
The Untouchables '87
La Cage aux Folles 3: The Wedding '86
The Mission '86
Stalking Danger '86
Hundra '85
Red Sonja '85
Corrupt '84
Once Upon a Time in America '84
Fatal Error '83
Sahara '83
The Scarlet & the Black '83
Time to Die '83
Butterfly '82
Nana '82
The Thing '82
Treasure of the Four Crowns '82
White Dog '82
La Cage aux Folles 2 '81
Le Professionnel '81
Lovers and Liars '81
So Fine '81
The Tragedy of a Ridiculous Man '81
The Island '80
Windows '80
Almost Human '79
Sidney Sheldon's Bloodline '79
Days of Heaven '78
La Cage aux Folles '78
The Chosen '77
The Exorcist 2: The Heretic '77
Orca '77
The Desert of the Tartars '76
The Inheritance '76
Moses '76
The Human Factor '75
Leonor '75
Night Train Murders '75
Salo, or the 120 Days of Sodom '75
Torture Train '75
When Women Lost Their Tails '75
Arabian Nights '74
Autopsy '74
La Grande Bourgeoise '74
Le Secret '74
Master Touch '74
My Name Is Nobody '74
The Tempter '74
Allonsanfan '73
Massacre in Rome '73
Night Flight from Moscow '73
Sonny and Jed '73
'Tis a Pity She's a Whore '73
Bluebeard '72
A Fistful of Dynamite '72
Four Flies on Grey Velvet '72
Who Saw Her Die? '72
The Black Belly of the Tarantula '71
The Canterbury Tales '71
The Cat o' Nine Tails '71
Dirty Heroes '71
Divine Nymph '71
A Lizard in a Woman's Skin '71
Sacco & Vanzetti '71
Short Night of Glass Dolls '71
The Bird with the Crystal Plumage '70
Burn! '70
Cold Eyes of Fear '70
Companeros '70
The Decameron '70
The Family '70
Two Mules for Sister Sara '70
When Women Had Tails '70
Red Tent '69
Danger: Diabolik '68
Once Upon a Time in the West '68
Partner '68
Teorema '68
The Good, the Bad and the Ugly '67
The Hawks & the Sparrows '67
Hellbenders '67
Navajo Joe '67
The Rover '67
Secret Agent 00 '67
The Battle of Algiers '66
How I Learned to Love Women '66
Before the Revolution '65
For a Few Dollars More '65
Nightmare Castle '65
A Fistful of Dollars '64
Gunfight at Red Sands '63

John Morris(1926-)

The Lady in Question '99
Murder in a Small Town '99
Only Love '98
Ellen Foster '97
Scarlett '94
Carolina Skeletons '92
Dirty Dancing '87
Ironweed '87
Spaceballs '87
Target: Favorite Son '87
Clue '85
The Doctor and the Devils '85
The Woman in Red '84
Yellowbeard '83
The Elephant Man '80
In God We Trust '80
The In-Laws '79
The Scarlet Letter '79
Blazing Saddles '74
Young Frankenstein '74
The Twelve Chairs '70
The Producers '68

Trevor Morris(1970-)

The Marine 2 '09
The Hills Have Eyes 2 '07
The Lost Angel '04

Van Morrison(1945-)

Beyond the Clouds '95
Moondance '95
Lamb '85

Boris Morros(1891-1963)

The Big Broadcast of 1938 '38
College Swing '38
You and Me '38
Double or Nothing '37
Easy Living '37

Thomas Morse

The Sisters '05
Gangland '00
The Big Brass Ring '99
The Apostate '98
If I Die Before I Wake '98

Arthur Morton(1908-2000)

Pushover '54
The Nevadan '50

Bob Mothersbaugh(1952-)

How to Eat Fried Worms '06
200 Cigarettes '98

Mark Mothersbaugh(1950-)

Ramona and Beezus '10
Cloudy with a Chance of Meatballs '09
Fanboys '09
Nick & Norah's Infinite Playlist '08
Quid Pro Quo '08
Mama's Boy '07
The Dog Problem '06
How to Eat Fried Worms '06
The Big White '05
First Descent '05
Herbie: Fully Loaded '05
Lords of Dogtown '05
The Ringer '05
Confessions of a Teenage Drama Queen '04
Envy '04
The Life Aquatic with Steve Zissou '04
Good Boy! '03
A Guy Thing '03
Rugrats Go Wild! '03
Thirteen '03
Sorority Boys '02
Welcome to Collinwood '02
Halloweentown 2: Kalabar's Revenge '01
The Royal Tenenbaums '01
Sugar & Spice '01
The Adventures of Rocky & Bullwinkle '00
Rugrats in Paris: The Movie '00
Drop Dead Gorgeous '99
It's the Rage '99
Best Men '98
Bongwater '98
Halloweentown '98
Quicksilver Highway '98
The Rugrats Movie '98
Rushmore '98
200 Cigarettes '98
Breaking Up '97
Dead Man on Campus '97
Men '97
The Big Squeeze '96
Happy Gilmore '96
The Last Supper '96
The Birdcage '95
Bottle Rocket '95
Revenge of the Nerds 2: Nerds in Paradise '87

William Motzing(1939-)

Young Einstein '89
The Coca-Cola Kid '84
Return of Captain Invincible '83

Rob Mounsey

Kings of South Beach '07
Dangerous Passion '95
Working Girl '88

Alain Mouysset

Last Hour '08
Wolves in the Snow '02

Michael Muhlfriedel

Player 5150 '08
R.S.V.P. '02
St. Patrick's Day '99
Plump Fiction '97

Nico Muhly

The Reader '08
Joshua '07

Dominic Muldowney(1952-)

Bloody Sunday '01
King Lear '98
Sharpe's Eagle '93
Sharpe's Rifles '93
Catherine Cookson's The Black Candle '92

Gerry Mulligan(1927-96)

I'm Not Rappaport '96
The Final Programme '73

John Murphy(1965-)

Armored '09
Crossing Over '09
The Last House on the Left '09
Sunshine '07
Basic Instinct 2 '06
Miami Vice '06
Guess Who '05
The Man '05
Millions '05
The Perfect Score '04
All About the Benjamins '02
City by the Sea '02
Friday After Next '02
New Best Friend '02
28 Days Later '02
Vacuuming Completely Nude in Paradise '01
Liam '00
Snatch '00
The Bachelor '99
One More Kiss '99
Lock, Stock and 2 Smoking Barrels '98
The Real Howard Spitz '98
Stiff Upper Lips '96
Solitaire for 2 '94

Lyn Murray(1909-89)

The Last of Mrs. Lincoln '76
Snow White and the Three Stooges '61
The Bridges at Toko-Ri '55
Prowler '51

Sean Murray

Firetrap '01
The Legend of Cryin' Ryan '98

Jennie Muskett

American Girl: Chrissa Stands Strong '09
Material Girls '06
The State Within '06
The Prince & Me '04
The Twelve Days of Christmas Eve '04
Dead Gorgeous '02
B. Monkey '97

Michel Musseau

After Sex '97
Celestial Clockwork '94

Romano Musumarra(1956-)

L'Eleve '95
Faceless '88

Selma Mutal

Undertow '10
The Milk of Sorrow '09

Personal Best '82
Cutter's Way '81
Cruising '80
Heart Beat '80
Hardcore '79
Blue Collar '78
Heroes '77
One Flew Over the Cuckoo's Nest '75
The Exorcist '73
Greaser's Palace '72
Performance '70
Village of the Giants '65

Dana Niu

Hurt '09
Conjurer '08

Tom Noonan(1951-)

The House of the Devil '09
The Wife '95
What Happened Was... '94

Erik Nordgren(1913-92)

The Emigrants '72
The Devil's Eye '60
The Virgin Spring '59
Wild Strawberries '57
The Seventh Seal '56

John E. Nordstrom

Two Tickets to Paradise '06
Nearing Grace '05
Black Cloud '04

Per Norgard

Royal Deceit '94
Babette's Feast '87

Alex North(1910-91)

The Last Butterfly '92
The Penitent '88
The Dead '87
Good Morning, Vietnam '87
Death of a Salesman '86
Prizzi's Honor '85
Under the Volcano '84
Dragonslayer '81
Carny '80
Wise Blood '79
The Word '78
Rich Man, Poor Man '76
Bite the Bullet '75
The Passover Plot '75
Journey into Fear '74
Once Upon a Scoundrel '73
Pocket Money '72
Willard '71
A Dream of Kings '69
The Devil's Brigade '68
The Shoes of the Fisherman '68
Who's Afraid of Virginia Woolf? '66
The Agony and the Ecstasy '65
Cheyenne Autumn '64
The Outrage '64
Cleopatra '63
All Fall Down '62
The Children's Hour '61
The Misfits '61
Spartacus '60
Hot Spell '58
The Long, Hot Summer '58
Stage Struck '57
The Bad Seed '56
The King and Four Queens '56
The Rainmaker '56
Daddy Long Legs '55
I'll Cry Tomorrow '55
The Racers '55
The Rose Tattoo '55
Desiree '54
Les Miserables '52
The Member of the Wedding '52
Viva Zapata! '52
Death of a Salesman '51
A Streetcar Named Desire '51

Craig Northey

Dog Park '98
Kids in the Hall: Brain Candy '96

Julian Nott

Heavy Petting '07
Wallace & Gromit in The Curse of the Were-Rabbit '05
P.D. James: Death in Holy Orders '03
Gentlemen's Relish '01
My Mother's Courage '95
A Man of No Importance '94

Michael Nyman(1944-)

Never Forever '07
The Libertine '05
Tristram Shandy: A Cock and Bull Story '05
Nathalie '03
The Claim '00
The End of the Affair '99
Ravenous '99
Wonderland '99
Gattaca '97
The Ogre '96
Carrington '95
Mesmer '94
The Piano '93
The Hairdresser's Husband '92
Prospero's Books '91
The Cook, the Thief, His Wife & Her Lover '90
A Zed & Two Noughts '88
Drowning by Numbers '87
Cold Room '84
The Draughtsman's Contract '82

Molly Nyman

A Mighty Heart '07
Hard Candy '06
The Road to Guantanamo '06

Paul Oakenfold(1963-)

Nobel Son '08
Nothing Like the Holidays '08

Arlon Ober(1943-2004)

Crimewave '85
Eating Raoul '82

John O'Brien(1962-)

Vince Vaughn's Wild West Comedy Show '06
Made '01

Richard O'Brien(1942-)

Return of Captain Invincible '83
Shock Treatment '81
The Rocky Horror Picture Show '75

Oscar Cardozo Ocampo(1942-2001)

Deathstalker '83
Funny, Dirty Little War '83

Dustin O'Halloran

An American Affair '09
Remember the Daze '07

Erin O'Hara

Day Zero '07
Sicko '07

Patrick O'Hearn(1954-)

Silent Tongue '92
White Sands '92
Heaven Is a Playground '91

Phil Ohman(1896-1954)

Dick Tracy vs. Cueball '46
Renegade Trail '39

Charles Olins

The Hive '08
Blood Monkey '07
Croc '07
In the Spider's Web '07

William Olvis

Steal Big, Steal Little '95
Separate Lives '94
Red Rock West '93
The Comrades of Summer '92
29th Street '91
El Diablo '90

Yuji Ono(1941-)

The Castle of Cagliostro '80
Murders in the Doll House '79
Proof of the Man '77

Steve O'Reilly

Into the Fire '05
Into the Fire '05

Norman Orenstein

Diary of the Dead '07
Stir of Echoes 2: The Homecoming '07
Cube: Zero '04
Gone Dark '03
American Psycho 2: All American Girl '02
Cube 2: Hypercube '02
Danger Beneath the Sea '02
Prisoner of Love '99
The First 9 1/2 Weeks '98
Sanctuary '98
Mask of Death '97
Bounty Hunters '96
Downhill Willie '96

Robert G. Orpin

Girls Are for Loving '73
The Abductors '72
Ginger '72

Buxton Orr(1924-97)

First Man into Space '59
Corridors of Blood '58
Fiend without a Face '58
The Haunted Strangler '58

Riz Ortolani(1931-)

Incantato '03
The Best Man '97
The Story of Boys & Girls '91
The New Gladiators '83
Cannibal Holocaust '80
Love by Appointment '76
Escape from Death Row '73
Confessions of a Police Captain '72
Dead Are Alive '72
Don't Torture a Duckling '72
The Valachi Papers '72
Madron '70
McKenzie Break '70
Liberators '69
Anzio '68
Apache's Last Battle '64
Castle of Blood '64
The Seventh Dawn '64
Mondo Cane '63

Mark Orton

The Loss of a Teardrop Diamond '08
The Real Dirt on Farmer John '06
Sweet Land '05

Atli Orvarsson

The Code '09
The Fourth Kind '09
Babylon A.D. '08
Vantage Point '08
The Last Confederate: The Story of Robert Adams '05

Jason Osborn

The Triumph of Love '01
High Season '88

Yoshihide Otomo(1959-)

The Day the Sun Turned Cold '94
Summer Snow '94
The Blue Kite '93

Nicholas O'Toole

How to be a Serial Killer '08
Fast Girl '07
Valley of the Heart's Delight '07
Outfoxed: Rupert Murdoch's War on Journalism '04

John Ottman(1964-)

Astro Boy '09
Orphan '09
Valkyrie '08
Fantastic Four: Rise of the Silver Surfer '07
The Invasion '07
Superman Returns '06
Fantastic Four '05
Hide and Seek '05
House of Wax '05
Imaginary Heroes '05
Kiss Kiss Bang Bang '05
Cellular '04
Gothika '03
X2: X-Men United '03
Brother's Keeper '02
Eight Legged Freaks '02
Point of Origin '02
Pumpkin '02
Trapped '02
Bubble Boy '01
Urban Legends 2: Final Cut '00
Goodbye, Lover '99
Lake Placid '99
Halloween: H20 '98
Apt Pupil '97
Incognito '97
Snow White: A Tale of Terror '97
The Cable Guy '96
The Usual Suspects '95
Public Access '93

Marc Ouellette

The Sign of Four '01
The Hound of the Baskervilles '00

Atli Ovarsson

Season of the Witch '10
Lansdown '01

Blair Packham

Hollywood North '03
Triggermen '02

Jose Padilla(1889-1960)

Cuban Blood '03
Ibiza Dream '02
Private Manoeuvres '83

Gene Page(1940-98)

Blacula '72
Brewster McCloud '70

Jimmy Page(1944-)

Death Wish 3 '85
Death Wish 2 '82

Hayes Pagel(1910-92)

The Phantom Planet '61
Prison Break '38

Woody Pak

Crystal River '08
Miss Monday '98

Jeremy Parise

Jack and Jill vs. the World '08
How to Eat Your Watermelon in White Company (and Enjoy It) '05

Alan Parker

Alex Rider: Operation Stormbreaker '06
Victoria & Albert '01
Britannic '99
Oktober '98
Rhodes '97
The Phoenix and the Magic Carpet '95
What's Eating Gilbert Grape '93
American Gothic '88

Clifton Parker(1905-89)

Damn the Defiant '62
Sink the Bismarck '60
Sea of Sand '58
Curse of the Demon '57
Tarzan and the Lost Safari '57
Tarzan's Hidden Jungle '55
Sailor of the King '53
The Gift Horse '52
Blanche Fury '48
Johnny Frenchman '46

Dean Parker

The Cry: La Llorona '07
The Unseen '05

Jim Parker(1934-)

Dr. Bell and Mr. Doyle: The Dark Beginnings of Sherlock Holmes '00
A Rather English Marriage '98
Moll Flanders '96
The Final Cut '95
Body & Soul '93
House of Cards '90
Mapp & Lucia '85

Van Dyke Parks(1943-)

Dark Matter '07
Pictures of Hollis Woods '07
The Company '03
Charms for the Easy Life '02
Monday Night Mayhem '02
In the Time of the Butterflies '01
Harlan County War '00
Shadrach '98
Oliver Twist '97
Bastard out of Carolina '96
Private Parts '96
The Summer of Ben Tyler '96
One Christmas '95
Wild Bill '95
The Two Jakes '90
Casual Sex? '88
Club Paradise '86

Stephen Parsons

Conspiracy of Silence '03
Another 9 1/2 Weeks '96
Split Second '92

Arvo Part(1935-)

Red Lights '04
Gerry '02
Hamsun '96
Rachel River '87

Antony Partos

Disgrace '08
The Silence '06
Garage Days '03
Walking on Water '02
Soft Fruit '99

Johnny Pate(1923-)

Every Girl Should Have One '78
Bucktown '75

Shawn Patterson(1965-)

The Bible and Gun Club '96
The Demolitionist '95

Alex Pauk

The Five Senses '99
Last Night '98

Michael Pavlicek(1956-)

The Scarlet Pimpernel '99
The Scarlet Pimpernel 2: Mademoiselle Guillotine '99
The Scarlet Pimpernel 3: The Kidnapped King '99

Jan Pawluskiewicz

Hero of the Year '85
Fever '81

Don Peake(1940-)

Body Count '95
Hard Justice '95
Solar Force '94
The People under the Stairs '91
The Hills Have Eyes '77

Steve Pecile

Universal Soldier 2: Brothers in Arms '98
Universal Soldier 3: Unfinished Business '98

Al Pellegrini

The Choppers '61
Heroes Die Young '60

Krzysztof Penderecki

Katyn '07
The Saragossa Manuscript '65

Michael Penn(1958-)

Solitary Man '10
Sunshine Cleaning '09
That Evening Sun '09
American Teen '08
The Last Kiss '06
Melvin Goes to Dinner '03
The Anniversary Party '01
Boogie Nights '97
Hard Eight '96

Hector Pereira

It's Complicated '09
Beverly Hills Chihuahua '08
Illegal Tender '07
Suburban Girl '07
Ask the Dust '06
Blind Dating '06
Curious George '06
Two Weeks '06
Dirty Dancing: Havana Nights '04
Haven '04
Real Women Have Curves '02

Jorge Perez

The Monster Demolisher '60
The Criminal Life of Archibaldo de la Cruz '55

Michael Perilstein

Winterbeast '92
Hollywood Chainsaw Hookers '88

Coleridge-Taylor Perkinson

Talk to Me '84
A Woman Called Moses '78

Payont Permsith

Diary '06
Re-Cycle '06
The Eye 3 '05
The Eye 2 '04

Tyler Perry(1969-)

Madea's Family Reunion '06
Diary of a Mad Black Woman '05

William Perry

The Innocents Abroad '84
The Private History of a Campaign That Failed '81
Sparrows '26

Alexander Peskanov

Killing Hour '84
He Knows You're Alone '80

Jean-Claude Petit(1943-)

A Loving Father '02
Lumumba '01
Beaumarchais the Scoundrel '96
The Horseman on the Roof '95
Foreign Student '94
My Life and Times with Antonin Artaud '93
Lady Chatterley '92
The Playboys '92
Uranus '91
Cyrano de Bergerac '90
Jean de Florette '87
Manon of the Spring '87
L'Addition '85

Laurent Petitgand

Beyond the Clouds '95
Faraway, So Close! '93

Mark Petrie

Farmhouse '08
Lake Dead '07

Barrington Pheloung(1954-)

When Did You Last See Your Father? '07
Little Fugitive '06
Shopgirl '05
Hilary and Jackie '98
The One That Got Away '96
Saint-Ex: The Story of the Storyteller '95
Catherine Cookson's The Cinder Path '94
The Mangler '94
Shopping '93
Truly, Madly, Deeply '91

Art Phillips(1955-)

Bullet Down Under '94
Possession '81

Britta Phillips

Just Like the Son '06

The Squid and the Whale '05

John Phillips(1935-2001)

The Myth of Fingerprints '97
River Street '95
The Man Who Fell to Earth '76

Steven R. Phillips

Bait Shop '08
Larry the Cable Guy: Health Inspector '06

Stu Phillips

Battlestar Galactica '78
How to Seduce a Woman '74
Jud '71
Beyond the Valley of the Dolls '70
The Losers '70
The Gay Deceivers '69
Run, Angel, Run! '69
Hell's Angels on Wheels '67
Dead Heat on a Merry-Go-Round '66

Martin Phipps

Wallander: Firewall '08
Wallander: One Step Behind '08
Wallander: Sidetracked '08
Oliver Twist '07
Persuasion '07
Sense & Sensibility '07
The Flying Scotsman '06
The Line of Beauty '06
Ruby in the Smoke '06
The Debt '03

Piero Piccioni(1921-2004)

Three Brothers '80
Swept Away... '75
Seduction of Mimi '72
Light at the Edge of the World '71
Camille 2000 '69
Murder for Sale '68
10th Victim '65
Mafioso '62
Il Bell'Antonio '60

Franco Piersanti(1950-)

My Brother Is an Only Child '07
Don't Tell '05
Without Evidence '96
Lamerica '95
Mille Bolle Blu '93
The Stolen Children '92

Nicholas Pike(1955-)

The Contractor '07
Riding the Bullet '04
Feardotcom '02
Return to Me '00
Delivered '98
Star Kid '97
Telling Lies in America '96
Attack of the 50 Ft. Woman '93
Blank Check '93
Perfect Family '92
Sleepwalkers '92
Mission Manila '87

Antonio Pinto

City of Men '07
Love in the Time of Cholera '07
Perfect Stranger '07
10 Items or Less '06
Lord of War '05
Collateral '04
Cronicas '04
City of God '02
Behind the Sun '01
Central Station '98

Nicola Piovani(1946-)

Avenue Montaigne '06
Pinocchio '02
In Love and War '01
Running Free '00
The Son's Room '00
Life Is Beautiful '98
A Month by the Lake '95
Caro Diario '93
Fiorile '93
Jamon, Jamon '93
Night Sun '90
Palombella Rossa '89
Good Morning, Babylon '87
Intervista '87
Ginger & Fred '86
Kaos '85
The Night of the Shooting Stars '82
Primal Impulse '74

Douglas Pipes

Trick 'r Treat '08
Monster House '06

Gianfranco Plenizio(1931-)

Django Strikes Again '87
And the Ship Sails On '83

Amotz Plessner(1962-)

Road House 2: Last Call '06
Deal of a Lifetime '99

Michael Richard Plowman(1965-)

Ace of Hearts '08
Never Cry Werewolf '08
Alien Agent '07
Something Beneath '07
The Invitation '03
He Sees You When You're Sleeping '02
Trucks '97

Edward Plumb(1907-58)

Peter Pan '53
The Woman Who Came Back '45
Bambi '42

Terry Plumeri

Love Takes Wing '09
The Last Letter '04
Route 666 '01
Diplomatic Siege '99
Storm Trooper '98
Watchers Reborn '98
The Corporation '96
The Wasp Woman '96
Raging Angels '95
Death Wish 5: The Face of Death '94
Teenage Bonnie & Klepto Clyde '93
Lower Level '91
Sometimes They Come Back '91
Body Chemistry '90
Black Eagle '88

The Pogues

Straight to Hell '87
Sid & Nancy '86

Basil Poledouris(1945-2006)

The Legend of Butch & Sundance '04
Crocodile Dundee in Los Angeles '01
Cecil B. Demented '00
If These Walls Could Talk 2 '00
For Love of the Game '99
Les Miserables '97
Starship Troopers '97
Switchback '97
Breakdown '96
Celtic Pride '96
The War at Home '96
Free Willy 2: The Adventure Home '95
It's My Party '95
Under Siege 2: Dark Territory '95
Lassie '94
On Deadly Ground '94
Serial Mom '94
Free Willy '93
Hot Shots! Part Deux '93
Lone Justice '93
Wind '92
Harley Davidson and the Marlboro Man '91
RoboCop 3 '91
White Fang '91
Flight of the Intruder '90
The Hunt for Red October '90
Quigley Down Under '90
Farewell to the King '89
Lonesome Dove '89
Wired '89
Cherry 2000 '88
The Spellbinder '88
Split Decisions '88
No Man's Land '87
RoboCop '87
Iron Eagle '86
Flesh and Blood '85
The Amazons '84
Conan the Destroyer '84
Making the Grade '84
Protocol '84
Red Dawn '84
Single Bars, Single Women '84
Conan the Barbarian '82
Summer Lovers '82
Whale for the Killing '81
The Blue Lagoon '80
Defiance '79
Big Wednesday '78

Zoe Poledouris(1973-)

Teenage Caveman '01
Cecil B. Demented '00

Jocelyn Pook(1960-)

The Merchant of Venice '04
How I Killed My Father '03
The In-Laws '03
Time Out '01
Butterfly Collectors '99
Eyes Wide Shut '99

Iggy Pop(1947-)

Repo Man '83
Rock & Rule '83

Conrad Pope

The Rising Place '02
Pavilion of Women '01
Lloyd '00
The Set Up '95
Project Metalbeast: DNA Overload '94

Steve Porcaro(1957-)

Carolina Moon '07
Cougar Club '07
Montana Sky '07
The Wizard of Gore '07
Killing Emmett Young '02
A Season on the Brink '02
Head Over Heels '01
My First Mister '01
Metro '96

Michel Portal(1935-)

You'll Get Over It '02
The Machine '96
Dr. Petiot '90
Max, Mon Amour '86
The Return of Martin Guerre '83

Cole Porter(1891-1964)

Evil under the Sun '82
High Society '56
Panama Hattie '42
Rosalie '38
Born to Dance '36

Lew Porter(1892-1956)

Flying Wild '41
Texas Trouble '41
Billy the Kid in Texas '40
Lightning Strikes West '40
Range Busters '40
Up in the Air '40
Phantom Rancher '39
Six Gun Rhythm '39
The Rangers' Roundup '38
Range Riders '35

Rachel Portman(1960-)

Grey Gardens '09
The Duchess '08
The Sisterhood of the Traveling Pants 2 '08
Infamous '06
The Lake House '06
Because of Winn-Dixie '05
Oliver Twist '05
The Manchurian Candidate '04
The Human Stain '03
Mona Lisa Smile '03
Hart's War '02
Nicholas Nickleby '02
The Truth About Charlie '02
The Emperor's New Clothes '01
American Women '00
Chocolat '00
The Legend of Bagger Vance '00
The Cider House Rules '99
Ratcatcher '99
Beloved '98
Home Fries '98
The Other Sister '98
Addicted to Love '96
The Adventures of Pinocchio '96
Emma '96
Marvin's Room '96
Palookaville '95
A Pyromaniac's Love Story '95
Smoke '95
To Wong Foo, Thanks for Everything, Julie Newmar '95
War of the Buttons '95
Only You '94
The Road to Wellville '94
Sirens '94
Benny & Joon '93
Used People '92
Antonia and Jane '91
Where Angels Fear to Tread '91
Oranges Are Not the Only Fruit '89
High Hopes '88
Young Charlie Chaplin '88
Sharma & Beyond '84

Mike Post

The Poker House '09
The Invasion of Johnson County '76

Randall Poster

The Pink Panther '06
The Bad News Bears '05
Fun With Dick and Jane '05
The Life Aquatic with Steve Zissou '04
Kiss Me, Guido '97

Sally Potter(1947-)

Yes '04
The Tango Lesson '97

Yuri Potyeyenko

Day Watch '06
Night Watch '04

Andrew Powell(1949-)

Rocket Gibraltar '88
Ladyhawke '85

John Powell(1963-)

Green Zone '10
How to Train Your Dragon '10
Jonah Hex '10
Ice Age: Dawn of the Dinosaurs '09
Bolt '08
Dr. Seuss' Horton Hears a Who! '08
Hancock '08
Jumper '08
Kung Fu Panda '08
Stop-Loss '08
The Bourne Ultimatum '07
P.S. I Love You '07
Happy Feet '06
Ice Age: The Meltdown '06
United 93 '06
X-Men: The Last Stand '06
Be Cool '05
Mr. & Mrs. Smith '05
Robots '05
Alfie '04
The Bourne Supremacy '04
Mr. 3000 '04
Stealing Sinatra '04
Agent Cody Banks '03
Gigli '03
The Italian Job '03
Paycheck '03
The Adventures of Pluto Nash '02
The Bourne Identity '02
Drumline '02
Two Weeks Notice '02
Evolution '01
Eye See You '01
I Am Sam '01
Just Visiting '01
Rat Race '01
Shrek '01
Chicken Run '00
The Road to El Dorado '00
Chill Factor '99
Forces of Nature '99
Antz '98
Face/Off '97

Reg Powell

Poison Ivy 3: The New Seduction '97
Forbidden Zone: Alien Abduction '96
ShadowZone: The Undead Express '96
Baja '95
The Pathfinder '94
Pet Shop '94
Test Tube Teens from the Year 2000 '93
The Banker '89

Pray for Rain

Car 54, Where Are You? '94
Floundering '94
Straight to Hell '87
Sid & Nancy '86

Roberto Pregadio

Invincible Barbarian '83
Place in Hell '69

Zbigniew Preisner(1955-)

A Woman in Berlin '08
A Secret '07
The Beautiful Country '04
It's All About Love '03
Between Strangers '02
Aberdeen '00
Dreaming of Joseph Lees '99
The Last September '99
FairyTale: A True Story '97
The Island on Bird Street '97
Feast of July '95
Elisa '94
Mouvements du Desir '94
Trois Couleurs: Blanc '94
Trois Couleurs: Rouge '94
When a Man Loves a Woman '94
The Secret Garden '93
Trois Couleurs: Bleu '93
Damage '92
At Play in the Fields of the Lord '91
The Double Life of Veronique '91
Eminent Domain '91
Europa, Europa '91
The Decalogue '88
I Like Bats '85

Tony Prendatt

Loving Jezebel '99
Colorz of Rage '97

Don Preston(1932-)

Blood Diner '87
Eye of the Tiger '86
Android '82

Andre Previn(1929-)

Rollerball '75
Jesus Christ, Superstar '73
The Music Lovers '71
Paint Your Wagon '69
The Fortune Cookie '66
Inside Daisy Clover '65
Dead Ringer '64
Goodbye Charlie '64
Kiss Me, Stupid! '64
Irma La Douce '63
The Four Horsemen of the Apocalypse '62
Long Day's Journey into Night '62
Two for the Seesaw '62
All in a Night's Work '61
One, Two, Three '61
Bells Are Ringing '60
Elmer Gantry '60
Designing Woman '57
Silk Stockings '57
The Catered Affair '56
Fastest Gun Alive '56
It's Always Fair Weather '55
Kismet '55
Bad Day at Black Rock '54
The Girl Who Had Everything '53
Give a Girl a Break '53
Kiss Me Kate '53
Small Town Girl '53
Cause for Alarm '51
Kim '50
Tension '50
Three Little Words '50
Challenge to Lassie '49
The Sun Comes Up '49

Charles Previn(1888-1973)

Broadway '42
The Ghost of Frankenstein '42
Buck Privates '41
The Wolf Man '41
If I Had My Way '40
Junior G-Men '40
Spring Parade '40
My Man Godfrey '36

Alan Price(1941-)

Britannia Hospital '82
O Lucky Man! '73

Henry Price

See Andre Brummer

Jonathan Price

Rustin '01
Bloodstream '00
Vampire Night '00
Merchants of Death '99
Vampires of Sorority Row: Kickboxers From Hell '99
Decay '98

Michael Price

Wild Child '08
Lethal Dose '03

Prince(1958-)

Girl 6 '96
Batman '89
J.D.'s Revenge '76

Sergei Prokofiev(1891-1953)

Ivan the Terrible, Part 2 '46
Ivan the Terrible, Part 1 '44
Alexander Nevsky '38

Craig Pruess

The Mistress of Spices '05
Bend It Like Beckham '02
What's Cooking? '00
Bhaji on the Beach '94

Sacha Puttnam

Octane '07
The Confessional '95

Xiao-Song Qu

Pushing Hands '92
Life on a String '90
The Horse Thief '87

Donald Quan

Cybercity '99
Falling Fire '97
Future Fear '97
Carver's Gate '96

Eduardo Quiroz

The Damned '06
San Franpsycho '06

Peer Raben(1940-)

Eros '04
2046 '04
Querelle '83
Veronika Voss '82
Berlin Alexanderplatz '80
The Marriage of Maria Braun '79
Despair '78
In a Year of 13 Moons '78
The Stationmaster's Wife '77
I Only Want You to Love Me '76
Satan's Brew '76
Fear of Fear '75
Tenderness of the Wolves '73

The American Soldier '70
Beware of a Holy Whore '70
Whity '70
Love Is Colder Than Death '69

Trevor Rabin(1954-)
The Sorcerer's Apprentice '10
G-Force '09
Race to Witch Mountain '09
12 Rounds '09
Get Smart '08
Hot Rod '07
National Treasure: Book of Secrets '07
Flyboys '06
Glory Road '06
Gridiron Gang '06
The Guardian '06
Snakes on a Plane '06
Coach Carter '05
Dominion: Prequel to the Exorcist '05
The Great Raid '05
Exorcist: The Beginning '04
National Treasure '04
Torque '04
Bad Company '02
The Banger Sisters '02
American Outlaws '01
The One '01
Rock Star '01
Texas Rangers '01
Gone in 60 Seconds '00
Remember the Titans '00
The 6th Day '00
Whispers: An Elephant's Tale '00
Deep Blue Sea '99
Armageddon '98
Enemy of the State '98
Jack Frost '98
Con Air '97
Homegrown '97
The Glimmer Man '96

Paul Rabjohns
Cash Crop '01
The Last Minute '01
Children of the Corn 5: Fields of Terror '98
The Colony '98

Didier Rachou
Powder Blue '09
Her Best Move '07
How to Rob a Bank '07
Moving McAllister '07

Karyn Rachtman(1964-)
Pulp Fiction '94
Reservoir Dogs '92

Stephen Rae
The Road from Coorain '02
The Well '97
Dead Heart '96
Blackwater Trail '95

Peter Rafelson
Deal '08
Heart of the Beholder '05

Robert O. Ragland(1931-)
Top of the World '97
Alien Chaser '96
Plato's Run '96
Warhead '96
The Fear '94
The Raffle '94
Messenger of Death '88
Rooster: Spurs of Death! '83
Brainwaves '82
Q (The Winged Serpent) '82
Only Once in a Lifetime '79
Project: Kill! '77
Grizzly '76
The Thing with Two Heads '72

A.R. Rahman(1966-)
Couples Retreat '09
Slumdog Millionaire '08
Water '05
Warriors of Heaven and Earth '03
Lagaan: Once upon a Time in India '01
Earth '98
Fire '96

Ralph Rainger(1901-42)
The Big Broadcast of 1938 '38
Waikiki Wedding '37
Ruggles of Red Gap '35
Here is My Heart '34
Kiss and Make Up '34
Little Miss Marker '34
Six of a Kind '34
She Done Him Wrong '33

David Raksin(1912-2004)
Night Tide '63
Separate Tables '58
Big Combo '55
Suddenly '54
The Bad and the Beautiful '52
Pat and Mike '52
Forever Amber '47
The Secret Life of Walter Mitty '47
Laura '44
Just Off Broadway '42
The Man Who Wouldn't Die '42
The Undying Monster '42
San Quentin '37

J. Ralph
The Cove '09
Lucky Number Slevin '06

Ron Ramin
Charlie & Me '08
Meltdown '06
Fatal Error '99
Rent-A-Kid '95
Christy '94

Kennard Ramsey
Freeway 2: Confessions of a Trickbaby '99
Ringmaster '98

David Raskin(1912-2004)
It's a Big Country '51
Whirlpool '49
Daisy Kenyon '47
Dr. Renault's Secret '42

Eldon Rathburn(1916-)
Canada's Sweetheart: The Saga of Hal C. Banks '85
Who Has Seen the Wind? '77
Railrodder '65

Manish Raval
Smother '08
Special '06

Roy J. Ravio
Fire on the Amazon '93
Terrorgram '90

Satyajit Ray(1921-92)
Distant Thunder '73
The Adversary '71
Days and Nights in the Forest '70
Shakespeare Wallah '65
Charulata '64
The Big City '63
Two Daughters '61
Jalsaghar '58

Chris Rea(1951-)
Parting Shots '98
Parting Shots '98

J.A.C. Redford(1953-)
Grace & Glorie '98
What the Deaf Man Heard '98
D3: The Mighty Ducks '96
A Kid in King Arthur's Court '95
Bye Bye, Love '94
D2: The Mighty Ducks '94
Heavyweights '94
Extremities '86

Les Reed(1929-)
Parting Shots '98
Creepshow 2 '87
One More Time '70
The Girl on a Motorcycle '68

Alan Reeves
To Walk with Lions '99
For Hire '98
Bleeders '97
Jack London's The Call of the Wild '97
Natural Enemy '96
A Young Connecticut Yankee in King Arthur's Court '95
Young Ivanhoe '95
Dr. Bethune '90

Vernon Reid(1958-)
Five Fingers '06
Paid in Full '02

Niki Reiser(1958-)
My Fuhrer '07
Go for Zucker '05
Nowhere in Africa '02
The Trio '97
Beyond Silence '96

Brian Reitzell(1966-)
Shrink '09
30 Days of Night '07
Stranger Than Fiction '06
Friday Night Lights '04

Joe Renzetti(1941-)
Blondes Have More Guns '95
Basket Case 3: The Progeny '92
South Beach '92
Basket Case 2 '90
Frankenhooker '90
Child's Play '88
Wanted Dead or Alive '86
Diary of a Teenage Hitchhiker '82
Dead and Buried '81
Tut & Tuttle '81
Exterminator '80
The Buddy Holly Story '78

Sam Retzer
American Son '08
Stomp the Yard '07

Graeme Revell(1955-)
Pineapple Express '08
The Ruins '08
Street Kings '08
Awake '07
Darfur Now '07
Marigold '07
Planet Terror '07
Bordertown '06
Goal! The Dream Begins '06
Goal! The Dream Begins '06
Man of the Year '06
The Adventures of Sharkboy and Lavagirl in 3-D '05
Aeon Flux '05
Assault on Precinct 13 '05
The Fog '05
Harsh Times '05
Sin City '05
The Chronicles of Riddick '04
Walking Tall '04
Daredevil '03
Freddy vs. Jason '03
Open Water '03
Out of Time '03
Below '02
Collateral Damage '02
High Crimes '02
Human Nature '02
Anne Frank: The Whole Story '01
Blow '01
Double Take '01
Lara Croft: Tomb Raider '01
Dune '00
Pitch Black '00
Titan A.E. '00
Bats '99
Buddy Boy '99
Gossip '99
Idle Hands '99
The Insider '99
Three to Tango '99
All I Wanna Do '98
The Big Hit '98
Bride of Chucky '98
Dennis the Menace Strikes Again '98
Lulu on the Bridge '98
The Negotiator '98
Phoenix '98
The Siege '98
Chinese Box '97
The Saint '97
Spawn '97
Suicide Kings '97
The Craft '96
The Crow 2: City of Angels '96
Fled '96
Race the Sun '96
The Basketball Diaries '95
From Dusk Till Dawn '95
Killer: A Journal of Murder '95
Mighty Morphin Power Rangers: The Movie '95
Strange Days '95
The Tie That Binds '95
Down Came a Blackbird '94
No Escape '94
Street Fighter '94
Tank Girl '94
Boxing Helena '93
The Crow '93
The Crush '93
Ghost in the Machine '93
Hard Target '93
Hear No Evil '93
Body of Evidence '92
The Hand that Rocks the Cradle '92
Love Crimes '92
Traces of Red '92
Till There Was You '91
Until the End of the World '91
Child's Play 2 '90
Psycho 4: The Beginning '90
Dead Calm '89
Spontaneous Combustion '89

Victor Reyes
Buried '10
Lisboa '99

David Reynolds
Heavens Fall '06
In Her Line of Fire '06
Cruel Intentions 3 '04
How to Make a Monster '01
She Creature '01

Tim Rice(1944-)
Jesus Christ Superstar '00
Joseph and the Amazing Technicolor Dreamcoat '00
The Road to El Dorado '00
Evita '96
The Lion King '94
Aladdin '92

Freddie Rich(1898-1956)
A Walk in the Sun '46
Stage Door Canteen '43

Joel J. Richard
The Andromeda Strain '08
Pope Dreams '06
Between '05

Griffin Richardson
Diminished Capacity '08
Winning Girls Through Psychic Mind Control '02

Craig Richey
The September Issue '09
Wonderful World '09
Gardens of the Night '08
The King of Kong: A Fistful of Quarters '07
Friends with Money '06
The Gymnast '06
Lovely & Amazing '02

William Richter
Net Games '03
Social Misfits '00

Hualampong Riddim
The Judgement '04
Last Life in the Universe '03

Nelson Riddle(1921-85)
America at the Movies '76
That's Entertainment, Part 2 '76
The Great Gatsby '74
Hell's Bloody Devils '70
Batman '66
Marriage on the Rocks '65
Paris When It Sizzles '64
Robin and the 7 Hoods '64
Four for Texas '63
Lolita '62
Ocean's 11 '60

Chris Ridenhour
The Land That Time Forgot '09
Mega Shark Vs. Giant Octopus '09
Supernova '09

Stan Ridgway(1954-)
Spent '00
Race '99
Speedway Junky '99
Futurekick '91

Ralph Rieckermann
Brotherhood of Blood '08
Loaded '08
Bram Stoker's Way of the Vampire '05
Purple Heart '05
Death Valley: The Revenge of Bloody Bill '04

Hugo Riesenfeld(1879-1939)
Roarin' Lead '37
It Happened in New Orleans '36
Hell's Angels '30
Alibi '29
Evangeline '29

Ned Rifle
See Hal Hartley

Tony Riparetti
Interceptor Force 2 '02
Postmortem '98
Mean Guns '97
Adrenalin: Fear the Rush '96
Fast Money '96
Nemesis 3: Time Lapse '96
Omega Doom '96
Spitfire '94
Brain Smasher... A Love Story '93
Bloodmatch '91

Nicholas Rivera
Guilty by Association '03
Dead Sexy '01
Godmoney '97
Little Witches '96
Saturday Night Special '92
Project A '83

David Robbins(1955-)
War, Inc. '08
King of California '07
Mirror Wars: Reflection One '05
How to Kill Your Neighbor's Dog '01
The Prime Gig '00
The Cradle Will Rock '99
Everything That Rises '98
Savior '98
Dead Man Walking '95
Fast Getaway 2 '94
Twenty Bucks '93
Bob Roberts '92

Richard Robbins(1940-)
The White Countess '05
Le Divorce '03
The Mystic Masseur '01
The Golden Bowl '00
Cotton Mary '99
Place Vendome '98
A Soldier's Daughter Never Cries '98
The Proprietor '96
Surviving Picasso '96
Jefferson in Paris '94
The Remains of the Day '93
Howard's End '92
The Ballad of the Sad Cafe '91
Mr. & Mrs. Bridge '90
Slaves of New York '89
Maurice '87
Sweet Lorraine '87
A Room with a View '86
Heat and Dust '82

Andy Roberts(1946-)
Face '97
Priest '94

Bruce Roberts
Flawless '99
The Crazies '73

Eric N. Robertson(1948-)
Full Disclosure '00
Captains Courageous '95
Black Fox: Good Men and Bad '94
Black Fox: The Price of Peace '94
Broken Lullaby '94
Millennium '89

Robbie Robertson(1943-)
Any Given Sunday '99
Jimmy Hollywood '94
The Color of Money '86
King of Comedy '82
Raging Bull '80

Leo Robin(1900-84)
Gentlemen Prefer Blondes '53
Two Tickets to Broadway '51
The Big Broadcast of 1938 '38
Waikiki Wedding '37
Here is My Heart '34

Earl Robinson
Maybe I'll Come Home in the Spring '71
A Walk in the Sun '46

J. Peter Robinson
The Bank Job '08
S.I.S. '08
Shelter '07
The Hades Factor '06
The World's Fastest Indian '05
15 Minutes '01
Detroit Rock City '99
Don't Look Down '98
Mr. Nice Guy '98
Firestorm '97
Jackie Chan's First Strike '96
Rumble in the Bronx '96
Vampire in Brooklyn '95
Wes Craven Presents Mind Ripper '95
Highlander: The Final Dimension '94
Wes Craven's New Nightmare '94
The Day My Parents Ran Away '93
Undesirable '92
Wayne's World '92
Blind Fury '90
Cadillac Man '90
Cocktail '88
The Believers '87

Peter Manning Robinson
The '70s '00
Where the Truth Lies '99
The Con '98
Family of Cops 2: Breach of Faith '97
Flypaper '97
The Stepsister '97
Sometimes They Come Back... Again '96
The Spree '96
Family of Strangers '93

Guido Robuschi(1926-)
Caesar the Conqueror '63
Fire Monsters Against the Son of Hercules '62

Milan Roder
The Lives of a Bengal Lancer '35
The Song of Songs '33

Nile Rodgers(1952-)
Beverly Hills Cop 3 '94
Blue Chips '94

Grind '03
The New Guy '02

Hans J. Salter(1896-1994)

Come September '61
Follow That Dream '61
The Gunfight at Dodge City '59
Abbott and Costello Meet the Mummy '55
The Far Horizons '55
Creature from the Black Lagoon '54
The 5000 Fingers of Dr. T '53
Duel at Silver Creek '52
Abbott and Costello Meet the Invisible Man '51
Tomahawk '51
Borderline '50
Love from a Stranger '47
The Brute Man '46
Dressed to Kill '46
Magnificent Doll '46
Can't Help Singing '45
His Butler's Sister '44
The Invisible Man's Revenge '44
The Mummy's Ghost '44
The Amazing Mrs. Holiday '43
Timber! '42
Hold That Ghost '41
Horror Island '41
It Started with Eve '41
The Wolf Man '41
The Mummy's Hand '40
The Tower of London '39

Bennett Salvay

Peaceful Warrior '06
Jeepers Creepers 2 '03
Jeepers Creepers '01
Love Stinks '99
Rites of Passage '99

Leonard Salzedo(1921-2000)

Sea Wife '57
Race for Life '55
Unholy Four '54

Jeremy Sams(1957-)

Enduring Love '04
The Mother '03
Persuasion '95

David Sanborn(1945-)

Lethal Weapon 4 '98
Lethal Weapon 3 '92
Lethal Weapon 2 '89

Buck Sanders

The Hurt Locker '08
Max Payne '08

Bernardo Sandoval

Daughter of Keltoum '01
Western '96

Anton Sanko

Delirious '06
One Last Thing '05
Saving Face '04
Scotland, PA '02
Dee Snider's Strangeland '98
Eye of the Storm '98
Ripe '97
An Occasional Hell '96
Live Nude Girls '95
Sex and the Other Man '95
Girl in the Cadillac '94
Party Girl '94

Dana Sano

The Man '05
Monster-in-Law '05
Little Odessa '94

Gustavo Santaolalla

Babel '06
Brokeback Mountain '05
North Country '05
The Motorcycle Diaries '04
21 Grams '03
Amores Perros '00

Frank Sanucci(1901-91)

The Pioneers '41
Stunt Pilot '39

Prison Break '38

Chris Saranec

Hourglass '95
Huck and the King of Hearts '93

Philippe Sarde(1945-)

The Girl on the Train '09
The Witnesses '07
On Guard! '03
Strayed '03
Alice et Martin '98
Lucie Aubrac '98
Les Voleurs '96
Nelly et Monsieur Arnaud '95
Ponette '95
The Favorite Son '94
Revenge of the Musketeers '94
Uncovered '94
Ma Saison Preferee '93
L.627 '92
I Don't Kiss '91
The Old Lady Who Walked in the Sea '91
Lord of the Flies '90
Lost Angels '89
Music Box '89
Every Time We Say Goodbye '86
Joshua Then and Now '85
Fort Saganne '84
Lovesick '83
Tales of Ordinary Madness '83
I Married a Dead Man '82
Beau Pere '81
Coup de Torchon '81
Ghost Story '81
Hotel America '81
Loulou '80
Buffet Froid '79
The Devil, Probably '77
Madame Rosa '77
Spoiled Children '77
Barocco '76
The Tenant '76
Vincent, Francois, Paul and the Others '76
The Judge and the Assassin '75
No Problem '75
Lancelot of the Lake '74
The Last Train '74
The Clockmaker '73
La Grande Bouffe '73
Cesar & Rosalie '72

David Sardy

Zombieland '09
21 '08

Kevin Sargent

Ballet Shoes '07
Fakers '04
Crush '02

Masaru Sato(1928-99)

The Silk Road '92
Forest of Little Bear '87
Irezumi '83
The Wolves '82
Toward the Terra '80
Nomugi Pass '79
Goyokin '69
Samurai Banners '69
Son of Godzilla '66
High & Low '62
Sanjuro '62
Yojimbo '61
The Bad Sleep Well '60
The Hidden Fortress '58
The Lower Depths '57
Throne of Blood '57
Godzilla Raids Again '55

Jordi Savall(1941-)

Jeanne la Pucelle '94
Tous les Matins du Monde '92

Carlo Savina(1919-2002)

The Sicilian Connection '85
Perfect Crime '79
Fury '78
Lisa and the Devil '75
Animal Called Man '72
And God Said to Cain '69

A Long Ride From Hell '68
Samson Against the Sheik '62
Beauty on the Beach '61
Girl Under the Sheet '61

Nitin Sawhney(1964-)

The Namesake '06
Pure '02

Paul Sawtell(1906-71)

Faster, Pussycat! Kill! Kill! '65
Island of the Blue Dolphins '64
The Last Man on Earth '64
Jack the Giant Killer '62
Misty '61
Voyage to the Bottom of the Sea '61
The Cosmic Man '59
The Fly '58
The Hunters '58
It! The Terror from Beyond Space '58
Kronos '57
Stopover Tokyo '57
Rage at Dawn '55
Tarzan and the She-Devil '53
Another Man's Poison '52
Kansas City Confidential '52
Tarzan's Savage Fury '52
Gunplay '51
Armored Car Robbery '50
Riders of the Range '50
Storm over Wyoming '50
Tarzan and the Slave Girl '50
The Clay Pigeon '49
Mysterious Desperado '49
Raw Deal '48
Dick Tracy Meets Gruesome '47
Dick Tracy's Dilemma '47
T-Men '47
Mr. Winkle Goes to War '44
Calling Dr. Death '43
Manhunt in the African Jungles '43

Mark Sayfritz

The Shepherd: Border Patrol '08
Second in Command '05

Walter Scharf(1910-2003)

Blind Ambition '79
Walking Tall '73
Ben '72
Journey Back to Oz '71
Willy Wonka & the Chocolate Factory '71
The Cheyenne Social Club '70
Funny Girl '68
The Nutty Professor '63
Pocketful of Miracles '61
The Bellboy '60
King Creole '58
Loving You '57
Rock-A-Bye Baby '57
Three Violent People '57
Buccaneer's Girl '50
Casbah '48
Fighting Seabees '44

Johnny Lee Schell

The Forsaken '01
Outside Ozona '98
Black Day Blue Night '95

Vladimir Scherbachov

Peter the First: Part 2 '38
Peter the First: Part 1 '37

Dominik Scherrer

Dracula '06
Scenes of a Sexual Nature '06

Prof. Peter Schickele(1935-)

Oh! Calcutta! '72
Silent Running '71

Lalo Schifrin(1932-)

Rush Hour 3 '07
The Bridge of San Luis Rey '05

After the Sunset '04
Bringing Down the House '03
Rush Hour 2 '01
Rush Hour '98
Tango '98
Money Talks '97
Scorpion Spring '96
Manhattan Merenque! '95
The Beverly Hillbillies '93
F/X 2: The Deadly Art of Illusion '91
The Dead Pool '88
The Fourth Protocol '87
Black Moon Rising '86
A.D. '85
Mean Season '85
Doctor Detroit '83
The Osterman Weekend '83
The Sting 2 '83
Sudden Impact '83
Tank '83
Amityville 2: The Possession '82
Class of 1984 '82
The Seduction '82
Buddy Buddy '81
Caveman '81
The Big Brawl '80
Brubaker '80
The Competition '80
The Nude Bomb '80
When Time Ran Out '80
The Amityville Horror '79
Boulevard Nights '79
The Concorde: Airport '79 '79
Escape to Athena '79
Love and Bullets '79
The Cat from Outer Space '78
The Manitou '78
Day of the Animals '77
The Eagle Has Landed '77
Rollercoaster '77
Telefon '77
St. Ives '76
Sky Riders '76
Special Delivery '76
Voyage of the Damned '76
The Four Musketeers '75
Charley Varrick '73
Enter the Dragon '73
Hit! '73
Magnum Force '73
Joe Kidd '72
Prime Cut '72
Rage '72
Dirty Harry '71
THX 1138 '71
The Beguiled '70
Kelly's Heroes '70
Hell in the Pacific '69
The Brotherhood '68
Bullitt '68
Coogan's Bluff '68
Cool Hand Luke '67
The President's Analyst '67
Murderers' Row '66
Murderers' Row '66
The Cincinnati Kid '65
Joy House '64

Eban Schletter

Coffee Date '06
Dumb and Dumberer: When Harry Met Lloyd '03

Norbert J. Schneider(1950-)

Brother of Sleep '95
Stalingrad '94

Alfred Schnittke(1934-98)

The Ninth Day '04
The Ascent '76
Commissar '68

Gaili Schoen

Festival at Cannes '02
Deja Vu '98

Peter Scholes

The Tattooist '07
Desperate Remedies '93

Rudolph (Rudy) Schrager(1900-83)

The Last Voyage '60
High Lonesome '50

Great Dan Patch '49
The Green Promise '49
Coroner Creek '48
Fear in the Night '47
Swamp Fire '46

Walter Schumann(1913-58)

The Night of the Hunter '55
Africa Screams '49
Buck Privates Come Home '47

Paul Schutze

The Siege of Firebase Gloria '89
The Tale of Ruby Rose '87

Arthur Schwartz(1900-84)

The Band Wagon '53
Dangerous When Wet '53

David Schwartz

Gonzo: The Life and Work of Dr. Hunter S. Thompson '08
True Confessions of a Hollywood Starlet '08
You Stupid Man '02
Two of Us '00
My Little Assassin '99
Magic in the Water '95

Stephen Schwartz(1948-)

Gepetto '00
The Hunchback of Notre Dame '96
Pocahontas '95
Pippin '81
Godspell '73

Garry Schyman

NightScreams '97
Robin Cook's Terminal '96
Tornado! '96
Revenge of the Nerds 3: The Next Generation '92
Hitz '89

Louis Sclavis

One Day You'll Understand '08
Apres Lui '07
A Song of Innocence '05
Kadosh '99

Gary Stevan Scott

3 Ninjas Knuckle Up '95
Play Nice '92

John Scott(1930-)

The Mill on the Floss '97
Rudyard Kipling's the Second Jungle Book: Mowgli and Baloo '97
The Scarlet Tunic '97
20,000 Leagues Under the Sea '97
Deadly Voyage '96
Detonator 2: Night Watch '95
Walking Thunder '94
Becoming Colette '92
Ruby '92
Lionheart '90
Winter People '89
Shoot to Kill '88
The Whistle Blower '87
Mountbatten: The Last Viceroy '86
Inseminoid '80
North Dallas Forty '79
The People That Time Forgot '77
Billy Two Hats '74
Doctor in Clover '66

Nathan Scott

Lassie: Well of Love '70
The Kid From Cleveland '49

Patrick John Scott

Sinful Intrigue '95
Cop-Out '67

Tom Scott(1948-)

An Unexpected Family '96
A Mother's Prayer '95
Deconstructing Sarah '94
Percy & Thunder '93

Final Notice '89
Soul Man '86
The Sure Thing '85
Stir Crazy '80
Conquest of the Planet of the Apes '72
Firehouse '72

Vincent Scotto(1876-1952)

Pepe Le Moko '37
Cesar '36
The Baker's Wife '33
Fanny '32

Michelle Scullion

Jack Brown, Genius '94
Bad Taste '88

Peter Sculthorpe(1929-)

Burke & Wills '85
Age of Consent '69

Humphrey Searle(1915-82)

The Haunting '63
The Abominable Snowman '57

Eckart Seeber(1963-)

Bram Stoker's Shadowbuilder '98
The Prisoner '90

Maurice Seezer

Get Rich or Die Tryin' '05
In America '02
Disco Pigs '01
The Boxer '97

Brad Segal

Crazylove '05
National Lampoon's Holiday Reunion '03
Isaac Asimov's Nightfall '00

Misha Segal

Santa Baby '06
Encrypt '03
A Girl of the Limberlost '90
The Phantom of the Opera '89
The New Adventures of Pippi Longstocking '88
The Last Dragon '85

Bernardo Segall(1911-93)

Moon of the Wolf '72
Loving '70
The Great St. Louis Bank Robbery '59

Gregorio Garcia Segura

Icebox Murders '82
The 317th Platoon '65

Ilona Sekacz(1948-)

Wondrous Oblivion '06
Solomon and Gaenor '98
Mrs. Dalloway '97
Under the Skin '97
Antonia's Line '95
Northanger Abbey '87

Gyorgy Selmeczi(1952-)

Flowers of Reverie '84
Daniel Takes a Train '83
Time Stands Still '82
Angi Vera '78

Dov Seltzer(1932-)

The Mummy Lives '93
Hanna's War '88
The Uranium Conspiracy '78
Eagles Attack at Dawn '70

Albert Sendrey(1911-2003)

Bloody Wednesday '87
Father's Little Dividend '51
Royal Wedding '51

Jean-Marie Senia(1947-)

Diary of a Seducer '95
Cross My Heart '91
Red Kiss '85
Man in the Silk Hat '83

Stop! or My Mom Will Shoot '92
Father of the Bride '91
Ricochet '91
Soapdish '91
Back to the Future, Part 3 '90
Predator 2 '90
Young Guns 2 '90
The Abyss '89
Back to the Future, Part 2 '89
Downtown '89
She's Out of Control '89
She's Out of Control '89
Tales from the Crypt '89
Mac and Me '88
My Stepmother Is an Alien '88
Who Framed Roger Rabbit '88
Outrageous Fortune '87
Overboard '87
Predator '87
American Anthem '86
The Clan of the Cave Bear '86
Critical Condition '86
Delta Force '86
Flight of the Navigator '86
No Mercy '86
Back to the Future '85
Cat's Eye '85
Fandango '85
Summer Rental '85
Romancing the Stone '84
The Amazing Dobermans '76
Las Vegas Lady '76

Samuel Sim

Emma '09
House of Saddam '08

Zoran Simjanovic(1946-)

Cabaret Balkan '98
Tito and Me '92
When Father Was Away on Business '85

Carly Simon(1945-)

Piglet's Big Movie '03
Postcards from the Edge '90
Working Girl '88
Heartburn '86

Marty Simon

No Alibi '00
Stranger in the House '97
Tales from a Parallel Universe: Eating Pattern '97
Tales from a Parallel Universe: Giga Shadow '97
Tales from a Parallel Universe: I Worship His Shadow '97
Tales from a Parallel Universe: Super Nova '97
The Ultimate Weapon '97
Marked Man '96
The Wrong Woman '95
George's Island '91
Scanners 2: The New Order '91

Tim Simonec

A Rumor of Angels '00
Suicide Kings '97

Claudio Simonetti(1952-)

Mother of Tears '08
Masters of Horror: Jenifer '05
Opera '88
Welcome to Spring Break '88
Demons '86
Cut and Run '85
El Barbaro '84
Conquest '83
Unsane '82

Rob Simonsen

(500) Days of Summer '09
Management '09

Mike Simpson

Stick It '06
Freddy Got Fingered '01
Saving Silverman '01
Road Trip '00

Marlin Skiles(1906-81)

Gunfight at Comanche Creek '64
King of the Wild Stallions '59
Man From God's Country '58
Queen of Outer Space '58
Canyon River '56
An Annapolis Story '55
Flight to Mars '52
Dead Reckoning '47
She Wouldn't Say Yes '45
A Thousand and One Nights '45
Manhunt in the African Jungles '43

Frank Skinner(1897-1968)

Madame X '66
Shenandoah '65
Portrait in Black '60
Battle Hymn '57
Man of a Thousand Faces '57
Tarnished Angels '57
Away All Boats '56
All That Heaven Allows '55
Because of You '52
The World in His Arms '52
Bedtime for Bonzo '51
Double Crossbones '51
Francis Goes to the Races '51
Harvey '50
Francis the Talking Mule '49
Abbott and Costello Meet Frankenstein '48
I'll Be Yours '47
Black Angel '46
Canyon Passage '46
Pillow of Death '45
The Amazing Mrs. Holiday '43
Saboteur '42
Sherlock Holmes and the Secret Weapon '42
Back Street '41
The Flame of New Orleans '41
Never Give a Sucker an Even Break '41
The Wolf Man '41
My Little Chickadee '40
Seven Sinners '40
Destry Rides Again '39
First Love '39
The Tower of London '39

Cezary Skubiszewski

Death Defying Acts '07
After the Deluge '03
Strange Fits of Passion '99
Lilian's Story '95

Rod Slane

Revenge '86
Blood Cult '85

Ivor Slaney(1921-98)

The Strange Case of the End of Civilization As We Know It '93
Death Ship '80
The Terror '79
Alien Prey '78
No Smoking '55
Blackout '54
Heat Wave '54
Scarlet Spear '54
Terror Street '54
Unholy Four '54
Three Stops to Murder '53
The Gambler & the Lady '52
Scotland Yard Inspector '52

Christopher Slaski(1974-)

Piano Tuner of Earthquakes '05
Beyond the Sea '04

Michael Small(1939-2003)

The Golden Spiders: A Nero Wolfe Mystery '00
Poodle Springs '98
Mountains of the Moon '90
1969 '89
Black Widow '87
Jaws: The Revenge '87
Orphans '87
Brighton Beach Memoirs '86
The Postman Always Rings Twice '81
The Lathe of Heaven '80
Comes a Horseman '78
Marathon Man '76
Night Moves '75
The Stepford Wives '75
The Parallax View '74
Love and Pain and the Whole Damn Thing '73
Klute '71

Bruce Smeaton(1938-)

A Cry in the Dark '88
Roxanne '87
Undercover '87
Eleni '85
The Naked Country '85
Plenty '85
Iceman '84
The Winds of Jarrah '83
Barbarosa '82
Grendel, Grendel, Grendel '82
1915 '82
The Chant of Jimmie Blacksmith '78
Circle of Iron '78
The Devil's Playground '76
Picnic at Hanging Rock '75
The Cars That Ate Paris '74

B.C. Smith

The Other End of the Line '08
Beer League '06
Outsourced '06
Ellie Parker '05
Kids in America '05
Standing Still '05
A Thief of Time '04
Coyote Waits '03
Skins '02
Finder's Fee '01
Deadlocked '00
Mercy '00
The Mod Squad '99
Around the Fire '98
Smoke Signals '98

Joseph Smith

Animal Instincts '92
Secret Games '92

Michael W. Smith(1957-)

The Second Chance '06
Joshua '02

Paul J. Smith(1906-85)

The Parent Trap '61
Pollyanna '60
The Great Locomotive Chase '56
20,000 Leagues under the Sea '54
The Strange Mrs. Crane '48
Fun & Fancy Free '47
Snow White and the Seven Dwarfs '37

Stanley A. Smith

The Gospel '05
Catfish in Black Bean Sauce '00

Neil Smolar

Varian's War '01
The Boys of St. Vincent '93

David Snell(1897-1967)

Killer McCoy '47
Grand Central Murder '42
Billy the Kid '41
The Secret of Dr. Kildare '39

Mark Snow(1946-)

The X Files: I Want to Believe '08
Private Fears in Public Places '06
Another Woman's Husband '00
Dirty Pictures '00
Crazy in Alabama '99
Disturbing Behavior '98
The X-Files '98
Down, Out and Dangerous '95
Frame by Frame '95
A Good Day to Die '95
Oldest Confederate Widow Tells All '95
A Stranger in Town '95
Dead Badge '94
Playmaker '94
The Substitute Wife '94
High Stakes '93
Take Down '92
Archie: Return to Riverdale '90
In the Line of Duty: A Cop for the Killing '90
Jake Speed '86
High Risk '81
The Boy in the Plastic Bubble '76

Curt Sobel

A Cool, Dry Place '98
Body Count '97
Treacherous Crossing '92
Alien Nation '88
The Flamingo Kid '84

Johan Soderqvist(1966-)

Let the Right One In '08
Things We Lost in the Fire '07
After the Wedding '06
Brothers '04
Like It Never Was Before '95

Stephen Sondheim(1930-)

Sweeney Todd: The Demon Barber of Fleet Street '07
Gypsy '93
Dick Tracy '90
Postcards from the Edge '90
Sunday in the Park with George '86
Sweeney Todd: The Demon Barber of Fleet Street '84
Reds '81
Stavisky '74
Gypsy '62
West Side Story '61

Sonic Youth

The Heart Is Deceitful Above All Things '04
Demonlover '02

Lodovico Sorret

See Tom Noonan

Matt Sorum(1960-)

Now You Know '02
Fish in a Barrel '01

Ondrej Soukup(1951-)

Dark Blue World '01
Kolya '96

Tim Souster(1943-94)

Traffik '90
Slugs '87

Kent Sparling

Seventh Moon '08
The Princess of Nebraska '07

David Spear(1953-)

Mortuary Academy '91
Ratings Game '84
The Creature Wasn't Nice '81

Eric Spear(1908-66)

Meet Mr. Callaghan '54
The Stranger from Venus '54
The Shadow Man '53

Mischa Spoliansky(1898-1985)

Hitler: The Last Ten Days '73
Happy Go Lovely '51
The Happiest Days of Your Life '50
Mr. Emmanuel '44
Secret Mission '42
King Solomon's Mines '37

John Sponsler(1965-)

The Stray '00
Y2K '99

Robert Sprayberry

Bodily Harm '95
Widow's Kiss '94
Quick '93
Where the Red Fern Grows: Part 2 '92
Video Murders '87

Willy Stahl

Dark Mountain '44
Navy Way '44

Ringo Starr(1940-)

Let It Be '70
Yellow Submarine '68
Magical Mystery Tour '67
Help! '65

Scott Starrett

Between Love & Goodbye '08
Dim Sum Funeral '08

Michael Stearns(1940-)

Temptress '95
Baraka '93

Andrew Stein

Death Sport '78
Hollywood Boulevard '76

Herman Stein(1915-2007)

King Kong vs. Godzilla '63
Shame '61
This Island Earth '55
It Came from Outer Space '53
Law and Order '53

Ronald Stein(1930-88)

The Rain People '69
Spider Baby '64
Dementia 13 '63
The Haunted Palace '63
The Terror '63
Premature Burial '62
Atlas '60
Dinosaurus! '60
The Ghost of Dragstrip Hollow '59
Legend of Tom Dooley '59
Attack of the 50 Foot Woman '58
Invasion of the Saucer Men '57
Reform School Girl '57
Sorority Girl '57
The Undead '57
The Gunslinger '56
It Conquered the World '56
The Phantom from 10,000 Leagues '56
Day the World Ended '55

Fred Steiner

Black Brigade '69
Hercules and the Princess of Troy '65

Max Steiner(1888-1971)

Those Calloways '65
A Distant Trumpet '64
Spencer's Mountain '63
Rome Adventure '62
Parrish '61
The Sins of Rachel Cade '61
Susan Slade '61
Cash McCall '60
Ice Palace '60
The FBI Story '59
The Hanging Tree '59
John Paul Jones '59
A Summer Place '59
Darby's Rangers '58
Marjorie Morningstar '58
Band of Angels '57
China Gate '57
Escapade in Japan '57
All Mine to Give '56
Death of a Scoundrel '56
Helen of Troy '56
Run of the Arrow '56
The Searchers '56
Battle Cry '55
Hell on Frisco Bay '55
The McConnell Story '55
The Caine Mutiny '54
King Richard and the Crusaders '54
By the Light of the Silvery Moon '53
The Desert Song '53
So This Is Love '53
Trouble along the Way '53
The Iron Mistress '52
Miracle of Our Lady of Fatima '52
Springfield Rifle '52
Close to My Heart '51
Distant Drums '51
Jim Thorpe: All American '51
On Moonlight Bay '51
Room for One More '51
Caged '50
The Flame & the Arrow '50
Rocky Mountain '50
Adventures of Don Juan '49
Beyond the Forest '49
Flamingo Road '49
The Fountainhead '49
White Heat '49
Johnny Belinda '48
Key Largo '48
My Girl Tisa '48
Silver River '48
South of St. Louis '48
Treasure of the Sierra Madre '48
Winter Meeting '48
Life with Father '47
Pursued '47
The Beast with Five Fingers '46
The Big Sleep '46
Cloak and Dagger '46
The Man I Love '46
My Reputation '46
Night and Day '46
A Stolen Life '46
Tomorrow Is Forever '46
The Verdict '46
The Corn Is Green '45
Mildred Pierce '45
Rhapsody in Blue '45
Roughly Speaking '45
San Antonio '45
Saratoga Trunk '45
The Adventures of Mark Twain '44
Arsenic and Old Lace '44
Passage to Marseilles '44
Since You Went Away '44
Mission to Moscow '43
This Is the Army '43
Watch on the Rhine '43
Captains of the Clouds '42
Casablanca '42
Desperate Journey '42
In This Our Life '42
Now, Voyager '42
The Bride Came C.O.D. '41
Dive Bomber '41
The Great Lie '41
Sergeant York '41
They Died with Their Boots On '41
All This and Heaven Too '40
City for Conquest '40
Dr. Ehrlich's Magic Bullet '40
The Letter '40
Santa Fe Trail '40
Virginia City '40
Confessions of a Nazi Spy '39
Dark Victory '39
Dodge City '39
Each Dawn I Die '39
Gone with the Wind '39
Intermezzo '39
Oklahoma Kid '39
The Old Maid '39
They Made Me a Criminal '39
The Adventures of Tom Sawyer '38
Amazing Dr. Clitterhouse '38
Angels with Dirty Faces '38
Crime School '38
Dawn Patrol '38
Four Daughters '38
Jezebel '38
The Sisters '38
Kid Galahad '37
The Life of Emile Zola '37

The Vertical Ray of the Sun '00
Cyclo '95
The Scent of Green Papaya '93

Timbaland(1971-)
30 Years to Life '01
Romeo Must Die '00

Michael Timmins
Niagara, Niagara '97
The Boys Club '96

Nikolai Timofeyev
The Inspector General '52
Baltic Deputy '37

Dimitri Tiomkin(1899-1979)
The War Wagon '67
36 Hours '64
The Guns of Navarone '61
Town without Pity '61
The Alamo '60
The Sundowners '60
Rio Bravo '59
The Young Land '59
The Old Man and the Sea '58
Gunfight at the O.K. Corral '57
Night Passage '57
Friendly Persuasion '56
Dial "M" for Murder '54
The High and the Mighty '54
I Confess '53
Angel Face '52
Bugles in the Afternoon '52
High Noon '52
Strangers on a Train '51
The Thing '51
Cyrano de Bergerac '50
Champion '49
D.O.A. '49
Home of the Brave '49
The Dude Goes West '48
Portrait of Jennie '48
Red River '48
The Long Night '47
Angel on My Shoulder '46
Duel in the Sun '46
It's a Wonderful Life '46
The Bridge of San Luis Rey '44
Shadow of a Doubt '43
The Corsican Brothers '42
A Gentleman After Dark '42
Twin Beds '42
Flying Blind '41
Meet John Doe '41
Lucky Partners '40
The Westerner '40
Mr. Smith Goes to Washington '39
Only Angels Have Wings '39
Spawn of the North '38
Lost Horizon '37
Mad Love '35

George Aliceson Tipton
Hit Lady '74
Phantom of the Paradise '74

Tony Tisdale
Love and Mary '07
The Night of the White Pants '06

Martin Todsharow(1967-)
Agnes and His Brothers '04
Guys and Balls '04

Tomandandy
The Good Guy '10
The Strangers '08
P2 '07
The Covenant '06
The Hills Have Eyes '06
Right at Your Door '06
Love, Ludlow '05
American Meltdown '04
Freshman Orientation '04
Mean Creek '04
The Mothman Prophecies '02
The Rules of Attraction '02
Waking the Dead '00
Arlington Road '99

Peter Tomashek
Final Approach '04
Destination Vegas '95

Isao Tomita(1932-)
The Hidden Blade '04
The Twilight Samurai '02

Ed Tomney
Persons Unknown '96
Safe '95
Carnosaur 2 '94
Night of the Warrior '91

Pinar Toprak
Breaking Point '09
Wyvern '09
Ba'al: The Storm God '08
Sinner '07
Behind Enemy Lines 2: Axis of Evil '06

Cieri Torjussen
Soul's Midnight '06
Dracula 3: Legacy '05

David Torn(1953-)
Saint John of Las Vegas '09
The Line '08
The Wackness '08
Lars and the Real Girl '07
Believe in Me '06
Friday Night Lights '04
The Order '03

Colin Towns
Half Broken Things '07
Ghostboat '06
Crimson Rivers 2: Angels of the Apocalypse '05
Goodbye, Mr. Chips '02
Catherine Cookson's The Secret '00
Catherine Cookson's Tilly Trotter '99
Essex Boys '99
Maybe Baby '99
The Waiting Time '99
Retribution '98
Catherine Cookson's The Wingless Bird '97
Ivanhoe '97
The Sculptress '97
Space Truckers '97
Catherine Cookson's The Girl '96
Catherine Cookson's The Moth '96
Catherine Cookson's The Rag Nymph '96
Catherine Cookson's The Tide of Life '96
The Crow Road '96
The Buccaneers '95
Captives '94
Catherine Cookson's The Dwelling Place '94
The Puppet Masters '94
The Blackheath Poisonings '92
Clarissa '91
Catherine Cookson's The Fifteen Streets '90
Fellow Traveler '89
Getting It Right '89
Bellman and True '88
Vampire's Kiss '88
Born of Fire '87
Knights & Emeralds '87
Rawhead Rex '87
Shadey '87
Slayground '84
Full Circle '77

Ed Townsend(1929-)
Fist '76
Homeboy '75

Pete Townshend(1945-)
The Kids Are Alright '79
Quadrophenia '79
Tommy '75

Shaun Tozer
Hardwired '09
Hard Core Logo '96

Stephen Trask
Cirque du Freak: The Vampire's Assistant '09
Sex Drive '08
Feast of Love '07
The Savages '07
American Dreamz '06
In the Land of Women '06
A Hole in One '04
How to Lose Your Lover '04
In Good Company '04
Camp '03
MTV's Wuthering Heights '03
The Station Agent '03
Hedwig and the Angry Inch '00

Michael Tremante
Sex Positive '09
The Village Barbershop '08
Blue Blood '07
Zombie Honeymoon '04

Fiachra Trench(1941-)
The Boys and Girl From County Clare '03
A Love Divided '01
Moondance '95

Gregory Tripi
Hydra '09
Termination Point '07

Ernest Troost
Front of the Class '08
Crashing '07
Fallen Angel '03
The Home Front '02
The Seventh Stream '01
Beat '00
The Runaway '00
A Lesson Before Dying '99
One Man's Hero '98
Saint Maybe '98
Calm at Sunset '96
The Canterville Ghost '96
Tremors '89
Dead Heat '88

Armando Trovajoli(1917-)
The Family '87
A Special Day '77
Down & Dirty '76
The Scent of a Woman '75
Hired to Kill '73
Hit Men '73
The Valachi Papers '72
The Libertine '69
Assassination in Rome '65
Boccaccio '70 '62
Mole Men Against the Son of Hercules '61
Two Women '61
The Unfaithfuls '60

Tim Truman
Angel's Dance '99
Boogie Boy '98
Retroactive '97
Good Luck '96
Marshal Law '96
Sketch Artist 2: Hands That See '94
Mikey '92
South Central '92
The Reluctant Agent '89

Marc Tschantz
The West Wittering Affair '05
Fun '94

Toshiaki Tsushima
Shogun's Samurai—The Yagyu Clan Conspiracy '78
The Street Fighter '74
The Green Slime '68
Legends of the Poisonous Seductress 1: Female Demon Ohyaku '68

Jonathan Tunick(1938-)
The Birdcage '95
I Am the Cheese '83
Fort Apache, the Bronx '81

Tom Tykwer(1965-)
The International '09
Paris, je t'aime '06
Perfume: The Story of a Murderer '06
The Princess and the Warrior '00
Run Lola Run '98
Winter Sleepers '97

Brian Tyler
The Expendables '10
Dragonball: Evolution '09
Fast & Furious '09
The Final Destination '09
The Killing Room '09
Law Abiding Citizen '09
Bangkok Dangerous '08
Eagle Eye '08
The Lazarus Project '08
Rambo '08
Aliens vs. Predator: Requiem '07
Partition '07
War '07
Annapolis '06
Bug '06
The Fast and the Furious: Tokyo Drift '06
Constantine '05
The Greatest Game Ever Played '05
The Big Empty '04
The Final Cut '04
Godsend '04
Paparazzi '04
Bubba Ho-Tep '03
Children of Dune '03
Darkness Falls '03
The Hunted '03
Timeline '03
Frailty '02
John Carpenter Presents Vampires: Los Muertos '02
Last Call: The Final Chapter of F. Scott Fitzgerald '02
Nobody's Baby '01
Four Dogs Playing Poker '00
Panic '00
Terror Tract '00
The 4th Floor '99
The Settlement '99
Simon Sez '99
Sirens '99
Final Justice '98
Six-String Samurai '98

Christopher Tyng
Finding Amanda '08
Bookies '03
The Diamond of Jeru '01
Seven Girlfriends '00
The Bumblebee Flies Anyway '98
The Associate '96
Cadillac Ranch '96
Kazaam '96
Crosscut '95
The Little Death '95
Across the Moon '94
National Lampoon's Attack of the 5 Ft. 2 Women '94
Unveiled '94

Steve Tyrell
These Old Broads '01
20 Dates '99
Once Upon a Time ... When We Were Colored '95
Out of Sync '95
T Bone N Weasel '92
Getting It Right '89

Nerida Tyson-Chew
Anacondas: The Hunt for the Blood Orchid '04
Visitors '03
Mr. Accident '99
Under the Lighthouse Dancing '97
Brilliant Lies '96
Twisted '96
Sorrento Beach '95

Deddy Tzur
Heaven's Fire '99
Termination Man '97

Giovanni Ullu
Emmanuelle, the Queen '79
Emmanuelle's Daughter '79

Shingeru Umebayashi(1951-)
Incendiary '08
Curse of the Golden Flower '06
House of Flying Daggers '04
2046 '04
Zhou Yu's Train '02
In the Mood for Love '00

Pierro Umiliani(1926-2001)
Lady of the Evening '75
Five Dolls for an August Moon '70
Big Deal on Madonna Street '58

Nick Urata
I Love You Phillip Morris '10
The Joneses '10
Fling '08

Teo Usuelli(1930-)
Amuck! '71
Dillinger Is Dead '69
Saul and David '64

Steve Vai(1960-)
P.C.U. '94
Crossroads '86

Jean-Louis Valero
The Romance of Astrea and Celadon '07
Boyfriends & Girlfriends '88
Summer '86
The Aviator's Wife '80

Paleis Van Boem
Nothing to Lose '08
Character '97

Nathan Van Cleave(1910-70)
Robinson Crusoe on Mars '64
Rhubarb '51

Pierre Van Dormael(1952-)
The Eighth Day '95
Toto le Heros '91

James Van Heusen(1913-90)
Journey Back to Oz '71
Robin and the 7 Hoods '64
Welcome Stranger '47
The Road to Utopia '46
The Bells of St. Mary's '45

Roger van Otterloo
Soldier of Orange '78
Katie Tippel '75

Georges Van Parys(1902-71)
Diabolique '55
Les Grandes Manoeuvres '55
Nana '55
The Earrings of Madame De... '54
Beauties of the Night '52
Casque d'Or '52
Fanfan la Tulipe '51

Melvin Van Peebles(1932-)
Tales of Erotica '93
Sweet Sweetback's Baadasssss Song '71
Watermelon Man '70

David Van Tiegham
Eye of God '97
Working Girls '87

John Van Tongeren
Princess Protection Program '09
WarGames 2: The Dead Code '08
Twitches Too '07
The Initiation of Sarah '06
Twitches '05
The Cheetah Girls '03
Malibu's Most Wanted '03

Kenny Vance(1943-)
The Heart of Dixie '89
Hairspray '88

Vangelis(1943-)
Alexander '04
Francesco '93
Bitter Moon '92
1492: Conquest of Paradise '92
Third Solution '89
Antarctica '84
The Bounty '84
Blade Runner '82
Missing '82
Chariots of Fire '81

Ross Vannelli
Children On Their Birthdays '02
The Void '01
Wounded '97
The Final Cut '96
Snowboard Academy '96

C.J. Vanston
For Your Consideration '06
A Mighty Wind '03
Best in Show '00
Almost Heroes '97

Varouje
Expect No Mercy '95
Jungleground '95
Fearless Tiger '94

Didier Vasseur
A Business Affair '93
Face the Music '92

Ben Vaughn
The Independent '00
Psycho Beach Party '00
Lewis and Clark and George '97
Black Mask '96

Fernando Velazquez
The Orphanage '07
Savage Grace '07

Rene Veldsman
Queen's Messenger II '01
Woman of Desire '93

Caetano Veloso(1942-)
Orfeu '99
Tieta of Agreste '96
O Quatrilho '95

James L. Venable
I Hope They Serve Beer in Hell '09
An American Carol '08
Superhero Movie '08
Zack and Miri Make a Porno '08
The Last Days of Summer '07
Clerks 2 '06
Scary Movie 4 '06
Deuce Bigalow: European Gigolo '05
Venom '05
Eurotrip '04
Jersey Girl '04
Scary Movie 3 '03
Jay and Silent Bob Strike Back '01
Iron Monkey '93

Giovanni Venosta(1961-)
Days and Clouds '07
Agata and the Storm '04
Bread and Tulips '01

Michael Vickers(1941-)
At the Earth's Core '76
Dracula A.D. 1972 '72

Joseph Vitarelli
John Adams '08
Kit Kittredge: An American Girl '08
And Starring Pancho Villa as Himself '03
My Architect: A Son's Journey '03
Nobody's Baby '01
Excellent Cadavers '99
Kissing a Fool '98
The Pentagon Wars '98
She's So Lovely '97
Commandments '96
Evil Has a Face '96
The Substance of Fire '96
The Invaders '95
Tall, Dark and Deadly '95

The Last Seduction '94
Big Man on Campus '89
How I Got into College '89

Alessio Vlad(1955-)
Callas Forever '02
Tea with Mussolini '99
Besieged '98
Jane Eyre '96

Roman Vlad(1919-)
The Ghost '63
The Horrible Dr. Hichcock '62
And the Wild, Wild Women '59
Where the Hot Wind Blows '59
I, Vampirj '56
Beauty and the Devil '50
The Walls of Malapaga '49

Henny Vrienten(1948-)
Left Luggage '98
The Vanishing '88

Popul Vuh
Cobra Verde '88
Fitzcarraldo '82
Nosferatu the Vampyre '79
Heart of Glass '74
Aguirre, the Wrath of God '72

Gyorgy Vukan
Hanussen '88
The Fifth Seal '76

Waddy Wachtel
Paul Blart: Mall Cop '09
The House Bunny '08
Strange Wilderness '08
The Benchwarmers '06
Grandma's Boy '06
The Last Request '06
Dickie Roberts: Former Child Star '03
Joe Dirt '01

Reinhardt Wagner
Mortal Transfer '01
Marquis '90

Tommy Wai
Seoul Raiders '05
New Police Story '04
Drunken Monkey '02
Special Unit 2002 '01
Time and Tide '00

Tom Waits(1949-)
Big Bad Love '02
Night on Earth '91
Down by Law '86
Streetwise '84
One from the Heart '82
On the Nickel '80

Adolfo Waitzman
Flying from the Hawk '86
Blue Jeans and Dynamite '76

Rick Wakeman(1949-)
Bullet to Beijing '95
Creepshow 2 '87
Crimes of Passion '84
The Burning '82
Lisztomania '75

Nathan Waks
Kangaroo '86
My Brilliant Career '79

Adam Walacinski
Pharaoh '66
Mother Joan of the Angels '60

Chris Walden
Alien Siege '05
Crimson Force '05

Dana Walden
Killing Obsession '94
Molly and Gina '94
Wyatt Earp: Return to Tombstone '94
My Mom's a Werewolf '89

W.G. Snuffy Walden(1950-)
Homecoming '96
Homage '95
Stephen King's The Stand '94
The Good Fight '92
The Chase '91

Shirley Walker(1945-2006)
Black Christmas '06
Final Destination 3 '06
Final Destination 2 '03
Willard '03
Disappearance '02
Final Destination '00
Asteroid '97
The Crying Child '96
Escape from L.A. '96
Turbulence '96
It Came from Outer Space 2 '95
Batman: Mask of the Phantasm '93

P.T. Walkley
Purple Violets '07
The Groomsmen '06
Looking for Kitty '04

Oliver Wallace(1887-1963)
Big Red '62
Nikki, the Wild Dog of the North '61
Old Yeller '57
Peter Pan '53
The Adventures of Ichabod and Mr. Toad '49
Fun & Fancy Free '47
Dumbo '41

Rob Walsh
The Darwin Conspiracy '99
Revenge of the Ninja '83

Jeff Walton
Paper Bullets '99
Hybrid '97
Invisible Dad '97
Invisible Mom '96
Prey of the Jaguar '96
Attack of the 60-Foot Centerfold '95
Jack-O '95
Fatal Justice '93

William Walton(1902-83)
Battle of Britain '69
Hamlet '48
Henry V '44
The Foreman Went to France '42
Spitfire '42
As You Like It '36

Gast Waltzing(1956-)
George and the Dragon '04
The Enemy '01
New World Disorder '99

Bill Wandel(1969-)
Octopus 2: River of Fear '02
Shark Attack 3: Megalodon '02
After the Storm '01
Crocodile 2: Death Swamp '01

Michael Wandmacher(1967-)
Piranha 3D '10
My Bloody Valentine 3D '09
Never Back Down '08
Punisher: War Zone '08
The Killing Floor '06
Cry_Wolf '05
From Justin to Kelly '03
Max Keeble's Big Move '01
On the Borderline '01
Modern Vampires '98
The Legend of Drunken Master '94
Twin Dragons '92

Eddie Wang
House of Traps '81
The Master '80

Fu-ling Wang
Chinese Connection '73
Fists of Fury '73
Sword Masters: Brothers Five '70
The Wandering Swordsman '70
Have Sword, Will Travel '69
Vengeance is a Golden Blade '69
Golden Swallow '68
The Cave of the Silken Web '67

Nathan Wang
Minutemen '08
Van Wilder: Freshman Year '08
The Final Season '07
Flight of the Living Dead: Outbreak on a Plane '07
The Game Plan '07
She's the Man '06
Come as You Are '05
Jackie Chan's Who Am I '98
Natural Causes '94

Thomas Wanker(1973-)
2012 '09
Dresden '06
RFK '02
The Tunnel '01

Kenneth Wannberg
Vanishing Act '88
Blame It on Rio '84
The Philadelphia Experiment '84
Losin' It '82

Stephen Warbeck(1953-)
Vanilla Gorilla '09
The Other Man '08
Flawless '07
Goal 2: Living the Dream '07
Alpha Male '06
On a Clear Day '05
Proof '05
Two Brothers '04
The Memory of a Killer '03
Birthday Girl '02
Captain Corelli's Mandolin '01
Charlotte Gray '01
Gabriel & Me '01
Billy Elliot '00
Quills '00
Very Annie Mary '00
A Christmas Carol '99
Heart '99
Mystery Men '99
Shakespeare in Love '98
Mrs. Brown '97
My Son the Fanatic '97
Different for Girls '96
Element of Doubt '96
Brothers in Trouble '95
Sister My Sister '94

Christopher Ward
The Natalee Holloway Story '09
John John in the Sky '00

Edward Ward(1900-71)
It Happened on 5th Avenue '47
The Climax '44
Cobra Woman '44
The Phantom of the Opera '43
Cheers for Miss Bishop '41
Dance, Girl, Dance '40
The Son of Monte Cristo '40
The Last Gangster '37
Night Must Fall '37
Wife Versus Secretary '36
The Mystery of Edwin Drood '35

Dean Wareham
Just Like the Son '06
The Squid and the Whale '05

Harry Warren(1893-1981)
Marty '55
The Barkleys of Broadway '49
The Harvey Girls '46
Yolanda and the Thief '45
That Night in Rio '41
Gold Diggers in Paris '38
42nd Street '33

Mervyn Warren(1964-)
A Raisin in the Sun '08
Honey '03
Marci X '03
A Walk to Remember '02
The Wedding Planner '01
Steel '97
The Wharf Rat '95

Julian Wass
The Freebie '10
Noah's Arc: Jumping the Broom '08

Michiaki Watanabe
Along with Ghosts '69
100 Monsters '68
Shinobi no Mono 2: Vengeance '63
Shinobi no Mono '62
The Ghost of Yotsuya '58

David Waters
Body and Soul '98
Rescue Me '93

Mark Watters
Doug's 1st Movie '99
Aladdin and the King of Thieves '96
All Dogs Go to Heaven 2 '95
The Pebble and the Penguin '94

Franz Waxman(1906-67)
Cimarron '60
Sunrise at Campobello '60
Beloved Infidel '59
The Nun's Story '59
Run Silent, Run Deep '58
Peyton Place '57
Sayonara '57
Spirit of St. Louis '57
Mister Roberts '55
Rear Window '54
The Silver Chalice '54
A Lion in the Streets '53
Stalag 17 '53
A Place in the Sun '51
The Furies '50
Night and the City '50
Sunset Boulevard '50
Sorry, Wrong Number '48
Nora Prentiss '47
The Paradine Case '47
The Unsuspected '47
Humoresque '46
God is My Co-Pilot '45
Objective, Burma! '45
Pride of the Marines '45
Air Force '43
Woman of the Year '42
Dr. Jekyll and Mr. Hyde '41
Suspicion '41
Boom Town '40
The Philadelphia Story '40
Rebecca '40
Strange Cargo '40
Honolulu '39
Three Comrades '38
Devil Doll '36
Next Time We Love '36
The Bride of Frankenstein '35
Mauvaise Graine '33

Roger Webb(1934-)
Riders '88
Boy in Blue '86
Au Pair Girls '72

Roy Webb(1888-1982)
Teacher's Pet '58
Top Secret Affair '57
The First Texan '56
Marty '55
Houdini '53
Second Chance '53
At Sword's Point '51
Fixed Bayonets! '51
Flying Leathernecks '51
Hard, Fast and Beautiful '51
Where Danger Lives '50
My Friend Irma '49
Out of the Past '47
Notorious '46
The Spiral Staircase '46
Bedlam '45
Dick Tracy, Detective '45
Fighting Seabees '44
The Master Race '44
Murder, My Sweet '44
The Seventh Cross '44
Zombies on Broadway '44
The Ghost Ship '43
I Walked with a Zombie '43
The Leopard Man '43
Cat People '42
I Married a Witch '42
The Magnificent Ambersons '42
Abe Lincoln in Illinois '40
My Favorite Wife '40
Love Affair '39
A Man to Remember '39
Room Service '38
Inside the Lines '30

Matthias Weber(1961-)
Crossover '06
Alien Siege '05
Crimson Force '05
D.R.E.A.M. Team '99

Paul Francis Webster(1907-84)
The Alamo '60
Calamity Jane '53

Konstantin Wecker(1947-)
The White Rose '83
Sisters, Or the Balance of Happiness '79

Craig (Shudder to Think) Wedren
The Kids Are All Right '10
Role Models '08
Reno 911! Miami '07
The Ten '07
Beautiful Ohio '06
The Baxter '05
P.S. '04
School of Rock '03
Laurel Canyon '02
Roger Dodger '02
Wet Hot American Summer '01
First Love, Last Rites '98
High Art '98

Cynthia Weil(1937-)
Syriana '05
All Dogs Go to Heaven 2 '95

Kurt Weill(1900-50)
The Three Penny Opera '62
One Touch of Venus '48
The Threepenny Opera '31

Larry Wellington
The Wizard of Gore '70
Just for the Hell of It '68
She-Devils on Wheels '68
The Girl, the Body and the Pill '67
Gruesome Twosome '67
2000 Maniacs '64

Richard Wells
Mutant Chronicles '08
Razor Blade Smile '98

John Welsman
In His Father's Shoes '97
Double Play '96
Looking for Miracles '90

Brahm Wenger
Santa Buddies '09
Snow Buddies '08
Space Buddies '08
Air Bud 6: Air Buddies '06
MXP: Most Xtreme Primate '03
MVP (Most Valuable Primate) '00
The Duke '99
Air Bud 2: Golden Receiver '98
Air Bud '97
Hollow Point '95

Guo Wenjing
Riding Alone for Thousands of Miles '05
Blush '95

Rick Wentworth
The Alchemists '99
How to Get Ahead in Advertising '89

Lars Johan Werle(1926-2001)
Hour of the Wolf '68
Persona '66

Walter Werzowa(1960-)
Cherry Falls '00
Sweet Jane '98
Back to Back '96

Jim West
Lady Dragon 2 '93
Lady Dragon '92

Paul Westerberg(1959-)
Open Season '06
Singles '92

Tim Westergren
Defying Gravity '99
The Last Best Sunday '98

Cody Westheimer
National Lampoon Presents Cattle Call '06
Devon's Ghost: Legend of the Bloody Boy '05

Nigel Westlake(1958-)
Miss Potter '06
The Nugget '02
Babe: Pig in the City '98
A Little Bit of Soul '97
Babe '95
Children of the Revolution '95

Robert Whaley
The Jimmy Show '01
Joe the King '99

Harold Wheeler(1943-)
Blood Brothers '97
Love! Valour! Compassion! '96
Straight out of Brooklyn '91

Bill Whelan(1950-)
Dancing at Lughnasa '98
Some Mother's Son '96
Two by Forsyth '86

David Whitaker(1931-)
Lemming '05
With a Friend Like Harry '00
Sword & the Sorcerer '82
Dr. Jekyll and Sister Hyde '71

Daniel White(1912-97)
Don Quixote '92
Revenge in the House of Usher '82
Female Vampire '73
Rites of Frankenstein '72

John Clifford White
Macbeth '06
Talk '94
Romper Stomper '92

Philip White
The Keeper '09
Against the Dark '08

Stacy Widelitz
Prayer of the Rollerboys '91
Phantom of the Mall: Eric's Revenge '89
Return to Horror High '87

Frederik Wiedmann
Beneath '07
The Indian '07
Return to House on Haunted Hill '07

Jean Wiener(1896-1982)
A Gentle Woman '69
Grisbi '53
Rendez-vous de Juillet '49
The Crime of Monsieur Lange '36
The Lower Depths '36

Scott Wilk
Plain Clothes '88
Valley Girl '83

K. Alexander (Alex) Wilkinson
Avalanche '99
Stealth Fighter '99
Inferno '98
Double Edge '97
Pure Danger '96
Street Corner Justice '96
Deadly Past '95
Forbidden Games '95
The Sweeper '95

Marc Wilkinson(1929-)
The Fiendish Plot of Dr. Fu Manchu '80
If... '69

John Willett
Case 39 '10
Brother's Keeper '02

Alan Williams
Soul Assassin '01
Santa and Pete '99
Asylum '97

David Williams(1971-)
Manticore '05
Benedict Arnold: A Question of Honor '03
Supernova '99
Shelter '98
Wishmaster 2: Evil Never Dies '98
Phantoms '97
The Prophecy 2: Ashtown '97
Children of the Corn 4: The Gathering '96
The Killing Jar '96
No Way Back '96
The Prophecy '95
American Yakuza '94

John Williams(1932-)
Indiana Jones and the Kingdom of the Crystal Skull '08
Memoirs of a Geisha '05
Munich '05
Star Wars: Episode 3—Revenge of the Sith '05
War of the Worlds '05
Harry Potter and the Prisoner of Azkaban '04
The Terminal '04
Catch Me If You Can '02
Harry Potter and the Chamber of Secrets '02
Minority Report '02
Star Wars: Episode 2—Attack of the Clones '02
A. I.: Artificial Intelligence '01
Harry Potter and the Sorcerer's Stone '01
The Patriot '00
Angela's Ashes '99
Star Wars: Episode 1—The Phantom Menace '99
Saving Private Ryan '98
Stepmom '98
Amistad '97
The Lost World: Jurassic Park 2 '97
Seven Years in Tibet '97
Rosewood '96
Sleepers '96
Nixon '95
Sabrina '95
Jurassic Park '93
Schindler's List '93
Far and Away '92
Home Alone 2: Lost in New York '92
Hook '91
JFK '91
Home Alone '90
Presumed Innocent '90
Stanley and Iris '90
Always '89
Born on the Fourth of July '89
Indiana Jones and the Last Crusade '89
The Accidental Tourist '88
Empire of the Sun '87
Superman 4: The Quest for Peace '87
The Witches of Eastwick '87
SpaceCamp '86
Indiana Jones and the Temple of Doom '84
The River '84
Jaws 3 '83
Return of the Jedi '83
Superman 3 '83
E.T.: The Extra-Terrestrial '82
Monsignor '82
Yes, Giorgio '82
Heartbeeps '81
Raiders of the Lost Ark '81
The Empire Strikes Back '80
Superman 2 '80
Dracula '79
1941 '79
The Deer Hunter '78
The Fury '78
Jaws 2 '78
Superman: The Movie '78
The Swarm '78
Black Sunday '77
Close Encounters of the Third Kind '77
Star Wars '77
Family Plot '76
Midway '76
Missouri Breaks '76
The Eiger Sanction '75
Jaws '75
Conrack '74
Earthquake '74
The Sugarland Express '74
The Towering Inferno '74
Cinderella Liberty '73
The Long Goodbye '73
Man Who Loved Cat Dancing '73
The Paper Chase '73
Psychopath '73
Tom Sawyer '73
The Cowboys '72
Images '72
Pete 'n' Tillie '72
The Poseidon Adventure '72
Fiddler on the Roof '71
Daddy's Gone A-Hunting '69
Goodbye, Mr. Chips '69
The Reivers '69
Sergeant Ryker '68
A Guide for the Married Man '67
Heidi '67
Valley of the Dolls '67
How to Steal a Million '66
The Rare Breed '66
None But the Brave '65
The Killers '64
Gidget Goes to Rome '63
Diamond Head '62

Joseph Williams(1960-)
Category 7 : The End of the World '05
Category 6 : Day of Destruction '04
Momentum '03
Judgment Day '99
From Dusk Till Dawn 2: Texas Blood Money '98
Never 2 Big '98
Body Count '97
Embrace of the Vampire '95
Poison Ivy 2: Lily '95

Ken Williams
Firefight '03
Crash & Byrnes '99
The Crimson Code '99
In the Company of Men '96

Patrick Williams(1939-)
Power and Beauty '02
Blonde '01
Jesus '00
The Thin Blue Lie '00
A Cooler Climate '99
Change of Heart '98
Kiss the Sky '98
A Knight in Camelot '98
Julian Po '97
My Very Best Friend '96
That Old Feeling '96
A Weekend in the Country '96
The Grass Harp '95
Kingfish: A Story of Huey P. Long '95
Getting Gotti '94
Blind Spot '93
Geronimo '93
The Cutting Edge '92
Jewels '92
Cry-Baby '90
In the Spirit '90
Violets Are Blue '86
All of Me '84
Some Kind of Hero '82
The Toy '82
Used Cars '80
Breaking Away '79
Cuba '79
I Wonder Who's Killing Her Now? '76
Sssssss '73
Evel Knievel '72

Paul Williams(1940-)
The Muppet Christmas Carol '92
The Muppet Movie '79
The End '78
The Boy in the Plastic Bubble '76
Bugsy Malone '76
A Star Is Born '76
Phantom of the Paradise '74

Robert Williamson
Gamer '09
The Midnight Meat Train '08
Pathology '08

Hal Willner(1957-)
Finding Forrester '00
Kansas City '95
Theremin: An Electronic Odyssey '95

Meredith Willson(1902-84)
The Unsinkable Molly Brown '64
The Music Man '62
The Little Foxes '41
The Great Dictator '40

Nancy Wilson(1954-)
Elizabethtown '05
Vanilla Sky '01
Almost Famous '00
Jerry Maguire '96
Say Anything '89

Stanley Wilson(1915-70)
The Beatniks '60
Iron Mountain Trail '53
Border Saddlemates '52
Government Agents vs. Phantom Legion '51
Silver City Bonanza '51
Thunder in God's Country '51
Missourians '50
Night Riders of Montana '50
Pioneer Marshal '49
Radar Patrol vs. Spy King '49

David Wingo
Gentlemen Broncos '09
Great World of Sound '07
All the Real Girls '03

Austin Wintory
Grace '09
Make the Yuletide Gay '09

Ari Wise
School of Life '06
Tokyo Cowboy '94

Debbie Wiseman(1963-)
Vampire Killers '09
Flood '07
Jekyll '07
Middletown '06
Freeze Frame '04
The Truth About Love '04
Othello '01
Dead of Night '99
The Guilty '99
Wilde '97
Female Perversions '96
Haunted '95
Tom & Viv '94

Dave Wittman
Fighting '09
The Tripper '06

Charles Wolcott
Blackboard Jungle '55
It's a Big Country '51

Peter Wolf
The Hollywood Sign '01
The NeverEnding Story 3: Escape from Fantasia '94
Weekend at Bernie's 2 '93

Tom Wolfe
Smother '08
Special '06

Michael Wolff(1954-)
The Tic Code '99
Who's the Man? '93

Cacine Wong
Running on Karma '03
The Executioners '93

James Wong(1940-2004)
Once Upon a Time in China '91
A Bullet in the Head '90

Raymond Wong(1948-)
Running Out of Time 2 '06
Kung Fu Hustle '04
Shaolin Soccer '01

John Wooldridge(1919-58)
Angels One Five '54
The Woman in Question '50

Lyle Workman(1957-)
The Goods: Live Hard, Sell Hard '09
Forgetting Sarah Marshall '08
Yes Man '08
Superbad '07
The 40 Year Old Virgin '05
Made '01

Arthur Wright
Dolemite 2: Human Tornado '76
Dolemite '75

Wai Lap Wu
Once Upon a Time in China III '93
Twin Warriors '93

Alex Wurman(1966-)
Extraordinary Measures '10
The Switch '10
Bernard and Doris '08
$5 a Day '08
Four Christmases '08
The Promotion '08
What Doesn't Kill You '08
National Lampoon's The Stoned Aged '07
The Nines '07
Run, Fatboy, Run '07
Talladega Nights: The Ballad of Ricky Bobby '06
A Lot Like Love '05
Anchorman: The Legend of Ron Burgundy '04
Criminal '04
Hollywood Homicide '03
Normal '03
Confessions of a Dangerous Mind '02
Thirteen Conversations About One Thing '01
Sleep Easy, Hutch Rimes '00
No Vacancy '99
Play It to the Bone '99
Bloodsport 4: The Dark Kumite '98
Footsteps '98
French Exit '97
Eat Your Heart Out '96

David Wurst
Walking Tall: Lone Justice '07
Black Dawn '05
The Foreigner '03
Agent Red '00
Mach 2 '00
Rangers '00
Counter Measures '99
Final Voyage '99
Fugitive Mind '99
Nautilus '99
Restraining Order '99
The White Raven '98
The Haunted Sea '97
Scorpio One '97
Crash Dive '96
The Last Assassins '96
Where Truth Lies '96
The Death Artist '95
Dillinger and Capone '95
Machine Gun Blues '95
The Crazysitter '94
Bloodfist 5: Human Target '93

Eric Wurst
Walking Tall: Lone Justice '07
Black Dawn '05
The Foreigner '03
Agent Red '00
Mach 2 '00
Rangers '00
Counter Measures '99
Final Voyage '99
Fugitive Mind '99
Nautilus '99
Restraining Order '99
The White Raven '98
The Haunted Sea '97
Scorpio One '97
Crash Dive '96
The Last Assassins '96
Where Truth Lies '96
The Death Artist '95
Dillinger and Capone '95
Machine Gun Blues '95
The Crazysitter '94
Bloodfist 5: Human Target '93

Danny Wyman
The Lawnmower Man '92
Hell Night '81

Ivan Wyszogrod
Chronicle of an Escape '06
What Your Eyes Don't See '99

Masao Yagi
Legend of the Dinosaurs and Monster Birds '77
Horrors of Malformed Men '69

Seiichi Yamamoto
Ichi the Killer '01
Adrenaline Drive '99

Gabriel Yared(1949-)
Amelia '09
Coco Chanel & Igor Stravinksy '09
Shanghai '09
Adam Resurrected '08
A Room With a View '08
1408 '07
Breaking and Entering '06
The Lives of Others '06
Shall We Dance? '04
Bon Voyage '03
Cold Mountain '03
Sylvia '03
Possession '02
Autumn in New York '00
The Next Best Thing '00
The Talented Mr. Ripley '99
City of Angels '98
Message in a Bottle '98
The Wings of the Dove '97
The English Patient '96
Black Water '94
The Lover '92
Camille Claudel '89
Romero '89
Clean and Sober '88
Light Years '88
Betty Blue '86
Trade Secrets '86
Moon in the Gutter '83
Every Man for Himself '79

Goro Yasukawa
Flower & Snake 2 '05
Masked Rider—The First '05
Flower & Snake '04
Gonin 2 '96

Peyman Yazdanian
Spring Fever '09
Lost in Beijing '07
Summer Palace '06
Crimson Gold '03

Dwight Yoakam(1956-)
South of Heaven, West of Hell '00
Chasers '94

Christopher Young(1954-)
Creation '09
Drag Me to Hell '09
The Informers '09
Love Happens '09
The Uninvited '09
When in Rome '09
Sleepwalking '08
Untraceable '08
Ghost Rider '07
Lucky You '07
Spider-Man 3 '07
The Grudge 2 '06
Beauty Shop '05
The Exorcism of Emily Rose '05
An Unfinished Life '05
The Core '03
Runaway Jury '03
Shade '03
The Country Bears '02
Bandits '01
The Glass House '01
The Shipping News '01
Sweet November '01
Swordfish '01
The Big Kahuna '00
Bless the Child '00
The Gift '00
Wonder Boys '00
Entrapment '99
The Hurricane '99
In Too Deep '99
Hush '98
Judas Kiss '98
Rounders '98
Urban Legend '98
Hard Rain '97
Murder at 1600 '97
Head Above Water '96
Set It Off '96
Unforgettable '96
Copycat '95
Murder in the First '95
Norma Jean and Marilyn '95
Species '95
Tales from the Hood '95
Virtuosity '95
Judicial Consent '94
Dream Lover '93
Rapid Fire '92
Bright Angel '91
The Dark Half '91
Last Flight Out: A True Story '90
Barbarian Queen 2: The Empress Strikes Back '89
The Fly 2 '89
Bat 21 '88
Hellbound: Hellraiser 2 '88
Flowers in the Attic '87
Hellraiser '87
Invaders from Mars '86
Barbarian Queen '85
The Power '80

Neil Young(1945-)
Neil Young: Heart of Gold '06
Dead Man '95
Where the Buffalo Roam '80

Victor Young(1901-66)
China Gate '57
Around the World in 80 Days '56
The Brave One '56
The Conqueror '56
Run of the Arrow '56
The Tall Men '55
Johnny Guitar '53
Shane '53
The Quiet Man '52
The Star '52
The Lemon Drop Kid '51

The **Video Sources** section provides full contact information, including address, phone, fax and toll-free numbers, as well as web site address and e-mail when available, for mail order and retail resources for videos reviewed in this book. They are listed alphabetically. Some of the videos have no currently known distributor, but copies may still be available. Others are **On Moratorium**, meaning their distributor, or more likely, their producer, has pulled them out of circulation for a certain amount of time. These videos may still be available from local or mail sources because they were distributed at one time. Many video stores provide an ordering service. If your local video store doesn't have a title you want, you can ask them to order it for you, or you can find someone here who will. To find additional web-based and specialty distributors, please check our **Web Site Guide**.

AMAZON.COM
United States
HomePage: www.amazon.com

ANCHOR BAY ENTERTAINMENT
1699 Stutz Dr.
Troy, MI 48084
248-816-0909
800-786-8777
Fax: 248-816-3335
HomePage: www.anchorbayentertainment.com

ANIMEIGO INC.
PO Box 989
Wilmington, NC 28402-0989
910-251-1850
800-242-6463
Fax: 910-763-2376
Email: questions@animeigo.com **HomePage:** www.animeigo.com

ARTISAN ENTERTAINMENT
2700 Colorado Ave., Ste. 200
Santa Monica, CA 90404
310-449-9200
Fax: 310-255-3730
HomePage: www.artisanent.com

THE ASYLUM
1012 North Sycamore Ave.
Los Angeles, CA 90038
323-850-1214
Fax: 323-850-1218
Email: asylumthe@aol.com
HomePage: www.theasylum.cc

BAKER & TAYLOR INC.
2709 Water Ridge Pkwy., Ste. 500
Charlotte, NC 28217
800-775-1800
Email: btinfo@btol.com
HomePage: www.btol.com

BIJOU VIDEO
1349 N. Wells
Chicago, IL 60610
312-943-5397
800-932-7111
Fax: 312-337-1270
HomePage: www.bijouworld.com

BLOCKBUSTER ENTERTAINMENT CORP.
1201 Elm St.
Dallas, TX 75270
214-854-3000
800-733-1939
Fax: 214-866-2250
HomePage: www.blockbuster.com

BMG ENTERTAINMENT
1540 Broadway
New York, NY 10036-4039
212-930-4000
HomePage: www.bmg.com

CENTRAL PARK MEDIA/U.S. MANGA CORPS
331 W. 57th St., Ste. 554
New York, NY 10019
212-977-7456
800-833-7456
Fax: 212-977-8709
Email: info@teamcpm.com
HomePage: www.centralparkmedia.com

CINEMA CLASSICS
167 7th Ave.
New York, NY 10014
212-667-1027
Email: cclassics@cinemaclassics.com
HomePage: cinemaclassics.com

CINEMA EPOCH
10940 Wilshire Blvd., 16th Fl.
Los Angeles, CA 90024
310-443-4244
Email: info@cinemaepoch.com **HomePage:** www.cinemaepoch.com

THE CINEMA GUILD
115 West 30th St., Ste. 800
New York, NY 10001
212-685-6242
800-723-5522
Fax: 212-685-4717
Email: info@cinemaguild.com **HomePage:** www.cinemaguild.com

CINEQUEST
United States
408-995-5033
Fax: 408-995-5713
Email: info@cinequest.org
HomePage: www.cinequestonline.org

CITY LIGHTS HOME ENTERTAINMENT
6 E. 39th St.
New York, NY 10016
212-679-4400
Fax: 212-679-3819
HomePage: www.citylightsmedia.com

COAST TO COAST VIDEO
318 W. 38th St.
New York, NY 10018
718-859-8464
800-221-3420

COLUMBIA HOUSE VIDEO LIBRARY
1400 N. Fruitridge Ave.
Terre Haute, IN 47811-0100
800-457-0866
Email: customerservice@columbiahouse.com
HomePage: www.columbiahouse.com

CRITERION COLLECTION
215 Park Ave. S, 5th Fl.
New York, NY 10003
Email: mulvaney@criterion.com **HomePage:** www.criterionco.com

CRITICS' CHOICE VIDEO & DVD
PO Box 1350
Ottawa, IL 61350-6350
800-993-6357
Email: vcatalog@ccvideo.com **HomePage:** www.ccvideo.com

DISCOUNT VIDEO TAPES, INC./ HOLLYWOOD'S ATTIC
PO Box 7122
Burbank, CA 91510
818-843-3366
800-253-9612
Fax: 818-843-3821
Email: wwwjr@hollywoodsattic.com
HomePage: www.hollywoodsattic.com/blackart.htm

FACETS MULTIMEDIA, INC.
1517 W. Fullerton Ave.
Chicago, IL 60614
773-281-9075
800-331-6197
Fax: 773-929-5437
Email: sales@facets.org
HomePage: www.facets.org

FANGORIA
1372 Broadway, 2nd Floor
New York, NY 10018
HomePage: www.fangoria.com

FILM THREAT VIDEO
5042 Wilshire Blvd., P.M.B. 1500
Los Angeles, CA 90036
818-248-4549
800-795-0969
Fax: 818-248-4533
HomePage: www.filmthreat.com

HEN'S TOOTH VIDEO
2805 E State Blvd.
Fort Wayne, IN 46805
360-527-9888
800-668-4344
HomePage: www.henstoothvideo.com

IFC FILMS
11 Penn Plz., 15th Fl.
New York, NY 10001
917-542-6200
Email: ifcfilmsinfo@ifcfilms.com **HomePage:** www.ifcfilms.com

KIM'S VIDEO
124 First Ave.
New York, NY 10009
212-533-7390
800-617-KIMS
Fax: 212-533-5396
Email: info@kimsvideo.com
HomePage: www.kimsvideo.com

KINO INTERNATIONAL
333 W. 39th St., Ste. 503
New York, NY 10018
212-629-6880
800-562-3330
Fax: 212-714-0871
Email: contact@kino.com
HomePage: www.kino.com

LUMINOUS FILM & VIDEO WURKS
PO Box 289
Hampton Bays, NY 11946
631-731-4864
Email: info@lfvw.com
HomePage: www.lfvw.com

A MILLION AND ONE WORLD-WIDE VIDEOS
1239 Pine Creek Dr.
Woodstock, GA 30188
800-849-7309
Email: worldwidevideos@comcast.net **HomePage:** www.wwvideos.com

MONDO MACABRO
Boum Productions Ltd.
PO Box 6465
Bridgeport, Dorset DT6 6DU, United Kingdom
Email: mmusa4@boumproductions.com
HomePage: www.boumproductions.com

MONTEREY HOME VIDEO
566 St. Charles Dr.
Thousand Oaks, CA 91360-3953
805-494-7199
800-424-2593
Fax: 805-496-6061
Email: customerservice@montereymedia.com
HomePage: www.montereymedia.com

MOVIES UNLIMITED
3015 Darnell Rd.
Philadelphia, PA 19154
215-637-4444
800-668-4344
Fax: 215-637-2350
Email: movies@

moviesunlimited.com
HomePage: www.moviesunlimited.com

NAVARRE CORP.
7400 49th Ave. N.
New Hope, MN 55428
763-535-8333
800-728-4000
Fax: 763-533-2156
Email: info@navarre.com
HomePage: www.navarre.com

NOSTALGIA COLLECTIBLES
58 Grove St.
Gaylordsville, CT 06755
860-350-8970
Email: foviatt@snet.net

NOSTALGIA FAMILY VIDEO/HOLLYWOOD'S ATTIC
PO Box 606
Baker City, OR 97814
800-784-3362
Email: info@nostalgiafamilyvideo.com
HomePage: www.nostalgiafamilyvideo.com

RHINO ENTERTAINMENT
10635 Santa Monica Blvd., 2nd Fl.
Los Angeles, CA 90025-8300
Fax: 818-562-9223
Email: drrhino@rhino.com
HomePage: www.rhino.com

SCARECROW VIDEO
5030 Roosevelt Way NE
Seattle, WA 98105
206-524-8554
800-700-8554
Fax: 206-524-4851
Email: scarecrow@scarecrow.com **HomePage:** www.scarecrow.com

SHOUT! FACTORY
2042-A Armacost Ave.
Los Angeles, CA 90025
310-442-5047
Fax: 310-442-5000
Email: info@shoutfactory.com **HomePage:** www.shoutfactory.com

SIGNALS VIDEO
1000 Westgate Dr.
St. Paul, MN 55114
800-669-5225
Fax: 800-454-3718

SINISTER CINEMA
PO Box 4369
Medford, OR 97501-0168
541-773-6860
Fax: 541-779-8650
Email: scinema@qwest.net
HomePage: www.sinistercinema.com

SOMETHING WEIRD VIDEO
PO Box 33664
Seattle, WA 98133
425-290-5830
888-634-3320
HomePage: www.somethingweird.com

SUN VIDEO
15 Donnybrook
Demarest, NJ 07627
201-784-0662
Fax: 201-784-0665

Email: hs@methodsworkshop.com

SUNDANCE CHANNEL
1633 Broadway
New York, NY 10019
212-708-1500
Email: feedback@sundancechannel.com
HomePage: www.sundancechannel.com

TAPEWORM VIDEO DISTRIBUTORS
25876 The Old Road 141
Stevenson Ranch, CA 91381
661-257-4904
Fax: 661-257-4820
Email: sales@tapeworm.com **HomePage:** www.tapeworm.com

TARTAN VIDEO
8322 Beverly Blvd., Ste. 300
Los Angeles, CA 90048
323-655-9300
Fax: 323-655-9301
Email: info@tartanvideo.com **HomePage:** www.tartanvideousa.com

THOMAS VIDEO
4732 Rochester Rd.
Royal Oak, MI 48073
248-280-2833
Fax: 248-280-4463
Email: vgmr@thomasvideo.com **HomePage:** www.thomasvideo.com

TIMELESS MEDIA GROUP
PO Box 22738
Eugene, OR 97402
800-547-6014
HomePage: www.timelessvideo.com

UNEARTHED
201 Brigadoon Dr.
Clearwater, FL 33759
Email: heneverdies@aol.com **HomePage:** www.unearthedfilms.com

VIDEO COLLECTIBLES
PO Box 385
Lewiston, NY 14092-0385
800-268-3891
Fax: 800-269-8877
Email: info@collectablesdirect.com
HomePage: www.collectablesdirect.com

VIDEO CONNECTION
3123 W. Sylvania Ave.
Toledo, OH 43613
419-472-7727
Fax: 419-472-2655

VIDEO LIBRARY
4040 Locust St.
Philadelphia, PA 19104
800-669-7157
Fax: 215-248-5627
Email: rentals@vlibrary.com
HomePage: www.vlibrary.com

VIDEO VAULT
113 S. Columbus St.
Old Town
Alexandria, VA 22314
800-VAU-LT66
Fax: 703-836-5720
Email: flix@videovault.com
HomePage: www.videovault.com

WARNERARCHIVE.COM
United States
HomePage: www.wbshop/Warner-Archive

Web Site Guide

The Internet is an important resource for movie information, appreciation, and (especially) obsession. For your web surfing enjoyment, we have compiled a comprehensive list of many of the top entertainment websites that will expand your movie knowledge. If you're looking for information on how to make your own film, there are sites for that, too. The guide is divided into seven categories: cult movie resources; film magazines; film studios; filmmaker resources; film reviews; general entertainment; and video outlets. The sites are listed alphabetically within each category, and each site includes name and URL address information. The general information websites briefly describe what you can expect to find. Just as you can spend hours flipping through *Videohound,* you can spend hours cruising the web with the sites listed below since a majority of these homepages can link you to other sites.

CULT MOVIE RESOURCES

Alamo Drafthouse
www.alamodrafthouse.com/
Web site devoted to a chain of Austin, Texas movie theatres that *Entertainment Weekly* calls "the best theatre in America." Check out their unbelievably cool theme screenings and Quentin Tarantino-sponsored film festival

Alien Almanac
http://www.alienalmanac.com/
Caters to fans of fantasy, horror, and scifi movies.

Allsubs
http://www.allsubs.org/
Online database of downloadable subtitles for films in various languages.

Animated News
http://www.animated-news.com/
Animation and CGI news (all animation not just Japanese anime).

Animation Insider
http://www.animationinsider.net/
More Animation and anime news.

The Animation Podcast
http://animationpodcast.com/
Weekly interviews and artists in the Animation Industry.

Anime Daze
http://www.animedaze.com/
Animation news, reviews, and FAQ.

Anime Mojo
http://www.animemojo.com/
More Anime news.

Anime News Network
http://www.animenewsnetwork.com/
Yet more Anime news and a handy encyclopedia of anime related terms.

Anime News Service
http://www.animenewsservice.com/
And still more Anime news.

AsianCineFest
http://asiancinefest.blogspot.com/
News and reviews of asian films and other media.

The Asian DVD Guide
http://asiandvdguide.com/
Rejoice, O ye fans of asian cinema!

Asian Film Reviews
http://www.asianfilmreviews.com/
Reviews of Asian films by David Hough.

Asian Media Wiki
http://asianmediawiki.com/Main_Page
Wikipedia style database of Asian film.

Asian Movie Database
http://www.asiandb.com/
A database of all asian film, not just the genre films so many in the states love.

Asian Movie Pulse
http://www.asianmoviepulse.com/
News of upcoming Asian film releases, along with reviews, a discussion forum, and profiles of major stars and directors.

Asia Shock
http://asiashock.blogspot.com/
Online blog reviewing current asian films, with an emphasis on genre films.

ASIFA Hollywood Animation Archive
http://www.animationarchive.org/
Blog dedicated to archiving animation for the benefit of the public and the industry.

Astounding B Monster Web
www.bmonster.com
Covers all genres of B-movies; includes reviews, top-ten lists, interviews, etc.

Atomic Monsters
http://www.atomicmonsters.com/
Fan site for fifties drive in B movies, with reviews and articles.

B-Independent
http://www.b-independent.com/
Online site for news and reviews of cult and indie films, and interviews with directors and actors.

B-Movie Central
http://www.bmoviecentral.com/
Reviews and articles on classic B Movies. Also has links to many other genre sites.

B-Movie Theater
http://www.b-movie.com/
Home of SRS Cinema and the B Movie Fest, along with news and reviews of B films and a movie store.

Bad Cinema Diary
http://www.cathuria.com/bcd/
Illustrated reviews of bad, low budget, and just plain unexplainable movies.

Bad Movie Planet
http://www.badmovieplanet.com/
Reviews of little known, low budget, and sometimes just plain godawful B films.

Bad Movies
www.badmovies.org
Reviews bad movies in a good way (clever, funny, witty). Includes reviews by visitors to the site. Rating system is from five teardrops ("pinnacle of bad movies") to a skull ("this is gonna hurt, lots.")

Badazz Mofo
http://www.badazzmofo.com/
Weblog of pop culture.

Best Horror Movies
http://www.best-horror-movies.com/
Site made for fans of horror films.

Beyond Hollywood
http://www.beyondhollywood.com/
Reviews of asian, horror, foreign, and genre films. Beware popups.

Black Hole DVD Reviews
http://blackholereviews.blogspot.com/
Reviews of various types of foreign and genre films currently on DVD.

Blaxploitation
http://funkmasterj.tripod.com/blax.html
List of sites ad articles written about the genre.

Bloody-Disgusting.com
www.bloody-disgusting.com
Interviews, reviews, features--anything your sick little mind might want to know about the Horror film genre

Blue Moon Rising
http://bluemoonrising.com/
News and reviews of fantasy films, animation, books, and other media.

Bollywood.com
http://www.bollywood.com/
Bollywood music and movie reviews and information.

Bollywood Hungama
http://www.bollywoodhungama.com/
News on all things Bollywood.

Bollywood World
http://www.bollywoodworld.com/
News, reviews and interviews of Bollywood films and professionals.

Bob Burns
http://bobburns.mycottage.com/
Bob's web site has a lot of neat stuff, but none quite as neat as his amazing links section.

Bottom of the Barrel
http://www.bottomofthebarrel.net/
News and reviews of truly the most godawful B movies of all time.

Brian's Drive-In Movie Theater
http://www.briansdriveintheater.com/index.html
. Has Photos and information on B movie actors/actresses from the 30's to the 80's. Also has a very extensive links section.

Brimstone Pit
http://www.living-dead.com/
Science Fiction and Horror film database.

British Horror Films
http://www.britishhorrorfilms.co.uk/
Site dedicated to British horror movies. There really aren't enough of them you know.

Bruce Campbell Online
www.bruce-campbell.com/
Home page of the Tom Cruise of cult movie actors, Bruce Campbell, the star of director Sam Raimi's *Evil Dead* series. Site features frequently updated Bruce-News, a filmography, and a schedule of public appearances

Buried
http://www.buried.com/
Horror film and fiction news, reviews, and interviews.

Cartoon Brew
http://www.cartoonbrew.com/
Cartoons and animation resource site.

Cinedelica
http://www.cinedelica.com/1970s/

Archive of cult films on DVD.

Cinema Strikes Back
http://www.cinemastrikesback.com/
News, reviews, interviews, and film festival reports. Specializes in genre, cult, and foreign films.

Cinematical
http://www.cinematical.com/
News and reviews of independent and genre films.

City on Fire
http://www.cityonfire.com/
Reviews of Hong Kong and martial arts cinema.

Classic Horror
http://classic-horror.com/
Reviews of classic and modern horror movies. Also has small profiles of famous actors, directors, and effects artists in the genre.

Classic Horror Film Board
http://monsterkidclassichorrorforum.yuku.com/bmonsterkidclassichorrorforum
Bela Lugosi demands you visit the forum. You will look into his spoookity hypnotic eyes....

Classic Scifi
http://www.classicscifi.com/
Contrary to the site's title it also reviews modern scifi movies.

Cold Fusion Reviews
http://www.coldfusionvideo.com/
Reviews of B-movie and genre flicks.

ComicBookMovie.com
http://www.comicbookmovie.com/
Page devoted to comic book films.

Comics2Film
http://www.comics2film.com/
Blog on comics in film and television.

Cult Media Studies
http://cultmediastudies.ning.com/
An online academic community devoted to the study of cult films and media.

Cult Movies Info
www.cultmovies.info/
Offers searchable reviews and summaries of cult movies, categorized into such sub-groups as European Horror Cinema and U.S. Horror Directors

Cult Sirens
http://www.cultsirens.com/
Dedicated to scream queens, and the leading ladies of exploitation films.

Cyberpunk Review
http://www.cyberpunkreview.com/
Reviews of cyberpunk films along with a little conspiracy theory.

Dark Angel's Horror Realm
http://usersites.horrorfind.com/home/horror/realm/
British site for news and reviews of horror films, including a history of the genres battles with censorship.

Dark Hollywood
http://richlabonte.net/darkhollywood/
Classic mysteries, noir, horror, and Hitchcock.

DavidLynch.com
www.davidlynch.com/
Membership site hosted by Emperor Weirdo himself, David Lynch. Contains original films and content as well as a daily weather report from Lynch.

Dead Harvey
http://deadharvey.blogspot.com/
Blog on the independent horror film scene with resources for aspiring filmmakers.

Den of Geek
http://www.denofgeek.com/
News and reviews of films, television, comics, and games from a geek perspective.

Dread Central
http://www.dreadcentral.com/index.php
Horror film, DVD, and book reviews with a forum and several podcasts.

Dreams: The Terry Gilliam Fanzine
www.smart.co.uk/dreams/
Managed by Phil Stubbs, this is the ultimate online resource for anything having to do with ex-Python and notorious film director Terry Gilliam

Eat My Brains
http://www.eatmybrains.com/index.php
Originally a zombie only horror film site, it is slowly including the horror genre as a whole.

E. Favata's Comic Book Movies
http://www.efavata.com/CBM/
News and rumors of current and upcoming comic book films.

Eccentric Cinema
http://www.eccentric-cinema.com/
Lists upcoming cult films on DVD, reviews, and even has a store.

European Film Review
http://www.erratica.co.uk/
If you like European exploitation cinema, you'll like this site.

Extraordinary Movie and Video Guide
http://www.emvg.net/
Reviews and interviews focusing on amateur, genre, independent, and underground films and film makers.

Faces of Death
www.facesofdeath.com/
If you're itching for production information on the Faces of Death video series, then look no further.

Fantastic Movie Musings and Ramblings
http://www.scifilm.org/
Sci-fi, fantasy, and horror movies. Has reviews, and upcoming movie and DVD news.

Far East Films
http://www.fareastfilms.com/
News and reviews of asian films (and occasionally some animation).

FEARnet
http://www.fearnet.com/
Has a rotating selection of streaming horror films.

Also has news, trailers, and behind the scenes stuff.

Flubtitles
http://www.flubtitles.com/
Bizarrely mistranslated dialogue from HK cinema.

Frankenstein
http://www.frankensteinfilms.com/
Dedicated to all things Frankenstein, especially movies.

Giant Monsters Attack
http://giantmonstersattack.blogspot.com/
Blog covering the appearance of giant monsters in films, television, comics, and other media.

Giant Monster Movies
http://www.giantmonstermovies.com/
Database of giant monster films from all over the world. Also has the infamous Today in G-History archives.

Girls With Guns
http://www.girlswithguns.org/
For the action heroine fan in everyone.

God Among Directors
www.godamongdirectors.com/
Series of web sites devoted to such indie luminaries as Quentin Tarantino, John Woo, Robert Rodriguez, Martin Scorsese, and Kevin Smith

Godzilla Asylum
http://godzillaasylum.blogspot.com/
Reviews of giant monster films on DVD with an accent on the Big G..

Godzilla Temple
www.godzillatemple.com/
A home page devoted to the glory of the world's finest man-in-suit, Godzilla. Showcases reviews, audio and video clips, and an exhaustive Godzilla FAQ

Hammer House of Horror
http://www.fortunecity.com/lavendar/judidench/339/
Fan webring for the classic Hammer horror films.

Han Cinema
http://www.hancinema.net/index.php
Online database and news site for Korean films.

Harvey Deneroff
http://deneroff.com/blog/
Blog on animated films from around the world.

Henshin Online
http://www.henshinonline.com/
News and reviews of Japanese fantasy and sci-fi films.

Holywood: Christian Entertainment Reviews
http://www.bettybowers.com/holywood.html
Mock film reviews from Betty Bowers and her Landover Baptist Church, themselves a parody of religion.

Hong Kong Cinemagic
http://www.hkcinemagic.com/en
Database and resource site for fans of HK films.

Hong Kong Movie Database
http://www.hkmdb.com/
Database of Hong Kong cinema in Chinese and English.

Horror Asylum
http://www.horror-asylum.com/
Reviews of horror films and DVD releases.

Horror DVDs
http://www.horrordvds.com/
Upcoming horror film releases, links, and a neat forum.

Horror Movies.ca
http://www.horror-movies.ca/
Massive Canadian horror film site.

Horror Movies That Suck
http://www.horrormoviesthatsuck.com/
Reviews of bad horror films.

Horror Stew
http://www.horrorstew.com/
Horror clips and articles.

Horrorfind
http://www.horrorfind.com/
A search engine dedicated to all things horror, including films.

Horrorhound
http://www.horrorhound.com/
Horror movie news and reviews.

Horror Movies!
horrormovies.com
Everything you ever wanted to know about horror flicks: films, cast, crew, locations, makeup, etc.

House of Horrors
http://www.houseofhorrors.com/
Horror film news, reviews, and interviews.

Japanese Horror Movie Database
http://jhmd.jp/
In English and Japanese.

Joe Bob Report
www.joebobbriggs.com/
Home page of the most prolific bad movie critic of our time, King of the Drive-In, Joe Bob Briggs. Site features archives of Briggs' reviews of schlock classics and his hilarious Ultimate B-Movie Guide

Kaiju Direct Website Directory
http://www2.arkansas.net/~gsraptor/guide.html
A list of websites devoted to Japanese sci-fi and fantasy film.

Kaiju Fan
http://www.historyvortex.org/KaijuFan.html
A very thorough giant monster history site.

Kaiju Headquarters
http://www.kaijuhq.org/index2.html
Hail Godzilla!

Kaijuphile
http://www.kaijuphile.com/
Portal to 5 other websites on giant monsters.

Keyframe
http://www.keyframeonline.com/
Information resource for animation in all its forms.

Korean Film
http://www.koreanfilm.org/
Online database and news site for Korean cinema that includes a history of Korean film, several essays, and a discussion board.

Kung-Fu Cinema
http://www.kungfucinema.com/
Reviews and news on asian films with an emphasis on martial arts and fighting films.

Ladies of the Evil Dead
www.ladiesoftheevildead.com/
Site run by the three actresses who all died horrible deaths in Sam Raimi's original *Evil Dead*. Granted, they're no Bruce Campbell, but they will sell you suggestive pictures and happily show up to your nerd convention for a price.

Last Drive-In on the Left
http://www.lastdriveinontheleft.com/
Incredibly fun site if you're a fan of drive-in cult and horror movies. Has upcoming DVD releases and reviews, ads, and trailers.

Love and Bullets
http://www.loveandbullets.com/
Reviews of Hong Kong films on DVD, and comparisons of quality between different releases.

Love HK Film
www.lovehkfilm.com/
Fans of Jackie Chan and John Woo will love this comprehensive site, which offers copious information on the Hong Kong film industry. Includes an update of new Hong Kong films, filmographies, interviews, reviews, and a searchable database of Hong Kong actors and actresses

The Midnight Eye
http://www.midnighteye.com/
Reviews of Japanese cinema, and interviews with directors.

The Missing Link
http://www.missinglinkhorrorclassics.co.uk/
British site devoted to horror films from the 50's and before.

M.J. Simpson
http://www.mjsimpson.co.uk/
News and reviews of horror and scifi films by former staff writer for SFX magazine.

Mondo Digital
http://www.mondo-digital.com/
DVD, video, and theatrical reviews of horror movies and unusual films (especially foreign ones).

Monster Island News
http://robojapan.blogspot.com/
Blog for the comic book, sci-fi, and Godzilla fan in you.

Monsters A-Go-Go
http://www.monstersagogo.com/
Monster movie blog and reviews.

Muppet Central
www.muppetcentral.com
The coolest and most comprehensive fan-made resource to Jim Henson's ageless creations, *The Muppets*

No Place for a Woman: The Family in Film Noir
http://www.lib.berkeley.edu/MRC/noir/np09epi.html
Reports on the implications that film noir has had on society. The author, John Blaser, pinpoints the role that women and family have in this genre. Subtopics include "Pro-family Messages in Film Noir" and "Women's Anti-Family Function in Film Noir."

Origins of American Animation
http://memory.loc.gov/ammem/oahtml/oahome.html
Library of Congress site chronicling the history of Animation in the states.

Pit of Horror
http://www.pitofhorror.com/
Covers horror film news, and reviews some films.

Planet of Dinosaurs
http://www.wsu.edu/~delahoyd/dinosource.html
Your resource for dinosaurs in movies.

Planet Origo
http://www.planetorigo.com/index.php?s=O7fAqK7icAmb0LNn&
Online store and review site for science fiction and fantasy films, and music.

Polish Movie Posters
www.polishposter.com/
Check out this archive of original movie poster artwork from Poland and marvel at how scary Polish advertising can be. Their *Weekend at Bernie's* poster looks like something out of *Eraserhead*.

Prison Flicks
http://www.prisonflicks.com/
Ummm...yeah.

Professor Neon's TV and Movie Mania
www.vortex.com/ProfNeon.html
Covers a gamut of information on film, television, radio, and the cable industry. When it comes to films, the Professor leans more to sci-fi, cult, and weird stuff.

Pulp Movies
http://www.pulpmovies.com/
Inspiring and informational blog on cult cinema.

The Pulsing Cinema
http://www.pulsingcinema.com/
News on foreign horror and crime films.

Quiet Earth
http://www.quietearth.us/
Film reviews with an emphasis on post apocalyptic movies.

Science Fiction Filmsite
http://www.umich.edu/~umfandsf/film/
Uses stills and clipz to analyze the realm of science in scfi movies.

Sci-fi Japan
http://www.scifijapan.com/

News and reviews of oriental sci-fi, horror, and fantasy films and dvd releases.

Sci-Fi Movie Page
http://www.scifimoviepage.com/
Sci-fi movie reviews, articles, scripts, and trailers.

Scifi-Movies
http://www.scifi-movies.com/
Huge database of science fiction films and television series.

Sci-Fi Trivia Real
http://www.realmovietrivia.com/
Insider trivia and neat info on popular science fiction movies.

Scifispace
http://www.scifispace.com/
Movie reviews and a directory of stores selling sci-fi stuff in each state!

Sciflicks
http://www.sciflicks.com/
Massive database on sci-fi movies.

Shivers of Horror
http://www.shiversofhorror.com/
Forum for horror movies, and a second site devoted to the Friday the 13th movies.

Shock Cinema
http://www.shockcinemamagazine.com/
Online version of magazine catering to fans of bizarre and unconventional cinema.

Slice of SciFi
http://www.sliceofscifi.com/
News and review site for science fiction films that also includes tech news.

The Spinning Image
http://www.thespinningimage.co.uk/index.asp
News, articles, and reviews of cult films from the world over.

Stomp Tokyo
www.stomptokyo.com
Reviews and salutes all manner of schlock and trash cinema on a 5-David Hasselhoff scale.

Superhero Flix
http://www.superheroflix.com/
Covers all superhero and comic related films and television.

Superhero Hype
http://www.superherohype.com/
Comics and some horror movies on the screen and DVD.

Tabula Rasa
http://www.tabula-rasa.info/
A history of horror in Australia, including horror movies.

They're Coming To Get You Barbara
http://www.theyrecoming.com/
Horror film reviews by two sisters who are fans of the genre. They also have some of the most disturbing cakes of all time.

Toho Kingdom
http://www.tohokingdom.com/
Oriental film news and reviews.

Unfilmable
http://unfilmable.blogspot.com/
Blog reviewing all films Lovecraftian in theme.

Upcoming Horror Movies
http://www.upcominghorrormovies.com/
Trailers, image gallery, reviews, etc.

Vampyre's Online
www.vampyres-online.com
Regularly updated database of almost every vampire film ever made, including such obscure treats as *Blacula Lives Again!* and *Wanda Does Transylvania.*

The Video Graveyard
http://www.thevideograveyard.com/
Horror movie reviews and trailers.

FILM FESTIVALS

ACB Sacramento Film and Music Festival
w http://www.sacfilm.com/akimbo.html
A centerpiece for the arts community of Sacramento and a celebration of both visual and musical works from around the world

ACE Film Festival
http://www.acefest.com/
Presented by New York Foundation for the Arts.

Adelaide Film Festival
http://www.adelaidefilmfestival.org/
International film festival held in Australia.

AFI Los Angeles International Film Festival (USA)
www.afi.com/onscreen/AFIFEST
Features attractions from this huge film festival held every October. Also lists synopses of the films appearing each year

African Diaspora Film Festival
nyadff.org/
Highlights the works of African-American filmmakers.

After Dark Horrorfest
http://www.horrorfestonline.com/
Three day festival premiering horror films nationwide.

Angel Film Festival
http://www.angelfilmfestival.org/
Competition for Independent Short Films in Islington, London.

Anima
http://www.animatv.be/
Annual European cartoon and animation festival.

Animex
http://www.animex.net/
International festival of animation and computer games.

Ann Arbor Film Festival
aafilmfest.org/
Not-for-profit festival showcases independent and experimental films.

Annecy International Animated Film Festival and Market
http://www.annecy.org/home/?Page_ID=1
Click on the small British flag in the top left corner for the English language site.

Arab Film Festival
http://www.aff.org/
Californian festival of Arabic film.

Arizona State University Art Museum Short Film and Video Festival
http://asuartmuseum.asu.edu/filmfest/index.html
Short films from directors with varying levels of experience.

Ashland Independent Film Festival
www.ashlandfilm.org/
Supports independent film and film education.

Aspen Filmfest
http://www.aspenfilm.org/
Indie and short film festivals.

Atlanta Film Festival
http://www.atlantafilmfestival.com/
Features animation, shorts, docs, narrative, and full length films.

Atlantic Film Festival
http://www.atlanticfilm.com/
Festival for International and Canadian film.

Austin Film Festival
www.austinfilmfestival.com/

Bangkok International Film Festival
http://www.bangkokfilm.org/
Annual festival held by the government of Thailand.

Beirut Film Foundation Mideast Film Festival
http://www.beirutfilmfoundation.org/
Festival encouraging young filmmakers in the Middle East.

Belize International Film Festival
http://www.belizefilmfestival.com/
Showcases Caribbean and Central American film.

Bergen International Film Festival
http://www.biff.no/2009/en/
Annual filmfest held in Norway.

Berlin Film Festival
berlinale.de/
Lists production information on all the films featured in this festival.

Bermuda International Film Festival
http://www.bermudafilmfest.com/
Annual film festival and charity event.

Bicknell International Film Festival
http://www.thebiff.org/
Utah's festival o' bad movies.

Bicycle Film Festival
http://www.bicyclefilmfestival.com/
Festival celebrating the bicycle in film, music, and art.

Big Bear Lake International Film Festival
http://www.bigbearlakefilmfestival.com/
California event showing indies, shorts, animation, and documentaries.

The Big Dam Festival
http://www.bigdamfilmfestival.blogspot.com/
Independent film festival in Quincy, Illinois.

Big Island Film Festival
http://www.bigislandfilmfestival.com/
Narrative independent filmfest in Hawaii.

Big Muddy Film Festival
http://bigmuddyfilm.com/
Independent film festival held in Illinois.

Boomtown Film and Music Festival
http://www.boomtownfestival.com/index/The_2009_Boomtown_Film_%26_Music_Festival.html
Festival of films and music held in Beaumont, Texas.

Boston Irish Film Festival
www.irishfilmfestival.com/

Boston Motion Picture Awards
http://www.bostonawards.com/
Promotes independent films and filmmakers.

Boston Science Fiction Film Festival
http://www.bostonsci-fi.com/
Annual event playing at various venues in Boston.

Bratislava International Film Festival
http://www.iffbratislava.sk/index.php?id=232&L=1
Film festival held in the capital of Slovakia

Cajun and Zydeco Film Festival
http://www.bayouprod.com/
Celebration of Southern Louisiana culture held every year in Saulieu, France.

Calgary International Film Festival
www.calgaryfilm.com

Cannes Film Festival
www.festival-cannes.fr/
Searchable site with each year's film schedule, a FAQ, and jury and press information

Chicago Asian American Showcase
http://www.faaim.org/
Promoting Asian American films.

Chicago International Film Festival
www.chicagofilmfestival.org
Answers questions in the area of awards, entries, juries, and transportation.

Chicago International Children's Film Festival
www.cicff.org/

Chicago Lesbian and Gay International Film Festival
www.reelingfilmfestival.org/
Offers a rundown of films featured in this alternative film festival.

Chicago Underground Film Festival
www.cuff.org/

Chris Awards
http://www.chrisawards.org/
Columbus International Film and Video Festival.

Cine Las Americas
http://www.cinelasamericas.org/
Latino film festival in Texas.

Cine Sin Fin
http://www.alabrava.com/
Chicano film festival in East L.A.

Cine Tropical
http://www.cinematropical.com/
Open air celebration of Latin American films, food, culture, and music.

Cinecon
http://www.cinecon.org/
Hollywood event screening silent and early talking films.

Cinefest Sudbury
http://www.cinefest.com/
Annual Canadian film festival.

Cinevent Classic Film Convention
http://www.cinevent.com/
Annual event in Columbus, Ohio.

Cinema St. Louis
http://cinemastlouis.org/
10 day festival showing foreign film, shorts, documentaries, and American Indie movies.

Cinema Rome Filmfest
http://www.romacinemafest.it/romacinemafest/
Annual Roman film festival.

Cleveland International Film Festival
clevelandfilm.org

Danville International Children's Film Festival
http://www.caiff.org/danville/index.html
Films by and for children.

DC Shorts
http://www.dcshorts.com/
Short film festival in Washington, DC.

DC Independent Film Festival
www.dciff.org

Dead By Dawn
http://www.deadbydawn.co.uk/
Annual UK horror festival held in Edinburgh.

Denver International Film Festival
www.denverfilm.org
Besides information on the entries, this site offers insight into the Denver Film Society

DepicT
http://www.depict.org/
Competition for films with a running time of 90 seconds or less.

Digital Gun Awards
http://www.digitalgunawards.com/
Competition for films made within 3 days.

The Directors Cut
http://www.thedirectorscut.org/
International filmfest in New York screening short films, trailers, and documentaries.

Donostia Horror and Fantasy Film Festival
http://www.donostiakultura.com/terror/
Genre festival in San Sebastian, Spain.

Dundee Mountain Film Festival
http://www.dundeemountainfilm.org.uk/
UK's longest running mountain film festival.

East Lansing Film Festival
www.elff.com/

Edinburgh International Film Festival
http://www.edfilmfest.org.uk/
Originally began as a documentary festival after WWII, EIFF is now the worlds longest running film festival.

Edmonton International Film Festival
http://www.edmontonfilmfest.com/
Annual independent film festival in Canada.

Eerie Horrorfest
http://www.eeriehorrorfest.com/
Held in (are you ready for it?) Erie, Pennsylvania.

Emergeandsee
http://www.emergeandsee.org/cms/website.php
London based event showing student films.

Epic Summer Film Festival
http://www.epicsummer.org/
Festival held each summer for short outdoor adventure films.

Everett Womens Film Festival
http://www.everetttheatre.org/film_festival.html
Washington event featuring films by women directors.

Fairy Tales International Queer Film Festival
http://www.fairytalesfilmfest.com/
Canadian event presenting films by and/or about the gay,lesbian,bi, transgender, and twin spirited community.

Festival Focus
http://www.festivalfocus.org/
Database of film festivals.

Festival of Fantastic Films
http://fantastic-films.com/festival/
Manchester film festival showing scifi, horror, and fantasy films.

FIFA
http://www.artfifa.com/
Festival of films about art.

FIKE
http://www.fikeonline.net/
International short film festival in Evora, Portugal.

Film Festival Deadlines
http://www.cooblae.nl/film-festival-deadlines/Deadlines-Holland-Film-Accredited.html
Calendar of deadlines for major film festival submissions, and a database of festivals.

Film Festival Server
http://www.filmfestivals.com/index.shtml
Searchable database of international film and video festivals.

Film Festival Source
http://www.filmfestivalsource.com/
Directory of film festivals, indexed by category, title, or country.

Film Festival Today
http://www.filmfestivaltoday.com/
Magazine covering the film festival circuit.

Film Festival Zlin
http://www.zlinfest.cz/cs/
International children's film festival.

Filmfest DC
http://www.filmfestdc.org/
Premieres international cinema in Washington DC.

Film Your Issue
http://whatsyourissue.tv/index.shtml
Short film competition wherein the contestants make films about a political or social issue important to them.

Filmfest Munchen
http://www.filmfest-muenchen.de/
Annual summer film festival in Germany.

Flickerfest
http://www.flickerfest.com.au/
Australian international short film festival.

Flicker Festival
http://www.flickerfestival.com/
Bi-monthly non-competitive Super 8 and 16mm short film festivals.

Flicker Los Angeles
http://www.flickerla.com/
LA chapter of the Flicker Festival.

Flicker New York
http://www.flickernyc.com/
New York chapter of the Flicker Festival.

Flicker Richmond
http://www.rmicweb.org/flicker/
Richmond chapter of the Flicker Festival.

Flying 5 Film Awards
http://www.flyingfives.co.nz/
New Zealand indie film competition for films or videos of 5 minutes or less.

Fort Williams Mountain Film Festival
http://www.mountainfilmfestival.co.uk/
Festival from the Scottish highlands focusing on mountain based films and photography.

48 Hour Film Project
http://www.48hourfilm.com/
Film competition for films done entirely within 48 hours.

Frameline
http://www.frameline.org/festival/index.aspx
San Francisco based international gay and lesbian film festival.

Fredrikstad Animation Festival
http://www.animationfestival.no/index_eng.shtml
Nordic and Baltic that highlights international and local animated films.

Free Form Film Festival
http://www.freeformfilm.org/
Traveling collection of outsider film and video works.

Freeze Frame
http://www.freezeframeonline.org/eng-about-us/
International festival of children's films held in Canada.

French Film Festival UK
http://www.frenchfilmfestival.org.uk/
British festival of French cinema.

Frightfest
http://www.frightfest.co.uk/
Annual fantasy and horror film festival in London.

Fukuoka International Film Festival
http://www.focus-on-asia.com/english/index.html
Focuses on Asian films.

Full Frame Documentary Film Festival
http://www.fullframefest.org/
Large Documentary fest in the states.

FW:FWD
http://www.fwfwd.org/
Online exhibit of winning films from a competition for viral short films.

Galway Film Fleadh
http://www.galwayfilmfleadh.com/
Along with this film festival, Galway hosts Irelands only film market.

Goteborg International Film Festival
http://www.goteborg.filmfestival.org/filmfestival/
Festival of features, shorts, and documentaries held in Sweden.

Harlan Jacobson's Talk Cinema
http://www.talkcinema.com/
Shows independent and foreign films before their release.

Harmony Film Festival
http://www.harmonyfilmfest.com/2007/
Short film festival dedicated to promoting peace and harmony.

Hartford Jewish Film Festival
http://www.hjff.org/
Showcases films highlighting the jewish international experience.

Havana Film Festival in New York
http://www.hffny.com/2008/index.php
New York festival celebrating Latin American film.

Hawaii International Film Festival
www.hiff.org/

Heartland Film Festival
http://www.trulymovingpictures.org/FilmFestival/Pages/default.aspx

Holland Animation Film Festival
http://haff.awn.com/?page=home&id=0&lang=en&sub=&anim=&film=&letter=
Biennial international animation festival.

Hollywood Black Film Festival
http://www.hbff.org/
Annual festival highlighting the works of black filmmakers.

Hollywood International Student Film Festival
http://www.isffhollywood.org/
Student films from elementary school to college.

Hong Kong International Film Festival
www.hkiff.org.hk/
Film Festival in Hong Kong

Hong Kong Jewish Film Festival
http://www.hkjewishfilmfest.org/
Asia's festival of the Jewish culture.

H.P. Lovecraft Film Festival
http://www.hplfilmfestival.com/
Promotes cinematic adaptations of weird tales from professional and amateur filmmakers.

Huesca Film Festival
http://www.huesca-filmfestival.com/index_E.html
Argentinian short film festival.

Hull Film Festival
http://www.hullfilm.co.uk/
Short film festival in UK

Human Rights Watch International Film Festival
www.hrw.org/iff/
Highlights films dealing with the worldwide struggle for Human Rights

Humboldt International Film Festival
http://www.humboldt.edu/~filmfest/
Student run film festival at HSU showing Super 8 and 16mm short films.

IF Istanbul
http://2010.ifistanbul.com/en
Indie film festival held in Istanbul.

Image Out Rochester Lesbian & Gay Film & Video Festival
www.imageout.org
Highlights films dealing with gay and lesbian issues

Imagenation
http://www.imagenationfilmfestival.org/pages/main.htm
Year-round film festival promoting independent art-house films about the African Diaspora.

Image+Nation
http://www.image-nation.org/2007/index-choix.php
LGBT festival held in Montreal.

Images Festival
http://www.imagesfestival.com/
Experimental film festival held every spring in Toronto.

Independent Film Festival of Boston
http://www.iffboston.org/
Indie filmfest held in, of course, Boston.

Independent Lens Online Shorts Festival
http://www.pbs.org/independentlens/insideindies/shortsfest/
Annual online festival of shsort films from the PBS series.

Indianapolis International Film Festival
http://indyfilmfest.org/
Midwest filmfest screening feature and short films.

Indiefest
http://www.indiefestchicago.com/
Combines a film festival, screenwriting contest, film and script markets, and a 10 day party.

The Indie Gathering
http://theindiegathering.com/
Independent film festival in Cleveland, Ohio.

Indian Film Festival of Los Angeles
http://www.indianfilmfestival.org/
LA event showcasing films about India.

Inside Film Online
http://www.insidefilm.com/
Festival news, listings, and articles.

Inside Out
http://www.insideout.on.ca/festival09/index.html
GLBT festival in Toronto.

International Buddhist Film Festival
http://www.ibff.org/
Films about Buddhist culture, history, etc.

International Experimental Cinema Exposition
http://www.experimentalcinema.com/
Experimental film festival and workshop.

International Festival of Cinema and Technology
http://ifct.org/
Touring fim festival that seeks to showcase undiscovered films.

International Film Festival Innsbruck
http://www.iffi.at/
Austrian festival showing contemporary and classic films.

International Film Festival of India
http://iffi.nic.in/
Annual festival and competitions held in Goa, India.

International Film Festival of Kerala
http://www.keralafilm.com/
Annual film festival held in India.

International Hamburg Short Film Festival
http://www.shortfilm.com/index.php?id=shortfilmcom&L=1
Film festival and workshop.

International Short Film Festival Winterthur
http://www.kurzfilmtage.ch/Default.aspx
Short film festival held in Winterthur.

International Wildlife Film Festival
http://www.wildlifefilms.org/
Film festival dedicated to wildlife and it's conservation.

International Womens Film Festival Dortmund/Cologne
http://www.femmetotale.de/indexe.html
Films by women, or featuring women.

Internationale Kurtzfilmtage Oberhausen
http://www.kurzfilmtage.de/
Short film competition from Oberhausen Germany.

Inverness Film Festival
http://www.invernessfilmfestival.com/
Scottish film festival that shows international films as well as gaelic language films.

ION International Short Film Festival
http://www.ionfilmfest.com/
Promotes digital and short films.

Israel Film Festival
http://www.israelfilmfestival.com/iff07/
Showing subtitled films in LA, New York, and Miami.

Italian Film Festival
http://www.italianfilm.com/
Held every year in Marin County, California.

It's All True
http://www.itsalltrue.com.br/2010/index.asp
Brazilian international documentary film festival.

Ivy Film Festival
http://www.ivyfilmfestival.com/
Film festival for students, run by students.

Jackson Hole Wildlife Film Festival
http://www.jhfestival.org/
Nature festival in Grand Teton National Park.

James River Film Festival
http://www.rmicweb.org/jrff/index.html
Indie film and video festival in Virginia.

John Hopkins Film Fest
http://www.hopkinsfilmfest.com/
Baltimore festival showing classics, independent films, and new movies.

Kansas City Filmmakers Festival
http://www.kcjubilee.org/
Competitive indie festival.

Kansas International Film Festival
http://www.kansasfilm.com/
Shows independent and classic cinema.

Kansas Silent Film Festival
http://www.kssilentfilmfest.org/
Annual silent film festival in Wichita, Kansas.

Karlovy Vary International Film Festival
http://www.kviff.com/en/news/
Held in the Czech spa town of Karlovy Vary and usually includes a visit by Czech President Vaclav Havel.

Kingston Canadian Film Festival
http://www.kingcanfilmfest.com/
Showcases strictly Canadian films.

LA Femme Film Festival
http://www.lafemme.org/
Focuses on works by female filmmakers.

Lake Arrowhead Film Festival
http://www.lakearrowheadfilmfestival.com/
Screens vintage films.

Last Remaining Seats
http://laconservancy.org/remaining/index.php4
Classic films shown in downtown LA.

Latino Film Festival of the San Francisco Bay Area
www.latinofilmfestival.org/

Leeds International Film Festival
http://www.leedsfilm.com/
Features and shorts from around the world, along with music, comic art, and more.

Leuven Kort Film Festival
http://www.kortfilmfestival.be/
Flemish and European shorts, music videos, and animations.

Locarno International Film Festival
http://www.pardo.ch/index.jsp
Annual Italian event.

London Film Festival
www.lff.org.uk/

London Lesbian and Gay Film Festival
http://www.llgff.org.uk/
LGBT festival in London England.

London Lesbian Film Festival
http://www.llff.ca/
Celebrating lesbian film making in Canada.

Lone Pine Film Festival
http://www.lonepinefilmfestival.org/index.asp
Festival featuring movies filmed in or around Lone Pine California.

Long Island Film Festival
http://www.lifilm.org/
Indie film festival at Long Island.

Long Island Gay and Lesbian Film Festival
http://www.ligff.org/
Has a "Make your own gay movie" contest.

Los Angeles Film Festival
www.lafilmfest.com/

Los Angeles International Short Film Festival
http://www.lashortsfest.com/video_list.asp
International short filmfest held in LA.

Los Angeles Latino International Film Festival
www.latinofilm.org
Co-founded by Edward James Olmos, this festival awards cash prizes to outstanding American, Latin-American, and Spanish filmmakers.

Lost Film Festival
http://www.lostfilmfest.com/
Traveling festival of underground films.

LUCAS
http://www.lucasfilmfestival.de/
Children's film festival held in Frankfurt Germany.

Lund International Fantastic Film Festival
http://www.fff.se/english/index.asp
Scandinavia's largest fantasy filmfest.

Madcat Women's International Film Festival
http://www.madcatfilmfestival.org/
Independent and experimental films by women.

Magnolia Independent Film Festival
http://www.magfilmfest.com/
Held in Mississippi.

Main Line Film Festival
http://www.mainlinefilmfestival.com/
Short film festival held in Wayne, Pennsylvania.

Maine International Film Festival
www.miff.org
Includes 100 screenings of new, old, and student films in a non-competitive, free-spirited atmosphere.

Maine Jewish Film Festival
http://www.mjff.org/
Features and documentaries on Jewish themes.

Majestic Theatre Silent Film Festival
http://www.majestic.spiderweb.com.au/
Silent film festival held in Australia.

Malibu International Film Festival
http://www.malibufilmfestival.org/
Held every year during the American Film Market.

Manhattan Short Film Festival
http://www.msfilmfest.com/
New York based festival.

Mardi Gras Film Festival
http://www.queerscreen.com.au/j/index.php
Gay and Lesbian film festival in Australia.

Margaret Mead Film and Video Festival
http://www.amnh.org/programs/mead/
Largest ethnographic/documentary film festival in US.

Maryland Film Festival
http://www.md-filmfest.com/
Features restored classics, indies, docs, shorts, and full length films.

Maui Film Festival
http://www.mauifilmfestival.com/
Annual film festival in Hawaii.

Melbourne Film Festival
http://www.melbournefilmfestival.com.au/
Annual international Australian film festival.

Melbourne International Animation Festival
http://www.miaf.net/
Showcase for animated films in Australia.

Melbourne Queer Film Festival
http://www.melbournequeerfilm.com.au/
Features, shorts, and experimental films.

Meniscus Film Festival
http://www.meniscusfilms.com/
Promotes independent films and filmmaking.

Method Fest
http://www.methodfest.com/
Indie showcase in Burbank California.

Miami Gay and Lesbian Film Festival
http://www.miamigaylesbianfilm.com/
Gay film and video festival in Florida.

Miami Latin Film Festival
www.miamifilmfestival.com/

Milan International Film Festival
http://www.miff.it/
Italian film festival.

Mill Valley Film Festival
http://www.mvff.com/
Sponsored by California Film Institute.

MIX NYC
http://www.mixnyc.org/
Experimental gay and lesbian film festival.

Molodist International Film Festival
http://www.molodist.com/en/
Annual festival held in Kyiv, Ukraine.

Monaco International Film Festival
http://www.monacofilmfestival.net/
Film competition held in Monaco.

Montreal World Film Festival
www.ffm-montreal.org/fr_index.html
Offers a rundown of the festival in both English and French.

Moondance International Film Festival
www.moondancefilmfestival.com/
Promotes and encourages the best work in screenwriting, filmmaking, stage plays, radio plays, TV scripts, musical scores, lyrics, librettos, musical videos, puppetry theatre, and short stories.

Mountainfilm Festival
http://www.mountainfilm.org/
Celebrates cultures of the mountain communities.

Moves
http://www.movementonscreen.org.uk/
Arts group exploring movement through film, video, and installations.

Museum of Television and Radio TV Documentary Festival
http://www.paleycenter.org/events/ss-07fall/ny-docfest.htm
Showcase for television documentaries.

Muskegon Film Festival
http://www.muskegonfilmfestival.com/
Michigan event showing features and student films.

Nantucket Film Festival
http://www.nantucketfilmfestival.org/
Shows films of various length and genre, studio or indie.

Nashville Independent Film Festival
http://www.nashvillefilmfestival.org/
Tennessee festival showing films of all genres.

New Jersey Film Festival
http://www.njfilmfest.com/
Indie, classic, international, and experimental films.

New Jersey Jewish Film Festival
http://www.njjff.org/
Jewish themed festival in the Garden State.

New Orleans Film Festival
http://www.nuff.no/
Features, shorts, documentaries, and music videos.

Newport Beach Film Festival
http://www.newportbeachfilmfest.com/
Features, shorts, documentaries, and animation from around he world.

Newport Film Festival
http://www.newportbeachfilmfest.com/
International features, shorts, documentaries, and classics.

New York City Independent Horror Film Festival
http://www.nychorrorfest.com/
Indie horror movies.

New York Film Festival
http://www.filmlinc.com/nyff/nyff.html
International features and shorts.

New York International Childrens Film Festival
http://www.gkids.com/
Showcase of childrens films.

New York International Independent Film and Video Festival
http://www.nyfilmvideo.com/
For independent, low budget, and non-mainstream artists.

New York International Latino Film Festival
http://www.nylatinofilm.com/
Films made by, featuring, and/or about the Latino community.

New Zealand International Film Festivals
http://www.nzff.co.nz/
Films from around the world.

NextFrame
http://nextframe.org/
University of Film and Video Association's touring festival of international student films.

Niagara Indie Film Fest
http://www.niagaraindiefilmfest.org/
Showcase for Canadian independent film and video.

Noir City
http://www.filmnoirfoundation.org/
Classic film noir movies in San Francisco.

Nordic Youth Film Festival
http://www.nuff.no/
Films by young people for young people.

Northampton Independent Film Festival
http://www.niff.org/
Celebrates independent filmmaking.

Northwest Film and Video Festival
http://www.nwfilm.org/
Foreign, classic, experimental, and independent films.

NSI FilmExchange
http://www.nsi-canada.ca/
Short and feature films from Canada.

NYC Midnight Movie Making Madness
http://www.nycmidnight.com/
Competition for digital films.

Ohio Independent Film Festival
www.ohiofilms.com/

Omaha Film Event
http://www.omahafilmevent.com/
Presents screenings of classic films.

One World International Human Rights Film Festival
http://oneworld.cz/ow/festival/index.php
Features films on the themes of human rights and freedoms.

Ottawa International Animation Festival
http://ottawa.awn.com/
Largest animated film festival in North America.

Out In Africa
http://www.oia.co.za/
Gay and Lesbian festival in Johannesberg.

Out On Film
http://www.outonfilm.com/
LGBT film festival in Georgia.

Out On Screen
http://www.outonscreen.com/
Vancouver Queer film and video festival.

Out Takes Dallas
http://www.outtakesdallas.org/
Gay and Lesbian Film Festival from Texas.

Out Takes-New Zealand
http://www.outtakes.org.nz/
Gay films in New Zealand.

Outdoor Film Festival at NIH
http://www.filmfestnih.org/
Picnic and film festival to benefit charity.

Over The Fence
http://www.overthefence.com.au/
Australian comedy festival.

Ozark Foothills Film Fest
http://www.ozarkfoothillsfilmfest.org/
Festival sponsored by the Foothills Film Society.

Palm Beach International Film Festival
http://www.pbifilmfest.org/
Showcases student and international films.

Palm Springs International Film Festival
http://www.psfilmfest.org/index.aspx
Has both an feature and a short film festival.

Pan African Film Festival
http://www.paff.org/
LA festival showing African American themed films.

Park City Film Music Festival
http://www.parkcityfilmmusicfestival.com/
Dedicated to music in film. Has screenings, and a competition.

Perspektive
http://www.fitame.de/index2.php?lang=en
International human rights oriented film festival held in Nuremberg.

Philadelphia International Gay and Lesbian Film Festival
http://piglff.bside.com/2007/
Largest Gay and Lesbian filmfest on the East Coast.

Philadelphia Film Festival
http://www.filmadelphia.org/
Annual event put on by Philadelphia Film Society.

Phoenix Film Festival
http://www.phoenixfilmfestival.org/pages/
Annual film event in Arizona.

Picture This Film Festival
http://www.ptff.org/
Highlights films for, by, and about people with disabilities

Pioneer Valley Jewish Film Festival
http://www.pvjff.org/
3 week event in Massachusetts.

Pittsburgh Lesbian and Gay Film Festival
http://www.pilgff.org/
Annual celebration of LGBT films.

Planet in Focus
http://www.planetinfocus.org/
Environmental film and video festival based in Toronto.wow

Polish Film Festival in LA
http://www.polishfilmla.org/
Also has info on other Polish events and films.

Portland International Short Short Film Festival
http://www.zonkerfilms.com/
Films of 10 minutes or less.

Portland Underground Film Festival
http://www.clintonsttheater.com/puff/
Shows experimental and underground films.

Portobello Film Festival
http://www.portobellofilmfestival.com/
Primarily British independent films and video.

Port Townsend Film Festival
http://www.ptfilmfest.com/
Independent film festival in Washington.

Projections d'Argile
http://www.fifav.fr/?lg=EN&PHPSESSID=6373d4cad3bac1b
French festival of films about ceramics and glass.

Providence Latin American Film Festival
http://www.plaff.org/
Competition held in Rhode Island.

Pusan International Film Festival
http://www.piff.org/intro/default.asp?lang=eng
Annual festival held in South Korea.

Q Cinema
http://www.qcinema.org/
Fort Worth's Gay and Lesbian film festival.

RAI Festival of Ethnographic Film
http://www.raifilmfest.org.uk/
Film festival sponsored by the Royal Anthropological Institute.

Raindance Film Festival
http://www.raindance.co.uk/site/
Independent festival by filmmakers for filmmakers.

Real to Reel Film Festival
http://www.ccartscouncil.org/realtoreel/
Independent film festival in North Carolina.

Red Bank International Film Festival
http://www.lauragesin.net/RBIFF/
New Jersey film festival showing documentaries, animation, foreign, shorts, and features.

Red Rock Film Festival
http://www.ophilia.com/
Utah film festival showing movies of all genres.

Red Shift Festival
http://www.rsfest.com/
Dedicated to Russian filmmakers and animators living abroad.

Reel Affirmations
http://www.reelaffirmations.org/
International gay and lesbian film festival in Washington DC.

ReelWorld Film Festival
http://www.reelworld.ca/
Toronto festival showcasing diverse types of film and video.

Reggio Film Festival
http://www.reggiofilmfestival.com/
Italian short film festival.

Rehoboth Beach Independent Film Festival
http://www.rehobothfilm.com/Festival.html
Sponsored by the Rehoboth Beach Film Society.

Rencontres Internationales Paris Berlin
http://www.art-action.org/en_index.htm
Fim, art, and music festival in France and Germany.

Reno Film Festival
http://www.renofilmfestival.com/
Gambling and movies. MWUHAHA!!! But seriously, avoid the gambling...

Revelation Perth International Film Festival
http://www.revelationfilmfest.org/
Australian festival showing works from the indie, film fest, and underground

Reykjavik International Film Festival
http://www.filmfest.is/?L=1
International film and documentary festival.

Rhode Island International Film Festival
http://www.film-festival.org/
International film festival in Providence. They also hold a horror festival.

RiverRun International Film Festival
http://www.riverrunfilm.com/
International festival for indie films in North Carolina.

Rochester International Film Festival
http://www.rochesterfilmfest.org/
Independent film festival in New York.

Rocky Mountain Women's Film Festival
http://www.madcatfilmfestival.org/
Annual festival profiling films by and about women.

Roger Ebert's Film Festival
http://www.ebertfest.com/
Annual spring festival of movies that Roger Ebert has seen.

Roma Independent Film Festival
http://www.riff.it/
Indie film festival in Italy

Rosebud Film and Video Festival
http://www.rosebudact.org/
Held in Washington, DC.

Rossland Mountain Film Festival
http://rosslandfilmfest.com/
Canadian film festival focusing on local artists.

Rotterdam International Film Festival
http://www.filmfestivalrotterdam.com/nl/
Shows worldwide independent and experimental films.

Roxbury Film Festival
http://www.roxburyfilmfestival.org/
Showcases films written, produced, or directed by persons of color.

Rural Route Film Festival
http://www.ruralroutefilms.com/
Specializes in films dealing with rural locales and people.

Sacramento Film and Music Festival
http://www.sacfilm.com/
Shorts, features, student films, and music videos.

Sacramento Film Festival
http://www.sacramentofilmfestival.com/
Premieres films that haven't been seen in California before.

Sacramento French Film Festival
http://www.sacramentofrenchfilmfestival.org/
Canadian festival celebrating historic and modern French cinema.

Sacramento Horror Film Festival
http://www.sachorrorfilmfest.com/
Californian horror and scifi film festival.

Sacramento International Gay and Lesbian Film Festival
http://siglff.org/
Canadian film festival for gay and lesbian film.

St. Barth Film Festival
http://www.stbarthff.org/2007/welcome.html
Films covering the Caribbean experience and life.

Salon Des Refuses Atlantique
http://rejectsalon.tripod.com/
Film festival of films rejected by the Atlantic Film Festival

San Antonio Underground Film Festival
http://www.safilm.com/
California film competition.

San Diego Asian Film Festival
www.sdaff.org/

San Diego International Film Festival
http://www.sdff.org/
Competition for documentaries, short films, and music video. Also presents films by Native American and Women filmmakers.

San Diego Latino Film Festival
http://www.sdlatinofilm.com/
Celebration of Latin film, art, and music.

San Diego Women's Film Festival
http://www.sdwff.org/
California's longest running women's film festival.

San Francisco Asian American Film Festival
http://asianamericanmedia.org/
Films about the Asian American experience

San Francisco Black Film Festival
http://www.sfbff.org/
Festival celebrating African-American cinema and the African cultural Diaspora.

San Francisco Independent Film Festival
http://www.sfindie.com/
Features American indie films and short animation.

San Francisco International Film Festival
http://www.sffs.org/
Sponsored by the San Francisco Film Society.

San Francisco International Lesbian & Gay Film Festival
http://www.frameline.org/festival/index.aspx
Annual celebration of diversity in SF.

San Francisco Jewish Film Festival
http://sfjff.org/site/pages/index.php
Shows international jewish films and also has a database of films online.

San Francisco Silent Film Festival
http://www.silentfilm.org/
Annual celebration of silent films in California.

San Luis Obispo International Film Festival
http://www.slofilmfest.org/2010/index.shtml
Competitive event in California.

San Sebastian Film Festival
http://www.sansebastianfestival.com/
Annual European festival.

Santa Barbara International Film Festival
http://www.sbfilmfestival.org/
Shows features, shorts, animation, documentaries, and indie films.

Santa Cruz Film Festival
http://www.santacruzfilmfestival.com/
Indie film festival in California.

Santa Fe Film Festival
http://www.santafefilmfestival.com/
Premieres new local and foreign films and has several mini-festivals.

Sao Paulo International Film Festival
http://www.mostra.org/home.php?x=1&language=en
Held yearly in Brazil.

Sapporo Shortfest
http://www.sapporoshortfest.jp/
Annual short film festival held in Sapporo, Japan.

Sarajevo Film Festival
http://www.sff.ba/content.php/en/main?set_culture=en
International showcase of films.

Sarasota Film Festival
http://www.sarasotafilmfestival.com/
Also shows movies and holds events year round.

Savanna Film and Video Festival
http://www.scad.edu/filmfest/
Independent festival in Georgia.

Sci-Fi-London
http://www.sci-fi-london.com/
Science Fiction and fantasy film in Britain.

Scinema
http://www.csiro.au/scinema/
Science films from students and professionals.

Scottsdale International Film Festival
http://www.scottsdalefilmfestival.com/
Arizona festival that premiers newer films.

Screamfest LA
http://www.screamfestla.com/
SciFi/Horror film and screenplay festival/competition in LA.

Scrittura e Immagine
http://www.scritturaeimmagine.it/english_home.html
Italian festival of films inspired by literary works.

Seattle International Film Festival
www.seattlefilm.com/
Enables you to look at photo stills from the festival, listen to audio speeches, and check out some internet broadcasts

Sedona International Film Festival and Workshop
http://www.sedonafilmfestival.com/
Independent film showcase and workshop.

Seoul Net Festival
http://www.senef.net/
Korean showcase for digital film.

SF Shorts
http://www.sfshorts.org/
Short films from around the world.

Shadow Documentary Film Festival
http://www.shadowfestival.nl/
Documentary film festival held in the Netherlands.

Shanghai International Film Festival
http://www.siff.com/
Annual event held every June in China.

Sheffield International Documentary Festival
https://sheffdocfest.com/
Documentary festival held in the UK.

The Shoot Out
http://www.theshootoutboulder.com/
Competition of short films produced within 24 hours.

Short Cuts
http://www.shortcuts.in/
Premiers shorts and documentaries in India.

Shorts Film Festival
http://www.shortsfilmfestival.com/
Australian festival of short film.

Short Shorts Lounge
http://www.shortshorts.org/
Japanese born short film festival

Shriek Fest
http://www.shriekfest.com/
Scifi/horror film festival in LA.

Sidewalk Moving Picture Festival
http://www.sidewalkfilm.org/
Shows narrative features, documentaries, shorts, and a competition for teens.

Silent Clowns Film Series
http://www.silentclowns.com/
Show of silent comedies presented by the New York Historical Society.

Silver Lake Film Festival
http://silverlakefilmfestival.org/
Independent and alternative films from the world over, plus it highlights local LA filmmakers.

Silverdocs
http://www.silverdocs.com/
Documentary festival sponsored by the American Film Institute and the Discovery Channel.

Singapore International Film Festival
http://www.filmfest.org.sg/index.php
Shows features, shorts, animation, and documentaries.

Slamdance Film Festival
www.slamdance.com/

Slapstick
http://www.slapstick.org.uk/
Classic silent film comedies.

SNOWYfest International Film Festival
http://www.snowyfest.com/
Competitions for international and local films at Australian ski resort.

Sound Unseen
http://www.soundunseen.com/
Underground films and documentaries about music.

South Asian Film Festival
http://www.thirdi.org/festival/
Indian arthouse classics, documentaries, and independent films from South Asia.

Sport Movies and TV International Film Festival
http://www.sportmoviestv.com/
Italian celebration of sports related film.

Sprout Film Festival
http://www.gosprout.org/FilmFestival.html
Film and video devoted to developmental disabilities.

Stockholm Film Festival
http://www.stockholmfilmfestival.se/
International Swedish film festival.

Straight 8
http://www.straight8.net/
Competition to make a three minute film on one cartridge of Super 8, with no editing. The results are shown at Cannes and other film festivals.

Studentfilms
http://www.studentfilms.com/
Online showcase of student short films.

Stuttgart International Festival of Animated Film
http://www.itfs.de/
Competition for animators 30 or younger.

Sundance-A Festival Virgin's Guide
http://www.sundanceguide.net/
Online companion to a guide about the festival.

Sundance Film Festival
http://www.sundance.org/festival/
Official site may not be as exciting as actually rubbing elbows among the hot talent, but it does come close. Sections include a daily report, listings of films competing, and a guide for getting around. Also has an archive for past festivals.

Swindon Film Festival
http://swindonfilmfestival.org/
Annual UK film festival.

SXSW
http://www.sxsw.com/
South by Southwest is an annual film, music, and multimedia festival held in Austin, Texas.

Sydney Film Festival
http://www.sydneyfilmfestival.org/index_flash.asp
Showcase for local and international films in Australia.

Syracuse International Film and Video Festival
http://www.syrfilm.com/
Film competition in New York.

Taiwan International Ethnographic Film Festival
http://www.tieff.sinica.edu.tw/
Films about the aboriginal peoples of the world.

Tampa International Gay and Lesbian Film Festival
https://www.tiglff.com/index.cfm
GLBT film festival from Florida.

Teddy Award
http://www.teddyaward.org/
Gay and Lesbian film awards in Berlin.

Telluride Film Festival
www.telluridefilmfestival.org/
Clint Eastwood calls this film festival the "best", and who are you to argue with the Outlaw Josey Wales?

Terror Film Festival
http://www.terrorfilmfestival.net/
Scifi/fantasy/horror festival held in Philadelphia, PA.

Texas Fear Fest
http://www.txfearfest.com/
Texas based horror festival.

Thessaloniki International Film Festival
http://www.filmfestival.gr/default.aspx?lang=en-US
Annual fall event in Greece.

Three Rivers Film Festival
http://3rff.com/
Showcases documentaries, films from Pittsburgh, American independents, shorts, classics, and international movies.

Tiburon International Film Festival
http://www.tiburonfilmfestival.com/
California event promoting heightened cultural awareness.

Tirana Film Fest
http://www.tiranafilmfest.com/
Albanian festival with shorts, fiction, documentaries, and animation.

Tokyo International Lesbian and Gay Film Festival
http://tokyo-lgff.org/2009/e/index.html
Festival is in Japan, but most films are open to English audiences.

Toofy Film Fest
http://www.toofy.com/
Colorado festival for indie filmmakers only.

Torino Film Festival
http://www.torinofilmfest.org/
Italian shorts, documentaries, and premieres.

Toronto Jewish Film Festival
http://www.tjff.com/
Films, documentaries, and shorts about jewish culture and identity.

Toronto International Film Festival
http://www.torontointernationalfilmfestival.ca/
Take off to the Great White North and enjoy one of the largest film festivals in North America

Toronto Online Film Festival
http://www.torontoonlinefilmfestival.com/
Feature films, shorts, animation, commercials, and music videos.

Tranny Fest
http://www.trannyfest.com/
Transgender film and video festival.

Trash Film Orgy
http://trashfilmorgy.com/
Bizarre film festival of some of the weirdest, goriest, and most disturbing films ever.

Traverse City Film Festival
http://www.traversecityfilmfest.org/
Founded by Michael Moore.

Trenton Film Festival
http://www.trentonfilmfestival.org/
Narrative films, documentaries, shorts, foreign movies, animation, and experiments.

Tribeca Film Festival
www.tribecafilmfestival.org/
Co-founded by Robert De Niro in 2002, this uber-trendy lower Manhattan film fete has evolved into one of the most respected festivals in the country

TromaDance Film Festival
www.tromadance.com

Tropfest
http://www.tropfest.com/
Worlds largest short film festival held in Australia.

Tucsonfilm
http://www.tucsonfilm.com/
Annual short film festival in Arizona.

Twin Rivers Multimedia Festival
http://www.twinriversmediafestival.com/
Festival encompassing film, video, and internet media formats.

UK Jewish Film Festival
http://www.ukjewishfilmfestival.org.uk/
Features jewish short films and features, and holocaust education.

United Nations Association Film Festival
http://www.unaff.org/
Documentaries about human rights, the environment, racism, homelessness, war, and women's issues.

USA Film Festival
http://www.usafilmfestival.com/
Nonprofit dedicated to recognizing excellence in film.

Uppsala International Short Film Festival
http://www.shortfilmfestival.com/
Swedish short film event. Click on flag in top right corner for English version.

Urbanworld Film Festival
http://www.uwff.com/
Features, shorts, and documentaries by African-American, Latin, and Asian people.

US International Film and Video Festival
http://www.filmfestawards.com/
Competition for documentary, educational, corporate, student, and entertainment films.

Vail Film Festival
http://www.vailfilmfestival.org/
Dedicated to American indie films, showing features, shorts, documentaries, tv pilots, commercials, and sports.

Valladolid International Film Festival
http://www.seminci.es/index.php
Annual Italian event.

Valley Film Festival
http://www.valleyfilmfest.com/
Indie filmfest in San Fernando Valley.

Vancouver Asian Film Festival
http://www.vaff.org/
Forum for North American Asian filmmakers.

Vancouver International Film Festival
http://www.viff.org/
Large competition for international and Canadian film.

Vancouver Jewish Film Festival
http://www.vijff.com/
Canada's longest running Jewish film festival.

Vancouver Latin American Film Festival
http://www.vlaff.org/
Canadian festival for Latin American cinema.

VCU French Film Festival
http://www.frenchfilm.vcu.edu/
French films premiered in Virginia.

Venice Film Festival
www.veneziafilmfestival.com/
Includes information on the film festival, as well as news on other cultural activities happening in Venice.

Victoria Independent Film and Video Festival
http://victoriafilmfestival.com/
Competition in British Columbia.

Viennale
http://www.viennale.at/
International film festival held in Austria.

Virginia Film Festival
http://www.vafilm.com/
Weekend long annual event in Charlottesville.

Visions du Reel
http://www.visionsdureel.ch/
International documentary festival in Switzerland.

Vistas Film Festival
http://www.vistasfilmfestival.org/
International event for Hispanic cinema in Texas.

Viva Film Festival
http://www.vivafilmfestival.com/
Spanish and Latin American film festival in Manchester.

Washington DC Independent Film Festival
http://www.dciff.org/
Annual competition for indie films.

Washington Jewish Film Festival
http://washingtondcjcc.org/center-for-arts/film/WJFF/
Celebration of Jewish culture, films, and filmmakers.

Webcuts
http://www.webcuts.org/2010/index-en.html
Annual internet short film festival from Berlin.

West Virginia International Film Festival
http://www.wviff.org/
West Virginia's Official State Film Festival.

Westchester Film Festival
http://www.westchesterfilmfestival.com/
Annual showcase of films of 60 minutes or less.

Westport Youth Film Festival
http://www.westportyouthfilmfest.org/
Features the work of high school filmmakers.

Where Is The Love
http://www.whereisthelove.ro/index.php?l=ro
Romanian international short film festival.

Wildscreen
http://www.wildscreen.org.uk/
UK event promoting nature films.

Wild and Scenic Environmental Film Festival
http://www.wildandscenicfilmfestival.org/
Nevada celebration of environmental and adventure films.

Wildlife Film Makers
http://www.wildlife-film.com/
Festival and website dedicated to wildlife filmmakers worldwide.

Wildlife Vaasa
http://wildlife.vaasa.fi/
Finnish competition for nature films.

Wild West Film Festival
http://www.wildwestfilmfest.com/
48 hour film competition in Kansas.

Williamsburg Brooklyn Film Festival
http://www.wbff.org/
Festival for new independent filmmakers.

Wine Country Film Festival
http://www.winecountryfilmfest.com/
Open air film screenings in California with food and wine events.

Woods Hole Film Festival
http://www.woodsholefilmfestival.com/
Cape Cod event for New England based independent film makers.

Woodstock Film Festival
http://www.woodstockfilmfestival.com/
Concerts and independent films.

Women Make Waves Film/Video Festival
http://www.wmw.com.tw/en/

Women's Film Festival
http://www.womensfilmfestival.org/
Benefit for he Women's Crisis Center in Windham County, Vermont.

WorldFest
http://www.worldfest.org/
International independent and short film festival in Houston, Texas.

Yamagata International Documentary Film Festival
http://www.yidff.jp/home-e.html
Documentary festival held in Japan.

Yorkton Short Film and Video Festival
http://www.yorktonshortfilm.org/
Canada's oldest short film festival.

Zagreb Film Festival
http://www.zagrebfilmfestival.com/
Croatian festival for shorts, documentaries, and features.

Zanzibar International Film Festival
http://www.ziff.or.tz/
Large cultural event in East Africa.

Zinebi
http://www.zinebi.com/zinebi51/
International festival of documentaries and short films held in Spain.

FILM MAGAZINES

Animation Journal
http://www.animationjournal.com/
A scholarly journal on animation history and theory. Yikes.

Animation Magazine
http://www.animationmagazine.net/
Magazine on animation.

Box Office
http://www.boxoffice.com/
One of the first trade publications to go online, reporting the latest on current films and films in production.

Cinefex
www.cinefex.com/
Online version of the renowned special-effects magazine. Offers synopses of articles, back issues, and a cover archive. Issues are indexed by artist, company, and film name.

CinemaSpace
cinemaspace.berkeley.edu/
Journal dedicated to all aspects of cinema and new media. Covers such areas as film theory, criticism, multimedia lectures, and the film program at UC Berkeley.

Empire Online
www.empireonline.co.uk
The web companion to the U.K.'s coolest film magazine

Entertainment Weekly
http://www.ew.com/ew
Vast amount of content from the best-selling movie, TV, and pop culture weekly

Fangoria
www.fangoria.com
Scream in terror thanks to original content and reviews from the world's leading horror film magazine

Film Threat
www.filmthreat.com
The irreverent film magazine may be out of circulation, but this site is the next best thing.

Frames Per Second
http://www.fpsmagazine.com/
Reviews and articles on animation.

G-Fan
http://www.g-fan.com/
Magazine and site devoted to japanese giant monster films and their loving fans.

The Hollywood Reporter
www.hollywoodreporter.com/
Provides the latest scoop on all major studio happenings.

iF Magazine
www.ifmagazine.com
Online magazine for indie filmmakers. Provides news, movie reviews, and columns.

Images
http://www.imagesjournal.com/index.html
Online film journal published quarterly, though the site itself updates with movie reviews weekly.

Millennium Film Journal
mfj-online.org/
Presents articles about independent, experimental, and avant-garde cinema, video, and, more recently, works that use newer technologies. Also has an archive for past issues.

Movieline
www.movieline.com/
Online version of the entertainment and interview magazine.

Premiere
www.premieremag.com/
Online version of the leading entertainment magazine

Rue Morgue
http://www.rue-morgue.com/
Magazine devoted to horror in culture and entertainment.

Scars Magazine
http://scarsmagazine.com/
Horror film magazine and website with several blogs from people in the industry.

Screem
http://screemag.com/
magazine devoted to bizarre cinema, mostly in the horror genre.

Shivers
http://www.visimag.com/shivers/
UK magazine devoted to horror in entertainment.

Time Out
www.timeout.com/
Provides a rundown of many cultural and art events happening around the world.

Unbound Zine
http://www.unboundzine.com/index.html
Indie horror fanzine that has mushroomed into a news and review site for horror movies.

Variety
www.variety.com
The classic trade magazine brings industry news, reviews, and box office info to the web

FILM STUDIOS

Dreamworks SKG
www.dreamworks.com/
Browse info on upcoming movie, TV, and music projects from one of the best-known studios in Hollywood

Focus Features
www.focusfeatures.com
Check out the home page of one of the major players in modern independent cinema. Includes a link to their more commercial arm, Rogue Pictures

Lionsgate Films
www.lionsgatefilms.com/
Takes you behind the scenes of their latest releases and gives you a glimpse of future films.

MGM Lion's Den
www.mgmua.com/
Home of the revamped *ShowGirls* site, also has coverage on the huge distributor's large slate of theatrical releases. Divided into MGM's niches, such as MGM television and home video.

Miramax
www.miramax.com/
Walk into a smorgasbord of Miramax's post-Weinstein delectables. Click on their week's specials and get a glimpse into their upcoming and current releases.

MPI Home Video
www.mpimedia.com/
Answers questions on availability for MPI video releases.

New Line Cinema
www.newline.com/
Displays their current and upcoming releases.

Newmarket Films
www.newmarketfilms.com/
Up-and-coming indie studio responsible for releasing everything from *Passion of the Christ* to *Memento*.

Paramount Pictures
www.paramount.com/
Click on any of the film icons to receive information on production and cast.

Pixar Animation Studios
www.pixar.com/
There's a reason why Disney bought Pixar--they've consistently put out the best animated movies of the past twenty years. Click around their web site and learn volumes about how they develop their award-winning CGI animated features.

Sony Classics
www.sonyclassics.com/
Focuses on Sony's independent releases and offers links to other sites.

Sony Pictures Entertainment
www.sonypictures.com/
Sony (which includes Columbia and TriStar) gives you the latest on their crop of films. Along with film and studio information, you can enter their contests to win movie t-shirts or trips to a Hollywood premiere.

Troma
www.troma.com/
With its #1 citizen, Toxie, welcoming you, indulge in the finest in camp cinema. Features information on such classics as *Toxic Avenger, Class of Nuke'em High* and *Sgt. Kabukiman NYPD.*

Twentieth Century Fox Home Entertainment
http://www.foxmovies.com/
Promotes the studio's library of films, listing films currently in theaters or that are coming soon..

United International Pictures
www.uip.com/
Comes in a variety of languages and has materials on their films which can be downloaded.

Universal Studios
www.universalstudios.com
Learn all about the upcoming films and awesome theme park rides of Universal Studios

Walt Disney Studios
http://home.disney.go.com/index
Divided into nine categories where you can find the latest on Disney books, home video, movies, music, shopping, software, television, theater and theme parks.

Warner Brothers
www.movies.warnerbros.com/
Get the latest on WB's films, TV programs, music, merchandise, DC comics and kid's programming.

Weinstein Company
www.weinsteinco.com/
Powerful producer brothers Harvey and Bob Weinstein left Miramax (the Disney arthouse wing they founded) and formed their own production company. Check out the inside info on their upcoming releases.

FILMMAKER RESOURCES

Adrienne Shelly Foundation
www.adrienneshellyfoundation.org
Founded in memory of actress/director/writer/indie icon Adrienne Shelly by her husband Andy Ostroy. Goal is to fund and mentor female filmmakers.

American Film Institute
www.afi.com/education/
The American Film Institute created this site to further its cause of finding talent that will prolong the life of art and film. The site lists the various courses, study facilities, and grants that this non-profit organization offers.

American Zoetrope
www.zoetrope.com/
A virtual tour of Francis Ford Coppola's Zoetrope Studios, which offers screenwriting contests and seminars as well as post-production information

Assn. of Independent Video and Filmmakers (AIVF)
http://www.aivf.org/
Resource that offers information on festivals and self distribution.

The Clay and Stop Motion Animation How-To Page
http://www.animateclay.com/
Tutorials and community based around stop motion animation.

Daily Script
www.dailyscript.com/
Don't know how to write a blockbuster screenplay? Check out this online archive of hundreds of TV and movie scripts and see how it's done

Film-Makers.com
www.film-makers.com
Offers hundreds of links to film resource sites.

Filmmaking.net
www.filmmaking.net/
Features a comprehensive film schools database and an internet filmmaker's FAQ

Film Underground
www.cyberfilmschool.com/
Want to become the next Quentin or Spike, but can't afford film school? Try this informative and entertaining venue that teaches the tricks of the trade in areas such as screenwriting, cinematography, and producing.

Independent Film & Television Alliance (IFTA)
www.ifta-online.org/
Formerly known as the American Film Marketing Association, this group speaks to those who exclusively license, distribute, and produce independent films.

Industry Central
http://www.industrycentral.net/
Links to film industry related sites.

KORDA
http://korda.obs.coe.int/web/search_aide.php
Database for public funding and support schemes for films made in the European Union.

Mandy's Film and Television Production Directory
www.mandy.com/
An international geographical listing of film technicians, facilities, and producers. Helpful site for anyone looking for a film crew.

Screenwriter's Online
www.screenwriter.com/
Invites novice screenwriters to interact with industry veterans.

Screenwriter's Utopia
www.screenwritersutopia.com/
A screenwriter's one-stop resource site. Learn about the format and structure of scripts, how to market your script, network among your peers, receive tips from the pros, and become informed of the latest events and seminars.

Script Zone
www.ScriptZone.com
Offers script consulting and analysis services, providing solutions to creative problems and analyzing strengths and weaknesses in a script

Stop Motion Animation
http://www.stopmotionanimation.com/
Tutorials on stop motion animation and puppet making.

Trigger Street
www.triggerstreet.com
Founded by scary character actor Kevin Spacey, this site allows fledgling screenwriters and directors to solicit feedback on their works

FILM REVIEWS

Attack of the 50 Foot DVD
http://www.50footdvd.com/
Covers and reviews cult, horror, and sci-fi films on DVD.

Back Row Reviews
http://www.backrowreviews.com/
James Dawson reviews films that, well, mostly suck.

Bigfanboy
http://bigfanboy.com/wp/
News, reviews, and interviews of current film (and some not so current film).

Chip Remington's World of Movies
http://www.chipremington.com/
Slightly mocking reviews of films by a slightly mocking man.

Choice Review
http://movie-review-sites.choice-review.com/
A review site that reviews movie review sites (say that one fast a few times).

Choking on Popcorn
http://www.chokingonpopcorn.com/
Originally the blog of two friends who decided to review whatever film they watched it has now expanded to include a review team.

CinemaReview
http://www.cinemareview.com/
Includes detailed synopses and content ratings, and sometimes images from the film.

Classic B-Movies on Video
http://www3.sympatico.ca/bmovieguy/
Reviews of classic B films, and where you can find them on tape or DVD.

Cranky Critic
http://www.crankycritic.com/
Rates movies in a way that will speak to people: i.e. was the film worth the price of the ticket it cost to see it.

Crazy for Cinema
www.crazy4cinema.com/
Straightforward, down-to-earth reviews by an ardent movie fan.

Deep Focus
www.deep-focus.com
Offers up five years worth of reviews by New York cinephile Bryant Frazer, listed alphabetically or by grade.

Digital Monster Island
http://www.digitalmonsterisland.com/
Reviews of giant monster movies on DVD.

DVD Cult
http://www.dvdcult.com/
Cult films on DVD and an awesome links section.

DVD Drive-In
http://www.dvddrive-in.com/
Reviews and announces upcoming sci-fi, horror, and cult films being released on DVD.

DVD Maniacs
http://www.dvdmaniacs.net/
Cult films on DVD.

DVD Movie Guide
http://www.dvdmg.com/index.shtml
Reviews upcoming films on DVD.

DVD Review
http://www.dvdreview.com/
DVD (and high definition DVD) news, reviews, and easter eggs.

Four Word Film Reviews
www.fwfr.com
Movies summed up in four words

Haiku Movie Reviews
www.wunderland.com/WTS/Ginohn/poetry/HMRlist.html
Movie reviews (really short ones) in Haiku form.

Kids in Mind
www.kidsinmind.com
Reviews movies with an eye toward whether or not they're suitable for the kiddies. Offers a sex, violence, and language rating system for parents.

The Man Who Viewed Too Much
www.panix.com/~dangelo/
A New York screenwriting student with a soft touch for the art house fluff and mediocre gems, like *Joe Versus the Volcano.*

Metacritic
www.metacritic.com
Compiles and provides links to new and recent release movie reviews from various magazines and newspapers, creating an overall rating (on a 1-100 scale) based on the consensus of the reviews. Also reviews DVD/video releases, music, books, and video games in the same way.

Mrs. Giggles
http://www.mrsgiggles.com/movies/index.html
Reviews by what we assume is someone's persnickety grandma...

Movie Deaths Database
http://www.moviedeaths.com/
Film reviews and a database about death in Hollywood films. Two subjects that naturally go together.

The Movie Mom's Guide to Movies and Videos for Families
http://blog.beliefnet.com/moviemom/
Created by movie critic and mother, Nell Minow, who gives critiques and advice on how to get children to watch movies that aren't doused in violence.

Movie Reviews by Joan Ellis
www.joanellis.com/
Film critic Joan Ellis puts her acerbic and astute observations on the Internet as she examines the cultural innuendoes in current film.

Movie Review Query Engine
www.mrqe.com
Allows you to search on any movie and find all available reviews appearing in the Usernet group *rec.arts.movies.reviews*

The Movies Made Me Do It
http://www.moviesmademe.com/home
Film reviews, usually genre or not so mainstream films.

Mr. Cranky Rates the Movies
www.mrcranky.com
The joke here is that this guy doesn't like *any* movie, hence the name Cranky. His rating scale is based on bombs and his followers (code names Lizard, and Philm Pham, just to name a few) are as nutty as his reviews.

Onion A.V. Club
www.avclub.com/
Spin-off of the popular satirical newspaper that features movie and DVD reviews, filmmaker interviews, and more

The Onliner
http://www.theoneliner.com/
Sardonic movie reviews done as only the British can do them.

Out Magazine Movie Reviews
www.out.com/
Online version of the magazine that includes movie reviews and commentary on gay and lesbian cinema.

Roger Ebert
http://rogerebert.suntimes.com/
Newspapers, books, television, now Ebert storms the web. Offers his newspaper film reviews, with a searchable archive that goes back to 1985.

Rotten Tomatoes
www.rottentomatoes.com/
Collects reviews of newly released movies from various newspapers and ranks the overall critical reaction to the film.

Teen Movie Critic
www.dreamagic.com/roger/teencritic.html
Teenaged movie buff from Minnesota offers his thoughts on current theatrical releases. Also has a link to a listing of many video rental stores around America.

VideoHound's Golden Movie Retriever
movieretriever.com
Our very own web site! The Hound's famous reviews, plus community features and blogs from the Editors of VideoHound's Golden Movie Retriever

The Voice of Reason
http://www.thevoiceofreason.com/ComedyMovieWatch/
Most very definitely not entirely serious movie reviews.

Women Studies Film Reviews
www.mith2.umd.edu/WomensStudies/FilmReviews/
Movie reviews with a feminist angle written by Florida radio personality Linda Lopez McAlister and film scholar Cynthia Fuchs.

GENERAL ENTERTAINMENT

Academy of Motion Picture Arts and Sciences
www.oscars.org/
Site proves that the AMPAS does more than just hand out gold statuettes every year. This homepage reveals this organization's dedication to spreading the love of film around the world. Includes information on AMPAS's various fellowships, educational, and historical activities.

Ain't It Cool News
www.aintitcool.com

Get the latest on upcoming releases before they even hit theaters with website originator Harry Knowles's inside scoop on their test screenings. He's the geekiest of web master film fanatics, but his information is usually fairly reliable.

American Memory
lcweb2.loc.gov/papr/mpixhome.html
Collection of historical film stock that can be downloaded from the Library of Congress. Time frame is from 1897 to 1916 and includes such archival footage as President William McKinley's funeral and "actuality films" showing panoramic views of old San Francisco policemen and firemen in action.

Angry Alien Productions
http://www.angryalien.com/
Movies re-enacted within 30 seconds....with bunnies. We'd like to say more, but we're speechless.

The Big Cartoon Database
http://www.bcdb.com/
Like IMDB, but for cartoons.

The Black Film Center/Archive
http://www.indiana.edu/~bfca/
An academic reference devoted to sharing resources on black cinema.

Black Films
www.blackfilm.com
Provides a forum for filmmakers, scholars, and organizations to discuss and express their artistic views. Includes info on upcoming releases, films in production, casting calls, jobs, and film festivals. There's also a gallery of film clips.

Black Flix
www.blackflix.com
Highlights the contributions of black movie stars, filmmakers, writers, and directors whom mainstream reviews and web sites often overlook.

Blockbuster Entertainment
www.blockbuster.com
Explores all the goodies the rental chain has to offer as well as their latest contests or sweepstakes

Bob World Film Database
http://www.bobworld.me.uk/
Continuing the tradition of quirky movie databases Bob World is all about films in which the female lead has a "bob" hairstyle.

Box Office Guru
www.boxofficeguru.com
Classic site devoted to box office results. See what came in first this week or check out their database of film grosses for over 2,700 movies

Box Office Mojo
http://www.boxofficemojo.com/
Similar to the above.

Box Office Prophets
http://www.boxofficeprophets.com/
Blogs, reviews, and research tools for movie buffs.

Bright Lights Film Journal
http://www.brightlightsfilm.com/index.html
Film blog and articles.

Britfilms
http://www.britfilms.com/
The official online database of British films.

British Cinema Greats
http://www.britishcinemagreats.com/
Online database of British film information.

Bugs Bunny Burrow
http://www.bugsbunnyburrow.com/
Site devoted to classic cartoons.

Celluloid Dreams
http://www.celluloiddreams.net/
web site for the Celluloid Dreams radio show. Features interviews, reviews, and interesting movie topics.

Cine Fantom
framework.v2.nl/archive/archive/node/text/default.xslt/nodenr-132348
Examines Russian experimental films and videos.

Cinema Blend
http://www.cinemablend.com
One of the Hound's FAVORITE places for movie news on the net. CB features thousands of mildly interesting, occasionally exciting editorials, reviews, reports, previews, and half-crazed rants, perfect for the film literate or merely film curious.

Cinema Confidential
http://www.cinecon.com/
News, reviews, interviews, and gossip. Also has trailers for upcoming films.

Cinema Sites
http://www.cinema-sites.com/
Directory of film and television related sites.

Cinemaniac
http://frank.mtsu.edu/~jpurcell/Cinema/maincinema2.htm
Collection of links to cinema related sites online.

Cinematic Happenings Under Development (CHUD)
www.chud.com
Offers gossip, news, and previews on upcoming films and projects in development.

Cinemorgue
http://www.cinemorgue.com/
List of actors/actresses who have died onscreen with descriptions of the events. Kinda creepy.

Clamen's Movie Information Collection
http://www.cs.cmu.edu/afs/cs.cmu.edu/user/clamen/misc/movies/
One man's personal collection of links to film related sites.

Classic Film Guide
http://www.classicfilmguide.com/
Reviews of silent and classic films, along with a FAQ.

Classic Hollywood Biographies
http://www.classichollywoodbios.com/
Also has many magazine covers featuring stars of the times.

Classic Movie Favorites
http://www.classicmoviefavorites.com/
Impressive effort by one tireless fan.

Classic Movies
http://www.classicmovies.org/
Articles, links, and a forum.

Classic Movies Online
http://www.classiccinemaonline.com/1/
Blog that streams classic and silent films online.

Classic Noir Online
http://www.classicnoir.com/
For fans of classic films and film noir.

Cliffhanger Corner
http://members.tripod.com/~fedora_2/
Fan page devoted to the old cliffhanger serials.

ComingSoon.net
www.comingsoon.net
Presents news, features, interviews, and images of upcoming movies, updated daily

The Complete Index to World Film
http://www.citwf.com/index.htm
Searchable database of films, actors, and professionals in the film industry compiled by Alan Goble.

Couch Cowboy
http://www.couchcowboy.com/
Classic cowboy films.

Cowboy Pal
http://www.cowboypal.com/
Silver screen cowboy films.

Counting Down
www.countingdown.com
Posts gossip, news, and features on upcoming movies.

Creepy Classics
http://www.creepyclassics.com/
Lists upcoming classic sci-fi and horror films on DVD. Also sells them.

Dark City
http://www.eskimo.com/~noir/
Dedicated to all things noir.

Dark Horizons
www.darkhorizons.com
Movie rumors are aplenty here and it's updated regularly. The site is regulated by Garth (yes, Garth) Franklin, an Australian entertainment journalist

The Darkside of the Web
www.darklinks.com
Specializes in shedding light on the bizarre and creepy in film.

Dart Movies
http://www.crowsdarts.com/movies/movies.html
A list of films (and the specific scenes in them) that involve throwing darts.

The Deadbolt
www.thedeadbolt.com
This ultimate hub site collects daily links related to the coolest in movies, music, entertainment, and more--plus they offer their own original reviews, features, and interviews. One-stop shopping for internet media addicts.

Defamer
www.defamer.com
Frequently updated blog-style gossip rag, airing out all of Hollywood's dirty laundry

Dermatology in the Cinema
www.skinema.com/
Proof that anything can go on the Web. Exposes how skin afflictions are handled in films. Broken down in three categories: "Representation of Evil"; "Actors with Skin Findings"; and "Realistic and Sympathetic Portrayals." Informative and healthy.

Digitally Obsessed
www.digitallyobsessed.com
Provides information, reviews, contests, and inside information on new DVD releases.

Don Markstein's Toonopedia
http://www.toonopedia.com/
Cartoon Reference site run by the former editor of Comics Revue.

Drive-Ins
http://www.drive-ins.com/
Drive-In movie theater database.

DriveIn Movie
http://www.driveinmovie.com/mainmenu.htm
List of Drive-Ins and some of their history.

Drive-In Theater
http://www.driveintheater.com/index.htm
Lists all remaining drive-in theaters by state and county.

DVD Demystified
http://dvddemystified.com/
Home of the exhaustive DVD FAQ, a guide to everything you wanted to know about DVD's and a lot of things you had no idea about.

DVD Easter Eggs
www.dvdeastereggs.com
Shows how to get to hidden features, or "easter eggs," that are hidden in some DVDs.

DVD File
www.dvdfile.com
Get the 411, in exhaustive detail, on all current and future DVD releases

E! Online
www.eonline.com
Filled with tons of entertainment news, this is a fun site to visit come Oscar time, thanks to their habit of creating online games at the expense of the stars not nominated

Eggheaven 2000
http://www.eggheaven.com/
Shows easter eggs (hidden features) in a variety of products, including easter eggs.

The 80's Movies Rewind
http://www.fast-rewind.com/
Reviews, trivia, plot synopses, and more in this homage to eighties cinema.

The Electronic Urban Report
www.EURweb.com/
Supports the positive images of African Americans in film and offers the latest celebrity news on the top black stars.

Fake Film Database
http://www.appallingtrash.com/
Database of movie parodies.

The Felixes
http://www.thefelixes.com/
Devoted to skewering the Oscars.

Fiction Into Film Database
http://www.fifdb.com/
Database of films and television based on fictional works.

Film and Video Resources
http://guides.lib.umich.edu/aml
Created by the folks at the University of Michigan School of Information and Library Studies, this site leads you to many of the textual resources available that deal with film and video. Organized according to reviews, filmographies, discussions and other databases.

Film Forum
www.filmforum.com/
Showcases the latest releases in New York's leading independent movie house. Offers premiere information on independent features and repertory programming.

Film Jerk
http://www.filmjerk.com/
Despite the name, they seem like nice people.

Film Monthly
http://www.filmmonthly.com/
News, reviews, and articles. Has an emphasis on genre films.

Film Noir
http://www.crimeculture.com/Contents/Film%20Noir.html
The Crime Culture websites historical guide to film noir.

Film Noir, Suspense, and Classic Action Movies
http://www.suspense-movies.com/
Huzzah for Carol Landis!

Film Resources on the Web
http://www.duke.edu/~kennethl/filmsite.html
Links to movie resources an sites on the web.

Film Sound Cliches
http://www.filmsound.org/cliche/
Popular movie sound clichés and logic flaws, and some articles on sound in films.

FilmJabber
http://www.filmjabber.com/
A blog with movie and fim reviews, trailers from upcoming films, and photos and posters.

The Filmmaker's Exam
http://www.rinkworks.com/filmmaker/
Test yourself to see if your movie is a stinker.

Films 101
http://www.films101.com/
Database fo films chosen by critics and filmmakers to be the best in their genre.

FilmScape
http://www.filmscape.co.uk/
Games and quizzes involving movie quotes and taglines.

FilmSpot
http://www.cinemaspot.com/
Site listing film related resources and sites.

Find Your Video Store
http://www.myvideostore.com/content/store/search.html
Enter your zip code into their search engine to find movie stores in your area.

A Fistful of Westerns
http://website.lineone.net/~braithwaitej/
Website specializing in the old spaghetti westerns.

555 List
http://home.earthlink.net/~mthyen/
Mind numbing list of all the fictional 555 numbers used in movies.

FlixFind
http://www.flixfind.com/Weblog/
Directory of links to (mostly) current films.

Flubs of Jurassic Park
http://www.bigwaste.com/library/jurassicflubs/
Several pages of mistakes from the dinosaur movie.

The Flying Inkpot's Incredible Movie Links Page
http://inkpot.com/movielinks/
Gotta love the name.

The Force
www.theforce.net
Articles, gossip, news, fan submissions on all things Star Wars.

Former Child Star Central
http://members.tripod.com/~former_child_star/
Whatever became of those ex-kiddie celebs? Doin' time? Stemmin' for change? Find out here.

ForMovies
http://formovies.com/
Movie news and trivia, and a directory of local video stores allowing users to search them for a specific title.

Garners Movie Classics
http://www.garnersclassics.com/
Collection of movies sorted by genre. Click on he icons by each one's name to see quotes or hear audio clips. Also has some one word reviews of recent films.

German-Hollywood Connection
http://www.germanhollywood.com/

Site about the impact the Germans, Austrians, and Swiss have had on Hollywood and it's films with essays on everything from Noir to Tarzan.

Glamour Girls of the Silver Screen
http://www.glamourgirlsofthesilverscreen.com/
Images and profiles of famous actresses from the 40's to the 60's.

Gods of Film Making
http://www.ambidextrouspics.com/
Bios of filmmakers.

Golden Age Cartoons
http://www.goldenagecartoons.com/
Central site for 7 dedicated carton historians who have banded together.

Golden Silents
http://www.goldensilents.com/
Bios and film clips from Hollywood's Silent Age.

The Golden Years
http://www.thegoldenyears.org/
Films from 1939 to 1969.

Go2flix
http://www.go2flix.com/
Links to films playing now, upcoming theater and DVD releases, Oscar info, etc.

The Hot Button
www.thehotbutton.com
Critic Dave Poland discusses Hollywood gossip, future films, and weekly box office reports.

Hollywood Elsewhere
www.hollywood-elsewhere.com
Movie journalist Jeffrey Wells posts articles on upcoming films, the movie industry, and the vagaries of Hollywood.

Hollywood Online
www.hollywood.com
Feast your eyes at movie trailers, movie trivia, movie chat, vote on the latest contest, or check out some real estate in California.

Hollywood Sign
www.hollywoodsign.org/
Offers snapshots and a historical overview of the world famous Hollywood sign

I Know the Ending
http://www.iknowtheending.com/
Humorous synopses of films consisting of 2 sentences that give away the ending.

IGN
www.ign.com
Testosterone fueled site focuses on sci-fi, wrestling, and video games. Movie fans will find interviews, features, opinions, and trivia in three film areas.

IndieFilms
www.indiefilms.com
An easy, inexpensive way to distribute any feature, short, or documentary film you've made. Allows independent filmmakers to make contact with potential investors and distributors.

IndieWire
www.indiewire.com
Up-to-date info on the latest in independent film festivals and wide releases

Insultingly Stupid Movie Physics
www.intuitor.com/moviephysics/
Rails on scenes from movies that disregard the laws of physics and explains why they're impossible. Lists generic "bad movie physics," examples of cliches that show up in movie after movie, as well as serious scientific gaffes.

International Film and Video Center
http://www.ifvc.com/home.htm
Film database, links to film festivals, and they produce their own films and documentaries.

The Internet Entertainment Network
www.hollywoodnetwork.com/dealmaking/index.html
Enables you to become a member of the Screenwriters, Producers, or Writers Network. Divided into various sites like dealmaking, box office, in-production, and script sales.

The Internet Movie Database
www.imdb.com
The mother of all entertainment databases. Users can frequently update the information and submit their own film reviews. With thousands of movies stored in its database, you can search by title, actor, director, country, and even by character name.

Jam! Movies
jam.canoe.ca/Movies/
Canadian movie site with daily entertainment news and information.

James Bond
www.klast.net/bond/
Bond arrives, shaken not stirred, onto the internet. Includes a rundown of every Bond film, villains and their famous lines, Bond trivia, and links to other Bond sites

Jerry Beck's Cartoon Research
http://www.cartoonresearch.com/
Comprehensive resource for animation.

Julie's Cinematic Slip-Ups
http://www.reocities.com/hollywood/2549/slips.html
Julie takes on Hollywood.

Latino Review
www.latinoreview.com
Film news, rumors, and interviews directed towards the English-speaking Latin-American audience

Locate TV
http://www.locatetv.com/
Type the name of an actor, film, or TV show into their search engine and it will tell you where you can see it on DVD, television, or online.

Lumiere
http://lumiere.obs.coe.int/web/search/
Record of annual film ticket sales of films released in Europe since 1996. Entries include a breakdown by individual country.

Martin's Film Noir Page
www.martinsfilmnoir.com/
Extensive site on the popular genre of film noir

Media Resource Center
http://www.lib.berkeley.edu/MRC/level2.html
List of resources for movie fans and makers.

Medium Rare
http://www.mediumraretv.org/
Website devoted to quality film and television that is often overlooked.

Meredy's Place
http://www.meredy.com/
Classic movie trivia site.

The Midnight Palace
http://www.midnightpalace.com/
A forum, articles, and reviews on films from before 1956.

Moderntimes
http://www.moderntimes.com/
Has, among other things, a history of how B films began to exist.

Motion Pictures Association of America (MPAA)
www.filmratings.com
Tells what a film is rated and why it received that rating.

Mov.ie
http://mov.ie/
Links to the official sites of movies.

Movie-A-Minute
http://www.rinkworks.com/movieaminute/
Humorous synopses of films.

The Movie Cliches List
www.moviecliches.com/
A vast list of common film stereotypes and instances that stifle logic. Divided into over fifty topics including bodily functions, minorities, teenagers, and wood. A growing site since people can submit their own materials.

Movie Mistakes
www.movie-mistakes.com
Identifies mistakes of continuity, fact, and omission in movies.

Movie Musicals: From Stage to Screen
http://www.geocities.com/TelevisionCity/Studio/8849/moviemusicals.htm
Reference site for those curious about stage musicals later made into films.

Movie Poster Web Page
www.musicman.com/mp/mp.html
No, you're not seeing double. This one is a catalog of movie posters available for sale. Includes foreign films.

The Movie Posters Archive
www.filmsondisc.com/movieposterarchives.htm
An online vault of old movie posters, categorized by lead actor

The Movie Show on Radio
www.lifestyletalkradio.com/movieshow/
Site for the syndicated Movie Show on Radio. Includes info on air times and stations that carry the show in various markets, as well as profiles of the hosts.

The Movie Sounds Page
www.moviesounds.com/
Download various sound bites from famous flicks and link to other sites.

Movie Theology
http://www.cmu.ca/library/faithfilm.html
Directory of websites offering film information from a Christian perspective.

MovieClicks
http://www.movieclicks.com/index.shtml
Whenever a film is released now odds are it also has a website. This site helps you find those websites.

Moviepooper
http://www.moviepooper.com/
Collection of spoilers revealing the ends of movies.

Movies.com
http://movies.go.com/
Trailers, clips, and reviews of upcoming films. Also reviews films coming out on DVD.

MovieTrailer
http://www.movietrailer.tv/
Online directory of Movie Trailers.

MovieWEB
movieweb.com/
Groups together info from every film studio and offers production data and still photos of their new releases. Also offers the latest box office statistics.

Musicals 101
http://www.musicals101.com/
A history of musical theatre and film.

Netflix
www.netflix.com/
The coolest mail-order DVD rental service around. Browse through their 75,000 title movie catalog and enjoy DVDs delivered right to your mailbox.

New York Film Annex
http://www.nyfavideo.com/index.htm
Dedicated to genre films of all kinds.

Nitpickers
www.nitpickers.com
Points out mistakes, omissions, and equipment sightings in movies.

Not Starring
http://www.notstarring.com/
A database of your favorite stars and the movie roles they didn't get.

NothingButMovies
http://www.nothingbutmovies.com/
Links to film related resources divided by category.

The Old Corral
http://www.b-westerns.com/
B movie westerns. Strange cowboy get-ups included

OpenFlix
http://www.openflix.com/
Listing of films in the public domain and how to get them.

Original Gangsters
http://www.dirtysquatters.com/evocrim/og/
Gangster movies in all their glory.

Pathfinder
www.pathfinder.com
Created by Time Warner, this site links to their variety of magazines that check the pulse of popular culture such as *People, Vibe, Groove* and *Entertainment Weekly*.

The Picture Show Man
http://www.pictureshowman.com/
The history of films from 1890 to 1960.

Planet Indie Independent Film Directory
http://www.planetindie.com/
Blog and directory of sites about independent film.

Prelinger Archives
http://www.archive.org/details/prelinger
Archive dedicated to the collection of historic films that haven't been collected elsewhere.

Projections
http://www.futuristmovies.com/
A site dedicated to films depicting the future.

Pulp Phantom
ulink.net/crossroads/phantom/
What if Quentin Tarantino had written Phantom Menace? Animated series shows you what it might look like.

Ravin' Maven
http://www.themave.com/
Collection of mini-sites devoted to classic actors and actresses.

Razzies
www.razzies.com/
Visitors can vote for the "Golden Raspberry Awards" for the year's worst films and performances.

Real Movie News
http://www.realmovienews.com/
News, reviews, trailers, etc.

Reel Classics
http://www.reelclassics.com/
Classic films, actors, filmmakers, and more.

Reel Faces
http://www.chasingthefrog.com/reelfaces/reel_faces.php
Looks at films based on real life events and people and compares them to actual events.

Running in Films
http://www.runningmovies.com/
A very comprehensive database of films that contain scenes of running. No seriously.

Scary Duck
http://scaryduck.blogspot.com/search/label/Condensed%20films
Clever and funny synopses of films done in L33tspeak.

The Serial Squadron
http://www.serialsquadron.com/
The cliffhanger serial appreciation society.

Shobary's Spaghetti Westerns
http://spaghettiwesterns.1g.fi/
Even has a bloopers section!

Silent and Sound Cliffhanger Serials
http://www.themaverick.us/home/serial.html
Lists serials by year, A-Z, and by studio.

Silent Era
http://www.silentera.com/
Scads of info on Silent Films, including what is available on DVD.

Silent Ladies and Gents
http://www.silentladies.com/Ladies.html
Large image galleries of silent film stars, and profiles of the studios of the era.

Silents Are Golden
http://www.silentsaregolden.com/
Devoted to silent movies, and the idea that they are...well, you know

The Silent Western
http://xroads.virginia.edu/~hyper/hns/westfilm/west.html
Chronicles the history of the old silent westerns.

Slipups
http://www.slipups.com/
Highlights amusing oopsies in film.

Smoke Free Movies
http://pages.videotron.com/abc/films-movies/
Listing of films where in there is no one smoking for those offended by cigarettes. In French and English.

Snopes: Movies
http://www.snopes.com/movies/
Snopes is the ultimate hoax and urban legends reference page, and thankfully for us they have a movie section.

Sports In Movies
http://www.sportsinmovies.com/
Dedicated to sports films and their fans.

Spout
http://www.spout.com/
Community for discussing movies, and you can buy them as well.

Surf Classics
http://www.surfclassics.com/
Site devoted to lobby cards and posters for surf movies from the 60's.

Teddy Blues Bunkhouse
http://www.wildwestweb.net/
Extensive source on the old west and westerns.

Temporal Anomalies In Time Travel Movies
http://www.mjyoung.net/time/
Now this site is fun.

Theater Hopper
http://theaterhopper.com/
Web comic about movies with some film reviews.

Those Golden Movie Musicals
http://www.classicmoviemusicals.com/
Dedicated to classic musicals.

Todd Gault's Serial Experience
http://www.serialexperience.com/
The old cliffhangers have many fans.

Toons At War
http://www.toonsatwar.blogspot.com/
Blog exploring the history of Walt Disney Studios during WWII

The Top 100
movieweb.com/movie/top25.html
Anxious to see if a certain movie has broken any box office records during its opening week? This site provides the box office ranking of all current releases. Updated every Thursday.

U.C. Berkeley Film Studies Science Fiction Page
cinemaspace.berkeley.edu/Resources/scifi2.html
For avid sci-fi film buffs, site has separate pages for such classics as *Blade Runner, Star Trek, Alien, Star Wars*, and other genre related sites.

VaRaces
http://www.varaces.com/
The Movie Car Chase Database.

VideoHelp
http://www.videohelp.com/
Ostensibly a site on how to make your own DVD's, it also has reviews of DVD players, specifically how to access the hidden menu's that will allow you to play DVD's of any region code.

Welcome to Silent Movies
http://www.welcometosilentmovies.com/
News on silent films available on VFS and DVD, and articles of various sorts.

The Western Posters Page
http://www.westernposterpage.com/
Seller of reproductions of posters from the classic western films.

Westerns
http://www.lewestern.com/
The Western movie internet database.

Where Did They Film That
http://www.wheredidtheyfilmthat.co.uk/
Location listings for films shot in the UK or Ireland.

Whoops! Movie Goofs
http://www.jonhs.com/moviegoofs/
Alphabetical list of films with some tragic errors, and explanations of them.

Women In Animation
http://wia.animationblogspot.com/
Professional non-profit group established to help the advancement of women in the animation industry.

World War 2 On Film
http://www.geocities.com/warmoviedatabase/
For our war film fans!

The Worldwide Guide to Movie Locations
http://www.movie-locations.com/
Photographic history of the locales of movie shoots. Can be searched by place, film, or cast member.

Yahoo Upcoming Movies
movies.yahoo.com/mv/upcoming/
Provides info on upcoming releases (including release dates, cast, and crew), as well as movies in production or scheduled for release in the next 1-2 years.

VIDEO OUTLETS

Amazon.com
www.amazon.com
The largest online store on the internet, with a huge DVD catalog and options to pre-order releases or buy used copies of out-of-print movies

Anchor Bay Entertainment
www.anchorbayentertainment.com/
One of the leading independent suppliers of movie and TV DVDs, particularly known for their horror catalog

AnimEigo
www.animeigo.com
Japanese animation and classic samurai films, including extensive translation notes on cultural quirks in the film that would otherwise be lost on western viewers.

BBC America Shop
http://www.bbcamericashop.com/
For your British tv and film needs.

Best Video
www.bestvideo.com
With over 24,000 titles, you can search their inventory via various topics and subject categories.
Also includes brief monthly reviews of current releases

Big Vision Entertainment
http://www.bigvisionentertainment.com/
Specializes in several niches, most notably wrestling and mma.

Bombshells
http://www.bombshells.com/
Profiles and picture galleries of actresses from the 30's to the 50's.

Captain Bijou
http://www.captainbijou.com/
Video and DVD sales, and all sorts of posters and memorabilia.

Carpel Video
www.carpelvideo.com/
If you're only interested in purchasing blank and recycled video tapes, then you've hit the jackpot with this site.

CD Universe
http://www.cduniverse.com/
Primarily a music seller, but it also carries DVD's.

Christmas Movies
http://www.christmasmovies.us/
Xmas films only, other holidays need not apply.

Cinematrix Releasing/ Unknown Productions
www.unknownproductions.com
Distributes the films of Unknown Productions, including *Vampires of Sorority Row* and *Club Dead*

The Criterion Collection
http://www.criterion.com/asp/
Collection of classic and contemporary films considered to be important.

Critics' Choice Video & DVD
www.ccvideo.com
Online ordering service. Includes new release, upcoming releases, classics, kids video, and bargain sections.

DDD House
http://www.dddhouse.com/v3/index.php
English language version of the Asian site. Carries DVD, VCD, games, and other stuff. Please make sure to pay attention to the Region Code and Format of your order to ensure it plays on your DVD player.

Deep Discount DVD
www.deepdiscountdvd.com
Online ordering service, with a lowest price guarantee, for DVD releases

DVD Asian
http://www.dvdasian.com/
Specializes in asian films (and not just from Japan and China). Please make sure to pay attention to the Region Code and Format of your order to ensure it plays on your DVD player.

DVD Concept
http://www.dvdconcept.com/
Sells Region 1 and 2 DVD's. Please make sure to pay attention to the Region Code and Format of your order to ensure it plays on your DVD player.

DVD Plus
http://www.dvd-plus.com/
Large DVD seller in Canada.

Draculina
http://www.draculina.com/
Magazine publisher that also carries some niche horror and exploitation films.

DVD Empire
http://www.dvdempire.com/

Facets
http://www.facets.org/
Distributor to hard to find art, cult, and foreign videos. Please make sure to pay attention to the Region Code and Format of your order to ensure it plays on your DVD player.

Family Home Video
http://www.familyvideo.com/catalog/
Online ordering service for over 25,000 titles that are also linked to the Internet Movie Database.

HBO Home Video Online
www.hbo.com
Along with information of their productions released on video, this site includes program summaries, sound and video clips, and celebrity photos.

Image Entertainment
http://www.image-entertainment.com/
Films of all kinds, many of which are hard to find.

iNetVideo
http://www.inetvideo.com/store/home.php
Sells movies, music, and games.

J Store
http://japanimation.com
Anime and Japanese products.

Kino on Video
www.kino.com/
Kino International showcases a breadth of films from world cinema.

Manga Video
www.manga.com/
Spin-off retailer site offering comic books, soundtracks, and fan club information.

Mondo Macabro DVD
http://www.mondomacabrodvd.com/
Foreign horror and exploitation film.

Moviesville
http://www.moviesville.com/
English language version of Chinese site. Please make sure to pay attention to the Region Code and Format of your order to ensure it plays on your DVD player.

On Reel.com
www.reel.com
Video distributor based out of Berkeley, California that categorizes films under uncanny subcategories. Hmmm, that sounds familiar. Holds over 85,000 titles.

Out of Print Movies
http://www.outofprintmovies.com
They will search for out of print films for you, but they don't claim to be cheap.

PicPal: Picture Palace
picpal.com/
Enormous online catalog that has a comprehensive and searchable database for its 36,000+ titles. Also has special features including a magazine rack and a place for international cinema.

Rare Hollywood
http://www.rarehollywood.com/
Specialists in finding rare and out of print films. They also sell Hollywood memorabilia and posters.

RightStuf
http://www.rightstuf.com/rssite/
Importer of Japanese merchandise, films, and anime.

Robert's Hard to Find Videos
http://robertsvideos.com/
Video catalog searchable by genre as well as format.

Russ Meyer Films International
http://www.rmfilms.com/
The man who gave many large busted women their first acting roles.

Scarecrow Video
http://www.scarecrow.com/
Rare and hard to find films for sale or rent.

Sci-Fi Station
http://www.scifistation.com/
Classic and modern science fiction films and collectibles.

Science Fiction Continuum
www.sfcontinuum.com/
Guide to a diverse collection of sci-fi and horror films as well as animation, television and UFO documentaries on video and DVD. Please make sure to check the Region/Format to make sure it plays on your DVD player.

Silent Film Sources
http://www.cinemaweb.com/silentfilm/
Resources for finding silent films.

Synapse Films
http://synapse-films.com/
Horror, scifi, indie, and cult films.

Tampoo
http://www.tampoo.com/
Videos, DVD's, CD's, and video games.

Tartan Video USA
www.tartanvideousa.com
Surf the web site of the distributor responsible for bringing some of the freakiest films from Japan, Hong Kong, Korea, and the rest of Asia to the good ol' US of A.

Tempe Entertainment
http://www.tempevideo.com/index.html
Direct to video horror and scifi movies.

Thomas Video
www.thomasvideo.com
Having difficult finding that obscure, and admit it, disgusting film you remember seeing when you were younger? Well, take all inquiries to Thomas Video, who specializes in those hard to find videos. Site also includes monthly spotlights on such indie pioneers as Mario Bava, Larry Cohen, and Japanese director Seijun Suzuki.

Turner Classic Movies
http://www.tcm.com/index.jsp
Aside from it's catalog the site also has trailers and clips from classic films.

The Video Collection
http://www.videocollection.com/
Video sales, searchable by genre.

Wolfe Video
www.wolfevideo.com
Online video outlet specializing in gay and lesbian themed films.

Xploited Cinema
http://xploitedcinema.com/catalog/index.php
Imported cult, exploitation, horror, and arthouse dvd's. Please make sure to pay attention to the Region Code and Format of your order to ensure it plays on your DVD player.

Zoom Movie
http://www.zoommovie.com/
Asian films, and Japanese animation. Please make sure to pay attention to the Region Code and Format of your order to ensure it plays on your DVD player.